ENCYCLOPÆDIA
BRITANNICA

MICROPÆDIA

The Encyclopædia Britannica
is published with the editorial advice
of the faculties of the University of Chicago;
a committee of persons holding
academic appointments at the universities
of Oxford, Cambridge, London, and Edinburgh;
a committee at the University of Toronto;
and committees drawn from members of the faculties
of the University of Tokyo
and the Australian National University.

THE UNIVERSITY OF CHICAGO

"Let knowledge grow from more to more
and thus be human life enriched."

The New Encyclopædia Britannica

Volume 1

MICROPÆDIA

Ready Reference

FOUNDED 1768
15 TH EDITION

Encyclopædia Britannica, Inc.
Robert P. Gwinn, Chairman, Board of Directors
Charles E. Swanson, President
Philip W. Goetz, Editor-in-Chief

Chicago
Auckland/Geneva/London/Manila/Paris/Rome
Seoul/Sydney/Tokyo/Toronto

First Edition	1768-1771
Second Edition	1777-1784
Third Edition	1788-1797
Supplement	1801
Fourth Edition	1801-1809
Fifth Edition	1815
Sixth Edition	1820-1823
Supplement	1815-1824
Seventh Edition	1830-1842
Eighth Edition	1852-1860
Ninth Edition	1875-1889
Tenth Edition	1902-1903

Printed in U.S.A.

Library of Congress Catalog Card Number: 83-83118
International Standard Book Number: 0-85229-423-9

How to use the MICROPAEDIA

The 12 volumes of the MICROPAEDIA contain tens of thousands of shorter articles on specific persons, places, things, and ideas arranged in alphabetical order. The MICROPAEDIA can be used as an information resource on its own; and it can function as support for the longer articles in the MACROPAEDIA (to which it refers when it is appropriate to do so). The MICROPAEDIA in turn is supported by references in the INDEX and by the lists of suggested readings in the PROPAEDIA. Finally, the MICROPAEDIA is the portion of the *Encyclopædia Britannica* best suited for the reader who wishes to browse among the countless subjects in all fields of human learning and history in all times and places.

Alphabetization. Entry titles are alphabetized according to the English alphabet, A to Z. All diacritical marks (such as in ö, ł, or ñ) and foreign letters without parallels in English (such as ayn [ʿ] and hamza [ʾ]) are ignored in the alphabetization. Apostrophes likewise are ignored. Titles beginning with a number, such as "**1812, War of,**" are alphabetized as if the number were written out ("**Eighteen-twelve, War of**").

Alphabetization proceeds according to the "word-by-word" principle. Thus, "**Mount Vernon**" precedes "**mountain**"; any "**John**" entry precedes "**John Henry,**" which in turn precedes "**Johne's disease.**" Any character or string of characters preceding a space, hyphen, dash, or virgule is treated as a word and alphabetized accordingly. Thus, "**De Broglie**" precedes "**debenture,**" "**J/psi particle**" precedes "**jack,**" and "**jack-o'-lantern**" precedes "**jackal.**" Titles with identical spellings are arranged in the following order: (1) persons, (2) places, (3) things.

For many rulers and titled nobility, chronological order, as well as alphabetical order, governs placement. Rulers of the same given name (*e.g.,* William) may be grouped together, separate from other entries, and indicated by the symbol •. They may be subgrouped alphabetically by country and, within each country, arranged chronologically ("**William I,**" "**William II,**" etc.). Nobility or peers of the same titled name (*e.g.,* "**Essex, EARLS OF**") are similarly grouped together, separate from other entries; they are indicated by the symbol • and arranged chronologically.

Places with identical names are in alphabetical order according to the countries in which they are located, with entries on physical features following cities and other political units. Identical place-names in the same country are alphabetized according to the alphabetical order of the state, province, or comparable political subdivision in which they are found. Physical features with identical names that lie on or that cross national borders are alphabetized by the continent in which they are found.

Entry arrangement. The titles of entries are arranged according to the forms commonly found in indexes and dictionaries, with some special conventions.

Entry titles for certain physical features, institutions, structures, events, and concepts are ordinarily inverted to place the substantive word first. Thus, the Bay of Bengal is entered as "**Bengal, Bay of**"; the Bank of England as "**England, Bank of**"; the Tower of London as "**London, Tower of**"; the Siege of Vienna as "**Vienna, Siege of**"; and the balance of power as "**power, balance of.**" If the name of a physical feature, institution, structure, event, or concept has two or more descriptors, it is entered under the descriptor appearing first. Thus, the Episcopal Church in Scotland is entered as "**Episcopal Church in Scotland**" (not "**Scotland, Episcopal Church in**"); the Leaning Tower of Pisa as "**Leaning Tower of Pisa**"; and the kinetic theory of gases as "**kinetic theory of gases.**"

The entries for most Western persons are arranged so that one can read a name in correct order by beginning after the first comma, proceeding to the end of the boldface type, returning to the beginning word or words, and proceeding forward to the first comma. Thus, the entry "**March, Patrick Dunbar, 2nd earl of,**" is read "Patrick Dunbar, 2nd earl of March"; the entry "**Orléans, Louis, duc d',**" is read "Louis, duc d'Orléans." Names of Far Eastern origin are given in Oriental order, with the surname preceding the personal name (*e.g.,* "**Tojo Hideki,**" "**Chou En-lai,**" "**Nguyen Cao Ky**").

Cross-references. Some cross-reference entries appear in the MICROPAEDIA for the purpose of leading a reader from names that are familiar to alternate names that may not be. Cross-references also appear frequently within or at the ends of standard entries, where they are identified by *see, see also, see under, q.v.* (*quod vide,* "which see"), or *qq.v.* (*quae vide,* "which see," plural).

Certain entries serve both as relatively brief essays on general subjects and as cross-references to the same subjects treated at greater length and in greater depth in the MACROPAEDIA. Such an entry (*e.g.,* "**radar**") begins with a definition of the subject and then provides the following cross-reference: "A brief treatment of radar follows. For full treatment, *see* MACROPAEDIA: Measurement and Observation."

Entries on certain broad subjects (*e.g.,* "**music**") direct the reader to several relevant articles in the MACROPAEDIA and also to the PROPAEDIA for listings of related articles in the MICROPAEDIA.

Abbreviations. Abbreviations used in the MICROPAEDIA are given in a list that appears at the end of every MICROPAEDIA volume.

a-ak (ancient East Asian music): *see* gagaku.

a cappella (Italian: "in the church style"), performance of a polyphonic (multipart) musical work by unaccompanied voices. The term is often associated with the church-music style of the 15th and 16th centuries, although such music was by no means always sung without instrumental doubling of or substitution for the voices.

A-ch'eng, Pinyin ACHENG, formerly (until 1909) ASHIHHO, city in Heilungkiang Province (*sheng*), China. It is a county (*hsien*) seat in Sung-hua-chiang Prefecture (*ti-ch'ü*). Located southeast of Harbin (Ha-erh-pin) in the basin of the A-shih Ho (river), it is a collecting and commercial centre for a rich agricultural district that supplies part of Harbin's food supply. A-ch'eng is also an industrial centre with brickworks, engineering works specializing in electrical equipment and other machinery, and various industries based on local agricultural production, such as breweries, sugar refineries, and a flax-processing plant. A-ch'eng also developed a small iron industry in the late 1950s. Most of its industries are closely integrated with those in Harbin, of which it is virtually a satellite city.

To the south of A-ch'eng are the remains of an ancient walled city known as Pai-ch'eng, or Pei-ch'eng, which is thought to be the remains of Hui-ning, the capital of the Chin (Juchen) dynasty from 1122 to 1234 and a subsidiary capital after 1173. Pop. (mid-1970s est.) 50,000–100,000.

A-erh-chin Mountains, also called ALTYN TAGH, Wade–Giles romanization A-ERH-CHIN SHAN, Pinyin ALTUN SHAN, mountain range in southern Sinkiang Uighur Autonomous Region, China. Branching off from the great Kunlun Mountains at about longitude 84° E, the range runs from southwest to northeast to form the boundary between the Tarim Basin to the north and the minor basin of A-ya-k'o-k'u-mu Hu (lake) and the Tsaidam Basin areas of interior drainage to the south.

The range falls into three divisions. The southwest section, bordering the Kunlun, is extremely rugged and complex; some ranges and peaks rise to heights of more than 20,000 ft (6,100 m) and are covered with perpetual snows. The central portion, forming the border of the western Tsaidam Basin, is lower, averaging about 13,000 ft in height, and is much narrower. The eastern section, in which the range joins the Nan Shan (mountains), is again higher, with peaks of 16,500 ft; it is structurally more complicated, consisting of a series of short ranges, the axes of which gradually adapt to the main northwest-to-southeast axis of the Nan Shan system.

There are very few rivers, because the area is one of extreme aridity, particularly in its central section. In the west various small streams run off into the Takla Makan Desert in the north, into the A-ya-k'o-k'u-mu Hu to the south, or into the western Tsaidam Basin. The main pass is the Tang-chin Shan-k'ou at the eastern end, which is crossed by a motor road between eastern Sinkiang (via Kansu Province), the Tsaidam Basin, and the Tibetan Autonomous Region (via Tsinghai Province).

A-Ku-Ta (founder of Chin dynasty): *see* T'ai Tsu.

A-kuei, Pinyin AGUI (b. Sept. 7, 1717, China—d. Oct. 10, 1797, Peking), famous general and official during the middle years of the Ch'ing dynasty (1644–1912).

The scion of a noble family, A-kuei directed expeditions that quelled uprisings in the western provinces of Szechwan and Kansu, conquering Ili and Chinese Turkestan, areas on China's northwestern frontier that are today part of the Sinkiang Uighur Autonomous Region. In addition, he helped subjugate Burma, making it a Chinese tributary state, and directed the campaign to stabilize China's position on the recently conquered island of Taiwan. He was one of the Emperor's most trusted ministers, serving until his 80th year as a senior member of the government's administrative cabinets, the Grand Council and the Grand Secretariat.

A-mdo, also called MDO-SMAD, one of three regions into which the area of Central Asia inhabited by Tibetans is traditionally divided. During the 7th to the 9th centuries, the central Tibetan kingdom was extended until it reached the Tarim Basin on the north, China on the east, India and Nepal on the south, and Kashmir on the west. The newly-added dominions to the east and northeast were called Mdo-Khams. The A-mdo region, constituting the northeastern part of ethnic Tibet, reached from the Huang Ho (river) northeastward to Mchod-rten dkarpo (now in Kansu Province, China). It passed under Manchu control in 1724 following the suppression of a Mongol revolt and was officially incorporated into the Chinese provincial system as part of Tsinghai Province in 1928.

A-pao-chi, Pinyin ABAOJI, posthumous dynastic name LIAO T'AI TSU, Pinyin LIAO TAI ZU (d. 926, China), leader of the nomadic Mongol-speaking Khitan tribes who occupied the northwest border of China.

Elected to a three-year term as great khan of the Khitans, A-pao-chi refused to resign at the end of his three years but made himself king of the Khitan nation. After the deposition in 907 of the last T'ang ruler of China, A-pao-chi made himself emperor and by 916 had set up a Chinese-style dynasty, with his son as heir apparent. He organized his followers into fighting units known as *ordos* (similar to what Westerners later called a horde) and then joined 12 *ordos* into an administrative district.

In 926 in return for aiding the founder of the Later Chin dynasty (936–947) in the Chin ruler's conquest of North China, A-pao-chi was given the northeast corner of Hopeh Province, an area inside the Great Wall encompassing the present site of Peking. After the death of A-pao-chi, the Khitans began to take on further Chinese mannerisms, and in 947 they proclaimed the Liao dynasty (947–1125), naming A-pao-chi as their dynastic founder with the posthumous title of T'ai Tsu (Grand Progenitor).

A-p'i-ta-mo chü-she lun: *see* Abhidharmakośa.

a posteriori knowledge, in Western philosophy since the time of Kant, knowledge derived from experience, as opposed to a priori knowledge, which is independent of all particular experiences. *See* a priori knowledge.

a priori knowledge, in Western philosophy since the time of Kant, knowledge that is independent of all particular experiences, as opposed to a posteriori knowledge, which derives from experience alone. The Latin phrases *a priori* ("from the earlier") and *a posteriori* ("from the later") were used in philosophy originally to distinguish between arguments from causes and arguments from effects.

The first recorded occurrence of the phrases is in the writings of the 14th-century logician Albert of Saxony. Here an argument a priori is said to be "from causes to the effect" and an argument a posteriori to be "from effects to causes." Similar definitions were given by many later philosophers down to and including Leibniz, and the expressions still occur sometimes with these meanings in nonphilosophical contexts. Thus a man might be said to argue a priori if he inferred the guilt of an accused person from the fact that he had been convicted many times before. It should be remembered, however, that medieval logicians used the word "cause" in a wide sense corresponding to Aristotle's *aitia* and did not necessarily mean by *prius* something earlier in time. This point is brought out by the use of the phrase *demonstratio propter quid* ("demonstration on account of what") as an equivalent for *demonstratio a priori* and of *demonstratio quia* ("demonstration that, or because") as an equivalent for *demonstratio a posteriori.* Hence the reference is obviously to Aristotle's distinction, knowledge of the ground or explanation of something and knowledge of the mere fact.

It was probably their connection with this antithesis between necessity and fact that made the phrases a priori and a posteriori seem suitable for use in the context in which Kant employed them in his *Critique of Pure Reason.* What we claim to know without recourse to experience is always some necessary truth such as a theorem of mathematics, whereas that which is known only from experience is not seen to be necessary.

Although the use of a priori to distinguish knowledge such as that which we have in mathematics is comparatively recent, the interest of philosophers in that kind of knowledge is almost as old as philosophy itself. No one finds it puzzling that he can acquire information by looking, feeling, or listening, but philosophers who have taken seriously the possibility of learning by mere thinking have often considered that this requires some special explanation. Plato maintained in his *Meno* and in his *Phaedo* that the learning of geometrical truths was only the recollection of knowledge possessed in a previous existence when we could contemplate the eternal ideas, or forms, directly. Augustine and his medieval followers, sympathizing with Plato's intentions but unable to accept the details of his theory, declared that the ideas were in the mind of God, who from time to time gave intellectual illumination to men. Descartes, going further in the same direction, held that all the ideas required for a priori knowledge were innate in each human mind. For Kant the puzzle was to explain the possibility of a priori judgments that were also synthetic (*i.e.,* not merely explicative of concepts), and the solution that he proposed was the doctrine that space, time, and the categories (*e.g.,* causality), about which we were able to make such judgments, were forms imposed by the mind on the stuff of experience.

In each of these theories the possibility of a priori knowledge is explained by a suggestion that we have a privileged opportunity for studying the subject matter of such knowledge. The same conception recurs also in the very un-Platonic theory of a priori knowledge first enunciated by Thomas Hobbes in his *De Corpore* and adopted in the 20th century by the logical empiricists. According to this theory statements of necessity can be made a priori because they are merely by-products of our own rules for the use of words. In favour of this conventionalist view it may be said that any truth that we know a priori must indeed be certifiable by reference to the rules which determine the meanings of the words or other signs in which it is expressed. But it is by no means obvious that such rules are all arbitrary.

A&P: *see* Great Atlantic & Pacific Tea Company, Inc.

AA: *see* Alcoholics Anonymous.

AAA: *see* Agricultural Adjustment Administration; Amateur Athletic Association.

Aabenraa (Denmark): *see* Åbenrå.

Aachen, Dutch AKEN, French AIX-LA-CHAPELLE, city, Nordrhein-Westfalen *Land* (North Rhine-Westphalia state), northwestern

West Germany. Its municipal boundaries coincide on the west with the frontiers of Belgium and The Netherlands. It was a Roman spa, called Aquisgranum, and rose to prominence in the 8th century as the favourite residence of Charlemagne, becoming the second city of his empire and a centre of Western culture and learning. From the coronation of Otto I in 936 until the 16th century, most German kings were crowned at Aachen. Fortified in the late 12th century and granted municipal rights in 1166 and 1215, Aachen became a free imperial city *c.* 1250.

Elisenbrunnen, a spa, with Aachen cathedral in the background, Aachen, W.Ger.
Hans Huber

It began to decline in the 16th century because of its insecure position near the French frontier and its distance from the centre of the Holy Roman Empire. The coronation site was changed to Frankfurt am Main in 1562.

Aachen was the scene of several peace conferences, including those ending the War of Devolution (1668) and the War of the Austrian Succession (1748). Occupied by the French in 1794 and annexed by France in 1801, it was given to Prussia after the Congress of Vienna (1814–15). The Congress of Aix-la-Chapelle, sealed in 1818, was one of those that regulated the affairs of Europe after the Napoleonic Wars. The city was occupied for a period by the Belgians after World War I; it suffered severe damage in World War II and was the first large German city to fall to the Allies (Oct. 20, 1944).

The noteworthy medieval churches of St. Foillan, St. Paul, and St. Nicholas were demolished or heavily damaged in World War II, but there has been much reconstruction. The Rathaus (town hall), built *c.* 1530 on the ruins of Charlemagne's palace and containing the magnificent hall of the emperors, has been restored.

The cathedral suffered relatively little damage. It incorporates two distinct styles: the Palace Chapel of Charlemagne (built 790–805), modelled on S. Vitale at Ravenna, is Carolingian-Romanesque; and the choir (*c.* 1355) is Gothic. In the gallery (Hochmünster) around the chapel is the marble *Königsstuhl* (royal chair) of Charlemagne, long used for coronations. Charlemagne's tomb is marked by a stone slab over which hangs a bronze chandelier presented by Frederick I Barbarossa in 1168. The rich cathedral treasury contains examples of fine medieval workmanship and sacred relics that are displayed to pilgrims about every seven years.

Other notable landmarks are the Suermondt Museum of Art and the fountain, surmounted by a statue of Charlemagne, in the market square. The Aachen Museum of the International Press deals with newspapers from the 16th century on. There are numerous educational institutions, including the Rhenish-Westphalian Technical University, founded in 1870. The sulfur springs are much frequented; Schwertbad-Quelle, in the suburb of Burtscheid, is the warmest in Germany (169° F [76° C]).

Aachen is a rail hub and the industrial and commercial centre of a coal-mining region; almost every branch of the iron and steel industry functions in the vicinity. Other products include textiles, furniture, glass, machinery, and needles and pins. Pop. (1983 est.) 245,000.

Aaiún (Western Sahara): *see* El Aaiún.

Aakjær, Jeppe (b. Sept. 10, 1866, Aakjær, Den.—d. April 22, 1930, Jenle), poet and novelist, leading exponent of Danish regional literature and of the literature of social consciousness.

Aakjær grew up in the Jutland farming area and so was well aware of the harsh conditions endured by farm labourers in his country. His early novels deal primarily with this theme. As a young man he went to study in Copenhagen, earning his living as a proofreader and later as a journalist. *Vredens børn, et tyendes saga* (1904; "Children of Wrath: A Hired Man's Saga"), which is considered to be his most powerful novel, was a strong plea for the betterment of the farm labourer's lot. The book initiated much public discussion and helped lead the way to some minimal reforms. He was best known, however, for his poems, especially those collected in *Fri felt* (1905; "Free Fields") and *Rugens sange* (1906; "Songs of the Rye"). A number of modern Danish composers have set Aakjær's poems to music; his "Jens Vejmand" (music by Carl Nielsen) is virtually a modern folk song. Only a few of his poems have been translated into English.

Aalborg (Denmark): *see* Ålborg.

Aalen, city, Baden-Württemberg *Land* (state), southern West Germany, on the Kocher River, at the northern foot of the Schwäbische Alb (Swabian Alps), north of Ulm. It originated around a large Roman fort, much of which remains; nearby are the remains of the Roman *limes* (frontier wall). It became a free imperial city in 1360 and was severely damaged by fire in 1634. It passed to Württemberg in 1802. The old city hall dates from 1636 and the church of St. Nikolaus from 1765. The Limesmuseum of Roman relics was opened in 1964. In 1975 the adjoining city of Wasseralfingen was annexed to Aalen, enlarging it by nearly a third. A communications centre, Aalen also has metal, textile, and chemical industries. Pop. (1983 est.) 62,790.

Aʿālī an-Nīl, English UPPER NILE, *mudīrīyah* (province), Southern Region, central Sudan, bounded by an-Nīl al-Azraq province on the east, Ethiopia on the east and southeast, Junqalī province on the south, al-Buḥayrah province on the south and southwest, and Kurdufān al-Janūbīyah and al-Baḥr al-Abyaḍ provinces on the north. Covering an area of 45,231 sq mi (117,148 sq km), it was formed in 1975 from the northern part of the former province of the same name.

The southern boundary of Aʿālī an-Nīl province marks the end of as-Sudd region of enormous swamps produced by the Baḥr (river) al-Jābal. That river is joined from the west at Lake No by the Baḥr al-Ghazāl, and then flows eastward toward Malakāl. It is joined south of Malakāl by the River Sobat, which rises in the mountains of Ethiopia. Together these two rivers form the White Nile that flows northward through the province. Permanent swamps have been formed along the River Sobat.

Surface finds suggest settlements along the banks of the White Nile in Neolithic times. The rising Muslim Funj dynasty in northern Sudan, with its capital at Sennār, came into contact with the people of the area in the 16th century AD. Egyptian rule was established in the first quarter of the 19th century. Exploration of the southern Sudan, beginning in 1851, paved the way for the spread of both Islāmic and Christian influences. In 1881 a revolt against the Egyptians was led by al-Mahdī, a religious reformer and Sudanese political leader. The Mahdists ruled until 1898, when they were defeated by Anglo-Egyptian forces. Subsequently, the province was incorporated into the Anglo-Egyptian Condominium in 1899. In 1920 the province, which had been called Fashoda, was renamed the Upper Nile and became part of independent Sudan in 1956.

The vegetation in Aʿālī an-Nīl province consists of short grass, scattered large trees, and scrub acacia. Cattle raising dominates the economy. Subsidiary food crops such as *durra* (sorghum), corn (maize), and millet are raised, and spear fishing is practiced. Household industry produces dairy products, processed hides and skins, and leather goods. A road roughly parallelling the White Nile links Malakāl, the provincial capital, with ar-Rank. The population is mainly Nilotic including the Dinka, Nuer, Shilluk and Auak, and some Sudanic groups; the languages spoken are mostly Nilotic. Pop. (1976 est.) 550,000.

Aalsmeer, *gemeente* (municipality), Noord-holland *provincie* (province), western Netherlands, southwest of Amsterdam, on the Ring Canal and Westeinder Lake, a remnant of Haarlem Lake. The older part of the town is on peaty soil at about sea level, surrounded by polders with loamy soil 9–15 ft (3–5 m) below sea level. Once known for its eels, whence its name (*aal*, "eel"; *meer*, "lake"), it is the flower-growing centre of The Netherlands, with numerous nurseries, the largest flower auction in the world, and a state experimental station for floriculture. Blooms include carnations, roses, lilacs, freesias, chrysanthemums, and potted plants such as cyclamens and begonias. Many flowers are exported by air, and there is a thriving trade in seeds and nursery plants. Pop. (1983 est.) 20,477.

Aalst (Flemish), French ALOST, municipality, East Flanders province, north central Belgium, on the Dender River, southeast of Ghent. The town hall (begun in the middle of the 12th century), with its 52-bell carillon, is the oldest in Belgium, and its archives include 12th-century manuscripts. Ravaged by fire in 1360, the town hall was subsequently rebuilt and its 13th-century belfry restored in the 15th century. The first printing shop in the Low Countries was established there in 1473 by Thierry Martens (later a professor at the University of Louvain). The French took Aalst in 1667 during the War of Devolution that gave southern Flanders to France. The Germans occupied the town in both world wars. Industry is dominated by the manufacture of textiles, clothing, and textile machinery. The surrounding region supplies hops for long-established breweries. The unfinished Gothic St. Martin's Church (begun *c.* 1480) has vault paintings, a picture by Rubens, and a remarkable tabernacle (1605) containing sculptures executed by Hieronymus Duquesnoy the Elder. Pop. (1983 est.) mun., 78,068.

Aalto, (Hugo) Alvar (Henrik) (b. Feb. 3, 1898, Kuortane, Russian Fin.—d. May 11, 1976, Helsinki), Finnish architect, city planner, and furniture designer, whose international reputation rests on a distinctive blend of modernist refinement, indigenous materials, and personal expression in form and detail. His mature style is epitomized by the Säynätsalo, Fin., town hall group (1950–52).

Early work. Aalto's architectural studies at the Technical Institute of Helsinki in Otaniemi, Fin., were interrupted by the Finnish War of Independence, in which he participated. Following his graduation in 1921, Aalto toured Europe and upon his return began practice in Jyväskylä, in central Finland. In 1927 he moved his office to Turku, where he worked in association with Erik Bryggman until 1933, the year in which he moved to

Aalto, 1970

By courtesy of the Consulate General of Finland, New York City

Helsinki. In 1925 he married Aino Marsio, a fellow student, who served as his professional collaborator until her death in 1949. The couple had two children.

The years 1927 and 1928 were significant in Aalto's career. He received commissions for three important buildings that established him as the most advanced architect in Finland and brought him worldwide recognition as well. These were the Turun Sanomat Building (newspaper office) in Turku, the tuberculosis sanatorium at Paimio, and the Municipal Library at Viipuri (now Vyborg). His plans for the last two were chosen in a competition, a common practice with public buildings in Finland. Both the office building and the sanatorium emphasize functional, straightforward design and are without historical stylistic references. They go beyond the simplified classicism common in Finnish architecture of the 1920s, resembling somewhat the building designed by Walter Gropius for the Bauhaus school of design in Dessau, Ger. (1925–26). Like Gropius, Aalto used smooth white surfaces, ribbon windows, flat roofs, and terraces and balconies.

The third commission, the Viipuri Municipal Library, although exhibiting a similar dependence on European prototypes by Gropius and others, is a significant departure marking Aalto's personal style. Its spatially complex interior is arranged on various levels. For the auditorium portion of the library Aalto devised an undulating acoustic ceiling of wooden strips, a fascinating detail that, together with his use of curved laminated wood furniture of his own design, appealed both to the public and to those professionals who had held reservations about the clinical severity of modern architecture. The warm textures of wood provided a welcome contrast to the general whiteness of the building. It was Aalto's particular success here that identified him with the so-called organic approach, or regional interpretation, of modern design. He continued in this vein, with manipulation of floor levels and use of natural materials, skylights, and irregular forms. By the mid-1930s Aalto was recognized as one of the world's outstanding modern architects; unlike many of his peers, he had an identifiable personal style.

Finnish pavilions for two world's fairs (Paris, 1937; New York City, 1939–40) further enhanced Aalto's reputation as an inventive designer of free architectural forms. In these designs, both chosen in competition, he continued to use wood for structure and for surface effects. Also during this period, in 1938, the Museum of Modern Art in New York City held an exhibition of his work, showing furniture that he had designed and photographs of his buildings.

Aalto's experiments in furniture date from the early 1930s, when he furnished the sanatorium at Paimio. His furniture is noted for its use of laminated wood in ribbonlike forms that serve both structural and aesthetic ends. In 1935 the Artek Company was established by Aalto and Mairea Gullichsen, the wife of the industrialist and art collector, to manufacture and market his furniture. The informal warmth of Aalto's interiors is best seen in the much admired country home Villa Mairea, which he built for the Gullichsens near Noormarkku, Fin.

Mature style. The decade of the 1940s was not productive; it was disrupted by war and saddened by his wife's death. In 1952 he married Elissa Mäkiniemi, a trained architect, who became his new collaborator.

Aalto's commissions after 1950, in addition to being greater in number, were more varied and widely dispersed: a high-rise apartment building in Bremen (1958), a church in Bologna (1966), an art museum in Iran (1970). His continuing work in Finland, however, remained the measure of his genius. Many of his projects involved site planning of building groups. Two such projects were the master plans of colleges at Otaniemi (1949–55) and at Jyväskylä (1952–57). Aalto's experience in planning originated early with such industrial commissions as the Sunila cellulose factory (1936–39, extended 1951–54), which included workers' housing and was a triumph of comprehensive planning.

The single work that epitomizes Aalto's mature style is perhaps the Säynätsalo town hall group. Modest in scale in its forest setting, it nonetheless asserts a quiet force. Its simple forms are in red brick, wood, and copper, all traditional materials of Finland. Viewing it, a person feels the achievement of a perfect building, in that the essence of the time, the place, the people, and their purpose is brought into focus by the awareness of the architect.

Aalto received many honours. He was a member of the Academy of Finland (Suomen Aketemia) and was its president from 1963 to 1968; he was a member of the Congrès Internationaux d'Architecture Moderne from 1928 to 1956. His awards included the Royal Gold Medal for Architecture from the Royal Institute of British Architects (1957) and the Gold Medal from the American Institute of Architects (1963).

Assessment. Aalto, whose work exemplifies the best of 20th-century Scandinavian architecture, was one of the first to depart from the stiffly geometric designs common to the early period of the modern movement and to stress informality and personal expression. His style is regarded as both romantic and regional. He used complex forms and varied materials, acknowledged the character of the site, and gave attention to every detail of building. Aalto achieved an international reputation through his more than 200 buildings and projects, ranging from factories to churches, a number of them built outside Finland.

Aalto's preliminary plans were freely sketched, without the use of T-square and triangle, so that the unfettered creative urge for inventive shapes and irregular forms was allowed full play before functional relationships and details were resolved. The absence of theoretical rigidity revealed itself in his final designs, which happily retained the spontaneity and individuality of his early sketches. As a Swiss art historian expressed it, he dared "the leap from the rational–functional to the irrational–organic." Since Aalto's staff was small (some six to eight architects), all of the work bore the imprint of his personality.

Aalto wrote little to explain his work, but his architecture conveyed a variable, lively temperament, free from dogma and without monotony. His work was said to express the spirit of Finland and its people, primitive yet lyrical. His friendships with such artists as Fernand Léger, Jean Arp, and Constantin Brancusi may have nourished his fondness for curvilinear shapes. While his work was never compulsively innovative, neither was it static. His late designs showed an increased complexity and dynamism that some regarded as incautious. In particular, his work of the late 1960s and early 1970s was marked by splayed, diagonal shapes and clustered, overlapping volumes. Energy and imagination were ever present. (H.F.K.)

MAJOR WORKS. Turun Sanomat Building, Turku, Fin. (1930); Municipal Library at Viipuri, now Vyborg in the Russian Soviet Federated Socialist Republic (designed 1927, built 1930–35, destroyed 1943); Sulfate Paper Mill at Toppila, Fin. (1931); Sanatorium at Paimio, Fin. (1933); cellulose factory at Sunila, Kotka, Fin. (1936–39; extended 1951–54); Villa Mairea (Gullichsen House) near Noormarkku, Fin. (1938–39); sawmill at Varkaus, Fin. (1945); Baker House (senior dormitory), Massachusetts Institute of Technology, Cambridge, Mass. (1947–48); town hall group, Säynätsalo, Fin. (1950–52); House of Culture, Helsinki (1955–58); house for Louis Carré, Bazoches, Fr. (1956–58); church at Vuoksenniska, Imatra, Fin. (1956–58); Nordjyllands Kunstmuseum, Ålborg, Den. (1958–72); post and telegraph office, Baghdad (1958); Community Centre, Wolfburg, Ger. (1959–62); Community Centre, Seinäjoki, Fin. (1962; theatre added, 1967); Edgar J. Kaufmann Conference Rooms, Institute of International Education, New York City (1964–65); Mount Angel Abbey Library, near Salem, Ore. (1967–70); Finlandia Hall, Helsinki (1971, enlarged 1974); Taidemuseo, Jyväskylä, Fin. (1973, later called the Alvar Aalto Museum).

BIBLIOGRAPHY. A definitive review of Aalto's work, extremely well illustrated with photographs and plans, is the two-volume work edited by Karl Fleig: *Alvar Aalto* (1963) and *Alvar Aalto 1963–1970* (1971). A brief essay by Farederick Gutheim, *Alvar Aalto* (1960), contains descriptive and critical comments as well as many photographs. A similar book is George Baird, *Alvar Aalto* (1970). A substantial chapter on Aalto appears in Sigfried Giedion, *Space, Time and Architecture,* 5th ed. rev. (1967), and is an excellent critical treatment of Aalto's architecture. No purely biographical work exists.

Aarau, capital of Aargau canton, northern Switzerland, at the southern foot of the Jura Mountains, on the right bank of the Aare River, west of Zürich. Founded about 1240 by the counts of Kyburg, it passed to the Habsburgs in 1264 and was taken by the Bernese in 1415. In 1798 it became the capital of the Helvetian Republic. Notable landmarks include several 13th-century towers, the town church (1471), the town hall (1762), and a cantonal library, containing a Bible with marginal notes made by the religious reformer Huldrych Zwingli. To the northeast is the ruined Habsburg, or Habichtsburg (Hawk's Castle), the original home of the Habsburg family. The medieval Lenzburg castle, located east of Aarau, houses a historical museum and a conference centre. There is considerable industry in the newer parts; manufactures include electrical goods, bells, precision instruments, shoes, cotton textiles, and chemicals. The population is largely German speaking and nearly 75 percent Protestant. Pop. (1983 est.) 15,710.

aardvark, also called AFRICAN ANT BEAR (*Orycteropus afer*), heavily built mammal, ranging south of the Sahara in forest or plain, that constitutes the family Orycteropodidae and the order Tubulidentata. The name aardvark—Afrikaans for "earth pig"—refers to its stout, piglike body, up to 180 centimetres (6 feet) long, including the 60-cm tail. Its coat varies from glossy black and full to sandy yellow and scant. The aardvark has a long snout, rabbitlike ears, and short legs. The toes are long and equipped with large, flattened claws; the second and third toes are united by a web of tissue.

One young is born in summer. The aardvark

excavates a burrow, in which it rests by day. It ventures out at night to rip open ant and termite nests and rapidly lap up the routed insects, using its sticky 30-cm-long tongue. Although not aggressive, the aardvark can fend off such formidable attackers as lions and leopards by parrying with its claws.

Aardvark (*Orycteropus afer*)

Shostal—EB Inc.

Formerly classified with the true anteaters, sloths, and armadillos in the order Edentata, aardvarks differ from them and from all other mammals in having permanent teeth traversed by tubules that radiate from a central pulp cavity; hence, the ordinal name Tubulidentata.

The tubulidentate line may be 60,000,000 years old. Fossil relatives have been uncovered in the southwestern Soviet Union, the Aegean island of Samos, and southern France. The relationship of tubulidentates to other orders of mammals remains to be settled.

aardwolf (*Proteles cristatus*), African carnivore generally placed in the family Hyaenidae but separated by some authorities as the family Protelidae. The aardwolf, whose name in Afrikaans means "earth wolf," resembles a small striped hyena. It is yellowish with vertical black stripes and a bushy, black-tipped tail, and it bears a long, coarse mane of erectile hairs along the length of its back.

Aardwolf (*Proteles cristatus*)

Simon Trevor—Bruce Coleman Ltd.

It has longer front than hind legs, large ears, a pointed muzzle, and weak jaws and teeth. Length varies from 55 to 80 centimetres (22 to 32 inches) exclusive of the 20- to 30-cm tail.

The aardwolf lives in the dry, open parts of eastern and southern Africa. It is nocturnal, lives in a burrow, and feeds largely on termites. It is usually solitary but may forage in small packs. The litter generally consists of three or four young. The aardwolf is harmless and shy; when attacked, as by dogs, it emits a musky-smelling fluid and may fight.

Aare River, also spelled AAR, tributary of the Rhine and the longest stream (183 mi [295 km]) entirely within Switzerland; it drains an area of 6,865 sq mi (17,779 sq km). The river rises in the Aare Glacier of the Berner Alpen in Bern canton, below the Finsteraarhorn and west of the Grimselpass. Below the Handegg Falls, the Aare drains the Upper Aare Valley, and flowing north past Meiringen, the river cuts through the scenic Aare Gorge; after turning west, it expands into the glacial Lake Brienz. The river is canalized at Interlaken above its entry into Lake Thun, at the lower end of which the river flows northwest in a deeply entrenched valley and almost encircles the medieval core of the city of Bern. It turns west to Lake Wohlen and then flows north to Aarberg, where it is diverted west by the Hagneckkanal into Lake Biel. Continuing northeastward, the river parallels the foot of the Jura Mountains. Below Brugg, the Reuss and Limmat rivers join the Aare before it enters the Rhine River at Koblenz, W.Ger.

Aargau (German), French ARGOVIE, canton, northern Switzerland, bordering West Germany to the north and bounded by the half canton of Basel-Laandschaft and by Solothurn canton to the west, Luzern canton to the south, and Zug and Zürich cantons to the east. It has an area of 542 sq mi (1,405 sq km) and forms the northeastern section of the great Swiss Plateau between the Alps and the Jura Mountains, taking in the lower course of the Aare River, whence its name. Its valleys alternate with pleasantly wooded hills. In 1415 the region was taken by the Swiss Confederation from the Habsburgs, whose ancestral seat was near Aarau (*q.v.*), now the cantonal capital. Bern kept the southwestern portion. In 1798 the Bernese part became Aargau canton of the Helvetic Republic, and the remainder formed the canton of Baden. In 1803 the two halves (and Frick, ceded to the Helvetic Republic by Austria in 1802) were united and admitted to membership of the Swiss Confederation as Aargau canton.

One of the most fertile parts of Switzerland, it includes among its principal economic activities agriculture, dairying, fruit and cereal growing, and straw plaiting. Industries include electrical engineering, the manufacture of precision instruments, textiles, cement, and cigars, and the mining and refining of salt. Two nuclear power stations are in operation at Beznau. The picturesque landscape, ancient castles, and rich museums of the canton attract considerable tourist traffic, as do the hot springs at Schinznach Bad and Baden. The population is almost exclusively German-speaking with a small Protestant majority. Pop. (1983 est.) 459,077.

Aarhus (Denmark): *see* Århus.

Aarlen (Belgium): *see* Arlon.

Aaron (fl. *c.* 14th century BC), the traditional founder and head of the Jewish priesthood, who, with his brother Moses, led the Israelites out of Egypt. The figure of Aaron as it is now found in the Pentateuch is built up from several sources of traditions. In the Talmud and Midrash he is seen as the leading personality at the side of Moses. He has appeared in different roles in Christian thought.

Life. Aaron is described in the Old Testament book of Exodus as a son of Amram and Jochebed of the tribe of Levi, three years older than his brother Moses. He acted together with his brother in the desperate situation of the Israelites in Egypt and took an active part in the Exodus. Although Moses was the actual leader, Aaron acted as his "mouth." The two brothers went to the Pharaoh together, and it was Aaron who told him to let the people of Israel go, using his magic rod in order to show the might of Yahweh. When the Pharaoh finally decided to release the people, Yahweh gave the important ordinance of the Passover, the annual ritual remembrance of the Exodus, to Aaron and Moses. But Moses alone went up on Mt. Sinai, and he alone was allowed to come near to Yahweh. Moses later was ordered to "bring near" Aaron and his

Aaron, detail of a 3rd-century fresco from the synagogue at Doura-Europus, Syria; in the National Museum, Damascus

By courtesy of the Direction Generale des Antiquities et des Musees, Damascus

sons, and they were anointed and consecrated to be priests "by a perpetual statute." Aaron's sons were to take over the priestly garments after him. Aaron is not represented as wholly blameless. It was he who, when Moses was delayed on Mt. Sinai, made the golden calf that was idolatrously worshipped by the people.

Once a year, on Yom Kippur (the Day of Atonement), Aaron was allowed to come into the Holy of Holies, the most sacred part of the tabernacle, or sanctuary, in which the Hebrew tribes worshipped, bringing his offering. Together with his sister, Miriam, Aaron spoke against Moses because he had married a foreigner (a Cushite woman); but, as in the episode of the golden calf, the narrative tells how Aaron was merely reproved, though Miriam was punished, for the offense. In the rebellion of Korah the Levite, however, Aaron stood firmly at the side of Moses. According to Numbers 20, Aaron died on the top of Mt. Hor at the age of 123; in Deuteronomy 10, which represents another tradition, he is said to have died in Moserah and was buried there.

Aaron is a central figure in the traditions about the Exodus, though his role varies in importance. At the beginning he seems to be coequal with Moses, but after the march out of Egypt he is only a shadow at Moses' side. Moses is obviously the leading figure in the tradition, but it is also clear that he is pictured as delegating his authority in all priestly and cultic matters to Aaron and "his sons."

Aaron and the biblical critics. Scholars have long been aware that the figure of Aaron as it is now found in the Pentateuch, or first five books of the Old Testament, is built up from several sources or layers of traditions. According to Julius Wellhausen, a German biblical scholar, and his followers, the Yahwist source was the oldest one, followed in order by the Elohist, Deuteronomist, and Priestly code. Scholars have attributed the passages about Aaron to one or the other of these sources. Although their results differ, they do agree in ascribing about 90 percent of the material about Aaron to the Priestly source. According to Wellhausen, Aaron was not mentioned at all in the Yahwist narrative, but he may have been inserted by later redactors. It was Moses who was the hero of the priests before the exile, and it was Joshua, not Aaron, who officiated in the tabernacle.

Other scholars, such as Sigmund Mowinckel, believe that the narrative about the golden calf, which presents Aaron in an unfavourable light, was part of the ancient tradition in the Yahwist work, being the only passage in it that mentions him. This narrative, according to these scholars, originally came from the northern kingdom of Israel and described Aaron as the ancestor of the priests in northern Israel; later it was rewritten in a way defamatory to Aaron. But there are also features in the narrative that may indicate that a later source (or traditionist), the Elohist, tried to excuse Aaron and to put the main responsibility on the people. The Elohist narrator was credited with making Aaron the brother and helper of Moses, who stood at the side of Moses in the conflict with the Pharaoh and assisted him as a leader in battles and in the cult. It may also be the Elohist who provides the unfavourable story about Aaron's objection to Moses' wife. On the other hand, it seems to be the same narrator who mentions Aaron at the side of Moses in the revolt at Meribah, but here also Aaron, together with Moses, is actually reproached. There is reason to believe that Aaron was not mentioned in the Deuteronomist work by the original author but that his name has been added by a redactor. The main bulk of the traditions about Aaron and the frequent addition of "and Aaron" after the mention of Moses are found in the Priestly source, which was written at a time when the priests had a more dominant position in Judah than they had before the exile. By then Moses had ceased to be the hero of the priests, and Aaron had taken over that role.

Many modern scholars prefer to speak of traditions and layers of traditions where their predecessors spoke of sources, but, apart from this terminology, the view concerning Aaron has not greatly changed. There have been new attempts, however, to see the contrasting figures of Moses and Aaron in a new light. It has been suggested that the traditions about Moses represent a southern Judaean tradition, while the old traditions about Aaron originated in the northern kingdom. It has also been indicated that the traditions about Moses are primarily concerned with a prophet, while those about Aaron are connected with priesthood. There may be a kernel of truth in all these suggestions, as also in the theory of Ivan Engnell that Moses represents the royal ideology while Aaron stands for priesthood, and priesthood alone. The standing struggle between the king and the leading priests is reflected both in the laws and in the narratives of the historical books.

Aaron in later Jewish and Christian thought. Aaron continued to live as a symbol in Jewish religion and traditions, and the position of the priests was strengthened after the exile. Also, in the Qumrān sect, a Jewish community that flourished in the era immediately before and contemporary with the birth of Christianity, Aaron was a symbol for a strong priesthood, as can be seen from the Dead Sea Scrolls. At the end of time, men of the community should be set apart, as a select group in the service of Aaron. Only the sons of Aaron should "administer judgment and wealth," and according to the *Manual of Discipline* two messiahs were expected, one of Aaron, the priestly one, and one of Israel. According to a fragment found near Qumrān, the priest would have the first seat in the banquets in the last days and bless the bread before the Messiah of Israel. Here "the sons of Aaron" have the highest position.

In Talmud and Midrash (Jewish commentative and interpretative writings), Aaron is seen less as a symbol than as the leading personality at the side of Moses. The relationship between the two brothers is painted as prototypical in the *Haggada* ("Narrative"—the nonlegal parts of Talmud and Midrash). Rabbi Hillel, the great liberal sage, praised Aaron as peace loving, a man of goodwill, who wanted to teach his fellow men the Law.

In Jewish exegesis little is said about him, though he is mentioned as a man who created peace among men. Many attempts have been made to explain the episode of the golden calf. According to some exegetes, Aaron had to make the calf in order to avoid being killed. In the early 14th century, Gersonides explained that this would have been fatal not only for Aaron but even more for the people. Earlier, in the 11th century, Rashi contended that the calf was a symbol of the leader, Moses, who was at that time on the mountain. The relationship between Moses and Aaron is also discussed in the Talmud. Some traditionists have wondered why Aaron, and not Moses, was appointed high priest. The answer has been found in an indication that Moses was rejected because of his original unwillingness when he was called by Yahweh. It also seems to have been hard for some traditionists to accept that Aaron was described as older than Moses. The death of Aaron is related in the Midrash *Petirat Aharon.*

The first Christian communities admitted that Aaron, "the sons of Aaron," or "the order of Aaron" were symbols of the highest priesthood. But in the Letter to the Hebrews, Christ is described as a high priest according to the order of Melchizedek, which was set against "the order of Aaron." Of the Church Fathers, Cyril of Alexandria says that Aaron was divinely called to a priesthood in spirit and in truth and that he was a type of Christ. Gregory the Great translates the name Aaron as "mountain of strength" and sees in him a redeemer who mediated between God and man. (A.S.K.)

BIBLIOGRAPHY. F.S. North, "Aaron's Rise in Prestige," in *Zeitschrift für die alttestamentliche Wissenschaft,* 66:191–199 (1954), is a short paper discussing Aaron's position; Roland De Vaux, *Les Institutions de l'Ancien Testament,* 2 vol. (1958–60; *Ancient Israel: Its Life and Institutions,* 2nd ed., 1965), a comprehensive work, also gives a picture of Aaron and his place in ancient Israelite life and cult. Walter Beyerlin, *Herkunft und Geschichte der Ältesten Sinaitraditionen* (1961; *Origins and History of the Oldest Sinaitic Traditions,* 1966), is mostly concerned with the traditions behind the story of Moses and Aaron. Harold H. Rowley, *Worship in Ancient Israel* (1967), gives a picture of religious life in Israel, including Aaron and his role. Bertil Gärtner, *The Temple and the Community in Qumran and the New Testament* (1965), treats the religious cult in the Qumrān society, in which "Aaron" was synonymous with the chief priest.

Aaron, Hank, byname of HENRY LOUIS AARON (b. Feb. 5, 1934, Mobile, Ala., U.S.), U.S. professional baseball player who, during 23 seasons in the major leagues, surpassed batting records that had been set by some of the greatest hitters in the game, including Babe Ruth, Ty Cobb, and Stan Musial.

Aaron, a righthander six feet tall and weighing 180 pounds, began his professional career in 1952, playing a few months as a shortstop with the Indianapolis Clowns of the Negro American League. His contract was bought by the Boston Braves of the National League, who assigned him to minor-league teams, first at Eau Claire, Wis., then at Jacksonville, Fla. He joined the Braves, who meanwhile had moved to Milwaukee, in 1954, thereafter playing mostly as an outfielder. In 1956 he won the league batting championship with an average of .328 and in 1957, leading his team to victory in the World Series, was named the league's most valuable player. Before the Braves moved to Atlanta, at the end of 1965, Aaron had hit 398 home runs. In Atlanta on April 8, 1974, he hit his 715th, breaking Babe Ruth's record, which had stood since 1935. After the 1974 season, he was traded to the Milwaukee Brewers of the American League. After the 1976 season, Aaron retired as a player and rejoined the Atlanta Braves as vice president in charge of player development and scouting. He was elected to the Baseball Hall of Fame on Jan. 13, 1982.

Hank Aaron
Pictorial Parade

Aaron's batting records include totals of 755 home runs, 1,477 extra-base hits, 2,297 runs batted in, and 12,364 times at bat in 3,298 games. His hits (3,771) and runs scored (2,174) were exceeded only by Ty Cobb. Aaron's lifetime batting average was .305.

Consult the INDEX *first*

Aaron ben Elijah (b. 1328/30, Nicomedia, Ottoman Empire—d. 1369), theologian of Constantinople (now Istanbul), the only scholar to seek a philosophical basis for Karaite beliefs. Karaism, a Jewish movement originating in 8th-century Persia, rejected the oral tradition and challenged the authority of the Talmud, the rabbinical compendium of law, lore, and commentary.

Aaron ben Elijah's views are summarized in his compilation of Karaite lore, in three books. In the first book, *'Etz ḥayyim* (1346; "Tree of Life"), modelled after the 12th-century Jewish philosopher Maimonides' *More nevukhim* ("Guide of the Perplexed"), he attempts to create a Karaite counterpart to Maimonides' Aristotelian outlook. In the second book, *Gan Eden* (1354; "The Garden of Eden"), he attempts to justify the Karaite code of law. The third book, *Keter Torah* (1362; "Crown of Law"), is a commentary on the Pentateuch, based on literal interpretations of the text.

Aaronic priesthood, in the Church of Jesus Christ of Latter-day Saints, the lesser of the two categories of priests, concerned principally with church finances and administration. *See* Mormon.

Aasen, Ivar (Andreas) (b. Aug. 5, 1813, Sunnmøre, Nor.—d. Sept. 23, 1896, Kristiania), language scholar and dialectologist, who constructed Landsmål (now called Nynorsk, or New Norwegian), one of the two official languages of Norway.

After learning Old Norwegian, Aasen surveyed the contemporary Norwegian dialects, which he judged to be the true offshoots of Old Norwegian, rather than the Danish-influenced written language of Norway. The results of his research were published in *Det norske folkesprog grammatik* (1848; "Grammar of the Norwegian Dialects") and *Ordbog over det norske folkesprog* (1850; "Dictionary of the Norwegian Dialects"), texts that prepared the way for the wide cultivation of Landsmål. Believing that the proper literary language for Norway's writers should be more purely Norwegian than the official Dano-Norwegian, Aasen composed poems and plays in his composite dialect and continued to enlarge and improve his grammar and dictionary. In 1864 his definitive grammar was published, followed in 1873 by the definitive dictionary of Landsmål. With certain modifications, the language Aasen constructed, which bears the most resemblance to Norway's western dialects, rapidly gained national importance, eventually achieving co-official status with Dano-Norwegian. Quite early in his career (1842) Aasen received a stipend to enable him to give his entire attention to his linguistic investigations.

AATUF: *see* All-African Trade Union Federation.

AAU: *see* Amateur Athletic Union of the United States.

ABA: *see* American Basketball Association.

Aba, town, Imo State, southern Nigeria, on the west bank of the Aba River, at the intersection of roads from Port Harcourt, Owerri, Umuahia, Ikot Ekpene, and Ikot Abasi (Opobo). Aba was a traditional market town for the Ibo people of the tropical rain forest before the establishment of a British military post there in 1901. With the construction of the railway in 1915 from Port Harcourt (36 mi [58 km] southwest), it became a major collecting point for agricultural produce (especially palm oil and palm kernels). Aba was the site of the Women's Riot against taxes in 1929. By the 1930s it was a settled urban community and is now the state's largest industrial and commercial centre. An 18.5-mi pipeline from the Imo River natural-gas field provides power for Aba's industrial estate, which lies north of the town between the river and the railroad sidings. Textiles, pharmaceuticals, soap, plastics, cement, footware, and cosmetics are manufactured. There are also a brewery and a distillery. Aba is the seat of a school of arts and science, secondary schools, a teacher-training college, and several technical and trade institutes. It has a government general hospital with a school of nursing, a psychiatric hospital, a school of hygiene, the Aba Institute of Child Health, and private hospitals. The town is noted for its handicrafts, has a television station, and is the headquarters of a local government council. Pop. (1983 est.) 216,000.

abaca (*Musa textilis*), plant of the family Musaceae, and its fibre, second in importance among the leaf fibre (*q.v.*) group. Abaca fibre, unlike most other leaf fibres, is obtained from the plant leaf stalks (petioles). Although sometimes known as Manila hemp, Cebu hemp, or Davao hemp, the abaca plant is not related to true hemp.

The plant, native to the Philippines, achieved importance as a source of cordage fibre in the 19th century. In 1925 the Dutch began cultivation in Sumatra, and the U.S. Department of Agriculture established plantings in Central America. A small commercial operation was started in British North Borneo (now Sabah, part of Malaysia) in 1930. During World War II, with Philippine abaca no longer available to the Allies, American production greatly increased.

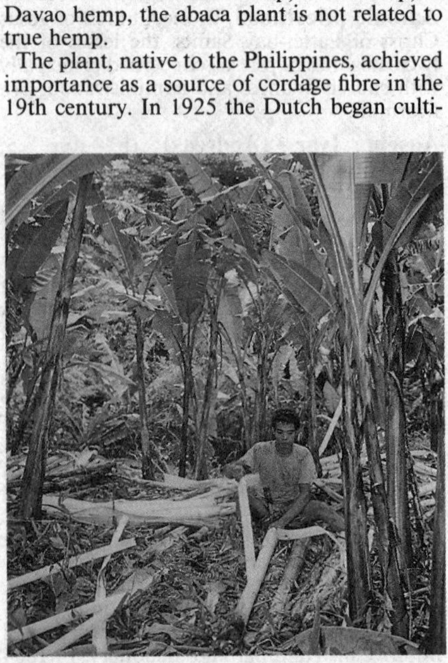

Stripping fibre from abaca (*Musa textilis*) in the Philippines

Charles W. Miller—Shostal Associates/EB Inc.

The plant, closely related to and resembling the banana plant (*Musa sapientum*), grows from rootstock that produces up to about 25 fleshy, fibreless stalks, forming a circular cluster called a mat, or hill. Each stalk is about 2 inches (5 centimetres) in diameter and produces about 12 to 25 leaves with overlapping leaf stalks, or petioles, sheathing the plant stalk to form a herbaceous (nonwoody) false trunk, about 12 to 16 inches in diameter. The oblong, pointed leaf blade topping each petiole is bright green on the upper surface and yellowish green below and grows to about 3 to 8 feet (1 to 2.5 metres) in length and 8 to 12 inches in width at its widest portion.

The first petioles grow from the plant stalk base; others develop from successively higher points on the stalk, so that the oldest leaves are on the outside and the youngest on the inside, extending to the top, which eventually reaches a height of 15 to 25 feet. The position of the petiole determines its colour and the colour of the fibre it yields, with outer sheaths being darkest and inner sheaths lightest. When the plant stalk has its full complement of sheathing petioles, a large flower spike emerges from its top. The small flowers, cream to dark rose in colour, occur in dense clusters; the inedible, banana-shaped fruits, about 3 inches long and $^3/_4$–1 inch in diameter, have green skins and white pulp; the seeds are fairly large and black.

Plants grow best in fairly rich, loose, loamy soil, with good drainage, and at elevations below 1,500 feet. Suitable temperatures average 80° to 85° F (27° to 29° C), not falling below 70° F (21° C); desirable rainfall is evenly distributed, averaging 100 to 110 inches per year; and winds must be gentle to avoid toppling the shallow-rooted plants. Propagation is mainly from pieces of mature rootstock, planted 8 to 10 feet apart, usually at the start of the rainy season. Within 18 to 24 months after planting, two to three of the plant stalks in each mat are ready for harvesting, and two to four stalks can be harvested at intervals of four to six months thereafter. The stalk, with its surrounding petioles, is cut off close to the ground, usually at the time of blossoming. Petiole size and number increase as the plant grows older, reaching a maximum in the sixth year and beginning to decline in the eighth. Plants are generally replaced within 10 years.

In the Philippines the fibre-bearing outer layer is usually removed from the petiole by a tuxying operation in which strips, or tuxies, are freed at one end and pulled off. In the cleaning operation that follows, pulpy material is scraped away by hand or machine, freeing the fibre strands, which are dried in the sun. In machine decortication, widely practiced in Central America, the stalks, cut into lengths of 2 to 6 feet, are crushed and scraped by machine, and the fibre strands are dried mechanically.

The strands average 3 to 9 feet in length, depending upon petiole size and the processing method employed. The lustrous fibre ranges in colour from white through brown, red, purple, or black, depending upon plant variety and stalk position; and the strongest fibres are obtained from the outer sheaths.

Abaca fibre, valued for its strength, flexibility, buoyancy, and resistance to damage in saltwater, is chiefly employed for ships' hawsers and cables, fishing lines, hoisting and power-transmission ropes, well-drilling cables, and fishing nets. Some abaca is used in carpets, table mats, and paper. Inner fibres can be used without spinning to manufacture lightweight, strong fabrics, mainly used locally for garments, hats, and shoes.

abacus, plural ABACI, or ABACUSES, calculating device, probably of Babylonian origin, long important in commerce, and the ancestor of the modern calculating machine and computer.

The word is probably derived, through its Greek form *abakos,* from a Semitic word such as the Hebrew *ibeq* ("to wipe the dust"; noun *abaq,* "dust"). The sand ("dust") surface, apparently used for general writing purposes, probably evolved into the board marked with lines and equipped with counters whose positions indicated numerical values—*i.e.,* ones, tens, hundreds, and so on. In the Roman abacus the board was given grooves to facilitate moving the counters in the proper files. Another form, common today, has the counters strung on wires.

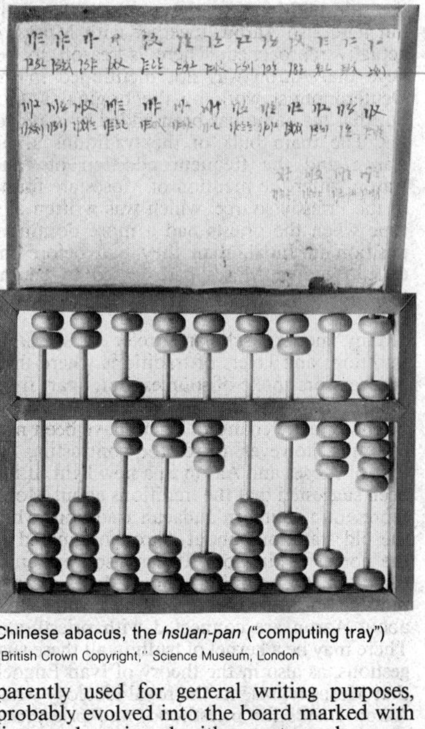

Chinese abacus, the *hsüan-pan* ("computing tray")

"British Crown Copyright," Science Museum, London

In the Chinese abacus shown, each of the two beads in the upper section of the frame represents five units, and each of the five beads in the lower section one unit (of the numerical order represented by the file). In performing addition, appropriate beads are moved to the dividing bar. The number represented on the bar in the picture is 7,230,189.

The abacus, generally in the form of a large calculating board, was in universal use in the Middle Ages throughout the European and Arab worlds as well as in Asia. It reached Japan in the 16th century. The introduction of the Hindu-Arabic notation, with its place value and zero, gradually replaced the abacus, though it was still widely used in Europe as late as the 17th century and survives today in the Middle East and Japan; an expert practitioner can compete against many modern mechanical calculating machines.

Abadan, Persian ĀBĀDĀN, Arabic ʿABBĀDĀN, city, Khūzestān *ostān* (province), Iran, on an island of the same name in the Shatt (river) al-Arab, 33 mi (53 km) from the Persian Gulf. Reputedly founded by a holy man, ʿAbbād, in the 8th century, Abadan was a prosperous coastal town in the ʿAbbāsid period, known for its salt and woven mats. The extension of the delta of the Shatt al-Arab by silt deposition caused the gulf to recede. By the time the town was visited by the Arab geographer Ibn Baṭṭūṭah in the 14th century, it was described as little more than a large village in a flat, salty plain.

Persia and the Ottomans long disputed its

Oil refineries, Abadan, Iran
Charles Lenars

possession, but Persia acquired it in 1847. Its village status remained unchanged until 1909, when the Anglo-Persian Oil Company (its Iranian properties nationalized in 1951 as the National Iranian Oil Company) established its pipeline terminus refinery there. There was fighting between the local people and Iranian troops in 1978. During Iran–Iraq hostilities, the oil refineries were bombed and the city was encircled by Iraqis in 1980. With an economy that has been centred on petroleum refining and shipping, Abadan is served by pipelines from oil fields to the north; pipelines have been constructed also to Tehrān and to Shīrāz. Abadan also has an international airport. The city has several well-built compounds for the oil company's staff, which contrast with a lively local bazaar and poor housing quarters for unemployed immigrants. Abadan has a museum, with a collection illustrating Iranian history, and the Abadan Institute of Technology (1939). Pop. (1976) 296,081.

Abae, ancient town in the northeast corner of Phocis, Greece, where one of the oracles of Apollo was consulted by the Lydian king Croesus. Although the Persians sacked and burned the temple in 480 BC, the oracle was still consulted; *e.g.,* by the Thebans before the Battle of Leuctra (371 BC). The temple, burned again during the Sacred War (355–346 BC), was partly restored by the Roman emperor Hadrian. Ruins of the town walls and the acropolis remain on the town's site.

Abaha (people): *see* Ha.

Abahai, reign titles (Wade–Giles romanization) T'IEN-TS'UNG and CH'UNG-TE (b. Nov. 28, 1592, Manchuria—d. Sept. 21, 1643, Manchuria), Manchurian tribal leader who, in 1636, became emperor of the Manchus, Mongols, and Chinese in Manchuria and, for his family, adopted the name of Ch'ing.

Abahai was the eighth son of Nurhachi (1559–1626), the great Manchu leader who extended his people's rule over the tribes of the Inner Asian steppes and organized his tribesmen into a bureaucratic Chinese-style state. Soon after his father's death, Abahai eliminated his brothers as rivals and consolidated his personal rule. He was successful largely because of his extraordinary ability as a military leader. He led armies into Inner Mongolia and Korea and made those countries vassal states of the Manchus. With the increased monetary and food supplies available from Korea and with the additional manpower and horses from the Mongols, he perfected the military machine known as the Eight Banners. After four expeditions he finally occupied the formerly Chinese-controlled Amur region of northern Manchuria and three times broke through the Great Wall on raids into North China.

As more Chinese were captured and taken into Manchu service, the government was able to duplicate more exactly the organizational structure of its Chinese counterpart. Thus other talented Chinese were induced to join. On the advice of his Chinese advisers, Abahai changed his dynastic name from Chin to Ch'ing (Pure) and began the conquest of China. Although he died before his goal was realized, his reign greatly strengthened the foundations of Manchu rule. A year after his death the Manchus conquered Peking, the capital of China's Ming dynasty, and a short time later subdued the remainder of the country.

Abaiang Atoll, also spelled APAIANG, also called APIA, formerly CHARLOTTE ISLAND, coral atoll of the Gilbert Islands, part of Kiribati, in the west central Pacific Ocean. Comprising six islets in the northern Gilberts with a total land area of 6 sq mi (16 sq km), the atoll has a lagoon (16 mi by 5 mi) that provides sheltered anchorage. Capt. Thomas Gilbert, its European discoverer (1788), named it Matthew's Island, after the owner of his ship, the "Charlotte." He called the lagoon Charlotte Bay and the main islet Point Charlotte. Subsequent errors in identification led to the island's being known as Charlotte Island. The area's first influential missionary, the American Hiram Bingham, arrived there in 1857. The atoll, occupied by the Japanese in 1941–43, was subsequently used by U.S. forces as a base for attacking the Marshall Islands. The administrative centre and main village is Taburao. Copra is exported. Pop. (1983 est.) 3,775.

Abailard, Pierre (theologian): *see* Abelard, Peter.

Abakaliki, town, Anambra State, southeastern Nigeria, at the intersection of roads from Enugu, Afikpo, and Ogoja. An agricultural trade centre (yams, cassava, rice, and palm oil and kernels) for the Ibo people, the town lies in an area known for its lead, zinc, and limestone deposits. Although lead has been mined since precolonial times, the deposits are worked only when the world market price is high. Limestone is quarried for the cement plant at Nkalagu, 22 mi (35 km) west-northwest. The town has several hospitals and secondary schools. It is the headquarters of a local government council. Its government farm promotes egg and poultry production. Pop. (1983 est.) 51,400.

Abakan, formerly (until 1931) UST-ABAKANSKOE, city and administrative centre of Khakass autonomous *oblast* (region), south central Russian Soviet Federated Socialist Republic, on the left bank of the Abakan River near its confluence with the Yenisey. The starting point of a southern Siberian railway line (opened in 1960), it is connected with Novokuznetsk and thence to Barnual, Akmolinsk, and Magnitogorsk. The city has metalworking, footwear, and food-processing industries, and coal and iron ore are mined in the vicinity. The construction of a dam and hydroelectric station on the Yenisey, upstream from Abakan, was expected to make the city the centre of a huge industrial region. Pop. (1982 est.) 140,000.

abalone, any of several marine snails of the subclass Prosobranchia (class Gastropoda) comprising the genus *Haliotis* and family Haliotidae, in which the dishlike shell has a row of holes on the outer edge. The large foot of the abalone is eaten as a steak. Abalones frequent the coasts of the northern Pacific Ocean, Australia, and South Africa. Largest is the 30-centimetre (12-inch) red abalone (*H. rufescens*) of the U.S. western coast.

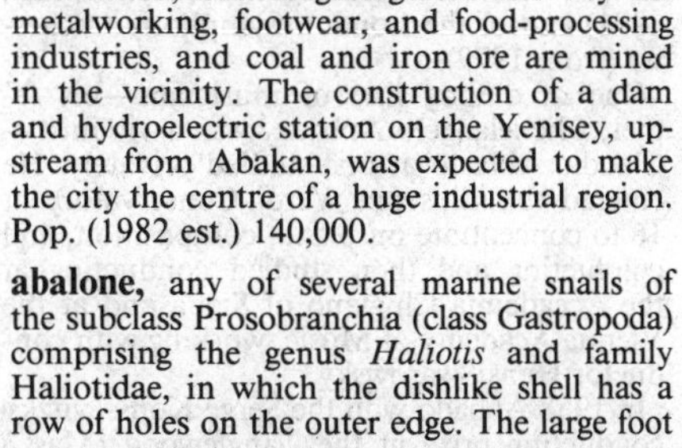

Abalone (*Haliotis*)
Jacques Six

Abancay, capital of Abancay province and of Apurímac department, southern Peru, on the eastern bank of the Río Marino at 7,798 ft (2,377 m) above sea level, in a cool, dry intermontane basin. The exact date of the founding of Abancay (from the Quechua Indian *amankay,* the name of a wild flower similar to a white lily) is unknown, but it was a leading commercial centre during the colonial era (1533–1821). Proclaimed a town in 1873, it was given city status in 1874. In addition to its political, religious, and commercial significance, Abancay is the agricultural and industrial centre of much of Apurímac. The growing and milling of sugar, liquor and rum distilling, copper mining, and sericulture are important.

About 300 mi (480 km) east-southeast of Lima, Abancay is fairly isolated; roads link it to the Andean cities of Ayacucho and Cuzco and to the coastal Pan-American Highway at Nazca. Pop. (1981 prelim.) city, 19,807; province, 61,863.

abandonment, in Anglo-American property law, the relinquishment of possession of property with an intent to terminate all ownership interests in that property. Abandonment may occur by throwing away the property, by losing it and making no attempt to retrieve it, by vacating the property with no intention of returning to it, or by any other act manifesting a complete disclaimer of ownership in the property. The general effect of abandonment is to give full ownership of the property to the first taker.

In the French and civil-law systems, the term abandonment is more technical and means the surrender by a debtor of his property to be used in satisfaction of claims by his creditors.

Abaoji (Mongol ruler): *see* A-pao-chi.

Abariringa Atoll (Kiribati): *see* Kanton Atoll.

Abasiyanık, Sait Faik (b. 1907, Adapazarı, Ottoman Empire—d. May 11, 1954, Istanbul), short-story writer, a major figure in modern Turkish literature.

Educated in Constantinople and Bursa, he spent four years in France, from 1931 to 1935, mainly in Grenoble. On his return to Turkey, he began to publish his short stories in *Varlık* ("Existence"), the leading avant-garde periodical.

Abasiyanık's stories were written in a style new to Turkish literature; despite their formlessness and lack of a conventional story line, they convey in a single, compelling episode a wide range of human emotions. In 1936 he published his first volume of short stories, *Semaver* ("The Samovar"). A dozen others followed, including *Lüzumsuz adam* (1948; "The Useless Man"), *Kumpanya* (1951; "The Company"), and *Alemdağda var bir yilan* (1953; "There's a Snake at Alem Mountain"). He also wrote an experimental novel, *Bir takım insanlar* (1952; "A Group of People"), which was censored because it dealt strongly with class differences.

Abate, Niccolò dell' (Italian painter): *see* Abbate, Niccolò dell'.

abatement, in law, interruption of a legal proceeding upon the pleading by a defendant of a matter that prevents the plaintiff from going forward with the action at that time or in that form. Pleas in abatement raise such matters as objections to the place, mode, or time of the plaintiff's claim. At one time, abatement of proceedings in equity differed from abatement in law, in that the former merely suspended the action, subject to revival when the defect was cured, whereas the latter terminated it, although the plaintiff could start the action anew. The latter is now the more common usage.

The term abatement is also used in law to mean the removal or control of annoyance, as in nuisance or noise abatement.

Abauzit, Firmin (b. Nov. 11, 1679, Uzès, Fr.—d. March 20, 1767, Geneva), theologian remembered for his contribution to an updated French version of the New Testament and other religious writings.

In order to help Abauzit flee the religious tyranny that was taking root in France during the 17th century, his mother arranged his escape to Switzerland. In his later years,

Abauzit, detail of an oil painting by Robert Gardelle, 1741; in the Bibliothèque Publique et Universitaire, Geneva

By courtesy of the Bibliotheque Publique et Universitaire, Geneva; photograph, Jean Arlaud

he travelled extensively and visited Germany, the Netherlands, and England, and along the way he met such prominent people as Pierre Bayle and Isaac Newton. In 1723 Abauzit was offered a professorship at a university in Geneva, which he turned down, but in 1727 he accepted an offer to work as a librarian there. In the same year, he was made a Swiss citizen. His article "Apocalypse" was printed in the *Encyclopédie,* edited by Diderot, the French philosopher and man of letters.

Abāy (Africa): *see* Blue Nile River.

Abaza language, language spoken in the Karachay-Cherkess Autonomous Oblast in the western part of the northern Caucasus; Abaza is related to Abkhaz, Adyghian, Kabardian (Circassian), and Ubykh, which constitute the Abkhazo-Adyghian, or Northwest Caucasian, language group. These languages are noted for the great number of distinctive consonants and the limited number of distinctive vowels in their sound systems. Abaza, like Abkhaz, has no grammatical cases. Abaza is written as well as spoken.

Abba Mari ben Moses ben Joseph: *see* Astruc of Lunel.

ʿAbbādid DYNASTY, Muslim Arab dynasty of Andalusia that arose in Seville in the 11th century, in the period of the party kingdoms (*ṭāʾifahs*) following the downfall of the caliphate of Córdoba.

In 1023 the *qāḍī* (religious judge) Abū al-Qāsim Muḥammad ibn ʿAbbād declared Seville independent of Córdoba. His son ʿAbbād, known as al-Muʿtaḍid (1042–69), forcibly annexed the minor kingdoms of Mertola, Niebla, Huelva, Saltés, Silves, and Santa María de Algarve.

A poet and patron of poets, al-Muʿtaḍid also had a reputation for ruthlessness and cruelty; in 1053 he suffocated a number of Berber chiefs of southern Andalusia in a steam bath in Seville, then seized their kingdoms of Arcos, Morón, and Ronda.

The last member of the dynasty, the poet-king Muḥammad ibn ʿAbbād al-Muʿtamid (1069–95), made Seville a brilliant centre of Spanish Muslim culture. In 1071 he took Córdoba, maintaining a precarious hold on the city until 1075; he held it again, 1078–91, while Ibn ʿAmmār, his vizier and fellow poet, conquered Murcia.

The ʿAbbādids' position was weakened, however, by an outbreak of hostilities with the Castilian king Alfonso VI; Christian progress in Aragon and Valencia and the fall of Toledo (1085), together with pressure from religious enthusiasts at home, forced al-Muʿtamid to seek an alliance with Yūsuf ibn Tāshufīn of the Almoravid dynasty. Despite ʿAbbādid support of Ibn Tāshufīn at the Battle of az-Zallāqah in 1086, Ibn Tāshufīn later turned against his ally and besieged Seville; the city was betrayed by Almoravid sympathizers in 1091 after a heroic defense by al-Muʿtamid.

Abbadie, Antoine-Thomson d' and Arnaud-Michel d' (respectively, b. Jan. 3, 1810, Dublin—d. March 19, 1897, Pirinei, Italy; b. July 24, 1815, Dublin—d. Nov. 13, 1893, Urrugne, Fr.), French brothers, geographers and travellers who conducted extensive investigations of the geography, geology, archaeology, and natural history of Ethiopia.

Their expedition began when they landed at Mitsiwa (Massawa) in 1838 and ended when they returned to France in 1848. Antoine d'Abbadie published a classified list and description of 234 Ethiopian manuscripts (1859), topographical findings (1860–73), and part of a geography of Ethiopia (1890). He became involved in controversies regarding his geographical findings, but subsequent explorers proved that his statements were correct, though he erred in contending that the Blue Nile was the main headstream of the Nile. In 1873 he published, along with findings from his stay in Ethiopia, the results of a scientific mission to Brazil made in 1836.

Arnaud d'Abbadie, in addition to his main Ethiopian venture, visited the country again in 1853. A general account of the expedition that he undertook with his brother was included in his work *Douze ans de séjour dans la Haute Éthiopie* (1868; "Twelve Years in Upper Ethiopia").

Abbado, Claudio (b. June 26, 1933, Milan), Italian conductor and music director (from 1968) at La Scala and principal conductor of the Vienna Philharmonic Orchestra (from 1971) and of the London Symphony Orchestra (from 1979).

One of a long line of musicians—his father, Michelangelo Abbado, was a violinist—Claudio Abbado at first studied privately. He entered the Giuseppe Verdi Conservatory at 16 to concentrate on piano, composition, and conducting and then studied conducting at the Accademia Chigiano of Siena and at the Vienna Academy of Music, working with conductor Hans Swarowsky.

In 1958 Abbado won the Serge Koussevitzky conducting prize at the Tanglewood (Mass.) Festival and in 1963 the Dimitri Mitropoulos conducting prize. He made his British debut in 1965, leading the Hallé Orchestra in Manchester, and in 1966 he began his long association with the London Symphony Orchestra; he directed it regularly before he succeeded André Previn as principal conductor in 1979. Abbado often conducted at La Scala, Milan; during a visit of the La Scala company to Covent Garden in 1976, he received wide public and critical praise, especially for his performance of Verdi's opera *Simon Boccanegra.* He made many visits to the U.S., a long-time association with the Boston and Chicago symphony orchestras leading to a host of memorable concerts and albums.

Abbah Quṣūr (Tunisia): *see* Althiburos.

ʿAbbas, name of rulers grouped below by country and indicated by the symbol •.

EGYPT

•**ʿAbbās I** (b. 1813—d. July 13, 1854, Banhā, Egypt), khedive (viceroy) of Egypt under the Ottomans from 1848 to 1854. During his reign he deliberately opposed change, such as the Western-inspired reforms initiated by his grandfather Muḥammad ʿAlī Pasha (viceroy 1805–48).

ʿAbbās, distrustful of Europeans and European-educated Egyptians, reacted to the reforms of Muḥammad ʿAlī by closing down or neglecting the public and military schools and factories. He reduced the armed forces, stopped the construction of the Delta Dam, and opposed the construction of the Suez Canal that had been proposed by the French. He allowed the construction, however, of the Alexandria–Cairo Railway by the British, who in return assisted him in his dispute with the Ottoman government over the application of the Western-inspired reforms (*tanzimat*) in Egypt. Although he was opposed to the reforms, ʿAbbās showed his loyalty by sending an expeditionary force to assist the Ottomans in the Crimean War (1853); he also abolished the state trade monopolies, which had defied the Ottoman treaties with the European powers.

Although ʿAbbās' aversion to reforms won him the reputation of a reactionary, his curtailment of government spending benefitted the poorer classes, who received tax remissions and suffered less from compulsory labour and conscription into the army. A man of secretive nature, ʿAbbās lived in isolation in his palace at Banhā, where he was strangled by two of his servants.

•**ʿAbbās II,** also called ʿABBĀS ḤILMĪ PASHA (b. July 14, 1874, Alexandria—d. Dec. 20, 1944, Geneva), last khedive (viceroy) of Egypt, from 1892 to 1914, when British rule was established. His opposition to British hegemony over Egypt made him prominent in the nationalist movement.

At the beginning of his reign, ʿAbbās attempted to rule independently of Lord Cromer, the British agent and consul general in Egypt. Encouraged by popular discontent with the increasing British influence over Egypt and by the enthusiastic support of the nationalists, he appointed a prime minister who was well-known for his opposition to the British. When in 1894 he criticized the military efficiency of the British troops, Lord Cromer took steps to curb the Viceroy's independence of action.

After 1894, although ʿAbbās no longer headed the nationalist movement, he provided financial assistance to the pan-Islāmic and anti-British daily newspaper *al-Muʿayyad.* When in 1906 the nationalists demanded constitutional government for Egypt, however, ʿAbbās, now reconciled with the British, rejected their demands. The following year he agreed to the formation of the National Party, headed by Muṣṭafā Kāmil, to counter the Ummah Party of the moderate nationalists, which was supported by the British. With the appointment of Lord Kitchener as consul general (1912–14), the leaders of the National Party were exiled or imprisoned, and ʿAbbās' authority was curtailed.

At the beginning of World War I ʿAbbās issued an appeal to the Egyptians and the Sudanese to support the Central Powers and to fight the British. On Dec. 18, 1914, Britain declared Egypt its protectorate and deposed ʿAbbās the following day. His uncle Ḥusayn Kāmil (reigned 1914–17) replaced him and assumed the title of sultan. In 1922, when Egypt was declared independent, ʿAbbās lost all rights to the throne. He passed the rest of his life in exile, mainly in Switzerland.

PERSIA

•**ʿAbbās I,** byname ʿABBĀS THE GREAT (b. Jan. 27, 1571—d. Jan. 19, 1629), *shāh* of Persia from 1588 to 1629, who strengthened the Ṣafavid dynasty by expelling Ottoman and Uzbek troops from Persian soil and by creating a standing army. He also made Isfahan the capital of Persia and fostered commerce and the arts, so that Persian artistic achievement reached a high point in his reign.

ʿAbbās I, detail of a painting by the Mughal school of Jahāngīr, *c.* 1620; in the Freer Gallery of Art, Washington, D.C.

By courtesy of the Smithsonian Institution, Freer Gallery of Art, Washington, D.C.

Life. The third son of Solṭān Moḥammad Shāh, ʿAbbās came to the throne in October 1588, at a critical moment in the fortunes of the Ṣafavid dynasty. The weak rule of his semi-blind father had allowed the emirs, or chiefs, of the Turkmen tribes, who had brought the Ṣafavid to power and still constituted the backbone of Ṣafavid military strength, to usurp the authority of the *shāh.* Moreover, the intertribal factionalism of these Turkmens (known as Kizilbash [Red Heads] because of the distinctive red headgear they had adopted to mark their adherence to the Ṣafavids) had so weakened the state that its traditional enemies, the Ottoman Turks to the west and the Uzbeks to the east, had been able to make large inroads into Persian territory.

Shāh ʿAbbās thus had two immediate tasks: to reassert the authority of the monarchy and to expel Ottoman and Uzbek troops from Persian soil. Since he was unable to fight a war on two fronts simultaneously, in 1589–90 he signed a peace treaty with the Ottomans, thus freeing himself for an offensive against the Uzbeks. By the treaty, large areas in west and northwest Persia were ceded to the Ottomans. Despite the breathing space thus gained, ʿAbbās for 10 years was unable to launch a major offensive against the Uzbeks, and Iran suffered further loss of territory both to the Uzbeks and to the Mughals of India.

The delay was caused by ʿAbbās' decision to create a standing army—a concept novel to Ṣafavid kings, who traditionally levied armies in time of need from the tribal cavalry. The creation of a standing army immediately caused a budgetary problem, because the old tribal cavalry had been paid from the revenues of the provinces governed by Kizilbash chiefs. ʿAbbās solved the problem in the short term by bringing a number of these provinces directly under the control of the Shāh; the taxes in these new "crown" provinces were remitted to the royal treasury. In the long run the inevitable result of this policy, the reduction in the numbers of Kizilbash troops, seriously weakened the country's military strength.

The new standing army was composed mainly of Georgians, Armenians, and Circassians, who had been brought to Persia as prisoners during the reign of ʿAbbās' grandfather, and their descendants. After their conversion to Islām, they were trained for service either in the army or in the administration of the state or the royal household. Shāh ʿAbbās felt he could rely on the loyalty of these *ghulāms* ("slaves") of the *shāh,* as they were known, and he used them to counterbalance the influence of the Kizilbash, whom he distrusted. *Ghulāms* soon rose to high office and were appointed governors of crown provinces.

Eventually, ʿAbbās was able to take the offensive against his external foes. In 1598 he inflicted a major defeat on the Uzbeks and regained control of Khorāsān. From 1602 onward he conducted a series of successful campaigns against the Ottomans and recovered the territory lost to them.

After his great victory over the Uzbeks, ʿAbbās transferred the capital from Kazvin to Isfahan. Under his guidance, Isfahan rapidly became one of the most beautiful cities in the world. He adorned the city with many mosques and theological colleges and constructed numerous caravansaries and public baths. He laid out the city with spacious boulevards and a splendid square. The Shāh's building energies were not confined to Isfahan; the extension and restoration of the famous shrine at Meshed and the construction, along the swampy littoral of the Caspian Sea, of the celebrated stone causeway, designed to give access to his favourite winter retreats, were among his most notable achievements.

To Isfahan came ambassadors from European countries, merchants seeking to establish trade relations, representatives of foreign monastic orders seeking permission to found convents at Isfahan and elsewhere, and gentlemen of fortune, such as the brothers Sir Anthony and Sir Robert Sherley—the former an adventurer, the latter a loyal servant of the Shāh who distinguished himself in the wars against the Ottomans. The reign of Shāh ʿAbbās was a period of intense commercial and diplomatic activity, and, in the Persian Gulf, the Portuguese, the Dutch, and the English strove to make themselves masters of trade there and in the Indian Ocean.

ʿAbbās' reign also marks a peak of Persian artistic achievement. Under his patronage, carpet weaving became a major industry, and fine Persian rugs began to appear in the homes of wealthy European burghers. Another profitable export was textiles, which included brocades and damasks of unparalleled richness. The production and sale of silk was made a monopoly of the crown. In the illumination of manuscripts, bookbinding, and ceramics, the work of the period of ʿAbbās is without equal; in painting it is among the most notable in Persian history.

Assessment. Shāh ʿAbbās ruled with a passionate zeal for justice and the welfare of his subjects. He frequented teahouses and other meeting places of the ordinary people in order to learn of extortion and oppression on the part of his officials; his punishment of corrupt officials was swift. He showed unusual religious tolerance, granting privileges to many Christian groups.

The dark side of his character was reserved for his own sons and members of his own family. The experiences of his youth, when he was marked for execution by his uncle, Shāh Esmāʿīl II, had left him with a morbid fear of conspiracy. Originally, he followed the practice of his predecessors in appointing the princes of the blood royal as provincial governors, but after a series of revolts and intrigues in favour of his sons, the royal princes were confined to the harem, where their only companions were women and eunuchs. As his obsessive fear of assassination increased, ʿAbbās began to put to death or to blind any member of the royal family who caused him anxiety in this regard. In this way, one son was executed (an act that caused ʿAbbās bitter remorse) and two were blinded, and his father and brothers were blinded and imprisoned. ʿAbbās died without an heir capable of succeeding him.

Though ʿAbbās possessed great stature as a monarch—even in an age notable for its outstanding rulers—his great achievement in first saving the Ṣafavid Empire from collapse and then raising it to new heights of splendour is marred by his treatment of his own family and the fact that his reforms contained within them the seeds of the future decay of both dynasty and state. (R.M.Sa.)

BIBLIOGRAPHY. L.L. Bellan, *Chah ʿAbbâs I: sa vie, son histoire* (1932), the only biography of Shāh ʿAbbās I in any European language—generally accurate; R.M. Savory, "ʿAbbās I" in the *Encyclopaedia of Islam,* new ed., vol. 1, pp. 7–8 (1960); for general background to the period of Shāh ʿAbbās, the reader is referred to: J. Chardin, *Voyages du Chevalier Chardin,* 4th ed., 4 vol. (1811); Sir John Malcom, *The History of Persia from the Early Period to the Present Time,* 2 vol. (1815); and V. Minorsky, *Tadhkirat al-Mulūk* (1943), especially the introduction, commentary, and appendixes.

Abbas, Ferhat (b. Aug. 24, 1899, Taher, near Constantine, Alg.), politician and leader of the national independence movement who served as the first president of the Provisional Government of the Algerian Republic.

Ferhat Abbas

Camera Press Ltd.—Pictorial Parade/EB Inc.

Son of a Muslim official in the Algerian civil service, Abbas received an entirely French education at Philippeville (now Skikda) and Constantine and at the University of Algiers. After two years' service with the French Army, he became a pharmacist at Sétif and was elected first to the municipal council of Sétif and then to the general council in Constantine. Early in his political career, he advocated collaboration with the French, the assimilation of the "native element in French society," and the abolition of colonialism to bring about the emancipation of the Algerian Muslims as French citizens. Disillusioned by the French in 1938, he organized the Union Populaire Algérienne, which proposed equal rights for French and Algerians while preserving the Algerian culture and language. Nevertheless, at the outbreak of World War II, Abbas enlisted in the medical corps of the French Army.

On Feb. 10, 1943, the "Manifesto of the Algerian People," prepared by Abbas, was proclaimed. It was subsequently presented to the French and the Allied authorities in North Africa. The manifesto, which reflected a fundamental change in its author's political position, not only condemned French colonial rule but also called for the application of the principle of self-determination and demanded an Algerian constitution granting equality to all inhabitants of Algeria. In May, Abbas, along with a number of his colleagues, wrote an addendum to the manifesto, which envisioned a sovereign Algerian nation. It was presented to the French on June 26. On its rejection by the French governor general, Ferhat Abbas and an Algerian working-class leader, Messali Hadj, formed the Amis du Manifeste et de la Liberté (AML; Friends of the Manifesto and Liberty), which envisioned an Algerian autonomous republic federated to a renewed, anti-colonial

France. After the suppression of the AML and a year's imprisonment, in 1946 he founded the Union Démocratique du Manifeste Algérien (UDMA; Democratic Union of the Algerian Manifesto), which advocated cooperation with France in the formation of the Algerian state. Abbas' moderate and conciliatory attempts failed to evoke a sympathetic response from the French colonial officials, however, and in 1956 he escaped to Cairo to join the Front de Libération Nationale (FLN), an Algerian organization committed to revolutionary struggle for independence from France.

On Sept. 18, 1958, the Provisional Government of the Algerian Republic was formed with Ferhat Abbas as president. He resigned in 1961 but was elected president of the Algerian Constituent Assembly in 1962, when Algeria gained independence. Despite his political alliance with the revolutionary and Socialist FLN, he remained an exponent of parliamentary institutions and constitutionalism. To protest the drafting of the Algerian constitution by the FLN outside the Constituent Assembly, he resigned his post as the assembly's president in August 1963 and was expelled from the FLN. An opponent of the then-president, Ahmed Ben Bella, he was placed under house arrest in 1964 but was released the following year.

Ferhat Abbas described the Algerian War of Independence in *La Nuit coloniale* (1962; "The Colonial Night"). He is also the author of *Le Jeune Algérien: de la colonie vers la province* (1931; "The Young Algerian: From Colony to Province") and *Autopsie d'une guerre* (1980; "Autopsy of a War"). Further information about Ferhat Abbas may be found in David C. Gordon's *Passing of French Algeria* (1966) and Joan Gillespie's *Algeria: Rebellion and Revolution* (1960).

'Abbās Ḥilmī Pasha: *see* 'Abbās II (Egypt).

'Abbās Mīrzā (b. September 1789, Navā, Qājār Iran—d. Oct. 25, 1833, Meshed), crown prince of the Qājār dynasty of Iran who introduced European military techniques into his country.

Although he was not the eldest son of Fatḥ 'Alī Shāh (1797–1834), 'Abbās Mīrzā was named crown prince and appointed governor of the province of Azerbaijan in 1798 or 1799. When war broke out between Russia and Iran in 1804, he was made commander of the Iranian expeditionary force of 30,000 men. The war (1804–13) resulted in the loss of most of Iran's Georgian territory and showed 'Abbās Mīrzā the necessity of reforming the Qājār military forces. He began sending Iranian students to Europe to learn Western techniques; a first group was sent to England in 1811 and a second group followed in 1815. In 1812 a printing press was established in Tabriz, the capital of Azerbaijan, and the translation of European military handbooks was encouraged. A gunpowder factory and an artillery foundry were also started in Tabriz.

The new army was drilled by British military advisers, who taught such tactics as the use of infantry formations and close cooperation between infantry and artillery. This army distinguished itself in campaigns against the Ottoman Turks in 1821–23. During the second Russo-Iranian war (1826–28) 'Abbās Mīrzā again led the Iranian forces. In the first year of the war he was able to recapture all of Iran's lost territory; his new army, especially the artillery arm, was more than a match for the Russian troops. In the end, however, Russian numerical superiority and discipline, coupled with Fatḥ 'Alī Shāh's refusal to reinforce and replace 'Abbās Mīrzā's losses, led to a disastrous defeat. At the cessation of hostilities (1828), Iran had lost all its Georgian and Caucasian territories.

'Abbās Mīrzā was shattered by this defeat. He lost interest in military reform and spent the last five years of his life trying to maintain his own position as crown prince and feuding with his many brothers. Broken in spirit as well as in health, he died leading a punitive expedition against rebels in Khorāsān.

'Abbāsid DYNASTY, second of the two great dynasties of the Muslim Empire of the Caliphate. It overthrew the Umayyad caliphate in AD 750 and reigned as the 'Abbāsid caliphate until destroyed by the Mongol invasion in 1258.

The name is derived from that of the uncle of the Prophet Muḥammad, al-'Abbās (died *c.* 653), of the Hāshimite clan of the Quraysh tribe in Mecca. From *c.* 718, members of his family worked to gain control of the empire, and by skillful propaganda won much support, especially from Shī'ī Arabs and Persians in Khorāsān. Open revolt in 747, under the leadership of Abū Muslim, led to the defeat of Marwān II, the last Umayyad caliph, at the Battle of the Great Zāb River (750) in Mesopotamia and to the proclamation of the first 'Abbāsid caliph, Abū al-'Abbās as-Saffāḥ.

Under the 'Abbāsids the caliphate entered a new phase. Instead of focussing, as the Umayyads had done, on the West—on North Africa, the Mediterranean, and southern Europe—the caliphate now turned eastward. The capital was moved to the new city of Baghdad, and events in Persia and Transoxania were closely watched. For the first time the caliphate was not coterminous with Islām; in Egypt, North Africa, Spain, and elsewhere, local dynasties claimed caliphal status. With the rise of the 'Abbāsids the base for influence in the empire became international, emphasizing membership in the community of believers rather than Arab nationality. Since much support for the 'Abbāsids came from Persian converts, it was natural for the 'Abbāsids to take over much of the Persian (Sāsānian) tradition of government. Support by pious Muslims likewise led the 'Abbāsids to acknowledge publicly the embryonic Islāmic law and to profess to base their rule on the religion of Islām. Between 750 and 833 the 'Abbāsids raised the prestige and power of the empire, promoting commerce, industry, arts, and science, particularly during the reigns of al-Manṣūr, Hārūn ar-Rashīd, and al-Ma'mūn. Their temporal power, however, began to decline when al-Mu'taṣim introduced non-Muslim Berber, Slav, and especially Turkish mercenary forces into his personal army. Although these troops were converted to Islām, the base of imperial unity through religion was gone, and some of the new army officers quickly learned to control the caliphate through assassination of any caliph who would not accede to their demands.

The power of the army officers had already weakened through internal rivalries when the Iranian Būyids entered Baghdad in 945, demanding of al-Mustakfī (944–946) that they be recognized as the sole rulers of the territory they controlled. This event initiated a century-long period in which much of the empire was ruled by local secular dynasties. In 1055 the 'Abbāsids were overpowered by the Seljuqs, who took what temporal power may have been left to the caliph but respected his position as religious leader, restoring the authority of the caliphate, especially during the reigns of al-Mustarshid (1118–35), al-Muqtafī, and an-Nāṣir. Soon after, in 1258, the dynasty fell during a Mongol siege of Baghdad.

Abbate, Niccolò dell', Abbate also spelled ABATE (b. *c.* 1512, Modena, Duchy of Modena—d. 1571, Fontainebleau, Fr.), painter of the Bolognese school who, along with others, introduced the post-Renaissance Italian style of painting known as Mannerism to France and helped to inspire the French classical school of landscape painting.

He began his career in Modena as a student of the sculptor Antonio Begarelli. His "Martyrdom of St. Peter and St. Paul" in the church of S. Pietro, Modena (1547), probably established his reputation. During his stay in Bologna (1548–52), his style matured, influenced by his contemporaries Correggio and Parmigianino. His stucco-surface landscapes in the Poggi (now Palazzo dell'Università) survive to show his understanding of nature.

In 1552 Abbate was called to the court of the king of France, Henry II, at Fontainebleau, and remained in France for the rest of his life. With Francesco Primaticcio he composed immense murals, most of them later lost. His easel works, which included an enormous number of lyrical landscapes based upon pagan themes, were burned in 1643 by the Austrian regent, Anna. Among his later paintings executed for Charles IX were a series of landscapes with mythologies that influenced the 17th-century French painters Claude Lorrain and Nicolas Poussin. He also designed a series of tapestries, "Les Mois arabesques," and some of his designs were adopted by the painted enamel industry of Limoges. His last works are believed to be 16 murals (1571) in which he was assisted by his son, Giulio Camillo. His work in France is recognized as a principal contribution to the first significant,

"The Story of Aristaeus," oil painting by Niccolò dell'Abbate; in the National Gallery, London

By courtesy of the trustees of the National Gallery, London; photograph, A.C. Cooper Ltd.

wholly secular movement in French painting, the Fontainebleau style.

Abbazia (Yugoslavia): *see* Opatija.

Abbe, Cleveland (b. Dec. 3, 1838, New York City—d. Oct. 28, 1916, Chevy Chase, Md., U.S.), meteorologist who pioneered in the foundation and growth of the U.S. Weather Bureau, later renamed the National Weather Service.

Trained as an astronomer, he was appointed director of the Cincinnati (Ohio) Observatory in 1868. His interest gradually turned to meteorology, however, and he inaugurated a public weather service that served as a model for the national weather service, which was organized shortly thereafter as a branch of the Signal Service. In 1871 he was appointed chief meteorologist of the branch (which in 1891 was reorganized under civilian control as the U.S. Weather Bureau) and served in that capacity for more than 45 years.

Abbe, Ernst (b. Jan. 23, 1840, Eisenach, Grand Duchy of Saxe-Weimar-Eisenach—d. Jan. 14, 1905, Jena, Ger.), physicist whose theoretical and technical innovations in optical theory led to great improvements in microscope design (such as the use of a condenser to provide strong, even illumination, introduced in 1870) and clearer understanding of magnification limits. He discovered the optical formula now called the Abbe sine condition, one of the requirements that a lens must satisfy if it is to form a sharp image, free from the blurring or distortion caused by coma and spherical aberration.

In 1863 he joined the University of Jena, rising to professor of physics and mathematics (1870) and director of the astronomical and meteorological observatories (1878). In 1866 he became research director of the Zeiss optical works. Two years later Abbe invented the apochromatic lens system for microscopes, which eliminates both the primary and secondary colour distortion of light.

In 1891 Abbe set up and endowed the Carl Zeiss Foundation for research in science and social improvement. Five years later he reorganized the Zeiss optical works into a cooperative, with management, workmen, and the university sharing in the profits.

abbess, the title of a superior of certain communities of nuns following the Benedictine Rule, of convents of the Second Order of St. Francis (Poor Clares), and of certain communities of canonesses. The first historical record of the name is on a Roman inscription dated *c.* 514.

To be elected, an abbess must be at least 40 years old and a professed nun for at least 10 years. She is solemnly blessed by the diocesan bishop in a rite similar to that of the blessing of abbots. Her blessing gives her the right to certain pontifical insignia: the ring and sometimes the crosier.

In medieval times abbesses occasionally ruled double monasteries of monks and nuns and enjoyed various privileges and honours. *See also* abbot.

Abbeville, town, Somme *département,* Picardie region, northern France, near the mouth of the canalized Somme, northwest of Amiens. Stone Age artifacts unearthed by Boucher de Crèvecoeur de Perthes in 1844 attesting to early occupation of the site are displayed at the Musée Boucher-de-Perthes. The town originated as Abbatis Villa, a 9th-century dependency of the abbots of Saint-Riquier, and was chartered in 1184. Under the English (1272–1435), it was capital of Ponthieu. Louis XII's marriage (1514) to Mary, sister of Henry VIII of England, took place there.

The Gothic church of Saint-Vulfran (15th–17th centuries) and the town hall with its 13th-century tower survived air bombardment during World War II.

Gothic church of Saint-Vulfran, Abbeville, Fr.
Club Iris

Abbeville has carpet factories (dating from the 17th century), sugar refineries, breweries, and ironworks. Pop. (1982) 24,825.

Abbeville, town, seat (1854) of Vermilion Parish, southern Louisiana, U.S., on the Vermilion River, 20 mi (32 km) south-southwest of Lafayette. Founded in 1843 by a Capuchin missionary, Père A.D. Mégret, who patterned it after a French Provençal village, it was first called La Chapelle and was settled by Acadians and Mediterranean immigrants. St. Marie Madeleine Church (1910) now occupies the site of Mégret's chapel, which was destroyed by fire in 1854. A trade centre for agricultural produce (especially rice) and seafood, it provides services for nearby oil and gas fields. Abbeville is linked with the Gulf of Mexico via the Freshwater Bayou Deepwater Channel. Avery Island, with a bird sanctuary and salt dome, is 15 mi (24 km) southeast. Inc. town, 1850. Pop. (1980) 12,391.

Abbeville, city, seat of Abbeville County, northwestern South Carolina, U.S. French Huguenots in 1764 settled the site, which was named for Abbeville, Fr., by John de la Howe. The city is regarded by some as the "Cradle and the Grave of the Confederacy"; it was there that a secessionist meeting was held (Nov. 22, 1860, on what is now Secession Hill) and there that the Confederate president, Jefferson Davis, held one of his last Cabinet meetings (May 2, 1865, at Burt House). John C. Calhoun was born on an outlying farm. A textile-based economy prevails. The Sumter National Forest is nearby. Inc. 1895. Pop. (1980) 5,863.

Abbevillian industry, prehistoric stone-tool tradition generally considered to represent the oldest occurrence in Europe of a bifacial (hand-ax) technology. The Abbevillian industry dates from an imprecisely determined part of the Middle Pleistocene, somewhat less than 700,000 years ago. It was recovered from high terrace sediments of the lower Somme valley, in a suburb of Abbeville, Fr. The distinctive stone tools include massive core-tools (hand-axes), bifacially flaked, with deep flake scars and sinuous or jagged edges, along with thick, usually unretouched, flakes. The assemblage is usually considered closely related to the Acheulian industry and may, in fact, represent merely a variant or temporal expression of it. *See also* Acheulian industry.

abbey, group of buildings housing a monastery or a convent, centred on an abbey church or a cathedral and under the direction of an abbot or an abbess. In this sense, an abbey consists of a complex of buildings serving the needs of a self-contained religious community. The term abbey is also used loosely to refer to priories, smaller monasteries under a prior. In England, since the dissolution of the monasteries under Henry VIII, all that remains in many cases is the abbey church, now simply called an abbey; Westminster Abbey is the best known example.

Monasteries originally developed in the Middle East and Greece from the earlier streets of hermits' huts, or lauras. Walls were built for defense, and the cells were later constructed against the walls, leaving a central space for church, chapels, fountain, and dining hall, or refectory. This Eastern type of monastery can be seen at Mt. Athos in Greece.

The first European abbey was Montecassino (*see* Cassino) in Italy, founded in 529 by St. Benedict of Nursia, who wrote the order that formed the basic foundation of monastic life in the Western world. His plan for an ideal abbey was circulated (about 820) to orders throughout Europe, and abbeys were generally built in accord with it in subsequent centuries. The cloister (*q.v.*) linked the most important elements of the abbey together and also served the monks for their contemplative meditation; it was usually an open, arcaded court, surfaced with grass or paving and sometimes with a fountain in the centre. The side adjoining the nave of the church had book presses and formed an open-air but sheltered library.

The ruins of Fountains Abbey, a Cistercian monastery founded in the 12th century, near Ripon, North Yorkshire, England
Andy Williams

The dormitory was often built over the refectory on the east side of the cloister and was linked to the central church by a "day-stair," which led to the arcaded cloister and so into the church, and by a "night-stair," which led directly to the church. To one side of the latter passage there was sometimes a "warming room," where the monks could warm themselves before entering the unheated church for midnight mass. The church assembly room, the chapter house (*q.v.*), was often attached to the chancel near the eastern side of the cloister.

The western side of the cloister provided for dealings with the outside world. There was the almonry, for example, where gifts of money or clothing were made to the poor, and guest rooms, lay brothers' quarters, cellars, and stables. The abbot's rooms were near the gatehouse, which controlled the only opening to the outer courtyard, where the general public was permitted. In wet weather or under the hot summer sun, the worshippers assembled before mass under an arcaded porch, or galilee (*see* porch), which was often added to the west end of the church. On the south side of the cloisters were workshops for smiths, enamellers, coopers, shoemakers, and saddlers; a central kitchen; and a brewery.

An important building within the inner walls housed the novitiate and the infirmary. In the manner of an early isolation hospital, it had its own chapel, bathhouse, refectory, kitchen, and garden. The doctor's house, with its physic garden of essential medicinal herbs and with small sickrooms, was nearby.

Buildings for the intensive agriculture practiced by most orders were to the south of the other buildings.

In the 12th and 13th centuries, many abbeys were built in England, Scotland, Spain, Italy, Germany, and Austria. In France the monastic movement flourished to a greater extent than in any other country. Perhaps the most remarkable abbey was established by the Benedictines on the rocky island of Mont-Saint-Michel (*q.v.*) in 966. The buildings spiralled around the rock, finally rising to a pinnacle above it with the church, rooftop cloister, refectory, and terraced garden. A good Western example of the eremetical style—*i.e.*, tending toward the pattern of Eastern monasticism, with individual hermit cells—is the Carthusian monastery of Porte-Sainte-Marie near Clermont-Ferrand. The Cistercian tenet of simplicity is seen at the well-preserved abbey of Fontenay, with its low, straightforward church and almost entire absence of decoration.

Abbey, Edwin Austin (b. April 1, 1852, Philadelphia—d. Aug. 1, 1911, London), U.S. painter and one of the foremost illustrators of his day.

While working as an illustrator for the publishing house of Harper and Brothers, New York City, Abbey was sent to England to gather material for illustrations of the poems of Robert Herrick. These were followed by illustrations for works of Oliver Goldsmith and Shakespeare. He spent many of his most productive years in England, where he was elected (1883) to the Royal Institute of Painters in Water-Colours. He became a member of the National Academy of Design in 1902. His later works include decorative schemes for several public buildings, among them the state capitol at Harrisburg, Pa., and the official picture of the coronation of King Edward VII of England (1902).

Abbey Theatre, Dublin theatre, effectively established in 1902. It grew out of the Irish Literary Theatre (founded in 1898 by W.B. Yeats and Lady Gregory and devoted to fostering Irish poetic drama), which in 1902 was taken over by the Irish National Dramatic Society, led by W.G. and Frank J. Fay and formed to present Irish actors in Irish plays. In 1903 this became the Irish National Theatre Society, with which many leading figures of the Irish literary renaissance were closely associated. The quality of its productions was quickly recognized, and in 1904 an Englishwoman, Annie Horniman, a friend of Yeats, paid for the conversion of an old theatre in Abbey Street, Dublin, into the Abbey Theatre. The Abbey opened in December of that year with a bill of plays by Yeats, Lady Gregory, and J.M. Synge (who joined the other two as co-director). Founder members included the Fays, Arthur Sinclair, and Sara Allgood.

The Abbey's staging of J.M. Synge's satire *The Playboy of the Western World*, on Jan. 26, 1907, stirred up so much resentment in the audience over its portrayal of the Irish peasantry that there was a riot. When the Abbey players toured the United States for the first time in 1911, similar protests and disorders were provoked when the play opened in New York City and Philadelphia.

The years 1907–09 were difficult times for the Abbey. Changes in personnel affected the management of the theatre, and the Fay brothers, whose commitment to nationalistic and folk drama conflicted with Yeats's art-theatre outlook, departed for the United States. Horniman withdrew her financial support, and the management of the theatre changed hands several times with little success until the post was filled by the playwright-director Lennox Robinson in 1910. The onset of World War I and the Irish Rebellion of 1916 almost caused the closing of the theatre. Its luck changed, however, in 1924 when it became the first state-subsidized theatre in the English-speaking world. The emergence of the playwright Sean O'Casey also stimulated new life in the theatre, and from 1923 to 1926 the Abbey staged three of his plays: *The Shadow of a Gunman, Juno and the Paycock,* and *The Plough and the Stars,* the last a provocative dramatization of the Easter Rising of 1916. In the early 1950s the Abbey company moved to the nearby Queen's Theatre after a fire had destroyed its playhouse. A new Abbey Theatre, housing a smaller, experimental theatre, was completed in 1966 on the original site. Although the Abbey has broadened its repertory, it continues to rely primarily on Irish plays.

abbot, official title of the superior of a monastic community that follows the Benedictine Rule (Benedictines, Cistercians, Camaldolese, Trappists) and of certain other orders (Premonstratensians, canons regular of the Lateran). The word derives from the Aramaic *ab* ("father") or *aba* ("my father"), which in the Septuagint (the Greek translation of the Old Testament) and in New Testament Greek was written *abbas.* Early Christian Egyptian monks renowned for age and sanctity were called *abbas* by their disciples, but, when monasticism became more organized, superiors were called *proestos* ("he who rules") in the East and the Latin equivalent, *praepositus,* in the West.

St. Benedict of Nursia (*c.* 480–*c.* 547) restored the word *abbas* in his rule, and to this early concept of spiritual fatherhood through teaching he added the concept of *patria potestas,* authority wielded by a father according to Roman law. Thus, the abbot has full authority to rule the monastery in both temporal and spiritual matters.

An abbot is elected by the chapter of the monastery in secret ballot. He must be at least 30 years old, of legitimate birth, professed at least 10 years, and an ordained priest. He is elected for life except in the English congregation, where he is elected for a term of 8–12 years. The election must be confirmed by the Holy See or by some other designated authority. The bishop of the diocese in which the monastery is situated confers the abbatial blessing, assisted by two abbots.

Chief among the privileges of an abbot are the power to administer tonsure and minor orders to his own subjects and the right to celebrate the liturgy according to pontifical rite, to give many blessings normally reserved to a bishop, and to use the pontifical insignia.

In Eastern monasticism, self-governing monasteries are ruled by several elder monks, whose leader is called abbot. *See also* abbess.

Abbot, C(harles) G(reeley) (b. May 31, 1872, Wilton, N.H., U.S.—d. Dec. 17, 1973, Washington, D.C.), astrophysicist who served (1928–44) as secretary of the Smithsonian Institution. Abbot is thought to have been the first scientist to suspect that the radiation of the Sun might vary over time. His continued studies of solar radiation led him to discover, in 1953, a connection between solar variations and weather on Earth, allowing general weather patterns to be predicted as many as 50 years in advance. For his research in solar radiation, Abbot earned the Draper Gold Medal of the National Academy of Science in 1910 and the Rumford Medal of the American Academy of Arts and Sciences in 1916.

Abbotsford, former home of the 19th-century novelist Sir Walter Scott, situated on the right bank of the River Tweed, district of Roxburgh, Borders region, Scotland. Scott purchased the original farm, then known as Carley Hole, in 1811 and transformed it (1817–25) into a Gothic-style baronial mansion. The surrounding area was a major source of inspiration for the author's historical novels.

Home of Sir Walter Scott, Abbotsford, Roxburgh
Colour Library International

Still the home of Scott's direct descendants, Abbotsford remains virtually unchanged; it contains Scott's valuable library, family portraits, and an interesting collection of historical relics and is open to the public during the summer.

Abbott, Berenice (b. July 17, 1898, Springfield, Ohio, U.S.), photographer best known for preserving the works of photographer Eugène Atget and for her photographic documentation of New York City in the late 1930s.

In 1918 Abbott left Ohio for New York City, where she independently studied drawing and sculpture until 1921. She studied sculpture briefly in Berlin and then became an assistant to Man Ray in Paris. While in Paris she came into contact with Atget, whose work was at the time virtually unknown. In 1925 Abbott set up her own photography studio and made several well-known portraits of Parisian expatriates, artists, writers, and aristocrats, including Peggy Guggenheim, James Joyce, Djuna Barnes, Jean Cocteau, Leo Stein, and Atget. After Atget's death in 1927, Abbott retrieved his prints and negatives from certain destruction and classified them, and in the following years she dedicated herself to promoting his work.

She remained in Paris until 1929, at which time she returned to New York City. Freelancing for a time, Abbott began photographing the city. She accepted a job with the

Federal Art Project of the Works Progress Administration (WPA) in 1935. Until the end of the decade she documented the city's changing character; *Changing New York* was published in 1939 (reissued as *New York in the Thirties*, 1973).

During the next two decades Abbott experimented with photography as a tool for the illustration of scientific phenomena such as magnetism and motion. She also continued to document the landscape around her; for one project she photographed scenes along U.S. Route 1 from Florida to Maine. In addition to collections of her photographs, Abbott's publications include a monograph on photographer Lisette Model, a photography guide, two monographs on Atget, and several articles on aspects of photography.

Abbott, Bud; and Costello, Lou, in full WILLIAM A. ABBOTT and LOUIS FRANCIS CRISTILLO (respectively b. Oct. 2, 1896, Asbury Park, N.J., U.S.—d. April 25, 1974, Woodland Hills, Calif.; b. March 6, 1908, Paterson, N.J., U.S.—d. May 9, 1959, Beverly Hills, Calif.), popular comedic partnership on stage, radio, television, and in motion pictures between 1929 and 1957.

Abbott was born into a theatrical family and operated burlesque houses and worked in box offices before he met Costello. Costello worked as an actor, prizefighter, and motion-picture stuntman before becoming a comedian in burlesque and vaudeville. Their partnership began when Costello's regular straight man fell ill during an engagement at the Empire Theatre in New York City. Abbott, who was working in the box office, offered to substitute. They worked so well together that Abbott played straight man to Costello's buffoon from then on.

In 1938 Abbott and Costello gave their first performance on radio. The duo made their Broadway debut the following year in *The Streets of Paris.* Their first motion-picture comedy, *Buck Privates,* released in 1941, became a popular hit and was followed by eight other comedies in the next two years. Their most famous vaudeville routine, which they performed on television many times, was a farcical baseball commentary entitled "Who's on First?"

Abbott, Grace (b. Nov. 17, 1878, Grand Island, Neb., U.S.—d. June 19, 1939, Chicago), social worker, public administrator, educator, and reformer who was especially important in the field of child-labour legislation.

In 1908 she became director of the newly formed Immigrants' Protective League, Chicago, and lived for a time at Hull House, the pioneer settlement house founded by Jane Addams, with whom she was closely associated. In a series of weekly articles ("Within the City's Gates," 1909–10) in the Chicago *Evening Post,* she attacked the exploitation of immigrants. Later she wrote *The Immigrant and the Community* (1917).

As director of the child-labour division, U.S. Children's Bureau (1917–19), she administered the first federal statute limiting the employment of juveniles, the Keating–Owen Act (1916). This law was declared unconstitutional by the U.S. Supreme Court in 1918, but she secured a continuation of its policy by having a child-labour clause inserted into all war-goods contracts between the federal government and private industries. Subsequently she was director of the entire Children's Bureau (1921–34). She worked hard to secure public approval of a constitutional amendment against child labour, submitted to the states in 1924 but never ratified. While serving as professor of public welfare at the University of Chicago (1934–39), she was also U.S. delegate to the International Labour Organisation (1935, 1937). Her book *The Child and the State* (2 vol.) appeared in 1938.

Her sister Edith Abbott (1876–1957) was dean of the University of Chicago School of Social Service Administration (1924–42).

Abbott, Jacob (b. Nov. 14, 1803, Hallowell, Maine, U.S.—d. Oct. 31, 1879, Farmington, Maine), teacher and writer, best known for his many books for young readers, including the "Rollo" series.

Abbott attended Hallowell Academy and Bowdoin College and studied at Andover Newton Theological School. After teaching at Amherst College, he moved in 1829 to Boston, where he founded and was the first principal of the Mount Vernon School, a secondary school for girls.

Abbott was sole author of 180 books and co-author or editor of 31 others, notably the "Rollo" series (28 vol.). To accompany the earlier books (*Rollo at Work, Rollo at Play*), Abbott wrote a volume for teachers, *The Rollo Code of Morals; or, The Rules of Duty for Children, Arranged with Questions for the Use of Schools* (1841). In following Rollo's travels about the world with his all-knowing Uncle George, the young reader could improve his knowledge of ethics, geography, science, and history. Abbott also wrote 22 volumes of biographical histories and the *Franconia Stories* (10 vol.).

Abbott, Sir John (Joseph Caldwell) (b. March 12, 1821, St. Andrews, Lower Canada—d. Oct. 30, 1893, Montreal), lawyer, statesman, and prime minister of Canada from 1891 to 1892.

Educated at McGill University, Montreal, Abbott became a lawyer in 1847 and was made queen's counsel in 1862. A recognized authority on commercial law in Lower Canada (now in Quebec), he served as dean of the McGill faculty of law from 1855 to 1880. He was elected to the Legislative Assembly of the then united province of Canada in 1857 and continued to represent his native county, Argenteuil, until 1887, except during 1874–80. In 1862 he served briefly as solicitor general in the Liberal administration of Sir John Macdonald and Louis Sicotte, before going over to the Conservatives in 1865.

As legal adviser to the shipping magnate Sir Hugh Allan, Abbott was implicated in the Pacific Scandal of 1873, in which Prime Minister Macdonald was accused of awarding a railway construction contract to Allan in return for campaign funds. Abbott accordingly was defeated in the 1874 election and was not reelected to the House of Commons until 1880. Seven years later he was appointed to the Senate, in which he was made government leader.

On the death of Macdonald in June 1891, Abbott was compromise choice for prime minister, but he resigned the following year because of ill health. He was knighted in 1892.

Abbott, Lyman (b. Dec. 18, 1835, Roxbury, Mass., U.S.—d. Oct. 22, 1922, New York City), Congregationalist minister and a leading exponent of the Social Gospel movement.

Abbott left law practice to study theology and was ordained in 1860. After serving in two pastorates he became associate editor of *Harper's Magazine* and in 1870 editor of the *Illustrated Christian Weekly.* In 1876 he joined Henry Ward Beecher's *Christian Union,* a nondenominational religious weekly, and in 1881 became its editor in chief. He succeeded in 1888 to Beecher's pulpit in the Plymouth Congregational Church, Brooklyn, where he served until 1899.

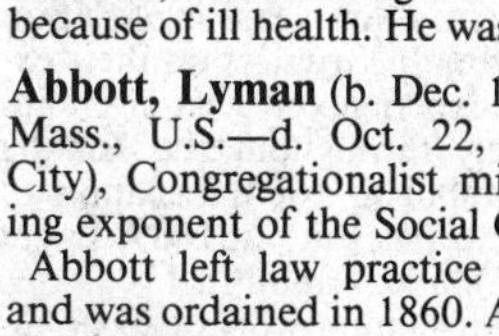

Lyman Abbott, 1901

By courtesy of the Library of Congress, Washington, D.C.

Abbott early became interested in industrial problems. Under his editorship the *Christian Union* (renamed *Outlook* in 1893) promulgated the Social Gospel, which sought to apply Christianity to social and industrial problems. His *Christianity and Social Problems* (1897), *The Rights of Man* (1901), *The Spirit of Democracy* (1910), and *America in the Making* (1911) present his moderate sociological views, which rejected both Socialism and laissez-faire economics.

On other problems Abbott presented the viewpoint of liberal evangelical Protestantism. He sought to interpret, rather than condemn, the effect of the theory of evolution on religion. Abbott also popularized the objective scholarly study of the Bible.

Abbottābād, city, headquarters of Abbottābād District, Hazāra Division, NorthWest Frontier Province, Pakistan, northeast of Rāwalpindi. A hill station (4,120 ft [1,256 m]), it lies on a saucer-shaped plateau at the southern corner of the Rāsh (Orāsh) Plain and is the gateway to the picturesque Kāgān Valley. Connected by road with the Indus Plain and Kashmir and by railhead (at Haveliān, 10 mi [16 km] south) with Peshāwar, it serves as a district market centre. Founded in 1853 and named after Maj. James Abbott, the first British deputy commissioner of Hazāra, it contains two parks, a preparatory school, two colleges affiliated with the University of Peshāwar, and a forest research centre. The Pakistan Military Academy is at Kākul, 5 mi northeast. Three major iron-ore deposits are located nearby, at Langrial, Galdanian, and on the city's eastern outskirts; reserves exceed 100,000,000 tons.

Abbottābād District, mountainous to the north and east, is densely forested in the eastern part with silver fir, pine, and hardwood trees. It borders Jammu and Kashmir state to the east and Mānsehra District to the north, and the Indus River forms part of its western boundary; the district is drained by the Siran and Dor rivers. The Tarbela Dam, located on the Indus River near its junction with the Siran, is the world's largest rockfill dam. Completed in 1976, it is 485 ft high and about 9,000 ft wide at its crest; it was built for flood control, irrigation, and the production of hydroelectricity. Wheat, barley, and corn (maize) are the principal crops. Fruits (plums, apples, apricots, melons, and oranges), tobacco, and vegetables are grown. Harīpur, 20 mi southwest of Abbottābād city on the railway spur to Haveliān, is a major centre for telecommunications. A telephone factory, a telecommunications research centre, and other associated corporations are located in Harīpur, which also has a cement factory, a textile mill, a flour mill, and a turpentine factory. Pashtun Jadoon are the main ethnic group in the district. Pop. (1981 prelim.) city, 66,000; district, 1,150,000.

abbreviation, in communications, especially written, the process or result of representing symbolically a word or group of words by part of the whole.

A list of abbreviations used in the MICROPAEDIA may be found at the end of each volume of the MICROPAEDIA. A more comprehensive list, which includes abbreviations used in the INDEX and in all other parts of the *Ency-*

clopædia Britannica, may be found in the INDEX.

Abbreviations take many forms and can be found in ancient Greek inscriptions, in medieval manuscripts (*e.g.,* "DN" for "Dominus Noster"), and in the Qur'ān. Cicero's secretary, Marcus Tullius Tiro, devised many abbreviations that have survived to modern times, such as the ampersand, &, for *et* (Latin "and"). But it was the so-called information explosion of the 20th century that made abbreviation a common practice in communication.

A major factor in the trend toward abbreviation is that of economy. In telegraphy, for example, as well as in computerized communications, the extra time, space, and materials required for rendering long words and phrases is an important concern. Fortunately, redundancy of information exists in all speech, and this redundancy increases dramatically if the context is not known or if the message is long. Scientific studies indicate that up to 75 percent of all information in relatively long communications is redundant, and this makes abbreviation not only possible but convenient.

Another factor in the development of abbreviations is the proliferation of new products and organizations that need to be named. Long descriptive terms can be turned into shorter, more manageable units mnemonically.

The need for speed in shorthand and the desire to avoid redundancy in codes makes abbreviation an important element in stenography and cryptography as well.

There are several important forms of abbreviation. One form entails representing a single word either by its first few letters (as "n" for "noun," or "Co." for "Company"), by its most important letters (as "Ltd." for "Limited"), or by its first and last letters (as "Rd." for "Road"). These abbreviations are usually spoken as the whole word they represent (though Ltd. is sometimes spoken as "el-tee-dee").

Truncation is especially common in popular speech, as, for example, "Mets" for "Metropolitans."

The combination of the first syllables or letters of component words within phrases or within names having more than one word is common and often produces acronyms, which are pronounced as words and which often cease to be considered abbreviations. Examples are "Chisox" for "Chicago White Sox" and "Flak" from "*Flugzeugab-wehrkanone*" (German "antiaircraft cannon"). Such combinations are especially common in the U.S. military, which has provided "COMFLOGWING" for "Commander Fleet Logistics Air Wing," and in the Soviet Union, which produced "Narkomvneshtorg" for "Narodny Komissariat Vneshney Torgovli" (Russian "People's Commissariat of Foreign Trade"). Other popular acronyms are the well-known "radar" ("radio detecting and ranging") and "snafu" ("situation normal, all fouled up").

Acronyms are to be distinguished from initialisms such as U.S.A. and NCAA, which are spoken by reciting their letters.

The symbolic notations used in mathematics and other sciences may also be considered as forms of abbreviation.

ABC: *see* American Broadcasting Companies, Inc.

ABC, tabloid daily newspaper published in Madrid and long regarded as one of Spain's leading papers. It was founded as a weekly in 1903 by one of the country's most distinguished journalists, Torcuato Luca de Tena y Alvarez-Ossorio, who later (1929) was made the Marqués de Luca de Tena by King Alfonso XIII in recognition of his accomplishments with *ABC.* The paper became a daily in 1905 and since 1929 has published a Seville edition.

ABC was monarchist in orientation from its founding, and during the Spanish Civil War it was taken over by the Republican government—nominally in 1931 and then, after several months' suspension in 1932 and continued resistance to censorship, completely in 1936. It was returned to private control under Franco in 1939 but remained critical of government excesses, although it did support the Franco regime.

ABC has always been noted for its graphics; it was a heavy user of photography from its inception and, in more recent times, has won wide acclaim for its coverage of Spanish culture and the arts, including special features by some of Spain's leading literary and artistic figures.

ABC art: *see* Minimal art.

Abchazija (Georgian S.S.R.): *see* Abkhaz Autonomous Soviet Socialist Republic.

Abchazskaja Avtonomnaja Sovetskaja Socialističeskaja Respublika (Georgian S.S.R.): *see* Abkhaz Autonomous Soviet Socialist Republic.

Abd al-Aziz, in full ʿABD AL-ʿAZĪZ IBN AL-ḤASAN IBN MUḤAMMAD AL-ḤASANĪ AL-ʿALAWĪ (b. Feb. 24, 1878, or Feb. 18, 1881—d. June 10, 1943, Tangier, Mor.), sultan of Morocco from 1894 to 1908, whose reign was marked by an unsuccessful attempt to introduce European administrative methods in an atmosphere of increasing foreign influence.

After the death in 1900 of his grand vizier, Ba Ahmed (Ahmad ibn Musa), Abd al-Aziz sought European advice in an attempt to modernize the country and in particular to reform the methods of taxation. These endeavours, defeated because of the complete lack of administrators trained in modern practices, caused great resentment among influential notables of the old school. Abd al-Aziz' brother, Moulay Hafid (Abd al-Hafid), raised the standard of revolt in Marrakech in 1907 and defeated Abd al-Aziz in battle on Aug. 19, 1908. Two days later the Sultan abdicated. Pensioned by his brother, he spent the rest of his life at Tangier. The Franco-Spanish occupation of Morocco followed his abdication by four years.

ʿAbd al-ʿAzīz ibn ʿAbd ar-Raḥmān ibn Fayṣal ibn Turkī ʿAbd Allāh ibn Muḥammad Āl Saʿūd (Arab leader): *see* Ibn Saʿūd.

ʿAbd al-Ghanī (ibn Ismāʿīl) an-Nābulusī (b. March 19, 1641, Damascus—d. March 5, 1731), mystic prose and verse writer on the cultural and religious thought of his time.

Orphaned at an early age, he joined the mystical orders of the Qādirīyah and the Naqshbandīyah. He then spent seven years in isolation in his house, studying the mystics on their expression of divine experiences. ʿAbd al-Ghanī travelled extensively throughout the Islāmic world, visiting Istanbul in 1664, Lebanon in 1688, Jerusalem and Palestine in 1689, Egypt and Arabia in 1693, and Tripoli in 1700.

His more than 200 written works can be divided into three categories: Ṣūfism (mysticism, largely within the main body of Islām, the Sunnīs); travel accounts; and miscellaneous subjects, including prophecy and the question of the lawfulness of the use of tobacco. The main component in his Ṣūfī writing is the concept of *waḥdat al-wujūd* ("divine existential unity" of God and the universe and, hence, of man). His travel accounts are the most important of his writings; the descriptions of his journeys provide vital information on the customs, beliefs, and practices of the peoples and places he visited.

Abd al-Hafid (b. 1875, Fès, Mor.—d. 1937, Enghien-les-Bains, Fr.), sultan of Morocco, 1908–12, the brother of Sultan Abd-al-Aziz IV, against whom he revolted in 1908. With Marrakech, the southern capital, his, Abd al-Hafid routed his brother's forces and pensioned off the Sultan. Recognized as sultan by the Western powers (1909), Abd al-Hafid invoked French aid against another pretender in 1912 and then was forced to recognize a French protectorate over Morocco.

To make the best use of the Britannica, consult the INDEX *first*

ʿAbd al-Ilāh (b. 1913, aṭ-Ṭāʾif, Arabia—d. July 14, 1958, Baghdad), regent of Iraq (1939–53) and crown prince to 1958.

Son of the Hāshimite king ʿAlī ibn Ḥusayn of the Hejaz (northwestern Arabia), who was driven from Arabia by Ibn Saʿūd, ʿAbd al-Ilāh accompanied his father to Iraq in 1925. Upon King Ghāzī's death in 1939, he was appointed regent for his four-year-old cousin and nephew, Fayṣal II. ʿAbd al-Ilāh ruled Iraq for 14 turbulent years, loyally serving the throne and supporting the Allies during World War II. In April 1941, faced with an uprising of army officers led by Rashid Ali al-Gailani, who was sympathetic to Germany and Italy,

ʿAbd al-Ilāh
BBC Hulton Picture Library

the Regent was forced to leave Iraq. With British assistance, however, the revolt was suppressed by the end of May, and ʿAbd al-Ilāh returned to Baghdad. Thereafter, in close collaboration with Nuri as-Said, he pursued a policy of moderate Iraqi nationalism and maintained strong ties with the West. When King Fayṣal reached legal age on May 23, 1953, the Regent relinquished his functions but remained as the young king's chief adviser and companion until both were killed during the Iraq revolution of 1958.

ʿAbd al-Karīm Qasim (Iraqi soldier): *see* Kassem, Abdul Karim.

ʿAbd al-Karīm Quṭb ad-Dīn ibn Ibrāhīm al-Jīlī: *see* Jīlī, al-.

ʿAbd al-Malik, in full ʿABD AL-MALIK IBN MARWĀN (b. 646/647, Medina, Arabia—d. October 705, Damascus), fifth caliph (685–705) of the Umayyad Arab dynasty centred in Damascus. He reorganized and strengthened governmental administration and, throughout the empire, adopted Arabic as the language of administration.

Life. ʿAbd al-Malik spent the first half of his life with his father, Marwān ibn al-Ḥakam, fourth Umayyad caliph, in Medina, where he received religious instruction and developed friendly relations with the pious circles of that city that were to stand him in good stead in his later life. At the age of 16, he was entrusted by his kinsman, the caliph Muʿāwiyah, with administrative responsibilities. He remained at Medina until 683, when he and his father were driven out of the city by Medinese rebels in revolt against the central government in Damascus. He then met the Syrian Umayyad army that was marching on Medina and gave its commander advice about the best means of attacking the city, advice that was followed and proved successful. When the caliph Yazīd died in November 683, Marwān was proclaimed caliph in 684 and was able to effect a partial rally of Umayyad rule but at the cost of a bitter feud that arose between northern and southern Arab tribes. When Marwān died in 685 and ʿAbd al-Malik succeeded to the caliphate, the forces opposing the Umayyads were still formidable.

There were, first, the northern Arab tribes who, under their leader Zufar, were holding out in northern Syria and Iraq. They were finally pacified only in 691. The second focus of resistance was in Iraq, where three main groups, opposed to each other but united in their resistance to the Umayyads, held sway: the Khārijites, the Shīʿah, and the forces of the anticaliph ʿAbd Allāh ibn az-Zubayr, who was proclaimed caliph in Mecca in 685 and had received at least nominal allegiance from many provinces. The initial attempts by the former Umayyad governor of Iraq, ʿUbayd Allāh ibn Ziyād, to regain the province failed, and he was killed by the Shīʿah in 686. For three years ʿAbd al-Malik made no further attempt to interfere in Iraq but bided his time as the various groups in Iraq exhausted themselves in internecine warfare. Muṣʿab, the brother of the anticaliph Ibn az-Zubayr, defeated the Shīʿah in 687 but then had to deal with the Khārijites, committing a large part of his forces.

ʿAbd al-Malik first took the field against Muṣʿab in 689 but had to turn back to quell a rebellion in Damascus. In the following year, the campaign again proved fruitless. Only after the defeat of the northern Arab tribes in 691 was ʿAbd al-Malik finally able to face Muṣʿab. The decisive battle took place at Dayr al-Jā Thalīq. The forces of Muṣʿab were weakened by their wars against the Khārijites, and ʿAbd al-Malik bribed many of them to desert Muṣʿab, who was then killed in battle. The whole of Iraq now fell into his hands, and the only remaining centre of opposition was the now aging anticaliph, Ibn az-Zubayr. ʿAbd al-Malik publicly chided him for his temerity and then sent his famous governor al-Ḥajjāj to Arabia. Al-Ḥajjāj besieged Ibn az-Zubayr in Mecca and killed him in September 692. The Muslim community was finally unified.

At first, the reestablishment of Umayyad rule was more apparent than real. The Khārijites were still either restless or in open revolt. The Khārijites in Persia were especially dangerous. It was only after ʿAbd al-Malik had appointed al-Ḥajjāj to govern Basra that campaigns against them began to prove successful (the Persian Khārijites were finally wiped out in 697). But north of Kūfah, another Khārijite trouble centre developed. In 695 these Khārijites captured Mosul and occupied large areas of central Iraq. Al-Ḥajjāj, leading his Syrian troops, defeated them too in 697. The Khārijite movement, however, remained strong, especially among the Bakr tribes between Mosul and Kūfah.

Al-Ḥajjāj had now become governor of all the eastern provinces. He was a ruthless and efficient administrator, intent upon pacifying all the provinces entrusted to him by ʿAbd al-Malik. A great Muslim army, led by an Arab aristocrat, Ibn al-Ashʿath, and operating in the Afghanistan region, mutinied, swore allegiance to its commander, and turned back to Iraq. Al-Ḥajjāj, with the aid of Syrian reinforcements, was able to defeat the rebels, and their leader was murdered in 704 in Afghanistan. Al-Ḥajjāj, realizing that he could no longer trust the Iraqis, built a new city, Wāsiṭ, which he planned as a garrison city for Syrian troops and as his private residence. Thereafter, he ruled Iraq as enemy territory.

Under ʿAbd al-Malik, the conquest of North Africa was resumed in 688 or 689. There, the Arabs were opposed by both the native Berbers and the Byzantines. The governor appointed by ʿAbd al-Malik succeeded in winning the Berbers over to his side and then captured Carthage, seat of the Byzantine province, in 697. Other coastal cities fell, and the work of pacification and Islāmization continued apace. ʿAbd al-Malik also resumed campaigns against the Byzantines in Anatolia in 692, but no permanent conquest ensued. These campaigns were partly designed to keep the Syrian troops fit.

Assessment. In general, Umayyad rule was greatly strengthened by ʿAbd al-Malik, who enjoyed good relations with the Medinese religious circles, an element with considerable moral influence in the Islāmic world. ʿAbd al-Malik was more pious than any of his Umayyad predecessors. His long sojourn in Medina had enabled him to know the sentiments of Medinese religious scholars. As caliph, he treated them respectfully, and his private life was close to their ideals. As a result, many were to abandon their earlier opposition to Umayyad rule.

ʿAbd al-Malik adopted Arabic instead of the local languages as the language of administration. Government officials had been mostly non-Muslim, but the measures of ʿAbd al-Malik enabled Arab Muslims more easily to control affairs of government. A new Muslim currency was also struck, modelled on Greek and Persian coinage, but with Muslim inscriptions. A wave of Islāmization set in, but the privileged position of the Arabs was maintained. In fact, the problem of non-Arab Muslims grew more acute and was to become one of the main threats to Umayyad rule in later years.

The Umayyad family lived in Damascus and surrounded the Caliph. Many of them were appointed as governors, but many were also recalled for inefficiency. ʿAbd al-Malik enjoyed the support of his clan, but he was more autocratic than Muʿāwiyah, the first Umayyad caliph, with whom he is often compared. He abandoned the policy of consulting with a council of advisers and reserved all major decisions for himself. Despite his religious interests and ideals (*e.g.,* he built the Dome of the Rock in Jerusalem), he was a master politician. In Syria he succeeded in placating the northern Arab tribes, to the chagrin of the southern Arabs.

ʿAbd al-Malik was a shrewd judge of character. His choice of al-Ḥajjāj as viceroy of the East was a wise one, and he supported his lieutenant loyally. In appearance, he was dark, thickset, and had a long beard. He was nicknamed "Dew of the Stone" for his miserliness. The sources describe him as eloquent in his speech and a lover of poetry. He maintained his calm during periods of crisis and was decisive in his opinions but was capable of great cruelty if necessary. He pursued his enemies relentlessly and closely supervised all affairs of state.

Shortly before his death the question of succession became acute. His brother, ʿAbd al-ʿAzīz, governor of Egypt, had been designated by their father to succeed ʿAbd al-Malik. Against the advice of his courtiers, ʿAbd al-Malik had begun to take steps to exclude his brother from succession in favour of his own children. He had tried to pressure ʿAbd al-ʿAzīz to renounce his claims but without success. Luckily for ʿAbd al-Malik, ʿAbd al-ʿAzīz died in May 705. ʿAbd al-Malik now felt free to name three of his own children to succeed him, al-Walīd, Sulaymān, and Yazīd. ʿAbd al-Malik died in Damascus shortly thereafter and was succeeded without difficulty by his eldest son, al-Walīd. (T.Kh.)

BIBLIOGRAPHY. The best account of ʿAbd al-Malik's reign is in J. Wellhausen, *Das arabische Reich und sein Sturz* (1902; *The Arab Kingdom and Its Fall,* 1927). Also useful are Sir William Muir, *The Caliphate: Its Rise, Decline, and Fall,* new ed. (1924); and P.K. Hitti, *History of the Arabs,* 10th ed. (1970).

ʿAbd al-Muʾmin, in full ʿABD AL-MUʾMIN IBN ʿALI (b. Tagra, Kingdom of the Ḥammādids—d. 1163, Rabat, Almohad Empire), Berber caliph of the Almohad dynasty (reigned 1130–63), who conquered the North African Maghrib from the Almoravids and brought all the Berbers under one rule.

Life. ʿAbd al-Muʾmin came from a humble family: his father had been a potter. He seems to have been well instructed in the Muslim faith and must have had a good knowledge of Arabic, for he wished to continue his studies at one of the centres of Muslim learning in the East. A chance meeting with Ibn Tūmart, a Berber religious reformer, made him abandon this idea and begin his brilliant career.

Around 1117, Ibn Tūmart, the founder of the Almohad movement, was returning from a long stay in the East. He landed at Mahdīyah in Tunisia and began a journey to southern Morocco, his native country. Wherever he stopped along the way, he proclaimed a twofold message: strict adherence to the doctrine of the oneness of God (hence the name Almohads or al-Muwaḥḥidūn, Unitarians) and scrupulous observance of Islāmic law. ʿAbd al-Muʾmin heard Ibn Tūmart preach at Mellala, near Bejaïa, Alg. He was an attentive listener and from that time attached himself to the man who had revealed to him the true doctrine.

ʿAbd al-Muʾmin does not seem to have played any special role among Ibn Tūmart's disciples during the slow journey that took them to Marrakech. But when his master declared his opposition to the ruling Almoravid regime, proclaimed himself the *mahdī* ("divinely guided one"), and took refuge in the remote High Atlas region, ʿAbd al-Muʾmin went with him. Ibn Tūmart won a following in the mountains and founded a small Almohad state there, centred on the village of Tinmel. When al-Bashīr, the reformer's second in command, was killed in an attack on Marrakech, ʿAbd al-Muʾmin took his place and became Ibn Tūmart's designated successor. The *mahdī* died in 1130. His death was kept secret at first to allow ʿAbd al-Muʾmin—a stranger to the High Atlas—time to win support from the Almohad leaders. When he was proclaimed leader of the Almohads, he assumed the prestigious title of caliph.

His first task was to carry on the struggle against the Almoravids. Learning from the failure at Marrakech, he realized that he must conquer Morocco from the mountains. On the plains, the Christian knights who served the Almoravids could easily repulse the Almohads' Berber infantry. He spent the next 15 years winning control of the High Atlas, Middle Atlas, and Rif regions, finally moving into his native country, north of Tlemcen.

Near that town, the Almoravids, having suffered the loss of Reverter, the leader of their Catalan mercenaries, were defeated by ʿAbd al-Muʾmin in open battle in 1145. The Almohad forces then moved west, subjugating Morocco's Atlantic coastal plain. They then laid siege to Marrakech and took it by storm in 1147, massacring the Almoravid inhabitants.

Arab historians have left a description of the man who had now become master of Northwest Africa. He was a sturdy Berber of medium height, with dark hair and regular features. A good soldier, with great courage and endurance, he was at the same time learned in Islām and a gifted orator. Although he had personal charm and could, when necessary, show patience and moderation, he was at times as harsh as his master, Ibn Tūmart. When a revolt broke out in the Atlantic plain area following the capture of Marrakech, he conducted a methodical purge there in which more than 30,000 people were executed.

ʿAbd al-Muʾmin left neither memoirs nor a political testament; his ideas must be deduced from his actions. His newfound power and his very success raised problems that demanded immediate solutions.

The capture of Marrakech posed the moral question of whether to abandon this city founded by the Almoravid heretics, whom he had exterminated without pity. He contented himself with destruction of their palace and mosques and retained Marrakech as the capital of his new empire.

Soon he had to choose between two imperial policies: to complete the conquest of North Africa or to concentrate his energies on Spain, where the Christians were threatening the former Almoravid domains. Showing good judgment as well as feeling for his native country, he gave priority to North Africa.

In 1151 he subjugated the area around Constantine and on his way home fought a battle near Sétif against a coalition of Arab tribes that had been wandering over the Berber country for a century, gradually destroying its peasant and sedentary way of life. ʿAbd al-Muʾmin was victorious, but instead of punishing these people who had showed themselves to be the worst enemies of the Berbers and the Almohad government, he came to rely on them to strengthen his dynasty against opposition from the family of Ibn Tūmart. He also wished to use the Arab cavalry in his holy war against the Christians in Spain.

In 1158–59 ʿAbd al-Muʾmin conquered Tunisia and Tripolitania. This marked the zenith of Berber power in Islām: a Berber caliph reigned over all of North Africa west of Egypt, and his authority was acknowledged by most of Muslim Spain as well.

ʿAbd al-Muʾmin's government. Even while he was pursuing his conquest, ʿAbd al-Muʾmin had established a central government for his empire. To the traditional clan organization of the Maṣmudah and other Berber peoples supporting the Almohads he added an organization to promote the spread of Almohad doctrine and a central administration (the *makhzan*) modelled on those of Muslim Spain, which was staffed largely by Spanish Muslims. A government land registry was improvised to assure the dynasty regular revenue. ʿAbd al-Muʾmin fully accepted the responsibilities of an art patron, but remembering the puritanical austerity of Ibn Tūmart, he sometimes imposed on the mosques built for him by Andalusian artisans a plainness that became more precious than the prevailing elaborate ornamentation.

ʿAbd al-Muʾmin died in 1163. His work, faithfully carried on by his successors Abū Yaʿqūb Yūsuf (reigned 1163–84) and Abū Yūsuf Yaʿqūb al-Manṣūr (1184–99), was maintained for more than half a century. Disturbances caused by the rebellious Arab tribes impoverished the country without endangering the dynasty. After their defeat by the Spanish Christians at Las Navas de Tolosa in 1212, however, the Almohads began to decline, and their empire soon disintegrated.

Though in the long run ʿAbd al-Muʾmin's successors proved unable to perpetuate his achievements, he himself had written one of the most glorious chapters in the history of the Muslim West. (H.-L.-É.T.)

BIBLIOGRAPHY. Information about ʿAbd al-Muʾmin and his work may be found in the general histories by Henri Terrasse, *Histoire du Maroc,* vol. 2, pp. 261–316 (1950); and Ambrosio Huici Miranda, *Historia política del Imperio Almohade,* 2 vol. (1956–57), both with numerous bibliographic references.

ʿAbd al-Qādir al-Jīlānī (b. 1077/78, Nif, Persia—d. 1166, Baghdad), founder of the Qādirīyah order of the mystical Ṣūfī branch of Islām.

He studied Islāmic law in Baghdad and was introduced to Ṣūfism rather late in life, first appearing as a preacher in 1127. His great reputation as a preacher and teacher attracted disciples from the entire Islāmic world, and he is said to have converted numerous Jews and Christians to Islām. As a thinker, his achievement was to have reconciled the mystical nature of the Ṣūfī calling with the sober demands of Islāmic law. His concept of Ṣūfism was that of a holy war or *jihād* waged against one's own will in order to conquer egotism and worldliness and to submit to God's will. Numerous legends of his saintliness arose after his death, and he retains a popular following among those who consider him a divine mediator.

ʿAbd al-Qādir ibn Muḥyī ad-Dīn ibn Mustafā al-Ḥasanī al-Jazāʾirī (Algerian leader): *see* Abdelkader.

ʿAbd al-Wādid DYNASTY, also called ZAYYĀNID DYNASTY, or BANŪ ZAYYĀN, dynasty of Zanātah Berbers (1236–1550), successors to the Almohad empire in northwestern Algeria. In 1236 the Zanātahs, loyal vassals to the Almohads, gained the support of other Berber tribes and nomadic Arabs and set up a kingdom at Tilimsān (Tlemcen), headed by the Zanātah *amīr* Yaghmurāsan (ruled 1236–83). Yaghmurāsan was able to maintain internal peace through the successful control of the rival Berber factions, and, in the face of the Marīnid threat in the west, he allied with the Sultan of Granada and the King of Castile.

After his death, however, the Marīnid sultan Abū Yaʿqūb besieged Tilimsān for eight years (1298–1306). The city was finally taken in 1337 by Abū al-Ḥasan, and a 10-year period of Marīnid domination followed. Recaptured by the ʿAbd al-Wādids in 1348, Tilimsān was again stormed by the Marīnids in 1352, who ruled for another seven years.

ʿAbd al-Wādid attempts at expansion eastward into Ḥafṣid Tunis also proved disastrous, and, for a time in the early 15th century, they were virtual vassals of the Ḥafṣid state. The kingdom's chronic weakness may be traced to its lack of geographical and cultural unity, the absence of fixed frontiers, and constant internal rebellions. It further suffered from a shortage of manpower, having to rely on intractable Arab nomads for soldiers. Its economic prosperity was based on the position of Tilimsān along the trade route between the Mediterranean ports and Saharan oases. The ʿAbd al-Wādid state collapsed in 1550, when Tilimsān was seized by the Ottoman Turks after a half century of alternating Spanish–Turkish suzerainty.

ʿAbd Allāh (Arabic personal name): *see under* Abdullah, except as below.

ʿAbd Allāh, in full ʿABD ALLĀH IBN MUḤAMMAD AT-TAʿĀʾISHĪ, also called ʿABDULLAHI (b. 1846, Sudan—d. Nov. 24, 1899, Kordofan), political and religious leader who succeeded Muḥammad Aḥmad—al-Mahdī—as head of a religious movement and state within the Sudan.

ʿAbd Allāh followed his family's vocation for religion. In about 1880 he became a disciple of Muḥammad Aḥmad, who announced that he had a divine mission, became known as al-Mahdī, and appointed ʿAbd Allāh a caliph (*khalīfah*). When al-Mahdī died in 1885, ʿAbd Allāh became leader of the Mahdist movement. His first concern was to establish his authority on a firm basis. Al-Mahdī had clearly designated him as successor, but the Ashraf, a portion of al-Mahdī's supporters, tried to reverse this decision. By promptly securing control of the vital administrative positions in the movement and obtaining the support of the most religiously sincere group of al-Mahdī's followers, ʿAbd Allāh neutralized this opposition. ʿAbd Allāh could not claim the same religious inspiration as had al-Mahdī, but, by announcing that he received divine instruction through al-Mahdī, he tried to assume as much of the aura as was possible.

ʿAbd Allāh believed he could best control the disparate elements that supported him by maintaining the expansionist momentum begun by al-Mahdī. He launched attacks against the Ethiopians and began an invasion of Egypt. But ʿAbd Allāh had greatly overestimated the support his forces would receive from the Egyptian peasantry and underestimated the potency of the Anglo-Egyptian military forces, and in 1889 his troops suffered a crushing defeat in Egypt.

A feared Anglo-Egyptian advance up the Nile did not materialize. Instead ʿAbd Allāh suffered famine and military defeats in the eastern Sudan. The most serious challenge to his authority came from a revolt of the Ashraf in November 1891, but he kept this from reaching extensive proportions and reduced his opponents to political impotence.

During the next four years, ʿAbd Allāh ruled securely and was able to consolidate his authority. The famine and the expense of large-scale military campaigns came to an end. ʿAbd Allāh modified his administrative policies, making them more acceptable to the people. Taxation became less burdensome. ʿAbd Allāh created a new military corps, the *mulazimiyah,* of whose loyalty he felt confident.

But in 1896 Anglo-Egyptian forces began their reconquest of the Sudan. Although ʿAbd Allāh resisted for almost two years, he could not prevail against British machine guns. In September 1898 he was forced to flee his capital, Omdurman, but he remained at large with a considerable army. Many Egyptians and Sudanese resented the Condominium Agreement of January 1899, by which the Sudan became almost a British protectorate, and ʿAbd Allāh hoped to rally support. But on Nov. 24, 1899, a British force engaged the Mahdist remnants, and ʿAbd Allāh died in the fighting.

ʿAbd Allāh, Khawr, estuary (*khawr*) separating Kuwait and Iraq, probably a drowned river mouth of the Shatt (stream) al-Arab, whose mouth is now farther north and forms the southeastern part of the border between Iraq and Iran. It extends into Iraqi territory in the form of the Khawr az-Zubayr, on which the Iraqi port of Umm Qaṣr is located and which is linked by canal northwestward to the Tigris–Euphrates River System. The Khawr ʿAbd Allāh borders the northeastern coast of the Jazīrat (island) Būbiyān and the northern coast of Jazīrat Warbah. Both islands are generally considered to be part of Kuwait, but are also claimed by Iraq.

ʿAbd Allāh ibn al-ʿAbbās, also called IBN ABBĀS, byname AL-ḤIBR ("the Doctor"), or AL-BAḤR ("the Sea") (b. *c.* 619—d. 687/688, aṭ-Ṭāʾif, Arabia), a companion of the prophet Muḥammad, one of the greatest scholars of early Islām, and the first exegete of the Qurʾān.

In the early struggles for the caliphate, Ibn ʿAbbās supported ʿAlī and was rewarded with the governorship of Baṣra. Subsequently he defected and withdrew to Mecca. During the reign of Muʿāwiyah he lived in the Hejaz, going to Damascus, the capital, only occasionally. After the death of Muʿāwiyah, he opposed ʿIbn az-Zubayr, whom he refused to recognize as caliph, and was forced to flee to aṭ-Ṭāʾif, where he died.

He gathered information concerning the words and deeds of Muḥammad from other companions and gave classes on interpretation of the Qurʾān, his commentaries on which were later collected. In Islāmic law, he is considered the principal authority among the Meccan Companions, and numerous traditions (*ḥadīth*) were transmitted on his authority or on that of those who knew him.

ʿAbd Allāh ibn al-Ḥusayn: *see* Abdullah.

ʿAbd Allāh ibn az-Zubayr (b. May 624, Medina, Arabia—d. November 692, Mecca), leader of a rebellion against the Umayyad ruling dynasty of the Islāmic empire, and the most prominent representative of the Muslim nobility of faith, which resented the Umayyad assumption of caliphal authority.

As a youth Ibn az-Zubayr went on many of the military campaigns that marked the initial expansion of Islām, and in 651 he was nominated by the caliph (the titular leader of the Islāmic empire) ʿUthmān to aid in compiling an official recension of the Qurʾān. Subsequently remaining politically inactive, he took little part in the civil wars that followed the death of ʿUthmān in 656. Resenting the Umayyad victory that resulted from the civil wars, he refused to take an oath of allegiance to Yazīd, the son and heir presumptive of Muʿāwiyah, the first Umayyad caliph. When Yazīd became caliph in 680, Ibn az-Zubayr still refused the oath of allegiance and fled to Mecca. There he secretly gathered an army. Yazīd learned of this and dispatched forces of his own, which besieged Ibn az-Zubayr in Mecca. In 683 Yazīd died, and the besieging army withdrew. Ibn az-Zubayr was left in peace until 692, when the caliph ʿAbd al-Malik sent an army to Mecca to force him to submit. Mecca was again besieged, and Ibn az-Zubayr was killed in the fighting.

ʿAbd Allāh ibn Lutf Allāh ibn ʿAbd ar-Rashīd al-Bihdādīnī Ḥāfiẓ-i Abrū: *see* Ḥāfiẓ-i Abrū.

Abd ar-Rahman, also called ʿABD AR-RAḤMĀN IBN HISHĀM (b. 1789/90—d. Aug. 28, 1859, Meknès, Mor.), 24th ruler of the ʿAlawī dynasty of Morocco, whose reign was marked by both peaceful and hostile contacts with European powers.

Having succeeded to the throne without internal conflict, he became an able administrator and active builder of public works. During his long reign his authority was often challenged by dissident tribes and disaffected notables; he suppressed revolts in 1824, 1828, 1831, 1843, 1849, and 1853.

The more serious challenge to his kingdom came from abroad. The traditional policy of the ʿAlawīs of encouraging piracy to raise funds led to conflict with the European powers. As a reprisal for seizing their ships, the English blockaded Tangier, and the Austrians bombarded the ports of Arzila, Larache (al-ʿArāʾish), and Tétouan. The port of Salé was bombarded in 1851, again as a reprisal for Moroccan piracy. Abd ar-Rahman attempted to expand his influence eastward by supporting Abdelkader, leader of Algerian resistance against the French. This policy led to a disastrous war with France in 1844. By the Treaty of Tangier, October 1844, Abd ar-Rahman was obliged to recognize France's dominant position in Algeria. During his reign, however, he also signed a number of commercial treaties with the European powers, and he preserved Moroccan independence by his astute diplomacy.

ʿAbd ar-Raḥmān I, also called AD-DĀKHIL RAḤMĀN (fl. 750–788), member of the Umayyad ruling family of Syria who founded an Umayyad dynasty in Spain.

When the ʿAbbāsids overthrew the Umayyad caliphate in 750 and sought to kill as many of the Umayyad family as possible, ʿAbd ar-Raḥmān fled, eventually reaching Spain. The Iberian Peninsula had for some time been occupied by Muslim Arab forces, and he saw political opportunity for himself in the rivalries of the Qais and Yaman, the dominant Arab factions there. By shifting alliances and using mercenary support, he placed himself in a position of power, attacking and defeating the Governor of al-Andalus in 755 and making Córdoba his capital. As news of his success spread eastward, men who had previously worked in the Umayyad administrative system came to Spain to work with ʿAbd ar-Raḥmān, and his administrative system came to resemble that formerly operative in Damascus.

ʿAbd ar-Raḥmān secured his realm against external attack by defeating armies sent by Charlemagne and the ʿAbbāsid caliph. Although he faced a series of rebellions by Muslim Spaniards, Berbers from the mountainous areas, and various Arab clans, his authority and dynasty remained firmly in power.

ʿAbd ar-Raḥmān II, fourth Umayyad ruler of Muslim Spain who enjoyed a reign (822–852) of brilliance and prosperity, the importance of which has been underestimated by some historians.

ʿAbd ar-Raḥmān II was the grandson of his namesake, founder of the Umayyad dynasty in Spain. His reign was an administrative watershed. As the influence of the ʿAbbāsid Caliphate, then at the peak of its splendour, grew, Córdoba's administrative system increasingly came into accord with that of Baghdad, the ʿAbbāsid capital. ʿAbd ar-Raḥmān carried out a vigorous policy of public works, made additions to the Great Mosque in Córdoba, and patronized poets, musicians, and men of religion. Although palace intrigues surrounded his death in 852, they did not diminish his accomplishments.

ʿAbd ar-Raḥmān III, byname AN-NĀṢIR LI-DĪN ALLĀH (Arabic: Victor for the Religion of Allah), in full ʿABD AR-RAḤMĀN IBN MUḤAMMAD IBN ʿABD ALLĀH IBN MUḤAMMAD IBN ʿABD AR-RAḤMĀN IBN AL-ḤAKAM AR-RABḌĪ IBN HISHĀM IBN ʿABD AR-RAḤMĀN AD-DĀKHIL (b. January 891—d. Oct. 15, 961, Córdoba), first caliph and greatest ruler of the Umayyad Arab Muslim dynasty of Spain. He reigned as hereditary *amīr* (prince) of Córdoba from October 912 and took the title of caliph in 929.

Accession as amīr. ʿAbd ar-Raḥmān succeeded his grandfather ʿAbd Allāh as *amīr* of Córdoba in October 912 at the age of 21. Because of his intelligence and character he had been the obvious favourite of his grandfather, who had designated him heir presumptive in preference to the other royal princes. In appearance he is described as having been light-skinned, handsome, thickset, and short-legged. He appeared to be very short when he walked but was imposing on horseback.

Public homage was paid to him in Córdoba immediately after his accession. He set about at once and with great energy to restore the authority of Córdoba in Spain—an authority that had been curtailed during the latter years of the reign of his grandfather by a host of rebels entrenched in mountain forts throughout the land. Ten days after his accession he had the head of the first rebel exhibited in Córdoba. Thereafter, for a score or so of years, he led almost annual expeditions against the rebels, first in southern and later in central and eastern Spain.

His greatest enemy was a crypto-Christian rebel, ʿUmar ibn Ḥafṣūn, lord of Bobastro. ʿAbd ar-Raḥmān's strategy was one of continuous harassment of Ibn Ḥafṣūn's forts. Beginning with the campaign of Monteleón, ʿAbd ar-Raḥmān captured 70 forts in the provinces of Elvira, Granada, and Jaén—all of which had been directly or indirectly controlled by Ibn Ḥafṣūn. In 913 Seville was captured, followed by Algeciras, Rayyu, Sidonia, and Carmona. When Ibn Ḥafṣūn died in 917, the rebellion collapsed. His children were captured or killed, and the centre of the rebellion, Bobastro, was finally stormed in 928. In 933 Toledo fell after a bitter siege, and, with its fall, the last Muslim centre of resistance to Córdoban hegemony disappeared.

Campaigns against the Christians. Meanwhile, ʿAbd ar-Raḥmān also had to check threats from the Christian north. The main danger came from the Kingdom of Leon. An expedition commanded by Ordoño II, then vassal king of Galicia and later king of Leon, into Muslim territory in the summer of 913, especially his sack of Evora (Talavera) and the massacre of its Muslim population, produced widespread resentment in Muslim Spain. ʿAbd ar-Raḥmān decided to counterattack, which he began in earnest in 920, leading the campaign of Muez in person. He captured the forts of Osma and San Esteban de Gormaz and then inflicted a crushing defeat on the combined armies of Leon and Navarre at Valdejunquera on July 26, 920. Four years later, in the spring of 924, he led another campaign into Navarre and sacked the capital, Pamplona. With these two campaigns, ʿAbd ar-Raḥmān was able to secure his frontiers with Christian Spain for the next seven years. But the next king of Leon, Ramiro II, who ascended the throne in 932, proved a formidable adversary and began immediately to mount attacks against Muslim territory. The encounter between the two rulers finally took place in 939, when, at the so-called ditch of Simancas, Ramiro severely defeated the Muslims and ʿAbd ar-Raḥmān narrowly escaped with his life. After that defeat ʿAbd ar-Raḥmān resolved never to take personal charge of another expedition. The Christian victory, however, was not followed up. When Ramiro died in 950, and civil war broke out in the Christian territories, ʿAbd ar-Raḥmān made good his earlier losses so thoroughly that in 958 Sancho, exiled king of Leon, Garcia Sánchez, king of Navarre, and his mother, Queen Toda, all paid personal homage to ʿAbd ar-Raḥmān in Córdoba.

In North Africa the policy of ʿAbd ar-Raḥmān was directed against the Fāṭimids in al-Qayrawān (now in modern Tunisia). In order to check their control over North Africa he financed rebellions against them and sent naval expeditions to sack the coastal cities. The city of Ceuta was fortified in 931 as a base of operations in North Africa. Toward the end of his reign, however, Fāṭimid power increased, and the Fāṭimid general Jawhar was able to repulse the allies of ʿAbd ar-Raḥmān. The struggle with the Fāṭimids, however, was inconclusive and was to continue throughout the 10th century.

As a result of his early successes, and probably at his own suggestion, some of his court poets urged ʿAbd ar-Raḥmān to adopt the title of caliph. He assumed that dignity in 929, shortly after the fall of Bobastro, and chose the honorific title an-Nāṣir li-Dīn Allāh (He Who Fights Victoriously for the Religion of God). His reasons were, internally, to enhance his prestige and, externally, to counter the Fāṭimid claim to this honour.

Significance. The consolidation of power brought great prosperity to Muslim Spain—one indication of which was his building of a mint where pure gold and silver coins were struck. ʿAbd ar-Raḥmān was also a great builder; he renovated and added considerably to the Great Mosque at Córdoba and to the royal palace. At vast expense he built a new royal city, Madīnat az-Zahrāʾ, to house his household and government. He kept a very strict control over the affairs of state and his civil service, changing his governors frequently to avoid the growth of local dynasties. In 949 he executed his own son for conspiring against him.

Christian and Jewish communities flourished during his tolerant reign. His fame spread so far beyond his domains that Córdoba by the end of his reign enjoyed almost as much fame as Constantinople in the Mediterranean world. In Córdoba he received emissaries from such distant rulers as Otto I of Germany and the Byzantine emperor. Córdoba was said to have contained 3,000 mosques and more than 100,000 shops and houses. His reign, the second longest of any Muslim caliph, afforded his wise and courageous policies the fullest chance of development. (T.Kh.)

BIBLIOGRAPHY. The best account of ʿAbd ar-Raḥmān's reign is in E. Lévi-Provencal, *Histoire de l'Espagne musulmane*, vol. 2, pp. 1–164 (1950). Also useful are W.M. Watt, *A History of Islamic Spain* (1965); and S. Lane-Poole, *The Story of the Moors in Spain* (1886; reprinted as *The Moors in Spain*, 1967).

Abd el-Kader (Algerian leader): *see* Abdelkader.

Abd el-Krim, in full MUḤAMMAD IBN ʿABD AL-KARĪM AL-KHAṬṬĀBĪ (b. 1882, Ajdir, Mor.—d. Feb. 6, 1963, Cairo), leader of a resistance movement against Spanish and French rule in North Africa and founder of the short-lived Republic of the Rif (1921–26). A skilled tactician and a capable organizer, he led a liberation movement that made him the hero of the Maghrib (northwest Africa). Designated by Ho Chi Minh as the "precursor" of armed struggle for independence, Abd el-Krim was defeated only by the military and technological superiority of the colonial powers.

Son of an influential member of the Berber tribe Banū Uriaghel, Abd el-Krim received a Spanish education in addition to the traditional Muslim schooling. He was employed as a secretary in the Bureau of Native Affairs. In 1915 he was appointed the *qāḍī al-quḍāt,* or chief Muslim judge, for the district of Melilla, where he also taught at a Hispano-Arabic school and was the editor of an Arabic section of *El Telegrama del Rif.*

During his employment with the Spanish protectorate administration he began to be disillusioned with Spanish rule, eventually opposed Spanish policies, and was imprisoned. He escaped and in 1918 was made chief Muslim judge at Melilla again, but he left the post in 1919 to return to Ajdir.

Soon Abd el-Krim, joined by his brother, who later became his chief adviser and commander of the Rif army, was organizing tribal resistance against foreign domination of Morocco. In July 1921 at Annoual he defeated a Spanish army and pursued it to the suburbs of Melilla. At that time the Republic of the Rif was founded with Abd el-Krim as its president. Overcoming tribal rivalries, he began organizing a centralized administration based upon traditional Berber tribal institutions. He defeated another Spanish army in 1924; in 1925 he almost reached the ancient city of Fès in his drive against French forces that had captured his supply base in the Wargha valley.

Faced with Abd el-Krim's successes and seeing in his movement a threat to their colonial possessions in North Africa, the Franco-Spanish conference meeting in Madrid decided upon joint action. As a Spanish force landed at Alhucemas near Ajdir, a French army of 160,000 men under Marshal Philippe Pétain attacked from the south. Confronted with this combined Franco-Spanish force of 250,000 men with overwhelming technological superiority, Abd el-Krim surrendered on May 27, 1926, and was exiled to the island of Réunion in the Indian Ocean. Receiving permission in 1947 to live in France, he left Réunion and was granted political asylum en route by the Egyptian government; for five years he presided over the Liberation Committee of the Arab West (sometimes called the Maghrib Bureau) in Cairo. After the restoration of Moroccan independence, King Muhammad V invited him to return to Morocco, which he refused to do as long as French troops remained on North African soil. Further information about Abd el-Krim may be found in David S. Woolman's *Rebels in the Rif: Abd el Krim and the Rif Rebellion* (1968) and in Rupert Furneaux's *Abdel Krim: Emir of the Rif* (1967).

ʿAbd-uṣ-Ṣamad, Khwāja (fl. 16th century), Persian painter who, together with Mīr Sayyid ʿAlī, was one of the first members of the imperial atelier in India and is thus credited with playing a strong part in the foundation of the Mughal school of miniature painting (*see* Mughal painting).

He was born in Shīrāz, Fārs, into a family of good social standing; the dates of his birth and of his death are not known. He had already gained a reputation as a calligrapher as well as a painter when he met the emperor Humāyūn, who was in exile in Persia. At Humāyūn's invitation, he followed him to India in 1548, first to Kābul and later to Delhi. He instructed both Humāyūn and his young son, the future emperor Akbar, in drawing. Among his students while he was superintendent of Akbar's atelier were Dasvant and Basāvan, Hindus who became two of the most renowned Mughal painters. ʿAbd-uṣ-Ṣamad received many honours from Akbar. In 1576 he was appointed master of the mint, and in 1584 at the end of his career he was made dewan (revenue commissioner) of Multān.

Among ʿAbd-uṣ-Ṣamad's greatest achievements was the supervision, together with his fellow Persian Mīr Sayyid ʿAlī, of a large part of the illustrations of the *Dāstān-e* ("Stories of") *Amīr Ḥamzeh,* a series that numbered about 1,400 paintings, all of unusually large size. As none of the paintings is signed, it is not certain whether he himself did any of them. Among the miniatures bearing his signature is one in the Royal Library in the Golestān Palace, Tehrān, depicting Akbar presenting a miniature to his father, Humāyūn. The work, though Persian in its treatment of many details, hints of the Indian style to come, evident in the realistic presentation of the life of the court. A more thoroughly Indianized version of ʿAbd-uṣ-Ṣamad's painting style is found in an illustrated manuscript of the *Khamseh* of Neẓāmī dated 1595, now part of the collection of the British Museum.

Abdālī: *see* Durrānī.

ʿAbdali Sultanate, former semi-independent state in the southern Arabian Peninsula, in what is now Yemen (Aden). Located just north of Aden city, it was one of the most important tribal areas of the Aden Protectorate, the forerunner of independent Yemen (Aden); its capital was Laḥij. The sultanate was earlier tributary to Yemen (now Yemen [Ṣanʿāʾ]), but gained its independence in 1728. The ʿAbdali tribal people then seized Aden and remained independent until 1839, when they signed the first of several treaties with the British that led to the formation of the Aden Protectorate. The sultanate was held by the Turks during World War I. The Ṣubayḥī (Subeihi) tribal area to the west came under ʿAbdali jurisdiction in 1948, and the sultanate became part of Yemen (Aden) in 1967. The lands comprise a fertile area that has a settled population and produces fruit, grain, and other crops.

Abdallah (Arabic personal name): *see under* ʿAbd Allāh, or Abdullah.

Abdelkader, also spelled ABD EL-KADER, or ABDUL-QADIR, Arabic in full ʿABD AL-QĀDIR IBN MUHYĪ AD-DĪN IBN MUṢṬAFĀ AL-ḤASANĪ AL-JAZĀʾIRĪ (b. Sept. 6, 1808, Guetna, near Mascara, Alg.—d. May 26, 1883, Damascus), *amīr* of Mascara (from 1832), the military and religious leader who founded the Algerian state and led the Algerians in their 19th-century struggle against French domination (1840–46).

Early career. His physical handsomeness and the qualities of his mind had made Abdelkader popular even before his military exploits. Of medium height, lithe and elegant, with regular features and a black beard, his demeanour was exceptionally refined, and his life-style simple. He was known as a religious and educated man who could excite his co-religionists with his poetry and oratorical eloquence.

Algeria was an Ottoman regency when the French Army landed there in 1830. The government was controlled by a dey (governor) and by the Turkish Janissaries who had chosen him. These rulers, supported by the Kouloughlis (people of mixed Turkish and Algerian ancestry) and by certain privileged tribes, and aided by the fact that they were of the same religion as the people, long held Algeria firmly in their grip.

Nevertheless, the Algerians detested them, and there were continual rebellions in the early 19th century. As a result, the country was left too divided to oppose the Christian invaders.

The western tribes laid siege to Oran and tried to organize themselves, unified by their common Muslim religious sentiment, which was cultivated by the schoolmasters and particularly by members of the religious brotherhoods. The leader of one of the brotherhoods, Mahieddin, director of the *zāwiyah* (religious school) near Mascara, was asked to lead the harassment of the French troops in Oran and Mostaganem.

In November 1832 the aging Mahieddin had his young son Abdelkader elected in his place. The youth, already renowned for his piety and military prowess, took over the war of harassment. The ensuing Desmichels Treaty of 1834 gave him the whole interior of the Oran, with the title commander of the believers. In a move to unify his new territories, Amīr Abdelkader, taking advantage of this treaty, imposed his rule on all the tribes of the Chelif, occupied Miliana and then Médéa, and succeeded in defeating Gen. Camille Trézel at Macta. Although pressed by generals Bertrand Clauzel and T.R. Bugeaud, he managed to rally support from Algerians who had become indignant over the French use of violence. By able negotiation, he convinced General Bugeaud to sign the Treaty of Tafna (1837), which further increased his territory and made him master of the whole interior of Oran and the Titteri, with the French having to be content with a few ports.

Creation of a new state. In two years the Amīr had organized a true state, the capital of which was sometimes Mascara and sometimes the fortress of Tiaret (now Tagdempt). He established juridical equality among population groups by suppressing the privileges of the warlike tribes (*makhzen*) and by imposing equal taxes on all his subjects. First he extended his influence to the Sahara by fighting at-Tijīnī, who dominated the southern oases, and rallying the desert peoples to him. Then he strengthened his authority in the valley of the Chelif and in the Titteri as far as the borders of the province of the east, where he was resisted by the bey of Constantine, Hajj Ahmed. He also exacted harsh punishment of the Kouloughlis of Zouatna, who had joined the French. By the winter of 1838, his authority extended across the borders of Kabylie and, in the south, from the oasis of Biskra to the Moroccan border. To destroy the power of at-Tijīnī, he besieged his capital, Aïn Mahdi, for six months and demolished it, while all the Saharan tribes paid him homage.

Abdelkader was an absolute leader who only rarely called in the grandees to advise him. Algerian religious sentiment was his support, the one force that could bring his subjects together and unify them in the face of the invader. But that did not prevent him from employing competent persons of all nationalities, whether Jews or Christians, to help him build a modern state. The best known of these Europeans was the future diplomat Léon Roches, who later recounted his adventures in a fanciful book, *Trente-deux ans à travers l'Islam* ("Thirty-two Years Through Islām"). Abdelkader organized a regular army of approximately 2,000 men, to be supported by either volunteers or contingents furnished by the tribes. As towns near French territory would have been too vulnerable, he fortified interior sites, such as Sebdou, Saïda, Tiaret, Taza, and Boghar, where he opened arsenals, warehouses, and workshops, and where he stored surplus crops whose sales were to finance his arms purchases, mainly in England. He set up a new administration, with officials on fixed salaries. He taught his people austerity and set a personal example, living without ceremony in a tent. By expanding education, he slowly spread the concepts of independence and nationality to his people.

When the columns of the Duc d'Orléans crossed the Iron Gates, the Amīr took it as a violation of the territories granted him by the Treaty of Tafna. Even though he was still far from having completed his own work of organization, he made a surprise attack and destroyed the French colonization of the Mitidja Plain. From then on the war languished until General Bugeaud was named governor general in 1840. Bugeaud convinced the French government to arm him for the conquest of all Algeria. The resulting war was bitter and lasted seven years. The Amīr avoided big battles, preferring to use his rifle-armed cavalry in incessant skirmishes, from which it would retreat almost as soon as it had fired. But he was fighting a French army composed of infantry organized by Bugeaud into extremely mobile columns, and he had to contend with the devastation of the countryside practiced by Bugeaud and his lieutenants so as to force the starving inhabitants to desert their leader.

In 1841 the French destroyed the Amīr's fortified sites, and he was forced to become a nomad in the interior of Oran. The following year he lost Tlemcen, and communication with his Moroccan allies became difficult. Yet, despite further reverses and French penetration in the south, he succeeded in reaching Morocco. But after Bugeaud's defeat of the Moroccans at Isly, the Sultan was forced to hold Abdelkader in the midst of his empire. The Amīr, however, proved to have unflagging energy. Taking advantage of a revolt in the Dahra, he reentered Algeria, took the Sidi Brahim outpost, and penetrated deep into the interior, all the while escaping the pursuing French columns.

Surrender to the French. In July 1846, with only a handful of men left, Abdelkader again took refuge in Morocco, the Sultan of which by then considered him to be a burden. Deprived of this last area of support, Abdelkader returned to Algeria and with great dignity turned himself over to Gen. Christophe de Lamoricière and to Bugeaud's successor, King Louis-Philippe's son, the Duc d'Aumale, who promised him transport to the East.

Louis-Philippe, however, failed to respect his son's promise. Abdelkader was held prisoner in France, first at the Château de Pau, where he learned the principles of Freemasonry, and later at Amboise. It was the prince-president Louis-Napoléon who, in 1852, authorized his return to Bursa and then to Damascus, where he led an exemplary life and wrote *Rappel à l'intelligent, avis à l'indifférent* ("Call to the Intelligent, Warning to the Indifferent"). The French government provided him with a large pension and with a Kabyle guard and even attempted to obtain a throne for him somewhere between Turkey and Egypt, which they wished to remove from Ottoman control. At the time of the 1871 Algerian insurrection, he disowned one of his sons who had tried to arouse the tribes of southern Constantine. When he died, he was respected by all. French efforts to make him the symbol of Algerian support for colonial rule were erroneous. Abdelkader believed he was carrying out God's will in admitting that his political role had ended. Present-day Algerians consider him to be the greatest hero of their people.

(M.E.)

BIBLIOGRAPHY. Paul Azan, *L'Émir Abd el Kader, 1808–1883, du fanatisme musulman au patriotisme français* (1925), the most complete work, but currently out of date; Marcel Emerit, *L'Algérie à l'époque d'Abd-el-Kader* (1951), documents and commentaries; René Gallissot, "Abd el-Kader et la nationalité algérienne," *Revue Historique,* 233:339–368 (1965); Charles Henry Churchill, *The Life of Abdel Kader, Ex-Sultan of the Arabs of Algeria* (1867).

Abdera, in ancient Greece, town on the coast of Thrace near the mouth of the Néstos River. The people of Teos, evacuating Ionia when it was overrun by the Persians under Cyrus (*c.* 540 BC), succeeded in establishing a colony there that developed a brisk trade with the Thracian interior. Abdera was a prosperous member of the Delian League in the 5th century but was crippled early in the 4th century BC by Thracian incursions and declined sharply in importance. The philosophers Protagoras and Democritus were citizens of Abdera. The site is occupied by the modern town of Ávdhira, Greece.

abdominal cavity, largest hollow space of the body. Its upper boundary is the diaphragm, a sheet of muscle and connective tissue that separates it from the chest cavity; its lower boundary is the upper plane of the pelvic cavity. Vertically it is enclosed by the vertebral column and the abdominal and other muscles. The abdominal cavity contains the greater part of the digestive tract, the liver and pancreas, the spleen, the kidneys, and the adrenal glands located above the kidneys.

The abdominal cavity is lined by the peritoneum, a membrane that covers not only the inside wall of the cavity (parietal peritoneum) but also every organ or structure contained in it (visceral peritoneum). The space between the visceral and parietal peritoneum, the peritoneal cavity, is a potential space only, normally containing a small amount of serous fluid that permits free movement of the viscera inside the peritoneal cavity. This motion is particularly true of the gastrointestinal tract. The peritoneum, by connecting the visceral with the parietal portions, assists in the support and fixation of the abdominal organs. The diverse attachments of the peritoneum divide the abdominal cavity into several compartments, of which the compartment called the lesser sac is of particular importance; it is located behind the stomach and is connected to the rest of the peritoneal cavity, the greater sac, by the foramen (opening) of Winslow.

Some of the viscera are attached to the abdominal walls by broad areas of the peritoneum, as is the pancreas. Others—*e.g.* the liver—are attached by folds of the peritoneum and ligaments, usually poorly supplied by blood vessels.

The peritoneal ligaments are actually rather strong peritoneal folds, usually connecting viscera to viscera or viscera to the abdominal wall; their name usually derives from the structures connected by them (*e.g.*, the gastrocolic ligament, connecting the stomach and the colon; the splenocolic ligament, connecting the spleen and the colon), or from their shape (*e.g.*, round ligament, triangular ligament).

The mesenteries are folds of peritoneum that are attached to the wall of the abdomen and enclosing viscera. They are richly supplied with vessels that carry blood to or from the organs they enfold. The three most important mesenteries are the mesentery for the small intestines; the transverse mesocolon, which attaches the transverse portion of the colon to the back wall of the abdomen; and the mesosigmoid, which enfolds the sigmoid portion of the colon.

The omenta are folds of peritoneum enclosing nerves, blood vessels, lymph channels, and fatty and connective tissue. There are two omenta: the greater omentum hangs down from the small intestine like an apron; the lesser omentum is much smaller and extends between the stomach and the liver.

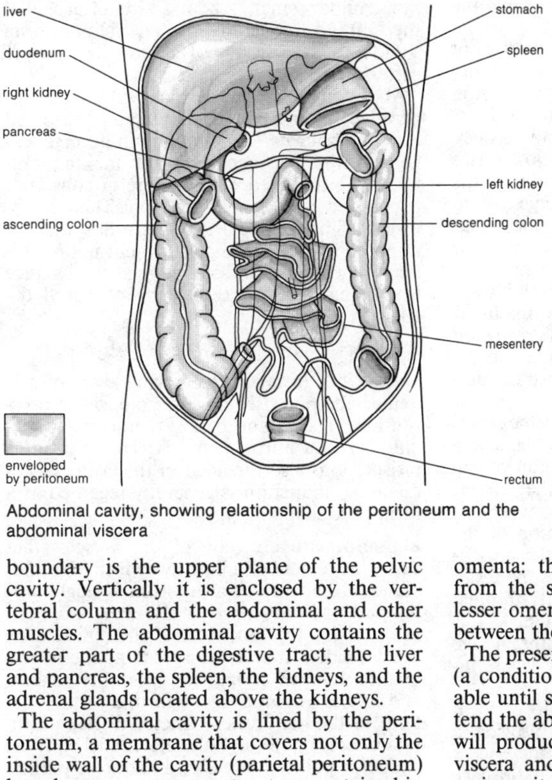

Abdominal cavity, showing relationship of the peritoneum and the abdominal viscera

The presence of fluid in the peritoneal cavity (a condition known as ascites) is not noticeable until such a volume is attained as to distend the abdomen. The accumulation of fluid will produce pressure against the abdominal viscera and veins and also against the thoracic cavity by pressing upon the diaphragm. Treatment is directed toward alleviation of the cause. Decrease in portal vein pressure in many cases relieves the ascites that accompanies cirrhosis. Chylous ascites is best treated by closure of the leaking lymphatic vessel. Adequate treatment of heart failure will usually produce regression of the ascites that the heart failure has caused.

Peritonitis, another disorder, is usually secondary to an inflammatory process elsewhere, which may come from an adjacent structure or organ; may be introduced from the outside by surgery or by injury; may come from organs in the abdomen; or may be borne by the bloodstream or the lymphatics. The most common origin of peritonitis is the gastrointestinal tract. Peritonitis may be acute or chronic, generalized or localized, and may be due to one agent or to a number of them. It is secondary to perforation of the intestines, for example. The severity of the reactions is related, at least in part, to the extent of the peritoneal contamination. In localized peritonitis, the surrounding structures, mainly the greater omentum, will enclose the infected area and temporarily control the infection. If no treatment is started, the infection may progress throughout the entire abdominal cavity. Often the period in which the peritonitis is localized is short, and the peritoneal inflammation becomes generalized with great rapidity.

Control of the source of inflammation, either by surgical or by medical means, is followed by remission of all evidence of peritoneal inflammation or infection or by formation of localized abcesses inside of the peritoneal cavity. Antibiotic therapy has considerably decreased the incidence of the latter complication. When an abscess does develop, antibiotic therapy and adequate external drainage are necessary. The most frequent sites for development of abscesses are the spaces between the diaphragm and the pelvic cavity.

abdominal muscle, any of the muscles of the anterolateral walls of the abdominal cavity, composed of three flat muscular sheets, from without inward: external oblique, internal oblique, and transverse abdominis, supplemented in front on each side of the midline by rectus abdominis.

For a depiction of the abdominal muscles in human anatomy, shown in relation to other parts of the body, *see* the colour Trans-Vision in the PROPAEDIA: Part Four, Section 421.

The first three muscle layers extend between the vertebral column behind, the lower ribs above, and the iliac crest and pubis of the hip bone below. Their fibres all merge toward the midline, where they surround the rectus abdominis in a sheath before they meet the fibres from the opposite side at the linea alba. Strength is developed in these rather thin walls by the crisscrossing of fibres. Thus, the fibres of the external oblique are directed downward and forward, those of the internal oblique upward and forward, and those of the transverse horizontally forward.

Around the rectus abdominis, which extends from the pubis upward to the ribs, the above muscles are all fibrous. In the region of the groin, between the pubic bone and the anterior superior iliac spine, a specialized arrangement of these fibres permits the formation of the inguinal canal, a passage through the muscular layers. This develops at birth as the testes descend out of the abdominal cavity through its wall into the scrotum. In the female this is replaced by a fibrous cord from the uterus. This gap is a potentially weak area where inguinal hernias can occur.

The muscles of the abdominal walls perform a variety of functions: (1) They provide a tonic, elastic muscular support for the viscera and, by their recoil, pull down the rib cage in expiration. (2) They contract against blows to form a rigid protective wall for the viscera. (3) When the glottis is closed and the thorax and pelvis are fixed, these muscles take part in the expulsive efforts of urination, defecation, childbirth, vomiting, and of singing and coughing. (4) When the pelvis is fixed, they initiate the movement of bending the trunk forward. Thereafter, gravity comes into play, the abdominal muscles relax, and the muscles of the back then take on the strain. (5) Conversely, the abdominal muscles come into play in preventing hyperextension. (6) When the thorax is fixed, the abdominal muscles can pull up the pelvis and lower limbs. (7) The muscles of one side can bend the vertebral column sideways and assist in its rotation.

ʿAbdor Raḥmān Khān (b. *c.* 1844, Kābul, Afg.—d. 1901, Kābul), *amīr* of Afghanistan (1880–1901) who played a prominent role in the fierce and long-drawn struggle for power waged by his father and his uncle, Aʿẓam Khān, against his cousin Shīr ʿAlī, the successor of Dōst Moḥammad Khān.

ʿAbdor Raḥmān was the son of Afzal Khān, whose father, Dōst Moḥammad Khān, had established the Barakzāi dynasty in Afghanistan. Shīr ʿAlī's victory in 1869 drove ʿAbdor Raḥmān into exile in Russian Turkistan, where he lived at Samarkand until Shīr ʿAlī's death in 1879, a year after the outbreak of the war between the British and the Afghans. ʿAbdor Raḥmān returned to Afghanistan in 1880, was heartily welcomed by his people, and remained in northern Afghanistan until the British negotiated a settlement recognizing ʿAbdor Raḥmān as *amīr* in return for his acknowledgment of the British right to control his foreign relations. ʿAbdor Raḥmān pacified the country and consolidated his authority. During the years 1880–87, he crushed a revolt by the powerful Ghilzai tribe and an unexpected rebellion led by his cousin Isḥāq Khān; he also decisively defeated Shīr ʿAlī's son Ayūb, who raided intermittently from his base in Herāt.

ʿAbdor Raḥmān's reign is notable for the agreement reached on the demarcation of Afghanistan's northwestern border with Russia, the result of talks held near Kābul in 1893 with a British delegation led by Sir Mortimer Durand, under which ʿAbdor Raḥmān accepted the Durand line as his frontier, relinquishing some hereditary rights over the tribes on the eastern border.

ʿAbdor Raḥmān also reorganized the administrative system of the country and initiated internal reforms. He brought in foreign experts, imported machinery for making munitions, introduced manufacture of consumer goods and new agricultural tools, and established Afghanistan's first modern hospital. He imposed an organized government upon a divided population and maintained the balance in dealing with the British in India and the Russian Empire.

Abdu (city, ancient Egypt): *see* Abydos.

abduction, in law, the carrying away of any female for purposes of concubinage or prostitution. The taking of a girl under a designated age for purposes of marriage is in most jurisdictions also included in the crime of abduction. Abduction is generally regarded as a form of kidnapping (*q.v.*).

abductor muscle, any of the muscles that cause movement of a limb away from the midplane of the body or away from a neighbouring part or limb (*compare* adductor muscles), as in raising the arms to the side (effected by the deltoideus muscle) or spreading the fingers or toes. In man certain muscles of the hands and feet are named for performing this function. In the hand, the abductor digiti minimi manus acts upon the little finger, and both the abductor pollicis longus and abductor pollicis brevis act upon the thumb. The corresponding foot muscles are the abductor digiti minimi pedis and the abductor hallucis, which act on the little and great toes, respectively.

ʿAbduh, Muḥammad (b. 1849, Nile Delta area, Egypt—d. July 11, 1905, near Alexandria), religious scholar, jurist, and liberal reformer, who led the late 19th-century movement in Egypt and other Muslim countries to revitalize Islāmic teachings and institutions in the modern world. As *muftī* (Islāmic legal counsellor) for Egypt (from 1899), he effected reforms in Islāmic law, administration, and higher education and, although resisted by conservatives, broke the rigidity of Muslim ritual, dogma, and family ties. His writings include the "Treatise on the Oneness of God" and a commentary on the Qurʾān.

Life. ʿAbduh attended the mosque school in Ṭanṭā and subsequently al-Azhar University in Cairo, receiving the degree of *ʿālim* (scholar) from the latter in 1877. After an early infatuation with mysticism, in 1872 he fell under the influence of Jamāl ad-Dīn al-Afghānī, the revolutionary pan-Islāmic preacher of Persian origin who had settled in Cairo and who stimulated ʿAbduh's interest in theology, philosophy, and politics. In punishment for political activity, Afghānī was expelled from Egypt in 1879 and ʿAbduh was exiled to his village, but the next year ʿAbduh's fortunes changed. He became editor of the government's official gazette, which he made a platform for preaching resistance to Anglo-French political encroachment and the need for social and religious reform. He was implicated in ʿUrābī Pasha's rebellion against foreign control in 1882 and, following the British military occupation of Egypt, was exiled. Rejoining Afghānī in Paris for several months in 1884, ʿAbduh helped his mentor publish the revolutionary journal *al-ʿUrwat alwuthqā* ("The Firmest Bond"), which was smuggled to Egypt, India, and elsewhere. After brief visits to England and Tunisia, ʿAbduh settled for three years in Beirut and taught in an Islāmic college there.

In 1888 ʿAbduh was permitted to return to Egypt, where he began a judicial career that spanned the rest of his life. He was appointed a judge in the National Courts of First Instance, then in 1891 at the Court of Appeal; in 1899, with British help, he became *muftī* of Egypt. In the latter post he effected several reforms in the administration of Islāmic law and of religious endowments. He also issued advisory opinions to private petitioners, including such controversially liberal judgments as the permissibility of eating meat slaughtered by Christian and Jewish butchers and of accepting interest paid on loans. ʿAbduh also lectured at al-Azhar and, against much conservative opposition, induced reforms in the administration and curriculum of that ancient institution. He established a benevolent society that operated schools for poor children. He served on the Legislative Council, preaching political cooperation with Britain and a long-term effort to bring about legal and educational reforms in Egypt; these views, differing markedly from those he had espoused earlier in life under Afghānī's influence, earned him the approval of Lord Cromer, the British Resident, but also the hostility of the khedive (ruling prince) ʿAbbās Ḥilmī and of the nationalist leader Muṣṭafā Kāmil. Late in life ʿAbduh learned French and pursued an interest in European thought.

Achievements. In addition to his numerous articles in the official gazette and *al-Urwat al-wuthqā*, ʿAbduh's most important writings included *Risālat at-tawḥīd* ("Treatise on the Oneness of God"); a polemic on the superiority of Islām to Christianity in its inherent receptivity to science and civilization; and a fragmentary commentary on the Qurʾān, completed after his death by a disciple. In theology ʿAbduh sought to establish the harmony of reason and revelation, the freedom of the will, and the primacy of the ethical implications of religious faith over ritual and dogma. He deplored the blind acceptance of traditional doctrines and customs and asserted that a return to the pristine faith of the earliest age of Islām not only would restore the Muslims' spiritual vitality but would provide an enlightened criterion for the assimilation of modern scientific culture.

In matters of Islāmic law, which governed Muslim family relationships, ritual duties, and personal conduct, ʿAbduh tried to break through the rigidities of scholastic interpretation and to promote considerations of equity,

welfare, and common sense, even if this occasionally meant disregarding the literal texts of the Qurʾān. From his death to the present day ʿAbduh has been widely revered as the chief architect of the modern reformation of Islām.
(M.H.K.)

BIBLIOGRAPHY. The only full-length biography of ʿAbduh is Muḥammad Rashīd Riḍā, *Tarīkh al-Ustādh al-Imām ash-Shaikh Muḥammad Abduh*, vol. 1 (in Arabic; 1931). Charles C. Adams' classic, *Islam and Modernism in Egypt* (1933), deals at length with Riḍā and other followers of ʿAbduh. A substantial analysis of ʿAbduh's thought and legacy is found in Malcolm H. Kerr, *Islamic Reform: The Political and Legal Theories of Muhammad ʿAbduh and Rashīd Riḍā* (1966); Elie Kedourie, *Afghani and ʿAbduh* (1966), portrays ʿAbduh as a clandestine religious and political subversive. An authoritative summary of ʿAbduh's life and work is by Joseph Schacht in *The Shorter Encyclopaedia of Islam* (1953).

Abdul (Arabic personal name, combining form): *see under* ʿAbd al-.

Abdul-Jabbar, Kareem, also called (until 1971) LEW ALCINDOR, byname of FERDINAND LEWIS ALCINDOR, JR. (b. April 16, 1947, New York City), collegiate and professional basketball player, who as a 7 ft 1³/₈ in. centre dominated the game.

As a schoolboy Alcindor first excelled at baseball, ice skating, and swimming, but by the eighth grade he was concentrating on basketball. He played for Power Memorial Academy (at 6 ft 8 in.) on the varsity for four years. His total of 2,067 points set a New York City high school record. At the University of California at Los Angeles (UCLA) in 1965 he worked on increasing his stamina and developed a dunk shot (jumping and thrusting the ball through the net from above the rim). He played on three National Collegiate Athletic Association championship teams (1966–68) and set a UCLA scoring record with 56 points in his first game. All attempts to guard him failed and he scored 61 points in his best game. During his stay at UCLA, the team lost only two games.

Alcindor joined the National Basketball Association (NBA) Milwaukee Bucks in 1969, and was rookie of the year (1970). In 1971 the Bucks won the NBA championship, and Alcindor led in scoring (2,596 points) and game point average (31.7); he also led in these statistics in 1972 (2,822 points; 34.8). In 1971, Alcindor, who had converted to Islām while at UCLA, took his Arabic name. In 1975 he was traded to the Los Angeles Lakers. In 1984 he surpassed Wilt Chamberlain's career scoring total of 31,419 points.

Abdul-Qadir (Algerian leader): *see* Abdelkader.

Abdul Rahman, Tuanku (King) (b. Aug. 24, 1895, Sri Menanti, Malaya—d. April 1, 1960, Kuala Lumpur), first supreme chief of state of the Federation of Malaya. After the declaration of independence from Great Britain in 1957, the *tuanku* became the first head of state, or Paramount Ruler, elected by and from the Malay rulers for a five-year term. He died before completion of his term.

Son of Tuanku Mohammed, ruler of the state of Negri Sembilan, Abdul Rahman in 1925 accompanied his father to England, where he remained to study law; he was called to the bar from the Inner Temple in 1928. After returning to Malaya, he held a variety of posts in the civil service. On the death of his father in 1933, he succeeded to the throne of Negri Sembilan.

Abdul Rahman was a retiring and kindly man who learned from his father a deep respect for constitutional law and sympathy for his people. (He should not be confused with Tunku Abdul Rahman, who was independent Malaya's first prime minister.)

Abdul Rahman Putra Alhaj, Tunku (Prince) (b. Feb. 8, 1903, Alor Star, Kedah, Malaya), first prime minister of independent Malaya (1957–63) and then of Malaysia (1963–70), under whose leadership the newly formed government was stabilized.

Tunku Abdul Rahman
Camera Press

After studies in England (1920–31), he returned to Malaya to enter the Kedah civil service. In 1947 he returned to England, was called to the bar in 1949, and was appointed a deputy public prosecutor in the Malayan Federal Legal Department, a post he resigned in 1951 to begin a political career. He became president of the United Malays National Organization (UMNO) and effected the alliance of UMNO with the Malayan Chinese Association (1951) and with the Malayan Indian Congress (1955). His Alliance Party won an overwhelming majority in the election of 1955, and Abdul Rahman became chief minister and home minister.

The mission he led to London (January 1956) to negotiate for independence secured immediate internal self-government and the pledge of independence by August 1957. When Malaya became independent, he became its first prime minister and foreign minister, and he continued in that post when the federation of Malaysia was formed in 1963.

In September 1970, one year after the outbreak of riots between the Chinese and the Malays following an election in which the Chinese had made gains, Abdul Rahman relinquished his post as prime minister and was succeeded by Abdul Razak.

His autobiography, *Looking Back: Monday Musings and Memories*, was published in 1977.

Abdul Razak bin Hussein, Tun Haji (b. March 11, 1922, Pekan, Pahang State, Federated Malay States—d. Jan. 14, 1976, London), prime minister, foreign minister, and defense minister of Malaysia from 1970 to 1976.

A lawyer by training, he joined the civil service in 1950, entered politics in 1955, and was a key figure in gaining his country's independence from Britain in 1957. As deputy prime minister and defense minister (1957–70) and as minister of rural development (1959–69) under Tunku Abdul Rahman, first prime minister of independent Malaya (Malaysia from 1963), Abdul Razak was largely responsible for the country's progress in rural and national development. Appointed head of the National Operations Council set up with emergency powers in 1969, he steered the country through that year's violent disturbances between Malays and Chinese. As prime minister from 1970, he pursued a policy of nonalignment, in furtherance of which he established relations with Communist China in 1974.

In 1959 he was awarded the Seri Maharaja Mangku Negara, one of Malaya's (and Malaysia's) highest honours, which carries the title of *tun.*

Abdülaziz, in full ABDÜLAZIZ OGLU MAHMUD II (b. Feb. 9, 1830, Constantinople—d. June 4, 1876, Constantinople), Ottoman sultan (1861–76) who continued the westernizing reforms initiated by his predecessors until 1871, after which his reign took an absolutist turn.

Like his brother Abdülmecid I, whom he succeeded as sultan on June 25, 1861, Abdülaziz was an ardent admirer of the material progress in western Europe. Educated in the Ottoman tradition, however, he could not always accept the adoption of Western institutions and customs. Abdülaziz was a member of the Mawlawiyah (Mevlevi) order of dervishes (Muslim mystics).

Between 1861 and 1871, reforms were continued under the leadership of Abdülaziz' able chief ministers, Fuad Paşa and Âli Paşa. New administrative districts (*vilayets*) were set up (1864); on French advice a council of state was established (1868); public education was organized on the French model and a new university founded; and the first Ottoman civil code was promulgated. Abdülaziz cultivated good relations with France and Great Britain and was the first Ottoman sultan to visit western Europe.

By 1871 Abdülaziz' ministers Ali and Fuad were dead, and France, his western European model, had been defeated by Germany. Abdülaziz, willful and headstrong, without powerful ministers to limit his authority, became the effective ruler and placed greater emphasis on the Islāmic character of the empire. In foreign policy, he turned to Russia for friendship, as turmoil in the Balkan provinces continued.

Abdülaziz, detail of a portrait by an unknown artist, 19th century; in the Topkapı Palace Museum, Istanbul
Sonia Halliday

When insurrection in Bosnia and Hercegovina spread to Bulgaria (1876), ill feeling mounted against Russia for its encouragement of the rebellions. The crop failure of 1873, the Sultan's lavish expenditures, and the mounting public debt had also heightened public discontent. Abdülaziz was deposed by his ministers on May 30, 1876; his death a few days later is attributed to suicide.

Abdülhak Hâmid (Tarhan) (b. Feb. 2, 1852, Constantinople—d. April 12, 1937, Istanbul), poet and playwright, considered one of the greatest Turkish Romantic writers, and instrumental in introducing Western influences into Turkish literature.

Born into a family of famous scholars, Hâmid was educated in Istanbul and in Paris. Later in Tehrān, he studied Arabic and Persian poetry. Following in his father's footsteps, Hâmid became a diplomat, holding posts in Paris, Greece, Bombay, The Hague, London, and Brussels. In 1908 he became a member of the Turkish Senate and after World War I, after a stay in Vienna, returned to Turkey, where he was elected a member of the Grand National Assembly in 1928. A follower of the

Tanzimat (a 19th-century Turkish political reform movement) school of literature and inspired by his patriotic predecessor, the Young Ottoman writer Namık Kemal, Abdülhak Hâmid's plays exhibit a strong French influence. Deeply moved by the death of his wife, he dedicated many poems to her, such as his famous "Makber" ("The Tomb"), written in 1885. His best dramas, notable among which are *Tarik* and *Ibn-i Musa*, feature personages in Muslim history and are written in prose and poetry, although *Finten* (1887) deals with London society. This sensitive poet paved the way for more radical literary reform. He was given a national funeral.

Abdülhamid I (b. March 20, 1725—d. April 7, 1789), Ottoman sultan from 1774 to 1789 who concluded the war with Russia by signing the humiliating Treaty of Küçük Kaynarca. By the terms of the treaty, Russia obtained the fortresses on the coast of the Sea of Azov, the area between the Dnepr and Bug rivers, and navigation and commercial privileges in the Ottoman Empire. Bukovina was ceded to Austria in 1775. Russia annexed the Crimea (an Ottoman vassal state) in 1783 and planned to partition the Ottoman Empire. Confronted with Russian designs, Abdülhamid in 1787 declared war, which was not ended until after his death.

A pious and benevolent man with a keen interest in state affairs, he favoured reform and appointed able grand viziers to whom he entrusted wide powers. He initiated army reforms and opened the Imperial Naval Engineering School. He also endeavoured to strengthen the central government against provincial rulers, particularly in Syria, Egypt, and Iraq.

Abdülhamid II (b. Sept. 21, 1842, Constantinople—d. Feb. 10, 1918, Constantinople), Ottoman sultan from 1876 to 1909, under whose autocratic rule the reform movement of Tanzimat (Reorganization) reached its climax and who adopted a policy of pan-Islāmism in opposition to Western intervention in Ottoman affairs.

Abdülhamid II, oil painting by an unknown artist

By courtesy of the Topkapi Sarayi Museum, Istanbul

A son of Sultan Abdülmecid I, he came to the throne at the deposition of his mentally deranged brother, Murad V, on Aug. 31, 1876. He promulgated the first Ottoman constitution on Dec. 23, 1876, primarily to ward off foreign intervention at a time when the Turks' savage suppression of the Bulgarian uprising (May 1876) and Ottoman successes in Serbia and Montenegro had aroused the indignation of Western powers and Russia. After a disastrous war with Russia (1877), Abdülhamid was convinced that little help could be expected from the Western powers without their intrusion into Ottoman affairs. He dismissed the Parliament, which had met in March 1877, and suspended the constitution in February 1878. Thenceforth for 40 years he ruled from his seclusion at Yıldız Palace (in Constantinople), assisted by a system of secret police, an expanded telegraph network, and severe censorship.

After the French occupation of Tunisia (1881) and assumption of power by the British in Egypt (1882), Abdülhamid turned for support to the Germans. In return, concessions were made to Germany, culminating in permission (1899) to build the Baghdad Railway. Eventually, the suppression of the Armenian revolt (1894) and the turmoil in Crete, which led to the Greco-Turkish War of 1897, once more resulted in European intervention.

Abdülhamid used pan-Islāmism to solidify his internal absolutist rule and to rally Muslim opinion outside the empire, thus creating difficulties for European imperial powers in their Muslim colonies. The Hejaz Railway (*q.v.*), financed by Muslim contributions from all over the world, was a concrete expression of his policy.

Internally, the most far-reaching of his reforms were in education; 18 professional schools were established; Darülfünun, later known as the University of Istanbul, was founded (1900); and a network of secondary, primary, and military schools was extended throughout the empire. Also, the Ministry of Justice was reorganized, and railway and telegraph systems were developed.

Discontent with Abdülhamid's despotic rule and resentment against European intervention in the Balkans, however, led to the military revolution of the Young Turks in 1908. After a short-lived reactionary uprising (April 1909), Abdülhamid was deposed, and his brother was proclaimed sultan as Mehmed V.

Studies of Abdülhamid include *Life of Abdul-Hamid* (1917), by Sir E. Pears, and *The Sultan: The Life of Abdul Hamid* (1958), by Joan Haslip.

Abdulla, Muhammed Said (b. April 25, 1918, Zanzibar, Tanz.), African novelist and the father of Swahili popular literature.

Abdulla, after completing his formal education, began his career as an inspector in the Colonial Health Department. After 10 years there, however, he decided to become a journalist. In 1948 he was made editor of the newspaper *Zanzibari*, and during the next decade he also served as assistant editor of *Al Falaq*, *Al Mahda*, and *Afrika Kwetu*. In 1958 he became editor of *Mkulima*, the national agricultural magazine, where he served until his retirement in 1968.

Coinciding with his shift to *Mkulima* was Abdulla's first success as a writer of fiction. His "Mzimu wa Watu wa Kale" ("Shrine of the Ancestors") won first prize in the Swahili Story-Writing Competition of 1957–58, conducted by the East African Literature Bureau, and was published as a novel in 1960. In this work, Abdulla introduced his detective hero, Bwana Msa—loosely based on Sir Arthur Conan Doyle's Sherlock Holmes—and other characters who recur in most of his subsequent novels, which include *Kisiwa cha Giningi* (1968; "The Well of Giningi"), also a prizewinner; *Duniani Kuna Watu* (1973; "In the World There Are People"); *Siri ya Sifuri* (1974; "The Secret of the Zero"); *Mke Mmoja Waume Watatu* (1975; "One Wife, Three Husbands"); and *Mwana wa Yungi Hulewa* (1976; "The Devil's Child Grows Up"). With each new title, Abdulla's work developed in complexity and sophistication of plot; his use of the Swahili language is admired throughout East Africa, and his works—reprinted several times—are widely used as school texts. The novels characteristically pit the hero's powers of reason against a web of ignorance and superstition that serves to conceal the true nature of the narrative conflict.

Abdullah (Arabic personal name): *see under* ʿAbd Allāh, except as below.

Abdullah, in full ʿABD ALLĀH IBN AL-ḤUSAYN (b. 1882, Mecca—d. July 20, 1951, Jerusalem), statesman who became the first ruler (1946–51) of the independent Arab kingdom of Jordan.

Abdullah, the second son of Ḥusayn ibn ʿAlī, the ruler of the Hejaz, was educated in Istanbul. After the Turkish Revolution of 1908 he represented Mecca in the Ottoman Parliament. Early in 1914 he joined the nationalist Arab movement, which sought independence for Arab territories in the Ottoman Empire. In 1915–16 he played a leading role in clandestine negotiations between the British in Egypt and his father that led to the proclamation (June 10, 1916) of the Arab revolt against the Ottomans.

With dubious legality Abdullah was proclaimed constitutional king of Iraq on March 8, 1920, by the so-called Iraqi Congress in Damascus. But he declined the Iraqi throne, which in August 1921 was given to his brother Fayṣal I. After French troops drove Fayṣal out of Damascus (July 1920), Abdullah occupied Transjordan and threatened to attack Syria. He was successful in gradually negotiating the legal separation of Transjordan from the Palestine mandate.

The creation of a united Arab kingdom encompassing Syria, Iraq, and Transjordan was Abdullah's ambition. During World War II, he actively sided with Great Britain, and his army—the Arab Legion—took part in the British occupation of Syria and Iraq in 1941. In 1946 Transjordan became independent, and he was crowned in Amman on May 25, 1946. He was the only Arab ruler prepared to accept the United Nations' partitioning of Palestine into Jewish and Arab states (1947). In the war with Israel in May 1948, his armies occupied the West Bank of the Jordan River and captured Old Jerusalem. Two years later he annexed the West Bank territory into the kingdom of Jordan, a move that angered his former Arab allies, Syria, Saudi Arabia, and Egypt, which wanted to see the creation of a Palestinian Arab state on the West Bank. His popularity at home declined, and he was assassinated by a Palestinian nationalist.

Abdullah, Sheikh Muhammad, byname LION OF KASHMIR (b. Dec. 5, 1905, Soura, near Srinagar, Kashmir, India—d. Sept. 8, 1982, Srinagar, Jammu and Kashmir), a prominent figure in India's struggle for independence, who fought for the rights of Kashmir and won for it a semiautonomous status within India.

Abdullah was educated at the Prince of Wales College (Jammu) and the Islamia College (Lahore) and received an M.S. degree in physics from Aligarh Muslim University in 1930. He championed the rights of the Muslim majority of the state during British rule in India and fought against the discrimination exercised by the Hindu ruling house. After Abdullah served the first of many terms of imprisonment in 1931, he founded the Kashmir Muslim (later National) Conference. He supported the concept of a secular state, and when India was granted independence he strongly opposed the idea of joining Muslim Pakistan.

In 1948 Abdullah became prime minister of Kashmir. Despite his early support for Indian leader Jawaharlal Nehru, many Indians believed that Abdullah's ultimate aim was succession to the presidency; therefore, in 1953 he was dismissed and imprisoned. During the next 11 years he refused to pledge his loyalty to India and spent most of the time under detention. When he was released by Nehru in 1964, he received an enthusiastic reception from his people. In subsequent talks with the Indian government, he worked out the basis of a possible solution to the Kashmir problem.

He was dispatched on a foreign tour to gain the goodwill of Pakistan and Algeria, but India's relations with Pakistan had by then deteriorated and Abdullah's foreign tour was seen as seditious. At the same time his support in Kashmir had been eroded by the apparent lack of progress in negotiations with India. Abdullah was again arrested and not released until 1968. From then until his appointment as chief minister of Jammu and Kashmir in 1975, his Plebiscite Front gained some successes but lost to the Congress Party in the 1972 elections. His relations with Indian Prime Minister Indira Gandhi were sometimes strained, but he persuaded her to allow Kashmir a form of autonomy. Abdullah's government was later accused of corruption but, though his popularity waned, he was still admired for his outstanding contribution to the cause of Kashmiri national rights.

Abdullah bin Abdul Kadir, Munshi (b. 1796, Malacca, Malaya—d. 1854, Jidda, Turkish Arabia), Malayan-born writer who, through his autobiographical and other works, played an important role as a progenitor of modern Malay literature.

Of mixed Arab (Yemeni) and Tamil descent, and Malayo-Muslim culture, Abdullah was born and grew up in a Malacca newly British, and spent most of his life interpreting Malay society to Westerners and vice versa. Styled *munshi* (teacher) from an early age, in recognition of his teaching Malay to Indian soldiers of the Malacca garrison (and later to a whole generation of British and American missionaries, officials, and businessmen), he rapidly became an indispensable functionary in the fledgling Straits Settlements. He was copyist and Malay scribe for Sir Stamford Raffles from 1908, translator of the Gospels and other texts into Malay for the London Missionary Society establishment in Malacca from 1815, and 20 years later printer to the press of the American Board of Missions in Singapore.

An American missionary, Alfred North, seems to have encouraged Abdullah in 1837, on the strength of a lively account published in that year of North's experiences on a voyage up the east coast of Malaya, to embark on the story of his life. Completed in 1843, under the title *Hikayat Abdullah* ("Abdullah's Story"), it was first published in 1849; it has been reprinted many times and translated into English and other languages. Its chief distinction—beyond the vivid picture it gives of his life and times—was the radical departure it marked in Malay literary style. In contrast to the largely court literature of the past, the *Hikayat Abdullah* provided a lively and colloquial descriptive account of events and people with a freshness and immediacy hitherto unknown. Abdullah's criticisms of his own society, and his eagerness to embrace standards set by the West (though he remained a staunch Muslim), have caused him to be treated with some caution by a more recent generation of nationalists, but he continues to be widely acknowledged as the father of modern Malay literature.

ʽAbdullahi (Sudanese leader): *see* ʽAbd Allāh.

Abdülmecid, also spelled ABDUL-MEDJID, or ABDUL-MEJID, name of Ottoman sultans grouped below chronologically.

Abdülmecid I (b. April 25, 1823, Constantinople—d. June 25, 1861, Constantinople), Ottoman sultan from 1839 to 1861 who issued two major social and political reform edicts known as the Hatt-ı Şerif of Gülhane (Noble Edict of the Rose Chamber) in 1839 and the Hatt-ı Hümayun (Imperial Edict) in 1856, heralding the new era of Tanzimat (Reorganization) that won the respect of Europeans.

Well educated, liberal minded, and the first sultan to speak French, Abdülmecid continued the reform program of his father, Mahmud II, and was strongly assisted by his ministers Mustafa Reşid Paşa, Mehmed Emin Âli Paşa, and Fuad Paşa. The reform edicts were in part directed toward winning the support of European powers. The edicts proclaimed the equality of all citizens under the law and granted civil and political rights to the Christian subjects. The main purpose of the reforms, however, remained the preservation of the Ottoman state. The army was reorganized (1842) and conscription introduced; new penal, commercial, and maritime codes were promulgated; and mixed civil and criminal courts with European and Ottoman judges were established. In 1858 a new land law confirming the rights of ownership was introduced, and an attempt was made to establish a new system of centralized provincial administration. The Sultan's educational reforms included the formation of a Ministry of Education, military preparatory schools, and secondary schools and the establishment of an Ottoman school in Paris (1855).

Abdülmecid's foreign policy was directed toward maintaining friendly relations with the European powers to preserve the territorial integrity of the Ottoman state. He ascended the throne as a mere boy a few days after the Ottoman defeat by the Viceroy of Egypt at the Battle of Nizip (*q.v.*; June 1839). Only an alliance of European powers (excluding France)

Abdülmecid I, detail of a portrait by an unknown artist, 19th century; in the Topkapı Saray Museum, Istanbul
Sonia Halliday

saved the Ottomans from accepting disastrous terms from Egypt (Treaty of London, July 1840). In 1849 Abdülmecid's refusal to surrender Lajos Kossuth and other Hungarian revolutionary refugees to Austria won him the respect of European liberals. Finally, in 1853 the Ottomans were assisted by France, Great Britain, and Sardinia in the Crimean War against Russia and were admitted as participants in the Treaty of Paris (1856).

The European powers, however, while insisting on reforms aimed toward the Christians and minorities in the Ottoman Empire, obstructed the Sultan's efforts at centralization or at recovering power in Bosnia and Montenegro in the Balkans. They also forced the Ottomans to grant autonomy in Lebanon (1861), while the effect of the Treaty of Paris was to unify the Danubian principalities, paving the way for the independence of Romania (1878).

Abdülmecid restored Hagia Sophia, built the Dolmabahçe Palace, and founded the first French theatre in Constantinople. *See also* Âli Paşa, Mehmed Emin; Reşid Paşa, Mustafa.

Abdülmecid II (b. May 30, 1868, Constantinople—d. Aug. 23, 1944, Paris), the last caliph and crown prince of the Ottoman dynasty of Turkey.

Following Ottoman custom, he was confined to the palace until he was 40, during which time his father, Abdülaziz, and three of his cousins reigned. When his fourth cousin took the throne as Mehmed VI in 1918, Abdülmecid became crown prince. He was elected caliph by the Grand National Assembly on Nov. 18, 1922, after the sultanate was abolished; and he lost his title of crown prince after Mehmed left Constantinople on the assumption of power by the Young Turks under Mustafa Kemal (Atatürk). Although the caliphate was severed from all political power, Abdülmecid, a gentle and scholarly man, was the living symbol of Turkey's link to the

Abdülmecid II, portrait by an unknown artist, 20th century; in the Topkapı Saray Museum, Istanbul
Sonia Halliday

Islāmic-Ottoman past. The forces of tradition and the opponents of Mustafa Kemal's regime rallied around him. Mustafa Kemal, determined to break with the Islāmic past, first proclaimed the Turkish Republic (Oct. 29, 1923), and on March 3, 1924, the Grand National Assembly abolished the caliphate. The next day Abdülmecid was exiled.

Abe Isoo (b. March 1, 1865, Fukuoka, Japan—d. Feb. 10, 1949, Tokyo), one of the founders of the Japanese Socialist movement and titular head of the Social Mass Party (Shakai Taishūtō) from its inception in 1932 until 1940. He is also remembered for introducing the game of baseball to Japan.

Abe was attracted to socialism while studying for the ministry in the United States, where he graduated from the Hartford (Conn.) Theological Seminary. He returned to Japan in 1899 and two years later became a professor at Tokyo Semmon Gakkō (later Waseda University), a position he held for 25 years. He helped the embryonic Japanese labour movement and played a part in the founding of the Social Democratic Party (1899), which was suppressed almost immediately by the government. A pacifist, Abe opposed the Russo-Japanese War (1904–05); when the antiwar newspaper *Heimin shimbun* ("People's Weekly News") was banned, Abe started his own magazine, *Shinkigen* ("A New Era"), as a platform to promote parliamentary socialism rooted in Christian humanism.

After the war Abe objected to the takeover of the Socialist movement by radical anarcho-syndicalist groups and to their terrorist activities, and in consequence he retired from politics and devoted himself to educational causes.

After World War I Abe again became active in Socialist activities; he established the Fabian Society of Japan (1921), and five years later he resigned from the university to become secretary general of the new People's Socialist Party. In 1928 he was elected to the first of his five terms in the lower house of the Japanese Diet. When his party reorganized in 1932 as the much more popular Social Mass Party, he became chairman of its executive committee. He resigned in 1940, however, over the issue of cooperation with the government's militaristic policies; the government dissolved the party soon after. In his last years, after World War II, Abe became an adviser to the Socialist Party.

Abe Kōbō, pseudonym of ABE KIMIFUSA (b. March 7, 1924, Tokyo), novelist and playwright noted for his use of bizarre and allegorical situations to underline the isolation of the individual man.

He grew up in Mukden, in Manchuria, where his father, a physician, taught at the medical college. The youngster was interested in insect collecting, mathematics, and the writings of Dostoyevsky, Heidegger, Jaspers, Kafka, Nietzsche, and Poe. Abe went to Japan in

Abe Kōbō

By courtesy of the International Society for Educational Information, Tokyo

1941 and in 1943 began studying medicine at the University of Tokyo but returned to Manchuria to face the end of World War II. Repatriated to Japan, he was graduated in medicine in 1948 but never practiced. He started writing poetry, publishing in 1947 *Mumei shishū* ("Poems of an Unknown Poet") at his own expense. The critical acceptance of his novel *Owarishi michi no shirube ni* ("The Road Sign at the End of the Street") in 1948 established his reputation.

Among his important novels, many of which have been called Kafkaesque, are *Suna no onna* (1962; *The Woman in the Dunes,* 1964), which was adapted into an internationally successful film; *Daiyon kampyōki* (1959; *Inter Ice Age 4,* 1970); *Tanin no kao* (1964; *The Face of Another,* 1966); *Moetsukita chizu* (1967; *The Ruined Map,* 1969); *Hako otoko* (1973; *The Box Man,* 1974); and *Mikkai* (1977; *Secret Rendezvous,* 1979). Of his many plays, which met with great success in Japan, *Tomodachi* (1967; *Friends,* 1969) and a few others were performed in English, in Honolulu. He directed his own theatre company in Tokyo, for which he wrote several plays each season. Politically, Abe was a leftist and a former member of the Japanese Communist Party, from which he was expelled after he wrote a book of scathing reportage about his travels in eastern Europe in 1956.

Abe Masahiro (b. Dec. 3, 1819, Edo, Japan—d. Aug. 6, 1857, Edo), statesman who negotiated the opening of Japan to trade and communication with Western nations after the arrival of Commo. Matthew C. Perry and his U.S. Navy fleet.

Born into an influential noble family, Abe was only 25 years old when he was appointed head of the *rōjū* (senior councillors), the highest administrative office under the shogun, or hereditary military dictator of Japan. The government had previously been in the hands of a group of conservative reformers whose attempts to restore the past virtues of the Japanese state had created considerable unrest among the population; Abe's first years in power were marked by his successful attempt to alleviate the discontent caused by these changes. Western ships had begun to appear off the Japanese coast in the early 19th century, however, and Abe, determined to preserve Japan's traditional isolationism, worked to strengthen coastal defenses. He welcomed Western learning only as a means of increasing Japan's military and economic potential.

When Perry's fleet arrived in 1853, it was readily apparent that Japanese armaments were no match for the U.S. warships. After Perry returned the following February, Abe signed the Treaty of Kanagawa (March 31, 1854), opening Japan to limited communication with the United States. Similar treaties were concluded with Great Britain, Russia, and The Netherlands in the following months. Meanwhile, fuelled by the seeming weakness of the shogunate, the movement for the restoration of power to the old Imperial family began to grow, and Abe, overwhelmed by criticism that he had betrayed his country, was forced to relinquish much of his power; thereafter he devoted himself exclusively to internal affairs.

Abéché, town, seat of Ouaddaï *préfecture,* eastern Chad, central Africa, between the wadis Chao and Sao. Historically it was the site of the capital of the Muslim sultanate of Ouaddaï (*q.v.*), which dominated much of the area of Chad before French conquest was accomplished in 1912. The remains of the ancient capital include a palace, tombs of former sultans, and the ruins of a mosque, all surrounded by a thick wall. The town has many mosques.

Abéché is surrounded by savanna-type terrain that is an important cattle-raising area, but the distance from suitable markets hinders development of the cattle industry. Abéché is linked by main road to the capital, N'Djamena (formerly Fort-Lamy), Sarh (formerly Fort-Archambault), and The Sudan. The Lycée Franco-Arabe (a secondary school) is in the town, which has an airport and a hospital and supports some light industry, including the manufacture of camel-hair blankets. Pop. (1978 est.) 50,000.

Abeel, John (Seneca Indian leader): *see* Cornplanter.

Abegg, Richard Wilhelm Heinrich (b. Jan. 9, 1869, Danzig, Prussia—d. April 3, 1910, Köslin, Ger.), physical chemist whose work contributed to the understanding of valence (the capacity of an atom to combine with another atom) in light of the newly discovered presence of electrons within the atom.

Abegg became professor of chemistry at the University of Breslau, Ger., in 1897, and two years later gained the chair of chemistry at the Technische Hochschule, Breslau. From his study of valence, he concluded that for the most stable configuration, the number of electrons in the outer group of an atom is eight, which is the number found in the inert gases.

Abel, in the Old Testament, second son of Adam and Eve, who was slain by his older brother, Cain (Gen. 4:1–16). According to Genesis, Abel, a shepherd, offered the Lord the firstborn of his flock. The Lord respected Abel's sacrifice but did not respect that offered by Cain. In a jealous rage, Cain murdered Abel. Cain then became a fugitive because his brother's innocent blood put a curse on him.

The storyteller in Genesis assumes a world of conflicting values, and he makes the point that divine authority backs self-control and brotherhood but punishes jealousy and violence. Cain had not mastered sin (v. 7); he had let it master him. The narrator takes a somber look at the human condition, seeing a dangerous world of Cains and Abels. Nevertheless, God is on the side of the martyrs; he avenges their deaths in the ruin of the Cains. In the New Testament the blood of Abel is cited as an example of the vengeance of violated innocence (Matt. 23:35; Luke 11:51).

Abel, Sir Frederick Augustus (b. July 17, 1827, Woolwich, London—d. Sept. 6, 1902, Westminster, London), chemist and explosives specialist who, with the British chemist Sir James Dewar, invented cordite (1889), later adopted as the standard explosive of the British Army. Abel also made studies of dust explosions in coal mines, invented a device for testing the flash point of petroleum, and found a way to prevent guncotton from exploding spontaneously.

Abel studied chemistry at the Royal Polytechnic Institution and in 1845 became one of the original 26 students of A.W. von Hofmann at the Royal College of Chemistry. In 1852 he was appointed lecturer in chemistry at the Royal Military Academy in Woolwich, succeeding Michael Faraday, who had held that post since 1829. From 1854 until 1888 Abel served as ordnance chemist at the Chemical Establishment of the Royal Arsenal at Woolwich, establishing himself as the leading British authority on explosives.

He was elected a fellow of the Royal Society in 1860, knighted in 1883, and created a baronet in 1893.

Abel, John Jacob (b. May 19, 1857, Cleveland—d. May 26, 1938, Baltimore), pharmacologist and physiological chemist who made important contributions to a modern understanding of the ductless, or endocrine, glands. He isolated adrenaline in the form of a chemical derivative (1897) and crystallized insulin (1926). He also invented an artificial kidney.

Abel taught at the University of Michigan, Ann Arbor (1891–93), and at Johns Hopkins University, Baltimore (1893), and directed the Laboratory for Endocrine Research (1932). He edited the *Journal of Pharmacology and Experimental Therapeutics* from 1909 to 1932.

Abel, Karl Friedrich (b. Dec. 22, 1723, Cöthen, Duchy of Anhalt-Cöthen—d. June 20, 1787, London), symphonist of the pre-Classical school and one of the last virtuosos of the viola da gamba.

After playing in the Dresden court orchestra (1748–58) he went to London in 1759 and became chamber musician to Queen Charlotte in 1765. When J.C. Bach arrived in London in 1762 they became friends and established

Karl Friedrich Abel, engraving by A. Saint-Aubin after a portrait by C.-N. Cochin, 1781

J.P. Ziolo

the "Bach and Abel" concerts that included the first public performances in England of Haydn's symphonies. Abel wrote about 40 symphonies, one of which, the so-called Köchel 18, was long attributed wrongly to the youthful Mozart.

Abel, Niels Henrik (b. Aug. 5, 1802, island of Finnøy, near Stavanger, Nor.—d. April 6, 1829, Froland), Norwegian mathematician, a pioneer in the development of several branches of modern mathematics.

Abel was the son of a poor Protestant minister. Soon after Abel was born, his family moved to the parish of Gjerstad, near the town of Risør (southeast Norway), where the boy grew up. In 1815, when he entered the cathedral school in Oslo, his mathematical talent was recognized by a teacher who introduced him to the classics in mathematical literature and proposed original problems for

Niels Henrik Abel, lithograph after a drawing by Johan Gørbitz, 1826

By courtesy of the Royal Norwegian Embassy, Washington, D.C.

solution. Thoroughly challenged, Abel studied the works of the 17th-century English mathematician and physicist Isaac Newton and the contemporary mathematicians Leonhard Euler (German), Joseph-Louis Lagrange (French), and Carl Friedrich Gauss (German) and learned to detect gaps in their mathematical reasoning.

Although when Abel's father died in 1820 the family was left in straitened circumstances, the boy was able to enter the University of Christiania (Oslo) in 1821 because his teacher contributed and raised funds. He obtained a preliminary degree from the university in 1822 and continued his studies independently with further subsidies obtained by his teacher.

His first papers, published in 1823 in the new periodical *Magazin for Naturvidenskaberne,* were on functional equations and integrals, his solution of an integral equation being the first. Abel's friends urged the Norwegian government to grant him a fellowship for study in Germany and France. While waiting for the royal decree to be issued, in 1824 he published at his own expense his proof of the impossibility of solving algebraically the general equation of the fifth degree, which he hoped would bring him recognition. He sent the pamphlet to Gauss, who dismissed it, failing to recognize that the famous problem had indeed been settled.

Abel spent the winter of 1825–26 with Norwegian friends in Berlin, where he met August Leopold Crelle, civil engineer and self-taught enthusiast of mathematics, who became his close friend and mentor. With Abel's warm encouragement, Crelle founded the *Journal für die reine und angewandte Mathematik* ("Journal for Pure and Applied Mathematics"), the first volume of which (1826) contains papers by Abel, including a more elaborate version of his work on the quintic equation. Other papers dealt with equation theory, functional equations, integration in finite forms, and problems from theoretical mechanics.

Abel's early mathematical training had been in the formal school typified by Euler. In Berlin new directions in mathematics stimulated him to do further independent work. Soon distracted socially, however, Abel travelled throughout Europe.

Arriving in Paris in the summer of 1826, he called on the foremost mathematicians and completed a memoir on transcendental functions. In this major work he presented a theory of integrals of algebraic functions, in particular the result known as Abel's theorem: there is a finite number, or genus, of independent integrals of this nature. This theorem forms the basis for the later theory of Abelian integrals and Abelian functions. Abel was accepted with restrained civility in Paris, for his work was still unknown. He submitted his memoir for presentation to the Academy of Sciences, hoping that it would establish his reputation, but he waited in vain. Before leaving Paris, thinking he had a persistent cold, Abel consulted a physician, who informed him he had tuberculosis.

Abel returned to Norway heavily in debt. He subsisted by tutoring, by receiving a small grant from the university, and, in 1828, by accepting a substitute-teaching position. His poverty and ill health did not decrease his production; he wrote a great number of papers during this period, principally on equation theory and elliptic functions. Among them are the theory of the Abelian equations with Abelian groups. He rapidly developed the theory of elliptic functions in competition with Karl Gustav Jacobi.

By this time Abel's fame had spread to all mathematical centres, and strong efforts were made to secure a suitable position for him by a group from the French Academy, who addressed Bernadotte, the king of Norway-Sweden; Crelle worked to secure a professorship for him in Berlin.

In the fall of 1828, Abel became seriously ill, and his condition deteriorated on a sled trip at Christmas time to visit his fiancée at Froland, where he died. The French Academy of Sciences published his memoir in 1841.

BIBLIOGRAPHY. The *Oeuvres complètes de N.H. Abel* (1839; new ed., 2 vol., 1881) contains all his works. For biographical discussions, see Oystein Ore, *Niels Henrik Abel, Mathematician Extraordinary* (1957), with bibliography; Eric T. Bell, *Men of Mathematics* (1937, reprinted 1961); and Ganesh Prasad, *Some Great Mathematicians of the Nineteenth Century,* vol. 1 (1933).

Abel, Rudolf (Ivanovich) (b. *c.* 1902, Moscow—d. Nov. 15, 1971, Moscow), Soviet intelligence officer convicted in the U.S. in 1957 for conspiring to transmit military secrets to the U.S.S.R. and exchanged in 1962 for U.S. aviator Francis Gary Powers, who had been imprisoned as a spy in Russia since 1960.

Abel, who held the rank of colonel and was believed to be a member of the Soviet intelligence agency known as KGB, was arrested in New York City on June 21, 1957. Although he never acknowledged that he was a spy, he admitted that he entered the U.S. illegally in 1948. Under the name of Emil R. Goldfus, he lived for some time as an artist and photographer in a Brooklyn studio apartment, where he concealed shortwave radio transmitting and receiving equipment. On Oct. 25, 1957, a federal district court in Brooklyn found him guilty of espionage, relying in part on testimony by Soviet Lieut. Col. Reino Hayhanen, who had defected to the West and who stated that he had been Abel's chief co-conspirator in the U.S. The court sentenced Abel to 30 years' imprisonment.

The U.S. government then used Abel to secure the release of Powers, whose Lockheed U-2 high-altitude reconnaissance aircraft had been forced down near Sverdlovsk, in the central U.S.S.R., on May 1, 1960. Pres. John F. Kennedy commuted the sentence, and, on Feb. 10, 1962, in a melodramatic ceremony on a bridge between West Berlin and East Germany (Potsdam), Abel was exchanged for Powers and Frederic L. Pryor, a U.S. student who had been held without charge in East Germany since August 1961.

Abel, Theodora Mead (b. Sept. 9, 1899, Newport, R.I., U.S.), U.S. educator who combined the disciplines of sociology and psychology in her work.

She was educated at Vassar College, where she received her B.A. (1921), Columbia University, where she received her M.A. (1922), and the University of Paris, where she received a diploma in psychology (1923). She obtained her Ph.D. from Columbia University (1925). Abel taught at numerous universities, including the University of Illinois (1925–26), Sarah Lawrence College (1929–33), and the Manhattan Trade School for Girls. From 1940 to 1946 she was chief psychologist for the New York State Department of Mental Hygiene and from 1947 to 1971 was director of psychology at the New York City Post-graduate Center for Mental Health. In 1971 she became a clinical psychiatrist at the medical school of the University of New Mexico, in Albuquerque. She was presented the Psychologist of the Year award from the New York Society of Clinical Psychologists (1972).

Her writings include co-authorship of *The Subnormal Adolescent Girl* (1940), *Facial Deformities and Plastic Surgery* (1954), *Psychological Testing in Cultural Contexts* (1973), and *Culture and Psychotherapy* (1975).

Abel Tasman National Park, wildlife preserve in northwestern South Island, New Zealand. Established in 1942, it was named for Abel Tasman, the Dutch navigator. With an area of 55,998 ac (22,656 ha), it extends inland for about 6 mi (10 km) from the beaches of Tasman Bay on its western shores between Separation Point and Marahau Inlet, about 50 mi (80 km) northwest of Nelson. The park includes the Tata Islands in Golden Bay and Tonga, Adele, and Fisherman islands in Tasman Bay. The Wainui, Awapoto, Awaroa, and Falls are the most important rivers in the park, which is largely covered in shrubland and pasture, although there are rain forests in the Lower Wainui Valley, Pigeon Saddle, Totaranui–Anapai, and Lower Falls River areas consisting of beech, rata, matai, miro, hinau, and tussock.

The park is unique in New Zealand in that its bush-clad slopes show a mixture of the vegetation typical of both North and South Islands, a phenomenon found nowhere else. Birdlife includes petrel, shag, penguin, gull, tern, heron, and numerous other varieties. Animal life includes deer, goat, wild pig, and opossum. Fishing, shell collecting, sailing, boating, swimming, hiking, and hunting (by permit) all provide recreation to visitors. The park's headquarters are at Totaranui.

Abelard, Peter, French PIERRE ABÉLARD, or ABAILARD, Latin PETRUS ABAELARDUS, or ABEILARDUS (b. 1079, Le Pallet, near

Abelard, with Héloïse, miniature portrait by Jean de Meun, 14th century; in the Musée Condé, Chantilly, Fr.

By courtesy of the Musee Conde, Chantilly, Fr.; photograph, Giraudon—Art Resource

Nantes, Brittany—d. April 21, 1142, Priory of Saint-Marcel, near Chalon-sur-Saône, Burgundy), French theologian and philosopher best known for his solution of the problem of universals and for his original use of dialectics. He is also known for his poetry and for his celebrated love affair with Héloïse.

Early life. The outline of Abelard's career is well known, largely because he described so much of it in his famous *Historia calamitatum* ("History of My Troubles"). He was born the son of a knight in Brittany south of the Loire. He sacrificed his inheritance and the prospect of a military career in order to study philosophy, particularly logic, in France. He provoked bitter quarrels with two of his masters, Roscelin of Compiègne and Guillaume de Champeaux, who represented opposite poles of philosophy. Roscelin was a Nominalist who asserted that universals are nothing more than mere words; Guillaume in Paris upheld a form of Platonic Realism according to which universals exist. Abelard in his own logical writings brilliantly elaborated an independent philosophy of language. While showing how words could be used significantly, he stressed that language itself is not able to demonstrate the truth of things (*res*) that lie in the domain of physics.

Abelard was a peripatetic both in the manner in which he wandered from school to school at Paris, Melun, Corbeil, and elsewhere and as one of the exponents of Aristotelian logic who were called the Peripatetics. In 1113 or 1114 he went north to Laon to study theology under Anselm of Laon, the leading biblical scholar of the day. He quickly developed a strong contempt for Anselm's teaching, which he found vacuous, and returned to Paris. There he taught openly but was also given as a private pupil the young Héloïse, niece of one of the clergy of the cathedral of Paris, Canon Fulbert. Abelard and Héloïse fell in love and had a son whom they called Astralabe. They then married secretly. To escape her uncle's wrath Héloïse withdrew into the convent of Argenteuil outside Paris. Abelard suffered castration at Fulbert's instigation. In shame he embraced the monastic life at the royal abbey of Saint-Denis near Paris and made the unwilling Héloïse become a nun at Argenteuil.

Career as a monk. At Saint-Denis Abelard extended his reading in theology and tirelessly criticized the way of life followed by his fellow monks. His reading of the Bible and of the Fathers of the Church led him to make a collection of quotations that seemed to represent inconsistencies of teaching by the Christian Church. He arranged his findings in a compilation entitled *Sic et non* ("Yes and No"); and for it he wrote a preface in which, as a logician and as a keen student of language, he formulated basic rules with which students might reconcile apparent contradictions of meaning and distinguish the various senses in which words had been used over the course of many centuries. He also wrote the first version of his book called *Theologia,* which was formally condemned as heretical and burned by a council held at Soissons in 1121. Abelard's dialectical analysis of the mystery of God and the Trinity was held to be erroneous, and he himself was placed for a while in the abbey of Saint-Médard under house arrest. When he returned to Saint-Denis he applied his *Sic et non* methods to the subject of the abbey's patron saint; he argued that St. Denis of Paris, the martyred apostle of Gaul, was not identical with Denis of Athens (also known as Dionysius the Areopagite), the convert of St. Paul. The monastic community of Saint-Denis regarded this criticism of their traditional claims as derogatory to the kingdom; and, in order to avoid being brought for trial before the king of France, Abelard fled from the abbey and sought asylum in the territory of Count Theobald of Champagne. There he sought the solitude of a hermit's life but was pursued by students who pressed him to resume his teaching in philosophy. His combination of the teaching of secular arts with his profession as a monk was heavily criticized by other men of religion, and Abelard contemplated flight outside Christendom altogether. In 1125, however, he accepted election as abbot of the remote Breton monastery of Saint-Gildas-de-Rhuys. There, too, his relations with the community deteriorated, and, after attempts had been made upon his life, he returned to France.

Héloïse had meanwhile become the head of a new foundation of nuns called the Paraclete. Abelard became the abbot of the new community and provided it with a rule and with a justification of the nun's way of life; in this he emphasized the virtue of literary study. He also provided books of hymns he had composed, and in the early 1130s he and Héloïse composed a collection of their own love letters and religious correspondence.

Final years. In about 1135 Abelard went to the Mont-Sainte-Geneviève outside Paris to teach, and he wrote in a blaze of energy and of celebrity. He produced further drafts of his *Theologia* in which he analyzed the sources of belief in the Trinity and praised the pagan philosophers of classical antiquity for their virtues and for their discovery by the use of reason of many fundamental aspects of Christian revelation. He also wrote a book called *Ethica* or *Scito te ipsum* ("Know Thyself"), a short masterpiece in which he analyzed the notion of sin and reached the drastic conclusion that human actions do not make a man better or worse in the sight of God, for deeds are in themselves neither good nor bad. What counts with God is a man's intention; sin is not something done (it is not *res*); it is uniquely the consent of a human mind to what it knows to be wrong. Abelard also wrote *Dialogus inter philosophum, Judaeum et Christianum* ("Dialogue Between a Philosopher, a Jew, and a Christian") and a commentary on St. Paul's letter to the Romans, the *Expositio in Epistolam ad Romanos,* in which he outlined an explanation of the purpose of Christ's life, which was to inspire men to love him by example alone.

On the Mont-Sainte-Geneviève Abelard drew crowds of pupils, many of them men of future fame, such as the English humanist John of Salisbury. He also, however, aroused deep hostility in many by his criticism of other masters and by his apparent revisions of the traditional teachings of Christian theology. Within Paris the influential abbey of Saint-Victor was studiously critical of his doctrines, while elsewhere William of Saint-Thierry, a former admirer of Abelard, recruited the support of Bernard of Clairvaux, perhaps the most influential figure in Western Christendom at that time. At a council held at Sens in 1140, Abelard underwent a resounding condemnation, which was soon confirmed by Pope Innocent II. He withdrew to the great monastery of Cluny in Burgundy. There, under the skillful mediation of the abbot, Peter the Venerable, he made peace with Bernard of Clairvaux and retired from teaching. Now both sick and old, he lived the life of a Cluniac monk. After his death, his body was first sent to the Paraclete; it now lies alongside that of Héloïse in the cemetery of Père-Lachaise in Paris. Epitaphs composed in his honour suggest that Abelard impressed some of his contemporaries as one of the greatest thinkers and teachers of all time. (D.E.L.)

BIBLIOGRAPHY. *The Letters of Abelard and Héloïse* have been translated into English by C.K. Scott Moncrieff (1925, reprinted 1964) and by J.T. Muckle (1947), who has also published separately a translation of *The Story of Abelard's Adversities* (1954). The historical novel *Peter Abelard,* by Helen Waddell (1933), is justly popular and has been reprinted many times. More general studies are Étienne Gilson, *Héloïse et Abélard* 938; *Heloise and Abelard,* 1953); and Lief Grane, *Pierre Abélard* (1964; *Peter Abelard,* 1970). Information concerning editions of Abelard's writings and studies of his thought may be found in D.E. Luscombe's edition and English translation of *Peter Abelard's "Ethics"* (1971). On the reception of Abelard's thought and teaching in his own time, see D.E. Luscombe, *The School of Peter Abelard* (1969). The best study of Abelard's philosophy is Jean Jolivet, *Arts du langage et théologie chez Abélard* (1969).

Abell, A(runah) S(hepardson) (b. Aug. 10, 1806, East Providence, R.I., U.S.—d. April 19, 1888, Baltimore), newspaper editor and publisher, and founder, with two other investors, of the Philadelphia *Public Ledger* and the Baltimore *Sun.*

Abell left school at the age of 14 to become a clerk in a store dealing in West Indian wares. He had hoped to become a printer, and in 1822 he was taken on as an apprentice by the *Providence Patriot.* He set up shop as a printer in Boston and then in New York. He came to the conclusion that Philadelphia was a likely market for a new penny paper. He and his partners, William M. Swain and Azariah H. Simmons, founded the *Public Ledger* in 1836. Within two years the paper had absorbed the rival Philadelphia *Transcript.* Meanwhile, in 1837, Abell and his partners founded the Baltimore *Sun,* which had 12,000 subscribers after a year. Both the *Public Ledger* and the *Sun* were oriented to the working man, but whereas the *Ledger* dealt freely in scandal and sensation, the *Sun* did not. As manager of the *Sun,* Abell, in cooperation with the publishers of the New Orleans *Daily Picayune,* established a "pony express" of relay riders between Baltimore and New Orleans to speed the transmission of news. In a historic "news beat," the express delivered in Baltimore the news of the U.S. Army victory at Vera Cruz, Mexico, before the U.S. government had learned of it. Abell then sent word of the victory by telegram to Pres. James K. Polk. He had encouraged Samuel F.B. Morse in developing the telegraph and was one of its most enthusiastic pioneer users.

An innovator who stressed technical progress, Abell used telegraph machines and carrier pigeons to speed news transmission. Under his direction, the Baltimore *Sun* became the first American newspaper to install a rotary press. In 1861, when the Civil War began, the *Sun* had a circulation estimated at 30,000. Abell directed the *Sun* until his death.

Abell, Kjeld (b. Aug. 25, 1901, Ribe, Den.—d. March 5, 1961, Copenhagen), dramatist and social critic, best known outside Denmark for two plays, *Melodien der blev væk* (1935; English adaptation, *The Melody That Got Lost,* 1939) and *Anna Sophie Hedvig* (1939; Eng. trans., 1944), which defends the use of force by the oppressed against the oppressor.

Abell studied political science but afterward began a career as a stage designer in Paris. He then went on to become Denmark's most unconventional man of the theatre, not only as an original dramatist but also as a stage designer who made full use of the technical apparatus of the theatre to achieve new and striking scenic effects, as in *Daga paa en Sky* (1947; "Days on a Cloud") and *Skrige* (1961; "The Scream").

abelmosk (plant): *see* musk mallow.

Abelson, Philip Hauge (b. April 27, 1913, Tacoma, Wash., U.S.), physical chemist who proposed the gas diffusion process for separating uranium-235 from uranium-238 and in collaboration with the U.S. physicist Edwin M. McMillan discovered the element neptunium.

In 1939–41 Abelson was assistant physicist in the department of terrestrial magnetism of the Carnegie Institution of Washington, D.C. There he began investigating a material that emitted beta rays (electrons) and that was produced by irradiating uranium with neutrons. After joining forces with McMillan, he proved the material to be a new element, later named neptunium.

During World War II Abelson worked with the Naval Research Laboratory, Washington, D.C. His uranium-separation process proved essential to the development of the atomic bomb. At the end of the war his report on the feasibility of building a nuclear-powered submarine gave birth to the U.S. program in that field.

In 1946 Abelson returned to the Carnegie Institution and pioneered in utilizing radioactive isotopes. As director of the Geophysics Laboratory of the Carnegie Institution from 1953 to 1971, he found amino acids in fossils, and fatty acids in rocks more than 1,000,000,000 years old. He was president of the Carnegie Institution from 1971 to 1978 and trustee from 1978. In 1962 he became editor of *Science,* the weekly publication of the American Association for the Advancement of Science.

Abemama Atoll, also spelled APAMAMA, formerly ROGER SIMPSON ISLAND, coral atoll of the northern Gilbert Islands, part of Kiribati, in the west central Pacific Ocean. Capt. Charles Bishop, who discovered the atoll in 1799, named it Roger Simpson Island for one of his associates. Seat of the area's ruling family in the 19th century, the atoll was the site of the formal British annexation of the island group in 1892. Occupied by Japanese forces from 1942 to 1943, Abemama became a U.S. military base for the following two years. Administrative headquarters of the atoll, which has a good anchorage, is at Tabontebike. There is also a hospital and airfield. Copra is exported. Pop. (1983 est.) 2,710.

Abengourou, town, administrative headquarters (since 1969) of Abengourou *département*, eastern Ivory Coast, on the road from Abidjan (the national capital) to Ghana. The major trading centre for a productive forest region, it is also the residence of the Anyi (Agni) paramount chief, who is the present king of Indénié (an Anyi kingdom founded in the mid-18th century). The king's official residence (built in 1882) is decorated with Indénié relics and tapestries. Abengourou has an agricultural–vocational-training institute and research station for coffee and cocoa, the region's major crops, which are sent to Abidjan (100 m [161 km] south-southwest) for export. The town is the seat of a Roman Catholic bishop, several schools, and one of the largest hospitals in the interior. Pop. (1975) town, 31,239; (1979 est.) *département*, 175,522.

Åbenrå, also spelled AABENRAA, city, seat of Sønderjyllands *amtskommune* (county), southeastern Jutland, Denmark, at the head of Åbenrå Fjord. First mentioned in the 12th century when attacked by the Wends, it was granted a charter (1335) and grew from a fishing village into a thriving port in the 17th and 18th centuries. Medieval landmarks include the St. Nikolaj Kirke (a 13th-century church; restored 1949–56) and Brøndlund Slot (a fortress, begun 1411, rebuilt 1807). The city was German from 1864 until a plebiscite in 1920 and was known as Apenrade. Åbenrå is a marketing centre with a large import trade and the largest port in southeastern Jutland. Local industries include machinery production, food processing, pipe-organ building, and fishing. Pop. (1981) city, 15,341; (1982 est.) mun., 21,185.

Abensperg und Traun, Otto Ferdinand, Graf von (count of): *see* Traun, Otto Ferdinand, Graf von Abensperg und.

Abeokuta, town, capital of Ogun State, southwestern Nigeria, on the east bank of the Ogun River, around a group of rocky outcroppings (altitude 600 ft [180 m]) that rise above the surrounding wooded savanna. It lies on the main railway (1899) from Lagos, 48 mi (78 km) south, and on the older trunk road from Lagos to Ibadan; it also has road connections to Ilaro, Shagamu, Iseyin, and Kétou (Benin).

Abeokuta ("refuge among rocks") was founded *c.* 1830 by Sodeke (Shodeke), a hunter and leader of the Egba refugees who fled from the disintegrating Oyo Empire. The town was also settled by missionaries (in the 1840s) and by Sierra Leone Creoles, who later became prominent as missionaries and as businessmen. Abeokuta's success as the capital of the Egbas and as a link in the Lagos–Ibadan oil-palm trade led to wars with Dahomey (now Benin). In the battle at Abeokuta in 1851, the Egba, aided by the missionaries and armed by the British, defeated King Gezo's Dahomeyan army (unique in West African history for its common practice of using women warriors). Another Dahomeyan attack was repulsed in 1864. Troubles in the 1860s with the British in Lagos led the Egba to close the trade routes to the coast and to expel (1867) its missionaries and European traders. Following the Yoruba civil wars (1877–93), in which Abeokuta opposed Ibadan, the Egba *alake* ("king") signed an alliance with the British governor, Sir Gilbert Carter, that recognized the independence of the Egba United Government (1893–1914). In 1914, the kingdom was incorporated into the newly amalgamated British Colony and Protectorate of Nigeria. The Abeokuta riots of 1918 protested both the levying of taxes and the "indirect rule" policy of Lord Frederick Lugard, the British governor general, which made the *alake,* formerly *primus inter pares* ("first among equals"), the supreme traditional leader to the detriment of the other quarter chiefs.

Modern Abeokuta is an agricultural trade centre (rice, yams, cassava, corn [maize], palm oil and kernels, cotton, fruits, vegetables) and an exporting point for cocoa, palm produce, fruits, and kola nuts. Rice and cotton were introduced by the missionaries in the 1850s, and cotton weaving and dyeing (with locally grown indigo) are now traditional crafts of the town. Abeokuta is the headquarters for the Federal Ogun–Oshin River Basin Authority with programs to harness land and water resources for Lagos, Ogun, and Oyo states for rural development. Irrigation, food processing, and electrification projects are included. Local industry is limited, but now includes fruit-canning plants, a plastics factory, a brewery, and an aluminum-products factory. South of the town are the Aro granite quarries, which provide building materials for much of southern Nigeria, and a cement plant at Ewekoro (18 mi south).

Abeokuta is a walled town. Notable buildings include the Ake (the residence of the *alake*), Centenary Hall (1930), and several churches and mosques. It is the headquarters of a local government council. Secondary schools and primary teachers' colleges are now supplemented by the Federal Advanced Teachers Training College for secondary teachers and Ogun State Polytechnic at Abeokuta. The town is served by several hospitals. Pop. (1983 est.) 308,800.

Aberbrothock (Scotland): *see* Arbroath.

Aberconwy, district, Gwynedd County, northwestern Wales. It was created in 1974, covers an area of 234 sq mi (606 sq km), and extends from the rugged Penmaenmawr headland southward along both sides of the River Conwy to its source, Lake Conwy. Aberconwy district is bordered by the districts of Arfon and Dwyfor to the west, Meirionnydd to the south, and Colwyn to the east. A Neolithic stone-axe-making site was discovered near the town of Penmaenmawr, and the remains of a Bronze Age stone circle are located on the crest of a hill above the town. Conwy Castle (1283), built on the River Conwy estuary by Edward I of England, was a vital link in a chain of English strongholds in the then newly invaded North Wales. The castle guarded the entrance to the once navigable River Conwy and dominated coastal access to the region of old Caernarfonshire and the Isle of Anglesey. Battles between the English and Welsh were waged periodically in the area until the early 1400s, when a battle between the English and Owen Glendower's Welsh forces caused such destruction in the town of Llanrwst that afterward grass was reputed to have grown in the streets of the deserted town.

The tourism industry dominates the economy of modern Aberconwy district. The coastal resorts of Conwy, Penmaenmawr, Llanfairfechan, and Llandudno all have comprehensive entertainment and accommodation facilities, as well as lengthy sand beaches. Llandudno also serves as the administrative seat for the district. Snowdonia National Park covers most of the hinterland, and numerous visitors are attracted each year to the mountain resort of Betws-y-Coed, for its celebrated waterfalls. The stone statue of a rabbit checking its watch, located on the western promenade of Llandudno, commemorates the part the town played in inspiring Lewis Carroll's *Alice's Adventures in Wonderland* (1865). Northern Aberconwy is traversed by both a railroad, upon which construction was not begun until 1845 owing to the nearly impenetrable Penmaenmawr headland, and a highway. Pop. (1981) 52,414.

Abercrombie, James, Abercrombie also spelled ABERCROMBY (b. 1706, Glassaugh, Banffshire, Scot.—d. April 23/28, 1781, Stirling, Stirlingshire), British general in the French and Indian Wars, commander of the British forces in the failed attack on the French at Ticonderoga.

A lieutenant colonel of the Royal Scots early in his military career, Abercrombie was promoted to colonel in 1746 and served in the Flemish campaign in the War of Austrian Succession. Promoted to major general in 1756, he was ordered to accompany Lord Loudoun to America as his second in command. Abercrombie's first independent command came in December 1757 when William Pitt, at the insistence of George III, made him commander in chief. His title notwithstanding, his actions were largely determined by the ministry in London. With Augustus Lord Howe as his second in command, Abercrombie was directed to take Ft. Ticonderoga by way of preparation for an assault on Montreal. Although he had a force of 15,000 British and colonial troops, Abercrombie was defeated by General Montcalm's army of 3,600 at Ticonderoga in July 1758. In September, Pitt recalled Abercrombie and gave his command to Jeffrey Amherst.

Despite his failure, Abercrombie was promoted to lieutenant general in 1759 and general in 1772. His remaining years were spent in Parliament, as deputy governor of Stirling Castle, and on his estate at Glassaugh, Banffshire.

A list of the abbreviations used in the MICROPAEDIA *will be found at the end of this volume*

Abercrombie, Lascelles (b. Jan. 9, 1881, Ashton upon Mersey, Cheshire, Eng.—d. Oct. 27, 1938, London), poet and critic who was associated with Georgian poetry (*q.v.*).

He was educated at Malvern College, Worcestershire, and Owens College, Manchester, after which he became a journalist and began to write poetry. His first book, *Interludes and Poems* (1908), was followed by *Mary and the Bramble* (1910), a dramatic poem—*Deborah*—and *Emblems of Love* (1912), and the prose work *Speculative Dialogues* (1913). All were marked by lyric power, lucidity, love of natural beauty, and mysticism.

After World War I, in which he served

as a munitions examiner, Abercrombie was appointed to the first lectureship in poetry at the University of Liverpool. As professor of English literature at Leeds (1922–29) and London (1929–35) and as reader in English literature at Oxford University (1935–38), he showed keen critical and philosophical powers. His critical works include *An Essay Towards a Theory of Art* (1922) and *Poetry, Its Music and Meaning* (1932). *Collected Poems* (1930) was followed by his most mature poetic work, *The Sale of St. Thomas* (1931), a poetic drama.

Abercrombie & Fitch Co., retail sporting goods concern originally based in New York City, famed for its wide range of expensive and often exotic sporting equipment and attire from tennis shoes to elephant guns. For half a century and more the store's apparel, guns and tackle, and impedimenta were the image of correctness and opulence, inspiring the humorist Ed Zern to lampoon a perfectly accoutred angler as an "Abercrombie and Fitcherman." When it expanded, the firm confined its new branch stores to downtown areas of large cities and to resort areas. In the early 1970s Abercrombie & Fitch attempted to widen its customer base by adding less expensive items to its usual stock and finally by moving into the suburbs, where other stores had been building for some time. Although these steps did attract new customers, they came too late; Abercrombie & Fitch was in financial trouble and filed for bankruptcy in 1977. The name was purchased for use by a new chain of stores featuring some items reminiscent of the old Abercrombie & Fitch as well as merchandise of broader appeal.

Aberdare, Welsh ABERDÂR, industrial town, Cynon Valley district, Mid Glamorgan county, Wales, on the River Cynon. The community dates from the Middle Ages; its Church of Saint John was built about 1189. Aberdare's main growth in the 19th century was based on iron ore (first ironworks, 1799) and coal, particularly steam coal for export after 1836. A branch (1811) of the Glamorganshire Canal and, later, railways provided outlets to the South Wales coast. In the 20th century the town's iron industry ceased, and coal mining declined in the vicinity. Aberdare now serves as the chief shopping and service centre for the Cynon Valley. Modern industries include the manufacture of cables, smokeless fuel, and, at Hirwaun to the northwest, light engineering and electrical products. Pop. (1981 prelim.) 36,621.

Aberdare Range, mountain range, forming a section of the eastern rim of the Great Rift Valley in west central Kenya, East Africa, northeast of Naivasha and Gilgil, and just south of the Equator. The range has an average height of 11,000 ft (3,350 m) and culminates in Oldoinyo Lesatima (13,120 ft) and Ilkinangop (12,816 ft). The Aberdares slope gradually east and southeast, providing a fine example of an immature, consequent drainage pattern, before the ground rises again to the cone of Mt. Kenya (17,058 ft).

Aberdaugleddyf (Wales): *see* Milford Haven.

Aberdeen, also called ABERDEENSHIRE, former county of Scotland, projecting eastward into the North Sea. It was the seventh largest and most easterly of Scotland's counties.

Since the reorganization of 1975, Aberdeen is included in the districts of Banff and Buchan, Gordon, City of Aberdeen, and Kincardine and Deeside, of Grampian (*q.v.*) region.

Aberdeen, historic royal burgh, on Scotland's North Sea coast, astride the Rivers Dee and Don. It is a busy seaport, the main centre of the Scottish fishing industry and the commercial capital of northeastern Scotland. During the 1970s Aberdeen (Gaelic *aber,* "mouth"; *deen,* "of the Dee") developed rapidly as the principal centre in the U.K. of the North Sea oil industry and its associated service and supply industries. As the City of Aberdeen, it is a district, area 71 sq mi (184 sq km), in Grampian region.

Its popular name, Granite City, reflects the prevalence of granite buildings. Aberdeen originated as two separate burghs, Old Aberdeen, the cathedral and university settlement on the Don, and New Aberdeen, the adjoining trading and fishing village on the Dee. Old Aberdeen, reputedly founded in 580 by St. Machar, a disciple of St. Columba, the Celtic missionary, subsequently became the seat of the bishopric of Aberdeen and was virtually destroyed by the English in 1336. The present Cathedral of St. Machar (begun 1424) is a fortified granite building. Royal charters granted in 1489 and 1498 created the community a "free burgh" with the church as its administrator. Remnants of this ecclesiastical power survived until 1891, when the episcopal burgh was incorporated with New Aberdeen to form the present city. The oldest surviving charter (1179) confers several trade privileges on the burgesses of Aberdeen. The Great Charter (1638) confirmed the burgh's ancient rights.

Some of the oldest streets, dating from the 13th and 14th centuries, still survive near Castlegate (the historic marketplace and commercial heart of the modern city). Castlegate still contains a fine old Market (City) Cross (1686). Nearby are two ancient houses, Provost Skene's House (17th century), now a local history museum, and Provost Ross's House (1593).

The parish Church of St. Nicholas (Union Street) is divided into two parts: the West Church, built in 1755 by James Gibbs, is separated from the East Church (built in 1838 by Archibald Simpson) by the original 13th-century transept and steeple. Two medieval bridges have survived, the Brig o' Balgownie (1320), spanning the Don, and the Old Bridge of Dee (1527).

Union Street, Aberdeen's broad central thoroughfare, contains many fine examples of the use of local granite. The imposing modern municipal buildings, incorporating the tower and spire of the medieval tollbooth, contain valuable charters, relics, and the most complete documentary record of any Scottish burgh. Other significant buildings include the neoclassical Music Hall (1822) and Marischal College (Broad Street), reputedly the world's largest granite building, begun in 1844 by Archibald Simpson.

The University of Aberdeen was formed in 1860 by the union of two medieval colleges: King's College, a Roman Catholic institution founded in 1494, and the Protestant Marischal College, founded in 1593. Other educational institutions include Robert Gordon's Institute of Technology, the College of Education, and colleges of agriculture, fisheries (Torry Research Station), soil (Macaulay Institute for Soil Research), and animal nutrition (Rowett Research Institute). Aberdeen's old Grammar School was a medieval foundation.

Aberdeen is an important route centre by road, rail, sea, and air (Dyce Airport is 6 mi [10 km] north). The original harbour, the Dee estuary, has been continually improved. It is now the chief port of northern Scotland, trading mainly with Scandinavia and the Baltic, and Scotland's premier fishing port since the development of steam and diesel trawling. Typical port industries—chemicals, fertilizers, and engineering, including Britain's largest granite exporting industry—exist alongside a flourishing tourist industry. The North Sea oil boom of the 1970s benefitted Aberdeen more than any other city of Scotland, bringing more than 200 new companies and 6,000 new foreign residents and financing construction of housing, offices, and schools; revenues of the port of Aberdeen increased 15-fold during the early 1970s. Some 800 ac (324 ha) of industrial land were allocated to attract industry associated with oil technology. Pop. (1981) 203,927.

Aberdeen, town, Harford County, northeastern Maryland, U.S., near Chesapeake Bay, 26 mi (42 km) northeast of Baltimore. Settled about 1800, it was named for the city in Scotland. Aberdeen is the principal trading centre for the nearby 75,000-ac (30,000-ha) Aberdeen Proving Ground, a U.S. army test site for guns, ammunition, and military vehicles, where one of the world's greatest collections of weapons is displayed in the Army Ordnance Museum. There is some light manufacturing. Inc. 1892. Pop. (1980) 11,533.

Aberdeen, city, seat (1880) of Brown County, northeastern South Dakota, U.S., in the James River Valley. Established in 1880 as a railway junction, it was named for Aberdeen in Scotland by Alexander Mitchell, president of the Chicago, Milwaukee, and St. Paul Railroad. The city is now the financial and trading centre for a wide agricultural area and has some light manufacturing. The autumn pheasant-hunting season augments the economy. It is the home of Northern State College (1901) and Presentation (junior) College (1951). Author Hamlin Garland, known for his autobiographical "Middle Border" series, and L. Frank Baum, who wrote *The Wonderful Wizard of Oz,* spent their early years in Aberdeen. Inc. town, 1882; city, 1883. Pop. (1980) 25,956.

Aberdeen, George Hamilton-Gordon, 4th earl of, original name GEORGE GORDON (b. Jan. 28, 1784, Edinburgh—d. Dec. 14, 1860, London), twice British foreign secretary and prime minister (1852–55), who headed a government that involved Great Britain in the Crimean War against Russia (1853–56).

Aberdeen, detail of an oil painting by Sir Thomas Lawrence, 1828; in the collection of Viscount Cowdray

By courtesy of the Scottish National Portrait Gallery, Edinburgh

Orphaned at age 11, George Gordon (who added his deceased first wife's family name to his own surname in 1818) was reared by his guardians, the politicians William Pitt the Younger and Henry Dundas (afterward Viscount Melville), and inherited the earldom from his grandfather in 1801. In the government of the Duke of Wellington, he was chancellor of the duchy of Lancaster (January–June 1828) and foreign secretary (June 1828–November 1830), while in the brief first administration of Sir Robert Peel (November 1834–April 1835), he was secretary for war and the colonies. As foreign secretary again (September 1841–July 1846) in Peel's second government, Aberdeen settled long-standing disputes over the eastern and western boundaries between Canada and the United States, by the Webster–Ashburton Treaty (1842) and the Oregon Treaty (1846), respectively.

On Dec. 28, 1852, Aberdeen formed a coalition Cabinet of Peelites (of whom he had been acknowledged leader after Peel's death in 1850), Whigs, and a Radical. In 1853, as his ministry reluctantly neared war with Russia over conflicts of interest in the Middle East, his indecision hampered the peacekeeping efforts of his foreign secretary, the 4th Earl of Clarendon. War became inevitable after Aberdeen and Clarendon sent the British fleet to Constantinople (September 23) and then, three months later, into the Black Sea. Both Great Britain and France declared war against Russia on March 28, 1854. Although he was ill informed by the British generals in the Crimea, Aberdeen was constitutionally responsible for their mistakes, and he resigned on Jan. 29, 1855.

The Earl of Aberdeen (1893) was written by his son Arthur Hamilton-Gordon, 1st Baron Stanmore, a noted British colonial governor. Lady Frances Balfour wrote *The Life of George, Fourth Earl of Aberdeen*, 2 vol. (1923).

Abergavenny, Welsh Y FENNI, town, Monmouth district, Gwent county, Wales, at the confluence of the rivers Gavenny and Usk. The strategic nature of this site, guarding a main valley corridor between the Black Mountains and the Brecon Beacons into South Wales, was recognized by Romans, who built Gobannium, a legionary fortress, and Normans, who built an 11th-century castle. The market town that grew under the castle's protection was attacked at various times over the next 500 years. Abergavenny held important cattle and horse fairs in the 18th and 19th centuries and developed some flannel making; it never participated in the industrial growth of the coalfield towns to the west. A service centre and attractive holiday resort, it also became a residential base for commuters employed in other nearby Gwent centres. Pop. (1981 prelim.) 9,390.

Aberhart, William (b. Dec. 30, 1878, near Kippen, Ont., Can.—d. May 23, 1943, Vancouver, B.C.), during and after the Great Depression, the first Social Credit Party premier of Alberta.

Trained as a teacher, Aberhart was a high school principal in Calgary, Alta. (1915–35). In 1918 he founded the Calgary Prophetic Bible Institute and in 1932 employed his evangelical rhetoric in promoting the unorthodox Social Credit monetary-reform and political theories of Clifford Douglas.

In order to solve economic problems and to build a new society, Aberhart proposed to issue dividends (social credit) to each person, based on the real wealth of the province. After the 1935 provincial election in which the Social Credit Party candidates won 56 of the 63 assembly seats, he was made premier and minister of education, and he determined to make Alberta an example of the Social Credit system. The necessary enabling legislation, however, was declared unconstitutional and disallowed by the federal government. Aberhart nonetheless continued in office, directing Alberta's economy along orthodox financial lines, until his death.

Aberhonddu (Wales): *see* Brecon.

Aberpennar (Wales): *see* Mountain Ash.

aberration, in optical systems, such as lenses and curved mirrors, the deviation of light rays through lenses, causing images of objects to be blurred. In an ideal system, every point on the object will focus to a point of zero size on the image. Practically, however, each image point occupies a volume of finite size and unsymmetrical shape, causing some blurring of the whole image. Unlike a plane mirror, which yields images free of aberrations, a lens is an imperfect image producer, becoming ideal only for rays passing through its centre parallel to the optical axis (a line through the centre, perpendicular to the lens surfaces). The equations developed for object–image relations in a lens having spherical surfaces are only approximate and deal only with paraxial rays; *i.e.,* rays making only small angles with the optical axis. When light of only a single wavelength is present, there are five aberrations to be considered, called spherical aberration, coma, astigmatism, curvature of field, and distortion. A sixth aberration found in lenses (but not mirrors), chromatic aberration, results when light is not monochromatic (not of one wavelength).

In spherical aberration, rays of light from a point on the optical axis of a lens having spherical surfaces do not all meet at the same image point. Rays passing through the lens close to its centre are focussed farther away than rays passing through a circular zone near its rim. For every cone of rays from an axial object point meeting the lens there is a cone of rays that converges to form an image point, the cone being different in length according to the diameter of the circular zone. Wherever a plane at right angles to the optical axis is made to intersect a cone, the rays will form a circular cross section. The area of the cross section varies with distance along the optical axis, the smallest size known as the circle of least confusion. The image most free of spherical aberration is found at this distance.

Coma, so called because a point image is blurred into a comet shape, is produced when rays from an off-axis object point are imaged by different zones of the lens. In spherical aberration, the images of an on-axis object point that fall on a plane at right angles to the optical axis are circular in shape, of varying

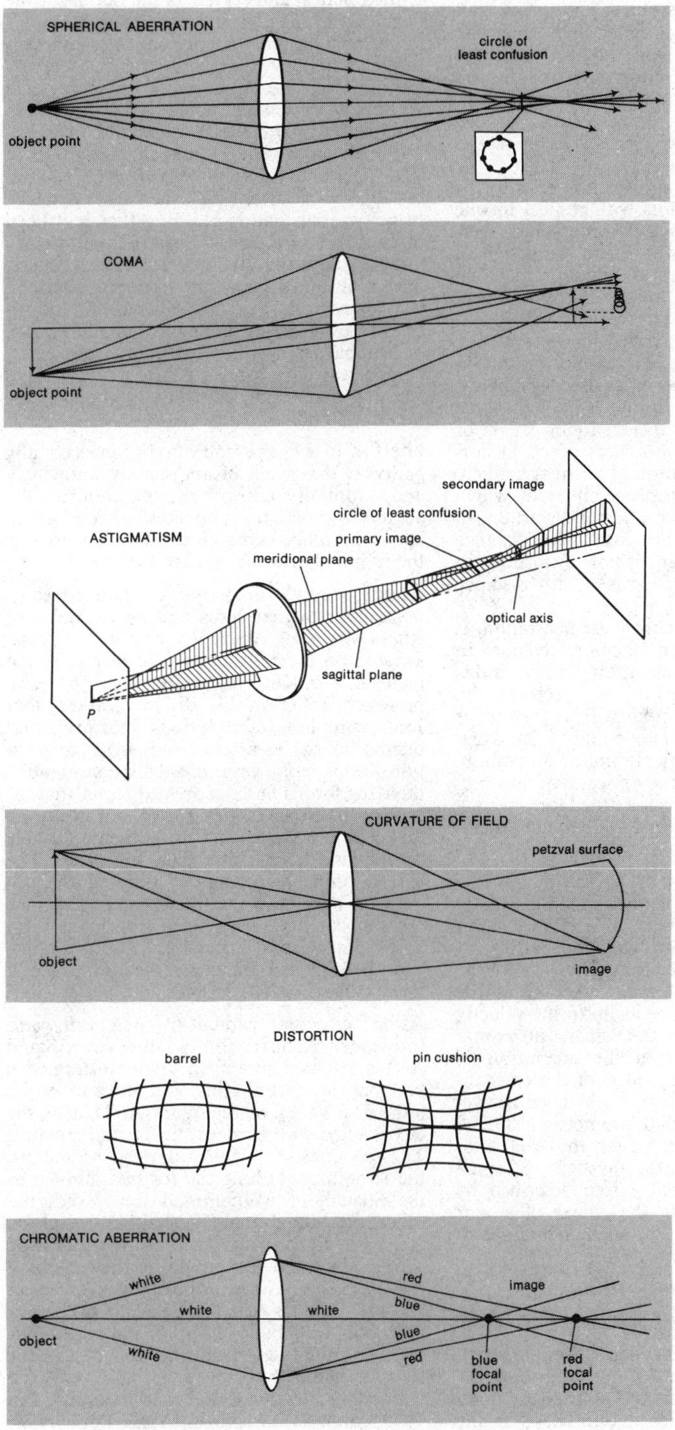

Several types of aberration

Diagram of astigmatism from F.W. Sears, *Optics* (1949); Addison-Wesley, Reading, Mass.

size, and superimposed about a common centre; in coma, the images of an off-axis object point are circular in shape, of varying size, but displaced with respect to each other. The accompanying diagram shows an exaggerated case of two images, one resulting from a central cone of rays and the other from a cone passing through the rim. The usual way for reducing coma is to employ a diaphragm to eliminate the outer cones of rays.

Astigmatism, unlike spherical aberration and coma, results from the failure of a single zone of a lens to focus the image of an off-axis point at a single point. As shown in the three-dimensional schematic the two planes at right angles to one another passing through the optical axis are the meridian plane and the sagittal plane, the meridian plane being the one containing the off-axis object point. Rays not in the meridian plane, called skew rays, are focussed farther away from the lens than those lying in the plane. In either case the rays do not meet in a point focus but as lines perpendicular to each other. Intermediate between these two positions the images are elliptical in shape.

Curvature of field and distortion refer to the location of image points with respect to one another. Even though the former three aberrations may be corrected for in the design of a lens, these two aberrations could remain. In curvature of field, the image of a plane object perpendicular to the optical axis will lie on a paraboloidal surface called the Petzval surface (after József Petzval, a Hungarian mathematician). Flat image fields are desirable in photography in order to match the film plane and projection when the enlarging paper or projection screen lie on a flat surface. Distortion refers to deformation of an image. There are two kinds of distortion, either of which may be present in a lens: barrel distortion, in which magnification decreases with distance from the axis, and pincushion distortion, in which magnification increases with distance from the axis.

The last aberration, chromatic aberration, is the failure of a lens to focus all colours in the same plane. Because the refractive index is least at the red end of the spectrum, the focal length of a lens in air will be greater for red and green than for blue and violet. Magnification is affected by chromatic aberration, being different along the optical axis and perpendicular to it. The first is called longitudinal chromatic aberration, and the second, lateral chromatic aberration.

aberration, constant of, in astronomy, the maximum amount of the apparent yearly aberrational displacement of a star or other celestial body, resulting from the Earth's orbital motion around the Sun. The value of the constant, about 20.49″ of arc, depends on the ratio of Earth's orbital velocity to the velocity of light. James Bradley, the British astronomer who in 1728 discovered the aberration of starlight, estimated the value of the constant at about 20″ and from this calculated the velocity of light at 295,000 kilometres (183,300 miles) per second, within a few thousand kilometres per second of the presently accepted value. The aberrational ellipse described by the image of a star in the course of a year has a major axis equal in angular distance to twice the constant of aberration.

Abertawe (Wales): *see* Swansea.

Aberteifi (Wales): *see* Cardigan.

Abertillery, town, Blaenau Gwent district, Gwent county, Wales, in the valley of the Ebbw River. Coal mining has been its main economic interest since about 1850; in the late 19th century it also had a small tinplate industry. Nantyglo, to the north, was the site of famous ironworks. Some light manufacturing has been introduced to Abertillery since the 1930s, mostly with government assistance. Pop. (1981 prelim.) 19,319.

Aberystwyth, coastal town, seat of Ceredigion district, Dyfed county, Wales, where the River Rheidol flows into Cardigan Bay. Traces of extensive Iron Age earthworks have been found on the hill Pen Dinas, which overlooks the old port and town. The medieval walled town grew around the castle erected by the Normans (1277) on a rocky headland immediately north of the mouth of the River Rheidol, into which the mouth of the River Ystwyth has also been diverted. The town spread northward along the coast, especially after the coming of railways. The port, now virtually unused, once handled coastal, Irish, and even transatlantic shipping (Welsh emigrants, for example, would sail direct for the United States) and served as the outlet for the once-flourishing Cardiganshire lead mines.

The town has grown since the late 19th century as a holiday resort and rural service centre and is the headquarters of many regional services of west Wales. Established by English conquerors in the Welsh heartland, Aberystwyth has become a principal stronghold of Welsh culture. The founder college of the University of Wales was established there in 1872, in a Victorian gothic building that had been constructed as a hotel. Post-1945 university buildings and the National Library of Wales, one of Britain's copyright libraries, overlook the town from Penglais Hill to the north-east. In the Rheidol Valley the inland hamlet of Llanbadarnfawr has become a suburb; its church was once a great centre of Dark Ages learning and Celtic Christianity. Pop. (1981 prelim.) 8,666.

abettor, in law, a person who becomes equally guilty in the crime of another by knowingly and voluntarily aiding the criminal during the act itself. An abettor is one kind of accomplice (*q.v.*), the other being an accessory, who aids the criminal prior to or after the crime.

Abgar legend, in early Christian times, a popular myth that Jesus had an exchange of letters with King Abgar V Ukkama of Edessa, situated on the northern fringe of the Syrian plateau. The King reputedly wrote to Jesus, professed belief in his divinity, asked that Jesus cure him of a serious infirmity, and offered his city as a safe refuge from persecution. In his reply, Jesus allegedly commended the King for his faith, expressed regret that his mission in life precluded a visit, but promised that after his Ascension into heaven a disciple would visit Edessa and heal the King. The letters, probably composed early in the 4th century, have been considered spurious since the 5th century. They were translated from Syriac into Greek, Armenian, Latin, Arabic, and other ancient languages, clear evidence of the popularity of the legend.

Abhā, city and capital of ʿAsīr *minṭaqah* (province), Abhā region, southwestern Saudi Arabia, situated on a plain at the western edge of Jabal (mount) al-Hijāz and surrounded by hills. The valley of the Wādī Abhā near the city is filled with gardens, fields, and streams. The city consists of four quarters: Manadhir, the largest, containing the fortress, known as the Shadah of Muḥammad ibn ʿAyād; the others are Muqabil; al-Khashah; and al-Qura. Abhā was freed from Ottoman rule following World War I and brought under the control of the Wahhabis, a Muslim puritanical group, in 1920 by ʿAbd al-ʿAziz ibn Saʿud. It is characterized by forts built on top of the neighbouring hills. Abhā lies 50 mi (80 km) east of the Red Sea and 528 mi southwest of Riyadh, the national capital. A coastal road, completed in 1979, connects Jiddah with Abhā. Pop. (1974) 30,150.

Abhayagiri, important ancient Theravāda Buddhist monastic centre (*vihāra*) built by King Vaṭṭagāmaṇi Abhaya (29–17 BC) on the northern side of Anurādhapura, the capital of Ceylon (Sri Lanka) at that time. Its importance lay, in part, in the fact that religious and political power were closely related, so that monastic centres had much influence on the secular history of the nation. But it is also important in the history of Theravāda Buddhism itself. Originally associated with the nearby Mahāvihāra ("Great Monastery"), which was the traditional centre of religious and civil power built by Devānanpiya-Tissa (307–267 BC), Abhayagiri seceded from the Great Monastery toward the end of Vaṭṭagāmaṇi's reign in a dispute over the relations between monks and the lay community and the use of Sanskrit works to augment Pāli texts as scripture.

Although viewed as heretical by the monks at the Great Monastery, the Abhayagiri monastery advanced in prestige and wealth under the patronage of King Gajabāhu I (AD 113–135). It subsequently suffered in the reign of Goṭhābhaya (223–267), who supported the religious and secular activities of the Great Monastery. Abhayagiri again flourished briefly under King Mahāsena (227–304), who later in his life changed his allegiance to the Great Monastery and destroyed the books held by the Abhayagiri monks. The Abhayagiri monastery never recovered, and the Great Monastery then remained in religious and political power until the 11th century. *See also* Mahāvihāra.

Abhdisho bar Berikha, also called EBEDJESUS OF NISIBIS (d. November 1318), Syrian Christian theologian and poet who was the last important representative of the Nestorian tradition, a theological school emphasizing a rational, critical interpretation of early Christian doctrine. The sect, centred in ancient Antioch, countered the speculative mysticism then prevalent in Alexandria and Jerusalem.

Appointed bishop of Shiggar and Beth-Arabaye (Syria) about 1285, Abhdisho became, by 1291, metropolitan (senior bishop over a larger province) of Nisibis (now Nusaybin, Tur.) and Armenia. Most notable of his works is *Margaritha vitae* ("The Pearl of Life"), considered to be one of the most comprehensive statements of late Nestorian teaching. The "Pearl" focussed on the issue of Christ's psychological identity. Reacting against the pietistic element of Greek and Oriental Christianity, which accented Christ as simply the divinity in human form rather than as a distinct individual, Abhdisho argued that Jesus experienced completely the biological and psychological functions of an integral, human person in feelings, mind, and will. Such a view was motivated by the Nestorian concern for an effective and authentic meaning to Christ's moral example and sacrifice on behalf of the human race.

Abhdisho also wrote the metrically structured *Catalogue* (1316), which is not only a list of his own works but also the best reference known for the writings of Nestorian Syrian and Greek churchmen-theologians and a valuable source on Syrian literary life.

abhibhvāyatana (Sanskrit: "total mastery over the senses"), Pāli ABHIBHĀYĀTANA, in Buddhist philosophy, one of the preparatory stages of meditation, in which the senses are completely restrained. In Buddhist canons, *abhibhvāyatana* is divided into eight substages during which man comes to realize that physical forms in the external world are different from himself, thus freeing himself from attachment to the sense objects. These stages become bases for man's deliverance from sensual pleasures and pains, which are understood to be sufferings.

Abhidhamma Piṭaka (Pāli: "Basket of Special Doctrine," or "Further Doctrine"), Sanskrit ABHIDHARMA PIṬAKA, the third—and historically the latest—of the three "baskets," or collections of texts, that together comprise the Pāli canon of Theravāda Buddhism, the form predominant in Southeast Asia and Sri Lanka (Ceylon). The other two collections are *Sutta* ("Discourse"; Sanskrit *Sūtra*) and *Vinaya* ("Discipline") *Piṭaka*s. Unlike *Sutta* and *Vinaya,* the seven *Abhidhamma* works are not generally claimed to represent the words of the Buddha himself but of disciples and great scholars. Nevertheless, they are highly venerated, particularly in Burma.

These are not systematic philosophical treatises but a detailed scholastic reworking, according to schematic classifications, of doctrinal material appearing in the *Sutta*s. As such they represent a development in a rationalistic direction of summaries or numerical lists that had come to be used as a basis for meditation—lists that, among the more mystically inclined, contributed to the *Prajñāpāramitā* ("Perfection of Wisdom") literature of Mahāyāna Buddhism, the form predominant in East Asia. The topics dealt with in *Abhidhamma* books include ethics, psychology, and epistemology.

As the last major division of the canon, the *Abhidhamma* corpus has had a checkered history. It was not accepted as canonical by the Mahāsaṅghika (Sanskrit: Great Community) school, the forerunners of Mahāyāna. Another school included within it most of the *Khuddaka Nikāya* ("Short Collection"), the latest section of the *Sutta Piṭaka.* And various Mahāyāna texts have been classified as *Abhidhamma,* including the *Prajñāpāramitā-sūtra*s in Tibet and, in China, the *Diamond Sūtra.*

The Pāli *Abhidhamma Piṭaka* encompasses the following texts, or *pakaraṇa*s: (1) *Dhammasaṅgaṇi* ("Summary of Dharma"), a psychologically oriented manual of ethics for advanced monks but long popular in Ceylon; (2) *Vibhaṅga* ("Division," or "Classification"—not to be confused with a *Vinaya* work or with several *sutta*s bearing the same name), a kind of supplement to the *Dhammasaṅgaṇi,* treating many of the same topics; (3) *Dhātukathā* ("Discussion of Elements"), another supplementary work; (4) *Puggalapaññatti* ("Designation of Person"), largely a collection of excerpts from the *Aṅguttara Nikāya* of the *Sutta Piṭaka,* classifying human characteristics in relation to stages on the Buddhist path; generally considered the earliest *Abhidhamma* text; (5) *Kathāvatthu* ("Points of Controversy"), attributed to Moggaliputta, president of the third Buddhist Council (3rd century BC), the only work in the Pāli canon assigned to a particular author; historically one of the most important of the seven, the *Kathāvatthu* is a series of questions from a heretical (*i.e.,* non-Theravāda) point of view, with their implications refuted in the answers; the long first chapter debates the existence of a soul; (6) *Yamaka* ("Pairs"), a series of questions on psychological phenomena, each dealt with in two opposite ways; (7) *Paṭṭhāna* ("Activations," or "Causes"), a complex and voluminous treatment of causality and 23 other kinds of relationships between phenomena, mental or material.

Abhidhammattha-saṅgaha (Pāli: "Summary of the Meaning of *Abhidhamma*"), probably the most important Buddhist manual of psychology and ethics. A highly popular primer, or digest, of the *Abhidhamma* corpus (the scholastic section of the canon) of the Theravāda tradition, it was composed in India or in Burma, the chief centre for *Abhidhamma* studies. Written in Pāli by the monk Anuruddha, it dates from no earlier than the 8th century AD and probably from the 11th or 12th.

This is a handbook rather than an expository work; it is extremely condensed, dealing in less than 50 pages with the entire contents of the seven texts of the *Abhidhamma Piṭaka.* It is the most widely read work of its kind, is held in very high esteem, especially in Burma and Sri Lanka (Ceylon), and has been the subject of an extensive exegetical literature in the centuries since its composition.

The subject matter of the *Abhidhammattha-saṅgaha* includes enumerations of 89 classes of consciousness, 52 mental properties in various combinations, the qualities of matter, the kinds of relations between phenomena, the varieties of rebirth, and a number of meditation exercises. The purpose of all this analysis is to elicit a realization of the impermanence of all things, leading to Enlightenment and emancipation.

Abhidhammāvatāra (Pāli: "Coming of *Abhidhamma*"), the earliest effort at systematizing, in the form of a manual, the doctrines dealt with in the *Abhidhamma* (scholastic) section of the Theravāda Buddhist canon. It was written in Pāli, apparently in the 5th century, by the poet and scholar Buddhadatta in the region of the Kāverī River, in southern India.

Following the closing of the canon in the final centuries BC, a number of commentaries (known in Pāli as *aṭṭhakathā*) on particular canonical texts appeared and culminated in those produced by Buddhadatta's contemporary, Buddhaghosa. In the *Abhidhammāvatāra* Buddhadatta then both summed up and gave an original systematization to that part of the commentary literature dealing with *Abhidhamma.* (Among his other works is the *Vinaya-vinicchaya* ["Analysis of the Vinaya"], which similarly summarizes the commentaries on the *vinaya* [monastic discipline] section of the canon.)

The *Abhidhammāvatāra* is written largely in verse and has 24 chapters. To a certain extent it was superseded in the 12th century by Anuruddha's *Abhidhammattha-saṅgaha.*

Abhidharma Piṭaka: *see* Abhidhamma Piṭaka.

Abhidharmakośa, also called ABHIDHARMAKOŚA-ŚĀSTRA (Sanskrit: "Treasury of Higher Law"), Chinese A-P'I-TA-MO CHÜ-SHE LUN, Japanese ABIDATSUMA-KUSHA-RON, encyclopaedic compendium of *Abhidharma* (scholasticism), the position of which within Buddhism has been likened to that of St. Thomas Aquinas' *Summa theologiae* for Roman Catholicism.

Its author, Vasubandhu, who lived in the 4th or 5th century in the northwestern part of India, wrote the work while he was still a monk of the Sarvāstivāda (Doctrine That All Is Real) order, before he embraced Mahāyāna, on whose texts he was later to write a number of commentaries. As a Sarvāstivāda work the *Abhidharmakośa* is one of few surviving treatments of scholasticism not written in Pāli and not produced by Theravādins, who follow the Pāli canon. The product of both great erudition and considerable independence of thought, the *Abhidharmakośa* authoritatively completed the systematization of Sarvāstivāda doctrine and at the same time incorporated Mahāyānist tendencies.

Translated into Chinese within a century or two, the *Abhidharmakośa* has been used in China, Japan, and Tibet both as a standard introduction to the Hīnayāna Buddhism of the southern countries and as a great authority in matters of doctrine. In China it provided the basis for the Abhidharma (Chinese Chü-she; Japanese Kusha) sect. The work has inspired numerous commentaries. It also provides scholars with a unique amount of information on the doctrinal differences between ancient Buddhist schools.

The text is composed of 600 stanzas of poetry plus the equivalent of 8,000 stanzas of prose commentary supplied by the author himself. As an introduction to the seven *Abhidharma* treatises in the Sarvāstivāda canon and a systematic digest of their contents, the *Abhidharmakośa* deals with a wide range of philosophical, cosmological, ethical, and salvational doctrine.

abhijñā (Sanskrit: "supernatural knowledge"), Pāli ABHIÑÑĀ, in Buddhist philosophy, miraculous power obtained especially through meditation and wisdom. Usually five kinds of *abhijñā* are enumerated: the ability (1) to travel any distance or take on any form at will; (2) to see everything; (3) to hear everything; (4) to know another's thoughts; (5) to recollect former existences. A sixth power, freedom by undefiled wisdom, is exclusively the prerogative of Buddhas and *arhats* (saints). An earlier enumeration of three knowledges (*tisro-vidyā*s) consists of this sixth *abhijñā* together with the powers of recollecting previous existences and of seeing everything and thus knowing the future destinies of all beings.

The first five *abhijñā*s enumerated in Buddhism are identical with the *siddhi*s (miraculous powers) known to Indian ascetics in general. Patañjali, for example, mentions them in his *Yoga-sūtra* (the classical exposition of Yoga) as magical virtues of meditation. Goblins and deities are said to be endowed naturally with such powers.

Attainment of the *abhijñā*s by monks is possible only through continual meditation directed toward the final goal of perfect freedom; the powers themselves are regarded as indications of spiritual progress. According to the Buddha, however, indulgence in the *abhijñā*s is to be avoided, since their use is a powerful distraction from the path toward Enlightenment, which is the sixth *abhijñā* and the final goal.

Abhijñānaśakuntalā (Sanskrit play): *see* Śakuntalā.

Abhinavagupta (fl. 1014, Kashmir, India), philosopher, ascetic and aesthetician, and outstanding representative of the "recognition" (*pratyabhijñā*) school of Kashmiri Saivite monism. This school conceived of the god Śiva (the manifestation of ultimate reality), the individual soul, and the universe as essentially one; *pratyabhijñā* refers to the way of realizing this identity. Abhinavagupta was a prolific writer on philosophy and aesthetics. Among his most notable philosophic works are the *Īśvara-pratyabhijñā-vimarśinī* and the more detailed *Īśvara-pratyabhijñā-vivṛti-vimarśinī,* both commentaries on *Īśvara-pratyabhijñā* ("Recognition of God"), by Utpala, an earlier philosopher of the *pratyabhijñā* school.

Abhisamayālaṅkārāloka (Sanskrit: "Illumination of the *Abhisamayālaṅkāra*"), important contribution to exegetical literature on the *Prājñāpāramitā-* ("Perfection of Wisdom") *sūtra*s of the Mahāyāna Buddhist tradition and one of the texts most often studied in Tibetan monasteries.

The *Prajñāpāramitā-sūtra*s, with their emphasis on the doctrine of ontological "emptiness" and the attainment of Nirvāṇa through perfect wisdom, had been systematized in a terse commentary known as the *Abhisamayālaṅkāra.* (*Abhisamaya* means either "insight" or "uniting" and designates Buddhist training toward Enlightenment; *alaṅkāra* is a literary form in verse.) This latter text required its own commentaries, which continued to be produced in Tibet into modern times. It was paraphrased in the present treatise, the *Abhisamayālaṅkārāloka,* which also offered a detailed commentary on the *Aṣṭasāhasrikā* ("8,000-Verse") *Prajñāpāramitā.*

The author was Haribhadra. He wrote around AD 750, and his text was translated from Sanskrit into Tibetan in the 10th or 11th century.

abhiṣeka (Sanskrit: "sprinkling"), in esoteric Buddhism, a purificatory or initiatory rite in which a candidate is sprinkled with water or other liquid, signifying a change in status.

Originally, *abhiṣeka* was an integral part of the ancient Indian royal consecration rite. Water from the four oceans was poured out of golden jars onto the head of the seated monarch during his accession ceremony and also during the investiture ceremony of his heir apparent.

In Tantric, or esoteric, Buddhism, the *abhiṣeka* rite is a necessary prelude to initiation into mystical teaching or rites. Four classes of *abhiṣeka* are known, each of them associated with one of the four *Tantras* (teachings) suitable to four groups of people with progressively superior levels of sensibility. They are the master consecration, secret consecration, knowledge of *prajñā* ("wisdom"), and the fourth consecration.

Abiathar, in the Old Testament, son of Ahimelech, priest of Nob. The sole survivor of a massacre carried out by Doeg, he fled to David and remained with him throughout his wanderings and reign and supported Adonijah against Solomon. Abiathar probably represents an early rival house to that of Zadok, the official priestly family of Jerusalem down to the Exile (I Sam. 22:20–23; II Sam. 15:24–37; and I Kings 2:26–27).

ʿAbīd al-Bukhārī, also called BUĀKHAR, army of Saharan blacks organized in Morocco by the ʿAlawī ruler Ismāʿīl (reigned 1672–1727). Earlier rulers had recruited black slaves (Arabic *ʿabīd*) into their armies, and these men or their descendants eventually formed the core of Ismāʿīl's guard.

The *ʿabīd* were sent to a special camp at Mechraʿ er-Remel to beget children. The communal children, male and female, were presented to the ruler when they were about 10 years old and proceeded to a prescribed course of training. The boys acquired such skills as masonry, horsemanship, archery, and musketry, whereas the girls were prepared for domestic life or for entertainment. At the age of 15 they were divided among the various army corps and married, and eventually the cycle would repeat itself with their children.

Ismāʿīl's army, numbering 150,000 men at its peak, consisted mainly of the "graduates" of the Mechraʿ er-Remel camp and supplementary slaves pirated from black Saharan tribes, all foreigners whose sole allegiance was to the ruler. The *ʿabīd* were highly favoured by Ismāʿīl, well paid, and often politically powerful; in 1697–98 they were even given the right to own property.

After Ismāʿīl's death the quality of the corps could not be sustained. Discipline slackened, and as preferential pay was no longer forthcoming, the *ʿabīd* took to brigandage. Many left their outposts and shifted into the cities, and others became farmers or peasants. Those who remained in the army were an unstable element, ready for intrigue. Under strong rulers, the ʿAbīd al-Bukhārī were periodically reorganized, though they never regained their former military and numerical strength. The *ʿabīd* were finally dissolved late in the 19th century, with only a nominal number retained as the king's personal bodyguard.

Abidatsuma-kusha-ron: *see* Abhidharmakośa.

Abidjan, chief port, capital, and largest city of Ivory Coast, on the Ébrié Lagoon, separated from the Gulf of Guinea and the Atlantic by the Vridi Plage sandbar. A village in 1898, it became a town in 1903. A rail terminus from 1904, Abidjan first depended on the meagre facilities of Port-Bouët on the sandbar's ocean shore. It succeeded Bingerville as capital of the French Ivory Coast colony in 1934 and retained that position after independence in 1960. Districts within the city include Plateau, Cocody (site of the University of Abidjan), Treichville, Adjame, Koumassi, and Marcory.

Abidjan and the Ébrié Lagoon, Ivory Coast

Q. Picou—De Wys Inc.

The Vridi Canal opened the lagoon to the sea in 1950, and the city soon became the financial centre of French-speaking West Africa. The first of two bridges linking the mainland to Petit-Bassam Island was built in 1958. Abidjan's modern deepwater port exports coffee, cocoa, timber, bananas, pineapples, and manganese. From the administrative and business sectors on the mainland, the city stretches southward to the industrial area on Petit-Bassam and the mineral and petroleum docks along the Vridi Canal. There are a number of wide, shady streets and gardened squares in the city; its university (1964) lies on the eastern mainland. Abidjan has a museum of traditional Ivorian art, a national library, and several agricultural and scientific research institutes. The city is a communications centre and the site of an international airport (at Port-Bouët, an autonomous municipality within Abidjan). North of the city is the Parc National du Banco, a magnificent tropical rain forest. Pop. (1981 est.) 1,400,000.

abietic acid, the most abundant of several closely related organic acids that comprise most of rosin, the solid portion of the oleoresin of coniferous trees. Commercial abietic acid is usually a glassy or partly crystalline, yellowish solid, melting at temperatures as low as 85° C (185° F). It belongs to the diterpene group of organic compounds (compounds derived from four isoprene units).

Rosin has been used for centuries for caulking ships. In modern times methods have been developed for improving the properties of the rosin acids, which are soft, tacky, and low melting, and subject to rapid deterioration by oxidation in air. Stability is greatly increased by heat treatment.

Rosin acids are converted into ester gum by reaction with controlled amounts of glycerol or other polyhydric alcohols. Ester gum has drying properties and is used in paints, varnishes, and lacquers.

Abigail (Hebrew: My Father Rejoices), in the Old Testament, the wife of Nabal of southern Judah, on whose death she became one of the first wives of David (I Sam. 25) and the mother of his son Chileab. The name Abigail was also borne by David's sister (I Chron. 2:16 fol.), the mother of Amasa, commander of the army of Absalom. From the former (self-styled "handmaid"; I Sam. 25:25 fol.) is derived the colloquial use of the word for a waiting woman.

Abildgaard, Nicolai Abraham, also spelled NIKOLAJ-ABRAHAM ABILGAARD (b. Sept. 11, 1743, Copenhagen—d. June 4, 1809, Frederiksdal, Den.), the most renowned Danish painter of the late 18th century and one of the early Neoclassicists.

Abildgaard studied in Rome during 1772–77, where he was primarily influenced by antique sculpture and Roman wall paintings. His style was classical, though with a romantic trend, and he had a remarkable sense of colour. Many of his paintings are melodramatic interpretations of episodes from ancient literature. He taught at the Danish Royal Academy of Fine Arts, of which he became director in 1789. Bertel Thorvaldsen, the prominent Danish sculptor, was his pupil.

Abilene, city, seat (1861) of Dickinson County, east central Kansas, U.S., on the Smoky Hill River. Settled in 1858 and known as Mud Creek, it was named *c.* 1860 for the biblical Abilene (which means "grassy plain"). Development was slow until Joseph McCoy, a cattle entrepreneur and later mayor of Abilene, selected it for the northern terminus of the Texas cattle drives in 1867, the year the Kansas Pacific Railroad reached this point. The biggest year of cattle drives to Abilene over the Chisholm Trail was 1871, when more than 5,000 cowboys driving 700,000 cows arrived at the yards. With the prosperity of the cattlemen came an era of lawlessness. Famed gunman James Butler (Wild Bill) Hickok served as marshal in 1871. The appearance of homesteaders and fenced ranges discouraged the Texas cattle trade, much of which was diverted to Wichita. Abilene is still a shipping point for livestock, as well as for grain and other agricultural products, and it has some light industry. Pres. Dwight D. Eisenhower spent his boyhood in Abilene, and he is buried at the Eisenhower Center, which also encompasses his family home and library. Inc. 1869. Pop. (1980) 6,572.

Place of Meditation, Eisenhower Center, Abilene, Kan.

Alan Pitcairn from Grant Heilman—EB Inc.

Abilene, city, seat (1883) of Taylor County (and partly in Jones County), west central Texas, U.S., on low, rolling plains, 153 mi (246 km) west of Fort Worth. Founded in 1881 as the new railhead (Texas and Pacific Railway) for the overland Texas cattle drives, it took not only the business of the previous railhead, Abilene, Kan., but also its biblical name as well. The economy, originally based solely on livestock and agriculture, has expanded to include industry. Petroleum and natural gas are produced in a 22-county area, of which Abilene is the centre. Manufactures include light machinery, aerospace structures, and band instruments. Abilene is the site of Hardin–Simmons University (1891), Abilene Christian University (1906), and McMurry College (1923). Dyess Air Force Base is adjacent (southwest). The West Texas Fair, rodeos, and livestock shows are annual events. Old Abilene Town (northeast) is a reconstructed Texas frontier town. Inc. 1881. Pop. (1980) city, 98,315; metropolitan area (SMSA), 139,192.

Abingdon, parish (town), Vale of White Horse district, county of Oxfordshire, England, south of Oxford at the confluence of the River Thames and the River Ock. The town was founded by the Saxons and grew up around a Benedictine abbey that was established in 676. In 1556, after the abbey had been dissolved, Abingdon was granted its first royal charter. The abbey remains include a Perpendicular gateway and the restored Checker Hall, which is now used as an Elizabethan-style theatre. The arched bridge over the Thames (1416; widened 1929) provides a view of the Early English tower and Perpendicular spire of St. Helen's Church. The county hall (1677–80) houses a museum collection. St. Nicholas' Church, the west front of which was built in 1180, stands nearby. Schools in the town include Abingdon (Roysse's) School—one of the oldest public (independent) schools in England—and Radley College (1847). The town also has a number of light industries and is a popular Thames-side resort. Pop. (1981 prelim.) 22,686.

Abingdon, town, seat of Washington County, southwestern Virginia, U.S., in the Appalachian Mountains, near the Tennessee line, 15 mi (24 km) northeast of Bristol. Settled *c.* 1765, it was the site of Black's Fort (1776), a settlers' haven from Indian attacks. It was incorporated as Abingdon in 1778; the name has been variously attributed to Lord Abingdon, Daniel Boone's home in Pennsylvania, and Mary Washington's hometown. During the Civil War it suffered severely at the hands of Union troops under Gen. George Stoneman. A resort town, Abingdon is also the state's largest burley tobacco market, and it holds livestock auctions. It is well known for its handicrafts and chinaware. The Barter Theatre, now the state theatre of Virginia, was founded (1933) during the Depression period, with admission tickets being bartered for food. The Virginia Highlands Festival is held annually in Abingdon. Virginia Highlands Community College opened there in 1969. Pop. (1980) 4,318.

Abingdon Island (Galápagos Islands): *see* Pinta, Isla.

Abington, town (township), Plymouth County, eastern Massachusetts, U.S., 20 mi (32 km) southeast of Boston. Known as Manamooskeagin (Land of Many Beavers) to the Indians, it was settled in 1668, incorporated in 1712, and named for Abington, Eng. An iron foundry was established there in 1769, and about 1815 Jesse Reed invented a machine that mass-produced tacks, thus enabling the footwear industry to thrive. Abington is reputed to have produced 50 percent of all the boots worn by the Federal army in the Civil War. From 1846 to 1865 it was a centre of the Abolitionist movement. Now primarily residential, it has some light manufacturing, notably printing and machine-tool industries. Ames Nowell State Park is nearby. Pop. (1980) 13,517.

Abington, urban township, Montgomery County, southeastern Pennsylvania, U.S., a northern suburb of Philadelphia, encompassing the communities of Ardsley, Glenside, McKinley, Noble, North Glenside, and Roslyn. Organized in the 1700s, it became a station on the North Pennsylvania Railroad in 1855. During the Revolutionary War, it was the site of the Whitemarsh Encampment of the American Army, and a skirmish with the British took place at nearby Edge Hill. Manufactures include pressed steel, chemicals, and metal and plastic products. The Ogontz campus of Pennsylvania State University opened (1950) in Abington. Inc. 1906. Pop. (1980) 59,084.

Abington, Fanny, *née* FRANCES BARTON (b. 1737, London—d. March 4, 1815, London), actress admired both for her craft and for her leadership in fashion.

She was at first a flower girl, hence her later nickname, Nosegay Fan, and street singer. Employment by a French milliner gave her taste in dress and a knowledge of French that she later found useful. She first appeared on the stage at the Haymarket Theatre, London, in 1755. In 1756 she joined the Drury Lane company but was overshadowed by Hannah Pritchard and Kitty Clive. After an unfortunate marriage to her music master in 1759, she was known as Mrs. Abington. She spent five successful years in Ireland and was then invited by David Garrick to rejoin Drury Lane. There she remained for 18 years, creating many important roles, among them Lady Teazle in Sheridan's *School for Scandal* (1777). She was equally successful in tragedy and comedy. In 1782 Mrs. Abington went from Drury Lane to Covent Garden. She left the stage in 1790, returning in 1797 for another two years. She was a leader of fashion, and a headdress of hers called the Abington cap was very widely worn.

abiogenesis: *see* spontaneous generation.

Abipón, South American Indian people who formerly lived on the lower Bermejo River in the Argentine Chaco. They spoke a language (also called Callaga) belonging to the Guaycuruan group of the Guaycurú–Charruan languages (*see* Guaycuruan languages). The Abipón were divided into three dialect groups: the Nakaigetergehè (Forest People), the Riikahè (People of the Open Country), and the Yaaukanigá (Water People). About 1750 their numbers were estimated at 5,000, but in the second half of the 19th century they became extinct as a people.

Semi-nomadic bands of Abipón hunted, fished, gathered food, and practiced a limited degree of agriculture before the introduction of the horse. The latter event transformed the whole social system of the Chaco. Agriculture was practically abandoned, and semi-wild cattle, rhea, guanaco, deer, and peccary were hunted on horseback. Abipón horsemen also raided Spanish farms and ranches, even threatening large cities such as Asunción and Corrientes.

By 1750 the Jesuits had settled the Abipón on missions that later became the Argentine cities of Reconquista and Resistencia. Military pacification in the 19th century circumscribed the Abipón hunting grounds. Many of them were slaughtered, and others were assimilated into the general population.

Abitibi River, river, northeastern Ontario, Canada. From its source in the shallow 360-sq-mi (930-sq-km) Abitibi Lake, lying across the Ontario–Quebec border, the river descends 868 ft (265 m) as it flows generally northward for 340 mi (550 km) to join the Moose River and empty into the southern end of James Bay. The heavily forested Abitibi Valley supports an extensive pulp and paper industry, centred at Iroquois Falls. Gold mining has long been important in the lake region, and tourism has become increasingly significant in the economy. The valley is served by the Ontario Northland and Canadian National railways. Abitibi is an Algonkian Indian term (*abitah* ["middle"] and *nipi* ["water"]) describing the lake's midway location on an old canoe route between the Ottawa Valley and James Bay.

Abkhaz Autonomous Soviet Socialist Republic, Russian ABKHAZSKAYA AVTONOMNAYA SOVETSKAYA SOTSIALISTCHESKAYA RESPUBLIKA, also spelled ABCHAZSKAJA AVTONOMNAJA SOVETSKAJA SOCIALISTIČESKAJA RESPUBLIKA, also called ABKHAZIYA, also spelled ABCHAZIJA, administrative division of the Georgian Soviet Socialist Republic, between the Black Sea and the crest line of the Great Caucasus range (Bolshoy Kavkaz), covering an area of 3,300 sq mi (8,600 sq km).

Bordering the eastern shores of the Black Sea, the republic consists of a narrow coastal lowland broken by mountain spurs, rising to a hilly foreland zone of eroded marine and river terraces that merge into the steep slopes of the Caucasus.

Near-subtropical conditions prevail in the lowland, where the average January temperature remains above freezing point and annual rainfall is 47 to 55 in. (1,200 to 1,400 mm). On the mountain slopes climatic conditions are more severe, and rainfall ranges from 80 to 120 in. The subtropical soils (yellow earths and *terra rossa*) bear a luxuriant vegetation of more than 1,500 species. Wide areas of the lowland and foreland zones have been cleared of the forests of oak, beech, and hornbeam that once covered Abkhaziya, while in the mountains conifers give way to meadows, and the snow line begins at 9,000 ft (2,750 m).

The Abkhaz were vassals of the Roman Empire when they became Christian under Justinian I (*c.* 550). In the 8th century the independent Kingdom of Abkhazia was formed. Later a part of Georgia, it secured its independence in 1463 only to come under the Ottoman Empire in the 16th century when Islām replaced Christianity. In 1810 a treaty with Russia was signed acknowledging a protectorate. Russia annexed Abkhazia in 1864, and the Soviet authorities proclaimed its autonomy as a region in 1919 and raised it to the status of a republic in 1921.

The Abkhaz form about one-sixth of the republic's population, being outnumbered by Georgians (44 percent) and Russians (16 percent) and slightly exceeding Armenians (15 percent) in number. Most of the population is concentrated in the coastal lowland, where the larger settlements are located—the capital, Sukhumi (*q.v.*), Ochamchira, and the resort centres of Gagra and Novy Afon. Although the amount of arable land is small, agriculture is the predominant economic activity. In the foreland zone the best tobacco in the Soviet Union is grown; the coastal zone is noted for its tea, silk, and fruits. Oil is extracted from the nut of the tung tree, which is widely grown along with eucalyptus and bamboo. Grapes have been cultivated since ancient times. Inland, on the higher slopes, timber production is the major occupation. Coal mining centres on Tkvarcheli, the largest inland city. Power is supplied by several hydroelectric plants. The coastal resorts and Lake Ritsa are popular holiday and convalescent centres. The main line of communication in the republic is the electrified railway along the coast, with a branch to Tkvarcheli. Roads also parallel the coast and lead inland to Lake Ritsa and along the Kodori and Bzyb valleys. Pop. (1982 est.) 513,000.

Consult the INDEX *first*

Abkhazo-Adyghian languages, also called NORTHWEST CAUCASIAN LANGUAGES, group of languages spoken primarily in the northwestern part of the Caucasus Mountains. The languages of this group—Abkhaz, Abaza, Adyghian, Kabardian (Circassian), and the nearly extinct Ubykh—are noted for the great number of distinctive consonants and limited number of distinctive vowels in their sound systems.

Ableman v. Booth (1859), case in which the U.S. Supreme Court upheld both the constitutionality of the Fugitive Slave Act and the supremacy of the federal government over state governments.

Sherman Booth was an Abolitionist newspaper editor in Wisconsin who had been sentenced to jail by a federal court for assisting a runaway slave—a clear violation of the 1850 Fugitive Slave Act, which required all Americans to cooperate in the capture and return of escaped slaves. Wisconsin (as well as several other Northern states), however, had responded to the federal act by passing a "personal liberty law," severely impeding enforcement by federal authorities of the Fugitive Slave Act within its borders.

As a consequence, Booth was released on a writ of habeas corpus, issued by a judge of the Wisconsin Supreme Court. U.S. District Marshal Ableman, however, obtained a writ of error from the U.S. Supreme Court in order to have the state court's action reviewed. The Supreme Court rendered a unanimous opinion reversing the Wisconsin court. Chief Justice Roger B. Taney's opinion denied the right of state courts to interfere in federal cases, prohibited states from releasing federal prisoners through writs of habeas corpus, and upheld the constitutionality of the Fugitive Slave Act.

ablution, in religion, a prescribed washing of part or all of the body or of possessions, such as clothing or ceremonial objects, with the intent of purification or dedication. Water, or water with salt or some other traditional ingredient, is most commonly used, but washing with blood is not uncommon in the history of religions, and urine of the sacred cow has been used in India.

The devout follower of Shintō, for example, rinses hands and mouth with water before approaching a shrine. Monks of the Theravāda Buddhist tradition wash themselves in the monastery pool before meditation. The upper-caste Hindu bathes ceremonially in water before performing daily morning worship (*pūjā*) in the home. Jewish law requires ritual immersion of their whole bodies by women prior to marriage and after menstruation, as well as by new converts to Judaism. Washing of the hands after rising in the morning and before meals that include bread are also examples of ablution in Judaism. The Roman Catholic priest (and priests of some Orthodox churches) celebrating the eucharistic liturgy prepares himself by ritual washing of his hands in the lavabo. Seven days after Baptism those newly baptized in Eastern Orthodox churches often go through a ceremony in which holy oil is washed from the forehead. Among some of the Brethren sects in the rural United States, ceremonial foot washing is performed on certain occasions. Muslim piety requires that the devout wash their hands, feet, and face before each of the five daily prayers; the use of sand is permitted where water is unavailable.

Like most ritual acts, ablution may carry a wide range of meanings to those who perform it. The stain of ritual uncleanness may be felt to be as real as contamination with unseen germs is for the medically minded; the act of cleansing may be only a gesture, symbolic of desired purity of soul. Or, as Carl Jung and others have suggested in studies of unconscious elements in religious symbolism, both objective and subjective aspects may be fused in the ritual act.

Abnaki, also called WABANAKI, a confederacy of Algonkian-speaking Indian tribes in northeast North America, which was organized to furnish resistance and protection against the Iroquois League, especially the Mohawk, of what is now northern New York state. In its earliest known organization it consisted of tribes east and northeast of present New York: Malecite in present New Brunswick; Passamaquoddy and Penobscot in present Maine; and tribes in present Vermont and New Hampshire. Later it included some eastern tribes as far south as the Delaware tribe.

Although they relied primarily on hunting and fishing, some corn (maize) was grown throughout the coastal region, more intensively from north to south. In the north the typical dwelling was the birch-bark-covered wigwam occupied by several families. The birch-bark canoe was in general use. Game was taken in snares and traps and by bow and arrow. Each tribe consisted of small bands under a headman, or civil chief, who advised but had little compulsory authority; there was a separate war chief. A general council of all the men and women decided matters relating to war; a grand council of chiefs and representatives of each family decided other questions of importance to the group. There was institutionalized comradeship with mutual responsibility, which united two men for life. Belief in a culture hero who will return to help the people in time of great need persists to the present.

Chiefly as a result of missionary influence, beginning in the 17th century the Abnaki favoured French interests and carried on a war against the English. After several severe defeats in 1724 and 1725, the Abnaki were reduced in number, and most withdrew to Canada, eventually settling at Saint-François-du-Lac in Quebec. The population in the late 20th century was about 5,000.

Abney, Sir William de Wiveleslie (b. July 24, 1843, Derby, Derbyshire, Eng.—d. Dec. 3, 1920, Folkestone, Kent), a specialist in the chemistry of photography, especially noted for his development of a photographic emulsion that he used to map the solar spectrum far into the infrared.

Abney
BBC Hulton Picture Library

Commissioned in the Royal Engineers (1861), he taught chemistry and photography at the School of Military Engineering at Chatham. He succeeded to various educational posts there and elsewhere.

In 1874 Abney made the first quantitative measurements of the action of light on photographic materials. In 1880 he discovered the photographic developing properties of hydroquinone. Elected to the Royal Society (1876), he also held posts with other learned societies and won various honours. He was knighted in 1900.

abnormal psychology: *see* psychopathology.

Åbo (Finland): *see* Turku.

Åbo, Treaty of (1743), peace settlement that concluded the Russo-Swedish War of 1741–43 by obliging Sweden to cede a strip of southern Finland to Russia and to become temporarily dependent on Russia. As a result of the Great Northern War (Treaty of Nystad, 1721), Sweden had lost Estonia, Livonia, Ingria, and part of Karelia to Russia. In 1741 Sweden reached a secret understanding (through French mediators) with Elizabeth, a daughter of Peter I the Great; Elizabeth agreed to return the Baltic territories to Sweden in exchange for Swedish support in her efforts to seize the Russian throne from the infant emperor Ivan VI. In July 1741 the Swedes declared war on Russia, announcing that they would withdraw when Elizabeth became the Russian empress. Although they lost a major battle at Vilmanstrand (August 1741), the Swedes advanced toward St. Petersburg; their threat to the Russian capital enabled Elizabeth to stage a successful coup d'etat (Dec. 6 [Nov. 25, old style], 1741); thereupon the Swedes retreated into Finland.

But Elizabeth reneged on the agreement. Russian troops conquered Helsingfors and Åbo (modern Turku, then the capital of Finland) and occupied a large portion of Finland. Hostilities ended in 1742; Russia, taking advantage of a succession crisis in Sweden, offered to return most of Finland if Sweden would accept the Russian-supported candidate—Adolf Frederick of Holstein-Gottorp-Eutin—as heir apparent.

The Swedes agreed; the final settlement, signed at Åbo (August 1743), gave Russia a strip of southern Finland that included the cities of Vilmanstrand and Frederikshamn. Russian troops were to leave the remainder of Finland when Adolf Frederick was officially designated crown prince; in the meantime, Russian forces were to be allowed to occupy Sweden to make sure that nothing interfered with his selection. Russia was thus able to exert a tremendous influence on Swedish affairs. But after the peace settlement, Russian influence was short-lived; all the Russian troops were withdrawn from Sweden by July 1744, and Adolf Frederick quickly ended his dependence on Russia.

The territorial provisions of the treaty were longer lasting. In 1788, while Russia was at war with Turkey, Sweden tried to alter the treaty's provisions. King Gustav III, demanding the return of Karelia and Finland, declared war on Russia (June 1788). Although the Swedes presented a threat to St. Petersburg and won a major victory at Svenskund (July 9–10, 1790, new style), the Treaty of Värälä (August 1790) restored the prewar (1788) borders, which remained as they had been set by the Treaty of Åbo until 1809 (Treaty of Frederikshamn).

ABO blood group system, method of classifying human blood on the basis of the inherited properties of red blood cells (erythrocytes) as determined by their possession or lack of the so-called antigens A (including A_1 and A_2) and B. Persons may, thus, have type A, type B, type O, or type AB blood. (Antigens of other blood group systems may also be present.)

An antigen is a substance that can, in certain circumstances, excite the production of a corresponding antibody. An antibody is a substance capable of reacting specifically with particular antigens. Blood group antigens are carried on the surface of the red cells.

Blood containing red cells with type A antigen on their surface has in its serum (fluid) antibodies against type B red cells. If, in transfusion, type B blood is injected into persons with type A blood, the red cells in the injected blood are destroyed by the antibodies in the recipient's blood. In the same way, type A red cells are destroyed by anti-A antibodies in type B blood. Type O blood can be injected into persons with type A, B, or O blood unless there is incompatibility with respect to some other blood group system also present. Persons with type AB blood can receive type A, B, or O blood.

Blood group O is commonest throughout the world, reaching a frequency of 100 percent in Amerindians of South and Central America and in the southern two-thirds of the United States. Type B is high in Asia, with a maximum in Northern India; it is low in Europe and Africa and absent among American Indians and in most Australian Aborigines. Type A_1 is common all over the world and appears to exist to the exclusion of type A_2 among the Australian Aborigines and Eskimos and in parts of Indonesia, the Pacific, India, Canada, and the northern United States. The world high occurs among the Blackfoot and Blood Indians and surrounding tribes in Alberta and Montana; this concentration in a continent otherwise so strongly type O is a puzzle that some scholars believe is evidence for repeated waves of migration into the New World from Asia. Gene A_2 reaches a frequency of 50 percent in certain Lapps; it is uncommon or rare elsewhere.

Stomach cancer is 20 percent more frequent in persons of type A than in people of types O or B; pernicious anemia and possibly bronchopneumonia in infants are also associated with type A. Type O is associated with a 40 percent higher frequency of duodenal ulcer, especially in persons who do not secrete water-soluble antigen (nonsecretors); gastric ulcer is also more frequent in type O individuals. Erythroblastosis fetalis (*q.v.*) occurs in offspring of ABO-incompatible matings, particularly when the mother is O and the father A; early loss of embryos is also increased in ABO-incompatible matings.

The ABO antigens are developed well before birth and remain throughout life. ABO antibodies are acquired passively from the mother before birth, but by three months the infant is making his own—it is believed the stimulus for such antibody formation is from contact with ABO-like antigenic substances in nature.

Åbo och Björneborgs län (Finland): *see* Turku ja Pori.

Aboisso, town, administrative headquarters (since 1969) of Aboisso *département*, southeastern Ivory Coast, at the head of navigation on the Bia River. An early trading post of the Anyi (Agni) people on the caravan route east to Ashanti (Asante), it declined in the late 19th century with the delineation of colonial boundaries by the French and British. It survived as a trade centre for the produce of the surrounding tropical rain forest and now sends coffee, cocoa, bananas, and timber (mahogany and sipo) to Abidjan, 22 mi (35 km) west, for export. Aboisso has a government hospital (1963) and a Roman Catholic mission. Pop. (1975) town, 14,272; (1979 est.) *département*, 146,551.

Abolition Movement (*c.* 1783–1888), in western Europe and the Americas, the movement chiefly responsible for creating the emotional climate necessary for ending the transatlantic slave trade and chattel slavery. Between the 15th and 19th centuries, an estimated total of 15,000,000 Africans were forcibly transported to the Americas. Abolitionist pressure first succeeded in bringing about an end to this traffic by the early decades of the 1800s, but widespread smuggling continued until 1862. Anti-slavery forces were triumphant when slavery was abolished in the British West Indies by 1838 and in French possessions 10 years later.

The situation in the United States was more complex because slavery was a domestic rather than a colonial phenomenon, being the social and economic base of the aristocracy of 11 Southern states. Reacting to Abolitionist attacks branding its "peculiar institution" as brutal and immoral, the South had intensified its system of slave control, particularly after the Nat Turner revolt of 1831. By this time, U.S. Abolitionists realized the failure of gradualism, persuasion, and such projects as resettlement of Afro-Americans in Liberia by the American Colonization Society (*q.v.*), founded in 1817. Many Abolitionists were already actively involved in other social reform movements, but because of its enormity, the issue of slavery came to eclipse other causes. Probably the best known Abolitionist was the aggressive agitator William Lloyd Garrison, founder of the American Anti-Slavery Society (*q.v.*; 1833–70). Others, drawn from the ranks of the clergy, included Theodore Dwight Weld and Theodore Parker; from the world of letters, John Greenleaf Whittier, James Russell Lowell, and Lydia Maria Child; and from the free black community, such articulate former slaves as Frederick Douglass and William Wells Brown. Abolition was not a popular cause even in the North, where its adherents met with continual persecution and assault; editor Elijah P. Lovejoy was murdered by a mob at Alton, Ill. (1837).

A number of factors combined to give the movement increased momentum. In addition to the question of slave versus free white labour in new Western territories, there was revulsion at the ruthlessness of slavehunters under the Fugitive Slave Law (1850) and the far-reaching emotional response to Harriet Beecher Stowe's anti-slavery novel, *Uncle Tom's Cabin* (1852). Jolted by the raid (1859) of Abolitionist extremist John Brown on Harpers Ferry (*q.v.*), the South became convinced that its entire way of life, based on race supremacy, was irretrievably threatened by the election of Pres. Abraham Lincoln (November 1860). The Civil War that followed began as a sectional power struggle to preserve the Union but finally resulted in the emancipation of almost 4,000,000 human beings (1863, 1865).

The failure of U.S. Abolitionist idealism lay in the absence of practical plans for restructuring a whole society. The humanitarian effort channelled into educational, economic, and civil activities of the Freedmen's Bureau (1865–72), created by Congress as a main arm of Reconstruction, was piecemeal and ameliorative rather than substantive. Despite the efforts of certain radical Republicans in Congress, the critical needs of land redistribution and lasting political control eluded the Abolitionist remnant genuinely concerned with the welfare of the blacks, and Reconstruction drew to an end in 1877.

Under the pressure of worldwide public opinion, slavery was completely abolished throughout the Western Hemisphere by 1900.

Abomey, town and administrative capital of Zou province, southern Benin (formerly Dahomey), West Africa. Probably founded in the early 17th century, it soon became the capital of the Kingdom of Abomey (later Dahomey), which dominated production and trade with the European enterprises on the Dahomey, or Slave Coast, until the late 19th century. The town is located in an area where palmnuts and groundnuts (peanuts) are grown; it is connected by road and rail to Cotonou, the nation's main commercial centre, and to Porto-Novo, the capital. The Royal Palace, the tombs of the kings, and a historical museum are maintained in Abomey. Pop. (1982 est.) 54,418.

Abominable Snowman, Tibetan YETI, mythical monster supposed to inhabit the Himalayas at about the level of the snow line. Though reports of actual sightings of such a creature are rare, certain mysterious markings in the snow have traditionally been attributed to it. Those not caused by lumps of snow or stones falling from higher regions and bouncing across the lower slopes have probably been produced by bears. At certain gaits bears place the hindfoot partly over the imprint of the forefoot, thus making a very large imprint that looks deceptively like an enormous human footprint positioned in the opposite direction.

Abong Mbang, also spelled ABONG-M'BANG, port and capital of Haut-Nyong department, East province, Cameroon, on the upper Nyong River, at the head of seasonal river navigation from Mbalmayo. Timber (especially mahogany), tobacco, and coffee are major products in the area; bricks are manufactured locally. The Dja game reserve to the south attracts tourists. An infirmary, a leprosarium, a bank, and an airfield serve the town. Pop. (1981 est.) 8,127.

Abonnema, also spelled ABONEMA, fishing and palm-oil port, Rivers State, southern Nigeria, on the Sombreiro River. It is a traditional trade centre of the Ijaw people, handling cassava, taro, fish, palm produce, plantains, and yams. There also is an oil-palm-processing plant. Its port is now combined with that of Degema, 2 mi (3 km) upstream. Abonnema has a secondary school. Pop. (1971 est.) 22,004.

Aboriginal cultures, Australian: *see* Australian Aboriginal cultures.

Aborigine, Australian: *see* Australian Aborigine.

abortion, the expulsion of a fetus from the uterus before it has reached the stage of viability (in human beings, usually about the 20th week of gestation). An abortion may occur spontaneously, in which case it is also called a miscarriage (*q.v.*), or it may be brought on purposefully, in which case it is often called an induced abortion.

Spontaneous abortions, or miscarriages, may be caused by a number of factors, including disease, trauma, or genetic or biochemical incompatibility of mother and fetus. Occasionally a fetus dies in the uterus but fails to be expelled; this condition is termed a missed abortion.

Induced abortions may be performed for reasons that fall into four general categories: to preserve the life or physical or mental well-being of the mother; to prevent the completion of a pregnancy that has resulted from rape or incest; to prevent the birth of a child with serious deformity, mental deficiency, or genetic abnormality; or to exercise birth control, that is, to keep from having a child for social or economic reasons. Abortions performed for any of the reasons in the first two categories are often termed therapeutic or justifiable abortions.

Numerous medical techniques exist for performing abortions. During the first trimester (up to about 12 weeks after conception) curettage or suction may be used to remove the contents of the uterus. From 12 to 19 weeks the injection of a saline solution may be used to trigger uterine contractions; alternatively, the administration of prostaglandins by injection, suppository, or other method may be used to induce contractions, but these substances may cause severe side effects. Hysterotomy, the surgical removal of the uterine contents, may be used during the second trimester or later. In general, the more advanced the pregnancy the greater the risk of mortality or serious complications following an abortion.

Whether and to what extent induced abortions should be permitted, encouraged, or severely repressed is a social issue that has divided theologians, philosophers, and legislators for centuries. Abortion (as well as infanticide) was apparently a common and socially accepted method of family limitation in the Greco-Roman world. Although Christian theologians early and vehemently condemned abortion, the application of severe criminal sanctions to deter its practice became common only in the 19th century. In the 20th century such sanctions were modified in one way or another in various countries, beginning with the Soviet Union in 1920 and with Japan and several Eastern European and Scandinavian countries in the 1950s. A broad social movement for the relaxation or elimination of restrictions on the performance of abortions led to the passing of liberalized legislation in several states in the United States during the 1960s. The U.S. Supreme Court ruled in *Roe*

v. *Wade* (1973) that unduly restrictive state regulation of abortion was unconstitutional but failed to write specific guidelines for acceptable legislation. A counter-movement for the restoration of strict control over the circumstances under which abortions might be permitted soon sprang up, and the issue became entangled in social and political conflict.

Opponents of abortion, or of abortion for any reason other than to save the life of the mother, argue on religious or humanistic grounds that there is no rational basis for distinguishing the fetus from a newborn infant; each is totally dependent and potentially a member of society, and each possesses a degree of humanity. Proponents of liberalized regulation of abortion hold that, at least during its first three or four months, the fetus exhibits few if any human characteristics; that public opinion favours making abortion available for a range of reasons; and that the alternative to legal, medically supervised abortion is illegal and demonstrably dangerous abortion. The public debate of the issue has demonstrated the enormous difficulties experienced by political institutions in grappling with moral and ethical problems.

abortion, epizootic (animal disease): *see* vibriosis.

Aboukir Bay (Mediterranean Sea): *see* Abū Qīr, Khalīj.

Abqaiq, Arabic BUQAYQ, town, ash-Sharqiyah *minṭaqah* (province), ash-Sharqīyah region, eastern Saudi Arabia, lying in the southern end of the Abqaiq oil field, one of the largest and most productive in the kingdom, about 25 mi (40 km) from the Persian Gulf. It grew rapidly following the discovery of the field in 1940. By 1950 it was the southern terminus of the Tapline (Trans-Arabian Pipeline), a 1,068-mi-long pipeline from Ṣaydā (Sidon), Lebanon; the following year it was linked to Riyadh and ad-Dammām by rail. Oil facilities include pumping stations, gas–oil separator plants, and pipelines to aẓ-Ẓahrān (Dhahran), Ra's Tannūrah (Ras Tanura), and the al-Ghawār oil field.

Abra, interior province, northwestern Luzon, Philippines. Hilly and mountainous, it is populated mostly by Ilocanos; Apayos and Tinggians, both mountain peoples, are the largest minorities. Its area is 1,535 sq mi (3,976 sq km). The provincial capital is Bangued, located on the floodplain of the Abra River; other population centres include Lagayan, La Paz, Dolores, and Manabo. Rice, tobacco, and corn (maize) are cultivated in the valleys, and lumbering is important on the slopes. Pop. (1980) 160,198.

Abraha, also spelled ABREHA (fl. 6th century AD), long-reigning Christian Ethiopian king of southern Arabia (the independence of which he prolonged), who led an expedition against Mecca in the same year as Muḥammad's birth, *c.* 570. Muslims believe that Mecca escaped capture through a miracle; possibly Abraha's army contracted smallpox.

Abraham, Hebrew AVRAHAM, also called ABRAM, Hebrew AVRAM (fl. early 2nd millennium BC), first of the Hebrew patriarchs and a figure revered by the three great monotheistic religions: Judaism, Christianity, and Islām. According to the biblical book of Genesis, Abraham left Ur, in Mesopotamia, because God called him to found a new nation in an undesignated land that he later learned was Canaan. He obeyed unquestioningly the commands of God, from whom he received repeated promises and a covenant that his "seed" would inherit the land.

The critical problem of a "biography" of Abraham. There can be no biography of Abraham in the ordinary sense. The most that can be done is to apply the interpretation of modern historical finds to biblical materials so as to arrive at a probable judgment as to the background and patterns of events in his life. This involves a reconstruction of the patriarchal age (of Abraham, Isaac, Jacob, and Joseph; early 2nd millennium BC), which until the end of the last century was unknown and considered virtually unknowable. It was assumed, based on a presumed dating of hypothetical biblical sources, that the patriarchal narratives in the Bible were only a projection of the situation and concerns of a much later period (9th–5th century BC) and of dubious historical value.

Several theses were advanced to explain the narratives; *e.g.,* that the patriarchs were mythical beings or the personifications of tribes or folkloric or etiological (explanatory) figures created to account for various social, juridical, or cultic patterns. However, after World War I, archaeological research made enormous strides with the discovery of monuments and documents, many of which date back to the period assigned to the patriarchs in the traditional account. The excavation of a royal palace at Mari, an ancient city on the Euphrates, for example, brought to light thousands of cuneiform tablets (official archives and correspondence and religious and juridical texts) and thereby offered exegesis a new basis, which specialists utilized to show that, in the biblical book of Genesis, narratives fit perfectly with what, from other sources, is known today of the early 2nd millennium BC, but imperfectly with a later period. A biblical scholar in the 1940s aptly termed this result "the rediscovery of the Old Testament."

Thus, there are two main sources for reconstructing the figure of father Abraham: the book of Genesis, from the genealogy of Terah, Abraham's father, and his departure from Ur to Harran in chapter 11 to the death of Abraham in chapter 25; and recent archaeological discoveries and interpretations, concerning the area and era in which the biblical narrative takes place.

The biblical account. According to the biblical account, Abram (The Father [or God] Is Exalted), who is later named Abraham (The Father of Many Nations), a native of Ur in Mesopotamia, is called by God (Yahweh) to leave his own country and people and journey to an undesignated land, where he will become the founder of a new nation. He obeys the call unquestioningly and (at 75 years of age) proceeds with his barren wife, Sarai, later named Sarah (Princess), his nephew Lot, and other companions to the land of Canaan (between Syria and Egypt).

There the childless septuagenarian receives repeated promises and a covenant from God that his "seed" will inherit the land and become a numerous nation. He not only has a son, Ishmael, by his wife's maidservant Hagar but, at 100 years of age, by Sarah, a legitimate son, Isaac, who is to be the heir of the promise. Yet, he is ready to obey God's command to sacrifice Isaac, a test of his faith, which he is not required to consummate in the end because God substitutes a ram. At Sarah's death, he purchases the cave of Machpelah near Hebron, together with the adjoining ground, as a family burying place. It is the first clear ownership of a piece of the promised land by Abraham and his posterity. Toward the end of his life, he sees to it that his son Isaac marries a girl from his own people back in Mesopotamia rather than a Canaanite woman. He dies at the age of 175 and is buried next to Sarah in the cave of Machpelah.

Abraham is pictured with various characteristics: a righteous man, with wholehearted commitment to God; a man of peace (in settling a boundary dispute with his nephew Lot), compassionate (he argues and bargains with God to spare the people of Sodom and Gomorrah), and hospitable (he welcomes three visiting angels); a quick-acting warrior (he rescues Lot and his family from a raiding party); and an unscrupulous liar to save his own skin (he passes off Sarah as his sister and lets her be picked by the Egyptian pharaoh for his harem). He appears as both a man of great spiritual depth and strength and a person with common human weaknesses and needs.

The Genesis narrative in the light of recent scholarship. The saga of Abraham unfolds between two landmarks, the exodus from "Ur of the Chaldeans" (Ur Kasdim) of the family, or clan, of Terah and "the purchase of" (or "the burials in") the cave of Machpelah. Tradition seems particularly firm on this point. The Hebrew text, in fact, locates the departure specifically at Ur Kasdim, the Kasdim being none other than the Kaldu of the cuneiform texts at Mari. It is manifestly a migration of which one tribe is the centre. The leader of the movement is designated by name: Terah, who "takes them out" from Ur, Abram his son, Lot the son of Haran, another son of Terah, and their wives, the best known being Sarai, the wife of Abram. The existence of another son of Terah, Nahor, who appears later, is noted.

Most scholars agree that Ur Kasdim was the Sumerian city of Ur, today Tall al-Muqayyar (or Mughair), about 200 miles (300 kilometres) southeast of Baghdad in Lower Mesopotamia, which was excavated with great success from 1922 to 1934. It is certain that the cradle of the ancestors was the seat of a vigorous polytheism whose memory had not been lost and whose uncontested master in Ur was Nanna (or Sin), the Sumero-Akkadian moon god. "They served other gods," Joshua, Moses' successor, recalled, speaking to their descendants at Shechem.

After the migration from Ur (*c.* 2000 BC), the reasons for which are unknown, the first important stopping place was Harran, where the caravan remained for some time. The city has been definitely located in Upper Mesopotamia, between the Tigris and the Euphrates, in the Balikh Valley, and can be found on the site of the modern Harran in Turkey. It has been shown that Harran was a pilgrimage city, for it was a centre of the Sin cult and consequently closely related to the moon god cult of Ur. The Mari tablets have shed new light on the patriarchal period, specifically in terms of the city of Harran.

There have been many surprising items in the thousands of tablets found in the palace at Mari. Not only are the Ḥapiru ("Hebrews") mentioned but so also remarkably are the Banu Yamina ("Benjaminites"). It is not that the latter are identical with the family of Benjamin, a son of Jacob, but rather that a name with such a biblical ring appears in these extrabiblical sources in the 18th century BC. What seems beyond doubt is that these Benjaminites (or Yaminites, meaning "Sons of the Right," or "Sons of the South," according to their habits of orientation) are always indicated as being north of Mari and in Harran, in the temple of Sin.

The Bible provides no information on the itinerary followed between Ur and Harran. Scholars think that the caravan went up the Euphrates, then up the Balikh. After indicating a stay of indeterminate length in Harran, the Bible says only that Terah died there, at the age of 205, and that Abraham was 75 when he took up the journey again with his family and his goods. This time the migration went from east to west, first as far as the Euphrates, which they may have crossed at Carchemish, since it can be forded during low-water periods.

Here again, the Mari texts supply a reference, for they indicate that there were Benjaminites on the right bank of the river, in the lands of Yamhad (Aleppo), Qatanum (Qatna), and Amurru. Since the ancient trails seem to have been marked with sanctuaries, it is noteworthy that Nayrab, near Aleppo, was, like Harran and Ur, a centre of the Sin cult and that south of Aleppo, on the road to Ḥamāh, there is still a village that bears the name of Benjamin. The route is in the direction of the "land of Canaan," the goal of the journey. If the tribe made a slight detour then, since it was to settle in Sichem (Shechem) and pass on to Damascus, this would explain the presence of a foreigner, Eliezer, a native of Damascus, who became the "servant" of Abraham, a sort of majordomo or steward, having authority over Abraham's entire household. However, this is uncertain, for the text is unreliable, specifically on the subject of the origins of the steward, whose name, Eliezer (My God Is Help), presents no difficulty.

If a stop in Damascus is assumed, the caravan must next have crossed the land of Bashan (the Ḥawrān of today), first crossing the Jabboq, then the Jordan at the ford of Dāmiyā, arriving in the heart of the Samaritan country, to reach at last the plain of Shechem, today Balāṭah, at the foot of the Gerizim and Ebal mountains. Shechem was at the time a political and religious centre, the importance of which has been perceived more clearly as a result of recent archaeological excavations.

From the mid-13th to the mid-11th century BC, Shechem was the site of the cult of the Canaanite god Ba'al-Berit (Lord of the Covenant); at this site a magnificent *matzeva* (sacred stone pillar) was discovered. There was also the "oak of Moreh" mentioned in the account of Abraham's journey to Shechem, an essential element in the local Semitic cult. The architecture uncovered by archaeologists, at least that of the palace, would date to the 18th century BC, in which the presence of the patriarchs in Shechem is placed.

The next stopping place was in Bethel, identified with present-day Baytīn, north of Jerusalem. Bethel was also a holy city, whose cult was centred on El, the Canaanite god par excellence. Its name does not lend itself to confusion, for it proclaims that the city is the *bet,* "house," or temple, of El (God). The Canaanite sanctuary was taken over without hesitation by the patriarchs, who built their altar there and consecrated it to Yahweh, at least if the Yahwistic tradition in Genesis is to be believed. Certainly this memory remained particularly alive in the hearts of the Israelites. Bethel remained for centuries the sanctuary par excellence for them. Even more than Abraham, they associated Jacob with it when, on the road to Harran, he had the dream of the ladder. But if Jacob stopped to spend the night in this place, it was because the spot had been marked in the past by the presence of an ancestor, namely, Abraham.

The latter had not yet come to the end of his journey. Between Shechem and Bethel he had gone about 31 miles. It was about as far again from Bethel to Hebron, or more precisely to the oaks of Mamre, "which are at Hebron" (according to the Genesis account). The location of Mamre has been the subject of some indecision. At the present time, there is general agreement in setting it 1.5 miles northwest of Hebron at Rāmat al-Khalīl, an Arabic name which means the Heights of the Friend, the friend (of God) being Abraham.

Mamre, where there was an oak (if not a grove of oaks), marked the site of Abraham's encampment, but this did not at all exclude episodic travels in the direction of the Negeb, to Gerar and Beersheba. Life was a function of the economic conditions of the moment, of pastures to follow and to find, and thus the patriarchs moved back and forth between the land of Canaan and the Nile delta. They remained shepherds and never became cultivators.

It was in Mamre that Abraham received the revelation that his race would be perpetuated, and it was there that he learned that his nephew Lot had been taken captive. The latter is an enigmatic episode, an "erratic block" in a story in which nothing prepared the way for it. Suddenly, the life of the patriarch was inserted into a slice of history in which several important persons ("kings") intervene: Amraphel of Shinar, Arioch of Ellasar, Ched-or-laomer of Elam, and Tidal of Goiim. Scholars of previous generations tried to identify these names with important historical figures—*e.g.,* Amraphel with Hammurabi of Babylon—but little remains today of these suppositions. The whole of chapter 14 of Genesis, in which this event is narrated, differs completely from what has preceded and what follows. It may be an extract from some historical annals, belonging to an unknown secular source, for the meeting of Melchizedek, king of Salem and priest of God Most High (El 'Elyon), and Abraham is impressive. The king-priest greets him with bread and wine on his victorious return and blesses him in the name of God Most High.

In this scene, the figure of the patriarch takes on a singular aspect. How is his religious behaviour to be characterized? He swears by "the Lord God Most High"—*i.e.,* by both Yahweh and El 'Elyon. It is known that, on the matter of the revelation of Yahweh to man, the biblical traditions differ. According to what scholars call the Yahwistic source (J) in the Pentateuch (the first five books of the Bible), Yahweh had been known and worshipped since Adam's time. According to the so-called Priestly source (P), however, the name of Yahweh was revealed only to Moses. It may be concluded that it was probably El whom the patriarchs, including Abraham, knew.

As noted before, in Mesopotamia the patriarchs worshipped "other gods." On Canaanite soil, they met the Canaanite supreme god, El, and adopted him, but only partially and nominally, bestowing upon him qualities destined to distinguish him and to assure his preeminence over all other gods. He was thus to become El 'Olam (God the Everlasting One), El 'Elyon (God Most High), El Shaddai (God, the One of the Mountains), and El Ro'i (God of Vision). In short, the god of Abraham possessed duration, transcendence, power, and knowledge. This was not monotheism but monolatry (the worship of one among many gods), with the bases laid for a true universalism. He was a personal god too, with direct relations with the individual, but also a family god and certainly still a tribal god. Here truly was the "God of our fathers," who in the course of time was to become the "God of Abraham, Isaac, and Jacob."

It is not surprising that this bond of the flesh should still manifest itself when it came to gathering together the great ancestors into the family burial chamber, the cave of Machpelah. This place is venerated today in Hebron, at the Ḥaram al-Khalīl (Holy Place of the Friend), under the mosque, and seems to have retained all its mystery. Abraham, "the friend of God," was forevermore the depositary of the promise, the beneficiary of the Covenant, sealed not by the death of Isaac but by the sacrifice of the ram that was offered up in place of the child on Mount Moriah.

(A.Pa.)

BIBLIOGRAPHY. A study of the patriarch Abraham is based on scriptural documentation and particularly on Genesis. One should therefore first consult a critical translation of the first book of the Old Testament as one finds in a basic work such as Ephraim A. Speiser (ed. and trans.), *Genesis: Introduction, Translation, and Notes,* "Anchor Bible" (1964). Also worthwhile are the atlases and albums that give illustrated introductions: L.H. Grollenberg, *Atlas van de Bijbel,* 3rd ed. (1955; *Atlas of the Bible* 1956); and G.E. Wright and F.V. Filson (eds.), *The Westminster Historical Atlas to the Bible,* rev. ed. (1956). Articles under "Abraham" in several dictionaries on the Bible, such as *The Interpreter's Dictionary of the Bible* (1962) and *The Westminster Dictionary of the Bible* (1944), are also useful.

The world of the patriarchs has called forth numerous works, among which these take into account the most recent archaeological discoveries: H. Cazelles, "Patriarches" in *Supplément au Dictionnaire de la Bible,* 7 (1961); William F. Albright, *The Biblical Period from Abraham to Ezra* (1963); H.H. Rowley, "Recent Discovery and the Patriarchal Age," *Bulletin of the John Rylands Library,* 32:44–79 (1949); Roland de Vaux, "Les Patriarches hébreux et les découvertes modernes," *Revue Biblique* (1946–49); and *Les Institutions de l'Ancien Testament,* 2 vol. (1958–60; *Ancient Israel: Its Life and Institutions,* 2nd ed., 1965). Centred on the city of Ur and the discoveries that were made there is Sir Leonard Woolley, *Abraham: Recent Discoveries and Hebrew Origins* (1936); some of his analogies must be rejected. On the texts gathered at Mari and dating from the 18th century BC, which are of very great importance for biblical exegesis, see G. Dossin, "Benjaminites dans les textes de Mari," *Mélanges syriens,* 2:981–996 (1939); and J.R. Kupper, *Les Nomades en Mésopotamie au temps des rois de Mari* (1957). A. Parrot, *Abraham et son temps* (1962; *Abraham and His Times,* 1968), presents a synthesis of the double archaeological and epigraphical documentation. John Van Seters, *Abraham in History and Tradition* (1975), includes a bibliography.

Abraham BEN MEIR IBN EZRA (Spanish-Jewish philosopher): *see* ibn Ezra, Abraham ben Meir.

Abraham, Karl (b. May 3, 1877, Bremen, Ger.—d. Dec. 25, 1925, Berlin), psychoanalyst whose studies on the role of infant sexuality in character development and mental illness continue to be basic in the field of psychoanalysis.

While serving as an assistant to the psychiatrist Eugen Bleuler at the Burghölzi Mental Hospital in Zürich (1904–07), Abraham met the psychoanalyst Carl Jung and made his initial acquaintance with the ideas of Sigmund Freud. His first psychoanalytic paper dealt with childhood sexual trauma in relation to the symptoms of schizophrenia.

Entering psychoanalytic practice at Berlin (1907), where he helped to establish the first branch of the International Psychoanalytic Institute (1910), he began work that was to enrich the theory of symbols and myths. In a major paper (published in 1909) he connected myths with dreams and viewed both as wish-fulfillment fantasies.

Abraham devoted himself chiefly to pioneering efforts in the psychoanalytic treatment of manic-depressive psychosis. He suggested that the libido, or sexual drive, develops in six stages: earlier oral, oral-sadistic, anal expulsive, anal retentive, phallic, and adult genital. If an infant's development becomes arrested at any of the earlier stages, mental disorders will most likely result from a libidinal fixation at that level.

Abraham's most important work, *A Short Study of the Development of the Libido, Viewed in the Light of Mental Disorders,* was published in German in 1924 and appeared in English in his *Selected Papers* (1953). "Character-Formation on the Genital Level of Libido-Development," also contained in the *Selected Papers,* is a translation of his last major paper (1925).

Abraham, Plains of, also called HEIGHTS OF ABRAHAM, French PLAINES D'ABRAHAM, plains in Québec region, southern Quebec province, Canada, at the western edge of the city of Quebec, overlooking the St. Lawrence River. The plateau was the scene of a battle (Sept. 13, 1759) between the French under the Marquis de Montcalm and the British under James Wolfe in which both leaders were killed, but which secured Quebec for the British. Named for Abraham Martin, a ship's pilot who formerly owned part of the land, the plains are now a national historic park.

Abraham bar Hiyya, also called ABRAHAM BAR HIYYA HA-NASI (Hebrew: the Prince) (b. *c.* 1065—d. *c.* 1136), Spanish Jewish philosopher, astronomer, astrologer, and mathematician who led in the revival of Hebrew as the written language of Jews in the western Mediterranean. He is sometimes known by the name Savasorda, a corruption of an Arabic term indicating that he held some kind of civic office in the Muslim administration of Barcelona.

In addition to translating scientific books from Arabic into Hebrew, he also wrote a number of original works, among them a scientific encyclopaedia (the first in the Hebrew language) and a book on mathematics, *Ḥibbur ha-Meshiḥah ve-ha-Tishboret* ("Treatise on Measurement and Calculation"), which, in its Latin translation, *Liber Embadorum* (1145), became a principal textbook in western European schools. Other notable works by Abraham include the philosophical treatise *Hegyon ha-Nefesh ha-Aẓuva* (Eng. trans. *Meditation of the Sad Soul,* 1969), which dealt with the nature of good and evil, ethical conduct, and repentance, and *Megillat ha-Megalleh* ("Scroll of the Revealer"), in which he outlined his view of history, based on astrology and purporting to forecast the messianic future.

Abraham Lincoln Battalion, a force of volunteers from the United States who served on the Republican side in the Spanish Civil War from February 1937 until November 1938. All seven International Brigades (*q.v.*)—each composed of three or more battalions—were formed by the Comintern (Communist International), beginning in late 1936, and all were disbanded by late 1938 as the war neared an end. Like the European battalions, the American one was composed largely of Communists; but, unlike the Europeans, the majority of Americans were students, and none had previously seen military service. Briefly in 1937 there was a second American force, the George Washington Battalion, but the casualties of both were so heavy that in mid-year the two were merged. As time went on, other nationalities were admitted to the Lincoln Battalion so that, by late 1938, Spaniards outnumbered Americans in the battalion three to one. Its first and perhaps most noted commander was Robert Merriman (1915–38), the son of a lumberjack and a graduate of the University of Nevada, who rose to the rank of major and became chief of staff of the XVth International Brigade (which included the Lincoln Battalion); he fought in several battles and was killed in action. Of the total of about 2,800 American volunteers, about 900 were killed.

Abrahams, Israel (b. Nov. 26, 1858, London—d. Oct. 6, 1925, Cambridge, Cambridgeshire, Eng.), one of the most distinguished Jewish scholars of his time, who wrote a number of enduring works on Judaism, particularly *Jewish Life in the Middle Ages* (1896). Although of strict Orthodox upbringing, Abrahams was later among the founders of the Liberal movement, an Anglo-Jewish group, somewhat synonymous with U.S. Reform, that stressed the universality of Jewish ethics, minimized ritual and custom, and originally eschewed Zionism.

In 1902, after teaching for several years at Jews' College, London, he was appointed reader in Talmudics (rabbinic literature) at Cambridge, a post he retained until his death. From 1888 to 1908 he was editor, jointly with the Anglo-Jewish scholar Claude G. Montefiore, of the *Jewish Quarterly Review.*

In *Jewish Life in the Middle Ages,* Abrahams concluded that there was no medieval period in Jewish history but that Christian medievalism had a lasting effect on the Jews, particularly in the sense of deepening the process of Jewish isolation from society; the work covers every facet of Jewish life of the times, including the functions of the synagogue, social customs and community organization, occupations and amusements, and Jewish–Christian relationships. *Studies in Pharisaism and the Gospels,* 2 vol. (1917–24), includes a series of essays based on an examination of the way in which Judaism is treated in the New Testament. Among his works on Jewish writings is *Chapters on Jewish Literature* (1899), a survey covering the period from the fall of Jerusalem in AD 70 to the death of the Jewish philosopher Moses Mendelssohn in 1786.

Abrahams, Peter (Henry) (b. March 19, 1919, Vrededorp, near Johannesburg), most prolific of South Africa's black prose writers, whose early novel *Mine Boy* (1946) was the first to emphasize the dehumanizing effect of apartheid upon South African blacks.

Abrahams left his country at the age of 20, first settling in Britain and then in Jamaica; nevertheless, most of his novels and short stories are based on his early experiences in South Africa. *Mine Boy,* for example, tells of a country youth thrown into the alien and oppressive culture of a large South African industrial city, and his semi-autobiographical *Tell Freedom: Memories of Africa* (1954; new ed. 1970) deals with the related theme of his struggles as a youth in the slums of Johannesburg. *The Path of Thunder* (1948; translated into nearly 30 languages) depicts a young "mixed" couple who love under the menacing shadow of enforced segregation. *Wild Conquest* (1950) follows the great northern trek of the Boers, and *A Night of Their Own* (1965) sets forth the plight of the Indian in South Africa. The novel *A Wreath for Udomo* (1956; new ed. 1971) and the travel book *This Island Now* (1966; new ed. 1971) are set in West Africa and the Caribbean, respectively.

In the late 1950s, inspired by his visit to Jamaica to gather materials for an official report on the British West Indies, Abrahams moved his family to the island. There he became editor of the *West Indian Economist* and took charge of the daily radio news network, West Indian News, until 1964, when he gave up most of his duties so that he could devote himself full time to writing. Many of his earlier works were reissued or translated into other languages in the 1960s and early 1970s, as his reading public steadily widened. A biography by Michael Wade, *Peter Abrahams,* was published in 1971.

Abram (Jewish patriarch): *see* Abraham.

Abramovitz, Max (b. May 23, 1908, Chicago), architect who designed the Law School at Columbia University and Philharmonic Hall of the Lincoln Center for the Performing Arts, New York City, both completed in 1962.

He was educated at the University of Illinois (B.S. 1929), Columbia University (M.S. 1931), and the École des Beaux-Arts in Paris (1932–34). He was a partner with Wallace K. Harrison (1945–76) and from 1976 in the firm of Abramovitz-Harris-Kingsland, Architects, of New York City. He served (1947–52) as deputy director of the United Nations Headquarters Planning Office and in 1955 became supervising architect at Brandeis University, where he designed the interfaith chapel group (1955) and the Master Plan and Academic Buildings (1970). His Krannert Center for the Performing Arts at the University of Illinois, Urbana, opened in 1969.

Abramowitsch, Shalom Jacob: *see* Mendele Mokher Sefarim.

Abrantès, Andoche Junot, duc d' (duke of): *see* Junot, Andoche.

Abrantès, Laure Junot, duchesse d': *see* Junot, Laure, duchesse d'Abrantès.

abrasax (in Gnosticism): *see* abraxas.

abrasion platform: *see* wave-cut platform.

abrasive, relatively hard natural or synthetic material used to grind or polish materials softer than itself. Grinding wheels, oilstones, and sandpaper are common examples of abrasives. The high-precision components and extremely smooth surfaces essential in modern machine tools, electronic equipment, and spacecraft can be obtained only through abrasive grinding operations. Most household cleansers use a mild abrasive to supplement the action of soap or detergent.

A brief treatment of abrasives follows. For full treatment, *see* MACROPAEDIA: Glass and Ceramic, Industrial.

The use of abrasives dates to prehistoric times, when stone tools and weapons were shaped by rubbing them against harder stones. Drawings in ancient Egyptian tombs show the polishing of jewelry and vases with abrasives. In later historical times, craftsmen used natural abrasive stones shaped into wheels, such as grindstones and mill wheels, and into blocks for use by hand for sharpening scythes, knives, axes, and woodworking tools. Powdered abrasives were used for polishing in much the same manner as they were employed by the Egyptians. It was not until late in the 19th century, when it became necessary to work with harder metals and to closer tolerances, that abrasives assumed a major role in the manufacturing industry.

Some natural abrasives are mined widely throughout the world; these include flint, a form of quartz that is the most common material used for sandpaper, and sand, which is naturally granulated quartz, used in sandblasting and other abrasive processes. Another fairly common natural abrasive is pumice, or hardened lava foam, which is widely used in metal polishes and scouring powders. Corundum and emery, which are natural forms of aluminum oxide, occur less commonly, as does garnet. Others occur only in relatively limited areas; diamonds, for example, are mined principally in South Africa and to a much lesser extent in Australia and South America. The diamonds and other precious stones used as abrasives are not of gem quality.

In the 20th century various synthetic abrasives, including silicon carbide (produced under such trade names as Carborundum, Crystolon, and Carbolon), synthetic diamonds, boron carbide, and artificial aluminum oxide, were developed with improved and more uniform characteristics, and new machines were designed to utilize these abrasives to best advantage. Natural abrasives are still widely used in some applications, but in industrial grinding they have been largely replaced by synthetics.

Abrasives intended for industrial use are first crushed into a powder, which may then be mixed with a liquid or paste, pressed into wheels or blocks, or glued to the surface of paper or cloth.

Consult the INDEX *first*

abraxas, also spelled ABRASAX, sequence of Greek letters considered as a word and formerly inscribed on charms, amulets, and gems in the belief that it possessed magical qualities. In the 2nd century, some Gnostic and other dualistic sects, which viewed matter as evil and the spirit as good and held that salvation came through esoteric knowledge, or gnosis, personified Abraxas and initiated a cult sometimes related to worship of the sun god. Basilides of Egypt, an early 2nd-century Gnostic teacher, viewed Abraxas as the supreme deity and the

Abraxas stone

By courtesy of the trustees of the British Museum

source of divine emanations, the ruler of all the 365 heavens or circles of creation—one for each day of the year. The number 365 corresponds to the numerical value of the seven Greek letters that form the word abraxas.

Abreha (Arab ruler): *see* Abraha.

Abreu, (João) Capistrano de (b. Oct. 23, 1853, Maranguape, Braz.—d. Aug. 13, 1927, Rio de Janeiro), historian best known for his large-scale interpretive work on the colonial history of Brazil.

After serving at the Biblioteca Nacional do Rio de Janeiro (1875–83), Abreu became professor of history at the Colégio Dom Pedro II in 1883. Influenced by the sociological systems of Auguste Comte and Herbert Spencer and the historical enterprises of Henry Buckle and Hippolyte Taine, Abreu wrote the *Capítulos de História Colonial* (1907; "Chapters of Colonial History"), his greatest work, as a broad treatment of Brazilian colonization from 1500 to 1800. His original emphasis on the culture of indigenous groups was an early and significant ethnological interpretation of the European settlement of Brazilian backlands. Abreu wrote additional works on linguistics, translated German and French documents on Brazilian history, and edited the writings of the eminent historian Francisco Adolfo de Varnhagen.

Abruzzi, also called ABRUZZO, region, central Italy, fronting the Adriatic Sea and comprising the provinces of L'Aquila, Chieti, Pescara, and Teramo. Most of the region's area of 4,168 sq mi (10,794 sq km) is mountainous or hilly, except for such intermontane basins as those of L'Aquila, Sulmona, and Fucino. The Apennines, chiefly of limestone and the dominant physical feature, consist of three chains trending northwest–southeast, of which the easternmost, including the Gran Sasso d'Italia (9,560 ft [2,914 m]) and Maiella groups, is the highest. From the Gran Sasso, sand and clay hills present a gradual slope eastward to the narrow Adriatic shoreline. The few small coastal harbours have little economic importance for fishing or commerce. The principal rivers (the Tronto, Pescara, Sangro, and Trigno) drain to the Adriatic, providing irrigation in their lower courses. The course of these streams is irregular and, because of massive deforestation on the upper slopes, floods and landslides occur frequently during the spring and fall rains.

The ancient Italic tribes that once inhabited the region long resisted conquest and retained their own character even after Roman rule was imposed on them. The name of the region, originally Aprutium, is believed to have come from that of one of the ancient tribes, the Praetutii. Under Lombard rule during the early Middle Ages, the Abruzzi was controlled by the Duchy of Spoleto, and Molise (the region to the south) by the Duchy of Benevento. The Normans established themselves in the area in the 12th century, and the region sided with the Hohenstaufens in their long struggle with the papacy. After the fall of the Hohenstaufen dynasty in the 13th century, Abruzzi and Molise came under the Angevin dynasty (House of Anjou), Spanish, and Bourbon rulers of the Kingdom of Naples (and were divided into Abruzzo Ulteriore I, Abruzzo Ulteriore II, Abruzzo Citra, and Molise). As Abruzzi e Molise, they became part of the Kingdom of Italy in 1860, and in 1965 were divided into the separate regions of Abruzzi and Molise (*q.v.*). The regional capital is L'Aquila (*q.v.*).

The rugged terrain of Abruzzi long hindered its economic development. The construction of a motorway from the west to L'Aquila and Arezzo, later extended to the Adriatic coast, opened the region to the rest of Italy. Agriculture is mainly of local importance, except in the intensively cultivated intermontane basins. Wheat, grapes, fruit, and olives are the most widespread crops, while tobacco, sugar beet, and saffron represent the cash crops. Livestock raising has been the mainstay of a large part of the region; migratory herding (transhumance) of sheep from mountain pastures in the Abruzzi to lowland winter pastures outside of the region continues although on a slowly decreasing scale. Pigs are raised and the region's smoked ham and sausages are well known. Industrial development, concentrated chiefly in the provincial capitals, is slight, being limited to small-scale food industries and artisan crafts, with some woollen manufacture. The main rail artery is the Rome–Pescara line, and there are local rail connections, slowly losing traffic to buses and trucks. Tourism is increasing in the coastal resorts, but is not yet a major economic factor. Pop. (1981 prelim.) 1,215,136.

Abruzzi, Luigi Amedeo Giuseppe Maria Ferdinando Francesco, duca d' (duke of) (b. Jan. 29, 1873, Madrid—d. March 18, 1933, Abruzzi City, near Mogadiscio, Italian Somaliland), mountaineer and explorer whose ventures ranged from Africa to the Arctic.

The son of King Amadeus of Spain (who was also the duca d'Aosta in Italy), Abruzzi was the first to ascend Mt. St. Elias in Alaska (1897). His 1899 Arctic expedition reached latitude 86°34′ N—a record for the time. In 1906 he was first to scale the highest summits of the Ruwenzori Range in east central Africa. His expedition provided detailed knowledge of the geology, topography, and glaciology of the range; it mapped the range and named its major peaks, passes, and glaciers. In 1909 Abruzzi climbed the world's second highest mountain, K2, in the Himalayas in Kashmir, to a height of more than 20,000 feet (6,000 metres). During World War I he held a naval command in the Adriatic until 1917. He was later involved in exploration and colonization in Italian Somaliland.

Abruzzo, Ben L. (b. June 9, 1930, Rockford, Ill., U.S.), balloonist who, with three crew mates, made the first transpacific balloon flight and the longest nonstop balloon flight in the "Double Eagle V."

Abruzzo received his B.S. degree in business administration from the University of Illinois (Urbana-Champaign) in 1952 and served two years in the U.S. Air Force at Kirtland Air Force Base in Albuquerque, N.M. (1952–54). He settled in Albuquerque and became a real-estate developer. He, as well as his wife and children, became active in skiing, boating, sailing, tennis, flying, and ballooning. In 1978 Abruzzo, with Maxie Anderson (*q.v.*) and Larry Newman, made the first transatlantic balloon flight in the "Double Eagle II." In 1979 Abruzzo and Anderson won the Gordon Bennett race in the "Double Eagle III."

The transpacific flight, with Abruzzo as captain and teammates Larry Newman and Ron Clark, both of Albuquerque, and Rocky Aoki, a Japanese-American restaurateur from Miami, who partly financed the flight, was launched from Nagashima, Japan, on Nov. 10, 1981. The balloon landed, 84 hr, 31 min later, in the Mendocino National Forest in California on November 12. The flight covered 9,244 kilometres (5,768 miles), the longest balloon flight in history.

Abruzzo held nine world balloon records, more than any other balloonist.

ABS: *see* American Bible Society.

Absalom (fl. *c.* 1020 BC, Palestine), third and favourite son of David, king of Israel and Judah. The picture of Absalom presented in II Sam. 13–19 suggests that he was the Alcibiades of the Old Testament, alike in his personal attractiveness, his lawless insolence, and his tragic fate. He is first mentioned as murdering his half brother Amnon, David's eldest son, in revenge for the rape of his full sister Tamar. For this deed he was driven into banishment, but he was eventually restored to favour through the good offices of Joab. Later, when some uncertainty seems to have arisen as to the succession, Absalom organized a revolt. For a time he seemed to be completely successful; David, with a few followers and his personal guard, fled across the Jordan, leaving to Absalom Jerusalem and the main portion of the kingdom. The usurper pursued the fugitives with his forces but was completely defeated in "the forest of Ephraim" (apparently west of Jordan) and killed by Joab, who found him caught by the hair in an oak tree. To the affectionate, chivalrous heart of David, the loss of his son, worthless and treacherous as he was, brought grief which more than outweighed his own safety and restoration.

Absalon (b. *c.* 1128, Fjenneslev, Den.—d. March 21, 1201, Sorö), archbishop, statesman, and close adviser of the Danish kings Valdemar I and Canute IV.

Scion of a powerful Zealand family, Absalon helped his childhood friend gain the Danish throne as Valdemar I (1156–57) and was named bishop of Roskilde in 1158. As the King's closest adviser, he initially supported Valdemar's alliance with Frederick I Barbarossa, Holy Roman emperor, against Pope Alexander III. By 1167, Absalon and Valdemar had become reconciled with the Pope.

Absalon helped end the Wend (Slav) threat to Danish shipping by leading a campaign in 1169 that captured the Wend stronghold of Rügen. The incorporation of Rügen into Absalon's diocese of Roskilde initiated a period of Danish supremacy in northern Germany that lasted until 1225. At that time he also directed the building of a fortress at Havn, which later developed into Copenhagen. He was a key advocate of the canonization of Valdemar's father, Canute Lavard, and of the coronation of Valdemar's son Canute IV as joint king (1170), which established the hereditary rights of the Valdemar dynasty.

Elected archbishop of Lund in 1177, Absalon served as the guardian of Canute IV and guided him to a position of independence from Frederick I after Canute became sole ruler in 1182. The expedition that Absalon headed to the southern Baltic coast in 1184 led to Danish control of Pomerania and Mecklenburg. He subsequently returned to his church duties.

Absaroka Range, mountain segment of the northern Rocky Mountains, in northwestern Wyoming and southern Montana, U.S. Extending in a northwest–southeast direction, the range is 170 mi (270 km) long and 50 mi wide. A large plateau, the result of volcanic action, was uplifted in the area, and stream and glacial erosion have produced spectacular features. Eight summits exceed 12,000 ft (3,700 m), including Francs Peak (13,140 ft), the highest point. The range is a source for

Ramshorn Peak (centre) in the Absaroka Range, Shoshone National Forest, northwestern Wyoming
Russell Lamb

headstreams of the Bighorn River and embraces portions of the Gallatin, Shoshone, and Custer national forests and the extreme northeastern part of Yellowstone National Park. Granite Peak (12,799 ft), the highest point in Montana, is in the Beartooth Range, a northeastern spur of the Absarokas.

abscisic acid, plant hormone, a major function of which is to inhibit growth. It derives its name from abscission, or the separation and fall of leaves, which it promotes. Probably universally distributed in higher plants, abscisic acid also has a variety of other functions—*e.g.,* it stimulates the development of dormancy in buds and promotes the formation of potato tubers. It also has an inhibiting effect on cell elongation.

absentee ownership, originally, ownership of land by proprietors who did not reside on the land or cultivate it themselves but enjoyed income from it. The term absentee ownership has assumed a social connotation not inherent in its literal meaning, based on the assumption that absentee owners lack personal interest in and knowledge of their lands and tenants.

Absentee ownership has been a social and political issue for centuries in many parts of the world. It was, for example, a basis for the criticism directed at a portion of the court nobility in pre-Revolutionary France and was also prominent in the debates concerning the exploitation of Irish tenants by English absentee owners in the 19th century. It continues to be a crucial economic issue in the land reform programs of many less developed countries.

absentee voting, electoral process that enables persons who cannot to appear at their designated polling places to vote from another location. The usual method of absentee voting is by mail, although provision is sometimes made for voting at prescribed places in advance of the polling date. Absentee voting requires special administrative arrangements to ensure the secrecy and legitimacy of the ballots cast. Within these basic provisions there are variations in detail from country to country.

In all of the European countries, the United States, Canada, and Australia (where voting is compulsory), provisions are made for the casting of absentee votes. Because the proper use of absentee voting facilities is related to literacy, in countries where illiteracy is fairly widespread, absentee voting is either not allowed, as in Zaire and Burkina Faso, or allowed only with restrictions, as in India, Malaysia, and Jamaica.

Where qualifications for electors are not primarily geographical, the postal vote may be the normal form of voting. Such is the case in the voting for university seats in the Senate of the Republic of Ireland. In European countries in which elections are held on Sundays, persons travelling for pleasure are permitted to cast their votes at polling places other than those where they are registered, provided that they have first obtained a permit from the election officials. They must, however, cast their ballots for candidates from their own constituencies.

absinthe, flavoured, distilled liquor, yellowish green in colour, turning to cloudy, opalescent white when mixed with water. Highly aromatic, this liqueur is dry and somewhat bitter in taste. Absinthe is made from a spirit high in alcohol, such as brandy, and marketed with alcoholic content of 68 percent by volume. Wormwood (*Artemisia absinthium*) is the chief flavouring ingredient; other aromatic ingredients include licorice, usually predominating in the aroma, hyssop, fennel, angelica root, aniseed, and staranise. The beverage was first produced commercially in 1797 by Henry-Louis Pernod, who purchased the formula from a French exile living in Switzerland.

Wormwood came to be considered dangerous to health, supposedly causing hallucinations, mental deterioration, and sterility, although some authorities suggest that any harmful effects of the liquor are caused by its high alcohol content and not its other ingredients. Absinthe manufacture was prohibited in Switzerland in 1908, in France in 1915, and eventually in many other countries. In 1918 Pernod Fils established a factory in Tarragona, Spain, to manufacture both absinthe and a similar beverage, without wormwood, for export to those countries prohibiting true absinthe. Beverages developed as substitutes, similar in taste but lower in alcohol content and without wormwood, are known by such names as anis, or anisette, pastis, ouzo, or raki. Anis and pastis are also popularly known under such trade names as Pernod, Pernod 45, and Ricard.

Absinthe is usually served diluted with water and ice and may be used to flavour mixed drinks. The classic absinthe drink, the absinthe drip, is served in a special drip glass, allowing water to slowly drip through a sugar cube into the liquor. Pastis also turns cloudy white when mixed with water, and anis turns to a cloudy, greenish-tinged white.

absolute humidity, the concentration of water vapour per unit volume of moist air. It is usually expressed in units of grams of water vapour per cubic metre. *See* humidity.

absolute Idealism, a philosophical theory chiefly associated with G.W.F. Hegel and Friedrich Schelling, both German Idealist philosophers of the 19th century, Josiah Royce, a U.S. philosopher, and others, but, in its essentials, the product of Hegel. Absolute Idealism can generally be characterized as including the following principles: (1) the common everyday world of things and embodied minds is not the world as it really is but merely as it appears in terms of uncriticized categories; (2) the best reflection of the world is not found in physical and mathematical categories but in terms of a self-conscious mind; and (3) thought is the relation of each particular experience with the infinite whole of which it is an expression, rather than the imposition of ready-made forms upon given material.

Idealism for Hegel meant that the finite world is a reflection of mind, which alone is truly real. He held that limited being (that which comes to be and passes away) presupposes infinite unlimited being, within which the finite is a dependent element. In this view, truth becomes the relationship of harmony or coherence between thoughts, rather than a correspondence between thoughts and external realities. As one proceeds from the confusing world of sense experience to the more complex and coherent categories of science, the Absolute Idea, of which all other abstract ideas are merely a part, is approached. Hegel also held that this increasing clarity is evident in the fact that later philosophy presupposes and advances from earlier philosophy, ultimately approaching that to which all things are related and which is nevertheless self-contained; *i.e.,* the Absolute Idea.

Schelling, though similar to Hegel in that he also believed in the Absolute Idea, differed from him in identifying the Absolute as the undifferentiated, or featureless, unity of opposites. Thus, in the state of intellectual intuition, subject and object, being opposites, are lost in the anonymity of the Absolute. Hegel attacked this position in his *Phänomenologie des Geistes* (1807; *Phenomenology of Mind,* 2nd ed. 1931).

Royce proposed that human minds are fragments of the Absolute, yet somehow remain separate selves and persons. He held that individual selves (as parts of the Absolute) are able, through the fundamental virtue of loyalty, to seek their ever increasing and ever widening meaning and identify with it, thus approaching the Absolute.

Hegel's Idealism formed the basis of the absolute Idealism of many philosophers (including F.H. Bradley and Bernard Bosanquet), who made absolute Idealism a dominant philosophy of the 19th century.

absolute reaction rates, theory of (chemistry): *see* transition-state theory.

absolute zero, temperature at which a thermodynamic system has the lowest energy. It corresponds to −273.15° on the Celsius scale and to −459.67° on the Fahrenheit scale.

The notion that there is an ultimately lowest temperature was suggested by the behaviour of gases at low pressures: it was noted that gases seem to contract indefinitely as the temperature is decreased. It appeared that an ideal gas (*see* gas, perfect) at constant pressure would reach zero volume at what is now called the absolute zero of temperature. Any real gas actually condenses to a liquid or a solid at some temperature higher than absolute zero; and, therefore, the ideal gas law is only an approximation to real gas behaviour. As such, however, it is extremely useful.

The concept of absolute zero as a limiting temperature has many thermodynamic consequences. For example, all molecular motion does not necessarily cease at absolute zero, but none is available for transfer to other systems, and it is therefore correct to say that the energy at absolute zero is minimal.

Any temperature scale having absolute zero for its zero point is termed an absolute temperature scale. By international agreement, the Kelvin, or thermodynamic, scale is the standard for a scale of this type and is the basis for all scientific temperature measurements. Its fundamental unit, the kelvin (symbol K written without a degree sign [°]), is defined as 1/273.16 of the triple point of pure water—*i.e.,* the temperature at which the liquid, solid, and gaseous forms of the substance can be maintained simultaneously. In effect, the interval between this triple point and absolute zero comprises 273.16 kelvins.

Another absolute temperature scale used in the United States (primarily for engineering applications) is the Rankine scale. Although the zero point of the Rankine scale is also absolute zero, Rankine temperatures differ from Kelvin temperatures. This is because the basic unit of the scale, the degree Rankine (° R), is 5/9 of the kelvin (*e.g.,* the freezing point of water is 273.15 K and 491.67° R). For coverage of empirical temperature scales, *see* Celsius temperature scale; Fahrenheit temperature scale.

absolution, in the Christian religion, a pronouncement of remission of sins to the penitent. In the several Christian traditions, interpretations of absolution vary in relation to two issues: the designations of penance as a sacrament and of the ministry as a priesthood. In Roman Catholicism, in which penance is a sacrament and the minister is a priest, absolution grants release from the guilt of sin to the sinner who is truly contrite, confesses his sin to a priest, and promises to perform satisfaction to God. The doctrine is similar in Eastern Orthodox teaching; but in place of the Western formula, "I absolve thee from thy sins in the name of the Father and of the Son and of the Holy Spirit," Eastern churches generally employ a formula such as "May God, through me, a sinner, forgive thee . . . ."

In Anglican and in Lutheran usage, formulas of absolution have ranged from the declaratory "I forgive you all your sins" or "I forgive thee," in the Visitation of the Sick, to "Almighty God, have mercy upon you, and forgive you all your sins." Some Anglican writers distinguish three forms of absolution: declaratory, intercessory, and judicial.

In keeping with their doctrines of the ministry and of the sacraments or ordinances, other Christian traditions have confined absolution to prayers for forgiveness and the announcement of God's willingness to forgive all those who truly repent of their sins. Absolution, therefore, is neither a judicial act nor a means by which the forgiveness of sins is conferred but is, instead, a statement of divine judgment and divine forgiveness. Nevertheless, a formula for the public confession of sins and the public pronouncement of forgiveness is included somewhere in the liturgies of most Christian groups.

absolutism, the political doctrine and practice of unlimited, centralized authority and absolute sovereignty, as vested especially in a monarch. The essence of such a system is that the ruling power is not subject to regularized challenge or check by any other agency, be it judicial, legislative, religious, economic, or electoral. Louis XIV, who ruled France during the late 17th and early 18th centuries, furnished the most familiar assertion of absolutism when he said, *"L'état, c'est moi"* ("I am the state").

Varying in form, political absolutism has prevailed in much of the world over long periods of time. However, the form originating early in modern European history became the prototype. Its character was definitely monarchical, based on the strong individual leaders of new nation-states created at the breakup of the medieval order. The power of these states was closely associated with the power of their kings; and, in order to strengthen both, it was necessary to curtail the restraints on centralized government that had been exercised by the church, feudal lords, and medieval customs generally. By claiming the absolute authority of the state against such former restraints, the monarch as head of state claimed his own absolute authority as well.

By the 16th century monarchical absolutism was coming to prevail in much of western Europe, and it was widespread in the 17th and 18th centuries. Besides France, whose absolutism was epitomized by Louis XIV, well-known illustrations may be drawn from Spain, Prussia, and Tudor England.

In defense of monarchical absolutism, the simplest argument was that kings derived their authority from God—"the divine right of kings." This view could justify even tyrannical rule as divinely ordained punishment, administered by rulers, for man's sinfulness. In its origins, the divine right theory may be traced to the medieval conception of God's award of temporal power to the political ruler, while spiritual power was given to the head of the Roman Catholic Church. However, the new national monarchs asserted their authority in all matters and tended to become heads of church as well as state. Their power was absolute in a way that was impossible for medieval monarchs confronted by a church that was essentially a rival centre of authority.

More pragmatic arguments than that of divine right were also advanced in behalf of absolute monarchy. Complete obedience to a single will was said to be essential to order and security; the alternative was the chaos believed to flow from challenging or dividing political power. In so justifying submission by subjects on the ground of self-interest, the most elaborate statement was made in the 17th-century work *Leviathan* by Thomas Hobbes. The monopoly of political power is also justified by a presumed knowledge of absolute truth. Neither the sharing of power nor limits on its exercise appear valid to those who believe that they know, and know absolutely, what is right.

absorption, in wave motion, the transfer of the energy of a wave to matter as the wave passes through it. The energy of an acoustic, electromagnetic, or other wave is proportional to the square of its amplitude—*i.e.,* the maximum displacement or movement of a point on the wave; and, as the wave passes through a substance, its amplitude steadily decreases. If there is only a small fractional absorption of energy, the medium is said to be transparent to that particular radiation, but if all the energy is lost the medium is said to be opaque. All known transparent substances show absorption to some extent. For instance, the ocean appears to be transparent to sunlight near the surface, but it becomes opaque with depth.

Substances are selectively absorbing—that is, they absorb radiation of specific wavelengths. Green glass is transparent to green light but opaque to blue and red; hard rubber is transparent to infrared and X-rays but opaque to visible light. Thus, radiation of an unwanted wavelength may be removed from a mixture of waves by letting them pass through an appropriate medium. Substances especially chosen and shaped into devices, such as a disk of coloured glass, for absorbing a particular wavelength or band of wavelengths are called filters.

As radiation passes through matter, it is absorbed to an extent depending on the nature of the substance and its thickness. A homogeneous substance of a given thickness may be thought of as consisting of a number of equally thin layers. Each layer will absorb the same fraction of the energy that reaches it. The diagram shows a beam of waves passing from left to right through a series of layers (d_1, d_2, d_3, d_4) of a medium. If the fractional absorption is taken as 50 percent, or $^1/_2$, after the beam passes through the first layer d_1, its initial energy (E_0) will be reduced to $E_0/2$. One-half the energy $E_0/2$ will be absorbed passing through layer d_2, and the beam will enter layer d_3 with energy $^1/_2$ ($E_0/2$) or ($E_0/$ 4). Similarly, each successive layer absorbs one-half of the energy it receives. Thus for radiation of a given wavelength, an infinitesimally thin layer will reduce the energy of

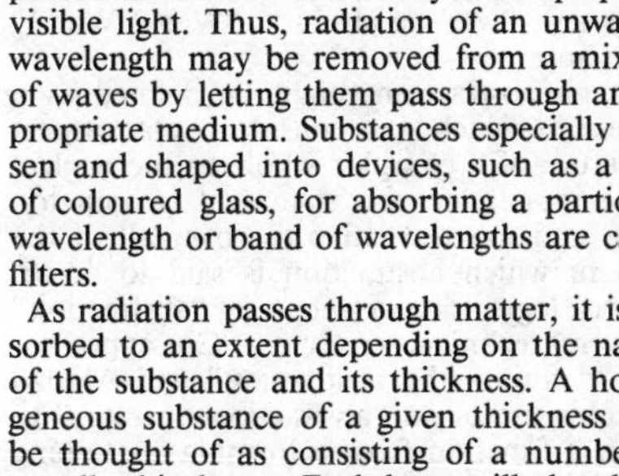

Absorption

From *Modern College Physics* by Harvey E. White © Litton Educational Publishing, Inc. Reprinted by permission of Van Nostrand Reinhold Company

a wave by a fractional amount that is proportional to the thickness of the layer. The change in energy as the wave passes through a layer is a constant of the material for a given wavelength and is called its absorption coefficient.

absorption edge, in physics, abrupt increase in the degree of absorption of electromagnetic radiation by a substance as the frequency of the radiation is increased. Absorption edges are particularly characteristic of the behaviour of X-rays and are related to the sharply defined levels of energy that electrons occupy in atoms.

Abstbessingen faience, tin-glazed earthenware produced in a factory in the village of Abstbessingen, in Thuringia, which flourished probably from the first half of the 18th century to about 1816. A hayfork factory mark indicates the patronage of the Prince of Schwarzburg. Ordinary wares such as flower vases, tankards, and jugs are thick-bodied, with a creamy glaze; and decorations either in blue or polychrome are common. Although

Abstbessingen faience butter dish in the form of a tortoise, Thuringia, Ger., *c.* 1755; in the Victoria and Albert Museum, London

By courtesy of the Victoria and Albert Museum, London; photograph, EB Inc.

a few ambitious pieces were made, such as vases with reserved panels (kept plain for later decoration, usually by hand), Abstbessingen remained a modest imitator of the more important German court factories.

abstract art, 20th-century nonfigurative painting, sculpture, and art of related media. The trends of modern art toward a diminished importance of representation gave significant emphasis to the purely abstract qualities of form, colour, line, and surface.

Abstract art is based on the proposition that these formal attributes have sufficient intrinsic beauty and expressiveness. Deliberately avoiding the use or concealing the identity of any recognizable form of reality, abstract art is a complete rejection of representational subjects, a total reliance on aesthetic elements.

Abstract Expressionism, post-World War II art movement centring on a group of American artists that by the 1950s had become the dominant (but by no means the only) force in American art. The group included Jackson Pollock, Willem de Kooning, Franz Kline, Jack Tworkov, Bradley Walker Tomlin, Philip Guston, Robert Motherwell, Adolf Gottlieb, William Baziotes, Clyfford Still, James Brooks, Mark Rothko, Barnett Newman, Ad Reinhardt, Arshile Gorky, and Mark Tobey. Although it is the accepted designation, "Abstract Expressionism" is not an accurate description of the body of work created by these artists, for not all of it is abstract and not all is Expressionist, and, in fact, there are almost as many different styles as there are artists. The Abstract Expressionist movement is better characterized as an approach that involves complete freedom from all traditional aesthetic and social values in favour of a free, spontaneous personal expression. It represents a sharp contrast to the documentary approach of Social Realism (*q.v.*), which previously had dominated 20th-century American painting. The term was first applied by his contemporaries to the early 20th-century paintings of the Russian artist Wassily Kandinsky, which express feeling and emotion through colour and nonobjective, or nonrepresentational, form.

"Composition," Abstract Expressionist painting by Willem de Kooning, oil on canvas, 1955; in the Solomon R. Guggenheim Museum, New York City

By courtesy of the Solomon R. Guggenheim Museum, New York City

In spite of the diversity of the Abstract Expressionist movement, three general approaches can be distinguished. One, called Action painting (*q.v.*), is characterized by a loose, rapid handling of paint in sweeping brushstrokes and in techniques partially dictated by chance, such as dripping or spilling the paint directly onto the canvas in a spontaneous manner reminiscent of the Automatic painting of the "organic Surrealists" (*see* Surrealism). In Action painting the aesthetic accomplishment lies in the interaction between the artist and his materials; the act of painting, the moment of spontaneous creative activity, is more important than the finished work, which serves primarily as a notation of the instinctive process that had produced it and thus as a revelation of the artist's inner creative forces. Pollock, the dean of Abstract Expressionism, first practiced Action painting by dripping commercial paints on raw canvas. De Kooning, many of whose works, like his series "Woman," retain figurative images, uses extremely vigorous and expressive brushstrokes that require the use of the artist's entire arm. Kline's paintings, consisting of powerful, sweeping black strokes on a white canvas, are the nonobjective expressions of states of mind. Other important Action painters are Tworkov and Tomlin.

The works of another group of Abstract Expressionist painters are executed in a style that came to be known as Abstract Impressionism. Guston is the most notable of this group. His works, characterized by a more lyrical, less passionate imagery of bright colours and fluid shapes, are less spontaneous and more manipulated toward a preconceived end than the works of the Action painters.

A third approach encompassed within Abstract Expressionism involves the use of either well-defined abstract images or large areas of pure colour in paintings whose surfaces are controlled to a considerable degree. The most prominent of the abstract imagists is Motherwell, whose paintings often consist of black ovoid shapes suspended between heavy black verticals on a white ground. Other major artists who painted in this mode are Still, Brooks, Gottlieb, and Baziotes, whose images are more expressive of specific, if sometimes obscure, ideas. The outstanding colour-field painter is Rothko, most of whose works consist of large-scale combinations of soft-edged, solidly coloured rectangular areas that tend to engulf the viewer. Newman and Reinhardt take a more intellectual approach to colour, delineating their stripes and rectangles with hard edges. Most of the artists of this third group of Abstract Expressionists—whether through colour, line, or shape—create a unique abstract image, a mysterious presence that, by its very simplicity, evokes complex responses. In the course of the 1950s, Abstract Expressionism increasingly followed the lead of this group and, by 1960, the movement was generally characterized by a rebellion against the impulsiveness of the more irrationally inspired Action painters.

Two major Abstract Expressionists who fit into none of these categories are Gorky, a former Surrealist and pioneer of the Abstract Expressionist movement, who uses undefined, suggestive biomorphic shapes for emotional impact, and Tobey, whose works include carefully controlled, luminous abstractions of outer space.

abstraction, the mental process of isolating a common element or explicating a relationship possessed by a number of things. Thus, when it was discovered that certain bodies allow electricity to flow through them, they came to be known as conductors of electricity, and the property that they shared in common was called conductivity—an abstract term, or abstraction. The concept of conductivity is called by some an abstract idea.

Abstraction may also occur when observation of a single thing leads to the detection of some property that can be shared by others. Thus, when it was discovered that blood did not clot normally in a certain individual, the condition was described by the abstract term "hemophilia."

"Abstract" is contrasted with "concrete" (*q.v.*) inasmuch as the latter refers to a particular thing; *e.g.,* "war" is abstract, "World War I" is concrete.

Though abstraction might be defined as a process in which one considers some aspect or feature of a complex whole to the neglect of the remainder, this statement is both too vague and too restrictive to cover all of the cases in which abstraction is said to occur. Modern logic, for example, uses "abstraction" in several technical senses: *e.g.,* Giuseppe Peano's "definition by abstraction" and Alonzo Church's use of an "abstraction operator" to obtain a function from a formula containing a free variable.

Abstraction-Création, group composed predominantly of French painters led by Georges Vantongerloo and Auguste Herbin who promoted the principles of pure abstraction in art from 1931 to 1936. These abstractionists were devoted, in theory if not in practice, to the pure use of the basic formal elements of painting, colour and form, depicted pictorially as flat, brightly coloured geometric shapes.

The immediate predecessor of the Abstraction-Création group was the Cercle et Carré (Circle and Square) group, founded by Michel Seuphor and Joaquin Torres-Garcia in 1930. An international exhibit held in April of that year included the works of Jean Arp, Wassily Kandinsky, Le Corbusier, Fernand Léger, Piet Mondrian, Kurt Schwitters, Joseph Stella, Torres-Garcia, and Vantongerloo, the leaders in avant-garde artistic expression. Although the membership was quite diverse in terms of practicing styles, the overriding philosophy favoured a pure form of abstraction. In 1931, *Abstraction-Création,* a periodical published by Herbin and Helion, took over the Cercle et Carré's mailing list; and the new Abstraction-Création group, with as many as 400 members, carried on in the direction of geometric abstraction until 1936. It was located in Paris and hence received the active membership of Kandinsky and Naum Gabo, both of whom were living there at the time. It was succeeded after World War II by the Salon des Réalités Nouvelles (Salon of New Realities). The Abstraction-Création group, in preserving the principle of pure geometric abstraction, was ultimately important to the development, in mid-century, of colour-field painting and, in the 1950s and 1960s, of Op art.

Absurd, Theatre of the, dramatic works of certain European and U.S. dramatists of the 1950s and early '60s who agreed with the Existentialist philosopher Albert Camus' assessment, in his essay "The Myth of Sisyphus" (1942), that the human situation is essentially absurd, devoid of purpose. The term is also loosely applied to those dramatists and the production of those works. Though no formal Absurdist movement existed as such, dramatists as diverse as Samuel Beckett, Eugène Ionesco, Jean Genet, Arthur Adamov, Harold Pinter, and a few others shared a pessimistic vision of humanity struggling vainly to find a purpose and to control its fate. Mankind in this view is left feeling hopeless, bewildered, and anxious.

The ideas that inform the plays also dictate their structure. Absurdist playwrights, therefore, did away with most of the logical structures of traditional theatre. There is hardly any dramatic action as conventionally understood; however frantically the characters perform, their busyness serves to underscore the fact that nothing happens to change their existence. In Beckett's *En Attendant Godot* (*Waiting for Godot*), first performed 1953, plot is eliminated, and a timeless, circular quality emerges as two lost creatures, usually played as tramps, spend their days waiting—but without any certainty of whom they are waiting for or of whether he, or it, will ever come. Language in an Absurdist play is often dislocated, full of cliches, puns, repetitions, and non sequiturs. The characters in Ionesco's *La Cantatrice Chauve* (*The Bald Soprano*), first performed in 1950, sit and talk, repeating the obvious until it sounds like nonsense, thus revealing the inadequacies of verbal communication. The combination of ridiculous, purposeless behaviour and talk gives the plays a sometimes dazzling comic surface, but there is an underlying serious message of metaphysical distress. Here we see reflected the influence of comic tradition drawn from such sources as commedia dell'arte, vaudeville, and music-hall combined with such theatre arts as mime and acrobatics. At the same time the impact of ideas as expressed by the Surrealist, Existentialist, and Expressionist schools and the writings of Franz Kafka is evident.

Originally shocking in its flouting of theatrical convention while popular for its apt expression of the preoccupations of our age, the Theatre of the Absurd declined somewhat by the mid-1960s; some of its innovations had been absorbed into the mainstream of theatre even while serving to inspire a new avant-garde to further experiments. Some of the chief authors of the Absurd have sought new directions in their art, while others continue to work in the same vein.

Abū ʿAbd Allāh al-Ḥarith ibn Asad al-ʿAnazī al-Muḥāsibī: *see* Muḥāsibī, al-.

Abū ʿAbd Allāh Mālik ibn Anas ibn al-Ḥārith al-Aṣbaḥī (Muslim legist): *see* Mālik ibn Anas.

Abū ʿAbd Allāh Muḥammad XI (king of Granada): *see* Muḥammad XI.

Abū ʿAbd Allāh Muḥammad al-Qudā ʿī: *see* Ibn al-Abbār.

Abū ʿAbd Allāh Muḥammad ibn ʿAbd Al-lāh al-Lawātī aṭ-Ṭanjī ibn Baṭṭūṭah (Arab traveller): *see* Ibn Baṭṭūṭah.

Abū ʿAbd Allāh Muḥammad ibn Idrīs ash-Shāfiʿī (Muslim legist): *see* Shāfiʿī, Abū ʿAbd Allāh ash-.

Abū ʿAbd Allāh Muḥammad ibn Ismāʿīl al-Bukhārī: *see* Bukhārī, al-.

Abū ʿAbd Allāh Muḥammad ibn Jābir ibn Sinān al-Battānī al-Ḥarrānī as-Ṣābiʾ: *see* Battānī, al-.

Abū ʿAbd Allāh Muḥammad ibn Muḥammad ibn ʿAbd Allāh ibn Idrīs al-Ḥammūdī al-Ḥasanī al-Idrīsī (Arab geographer): *see* Idrīsī, ash-Sharīf al-.

Abū ʿAbd Allāh Muḥammad ibn ʿUmar ibn al-Ḥusayn Fakhr ad-Dīn ar-Rāzī (Muslim theologian): *see* Fakhr ad-Dīn ar-Rāzī.

Abū ʿAbdollāh Jaʿfar ebn Moḥammad: *see* Rūdakī.

Abū al-ʿAbbās ʿAbd Allāh al-Maʾmūn ibn ar-Rashīd (caliph): *see* Maʾmūn, al-.

Abū al-ʿAbbas al-Walīd ibn Yazīd ibn ʿAbd al-Malik ibn Marwān: *see* Walīd ibn Yazīd, al-.

Abū al-ʿAbbās as-Saffāḥ (b. 722–d. 754, al-Anbār), Islāmic caliph (reigned 749–754), first of the ʿAbbāsid dynasty, which was to rule over eastern Islām for approximately the next 500 years. The ʿAbbāsids were descended from an uncle of Muḥammad and were cousins to the ruling Umayyad dynasty. The Umayyads were weakened by decadence and an unclear line of succession, and enjoyed little popular support, prompting the ʿAbbāsids to declare open revolt in 747. When Abū al-ʿAbbās assumed the caliphate in 749, he began a campaign of extermination against the Umayyads, the ʿAlids, other ʿAbbāsid leaders who had become too popular, and all other claimants to power. He named himself as-Saffāḥ, "the blood-shedder," because of his savage attacks. He established a firm legal and dynastic base for the ʿAbbāsids. His successor moved the caliphate to Baghdad.

Abū al-ʿAlāʾ: *see* Maʿarrī, al-.

Abū al-ʿAtāhiyah, original name ABŪ ISḤĀQ ISMĀʿĪL IBN AL-QĀSIM IBN SUWAYD IBN KAYSĀN (b. 748, al-Kūfah or ʿAyn at-Tamr, Iraq—d. 825/826, Baghdad), first Arab poet of note to break with the conventions established by the pre-Islāmic poets of the desert and to adopt a simpler and freer language of the village.

Abū al-ʿAtāhiyah (Father of Craziness) came from a family of *mawlā*s, poor non-Arabs who were clients of the ʿAnaza Arab tribe. The family's poverty prevented Abū al-ʿAtāhiyah from receiving a formal education, which may account for his subsequently original and untraditional poetic style. He began to write *ghazal*s (lyrics) in his early years in al-Kūfah; they later gained him notoriety as well as the favour of the ʿAbbāsid caliph Hārūn ar-Rashīd. Abū al-ʿAtāhiyah's fame, however, rested on the ascetic poems of his later years, the *Zuhdīyāt* (Ger. trans. by O. Rescher, 1928), collected in 1071 by the Spanish scholar Ibn ʿAbd al-Barr. The *Zuhdīyāt* gave vent to his feelings of social resentment in verses depicting the levelling of the rich and powerful by the horrors of death. These found an enthusiastic following among the masses.

Despite suggestions of heresy in his verse, probably attributable to his lack of religious training and unfettered style, Abū al-ʿAtāhiyah's poetry enjoyed immense popularity and was frequently set to music.

Abū al-Faraj (medieval Syrian scholar): *see* Bar Hebraeus.

Abū al-Faraj al-Iṣbahānī, in full ABŪ AL-FARAJ ʿALĪ IBN AL-ḤUSAYN AL-QURASHĪ AL-IṢBAHĀNĪ, also called AL-IṢFAHĀNĪ (b. 897, Isfahan, Iran—d. Nov. 20, 967, Baghdad), literary scholar who composed an encyclopaedic and fundamental work on Arabic song, composers, poets, and musicians.

Abū al-Faraj was a descendant of Marwān II, the last Umayyad caliph of Syria. Despite the enmity of this family and the ʿAlids, he was a Shīʿī Muslim, upholding the rights of the descendants of the Prophet Muḥammad's son-in-law ʿAlī to the caliphate. He spent most of his life in Baghdad where he enjoyed the patronage of the Būyid *amīr*s.

Kitāb al-aghānī ("The Book of Songs"), his major work, contains songs, biographical information, and much material on the life and customs of the early Arabs and of the Muslim Arabs of the Umayyad and ʿAbbāsid periods.

Abū al-Faraj also wrote *Maqātil aṭ-Ṭālibīyīn wa-akhbaruhum* ("The Slaying of the Ṭālibīs"), comprising biographies of the Shīʿah martyrs descended from ʿAlī and his father, Abu Ṭālib.

Abū al-Fidāʾ, in full ABŪ AL-FIDĀʾ ISMĀʿĪL IBN ʿALĪ AL-MĀLIK AL-MUʾAYYAD ʿIMAD AD-DĪN, also called ABULFEDA (b. Nov. 1273, Damascus—d. Oct. 27, 1331, Ḥamāh, Syria), Ayyūbid dynasty historian and geographer who became a local sultan under the Mamlūk Empire.

Abū al-Fidāʾ was a descendant of Ayyūb, the father of Saladin, founder of the Ayyūbid dynasty that had been supplanted by the Mamlūks in Egypt and elsewhere before his birth. In 1285, he accompanied his father and his cousin (prince of Ḥamāh and a Mamlūk client) to Mamlūk sieges of Crusader strongholds. Abū al-Fidāʾ served the Mamlūk governor of Ḥamāh until he was made first governor of Ḥamāh (1310), then prince for life (1312). In 1320, after making a pilgrimage to Mecca with the Mamlūk sultan al-Nāṣir Muḥammad, he became al-Malik al-Muʾayyad, with the rank of sultan; and he continued to rule Ḥamāh until his death. His son Muḥammad succeeded him.

Abū al-Fidāʾ was a patron of scholars and a scholar himself. His two major works were a history, *Mukhtaṣar taʾrīkh al-bashar* ("Brief History of Man"), spanning pre-Islāmic and Islāmic periods to 1329; and a geography, *Taqwīm al-buldān* (1321; "Locating the Lands"). Both works were compilations of other authors, arranged and added to by Abū al-Fidāʾ, rather than original treatises. Popular in their day in the Middle East, they were much used by 18th- and 19th-century European Orientalists before earlier sources became available.

Abū al-Ghāzī Bahādur, also spelled ABULGHAZI BAHADUR (b. Aug. 24, 1603, Urgench, Khanate of Khiva—d. 1663, Khiva), khan (ruler) of Khiva and one of the most prominent historians in Chagatai Turkish literature.

The son of ʿArab Muḥammad Khan, Abū al-Ghāzī spent most of his early life in Urgench. When his father died and a dynastic struggle arose among Abū al-Ghāzī and his brothers for the succession to the throne, he was compelled to flee to the Ṣafavid court of Iran in the city of Isfahan, where he lived in exile from 1629 to 1639. While in exile he studied history, examining Persian and Arabic historical sources. In 1644/45, Abū al-Ghāzī finally succeeded to the throne of Khiva, reigning for about 20 years, carrying on intermittent wars with the Turkmen, the Uzbeks of Bukhara, the Kalmyks, Russia, and Iran.

The historical works for which he is most famous are *Shajare-i Tarākime*, or *Şecere-i Terakime* (1659; "The Genealogical Tree of the Turkmen"), written in Chagatai Turkish, mainly a compilation from the Persian historian Rashīd ad-Dīn (died 1318) and the semilegendary oral traditions of the Turks, and the *Shajare-i Turk* ("The Genealogical Tree of the Turks"), left incomplete and finished by his son, Abū al-Muẓaffar Anūsha Muḥammad Bahādur, in 1665. This work is mainly a history of the Shaybānid dynasty (mid-15th century–1665); it is not considered reliable because the author wrote from memory without using sources. The introduction is interesting for relating traditional material on Genghis Khan and his sons. The work became well known in Europe by the 18th century through German, French, Russian, Latin, and English translations.

Abū al-Ḥasan (fl. early 17th century, Delhi), one of the leading Mughal painters of the emperor Jahāngīr's atelier, honoured by the Emperor with the title Nādir-uz-Zamān (the Wonder of the Age).

He was the son of Āqā Reẓā of Herāt, who took employment with Jahāngīr (ruled 1605–27) before his accession to the throne. Abū al-Ḥasan was trained in painting under the careful tutelage of the Emperor, who praised him as having "no rival or equal" and took pride in having personally formed him at his court. Paintings of his that have survived include the famous chinar tree with squirrels in the India Office Library, and a large number of superb portraits. His study of European prints may have reinforced his naturalism and sympathy for his subjects. He is known to have worked early in the reign of Shāh Jahān (ruled 1628–57/58).

Abū al-Ḥasan al-Ashʿarī (Arab theologian): *see* Ashʿarī, Abū al-Ḥasan al-.

Abū al-Ḥasan ʿAlī (b. *c.* 1297—d. May 24, 1351, Hintato, Mor.), Marīnid sultan of Morocco (ruled 1331–51) who increased the territories of his dynasty and, for a brief time, created a united North African empire.

In 1331 Abū al-Ḥasan succeeded his father, Abū Saʿīd, to the throne. With the goals of expelling the Christians from Spain and uniting all the Islāmic lands of North Africa, Abū al-Ḥasan attacked and captured Algeciras and Gibraltar in Spain (1333). He next attacked the Algerian territories of the ʿAbd al-Wādid dynasty and after a three-year siege took the strategic town of Tlemcen (1337). Taking advantage of the internal weakness of Spain, he won a brilliant naval victory in the Strait of Gibraltar on April 5, 1340, but was defeated six months later at the Battle of Rio Salado and was forced to abandon his "holy war" against Spain.

Abū al-Ḥasan expanded his influence in Tunisia and married a daughter of Abū Bakr, the Ḥafṣid ruler of Tunisia, which by 1342 had become a virtual vassal state. After Abū Bakr's death he invaded Tunisia and captured Tunis (Sept. 15, 1347), but in the following April he was badly defeated by a confederation of Tunisian tribes at Kairouan. Forced to flee Tunisia by sea during December 1349, he landed at Algeria in January and set out for Morocco to put down a rebellion led by his son Abū ʿInān. Deserted by his troops, he abdicated in favour of Abū ʿInān in 1351, dying shortly afterward of an infected wound.

Abū al-Ḥasan ʿAlī al-Masʿūdī (Arab historian): *see* Masʿūdī, al-.

Abū al-Ḥasan ʿAlī ibn Hilāl ibn al-Bawwāb: *see* Ibn al-Bawwāb.

Abū al-Ḥasan ʿAli ʿIzz ad-Dīn ibn al-Athīr: *see* Ibn al-Athīr.

Abū al-Ḥusayn Muslim ibn al-Ḥajjāj al-Qushayrī: *see* Muslim ibn al-Ḥajjāj.

Abu al-Majd Majdud ibn Adam: *see* Sanāʾi.

Abū al-Mughīth al-Ḥusayn ibn Manṣūr al-Ḥallāj (Islāmic mystic): *see* Ḥallāj, al-.

Abū al-Mundhir: *see* Hishām ibn (Muḥammad) al-Kalbī.

Abū al-Qāsim, also spelled ABUL KASIM, in full ABŪ AL-QĀSIM KHALAF IBN ʿABBĀS AZ-ZAHRĀWĪ, Latin ALBUCASIS (b. *c.* 936, near Córdoba—d. *c.* 1013), Islām's greatest medieval surgeon, whose comprehensive medical text, combining Eastern and classical teachings, shaped European surgical procedures until the Renaissance. Court physician to ʿAbd ar-Raḥmān III an-Nāṣir, the most respected and successful of the Spanish caliphs, Abū al-Qāsim wrote *at-Taṣrīf liman ʿajazʿan at-Taʾālīf* ("The Method"), a medical work in 30 parts. While much of the text was based on the works of earlier authorities, especially the *Epitomae* of the 7th-century Byzantine physician Paul of Aegina, it contained many original observations, including the earliest known description of hemophilia. The last chapter, with its drawings of more than 200 instruments, constitutes the first illustrated, independent work on surgery.

Although *at-Taṣrīf* was largely ignored by physicians of the eastern caliphate, the surgical treatise had tremendous influence in Christian Europe. Translated into Latin in the 12th century by the scholar Gerard of Cremona, it stood for nearly 500 years as the leading textbook on surgery in Europe, preferred for its concise lucidity even to the works of the classic Greek medical authority Galen.

Abū al-Qāsim Muḥammad ibn ʿAbd Allāh ibn ʿAbd al-Muṭṭalib ibn Hāshim: *see* Muḥammad.

Abū al-Wafāʾ (al-Būzajānī), also spelled ABUL WEFA (b. 940, Buzjan, Iran—d. 998, Baghdad), astronomer and one of the greatest of Muslim mathematicians, who made important contributions to the development of trigonometry. He worked in an observatory in Baghdad, where he built the first wall quadrant for observing the stars. He did not, as is sometimes claimed, discover the inequality in the Moon's motion, later called variation, but, in his work on lunar theory, he utilized the tangent and cotangent trigonometric functions and calculated tables for them. He also invented the secant and cosecant functions, proved the generality of the sine theorem for spherical triangles, and devised a new method of calculating sine tables.

He translated and wrote commentaries, since lost, on the works of the Greek mathematicians Euclid and Diophantus and on those of the Arabic mathematician al-Khwarizmi. Abū al-Wafāʾ also wrote *Kitāb fīmā yaḥtāj ilayh al-kuttāb wa al-ummāl min ʿilm al-ḥisāb* ("Book on What Is Necessary from the Science of Arithmetic for Scribes and Businessmen") and *Kitāb fīmā yaḥtāj ilayh al-sānī ʿmin al-aʿmāl al-Handasīyha* ("Book on What Is Necessary from Geometric Construction for the Artisan").

Abū al-Walīd Muḥammad ibn Aḥmad ibn Muḥammad ibn Rushd (Islāmic philosopher): *see* Averroës.

Abū ʿAlī al-Ḥasan ibn al-Haytham: *see* Alhazen.

Abū ʿAlī al Ḥusayn ibn ʿAbd Allāh ibn Sīnā (Persian scientist): *see* Avicenna.

Abū ʿAlī Ḥasan ibn ʿAlī (Persian vizier): *see* Niẓām al-Mulk.

Abū ʿAli Muḥammad ibn ʿAlī ibn Muqlah: *see* Ibn Muqlah.

Abu aṭ-Ṭayyib Aḥmad ibn Ḥusayn al-Mutanabbī: *see* Mutanabbī, al-.

Abū Ayyūb Sulaymān ibn Yaḥyā ibn Gabirūt (Hebrew poet): *see* Ibn Gabirol.

Abu Bakar (b. 1843?—d. June 4, 1895, London), great modern sultan of the Malay state of Johore (now part of Malaysia) from 1885 to 1895. He maintained independence from Britain and stimulated economic development in Johore at a time when most Southeast Asian states were being incorporated into European colonial empires.

Under the terms of an 1824 British treaty, supplemented by an agreement in 1855, the Malay state of Johore was ruled not by the sultan but by a lower-ranking official called a *temenggong.* These arrangements reflected the actual power distribution in Johore and were in part an outgrowth of British machinations in acquiring Singapore in 1819. Abu Bakar, who became *temenggong* in 1862, was the third ruler under that agreement. He elevated his title to maharaja in 1868, and in 1885 he was acknowledged by Great Britain as sultan of Johore, disestablishing the former sultan's lineage. An able and clever ruler, he did much to promote trade, investment, and agriculture in his state. In particular he encouraged the development of gambir and pepper plantations. Western in his interests, he lived in the British colony of Singapore, and, in his conduct of Johore's internal affairs (Britain had control of Johore's foreign affairs under terms of an 1861 agreement), he made use of Western advisers and methods. This practice stood him in good stead in persuading the British that the government of Johore was stable and just. He also elicited British positions on important issues and established his own policy accordingly, temporizing and compromising when necessary. Thus, he not only maintained his independence but he also strengthened his position vis-à-vis other Malay rulers.

Abū Bakr, also called AṢ-ṢIDDĪQ (the Upright) (b. *c.* 573—d. Aug. 23, 634), Muḥammad's closest companion and adviser, succeeding to his political and administrative functions, thereby initiating the office of the

Abū Bakr (second figure on left), miniature from an illuminated manuscript; in the British Library (MS. Or. 371)

By courtesy of the trustees of the British Library

caliphate. Of a minor clan of the ruling merchant tribe of Quraysh at Mecca, he is said to have been the first male convert to Islām. Abū Bakr's prominence in the community was clearly marked by Muḥammad's marriage to his young daughter ʿĀʾishah and again by Muḥammad's choosing Abū Bakr as his companion on the journey to Medina (*hijrah,* 622).

In Medina he was Muḥammad's chief adviser (622–632) but functioned mainly in conducting the pilgrimage to Mecca in 631 and leading the public prayers in Medina during Muḥammad's last illness.

On Muḥammad's death (June 8, 632), the Muslims of Medina resolved the crisis of succession by accepting Abū Bakr as the first *khalīfat rasūl Allāh* ("deputy or successor of the Prophet of God," or caliph). In his rule (632–634), he suppressed the *riddah* ("apostasy"), tribal political and religious uprisings, bringing central Arabia under Muslim control; then by undertaking direct expansion from Arabia into Iraq and Syria he began the Muslim conquests.

Abū Bakr Muḥammad ibn ʿAbd al-Malik ibn Muḥammad ibn Muḥammad ibn Ṭufayl al-Qaysī (Moorish philosopher and physician): *see* Ibn Ṭufayl.

Abū Bakr Muḥammad ibn Yaḥyā ibn al-Sāyigh al-Tujībī al-Andalusī al-Saraqustī (Arabic philosopher): *see* Avempace.

Abū Bakr Muḥammad ibn Zakarīyāʾ ar-Rāzī (physician): *see* Rāzī, ar-.

Abu Dhabi, Arabic ABŪ ẒABY, constituent emirate of the United Arab Emirates (formerly Trucial States, or Trucial Oman). Though its international boundaries are disputed, it is unquestionably the largest of the country's seven constituent emirates with an area of about 30,000 sq mi (77,700 sq km), or more than three-fourths of the area of the entire federation. Its rich oil fields, both onshore and in the Persian Gulf, make it, with neighbouring Dubai, one of the nation's two most prosperous emirates.

Abu Dhabi fronts the Gulf on the north for about 280 mi (450 km). The desolate coast has many areas of *sabkhah* ("salt marsh") and numerous offshore islands. Abu Dhabi borders Qatar (west); Saudi Arabia (south); and Oman, formerly Muscat and Oman (east). Internally it half-surrounds Dubai and has a short frontier with Sharjah.

Since the 18th century the Āl bū Falāh clan of the Banī Yās has been in power; their earliest seat was in the al-Jiwāʾ (al-Liwāʾ) oasis district. In 1761 they found wells of potable water at the site of Abu Dhabi town on the coast and made their headquarters there from 1795. Because Abu Dhabi's traditional rivals were the Qawāsim pirates of Ras al-Khaimah and Sharjah shaykhdoms, and because the pirates were hostile to the Sultanate of Muscat and Oman, Abu Dhabi's rulers at first allied themselves with the sultanate. In the 19th century, however, territorial conflicts developed between Abu Dhabi, Muscat and Oman, and the expanding power of the Wahhābī of Najd, ancestors of the present ruling dynasty of Saudi Arabia. These conflicts led to border disputes, most still unsettled; that over the al-Buraymī oasis region is the most serious.

Although not considered a pirate state, Abu Dhabi signed the British-sponsored General Treaty of Peace (1820), the maritime truce (1835), and the Perpetual Maritime Truce (1853). By the terms of the Exclusive Agreement of 1892, its foreign affairs were placed under British control. During the long rule of Shaykh Zayd ibn Khalīfah (1855–1908), Abu Dhabi was the premier power of the Trucial Coast, but in the early 20th century it was outpaced by Sharjah and Dubai. When Britain proposed withdrawal from the Persian Gulf (1968), Abu Dhabi, together with the other Trucial States, Bahrain, and Qatar, negotiated to form a nine-member federation. The latter two states, however, became separately independent (1971); Britain abrogated its earlier treaties with the Trucial States, and the new United Arab Emirates, of which Abu Dhabi is a leading member, came into being. Abu Dhabi town was made the provisional national capital for five years (1971–76), extended, together with the United Arab Emirates' interim constitution, a further five years in July 1976.

Abu Dhabi's economic base rests almost entirely on crude oil production. Petroleum was discovered in 1958 at the submarine field of Umm Shaif, about 75 mi (125 km) offshore at a depth of almost 9,000 ft (2,750 m). This oil is pumped through a submarine pipeline to previously desolate Dās Island, about 20 mi west, where the emirate's main offshore tanker terminal was built, with airstrip, gas liquefaction plant, and ancillary facilities; exports began in 1962. Principal onshore production is from the Murban, or Bāb ʿAṣab, and Bū Ḥāssah fields, the centres of which are in the central part of the state, 25 to 40 mi from the coast. Pipelines connect these with a coastal terminal to the northwest at Jabal az-Ẓannah (Jabal Danna). Other offshore fields are at the bank of Ruqq az-Zaqqūm (Rak az-Zakum), just northwest of Abu Dhabi town and connected by submarine pipeline to Dās Island, and at Fatḥ (Fateh or Fatta), about 55 mi north of Abu Dhabi town in the open Gulf. The state's total oil reserves are estimated at 30,000,000,000 barrels; production in the early 1980s was at a rate of about 511,-000,000 barrels annually.

Abu Dhabi's revenues from oil royalties give it one of the world's highest per capita incomes; in addition to internal modernization, it has lent some of its wealth to its less prosperous sister states in the United Arab Emirates, to other countries in the Arab world, and to developing countries elsewhere. An Arid Lands Research Centre at as-Sadīyāt near Abu Dhabi town seeks improved methods of vegetable growing. Pop. (1968) 46,375; (1975) 235,662; (1980) 450,732.

Abu Dhabi, Arabic ABŪ ẒABY, town, capital of Abu Dhabi emirate, one of the United Arab Emirates (formerly Trucial States, or Trucial Oman), and the provisional (1971–81) capital of that federation. The town occupies most of a small triangular-shaped island of the same name, just off the Persian Gulf coast and connected to the mainland by a short bridge. Formerly an undeveloped town of only local importance, Abu Dhabi emirate's oil revenues have enabled it to develop into a modern settlement, with many of the material characteristics of Western civilization.

No settlement existed at Abu Dhabi town before 1761, when tribesmen of the Āl bū Falāh clan of the Banī Yās, rulers of Abu Dhabi then as now, settled there. They moved their headquarters to this coastal islet from the inland al-Jiwāʾ (al-Liwāʾ) oases in 1795. Through most of the 19th and early 20th centuries, the town, though capital of one of the chief shaykhdoms of the Trucial Coast, yielded pride of place in trade and economic importance to Dubai town and Sharjah town, capitals of neighbouring Trucial shaykhdoms. At the beginning of the 20th century, Abu Dhabi town's population was estimated at 6,000; pearl diving from the rich offshore banks, and some local trade (chiefly in the hands of Persians and Hindus), sustained the economy. Pearling declined with the development of the Japanese cultured pearl industry and the worldwide economic depression beginning in 1929.

The discovery (1958) and commercial production (since 1962) of the rich oil fields of Abu Dhabi emirate revolutionized the political and economic position of Abu Dhabi town. Great Britain, as the protecting power of the then Trucial States, established a separate Political Agency at the town in 1961, removing the shaykhdom from dependence on the Political Agent at Dubai town. As capital of the chief oil-producing state in the region, Abu Dhabi town had large sums available for urban development. The town modernized slowly, however, because of the extremely conservative policies of Shaykh Shakhbūṭ ibn Sulṭān (ruler 1928–66). In the latter year, he was deposed in favour of his younger brother Zayd ibn Sulṭān, former governor of the Abu Dhabi-controlled portion of al-Buraymī oasis. Shaykh Zayd began developing a road network radiating from Abu Dhabi town and had a seawall built along the northern end of the island containing the town. Under an ambitious five-year development plan, inaugurated in 1968, the town was thoroughly modernized. Electricity, running water, and a central sewage system were installed; modern government buildings, hotels, housing projects, and a new port extension were built. An oil refinery on nearby Umm an-Nār Island began production in 1976. Abu Dhabi's international airport is at the south end of the island. Light industry is concentrated at nearby Musafah. Just northeast of the town, on the previously desolate island of as-Sadīyāt, the government has developed an Arid Lands Research Centre; with U.S. technical assistance and ample amounts of desalinated irrigation water, large crops of vegetables have been produced. Motor roads link Abu Dhabi town with Dubai town (northeast), al-ʿAyn (al-Ain) oasis (east), and Qatar (west).

When Britain finally left the Persian Gulf, and the United Arab Emirates achieved political independence (December 1971), a compromise decision placed the federal capital at Abu Dhabi town for a period of five years (1971–76), renewed until 1981. It was proposed to build a new national capital thereafter at a previously uninhabited site on the boundary of Abu Dhabi and Dubai emirates or to make al-ʿAyn (al-Ain) the new site. Pop. (1980) 242,975.

Abū Ḥabbah (Iraq): *see* Sippar.

Abū Ḥāmid Muḥammad ibn Muḥammad aṭ-Ṭūsī al-Ghazālī (Muslim mystic): *see* Ghazālī, al-.

Abū Ḥanīfah, in full ABŪ ḤANĪFAH AN-NUʿMĀN IBN THĀBIT (b. 699, Kūfah, Iraq—d. 767, Baghdad), Muslim jurist and theologian whose systematization of Islāmic legal doctrine was acknowledged as one of the four canonical Islāmic schools of law. He eschewed any political involvements, steadfastly refusing a judgeship, and thus incurred the persecution of the Umayyad and ʿAbbāsid dynasties. The school of Abū Ḥanīfah acquired such prestige that its doctrines were applied by a majority of Muslim dynasties. Even today it is widely followed in India, Pakistan, Turkey, China, Central Asia, and Arab countries.

Abū Ḥanīfah was born in Kūfah, an intellectual centre of Iraq. He belonged to the *mawālī*, the non-Arab Muslims, who pioneered intellectual activity in Islāmic lands. The son of a merchant, young Abū Ḥanīfah took up the silk trade for a living and earned renown for honest dealing. It provided him with a steady and handsome income, out of which he donated generously to charity, helping scholars particularly.

Abū Ḥanīfah had a well-rounded education. In early youth he was attracted to theological debates, in which his sharp wit and logical mind won him laurels. Disenchanted with theology, he turned to law and for about 18 years was a disciple of Ḥammād (died 738), then the most noted Iraqi jurist. After Ḥammād's death, he became his successor. He also learned from several other scholars, notably the Meccan traditionist ʿAṭāʾ (died *c.* 732) and the founder of the Shīʿī law, Jaʿfar aṣ-Ṣādiq (died 765). Abū Ḥanīfah's mind was also matured by extensive travels, contacts with a variety of people, exposure to the stimulating influences of the heterogeneous, dynamic, and advanced society of Iraq, and conversance with business practices.

Tall, of medium weight, Abū Ḥanīfah was impressive in his bearing and dignity. He had a serious and sober disposition and was known for piety and religious earnestness and devotion. Having an independent income, he neither needed nor cared for governmental patronage, and this helped Islāmic law develop independently of political authority. His independence and fearlessness, his disregard for worldly vanities, and, above all, his piety made him a paragon of Muslim scholarship.

By Abū Ḥanīfah's time a vast body of legal doctrines had accumulated as a result of the endeavour to apply Islāmic norms to legal problems. The disagreements in these doctrines had rendered the development of a uniform code, based on sound principles, a need of the hour. Abū Ḥanīfah responded by thoroughly scrutinizing the current doctrines in collaboration with his students, several of them outstanding scholars. He had each legal problem discussed thoroughly before formulating doctrines definitively.

Being a speculative jurist, Abū Ḥanīfah brought about systematic consistency in legal doctrines. In his doctrines, emphasis shifts from material to systematic considerations. Again and again he disregarded established practices and considerations of judicial and administrative convenience in favour of systematic and technical legal considerations. His legal acumen and juristic strictness were such that Abū Ḥanīfah reached the highest level of legal thought achieved up to his time. Compared with his contemporaries, the Kufan Ibn Abī Laylā (died 765), the Syrian Awzāʿī (died 774), and the Medinese Mālik (died 795), his doctrines are more carefully formulated and systematically consistent and his technical legal thought more highly developed and refined.

Before Abū Ḥanīfah's time, doctrines had been formulated mainly in response to actual problems, whereas he attempted to solve problems that might arise in the future. By the introduction of this method—a characteristic of Abū Ḥanīfah—the area of law was considerably enlarged. The method presupposed advanced legal thought—thought that was further refined by the practice of this method. It was presumably because of this, coupled with Abū Ḥanīfah's somewhat rationalist orientation and his reserve about traditions that were not highly authenticated, that his school was denounced as the school of *raʾy* (independent opinion) as opposed to that of Ḥadīth (authoritative tradition). This, however, was a polemical allegation rather than an objective statement of the school's standpoint.

Although it was not Abū Ḥanīfah's primary concern, his contribution to theology was also significant. He took distinct and moderate positions on several theological questions, stimulating the development of the Māturīdī school.

Thanks to his temperament and academic preoccupation, Abū Ḥanīfah took no direct part in court politics or power struggles, notwithstanding his obvious antipathy toward the Umayyads and ʿAbbāsids, the ruling dynasties of that time. His sympathies lay with the ʿAlids, whose revolts he openly supported with both words and money. This fact partly explains why Abū Ḥanīfah adamantly refused to accept a judgeship and, consequently, suffered severe persecution under both the dynasties. (Z.I.A.)

BIBLIOGRAPHY. For bibliographical information on Abū Ḥanīfah, see the article by J. Schacht in the *Encyclopaedia of Islam,* vol. 1 (1960); and *An Introduction to Islamic Law* (1964). For most authentic sources of Abū Ḥanīfah's legal doctrines, see the works of his disciples, Abū Yūsuf (d. 798) and al-Shaybānī (d. 805). For theological doctrines, see A.J. Wenswinck, *The Muslim Creed* (1932); and J.A. Williams (ed.), *Islam* (1961).

Abū Ḥudhayfah (Muslim theologian): *see* Wāṣil ibn ʿAṭāʾ.

Abū ʿImran Mūsā ibn Maymūn ibn ʿUbayd Allāh (Jewish philosopher): *see* Maimonides, Moses.

Abū ʿĪsā Muḥammad ibn ʿĪsā ibn Sawrah ibn Shaddād at-Tirmidhī (9th-century Arab scholar): *see* Tirmidhī, at-.

Abū Isḥāq Ibrāhīm ibn Sayyār ibn Hanī' an-Naẓẓām (Muslim theologian): *see* Naẓ-ẓām, **Ibrāhīm an-**.

Abū Isḥāq Ismāʿīl ibn al-Qāsim ibn Suwayd ibn Kaysān (Arab poet): *see* Abū al-ʿAtāhiyah.

Abū Jaʿfar Abd Allāh al-Manṣūr ibn Muḥammad (caliph): *see* Manṣūr, al-.

Abū Jaʿfar Muḥammad ibn Jarīr aṭ-Ṭabarī (Muslim scholar): *see* Ṭabarī, aṭ-.

Abū Jirāb, also spelled ABU GURAB, ancient Egyptian site, about one mile (1.6 kilometres) north of Abū Ṣīr, between Ṣaqqārah and Giza; it is known as the location of two 5th-dynasty (*c.* 2494–*c.* 2345 BC) sun temples. The first part of the 5th dynasty is recognized as a period of unusually strong emphasis on the worship of the sun god Re, contemporary inscriptions

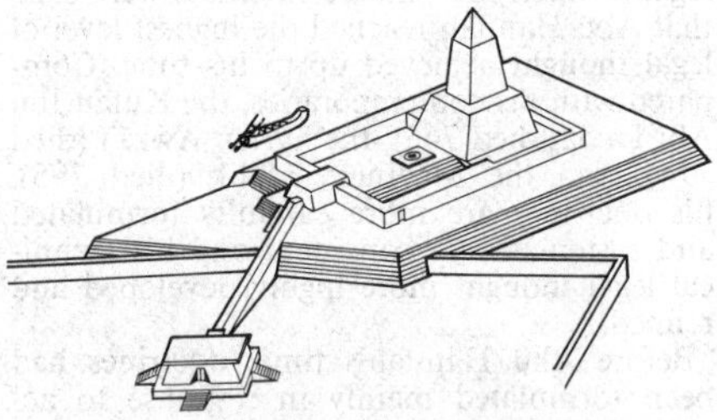

Reconstruction of the sun temple of King Neuserre

From I.E.S. Edwards, *The Pyramids of Egypt* (Copyright © I.E.S. Edwards, 1947, 1961); Penguin Books Ltd.

recording that six sun temples were built. Only those of King Userkaf (*c.* 2460–*c.* 2455) and King Neuserre (*c.* 2422–*c.* 2411), however, have been found and excavated, the latter one better preserved because it was built entirely of stone. The temple of King Neuserre originally consisted of a large unroofed platform surrounded by storerooms, cult chambers, and an altar. In the rear, resting on a rectangular podium, was a squat obelisk, about 56 feet (18 metres) in height and perhaps signifying radiating sunbeams. A long covered passage approached the platform and was decorated with some of the most beautifully sculptured and painted scenes remaining from the Old Kingdom.

Abū Kālījār al-Marzubān ibn Sulṭān ad-Dawlah, also called MUḤYĪ'AD-DĪN (b. May/June 1009, Basra, Iraq—d. October 1048, Khannāb, Kermān), ruler of the Būyid dynasty from 1024, who for a brief spell reunited the Būyid territories in Iraq and Iran.

When his father, Sulṭān ad-Dawlah, died in December 1023/January 1024, Abū Kālījār's succession to the Sultan's Iranian possessions of Fārs and Khuzistan was challenged by his uncle Abū al-Fawāris, the ruler of Kerman, to the west. By 1028 Abū Kālījār was victorious and added Kerman to his domains. In the meantime (1027) he had attacked the Iraqi lands of another uncle, Jalāl ad-Dawlah, and had precipitated a civil war between the Iraqi and the Iranian branches of the Būyid family that lasted until 1037, when the two made peace. With the death of his uncle in March 1044, Abū Kālījār was recognized as the Būyid ruler in Iraq.

In the face of the growing challenge of the Seljuq Turks, Abū Kālījār fortified his capital Shīrāz, in Fārs (1044), and three years later entered a marriage alliance with the Seljuq ruler Toghrïl Beg. In 1048, however, Toghrïl broke the alliance and attacked. Abū Kālījār died leading a force against the Seljuqs, who by 1062 completed their occupation of Būyid territories.

Abu 'l-Faḍl ʿAllāmī, Abu 'l-Faḍl also spelled ABU-L-FAẒL (b. Jan. 14, 1551, Āgra, India—d. Aug. 22, 1602), historian, military commander, secretary, and theologian to the Mughal emperor Akbar.

Abu 'l-Faḍl ʿAllāmī studied with his father, Shaykh Mubārak Nāgawrī, a distinguished scholar, and after teaching in his father's school was presented to Akbar in 1574 by the poet Fayẓī, Abu 'l-Faḍl's older brother. Through his criticism of the traditional Muslim religious leaders, he influenced the development of Akbar's religious synthesis. He opposed the narrow-mindedness of the religious leaders and their preoccupation with outward forms instead of the transcendent God. Abu 'l-Faḍl had immense influence at court. Appointed a military commander in the Deccan in 1599, he distinguished himself both as a soldier and as an administrator. He was called back to court during a rebellion of Akbar's son Salīm (afterward the emperor Jahāngīr) but, at the instigation of Salīm, was stopped en route and assassinated.

Abu 'l-Faḍl's major literary achievement was a history of Akbar and his ancestors, *Akbar-nāmeh* (Eng. trans. by H. Beveridge, *The Akbarnāma of Abu-l-Fazl,* 1907–39), concluded by the *Āīn-e Akbarī* (Eng. trans. by H.F. Blochmann and H.S. Jarrett, *ʿAin-i-Ākbari of Abul Fazl-i-ʿĀllami,* 1927–49). *Āīn-e Akbarī* is in three parts: (1) a manual of government operations from the jewel office and elephant stables to the army and tax collection; (2) a description and short history of Akbar's 12 provinces; and (3) an account of Hindu culture and sciences. He is said to have translated the Bible into Persian. Collections of Abu 'l-Faḍl's letters are also extant.

Abu Madi, Iliya (b. *c.* 1890, al-Muḥaydithah, Lebanon—d. 1957), Arab poet and journalist who spent much of his life in the United States.

When he was 11 years old, Abu Madi moved with his family from their mountain village in Lebanon to Alexandria, Egypt. As a young man he earned money selling cigarettes. He published his first collection of poetry in Alexandria in 1911. The following year he migrated to the United States, settling in Cincinnati, where he worked with his brother. In 1916, he moved to New York City and began editing several Arabic newspapers and magazines, which were supported by New York City's Arab community. He worked for 10 years with the magazine *Mir'āt al-gharb* ("Mirror of the West") and married the owner's daughter. In 1929 he started his own bimonthly magazine, *as-Samīr* ("The Companion"), which he expanded into a daily newspaper in 1936 and continued to publish until his death.

Abu Madi published a collection of poetry in 1916 and a second, *al-Jadāwil* ("Streams"), in 1927. *Al-Khamā'il* (1946; "Thickets") was printed in Beirut, as was the posthumous *Tibr wa-turāb* (1960; "Ore and Dust"). The popularity of his poetry was based on his expressive and natural use of language, his mastery of the traditional patterns of Arabic poetry, and the relevance of his ideas to contemporary Arab readers.

Abū Manṣūr Muḥammad ibn Maḥmūd al-Ḥanafī al-Mutakallim al-Māturīdī as-Samarqandī (Muslim theologian): *see* Māturīdī, Abū Manṣūr Muḥammad al-.

Abū Manṣūr Sebüktigin (ruler, Afghanistan): *see* Sebüktigin.

Abū Maʿshar: *see* Albumazar.

Abū Muʿīn Nāṣir-i Khusraw al-Marvāzi al-Qubādiyānī (Persian poet): *see* Nāsir-i Khusraw.

Abū Muḥammad ʿAbd Allāh ibn Muslim ad-Dīnawarī ibn Qutaybah: *see* Ibn Qutaybah.

Abū Muḥammad al-Ḥasan ibn Aḥmad al-Hamdānī: *see* Hamdānī, al-.

Abū Muḥammad al-Kūmī (Berber caliph): *see* ʿAbd al-Mu'min (ibn ʿAli ibn Makhlūf ibn Yuʿlā ibn Marwān).

Abū Muḥammad al-Qāsim ibn ʿAli al-Ḥarīrī: *see* Ḥarīrī, al-.

Abū Muḥammad ʿAlī ibn Aḥmad ibn Saʿīd ibn Ḥazm (Muslim historian): *see* Ibn Ḥazm.

Abū Mūsā Jabir ibn Ḥayyān (alchemist): *see* Jābir ibn Ḥayyān, Abū Mūsā.

Abū Muslim (d. February 755), leader of a revolutionary movement in Khorāsān who, while acting as an agent for the ʿAbbāsid family, was instrumental in the downfall of the Umayyad caliphate and in placing the ʿAbbāsids on the throne.

There are numerous versions of Abū Muslim's background, but it seems most likely that he was descended from a slave of Persian origin, and was therefore a *mawālī* (non-Arab Muslim, accorded lowly status under the Umayyads). The emissary of the ʿAbbāsid imām, who was briefly incarcerated, met Abū Muslim while in prison (741) and later arranged for his release. Abū Muslim was instructed by the imām and then sent to Khorāsān (745–46) to instigate a revolt.

Abū Muslim proved to be an energetic and capable leader. Overcoming the initial resentment caused by his obscure origin, he took advantage of the deep social divisions rife in Khorāsān, where the ʿAbbāsids had carefully intrigued and disseminated propaganda against the Umayyads for 20 years. Recruiting from various discontented or dispossessed social groups, Abū Muslim created a coalition of rebellious Arabs and Iranians; the distinctions between Arab and non-Arab were blurred as he managed to syncretize local tradition and Iranian culture with Islāmic religion.

On June 15, 747, Abū Muslim raised the banner of revolution and the revolt quickly spread throughout Khorāsān and to other provinces, with Abū Muslim as the chief military organizer. The revolt triumphed when the last Umayyad caliph, Marwān II, was defeated and killed (750) and as-Saffāḥ became the first ʿAbbāsid caliph (749). Abū Muslim was given the governorship of Khorāsān in reward for his services. The ʿAbbasids still depended on him to keep order, and Abū Muslim served his patrons well by defeating both internal and external enemies.

Although the ʿAbbāsids were in large part enthroned owing to Abū Muslim's military victories and political prowess, they became leery of a vassal with so much power and popularity. With the accession of the second ʿAbbāsid caliph (754), the morbidly suspicious al-Manṣūr, Abū Muslim's downfall was certain. After having Abū Muslim quell an uprising led by a rebellious uncle, al-Manṣūr stripped away the governorship of Khorāsān from him. When Abū Muslim arrived at court, al-Manṣūr had him treacherously put to death, thus eliminating a potential rival for the throne. The unavenged death of Abū Muslim, already a legendary hero to the population, inspired many later uprisings and revolts.

Abū Naṣr, Aḥmad Shāh Bahādur Mujāhid-ud-Dīn: *see* Aḥmad Shāh.

Abū Nuwās, also spelled ABŪ NU'ĀS, in full ABŪ NUWĀS AL-ḤASAN IBN HĀNI' AL-ḤAKAMĪ (b. *c.* 747–762, Ahvāz, Iran—d. *c.* 813–815, Baghdad), important poet of the early ʿAbbāsid period (750–835).

Abū Nuwās, of mixed Arab and Persian heritage, studied in Basra and al-Kūfah, first under the poet Wālibah ibn al-Ḥubāb, later under Khalaf al-Aḥmar. He also studied the Qur'ān (Islāmic sacred scripture), Ḥadīth (traditions relating to the life and utterances of the Prophet), and grammar and is said to have spent a year with the Bedouins in the desert to acquire their traditional purity of language.

Abū Nuwās' initial appearance at the ʿAbbāsid court in Baghdad met with little success; his alliance with the Barmakids, the ʿAbbāsid viziers, forced him to seek refuge in Egypt when the Barmakid dynasty collapsed. On his return to Baghdad, however, his panegyrics earned the favour of the caliphs Hārūn ar-Rashīd and al-Amīn, and he enjoyed great success in the ʿAbbāsid court until his death.

The language of Abū Nuwās' formal odes (*qaṣīdahs*) is grammatically sound and based on the old Arab traditions; his themes, however, are drawn from urban life, not the desert. He is particularly renowned for his poems on wine (*khamrīyāt*) and pederasty. His verse is laced with humour and irony, reflecting the genial, yet cynical outlook of the poet, who spent much of his life in pursuit of pleasure.

Abū ol-Qasem Manṣūr (Persian poet): *see* Ferdowsī.

Abū Qīr, Khalīj, also called ABUKIR BAY, or ABOUKIR BAY, semicircular inlet of the Mediterranean Sea, lying between Abū Qīr Point (southwest) and the mouth of the Rosetta Branch (northeast) of the Nile River Delta, in al-Buḥayrah *muḥāfaẓah* (governorate), Lower Egypt. The bay was the scene of a famous battle of the Nile (1798) in which an English fleet under Rear Adm. Sir Horatio Nelson defeated the Napoleonic fleet. A natural gas field, developed offshore in the late 1970s, provides energy for industries around Alexandria and in al-Buḥayrah *muḥāfaẓah.*

Abū Ruwaysh, also spelled ABU ROASH, ancient Egyptian site of a 4th-dynasty (*c.* 2613–*c.* 2494 BC) pyramid built by Djedefre, usually considered the third of the seven kings of that dynasty. The site is about five miles (eight kilometres) northwest of Giza (al-Jīzah) on the west bank of the Nile. Of the pyramid superstructure very little remains, and some scholars believe that it was never finished—a theory reinforced by the fact that the walls of the mortuary temple next to the pyramid were hastily made of mud brick instead of the usual cut stone; the complex was also deliberately ransacked, as Djedefre was involved in a dynastic struggle. Nothing remains of the pyramid's valley temple, but the causeway from it to the mortuary temple can still be traced.

An Early Dynastic (*c.* 3100–*c.* 2690 BC) private cemetery has also been found at Abu Roash.

Abū Saʿīd ʿAbd al-Malik ibn Qurayb al-Asmaʿī: *see* Aṣmaʿī, al-.

Abū Saʿīd ibn Abī al-Ḥasan Yasār al-Baṣrī: *see* Ḥasan al-Baṣrī, al-.

Abū Shahrayn (Iraq): *see* Eridu.

Abu Simbel, also spelled ABŪ SUNBUL, site of two temples built by the Egyptian king Ramses II (ruled *c.* 1304–*c.* 1237 BC); the four colossal statues of Ramses in front of the main temple are one of the most spectacular examples of ancient Egyptian art. The temples were salvaged from the rising waters of the Nile River by a complex engineering feat in the 1960s.

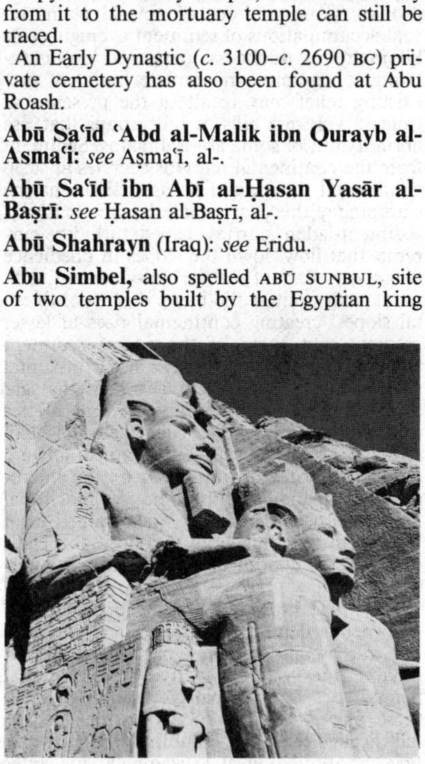

Sandstone figures of Ramses II in front of the main temple at Abu Simbel
By courtesy of Air France

Carved out of a sandstone cliff on the west bank of the Nile, south of Korosko (modern Kuruskū) in the Aswān governorate of Egypt, near the Sudanese frontier, the temples were unknown to the outside world until their rediscovery in 1813. They were first explored in 1817 by the early Egyptologist Giovanni Battista Belzoni.

The 67-foot (20-metre) seated figures of Ramses were set against the recessed face of the cliff, two on either side of the entrance to the main temple. Carved around their feet were small figures representing Ramses' queen, Nefertari, and their children. Graffiti inscribed on the southern pair by Greek mercenaries serving Egypt in the 6th century BC have provided important evidence of the early history of the alphabet. The temple itself, dedicated to the sun gods Amon-Re and Re-Horakhte, consisted of three consecutive halls extending 185 ft into the cliff, decorated with more figures of the King and with painted reliefs showing his life and achievements. It was built so that, on certain days of the year, the first rays of the morning sun would penetrate its whole length and even illuminate the shrine in its innermost sanctuary.

Just to the north of the main temple was a smaller one, dedicated to Nefertari for the worship of the goddess Hathor and adorned with 35-ft statues of the King and Queen.

When the reservoir created by the construction of the nearby Aswān High Dam threatened to submerge Abu Simbel in the early 1960s, the United Nations Educational, Scientific and Cultural Organization (UNESCO) and the Egyptian government sponsored a project to save the site. Between 1964 and 1966 a work force and an international team of engineers and scientists, supported by funds from more than 50 countries, dug away the top of the cliff and completely disassembled both temples, reconstructing them on high ground 200 ft above the riverbed.

Where the same name may denote a person, place, or thing, the articles will be found in that order

Abū Ṣīr, in Egypt, ancient site between Giza (al-Jīzah) and Ṣaqqārah where several 5th-dynasty (*c.* 2494–*c.* 2345 BC) kings built their pyramids. The pyramids were poorly constructed and are now in a state of disrepair. The adjoining mortuary temples are notable for their elaborate sculptured wall reliefs and columns in the forms of palm, lotus, and papyrus plants. Near their pyramids a number of the kings built sanctuaries with obelisks dedicated to Re, the sun god; only those of King Userkaf and King Neuserre have been excavated.

Abū Sunbul (Egypt): *see* Abu Simbel.

Abū Tammām, in full ABŪ TAMMĀM ḤABĪB IBN AWS (b. 804, near Damascus—d. *c.* 845, Mosul, Iraq), poet and editor of an anthology of early Arabic poems known as the *Ḥamāsah.*

Abū Tammām changed his Christian father's name of Thādhūs to Aws and invented for himself an Arab genealogy. In his youth he worked in Damascus as a weaver's assistant but on going to Egypt began to study poetry. It is not certain when he began to write verse, but by the time of the caliph al-Muʿtaṣim (reigned 833–842) he had established a small reputation. This was greatly enlarged through his association with al-Muʿtaṣim's court, where he became the most acclaimed panegyrist of his day. He travelled to Armenia and Nīshāpūr, Iran, and on his return from Iran stopped in Hamadan, where he began compiling his *Ḥamāsah.*

Abū Tammām's divan, or collection of poems, generally deals with contemporary events of historical significance. In his own day it was variously judged by the Arab critics; while his command and purity of language were generally recognized, many deprecated his excessive use of tortuous poetical devices.

Abū ʿUbādah al-Walīd ibn ʿUbayd Allāh al-Buḥturī: *see* Buḥturī, al-.

Abū-ul-Fatḥ Jalāl-ud-Dīn Muḥammad Akbar (Mughal emperor): *see* Akbar.

Abū ʿUthman ʿAmr ibn Baḥr ibn Maḥbūb al-Jāḥiẓ: *see* Jāḥiẓ, al-.

Abū Yūsuf Yaʿqūb al-Manṣūr (Muslim ruler of Spain and North Africa): *see* Manṣūr, Abū Yūsuf Yaʿqūb al-.

Abuja (town and emirate, Nigeria): *see* Suleja.

Abuja, federal capital territory, central Nigeria, created in 1976 from a northwestern part of former Benue-Plateau State, a southeastern part of former North-Western State, and a northeastern part of former Western State. The territory has an area of 2,824 sq mi (7,315 sq km) located north of the confluence of the Niger and Benue rivers. It is bordered by the states of Niger to the west and northwest, Kaduna to the northeast, Plateau to the east and south, and Kwara to the southwest. Abuja, the new federal capital and a planned modern city under construction in the early 1980s, is located near the centre of the territory.

The region is underlain by crystalline rocks consisting of granites and gneisses. The vegetation is mainly savanna with limited forest areas. Agriculture, the economic mainstay, produces yams, millet, corn (maize), sorghum, and beans. The population comprises the Gwaris, Koro, Ganagana, Gwandara, Afo, and Bassa ethnic groups, predominantly dairy farmers. Hausa and Fulani also live in the territory. Mineral resources include clay, tin, feldspar, gold, iron ore, lead, marble, and talc. Abuja city has an airport and major road connections.

Abuja, planned modern city and proposed new federal capital of Nigeria, in the central part of the Abuja Federal Capital Territory (created 1976), located about 300 mi (480 km) northwest of Lagos, the present capital. In the early 1980s, the new capital city (designed by the Department of Architecture, Ahmadu Bello University in Zaria), was being built and developed in the grass-covered Chukuku Hills. The site was chosen because of its central location, easy accessibility, salubrious climate, low population density, and the availability of land for future expansion. It is the first planned city to be built in Nigeria. Abuja lies at 1,180 ft (360 m) above sea level and has a cooler climate and less humidity than is found in Lagos. The city was planned with a projected population of 20,000 in the early stage and is divided into two zones. The central area contains the National Assembly, the city hall, national cultural institutes, and other government related offices. The other zone provides residential accommodation (5,000 housing units were completed in the early 1980s), shopping facilities, and other modern amenities. Abuja has an airport and expressways connect the new capital with other state capitals. High-tension power lines conduct electricity to the city from Shiroro Dam, on the Niger River, 46 mi (75 km) southwest of Abuja.

Abukir Bay (Mediterranean Sea): *see* Abū Qīr, Khalīj.

Abukuma-sammyaku (Japanese: Abukuma Mountains), range in northern Honshu, Japan, extending for 106 mi (170 km) north to south and paralleling the Pacific coast of Fukushima Prefecture (*ken*), Tōhoku Region (*chihō*). Its southern end extends into Ibaraki Prefecture of Kantō Region. The mountains are 30 mi wide and are sphenoidal, or wedge shaped. They consist of schistose granite and granodiorite, occasionally accompanied by slate, sandstone, and limestone.

The mountains are also referred to as the Abukuma-kōgen (Abukuma Plateau) because much of the original surface in the south has been obliterated by erosion and broken by several parallel fault valleys that run from north-northwest to south-southeast. Ōtakine-san (Mt. Ōtakine) is the highest point in the range; it rises to 3,914 ft (1,193 m) above the surrounding eroded surfaces, which average 2,950 ft in elevation. Since ancient times a main highway has followed the pass between these mountains and the Mikuni-sammyaku from the Kantō Plain to Tōhoku Region. The eastern piedmont hills contain the Jōban coalfields, which are developing as a new industrial district.

Abul Kasim: *see* Abū al-Qāsim.

Abul Wefa (Persian mathematician): *see* Abū al-Wafā' (al-Būzajānī).

Abulfeda: *see* Abū al-Fidā'.

Abulghazi Bahadur (Uzbek ruler and historian): *see* Abū al-Ghāzī Bahādur.

Abumeron: *see* Ibn Zuhr.

Abuná River, Spanish RÍO ABUNÁ, Portuguese RIO ABUNÃ, headwater of the Amazon, rising in several streams, east of the Cordillera Oriental of the Andes. The navigable river flows for about 200 mi (320 km) northeast through rain forests, forming Bolivia's northern border with Brazil. It joins the Río Madeira, a tributary of the Amazon, at Manoa, Bolivia. Rubber, Brazil nuts, quinine, and other forest products are the principal items of commerce in the sparsely inhabited Abuná region.

Abung (people): *see* Lampong.

Abutilon, genus of about 150 species of herbaceous plants and partly woody shrubs, of the mallow family (Malvaceae), native to tropical and warm temperate areas. It includes several species used as houseplants and in gardens for their white to deep-orange, usually nodding, five-petalled blossoms.

A. hybridum, sometimes called Chinese lantern, is planted outdoors in warm regions and grown in greenhouses elsewhere. The trailing abutilon (*A. megapotamicum*), often grown as a hanging plant, is noted for its nodding, yellowish-orange, closed flowers; it has a handsome variegated-leaved variety. *A. pictum,* a shrub reaching a height of 4.5 metres (15 feet), often called parlor, or flowering, maple, is grown as a houseplant. An important fibre plant in China is *A. theophrastii,* called China jute; it is a field weed in the U.S., where it is called velvet leaf (*q.v.*), or Indian mallow.

Abuza, Sophie (U.S. singer): *see* Tucker, Sophie.

Abyaḍ, al-Baḥr al- (The Sudan): *see* White Nile River.

Abyān, *muḥāfaẓah* (governorate), southern Yemen (Aden), on the Gulf of Aden; it was formerly called *al-muḥāfaẓah ath-Thālithah,* (the third governorate). It embraces an area of 8,297 sq mi (21,489 sq km). Abyān is bounded by Shabwah *muḥāfaẓah* to the north and east and by Yemen (Ṣan'ā') to the north. In the north, the elevation reaches 8,248 ft (2,514 m). The aridity of the mountainous highland limits economic activity to nomadic herding in the north. The southwestern corner of the governorate, along the gulf coast, is one of the major cotton-producing areas in the country. Zinjibār is the provincial capital. Pop. (1973 prelim.) 291,376.

Abydos, Egyptian ABDU, Coptic EBOT, modern AL-'ARABAT AL-MADFUNA, prominent sacred city and one of the most important archaeological sites of ancient Egypt. The site, located west of the Nile near al-Balyanā, was a royal necropolis of the first two dynasties and later a pilgrimage centre for the worship of Osiris.

The history of Abydos, intimately associated with the political and religious development of Egypt itself, dates to the beginnings of Egyptian history. Excavations there at the end of the 19th century by Emile-Clément Amélineau and Sir Flinders Petrie uncovered a series of pit tombs, apparently belonging to the kings of the first two dynasties of Egypt. The correctness of this identification, however, was questioned when tombs were uncovered at Ṣaqqārah of far greater size and richness and containing objects bearing the same royal names as those at Abydos. Some of the 2nd-dynasty pharaohs, however, may have been buried at Abydos, and they built imposing brick funerary enclosures at the northwestern end of the necropolis area.

The tutelary deity of the necropolis city was the jackal god, called Khenti-amentiu in the Old Kingdom; in the 5th dynasty, however, his cult was gradually absorbed by that of the god Osiris. Abydos became a place of pilgrimage for pious Egyptians, who desired above all else to be buried as close as possible to the tomb of Osiris at Abydos. For those who could not afford the expense, steles were set up, inscribed with the dead man's name and titles and a prayer to the god. The pharaohs, encouraging the cult of the deified king at Abydos, took special care to embellish and enlarge the temple of Osiris there. Some pharaohs had a cenotaph or a mortuary temple at Abydos. The temple of Seti I was one of the most beautiful of all the temples of antiquity. Its plan was unique, for it has seven sanctuaries, approached through two broad hypostyle halls. In a long gallery leading to other rooms was a relief showing Seti and his son Ramses making offerings to the cartouches of 76 of their dead predecessors beginning with Menes. This is the so-called Abydos list of kings.

Only 26 feet (8 metres) behind the temple of Seti I was a remarkable structure known as the Osireion, but probably in reality Seti's cenotaph. This curious monument was an underground vaulted hall containing a central platform with 10 monolithic pillars surrounded by a channel of water. Perhaps the whole was an allegory in stone of the primeval hill amid the waters of the deep.

Abydos, ancient Anatolian town located just northeast of the modern Turkish town of Çanakkale on the east side of the Dardanelles (Hellespont) in Çanakkale *il* (province). Probably originally a Thracian town, it was colonized about 670 BC by the Milesians. There Xerxes crossed the strait on his bridge of boats to invade Greece in 480 BC. Abydos is celebrated for its vigorous resistance to Philip V of Macedon (200 BC) and for the legend of Hero and Leander (*q.v.*). It survived until late Byzantine times as the toll station of the Hellespont.

abyssal gap: *see* submarine gap.

abyssal hill, small, topographically well-defined submarine hill that may rise from several metres to several hundred metres above the abyssal seafloor, in water 3,000 to 6,000 metres (10,000 to 20,000 feet) deep. Typical hills have diameters of several to several hundred metres. Abyssal-hill provinces, areas of abyssal seafloor occupied exclusively by such hills, characteristically occur seaward of the smooth abyssal plains at the bases of continental rises. Isolated hills and groups of hills also protrude from abyssal-plain surfaces, and the base of an abyssal-plain accumulation of sediment, as revealed by sub-bottom seismic profiling, generally matches the undulating topography and relief of abyssal-hill provinces.

Abyssal hills, although generally veneered with marine sediments, probably are identical in composition and origin to the extrusive basaltic prominences on the upper flanks of mid-oceanic ridges and rises. Thus, it is believed that abyssal hills underlie most of the ocean floor, locally buried by accumulations of abyssal sediment. In the Atlantic Ocean, long abyssal-hill provinces parallel both flanks of the Mid-Atlantic Ridge along most of its length. The Pacific Ocean has a smaller supply of continental sediment than the Atlantic Ocean, and numerous trenches and local rises separate the main ocean floor from the continents, preventing the seaward transport of sediment; consequently, between 80 and 85 percent of the Pacific abyssal floor is occupied by abyssal hills.

abyssal plain, flat seafloor area at an abyssal depth (3,000 to 6,000 metres [10,000 to 20,000 feet]), generally adjacent to a continent. These submarine surfaces vary in depth only from 10 to 100 centimetres per kilometre of horizontal distance. Irregular in outline but generally elongate along continental margins, the larger plains are hundreds of kilometres wide and thousands of kilometres long. In the North Atlantic the Sohm Plain alone has an area of approximately 900,000 square kilometres (350,000 square miles). The plains are largest and most common in the Atlantic Ocean, less common in the Indian Ocean, and even rarer in the Pacific, where they occur mainly as the small, flat floors of marginal seas or as the narrow, elongate bottoms of trenches.

The plains are thought to be the upper surfaces of land-derived sediment that accumulates in abyssal depressions, thus modifying irregular preexisting topography. Seismic profiles (cross sections) of abyssal plains reveal accumulations of sediment averaging one kilometre in thickness, deposited on undulating topography. Incomplete burial of preexisting relief may result in the presence of isolated volcanic hills or hill groups that rise abruptly out of some abyssal plains. Sediment from the continental margins accretes at steep continental slopes, and occasional submarine slumping of this coarse material creates dense, sediment-laden slurries, called turbidity currents, that flow down the slopes in obedience to gravity. Part of the turbidity-current sediment settles out at the bases of the continental slopes, creating continental rises of lesser gradient, but some of the coarse sediment reaches the abyssal depressions. Horizontal silty, sandy, and even gravelly beds that are fractions of a centimetre to several metres thick comprise 2 to 90 percent of abyssal-plain sediment. Many such layers demonstrably are of shallow-water organisms—*e.g.,* the microscopic protozoan Foraminifera. An individual layer may be progressively finer grained from bottom to top; this grading reflects the bed's origin as the deposit of a single turbidity current.

The coarse layers are interbedded with homogeneous deposits of fine-grained clay and the microscopic remains of organisms that inhabit the waters overlying the abyssal plains. Between turbidity-current episodes these fine-grained sediments are believed to fall through the water column particle by particle, accumulating at exceedingly slow rates (a millimetre to several centimetres per 1,000 years). Alternatively, it has been proposed that deep-sea clay deposits may be brought to abyssal plains continuously by slowly flowing, diffusely turbid bottom waters that originate in turbulent, shallow nearshore areas.

abyssal zone, portion of the ocean deeper than about 2,000 metres (6,600 feet) and shallower than about 6,000 m (20,000 ft). The zone is defined mainly by its extremely uniform environmental conditions, as reflected in the distinct life forms inhabiting it. The upper boundary is conveniently defined between the abyssal zone and the overlying bathyal zone as the depth at which the water temperature is 4° C (39° F); this depth varies between 1,000 and 3,000 m. Waters deeper than 6,000 m are characterized by their own unique faunal assemblages and are treated separately as the hadal realm by ecologists.

The abyssal realm is the largest environment for Earth life, covering 300,000,000 square kilometres (115,000,000 square miles), about 60 percent of the global surface and 83 percent of the area of oceans and seas.

Abyssal waters originate at the air–sea interface in polar regions, principally the Antarctic. There, the cold climate produces sea ice and residual cold brine. Because of its high density, the brine sinks and slowly flows along the bottom toward the Equator. Abyssal salinities range narrowly between 34.6 and 35.0 parts per thousand, and temperatures are mostly between 0° and 4° C, although deep basins isolated from the polar regions by submarine topographic barriers have warmer abyssal waters and, consequently, no true abyssal fauna. Pressure increases by about one atmosphere (approximately 14.7 pounds per square inch at sea level) with each 10-m increment in depth; thus, abyssal pressures range between 200 and 600 atmospheres. Pressure presents few problems for abyssal animals, however, because the pressures within their bodies are the same as those outside them.

The concentrations of nutrient salts of nitrogen, phosphorus, and silica are very uniform in abyssal waters and are much higher than in overlying waters. Abyssal and hadal waters are the reservoir for these salts from decomposed biologic materials at the end of the oceanic food chain, and the lack of sunlight prevents their uptake by photosynthesis.

The oxygen content of abyssal water depends entirely upon the amounts dissolved into it at its polar site of origin and the absence of photosynthesis, which precludes the introduction of new oxygen at depth. Abyssal waters retain several cubic centimetres of dissolved oxygen per litre, because the sparse animal populations do not consume oxygen faster than it is introduced into the abyssal zone. Abyssal life is concentrated at the very bottom, however, and the water nearest the seafloor may be essentially depleted in oxygen.

The abyssal realm is very calm, being far removed from such energetic phenomena as storms that agitate the ocean at the air–sea interface. These low energies are reflected in the character of abyssal sediments. Near land the sediment may contain significant amounts of coarse material derived from the continents; more typically, the abyssal realm is far enough from land so that the sediment is composed predominantly of microscopic plankton remains produced in the food chain in the overlying waters, from which they settle. Abyssal sediment in waters shallower than 4,000 m in equatorial to temperate regions is composed primarily of the calcareous shells of foraminiferan zooplankton and of phytoplankton such as coccolithophores. Below 4,000 m, calcium carbonate tends to dissolve, and the principal sediment constituents are brown clays and the siliceous remains of radiolarian zooplankton and phytoplankton such as diatoms. Radiolaria and diatoms also are found abundantly in high latitudes and dominate the abyssal deposits of Antarctica and the northernmost Pacific.

Abyssal fauna, although very sparse and embracing relatively few species, include areally widespread representatives of all major marine invertebrate phyla and several kinds of fish, all adapted to an environment marked by no diurnal or seasonal changes, high pressures, darkness, calm water, and soft sediment bottoms. These animals tend to be gray or black, delicately structured, and unstreamlined. Mobile forms have long legs; and animals attached to the bottom have stalks, enabling them to rise above the water layer nearest the bottom, where oxygen is scarce. Abyssal crustaceans and fish may be blind. With increasing depth, carnivores and scavengers become less abundant than animals that feed on mud and suspended matter. Abyssal animals are believed to reproduce very slowly.

Abyssinia: *see* Ethiopia.

Abyssinian, breed of domestic cat, probably of Egyptian origin, that has been considered to approximate the sacred cat of ancient Egypt more closely than any other living cat. The Abyssinian is a lithe cat with relatively slender legs and a long, tapering tail. The short, finely textured coat is ruddy reddish brown, with individual hairs of the back, sides, chest, and tail distinctively ticked, or tipped, with bands of black or brown. The nose is red, the eyes are hazel, green, or gold, and the tail tip and backs of the hindlegs are black. The Abyssinian is noted for being affectionate and quiet, though generally shy with strangers.

Abyssinian
John Gajda—EB Inc.

Abyssinians: *see* Amhara and Tigre.

ac: *see* alternating current.

Acacia, genus of perhaps 800 species of trees and shrubs, of the mimosa family (Mimosaceae), mostly native to warmer regions, particularly Australia (where they are called wattles) and Africa. The leaves are usually bipinnate (*i.e.,* the leaflets of the compound leaves are compound). Some species have thorny twigs. The small, often fragrant flowers are arranged in rounded or elongated clusters. The podlike fruits are either flattened or cylindrical, often exhibiting constrictions between the seeds.

A. senegal, native to tropical Africa, yields true gum arabic, a substance used in adhesives, pharmaceuticals, inks, confections, and other industrial products. Useful gums are also obtained from other species. The bark of most acacias is rich in tannin, used in tanning and in dyes, inks, pharmaceuticals, and other products. A few acacias produce valuable timber. Chief among these are Australian blackwood (*A. melanoxylon*); yarran (*A. homalophylla*), also of Australia; and *A. koa* of Hawaii. Sweet acacia (*A. farnesiana*), native to the southwestern U.S. and introduced into India and Europe, bears fragrant yellow flowers used in making perfume. Many of the Australian species have been widely introduced elsewhere as cultivated small trees valued for their spectacular floral displays.

(Top) Sydney golden wattle (*Acacia longifolia*) and (bottom) camel's-thorn (*Acacia giraffae*) with social weaver's nest
(Top) Douglas Baglin, (bottom) Gerald Cubitt

Acacian Schism (484–519), split between the patriarchate of Constantinople and the Roman See, occasioned by the issuance of an edict by Byzantine patriarch Acacius that was considered inadmissible by Pope Felix III.

Seeking greater autonomy for the Eastern Orthodox Church and supremacy of Constantinople over the Byzantine world, Acacius drew up the edict, the *Henotikon* (Greek: "Edict of Union"), incorporating the decisions of the general Councils of Nicaea (325) and Constantinople (381). Although recognizing Christ's divinity, the *Henotikon* omitted the orthodox distinction of Christ's human and divine essences, as enunciated by the Council of Chalcedon (451). Supported by the emperor Zeno, Acacius sought to obtain the assent of all Byzantine Christian communities to his conciliatory *Henotikon.* He had neglected to consult Rome, however, and was deposed by Pope Felix III in an excommunication, reaffirmed and broadened in 485 to embrace all of Acacius' accomplices, including a substantial part of the Byzantine hierarchy. Acacius died unreconciled, having struck mention of the bishop of Rome from the prayers of the Orthodox liturgy.

The condemnation by Pope Felix precipitated the Acacian Schism, which, though resolved in 519, nevertheless established Byzantine autonomy and fostered an alienation that culminated in the definitive Schism of 1054.

Academia, Bahia de la: *see* Academy Bay.

academic freedom, the freedom of teachers and students to teach, study, and pursue knowledge and research without unreasonable interference or restriction from law, institutional regulations, or public pressure. Its basic elements include the freedom of teachers to inquire into any subject that evokes their intellectual concern; to present their findings to their students, colleagues, and others; to publish their data and conclusions without control or censorship; to teach in the manner they consider professionally appropriate; and to act in their private lives with all the rights and liberties enjoyed by other citizens. For students, the basic elements include the freedom to study subjects that concern them; to form conclusions for themselves and express their opinions; and to enjoy all the common rights and liberties of other citizens.

According to its proponents, the justification for academic freedom thus defined lies not in the comfort or convenience of teachers and students but in the benefits to society; *i.e.*, the long-term interests of a society are best served when the educational process leads to the advancement of knowledge, and knowledge is best advanced when inquiry is free from restraints by the state, by the church or other institutions, or by special-interest groups.

The foundation for academic freedom was laid by the medieval European universities, even though their faculties met periodically to condemn colleagues' writings. Protected by papal bulls and royal charters, the universities became legally self-governing corporations with the freedom to organize their own faculties, control admissions, and establish standards for graduation.

After the Reformation, the rise of the European nation-states constituted a threat to the universities' autonomy. Professors were subject to governmental authority and were liable to have to teach only what was acceptable to the government in power. Thus began a tension that has continued to the present. Some states permitted or encouraged academic freedom and set an example for subsequent emulation. For example, the University of Leiden in Holland (founded in 1575) provided great freedom from religious and political restraints for its teachers and students. The University of Göttingen in Germany became a beacon of academic freedom in the 18th century, and with the founding of the University of Berlin in 1811 the basic principles of *Lehrfreiheit* (freedom to teach) and *Lernfreiheit* (freedom to learn) were firmly established and became the model that inspired universities elsewhere.

Academic freedom is never unlimited. The general laws of society, including those concerning obscenity, pornography, and libel, apply also to academic discourse and publication. Teachers are more free within their disciplines than outside them. The more highly trained teachers are, the more freedom they are likely to be afforded: university professors tend to experience fewer restrictions than elementary school teachers. Similarly, students are ordinarily granted increasing freedom as they move through the academic system. Teachers in small towns can usually expect more interference in their teaching than teachers in large cities. Academic freedom is liable to contract in times of war, economic depression, or political instability.

In countries without democratic traditions, academic freedom may be unreliably granted and unevenly distributed. It exists, at the university level, in Communist countries, most markedly in fields such as mathematics, natural sciences, linguistics, and archaeology, fields in which innovative and fruitful work has been done in those countries. From a Western point of view academic freedom in such countries appears to be largely absent in the social sciences, arts, and humanities. In other countries, the situation may be better but it is never certain. In Germany, for example, where the tradition of academic freedom was strongest, a virtually complete eclipse of academic freedom came in the 1930s. In the United States, the history of academic freedom has been marred by requirements of "loyalty" oaths. State requirements for such oaths date from the Great Depression of the 1930s, when many states required them of their teachers. In the anti-Communist hysteria of the 1950s, loyalty oath requirements proliferated; many teachers were dismissed without due process, and freedom of inquiry was seriously hampered. Under the National Defense Education Act of 1958, students were required to sign a loyalty oath in order to receive a government loan.

Academic Town (Russian S.F.S.R.): *see* Akademgorodok.

Académie des Sciences (France): *see* Sciences, Académie des.

Académie Française, French literary academy, established by Cardinal de Richelieu in 1634 and incorporated in 1635, and existing, except for an interruption during the era of the French Revolution, to the present day. Its original purpose was to maintain standards of literary taste and to establish the literary language. Its membership is limited to 40. Though it has often acted as a conservative body, opposed to innovations in literary content and form, its membership has included most of the great names of French literature; *e.g.*, Corneille, Racine, Voltaire, Chateaubriand, Hugo, Renan, and Bergson. Among numerous European literary academies, it has consistently retained the highest prestige over the longest period of time.

Académie Nationale de Musique: *see* Paris Opéra.

academy, school or place of learning or any association formed for literary, artistic, musical, or scientific pursuits. The word academy is derived from the name of an olive grove outside ancient Athens where Plato taught philosophy. Gradually the term acquired the general meaning of a higher school and in that sense it was used by Ptolemy I in Alexandria and by Spanish Muslim caliphs, Charlemagne, Alfred the Great, and others.

At the close of the Middle Ages academies began to be formed in Italy, first for the study of classical and then Italian literature. One of the earliest was the Platonic Academy founded in Florence in 1442 by Cosimo de' Medici. The most famous of these institutions from the Renaissance was the Accademia della Crusca (1582). The Calvinists in France, Switzerland, and the Netherlands called their higher institutions academies until the 18th century, when the term university was generally adopted. In modern times many institutions for higher learning in special subjects such as naval, military, agricultural, fine arts, music, or commerce have been called academies.

Learned societies for the advancement of arts, literature, or science have been established in most European countries and have acquired the status of national academies. Their influence was greatest during the 17th and 18th centuries but declined during the 19th because of their tendency to resist new and unorthodox developments.

Academy, Greek, originally an olive grove outside Athens, said to be dedicated to the hero Akadēmos, where Plato began teaching *c.* 387 BC; it was for 900 years a Platonic school of philosophy distinguished from that of the Peripatetic followers of Aristotle.

The Academy underwent various phases, arbitrarily classified as follows: the Old Academy, under Plato and his immediate successors as scholarchs (heads), when the philosophy thought there was moral, speculative, and dogmatic; the Middle Academy, begun by Arcesilaus (316/315–*c.* 241 BC), who introduced a nondogmatic Skepticism; and the New Academy, founded by Carneades (2nd century BC), which ended with the scholarch Antiochus of Ascalon (died 68 BC), who effected a return to the dogmatism of the Old Academy. Thereafter, the Academy was a centre of Middle Platonism and Neoplatonism until it was closed, along with other pagan schools, by the Roman emperor Justinian in AD 529.

Academy Bay, Spanish BAHIA DE LA ACADEMIA, at the south end of Santa Cruz (Indefatigable) Island (one of the Galápagos Islands), about 600 mi (965 km) west of Ecuador, in the eastern Pacific Ocean. Named in 1905 by the California Academy of Sciences Expedition, it is the site of the Charles Darwin Research Station (established in 1959 to study and preserve the archipelago's flora and fauna) and serves as a harbour for small craft. It was from there that the stranded Norwegian crew of the abandoned ship "Alexandra" was rescued in 1906. Subsistence agriculture and lobster freezing are the main economic activities.

Academy of Sciences of the U.S.S.R., Russian AKADEMIYA NAUK S.S.S.R., highest scientific society and principal coordinating body for research in natural and social sciences, technology, and production in the Soviet Union. Composed of outstanding Russian scholars who are elected to the academy, membership is of three types—academicians, corresponding members, and foreign members. The academy is also devoted to training students and to publicizing scientific achievements and knowledge. It maintains ties with many international scientific institutions and collaborates with foreign academies, particularly those of the socialist countries. Under the Council of Ministers of the U.S.S.R., the academy directs the research of the academies of sciences of the Union republics, other scientific institutions, and institutions of higher education. Its chief administrative organ, the elected General Assembly, resolves questions of the academy's activities and membership. The society's many divisions are directed by its Presidium under four sections: physical-technical and mathematical sciences; chemotechnical and biological sciences; earth sciences; and social sciences.

Founded in St. Petersburg in 1724 by Peter I the Great, the academy was opened in 1725 by his widow Catherine I as the Academy of Sciences and Arts. Subsequently known under various names, it assumed its present name in 1925. In its early decades, foreign scholars, notably the Swiss mathematicians Leonhard Euler and Daniel Bernoulli, worked in the academy. The first Russian member was Mikhail Vasilyevi Lomonosov, scientist and poet, who was elected in 1742 and contributed extensively to many branches of science. The society's highest prize, the Lomonosov Medal, bears his name.

Under the tsars, the academy was headed by members of court circles and controlled a small number of institutions. After 1917 the academy chose its president and expanded its activities as new scientific institutions arose throughout the Soviet Union. By 1934, when it transferred from Leningrad (formerly St. Petersburg) to Moscow, it embraced 25 institutes. By the late 20th century, the academy directed more than 260 institutions, including laboratories, naval institutes, observatories, research stations, and scientific societies. Its branches were spread throughout the Union republics.

Acadia, French ACADIE, North American Atlantic seaboard possessions of France in the 17th and 18th centuries. Centred in what is now Nova Scotia, Acadia was probably intended to include the other present Maritime Provinces of Canada as well as parts of Maine and Quebec.

The first organized French settlement in Acadia was founded in 1604 on an island in Passamaquoddy Bay, on the present U.S.–Canadian border, by Pierre de Monts and Samuel de Champlain. In 1605 the colony was moved to Port Royal (now Annapolis Royal, Nova Scotia), and that settlement became the centre of Acadia's future. Because the French claimed for Acadia lands also claimed by England, the colony was continually contested by both nations. In 1613 Port Royal was destroyed and its inhabitants were dispersed by an English military expedition from Virginia.

In 1621, James VI of Scotland awarded the lands of Acadia to Sir William Alexander for the purpose of founding the colony of Nova Scotia. In 1632 King Charles I of England ceded Acadia back to France, and, under the Company of New France, a renewed period of French colonization followed. A bitter struggle for power broke out in 1636 between two of the leading French officials of the colony—a struggle that eventually resulted in a local civil war. Acadia was under English rule from 1654 to 1670 and then reverted again to French rule and remained under French control for the next 40 years.

On Oct. 16, 1710, Port Royal was captured by the British. The Treaty of Utrecht (1713) gave Nova Scotia to Great Britain but left Cape Breton Island and Île St. Jean (from 1799 Prince Edward Island) with France. In 1755 many Acadians were deported because of the imminence of war with France, the question of Acadian neutrality, and the possibility of revolt. The long narrative poem *Evangeline* by Henry Wadsworth Longfellow deals with this expulsion and the subsequent settlement of a group of Acadians in Louisiana. At the conclusion of the French and Indian Wars in 1763, Île St. Jean and Cape Breton Island also formally came under British rule; the province of New Brunswick was separated from Nova Scotia in 1784. Some Acadians, and descendants of the group have formed a distinctive part of the population in some areas. *See also* Cajun.

Acadia National Park, park on the Atlantic coast of Maine, U.S., astride Frenchman Bay. It has an area of 60 sq mi (155 sq km) and was originally established as Sieur de Monts National Monument (1916). It became the first national park in the eastern United States, as Lafayette National Park in 1919, renamed Acadia in 1929 to preserve the historic name given to the region by the De Monts Commission in 1604.

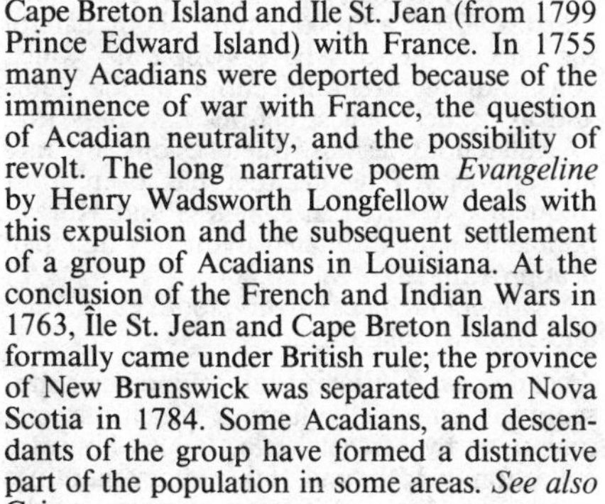

Great Head from Mount Desert Island, Acadia National Park, Maine

Josef Muench

Acadia National Park mainly comprises a rugged forested area on Mount Desert Island (*q.v.*), dominated by Cadillac Mountain and including Anemone Cave and Sieur de Monts Spring (site of the Nature Center and Abbe Museum, which displays Indian relics). Other segments include half of Isle au Haut, with its spectacular cliffs, and the Schoodic Peninsula on the mainland. Situated at the crossroads of northern and temperate zones, Acadia is biologically rich with about 50 species of birds and more than 500 kinds of flowering plants, while its cold, shallow gulf environment provides the area with an abundance of marine life.

Acadian orogeny, a mountain-building event that affected the northern portion of the Appalachian Geosyncline from New York to Newfoundland in Devonian time (the Devonian Period began 395,000,000 years ago and ended 345,000,000 years ago). Orogeny began during the Early Devonian in Gaspé, spread westward throughout Devonian time, and affected the western margins of the geosyncline in Late Devonian time. The orogeny was most intense in the Merrimac area in southern New England, in Maine, and extending northward to the Central Volcanic Belt of Newfoundland. Evidence for the Acadian orogeny consists of abundant angular unconformities (nonparallel strata) and igneous intrusions, regional metamorphism, and deformation of pre-Devonian and Devonian rocks; additionally, the westward spread of clastic sedimentary wedges and red beds probably resulted from Acadian uplift in the interior portions of the geosyncline. The Catskill Delta in New York and eastern Pennsylvania represents the westernmost and best developed of these clastic wedges.

The cause of the Acadian orogeny has been ascribed by advocates of the theory of plate tectonics to the collision of the northeastern portion of the North American Plate with western Europe.

Acajutla, Pacific seaport, Sonsonate department, El Salvador. Spanish conquistadores defeated the Indians there in 1524, and it later flourished as a colonial port. The old town has been rebuilt inland to make room for new port facilities. Acajutla is El Salvador's principal port and handles much of its coffee exports and shipments of sugar and balsam. It has an oil refinery and a fertilizer plant. Fish- and shell-processing industries and summer beach-resort facilities are also economic assets. Pop. (1980 est.) mun., 40,342.

Acámbaro, city, southeastern Guanajuato state, north central Mexico. It lies on the Río Lerma, in the central plateau, at 6,388 ft (1,947 m) above sea level. A Spanish settlement was founded there in 1526 on the site of a small Tarascan Indian village. With the construction of the Solís Reservoir, irrigation water became available to bring land under cultivation. Corn (maize), beans, wheat, and chick-peas are the principal crops. Cattle, sheep, and pig raising are also important. Much of Acámbaro's importance derives from its function as a rail and highway junction 45 mi (70 km) south of Celaya and 172 mi west-northwest of Mexico City. Pop. (1970) 32,257.

Acanthaceae, one of 18 families in the figwort order of flowering plants (Scrophulariales), containing about 250 genera and at least 2,500 species distributed mostly in tropical and subtropical regions of the world. Most are herbs or shrubs, but climbers (vines) and trees occur. The range of habitats extends from marshes to extremely dry situations, but most are found in damp tropical forests.

The family is characterized by simple leaves arranged in opposite pairs on the twigs, cystoliths (enlarged cells containing crystals of calcium carbonate) in streaks or protuberances in the vegetative parts, and bilaterally symmetrical, bisexual flowers that are usually

Acanthaceae, (top) *Jacobinia magnifica,* (centre) zebra plant (*Aphelandra squarrosa*), (bottom) *Acanthus spinosus*

(Top) Sven Samelius, (centre) Kitty Kohout from Root Resources—EB Inc., (bottom) B. Alfieri from the Natural History Photographic Agency—EB Inc.

crowded together in clusters and individually enclosed by leaflike bracts, often coloured and large. Sepals and petals number five or four each and are fused into tubular structures called the calyx and corolla. There are usually four or two stamens that arise from the corolla tissues and extend beyond the mouth of the flower; often there are one to three sterile stamens (staminodes). The pistil is superior (*i.e.*, positioned above the attachment point of the other flower parts) and consists of two fused ovule-bearing segments (carpels) enclosing two chambers (locules), each of which has two to many ovules in two rows along the central axis of the ovary. Seeds are borne on hooks on the placenta.

The group is mainly of horticultural interest and includes such ornamentals as bear's-breech (*Acanthus mollis*), clock vine (*Thunbergia*), shrimp plant (*Beloperone guttata*), and caricature plant (*Graptophyllum pictum*). The largest genera include *Jacobinia* (about 300 species), *Stobilanthes* (250), *Barleria* (230), *Aphelandra* (200), *Thunbergia* (200), *Dicliptera* (150), *Hypoestes* (150), *Blepharis* (100), *Dyschoriste* (100), *Lepidagathis* (100), and *Hygrophila* (80).

Acanthisittidae (bird family): *see* Xenicidae.

acanthocephalan: *see* spiny-headed worm.

acanthus, in architecture and decorative arts, a stylized ornamental motif based on a characteristic Mediterranean plant with jagged leaves, *Acanthus spinosus* (for illustration, *see* Acanthaceae). It was first used by the Greeks in the 5th century BC on temple roof ornaments, on wall friezes, and on the capital of the Corinthian column. One of the best examples of its use in the Corinthian order is the Erechtheum on the Athenian Acropolis. Later, the Romans used the motif in their Composite order, in which the capital of the column is a three-dimensional combination of spirals resembling rams' horns and full-bodied acanthus leaves. The acanthus leaf has been a popular motif in carved furniture decoration since the Renaissance.

Acapulco, in full ACAPULCO DE JUÁREZ, resort and port, Guerrero state, southwestern Mexico. Situated on a deep, semicircular bay, Acapulco has the best harbour on the Pacific coast of Mexico and one of the finest natural anchorages in the world. The town lies on a narrow strip of land between the bay and the steeply rising mountains that encircle it. From May to November the climate is hot and humid, but from December through April it is warm and pleasant. The harbour was discovered by Hernán Cortés in 1531, and a settlement was founded in 1550. It was designated a city in 1599. Acapulco was a main depot for Spanish colonial fleets plying between Mexico and the Orient, especially Manila, and continued to be a port of call for steamship lines between Panama and San Francisco and a major export point for coffee, sugar, and other products of the interior.

Acapulco has become the "Riviera of Mexico" for tourists attracted by the climate, the many luxurious hotels, excellent beaches, and deep-sea fishing. More than 300,000 visitors go there annually. No railroads connect to Acapulco, but the paving in 1940 of the Taxco–Acapulco link of the highway from Cuernavaca and Mexico City (288 mi [463 km] to the north-northeast) and frequent air service make it easily accessible. A summer school for foreigners, founded in 1955, provides tourists with courses on Mexican arts and archaeology.

Local industry is limited to the manufacture of woven sombreros, shellwork, confectionery, and other tourist-based products. Local historical attractions include the 18th-century Fort of San Diego, which houses a regional museum. Pop. (1980) 335,000.

The harbour at Acapulco, Mex.
Victor Englebert

Acaraí Mountains, also spelled ACARAHY or AKARAI, Portuguese SERRA ACARAÍ, low range on the border of Brazil (Pará state) and southern Guyana. The mountains, which rise to about 2,000 ft (600 m) above sea level, run in an east–west direction for about 80 mi (130 km) and form part of the northern watershed of the Amazon Basin. The whole area is covered with dense tropical rain forest and was mapped by satellite in the late 1970s.

acaricide: *see* miticide.

Acarie, Barbe-Jeanne Avrillot, Mme (French mystic): *see* Mary of the Incarnation.

Acarigua, city, northern Portuguesa state, northwestern Venezuela. Formerly the state capital, Acarigua is a principal commercial centre of the northern portion of the Llanos (plains), in which cattle, sugarcane, cotton, corn (maize), and rice are the principal products. Industries in the city include sawmilling and dairying. Acarigua is accessible by air and by highway from Guanare, the state capital, 50 mi (80 km) to the southwest, and from Barquisimeto, capital of Lara state, 50 mi north-northwest. The city has been designated a rail centre under Venezuela's railway expansion plan. Pop. (1981 est.) 126,000.

Acarina, subclass of the arthropod class Arachnida that includes the mite and tick (*qq.v.*).

Acarnania, district of ancient Greece bounded by the Ionian Sea, the Ambracian Gulf, Mt. Thyamus, and the Achelous River. Corinth founded several colonies on the coast of Acarnania in the 7th and 6th centuries BC. Originally a tribal unit, Acarnania developed into a federal state with generals and other magistrates, a council, and an assembly by the late 5th century; its capital was at the city of Stratus. With Athenian help, in the early years of the Peloponnesian War it repulsed Corinthian and Spartan attacks and enlarged its territory. In 388 it was compelled by Sparta to give up the Athenian alliance. It later came under Athenian, Theban, and Macedonian rule. In 314 the Acarnanians established a confederation of newly founded cities; but frontier disputes with Aetolia culminated in the partition of their country between Aetolia and Epirus (*c.* 243). The Epirote part of Acarnania recovered its independence in 231 and set up a new confederacy. By allying with Philip V of Macedon it succeeded in recovering some of its former territory. When Rome overthrew the Macedonian dynasty (167 BC), it deprived Acarnania of Leucas, the capital of the revived confederacy, and compelled it to send hostages to Rome; but the confederacy, with its capital at Thyrrheum, survived until Augustus incorporated many Acarnanians into his new city, Nicopolis Actia; the rest were included in the province of Achaea. In modern Greece Acarnania is linked with Aetolia in the *nomós* (department) Aitolía kai Akarnanía.

Consult the INDEX *first*

acatalasia, rare hereditary metabolic disorder caused by lack of the organic catalyst or enzyme called catalase. Although a deficiency of catalase activity is noted in many tissues of the body, including the red blood cells, bone marrow, liver, and skin, only about half of the affected persons have symptoms, which consist of recurrent infections of the gums and associated oral structures that may lead to gangrenous lesions. Such lesions are rare after puberty. The disorder has been most frequently reported in Japanese and Korean populations; its estimated frequency in Japan is approximately 2 in 100,000.

Treatment includes surgery, tooth extraction, and antimicrobial therapy.

Accademia, Galleria dell' (Florence), museum of art chiefly famous for its several sculptures by Michelangelo. It also houses a collection of 15th- and 16th-century paintings and a large body of Tuscan paintings of the 13th to the 16th century.

It was founded in 1784 by the grand duke Pietro Leopoldo and was subsequently enlarged. The main hall is devoted to 16th-century tapestries from Florence and Brussels.

Accademia della Crusca (literary academy): *see* Crusca, Accademia della.

Accademia dell'Arcadia (literary academy): *see* Arcadia, Accademia dell'.

Accademia di Venezia, Gallerie dell' (Venice), museum of art housing an unrivalled collection of paintings from the Venetian masters of the 13th through 18th century. There are outstanding works by Bellini, Giorgione, Titian, Tintoretto, Tiepolo, and Canaletto.

The galleries occupy the former monastery, church, and school of Sta. Maria della Carità. The core of the collection was assembled in 1756.

Accadian language: *see* Akkadian language.

acceleration, time rate at which a velocity is changing. Because velocity has both magnitude and direction, it is called a vector quantity; acceleration is also a vector quantity and must account for changes in both the magnitude and direction of a velocity. The velocity of a point or an object moving on a straight path can change in magnitude only; on a curved path, it may or may not change in magnitude, but it will always change in direction. This condition means that the acceleration of a point moving on a curved path can never be zero.

If the velocity of a point moving on a straight path is increasing (*i.e.,* if the speed, which is the magnitude of the velocity, is increasing), the acceleration vector will have the same direction as the velocity vector. If the velocity is decreasing (that is, the point or object is decelerating), the acceleration vector will point in the opposite direction. The average acceleration during a time interval is equal to the total change in the velocity during the interval divided by the time interval. The acceleration at any instant is equal to the limit of the ratio of the velocity change to the length of the time interval, as the time interval approaches zero.

When a point moves on a curved path, the component of the acceleration that results from the change in the direction of the velocity vector is perpendicular to the velocity vector and is directed inward, to the concave side of the path; its magnitude is given by the square of the velocity divided by the radius of curvature r of the path: $\mathbf{v}^2/r$. The change in the magnitude of $\mathbf{v}$ may be represented by another vector (that is, a second component of the acceleration) collinear with $\mathbf{v}$ and in the same direction if $\mathbf{v}$ is increasing and the opposite direction if $\mathbf{v}$ is decreasing. If velocity is stated in metres per second, acceleration will be stated in metres per second per second.

acceleration stress, physiological changes that occur in the human body in motion as a result of rapid increase of speed. Rapid acceleration and surges in acceleration are felt more critically than are gradual shifts. Pilots are especially subject to the effects of acceleration because of the high speeds at which they travel. Acceleration forces are measured in units of gravitational acceleration, or *g*. A force of three *g*, for example, is equivalent to an acceleration three times that of a body falling near the Earth.

Three kinds of acceleration stress are distinguished—positive, negative, and transverse—according to the position of the body with relation to the direction of acceleration.

Positive acceleration stress. Positive acceleration stress occurs when the direction of acceleration is along the long axis of the body from head to foot. As acceleration increases the force exerted on the pilot from one *g* to two *g*, there is an awareness of increased pressure and a general feeling of heaviness in the seat, hands, and feet. Three and four *g* further increase this sensation, and movement of the extremities becomes difficult; unless the trunk and head are supported, it may be difficult to keep them erect. The internal organs are pulled down in the body cavity and blood pressure falls. Eyesight may become limited, or there may be total blackout. The legs may feel congested and may have muscle cramps. Breathing may become difficult. If the acceleration is uneven or if the pilot is inexperienced, there may be mental confusion and disorientation. Unconsciousness can occur when the force exerted is from three to five *g*.

When acceleration is in the direction from head to feet, the blood is forced to the lower part of the body, and unconsciousness occurs when the brain fails to receive enough oxygen. Increased pressure in the extremities can cause rupture of the small blood vessels of the skin. The more gradual the acceleration, the less will be the fall in blood pressure, since the circulatory system is capable of making adjustments; but it takes about five seconds before this mechanism becomes fully activated.

There are seldom any aftereffects of acceleration in the direction from head to feet except for a few moments of mental confusion. There is usually no pain, though there may be some discomfort. Repeated exposures to such acceleration do not usually have permanent effects.

Negative acceleration stress. Negative acceleration stress occurs when the direction of acceleration is from feet to head. This causes a slight displacement of the internal organs in the abdomen and chest and a rush of blood to the face accompanied by the feeling of congestion. As the acceleration increases the congestion increases and throbbing pains are felt throughout the head. When the force is from 3 to 4.5 *g*, the eyes feel as though they are protruding, and there is a gritty feeling under the eyelids because of swelling in the small blood vessels. There may be temporary loss of vision or all objects may appear red; this latter condition is known as "red-out." The mental confusion that develops at high accelerations may lead to unconsciousness.

In acceleration in the direction from feet to head the blood pressure in the skull rises. In order to relieve the pressure in the skull the velocity of the blood flow to the rest of the body must be increased. Temporary cardiac arrest may occur at around 5 *g*. Respiration is also impaired because of the pressure upon the lungs from the abdominal contents and the muscular diaphragm (the wall between the chest and the abdomen). Bleeding can occur under the skin of the face; weak arteries or veins in the head region can rupture while under such stress. The average endurable times for negative stress are a few seconds at 5 *g*, 15 seconds for 4.5 *g*, and around 30 seconds for 3 *g*. Stunt fliers and pilots experienced with accelerations in the direction from feet to head seem to tolerate its effects better than new or inexperienced fliers.

Transverse acceleration stress. Transverse acceleration stress occurs when the direction of acceleration is sideways with relation to the long axis of the body. The effects of transverse acceleration are not as great as those of equivalent forces in the previous two cases. Thus, the position in which a pilot lies on his back at right angles to the direction of flight seems to be best for the high accelerations required to reach orbital velocity and reentry decelerations in manned space flight. Accelerations up to 6 *g* directed across the body produce only the sensations of increased pressure on that part of the body that supports the weight. As the force increases toward 8 *g*, breathing may become difficult because of the compression of the abdomen and chest. Accelerations of up to 12 *g* can be tolerated in transverse acceleration without undue discomfort or visual disorders. There may, however, be a slight increase in heart rate and blood pressure, and the blood oxygenation level seems to decrease with pressure.

It is speculated that future space flights may have acceleration forces of 15–20 *g* for one to two minutes and that additional protective measures may prove to be necessary. Breathing pure oxygen increases the blood's oxygen saturation level, and it is thought that certain heart stimulants may help to increase the heart output without affecting blood pressure, so that the circulatory system's capacity under stress is increased.

accelerator, in the rubber industry, any of numerous chemical substances that cause vulcanization (*q.v.*) of rubber to occur more rapidly or at lower temperatures. Many classes of compounds act as accelerators, the most important being organic materials containing sulfur and nitrogen, especially derivatives of benzothiazole.

The use of alkaline compounds of metals as vulcanization accelerators was cited in the original patent of the vulcanization process, granted to Charles Goodyear in 1844; magnesium oxide, zinc oxide, and basic lead carbonate were used until early in the 20th century, when the superiority of aniline, an organic compound, was discovered. Despite its toxicity, aniline was used as an accelerator for several years. Thiocarbanilide, less poisonous than aniline, succeeded it as the most important accelerator until it was displaced by mercaptobenzothiazole (MBT) about 1925. Compounds related to MBT have proved especially useful in vulcanizing synthetic rubbers.

During vulcanization the accelerator apparently converts the sulfur into a compound that reacts more rapidly with rubber than does sulfur itself. An alternative possibility is that the accelerator reacts first with the rubber, changing it into a form that combines rapidly with sulfur.

accelerator, particle: *see* particle accelerator.

accelerometer, instrument that measures the rate at which the velocity of an object is changing (*i.e.,* its acceleration). Acceleration cannot be measured directly. An accelerometer, therefore, measures the force exerted by restraints that are placed on a reference mass to hold its position fixed in an accelerating body. Acceleration is computed using the relationship between restraint force and acceleration given by Newton's second law: force = mass x acceleration.

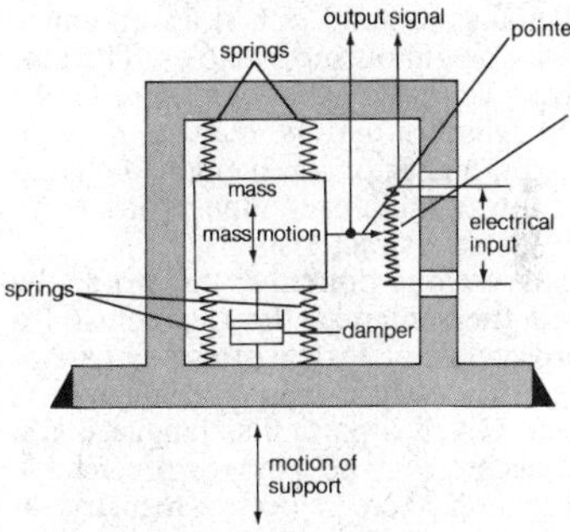

Accelerometer

The output of an accelerometer is usually in the form of either a varying electrical voltage or a displacement of a moving pointer over a fixed scale. The figure shows an accelerometer of the former type, called a spring-mass accelerometer. This device incorporates a mass suspended by four precisely designed and matched springs; movement of the mass is restrained by a damper. The accelerometer housing is solidly attached to the moving object.

As the object accelerates, inertia causes the suspended mass to lag behind as its housing moves ahead (accelerates with the object). The displacement of the suspended mass within its housing is proportional to the acceleration of the object. This displacement is converted to an electrical output by a pointer fixed to the mass moving over the surface of a potentiometer attached to the housing. Since the current supplied to the potentiometer remains constant, the movement of the pointer causes the output voltage to vary directly with the acceleration.

Specially designed accelerometers are used in applications as varied as control of industrial vibration test equipment, detection of earthquakes (seismographs), and input to navigational and inertial guidance systems. The design differences are primarily concerned with the method used to convert acceleration to a proportional electrical voltage. These methods include the direct pressure of a mass on a piezoelectric crystal and the electrically sensed displacement of a damped pendulum.

accent, also called STRESS, in music, momentary emphasis on a particular rhythmic or melodic detail; accent may be implied or specifically indicated, either graphically for example, >, —) or verbally (*sforzato*, abbreviated *sfz*). In metrically organized music, accents serve to articulate rhythmic groupings, especially in dances where regular accentuation facilitates the patterning of steps. As a rule, the heaviest accent falls on the first beat of the measure (actually it is the accent that determines where the measure begins). In compound metres a lesser accent marks the beginning of the second half of the measure (*e.g.*, the third beat in $\frac{4}{4}$ or the fourth in $\frac{6}{8}$).

Entire measures, also, may be subject to greater or lesser accentuation, which contributes vitally to meaningful phrasing, especially in periodically structured music. Dynamic accents, realized through a temporary increase in sonorous volume, are to be distinguished from agogic accents, produced by slight durational extensions. Regular implied accents may be temporarily displaced through the process known as syncopation (*q.v.*). In a typical instance, the accent on the first beat will be suppressed by a quarter rest followed by a half note (in $\frac{4}{4}$). Or, instead of being replaced by a rest, the first beat may be tied across the bar line to the last note of the preceding measure.

accent, in phonetics, that property of a syllable which makes it stand out in an utterance relative to its neighbouring syllables. The emphasis on the accented syllable relative to the unaccented syllables may be realized through greater length, higher or lower pitch, a changing pitch contour, greater loudness, or a combination of these characteristics.

Accent has various domains: the word, the phrase, and the sentence. Word accent (also called word stress, or lexical stress) is part of the characteristic way in which a language is pronounced. Given a particular language system, word accent may be fixed, or predictable (*e.g.*, in French, where it occurs regularly at the end of words, or in Czech, where it occurs initially), or it may be movable, as in English, which then leaves accent free to function to distinguish one word from another that is identical segmentally (*e.g.*, the noun permit versus the verb permit). Similarly, accent can be used at the phrasal level to distinguish sequences identical at the segmental level (*e.g.*, "light housekeeping" versus "lighthouse keeping," or "blackboard" versus "black board"). Finally, accent may be used at the sentence level to draw attention to one part of the sentence rather than another (*e.g.*, "What did you sign?" "I signed a *contract* to do some light housekeeping." versus "Who signed a contract?" "*I* signed a contract to do some light housekeeping.").

accentor, any of the 12 species of the bird genus *Prunella,* constituting the Old World family Prunellidae (order Passeriformes). They have thrushlike bills and rounded wings, and they frequently hop or move with a peculiar motion that has given them another name, shufflewing.

Accentors breed chiefly in mountains but winter at lower elevations. A widespread lowland species is the dunnock, or hedge sparrow (*P. modularis*), which nests in hedges and shrubbery evergreens. A typical member is the alpine accentor (*P. collaris*), of northwestern Africa and from Spain to Japan; 18 centimetres (7 inches) long and mostly brown, it has reddish-spotted flanks and a heavily stippled throat (sexes alike). In courtship the male warbles from a station near the ground or may ascend, larklike.

acceptance, short-term credit instrument consisting of a written order requiring a buyer to pay a specified sum at a given date to the seller, signed by the buyer as an indication of his intention to honour his obligation. Acceptances are used in financing export and import operations and in some domestic transactions involving staple commodities.

An exporter of goods, for example, may send such an order to pay to the buyer, who signs it to indicate his acceptance of the obligation and returns it to the exporter. The exporter can then obtain his payment promptly by selling the bill (or acceptance) to his bank at a discount. The buyer has obtained time (until the bill's maturity date) to dispose of the goods and obtain the funds to meet his obligation. This is known as a self-liquidating transaction, and this characteristic has given trade acceptances excellent credit standing (with consequent widespread use) in many countries. The acceptance market therefore provides investors with a means of employing temporarily excess funds for short periods of time with a minimum of risk.

If a bill of exchange is accepted by the buyer of the goods, it is known as a trade acceptance. If the bill is drawn against and accepted by a bank (commonly done when the buyer is not a widely known firm), it is called a banker's acceptance.

Accesi, Compagnia degli, company that performed commedia dell'arte (improvised popular Italian comedy) in the early 1600s. The name means "the stimulated." Leadership was provided by Tristano Martinelli (famous for his portrayal of Arlecchino, the mischievous servant) and Pier Maria Cecchini (known as the leading interpreter of the character Fritellino, as well as the author of valuable texts on the proper performance of commedia dell'arte).

The Accesi joined for a time with the Fedeli, another great Italian company under the direction of Giovambattista Andreini, but the wives of Cecchini and Andreini quarrelled, and the companies separated. The Accesi was one of the commedia troupes that became popular with European royalty and was known as the troupe of the duke of Mantua. The company was well received in the Habsburg empire at both Linz and Vienna and appeared several times in France, playing in Fontainebleau and such locations as the Hôtel de Bourgogne.

accessory, in law, a person who becomes equally guilty in the crime of another by knowingly and voluntarily aiding the criminal prior to or after the crime. An accessory is one kind of accomplice (*q.v.*), the other being an abettor, who aids the criminal during the act itself.

accessory mineral, any mineral in an igneous rock not essential to the naming of the rock. When it is present in small amounts, as is common, it is called a minor accessory. If the amount is greater or is of special significance, the mineral is called a varietal, or characterizing, accessory and may give a varietal name to the rock (*e.g.*, the mineral biotite in biotite granite). Accessory minerals characteristically are formed during the solidification of the rocks from the magma; in contrast are secondary minerals, which form at a later time through processes such as weathering by hydrothermal alteration. Common minor accessory minerals include topaz, zircon, corundum, fluorite, garnet, monazite, rutile, magnetite, ilmenite, allanite, and tourmaline. Typical varietal accessories include biotite, muscovite, amphibole, pyroxene, and olivine.

acciaccatura, in music, ornamental note sometimes confused with appoggiatura (*q.v.*).

Acciaiuoli, Niccolò (b. Sept. 12, 1310, Montegufoni, near Florence—d. Nov. 8, 1365, Naples), statesman, soldier, and grand seneschal of Naples who enjoyed a predominant position in the Neapolitan court.

Of a prominent and wealthy Florentine family, Acciaiuoli went to Naples in 1331 to direct the family's banking interests. In 1335 King Robert made him a knight, entrusted him with the care of his nephew Louis of Taranto, and bestowed upon him a series of fiefs in Apulia and in Greece.

After playing a major role in arranging the marriage between Louis of Taranto and Queen Joan I of Naples in 1347, Acciaiuoli became one of the most powerful men in the kingdom, being named grand seneschal in 1348. He defended Louis and Joan against the attack of Louis I of Hungary, who was seeking revenge for the assassination of his brother Andrew, Joan's first husband. Acciaiuoli finally regained the kingdom, having Louis of Taranto crowned king (May 27, 1352).

Acciaiuoli then led the conquest of almost all of Sicily (1356–57), put down a barons' revolt, and conquered Messina, for which he was created count of Malta and Gozo. In 1358 he defended Achaea, which was menaced by the Turks and the Catalans, and for this he was created lord of Corinth. He later consolidated his power in Messina, but following Louis of Taranto's death (1362), he returned to Naples in 1364 to defend Joan against another baronial revolt.

accidence: *see* inflection.

accidental, in music, sign placed immediately to the left of a note to show that the note must be changed in pitch. A sharp (♯) raises a note by a semitone; a flat (♭) lowers it by a semitone; a natural (♮) restores it to the original pitch. Double sharps (×) and double flats (♭♭) indicate that the note is raised or lowered by two semitones. A single natural cancels a double sharp or flat; a natural next to a sharp or flat (as ♮♯) cancels half of a double sharp or flat. Sharps or flats that are placed at the beginning of a musical staff indicate the tonality, or key, of the music and are not considered accidentals.

Accidentals were first applied to the note B, by about the 10th century. To fulfill certain theoretical and aesthetic rules, B was sometimes flatted and, later, F was sometimes sharped. At first there was no sign for a natural; a sharp (written ♯ or ♮) cancelled a flat, a flat cancelled a sharp. By the late Renaissance, E♭, A♭, and C♯ were fairly common. Accidentals applied to all notes became increasingly common in music of subsequent periods.

accipiter, any bird of the genus *Accipiter,* largest genus of the birds of prey, consisting of about 50 species of falconiform birds, or "bird" hawks, of the family Accipitridae. Sometimes accipiters are referred to as the "true" hawks. They have broad, short wings and comparatively long legs and tail. They range in size from the little sparrowhawk

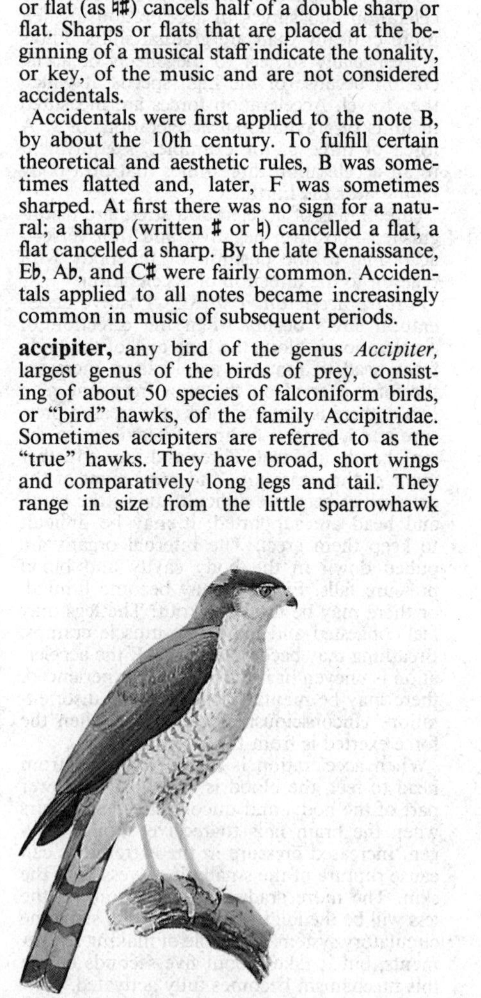

Sharp-shinned hawk (*Accipiter striatus*)
Albert E. Gilbert

(*A. minullus*) of Africa, slightly larger than a thrush, to the northern goshawk (*A. gentilis*), about 60 centimetres (2 feet) long.

Accipiters occur in forested areas throughout the world. They build soft-lined nests of sticks in tall trees. The three to five brown-blotched white eggs are incubated for four to five weeks by the female. The young fledge after five or six weeks. *See also* hawk; goshawk; sparrowhawk.

Accius, Lucius, Accius also spelled ATTIUS (b. 170 BC, Pisaurum, Umbria, Italy?—d. *c.* 86 BC), one of the greatest of the Roman tragic poets, in the view of his contemporaries. His plays (more than 40 titles are known, and about 700 lines survive) were mostly free translations from Greek tragedy, many from Euripides, with violent plots, flamboyant characterizations, and forceful rhetoric. His tragedies were performed until the end of the republic (*c.* 30 BC). Their themes were those of classical legend, particularly the Troy cycle, but Accius also composed two historical plays, *Decius* and *Brutus*, based on Roman history.

He also wrote several treatises: the *Didascalica*, a work on the history of Greek and Latin poetry; and *Annales*, which seems to deal with the calendar. Gellius, Varro, and other later grammarians refer to his observations on grammar and orthography. Cicero records having met Accius in his youth and having seen his plays. He quoted with admiration the famous line from Accius' *Atreus*, "*Oderint, dum metuant!*" ("Let them hate so long as they fear"), a motto that is said to have appealed to the tyrant Caligula.

acclimatization, any of the numerous gradual, long-term responses of an organism to changes in its environment. Such responses are more or less habitual and reversible should environmental conditions revert to an earlier state.

The numerous sudden changes that evoke rapid and short-term responses via the nervous and hormonal systems are not examples of acclimatization. An individual organism can regulate its internal processes rapidly to sustain itself within the usual range of environmental changes that it encounters hourly or daily. But this rapid regulation, or homeostasis, is limited in its operation to a small range of environmental variations. Homeostatic regulation usually cannot meet effectively large environmental changes such as those that would allow a plant or animal living in the warmth of summer to function in the cold of winter. As summer wanes, organisms change their substance and their habits in seeming anticipation of the coming winter. This gradual adjustment to conditions is acclimatization.

In contrast to changes that occur during growth and development, acclimatization, as defined above, refers to an adaptive change that is reversible when conditions return to their former condition. Acclimatization does not leave a lasting impression upon the genetic mechanisms of the acclimatized organism. The adaptation of populations to change that effects evolution by the selection of genetic capability is a different process from the acclimatization of an individual.

In dealing with acclimatization, the influence of climate upon life can be treated under headings of adjustments to temperature, humidity, salinity, light, pressure, and certain chemical substances in the environment. Because organisms do not have unlimited combinations of adaptations, they may use a similar process to adapt to changes of different origins. For example, in acclimatization to the low pressure of oxygen (hypoxia) in high mountains, animals, including man, improve the capacity of blood to transport oxygen by increasing the number of red blood cells (polycythemia); in the chronic disease emphysema, the inadequate supply of oxygen to the lungs is to some degree compensated for by a similar polycythemia.

Because animals and plants can be successfully introduced to new regions, it can be said that species do not necessarily thrive at their best potential in their native regions. Thus acclimatization does not invariably mean that a plant or animal is adapted to function at its maximum rate. In the hot summer, acclimatized birds and mammals often rest in the shade, and in winter cold some animals and all plants become dormant. At extreme limits an organism may suffer some impairment of vigour, but it survives; if the impairment is overt, acclimatization is considered inadequate.

Although acclimatization commonly requires modification of activity, the adaptive changes permit an organism to exploit regions of great seasonal variation and, on occasion, to move in wholly new environments. Only the individuals that acclimatize can survive to produce progeny from which a new population may become established. Ability to become acclimatized differs greatly among species of plants and animals. Some breeds of domesticated animals and cultivated plants are quite versatile in this ability, whereas others are narrowly restricted.

An interesting characteristic of seasonal acclimatization appears in animals and plants that become adjusted to cold beyond that which they are likely to encounter. Not only does acclimatization prepare them with a margin of safety but some microorganisms, insects, and plants tolerate experimental exposure at temperatures far colder or warmer than ever occur in nature. It seems strange that adaptability enables these organisms to be prepared to encounter conditions beyond their natural experience.

Another surprising characteristic of acclimatization is its anticipatory nature—it can develop before the change occurs. It would seem that anticipation of the need for change would be required in order to make the slow physiological preparations for climatic changes that often set in very suddenly. Anticipation of acclimatization seems to require a sense of time by which the coming environmental conditions can be predicted. Length of day is one external signal, but it seems to impinge upon intrinsic rhythms that provide clues from within as to the passage of time.

Although acclimatization refers basically to adaptation to climate, the term can also be used to describe the adjustments that a person makes to urban, social, or political conditions or the adaptation of a population of plants to conditions of cultivation or of an animal to the unnatural conditions of captivity. Adaptations to strange or artificial conditions, however, are often difficult to describe, and only in a few cases can such adaptations be compared with acclimatization.

accompaniment, in music, auxiliary part or parts of a composition designed to support the principal part or to throw it into relief. In secular medieval music and in much folk and non-European music, instrumental accompaniments for singers consist of unison or octave duplications of the melody (sometimes with slight differences, creating heterophony, the simultaneous performance of variant versions of the same melody), of novel rhythmic features, or of a drone (sustained note or notes) played on wind or stringed instruments. In 16th-century European music, solo songs were sung with simple lute accompaniments, both chordal and contrapuntal (using interwoven melodic lines); notable examples include the songs of the English composer John Dowland and the French *airs de cour* (courtly songs or airs).

The beginning of the 17th century saw the introduction of the thorough bass, or basso continuo, a type of harmonic accompaniment improvised at the harpsichord or organ and based on chords that the composer indicated by figures. By the 18th century, thorough bass accompaniments designed to support either a soloist, as in the sonatas and solo cantatas of J.S. Bach, or an instrumental ensemble, as in the operas of the Italian composer Alessandro Scarlatti, demanded from the performer a high degree of ornamental and contrapuntal invention. The accompaniment thus assumed a role as important as that of the soloist.

The term obbligato accompaniment came to be applied to accompaniments of this type, as opposed to ad libitum accompaniment, the unessential ornamentation or the optional reduplication of a part, performed on a secondary instrument. Obbligato accompaniments were sometimes written out, among them one originally improvised by Bach for a movement of his *Sonata in B Minor* for flute and harpsichord. In the second half of the 18th century the obbligato accompaniment assumed a primary role, gaining increased complexity and musical substance while the solo instrument was reduced to the role of an ad libitum accompaniment. Thus, Mozart followed the example of a contemporary composer, Johann Schobert, in writing four sonatas for harpsichord accompanied by the violin.

The influence of the obbligato style of the late 18th century is suggested in Beethoven's statement "I came into the world with obbligato accompaniment." Obbligato style persisted into the 19th century in both solo and concerted works of the Romantic composers, in which accompaniments became even more elaborate and expressive. The expressive resources of the piano allowed the accompaniments of Schubert to illustrate pictorial or psychological aspects of the texts of his lieder ("songs"). His example was followed in the lieder of Schumann, Brahms, and Hugo Wolf. Piano accompaniments in works for string or wind instruments acquired the status of a concerted part. Orchestral accompaniment was greatly developed in the Romantic concerto and in songs and song cycles with orchestra by numerous composers from Hector Berlioz (1803–69) to Alban Berg (1885–1935) and Benjamin Britten (1913–76).

The art of piano accompaniment flourished chiefly in response to the demands in the 19th century of the German lied and the French *mélodie.* Qualities of poetic and musical insight and also of ensemble playing distinguish the piano accompanist's art, which resembles the art of performance in chamber music. In the 20th century, accompanists such as the English pianist Gerald Moore and the Dutch pianist Coenraad Valentyn Bos developed the art by their sensitive attitude to the soloist and by their power to interpret the composer's intention. Both Moore and Bos have written valuable books on the art of accompaniment.

accomplice, in law, a person who becomes equally guilty in the crime of another by knowingly and voluntarily aiding the other to commit the offense. An accomplice is either an accessory or an abettor. The accessory aids a criminal prior to his crime, whereas the abettor aids him during the act itself.

An abettor is one who is present actually or constructively at the commission of a crime and incites, encourages, or assists the offender in his act. One may assist the offender by failing to try to prevent the offense, when a duty to act is imposed by law.

An accessory is one who is not present during the commission of the offense but who assists, procures, encourages, or counsels the offender prior to the crime. In most jurisdictions the accessory must perform an act of assistance, and there must be evidence that he intended to facilitate the crime. Thus, the owner of a sporting-goods store will not be guilty of murder if he sells a rifle to one who subsequently commits murder with it.

The terms accessory and abettor derive from the English common law, which distinguished between accomplices and principals in assessing guilt for crime. Modern statutes abolish these differences, consider all accomplices as principals, and punish all equally. It is no longer necessary to prove which kind of an accomplice a person is or to find the principal guilty before the accomplice can be convicted. Once a crime has been committed and a party is shown to have contributed to its commission, he may be punished as a principal.

The statutes continue to recognize a separate offense—that of being an "accessory after the fact." Such an offender is one who harbours, protects, or assists a person who has already committed an offense or is charged with committing an offense. Usually the offense must be a felony. Punishment for an accessory after the fact is universally less than that for the principal offender, except in cases of sedition or treason. *See also* solicitation.

accordion, French ACCORDÉON, German ZIEHHARMONIKA, free-reed portable musical instrument, patented in 1822 under the name *Handäoline* by Friedrich Buschmann in Berlin and in 1829 under the name *Akkordion* (German: "harmony") by Cyril Demian in Vienna. The free reed of an accordion is a metal tongue fastened over a slot accurately cut in a metal frame. The reed is sprung up above its frame and vibrates when air flows around it from this upper side; airflow in the opposite

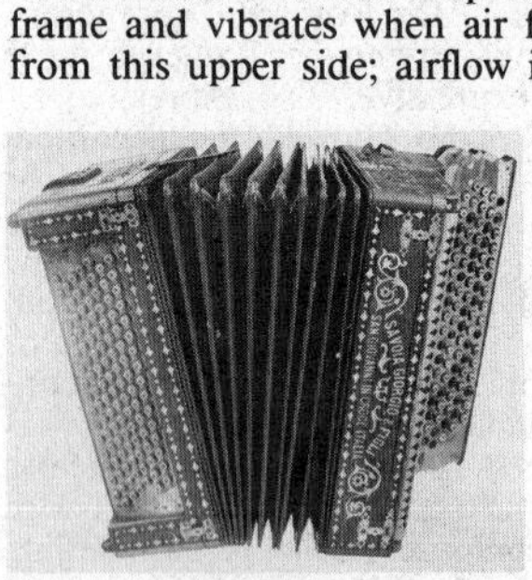

Italian accordion, 19th century
Richard Saunders—Scope Associates, Inc.

direction does not cause vibration. The reed sounds a definite pitch and can be tuned by filing near the free end to raise the pitch and near the fixed end to lower it. In an accordion, a bellows is fastened between two oblong wooden structures that carry the reeds. Wind is admitted to the reeds selectively through pallet valves controlled by a keyboard or set of finger buttons. Each key or button admits wind to a pair of reeds, one of which is mounted to sound on the press of the bellows, the other, on the draw.

In some accordions, including the earliest ones, the paired reeds sound adjacent notes of the scale, so that a button will give, for instance, G on the press and A on the draw ("single action"). With a single action, 10 buttons suffice for a diatonic (seven-note scale) compass of more than two octaves, with each note available with a bellows movement in one direction only. For the left hand there are typically two keys, or basses, one providing a bass note, the other a major chord. These sound the tonic (keynote and chord) on the press and the dominant (fifth note and chord) on the draw in the tonality (key) of the melody reeds.

This single action has been developed, chiefly in Austria and Switzerland, by adding a second row of buttons giving the F scale (the first-row scale being C), so arranged that almost every note of the diatonic series is available both with a C-row button on the press and an F-row button on the draw, or vice versa. Semitones are provided by additional rows, and the number of basses is increased.

The piano accordion, with piano-style keyboard for the right hand, was patented by M. Bouton of Paris in 1852 and was later perfected in Italy by Mariano Dallapé. In its "double action," the two reeds of each pair are tuned to the same note, thus making every note and bass available from the same key with both directions of bellows movement. Steel reeds, instead of brass, give a steadier pitch. Couplers or "registers," developed by the 1930s, bring into action extra sets of reeds, one pitched an octave below the main set and another off-tuned from the main set to give a tremulant through "beating" (sound-wave interference). Other registers may include a high-octave set and a second tremulant. Each set may be used alone or with others.

The left-hand provision is also extended, with up to 140 basses actuated by seven rows of buttons. Two rows give bass notes arranged in cyclic order of tonalities (D, G, C, F, etc.), one row being offset against the other at the interval of a major third for convenience in fingering melodic passages in the bass. The other rows give three-note chords, respectively, major and minor triads and dominant and diminished sevenths. There are up to five registers for the basses, causing each bass note to sound over as many as five octaves if desired and each chord to sound in three.

A variant of the accordion is the bandoneon, a double-action instrument with square shape and finger buttons, invented by Heinrich Band of Krefeld, Ger., and the leading solo instrument in modern Argentine tango orchestras. For precursors of the free-reed instruments, *see* sheng; for other types, *see* concertina; harmonica; harmonium.

Accorso, Francisco (legal scholar): *see* Accursius, Franciscus.

account payable, any amount owed by a company as the result of a purchase of goods or services from another company on a credit basis. Under a trade-credit arrangement, the purchasing company, after placing its order with the seller, receives the goods and an invoice denoting the price of the goods and the terms for payment. The purchasing firm does not send a trade acceptance or promissory note for payment but enters the amount owed as a current liability in its accounts.

Companies incur this type of short-term debt primarily to finance their inventories; if inventory turnover is rapid within an industry, a company may be expected to have large accounts payable. Within any given industry, smaller companies are more likely to make use of this type of trade credit because they are less able to pay cash and take advantage of discounts than larger companies and have fewer sources of credit open to them.

Accounts payable are a customary means of conducting domestic trade in the U.S. In international trade and in the domestic trade of many European countries, the use of the acceptance and promissory note is common. *Compare* account receivable.

account receivable, any amount owed to a business by a customer as a result of a purchase of goods or services from it on a credit basis. The company making the sale does not receive an acceptance or promissory note (*qq.v.*) from the purchaser but merely enters the amount due as a current asset in its books. Accounts receivable constitute a major portion of the assets of many companies and tend to vary directly with sales.

Accounts receivable may be sold to finance companies or pledged as collateral to obtain loans from commercial banks or finance companies. This kind of financing differs from factoring (*q.v.*) in that the company's customers are not notified that their accounts have been sold or pledged as collateral, and the company remains responsible for credit losses. This type of financing is frequently employed by smaller companies that cannot obtain additional credit from commercial banks and have no other highly liquid assets to offer as security.

Although it offers a flexible source of credit, varying with the volume of sales, accounts-receivable financing is considered a relatively expensive form of borrowing. *Compare* account payable.

accounting, the systematic development and analysis of information about the economic affairs of an organization. Every business and many organizations that are not businesses, up to and including nations, are continually engaged in transactions involving money or goods or both. Interested and responsible parties must have access to the information necessary for assessing the organization's economic status and performance.

A brief treatment of accounting follows. For full treatment, *see* MACROPAEDIA: Accounting.

The actual recording and summarizing of financial transactions in accordance with well-established procedures is known as bookkeeping (*q.v.*). When the data thus produced are abstracted in reports (typically produced on an annual basis) published for the use of persons outside the organization—stockholders, creditors, brokers, government officials, and others—the process is called financial accounting. The process of producing reports (typically on a monthly basis) for the use of the management of the organization in planning and monitoring activities is called managerial accounting. Accounting systems also serve to produce the internal financial documents needed in the ordinary course of operations, to institute systems of internal controls for the protection of the organization's assets, and to provide data needed for tax returns and other legally required reporting.

The periodic reports generated in financial accounting are usually four in number: the balance sheet, which summarizes, as of a specified date, the assets or resources controlled by the firm, the liabilities of the firm to creditors, and the owners' equity, that is, the funds provided by the owners (usually in exchange for shares of capital stock) plus the sum of earnings retained by the organization; the income statement, which reports the gross proceeds of the organization's operations for a specified period, the expenses incurred in those operations, and the net proceeds; the statement of changes in retained earnings, which details the disposition of net income between dividends paid to shareholders and the addition to retained earnings for the period in question; and the statement of sources and uses of funds, which analyzes the flow of funds (typically defined as cash or as working capital) into and out of the organization during the period.

A large number of conventions and practical guidelines govern the difficult questions of valuing assets, distributing the costs of assets over time (a process known as amortization, or depreciation), measuring income, matching expenses to corresponding revenues, and adjusting costs for changes in the purchasing power of money. The reports prepared for an organization by its accountant are ordinarily reviewed by outside auditors for completeness, accuracy, and adherence to conventional practices; these auditors are independent accountants who in the United States bear the title of certified public accountant (CPA) and in Great Britain are known as chartered accountants.

Managerial accounting aims to provide management with reliable and timely information on the various costs of operations and on standards with which those costs can be compared, to assist in the development of budgetary plans and in the measurement of performance against those plans, and to analyze the results of operations (in businesses, profits). The forecasts of cash requirements for given kinds and levels of operations that are provided by accountants to managers are essential to assure that the organization will remain liquid—able to meet its obligations as they fall due—while quantified profit plans form an integral part of any rational business strategy.

accounting machine, also called BOOKKEEPING MACHINE, office machine capable of performing normal bookkeeping functions, such as tabulating in vertical columns, performing arithmetic functions, and typing horizontal rows. The billing machine is a class of accounting machine designed to typewrite names, addresses, and descriptions, to multiply and extend, to compute discounts, and to add net total, posting the requisite data to the proper accounts, and so to prepare a customer's bill automatically once the operator has entered the necessary information.

Early accounting machines were marvels of mechanical complexity, often combining a typewriter and various kinds of calculator elements. The refinements in speed and capacity made possible by advances in electronics technology quickly reduced the size, noise, and operating complexity of these machines. Many of the newer "generations" of accounting machines are operated by a computer to which they are permanently connected.

Accra, capital and largest city of Ghana, on the Gulf of Guinea (Atlantic Ocean). The city lies partly on a cliff, 25 to 40 ft (8 to 12 m) high, and is backed by the undulating Accra plains. The land, being flat, floods readily. Its susceptibility to faulting is the cause of frequent earthquakes.

When the Portuguese first settled on the coast of what is now Ghana in 1482, the present site of Accra was occupied by several villages of the Ga tribe, ruled from a parent settlement, Ayaso (Ayawaso), located about 15 mi (24 km) north. Between 1650 and 1680 the Europeans built three fortified trading posts—Ft. James (English), Ft. Crevecoeur (Dutch), and Christiansborg Castle (Danish). While these European posts were being constructed, Ayaso was destroyed in a tribal war, and its population, together with that of the other major Ga towns on the Accra plains, was drawn to the coast by the prospect of profitable trade with the Europeans. As a result, three coastal villages—Osu (Christiansborg), Dutch Accra (later called Ussher Town), and James Town—sprang up, becoming the nuclei of what was to be Accra. The name Accra itself is a corruption of the Akan word *nkran.* It refers to the black ants that abound in the vicinity. It came to be applied to the inhabitants of this part of the Accra plains.

Accra grew into a prosperous trading centre. The Danes and the Dutch left the region in 1850 and 1872, respectively, and in 1877 Accra became the capital of the British Gold Coast colony. In 1898 a municipal council was formed to improve the town. By the 1930s Accra was systematically laid out.

Accra is the administrative, economic, and educational centre of Ghana. The city contains the head offices of all of the large banks and trading firms, the insurance agencies, the electricity corporation, the general post office, the large open markets to which most of the food supply comes, and the Accra Central Library.

In addition to the forts, important buildings include the Korle Bu General Hospital, which also houses the Ghana Medical School; the Holy Spirit (Roman Catholic), Holy Trinity (Anglican), and Methodist cathedrals; the national archives; and the national musuem. Also located in the city are the offices of the Council for Scientific and Industrial Research and the Ghana Academy of Arts and Sciences. The University of Ghana (1948) is located at Legon, to the north. In addition, there is a football stadium and a race course in the city. Independence Arch, in Black Star Square, is used for ceremonial parades.

Accra has well-paved roads and a good municipal bus service. A transportation hub, the city is also connected by rail to Kumasi, in the interior, and to the port city of Tema, 17 mi to the east, which has taken over Accra's port function. Accra is a terminus of the internal air service and has Ghana's only international airport, Kotoka International Airport. The chief manufactures are processed food, lumber, and textiles. Pop. (1982 est.) city, 1,045,-381; (1980) metropolitan area, 1,142,690.

acculturation, the processes of change in artifacts, customs, and beliefs that result from the contact of societies with different cultural traditions. The term is also used to refer to the results of such changes.

Two major types of acculturation may be distinguished based on two classes of conditions under which changes take place. A free "borrowing" and modification of cultural elements may occur when people of different cultures maintain an interchange without the exercise of military or political domination of one group by another. These new elements may be integrated into the existing culture in a process called incorporation. The unconquered Navajo Indians, in frequent and varied contact with Spanish colonists in the 18th century, selected elements of Spanish culture such as clothing and metalworking techniques that were integrated into their own culture in their own way.

Directed change, the second type of acculturation, takes place when one people establishes dominance over another through military conquest or political control. Directed change characterized the Roman conquest of the Mediterranean region and western Europe, the American conquest of the North American Indians, the European domination of Africa, and many other political expansions.

Directed culture change, like incorporation, involves selection and modification, but the processes are more varied and the results more complex because they result from the interference in one cultural system by members of another. The processes that operate under conditions of directed change include assimilation, the almost complete replacement of one culture by another; cultural fusion, a new synthesis of cultural elements differing from both precontact cultures; and reaction against aspects of the dominant culture.

Accursius, Franciscus (Latin), Italian FRANCISCO ACCORSO (b. *c.* 1182, Bagnolo, Tuscany—d. *c.* 1260, Bologna), the leading jurist of the 13th century, a legal scholar responsible for the renovation of Roman law. He was the last of a series of legal glossators (annotators) of Justinian's compilation of Roman law, his authoritative *Glossa ordinaria,* also called the *Glossa magna* (the "Great Gloss"; 1220–50), so far surpassing the glosses of earlier scholars that those works were rendered obsolete. For the next 500 years the *Glossa* of Accursius remained an indispensable complement to the texts of Roman law.

A professor at the University of Bologna, Accursius had access to the many legal works of the Romans that had been brought from Ravenna in the 11th century, when the institution at Bologna was first established as a law school. One result of Accursius' definitive compilation was the popularity of Roman law as a course of study during the Renaissance period. Accursius' interpretations of Roman law influenced the development of later European legal codes, among them the Code Napoleon, or French Civil Code, enacted in the early 19th century.

accused, rights of, in law, rights and privileges of a person accused of a crime, guaranteeing him a fair trial. These rights were initially (generally from the 18th century on) confined primarily to the actual trial itself, but in the second half of the 20th century many countries have begun to extend them to the periods before and after the trial.

All legal systems provide, at least on paper, guarantees that insure certain basic rights of the accused. These include right to trial by jury (unless jury trial is waived), to representation by counsel (at least when he is accused of a serious crime), to present witnesses and evidence that will enable him to prove his innocence, and to confront (*i.e.,* cross-examine) his accusers, as well as freedom from unreasonable searches and seizures and freedom from double jeopardy.

Certain very general rights are attached to the process. An accused person must not be allowed to languish indefinitely in jail but must be given a speedy trial. Involved with this issue are the rights to a reasonable bail and prohibitions against being detained for more than a specified time without bail.

The most important right has been the right to be represented by counsel. During the second half of the 20th century this right has been extended to cover the time when a person is arrested until final appeal. Different countries set different times at which an accused must be provided with counsel as well as different types of crimes for which counsel must be provided if the accused is indigent. The United States has made the most far-reaching changes in this area and has set a pattern that other nations have begun to emulate. Essentially, the U.S. system stipulates that the accused has the right to counsel from the time that he is taken into custody until all appeal is exhausted. The Supreme Court has ruled, moreover, that where the accused is indigent, the right to counsel must be implemented by the provision of a court-appointed lawyer in the case of all crimes for which punishment may be imprisonment. Further, at the time of his arrest the accused must be notified of both this right to counsel and the right not to answer any questions that might produce evidence against him (*see* Miranda v. Arizona). Both rights were introduced to prevent the police from extracting involuntary confessions to be used as evidence in court.

In civil-law countries such as France and Germany, there is less emphasis on the importance of the confession as evidence. It is considered merely as one piece of evidence. Because confessions are not as important, rights to counsel and to remain silent are less clearly defined. As a result, particularly in France, certain abuses have existed during the period of interrogation.

Other important rights guaranteed to the accused are those that protect him from illegally gathered evidence, be it from search and seizure (*q.v.*) or electronic eavesdropping (*q.v.*). Also important are the rights to appeal, which vary from country to country (*see* appeal).

Aceh, also spelled ACHEH, ACHIN or ATJEH, *daerah istimewa* (special district) of Sumatra, Indonesia, forming the northern extremity of the island. The boundary with Sumatera Utara *propinsi* (North Sumatra province) to the east extends north–south from Salahaji on the eastern coast just north of Teluk (bay) Aru to a point on the western coast about midway between Singkilbaru and Barus. Aceh, covering an area of 21, 387 sq mi (55,392 sq km), is mountainous, with Gunung (mount) Abongabong rising to an elevation of 9,793 ft (2,985 m). Except in the extreme north, there is a fairly wide coastal plain and the rivers are short and have little value for shipping.

The west central and southwestern coasts are dotted with swamps. The interior volcanic mountains are covered by temperate and tropical rain forests including stemless palm, oak, conifers, and laurel. Mosses and herbaceous plants carpet the ground and the lower trunks of trees.

Pole, a Buddhist state that flourished *c.* AD 500 in northern Sumatra, was visited by Arab, Indian, and Chinese merchants and pilgrims. In the 13th century, Aceh became the first Muslim stronghold in the archipelago and was visited by English explorers (in 1591) and by the Dutch. Its power reached its height in the time of Sultan Iskandar Muda (1607–36). In that period there were frequent wars with the Portuguese at Malacca, and the Portuguese fleet was defeated at Bintan in 1614. The Dutch (1599) and the English (1602) tried unsuccessfully to establish trading settlements in Aceh. After a short-lived alliance (1641) with the Dutch, the sultanate of Aceh declined in influence. After the Napoleonic Wars, when the East Indies were restored to the Netherlands, the British tried to keep Dutch influence out of Aceh, and an 1824 treaty stipulated that no hostile actions be undertaken. This reservation was withdrawn in 1873, the Dutch occupied Banda Aceh city, and more than 25 years of open warfare (the Aceh War) ensued between the Achinese and the Dutch. Tuanku Danel Syah, the Achinese Sultan, surrendered to the Dutch in 1903 and was exiled in 1905. Until the end of Dutch colonial rule, however, the area was never fully pacified. In 1942 Aceh revolted once more against the Dutch, shortly before the area was occupied by the Japanese. In 1945 a civil war between pro-republican forces (led by the Ulamas) and the aristocratic administrators (the Uleebalangs) erupted after the Japanese withdrew. Aceh became an autonomous province in 1949 and amalgamated with Sumatera Utara province in 1950. Under the Indonesian republic the people continued to be restive, with open rebellion in 1953; and the creation of Aceh as a special district, administratively equal with the country's other provinces, in 1956 did not solve the problem.

The Achinese, a people of Malay stock who are devout Muslims, occupy the lowlands and adjoining hills and constitute more than 90 percent of the population. In the highlands live the Gajo, also Muslims but related to the Batak. Rice is the food staple together with corn (maize), sweet potatoes, yams, and pulses (legumes). Pepper, copra, areca nuts, and rubber are the chief exports. Bauxite and coal are mined. There are some oil fields and increasingly important natural gas fields on the eastern coast; Lhokseumawe is being developed as a petroleum and liquefied-natural-gas terminal to facilitate the exploitation of these deposits. Industries and crafts produce processed foods, textiles, metalware, gold jewelry and filigree work, wood carvings, and engraved metal products. During the Dutch period a narrow-gauge railway serviced the eastern coast between Kutaradja (Banda Aceh) and Medan; this railway has fallen into disrepair, and only isolated portions are used. Principal ports are Ulseelheue, Sigli, Lhokseumawe, and Idfi, but large vessels can use the free port of Sabang on Pulau (island) We, 50 mi (80 km) north of Uleelheue. The capital of the province, Banda Aceh (formerly Kutaradja), is on the Krueng (river) Aceh, 3 mi from the sea, and is connected by a major road with Medan. The district has four wildlife sanctuaries. Pop. (1980) 2,611,271.

Aceraceae, the maple family of flowering plants, in the order Sapindales, comprising about 200 species of trees and shrubs in 2 genera, *Dipteronia* (2 species) of central and southern China, and *Acer,* the maples, widely

Hedge maple (*Acer campestre*)
A to Z Botanical Collection—EB Inc.

distributed in the Northern Hemisphere, crossing the Equator only in Malaysia. In *Dipteronia* the seed is surrounded by a wing; in *Acer* it is winged only on the back. Leaves of maples are opposite, simple, or compound (divided into separate leaflets), and usually toothed or lobed. The small, clustered flowers are mostly unisexual and are sometimes without petals. The fruit, a samara (a winged nutlet), splits into two (rarely three) winged,

Bigleaf maple (*Acer macrophyllum*)
R.F. Thorne

one-seeded parts. Many maples are cultivated for ornament and shade. Maples have a watery, sweet sap that in some species, especially sugar maple (*A. saccharum*), is used to make syrup and sugar. Certain species of *Acer* are also important timber trees. *See also* box elder; maple.

Acernus (poet): *see* Klonowic, Sebastian (Fabian).

acerola: *see* Barbados cherry.

A list of the abbreviations used in the MICROPAEDIA *will be found at the end of this volume*

acervulus, an open, saucer-shaped asexual fruiting body found in fungi (division Mycota). Always developed below the epidermis of the host tissue, it bears conidiophores (specialized filaments, or hyphae) that form conidia (spores).

Acestes, in Greek mythology, legendary king of Segesta (Greek Egesta) in Sicily. His mother, Egesta, had been sent from Troy by her parents to save her from being devoured by a sea serpent. Going to Sicily she met the river god Crimisus, by whom she became the mother of Acestes.

Acestes appears notably in the *Aeneid;* his function is to emphasize the mythological connection of Sicily with Troy; in Greek legend Aeneas, whose descendants founded Rome, travelled no farther than Sicily. Acestes brought the funeral games of Anchises, Aeneas' father, to a climax by shooting into the air an arrow that became a comet, a sign of Anchises' eternal life.

Acetabularia, genus of one-celled, umbrella-like green algae found in subtropical seas and sometimes called the "mermaid's wine glass." At the top of the tall, slender stalk, 0.5 to 10 centimetres (0.2 to 3.9 inches) long, is a ring of branches that may fuse to form a cap. Near the base of its stalk, *Acetabularia* has a large nucleus that divides many times when the alga matures and reproductive structures form; streaming cytoplasm carries the daughter nuclei to the saclike sporangium or umbrella lobe. Because part of one species can be

Acetabularia from Cholla Bay, Mex.
Robert W. Hoshaw—EB Inc.

grafted onto another, *Acetabularia* has been used to study the genetic control of growth and development.

acetaldehyde, also called ETHANAL (CH_3CHO), an aldehyde used as a starting material in the synthesis of acetic acid, *n*-butyl alcohol, ethyl acetate, and other chemical compounds. It is manufactured by the oxidation of ethyl alcohol and by the hydration of acetylene. Pure acetaldehyde is a colourless, flammable liquid with pungent, fruity odour; it boils at 20.8° C.

acetaminophen, drug used as an alternative to aspirin to relieve mild pain, such as tension headache and pain in joints and muscles, and to reduce fever. It is formed in the body from acetanilide or phenacetin, which were formerly common drugs, and is responsible for their analgesic effects. It lacks many side effects of aspirin, but overdosages can cause fatal hepatic damage. Unlike aspirin, it has a weak antiinflammatory effect. For prolonged use, aspirin and sodium salicylate are considered safer.

acetanilide, synthetic organic compound introduced in therapy in 1886 as a fever-reducing drug. Its effectiveness in relieving pain was discovered soon thereafter, and it was used as an alternative to aspirin for many years in treating such common complaints as headache, menstrual cramps, and rheumatism. Excessive or prolonged use engenders toxic side effects: it interferes with the function of hemoglobin, the oxygen-carrying pigment of the blood. In the body acetanilide is mostly converted to acetaminophen, which has replaced acetanilide in therapy because it is less likely to induce blood disorders (though overdoses of it can damage the liver).

acetate (textile): *see* cellulose acetate.

acetic acid, also called ETHANOIC ACID (CH_3COOH), the most important of the carboxylic acids. A dilute solution of acetic acid produced by fermentation and oxidation of natural carbohydrates is called vinegar (*q.v.*); a salt, ester, or acylal of acetic acid is called acetate. Industrially, acetic acid is used in the preparation of metal acetates, used in some printing processes; vinyl acetate, employed in the production of plastics; cellulose acetate, a major ingredient in photographic films and textiles; and volatile organic esters (such as ethyl and butyl acetates), which are widely used as solvents for resins, paints, and lacquers. Biologically, acetic acid is an important metabolic intermediate, and it occurs naturally in body fluids and plant juices.

Besides that produced as vinegar, vast amounts of acetic acid are prepared synthetically. In one common process acetylene is hydrated to acetaldehyde, which is then oxidized to acetic acid. Ethyl alcohol also is converted industrially to acetic acid by oxidation.

Pure acetic acid, often called glacial acetic acid, is a corrosive, colourless liquid (boiling point, 117.9° C; melting point, 16.6° C), completely miscible with water.

acetoacetic ester: *see* ethyl acetoacetate.

acetone, also called 2-PROPANONE, or DIMETHYL KETONE (CH_3COCH_3), the simplest representative of the aliphatic ketones and a widely used solvent. Because of its ability to dissolve cellulose acetates and nitrates, acetone is used extensively in the manufacture of artificial fibres and explosives. It is also employed as a starting material in the synthesis of many compounds. Physiologically, acetone is a minor constituent of normal blood and urine; in diabetic patients it is produced in large amounts.

Acetone is prepared commercially on a large scale by the dehydrogenation of isopropyl alcohol.

Pure acetone is a colourless, fragrant, flammable, mobile liquid boiling at 56.2° C.

acetophenetidin, also called PHENACETIN, aniline derivative used as a mild analgesic. This drug, which has antipyretic (fever-reducing) as well as analgesic effects, may be used alone or in combination with aspirin and either caffeine or codeine; such combinations are called APC mixtures. Because of the possible kidney damage that may be caused by high doses and prolonged use of acetophenetidin, aspirin is sometimes used as a substitute, even though the latter may cause some gastrointestinal irritation.

acetophenone ($C_6H_5COCH_3$), an organic compound used as an ingredient in perfumes and as a chemical intermediate in the manufacture of pharmaceuticals, resins, flavouring agents, and a form of tear gas. It also has been used as a drug to induce sleep.

The compound can be synthesized from benzene and acetyl chloride, but it is prepared commercially by the air oxidation of ethylbenzene.

acetylcholine (ACh), an ester of choline and acetic acid that is the transmitter substance at many nervous synapses and at the motor end-plate of vertebrate muscles (*see* end-plate potential). When a nerve impulse arrives at the nerve ending, ACh, which is stored there in the form of granules, is released and combines with a receptor molecule in the postsynaptic membrane or the end-plate membrane of a muscle fibre. Here, it changes the permeability of the membrane, and a change in the nature of a generator potential results. The effects of successive nerve impulses accumulate if they arrive at a sufficiently high frequency. The ACh is destroyed by an enzyme, acetylcholin-esterase, and thus is effective only briefly. Inhibitors of the enzyme, however, prolong the lifetime of ACh itself.

ACh was first isolated around 1914; its functional significance was first established around 1920 by Otto Loewi, a German physiologist and Nobel laureate, when he showed that ACh is the substance liberated when the vagus nerve is stimulated, causing slowing of the heartbeat. Subsequently he and others showed that ACh is also liberated as transmitter at the motor end-plate of striated (voluntary) muscles of vertebrates, and it has since been identified as transmitter at many neural synapses and in many invertebrate systems as well.

acetylene, also called ETHYNE, the simplest and best known member of the hydrocarbon series containing one or more pairs of carbon atoms linked by triple bonds, called the acetylenic series, or alkynes. It is a colourless, inflammable gas widely used as a fuel in oxyacetylene welding and cutting of metals and as raw material in the synthesis of many organic chemicals and plastics.

Pure acetylene is a colourless gas with a pleasant odour; as prepared from calcium carbide it usually contains traces of phosphine that cause an unpleasant garlic-like odour. Acetylene can be decomposed to its elements with the liberation of heat. The decomposition may or may not give rise to explosions, depending on conditions. Pure acetylene under pressure in excess of about 15 pounds per square inch or in liquid or solid form explodes with extreme violence.

Mixtures of air and acetylene are explosive over a wide range, from about 2.5 percent air in acetylene to about 12.5 percent acetylene in air. When burned with the correct amount of air, acetylene gives a pure, white light, and for this reason it was used for illumination in locations where electric power was not available; *e.g.,* buoys, miners' lamps, and road signals. The combustion of acetylene produces a large amount of heat, and, in a properly designed torch, the oxyacetylene flame attains the highest flame temperature (about 6,000° F or 3,300° C) of any known mixture of combustible gases.

The hydrogen atoms in acetylene can be replaced by metallic elements to form acetylides; *e.g.,* acetylides of silver, copper, or sodium. The acetylides of silver, copper, mercury, and gold are detonated by heat, friction, or shock. In addition to its reactive hydrogen atom, the carbon–carbon triple bond can readily add halogens, halogen acids, hydrogen cyanide, alcohols, amines, and amides. Acetylene can also add to itself or to aldehydes and ketones. Many of the reactions mentioned above are used for the commercial manufacture of various industrial and consumer products, such as acetaldehyde, the synthetic rubber neoprene, water-base paints, vinyl fabric and floor coverings, dry-cleaning solvents, and aerosol insecticide sprays. Acetylene is produced by any of three methods: by reaction of water with calcium carbide, by passage of a hydrocarbon through an electric arc, or by partial combustion of methane with air or oxygen.

acetylene tetrachloride: *see* tetrachloroethane.

acetylsalicylic acid, also called ASPIRIN, mild analgesic useful in the relief of headache and muscle and joint aches. Because it is so effective in reducing the swelling and pain associated with rheumatoid arthritis, aspirin is the drug of choice in the treatment of this disease. Moreover, when given in high doses to patients suffering from rheumatic fever, aspirin causes a dramatic lowering of the fever and also relieves the pain and swelling of the joints, prominent symptoms of the acute phase of the disease. In cases of mild infection, aspirin has some value in the reduction of fever and the relief of pain that may accompany the infection; it does not, however, modify or shorten the duration of a disease.

Other salicylates commonly used as analgesics are sodium salicylate and salicylamide. Like aspirin, the former is used in the treatment of rheumatic fever, but it has the undesirable side effect of causing a greater amount of gastrointestinal irritation than does aspirin. Salicylamide, on the other hand, causes less gastrointestinal irritation than aspirin, but its analgesic and anti-inflammatory activities are not as great.

Acevedo Díaz, Eduardo (b. April 20, 1851, Villa de la Unión, Uruguay—d. June 18, 1921, Buenos Aires), writer and politician, commonly adjudged Uruguay's first novelist. Active in revolutionary movements, he did most of his writing while in exile. His works include a trilogy of historical novels concerned with the Uruguayan wars for independence: *Ismael* (1888), *Nativa* (1890), and *Grito de gloria* (1894; "Shout of Glory"). *Soledad* (1894; "Solitude"), his masterpiece, had a continuing influence on gaucho novelists in Uruguay and Argentina.

Acey-Deucey, dice board game, a variant of Backgammon, much played in the U.S. Navy, Marine Corps, and merchant marine. For the basic play of the game, *see* Backgammon.

Acey-Deucey differs from standard Backgammon in that all pieces begin off the board. Each player must enter all 15 pieces before advancing any of them and must bring at least one home before he may hit an opponent's blot. Also, pieces need not be borne off by exact number; a piece may be taken off from the space that is next highest to the number thrown.

The terminology of Acey-Deucey differs from that of Backgammon. The bar is called the fence; hitting is called booting, or kicking; and the blockage of six consecutive points is called a Hindenberg Line, reflecting the game's popularity in World War I.

The dice combination of 1 and 2, called acey-deucey, has special significance. Upon throwing acey-deucey, the player first moves a piece the three spaces to which he is entitled. He then selects any doublet and moves accordingly, mindful that a doublet, as in Backgammon, is taken twice over. He then rolls again. If a player is unable to use any part of the acey-deucey roll, however, he forfeits the rest of his turn. The game may be played on a Backgammon board or an Acey-Deucey mat, the mat being more practical on a rolling and pitching ship.

In European Acey-Deucey, the player throwing Acey-Deucey selects a doublet but, instead of taking it twice over, moves the doublet and its complement, the number on the die's extra opposite face.

Achab: *see* Ahab.

Achaea, Modern Greek AKHAIA, region of ancient Greece on the north coast of the Peloponnese, south of the Gulf of Corinth (Korinthiakós, Kólpos). In ancient times it was bounded on the west by Elis (modern Ilía), on the south by Mount Erymanthus (Óros Erýmanthos) and Arcadia, and on the east by Sicyon (modern Sikión). The hilly coastal region corresponds almost to the modern *nomós* (department) of Akhaia, whose administrative capital is Pátrai, although the eastern boundary now falls west of Mount Kyllene (*Óóros* Killíni). The highway and railway from Athens to Pátrai follows the north coast of the Peloponnese.

Early in the 4th century BC the 12 cities of Achaea formed the Achaean League, a military alliance. In Hellenistic times, the League admitted non-Achaean allies and became the chief political power in Greece. It went over to Rome in 198 BC but was dissolved by the Romans in 146 BC, after which it was annexed to the Roman province of Macedonia. In 27 BC it became the centre of the Roman senatorial province of Achaea which included all of Greece south of Thessaly. After various invasions and dismemberments in the Middle Ages, Achaea was conquered by the Turks in 1460. It was in the monastery of Ayía Lavra near Kalávrita in this province that the standard of the Greek Revolution was raised in 1821. Achaea was liberated from the Turks in 1828.

The name Achaea was also applied in antiquity to a region west of the Gulf of Pagasae (Pagasitikós Kólpos) in southern Thessaly, which was known as Achaea Phthiotis. Also in Mycenaean times the name referred to the whole Peloponnese. Pop. (1981) *nomós,* 275,193.

Achaean, Greek ACHAIOS, any of the ancient Greek people, identified in Homer, along with the Danaoi and the Argeioi, as the Greeks who besieged Troy. Their area as described by Homer—the mainland and western isles of Greece, Crete, Rhodes, and adjacent isles, except the Cyclades—is precisely that covered by the activities of the Mycenaeans in the 14th–13th centuries BC, as revealed by archaeology. From this and other evidence, some authorities have identified the Achaeans with the Mycenaeans. Other evidence suggests that the Achaeans did not enter Greece until the so-called Dorian invasions of the 12th century BC. It seems at least possible that Homer's Achaean chiefs, with their short genealogies and their renown for infiltrating into Mycenaean kingships by way of military service and dynastic marriages, held power in the Mycenaean world only for a few generations in its last, warlike, and semibarbarous phase, until replaced by the Dorians, their relatively close kindred. The Achaeans of the northern Peloponnese in historic times were reckoned by Herodotus to be descendants of these earlier Achaeans. The name Ahhiyawa, occurring in Hittite documents of the 14th and 13th centuries BC, has sometimes been identified with the Achaeans, but this is disputed.

Achaean League, 3rd-century-BC confederation of the towns of Achaea in ancient Greece. The 12 Achaean cities of the northern Peloponnese had organized a league by the 4th century BC to protect themselves against piratical raids from across the Corinthian Gulf, but it fell apart after the death of Alexander the Great. The 10 surviving cities renewed their alliance around the shrine of Zeus Homarios, near Aegium, in 280 BC, and under Aratus of Sicyon, the league gained strength by the inclusion of his city, and later other non-Achaean cities, on equal terms.

League activity initially centred on the expulsion of the Macedonians and the restoration of Greek rule in the Peloponnese. After this was successfully accomplished, Achaea faced the danger of complete disintegration before the assaults of the Spartan king Cleomenes III, who also aimed at control of the Peloponnese. To counteract the Spartan threat, Aratus appealed to Macedonia, and Antigonus Doson and his troops subdued Sparta, making it a Macedonian ally, and renewed the Macedonian hold over Greece (224–221). In the Second Macedonian War, Achaea joined Rome (198), which led to the incorporation of nearly the whole Peloponnese and the dissolution of the confederacy (146). A smaller league, however, was set up soon afterward and continued into the Roman imperial age.

Under a federal constitution, the city-states in the league had maintained their internal independence within the framework of an organized central administration; only in foreign affairs and war was their competence restricted. The league also made noteworthy progress in the institution of representative government, despite a high minimum age (30 years) for membership in the assembly and no remuneration for attendance, which left officeholding and power to the wealthy. There was a representative council (*boulē*), possibly elected on a proportional system. Regular meetings of council and assembly were held throughout the year to transact normal business, and at all times irregular meetings could be summoned to debate such questions as war or alliance. After 200, when the primary assembly was convened only for this purpose or on the instructions of the Roman Senate, the council governed Achaea.

Achaemenes, Old Persian HAKHAMANISH (fl. early 7th century BC), eponymous ancestor of the Persian Achaemenid dynasty; he was the father of Teispes (Chishpish) and an ancestor of Cyrus II the Great and Darius I the Great. Although Achaemenes probably ruled only Parsumash, a vassal state of the kingdom of Media, many scholars believe that he led armies from Parsumash and Anshan (Anzan, northwest of Susa in Elam) against the Assyrian king Sennacherib in 681. Teispes was called "king of the city Anshan."

Achaemenes, Old Persian HAKHAMANISH (d. *c.* 460 BC, Papremis, Egypt), son of the Achaemenid king Darius I of Persia. After the first rebellion of Egypt (484), he was appointed satrap (governor) of Egypt by his brother Xerxes I; he also commanded the Egyptian contingent of the Achaemenid fleet defeated by the Greeks at the Battle of Salamis (480). Little more is known of Achaemenes' career until he was defeated and slain in battle by Inaros, the leader of the second rebellion of Egypt against Achaemenid rule.

Achaemenian DYNASTY, also called ACHAEMENID, Persian HAKHAMANISHIYA (559–330 BC), ancient Iranian dynasty whose kings founded and ruled the Achaemenian Empire. Achaemenes (Persian Hakhamanish), the Achaemenians' eponymous ancestor, is presumed to have lived early in the 7th century BC, but nothing is known of his life. From his son Teispes two lines of kings descended. The kings of the older line were Cyrus I, Cambyses I, Cyrus II the Great, and Cambyses II. After the death of Cambyses II (522 BC) the junior line came to the throne with Darius I. The dynasty became extinct with the death of Darius III, following his defeat (330 BC) by Alexander the Great.

Probably the greatest of the Achaemenian rulers were Cyrus II (reigned 559–*c.* 529 BC), who actually established the empire and from whose reign it is dated; Darius I (522–486), who excelled as an administrator and secured the borders from external threats; and Xerxes I (486–465), who completed many of the buildings begun by Darius. During the time of Darius I and Xerxes I, the empire extended as far west as Macedonia and Libya and as far east as the Hyphasis (Beās) River; it stretched to the Caucasus Mountains and the Aral Sea in the north and to the Persian Gulf and the Arabian Desert in the south.

The Achaemenian rule of conquered peoples was generally liberal; the empire itself was divided into provinces (satrapies), each administered by a satrap who underwent frequent inspections by officials reporting directly to the king.

Royal inscriptions were usually trilingual, in Old Persian, Elamite, and Akkadian; Aramaic, however, with its alphabetic script, was employed throughout the empire for imperial administration and also for diplomatic correspondence.

Building activity was extensive during the height of the empire, and of the several Achaemenian capitals, the ruins at Pasargadae and at Persepolis (*qq.v.*) are probably the most outstanding. Although very little free-standing monumental sculpture remains from Achaemenian times, the reliefs and the great number of small objects present a remarkably unified style for the period. Metalwork, especially in gold, was highly developed, and a variety of carefully executed examples survive, including rhytons, daggers, jewelry, and animal sculptures.

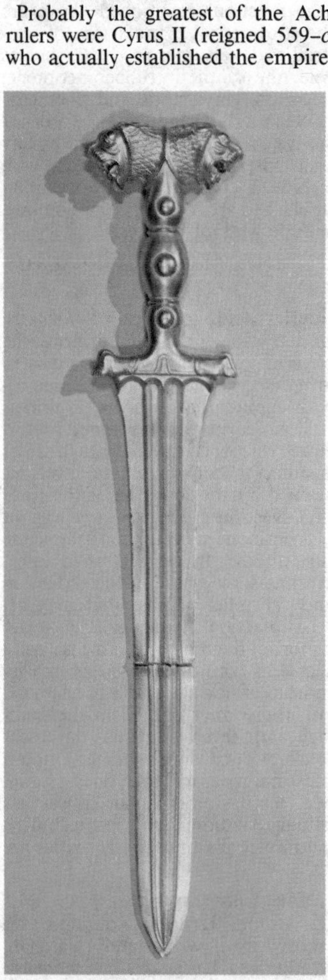

Achaemenian gold dagger, 5th century BC; in the Metropolitan Museum of Art, New York City

By courtesy of the Metropolitan Museum of Art, New York City, Dick Fund, 1954

Achaemenid DYNASTY, the Persian 27th dynasty of Egypt (525–404 BC), founded by Cambyses II of Persia and named after his family of the Achaemenids.

The policy of the Achaemenid kings seems to have been conciliatory to national beliefs and sentiments. There are conflicting views of Cambyses' reign. The courtier Udjahorresne depicts an ideal ruler in the pharaonic tradition; Herodotus, viewing the past through the eyes of a nationalistic priesthood, draws a savage tyrant. Certainly Darius (reigned 522–486 BC) proved himself a beneficent ruler and, in a visit to Egypt, displayed his consideration for the religion of the country. In the great oases he developed agriculture and built temples. The annual tribute imposed on the satrapy of Egypt and Cyrene was heavy, but it was probably raised with ease. The canal from the Nile to the Red Sea was completed or repaired, and commerce flourished. At the very end of his reign, however, several years after the disaster of Marathon, Egypt was induced to rebel. Xerxes (reigned 486–465 BC) put down the revolt with severity.

The disorders that marked the accession of his successor, Artaxerxes (reigned 465–425 BC), gave Egypt another opportunity to rebel, aided by an Athenian force. After two years, having diverted the river from its channel, the Achaemenids captured and burned the Athenian ships and quickly ended the rebellion. The reigns of Xerxes II and Darius II are marked by no recorded incident in Egypt until a revolt (*c.* 410 BC) interrupted the Persian domination; by 404 BC Egypt had regained its independence under Amyrtaeus of Sais.

Achagua, South American Indian people of Venezuela and eastern Colombia. They speak a language of the Maipurean Arawakan group. Traditionally, the Achagua had typical tropical forest economies, living in large villages and growing bitter cassava and other crops. Their villages were palisaded for defense against enemy raiders such as the Chibcha (*q.v.*). The Achagua themselves were somewhat warlike; they were one of the few native South American people to poison arrows with curare.

Achagua social organization was distinguished by numerous lineages named for animals such as the serpent, bat, jaguar, and fox.

Each such unit occupied one communal house in the village. The Achagua were polygynous, each man aiming to have three or four wives. The chiefs also maintained concubines. The wives were legally equal, and each cultivated her own separate field. Women were excluded from the men's house and from a number of religious ceremonies. The Achagua believed in a supreme being, in a god of the fields, a god of riches, and gods of earthquakes, of madness, and of fire. They also worshipped lakes.

Achaios (member of an ancient people): *see* Achaean.

Achaz (king of Judah): *see* Ahaz.

Achdar, Gebel el- (Libya): *see* Akhḍar, al-Jabal al-.

Acheampong, Ignatius Kutu (b. Sept. 23, 1931, Kumasi, Gold Coast—d. June 16, 1979, Accra, Ghana), Ghanaian army officer, who, after leading a military revolt that overthrew the government of Kofi Busia, became Ghana's chief of state in 1972. In July 1978 he was forced to resign, and the following June he and his successor, Lieut. Gen. F.W.K. Akuffo, were executed after a coup led by young officers, whose Armed Forces Revolutionary Council returned Ghana to civilian rule in September 1979.

Achebe, Chinua (b. Nov. 16, 1930, Ogidi, Nigeria), prominent Ibo novelist acclaimed for his unsentimental depictions of the social and psychological disorientation accompanying the imposition of Western customs and values upon traditional African society. His concern was with emergent Africa at its moments of crisis, his novels ranging in subject matter from the first contact of an African village with the white man to the educated African's attempt to create a firm moral order out of the changing values in a large city.

Educated in English at the University of Ibadan, Achebe taught for a short time before joining the staff of the Nigerian Broadcasting Corporation in Lagos, where he served as director of external broadcasting during 1961–66. In 1967 he launched a publishing company at Enugu with the poet Christopher Okigbo, who died shortly thereafter in the Nigerian civil war. In 1969 Achebe toured the United States with his fellow writers Gabriel Okara and Cyprian Ekwensi, lecturing at universities. Upon his return to Nigeria he was appointed research fellow at the University of Nigeria and became professor of English there in 1973. He was director (from 1970) of two Nigerian publishers, Heinemann Educational Books Ltd. and Nwankwo-Ifejika Ltd.

Things Fall Apart (1958), Achebe's first novel, concerns traditional Ibo life at the time of the advent of missionaries and colonial government in his homeland. His principal character cannot accept the new order, even though the old has already collapsed. In *No Longer at Ease* (1960) he portrayed newly appointed civil servant, recently returned from university study in England, who is unable to sustain the moral values he believes to be correct in the face of the obligations and temptations of his new position.

In *Arrow of God* (1964), set in the 1920s in a village under British administration, the principal character, the chief priest of the village, whose son becomes a zealous Christian, turns his resentment at the position he is placed in by the white man against his own people. Achebe's fourth novel, *A Man of the People* (1966), attacks injustice in a satirical exposé of corrupt government practices and politicians in newly independent Africa.

Achebe also published several collections of short stories; a children's book called *How the Leopard Got His Claws* (1973; with John Iroaganachi); two books of poems, *Beware, Soul-Brother* (1971) and *Christmas in Biafra* (1973); and a book of essays, *Morning Yet on Creation Day* (1975). His novels have been translated into many languages.

Achelous River, Modern Greek AKHELÓÖS POTAMÓS, also called ASPROPÓTAMOS, one of the longest rivers in Greece, rising in the Pindus Mountains of central Epirus (Ípiros) and dividing Aetolia from Acarnania. It debouches into the Ionian Sea after a course of 140 mi (220 km), mostly through gorges. Well above Agrínion two hydroelectric dams were built to harness the waters of the river and its tributaries. One is at Kastraki; the other, at Kremasta, is the highest (490 ft [150 m]) earth-fill dam in Europe. At the mouth of the river, where it is less than 2 ft deep, a number of small islands, the Ekhinádhes, have been enveloped by the silt. The name Aspropótamos (White River) is given to several other rivers in Greece, and the name Achelous appears in cult and in Greek mythology as that of the typical river god.

Achenbach, Andreas (b. Sept. 29, 1815, Kassel, Hesse—d. April 1, 1910, Düsseldorf, Ger.), landscape painter, a pioneer of the German realist school. He studied at the Düsseldorf academy under Johann Wilhelm Schirmer, but emancipated himself from the contemporary school of landscapists that delighted in the representation of romantic scenery. He was the first artist of the Düsseldorf school to paint nature for its own sake. His pictures of the stormy North Sea, of Dutch canal scenes, and of Rhineland villages contrasted favourably with the sentimental landscapes of his contemporaries. His brother Oswald was also a painter.

Achenbach, Oswald (b. Feb. 2, 1827, Düsseldorf, Prussia—d. Feb. 1, 1905, Düsseldorf, Ger.), landscape painter of the Düsseldorf school who is distinguished for his colourful renderings of the Bay of Naples, of Rome, and of Venice. He broke away from the traditional classicist interpretation of these scenes and revelled in strong and glowing colour effects. His more famous brother, Andreas, influenced his work.

achene, dry, one-seeded fruit lacking special seams that split to release the seed. The seed coat is attached to the thin, dry ovary wall (husk) by a short stalk, so that the seed is easily freed from the husk, as in buckwheat. The fruits of many plants in the buttercup family and the rose family are achenes.

Achernar, also called ALPHA ERIDANI, brightest star in the southern constellation Eridanus and one of the 10 brightest stars in the sky, with an apparent visual magnitude of 0.47. It lies about 60 or 70 light-years from the Earth. The name probably derives from an Arabic phrase meaning "the end of the river," in which the river referred to is the constellation.

Acheron, river in Thesprotía in Epirus, Greece, that was thought in ancient times to go to Hades because it flowed through dark gorges and went underground in several places; an oracle of the dead was located on its bank. In Greek mythology it is a river in Hades, and the name sometimes refers to the lower world generally. Several other rivers in Greece are also called Acheron, which traditionally means River of Woe.

Acheson, Archibald: *see* Gosford, Archibald Acheson, 2nd earl of.

Acheson, Dean (Gooderham) (b. April 11, 1893, Middletown, Conn., U.S.—d. Oct. 12, 1971, Sandy Spring, Md.), U.S. secretary of state (1949–53) and adviser to four presidents, who became the principal creator of U.S. foreign policy in the Cold War period following World War II, during which he helped to create the Western alliance in opposition to the Soviet Union and other Communist nations.

A graduate of Yale and of Harvard Law School, Acheson served for two years as private secretary to Supreme Court Justice Louis Brandeis. In 1921 he joined a law firm in Washington, D.C. His first government post was under Roosevelt as undersecretary of the Treasury in 1933; he entered the Department of State in 1941 as an assistant secretary and was undersecretary from 1945 to 1947.

Dean Acheson

By courtesy of the National Archives, Washington, D.C.

One of Acheson's first responsibilities in 1945 was to secure Senate approval for U.S. membership in the United Nations. After 1945 he became a convinced anti-Communist, a position that was the dominant influence on his later conduct of foreign policy. Believing that the Soviet Union sought expansion in the Middle East, he shaped what came to be known as the Truman Doctrine (1947), pledging immediate military and economic aid to the governments of Greece and Turkey. In the same year he outlined the main points of what became known as the Marshall Plan.

Appointed secretary of state by Pres. Harry S. Truman in January 1949, Acheson promoted the formation of the North Atlantic Treaty Organization (NATO), the first peacetime defensive alliance ever entered into by the U.S.

Despite his strong stance in what he conceived to be a global confrontation with Communism, Acheson—because he had been associated with high government circles during the period when Communist parties were taking over many European countries—was the target of attack by foreign-policy critics within both political parties. His enemies were particularly inflamed when, during the congressional hearings of Sen. Joseph R. McCarthy on subversive activities (1949–50), Acheson refused to fire any of his State Department subordinates. His most widely publicized remark was, "I will not turn my back on Alger Hiss"—a former State Department officer later convicted of perjury in denying that he had engaged in espionage in the 1930s.

Demands for Acheson's resignation increased after the entry of Communist China into the Korean War (1950–53). The storm of public controversy erupted more violently after the President removed Gen. Douglas MacArthur as commander of forces in Korea. Acheson subsequently established the policies of nonrecognition of China and aid to the Nationalist regime of Gen. Chiang Kai-shek on Taiwan; later he also supported U.S. aid to the French colonial regime in Indochina.

After leaving office he returned to private law practice but continued to serve as foreign-policy adviser to successive presidents. His account of his years in the Department of State, *Present at the Creation*, won the Pulitzer Prize in history in 1970. Other works include *Power and Diplomacy* (1958), *Morning and Noon* (1965), *The Korean War* (1971), and *Grapes from Thorns* (posthumous, 1972).

Acheson, Edward Goodrich (b. March 9, 1856, Washington, Pa., U.S.—d. July 6, 1931,

New York City), inventor who discovered Carborundum and perfected a method for making graphite.

He joined Thomas A. Edison's staff in 1880 and helped to develop the incandescent lamp at Edison's laboratories at Menlo Park, N.J. In 1881 he installed the first electric lights for Edison in Italy, Belgium, and France. Upon returning to the U.S., Acheson quit Edison and in 1884 began his own experiments on methods for producing artificial diamonds in an electric furnace. He heated a mixture of clay and coke in an iron bowl with a carbon arc light and found some shiny, hexagonal crystals (silicon carbide) attached to the carbon electrode. Because he at first mistakenly thought the crystals were a compound of carbon and alumina from the clay, he devised the trade name Carborundum, after corundum, the mineral composed of fused alumina. In 1893 he received a patent on this highly effective abrasive.

Later, while studying the effects of high temperature on Carborundum, he found that the silicon vaporizes at about 7,500° F (4,150° C), leaving behind graphitic carbon. He was granted a patent for this process in 1896. In all, he received 69 patents and organized several firms to commercialize his inventions, including The Carborundum Company, Niagara Falls, N.Y.

Acheulian industry, Acheulian also spelled ACHEULEAN, long-lived (more than 1,000,000 years), first standardized tradition of toolmaking of *Homo erectus* and early *Homo sapiens*. Acheulian (from the type site, Saint-Acheul, in Somme *département*, in northern France) tools were made of stone with good fracture characteristics, including chalcedony, jasper, and flint; in regions lacking these, quartzite might be used. During the Acheulian, the presence of good tool stone was probably an important determining factor in the distribution of man. In the later stages man learned to bring stone from distant areas and thus became freer in his choice of homesites. "Tool kits" that differ in tool types reflect the varying adaptations made by Early Stone Age man to different environments.

The most characteristic Acheulian tools are termed hand axes and cleavers. Considerable improvement in the technique of producing hand axes occurred over a period of about 1,000,000 years; anthropologists sometimes distinguish each major advance in method by a separate number or name. Early Acheulian tool types are called Abbevillian (especially in Europe); the last Acheulian stage is sometimes called Micoquian. Industries that existed at the same time and overlapped in geographical range, but specialized in flake tools and lacked hand axes, are known as Clactonian (England) and Tayacian (western and central Europe). Acheulian industries are found in Africa, Europe, the Middle East, and Asia as far east as Calcutta (the Far East was characterized by a tool tradition called the chopper chopping-tool industry). The earliest hand axes, such as those found with *Homo erectus* in Bed II at Olduvai Gorge in Tanzania, were crude pointed bifaces—chips were removed from both sides of a core by rapping it against a set "anvil" stone to form a sinuous cutting edge all around. In the next step a hammerstone replaced the "anvil," and the whole surface of the core was flaked away to form an oval implement with relatively straight edges. Small flakes were sometimes removed from the edges to further straighten them. Later still the hammerstone was replaced by bone or wood "hammers," which removed smaller, flatter flakes and resulted in a smoother tool with a sharp, straight edge. A sinuous edge could be produced purposefully, resulting in a "saw." In the late Acheulian, hand axes were pointed, and the butt end was often only roughly finished. Cleavers were large tools with one end squared off to form an axelike cutting edge.

In addition to hand axes and cleavers, the Acheulian industry included choppers and flakes. The latter were produced from a prepared core and could be used as knives without further change or could be chipped to make side-scrapers, burins, and other implements. Though bone and wood were probably also used as tools, little evidence of them remains, and no discussion of style can be attempted. At the beginning of the Fourth (Würm) Glacial Period, Acheulian industries were gradually replaced by (graded into) the Levalloisian stone-flaking technique and the Mousterian industry in Europe and Fauresmith and Sangoan industries in Africa.

Achill, mountainous island off the west coast of Ireland, joined to the mainland by a bridge across Achill Sound. Its area is 56 sq mi (145 sq km), and its highest points are the quartzite peaks of Slieve Croaghaun (2,192 ft [668 m]) and Slieve More (2,204 ft [672 m]). The landscape is dominated by wild moorlands and spectacular coastal scenery. Farming and fishing provide some livelihood; supplementary income is obtained from tourism and by migration of agricultural labourers to England and Scotland in summer. The ruins of Kildavnet, a 12th-century church, are in the vicinity. Pop. (1981) 3,101.

Achilles, in Greek mythology, son of the mortal Peleus, king of the Myrmidons, and the Nereid, or sea nymph, Thetis. He was the bravest, handsomest, and greatest warrior of the army of Agamemnon in the Trojan War. According to Homer, Achilles was brought up by his mother at Phthia with his cousin and inseparable companion Patroclus. One of the non-Homeric tales of his childhood relates that Thetis dipped Achilles in the waters of the River Styx, by which he became invulnerable, except for the part of his heel by which she held him: the proverbial "heel of Achilles."

The later mythographers related that Peleus, having received an oracle that his son would die fighting at Troy, sent Achilles to the court of Lycomedes on Scyros, where he was dressed as a girl and kept among the King's daughters (one of whom, Deïdamia, bore him Neoptolemus). On the warning of the soothsayer Calchas that Troy could not be taken without Achilles, the Greeks searched for and found him.

Achilles killing Penthesilea during the Trojan War, interior of an Attic cup, *c.* 460 BC; in the Antikensammlungen, Munich

The Mansell Collection

During the first nine years of the war, Achilles ravaged the country around Troy and took 12 cities. In the 10th year a quarrel with Agamemnon occurred when Achilles insisted that Agamemnon restore Chryseis, his prize of war, to her father, a priest of Apollo, in order to appease the wrath of Apollo, who had decimated the camp with a pestilence. An irate Agamemnon then recouped his loss by depriving Achilles of his favourite slave, Briseis.

Achilles refused further service, and consequently the Greeks floundered so badly that at last Achilles allowed Patroclus to impersonate him, lending him his chariot and armour. Hector (the eldest son of King Priam of Troy) slew Patroclus, and Achilles, having finally reconciled with Agamemnon, obtained new armour from the god Hephaestus and slew Hector. The poet Arctinus in his *Aethiopis* took up the story of the *Iliad* and related that Achilles, having slain the Ethiopian king Memnon and the Amazon Penthesilea, was himself slain by Paris (*q.v.*), whose arrow was guided by Apollo.

Achilles was worshipped in many places, including Leuke, Sparta, Elis, and especially Sigeum on the Hellespont.

Achilles Painter (fl. 5th century BC), Athenian vase painter known by and named for an amphora attributed to him with a painting of "Achilles and Briseis." The amphora is now in the Vatican Museums. His period of activity coincides with the Parthenon sculptures and with the administration of Pericles.

Achilles holding a spear, front of the "Achilles and Briseis" red-figure amphora by the Achilles Painter, *c.* 450 BC; in the Vatican Museums

Photograph by the Vatican Museums

The "Achilles and Briseis" amphora is a red-figure vase (that is, the figures are painted in red against a glazed black background). The vase dates from *c.* 450 BC and is among the finest surviving examples of vase painting from the Classical period.

In addition to red-figure pottery, the Achilles Painter is praised for his white-ground lekythoi (funerary vases on which the figures are painted in colour against a white background). The white-ground lekythoi are currently believed to be the most reliable source information about monumental Greek paintings of the Classical period. The original monumental paintings do not survive and are known only through the writings of the ancients.

More than 200 vase paintings have been attributed to the Achilles Painter on the basis of the style of the "Achilles and Briseis." Among them are: lekythoi of "Girl Bringing a Casket to Her Mistress" (Boston Museum of Fine Arts); "Youth Bidding Farewell to Wife" (Athens); and "Warrior Arming" (British Museum). The Achilles Painter is cited for his delicately drawn, gentle, pensive, almost melancholy figures.

Achilles paradox, in logic, a sophism of the 5th-century-BC Greek philosopher Zeno. Not a true paradox, the sophism posits that if Achilles, who is capable of running 10 yards a second, races with a tortoise that can run 5 yards a second, and if Achilles gives the tortoise a 10-yard handicap, Achilles can never catch the tortoise. Zeno's argument rested on the presumption that whenever Achilles reaches a point where the tortoise had been, the tortoise would have moved on. *See also* paradoxes of Zeno.

Achilles Tatius (fl. 2nd century AD, Alexandria), teacher of rhetoric and author of *Leucippe and Cleitophon*, one of the Greek prose romances that influenced the development of the novel centuries later. A story of two lovers' improbable adventures, hairbreadth escapes, and eventual reunion, it is unusual in being narrated by the hero, Cleitophon. Achilles is ingenious in inventing *coups de théâtre* (Leucippe thrice is thought to have died but reappears alive). The romance was admired by Byzantine critics and widely translated in the Renaissance.

Achillini, Alessandro (b. Oct. 29, 1463, Bologna, Papal States—d. Aug. 2, 1512, Bologna), philosopher, physician, an advocate of the teachings of William of Ockham. Achillini was educated at the University of Bologna, where he taught philosophy and medicine from 1484 to 1512, except for two years at Padua. Although sometimes classed as a strict Averroist, an adherent of the Arabic philosophy of Averroës (1126–98) asserting the supremacy of reason over faith, Achillini reflected other influences. Achillini's complete works were published in 1508.

Achin (Indonesia): *see* Aceh.

Achinese, also spelled ATJEHNESE, one of the main ethnic groups on the island of Sumatra, Indonesia. They were estimated to number roughly 2,100,000 in the mid-1970s. They speak a language of the Austronesian (Malayo-Polynesian) family.

The Achinese were ruled by Indian princes prior to AD 500, and in the 13th century they became the first people in the archipelago to adopted Islām. After expelling the Portuguese in the 17th century, the sultanate of Acheh (Atjeh) was dominant in northern Sumatra until 1904, when the sultanate was conquered by the Dutch. The Achinese, however, were never fully subdued. Although they are now part of the Indonesian republic, they remain restive and are administered within a special district.

Western influence is evident in public buildings and in the homes of the well-to-do. Otherwise the native type of dwelling prevails, consisting of a three-room structure of wood raised high above the ground on pilings.

Descent is traced through both the maternal and paternal lines. A married couple goes to live with the bride's family. The position of women is high, and they do not wear veils. Their dress consists of a skirt over trousers, a jacket and scarf, and many ornaments. The man wears a jacket or shoulder cloth and trousers of great width.

Achinese War (1873–1904), an armed conflict between The Netherlands and the Muslim state of Acheh (now Aceh) in northern Sumatra that resulted in Dutch conquest of the Achinese and, ultimately, in Dutch domination of the entire region. In 1871 The Netherlands and Britain had signed a treaty that recognized Dutch influence in northern Sumatra in return for Dutch confirmation of Britain's right of equal trade in the Indies.

The Dutch, considering Acheh as within their sphere of influence, decided to conquer the area and sent two expeditions to Acheh in 1873. The palace was seized and shortly afterward the Sultan died. The Dutch suspended military operations and concluded a treaty with the new sultan, who recognized Dutch sovereignty over the area. He was unable to control his subjects, however, and Dutch forces became involved in a prolonged guerrilla war in the countryside. This war, however, drained the colonial treasury, and public opinion in The Netherlands became increasingly critical of the colonial administration.

The administration later realized that their ignorance of the region had led them to commit serious errors. C. Snouck Hurgronje, professor of Islāmic studies at the University of Leyden, was invited to undertake a thorough study of Acheh and published a book in 1893–94 on the Achinese. A "castle strategy," which provided fortified bases for the Dutch troops, was then introduced. Under the leadership of J. B. van Heutsz, who was appointed military and civil governor of Acheh in 1899, the kingdom was quickly subdued. The conquest of the entire region was accomplished by van Heutsz in 1904.

Achinsk, also spelled AČINSK, city, Krasnoyarsk *kray* (territory), south central Russian Soviet Federated Socialist Republic, on the Chulym River, a tributary of the Ob. It was founded in 1621 and chartered in 1782. Important as a river-road transfer point until rail lines were constructed, it gained economic importance when an alumina plant was put into production in 1969 and when an oil refinery began operation at Kritovo, 15 mi (24 km) west of Achinsk, in the late 1970s. The Kansk-Achinsk coal basin was also being developed in the early 1980s. The city has clothing, furniture, and brick factories. Pop. (1983 est.) 120,000.

Achitophel (Old Testament): *see* Ahithophel.

Achmed, also spelled ACHMET (Arabic personal name): *see under* Ahmed, or Ahmad.

Acholi, also spelled ACOLI, also called GANG, or SHULI, ethnolinguistic group of northern Uganda and southernmost Sudan. They speak an Eastern Sudanic language of the Chari-Nile branch of the Nilo-Saharan family and are culturally and historically related to the neighbouring Lango. Like the Luo and Anuak peoples, the Acholi are believed to have migrated from an area to the southwest three or four centuries ago.

The Acholi have small chiefdoms of one or more villages, each containing several patrilineal clans. Chiefs (*rwot*) are chosen from one lineage. Formerly villages were substantial and stockaded; since the 19th century Acholi have split into small hamlets of patrilineal kin.

The Acholi maintain herds of sheep and cattle, but are not as committed to pastoralism as some Nilotic peoples are. Millet is the staple food of the Acholi, and tobacco is grown for trade. Corn (maize), sorghum, beans, squash, peanuts (groundnuts), and other savanna crops are also grown. Hunting tracts are owned by clans, and communal and other specialized hunting methods are practiced. Stream and swamp fishing is also important.

Acholi were considered a martial people by the British, and many joined the military. Under Pres. Idi Amin (1971–79), the Acholi were severely persecuted and their men systematically executed for their past association with the colonial army and their ties of kinship and ethnicity with Pres. Milton Obote (1962–71, 1980–). After Amin's overthrow the Acholi became victims of marauding bands of soldiers and bandits, and also suffered from famine and drought.

Achomawi and Atsugewi, two American Indian groups living along the Pit River and its tributaries in far northern California. They spoke mutually unintelligible languages of the Palaihnihan family of Hokan stock but were otherwise culturally almost identical. Most of their region comprised dry highlands of barren waste lava, and only narrow areas along streams were generally habitable. Some areas were so wanting in what were the usual northern Californian Indian staples—acorns and salmon—that many villages had to rely more on hunting the scarce deer and other game and gathering edible roots and seeds.

The Achomawi and Atsugewi comprised various communities of peoples grouped in villages scattered in the several drainage basins. They lived, in summer, usually in lean-tos or huts of brush and, in winter, usually in oblong or oval houses formed of poles and bark with sometimes an earth covering. The most important dwelling was the large sweat house, used also as a ceremonial lodge, council chamber, and dwelling for certain important families. Each settlement had a chief. Notable manufactures included the basketry common to most northern Californians, as well as the dugout pine and cedar canoes. Among some groups there is known to have been a first salmon ceremony, designed to increase the year's salmon run; and the powers of shamans to cure by ritual were accepted by all groups.

achondrite, any stony meteorite containing no chondrules (rounded granules of cosmic origin). Achondrites, comprising about 4 percent of the known meteorites, are similar in appearance to terrestrial igneous rocks low in silica content, such as basalts, peridotites, and pyroxenites. They may have crystallized from a melt similar to the terrestrial magma that formed basic and ultrabasic igneous rocks; it is possible that they were derived from the melting and fractional crystallization of parent bodies having the overall composition of chondrites. Achondrites are classified into the following groups according to their mineralogy: angrites, aubrites, chassignites, diogenites, eucrites, howardites, nakhlites, shergottites, and ureilites. *See also* chondrite.

achondroplasia, also called CHONDRODYSTROPHIA FETALIS, hereditary disorder characterized by a lack of cartilage cells. As a consequence, bones that depend on cartilage models for development cannot grow (*see* bone development). Achondroplasia is the most common cause of dwarfism. In those afflicted with the disease, the limbs are very short (fingers reach only to hips), but the trunk is almost normal in size. The head is enlarged because of some overgrowth of the vault bones following premature closure of sutures at the base of the skull. There is usually a bulging forehead, saddle nose, protruding full-sized jaw, deeply incurved lower back with prominent buttocks, and a narrow chest; women may have narrow pelves and subsequent difficulty in childbirth.

Achondroplastic dwarfs are of normal intelligence and have otherwise normal health. This disease has been known since antiquity—in Egypt the god Ptah was depicted as an achondroplastic dwarf; until recently, affected individuals were in demand as court jesters and soothsayers.

achroite, colourless alkali tourmaline of gem quality. *See* tourmaline.

Achtyrka (Ukrainian S.S.R.): *see* Akhtyrka.

acid, any substance that in water solution tastes sour, changes the colour of certain indicators (*e.g.,* reddens blue litmus paper), reacts with some metals (*e.g.,* iron) to liberate hydrogen, reacts with bases to form salts, and promotes certain chemical reactions (acid catalysis). Examples of acids include the inorganic substances known as the mineral acids—sulfuric, nitric, hydrochloric, and phosphoric acids—and the organic compounds belonging to the carboxylic acid, sulfonic acid, and phenol groups. Such substances contain one or more hydrogen atoms that, in solution, are released as positively charged hydrogen ions (*see* Arrhenius theory).

Broader definitions of an acid, to include substances that exhibit typical acidic behaviour as pure compounds or when dissolved in solvents other than water, are given by the Brønsted–Lowry theory (*q.v.*) and the Lewis theory (*q.v.*). Examples of nonaqueous acids are sulfur trioxide, aluminum chloride, and boron trifluoride. *Compare* base.

acid–base catalysis, acceleration of a chemical reaction by addition of an acid or a base, the acid or base not being consumed in the reaction itself. The catalytic reaction may be acid-specific (acid catalysis), such as the decomposition of the sugar sucrose into glucose and fructose in sulfuric acid; or base-specific (base catalysis), such as the addition of hydrogen cyanide to aldehydes and ketones in the presence of sodium hydroxide. Many reactions are catalyzed by both acids and bases.

The mechanism of acid- and base-catalyzed reactions is explained in terms of the Brønsted-Lowry concept of acids and bases as one in which there is an initial transfer of protons from an acidic catalyst to the reactant or from the reactant to a basic catalyst. In terms of the Lewis theory of acids and bases, the reaction entails sharing of an electron pair donated by a base catalyst or accepted by an acid catalyst.

Acid catalysis is employed in a large number of industrial reactions, among them the conversion of petroleum hydrocarbons to gasoline and related products. Such reactions include decomposition of high-molecular-weight hydrocarbons (cracking) using alumina–silica catalysts (Brønsted-Lowry acids), polymerization of unsaturated hydrocarbons using sulfuric acid or hydrogen fluoride (Brønsted-Lowry acids), and isomerization of aliphatic hydrocarbons using aluminum chloride (a Lewis acid).

Among industrial applications of base-catalyzed reactions is the reaction of diisocyanates with polyfunctional alcohols in the presence of amines, used in the manufacture of polyurethane foams.

acid–base reaction, a type of chemical process typified by the exchange of one or more hydrogen ions, H^+, between species that may be neutral (molecules, such as water, H_2O; or acetic acid, CH_3CO_2H) or electrically charged (ions, such as ammonium, NH_4^+; hydroxide, OH^-; or carbonate, CO_3^{2-}). It also includes analogous behaviour of molecules and ions that are acidic but do not donate hydrogen ions (aluminum chloride, $AlCl_3$, and the silver ion Ag^+).

A brief treatment of acid–base reactions follows. For full treatment, *see* MACROPAEDIA: Chemical Reactions.

Typical acid–base reactions can be represented by the equation:

$$\text{Acid}_1 + \text{Base}_2 \rightleftharpoons \text{Base}_1 + \text{Acid}_2$$
$$\text{or } HA + B \rightleftharpoons A^- + BH^+,$$

where A^- and B are conjugate bases of the acids HA and BH^+, respectively; similarly, HA and BH^+ are the conjugate acids of the bases A^- and B.

In such generalized equations the presence or absence of an electric charge on any particle does not necessarily indicate the net charge on the particle in question. It merely shows that an acid has one more positive or one less negative charge than its conjugate base, and conversely that a base has one less positive charge or one more negative charge than its conjugate acid.

Among the most important reactions involving acids and bases are their dissociation in water and their dissociation in nonaqueous solvents, the self-dissociation of amphoteric solvents, neutralization, and the hydrolysis of salts.

When a molecular acid, such as acetic acid, is in an aqueous solution, water acts as a base, or proton acceptor, as in the equation

$$CH_3CO_2H + H_2O \rightleftharpoons CH_3CO_2^- + H_3O^+.$$

When a base is in an aqueous solution, water acts as an acid, or proton donor, as in the equation

$$H_2O + NH_3 \rightleftharpoons OH^- + NH_4^+.$$

The dissociation of acids and bases in nonaqueous solvents is analogous to the comparable reactions in water. The dissociation of acetic acid in methanol, for example, may be represented by the equation

$$CH_3CO_2H + CH_3OH \rightleftharpoons CH_3CO_2^- + CH_3OH_2^+.$$

Amphoteric solvents, such as water and liquid ammonia, have both acidic and basic properties. The self-dissociation of water may be given as an example:

$$H_2O + H_2O \rightleftharpoons OH^- + H_3O^+.$$

Neutralization. When an acid and a base neutralize one another, the hydronium ion (H_3O^+) and hydroxide ion (OH^-) combine to form water; if equivalent quantities of the two materials are present, the reaction proceeds essentially to completion because water is only slightly dissociated into ions. The chemical equation for the reaction between potassium hydroxide and hydrochloric acid is written

$$K^+ + OH^- + H_3O^+ + Cl^- \rightleftharpoons K^+ + Cl^- + 2H_2O,$$

which may be simplified to

$$OH^- + H_3O^+ \rightleftharpoons 2H_2O,$$

where the potassium and chloride ions, which do not really enter into the chemical reaction, are omitted. These ions, however, are present after the neutralization; with the water produced by the neutralization and the excess water present as a solvent, the ions form a solution of potassium chloride (a salt).

Many acids ionize in water to give more than one hydronium ion; these are called polybasic acids because each molecule of acid can neutralize more than one molecule of base. For example, sulfuric acid is dibasic; it ionizes in two steps:

$$H_2SO_4 + H_2O \rightleftharpoons H_3O^+ + HSO_4^-$$
$$HSO_4^- + H_2O \rightleftharpoons H_3O^+ + SO_4^{2-}$$

and forms two series of salts, corresponding to $NaHSO_4$ and Na_2SO_4; phosphoric acid (H_3PO_4) is tribasic and forms three series of salts. Bases that can ionize to give more than one hydroxide ion per molecule are called polyacid bases.

Hydrolysis of salts. The aqueous solutions of many salts have acidic or basic properties. This phenomenon, termed hydrolysis, can be understood as a result of the acidic properties of cations derived from weak bases, and the basic properties of anions derived from weak acids.

Ionization constant. Acids which in aqueous solution are largely dissociated into ions are called strong acids; those which under similar conditions are only slightly dissociated are called weak acids.

In water, any acid HA is ionized according to the equation

$$HA + H_2O \rightleftharpoons H_3O^+ + A^-.$$

The equilibrium constant for the reaction is represented by the equation

$$\frac{[H_3O^+][A^-]}{[HA]} = K_a,$$

where the expressions in brackets represent the activities of the acid and its ions. A strong acid then is one with a large value for its ionization constant K_a; indeed, the value of this constant is a quantitative measure of the strength of the acid in question. The more dilute the solution, the more extensively is the acid ionized. If it is possible by some analytical technique to determine the concentration of hydronium ions in solution, where the gross concentration of ionized and unionized acid is known, K_a may be computed.

acid dye, any bright-coloured synthetic organic compound whose molecule contains two groups of atoms: one acidic, such as a carboxylic group, and one colour-producing, such as an azo or nitro group. Acid dyes are usually applied in the form of their sodium salts—chiefly on wool but also on silk and, to a limited extent, in combination with a mordant, or fixing agent, on cotton and rayon. These dyestuffs produce bright shades in a wide range of colours, usually with good fastness to light and washing.

acid halide, neutral compound that reacts with water to produce an acid and a hydrogen halide. Acid halides are ordinarily derived from acids or their salts by replacement of hydroxyl groups by halogen atoms. The most important organic acid halides are the chlorides derived from carboxylic acids and from sulfonic acids. The carboxylic acid chlorides, called acyl halides, are generally more reactive than the sulfonic acid chlorides, called sulfonyl chlorides.

The acyl halides are highly reactive substances used primarily in organic syntheses to introduce the acyl group. They react with water, ammonia, and alcohols to give carboxylic acids, amides, and esters, respectively.

Most acyl halides are liquids insoluble in water. They have sharp odours and irritate the mucous membranes. Sulfonyl chlorides (RSO_2Cl) react with ammonia to form sulfonamides, including the sulfa drugs.

Common halides of inorganic acids include chlorosulfuric acid ($ClSO_3H$) and sulfuryl chloride (SO_2Cl_2), corresponding to the replacement of one or both hydroxyl groups of sulfuric acid, H_2SO_4 or $SO_2(OH)_2$; thionyl chloride ($SOCl_2$), the chloride of sulfurous acid; phosphorus trichloride (PCl_3), the chloride of phosphorous acid; and phosphorus oxychloride ($POCl_3$, also called phosphoryl chloride), the chloride of phosphoric acid.

acid rain, form of precipitation containing a heavy concentration of sulfuric and nitric acids. The term is also commonly applied to snow, sleet, and hail that manifest similar acidification. Such precipitation has become an increasingly serious environmental problem in many areas of North America and Europe. Although this form of pollution is most severe in and around large urban and industrial areas, substantial amounts of acid precipitation may be transported great distances.

The process that results in the formation of acid rain generally begins with emissions into the atmosphere of sulfur dioxide and nitrogen oxide. These gases are released by automobiles, certain industrial operations (*e.g.,* smelting and refining), and electric power plants that burn such fossil fuels as coal and oil. The gases combine with water vapour in clouds to form sulfuric and nitric acids. When precipitation falls from the clouds, it is highly acidic, having a pH value of about 5.6 or lower. (The term pH is defined as the negative logarithm of the hydrogen ion concentration in kilograms per cubic metre. The pH scale ranges from 0 to 14, with lower numbers indicating increased acidity.) At several locations in the eastern United States and western Europe, pH values between 2 and 3 have been recorded. In areas such as Los Angeles, San Francisco, and Whiteface Mountain in New York, fog is often 10 or more times as acidic as the local precipitation.

Precipitation and fog of high acidity contaminate lakes and streams; they are particularly harmful to fish and other aquatic life in regions with thin soil and granitic rock, which provide little buffering to acidic inputs. It also has been discovered that aluminum is leached from the soil in such regions subjected to acid precipitation, and that dissolved aluminum seems to be extremely toxic to aquatic organisms. All forms of acid precipitation have been found to damage various kinds of vegetation, including agricultural crops and trees, chiefly by inhibiting nitrogen fixation and leaching nutrients from foliage. In addition, these pollutants can corrode the external surfaces of buildings and other man-made structures.

acidosis, abnormally high level of acidity, or low level of alkalinity, in the body fluids, including the blood. Acidosis may be respiratory or metabolic in origin. The former results from excess retention of carbon dioxide because of faulty oxygen–carbon dioxide exchange in the lungs. The latter may result from the inability of diseased kidneys to excrete the acids produced within the body. It may also accompany diabetes mellitus, severe diarrhea, or starvation, conditions that involve either the accumulation of acids in the system or the loss of alkali. *Compare* alkalosis.

Aciéries Réunies de Burbach-Eich-Dudelange: *see* ARBED.

Ačinsk (Russian S.F.S.R.): *see* Achinsk.

Acireale, town and episcopal see, Catania province, eastern Sicily, Italy, on terraces above the Ionian Sea at the foot of Mt. Etna, just north-northeast of Catania. Known as Aquilia by the Romans, the town was called Reale by Philip IV of Spain in 1642. The first part of its name is derived from the ancient Acis River, which according to legend welled forth at the death of the shepherd Acis, beloved by the Nereid (sea nymph) Galatea and slain by the Cyclops Polyphemus, a one-eyed giant. Much of the present town was built after the earthquake of 1693. Notable landmarks include the cathedral (1597–1618), with a modern facade; the Baroque church of S. Sebastiano; the town hall (1659) containing a library, museum, and picture gallery; an observatory; a fruit experimental station; and the sulfur springs called Terme di Santa Venera.

A noted spa since Roman times, Acireale is a climatic and mineral water resort with a fine beach. Mineral water, wine, and citrus fruit are exported, and textiles and leather goods are produced. Pop. (1981 prelim.) mun., 47,888.

ackee (tree): *see* akee.

Ackermann, Konrad Ernst (b. Feb. 1, 1710/12?, Schwerin, Mecklenburg—d. Nov. 13, 1771, Hamburg), actor-manager, a leading figure in the development of German theatre.

Attracted to the theatre by reading Molière and Holberg, although he was a trained scientist and surgeon, he joined the company of Johann Friedrich Schönemann in Lüneburg in 1740. Schönemann specialized in German adaptations of the French plays of Corneille, Racine, Molière, and Voltaire, and Ackermann's initial training as an actor was along formal lines. In 1749 he married Sophie Charlotte Schröder, the leading lady of Schönemann's company, and with her and a good troupe toured in Russia, the Baltic states, and East Prussia for many years, until the Seven Years' War forced him to move to the south and into Switzerland.

Gradually Ackermann developed a taste for domestic drama and a technique for parts in which he could mingle the comic and the sentimental. In 1765, with Konrad Ekhof (*q.v.*) in his company, he built a modest playhouse in Hamburg. By opening night he was heavily in debt, dissension gripped his company, and the next year he had to lease his theatre, not regaining control over it until two years later. Shortly before his death he turned the management over to his stepson, Friedrich Ludwig Schröder, who was to bring Shakespeare to the German stage.

Ackermann, Louise-Victorine, *née* CHOQUET (b. Nov. 30, 1813, Paris—d. Aug. 2, 1890, Nice, Fr.), French poet who is best known for works characterized by a deep sense of pessimism.

Educated by her father in the philosophy of the Encyclopédistes, she travelled to Berlin in 1838 to study German and there married (1843) Paul Ackermann, an Alsatian philologist. Two years later her husband died, and she went to live with her sister at Nice. There she wrote *Contes en vers* (1855; "Stories in Verse") and *Contes et poésies* (1862; "Stories and Poetry"), but her real reputation rests on the *Poésies, premières poésies, poésies philosophiques* (1874; "Poetry, First Poetry, Philosophical Poetry"), a volume of sombre and powerful verse, expressing her revolt against human suffering.

Aclla Cuna (Inca religion): *see* Chosen Women.

Acmeist, Russian AKMEIST, plural AKMEISTY, member of a small group of early-20th-century Russian poets reacting against the vagueness and affectations of Symbolism. It was formed by the poets Sergey Gorodetsky and Nikolay S. Gumilyov. They reasserted the poet as craftsman and used language freshly and with intensity. Centred in St. Petersburg (now Leningrad), the Acmeists were associated with the review *Apollon* (1909–17). In 1912 they founded the Guild of Poets, whose most outstanding members were Anna Akhmatova and Osip Mandelstam. Because of their preoccupation with form and their ivory-tower aloofness, the Acmeists were regarded with suspicion by the Soviet regime. Gumilyov was executed in 1921 for his alleged activities in an anti-Soviet conspiracy. Akhmatova was silenced during the most productive years of her life, and Mandelstam died after long internment in a concentration camp.

acne, any inflammatory disease of the sebaceous, or oil, glands of the skin. There are some 50 different types of acne. In common usage, the term acne is frequently used alone to designate acne vulgaris, or common acne, probably the most prevalent of all chronic skin disorders.

Acne vulgaris results from an interplay of heredity factors, hormones, and bacteria. In susceptible individuals, it begins in the teen years, being caused by overactive sebaceous glands, which are stimulated by the upsurge in the circulating level of male sex hormones that accompanies the onset of puberty. The primary lesion of acne vulgaris is the comedo, or blackhead, which consists of a plug of sebum (the fatty substance secreted by a sebaceous gland), cell debris, and microorganisms (especially the bacterium *Propionibacterium acnes*) filling up a hair follicle. Comedones may be open, their upper or visible portion being darkened by oxidative changes; or they may be closed (*i.e.,* not reaching the surface to be extruded), in which case, they may be starting points for pustules and deep inflammatory lesions.

The severity of acne is divided generally into four grades. In grade I, comedones may be sparse or profuse but there is little or no inflammation. In grade II, comedones are intermingled with superficial pustules and papules (small, solid, usually conical elevations). The lesions are ordinarily confined to the face and do not produce significant scarring, unless there has been continued scratching and picking. At this stage, topical (locally applied) medication is reasonably effective. Complete spontaneous remission is ordinarily seen within one to two years. In grades III and IV, the acne is characterized by comedones and pustules and deeper inflamed nodules, which are thought to result from the rupture of the sebaceous duct, with extrusion of sebum and bacterial products into the skin tissue. The lesions are likely to extend from the face to the neck and upper trunk and to produce a permanent scarring of the skin.

The course of acne vulgaris is variable, persistence being ordinarily directly related to the severity of the lesions, although changes of climate and emotional stress may markedly improve or exacerbate the acne lesions. Methods of treatment vary from topical medication to sunlight and ultraviolet light, antibiotics, and hormones. In a high proportion of cases, however, the tendency is toward spontaneous cure over several months.

Acoli (people): *see* Acholi.

acolyte (from Greek *akolouthos,* "server," "companion," or "follower"), in the Roman Catholic Church, a ministry in which a person is installed in order to assist the deacon and priest in liturgical celebrations, especially the eucharistic liturgy. The first probable reference to the office dates from the time of Pope Victor I (189–199), and it was mentioned frequently in Roman documents after the 4th century. Acolytes also existed in North Africa but were unknown outside Rome and North Africa until the 10th century, when they were introduced throughout the Western Church. The Council of Trent (1545–63) defined the order and hoped to reactivate it on the pastoral level, but it became only a preparatory rite, or minor order, leading to the priesthood. A *motu proprio* of Pope Paul VI (effective Jan. 1, 1973) decreed that the office of acolyte should no longer be called a minor order but a ministry and that it should be open to laymen.

In the Eastern Church, the order of acolytes was not accepted. In Anglican and Lutheran churches, acolytes are generally lay persons who light the candles at church services.

Acoma, Indian pueblo, Valencia County, west central New Mexico, U.S., 55 mi (89 km) west-southwest of Albuquerque, known as the "Sky City." Its inhabitants live in terraced dwellings made of stone and adobe atop a precipitous sandstone butte 357 ft (109 m) high. They have always engaged in farming (on the plains below) and pottery making. Believed to be the oldest continuously inhabited place in the U.S. (since the 10th century), it was described by the conquistador Coronado in 1540 as the strongest defensive position in the world. The massive mission church of San Esteban Rey was built 1629–41; its 30-ft log beams were carried from the Cebolleta Mountains (30 mi southwest), and with dirt for its graveyard, were hauled up from below. Access is now gained either by a staircase cut into the rock or by a vehicle road. The pueblo's name comes from the Keresan Indian language: *ako* meaning "white rock" and *ma,* "people." About 3 mi northeast *katzimo,* or the Enchanted Mesa, another butte rising 430 ft above the surrounding plain, is believed by the Acoma Indians to be the dwelling place of their nature gods.

Acominatus, Nicetas: *see* Choniates, Nicetas.

Aconcagua, Mount, Spanish CERRO ACONCAGUA, mountain in Argentina. It is commonly regarded as the highest summit in the Western Hemisphere, rising 22,831 ft (6,959 m) above sea level. Aconcagua lies in the northern Andes, its peak in Mendoza province, in northwestern Argentina, but its western flanks build up from the coastal lowlands of Chile, just north of Santiago. It is of volcanic origin, but it is not itself a volcano. The first attempted ascent, made in 1883, failed; the summit was first reached in 1897 by Matthias Zurbriggen.

Aconcagua River, Spanish RÍO ACONCAGUA, river in central Chile. It rises in the Andes in the northwestern foothills of the Cerro Aconcagua and flows westward from the Argentine border area through Valparaíso region to enter the Pacific north of Viña del Mar after a course of 120 mi (190 km). Much of the Chilean trackage of the Transandine Railway to Mendoza, Arg., follows the river valley. San Felipe is the chief city on the river.

Aconcio, Giacomo, Aconcio also spelled ACONZIO, Latin JACOBUS ACONTIUS (b. Sept. 7, 1492, Trent, Tirol—d. 1566?, England), advocate of religious toleration during the Reformation whose revolt took a more extreme form than that of Lutheranism.

Aconcio served as secretary to Cristoforo Madruzzo, a liberal cardinal. When the more conservative Paul IV became pope, he repudiated Roman Catholic doctrine, left Italy, and eventually found refuge in England. He arrived soon after the accession of Queen Elizabeth I (1558).

On his arrival in London, Aconcio joined the Dutch Reformed Church; before reaching England, however, he had published a treatise on methods of scientific investigation, and his critical spirit made it difficult for him to remain within any of the recognized religious societies of his time. He was subsequently excluded from the sacraments, partly because he was considered to hold Anabaptist (baptism of adult believers) and Arian (anti-Trinitarian) opinions and partly because he defended the radical pastor, Adrian Haemstede, who had previously been excommunicated.

In his *Satanae stratagemata* (1565) Aconcio identified the dogmatic creeds that divide the church as the "strategems of Satan." In the hope of finding a common denominator for the various creeds, he sought to reduce dogma to a minimum. A study of the man and his doctrine is found in Charles O'Malley's *Jacopo Aconcio, uomini e dottrine* (1955).

aconite, any member of two genera of perennial herbs of the buttercup family (Ranunculaceae): *Aconitum* are summer-flowering poisonous plants (*see* monkshood); *Eranthis* are spring-flowering ornamentals (*see* winter aconite).

Açores, Arquipélago dos (Atlantic Ocean): *see* Azores.

acorn and nut weevil, any of certain members of the insect family Curculionidae (order Coleoptera). Nut weevils (*e.g.,* Balaninus) have extremely long and slender snouts, which in females can be almost twice the body length. Eggs are deposited in holes bored in the nut.

These weevils are common in both Europe and North America. Different species prefer certain nuts: *Curculio proboscides* attacks large chestnuts, for example, and *C. rectus* and *C. baculi* feed on acorns.

Nut weevil (*Balaninus nucum*)
Jacques Six

acornworm, also called ENTEROPNEUST, any of the soft-bodied invertebrates of the class Enteropneusta, phylum Hemichordata. The front end of these animals is shaped like an acorn, hence their common name. The "acorn" consists of a proboscis and a collar that may be used to burrow into soft sand or mud. Length varies from about 5 centimetres (about 2 inches) in certain *Saccoglossus* species to more than 180 centimetres (about 6 feet) in *Balanoglossus gigas.*

Acornworm (*Dolichoglossus kowalewskii*)
Walter Dawn

Acornworms live along the seashore and in water to depths of more than 3,200 metres (10,500 feet). Most live in U-shaped burrows, but some deep-water species swim freely over the bottom. Food is filtered from seawater that passes into the mouth and out through the gill slits. Some species secrete a slime that is swept into the mouth by cilia, or tiny hairs, carrying food particles with it.

Paired gonads lie next to the gills, which lie behind the collar. Females of some species lay a few large eggs with much yolk; others lay many small eggs with little yolk. Some hatch into miniature acornworms; others hatch into an immature form called tornaria larva.

acosmism, in philosophy, the view that God is the sole and ultimate reality and that finite objects and events have no independent existence. Acosmism has been equated with pantheism, the belief that everything is God. G.W.F. Hegel coined the word to defend Benedict de Spinoza, who was accused of atheism for rejecting the traditional view of a created world existing outside God. Hegel argued that Spinoza could not be an atheist because pantheists hold that everything is God, whereas atheists exclude God altogether and make a godless world the sole reality. Furthermore, pantheism is not acosmistic inasmuch as it regards man from the standpoint of the universe, rather than the universe from that of man. Nevertheless, because Spinoza's cosmos is part of God, it is not what it seems to be. He is acosmistic insofar as "non-cosmic" seems to deny the cosmos, a position, however, very alien to Spinoza's thought.

Acosmism has also been used to describe the philosophies of Hindu Vedānta, Buddhism, and Arthur Schopenhauer; and Johann Gottlieb Fichte used the term to defend himself against accusations similar to those levelled against Spinoza.

Acosta, José de (b. 1539, Medina del Campo, Spain—d. Feb. 15, 1600, Salamanca), Jesuit theologian and missionary to the New World, chiefly known for his *Historia natural y moral de las Indias,* the earliest survey of the New World and its relation to the Old. His works, missionary and literary, mark the end of the period of the religious and scientific incorporation of the newly discovered lands into Western culture.

Acosta joined the Jesuits in 1551, going as a missionary to Peru in 1571. Having been provincial of his order there (1576–81), he was appointed theological adviser to the council of Lima (1582), later writing a catechism in local Indian languages, the first book printed in Peru. On returning to Spain in 1587, he wrote *Historia natural y moral de las Indias* (1590; *Natural and Moral History of the Indies,* 1604), which attempted to place his observations of the physical geography and natural history of Mexico and Peru (including the aboriginal religious and political institutions) in the context of contemporary Jesuit and scientific thought and is especially valuable as a firsthand account.

Acosta led the opposition to Claudio Acquaviva (the general of the Jesuits), helping to call the fifth Jesuit congregation to redress alleged grievances. The reformers' proposals were rejected and Acosta was imprisoned (1592–93). After submitting in 1594 Acosta became superior of the Jesuits at Valladolid and rector of the Jesuit college at Salamanca (1598), where he remained until his death.

Acosta's other significant study is the *De procuranda indorum salute* (1588), a systematic examination of missionary problems in the New World.

Acosta, Uriel, original name GABRIEL DA COSTA (b. *c.* 1585, Oporto, Port.—d. April 1640, Amsterdam), freethinking rationalist who became an example among Jews of one martyred by the intolerance of his own religious community. He is sometimes cited as a forerunner of the renowned philosopher Benedict de Spinoza.

The son of Marranos (Spanish and Portuguese Jews forcibly converted to Roman Catholicism), he was treasurer of a cathedral chapter but became a convert to Judaism after reading the Old Testament. He persuaded his family to flee with him to Amsterdam, where Jews were not persecuted. After circumcision, he took Uriel as his given name.

When he discovered the discrepancy between biblical Judaism and the Judaism of Amsterdam as then practiced, he attacked the city's rabbinic authorities (1616) and was excommunicated. Nevertheless, he published (1624) a book that, among other heresies, denied the immortality of the soul and its resurrection and attacked Christian dogma as well as Judaism. As a result, the civil authorities fined and imprisoned him as an enemy of religion, and his book was burned. In 1633 Acosta publicly recanted, to become, in his phrase, "an ape among apes"; but he secretly rejected revealed religion, advocating a faith based on natural law and reason. Accused of dissuading some Christians from converting to Judaism, he was excommunicated by the rabbis a second time. After years of ostracism, he again recanted (1640). He was forced to confess his sins in a humiliating ceremony at the threshold of the synagogue. Soon thereafter he wrote a short biographical sketch, *Exemplar Humanae Vitae* (1687; "Example of a Human Life"), and took his own life.

acouchi, either of two species of South American rodents of the genus *Myoprocta,* family Dasyproctidae, which resemble the related agouti (*q.v.*). Weighing 600 to 1,300 grams (21 to 45½ ounces), acouchis range in size from 32 to 38 centimetres (12½ to 15 inches) long, with 4.5- to 7-cm tails that are white-haired below. The acouchi's coarse fur is reddish or greenish, with yellowish patches on the side of the head. Acouchis eat sitting on their haunches, horde extra food, and stamp their feet when alarmed.

acoustic impedance, absorption of sound in a medium, equal to the ratio of the sound pressure at a boundary surface to the sound flux (flow velocity of the particles or volume velocity, times area) through the surface. In analogy to electrical circuit theory, pressure corresponds to voltage, volume velocity to current, and acoustic impedance is expressed as a complex number, the real part being referred to as the resistance and the imaginary part the reactance.

acoustic interferometer, device for measuring the velocity and absorption of sound waves in a gas or liquid. A vibrating crystal creates the waves that are radiated continuously into the fluid medium, striking a movable reflector placed accurately parallel to the crystal source. The waves are then reflected back to the source. The strength of the standing wave pattern set up between the source and the reflector as the distance between source and reflector is varied, or as the frequency is varied, indicates the absorption by the medium. The velocity at which the waves travel may be determined from the distance between the peaks in the pattern of standing waves. This method has been brought to a high degree of accuracy and has been used for determining the characteristics of seawater for sonar applications.

acoustic meatus, external: *see* external auditory canal.

acoustic nerve: *see* vestibulocochlear nerve.

acoustic neuroma, benign tumour on the vestibulocochlear nerve (also called acoustic nerve) near its point of entry into the inner ear. The tumour, though benign, may spread into the brain cavity if not detected in its first stages. Early symptoms include mild unilateral hearing impairment, tinnitus (ringing in the ear), and sometimes dizziness. If the tumour has extended into the brain cavity, headache and paralysis are experienced. Treatment of acoustic neuroma is surgical excision.

acoustic trauma, physiological changes in the body caused by sound waves. Sound waves cause variations in pressure, the intensity of which depends upon the range of oscillation, the force exerting the sound, and the distribution of waves. In aerospace medicine the major producers of noise are aircraft and space vehicle propulsion units.

Excessive noise exposures can cause hearing loss and produce physical damage to the components of the ear. The ability to interpret sounds can decrease as a result of continuous exposures to sound waves of sufficient intensity and duration. Hearing loss can be caused by damage to the middle ear, tympanic (eardrum) membrane, and inner ear. The hair cells that line the inner ear and take part in the process of hearing can be irreversibly damaged by excessive noise levels. Intense sound blasts can rupture the tympanic membrane and dislocate or fracture the small bones of the middle ear. Hearing loss that comes from middle ear damage can sometimes be corrected. A ruptured membrane usually heals in time, restoring most of the hearing loss. The small bones of the ear may be repaired or replaced by surgery. Pain felt in the ears from sound waves usually originates in the middle ear and serves as a warning that the threshold for damage has been reached.

Nonauditory effects of acoustic energy can also occur; most of these can be prevented by use of ear protection devices. Intense low-frequency energy can affect the chest, abdomen, eyes, and sinus cavities, causing concern, anxiety, pain, and fatigue. The body's equilibrium is partially controlled by the vestibular system in the ears; high-level noise may cause disorientation, motion sickness, and dizziness. High-speed, low-altitude flight causes vibrations as well as intense noise levels; both factors can make oral communication difficult or impossible. Sudden unexpected changes in noise levels may cause a startle response and distraction. Noise does not usually affect the speed at which work is performed; it may increase the number of errors, however. More constant noises of moderate to high levels cause stress, fatigue, and irritability.

acoustical engineering, branch of engineering practice concerned with the control of sound in the environment. The sounds being controlled may be wanted or unwanted, and the control exerted may be intended to enhance or suppress them. Techniques of acoustical engineering may be employed in the home, in the office, in factories, in public buildings, and in concert halls.

A brief treatment of acoustical engineering follows. For full treatment, *see* MACROPAEDIA: Sound.

Sound is one of the pervasive elements of man's environment. The sound in any given setting is characterized by a number of qualities, including intensity or loudness, information content, reverberation, clarity, and so on. The acoustical engineer attempts to find optimal values of these qualities for particular settings and purposes and then to design physical means for attaining those values.

In a factory the chief acoustical problem may be the suppression of machine noise, and various design tactics may be employed to accomplish that end. In an office building the problem may be to introduce noise of a certain sort and at a certain level in order to provide a degree of privacy for conversation. Buildings near airports need to be insulated against outside sound, and the techniques used to do so will differ markedly from those used to shield an office building or private home from traffic noise in the city.

The best known application of acoustical engineering is in the design of halls and auditoriums where the quality of sound is of critical importance. The characteristics of loudness and distribution of sound, reverberation time, and balance of direct and reflected sound will have different optimal values depending on the specific kinds of sounds concerned—speech, music, or a combination of both—and will all depend on such design variables as the form and dimensions of the hall, the materials used to finish the walls and especially the ceiling, the arrangement of seats and the materials used to cover them, the placement of special reflecting surfaces, the use of amplification, and the presence of such stage furnishings as curtains and draperies.

acoustics, the science concerned with the production, control, transmission, reception, and effects of sound.

A brief treatment of acoustics follows. For full treatment, *see* MACROPAEDIA: Sound.

Acoustics is generally divided into several branches, the principal ones of which are architectural acoustics and environmental acoustics. Other significant fields include musical acoustics, which deals with the principles governing the operation and design of musical instruments and the way musical sounds affect listeners; engineering acoustics, which is concerned chiefly with the development of high-fidelity sound recording and reproduction systems; and ultrasonics, which involves research into acoustical phenomena whose vibration rate is above the audible range (*i.e.,* roughly 20,000 hertz) and their application in industry and biomedical science.

Architectural acoustics focusses on the behaviour of sound waves in closed spaces and on those factors crucial to creating optimal acoustical conditions for different applications. It contributes significantly to both the design and construction of concert and lecture halls, theatre and church auditoriums, and the like. Architectural acoustics technology involves many special techniques and equipment, as for example the use of strategically positioned sound-reinforcing systems. It also makes extensive use of computer simulation models for determining the appropriate acoustical properties of specific halls and buildings.

Environmental acoustics deals primarily with the problem of noise control. Noise from jet aircraft, factories, heavy construction machinery, and automobiles has become a problem in large urban areas. Control of such forms of noise pollution ranges from efforts to produce quieter machines through the use of absorbent mountings to more careful fabrication of moving parts so as to reduce vibrations that give rise to noise. Noise in office and residential buildings has been curbed by the utilization of improved insulation materials in walls, the erection of suitably designed room partitions, and other procedures.

Acquaviva, Claudio: *see* Aquaviva, Claudio.

acquired character, in biology, modification in structure or function acquired by an organism during its life, caused by environmental factors. With respect to higher organisms, there is no evidence that such changes are transmissible genetically—the view associated with Lamarckism—but, among protozoans and bacteria, certain induced changes are heritable. *See also* Lamarckism.

acquired immune deficiency syndrome (AIDS), disease that destroys the immune system of the human body. The disease was first diagnosed in 1979 in the United States, and incidence increased dramatically after its identification, with a death rate of about 40 percent.

A large majority of those diagnosed as having AIDS are previously healthy homosexual males who have engaged in extensive sexual contact with a variety of partners. The syndrome also has been diagnosed among intravenous drug abusers, hemophiliacs treated with medication derived from donated blood and persons who have received blood transfusions, Haitians and Haitian immigrants, heterosexual females whose male sexual partner has AIDS, children of high-risk families, and infants born to mothers who are drug abusers. Extensive research of social and physical contacts among these groups has sought to aid medical determination of the cause and transmission of the disease. Much evidence has pointed toward a viral agent, and researchers have identified two closely related viruses that are suspected of causing AIDS. These viruses, which may in fact be the same organism, infect the T-lymphocytes, an important component of the immune system.

Early and nonspecific symptoms of AIDS include severe weight loss, intermittent fevers, fatigue, weakness, malaise, and enlargement of lymph glands. As the immune system deteriorates, persons with AIDS develop recurrent or chronic infections with organisms that are tolerated by the normal, healthy individual but that in the AIDS victim can lead to massive infection and death. Persons with AIDS are also at an increased risk for the development of malignancies, including lymphomas and squamous-cell carcinomas. Kaposi's sarcoma, a previously rare, but treatable, cancer characterized by dark blue or purplish spots on the skin of the extremities, has been diagnosed and has been fatal in a disproportionately high number of AIDS victims.

Antibiotics are used to treat specific infections in AIDS victims, and malignancies are treated appropriately. Death usually results from infections that no longer respond to treatment or for which no treatment is known.

acquittal, in criminal law, acknowledgment by the court of the innocence of the defendant or defendants. Such a judgment may be made by a jury in a trial or by a judge who rules that there is insufficient evidence either for conviction or for further proceedings. An acquittal removes all guilt in law. An acquittal "in fact" occurs when a jury finds the defendant not guilty. An acquittal "in law" occurs through the mere operation of law. For instance, if the principal in a case is acquitted, an accessory also is deemed acquitted in law.

Acquittal has other meanings. In the Middle Ages it was an obligation of an intermediate lord to protect his tenants against interference from his own overlord. The term is also used in contract law to signify a discharge or release from an obligation.

Acrasieae, class name for cellular SLIME MOLDS (division Myxomycophyta). The class contains a single order, Acrasiales, and about a dozen species. The vegetative phase of these slime molds consists of amoeba-like cells (myxamoebas) that group together ultimately to form a fruiting (reproductive) structure.

Acre, westernmost *estado* (state) of Brazil. Acre covers the southwesternmost part of Brazil's Hiléia (Hylea), the forest zone of the Amazon River basin. Bounded north by Amazonas state, it has western and southern frontiers with Peru and southeastern with Bolivia and has an area of 58,915 sq mi (152,589 sq km). The capital is Rio Branco on the Rio Acre in the eastern part of the state. The state's name is derived from that of the Rio Acre, which seems to be of Indian origin. Covered by tropical rain forest, Acre produces the highest quality rubber in Brazil.

Portuguese explorers, making their way through the immense Amazon forest from the Atlantic estuary of the Amazon River, did not reach Acre before the middle decades of the 18th century, when there were no settled inhabitants but only roving bands of Indians. Under the Brazilian Empire, more expeditions began to penetrate the territory in the 1850s and 1860s; and although the whole area was ceded by Brazil to Bolivia in 1867 (by the Treaty of Ayacucho), the rubber boom of the following decades attracted more and more immigrants from northeastern Brazil. In 1899, during a local revolution, an independent Republic of Acre was proclaimed by Luís Gálvez Rodríguez, a Spanish adventurer, but this regime was short-lived. After further vicissitudes, negotiations sponsored by Brazil's foreign minister culminated in 1903 in the Treaty of Petrópolis, whereby Acre was reincorporated with Brazil. The frontier with Peru was agreed upon in 1909. Organized at first as a territory, Acre achieved statehood in 1962.

With an average elevation of 600 ft (183 m) above sea level, the land slopes gently down toward the Amazonian Plain from the higher ground in the west and south. An average annual temperature of 77° F (25° C) and an annual rainfall of 79–98 in. (2,000–2,500 mm) makes the climate warm and humid. The forest is traversed by headstreams of two of the Amazon's major tributaries, the Juruá and the Purus. The principal trees of the forest are rubber and Brazil nut. The fauna include peccaries (piglike animals), red deer, capybaras (rodents with no tail and partly webbed feet), agoutis (short-haired, short-eared rodents), and tapirs (large, hoofed quadrupeds).

The local Indian tribes are few and small, most of Acre's population consisting of immigrants, or descendants of immigrants, from northeastern Brazil. The overwhelming majority of the people live on the rivers and tracks that give access to the raw materials of the forests; the remainder live in the towns. The largest city is Rio Branco. Other major towns are Cruzeiro do Sul, Sena Madureira, Tarauacá, and Feijó. The common language is Portuguese, the predominant religion Roman Catholicism. Amoebic dysentery, malaria, and leprosy are the major endemic diseases.

Acre's chief natural resource is rubber, which constitutes the majority of the state's exports; it is Brazil's leading producer of that commodity. Brazil nuts are the next most important natural product of the forest.

Agriculture, which is only of the subsistence type, is concerned with short-cycle crops, chiefly cassava (manioc), corn (maize), and beans. Zebus (humped oxen) are being raised on the open-range system, but this activity is still at an early stage; pigs and chickens are bred quite widely.

Rivers are the main channels of communication. Rio Branco is connected with Manaus, capital of Amazonas, by the Rio Acre-Purus-Amazon linkage and with Brasília—the federal capital—by a land highway; there are also air services connecting Rio Branco with both places. Pop. (1980 prelim.) 306,893.

Acre (Israel): *see* ʿAkko.

acre, unit of land measurement in the British Imperial and U.S. Customary systems, equal to 43,560 square feet, or 160 square rods. One acre is equivalent to 0.4047 hectares (4,047 square metres). Derived from the Latin *ager* ("field"), the term acre originated in the primitive technique of measuring land by the oxen needed to plough it or the seed needed to sow it. The Anglo-Saxon acre was defined as a strip of land $1 \times \frac{1}{10}$ furlong, or 40 x 4 rods (660 x 66 feet). "Acre" gradually came to mean a piece of land of any shape measuring the present 4,840 square yards. Larger variant acres include the Scottish, the Irish, and the Cheshire.

Acre River, Portuguese RIO ACRE, river, chiefly in western Brazil, rising on the Peruvian border, along which it continues eastward to form part of the Brazil–Bolivia border. Turning north at Brasiléia, the remainder of its 400-mi (645-km) course flows in a north-northeasterly direction, through the Brazilian states of Acre and Amazonas, to join the Rio Purus, a tributary of the Amazon, at Bôca do Acre. It was formerly called the Aquiri.

acriflavine, dye obtained from coal tar, introduced as an antiseptic in 1912 by the German medical-research worker Paul Ehrlich and used extensively in World War I to kill the parasites that cause sleeping sickness. The hydrochloride and the less irritating base, neutral acriflavine, both are odourless, reddish-brown powders used in dilute aqueous solutions primarily as topical antiseptics or given orally as urinary antiseptics. Once used in the treatment of gonorrhea, acriflavine has been replaced by the antibiotics.

acrobatics (Greek: "to walk on tip-toe," or "to climb up"), the specialized and ancient art of jumping, tumbling, and balancing, often later with the use of such apparatus as poles, one-wheel cycles, balls, barrels, tightropes, trampolines, and flying trapezes.

In 1859 the invention of the flying trapeze by J. Léotard, as well as Charles Blondin's crossing of Niagara Falls on a tightrope, rekindled public interest in aerial gymnasts and acrobats. Although the trapeze had never been seen before, ropedancing can be traced back to ancient Greece.

By the turn of the century, acrobatics were important in the circus. About 1900 the Scheffers, Craggs, Hanlon-Voltas, Sandow, Lauck and Fox, Cinquevalli, Caicedo, and the Potters were the most prominent European and U.S. acrobats. Later, the Concellos and Codonas on the flying trapeze, Con Colleano on the tightwire, and the juggler Enrico Rastelli captivated audiences with their skill and daring. Popular mid-20th-century acrobats were the Wallendas, a family of high-wire artists originally from Germany. Traditionally, acrobatics and tumbling were the province of eastern Europeans.

Acrobatics are performed in fairgrounds, circuses, and theatres. They are also related to movements of modern gymnastics and of certain theatre genres, such as the Peking Opera.

acrocephalosyndactyly, also called APERT'S SYNDROME, congenital malformation of the skeleton, affecting the skull, hands, and feet, first described by the French pediatrician Eugène Apert. The head is shortened front-to-back and appears pointed (acrocephaly) because of premature closing of the cranial sutures between the individual bones that make up the skull. The bones and skin of the hands and feet are fused (syndactyly), reducing the normal complement of fingers and toes; in some cases, all five digits may fuse. The skull deformity causes the eyes to appear to bulge because the orbits are shallower than normal. *See also* craniosynostosis.

acrocyanosis, uneven reddish-blue discoloration of the hands caused by spasms in arterioles (small arteries) of the skin. Less commonly the feet are affected. The fingers, or toes, are usually cold and sweat copiously. The condition may be the result of an endocrine disorder or of some anxiety state. It is most common in adolescents and those in the 20s and usually improves with age.

acrolith, statue, especially ancient Greek, in which the trunk of the figure was of wood and the head, hands, and feet of marble. The wood was either gilded or covered by real or metal drapery. Acroliths are known from the descriptions of Pausanias, a 2nd-century-AD Greek geographer and traveller, who mentions, for example, Phidias' acrolith of Athena at Plataea. This form of sculpture was practiced at least as late as the 4th century BC.

acromegaly, growth and metabolic disorder characterized by enlargement of the skeletal extremities. It is the result of overproduction of pituitary growth hormone (somatotropin) after maturity, caused by a tumour of the pituitary gland. Acromegaly is often associated with the abnormal growth in stature known as pituitary gigantism (*see* gigantism).

The onset of acromegaly is gradual. Hands and feet become enlarged; facial features are exaggerated as the jaw lengthens and the nose and brow ridge grow thicker; the skin thickens; and most internal organs enlarge. Headache, excessive sweating, and high blood pressure are other manifestations.

Acromegalic individuals are likely to develop congestive heart failure, particularly when blood pressure becomes high. Muscle weakness is frequent because muscle overgrowth produced by growth hormone decreases their capacity for work. At times, excessive overgrowth of bone edges involves the joints and produces pain. The bones may become thin and porous—a condition known as osteoporosis. Diabetes mellitus appears in 20 to 40 percent of acromegalic individuals because excesses of growth hormone block the action of insulin. If the pituitary tumour enlarges, it can produce visual-field defects, blindness or paralysis of the eye muscles, and can injure the posterior pituitary gland or the hypothalamus. Also, hemorrhage into the tumour can produce sudden loss of vision.

Acromegaly may be treated by surgical removal of the pituitary tumour or destruction of it by X-ray irradiation or liquid nitrogen. Rarely, the pituitary tumour will cease to secrete growth hormone because of a spontaneous hemorrhage or a blockage of the blood supply. Decreases in acromegalic manifestations and amelioration of diabetes mellitus have followed therapy with female hormones—estrogen or medroxyprogesterone—which reduce the secretion of growth hormone. For those treated by pituitary surgery, irradiation, or other measures and for those who spontaneously develop deficits of gonadal, thyroidal, or adrenocortical hormones, replacement-hormone therapy is necessary.

acropolis, central, defensively oriented district in ancient Greek cities, located at the highest point and containing the chief municipal and religious buildings. Because the founding of a city was a religious act, the establishment of a local home for the gods was a basic factor in Greek city planning. From both a religious and a military point of view, a hilltop site was highly desirable: militarily, because an acropolis had to be a citadel; religiously, because a hill was imbued with natural mysteries—caves, springs, copses, and glens—that denoted the presence of the gods.

The Acropolis, Athens, second half of the 5th century BC, with the Parthenon at centre and the Erechtheum at left

Toni Schneiders

Athens has the best known acropolis, built during the second half of the 5th century BC. The Athenian acropolis, located on a craggy, walled hill, was built as a home of Athena, the patron goddess of the city. The structures that survive consist of the Propylaea (*q.v.*), the gateway to the sacred precinct; the Parthenon (*q.v.*), the chief shrine to Athena and also the treasury of the Delian League; the Erechtheum (*q.v.*), a shrine to the agricultural deities, especially Erichthonius; and the Temple of Athena Nike (*q.v.*), an architectural symbol of the harmony with which the Dorian and Ionian peoples lived under the government of Athens.

Acropolites, George (b. 1217, Constantinople—d. 1282, Constantinople), Byzantine scholar and statesman, the author of *Chronikē syngraphē*, a history of the Byzantine Empire from 1204 to 1261. He also played a major diplomatic role in the attempt to reconcile the Greek and Latin churches.

Acropolites was raised at the imperial court, then at Nicaea in Asia Minor. Entrusted with important state missions under the emperor John III Ducas Vatatzes and his successors, Theodore II Lascaris and Michael VIII Palaeologus, he was in 1244 appointed grand logothete (chancellor). Named governor of the western provinces by Theodore II, Acropolites was engaged (1257) as commander in the field against Michael Angelus, despot of Epirus. Later captured but released, he returned to Constantinople when it was retaken from the crusaders (1261). He represented Michael VIII in the negotiations for the reunion of the Western and Byzantine churches that culminated in the second Council of Lyon (1274) at which, in the Emperor's name, he acknowledged the supremacy of Rome. In 1282 he was sent on an embassy to John II, emperor of Trebizond, and died not long after his return.

Acropolites' history of the Byzantine Empire reveals his firsthand knowledge of events. He also wrote theological and rhetorical works as well as some poems.

acrostic, short verse composition, so constructed that the initial letters of the lines, taken consecutively, form words. The term is derived from the Greek words *akros*, "at the end," and *stichos*, "line," or "verse."

The word was first applied to the prophecies of the Erythraean Sibyl, which were written on leaves and arranged so that the initial letters of the leaves always formed a word. Acrostics were common among the Greeks of the Alexandrine period, as well as with the Latin writers Ennius and Plautus, many of the arguments of whose plays were written with acrostics on their respective titles. Medieval monks were also fond of acrostics, as were the poets of the Middle High German and Italian Renaissance periods.

The term acrostic is also applied to alphabetical, or abecedarian, verses, each line after the first, which begins with *a*, using a succeeding letter of the alphabet. Examples of these are some of the Psalms (in Hebrew), such as Psalms 25 and 34, where successive verses begin with the letters of the Hebrew alphabet in order.

Double acrostics are puzzles constructed so that not only the initial letters of the lines but in some cases also the middle or last letters form words. In the United States, the Double Crostic puzzle, devised by Elizabeth Kingsley for the *Saturday Review* in 1934, had an acrostic in the answers to the clues giving the author and title of a literary work; the letters, keyed by number to blanks like those of a crossword puzzle, spelled out a quotation.

acroterion, in architecture, decorative pedestal for an ornament or statue placed at the gable end, or pediment, of a Greek temple; the term has also been extended to refer to both the pedestal and the statue or ornament that stands on it. Originally a petal-shaped ornament with incised pattern, such as the honeysuckle, was placed on the ridge and at the eaves at either side of the pediment. Later this ornamentation was developed into groups of statuary, as at the Temple of Apollo (420 BC) on the island of Delos; the crowning group is dominated by Eos, the dawn, being lifted up by the handsome god Cephalus. At first, acroteria were made of terra-cotta, as were the roof tiles; later they were made of stone. The acroteria of the Apollo temple are made of beautiful semitranslucent Pentelic marble.

The acroterion is sometimes incorporated into the design of furniture; for example, it can be placed in the broken pediment of a secretary bookcase.

Acroteria

From M.S. Briggs, *Everyman's Concise Encyclopaedia of Architecture*; E.P. Dutton and Co., Inc., and J.M. Dent & Sons Ltd.

Acrux (star): *see* Alpha Crucis.

acrylic compound, any of a class of synthetic plastics, resins, and oils used to manufacture many products. By varying the starting reagents and the process of forming, a material may be produced that is hard and transparent, soft and resilient, or a viscous liquid. Acrylic compounds are used to make molded structural and optical parts, jewelry, adhesives, coating compounds, and textile fibres. Orlon and Acrilan are trademark names of acrylic fibres; Lucite (*q.v.*) and Plexiglas are glasslike acrylic materials. *See also* vinyl compounds.

acrylic painting, painting executed in the synthetic medium of acrylic resins. Acrylics dry rapidly, serve as a vehicle for any kind of pigment, and are capable of giving both the transparent brilliance of watercolour and the density of oil paint. They are considered to be less affected by heat and other destructive forces than is oil paint. Because of all these desirable characteristics, acrylic paints became immediately popular with artists when they were first commercially promoted in the 1960s.

Act of ——: *see under* substantive word (*e.g.*, Settlement, Act of), except as below.

Act of Parliament clock, plain, hanging, weight-driven wall clock with a large wooden, painted or lacquered dial. The term Act of Parliament clock was applied incorrectly to these timepieces, which were thought to have been displayed by innkeepers to save their customers from paying a five-shilling duty on clocks in Great Britain, introduced in 1797 by the English prime minister William Pitt the Younger. (Many clocks were disposed of by their owners, and the effect on the clock-making industry was so disastrous that the act was repealed the following year.) Actually,

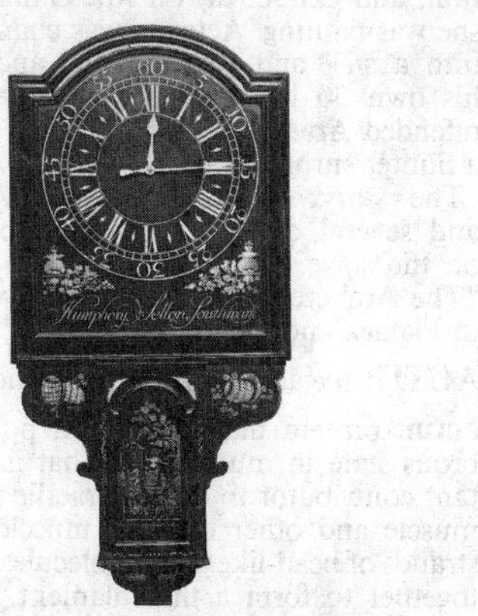

Act of Parliament clock, painted wood with gilt enrichments, English, mid-18th century; in the Victoria and Albert Museum, London

By courtesy of the Victoria and Albert Museum, London

these clocks were first displayed in inns during the mid-18th century (before the duty was imposed), probably for the convenience of passengers when coaches began to run on a definite timetable, and are more correctly called tavern, or coaching inn, clocks.

Acta (Latin: Acts), in ancient Rome, minutes of public business and gazette of political and social events. They were in two forms: *Acta Senatus* and *Acta diurna*.

The *Acta Senatus* or *Commentarii Senatus* were the minutes of the proceedings of the Senate. The emperor Augustus continued to keep them but forbade their publication. From the reign of his successor, Tiberius, in the 1st century AD, a young senator drew up the *Acta*, which were kept in the imperial archives and public libraries. Special permission was necessary in order to examine them.

The *Acta diurna, Acta populi,* or *Acta publica* grew out of Julius Caesar's arrangements for the publishing of official business and matters of public interest. Under the empire (after 27 BC) the *Acta diurna* constituted a type of daily gazette, thus to some extent filling the place of the modern newspaper.

Actaeon, in Greek mythology, son of the god Aristaeus and Autonoë (daughter of Cadmus, the founder of Thebes in Boeotia); he was a Boeotian hero and hunter. According to Ovid's *Metamorphoses,* having accidentally seen Artemis (goddess of wild animals, vegetation, and childbirth) on Mt. Cithaeron while she was bathing, Actaeon was changed by her into a stag and was pursued and killed by his own 50 hounds. In another version, he offended Artemis by boasting that his skill as a hunter surpassed hers.

The story was well known in antiquity, and several of the tragic poets presented it on the stage (*e.g.,* Aeschylus' lost *Toxotides,* "The Archeresses"). Actaeon was worshipped in Plataea and Orchomenus.

ACTH: *see* adrenocorticotropic hormone.

actin, protein that exists in a polymeric, fibrous state in muscles and that is an important contributor to the contractile property of muscle and other cells. In muscle, two long strands of bead-like actin molecules are twisted together to form a thin filament, bundles of which alternate and interdigitate with bundles of thick filaments formed of myosin, another fibrous protein. Two other muscle proteins, tropomyosin and troponin, regulate the temporary fusion of actin and myosin; this fusion results in the contraction of muscle.

Actin and myosin have been found in dozens of other (non-muscle) cells, and are believed to be responsible for the contractile properties of animal cells generally.

acting, the creating of another character, usually in a dramatic performance. The word comes from the Latin *actus,* "a doing, or performance." Mystery surrounds the art of acting because it is hard to supply a reliable formula of how to act or what makes an actor. Even many of the world's greatest actors have been unable to understand the process themselves.

A brief treatment of acting follows. For full treatment, *see* MACROPAEDIA: Theatre, The Art of the.

Part of the confusion over the definition of acting derives from the open-ended way in which Western plays are staged. Innumerable choices confront the actor in his interpretation of the character, the dynamics of the movement, and the way he will speak the text. The traditional Asian actor, on the other hand, is faced with comparatively few choices. He must master each role down to the minutest details according to a tradition refined over centuries by the subtle innovations of great actors. Within that rigid physical and vocal framework, he is then free to concentrate on spontaneity.

The ephemeral nature of acting also makes it difficult to place in a historical context. A performance exists only for the length of the play and has to be re-created each night. Until the advent of motion pictures and sound recording, there was no way of fixing a performance for all time, so there are only the written descriptions and paintings of contemporaries to indicate what the great actors of the past might have been like.

Most discussion on the craft of acting centres on an effort to understand relationships between the technical skill an actor requires and the sensibilities that lie beneath them, since the actor is both the instrument and the player. The most direct example of this is the question of an actor's emotion: How much of what an actor projects is genuine emotion and how much is feigned?

The history of acting has been paralleled by a search for systems that will lead to a more reliable understanding of the creative process that makes an actor. Aristotle doubted that acting could be taught at all, and more than 2,000 years later this is still a favourite controversy among theoreticians. Denis Diderot's 18th-century essay *Paradox of Acting* stressed the need for control, concluding that if the actor is to move the audience, he must himself remain unmoved. How the actor could achieve this on cue several nights running remained to Diderot an unsolved problem.

It was left to the Russian director Konstantin Stanislavsky in the late 19th century to suggest how the actor might recapture those moments when a performance had been truly inspired. Basing his work on an understanding of human psychology, Stanislavsky developed the concept of "affective memory." By focussing on a deep emotional experience in his past, the actor could learn to stimulate a similar emotional state in the present and to channel it to the requirements of a particular scene. Stanislavsky also drew attention to the importance of subtext, the nuances that lay beneath the lines.

Some of Stanislavsky's ideas were adopted in the mid-20th century by Lee Strasberg at the Actors' Studio in New York City and popularized as "the method." This was partly based on misunderstanding, because Stanislavsky's writings in which he stressed the need for technique were not then available in translation. Nevertheless, the movement produced many fine screen actors.

The major influence on acting after Stanislavsky was the German dramatist Bertolt Brecht. He saw characters as representatives of the class struggle and required his actors to stand outside themselves in order to present more objectively the arguments of the play. A third influence was Jerzy Grotowski, the Polish director who in the 1960s introduced a new level of intensity to acting achievable through fiercely rigorous training of the voice and body. All three of these directors emphasized a more disciplined approach to the craft of acting through which the actor could build what Grotowski called "the physical score" of the role. Like the Asian actor, he would then be free to find a spontaneity without the performance losing its shape.

The main areas of training today are in vocal and physical work. Vocal training aims to help the actor develop strength, expressiveness, and flexibility of voice so that he may portray a variety of characters. Similarly, physical training works to make the body supple and expressive. Physically the actor must operate in a state of concentrated alertness, for which he must find a balance between tension and relaxation. Improvisation, a favourite device of Stanislavsky's, is still at the core of the psychological aspects of training. It helps develop a sense of truthfulness in performance and encourages the actor to listen and respond naturally to his partner.

The rehearsal process is a period of collaboration with the director and fellow actors to arrive at an interpretation for the character and the play as a whole. This is the time when the actor shapes his creation, testing and revising it until he arrives at a finished, repeatable work. Even after the opening night, a performance should continue to grow as the actor makes new discoveries within what he has created.

With renewed interest during the 20th century in the broad span of world theatre, there has been much preoccupation with the question of style—the overall point of view of the interpretation. The way the world of Shakespeare, Molière, or Chekhov is re-created for a modern audience determines the style of the acting. Since our theatre is not fixed, style is subject to change, which can consequently make vintage performances seem old-fashioned because the point of view will be different for each generation.

In motion pictures and television the principles of acting are the same as they are for the stage, though truthfulness is even more crucial because the camera in close-up will easily expose any lack of concentration. In motion pictures, editing makes possible a composite performance compiled from several "takes," which has meant that some screen idols have succeeded on the screen through natural charm and looks alone. This is partly why screen actors often lack the technical skills to work in the live theatre, whereas most skilled stage actors can successfully adapt to motion pictures and television.

A list of the abbreviations used in the MICROPAEDIA *will be found at the end of this volume*

---

actinide, any of a series of 15 consecutive chemical elements in the periodic table from actinium to lawrencium (atomic numbers 89–103).

A brief treatment of the actinides follows. For full treatment, *see* MACROPAEDIA: Chemical Elements. *See also* MICROPAEDIA for entries on each member of the series.

All the actinide elements are heavy metals that are unstable toward radioactive decay. Only four of them—actinium, thorium, protactinium, and uranium—occur in nature in appreciable quantities. The remaining 11 members from neptunium to lawrencium, which are frequently classified as transuranium elements, are produced artificially by bombardment of other related elements with high-energy particles (*see* transuranium element). Uranium (or more properly its isotope uranium-235) is by far the most important actinide because of its fissionability—that is, the tendency of its nucleus to split into fragments of almost equal mass. The result of this fission is the release of large amounts of energy.

The actinide elements have a similar electronic structure, which is reflected by strong affinities in their chemical properties and behaviour. Actinides generally show several oxidation states. (When an element combines with others to form a compound, the number of electrons of its atoms that can be involved in the bonds of that particular compound is called the oxidation state of the element.) Most common among the actinides are the +3 and +4 oxidation states. The actinides in both these states bear a distinct resemblance to members of the lanthanide series in identical states. The lanthanides consist of the rare-earth elements with atomic numbers 57–71 (*see* rare-earth element).

actinium (Ac), radioactive chemical element, in Group IIIb of the periodic table, atomic number 89. Actinium was discovered (1899) by André-Louis Debierne in pitchblende residues left after the Curies had extracted radium, and was also discovered (1902) independently by Friedrich Otto Giesel. A ton of pitchblende ore contains about 0.15 milligram of actinium. The rare and silvery-white metal is extremely radioactive, glowing blue in the dark.

The commonest isotope of actinium is actinium-227; the others, natural and artificial, are too short-lived to accumulate in macroscopic quantity. Actinium-227, one of the decay products of uranium-235, has a 21.6-year half-life and in turn decays almost entirely to thorium-227, but about 1 percent decays to francium-223. This whole disintegration chain with its branches is called the actinium decay series.

Actinium, the ions of which in solution are colourless, exhibits an oxidation state of +3, closely resembling the rare-earth lanthanide elements in its chemical properties, and is the prototype of a second rare-earth-like series, the actinide elements.

atomic number	89
stablest isotope	227
valence	3
electronic config.	2-8-18-32-18-9-2 or $(Rn)6d^17s^2$

actinium series, set of unstable heavy nuclei comprising one of the four radioactive series (*q.v.*).

actinolite, an amphibole mineral in the tremolite–actinolite–ferrotremolite series of calcium, magnesium, and iron silicates. The minerals in this series are abundant in low-grade, regionally metamorphosed rocks. Tremolite may weather to talc, and both tremolite and actinolite may alter to chlorite or carbonates. For chemical formula and detailed physical properties, *see* amphibole (table).

The fibres of the magnesium-rich members are economically important as asbestos; these varieties, which are sometimes called amphibole asbestos, are the material to which the name asbestos was originally given. The fibres are fine and silky and have appreciable tensile strength; those occurring in thin, felted sheets of interwoven fibres are referred to as mountain leather; in thicker sheets, mountain cork; and in compact masses resembling dry wood, mountain wood. Nephrite (*q.v.*), a gem-quality variety in this series, is a form of jade.

actinometer, in chemistry, a substance or a mixture of substances that reacts through the action of light and that, because of the easily determined quantitative relationship between the extent of the reaction and the energy of the absorbed light, is used as a standard for measurement of light energies involved in photochemical work.

A typical actinometer is a liquid solution of oxalic acid containing uranyl sulfate. Light in the wavelength range of about 2080 to 4350 angstroms (ultraviolet to violet light) decomposes the oxalic acid (through a complex process involving initial absorption of the light energy by the uranyl ion) into a mixture of carbon dioxide, carbon monoxide, and water. A standard solution is generally irradiated with light of the proper wavelength and of known intensity, and the quantity of oxalic acid decomposed is accurately measured by titration with potassium permanganate. The experimentally determined relationship between the quantity of oxalic acid transformed and the quantity of light energy absorbed can then be used as a scale from which to predict either quantity when the other is known or measured.

In addition to the oxalic acid–uranyl sulfate solution, other substances commonly used as chemical actinometers include acetone, hydrogen bromide, carbon dioxide, and a solution of ferrioxalate in sulfuric acid.

actinomycete, moldlike bacterium of the order Actinomycetales, a group of microorganisms noted for a filamentous and branching growth pattern, which results, in most forms, in an extensive colony, or mycelium. Many species occur in soil and are harmless to animals and higher plants; others are important pathogens.

Many authorities recognize eight families, one of which, the Mycobacteriaceae, includes *Mycobacterium tuberculosis,* the cause of tuberculosis (*q.v.*) in man, and *M. leprae,* the agent of leprosy (*q.v.*; also called Hansen's disease). Others of the genus *Mycobacterium* cause tuberculosis-like diseases in other animals.

Within the family Actinomycetaceae are many bacteria that aid in the decay of plant and animal material in soil. The family Streptomycetaceae includes *Streptomyces* species, soil bacteria, many of which form antibiotics (*e.g.,* streptomycin). The Actinoplanaceae is a little-known family of aquatic bacteria that forms mycelia on plant and animal surfaces. The remaining families in the order are Frankiaceae, Dermatophilaceae, Nocardiaceae, and Micromonosporaceae.

actinomycosis, a noncontagious fungal infection of man and cattle caused by two anaerobic species of the genus *Actinomyces* and characterized by multiple painful, hard swellings filled with pus, most often seen on the face, neck, chest, and abdomen. *Actinomyces bovis* is responsible for the disease in cattle and *Actinomyces israeli* for that in man.

In man the organism lives chiefly in the mouth and bowel, growing best in the absence of oxygen, and disease is produced by direct invasion of devitalized tissues. Lesions of the neck and face (cervicofacial actinomycosis), notably the jaw, which account for about one-half of all cases, may appear following a wound in the mouth or a tooth extraction, and lesions of the abdomen may follow appendicitis or perforation of the stomach or large intestine. Infection of the lungs and surrounding structures (thoracic actinomycosis) may result from inhalation of the organism into the air passages and is usually associated with weight loss, night sweats, coughing, and high fever. In rare cases, the disorder may involve the brain, heart valves, or extremities; it may also be disseminated, via the bloodstream, in which case lesions appear in most parts of the body. Treatment is with antibiotics; surgical drainage or excision of accessible lesions are valuable adjuncts.

actinomyxidian, any parasitic protozoan of the small cnidosporidian order Actinomyxida; it inhabits the alimentary canal of certain aquatic worms. The characteristic spores develop in the host's gut after the union of large and small gametes. Spores contain three polar filaments (possibly anchoring devices) enclosed in capsules and one to many infective sporozoites. The spore is protected by a membrane composed of three parts, each of which may be elongated into a hook or other process. The representative species *Triactinomyxon ignotum* lives in the marine worm *Tubifex* and has spore valves that are elongated into three large hooks.

action, in theoretical physics, an abstract quantity that describes the overall motion of a physical system. Motion, in physics, may be described from at least two points of view: the close-up view and the panoramic view. The close-up view involves an instant-by-instant charting of the behaviour of an object. The panoramic view, on the other hand, reveals not only a complete picture of the actual behaviour of an object but also all the possible routes of development connecting an initial situation with a final situation. From the panoramic view, each route between the two situations is characterized by a specific numerical quantity called its action. Action may be thought of as twice the average kinetic energy of the system multiplied by the time interval between the initial and final position under study, or again as the average momentum of the system multiplied by the length of the path between the initial and final positions.

The value of the action for any actual motion of a system between two configurations is always a minimum or a maximum. In most instances, the behaviour of the system follows the path of minimum, or least, action. In an optical system, such as a microscope, light travels along the path of least action as it undergoes bending in the lenses. For light, action is proportional to the time of travel, so that the light travels the path that takes the least time.

With the beginning of quantum theory (1900), the concept of action took on a new importance. In describing the behaviour of molecular or atomic particles, a previously unsuspected restriction had to be invoked. Only those states of motion are possible in which actions are whole-number multiples of a certain very small number, known as Planck's constant, named for the German scientist Max Planck, who first proposed a discrete, or quantized, behaviour for objects of subatomic dimensions. Thus Planck's constant is the natural unit, or quantum, of action.

Action Française (French: French Action, or Enterprise), influential right-wing antirepublican group in France during the first 40 years of the 20th century; also the name of a daily newspaper (published from March 21, 1908, to Aug. 24, 1944) that expressed the group's ideas.

The Action Française movement originated at the close of the 19th century to champion the antiparliamentarian, anti-Semitic, and strongly nationalist views inspired by the controversy over the Dreyfus affair. Its leader, Charles Maurras, formulated the doctrine of integral nationalism that sought a restoration of the monarchy, considered the only institution capable of unifying strife-torn French society. Widely supported by Roman Catholics, small businessmen, and professional men, the movement, though based on a return to the past, was revolutionary in advocating violent overthrow of the parliamentary Third Republic (1870–1940). The disruptive tactics of the Action Française and its youth group, the Camelots du Roi (Hucksters of the King), brought it to prominence among right-wing groups prior to World War I.

The Action Française reached its apogee following World War I, when nationalist feeling was strong, but suffered a severe setback in 1926, when it was publicly condemned by the papacy. Yet it was still powerful enough to lead a serious attack on the republic in 1934. Because of its association with the German collaborationist Vichy government (1940–44), the Action Française was discredited and ceased to exist after World War II.

Action painting, direct, instinctual, and highly aggressive kind of art that involves the spontaneous application of vigorous, sweeping brushstrokes and the chance effects of dripping and spilling paint onto the canvas. The term was coined by the American art critic Harold Rosenberg to characterize the work of a group of American Abstract Expressionists (*see* Abstract Expressionism) who utilized the method from about 1950. Action painting is distinguished from the carefully preconceived work of the "abstract imagists" and "colour-field" painters, which constitutes the other major direction implicit in Abstract Expressionism and resembles Action painting only in its absolute devotion to unfettered personal expression free of all traditional aesthetic and social values.

"Untitled," Action painting by Jackson Pollock, oil and enamel on metal, 1948; in the Mr. and Mrs. Willard Gidwitz Collection, Illinois
By courtesy of the Sidney Janis Gallery, New York

The works of the Action painters Jackson Pollock, Willem de Kooning, Franz Kline, Bradley Walker Tomlin, and Jack Tworkov reflect the influence of the Automatic techniques developed in Europe in the 1920s and 1930s by the Surrealists (*see* Surrealism). While Surrealist Automatism (*q.v.*), which consisted of various chance effects and psychically inspired scribblings recorded without the artist's conscious control, was primarily designed to awaken unconscious associations in the viewer, the automatic approach of the Action painters was primarily a means of giving the artist's instinctive creative forces free play and of revealing these forces directly to the viewer. In Action painting the act of painting itself, being the moment of the artist's creative interaction with his materials, is more significant than the finished work.

Although it is generally recognized that Jackson Pollock's abstract drip paintings, executed from 1947, opened the way to the bolder, gestural techniques that characterize Action painting, it was the vigorous brushstrokes of de Kooning's biomorphic "Woman" series, begun in the early 1950s, that successfully evolved a richly emotive, expressive style.

Action painting was of major importance throughout the 1950s in Abstract Expressionism, the most influential art movement at the time in the United States. By the end of the decade, however, leadership of the movement had shifted to the colour-field and abstract imagist painters, whose followers in the 1960s rebelled against the irrationality of the Action painters. *See also* Tachism.

action potential, the brief (about one-thousandth of a second) reversal of electrical polarity of the membrane of a nerve-cell fibre in response to a stimulus. It gives rise to the nerve impulse. Sometimes called a propagated potential because a wave of excitation is actively transmitted along a nerve-cell fibre, an action potential is conducted at speeds that range from 1 to 100 metres (3 to 300 feet) per second, depending on the properties of the fibre and its environment.

When an action potential occurs in a nerve-cell fibre (*i.e.,* upon stimulation), the inside of a short segment of the fibre becomes positively charged, the opposite of the situation inside the resting nerve cell. This change in voltage across the short section of the cell membrane during an action potential is passed on to the adjacent section, so that the impulse moves along the fibre. The action potential appears to be caused by the movement of ions (charged atoms), across the cell membrane. Both the interior of the nerve cell and the fluid that surrounds the cell contain various ions. In its resting state, the interior of the nerve cell is rich in potassium ions and poor in sodium ions in relation to the surrounding fluids. Following stimulation by a chemical transmitter substance (such as acetylcholine), there is a transient increase in the permeability of the nerve-cell membrane to sodium ions, thus allowing them to enter the cell. The inward movement of sodium ions, which carry a positive charge, is believed to be responsible for the action potential.

If the entry of sodium ions into the fibre were not balanced by the exit of some other ion of similar charge, an action potential could not decline from its peak value and return to the resting potential. The falling phase of the action potential appears to be caused by an increase in the membrane permeability to potassium ions, which allows a charge approximately equal to that brought into the cell (as sodium ions) to leave in the form of potassium ions. Subsequently, sodium ions are actively pumped out of the nerve cell and potassium ions are pumped into it, thereby restoring the original ion concentrations and readying the cell for a new action potential. The Nobel Prize for Physiology or Medicine was awarded in 1963 to A.L. Hodgkin, A.F. Huxley, and Sir John Eccles for formulating these ionic mechanisms involved in nerve cell activity.

Actium, Battle of (Sept. 2, 31 BC), battle on a promontory in the north of Acarnania, Greece, where Octavian, by his decisive victory over Mark Antony, became the undisputed master of the Roman world. Octavian cut Antony's communications with the Peloponnese by occupying Patrae and Corinth.

Either hoping to win at sea because he was outmanoeuvred on land, or else simply trying to break the blockade, Antony followed Cleopatra's advice to employ the fleet. He drew up his ships outside the bay, facing west, with Cleopatra's squadron behind. The battle action is not certain, but it ended when Antony signalled to Cleopatra to escape; he then broke off and with a few ships managed to follow her. His land forces and the remainder of his fleet surrendered to Octavian.

activated-complex theory: *see* transition-state theory.

activated-sludge method, sewage-treatment process in which sludge (*q.v.*), the accumulated, bacteria-rich deposits of settling tanks and basins, is seeded into incoming waste water and the mixture agitated for several hours in the presence of an ample air supply. Suspended solids and many organic solids are absorbed or adsorbed by the sludge, while organic matter is oxidized by the microorganisms. In the process, gas is produced that is rich in methane, which is sometimes extracted and burned to raise the temperature of the mixture and accelerate the action, or used for other purposes. The sludge is then separated out in a settling tank.

Articles are alphabetized word by word, not letter by letter

activation, also called AROUSAL, in psychology, the stimulation of the cerebral cortex into general wakefulness or attention. Activation proceeds from various parts of the brain, but mainly from the reticular formation, the nerve network in the mid-brain that monitors ingoing and outgoing sensory and motor impulses. Activation, however, is not the same as direct cortical stimulation by specific sense receptors, such as being awakened by noises. It involves a complex of impulses both internal and external to the body.

activation analysis, a method of chemical analysis in which the sample is subjected to irradiation, usually by a beam of neutrons, that renders it radioactive; measurement of the radioactivity then indicates the identity and proportions of the chemical elements present in the sample.

activation energy, in chemistry, the minimum amount of energy required to activate atoms or molecules to a condition in which they can undergo chemical transformation or physical transport. In terms of the transition-state theory (*q.v.*), the activation energy is the difference in energy content between atoms or molecules in an activated or transition-state configuration and the corresponding atoms and molecules in their initial configuration. The activation energy is usually represented by the symbol E in mathematical expressions for such quantities as the reaction-rate constant, $k = A\exp(-E/RT)$, and the diffusion coefficient, $D = D_o\exp(-E/RT)$.

Activation energies are determined from experimental rate constants or diffusion coefficients measured at different temperatures.

activity, in radioactive decay processes, the number of disintegrations per second, or the number of unstable atomic nuclei that decay per second in a given sample. Activity is determined by counting, with the aid of radiation detectors and electronic circuits, the number of particles and photons (pulses of electromagnetic energy) ejected from a radioactive material during a convenient time interval. This experimental count, however, must be interpreted in the light of a thorough knowledge of the particular manner of radioactive decay in the sample material, because some sources emit more than one particle or photon per disintegration.

The international unit for expressing activity is the curie (abbreviated Ci), exactly equal to 3.7×10^{10} disintegrations per second and very nearly equivalent to the activity of one gram of naturally occurring radium, the old standard curie (abbreviated C).

activity coefficient, in chemistry, the ratio of the chemical activity of any substance to its concentration. The measured concentration of a substance may not be an accurate indicator of its chemical effectiveness, as represented by the equation for a particular reaction, in which case an activity coefficient is arbitrarily established and used instead of the concentration in calculations. In solutions, the activity coefficient is a measure of how much a solution differs from an ideal solution—*i.e.,* one in which the effectiveness of each molecule is equal to its theoretical effectiveness.

Acto Adicional of 1834, amendment to the Brazilian constitution of 1824, whereby some of the extremely centralist and authoritarian aspects of that charter were abolished. It was enacted as a concession to federalists and republicans who threatened to break the nation asunder.

The abdication of the unpopular Brazilian emperor Pedro I in 1831 precipitated the surfacing of violently opposed factions and civil wars—in Pará in 1831, in Minas Gerais in 1833, and in Maranhão and Mato Grosso in 1834. The constitution, which on the whole remained in effect until the inception of the First Republic in 1889, had been drawn up by a council of state appointed by Pedro I. The extensive powers it gave to the emperor, referred to as the *poder moderador* ("mediative power"), included the appointment of the members of the upper house of Parliament for life from lists of nominees prepared by special electors; the convening and dissolving of the lower house of Parliament, composed of popularly elected representatives; and the right to veto parliamentary acts, although a veto could be overridden if Parliament repassed the measure in three consecutive sessions. Moreover, the popularly elected provincial and municipal assemblies were dominated by imperially appointed presidents.

The Acto Adicional eliminated the reactionary Council of State. It also replaced a three-member regency, which had been instituted for the minority (1831–40) of Pedro II, with a single regent, to make the government more efficient. The amendment also created provincial legislatures, allowed for provincial control over primary and secondary education, and ended the entailing of estates.

Opposition to the central government continued, however, even after the reform: slaves in Bahia revolted in 1835, Maranhão broke out in revolts once again, and a 10-year revolt in Rio Grande do Sul, called the Guerra dos Farrapos (War of the Ragged Ones), began in 1835.

Acton (of Aldenham), John Emerich Edward Dalberg Acton, 1st Baron, 8TH BARONET (b. Jan. 10, 1834, Naples—d. June 19, 1902, Tegernsee, Bavaria, Ger.), English Liberal historian and moralist, the first great modern philosopher of resistance to the evil state, whether its form be authoritarian, democratic, or socialist. A comment that he wrote in a letter, "Power tends to corrupt, and absolute power corrupts absolutely," today has become a familiar aphorism. He succeeded to the baronetcy in 1837, and he was raised to the peerage in 1869.

Life. Acton was the only son of Sir Ferdinand Richard Edward Acton (1801–37) by his marriage to Marie Louise Pelline von Dalberg, heiress to a very respectable German title. In 1840 his widowed mother married Lord Leveson, the future Lord Granville and Liberal foreign secretary, an alliance that brought Acton early into the intimate circle of the great Whigs. Educated at Oscott College, Warwickshire, he went to Munich to study under the German Catholic Church historian Johann Joseph Ignaz von Döllinger, who grounded him in the new German methods of historical research.

Having spent much time in the United States and Europe, he returned to England, settled at the family seat in Aldenham, Shropshire, and was elected to the House of Commons for Carlow, Shropshire, in 1859. In the same year he became editor, following John Henry Newman, of the Roman Catholic monthly the *Rambler,* but this experience was unfortunate. He himself believed that a rigorously scientific history would ultimately strengthen the church and that Christian doctrine would be harmonized with the findings of history. When Pius IX indicated that it was wrong, though not heretical, to reject the opinion of the Roman congregations, Acton did not dispute the Pope's authority but held that it condemned the intellectual independence of his journal (by then called the *Home and Foreign Review*) and so laid down the editorship in 1864.

1st Baron Acton of Aldenham, oil painting by Franz von Lenbach; in the National Portrait Gallery, London

By courtesy of the National Portrait Gallery, London

Though he was no upholder of the papacy's temporal power and was ready to denounce its unfortunate effects on the course of history, he was firmly attached to Catholicism. Unlike Döllinger, he remained faithful to the Catholic Church after 1870, when the Vatican Council formulated the doctrine of papal infallibility. He regarded "communion with Rome as dearer than life."

In 1865 he married Marie von Arco-Valley, daughter of a Bavarian count, by whom he was to have one son and three daughters.

His parliamentary career had ended in 1865—he was an almost silent member—but his friendship with William Gladstone, the Liberal leader and prime minister, was of great consequence for the minds of both men. The poet and educationist Matthew Arnold used to say that "Gladstone influences all around him but Acton; it is Acton who influences Gladstone." He claimed, in fact, to be the author of the Home Rule policy for Ireland.

Acton was raised to the peerage on Gladstone's recommendation in 1869, and in 1892 Gladstone repaid his services as adviser by having him made a lord-in-waiting to Queen Victoria.

After 1870 Acton wrote little, his only notable publications being a masterly essay in the *Quarterly Review* (January 1878) on "Democracy in Europe"; two lectures delivered at Bridgnorth in 1877 on *The History of Freedom in Antiquity* and *The History of Freedom in Christianity* (both published in 1907)—these last the only tangible portions put together by him of his long-projected "History of Liberty"—and an essay on modern German historians in the first number of the *English Historical Review,* which he helped to found (1886). In 1895, on the death of Sir John Seeley, the prime minister Lord Rosebery had him appointed to the regius professorship of modern history at Cambridge. His inaugural *Lecture on the Study of History* (published in 1895) made a great impression in the university, and his influence on historical study was felt. He delivered two valuable courses of lectures, on the French Revolution and on modern history, but it was in private that the influence of his teaching was most marked.

In 1899 and 1900 he devoted much of his energy to coordinating the project of *The Cambridge Modern History,* a monument of objective, detailed, collaborative scholarship.

His efforts to secure, direct, and coordinate contributors for the project exhausted him. Suffering from the effects of a paralytic stroke that he had suffered in 1901, Acton withdrew to a Bavarian property belonging to his wife's family at Tegernsee.

Assessment. His life, as stated in his own words, "is the story of a man who started in life believing himself a sincere Catholic and a sincere Liberal; who therefore renounced everything in Catholicism which was not compatible with Liberty and everything in Politics not compatible with Catholicism."

A stern critic of nationalism, his liberalism was rooted in Christianity. "I fully admit that political Rights proceed directly from religious duties, and hold this to be the true basis of Liberalism." For him, conscience was the fount of freedom, and its claims were superior to those of the state. "The nation is responsible to Heaven for the acts of the State." If democracy could not restrain itself, liberty would be lost. The test of a country's freedom was the amount of security enjoyed by minorities. For Acton, in his judgment of politics as of history, morality was fundamental. He was the great modern philosopher of resistance to the evil state.

Civilized, cosmopolitan, rich, learned, and widely connected, he is remembered as much for his few historical writings as for his prescient concern with the problems of political morality. (A.W.J.)

BIBLIOGRAPHY. Gertrude Himmelfarb, *Lord Acton: A Study in Conscience and Politics* (1952), an excellent intellectual biography; George Fasnacht, *Acton's Political Philosophy* (1953), and Lionel Kochan, *Acton on History* (1954), two competent, specific studies; Hugh MacDougall, *The Acton-Newman Relations* (1962).

Acton, Sir John Francis Edward, 6TH BARONET (b. June 1736, Besançon, Fr.—d. Aug. 12, 1811, Palermo), commander of the naval forces of Tuscany and then of Naples who as prime minister of Naples allied that kingdom with England and Austria in the period of the French Revolution.

Finding the French Navy unappreciative of his skills, Acton, the son of an expatriate Englishman, joined the forces of Peter Leopold (later Holy Roman emperor Leopold II), grand duke of Tuscany, and distinguished himself by commanding a Tuscan squadron when Spain and Tuscany joined forces against Algeria (1774). In 1779 Peter Leopold's brother-in-law Ferdinand IV of Naples invited Acton to reorganize the Neapolitan fleet, of which Acton soon became commander.

A favourite of Ferdinand's wife, Maria Carolina, he rose rapidly, disposing of all rivals, becoming minister of the navy, of war, of finance, and finally prime minister with almost absolute powers. His English and Austrian alliances weakened the traditional ruling class and the clergy, which had close ties with Spain. In addition, he engaged Naples in a long struggle against the French Revolution, the liberal ideals of which he opposed.

When the French attacked Naples in 1798, Acton fled to Sicily with the King and Queen aboard the ship of Horatio Nelson, the British admiral. Naples was declared the Parthenopean Republic, but when Ferdinand regained control of Naples five months later, he instituted a reign of terror against those who had supported the French, for which Acton and Nelson must bear principal responsibility.

Acton stayed in power with only one brief interruption until the French attacked Naples again in 1806, and then he fled to Sicily with the royal family. He was the grandfather of the 1st Baron Acton, the renowned 19th-century historian.

actor-manager system, method of theatrical production dominant in England and the U.S. in the 19th century, consisting of a permanent company formed by a leading actor who chose his own plays, took a leading role in them, and handled business and financial arrangements. The advantages of this system became apparent in the 18th century when successful actor-managers such as Colley Cibber and David Garrick achieved performance standards superior to those achieved by theatre owners who hired occasional casts for individual plays. In the 19th century great actor-managers such as William Charles Macready, Sir Henry Irving, Madame Vestris, and Sir Herbert Beerbohm Tree maintained high standards. Shakespeare was an ever-popular staple in their repertoires because it afforded the actor-manager an opportunity for his interpretation of a famous role such as Shylock, Iago, or Richard III. The era of the actor-manager, however, was geared to star performances, and often the actor's most famous performance was in an inferior literary work, such as Sir Henry Irving's role in the horror play *The Bells.* The trend toward realism, partly the result of controlled lighting that allowed for the darkening of the auditorium, thus creating an aesthetic distance between actor and audience, led to the decline of personality-dominated plays. The actor-manager was replaced first by the stage manager, who unified the various effects of the performance from the point of view of an onlooker, and later by the more creative director, who imposed his own interpretation on the play.

Actors Studio, prestigious professional actors' workshop in New York City whose members have been among the most influential performers in American theatre and film since World War II. It is one of the leading centres for the Stanislavsky method of dramatic training. Founded in New York City in 1947 by directors Cheryl Crawford, Elia Kazan, and Robert Lewis, it provides a place where actors can work together without the pressures of commercial production or the duress of long runs. Actors Studio membership, which is for life, is by invitation; from 1,000 auditions, six or seven new members are chosen each year. Lee Strasberg was director from 1948 to 1982. In 1962 a production company was added to its activities, and later a western workshop was opened in Los Angeles. Strasberg extended the teachings of Stanislavsky and developed what came to be recognized as "the Method." In 1980 the theatre in the Actors Studio, New York City, was named the Lee Strasberg Theatre.

Acts of the Apostles, fifth book of the New Testament, a valuable history of the early Christian Church. Acts was written in Greek, presumably by the Evangelist Luke, whose Gospel concludes where Acts begins, namely, with Christ's Ascension into heaven. Acts was apparently written in Rome, perhaps between AD 70 and 90, though some think a slightly earlier date is also likely. After an introductory account of the descent of the Holy Spirit on the Apostles at Pentecost (interpreted as the birth of the church), Luke pursues as a central theme the spread of Christianity to the Gentile world under the guiding inspiration of the Holy Spirit. He also describes the church's gradual drawing away from Jewish traditions. The missionary journeys of St. Paul are given a prominent place, because this close associate of Luke was the preeminent Apostle to the Gentiles. Without Acts, an accurate picture of the primitive church would be impossible to reconstruct; with it, the New Testament letters of Paul are far more intelligible. Acts concludes rather abruptly after Paul has successfully preached the gospel in Rome, then the acknowledged centre of the Gentile world.

actuary, one who calculates insurance risks and premiums. He computes the probability of the occurrence of various contingencies of human life, such as birth, marriage, sickness, unemployment, accidents, retirement, and death. He also evaluates the hazards of property damage or loss and the legal liability for the safety and well-being of others.

Most actuaries are employed by insurance companies. They make statistical studies to establish basic mortality and morbidity tables, develop corresponding premium rates, establish underwriting practices and procedures, determine the amounts of money required to assure payment of benefits, analyze company earnings, and counsel with the company accounting staff in organizing records and statements. In many insurance companies the actuary is a senior officer.

Some actuaries serve as consultants, and some are employed by large industrial corporations and governments to advise on insurance and pension matters.

Acuff, Roy (Claxton) (b. Sept. 15, 1903, Maynardsville, Tenn., U.S.), U.S. vocalist, songwriter, and fiddler, called the "King of Country Music," who in the mid-1930s reasserted the mournful musical traditions of southeastern rural whites and became a national radio star on the "Grand Ole Opry" broadcasts.

Turning his attention to music after an aborted baseball career, Acuff gained immediate popularity with his recordings of "The Great Speckled Bird" and "The Wabash Cannonball," his theme song. By the early 1940s his sincere singing style, backed by the traditional sound of the Smoky Mountain Boys, was earning him $200,000 per year.

In 1942 he organized Acuff-Rose Publishing Company, the first publishing house exclusively for country music, with songwriter Fred Rose. From the mid- to late 1940s Acuff appeared in several movies, entertained U.S. troops, and made foreign tours. Following an unsuccessful bid for the Tennessee governorship in 1948, Acuff continued to record extensively through the 1950s into the 1980s, lending authenticity to the new boom in country music with such albums as *Will the Circle Be Unbroken,* performed with the Nitty Gritty Dirt Band.

In 1962 Acuff was elected the first living member of the Country Music Hall of Fame.

Aculeata, any stinging insect, originally of the suborder Apocrita (*q.v.*), order Hymenoptera. The rest of the Apocrita were known as Parasitica. Because distinctions between Parasitica and Aculeata were difficult to define, the names have been discontinued.

Some Aculeata species, for example, were parasitic in habit, and some Parasitica species were plant eaters. The noun and adjective aculeate, however, continues to be used to refer to any stinging insect.

Acuña (Mexico): *see* Ciudad Acuña.

acupuncture, ancient medical technique for relieving pain, devised many centuries ago by the Chinese and practiced today in many areas of the world. Modern Chinese surgeons have used acupuncture as a form of anesthesia, employing ancient charts that indicate points of the body at which brass-handled needles may be inserted. In 1971 two U.S. scientists observed the surgical removal of an ovarian cyst under acupuncture anesthesia in Peking. They reported that the needles were inserted in the patient's wrists and that she remained totally conscious with no evidence of discomfort. Since then many similar operations have been witnessed by other Western medical observers.

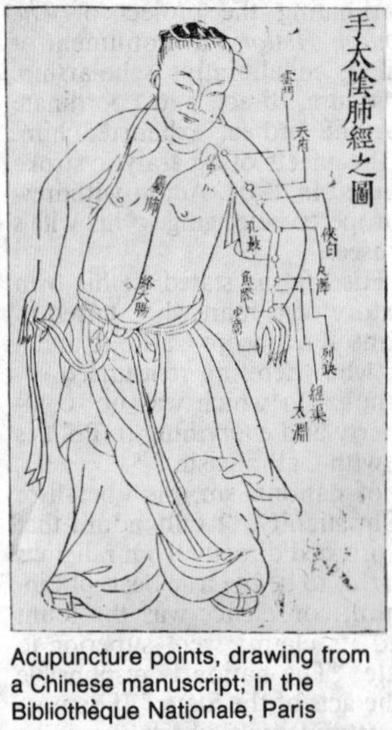

Acupuncture points, drawing from a Chinese manuscript; in the Bibliothèque Nationale, Paris

By courtesy of the Bibliotheque Nationale, Paris

Even the Chinese do not have a full explanation for the effectiveness of acupuncture, although they have observed that inserting a needle at one point of the body sets up a specific reaction at a second point. Acupuncture in the West has traditionally been considered a metaphysical treatment—illness is supposed to be the result of an imbalance of the body's forces. Western observers who reject the validity of acupuncture draw an analogy from early Western medical practice in bloodletting, which was claimed to control body humours and so remove putrefactions and redirect energy. Others who credit its efficacy but do not understand it suggest that it may liberate interferons. Acupuncture is supposed to stimulate or mute body forces and thereby prevent or control disease. Traditionally, it has been used to treat malaria, stomach upsets, and rheumatic or arthritic disease, to restore hearing for deaf-mutes, and to induce sleep.

ad: *see* advertisement.

Ad-Daffah Al-Gharbīyah: *see* West Bank.

Ad-Damar (The Sudan): *see* Dāmir, ad-.

Ad-Dār al-Bayḍā' (prefecture, Morocco): *see* Casablanca.

ad valorem tax, any tax imposed on the basis of the monetary value of the taxed item. Literally the term means "according to value." Traditionally, most customs and excises had "specific" rates; the tax base was defined in terms of physical units such as gallons, pounds, or individual items.

Ad valorem rates, which have come into increased use, have the important advantage of adjusting the tax burden according to the amount the consumer spends on the taxed items. They thus avoid the serious discrimination of specific rates against the low-priced varieties of the commodities. The primary difficulty with the ad valorem taxation, especially in the case of tariffs, is in establishing a satisfactory value figure.

Sales taxes of broad scope must of necessity have ad valorem rates. Property taxes are sometimes considered ad valorem taxes, since the rates are applied to the value of the property, as distinguished from special assessments, which are frequently imposed on a specific unit (*e.g.,* front footage) basis.

Ada, city, seat (1907) of Pontotoc County, south central Oklahoma, U.S., on Clear Boggy Creek, south of the Canadian River. It was named for the daughter of the first postmaster, William J. Reed, who built a log store there in 1889. The railroad arrived in 1900, and the city developed as a marketing and trading centre for a large cattle and grain area. The discovery of oil in the vicinity contributed to Ada's economic growth. Fine silica sand and limestone quarries nearby provide the raw materials for glass and cement industries. Plastics, auto parts, and clothing are also manufactured. The large Fitts Oil Field and the Robert S. Kerr Water Research Center are south of the city.

Ada is the seat of East Central Oklahoma State University (1909); at the campus entrance is a giant *Callixylon,* a fossilized tree stump dating from the Devonian Period (between 395,000,000 and 345,000,000 years ago). Inc. 1901. Pop. (1980) 15,902.

Ada group, ivory carvings and a group of about 10 illuminated manuscripts, dating from the last quarter of the 8th century, the earliest examples of the art of the Court School of Charlemagne. The group is named after a Gospel book (*c.* 750; Trier, Cathedral Treasury) commissioned by Ada, supposed half sister of Charlemagne. These earliest manuscripts of the Carolingian period, which initiated a revival of Roman classicism, are

"St. Matthew," page from the Ada Codex, *c.* 890; in the Stadtbibliothek Trier, W.Ger. (MS. 22, fol. 15r.)

By courtesy of the Stadtbibliothek Trier, W.Ger.

clearly more monumental in conception and more ambitious in the treatment of the human figure than previous Hiberno-Saxon or Merovingian manuscripts; but, as can be seen in the Godescalc Gospels (*c.* 780; Paris, Bibliothèque Nationale), they continue traditions from these other arts in their basically linear presentation, with a lack of concern for volume and spatial relationships.

Adab, modern BISMĀYAH, ancient Sumerian city located south of Nippur (modern Niffer or Nuffar) in Kūt al-Imāra *muḥāfaẓah* (governorate), Iraq. Excavations (1903–04) by the American archaeologist Edgar James Banks revealed buildings dating from the prehistoric period to the reign of Ur-Nammu (reigned 2112–2095 BC). Adab was important only up to about 2000. The Sumerian

Alabaster head of a man wearing a turban, from Adab, Akkadian period, *c.* 24th century BC; in the Oriental Institute, the University of Chicago

By courtesy of the Oriental Institute, the University of Chicago

king list ascribed to it one of the early dynasties, comprising only one king, Lugal-anne-mundu, said to have reigned for 90 years; according to his position on the list this would have been about 2400. At almost all other times Adab was ruled by kings who controlled all or most of Babylonia (southern Mesopotamia). The principal deity of the city was the goddess Ninhursag.

adab, Islāmic concept that became a literary genre distinguished by its broad humanitarian concerns; it developed during the brilliant height of ʿAbbāsid culture in the 9th century and continued through the Muslim Middle Ages.

The original sense of the word was simply "norm of conduct," or "custom," derived in ancient Arabia from ancestors revered as models. As such practice was deemed praiseworthy in the medieval Muslim world, *adab* acquired a further connotation of good breeding, courtesy, and urbanity.

Parallel to and growing out of this expanded social meaning of *adab* there appeared an intellectual aspect. *Adab* became the knowledge of poetry, oratory, ancient Arab tribal history, rhetoric, grammar, philology, and non-Arab civilizations that qualified a man to be called well-bred, or *adīb.* Such men produced a vast and erudite *adab* literature, concerned with man and his achievements and written in a style rich in vocabulary and idiom, and usually expressive and flexible. They included such writers as the 9th-century essayist al-Jāḥiẓ of Basra and his 11th-century follower Abū Ḥayyān at-Tawḥīdī; the 9th-century Kūfan critic, philologist, and theologian Ibn Qutaybah; and the 11th-century poet al-Maʿarrī.

As the golden age of the ʿAbbāsids declined, however, the boundaries of *adab* narrowed into belles lettres: poetry, elegant prose, anecdotal writing (*maqāmāt*). In the modern Arab world *adab* merely signifies literature.

Adad, weather god of the Babylonian and Assyrian pantheon. The name Adad may have been brought into Mesopotamia toward the end of the 3rd millennium BC by Western (Amorite) Semites. His Sumerian equivalent was Ishkur (*q.v.*) and the West Semitic was Hadad (*q.v.*).

An Assyrian governor standing before the deities Adad (centre) and Ishtar (left), limestone relief from Babylon, 8th century BC; in the Museum of Oriental Antiquities, Istanbul

Weidenfeld & Nicolson Ltd.

Adad had a twofold aspect, being both the giver and the destroyer of life. His rains caused the land to bear grain, wine, and food for his friends; hence his title Lord of Abundance. His storms and hurricanes, evidences of his anger against his foes, brought darkness, want, and death. The bull and the lion were sacred to him. Adad's father was the heaven god Anu, but he is also designated as the son of Bel, Lord of All Lands and god of the atmosphere. His consort was Shalash, which may be a Hurrian name. The symbol of Adad was the cypress, and six was his sacred number. In Babylonia, Assyria, and Aleppo in Syria, he was also the god of oracles and divination. Unlike the greater gods, Adad quite possibly had no cult centre peculiar to himself, although he was worshipped in many of the important cities and towns of Mesopotamia, including Babylon and Ashur, the capital of Assyria.

ʿādah (Arabic: "custom"), in Islāmic law, a local custom that is given a particular consideration by judicial authorities even when it conflicts with some principle of canon law (Sharīʿah); in Indonesia it is known as *adat,* in North Africa it is *ʿurf,* and in East Africa, *dustūr.* Muslim communities developed their *ʿādah*s before accepting Islām and did not abandon them entirely afterward. Thus in Indonesian Minangkabau, where many Muslims still retain old Hindu or pagan traditions, a matriarchate is recognized, contrary to the Sharīʿah; in parts of India, Muslims adopt children, forbidden by canon law, and then again circumvent the Sharīʿah by providing them with an inheritance. Such *ʿādah*s are accepted by religious courts as legitimate local laws that must be respected by others. Each community has developed its own norms for handling disputes and these may often disagree with standard religious teachings. Nevertheless authorities condone various religious customs to foster harmony and peace in the community.

Adair, John (b. *c.* 1655—d. *c.* 1722, London?), Scottish surveyor and cartographer whose maps established a standard of excellence for his time and probably inspired the early 18th-century surveys of Scotland. Between 1680 and 1686 he completed maps of the counties adjoining the River Forth as well as charts of the Firth of Forth, the River Clyde, and the west of Scotland. Manuscripts of these are in the National Library of Scotland and other libraries. Other maps and charts prepared by Adair also exist in manuscript. In 1703 he published the first part of his *Description of the Sea-coast and Islands of Scotland, With Large and Exact Maps, for the Use of Seamen.* The second part was never printed. Judging from his scrupulous delineations, Adair's search for perfection may have delayed completion of his work, but he was also hampered by the inadequacy of the public funds available for his work. In 1723 an annuity was granted to his widow for unpublished manuscripts that were later deposited in the Bodleian Library, Oxford, and in the British Museum.

Adair v. the United States (1908), case in which the Supreme Court upheld "yellow dog" contracts forbidding workers from joining labour unions. William Adair of the Louisville and Nashville Railroad fired O.B. Coppage for belonging to a labour union, an action in direct violation of the Erdman Act of 1898, which prohibited railroads engaged in interstate commerce from requiring workers to refrain from union membership as a condition of employment. In 1908 the Supreme Court decided in a 6 to 2 vote that the Erdman Act was unconstitutional. The court held that the act represented an unreasonable violation of the due process clause of the Fifth Amendment, which guaranteed freedom of contract and property rights; moreover, according to the majority, Congress' constitutional authority over interstate commerce did not extend to matters of union membership.

Adal (people): *see* Afar.

Adal, historic Islāmic state of eastern Africa, in the Danakil-Somali region southwest of the Gulf of Aden, with its capital at Harer (now in Ethiopia). Its rivalry with Christian Ethiopia began in the 14th century with minor border raids and skirmishes. In the 16th century, Adal rose briefly to international importance by launching a series of more serious attacks. The first phase, in which the forces of Adal were led by Mahfuz, governor of Zeila on the Gulf of Aden, ended in 1516, when Mahfuz and many of his followers were killed in an Ethiopian ambush.

Within a few years there emerged a new leader, Ahmed Gran (Ahmed the Left-handed). He gathered a following of Muslim nomads for a *jihād,* or religious war, against Ethiopia. They swept into the highlands, drove the Ethiopian emperor into exile, forced massive conversions, and by 1533 controlled most of central Ethiopia. They destroyed churches and monasteries. The fugitive emperor appealed to Portugal for help. Four hundred Portuguese musketeers landed at Mitsiwa in 1541. Adal then took on reinforcements as well: 900 Arab, Turkish, and Albanian musketeers, plus some canon. Adal's successes continued until Gran was killed in a battle near Lake Tana in 1543. The Oromo (Galla) invasions of the later 16th century put an end to Adal's power. Its rulers fled north into the desert, their nomadic followers lost any semblance of unity, and Adal was reduced to insignificance.

Adalbero OF ARDENNES, also called ADALBERO OF REIMS, French ADALBÉRON D'ARDENNE, or ADALBÉRON DE REIMS (d. January 989), archbishop of Reims who, by declaring the Frankish crown to be elective rather than hereditary, paved the way for the accession of Hugh Capet in place of the Carolingian claimant, Charles, duke of Lower Lorraine.

Adalbero, a native of Lorraine, had opposed the attempts of the Carolingian king of France, Lothair, to gain Lorraine from the emperor Otto II. Accused of treason, he was summoned by Louis V (986–987), Lothair's son and successor, to appear at an assembly of the leading Franks at Compiègne. But Louis's sudden death prevented the trial from taking place; instead, Adalbero denounced Charles of Lorraine, uncle of Louis, as unfit to succeed to the Frankish throne and supported the candidacy of Hugh Capet. Duly elected, Hugh was crowned by Adalbero in July 987 at Noyon.

Consult the INDEX *first*

Adalbert, Italian ADALBERTO (d. *c.* 966), Lombard king of Italy who shared the throne for 11 years with his father, Berengar II, and after Berengar's exile continued his father's struggle against the German king and Holy Roman emperor Otto I.

Adalbert joined his father in 946–947 in fighting the co-kings of Italy, Hugh of Provence and his son Lothair. After Lothair's death in 950, Adalbert was crowned with Berengar at Pavia. When Lothair's widow, Adelaide, refused to marry Adalbert and Berengar imprisoned her, Otto I marched into Italy in 951 to rescue and marry her. After Otto's return to Germany, Berengar and Adalbert resumed the throne and in August 952 swore homage to Otto.

In 956 Otto sent his son Liudolf against Berengar and Adalbert, but, when Liudolf died of malaria after a temporary victory, the co-kings continued to rule. When Otto again invaded Italy and was crowned emperor (962) by the Pope, Adalbert fled to Provence.

Returning to Italy in the autumn of 963, Adalbert was summoned to Rome by Pope John XII, who had quarrelled with Otto and now offered his support to Adalbert. Adalbert and the Pope fled when Otto marched on Rome, installing a new pope, Leo VIII. With Otto back in Germany, Adalbert assumed the throne again. In 965 an army sent by Otto drove Adalbert from Pavia; the following autumn Otto inflicted a final crushing defeat on him and his supporters.

Adalbert, also spelled ADELBERT (b. *c.* 1000—d. March 16, 1072, Goslar, Saxony), German archbishop, the most brilliant of the medieval prince bishops of Bremen, and a leading member of the royal administration. The youngest son of Frederick, count of Goseck (on the Saale River), Adalbert attended the cathedral school at Halberstadt, becoming subsequently subdeacon and, in 1032, canon. In May 1043 he was appointed archbishop of Hamburg–Bremen by the German king, later the emperor Henry III. High in the Emperor's favour, Adalbert tried to increase the influence of his archbishopric and to make Bremen a patriarchal see for northern Europe. Pope Leo IX, however, though he made Adalbert his vicar for the northern countries in 1053, never allowed him to exercise the authority that he desired.

Adalbert's secular ambitions involved him in conflict with the Saxon nobles and especially with the House of Billung. After the Emperor's death in 1056, the lands of his bishopric were ravaged by Bernard II Billung, and Adalbert had to flee to Goslar, where he gained considerable influence in imperial politics during the minority of Henry IV, whom he served as guardian and tutor. Henry granted Adalbert extensive powers in Saxony in 1063 but was obliged to dismiss him as royal adviser in 1066 because of the protests of the nobility. Although he was frequently at court after 1069, Adalbert never regained his political ascendancy. He was buried in the cathedral he had built at Bremen, a city he had made important.

Adalbert, SAINT, original name VOJTĚCH (b. 956, Libice?, Bohemia—d. April 23, 997, near Gdańsk, Pol.; canonized 999; feast day, April 23), first bishop of Prague of Czech origin. Descended from the Slavník princes of Bohemia, he was trained in theology at Magdeburg (now in East Germany). At his confirmation he received his name from St. Adalbert, first archbishop of Magdeburg.

As bishop (elected 982), Adalbert promoted the political aims of Boleslav II, prince of Bohemia, by extending the influence of the church beyond the borders of the Czech kingdom. He tried to improve the standards of church life but found little understanding among his countrymen for his lofty ideals.

Critical of the superficial attitude to Christianity prevalent in the country, Adalbert departed in 988 with the intention of leading the ascetic life of a monk. On papal orders he returned in 992 to find little change. He came into sharp conflict with some of the nobility and was probably drawn into the growing feuds between the Czech kings and the Slavník princes. Disillusioned, in 994 he left Bohemia again to become a missionary along the Baltic Coast, where he was martyred three years later. An account of Adalbert's life was written by his friend and disciple St. Bruno of Querfurt.

Adam BROTHERS (b. Nancy, Fr.; fl. 18th century), three French brothers who sculptured many monuments for the French and Prussian royal residences. They were exponents of a style that employed the textures of shells, corals, and perforated rocks. Lambert-Sigisbert Adam (1700–59) created sculptures for King Louis XV of France and Frederick the Great of Prussia. Nicolas-Sébastien Adam (1705–78) sculptured for Stanislas I Leszczyński, father-in-law of Louis and former king of Poland. François-Gaspard-Balthasar Adam (1710–61) was responsible for works at Frederick's royal palace of Sans Souci near Potsdam (now in East Germany) and at Potsdam itself.

Adam DE LA HALLE, byname ADAM LE BOSSU, or ADAM THE HUNCHBACK (b. *c.* 1250, Arras, Fr.—d. *c.* 1306, Naples), poet, musician, and innovator of the earliest French secular theatre. His *Jeu de la feuillée* ("Play of the Greensward") is a satirical fantasy based on his own life, written to amuse his friends in Arras upon his departure for Paris to pursue his studies; *Le Congé* ("The Leave Taking") expresses his sorrow at leaving his wife and his native Arras. As court poet and musician to the Comte d'Artois, he visited Naples and became famous for his polyphony as well as his topical productions considered the predecessors of comic opera. *Jeu de Robin et de Marion* is a dramatization of the pastoral

Adam de la Halle, detail from a manuscript, 1278; in the Bibliothèque Municipale d'Arras, France (MS. No. 657)

By courtesy of the Bibliotheque Municipale d'Arras, France

theme of a knight's wooing of a pretty shepherdess, with dances and peasants' dialogue. *Jeu du pélérin* ("Play of the Pilgrim") mocks his friends for forgetting him.

Adam OF BREMEN (fl. 11th century), German historian whose work on the archbishops of Hamburg–Bremen provides valuable information on German politics under the Salian emperors and is also one of the great books of medieval geography.

Of Franconian origin, he was probably educated at the cathedral school in Bamberg but was introduced in 1066 or 1067 into the cathedral chapter at Bremen by Archbishop Adalbert. In 1069 Adam was head of the Bremen cathedral school.

Adam began his *Gesta Hammaburgensis ecclesiae pontificum* (*History of the Archbishops of Hamburg-Bremen,* 1959) after Adalbert's death (1072). Comprising four books, it is a major source of knowledge of the archdiocese of Hamburg–Bremen and of Adalbert. In Book III a candid and vivid description of the Archbishop's personality and activities leads to an account of the German political affairs of the time. Book IV gives a "description of the islands of the north," and besides dealing with Russia, the countries of the Baltic peoples, Scandinavia, Iceland, and Greenland, Adam makes the earliest known reference to Vinland, that part of North America reached by Leif Eriksson.

Adam REX MENESTRALLUS (poet): *see* Adenet le Roi.

Adam THE HUNCHBACK (poet): *see* Adam de la Halle.

Adam, Adolphe-Charles (b. July 24, 1803, Paris—d. May 3, 1856, Paris), composer whose music for the ballet *Giselle* (1841) is notable for its dramatic power. It has retained its popularity with dancers and audiences to the present day. Adam wrote more than 60 operas, the best of which are generally considered to be *Le Postillon de Longjumeau* (1836) and *Giralda* (1850). In his ballets, which he composed for production in London, Berlin, and St. Petersburg, as well as Paris, he subordinated the music to choreographic demands. His works were successful in their own day, but few of them are regularly revived.

Adam, Paul (b. Dec. 7, 1862, Paris—d. Jan. 1, 1920, Paris), author whose early works exemplify the Naturalist and Symbolist schools and who later won considerable reputation for his historical and sociological novels. Publication of his first Naturalist novel, *Chair* *molle* (1885), led to his being prosecuted; his second, *Le Thé chez Miranda* (1886), written with Jean Moréas, is an early example of Symbolism. In 1899, with *La Force,* he began a series of novels depicting French life during the period 1800–30; the last, *Au soleil de Juillet,* appeared in 1903. He travelled widely and wrote two books on his American journeys, *Vues d'Amérique* (1906) and *Le Trust* (1910). His autobiography, in the form of a novel, *Jeunesse et amours de Manuel Héricourt,* appeared in 1913.

Adam, Robert (b. July 3, 1728, Kirkcaldy, Fife, Scot.—d. March 3, 1792, London), Scottish architect and designer who, with his brother James, transformed Palladian Neoclassicism in England into the airy, light, elegant style that bears their name. His major architectural works included public buildings (especially in London), and his designs were used for the interiors of such country mansions as Syon House, Middlesex (1762–69).

Early life. Robert was the second son of William Adam, the foremost Scottish architect of his time. William, who as Master Mason to the Ordnance in North Britain supervised the design of military buildings, also designed numerous country houses in a conservative Palladian style—the modified classic Roman style that was originally developed by the 16th-century architect Andrea Palladio. The Adam children grew up in the cultured atmosphere of a propertied and well-connected 18th-century family. Shortly after Robert's birth the family moved to Edinburgh, where, at the age of six, he entered the Edinburgh High School. In 1743 he enrolled at Edinburgh College (now University of Edinburgh), but in 1745 he abandoned his studies and the following year entered his father's offices as an apprentice and assistant.

William Adam died in 1748, and his post as Master Mason to the Board of Ordnance passed to his eldest son, John, who took Robert into partnership. In the succeeding few years both benefitted from the lucrative contracts that resulted from the appointment. Besides building Ft. George in the Moray Firth near Inverness, the Adam brothers were also engaged to complete the interior of the Earl of Hopetoun's house. In their interiors the brothers introduced into Scotland a new, lighter, almost Rococo, style of decoration. The other important private commission of these years was Dumfries House, Ayrshire, for Lord Dumfries.

European influences. In 1754 Robert, who by then considered himself to be worth £5,000, was invited to accompany the Honourable Charles Hope, the Earl's younger brother, to Italy. He thus had the opportunity to realize the dream he had been saving for since his father's death, and, just as important, he had the social advantages of travelling with the brother of an earl. He was as much concerned with meeting young noblemen abroad as with acquiring more architectural knowledge from a study of the monuments of Roman antiquity. The letters he wrote to his family during his years abroad give a picture of Robert as a madly ambitious young man, an arrogant social climber, and yet still a dedicated artist.

He met Charles Hope in Brussels, and they proceeded to Paris, where Robert fitted himself out in the latest fashions and set out to "lay in a stock of good acquaintance that may be of use to me hereafter." After fewer than three weeks in Paris, they set off for Italy via the south of France, visiting en route the Roman sites of Nîmes, Arles, the Pont du Gard, and Montpellier. They reached Genoa early in January 1755 and proceeded to Florence via Leghorn. Arriving at the end of the month, they were immediately caught up in the social whirl for which Robert had hoped.

While in Florence, Robert met a man who was to have an important professional influence upon him. This was the talented young French architect and draftsman Charles-Louis Clérisseau, who agreed to accompany him on his tour as instructor and draftsman. Clérisseau had been a student at the French Academy in Rome but had left in 1754 after a dispute with its director. As a result of his friendship with Clérisseau, Robert came in contact with avant-garde architectural theory in Rome. "I hope," he wrote, "to have my ideas greatly enlarged and my taste formed upon the solid foundation of genuine antiquity." Clérisseau agreed to

> serve [him] as an antiquarian . . . teach [him] perspective and drawing . . . [and] give [him] copies of all [Clérisseau's] studies of the antique, basreliefs and other ornaments. . . .

Adam left Florence in February 1755 and travelled to Rome, where he had to decide whether to devote himself to elegant society or to architecture:

> If I am known in Rome to be an architect, if I am seen drawing or with a pencil in my hand, I cannot enter into genteel company who will not admit an artist or, if they do admit him, will very probably rub affronts on him in order to prevent his appearing at their card-playing, balls and concerts.

He had to decide: "Shall I lose Hope and my introduction to the great, or shall I lose Clérisseau and my taste for the grand?"

He quarrelled with Hope, and the two separated. Taking rooms for himself and Clérisseau, Robert settled down to serious study, visiting, sketching, and measuring the monuments of antiquity. Among the important figures he met in Rome were the art collector Cardinal Albani and the engraver Giambattista Piranesi, who dedicated an engraving and a book to him.

In May 1757 Adam and Clérisseau left Rome and travelled to Dalmatia via Venice to visit the ruins of Diocletian's palace at Spalato (Split). Adam felt he

> could not help considering my knowledge of Architecture as imperfect, unless I should be able to add the observation of a private edifice of the Ancients to my study of their public works.

They spent five weeks at Spalato, preparing the drawings that were eventually to be published in 1764 as the *Ruins of the Palace of the Emperor Diocletian at Spalato in Dalmatia.*

Robert Adam, oil painting by an unknown artist; in the National Portrait Gallery, London
By courtesy of the National Portrait Gallery, London

The Adam style. Having nearly exhausted his money and anxious to return to England, Robert had to forgo the pleasures of further expeditions to Greece and Egypt. He returned to London in January 1758, his head full of details of Roman antiquities. The current Palladian style was losing its appeal, and the public was ready for a new architectural style. Adam lost no time in making his reputation, and by the mid 1760s he had, with the help of his younger brother James, who joined him in London in 1763, created and fully developed the Adam style. That style, which he and James later claimed had "brought about, in this country . . . a kind of revolution in the whole system of this useful and elegant art," was marked by a then new lightness and freedom in the use of the classical elements of architecture. In the Royal Society of Arts building (1772–74), for instance, Adam combined an Ionic pilaster—a rectangular column with scroll-like ornaments projecting from a wall—with a Doric entablature—the upper section of a wall designed in the oldest, simplest Greek style, a liberty a Palladian would never have dared take. This new style consisted basically of a fresh combination of many architectural elements. The various influences included the Palladianism of Lord Burlington and William Kent, both architects; the movement and vigour of the architecture of Sir John Vanbrugh; contemporary French influence, discernible particularly in details, planning, and furniture design; Roman archaeological influences; and the influence of Italian Renaissance decoration, particularly the fanciful ornamentation of the 16th century. Adam's genius was thus a result not of isolated influences but of the synthesis of various lines of development. The Adam style was essentially a decorative style, and it is as a designer of interiors that Adam is chiefly remembered. He gave meticulous attention to every part of each room, from the carpets to the most unobtrusive decoration.

Robert's first important work in London was the Admiralty Screen (1758). Through the influence of Lord Bute, a friend of the King, he was appointed Architect of the King's Works in November 1761 along with Sir William Chambers, his principal architectural rival. By the early 1760s he had many domestic commissions; almost without exception these consisted of the completion or redecoration of earlier houses. It was ironic that despite his fame and ability Adam was rarely called upon to build completely new houses, nor was he to realize his grandiose ideas for public buildings until the very end of his life.

The first Adam interiors at Hatchlands, Surrey (1758–61), and Shardeloes, Buckinghamshire (1759–61), were still near-Palladian. But by 1761 his mature style was developing, and important commissions from this time include Harewood, Yorkshire; Croome Court, Worcestershire; Kedleston Hall, Derbyshire; Bowood, Wiltshire; and Osterley Park, Middlesex. In 1762 he was employed to redesign the interior of Syon House, Middlesex.

Robert produced an important plan that proposed filling an old centre court with a vast domed pantheon-like hall; it was not executed, however. The entrance hall of Syon, based on a basilica—a rectangular building divided into three areas by two rows of columns—with its half-domed ends, is one of the most significant Neoclassical interiors in England. Other houses from this early phase include the first completely new house, Mersham-le-Hatch, Kent (1762–72); Lansdowne House, Berkeley Square, London (1762–68); Luton Hoo, Bedfordshire (1766–75); Newby Hall, Yorkshire (*c.* 1767–85); and Kenwood, London (1767–68).

The south front of Kedleston Hall provides an example of Adam's exterior treatment. His theme of a triumphal arch as the exterior expressions of the great domed interior hall is the first use of this particular Roman form in domestic architecture. The double portico (an open space created by a roof held up by columns) at Osterley Park, derived from the

Portico of Octavia, Rome, is a similar Neo-classical motif.

In 1768 Robert and James Adam leased a site on the Thames for a speculative development to be known as the Adelphi (it was almost totally destroyed in 1936). They invested a large sum on embanking the site and building several terraces of houses (1768–72) in which the Adam interior style of slim pilasters supporting a shallow frieze and cornice—the middle and uppermost sections of an entablature—was brought out of doors. It was, however, a financial disaster. In 1773 they again speculated unsuccessfully in a group of stuccoed terraces in Portland Place, London.

The Adams built three major London houses in the early 1770s, which were superb examples of their mature style—No. 20, St. James's Square for Sir Watkin Williams-Wynn (1772–74); No. 20, Portman Square for the Countess of Home (1775–77; now the Courtauld Institute of Art); and Derby House in Grosvenor Square for the Earl of Derby (1773–74; demolished 1862).

In 1773 they published the first volume of *The Works in Architecture of Robert and James Adam.* A second volume followed in 1779 and a third was published posthumously in 1822. In the preface to the first volume they explain their idea of "movement," an essential aspect of the Adam style:

> *Movement* is meant to express, the rise and fall, the advance and recess, with other diversity of form, in the different parts of a building, so as to add greatly to the picturesque of the composition.

By 1780 Robert Adam's popularity was beginning to decline, and Horace Walpole, after visiting the architect Henry Holland's new Carlton House, wrote, "How sick one shall be, after this chaste palace, of Mr. Adam's gingerbread and sippets of embroidery."

Neo-Gothic work. Robert Adam designed and built a number of romantic Neo-Gothic castles, mostly dating from the 1780s, in Scotland. The most important of the castles is Culzean, Ayrshire, for the earls of Cassilis (1777–90). Another important work in the Gothic style was the interior at Alnwick Castle, Northumberland (*c.* 1770–80; destroyed in the 19th century).

Toward the end of his life, Robert built the Register House, Edinburgh (1772–92), in which he at last realized the conception of a monumental domed hall within a square, envisaged at Syon some years earlier; and in 1789 he designed the University of Edinburgh, whose entrance front is perhaps his most successful exterior. At Fitzroy Square, London (1790), and Charlotte Square, Edinburgh (1791), he experimented for the last time with the introduction of movement into street architecture.

Robert Adam was buried in Westminster Abbey. The bulk of the nearly 9,000 drawings he left were purchased by the architect Sir John Soane in 1833 and are now in the Soane Museum, London.

Furniture design. As a designer of furniture, Adam played a leading role. The furniture style he evolved, popularized by the cabinetmaker George Hepplewhite, was always meant to harmonize with the rest of the interiors. In this field, too, he was prolific, turning his hand to everything from organ cases and sedan chairs to saltcellars and door fittings. It is one of the outstanding features of an Adam interior that everything, even the smallest detail, was part of the unified scheme created by the architect. (S.Mi.)

MAJOR WORKS. *Public buildings.* Screen wall to the Admiralty, London (1760; mutilated 1827, since restored); Gunton Church, Norfolk (1769); Pulteney Bridge, Bath, Somerset (1769–74); Chandos House, Portland Place, London (1770–71); Royal Society of Arts, London (1772–74); Register House, Edinburgh (1772–92); Mistley Church, Essex (1776; demolished except for twin towers, 1870); Portland Place, London (1776–*c.* 1780; partly rebuilt or demolished).

Country houses. Shardeloes, Buckinghamshire, portico, interior decorations, and stables (1759–61); Harewood House, Yorkshire, modified John Carr's designs and designed the interiors (1759–71; house much altered, 1843–50); Osterley Park, Middlesex, remodelling of interior (1761–80); Syon House, Middlesex, remodelling of interior (1762–69); Mersham-le-Hatch, Kent (1762–72); Kedleston Hall, Derbyshire (*c.* 1765–70); Luton Hoo, Bedfordshire (1766–75; altered *c.* 1816; reconstructed after a fire in 1843); Nostell Priory, Yorkshire, redecoration (1766–85); Kenwood House, Hampstead, London, remodelling (1767–68); Newby Hall, Yorkshire, added porch and wings and remodelled library (*c.* 1767–85); Saltram House, Devon, decoration (1768 and 1779); Culzean Castle, Ayrshire (1777–90).

Town houses. Lansdowne House, Berkeley Square, London (1762–68); Adelphi Buildings, Strand, London (1768–72, demolished); 20, St. James's Square, London (1772–74); Derby House, Grosvenor Square, London (1773–74, demolished); Home House, 20, Portman Square, London (1775–77).

Writings. Ruins of the Palace of the Emperor Diocletian at Spalato in Dalmatia (1764); *The Works in Architecture of Robert and James Adam,* 3 vol. (1773–1822).

BIBLIOGRAPHY. A.T. Bolton, *The Architecture of Robert and James Adam,* 2 vol. (1922), the standard work on the subject, with comprehensive lists of works and many illustrations; John Fleming, *Robert Adam and His Circle* (1962), an excellent biographical work based on original letters; Eileen Harris, *The Furniture of Robert Adam* (1963), the best and most complete account of Adam's activity as a furniture designer; Damie Stillman, *The Decorative Work of Robert Adam* (1966), an account of Adam's work in the field of interior decoration, well-illustrated with original drawings; and Doreen Yarwood, *Robert Adam* (1970), a popular biography concentrating on Adam the man rather than the artist.

Adam, Roi (poet): *see* Adenet le Roi.

Consult the INDEX *first*

Adam and Eve, the original human couple in the Hebrew Bible. Their story is told in two different accounts of creation in the book of Genesis. The first account, although it is now generally regarded as more recent in origin, is found in Gen. 1:1–2:4; the second, older account, which includes the story of the sin and fall of man, is found in Gen. 2:4–3:24.

Adam (*adham*), one of several Hebrew words meaning "man," is generally used in a collective sense to designate the human species. This is the way it is used in Gen. 1:26–27 in the first creation account, where there is nothing to suggest that an individual pair is meant. The definite article is used with the word in the second account ("the man"), but the English translations mostly use the proper name ("Adam") in these passages. Eve (Hebrew *ḥawwa*) is given to the first woman as a personal name in Gen. 3:20. The name is commonly explained through its assonance with the Hebrew word for life, *ḥayyim;* this etymology, however, is often questioned.

Chapters 2 and 3 of Genesis relate the creation of a single man from the soil or clay and his location in a garden called Eden; the creation of the animals, which are named by the man; the creation of a single woman from the body of the man to be a companion for him; the woman's temptation by a serpent and the temptation of the man by her; the eating of the forbidden fruit of the tree of the knowledge of good and evil; the curse of the serpent (it will have to crawl on its belly and will be at enmity with the woman's descendants), of the woman (she will have to undergo pain during childbirth and will be subject to her husband), and of the man (he will have to suffer and toil for a living and will eventually die); and the expulsion of the two from Eden. At this point, in the conception of the author, historical experience begins. After the expulsion, Adam and Eve had several children, including Cain and Abel and Seth.

Most biblical scholars now view the Genesis story not as a natural history but as an expression of the authors' beliefs concerning the relationship of man with the universe and with God the Creator. The composition is properly called a myth of origins ("myth" meaning an imaginative expression of basic truth). "The Man" and "the Woman" are typical figures, and the human adventure is foreshadowed in their experience. It is possible, by comparison and contrast with other ancient Near Eastern literature, to recognize and interpret most of the imagery used in the story, although biblical scholars differ in interpretations.

The Hebrew Bible does not elsewhere refer to the Adam and Eve story, except for the purely genealogical reference in I Chronicles 1:1. Allusions occur in the apocryphal books (*i.e.,* highly regarded but noncanonical books for Jews and Protestants; deuterocanonical books for Roman Catholics and Orthodox). The story was more popular among the writers of the pseudepigrapha (*i.e.,* noncanonical books for all traditions), which include the *Life of Adam and Eve,* told with much embellishment.

In the New Testament Adam is a figure of some theological importance in the Pauline writings. Paul sees Adam as a forerunner to Christ, "a type of the one who was to come" (Romans 5:12). As Adam initiated the life of man upon earth, so Christ initiates the new

Ivory relief of Adam in the Garden of Eden, 4th century; in the Bargello, Florence

Alinari

life of man. Because of the sin of Adam, death came upon all men; because of the righteousness of Christ, life is given to all men. Thus, in Paul's theology, it was Adam's sin and not failure to observe the Law of Moses that made the Gentiles sinners; therefore, Jews and Gentiles alike stand in need of the grace of Christ. It is likely that this Pauline rereading of Genesis is responsible for his emphasis upon the universality and the gratuity of the redemption wrought by God the Father in Christ.

Adam and Eve, Life of, pseudepigraphal work (a noncanonical writing that in style and content resembles authentic biblical works), one of numerous Jewish and Christian stories that embellish the account of Adam and Eve as given in the Old Testament book of Genesis. Because biography was an extremely popular literary genre during the late Hellenistic period of Judaism (3rd century BC to 3rd century AD), legends of biblical figures were numerous. But all surviving Haggada (folk stories and anecdotes) about Adam and Eve are Christian works and are preserved in a number of ancient languages (*e.g.,* Greek, Latin, Ethiopic). Although all Aramaic and Hebrew texts have been lost, the basic material was presumably of Jewish authorship. Extant versions of the *Life of Adam and Eve* have consequently been used to reconstruct the supposed original, which was probably composed sometime between 20 BC and AD 70, because the apocalyptic portion of the work (chapter 29) seems to imply that the Herodian Temple of Jerusalem was functioning when the book was written. The book is primarily noteworthy for its imaginative retelling of the biblical story and for its inclusion of visions and angelology, both characteristic features of Hellenistic religious writing. The detailed descriptions of the penances that Adam and Eve inflicted upon themselves after their expulsion from Eden suggest an ascetic influence.

Adamawa, traditional emirate in Gongola State, eastern Nigeria. The emirate was founded by Modibbo ("the learned one") Adama, a Fulani warrior and scholar who received a flag from Shehu (Sheikh) Usman dan Fodio in 1806 and who began a Fulani *jihād* ("holy war") in 1809 against the various non-Muslim peoples. Adama moved the capital of his kingdom, which was then known as Fumbina (Fombina), from Gurin (27 mi [43 km] east-southeast of Yola town) to nearby Ribadu in 1830 and to Jobolio in 1839 and, finally, in 1841, to Yola, which has since remained the seat of the emirate. At his death, in 1848, Fumbina extended over parts of present-day eastern Nigeria and most of northern Cameroon; even as the easternmost emirate of the Fulani empire, however, it was required to pay annual tribute (mostly in slaves) to the sultans at Sokoto, the Fulani capital, 555 mi west-northwest.

Adama was succeeded by four of his sons. Lamido (Lord) Hamman (usually known as Lawal [Lauwal, Lowal]) consolidated Fulani control during his reign (1848–72). During the weak rule of Sanda (Saanda), the Royal Niger Company established trading posts along the Benue River in Adamawa; when Emir Zubeiru (1890–1901) tried to force the British to leave Yola in 1901, British troops captured the town and compelled him to flee. After Adamawa was partitioned in 1901 between British Northern Nigeria and German Kamerun (Cameroon), Bobbo Ahmadu (Bobo Amadu), Adama's fourth son, became *amīr* of Yola in the British section of the state. Despite German attempts to change tradition, Ahmadu and his successors' titular suzerainty as *lamido* of Adamawa was recognized by the Fulani across the frontier.

Yola province was created in 1901 and was a battleground (1914–16) between British and German forces. Part of the German colony was incorporated as a United Kingdom trusteeship by a League of Nations mandate in 1922 and was mainly administered by Yola province and the *lamido.* In the general reorganization of the northern provinces in 1926 Yola and Muri provinces were roughly joined to form Adamawa province. Adamawa remained Nigeria's third largest province (31,786 sq mi [82,325 sq km]) until 1961, when the peoples of the United Nations Trust Territory of Northern Cameroons (whose share of Adamawa was 10,970 sq mi) voted to join Nigeria only if they were allowed to form a new (later Sardauna) province. The area of the emirate is now largely a part of Gongola State.

Besides the dominant Fulani, Adamawa is mainly inhabited by the Mumuye, Higi, Kapsiki, Chamba, Margi (Marghi), Hausa, Kilba, Gude, Wurkum, Jukun, and Bata (Batta) peoples. There are also, however, sizable clusters of Bachama, Kanuri, Longuda, Mbula, Vere, and Yungur peoples. All these groups except the trader Hausa population are primarily engaged in farming and herding, but fishing is also important along the riverbanks. Peanuts (groundnuts) and cotton are exported, as are cattle, dyed skins, and gum arabic.

The area is almost entirely a savanna region and is drained by the Benue River and several of its tributaries, including the Gongola, the Taraba, and the Pai. Yola, Jimeta, Numan, and Jalingo are the chief market centres.

Adamawa-Eastern languages, branch of the Niger-Congo family of languages spoken in east central Nigeria, northern Cameroon, much of the Central African Republic, and northern Zaire between the Congo and Ubangi rivers. At least one of the languages (Gbaya) is spoken by several million people. Linguists usually divide the Adamawa-Eastern group of languages into two subgroups: Adamawa (spoken in Nigeria and Cameroon) and Eastern (spoken in Zaire and the Central African Republic). *See also* Niger-Congo languages.

Adamawa Plateau, also spelled ADAMAOUA PLATEAU, volcanic upland in west central Africa. Chiefly in north central Cameroon, part of the area, known as the Gotel Mountains, is in southeastern Nigeria. It is the source of the Benue River. The plateau's highest elevations are more than 8,700 ft (2,650 m) above sea level. Many craters and small lakes attest to the region's volcanic origin. Vegetation is chiefly savanna, with some tropical woodlands; the economy is based on pastoralism, with subsistence agriculture, and there are also some cattle ranches. Some tin deposits are exploited, and exploitation of bauxite deposits began in 1976–77. The region is named for Modibbo Adama (died 1847/48), who temporarily united the Fulani people under a central government.

adamellite: *see* quartz monzonite.

Adamic, Louis (b. March 23, 1899, Blato, Slovenia, Austria-Hungary—d. Sept. 4, 1951, near Riegelsville, N.J., U.S.), novelist and journalist who wrote about the experience of U.S. minorities, especially immigrants, in the early 1900s.

Adamic immigrated to the U.S. from Yugoslavia at age 14 and was naturalized in 1918. He wrote about what he called the failure of the American melting pot in *Laughing in the Jungle* (1932). He returned to Yugoslavia on a Guggenheim Fellowship and wrote about the experience in *The Native's Return* (1934), the story of a man who finds he cannot slip comfortably into his former life. Two successful sequels, *Grandsons* (1935) and *Cradle of Life* (1936), were followed by his first novel, *The House in Antigua* (1937). His following book, *My America* (1938), a mixture of memoir and social philosophy, outlines his dream of a unified American people.

Adamic believed America had great potential but that tensions between ethnic minorities and the status quo were near crisis. Starting in 1940 he edited *Common Ground,* a magazine that analyzed the interracial culture of the United States.

An intensely political man, Adamic suffered greatly because of the fragmentation of Yugoslavia, and he called for U.S. immigrants to take democracy back to Eastern Europe. Labelled subversive by some, he supported Tito. Adamic was found shot to death, with a rifle in his hands; murder was suspected because of his political views, but the official cause of death was finally determined to be suicide caused by overwork and anxiety.

Adamnan, SAINT, also called ADOMNAN, or EUNAN (b. *c.* 628, County Donegal, Ire.—d. 704; feast day September 23), abbot and scholar, particularly noted as the biographer of St. Columba.

Nothing is known of Adamnan's early life. In 679 he was elected abbot of Iona, the ninth in succession from St. Columba, the founder. While on a visit to Northumbria he adopted the Roman rules on the tonsure and for determining the date of Easter that had been accepted for England at the Synod of Whitby in 663/664. He failed, however, to enforce the changes at Iona. He then travelled much in Ireland to promote the observance of the Roman Easter, but he was never able to persuade his own community. At the council of Birr in County Offaly, he succeeded in ameliorating the condition of women, particularly by exempting them from military service; he also made regulations protecting children and clerics; these reforms became known as the Law of Adamnan.

Adamnan's *Vita S. Columbae,* in which he describes the saint's prophecies, miracles, and visions, is one of the most important hagiographies ever written. He was also the author of *De locis sanctis* ("Concerning the Sacred Places"), a narrative of the pilgrimage (*c.* 680) made to the Holy Land by the Frankish bishop Arculf, who, forced by storms to the west coast of Britain, became Adamnan's guest. Adamnan is the subject of *Adamnan's Vision* (*Fís Adamnáin*), an Irish tale of the 10th or 11th century describing the glories of heaven and the sufferings of the damned as seen by his own soul.

Adamnan, Vision of, Irish Gaelic FÍS ADAMNÁIN, in the Gaelic literature of Ireland, one of the earliest and most outstanding of medieval Irish visions. This graceful prose work dates from the 10th century and is preserved in the later *Book of the Dun Cow* (*q.v.; c.* 1100). Patterned after pagan voyages (*imramha*) to the otherworld, *The Vision of Adamnan* vividly describes the journey of Adamnan's soul, guided by an angel, first through a delightful, fragrance-filled heaven; through the seven stages through which a sinful soul passes to reach perfection; and then through the monster-ridden Land of Torment. It is often attributed, erroneously, to St. Adamnan (*c.* 625–704), the abbot of Iona.

Adamov, Arthur (b. Aug. 23, 1908, Kislovodsk, Russia—d. March 16, 1970, Paris), avant-garde writer, a founder and one of the most important playwrights of the Theatre of the Absurd.

In 1912 his wealthy Armenian family left Russia and settled in Freudenstadt, Germany. He was subsequently educated in Geneva, Mainz, and Paris, where, having mastered French, he settled in 1924, associating with Surrealist groups. He edited a periodical, *Discontinuité,* and wrote poetry. In 1938 he suffered a nervous breakdown, later writing *L'Aveu* (1938–43; "The Confession"), an autobiography that revealed his tortured conscience, delving into a terrifying sense of alienation and preparing his personal, neurotic stage for some of the most powerful of all Absurdist dramas. He spent almost a year of World War II in the internment camp of Argelès, Fr. A severe depression followed.

Strongly influenced by the Swedish dramatist August Strindberg—with whose own mental crisis Adamov identified—and by Franz Kafka, he began writing plays in 1947. Believing that God is dead and that life's meaning is unobtainable, Adamov turned to a private, metaphysical interpretation of Communistic ideals. His first play, *La Parodie,* features a handless clock that looms eerily over characters who are constantly questioning one another about time. The world of the play is a parody of man, whom Adamov saw as helplessly searching for life's meaning, which, although it exists, is tragically inaccessible to him. In *L'Invasion,* he attempted to depict the human situation more realistically; it impressed André Gide and the director Jean Vilar, and, under Vilar's direction, it opened in Paris in 1950, with his third play, *La grande et la petite manoeuvre.* The latter reveals the influence of his friend, Antonin Artaud, theoretician of the "theatre of cruelty."

Le Professeur Taranne (performed 1953) was about a university professor unable to live up to his public role; though the play is dictated by the absurd logic of a dream, the construction and characterizations are firm and clear. In his best known play, *Le Ping-pong* (performed 1955), the powerful central image is that of a pinball machine to which the characters surrender themselves in a never-ending, aimless game of chance, perfectly illustrating man's adherence to false objectives and the futility of his busy endeavours. Adamov's later plays (*Paolo Paoli,* 1957; *Le Printemps 71,* 1961; *La Politique des restes,* 1963) embodied radical political statements, though his interest in dramatic experimentation continued. Finally admitting that life was not absurd but merely difficult, he committed suicide. In a preface to *Théâtre II* (1955), his second volume of plays, Adamov describes his attitudes toward his work and comments on his career.

Adams, urban town (township), Berkshire County, northwestern Massachusetts, U.S., at the foot of Mt. Greylock (3,491 ft [1,064 m]), on the Hoosic River, 13 mi (21 km) north-northeast of Pittsfield. Founded by Quakers in 1766, it was known as East Hoosuck until 1778, when it was incorporated and renamed for the Revolutionary War hero Samuel Adams. Local limestone and marble quarries supplied early building stone industries, and waterpower from the Hoosic led to the manufacture of textiles and paper. Mt. Greylock (highest point in the state, crowned by a 90-ft granite war memorial) and nearby state forests, parks, and ski resorts make Adams a year-round tourist base. The town's Quaker meetinghouse dates from 1784. The birthplace (*c.* 1810) of the pioneer woman suffragist Susan B. Anthony is preserved. North Adams is 5 mi north. Pop. (1980) 10,381.

Adams FAMILY, Massachusetts family with deep roots in American history whose members made major contributions to the nation's political and intellectual life for more than 150 years.

Established in America by Henry Adams, who emigrated from England to Massachusetts Bay Colony in about 1636, the family made no special mark until the time of John Adams (*q.v.*; 1735–1826). Perhaps the most profound political philosopher of the Revolutionary and Early National periods of U.S. history, Adams also served as the country's second president (1797–1801). His wife, Abigail (*q.v.*; 1744–1818) left a voluminous correspondence testifying to her wit, literary capabilities, and political insight. John's cousin Samuel Adams (*q.v.*; 1722–1803) was the firebrand of Revolutionary Boston, constantly organizing protests against British policies and shrewdly directing public opinion toward the goal of independence.

John Quincy Adams (*q.v.*; 1767–1848), son of John and Abigail, like his father served four unhappy years as president of the United States (1825–29). More than for his presidency, perhaps, he is best remembered for his diplomatic skills, which resulted in the acquisition of Florida and in the Monroe Doctrine, and for his heroic championing of antislavery petitions while a member of the U.S. House of Representatives. His son, Charles Francis Adams (*q.v.*; 1807–86), continued the battle against slavery as a congressman and as a leader of the Free-Soil Party. During the Civil War he demonstrated his own diplomatic genius while U.S. minister to Great Britain, preventing British recognition of and possible alliance with the Confederacy.

Except for a grandson of Charles Francis Adams—Charles Francis Adams III (1866–1954), who served as secretary of the navy during the Herbert Hoover administration—subsequent generations of the Adams family refrained from participation in public life. Charles Francis Adams, Jr. (1835–1915), was a businessman who for a time was president of the Union Pacific Railroad and who later retired to write a biography of his father and on other historical subjects. His two brothers, Henry Adams (*q.v.*; 1838–1918) and Brooks Adams (*q.v.*; 1848–1927), were also historians, as well as profound social critics. Henry Adams, in particular, ranks as one of the truly great American writers since the Civil War.

Other Adamses have been prominent lawyers, financiers, and corporation executives. Family characteristics of physical stature (short and stout), psychology (introspective and driven by guilt), and intellectual capacity remained remarkably consistent over the decades.

Adams, Abigail, *née* SMITH (b. Nov. 22 [Nov. 11, old style], 1744, Weymouth, Mass.—d. Oct. 28, 1818, Quincy, Mass., U.S.), prolific letter writer whose correspondence gives an intimate and vivid portrayal of life in the young republic; she was the wife of John Adams, second president of the U.S. (1797–1801), and mother of John Quincy Adams, sixth president (1825–29).

Although her formal education was meagre, Abigail Adams was remarkably knowledgeable and an avid reader of history. Her marriage in 1764 to John Adams, a young Boston lawyer, began a lifetime partnership of support and mutual respect that many considered an ideal union. For 10 years beginning in 1774, after the birth of four children, Mrs. Adams was

Abigail Adams, detail of a portrait by Ralph Earl, 1785; in the collection of the New York State Historical Association

By courtesy of the New York State Historical Association, Cooperstown

largely separated from her husband at the family home in Quincy, while he attended to federal business at the Continental Congress in Philadelphia. The enforced separation evoked a stream of letters, leading to the flowering of Mrs. Adams' genius as a correspondent. Her artless spontaneity brought the times to life with a charming blend of comments on minutiae of the day with observations on the momentous events of the Revolutionary period. She strongly supported the necessity of colonial independence from England, espoused the cause of women's rights, especially with regard to educational opportunities, and vigorously opposed slavery.

Following the peace treaty of 1783, Mrs. Adams joined her husband abroad while he served in diplomatic posts in Paris, The Hague, and London. Her letters to friends and family at home again provide a colourful commentary on manners and customs.

During the 12-year period when John Adams served as vice president and president of the United States (1789–1801), she moved back and forth between Massachusetts and Philadelphia (the temporary capital)—once more filling in the absences with her flowing commentary. In mid-November 1800 she became briefly the first mistress of the White House, newly built on the Potomac River in Washington, D.C.

The Adamses spent the next 17 years in quiet retirement at the family home. Successive printings of Mrs. Adams' letters (1840, 1876, 1947, 1963) periodically revived public appreciation of her contribution to the original source material of the early American period. Her biography was written by Laura E. Richards (1917) and by Janet Whitney (1947). *Dearest Friend: A Life of Abigail Adams* by Lynne Withey was published in 1981.

Adams, Ansel (b. Feb. 20, 1902, San Francisco—d. April 22, 1984, Carmel, Calif.), photographer especially known for technical innovations and masterly representations of the dramatic sweep of mountainous terrain.

Originally a student of music, Adams pursued photography as an avocation until 1927. In that year he published his first portfolio, *Parmellian Prints of the High Sierras,* photographs in the style of the Pictorialists, who imitated Impressionistic painting by suppressing detail in favour of soft, misty effects often achieved in the darkroom.

In 1930 Adams was so impressed by the U.S. photographer Paul Strand, whose photographs emphasized beauty of tone and sharp detail, that he adopted Strand's approach, called "straight photography." With Willard Van Dyke, Adams in 1932 formed Group f.64, an association of photographers who used large cameras and small apertures to capture nature's infinite variety of light and textures. Holding as paragons the crisp brilliance of daguerreotypes and the landscapes of the 19th-century photographers Timothy H. O'Sullivan and William Henry Jackson, Adams became one of the outstanding technicians in the history of photography. In 1935 he published *Making a Photograph,* the first of many books on photographic technique, illustrated with reproductions of his own prints.

In 1941 Adams began making photo-murals for the U.S. Department of the Interior. Forced by the large scale of this work to master the light and space of such immense landscapes as "Moonrise, Hernandez, New Mexico" (1941), he developed the zone system, a method of predetermining precisely what tone each part of the scene to be photographed will produce in the final print.

Throughout his career, Adams worked to increase public acceptance of photography as a fine art. In 1940 he helped found the world's first museum collection of photographs at the Museum of Modern Art in New York City, and in 1946 he established at the California School of Fine Arts in San Francisco—the first academic department to teach photography as a profession.

An ardent conservationist since adolescence, Adams served from 1936 as a director of the Sierra Club. Many of his photographic books, such as *My Camera in the National Parks* (1950), *This Is the American Earth* (1960), and *Photographs of the Southwest* (1976), are collections from the years he spent photographing the wildernesses of the United States, and are pleas for their preservation. Several general anthologies of his work, including *Ansel Adams: Images, 1923–1974* (1974) and *The Portfolios of Ansel Adams* (1977), have also been published.

Adams, Brooks (b. June 24, 1848, Quincy, Mass., U.S.—d. Feb. 13, 1927, Boston), historian who questioned the success of democracy in the U.S. and who related the march of civilization to the westward movement of trade centres.

Adams graduated from Harvard in 1870 and practiced law in Boston until 1881. Son of the diplomat Charles Francis Adams and grandson of Pres. John Quincy Adams, he was enabled by a substantial inheritance to travel extensively in Europe, the Middle East, and India.

Adams was particularly close to his brother Henry, a distinguished historian. Through an active correspondence they developed the idea—revolutionary at the time—that by its nature and substance U.S. democracy was foreordained to degradation and decay. In 1895 he published his *Law of Civilization and Decay*, in which he expounded his theory of history. It held that the centre of trade had consistently followed a westward movement from the ancient crossroads in the East to Constantinople, Venice, Amsterdam, and finally to London, in accord with a law relating to the density of populations and the development of new and centralizing techniques of trade and industry.

His *America's Economic Supremacy* (1900) accurately foresaw that within 50 years there would be in the world only two powers, Russia and the United States, the latter possessing economic supremacy. In 1913 he published *The Theory of Social Revolutions,* a study of defects in the American form of government, developing the idea of the imminent danger in the existence of great wealth that exerted private power but declined to accept responsibility. After Henry Adams' death, Adams prepared for publication his brother's book *The Degradation of the Democratic Dogma* (1919), for which he wrote the introduction—a kind of family chronicle that began with John Quincy Adams' troubles and ended with the renunciation by the two grandsons of the democratic dogma.

For most of his life Adams had been an agnostic and a profound skeptic; the roots of his Puritan ancestry were deep, however, and he returned in his last years to the church at Quincy to publicly profess his faith.

Adams, Charles Follen (b. April 21, 1842, Dorchester, Mass., U.S.—d. March 8, 1918, Roxbury, Mass.), U.S. regional humorous poet, best known for his Pennsylvania German dialect poems.

During the American Civil War he was wounded and taken prisoner. In 1872 he began writing humorous verses for periodicals and newspapers in a Pennsylvania German dialect. Collections of his verse are *Leedle Yawcob Strauss, and Other Poems* (1877) and *Dialect Ballads* (1888). His complete poetical writings, *Yawcob Strauss, and Other Poems,* with illustrations by "Boz," were published in 1910.

Adams, Charles Francis (b. Aug. 18, 1807, Boston—d. Nov. 21, 1886, Boston), U.S. diplomat who played an important role in keeping Britain neutral during the U.S. Civil War (1861–65) and in promoting the arbitration of the important "Alabama" claims.

The son of Pres. John Quincy Adams and the grandson of Pres. John Adams, Charles was early introduced to a cosmopolitan way of life when his father was appointed minister to Russia in 1809. He graduated from Harvard in 1825, and then, during his father's presidency (1825–29), lived for two years in the White House, studying law and moving freely among the political leaders of the period.

Charles Francis Adams
By courtesy of the Library of Congress, Washington, D.C.

In the 1840s Adams served for six years as a member of the Massachusetts legislature and as the editor of a party journal, the *Boston Whig.* He felt, however, that the Whigs should take a more forthright position against the extension of slavery into the territories, and when, in 1848, the so-called Conscience Whigs broke with the party to form the antislavery Free-Soil Party, Adams received the vice-presidential nomination of the new coalition.

The emergence of the Republican Party in 1856 offered Adams the permanent political affiliation he was seeking, and he was elected to the U.S. Congress from his father's old district in 1858. When the Republicans won at the polls two years later, Adams was named ambassador to Great Britain by his close friend William H. Seward, the new secretary of state.

Civil war broke out in April 1861, and, when Adams arrived in London the following month, he found that Great Britain had already recognized Confederate belligerency. So much sympathy was shown in England for the South that Adams' path for the next seven years was strewn with difficulties, but his logic, reserve, and directness appealed to the British, and gradually he won their support.

His main mission was to prevent the British from abandoning neutrality, and, with the issuance of the Emancipation Proclamation (Jan. 1, 1863), the immediate danger of diplomatic recognition of the South was over. Adams then laboured to prevent the building or the outfitting at British shipyards of privateers for Confederate use. He had not been able to prevent the sailing (May 1862) of the highly effective commerce destroyer "Alabama," but his vigorous protestations of the obligations of neutrals succeeded in preventing further launchings. Furthermore, he persistently argued the British government's responsibility for the estimated $6,000,000 worth of damage done by the "Alabama" to Federal merchant vessels. During this long and taxing period in Anglo-American relations, Adams' judicious and balanced conduct greatly enhanced the reputation of his country abroad.

From 1871 to 1872 Adams served as U.S. arbiter on the international commission that met at Geneva to settle the "Alabama" claims. His name is inseparable from this seminal work in forwarding the concept of world law through arbitration. He edited *Works of John Adams* (1850–56) and *Memoirs of John Quincy Adams* (1874–77). His biography was written in 1900 by his son, Charles Francis Adams, Jr. A more recent work is Martin B. Duberman's biography, published in 1961.

Adams, Franklin Pierce, byname F.P.A. (b. Nov. 15, 1881, Chicago—d. March 23, 1960, New York City), U.S. newspaper columnist, translator, poet, and radio personality whose humorous syndicated column "The Conning Tower" earned him the reputation of godfather of the contemporary newspaper column. He wrote primarily under his initials, F.P.A.

Adams' newspaper career began in 1903, with the *Chicago Journal.* The next year he went to New York, where he wrote for several newspapers. From 1913 to 1937 his column, "The Conning Tower," appeared in the *Herald Tribune* and several other New York newspapers, interrupted only during the years of World War I, when Adams wrote a column for *Stars and Stripes,* and from 1923 to 1931, when he worked for the New York *World* until it ceased publication. Witty and well-written, his columns consisted of informal yet careful critiques of the contemporary U.S. scene. His column also included writing by such authors as Dorothy Parker and Sinclair Lewis. His Saturday columns imitated the language and style of Samuel Pepys' diary, and Adams is credited with a renewal of interest in Pepys. Reprints were collected in *The Diary of Our Own Samuel Pepys* (1935).

Adams' poetry is light and conventionally rhymed. He hated free verse and was never slow in expressing this opinion. His verse is collected in 10 volumes, beginning with *Tobogganing on Parnassus* (1911); the final volume, *The Melancholy Lute* (1936), is Adams' selection from 30 years of his writing.

In 1938, Adams became one of the panel of experts on the radio show "Information, Please." He achieved almost instant popularity for his humour and erudition, and his name became something of a household word in the 1930s, '40s, and '50s.

Adams, Henry (Brooks) (b. Feb. 16, 1838, Boston—d. March 27, 1918, Washington, D.C.), historian, man of letters, and author of one of the outstanding autobiographies of Western literature, *The Education of Henry Adams.*

Adams was the product of Boston's Brahmin class, a cultured elite that traced its lineage to Puritan New England. He was the great-grandson of John Adams and the grandson of John Quincy Adams, both presidents of the United States. The Adams family tradition of leadership was carried on by his father, Charles Francis Adams (1807–86), a diplomat, historian, and congressman. His younger brother, Brooks (1848–1927), was also a historian; his older brother, Charles Francis, Jr. (1835–1915), was an author and railroad executive. Through his mother, Abigail Brown Brooks, Adams was related to one of the most dis-

Henry Adams
By courtesy of Harvard University Archives

tinguished and wealthiest families in Boston. Tradition ingrained a deep sense of morality in Adams. He never escaped his heritage and often spoke of himself as a child of the 17th and 18th centuries who was forced to come to terms with the new world of the 20th century.

Adams was graduated from Harvard in 1858 and, in typical patrician fashion, embarked upon a grand tour of Europe in search of amusement and a vocation. Anticipating a career as an attorney, he spent the winter of 1859 attending lectures in civil law at the University of Berlin. With the outbreak of the U.S. Civil War in 1861, Pres. Abraham Lincoln appointed Adams' father minister to England. Henry, age 23, accompanied him to London, acting as his private secretary until 1868.

Returning to the United States, Adams travelled to Washington, D.C., as a newspaper correspondent for *The Nation* and other leading journals. He plunged into the capital's social and political life, anxious to begin the reconstruction of a nation shattered by war. He called for civil service reform and retention of the silver standard. Adams wrote numerous essays exposing political corruption and warning against the growing power of economic monopolies, particularly railroads. These articles were published in *Chapters of Erie and Other Essays* (1871). The mediocrity of the nation's "statesmen" constantly irritated him. Adams liked to repeat Pres. Ulysses S. Grant's remark that Venice would be a fine city if it were drained.

Adams continued his reformist activities as editor of the *North American Review* (1870–76). Moreover, he participated in the Liberal Republican movement. This group of insurgents, repelled by partisanship and the scandals of the Grant administration, bolted the Republican Party in 1872 and nominated the Democrat Horace Greeley for president. Their crusade soon foundered. Adams grew disillusioned with a world he characterized as devoid of principle. He was disgusted with demagogic politicians and a society in which all became "servant[s] of the powerhouse." Americans, he wrote, "had no time for thought; they saw, and could see, nothing beyond their day's work; their attitude to the universe outside them was that of the deep-sea fish." His anonymously published novel *Democracy, an American Novel* (1880) reflected his loss of faith. The heroine, Madeleine Lee, like Adams himself, becomes an intimate of Washington's political circles. As confidante of a Midwestern senator, Madeleine is introduced to the democratic process. She meets the President and other figures who are equally vacuous. After her contact with the power brokers, Madeleine concluded: "Democracy has shaken my nerves to pieces."

In 1870 Charles W. Eliot, president of Harvard College, appointed Adams professor of medieval history. He was the first American to employ the seminar method in teaching history. In 1877 he resigned to edit the papers of Thomas Jefferson's treasury secretary, Albert Gallatin. Pursuing his interest in U.S. history, Adams completed two biographies, *The Life of Albert Gallatin* (1879) and *John Randolph* (1882). He continued to delve into the nation's early national period, hoping to understand the nature of an evolving American democracy. This study culminated in his nine-volume *History of the United States of America* during the administrations of Jefferson and Madison, a scholarly work that received immediate acclaim after its publication (1889–91). In this work he explored the dilemma of governing an egalitarian society in a political world in which the predominant tendency was to aggrandize power. In 1884 Adams wrote another novel, *Esther*. Published under a pseudonym, *Esther* dealt with the relationship between religion and modern science, a theme that engaged Adams throughout his life.

Adams was stunned when, in 1885, his wife of 13 years, Marian Hooper, committed suicide. Distraught, he arranged for the sculpture of a mysterious, cloaked woman to be placed upon her grave. The union had produced no children, and Adams never remarried. After his wife's death, Adams began a period of restless wandering. He travelled the globe from the South Sea islands to the Middle East. Gradually the circuit narrowed to winters in Washington and summers in Paris.

Though Adams referred to his existence during this period as that of a "cave-dweller," his life was quite the opposite. From the 1870s until his last years, intellectuals gravitated to his home to discuss art, science, politics, and literature. Among them were the British diplomat Sir Cecil Arthur Spring-Rice, the architect Henry Hobson Richardson, and Sen. Henry Cabot Lodge. His closest friends were the geologist Clarence King and the diplomat John Hay. Adams and King were inseparable. Their letters remain a rich source of information on everything from gossip to the most current trends of thought.

While in France, Adams pushed further into the recesses of history in search of "a fixed point . . . from which he might measure motion down to his own time." That point became medieval Christendom in the 13th century. In *Mont-Saint-Michel and Chartres* (printed privately, 1904; published, 1913) he described the medieval world view as reflected in its cathedrals. These buildings, he believed, expressed "an emotion, the deepest man ever felt—the struggle of his own littleness to grasp the infinite." Adams' attraction to the Middle Ages lay in the era's ideological unity; a coherence expressed in Catholicism and symbolized by the Virgin Mary.

The Education of Henry Adams (printed privately, 1906; published 1918) was a companion volume to *Chartres*. The *Education* remains Adams' best known work and one of the most distinguished of all autobiographies. In contrast to *Chartres*, the *Education* centred upon the 20th-century universe of multiplicity, particularly the exploding world of science and technology. In opposition to the medieval Virgin, Adams saw a new godhead—the dynamo—symbol of modern history's anarchic energies. The *Education* recorded his failure to understand the centrifugal forces of contemporary life. The book traced Adams' confrontations with reality as he moved from the custom-bound world of his birth into the modern, existential universe in which certainties had vanished.

Neither history nor education provided an answer for Henry Adams. Individuals, he believed, could not face reality; to endure, one adopts illusions. His attempt to draw lines of continuity from the 13th to the 20th century ended in futility. Adams concluded that all he could prove was change.

In 1908 Adams edited the letters and diary of his friend John Hay, secretary of state from 1898 to 1905. His last book, *The Life of George Cabot Lodge*, was published in 1911. In two speculative essays, "Rule of Phase Applied to History" (1909) and *Letter to American Teachers of History* (1910), Adams calculated the demise of the world. Basing his theory on a scientific law, the dissipation of energy, he described civilization as having retrogressed through four stages: the religious, mechanical, electrical, and ethereal. The cataclysm, he prophesied, would occur in 1921. How literally Adams intended his prediction remains a point of dispute.

In 1912, at the age of 74, Adams suffered a stroke. His haunting fear of senility became real for a short time. For three months he lay partially paralyzed, his mind hovering between reason and delirium. He recovered sufficiently, however, to travel to Europe once again. When he died, in his sleep in his Washington home, he was, according to his wish, buried next to his wife in an unmarked grave. In 1919 he was posthumously awarded a Pulitzer Prize for the *Education*.

Adams is noted for an ironic literary style coupled with a detached, often bitter, tone. These characteristics have led some critics to view him as an irascible misfit. They contend that his fascination with the Middle Ages and his continuous emphasis upon failure were masks behind which he hid a misanthropic alienation from the world. More sympathetic commentators see Adams as a romantic figure who sought meaning in the chaos and violence of the 20th century. As Adams described it, he was in pursuit of ". . . a world that sensitive and timid natures could regard without a shudder." (C.McH.)

BIBLIOGRAPHY. Henry Adams, *The Degradation of the Democratic Dogma* (1919, reprinted 1969), a collection of Adams' theoretical essays with a lengthy introduction by his brother Brooks; "The Great Secession Winter 1860–1861," *Proceedings*, Massachusetts Historical Society, 43:656–687 (1909–10), an essay, written during the secession crisis of 1860–61 but not published for 50 years, which analyzed the political developments that led to the Civil War; *Essays in Anglo-Saxon Law* (1876), a collection of studies in early British history written by Adams and his seminar students; *Historical Essays* (1891), a reprint of articles Adams had previously published in various journals; and introductions to *Documents Relating to New England Federalism* (1877), which shed light on the politics of the early national period; Ernest Samuels (ed.), *The Education of Henry Adams* (1973), is the definitive edition in which collation is made between the privately printed text and the revised text of the published edition. Worthington Chauncey Ford (ed.), *A Cycle of Adams Letters, 1861–1865*, 2 vol. (1920, reprinted in 1 vol. 1969), *Letters of Henry Adams, 1858–1891* (1930, reprinted 1969), and *Letters of Henry Adams, 1892–1918* (1938, reprinted 1969), all contain a rich selection of Adams' letters; Ernest Samuels, *The Young Henry Adams* (1948), *Henry Adams: The Middle Years* (1958), and *Henry Adams: The Major Phase* (1964), the most comprehensive and distinguished biography of Adams; J.C. Levenson, *The Mind and Art of Henry Adams* (1957), an unexcelled interpretative work centring upon both the man and his writings; Melvin Lyon, *Symbol and Idea in Henry Adams* (1970), an examination of the problem of illusion and reality, which Adams often expressed through symbols, as seen in his six major works; Vern Wagner, *The Suspension of Henry Adams: A Study of Manner and Matter* (1969), a discussion of Adams' writing style as an example of unique literary artistry; Frederic Cople Jaher, *Doubters and Dissenters: Cataclysmic Thought in America, 1885–1918* (1964), a critical study of Adams, seeing him as a displaced Brahmin afloat in an industrialized world he was helpless to understand; William Dusinberre, *Henry Adams: The Myth of Failure* (1980), is a reconsideration.

Adams, Herbert Baxter (b. April 16, 1850, Shutesbury, Mass., U.S.—d. July 30, 1901, Amherst, Mass.), historian and educator, one of the first to use the seminar method in U.S. higher education and one of the founders of the American Historical Association.

The son of a successful merchant and manufacturer, Adams graduated from Amherst College, Massachusetts, in 1872 and attended lectures in Germany between 1874 and 1876 at Göttingen, Berlin, and Heidelberg, receiving his Ph.D. from the latter in July 1876. His stay in Germany had two results. It started him on the road, in his own historical work, toward a "germ theory of politics," which traced American political institutions to their supposed origin in early Anglo-Saxon village institutions; and it convinced him of the superior quality of scholarship and instruction possible in the seminar method of teaching.

Herbert Adams

By courtesy of the Library of Congress, Washington, D.C.

When Adams joined the faculty of Johns Hopkins University, Baltimore, in 1876, he was influential in instituting a seminar in history that became an important model for American higher education. Named secretary of the newly formed American Historical Association in 1884, Adams extended his activities to the editing of publications by the U.S. Bureau of Education.

While Adams' own scholarship and criticism were relatively undistinguished, his enthusiasm and interest were highly influential on his students, among them the future U.S. president Woodrow Wilson and the eminent historian Frederick Jackson Turner.

Where the same name may denote a person, place, or thing, the articles will be found in that order

Adams, John (b. Oct. 30 [Oct. 19, old style], 1735, Braintree, Mass.—d. July 4, 1826, Quincy, Mass., U.S.), first vice president (1789–97) and second president (1797–1801) of the United States, who earlier had served the American independence movement as a politician and political theorist, influencing the content of state constitutions. He also served as a diplomat during and immediately after the American Revolution.

Early life. John Adams was the eldest of three sons of Deacon John Adams, a farmer and selectman, and Susanna Boylston of Braintree, Mass. There he grew up, relishing all the outdoor joys of boyhood, and was educated for college. After graduating in 1755 from Harvard, he studied law in Worcester in the office of James Putnam, a sophisticated and learned man, in whose household he lived while teaching grammar school. Having returned to Braintree in 1758 and been admitted to the Boston bar, Adams in 1764 married Abigail Smith, a minister's daughter of neighbouring Weymouth who had important family connections that were to benefit his practice.

Intelligent, vivacious, and witty, Abigail composed brilliant letters that together with an uninhibited diary kept by Adams reveal the earthy culture of the New England countryside of the time and its avidity for manners and learning. In this remarkably self-revealing diary, Adams exhibits a talent for the delineation of character in others. A bundle of contradictions himself, he was sometimes outspoken to the point of rudeness, but at other times scholarly and urbane; irascible, jealous, and suspicious, he was also playful and tender.

As a young lawyer Adams was not only proud of his learning but apparently ambitious of being in print. In this he succeeded in 1763 by making contributions simultaneously to different newspapers, so that, as has been remarked, "he was carrying on a dialogue with himself in the two leading Boston papers." This was at the time when "sides" were beginning to be formed in Massachusetts politics, the radical wing of colonial opposition to British measures being led by James Otis, Jr., a popular leader at the bar. Adams had long admired Otis, particularly his eloquent defense of the rights of the colonists in the Writs of Assistance case (1761), in which he argued the unconstitutionality of any writ that entitled customhouse officers to search colonists' homes for smuggled goods without specific evidence. Adams remembered this issue in his old age as the one that signalled the opening of the contest with Great Britain. Doubtless his recollection of the incident was somewhat dramatized, but it inspired him with zeal for the cause of the patriots, and there can be no doubt about his own vigorous participation in the crisis four years later over the Stamp Act, a British revenue law that required publications and documents in the American colonies to bear a stamp. Although he opposed the riots associated with the act, he regarded it as illegal because the colonists had not consented to it. This argument resulted in his famous articles in the *Boston Gazette,* beginning in August 1765, which were reprinted in London in 1768 as *A Dissertation On the Canon and Feudal Law.* The *Dissertation* argued that the opposition of the New England colonies to the Stamp Act was a part of the protest of New World individualism against Old World collective authority. In 1768 Adams moved his family from Braintree to Boston, where he was introduced into the practice of the Superior Court by Chief Justice Thomas Hutchinson (1711–80), later governor of Massachusetts, a man for whom Adams, somewhat paradoxically, bore the utmost dislike. In 1770 Adams courageously participated in the defense of the British soldiers accused of murder in the so-called Boston Massacre. Attempting to enforce the Townshend Acts, which imposed import duties on glass, lead, tea, paper, and paint, the soldiers became involved in a riot that resulted in the deaths of five persons. Public sentiment was against the accused. The trial, however, resulted in the acquittal of the commanding officer and most of the soldiers.

John Adams, oil painting by Gilbert Stuart, 1826; in the National Collection of Fine Arts, Washington, D.C.

By courtesy of the National Collection of Fine Arts, Smithsonian Institution, Washington, D.C.

Adams' public career received a setback in 1771. His law practice had recently been enlarged to the point where he had to hire two clerks, but, suffering a brief relapse in health, he moved back to Braintree and made a long horseback trip "to take the waters" at Stafford Springs. Apparently much improved, he returned to Boston in 1772 to earn a living for his growing family, a girl born in 1765 and his first son, John Quincy, in 1767. His private interests, however, were soon again being sacrificed to public ends, for he was elected to serve in the Massachusetts House of Representatives.

Continental Congress. In August 1774 Adams journeyed to Philadelphia with the Massachusetts delegation to the First Continental Congress, the first federal legislature of the 13 colonies. Entries in his diary give a rare insight into the composition of that body, which clearly yielded to the radicals in giving first place to grievances rather than to plans for reconciliation with Britain. Here, Adams served as an outspoken but shrewd member for three stormy years. Meantime, in early 1775 he published letters in the *Boston Gazette* under the pseudonym Novanglus, which were rebuttals to letters by the Loyalist writer Daniel Leonard, or "Massachusettensis." Novanglus, not unlike Thomas Jefferson in his "Summary View" of the previous year, emphasized an advanced stage in revolutionary thought: that the colonies having always been outside the realm had never properly been subject to imperial control by Parliament.

Only the personal tie with the sovereign now remained, and this Adams proceeded to sever. In the Second Continental Congress, in June 1775, he nominated George Washington of Virginia to be commander in chief of the almost nonexistent army, a move that he hoped would gain Virginia's support for the Revolutionary policies. A year later, he seconded the resolution of Richard Henry Lee of Virginia "that these United Colonies are, and of a right ought to be, free and independent States" and on June 11, 1776, was appointed to serve on a committee to draft a declaration of independence. The Declaration, written primarily by Thomas Jefferson, was defended on the floor of Congress primarily by Adams. Meanwhile, he had had altercations with some of the more conciliatory members of that body, notably with John Dickinson of Delaware, whom he had described in an imprudent letter, captured and gleefully published by the British, as a "piddling genius." His dislike of hesitant congressmen was accompanied by mixed feelings about a newly arrived journalist, Thomas Paine, the Englishman, whose "Common Sense" nevertheless hastened the cause of independence that Adams strongly favoured in 1776. At a time of general confusion, Adams' *Thoughts On Government* was circulated by several of his colleagues for use throughout the colonies in the making of new constitutions.

Revolutionary politics. Between 1776 and 1778 Adams divided his time in promoting the Revolutionary cause and in serving on numerous congressional committees, including one to create a navy and one to review foreign affairs. The Revolutionaries had begun to hope that they could improve their position by involving France with its old enemy, Britain. Late in 1777, Adams was named by Congress to serve with Benjamin Franklin as a joint commissioner to France, replacing Silas Deane, an original American commissioner whose loyalty to the Revolutionary cause had been called into question. Adams sailed on a continental frigate in February, together with his eldest son, 11-year-old John Quincy Adams. In France he learned that Franklin had already successfully concluded a French alliance, and later in the year, when the joint American commission in France was dissolved, he returned home, leaving Franklin in sole charge. He arrived in America in the summer of 1779, in time to play a major role in the drafting of the most famous of all Revolutionary state constitutions—that of

Massachusetts in 1780—along lines that he considered the proper divisions of functions: "that it may be a government of laws and not of men." He reacquainted himself with congressional politics and again found himself the questionable beneficiary of the old quarrel over Deane. Appointed one of the commissioners to negotiate commercial treaties and to make peace with Great Britain, it was clear that Adams' friends in Congress were noticeably not of the "pro-French" faction but advocates of the blunt, frank school of "shirtsleeve" diplomacy.

Once again he had to set out on a long and perilous journey, again taking John Quincy with him and a younger son, Charles, and again leaving his wife to run the farm at Braintree. It was a major separation in the lives of the Adamses, not to be healed until six years later when Abigail and her 18-year-old daughter sailed to rejoin the family at Auteuil, near Paris. This was after Adams, together with John Jay, one of the peace commissioners appointed by Congress, and Franklin, had helped bring about a final peace with Britain and had negotiated several badly needed congressional loans in Holland. In 1785 he was made the first U.S. minister to the court of St. James's and moved with his family to England.

Foreign service. In middle age John Adams thus entered into a career in foreign service in which his son and grandson were also one day to win distinction. The transformation of the Braintree lawyer into an envoy capable of dealing with experienced European diplomats was, however, less astonishing than it seems. Although his long years of foreign residence were later to influence American public opinion to the effect that the "Duke of Braintree" had become an aristocrat, such vilification was always basically political. John Adams the envoy was essentially the same blunt New Englander he had always been, and what he principally learned abroad between 1778 and 1788 seems to have been to distrust French politics of the Old Regime (preceding the French Revolution of 1789) and the morals of Europeans, generally; neither idea was wholly new.

While minister to Great Britain, and a year before he returned to America, Adams published his *Defence of the Constitutions of Government of the United States of America* (1787), expressing himself strongly along what some people considered to be "aristocratic" lines—as in the suggestion that "the rich, the well-born and the able" would have to compose the upper chamber of a republic if it were to survive. The work was filled with learned and frequently unacknowledged extracts from an awesome range of writers on government and human nature. Yet despite all its pretentiousness, it merely emphasized ideas held by Adams since 1776 at least—that all branches of government should be separated and that the legislature itself should be two-chambered. It was a scholar's view, based more or less upon what the French political philosopher Montesquieu had once understood to be the makeup of the British government and its system of checks and balances. The political reputation of the *Defence* became an important factor in explaining some of the political difficulties experienced by John Adams in later years. More importantly, the first volume of the *Defence* had arrived in America in time to influence the members of the Philadelphia Convention had they so desired. Offended by the aristocratic tone of the work, many electors failed to cast their votes for Adams in the presidential election of 1789. While George Washington received 69 votes, or one of the two votes cast by every elector, Adams received only 34 of the remaining 69 votes, the second largest number, and was thus declared vice president.

Vice presidency and presidency. The differences of opinion among the members of the new government over the policies to be pursued resulted in the formation of two political groups: the Federalists—the conservative faction led by Alexander Hamilton, which advocated a strong, centralized government and favoured industry, landowners, and merchants—and the Democratic-Republicans, led by Thomas Jefferson, who emphasized personal liberty and limited powers for the federal government. Adams had been a supporter of the new Federal plan for a republic from the first, and although he was less conservative than many others in the party, he became one of the leading Federalists. As vice president, moreover, he was to think of himself, somewhat pompously, as a lightning rod for the whole national experiment. He even fancied himself at one time as a "whipping boy" for some of Hamilton's measures, although his agrarian nature eventually rebelled against the consequence of those policies. The newspaper publication of his *Discourses on Davila* alienated Hamilton, who criticized the work for fear it might bring the federal experiment into disrepute, while Jefferson, on the other hand, thought it verged on promulgating a hereditary monarchy and aristocracy.

It was no doubt symptomatic of a certain unpopularity of Adams that he could secure only about half of the electoral votes possible in the elections of 1789 and 1792. His eight years under Washington were politically insignificant, although as presiding officer in the Senate, "His Rotundity" (as his detractors called him) invariably voted in a Federalist direction when breaking ties. Not until 1796, when he was selected by a congressional caucus to succeed Washington, did opposition in his own party become apparent. The fact that he received only a few more electoral votes than Jefferson was due in part to the number of votes cast for another Federalist, Thomas Pinckney of South Carolina, the recently successful envoy to Spain and a favourite with party leaders. Thus, Adams began his term as president with deep suspicions not only about Jefferson but about Hamilton and his followers as well. Nevertheless, he kept the Cabinet of Washington more or less intact until 1800, despite the fact that several of its members relied upon the advice of Hamilton, Washington's brilliant secretary of the treasury, who was now trying to rehabilitate his fortunes in law practice in New York. The retention of most members of Washington's Cabinet was a serious mistake that was partly due to Adams' continuing inability to grasp the significance of "parties." He proudly thought of himself like Washington, as a leader of the whole country.

The Adams administration went from crisis to crisis, for the French Revolutionists were threatening to create a new imperium in Europe, and in America they were stirring up their numerous admirers. Adams had been appalled by the nature of this new revolutionary upheaval from the beginning, so different, as he saw it, from what had happened in America. Together with his son John Quincy he had taken up the gauntlet seemingly thrown down by Jefferson in 1791, when the latter had endorsed the publication in America of Tom Paine's "Rights of Man," which defended the French Revolution. But if Adams was angered by his Francophile critics, Abigail was outraged, for criticism of her husband was to her little less than treason. Adams did not originate the Alien and Sedition Acts in 1798, which were designed to restrict the activities of friends of Revolutionary France who either hoped to come to America or were already there, but he did sign them into law, and doubtless with Abigail's hearty concurrence. Hating militarism, he decided in 1799 not to go to war with France but to reopen negotiations. This decision drew the sting from the extremists, many of whom now saw Adams himself as the enemy. Adams seems to have been more friendly to moderate Federalists than he himself realized. More popular than his own party, he was defeated for reelection in 1800 not only by the strategy of the opposition, the Democratic-Republican Party led by Jefferson and Aaron Burr, but also by the reluctant endorsement of Hamilton, who retaliated against Adams' conciliatory policy toward France, by which war was averted. In office to the bitter end, March 3, 1801, he signed in a number of "midnight judges," under an act reforming the national judiciary that he had recommended, having already appointed his secretary of state, John Marshall of Virginia, as chief justice. Thus, Adams attempted to keep Federalists in control of the national judiciary, at least, and he hurried from the capital without greeting Thomas Jefferson, the new president. He was to remember his critics with great bitterness.

Retirement. Adams retired to Quincy and lived on into a vigorous old age, composing parts of an "Autobiography" on three different occasions and in varying moods; writing innumerable letters to set people straight about the Revolution; heaping coals of fire on the head of his neighbour and former friend, Mercy Otis Warren, for the misinformation allegedly conveyed in her *History . . . of the American Revolution*; rejoicing in the size of his manure pile; enjoying his tankard of hard cider each morning before breakfast; and glorying in the diplomatic success and political eminence of his son, John Quincy Adams. Even after Abigail's death in 1818, he strove to maintain an active life, taking walks in the countryside, dictating to dutiful nieces, and enjoying the role of a senior citizen become a sage.

Gilbert Stuart's portrait of Adams in his 89th year shows him in characteristically bold mood but shrunken frame, obviously in need of teeth, his palsied fingers transparently thin. His last great joy was the elevation of his son to the presidency in 1825. He died 50 years to the day after the formal Declaration of Independence, on the same day and only a few hours after the death of Thomas Jefferson, the one-time friend and collaborator who had become his political enemy only to become reconciled again late in life. (R.A.E.)

BIBLIOGRAPHY. Page Smith, *John Adams,* 2 vol. (1962), is an exhaustive modern account, enriched with details from the microfilm of the Adams Family Papers. The Adams Family Papers have also provided the raw material for the modern edition of the *Diary and Autobiography of John Adams,* ed. by L.H. Butterfield *et al.,* 4 vol. (1961), supplemented by *The Earliest Diary of John Adams* (1966). These bring up to date the 19th-century edition by Charles Francis Adams of his grandfather's major writings, *The Works of John Adams, Second President of the United States: With a Life of the Author,* 10 vol. (1850–56). The opening portions of the *Life* in this edition were written by John Adams' son, John Quincy Adams, the 6th president.

Adams, John Couch (b. June 5, 1819, Laneast, Cornwall, Eng.—d. Jan. 21, 1892, Cambridge, Cambridgeshire), British mathematician and astronomer, one of two people who independently discovered the planet Neptune. On July 3, 1841, Adams had entered in his journal: "Formed a design in the beginning of this week of investigating, as soon as possible after taking my degree, the irregularities in the motion of Uranus . . . in order to find out whether they may be attributed to the action of an undiscovered planet beyond it. . . ." In September 1845 he gave James Challis, director of the Cambridge Observatory, accurate information on where the new planet, as yet unobserved, could be found; but unfortunately the planet was not recognized at Cambridge until much later, after its discovery at the Berlin Observatory on Sept. 23, 1846.

Adams also showed (1866) that the Leonid meteor shower had an orbit closely matching that of a comet (1866 I). He described the Moon's motion more exactly than had Pierre-Simon Laplace and studied terrestrial magnetism.

After being made professor of mathematics at the University of St. Andrews (Fife) in 1858 and Lowndean professor of astronomy and geometry at Cambridge in 1859, he became director of Cambridge Observatory in 1861.

Adams, John Quincy (b. July 11, 1767, Braintree, Mass.—d. Feb. 23, 1848, Washington, D.C.), eldest son of Pres. John Adams and sixth president of the United States (1825–29). In his pre-presidential years he was one of America's greatest diplomats (formulating, among other things, what came to be called the Monroe Doctrine); in his post-presidential years (as U.S. congressman, 1831–48) he conducted a consistent and often dramatic fight against the expansion of slavery.

John Quincy Adams, daguerreotype by A.S. Southworth and J.J. Hawes

By courtesy of the Metropolitan Museum of Art, New York, gift of I.N. Phelps Stokes, Edward S. Hawes, Alice Mary Hawes, Marion Augusta Hawes, 1937

Early life and career. John Quincy Adams entered the world at the same time his maternal great-grandfather, John Quincy, for many years a prominent member of the Massachusetts legislature, was leaving it; hence his name. He grew up as a child of the American Revolution. He watched the Battle of Bunker Hill from Penn's Hill and heard the cannons roar across the Back Bay. His patriot father, at that time a delegate to the Continental Congress, and his patriot mother, one of the intellectual women of those times, had a strong molding influence on his education after the war had deprived Braintree of its only schoolmaster. In 1778 and again in 1780 the boy accompanied his father to Europe. He studied at a private school in Paris in 1778–79 and at the University of Leiden in 1780. Thus, at an early age he acquired an excellent knowledge of the French language and a smattering of Dutch. In 1780, also, he began to keep regularly the diary that forms so conspicuous a record of the doings of himself and his contemporaries through the next 60 years of American history.

In 1781, at the age of 14, he accompanied Francis Dana, United States envoy to Russia, as his private secretary and interpreter of French. Dana, after lingering for more than a year in St. Petersburg, was not received by the Russian government; and in 1782 Adams, returning by way of Scandinavia, Hanover, and the Netherlands, joined his father in Paris. There he acted, in an informal way, as an additional secretary to the American commissioners in the negotiation of the treaty of peace that concluded the American Revolution. Instead of remaining in London with his father, who had been appointed United States minister to the Court of St. James's, he chose to return to Massachusetts, where he was graduated from Harvard College in 1787. He then read law at Newburyport under the tutelage of Theophilus Parsons, and in 1790 he was admitted to the bar in Boston. While struggling for a practice, he wrote a series of articles for the newspapers in which he controverted some of the doctrines in Thomas Paine's "Rights of Man." In another later series he ably supported the neutrality policy of George Washington's administration as it faced the war that broke out between France and England in 1793. These articles were brought to President Washington's attention and resulted in Adams' appointment as U.S. minister to the Netherlands in May 1794.

The Hague was then the best diplomatic listening post in Europe for the war of the first coalition against Revolutionary France. Young Adams' official dispatches to the Secretary of State and his informal letters to his father, who was now the vice president, kept the government well informed of the diplomatic activities and wars of the distressed Continent and the danger of becoming involved in the European vortex. These letters were also read by President Washington: some of Adams' phrases, in fact, appeared in Washington's "Farewell Address" of 1796. During the absence of the regular minister at London, Thomas Pinckney, Adams transacted public business with the British Foreign Office relating to exchange of ratifications of the Jay Treaty of 1794 between the United States and Great Britain. In 1796 Washington, who came to regard young Adams as the ablest officer in the foreign service, appointed him minister to Portugal, but before his departure his father, John Adams, became president and changed the young diplomat's destination to Prussia.

John Quincy Adams was married in London in 1797, on the eve of his departure for Berlin, to Louisa Catherine Johnson (1775–1852), daughter of the United States consul Joshua Johnson, a Marylander by birth, and his wife, Katherine Nuth, an Englishwoman.

While in Berlin, Adams negotiated (1799) a treaty of amity and commerce with Prussia. Recalled from Berlin by President Adams after the election of Thomas Jefferson to the presidency in 1800, the younger Adams reached Boston in 1801 and the next year was elected to the Massachusetts Senate. In 1803 the Massachusetts legislature elected him as a member of the Senate of the United States.

Break with the Federalists. Up to this time John Quincy Adams was regarded as belonging to the Federalist Party, but he found its general policy displeasing. He was frowned upon as the son of his father by the followers of Alexander Hamilton and by reactionary groups, and he soon found himself practically powerless as an unpopular member of an unpopular minority. Actually he was not then, and indeed never was, a strict party man; all through his life, ever aspiring to higher public service, he considered himself a "man of my whole country." Adams arrived in Washington too late to vote for ratification of the treaty for the purchase of Louisiana, opposed by the other Federalist senators, but he voted for the appropriations to carry it into effect and announced that he would have voted for the purchase treaty itself. Nevertheless, he joined his Federalist colleagues in voting against a bill to enable the President to place officials of his own appointment in control of the newly acquired territory; such a bill, Adams vainly protested, overstepped the constitutional powers of the presidency, violated the right of self-government, and imposed taxation without representation. In December 1807 he supported President Jefferson's suggestion of an embargo prohibiting all foreign commerce (an attempt to gain British recognition of American rights) and vigorously urged instant action, saying: "The President has recommended the measure on his high responsibility. I would not consider, I would not deliberate; I would act!" Within five hours the Senate had passed the embargo bill and sent it to the House of Representatives. Support of this measure, hated by the Federalists and unpopular in New England because it stifled the region's economy, cost Adams his seat in the Senate. His successor was chosen on June 3, 1808, several months before the usual time of electing a senator for the next term, and five days later Adams resigned. In the same year he attended the Republican congressional caucus, which nominated James Madison for the presidency, and thus allied himself with that party. From 1806 to 1809 Adams was Boylston professor of rhetoric and oratory at Harvard College.

In 1809 President Madison sent Adams to Russia to represent the United States at the court of the tsars. He arrived at St. Petersburg at the psychological moment when the Tsar had made up his mind to break with Napoleon. Adams therefore met with a favourable reception and a disposition to further the interests of American commerce in every possible way. From this vantage point he watched and reported Napoleon's invasion of Russia and the final disastrous retreat and dissolution of France's *grande armée.* On the outbreak of the war between the United States and England in 1812, he was still at St. Petersburg. That September the Russian government suggested that the Tsar was willing to act as mediator between the two belligerents. Madison precipitately accepted this proposition and sent Albert Gallatin and James Bayard to act as commissioners with Adams, but England would have nothing to do with it. In August 1814, however, these gentlemen, with Henry Clay and Jonathan Russell, began negotiations with English commissioners that resulted in the signing of the Treaty of Ghent on December 24 of that year. Adams then visited Paris, where he witnessed the return of Napoleon from Elba, and next went to London, where, with Clay and Gallatin, he negotiated (1815) a "Convention to Regulate Commerce and Navigation." Soon afterward he became U.S. minister to Great Britain, as his father had been before him, and as his son, Charles Francis Adams, was to be after him. After accomplishing little in London, he returned to the United States in the summer of 1817 to become secretary of state in the Cabinet of Pres. James Monroe. This appointment was primarily because of his diplomatic experience but also because of the President's desire to have a sectionally well-balanced Cabinet in what came to be known as the Era of Good Feeling.

Secretary of state. As secretary of state, Adams played the leading part in the acquisition of Florida. Ever since the acquisition of Louisiana, successive administrations had sought to include at least a part of Florida in that purchase. In 1819, after long negotiations, Adams succeeded in getting the Spanish minister to agree to a treaty in which Spain would abandon all claims to territory east of the Mississippi, the United States would relinquish all claim to what is now Texas, and a boundary of the United States would be drawn (for the first time) from the Atlantic to the Pacific Ocean. This Transcontinental Treaty was perhaps the greatest victory ever won by a single man in the diplomatic history of the United States. Adams himself was responsible for the idea of extending the country's northern boundary westward from the Rocky Mountains to the Pacific—considered a stroke of diplomatic genius. To use his own word, it marked a triumphant "epocha" in U.S. continental expansion. Before the Spanish government ratified the Transcontinental Treaty in 1819, however, Mexico (including Texas) had thrown off allegiance to the mother country, and the United States had occupied Florida by force of arms. As secretary of state, Adams was also responsible for conclusion of the treaty of 1818 with Great Britain, laying down the northern boundary of the United States from the Lake of the Woods to the Rocky Mountains along the line of 49° N latitude. Years later, as a member of the House of Representatives he supported 49° N latitude as the boundary of Oregon from the Rocky Mountains to the Pacific Ocean: "I want that country for our Western pioneers." Polk's Oregon treaty of 1846 drew that boundary along the line of 49°. The Monroe Doctrine rightly bears the name of the president who in 1823 assumed the responsibility for its promulgation, but it was the work of John Quincy Adams more than of any other single man.

Presidency and feud with Jackson. As President Monroe's second term drew to a close in 1824, there was a lack of good feeling among his official advisers, three of whom—Secretary of State John Quincy Adams, Secretary of War John C. Calhoun, and Secretary of the Treasury William H. Crawford—aspired to succeed him in his high office. Henry Clay, speaker of the House, and Gen. Andrew Jackson were also candidates. Calhoun was nominated for the vice presidency. Of the other four, Jackson received 99 electoral votes for the presidency, Adams 84, Crawford 41, and Clay 37; because no one had a majority, the decision was made by the House of Representatives, which was confined in its choice to the three candidates who had received the largest number of votes. Clay, who had for years assumed a censorious attitude toward Jackson, cast his influence for Adams, whose election was thereby secured on the first ballot. A few days later Adams offered Clay the office of secretary of state, which was accepted. The charge of "bargain and corruption" followed, and the feud thus created between Adams and Jackson greatly influenced the history of the United States.

Up to this point Adams' career had been almost uniformly successful, but his presidency (1825–29), during which the country prospered, was in most respects a political failure because of the virulent opposition of the Jacksonians. In 1828 Jackson was elected president over Adams. It was during Jackson's administration that irreconcilable differences developed between the followers of Adams and the followers of Jackson, the former becoming known as the National Republicans, who, with the Anti-Masons, were the precursors of the Whigs. In 1829 Adams retired to private life in the town of Quincy, but only for a brief period; in 1830, supported largely by members of the Anti-Mason movement (a political force formed initially in opposition to Freemasonry), he was elected a member of the national House of Representatives. When it was suggested to him that his acceptance of this position would degrade a former president, Adams replied that no person could be degraded by serving the people as a representative in Congress or, he added, as a selectman of his town. He served in the House of Representatives from 1831 until his death, in 1848. But he had not abandoned his hopes for a reelection to the presidency—whether as nominee of the Anti-Masonic Party (in which he was very active as long as that party had political possibilities) or of the National Republican Party or of a union of both or even of the later Whig Party—always in his own mind as a "man of the whole nation." Gradually, these hopes faded.

Second career in Congress. His long second career in Congress was at least as important as his earlier career as a diplomat. Throughout, he was conspicuous as an opponent of the expansion of slavery and was at heart an Abolitionist, though he never became one in the political sense of the word. In 1839 he presented to the House of Representatives a resolution for a constitutional amendment providing that every child born in the United States after July 4, 1842, should be born free; that, with the exception of Florida, no new state should be admitted into the Union with slavery; and that neither slavery nor the slave trade should exist in the District of Columbia after July 4, 1845. The "gag rules," a resolution passed by Southern members of Congress against all discussion of slavery in the House of Representatives, effectively blocked any discussion of Adams' proposed amendment. His prolonged fight for the repeal of the gag rules and for the right of petition to Congress for the mitigation or abolition of slavery was one of the most dramatic contests in the history of Congress. These petitions, from individuals and groups of individuals from all over the northern states, were increasingly sent to Adams, and he dutifully presented them. Adams contended that the gag rules were a direct violation of the First Amendment to the federal Constitution, and he refused to be silenced on the question, fighting indomitably for repeal, in spite of the bitter denunciation of his opponents. Each year the number of anti-slavery petitions received and presented by him grew in great numbers. Perhaps the climax was in 1837 when Adams presented a petition from 22 slaves and, threatened by his opponents with censure, defended himself with remarkable keenness and ability. At each session the majority against him decreased until, in 1844, his motion to repeal the then standing 21st (gag) rule of the House was carried by a vote of 108 to 80, and his long battle was over.

Another spectacular contribution of Adams to the anti-slavery cause was his championing of the cause of the Africans of the slave ship "Amistad"—slaves who had mutinied and escaped from their Spanish owners off the coast of Cuba and brought the slave ship into United States waters near Long Island. Adams defended these Negroes as freemen before the Supreme Court in 1841 against efforts of the administration of Pres. Martin Van Buren to return them to their masters and to inevitable death. Adams won their freedom.

As a member of Congress—in fact, throughout his life—Adams supported the improvement of the arts and sciences and the diffusion of knowledge; and he did much to conserve the bequest of James Smithson (an eccentric Englishman) to the United States and to create and endow the Smithsonian Institution with the money from Smithson's estate.

Perhaps the most dramatic event in Adams' life was its end. On Feb. 21, 1848, in the act of protesting an honorary grant of swords by Congress to the generals who had won what Adams considered a "most unrighteous war" with Mexico, he suffered a cerebral stroke, fell unconscious to the floor of the House, and died two days later in the Capitol building. His obsequies in Washington and in his native Massachusetts assumed the character of a countrywide pageant of mourning.

Personality. Few men in American public life have possessed more independence, more public spirit, and more ability than did Adams; but throughout his political career he was handicapped by a certain personal reserve and austerity and coolness of manner, which prevented him from appealing to the imaginations and affections of the people. He had few intimate friends, and not many men in American history have been regarded, during the period of their lifetime, with so much hostility or attacked with so much rancour by their political opponents. (S.F.Be.)

BIBLIOGRAPHY. C.F. Adams (ed.), *Memoirs of John Quincy Adams, Comprising Portions of His Diary from 1795 to 1848* (1874–77, reprinted 1969); J.T. Morse, *John Quincy Adams* (1883; new ed. 1899); Dexter Perkins, "John Quincy Adams," in *American Secretaries of State and Their Diplomacy,* vol. 4 (1928, reprinted 1963); Bennett Champ Clark, *John Quincy Adams, "Old Man Eloquent"* (1932). Two basic volumes by Samuel Flagg Bemis, *John Quincy Adams and the Foundations of American Foreign Policy* (1949) and *John Quincy Adams and the Union* (1956), utilized the archives of the Adams family.

Adams, Léonie (Fuller) (b. Dec. 9, 1899, Brooklyn, N.Y., U.S.), American poet and educator whose verse interprets emotions and nature with an almost mystical vision.

After graduating from Barnard College (A.B., 1922), she became editor of *The Measure,* a literary publication, in 1924 and was persuaded to publish a volume of poetry, *Those Not Elect,* in 1925. She began to teach the writing of poetry in New York City and in 1932 edited *Lyrics of François Villon.* Winner of Guggenheim fellowships in 1928 and 1930, she lectured at various U.S. colleges and universities over the years, served as poetry consultant for the Library of Congress (1948–49), and was Fulbright lecturer in France (1955–56). She won a National Institute of Arts and Letters grant in Literature (1949) and won various poetry awards thereafter. *Poems, a Selection* (1954) won the Bollingen Prize for Poetry in 1955.

Adams, Marian, *née* HOOPER, byname CLOVER (b. Sept. 13, 1843, Boston—d. Dec. 6, 1885, Washington, D.C.), social arbiter and accomplished photographer.

After her marriage to the historian Henry Adams in 1872, Marian Hooper Adams presided over an intellectual salon in Boston. When the couple moved to Washington, D.C., in 1877, they made their home a centre for the intellectual and political elite of that city. There Mrs. Adams also became one of the first women to cultivate a serious interest in photography; her portraits of the historian George Bancroft and the statesman John Hay were particularly notable.

After the death of her father in 1885, Adams sank into a deep depression; she eventually committed suicide. The bronze monument commissioned for her grave in Washington's Rock Creek Cemetery was executed by Augustus Saint-Gaudens and is generally acknowledged his masterpiece. Sometimes called "Grief," it depicts a seated, cowled figure. Henry Adams was buried next to his wife in 1918.

Marian Adams' letters to her father were published in 1936 as *The Letters of Mrs. Henry Adams.* A biography by Otto Friedrich, *Clover,* was published in 1979; *The Education of Mrs. Henry Adams,* by Eugenia Kaledin, appeared in 1981.

Adams, Maude, original name MAUDE KISKADDEN (b. Nov. 11, 1872, Salt Lake City, Utah, U.S.—d. July 17, 1953, Tannersville, N.Y.), actress, best known for her portrayals of Sir James Barrie's heroines.

Her mother, whose maiden name she adopted, was leading lady of the Salt Lake City stock company. From Adams' first triumph at the age of five as Little Schneider in *Fritz* at the San Francisco Theatre, she played child roles. In 1888 she joined E.H. Soth-

Maude Adams in *L'Aiglon*, 1901

By courtesy of the Library of Congress, Washington, D.C.

ern as ingenue. From her appearance in C.H. Hoyt's *Midnight Bell* (1889), her popularity grew rapidly. The next year Charles Frohman cast her in William Gillette's *All the Comforts of Home*, and when John Drew left Augustin Daly for the Frohmans in 1892 she became his leading lady for five years. From 1897 she was for many years a Frohman star, especially successful in *The Little Minister, Peter Pan, What Every Woman Knows, Quality Street*, and *A Kiss for Cinderella*. She also played the Shakespearean roles of Juliet, Viola, and Rosalind, and Joan of Arc in Schiller's *Die Jungfrau von Orleans*. She left the stage in 1918, experimented for a time with stage lighting, returned in 1931 as Portia to Otis Skinner's Shylock, and made her last appearance as Maria in *Twelfth Night* in 1934. She became professor of dramatic art at Stephens College, Columbia, Mo., in 1937. Phyllis Robbins' *Maude Adams: An Intimate Portrait* was published in 1956.

Adams, Robert (b. *c.* 1791, Ireland—d. Jan. 13, 1875, Dublin), clinician noted for his contributions to the knowledge of heart disease and gout. In 1827 he described a condition characterized by a very slow pulse and

Robert Adams, drawing by an unknown artist

By courtesy of the Royal College of Surgeons, Dublin

by transient giddiness or convulsive seizures, now known as the Adams-Stokes disease or syndrome.

Educated at Trinity College, Dublin, Adams studied medicine in Europe and then returned to Dublin, where he established his practice and served as surgeon to the Jervis Street and Richmond hospitals. In 1861 he was appointed surgeon to the queen in Ireland and regius professor of surgery at the University of Dublin.

Adams, Roger (b. Jan. 2, 1889, Boston—d. July 6, 1971, Champaign, Ill., U.S.), chemist and teacher known for determining the chemical constitution of such natural substances as chaulmoogra oil (used in treating leprosy), the toxic cottonseed pigment gossypol, marihuana, and many alkaloids. He also worked in stereochemistry and with platinum catalysts and the synthesis of medicinal compounds.

Receiving his Ph.D. from Harvard University (1912), Adams studied in Germany and taught briefly at Harvard. In 1916 he went to the University of Illinois, becoming professor of organic chemistry (1919) and head of the chemistry department (1926). A consultant to the chemical industry, he also served as a scientific adviser to the government during World War II. He accepted a research professorship (1954) and retired in 1957. His many honours include the American Chemical Society's Priestley Medal (1946).

Adams, Samuel (b. Sept. 27 [Sept. 16, old style], 1722, Boston—d. Oct. 2, 1803, Boston), politician of the American Revolution, leader of the Massachusetts "radicals," who was a delegate to the Continental Congress (1774–81) and a signer of the Declaration of Independence. He was later lieutenant governor (1789–93) and governor (1794–97) of Massachusetts.

Samuel Adams, oil portrait by John Singleton Copley, *c.* 1700–72; in the Museum of Fine Arts, Boston

By courtesy of the Museum of Fine Arts, Boston, deposited by the City of Boston

Early career. A second cousin of John Adams, second president of the United States, Samuel Adams was graduated from Harvard College in 1740 and briefly studied law; he failed in several business ventures. As a tax collector in Boston, he neglected to collect the public levies and to keep proper accounts, thus exposing himself to suit.

Although unsuccessful in conducting personal or public business, Adams took an active and influential part in local politics. By the time the English Parliament passed the Sugar Act (1764) taxing molasses for revenue, Adams was a powerful figure in the opposition to British authority in the Colonies. He denounced the act, being one of the first of the colonials to cry out against taxation without representation. He played an important part in instigating the Stamp Act riots in Boston that were directed against the new requirement to pay taxes on all legal and commercial documents, newspapers, and college diplomas.

Commitment to American independence. His influence was soon second only to James Otis, the lawyer and politician who gained prominence by his resistance to the revenue acts. Elected to the lower house of the Massachusetts general court from Boston, Adams served in that body until 1774, after 1766 as its clerk. In 1769 Adams assumed the leadership of the Massachusetts radicals. There is some reason to believe that he had committed himself to American independence a year earlier. John Adams may have erred in ascribing this extreme stand to his cousin at so early a time, but certainly Samuel Adams was one of the first American leaders to deny Parliament's authority over the Colonies; and he was also one of the first—certainly by 1774—to establish independence as the proper goal.

John Adams described his cousin as a plain, modest, and virtuous man. But in addition, Samuel Adams was a propagandist who was not overscrupulous in his attacks upon British officials and policies, and a passionate politician as well. In innumerable newspaper letters and essays over various signatures, he described British measures and the behaviour of royal governors, judges, and customs men in the darkest colours. He was a master of organization, arranging for the election of men who agreed with him, procuring committees that would act as he wished, and securing the passage of resolutions that he desired.

During the crisis over the Townshend duties (1767–70), the import taxes on previously duty-free products proposed by Cabinet Minister Charles Townshend, Adams was unable to persuade the Massachusetts colonists to take extreme steps, partly because of the moderating influence of Otis. British troops sent to Boston in 1768, however, offered a fine target for this propaganda, and Adams saw to it that they were portrayed in the colonial newspapers as brutal soldiery oppressing citizens and assailing their wives and daughters. He was one of the leaders in the town meeting that demanded and secured the removal of the troops from Boston after some British soldiers fired into a mob and killed five Americans. When news came that the Townshend duties, except for that on tea, had been repealed, his following dwindled. Nevertheless, during the years 1770–73, when other colonial leaders were inactive, Adams revived old issues and found new ones; he was responsible for the foundation (1772) of the committee of correspondence of Boston that kept in contact with similar bodies in other towns, in whose establishment he also had a hand. These committees later became effective instruments in the fight against the British.

The passage by Parliament of the Tea Act of 1773, which granted the East India Company a monopoly on tea sales in the Colonies, gave Adams ample opportunity to exercise his remarkable talents. Although he did not participate in the Boston Tea Party, he was undoubtedly one of its planners. He was again a leading figure in the opposition of Massachusetts to the execution of the Intolerable (Coercive) Acts passed by the British Parliament in retaliation for the dumping of tea in Boston Harbor; and as a member of the First Continental Congress, which spoke for the 13 Colonies, he insisted that the delegates take a vigorous stand against Britain. A member of the provincial congress of Massachusetts in 1774–75, he participated in making preparations for warfare should Britain resort to arms. When the British troops marched out of Boston to Concord, Adams and the president of the Continental Congress, John Hancock, were staying in a farmhouse near the line of march; and it has been said that the arrest of the two men was one of the purposes of the expedition. But the troops made no effort to find them, and British orders called only for destruction of military supplies gathered at Concord. When Gen. Thomas Gage issued an offer of pardon to the rebels some weeks later, however, he excepted Adams and Hancock.

Membership in Continental Congress. As a member of the Continental Congress, in which he served until 1781, Adams was less conspicuous than he was in town meetings and the Massachusetts legislature, for the congress contained many men as able as he. He and John Adams were among the first to call for a final separation from Britain, both signed the Declaration of Independence, and both exerted considerable influence in the congress.

Adams was a member of the convention that framed the Massachusetts constitution of 1780 and also sat in the convention of his state that ratified the Federal Constitution. He was at first an anti-Federalist who opposed the ratification of the Constitution for fear that it would vest too much power in the federal government but finally abandoned his opposition when the Federalists promised to support a number of future amendments, including a bill of rights. He was defeated in the first congressional election. Returning to political power as a follower of Hancock, he was lieutenant governor of Massachusetts from 1789 to 1793 and governor from 1794 to 1797. When national parties developed, he affiliated himself with the Democratic Republicans, the forerunner of the Democratic Party. After being defeated as a presidential elector favouring Thomas Jefferson in 1796, he retired to private life. (J.R.Al.)

BIBLIOGRAPHY. The best biography of Samuel Adams is John C. Miller, *Sam Adams: Pioneer in Propaganda* (1936). There are several others: William V. Wells, *The Life and Public Services of Samuel Adams*, 3 vol. (1865); James K. Hosmer, *Samuel Adams* (1885); Ralph V. Harlow, *Samuel Adams: Promoter of the American Revolution* (1923); and Stewart Beach, *Samuel Adams: The Fateful Years, 1764–1776* (1965). Many of Samuel Adams' writings have been lost or destroyed, but a substantial collection of them, edited by Harry A. Cushing, *The Writings of Samuel Adams*, 4 vol., was published in 1904–08.

Adams, Samuel Hopkins (b. Jan. 26, 1871, Dunkirk, N.Y., U.S.—d. Nov. 15, 1958, Beaufort, S.C.), journalist and author of more than 50 books of fiction, biography, and exposé.

He graduated from Hamilton College in 1891 and was with the *New York Sun* until 1900; from 1901 to 1905 he was associated in various editorial and advertising capacities with McClure's syndicate and *McClure's Magazine*.

One of the so-called muckrakers of the period, Adams contributed to *Collier's, the National Weekly* in 1905 a series of articles exposing quack patent medicines, followed by *The Great American Fraud* (1906), which furthered the passage of the Pure Food and Drug Act in 1906. In 1915–16 in the *New York Tribune*, he exposed dishonourable practices in advertising. The novel *Revelry* (1926) and a biography of Warren G. Harding, *Incredible Era* (1939), set forth the scandals of the Harding administration. Adams also wrote biographies of Daniel Webster (*The Godlike Daniel*, 1930) and of Alexander Woollcott (1945). Several of his novels became movie scenarios, notably *It Happened One Night* (1934) and a musical, *The Harvey Girls* (1942). *Grandfather Stories* (1955) was based on reminiscences of his grandfather in upper New York State. He also wrote under the name Warner Fabian.

Adams, Walter (Sydney) (b. Dec. 20, 1876, Syria—d. May 11, 1956, Pasadena, Calif., U.S.), astronomer best known for his spectroscopic studies. With the spectroscope he investigated sunspots and the rotation of the Sun, the velocities and distances of thousands of stars, peculiar stars (*e.g.*, the dwarf companion of Sirius), and planetary atmospheres.

Born of missionary parents who returned to the U.S. when he was eight years old, he studied astronomy at Dartmouth College, Hanover, N.H., the University of Chicago, and the University of Munich. In 1904 he became a member of the original staff of Mt. Wilson Observatory in California, where he served as director from 1923 to 1946. Adams took an important part in planning the 200-inch telescope for the Palomar Mountain Observatory.

Walter Adams

By courtesy of Hale Observatories, Pasadena, Calif., and the Niels Bohr Library, American Institute of Physics, New York

Adams, William (b. 1564, Gillingham, Kent, Eng.—d. May 16, 1620, Japan), navigator, merchant-adventurer, and the first Englishman in Japan.

In 1598 he shipped as pilot major with five Dutch ships bound from Europe for the East Indies via the Straits of Magellan. The trouble-ridden fleet was scattered, and in April 1600 the "Charity," her crew sick and dying, anchored off southern Japan. Adams was summoned to Ōsaka, where the Shogun was so impressed with Adams' knowledge of ships and shipbuilding that he presented him with an estate. Around 1613 he helped to establish an English trading factory for the East India Company. Refused permission to return to England, he settled permanently in Japan, married a Japanese woman (though he had an English wife and family), and was given a title. A Tokyo street, Anjin-chō, was named in his honour.

Adams' career in Japan was the inspiration for James Clavell's best-selling novel *Shogun* (1975).

Adams, William Taylor, pseudonym OLIVER OPTIC (b. July 30, 1822, Medway, Mass., U.S.—d. March 27, 1897, Boston), American teacher and author of juvenile literature, best known for his children's magazine and the series of adventure books that he wrote under his pseudonym.

Although he never graduated from college, Adams was a teacher and principal in Boston elementary schools for more than 20 years. Under the pen name Oliver Optic, he wrote stories for boys, and in 1865 he resigned his position as a principal to pursue his writing full time. Soon after that he began *Oliver Optic's Magazine for Boys and Girls* (1867–1875), which enjoyed great popularity.

Adams was a prolific writer, producing about a thousand magazine and newspaper stories and well over a hundred full-length books. His books are written in series and take young heroes through exotic and educational adventures. His characters travel much and are well mannered, athletic, and patriotic, and the stories are laced with a strong moral. Adams' books were popular with girls as well as boys, although girls appeared infrequently as characters in his writing.

Critics charge that, to the adult reader, Adams' books reveal careless writing and are remarkable only for their vivid narratives.

Adams Bridge, also called RAMA'S BRIDGE, chain of shoals, between the islands of Mannar, near northwestern Sri Lanka and Rāmeswaram, off the southeastern coast of India. It is 30 mi (48 km) long and separates the Gulf of Mannar (southwest) from the Palk Strait (northeast). Some of the sandbanks are dry, and nowhere are the shoals deeper than 4 ft (1 m); thus, they seriously hinder navigation. Dredging operations, now abandoned, were begun as early as 1838 but never succeeded in maintaining a channel for any vessels except those of light draft. Geological evidence suggests that Adams Bridge represents a former land connection between India and Sri Lanka. Traditionally, it is said to be the remnant of a huge causeway, constructed by Rāma, the hero of the Hindu epic *Rāmāyaṇa*, to facilitate passage of his army from India to Ceylon for the rescue of his abducted wife, Sītā. According to Muslim legend, Adam crossed there to Adams Peak, Ceylon, atop which he stood repentant on one foot for 1,000 years.

Adams–Onís Treaty: *see* Transcontinental Treaty.

Adams Peak, mountain in southwestern Sri Lanka (Ceylon), 7,360 ft (2,243 m) high and 11 mi (18 km) northeast of Ratnapura; it is located on the boundary between Central and Sabaragamuwa provinces in the Sri Lanka hill country. Because of a large hollow resembling a human footprint on the summit, it is venerated as a holy place by Buddhists, Muslims, and Hindus, who regard it as the footprint of the Buddha, Adam, and Śiva, respectively. Many pilgrims of all faiths visit the peak every year. Heavy chains on the mountain's southwestern face, said to have been placed there by Alexander the Great, mark the route to the summit.

Adams Peak, Sri Lanka

Ed Lark—Artstreet

adamsite, in chemical warfare, sneeze gas developed by the United States and used during World War I. Adamsite is an arsenical, diphenylaminechlorarsine, and is an odourless crystalline organic compound employed in vaporous form as a lung irritant. It appears as a yellow smoke that irritates eyes, lungs, and mucous membranes and causes sneezing, vomiting, and acute discomfort in the nose, throat, and chest. Eventually severe nausea develops, with headache, general physical weakness, and despondency. The effect lasts almost 12 hours. The only protection is a good mechanical filter.

Adamson, Robert: *see* Hill, David Octavius, and Adamson, Robert.

ʿAdan (Yemen [Aden]): *see* Aden.

ʿAdan, *muḥāfaẓah* (governorate) southern Yemen (Aden), on the Gulf of Aden; it was formerly called *al-muḥāfaẓah al-Ūlā* (the first governorate). It is bounded by the *muḥāfaẓah* (governorates) of Tuban on the east and north and Abyān on the west. ʿAden is the smallest governorate of the country, and has an area of 2,695 sq mi (6,980 sq km). It encompasses a low, arid plain with rugged terrain. Agriculture is sustained through irrigation. There are several impressive water reservoirs from the 1st century AD in Kraytar (near Aden) that were carved out of solid rock and connected to one another by canals. Main crops are vegetables and fruits; chicken farming is increasing. Industrial activities centre around the port of Aden, which is the national and provincial capital; they include petroleum refining, salt production, fish processing, cotton manufacturing, and shipbuilding. Pop. (1973 prelim.) 291,376.

Adan le Menestrel (poet): *see* Adenet le Roi.

Adana, city, capital of Adana *il* (province), southern Turkey, in the plain of Cilicia, on the Seyhan Nehri (the ancient Sarus River). An agricultural and industrial centre and the nation's fourth largest city, it probably overlies a Hittite settlement dating from about 1400 BC; and its history has been profoundly influenced by its location at the foot of the Taurus Mountain passes leading to the Syrian plains. Conquered by Alexander the Great in 335–334 BC, it came under ʿAbbāsid Arabs at the end of the 7th century AD and changed hands intermittently in the next 600 years until the establishment of the Turkmen Ramazan dynasty in 1378. The Ramazan rulers retained control of local administration even after Adana was conquered by the Ottoman sultan Selim I in 1516, and they enjoyed the favour of Selim's successor, Süleyman I the Magnificent. In 1608 Adana was reconstituted as a province under direct Ottoman administration. Between 1832 and 1840 it fell under the rule of the rebellious Ottoman viceroy of Egypt, Muḥammad ʿAlī Pasha. Adana became a provincial capital in 1867. Historical monuments date from as early as the 2nd century AD.

Adana's prosperity has long come from the fertile valleys behind it and its position as a bridgehead on the Anatolian-Arabian trade routes. A centre of the Turkish cotton industry, it manufactures textiles, cement, agricultural machinery, and vegetable oils. Adana lies on the Istanbul–Baghdad railway and is connected by a branch line to the Mediterranean port of Mersin, 32 mi (51 km) southwest, through which its products are shipped. Çukurova University was established at Adana in 1973.

Adana *il,* 7,138 sq mi (18,487 sq km) in area, extends northward from the Mediterranean coast to the inner slopes of the Taurus Mountains. The northern part is rugged and sparsely populated; in the south, the densely populated plains of Adana and Ceyhan are drained by the Ceyhan and Seyhan rivers. Industrialization has been rapid in recent years; but Adana still remains an agricultural province producing cotton, rice, sesame, oats, and citrus fruits. Pop. (1980) city, 574,515; (1982 est.) *il,* 1,578,301.

Adangme, people occupying the coastal area of Ghana from Kpone to Ada, on the Volta River, and inland along the Volta; they include the Ada, Kpone, Krobo, Ningo, Osuduku, Prampram, and Shai, all speaking variants of Ga-Adangme of the Kwa branch of Niger-Congo languages.

The chief Adangme occupation is farming, based on the *huza* system, in which a tract of land is purchased by a group of people, usually kinsmen; the tract is then subdivided among the purchasers according to the amount each has paid, and the individual thereafter has complete control of his own section. Negotiations with the seller are carried out by an elected *huzatse* ("father of the *huza*"), who later acts as the *huza* leader and representative. Millet was formerly the staple food, but more common crops now include cassava, yam, maize, plantain, cocoa, and palm oil.

The Adangme are organized into clans based on patrilineal descent; the clans are subdivided into localized patrilineages, the basic units of Adangme political organization. Lineage members generally return to the traditional lineage home from the *huza* farms several times a year to participate in the festivals of their lineage gods. There are also many annual festivals.

Adanson, Michel (b. April 7, 1727, Aix-en-Provence, Fr.—d. Aug. 3, 1806, Paris), botanist who devised a natural system of classification and nomenclature of plants, based on all their physical characteristics, with an emphasis on families.

In 1749 Adanson left for Senegal to spend four years as an employee with the Compagnie des Indes, a trading company. He returned with a large collection of plant specimens, some of which became part of the royal collection under the supervision of the naturalist Georges Buffon; most of them now belong to the Muséum National d'Histoire Naturelle. He published *Histoire naturelle du Sénégal* (1757), describing the flora of Senegal, and a survey of mollusks.

Familles des plantes (1763) described Adanson's classification system for plants, which was much opposed by Linnaeus, the Swedish botanist. Adanson's classification of mollusks, a group that he originally described, was based on anatomical characters. Adanson also introduced the use of statistical methods in botanical classification and studied electricity in torpedo fish and the regeneration of limbs and heads in frogs and snails. Although Adanson was well known to European scientists, his system of classification was not widely successful, and it was superseded by the Linnaean system.

Adapa, in Mesopotamian mythology, legendary sage and citizen of Eridu, a Sumerian city the ruins of which are in southern Iraq. Endowed with vast intelligence by Ea (Sumerian Enki), the god of wisdom, he became the hero of a myth in which he was denied immortality. The myth relates that Adapa, who had broken the wings of the south wind, was summoned by the sky god, Anu (Sumerian An), to receive punishment. Jealous Ea cautioned Adapa not to touch the bread and water that would be offered him. The two heavenly doorkeepers, Tammuz and Ningishzida, however, interceded for him, and Anu, in a change of mind, offered him the bread and water of eternal life, which he refused; thus mankind became mortal.

Adapazarı, city, capital of Sakarya *il* (province), northwestern Turkey, in a fertile plain west of the Sakarya Nehri (river), on the old military road from Istanbul. The region came under Ottoman control in the early 14th century, and the city acquired its present name at the end of the 18th century. An agricultural and industrial centre, Adapazarı is connected by a branch line to the main Anatolian railway system by which its wheat, tobacco, fruits, and vegetables are sent to the Istanbul markets. The city has a large sugar beet-processing plant. A stone bridge built during the reign of the Roman emperor Justinian is the only surviving ancient monument. Pop. (1980) 130,977.

adaptation, in biology, process by which an animal or plant becomes fitted to its environment; it is the result of natural selection acting upon heritable variation. Even the simpler organisms must be adapted in a great variety of ways: in their structure, physiology, and genetics; in their locomotion or dispersal; in their means of defense and attack; in their reproduction and development; and in other respects.

Accurate adaptations may involve migration to, or survival in, favourable conditions of, for example, temperature. Alternatively, organisms may manufacture their own environment, as do the mammals, for example, which are precisely adjusted to their optimum temperature. To be useful, adaptations must often occur simultaneously in a number of different parts of the body. A change from a more carnivorous to a more vegetarian diet necessitates alterations not only of the digestive system but also in habit and defense mechanisms.

Some of the most fundamental biological adaptations are chemical and genetic. The conditions in which the cells of the body can live are restricted and have changed little since life first arose in the sea. Exploitation of fresh water and of land was possible only through the evolution of adaptive mechanisms capable of maintaining at least a semblance of the original constitution of body fluids.

adaptive radiation, evolution of an animal or plant group into a wide variety of types adapted to specialized modes of life. A striking example is the radiation, beginning in the Tertiary Period (beginning 65,000,000 years ago), of basal mammalian stock into forms adapted to running, leaping, climbing, swimming, and flying.

adaptive value (genetics): *see* Darwinian fitness.

Adare (people): *see* Hareri.

adat, customary law of the indigenous peoples of Malaysia and Indonesia. It was the unwritten, traditional code governing all aspects of personal conduct from birth to death. Two kinds of Malay *adat* law developed prior to the 15th century: Adat Perpateh developed in a matrilineal kinship structure in areas occupied by the Minangkabau people in Sumatra and Negri Sembilan; Adat Temenggong originated in bilaterally based territorial social units. Both *adat* forms were markedly transformed by Islamic and later European legal systems.

Adat Perpateh emphasized law based on group responsibility. Criminal or civil offenses were not differentiated. Punishment stressed compensation rather than retribution. A crime was absolved by payment in kind, for example, or by a reconciliation feast given to the aggrieved person. Payment was enforced by community pressure. Mutilation and death penalties rarely were invoked. Acceptance of circumstantial evidence was a prominent feature of Adat Perpateh.

Prior to Islāmic influence Adat Temenggong consisted of a mixture of Hindu law and native custom. It encompassed civil, criminal, constitutional, and maritime law and invoked torture, amputation, or even death as punishment for offenses.

Both *adat* systems continued into the 20th century, until formalized European jurisprudence largely displaced them.

Adda River, Italian FIUME ADDA, river, in the Lombardia (Lombardy) region of northern Italy, issuing from small lakes in the Rhaetian Alps at 7,660 ft (2,335 m). It flows southward from Bormio to Tirano, where it turns west past Sondrio to enter Lake Como near its northern end after a course of 194 mi (313 km). The river's upper course is known as the Valtellina (*q.v.*). Leaving Lake Como at Lecco, it crosses the Pianura Lombarda (Lombardy Plain), flowing past Lodi and forming the Milano–Cremona provincial boundary before joining the Po River just upstream from Cremona city. The drainage basin of the Adda covers 3,000 sq mi (7,800 sq km), and its average flow in the lower course, navigable for 50 mi, is about 8,800 cu ft (250 cu m) per second, varying between 600 and 28,000. It is used extensively for hydroelectric power in the Valtellina and for irrigation on the Pianura Lombarda. Historically the Adda (Addua) was a strategic defense line in many wars as early as the Roman period.

Addams, Charles (Samuel) (b. Jan. 7, 1912, Westfield, N.J., U.S.), cartoonist whose drawings, known mostly through *The New Yorker* magazine, became famous in the U.S. as examples of macabre humour.

Addams attended various schools from 1929

to 1932; thereafter, aside from a brief period as a commercial artist, he was a free-lance cartoonist, selling his first work to *The New Yorker* in 1933. His cartoons began to attract wide popular attention about 1940. Addams' early cartoons were concerned with sex and parodied clubmen, but many of his later

Cartoon by Charles Addams, 1965

Drawing by Chas. Addams; © 1965 The New Yorker Magazine, Inc.

ones dealt with a family of monsters whose activities travestied those of a conventional family; *e.g.*, parent monsters beam approval as their children behead a doll with a toy guillotine. Addams' monster characters were the basis of "The Addams Family," a popular television series in the mid-1960s. Collections of his cartoons include *Drawn and Quartered* (1942), *Addams and Evil* (1947), *Monster Rally* (1950), *Homebodies* (1954), *Nightcrawlers* (1957), *Dear Dead Days* (1959), *Black Maria* (1960), *The Charles Addams Mother Goose* (1967), *My Crowd* (1970), *Chas. Addams Favorite Haunts* (1976), and *Creature Comforts* (1981).

Addams, Jane (b. Sept. 6, 1860, Cedarville, Ill., U.S.—d. May 21, 1935, Chicago), social reformer and pacifist, co-winner (with Nicholas Murray Butler) of the Nobel Prize

Jane Addams

By courtesy of the University of Illinois at Chicago, Jane Addams Memorial Collection

for Peace in 1931, who is probably best known as the founder of Hull House, Chicago, one of the first social settlements in North America.

After graduation from Rockford (Ill.) College in 1881, Addams entered the Woman's Medical College, Philadelphia, but her health failed, and for two years she was an invalid. Then (1883–85, 1887–88) she travelled extensively in Europe, visiting the Toynbee Hall settlement house (founded 1884) in the Whitechapel industrial district of London. Upon returning to the U.S., she and her travelling companion, Ellen Gates Starr, determined to create something like Toynbee Hall. In a working-class district in Chicago, they acquired a large vacant residence built by Charles Hull in 1856, and, calling it Hull House, they moved into it on Sept. 18, 1889. Eventually the settlement included 13 buildings and a playground, as well as a camp near Lake Geneva, Wis. Many prominent social workers and reformers—Julia Lathrop, Florence Kelley, Grace and Edith Abbott—came to live at Hull House, as did others who continued to make their living in business or the arts while helping Addams in settlement activities.

Facilities at Hull House included a day nursery, a gymnasium, a community kitchen, and a boarding club for working girls. Hull House offered college-level courses in various subjects; furnished training in art, music, and crafts such as bookbinding; and sponsored one of the earliest little-theatre groups, the Hull House Players. In addition to services and cultural opportunities for the largely immigrant population of the neighbourhood, Hull House afforded an opportunity for young social workers to acquire training.

Jane Addams worked with labour and other reform groups for the first juvenile-court law, tenement-house regulation, an eight-hour working day for women, factory inspection, and workmen's compensation. She also strove for justice for the immigrant and the Negro, advocated research to determine the causes of poverty and crime, and supported woman suffrage. In 1910 she became the first woman president of the National Conference of Social Work, and in 1912 she took an active part in the Progressive Party's presidential campaign for Theodore Roosevelt. At The Hague in 1915 she was chairman of the International Congress of Women, following which was established the Women's International League for Peace and Freedom.

Establishment of the Chicago campus of the University of Illinois in 1963 forced the Hull House Association to relocate its headquarters. Most of its original buildings were demolished, but the Hull residence itself was preserved as a monument to Jane Addams.

Among Miss Addams' books are *Democracy and Social Ethics* (1902), *Newer Ideals of Peace* (1907), *Twenty Years at Hull-House* (1910), and *The Second Twenty Years at Hull-House* (1930).

addax (*Addax nasomaculatus*), desert-dwelling antelope, family Bovidae (order Artiodactyla), once found throughout the Sahara but

Addax (*Addax nasomaculatus*)

Kenneth W. Fink—The National Audubon Society Collection/Photo Researchers

now much reduced in numbers and distribution and threatened with extinction from overhunting. A heavy-bodied, short-legged, gregarious antelope, the addax is characterized by broad hooves adapted to travel in loose sand and by long, spirally twisted horns, present in both sexes. It stands about 1 metre (39 inches) at the shoulder and is grayish in summer, darker in winter. Legs, underparts, and a patch on the face are white, and there is a tuft of dark hair on the forehead.

adder, any of several venomous snakes of the viper family, Viperidae, and the death adder, a viperlike member of the cobra snake family, Elapidae. The name may also be used for certain other snakes, such as the hognose snake (*q.v.*), a harmless North American species. Among the adders of the viper family are the common adder (*Vipera berus*), the puff adders (several species including *Bitis arietans*), and the night adders (four species of *Causus*).

Common adder (*Vipera berus*)

Walther Rohdich—Annan Photo Features

The common adder, or European viper, the serpent often mentioned in works of literature, is a stout-bodied snake that is widely distributed across Europe and Asia, even ranging north of the Arctic Circle in Norway. It grows to a maximum length of approximately 80 centimetres (30 inches) and is usually gray with a black zigzag band on the back and black spots on the sides. Its bite is rarely fatal to man.

The puff and night adders are terrestrial African vipers. The puff adder (so named because it gives warning by inflating its body

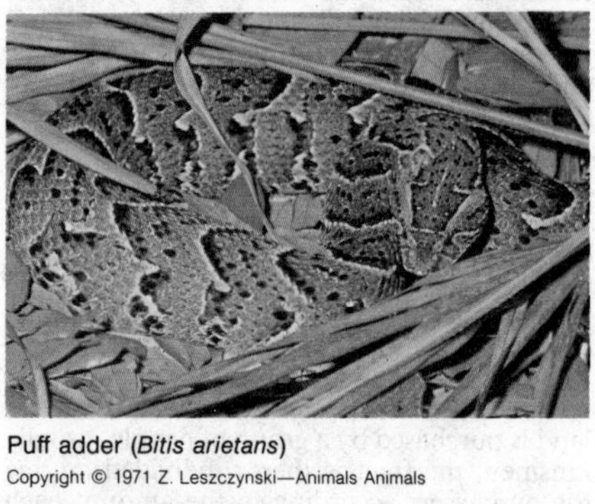

Puff adder (*Bitis arietans*)

Copyright © 1971 Z. Leszczynski—Animals Animals

and hissing loudly) is a large, extremely venomous snake found in the semi-arid regions of Africa and Arabia. It is about 1 to 1.5 metres (3 to 5 feet) long and is gray to dark brown with thin yellow chevrons on its back. A thick-bodied snake with a potentially lethal bite, it tends to stay put, rather than flee, when approached. Night adders are small, relatively slender vipers found south of the Sahara. They are gray with darker blotches, up to about one metre long, and are characterized by small fangs and a relatively weak venom that is unlikely to cause more than pain and swelling in man. Two of the four species, *C. rhombeatus* and *C. resimus,* have long venom glands that extend back from the head into the body cavity.

The death adder (*Acanthophis antarcticus*) is found in Australia and nearby islands, though not in Tasmania, in a variety of habitats. The desert death adder, *A. pyrrhus*, is found only in the deserts and ranges of central and Western Australia. Although they are related to the slender-bodied cobras, adders are viper-like in appearance, with thick bodies, short tails, and broad heads. They are about 45 to 90 cm (18 to 35 in.) long and are gray or brownish with darker crosswise bands. The death adder is a dangerous snake that has a potent venom that can cause death in about one-half of untreated cases.

Adderly, Herb, byname of HERBERT ANTHONY ADDERLEY (b. June 8, 1939, Philadelphia), U.S. professional National Football League (NFL) football defensive cornerback who was also a kickoff return specialist.

Adderley was graduated from Michigan State University (East Lansing) and joined the Green Bay Packers as their first draft choice in 1961. He played for them until he was traded to the Dallas Cowboys in 1969. In 1973, his final season, he played for the Los Angeles Rams and the New England Patriots. Adderley scored six touchdowns after interceptions in one season and made a 60-yd touchdown run after an interception in the 1968 Super Bowl. He played in four Super Bowl games (Green Bay, 1967–68, and Dallas, 1971–72). He was elected to the football Hall of Fame in 1980.

adding machine, a type of calculator (*q.v.*) used for performing simple arithmetical operations.

Addington, Henry: *see* Sidmouth, Henry Addington, 1st Viscount.

Addis Ababa, also spelled ADDIS ABEBA, capital and largest city of Ethiopia and of Shewa province. It is located on a well-watered plateau surrounded by hills and mountains, in the geographical centre of the country.

Only since the late 19th century has Addis Ababa been the capital of the Ethiopian state. Its immediate predecessor, Entoto, was situated on a high tableland and was found to be unsatisfactory because of extreme cold and an acute shortage of firewood. The empress Taitu, wife of Emperor Menelik II (reigned 1889–1913), persuaded the Emperor to build a house near the hot springs at the foot of the tableland and to grant land in the area to members of the nobility. The city was thus founded in 1887 and was named Addis Ababa (New Flower) by the Empress.

In its first years the city was more like a military encampment than a town. The central focus was the Emperor's palace, which was surrounded by the dwellings of his troops and of his innumerable retainers. As the population increased, firewood became scarce. In 1905 a large number of eucalyptus trees were imported from Australia; the trees spread and provided a forest cover for the city.

Addis Ababa was the capital of Italian East Africa from 1935 to 1941. Modern stone houses were built during this period, particularly in the areas of European residence, and many roads were paved. Other innovations included the establishment of a water reservoir at Gefarsa to the west and the building of a hydroelectric station at Akaki to the south. There were only limited changes in Addis Ababa between 1941 and 1960, but development has been impressive since then.

Addis Ababa is the educational and administrative centre of Ethiopia. It is the site of Addis Ababa University and contains several teacher-training colleges and technical schools. Also located in the city are the Museum of the Institute of Ethiopian Studies (operated by the university), the National School of Music, the National Library and Archives, palaces of former emperors, and governmental ministries. Several international organizations have their headquarters in the city; the most important are the Organization of African Unity and the United Nations Economic Commission for Africa, both located in Africa Hall.

Manufactured goods include textiles, shoes, food, beverages, wood products, plastics, and chemical products. Most of the country's service industries are also located in the city.

The bulk of the export and import trade of Ethiopia is channelled through Addis Ababa on its way to or from the ports of Djibouti, on the Gulf of Aden, or Aseb (Assab), on the Red Sea. The city is also the collection and distribution centre for much of the country's internal trade. The Mercato, located in the west, is one of the largest open-air markets in Africa. The Piazza in the central city contains the more expensive European-style shopping centres. Banking and insurance services are concentrated in Addis Ababa, and there is a small but growing stock exchange.

Addis Ababa is the hub of the nation's transportation network. Several roads connect it to other major cities; the only railway runs to Djibouti. The city is also served by an international airport.

Formally designated recreational areas are limited, but there are many open spaces suitable for recreational purposes. A small zoo is located in a park near the university, and the lake region, which is a short drive to the south, has facilities for boating, water-skiing, bathing, and bird-watching. The most popular spectator sport is soccer. Basketball, volleyball, and other sports are also played, chiefly by school teams. Pop. (1982 est.) 1,408,068.

Addison (of Stallingborough), Christopher Addison, 1st Viscount, also called (1937–45) BARON ADDISON OF STALLINGBOROUGH (b. June 19, 1869, Hogsthorpe, Lincolnshire, Eng.—d. Dec. 11, 1951, West Wycombe, Buckinghamshire), British surgeon and statesman, prominent in both Liberal and Labour governments between the wars and after World War II.

Educated at Trinity College, Harrogate, Yorkshire, and at St. Bartholomew's Hospital Medical College, London, he was subsequently an anatomy lecturer at "Bart's," professor of anatomy at University College, Sheffield, and, in 1901, Hunterian professor at the Royal College of Surgeons, London. Elected Liberal member of Parliament in 1910, he was parliamentary secretary to the Board of Education, 1914–15, and minister of munitions, 1916–17, minister in charge of postwar reconstruction, 1917, and first minister of health, 1919–21. He promoted an ambitious state-subsidized housing scheme, which caused an outcry against the heavy burden upon the taxpayer it would involve and which strained the hitherto close relations between himself and David Lloyd George, the prime minister. In 1921 Addison was transferred to a ministry without portfolio and in the same year he resigned from the government altogether.

In 1922 he transferred his allegiance to the Labour Party; in the same year he published *The Betrayal of the Slums* and, in 1926, *Practical Socialism.* In the 1929 general election Addison was returned to Parliament, in the Labour interest, and the new prime minister, Ramsay MacDonald, appointed him successively parliamentary secretary to the Ministry of Agriculture and Fisheries (1929–30) and minister of agriculture and fisheries (1930–31). In 1937 he was created a baron, and when the Labour Party was returned to power in 1945 he was elevated to a viscountcy and appointed dominions secretary, remaining in charge when this department became the Commonwealth Relations Office in 1947. In the same year, however, he asked to be relieved of some of his heavy duties because of his responsibilites as leader of the House of Lords, and he was appointed lord privy seal. In 1948–49 he was paymaster general. When in March 1951 Herbert Morrison became foreign secretary, Addison succeeded him as lord president of the council.

Addison, Joseph (b. May 1, 1672, Milston, Wiltshire, Eng.—d. June 17, 1719, London), essayist, poet, and dramatist, who, with Richard Steele, was a leading contributor to and guiding spirit of the periodicals *The Tatler* and *The Spectator*. His writing skill led to his holding important posts in government while the Whigs were in power.

Early life. Addison was the eldest son of the Rev. Lancelot Addison, later archdeacon of Coventry and dean of Lichfield. After schooling in Amesbury and Salisbury and at Lichfield Grammar School, he was enrolled at the age of 14 in the Charterhouse in London. Here began his lifelong friendship with Richard Steele, who later became his literary collaborator. Both went on to Oxford, where Addison matriculated at Queen's College in May 1687. Through distinction in Latin verse he won election as Demy to Magdalen College in 1689 and took the degree of M.A. in 1693. He was a fellow from 1697 to 1711. At Magdalen he spent 10 years as tutor in preparation for a career as a scholar and man of letters. In 1695 *A Poem to his Majesty* (William III), with a dedication to Lord Keeper Somers, the influential Whig statesman, brought favourable notice not only from Somers but also Charles Montague (later earl of Halifax), who saw in Addison a writer whose services were of potential use to the crown. A treasury grant offered opportunity for travel and preparation for government service. Much of his Latin verse had been published in the second volume of *Musarum Anglicanarum Analecta* (1699), which Addison himself edited. He had also attained distinction by contributing the preface to Virgil's *Georgics,* in John Dryden's great translation of 1697.

Joseph Addison, oil painting by M. Dahl, 1719; in the National Portrait Gallery, London

By courtesy of the National Portrait Gallery, London

The European tour (1699–1704) enabled Addison not only to become acquainted with English diplomats abroad but also to meet contemporary European men of letters and to observe at first hand the background of the Latin poets. His letters from Paris record visits to such celebrities as the literary critic Boileau, who was the most famous French poet of his day, and to Nicolas Malebranche, the philosopher, as well as his impressions of French drama and opera. He spent the year 1701 in leisurely travel in Italy, viewing ancient ruins, mountains, and rivers, as well as statues, paintings, and medals, against the background of Horace and Virgil, Claudian and Silius Italicus, who were to figure in his *Remarks on Several Parts of Italy* (1705; rev. 1718). *A Letter from Italy* (1704), a poetic epistle to Lord Halifax, records his delight in surveying these "poetic fields." The prose *Remarks,* addressed to Lord Somers, reveals not only his interest in the arts but also a true Whig's hatred of despotic power and the concentration of wealth in the papal treasury, contrasted with the widespread poverty of the people. From Italy Addison crossed the Alps at Mont Cenis into Switzerland, where, in Geneva, he learned in March 1702 of the death of William III and the consequent loss of power of his two chief patrons, Somers and Halifax. Instead of returning to England, therefore, he remained in Switzerland through the summer and then made an extended tour to Vienna, Dresden, Hanover (for a visit to the electress Sophia, the mother of the future king George I of England), and Hamburg, finally reaching Holland. There he lingered nearly a year, with visits to such men of letters as the French philosopher and critic Pierre Bayle and contacts with Englishmen in Amsterdam, including the publisher Jacob Tonson (who was then in Holland arranging for the first English publication of Bayle's great *Dictionary*), before returning to England in 1704.

Government service. In London Addison renewed his friendship with Somers and Halifax and other members of the Kit-Cat Club, founded by Tonson as an association of prominent Whig leaders and literary figures of the day—among them Steele, William Congreve, Sir John Vanbrugh, and Sir Samuel Garth. In August of this year London was electrified by the news of the Duke of Marlborough's sweeping victory over the French at Blenheim, and Addison was approached by government leaders to write a poem worthy of the great occasion. Even before the final draft was completed, Addison was appointed commissioner of appeals in excise, a sinecure left vacant by the death of John Locke. *The Campaign,* addressed to Marlborough, was published on December 14 (though dated 1705), the very day the Duke returned in triumph to London. By its rejection of conventional classical imagery (what Dr. Johnson called its "rational and manly contempt of fiction") and its effective portrayal of Marlborough's military genius, it was an immediate success, and three editions were sold before the year's end. It perfectly expressed the nation's great hour of victory.

The Whig success in the election of May 1705, which saw the return of Somers and Halifax to the Privy Council, brought Addison increased financial security in an appointment as under secretary to the secretary of state for southern affairs, a position of considerable administrative importance, with an income of more than £500 a year. With an office at the Cockpit (the government offices in Whitehall), Addison found himself in a busy and lucrative post, involving correspondence with diplomats abroad and a variety of business at home. Early in 1706 he accompanied Halifax to the court of Hanover to discuss details of the Act of Settlement, providing for the Hanoverian succession upon the death of Queen Anne; here and in Holland contacts were renewed with Bayle, the German philosopher Leibniz, and other men of letters. Addison's retention in a new, more powerful Whig administration in the autumn of 1706 reflected his further rise in government service.

At this time he began to see much of Steele, helping him write *The Tender Husband* (1705), for which he also provided a prologue; when the play was published it carried a dedication to Addison in honour of "an inviolable friendship." In practical ways Addison also assisted Steele with substantial loans and the appointment as editor of the official London *Gazette.* Moreover, as under secretary, Addison frequently supplied him with material for the paper. He lodged with Steele during the summer of 1707, until the latter's marriage in September, when Addison moved to larger quarters.

As a challenge to the popularity of Italian opera, Addison chose to write an opera in English centred on the legend of "fair Rosamond" and set in Woodstock Park, site of Marlborough's Blenheim Palace. For the music he engaged Thomas Clayton, composer of *Arsinoe, Queen of Cyprus*—an unfortunate choice as it turned out; when *Rosamond* was staged at Drury Lane (March 4, 1707), it ran for only three nights. The libretto itself was well constructed and the lyrics light and effective. Later in the century, with new music by Thomas Augustine Arne, it in fact proved very popular.

In 1708 Addison was elected to Parliament for Lostwithiel in Cornwall and later in the same year was made secretary to the Earl of Wharton, the new lord lieutenant of Ireland. Addison's post was in effect that of secretary of state for Irish affairs, with a revenue of some £2,000 a year. In addition to routine duties as Irish secretary, he was responsible to the crown for much official policy in Ireland, where such delicate matters as the Test Act, the laws against Roman Catholics, and the settlement of the Protestant palatines required a tactful and firm hand. He was elected a member of the Irish Parliament, taking his seat as representative for Cavan on May 15, 1709. He also interested himself in the preservation and arrangement of the Irish public records, purchasing the office of keeper of the records in Bermingham's Tower, which he developed into a responsible office with an annual salary of £400.

Addison served as Irish secretary for the two years during which Wharton was lord lieutenant, residing in Dublin Castle from April to September 1709 and from May to August 1710, spending the winter months in England. It was during his term as Irish secretary that his friend Steele began publishing *The Tatler,* which appeared three times a week under the pseudonym of Isaac Bickerstaff. The first number appeared on April 12, 1709, while Addison was still in England, but while still in Ireland, Addison began contributing to the new periodical. Back in London in September 1709, he supplied most of the essays during the winter of 1709–10 before returning to Ireland in May.

Years of Tory dominance. The year 1710 was marked by the overturn of the Whigs from power and a substantial Tory victory at the polls. Although Addison easily retained his seat in the Commons—this time for Malmesbury in Wiltshire—his old and powerful patrons were again out of favour, and for the first time since his appointment as under secretary in 1705, Addison found himself without employment. He was thus able to devote even more time to literary activity and to cultivation of personal friendships not only with Steele and other Kit-Cats but, for a short period, with Jonathan Swift—until Swift's shift of allegiance to the rising Tory leaders resulted in estrangement. Addison continued contributing to the final numbers of *The Tatler,* which Steele finally brought to a close on Jan. 2, 1711.

Thanks to Addison's help *The Tatler* was an undoubted success, although it had met with criticism because of Steele's attacks on the new Tory government. By the end of 1710 Steele had enough material for a collected edition of *The Tatler;* thereupon, he and Addison decided to make a fresh start with a new periodical. *The Spectator,* appearing six days a week, from March 1, 1711, to Dec. 6, 1712, offered a wide range of material to its readers, from discussion of the latest fashions to serious disquisitions on criticism and morality, including Addison's weekly papers on *Paradise Lost* and the series on the "pleasures of the imagination." In bringing learning "out of closets and libraries, schools and colleges, to dwell in clubs and assemblies, at tea-tables, and in coffee-houses," *The Spectator* was eminently successful—as shown by the great variety of letters from readers and the steadily increasing number of advertisements printed. More than 3,000 copies were published daily, and the 555 numbers were then collected into seven volumes. Two years later (from June 18 to Dec. 20, 1714) Addison published 80 additional numbers, with the help of two assistants, and these were later reprinted as volume eight.

Addison's other notable literary production, while in the political wilderness during the years of Tory dominance, was his tragedy *Cato.* Performed at Drury Lane on April 14, 1713, the play was a resounding success—largely, no doubt, because of the political overtones that both parties read into the play. To the Whigs Cato seemed the resolute defender of liberty against French tyranny; while the Tories were able to interpret the domineering Caesar as a kind of Roman Marlborough whose military victories were a threat to English liberties. The play enjoyed an unusual run of 20 performances in April and May 1713, eight editions were sold within the year, and it continued to be performed, read, and quoted throughout the century.

Later years. With the death of Queen Anne on Aug. 1, 1714, and the accession of George I, Addison's political fortunes rose. He was appointed secretary to the regents (who governed until the arrival of the new monarch from Hanover) and in April 1717 was made secretary of state. Ill health, however, prevented his taking a very active part in government affairs, and he resigned the office the following year. Meanwhile, he had married the dowager countess of Warwick and spent the remaining years of his life in comparative affluence at Holland House in Kensington. A series of political essays, *The Free-Holder, or Political Essays,* was published from Dec. 23, 1715, to June 29, 1716, and his comedy *The Drummer* was produced at Drury Lane on March 10, 1716. The dispute over Lord Sunderland's bill for restricting the peerage, in which Addison and Steele took opposing sides, unfortunately estranged the two friends during the last year of Addison's life. He was buried in Westminster Abbey, near the grave of his old patron and friend Lord Halifax.

As a writer he produced one of the great tragedies of the 18th century in *Cato* and brought to perfection the periodical essay in his journal, *The Spectator.* As a civil servant he became an influential supporter of the Whigs (who sought to further the constitutional principles established by the Revolution of 1688) in a number of government posts, finally becoming secretary of state under George I. He achieved early fame as a writer of Latin and English verse, but it was his poem on the Battle of Blenheim that brought him to the attention of Whig leaders and paved the way to government employment and literary fame. Dr. Johnson's praise of *The Spectator* as a model of prose style established Addison as one of the most admired and influential masters of prose in the language. (D.F.B.)

MAJOR WORKS. *Poems.* "Letter from Italy" in Dryden's fifth miscellany (1704); The Campaign (1705); Latin verse in vol. 2 of *Musarum Anglicanarum Analecta,* ed. by Addison (1699).

Dramatic works. *Rosamond: An Opera* (1707); *Cato: A Tragedy* (1713); *The Drummer; or, the Haunted-House, a Comedy* (1716).

Periodical essays. *The Tatler* (1709–11), about 42 numbers; *The Whig Examiner* (1710), all 5 numbers; *The Spectator* (1711–12), 251 numbers; *The Guardian* (1713), 53 numbers; *The Lover* (1714), 2 numbers; *The Reader* (1714), 2 numbers; *The Spectator,* 2nd series (1714), 25 numbers; *The Free-Holder, or Political Essays* (1715–16), all 55 numbers; *The Old Whig* (1719), both numbers.

Other prose works. *Remarks on Several Parts of Italy* (1705); *The Present State of the War* (1708); *The Late Tryal and Conviction of Count Tariff* (1713).

BIBLIOGRAPHY. Addison's works were published with a life by Thomas Tickell, 4 vol. (1721; reprinted 1730, 1741, 1804); and by John Baskerville (1761); edited with notes by Richard Hurd, 6 vol. (1811); and in Bohn's British Classics, 6 vol. (1854–56, frequently reprinted); and by G.W. Greene, 6 vol. (1856). The standard modern edition of the *Miscellaneous Works* (poems, plays, and prose, omitting the periodical essays) is by A.C. Guthkelch, 2 vol. (1914). Addison's *Letters* were edited by Walter Graham (1941). The definitive edition of *The Spectator* is by Donald F. Bond, 5 vol. (1965), who has also edited *Critical Essays from the Spectator* (1970). The standard biography is Peter Smithers, *The Life of Joseph Addison*, 2nd ed. (1968).

Addison, Thomas (b. April 1793, Longbenton, Northumberland, Eng.—d. June 29, 1860, Bristol, Gloucestershire), physician after whom Addison's disease, a metabolic dysfunction caused by atrophy of the adrenal cortex, and Addison's (pernicious) anemia were named. He was the first to correlate a set of disease symptoms with pathological changes in one of the endocrine glands.

In 1837 Addison became a full physician at Guy's Hospital, London, and a joint lecturer on medicine with Richard Bright, with whom he wrote *Elements of the Practice of Medicine* (1839). He gave a preliminary account in 1849 of the two diseases named after him and in 1855 wrote *On the Constitutional and Local Effects of Disease of the Supra-Renal Capsules.* He was author, with John Morgan, of *An Essay on the Operation of Poisonous Agents upon the Living Body* (1829), the first English book on the subject.

Addison's anemia: *see* pernicious anemia.

Addison's disease, also called ADRENAL CORTICAL INSUFFICIENCY, insidious disease caused by progressive atrophy of the cortex of the adrenal glands. Most of the cortex is destroyed before the symptoms of the disease become apparent. The symptoms—which include weakness, abnormal skin and mucous pigmentation, weight loss, low blood pressure, and gastrointestinal upset—are caused by lack of hydrocortisone (a substance secreted by the cortex of the adrenal glands) and overproduction of pituitary hormones. Replacement of the lacking hydrocortisone with drugs known as adrenal corticosteroids restores normal health.

In the mid-19th century, when the disorder was first recognized, the atrophy was attributed to tuberculosis, which remains the second leading cause of Addison's disease. More than half of all cases are now believed to result from destruction of the adrenal cortex by the body's own antibodies in an autoimmune reaction.

Consult the INDEX *first*

addition reaction, any of a class of organic chemical reactions that produce an increase in the number of atoms or groups of atoms attached to at least one carbon atom in the molecule.

In certain organic molecules the carbon atoms can be bonded to as many as four atoms or groups of atoms. When there are fewer than four atoms available for bonding, the carbon atoms become triply or doubly bonded to one of two or three atoms, as in alkenes ($>C=C<$), aldehydes and ketones ($>C=O$), and alkynes ($-C\equiv C-$). An addition reaction may be visualized as a process by which double or triple bonds between atoms are fully or partially broken in order to accommodate additional atoms or groups of atoms in the molecule. Addition reactions to alkenes and alkynes are sometimes called saturation reactions, deriving from the description of carbon atoms with the maximum number of attached groups as saturated carbons.

A typical addition reaction may be illustrated by the hydrobromination of propene (an alkene), for which the equation is

$$CH_3CH=CH_2+HBr \longrightarrow CH_3C^+HCH_3+Br^- \longrightarrow CH_3CHBrCH_3.$$

The reaction proceeds in two stages: first, the hydrogen atom component of hydrogen bromide (the positively charged component) adds to one of the pair of carbon atoms joined by double bonds—in this case, the less alkylated carbon atom—followed by addition of the bromine atom (the negatively charged component) to the other carbon atom. In addition reactions to aldehydes and ketones, the sequence of events is reversed; *i.e.*, the initial step is addition of the negatively charged component of the reagent to the carbon atom, followed by addition of the positively charged component to the oxygen atom. Thus, the reaction of a ketone ($RCH_3C=O$, where R is an alkyl group) with hydrogen cyanide proceeds as follows:

$$RCH_3C=O+HCN \longrightarrow \underset{\textstyle CN}{RCH_3C}-O^- + H^+ \longrightarrow \underset{\textstyle CN}{RCH_3C}-OH.$$

The hydrobromination of propene or, in general, the addition to alkenes is said to be initiated by electron-seeking (electrophilic) reagents, while the additions to alkynes, aldehydes and ketones are said to be initiated by electron-rich (nucleophilic) reagents. Other forms of addition reactions include: catalyzed addition reactions, such as the self-addition of alkenes (catalyzed by acids) or the hydrogenation of alkenes, aldehydes, and ketones (catalyzed by metals); addition reactions with formation of cyclic or ring compounds; and addition reactions that proceed by chain mechanisms.

additive, in foods, any of numerous chemical substances added to foods to produce specific desirable effects. The term additive may also be expanded to include substances—possibly useless or deleterious—that enter foods unintentionally (*see* below). Additives include such substances as artificial or natural colourings and flavourings; stabilizers, emulsifiers, texturizers, and thickeners; preservatives; flavour enhancers; and supplementary nutrients. Salt, used for centuries to preserve meat, is an additive, as are baking soda, vinegar, and many spices commonly used in home food preparation.

In commercial food processing additives may be used for aesthetic reasons (to improve colour or consistency) or for considerations of health (to retard spoilage or to increase nutritional value). Some artificial flavourings and colourings are used for economic reasons, because they are cheaper than the natural ingredients. Other chemicals are added to extend the shelf life of products; for example, humectants, which help to retain moisture; anticaking agents, which maintain the free-flowing qualities of salt, sugar, and similar products; and release agents, used to prevent confections and baked goods from sticking to their wrappings. While many additives are beneficial—or, at least, harmless—others have the effects of reducing nutritional value or concealing inferior raw materials or processing.

In the United States, prior to 1958, any such substance added to food by manufacturers or producers was assumed to be safe unless proven otherwise. Since that time, however, many additives have come under scrutiny as possible causes of cancer (carcinogens), birth defects (teratogens), and conditions such as the behaviour syndrome in children known as hyperactivity. Thus, the U.S. government, along with many others, became involved in regulating the use of additives, both to protect public health and to avoid consumer deception.

Incidental additives, or contaminants, are substances that enter food inadvertently or accidentally during production, processing, or handling. Pesticides used to protect crops may leave residues in foods, as may drugs added to livestock feed to control disease and improve meat yield. Legislation often establishes limits for such residue in food products. Maximum levels may also be specified for chemicals employed in packaging materials, which may actually introduce toxic substances into the products they contain.

For more information on additives, *see* emulsifier; food colouring; food flavouring; nutritional supplement; preservative.

Addo Elephant National Park, national park in southern Cape Province, South Africa, lying in the Sundays River Valley south of the Suurberge range, north of Port Elizabeth. It has an area of 26.5 sq mi (69 sq km). The park, established in 1931, is largely covered with dense, impenetrable evergreen scrub and preserves a band of about 100 elephants, remnant of a great herd that roamed the area before an extermination campaign was started by landowners in 1919. It is also the habitat of hippopotamuses, scarce Cape buffalo, several species of transplanted antelope, black rhinoceroses from Kenya, and numerous small birds, mammals, and reptiles. Headquarters are at Port Elizabeth.

adductor muscle, any of the muscles that draw a part of the body toward its median line or toward the axis of an extremity (*compare* abductor muscles), particularly three powerful muscles of the human thigh—adductor longus, adductor brevis, and adductor magnus. Originating at the pubis and the ischium (lower portions of the pelvis—the hipbone), these ribbonlike muscles are attached along the femur (thighbone). Their primary action is adduction of the thigh, as in squeezing the thighs together; they also aid in rotation and flexion of the thigh.

For a depiction of the adductor brevis and adductor longus in human anatomy, shown in relation to other parts of the body, *see* the colour Trans-Vision in the PROPAEDIA: Part Four, Section 421.

Other muscles named for this function include the adductor pollicis, which draws in and opposes the thumb, and the adductor hallucis, which acts on the great toe.

Ade, George (b. Feb. 9, 1866, Kentland, Ind., U.S.—d. May 16, 1944, Brook, Ind.), playwright and humorist whose *Fables in Slang* summarized the kind of wisdom accumulated by the country boy in the city.

Graduated from Purdue University, he was on the staff of the *Chicago Record* from 1890 to 1900. Characters introduced in his widely acclaimed editorial-page column, "Stories of the Streets and of the Town," became the subjects of his early books, *Artie* (1896), *Pink Marsh* (1897), and *Doc Horne* (1899). His greatest recognition came with *Fables in Slang* (1899), a national best-seller that was followed by a weekly syndicated fable and by 11 other books of fables. The fables, which contained only a little slang, were, rather, examples of the vernacular.

In 1902 Ade's light opera *The Sultan of Sulu* began a long run in New York, followed by such successful comedies as *The County Chairman* (1903) and *The College Widow* (1904). He was recognized as one of the most successful playwrights of his time. He established an estate near Brook, Ind., which became his permanent home. He wrote many motion-picture scripts and, during the Prohibition era, what many called one of his most amusing books, *The Old Time Saloon* (1931).

Adelaer, also spelled ADELER (Norwegian: Eagle), byname of CORT, or CURT, SIVERTSEN, Italian CURZIO SUFFRIDO (b. Dec. 16, 1622, Brevik, Nor.—d. Nov. 5, 1675, Copenhagen), Norwegian-born seaman and naval officer, distinguished in Venetian and in Danish naval history.

He entered the Dutch navy in 1639 as an *adelborst* ("cadet") and served under Martin van Tromp but in 1642 moved into Venetian service, where he was known as Curzio Suffrido Adelborst. He soon distinguished himself and in 1650 was sent to patrol the Dardanelles. On May 16, 1654, his Venetian squadron took part in the Battle of the Dardanelles, when his ship alone sank 15 Turkish galleys; and on the following day he compelled the surrender of the Turks at Tenedos. In 1659 he was made a knight of St. Mark and given a pension for life (heritable to the first three generations of his descendants), and in 1660 he became lieutenant admiral of the Venetian fleet.

Two years later, in 1662, he returned to Denmark as admiral of the Danish fleet, receiving at the same time various honours and revenues from Frederick III. His most important work was the refitting and reorganization of the fleet. In 1665 he received an invitation to command the Dutch fleet against England, but this he refused. He was ennobled by Frederick III in 1666 and was sent to India to negotiate with the court of Coromandel three years later (1669–70). Under Christian V he was appointed to command the Danish fleet against Sweden but died before the expedition.

Adelaide, capital of the state of South Australia. Situated at the base of the Mt. Lofty Ranges, 9 mi (14 km) inland from the centre of the eastern shore of the Gulf St. Vincent, it has a Mediterranean climate with hot summers (February mean temperature 74° F [23° C]), cool winters (July mean 54° F [12° C]),

Park lands along the Torrens River, Adelaide, South Australia
Picturepoint

and an average annual rainfall of 21 in. (530 mm). The site, chosen in 1836 by William Light (the colony's first surveyor general), is on slightly rising ground along the Torrens River, which divides it into a southern business district and a northern residential section. The city is separated from its suburbs by extensive areas of parklands. Named for Queen Adelaide, consort of the British king William IV, it was incorporated as Australia's first municipal government in 1840 and became a city in 1919, when it gained a lord mayoralty.

The fertility of the surrounding plains, easy access to the Murray lowlands to the east and southeast, and the presence of mineral deposits in the nearby hills all contributed to the city's growth. As an early agricultural marketing centre, it handled wheat, wool, fruits, and wine. Adelaide, aided by its central position and a ready supply of raw materials, has since become industrialized, with factories producing automobile components, machinery, textiles, and chemicals. An oil refinery was completed in 1962 at Hallet Cove, south of Adelaide near Port Noarlunga; a second oil refinery has also been completed. Adelaide is connected by pipeline with the Gidgealpa natural gas fields in Cooper Basin, northeastern South Australia. A focus of rail, sea, air, and road transportation, Adelaide receives the bulk of the products of the lower Murray River Valley, which has no port at its mouth. Adelaide's own harbour facilities are at Port Adelaide, 7 mi northwest.

Notable city landmarks include the university (founded in 1874), Parliament and Government houses, the Natural History Museum, and two cathedrals—St. Peter's (Anglican) and St. Francis Xavier's (Roman Catholic). The biennial Adelaide Festival of Arts (1960) was the first international celebration of its kind to be held in Australia. Pop. (1981) city, 12,656; metropolitan area, 882,520.

Adelaide, SAINT, German ADELHEID DIE HEILIGE (b. 931—d. Dec. 16, 999, Seltz, Alsace; feast day December 16), consort of the Western emperor Otto I and, later, regent for her grandson Otto III who helped strengthen the German church while subordinating it to imperial power.

Daughter of Rudolf II (d. 937), king of Burgundy, and Bertha of Swabia, Adelaide was married (947) to Lothair, who succeeded his father, Hugh of Arles, as king of Italy in the same year. After Lothair died (950), Berengar of Ivrea, his old rival, seized the Italian throne and imprisoned her (April 951) at Garda. After her escape four months later, she asked the German king Otto I the Great to help her regain the throne. Otto marched into Lombardy (September 951), declared himself king, and married her (December 951). They were crowned emperor and empress by Pope John XII in Rome in 962. She devoted her time to promoting Cluniac monasticism (a reform of the Benedictine order) and to strengthening the allegiance of the German church to the emperor.

After Otto's death (May 7, 973), Adelaide exercised influence over her son Otto II until their estrangement in 978, when she left the court and lived in Burgundy with her brother King Conrad. At Conrad's urging she became reconciled with her son, and, before his death in 983, Otto appointed her his regent in Italy. With her daughter-in-law, Empress Theophano, she upheld the right of her three-year-old grandson, Otto III, to the German throne. She lived in Lombardy from 985 to 991, when she returned to Germany to serve as sole regent after Theophano's death (991). She governed until Otto III came of age (994), and, when he became Holy Roman emperor in 996, she retired from court life, devoting herself to founding churches, monasteries, and convents. Miracles reportedly occurred at her tomb at Seltz.

Adelaide River, river in northwestern Northern Territory, Australia, rising in the hills west of Brock's Creek and flowing (with marked summer increases in volume) for 110 mi (180 km) northeastward to Adam Bay, an inlet of the Timor Sea on Clarence Strait. From its mouth, 32 mi northeast of Darwin, it is navigable for 80 mi. The river was reached in 1839 by L.R. Fitzmaurice of the ship HMS "Beagle" and named after the dowager queen Adelaide. It was explored by John McDouall Stuart in 1862, and the first settlement along its banks was Escape Cliffs (1864–67). Since the 1890s the fertile black soils lining the Adelaide's lower reaches have been used for agricultural experiments: vegetables (1939–45) and subsequent rice- and cattle-farming projects. The town of Adelaide River, located where the Stuart Highway and North Australia Railway cross the stream, 50 mi south of Darwin, is a tourist base for the Rum Jungle and Daly River districts.

adelantado (Spanish: "one who goes before"), representative of the kings of Castile, who in the early Middle Ages headed military expeditions and, from the reign of Ferdinand III (1217–52) until the 16th century, held judicial and administrative powers over specific districts. Greater *adelantados* (*adelantados mayores*) served as appeal judges and in times of war were responsible for organizing their territories' armies. Lesser *adelantados* (*adelantados menores*) held similar powers, but they were often stationed along the frontiers, becoming known as *adelantados fronterizos,* and figured prominently in the military conquest of the Americas. In the 16th century the office was replaced by that of alcalde (magistrate).

Adelard OF BATH (fl. early 12th century), English Scholastic philosopher and early interpreter of Arabic scientific knowledge who translated into Latin an Arabic version of Euclid's *Elements*, which for centuries served as the chief geometry textbook in the West. Adelard studied and taught in France and travelled in Italy, Cilicia, Syria, Palestine, and perhaps also in Spain (*c.* 1110–25) before returning to Bath and becoming a teacher of the future king Henry II. In his Platonizing dialogue *De eodem et diverso* ("On Sameness and Diversity"), his atomism and his attempt to reconcile the reality of universals with that of the individual distinguish him from other Platonists. His *Quaestiones naturales* (76 discussions of human nature, meteorology, astronomy, botany, and zoology) are based on Arabic science. His other writings include works on the abacus, the astrolabe, and a translation of an Arabic astronomical table.

Adelbert (German archbishop): *see* Adalbert.

Adeler (Norwegian seaman): *see* Adelaer.

Adelheid DIE HEILIGE: *see* Adelaide, Saint.

Adélie Coast, also called ADÉLIE LAND, part of the coast of Wilkes Land in eastern Antarctica, extending from Claire Coast (west) to George V Coast (east). The region is an ice-covered plateau rising from the Indian Ocean and comprising an area of about 150,000 sq mi (390,000 sq km). Discovered in 1840 by the French explorer Jules-Sébastien-César Dumont d'Urville, who named it after his wife, it is the basis of France's claim on the continent between longitude 136° and 142° E; administratively it is a part of Terres Australes et Antarctiques Françaises (*q.v.*). The French meteorological station Dumont d'Urville base was established in 1952 at Géologie Archipelago, replacing the original station of Port-Martin (founded 1950), which was destroyed by fire.

Adelsberg (Yugoslavia): *see* Postojna.

Adelung, Johann Christoph (b. Aug. 8, 1732, Spantekow, Prussia—d. Sept. 10, 1806, Dresden, Saxony), one of the most influential German-language scholars before Jacob Grimm; his grammars, dictionary, and works on style helped to standardize the language, establish its principles of spelling, and refine its idiom.

He engaged in private research from 1761 to 1787, when he became principal librarian to the elector of Saxony at Dresden, a post he retained to the end of his life.

Adelung's *Versuch eines vollständigen Grammatisch-kritischen Wörterbuches der hochdeutschen Mundart* (1774–86; "Attempt at a Complete Grammatical-Critical Dictionary of the High German Dialect") revealed an intimate knowledge of the history of dialects basic to modern German. At the time of his death, he was still at work on *Mithridates, oder allgemeine Sprachenkunde,* 3 vol. (1806–17; "Mithridates, or General Linguistics"), in which he affirmed the relation of Sanskrit and the major European languages and also collected the Lord's Prayer in some 500 languages and dialects.

Adémar OF MONTEIL, also called ADÉMAR OF PUY: *see* Adhémar of Monteil.

Aden, Arabic ʿADAN, national capital and capital of ʿAdan *muḥāfaẓah* (governorate), Yemen (Aden), situated on the Gulf of Aden and on a peninsula enclosing the eastern side of Bandar at-Tawāhī (Aden Harbour). The former administrative capital of the nation, Madīnat ash-Shaʿb, lies on the western side. The city has been a trade centre since antiquity and is mentioned in the Bible. During the 16th century it came under Ottoman control; the British established themselves there by treaty in 1802. Under Britain, Aden became a coaling station on the sea route to India, and in 1937 it was made a crown colony. In 1953 an oil refinery was built at Little Aden, on the western side of the bay.

Commercial harbour at Aden, Yemen (Aden)
Charles Harbutt—Magnum

Aden became partially self-governing in 1962 and was incorporated in the Federation of South Arabia in 1963. It then became involved in a struggle between two rival nationalist groups before finally becoming part of the independent republic in 1967. It was made the national capital in 1968.

The contemporary city consists of three sections: Crater, the old commercial quarter; at-Tawāhī, the business section; and Maʿallah, the native harbour area. Its economy is based almost entirely on its functions as a commercial centre for nearby states and as a refuelling stop for ships; the latter activity declined considerably during the closure of the Suez Canal (1967–75) and still has far below its former level of traffic. The city has some small industries, including light manufacturing, evaporation of seawater to obtain marine salt, and boatbuilding. Aden was a free port, with no customs duties, until 1970, when duties were imposed. There is an international airport at Khaur Maksar, a former Royal Air Force (RAF) base just north of Aden. The University of Aden was opened in 1970. Pop. (1981 est.) 365,000.

Aden, Gulf of, deepwater basin that forms a natural sea link between the Red Sea and the Arabian Sea. Named after the seaport of Aden, in Yemen (Aden), at its western end, the gulf is situated between the coasts of Arabia and the Horn of Africa. To the west, it narrows into the Gulf of Tadjoura; its eastern geographic limits are defined by the meridian of Cape Guardafui (51°16′ E). In oceanographic and geologic terms, however, it extends to the eastern limits of the continental shelf beyond the Kuria Muria Islands to the north and the island of Socotra to the south, covering an area of some 205,000 sq mi (530,000 sq km). Its total length, measured from east-northeast to west-southwest, is 920 mi (1,480 km), and its mean width, measured from north-northeast to south-southwest is 300 mi.

The dominant relief feature is the Sheba Ridge, an extension of the ridge system of the Indian Ocean, which extends along the middle of the gulf. The rough topography of the ridge includes a well-defined median valley that is continually offset by faults running approximately northeast to southwest. The largest of these faults forms the Alula-Fartak Trench, in which is found the gulf's maximum recorded depth of 17,586 ft (5,360 m). The Sheba Ridge is flanked on both sides by sediment-filled basins that reach depths of 13,000 ft at the mouth of the gulf. To the west, the ridge gives way to a relatively shallow east–west-trending valley known as the Tadjoura Trench.

The main factor in the gulf's geologic formation is the spreading of the sea floor away from the Sheba Ridge axis. The African and Arabian continents split initially along the present continental margins either in the late Eocene Epoch (38,000,000 to 54,000,000 years ago) or else in the Oligocene Epoch (26,000,000 to 38,000,000 years ago). They have since drifted apart in a direction parallel to the gulf's faults.

The gulf is underlain by an oceanic crust, and the Sheba Ridge is characterized by shallow earthquake activity, high heat flow, fresh lavas, and a thin or absent sedimentary cover. The evolution of the gulf is also linked with the geological evolution of the East African Rift Valley and of the Red Sea.

Sediment thicknesses increase away from the Sheba Ridge toward the continental shelf, especially in the region south of the Wādī Ḥaḍramawt (a seasonal river that drains into the gulf from the Arabian Peninsula), where a thickness of about one mile is found. Brown, green, and gray muds—characteristic of materials originating on land—predominate near the coasts. The basins are filled mainly with material from the coastal margins, eroded by turbid water currents, while sediments formed in deep water far from land predominate on the Sheba Ridge. A slight amount of wind-blown material is also present.

The intensive exchange of water between the Red Sea, the Gulf of Aden, and the Arabian Sea, as well as strong evaporation and monsoon (rain-bearing) winds that constitute part of the air flow, all assist in the formation of a complex water structure. The surface layer is highly saline, and eddies complicate its flow pattern. During the northeast monsoon from November to March, the surface temperature is fairly uniform—between 77° and 82° F (25° and 28° C). During the stronger southwest monsoon from May to September, however, horizontal temperature gradients develop, with temperatures ranging from 77° to 88° F (25° to 31° C). In the subsurface layer, at depths of from 300 to 2,000 ft, slightly less saline water flows from the Arabian Sea and passes into the Red Sea through the straits of Bab el-Mandeb. This flow is reversed below 2,500 ft in a highly saline layer that originates in the Red Sea. A low temperature and salinity layer occurs at depths of from 3,000 to 6,000 ft down to the bottom in the east but only in the depressions to the west.

Marine life is rich in both the quantity and the variety of its species. Seasonally variable upwelling of waters in the coastal zone provides the surface layer with a considerable supply of nutrient elements, which produce an abundant growth of plankton. Sardines and mackerel abound in these areas of upwelling. The main open-sea fish are dolphin, tuna, billfish, and sharks. Whales are frequently sighted. The gulf provides a breeding ground for sea turtles, and rock lobster are abundant.

Despite a lack of large-scale commercial fishing facilities, the coastline supports many isolated fishing towns and villages. Local fishing takes place close to the shore; sardines, tuna, kingfish, and mackerel make up the bulk of the annual catches. Crayfish and sharks are also fished locally, while survey ships have occasionally pulled in exceptional catches of fish.

BIBLIOGRAPHY. The morphology, geology, and geophysics of the gulf and its surrounding areas are comprehensively covered in various articles in the *Phil. Trans. R. Soc.,* Series A, vol. 267, no. 1181 (1970), which also contains up-to-date bathymetric and magnetic charts of the gulf itself. The hydrological structure of the water mass is described by V.A. Khimitsa in *Oceanology,* 8:318–322 (1968); while its physical and chemical properties are covered in the *University of California, Institute of Marine Resources Report, I.M.R. Reference 67–12* (1967). Biology is not covered by any standard text but fishery data is reported in the *Commercial Fisheries Review* (monthly).

Adena culture, culture of various communities of ancient North American Indians, *c.* 500 BC–AD 100, centred in what is now southern Ohio. Groups in Indiana, Kentucky, West Virginia, and possibly Pennsylvania bear similarities and are roughly grouped with the Adena culture. (The term Adena derives from the Adena Mound near Adena, Ohio.)

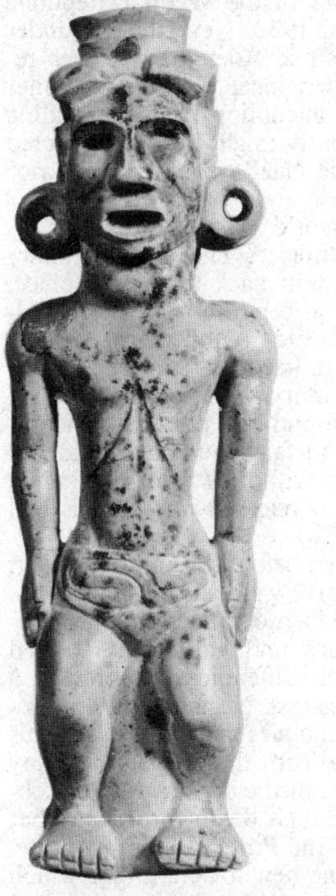

Stone pipe carved in the form of a human figure, found in the Adena Mound near Chillicothe, Ohio
By courtesy of the Ohio Historical Society

The Adena usually lived in villages containing circular houses with conical roofs, constructed of poles, willows, and bark, though some had rock shelters. They subsisted by hunting, fishing, and gathering wild plant foods. Their utensils consisted of such items as stone hoes, axes, and projectiles, stone smoking pipes, and simple pottery. Adena ornaments of copper, mica, and seashells attest to trade with faraway peoples.

Adenauer, Konrad (b. Jan. 5, 1876, Cologne—d. April 19, 1967, Rhöndorf, W.Ger.), first chancellor of the Federal Republic of Germany (1949–63), presiding over its reconstruction after World War II. A Christian Democrat and firmly anti-Communist, he supported NATO, and he worked to reconcile Germany with its former enemies, especially France.

Early career. The son of a Cologne civil servant, Adenauer grew up in a Roman Catholic family of simple means in which frugality, fulfillment of duty, and religious dedication were stressed. He studied jurisprudence and political science at the universities of Freiburg, Munich, and Bonn. In 1906 he was elected to the Cologne City Council and, in 1917, during World War I, was chosen *Oberbürgermeister,* or lord mayor, of the city. From 1920 he served as a member of the Staatsrat (the central organ representing the diets of the Prussian provinces) and in 1928 was elected its speaker. Politically, he belonged to the Centre Party, which in Cologne was long the leading political force. The largest part of German Catholicism became politically entrenched in it. The conflict between Bismarck and the Vatican had caused the state and German Catholicism to become critically and widely separated. In the Rhineland at that time, Catholicism was submerged in the reservations of the German states, which had come under Prussian rule only in the 19th century.

Such influences and moods were shared with Adenauer, but they do not explain why he never seized on the opportunities offered by the Centre Party to play a formative role in German politics in the Weimar Republic between 1919 and 1933. Nevertheless, under the Weimar Republic Adenauer's career remained confined to local politics; his inner aloofness and his alienation from the leading men of his own party might have contributed to this. During the Nazi regime he was twice imprisoned.

At the end of World War II, Adenauer returned to his birthplace. The Allied military authorities called him back to his old office, but, before he could begin his task of rebuilding the beautiful, old, bomb-shattered city, Adenauer was dismissed by Sir John Barraclough, British military governor of the North Rhine area, who found him politically incompetent. This second fall from power did not cause Adenauer to withdraw from public life. On the contrary, it released him for his real mission.

Chancellor. Even before the end of the war, a new political party was being formed—the German Christian Democratic Union (CDU)—in which Catholics and Protestants buried their long-standing differences to present a common front against Nazism and to promote Christian principles in government. This movement sprang from the insights of many that the old parties of the civil camp were obsolete and were in their death throes and that the Catholics and the Protestants must unite. This was something new for Germany, which for centuries following the Reformation had created a climate in which the two communities encountered each other often polemically or at a respectful distance. Adenauer was now able to play an important role in the formation of the new party, and in 1946 he became its chairman. He had always had a sharp eye for the possibilities and necessities of political tactics. The CDU began expanding in the four zones of the Allied occupation. As the Soviet Union began increasingly to obstruct the Allied Control Council, the Western Allies decided to give their three occupation zones a federal-state organization. Adenauer became president of the Parlamentarischer Rat (Parliamentary Council), the task of which was to work out a provisional constitution for the intended Federal Republic. The first Bundestag elections took place in August 1949. The CDU won with a narrow majority over the opposition Social Democratic Party (SPD), and Adenauer was appointed chancellor.

As a result of his upbringing and education, Adenauer was always opposed to Socialist ideas. He rejected the notion of an egalitarian mass society, arguing that it would not allow legitimate leadership to emerge. His leading political theme was individualism under the rule of law. He was imbued with the conviction that the state must guarantee its citizens optimal room for independent intellectual and economic development, as well as absolute protection under the law. In these views Adenauer reflected the Roman Catholic social teachings of Pope Leo XIII.

The political platform of the CDU, however, went beyond Adenauer's ideas; it advocated some programs of a Socialist nature. In the controversies that resulted from his party's social program, Adenauer restrained himself—both as chairman of the party and as a government official—from interference. Such restraint was not entirely in keeping with his nature and position.

But Konrad Adenauer was not a politician with merely private interests; he was quite pragmatic in his approach. He was willing to compromise on domestic programs with which he philosophically disagreed so that he could promote the unity of the country and give West Germany an important place in the European community.

Adenauer
©Karsh—Woodfin Camp and Associates

Indeed, the focus of his interest throughout his career lay in foreign affairs. He viewed the expansion of Communist rule into the heart of Europe as a direct threat to the West and its values. He had no faith in the possibility of peaceful coexistence with the Communist world and felt the need for tough opposition to any aggressive military threats from the Communist bloc. He considered as irreconcilable the principal differences between individualistic rule of law and totalitarian dictatorship and between Humanistic–Christian teachings and Communist social regimentation. He therefore became a strong advocate of the politics of containment. He was not, however, an opponent of the relaxation of tensions. Under the circumstances, he felt that a policy of appeasement was utterly illusory, if not traitorous. Except for the period during which Nikita S. Khrushchev was in power in the Soviet Union, Adenauer believed the Communist bloc to be a direct military threat that could only be held in check by superior deterrent forces. As a result, he energetically supported German contributions to the North Atlantic Treaty Organization (NATO) and its nuclear arsenal, and he would have preferred the development of a European defense community. He saw in its creation one of the most promising instruments for imparting to Europe a new order and character. A prerequisite for this defense community was the reconciliation of Germany with its neighbours, especially France, and Adenauer worked for this with all his strength.

During Adenauer's chancellorship his opponents demanded that Germany be neutralized and placed in a position of nonalignment between the Eastern and Western blocs. But Adenauer and his party won all major elections because they declared that the risks to security in such a policy would be intolerable. Behind this position was a decision made by the CDU and its party leaders to guide Germany out of its historically vulnerable position between East and West by making the nation an intrinsic part of a united Europe.

To the end of his life, Adenauer was reproached, unfairly, for not having seriously desired the reunification of Germany, but he believed that it was impossible to come to terms with the Soviet Union. In addition, he had made his decision to bring German policies into alignment with those of the West.

In 1963 Adenauer turned over the chancellorship to Ludwig Erhard, who claimed much credit for the "miracle" of Germany's economic recovery after the war.

There were no political reasons for his decision to step down from office; rather, it was his belief that at age 88—after 14 years in national government—he had grown too old to lead the nation. Thereafter, he began to write his memoirs. Nevertheless, he continued as chairman of the CDU until March 1966.

Personal characteristics. That Adenauer was able to hold his demanding office into the ninth decade of his life bespeaks his excellent physical, mental, and spiritual constitution, his first-class staff, and loyal party. Equally important—and in many instances even more important—were the congenial relations he enjoyed with the American and European statesmen, particularly U.S. secretary of state John Foster Dulles and French president Charles de Gaulle. Adenauer's open and undisguised warmth toward these statesmen belies the charge that he was a cold and suspicious individual. He was merely a sober man of great sensibility who despised wishful thinking, which he held to be especially dangerous for Germany. His use of language served him in his political goals, for it was sharpened to be intelligible and convincing to the common man; and its simplicity emphasized his authority.

In his personal life, Adenauer was unpretentious and extremely disciplined. His family was gathered around him, and he was its patriarch. He was married twice and was twice widowed. He ate little, detested smoking, and loved to work in his large garden. He cultivated a deepened appreciation for painting, and several works of old masters adorned the walls of his own home as well as his official residence—the Schaumburg Palace. As a rule, his day began early and ended late, for he required little sleep.

On Adenauer's death, the friends and opponents of the past who visited West Germany to pay a last farewell included the leaders of the United States and France, as well as many other heads of state, including David Ben-Gurion of Israel. (Eu.G.)

BIBLIOGRAPHY. Konrad Adenauer, *Erinnerungen,* 4 vol. (1965–68), his autobiography encompassing the years 1945 to 1963; Rudolf Morsey and Konrad Repgen (eds.), *Adenauer-Studien,* vol. 1 (1971), contributions by four German historians and political scientists on the politics and personality of Adenauer; Paul Weymar, *Konrad Adenauer* (1955), an authorized popular biography that provides the best description of his life.

Adenet LE ROI, also called ROI ADAM, LI ROIS ADENES, ADAN LE MENESTREL, or ADAM REX MENESTRALLUS (b. *c.* 1240—d. *c.* 1300), poet and musician, interesting for the detailed documentary evidence of his career as a household minstrel.

He received his training in the court of Henry III, duke of Brabant, at Louvain; after his patron's death in 1261, his fortunes wavered, owing to dynastic rivalries and the growth of Flemish literature at court, until in 1268 or 1269 he entered the service of Guy of Dampierre, heir to the county of Flanders, as principal minstrel (whence his title *roi—i.e.,* "king of minstrels"). Adenet accompanied Guy in 1270–71 on the Tunisian crusade, and his poems contain many precise references to parts of their return through Sicily and Italy. Of his rather pallid and unoriginal written work, three chansons de geste (*q.v.*) are preserved: *Buevon de Conmarchis, Les Enfances Ogier* ("The Youthful Exploits of Ogier the Dane," part of the Charlemagne legends), and *Berte aus grans piés* ("Berta of the Big Feet"). Also extant is *Cléomadès,* a romance about a flying wooden horse, written at the suggestion of Marie de Brabant, daughter of his old patron and queen of Philip III of France.

adenine, organic compound belonging to the purine family, occurring free in tea or combined in many substances of biological importance, including the nucleic acids, which govern hereditary characteristics of all cells.

Partial decomposition of ribonucleic and deoxyribonucleic acids yields mixtures from which the compounds adenylic acid and deoxyadenylic acid, respectively, may be separated. These acids, called nucleotides, are phosphate esters of adenosine and deoxyadenosine, which are smaller units (nucleosides) composed of adenine and either ribose or deoxyribose.

Compounds of adenine include vitamin B_{12}, active against pernicious anemia, and adenosine triphosphate and other coenzymes (substances that act in conjunction with enzymes).

adenoiditis, inflammation and swelling of the adenoids, the lymphatic tissue in the back wall of the nasopharynx; this is the upper part of the throat and opens into the nasal cavity proper. Adenoiditis, typically a children's disease, results from infection, which may be associated with a common cold or with infection of the tonsils. The affected child may experience chills, a general feeling of ill health, blocked nasal passages, and earache. In treatment antibiotics are administered. If the adenoids remain swollen and block the airways they may be removed surgically. *See also* tonsillitis.

adenosine triphosphate (ATP), coenzyme (so called because it functions with an enzyme) in many enzyme-catalyzed reactions in animals, plants, and microorganisms. The energy-rich molecule ATP functions as the carrier of chemical energy from the energy-yielding oxidation of foodstuffs to the energy-demanding processes within cells. It is converted to adenosine diphosphate (ADP) and inorganic phosphate or to adenosine monophosphate (AMP) and inorganic pyrophosphate in such energy-requiring processes as the performance of chemical, electrical, and osmotic work.

There are three metabolic sources of ATP: fermentation (*q.v.*), the tricarboxylic acid cycle (*q.v.*), and oxidative phosphorylation coupled to the transfer of electrons (negatively charged particles). *See also* respiration, cellular.

adenovirus, any of a group of viruses constituting the family Adenoviridae, discovered in the 1950s, including about 30 types that cause sore throat and fever in humans, hepatitis in dogs, and several diseases in fowl, mice, cattle, pigs, and monkeys. The virus particle lacks an outer membrane; is spheroidal, about 70 nanometres (nm; 1 nm $= 10^{-9}$ metre) across; is covered with 252 regularly arranged protein subunits called capsomeres; and contains a core of deoxyribonucleic acid (DNA) wrapped in a protective coat of protein. Adenoviruses develop within the nuclei of infected cells, wherein they often can be observed packed in an apparently crystalline arrangement. *See also* common cold.

adenovirus infection, acute mucous-membrane infection of the upper respiratory tract, eyes, and frequently the regional lymph nodes, bearing considerable resemblance to the common cold. Like the cold viruses, adenoviruses are often found in latent infections in clinically healthy persons. There are more than 30 different members of the adenovirus group, but only a few commonly cause illness in man; it is thus possible to prepare a vaccine against these viruses. In contrast, there are more than 100 cold viruses, all of which are fairly commonly found as disease agents; this great number makes the development of a vaccine for the common cold virtually impossible.

Adeodatus I: *see* Deusdedit, Saint.

Adeodatus II (b. Rome—d. June 17, 676), pope (672–676) who was the first pontiff to date events in terms of his reign, which began with his election on April 11, 672.

Adeodatus played no known role in the political events of the day or in the liquidation of Monothelitism (a heresy teaching that Christ had only one will), although he did defend orthodoxy. He devoted his attention to restoring churches in a state of disrepair. A Benedictine monk, he took the Abbey of St. Peter and St. Paul (St. Augustine's) under his protection; he improved the Monastery of St. Erasmus; and he seems to have recognized the exemption of the Abbey of St. Martin of Tours from episcopal authority. Some hagiographers style him "Saint" and give him June 26 as a feast day, but the Bollandists, who edit and publish the *Acta Sanctorum,* insist that he had no cult and therefore is not entitled to a feast day.

Ader, Clément (b. Feb. 4, 1841, Muret, Fr.—d. March 5, 1926, Toulouse), self-taught engineer, inventor, and a pioneer of flight before the Wright brothers.

An enthusiast of aviation from early youth, in the war of 1870 Ader constructed a balloon at his own expense. In 1876 he quit his job in the Administration des Ponts et Chaussées to make more money to support his hobby. His early inventions in the electrical communications field included a microphone and a public-address device. He then devoted himself to the problem of flying machines that were heavier than air, and in 1890 he constructed a steam-powered, bat-winged monoplane, which he named the "Eole" (Greek Aeolus, God of the Wind). On October 9 he flew it a distance of 50 metres (160 feet) on a friend's estate near Paris. The steam engine was unsuitable for sustained and controlled flight, which required the gasoline engine; nevertheless, Ader's short hop was the first demonstration that a machine that was heavier than air could leave the ground.

Adere (people): *see* Hareri.

Adernò (Sicily): *see* Adrano.

adhān (Arabic: "announcement"), the Muslim call to Friday public worship and to the five daily hours of prayer. It is proclaimed by the *mu'adhdhin* (muezzin), a servant of the mosque chosen for good character, as he stands at the door or side of a small mosque or in the minaret of a large one.

The *adhān* was originally a simple "Come to prayer," but, according to tradition, Muḥammad consulted his followers with a view to investing the call with greater dignity. The matter was settled when ʿAbd Allāh ibn Zayd dreamed that the faithful should be summoned by a crier. The standard Sunnī *adhān* can be translated as: "Allāh is most great. I testify that there is no god but Allāh. I testify that Muḥammad is the prophet of Allāh. Come to prayer. Come to salvation. Allāh is most great. There is no god but Allāh." The first phrase is proclaimed four times, the final phrase once, and the others twice, the worshippers making a set response to each phrase.

Ad'har (Scotland): *see* Ayr.

Adhémar DE CHABANNES (b. 988, Limousin, Aquitaine—d. 1034), Frankish chronicler whose major work, *Chronicon Aquitanicum et Francicum,* traces the history of Aquitaine, the southwestern area of France, and of the Franks from the times of the legendary king Pharamond.

The first two books of Adhémar's history are of little value because his sources were severely limited. The third book, however, contains a reasonably accurate history of western France between 814 and 1028. Adhémar seems to have been more concerned about the development of his narrative than the accuracy of his dates. He also invented the famous dialogue between Hugh Capet, the first Capetian king of France, and his vassal in which Hugh asked his vassal, "Who made you duke?" and received the response, "Who made you king?" Adhémar's works were critically edited by J. Chavanon (1897) and his minor works published by J.-P. Migne in *Patrologia Latina* (vol. 141, 1853).

Adhémar OF MONTEIL, also called ADHÉMAR OF PUY, Adhémar also spelled ADÉMAR, or AIMAR (d. Aug. 1, 1098, Antioch, Syria), French bishop, papal legate, and one of the leaders of the First Crusade.

Bishop of Le Puy from 1077, he made a pilgrimage to the East in 1086–87. Responding to Pope Urban II's call in November 1095 for a holy expedition to the East, he was appointed papal legate and leader of the crusade. Wounded and temporarily captured, he recovered and entered Constantinople with Raymond IV of Toulouse and his troops and had friendly audiences with the Byzantine emperor and with Greek ecclesiastics. With the patriarch Symeon II of Jerusalem, who was in exile in Cyprus, he appealed to the West for more crusaders. Adhémar did not preach Western papal supremacy, despite Urban II's plans for such a policy, but by effectively directing many battles, as well as organizing relief for poor pilgrims and ordering repentance fasts for the crusaders, he proved to be a forceful, unifying leader. His death from the plague left the Crusade without a leader and widened the breach between Rome and Constantinople.

adhesive, substance used to join separate materials through surface attachment.

A brief treatment of adhesives follows. For full treatment, *see* MACROPAEDIA: Adhesives.

Egyptians used glue in woodworking 3,300 years ago and also used flour paste in the production of papyrus. Several other organic materials, including beeswax and vegetable resins, were important as adhesives in ancient and medieval industries, and the development of glues and sealants (protective coatings) derived from animal tissue greatly improved the efficiency of wood and paper manufacture. During the 19th century, there were advances in adhesive technology, the introduction of rubber-based products being an especially significant development. It has been during the 20th century, however, that the most revolutionary changes in the industry have occurred, due primarily to the invention of synthetic resins and compounds.

Modern research indicates that adhesion occurs on a minute and intimate molecular level. This explanation, called the adsorption theory, holds that adhesion depends on the same molecular attraction that binds all solid matter; any two materials can thus theoretically adhere if placed in close enough molecular proximity. Other factors, however, such as tensile strength, evaporative properties, and flexibility, determine the applicability of a material as a practically useful adhesive.

Most adhesives, both organic and synthetic, are polymers. Polymers consist of giant, complex molecules formed by the union of many simpler molecules, called monomers.

Polymeric substances offer a great degree of strength and flexibility, two necessary attributes of any sophisticated adhesive.

The two most important types of modern adhesives are thermoplastic and thermosetting adhesives. The thermoplastics provide strong, durable adhesion at normal temperature, but can be softened by heating for manipulation and reconfiguration. Cooling produces rehardening without chemical deterioration or alteration. Thermosetting adhesives form permanent bonds that are heat-resistant and insoluble; they cannot be modified without undergoing a chemical change. These adhesives are extremely useful in industry, especially aircraft and aerospace technology. Other common types are contact cements, usually applied to both bonding surfaces; hot melt adhesives, used exclusively in a molten state; pressure-sensitive adhesives, carried on sheets or tapes; and remoistenable adhesives, in which a solution is applied to a backing, allowed to dry, and then reactivated by water.

Natural adhesives are made from both animal and vegetable materials. Animal glues are generally a preparation of collagen, the primary component protein of mammalian bone and skin. These substances are still used in the production of wood and paper materials. Other important mammalian glues are refined from casein, a milk protein, and from blood albumin. Vegetable adhesives are those adhesives extracted from plants that also are soluble or dispersable in water. Starches, obtained from a number of grains and vegetables, form the base material for many such adhesives. Another group, the natural gums, include agar, a colloid (minute particle suspension) of marine plants; algin, a derivative of seaweed; and gum arabic, extracted from the acacia tree.

Although natural adhesives are less expensive to produce, most important modern adhesives are synthetic. Based on complex polymeric compounds, synthetic adhesives are strong, heat-resistant, and durable. They are easily modified to suit specific functions and can be manufactured in a constant and uniform manner. The two principal types of synthetic adhesives are thermoplastic resins, including vinyl resins and cellulose derivatives, and several types of thermosetting resins.

A third group, elastomeric adhesives, are made from both natural and synthetic products.

Ādi-Buddha, among some sects of Mahāyāna Buddhism, the first, or self-existing, Buddha, from whom are said to have evolved the five Dhyāni-Buddhas (*see* Dhyāni-Buddha). Though the concept of an Ādi-Buddha was never generally popular, a few groups, particularly in Nepal, Tibet, and Java, elevated Vairocana to the position of Ādi-Buddha or named a new deity, such as Vajradhara or Vajrasattva, as the supreme lord. The Ādi-Buddha is represented in painting and sculpture as a crowned Buddha, dressed in princely garments and wearing the traditional ornaments of a *bodhisattva* ("Buddha-to-be").

Ādi Granth (Punjabi: The First Book), the sacred scripture of Sikhism, a religion of India. The book (also known as *Granth*, or *Granth Sahib*) is a collection of nearly 6,000 hymns of the Sikh Gurūs (religious leaders) and various early and medieval saints of different religions and castes.

The *Ādi Granth* is the central object of worship in all *gurdwārās* or Sikh houses of worship and is accorded the reverence paid a living Gurū. It is ritually opened in the morning and wrapped up and put away for the night. On special occasions continuous readings of it are held, which last from 2 to 15 days. On the birthdays of the Gurūs or anniversaries

Priest worshipping the *Ādi Granth*
Foto Features

commemorating Sikh martyrs, the *Granth* is sometimes taken out in procession.

The first version of the book was compiled by the fifth Sikh Gurū, Arjun, at Amritsar in AD 1604. He included his own hymns and those of his predecessors, the Gurūs Nānak, Aṅgad, Amar Dās, and Rām Dās, and a selection of devotional songs of both Hindu and Islāmic saints (notably the poet Kabīr). In AD 1704 the tenth and last Gurū, Gobind Singh, added the hymns of his predecessor, Gurū Tegh Bahādur (the sixth, seventh, and eighth Gurūs did not write hymns), and enjoined that after his own death the *Granth* would take the place of the Gurū. The book opens with the *Mūl Mantra* (basic prayer), which is a declaration of the nature of God as Truth, followed by the *Japjī* (Recital), the most important Sikh scripture, written by the founder of the Sikh religion, Gurū Nānak. The hymns are arranged according to the musical modes (ragas) in which they are meant to be sung. The language is mostly Punjabi or Hindi, interspersed with Marathi, Persian, and Arabic words.

After the death of Gurū Gobind Singh his own hymns and other writings were compiled into a book known as the *Dasam Granth* (*q.v.*).

adiabatic demagnetization, process by which the removal of a magnetic field from certain materials serves to lower their temperature. This procedure, proposed by the U.S. and Dutch chemists, respectively, William Francis Giauque (1927) and Peter Debye (independently, 1926), provides a means for cooling an already cold material (around 1 K) to a small fraction of 1 K.

The mechanism involves a material in which some aspect of disorder of its constituent particles exists at 4 K or below (liquid helium temperatures). Magnetic dipoles, *i.e.,* atoms that have poles like bar magnets, in a crystal of paramagnetic salt—for example, gadolinium sulfate, $Gd_2(SO_4)_3 \cdot 8H_2O$—have this property of disorder in that the spacing of the energy levels of the magnetic dipoles is small compared with the thermal energy. Under these conditions the dipoles occupy these levels equally, corresponding to being randomly oriented in space. When a magnetic field is applied, these levels become separated sharply; *i.e.,* the corresponding energies are widely different, with the lowest levels occupied by dipoles most closely aligned with the applied field. If the magnetic field is applied while the paramagnetic salt is in contact with the liquid helium bath (an isothermal process in which a constant temperature is maintained), many more dipoles will become aligned, with a resultant transfer of thermal energy to the bath. If the magnetic field is decreased after contact with the bath has been removed, no heat can flow back in (an adiabatic process), and the sample will cool. Such cooling corresponds to the dipoles remaining trapped in the lower energy states (*i.e.,* aligned). Temperatures from 0.3 K to as low as 0.0015 K can be reached in this way.

Much lower temperatures can be attained by an analogous means called adiabatic nuclear demagnetization. This process relies on ordering (aligning) nuclear dipoles (arising from nuclear spins), which are at least 1,000 times smaller than those of atoms. With this process, temperatures of the ordered nuclei as low as 16 microdegrees (0.000016 degree) absolute have been reached.

adiabatic process, in thermodynamics, change occurring within a system as a result of transfer of energy to or from the system in the form of work only. A rapid expansion or contraction of a gas is very nearly adiabatic. Any process that occurs within a container that is a good thermal insulator is also adiabatic. Adiabatic processes are characterized by an increase in entropy, or degree of disorder, if they are irreversible and by no change in entropy if they are reversible. Adiabatic processes cannot decrease entropy.

Adiabene, petty kingdom, vassal to the Parthian Empire (247 BC–AD 224) in northern Mesopotamia (now Iraq); its capital was Arba-ilu (Arbela; modern Irbīl). In the 1st century AD its royal family embraced Judaism; the queen mother Helena (died AD 50), famous for her generosity to the Jews and the Temple, and her sons Monobazus II and Izates II were buried in the Tombs of the Kings at Jerusalem. Adiabene was frequently attacked by the Romans during their campaigns against the Parthians.

Adiantaceae, one of several families in the fern order Pteridales. It consists of several genera with about 200 species distributed throughout the world but especially found in tropical America. Among the best known species of the group is the maidenhair fern (*Adiantum capillus-veneris*). Many other species are grown as indoor and greenhouse ornamentals.

Maidenhair fern (*Adiantum capillus-veneris*)
Grant Heilman—EB Inc.

Another classification system, which places the family in the order Polypodiales, includes several other genera, such as *Cheilanthes* (lip ferns [*q.v.*]), *Pellaea* (cliffbrakes [*q.v.*] and button ferns), *Ceratopteris* (aquarium ferns), *Vittaria* (shoestring ferns), and many others. The family thus conceived contains about 15 to 22 genera and 900 species.

The family is characterized by spore-producing structures (sporangia) in lines along the veins of the leaves or at the vein tips, either without a protective covering (indusium), in grooves, or covered by the rolled leaf margin, a condition called a false indusium.

adiaphorism (from Greek *adiaphora,* "indifferent"), in Christian theology, the opinion that certain doctrines or practices in morals or religion are matters of indifference because they are neither commanded nor forbidden in the Bible. Two adiaphorist controversies occurred in Germany after the Reformation.

The first controversy arose over the religious compromise between the Lutheran theologians of Wittenberg, primarily Philipp Melanchthon, and Saxony's civil and ecclesiastical leaders. The elector Maurice of Saxony succeeded in making the Wittenberg theologians accept, for political reasons, the Leipzig Interim (December 1548), which sanctioned the jurisdiction of Roman Catholic bishops and observance of certain rites (such as extreme unction and confirmation), while all were to accept the doctrine of justification by faith, the added word "alone" being treated as one of the *adiaphora*. Matthias Flacius Illyricus, a Lutheran Reformer and church historian, passionately opposed this policy on the grounds that under political pressure no *adiaphora* could be accepted, and, therefore, no concession could be allowed.

In practice the controversy was ended in September 1555 by the religious Peace of Augsburg, when Lutheranism was acknowledged as a legitimate religion. The theoretical question of *adiaphora*, however, continued to be debated by Protestants. The Formula of Concord (1577), a Lutheran confession, attempted to settle the matter by stating that rites and ceremonies that were matters of religious indifference could not be imposed during times of controversy.

Another adiaphorist controversy occurred in the field of morals in 1681, when Pietists opposed the building of a theatre in Hamburg. They denounced worldly amusements as anti-Christian, whereas Lutherans generally defended Christian freedom in such matters.

Adige River, Italian FIUME ADIGE, Latin ATHESIS, German ETSCH, longest stream of Italy after the Po, rising in the north from two Alpine mountain lakes below Passo (pass) di Resia and flowing rapidly through the Val (valley) Venosta south and east past Merano and Bolzano. Having received the waters of the Isarco River at Bolzano, the Adige turns south to flow through the Trentino-Alto Adige region in its middle course, known as the Val (valley) Lagarina. Entering the Po lowland near Verona, it veers southeast and, after several long meanders, enters the Adriatic Sea just south of Chioggia and north of the Po Delta after a course of 255 mi (410 km). It drains a basin of 4,710 sq mi (12,200 sq km), and in its lower course, near the sea, the average flow is about 9,000 cu ft (255 cu m) per second, varying from a maximum of 70,500 to a minimum of 2,000.

In early Christian times the river's course was probably several miles farther north until, in about AD 589, the river broke through its banks and built its present course. The dikes constructed during the past several centuries have had to be raised several times; the last 50 mi or so of the river's course are entirely man-made. The Adige supplies hydroelectric power in its upper Alpine section and irrigation for the Veneto in its lower course. Floods, as in 1951 and 1966, do great damage and require constant control of the river bank.

Adigei autonomous oblast (Russian S.F.S.R.): *see* Adygey autonomous oblast.

ʿĀdil Shāhī DYNASTY (1489–1686), ruling family of the kingdom of Bijāpur, India, one of the two principal successor states to the Muslim sultanate of Bahmanī in the Deccan. The dynasty strongly resisted the Mughal advance southward in the 17th century until it was extinguished by Aurangzeb with the capture of Bijāpur in 1686. It was named after its founder, Yūsuf ʿĀdil Shāh, said to have been a son of the Ottoman sultan Murad II. He introduced a form of Islām but practiced toleration. At the end of his reign, Goa was lost (1510) to the Portuguese. After constant wars a coalition of Bijāpurand with the three other Muslim Deccan states—Golconda, Bīdar, and Ahmadnagar—overthrew the Hindu Vijayanagar empire, threatening from the south, at Talikota in 1565.

The dynasty's greatest period was during the reign of Ibrāhīm ʿĀdil Shāh II (1579–1626), who extended his frontier as far south as Mysore and was a skillful administrator and a generous patron of the arts. He reverted to the Sunnī form of Islām but remained tolerant of other religions, including Christianity. Thereafter, increasing weakness permitted Mughal encroachment and the successful revolt of the Marāthā Śivajī, who killed the Bijāpur general Afzal Khān and scattered his army. The dynasty left a tradition of cosmopolitan culture and artistic patronage, whose architectural remains are to be seen in the capital city of Bijāpur.

Ādilābād, formerly EDLĀBĀD, town, administrative headquarters of Ādilābād district, northern Andhra Pradesh state, southern India. It is an agricultural trade centre 160 mi (260 km) north of Hyderābād, on the Nāgpur–Hyderābād section of the Vārānasi–Kanniyākumāri National Highway. Nearby, at Māhūr (Mahārāshtra state), is a fort dating from the Bahmanī and ʿImād Shāhī dynasties (14th–16th century).

The district (6,229 sq mi [16,133 sq km]) is on a well-forested plateau (2,000 ft [600 m] high) between the Godāvari and Penganga rivers. Teak and ebony are commercially lumbered. Agriculture and mining are significant in the local economy. Rice, sorghum, and wheat rank among the major crops, and coal, talc, and limestone are mined. Asifābād is a commercial centre in the district. Pop. (1981) town, 53,482; district, 1,639,003.

Ādinātha: *see* Ṛṣabhanātha.

adipose cell, also called FAT CELL, connective tissue cell specialized to synthesize and contain large globules of fat. Adipose cells can accept fatty acids from the blood and convert them into globules of fats. These fat deposits together make up adipose tissue, which serves as the body's storehouse for fats not immediately necessary in metabolic processes. The main areas of adipose tissue are beneath the skin (subcutaneous fat deposits), between layers of muscle fibre, and around the internal organs.

adiposogenital dystrophy: *see* Fröhlich's syndrome.

Adirondack Mountains, mountains in northeastern New York, U.S., extending southward from the St. Lawrence Valley and Lake Champlain to the Mohawk Valley. Although often included in the Appalachian System, the mountains are related geologically to the Laurentian Highlands of Canada and were formed by a fracturing of the Earth's crust (faulting) and long years of erosion. The region, covering 5,000 sq mi (13,000 sq km) and circular in outline, is made up of about 100 unconnected peaks ranging in height from 1,200 ft (370 m) to 5,000 ft above sea level. While they are primarily rounded in shape, several of the higher peaks (Mt. Marcy, 5,344 ft, and Mt. Whiteface, 4,865 ft) reveal bare rock walls in vertical escarpments. The action of retreating glaciers during the last ice age left the area covered by glacial till (clay, sand, gravel, and boulders intermingled) and created the many spectacular gorges, waterfalls, lakes, ponds, and swamps for which the region is noted. More than 200 lakes of irregular shape dot the landscape, many of which were recognized in the early 1980s as having been ecologically damaged by "acid rain." Numerous fishing streams radiate from the centre of the region to drain into the St. Lawrence, Hudson, and Mohawk rivers and Lakes Ontario and Champlain.

A large part of the region became Adirondack Park in 1892, an unspoiled wilderness which inspired Emerson's poem "The Adirondacks" (1858). The mountains are covered with spruce, hemlock, and pine forests, interspersed with hardwoods on the lower slopes. The state-owned Adirondack Forest Preserve now comprises more than 2,400,000 ac (970,000 ha) within the park and is a popular tourist area. Numerous parks and private resort communities provide facilities for camping, bathing, hiking, and canoeing. Historical landmarks are at Ft. Ticonderoga, Saratoga, Lake George, and Plattsburgh. Winter sports include Olympic ski and bobsled runs. Good roads provide access to nearly all parts of the area, and a memorial highway approaches the summit of Mt. Whiteface, near Lake Placid. There are no immediate large cities but the moderate, invigorating climate has encouraged development of resort villages and sanatoriums, especially around the Saranac River and Lake Placid. Lumbering and mining (iron and graphite), once major industries, have been considerably restricted by state control. The Adirondack Museum, near Blue Mountain Lake, houses relics of man's activities in the mountains since colonial times.

The Adirondacks were seen by Samuel de Champlain in 1609 and named for a local Indian tribe, referred to as "tree eaters."

adit, horizontal opening, or entrance, made from the Earth's surface, usually to intersect a seam of coal or a mineral vein. An adit is frequently called a tunnel, a term more properly reserved for a working open at both ends, such as through a mountain or a ridge. Adits are often driven during tunnel construction to drain water from the workings.

Adits can be driven only in hilly country where the portal will be at such an elevation as to provide an adequate slope for water to flow out and to favour removal of coal or ore.

Where either a vertical shaft or an adit can be used to reach a mineral deposit, both the generally lower cost of driving an adit and the saving in the cost of pumping water and hoisting the coal or ore through the shaft dictate in favour of the adit. Consequently adits as long as one or two miles are often economically feasible.

The cross section of adits is square, round, elliptical, or—more commonly—horseshoe shaped. The diameter is usually just enough to allow a man to stand erect or to allow passage of haulage equipment. The walls may be of the natural rough rock or may be lined with concrete, masonry, wood, or steel.

Aditi (Sanskrit: the boundless), in the Vedic phase of Hindu mythology, the personification of the infinite, and the mother of a group of celestial deities, the Ādityas. As a primeval goddess, she is referred to as the mother of many gods, including Vishnu in his dwarf incarnation, and, in a later reappearance, Krishna. She supports the sky, sustains all existence, and nourishes the earth. It is in the latter sense that she is often represented as a cow.

Her sons, the Ādityas, are of uncertain number and identity. Varuṇa is their chief, and they are called like him "Upholders of *ṛta* ('divine order')." One hymn names them as Varuṇa, Mitra, Aryaman, Dakṣa, Bhaga, and Aṃśa. Sometimes Dakṣa is excluded and Indra, Savitṛ (the sun), and Dhātṛ are added. Occasionally the term is extended to include all the gods. In later periods their number is increased to 12, and they are linked to the 12 solar months of the year. Āditya in the singular form is a name of the sun.

Adıyaman, formerly HÜSNÜMANSUR, Arabic ḤIṢN MANṢŪR, city, capital of Adıyaman *il* (province) in a valley of southeastern Turkey. Founded in the 8th century by the Umayyad Arabs near the site of ancient Perre, Ḥiṣn Manṣūr was later fortified by Caliph Hārūn ar-Rashīd and became the chief town of the area, replacing Perre. Ruled successively by the Byzantines, Seljuq Turks, and the Turkmen Dulkadir dynasty after the Arabs, it was incorporated into the Ottoman Empire near the end of the 14th century. Under the Turkish Republic, it was renamed Adıyaman in 1926 and was an *ilçe* of Malatya *il* until the establishment of the present *il* in 1954. The ruins of Perre are just to the north. The city is a local market for the agricultural products of the area.

Adıyaman *il*, with an area of 3,039 sq mi (7,871 sq km), has a mountainous northern section and series of fertile plateaus drained by the Euphrates River and its tributaries. Many of the residents are Kurds. Products include cereals, cotton, tobacco, pistachio nuts, and grapes. It was once part of the Commagene kingdom, and landmarks dating from that period include the ruins of Samosata (modern Samsat [*q.v.*]) and a monumental funerary sanctuary built by Antiochus I (*c.* 69–*c.* 34 BC) on the summit of Mt. Nemrut about 9,700 ft (2,950 m) above sea level. Pop. (1980) city, 53,219; (1982 est.) *il*, 374,808.

adjective law: *see* procedural law.

adjustment, in psychology, the behavioral process by which humans and other animals maintain an equilibrium among their various needs or between their needs and the obstacles of their environments. A sequence of adjustment begins when a need is felt and ends when it is satisfied. A hungry man, for example, is stimulated by his physiological state to seek food. He eats and thereby reduces the stimulating condition that impelled him to activity. He is then adjusted to this particular need.

Social adjustments are similar. In most cultures people want to be recognized and approved by their fellows. When a man is criticized, that need is thwarted. In response, he may try various ways to regain approval; or he may belittle the critic or argue that someone else is to blame. The latter behaviours do not really bring approval, but they are adjustments of a sort because they tend to reduce the man's feeling of distress.

In general, the adjustment process involves four parts: (1) a need or motive in the form of a strong persistent stimulus; (2) the thwarting or nonfulfillment of this need; (3) varied activity, or exploratory behaviour; and (4) some response that removes or at least reduces the initiating stimulus and completes the adjustment.

Every person experiences some thwarting through frustration and conflict but is able to solve most problems with his own resources. A person engages in exploratory behaviour, trying one act and then another until he discovers one that overcomes the frustration, resolves the conflict, or at least reduces its intensity.

adjuvant, substance that enhances the effect of a particular medical treatment. Administration of one drug may enhance the effect of another. In anesthesia, for example, sedative drugs are customarily given before an operation to reduce the quantity of anesthetic drug needed. In immunology an adjuvant is a substance that increases the body's reaction to a foreign substance. The reaction to diphtheria toxoid—modified form of the toxin, or poisonous substance, produced by the organism that causes diphtheria—is increased, for example, if the toxoid is adsorbed (attached) to particles of aluminum hydroxide or aluminum phosphate.

Adkins v. Children's Hospital, U.S. Supreme Court case, decided in 1923, in which the court invalidated a board established by Congress to set minimum wages for women workers in the District of Columbia. Congress in 1918 had authorized the Wage Board to ascertain and fix adequate wages for women employees in the nation's capital.

The court ruled in a 5–3 vote that the law authorizing the Wage Board infringed upon Fifth Amendment guarantees of life, liberty, and property. Employer and employee, according to the majority opinion, had a constitutional right to contract in whatever manner they pleased. Thus, the establishment of the Wage Board was an unjustified interference with the freedom of contract.

In their dissent, justices Taft, Holmes, and Sanford argued that Congress had the policing power to correct recognizable evils. The effects of *Adkins* v. *Children's Hospital* were reversed in *West Coast Hotel Company* v. *Parrish* (1937), when the Supreme Court overturned the position adopted by the court's conservative majority.

Adler, Alfred (b. Feb. 7, 1870, Penzing, Austria—d. May 28, 1937, Aberdeen, Aberdeenshire, Scot.), psychiatrist whose influential system of individual psychology introduced the term inferiority feeling, later widely and often inaccurately called inferiority complex; he developed a flexible, supportive psychotherapy to direct those emotionally disabled by inferiority feelings toward maturity, common sense, and social usefulness.

Alfred Adler

By courtesy of the Osterreichische Nationalbibliothek, Vienna

Throughout his life Adler's strong awareness of social problems served as a principal motivation in his work. From his earliest years as a physician (M.D., University of Vienna Medical School, 1895), he stressed consideration of the patient in relation to his total environment, and he began developing a humanistic, holistic, organismic approach to human problems.

About 1900 Adler began to explore psychopathology within the context of general medicine and in 1902 became closely associated with Sigmund Freud. Gradually, however, differences between the two became irreconcilable, notably after the appearance of his *Studie über Minderwertigkeit von Organen* (1907; *Study of Organ Inferiority and Its Psychical Compensation,* 1917), in which he suggested that persons try to compensate psychologically for a physical disability and its attendant feeling of inferiority. Unsatisfactory compensation, he continued, results in neurosis, any of a number of functional disorders of the mind or emotions. In 1908 he argued that the aggressive drive, or instinct, is primary, other drives being subordinate to it. Two years later he asserted that the critical human reaction to feelings of inferiority is the "masculine protest," or attempt to overcome socially conditioned feelings of weakness associated with femininity. He disagreed with Freud that sexual conflicts in early childhood cause mental illness, and he further came to confine sexuality to a symbolic role in human strivings to overcome feelings of inadequacy. More outspokenly critical of Freud in 1911, Adler and a group of followers severed ties with Freud's circle and began developing individual psychology, first outlined in *Über den nervösen Charakter* (1912; *The Neurotic Constitution,* 1917). The system was elaborated in later editions of this work and in other writings, such as *Menschenkenntnis* (1927; *Understanding Human Nature,* 1918).

Adler's individual psychology maintains that man's principal motive, a striving for perfection, may become a striving for superiority and thus an overcompensation for a feeling of inferiority. Man's opinion of self and the world influences all his psychological processes. Because all important life problems are social, the individual must be considered within the social context. His socialization is achieved through development of innate social instinct. The personality structure of the unique individual, including his unique goal and ways of striving for it, constitutes his life-style, which lies more or less outside his awareness. A self-consistent unity, the individual subordinates specific drives and emotions to his life-style. Life-style forms in early childhood, important factors being birth order, physical inferiority, and neglect or pampering. Mental health is characterized by reason, social interest, and self-transcendence; mental disorder by feelings of inferiority and self-centred concern for one's safety and superiority or power over others. Psychotherapy, in which physician and patient discuss problems as equals, should encourage sound human relationships and strengthened social interest.

In 1921 Adler established the first child-guidance clinic in Vienna, soon opening and maintaining about 30 more there under his direction. Regarding the education of children as essential for perpetuating social values, he tirelessly fostered sound child guidance; and in his clinics children, parents, and teachers were counselled before interested observers.

Adler first went to the United States in 1926 and became visiting professor at Columbia University in 1927. He was appointed visiting professor of the Long Island College of Medicine in New York in 1932. In 1934 the government in Austria closed his clinics. Many of his later writings, such as *What Life Should Mean to You* (1931), were directed to the general reader. H.L. and R.R. Ansbacher edited *The Individual Psychology of Alfred Adler* (1956) and *Superiority and Social Interest* (1964).

BIBLIOGRAPHY. Phyllis Bottome, *Alfred Adler: Apostle of Freedom* (1939); Rudolf Dreikurs, *Fundamentals of Adlerian Psychology* (1950); Hertha Orgler, *Alfred Adler* (1939).

Adler, Cyrus (b. Sept. 13, 1863, Van Buren, Ark., U.S.—d. April 7, 1940, Philadelphia), scholar, educator, editor, and Conservative Jewish leader who had great influence on U.S. Jewish life in his time.

Adler received his Ph.D. in Semitics in 1887 from Johns Hopkins University, where he later taught Semitic languages. In 1892 he founded the American Jewish Historical Society, of which he was president from 1898 until 1922. For the Jewish Publication Society of America, he planned the *American Jewish Year Book*, which he edited from its first year, 1899, until 1905 and again in 1916. Under his chairmanship, the Bible Committee of the Jewish Publication Society published the first authoritative Jewish translation of the Hebrew Scriptures in the English language (1917).

Adler helped develop the Jewish Theological Seminary in New York City, an institution for research in Judaica and the training of rabbis; he did so principally by bringing Solomon Schechter from Europe, in 1902, to head the institution. In 1908 Adler became the first president of Dropsie College for Hebrew and Cognate Learning, in Philadelphia. There Adler published and edited the *Jewish Quarterly Review*, which had been previously printed in England. With Schechter, in 1913, he created the United Synagogue of America, a laymen's organization that remains the chief organ of Conservative Judaism in the U.S. When Schechter died in 1915, Adler became acting president of the Jewish Theological Seminary and from 1924 until his death served as president. During his tenure, the seminary accumulated one of the world's foremost collections of Judaica.

Adler, Dankmar (b. July 3, 1844, Stadtlengsfeld, Prussia—d. April 16, 1900, Chicago), architect and engineer whose partnership with Louis Sullivan was perhaps the most famous and influential in U.S. architecture.

Chicago Stock Exchange designed by Dankmar Adler, 1897, demolished 1972
Chicago Architectural Photographing Co.

Adler emigrated to the United States in 1854 and settled in Detroit, where he began his study of architecture in 1857. Later Adler moved to Chicago, where he became a draftsman in the office of Augustus Bauer. The American Civil War interrupted his career, and upon his return to Chicago in 1865 he held a succession of positions in the offices of Bauer, A.J. Kinney, and Edward Burling. The first of his important buildings was the Central Music Hall in Chicago, in which he made initial use of his knowledge of acoustics.

In 1881 the partnership of Adler and Sullivan was founded. The commercial buildings which they designed—particularly the Auditorium (Chicago), Wainwright (St. Louis), and Guaranty (Buffalo)—constituted a new architectural style with the essential features of modern building art. Adler acted as engineering designer and administrator, Sullivan as planner and artist. The association ended in July 1895.

Adler wrote extensively on the technical and legal aspects of architecture and building construction. His most important paper is "The Influence of Steel Construction and Plate Glass upon the Development of Modern Style" (1896).

Adler, Felix (b. Aug. 13, 1851, Alzey, Hesse-Darmstadt—d. April 24, 1933, New York City), educator and founder of the Ethical Movement.

The son of a rabbi, Adler emigrated to the United States with his family in 1856 and graduated from Columbia College in 1870. After study at Berlin and Heidelberg, he became professor of Hebrew and Oriental literature at Cornell University, Ithaca, N.Y. In 1902 he

Felix Adler
By courtesy of The Society for Ethical Culture in the City of New York

was appointed professor of political and social ethics at Columbia University.

In 1876 Adler established in New York City the Society for Ethical Culture. This marked the beginning of the Ethical Movement, the aim of which was to assert the importance of the moral factor in all life's relations, without regard to considerations of a supreme being.

Adler took a prominent part in social reform movements, such as the erection of model tenement houses and the abolition of child labour. Among his writings are *Creed and Deed* (1877), *The Moral Instruction of Children* (1892), *The World Crisis and Its Meaning* (1915), *An Ethical Philosophy of Life* (1918), and *The Reconstruction of the Spiritual Ideal* (Hibbert lectures at Oxford, 1923).

Consult the INDEX *first*

Adler, Guido (b. Nov. 1, 1855, Eibenschütz, Moravia, Austrian Empire—d. Feb. 15, 1941, Vienna), Austrian musicologist and teacher who was one of the founders of modern musicology.

Adler's family moved to Vienna in 1864, and four years later he began to study music theory and composition with Josef Anton Bruckner at the Vienna Conservatory. Intending to pursue a career in law, Adler studied at the University of Vienna, receiving a doctoral degree in 1878. During this period he gave a series of lectures on Wagner at the university (later published as *Richard Wagner,* 1904) and, in cooperation with Felix Mottl, established the Akademischer Wagnerverein.

Influenced by the writings of outstanding contemporaries in the field of music history, Adler abandoned law for the study of music history; he wrote a dissertation on Western music before 1600 and was awarded a Ph.D. in 1880. The next year he became an instructor, lecturing on the history of harmony. In collaboration with Philipp Spitta and K.F.F. Chrysander, Adler founded the *Viertel-jahrsschrift für Musikwissenschaft* ("Quarterly of Musicology") in 1884. The following year he was appointed professor of musicology at the German University at Prague.

In 1888 he recommended that the Austrian government publish an edition of great Austrian music. This project came into being as the *Denkmäler der Tonkunst in Österreich* ("Monuments of Music in Austria"), and Adler was its general editor from 1894 to 1938, producing 83 of the more than 130 volumes in the series.

Adler was elected president (1892) of the Central Committee of the International Music and Theatre Exhibition in Vienna. In 1898, Adler became professor of music history at the University of Vienna, where he founded an institute devoted to musicological research. His lectures were popular and were attended by many students from distant parts of Europe. A considerable number of his pupils later attained fame as composers or musicologists. In addition to music history, Adler's interests extended to contemporary music; he developed a close friendship with Mahler, about whom he published a book in 1916, and he also admired the work of Arnold Schoenberg.

As one of the earliest musicologists, Adler articulated the major principles and methods of the new discipline as it was taking form in the late 19th century; he was the first music historian to emphasize style criticism in research. His attitudes and procedures are evident in the *Handbuch der Musikgeschichte* ("Handbook of Music History"), of which he became the editor in 1924.

Adler, Larry, byname of LAWRENCE CECIL ADLER (b. Feb. 10, 1914, Baltimore), harmonica player generally considered to be responsible for the elevation of the mouth organ to concert status in the world of classical music.

Adler's family was not particularly musical, but their observance of Orthodox Judaism provided access to religious music. By age 10 he was the youngest cantor in Baltimore, although unhappy in school and considered to be overly pious by his peers. By feigning a nervous breakdown, he convinced his parents to let him enroll in the Peabody Conservatory of Music, but he was soon dismissed as untalented. The rebuff made him even more determined. At age 11, without his parents' consent, he ordered a piano for their home, which he then persuaded them to accept. He also began playing the mouth organ. Unable to read music, he listened assiduously, buying records and concert tickets with money earned by selling magazines.

In 1927 he won the Maryland National Harmonica Championship, playing a Beethoven minuet. The following year in New York City he accompanied early motion picture cartoons and performed vaudeville routines dressed as a vagabond. He had played in both musicals and motion pictures before he was invited to play with an orchestra. His solo debut took place in 1939 with the symphony orchestra of Sydney, Australia. Adler did not learn to read music until 1940, when the French composer Jean Berger wrote a harmonica concerto for him. Ralph Vaughan Williams, Darius Milhaud, and others wrote musical scores for Adler. Accused of Communist sympathies and blacklisted during the ascendancy of U.S. Sen. Joseph R. McCarthy, Adler was unable to find work and took up residence in England.

He wrote musical scores for motion pictures and television and also wrote several books, including *How I Play* (1937) and *Larry Adler's Own Arrangements* (1960).

Adler, Mortimer J(erome) (b. Dec. 28, 1902, New York City), philosopher, educator, editor, and advocate of adult and general education by study of the great writings of the Western world.

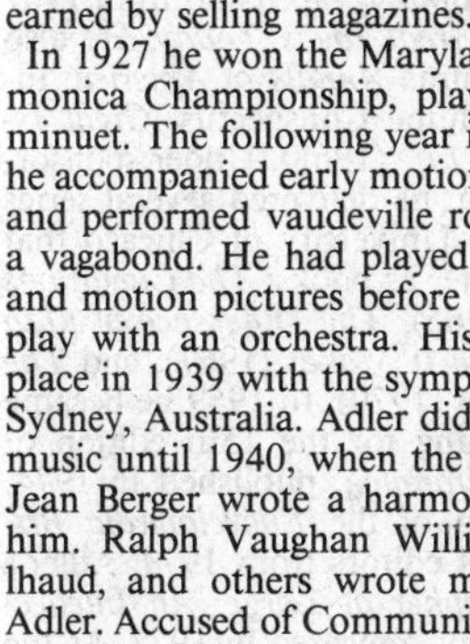

Mortimer Adler

While still in public school he was taken on as a copy boy by the New York *Sun*, where he stayed for two years doing a variety of editorial work full time. He then attended Columbia University, completed his coursework for a bachelor's degree, but did not receive a diploma because he had refused physical education (swimming). He stayed at Columbia to teach and earn a Ph.D. (1928) and then became professor of the philosophy of law at the University of Chicago. There, with Robert M. Hutchins, he led in the pursuit of liberal education through regular discussions based on reading great books. He had studied under John Erskine in a special honours course at Columbia in which the "best sellers of ancient times" were read as a "cultural basis for human understanding and communication."

Adler was associated with Hutchins in editing the 54-volume *Great Books of the Western World* (1952) and conceived and directed the preparation of its two-volume index of great ideas, the *Syntopicon*.

In 1952 Adler became director of the Institute for Philosophical Research (initially in San Francisco and from 1963 in Chicago), which prepared *The Idea of Freedom*, 2 vol. (1958–61). His books include *How to Read a Book* (1940; rev. ed. 1972); *A Dialectic of Morals* (1941); *The Capitalist Manifesto* (with Louis O. Kelso, 1958); *The Revolution in Education* (with Milton Mayer, 1958); *Aristotle for Everyone* (1978); *How to Think About God* (1980); and *Six Great Ideas* (1981).

With Hutchins, Adler edited for Encyclopædia Britannica, Inc., the 10-volume *Gateway to the Great Books* (1963) and from 1961 an annual, *The Great Ideas Today*. He also edited the 20-volume *Annals of America*, including a two-volume Conspectus, *Great Issues in American Life* (1968). Under sponsorship of Britannica, he delivered several series of lectures at the University of Chicago that were published later as books: *The Conditions of Philosophy* (1965), *The Difference of Man and the Difference It Makes* (1967), and *The Time of Our Lives* (1970). In 1969 he became director of planning for the 15th edition of *Encyclopædia Britannica*, published in 1974. He was chairman of the *Encyclopædia Britannica*'s board of editors from 1977. Adler's memoirs, *Philosopher at Large: An Intellectual Autobiography*, appeared in 1977. As the spokesman for a group of noted educators he wrote, after months of study and debate, *The Paideia Proposal: an Educational Manifesto* (1982), calling for the abolition in U.S. schools of multitrack educational systems, arguing that a single elementary and secondary school program for all students would ensure the upgrading of the curriculum and the quality of instruction to serve the needs of the brightest and to lift the achievement of the least advantaged. He proposed that specialized vocational or preprofessional training be given only after students had completed a full course of basic education in the humanities, arts, sciences, and language. Among many honours was the bestowal of his baccalaureate degree by Columbia University 60 years after the fact in May 1983.

Adler, Nathan Marcus (b. Jan. 15, 1803, Hanover—d. Jan. 21, 1890, Brighton, East Sussex, Eng.), chief rabbi of the British Empire, who founded Jews' College and the United Synagogue. He became chief rabbi of Oldenburg in 1829 and of Hanover in 1830. On Oct. 13, 1844, he was elected chief rabbi in London. There he originated and carried out his scheme for a Jewish college for teachers (Jews' College, still in existence), which was founded in London on Nov. 11, 1855, with Adler himself as its first president. In 1860 he

Nathan Adler
The Mansell Collection

formulated a plan to establish a United Synagogue to bring all the British congregations under a central administration; this idea was realized in 1870, when Parliament passed the United Synagogue bill.

Adler, Victor (b. June 24, 1852, Prague—d. Nov. 11, 1918, Vienna), Austrian Social Democrat, the founder of a party representing all the diverse nationalities of Austria-Hungary.

Born into a wealthy Jewish family, Adler studied medicine at the University of Vienna,

Victor Adler, pastel drawing by L. Braun
By courtesy of the Bild-Archiv, Osterreichische Nationalbibliothek, Vienna

receiving his degree in 1881. While there, he became a member of Georg von Schönerer's German nationalist organization, a movement he left when its anti-Semitic character became more pronounced. After meeting the German Socialists Friedrich Engels and August Bebel while travelling in Germany, Switzerland, and England (1883), Adler became a dedicated Socialist. He remained a lifelong friend of and correspondent with Engels.

Adler founded and headed the Socialist weekly *Gleichheit* (1886–89, "Equality") and, after its ban, published the *Arbeiter Zeitung* ("Workers' Paper"), which became the Socialists' main organ. Chiefly responsible for the establishment of the united Social Democratic Party of Austria (December 1888–January 1889), in which he remained a leading figure until his death, he made it a multinational party advocating federalism and autonomy for the peoples of Austria-Hungary. He was elected to the Lower Austrian Landtag (Diet) in 1905 and quickly became a leader in the fight for universal suffrage (introduced in 1907).

The breakaway of the Czech Social Democrats in 1911 frustrated Adler's efforts to maintain a single, united party. During World War I, he worked for a peaceful settlement at the abortive Socialist conference in Stockholm (1917). Entering the new Austrian government in October 1918, he advocated the *Anschluss* (unification) of the rump Austrian state with Germany but died before he could pursue this project.

Adler Gebirge (eastern Europe): *see* Orlice Mountains.

Adlersparre, Georg, Greve (Count) (b. March 28, 1760, Hovermo, Swed.—d. Sept. 23, 1835, near Kristinehamn), political and social reformer who was a leader of the 1809 coup d'etat that overthrew Sweden's absolutist king Gustav IV.

Holding the rank of lieutenant colonel in the army, Adlersparre led a faction of officers that, with another group, the "men of 1809," deposed Gustav IV on March 13, 1809, after several years of planning. A liberal, Adlersparre had been moved to conspire against the monarch by Gustav's refusal to summon a Riksdag (estates general) during a decade of excessive taxation and disastrous wars. After the coup, however, Adlersparre retreated somewhat from his earlier liberalism and championed the strong monarchy that the new constitution was soon to provide. He served in the Council of State (1809–10) and then as governor of the county of Skaraborg (1810–24). In 1814 he declined the post of governor general of Norway (administered under the Swedish crown from 1814 to 1905), urging unsuccessfully that a Norwegian hold that office. Adlersparre also championed such social projects as prison reform.

ADLP (political party): *see* Australian Democratic Labor Party.

Admetus, in Greek legend, son of Pheres, king of Pherae in Thessaly. Having sued for the hand of Alcestis, the most beautiful of the daughters of Pelias, king of Iolcos in Thessaly, Admetus was first required to harness a lion and a boar to a chariot. The god Apollo, who served him, yoked the pair for Admetus, who thus obtained Alcestis. Finding that Admetus was soon to die, Apollo persuaded the Fates to prolong his life, on the condition that someone could be found to die in his place. Alcestis consented, but she was rescued by Heracles, who successfully wrestled with Death at the grave. The death and resurrection of Alcestis form the subject of many ancient reliefs and vase paintings, as well as the *Alcestis* of Euripides.

administrative law, the law regulating the powers, procedures, and acts of public administration. It applies to the organization, powers, duties, and functions of public officials and public agencies of all kinds. Its development has been concurrent with the modern growth in the functions of government and in bureaucracy and with the parallel expanding need for legal safeguards over them.

A brief treatment of administrative law follows. For full treatment, *see* MACROPAEDIA: Public Administration.

Of the powers delegated to administrative authorities by modern regulatory statutes, four types may be mentioned: (1) the *rulemaking power*, or the power to issue general rules and regulations having the force of law for the purpose of filling up the details of statutory policy; (2) the *licensing power*, or the power to grant or refuse, to renew, and to revoke licenses or permits which may be required by statute for the pursuit of such professions as law and medicine and the conduct of certain forms of business; (3) the *investigatory power*, or the power to require witnesses to testify and produce books, papers, and records for the purpose of acquiring the information needed for effective regulation; and (4) the *directing power*, or the power to issue, usually after notice and an opportunity to be heard, administrative orders by which a private party is required, in conformity with the governing statute, to do or refrain from doing specified things.

Whatever the public-service and control functions of the administrative system may be, however, their performance depends upon its also conducting auxiliary operations which relate to its organization as a going concern, provision for its personnel and matériel, and the financing, planning, and overall administrative management of its varied activities. Accordingly, the law must also establish rules to authorize and govern these auxiliary and managerial operations and the relations which the administrative system is to bear with respect to them to other parts of the government.

In the broadest sense, the problem of administrative law is an aspect of the central problem of political theory: the reconciliation of authority and liberty. More specifically, the purposes of legal control of public administration are: (1) to establish administrative authorities and enable them to carry out public policies designed to protect the public interest and (2) to safeguard private interests against administrative arbitrariness or excess of power.

It is important to remember, however, that in the larger view each of these interests includes the other as a factor. The public interest includes the welfare of all members of the community, those who are regulated no less than those for whose protection regulation is undertaken. Accordingly, the public interest itself suffers if those who are regulated become victims of administrative oppression. Yet it is equally true that the private interest of those who are regulated includes in the long run the public interest. They may profit in the short run if the law renders ineffective those administrative efforts designed to prevent their exploitation of the public; but by the same token it may render ineffective their protection against forms of exploitation indulged in by others. The aim of administrative law is thus to attain a synthesis of public and private interests in terms of the social and economic circumstances and ideals of the age.

Administrative law has a valuable contribution to make as an instrument for controlling the bureaucracy. In social democratic regimes, political and judicial control of administration are regarded as complementary, but distinct. The former is concerned with questions of policy and the responsibility of the executive for administration and expenditure. The latter is concerned with inquiring into particular cases of complaint. Administrative law does not include the control of policy by ministers or the head of state. In the people's democracies of eastern Europe, however, this distinction does not exist. The control exercised by an elected council or a presidium over a similar body at the next lower level of government is regarded as a form of legal control over administration. Internal methods of control are also regarded as falling within the ambit of administrative law. These include an appeal from the decision of an official to a higher official within the same organization or an appeal to a higher administrative unit. A distinctive feature of the socialist countries of eastern Europe is that there is no definition of the powers of governmental organs at different levels. They are all assumed to be unlimited in scope but always subject to an equally unlimited right of intervention and restraint by the corresponding organ at the next higher level of government. This contrasts with the explicit definition of powers at each level of government which is found in the Western-type democracies. The admixture of political and legal control results in administrative law having a loose and imprecise meaning in the people's democracies of eastern Europe.

admiral, the title and rank of a senior naval officer, often referred to as a flag officer, who commands a fleet or group of ships of a navy or who holds an important naval post on shore. The term is sometimes also applied to the commander of a fleet of merchant vessels or fishing ships.

The title has an ancient lineage. It apparently originated before the 12th century with Muslim Arabs, who combined *amīr* ("commander"), the article *al,* and *baḥr* ("sea") to make *amīr-al-baḥr.* Shortened to *amiral,* it was adopted for naval use by the Sicilians. The French copied the word from the Genoese during the Seventh Crusade (1248–54). The Latin word *admirabilis* ("admirable") may have helped to produce the title admiral for the commander of the Cinque Ports in England before the end of the 13th century.

In Europe it became the title of a great officer of the crown: in France as *grand amiral,* in Spain as *almirante mayor,* and in England as lord high admiral. The noblemen who held these posts were not seamen and did not command at sea except on rare occasions; they were heads of departments that administered naval affairs. They were responsible for providing ships for war, and their duties usually brought them large fees. They also had jurisdiction in legal cases of the types afterward handled by admiralty courts.

By 1620 the word admiral was used in England to denote a commander at sea. In that year the fleet was formed into three squadrons with the admiral commanding the centre squadron, his ships flying red ensigns. The vice admiral in the van squadron flew white ensigns, and the rear admiral flew blue ensigns in his squadron.

In the U.S. Navy a fleet admiral ranks with a general of the army or general of the air force. Admiral ranks with general, vice admiral with lieutenant general, and rear admiral with major general. Rank insignia for U.S. or British admirals consist of a broad gold stripe encircling the lower sleeve with one or more (depending on rank) narrower stripes above it.

admiral, any of several butterfly species belonging to the family Nymphalidae (order Lepidoptera), colourful, fast-flying, and much prized by collectors. The migratory red admiral (*Vanessa atalanta*), widespread in Europe, Scandinavia, and North Africa, feeds on stinging nettles. The Indian red admiral, *V. indica,* found in the Canary Islands as well as India, is distinguished by a red band on the fore wings wider than that of *V. atalanta.* A Eurasian species, the white admiral (*Basilarchia arthemis* or *Limenitis camilla*), distributed from Great Britain across the Continent to Japan, feeds on honeysuckle.

Red admiral (*Vanessa atalanta*)

William E. Ferguson

Admiral carpet, any of a series of 15th-century carpets handwoven in Spain, probably at Letur or at Liétor in Murcia. The carpets were made with the Spanish knot, on a single warp. In most cases they show heraldic shields with coats of arms against a background diaper of small octagons, many of which contain eight-pointed stars; the shields of some of these carpets bear the blazons of members of the Enríquez family, hereditary admirals of Castile, and others show the arms of Maria of Castile, queen of Aragon. Other Admiral carpets display merely the diapered ground, without shields. The borders are complex, the outermost stripe usually a deformation of Kūfic script interspersed with tiny stylized animals, birds, and human figures.

Many of these carpets originally were very long but were shortened in the course of their use in the convents upon which they were bestowed in the 15th century and where they were preserved until removed to museums. Admiral carpets appear in several Spanish paintings, in a fresco painted about 1346 at Avignon, and in Hans Holbein the Younger's painting "Solothurn Madonna" (1522; Museum der Stadt Solothurn, Switzerland).

Heraldic shield with the coat of arms of Admiral Fadrique Enríquez, detail of an Admiral carpet, 15th century; in the Philadelphia Museum of Art

By courtesy of the Philadelphia Museum of Art, The Joseph Lees Williams Memorial Collection; photograph, Otto E. Nelson—EB Inc.

Admiral's Cup, racing trophy awarded to the winner of a biennial international competition among teams of sailing yachts; it was established in 1957 by the Royal Ocean Racing Club (RORC) of Great Britain. Teams of three yachts rated at 25 to 70 feet (8 to 21 metres) by RORC rules (formerly 30 to 60 feet waterline length) represent each nation in four races, two short and two long, culminating in the 605-mile (975-kilometre) Fastnet Cup Race, for one of the most prized ocean-racing trophies. *See* Sporting Record: *Yachting.*

Admiral's Men, a theatrical company in Elizabethan and Jacobean England. About 1576–79 they were known as Lord Howard's Men, so called after their patron Charles Howard, 1st earl of Nottingham, 2nd Baron Howard of Effingham. In 1585 he became England's Lord High Admiral, and the company changed its designation to "Admiral's Men." It was later known successively as Nottingham's Men, Prince Henry's Men, and the Elector Palatinate's (Palsgrave's) Men.

The chief actor of the Admiral's Men was Edward Alleyn; their manager and effectively their employer until his death in 1616 was Philip Henslowe (*q.v.*), whose *Diary,* covering the years 1592 to 1603, documents the Elizabethan theatre and its organization. The company disbanded in 1625.

admiralty: *see* maritime law.

Admiralty, High Court of: *see* High Court of Admiralty.

Admiralty Inlet, one of the world's longest, between Brodeur and Borden peninsulas and indenting for 230 mi (370 km) the northwest coast of Baffin Island in the Northwest Territories, Canada. The inlet leading southward from Lancaster Sound of Baffin Bay is 2 to 20 mi wide, with a shoreline that rises abruptly about 1,000 to 1,500 ft (300 to 460 m). Arctic Bay, a mineral exploration and hunting base, is on its northeastern shore.

Admiralty Islands, in Papua New Guinea, extension of the Bismarck Archipelago comprising a group of about 40 islands, in the southwestern Pacific, 380 mi (610 km) northwest of Rabaul, New Britain. The volcanic Manus Island (*q.v.*) constitutes the majority of its land area.

Possibly explored by the Spaniard Álvaro Saavedra in 1528, the group was sighted by the Dutch navigator Willem Schouten in 1616 and named by the British captain Philip Carteret in 1767. Constituted part of a German protectorate in 1884, the islands were captured by Australia in 1914 and were included in the territory mandated to that nation in 1921. They were occupied by Japan from 1942 to 1944 and made part of the UN Trust Territory of New Guinea in 1946. When Papua New Guinea attained its independence in 1975, the islands became part of that country.

The economy is primarily agricultural, consisting of copra production and some coffee growing. Copper deposits were located on Manus Island in 1972. The indigenous population, which is Melanesian, engages in fishing and local trading. Many are adherents of the cargo cult founded by the prophet Paliau after World War II. Pop. (1980 prelim.) 25,844, almost all of whom live on Manus Island.

admiralty law: *see* maritime law.

Admonition to Parliament, Puritan manifesto, published in 1572, that demanded that Queen Elizabeth I restore the "purity" of New Testament worship in the Church of England and eliminate the remaining Roman Catholic elements and practices from the Church of England. Reflecting wide Presbyterian influence among Puritans, the admonition advocated greater direct reliance on the authority of the Scriptures and also church government by ministers and elders rather than by a higher order of clergy (bishops). The Queen, however, resisted this document. The leader of the Presbyterians, Thomas Cartwright, was removed from his position at Cambridge University and any of the clergy who refused to conform to the compulsory form of worship that had been promulgated by Elizabeth in 1559 (as the Act of Uniformity) lost their pulpits or were imprisoned.

Ado-Ekiti, town, Ondo State, southwestern Nigeria, in the Yoruba Hills (altitude 1,650 ft [503 m]), at the intersection of roads from Akure, Ilawe, Ilesha, Ila (Illa), and Ikare. An important urban and industrial centre of the region, it was founded by the Ekiti people, a Yoruba subgroup whose members belonged to the Ekiti–Parapo, a late 19th-century confederation of Yoruba peoples that fought against Ibadan, 92 mi (148 km) west-southwest, for control of the trade routes to the coast. Ado-Ekiti became the site of a large textile mill in 1967—its occupants having a long-standing tradition of cotton weaving. The town also makes shoes and pottery and is a collecting point for the commercial crops of tobacco, cocoa, palm oil and kernels, and cotton. Yams, cassava, corn (maize), upland rice, fruits, pumpkins, palm produce, and okra are marketed locally. The town has several secondary schools, a government hospital, and a livestock station. It is also the headquarters of a local government council. Pop. (1983 est.) 265,800.

adobe, Spanish word for sun-dried clay bricks, or a structure built from such bricks, or the clay soil from which the bricks are made.

Adobe clay is basically calcareous and sandy, having good plastic qualities and drying to a hard uniform mass. Its use, or that of clays with similar properties, dates back thousands of years in several parts of the world, especially areas with arid or semi-arid climate, in North Africa, Spain, and the Middle East in the Eastern Hemisphere, and from the United States Southwest to Peru in the Western Hemisphere. American Indians built walls by the hand manipulation of the plastic clay into courses, or layers, allowing each course to dry before adding the next.

The usual method of making adobe bricks consists of wetting a quantity of suitable soil and allowing it to stand for a day or more to soften and break up clods. A small quantity of straw or other fibrous material is added, and the materials are mixed with a hoe or similar implement. The mass is then trampled with the bare feet.

When it is brought to the proper consistency, the adobe is shaped into bricks in simple molds. The molds, made of smooth lumber or sheet metal, are four-sided and open at the top and bottom. Although they vary widely in size, depending on the intended use of the finished brick, they are usually from 3 to 5 inches (8 to 13 centimetres) thick, 10 or 12 inches wide, and 14 to 20 inches long. The bricks are allowed to dry partially while flat on the ground; then they are stacked on edge to permit more thorough and uniform drying.

Adobe walls are normally built on a solid, waterproof foundation of stone or concrete; otherwise the capillary action of groundwater may cause the lower courses to disintegrate. The bricks are laid in a mortar of the same material, then finished with a coat of adobe, or with lime or cement plaster. With proper construction and maintenance, an adobe wall may last centuries. Its chief advantages are its availability in dry regions, its cheapness, and its remarkable insulation properties.

adolescence, usually defined as the period of transition between childhood and adulthood. Although some writers equate adolescence with puberty and the cycle of physical changes culminating in reproductive maturity, adolescence is more commonly defined in psychological and social terms as beginning with pubescence and terminating vaguely with "adulthood." The term is a convenient label for a period in the life of an individual (approximately ages 12 to 20); such usage need make no commitment regarding the character of adolescent development or the specific nature of its causes (*e.g.*, pubescence).

A brief treatment of adolescence follows. For further treatment, *see* MACROPAEDIA: Growth and Development, Biological; Social Differentiation.

Any period of life tends to be characterized by a group of developmental problems that are biological, psychological, and social in origin and timing. Among those that typically but not necessarily occur during the second decade of life are adjustments in the areas of heterosexual relations, occupational orientation, the development of a mature set of values and responsible self-direction, and the breaking of close emotional ties to parents. In a sense, such developmental tasks define adolescence and represent areas in which satisfactory adjustments must be made if future psychological development is to be possible.

Authorities are not in agreement as to the nature of adolescence. To the popular mind and to many specialists, adolescence is presumed to be a psychologically stressful and critical period, characterized by a variety of special types of behaviour.

According to one viewpoint, essentially biological and stemming mainly from psychoanalytic literature, adolescence is initiated at pubescence by the sudden upsurge of sex feelings following a sexually tranquil period of latency. Adolescence is the period during which the individual learns to control and direct his sex urges; it ends when such control and direction are established. The whole process is presumed to be highly stressful emotionally and to give rise to a variety of behaviours, ranging from avoidance of the opposite sex to the writing of diaries, which are thought to be characteristic of adolescence and which serve to reduce the sex-generated anxiety. A biological view of adolescence implies a certain universality of occurrence.

Cultural views also assume adolescence to be a stressful period, but one that occurs only under certain circumstances. Because children generally are not given graded opportunities for maturing experiences compatible with their physical and intellectual development, they experience a sudden widening of their world during their teens. This encountering of new ideas, concepts, values, and types of people, and the sudden responsibility for self-determination and self-sufficiency, force an array of adjustments upon the comparatively inexperienced young person and generate much apprehensiveness and anxiety. Furthermore, the teenager has no defined role of his own in society but is caught in the ambiguous overlap between the reasonably clearly defined roles of childhood and adulthood. Sometimes treated as a child, sometimes expected to be adult, he is uncertain how to behave. Also, society serves to frustrate important psychological needs of the young person (*e.g.*, sex and desire for independence), thus generating aggression or other reactions, many of a socially disapproved type. In all the various cultural views, adolescence exists in the degree that such conditions prevail in a particular culture or a particular home.

Adolf, name of rulers grouped below by country and indicated by the symbol •.

Foreign-language equivalents:

Dutch	Adolf
German	Adolf
French	Adolphe

GERMANY/HOLY ROMAN EMPIRE

• **Adolf,** also called ADOLF, GRAF (count) VON NASSAU (b. *c.* 1250—d. July 2, 1298, Göllheim, near Worms), German king from May 5, 1292, to June 23, 1298, when he was deposed in favour of his Habsburg opponent, Albert I.

Adolf of Nassau (centre), ivory carving, 13th century; in the Germanisches Museum, Nürnberg

Archiv fur Kunst und Geschichte, West Berlin

Adolf, who was count of Nassau from 1277 and a mercenary soldier of repute, was chosen king at Frankfurt by the German electors, who preferred him to Albert as successor to Albert's father, Rudolf I, the first Habsburg king. After his coronation at Aachen on June 24, 1292, Adolf had to face exorbitant demands by his electors and the hostility of Albert, who as duke of Austria commanded great financial and territorial resources.

Adolf seized Meissen as a vacant fief and purchased the right of succession in Thuringia from the landgrave Albert. His alliance with King Edward I of England against France

(Aug. 24, 1294) brought him a cash subsidy, which he spent in defeating the landgrave's disinherited sons, Frederick the Dauntless and Dietzmann (Dietrich). The German electors, alarmed by Adolf's growing power, decided to transfer the crown to Albert, with whom they had been negotiating. Albert's large army was present at Mainz when the sentence of deposition was pronounced. Adolf attempted to regain the throne in battle against his rival's superior forces but was defeated and killed.

LUXEMBOURG

• **Adolf,** also called ADOLF, HERZOG (duke) VON NASSAU, in full ADOLF WILHELM AUGUST KARL FRIEDRICH (b. July 24, 1817, Biebrich, Nassau—d. Nov. 17, 1905, Hohenberg, Württemberg), duke of Nassau from 1839 to 1867, who, as grand duke of Luxembourg from 1890 to 1905, was the first ruler of the autonomous duchy.

Son of Duke William of Nassau-Weilburg and Charlotte of Saxony, Adolf became duke of Nassau upon his father's death (1839). Educated in Vienna and a military supporter of the Habsburgs, he sided with Austria against Prussia in the Seven Weeks' War (over hegemony in German affairs); and, upon the defeat of Austria (1866), Nassau was annexed by Prussia. He formally abdicated as duke of Nassau (Sept. 9, 1867) and was granted 8,500,000 thalers and a few castles as compensation. He served as regent of Luxembourg for King William III of The Netherlands in 1889; when the male line of Orange-Nassau ended with William III's death (1890) and the personal union between Luxembourg and The Netherlands ceased, the grand duchy reverted, according to the 1783 Nassau Succession Agreement, to him as the head of the ducal house of Nassau-Weilburg. Ruling until his death, he was succeeded by his son, Grand Duke William IV.

NASSAU

• **Adolf** (1817–1905): *see* Adolf (Luxembourg).

Adolf Frederick, German ADOLF FRIEDRICH, Swedish ADOLF FREDRIK (b. May 14, 1710, Gottorp, Schleswig—d. Feb. 12, 1771, Stockholm), king of Sweden from 1751 to 1771, son of Christian Augustus (1673–1726), duke of Schleswig-Holstein-Gottorp, and of Albertina Frederica of Baden-Durlach.

Adolf Frederick, detail from an oil painting by Lorenz Pasch the Younger; in Gripsholm Castle, Sweden

By courtesy of the Svenska Portrattarkivet, Stockholm

While Adolf Frederick was bishop of Lübeck (1727–50), he administered Holstein-Kiel (1739–45) during the minority of Duke Charles Peter Ulrich (afterward Peter III of Russia). In 1743 he was elected heir to the throne of Sweden by the "Hat" faction, which favoured a foreign policy that would regain Swedish hegemony in the Baltic. The Hats hoped by their choice to obtain better conditions of peace from the Russian empress Elizabeth, who was favourable to the House of Gottorp. He thus succeeded to the throne after the death of Frederick I (1751).

Most of the power during the new king's reign rested in the Riksdag (parliament). Twice he tried to free himself of its control: in his first attempt (1756) he nearly lost his throne, but in his second (1768–69)—with the assistance of his son, Crown Prince Gustav—he brought about the overthrow of the generally pro-Russian and pro-Prussian "Cap" Party in the Riksdag. The victorious Hats, however, reneged on their promise to increase the King's power.

Adolphe (French personal name): *see under* Adolf.

Adomnan, SAINT: *see* Adamnan, Saint.

Adonai (religious term): *see* Yahweh.

Ādoni, town, Kurnool district, western Andhra Pradesh state, southern India, located 140 mi (225 km) southwest of Hyderābād, on the Madras–Bombay railway route. Ādoni was once the stronghold for the rulers of the medieval Hindu kingdom of Vijayanagar. Muslims later controlled it until 1792, when a war between the British East India Company and Tippu Sultan resulted in its cession to the Niẓām of Hyderābād. A magnificent mosque (Jāmiʿ Masjid) was built in 1680. Ādoni manufactures cotton cloth and carpets. Pop. (1981) 108,939.

Adonias (Aguiar) Filho (b. Nov. 27, 1915, Itajuípe, Braz.), novelist, essayist, journalist, and literary critic whose works of fiction embrace universal themes within the provincial setting of Brazil's rural northeast.

His literary career began in the early 1930s under the aegis of the Neo-Catholic writers' group (Tasso da Silveira and Andrade Murici, among others) of Rio de Janeiro. Until the late 1940s he dedicated his energies principally to journalism in periodicals such as *O Correio da Manhã* and the *Revista do Brasil.* He subsequently established a column of literary criticism in the *Jornal de Letras* and began to publish translations of English-language fiction (notably the works of Graham Greene, Virginia Woolf, and William Faulkner).

For a time in the 1950s Adonias Filho served as director of the National Book Institute and worked in the National Theatrical Service. He subsequently became director of the National Library and was elected to the Brazilian Academy of Letters in 1965. In 1972 he was elected president of the Brazilian Press Association.

His career as a writer of fiction was launched in the 1940s with the publication of *Os Servos da Morte* (1946; "The Servants of Death"), the first of three novels depicting life in the cacao-growing region of northeastern Brazil. *Memórias de Lázaro* (1952; *Memories of Lazarus,* 1969) and *O Forte* (1965; "The Strong Man") complete the trilogy. In 1962 he published the novel *Corpo Vivo* ("Living Body"), which maintains the dreamlike ambience that characterizes the trilogy.

Adonis, in Greek mythology, a youth of remarkable beauty, the favourite of the goddess Aphrodite. Traditionally, he was the son of the Syrian king Theias by his daughter Smyrna (Myrrha). Charmed by his beauty, Aphrodite put the infant Adonis in a box and handed him over to the care of Persephone, the queen of the underworld, who afterward refused to give him up. An appeal was made to Zeus, the king of the gods, who decided that Adonis should spend a third of the year with Persephone and a third with Aphrodite, the remaining third being at his own disposal. Numerous variants of the legend exist.

The name Adonis is believed to be of Phoenician origin (from *adon,* "lord"), Adonis himself being identified with the Babylonian god Tammuz (*q.v.*). He is generally viewed by modern scholars as a vegetation spirit, whose death and rebirth represented the cycle of nature. Annual festivals called Adonia were held at Byblos and elsewhere to commemorate the death and resurrection of Adonis; the throwing of an effigy and other objects into the water was supposed to procure rain. A

"Venus and Adonis," oil painting by Titian, 16th century, showing Aphrodite (Roman Venus) and Adonis; in the National Gallery of Art, Washington, D.C.

By courtesy of the National Gallery of Art, Washington, D.C., Widener Collection

special feature of the Athenian festival was the "Adonis gardens," small pots of seeds specially cultivated for rapid growth and fading (the custom is still practiced by Christians in Cyprus).

adoption, the act of establishing a person as parent to one who is not in fact or in law his child. Adoption is so widely recognized that it can be characterized as an almost worldwide institution with historical roots traceable into antiquity.

In most ancient civilizations and in certain later cultures as well, the purposes served by adoption differed substantially from those emphasized in modern times. Continuity of the male line in a particular family was the main goal of these ancient adoptions. The importance of the male heir stemmed from political, religious, or economic considerations, depending on the culture. The person adopted invariably was male and often adult. In addition, the welfare of the adopter in this world and the next was the primary concern; little attention was paid to the welfare of the one adopted.

In contrast, contemporary laws and practices aim to promote child welfare and are regarded as one facet of the state's general program to protect its young. Although the desire to continue a family line or to secure rights to inheritance are still among the personal motives for adoption, society's interest now centres more on the creation of a parent–child relationship between a married couple and a young child. This attitude developed primarily in the period following World War I, when vast numbers of children were orphaned, and the number of illegitimate births increased. The desirability of adoption was further emphasized by developments in psychology and sociology that stressed the influence on child development of a stable family life. In the latter part of the 20th century, a decline in the number of children available for legal adoption stimulated changes in traditional restrictions on adult–child age differential, level of income, the mother's employment outside the home, and placements across religious and ethnic lines. Single-parent adoptions were accepted by a number of agencies.

Although adoption of adults is permitted in most countries, the legal provisions are generally formulated in terms of child adoption, and the adopter must usually be an adult. The laws typically provide for the consent of any older child (commonly one over 12 or 14 years), an investigation of the suitability of the prospective home according to criteria stated in the governing statute, and a probationary period of residence in the adoptive home.

In the matter of inheritance, laws differ considerably. As a general rule, the child may inherit from the adopting parents and they from him. Inheritance by the child from his natural parents, once commonplace, is increasingly prohibited, with the exception of adoption by stepparents. In addition, there has been a tendency to broaden the child's right to inherit from relatives of the adopting parents, although great variation appears among laws on this point.

Adoptionism, either of two Christian heresies; one developed in the 2nd and 3rd centuries and is also known as Dynamic Monarchianism (*see* Monarchianism); the other began in the 8th century in Spain and was concerned with the teaching of Elipandus, archbishop of Toledo.

Wishing to distinguish in Christ the operations of each of his natures, human and divine, Elipandus referred to Christ in his humanity as "adopted son" in contradistinction to Christ in his divinity, who is the Son of God by nature. The son of Mary, assumed by the Word, thus was not the Son of God by nature but only by adoption.

Opposition to this view of Christ was expressed, which led Pope Adrian I to intervene and condemn the teaching. Elipandus gained the support of Felix, bishop of Urgel, who eventually engaged in a literary duel with Alcuin of York over the doctrine.

In 798 Pope Leo III held a council in Rome that condemned the "Adoptionism" of Felix and anathematized him. Felix was forced to recant in 799 and was placed under surveillance. Elipandus remained unrepentant, however, and continued as archbishop of Toledo, but the Adoptionist view was almost universally abandoned after his death. It was temporarily revived in the 12th century in the teachings of Peter Abelard and his followers.

Adorno FAMILY, Genoese family prominent in the politics of the "popular" (democratic) dogeship (1339–1528), when the old aristocracy was exiled and new families seized power. Branches of the family became prominent in Flanders and Spain.

They acceded to real power in the 14th century when a revolution ended the rule of the old nobility and eventually inaugurated that of two families, the Adorno and the Fregoso, who contended for the office of doge for a century and a half. The Adorno contributed six doges to the Republic of Genoa. Gabriele, elected in 1363, served for seven years, was named imperial vicar by the emperor Charles IV in 1368, and was driven from power two years later by an uprising led by Domenico Fregoso. Eight years later the Adorno returned to office with Antoniotto I (died 1397), who was alternately ousted and reinstated until he was elected doge by a large majority in 1394. Rising factional strife, however, forced him to turn the city over to Charles VI of France.

Another Adorno doge, Agostino (served 1487–99), a faithful supporter of the Sforza dukes of Milan, relinquished his office when Louis XII of France conquered Milan. His son Antoniotto II came to power during the stormy early 16th century, ruling the city briefly in 1513 as vicar of the King of France, later transferring his allegiance to Spain, and becoming doge in 1522, when the Marquis of Pescara took Genoa for the Holy Roman emperor Charles V. Antoniotto's five-year rule ended in 1527, when Genoa was conquered by Andrea Doria for Francis I of France. Antoniotto retired to Milan, while Doria quarrelled with the French king and recaptured Genoa for Charles V.

A line of the Adorno in Flanders, founded by Obizzo (died 1307), a crusader in the forces of Count Guy of Dampierre, established itself in Bruges, Pietro (died 1409) serving as treasurer of the commune of Bruges and his sons Giacomo and Pietro establishing in Bruges in 1428 the Church of Jerusalem, a replica of the Church of the Holy Sepulchre in Jerusalem. Anselmo, son of the second Pietro, was treasurer of Bruges, travelled in Syria and Africa, and served as ambassador to Persia for Charles the Bold, duke of Burgundy, and as counsellor to King James II of Scotland. In Spain another branch of the family produced many soldiers and admirals.

In 1463 Giuliano Adorno married Caterina Fieschi (died 1510), a member of another famous Genoese family, who was canonized in 1737 as St. Catherine of Genoa.

Adorno, Theodor Wiesengrund (b. Sept. 11, 1903, Frankfurt am Main—d. Aug. 6, 1969, Visp, Switz.), German philosopher knowledgeable in sociology, psychology, and musicology and known for his contribution to the Frankfurt school of critical theory, which contributed to the German intellectual revival after World War II.

Musical training and a degree in philosophy from the liberal Johann Wolfgang Goethe University (1924) influenced his early writings, which emphasized aesthetic development as important to historical evolution and the search for "truth." In 1934, after teaching two years at the University of Frankfurt, Adorno, to escape the Nazi persecution of Jews, emigrated to England, where he taught at Merton College, Oxford, for three years, and then to the United States (1938), where he was musical director of the Princeton Radio Research Projects (1938–41) and co-director of the Research Project on Social Discrimination at the University of California, Berkeley (1941–48); he returned to the University of Frankfurt as a sociology professor in 1956. His later philosophical studies concentrated on social-critical analysis of intellectual movements that were based on Freudian-Marxist theory but stressed the individual and shunned authoritarianism. His major publications included *Dialektik der Aufklärung* (1947; *Dialectic of Enlightenment*), *Philosophie der neuen Musik* (1949; *Philosophy of Modern Music*), *The Authoritarian Personality* (1950, with others), and *Ästhetische Theorie* (1970; "Aesthetic Theory").

Adour River, river in southwestern France, rising in the central Pyrenees near the Col du Tourmalet, just south of the Pic du Midi de Bigorre and flowing in a curve, north, then west, to enter the Bay of Biscay just below Bayonne after a course of 208 mi (335 km). Draining a basin of 5,800 sq mi (15,000 sq km), it traverses the scenic Campan Valley and, after passing Bagnères de Bigorre, crosses the Tarbes plain. Beyond Tarbes the river feeds many irrigation canals, the most important of which is the Canal d'Alaric, which follows the right bank. Within Landes *département* the Adour flows west and southwest and is joined on the left by the Larcis, Gabas, Louts, Luy, and Gave de Pau, on the right by the Midouze. The Adour, navigable to Dax, enters the bay through an estuary made hazardous by a shifting sandbar.

Adowa (Ethiopia): *see* Adwa.

Adowa, Battle of, Adowa also spelled ADWA, Italian ADUA (March 1, 1896), military clash at Adowa, in north central Ethiopia, between the Ethiopian army of King Menelik II and Italian forces. The decisive Ethiopian victory checked Italy's attempt to build an empire in Africa comparable to that of the French or the British and left open to the French the prospect of expansion across Africa from the Atlantic to the Red Sea.

The death (in 1889) of the Ethiopian emperor Yohannes IV was followed by great disorder, during which the Italians helped Menelik of Shewa (Shoa) win the throne. Furthermore, the Treaty of Ucciali, which Italy had signed with Menelik in 1889, was interpreted by the Italian premier Francesco Crispi as implying the declaration of an Italian protectorate over Ethiopia. Accordingly, the Italian possessions in Africa were constituted (January 1890) as Colonia Eritrea.

Repudiating first, in September 1890, the ambiguous Article XVII of the treaty and then, in September 1893, the treaty altogether, Menelik prepared to combat the Italians' attempt to impose their dominion militarily. Italian victories at the beginning of the campaign were brilliant but fruitless, and at the end of 1895 large Ethiopian armies were threatening Italian outposts. The Italian governor of Eritrea, Gen. Oreste Baratieri, sighted Menelik's forces on Feb. 7, 1896, but remained inactive while the Ethiopians retired to Adowa; he even hinted at withdrawal. On February 28 Crispi sent Baratieri a furious telegram in an attempt to goad him into action. Desperately trying to retrieve his position, Baratieri advanced to Adowa with 20,000 men against an army four times that size; the Italian force, moreover, was disorganized and ill-equipped to fulfill its task. Humiliatingly routed on March 1, the Italians retreated through difficult terrain, harassed by a hostile population.

The Italian claim to a protectorate over all Ethiopia was thereafter abandoned; and the colony of Eritrea, finally delimited by a treaty of peace (September 1900), was reduced to a territory of about 80,000 square miles (200,000 square kilometres). In December 1906, Italy, France, and Great Britain signed an agreement regarding Ethiopian affairs.

Adrano, formerly (until 1929) ADERNÒ, town, Catania province, eastern Sicily, Italy, near the Fiume (river) Simeto on a lava plateau on the western slopes of Mt. Etna, northwest of Catania. It originated as the ancient town of Hadranon, founded *c.* 400 BC by Dionysius the Elder, tyrant of Syracuse, near a sanctuary dedicated to the Siculan god Adranus (Hadranus). Conquered in 263 BC by the Romans, who called it Adranum (Hadranum), it belonged in the Middle Ages to Count Roger I of Sicily. Emperor Frederick II made it a countship, and it was held from 1549 to 1812 by the Moncada, princes of Paternò. In 1929 it resumed the classical name, which had been corrupted to Adernò. There are ruins of the Greek walls and of baths and burial grounds. The restored 13th-century Norman castle and the convent of Sta. Lucia (founded in 1157 by Roger I) are also notable. Citrus fruits and grapes are cultivated locally and honey is made. Pop. (1981 prelim.) mun., 33,393.

Adrar, *wilāyah* (province, or *département*), southwestern Algeria, lying totally within the Sahara. Adrar province consists almost entirely of sand-dune-covered plains including part of the Grand Erg (sand dunes) Occidental in the north and the Erg Chech in the south except for the Plateau du Tademaït, a limestone and sandstone escarpment (*hamada*) in the northeast. Adrar *wilāyah* was created in 1974 with an area of 163,127 sq mi (422,498 sq km), and is bounded by Mauritania and Mali (south), and by the *wilāyāt* (provinces) of Béchar (northwest), and Laghouat and Tamanrasset (east). Nearly all of the inhabitants live in the vicinity of the Touat oases group in the northwestern part of the *wilāyah;* palm-grove settlements are strung out along Oued (wadi) Messaoud (called Oued Saoura farther north), an ancient streambed with intermittent flow. The desolate Tanezrouft region in the south was the site of the first French nuclear bomb test (1960). Principal oasis settlements include Adrar town, the *wilāyah* capital, Timimoun (or Timimoune; "Red Oasis"), and Reggane (Reggan). Dates, cereals, vegetables, figs, and almonds are grown in the oases, and a road connects Adrar town with Béchar town (391 mi [630 km] north) and Gao in Mali (891 mi south). Pop. (1980 est.) 167,557.

Adrar, formerly TIMMI, palm grove settlement, the largest of the Touat oasis group, and capital of Adrar *wilāyah* (province, or *département*), southwestern Algeria, in the Sahara. Adrar's historical name was given it by the local Berber people, the Timmi, who established their *ksar* (fortified village) here. The modern name is derived from the Berber *adrar* ("mountain"). It lies between the Erg (sand dunes) Chech and the Grand Erg Occidental near the streambed of the Oued (wadi) Messaoud. The medieval Adrar area was a strategic point on the trade route between North and West Africa. Its distinctive thick-walled red-wash architecture (which later spread to the Niger River valley) is characterized by saw-tooth crenellation.

The French captured Adrar from Moroccan forces in 1900, and in 1962 it became part of independent Algeria. The contemporary town is entered through a monumental gateway and has two main squares and rectangular avenues. Pop. (1977 prelim.) 7,057.

Adrar, traditional and administrative region of central Mauritania in West Africa. It consists of a low central massif with noticeable cliffs that rise to about 800 ft (240 m). The terrain is arid, almost totally unsuitable for cropping. There is, however, sufficient water at the base of the uplands to support date palm groves, and during the wetter part of the year there is cultivation of millet, sorghum, melons, and vegetables in gorges. The population of the Adrar (Berber for "mountain") formerly was nomadic. The capital of the region is at Atar. Historic sites include Ouadane, formerly a caravan and gold-trading centre, and Chinguetti, an ancient centre of learning and of Islām. Pop. (1977) 62,071.

adrenal cortical insufficiency: *see* Addison's disease.

adrenal gland, also called SUPRARENAL GLAND, either of two small and virtually identical triangular endocrine glands, one at the upper end of each kidney.

For a depiction of the adrenal glands in human anatomy, shown in relation to other parts of the body, *see* the colour Trans-Vision in the PROPAEDIA: Part Four, Section 421.

The adrenal glands show considerable species variation in size, shape, and nerve supply. In man each gland averages a weight of about 4.5 grams (0.16 ounce) and measures about 25 millimetres (1 inch) wide, 50 mm long, and 5 mm thick. In general each gland consists of two parts: an inner medulla, which produces adrenaline and noradrenaline (*q.v.*), and an outer cortex that secretes steroid hormones. The two parts are completely different in embryological origin, structure, and function.

In the adult human the cortex comprises about 90 percent of the gland. The cortex is made up of three structurally different concentric zones. From the outermost inward they are zona glomerulosa, zona fasciculata, and zona reticularis. The zona glomerulosa is principally responsible for the secretion of aldosterone. This steroid hormone is known as a mineralocorticoid—a regulator of sodium and potassium metabolism.

The inner two zones—fasciculata and reticularis—operate almost as a physiological unit and are controlled by ACTH (adrenocorticotropic hormone), a hormone secreted by the pituitary gland (*q.v.*). Their principal function is the secretion of cortisol and of some adrenal androgens, or male hormones. Cortisol has two primary roles: (1) gluconeogenesis—*i.e.,* the breakdown of protein to form glucose; and (2) an anti-inflammatory action. It also exerts a potent antiallergic action. Thus cortisol can reduce disease manifestations without having any direct effect on the causative agent.

The medulla of the adrenal gland is made up of columnar cells that secrete epinephrine and norepinephrine. These hormones belong to a class of chemicals called catecholamines, which are darkened when oxidized by potassium dichromate. The medulla, therefore, is frequently referred to as chromaffin tissue.

adrenaline and noradrenaline, also called EPINEPHRINE and NOREPINEPHRINE, separate, active principles secreted by the medulla of the adrenal glands (*q.v.*). They are also liberated at the ends of sympathetic nerve fibres, where they serve as chemical mediators for conveying the nerve impulses to effector organs. Chemically, the two compounds differ only slightly; and they exert similar pharmacological actions, which resemble the effects of stimulation of the sympathetic nervous system. They are, therefore, classified as sympathomimetic agents. The active secretion of the adrenal medulla contains approximately 80 percent adrenaline and 20 percent noradrenaline; but this proportion is reversed in the sympathetic nerves, which contain predominantly noradrenaline.

The purified, active compounds are used clinically and are obtained from the adrenal glands of domesticated animals or prepared synthetically. The administration of adrenaline results in an increase in blood pressure by increasing the rate and force of contraction of the heart and by constricting the peripheral blood vessels. It also dilates the bronchioles and in this way is an aid to respiration. Adrenaline exerts a metabolic effect manifested by a rise in blood glucose. Noradrenaline elicits similar responses, but its metabolic effects and actions on the heart are much less than those of adrenaline. The rise in blood pressure after the administration of noradrenaline is due to its powerful vasoconstrictor action.

Adrenaline is used in combination with local anesthetics because its vasoconstricting properties delay the absorption of the local anesthetics, and in this way it prolongs their activity and reduces their toxicity. It is useful in acute allergic disorders, such as drug reactions, hives, and hay fever. Occasionally it is applied as a local vasoconstrictor in the control of superficial hemorrhage from the skin and mucous membranes and to relieve the nasal congestion associated with certain allergic conditions.

Noradrenaline is administered by intravenous infusion to combat the acute fall in blood pressure associated with certain types of shock. Large doses of these compounds may result in such serious consequences as cerebral hemorrhage and cardiac abnormalities.

adrenergic drug, also called SYMPATHOMIMETIC DRUG, any member of a class of drugs affecting the nervous system. Adrenergic drugs stimulate the release of adrenaline or noradrenaline—neurotransmitters, or compounds that diffuse from the end of a stimulated nerve cell across a space called the synaptic cleft to a neighbouring nerve cell, which is thus stimulated. Adrenergic drugs may inhibit the metabolism of these neurotransmitters or may mimic their effects.

Adrenergics affect cardiac muscles and the muscles involved in blood-vessel elasticity and may exacerbate heart disease or urinary tract obstruction. They are used to treat systemic trauma, including bronchial asthma, shock, and cardiac arrest; to effect nasal decongestion and appetite suppression; and to relieve allergic disorders. They increase glandular secretions, increase the heart rate, and prolong the action of local anesthetics.

Adrenergic blocking drugs (*e.g.,* benzamine or propranolol) inhibit certain responses of sympathetic nerves to adrenaline or noradrenaline.

adrenergic nerve fibre, nerve fibre that releases the neurotransmitter norepinephrine at the synapse, or junction, between a nerve and its end organ, which may be a muscle, gland, or another nerve. Such fibres make up the sympathetic nervous system, one of two peripheral nervous systems controlling involuntary activities, such as digestion, respiration, and circulation.

Adrenergic fibres innervate smooth muscle, cardiac muscle, visceral glands, and various central nervous system structures and sense organs; their action on these organs is opposite to that of the cholinergic fibres of the parasympathetic system. Peripheral adrenergic neurons (nerve cells) integrate signals from other nerves of the central nervous system and peripheral sense organs; an adrenergic nerve impulse is triggered when one nerve fires repeatedly or when several nerves fire simultaneously.

adrenocorticotropic hormone (ACTH), also called CORTICOTROPIN, a polypeptide hormone formed in the pituitary gland that regulates the activity of the outer region (cortex) of the adrenal glands. In mammals the action of ACTH is limited to those areas of the adrenal cortex in which the glucocorticoid hormones—cortisol and corticosterone (*see* corticoid)—are formed. The secretion of ACTH by the pituitary is itself regulated by another polypeptide, a so-called corticotropin-releasing hormone (CRH), that is discharged from the hypothalamus in response to impulses transmitted by the nervous system.

adrenogenital syndrome, a complex of symptoms resulting from an excess secretion of androgenic 17-ketosteroids by the adrenal cortex. (The hormones called 17-ketosteroids further the development of secondary sexual characteristics—the growth of body hair, deepening of the voice, and so on.) The clinical signs and symptoms differ depending upon the age and sex of the person affected. In infantile adrenogenital syndromes, simple virilism is the result of a defect in the biosynthesis of cortical steroids. A deep melanin pigmentation is usually present, and, depending upon the location of the biosynthetic block (enzyme), there may be an abnormal loss of sodium, severe hypertension, lipoid hyperplasia, dehydrogenase deficiency, or a complete lack of steroid hormone production—not only adrenal cortical but also testicular or ovarian. The most severe defect of infantile syndromes is the one in which there is hyperplasia (increase in the number of cells) of the adrenal cortex and a great accumulation of cholesterol. Although both males and females can be affected, a genotypic male develops female external genitalia (because of the absence of androgenic influence); thus, steroid hormones are almost entirely absent. Of two other infantile adrenogenital syndromes, one leads to macrogenitosomia in the male and pseudohermaphroditism in the female, and the other causes severe salt retention leading to hypertension.

In the adult, excess of 17-ketosteroids may, since it causes masculinization, be relatively unnoticed in the male, but it brings about virilism in the female. She develops a male habitus, receding hairline (leading to baldness), facial and body hair, atrophic breasts, acne, enlargement of the clitoris, and an irreversible deepening of the voice. Menstruation and ovulation cease, and there is a heavy masculine musculature. Unlike Cushing's disease (*q.v.*) it causes the skin to thicken. The adrenogenital syndrome may be a result of adrenal cancer, hyperplasia, or adenoma.

Adret, Solomon ben Abraham, Hebrew RABBI SHLOMO BEN ABRAHAM ADRET, also called (by acronym) RASHBA (b. 1235, Barcelona—d. 1310, Barcelona), outstanding spiritual leader of Spanish Jewry of his time (known as El rab de España [the Rabbi of Spain]); he is remembered partly for his controversial decree of 1305 threatening to excommunicate all Jews under 25 (except medical students) who studied philosophy or science.

As a leading scholar of the Talmud, the rabbinical compendium of law, lore, and commentary, Adret received inquiries on Jewish law from all over Europe, and more than 3,000 of his responsa (replies) still remain. Besides providing cultural data on Adret's time, his responsa strongly influenced the later development of authoritative codes of Jewish law, such as the *Shulḥan ʿarukh* ("The Well-Laid Table") of the codifier Joseph Karo (1488–1575). Adret's many other writings include commentaries on the Talmud and polemics defending it against attacks by non-Jews.

Late in life, Adret became embroiled in a quarrel between the followers of the medieval Jewish philosopher Maimonides and the members of a conservative, antirationalist movement led by a zealot known as Astruc of Lunel (*q.v.*), who believed that the followers of Maimonides were undermining the Jewish faith by, for example, interpreting the Bible allegorically. It was Astruc who induced Adret to issue his famous decree against the study of philosophy and science. Although the ban itself did not bring about an end to such studies, it precipitated among Jews in Spain and southern France a bitter controversy that continued during Adret's last years.

Adrets, François de Beaumont, baron des (baron of) (b. 1512/13, Château of La Frette, Isère, Fr.—d. Feb. 2, 1587, La Frette), French military leader of the Wars of Religion, notorious for his cruelty.

During the reign of Henry II of France Adrets served with distinction in the royal army and became colonel of the "legions" of Dauphiné, Provence, and Languedoc. In 1562, however, he joined the Huguenots, probably from motives of ambition and personal dislike of the Catholic House of Guise. His campaign against the Catholics in 1562 was eminently successful. In June of that year Adrets was master of the greater part of Dauphiné. But his brilliant military qualities were marred by his atrocities. He exacted fierce reprisals on the Catholics after their massacres of the Huguenots at Orange. The garrisons that resisted him were butchered, and at Montbrison, in Forez, he forced 18 prisoners to precipitate themselves from the top of the keep. Having alienated the affections of the Huguenots by his pride and violence, he entered into communication with the Roman Catholics and declared himself openly in favour of conciliation. On Jan. 10, 1563, he was arrested on suspicion by some Huguenot officers and confined in the citadel of Nîmes. He was liberated at the Edict of Amboise in the following March and, distrusted alike by Huguenots and Catholics, retired to the Château of La Frette, where he died, a Catholic, 23 years later.

Adria, Latin ATRIA, or HADRIA, town and episcopal see of Rovigo province, in the Veneto region of northern Italy, on the Bianco Canale just east of Rovigo. Founded by the Etruscans or the Veneti of Brittany, it later became a Roman town and was a flourishing port on the Adriatic Sea (to which it gave its name) until the silting up of the Po and Adige deltas caused the sea (now 13½ mi [22 km] east) to recede from the town. It has a fine museum of antiques and an 18th-century cathedral. It is now an agricultural and commercial centre of the Polesine (delta district) with diversified manufactures. Pop. (1981 prelim.) mun., 21,704.

Adrian (Roman emperor): *see* Hadrian.

Adrian, also spelled HADRIAN, Latin ADRIANUS, or HADRIANUS, name of Roman Catholic popes, grouped below chronologically and indicated by the symbol •.

• Adrian I (b. Rome—d. Dec. 25, 795), pope from 772 to 795 whose relationship with Charlemagne symbolized the medieval ideal of union of church and state in a united Christendom.

An aristocrat by birth and having served popes Paul I and Stephen III (IV), he was elected on February 1 with the support of the Frankish party at Rome. As pope Adrian invoked Frankish aid against the Lombard king Desiderius, who had attacked the papal possessions and was threatening Rome. By Easter 774, Charlemagne was in Rome, having destroyed the Lombard kingdom. Thenceforth, Adrian's policies were determined by the Frankish alliance rather than by relations with the Byzantine emperors of Constantinople.

The relationship between Charlemagne and Adrian was characterized by amicable rivalry. Charlemagne used the church to hold his empire together and to enforce overlordship on the Papal States, while Adrian fought firmly but adroitly for ecclesiastical autonomy and painstakingly pieced together a papal domain that was not lost until the 19th century.

Adrian strongly opposed Adoptionism, the doctrine of the dual sonship of Christ, and condemned the teachings of Archbishop Elipandus of Toledo, Spain. Constantinople was conciliated by Adrian's cooperation in opposing the Iconoclasts in the second Council (787) of Nicaea. Adrian confirmed the council's decrees, but, partly because of faulty translation, they were attacked by Charlemagne. Despite their difference of opinion, the rulers remained in rapport. Charlemagne commemorated Adrian in an epitaph composed by the scholar Alcuin and preserved at St. Peter's in Rome.

• Adrian II (b. 792, Rome—d. Dec. 14, 872), pope from 867 to 872.

A relative of two previous popes, Stephen V and Sergius II, he was elected on December 14. Under his vigorous predecessor, St. Nicholas I, the papacy had reached a high point that Adrian could not maintain. Vacillatory and lacking continuity, he was snubbed by Charles II the Bald, king of France. He readmitted King Lothair II of Lorraine to communion, but Lothair's early death (869) created a difficult problem of succession in which Adrian ineffectually intervened. Adrian also had difficulties with the powerful archbishop Hincmar of Reims, Fr., by steadfastly upholding the unlimited right of bishops to appeal to the pope.

Adrian II, detail from a fresco, 11th century; in the lower basilica of S. Clemente, Rome

Alinari—Art Resource/EB Inc.

Adrian approved the use of the Slavic language in liturgy by SS. Cyril and Methodius. By making Methodius archbishop of Sirmium, Adrian won the Moravians' faithfulness.

Adrian's legates took part in the eighth ecumenical council and the fourth Council of Constantinople (869–870), which deposed the Byzantine patriarch Photius. For the sake of reuniting East with West, Adrian accepted the council's 21st canon, which gave the patriarch of Constantinople rank second to that of the Roman see. He refused, however, to sanction the transfer of the Bulgarians to the patriarchate of Constantinople, and Bulgaria was lost to the Roman Catholic Church during Adrian's pontificate.

• Adrian III, SAINT (b. Rome?—d. *c.* September 885, near Modena, Bishopric of Modena; canonized June 2, 1891; feast day July 8), pope from 884 to 885.

His brief pontificate came during troubled times. He died en route to the Diet of Worms after being summoned by the Frankish king Charles III the Fat to settle the succession to the empire and discuss the rising Saracen power. The motives for his veneration are practically unknown, but he was noted for having aided the Romans during a famine.

• Adrian IV, original name NICHOLAS BREAKSPEAR (b. 1100?, Abbot's Langley, near St. Albans, Hertfordshire, Eng.—d. Sept. 1, 1159, Anagni, near Rome), the only Englishman to occupy the papal throne (1154–59).

He became a canon regular of St. Ruf near Avignon, Fr., and *c.* 1150 Pope Eugenius III appointed him cardinal bishop of Albano, Italy. Eugenius sent him as legate to Scandinavia in 1152, where his mission to reorganize the hierarchy was so successful that on his return in 1154 he was elected pope (December 4). Adrian crowned Frederick Barbarossa as Holy Roman emperor in 1155, after Frederick had captured and handed over to him Arnold of Brescia, who had led a revolt in Rome.

The papal policy toward the Normans of southern Italy, however, aroused the Emperor's anger. Thereafter, the relations between Adrian and Frederick laid the groundwork for the struggle to come between Pope Alexander III and Frederick. Adrian refused to recognize William I the Bad, who had been crowned king of Sicily (1154). That step caused the Sicilians, after unsuccessfully attacking the papal possession of Benevento, to wage war in the southern Campania. Thereupon the Pope excommunicated William.

Adrian then marched to Benevento, during which time he received John of Salisbury, secretary to the Archbishop of Canterbury, and granted him the Donation of Ireland (known as the bull *Laudabiliter*), which supposedly gave Ireland to Henry II of England. Attacked for false representation, the bull was subsequently refuted. (Even if *Laudabiliter* is authentic, which is doubtful, it does not grant hereditary possession of Ireland to the English king.)

Meanwhile, in June 1156, peace was made with the Sicilians, and Adrian agreed to invest William, who in turn became the Pope's liege man, which further embittered Frederick.

• Adrian V, original name OTTOBONO FIESCHI, (b. Genoa—d. Aug. 18, 1276, Viterbo, Papal States), pope for about five weeks in 1276.

His uncle Pope Innocent IV appointed him cardinal. He was legate to England (1265–68), charged with establishing peace between the English king Henry III and the rebellious barons. Elected as successor to Innocent V on July 11, he died a little more than a month later, having, however, revoked the stern conclave regulations of Pope Gregory X. Dante in his *Purgatory* (XIX, 97–126) portrays him

Adrian V, detail from a tomb monument by Vassalletto Iacopo, 1276; in the church of St. Francis, Viterbo, Italy

Alinari—Art Resource/EB Inc.

as lamenting his avarice and acknowledging "how the great mantle weighs" and "so justice here holds us close."

•**Adrian VI,** original name ADRIAN FLORENSZ BOEYENS (b. March 2, 1459, Utrecht, Bishopric of Utrecht—d. Sept. 14, 1523, Rome), the only Dutch pope, elected in 1522. He was the last non-Italian pope until the election of John Paul II in 1978.

He studied at the University of Louvain, where he was ordained priest and became, successively, professor of theology, chancellor, and rector. The great Humanist Erasmus was one of his pupils. In 1507 the Holy Roman emperor Maximilian I appointed Adrian tutor of his grandson Charles (later Holy Roman emperor as Charles V), who afterward entrusted him to perform many of the highest offices.

Adrian VI, Flemish commemorative medallion, 16th century

By courtesy of the National Gallery of Art, Washington, D.C., the Samuel H. Kress Collection

He became bishop of Tortosa in 1516 and grand inquisitor of Aragon (1517) and Castile (1518); he was created cardinal in 1517. He was elected pope on January 9, 1522, and was crowned at Rome on August 31. Adrian took up the task of reforming the church with great earnestness, starting with the Curia, but could accomplish little in the face of opposition by the Italian cardinals, the German Protestants, and the Turkish armies.

Adrian, city, seat (1826) of Lenawee County, southeastern Michigan, U.S., on the Raisin River. Addison J. Comstock settled the site in 1826 as Logan and renamed it in 1828 for the Roman emperor Hadrian (the *H* was dropped in 1838). He built the Erie and Kalamazoo Railroad (1832–36, the first west of New York State) connecting Adrian and Toledo, Ohio (34 mi [55 km] southeast); its cars were horse drawn until replaced by a locomotive in 1837. An agricultural centre, the city has acquired some light industry (notably the manufacture of auto parts and aluminum, paper, and wood products). Adrian College was founded in 1845, and Siena Heights College in 1919. Inc. village, 1836; city, 1853. Pop. (1980) 21,186.

Adrian (of Cambridge), Edgar Douglas Adrian, 1st Baron (b. Nov. 30, 1889, London—d. Aug. 4, 1977, London), electrophysiologist who with Sir Charles Sherrington won the Nobel Prize for Physiology or Medicine in 1932 for discoveries regarding the nerve cell.

Adrian graduated in medicine in 1915 from Trinity College, Cambridge. After medical service during World War I, he spent the greater part of his professional life at Cambridge in research and teaching, and as master of Trinity College (1961–65) and chancellor of the University (1968–75).

Adrian researched nerve impulses from sense organs, amplifying variations in electrical potential and recording smaller potential changes than had been detectable previously. Later he recorded nerve impulses from single sensory endings and motor nerve fibres, measurements contributing to a better understanding of the physical basis of sensation and the mechanism of muscular control. After 1934 Adrian studied the electrical activity of the brain; his work on the variations and abnormalities of the changes known as the Berger rhythm opened new fields of investigation in epilepsy and in the location of cerebral lesions.

Lord Adrian, 1956

Keystone

He was president of the Royal Society (1950–55) and of the British Association for the Advancement of Science (1954). In 1942 he was awarded the Order of Merit and in 1955 a barony. Among his writings are *The Basis of Sensation* (1927), *The Mechanism of Nervous Action* (1932), and *The Physical Background of Perception* (1947).

Adrianople (Turkey): *see* Edirne.

Adrianople, Battle of, Adrianople also spelled HADRIANOPOLIS (Aug. 9, AD 378), battle fought at present Edirne, in European Turkey, resulting in the defeat of a Roman army commanded by the emperor Valens at the hands of the Germanic Visigoths led by Fritigern and augmented by Ostrogothic and other reinforcements. It was a major victory of barbarian horsemen over Roman infantry and marked the beginning of serious Germanic inroads into Roman territory.

The Goths annihilated the Roman army; by some accounts, the Romans lost 40,000 men. Valens, who had failed to await reinforcements from Gratian, his nephew and co-emperor, was killed on the battlefield. An accommodation (382) was reached with the Goths by Theodosius I, Valens' successor as Eastern co-emperor, whereby the Goths agreed to aid in the imperial defenses in exchange for annual food subsidies, establishing a pattern for later barbarian intrusions into the empire.

Adrianople, Treaty of (1829): *see* Edirne, Treaty of.

Adriatic Sea, Italian MARE ADRIATICO, arm of the Mediterranean Sea, lying between the Italian and Balkan peninsulas. The Strait of Otranto at its southeasterly limit links it with the Ionian Sea. It is about 500 mi (800 km) long with an average width of 100 mi, a maximum depth of 4,035 ft (1,324 m), and an area of 50,590 sq mi (131,050 sq km). The Adriatic has been of great importance in the historical development of Mediterranean Europe and is of considerable scientific interest in itself. Modern study of the Adriatic has been carried out mainly under the auspices of a dozen or so Italian scientific institutes and their Yugoslavian equivalents.

There is a striking contrast between its two shores. The Italian coast is relatively straight and continuous, having no islands, whereas the Balkan coast is full of both large and small islands, generally oblong in shape and running parallel to the continental shore. Many tortuous straits also form inlets between the islands similar to those of the Norwegian fjords and make the coastline very intricate.

The depths of the Adriatic near its shores bear a close relationship to the physiography of the adjacent coasts. Wherever such coasts are high and mountainous, the nearby sea depths are considerable, as in the case of the Istrian and Dalmatian areas of Yugoslavia. Where low and sandy shores are found, the nearby sea is shallow, as in the vicinity of Venice or, farther south, near the delta of the Italian Po River. Generally speaking, the waters are shallow all along the Italian coast. The site of maximum depth of the Adriatic Sea is situated south of the central area; average depth is 1,457 ft (444 m).

The Adriatic has two types of rather special sea bottoms, difficult to arrange in a rigorous classification but very common in the Mediterranean, namely, inlet-derived sediments and heat-altered sediments of the sea bottom proper. In general, the seabed consists of a yellowish mud and sand, containing fragments of shells, fossil mollusks, and corals. The main winds prevailing in the area are the bora, a strong northeast wind that blows from the nearby mountains into the sea, and a southeasterly wind named the sirocco that is less troublesome from a navigational point of view. During the six winter months, bora and sirocco alternate, with or without an interval of a few days calm. The tides of the Adriatic, which have been intensively studied, follow a complicated pattern, sweeping into the region from the south and being linked with those of the Ionian Sea.

The tidal range is about three ft, in contrast to the general Mediterranean tidal range of about 0.9 ft. The surface currents are chiefly influenced by the blowing winds, with currents spurred by north winds reaching a speed of four miles per hour.

Temperatures in the surface layers of the sea reach 75°–77° F (24°–25° C) during the month of August, and the minimum readings, some 50° F (10° C), are usually reached during January and February. In the northern Adriatic, river mouth temperatures are even lower because the waters are cooled by melting ice and snow. At greater depths (820–980 ft) the maximum temperatures fluctuate around 57° F (14° C) while minimum temperatures are about 52° F (11° C).

The Adriatic Sea, like the Mediterranean in general, is deficient in life; nutrient content, as indicated by the amount of phosphates and nitrates, is extremely low. Three main areas of marine life may nevertheless be recognized. In the northern Adriatic area significant winter cooling and a lowered salinity further impoverish the typical Mediterranean marine life. In the middle Adriatic area, life is much richer than further north, while the southern Adriatic area has its own distinctive forms of life.

Articles are alphabetized word by word, not letter by letter

adsorption, capability of all solid substances to attract to their surfaces molecules of gases or solutions with which they are in contact. Solids that are used to adsorb gases or dissolved substances are called adsorbents; the adsorbed molecules are usually referred to collectively as the adsorbate. An example of an excellent adsorbent is the charcoal used in gas masks to remove poisons or impurities from a stream of air.

Adsorption refers to the collecting of molecules by the external surface or internal surface (walls of capillaries or crevices) of solids or by the surface of liquids. Absorption, with which it is often confused, refers to processes in which a substance penetrates into the actual interior of crystals, of blocks of amorphous solids, or of liquids. Sometimes the word sorption is used to indicate the process of the taking up of a gas or liquid by a solid without specifying whether the process is adsorption or absorption.

Adsorption can be either physical or chemical in nature. Physical adsorption resembles the condensation of gases to liquids, depending on the physical, or van der Waals, force of attraction between the solid adsorbent and the adsorbate molecules. There is no chemical specificity in physical adsorption, any gas tending to be adsorbed on any solid if the temperature is sufficiently low or the pressure of the gas sufficiently high. In chemical adsorption, gases are held to a solid surface by chemical forces that are specific for each surface and each gas. Chemical adsorption occurs usually at higher temperatures than those at which physical adsorption occurs; furthermore, chemical adsorption is ordinarily a slower process than physical adsorption and, like most chemical reactions, frequently involves an energy of activation.

'Aḍud ad-Dawlah (b. 936—d. 983), greatest ruler (949–983) of the Iranian Būyid dynasty.

Becoming ruler of Fārs province in southern Iran in 944, he did not actually reign on his own until almost a decade later. But by 979 his authority extended, through inheritance and conquest, over all southern Iran and most of what is now Iraq. Famous for his public works, which included a dam still standing near Shīrāz, he also consolidated the internal security and administrative order of the dynasty and patronized arts and letters. *See also* Būyids.

'Aḍud ad-Dawlah Abū Shujā' Muḥammad ibn Dā'ūd ibn Čaghribeg: *see* Alp-Arslan.

'Aḍud al-Dawla, in full 'AḌUD AL-DAWLA ABŪ SHUJA' MUḤAMMAD IBN DĀ'ŪD CHAGHRIBEG (Turkish sultan): *see* Alp-Arslan.

adularia, a feldspar mineral that contains more than 80 percent potassium aluminosilicate ($KAlSi_3O_8$); it commonly forms colourless, glassy, prismatic, twinned crystals in low-temperature veins of acidic plutonic rocks and in cavities in crystalline schists. Typical occurrences include the schists of the central and eastern Alps.

Adularia and microcline are sometimes considered identical, differing only in the size of their twinned crystals: the twins, two sets of fine, tapering lamellae at right angles to each other that are microscopically visible in microcline, are supposedly present, but invisible, in adularia. Slight differences in refractive indices, specific gravity, temperature of their conversion tosanidine (a high-temperature form of potassium feldspar), and axial angle, however, indicate the existence of two different species.

'Adullam, ancient city and modern development region, in the upper part of ha-Shefela, central Israel. The mound of Tel 'Adullam or Ḥorbat (ruins of) 'Adullam (Arabic Tall ash-Shaykh Madhkūr), 22½ mi (36 km) southwest of Jerusalem, is generally accepted as the site of the ancient city. The earliest reference to 'Adullam is in the book of Genesis, which tells of the activities of Judah, son of Jacob, in the area (Gen. 38). After the exodus from Egypt and the Israelite conquest, 'Adullam was assigned to the tribe of Judah (Joshua 15:35). Later, during David's flight from King Saul, he and his followers took refuge in the fortified caves there (I Samuel 22:1–4). Following the division of the Jewish kingdom (10th century BC), Solomon's son, Rehoboam, first king of Judah, fortified 'Adullam, but it and the other fortified cities of Judah were taken by Pharaoh Sheshonk I (biblical Shishak), who ruled Egypt *c.* 935–914 BC.

In later centuries 'Adullam was reoccupied by the Jews after the Babylonian Exile (early 6th century BC); during the Hasmonean revolt (2nd century BC), Judas Maccabeus took the fortified city from Gorgias, one of Antiochus IV Epiphanes' generals (II Maccabees 12:38).

In modern Israel the name 'Adullam is given to the planned development region (Hebrew *ḥevel*) in the former (1949–67) "Jerusalem corridor," west of the capital. This hilly area, on the boundary of ha-Shefela and Har Yehuda (the Judaean Hills), includes the ancient site. Settlement commenced in 1958; several agricultural villages and rural subcentres were established. No main regional centre was built due to the area's proximity to Jerusalem, but most villages were clustered around three rural centres. Orchards are prominent in the northeastern part of the region, while field crops predominate in the southwest. Mixed light manufacturing has been located in some of the villages.

Adullamite, member of a group of English politicians who rebelled against their leaders in the Liberal Party and defeated the Reform Bill of 1866. Their name was derived from the biblical "cave" of Adullam (I Samuel 22:1), a refuge for the discontented. The Liberal politician John Bright applied the term to party rebels who opposed the extension of the franchise proposed by W.E. Gladstone and John Russell, 1st Earl Russell, in 1866. Some of the group of about 40 members of Parliament acted out of fear of losing their seats, but most agreed with their leader Robert Lowe (later Viscount Sherbrooke; *q.v.*) in his fear of the effects of democracy.

adult education, also called CONTINUING EDUCATION, any form of learning undertaken by or provided for mature men and women. It comprehends such diverse modes as independent study consciously pursued with or without the aid of libraries; broadcast programs or correspondence courses; group discussion and other "mutual aid" learning in study circles, colloquia, seminars or workshops, and residential conferences or meetings; and full- or part-time study in classes or courses in which the lecturer, teacher, or tutor has a formal leading role. Types of adult education can also be classified as follows:

1. Education for vocational, technical, and professional competence. (Such education may aim at preparing an adult for a first job or for a new job, or it may aim at keeping him up to date on new developments in his occupation or profession.)

2. Education for health, welfare, and family living. (Such education includes all kinds of education in health, family relations, consumer buying, planned parenthood, hygiene, child care, and the like.)

3. Education for civic, political, and community competence. (Such education includes all kinds of education relating to government, community development, public and international affairs, voting and political participation, and so forth.)

4. Education for "self-fulfillment." (Such education embraces all kinds of liberal education programs: education in music, the arts, dance, theatre, literature, arts and crafts, whether brief or long term. These programs aim primarily at learning for the sake of learning rather than at achieving the aims included in the other categories.)

5. Remedial education: fundamental and literacy education. (Such education is obviously a prerequisite for all other kinds of adult education and thus, as a category, stands somewhat apart from the other types of adult education.)

In reference to the fifth category, adults frequently need to compensate for inadequacies of earlier education. If they are not remedied, they inhibit recourse to modes of education that are "adult"—adult, that is, in terms of sophistication in modern society and not in terms of age. Such education is required most extensively in societies changing rapidly from a subsistence to an industrial economy and concurrently changing politically and socially. Mass literacy acquires a new importance in these nations of Asia, Africa, and Latin America, and the establishment of universal primary education becomes a social imperative. To prevent a "generation gap" in reading skills and education while an effective school system is being created for the young, governments must attempt to provide parallel facilities for adults. Even in countries with mature systems of childhood education, however, opportunities for higher or even sometimes secondary education are unequal among various regional, occupational, and social groups. Hence there are adult programs for completing high school or preparing for examinations normally taken at the end of secondary school. Even in so highly developed a country as Sweden it has been considered necessary in recent years not only to try to extend secondary education to more children but also to offer equivalent second chances for adults. The implication is that "remedial" adult education is needed in societies in all stages of development and not merely in the so-called developing countries.

Any classification of agencies and institutions involved in adult education must necessarily be arbitrary, given the great variety found not only among nations but within single nations. The following are the general types.

The folk high schools, first established in Denmark and now found in all Scandinavian countries, are residential schools in which young adults who have completed formal schooling and usually have had some subsequent work experience pursue at least several months of study. The study aims at furthering both moral and intellectual development and instilling an understanding of local and national traditions and conditions. Although at first they were independent or separate institutions, they are now frequently promoted or supported by communal boards of education. Although rarely exported with success in their pure form, the folk high schools have influenced the development of residential forms of adult education in countries as diverse as Canada, Kenya, India, and The Netherlands.

Nonresident adult education centres, the most widely distributed specialized institutes for adult education, are represented by "workers academies" in Finland, "palaces of culture" in the U.S.S.R. and some other Communist countries, "workers' universities" in Yugoslavia, "peoples' high schools" in West Germany and Austria, "adult education centres" in Great Britain, and "people's universities" in The Netherlands, Italy, and Switzerland. The distinguishing characteristics of these institutions are that they are independent of the general education authorities, at least in terms of programming; that student attendance is voluntary and part-time; and that teachers and administrators are either volunteers or professionals offering mainly part-time services. Traditionally these schools do not prepare students for examinations or offer training in advanced vocational skills. Typically the curriculum includes instruction in practical and domestic crafts, fine arts, music and drama, familial and social problem solving, and modern languages, as well as instruction designed to reinforce primary and secondary education. The workers' universities in Yugoslavia probably go furthest in trying to fuse these elements into an overall program to equip workers to play a role in the self-management of industrial and commercial enterprises.

Agricultural extension services, though almost wholly an American development, are conducted on a scale great enough to rate separate mention. The extension service of the U.S. Department of Agriculture conducts agricultural, home economics, and even public affairs programs in every county in the United States. It has had special significance in developing "demonstration" as a method of adult education, in emphasizing the adoption of new practices, and in providing a possibly appropriate model for newly developing countries.

The open university, a new British institution, is significant for its new dimension and sharp break with previous degree programs for adults. In some educationally advanced countries—such as Australia, New Zealand, Canada, and the United States—adults have long had opportunities to pursue part-time education leading to the award of university degrees, but these programs have usually been carbon copies of programs offered to regular undergraduates. The open university, in theory at least, aspires to a kind of universal higher education. It is intended to service only mature or older adults studying part-time; it has no standardized entry requirements; and it attempts to combine various educational technologies and techniques—correspondence instruction, mass-communication media, personal counselling, and short-term residential courses.

Commercial enterprises have provided correspondence courses or class instruction (part- or full-time) for adults who are usually seeking some form of vocational qualification (but who may, however, be simply seeking "self-improvement," as in speed-reading programs). Such schools may be licensed or supervised by state agencies (as in Sweden and The Netherlands), or they may be self-policing through associations offering accreditation. Some schools are nonprofit organizations. One interesting development has been Switzerland's *Klub-Schulen* ("club schools"), supported through the philanthropy of a commercial concern, the Migros trading organization, but operated on a nonprofit basis; the programs, furthermore, have no particular vocational emphasis.

Extension services include both public school programs for adults and the university extensions mentioned earlier. The school programs are administered by the public school systems, and they are popularly termed night schools because ordinarily they are housed in the same school buildings used in the daytime for school-age youth and also because some of the same teachers are often involved. (Much of the teaching, however, is also done by subject specialists not employed as schoolteachers.) Though often originating in efforts to remedy or supplement inadequate childhood education, many of these programs now cater to the same range of interests served by the "nonresident adult education centres" cited above. They often retain elements of vocational preparation at a less specialized level, generally for younger adults—for example, in commercial and trade skills.

The difficulties inherent in trying to provide adequate services to adults as a kind of marginal addition or afterthought to the education of children have led some local education authorities in Britain and the United States to design schools that can be used specifically for adults as well as children. The "village colleges" in Cambridgeshire and the Mott Foundation program in Flint, Mich., involve a pattern of separate staffing for adult and child education and of comprehensive planning that enables a very large adult program to be provided within the school system. Such developments require the recruitment and training of larger cadres of full-time adult education teachers than have been customary in the past. The further growth and sophistication of public provision is likely to be a marked feature of adult education in the future.

The extension services offered by institutions of higher learning are of two broad types. The British tradition, influential in most Commonwealth countries and former colonial territories, has emphasized the provision of noncredit courses of "liberal" studies. The North American tradition, found in countries influenced by the United States and Canada, places a larger emphasis on credit programs duplicating courses offered to regular undergraduates; such programs are offered via television or correspondence or in separate urban colleges. Both traditions seem in the process of modification—the British in the direction of offering more credit-earning and vocation-related refresher courses, the North American toward a wider acceptance of the provision of general liberal studies for the public at large and for specialized vocational groups. It is everywhere apparent that universities are assuming more responsibility for the continuance and renewal of education for the highly educated.

In addition to the various schools or services listed above, there are countless organizations whose main purposes may not be adult education but that offer some kind of instruction or leisure-time activities for adults. They include such bodies as the Young Men's Christian Association, the Young Women's Christian Association, political parties and labour unions (often operating through especially constituted "workers educational associations"), women's organizations such as the Norwegian Housewives League, and temperance organizations such as the International Order of Good Templars. Other agencies for which adult education is a related rather than a primary function are libraries, museums, botanical gardens, and the like. Not only do these agencies provide the means of individual self-education but also they frequently promote group activities or put their accommodations and resources at the disposal of adult education agencies. Finally there should be mentioned the advisory and instructional services offered by various social and welfare agencies in the fields of health, safety, marital guidance, family planning, and so forth.

adultery, sexual relations by a married person with someone other than the spouse. Prohibitions or taboos against adultery, written or customary, constitute part of the marriage code of virtually every society. Indeed, adultery seems to be as universal and, in some instances, as common as marriage.

The Code of Hammurabi (18th century BC) in Babylonia provided a punishment of death by drowning for adultery. In ancient Greece and in Roman law, the offending female spouse could be killed, but men were not severely punished. The Jewish, Islāmic, and Christian traditions are unequivocal in their condemnation of adultery. The culpability of men as well as women is more explicitly expressed in the New Testament and the Talmud than in the Old Testament or the Qur'ān.

The attitude toward adultery within different cultures varies widely. Whereas the traditional Senufo (Senoufo) and Bambara of West Africa, for instance, tacitly condone the honour crime of killing the adulterous female spouse and her companion, among the Kaka in Cameroon, a man may have sexual relations with the wives of certain relatives with impunity. Wife lending is part of Eskimo hospitality. Nonincestuous adultery is permitted by many South Sea island peoples, and among certain Pueblo Indian societies adultery is so common that it is tolerated if the act is kept secret.

Under ancient Hindu law, marriage was an indissoluble sacrament, and not even a wife's adultery could sever the legal tie and dissolve the marriage act. In the modern Hindu code, divorce will be granted to either offended party, but not for occasional violations; the spouse must actually be living in adultery with another.

In western Europe and North America, adultery is a ground for divorce. The diffusion of this principle, as well as Western notions of egalitarianism and modern expectations of mutual emotional support in marriage, has resulted in unprecedented pressure for equal marital rights for women in traditional African and Southeast Asian societies.

In many eastern European countries, adultery does not in itself constitute grounds for divorce; both partners must testify, under the principle of "general breakdown," that the offense results in the decline of those feelings of which marital unity is composed.

Adur, district, county of West Sussex, England. It is named for the River Adur, which cuts through the chalk ridge of the South Downs by way of an impressive water gap before entering the English Channel at Shoreham-by-Sea. The district is small, with an area of 16 sq mi (42 sq km); it occupies the lower valley of the river between the urban areas of Worthing to the west and Brighton-Hove to the east. Pop. (1982 est.) 58,300.

Aduwa (Ethiopia): *see* Adwa.

Advaita (Sanskrit: Nondualism, Monism), most influential of the schools of Vedānta, an orthodox philosophy of India. While its followers find its main tenets already fully expressed in the *Upaniṣads* and systematized by the *Vedānta-sūtras*, it has its historical beginning with the 7th-century thinker Gauḍapāda, author of the *Māṇḍūkya-kārikā*, a commentary in verse form on the late *Māṇḍūkya Upaniṣad.* Gauḍapāda builds further on the Mahāyāna Buddhist philosophy of Śūnyavāda (Emptiness).

He argues that there is no duality; the mind, awake or dreaming, moves through *māyā* ("illusion"); and only nonduality (*advaita*) is the final truth. This truth is concealed by the ignorance of illusion. There is no becoming, either of a thing by itself or of a thing out of some other thing. There is ultimately no individual self or soul (*jīva*), only the *ātman* (all-soul), in which individuals may be temporarily delineated just as the space in a jar delineates a part of main space: when the jar is broken, the individual space becomes once more part of the main space.

The medieval Indian philosopher Śaṅkara, or Śaṅkarācārya (Master Śaṅkara, *c.* 700–750), builds further on Gauḍapāda's foundation, principally in his commentary on the *Vedānta-sūtras*, the *Śārī-raka-mīmāṃsā-bhāṣya* ("Commentary on the study of the self"). Śaṅkara in his philosophy does not start from the empirical world with logical analysis but, rather, directly from the absolute (Brahman). If interpreted correctly, he argues, the *Upaniṣads* teach the nature of Brahman. In making this argument, he develops a complete epistemology to account for the human error in taking the phenomenal world for real. Fundamental for Śaṅkara is the tenet that the Brahman is real and the world is unreal. Any change, duality, or plurality is an illusion. The self is nothing but Brahman. Insight into this identity results in spiritual release. Brahman is outside time, space, and causality, which are simply forms of empirical experience. No distinction in Brahman or from Brahman is possible.

Śaṅkara points to scriptural texts, either stating identity ("thou art that") or denying difference ("There is no duality here"), as declaring the true meaning of a Brahman without qualities (*nirguṇa*). Other texts that ascribe qualities (*saguṇa*) to Brahman refer not to the true nature of Brahman but to its personality as God (Īśvara).

Human perception of the unitary and infinite Brahman as the plural and infinite is due to man's innate habit of superimposition (*adhyāsa*), by which a thou is ascribed to the I (I am tired; I am happy; I am perceiving). The habit stems from man's ignorance (*ajñāna, avidyā*), which can be avoided only by the realization of the identity of Brahman. Nevertheless, the empirical world is not totally unreal, for it is a misapprehension of the real Brahman. A rope is mistaken for a snake; there is only a rope and no snake, but, as long as it is thought of as a snake, it is one.

Śaṅkara had many followers who continued and elaborated his work, notably, the 9th-century philosopher Vācaspati Miśra. The Advaita literature is extremely extensive, and its influence is still felt in modern Hindu thought.

advection, change in a property of a moving air parcel because the parcel moves to a region where the property has a different value (*e.g.,* the change in temperature when a warm air parcel moves into a cool region). Commonly, advection is divided into horizontal and vertical components and differs from convection only in scale. Convection is transport by random thermally induced currents, whereas advection is transport by steady vertical currents.

Advent (from Latin *adventus,* "coming"), in the Christian Church, a period of preparation for the celebration of the birth of Jesus Christ at Christmas, and also of preparation for the Second Coming of Christ. It begins on the Sunday nearest to November 30 (St. Andrew's Day) and is the beginning of the church year. The date when the season was first observed is uncertain. Bishop Perpetuus of Tours (461–490) established a fast before Christmas that began on November 11 (St. Martin's Day), and the Council of Tours (567) mentioned an Advent season.

Although a solemn season, it is no longer kept with the strictness of Lent, as it once was. The Roman Catholic Church forbids the solemnization of marriage during Advent. In many countries it is marked by a variety of popular observances, such as the lighting of Advent candles.

Advent Christian Church, one of several Adventist churches that evolved from the teachings in the late 1840s of William Miller (1782–1849). It was organized in 1860. Doctrinal emphasis is placed on the anticipated Second Coming of Christ and on the Last Judgment, after which the wicked will be destroyed and the chosen will be resurrected to live in a restored paradise on Earth. It is congregational in polity and, unlike the Seventh-day Adventists, holds services on Sunday.

In 1964 the former Life and Advent Union merged with the Advent Christian Church.

Adventist (from Latin *adventus,* "coming"), member of any of a group of Protestant Christian churches, arising in the U.S. in the 19th century and rooted in Hebrew and Christian prophetism, messianism, and millennial expectations recorded in the Bible. Adventists believe that at Christ's Second Coming he will separate the saints from the wicked and inaugurate his millennial (1,000-year) Kingdom. *See* millennium.

History. It was in an atmosphere of millennialist revival in the U.S. that William Miller (1782–1849), a founder of the Adventists, began to preach. Miller, while an officer in the U.S. Army in the War of 1812, had become a skeptic. After a conversion, he began to study the books of Daniel and Revelation and to preach as a Baptist, the faith of his father. He concluded that Christ would come some time between March 21, 1843, and March 21, 1844, and was encouraged in his views by a number of clergymen (such as the reform-minded Joshua Himes of Boston) and numerous followers—about 100,000 according to some estimates.

Miller was accused of fanaticism because of his millenarianism, and he stressed the coming of Christ in conjunction with a fiery conflagration, which distressed his hearers. Christ, however, did not return on the first appointed date, so Miller and his followers set a second date, Oct. 22, 1844. The quiet passing of this day led to what is called the "Great Disappointment" among Adventists and the convening of a Mutual Conference of Adventists in 1845 to sort out problems. Those who met, however, found it difficult to shape a confession and form a permanent organization.

Among those who persisted after the failure of Miller's prophecy were Joseph Bates (1792–1872), James White (1821–81), and his wife, Ellen Harmon White (1827–1915). These Adventists, called Millerites in the press, believed that Miller had set the right date, but that they had interpreted what had happened incorrectly. Reading Daniel, chapters 8 and 9, they concluded that God had begun the "cleansing of the heavenly sanctuary,"—*i.e.,* an investigative judgment that would be followed by the pronouncing and then the execution of the sentence of judgment.

What actually began in 1844, then, in their view, was an examination of all of the names in the Book of Life. Only after this was completed would Christ appear and begin his millennial reign. Though they did not set a new date, they insisted that Christ's advent was "personal, visible, audible, bodily, glorious and premillennial" and imminent. They also believed that observance of the seventh day, Saturday, rather than Sunday, would help to bring about the Second Coming.

These Millerites founded a magazine in 1850—based on the earlier *Present Truth*—called the *Advent Review and Sabbath Herald* (now the *Review and Herald*), established a headquarters in Battle Creek, Mich., in 1855, and became an official denomination (Seventh-day Adventists) in 1863. Adventists believe that Mrs. White, a former Methodist, had received the gift of prophecy. She had visions, travelled and lectured widely in America, Europe, and Australia, and wrote prolifically, including the "Conflict of the Ages" series (5 vol., 1888–1917) and *Testimonies for the Church* (9 vol., 1855–1909).

Other Adventist bodies emerged in the 19th century as a direct or indirect result of the prophecy of William Miller. These include the Evangelical Adventists (1845), Life and Advent Union (1862), Church of God (Seventh Day, 1866), Church of God General Conference (Abrahamic Faith, 1888), and the Advent Christian Church. The latter is the largest among these small bodies. It was organized in 1860 by Jonathan Cummings (fl. *c.* 1852), a follower of Miller. Cummings stressed the teaching of conditional immortality. Because of sin, man forfeited immortality. At death he remains in a state of unconsciousness until Christ's Second Coming, when the faithful will enter into life and the unrighteous will suffer extinction.

The Advent Christians do not accept the teachings of Mrs. White as in any way prophetic. They also reject the teachings of the Seventh-day Adventists about sabbath observance and dietary laws. They are congregational in polity and coordinate work in the United States and throughout the world through the Advent Christian General Conference of America. In 1964 the Advent Christian Church united with the Life and Advent Union.

Adventist emphases may also be found among pentecostal and holiness groups that interpret the outpourings of the Holy Spirit, the manifestation of his gifts, and growth in sanctification as signs of the coming of Christ and his Kingdom. Charles Taze Russell (1852–1916), the founder of the Jehovah's Witnesses, came under the influence of Adventist ideas. His followers became known as Millennial Dawnists, who believed that this present world is under the reign of Satan and in conflict with Jehovah's (God's) rule. Millennial Dawnists considered it their responsibility to announce the Second Coming of Christ, which would be marked by the battle of Armageddon, in which Satan would be defeated, the faithful rewarded, and the wicked annihilated (*see also* Jehovah's Witnesses).

Beliefs and practices. Seventh-day Adventists share many basic beliefs held by most Christians. They accept the authority of the Old and New Testaments. They are Arminian (emphasizing man's choice and God's election) rather than Calvinist (emphasizing God's sovereignty) in their interpretation of Christ's atonement, and they argue that his death was "*provisionally* and *potentially* for all men," yet efficacious only for those who avail themselves of its benefits.

In addition to the emphasis upon the Second Advent of Christ, two other matters set them apart from other Christians. (1) They observe the seventh day, rather than the first day of the week, as the sabbath. This day, according to the Bible, was instituted by God since the creation, and the commandment concerning sabbath rest is a part of God's eternal law. (2) They also avoid eating meat and taking narcotics and stimulants, which they consider to be harmful. Though they appeal to the Bible for the justification of these dietary practices, they maintain that these are based upon the broad theological consideration that the body is the temple of the Holy Spirit and should be protected.

Adventists stress tithing and therefore have a high annual giving per capita that allows them to carry on worldwide welfare programs. Because of their unwillingness to work on Saturday, they have suffered some job discrimination. This has made them deeply concerned about religious liberty. In recent years, despite the church's traditional stand against ecumenism, consultations have been held between representatives of the Seventh-day Adventists and the World Council of Churches to discuss the relation of Adventists to the ecumenical movement.

Institutions. Sending out its first missionary, John Nevins Andrews (1829–83), in 1874, Seventh-day Adventism expanded into a worldwide movement. The General Conference, the main governing body, has its headquarters in Takoma Park, Washington, D.C., where it was moved in 1903 from Battle Creek. The meeting of the General Conference is held quadrennially and is made up of delegates from divisions, union and local, that are also called conferences. These local conferences provide pastoral oversight for the local congregations, which are governed by elected lay elders and deacons. The General Conference supervises the work of evangelism in more than 500 languages, a large parochial school system, and numerous medical institutions called sanitariums, of which the first was established in Battle Creek in 1866. Publishing houses are operated in many countries, and Adventist literature is distributed door to door by volunteers. (J.H.Sm.)

BIBLIOGRAPHY. Sylvester Bliss, *Memoirs of William Miller* (1853); LeRoy Edwin Froom, *The*

Prophetic Faith of Our Fathers, 4 vol. (1950–54), a rich description of Adventist literature by an Adventist, helpful for research; Arthur W. Spalding, *Origin and History of Seventh-Day Adventists* (1962); Don F. Neufeld *et al.* (eds.), *Seventh-Day Adventist Encyclopedia* (1966).

adventure bay pine: *see* celery-top pine.

adversary procedure, in law, one of the two methods of exposing evidence in court (the other being the inquisitorial procedure; *q.v.*).

The adversary procedure requires the opposing sides to bring out pertinent information and to present and cross-examine witnesses. This procedure is observed primarily in countries in which the Anglo-American legal system of common law predominates.

Under the adversary system, each side is responsible for conducting its own investigation. In criminal proceedings, the prosecution represents the people at large and has at its disposal the police department with its investigators and laboratories, while the defense must find its own investigative resources and finances. Both sides may command the attendance of witnesses by subpoena (*q.v.*). If the defendant is indigent, his attorney's opportunities for a broader investigation are limited by the provisions of the jurisdiction in which the trial is conducted. In criminal law under the adversary system, the accused is not present in grand jury indictment proceedings (no longer conducted in Great Britain and recommended by some authorities for eventual abolition in the United States). If an indictment is handed down by the grand jury, its proceedings are available to the defendant. Under civil law the adversary system works similarly, except that both plaintiff and respondent must prepare their own cases, usually through privately engaged attorneys.

In any adversary trial, the opposing sides present evidence, examine witnesses, and conduct cross-examinations, each in an effort to produce information beneficial to its side of the case. Skillful questioning can often produce testimony that can be made to take on various meanings. What seemed absolute in direct testimony can raise doubts under cross-examination. The skills of the attorneys are also displayed at the time of summation, especially in a jury trial, when their versions of what the jury has heard may persuade the jury to interpret the facts to the benefit of the side that is most persuasive.

In adversary proceedings before juries the judge functions as moderator and referee on points of law, rarely taking part in the questioning unless he or she feels that important points of law or fact must be made clearer. In a bench trial (without a jury) the judge makes findings of fact and damages (if any) as well as of law.

adverse possession, in Anglo-American property law, holding of property under some claim of right with the knowledge and against the will of one who has a superior ownership interest in the property. Its legal significance is traced back to the English common-law concept known as seisin, a possession of land by one who owns the property at least for the period of his life, having a complete right to possession of the property as against all others. The possession by any other under some claim of right to the land was known as disseisin. One who was disseised of his property could take the matter to the king's court through a legal action known as the assize of novel disseisin. If the land held by a disseisor was claimed by an heir of the original owner in seisin, the heir could bring a similar legal action known as the assize of mort d'ancestor. After the 17th century more expeditious legal actions were developed.

In the U.S., disseisin developed as the concept of adverse possession. Statutes of limitation in most of the U.S. states set time limits within which an owner can bring an action for possession, after which time an adverse possessor acquires a legal title to the land.

advertising, the techniques used to bring products, services, opinions, or causes to public notice for the purpose of persuading the public to respond in a certain way toward what is advertised. Most advertising involves promoting a good that is for sale, but similar methods are used to encourage people to drive safely, to support various charities, or to vote for political candidates, among many other examples. In many countries advertising is the most important source of income for the media (*e.g.,* newspapers, magazines, or television stations) through which it is conducted. In the non-Communist world advertising has become a multi-billion dollar business.

A brief treatment of advertising follows. For a full treatment, *see* MACROPAEDIA: Marketing and Merchandising.

In the ancient and medieval world such advertising as existed was conducted by word of mouth. The first step toward modern advertising came with the development of printing in the 15th and 16th centuries. In the 17th century weekly newspapers in London began to carry advertisements, and by the 18th century such advertising was flourishing.

The great expansion of business in the 19th century was accompanied by the growth of an advertising industry; it was that century, primarily in the United States, that saw the establishment of advertising agencies. The first agencies were, in essence, brokers for space in newspapers. But by the early 20th century agencies became involved in producing the advertising message itself, including copy and artwork, and by the 1920s agencies had come into being that could plan and execute complete advertising campaigns, from initial research to copy preparation to placement in various media.

There are eight principal media for advertising. Perhaps the most basic medium is the newspaper, which offers advertisers large circulations, a readership located close to the advertiser's place of business, and the opportunity to alter their advertisements on a frequent and regular basis. Magazines, the other chief print medium, may be of general interest or they may be aimed at specific audiences (such as people interested in outdoor sports or computers or literature) and offer the manufacturers of products of particular interest to such people the chance to make contact with their most likely customers. Many national magazines publish regional editions, permitting a more selective targeting of advertisements.

In Western industrial nations the most pervasive media are television and radio. Although in some countries radio and television are state-run and accept no advertising, in others advertisers are able to buy short "spots" of time, usually a minute or less in duration. Advertising spots are broadcast between or during regular programs, at moments sometimes specified by the advertiser and sometimes left up to the broadcaster. For advertisers the most important facts about a given television or radio program are the size and composition of its audience. The size of the audience determines the amount of money the broadcaster can charge an advertiser, and the composition of the audience determines the advertiser's choice as to when a certain message, directed at a certain segment of the public, should be run.

The other advertising media include direct mail, which can make a highly detailed and personalized appeal; outdoor billboards and posters; transit advertising, which can reach the millions of users of mass-transit systems; and miscellaneous media, including dealer displays and promotional items such as matchbooks or calendars.

For an advertisement to be effective its production and placement must be based on a knowledge of the public and a skilled use of the media. Advertising agencies serve to orchestrate complex campaigns whose strategies of media use are based on research into consumer behaviour and demographic analysis of the market area. A strategy will combine creativity in the production of the advertising messages with canny scheduling and placement, so that the messages are seen by, and will have an effect on, the people the advertiser most wants to address. Given a fixed budget, advertisers face a basic choice: they can have their message seen or heard by many people fewer times, or by fewer people many times. This and other strategic decisions are made in light of tests of the effectiveness of advertising campaigns.

There is no dispute over the power of advertising to inform consumers of what products are available. In a free-market economy effective advertising is essential to a company's survival, for unless consumers know about a company's product they are unlikely to buy it. In criticism of advertising it has been argued that the consumer must pay for the cost of advertising in the form of higher prices for goods; against this point it is argued that advertising enables goods to be mass marketed, thereby bringing prices down. It has been argued that the cost of major advertising campaigns is such that few firms can afford them, thus helping these firms to dominate the market; on the other hand, whereas smaller firms may not be able to compete with larger ones at a national level, at the local level advertising enables them to hold their own. Finally, it has been argued that advertisers exercise an undue influence over the regular contents of the media they employ—the editorial stance of a newspaper or the subject of a television show. In response it has been pointed out that such influence is counteracted, at least in the case of financially strong media firms, by the advertiser's reliance on the media to convey his messages; any compromise of the integrity of a media firm might result in a smaller audience for his advertising.

Where the same name may denote a person, place, or thing, the articles will be found in that order

---

advertising coloration, in animals, the use of biological coloration to make an organism unique and highly visible as compared with the background, thereby providing easily perceived information as to its location, identity, and movement. Such advertisement may serve the function of attracting individuals in order to enter into some advantageous interaction (*e.g.,* courtship for reproductive purposes) or of warning or repelling other organisms.

advisory opinion, in law, the opinion of a judge, a court, or a law official, such as an attorney general, upon a question of law raised by a public official or legislative body. Advisory opinions adjudicate nothing and are binding upon no one. Neither federal nor state courts in the United States issue advisory opinions, but such opinions are issued routinely by the attorneys general of the various states upon the request of the governor, legislators, or other state officials. The opinions typically refer to the legality of some contemplated official action. Advisory opinions originated very early in English law as a result of extralegal consultation of judges by the Crown or the House of Lords on questions that often were not even related to the law. The function of the opinions was wholly non- or extralegal.

advocate, in law, a person who is professionally qualified to plead the cause of another in a court of law. As a technical term, advocate is used mainly in those legal systems that derived from the Roman law. In Scotland the word refers particularly to a member of the bar of Scotland, the Faculty of Advocates. In France *avocats* were formerly an organized body of pleaders, while preparation of cases was done by *avoués;* today this distinction exists only before the appellate courts. In Germany, until the distinction between counsellor and pleader was abolished in 1879, the *Advokat* was the adviser rather than the pleader. The term has traditionally been applied to pleaders in courts of canon law, and thus in England those who practiced before the courts of civil and canon law were called advocates. In the United States the term advocate has no special significance, being used interchangeably with such terms as attorney, counsel, or lawyer. *See also* lawyer.

Advocates, Faculty of, the collective term designating the members of the bar of Scotland. Barristers are the comparable group in England (*see* barrister; solicitor). The faculty grew out of the Scots Act of 1532, which established the Court of Session in Scotland. The advocates had, and still have, the sole right of audience in the Court of Session and High Court of Justiciary. By immemorial custom, they have formed themselves into a self-governing faculty under annually elected officers. When properly instructed by an agency of the law, an advocate is bound and entitled to plead in any court in Scotland and also before the House of Lords, the Judicial Committee of the Privy Council, and committees of Parliament. *See also* Scottish law.

advocatus diaboli (Roman Catholic Church): *see* devil's advocate.

Adwa, also spelled ADOWA, or ADUWA, town, Tigrai province, northern Ethiopia, 6,500 ft (2,000 m) above sea level. It lies on the east-west highway between Aksum and Adi Grat at its junction with the road north to Asmera. Formerly the provincial capital, it is now a market centre (grains, honey, hides, coffee) for the Tigrai people. It is located 10 mi (16 km) west of an area of fantastic volcanic formations. On March 1, 1896, Emperor Menelik II defeated an Italian force there. Nearby are the ruins of Fremona, headquarters for the Portuguese Jesuits who came to Ethiopia in the 16th and 17th centuries. Pop. (1982 est.) 26,782.

Adwa, Battle of (1896): *see* Adowa, Battle of.

Ady, Endre (b. Nov. 22, 1877, Érmindszent, Hung., Austria-Hungary—d. Jan. 27, 1919, Budapest), greatest Hungarian lyric poet of the 20th century and considered by some the greatest of any century.

Ady was born into an impoverished but noble family. On leaving school he studied law

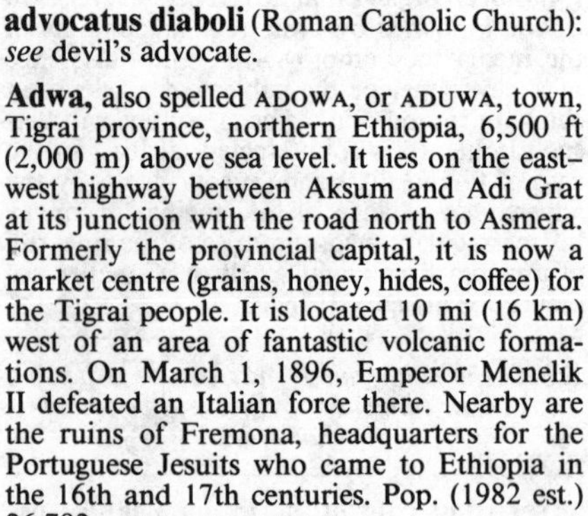

Ady
By courtesy of the Petofi Irodalmi Muzeum, Budapest

for a time, but in 1899 he published an insignificant volume of verse, *Versek*, and from 1900 until his death worked as a journalist. In 1903 he published another volume of poetry, *Még egyszer*, in which signs of his exceptional talent could be seen. With his next book, *Uj versek* (1906; "New Poems"), he burst into Hungarian literary life. Poetry in Hungary had been dormant at the end of the 19th and at the beginning of the 20th century, and imitations of Sándor Petőfi and János Arany were prevalent. None of the few original poets had been powerful enough to make an impression on the public, which was thus unprepared for the "new verses of a new era," as Ady described his work. These poems were revolutionary in form, language, and content; his unconventional though splendid language, with its unusual choice of adjectives, shocked the public. The outrage was furthered by the general tone of his poems. Ady's stay as a journalist in Paris had made Hungary seem to him narrow and materialistic, and in these poems he unleashed a storm of violent and insulting attacks upon his country. Though the artistic value of the "new poems" is beyond question, Ady became the target of onslaughts that soon developed into a political struggle, Ady being supported by the left-wing radicals, who hailed him as a prophet, and abused by right-wing nationalists.

In his later work, Ady abandoned gratuitous insult and attained a higher level of social and political censure. His understanding of his country, of its social and political ills, and of the sufferings inflicted by World War I inspired him to find new means of expressing pain and anger. By that time his failing health, undermined by a profligate life, was unable to stand up to the pressure of constant hard work. He had published 10 volumes of poetry in 12 years, as well as short stories and countless articles. He died a victim of alcoholism.

Ady's love of the Hungarian people was only one of his themes. His love poems are striking in their originality and their mystical approach to physical love. His religious poems, which seemed blasphemous to many, reveal his search for God "who is at the bottom of all things, to whom all the bells toll and on whose left I, alas, sit."

Adygey autonomous oblast, also spelled ADIGEI, also called ADYGEYA, administrative region, established in 1922, in Krasnodar *kray* (territory), Russian Soviet Federated Socialist Republic. Its area of 2,950 sq mi (7,600 sq km) extends from the Kuban River to the Caucasus foothills. It was formed for the Adyghian people, a branch of the Circassians (Cherkess), who make up about one-fifth of the total population. Apart from the foothills in the south, which are covered in deciduous forest, most of the *oblast* is an undulating plain with rich soils that are used almost wholly for agriculture. Corn (maize), wheat, sunflowers, hemp, tobacco, melons, potatoes, and other vegetables are grown. A local specialty is flowers, especially Crimean roses and lavender, grown for scent. On the marshy floodplain along the Kuban, some 20,000 ac (8,000 ha) have been reclaimed for market gardening. Industry is chiefly concerned with processing farm produce, but oil and natural gas are exploited near Maykop (*q.v.*), the administrative centre of the *oblast*. There is some timbering in the south. Pop. (1983 est.) 413,000.

adz, also spelled ADZE, hand tool for shaping wood. One of the earliest tools, it was widely distributed in Stone Age cultures in the form of a hand-held stone chipped to form a blade. By Egyptian times it had acquired a wooden haft, or handle, with a copper or bronze blade set flat at the top of the haft to form a T. In this form the adz continued to be the prime hand tool for shaping and trimming wood. A log or other piece of timber was laid on the ground or floor, and the carpenter stood

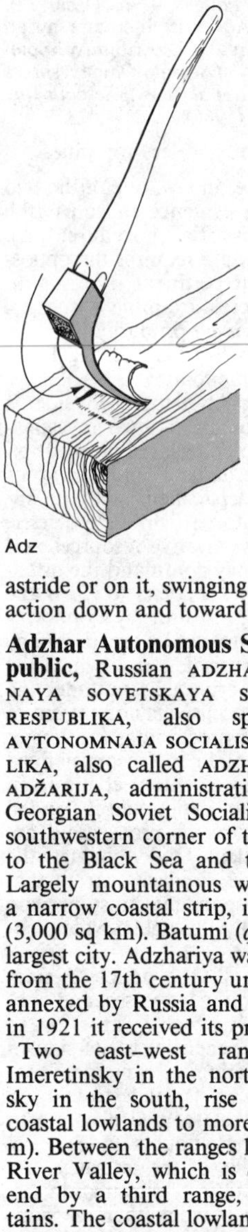

Adz

astride or on it, swinging the adz in a pick-like action down and toward himself.

Adzhar Autonomous Soviet Socialist Republic, Russian ADZHARSKAYA AVTONOMNAYA SOVETSKAYA SOTSIALISTICHESKAYA RESPUBLIKA, also spelled ADŽARSKAJA AVTONOMNAJA SOCIALISTICHESKAJA RESPUBLIKA, also called ADZHARIYA, also spelled ADŽARIJA, administrative division of the Georgian Soviet Socialist Republic, in the southwestern corner of that republic adjacent to the Black Sea and the Turkish frontier. Largely mountainous with the exception of a narrow coastal strip, it covers 1,150 sq mi (3,000 sq km). Batumi (*q.v.*) is the capital and largest city. Adzhariya was under Turkish rule from the 17th century until 1878, when it was annexed by Russia and attached to Georgia; in 1921 it received its present political status.

Two east–west ranges, the Adzhar-Imeretinsky in the north and the Shavshetsky in the south, rise from the Black Sea coastal lowlands to more than 9,200 ft (2,800 m). Between the ranges lies the Adzharistskali River Valley, which is closed at the eastern end by a third range, the Arsiyan Mountains. The coastal lowland area, which widens somewhat to the south of Batumi and again in the north around Kobuleti, has a humid subtropical climate with average January temperatures ranging from 41° F (5° C) to 46° F (8° C) and average August temperatures ranging from 70° F (21° C) to 73° F (23° C). The climate becomes more severe in the foothills and mountains as elevation increases; above 6,000 ft it is cold, and snow lies on the summits for six months. The highest rainfall average in any city of the Soviet Union occurs at Batumi, where 62 in. (1,600 mm) are recorded annually. Subtropical vegetation prevails in the lowland areas, and coniferous forests, scrub, and alpine meadows predominate on the mountain slopes.

The population of Adzhariya includes Georgians, Russians, Armenians, and the Adzhars themselves, a Georgian population Islāmicized under Turkish rule. Although the Adzhars are not a nationality distinct from other Georgians, they do represent a distinctive cultural fraction of the Georgian homeland. Of the total population, less than one-half is urban and two-thirds live in the coastal lowlands and foothills.

Subtropical crops, which form the basis of the republic's economy, include tea, citrus fruits, and avocados, tung trees (for oil), eucalyptus trees (camphor oil), and bamboo. Tobacco is grown in the higher areas, in which livestock raising is also important. Industrial development is concentrated around Batumi, the terminus of a pipeline from Baku on the Caspian Sea. Industrial activity includes oil refining, shipping and shipbuilding, food processing, light manufacturing, and the production of wine, plywood, furniture, and chemical pharmaceuticals. The republic is linked with the rest of the Georgian S.S.R. by a road over the Goderdzi Pass in the Arsiyan Mountains and by the Transcaucasian Railway, which runs north along the coast from Batumi, then eastward; and there are air services from Batumi to Tbilisi, Moscow, and other cities of the Soviet Union. Pop. (1983 est.) 371,000.

Adzopé, town, administrative headquarters (since 1969) of Adzopé *département*, southeastern Ivory Coast. A traditional market centre for the Attie people, it sends coffee, bananas, cocoa, and timber (mahogany, sipo) to Abidjan, 55 mi (89 km) south, for export. Adzopé is the site of Roman Catholic and Protestant missions, a government agricultural training institute (1964), a leprosy hospital, and a model housing project. Pop. (1975) town, 23,361; (1979 est.) *département*, 160,931.

Æ, pseudonym of GEORGE WILLIAM RUSSELL (b. April 10, 1867, Lurgan, County Armagh, Ire.—d. July 17, 1935, Bournemouth, Hampshire, Eng.), poet and mystic, a leading figure in the Irish literary renaissance (*q.v.*).

After attending the Metropolitan School of Art, Dublin, where he met the poet William Butler Yeats, Æ became an accounts clerk in a drapery store but left in 1897 to organize agricultural cooperatives. In 1894 he published the first of many books of verse, *Homeward: Songs by the Way.* His first volume of *Collected Poems* appeared in 1913 and a second in 1926. He was interested all his life in theosophy, the origins of religion, and mystical experience. *The Candle of Vision* (1918) is the best guide to his religious beliefs.

Aeacus, in Greek mythology, son of Zeus and Aegina, the daughter of the river god Asopus. His mother was carried off by Zeus to the island of Oenone, afterward called by her name. Aeacus was celebrated for justice and in Attic tradition became a judge of the dead, together with Minos and Rhadamanthus. His successful prayer to Zeus for rain during a drought was commemorated by a temple at Aegina, where a festival, the Aiakeia, was held in his honour.

AEC: *see* Atomic Energy Commission.

Aechmea, genus of epiphytes (plants that are supported by other plants and have aerial roots exposed to the humid atmosphere) of the pineapple family (Bromeliaceae), with more than 140 species distributed in South America. Spiny-edged leaves, usually about 30 to 60 centimetres (about 12 to 24 inches) long, grow in a rosette from the root. A spike of red and yellow flowers, often with blue tips, grows from the centre.

Urn plant (*Aechmea fasciata*)
Sven Samelius

Many species are grown as indoor ornamentals for their colourful foliage or showy flowers. The fibrous leaves of *A. magdalenae,* native to Central and South America, are made into rope and twine.

aecium, also called AECIDIUM, a cluster-cup or fruiting body of certain rust fungi (order Uredinales, division Mycota). Yellow to orange in colour, aecia develop after fertilization and bear one-celled spores (aeciospores, or aecidiospores). Aecia are usually found on lower leaf surfaces of plants.

Aedan (king of Dalriada): *see* Aidan.

Aedesius (d. 355), Greek philosopher whose ideas had their roots in Neoplatonism, a school of philosophy that grew out of the Idealism of Plato. Aedesius founded the so-called Pergamum school of philosophy, whose major concerns were theurgy (the magic practiced by some Neoplatonists who believed miracles could be worked by the intervention of divine and beneficent spirits) and the revival of polytheism. None of his writings has survived.

Aedilberct (Old English personal name): *see under* Aethelberht.

aedile, Latin AEDILIS, plural AEDILES (from Latin *aedes,* "temple"), magistrate of ancient Rome who originally had charge of the temple and cult of Ceres. At first the aediles were two officials of the plebs, created at the same time as the tribunes (494 BC), whose sanctity they shared. These magistrates were elected in the assembly of the plebs. In 366 two curule ("higher") aediles were created. These were at first patricians; but those of the next year were plebeians and so on year by year alternately until, in the 2nd century BC, the system of alternation between classes ceased. They were elected in the assembly of the tribes, with the consul presiding. The privileges of the curule aediles included a fringed toga, a curule chair, and the right to ancestral masks—privileges perhaps extended to the plebeian aediles after 100 BC. Aediles ranked between tribunes and praetors, a greater proportion of the curule ones attaining the consulship, but the office was not necessary for advancement in a senatorial career.

The functions of the aediles were threefold: first, the care of the city (repair of temples, public buildings, streets, sewers, and aqueducts; supervision of traffic; supervision of public decency; and precaution against fires); second, the charge of the provision markets and of weights and measures and the distribution of grain, a function for which Julius Caesar added two plebeian aediles called ceriales; third, organization of certain public games, the Megalesian and the Roman games being under the curule aediles and the Plebeian games as well as those of Ceres and Flora being under the plebeian. They had judicial powers and could impose fines.

Augustus transferred the care of the games and the judicial functions to the praetors and the care of the city to appointed boards and to the prefects of the watch and of the city. Under the imperial regime the office became a step in the senatorial career for plebeians until it disappeared after the reign of Alexander Severus in the 3rd century AD.

In Roman municipalities aediles were regular magistrates and are recorded as officials in associations and clubs.

Aedui, Celtic tribe of central Gaul (occupying most of what was later Burgundy), chiefly responsible for the diplomatic situation exploited by Julius Caesar when he began his conquests in 58 BC. The Aedui had been supported by Rome since 121 BC, but they were heavily defeated *c.* 61 BC by the Sequani and lost their revenue from tolls on the Arar (Saône) River. Appealing to Rome, they were rescued by Caesar, who made them his principal allies; under Augustus they became a *civitas foederata* ("allied state"), and a new capital was built at Augustodunum (Autun). In AD 21 they joined the Treveri in a revolt but were quickly crushed by the Roman army. In AD 48 the Aedui became the first tribe of Gallia Comata to send senators to Rome.

AEG-Telefunken AG, major West German electronics and electrical equipment combine involved in the production of power generation equipment, home and industrial electrical equipment, telecommunications equipment, industrial and electronics components, and home appliances. Headquarters are in Frankfurt am Main.

The company was founded in Berlin in 1883 when the German industrialist Emil Rathenau, with financial support from Siemens and Halske, another major German electrical company, founded the Deutsche Edison Gesellschaft für angewandte Electricität (German Edison Company for Applied Electricity).

In 1887 the company was renamed the Allgemeine Elektricitäts Gesellschaft (AEG), which became largely responsible for installing Germany's first electrical system. It strung transmission lines and built electric trolley systems all across Germany before 1900.

In 1941, AEG acquired Gesellschaft für elektrische Unternehmungen AG, an electric holding company, thus tightening its grip on the German electrical market. In 1966 Telefunken AG, formerly an AEG subsidiary, was integrated into AEG, changing the company name to Allgemeine Elektricitäts Gesellschaft-AEG-Telefunken. The present name was adopted in 1978.

In the latter part of the 20th century, AEG-Telefunken faced severe financial problems, which some analysts attributed to the company's decision to continue making high-priced consumer electronics goods such as stereos and television sets long after Telefunken's prices had been undercut by foreign competitors. The German government at first refused to bail the company out of its financial crisis, and in a 1979 plan gave AEG-Telefunken's creditor banks control of the company. Even though AEG's creditor banks wrote off the company's losses in 1981 and 1982, massive outstanding debts threatened AEG's survival, and the German government finally agreed to extend credit guarantees in 1982. The company tried to help itself out of its difficulties that same year by introducing a restructuring plan which would trim down AEG's size by selling several of its consumer goods units.

Aegadian Islands (Italy): *see* Egadi Islands.

Aegaeon (Greek mythology): *see* Briareus.

Aegates Insulae (Italy): *see* Egadi Islands.

Aegean Islands, Modern Greek NÍSOI AIYAÍOU, the multitude of Greek islands in the Aegean Sea between Greece and Turkey. Geographically, they can be arranged into seven principal groups, from north to south: (1) the Thrakikón Pélagos (Thracian Sea) group, including Thásos, Samothrace (Samothráki), and Lemnos; (2) the east Aegean group, including Lesbos (Lésvos), Chios, Ikaría, and Sámos; (3) the Northern Sporades, including Skyros, a group lying off Thessaly; (4) the Cyclades, which include Melos (Mílos), Páros, Náxos, Thera (Thíra), and Andros (Euboea [Évvoia], although technically an island, is considered a part of the Greek mainland and is connected to Attica by a bridge at Chalcís); (5) the Saronic Islands west of the Cyclades, lying 5 to 50 mi (8 to 80 km) from Piraeus: Salamís, Aegina (Aíyina), Póros, Hydra (Ídhra), and Spétsai; (6) the Dodecanese, a group of 13 islands transferred to Greece by Italy after World War II, the principal island and capital of which is Rhodes; (7) Crete and associated small islands, the largest Greek island and the southernmost land in Europe. Geographically, Crete, Kárpathos, and Rhodes form an arc of giant stepping-stones from Greece to the Turkish coast of Asia Minor. Together with Ikaría, Foúrnoi, and Sámos, the Dodecanese are also known as the Southern Sporades. The *dhiamerisma* (administrative region) of the Aegean Islands encompasses the *nomoí* (departments) of Cyclados, Dodecanese, Khíos, Lésvos, and Sámos.

So numerous are the islands of the Aegean that the name Archipelago was formerly applied to the sea. Structurally the Aegean is a much-faulted, submerged old land block hemmed in by younger fold mountains of Asia Minor that are subject to frequent earthquakes. Although many of the larger islands, such as Lesbos, Chios, Rhodes, and Crete, have fertile, well-cultivated plains, most are rocky and quite barren, with terraces to conserve the sparse soil. Typical of this landscape is the Cyclades group, the southernmost island of which, Thera, has a volcano last active in 1925. The northern islands are generally more wooded than the southern, except Rhodes. The chief products of the islands are wheat, wine, oil, mastic, figs, raisins, honey, vegetables, marble, and minerals; fishing is also important. Tourism generates increasing income, with visitors attracted to the villages of whitewashed houses and their handicrafts, as well as to the impressive monuments of the great prehistoric civilization that flourished here. *See also* articles on individual islands. Pop. (1981) 428,533.

Aegean Sea, Greek AIGAÍON PÉLAGOS, Turkish EGE DENIZ, an arm of the Mediterranean Sea, located between the Greek peninsula on the west and Asia Minor on the east. About 380 mi long and 186 mi wide, it has a total area of some 83,000 sq mi (214,000 sq km). The Aegean is connected through the straits of the Dardanelles, the Sea of Marmara, and the Bosporus with the Black Sea, while the island of Crete can be taken as marking its boundary on the south. The cradle of two of the great early civilizations, those of Crete (Kríti) and Greece, from which much of modern Western culture is derived, the Aegean Sea is also an important natural feature of the Mediterranean region, possessing several unique characteristics that make it of considerable scientific interest.

The Aegean has an intricate configuration and could well be considered as a bay within the eastern Mediterranean Basin, to which it is connected by the straits to the west and east of Crete. It also has a good connection with the Ionian Sea to the west, through the strait lying between the Peloponnese peninsula of Greece and Crete. Virtually throughout the Aegean area, numerous islands large and small emerge from the clear blue waters. These are the mountain peaks of Aegeis, the name given to a now submerged land mass. At the dawn of European history, these islands facilitated contacts between the people in this area and of three continents. Throughout the entire Aegean shoreline—that is, both the continental shores surrounding the Aegean Sea and those of the islands—bays, ports, and shelter creeks are also abundant. These also facilitated the task of seamen travelling in the Aegean Sea, making longer and longer voyages possible at a time when shipbuilding was in its infancy. No other maritime area of the Mediterranean has such shoreline development as compared with its size.

The maximum depth of the Aegean is to be found in the east of Crete, where it reaches 11,627 ft (3,543 m). The rocks making up the floor of the Aegean are mainly limestone, though often greatly altered by volcanic activity that has convulsed the region in relatively recent geological times. The richly coloured sediments in the region of the islands of Santoríni (Thíra) and Mílos, in the south Aegean, are particularly interesting. During the 1970s, Santoríni, in particular, became a topic of major international scientific importance, analysis of its surrounding sediments having been linked with a possible explanation of the ancient legend of the lost island of Atlantis.

North winds prevail in the Aegean Sea, although from the end of September to the end of May, during the mild winter season, these winds alternate with milder southwesterlies. The tides of the Aegean Basin seem to follow the movements of those in the eastern Mediterranean generally. The tide of Euripus (Porthmós Evrípou)—a strait lying between continental Greece and the island of Euboea (Évvoia), in the heart of the Aegean—is, however, extremely important, as it displays a tidal phenomenon of international significance, to which it has, in fact, lent its name. The euripus phenomenon—characterized by violent and uncertain currents—has been studied since the time of Aristotle, who first provided an interpretation of the term. Aegean currents generally are not smooth, whether considered from the viewpoint of either speed or direction. They are chiefly influenced by blowing winds. Water temperatures in the Aegean are influenced by the cold water masses of low temperature that flow in from the Black Sea to the northeast. In depths of up to about 1,600 ft, temperature fluctuates around 57°–64° F (14°–18° C), while it is practically steady around 57° F at sea level.

The Aegean Sea, like the Mediterranean in general, is the most impoverished large body of water known to science. The nutrient content, as indicated by the amount of phosphates and nitrates in the water, is on the whole poor: the less saline waters coming from the Black Sea have a distinct ameliorative influence, but the role of their fertility in the Mediterranean in general has been little studied. Generally, marine life in the Aegean Sea is very similar to that of the northern area of the western basin of the Mediterranean. In view of its limpidity and as a result of its hot waters, it is not surprising that the Aegean Sea accommodates large quantities of fish at the time of their procreating maturity. Such fish enter the Aegean from other areas, notably from the Black Sea.

Aegidius ROMANUS: *see* Giles of Rome.

Aegilops, genus of grasses (order Poales) that has become an agricultural contaminant. It grows with wheat, matures at the same time, and, unless care is taken, is harvested along with it.

One species was an ancestor of bread wheat. Its origin was in southeastern Turkey, northern Iraq, and western Iran.

Aegina, Modern Greek AÍYINA, island, one of the largest in the Saronic group of Greece, about 16 mi (26 km) south-southwest of Piraeus. With an area of about 32 sq mi (83 sq km), it is an *eparkhía* (province) of the *nomós* (department) of Piraeus. The northern plains and hills are cultivated with vines and olive, fig, almond, and pistachio trees, while along the east coast stretches a ridge of light volcanic rock known as trachyte. The highest point is conical Óros (mount) Áyios Ilías (ancient Mt. Pan Hellenion), at 1,745 ft (532 m). On the west coast the chief town and port, Aegina, lies over part of the ancient town of the same name.

Inhabited since Neolithic times (*c.* 3000 BC), the island became a leading maritime power after the 7th century BC because of its strategic position, and its silver coins became currency in most of the Dorian states. Economic rivalry with Athens led to wars and to close collaboration with Persia, but at the battle of Salamis

The temple of Aphaea, Aegina, Greece
Susan McCartney—Photo Researchers

(480 BC) the island sided with Athens and prevailed. The conspicuous bravery of the tiny Aeginetan contingent (only about 40 ships) was recognized by a prize for valour. Hostility with Athens was later resumed, and at the beginning of the Peloponnesian War the Athenians deported all of Aegina's population and replaced them with Athenian settlers (431). The refugees were settled by the Spartans in the region of Thyreatis in northern Laconia. The remnants were allowed to return from exile in 404 after the defeat of Athens, but Aegina never recovered from the blow. It fell with the rest of Greece to Macedon, then to the Romans in 133 BC. It regained some prosperity under Venice (1451), but was eclipsed by a pirate raid in 1537; from that time, except for another Venetian interlude, the island remained in Turkish hands until 1826, by which time it was again a modestly successful commercial centre. It was chosen as the temporary capital of independent Greece (1826–28), but afterward the increasing concentration of business in Athens forced a gradual decay. Today it is a holiday and weekend resort for Athenians, and the ancient pottery trade is still carried on.

Aegina's period of glory was the 5th century BC, as reflected by the legacy of sculpture and the poetry of Pindar. A fairly well-preserved 5th-century-BC temple to Aphaea (Aphaia), the ancient Aeginetan deity related to the Cretan Britomartis (Artemis), is situated on a wooded crest in the east of the island. Its Doric peripheral construction (having columns surrounding the building) of local gray limestone has been partially restored. Pop. (1981) 11,127.

Aegina, Gulf of (Greece): *see* Saronic Gulf.

aegirine, a pyroxene mineral, sodium and iron silicate ($NaFe^{+3}Si_2O_6$), that is commonly found in alkaline igneous rocks, particularly in syenites and syenite pegmatites. It also occurs in crystalline schists. Aegirine forms a continuous chemical series with aegirinaugite, in which calcium replaces sodium, and magnesium and aluminum replace iron. In this series, the name acmite is given to crystals with the composition $NaFeSi_2O_6$ as well as to the reddish-brown or greenish-black pointed

Aegirine crystals from Magnet Cove, Arkansas
By courtesy of the Field Museum of Natural History, Chicago; photograph, John H. Gerard—EB Inc.

crystals approximating that composition. Aegirine generally is restricted to the dark-green to greenish-black, blunt crystals of the same composition. For detailed physical properties, *see* pyroxene (table).

aegis, in ancient Greek dress, leather cloak or breastplate generally associated with Zeus, the king of the gods, and thus thought to possess supernatural power; Zeus's daughter Athena adopted the aegis for ordinary dress. Occasionally, another god used it—*e.g.*, Apollo in the *Iliad,* where it provoked terror. As early as Homer the aegis was something more than the ordinary goatskin cloak, for it was decorated with golden tassels. A stout hide of this sort could turn a blow, like a buffcoat, and thus it often appears as a piece of armour. Later, after improvised armour of this type went out of use, it was occasionally thought of as a metal corselet.

Aegithalidae, songbird family that includes the long-tailed tits (or titmice) of the Old World and the bushtits of North America. Both groups are sometimes considered subfamilies of the family Paridae (order Passeriformes). The eight species are small, arboreal insect-eaters with long, narrow tails; tiny bills; and silky, plain plumage. The nest is a thick-walled, hanging pouch with side entrance. The best known species is the common, long-tailed tit (*Aegithalos caudatus*) of Eurasia. It is pinkish and black, with white

Long-tailed tits (*Aegithalos caudatus*)
Hans Reinhard—Bruce Coleman Ltd.

head, and its tail makes up half of its 14-centimetre (6-inch) total length. One of the world's tiniest birds is the pygmy tit (*Psaltria exilis*) of Java, with head and body length of 7 cm (3 in.).

Aegospotami, Battle of (405 BC), naval victory of Sparta over Athens, final battle of the Peloponnesian War. The fleets of the two Greek rival powers faced each other in the Hellespont for four days without battle, until on the fifth day the Spartans under Lysander surprised the Athenians in their anchorage off Aegospotami. Conon, the Athenian commander, escaped with only 20 of his 180 ships, and the three or four thousand Athenians who were captured were put to death. The victory at Aegospotami enabled Lysander to proceed against Athens itself, forcing the Athenians to surrender in April 404.

Aehrenthal, Aloys (Leopold Johann Baptist), Graf Lexa von (Count Lexa of) (b. Sept. 27, 1854, Gross-Skal, Bohemia—d. Feb. 17, 1912, Vienna), foreign minister (1906–12) of the Austro-Hungarian Dual Monarchy, whose direction of the latter's annexation of Bosnia (1908) provoked an international crisis.

Entering the imperial foreign service as attaché in Paris (1877), Aehrenthal subsequently worked at the Austrian Foreign Office and later was appointed diplomatic counsellor at St. Petersburg (now Leningrad; 1888), ambassador to Romania (1895), and four years later ambassador to Russia. In 1906 he replaced Count Agenor Goluchowski as foreign minister. As aggressive as his predecessor was restrained, he revived the dormant foreign policy of the empire.

Aehrenthal's proclamation of the annexation of Bosnia (October 1908) raised the threat of war with Russia (whose foreign minister, Izvolsky, felt himself to have been deceived in his negotiations with Aehrenthal), inflamed the Austrophobe passions of Serbia, and incurred international censure. He consistently opposed suggestions of preventive war against Italy and Russia, however, and sought to reestablish good relations with Italy, Austria's nominal ally, by supporting Italian imperialist ambitions in Libya (1911). The generally assertive course of his foreign policy also led to a cooling of relations with Germany.

Aeizanas (Ethiopian king): *see* Ezana.

Aeken, Jeroen van: *see* Bosch, Hiëronymus.

Aelfheah, SAINT, Aelfheah also spelled ELPHEGE, ALPHAGE, or ALPHEGE; also called ELPHEGE THE MARTYR or GODWINE (b. 954, Gloucestershire?, Eng.—d. April 19, 1012, Greenwich, London; feast day, April 19), archbishop of Canterbury who became popularly venerated as a martyr after his death at the hands of the Danes.

Of noble birth, he entered the Benedictine abbey of Deerhurst, Gloucestershire, and later became a hermit at Bath, Somerset, where fervid followers elected him abbot. Aelfheah was a friend of Archbishop St. Dunstan of Canterbury, through whose influence he was named bishop of Winchester in 984. Aethelred II the Unready, king of the English, sent Aelfheah as ambassador to King Olaf I Tryggvason of Norway, who in 994 entered Britain and whom Aelfheah confirmed and allegedly persuaded not to invade England again.

In 1005 he became the 29th archbishop of Canterbury and immediately went to Rome to receive the pallium (symbol of metropolitan jurisdiction) from Pope John XVIII. Back in England, he called the Council of Enham (1009?) in a futile effort to halt the social demoralization caused by the devastating Danish invasions. On Sept. 8, 1011, the Danes began their sack of Canterbury and seized Aelfheah. He was ill-treated and held seven months without ransom, which he refused to pay with money that the poor would have had to supply as taxes. Aelfheah thereupon was slain by the Danes, after first being pelted with ox bones remaining from their feast.

He was first buried at St. Paul's, London, by order of King Canute of Denmark, England, and Norway; his body was removed to Canterbury in 1023 amid great splendour. From the earliest years after his death he was venerated as a martyr. The parish church of Greenwich is dedicated to him.

Aelfled (queen of Mercia): *see* Aethelflaed.

Aelfred (Old English personal name): *see under* Alfred.

Aelfric (fl. *c.* 955–*c.* 1010, Eynsham, Oxfordshire, Eng.), Anglo-Saxon prose writer, considered the greatest of his time. He wrote both to instruct the monks and to spread the learning of the 10th-century monastic revival. *Catholic Homilies,* written in 990–992, 2 vol. (1844–46), provided orthodox sermons, based on the Church Fathers. He also wrote a Latin grammar, hence his nickname Grammaticus, and *Lives of the Saints* (1881–1900).

Aelia Capitolina, city founded in AD 135 by the Romans on the ruins of Jerusalem, which their forces, under Titus, had destroyed in AD 70. The name was given after the Second Jewish Revolt (132–135), in honour of the emperor Hadrian (whose nomen, or clan name, was Aelius) as well as the deities of the Capitoline Triad (Jupiter, Juno, and Minerva). A sanctuary to Jupiter was built on the Temple Mount, and statues of Roman deities were erected in the city, in intentional violation of Old Testament law. The area was walled, and a large foreign population imported; Jews were generally forbidden entrance to the city. The present walls of the Old City of Jerusalem follow the layout of the Roman walls. The name was used until Christianity became the official religion of the Roman Empire in the 4th century.

Aelian, Latin in full CLAUDIUS AELIANUS (b. *c.* 170, Praeneste, near Rome—d. *c.* 235), Roman author and teacher of rhetoric, who spoke and wrote so fluently in Greek—in which language his works were written—that he was nicknamed "Honey-tongued." He was an admirer and assiduous student of the writings of Plato, Aristotle, Isocrates, Plutarch, Homer, and others, and his own works are valuable for preserving numerous excerpts from earlier writers. Aelian is chiefly remembered for his *On the Nature of Animals,* curious stories of birds and other animals often in the form of anecdote, folklore, or fable that pointed a moral, which set a pattern that continued in bestiaries and medical treatises through the Dark Ages. His *Various History* related anecdotes of men and customs and miraculous events. Fragments of other works survive.

Aelianus, also called AELIANUS TACTICUS, English AELIAN (fl. early 2nd century AD), Greek military writer residing in Rome whose manual of tactics exerted considerable influence on Byzantine, Muslim, and post-15th-century European methods of warfare.

Probably written in AD 106, Aelianus' *taktikē theōria* ("Tactical Theory"), based on the art of warfare as practiced by the Hellenistic successors of Alexander the Great, was an instruction manual on arming, organizing, deploying, and manoeuvring an army in the field. Consulting previous authorities on the subject, Aelianus dealt with a force composed mainly of armoured infantry of the Greek hoplite type, with auxiliary light infantry and cavalry screens. His influence is evident in the military writings of the Byzantine emperor Leo VI (886–912); an Arab translation of the *taktikē theōria* was made about 1350. Aelianus' detailed treatise became a valuable source of knowledge for European military writers of the 16th century, when infantry once again began to supersede cavalry as the decisive arm of the battlefield.

Aelius Donatus: *see* Donatus, Aelius.

Aelius Stilo: *see* Stilo Praeconinus, Lucius Aelius.

Aelle, also spelled AELLA, or AELLI (fl. late 5th century AD), Anglo-Saxon ruler who is credited with the foundation of the kingdom of the South Saxons, or Sussex. Aelle is said to have landed near Selsey Bill (in modern West Sussex) in 477. He immediately made war on the native Britons, and in 491 he and his son Cissa massacred a British garrison at the former Roman fort of Anderida (modern Pevensey, East Sussex). His subsequent fate is unknown, but the 8th-century historian Bede wrote that Aelle was the first king to be recognized as overlord of all the English peoples south of the Humber. Drawing on Bede, the 9th-century Anglo-Saxon Chronicle described Aelle as the first *bretwalda* ("ruler of Britain").

Aelle, also spelled AELLA, or AELLI (d. 588/90), first king of Deira in Scotland, whose people threw off the Bernician overlordship upon the death of Ida, king of Bernicia. Aelle became king in 559, while Ida's descendants continued to reign in the northern kingdom. On Aelle's death the Bernician king Aethelric again subdued Deira, but Aelle's son Edwin (*q.v.*) would return to rule as the most powerful English ruler of the age.

Aelred OF RIEVAULX, SAINT, Aelred also spelled AILRED, AETHELRED, or ETHELRED (b. *c.* 1110, Hexham, Northumberland, Eng.—d. Jan. 12, 1167, Rievaulx Abbey, Yorkshire), writer, historian, and outstanding Cistercian abbot who influenced monasticism in medieval England, Scotland, and France.

Of noble birth, Aelred was reared at the court of King David I of Scotland, whose life story he later wrote and for whom he was royal steward. He entered the Cistercian abbey of Rievaulx *c.* 1134, and from 1143 to 1147 he was abbot of Revesby in Lincolnshire. In late 1147 he became abbot of Rievaulx.

An adviser to kings as well as to ecclesiastics, Aelred in 1162 persuaded King Henry II of England to ally with King Louis VII of France in support of Pope Alexander III against the Holy Roman emperor Frederick I Barbarossa. Despite poor health, Aelred led a severely ascetic life and made numerous visits to Cistercian houses in England, Scotland, and France. His spirituality, his Christocentric doctrine, and, in particular, his writings—considered among the finest produced in England during the Middle Ages—highly influenced the Cistercians and earned him the title of "the Bernard of the north" (after the celebrated reformer Bernard of Clairvaux). By 1166 illness halted his missions. His feast day is celebrated by the Cistercians on February 3.

Aelred's surviving works deal with either devotion or history. *De spirituali amicitia* ("On Spiritual Friendship"), considered to be his greatest work, is a Christian counterpart of Cicero's *De amicitia* and designates Christ the source and ultimate impetus of spiritual friendship. His historical works include the incomplete *Genealogia regum Anglorum* ("Genealogy of the English Kings") and *Vita S. Eduardi Confessoris* ("Life of St. Edward the Confessor"), written in honour of the translation of St. Edward the Confessor's body in 1163, which he witnessed. His last work is *De anima* ("On the Soul").

T.E. Harvey's *St. Aelred of Rievaulx* appeared in 1932. *De spirituali* was translated in 1942 by Hugh Talbot, and in 1952 Talbot translated Aelred's *De anima* and various sermons. *De Jesu* was translated by G. Webb and A. Walker in 1956. Aelred's life history written by Walter Daniel, a contemporary monk, was translated in 1950 by F.M. Powicke as *Ailred of Rievaulx and His Biographer Walter Daniel.*

To make the best use of the Britannica, consult the INDEX *first*

Aemilian, Latin in full MARCUS AEMILIUS AEMILIANUS (b. Mauretania—d. 253, near Spoletium, Umbria), Roman emperor for three months in 253.

Aemilian was a senator and served as consul before receiving the command of the army of Moesia (in present eastern Yugoslavia) during the reign of the emperor Gallus (ruled 251–253). After turning back an invasion by the Goths, Aemilian rebelled against the Emperor in the summer of 253 and invaded Italy. When Gallus was killed by his own troops, Aemilian became his successor. A few weeks later the Roman forces of the Upper Rhine declared their commander, Valerian, emperor. Before the two sides came to battle, Aemilian was assassinated by his troops near Spoletium.

Aemilius Lepidus, Marcus: *see* Lepidus, Marcus Aemilius.

Aemilius Papinianus: *see* Papinian.

Aeneas, mythical hero of Troy and Rome, son of the goddess Aphrodite and Anchises. Aeneas was a member of the royal line at Troy and cousin of Hector. He played a prominent part in the war to defend his city against the Greeks, being second only to Hector in ability. Homer implies that Aeneas did not like his subordinate position, and from that suggestion arose a later tradition that Aeneas helped to betray Troy to the Greeks. The more common version, however, made Aeneas the leader of the Trojan survivors. In any case, he came through the war, available to compilers of Roman myth.

The association of Homeric heroes with Italy and Sicily goes back to the 8th century BC, and the Greek colonies founded there in that and the next century frequently claimed descent from leaders in the Trojan War. Legend connected Aeneas, too, with certain places and families, especially in Latium. As Rome expanded over Italy and the Mediterranean, its patriotic writers began to construct a mythical tradition that would at once dignify their land with antiquity and satisfy a latent dislike of Greek superiority. The fact that Aeneas, as a Trojan, represented an enemy of the Greeks and that tradition left him free after the war made him peculiarly fit for the part assigned him, *i.e.,* the founding of Roman greatness.

It was Virgil who gave the various strands of legend related to Aeneas the form they have possessed ever since. The family of Julius Caesar, and consequently of Virgil's patron Augustus, claimed descent from Aeneas, whose son Ascanius was also called Iulus. Incorporating these different traditions, Virgil created his masterpiece, the *Aeneid* (*q.v.*), the Latin epic whose hero symbolized not only the course and aim of Roman history but also the career and policy of Augustus himself. In the journeying of Aeneas from Troy westward to Sicily, Carthage, and finally to the mouth of the Tiber in Italy, Virgil portrayed the qualities of persistence, self-denial, and obedience to the gods that, to the poet, built Rome.

The death of Aeneas is described by Dionysius of Halicarnassus. After he had fallen in battle against the Rutuli, his body could not be found, and he was thereafter worshipped as a local god, *Juppiter indiges,* as Livy reports.

Aeneid (written *c.* 29–19 BC), epic poem by the Roman poet Virgil. It tells in 12 books of the legendary foundation of Lavinium (parent town of Alba Longa and of Rome) by Aeneas, a Trojan who had left the burning ruins of Troy to found under supernatural guidance a new city with a glorious destiny in the West.

Aeneas, taking his family, followers, and household gods, fled from Troy after the Greek victory; but in the confusion of leaving the burning city, his wife disappeared. Her ghost informed him that he was to go to a western land where the Tiber River flowed. He then started his long voyage, touching at Thrace, Crete, and Sicily, and meeting with many adventures that culminated in shipwreck on the coast of Africa near Carthage. There he was received by Dido, the widowed queen, to whom he told his story. They fell in love, and he lingered there until sharply reminded by Mercury that Rome was his goal. Guilty and wretched, he immediately abandoned Dido, who committed suicide, and sailed on until he finally reached the mouth of the Tiber. He was well received by Latinus, the king of the region, but other Italians, notably Latinus' wife and Turnus, leader of the Rutuli, resented the Trojan arrival and the projected marriage alliance between Aeneas and Lavinia, Latinus' daughter. War broke out, but the Trojans were successful and Turnus was killed. Aeneas then married Lavinia and founded Lavinium.

Aenesidemus (b. 1st century BC, Knossos, Crete), philosopher and dialectician of the Greek Academy who revived the Pyrrhonian principle of "suspended judgment" (*epoche*) as a practical solution to the vexing and "insoluble" problem of knowledge. In his *Pyrrhonian Discourses* Aenesidemus formulated 10 tropes in defense of Skepticism, four suggesting arguments that arise from the nature of the perceiver, two dealing with the thing perceived, and four concerning the relationship between the perceiver and the thing perceived.

Aenus (Europe): *see* Inn River.

Aeoliae, Insulae (Italy): *see* Eolie Islands.

aeolian: *see under* eolian, except as below.

Aeolian harp (from Aeolus, the Greek god of wind), stringed musical instrument played by the wind. It is made of a wooden sound box about 3 feet by 5 inches by 3 inches (1 metre by 13 centimetres by 8 centimetres) loosely strung with 10 or 12 gut strings varying in thickness and elasticity, usually tuned in unison. In the wind they vibrate in aliquot parts (*i.e.,* in halves, thirds, fourths . . .) thus sounding the octave, 12th, second octave, and succeedingly higher harmonics of the string's fundamental note, which is silent.

The principle of natural vibration of strings by the pressure of the wind has long been recognized. According to legend, King David hung his *kinnor* (a kind of lyre) above his bed at night to catch the wind, and in the 10th century, Dunstan of Canterbury was charged with sorcery when the wind produced sound from his harp.

Aeolian harp
The Mansell Collection

The first known Aeolian harp was constructed by Athanasius Kircher and was described in his *Musurgia Universalis* (1650). The Aeolian harp was popular in Germany and England during the Romantic movement. Two attempts to devise a keyboard version using a bellows were the *anémocorde* (1789), invented by Johann Jacob Schnell, and the *piano éolien* (1837), by M. Isouard.

Aeolian Islands (Italy): *see* Eolie Islands.

aeolipile, steam turbine invented *c.* AD 100 by Hero of Alexandria and described in his *Pneumatica.* The aeolipile consisted of a hollow sphere mounted so that it could turn on a pair of hollow tubes that provided steam to the sphere from a cauldron. The steam escaped from the sphere from one or more

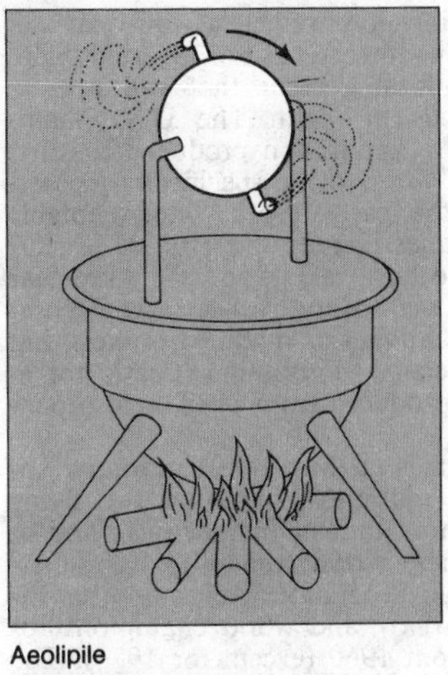

Aeolipile

By permission. From Webster's Third New International Dictionary © 1971 by G.&C. Merriam Co., Publishers of the Merriam-Webster Dictionaries

bent tubes projecting from its equator, causing the sphere to revolve. The aeolipile is the first known device to transform steam into rotary motion. Like many other machines of the time that demonstrated basic mechanical principles, it was simply regarded as a curiosity or a toy and was not used for any practical purpose.

Aeolis, also called AEOLIA, group of ancient cities on the west coast of Anatolia, which were founded at the end of the 2nd millennium BC by Greeks speaking an Aeolic dialect. The earliest settlements, located on the islands of Lesbos and Tenedos and on the mainland between Troas and Ionia, resulted from migrations during 1130–1000 BC. A second group of Aeolian settlements was colonized in the 7th century BC. At the end of the 6th century, Darius I incorporated Aeolis into one of the satrapies (provinces) of the Persian Empire.

Aeolus, in the works of Homer, controller of the winds and ruler of the floating island of Aeolia. In the *Odyssey* he gave Odysseus a favourable wind and a bag in which the unfavourable winds were confined. Odysseus' companions opened the bag; the winds escaped and drove them back to the island. Although he appears as a human in Homer, Aeolus later was described as a minor god.

Aeolus, in Greek mythology, mythical king of Magnesia in Thessaly, the son of Hellen (the eponymous ancestor of the true Greeks, or Hellenes) and father of Sisyphus (the "most crafty of men"). Aeolus' daughter Canace and son Macareus committed incest and then took their own lives. Their story provided the subject of Euripides' lost *Aeolus.* Aeolus gave his name to Aeolis, a territory on the western coast of Asia Minor.

aeon, also spelled EON (Greek: "age," or "lifetime"), in Gnosticism and Manichaeism, one of the orders of spirits, or spheres of being, that emanated from the Godhead and were attributes of the nature of the absolute; an important element in the cosmology that developed around the central concept of Gnostic dualism—the conflict between matter and spirit.

The first aeon was said to emanate directly from the unmanifest divinity and to be charged with a divine force. Successive emanations of aeons were charged with successively diminished force. Each Gnostic system explained aeons in its own way, but all concurred that aeons increased in number in proportion to their remoteness from the divinity and that lower aeons shared proportionately less in divine energy. At a certain level of remoteness, the possibility of error was said to invade the activity of aeons; in most systems, such error was responsible for the creation of the material universe. For many, Christ was the most perfect aeon, whose specific function was to redeem the error embodied in the material universe; the Holy Spirit was usually a subordinate aeon.

In certain systems, aeons were regarded positively as embodiments of the divine; in others, they were viewed negatively as vast media of time, space, and experience through which the human soul must painfully pass to reach its divine origin.

Aepinus, Franz Maria Ulrich Theodor Hoch (b. Dec. 13, 1724, Rostock, Mecklenberg-Schwerin—d. Aug. 10, 1802, Dorpat, Russia), physicist whose *Tentamen theoriae electricitatis et magnetismi* (1759; "An Attempt at a Theory of Electricity and Magnetism") was the first work to apply mathematics to the theory of electricity and magnetism.

Aepinus studied medicine before turning to physics and mathematics. His work in these new fields resulted in his election to the Berlin Academy of Sciences and, in 1757, led to a professorship of physics in St. Petersburg. He remained in St. Pétersburg until his retirement in 1798.

Aepinus' experiments led to the design of the parallel-plate capacitor, a device used to store energy in an electric field. He also discovered the electric properties of the mineral tourmaline and investigated pyroelectricity, the state of electrical polarization produced in tourmaline and various other crystals by a change of temperature. In addition, Aepinus studied the relation between conductors and nonconductors, extended Benjamin Franklin's one-fluid theory of electricity, and explained virtually all electric induction in terms of the attraction, repulsion, and flow of electricity in conductors.

Aepinus improved the microscope, and his essay on the effects of parallax in the transit of a planet across the Sun's disk excited great general interest, for it was published in 1764, between the dates of two transits of Venus.

Aepyornis, extinct genus of giant flightless birds found as fossils in Pleistocene and post-Pleistocene deposits on the island of Madagascar. Remains of *Aepyornis* are abundant; of the several known species, most were massively constructed, with four-toed feet and relatively small wings useless for flight. Characteristically, the skull in *Aepyornis* was of small size; the neck was long and slim. Some forms of *Aepyornis* attained very large size; *Aepyornis titan* stood more than 3 metres (10 feet) high. The fossilized remains of *Aepyornis* eggs are relatively common, both fragmented and intact; sometimes they contain the bones of embryonic young. The eggs of the giant forms were also large. One of the largest intact specimens is almost one metre (about three feet) in circumference and probably had a capacity of about nine litres (more than two gallons).

Aepyornis occurs relatively late in the geologic record and its ancestry is uncertain. The rather late appearance of *Aepyornis* in Madagascar, however, may represent a relict situation; the genus was probably much more widespread during earlier geologic time. Fragmentary remains of bone and eggshell are known from the Eocene deposits of northern Africa (the Eocene Epoch began 54,000,000 years ago and lasted 16,000,000 years); the fragments may represent forms that were closely related to the ancestors of *Aepyornis,* indicating the formerly wider distribution of the genus.

Aequi, ancient people of Italy originally inhabiting the region watered by the tributaries of the Avens River (modern Velino). Long hostile to Rome, they became especially menacing in the 5th century BC, advancing to the Alban Hills. Although repulsed by the Romans in 431, the Aequi were not completely subdued by Rome until the end of the Second Samnite War (304 BC), when they received *civitas sine suffragio* ("citizenship without voting rights"). The establishment of the Latin colony of Carsioli (302 BC) and the extension of the Via Valeria through the territory of the Aequi aided the rapid Romanization of that people.

Aer Lingus, national airline of Ireland, comprising two government-owned companies: (1) Aer Lingus Teoranta, incorporated in 1936 and operating air services within Ireland and between Ireland and Britain and continental Europe, and (2) Aerlinte Eireann Teoranta, incorporated in 1947 and operating air services between Ireland and the United States and Canada. Though legally separate and governed by separate boards of directors, the two companies share a common management. Headquarters are at Dublin Airport.

The airline's first route, inaugurated on May 27, 1936, extended from Dublin to Bristol and, in the same year, was extended to London. Other flights prior to World War II were routed to Liverpool and the Isle of Man. After the war, service was inaugurated to Paris and Amsterdam and eventually expanded to other European cities. The first transatlantic routes, from Dublin through Shannon International Airport to New York and Boston, were inaugurated in 1958; flights to Chicago and Montreal began in 1966.

aerarium, treasury of ancient Rome, housed in the Temple of Saturn and the adjacent *tabularium* (record office) in the Forum. Under the republic (*c.* 509–27 BC) it was managed by two finance magistrates, the urban quaestors, and controlled by the Senate. In theory all revenues were paid into the *aerarium,* and all public payments were made from it. In practice, money was moved from the provinces to the *aerarium* only if the province, after paying the governor's allowance, produced a surplus. Conversely, money was paid out of the *aerarium* only if the provincial revenue did not cover expenses. All accounts, however, had to be balanced with the *aerarium,* which was thus a central clearinghouse.

Under the principate (27 BC–AD 305) the *aerarium* gradually lost importance as the emperors, under whose seal most of the public money was spent, drew funds from provincial depots (*fisci*) and did not account to the *aerarium.* In AD 6 the emperor Augustus founded a second treasury, the *aerarium militare* (the old treasury was thereafter known as *aerarium Saturn,* eventually becoming the municipal treasury of the city of Rome). The new treasury's function was to pay bounties to discharged veterans or purchase land for them. It was supplied with funds from taxes (sales, inheritance, and property) collected by the Emperor's procurators.

aerial perspective, also called ATMOSPHERIC PERSPECTIVE, method of creating the illusion of depth, or recession, in a painting or drawing by modulating colour to simulate changes effected by the atmosphere on the colours of things seen at a distance. Although the use of aerial perspective has been known since antiquity, Leonardo da Vinci first used the term aerial perspective in his *Treatise on Painting,* in which he wrote: "Colours become weaker in proportion to their distance from the person who is looking at them." It was later discovered that the presence in the atmosphere of moisture and of tiny particles of dust and similar material causes a scattering of light as it passes through them, the degree of scattering being dependent on the wavelength, which corresponds to the colour, of the light. Because light of short wavelength—blue light—is scattered most, the colours of all distant dark objects tend toward blue; for example, distant mountains have a bluish cast. Light of long wavelength—red light—is scattered least; thus, distant bright objects appear redder because some of the blue is scattered and lost from the light by which they are seen.

Examples of aerial perspective have been found in Greco-Roman wall paintings and in Chinese paintings of the 8th century. The techniques had been lost from European art during the Middle Ages and was rediscovered by Flemish painters of the 15th century, whose development of oil painting permitted great sophistication and subtlety in the manipulation of pigment to produce complex colour effects.

Aerial perspective was popular with such 16th-century artists as Correggio and Titian, and it was used with considerable effect in the 17th century by Rubens, Claude Lorrain, and Hobbema. The technique reached its apogee in the 19th century in the paintings of J.M.W. Turner and of some of the Impressionists. The principles of aerial perspective also played an important part in the works of such 19th-century English watercolourists as John Sell Cotman and Richard Parkes Bonington. *See also* perspective.

aerial photography, technique of photographing the Earth's surface or features of its atmosphere with cameras mounted on aircraft, rockets, or satellites and other spacecraft.

For terrestrial mapping, aerial photographs usually are taken in overlapping series from an aircraft following a systematic flight pattern at a fixed altitude. Each photograph depicts an area that includes several control points, the locations of which are determined by ground surveying techniques. A technique known as photogrammetry, which involves the simultaneous projection of the overlapping views, makes possible the preparation of contour maps or three-dimensional models of the surface. Much information on rock type and structure, soils, vegetation, and hydrology can be obtained by a viewer trained to interpret terrain features. Views of cloud patterns obtained from orbiting satellites are valuable in weather forecasting.

aero-otitis: *see* ear squeeze.

aerobatics, the sport of flying an airplane through such unusual manoeuvres as rolls, loops, stalls, and spins. The term, derived in imitation of acrobatics, came into use during World War I to describe what had earlier been called stunt flying (*q.v.*). As an organized sport, rather than as an airshow attraction or a part of military aviation training, aerobatics began international competition in 1964.

A plane for aerobatics needs extra strength in construction, low weight, a wing that will develop lift in either upright or inverted flight, and fuel and oil systems that will operate in both kinds of flight. The U.S. Champion Aircraft Corporation produced the first post-World War II plane specifically for aerobatics in the early 1960s. Other notable aerobatic planes include the Yak (U.S.S.R.), the Zlin (Czechoslovakia), and the Akro Star (West Germany). Many planes in U.S. competition are antiques or modified trainers, but the Pitts Special, a sports and aerobatic home-built plane, produced from 1948, is also popular.

Competition is at three levels: primary, advanced, and unlimited, the latter two flying more and more difficult manoeuvres and at lower altitudes. World competition is supervised by the Fédération Aéronautique Internationale (FAI), and world championships were held from 1960 (except for 1974). The annual contest of the Experimental Aircraft Association (U.S.) is one of the largest. Aerobatic contests are held in a zone from 100 to 1,000 metres (328 to 3,280 feet) in altitude, 1,000 m long and 800 m wide. Teams, both men's and women's, have three to five pilots. Planes are piston-engined with from 150 to 350 horsepower. Judging is based on methods introduced by Spanish aerobatic flyer José L. Aresti.

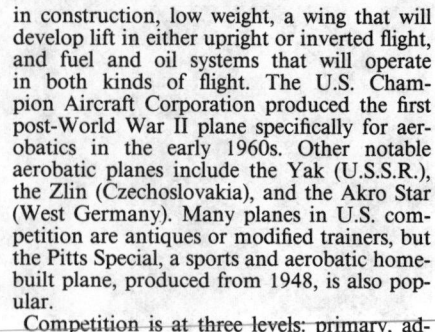

Aerial perspective
(Top) "Banks of the Seine in Autumn," Impressionist painting in oil by Alfred Sisley, in the Städelsches Kunstinstitut, Frankfurt, W.Ger.; (bottom) "Landscape with Flight into Egypt," oil painting by the Flemish painter Joachim Patinir, 1520, in the Koninklijk Museum voor Schone Kunsten, Antwerp, Belg.

By courtesy of (top) the Stadelsches Kunstinstitut, Frankfurt am Main, W. Ger., (bottom) Koninklijk Museum voor Schone Kunsten, Antwerp, Belg.

aerobe, an organism able to live and reproduce in the presence of free oxygen (*e.g.,* certain bacteria and certain yeasts). Organisms that grow in the absence of free oxygen are termed anaerobes; those that grow only in the absence of oxygen are obligate, or strict, anaerobes. Some species, called facultative anaerobes, are able to grow either with or without free oxygen. Certain others, able to grow in the presence of minute amounts of oxygen, are called microaerophiles.

aerobics, system of physical conditioning developed to increase the efficiency of the body's intake of oxygen. Typical aerobic exercises (*e.g.,* walking, running, swimming, dancing, and cycling) stimulate heart and lung activity long enough to produce beneficial changes in the body. A point-system chart is used to demonstrate the amount of energy expended on an exercise. As individuals progressively upgrade the quantity and quality of exercise, they can gauge their improvement through the point system. Aerobic charts have been developed for different age groups and for various types of exercise. The term was popularized in Kenneth H. Cooper's *Aerobics* (1968) and *The Aerobics Way* (1977).

aerodontalgia: *see* tooth squeeze.

aerodrome: *see* airport.

aerodynamics, branch of physics that deals with the motion of air and other gaseous fluids and with the forces acting on bodies passing through such a fluid. Aerodynamics seeks, in particular, to explain the principles governing the flight of aircraft, rockets, and missiles. It is also concerned with the design of automobiles, high-speed trains, and ships, as well as with the construction of such structures as bridges and tall buildings to determine their resistance to high winds.

Observations of the flight of birds and projectiles stirred speculation among the ancients as to the forces involved and the manner of their interaction. They, however, had no real knowledge of the physical properties of air, nor did they attempt a systematic study of those properties. Most of their ideas reflected a belief that the air provided a sustaining or impelling force. These notions were based to a large degree on the principles of hydrostatics (the study of the pressures of liquids) as they were then understood. Thus, in early times, it was thought that the impelling force of a projectile was associated with forces exerted on the base by the closure of the flow of air around the body. This conception of air as an assisting medium rather than a resisting force persisted for centuries, even though in the 16th century it was recognized that the energy of motion of a projectile was imparted to it by the catapulting device.

Near the end of the 15th century, Leonardo da Vinci observed that air offered resistance to the movement of a solid object and attributed this resistance to compressibility effects. Galileo later established the fact of air resistance experimentally and arrived at the conclusion that the resistance was proportional to the velocity of the object passing through it. In the late 17th century, Christiaan Huygens and Sir Isaac Newton determined that air resistance to the motion of a body was proportional to the square of the velocity.

Newton's work in setting forth the laws of mechanics marked the beginning of the classical theories of aerodynamics. He considered the pressure acting on an inclined plate as arising from the impingement of particles on the side of the plate that faces the airstream. His formulation yielded the result that the pressure acting on the plate was proportional to the product of the density of the air, the area of the plate, the square of the velocity, and the square of the sine of the angle of inclination. This failed to account for the effects of the flow on the upper surface of the plate where low pressures exist and from which a major portion of the lift of a wing is produced. The idea of air as a continuum with a pressure field extending over great distances from the plate was to come much later.

Various discoveries were made during the 18th and 19th centuries that contributed to a better understanding of the factors influencing the movement of solid bodies through air. The relationship of resistance to the viscous properties of a fluid, for example, was perceived in part by the early 1800s, and the experiments of the British physicist Osborne Reynolds in the 1880s brought into clearer view the significance of viscous effects.

Modern aerodynamics emerged about the time that the Wright brothers made their first powered flight (1903). Several years after their historic effort, Frederick W. Lanchester, a British engineer, proposed a circulation theory of lift of an airfoil of infinite span and a vortex theory of the lift of a wing of finite span. The German physicist Ludwig Prandtl, commonly regarded as the father of modern aerodynamics, arrived independently at the same hypotheses as Lanchester and developed the mathematical treatment. Prandtl's work, refined and expanded by subsequent investigators, formed the theoretical foundation of the field. Among others who played a prominent role in the development of modern aerodynamics was the Hungarian-born engineer Theodore von Kármán, whose contributions led to major advances in such areas as turbulence theory and supersonic flight.

Aeroflot, byname of GLAVNOE UPRAVLENIE GRAZHDANSKOGO VOZDUSHNOGO FLOTA (Russian: Main Civil Air Fleet Administration), Soviet state airline founded in 1928 (as Dobroflot) and reorganized in 1932 under its current name. Although few precise figures on passenger-miles and revenue are published, Aeroflot is the world's largest airline, with about 15 percent of all civil air traffic.

Dobroflot, or Dobrovolny Flot (Volunteer Fleet), the new government-owned company created by the first Five-Year Plan in 1928, grew out of two former concerns: Dobrolyot, or Rossiyskoye obshchestvo dobrovolnogo vozdushnogo flota (Russian Volunteer Air Fleet), founded in 1923, and Ukvozdukhput, or Ukrainian Airways, founded in 1925. These airlines together connected such cities as Moscow, Gorky, Kiev, Kharkov, and Odessa. After Dobroflot was reorganized as Aeroflot in 1932, progress was rapid; by 1935 Aeroflot's routes spanned the Soviet Union from Leningrad to Vladivostok, with a network of lines also extending southward to the Black Sea, the Caucasus, and Central Asia. By the 1980s Aeroflot was flying to all continents (including, on occasion, to Antarctica), serving most of the major cities of Europe, Africa, the Middle East, South and Southeast Asia, and the Far East, as well as a few cities of the Western Hemisphere.

In addition to its primary function of providing passenger and freight transportation, Aeroflot is responsible for such domestic operations as crop-spraying, surveying, fishery protection, rescue work, and ambulance service.

aerofoil (aircraft): *see* airfoil.

Aeroméxico, formerly (until 1971) AERONAVES DE MÉXICO, SA, Mexican airline founded in 1934 as a private corporation but, since 1959, completely owned by the Mexican government.

The first scheduled services began in 1934 between Mexico City and Acapulco. By 1940 Pan American Airways had acquired 40 percent of Aeronaves' holdings and, in the succeeding dozen years, merged several independent Mexican lines, improved equipment, and enlarged the route network. Pan American's holdings were gradually reduced, however (to accord with new requirements of Mexican laws governing foreign ownership), and in 1959 the Mexican government took over the airline's total stock. The current name was adopted in 1971. Over the years, more companies were acquired and more routes developed so that by 1980 Aeroméxico was servicing cities in Mexico, the United States, Canada, Europe, and South America.

aeronautical engineering, field of engineering concerned with the development, design, construction, testing, and operation of aircraft and space vehicles.

A brief treatment of aeronautical engineering follows. For full treatment, *see* MACROPAEDIA: Engineering.

Historically, aeronautical engineering traces its roots back to balloon flight, gliders, and airships. But the real expansion of activity came with the first mechanically powered and controlled flight of the Wright brothers' "Flyer" in December 1903 at Kitty Hawk in North Carolina.

During the 1960s the concept of aeronautical engineering was broadened to include all vehicles that operate above the surface of the Earth, in outer space as well as in the atmosphere. The terms aerospace engineering, or aeronautical and astronautical engineering, are sometimes used to describe this broadened discipline. In addition to space vehicles, all types of hovercraft are included in this field of engineering.

The principal technologies encompassed by aeronautical engineering are those of aerodynamics, propulsion, structures and stability, and control. The aeronautical engineering process begins in academic, industrial, and government research centres. Industrial designers, using the latest technological developments, propose an initial vehicle design calculated to satisfy the particular requirements specified. This initial design is followed by a long process, lasting months and sometimes years, in which the design and development of the many vehicle components are carried out by aeronautical engineers. The design process precedes the construction and testing of one or more prototype vehicles. Satisfactory completion of flight testing of prototypes is followed by quantity production and operation. Aeronautical engineers participate in all steps of these processes.

The history of aeronautical engineering has been prone to revolutionary leaps in technology, coupled with the slower but continual evolutionary development of basic processes. The metal monocoque fuselage, the cantilevered monoplane wing, the jet engine, supersonic flight, and space flight are such examples. In fact, the post-World War II period was one of rapid change in aeronautical engineering, as new knowledge in aerodynamics, structures, propulsion, stability, and control developed at increasing rates. Low-speed aerodynamics gave way to transonic, supersonic, and hypersonic aerodynamics; frame structures were replaced by thin, metallic shells that required the development of new aluminum, magnesium, titanium, and steel alloys; internal combustion engines were replaced by rocket and turbojet engines; and manual control developed into automatic control.

The practice of aeronautical engineering rests upon principles fundamental to all flight vehicles—a propulsion system with high thermodynamic and propulsive efficiencies, a structure of minimum weight and maximum strength, an external shape that is stable in flight with maximum aerodynamic efficiency, a precision control and guidance system, and a suitable design compromise among all these elements that allows the vehicle to achieve the required performance. An understanding of these principles depends upon knowledge of the engineering sciences: materials science, solid and structural mechanics, thermodynamics, fluid mechanics, and electrical science. In turn, the engineering sciences rest upon the basic sciences of physics, chemistry, and mathematics.

The largest employers of aeronautical engineers are the aircraft and aerospace industries and the supporting subcontractors associated with those industries. Aeronautical engineers employed in such activities are engaged in a wide variety of duties ranging from basic research on fundamental principles to hardware design and production.

The second largest employer in most countries is the government. Here the engineer's duties lie principally in research, development, and procurement. Aeronautical engineers are also employed to a limited extent by universities and airlines. Important engineering functions must be carried out by the airlines in acquiring new equipment and in the maintenance and operation of equipment.

Aeronaves de México, SA: *see* Aeroméxico.

aeronomy, study of the physics and chemistry of the upper atmosphere, including the distribution of temperature, density, and chemical constituents, and the chemical reactions that occur. Studies of aurora, airglow, the ionosphere, Van Allen radiation belts, cosmic rays, and radiative and photochemical phenomena exemplify the diverse subjects that properly come under the heading of aeronomy.

aerophone, any of a class of musical instruments in which a vibrating mass of air produces the initial sound. The basic types include woodwind, brass, and free-reed instruments, as well as instruments that fall into none of these groups, such as the bull-roarer and the siren. Bagpipes and organs are hybrids with different kinds of pipes. The word aerophone replaces the term wind instrument when an acoustically based classification is desired. *See also* chordophone; electrophone; idiophone; membranophone.

aeroplane: *see* airplane.

aerosinusitis (sinus malady): *see* sinus squeeze.

aerosol, a system of liquid or solid particles uniformly distributed in a finely divided state through a gas, usually air; aerosol particles play an important role in weather in the precipitation process, providing the nuclei upon which condensation or freezing takes upon which condensation or freezing takes place. They participate in chemical processes and influence the electrical properties of the atmosphere.

True aerosol particles range in diameter from a few millimicrometres to about one micrometre (equal to 10^{-4} centimetre). When smaller particles are in suspension, the system begins to acquire the properties of a true solution; for larger particles, the settling rate is usually so rapid that the system cannot properly be called a true aerosol. Nevertheless, the term is commonly employed, especially in the case of fog or cloud droplets and dust particles, which can have diameters of more than 100 micrometres.

In general, aerosols composed of particles larger than about 50 micrometres are unstable unless the air turbulence is extreme, as in a severe thunderstorm. Particles with a diameter of less than 0.1 micrometre are sometimes referred to as Aitken nuclei.

aerosol container, any package, usually a metal can or plastic bottle, designed to dispense its liquid contents as a mist or foam. This type of container was developed in 1941 by the U.S. Army for dispensing insecticides. Since that time a wide variety of products

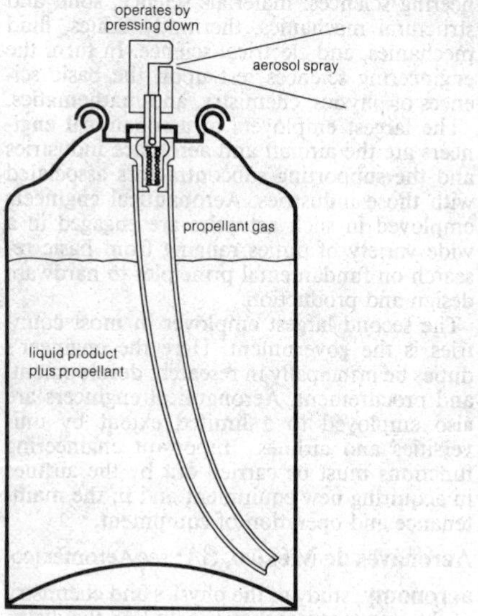

Cross section of a typical spray aerosol container

From *Kirk-Othmer Encyclopedia of Chemical Technology*, vol. 1 (copyright 1963); by permission of John Wiley & Sons, Inc.

ranging from disinfectants to whipping cream have been packaged in aerosol containers.

The most common type of aerosol container consists of a shell, a valve, a "dip tube" that extends from the valve to the liquid product, and a liquefied gas propellant under pressure. The liquid product is generally mixed with the propellant. When the valve is opened, this solution moves up the dip tube and out the valve. The propellant vaporizes as it is released into the atmosphere, dispersing the product in the form of fine particles. In foam packs, such as shaving cream, the propellant and product are present together as an emulsion. On release, the liquid vaporizes, whipping the whole into a foam.

Chlorofluorocarbons, often called Freons, were used extensively as propellants in aerosol spray products manufactured in the United States until 1978, when the federal government banned most uses of those compounds because of their potentially harmful environmental effect. Scientific studies indicated that chlorofluorocarbons released into the air rise up to the stratosphere, where they catalyze the decomposition of ozone molecules. The stratospheric ozone helps shield animal life from the Sun's intense ultraviolet radiation, which can cause skin cancer.

In compliance with the federal ban, U.S. manufacturers have substituted hydrocarbons, nitrous oxide, and carbon dioxide for chlorofluorocarbons in most aerosol products. They also have developed aerosol containers that use air pressure produced by hand-operated pumps instead of a propellant.

aerospace medicine, specialized branch of medical science concerned with medical problems encountered in connection with human flight in the atmosphere (aviation medicine) and beyond the atmosphere (space medicine).

The ultimate aim of this specialty is to promote the safety and effectiveness of humans while they are exposed to the stresses of aerospace flight, such as extreme temperatures, low atmospheric pressure, radiation, noise, vibrations, oxygen deprivation, and the strong forces of acceleration and deceleration. Other hazards of space flight include weightlessness, motion sickness, pilot fatigue, discomfort from hunger or sleepiness due to the absence of the Earth's day-and-night cycle, and psychological disturbances caused by confinement and isolation. These problems, however, are generally prevented by intensive preflight training in high-powered simulators and by careful design of equipment and spacecraft.

The 19th-century French physiologist Paul Bert is generally regarded as the father of modern aviation medicine. His classic observations of the effects of both high and low air pressure on balloonists were used extensively beginning in World War II and prompted a broad and vigorous program of research. In 1948 the first unit for space research in the world was established in the United States, and as major technological advances were made in space flight, space medicine became recognized as an important medical specialty.

Specialists in civil and military aerospace medicine establish and apply appropriate medical standards for the certification and selection of pilots and other flight personnel to assure that they have no physical limitations or medical conditions that could impair their performance. Physicians who are trained in aerospace medicine are known as flight surgeons.

Aerospace medical specialists plan and help to carry out flight crew training in first aid and in the prevention of illness and injuries among passengers; they also assist in training paramedical personnel in the aerial transportation of patients. Such specialists also apply the principles of preventive medicine to avert the spread of disease by air travel. In addition, they conduct postflight medical evaluations of astronauts to identify any adverse effects of space flight on the body. During space flight, they monitor physiologic responses of astronauts and advise them on the management of in-flight medical problems. Beyond the scope of clinical medicine, they often help to develop the vehicles, emergency systems, and protective equipment for manned aerospace flight.

aerotitis: *see* ear squeeze.

Aeschbacher, Hans (b. Jan. 18, 1906, Zürich), Swiss sculptor of severe and massive abstract forms.

Trained as a printer, he taught himself to draw and paint and began sculpting around the age of 30; his earliest pieces were figurative, composed mainly from terra-cotta and plaster. By 1945 he was working essentially with stone, and his sculptures became increasingly abstract, geometrical, and austere. With "Abstract Faces" (1945) Aeschbacher eliminated representational detail from his unified architectonic stone volumes. His predominant use of porous lava rock in the mid-1950s relieved some of the rigidity of his forms. Though his sculptures of the late '50s were less austere, Aeschbacher soon returned to the massive scale (some pieces 15 feet in height) and stern geometry of his previous work. "Explorer I," placed at the Zürich-Kloten Airport, is exemplary.

Aeschines (b. 390 BC—d. *c.* 314), Athenian orator who advocated peace with Philip II of Macedonia and who was a bitter political opponent of the statesman Demosthenes.

In 346 he, like Demosthenes, was a member of the embassies to Philip II that resulted in the peace of Philocrates. During the negotiations Aeschines changed his policy in favour of Macedonia, and after the peace had been concluded Demosthenes and Timarchus prepared to prosecute him for treason. In retaliation Aeschines successfully indicted Timarchus for gross immorality, and at his own trial in 343 he was acquitted by a narrow majority.

In 339, by provoking the council of the Delphic Amphictyony to declare a sacred war against the town of Amphissa, in Locris, Aeschines enabled Philip to enter central Greece as the champion of the Amphictyonic forces. The result was the defeat of Athens and Boeotia at Chaeronea, and the bitter hostility between Aeschines and Demosthenes worsened in the years that followed. In 336 Aeschines brought suit against a certain Ctesiphon for illegally proposing the award of a crown to Demosthenes in recognition of his services to Athens. The case, tried in 330, concluded with the overwhelming defeat of Aeschines, largely, no doubt, because of Demosthenes' brilliant speech for Ctesiphon ("On the Crown"). Aeschines left Athens for Rhodes, where he is said to have taught rhetoric.

Three of his speeches are extant: (1) in accusation of Timarchus; (2) in defense of his own conduct on the embassies to Philip; and (3) in accusation of Ctesiphon. These appear to have been the only speeches he wrote, as opposed to those he delivered extempore. They show a tendency to superlative expression and exaggeration, free use of rhetorical figures, variety of sentence construction, fondness for poetical quotations, and ready wit.

Aeschylus (b. 525/524 BC—d. 456/455 BC, Gela, Sicily), first of classical Athens' great tragic dramatists who raised the emerging art to great heights of poetry and theatrical power.

A brief account of the life and works of Aeschylus follows; for a full biography, *see* MACROPAEDIA: Greek Dramatists.

Aeschylus, the son of Euphorion, was born into an intensely political era and made political man the focus of his tragedies, in which humanitarian considerations conflict with personal ones. He fought and was wounded at Marathon (490 BC), where Athens defeated the invading Persians, and he again fought against the Persians when they invaded Greece in 480. His first prize in a dramatic contest was in 484 BC, followed 12 years later by his earliest extant work *Persai* (*Persians*).

After a visit to the court of Hieron I at Syracuse, Sicily, where Aeschylus wrote a pageant, *The Women of Etna*, he had a series of successes in the 460s and 450s with three trilogies, only one of which, the *Oresteia*, has survived complete. It consisted of *Agamemnon, Choephoroi* (*The Libation Bearers*), and *Eumenides* (*The Furies*). Of the Oedipus trilogy only *Hepta epi Theobas* (*Seven Against Thebes*) survives, and of the Danaid trilogy only *Hiketides* (*Suppliants*) survives. *Prometheus desmotes* (*Prometheus Bound*), possibly his last play and probably written as part of a trilogy, shows signs of having been influenced by the work of Sophocles.

Aeschylus went again to Sicily, where he died. He is credited with introducing the second actor, as well as spectacular scenic and costume effects, and he reduced the role of the chorus. His two sons, also tragedians, presented his works posthumously.

Aesculapius (Greek mythology): *see* Asclepius.

Aesir, Old Norse ÆSIR, singular ÁSS, in Scandinavian mythology, either of two main groups of deities, four of whom were common to the Germanic nations: Odin (*q.v.*), chief of the Aesir; Frigg (*q.v.*), Odin's wife; Tyr (*q.v.*), god of war; and Thor (*q.v.*), whose name was the Teutonic word for thunder. Some of the other important Aesir were Balder, Jörd, Heimdall, and Loki (*qq.v.*).

Aesop, the name traditionally assigned to the author of a collection of Greek fables; he is almost certainly a legendary figure. Various attempts were made in ancient times to establish him as an actual personage. Herodotus in the 5th century BC said that he had lived in the 6th century and that he was a slave, and Plutarch in the 1st century AD made him adviser to Croesus, the 6th-century-BC king of

Aesop, with a fox, from the central medallion of a kylix, *c.* 470 BC; in the Gregorian Etruscan Museum, the Vatican
Alinari—Art Resource/EB Inc.

Lydia. One tradition holds that he came from Thrace, while a later one styles him a Phrygian. An Egyptian biography of the 1st century AD places him on the island of Samos as a slave who gained his freedom from his master, thence going to Babylon as riddle solver to King Lycurgus, and, finally, meeting his death at Delphi. The probability is that Aesop was no more than a name invented to provide an author for fables centring on beasts, so that "a story of Aesop" became synonymous with "fable." The importance of fables lay not so much in the story told as in the moral derived from it.

The first known collection of the fables ascribed to Aesop was produced by Demetrius Phalareus in the 4th century BC, but it did not survive beyond the 9th century AD. A collection of fables that relied heavily on the Aesop corpus was that of Phaedrus, which was produced at Rome in the 1st century AD.

The fables may have been preserved in writing because it was convenient for speakers to have a collection of stories available for their use.

Not until Phaedrus were the Aesop stories meant to be read consecutively as literature. His treatment of them greatly influenced the way in which they were used by later writers, notably by the 17th-century French poet and fabulist Jean de La Fontaine.

Aesopus, Claudius, Claudius also spelled CLODIUS (fl. 1st century BC), most eminent of the Roman tragedians, contemporary and intimate friend of Cicero, whom he instructed in elocution, and regarded by Horace as the equal of the great Roman comic actor Roscius. Aesopus became completely absorbed in his roles; the biographer Plutarch mentions that, while playing the part of Atreus deliberating revenge, Aesopus forgot himself and in the heat of the moment struck and killed another actor. Aesopus made a last appearance in 55 BC at the dedication of the Roman ruler Pompey's new theatre; Cicero mentions that Aesopus was advanced in years at that time.

Aestheticism, movement in Europe in the late 19th century that centred on the doctrine that art exists for the sake of its beauty alone.

The movement began in reaction to prevailing utilitarian social philosophies and to what was perceived as the ugliness and philistinism of the industrial age. Its philosophical foundations were laid in the 18th century by Immanuel Kant, who postulated the autonomy of aesthetic standards from morality, utility, or pleasure. This idea was amplified by Goethe, J.L. Tieck, and others in Germany and by Samuel Taylor Coleridge and Thomas Carlyle in England. The movement was popularized in France by Madame de Staël, Théophile Gautier, and the philosopher Victor Cousin, who coined the phrase *l'art pour l'art* ("art for art's sake") in 1818.

In England, the artists of the Pre-Raphaelite Brotherhood, from 1848, had sown the seeds of Aestheticism, and the work of Dante Gabriel Rossetti, Edward Burne-Jones, and Algernon Charles Swinburne exemplified it in expressing a yearning for ideal beauty through conscious medievalism. The attitudes of the movement were also represented in the writings of Oscar Wilde and Walter Pater and the illustrations of Aubrey Beardsley in the periodical *The Yellow Book.* The painter James McNeill Whistler raised the movement's ideal of the cultivation of refined sensibility to perhaps its highest point.

Contemporary critics of Aestheticism included William Morris and John Ruskin and, in Russia, Leo Tolstoy, who questioned the value of art divorced from morality. The movement's worship of sensation also became increasingly disreputable. Yet the movement focussed attention on the formal aesthetics of art and contributed to the art criticism of Roger Fry and Bernard Berenson. It was unparochial in its affinities with the French Symbolist movement, fostered the arts and crafts movement, and sponsored Art Nouveau, with its decisive impact on 20th-century art.

aesthetics, also spelled ESTHETICS, branch of philosophy concerned with the nature of beauty, art, and taste, as well as with the creation and appreciation of art.

A brief treatment of Western aesthetics follows. For full treatment, including analogous concerns of Eastern philosophical traditions, *see* MACROPAEDIA: Aesthetics.

The word aesthetic comes from the Greek for "sensation," and its modern use derives from the philosopher Alexander Baumgarten, who in his *Reflections on Poetry* (1735) argued that sensation is an important ingredient in the judgment of beauty. This judgment is concerned only with appearances and the order contained in appearances. The name was then extended to cover everything that critics and philosophers of the 18th century had subsumed under the idea of taste, by which was meant the discriminating enjoyment of nature and art. In its modern form the subject owes its structure to Immanuel Kant, whose *Critique of Judgement* (1790) attempted to show the place occupied by the idea of beauty in a person's apprehension of the world. For Kant, aesthetic judgment is a fundamental capacity of reason. Without it, man should be deprived of an essential instrument of understanding and unable to conceive the transcendental nature of the world. With it, he is able to construct the necessary bridge between active and thinking natures and find in the heart of experience itself the intimation of a divine order that justifies and redeems conduct.

Among the central issues of aesthetics is that of the nature of aesthetic judgment itself and of its relation to moral judgment on the one hand and scientific judgment on the other. Philosophers have tended to agree that there is indeed a kind of thinking that concerns appearances alone and in which sensory experiences are inextricably mingled. Those who consider taste to be nothing more than arbitrarily rationalized preference would reject the term judgment altogether. Some philosophers, however, including Kant, argue that aesthetic judgment is founded in reason and that it is never simply a matter of unconsidered preference.

A second important question concerns the validity of the notion of a right and wrong in matters of taste. Some aestheticians believe that there is indeed a right and wrong, founded in criteria that all reasonable beings will recognize. Others argue that there is only the appearance of a right and wrong. Still others say that, although there is no absolute and objective answers to a question of taste, all aesthetic judgments can be defended by incorporating them into a canon, itself expressing the distilled wisdom and experience of a culture. Closely related to this issue is that of the role of aesthetic judgment in human life as a whole. Many philosophers, notably G.W.F. Hegel, follow Kant in thinking that the aesthetic is an essential dimension of human experience and that without it the human being is incomplete.

A fourth question concerns the state of mind appropriate to, or required by, aesthetic experience. Some philosophers maintain that aesthetic experience and judgment are possible only for the person who puts himself in a disinterested or distanced state of mind so as to cease all practical involvement with, and all theoretical curiosity toward, the objects of his attention. Others insist on the central place of the aesthetic in ordinary practical activity.

Finally, there are the philosophical issues raised by art itself. Some theorists argue that art is the only true object of aesthetic judgment. (Kant argued to the contrary, because for him nature was the only true object of aesthetic experience, art being in some way a "derived case.") As artistic forms and styles vary from tradition to tradition, so do the philosophical and critical frameworks in which art is perceived and analyzed. To varying degrees, these frameworks may posit fixed criteria by which genuine art is distinguished from imposture or superior works from inferior ones. These myriad notions of artistic value, together with the specialized vocabulary in which they are conveyed, are important as both tools and objects of aesthetic inquiry.

Aesthetics, in essence, seeks either to lay foundations for criticism or to show that such foundations are impossible. In the present century it has divided into contentious factions. Anglo-American philosophers tend to follow in the steps of Kant and to concentrate upon the analysis of the fundamental experiences and judgments involved in the apprehension of beauty. On the Continent, phenomenologists have been more concerned with the idea of the "meaning" of the work of art, as a significant human artifact, and structuralists have devoted their attention to the detailed construction of the work of art and to its resulting status as a "sign." Some Marxist critics have attempted to develop foundations for a criticism that relates the work of art systematically to the social conditions of its production or enjoyment. Others advocate the theory of "reception," which shows a partial return to the Kantian approach by transforming the aesthetic experience into the true subject of study.

Aeterni Patris, an encyclical issued by Pope Leo XIII on Aug. 4, 1879, which strengthened the position of the philosophical system of the medieval Scholastic philosopher-theologian St. Thomas Aquinas and soon made Thomism the dominant philosophical viewpoint in Roman Catholicism.

Aethelbald, also spelled ETHELBALD (d. 757, Seckington, Eng.), king of the Mercians from 716, who became the chief king of a confederation including all the Anglo-Saxon kingdoms between the River Humber and the English Channel. His predominance was made possible by the death of the strong king Wihtred of Kent (725) and the abdication of Ine of Wessex (726). During Aethelbald's reign, London passed from East Saxon to Mercian control. Although generous to the Church, he was rebuked in a letter (746 or 747) from Boniface and other Anglo-Saxon missionary bishops in Germany for his loose living and his violation of ecclesiastical prerogatives. In 749 he freed churches from all public financial responsibilities except bridge repair and fortress building. His charters use the regnal style "king of Britain." He was murdered by his retainers.

Aethelbald, also spelled ETHELBALD (d. 860), king of Wessex (from 855/856), the son of Aethelwulf, with whom he led the West Saxons to victory against the Danes at Aclea (851). He reportedly rebelled against his father either before (855) or on the latter's return from Rome in 856 and deprived him of Wessex, which he ruled until his death. On his father's death in 858 he married his stepmother Judith.

Aethelberht I, also spelled ETHELBERHT, or AEDILBERCT (d. Feb. 24, 616), king of Kent (560–616) who issued the first code extant of Anglo-Saxon laws, a code that established the legal position of the clergy and many secular regulations. His marriage to Bertha (or Berhta), daughter of Charibert, king of Paris, and a Christian, may account for the tolerant reception he accorded Augustine and other missionaries dispatched to Kent by Pope Gregory the Great in 597. Aethelberht gave them a dwelling at Canterbury and later accepted Christianity himself, though he did not force it on his subjects. According to the English historian and theologian Bede, his kingdom included all of England south of the Humber, but probably only at the end of his reign.

Aethelberht, also spelled ETHELBERHT, or AEDILBERCT (d. 865/866), king of the West Saxons, or Wessex, who succeeded to the subkingdom of Kent during the lifetime of his father Aethelwulf and retained it until the death of his elder brother Aethelbald in 860, when he became sole king of Wessex and Kent, the younger brothers Aethelred and Alfred renouncing their claim. He ruled these kingdoms for five years. His reign was marked by two serious attacks on the part of the Danes, who destroyed Winchester in 860, in spite of the resistance of the ealdormen Osric and Aethelwulf with the levies of Hampshire and Berkshire, while in 865 they ravaged Kent.

Aethelflaed, also spelled ETHELFLEDA, or AELFLED, also called LADY OF THE MERCIANS (d. June 12, 918, Tamworth, Eng.), Anglo-Saxon ruler of Mercia in England.

The daughter of Alfred the Great, she helped her brother Edward the Elder, king of the West Saxons (ruled 899–924), conquer the Danish armies occupying eastern England. Aethelflaed became the effective ruler of Mercia some years before the death (911) of her husband, Aethelred, ealdorman of the Mercians. While Edward fortified (910–916) the southeast Midlands, Aethelflaed was building fortresses around Mercia. By 917 she and Edward were ready to launch a massive joint assault on the Danish positions. Aethelflaed quickly captured Derby, and in 918 she occupied Leicester, but she died before the campaign was successfully completed. Edward then claimed his sister's kingdom and completed the subjugation of the Danes. Because Aethelflaed had extended her influence into Wales and Northumbria, Edward was able to assert his authority over these regions as well. Thus, almost all of England came under his control.

Aethelfrith, also spelled ETHELFRITH (d. 616), king of Bernicia (from 592/593) and of Deira, which together formed Northumbria.

Aethelfrith was the son of Aethelric and grandson of Ida, king of Bernicia, and his reign marks the true beginning of the continuous history of a united Northumbria, and indeed of England. He married Acha, daughter of Aelle, king of Deira, whom his father succeeded in 588 or 590, expelling Aelle's son Edwin (*q.v.*).

In 603 Aethelfrith repelled the attack of Aidan, king of the Dalriada Scots, at Degsastan, defeating him with great loss. The appearance of Hering, son of Aethelfrith's predecessor, on the side of the invaders seems to indicate family quarrels in the royal house of Bernicia. Later in his reign, probably in 614, he defeated the Welsh in a great battle at Chester and massacred the monks of Bangor who were assembled to aid them by their prayers. This war may have been due partly to Aethelfrith's persecution of Edwin, but it had a strategic importance in the separation of the North Welsh from the Strathclyde Britons. In 616 Aethelfrith was defeated and slain at the River Idle by Raedwald, king of East Anglia, whom Edwin had persuaded to take up his cause.

To make the best use of the Britannica, consult the INDEX *first*

Aetheling, also spelled ATHELING, or ETHELING, an Old English word compounded of *aethele,* or *ethel,* meaning "noble," and *ing,* meaning "belonging to," and akin to the modern German words *Adel,* "nobility," and *adelig,* "noble." During the earliest years of the Anglo-Saxon rule in England the word was probably used to denote any person of noble birth. Its use was, however, soon restricted to members of a royal family, and in the Anglo-Saxon Chronicle it is used almost exclusively for members of the royal house of Wessex. It was occasionally used after the Norman Conquest to designate members of the royal family—*e.g.,* William the Aetheling, son and heir of King Henry I.

The earlier part of the word formed part of the name of several Anglo-Saxon kings—*e.g.,* Aethelbert, Aethelwulf, Aethelred—and was used obviously to indicate their noble birth.

Aethelred, also spelled ETHELRED, name of Anglo-Saxon rulers grouped below by country and indicated by the symbol •.

MERCIA

• **Aethelred** (d. 716, Bardney, Eng.), king of Mercia, who was a benefactor of many churches in his several provinces and at last retired to a monastery.

He succeeded his brother Wulfhere (*q.v.*) in 674 and early on spent most of his time in warfare. In 676 he ravished Kent, taking Rochester. In 679, in a battle on the banks of the Trent, he defeated the Northumbrians, taking the province of Lindsey. Aelfwine, the brother of Ecgfrith, king of Northumbria, was slain on this occasion, but at the intervention of Theodore, archbishop of Canterbury, Aethelred agreed to pay a wergild for the Northumbrian prince and so prevented further hostilities. Aethelred abdicated in 704, choosing his nephew Cenred as his successor. He then became abbot of Bardney.

WESSEX AND ENGLAND

• **Aethelred I** (d. April 871), king of Wessex and of Kent (865/866–871), son of Aethelwulf of Wessex.

By his father's will he should have succeeded to Wessex on the death of his eldest brother Aethelbald (d. 860). He seems, however, to have stood aside in favour of his brother Aethelberht, king of Kent, to whose joint kingdoms he succeeded in 865 or 866. Aethelred's reign was one long struggle against the Danes. In the year of his succession a large Danish force landed in East Anglia, and in the year 868 Aethelred and his brother Alfred went to help Burgred of Mercia against this host, but the Mercians soon made peace with their foes. In 871 the Danes encamped at Reading, where they defeated Aethelred and his brother, but later in the year the English won a great victory at "Aescesdun." A fortnight later they were defeated at Basing but partially retrieved their fortune by a victory at "Maeretun" (perhaps Marden in Wiltshire), though the Danes held the field. In the Easter of this year Aethelred died, perhaps of wounds received in the wars against the Danes, and was buried at Wimborne.

• **Aethelred II:** *see* Ethelred II.

Aethelred OF RIEVAULX, SAINT: *see* Aelred of Rievaulx, Saint.

Aethelstan: *see* Athelstan; Guthrum.

Aethelweard, also spelled ETHELWERD (d. 998?), English chronicler and ealderman of the western provinces (probably the whole of Wessex), a descendant of King Alfred's brother Aethelred. He wrote, in elaborate and peculiar Latin, a chronicle for his continental kinswoman, Matilda, abbess of Essen. In the printed version of the text, the chronicle stops in 975, but fragments of the burned manuscript show that it continued in this into the reign of Aethelred (978–1016). Up to 894 it is based on a version of the Anglo-Saxon Chronicle, more ancient than any now surviving; thereafter it is an independent authority. Aethelweard was the patron of Aelfric the homilist. The last certain mention of him is in 998.

Aethelwulf, also spelled ETHELWULF (d. 858), Anglo-Saxon king in England, the father of King Alfred the Great. As ruler of the West Saxons from 839 to 856, he allied his kingdom of Wessex with Mercia and thereby withstood invasions by Danish Vikings.

The son of the great West Saxon king Egbert (ruled 802–839), Aethelwulf ascended the throne four years after the Danes had begun

Aethelwulf, coin, 9th century; in the British Museum
Peter Clayton

large-scale raids on the English coast. In 851 he scored a major victory over a large Danish army at a place called Aclea in Surrey. Aethelwulf then married his daughter to the Mercian king Burgred (853), and in 856 he himself married the daughter of Charles II the Bald, king of the West Franks. Aethelwulf was deposed by a rival faction upon his return from a pilgrimage to Rome in 856, but he continued to rule Kent and several other eastern provinces until his death. In addition to Alfred the Great (ruled 871–899), three of Aethelwulf's other sons became kings of Wessex.

aether (physics): *see* ether.

Aethra, in Greek mythology, daughter of King Pittheus of Troezen, who married her to Aegeus, king of Athens. She became mother of Theseus by Aegeus or by Poseidon, who had ravished her in Troezen. (The two versions may reflect the ancient confusion of Aegeus with the sea god—*e.g.,* the Aegean Sea.)

Later she guarded Helen after she had been stolen from Sparta by Theseus; in retribution Aethra was carried to Sparta by the Dioscuri to be Helen's slave, thereafter following her to Troy. Freed after the 10 years' war, Aethra later killed herself in grief for her son.

Aëtius (fl. 4th century), Syrian bishop and heretic who, during the theological controversies over the Christian Trinity, founded the extreme Arian sect (*see* Arius) of the Anomoeans (*q.v.*). His name became a byword for radical heresy.

Originating probably near Antioch, Aëtius studied there under Arian masters while supporting himself as a goldsmith and a physician, rendering gratuitous service to the poor. As a student he wandered from one Syrian school to another and cultivated an acute facility in Aristotelian dialectical argument. Identifying theology with formal logic, Aëtius methodically provoked his disputants and then reduced them to silence with extremely stringent and subtle arguments. A contemporary Syrian theologian, Epiphanius, records that Aëtius expounded his doctrine in 300 close-knit syllogisms, 47 of which still exist.

Ordained a deacon at Antioch to teach Christian doctrine, Aëtius is said to have scandalized the faithful with his contention that from the aspect of divinity the Son was a totally different substance from the Father and was created from nothing. For this offense he was excommunicated. He then sought refuge with fellow Arians in Alexandria, Egypt, where he trained a disciple, Eunomius, also a bishop. Recalled to Antioch by the sympathetic Arian bishop Eudoxius, Aëtius nevertheless alienated the general membership of Arians by his extreme views and was condemned by some of his own heterodox colleagues at the church Council of Seleucia, near Antioch, in 359. The Arianizing Roman emperor Constantius II (337–361) thereupon exiled him to the wilderness of northeast Asia Minor. In 361 Aëtius was made a bishop by the emperor Julian the Apostate but never exercised territorial jurisdiction; he died in Constantinople *c.* 366.

Aetius, Flavius (b. Durostorum, Moesia Inferior—d. Sept. 21, 454), Roman general and statesman, the dominating influence over Valentinian III (emperor 425–455).

The son of a *magister equitum* ("master of the cavalry"), Aetius in his youth spent some time as a hostage with the Visigothic leader Alaric, and later with the Huns, thus acquiring valuable knowledge of the leading tribal peoples of his day. From 423 to 425 he supported the usurper John in Italy. After successful battles in Gaul against the Visigoths and the Franks, Aetius was appointed in 430 *magister utriusque militiae* ("master of both services"). On the death of his rival Bonifacius in 432, he quickly gained almost complete control over the young emperor Valentinian III. Aetius thereby became the dominant personality in the Western Empire. He was consul three times (432, 437, 446), a unique distinction for a commoner, and it was said that envoys from the provinces were no longer sent to the Emperor, but to Aetius. He was given the title of patrician in 433, and for several years thereafter fought continuously and successfully in Gaul against rebels and hostile tribes. In 435–437 he mercilessly destroyed the Burgundian kingdom at Worms (an event remembered in the *Nibelungenlied*, a German epic poem written *c.* 1200) and in 437–439 checked the Visigoths at Toulouse. He returned to Italy in 440. In 451 he joined with the Visigoths in defeating Attila in the Battle of the Catalaunian Plains, but when Attila invaded Italy in the following year, Aetius could do little to oppose him. At the height of his power Aetius was murdered by Valentinian at the instigation of Petronius Maximus, the future emperor.

Aetna (volcano, Sicily): *see* Etna (Mount).

Aetolia, also spelled Aitolia, district of ancient Greece, located directly north of the Gulf of Corinth and bounded by Epirus (north), Locris (east), and Acarnania (west). In modern Greece, Aetolia is linked with Acarnania in the department of Aitolía kai Akarnanía. Aetolia, particularly its cities Pleuron and Calydon, figures prominently in early legend. During the great migrations (1200–1000 BC) most of the region's early inhabitants were displaced; those tribes that remained still lived in open villages under petty kings in the 5th century BC and were dedicated to piracy. Their archers and slingers, however, repulsed an Athenian invasion in 426 BC, and by 367 they had organized into a federal state, the Aetolian League. In 27 BC Augustus incorporated Aetolia into the Roman province of Achaea. In the 15th century AD it passed successively under the rules of Albania, Venice, and, in 1450, Turkey. In the War of Greek Independence (1821–29), it was the scene of fierce fighting, notably the sieges of Mesolóngion (Missolonghi).

Aetolia and Acarnania, Modern Greek Aitolía kai Akarnanía, *nomós* (department)

The Achelous River, Aetolia and Acarnania *nomós*, Greece

Dimitri Papadimos

in west central Greece, with an area of 2,103 sq mi (5,447 sq km); the capital of the department is Mesolóngion on the Patraïkós Kólpos (gulf) in Aetolia. The *nomós* produces tobacco, wheat, oats, wine, and caviar; some livestock is raised. Its chief centres are Agrínion, Mesolóngion, Amfilokhía, and Návpaktos, the last at the mouth of the Gulf of Corinth.

Most of Acarnania is a large, irregular peninsula, the base being formed by a line of lakes and lagoons from Amfilokhía on the Amvrakikós Kólpos (ancient Ambracia), its northern limit, to Mesolóngion; the western limit is the Ionian Sea, along which the barren, limestone Akarnaniká Óri (mountains) predominate. In ancient Greece the Achelous River was the boundary with Aetolia; today its fertile basin, together with that of the Évinos Potamós (river), is the agricultural and population centre of the *nomós,* hinging on Agrínion and Mesolóngion. Límni (lake) Trikhonís supports a fishing (caviar) industry. In contrast, northern and eastern Aetolia is a complex of almost barren limestone peaks rising in the frontier ranges of Timfristós, Oxiá, and Vardhoúsia to more than 7,000 ft (2,100 m); but agriculture is supported. Pop. (1981) *nomós*, 219,764.

Aetolian League, federal state or "sympolity" of Aetolia, in ancient Greece. Probably based on a looser tribal community, it was well-enough organized to conduct negotiations with Athens in 367 BC. It became by *c.* 340 one of the leading military powers in Greece. Having successfully resisted invasions by Macedonia in 322 and 314–311, the league rapidly grew in strength during the ensuing period of Macedonian weakness, expanding into Delphi (centre of the Amphictyonic Council) and allying with Boeotia (*c.* 300).

It was mainly responsible for driving out a major Gallic invasion of Greece in 279. About 270 it gained an alliance with Antigonus Gonatas, king of Macedonia, which lasted until his death (240 or 239). In 245 the league confirmed its influence in central Greece by the defeat of the Boeotians at Chaeronea. By the end of the 3rd century the league's power extended to Cephallenia and several Aegean islands; soon afterward, however, it lost ground to Macedonia.

From 239 to 229 the league joined Achaea against Demetrius II of Macedonia, but the provinces of Thessaly that they seized on the death of Demetrius were promptly recovered by his successor, Antigonus Doson. Meanwhile, eastern Phocis and Boeotia detached themselves from the confederacy. Then Aetolian raids on Achaean territory (220) led to a war with Philip V of Macedonia and many members of Antigonus Doson's Greek League. Philip expelled the Aetolians from the Peloponnese and marched into Aetolia, sacking the federal capital of Thermum. He made peace with Aetolia in 217, but in 211 and 200–197 the Aetolians fought with Rome against Philip. When their cavalry prevailed at Cynoscephalae (197), the Romans handed over Dolopia, Phocis, and Eastern Locris to the Aetolians but withheld their former Thessalian possessions. Resentful, Aetolia attempted to fight Rome (192), soliciting the support of the Seleucid king Antiochus III; but Aetolian forces failed to hold Thermopylae and brought on the defeat of Antiochus at Magnesia. The Romans refused all compromises and in 189 BC restricted the league to Aetolia proper and assumed control of its foreign relations. The importance of the league as an independent state was at an end, and by the time of Sulla its functions were purely nominal.

The federal constitution of Aetolia, probably a model for that of the Achaean League, provided for two main ruling bodies: a primary assembly, composed of all adult male citizens and presided over by the annually elected general (*stratēgos*), which met at Thermum to elect officials and at various cities to transact other business; and a council (*boulē* or *synedrion*), to supervise administration, in which cities were represented in proportion to their populations. *Apoklētoi,* a small group of at least 30 who were assigned essential duties in wartime, assisted the *stratēgos,* who had complete control in the field. Leadership within the league was always kept in Aetolian hands, since the more distant states, linked to the confederacy by isopolity (potential citizenship), had full civil but no political rights.

Afan, district, West Glamorgan County, Wales. It was created in 1974, covers an area of 58 sq mi (151 sq km), and extends along the South Wales coast from Port Talbot in the north to the Kenfig Burrows in the south and reaches to the top of Afan Valley in the northeast. Afan district borders the districts of Rhondda and Ogwr to the east and Neath to the west and north.

Founded in 1147 by Robert, earl of Gloucester, Margam Abbey dominated the area during the Middle Ages and functioned as the local cultural and educational centre until its dissolution in 1537. Modern industry began in the area in 1770 with the establishment of copper smelting in Port Talbot, which became the outport for collieries in the Afan and Rhondna valleys.

Afan district today remains primarily industrial. Port Talbot, the administrative seat of the district, has developed into one of the largest towns in Wales. It is a major industrial and commercial centre, with a recently established petroleum chemicals plant and the largest tidal harbour facility (completed 1970) in Great Britain. The gigantic Margam Abbey steelworks are located just south of Port Talbot, and there is an oil refinery in Baglan, to the northwest.

The town of Aberavon, bounded by Port Talbot between the Bristol Channel and the mountains, has become a popular seaside resort. Other tourist attractions include the Afan Argoed Country Park, the Margam Country Park, and the Margam Abbey Museum, with an important collection of inscribed and sculptured early Christian memorial stones. The village of Pontrhydyfen, in eastern Afan, is the birthplace of the actor Richard Burton. The M4 Motorway extends through the district and along the northern edge of Port Talbot. Pop. (1982 est.) 53,800.

Afar, Amharic ADAL, Arabic DANAKIL, a people of the Horn of Africa who speak a language of the Cushitic branch of the Hamito-Semitic family. They live in northeastern Ethiopia and in Djibouti, where, with the Issas, they are the dominant people. It is thought that the Afars were the first of the present inhabitants of Ethiopia to elaborate their pastoral life into full-scale nomadism, descending from the highlands of southeast Ethiopia and migrating to the stony desert area of Danakil, the name used by surrounding tribes to identify them.

The Afars' subsistence economy depends on livestock, especially goats, some camels, and, more rarely, cattle. There are some exceptions, such as fishermen in the coastal areas and agriculturalists in the Assau oasis. The Afars also mine and export salt.

Proud, highly individualistic, and much feared by outsiders, the Afars are organized in patrilineal kin groups. Cooperation in larger units such as subtribe or tribe is induced only by warfare against other tribes or neighbouring peoples. Two distinct classes, the Asaimara (or Red Men) and the Adoimara (or White Men), constitute the landowning, titled nobles and the lower-class tenants, respectively.

Age-set societies exist wherein people of the same age group are subject to a chief who settles disputes among them. Beyond this, legal procedure consists of the rules for compensation for adultery—a system of fines to the

Afar nomads in Ethiopia
Victor Englebert—De Wys Inc.

injured husband or father—and revenge for homicide. Blood feuds are a principal, perennial, and costly occupation, except among the few sultanates, notably at Assau, in which despotic law is backed up with an army.

The Afars are nominally Muslim, but even a slight degree of orthodoxy in practice is attained only in the coastal regions and in the sultanates. The nomads of the interior are lax, and, though they hold Islām in great esteem, their own practices are imbued with the earlier Cushitic religion.

Afars and Issas (Africa): *see* Djibouti.

afebrile coryza: *see* common cold.

affections, doctrine of the, also called DOCTRINE OF AFFECTS, German AFFEKTENLEHRE, theory of musical aesthetics, widely accepted by late Baroque theorists and composers, that embraced the proposition that music is capable of arousing a variety of specific emotions within the listener. At the centre of the doctrine was the belief that, by making use of the proper standard musical procedure or device, the composer could create a piece of music capable of producing a particular involuntary emotional response in his audience.

These devices and their affective counterparts were rigorously cataloged and described by such 17th- and 18th-century theorists as Athanasius Kircher, Andreas Werckmeister, Johann David Heinichen, and Johann Mattheson. Mattheson is especially comprehensive in his treatment of the affections in music. In *Der vollkommene Capellmeister* (1739; "The Perfect Chapelmaster"), he notes that joy is elicited by large intervals, sadness by small intervals; fury may be aroused by a roughness of harmony coupled with a rapid melody; obstinacy is evoked by the contrapuntal combination of highly independent (obstinate) melodies. Carl Philipp Emanuel Bach (1714–88) and the Mannheim school were exponents of the doctrine.

It should be noted that the contemplation of the emotional aspect of music is not limited to the Baroque era but may be found throughout the history of music. It is an essential part of ancient Greek musical theory (the doctrine of ethos), it takes on a particular importance in the Romantic movement of the 19th century, and it also occurs in such non-Western music as the Indian raga. It was in the Baroque era, however, that theorists, influenced by the Enlightenment's tendency toward encyclopaedic organization of all knowledge, attempted to delineate music into affective categories.

affective disorder, mental disorder characterized by dramatic changes or extremes of mood. Affective disorders may include manic (elevated, expansive, or irritable mood with hyperactivity, pressured speech, and inflated self-esteem) or depressive (dejected mood with disinterest in life, sleep disturbance, agitation, and feelings of worthlessness or guilt) episodes, and often combinations of the two. Persons with an affective disorder may or may not have psychotic symptoms such as delusions, hallucinations, or other loss of contact with reality.

In manic-depressive disorders, periods of mania and depression may alternate with abrupt onsets and recoveries. Depression is the more common symptom, and many patients never develop a genuine manic phase, although they may experience a brief period of overoptimism and mild euphoria while recovering from a depression. The most extreme manifestation of mania is violence against others, while that of depression is suicide. Statistical studies have suggested a hereditary predisposition to the disorder, which commonly appears for the first time in young adults.

Manic-depressive disorders were described in antiquity by the 2nd-century Greek physician Aretaeus of Cappadocia and in modern times by the German psychiatrist Emil Kraepelin. The current term is derived from *folie maniaco-mélancholique,* which was introduced in the 17th century. *See also* manic-depressive psychosis.

affective fallacy, according to the followers of New Criticism (*q.v.*), the misconception that arises from judging a poem by the emotional effect that it produces in the reader. The concept of affective fallacy is a direct attack on impressionistic criticism, which argues that the reader's response to a poem is the ultimate indication of its value.

Those who support the affective criterion for judging poetry cite its long and respectable history, beginning with Aristotle's dictum that the purpose of tragedy is to evoke "terror and pity." Edgar Allan Poe stated that "a poem deserves its title only inasmuch as it excites, by elevating the soul." Emily Dickinson said, "If I feel physically as if the top of my head were taken off, I know that is poetry." Many modern critics continue to assert that emotional communication and response cannot be separated from the evaluation of a poem.

Affenkapelle ware (German: Monkey Orchestra), a series of figures created by the Meissen porcelain factory in Saxony (now in East Germany) *c.* 1747 and imitated later. Believed to be a parody of the Dresden Court Orchestra, the set was modelled by the Ger-

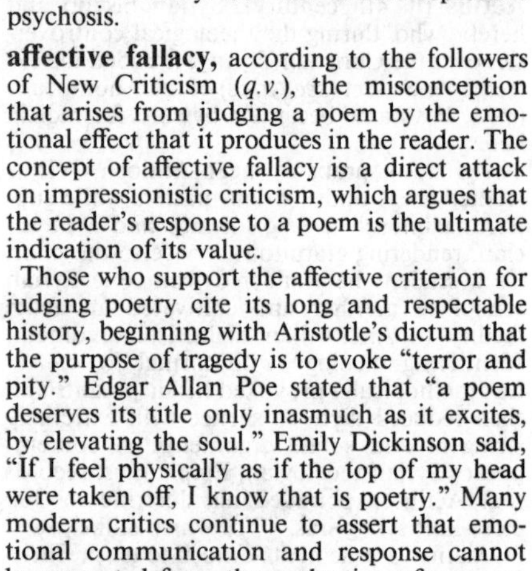

Hurdy-gurdy-playing monkey derived from one of Johann Joachim Kändler's Affenkapelle figures, Korniloff factory, St. Petersburg (now Leningrad), mid-19th century; in the Victoria and Albert Museum, London
By courtesy of the Victoria and Albert Museum, London; photograph, EB Inc.

man sculptors Johann Joachim Kändler and Peter Reinicke after fanciful singerie (monkeys in human costume) engravings by the French artists Jean-Antoine Watteau and Christophe Huet. Each musician, dressed in delicately coloured formal 18th-century costume, stands on a gilded scrollwork base of leaves and flowers; a male monkey conducts, four females sing, and each of the others plays a musical instrument. In 1753 Meissen supplied the Marquise de Pompadour with a "concert" of 19 players, which is the largest known surviving group, though there is evidence that a whole set might have numbered 25. The figures belong to the most brilliant period of Meissen porcelain, and Kändler's mastery of expression clearly transcends mere caricature. Among the many imitations that exist, most far less elegant than the original, are a set of five musical monkeys made in Chelsea (London) and sold there in 1756; figures from Fürstenberg (Germany) and Derby (England); and, 100 years later, a spirited hurdy-gurdy-playing monkey made by the Russian Korniloff factory and directly inspired by one of Kändler's figures.

affenpinscher, also called MONKEY TERRIER, breed of toy dog known since the 17th century. The affenpinscher stands 10 inches (26 centimetres) or less and weighs 7 to 8 pounds (3 to 3.5 kilograms). A sturdily built, terrier-like dog, it has small, erect ears, round black eyes, and a short, docked tail. Its wiry, preferably black coat is short on parts of the body but longer on the legs and on the face, where it produces the monkey-like expression for which the breed is named.

affidavit, a written statement of fact made voluntarily, confirmed by the oath or affirmation of the party making it, and signed before an officer empowered to administer such oaths. It names the place of execution and certifies that the person making the affidavit states certain facts and that he appeared before the officer on a certain date and "subscribed and swore" to the statement.

affirmation, in law, a form of safeguard against false testimony allowed in place of an oath (*q.v.*) to those who cannot, because of conscience, swear an oath. Quakers, Jehovah's Witnesses, and other persons who have conscientious scruples against taking an oath are allowed to make affirmation in any manner they may declare to be binding upon their consciences, in confirmation of the truth of testimony that they are about to give.

affirmative action, in the United States, active efforts that take into account race, sex, and national origin for the purpose of remedying and preventing discrimination. Under the landmark Civil Rights Act of 1964 and subsequent executive orders and judicial decisions, the federal government requires certain businesses and educational institutions that receive federal funds to develop affirmative action programs. The Office of Federal Contract Compliance and the Equal Employment Opportunity Commission (EEOC) monitor them.

Affirmative action has been criticized as "reverse discrimination" (usually against white males), but the U.S. Commission on Civil Rights argued until 1983 that only if society were operating fairly would measures that take race, sex, and national origin into account be "preferential treatment." After the Commission on Civil Rights was reorganized in late 1983, however, it took the opposite position; in January 1984 it approved a statement that "racial preferences merely constitute another form of unjustified discrimination." Elements of an affirmative action plan include a written policy, self-evaluation to identify deficiencies, steps to correct them on a timetable, and accountability by senior management.

In 1978, in *University of California Regents* v. *Bakke*, the U.S. Supreme Court held (5–4) that fixed quotas may not be set for places for minority applicants for medical school if white applicants are denied a chance to compete for those places. The court, however, said that professional schools may consider race as a factor in making decisions on admissions. In *United Steelworkers of America* v. *Weber* (1979), the court held (5–2) that employers and unions could conduct voluntary training programs designed to improve skills of minority employees even if qualified white employees were excluded, provided that the programs were "temporary," did not "trammel" white interests, and were intended to overcome "manifest racial imbalance." In *Fullilove* v. *Klutznick* (1980), the court found (6–3) that constitutional rights of white businessmen were not violated by the federal law requiring that 10 percent of funds for public works be allotted to qualified minority contractors.

The U.S. Commission on Civil Rights issued a report in November 1981: "Affirmative Action in the 1980s: Dismantling the Process of Discrimination."

affix, a grammatical element combined with a word, stem, or phrase that produces derived and inflected forms; there are three types of affixes—prefixes, infixes, and suffixes. A prefix occurs at the beginning of a word or stem (*sub*-mit, *pre*-determine, *un*-willing); a suffix at the end (wonder-*ful*, depend-*ent*, act-*ion*); and an infix occurs in the middle. English has no infixes, but they are found in American Indian languages, Greek, Tagalog, and elsewhere. Examples of English inflectional suffixes are illustrated by the *-s* of "cats," the *-er* of "longer," and the *-ed* of "asked." *See also* morphology.

Affleck, Thomas (b. 1745, Aberdeen, Aberdeenshire, Scot.—d. 1795, Philadelphia), cabinetmaker considered outstanding among the Philadelphia craftsmen working in the Chippendale style during the 18th century.

Probably trained in England, he settled in Philadelphia in 1763, producing tables, chairs, sofas, and case furniture for Gov. John Penn and other leading Philadelphia citizens. A Royalist sympathizer, he was arrested as a Tory in 1777 and banished to Virginia for more than seven months. His son, Lewis G. Affleck, unsuccessfully attempted to maintain the business after his father's death.

Works attributed to Affleck, showing the Marlborough-style leg (a straight, grooved type having a block foot) and elaborate carving characterizing his work, are in the Philadelphia Museum of Art; the Boston Museum of Fine Arts; and the Metropolitan Museum of Art, New York City.

affray, fighting in public in a way that endangers or alarms the people. Abusive and threatening words do not amount to an affray unless a fight results. *See also* disorderly conduct; disturbing the peace.

Affre, Denis-Auguste (b. Sept. 28, 1793, Saint-Rome-de-Tarn, Fr.—d. June 27, 1848, Paris), prelate, archbishop of Paris, and opponent of King Louis-Philippe, remembered for his brave attempt to end the June 1848 riots, in which he was accidentally slain.

Ordained priest in 1818, he became a Sulpician and a teacher of theology (1819). He successively became vicar general of the French dioceses of Luçon (1821), Amiens (1823), and Paris (1834) and in 1840 was named archbishop of Paris.

By 1827 Affre had become well known for his clerical reforms. His differences with Louis-Philippe began in 1843, and a long polemical debate over secondary education ensued in which Affre particularly defended academic freedom. He welcomed the establishment of the Second Republic in 1848 and the overthrow of Louis-Philippe on February 24 of that year. On the following June 23 the Parisian workers rose in an insurrection known as the June Days, which ended in bloodshed that grieved Affre. Led to believe that his personal intervention might restore

Affre, lithograph after a drawing by Krinowski, 19th century

By courtesy of the Bibliotheque Nationale, Paris

order, he entered the barricades in the workers' Saint-Antoine district on June 25. He had scarcely begun to speak when confused firing broke out. Struck by a stray bullet, he died two days later.

Among Affre's several canonical and philosophical works are *Essai historique et critique sur la suprématie temporelle du pape* (1829; "Historical Essay on the Temporal Supremacy of the Pope") and *Introduction philosophique à l'étude du Christianisme* (1845; "Philosophical Introduction to the Study of Christianity"). He had also edited the periodical *La France chrétienne,* which he helped found. Lucien Alazard's *Denis-Auguste Affre, archévêque de Paris,* appeared in 1905.

affreightment, contract for carriage of goods by water, "freight" being the price paid for the service of carriage. Such contracts are of immense importance to the world economy, forming the legal structure of the arterial traffic of the oceans.

Essentially, such a contract is an agreement between two parties, the carrier and the shipper. The carrier undertakes to carry the goods to a specified destination, and the shipper to pay the freight. There are two basic forms: the charter party, engaging the whole capacity of the ship for a single voyage or for a period of time, and the bill of lading, which is a receipt for goods taken on board for carriage. *See also* lading, bill of; charter party.

affricate, also called SEMIPLOSIVE, a consonant sound that begins as a stop (sound with complete obstruction of the breath stream) and concludes with a fricative (sound with incomplete closure and a sound of friction). Examples of affricates are the *ch* sound in English "chair," which may be represented phonetically as a *t* sound followed by *sh;* the *j* in English "jaw" (a *d* followed by the *zh* sound heard in French "jour" or in English "azure"); and the *ts* sound often heard in German and spelled with *z* as in "nazi."

Afghan: *see* Pashtun.

Afghan carpet, stout, long-wearing floor covering handwoven by the Afghan tribe of Turkmens of the Turkmen S.S.R. and Afghanistan. Afghan carpets are generally all wool or goat hair and made with the Senna (Sehna) knot. Usually in dull reds, these carpets show less white than the products of other Turkmens. Their gul, or basic tribal motif, is a large, parti-coloured, scalloped octagon or near octagon, full of forms like arrowheads or trilobate figures that resemble shamrocks. The guls alternate with other motifs, usually clusters of dark-blue, connected stars. The border may be a notched zigzag stripe.

A few "golden" Afghans, with a moderate use of yellow and orange, offer a contrast to

Octagonal motif, detail of an Afghan carpet from Russian Turkistan, late 19th century; in the Raoul E. Tschebull Collection
Collection of Raoul E. Tschebull; photograph, Otto E. Nelson—EB Inc.

their somber fellows. Small rugs are rarely seen except among an aniline-dyed recent Afghanistan production.

Afghan hound, breed of dog that originated in Egypt several thousand years before Christ and was later developed as a hunter in the rugged hill country of Afghanistan. The Afghan hunts by sight and has been used to pursue leopard and gazelle. It is adapted to rough country by the structure of its high, wide hipbones. A long-legged dog, it stands 24 to 28 inches (61 to 71 centimetres) and weighs 50 to 60 pounds (23 to 27 kilograms). It has floppy ears, a long topknot, and a long, silky coat, which may be of various but usually solid colours; it is especially heavy on the forequarters and hindquarters; and the tail is slim

Afghan hound
Sally Anne Thompson—EB Inc.

and carried in an upright curve. The overall appearance of the Afghan has been described as "aristocratic, with a farseeing expression."

Afghan interlude (1722–30), period in Iranian history that began with the Afghan conquest of Iran and ended with the defeat and death of the Afghan ruler Ashraf.

In 1722 Maḥmūd, an Afghan notable and former vassal of the Ṣafavids, attacked and captured Isfahan, the Ṣafavid capital. The capture of Isfahan marked the eclipse of the Ṣafavid dynasty. Maḥmūd proclaimed himself ruler of Iran in 1722, and in 1723 he put to death Shāh Solṭān Ḥoseyn, the former Ṣafavid ruler. Maḥmūd consolidated his gains in southern and southeastern Iran, and in 1725 he was succeeded by his cousin Ashraf. Ashraf attempted to conciliate the Iranians, but he was always regarded as the hated foreign invader.

In the meantime Peter the Great of Russia, who had long contemplated establishing a trade route to India via the countries east of the Caspian, invaded the north of Iran in 1722, ostensibly because of losses suffered by some Russian merchants during a tribal uprising there. At this the Ottomans moved into western and northwestern Iran to prevent the Russians from taking over Iranian territory next to Turkey. The confrontation threatened to blow up into war, but a settlement was negotiated in 1724. Russia held much of Iran's north and the Ottomans the west, with the northwestern regions partitioned between them; this was perhaps the first such imposition of precise boundaries by European powers on an Islāmic state. In the north Ṭahmāsp II—the representative of the ousted Ṣafavid dynasty—controlled the provinces of Māzandarān and Gīlān. In 1727 Ashraf negotiated a treaty with the Ottomans, accepting their annexation of western Iran; in return the Ottomans recognized Ashraf as ruler of Iran. In 1727 Ṭahmāsp II was joined by Nāder Qolī Khān, a leader of the Afshār tribe. Nāder (later ruled in 1736–47 as Nāder Shāh) set out to expel the Afghans and to reunify the former Ṣafavid domains. A brilliant general, Nāder defeated the Afghans in a series of battles; Ashraf was killed, and Nāder installed Ṭahmāsp II as *shāh* in Isfahan (1729). He continued operations against the Afghans until they were finally routed and expelled from Iran in 1730.

Afghan language: *see* Pashto language.

Afghan Wars (1839–42; 1878–80; 1919): *see* Anglo-Afghan Wars.

Afghanistan, officially DEMOCRATIC REPUBLIC OF AFGHANISTAN, Dari Persian DOWLAT-E JUMHŪRĪ-YE DIMUKRĀTIK-E AFGHĀNISTĀN, Pashto DA AFGHĀNESTĀN DIMUKRATIK JAMHURIYAT, landlocked country of south central Asia, covering an area of 252,100 sq mi (653,000 sq km). The capital is Kābul. The country extends about 600 mi (970 km) from north to south and about 800 mi from east to west, including the narrow 150-mi-long Wākhān Corridor connecting Afghanistan with China to the northeast; it is also bordered on the southeast by Pakistan, on the west by Iran, and on the north by the Soviet Union. The population in 1982 was estimated at 16,786,000, which excluded an estimated 4,000,000 refugees in surrounding countries who fled after the 1979 Soviet invasion.

The article that follows is a summary of significant detail about Afghanistan. Fuller treatment is provided in the following MACROPAEDIA articles. For geography and history, *see* Afghanistan; for information about the country and its history, peoples, and traditional cultures in their regional setting, *see* Asia.

For current history and for statistics on society and economy, *see* the article "World Affairs" and BRITANNICA WORLD DATA, respectively, in the *Britannica Book of the Year*.

The land. Afghanistan has three distinctive regions. The northern plain (roughly 40,000 sq mi) is the major agricultural area. The southwestern plateau (50,000 sq mi) consists primarily of desert and semidesert and includes the Rigestān desert. These regions are separated by the central highlands (160,000 sq mi), an extension of the Himalayan mountain chain, which includes the Hindu Kush range, often rising above 21,000 ft (6,400 m). The northeastern section of the central highlands (including the Wākhān Corridor) is geologically very active; more than a dozen earthquakes of moderate to great intensity have occurred in the vicinity of Kābul since 1900.

The Amu Darya (ancient Oxus River) forms the border to the north with the Soviet Union and extends nearly 1,600 mi from its source in the Himalayas to the Aral Sea. The 600-mi-long Helmand River provides, through its many irrigation projects, most of the agricultural water needs of the southwestern plateau region. The climatic zones of Afghanistan are dominated by the Himalayan mountains. The central highlands have a subpolar climate (winters below freezing and cool short summers), while most of the remainder is semi-arid steppe (cold winters and hot summers) or desert. Annual precipitation varies from less than 3 in. (75 mm) in the southwestern desert to more than 50 in. in the mountains, falling primarily in summer monsoons.

Much of Afghanistan has thin, infertile mountain and desert soils, but the northern plains region, with extensive loess soils, has some of the best agricultural land in Asia. About 12 percent of the country's land area is arable, and approximately one-third of that area is irrigated. The valley of the Kābul River between Kābul and Jalālābād, because of its relatively humid climate, supports a wide variety of trees and associated shrubs and bushes. While many mammalian species are represented in this region, increasing human demands on the land's resources are reducing

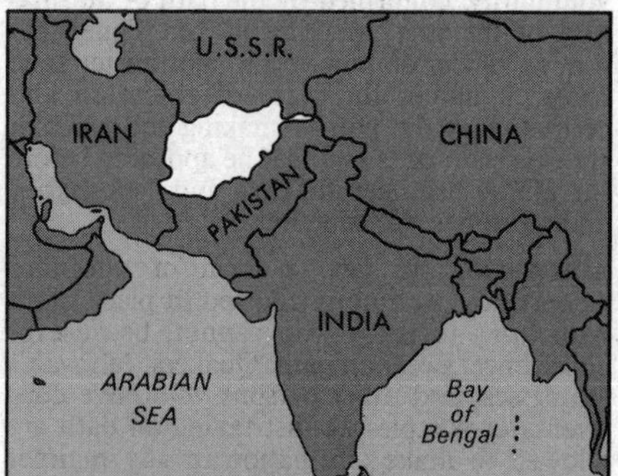

Afghanistan

their numbers (the Siberian tiger, which once roamed the banks of the Amu Darya, is nearly extinct).

Afghanistan has known deposits of iron, copper, lead, zinc, and other mineral resources that remained unexploited in the early 1980s. The only resource tapped in significant quantities is natural gas from a reserve in the northern plains estimated at almost 5,000,000,000,000 cu ft (140,000,000,000 cu m). Bituminous coal reserves are estimated at between 300,000,000 and 500,000,000 tons.

The people. Afghanistan's estimated population in mid-1982 was 16,786,000 (excluding some 4,000,000 refugees in surrounding countries) and in the year prior to the 1979 invasion had been growing at an annual rate of 2.5 percent. The birth rate (1978–79) was 46.2 per thousand and the registered death rate 2.2; the actual death rate was about 21.1 per thousand. Population density is 67 persons per sq mi (26 per sq km). The ratio of males to females is about 100 to 94.5. Afghanistan has a relatively young population—44 percent are under 15. About half of the Afghan people are of Pashtun ancestry followed by Tadzhik (about one-fourth of the total), Uzbek, and Hazara. The Pashtuns mainly inhabit the southern and eastern parts of the country. Most Pashtuns are sedentary, though some remain nomadic. The Tadzhiks, mostly farmers and artisans, live mostly in the northeast and in the west around Herat. The Uzbeks are mainly farmers living north of the Hindu Kush. The Hazaras are nomads who inhabit the central mountains.

The official languages of the country are Pashto (Pushtu) and Dari (a form of Persian), both Indo-European languages. Pashto is spoken by about half the population. Dari (or Farsi) is spoken by about a third of the population—mainly the Tadzhik, Hazara, Chahar Aimak, and Kizilbash peoples. Uzbek is spoken by about 1,000,000 persons in northern Afghanistan and Turkmen by some 300,000 in the same general area; both belong to the Ural-Altaic language family. Most of the people are Muslims. There are small numbers of Hindus, Sikhs, and Jews.

Infant mortality and morbidity are generally high; family health services have been incorporated into the basic health services in Kābul and surrounding areas, and services are being funded and implemented by the United Nations Fund for Population Activities. At the 1979 census about 13 percent of Afghanistan's more than 16,000,000 people were urban dwellers. Nearly one-fifth were nomads. Kābul, the national capital and largest city, had a population of 910,000 in the late 1970s; other urban centres include Qandahār, Herat, Mazār-e Sharīf, Jalālābād, and Kunduz. Most urban settlements are situated along the major circular road of the country that runs from Kābul southwestward to Qandahār, then northwest to Herat, northeast to Mazār-e Sharīf, and south back to Kābul. The rural population, distributed unevenly over the rest of the country, is mainly concentrated along the rivers. By 1982, an estimated 1,500,000 refugees had fled Afghanistan for Iran, and some 2,800,000 refugees sought asylum in Pakistan. The number of refugees fleeing Afghanistan into Pakistan continued to rise throughout 1983.

The economy. Afghanistan has a developing centrally planned economy, based largely on agricultural production. The gross national product (GNP) in 1979 amounted to U.S. $2,800,000,000, about $225 per capita. Annual growth of real GNP was only about 2.5 percent during the 1970s prior to the Soviet invasion. The GNP originated primarily in agricultural output followed by mining, manufacturing, electricity, gas, and water; services (including foreign transactions); and trade, restaurants, and hotels. Under Soviet influence, in the early 1980s nationalization was being extended to all sectors of the economy.

Cereal grains are grown on most of the cultivated land, including wheat, corn (maize), rice, and barley; vegetables, fruits, nuts, and cotton are also grown. Pistachios and other wild nuts grow in sufficient quantity to permit export. Arid rangeland and a small amount of good pasture occupy nearly four-fifths of Afghanistan's total land area. Animal husbandry, yielding meat and dairy products for local consumption, as well as leather and skins, and wool, is the predominant activity on these lands. Sheep and lambs are the most important livestock; cattle, donkeys, horses, and camels are also raised. More than two-thirds of the country's labour force is employed in agriculture and animal husbandry. Mining remains comparatively undeveloped, except for natural gas and coal. Metallic minerals are not mined extensively, although a high-grade iron-ore deposit is estimated at 2,000,000,000 tons. Cement, salt, nitrogen, asbestos, and barite are also produced.

Industrial products, based largely upon agricultural and pastoral resources, include cotton textiles, wool, rayon, and acetate fabrics. Phosphate fertilizers and cement are also produced. Traditional handicrafts remain important; among these woollen carpets constitute an important export.

Construction expenditures were focussed upon roads, factories, and basic infrastructure in the 1970s, but the sector was subsequently severely impaired by the war and the accompanying need for military construction.

Hydroelectric plants on Afghanistan's swiftly flowing rivers produce three-fourths of the country's electric power, but this resource is underutilized. Trade agreements of 1981 provided for the integration of the country's electrical grid with that of the Soviet Union.

Since the Soviet invasion, budget, revenue, and tax collection have increasingly been modelled along Soviet patterns. Much of the total revenue is raised from taxes and from loans from Soviet bloc countries and Soviet grants-in-aid. Nearly 60 percent of expenditures went to government ministries (of which one-third went for military and security expenses), and the rest was spent on development. Inflation, which had tripled prices between 1961–62 and 1978–79, fell to the 1961–62 levels in the years following the Soviet invasion.

Transportation is inadequately developed. There is only a 6-mi Soviet spur rail line, and only about 15 percent of the road network is paved. The war extensively damaged existing roads, bridges, and related structures. There are two international airports and a number of airfields.

Afghanistan's exports and imports were roughly equal in value in the early 1980s. Major exports include fruits and nuts, natural gas, and carpets. Major importers of Afghan goods were the Soviet Union, the United Kingdom, and Pakistan. Afghan imports include textile yarns and fabrics, and petroleum products. Major exporters to Afghanistan were the Soviet Union, Japan, and Iran.

Administrative and social conditions. Afghanistan is a one-party state ruled by the Parcham faction of the Soviet-supported People's Democratic Party of Afghanistan (PDPA). A provisional constitution adopted by the PDPA in 1980 provided for the eventual election of a Grand National Assembly. In the war that followed the Soviet invasion of 1979, governmental authority was challenged in many areas by rebels belonging to the Islāmic Alliance for the Liberation of Afghanistan, the Islāmic Party, and the Khalq faction of the PDPA. Some 40,000 government troops and 80,000 Soviet troops have acted to break rebel resistance and maintain PDPA rule.

The government's social welfare system provides free hospital treatment for all workers; the infant mortality rate in Afghanistan, however, remains extremely high, and life expectancy is only 40 years, one of the world's lowest figures. The country has a high incidence of tuberculosis, venereal disease, and of both bacillary and amebic dysentery; most of these diseases cannot be treated because of the lack of doctors and hospital facilities. Good progress, however, has been made toward lessening the incidence of cholera, typhoid fever, and typhus; and smallpox has been eradicated.

The literacy rate in Afghanistan is only 12 percent. A major goal of the PDPA is to raise the country's educational level, and in 1979 the government introduced free and compulsory education for children between the ages of 7 and 10. The war has hurt the development of higher education in Afghanistan; it is believed that most of the professors of Kābul University and the University of Nangarhar fled their posts during the fighting. The news media are under complete government control.

Cultural life. The highest artistic achievements in the Afghan heritage are probably those of the court of Maḥmūd of Ghazna (971–1030), under whom that city rivalled Baghdad; and those of the Timurid dynasty (15th century), which flourished in such centres as Herāt. Afghans still engage in traditional folksinging and dancing on religious and national feast days. Many modern painters draw direct inspiration from the Herāt school of the Timurid period.

History. The area covered by the modern state of Afghanistan has occupied for centuries a strategic meeting place of a variety of cultures. The Afghans were first mentioned under their modern name in a Muslim source dating from 982. The area was part of the Persian Achaemenian empire of Cyrus II the Great and was conquered in the 4th century BC by Alexander III the Great. After Alexander's death, part of the area came under Seleucid control and part under the Maurya Empire of northern India. The Seleucid satrapy of Bactria (Balkh) forged its own kingdom and created a unique fusion of Greek and Indian cultures.

During the 2nd century BC, Afghanistan became part of the empire of the Kushān King Kaniṣka (*c.* AD 78–144). The Kushāns propagated Mahāyāna Buddhism, and their cultural achievements have been documented in the excavations of their major cities of Bagrām, Delbarjin, and Sheberghān.

Hindu influence entered Afghanistan by way of the Persian Sāsānians; during the rule of the Ṣaffārids, *c.* 870, Islām became firmly entrenched. The Mongols under Genghis Khan invaded Afghanistan in 1219. The dissolution of his empire resulted in the rise of mostly independent principalities, and, until the 18th century, Afghanistan existed partly within the Mughal empire of India and the Ṣafavid of Persia.

In the early 1700s, the Persian leader Nāder Shāh took control of Aghanistan from the Mughals and was succeeded by his chief bodyguard Aḥmad Khān Abdālī, who assumed the name Aḥmad Shāh Durrānī. He consolidated his rule over Afghanistan and united it as one country.

After Durrānī's death (1773), the empire foundered because of recurring tribal and family loyalties, and the imperialist designs of Russia and Great Britain. Three distinct Anglo-Afghan wars in the 19th and early 20th centuries culminated in the Treaty of Rāwalpindi of 1919, granting Afghan independence.

The political instability continued, and in 1928 civil war broke out. The King was assassinated in 1933. The coup of 1973 ended the monarchy and established the Republic of Afghanistan, an initially leftist government. Another coup followed in 1978, when other leftists with Soviet support overthrew Pres. Mohammad Daud Khan. Widespread violence followed the 1978 coup, culminating in the murder of the president. In December 1979, the Soviet Union invaded Afghanistan and, following the execution of the prime minister, bolstered the new Marxist regime of the new Pres. Babrak Karmal. Armed resistance continued throughout the countryside and refugees poured into Pakistan and Iran.

AFL: *see* American Federation of Labor–Congress of Industrial Organizations; American Football League.

AFL–CIO: *see* American Federation of Labor–Congress of Industrial Organizations.

'Aflaq, Michel, 'Aflaq also spelled AFLAK (b. 1910, Damascus), social and political leader who played a major role in the Arab nationalist movement during and after World War II (1939–45).

'Aflaq first saw nationalism as centring upon the issue of imperialism; he especially resented the French, who after World War I (1914–18) held a mandate over Syria and Lebanon. In 1929–34, however, he studied at the University of Paris, and his political thinking took on a Marxist orientation. He came to believe that the nationalist struggle had to oppose both the native aristocracy and the foreign ruler. By 1940 he was ready to devote his full efforts to organizing a political party, although he did not officially establish the Ba'th Party until 1946. 'Aflaq's role was that of teacher, theorist, and organizer; he seldom held public office.

'Aflaq's political thinking linked the themes of unity, freedom, and Socialism. He saw unity as a regenerative process that would reform Arab society and character and as a vital creative force that would foster the emergence of a morally ideal, socialistic society. He saw final success as the product of a profound and nonviolent overthrow of the status quo.

Not until after 1955 did the Syrian political scene provide opportunity for the realization of 'Aflaq's dreams. With the conservative political parties fighting among themselves, 'Aflaq made a tactical alliance with the Communist Party and thus increased markedly the Ba'th's political influence. But he could not secure political dominance in the Syrian government, and he feared that the activities of the Communists might provoke right-wing repressions. Accordingly, he initiated moves that led in 1958 to a merger of Syria and Egypt to form the United Arab Republic (U.A.R.).

'Aflaq had expected Gamal Abdel Nasser, the president of Egypt, to allow the Ba'th to dominate the Syrian province of the U.A.R. But by 1960 the Ba'th had been reduced to political impotence. In 1961 Syria seceded from the U.A.R. 'Aflaq held himself and the Ba'th aloof from the ensuing violent criticism of Nasser and the conservative social and economic policies of the secessionist regime. The secessionist government was overthrown in 1963, and a government dominated by the Ba'th took power. At the same time a Ba'thist group effected a coup in Iraq. 'Aflaq began to coordinate movements between the two governments and to hold unity talks with Nasser. He distrusted Nasser, however, and wanted to strengthen Ba'thist rule in Iraq and Syria by simply identifying with the Egyptian's enormous prestige. The talks, however, brought no important results. 'Aflaq ceased to play an important role in Syrian politics after 1966 (when he moved to Lebanon) but continued to guide certain factions of the Ba'th Party in Iraq, Syria, and Lebanon.

Consult the INDEX *first*

Afonso, also spelled ALFONSO, name of rulers grouped below by country and indicated by the symbol •.

KONGO

• **Afonso I,** also called NZINGA MBEMBA (d. *c.* 1550), ruler of the Kongo Kingdom (in present Zaire and Angola), the first of a line of Portuguese vassal kings that lasted until the early 20th century. Nzinga Mbemba, who became the sixth *manikongo* (lord of the Kongo) in 1506 or 1507, encouraged the penetration of his country by the Portuguese that had begun under his predecessor, Nzinga Nkuwa. Becoming a Christian and adopting the Portuguese name Dom Afonso, he made an agreement (the *Regimento,* 1512) with Manuel I of Portugal by which the Kongo accepted Portuguese institutions, granted extraterritorial rights to Portuguese subjects, and supplied slaves to Portuguese traders.

PORTUGAL

• **Afonso I,** also called AFONSO HENRIQUES, byname AFONSO THE CONQUEROR, Portuguese AFONSO O CONQUISTADOR (b. 1109/11, Guimarães, Port.—d. Dec. 6, 1185, Coimbra), the first king of Portugal (1139–85), who conquered Santarém and Lisbon from the Muslims (1147) and secured Portuguese independence from Leon (1139).

Alfonso VI, emperor of Leon, had granted the county of Portugal to Afonso's father, Henry of Burgundy, who successfully defended it against the Muslims (1095–1112). Henry married Alfonso VI's illegitimate daughter, Teresa, who governed Portugal from the time of her husband's death (1112) until her son came of age. She refused to cede her power to him, but his party prevailed in the Battle of São Mamede, near Guimarães (1128). Though at first obliged as a vassal to submit to his cousin Alfonso VII of Leon, Afonso assumed the title of king in 1139.

By victory in the Battle of Ourique (1139) he was able to impose tribute on his Muslim neighbours; and in 1147 he further captured Santarém and, availing himself of the services of passing crusaders, successfully laid siege to Lisbon. He carried his frontiers beyond the Tagus River, annexing Beja in 1162 and Évora in 1165, but, in attacking Badajoz, he was taken prisoner, but then released. He married Mafalda of Savoy and associated his son, Sancho I, with his power. By the time of his death he had created a stable and independent monarchy.

• **Afonso II,** byname AFONSO THE FAT, Portuguese AFONSO O GORDO (b. 1185?, Coimbra, Port.—d. March 25, 1223, Coimbra), the third king of Portugal (1211–23), under whom the reconquest of the south from the Muslims was continued.

Afonso II was the son of King Sancho I and Queen Dulcia, daughter of Ramón Berenguer IV of Barcelona. His obesity seems to have been caused by illness in his youth, and he was unable to lead his forces. However, they distinguished themselves in the victory of Alfonso VIII of Castile at Las Navas de Tolosa (1212). This marked the decline of the Muslim Almohads, and Afonso II's army seized Alcacer do Sal in 1217.

Afonso II instituted inquiries into land titles, challenging the church and other landowners. This led to a long conflict with nobles and churchmen, and in 1219 the Archbishop of Braga excommunicated King and court and placed the kingdom under an interdict. These actions were confirmed by the papacy, but Afonso resisted until his death. He was succeeded by his son, Sancho II.

• **Afonso III** (b. May 5, 1210, Coimbra, Port.—d. Feb. 16, 1279, Lisbon), fifth king of Portugal (1248–79), who supplanted his brother, King Sancho II, and completed the reconquest of the Algarve from the Muslims.

The younger son of Afonso II and Urraeca, daughter of Alfonso VIII of Castile, Afonso emigrated and became, by marriage, count of Boulogne. His elder brother, Sancho II, was deposed by order of the Pope, who granted Afonso the crown. He returned to Portugal and was welcomed by the towns and the church. He reconquered the district of Faro in 1249 and shared the former Muslim region of Algarve with Castile.

His reign saw the first meeting of the Portuguese Cortes (parliament) in which the commoners of the municipalities were represented. Despite the help that he received from the Pope in becoming king, he took the same attitude as his predecessors about the repossession of church lands and was, like them, excommunicated. On his death, he was succeeded by his son Dinis.

• **Afonso IV,** byname AFONSO THE BRAVE, Portuguese AFONSO O BRAVO (b. Feb. 8, 1291, Lisbon—d. May 28, 1357, Lisbon), seventh king of Portugal (1325–57).

Afonso IV was the son of King Dinis and of Isabella, daughter of Peter II of Aragon. Afonso resented his father's generosity toward two illegitimate sons and in 1320 demanded to be given power, remaining in open revolt until May 1322. His mother reconciled them, but the conflict broke out again. When Dinis died, Afonso succeeded, but the quarrel was transferred to Castile, which sheltered his half brother. However, when the Marinid sultan of Morocco invaded Spain in 1340, Afonso IV led a force that joined Alfonso XI of Castile in the victory of the Salado River near Tárifa (Oct. 30, 1340).

In 1355 Afonso ordered the murder of Inês de Castro, the Galician mistress of his heir, the future Peter I, because he feared the influence of her family in Portugal. Peter rebelled, but Afonso finally was reconciled with him before his death.

• **Afonso V,** byname AFONSO THE AFRICAN, Portuguese AFONSO O AFRICANO (b. Jan. 15, 1432, Sintra, Port.—d. Aug. 28, 1481, Sintra), 10th king of Portugal (1438–81), known as the African from his campaigns in Morocco.

The son of King Edward (Duarte) and Queen Leonor, daughter of King Ferdinand I of Aragon, Afonso succeeded at the age of six. In 1440 his mother was deprived of the regency by his uncle Pedro, duque de Coimbra, whose daughter Isabella Afonso married. The regent was in turn challenged by a half brother, the Duque de Bragança, and was forced to fight, dying at Alfarrobeira (May 1449). Afonso remained much under the influence of others and distributed his favours rashly. In North Africa he conquered Alcácer Ceguer in 1458, failed to take Tangier in 1463, took Arzila in 1471, and finally took Tangier.

A widower, he married the young daughter of Henry IV of Castile and espoused her cause against Isabella and Ferdinand. Although he assumed the title of king of Castile, he was defeated at Toro in 1476. He then sailed for France, hoping to enlist the aid of Louis XI. This was refused, and he informed his son (later King John II) that he would abdicate and become a hermit in France. He was persuaded to return to Portugal in November 1477, but he renounced his reign and signed the Treaty of Alcáçovas (1479) abandoning any claim to Castile. He died before the Cortes could meet to ratify his abdication.

• **Afonso VI** (b. Aug. 21, 1643, Lisbon—d. Sept. 12, 1683, Sintra, Port.), king of Portugal, whose reign was marked by internal disputes between his partisans and those of his brother Pedro.

Afonso succeeded his father, John IV, in 1656, but his mother acted as regent until 1662. His reign saw a series of victories against Spain, including the battles of Ameixal (1663), Castelo Rodrigo (1664), and Montes Claros (1665), which in 1668 led to Spanish recognition of Portuguese independence. When Afonso's wife left him, their marriage was annulled on grounds of his incapacity. She married his brother, the future Peter II, who was declared Defender of the Realm. After surrendering the throne in 1667, Afonso was kept a virtual prisoner in the Azores and at Sintra until his death.

AFPFL (Burmese political party): *see* Anti-Fascist People's Freedom League.

Afrahat: *see* Aphraates.

Afram River, river, in southern Ghana, West Africa, rising in the Ashanti Region, 16 mi (26 km) northwest of Mampong, and flowing southeast into Lake Volta (formerly the Afram was a tributary of the Volta River) in Ghana's Eastern Region. It is about 55 mi (90 km) long. The river is important for fishing, despite its running dry from October to March, and it collects nearly all the drainage of the Kwahu Plateau. In the river valley the terrain is very flat and often flooded and swampy. Since the project to dam the Volta River for hydroelectric power (begun 1961; finished 1965), the lower Afram has become a busy arm of the impounded Lake Volta, serving as an important waterway.

Afranius, Lucius (b. Picenum—d. 46 BC, Africa), Roman general, a devoted adherent of Pompey the Great.

In 60 BC, chiefly by Pompey's support, he was raised to the consulship, in which office he proved himself incompetent to manage civil affairs. In the following year, while governor of Cisalpine Gaul, he obtained a triumph; and on the allotment of Spain to Pompey (55 BC), Afranius and Marcus Petreius were sent to govern it as legates.

On the rupture between Julius Caesar and Pompey, Afranius and Petreius were compelled, after a short campaign in which they were at first successful, to surrender to Caesar at Ilerda (49 BC). Caesar dismissed them on their promise not to serve again in the war. Afranius, however, went to join Pompey, and at the Battle of Pharsalus (48 BC) he had charge of Pompey's camp. On Pompey's defeat, Afranius, despairing of pardon from Caesar, went to Africa, and he was present at the disastrous Battle of Thapsus (46 BC), at which Caesar defeated the supporters of Pompey and gained control of Roman Africa. Although he escaped from the field with a strong body of cavalry, Afranius was afterward taken prisoner and was killed (according to varying accounts) either by seditious soldiers or at the command of Caesar.

Afrasian languages: *see* Hamito-Semitic languages.

Africa, second largest continent on Earth, embracing one-fifth of its land area and occupying 11,667,159 sq mi (30,217,894 sq km). The following article summarizes information about Africa; for full details, *see* MACROPAEDIA: Africa. From north to south, the continent is divided almost equally by the Equator, but because of the bulge formed by Western Africa, the greater part of Africa's territory lies northward. The continent is bounded on the north by the Mediterranean Sea, on the west by the Atlantic Ocean, on the east by the Red Sea and the Indian Ocean, and on the south by the confluence of the Atlantic and Indian oceans off the Cape of Good Hope. There are a number of islands associated with Africa; the largest of these, lying to the southeast, is Madagascar. In 1982 the population for the entire continent was estimated to be 504,882,000.

The land. Africa is largely composed of a vast rigid block of ancient rocks, forming the huge plateau regions of the African Shield that are higher at their coastward margins and drop along their local escarpments to form the continent's generally narrow coastal plains. The coastal lowlands widen inland at the Mozambique Lowland in the southeast, at the Mauritania-Senegal Basin in the northwest, at the Qattara Depression in the north, and at the Benadir Lowland along the Horn of Africa in the west. In contrast to the continent's average elevation of about 2,200 ft (670 m), the range of relief in Africa is nearly 20,000 ft, ranging from 19,340 ft (5,895 m) above sea level at Mt. Kilimanjaro in Tanzania to 512 ft below sea level at Lake Assal in Djibouti. The East African Rift System constitutes the most striking and distinctive relief feature of the continent; it is composed of a western branch (The Great Rift Valley) and an eastern branch (East African Rift Valley). Extending practically the length of the continent, the rift system forms the Red Sea basin; borders the Ethiopian Highlands (rising to heights of nearly 15,000 ft, comprising the continent's most extensive mountain system); and encompasses the extensive volcanic formations of the Virunga Mountains, before exiting into the Indian Ocean near the mouth of the Zambezi River in Mozambique. The Ruwenzori Range (Mountains of the Moon), rising to more than 16,000 ft in east central Africa, and the Drakensberg Mountains, rising to more than 11,000 ft along the southeastern coast, are among the continent's more dramatic highlands. Excepting the Atlas Mountains, along the northwestern coast, which rise to more than 13,000 ft, the northwestern third of the continent seldom exceeds 3,000 ft in elevation and generally lies between 500 and 1,000 ft. The Sahara, the world's largest contiguous desert, is roughly coincident with this lowland region and occupies more than one-fourth of Africa's total land area. The other major desert areas, the Namib and the Kalahari, lie in the southwestern extreme of the continent.

Africa's hydrology is dominated by the Nile (northward from the Equator) and the Congo (Central Africa) river basins, which together drain nearly one-fourth of the continent's land area. Lying at the divide of these two great watersheds are some of the world's most impressive lakes, formed within the deep valleys of Africa's great rift system and including Lake Victoria and Lake Tanganyika, third and seventh, respectively, among world lakes in surface area. The Niger river in West Africa and the Zambezi and Orange rivers in the south, along with their tributaries, account for much of the remaining external drainage area of the continent. Lake Chad, in the north, and the Okavango Swamp in the south lie within Africa's two major interior basins.

Africa's climate is dominated by its position astride the Equator. Temperatures are high for most of the year in the northern and southern tropical zones, but temperatures are modified by elevation in the mountains and on the coasts by the influence of ocean currents, *e.g.,* the cooling Benguela Current (southwest) and the warming Mozambique Current (southeast).

Only about 6 percent of the African continent is arable and nearly one-fourth is forested or wooded. The continent is well known for its wide variety of exotic animals. Big game animals are found roaming the savanna regions of the south and east and, to a lesser extent, in the savanna areas to the north. Some of the world's finest national parks were established as game reserves in Kenya, Uganda, Tanzania, Zambia, South Africa, and other countries.

Africa's share of some of the world's major mineral reserves was estimated in the early 1980s to include reserves of about a tenth of all petroleum, some 45 percent of the bauxite, 16 percent of the uranium, and 20 percent of the copper. The continent also has about two-thirds of the world's phosphorites and substantial reserves of iron ore, manganese, chromium, cobalt, platinum, and titanium.

The people. The population density of the continent is about 42 persons per sq mi (17 per sq km). Wide variations occur from country to country and within countries. The continent is a developing region with the associated demographic and social problems. Africa's efforts to achieve sustained economic growth have been plagued by the region's very high fertility levels, which negate most of the relatively modest economic growth that has been achieved by outpacing local economies. It is estimated that the continent's annual rate of population growth is about 2.9 percent, almost three times higher than real economic growth. Birth and death rates are as various as the countries within Africa's borders. Southern Africa, for example, has the lowest crude birth rate and an annual rate of growth of only about 2.2 percent. North, East, and Central Africa had annual rates of growth between 2.7 and 2.9 percent in the late 1970s, but the highest regional growth rate was reported in West Africa, with 3 percent.

The peoples inhabiting Africa probably speak more separate and distinct languages (800 to 1,000) than those of any other continent. The most homogeneous region, in terms of language, is North Africa, where Arabic is predominant from Egypt to Mauritania, as well as in The Sudan. Within the Maghrib, along the Mediterranean coast, reside Berber-(Hamitic-) speaking peoples, concentrated in Morocco and Algeria, but Arabic is also widely used.

The languages spoken by the sub-Saharan peoples are more numerous. With the exception of the Khoisan language family of southwestern Africa, the largest area of the sub-Sahara is inhabited by peoples speaking a number of languages known collectively as Bantu, the major subgroup of the Benue-Congo group of the Niger-Congo language family. Between the Arabic-dominated northern region and Bantu-speaking central and southern Africa reside groups speaking other languages of the Niger-Congo family. Close proximity to the Arabic culture of the Sahara has influenced black West Africans, and in a number of countries Islām is the predominant religion.

Nilo-Saharan peoples inhabit the Chad Basin (Saharan and Maba speakers), the Blue Nile basin (Koma speakers), and the upper middle Niger River region (Songhai speakers).

Chari-Nile-speakers reside along the middle Nile River, the White Nile, and the East African lakes. The forest-dwelling Pygmies, inhabiting various parts of central Africa, form a distinct ethnic and cultural group but have no distinctive language of their own. The Berbers of North Africa are Caucasoid and pursue a mixed agricultural and pastoral way of life. The vast majority of those who speak Bantu and other languages of the Niger-Congo family in western and central Africa are sedentary horticulturalists. Among the Bantu-speaking peoples of eastern and southern Africa, cattle raising plays an important economic role. Many Nilotic peoples in East Africa are sedentary horticulturalists.

In the southernmost parts of the continent peoples of European descent are found. Dutch (Boer) migrations began in the mid-17th century. The English first settled in what is now Zambia, Zimbabwe, and the East African Highlands in the 19th century. The Portuguese settled in Angola and Mozambique, while Germans settled South West Africa/Namibia.

The economy. Africa as a whole is a developing region; it may be divided into regions consisting of the more developed Mediterranean North African countries and Nigeria; the partly developed nations, including the Ivory Coast, Gabon, Réunion, Kenya, Zaire, Cameroon, Ghana, Zimbabwe, South West Africa/Namibia, and Mauritius; and the remaining less developed nations, except South Africa, which alone has an almost fully developed economy.

The continent's aggregate gross national product (GNP) was estimated in 1980 at $354,876,000,000, about $750 per capita. Average annual increase of the GNP (1970–79) was 0.9 percent. The GNP originates mainly from agriculture, services, industry and utilities, and mining and quarrying.

Agriculture produces about three-fourths of the continent's GNP but employs about two-thirds of the labour force. Traditional farming still predominates, though mechanization is slowly increasing. The leading cash crops include sugarcane, tomatoes, peanuts (groundnuts), bananas, oranges, cotton, grapes, coconuts and palm oil, olives, pineapples, coffee, and cacao. Subsistence crops include cassava, corn (maize), plantains, sorghum, millet, wheat, rice, sweet potatoes, potatoes, barley, watermelons, onions, and dry beans. Temperate and subtropical crops are grown primarily in northern and southern Africa, and in the highlands of Eastern

Africa, while tropical crops dominate in central and western Africa. Egypt, Nigeria, the Ivory Coast, Ghana, and Senegal are the leading crop producers. Many countries do not produce adequate domestic crops for national needs and must import food.

Rangeland and pastures occupy more than one-fourth of Africa's area, but they are marginal in the deserts of the north and south and overgrazed in the Sahel. Lower altitude pastures in Central Africa suffer from tsetse fly infestation. Cattle, sheep, goats, and pigs are the main livestock; in northern and eastern Africa camels, donkeys, and water buffaloes are widely used for transport and agricultural work. Dairying is limited overall, and most African countries must import dairy products; most North African countries also import meat.

About seven-eighths of the wood cut in Africa's vast forests is used as fuelwood. Forestry has been developed mainly in the Ivory Coast and Gabon, which lead in exports. Northern and southern Africa lack forests and must import nearly all wood supplies.

In the coastal states and in those states with reservoirs, fishing has developed into an important commercial industry and a source of exports.

Africa has rich but unevenly distributed mineral deposits. South Africa and four neighbouring countries produce three-fourths of the world's diamonds; South Africa, Ghana, and Zimbabwe produce more than half the gold. Petroleum and natural gas are produced in large quantities by Nigeria, Libya, Algeria, and Egypt.

Manufacturing contributes only about one-eighth of the continent's GNP, and half of that comes from the partly industrialized nations including South Africa, Zimbabwe, Swaziland, Morocco, and Senegal. Industrializing nations contributed another one-third.

Construction generates about 6 percent of the continental GNP. Tourism is important to many African nations as a source of revenue, and countries with well-developed tourist facilities include Tunisia, Morocco, Egypt, Botswana, Kenya, Zimbabwe, Algeria, and the Ivory Coast.

Africa receives developmental aid from a great variety of sources, largely determined by the individual countries' political orientation and international memberships.

Much of Africa suffers from inadequate transportation facilities; landlocked mid-continent countries are particularly affected. Although many countries have railway systems, problems arise from differing track gauges and from political hostilities. The principal rivers are navigable for long stretches and are an important part of the transportation network. Only about 27 percent of Africa's roads are paved.

Africa's exports exceeded imports (1979) by about $10,000,000,000, but most countries had negative trade balances; those with positive balances were major producers of petroleum, natural gas, or minerals—except for the Ivory Coast and Rwanda. The principal exports were petroleum and natural gas, food, beverages, and tobacco, and raw materials, sent mainly to the European Economic Community (EEC), the United States, and Eastern Europe and the Soviet Union. The principal imports were machinery and transport equipment, miscellaneous manufactured goods, food, beverages, and tobacco, and petroleum and natural gas, mainly obtained from the EEC, the Middle Eastern Organization of Petroleum Exporting Countries (OPEC), the United States, and Japan.

Administrative and social conditions. The predominant form of government in Africa is the one-party state controlled by either a socialist political organization or a group of military officers. Multi-party democracy is confined to Egypt, The Gambia, Mauritius, Nigeria, Senegal, Uganda, Zimbabwe, and South Africa (however, only whites may vote). Some African island territories remain under the control of European countries: Réunion and Mayotte (France), St. Helena (the United Kingdom), the Canary Islands (Spain), and the Madeira Islands (Portugal). On the mainland, the Western Sahara and South West Africa/Namibia had not achieved independence by the early 1980s.

Many present-day African legal systems are based on the laws introduced by European powers during the colonial era, though the countries of North Africa derive their laws from the tenets of Islām.

African leaders seek to develop a pan-African approach to the continent's political and military problems through the Organization of African Unity (OAU). Although classic colonial rule in Africa has ended, external powers continue to seek political and military influence there. African countries receive large amounts of economic and military aid from the contending world powers and their proxies; the Soviet Union, East Germany, Cuba, and France all maintain significant numbers of troops and military advisers on African soil. During the early 1980s, it was estimated that Cuba's military force in Africa numbered between 30,000 and 40,000.

Most African countries have yet to develop comprehensive systems of social welfare benefits. The more developed systems are found in South Africa and the North African countries of Egypt, Tunisia, and Algeria.

Health and sanitary conditions in Africa are generally poor, particularly outside the major metropolitan centres where there are doctors and hospitals. Africans in many parts of the continent suffer from starvation or malnutrition; the most prevalent diseases include malaria, dysentery, tuberculosis, whooping cough, typhoid fever, and gonorrhea. South Africa, Libya, and the Western Sahara are perhaps the only countries in Africa that do not have a serious shortage of doctors. High infant mortality rates are prevalent throughout much of the continent; some (*e.g.,* Guinea-Bissau) as high as 200 per 1,000 live births. Life expectancies may be as low as 40 years in the least developed countries or as high as 65 years in salubrious climates like that of Mauritius. Most African countries do not have compulsory education and are usually lacking enough trained teachers and adequate facilities. Only in the Congo, the Seychelles, Zimbabwe, and Mauritius are primary enrollment rates high (more than 90 percent).

The news media in most African countries are government-controlled. Freedom of the press (of varying degrees) is found in Egypt, Kenya, Morocco, Nigeria, the Ivory Coast, Mauritius, and Senegal.

Cultural life. The sociocultural traditions of northern Africa are both Arabic and Islāmic. The area is noted for its traditional arts of weaving, embroidery, metal engraving, and leather work. The dominant geometric and arabesque designs are presented in the stucco and tiles of the many mosques found throughout North Africa. Musical styles are basically Arabic and rely upon improvisation and embellishment of melody. To the traditional Arabic literary genres—poetry, essays, and historiography—have been added forms inspired by Middle Eastern and Western literary models.

In sub-Saharan Africa, dance, drama, and sculpture are among the more exciting and original of the area's many art forms; the dance in particular can be fiercely beautiful or tenderly expressive. Most of sub-Saharan Africa also has an active literary life, and authors and playwrights write in either the language of the former colonial power (to reach a wider audience) or in one of the vernacular languages. Works in the vernacular are particularly extensive in Swahili, Yoruba, and the Bantu languages of South Africa. Popular music is also vigorous, with many traditions represented. The "high life" music of the Guinea coast has found ready acceptance in Europe and North America.

History. The human race may well have originated in Africa. In much of the continent about 15,000,000 to 25,000,000 years ago there were various forms of the Dryopithecine apes believed by some scientists to be common ancestors of humans and recent apes. The hominid *Ramapithecus,* found in East Africa, dates from 14,000,000 years ago and *Australopithecus* from 5,000,000 years ago. The hominids *Homo habilis* and *Homo erectus* inhabited East, South, and Northwest Africa from about 1,000,000 years ago. Sometime after 60,000 years ago, there occurred a lowering of much of the continent's climatic temperatures and the appearance of *Homo sapiens.*

At the end of the Pleistocene Epoch (about 10,000 years ago), distinct indigenous African races had emerged. Africa's first great kingdom, that of Egypt, arose along the Nile, and from its unification in approximately 3000 BC, it flourished for nearly 3,000 years. With the Sumerian kingdom of Mesopotamia, it is indeed the cradle of civilization. The Phoenicians established a colony at Carthage (in present-day Tunisia), which outstripped Phoenicia itself and controlled the western Mediterranean for nearly 600 years. The whole of North Africa fell to the Romans after 146 BC, and its legacy lasted until the Arab Bedouin invasions of the 11th century AD.

Trading empires that controlled trans-Saharan trade in gold, kola nuts, and slaves developed in western Africa. The first empire of which there is extant knowledge was Ghana, with its capital at Kumbi, which flourished from the 5th to the 11th century AD. The same period saw the rise of the empire of Kanem-Bornu around Lake Chad, which reached the height of its power in the 17th century. Muslim empires to the west also flourished; the greatest of these were the Mali (*c.* 1250–1400) and its successor, the Songhai of Gao (*c.* 1400–1591).

In eastern and central Africa the emphasis was greater on trade with countries beyond Africa, particularly Arabia. By the 13th century, East African-Arab settlements had developed into powerful city states: Mogadishu, Mombasa, Lamu, Kilwa, and others. In the 16th century, they were destroyed by the Portuguese who in turn were ousted by the Omani Arabs; the Omanis established the slave-trading state of Zanzibar.

To the south was the Bantu-speaking empire of Mwene Matapa, and other dynasties arose inland from the East African coast. The kingdom of the Kongo was located near the mouth of the Congo River and others lay farther south.

Most of these empires depended on long-distance trade. They were weakened and in many cases destroyed by the early colonial powers from Europe and Arabia who coveted their trade and supplanted them, turning much of the trade to external rather than internal markets and creating new trade goods, notably slaves. Estimates of the number of slaves actually taken from Africa range from 30,000,000 to 100,000,000.

The Portuguese were the first Europeans to undertake systematic voyages of discovery along the African coast (15th century). The Dutch presence in South Africa dates from 1652, but European exploration of the interior was carried out mainly in the 19th century by British explorers Sir Richard Burton, David Livingstone, and Henry Stanley.

By 1884 the European powers began a scramble to partition Africa so that by 1920 every square mile except for Ethiopia, Liberia, and the Union of South Africa was under colonial rule or protection. Anti-colonial and independence movements developed and became widespread after 1950, and, one by one, the colonies became independent.

Africa, Roman province of, first African territory of Rome, at times roughly corresponding to modern Tunisia; it was acquired in 146 BC after the destruction of Carthage at the end of the Third Punic War.

Initially, the province comprised the territory subject to Carthage in 149 BC, an area of about 5,000 square miles (13,000 square kilometres), divided from the kingdom of Numidia in the west by a ditch and embankment running southeast from Thabraca (modern Ṭabarqah) to Thaenae (modern Thīnah). About 100 BC this boundary was extended further westward, almost as far as the present Algerian–Tunisian border.

The province grew in importance during the 1st century BC, when Julius Caesar and, later, the emperor Augustus founded a total of 19 colonies. Most notable among these was the new Carthage, which the Romans called Colonia Julia Carthago; it rapidly became the second city in the Western Roman Empire. Augustus extended Africa's borders southward as far as the Sahara and eastward to include Arae Philaenorum, at the southernmost point of the Gulf of Sidrah. In the west he combined the old province of Africa Vetus (Old Africa) with what Caesar had designated as Africa Nova (New Africa)—the old kingdoms of Numidia and Mauretania—so that the western boundary was the Ampsaga (modern Oued Rhumel) River in modern northeastern Algeria. The province generally retained those dimensions until the late 2nd century AD, when a new province of Numidia, created in the western end of Africa, was formally constituted under Septimius Severus. A century later Diocletian, in his reorganization of the empire, formed two provinces, Byzacena and Tripolitania, from the southern and eastern parts of the old province.

The original territory annexed by Rome was populated by indigenous Libyans who lived in small villages and had a relatively simple culture. In 122 BC, however, an abortive attempt by Gaius Sempronius Gracchus to colonize Africa aroused the interest of Roman farmers and investors. In the 1st century BC Roman colonization, coupled with Augustus' successful quieting of hostile nomadic movements, created conditions that led to four centuries of prosperity. Between the 1st and 3rd centuries AD, private estates of considerable size appeared, many public buildings were erected, and an export industry in cereals, olives, fruit, and hides flourished. Substantial elements of the urban Libyan population became Romanized, and many communities received Roman citizenship long before it was extended to the whole empire (212). Africans increasingly entered the imperial administration, and the area even produced an emperor, Septimius Severus (ruled AD 193–211). The province also claimed an important Christian Church, which had more than 100 bishops by AD 256 and produced such luminaries as the Church Fathers Tertullian, Cyprian, and St. Augustine of Hippo.

By the end of the 4th century, however, city life had decayed. The Germanic Vandals under Gaiseric reached the province in 430 and soon made Carthage their capital. Roman civilization entered a state of irreversible decline, despite the numerical inferiority of the Vandals and their subsequent destruction by the Byzantine general Belisarius in 533. When Arab invaders took Carthage in 697, the Roman province of Africa offered little resistance.

African ant bear: *see* aardvark.

African arts, the literary, performing, and visual arts of native Africa, particularly of sub-Saharan, or black, Africa. All the familiar media—sculpture, painting, textiles and other fabrics, costume, jewelry, architecture, music, dance, drama, and poetry—are found.

A brief treatment of African arts follows. For full treatment, *see* MACROPAEDIA: African Arts.

What gives art in Africa its special character is the generally small scale of most of its traditional societies, in which one finds a more immediate interrelationship between art and other social forms and its bewildering variety of styles, each developed in its own particular ecological, historical, and social circumstances. The contemporary artist in Africa, living and working in a modern, urban environment has, of course, all the richness of these cultural traditions to draw upon, even though he may employ different techniques and enjoy a different kind of patronage than did his traditional counterpart.

It is usual, but mistaken, to equate art in Africa with sculpture. The earliest evidence of art is provided by the engravings and paintings on rock surfaces in the Sahara spanning a period of about 5,000 years to the present day. Regarding visual art, Africa can be divided into three broad regions. The first is the area in which Islām and Oriental Christianity have linked Africa to the rest of the world in pre-colonial times. Architecture predominates among the visual arts. Included here are north and northeast Africa, extending southward to take in the magnificent mosques, built of mud, of Jenne and Mopti in Mali, the rock-hewn churches of Ethiopia, and the Islāmic monuments of coastal east Africa. The second is the area in which pastoral cultures predominate. Here, stress in the visual arts is laid upon personal adornment and upon the aesthetic values of cattle. This is also the area in which rock art is mainly to be found. Clearly, these two areas intersect in their trans-Saharan distribution; and from there this area extends through the grasslands of eastern and southern Africa. The third is the area that the agricultural peoples of western and central Africa share with the great river systems of the Niger and Zaire. Here sculpture predominates among the visual arts. These areas are by no means precisely demarcated, however, and it would be incorrect to assume that personal arts are of significance only to pastoralists.

Knowledge of the history of visual arts in Africa remains extremely fragmentary. The earliest known sculptures are the pottery heads and figures of the Nok culture of Nigeria (500 BC to AD 200). This also provides the earliest evidence for iron-working in sub-Saharan Africa, where the Iron Age follows directly upon the Stone Ages. The earliest evidence for the use of copper and its alloys comes from the Igbo village of Igbo-Ukwu, also in Nigeria, where sites of the 9th century AD have revealed a quantity of cast bronze regalia among other works of art. These bear no relationship in style either to the famous brass castings of the Yoruba city of Ife (11th–15th century) or to those of Benin (15th–19th century), both in Nigeria. Other examples of antique pottery sculpture include the heads from Lydenburg in South Africa dated to about AD 500. Sculptures in stone are known from Sierra Leone, probably the work of Sherbro carvers and datable to no later than the 16th century, and from the Kongo peoples of the area around the mouth of the Zaire river. In the 16th century, ivory was being carved with extraordinary skill at Benin and by the Sherbro of Sierra Leone. The earliest known sculptures in wood may be certain portrait statues of kings of the Kuba, central Zaire, thought to date from the 17th century. Some of the finest sculptures in wood date, however, only from the 1920s: for example, the works of Yoruba masters such as Olowe of Ise (d. 1939) and Areogun of Osi-Ilorin (*c.* 1880–1954). The earliest known textiles in sub-Saharan Africa are the bast fibre fragments from Igbo-Ukwu (9th century AD) and the cotton and woollen cloths found in the Tellem caves of the Bandiagara region of Mali (11th century and earlier). None of these artistic manifestations represents a beginning of any kind: each appears as fully developed in style.

The performing arts—dance, drama, and music—are at least as pervasive in African culture as the visual arts. Perhaps the most distinctive features of African music are the complexity of rhythmic patterning and the relationship between melodic form and language tone structure. Without this the text of a song is rendered meaningless; but even in purely instrumental music, melodic pattern is likely to follow speech tone.

The literary arts are probably the most universal and the most highly regarded of arts in Africa. They include myths, folktales, spells, proverbs, and, above all, poetry. These are the arts most inaccessible to outsiders, which probably explains why comparatively little attention has yet been paid to them. Most of these forms are oral, but written literatures have existed for several centuries in Hausa, Swahili, and Amharic. In the present century written literatures in other African as well as European languages have developed.

In many parts of Africa most people have some practical familiarity with techniques of manufacture and performance. Wherever there are professional artists, however, attitudes toward them vary considerably. The esteem an artist enjoys may have as much to do with the cultural role of art in that community as with his ability.

The masquerade is a complex art form employing all the other media. Masquerades may entertain, cure disease, be consulted as oracles, initiate boys to manhood, impersonate ancestors, judge disputes, or execute criminals. The mask is essentially a dramatic device enabling the performer to stand apart from his everyday role in the community. The complexity of masquerade and its related public festivities suggests that it is the sub-Saharan's principal art form.

A list of the abbreviations used in the MICROPAEDIA *will be found at the end of this volume*

African Development Bank (ADB), French BANQUE AFRICAINE DE DÉVELOPPEMENT, African organization established in September 1964 and operational beginning in July 1966. The Secretariat of the United Nations Economic Commission for Africa, together with a nine-member committee of experts from member states engineered the agreement, but the bank is not formally associated with the United Nations. Its membership includes 50 African states. The headquarters are in Abidjan, Ivory Coast.

The bank aims to spur both economic development and social progress among its members on an individual and a joint basis. It has five associated institutions through which public and private capital is channelled: the African Development Fund, the Nigeria Trust Fund, the African Reinsurance Corporation (Africare), the Société Internationale Financière pour les Investissements et le Développement en Afrique (SIFIDA), and the Association of African Development Finance Institutions (AADFI).

African Games, also called PAN-AFRICAN GAMES, or ALL-AFRICAN GAMES, international athletics (track and field) competition sponsored by the International Amateur Athletics

Federation (IAAF), first held in 1965. Attempts to hold such African games date back to the 1920s; and in the early 1960s "friendship" games were held, but only among formerly French-governed countries. Two later Games were postponed for political reasons after 1965; the second Games were held in 1973, and the number of participating countries rose from 29 to 35. Other athletic events were added such as boxing, cycling, basketball, handball, tennis, soccer, swimming, and volleyball. While the United Arab Republic won the most medals in the Games, world-class performances by blacks in the middle distance races drew international attention. The Games were next held in 1982.

African geographical race: *see* Negroid geographical race.

African Greek Orthodox Church, a religious movement in East Africa that represents a prolonged search for a Christianity more African and, its adherents say, more authentic than the denominational mission forms transplanted from overseas. It began when an Anglican in Uganda, Reuben Spartas, heard of the independent, all-black African Orthodox Church in the United States and founded his own African Orthodox Church in 1929. In 1932 he secured ordination by the U.S. church's archbishop from South Africa, whose episcopal orders traced to the ancient Syrian Jacobite (Monophysite) Church of India. After discovering that the U.S. body was heterodox, the African Church added the term Greek and from 1933 developed an affiliation with the Alexandrian patriarchate of the Greek Orthodox Church that culminated in its coming under the control of the first Greek missionary archbishop for East Africa in 1959. Also included were similar but larger churches that had arisen in central and western Kenya.

In 1966 tensions arising from missionary paternalism, inadequate material assistance, and young Greek-trained priests who were not particularly African-oriented led Spartas and his followers into secession. The new group, the African Orthodox Autonomous Church South of the Sahara (with some 7,000 members in Uganda), made unsuccessful approaches to other Greek patriarchates. These East African churches have asserted their African autonomy, shared in nationalist political activities, and accommodated to African customs (such as polygamy, ritual purificatory circumcision of females, and divination). At the same time their vernacular versions of the Liturgy of St. John Chrysostom, use of vestments and icons, and identification with Eastern Orthodoxy represent a search for connection with the primitive church.

A list of the abbreviations used in the MICROPAEDIA *will be found at the end of this volume*

African horse sickness (AHS), also called EQUINE PLAGUE, OR PERDESIEKTE, viral disease important in southern and equatorial Africa, transmitted by insects, especially *Culicoides* gnats. Dogs have contracted the disease by eating infected horsemeat. Symptoms occur within 10 days of viral invasion and include fever and localized fluid retention. Death may quickly occur from fluid-filled lungs, or the disease may assume a chronic form, ending in heart failure. There is no cure. Annual vaccination provides effective immunity.

African hunting dog, also called CAPE HUNTING DOG, OR HYENA DOG (*Lycaon pictus*), wild African carnivore that differs from the rest of the dog family (Canidae) in having only four toes on each foot. Its coat is short, sparse, and irregularly blotched with yellow, black, and white. The African hunting dog is about 76–102 centimetres (30–41 inches) long, exclusive of its 31–41-cm tail, stands about 60 cm at the shoulder, and weighs about 16–23 kilograms (35–50 pounds).

African hunting dogs (*Lycaon pictus*)
Christina Loke—Photo Researchers

Long-limbed with a broad, flat head, short muzzle, and large, erect ears, it hunts in packs of 15 to 60 or more and is found in most of Africa south and east of the Sahara, particularly in grasslands. It usually preys on antelopes and some larger game but has been hunted in settled regions for the damage it sometimes does to domestic livestock. The average number of young per litter appears to be about six; gestation periods of about 60 and 80 days have been noted.

African International Association: *see* Association Internationale Africaine.

African languages, languages indigenous to sub-Saharan Africa that belong to the Niger-Congo, Nilo-Saharan, Khoisan, and Hamito-Semitic language families. The number of African languages has been estimated to be from 800 to more than 1,000. Important sub-Saharan languages include Fulani, Yoruba, Igbo, and Zulu of the Niger-Congo family; Kunama, Shilluk, Dinka, and Nuer of the Nilo-Saharan family; and Galla, Somali, and Hausa of the Hamito-Semitic languages (*q.v.*). Lingua francas that incorporate Arabic and European loanwords include Swahili, Lingala, Fanagalo, and Sango.

A brief treatment of the African languages follows. For full treatment, *see* MACROPAEDIA: Languages of the World.

Since the mid-19th century, linguists have been facing the challenge of classifying African languages. In addition to the problems of searching for features that would demonstrate genetic relationships between languages and then substantiating chosen methods of classification, their task has been complicated by the facts that Africa is the most polyglot continent and that the borders between linguistic families are in some places very complex and indistinct. As a result, many different systems of grouping the languages were devised and, more often than not, rejected.

In 1963, however, the United States linguist Joseph Greenberg revised an earlier thesis and proposed a system of classification with which most linguists agree. According to Greenberg, all the native languages of Africa may be divided into four large families or stocks, which are considered to be independent of each other and which can be further divided into subgroups, member languages, and dialects. These four stocks are: Niger-Kordofanian (including Niger-Congo), Nilo-Saharan (including Chari-Nile), Khoisan, and Hamito-Semitic (Afro-Asiatic). Not included in this division is the language spoken in Madagascar, which belongs to the Austronesian family of languages.

The Niger-Kordofanian family consists of two branches of very disproportionate size: the small Kordofanian group in The Sudan and the vast Niger-Congo family, which covers almost all of western Africa south of the Sahara, as well as most of the Congo Basin and eastern and southern Africa.

The Niger-Congo family includes some 900 member languages and thousands of dialects. Fulani, the most widely spoken member language of the West Atlantic group (one of the six subgroups that make up the Niger-Congo family), is also the most grammatically complex. The 26 member languages that comprise the Mande subgroup are the most divergent from the rest so that the fundamental division within Niger-Congo is between Mande and all other groups. The 79 languages spoken in Burkina Faso (formerly Upper Volta) and parts of neighbouring states are known as the Voltaic (Gur) subgroup; and, of these, Mossi is the most important. The fourth subgroup, Kwa, includes Ga, Yoruba, Igbo, and 70 other member languages. Not much is known about the 112 languages that make up the Adamawa-Eastern subgroup, spoken mainly in the Central African Republic and parts of Cameroon and Zaire. Swahili, Kongo, Zulu, and 554 other languages belong to the Benue-Congo subgroup, which includes Bantu as a subdivision.

Nilo-Saharan is divided into six branches of unequal size and importance: Songhai, spoken in Mali and Niger along the Niger River; the Saharan group, comprising Kanuri, a language of Nigeria, Teda, spoken over a considerable part of the central Sahara, and Zaghawa of Chad and The Sudan; Maba, a small group of languages spoken in Chad; Koma, a group of little-known languages spoken in a relatively restricted portion of the Ethiopian–Sudan border area; Fur, a language of Darfur province of The Sudan; and by far the largest of the six branches, Chari-Nile, the family of languages spoken in areas surrounding the Nile and Chari rivers. Chari-Nile is further subdivided into four branches: Kunama, Berta, Central Sudanic, and Eastern Sudanic.

The Khoisan family of languages comprises approximately 12 languages that are spoken by the San (Bushmen) and Khoikhoin (Hottentots) of southern Africa. These languages are characterized by click sounds not found anywhere in the world outside Africa. Sandawe and Hadza, spoken in Tanzania, are usually included in the Khoisan family.

Hamito-Semitic, or Afro-Asiatic, covers all of northern Africa, while its Semitic branch extends into the adjoining areas of Asia. It is divided into five branches: Berber, of Morocco, Algeria, and parts of the Sahara; Ancient Egyptian, no longer in existence; Semitic, including Arabic, the Ethiopian Semitic languages, and Tigrinya, the language of Eritrea; Cushitic, consisting of five groups of languages spoken in northeastern Africa; Chadic, those languages spoken in northern Nigeria and surrounding areas.

Despite the fact that the languages of these four independent stocks differ greatly from one another in structure, certain common features can be discerned. Most sub-Saharan African languages are tonal: a change in pitch, for example, is often the only means of distinguishing two words that would sound exactly alike in all other circumstances. Tones are based on pitch levels usually two or three in number.

Many West African languages have noun classes: nouns are divided into classes, each marked by a pair of affixes (prefixes, suffixes, or both), one for the singular and one for the plural. For example, in Swahili, a Bantu language, the sentence "one sharp knife has been lost" would read *ki-su ki-kali ki-moja ki-me-pota. Su* ("knife") has *ki-* as its class prefix, and this is repeated before every word agreeing with *su.* The prefix *vi-* takes the place of *ki-* when "knives" is plural: *vi-su vi-kali vi-nane vi-me-potea* ("eight sharp knives have been lost").

Various African languages also have systems of verb derivation. In Swahili, from *pata* ("to obtain") the following derivatives may be formed, among others: *patana* ("to make an agreement"); *patanisha* ("to reconcile"); *patia* ("to obtain for somebody"); *patika* ("to be obtainable"); *patiliza* ("to vex someone"); *patilizana* ("to vex each other"). The meanings are generally but not always predictable.

Contact between people who do not speak the same language has necessitated the development of lingua francas, *i.e.,* languages that allow diverse groups to communicate with one another. Examples of such languages are Swahili in East Africa, Lingala in the Congo Basin, Sango in the Central African Republic, and Arabic in large areas of The Sudan. In some parts, English and French are also used as lingua francas, as are their pidgin versions.

African lion dog: *see* Rhodesian ridgeback.

African Methodist Episcopal Church, U.S. Methodist church, formally organized in 1816. It developed from a congregation formed by a group of blacks who withdrew in 1787 from St. George's Methodist Episcopal Church in Philadelphia because of discrimination. They built Bethel African Methodist Church in Philadelphia, and in 1799 Richard Allen (*q.v.*) was ordained minister of the church by Bishop Francis Asbury of the Methodist Episcopal Church. In 1816 Asbury consecrated Allen bishop of the newly organized African Methodist Episcopal Church.

Confined to the Northern states before the Civil War, the church spread rapidly in the South after the war. It supports an active home-missions program and has sent foreign missionaries to Africa and the West Indies.

The church is Methodist in doctrine and church government, and it holds a general conference every four years. It has about 2,200,000 members.

African Methodist Episcopal Zion Church, black Methodist church in the U.S., organized in 1821; it adopted its present name in 1848. It developed from a congregation formed by a group of blacks who in 1796 left the John Street Methodist Church in New York City because of discrimination. They built their first church (Zion) in 1800 and were served for many years by white ministers of the Methodist Episcopal Church. In 1821 a conference attended by representatives of six black churches and presided over by a white Methodist minister elected a black bishop, James Varick (1750–1828).

After the Civil War the church grew rapidly in the North and the South. Foreign-mission programs were established in South America, Africa, and the West Indies.

The church is Methodist in doctrine and church government; a general conference is held every four years. In 1980 nearly 1,350,000 members were reported.

African National Congress (ANC), South African political party and black nationalist organization, founded in 1912. It is the oldest of the nonwhite political bodies in South Africa and, since its banning by the government in 1961, has operated underground and outside South African territory.

Founded by blacks during parliamentary discussions of the restrictive Native Lands Act (1913), the ANC aimed at eliminating all colour bars and obtaining black representation in parliament. Over the years it sponsored protests, strikes, petitions, and marches, frequently becoming a target of police harassment and arrest. By the end of World War II the ANC had begun strong agitation against the pass laws; and, after the victory (1948) of the National Party with its doctrines of apartheid and white supremacy, ANC membership grew rapidly, rising to 100,000 in 1952, the year that Albert Lutuli (winner of the Nobel Peace Prize in 1960) was elected president general of the party.

In 1960 the Pan-African Congress, an ANC split-off, organized massive demonstrations against the pass laws. After police killed or wounded hundreds at Sharpeville, a suburb of Vereeniging, the ANC and PAC were outlawed. Denied legal avenues for political change, the ANC turned first to sabotage and then began to organize abroad for guerrilla warfare. Many new fighters joined the ANC after the Soweto uprising in 1976 when the police and army killed over 600 people. By the early 1980s ANC guerrilla activity was becoming a regular feature of South African life, the most dramatic being a series of car bomb attacks on Air Force headquarters that killed or wounded hundreds in 1983. The South African government in turn launched frequent attacks on alleged ANC bases abroad.

The most important ANC leaders in the 1980s included Oliver Tambo (in exile) and Nelson Mandela (imprisoned).

African oil palm (*Elaeis guineensis*), one of two species of tropical palms (family Palmae), a source of commercially valued oil. *See* oil palm.

African polecat: *see* zorille.

African Pygmy local race, a subgroup, roughly corresponding to a breeding isolate in genetics, of the Negroid (African) geographical race. There are three main populations of Pygmies: Western, Northern, and Southern. The Western Pygmies live in scattered groups in Cameroon, Gabon, Equatorial Guinea, the Congo (Brazzaville), Zaire, and part of the Central African Republic. The Northern Pygmies are those of the Ituri rain forest in eastern Zaire near Uganda. The Southern group ("Lake Kivu potters") are found in Rwanda and Burundi.

The chief physical traits of the Pygmies are short stature (averaging less than five feet)

Pygmies living near the Epulu River, Zaire
Hubertus Kanus—Rapho/Photo Researchers

with short legs and long arms, yellowish to reddish-brown skin, rather heavy body hair, wide nose with a low bridge, prognathous (projecting) jaw, and receding chin. The Pygmies are also notable in having the highest basal metabolism rate in the world. They resemble the Forest Negro local race in the high incidence of sickle-cell anemia. *See also* Negroid geographical race; pygmy.

African Trade Union Confederation (ATUC), international African trade union federation with a more pragmatic approach than that of the All-African Trade Union Federation (*q.v.*). It was formed in 1962 by a group of unions affiliated with the International Confederation of Free Trade Unions, the International Federation of Christian Trade Unions (now World Confederation of Labour), and some independents in reaction to the All-African group's strong stand against affiliating with those international organizations. The ATUC favours diversity among its members and supports their autonomy in affiliating with other international unions. Its general aims include a socialist African society, economic development, an African common market, and social security for workers.

African Trade Union Unity, Organization of (OATUU), French ORGANISATION DE L'UNITÉ SYNDICALE AFRICAINE (OUSA), labour organization founded in 1973 at Addis Ababa, Eth., on the initiative of the Organization of African Unity and replacing the former All-African Trade Union Federation (AATUF; founded in 1961) and the African Trade Union Confederation (ATUC; founded in 1962). The ATUC had had a more traditionally pragmatic approach than that of the AATUF, which was a militant supporter of African nationalism and considered affiliation with world trade-union confederations to be incompatible with the development of a Pan-African federation.

The OATUU in the late 1970s had as members trade-union movements in 31 countries on the continent; in 1977 it held a Pan-African conference in Luanda, Angola. Its aims are to build trade-union unity on the African continent, to coordinate the action of national union organizations, and to support, in general, the interests of the African working class. Its headquarters are in Accra, Ghana.

African trypanosomiasis: *see* sleeping sickness.

African Unity, Organization of (OAU), intergovernmental organization, established May 25, 1963, to which all African states (except South Africa and South West Africa/Namibia) have at some time belonged. (In 1978–79 the Comorros were briefly expelled because of a disputed government. In 1984 Morocco resigned and Zaire withdrew over the seating of the "Sahrawi Arab Democratic Republic," a Polisario rebel group at war with Morocco in the Western Sahara.)

The OAU's major practical achievements were mediation in the Algerian–Moroccan dispute (1964–65) and in the Somali–Ethiopia and Kenya–Somali border disputes (1965–67). Efforts to mediate in the civil war in Nigeria (1968–70) proved unavailing. In the 1980s the OAU attempted mediation to halt the civil war in Chad and proposed economic sanctions against South Africa to protest that country's policy of racism. The OAU maintains the "Africa group" at the United Nations through which many of its efforts at international coordination are channelled. The OAU has also brought about the joint cooperation of African states in the work of the "Committee of 77," which acts as a caucus of developing nations within the UN Conference on Trade and Development (UNCTAD).

The principal organ of the OAU is the annual assembly of heads of state and government. Between these summit conferences policy decisions are in the hands of a council of ministers, composed of foreign ministers of member states. The OAU's headquarters are in Addis Ababa, Eth.

African violet, flowering plant of the genus *Saintpaulia* (family Gesneriaceae, *q.v.*), especially *S. ionantha.* The genus consists of 12 species native to higher elevations in tropical eastern Africa. The plants are small, hairy, usually stemless herbs with crowded, long-stalked leaves.

African violet flowers are bilaterally symmetrical and violet, white, or pink in colour; they bloom throughout most of the year. Hundreds

African violet (*Saintpaulia ionantha*)
Maurice B. Cook

of horticultural varieties have been developed for their various flower colours and shapes, including half-sized miniatures and varieties developed for their foliage.

Africanthropus, genus name tentatively assigned to fragments of three human crania found in 1935 and 1938 by Ludwig Kohl-Larsen near Lake Eyasi in northern Tanzania. The fossils were originally thought to be of the same lower Pleistocene age as Java and Peking man because of a dubious reconstruction of the fragments. Evidence now indicates that the craniums represent remains with affinities to *Homo sapiens rhodesiensis,* commonly called Kabwe man (*q.v.*).

Africanus, Sextus Julius (b. *c.* AD 180, Jerusalem—d. *c.* 250), first Christian historian known to produce a universal chronology.

His life is not well documented, but evidence indicates that he travelled considerably in Asia, Egypt, and Italy, and later lived chiefly at Emmaus, in Palestine, where he served as prefect. He was named (*c.* 222) regional ambassador to Rome, when he became a protégé of the emperor Severus Alexander. Africanus' greatest work was *Chronographiai* (221), a five-volume treatise on sacred and profane history from the creation (which he placed at 5499 BC) to AD 221. Relying on the Bible as the basis of his calculations, he incorporated and synchronized Egyptian and Chaldaean chronologies, Greek mythology, and Judaic history with Christianity. His work raised the prestige of early Christianity by placing it within a historical context. He also wrote a critical work on genealogies of Christ as found in Matthew and Luke.

Afrīdī, Pashtun tribe inhabiting the hill country from the eastern spurs of the Safed Koh to the borders of the Peshāwar district in Pakistan. The Afrīdīs, whose territory straddles the Khyber Pass, are of uncertain origin. They have been identified with the Aparytae mentioned by Herodotus as living in the Peshāwar area—an identification that remains a matter of dispute.

Fighting between the Afrīdīs and the troops of the Mughal dynasty of India occurred frequently in the 16th and 17th centuries. In the 18th century the Afghan ruler Aḥmad Shāh Durrānī employed Afrīdīs in his armies, and his grandson Shāh Shojāʿ (reigned 1803–09) received both support and asylum from them.

British encounters with the Afrīdīs began during the first Anglo-Afghan War (1839–42), notably when Gen. George Pollock fought against them during his march to Kābul. After the British annexation of the Punjab in 1849, various methods were tried to keep the Khyber Pass open, including allowances, punitive expeditions such as those of 1878 and 1879 against the Kohāt and Khyber Afrīdīs, and the use of tribal militia (the Khyber Rifles). In 1893 the Afrīdīs of the Khyber region came under control by the Durand Line, which divided the tribal region between Afghanistan and the British Indian Empire.

During the 1930s the Indian Congress Party enlisted Afrīdī support for the militant anti-British Red Shirt Movement, an amalgam of pan-Islāmism and Indian nationalism. With independence, the Afrīdī lands in the North-West Frontier Province became a part of Pakistan, which thereafter faced an Afghan-supported movement for an independent Pakhtunistan, or Pashtun state.

Afrikaans language, also called CAPE DUTCH, West Germanic language of South Africa, developed from 17th-century Netherlandic (Dutch) by the descendants of the Dutch, German, and French colonists who settled in southern Africa before the British occupation in 1806. Along with English, it has been one of the two official languages of the Republic of South Africa since 1925. Although Afrikaans is very similar to Netherlandic, it is clearly a separate language, differing from Standard Netherlandic in its sound system and its loss of case and gender distinctions.

Afrikaans was adopted for use in schools in 1914 and in the Dutch Reformed Church in 1919. A distinct Afrikaans literature has evolved during the 20th century, and the first complete translation of the Bible into Afrikaans was published in 1933. *See also* Netherlandic language.

Afrikaner Bond (Afrikaans: Afrikaner League), also called AFRIKANDER BOND, the first political party of Cape Colony, southern Africa, founded by S.J. du Toit in 1880. In 1883 it amalgamated with J.H. Hofmeyr's Boeren Beschermings Vereeniging (Farmer's Protection Association). Du Toit attempted to create a pan-Afrikaner nationalist Bond with affiliated branches outside the Cape, but this effort foundered, and the unity of Afrikaners in the late 1890s owed more to British imperial intervention in southern Africa than to Bond policies. Under Hofmeyr's leadership, Bond advocated a broader nationalism that included the British. Although he never formed a Cabinet, as the majority leader in Cape House of Assembly Hofmeyr was able, through the judicious support of the English-speaking politicians, to protect Afrikaner interests and keep Cape Colony neutral during the South African War (1899–1902). In 1910 the Bond joined with Afrikaner parties in the rest of South Africa to form the South African National Party (later, the South Africa Party) and dissolved itself in 1911.

Afrique Équatoriale Française: *see* French Equatorial Africa.

Afrique Occidentale Française: *see* French West Africa.

Afro-Arabian Rift Valley (Africa): *see* East African Rift Valley.

Afro-Asiatic languages: *see* Hamito-Semitic languages.

AFSC: *see* American Friends Service Committee.

Afṭasid DYNASTY, Muslim Berber dynasty that ruled one of the party kingdoms (*ṭāʾifahs*) at Badajoz in western Spain (1022–94) in the period of disunity after the demise of the Umayyad caliphate of Córdoba. The Lower Frontier (modern central Portugal) had enjoyed a measure of autonomy after the death of the Umayyad caliph al-Ḥakam II (976), when it was ruled by his freed slave, Sābūr (976–1022). In 1022, at Sābūr's death, his minister ʿAbd Allāh ibn Muḥammad ibn Maslamah, who was known as Ibn al-Afṭas, seized control of the kingdom and, assuming the title al-Manṣūr (Made Victorious by God), ruled fairly peacefully until 1045. But trouble with the neighbouring ʿAbbādids of Seville, which had begun at the end of al-Manṣūr's rule, consumed the energies of his son Muḥammad al-Muẓaffar (reigned 1045–60). Constant warfare weakened Badajoz sufficiently to allow the Christian king Ferdinand I of Castile and Leon to extort tribute from al-Muẓaffar and then to capture the frontier garrisons of Viseu and Lamego (1057). Ferdinand also took Coimbra and the surrounding area as far north as the Douro River (1063), in present Portugal. ʿUmar al-Mutawakkil (reigned 1068–94) was also forced to pay tribute to Alfonso VI of Castile and Leon; and he made an unsuccessful attempt to annex Toledo, which was held by a rival Muslim dynasty (1080). When Toledo was eventually taken by Alfonso in 1085, al-Mutawakkil and several other Muslim kings appealed to the Almoravids of North Africa for assistance. Almoravid armies defeated Alfonso at az-Zallāqah near Badajoz (Oct. 23, 1086), establishing a foothold in Spain. Hence, al-Mutawakkil tried to bargain for Alfonso VI's support, but Badajoz fell to the Almoravids in 1094, and al-Mutawakkil and two of his sons were executed.

Aftenposten (Norwegian: "Evening Post"), morning and evening daily newspaper published in Oslo, one of the leading newspapers in Norway and in all Scandinavia.

It was established in 1860 by Christian Schibsted during the long period of turmoil between Norway's nominal independence of Denmark and its de facto independence of Sweden in 1905. The paper played a significant role in developing a sense of Norwegian nationhood, although it was not particularly involved in political agitation. Noted from its founding for the strength of its coverage of local and, increasingly, national news, *Aftenposten* has generally taken an editorial stance that is moderately conservative, although it considers itself politically independent. Like other papers in Norway, whose constitution explicitly provides freedom of the press, it is jealous of that freedom, and it was an early voice warning Norwegians of the dangers of Hitler's Germany.

When the Nazis invaded Norway in 1940, the paper's elevator operator, who had been a member of the "fifth column" of the traitorous Maj. Vidkun Quisling, took over *Aftenposten* from its editor, and, for the remainder of World War II, the paper was a Nazi propaganda organ. During the Nazi occupation, more than 60 editors of Norwegian newspapers were executed and 3,000 sent to concentration camps.

In its postwar era, *Aftenposten* has won wide note for the strength of its coverage of international news and of culture and the arts while retaining its outstanding strength in local and national affairs.

afterburner, second combustion chamber in a turbojet (*q.v.*) engine, immediately in front of the engine's exhaust nozzle. The injection and combustion of extra fuel in this chamber provides additional thrust for takeoff or for high-speed supersonic flight. In most cases the afterburner can nearly double the thrust of a turbojet engine. Since the jet nozzle must be larger when using the afterburner, an automatic, adjustable nozzle is an essential component of the afterburner system. Use of the afterburner sharply increases fuel consumption and therefore is usually restricted to high-speed military aircraft.

afterimage, visual illusion in which retinal impressions persist after the removal of a stimulus, believed to be caused by the continued activation of the visual system. The afterimage may be positive, corresponding in colour or brightness to the original image; or negative, being less bright or of colours complementary to the original. A common afterimage is the spot of light one sees after a flashbulb has been fired. The afterimage is the most readily observed of the class of phenomena known as aftersensations, or aftereffects.

afterpiece, supplementary entertainment presented after full-length plays in 18th-century England. Usually a short comedy, farce, or pantomime, these entertainments lightened the solemnity of Neoclassical drama and made the bill more attractive to audiences. Long theatre programs—including interludes of music, song, and dance—developed in the first 20 years of the 18th century, promoted primarily by John Rich at Lincoln's Inn Fields in order to compete with the Drury Lane. The addition of afterpieces to the regular program may also have been an attempt to attract working citizens, who often missed the early opening production and paid a reduced charge to be admitted later, usually at the end of the third act of a five-act play.

Before 1747, afterpieces were generally presented with old plays, but after that date, almost all new plays were accompanied by afterpieces as well. Although farce and pantomime were the most popular forms of afterpiece—the latter usually integrating classical themes with commedia dell'arte characters—other kinds of afterpiece were performed occasionally. These included processions, burlettas or burlesques, music, and ballad operas, which gained popularity after the success of John Gay's *Beggar's Opera* in 1728.

afterripening, also called DORMANCY, suspension of growth of the plant embryo during ripening of the seed. It results at least in part from rapid and extensive water loss because of the conversion of soluble nutrients to their stored forms. This interruption of growth, or the lack of it in the seeds of many tropical plants, may be an adaptation to seasonal and climatic changes. Afterripening provides for germination at the most favourable time, when conditions of moisture, temperature, and day length are most conducive to plant growth. *See also* germination.

Aftonian Interglacial Stage, major division of Pleistocene deposits and time in North America (the Pleistocene Epoch began about 2,000,000 years ago and ended about 10,000 years ago). The Aftonian Interglacial, a time of relatively moderate climatic conditions, followed the Nebraskan Glacial Stage and preceded the Kansan Glacial Stage, both times of widespread continental glaciation and relative cold. The Aftonian was named for deposits studied in the region of Afton, Iowa. In some places, the Aftonian deposits consist of ancient soils that may also include peat and wind-blown deposits; elsewhere, the deposits consist of sand and gravel deposited by streams.

Study of fossil invertebrates in some regions indicates that the Aftonian climate was warmer and drier than that of today. The end of the Aftonian was apparently a time of great difficulty for many mammalian forms; numerous genera became extinct. It is difficult to pinpoint the causes, but changing climatic conditions as well as the introduction of new, competing forms may have been responsible. The Aftonian is thought to be equivalent to the Günz-Mindel Interglacial Stage of the European Pleistocene chronology.

aftosa: *see* foot-and-mouth disease.

ʿAfula, largest city of the Plain of Esdraelon or Valley of Jezreel (Hebrew ʿEmeq Yizreʿel), northern Israel. Named for the Arab village of al-ʿAffūla, formerly at that site, it is sometimes called ʿIr Yizreʿel (City of Jezreel). Founded in 1925 on lands acquired by the American Zion Commonwealth, a land-development organization, it was the first planned urban settlement of Jewish Palestine. The city is situated at the junction of two main roads leading to Galilee and the north. One is the coastal road from Tel Aviv–Yafo; the other is the hill road from Jerusalem via Nābulus and Janīn. The latter route is largely in Israeli-occupied West Bank territory. ʿAfula was also a station on the former narrow-gauge branch of the Hejaz Railway, which ran through the plain, but it has been inactive and largely dismantled since World War II.

At its foundation, most of the city's natural hinterland was occupied by collective or cooperative settlements. These were independent of ʿAfula economically and socially, and most of them rejected urban society ideologically. As a result, the development of ʿAfula as a quasi-metropolitan centre was hindered. Only after 1948 did the population begin to grow, due to the settlement of large numbers of Jewish immigrants. A new section, ʿAfula ʿIllit (Upper ʿAfula), has been built on the slopes of Givʿat ha-More, about 3 mi (5 km) from the old central business district. In 1972 ʿAfula received municipality status.

ʿAfula has a large sugar-refining plant, textile mills, and a nylon-stocking factory. The Plain of Esdraelon's large regional hospital, with nursing school, is there, as are a teachers' college and numerous government offices. Pop. (1982 est.) 20,700.

Afyon Karahisar, also called AFYON, formerly KARA HİSAR-İ SAHİP, city, capital of Afyon Karahisar *il* (province), western Turkey, on the Akar Çayi (stream) at an elevation of 3,392 ft (1,034 m). In ancient times the town was called Akroïnos. It fell to the Seljuq Turks in the 13th century and was renamed Kara Hisar (Black Fortress) after the ancient fortress atop a cone of volcanic rock 660 ft above the town. Subsequently Afyon (Opium) was prefixed, reflecting the region's chief product. The town came under Ottoman rule briefly in 1392–1402 and then conclusively in 1428–29. It was heavily damaged in the Turkish War of Independence (1919–22), when it was occupied twice by Greek forces. Historical monuments include the partly ruined fortress (the landmark of the town), the 13th-century Ulu Cami (Great Mosque), and the Altıgöz Bridge built by the Seljuqs. The local archaeological museum is housed in an old theological school. An important railway junction on the Izmir–Ankara line, Afyon Karahisar is also well served by highways and air service linking it to all the major towns in Turkey.

Municipal buildings, Afyon Karahisar, Tur., overlooked by a massive trachytic rock with a ruined fortress on the summit

Thomas E. Bennek—Shostal/EB Inc.

Afyon Karahisar *il,* 5,519 sq mi (14,295 sq km) in area, has traditionally been the leading opium-poppy producing area in Turkey. Its other agricultural products include wheat, barley, potatoes, sugar beets, and livestock. Industry is confined to mohair, wool, carpets, cement, and marble. Pop. (1980) city, 74,562; (1982 est.) *il,* 603,796.

Afẕal od-Dīn Bādel Ebrāhim ebn ʿAlī Khāqānī Shīrvānī: *see* Khāqānī.

AG catalog, German in full ASTRONOMISCHE GESELLSCHAFT KATALOG (AGK; Astronomical Society Catalog), compilation of the positions of all stars brighter than the ninth magnitude, compiled by the Astronomische Gesellschaft of Germany. Friedrich W.A. Argelander, founder of the society, proposed the star catalog in 1867, and observatories around the world took part in the work. The first version of the *Astronomische Gesellschaft Katalog* (*AGK1*) covered the sky north of 18° south declination and was completely published by 1912. A second (*AGK2*), based on photographs rather than direct observations, was begun in the 1920s and published in the 1950s; a third (*AGK3*), including stars' proper motions (the rates at which their apparent positions change), appeared in the 1960s.

aga, also spelled AGHĀ, in Turkey, person of high rank or social position, especially during the era of the Ottoman Empire. Combined with the names of military units or administrative departments, it formed the official titles borne by the chief officers of the Janissaries and of the cavalry, by the principal members of the imperial household, and by the eunuchs controlling the sultan's harem. Later it was applied to officers of lower rank and, socially, as a term of respect, to heads of families and villages and to landowners. In republican Turkey the official title disappeared, the social use of the word surviving only among the lower classes.

As a title of respect, aga has also been used for Islāmic religious leaders, notably for the leader of the Ismāʿīlī sect of the Shīʿī Muslims.

Aga Khan, also spelled AGHA KHĀN, or ĀQĀ KHĀN, title of *imāms*, or spiritual leaders, of the Nizārī Ismāʿīlī sect of the Shīʿī Muslims, grouped below chronologically and indicated by the symbol •.

• **Aga Khan I,** personal name ḤASAN ʿALĪ SHĀH (b. 1800—d. April 1881), *imām,* or spiritual leader, of the Nizārī Ismāʿīlī sect of the Shīʿī Muslims. He claimed to be directly descended from ʿAlī, the son-in-law of the Prophet Muḥammad, and ʿAlī's wife Fāṭimah, Muḥammad's daughter, and also from the Fāṭimid caliphs of Egypt.

He was the governor of the Persian province of Kerman and was high in the favour of Fatḥ ʿAlī Shāh. The title Aga Khan (chief commander) was granted him in 1818 by the Shāh of Persia. Under Moḥammad Shāh, however, he felt his family honour slighted and rose in revolt in 1838 but was defeated and fled to India. He helped the British in the first Anglo-Afghan War (1839–42) and in the conquest of Sind (1842–43) and was granted a pension. After he had settled in Bombay, he encountered some opposition from a minority of his followers, who contested the extent of his spiritual authority and in a lawsuit challenged his control over the community's funds, but he won his case (1866).

• **Aga Khan II,** personal name ʿALĪ SHĀH (d. August 1885, Poona, India), eldest son of the Aga Khan I. In 1881 he succeeded his father as *imām,* or spiritual leader, of the Nizārī Ismāʿīlī sect of Shīʿī Muslims, and, during his short imamate, sought to improve the conditions of the community.

• **Aga Khan III,** personal name SULTAN SIR MOḤAMMED SHĀH (b. Nov. 2, 1877, Karachi, India—d. July 11, 1957, Versoix, Switz.), only son of the Aga Khan II. He succeeded his father as *imām* of the Nizārī Ismāʿīlī sect in 1885.

Under the care of his mother, a daughter of the ruling house of Persia, he was given an education not only Islāmic and Oriental but also Western. In addition to attending diligently to the affairs of his own community, he rapidly acquired a leading position among India's Muslims as a whole. In 1906 he headed the Muslim deputation to the viceroy, Lord Minto, to promote the interests of the Muslim minority in India. The Morley-Minto reforms of 1909 consequently provided for separate Muslim electorates. He served as president of the All-India Muslim League during its early years and initiated the fund for raising the Muslim college at Alīgarh to university status, which was effected in 1920.

When World War I broke out, the Aga Khan supported the Allied cause, but at the subsequent peace conference he urged that Turkey should be leniently treated. He played an important part in the Round Table conferences on Indian constitutional reform in London (1930–32). He also represented India at the World Disarmament Conference in Geneva in 1932 and at the League of Nations Assembly in 1932 and from 1934 to 1937. He was appointed president of the League in 1937. During World War II he lived in Switzerland and withdrew from political activity.

The Aga Khan was also well known as a successful owner and breeder of Thoroughbred racehorses.

• **Aga Khan IV,** personal name KARIM AL-HUSSAIN SHĀH (b. Dec. 13, 1937, Geneva), elder son of Prince Aly Khan by his first wife, the daughter of the 3rd Baron Churston. He succeeded to the imamate of the Nizārī Ismāʿīlī sect in 1957 at the death of his grandfather, the Aga Khan III. The new Aga Khan initiated visits to his scattered Ismāʿīlī peoples in the first year of his reign. He became a strong leader, ordering his followers to become citizens of the countries in which they resided and to leave countries where they faced trouble and persecution. He was known for his business acumen and led a consortium in the development of Costa Smeralda (Emerald Coast) on Sardinia as a resort. He continued his family's extensive horse-breeding enterprise.

Agadez, also spelled AGADES, *département,* northern Niger, almost entirely within the Sahara (desert) and bordered by the *départements* of Maradi, Zinder, and Diffa (south), Tahoua (west), and by Mali (west), Algeria and Libya (north), and Chad (east). With an area of 244,869 sq mi (634,209 sq km), it is Niger's largest *département,* comprising more than half of the country's area. The *département* receives less than 12 in. (300 mm) of annual rainfall, and therefore lies above the northern limit of non-irrigated cultivation in Niger. The general altitude of this vast landscape of sandy basins, low lateritic plateaus, isolated hills and sandstone bluffs varies from 1,000 to 3,300 ft (300 to 1,000 m). The Aïr massif, a 200-mi (325-km) Precambrian granite mountain range in the central north, cuts Agadez into two parts—Talak in the west and Ténéré in the east; elevations in the Aïr reach nearly 6,600 ft (2,000 m). Djado, Manguéni, and Tchigaï plateaus are in the northeast as are Dirkou, Séguédine, Bilma, and Fachi oases. The extremely arid climate, roughly north of 17° N, is characterized by less than 4 in. of rain (May to October) and summer temperatures of 110° F (43° C). Nomadic grazing is conducted in southern Agadez *département.* Important international sources of uranium are mined at Arlit (since 1971) and nearby Akouta (since 1978). Cassiterite (tin) and coal (since 1980) are mined further south near Agadez town, the departmental seat; salt making is important near the oasis of Bilma. A thermal plant at Ânou Ararene provides electricity to the uranium mines at Arlit and Akouta, and Agadez town. The Teda nomads occupy the northeastern oases, and the Tuareg and Fulani nomads in the southwest traditionally meet annually, in August, at I-n-Gall town, where a nomadic census is taken and first-aid is given by the national government. Pop. (1977) 124,657.

Agadez, also spelled AGADES, town, capital of Agadez *département,* northern Niger, West Africa, at the southern edge of the Aïr massif. It is a market town at a crossroads, 460 mi (740 km) northeast of Niamey, the national capital. Once the seat of a Tuareg sultanate (dating from the 15th century), it remains the centre for Tuareg pastoralists, who still wander over the arid plateau. Agadez handles their livestock and hides as well as some grains and vegetables. The School of Mines of the Aïr opened in Agadez in 1976, and uranium mining has become important. There is an airstrip. Pop. (1977) 20,475.

Mosque in Agadez, Niger
Picturepoint

Agadir, city, Atlantic port, provincial capital, and province, Sud region, Morocco.

The city lies 6 mi (10 km) north of the mouth of the Oued (river) Sous. Possibly the ancient Roman Portus Risadir, it was occupied by the Portuguese from 1505 to 1541, when it fell to the Saʿdian king of Sūs (Sous). After the Moroccan crisis of 1911, when the German gunboat "Panther" appeared offshore "to protect German interests," the city was occupied by French troops (1913). Modern growth began with the construction of the port (1914), development of the Sous plain, exploitation of inland mineral resources, and the fishing and fish-canning industries. In 1960, the city was virtually destroyed by two earthquakes, a tidal wave, and fire, which killed about 20,000 people. A new central city, including an industrial quarter and earthquake-proof buildings, was built to the south of the old town. The city is linked by road with Safi and Marrakech; it also has an international airport.

Agadir province has an area of 6,741 sq mi (17,460 sq km) and is bounded by Essaouira and Marrakech provinces (north), by Ouarzazate and Tata provinces (east), by Tiznit province (south), and by the Atlantic Ocean to the west. The plain of the east–west trending Oued Sous is enclosed by the Anti-Atlas mountains. Cereals (primarily barley), citrus fruits, olives, sheep, goats, and cattle are raised on the irrigated Sous plain; sheep and goats are grazed in the mountains. Pop. (1982) mun., 110,479; (1981 est.) province, 985,000.

Agadir Incident, event involving a German attempt to challenge French rights in Morocco by sending the gunboat "Panther" to Agadir in July 1911. The action incited the Second Moroccan Crisis (*see* Moroccan crises).

Agaie, town and traditional emirate, Niger State, west central Nigeria. The town lies at the intersection of roads from Bida, Baro, Tagagi, Lapai, and Ebba. Originally inhabited by the Dibo (Ganagana, Zitako), a people associated with the Nupe, it fell under the sway of Malam Baba, a Fulani warrior, in 1822. After Baba had extended his territory south to the Niger River, he requested the Amīr of Gwandu, the Fulani Empire's overlord of the western emirates, to establish a new emirate; in 1832 Baba's son Abdullahi was inaugurated as the first *amīr* of Agaie. Shortly after the chiefs of Agaie emirate had given military aid to Bida (the adjacent Fulani emirate to the west) in its campaign of 1897 against the Royal Niger Company, Agaie was occupied by the British. In 1908 the emirate, a 737-sq-mi (1,909-sq-km) area, became part of the newly created Niger Province within North-Western State after 1967 and part of Niger State in 1976. Its present population, still predominantly Nupe, is mainly engaged in farming.

Agaie town is a market centre (yams, sorghum, millet, rice, shea nuts, cotton, and peanuts [groundnuts]). Swamp rice, an especially important cash crop south and west of the town in the Niger's floodplains, is cultivated both on small farms and at the government's irrigated rice project at Loguma, 20 mi (32 km) south. Agaie is served by a health office and dispensary. Pop. (1972 est.) town, 13,766.

Agaja, also spelled AGADJA (b. *c.* 1673—d. 1740, Allada, Dahomey), third ruler of the West African kingdom of Dahomey (1708–40), who was able to extend his kingdom southward to the coast and who consolidated and centralized it through important administrative reforms.

The first part of Agaja's reign was by far the most successful. From 1708 to 1727 he carried out a series of expansionist wars, culminating in the takeover of the kingdom of Allada in 1724 and of the important coastal trading state of Whydah (Ouïdah) in 1727. In the second half of his reign, however, he was subject to the invasions of the powerful Oyo kingdom to the northeast.

The Oyo first invaded Dahomey in 1726, easily defeating Agaja's forces and burning his capital, Abomey, before returning home. They invaded Dahomey again in 1728, 1729, and 1730. Agaja and his men retreated or hid as the Oyo burned and pillaged. Finally, in 1730, Agaja was forced to come to terms and pay tribute. He also gave up his opposition to the slave trade, though he did insist on a royal monopoly. From 1730 until his death he maintained his capital at Allada, south of his former capital; once his territory seemed secure he concentrated on administrative reform, especially the creation of a bureaucracy under royal control. Internal dissension developed after 1735, however, partly because of the chiefs' resentment over the royal monopoly of the slave trade, and in 1737 this trade became free. Meanwhile, Agaja was evidently not able to keep up the annual tribute to the Oyo, who invaded his kingdom once more the year before his death.

Agalega Islands, two island dependencies (North Island and South Island) of Mauritius, in the western Indian Ocean. They lie about 600 mi (1,000 km) north of Mauritius and have a total land area of 27 sq mi (70 sq km). Copra and coconut oil are produced and exported, while some poultry and cattle are raised and vegetables grown for subsistence. The main village, Sainte Rita on South Island, has a school and a small hospital. There are some roads but few motor vehicles. Pop. (1983 prelim.) 350.

Agam, Yaacov, original name YAACOV GIPSTEIN (b. May 11, 1928, Rishon le-Zion, Palestine), pioneer and leading exponent of optical and kinetic art who first exhibited works of that nature in 1953 in Paris.

Agam's art demonstrates a concern with time, change, and movement; the viewer witnesses

Agam, 1972
Michele Vishny

a series of changes in colours and shapes created, in some instances, by his own movement and, in others, by rotation of the work itself or by the manipulation of light. Examples of his works are "Three Times Three Interplay" (1970–71; Juilliard School of Music, New York City) and "The Hundred Gates" (1972) in the gardens of Israel's presidential palace in Jerusalem. He also designed an enormous musical fountain in the Quartier de la Défense, Paris (1976).

Other works include "Jacob's Ladder," a 197-foot- (600-metre-) long ceiling painting (1964; convention centre, Jerusalem); a mural at Forum Leverkusen, West Germany (1969–70); the decoration of an anteroom at the Élysée palace, Paris (1971–72); a water–fire fountain (1972; Laclede Gas Building, St. Louis, Mo.); and a mural in Birmingham, Ala. (1979).

agama (*Agama*), any of about 60 species of lizards belonging to the family Agamidae (suborder Sauria). They are rather unspecialized "typical" lizards about 30 to 45 centimetres (12 to 18 inches) long exhibiting little development of crests or dewlaps. They inhabit rocky desert areas throughout Africa, southeastern Europe, and central India.

Hardun (*Agama stellio*)
John Markham

Agama agama, a common gray lizard with a red or yellow head, is well adapted to gardens and to the bush and grasslands. The hardun, *A. stellio*, which is common in northern Egypt, has a tail ringed with spiked scales, giving it a ferocious appearance.

Āgama (Sanskrit: Acquisition of Knowledge), any of a class of Hindu Tantric writings of medieval India that are sacred texts of the Śaivites, or followers of the lord Śiva (Shiva). They correspond to the other Tantric sectarian writings, the Vaiṣṇava Saṃhitās and the Śākta *Tantras*. They are often in the form of a dialogue between Śiva and his wife Pārvatī.

The Śaiva *Āgamas* probably began to emerge about the 8th century. For convenience scholars discuss the texts according to the four Śaivite sects that follow the Āgamic tradition. These are the Sanskrit school of Śaivasiddhānta, the Tamil Śaivas, the Kashmir Śaivas, and the Vīraśaivas, who are also known as the Liṅgāyats. The *Āgamas* give much information on the earliest codes of temple building, image making, and religious procedure.

Agamemnon, in Greek legend, king of Mycenae or Argos, son of Atreus (king of Mycenae) and his wife Aërope, and brother of Menelaus. After the murder of Atreus by Thyestes and his son Aegisthus, Agamemnon and Menelaus took refuge with Tyndareus, king of Sparta, whose daughters, Clytemnestra and Helen, they respectively married. By Clytemnestra, Agamemnon had a son, Orestes, and three daughters, Iphigeneia (Iphianassa), Electra (Laodice), and Chrysothemis. Menelaus succeeded Tyndareus, while Agamemnon recovered his father's kingdom.

After Paris (Alexandros), son of King Priam of Troy, carried off Helen, Agamemnon called on the princes of the country to unite in a war of revenge against the Trojans. He himself furnished 100 ships and was chosen commander in chief of the combined forces. The fleet assembled at the port of Aulis in Boeotia but was prevented from sailing by calms or contrary winds that were sent by the goddess Artemis because Agamemnon had in some way offended her. To appease the wrath of Artemis, Agamemnon was forced to sacrifice his own daughter Iphigeneia.

After the capture of Troy, Cassandra, the daughter of Priam, fell to Agamemnon's lot in the distribution of the prizes of war. On his return he landed in Argolis, where Aegisthus, who in the interval had seduced Agamemnon's wife, treacherously carried out the murder of Agamemnon, his comrades, and Cassandra. The Greek poet Aeschylus, however, attributed the murder to Clytemnestra alone. The murder was avenged by Orestes, who returned to slay both his mother and her paramour.

Agamemnon was possibly a historical character, the overlord of the Mycenaean or Achaean states of the Greek mainland. In Hellenistic times, at Sparta, he was worshipped under the title Zeus Agamemnon.

Agamidae, lizard family of about 325 species that typically have scaly bodies, well-developed legs, and a moderately long tail. The normal body size ranges from 10 to 15 centimetres (4 to 6 inches), and the tail is 20 to 30 cm long, though the family varies widely.

Most agamids occur in the tropical regions of the Old World. For more information on some important and interesting members, *see* agama, Calotes, *Chlamydosaurus* (frilled lizard), Draco (flying lizard), and moloch.

Agana, capital of the unincorporated U.S. outlying territory of Guam, situated at the centre of the west coast of the island on a sandy beach surrounding Agana Bay at the mouth of the small Agana River. A town of 10,000 inhabitants in 1940, it was completely destroyed in World War II. Its population has since increased slowly. Reconstruction has been hindered by the difficulty of determining ownership of many small plots of land. Agana Cathedral (Dulce Nombre de María) was rebuilt after World War II. Adjoining the cathedral is the Plaza de España and the Azotea, the only part of the original Spanish governor's palace still standing. Close by is Latte Stone Park, with latte stones (pillars that supported houses of the prehistoric Latte culture).

Tamuning, just northeast of Agana, and Piti,

Agana town and bay, Guam
Shostal—EB Inc.

to the southwest, have grown to be important business centres at the expense of the capital. Although it usually enjoys a mild climate, the town is struck almost every year by typhoons. Pop. (1980) 881.

agapē, common Greek noun ("love") given special significance in the New Testament, in which it is applied both to God's love for mankind, especially through Jesus Christ, and to man's reciprocal love for God, which necessarily extends to the love of one's fellowman. The Church Fathers used *agapē* in the sense of "love feast" to designate both a rite (using bread and wine) and a meal of fellowship to which the poor were invited. The historical relationship between the *agapē*, the Lord's Supper, and the Eucharist is still uncertain. Some scholars believe the *agapē* was a form of the Lord's Supper and the Eucharist the sacramental aspect of that celebration. Others interpret *agapē* as a fellowship meal held in imitation of gatherings attended by Jesus and his disciples; the Eucharist (emphasizing Christ's death) is believed to have been joined to this meal later but eventually to have become totally separated from it. The possibility that Jesus may have given a new significance to Jewish ritual gatherings of his day has complicated the problem of interpretation.

Agapetus, also spelled AGAPITUS, name of two Roman Catholic popes, grouped below chronologically and indicated by the symbol •.

• **Agapetus I,** SAINT (b. Rome—d. April 22, 536, Constantinople; feast days April 22, September 20), pope from 535 to 536. Of noble birth, he was an archdeacon at the time of his election (May 13, 535). At the urging of the Ostrogothic king Theodahad, he headed an unsuccessful mission to Constantinople to deter the emperor Justinian I from his plans to reconquer Italy. While there he secured the election of, and consecrated, Mennas as successor to the patriarch Anthimus I (*q.v.*), whom he deposed for his Monophysite beliefs (that Christ had but one nature). Agapetus' remains were brought back from Constantinople, where he died, and were buried in Rome.

• **Agapetus II** (b. Rome—d. December 955, Rome), pope from 946 to 955. Elected on May 10, 946, he was a wise and pious administrator who endeavoured to restore ecclesiastical discipline. The chief events of his pontificate included the spread of Christianity in Denmark, the settlement of the dispute over the see of Reims, and the German king Otto I's first success in Italy (951).

Agar (mother of Ishmael): *see* Hagar.

agar, also called AGAR-AGAR, gelatin-like product made primarily from the algae *Ge-*

(Top to bottom) A mushroom growing in groups or tufts, *Mycena leaiana* has a sticky cap and stalk; the oyster cap (*Pleurotus ostreatus*), which usually has a sessile growth habit (lacking a stem), grows in clumps that may weigh a pound (454 grams) or more; *Russula mariae*, which grows on soil or humus

(Top) William Cibula, (centre) Hal H. Harrison from Grant Heilman— EB Inc., (bottom) Larry C. Moon—Tom Stack & Associates

lidium and *Gracilaria* (red seaweeds). Best known as a solidifying component of bacteriological culture media, it is used also in canning meat, fish, and poultry; in cosmetics, medicines, and dentistry; as a clarifying agent in brewing and wine making; as a thickening agent in ice cream, pastries, desserts, and salad dressings; and as a wire-drawing lubricant. Agar is isolated from the algae as an amorphous and translucent product sold as powder, flakes, or bricks. It is produced chiefly in Japan, New Zealand, Australia, the United States, and the Soviet Union. Although agar is insoluble in cold water, it absorbs as much as 20 times its own weight. It dissolves readily in boiling water; a dilute solution is still liquid at 42° C (108° F) but solidifies at 37° C into a firm gel. In the natural state, agar occurs as a complex cell-wall constituent containing a complex carbohydrate (polysaccharide) with sulfate and calcium.

Agaricales, also called GILL FUNGI, a large and important order of fungi (division Mycota) in the class Basidiomycetes (*q.v.*). The group contains about 16 families and 4,000 species. The best known family, Agaricaceae, has spore-bearing cells (basidia) located on thin sheets called gills. The familiar commercially grown mushroom is a representative example: its fruiting structure (the mushroom proper) typically consists of a stalk (stipe) and a cap (pileus), which bears the gills on its underside. Best known of the agarics is the genus *Agaricus* (*Psalliota*), with some 60 species (*see* mushroom). The most prominent of the agarics are the edible meadow or field mushroom *A. campenstris* and the common cultivated mushroom *A. bisporus*.The family Amanitaceae contains many species which are poisonous (*see* Amanita).

Among the remaining families, the following members are of interest. *Clitocybe* is a cosmopolitan genus and contains with the poisonous *C. illudens,* the jack-o-lantern, which glows in the dark. This orange-yellow fungus of woods and stumps resembles the sought after edible species of *Cantharellus*, the chanterelle; the similarity emphasizes the need for careful identification by the mushroom gatherer. *Russula* has 275 species, many with caps of red, orange, yellow, or green. *Lactarius* has milky (hence the name) or bluish juice; the genus contains the edible *L. deliciosis* as well as several poisonous species. *Coprinus,* the ink caps, characteristically grow in clumps at the sides of roads and at the base of old stumps. They are characterized by bullet-shaped caps, black spores (which make the gills appear black), and their habit of liquefying when mature, leaving an inky mass. The majority are edible, a few are somewhat poisonous, and some are mildly toxic only when alcoholic beverages are consumed with the mushrooms.

Armillaria is a genus of about 40 cosmopolitan species. *A. mellea,* the edible honey mushroom, causes root rot in trees. Its yellowish clusters are often found at the bases of trees and stumps, and black shoe-string-like fungal filaments can be found in the decaying wood. *Armillaria ponderosa*, an edible mushroom with an interesting cinnamon flavor, is found in Northwest coastal forests; it is avidly collected by Japanese-Americans, who call it matsutake, after the matsutake of Japan (*Tricholoma matsutake*). *Tricholoma* also contains a number of inedible forms, including the very poisonous *T. pardinium. Pholiota* is found almost exclusively on wood. Some species are known to cause heartwood rot in trees. The cap and stalk of *P. squarrosa*, an edible mushroom, are covered with dense, dry scales. Among the shelf or bracket fungi growing from tree trunks is the oyster cap, *Pleurotus ostreatus,* so called because of its appearance. It is edible when young, but, as with most shelf and bracket fungi, it tends to become hard or leathery with

(Top to bottom) *Cortinarius cinnamomeus* occurs singly or in small groups under conifers; the shaggy parasol (*Lepiota rhacodes*) appears in humus and compost piles; *Lactarius* grows on soil; usually small, some *Psilocybe* species grow in dung

(Top to bottom) Larry C. Moon—Tom Stack & Associates, G.E. Hyde from the Natural History Photographic Society—EB Inc., Ervin Hillhouse, Ellen Trueblood

Scaly pholiota, (*Pholiota squarrosa*)
Stephen Dalton from the Natural History Photographic Agency—EB Inc.

age. The small *Marismium oreades* appears frequently in lawns (*see* fairy ring mushroom).

Agartala, town, capital of Tripura state, northeastern India, lying near the Bangladesh border in an intensively cultivated plain. Situated astride the Haroa River amid numerous villages, it is the commercial centre of the area. A maharaja's palace, a temple, and four colleges affiliated with the University of Calcutta are located there. Pop. (1981) 132,186.

Agarwālā, important mercantile caste in India, belonging to that group of merchants, bankers, landowners, and shopkeepers that are called Bania in northern and western India. According to caste tradition, its members are descended from a *nāga,* or snake goddess; hence, they do not molest snakes, and they observe a special form of snake worship that is peculiar to them. The caste goddess is Lakṣmī (Lakshmi), goddess of good fortune, who is thought to have blessed the original union of the snake goddess. The Gauḍa branch of northern Indian Brahmins act as priests for the Agarwālās, who tend to be orthodox in their conduct and diet. The majority are Vaiṣṇavas, worshippers of the god Vishnu, but about 14 percent of the caste members follow the Jaina religion.

Agassiz, Alexander (Emmanuel Rodolphe) (b. Dec. 17, 1835, Neuchâtel, Switz.—d. March 27, 1910, at sea), marine zoologist, oceanographer, and mining engineer who made important contributions to systematic zoology, to the knowledge of ocean beds, and to the development of a major copper mine.

Son of the Swiss naturalist Louis Agassiz, he joined his father in 1849 in the U.S., where he studied engineering and zoology at Harvard University. His early research on echinoderms (*e.g.,* starfish) resulted in his most significant work in the area of systematic zoology, the *Revision of the Echini* (1872–74).

From 1866 to 1869 Agassiz was the superintendent of a copper mine near Lake Superior, at Calumet, Mich.; he eventually became president of the mine, retaining that position until his death, by which time he had changed an initially unprofitable operation into the world's foremost copper mine. Agassiz instituted modern machinery and safety devices, pension and accident funds for miners, and sanitary measures for surrounding communities. He donated large sums to the Harvard Museum, of which he was curator from 1874 to 1885, and to other institutions engaged in advancing the study of biology.

Agassiz opened a private biological laboratory at Newport, R.I., soon after closing his father's experimental school of biology on Penikese Island, off the coast of Massachusetts, following the death of Louis Agassiz (1873). On a trip along the west coast of South America (1875), he discovered a coral reef 3,000 feet above sea level, an observation that appeared to contradict Charles Darwin's theory of coral-reef formation, in which he postulated a rate of coral formation identical with the rise of sea level. He continued his marine and coral-reef studies for more than 25 years, making expeditions in various waters, including the Caribbean, the South Pacific, and the Great Barrier Reef of Australia.

Agassiz, Elizabeth Cabot, *née* CARY (b. Dec. 5, 1822, Boston—d. June 27, 1907, Arlington Heights, Mass., U.S.), U.S. naturalist and educator who was the first president of Radcliffe College, Cambridge, Mass.

Her early career was in association with her husband, the Swiss naturalist Louis Agassiz, whom she married in 1850. Together they travelled on scientific expeditions, wrote scholarly works, and founded the Anderson School of Natural History, a marine laboratory on Penikese Island in Buzzard's Bay, Mass.

After her husband's death in 1873, Elizabeth Agassiz became interested in the idea of a college for women to be taught by the Harvard University faculty; a coordinate college would give women access to previously male-dominated educational resources. In 1879 she helped open the "Harvard Annex" in Cambridge and was named president when it was incorporated in 1882 as the Society for the Collegiate Instruction of Women. In 1894 the Annex became Radcliffe College. Agassiz served as president until 1899. She then became honorary president until 1903. Her writings include *A First Lesson in Natural History* (1859); with Louis Agassiz, *A Journey in Brazil* (1867); and *Louis Agassiz: His Life and Correspondence,* 2 vol. (1885).

Agassiz, Lake, largest of the ice-marginal lakes that once covered what are now parts of Manitoba, Ontario, and Saskatchewan in Canada, and North Dakota and Minnesota in the United States. It was present in the Pleistocene Epoch (a geological period dating back more than 2,000,000 years) during the last two phases of the Wisconsin Glacial Age, when the Laurentide Ice Sheet blocked the drainage of the northern Great Plains into what is today Hudson Bay. As a result, the waters of the Saskatchewan and other rivers backed up, forming the 700-mi- (1,100-km-) long by 200-mi-wide Lake Agassiz and the smaller lakes of Souris and Saskatchewan, which drained through various outlets (depending upon their water level) either into the Mississippi River (via the Minnesota River) or Lake Superior. With the retreat of the ice sheet, after nearly 1,000 years, a channel to the north (now the Nelson River) drained the 110,000-sq-mi (285,000-sq-km) Lake Agassiz into Hudson Bay, leaving lakes Winnipeg, Winnipegosis, and Manitoba, and Lake of the Woods (*qq.v.*) as remnants. The fine claylike silt that accumulated on the bottom of Agassiz is responsible for the fertility of the valleys of the Red and Souris rivers. The lake was named in 1879 after the Swiss-born naturalist and geologist Louis Agassiz, who conducted extensive studies on the movement of glaciers.

Agassiz, (Jean) Louis (Rodolphe) (b. May 28, 1807, Motier, Switz.—d. Dec. 14, 1873, Cambridge, Mass., U.S.), Swiss-born U.S. naturalist, geologist, and teacher who made revolutionary contributions to the study of natural science with landmark work on glacier activity and extinct fishes. He achieved lasting fame through his innovative teaching methods, which altered the character of natural science education in the United States.

Early life. Agassiz was the son of the Protestant pastor of Motier, a village on the shore of Lake Morat, Switzerland. In boyhood he attended the gymnasium in Bienne and later the academy at Lausanne. He entered the universities of Zürich, Heidelberg, and Munich and took at Erlangen the degree of doctor of philosophy and at Munich that of doctor of medicine.

As a youth he gave some attention to the ways of the brook fish of western Switzerland, but his permanent interest in ichthyology began with his study of an extensive collection of Brazilian fishes, mostly from the Amazon River, which had been collected in 1819 and 1820 by two eminent naturalists at Munich. The classification of these species was begun by one of the collectors in 1826, and when he died the collection was turned over to Agassiz. The work was completed and published in 1829 as *Selecta Genera et Species Piscium.* The study of fish forms became henceforth the prominent feature of his research. In 1830 he issued a prospectus of a *History of the Fresh Water Fishes of Central Europe,* printed in parts from 1839 to 1842.

The year 1832 proved the most significant in Agassiz's early career because it took him first to Paris, then the centre of scientific research, and later to Neuchâtel, Switz., where he spent many years of fruitful effort. While in Paris he lived the life of an impecunious student in the Latin Quarter, supporting himself and helped at times by the kindly interest of such friends as the German naturalist Alexander von Humboldt—who secured for him a professorship at Neuchâtel—and Baron Cuvier, the most eminent ichthyologist of his time.

Louis Agassiz, between 1855 and 1865
By courtesy of the Museum of Comparative Zoology, Harvard University

Already Agassiz had become interested in the rich stores of the extinct fishes of Europe, especially those of Glarus in Switzerland and of Monte Bolca near Verona, of which, at that time, only a few had been critically studied. As early as 1829 Agassiz planned a comprehensive and critical study of these fossils and spent much time gathering material wherever possible. His epoch-making work, *Recherches sur les poissons fossiles,* appeared in parts from 1833 to 1843. In it, the number of named fossil fishes was raised to more than 1,700, and the ancient seas were made to live again through the descriptions of their inhabitants. The great importance of this fundamental work rests on the impetus it gave to the study of extinct life itself. Turning his attention to other extinct animals found with the fishes, Agassiz published in 1838–42 two volumes on the fossil echinoderms of Switzerland, and later (1841–42) his *Études critiques sur les mollusques fossiles.*

From 1832 to 1846 he served as professor of natural history in the University of Neuchâtel. In Neuchâtel he acted for a time as his own publisher, and his private residence became a hive of activity with numerous young men assisting him. He now began his *Nomenclator Zoologicus,* a catalog with references of all the names applied to genera of animals from the beginning of scientific nomenclature, a date since fixed at Jan. 1, 1758.

In 1836 Agassiz began a new line of studies: the movements and effects of the glaciers of Switzerland. Several writers had expressed the opinion that these rivers of ice once had been much more extensive and that the erratic boulders scattered over the region and up to the summit of the Jura Mountains were carried by moving glaciers. On the ice of the Aar Glacier he built a hut, the "Hôtel des Neuchâtelois," from which he and his associates traced the structure and movements of the ice. In 1840 he published his *Études sur les glaciers,* in some respects his most important work. In it, Agassiz showed that at a geologically recent period Switzerland had been covered by one vast ice sheet. His final conclusion was that "great sheets of ice, resembling those now existing in Greenland, once covered all the countries in which unstratified gravel (boulder drift) is found."

Activities in the United States. In 1846 Agassiz visited the United States for the general purpose of studying natural history and geology there but more specifically to give a course of lectures at the Lowell Institute in Boston. The lectures were followed by another series in Charleston and, later, by both popular and technical lectures in various cities. In 1847 he accepted a professorship of zoology at Harvard University; and in 1850, after his first wife's death, he married Elizabeth Cabot Cary of Boston, who was well known as a writer and a promoter of women's education.

In the United States his chief volumes of scientific research were the following: *Lake Superior* (1850); *Contributions to the Natural History of the United States* (1857–62), in four quarto volumes, the most notable being on the embryology of turtles; and the *Essay on Classification* (1859), a brilliant publication, which, however, failed to grasp the fact that zoology was moving away from the doctrine of special creation toward the doctrine of evolution. Besides these extensive contributions there appeared a multitude of short papers on natural history and especially on the fishes of the U.S. His two expeditions of most importance were, first, to Brazil in 1865 and, second, to California in 1871, the latter trip involving both shores of South America. *A Journey in Brazil* (1868), written by Mrs. Agassiz and himself, gives an account of their experiences. His most important paper on U.S. fishes dealt with the group of viviparous surf fishes of California.

Agassiz was deeply absorbed in his cherished plan of developing at Harvard a comprehensive museum of zoological research. This institution, which was established in 1859 and ultimately grew into the present museum of comparative zoology, enjoyed his fostering care during the rest of his lifetime. In the U.S., Agassiz's industry and devotion to scientific pursuits continued, but two other traits now assumed importance. Quite possibly he was the ablest science teacher, administrator, promoter, and fund raiser in the U.S. in the 19th century. In addition, he was devoted to his students, who were in the highest sense co-workers with him.

Agassiz's method as teacher was to give contact with nature rather than information. He discouraged the use of books except in detailed research. The result of his instruction at Harvard was a complete revolution in the study of natural history in the U.S. The purpose of study was not to acquire a category of facts from others but to be able, through active contact with the natural world, to gather the needed facts. As a result of his activities, every notable teacher of natural history in the U.S. for the second half of the 19th century was a pupil either of Agassiz or of one of his students.

In the interests of better teaching and of scientific enthusiasm, he organized in the summer of 1873 the Anderson School of Natural History at Penikese, an island in Buzzards Bay. This school, which had the greatest influence on science teaching in America, was run solely by Agassiz. After his death it vanished.

Agassiz and Darwin. Because Agassiz was beyond question one of the ablest, wisest, and best informed of the biologists of his day, it may be asked why his attitude toward Darwin's *Origin of Species,* published in 1859, was cold and unsympathetic. It is likely that Agassiz's lifelong view of nature determined his attitude toward the new doctrine of evolution. Although Agassiz was quite familiar with the factual evidence concerning environmental change, variability, and hereditary modification on which Darwin built his arguments, he held that the organic world represented repeated interventions by the Supreme Being. Ordinary physical events on which Darwin relied, such as climatic and geologic change, and even glaciers, could bring about extinctions but not new species. The sequence in the fossil record from simple animals and plants in the ancient, deeper strata to the more complex, recent forms found near the surface represented a progressive development, Agassiz agreed, but these different animals and plants did not arise because of interactions between populations and external environmental changes, as Darwin argued. Agassiz maintained that since organisms arose by a series of independent and special creations, there could be no hereditary continuity between different types of organisms. Each species of plant and animal was a "thought of God," and homologies or anatomical similarities were "associations of ideas in the Divine Mind." Agassiz's view of nature was historically derived from the thought of Plato, for whom the unseen world had more reality than the world of sense experience. Agassiz, therefore, could not accept Darwin's conceptual view of nature, in which environmental events could evoke organic change.

(D.S.J.)

BIBLIOGRAPHY. The definitive biography is Edward Lurie, *Louis Agassiz: A Life in Science* (1960; abridged ed., 1967), a substantial, documented analysis of his scientific thought. It contains an extensively annotated bibliography relating to earlier biographical materials and particular aspects of his scientific career.

agate, common semiprecious silica mineral, a variety of chalcedony (*q.v.*) that occurs in bands of varying colour and transparency. Agate is essentially quartz, and its physical properties are in general those of that mineral. *See* silica mineral (table).

Banded agate
B.M. Shaub

Agate is found throughout the world. In the United States it is produced in several western states; Oregon, Washington, Idaho, and Montana are the chief sources of gemstones. Most agates occur in cavities in eruptive rocks or ancient lavas. These agates have a banded structure, successive layers being approximately parallel to the sides of the cavity. It is probable that they have been formed as follows. During cooling of the lava, steam and other gases form bubbles. The bubbles overtaken by solidification are frozen in, forming cavities. Long after the rock has solidified, water—carrying silica (*q.v.*) in solution, probably as alkali silicate—penetrates into the bubble and coagulates to a silica gel. Soluble components of the iron-bearing rock diffuse into the silica gel and produce the regular layers of iron hydroxide. Finally the whole mass gradually hardens with loss of water and crystallization of much of the silica as quartz or chert. During crystallization, the coloured bands are not disturbed. Varieties of agate are characterized by peculiarities in the shape and colour of the bands, which are seen in sections cut at right angles to the layers. In riband agate the bands appear as straight lines in cross section. Such agate, with white bands alternating with bands of black, brown, or red, is called onyx (*q.v.*). A ring or eye agate has concentric circular bands of different colours. A variety having included matter of a green colour, embedded in the agate and disposed in filaments and other forms suggestive of vegetable growth, is known as moss agate (*q.v.*).

The agate-working industry grew up centuries ago in the Idar-Oberstein district, now in West Germany, where agates were abundant. After 1900 most agates were supplied by Brazil and Uruguay. Most commercial agate is artificially stained so that stones unattractive because of their dull-gray tints become valuable for ornamental purposes.

Agate, James (Evershed) (b. Sept. 9, 1877, Pendleton, Lancashire, Eng.—d. June 6, 1947, London), drama critic for the London *Sunday Times* (1923–47), book reviewer for the *Daily Express,* novelist, essayist, diarist, and raconteur. He is remembered for his wit and perverse yet lovable personality, the sparkle and fundamental seriousness of his dramatic criticism, and his racy, entertaining diary, called, characteristically, *Ego*, 9 vol. (1935–49).

Educated at the Giggleswick and Manchester grammar schools, Agate went to London to become a journalist, working as drama critic for several papers. During World War I he served as an army officer. Between 1917, when, as he said, he "stormed London" with a lively account of an uneventful war, and 1949, 44 volumes of his drama, book, and film reviews, essays, novels, and surveys of the contemporary theatre for 1923–26 and 1944–45 had been published, not counting the nine volumes of *Ego.* He was perhaps one of the last of a long line of English dramatic critics to take for granted his position as arbiter of taste and was also one of the last outstanding journalists of a great age of English journalism.

Agate Fossil Beds National Monument, natural "depository" of an extinct animal community, on the Niobrara River, Sioux County, northwestern Nebraska, U.S., 40 mi (64 km) north of Scottsbluff. The beds were laid down as sedimentary deposits about 20,000,000 years ago (Miocene Epoch) and bear the remains of prehistoric mammals including the Diceratherium (two-horned rhinoceros), the Moropus (7 ft [2m] at the shoulders with a horselike head), and the Dinohyus (a large piglike beast). The site, named because of its proximity to rock formations containing agates, lies in the Carnegie and University hills. Established as a national monument in 1965, it covers an area of 2,269 ac (918 ha). Capt. James W. Cook was the first white man to discover the fossil bones *c.* 1878.

agateware, in pottery, 18th-century ware of varicoloured clay, with an overall marbled effect. It was sometimes called solid agate to distinguish it from ware with surface marbling. Agateware was probably introduced about 1730 by Dr. Thomas Wedgwood of Rowley's Pottery, Burslem, Staffordshire, Eng. The random mingling of coloured clays, such as red and buff, gave a broad veining to domestic

Agateware sauceboat, Whieldon type, Staffordshire, England, *c.* 1750; in the Victoria and Albert Museum, London

By courtesy of the Victoria and Albert Museum, London; photograph, EB Inc.

and ornamental pieces. The English potter Thomas Whieldon greatly improved agateware in the 1740s by using white clays stained with metallic oxides. Repeated mixing of different layers of brown, white, and green or blue clay yielded a striated marbling throughout the substance; the clay "cake," difficult to manipulate without blurring, was shaped in two-part molds, polished after firing, and glazed. A typical golden-yellow glaze is on early ware, but after about 1750 it is transparent or blue gray, being tinted by the cobalt in the blue-stained clay. Whieldon's agateware commenced with snuffboxes and knife shafts; and Josiah Wedgwood used the process at Etruria for classical onyx or pebbled vases closely imitating natural agate. Other makers of agateware were Thomas Astbury and Josiah Spode. It was an unsuitable medium for human figures but proved felicitous in models of cats or rabbits and for tableware. Its manufacture ceased in about 1780. Some agateware was made at continental factories—*e.g.,* Aprey près Langre (Haute Marne).

Agatha, Saint (fl. 3rd century AD?, Sicily; feast day February 5), legendary Christian saint and martyr, cited in the martyrology of St. Jerome, the Calendar of Carthage (*c.* 530), and other works. Palermo and Catania both claim to be her birthplace.

The traditional particulars of her martyrdom are of no historical value; according to them she resisted the advances of a Roman prefect sent by the emperor Decius to govern Sicily and was thereupon brutally tortured, her breasts being cut off (a condition reflected in her iconography). She was sent to the stake, but, according to some versions, as soon as the fire was lighted, an earthquake occurred, causing the people to insist upon her release; she then allegedly died in prison.

Agathias (b. *c.* 536, Myrina, Aeolis, Asia Minor—d. *c.* 582), Byzantine poet and author of a history, covering part of Justinian I's reign.

After studying law at Alexandria, he completed his training at Constantinople and practiced in the courts as an advocate. He wrote a number of short love poems in epic metre, called *Daphniaca,* and compiled an anthology of epigrams by earlier and contemporary poets, including his own. About 100 epigrams by Agathias have been preserved in the *Greek Anthology.* After the death of Justinian I (565), he began a history of his own times. This unfinished work in five books stands as the chief authority for the period 552–558.

Agathis, the genus of the dammar pines, pinelike plants of the family Araucariaceae. *Agathis* species range from the Philippines to Australia and New Zealand. Elsewhere some are grown as ornamental plants in warm areas or in greenhouses. Several species yield hard resins or gums (including kauri copal, Manila copal, and dammar resin) used primarily in making varnishes and other products such as patent leather and sealing wax.

Agatho, Saint (b. *c.* 577, Sicily—d. Jan. 10, 681; feast day January 10), pope from 678 to 681. A cleric at Rome, he was elected pope in June 678. He judged that St. Wilfrid, bishop of York, had been unjustly deprived and ordered his restoration, and he received the submission of Exarch Theodore of Ravenna, whose predecessors had aspired to autonomy.

Through legates, he participated in the sixth ecumenical council (680–681), in Constantinople, which condemned Monothelitism (belief that Christ had only one will) and accepted his definition of two wills, divine and human, in Christ. Agatho prevailed upon the Byzantine emperor Constantine IV to abolish the tax formerly exacted at the consecration of a newly elected pope. Agatho died during a plague that ravaged Rome.

Agathocles (b. 361 BC, Thermae Himeraeae, Sicily—d. 289), tyrant of Syracuse, in Sicily, from 317 to *c.* 304 and self-styled king of Sicily after *c.* 304. A champion of Hellenism, he waged war unsuccessfully against Carthage.

Agathocles moved from his native town to Syracuse about 343 and served with distinction in the army. Twice banished for attempting to overthrow the oligarchical party, he returned in 317 with an army, banished or murdered about 10,000 citizens (including the oligarchs), and set himself up as tyrant.

Agathocles then embarked on a long series of wars. His first campaigns (316–*c.* 313), against the other Sicilian Greeks, brought a number of cities, including Messana, under his control. Carthage, however, fearing for its own possessions in Sicily, sent a large force to the island. Thus the struggle that had gone on between the Sicilian Greeks and Carthage intermittently since the 6th century was renewed. In 311 Agathocles, defeated and besieged in Syracuse, saved himself by breaking through the blockade and attacking his enemy's homelands in Africa with considerable success until his defeat in 307. The peace he concluded in 306 was not unfavourable, for it restricted Carthaginian power in Sicily to the area west of the Halycus (Platani) River. Agathocles continued to strengthen his rule over the Greek cities of Sicily. By *c.* 304 he felt secure enough to assume the title king of Sicily, and he extended his influence into southern Italy and the Adriatic.

Agathocles' reign as king was peaceful, allowing him to enrich Syracuse with many public buildings. Dissension among his family about the succession, however, caused him in his will to restore liberty to the Syracusans, and his death was followed by a recrudescence of Carthaginian power in Sicily.

Agathon (b. *c.* 445 BC—d. *c.* 400 BC, Macedonia), an Athenian tragic poet whose first victory at the festival of the Great Dionysia, in which plays were presented and judged, was gained in 416 BC. The event is made, by Plato, the occasion for his dialogue *Symposium,* and the banquet, which is the setting of the dialogue, is placed in Agathon's house. Aristotle, in the *Poetics,* ascribes to Agathon two innovations. He wrote a play, possibly *The Flower,* in which the characters, instead of being derived from the stock of Greek mythology, were his own invention, and he changed the traditional function of the choral lyrics so that they became musical interludes in the action of the play instead of offering comment upon it. Aristophanes, in his play *The Thesmophoriazusae,* includes a parody of Agathon, but in another of his plays, *The Frogs,* calls him "a good [*agathos*] poet sorely missed by his friends." Agathon spent his last years at the court of Archelaus of Macedonia. Only some 40 lines of his writing are extant.

Agau, also spelled AGAW, an ancient people that settled in the northern and central Ethiopian Plateau; they are associated with the development of agriculture and animal husbandry in the area. The term Agau also refers to any of several contemporaneous groups that are either culturally similar or linked by a Cushitic language base. The Jewish Falasha (or "Black Jews") are believed to have descended from the Agau, and they retain some of the old Agau words in their religious vocabulary. Agau dialects are spoken in the mountainous region of Simen northeast of the City of Gonder and in the area southeast of Gonder. Awiya, a dialect spoken south of Lake Tana, is believed to contain the strongest similarities of any of the dialects to the ancient Agau language. Amharic also has many Agau elements and influences.

Agavaceae, the agave family of the flowering plant order Liliales, consisting of about 22 genera and at least 720 species of short-stemmed, often woody plants distributed throughout tropical, subtropical, and temperate areas of

Century plant (*Agave americana*)

Jim Annan

the world. Members of the family have narrow, lance-shaped, sometimes fleshy or toothed leaves that are clustered at the base of each plant. Most species have large flower clusters containing many flowers. The fruit is a capsule or berry.

Plants of the genus *Agave* are important primarily for the fibres obtained from their leaves. Sisal hemp, from *A. sisalana,* is the most valuable hard fibre. Henequen fibre is obtained from *A. fourcroyoides* and cantala, or Manila-Maguey fibre, from *A. cantala.* Some species of *Agave* contain a sap that is fermented to produce a cheesy-smelling, intoxicating drink. The century plant (*A. americana*) of southwestern North America is widely cultivated both indoors and outdoors for its 1.5- to 1.8-metre (5- to 6-foot) spiny leaves and 7.5- to 12-m flower cluster. The stemless plant produces its branched, yellow flower spike after 10 to 15 years and then dies, leaving small plants growing about its base. Many species of the genus *Yucca* are popular as ornamentals for their woody stems and spiny leaves. Some species of *Nolina* and *Dasylirion,* similar to yuccas except for taller flower clusters and narrow leaves, also are cultivated. Sotol (*Dasylirion acotrichum*), a short-stemmed plant, and

Nolina recurvata, the base of which is swollen and bottle-shaped, are the most common ornamentals. Red-leaved and broad-veined varieties of the tropical species *Cordyline indivisa, C. australis,* and *C. terminalis* are popular greenhouse and indoor pot plants. Other ornamentals of the family belong to the genera *Dracaena* and *Sansevieria.* Tuberose (*Polianthes tuberosa*) is cultivated for its volatile oil. It has spikes of white flowers.

Agazzari, Agostino (b. Dec. 2, 1578, Siena, Siena—d. April 10, 1640, Siena), composer famous for his treatise, *Del sonare sopra il basso,* one of the earliest instruction books for performing from the thorough bass.

He held positions in Rome and in 1630 became chapelmaster at Siena cathedral. He composed both in the *stile antico* of the late Renaissance and the *stile moderno* of the early Baroque.

In his thorough bass treatise (1607) he distinguishes between "melody" and "fundamental" instruments. The significance of that distinction is that it recognizes that, whereas usually in Renaissance music all voices of a composition were equally important, in the developing Baroque music upper (melody) and lower (bass) parts alternated in dominance, with relatively neutral, improvised inner parts.

Agboville, town, administrative headquarters (since 1969) of Agboville *département,* southeastern Ivory Coast, on the Abidjan–Ouagadougou railway and the Agnéby River. The chief trading centre for an agricultural region inhabited mainly by Abe (Abbe) people, it ships coffee, bananas, cocoa, and timber (mahogany, sipo) by rail and road to Abidjan, 45 mi (72 km) south-southeast, for export. At the handicraft centre in Agboville, Chinese instructors have taught Ivory Coast apprentices to make furniture from rattan, bamboo, and other tropical forest growths. Agboville has a government hospital (1963). Pop. (1975) 26,914.

Agdistis (religion): *see* Great Mother of the Gods.

Age, The, daily newspaper published in Melbourne and widely considered to provide the finest news coverage in Australia. It is highly regarded for its dedication to accuracy.

Originally established as an eight-page weekly in 1854 by the brothers John and Henry Cooke, it became a daily after being sold to Ebenezer and David Syme in 1856. Under David Syme's leadership the paper grew with the state of Victoria and became noted for its serious tone and liberal orientation.

The Age has consistently given particular attention to politics and economics. It has not hesitated to attack political leaders, among them Prime Minister Sir Robert Menzies (1894–1978), who nonetheless termed *The Age* his favourite paper.

age–area hypothesis, in anthropology, theory holding that the age of culture traits (elements of a culture) may be determined by examining their distribution over a large geographical area; the hypothesis states that widely distributed traits are older than those more narrowly distributed. It is based on the assumption that traits tend to diffuse outward in a circle from a single centre. Traits at the periphery are believed to have left the centre earlier than those closer to it and are therefore characteristic of an earlier period of the centre.

There are several problems with this hypothesis. Diffusion may be more rapid in one direction than in another. Modification in traits may make it difficult to determine the point of origin. Population movements may also disturb the distribution of traits. Some elements (*e.g.,* sociopolitical units) may be more subject to ecological adaptive pressure than others. In several cases in which historical data are available they contradict reconstructions based on the age–area hypothesis. At best, the hypothesis may be used in a delimited and historically unified area to determine the probability, rather than the certainty, of historic developments.

age distribution, also called AGE COMPOSITION, in population studies, the proportionate numbers of persons in successive age categories in a given population. Age distributions differ among countries mainly because of differences in the levels and trends of fertility. A population with persistently high fertility, for instance, has a large proportion of children and a small proportion of aged persons. A population, such as that of France, in which fertility has been low for a long time, has a smaller proportion of children and a larger proportion of aged persons. Changes in fertility have an immediate effect on numbers of children, but many years must pass before the change affects the numbers above childhood. Thus, a population that has experienced a recent decline in fertility tends to have relatively small numbers both of children and of aged persons and a large proportion of adults in the middle ages.

Age distributions have also been influenced in varying ways by migrations, war losses, and differences in mortality—though these effects are generally less important than the influence of variations in fertility. Yet, the migration of young adults, who bring children with them or soon have children in the area to which they move, is likely to swell the number both of adults in the middle ages and of children in the receiving country, while the proportion of aged persons remains low—with reverse effects on the population of an area from which there is a large net out movement.

age set, a formally organized group consisting of every male (or female) of comparable age. In those societies chiefly identified with the practice, a person belonged, either from birth or from a determined age, to a named set that passed through a series of stages, each of which had a distinctive status or social and political role. Each stage is usually known as an age grade.

Among the Nuer of the southern Sudan, the age sets (which were formed among males only) constituted a system of social stratification in which there was equality among members of the same age set and deference and subordination between junior and senior age sets. The sets were formed at approximately 10-year intervals by initiation ceremonies that marked the passage from boyhood to manhood, and each individual then remained for the rest of his life in the age set into which he had been initiated. The Nuer had no system of age grades apart from the original transition from boyhood to manhood, and there were no clearly defined activities assigned to each age set; a particular set advanced slowly to a position of acknowledged seniority as older sets died out.

In other tribal societies, age grades were found having a more specific allocation of activities to age sets in each grade; thus, the age-grade system might provide for the military training of the young and the organization of military expeditions. The Nandi tribe of Kenya had seven male age sets—two of boys, one of warriors, and four of elders. The warrior set, which was responsible for warfare and for tribal government, retained its position for about 15 years, after which it moved up to become one of the sets of elders, and the government was handed over to the next age set below it.

Among five of the Plains Indians of North America (Blackfoot, Atsina [Gros Ventre], Arapaho, Mandan, Hidatsa), there were ceremonial societies organized on the age-grading principle. It has been suggested that the prominence of age grading in these tribes (contrasted with its absence among other Plains Indians) may be partly attributable to the absence of any extensive division of labour or economic inequality in these tribes. Whereas such tribes as the Crow had large numbers of horses (in a warring and buffalo-hunting culture that demanded horses) and made their possession the chief basis of individual wealth and social status, the five tribes were relatively poor in horses, and age grades provided the basis of social stratification.

This idea is useful in considering the differences between tribal societies and other forms of society, including modern societies. In the last named—though age differences are recognized, particularly in youth movements and organizations—there is no formal and elaborate organization of the population in age sets and grades. It may thus be that social classification mainly in terms of sex and age belongs to an early period of social development, when obvious "natural" differences provide a means of differentiation, and that these factors lose their prominence with the more extensive division of labour and the growth of economic inequality.

Agedabia (Libya): *see* Ajdābiyah.

Agee, James (b. Nov. 27, 1909, Knoxville, Tenn., U.S.—d. May 16, 1955, New York City), poet, novelist, and writer for and about motion pictures. One of the most influential U.S. film critics in the 1930s and '40s, he applied rigorous intellectual and aesthetic standards to his reviews, which appeared anonymously in *Time* and signed in *The Nation.*

Agee grew up in Tennessee's Cumberland Mountain area, attended Harvard University, and wrote for *Fortune* and *Time* after he graduated in 1932. *Permit Me Voyage,* a volume of poems, appeared in 1934. For a proposed article in *Fortune,* Agee and the photographer Walker Evans lived for about six weeks among sharecroppers in Alabama in 1936. The article never appeared, but the material they gathered became a book, *Let Us Now Praise Famous Men* (1941), illustrated by Evans and accompanied by lyrical prose in which Agee dealt with both the plight of the people and his subjective reaction to it.

From 1948 until his death, Agee worked mainly as a film scriptwriter, notably for *The African Queen* (1951) and *The Night of the Hunter* (1955). *A Death in the Family* (1957), a novel about the effect of a man's sudden death on his six-year-old son and the rest of his family, and his novella *The Morning Watch* (1951), on the religious experiences of a 12-year-old boy, are both autobiographical. *A Death in the Family* was adapted for the stage as *All the Way Home* (1960). His other works include *Agee on Film* (1958), collected reviews; *Agee on Film II* (1960), consisting of five film scripts; and *Letters to Father Flye* (1962), a collection of his letters to a former teacher and lifelong friend.

Agekoyo (people): *see* Kikuyu.

Agen, town, capital of Lot-et-Garonne *département,* Aquitaine region, southwestern France, on the Garonne River at the foot of the Coteau de l'Ermitage (530 ft [162 m]), northwest of Toulouse. Mentioned by Caesar as Aginnum, capital of the Nitiobriges, it was captured by the Frankish king Clovis (509) and was the centre of the countship of Agenais (*q.v.*). SS. Faith (Foy) and Caprasius were martyred there in 303 under Diocletian. The cathedral of Saint-Caprais has a 12th-century apse, and Notre-Dame-des-Jacobins is an example of 13th-century Dominican construction. The museum occupies a group of Renaissance mansions. A network of narrow medieval streets contrasts with wide modern boulevards. Agen was the home of the

Agen, Fr., on the Garonne River
Editions "La Cigogne"—Hachette

Scaligers, eminent medieval scholars, and of Jacques Jasmin, the barber-poet. The town is an agricultural market centre, noted for fruits and vegetables. Industries include food processing, pharmaceuticals, and shoes. Pop. (1982) 31,239.

Agenais, also spelled AGENOIS, former province of France, of which Agen was the centre and to which the modern *département* of Lot-et-Garonne nearly corresponds.

The following article summarizes the political history of Agenais. For additional treatment of its geography and history, *see* MACROPAEDIA: France.

In ancient Gaul it was the country of the Nitiobriges, then a Gallo-Roman *civitas*, whose limits became those of the diocese of Agen. Having in general shared the fortunes of Aquitaine during the Merovingian and Carolingian periods, Agenais eventually became a hereditary countship. From the middle of the 10th century it was part of the demesne of the counts of Bordeaux, dukes of Gascony, from whom it passed in 1036 to Eudes of Poitiers, later duke of Aquitaine. After Eleanor of Aquitaine married Henry Plantagenet (later Henry II of England) in 1152, Agenais went to England; it later reverted to France (1249), but Edward I recovered it for England by the Treaty of Amiens (1279). The "general court of Agenais," first attested in the late 12th century, was one of the earliest representative institutions of the Middle Ages.

England and France alternately controlled Agenais during the Hundred Years' War (1337–1453) until the final retreat of the English gave the province to France. In 1578 the countship was given to Margaret of France (Marguerite de Valois) in part settlement of the dowry due on her marriage to Henry of Navarre (the future Henry IV of France). On her death (1615) it was finally reunited to the French crown. In the last years of the ancien régime Agenais was a *sénéchaussée* within the *gouvernement* of Guyenne and the intendance of Bordeaux. Since the late Middle Ages the country has been agriculturally rich, subject, however, to alternating phases of depopulation and immigration.

Agence France-Presse (AFP), French cooperative news agency, one of the world's great wire news services. It is based in Paris, where it was founded under its current name in 1944, but its roots go to the Bureau Havas, which was created in 1832 by Charles-Louis Havas, who translated reports from foreign papers and distributed them to Paris and provincial newspapers. In 1835 the Bureau Havas became the Agence Havas, the world's first true news agency. Stressing rapid transmission of the news, Agence Havas established the first telegraph service in France in 1845. Between 1852 and 1919 the agency worked in close collaboration with an advertising firm, the Correspondance General Havas. Staff correspondents for the agency were stationed in many world capitals by the late 1800s.

The German occupation of France suppressed Agence Havas in 1940, and many of its personnel were active in the underground. After the liberation of Paris in 1944, underground journalists emerged to set up Agence France-Press as a wire-service voice for liberated France. The postwar French government gave AFP the assets of Agence Havas, including the Paris building that became its headquarters. AFP quickly grew to join Reuters (United Kingdom), Tass (U.S.S.R.), and the U.S. agencies Associated Press (AP) and United Press International (UPI) as the world's leading news agencies. In addition to having bureaus in major French cities, it has bureaus and correspondents in important world capitals. Besides having contracts with AP, Reuters, and Tass for exchange of news reports, it sells a domestic French news report to most of the world's news agencies and provides its worldwide report to many of them. Within France it has a leased-wire circuit and distributes news to its foreign clients from Paris through radioteleprinter. AFP also has a photo service and a number of specialized news reports, several concerned with African matters.

agency, in law, the relationship that exists when one person or party (the principal) engages another (the agent) to act for him—*e.g.,* to do his work, to sell his goods, to manage his business.

A brief treatment of agency follows. For full treatment, *see* MACROPAEDIA: Business Law.

Early precedents for agency date back to Roman law, when slaves (though not true agents) were considered to be extensions of their masters and could make commitments and agreements for them. This was an outgrowth of the preference in Roman law to have relations between principals as direct as possible. Through the Middle Ages, legal writers in continental European civil-law countries attempted to change the concept with little success. It was in Anglo-Norman England around 1200, under the system of common law, that two special figures were created, greatly advancing the notion of agency. The *ballivus* and *attornatus* began as close relatives of the master–servant relationship. The *ballivus* handled commercial transactions and became in time a nearly independent land administrator for the principal. The *attornatus* represented parties in litigation and became the principal's sole representative before the court.

The servant–master aspect of agency relationships predominated for many centuries and still has a place. Technically speaking, an employee of an individual or of a business stands in a "servant" relationship to the employer and is considered an agent. The matter becomes a legal problem when the agent injures or wrongs a third party. A doctrine called *respondeat superior,* devised in 17th-century England, provides for the injured third party to hold the master/employer liable for the agent's actions, the rationale being that the employer controls the employee's behaviour and must therefore assume some responsibility for his or her actions. This liability is usually limited to acts occurring while the agent is acting "within the scope of his employment."

The great increase in shipping, banking, insurance, and mercantile transactions generally, which occurred in the later 18th and early 19th centuries, brought another kind of agency relationship to the fore. Ship's captains, insurance brokers, bank managers, factors, and salesmen were agents whose relationships to principals could not aptly be defined as servant to master. Legal scholarship of the 19th century, primarily in Europe, came to deem that the authority to effect legal transactions resides in certain agents independent of the specific contracts made with individual principals. This is a primary feature of modern agency laws in many countries. The relationship is seen in two parts. Its internal aspect is the bilateral agreement, the contract of agency, existing between agent and principal, which protects the rights of the principal to (1) receive the benefits of the agent's services and (2) be assured that only certain actions will be carried out. The external aspect is a unilateral act of "authorization" bestowed on agents according to their specified positions within a given legal system.

There is some variety among systems relating to this external relationship. In some countries, like France, Spain, Portugal, and Brazil, the agent's authorization is seen to be direct and not independent of the mandate given by the principal. This mandate, more closely akin to the servant–master relationship, often requires a certain degree of formality for its verification. In the U.S.S.R., for example, any authorization of an agent must be given in writing. On the other hand, the Scandinavian countries, Germany, Japan, Poland, Italy, and others take the more modern view that an agent's authority exists independent of a specific written mandate from the principal. Under such circumstances, an agent, given a general charge, has more flexibility to act for the principal's benefit; and in systems where complicated laws make access difficult to laymen, such flexibility is useful. For example, minors can exercise many rights through agency that are not available to them in person. Anglo-American law is of this latter school of legal thought.

One legal problem that may arise from an agent's external authority is known as "apparent authority," where an agent tries to use his independent authority to transact business that was not mandated in the internal relationship with a principal. Most courts in both continental European and Anglo-American law allow such agreements made with apparent authority, in order to protect the third party, although the principal may then want to take independent action against the agent based on the contract of agency binding their internal relationship which the agent overstepped.

The range of agency roles is broad in both continental European and Anglo-American systems. The "commercial agent" in continental countries may possess varying authority. A commission agent sells goods upon which a principal has basic claim, minus the agent's commission, but the agent may handle transactions any way he likes. A commercial agent handles the negotiation of contracts and can conclude them for the principal. A broker provides services of employment or placement on an entirely independent basis from the principal, and the salesman has a dependent relationship to the principal, who stands as a direct employer. In the Anglo-American system, agents known as factors and brokers manage transactions involving personal property. Brokers differ in never having physical possession of the property, only contract to them. Real estate agents can represent the principal in property sale negotiations but cannot transact deals affecting ownership. A large group of agents are those who manage businesses—administrators and managers. Their powers can be extensive. On an executive level, corporate directors determine entire policies for stockholder principals. Legal representatives, lawyers, use the knowledge of extensive training to do whatever they can for the benefit of a client, the principal.

agenesis, failure of all or part of an organ to develop during embryonic growth. Many forms of agenesis are consistently lethal, as when the entire brain is absent (anencephaly), but agenesis of one of a paired organ may create little disruption of normal function. Agenesis of the kidney, bladder, testicle, ovary, thyroid, and lung are known. Agenesis of the long bones of the arms or legs also may occur, called variously meromelia (agenesis of hands and feet), phocomelia (normal hands and feet but absence of the long bones), and amelia (complete absence of the limbs).

Agenesis often occurs because the embryonic tissue that gives rise to the affected organ, or an adjacent embryonic tissue, is missing. At many stages in development, one structure induces the formation of another; removing the first structure causes agenesis of the second. Other cases of agenesis have been associated with chemical exposure in the womb, as in the association between thalidomide and phocomelia.

Agenesis syndromes are frequently associated with other congenital anomalies. In renal agenesis (absence of one or both kidneys), the ureters also are usually absent, and sex organs may be abnormal. Affected children have wide-set eyes, large, low-set ears, and flattened nose (Potter's face). Agenesis of the bladder or of the penis, both rare malformations, also tend to be accompanied by other urogenital abnormalities. Agenesis of the lung may be unilateral, a relatively common defect, or bilateral, the latter occurring most frequently with acardia (failure of the heart to develop).

Agenois (French county): *see* Agenais.

Agent Orange, mixture of herbicides used by U.S. military forces during the Vietnam War to defoliate forested areas in which Viet Cong guerrilla forces concealed themselves. The defoliant, sprayed from low-flying aircraft, consisted of approximately equal amounts of the unpurified butyl esters of 2,4-dichlorophenoxyacetic acid (2,4-D) and 2,4,5-trichlorophenoxyacetic acid (2,4,5-T).

Agent Orange also contained small, variable proportions of 2,4,7,8-tetrachlorodibenzo-*p*-dioxin (commonly called "dioxin"), which is a by-product of the manufacture of 2,4,5-T. Exposure of laboratory animals to dioxin is associated with abnormally high incidences of abortions, skin diseases, and birth defects. Some persons have suffered similar disorders after returning to the U.S. from Vietnam and have claimed that their afflictions resulted from exposure to Agent Orange. Despite the difficulty of establishing conclusive proof that their claims were valid, Vietnam veterans brought a class-action lawsuit against the seven herbicide makers that produced Agent Orange for the U.S. military. The suit was settled out of court with the establishment of a $180,000,000 fund to compensate veterans and their families for disabilities thought to be caused by exposure to Agent Orange.

Ageo, city, Saitama Prefecture (*ken*), Honshu, Japan, on the terrace between the Ara-kawa (Ara River; west) and the Ayase-gawa (Ayase River; east). A former post town between Tokyo and Maebashi, Gumma Prefecture, it was connected to Tokyo (25 mi [40 km] south) in 1883. Ageo remained the centre of the neighbouring agricultural region until 1955, when the machinery, rubber, and metallurgy industries were developed. Industrialization contributed to a rapid increase in population. Pop. (1983 est.) 172,879.

Ageratum, genus of annual herbs of the family Asteraceae, about 30 species native to tropical America. They have toothed, oval leaves that are opposite each other on the stem; compact clusters of blue, pink, lilac, or white flowers; and small, dry fruits.

Dwarf varieties of the common garden ageratum (*A. houstonianum*) are used as edging

Ageratum houstonianum
Syndication International—Photo Trends

plants. Some ageratums are variously known as flossflower and pussy-foot.

Agesilaus II (b. *c.* 444 BC—d. 360, Cyrene, Cyrenaica), king of Sparta from 399 to 360 who commanded the Spartan army throughout most of the period of Spartan supremacy (404–371) in Greece. An excellent military tactician, he is usually cited as the embodiment of the aggressive Spartan spirit that sought to further Spartan interests at the expense of Hellenic unity.

He was born into the Eurypontid house (one of the two royal families of Sparta), son of King Archidamus II, and succeeded Agis II with aid from Lysander. At the time he assumed power, Sparta, which had defeated Athens in 404, was at war with Persia in Asia Minor. Sailing to Ephesus in 396, Agesilaus made a three months' truce with the Persians; during this interim he managed to shake off Lysander's control over him. Agesilaus then raided Phrygia in 396 and 394 and Lydia in 395. Meanwhile, a coalition of Thebes, Athens, Argos, and Corinth engaged Sparta in the Corinthian War (395–387). Agesilaus was recalled to fight in Greece (394), but he had been unable to prevent the formation of the huge Persian fleet that, after his departure, overwhelmingly defeated the Spartan navy at Cnidus. The Spartan king scored a minor victory over the coalition in 394 and fought near Corinth in 391–390 and in Acarnania in 389.

The peace of Antalcidas (387), which ended the war, included a clause guaranteeing the Greek cities their independence. Agesilaus used this clause as an excuse to force the dissolution of Thebes' Boeotian League. In two sieges (378 and 377) he reduced Thebes to near starvation. By refusing to allow the Thebans, at the peace conference of 371, to sign the treaty on behalf of all Boeotia, he precipitated the war with Thebes that began with the severe defeat of the other Spartan king, Cleombrotus, at Leuctra, in 371. This disaster signified the end of Spartan ascendancy and the beginning of a decade of Theban supremacy in Greece. Sparta was put on the defensive. Agesilaus twice rescued the city from attacks by the Theban commander Epaminondas, but took no part in the subsequent battle of Mantineia.

In 361 Agesilaus was abroad serving Tachos (also known as Zedhor), king of Egypt, but he quarrelled with the King and joined a revolt against him. Agesilaus died at age 84 on his way home from Egypt.

Agfa-Gevaert Group, German AGFA-GEVAERT GRUPPE, Dutch AGFA-GEVAERT GROEP, German and Belgian corporate group established in 1964 in the merger of Agfa AG of Leverkusen, W.Ger., and Gevaert Photo-Producten NV of Mortsel, Belg. The merger established twin operating companies, one German (Agfa-Gevaert AG) and one Belgian (Gevaert-Agfa NV, which in 1971 became Agfa-Gevaert NV). A controlling interest in the Group was purchased by Bayer AG in 1981.

The two principal factories of the group—located in Leverkusen (in Cologne) and Mortsel (near Antwerp)—produce photographic film and equipment, audio tape, and photocopying and duplicating systems. The group also has subsidiaries in other western European countries, the United States, Latin America, Japan, Australia, and New Zealand, as well as distributors worldwide.

Agfa, an abbreviation for Aktiengesellschaft für Anilinfabrikation (Corporation for Aniline Manufacture), was founded as a dye company in 1867 at Rummelsburger See near Berlin; it began producing film in 1908. From 1925 to 1945 it was a part of the German cartel, IG Farben (*q.v.*); in 1951 it became a partly-owned subsidiary of Bayer AG, one of the successors to IG Farben. Bayer AG acquired the remaining interest in Agfa AG from Gevaert Photo-Producten in 1981 in exchange for a minority share of Bayer stock. As a result of this arrangement, Bayer AG and Agfa AG together claim full ownership of the two operating companies of the Agfa-Gevaert Group—Agfa-Gevaert AG and Agfa Gevaert NV.

The history of Gevaert began in 1890, when Lieven Gevaert (1868–1935) started manufacturing photo paper in Antwerp; in 1920 the company he founded became Gevaert Photo-Producten NV.

Aggada (literature): *see* Haggada.

Aggeus (Old Testament prophet): *see* Haggai.

agglomerate, coarse fragmental rock produced by explosive volcanic action. Although similar in appearance to conglomerate, which is produced by sedimentary processes, it consists almost wholly of angular to subrounded lava fragments in a poorly sorted, tuffaceous matrix or in lithified volcanic dust or ash. Agglomerates are closely associated with lava flows.

The term is restricted by some to rocks composed of volcanic bombs, which are ejected in a liquid or plastic state, while the term volcanic breccia is applied only to fragmental accumulations that were erupted in a solid condition.

agglutinate, pyroclastic igneous rock formed from partly fused volcanic bombs. *See* bomb, volcanic.

agglutination, a grammatical process in which words are composed of a sequence of morphemes (word elements), each of which represents not more than a single grammatical category; this term is traditionally employed in the typological classification of languages. Turkish, Finnish, and Japanese are among the languages that form words by agglutination. The Turkish term *ev-ler-den* "from the houses" is an example of a word containing a stem and two word elements; the stem is *ev-* "house," the element *-ler-* carries the meaning of plural, and *-den* indicates "from." In Wishram, a dialect of Chinook (a North American Indian language), the word *ačimluda* ("he will give it to you") is composed of the elements *a-* "future," *-č-* "he," *-i-* "him," *-m-* "thee," *-1-* "to," *-ud-* "give," and *-a* "future."

Agglutinating languages contrast with inflecting languages, in which one word element may represent several grammatical categories, and also with isolating languages, in which each word consists of only one word element. Most languages are mixtures of all three types.

agglutinin, substance that causes particles to congeal in a group or mass, particularly a typical antibody that occurs in the blood serums of immunized and normal human beings and animals. When an agglutinin is added to a uniform suspension of particles (such as bacteria, protozoa, or red cells) that contains the specific surface structure (antigen) with which the agglutinin reacts, the suspended objects adhere to each other, form clumps, fall to the bottom, and leave the suspending diluent clear. This phenomenon of agglutination is a typical antigen–antibody reaction (*q.v.*)—highly specific, reversible, and involving small reacting groups on the surface of each.

A particular antibody is usually in greatest amount (titre) in individuals who have been immunized with the specific antigen by infection or by other active immunizing procedures. For this reason, agglutination is used as an indirect test for past or present infection or immunization with the specific antigen, as indicated by the presence of agglutinins in the serum. Conversely, serums containing agglutinins to known antigens can be used to identify various bacteria, red cells, and other particulate materials containing the specific antigen.

Isohemagglutinins, substances that agglutinate the red blood cells of others of the same species, are also found in man. Thus, there are four main blood groups, which differ with respect to two antigens, A and B, in the red blood cells and two isohemagglutinins, anti-A and anti-B, in the serum. Thus, in man, type O has neither antigen but both agglutinins; type A has A antigen and anti-B agglutinin, type B has B antigen and anti-A agglutinin, and type AB has both antigens but neither agglutinin. *See also* blood typing.

aggregate, in building and construction, material used for mixing with cement, bitumen, lime, gypsum, or other adhesive to form concrete or mortar. The aggregate gives volume, stability, resistance to wear or erosion, and other desired physical properties to the finished product. Commonly used aggregates include sand, crushed or broken stone, gravel (pebbles), broken blast-furnace slag, boiler ashes (clinkers), burned shale, and burned clay. Fine aggregate usually consists of sand, crushed stone, or crushed slag screenings; coarse aggregate consists of gravel (pebbles), fragments of broken stone, slag, and other coarse substances. Fine aggregate is used in making thin concrete slabs or other structural members and where a smooth surface is desired; coarse aggregate is used for more massive members.

aggression, in international relations, an act or policy of expansion carried out by one state at the expense of another by means of an unprovoked military attack. For purposes of reparation or punishment after hostilities, aggression has been defined in international law as any use of armed force in international relations not justified by defensive necessity, international authority, or consent of the state in which force is used. Numerous treaties and official declarations since World War I, including the Covenant of the League of Nations (article 10) and the Charter of the United Nations (article 39), have sought to prohibit acts of aggression to ensure collective security among nations. Since World War I the acceptance by most states of obligations to refrain from the use of force has often made it necessary for international forums to consider the problem of aggression in hostilities that have occurred. In such cases the League of Nations and the United Nations have usually followed the procedure of ordering a cease-fire and have considered a government an aggressor only if it failed to observe that order.

Such cease-fire orders marked the ending of hostilities between Turkey and Iraq in 1925, between Greece and Bulgaria in 1925, between Peru and Colombia in 1933, between Greece and its neighbours in 1947, between The Netherlands and Indonesia in 1947, between India and Pakistan in 1948, between Israel and its neighbours in 1949, between Israel, Great Britain, France, and Egypt in 1956, and between Israel, Jordan, and Egypt in 1970. None of these states was at the time declared an aggressor. On the other hand, Japan was found to be an aggressor in Manchuria in 1933, Paraguay in the Chaco area in 1935, North Korea and mainland China in Korea in 1950 and 1951, and the Soviet Union in Hungary in 1956, because they refused to observe cease-fire orders.

Other instances of military intervention have been widely considered aggression by opponents although not pronounced such by an international forum. These include the U.S.-supported Bay of Pigs invasion of Cuba in 1961, U.S. military intervention in the Dominican Republic in 1965, U.S. actions in Vietnam, North Vietnamese actions in South Vietnam and elsewhere in Indochina, and the invasion of Czechoslovakia in 1968 by the Soviet Union and its east European allies.

aggressive behaviour, any action of an animal that serves to injure an opponent or prey animal or to cause an opponent to retreat.

A brief treatment of aggressive behaviour follows. For full treatment, *see* MACROPAEDIA: Behaviour, Animal.

Animals develop their aggressive tendencies over time. A mouse, for example, shows a defensive posture only at 12 days of age and will not display an attack posture until one month old. Young animals often engage in play fighting with each other, mimicking adults in all but the final—and hurtful—steps. A kitten playing with an inanimate object is another example of a young animal rehearsing for more serious activity to come. In some mammals, juveniles may be recognized by a distinctive hair colour that allows them to act in ways forbidden to adults.

Sexual maturity is brought on by the secretion of sex hormones within the body, some of which are also associated with aggressive behaviour. Although many females are capable of aggression—to protect their young and to hunt—male sex hormones (androgens) are more closely associated with aggression. For example, red deer stags given the androgen testosterone at any time of the year will return to their regular mating grounds and will lose the velvet covering on their antlers in preparation for territorial battles, even in the absence of females.

An aggressive act may be caused by various stimuli. Within its own group, an animal must display aggressive postures to maintain its position within the hierarchy. The mere threat—manifested by ruffled feathers or teeth revealed in a snarl—is usually sufficient to maintain an already established social order. The pecking order of chickens is a well-known example of a hierarchy maintained where many animals share the same territory. If family groups are smaller, the boundaries of neighbouring territories may be established by bird calls or scent marking, but these would be insufficient if they could not be reinforced with a physical threat to keep out intruders.

Conspecific hostility (fighting with a member of one's own species) is also found just before the mating season, when males win their choice of females and territory. As in juvenile play fighting, the interests of the species are not served by actual combat, so that most animals in conspecific disputes have developed distinct postures that signify submission. The exposed throat of a dog, for example, will immediately inhibit attack; among some baboons, a male will indicate submission by assuming the receptive posture of a female in heat. Humans also have signs of submission, ranging from weeping in the face of an enemy to the formal presentation of one's neck to a sovereign's sword, but none of these measures brings about an instinctive halt to aggression as it does with other animals.

aggressive mimicry, a form of similarity between a predator and its prey or between a parasite and its host that evolves through the advantage gained by the predator or parasite. Alternatively, the aggressive mimic may imitate some other factor in the natural history of another species. Anglerfish, for example, possess a small, mobile, wormlike organ that can be waved in front of the fish on a slender rod; lured in by this organ, which they mistake for their own natural prey, smaller fish are eaten by the anglerfish.

A much-studied example of aggressive mimicry by a parasite is found in the eggs of the European cuckoo (*Cuculus canorus*), which closely resemble those of the small birds in whose nests the cuckoo lays its eggs. This resemblance is important for the acceptance of the cuckoo eggs by the hosts, which hatch and rear the young cuckoos.

āghā (title): *see* aga.

Agha Khān: *see* Aga Khan.

Āghā Mīrak (Persian painter): *see* Āqā Mīrak.

Āghā Moḥammad Khān (b. 1742, Gorgān, Qājār Iran—d. 1797, near Shusha), founder and first ruler of the Qājār dynasty of Iran (*see* Qājārs). Following the disintegration of the Ṣafavid Empire in 1722, Qājār tribal chieftains became prominent in Iranian affairs. In the 50 years prior to Āghā Moḥammad's coronation, various Qājār chieftains were serious contenders for the throne.

At the age of six Āghā Moḥammad was castrated on the orders of ʿĀdil Shāh to prevent him from becoming a political rival, but this disability did not hinder his career. In 1757 he became the de facto governor of the Azerbaijan province of northern Iran; the next year he succeeded his father as chief of the Qavānlū clan of the Qājārs. In 1762 he was captured by a rival chieftain and sent as a prisoner to Shīrāz, where he spent the next 16 years as a political hostage. In 1779 Āghā Moḥammad escaped and fled to Astarābād, the centre of Qavānlū authority. By 1785, when Tehrān was made the capital, he was the dominant political figure in northern Iran.

In 1796 Āghā Moḥammad led a successful expedition against the Christian Kingdom of Georgia (now in the U.S.S.R.), which was then reincorporated into Iran. Crowned the same year as *shāhanshāh* ("king of kings"), he attacked and conquered Khorāsān, the last centre of resistance to his authority; its blind ruler, Shāh Rokh (the grandson of Nāder Shāh), was tortured to death.

The civil war that led to the establishment of the Qājār dynasty, followed by Āghā Moḥammad's conquests, had serious consequences for the prosperity and economy of Iran. Many cities, such as Kerman, were completely sacked. In monetary matters Āghā Moḥammad was tightfisted. The extraordinary cruelty of his reign was in part a means to deter rebellion. During his reign his capital city of Tehrān grew from a village to a city of between 15,000 and 20,000 people. While leading a second expedition into Georgia, he was assassinated by two of his servants. The major legacy of his reign was a unified kingdom that survived until 1925. Two books on the subject are Sir Harford Jones Brydges' *Dynasty of the Kajars* (1833) and E. Pakravan's *Agha Mohammad Ghajar* (1953).

Aghlabid DYNASTY, also called BANŪ AL-AGHLAB, Arab Muslim dynasty that ruled Ifrīqīyah (Tunisia and eastern Algeria) from AD 800 to 909, nominally subject to the 'Abbāsid caliphs of Baghdad but in fact independent. Their capital city was Kairouan (al-Qayrawān), in Tunisia. The most interesting of the 11 Aghlabid *amīrs* were the energetic and cultured Ibrāhīm ibn al-Aghlab (ruled 800–812), founder of al-Abbasiyya (two miles south of Kairouan), who received an embassy from Charlemagne; Ziyādat Allāh I (817–838), who broke the rebellion of the Arab soldiery and sent it to conquer Sicily (which remained in Arab hands for two centuries); and Abū Ibrāhim Aḥmad (856–863), who commissioned many public works. During the 9th century the brilliant Kairouan civilization evolved. The Aghlabid *amīrs* maintained a splendid court, though at the cost of oppressive taxes; their public works for the conservation and distribution of water, however, contributed to the prosperity of a country that was on the whole peaceful. Their fleet was supreme in the central Mediterranean.

Articles are alphabetized word by word, not letter by letter

Agin-Buryat Autonomous Okrug, also spelled AGIN-BURIAT, formerly (until 1977) AGIN BURYAT NATIONAL OKRUG, administrative area (7,000 sq mi [19,000 sq km]) in Chita *oblast* (region), Russian Soviet Federated Socialist Republic, on the left bank of the lower Onon River, a headstream of the Amur. It was formed in 1937 for an exclave group of the Buryat people, who live chiefly east and south of Lake Baikal, although by the 1980s they comprised only about half of the population (the remainder being mostly Russian). The western half of the *okrug* consists of forested hilly country and the eastern half of steppe lowland. There are no towns, but three urban districts including Aginskoye, the administrative centre. The economy is essentially pastoral, and large herds of cattle and sheep are kept; spring wheat and oats are grown. Pop. (1983 est.) 72,000.

Agincourt, Battle of (Oct. 25, 1415), bloody victory of the English over the French in the middle period of the Hundred Years' War. Invading France from the estuary of the Seine in August 1415, Henry V of England took Harfleur in September and then decided to move through eastern Normandy, Ponthieu, and western Picardy to Calais. He had to march unexpectedly far inland to find a practicable ford over the Somme. When he had done so (October 19), large French forces under the constable Charles I d'Albret set out from Bapaume and from Péronne to intercept his retreat to the north. They finally caught the exhausted English army at Agincourt (Azincourt in the Pas-de-Calais); but the terrain there was thickly wooded, with only 1,000 yards' frontage of open ground, so that the French pursuers forfeited the advantage of their numerical superiority. Preliminary attacks by the cavalry were repelled by the English archers; and, when the main French assaults were launched by armoured men across a sodden field, the lightly equipped and more mobile archers engaged their flanks with swords and axes and cut the assailants down. Three hours of battle ended in disaster for the French. The Constable himself, 12 other members of the highest nobility, some 1,500 knights, and about 4,500 men-at-arms were killed on the French side, whereas the English losses were negligible.

aging, progressive physiological changes in an organism that lead to senescence, or a decline of biological functions and of the organism's ability to adapt to metabolic stress.

A brief treatment of aging follows. For full treatment, *see* MACROPAEDIA: Growth and Development of Living Organisms, The.

Many debilitating changes associated with old age in both humans and animals are now attributed to disease processes, such as atherosclerosis or Alzheimer's disease, which occur more frequently with advancing age, rather than to the natural aging process itself. Some deterioration of bodily functions, however, accompanies normal aging.

There are many theories about why senescence occurs, most postulating that small alterations in cellular functions accumulate to the point that they impair the function of the organism as a whole. It has been suggested that mutations occur with age in working cells, so that the proteins produced by the cells are no longer capable of normal functions. Insoluble substances called age pigments are also believed to build up in cells over time, eventually interfering with the cells' metabolism, and individual cells eventually wear out, causing breakdowns in organ function. Laboratory experiments have demonstrated that cells from complex organisms go through only a limited number of cell divisions before they die off, supporting the idea that cellular events can produce senescence. On the other hand, the effects of age on the organism as a whole are generally greater than on its component cells.

Aging in all organisms appears related to the reproductive cycle. In plants and animals that reproduce once, near the end of the life span, senescence is precipitous once the reproductive act has been completed. In organisms that reproduce several times, senescence is more gradual, beginning during the reproductive phase and continuing until death.

A major manifestation of senescence in mammals is the loss of lean body mass, often accompanied by increases in fat and body water. As part of this process, muscle tissue is steadily lost throughout adult life; thus, older individuals are often weaker and less able to exert themselves physically. As lean body mass decreases, the basal metabolic rate (the rate at which the body converts food into energy while at rest) also decreases.

Other significant changes take place in the connective tissues. In humans, aging causes a loss of calcium from the bones, increasing the fragility of the skeleton and slowing the rate of healing of fractures; this process, called osteoporosis, is particularly pronounced in women past the age of menopause. All mammals experience a general stiffening of connective tissues with age. Collagen, a fibrous protein found in bones, skin, and tendons, is constantly produced early in life as a soluble molecule that is converted to the sturdier, insoluble collagen by formation of chemical cross-links. As an organism grows older, the production of new collagen ceases, so that connective tissue consists increasingly of the stiffer insoluble form. This increased stiffness reduces the permeability of connective tissue to nutrients, hormones, and other substances, and contributes to reduced elasticity in the skin, causing wrinkle formation and increased skin fragility in elderly persons.

Similar changes occur in elastin, another fibrous protein found in the walls of the blood vessels and in the lungs. Stiffening of the elastin in blood vessels may contribute to high blood pressure by resisting blood flow, increasing the workload on a heart that has already been weakened by the loss of muscle mass. Stiffening of elastin and collagen in the lungs reduces their ability to expand during respiration, reducing the lung capacity. Disease may further complicate these natural consequences of aging in some individuals.

Changes in the nervous system associated with aging chiefly reflect the inability of nerve cells to renew themselves once the animal reaches adulthood. In humans the number of peripheral nerve fibres declines during adult life, and cells from the cerebral cortex may also be lost. The total number of nerve cells, however, is so great that these losses may not have functional effects.

Tissues that do retain the ability to renew themselves through most of life begin to lose that ability with age. These tissues contain fewer proliferative cells to replace dying cells, and the rate of cell division in those proliferative cells that remain may be reduced. Effects of this decline include reduced ability to heal wounds, to replenish blood cells lost to injury or disease, and to produce immune cells to combat infection. The declining proliferative capacity of reproductive cells may also end the reproductive life of females (menopause) and reduce the reproductive ability of males.

Plants also undergo senescence, exhibiting structural as well as functional deterioration. The characteristics altered by age include: leaf structure (*e.g.,* simple to compound), growth habit (*e.g.,* vining to treelike), stem composition (*e.g.,* soft to woody; thorny to smooth), and bark surface (*e.g.,* smooth to furrowed). The onset of reproductive capability in plants signals a change to the adult life habit; flowers are produced and fruiting occurs, but regenerative capacity (*e.g.,* ability to root from cuttings) declines.

Aginskoye, also spelled AGINSKOJE, administrative centre of Agin-Buryat autonomous *okrug* (area), Chita *oblast* (region), Russian Soviet Federated Socialist Republic, in the Aga Valley. The village was founded in 1811 but acquired urban district status only in 1959. It is a cultural centre of the *okrug* and has small food-processing industries. Pop. (latest est.) 7,200.

Agis I, early Spartan king, traditionally held to be the son of Eurysthenes (in legend, one of the twins who founded Sparta). Since the Agiad line of kings was named after him, Agis was perhaps a historical figure. The 4th-century Greek historian Ephorus attributes to Agis the capture of the city of Helos in Laconia and the reduction of the inhabitants to helot (serf) status.

Agis II (d. 400 or 398 BC), king of Sparta after *c.* 427 who commanded all operations of the regular army during most of the Peloponnesian War (431–404) against Athens.

In 418, while the inconclusive Peace of Nicias (421–415) was still in effect, Agis invaded the territory of Athens' ally Argos, but inexplicably made a truce and withdrew after cutting the Argive army off from its city. He escaped heavy penalties for his failure to press his advantage by promising more successful enterprises. He restored Spartan prestige a few weeks later when he defeated the Argive alliance at Mantineia.

In 413, after the war with Athens was formally resumed, Agis led the force that occupied Decelea in Attica. The historian Thucydides stressed the influence Agis exerted from there over Spartan policy. Though this occupation caused great hardship to Athens, it was Lysander's naval victory for Sparta that ended the war in 404. Agis took no part in the subsequent settlement at Athens. In 402 (or 400) war broke out between Sparta and Elis. Agis forced Elis' surrender in the spring of 400 (or 398) but died shortly afterward.

Agis III (d. 331 BC, near Megalopolis, Arcadia), Spartan king from 338 to 331 who rebelled unsuccessfully against Alexander the Great. A member of the Eurypontid house (one of the two royal families of Sparta), Agis succeeded to the throne of his father, Archidamus III. While Alexander was invading Anatolia, Agis, profiting from the Macedonian general's absence from Greece, led the Greek cities in revolt. With Persian money and 8,000 Greek mercenaries (refugees from the Persian army after the Battle of Issus, 333), he tried to hold Crete against Alexander. In 331 he raised a coalition in the Peloponnese and laid siege to Megalopolis. Alexander's regent, Antipater, made peace with the Thracians (with whom he had been warring), marched south, and won a hard-fought battle near Megalopolis (331). Agis was killed and Spartan resistance was broken.

Agis IV (b. *c.* 263 BC—d. 241), Spartan king 244–241 who failed in his attempt to reform Sparta's economic and political structure. He succeeded his father Eudamidas II, at the age of 19. Drawing upon the tradition of the Spartan lawgiver Lycurgus, Agis sought to reform a system that distributed the land and wealth unequally and burdened the poor with debt.

He proposed cancellation of debts and division of the Spartan homeland into 4,500 lots for citizens. By this time the number of full citizens had dwindled to 700. Full citizenship was to be extended to many Perioeci ("voteless free men") and foreigners, and 15,000 lots were to be distributed to the remaining Perioeci. In addition to these reforms, Agis sought the restoration of the Lycurgan system of military training.

Agis was supported by his wealthy mother and grandmother, who surrendered their property; by his uncle Agesilaus; and by Lysander, who was an ephor (magistrate with the duty of limiting the power of the king) in 243. When the rich, led by the other king, Leonidas II, defeated these proposals, Leonidas was deposed. The ephors of 242 tried to restore him to his throne, but they were replaced by a board headed by Agesilaus.

Agis then began to carry out the cancellation of debts while delaying the redistribution of land. He was called away from Sparta (241) when Aratus of Sicyon, temporarily Sparta's ally, requested aid in one of his wars. Upon his return, Agis found his supporters discontented with Agesilaus' rule and disillusioned by the delay of the reforms. Leonidas had regained power, supported by mercenaries. Rather than engage in war with Leonidas, Agis took sanctuary but was enticed out, summarily tried, and executed along with his mother and grandmother.

AGK (in astronomy): *see* AG catalog.

Aglauros, in Greek mythology, eldest daughter of the Athenian king Cecrops; she died with her sisters by leaping in fear from the Acropolis after seeing the infant Erechthonius, a human with a serpent's tail. The Roman poet Ovid, however, related that Aglauros was turned to stone by the god Mercury in retribution for her attempt to frustrate his abduction of Herse, Aglauros' youngest sister. Aglauros and her sisters (Herse and Pandrosos) were apparently at first fertility deities. Aglauros had a sanctuary on the Acropolis in which young men of military age swore an oath to her as well as to Zeus and to other deities. The honour, however, may have stemmed from another legend—that Aglauros had sacrificed herself for the city during a protracted war.

Aglipayan Church: *see* Philippine Independent Church.

Agnano, former volcanic crater lake, Napoli province, Campania region, southern Italy, in the Campi Flegrei volcanic region just west of Naples. The crater, about 4 mi (6 km) in circumference, was known to the Greeks and Romans for its thermal baths (Thermae Anianae), but the lake, drained in 1870, is believed to have been formed in the Middle Ages. There are numerous mineral springs of various temperatures, utilized by the large thermal establishment at Agnano Terme on the rim of the crater. A large hippodrome (arena) occupies the centre of the crater.

Agnatha, class of primitive, jawless fishes that contains the lampreys and hagfishes and some extinct groups.

A brief treatment of the Agnatha follows. For full treatment, *see* MACROPAEDIA: Fishes.

Living species of the Agnatha lack true jaws and body scales, and their skeleton is cartilaginous. They breathe oxygen with paired gills and have muscular, nervous, sensory, circulatory, and excretory systems similar to those of lower fishes. Certain species of the Agnatha, known from fossils, were among the first craniated (skulled) animals.

The body of a lamprey is elongated and eel-like. It has developed eyes, a nostril on the top of its head, a low dorsal fin, and a low caudal fin that extends around its tail. Lampreys use a disk of rasplike teeth to attach themselves to larger bony fish and feed off them parasitically. An anticoagulant released in their saliva aids in digestion. Breeding takes place in fresh water. Each egg hatches into a wormlike larva called an ammocoete, which burrows into the silt of the streambed, where it feeds on microscopic plants from the water. After three years the ammocoete undergoes metamorphosis, and upon reaching maturity the lamprey returns to marine waters to repeat the life cycle. Certain species remain in fresh water.

The hagfish also has a long, eel-like body. It lacks a dorsal fin, but the caudal fin extends to the dorsal and ventral sides of the body. Hagfishes have covered vestigial eyes and a nostril above their mouths; they seek food entirely by scent. One species, *Myxine glutinosa*, secretes an unappetizing slime from lateral glands when provoked.

Hagfishes usually burrow with their tails into sea bottoms, leaving only their heads protruding to scent prey; they generally feed on dead fish or soft-bodied invertebrates. The gonads of hagfishes contain both ovary and testes, but these fish are not hermaphroditic—only one of these organs will function. The eggs laid by the female hatch into small hagfishes.

Fossil orders include Osteostraci, Anaspida, Heterostraci, and Coelolepida. Osteostraci had a flatter body than that of the lamprey or hagfish and a heavy bone shield around its head and gills; it was probably a filter feeder. The body of anaspids was laterally compressed, suggesting that they were free-swimming rather than burrowing fish. The heterostracans were heavily armoured, with nostrils at each mouth corner, rather than the single nostril of lampreys and hagfishes. Little is known of the Coelolepida, an order that grew to 10 centimetres (4 inches) in length and flourished in the Upper Silurian Period (395,000,000 years ago).

Agnelli, Giovanni (b. Aug. 13, 1866, Villar Perosa, Piedmont, Italy—d. Dec. 16, 1945, Turin), founder of the Fiat (Fabbrica Italiana Automobili Torino) automobile company and the leading Italian industrialist of the first half of the 20th century.

Agnelli attended the military school at Modena, but he quit the army in 1889. In 1899 he was one of the prime movers in creating Fiat, which soon became an internationally renowned automobile manufacturer. During the First World War, Fiat ran its huge Turin plants at full speed, supplying the Italian military forces with armaments. The company also produced street cars, airplanes, railroad cars, tractors, and diesel engines. Often compared with Ford and Krupp and other industrial barons, Agnelli employed a work force that exceeded 30,000.

In 1921 workers seized the Fiat plants and hoisted the red flag of Communism over them. Agnelli responded by quitting the company, retiring to private life, and letting the workers try to run Fiat. In short order, 3,000 of them paraded to his office and asked him to return to the helm—a request to which he acquiesced.

Agnelli also established the ball- and roller-bearing industry in Italy (1907), and he was a chief mobilizer of the Italian war industry before and during World War II. In April 1945, however, the Italian Committee of National Liberation removed him—along with other top executives—from control of Fiat.

Agnelli, Giovanni (b. March 12, 1921, Turin, Italy), chairman of the automobile manufacturing company Fiat, Italy's largest private business enterprise, from 1966.

Grandson of Fiat's founder (also named Giovanni Agnelli), the younger Giovanni was brought up in affluence and groomed by his grandfather to run the family business. His father had died when he was 14 years old, making Giovanni—the oldest son—next in line to take over control of Fiat from his grandfather.

Agnelli resisted his grandfather's plea to take a safe job with Fiat during World War II, insisting instead upon seeing combat with the Italian army—first against the Russians and later against the Germans. After the war, Agnelli accepted his grandfather's advice to enjoy life to the fullest before settling down, and for several years Giovanni Agnelli was one of the world's leading playboys. A serious car crash in 1952, however, put an end to his days of racing automobiles.

By that time he was already head of the family's ball-bearing enterprise and vice chairman of Fiat's board of directors. In 1963 he took over as Fiat's managing director and, in 1966, succeeded to operational control of the company as chairman and chief executive officer. As such, he became one of the most powerful men in western Europe. In addition to making automobiles, Agnelli's industrial colossus had interests in insurance, shipping, oil refining, publishing, banking, retailing, athletic teams, hotels, food and drink purveyors, and factories that produce cement, chemicals, and plastics.

Agnelli, Umberto (b. Nov. 1, 1934, Lausanne, Switz.), Italian automotive executive and son of Edoardo Agnelli, the founder of Fiat Auto S.p.A.

After graduating from the University of Turin in law, Agnelli joined the family's automotive enterprise, Fiat. He assumed the presidency of Fiat France in 1965 and in five years doubled sales in that country. When he was made president of Fiat International, he increased Fiat sales and made the car the most popular in western Europe and doubled its sales in the United States. These successes pulled Agnelli out of the shadow of his brother Giovanni, 13 years his senior and the president of the parent firm.

After becoming Fiat's general manager, the younger Agnelli instituted progressive reforms for company workers. He offered flex-time, which allowed the workers to choose their own hours within limits. He became vice-chairman and managing director of the Turin-based corporation in 1979 and chairman of Fiat Auto at the same time. Besides manufacturing automobiles, the company acquired interests in banking, real estate, publishing, and insurance. Agnelli also served as a senator in Italy from 1976 to 1979.

Agnes, SAINT (b. *c.* 304, Rome—d. Rome; feast day January 21), virgin and patron saint of girls, who is one of the most celebrated Roman martyrs.

According to tradition, of uncertain value, Agnes was a beautiful girl, about 13 years old, who refused marriage, stating that she could have no spouse but Jesus Christ. Her suitors revealed her Christianity, and in punishment she was exposed in a brothel. Awed by her presence, all but one of the Roman youths left her untouched; in his attempt to violate her, the sole attacker was struck blind, whereupon she healed him with prayer. Suffering no harm, she was later murdered under the persecution of the Christians by the Roman emperor Diocletian and buried beside the Via Nomentana. On her feast day two lambs are blessed in the church of S. Agnese in Rome, and from their wool are made the pallia sent by the pope to archbishops as tokens of jurisdiction.

Agnew, Spiro T(heodore) (b. Nov. 9, 1918, Baltimore), 39th vice president of the United States, elected in 1968 and 1972 on the Republican ticket headed by Richard M. Nixon. He was historically the second person to quit the nation's second-highest office (John C. Calhoun was the first, in 1832) and the only one to resign under duress.

The son of a Greek immigrant who had shortened his name from Anagnostopoulos, Agnew studied law at the University of Baltimore and in 1947 began practicing law in a Baltimore suburb. In 1957 he was appointed to the Baltimore County Zoning Board of Appeals and in 1962 was elected Baltimore County Executive. Elected governor in 1967, he secured a graduated income tax, a strong antipollution law, the first open-housing law south of the Mason and Dixon Line, and repeal of the state's 306-year-old anti-miscegenation law. After the April 1968 race riots, however, Agnew lost black and liberal support when he strongly opposed civil disobedience, won sharply increased police powers, and approved health and welfare cuts.

Little known to the American public at the time of his nomination for the vice presidency in 1968, Agnew won national recognition soon after his election to office for his speeches attacking radical dissidents. He also criticized the news media for alleged lack of objectivity in covering news of the administration, characterizing his opponents as an "effete corps of impudent snobs" and "nattering nabobs of negativism."

Agnew's downfall began on Aug. 2, 1973, when U.S. Attorney George Beall of Baltimore informed the vice president that he was being investigated in connection with accusations of extortion, bribery, and income tax violations relating chiefly to his period as governor of Maryland. After declaring at first that he would not discuss the investigation, Agnew called the first of two television sessions to denounce as "damned lies" newspaper reports about the charges against him. On Oct. 10, 1973, however, faced with federal indictments, Agnew resigned the vice presidency. That same day Agnew made a dramatic surprise appearance in U.S. District Court in Baltimore. Standing before Judge Walter E. Hoffman, he pleaded *nolo contendere* to a single federal count of failing to report on his income tax return $29,500 in income that he had received in 1967, while governor of Maryland. Acknowledging that he knew that the plea amounted to a felony conviction, Agnew declared that he was resigning only because it was in the national interest. The judge fined Agnew $10,000 and sentenced him to three years' unsupervised probation, but he told Agnew that he would have sent him to prison if it were not for a personal appeal by the U.S. attorney general.

Agnew's *The Canfield Decision,* a novel about the downfall of a vice president, was published in 1976. *Go Quietly . . . or Else* (1980) is his defense of his political career and an attack on officials of the Nixon administration. After the state of Maryland had disbarred him in 1974, he turned to private business, becoming a consultant to foreign business concerns.

Agni (people): *see* Anyi.

Agni (Sanskrit: Fire), fire-god of the Hindus, second only to Indra in the Vedic mythology of ancient India. He is equally the fire of the

Agni with characteristic symbol of the ram, wood carving; in the Musée Guimet, Paris
Giraudon—Art Resource/EB Inc.

sun, of lightning, and of the hearth that men light for purposes of worship. As the divine personification of the fire of sacrifice, he is the mouth of the gods, the carrier of the oblation, and the messenger between the human and the divine orders. Agni is described in the scriptures as ruddy-hued and having two faces—one beneficent and one malignant. He has three or seven tongues, hair that stands on end like flames, three legs, and seven arms; he is accompanied by a ram. In the Rigveda he is sometimes identified with Rudra, the forerunner of the later god Śiva. Though Agni has no sect in modern Hinduism, his presence is invoked in many ceremonies, especially by Agnihotrī Brahmins, and he is the guardian of the southeast.

Agnihotri, Shiv Narayan (b. 1850, near Kānpur, Oudh Province, India—d. 1923, Lahore, Punjab Province), Hindu social reformer and founder of an atheistic society called Deva Samaj (Society of God).

At the age of 16 Agnihotri entered the government-sponsored Thompson Engineering College in Roorkee and in 1873 took a position as a drawing master in the Government School of Lahore. While still a student he and his wife first became interested in Vedanta studies, and later, in Lahore, became active members of the Brahmo Samaj (literally, Society of Brahmā, also translated as Society of God, a Hindu reform movement founded in Bengal). In 1882 he resigned his teaching position to work full time for the Brahmo Samaj.

Agnihotri's imperious nature and high-handed arrogance, however, irritated other members, and he finally resigned to form a new society, the Deva Samaj, which he ruled as *deva guru* ("divine teacher"). The Deva Samaj was at first a theistic society, but later its literature was withdrawn, and it reemerged as an atheistic society, emphasizing ethical conduct and confession of sins, but denying the existence of gods.

Agnihotri believed that a man must rise to the higher life, and, when he reaches a determined level, is placed beyond spiritual danger. He himself was recognized by his followers as on the highest plane possible, possessing supernatural powers, and was accorded many of the honours commonly paid to a deity.

Agnolo DI COSIMO: *see* Bronzino, Il.

Agnolo, Baccio d': *see* Baccio d'Agnolo.

Agnon, Shmuel Yosef, pseudonym of SAMUEL JOSEF CZACZKES (b. July 17, 1888—d. Feb. 17, 1970, Jerusalem), one of the greatest modern Hebrew novelists and short-story writers and, in 1966, recipient, with Nelly Sachs, of the Nobel Prize for Literature.

Born of a family of Polish Jewish merchants, rabbis, and scholars, he wrote at first (1903–06) in Yiddish and Hebrew, under his own name and various pseudonyms; but, soon after settling in Palestine in 1907, he took the surname Agnon and chose the language of the Bible in which to unfold his dramatic, visionary, sometimes almost too highly polished narratives.

Agnon's real literary debut was made with *Agunot* (1908; "Forsaken Wives"), his first "Palestinian" story. His first major work was the novel *Hakhnasat kala* (2 vol., 1919; *The Bridal Canopy,* 1937). Its hero, Reb Yudel Hasid, is the embodiment of every wandering, drifting Jew in the ghettos of the tsarist and Austro-Hungarian empires. His second novel, *Ore'ah Nata Lalun* (1938; *A Guest for the Night,* 1968), describes the material and moral decay of European Jewry after World War I; in 1950 it was awarded the Bialik Prize. His third and perhaps greatest novel, *'Tmol shilshom* (1945; "The Day Before Yesterday"), tackles the problem facing the Westernized Jew, of absorbing a wholly new material, mental, and moral climate—that of Israel, no longer the Promised but the Redeemed Land. This is neither a realistic story (like some of the early tales) nor a symbolic autobiography, yet it can be understood only in the light of Agnon's own actual and spiritual experience.

Agnon
By courtesy of the Nobel Foundation, Stockholm

All Agnon's works are the final result of innumerable Proust-like revisions, as is shown by the many manuscripts in existence and by the variety of the printed texts. Already there are two widely different versions of his collected works, one in 11 volumes (*Kol sipurav shel Sh. Y. Agnon,* vol. i–vi, Berlin, 1931–35; vii–xi, Jerusalem and Tel Aviv, 1939–52) and one in 8 volumes (Tel Aviv, 1953–62). The archaic structure of his prose presents great difficulties for the translator, yet even in translation his power is unmistakable.

Agnon edited an anthology of folktales inspired by the High Holidays of the Jewish year, *Yamin nora'im* (1938; *Days of Awe,* 1948), and a selection of famous rabbinic texts, *Sefer, sofer, vesipur* (1938). An autobiographical sketch appeared in 1958.Translations of his works include *In the Heart of the Seas* (1948; *Bilvav yamim*) and *Two Tales* (1966; *Edo ve'-Enam*).

agnosticism (from Greek *agnōstos,* "unknowable"), strictly speaking, the doctrine that man cannot know the existence of anything beyond the phenomena of his experience. The term has come to be equated in popular parlance with skepticism (*q.v.*) about religious questions in general, and in particular with the rejection of traditional Christian beliefs under the impact of modern scientific thought.

A brief treatment of agnosticism follows. For full treatment, *see* MACROPAEDIA: Religious and Spiritual Belief, Systems of.

Agnosticism both as a term and as a philosophical position gained currency through its espousal by Thomas Huxley, who seems to have coined the word agnostic (as opposed to "gnostic") in 1869 to designate one who repudiated traditional Judeo-Christian theism and yet disclaimed doctrinaire atheism, transcending both in order to leave such questions as the existence of God in abeyance.

From this definition and from the way the word has been used in ordinary speech it is evident that there are two related but nevertheless distinct viewpoints suggested by the term agnosticism. It may mean no more than the suspension of judgment on ultimate questions because not all the evidence has come in or because not all the evidence can ever come in. As doubt has been a path to faith in the thought of men such as St. Augustine, Pascal, and Kierkegaard, so agnosticism in this sense may be applied to the biblical interpretation of man's relation to God.

But Huxley's own elaboration on the term makes clear that this very biblical interpretation of man's relation to God was the intended polemic target of agnosticism. The suspension of judgment on ultimate questions for which it called was thought to invalidate Christian beliefs about "things hoped for" and "things not seen." Huxley's role in the struggle over the teachings of Charles Darwin helped to establish this connotation as the primary one in the definition of agnosticism. When such prominent defenders of the Darwinian hypothesis as Clarence Darrow likewise labelled themselves as agnostics, the writers of popular apologetic pamphlets found it easy to equate agnosticism with hostility to conventional Christian tenets.

By the second half of the 20th century, however, the field of the battle had shifted. Not the question of Christian evidences but the problem of evidence and verification as such had become the central issue among philosophers. Thus logical positivism, which bore certain resemblances to agnosticism in its refusal to speculate about ultimate and unknowable questions, also went beyond the agnosticism of Huxley.

Agnostus, genus of trilobites (an extinct group of aquatic arthropods) found as fossils in rocks of Early Cambrian to Late Ordovician age (between 430,000,000 and 570,000,000 years old). The agnostids were generally small, with only two thoracic segments and a large tail segment. *Agnostus* itself was only about 6 millimetres (0.25 inch) long and lacked eyes. The similarity of the anterior and posterior regions frequently makes the agnostids difficult to differentiate.

Agnostus, of Cambrian age, from Kinekulla, Swed.

By courtesy of the trustees of the British Museum (Natural History); photograph, Imitor

Agnus Dei (Latin), English LAMB OF GOD, designation of Jesus Christ in Christian liturgical usage. It is based on the saying of John the Baptist: "Behold, the Lamb of God, who takes away the sin of the world!" (John 1:29). In the Roman Catholic liturgy the Agnus Dei is employed in the following text: "Lamb of God, who takest away the sin of the world, have mercy upon us! Lamb of God, who takest away the sin of the world, have mercy upon us! Lamb of God, who takest away the sin of the world, grant us peace!" It comes between the Lord's Prayer and the Communion and sounds the themes of sacrifice and of adoration. Thus, it unites the sacrifice of the liturgy to the sacrifice of Christ on the Cross as the Lamb of God and calls to mind the sacrifice of the lamb in the cultus of the Old Testament. Both Anglican and Lutheran liturgies have retained the Agnus Dei in their eucharistic rites. It also appears as part of many of the litanies.

The name is also applied to figures of Christ as the Lamb of God, especially to waxen disks impressed with this figure and blessed by the pope.

Agobard, SAINT (b. 769/779, Spain—d. June 6, 840, Lyon; feast day June 6), archbishop of Lyon from 816, who was active in political and ecclesiastical affairs during the reign of the emperor Louis I the Pious. He also wrote theological and liturgical treatises.

Moving from Spain to southern Gaul in 782, he went to Lyon in 792 and was ordained priest in 804. As archbishop, he was frequently in conflict with the secular powers, opposing their interference in ecclesiastical elections, and attempting to free church lands from lay control. Having written a public justification of the deposition of Louis the Pious in 833, he lost his see when Louis was restored to his throne, but was reinstated at Lyon in 838.

Agobard wrote against the Adoptionist heresy (that Jesus was not the son of God by nature but by adoption) of Felix of Urgel (who was confined at Lyon from 800 to 818) and against the Jews. His zeal for reform led him to attack trial by ordeal and image worship, and his critical ability led him to deny the verbal inspiration of the Bible and to object to the invocation of saints.

agon, debate or contest between two characters in Attic comedy, constituting one of several formal conventions in these highly structured plays. The Old Comedy of Greece, introduced into Dionysian festivals in 487 BC and surviving in the works of Aristophanes, adhered to a rigid structure within which some variation was allowed. The plays begin with a *prologos,* which outlines the dilemma of the plot, followed by the *parados,* or chorus entrance, which in Aristophanic comedies often revealed the chorus dressed as animals. Next, a debate, or *agon,* develops between an actor and the chorus or between two actors, each supported by half the chorus. Representing opposing principles, the actors argue in a fashion similar to the dialectical dialogues of Plato. In Aristophanes' *The Clouds,* for example, the *agon* concerns right and wrong logic. Following the debate is the *parabasis,* or "coming forward," at which time the chorus steps forward to address the audience directly, speaking in the name of the poet and often haranguing the audience by attacking prominent people or social and political principles.

The probable source of the *agon* and the other elaborate conventions of Old Comedy is the mimetic ritual from which comedy evolved, namely ancient fertility rituals in which men attempted to imitate the life cycles of regeneration and rebirth.

agonism, also called AGONISTIC BEHAVIOUR, survivalist animal behaviour that includes aggression, defense, and avoidance. The term is favoured by biologists who recognize that the behavioral bases and stimuli for approach and fleeing are often the same, the actual behaviour exhibited depending on other factors, especially the distance to the stimulus.

Ethologists believe that the most general and probably the primary function of agonistic behaviour is to allow members of a species to regulate the spatial distribution of that species. It also may regulate access to both food supplies and mates.

In human societies, where verbal explanation is possible, agonistic behaviour can serve as a tool to bring about constructive activity as well as distinct antisocial, destructive acts. Some ethologists have suggested that many seemingly irrational human behaviours, such as war and murder, reflect the same instinctual mechanisms (territorial defense, for example) that leads to aggressive acts in many non-humans.

The view of human motivation as having instinctual components serves as a cornerstone for the controversial science of sociobiology. Agonistic behaviour, according to the sociobiologist, tends to occur only in those contexts where it improves the chances of the survival of an individual's genes, either through the individual's own efforts or those of his or her relatives. Thus, human competition may lead to the acquisition of more material resources which, in turn, may make a person a more desirable mating partner.

Agonistic behaviour, in both humans and non-humans, is greatly influenced by learning according to the general principles of classical and operant conditioning; agonistic behaviours are commonly learned through social modelling. *See also* social learning.

agora, in ancient Greek cities, an open space that served as a meeting ground for various activities of the citizens. The name, first found in the works of Homer, connotes both the assembly of the people as well as the physical setting; it was applied by the classical Greeks of the 5th century BC to what they regarded as a typical feature of their life: their daily religious, political, judicial, social, and commercial activity. The agora was located either in the middle of the city or near the harbour, which was surrounded by public buildings and by temples. Colonnades, sometimes containing shops, or stoae, often enclosed the space, and statues, altars, trees, and fountains adorned it. The general trend at this time was to isolate the agora from the rest of the town. Earlier stages in the evolution of the agora

Plaster model of the Agora, Athens, as it might have appeared in the 2nd century AD
American School of Classical Studies at Athens

have been sought in the East and, with better results, in Minoan Crete (for instance, at Ayiá Triádha) and in Mycenaean Greece (for instance, at Tiryns).

In the 5th and 4th centuries BC two kinds of agora existed. Pausanias, writing in the 2nd century AD, calls one type archaic and the other Ionic. He mentions the agora of Elis (built after 470 BC) as an example of the archaic type, in which colonnades and other buildings were not coordinated; the general impression created was one of disorder. The agora of Athens was rebuilt to this type of design after the Persian Wars (490–449 BC). The Ionic type was more symmetrical, often combining colonnades to form either three sides of a rectangle or a regular square; Miletus, Priene, and Magnesia ad Maeandrum, cities in Asia Minor, provide early examples. This type prevailed and was further developed in Hellenistic and Roman times. In this later period the agora influenced the development of the Roman forum and was, in turn, influenced by it. The forum, however, was conceived in a more rigid manner than the agora and became a specific, regular, open area surrounded by planned architecture.

The use of the agora varied at different periods. Even in classical times the space did not always remain the place for popular assemblies. In Athens the ecclesia, or assembly, was moved to the Pnyx (a hill to the west of the Acropolis), though the meetings devoted to ostracism were still held in the agora, where the main tribunal remained.

A distinction was maintained between commercial and ceremonial agoras in Thessaly and elsewhere (Aristotle, *Politics,* vii, II, 2). In the highly developed agora, like that of Athens, each trade or profession had its own quarter. Many cities had officials called *agoranomoi* to control the area.

The agora also served for theatrical and gymnastic performances until special buildings and spaces were reserved for these purposes. In Athens respectable women were seldom seen in the agora. Men accused of murder and other crimes were forbidden to enter it before their trials. Free men went there not only to transact business and to act as jurors but also to talk and idle—a habit often mentioned by comic poets. In exceptional circumstances a tomb in the agora was granted as the highest honour for a citizen.

Agostino DI DUCCIO (b. 1418, Florence—d. 1481?, Perugia, Papal States), early Renaissance sculptor whose work is characterized by its linear decorativeness. His early work shows the influence of Donatello and Michelozzo, whom he assisted in adorning SS. Annunziata in Florence.

Agostino's name is associated mainly with the wealth of sculptured decoration for the Tempio Malatestiano at Rimini, a building designed by L.B. Alberti. The only work in the Tempio with which he can certainly be associated is the Arca degli Antenati, and it is likely that his share was limited to the sculptures in the chapels of S. Sigismondo, the Sibyls, and the Infant Games and to some decorative carvings. Whether or not he also carved the much-superior reliefs in the chapels of the Planets and the Liberal Arts, he was profoundly influenced by the Neo-Attic style on which these were based. Agostino's other major work was the series of reliefs he executed for the facade of the Oratory of S. Bernardino at Perugia (*c.* 1457–61). His style—with its linear emphasis, cursive

Musician Angels, relief by Agostino di Duccio; in the Oratorio di San Bernardino, Perugia, Italy
SCALA—Art Resource/EB Inc.

drapery, and flat, schematic forms—lacks the fundamentally naturalistic intention of most Florentine sculpture of his time and owes its mannerisms largely to the Humanist environment of Rimini.

Agostino DI GIOVANNI (fl. first half of 14th century), late Gothic sculptor, best known for his work, with Agnolo di Ventura, on the tomb of Guido Tarlati.

Agostino is first heard of in Siena in 1310 and again lived there in 1340–43. After 1320 he was active with Agnolo at Volterra, where they executed a number of scenes from the lives of SS. Regulus and Octavian. The work of the two sculptors cannot be clearly differentiated. Between 1329 and 1332 they were jointly employed in the cathedral at Arezzo on the tomb of Tarlati. It displays a proficient technique, but its figures are stiff, heavy, and sometimes awkward. It is primarily important as a social document, delighting in the commonplaces of medieval life.

Agostino and Agnolo also were active as architects, and a number of buildings in Siena, including the Porta Romana and the church of S. Francesco, are conjecturally ascribed to them.

Agou, Mont (Togo): *see* Baumann, Pic.

Agoult, Marie (-Catherine-Sophie) de Flavigny, comtesse d' (countess of), pseudonym DANIEL STERN (b. Dec. 31, 1805, Frankfurt am Main—d. March 5, 1876, Paris), writer famous for her position in Parisian society in the 1840s and for her liaison with the composer Franz Liszt.

Mme d'Agoult was the daughter of the émigré Comte de Flavigny. In 1827 she married Col. Charles d'Agoult, 20 years her senior. She had early shown strength of will and enthusiasm for justice and freedom, and her marriage disappointed her expectations. Meeting Franz Liszt, she decided in 1834 to run away with him. Their relationship lasted till 1839, when Liszt felt that his musical career prevented a settled life. Their separation became permanent in 1844. Their daughter Cosima was the second wife of the composer Richard Wagner.

Returning to Paris in 1839, Mme d'Agoult began her career as a writer and in 1846 published a largely autobiographical novel, *Nélida.* She was a close friend of George Sand, whose views on morals, politics, and society she shared and in whose house she had lived for a time with Liszt. She also became the leader of a salon where the ideas that culminated in the Revolution of 1848 were discussed by the outstanding writers, thinkers, and musicians

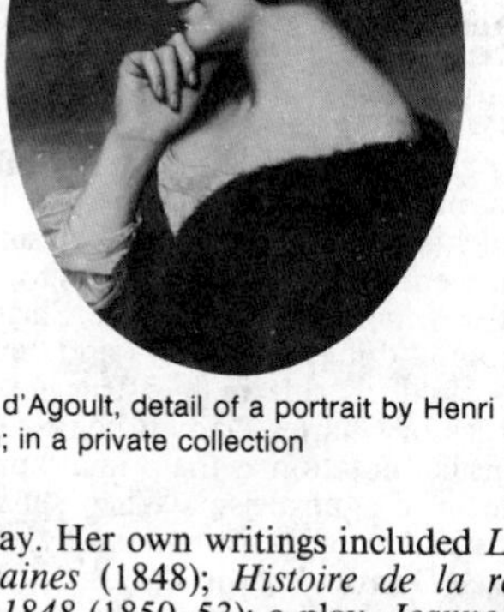

Madame d'Agoult, detail of a portrait by Henri Lehmann; in a private collection
J.E. Bulloz

of the day. Her own writings included *Lettres républicaines* (1848); *Histoire de la révolution de 1848* (1850–53); a play, *Jeanne d'Arc* (1857); a dialogue, *Dante et Goethe* (1866); and *Mes Souvenirs 1806–1833* (1877), supplemented by *Mémoires, 1833–1854* (1927), interesting for the light they throw on the social, literary, and musical circles of her time.

agouti (*Dasyprocta*), any of about half a dozen species of tropical American rodents belonging to the family Dasyproctidae (order Rodentia). Agoutis are 40 to 60 centimetres (16 to 24 inches) long. They have long bodies, small ears, vestigial tails, and slender feet with long, hooflike claws. The wiry fur is reddish brown to blackish, with the individual hairs banded in what is called the agouti pattern. Agoutis eat roots, leaves, and fruit, and occasionally damage sugarcane and banana plants. Two to four young are produced, after a gestation period of about three months, in a burrow among boulders or roots on the forest floor. Agoutis are swift, shy animals; their flesh is prized as food by the Indians.

The name agouti is also applied to the

Agouti (*Dasyprocta*)
Warren Garst—Tom Stack & Associates

acouchis (*Myoprocta*) of South America. Acouchis resemble agoutis, but are smaller and have short, white-tipped tails.

Āgra, city, administrative headquarters of Āgra district, Uttar Pradesh state, northern India, on the Yamuna (Jumna) River. Founded by Sikandar Lodī in the early 16th century, it was the Mughal capital during some periods of their empire. In the late 18th century the city fell successively to the Jāṭs, Marāṭhās, Mughals, the ruler of Gwalior, and, finally, to the British in 1803. It was the capital of Āgra (later North-Western) Province from 1833 to 1858.

Āgra is best known as the site of the Tāj Mahal (17th century). Other monuments include a 16th-century fort built by the emperor Akbar that contains the Pearl Mosque (Motī Masjid), constructed of white marble, and a palace, the Jahāngīrī Mahal. Also in Āgra are the Jāmiʿ Masjid, or Great Mosque, and an elegant tomb noted for its architectural style. To the northwest, at Sikandra, is the tomb of Akbar.

Āgra is a major road and rail junction and a commercial and industrial centre. Āgra University (1927) and six of its affiliated colleges are located in the city; the state mental hospital and Dayalbāgh, a colony of the Rādhā Soāmi sect, are in the suburbs.

Āgra district (1,859 sq mi [4,816 sq km] in area) consists almost entirely of a level plain, with hills in the extreme southwest. It is watered by the Yamuna River and the Āgra Canal; millet, barley, wheat, and cotton are among the crops grown. The deserted Mughal city of Fatehpur Sīkri is 23 mi (37 km) southwest of Āgra city. Pop. (1981) city, 747,318; metropolitan area, 1,007,043; district, 2,842,-942.

The Pearl Mosque (Motī Masjid) and the fort at Āgra, Uttar Pradesh, India
Picturepoint

Agramonte y Simoni, Aristides (b. June 3, 1868, Camagüey, Cuba—d. Aug. 19, 1931, New Orleans), physician, pathologist, and bacteriologist, a member of the Reed Yellow Fever Board of the U.S. Army that discovered (1901) the role of the mosquito in the transmission of yellow fever.

Agramonte was the son of a prominent physician killed while serving in the Cuban Army of Liberation. He was brought up in New York City and received his M.D. in 1892 from the College of Physicians and Surgeons of Columbia University. After his internship, he conducted research in pathology and bacteriology at Bellevue Hospital and with the New York City Department of Health. He was appointed an assistant surgeon with the U.S. Army from 1898 to 1902.

As professor of bacteriology and experimental pathology at the University of Havana (from 1900), member of the government board of infectious diseases, Cabinet secretary of health and charities, and medical practitioner for many of the Americans who lived in Havana, Agramonte was an influential leader of scientific medicine in Cuba. In 1931, he was appointed to head the new department of tropical medicine at the University of Louisiana Medical School, but he died while preparing to assume the position.

agranulocytosis, also called AGRANULOCYTIC ANGINA, acute infection characterized by severe sore throat, fever, and prostration and associated with an extreme reduction of the white blood cells (leukopenia), particularly the cell types known as neutrophils (neutropenia). In most cases, agranulocytosis appears to develop as a result of sensitization to certain drugs and chemicals; infection then follows as a consequence, not as a cause, of the profound neutropenia. First observed as a reaction to the coal-tar product aminopyrine, agranulocytosis is now known to be triggered by a variety of pain relievers, tranquillizers, antihistamines, anticonvulsants, sulfonamide derivatives, and antithyroid drugs. It affects only a small number of susceptible individuals. Treatment consists of the immediate and permanent withdrawal of the offending drug and control of the infection with antimicrobial medication.

Agrarian League, German BUND DER LANDWIRTE, extraparliamentary organization active under the German Empire from 1893. Formed to combat the free-trade policies, initiated in 1892, of Chancellor Leo Graf von Caprivi, it worked for farmers' subsidies, import tariffs, and minimum prices. Caprivi's successor promised to increase wheat tariffs; but by 1900 the Agrarian League had increased to 250,000 members, 50,000 more than its mid-1890s membership. By then it had largely captured the Conservative Party, which in the Reichstag (parliament) merely represented the economic self-interest of Germany's landed class. In 1902 another new chancellor restored agricultural tariffs (partly in return for support for legislation in naval expansion) to their 1892 levels, though this was insufficient for the league. In 1921 it became the Reichslandbund, or State Land League.

Agreda, María de, also called SISTER MARÍA DE JESÚS, original name MARÍA FERNÁNDEZ CORONEL (b. April 2, 1602, Agreda, Spain—d. May 24, 1665, Agreda), abbess and mystic. In 1620 she took her vows as a Franciscan nun and in 1627 became abbess of a Franciscan monastery in Agreda, retaining this office, except for a brief period, until her death.

Her virtues and holy life were universally acknowledged, but controversy arose over her mystical writings, her political influence, and her missionary activities. Her best known work is *The Mystical City of God* (1670), a life of the Virgin Mary ostensibly based on divine revelations granted to María. It was placed on the *Index Librorum Prohibitorum* in 1681, but the ban was lifted in 1747; Spanish theologians maintained from the start that most of the opposition arose from a misunderstanding of the Spanish text. Despite the book's evident historical, geographic, and chronological errors, scholars value it as an ascetic and mystical treatise.

In 1643 Philip IV of Spain, visited María, initiating a correspondence that was maintained until her death. Their letters dealt with spiritual and political matters and form a rich source for historians on Philip's reign.

María was noted for her encouragement of missionary activity, especially among the Franciscans. She frequently repeated that God had revealed to her his desire to convert the North American Indians and had assured the missionaries the reward of becoming apostles. Some thought her words fanciful, but many others accepted her assurances of success and took up mission work; among them was Junípero Serra, founder of California missions.

Ağrı, formerly KARAKÖSE, city, capital of Ağrı *il* (province), in the highlands of eastern Turkey. It lies 5,380 ft (1,640 m) above sea level in the valley of the Murat River, a tributary of the Euphrates River. The town is a centre for trade in livestock and livestock products and is a transit station on the main highway from Turkey to Iran.

Ağrı *il,* with an area of 4,436 sq mi (11,-488 sq km), is largely coextensive with the former *sancak* (district) of Bayezid under the Ottoman Empire. The *il* is named after Mt. Ararat (Turkish Ağrı Dağı), which occupies its northeastern section near its boundaries with Kars *il* and Iran. Stock raising and agriculture are the main activities. Kurds constitute half or more of the population. Pop. (1980) city, 40,532; (1982 est.) *il,* 381,624.

Ağrı Dağı (Turkey): *see* Ararat, Mount.

Agri Decumates, in antiquity, the Black Forest and adjoining areas of what is now southwestern West Germany between the Rhine, Danube, and Main rivers. The name may imply earlier occupation by a tribe with 10 cantons. The Romans under the Flavian emperors began annexing the area in AD 74 to secure better communications between the Rhine and Danube armies. According to Tacitus, the territory was previously inhabited by the Helvetii; later, Gauls settled there. The Romans were displaced from the Agri Decumates by the Alemanni *c.* AD 260.

Agri Decumates in the time of Augustus
Adapted from R. Treharne and H. Fullard (eds.), *Muir's Historical Atlas: Ancient, Medieval and Modern*, 9th ed. (1965); George Philip & Son Ltd., London

agribusiness, agriculture regarded as a business; more specifically, that part of a modern national economy devoted to the production, processing, and distribution of food and fibre products and by-products.

In highly industrialized countries, many activities essential to agriculture are carried on separately from the farm. These include the development and production of equipment, fertilizers, and seeds; in some countries the processing, storage, preservation, and delivery of products have also been separated from basic farming. In consequence, farming itself has become increasingly specialized and businesslike. Some business firms even raise crops, as in the case of a winery that operates its own vineyards or a large commercial producer of fast-frozen or canned vegetables that maintains its own farm. Many of these farms use extensive mechanization and computer technology to increase production.

In recent years, conglomerate companies that are involved in nonagricultural businesses have entered agribusiness by buying and operating large farms. Some food-processing firms that operate farms have begun to market fresh produce under their brand names.

Agricola, Alexander (b. 1446, Flanders—d. 1506, Valladolid, Spain), composer of the late Burgundian polyphonic school.

Agricola was educated in the Netherlands and entered the service of Charles VII of France. He later went to Milan and in 1474 was at the court of Lorenzo de' Medici. The same year he returned to the Netherlands. In 1500 he became chaplain and chanter to Philip the Fair of Burgundy, whom he accompanied to Spain. His works appear widely in contemporary printed music books and are noted for their rhythmic ingenuity. They include masses, motets, French chansons, and Italian carnival songs.

Agricola, Georgius (Latin), German GEORG BAUER (b. March 24, 1494, Clauchau, Saxony—d. Nov. 21, 1555, Chemnitz), German scholar and scientist known as "the father of mineralogy." While a highly educated classicist and humanist, well regarded by scholars of his own and later times, he was yet singularly independent of the theories of ancient authorities. He was indeed among the first to found a natural science upon observation, as opposed to speculation. His *De re metallica* dealt chiefly with the arts of mining and smelting; his *De natura fossilium,* considered the first mineralogy textbook, presented the first scientific classification of minerals (based on their physical properties) and described many new minerals, their occurrence and mutual relationships.

Life. Agricola was born of obscure parentage. From 1514 to 1518 he studied classics, philosophy, and philology at the University of Leipzig, which had recently been exposed to the Humanist revival. Following the custom of the times, he latinized his name to Georgius Agricola. After teaching Latin and Greek from 1518 to 1522 in a school in Zwickau, he returned to Leipzig to begin the study of medicine but found the university in disarray because of theological quarrels. A lifelong Catholic, he left in 1523 for more congenial surroundings in Italy. He studied medicine, natural science, and philosophy in Bologna and Padua, finishing with clinical studies in Venice.

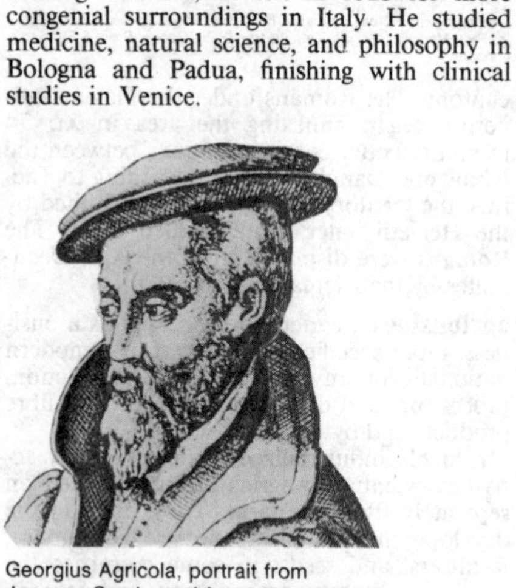

Georgius Agricola, portrait from Joannes Sambucus' *Icones veterum aliquot ac recentium medicorum philosophorumque . . .*; Antwerp, 1574

By courtesy of the Museum National d'Histoire Naturelle, Paris

For two years he worked at the Aldine Press in Venice, principally in preparing an edition of Galen's works on medicine (published in 1525). In this task he collaborated with John Clement, who had been Thomas More's secretary during the writing of *Utopia.* More's book may well have influenced Agricola to concern himself later with the laws and social customs of the Saxon mining district. In Italy he also met and won the friendship of the great scholar Erasmus, who encouraged him to write and later published several of his books. (Erasmus wrote an introduction to Agricola's first book, the mineralogical treatise *Bermannus.* Agricola shared that honour with More and only three other scholars.)

In 1526 he returned to Saxony, and from 1527 to 1533 he was town physician in Joachimsthal, a burgeoning mining town in the richest metal-mining district of Europe. Partly in the hope of finding new drugs among the ores and minerals of his adopted district (a hope eventually to be disappointed), he spent all his spare time visiting mines and smelting plants, talking to the better educated miners, and reading classical authors on mining. These years shaped the rest of his life and provided the subject matter for most of his books, beginning with *Bermannus; sive, de re metallica* (1530), a treatise on the Erzgebirge mining district. There are indications that he owned a share in a silver mine.

He appears not to have been particularly distinguished as a physician, though in this pursuit he made use of direct observation rather than of received authority. He introduced the practice of quarantine into Germany, and his books make many references to miners' occupational diseases. In 1533 he became town physician in Chemnitz, where he remained to the end of his life.

In 1546 Duke Maurice, elector of Saxony, appointed Agricola burgomaster (mayor) of Chemnitz. He also served as an emissary in the Protestant ruler Maurice's ambiguous negotiations with Charles V, the Holy Roman emperor. The religious wars of the period rapidly eroded the tolerance that had hitherto prevailed in the Protestant German states, a tolerance from which Agricola had benefitted. Apart from his diplomatic role, Agricola took only limited interest in politics. His youthful "Turkish Speech" of 1529, a vigorous call to the Holy Roman emperor Ferdinand I to undertake a war against the Turks, was a patriotic hymn to Germany and a call to political and religious unity. It made a great impression on the public and was often reprinted.

Chief works. Agricola's magnum opus, for which the treatise *Bermannus* was a prelude, was *De re metallica,* published posthumously in 1556. In it, among other things, Agricola surveys historical and classical allusions to metals and assesses the content and distribution of metal mines in antiquity. He treats the pattern of ownership and the system of law governing Saxon mines, together with the details of their day-to-day labour management. He was mainly concerned, however, with mining and metallurgy, and he discussed the geology of ore bodies, surveying, mine construction, pumping, and ventilation. There is much on the application of waterpower. He describes the assaying of ores, the methods used for enriching ores before smelting, and procedures for smelting and refining a number of metals; and he concludes with a discussion of the production of glass and of a variety of chemicals used in smelting operations.

In *De natura fossilium* (the book on which rests his right to be regarded as the father of mineralogy), Agricola offers a classification of minerals (called "fossils" at that time) in terms of geometrical form (spheres, cones, plates). He was probably the first to distinguish between "simple" substances and "compounds." In Agricola's day, chemical knowledge was almost nonexistent, and there was no proper chemical analysis (other than analysis of ores by the use of fire), so the classification of ores was necessarily crude.

In several other books, notably *De natura eorum quae effluunt ex terra* (1546) and *De ortu et causis subterraneorum* (1546), Agricola describes his ideas on the origin of ore deposits in veins and correctly attributes them to deposition from aqueous solution. He also describes in detail the erosive action of rivers and its effect in the shaping of mountains. His readiness to discard received authority, even that of classical authors, such as Aristotle and Pliny, is impressive.

Agricola's scholarly contemporaries regarded him highly. Erasmus prophesied in 1531 that he would "shortly stand at the head of the princes of scholarship." Later Goethe was to liken him to Francis Bacon. Melanchthon praised his "grace of presentation and unprecedented clarity." The mining engineer Herbert Hoover (later U.S. president), who translated *De re metallica* into English in 1912, regarded Agricola as the originator of the experimental approach to science, "the first to found any of the natural sciences upon research and observation, as opposed to previous fruitless speculation." (R.W.C.)

BIBLIOGRAPHY. No detailed life of Agricola has been published in English. A German biography is H. Hartmann, *Georg Agricola, 1494–1555* (1953). The most important source is the work published by the East German Academy of sciences on the occasion of the 400th anniversary of his death, *Georgius Agricola, 1494–1555, zu Seinem 400. Todestag 21. Nov.* (1955), which contains a number of essays on Agricola's life and work, including his diplomatic activity. F.D. Adams, *The Birth and Development of the Geological Sciences* (1938), is informative on Agricola's contribution to geology. Of his books, only *De re metallica* and *De natura fossilium* have as yet been translated into English.

Agricola, Gnaeus Julius (b. June 13, AD 40, Forum Julii, Gallia Narbonensis—d. Aug. 23, 93), Roman general celebrated for his conquests in Britain. His life is set forth by his son-in-law, the historian Tacitus.

After serving as military tribune under Suetonius Paulinus, governor in Britain (59–61), Agricola became, successively, quaestor in Asia (64), people's tribune (66), and praetor (68). In the civil war of 69 he took the side of Vespasian, who appointed him to a command in Britain. He was granted patrician status upon his return to Rome in 73 and served as governor of Aquitania (74–77). Appointed consul in 77, he was made governor of Britain. Agricola was in Britain from 77/78 to 84. After conquering portions of Wales, including the island of Mona (now Anglesey), he completed the conquest of what is now northern England. By the end of the third campaigning season, he had advanced into Scotland, establishing a temporary frontier of posts between the firths of the Clota and Bodotria (Clyde and Forth) rivers. The Romans crossed the Forth in 83 and defeated the Caledonians in a decisive battle at Mons Graupius. Agricola's permanent occupation of Scotland reached the fringe of the highlands, where he blocked the main passes with forts and placed a legionary fortress at Inchtuthil (near Dunkeld in Perthshire). Recalled to Rome after his victory, the general lived in retirement, refusing the proconsulship of Asia.

Agricola, Johann, original name JOHANN SCHNEIDER, Schneider also spelled SCHNITTER, Latin SARTOR (b. April 20, 1494, Eisleben, Saxony—d. Sept. 22, 1566, Berlin), Lutheran Reformer, friend of Martin Luther, and advocate of antinomianism, a view asserting that Christians are freed by grace from the need to obey the Ten Commandments. At Wittenberg, Agricola was persuaded by Luther to change his course of study from medicine to theology. Increasingly under Luther's influence, Agricola accompanied him as recording secretary to his Leipzig debate of 1519 with the scholar Johann Eck.

In 1525 Agricola helped introduce Lutheranism to Frankfurt and, in the same year, became head of the Latin school at Eisleben. There, he began to assert his antinomianism (Greek *anti,* "against"; *nomos,* "law"), condemning the law as an unnecessary carry-over from the Old Testament and as too similar to the Catholic stress on good works: "The Decalog (Ten Commandments) belongs in the courthouse, not in the pulpit. . . .To the gallows with Moses!" In 1527 he became more forceful, attacking the Reformer Philipp Melanchthon, an associate of Luther, for Lutheran inclusion of the law in Reformation theology. The conflict was enlarged when Agricola returned to Wittenberg in 1536, and Luther responded with five disputations and the treatise "Against the Antinomians." Under persecution for his attacks on Luther's position, in 1540 Agricola went to Berlin, where he retracted his views and in the same year was made court preacher by the Protestant prince Joachim II of Brandenburg. Shortly afterward he returned to Saxony but found himself no longer in Luther's trust.

In 1548, following Charles V's victory over the Protestants in his effort to unify the Holy Roman Empire, Agricola was selected by the Emperor as one of three theologians to draft a provisional religious settlement between Protestants and Catholics, a document that became known as the Augsburg Interim. His role earned Agricola the hatred of staunch Protestants, but he defended strict Lutheranism in other controversies and toward the end of his life considered himself to have won a substantial victory for Luther's views. Although criticized by some as vain and too morally weak to shun court favours, Agricola was a gifted theologian and administrator.

Agricola, Martin, original name MARTIN SORE, or SOHR (b. Jan. 6, 1486, Schwiebus, Silesia—d. June 10, 1556, Magdeburg, Archbishopric of Magdeburg), composer, teacher, and writer on music, one of the first musicians to concern himself with the needs of the Reformed churches and to publish musical treatises in the vernacular.

Agricola was self-taught, called to music "from the plough," as his chosen surname suggests. He worked at Magdeburg from about 1510 and in 1524 taught at the first Protestant school there. He published several treatises on music theory, most notably his *Musica instrumentalis deudsch* (1529). Much of the German musical vocabulary that he invented is still in use. His books give a valuable picture of the musical life of his time, particularly his descriptions of early 16th-century musical instruments. Most of his unpublished compositions are lost. His printed volumes include sacred music and many instrumental pieces that are transcriptions of vocal part-songs.

Agricola, Rodolphus, original name ROELOF HUYSMAN (b. 1443/44, Baflo, Groningen—d. Oct. 27, 1485, Heidelberg, Palatinate), Dutch Humanist who, basing his philosophy on Renaissance ideas, placed special emphasis on the freedom of the individual and the complete development of the self, from both an intellectual and a physical standpoint. His ideas influenced Erasmus, another Dutch Humanist.

Agricola studied in Groningen, Erfurt, Cologne, and Louvain, graduating from Louvain in 1465. While in his early 30s, he started to write, producing an oration in praise of philosophy (1476) and a life of Petrarch, the Italian poet and scholar (1477). During the following five years, he travelled between universities in northwestern Germany and the Netherlands. In 1484 he accepted an invitation from the bishop of Worms, Johann von Dalberg, to lecture on classical literature in Heidelberg. In the same year he wrote *De formando studio,* a book on education.

Agricultural Adjustment Administration (AAA), in U.S. history, major New Deal program to restore agricultural prosperity by curtailing farm production, reducing export surpluses, and raising prices. The Agricultural Adjustment Act (May 1933) was an omnibus farm relief bill embodying the schemes of the major national farm organizations. It established the Agricultural Adjustment Administration under Secretary of Agriculture Henry Wallace to effect a "domestic allotment" plan that would subsidize producers of basic commodities for cutting their output. Its goal was to achieve "parity" prices that would restore to the farmer purchasing power equivalent to that of an earlier base period (mainly 1909–14). In addition, the Commodity Credit Corporation, with a crop loan and storage program, was established to make price-supporting loans and purchases of specific commodities.

Although benefit payments to farmers totalled $1,500,000,000 by 1936, a rise in commodity prices was attributable mainly to severe drought conditions in 1933–36. In spite of its limited achievements, the early AAA program was favoured by most farmers. The Supreme Court declared the act unconstitutional in 1936, and Congress passed new agricultural legislation two years later based on the soil conservation concept. While farmers' cash income doubled between 1932 and 1936, it took the enormous demands of World War II to reduce the accumulated farm surpluses and to increase farm income significantly.

agricultural economics, the study of the allocation, distribution, and utilization of the resources used by and commodities produced by farming. The system of economic relations involved in agriculture includes the livelihoods of more than half the people on earth; in some areas, the proportion is as much as three-quarters of the general populace. Agricultural economics plays a role in the economics of development, for a continuous level of farm surplus is one of the wellsprings of technological and commercial growth.

A brief treatment of agricultural economics follows. For full treatment, *see* MACROPAEDIA: Rural Society, Modern.

The peasant farms of the past were largely self-sufficient, producing just enough foodstuffs for their cultivators, with perhaps a small surplus for the local market. Typically, a farmworker produced enough to feed three other people, two of whom were of the household. The excess might be used for rent or to buy supplies smallholders could not make for themselves. An average farmer planted small quantities of many different crops, thus ensuring that the members of the household were not completely dependent on the harvest of any one of them.

This description was true for the United States in the middle of the 19th century, and it still holds for many areas in the developing world, from Asia to Africa. Such farms are not, in any important way, connected to market economies. They are also not very productive, in part because of lack of information but more because they are usually neither fertilized nor irrigated adequately, and the soil is frequently exhausted from decades of intense cultivation. Production increases in underdeveloped regions arise only from increases in the amount of land tilled or the amount of labour employed per area of cropland. As the population grows, crops requiring more labour usually take the place of less labour-intensive crops. With low yields, peasant farmers are ever subject to famine and thus are reluctant to take risks on innovative methods.

However, given convincing demonstrations of the virtues of new methods or seed stocks, even the most traditional peasant farmers will readily change their ways, as was shown in the 1960s by the rapid adoption of improved agricultural techniques throughout the world. With investment in the fertilizers, insecticides, herbicides, irrigation systems, machinery, and high-yielding varieties of food crops that have been developed in the past century, yields per unit of land can be increased enormously. For instance, high-yield varieties of rice were not introduced in Bangladesh (then West Pakistan) until the 1968–69 growing season, yet one year later a fourth of the total crop came from the new strains.

The substitution of mechanical power for animal power and the increased use of fertilizers reduces the need for labour and land. In 1910 feeding the horses and mules that pulled farmers' plows required the output of more than one-fourth of the world's cropland, and nearly one-tenth of the work on farms involved caring for draft animals. Mechanizing agriculture ends farmers' dependence on these resources. By making land more productive, fertilizers also remove additional pressure to expand the amount of cultivation.

Rising harvests yield ever greater surpluses for the market, while the decreasing need for human labour pushes people out of the countryside and into the cities. The surplus enables other types of development to take place while drawing farmers into the larger market economy. Unlike peasant cultivators, farmers in developed nations are vulnerable to outside economic conditions. Farm prices are notoriously volatile, rising or falling by as much as one-third or one-half from year to year. Part of the reason for this extreme variability is the consumer's low level of response to agricultural price changes. To increase sales in other fields, it is often necessary only to reduce the price; in agriculture, however, large price reductions stimulate very little added demand. In addition, even if changes in demand do occur, farmers have limited ability to respond to them. They must plant on the basis of expectations; if their expectations are not borne out, they cannot do anything about it until the next harvest.

Dependent on the market, such farmers are caught between their relatively high fixed costs—machinery, fertilizer, feedstocks, interest, and so on—and their fluctuating income. As a result, farm incomes throughout the world still tend to be lower than incomes from nonfarm pursuits. Governments have tried a number of methods to make farming more rewarding. Among these are direct payments, limitations on production, tariffs and levies on food imports, and taking agriculture out of the market system altogether. In the United States farmers are frequently paid not to grow particular crops, thus preventing soil exhaustion and keeping the market from being glutted. Price supports are also offered for major crops including wheat, rice, cotton, and tobacco; if the market price falls below certain levels, the Commodity Credit Corporation (CCC) will buy farmers' crops, which are then usually distributed in economic aid programs.

The European Economic Community (EEC), or Common Market, has a complex agricultural policy for its 10 member nations. The EEC exacts levies on farm imports, driving their prices up until they reach the domestic levels. Using this system, Common Market farmers have been able to keep grain prices, for example, 60 to 90 percent higher than prevailing levels in North America. In the Soviet Union and most other Communist nations, agriculture has been collectivized. Markets were abolished, and each farm was simply required to produce an assigned quota, for which the state paid a set price. Before 1953, the year of Stalin's death, the Soviet state paid very low prices, and farm incomes were low, providing in effect a subsidy for industrialization. In the post-Stalin period prices have been raised significantly, and cultivators have fared better.

The effects of these various policies are difficult to assess. Although they have raised productivity in the nations where they have been applied, they have not always benefitted farmers. It is apparent that real income from agriculture has less to do with governmental policies than with the local level of economic development. Rising farm prices have often been offset by an increase in the number of farmers and the acreage put to the plow; in addition, they frequently have had the consequence of inducing farmers to spend more on fertilizers, machinery, and other costs, thus lowering their net income. The problem of maintaining growth in productivity, guarding the natural resources of the land, and adequately rewarding cultivators for their work in societies with advanced agricultural practices has not been fully solved.

agricultural sciences, the sciences dealing with farm production, including soil cultivation, crop growing and harvesting, animal husbandry, and, to some extent, the processing of plant and animal products to a marketable stage. The agricultural industry that is the focus of study includes farming, concerned with production; service industries, concerned with making or supplying machinery, buildings, fertilizers, and pesticides; and the first purchasers of farm products, such as processors, distributors, and marketing boards.

A brief treatment of agricultural sciences follows. For full treatment, *see* MACROPAEDIA: Agricultural Sciences.

In prehistoric times, religion and farming were closely allied. When agriculture was invented (about 8000–6000 BC), the first agricultural teachers were the priests. Apart from references in some ancient inscriptions, the first recorded instruction book was the *Works and Days* of Hesiod (probably 8th century BC). Like that of the priests, his instruction was largely seasonal and based on predictable astronomic events, thus: "Then after the Pleiades and the Hyades and the strength of Orion have set, then remember again to begin your seasonal ploughing." By the 16th century AD the link between religion or astronomy and agriculture was weaker, and the advent of printing led to many secular printed books, such as Thomas Tusser's *Points of Husbandry* (1557). In the 18th century, progressive landowners started early versions of the "field trials" of today. There was, however, no formal agricultural education or research until the end of the 18th century, when professorships of agriculture and rural economy were founded at Oxford (1790) and Edinburgh (1796) in the United Kingdom. Meanwhile, in France and Germany, Bernard Palissy (1510–89), Albrecht Thaer (1752–1828), S.F. Hermstädt (1760–1833), and in particular Jean-Baptiste Boussingault (1802–87), and Justus von Liebig (1803–73) were laying the foundations of agricultural research. In England, Rothamsted Experimental Station, the oldest research centre in continuous operation, and the Royal Agricultural College at Cirencester started before 1850. But probably the key date in the history of agricultural research and education is 1862, when the United States Congress set up the Department of Agriculture and provided for colleges (many now incorporated in state universities) of agricultural and mechanical arts in each state. This legislation heralded a movement that spread across the world from the second half of the 19th century onward; after World War II, it gathered increasing momentum.

Today there is scarcely a sovereign country that does not have practical colleges or courses and extension (*i.e.,* farmers' advisory) services, and at least one university with a faculty of agriculture. The disciplines of such a faculty may well include biochemistry, physics and agrometeorology, soil science, engineering, botany, crop physiology, animal physiology and nutrition, genetics, entomology, plant and animal pathology, economics and sociology, farming systems and production methods, human nutrition, and food processing (in the factory and in the home). Applied statistics and operational mathematics (*e.g.,* linear programming of least cost livestock rations) are essential research tools for these disciplines and permit a quantitative intellectual rigour that enables agricultural science to contribute to the basic natural and social sciences as much as it receives from them.

agriculture, the science or art of cultivating the soil, growing and harvesting crops, and raising livestock. The art of making land more productive is practiced throughout the world—in some areas by methods not far removed from the conditions of several thousands of years ago, in other areas with the aid of science and mechanization, as a highly commercial type of endeavour. Agriculture still drafts into its service more of the world's aggregate manpower than all other occupations combined.

Agriculture is treated in a number of articles in the MACROPAEDIA. For the history and principal treatments of the subject, *see* Agriculture, The History of; Farming and Agricultural Technology; Food Processing. For the economics and sociology of agriculture and farming, *see* Rural Society, Modern. For the academic and technological discipline, *see* Agricultural Sciences.

For a description of the place of agriculture in the circle of learning and for a list of both MACROPAEDIA and MICROPAEDIA articles on the subject, *see* PROPAEDIA: Part Seven, Division III.

For statistical data on farming and on crop and livestock production, *see* BRITANNICA WORLD DATA in the current *Britannica Book of the Year.*

Agriculture and Education, Institute of: *see* Brook Farm.

Agrigento, formerly (until 1927) GIRGENTI, Greek AKRAGAS, Latin AGRIGENTUM, capital of Agrigento province, near the south coast of Sicily, Italy. It lies on a plateau encircled by low cliffs overlooking the junction of the Drago (ancient Hypsas) and San Biagio (Akragas) rivers, dominated from the north by a ridge with twin peaks. A wealthy ancient city founded *c.* 581 BC by Greek colonists from

The Temple of Hera, Agrigento, Sicily
V. Dia—SCALA from Art Resource/EB Inc.

Gela, it was ruled 570–554 BC by the notorious tyrant Phalaris who was reputed to have had men roasted alive in a brazen bull; it reached its peak in 480 when the tyrant Theron, in alliance with Syracuse, won the decisive Battle of Himera, on the northern coast, over the Carthaginians. In 470 the tyranny was replaced by a democracy. Agrigento was the birthplace of the philosopher-politician Empedocles. Under the tyranny it was a considerable centre of the arts. Neutral in the struggle between Athens and Syracuse, it was ravaged by the Carthaginians in 406 BC. Refounded by the Greek general and statesman Timoleon in 338, it achieved some local importance in the early 3rd century BC, but was sacked by the Romans (262) and the Carthaginians (255) before falling finally to Rome in 210 BC. Under Roman rule its agricultural wealth and the exploitation of the nearby sulfur mines ensured a modest prosperity. In late antiquity its inhabitants withdrew to the relative security of the medieval hilltop town of Girgenti, the nucleus of modern Agrigento. Occupied and colonized by the Saracens in 828, Girgenti was captured in 1087 by the Norman conqueror of Sicily, Count Roger I, who established a Latin bishopric.

The plateau site of the ancient city is extraordinarily rich in Greek remains. A wall, with remnants of eight gates, can be traced from the two northern peaks (the Rock of Athena and the hill of Girgenti) to the ridge that carried the south line of the city's defenses. An almost continuous sacred area along this ridge has been excavated to reveal Agrigento's most famous remains, its seven Doric temples. The best preserved are two very similar peripteral, hexastyle temples conventionally, though wrongly, attributed to the goddesses Hera and Concordia; the latter temple, which lacks little but the roof, owes its remarkable preservation to having been converted into a church in AD 597. The temple of Zeus, in front of which stood a huge altar, was one of the largest and most original of all Doric buildings; it was still unfinished in 406 BC. Its ruins were quarried in 1749–63 to build the jetties of Porto Empedocle and very little is now standing. The sanctuary of Demeter and Persephone (formerly known as the temple of Castor and Pollux) is notable for many remains of archaic cult-buildings. There is a pre-Hellenic cave sanctuary at the foot of the cliffs where the temple of Demeter, underlying the church of S. Biagio, is found. There are also ruined temples of Hephaestus and Asclepius (Aesculapius); the "tomb of Theron," a late Hellenistic funerary monument; and the "Oratory of Phalaris," a *heroon* (heroic shrine) of the 1st century AD adjoining the 13th-century church of S. Nicola (the setting of Agrigento's native son Luigi Pirandello's play *Sagra del signore della nave*). A short distance to the east of the latter a considerable quarter of the Greek and Roman town has been excavated, but apart from extensive remains of aqueducts and cisterns, little is known of the Greek civil or domestic architecture. Earlier classical cemeteries lie beyond the walls.

Notable buildings of the medieval and modern city include the 14th-century cathedral, the 13th-century churches of S. Spirito and Sta. Maria dei Greci (overlying remains of a Doric temple), Baroque churches and palaces, and the rich archaeological museum. Illegal construction and landslides have caused damage to some local monuments, however.

Agrigento's economy is based on sulfur and potash mining, agriculture, and tourism. It is served by Porto Empedocle, 9 mi (15 km) southwest, the best harbour on the southwest coast of Sicily and Italy's principal sulfur port. Pop. (1981 prelim.) mun., 51,931.

Agrihan, formerly GRIGAN, or AGRIGAN, one of the Mariana Islands, part of the U.S. Commonwealth of the Northern Mariana Islands (internally self-governing in 1978), and part of the United Nations Trust Territory of the Pacific Islands. It lies in the western Pacific, 350 mi (563 km) north of Guam. An active volcano that last erupted in 1917, it has a total land area of 18 sq mi (47 sq km) and rises to 3,166 ft (965 m), the highest point in the commonwealth. Agrihan was the site of the last stand the indigenous Chamorros made against the Spaniards, who had occupied the Marianas late in the 17th century. In 1810, colonists from the United States and Hawaii established plantations, but they were expelled by the Spanish administration. Agrihan has some fertile highlands and phosphate deposits. Pop. (1980) Agrihan, including Alamagan and Pagan, 104.

agrimensoris (ancient Roman surveyors): *see* gromaticus.

agrimony, any plant of the genus *Agrimonia*, of the rose family (Rosaceae), especially *A. eupatoria*, an herbaceous, hardy perennial native to Europe but also cultivated in other temperate regions. *A. eupatoria* grows to about 90 centimetres (3 feet) tall and has alternate feather-formed leaves that yield a yellow dye.

Agrimony (*Agrimonia gryposepala*)
B.M. Shaub

The oval leaflets, about 2–6 centimetres (0.8–2.4 inches) long, have toothed margins. The small, stalkless yellow flowers are borne in a long terminal spike. The fruit is a bur about 0.6 cm (0.24 in.) in diameter.

Agrínion, agricultural town, west central Greece, the largest centre of the *nomós* (department) of Aetolia and Acarnania and capital of the *eparkhía* (province) of Trikhonidos, located 4 mi (6 km) northwest of Límni (lake) Trikhonís, about midway between the Ionian Sea and the Patraïkós Kólpos (gulf). Formerly called Vrakhóri (an abbreviation of Evrekori, "town of the Jews"), it has reverted under Greek rule to the name of an ancient Aetolian centre on the Achelous River that was just northwest of the present town. In 314 BC Agrínion received the assistance of the Macedonian king Cassander, who helped the Acarnanians reorganize their defense league against Aetolian aggression. Modern Agrínion, rebuilt after a destructive earthquake in 1887, is a tobacco-growing and processing centre; it is the terminus of a railway from Krionérion via Mesolóngion, the *nomós* capital, and has a commercial airport. Pop. (1981) 35,774.

Agrionia (from Greek *agrios,* "wild" or "savage"), Greek religious festival celebrated annually at Orchomenus in Boeotia and elsewhere in honour of the wine god Dionysus. The tradition is that the daughters of Minyas, king of Orchomenus, having despised the rites of the god, were driven mad by Dionysus and ate the flesh of one of their children; as punishment they were turned into bats or birds. At this festival it was originally the custom for the priest to pursue and kill a woman of the Minyan family at night.

Agrippa (fl. 1st or 2nd century AD), ancient Greek philosophical Skeptic. He is famous for his formulation of the five tropes, or grounds for the suspension of judgment, that summarize the method of Greek Skeptics generally. His five arguments held that (1) there is a clash of opinions, both in daily life and in the debates of philosophers; (2) nothing is self-evident, because that which is called a proof is merely a second proposition itself in need of demonstration, and so on ad infinitum; (3) both perception and judgment are relative in a double sense: each is relative to a subject, and each is affected by concomitant perceptions; (4) dogmatic philosophers seeking to avoid the infinite regression merely offer hypotheses that they cannot prove; and (5) philosophers are caught in the double bind by trying to prove the sensible by the intelligible and the intelligible by the sensible. Doubting both the evidence of the senses and the possibility of understanding, Agrippa concluded that men have no starting point for obtaining knowledge. Agrippa's 5 seem to have been based in part on the 10 tropes of the earlier Skeptic Aenesidemus, but Agrippa's Skepticism is more thorough, not limited to the sense perceptions that Aenesidemus questioned.

Agrippa, Marcus Julius: *see* Herod Agrippa I.

Agrippa, Marcus Vipsanius (b. 63 BC?—d. March, 12 BC, Campania), powerful deputy of Augustus, the first Roman emperor. He was chiefly responsible for the victory over Mark Antony at Actium in 31 BC, and during Augustus' reign he suppressed rebellions, founded colonies, and administered various parts of the Roman Empire. Of modest birth but not a modest man, Agrippa was disliked by the Roman aristocracy. In his own interest he scrupulously maintained a subordinate role in relation to Augustus, but he felt himself inferior to no one else.

Virtually nothing is known of his early life until he is found as the companion of Octavian (the future emperor Augustus) at Apollonia, in Illyria, at the time of Julius Caesar's murder in 44. Octavian, the adopted son of Caesar, returned with Agrippa to Italy to make his political claim as Caesar's heir. In 43 Agrippa is thought to have held the office of tribune of the plebs; presumably in this capacity he prosecuted the tyrannicide Cassius, then absent in the East. In the struggle for power after Caesar's death, Agrippa served as one of Octavian's key commanders. In 41–40 he fought against Mark Antony's brother Lucius. In 40 he held the post of praetor urbanus (magistrate mainly in charge of administration of justice at Rome) and was a major figure in negotiating a settlement between Octavian and Antony at Brundisium. During the next two years he was away on campaigns in Aquitania and on the Rhine. When he returned to Italy, he conspicuously refused to celebrate a triumph for his successes in the north, but in 37 he held the office of consul. In the spring of 37 Octavian and Antony came to an agreement at Tarentum, and it must have been then that Antony arranged the marriage of Agrippa to the daughter of Titus Atticus, a wealthy friend of Cicero.

Octavian's efforts to resist at sea the son of the republican general Gnaeus Pompey, Sextus Pompeius, had not met with success. Agrippa therefore took charge of the operations. He constructed a fine harbour at Puteoli in the Bay of Naples and then won, in 36, two decisive naval victories (at Mylae and Naulochus), which ended the threat from Pompeius. For this achievement Agrippa accepted the award of a golden crown. In 35–34 Octavian waged a vigorous campaign in Dalmatia, and in this Agrippa had a distinguished military role. In 33 Agrippa served as curule aedile (magistrate of public buildings and works) at Rome, even though it was a much lower post than the consulate that he had already held. He used the opportunity to win favour for Octavian by spending his own funds lavishly on building baths, cleaning sewers, and improving the water supply. When Octavian and Antony finally came into direct conflict at the Battle of Actium in 31, Agrippa commanded the fleet and was chiefly responsible for Octavian's victory.

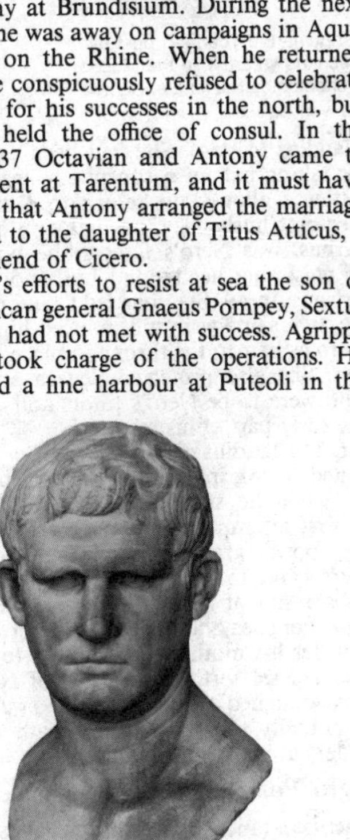

Marcus Vipsanius Agrippa, marble portrait bust, early 1st century BC; in the Louvre, Paris
Cliche Musees Nationaux, Paris

During Octavian's absence from Rome after Actium, Agrippa managed affairs in the city together with Maecenas, the great patron of poets. In 29–28 Agrippa and Octavian jointly conducted a census and carried out a purge of the Senate; in 28 and 27 Agrippa held the consulate again, both times with Octavian (from 27, Augustus) as his colleague. In 23, a year of constitutional crisis, Augustus fell ill and presented his signet ring to Agrippa, who seemed thus to be designated the Emperor's successor. Agrippa took Augustus' daughter Julia as his wife after divorcing a niece of Augustus (Marcella the Elder), who had replaced Atticus' daughter as his wife some four or five years previously.

Agrippa went immediately to Mytilene on the island of Lesbos, from which he administered affairs in the East. The nature of Agrippa's constitutional power (*imperium*) at this time is controversial. It has been argued whether the Senate in 23 gave him an *imperium* greater than that of any other provincial governor in the East (*imperium majus*). After Augustus' death Roman historians claimed that Agrippa's sojourn at Mytilene was a kind of exile as a result of Augustus' preference for his own nephew Marcellus. This appears implausible. Agrippa was soon back in Rome to act on behalf of the Emperor, who himself left for the East in 22. Before Augustus' return, in 19, Agrippa had left for Gaul and Spain. In Spain he finally subdued the recalcitrant Cantabrians.

Returning to Rome in 18, Agrippa received the power of a tribune (*tribunicia potestas*), which Augustus also possessed. Perhaps, too, he received an *imperium majus,* if he had not been granted it in 23. He participated in Augustus' celebration of the Secular Games at Rome in 17, after which he returned to the East as vicegerent of the Emperor. In 15 he accepted an invitation from Herod I the Great to visit Judaea; while in the East, he established colonies of veterans at Berytus and Heliopolis, in Lebanon. He next settled an uprising in the Bosporan kingdom on the Black Sea and set up the cultivated dynast Polemo as king. Herod led a fleet to support Agrippa in the Bosporan affair, and, when it was over, the two travelled together along the coast of western Asia Minor.

In 13 Agrippa's *tribunicia potestas* was renewed, and at this time without doubt he received (or had renewed) a grant of *imperium majus.* Troubles in Pannonia required his presence, but the rigours of the winter of 13–12 caused a fatal illness; he died in March of 12 BC. Augustus delivered a funeral oration in honour of his colleague; a fragment of that oration, in Greek translation, has recently come to light.

Agrippa deserved the honours Augustus heaped upon him. It is conceivable that without Agrippa, Octavian would never have become emperor. Rome remembered him for his generosity in attending to aqueducts, sewers, and baths; and in the mid-20s he completed the celebrated Pantheon. One of Agrippa's five children by Julia, Agrippina the Elder, was the mother of one emperor (Caligula) and the grandmother of another (Nero). Agrippa's autobiography is lost, but an extensive geographical commentary that he wrote influenced the extant works of the geographer Strabo and of Pliny the Elder. (G.W.Bo.)

BIBLIOGRAPHY. The best full-length study of Agrippa is Meyer Reinhold, *Marcus Agrippa* (1933). There is also an important account of him in Sir Ronald Syme's classic work, *The Roman Revolution* (1939). On problems arising from the new fragment of Augustus' funeral oration on Agrippa, see E.W. Gray, "The Imperium of M. Agrippa," *Zeitschrift für Papyrologie und Epigraphik*, 6:227–238 (1970).

Agrippa von Nettesheim, Heinrich Cornelius (b. Sept. 14, 1486, Cologne—d. Feb. 18, 1535, Grenoble, Fr.), court secretary to Charles V, physician to Louise of Savoy, exasperating theologian within the Catholic Church, military entrepreneur in Spain and Italy, acknowledged expert on occultism, and philosopher. His tempestuous career also included teaching at Dôle and Pavia universities, appointment as orator and public advocate at Metz (until denounced for defending an accused witch), banishment from Germany in 1535 (after battling with the inquisitor of Cologne), and imprisonment in France (for criticizing the Queen Mother).

Agrippa's *De occulta philosophia* added impetus to Renaissance study of magic and injected his name into early Faust legends. In this book he explained the world in terms of cabalistic analyses of Hebrew letters and Pythagorean numerology and acclaimed magic as the best means to know God and nature. About 1530 Agrippa outraged Charles V by publishing a scathing attack on occultism and all other sciences ("Of the Vanitie and uncertaintie of artes and sciences," trans. 1569) and thus served the Renaissance revival of Skepticism. Agrippa was jailed and branded as a heretic. After scuttling every type of scientific

Agrippa von Nettesheim, engraving by an unknown artist, 1527
Archiv fur Kunst und Geschichte, West Berlin

knowledge, he found peaceful refuge in a simple biblical piety.

Agrippina THE ELDER (b. *c.* 14 BC—d. Oct. 18, AD 33, the island of Pandateria, in the Tyrrhenian Sea), granddaughter of the emperor Augustus and a major figure in the succession struggles in the latter part of the reign of Tiberius (ruled AD 14–37).

Agrippina was married to Germanicus Caesar (great-nephew of Augustus and nephew and adopted son of Tiberius). She accompanied her husband to Germany and to the East, where he died at Antioch in AD 19. When the death of Tiberius' son Drusus in 23 brought her sons into direct line for the succession, she became the object of attacks by Sejanus, Tiberius' adviser, who had his own designs. Finally, in 29 she was exiled to Pandateria, where she died, either self-starved or, according to some, starved at Tiberius' order. Of her nine children by Germanicus, one son and three daughters survived her, the son becoming Tiberius' successor as the emperor Gaius Caligula (37–41). The most famous of her daughters was Agrippina, the mother of the emperor Nero. Several fine portraits of Agrippina have been preserved, the most famous being in the Capitoline Museum, Rome.

Agrippina THE YOUNGER (b. AD 15—d. 59), mother of the Roman emperor Nero and a powerful influence on him during the early years of his reign (54–68).

Agrippina was the daughter of the elder Agrippina, sister of the emperor Gaius, or Caligula (37–41), and wife of the emperor

Agrippina the Younger, bust by an unknown artist; in the Museo Archeologico Nazionale, Naples
Anderson—Mansell

Claudius (41–54). She had been exiled in 39 for taking part in a conspiracy against Gaius but was allowed to return to Rome in 41. Her first husband, Gnaeus Domitius Ahenobarbus, was Nero's father. She was accused of poisoning her second husband, Passienus Crispus, in 49. She married Claudius, her uncle, that same year and induced him to adopt Nero as heir to the throne in place of his own son. She also protected Seneca and Burrus, who were to be Nero's tutors and advisers in the early part of his reign.

In 54 Claudius died, perhaps after being poisoned by Agrippina. Because Nero was only 16 when he succeeded Claudius, Agrippina at first attempted to play the role of regent. Her power gradually weakened, however, as Nero came to take charge of the government. As a result of her opposition to Nero's affair with Poppaea Sabina, the Emperor decided to murder his mother. Inviting her to Baiae, he had her set forth on the Bay of Naples in a boat designed to sink, but she swam ashore. Eventually she was put to death on Nero's orders at her country house.

Agro Pontino (Italy): *see* Pontine Marshes.

agroikoi (ancient Greek social class): *see* geōmoroi.

agrostology, the branch of botany concerned with the study of grasses, especially their classification. In 1708 the German botanist Johann Scheuchzer wrote *Agrostographiae Helveticae Prodromus,* a taxonomic paper on grasses that some authors consider to mark the birth of agrostology. Many systems of classification followed this brief beginning. The earliest were based purely on external morphology of the plant, but later systems take into consideration the results of cellular, embryological, physiological, and histological studies.

Modern agrostologists investigate living populations of grasses to determine their genetic inheritance and adaptations to specific habitats. Biochemical studies are another promising tool in determining evolutionary relationships between groups of grasses.

Aguadilla, town and municipality, northwestern Puerto Rico. The town is a port on a wide bay formed on the south by the hills of Punta Higüero (Jiguera) and on the north by Punta Borinquen, the northwestern corner of the island. It was established as a town in 1775 and elevated to the royal rank of *villa* in 1861. The town is a processing and trading centre for a prosperous agricultural hinterland; products include cigars and straw hats. The town has a regional college of the University of Puerto Rico.

The municipality, with an area of 36 sq mi (93 sq km), has seven urban or partly urban and nine rural barrios (wards). It is an agricultural area producing sugar, coffee, fruits, tobacco, and cotton. Coastal roads link Aguadilla municipality with Mayagüez and San Juan, the capital, to which it also has a rail link. Aguadilla town has an airport. Pop. (1980) town, 22,039; mun., 54,606.

Aguán River, Spanish RÍO AGUÁN, river in northern Honduras, 150 mi (240 km) in length. After rising in the central highlands west of Yoro, it descends to the northeast between the Cerros de Cangreja and the Sierra de la Esperanza to the coastal lowlands, on which it forms a maze of channels and empties into the Caribbean Sea near the towns of Santa Rosa de Aguán and Limón. The lands along the river, although periodically devastated by banana diseases, floods, and hurricanes (particularly Fifi in 1974), were restored to banana cultivation with new disease-resistant varieties in the late 1970s. In the lower river valley, agricultural cooperatives shifted to raising citrus fruits, corn (maize), rice, and African palm for oil. Flood control works were started after the river burst its levees in 1977. A new highway links the river valley to the ports at Tela, La Ceiba, Trujillo, and Puerto Cortés. The railway paralleling the lower and middle valley of the Aguán, damaged by natural disasters, was restored to service and extended to Puerto Castilla in the late 1970s.

Aguarico River, Spanish RÍO AGUARICO, river, northeastern Ecuador, rising south of

The Aguarico River in the rain forests of El Oriente region, Ecuador
Reflejo—EB Inc.

Tulcán, capital of Carchi province, in the Andes mountains near the Ecuador–Colombia border, and flowing east-southeast for approximately 230 mi (370 km) to its juncture with the Río Napo at Pantoja. It is navigable for smaller boats. The Rio de Janeiro Protocol of 1942 fixed the lower course of the Aguarico (Rich Water) as part of the long-disputed Ecuador–Peru frontier. Although Ecuador unilaterally denounced the protocol in 1960, it has in practice observed its general provisions.

Aguascalientes, state, central Mexico. One of the country's smallest states (2,112 sq mi [5,471 sq km]), it occupies part of the central plateau between 3,300 and 10,000 ft (1,000 and 3,000 m) above sea level, extending from two spurs of the Sierra Madre eastward and southward to rolling fertile plains. It is well watered and has a mild, healthful climate, with light rainfall. The name, from the Spanish for "hot waters," stems from the many thermal springs in the vicinity.

Explored by Spaniards in the 16th century, Aguascalientes was a colonial mining centre. During the revolution of 1910–20 it was the scene of bitter fighting and was occupied by successive factions in the struggle. Since 1950, irrigation projects have greatly increased productivity of the land. The fertile valleys of the north and west are devoted to agriculture, and the plains to livestock raising. Corn (maize), cattle, horses, mules, and hides are exported to neighbouring states. Aguascalientes also grows excellent wines and fruits and is noted for its production of zinc, copper, gold, silver, and other minerals. The state has good rail and highway connections with all parts of Mexico. There is an airport at Aguascalientes (*q.v.*) city, the state capital. Pop. (1980) 519,000.

Aguascalientes, city, capital of Aguascalientes state, central Mexico. It stands on the central plateau at 6,194 ft (1,888 m) above sea level, on the left bank of the Río de Aguas-

La Parroquia church, Aguascalientes City, Mex.
Walter Aguiar—EB Inc.

calientes. Founded as a mining settlement in 1575 and designated a town in 1661, Aguascalientes was named capital when the state was created during the 1850s. It is sometimes called La Ciudad Perforada (The Perforated City) because of a labyrinth of tunnels excavated beneath it in pre-Columbian times by an unknown tribe. Aquascalientes is the centre of a fruit- and vegetable-growing region. It has important railroad repair shops, cotton and other textile factories, potteries, tobacco factories, distilleries, and other industries. The most notable of the city's many fine churches are San Juan de Dios, San Francisco, and La Parroquia, each of which possesses outstanding examples of colonial religious art. The city can be reached by rail, highway, or air. The Autonomous University of Aguascalientes was founded in 1973. Pop. (1980) 233,000.

ague tree: *see* sassafras.

Aguesseau, Henri-François d' (b. Nov. 27, 1668, Limoges, Fr.—d. Feb. 5, 1751, Paris), jurist who, as chancellor of France during most of the period from 1717 to 1750, made important reforms in his country's legal system.

The son of Henri d'Aguesseau, intendant (royal agent) of Languedoc, he was advocate general to the Parlement (high court of justice) of Paris from 1690 until 1700. As attorney general in that Parlement from 1700 to 1717, he opposed papal intervention in the affairs of the French Roman Catholic Church and resisted (though unsuccessfully) the promulgation in France of the bull *Unigenitus* (1713), which condemned the Jansenist faction in the church.

Philippe II, duc d'Orléans, regent for young King Louis XV (ruled 1715–74), made him chancellor and keeper of the seals in 1717, but Aguesseau's opposition to the government's financial policies caused the Duc to exile him to Fresnes in the following year. Recalled in 1720, Aguesseau reversed himself and helped promote acceptance of *Unigenitus.* Nevertheless, he again forfeited the chancellorship when Cardinal Guillaume Dubois became chief minister in 1722. In 1727 Aguesseau was reinstated as chancellor by the new chief minister, Cardinal André-Hercule de Fleury, who instructed him to continue the codification of French law begun under King Louis XIV (ruled 1643–1715).

Hence between 1731 and 1747 he obtained from Louis XV three important ordinances on donations, testaments, and successions. The Parlements prevented Aguesseau from extending the scope of his work, but he did improve court procedures and achieve greater uniformity in the execution of the laws.

Agui (Chinese general): *see* A-Kuei.

Aguilar, Grace (b. June 2, 1816, London—d. Sept. 16, 1847, Frankfurt am Main), poet, novelist, and writer on Jewish history and religion, best known for her numerous sentimental novels of domestic life. The most popular, *Home Influence* (1847), was the only one published during her lifetime. Although they evinced strong religious feeling, her novels were free of sectarian bias. In *The Spirit of Judaism* (1842) she attacked contemporary Judaism for its formalism and traditionalism.

Consult
the
INDEX
first

Aguinaldo, Emilio (b. March 23, 1869, near Cavite, Luzon, Phil.—d. Feb. 6, 1964, Manila), Filipino leader who fought first against Spain and later against the United States for the independence of the Philippines.

Born of Chinese and Tagalog parentage, he completed his education at the University of Santo Tomás, Manila. In August 1896 he was mayor of Cavite Viejo and was the local leader of the Katipunan, a revolutionary society that fought bitterly and successfully against the Spanish. In December 1897 he signed an agreement called the Pact of Biac-na-Bató with the Spanish governor general. He agreed to leave the Philippines and to remain permanently in exile on condition of a substantial financial reward from Spain coupled with the promise of liberal reforms. While in Hong Kong and Singapore he made arrangements with representatives of the American consulates and of Commo. George Dewey to return to the Philippines to assist the United States in the war against Spain.

Aguinaldo
Brown Brothers

Aguinaldo returned to the Philippines May 19, 1898, and announced renewal of the struggle with Spain. The Filipinos, who declared their independence of Spain on June 12, 1898, proclaimed a provisional republic, of which Aguinaldo was to become president; and in September a revolutionary assembly met and ratified Filipino independence. However, the Philippines, along with Puerto Rico and Guam, were ceded by Spain to the United States by the Treaty of Paris, Dec. 10, 1898.

Relations between the Americans and the Filipinos were unfriendly and grew steadily worse. On Jan. 23, 1899, the Malolos Constitution, by virtue of which the Philippines was declared a republic and which had been approved by the assembly and by Aguinaldo, was proclaimed. Aguinaldo, who had been president of the provisional government, was elected president.

On the night of February 4 the inevitable conflict between the Americans and Filipinos surrounding Manila was precipitated. Morning found the Filipinos, who had fought bravely, even recklessly, defeated at all points. While the fighting was in progress, Aguinaldo issued a proclamation of war against the United States, which immediately sent reinforcements to the Philippines. The Filipino government fled northward. In November 1899 the Filipinos resorted to guerrilla warfare, with all its devastating features.

After three years of costly fighting the insurrection was finally brought to an end when, in a daring operation led by Gen. Frederick Funston, General Aguinaldo was captured in his secret headquarters at Palanan in northern Luzon on March 23, 1901. Aguinaldo took an oath of allegiance to the United States, was granted a pension from the U.S. government, and retired to private life.

In 1935 when the commonwealth government of the Philippines was established in preparation for independence, Aguinaldo ran for president but was decisively beaten. He returned to private life until the Japanese invaded the Philippines in 1941. The Japanese used Aguinaldo as an anti-American tool. They caused him to make speeches, to sign articles, and to address a radio appeal to Gen. Douglas MacArthur on Corregidor to surrender in order to spare the flower of Filipino youth.

When the Americans returned, Aguinaldo was arrested and, together with others accused of collaboration with the Japanese, was held for some months in Bilibid Prison until released by presidential amnesty. As a token vindication of his honour, he was appointed by Pres. Elpidio Quirino as a member of the Council of State in 1950. In the later years of his life, he devoted his major attention to veterans' affairs, the promotion of nationalism and democracy in the Philippines, and the improvement of relations between the Philippines and the United States.

Aguirre, Lope de (b. *c.* 1518, Oñate, Spain—d. Oct. 27, 1561, El Tocuyo, New Spain), Spanish adventurer who is known chiefly for his role in the murders of the explorers Pedro de Ursúa and Fernando de Guzmán.

Nothing is known of Aguirre's life prior to 1544, when he arrived in Peru and took part in the Spanish suppression of Indian rebellions and in wars that continually broke out between the Spanish conquerors. On Sept. 26, 1560, he joined an expedition led by Ursúa to find the legendary kingdom of El Dorado, thought to be located at the headwaters of the Amazon River, in what is now western Brazil. Upon reaching the headwaters, Aguirre incited a rebellion in which Ursúa was killed. He then killed Guzmán, who had succeeded Ursúa, and took command of the expedition.

It was said that Aguirre had all those on the expedition who had opposed his plans, including several priests, put to death. He is then thought to have raided several towns in what is now Venezuela before he was finally caught and executed by the Spaniards. It is also believed that he killed his own daughter immediately prior to his capture.

Aguirre was considered to be a thoroughly disreputable character, and his name in colonial Spanish America practically became synonymous with cruelty and treachery.

Aguisy, Jean Grolier, vicomte d': *see* Grolier, Jean, vicomte d'Aguisy.

Agulhas, Cape, southernmost point of the African continent, 109 mi (176 km) southeast of Cape Town. Its name, Portuguese for Needles, refers to the rocks and reefs that have wrecked many ships. A lighthouse was established there in 1849. The Agulhas Banks are excellent for trawling. The cape's meridian (20° E) is the official boundary between the Indian and Atlantic oceans.

Agulhas Current, surface oceanic current, one of the fastest-flowing in any ocean, part of the westward-flowing South Equatorial Current that turns southward along the east coast of Africa and then eastward to join the flow from Africa to Australia. A small part of Agulhas water may, however, continue westward around the Cape of Good Hope into the Atlantic. The Mozambique Current, between Madagascar and Africa, also feeds the Agulhas Current. Only 60 mi (100 km) wide, the Agulhas Current is estimated to flow at a rate of 8 to 24 in. (20 to 60 cm) per second, its velocity depending on seasonal variations in South Equatorial Current velocity. Because it is fed from lower latitudes, the Agulhas Current is warm, ranging in temperature from 57° to 79° F (14° to 26° C) at the surface. Its salinity varies from 34.4 parts per thousand at 122° F (50° C) (at a depth equal to 3,900 ft) to 35.6 parts per thousand at 68° F (20° C) at the surface.

'aguna, also spelled AGUNAH (Hebrew: "deserted woman"), plural 'AGUNOT, or AGUNOTH, in Orthodox and Conservative Judaism, a woman who is presumed to be widowed but who cannot remarry because evidence of her husband's death does not satisfy legal requirements. The plight of the *'aguna* has generated voluminous and complex treatment in Halakhic literature. Although religious courts are not empowered to grant remarriage without indisputable evidence of the spouse's death, human considerations have led to a de facto relaxation of the law of evidence. The testimony of a single witness has thus been accepted as sufficient proof of death even when the body of the presumed deceased has not been recovered from, for example, a battlefield, the sea, or a disaster area.

An effort to solve the still vexing problem facing *'agunot* has, in some places, led to the introduction of a custom whereby soldiers sign a document authorizing a rabbinic court to grant a divorce should the soldier be officially declared missing in action and presumed dead.

Women who are victims of willful desertion are also called *'agunot* inasmuch as they are forbidden to remarry without a religious divorce that cannot be granted unilaterally to the wife by a religious court. Because of the severity of the biblical injunction against adultery and the possibility that a husband who was presumed dead might suddenly reappear, various proposed solutions to the problems of *'agunot* have enjoyed but limited acceptance. Even the great emergencies created by Jewish mass migrations at the beginning of the 20th century and the vast number of missing persons after the two World Wars and the Nazi holocaust have not led to universally accepted modifications of existing laws and practices.

Agung (d. 1645), third sultan of the central Javanese kingdom of Mataram who brought that kingdom to its greatest territorial and military power.

In the early years of Sultan Agung's reign, he consolidated the kingdom by subduing the autonomous trade-based coastal states of Padang and Tuban in 1619; Banjermasin, Kalimantan, and Sukadana in 1622; Madura in 1624; and Surabaya in 1625. Because Mataram's economy was based on agriculture, Sultan Agung, who was openly contemptuous of trade, maintained no significant naval forces. Dutch troops had conquered Jacatra (now Jakarta) in 1619 and established there a base they named Batavia. In 1629 the Sultan's forces attacked the city in an effort to drive out the Europeans, but superior Dutch naval forces succeeded in maintaining the Dutch position. This was the last major threat to the Dutch position in Java until after World War II.

After failing to conquer Batavia, Sultan Agung turned against the Balinese, then controlling Balambangan in East Java, in a "holy war" against infidels. His campaign was successful in Java, but he was unable to extend his power to the island of Bali itself. Bali thus retained its identity as a Hindu state in the midst of the predominantly Muslim states of the archipelago. Internally Sultan Agung introduced reforms to bring the judicial system more in line with Qur'ānic precepts and reformed the tax system. By the mid-18th century, however, the Dutch were sufficiently strong to put an end to Mataram as a great power by bringing about a division of the realm into two lesser kingdoms centring on Surakarta and Jogjakarta.

Agung, Abulfatah (d. 1692), ruler of the powerful Javanese kingdom and sultanate of Bantam from 1651 to 1683. He encouraged English and French trade but successfully opposed Dutch expansion into the area in the early part of his reign. In the 1670s, however, when he attempted to change the succession to his throne from his older son Sultan Haji to his younger son, Haji revolted and with Dutch help seized the throne. Haji had to pay war costs and grant a trade monopoly to the Dutch. Agung ended his days in captivity, and Bantam came under Dutch domination.

Agung, Mount, Bahasa Indonesia GUNUNG AGUNG, Dutch PIEK VAN BALI, volcano, northeastern Bali, Indonesia. The highest point in Bali, and the object of traditional veneration, it rises to 10,308 ft (3,142 m). In 1963 a neighbouring volcano, Gunung Batur, erupted after being dormant for 120 years; some 1,600 people were killed and 86,000 left homeless.

Agus Salim, Hadji (b. Oct. 8, 1884, Kota Gedang, Sumatra—d. Nov. 4, 1954, Jogjakarta, Indon.), Indonesian nationalist and religious leader from an upper class Minangkabau family, who played a key role during the 1920s in moderating the messianic and Communist element in the Muslim nationalist movement.

Agus Salim received a Dutch education through secondary school, after which he dealt with Dutch consular affairs in Jiddah, Arabia, where he became interested in reformist and modernist movements in Islām. In 1915 Salim joined the Sarekat Islām (Islāmic Association) and soon became a leading influence in that Indonesian nationalist group. His opposition to the messianic cult that had grown up around the group's central figure, Omar Said Tjokroaminoto, led to a deemphasis of mystical elements in the organization.

Salim, an evolutionary socialist, played an important role in the political conflicts of the early 1920s. His opposition to the use of force in resisting colonialism made him relatively acceptable to Dutch leaders. In 1921 he was the main non-Communist spokesman in the discussions over control of the labour movement that led to the Communist withdrawal from Sarekat Islām. After 1923 the organization came increasingly under Salim's control, and he directed it away from political activity and toward the pan-Islāmic movement. During the birth of Indonesian independence, Salim served briefly in 1946–47 as vice minister of foreign affairs.

Agusan del Norte, province, northeastern Mindanao, Philippines, bordering Butuan Bay (north) of the Mindanao Sea. Created in 1970 with the division of the former province of Agusan, it includes the lower course of the Agusan River. The province has an area of 1,000 sq mi (2,590 sq km). The economy is largely agricultural; abaca, tobacco, corn (maize), and fruits are the principal crops. About 90 percent of the people are Cebuano. The provincial capital is Butuan. Pop. (1980) 365,421.

Agusan del Sur, province, northeastern Mindanao, Philippines, created in 1970 from the former province of Agusan. Agusan del Sur has an area of 3,462 sq mi (8,966 sq km). The province includes the middle course of the Agusan River, where a substantial timber industry has developed. Rice, corn (maize), and sugarcane are among the most important agricultural products; rubber is also produced. The provincial capital is Prosperidad. The population is largely Cebuano. Pop. (1980) 265,030.

Agusan River, longest river in Mindanao, Philippines. It rises in Davao province in the southeast and flows northward for 240 mi (390 km) to enter Butuan Bay of the Mindanao Sea. The river forms a fertile valley 40 to 50 mi wide between the Central Mindanao Highlands (west) and the Pacific Cordillera (east). Important population centres are clustered around the bay and include Butuan, Cabadbaran, and Buenavista. Nasipit, west of Butuan, is the base for a large sawmilling operation and produces lumber, veneers, and wallboard.

Despite early Spanish contacts and missionary activities in the 17th century, most of the valley has remained sparsely settled by the Magahats, Mamanuas, Manobos, Higahons, Mandayas, and Bagobos. With the advent of logging and immigrant labourers, many of these groups have moved farther inland. Until the early 1960s, when a road was completed linking Butuan with Davao City to the south, the Agusan, which is navigable for 160 mi by small craft, was the only access route to the interior. Small trading villages grew up along the riverbanks; Esperanza and Talacogon are old trading stations located on natural levees.

The productive forest industry is concentrated along the Agusan's swampy middle course. Lumberjacks, merchants, and traders in the area live on huge log rafts anchored to giant trees. Vast plantations of coconut, rice, bamboo, and various fruits lie along its lower course. Farming and subsistence fishing are other economic activities. Rice is the leading food crop, and coconut is the main cash crop.

Agustin I: *see* Iturbide, Agustin de.

Agustini, Delmira (b. Oct. 24, 1886, Montevideo—d. July 6, 1914, Montevideo), one of the most important poets of South America. She was the first woman to deal boldly with the themes of sensuality and passion, and her poems have a force lacking from most other Modernist poetry. Her life ended tragically when she was murdered by her estranged husband. Her chief works are *El libro blanco* (1907; "The White Book"), *Cantos de la mañana* (1910; "Morning Songs"), *Los cálices vacíos* (1913; "Empty Chalices"), *El rosarío del Eros* (1924; "Eros' Rosary"), and *Obras completas* (1924; "Complete Works").

Ah Kin (Mayan: He of the Sun), the regular clergy of the Yucatec Maya. The Ah Kin are best known for their performance in the ritual sacrifice of victims, whose hearts were offered to the Mayan gods. The chief priest (Ah Kin Mai) served in the various capacities of administrator, teacher, healer, astronomer, adviser to the chief, and diviner. Priests specializing in prophecy were known as Chilans, but it is likely that Ah Kins and Chilans performed many of the same functions. Prophecy was aided by readings from hieroglyphic books and, possibly, drug-induced visions. Couples contemplating marriage as well as civic leaders consulted the Ah Kin on the prospects of their undertakings. The office of Ah Kin was hereditary, passing from priests to their sons, but training was also extended to the sons of the nobility who showed inclinations toward the priesthood.

Aḥa of Shabḥa (b. *c.* 680, probably at Shabḥa, near Basra, Iraq—d. *c.* 752), rabbinical scholar whose *She'eltot* ("Book of Problems"), published in Venice in 1566, was the first attempt to codify and explicate materials contained in the Babylonian Talmud. *She'eltot* was as original in its form as in its content. Written in Aramaic and unique in its organization, the text connects decisions of the Oral Law with those of the Written Law. The connections, many of them original, are concerned not only with ritualistic laws but also with man's ethical obligations. *She'eltot* itself came to be regarded as a literary model and was widely copied.

Ahab, also spelled ACHAB (reigned *c.* 874–*c.* 853 BC), 7th king of the northern kingdom of Israel, according to the Old Testament, and son of King Omri. His reign was generally peaceful, and by an alliance (through lineal intermarriage) with the southern kingdom of Judah he withstood the Assyrians. His wife Jezebel aroused strong opposition, especially from the prophet Elijah, by her worship of the Canaanite god Baal.

Aḥad Haʿam (Hebrew: One of the People), original name ASHER GINZBERG (b. Aug. 18, 1856, Skvira, near Kiev—d. Jan. 2, 1927, Tel Aviv, Palestine), Zionist leader whose concepts of Hebrew culture had a definitive influence on the objectives of the early Jewish settlement in Palestine and who was a major Hebrew stylist whose clarity and precision influenced modern Hebrew literature.

Reared in Russia in a rigidly Orthodox Jewish family, he mastered rabbinic literature but soon was attracted to the rationalist school of medieval Jewish philosophy and to the writings of the Haskala (Enlightenment), a liberal

Aḥad Haʿam

By courtesy of the Central Zionist Archives, Jerusalem

Jewish movement that attempted to integrate Judaism with modern Western thought.

At the age of 22, he went to Odessa, the centre of the Jewish nationalist movement known as Ḥovevei Ẓiyyon (Lovers of Zion). There he was influenced both by Jewish nationalism and by the materialistic philosophies of the Russian nihilist D.I. Pisarev and the English and French Positivists. After joining the central committee of Ḥovevei Ẓiyyon, he published his first essay, "Lo ze ha-derekh" (1889; "This Is Not the Way"), which emphasized the spiritual basis of Zionism and opened a new, controversial epoch in Jewish nationalist ideology.

In 1897, after two visits to Palestine, he founded the periodical *ha-Shiloaḥ*, in which he severely criticized the political Zionism of Theodor Herzl, the foremost Jewish nationalist leader of the time. Aḥad Haʿam remained outside the Zionist organization, believing that a Jewish state would be the end result of a Jewish spiritual renaissance rather than the beginning, although he supported the goal of a Jewish national centre in Palestine. Interpreting Jewish religious and ethical teachings as expressions of Jewish culture, he stressed that the national spirit was essential not only for Jewish survival in the Diaspora (*i.e.,* the settlements of Jews outside Palestine) but also as a means of expressing distinctly Jewish moral values in a Jewish state.

He was an intimate adviser to the Zionist leader Chaim Weizmann during the time Weizmann was playing a leading role in eliciting from the British government its Balfour Declaration of 1917, a document supporting a Jewish homeland in Palestine. His last years were spent in Palestine, editing his letters *Iggerot Aḥad Haʿam*, 6 vol. (1923–25; "Letters of Aḥad Haʿam"). Further letters, principally from the last phase of his life, and his memoirs were published in *Aḥad Haʿam: Pirqe zikhronot we-iggerot* (1931; "Collected Memoirs and Letters"). His essays comprise four volumes (1895, 1903, 1904, and 1913).

Though deeply affected by secular thought, he retained a passionate love for traditional Judaism, rejecting those thinkers who sought to re-create Jewish nationhood by a radical transformation of Jewish values. Although Aḥad Haʿam's high moral concerns had a tremendous impact on his contemporaries, Zionists of subsequent generations saw in his work an excess of rationalism.

Ahaggar, also spelled HOGGAR, large plateau in the north centre of the Sahara, on the Tropic of Cancer. Its height is above 3,000 ft (900 m) culminating in Mt. Tahat (9,852 ft). The plateau, about 965 mi (1,550 km) north to south and 1,300 mi east to west, is rocky desert composed of black volcanic (basalt) necks and flows rising above a pink granite massif. The main caravan route to Kano in northern Nigeria passes along the western margin through the important oasis town of Tamanrasset which is about 1,200 mi south of Algiers. Natural gas deposits have been found northwest of the plateau.

ahaṃkāra (Sanskrit: "I-saying, I-making"), in the dualist and evolutionist Sāṃkhya school of Hindu philosophy, one of the stages of development of the *prakṛti,* the original stuff of material nature, which evolves into the manifest world. *Ahaṃkāra* describes the erroneous judgment of the unrelated soul that it is related to the *prakṛti* by assuming an ego that knows and experiences it. The stage of *ahaṃkāra* follows in the evolution (and in the hierarchy of functions based on it) of the stage of *buddhi* ("awareness"); *i.e.,* the soul's becoming aware of the existence of a presence outside itself. From the "this-awareness" of the *buddhi* level evolves the "I-this-awareness" of the *ahaṃkāra* level. Henceforth, the soul mistakenly assumes that it is identical with the *prakṛti* and is bound to existence in transmigration, or series of reincarnations. Release (*mokṣa*) necessitates the eradication of the ego awareness and finally that of the *prakṛti* awareness.

Ahaz, also spelled ACHAZ, Assyrian JEHOAHAZ, king of Judah who became an Assyrian vassal (II Kings 16; Isa. 7–8). When Ahaz began his reign the kings of Damascus and Israel threatened him with war because he refused to join their alliance against Assyria. The account in Isaiah shows that Ahaz was sadly lacking both in faith and in an elementary understanding of his political situation. Isaiah apparently told the King that Assyria needed no inducement to put down the less powerful kings plotting against it; and that, in the meantime, Ahaz need not fear their talk of war and siege. But Ahaz, anxious and fearful, wanted to insure his security. He sought Assyrian protection, and thereby sacrificed Judah's religious freedom without improving its political situation.

Ahenobarbus, Gnaeus Domitius (d. 31 BC), Roman general who became one of the chief partisans of Mark Antony after Antony defeated the assassins of Julius Caesar.

Along with his father, Lucius Domitius Ahenobarbus, he had been a member of the party that took up arms in 49 in an unsuccessful attempt to prevent Caesar from seizing power. After the assassination of Caesar in 44 by a group led by Marcus Junius Brutus and Gaius Cassius Longinus, Ahenobarbus sided with the assassins and commanded their fleet. When they were defeated by the forces of Antony and Octavian (later the emperor Augustus) at Philippi in Macedonia in 42, Ahenobarbus held out as a privateer until he was reconciled with Antony in 40. From 40 until about 35 he served Antony as governor of Bithynia. He was consul at Rome in 32, when the final breach occurred between Antony and Octavian. Ahenobarbus then left Italy to join Antony in the east, but he opposed the Egyptian queen Cleopatra's dominance over Antony and deserted to Octavian shortly before Octavian defeated Antony and Cleopatra at Actium, Greece, in 31. Ahenobarbus died soon afterward, allegedly of remorse but possibly from a disease that he had contracted before the battle.

Ahenobarbus, Lucius Domitius (d. 48 BC, Pharsalus, Macedonia), a leader of the Optimates (conservative senatorial aristocracy) in the last years of the Roman Republic. After the powerful generals Julius Caesar, Gnaeus Pompey, and Marcus Licinius Crassus formed an unofficial ruling triumvirate in 60 BC, Ahenobarbus repeatedly resisted their designs. As candidate for the consulate of 55, he pledged that, if elected, he would remove Caesar from the command in Gaul. The triumvirs met this threat by developing a strategy that postponed Ahenobarbus' consulate until 54. By this time he was unable to challenge their power effectively. In January 49, however, the Senate outlawed Caesar and appointed Ahenobarbus to replace him in Gaul. Caesar then marched on Rome, precipitating a civil war.

Against the advice of Pompey, who had joined the senatorial camp, Ahenobarbus attempted to stop the invading army at Corfinium in central Italy. He was defeated and captured by Caesar but soon released. Immediately he raised a revolt against the Caesarians at Massilia (now Marseille) but died in battle against Caesar.

Ahenobarbus, Lucius Domitius (Roman emperor): *see* Nero.

Aḥer (Jewish heretic): *see* Elisha ben Abuyah.

Ahern, James (writer): *see* Herne, James A.

Ahhiyawa, also called AHHIYĀ, ancient kingdom in Anatolia that bordered on the Hittite Empire. The exact location of Ahhiyawa is not definitely known but may have been northwestern Anatolia, near the west coast of the Sea of Marmara in present-day Turkey. According to one theory, the people of Ahhiyawa may have been the Achaeans of Homer, early Mycenaean Greeks. Another represents them as ancestors of the Trojans. In any case, it seems quite certain that the Ahhiyawans were a powerful seafaring people.

Much of what is known about Ahhiyawa has been derived from Hittite (*q.v.*) texts. The earliest references to the kingdom occur in documents prepared during the reign of Suppiluliumas (*c.* 1380–46 BC). It seems that Ahhiyawa was a large and formidable kingdom with which the Hittites had good relations. Later documents indicate that members of the Ahhiyawan royal family travelled to the Hittite capital of Hattusas to study the charioteer's art and that a statue of the god of Ahhiyawa was brought to the Hittite king Mursilis II (reigned *c.* 1346–20 BC) to cure his illness. During the successionary struggles between Mursilis III and his uncle Hattusilis III in the late 13th century BC, the Ahhiyawans supported Mursilis. The Ahhiyawans apparently became a threat to the Hittite Empire during the reign of Tudhaliyas IV (*c.* 1250–20 BC), the son of Hattusilis, and were accused of aiding the rebellion of Millawanda, a Hittite tributary state.

Ahidjo, Ahmadou (b. August 1924, Garoua, Cameroon), first president of the United Republic of Cameroon, who served from 1960 to 1982. He presided over one of the few successful attempts at supra-territorial African unity: the joining of the southern half of the former British Cameroons with the larger French-speaking Cameroon.

A Muslim from the northern part of Cameroon, Ahidjo was a radio operator in the French colonial administration from 1941/42 to 1953. He was elected to the Cameroon territorial assembly in 1947 and reelected in 1952 and 1956. His early political career also included several years in France (1953–56) as the Cameroon member of the Assembly of the French Union. In the first Cameroon government (1957), he was vice premier and minister of the interior; when the first premier fell in early 1958, he formed his own party, the Union Camerounaise, and became the new premier.

Meanwhile, since 1956 the more radical, nationalist Union des Populations du Cameroun, which advocated immediate independence from France, had taken up arms against the French administration. Ahidjo, like his predecessor, used French troops to put down the rebels, but he also offered amnesty to those who would surrender. Many refused, however, and sporadic outbreaks of violence haunted Ahidjo for years. His initial program included immediate internal autonomy, a definite timetable for full independence, reunification with the British Cameroons, and cooperation with the French. He was able to attain independence in 1960 and the unification with the southern, British Cameroons in 1961, following a plebiscite.

In the elections held soon after independence, Ahidjo won only by a small majority, but, despite continuing small-scale violence, managed to build up a stable, relatively prosperous country. After being elected five consecutive times for the presidency (in what became a one-party state), he resigned on Nov. 6, 1982, claiming that he was suffering from "exhaustion." He was replaced by a Christian southerner, Paul Biya, who proceeded to oust Ahidjo from chairmanship of the ruling party in 1983.

After 1983 Ahidjo lived in exile in France, having been condemned to death in Cameroon for complicity in a plot against Biya. In April 1984 a military uprising was crushed, and Ahidjo was accused of responsibility for the revolt.

Ahikar, The Story of, folktale of Babylonian or Persian origin, about a wise and moral man who supposedly served as one of the chief counsellors of Sennacherib, king of Assyria (704–681 BC). Like Job, Ahikar was a prototype of the just man whose righteousness was ultimately rewarded by God. Betrayed by his power-hungry son, Ahikar was condemned to death, suffered severely, but was finally restored to his former position. The work is classified as pseudepigraphal—*i.e.,* a noncanonical book that in style and content resembles authentic biblical works. A considerable number of translations (among them Syriac, Arabic, Armenian, Ethiopic, Old Turkic, Greek, and Slavonic) indicate that the story of Ahikar was immensely popular in antiquity. The writing follows the memoir style used by official state writers rather than the "wisdom" genre of literature. Nevertheless, the story of Ahikar and his proverbial wisdom influenced the development of Jewish wisdom literature early in the Hellenistic period (3rd century BC to 3rd century AD), as is shown by similar ethical doctrines in the Old Testament books of Psalms and Ecclesiastes and in the apocryphal books of Tobit and Ecclesiasticus.

ahiṃsā (Sanskrit: "non-injury"), the fundamental ethical virtue of the Jainas of India, highly respected throughout the centuries by Hindus and Buddhists as well. In modern times, Mahatma Gandhi, the famous spiritual and political leader, developed his theory of passive resistance as a means of bringing about political change on the principle of *ahiṃsā.*

In Jainism, *ahiṃsā* is the standard by which all actions are judged. For a householder observing the small vows (*aṇuvrata*), the practice of *ahiṃsā* requires that he not kill any animal life, but for an ascetic observing the great vows (*mahāvrata*), *ahiṃsā* entails the greatest care to prevent him from knowingly or unknowingly being the cause of injury to any living substance. Living matter (*jīva*) includes not only human beings and animals but insects, plants, and atoms as well, and the same law governs the entire cosmos. The interruption of another *jīva*'s spiritual progress increases one's own *karman* and delays one's liberation from the cycle of rebirths. Many common Jaina practices, such as not eating or drinking after dark or the wearing of cloth mouth covers (*mukhavastrikā*) by monks, are based on the principle of *ahiṃsā.*

Though the Hindus and Buddhists never required so strict an observance of *ahiṃsā* as the Jainas, vegetarianism and tolerance toward all forms of life became widespread in India. The Buddhist emperor Aśoka in his inscriptions of the 3rd century BC stressed the sanctity of animal life. *Ahiṃsā* is one of the first disciplines learned by the student of *yoga* and is required to be mastered in the preparatory stage (*yama*), the first of the eight stages that lead to perfect concentration. In the late 19th and early 20th centuries Gandhi extended *ahiṃsā* into the political sphere as *satyāgraha.*

Ahīr, cattle-tending caste widespread in northern and central India. Considerable historical interest attaches to this caste, as its members are thought to be identical with the Ābhīras of Sanskrit literature, who are mentioned repeatedly in the great epic the *Mahābhārata.* Some scholars contend that these cattlemen, scattered over southern Rājasthān and Sind (now part of Pakistan), played a role of importance in the early development of the god Krishna as the cowherd, which has continued to be a significant aspect of the Krishna legend.

Ahiram: *see* Hiram.

Ahithophel, also spelled ACHITOPHEL, in the Old Testament, one of King David's most trusted advisers. He took a leading part in Absalom's revolt, and his defection was a severe blow to the King. Having consulted Ahithophel about his plans to proceed against David, Absalom then sought advice from Hushai, another of David's counselors. Hushai, who remained secretly loyal to the King, betrayed Absalom's cause by opposing Ahithophel's plan and proposing in its place a scheme of his own, which actually gave the advantage to David. This plan Absalom accepted. Ahithophel, realizing that Hushai had outwitted him, foresaw the disastrous defeat of Absalom's forces and took his own life (II Sam. 15:31–37; 16:20–17:23).

ahl al-Kitāb (Arabic: "people of the Book"), in Islāmic thought, those religionists such as Jews, Christians, and Zoroastrians who are possessors of divine books (*i.e.,* the Torah, the Gospel, and the Avesta), as distinguished from those whose religions are not based on divine revelations. The latter are an imprecisely identified group referred to as Sabaeans but also considered "people of the Book."

The Prophet Muḥammad gave many privileges to *ahl al-Kitāb* that are not to be extended to heathens. *Ahl al-Kitāb* are granted freedom of worship; thus, during the early Muslim conquests, Jews and Christians were not forced to convert to Islām and had only to pay a special tax for their exemption from military service. Muslim authorities are responsible for the protection and well-being of *ahl al-Kitāb*, for, according to a saying of the Prophet, "he who wrongs a Jew or a Christian will have myself [the Prophet] as his indicter on the day of judgment." After Muḥammad's death, his successors sent strict instructions to their generals and provincial governors not to interfere with *ahl al-Kitāb* in their worship and to treat them with full respect.

Muslim men are permitted to marry women from *ahl al-Kitāb* even if the latter choose to remain steadfast in their religion; Muslim women, however, are not allowed to marry Christians or Jews unless they convert to Islām.

Ahl-e Ḥaqq, English PEOPLE OF TRUTH, or MEN OF GOD, a secret, syncretistic religion, derived largely from Islām, whose adherents are found in western Iran, with enclaves in Iraq. They retain the 12 *imām*s of the Ithnā ʿAsharīyah sect and such aspects of Islāmic mysticism as the communal feast. Central to their religion, however, is a belief in seven successive manifestations of God. They further believe in the transmigration of souls, asserting that every person must pass through 1,001 incarnations, in the course of which he receives the proper reward for his actions. The ultimate purification, however (becoming "luminous"), is limited to those who in the initial creation were destined to be good and were made of yellow clay; those destined to be evil were made of black clay. On the Day of Judgment the good will enter Paradise and the wicked will be annihilated. The Ahl-e Ḥaqq rites, all communal, include animal sacrifice.

The chief source of information about the sect is the *Firqān al-Akhbār*, written in the late 19th or early 20th century by a member.

Ahlgren, Ernst: *see* Benedictsson, Victoria.

Ahlin, Lars (b. April 4, 1915, Sundsvall, Swed.), influential Swedish novelist of the 1940s and 1950s.

Tåbb med Manifestet (1943; "Tåbb with the Manifesto") presents many of the central ideas of Ahlin's writings. A young proletarian finds the Communist ideology unsatisfactory and reaches a better understanding of himself and the world through a secularized Lutheran theology wherein man is perceived without preconceptions and is judged according to his deeds. Man is viewed as unfathomable but is ultimately holy and in need of divine grace. Ahlin prefers not to judge his fictional characters but rather to present them with the utmost impartiality. Similar themes are found in a number of subsequent novels, of which *Min död är min* (1945; "My Death is Mine"), *Kanelbiten* (1953; "The Cinnamon Stick"), and *Natt i marknadstältet* (1957; "Night in the Booths of the Fair") are the best known.

Ahlin received a number of literary distinctions, among them the Prize of the Nine in 1960, the Great Novel Prize in 1962, and the Small Nobel Prize in 1966.

Ahmad (Arabic personal name): *see under* Ahmed, except as below.

Aḥmad, in full AḤMAD IBN MUṢṬAFA (b. 1806, Tunis—d. 1855, Ḥalq al-Wādī, Tunisia), 10th ruler of the Ḥusaynid dynasty of Tunisia.

Succeeding his brother as the ruler of Tunis in 1837, Aḥmad began at once to modernize his armed forces: Tunisian cadets were sent to France, a military and technical academy was established, and European instructors invited to Tunis. He organized a naval force with 12 frigates purchased from France. He sent 8,000–10,000 soldiers to fight with the allies (France, England, Sardinia, and the Ottoman Empire) against the Russians in the Crimean War (1853–56).

Also active in internal reform, Aḥmad in 1841 abolished the sale of Negro slaves and in 1846 slavery altogether, and he removed many disabilities endured by the Jews. In Carthage he founded a hospital and, in 1845, Saint-Louis College, which was open to boys of all faiths and was the beginning of secular education in Tunisia. To pay for his reforms, he increased taxation, but this led to revolts in 1840, 1842, and 1843.

Prior to his rule, Tunisia was nominally a part of the empire that was ruled by Ottoman Turks. Resisting their claims of sovereignty, he sought the help of France in order to assert his independence. In 1845 he was recognized by the Ottomans as an independent sovereign. He was succeeded in 1855 by his cousin Muḥammad, who reigned until 1859.

Ahmad, Mirza Ghulam: *see* Ghulam Ahmad, Mirza.

Aḥmad al-Manṣūr, also called AL-DHAHABĪ (the Golden) (b. 1549, Fès, Mor.—d. Aug. 20, 1603, Fès), sixth ruler of the Saʿdī dynasty, which he raised to its zenith of power by his policy of centralization and astute diplomacy. Al-Manṣūr resisted the demands of his nominal suzerain, the Ottoman sultan, by playing off the European powers, namely, France, Portugal, Spain, and England, against one another in order to preserve Moroccan independence.

Aḥmad al-Manṣūr succeeded his brother ʿAbd al-Malik in August 1578. During the early years of his rule a largely mercenary army was trained and led by Ottoman Turks. The administrative system of the government was centralized, and important state officials were given land assignments and exempted from taxation. A survey of property was made, and land revenue was collected directly. Agriculture and the sugar industry were developed. The capital city of Marrākush was restored to its former grandeur.

Aḥmad al-Manṣūr encouraged the immigration of artisans, and his court was noted for its splendour. The cities of Gao and Timbuktu, on the Sudanese trade route, were captured in 1591, thus diverting an immense amount of gold to the central treasury, which earned him the title al-Dhahabī.

He established trade and diplomatic relations with Spain, effectively breaking the monopoly held since 1585 by the Barbary Company, which had been formed by British merchants to control foreign trade.

Aḥmad Bābā, in full ABŪ AL-ʿABBĀS AḤMAD IBN AḤMAD AL-TAKRŪRĪ AL-MASSŪFĪ (b. Oct. 26, 1556, Arawān, near Timbuktu, Songhai Empire—d. April 22, 1627, Timbuktu), jurist, writer, and a cultural leader of the western Sudan.

A descendant of a line of jurists, Aḥmad Bābā was educated in Islāmic culture, including jurisprudence. When Timbuktu was conquered by the Sultan of Morocco in 1591, he was accused of refusing to recognize the Sultan's authority and of plotting a rebellion. In 1594 he was deported to the Moroccan capital of Marrakūsh. The conditions of his captivity were liberal, and he was allowed to teach and practice law. His *fatwā*s (legal opinions) dating from this period are noted for their clarity of thought and clear exposition of Islāmic judicial principles. He also compiled a biographical dictionary of the famous Mālikī (one of the four schools of Islāmic law) jurists; this work is still an important source of information concerning the lives of Mālikite jurists and Moroccan religious personalities.

When the Sultan of Morocco died in 1607, Aḥmad Bābā was allowed to return to his native city. He spent the last years of his life in scholarly pursuits, which included writing a treatise on the populations of the western Sudan and a grammar of Arabic that is still used in northern Nigeria.

Aḥmad ebn Buyeh: *see* Muʿizz ad-Dawlah.

Aḥmad Grāñ, real name AḤMAD IBN IBRĀHĪM AL-GHĀZĪ (b. *c.* 1506—d. 1543), leader of a Muslim movement that all but subjugated Ethiopia. At the height of his conquest, he held more than three-quarters of the kingdom, and, according to the chronicles, the majority of men in these conquered areas had converted to Islām.

Once Aḥmad Grāñ had gained control of the Muslim Somali state of Adal (Adel), where he installed his brother as a puppet king, he determined on a *jihād* (Islāmic holy war) against Christian Ethiopia. He created an army out of the masses of heterogeneous and nomadic Somalis who had joined him, motivated by religious zeal, the prospects of wealth, and possibly by population pressure caused by Arab immigration. He also made skillful use of firearms, introduced by the Turks, and employed a small body of Turkish troops.

Although Aḥmad Grāñ defeated an Ethiopian army in Adal in 1526–27, it was not until 1531 that he felt ready for a large-scale invasion. By 1535 he had conquered the southern and central areas of the state and had even invaded the northern highlands, leaving a trail of devastation behind him. The Ethiopian king and a few followers retreated and begged for Portuguese aid. But when a small Portuguese force tried to relieve them in 1541, they were first delayed and later soundly defeated by Aḥmad Grāñ, who had meanwhile been able to obtain Turkish reinforcements. The few remaining Portuguese, however, with the new Ethiopian ruler, Galawdewos (Claudius), were soon able to rearm themselves and rally a large number of Ethiopians. Aḥmad Grāñ, who had sent most of his Turkish troops back, was killed in the crucial battle that followed, and Galawdewos was able to regain his kingdom, though the conversion to Islām and reconversion of most of his subjects may have left a spiritual crisis less easily resolved.

Aḥmad ibn Ḥanbal (b. 780, Baghdad—d. 855, Baghdad), Muslim theologian, jurist, and martyr for his faith. He was the compiler of the Traditions of the Prophet Muḥammad (*Musnad*) and formulator of the Ḥanbalī, the most strictly traditionalist of the four orthodox Islāmic schools of law. His doctrine influenced such noted followers as the 13th–14th-century theologian Ibn Taymīyah, the Wahhābīyah, an 18th-century reform movement, and the Salafiyah, a 19th-century Egyptian movement rooted in tradition.

Life. Of pure Arab stock, Ibn Ḥanbal belonged to the tribe of Shaybān through both parents. He was still an infant when his father died at 30. When Ibn Ḥanbal was 15 he began to study the Traditions (Ḥadīth) of the Prophet Muḥammad. Seeking to learn from the great masters of his day, he travelled to the cities of Kūfah and Basra in Iraq; Mecca, Hejaz, and Medina in Arabia; and to the lands of Yemen and Syria. He made five pilgrimages to the holy city of Mecca, three times on foot. Ibn Ḥanbal led a life of asceticism and self-denial, winning many disciples. He had eight children, of whom two were well known and closely associated with his intellectual work: Ṣālih (died 880) and ʿAbd Allāh (died 903).

The central fact of Ibn Ḥanbal's life is the suffering to which he was subjected during the inquisition, known as *al-miḥnah,* ordered by the caliph al-Ma'mūn. But for this great trial, and the unflagging courage he displayed in the face of his persecutors, Ibn Ḥanbal would most likely have been remembered solely for his work on the Traditions. As it is, he remains to this day, in addition to his recognized stature as an expert on Traditions, one of the most venerated fathers of Islām, a staunch upholder of Muslim orthodoxy.

The inquisition was inaugurated in 833, when the Caliph made obligatory upon all Muslims the belief that the Qur'ān was created, a doctrine of the Muʿtazilites, a rationalist Islāmic school that claimed that reason was equal to revelation as a means to religious truth. The Caliph had already made public profession of this belief in 827. Heretofore, the sacred book had been regarded as the uncreated, eternal word of God. The inquisition was conducted in Baghdad, seat of the ʿAbbāsid caliphate, as well as in the provinces. It lasted from 833 to 848, a period involving the reign of four caliphs, ending during the caliphate of al-Mutawakkil, who returned to the traditionalist view.

At the risk of his life, Ibn Ḥanbal refused to subscribe to the Muʿtazilī doctrine. He was put in chains, beaten, and imprisoned for about two years. After his release he did not resume his lectures until the inquisition was publicly proclaimed at an end. Some orthodox theologians, to survive the ordeal, had recanted, and later claimed the privilege of dissimulation, *taqīyah,* as a justification for their behaviour. This is a dispensation granted in the Qur'ān to those who wish to avail themselves of it when forced to profess a false faith, while denying it in their hearts. Other theologians, following the example of Ibn Ḥanbal, refused to repudiate their beliefs.

In 833 Ibn Ḥanbal and another theologian, Muḥammad ibn Nūḥ, who had also refused to recant, were cited to appear for trial before Caliph al-Ma'mūn, who was in Tarsus (now in modern Turkey) at the time. They were sent off in chains from Baghdad; but shortly after beginning their journey, the Caliph died, and on their trip back to the capital, Ibn Nūḥ died.

Ibn Ḥanbal was ordered to appear before the new caliph, al-Muʿtaṣim. He was on trial for three days, and on the third day, after the learned men disputed with him, there followed a private conference with the Caliph who asked Ibn Ḥanbal to yield at least a little so that he might grant him his freedom. Ibn Ḥanbal made the same reply he had been making from the beginning of the inquisition; he would yield when given some ground for modifying his faith derived from the sources he regarded as authoritative, namely the Qurʾān and the Traditions of Muḥammad. Losing patience, the Caliph ordered that he be taken away and flogged. Throughout the flogging the Caliph persisted in his attempts to obtain a recantation, but to no avail. Ibn Ḥanbal's unflinching spirit was beginning to have its effect upon the Caliph; but the latter's advisers warned that if he desisted from punishing him, he would be accused of having opposed the doctrine of his predecessor al-Maʾmūn, and the victory of Ibn Ḥanbal would have dire consequences on the reign of the caliphs. But the Caliph's treatment of Ibn Ḥanbal had to be suspended, nevertheless, because of the mounting anger of the populace gathering outside the palace and preparing to attack it. Ibn Ḥanbal is reported to have been beaten by 150 floggers, each in turn striking him twice and moving aside. The scars from his wounds remained with him to the end of his life.

The inquisition continued under the next caliph, al-Wāthiq, but Ibn Ḥanbal was no longer molested, in spite of attempts on the part of his opponents to persuade the Caliph to persecute him. The new caliph, like his predecessor, was most likely influenced by the threat of a popular uprising should he lay violent hands on a man popularly held to be a saint. The momentum of the inquisition carried it two years into the reign of al-Mutawakkil, who finally put an end to it in 848.

Ibn Ḥanbal earned the greatest reputation of all the persons involved in the inquisition and the everlasting gratitude of the Muslim people. He is credited with having held his ground in the face of all odds, saving Muslims from becoming unbelievers. At his funeral the procession was estimated at more than 800,000 mourners.

Achievements. The most important of Ibn Ḥanbal's works is his collection of the Traditions of the Prophet Muḥammad. This collection was heretofore believed to have been compiled by the author's son (ʿAbd Allāh), but there is now evidence that the work was compiled and arranged by Ibn Ḥanbal himself. These Traditions were considered by Ibn Ḥanbal as a sound basis for argument in law and religion.

Historical scholarship regarding Ibn Ḥanbal and his school has suffered from a lack of sufficient documentation, among other things. There are, therefore, some opinions regarding Ibn Ḥanbal that bear closer scrutiny in the light of new documents and recent studies. Too much stress has been laid on the influence on him of the teachings of Shāfiʿī, the founder of the Shāfiʿī school, whom Ibn Ḥanbal apparently met only once. He had a high respect for Shāfiʿī but also for the other great jurists who belonged to other schools of law, without, for that matter, relinquishing his own independent opinions. He was against codification of the law, maintaining that canonists had to be free to derive the solutions for questions of law from scriptural sources, namely the Qurʾān and the *sunnah* (the body of Islāmic custom and practice based on Muḥammad's words and deeds). It was to this end that he compiled his great *Musnad,* wherein he registered all the traditions considered in his day acceptable as bases for the solution of questions, along with the Qurʾān itself.

The fact that the Ḥanbalī school was organized at all was due to the impact of Ibn Ḥanbal on his time. The other orthodox schools were already prospering in Baghdad when the Ḥanbalī school sprang up in their midst, drawing its membership from theirs. The lateness of the hour accounts for the relatively small membership attained by the Ḥanbalī school compared with the older schools. It is, however, not by the number of its members that the importance of the school and its originator should be judged but rather by their impact on the development of Islāmic religious history. In the Middle Ages the school acted as a spearhead of traditionalist orthodoxy in its struggle against rationalism. One of Ibn Ḥanbal's greatest followers, Ibn Taymīyah (1263–1328), was claimed by both the Wahhābīyah, a reform movement founded in the mid-18th century, and the modern Salafīyah movement, which arose in Egypt and advocated the continued supremacy of Islāmic law but with fresh interpretations to meet the community's changing needs. Ibn Ḥanbal himself is one of the fathers of Islām whose names have constantly been invoked against the forces of rationalism down through the ages.

(G.M.)

BIBLIOGRAPHY. For bibliography and information pertaining to Ibn Ḥanbal's works, see Fuat Sezgin, *Geschichte des arabischen Schrifttums,* vol. 1 (1967); for his life and works generally, see W.M. Patton, *Ahmed ibn Hanbal and the Mihna* (1897); and H. Laoust, "Le Hanbalisme sous le califat de Bagdad," in *Revue des Études Islamiques* (1959); and the *Encyclopaedia of Islam,* vol. 1 (1960). On Sufism in the Ḥanbalī school of thought, see G. Makdisi, "L'Isnad initiatique soufi de Muwaffaq ad-Din Ibn Qudama," in *L'Herne: Louis Massignon* (1970).

Aḥmad ibn Ibrāhīm al-Ghāzī: *see* Aḥmad Grāñ.

Aḥmad ibn Muḥammad ibn Abū Bakr ibn Saʿīd: *see* Shehu Ahmadu Lobbo.

Aḥmad ibn Ṭūlūn (b. September 835—d. March 884, Egypt), the founder of the Ṭūlūnid dynasty in Egypt, and the first Muslim governor of Egypt to annex Syria.

As a child Aḥmad was taken into slavery and placed in the private service of the ʿAbbāsid caliph (the titular leader of the Islāmic community) at Baghdad. Later he studied theology in the city of Tarsus. He rose in the administrative structure of the ʿAbbāsid government and in 868 became a lieutenant in the service of the governor of Egypt. In Egypt he saw that the real centre of authority lay with the minister of finance, and during the next years he struggled to bring that department under his control. He was successful, and himself became vice governor. Using a rebellion in Palestine as a pretext, he purchased a large number of slaves to increase the strength of his army, which formed the basis of his personal authority. In 882, using the pretext of a holy war against the Byzantine Empire, he annexed Syria. Aḥmad never went so far as to declare formal independence from the ʿAbbāsid caliph, but the autonomy of his rule was clearly a threat to the authority of the latter, and he ceased to send any tribute to the ʿAbbāsid government. The Caliph himself was preoccupied with other problems and was unable to spare the military forces necessary to bring Aḥmad into submission.

Aḥmad ibn Ṭūlūn, Mosque of, huge and majestic red brick building complex built in 876 by the Turkish governor of Egypt and Syria. It was built on the site of present-day Cairo and includes a mosque surrounded by three outer *ziyadah*s, or courtyards. Much of the decoration and design recalls the ʿAbbāsid architecture of Iraq. The crenellated outside walls have merlons that are shaped and perforated in a decorative pattern. The courtyards are lined with arcades of broad arches and heavy pillars. In the mosque and the courtyard the arches are decorated with elaborate designs in carved stucco. The roofed oratory of the mosque is divided by pillars into five long aisles or naves originally ornamented with panels of carved wood.

The building was restored several times, notably between 1296 and 1299, when the wall facing Mecca and the minaret—which has three floors, each in a different shape (square, spiral, and octagonal)—were rebuilt. It was used as a belt factory in the 18th century and was divided into shops in 1814. Classed as a historic monument in 1890, the mosque has since been completely restored.

Ahmad Khan, Sir Sayyid, Sayyid also spelled SYAD, or SYED, Ahmad also spelled AHMED (b. Oct. 17, 1817, Delhi—d. March 27, 1898, Alīgarh, India), Muslim educator, jurist, and author, founder of the Anglo-Mohammedan Oriental College at Alīgarh, Uttar Pradesh, India, and the principal motivating force behind the revival of Indian Islām in the late 19th century. His works, in Urdu, include *Essays on the Life of Mohammed* (1870) and commentaries on the Bible and on the Qurʾān. In 1888 he was made a Knight Commander of the Star of India.

Sayyid's family, though progressive, was highly regarded by the dying Mughal dynasty. His father, who received an allowance from the Mughal administration, became something of a religious recluse; his maternal grandfather had twice served as prime minister of the Mughal emperor of his time and had also held positions of trust under the East India Company. Sayyid's brother established one of the first printing presses at Delhi and started one of the earliest newspapers in Urdu, the principal language of the Muslims of northern India.

The death of Sayyid's father left the family in financial difficulties, and after a limited education Sayyid had to work for his livelihood. Starting as a clerk with the East India Company in 1838, he qualified three years later as a subjudge and served in the judicial department at various places.

Sayyid Ahmad had a versatile personality, and his position in the judicial department left him time to be active in many fields. His career as an author (in Urdu) started at the age of 23 with religious tracts. In 1847 he brought out a noteworthy book, *Āthār aṣṣanādīd* ("Monuments of the Great"), on the antiquities of Delhi. Even more important was his pamphlet, "The Causes of the Indian Revolt." During the Indian Mutiny of 1857 he had taken the side of the British, but in this booklet he ably and fearlessly laid bare the weaknesses and errors of the British administration that had led to dissatisfaction and a countrywide explosion. Widely read by British officials, it had considerable influence on British policy.

His interest in religion was also active and lifelong. He began a sympathetic interpretation of the Bible, wrote *Essays on the Life of Mohammed* (translated into English by his son), and found time to write several volumes of a modernist commentary on the Qurʾān. In these works he sought to harmonize the Islāmic faith with the scientific and politically progressive ideas of his time.

The supreme interest of Sayyid's life was, however, education—in its widest sense. He began by establishing schools, at Muradabad (1858) and Ghāzīpur (1863). A more ambitious undertaking was the foundation of the Scientific Society, which published translations of many educational texts and issued a bilingual journal—in Urdu and English.

These institutions were for the use of all citizens and were jointly operated by the Hindus and the Muslims. In the late 1860s there occurred developments that were to alter the course of his activities. In 1867 he was transferred to Benares, a city on the Ganges with great religious significance for the Hindus. This was the year in which an elaborate religio-political festival, the Hindu *melā,* was first organized at Calcutta, signifying a noteworthy attempt at separate communal organization of the Hindus. At about the same time a movement started at Benares to replace Urdu, the language cultivated by the Muslims, with Hindi. This movement and the attempts to substitute Hindi for Urdu in the publications of the Scientific Society convinced Sayyid that the paths of the Hindus and the Muslims must diverge. Thus, when during a visit to England (1869–70) he prepared plans for a great educational institution, they were for "a Muslim Cambridge." On his return he set up a committee for the purpose and also started an influential journal, *Tahdhīb al-Akhlāq* ("Social Reform"), for the "uplift and reform of the Muslim." A Muslim school was established at Alīgarh in May 1875, and, after his retirement in 1876, Sayyid devoted himself to enlarging it into a college. In January 1877 the foundation stone of the college was laid by the Viceroy. In spite of conservative opposition to Sayyid's projects, the college made rapid progress. In 1886 Sayyid organized the All-India Muhammadan Educational Conference, which met annually at different places to promote education and to provide the Muslims with a common platform. Until the founding of the Muslim League in 1906, it was the principal national centre of Indian Islām.

For the college, and even more for the conference, Sayyid was able to attract the elite of the Muslim intelligentsia, who not only helped his educational program but also transformed Urdu literature: poetry, historiography, fiction, and prose. Their efforts brought about a general awakening among Indian Muslims and instilled within them a renewed confidence and cohesion.

Sayyid advised the Muslims against joining active politics and to concentrate instead on education. Later, when some Muslims joined the Indian National Congress, he came out strongly against that organization and its objectives, which included the establishment of parliamentary democracy in India. He argued that in a country where communal divisions were all-important and education and political organization were confined to a few classes, parliamentary democracy would work only inequitably. Muslims, generally, followed his advice and abstained from politics until several years later when they had established their own political organization.

Sayyid Ahmad was a relic of the age of the great Mughals. Opinions differ regarding his politics, but most impartial observers praise his solid achievements. Under his leadership the disintegration of Muslim India was halted, and within a generation it was again prominent and influential. (S.M.I.)

BIBLIOGRAPHY. Altaf Husan Hali, *Hayat-i-Javid* (1901), the only comprehensive account of Sayyid Ahmad's life and work; G.F.I. Graham, *The Life and Work of Syed Ahmed Khan,* rev. ed. (1909), contains little biographical information beyond 1887, but is still a useful account. See also S.K. Bhatnagar, *History of the M.A.O. College, Aligarh* (1969); J.M.S. Baljon, *The Reforms and Religious Ideas of Sir Sayyid Ahmad Khan* (1949); and Hadi Hussain, *Syed Ahmed Khan: Pioneer of Muslim Resurgence* (1970).

Consult the INDEX *first*

Aḥmad Mūsa (fl. 14th century, Tabrīz, Azerbaijan), painter active at the court of the Il Khans at Tabrīz. He is said to have learned painting from his father and to have "drawn the veil from the face of painting and invented the art of the Persian miniature." He was active under Abū Saʿīd (ruled 1316–35), the last of the Mongol sultans in fact as well as name. He illustrated a *Kalila wa Dimna* (book of animal fables) and a book of the Miʿrāj (the miraculous journey of Muḥammad), which are probably now preserved in part in the "Conqueror's Albums" of the imperial Ottoman library at the Topkapı Palace at Istanbul. Aḥmad Mūsa's most famous pupil was Shams ad-Dīn, who painted at the court of the Jalāyir sultans of Baghdad in the latter part of the 14th century.

Aḥmad Shāh, in full AḤMAD SHĀH BAHĀDUR MUJĀHID-UD-DĪN ABŪ NAṢR (b. Dec. 24, 1725, Delhi—d. Jan. 1, 1775, Delhi), ineffectual Mughal emperor of India from 1748 to 1754, who has been characterized as a "good-natured imbecile," without personality, training, or qualities of leadership. He was entirely dominated by others, including the queen mother, Udham Bai, and the eunuch superintendent of the harem, the emperor's vicar Javīd Khān. Twice during his reign, the Afghan Aḥmad Shāh Durrānī plundered the northwest Punjab area, extorting money and land from him. At a demonstration by the Marāthās in Sikandarābād, he fled, abandoning the women of his family to captivity.

In 1750 Aḥmad Shāh's *wazīr* ("vizier"), Ṣafdar Jang, who had been defeated by Afghans of the Doab, joined the Marāthās of southwest India in attempting to gain the spoils of Aḥmad Shāh's empire. Aḥmad Shāh was blinded and deposed by the Marāthās and their allies in 1754, after which he lived in confinement until his death.

Aḥmad Shāh Durrānī (b. 1722?, Multān, Punjab—d. Oct. 16–23?, 1772, Toba Maʿrūf, Afg.), founder of the state of Afghanistan and ruler of an empire that extended from the Amu Darya to the Indian Ocean and from Khorāsān into Kashmir, the Punjab, and Sind. He united under a kind of federal republic a large number of warring tribes that through history had suffered domination by Greeks, Huns, Turks, and Mongols. Head of the central government, with full control of all departments of state in domestic and foreign affairs, both civil and military, the shah was assisted by a prime minister and a council of nine life-term advisers that he selected from the chiefs of the leading Afghan tribes. The shah exercised little control over provincial governors, however, and in towns and villages the local chief occupied the position of a feudal lord.

A member of the noble Sadōzai clan and the second son of Moḥammad Zamān Khān, a hereditary chief of the Abdālī tribe of Afghans, Aḥmad rose to command an Abdālī cavalry group under Nāder Shāh of Persia and, on Nāder Shāh's assassination, the Afghan chiefs elected Aḥmad as *shāh.* He was crowned in 1747 near Qandahār, where coins were struck in his name and where he set up his capital. Embarking on the conquest of regions held by ineffectual rulers, he invaded India nine times between 1747 and 1769, supposedly with no intention of founding an empire there. After an unopposed march to Delhi in 1757, he plundered that city, Āgra, Mathura, and Vṛndāvana.

Before an outbreak of cholera among his troops forced his return to Afghanistan, Aḥmad married Ḥazrat Baygam, daughter of the Indian Mughal emperor Muḥammad Shāh. His son Tīmūr remained behind as viceroy of the Punjab and married the daughter of India's puppet emperor ʿĀlamgīr II. Tīmūr was driven out in 1758 by a force of Sikhs, Mughals, and Marāthās, but in 1759–61 Aḥmad Shāh swept the Marāthās from the Punjab and destroyed their large army at Pānīpat, north of Delhi. In the 1760s he attempted four times to crush the Sikhs, but his empire was restive with serious revolts nearer home, and he lost control of the Punjab to them. He is buried in a mausoleum in Aḥmad Shāhī, the new capital he built.

Ahmadābād, also spelled AHMEDABAD, city, administrative headquarters of Ahmadābād district, Gujarāt state, west central India, on the Sābarmati River, north of Bombay. The city was founded in AD 1411 by the Muslim ruler of Gujarāt, Sultan Aḥmad Shāh, next to the older Hindu town of Asāwal. Ahmadābād grew larger and wealthier for a century, but dynastic decay and anarchy brought decline, and the city was captured in 1572 by the Mughal emperor Akbar. Renewed eminence under the Mughals ceased with the death of Aurangzeb in 1707. Further decline was arrested by the British annexation of Gujarāt in 1818. The city's first cotton mills were opened in 1859–61, and it has become the sixth most populous city and largest inland industrial centre in India. Ahmadābād became the temporary capital of Gujarāt state in 1960; the state administration was moved in 1970 to Gāndhīnagar.

The Jaina temple of Hāṭhīsingh in Ahmadābād, Gujarāt, India
Candida

In the city Hindu, Muslim, and Jaina architectures met, and its ancient architectural remains contrast sharply with modern mills and factories. An attractive feature of the city is Lake Kankaria, offering promenades, boating, a hill garden, and a museum designed by the architect Le Corbusier. Ahmadābād is the home of Gujarāt University (1949) and of the Lalbhai Dalpatbhai Institute for Indological Research.

About one-half of the city's population depends upon the cotton industry, with various other light manufactures. Roads lead to Bombay and central India, the Kāthiāwār Peninsula, and the Rājasthān border. It is a major junction on the Western Railway, with lines running to Bombay, Delhi, and the Kāthiāwār Peninsula.

Ahmadābād district occupies 3,362 sq mi (8,707 sq km) across the neck of the Kāthiāwār Peninsula. The northeast is dotted with low hills that gradually give way southwestward to a great plain, the only fertile area in the district. The chief crops are cotton, millet, wheat, and pulses. Parts of the district are wooded. The main rivers are the Sābarmati and its tributaries, which flow southward into the Gulf of Cambay. Pop. (1981) city, 2,129,799; metropolitan area, 2,548,057; district, 3,875,794.

Aḥmadī, al-, town and *muḥāfaẓah* (governorate) in southern Kuwait. The oasis town, capital of the *muḥāfaẓah,* was built after 1946 with the development of the oil field in which it is located. Al-Aḥmadī is the headquarters of the Kuwait Oil Company. Pipelines link it with Mīnā' (port) al-Aḥmadī, on the Persian Gulf to the east, where a refinery and tanker terminals are located. Al-Aḥmadī *muḥāfaẓah* is 1,984 sq mi (5,138 sq km) in area. Pop. (1980) town, 23,854; *muḥāfaẓah,* 232,643.

Aḥmadīyah, a modern Islāmic sect and the generic name for various Ṣūfī (Muslim mystic) orders. The sect was founded in Qādiān, the Punjab, India, in 1889 by Mirza Ghulam Aḥmad (*c.* 1839–1908), who claimed to be the *mahdī* (a figure expected by some Muslims at the end of the world), the Christian Messiah, an incarnation of the Hindu god Krishna, and a reappearance (*burūz*) of Muḥammad. The sect's doctrine, in some aspects, is unorthodox: for example, it is believed that Jesus feigned death and resurrection but in actuality escaped to India, where he died at the age of 120; also, *jihād* ("holy war") is reinterpreted as a battle against unbelievers to be waged by peaceful methods rather than by violent military means.

On the death of the founder, Mawlawi Nur-ad-Din was elected by the community as *khalīfah* ("successor"). In 1914, when he died, the Aḥmadiyah split, the original, Qadiani, group recognizing Ghulam Aḥmad as prophet (*nabī*) and his son Hadrat Mirza Bashir-ad-Dīn Mahmud Aḥmad (b. 1889) as the second caliph, the new Lahore society accepting Ghulam Aḥmad only as a reformer (*mujaddid*).

The Qadianis, residing chiefly in Pakistan (though there are communities in India and West Africa and to some extent in Great Britain, Europe, and the United States), are a highly organized community with a considerable financial base. They are zealous missionaries, preaching Aḥmadī beliefs as the one true Islām, with Muḥammad and Mirza Ghulam Aḥmad as prophets. In 1947, with the establishment of Pakistan, they officially relocated from Qādiān to Rabwah, Pakistan.

The Lahore group are also proselytizers, though more concerned in gaining converts to Islām than to their particular sect. Led from its inception to his death in 1951 by Mawlana Muhammad Ali, the sect has been active in English- and Urdu-language publishing and in liberalizing Islām.

Aḥmadīyah also designates several Ṣūfī orders, the most important of which is that of Egypt named after Aḥmad al-Badawī, one of the greatest saints of Islām (d. 1276). Al-Badawī achieved great fame for his knowledge of Islāmic sciences, but he eventually abandoned speculative theology and devoted himself to contemplation in seclusion. Soon he became known as a miracle-working saint and had thousands of followers. He arrived in Ṭanṭā (south of Cairo, Egypt) in 1236. His followers were also called Suṭūḥiyah from *aṣḥāb as-saṭḥ* (the people of the roof); according to one anecdote, when al-Badawī arrived at Ṭanṭā, he climbed upon the roof of a private house and stood motionless looking into the sun until his eyes became red and sore. This action was then imitated by some of his followers.

After al-Badawī's death, the Aḥmadīyah was headed by ʿAbd al-ʿĀl, a close disciple who kept the order under strict rule until his death in 1332. ʿAbd al-ʿĀl inherited the order's symbols: a red cowl, a veil, and a red banner that belonged to al-Badawī. Before his death, ʿAbd al-ʿĀl ordered a chapel built on al-Badawī's tomb, which was later replaced by a large mosque.

The Aḥmadīyah order, which is representative of the lower type of dervishes, faced great opposition from Muslim legalists, who, in general, opposed all Ṣūfism, and from political figures who felt threatened by the tremendous influence the order had on the masses. Under the Mamlūk dynasty, however, the head of the Aḥmadīyah at times enjoyed considerable privileges and was treated as a dignitary. During the Ottoman rule the Aḥmadīyah suffered from official neglect because of the powerful rivalry from Turkish orders, but this did not lessen in any way the deep veneration for al-Badawī among the Egyptians. The Aḥmadīyah is one of the most popular orders in Egypt, and the three yearly festivals in honour of al-Badawī are major celebrations. Numerous minor orders are considered branches of the Aḥmadīyah and are spread all over the Islāmic world. Among these are the Shinnāwīyah, the Kannāsīyah, the Bayyūmīyah, the Sallāmīyah, the Halabīyah, and the Bundārīyah.

Ahmadnagar, also spelled AHMEDNAGAR, town, administrative headquarters of Ahmadnagar district, Mahārāshtra state, western India, on the Sīna River. Known as Bhinar in early Yādava times, it was conquered by Malik Aḥmad Niẓām Shāh, founder of the Ahmadnagar dynasty, in 1490. It was later taken by the Mughals, Marāṭhās, and British. Chief among its historical sites are Aḥmad Niẓām Shāh's fort, in which Jawaharlal Nehru was imprisoned in the 1940s, and the Mughal palace and gardens. Connected by road and rail to Bombay, Pune (Poona), and Sholāpur, the town is a commercial centre whose major industries are cotton and leather processing. It has three colleges affiliated with the University of Poona.

Ahmadnagar district occupies 6,577 sq mi (17,035 sq km) in the upper Godāvari River Basin. The river forms the district boundary in the north, and several of its tributaries, including the Mula, traverse the northern parts of the district. The Sīna and Bhīma rivers flow southeastward to meet the Krishna River in Karnātaka state. All these rivers originate in the forested Sahyādri Hills of the Western Ghāts, which form the western boundary.

Agriculture is the mainstay of the district. Rainfall is extremely unreliable, however, and food scarcity is a perennial concern. Millet, wheat, and cotton are the district's chief dry crops, and sugarcane ranks as the most important irrigated crop. Industries include sugar processing and cotton ginning and pressing. The district is known for its Āyurvedic (traditional Indian) herbal medicines. Important tourist sites include the Bhandardara Dam and the religious centre at Shirdī. Pop. (1981) town, 143,937; metropolitan area, 181,210; district, 2,708,309.

Ahmadu Hammadi Bubu: *see* Shehu Ahmadu Lobbo.

Ahmadu Seku (d. 1898, Sokoto, Northern Nigeria), second and last ruler of the Tukulor empire in West Africa, celebrated for his resistance to the French occupation.

Succeeding his father, al-Ḥājj ʿUmar, in 1864, Ahmadu ruled over a great empire centred on the ancient Bambara kingdom of Segu, in present Mali. By the Treaty of Nango (1881) he granted France most-favoured-nation status. After the advance of the French to Kita and Bamako, he abandoned Segu as his capital and accepted a French protectorate (Treaty of Gouri, May 12, 1887). But Col. Louis Archinard took the offensive against him in 1888 and by 1891 had seized most of his strongholds.

Aḥmad ʿUrābī Pasha al-Miṣrī: *see* ʿUrābī Pasha.

Aḥmar, al-Baḥr al- (Asia): *see* Red Sea.

Ahmed (Arabic personal name): *see under* Ahmad, except as below.

Ahmed, also spelled ACHMED, or ACHMET, name of Ottoman sultans grouped below chronologically and indicated by the symbol •.

•Ahmed I (b. April 18, 1590, Manisa, Ottoman Empire—d. Nov. 22, 1617), Ottoman sultan from 1603 to 1617, whose authority was weakened by wars, rebellions, and misrule. The rebellions he was able to suppress; he executed some of the viziers and exiled many palace dignitaries for bribery and intrigue; and he introduced a new regulation for the improvement of land administration. The peace of Zsitvatörök (1606) that he signed with Austria was a blow to Ottoman prestige, and he was compelled to extend commercial privileges to France, Venice, and the Netherlands within his domains.

Ahmed I, being entertained by midgets in mock combat, miniature, early 17th century; in the Topkapı Saray Museum, Istanbul

By courtesy of the Topkapi Saray Museum, Istanbul

Ahmed was pious and made many donations, especially to the holy places of Mecca and Medina. He built the great Blue Mosque near the Church of Hagia Sophia. Of his seven sons, Osman II, Murad IV, and İbrahim I eventually succeeded to the throne.

•Ahmed II (b. Aug. 1, 1642—d. Feb. 6, 1695, Edirne, Ottoman Empire), Ottoman sultan (1691–95) whose reign was marked by the continuing war with the Holy League (Austria–Poland–Venice).

Soon after his accession to the throne, Ahmed's forces were defeated by the Austrians at Slankamen, Hung. The able grand vizier (chief minister) Fazıl Mustafa Köprülü died in the battle, and the Ottomans suffered substantial territorial losses in Hungary. In 1692 the Venetians attacked Crete and in 1694 captured Chios. In addition, Ahmed faced unrest in his Arab provinces of Syria, Hejaz, and Iraq. To find land for the nomadic Turkmen tribes, Ahmed encouraged tribal settlement in Anatolia and Syria and put an end to certain abuses in the Ottoman land administration system. Generally, however, Ahmed, who had been imprisoned in the palace before his accession, was unable to show any independence and remained under the influence of his courtiers.

•Ahmed III (b. 1673—d. 1736), sultan of the Ottoman Empire from 1703 to 1730. With Charles XII of Sweden, a refugee at his court, he was forced into war with Russia (1711–13) and came nearer than any other Turkish sovereign to breaking that power. Encircled near the Pruth (1711), the Russians had to agree to restore Azov, to destroy the Azovian forts, and to abstain from interference in Polish or Cossack affairs. In 1715 Ahmed directed the capture of the Morea (Peloponnesus) from the Venetians, but when Austria intervened, the Turks suffered reverses, losing Belgrade in 1717. Under the peace of Passarowitz (1718), which Ahmed made, Turkey retained its conquests from the Venetians but ceded Hungary and part of Serbia.

Deposed during the uprising led by Patrona Halil in 1730, Ahmed died in captivity in 1736. His reign is sometimes known as the Tulip

Ahmed III, attended by a son, portrait miniature by Levni, early 18th century; in the Topkapı Saray Museum, Istanbul

By courtesy of the Topkapi Saray Museum, Istanbul

Time because of the popularity of that flower in Constantinople in the early 18th century.

Ahmed, Fakhruddin Ali (b. May 13, 1905, Delhi—d. Feb. 11, 1977, New Delhi), statesman, president of India from 1974 to 1977.

The son of an Army doctor from Assam, Ahmed was educated in India and later studied history at Cambridge, graduating in 1927. After he returned to India, he was elected to the Assam legislature (1935). As the province's minister of finance and revenue in 1938, he was responsible for some radical taxation measures. On the outbreak of World War II in 1939 the Congress had a confrontation with British power, and Ahmed was jailed for a year. Soon after his release he was again imprisoned for another three and a half years, being released in April 1945.

In 1946 he was appointed advocate general of Assam and held the post for six years. After a term in the national Parliament, he returned to Assam politics until Prime Minister Indira Gandhi included him in her first Cabinet in January 1966. He held a variety of portfolios—irrigation and power, education, industrial development, and agriculture. Ahmed became India's fifth president in 1974. He was a soft-spoken man of quiet humour.

Ahmed Cevdet Paşa: *see* Cevdet Paşa, Ahmed.

Ahmed Haşim (b. 1884, Baghdad—d. June 4, 1933, Istanbul), writer, one of the most outstanding representatives of the Symbolist movement in Turkish literature.

Born into a prominent family long active in government service, Haşim developed his knowledge of French literature and his fondness for poetry at Galatasaray Lycée in Constantinople. After briefly studying law, he worked for the government tobacco offices. Later, except for a two-year period during which he taught French in Izmir, he served as an official government translator. After military service in World War I, he worked for the Ottoman Public Debt Administration and then took teaching positions at the Academy of Fine Arts, the School of Political Science, and the War Academy. In 1924 and 1928 he made trips to Paris during which he met leading French literary figures.

Haşim's early poetry was written in classical Ottoman style, but, after his study of the French Symbolist poets Baudelaire, Rimbaud, Mallarmé, and others, his poetic style changed. In 1909 he joined the Fecr-i âti (Dawn of the Future) literary circle but gradually drew apart from this group and developed his own style. Haşim, following the French masters, strove to develop the Turkish Symbolist movement. In a 1924 article on Turkish literature for the French publication *Mercure de France*, he stated that poetry is the intermediary language between simple speech and music. His work at times seems intentionally obscure, but, nevertheless, he creates images and moods of great beauty and sensitivity. Among his most famous poetry collections are *Göl saatleri* (1921; "The Hours of the Lake") and *Göl kuşları* ("The Birds of the Lake").

Ahmed Vefik Paşa (b. July 6, 1823, Constantinople—d. April 2, 1891, Constantinople), Ottoman statesman and scholar who presided over the first Ottoman Parliament (1877) and who is known for his contributions to Turkish studies.

Born into a family of diplomats, Ahmed Vefik was appointed (1849) imperial commissioner in the Danubian principalities and later ambassador to Persia and to France. He presided over the first Parliament and was twice appointed grand vizier (chief minister) for brief periods. In 1879 he became the *vali* (governor) of Bursa, where he sponsored reforms in sanitation and education and established the first Ottoman theatre.

Ahmed Vefik spent his leisure translating Molière's plays and compiling Turkish dictionaries and historical and geographical manuals. He edited the first *Salnâme* (Year Book) of the Ottoman Empire (1847), and in 1876 he published *Lehçe-i Osmanî* ("Language of the Ottomans"), a concise dictionary that emphasized pure Turkish and formed a basis for the works of other Turkish scholars.

After December 1882 he was confined, on Sultan Abdülhamid II's order, to his house at Rumeli Hisar on the Bosporus. His library was sold for the payment of his debts.

Ahmed Yesevi, also spelled AḤMAD YASAWĪ, Yesevi also spelled YASAVĪ (b. second half of the 11th century, Sayrām—d. 1166, Yasī), poet and Ṣūfī (Muslim mystic), an early Turkish mystic leader who exerted a powerful influence on the development of mystical orders throughout the Turkish-speaking world.

Very little is known about his life, but legends indicate that his father died when he was young and his family moved to Yasī, where he began his mystical teaching, hence his name. He is said to have gone to Bukhara to study with the great Ṣūfī leader Yūsuf Hamadhānī and other famous mystics. Finally he returned to Yasī. The extant work attributed to the poet is the *Divan-i hikmet* ("Book of Wisdom"), containing poems on mystical themes. Scholars believe that the work is probably not his. It is felt, however, that the poems in the *Divan* are similar in style and sentiment to what he wrote. The importance of Yesevi cannot be overestimated. Legends about his life were spread throughout the Turkish Islāmic world, and he developed a tremendous following. The conqueror Timur erected a magnificent mausoleum over his grave in 1397/98, to which pilgrims came, revering Yesevi as a saint.

Ahmed Yesevi wrote poetry for the people, and his mystical order was a popular brotherhood. Not only Islāmic but also ancient Turco-Mongol practices and customs were preserved in their ritual. His disciples formed many affiliated mystical associations that spread throughout the Turkish world. His poetry influenced Turkish literature a great deal, paving the way for the development of mystical folk literature.

Ahmedabad (India): *see* Ahmadābād.

Ahmedi, Taceddin, in full TACEDDIN (TAJ AD-DĪN) İBRAHIM IBN HIZR AHMEDI (b. 1334?, Anatolia—d. 1413, Amasya, Ottoman Empire), one of the greatest poets of 14th-century Anatolia.

As a young man, Ahmedi studied with the famous scholar Akmal ad-Din (al-Babarti) in Cairo. He then went to Kütahya, in Anatolia, and wrote for the ruler Amīr Süleyman (1367–86). Later he went to the court of the Ottoman sultan Bayezid I (1389–1403), and, at the Battle of Ankara, in which the Ottomans suffered a drastic defeat, Ahmedi apparently met the victor, the world conqueror Timur (Tamerlane [d. 1405]) and wrote a *qaṣīdah* ("ode") for him.

At the death of Sultan Bayezid, Ahmedi joined the monarch's son Süleyman Çelebi in the city of Edirne and presented him with panegyrics and one of his best known works, the *Iskendername* ("The Book of Alexander"), a work that he had dedicated originally to Amīr Süleyman of the house of Germiyan in Kütahya but that he revised and added to for many years. Modelled after the work of the great Persian poet Neẓāmī (d. 1209), Ahmedi's *Iskendername* is a poem of some 8,000 rhymed couplets (*mašnavī*), in which he uses the legend of Alexander as a framework for discourses on theology, philosophy, and history. The last part is regarded as an important early source for Ottoman history because the poet apparently based it on a very early chronicle that is no longer extant.

At the death of his patron, Süleyman Çelebi, in 1411, Ahmedi then wrote panegyrics for the new Ottoman sultan, Mehmet Çelebi I (d. 1421), until his own death in 1413.

In addition to the *Iskendername*, Ahmedi wrote a divan, or collection of poems; many *mašnavī*; a poem, *Cemşid u Hürşid*; and a didactic work, *Tervih al-Ervah* ("The Comfort of the Spirit").

Ahmednagar (India): *see* Ahmadnagar.

Ahmet Paşa Bursali (b. Edirne?, Ottoman Empire—d. 1496/97, Bursa), one of the most important figures in 15th-century Turkish literature.

Born into a prominent family, Ahmet Paşa received a classical Islāmic education and was appointed as a teacher in the *madrasah* ("religious college") in the city of Bursa. In 1451 he became judge of the city of Edirne. With the accession of Sultan Mehmet II (1451–81), he became *qāḍī ʿasker* ("military judge") and tutor to the Sultan and took part in the conquest of Constantinople in 1453. After falling out of favour with the Sultan, he spent many years in virtual exile in Bursa and then as governor of a number of Ottoman cities. With the accession of Sultan Bayezid II (1481–1512), however, he continued his career in government service until his death in 1496/97.

Principally a panegyrist, Ahmet Paşa wrote mainly *qaṣīdah*s ("odes") and *ghazal*s ("lyrics") and is considered the first master of classical poetry in Ottoman literature. The melodious poems in his divan, or collection of poems, had a strong influence on later Ottoman classical poets, securing for him an important place in Turkish literary history.

Ahmose, also spelled AHMOSIS, Greek AMASIS, name of Egyptian kings grouped below chronologically and indicated by the symbol •.

• **Ahmose I** (reigned *c.* 1570–46 BC), founder of the 18th dynasty, who completed his brother's expulsion of the Hyksos (Asiatic rulers of Egypt), invaded Palestine, and re-exerted Egypt's hegemony over Nubia, to the south.

Resuming the war of liberation against the Hyksos early in his reign, Ahmose crushed the foreigners' allies in Middle Egypt and, advancing down the Nile River, captured Memphis, the traditional capital of Egypt, near modern Cairo. While his mother, Queen Ahhotep, ran the government in Thebes, near modern Luxor, he undertook a waterborne operation against Avaris, the Hyksos capital, in the eastern Delta, followed by a land siege. When a rebellion flared in Upper Egypt, he hastened upriver to quell the rising, while the queen mother Ahhotep helped to contain it. Having put down the rising, he captured Avaris and then pursued the enemy to Sharuhen, a Hyksos stronghold in Palestine, which was reduced after a three-year siege.

Before advancing into Palestine, Ahmose, in three campaigns, advanced into Nubia, whose ruler had been an ally of the Hyksos. The rich gold mines of the south provided another incentive for Ahmose's expansion into Nubia.

After his borders were secure, Ahmose established an administration loyal to him in Egypt and granted lands to distinguished veterans of his campaigns and to members of the royal family. He reactivated the copper mines at Sinai and resumed trade with the cities of the Syrian coast, as attested by inscriptions recording the use of cedar found in Syria and by the rich jewelry from his reign. He restored neglected temples, erected chapels for his family, and planned more ambitious works, but he died soon afterward, leaving a prosperous and reunited Egypt.

• **Ahmose II** (reigned 570–526 BC), a member of the 26th dynasty, a general who seized the throne during a revolt against King Apries. The account of the 5th-century-BC Greek historian Herodotus reveals Ahmose as a shrewd and opportunistic ruler, who, while promoting Greek trade with Egypt, strictly regulated it.

Under Psamtik II (reigned 595–589 BC), Ahmose led the native Egyptian troops during an expedition south into Nubia. Later, in 570, after Apries' unsuccessful campaign against Cyrene, in modern Libya, the Egyptian troops mutinied, and when Ahmose was sent to pacify them the mutineers proclaimed him king. In the ensuing civil war the Egyptians under his command defeated Apries' Greek mercenaries. Ahmose, however, allowed Apries to live and later gave him a royal burial.

A fragmentary tablet of Nebuchadrezzar, king of Babylon, alludes to a campaign against Egypt in 568, but Ahmose was not affected adversely. He turned to diplomacy, securing an alliance with Cyrene by marrying a woman of that country and also seeking alliances in Greece. Herodotus tells of his friendship with Polycrates, tyrant of Samos, and also mentions his donation toward rebuilding the temple at Delphi. Nonetheless, to regulate Greek influence in Egypt he confined merchants to the city of Naukratis in the Nile Delta, southwest of his own capital.

Perhaps employing the fleet of his friend Polycrates, Ahmose reputedly subdued Cyprus, exacting tribute from it. Herodotus states that Ahmose allied himself with Croesus when the Lydian king was seeking assistance against Persia. Yet Persian power grew rapidly, and Ahmose died only one year before King Cambyses' invasion of Egypt.

Aho, Juhani, pseudonym of JOHANNES BROFELDT (b. Sept. 11, 1861, Lapinlahti, Russian Finland—d. Aug. 8, 1921, Helsinki), novelist and short story writer who began as a Realist but toward the end of his life made large concessions to Romanticism.

A country clergyman's son, Aho studied at Helsinki University, worked as a journalist, and was an active member of the liberal group Nuori Suomi ("Young Finland").

Aho's early realistic stories and novels humorously describe life in the Finnish backwoods he knew so well. His novel *Rautatie* (1884; "The Railway"), the story of an elderly couple's first railway trip, is a Finnish classic. Influenced by contemporary Norwegian and French writers—Ibsen, Bjørnson, Maupassant, and particularly Daudet—he described the life of the educated classes in *Papin tytär* (1885; "The Parson's Daughter") and *Papin rouva* (1893; "The Parson's Wife").

In the 1890s Aho was drawn toward romantic nationalism: the long novel *Panu* (1897) dealt with the struggle between paganism and Christianity in 17th-century Finland, and *Kevät ja takatalvi* (1906; "Spring and the Untimely Return of Winter"), with the national awakening of the 19th century. His soundest romantic work, *Juha* (1911), is the story of the unhappy marriage of a cripple in the Karelian forests. Aho's short stories, *Lastuja* (8 series, 1891–1921; "Chips"), have been most enduring; they are concerned with peasant life, fishing, and the wildlife of the lakelands. In these, as in his reminiscences of childhood, *Muistatko—?* (1920; "Do You Remember?"), Aho displays a quiet lyricism.

aholehole, any of the dozen species of fishes (class Osteichthyes) in the family Kuhliidae. One genus (*Kuhlia*) is strictly marine in the Indo-Pacific region, whereas representatives of the other two genera have only been discovered in freshwater habitats of Australia. Superficially the aholeholes resemble the sunfishes (family Centrarchidae) and are presumably closely related. The Hawaiian aholehole (*Kuhlia sandvicensis*) is restricted to coastal waters throughout the Hawaiian Islands. Its maximum length is about 30 centimetres (12 inches). Some species in the family reach lengths of 45 cm (18 in.).

Ahom, tribe that ruled much of Assam from the 13th century until the establishment of British rule in 1838. Their power in Assam reached its peak during the reign of King Rudra Singh (1696–1714). They originated in the Chinese province of Yunnan and began migrating into Indochina and upper Burma in the first centuries AD. Their original language is now extinct, and they speak Assamese.

Ahram, al- (Egyptian: "The Pyramids"), daily newspaper published in Cairo, long regarded as Egypt's most authoritative and influential newspaper.

It was founded in 1875 by two Lebanese-Christian brothers, Salim and Bishara Takla. As a daily from 1881, the paper became famous for its independence and objectivity, despite British censorship and control, and for its coverage of international news and nonpolitical news about Egypt and Egyptians. Its influence waned, however, after censorship tightened as Egyptian independence neared.

In the late 1950s *al-Ahram* came under the influence of the Egyptian government, and Pres. Gamal Abdel Nasser made his friend Muhammad Hassanin Haikil its editor. In 1960 Nasser nationalized the press, and *al-Ahram* became the de facto voice of the government. Haikil's influence on the paper was profound. He was an eloquent editorialist and a solid journalist, and he built the paper's prestige, its journalistic excellence, its makeup and technical operation to new levels. The paper had become the dominant daily in the Arab world. Haikil was removed as editor in 1974 when he lost the confidence of Pres. Anwar as-Sadat, but the qualities he had built into *al-Ahram* have remained.

Ahrāmāt al-Jīzah (ancient Egyptian pyramid field): *see* Giza, Pyramids of.

Ahriman, Avestan ANGRA MAINYU (Destructive Spirit), the evil spirit in the dualistic doctrine of Zoroastrianism. His essential nature is expressed in his principal epithet—Druj, "the Lie." The Lie expresses itself as greed, wrath, and envy. To aid him in attacking the light, the good creation of Ahura Mazdā, the Wise Lord, Ahriman created a horde of demons embodying envy and similar qualities. Despite the chaos and suffering effected in the world by his onslaught, believers expect Ahriman to be defeated in the end of time by Ahura Mazdā; confined to their own realm, his demons will devour each other, and his own existence will be quenched.

The modern Zoroastrians of India, the Parsis, tend to diminish the importance of Ahriman by explaining him away as an allegory of man's evil tendencies, thus restoring omnipotence to Ahura Mazdā.

AHS: *see* African horse sickness.

Aḥsā', al- (Saudi Arabia): *see* al-Hasa.

Aḥsā'ī, al-, in full SHAYKH AḤMAD IBN ZAYN AD-DĪN IBN IBRĀHĪM AL-AḤSĀ'Ī (b. 1753, al-Hasa, Arabia—d. 1826, near Medina), founder of the heterodox Shīʿī Muslim Shaykhī sect of Iran.

After spending his early years studying the Islāmic religion and travelling widely in Persia, in the Turkish provinces of Basra, Baghdad, and Mosul, and in Arabia, Shaykh Aḥmad in 1808 settled in Yazd, Persia, where he taught religion. His interpretation of the Shīʿī faith (one of the two major branches of Islām) soon attracted many followers. Although he was well received by Fatḥ ʿAlī Shāh, the reigning monarch in Tehrān, Shaykh Aḥmad's teachings aroused controversy among the orthodox religious leaders of the day. A central idea of Shīʿī Islām is that the greater *imām,* the leader of Islām, is descended from the male offspring of ʿAlī (the Prophet Muḥammad's son-in-law) and Fāṭimah (the Prophet's daughter) and is divinely appointed and divinely inspired. After 874 the spiritual functions of the *imām* were performed by *wakīls*, or agents, who were in contact with the *mahdī,* the last *imām* and a messianic deliverer. But following the death of ʿAlī ibn Muḥammad as-Sāmarrī' in 940, this direct contact between the community and the *mahdī* ceased. The Shīʿah believed that some day prior to the apocalyptic end of the world, the *mahdī* would establish a reign of justice.

This apocalyptic belief was strengthened by the prevailing social and economic conditions of Persia. At the beginning of the 19th century the country was recovering from the hardships of a cruel civil war that had preceded the establishment of the Qājār dynasty. The precarious temporal existence of the faithful led to a strong upsurge in millennialist anticipation of the coming of the *mahdī*.

Shaykh Aḥmad taught that at all times there must be direct human contact between the *mahdī* and the community and probably believed himself to be the medium of that contact. The doctrine brought him into conflict with the orthodox Shīʿī theologians of Basra, Baghdad, and Mosul, who regarded themselves as the spiritual caretakers of the community during the *mahdī*'s absence. The Shaykh's final breach with the established and orthodox Shīʿī theologians occurred in 1824, when he was formally denounced as an infidel. He was accused of having denied the physical resurrection of the Prophet Muḥammad and of having taught, instead, that the ascension of the Prophet was purely spiritual. The charge that he taught the divinity of ʿAlī remained unproved. Following his excommunication the Shaykh left the area and died during a pilgrimage to Mecca. He was succeeded as the leader of the Shaykhī sect by Sayyid Kāẓim Rashtī (d. 1843).

Ahuachapán, department, western El Salvador, with an area of 479 sq mi (1,240 sq km); except for the Pacific coastal plain, about 8 mi (13 km) wide, it comprises deep valleys and mountains, which include several volcanoes, the highest being Cerro Chichicastepeque (6,075 ft [1,852 m]). The Río de Paz, to the west, forms the boundary with Guatemala. Originally a Pipil Indian kingdom, it was made Ahuachapán department in 1869. Coffee is grown on volcanic slopes at altitudes of between 1,800 and 4,000 ft. Food crops, including corn (maize) and beans, and livestock, and blooms from Apaneca, the nation's flower garden, are supplied to all parts of the country. Salt deposits are worked along the coast. Industry is concentrated in the departmental capital of Ahuachapán (*q.v.*). Pop. (1981 est.) 241,323.

Ahuachapán, capital of Ahuachapán department, western El Salvador, on the small Río Molino (with a hydroelectric station) at the foot of La Lagunita Volcano. Originally called Güeciapam by the Indians, it was renamed Agüecha before becoming the town (1823) and the city (1862) of Ahuachapán. A manufacturing and distributing centre (the most important product being coffee), it is also noted for its mineral baths, drawn from thermal springs, notably below the nearby Malacatiupán Falls. A geothermal power plant, using heat from the springs, began operation in 1975. Pop. (1980 est.) mun., 69,852.

Ahuitzotl (d. 1503), eighth king of the Aztecs under whose reign (1486–1503) the Aztec empire reached its greatest extent.

The aggressive Ahuitzotl succeeded his brother, Tizoc, to the throne. He proved a fierce and merciless warrior, conquering tribes as far south as present-day Guatemala and Nicaragua and in territory along the Gulf of Mexico. Ahuitzotl was fond of war, and his military tactics consisted of forced marches, ambushes, and surprise attacks. His men feared and respected him, and their king, after conquering a foreign city, chose to camp with his men in lieu of a captured palace. Conquest brought enormous wealth to the Aztec empire as tribute poured in from all the vassal states. The capital of Tenochtitlán grew to such an extent that Ahuitzotl had another aqueduct built. He built the great temple of Malinalco as well. The king imposed tight bureaucratic control over the empire.

Ahuitzotl is known primarily for having occasioned the greatest orgy of sacrificial bloodletting in Aztec history. In 1487 the king decided to dedicate his new temple at Tenochtitlán. The ceremonies, lasting four days, consisted of prisoners of war forming four lines, each one extending over three miles. As the captives were marched up to the altar, priests and Aztec nobles, including Ahuitzotl, had the honour of cutting open their chests and tearing out their hearts. Approximately 20,000 prisoners were killed this way, while guests from the conquered provinces were asked to watch. Ahuitzotl was later killed when he hit his head on a stone lintel trying to escape the great flood that devastated Tenochtitlán in 1503.

ahura (religion): *see* asura.

Ahura Mazdā (Avestan: Wise Lord), also spelled ORMIZD, or ORMAZD, supreme god in ancient Iranian religion, especially in the religious system of the Iranian prophet Zoroaster (7th century–6th century BC). He was worshipped by the Persian king Darius I (reigned 522 BC–486 BC) and his successors as the greatest of all gods and protector of the just king.

Ahura Mazdā, symbol from a doorway of the main hall of the Council Hall, Persepolis, Persia

By courtesy of the Oriental Institute, the University of Chicago

According to Zoroaster, Ahura Mazdā created the universe and the cosmic order that he maintains. He created the twin spirits Spenta Mainyu and Angra Mainyu (Ahriman), the former beneficent, choosing truth, light, and life; the latter destructive, choosing the lie, darkness, and death. The struggle of the spirits against each other makes up the history of the world.

In the developed religion reflected in the Avesta, Ahura Mazdā is identified with the beneficent spirit and directly opposed to the destructive one. He is all-wise, bounteous, undeceiving, and the creator of everything good. The beneficent and evil spirits are conceived as mutually limiting, coeternal beings, the one above and the other beneath, with the world in between as their battleground. In late sources (3rd century AD onward) Zurvān (Time) is made father of the twins Ormazd and Ahriman (Angra Mainyu) who, in orthodox Mazdaism, reign alternately over the world until Ormazd's ultimate victory.

Something of this conception is reflected in Manichaeism, in which God is sometimes called Zurvān, while Ormazd is his first emanation, Primal Man, who is vanquished by the destructive spirit of darkness but rescued by God's second emanation, the Living Spirit.

Ahvāz, Arabic AHWĀZ, capital of Khūzestān *ostān* (province), Iran, on the Kārūn River, amid low sandstone hills. The town has been identified with Achaemenid Tareiana, a river crossing on the royal road connecting Susa, Persepolis, and Pasargadae. Ardashīr I, the Sāsānian king (224–241) who rebuilt the town, named it Hormuzd Ardashīr. He dammed the river, providing irrigation water, and the town prospered. When the Muslim Arabs conquered it in the 7th century, they renamed it Sūq al-Ahwāz (Market of the Hūzī). Ahwāz is the plural of Hūzī, or Khūzī, a local warlike tribe, as in Khūzestān (*q.v.*). Ahvāz continued to prosper under the Umayyads and ʿAbbāsids, when it was the centre of vast sugar plantations. It had begun to decline in the 19th century when the dam collapsed and nearly destroyed the town. The discovery of oil in Khūzestān in the 20th century brought new prosperity. The Iranian workers struck work in the oil fields in 1978. During Iran-Iraq hostilities, the city was attacked by Iraqi planes in 1980.

Since the late 19th century a new settlement, laid out in grid pattern—Bandar-e Nāṣer—has arisen on the left bank; steamers anchor there. New quarters, including the seat of government and the main railway station, have developed on the right bank, whereas workshops, stores, and workers' quarters originally built by the Anglo-Iranian Oil Company were north of the old centre. Ahvāz is a junction of two branches of the Trans-Iranian Railway; it is also connected with Abadan, Khorramshahr, Shūshtar, Dezfūl, and the oil fields by road and with Tehrān by air. The town was scheduled for industrialization under the Khūzestān development program. Jundi Shapūr University (1955) has instruction in Persian and English and has campuses in Lorestān and in the Persian Gulf. Pop. (1976) 329,006.

Ahvenanmaa (Finland): *see* Åland Islands.

Ahwa, town, administrative headquarters of The Dangs district, southeastern Gujarāt state, west central India, on a plateau at approximately 1,600 ft (490 m) above sea level. The hinterland yields timber and foodstuffs, which are traded in Ahwa. It is connected by road with Surat and Valsād.

aḥwāl (Islām): *see* ḥāl.

Ai, ancient Canaanite town destroyed by the Israelites under their leader Joshua (Josh. 7–8). Biblical references agree in locating Ai (Hebrew *ha-ʿAy*, The Ruin), just east of Bethel (modern Baytīn in Israeli-occupied Jordan). This would make it identical with the large Early Bronze Age site now called at-Tall. Excavations there (1933–35) by Judith Marquet-Krause uncovered a large temple and other remains of the 3rd millennium BC. That occupation ended *c.* 2500 BC, and there was no later reoccupation except briefly in the 12th–11th centuries BC. The biblical events, however, are usually assigned to a period between *c.* 1400 and 1200 BC. A widely accepted explanation is that early Israelite tradition identified the Canaanite town that was buried under the Israelite Bethel with the imposing ruins of the still earlier at-Tall, only one and a half miles to the east.

ai, any of several tree-dwelling mammals also known as three-toed sloths. *See* sloth.

Ai Ch'ing, Pinyin AI QING, also called (Wade-Giles romanization) CHIANG HAI-CH'ENG (b. 1910, Chinhua, Chekiang Province, China), Chinese poet committed to the doctrines of Mao Tse-tung and who held various literary and political posts until he was denounced as a rightist in 1957; he was finally cleared of that charge in 1961.

The son of a well-to-do landowner, Ai Ch'ing was encouraged to learn Western languages and studied in Paris from 1928 to 1932. He began to write poetry, which became increasingly more political; it reflected his concern for the common people of China and his agreement with the literary teachings of Mao. From 1949 to 1953 Ai Ch'ing worked on the editorial staff of the magazine *Jen-min wen-hsueh* ("People's Literature"). He served on various cultural committees until he was officially censured in 1957.

Ai Ch'ing remained silent for 21 years and was interned in labour camps in Heilungkiang and Sinkiang. He began publishing again in 1978. An advocate of free expression and the role of the writer as social critic, Ai Ch'ing used simple language and a free style in creating his socially oriented poems.

Ai-hui, also called (locally) HEI-HO, Pinyin AIHUI, or HEIHE, town on the Amur River in northern Heilungkiang Province (*sheng*), China. A county (*hsien*) seat and the administrative centre of the extensive Hei-ho Prefecture (*ti-ch'ü*), it controls the northwestern Heilungkiang region along the Amur River border with the Soviet Union.

The region was still largely covered with virgin forest and had few inhabitants until the 19th century. Ai-hui, originally a small village on the Amur, began to grow after the discovery of gold in the area in 1883, which precipitated a gold rush of impoverished peasants from farther south. Agricultural development began early in the 20th century but was slow, largely because of the harsh climate and short growing season. Later a lumber industry was established. The gold boom—which brought some 60,000 miners into the area and changed Ai-hui into a typical boom town with theatres, stores, and places of entertainment—caused its population to reach 50,000 during World War I. After the war the town changed into a commercial centre.

Under Japanese rule from 1931 to 1945, it was linked by rail to Nen-chiang and Pei-an to the south. These rail lines were destroyed after World War II. The town's transportation links consist of the Amur River and of a network of poor highways. It is, nevertheless, the commercial centre for a large area, and many small industries have been established there. Pop. (1957 est.) 24,000; (mid-1970s est.) 10,000–50,000.

Ai Qing (Chinese poet): *see* Ai Ch'ing.

Aias (Greek mythology): *see* Ajax.

Aichbühl, site of a Middle Neolithic settlement (end of the 3rd millennium BC) on the shores of the Federsee (Feder Lake) in southeastern Baden-Württemberg *Land* (state), southwestern West Germany. Foundations of 25 rectangular buildings arranged in an irregular row along the shoreline were uncovered in the peat wetland by R. Schmidt in 1930. Approximately twenty of the buildings were two-room houses averaging 16.5 by 26.0 feet (5 by 8 metres) in size, with walls built of split wooden posts arranged vertically. A central building, likely used for communal purposes, was approximately 66 by 66 ft (20 by 20 m); the remaining buildings were classified as storage houses. The economy was based primarily on hunting, supplemented by wheat and barley fields and livestock breeding. Small polished stone hatchets and bone implements were discovered around the site, and hearths and clay ovens were found in the houses. Aichbühl's ceramics were an unpainted Neolithic type common in southern Germany.

Aichi, prefecture (*ken*), central Honshu, Japan, on the Pacific coast. More than one-half of its area of 1,980 sq mi (5,127 sq km) lies within Nōbi-heiya (the Nōbi Plain) and two

Pleasure boats on the Kiso-gawa, Aichi Prefecture, Japan
Etsunori Arakawa—Orion Press

smaller plains to the east. The northwestern border with Gifu Prefecture is formed by the Kiso-gawa (Kiso River), sometimes known as the Nihon (Japan) Rhine. The irregular coast is marked by the peninsulas of Chita (west) and Atsumi (east), which enclose Mikawa-wan (Mikawa Bay) and lie within Mikawa-wan Quasi-national Park, a popular resort area.

During the Tokugawa era (1603–1867) the area that is now Aichi Prefecture was Japan's centre for cotton cultivation and manufacture. Its capital, Nagoya, and surrounding industrial suburbs now constitute the Chukyo Industrial Region, Japan's third-ranking industrial concentration, after Keihin and Hanshin. Textiles, ceramics, automobiles, machinery, plywood, chemicals, cloisonné, and processed foods are produced. Toyohashi is a major cotton and silk textile centre, and Seto is noted for its china. There are well-developed road and rail services; main port facilities are in Nagoya. Pop. (1983 est.) 6,356,000.

Aichinger, Gregor (b. 1564, Regensburg, Bishopric of Ratisbon—d. Jan. 21, 1628, Augsburg), composer of religious music during the stylistic transition from the late Renaissance to early Baroque.

Aichinger took holy orders and became organist to the family of Jakob Fugger at Augsburg from 1584. He visited Italy in 1584–87 and later, 1599–1600, went to Rome. His music is chiefly choral and ecclesiastical, set to Latin texts. It shows a conservative taste influenced by the Venetian school of composers, especially Giovanni Gabrieli, with whom he also studied. His motets were well known and frequently appeared in contemporary collections. His *Cantiones Ecclesiasticae* (1607) was one of the earliest German examples of the use of basso continuo.

aid, a tax levied in medieval Europe, paid by persons or communities to someone in authority. Aids could be demanded by the crown from its subjects, by a feudal lord from his vassals, or by the lord of a manor from the inhabitants of his domain.

A feudal lord could ask his vassals for an aid because they owed him help and counsel. In the course of time, however, the occasions on which a lord could ask for a subsidy came to be limited (1) to the knighting of his eldest son, (2) to the first marriage of his eldest daughter, (3) to the payment of his ransom, and sometimes (4) to his going on a crusade. These feudal aids were distinguished from the feudal relief, which was a tax due the lord by a new vassal upon entering into possession of a fief. They were also different, at least in origin, from scutage (*q.v.*), which was a payment in lieu of military service by a feudal tenant.

The aids that the lord of the manor could demand from the inhabitants of his domain, peasants as well as vassals, were called taille (*q.v.*) and developed into the royal taille, or tallage, a direct tax levied by sovereigns.

All over Europe princes had to resort to forms of direct taxation because the other revenues of the crown were insufficient, especially in emergencies. In Carolingian times (8th and 9th centuries), "gifts" were regularly offered to the king. In the later Middle Ages the crown negotiated with various sections of the population for aids. Thus in time of war, towns or communes would be asked for certain lump sums by the crown. It was up to them to collect the money from their citizens. Attempts to limit the amount that could be asked were occasionally made by communes but were never really successful against the overriding financial needs of the crown. Eventually these negotiations were carried on with representatives of the whole country meeting in "estates," where the amounts that could be obtained by the crown often depended on the relative strengths of the bargainers.

Aidan, also spelled AEDAN (d. *c.* 608), king of the Scottish kingdom of Dalriada, son of Gabran, king of Dalriada. He was crowned at Iona by St. Columba. Aidan refused to allow his kingdom to remain dependent on the Irish Dalriada; but, coming into collision with his southern neighbours, he led a large force against Aethelfrith, king of the Northumbrians, and was defeated at a place called Degsanstan, probably in Liddesdale.

Aidan, SAINT (b. Ireland—d. Aug. 31, 651, Bamburgh, Northumberland, Eng.; feast day August 31), apostle of Northumbria, monastic founder, first bishop of Lindisfarne, or Holy Island, off the coast of Northumberland.

Aidan was a monk at Iona, an island of the Inner Hebrides, when King Oswald of Northumbria requested that he be made bishop of the newly converted Northumbrians. Consecrated in 635, Aidan settled on Lindisfarne, where he established his church, monastery, and see near the royal stronghold of Bamburgh. Under his direction and that of his successors, Lindisfarne flourished as a leading ecclesiastical centre until the Danish invasions began in 793.

From Lindisfarne, Aidan evangelized northern England. He founded churches, monasteries, and, on Lindisfarne, a school for the training of ministers, among whom were Chad (first bishop of Lichfield), his brother Cedd (who converted the East Saxons), and Eata, abbot of Melrose. The celebrated Anglo-Saxon historian and theologian Bede praised Aidan for his learning, charity, and simplicity of life.

After Oswald's death in 641, Aidan's protector became the succeeding king, Oswin. He died soon after Oswin's martyrdom (Aug. 20, 651).

aide-de-camp (French: "camp assistant"), an officer on the personal staff of a general, admiral, or other high-ranking commander who acts as his confidential secretary in routine matters. On Napoleon's staff such officers were frequently of high military qualifications and acted both as his "eyes" and as interpreters of his mind to subordinate commanders, even on occasion exercising delegated authority. In modern times they are usually of junior rank and their duties largely social. Military, naval, and air force officers, frequently of high rank, who act as aides to chiefs of state, such as kings or presidents, are also called aides-de-camp. In many countries, the word adjutant is used for aide-de-camp and adjutant general for a royal aide-de-camp.

Aidoo, (Christina) Ama Ata (b. 1942, near Saltpond, Gold Coast), poet, playwright, and short-story writer whose work emphasizes the paradoxical nature of the African woman's role today.

Aidoo first published poetry while an honours student at the University of Ghana (B.A. 1964). She won early recognition with a problem play, *The Dilemma of a Ghost* (1964), in which a Ghanaian student returning home brings back his Afro-American wife to the traditional culture and the extended family he now finds restrictive. Their dilemma reflects Aidoo's characteristic concern with the "been-to" (African educated abroad), voiced again in her semi-autobiographical *Our Sister Killjoy; or, Reflections of a Black-Eyed Squint* (1966). Aidoo herself won a fellowship to Stanford University, Stanford, Calif.; returned to teach at Cape Coast; and subsequently accepted various visiting professorships in the United States and Kenya.

No Sweetness Here (1970), a collection of short stories, and *Anowa* (1970), another problem play, are concerned with Western influences on the role of women and on the individual in a communal society. Aidoo denies that Western education, which enables African women to gain secretarial and teaching jobs, actually emancipates them. She exposes exploitation of women who, as unacknowledged heads of households when war or unemployment leaves them husbandless, must support their children alone. A "been-to," single parent, and critic of European superficial trappings, Aidoo mirrored her own conflicts in her fiction. She ridiculed wigs, make-up, cigarettes, diplomas, and British English. She dropped the "Christina" of her name and mixed Akan expressions into her English without explanation.

AIDS (disease): *see* acquired immune deficiency syndrome.

Aigaion Pelagos: *see* Aegean Sea.

aigrette, tuft of long, white heron (usually egret) plumes used as a decorative headdress, or any other ornament resembling such a headdress. Such plumes were highly prized as ornaments in Oriental ceremonial dress. Jewelled aigrettes, at first made in the form of a tuft of plumes, became an adornment for turbans in Turkey, particularly during the Ottoman period (1281–1924).

Jewelled aigrettes were listed in royal collections at the end of the 16th and the beginning of the 17th centuries. During the 18th century, jewelled aigrettes were popular with fashionable European women, who wore them pinned in their hair to hold masses of curls at the back of the head. Diamonds in particular were often used to simulate the original white-plumed headdress.

Aigues-Mortes, town, Gard *département*, Languedoc-Roussillon region, southeastern France, southwest of Nîmes, on the Canal du

Rhône à Sète, with its own 3.5-mi (6-km) canal to the Gulf of Lion. Its name comes from *aquae mortuae,* the "dead waters" of the surrounding saline delta marshland. Built by Louis IX as the embarkation port for his two crusades (seventh, 1248; eighth, 1270), the little town is enclosed by crenellated and tower-strengthened walls 25 to 30 ft (8 to 9 m) high, which trace a rectangle roughly ½ by ¼ mi (800 by 400 m). The medieval town plan remains intact. Fishing is a source of revenue, although the port long ago silted up. The principal industry is extraction and processing of marsh salt. Pop. (1982) 4,106.

The walled town of Aigues-Mortes, Fr., on the Canal du Rhône à Sète
Club Iris

Aiguillon, Emmanuel-Armand (de Vignerot du Plessis) de Richelieu, duc d' (duke of) (b. July 31, 1720—d. Sept. 1, 1788, Paris), French statesman, whose career illustrates the difficulties of the central government of the *ancien régime* in dealing with the provincial Parlements and estates, the extent to which powerful ministers were at the mercy of court intrigue, and how French diplomacy suffered under Louis XV as a result of secret diplomacy.

In 1750 he succeeded to the peerage duchy of Aiguillon and in 1753 was appointed military commander for Brittany, where he was the chief representative in the province of the central government and so incurred the hostility of the Parlement of Rennes and of the provincial estates, which resisted the government's fiscal reforms of 1764–65. He also aroused the personal enmity of L. R. de Caradeuc de La Chalotais (*q.v.*), the powerful *procureur-général* of the Parlement. These quarrels led to his recall in 1766. Aiguillon, however, was a man of great ambition and, after the fall of the Duc de Choiseul, was appointed minister of foreign affairs (June 1771). He was closely associated with the chancellor, René de Maupeou, and with the controller-general, the abbé Joseph-Marie Terray, in the so-called triumvirate, which attempted to destroy the political powers of the Parlements. As foreign minister he was unable to prevent the rapid decline of French influence in central and northern Europe. Though this was partly due to the rising power of Prussia and Russia, he gave no firm direction to French diplomacy and could not save Poland from being partitioned in 1772. His only—dubious—success was the help he gave Gustavus III of Sweden in effecting his coup of 1772. He was dismissed from office on the accession of Louis XVI in 1774.

Aiguisy, Jean Grolier de Servières, vicomte d' (viscount of): *see* Grolier de Servières, Jean.

Aihole (India): *see* Aivalli.

Aiken, city, seat of Aiken County, western South Carolina, U.S., 17½ mi (28 km) northeast of Augusta, Ga. Chartered in 1835 and named for William Aiken, cotton merchant and builder of the Charleston–Hamburg Railroad, it was early a health resort. During the Civil War, Confederate forces of Gen. Joe Wheeler defeated Gen. Hugh J. Kilpatrick's Federal troops in the main street. By the turn of the century Aiken became (and remains) a winter colony for the wealthy, noted for equestrian sports, especially polo. It experienced a boom after 1950 with the building of the Savannah River Atomic Plant, 12 mi south, and has become a focus of regional industrialization (textiles, glass fibre, electrical equipment, kaolin mining). A branch campus of the University of South Carolina was established there in 1961. Also situated in the city is Aiken Technical College (1975). Hopeland Gardens, a 14.2-ac (5.7-ha) public garden on a former estate, is a local attraction. Pop. (1980) 14,978.

Aiken, Conrad (Potter) (b. Aug. 5, 1889, Savannah, Ga., U.S.—d. Aug. 17, 1973, Savannah), poet, short-story writer, novelist, and critic whose works, influenced by early psychoanalytic theory, are concerned largely with man's need for awareness, particularly self-awareness. In his view awareness must be pursued even if it leads to a confrontation with terror, as Aiken himself was confronted by the trauma in his childhood of finding the bodies of his parents after his father had killed his mother and committed suicide. He later wrote of this in his autobiography *Ushant* (1952).

Aiken
Brown Brothers

Educated at private schools and at Harvard, where he was a friend and contemporary of T.S. Eliot (whose poetry was to influence his own), Aiken divided his life almost equally between England and the U.S. until 1947, when he settled in Massachusetts. He played a significant role in introducing American poets to the British.

After three early collections of verse, he wrote, between 1915 and 1920, five "symphonies" in an effort to create poetry that would resemble music in its ability to express several levels of meaning simultaneously. Then came a period of narrative poems, several volumes of lyrics and meditations, and, after World War II, a return to musical form but with richer philosophical and psychological overtones. The best of his poetry is contained in *Collected Poems* (1953), including a long sequence "Preludes to Definition," which some critics consider his masterwork, and the frequently anthologized "Morning Song of Senlin."

Most of his fiction was written in the 1920s and '30s. Generally more successful than his novels of this period were his short stories, notably "Strange Moonlight" from *Bring! Bring!* (1925) and "Silent Snow, Secret Snow" and "Mr. Arcularis" from *Among the Lost People* (1934).

The Short Stories of Conrad Aiken were published in 1950, followed by *A Reviewer's ABC: Collected Criticism from 1916 to the Present* (1958) and *The Collected Novels* (1964).

Aiken, Howard Hathaway (b. March 9, 1900, Hoboken, N.J., U.S.—d. March 14, 1973, St. Louis, Mo.), mathematician who invented the Harvard Mark I, forerunner of the modern electronic digital computer.

Aiken did engineering work while he attended the University of Wisconsin, Madison. After completing his doctorate at Harvard University in 1939, he remained there for a short period to teach before undertaking war work for the U.S. Navy Board of Ordnance.

With three other engineers—Clair D. Lake, B.M. Durfee, and F.E. Hamilton—Aiken began work in 1939 on an automatic calculating machine that could perform any selected sequence of five arithmetical operations (addition, subtraction, multiplication, division, and reference to previous results) without human intervention. The first such machine, the Mark I, was completed by Aiken and his partners in February 1944: 51 feet (15.3 metres) long and 8 feet (2.4 metres) high, it weighed 35 tons (31,500 kilograms) and contained about 500 miles (800 kilometres) of wire and more than 3,000,000 connections. The Mark I was programmed to solve problems by means of a paper tape on which coded instructions were punched. Once so programmed, the calculator could be operated by persons with little training. The Mark I was used by the Navy for work in gunnery, ballistics, and design. Continuing his work, Aiken completed an improved all-electric Mark II in 1947. Recipient of many honours from the United States, France, The Netherlands, Belgium, and Germany, he also contributed numerous articles on electronics, switching theory, and data processing to scholarly journals.

aikido (Japanese: "way of spiritual harmony"), self-defense system that resembles the fighting methods jujitsu and judo in its use

A throw in an aikido match
Ken Brown

of twisting and throwing techniques and in its aim of turning an attacker's strength and momentum against himself. Pressure on vital nerve centres is also used. Aikido was developed to subdue, rather than maim or kill as in jujitsu and karate, but many of its movements can be deadly. Aikido especially emphasizes the importance of achieving complete mental calm and control of one's own body to master an opponent's attack. As in other Oriental martial arts, the development of courtesy and respect is an integral part of aikido training.

The basic skills of aikido originated, probably in Japan, in about the 14th century. In the early 20th century they were systematized in their modern form, through the work of the Japanese martial arts expert Ueshiba Morihei. There are no offensive moves in aikido. As taught by Ueshiba, it was so purely defensive an art that no direct contest between practitioners was possible. Later a student of Ueshiba, Tomiki Kenji, developed a competition style (known as Tomiki aikido) which incorporates aikido techniques. A competitor attempts to score points by swiftly touching an opponent with a rubber or wooden knife, and the other tries to avoid and disarm the attacker. The two alternate in wielding the knife. *See also* martial arts.

aileron, movable part of an airplane wing that is controlled by the pilot and permits him to roll the aircraft around its longitudinal axis, used primarily to bank the aircraft for turning. Ailerons have taken different forms through the years but are usually part of the

Ailerons (arrows) of a jet aircraft
By courtesy of the Boeing Co.

wing's trailing edge, near the tip. Their efficiency in lateral control made obsolete the Wright brothers' system of wing warping.

Ailey, Alvin, Jr. (b. Jan. 5, 1931, Rogers, Texas, U.S.), U.S. dancer, choreographer, and director of the Alvin Ailey American Dance Theater.

Ailey was first exposed to dance through the motion-picture musicals of the 1940s and, later, in classes with Lester Horton. Horton's Dance Theater provided Ailey with his first performance, in 1950. Following Horton's death in 1953, Ailey became director of the company until he moved to New York City in 1954. There he performed in various stage productions and studied acting with Stella Adler and dance with Martha Graham, Hanya Holm, and Charles Weidman, thus forming a diverse base for his future choreography.

In 1958 Ailey produced some concerts using his own works. From these roots his company grew into one of international fame. Ailey's choreography varies in style, but is typified in *Revelations*, an early work. Ailey was honoured with the Springarn Medal (1976), the Mayor's Award of Art and Culture (1977), and the Capezio Dance Award (1979).

Ailly, Pierre d' (b. 1350, Compiègne, Fr.—d. Aug. 9, 1420, Avignon), theologian, cardinal, and advocate of church reform whose chief aim was to heal the Great Schism of the Western Church (1378–1417). He advocated the doctrine of conciliarism—the subordination of the pope to a general council—and in 1381 he suggested convoking such a council in an effort to end the schism.

D'Ailly studied at the College of Navarre of the University of Paris, where he became a doctor of theology (1380). He became master of the college in 1384 and later was made chancellor of the university and the King's confessor and almoner (1389). He displeased the university, however, by supporting the antipope Benedict XIII, who appointed him bishop of Le Puy (1395) and then bishop of Cambrai (1397). He gradually broke with Benedict, who, with the Roman pope Boniface IX, refused to abdicate to heal the schism. D'Ailly then returned to his earler conciliar doctrine, which steadily became more extreme. He played a prominent part in the Council of Pisa (1409), which declared Benedict and the new Roman pope Gregory XII deposed and elected a third, the conciliar pope Alexander V, who was succeeded the following year by John XXIII. John made d'Ailly a cardinal (1411), bishop of Orange, and his legate to Germany (1413). But since the schism persisted, there being now three popes instead of two, d'Ailly favoured calling a new general council, which was convened at Constance (1414–18). He was influential in the decisions of Constance, which called for the abdication of John XXIII, condemned the Hussites (heretical followers of the Bohemian Reformer Jan Hus), supported conciliarism, and accepted a compromise on the roles of the council and the cardinals in order to elect a new pope, Martin V (November 1417). The possibility that d'Ailly might be elected pope was ruled out by a hostile coalition of Italians, Germans, and English. He retired to Avignon, where he was legate for Martin.

D'Ailly was the author of several influential works. Although many of his views on the constitution of the church were later rejected as heretical, particularly inasmuch as they were echoed by Protestant Reformers, they were adopted in his time as the only apparent way of ending the Great Schism. Interested in science, he advocated calendar reform (later effected by Pope Gregory XII) and wrote his *Image of the World,* which supported the idea that the East Indies could be reached by sailing west.

Ailred OF **RIEVAULX, SAINT**: *see* Aelred of Rievaulx, Saint.

AIM: *see* American Indian Movement.

Aimar OF **MONTEIL**, also called AIMAR OF PUY: *see* Adhémar of Monteil.

Aimoin (b. 960—d. 1010), French Benedictine monk whose history of the Franks was highly esteemed in the Middle Ages.

After his arrival at the abbey of Fleury-sur-Loire (between 979 and 985), he wrote about St. Benedict, completing the second and third books of the *Miracula Sancti Benedicti* in 1005 (the first book had been the work of an earlier writer). During this time he also wrote the biography of the abbot Abbon (d. 1004), who suggested that Aimoin compose a history of the Franks. His *Historia Francorum,* or *Libri IV de gestis Francorum,* was compiled from the texts from the Merovingian period, rewritten by Aimoin in better Latin. Later, 12th-century historians expanded and refined his history of the Franks. His lives of Abbon and St. Benedict were historically more valuable. Aimoin's description of Abbon's two trips to Rome, made because of political disagreements between the French king and the church, is one of the many important historical events of the 10th century recounted in his histories.

Aimorés Mountains, Portuguese SERRA DOS AIMORÉS, mountainous region divided between the states of Minas Gerais and Espírito Santo, eastern Brazil, occupying an area of about 3,900 sq mi (10,100 sq km). Mainly a crystalline hill upland, with an average elevation of 3,000 ft (900 m), the mountains are covered with semi-deciduous forest and are crossed by the Rio São Mateus and several smaller streams; the Rio Doce follows their southwestern border closely. Mantena (Gabriel Emílio) is the principal town.

A list of the abbreviations used in the MICROPAEDIA *will be found at the end of this volume*

Ain, *département*, Rhône-Alpes region, eastern France, in the angle between the Rhône and the Saône, and bordering Switzerland (north and east). Covering 2,222 sq mi (5,756 sq km), it is bisected by the Ain River flowing south to the Rhône and roughly separating the fertile Bresse and swampy Dombes lowlands from the Jura scarps (east). The latter are covered with pasture and timber. Bresse is a region of diversified farming and swine and poultry raising; horses and geese are bred in the pool-studded Dombes. The rest of Ain is concerned primarily with stock raising, cheesemaking, forest activities, and small manufacturing (notably textiles and plastics) based in Bourg (*q.v.*; the prefecture), Oyonnax, Bellegarde-sur-Valserine, Nantua, Jujurieux, Tenay, Saint-Rambert-en-Bugey, Trévoux, and Saint-Bernard. Hydropower is supplied by the Ain, Bienne, and Rhône. Other industries include diamond cutting, plastics, and precision machinery. Tourism is important locally. Ain's four *arrondissements* take their names from Bourg, Belley (a bishopric), Nantua, and Gex. Pop. (1982) 418,516.

Ain, al- (United Arab Emirates): *see* ʿAyn, al-.

Aïn Beïda, formerly DAOUD, town, Oum el-Bouaghi *wilāyah* (province, or *département*), Algeria, on a plateau (2,500–3,300 ft [750–1,000 m]) at the eastern edge of the Sétif plains. The plateau, once occupied by a large lake, now contains several shallow, saline lakes, called chotts. Sheltered on the east by wooded hills with the Djebel (mount) Tafrennt (20 mi [32 km] south) trending southwest to Khenchela, Aïn Beïda is in a grain-producing area irrigated by wells and springs.

Roman settlement is evidenced by remains of lead and copper mines in the neighbouring hills and inscriptions on display in the Public Garden. Aïn Beïda was founded as a French military post (two forts, 1848 and 1850) to control the powerful, arabized Harakta Berbers. It is a road and rail junction and trades in agriculture produce. There are saltworks at the Chott Garaet et-Tarf (11 mi southwest) and phosphate deposits nearby. Pop. (1977 prelim.) mun., 44,275.

Ain Jalut, Battle of (1260): *see* ʿAyn Jālūt, Battle of.

Ain River, river, eastern France, flowing 124 mi (200 km) southward from the Jura Plateau through Jura and Ain *départements.* It emerges from its gorge near Pont-d'Ain, having powered several hydroelectric stations (the largest of which is the Barrage de Vouglans), to cross the Dombes to join the Rhône. Its principal affluents include the Bienne and Albarine.

Aïn Salah (Algeria): *see* I-n-Salah.

Aïn Sefra, town, Saïda *wilāyah* (province, or *département*), Algeria, in the Saharan Atlas, 28 mi (45 km) east of the Moroccan border. It lies in a broad valley between Djebel (mount) Aïssa (7,336 ft [2,236 m]) and Djebel Mekter (6,765 ft), on either side of the usually dry Oued (wadi) Aïn Sefra.

Aïn Sefra was founded in 1881 as a French garrison town. The former European quarter, rebuilt after a disastrous flood in 1904, is clustered around the railway station on the north bank of the *oued*. An iron bridge leads to the southern section containing a former French military post and its neo-Moorish barracks. The oldest part of the town, with its traditional walled gardens, lies to the southwest. The market deals in sheep, wool, skins, and salt brought there by nomadic Berbers. Pop. (1977 prelim.) mun., 22,443.

Aïn Temouchent, town, Sidi bel Abbes *wilāyah* (province, or *département*), Algeria, on the right bank of the Oued (stream) Sennêne. It is bounded on the south by the Oued Temouchent, with the Monts (mountains) du Tessala in the background. On the site of the ruined Roman Albula and the later Arab settlement of Ksar ibn Senar, the town was founded in 1851 with the arrival of Spanish immigrants. It lies in a narrow valley and is surrounded by vineyards and orchards planted in fertile basaltic soils. Pop. (1977 prelim.) mun., 41,987.

Ainsworth, Henry (b. 1571, Swanton Morley, Norfolk, Eng.—d. 1622?, Amsterdam), Nonconformist theologian, Hebrew scholar, and a leader of the English Separatist colony in Amsterdam.

At first a Puritan, Ainsworth joined the Separatists who broke entirely with the Church of England. Driven abroad in the persecution of 1593, he settled in Amsterdam. When part of the London church of which Francis Johnson (then in prison) had been pastor was reassembled in Amsterdam, Ainsworth was chosen as its doctor, or teacher. In 1596 he drew up a confession of the church's faith, which he reissued in Latin in 1598. With Johnson, who rejoined the group in 1597, he composed in 1604 *An Apology or Defence of Such True Christians as Are Commonly but Unjustly Called Brownists* (after the Separatist Robert Browne). In 1610 Ainsworth was forced reluctantly to withdraw, with a large part of the church, from Johnson and his followers after a dispute over church government in which Ainsworth argued for congregational autonomy. From 1616 until his death, he devoted himself to writings that utilized his command of Hebrew, publishing the *Annotations* on several Old Testament books.

Ainsworth, William Harrison (b. Feb. 4, 1805, Manchester, Lancashire, Eng.—d. Jan. 3, 1882, Reigate, Surrey), author of popular historical romances that excelled in pageantry, movement, and historical accuracy. His historical novels include *The Tower of London* (1840), *Old St. Paul's, a Tale of the Plague and the Fire of London* (1841), *Windsor Castle: An Historical Romance* (1843), and *The Lancashire Witches* (1849).

William Harrison Ainsworth, detail of a portrait by Daniel Maclise, *c.* 1834; in the National Portrait Gallery, London

By courtesy of the National Portrait Gallery, London

Ainu, people living in Hokkaido, Sakhalin, and the Kuril Islands who are physically unlike their Mongoloid neighbours. The Ainu may be descendants of early Caucasoid peoples who were once widely spread over northern Asia. The original Ainu language, with a number of dialects, has been largely supplanted by Japanese.

Ainu couple in ceremonial dress, Hokkaido Island, Japan

By courtesy of the Consulate General of Japan, New York City

The Ainu formerly lived on all four of the major Japanese islands but were pushed northward over the centuries by the Japanese. Intermarriage and cultural assimilation have made the traditional Ainu virtually extinct. Of the approximately 12,000 persons on Hokkaido who are still considered Ainu, hardly any are purebloods and very few maintain the language and religion. Most of them now resemble the Japanese in physique.

The traditional Ainu were short-statured and brunette, with the most profuse body hair of any known human group. The men wore heavy beards, and the women had moustache-like tattooing around the mouth. They dressed in bark cloth or skin drapes, often decorated with geometric designs. They were hunters, fishermen, and trappers until the Japanese moved into Hokkaido and attempted to settle them in agriculture. Many of them now work in factories or as day labourers.

The traditional religion of the Ainu centred on local forces of nature, which were thought to have souls or spirits. The most important ritual in the Ainu religion involved the sacrifice of a bear.

air, mixture of gases comprising the Earth's atmosphere. The mixture contains a group of gases of nearly constant concentrations and a group with concentrations that are variable in both space and time. The atmospheric gases of steady concentration (and their proportions in percentage by volume) are as follows:

nitrogen (N_2)	78.084
oxygen (O_2)	20.946
argon (Ar)	0.934
neon (Ne)	0.0018
helium (He)	0.000524
methane (CH_4)	0.0002
krypton (Kr)	0.000114
hydrogen (H_2)	0.00005
nitrous oxide (N_2O)	0.00005
xenon (Xe)	0.0000087

The uniformity of composition is maintained by mixing associated with atmospheric motions; but above a height of about 90 kilometres (55 miles), diffusional processes become more important than mixing, and the lighter gases (hydrogen and helium, in particular) are more abundant above that level.

Of the gases present in variable concentrations, water vapour, ozone, carbon dioxide, sulfur dioxide, and nitrogen dioxide are of principal importance. The typical concentration ranges of these gases (in percentage by volume) are as follows:

water vapour (H_2O)	0 to 7
carbon dioxide (CO_2)	0.01 to 0.1 (average about 0.032)
ozone (O_3)	0 to 0.01
sulfur dioxide (SO_2)	0 to 0.0001
nitrogen dioxide (NO_2)	0 to 0.000002

Although present in relatively small amounts, these variable constituents may be extremely important for maintaining life on the surface of the Earth. Water vapour is the source for all forms of precipitation and, in addition, is an important absorber and emitter of infrared radiation. Similarly, carbon dioxide, besides being involved in the process of photosynthesis, is also an important absorber and emitter of infrared radiation. Ozone, present primarily in the region 10 to 50 kilometres (6 to 30 miles) above the Earth's surface, is an effective absorber of ultraviolet radiation from the Sun and effectively shields the Earth from all radiation of wavelengths less than 3,000 angstroms.

air (music): *see* ayre.

air bladder (fish): *see* swim bladder.

air brake, either of two kinds of braking systems. The first, used by railroad trains, trucks, and buses, operates by a piston driven by compressed air from reservoirs connected to brake cylinders. When air pressure in the brake pipe is reduced, air is automatically admitted into the brake cylinder. The first practical air brake for railroads was invented by George Westinghouse (*q.v.*) in the 1860s.

The term is also used to refer to the braking system used by aircraft and race cars. This brake consists of a flap or surface that can be mechanically projected into the airstream to increase the resistance of the vehicle to air and lower its speed.

Air Canada, airline established by act of the Canadian Parliament in the Trans-Canada Air Lines Act of April 10, 1937. Known for almost 28 years as Trans-Canada Air Lines, it assumed its current name on Jan. 1, 1965. All issued capital stock is owned by the Canadian National Railway Co. Air Canada's headquarters are in Montreal.

Initially flying a scheduled route between Vancouver, B.C., and Seattle, Wash., it so expanded its services that by 1980 it was reaching more than 60 communities throughout Canada and points in the United States, Bermuda, the Caribbean, the United Kingdom, and continental Europe. In 1966 it became the first North American airline to serve Moscow.

Venturex Limited, a wholly owned affiliate, operates charters and group-reception services. A subsidiary, Canac Consultants Limited, sells management and advisory services relating to air and surface transportation, hotels, and telecommunications. Air Canada owns an interest in Air Jamaica Limited, and in 1979 bought controlling interest in Nordair Ltd.

air-conditioning, the control of temperature, humidity, purity, and motion of air in an enclosed space, independent of outside conditions.

A brief treatment of air-conditioning follows. For full treatment, *see* MACROPAEDIA: Building Construction.

An early method of cooling air as practiced

in India was to hang wet grass mats over windows where they cooled incoming air by evaporation. Modern air-conditioning had its beginnings in the 19th-century textile industry, in which atomized sprays of water were used for simultaneous humidification and cooling.

In the early 20th century, Willis Carrier of Buffalo, N.Y., devised the "dew point control," an air-conditioning unit based on the principle that cooled air reaches saturation and loses moisture through condensation. Subsequent development of refrigerants in the early 1920s enabled the manufacture of light and efficient equipment, and in 1922 the first unit made expressly for human comfort was used in a motion-picture theatre. In the next decade, small air-conditioning units were used in railroad cars, and after World War II, the development of highly efficient refrigerants known as Freons (carbon compounds containing fluorine and chlorine or bromine) made air-conditioning a common phenomenon.

In a simple air conditioner, the refrigerant, in a volatile liquid form, is passed through a set of evaporator coils across which air inside the room is passed. The refrigerant evaporates and, in the process, absorbs the heat contained in the air. When the cooled air reaches its saturation point, its moisture content condenses on fins placed over the coils. The water runs down the fins and drains. The cooled and dehumidified air is returned into the room by means of a blower.

In the meantime the vaporized refrigerant passes into a compressor where it is pressurized and forced through condenser coils, which are in contact with outside air. Under these conditions the refrigerant condenses back into a liquid form and gives off the heat it absorbed inside. This heated air is expelled to the outside, and the liquid recirculates to the evaporator coils to continue the cooling process. In some units the two sets of coils can reverse functions so that in winter, the inside coils condense the refrigerant and heat rather than cool the room. Such a unit is known as a heat pump.

Alternate systems of cooling include the use of chilled water. Water may be cooled by refrigerant at a central location and run through coils at other places. In some large factories a version of the earlier air-washer systems is still used to avoid the massive amount of coils needed otherwise. Water may be sprayed over glass fibres and air blown through it. Dehumidification is achieved in some systems by passing the air through silica gel which absorbs the moisture, and in others, liquid absorbents cause dehydration. A phenomenon noted by French physicist J.-C.-A. Peltier in the early 19th century involves materials that conduct electricity but little heat; current passed through them causes a cooling effect.

The design of air-conditioning systems takes many circumstances into consideration. A self-contained unit, described above, serves a space directly. More complex systems, as in tall buildings, use ducts to deliver cooled air. In the induction system, air is cooled once at a central plant and then conveyed to individual units, where water is used to adjust the air temperature according to such variables as sunlight exposure and shade. In the dual-duct system, warm air and cool air travel through separate ducts and are mixed to reach a desired temperature. A simpler way to control temperature is to regulate the amount of cold air supplied, cutting it off once a desired temperature is reached.

Distribution of air is a concern because direct exposure to the cool air may cause discomfort. In some cases, cooled air needs to be slightly reheated before it is blown back into a room. One popular method of distribution is the ceiling diffuser, from which air is blown out along the ceiling level and allowed to settle down. The linear diffuser brings air through a plenum box or duct with a rectangular opening; louvers divert the down-flowing air. Other units are circular, and their fins radiate the air. Some ceilings are perforated to allow passage of cool air, and other ceilings are simply cooled so that basic ventilation can circulate the cool air.

air-cushion machine, also called GROUND-EFFECT MACHINE, or HOVERCRAFT, vehicle that operates on land or water with its weight supported by air pressure created between the craft and the ground surface. There are two classes of air-cushion machines: those that generate their own pressure differential irrespective of forward speed, called aerostatic craft (sometimes denoted by the acronym ACV, for air-cushion vehicle), and those that require forward speed before the pressure differential can be achieved, called aerodynamic ground-effect machines (GEM's).

A brief treatment of air-cushion machines follows. For full treatment, *see* MACROPAEDIA: Transportation.

Sir John Thornycroft of Britain was perhaps the first to conceive of an air-cushion vehicle. In the 1870s he theorized that if a ship had a plenum chamber (essentially an empty box, open at the bottom) for a hull and if that plenum chamber were pumped full of air, the ship would rise out of the water and move faster, since there would be reduced drag. He built models to test his idea and in 1877 took out a patent. Thornycroft discovered a problem with his concept, however, that for several decades hindered the development of a successful craft: how to keep the air cushion from escaping from under the craft.

It is generally agreed that in the 1950s Christopher Cockerell, also of Britain, was the first to devise a method of containing the air cushion. Instead of having a plenum chamber for a hull, Cockerell designed a craft with a slot running around the entire circumference of its bottom from which air could be jetted. The peripheral jets used to pump the air were angled inward slightly, so that the jetted air would mass under the craft and lift it. It was theorized that the force of these jets would create a curtain of air that would keep the air cushion from escaping.

In 1959 the world's first practical air-cushion vehicle, the SR.N1, was launched. This first model was able to carry only three passengers at relatively slow speeds and only over calm water or even ground. It differed from Cockerell's original plans in one major respect: it was found that force of the peripheral jets was not enough to contain the air-cushion, and so a rubberized "skirt" was suspended around the craft's perimeter. The special advantage of the skirt was that it helped to maintain the air cushion over uneven ground or in choppy water.

The skirt is one of the five main components of an air-cushion vehicle, the other four being the hull, engine, lift system, and propulsion system. In construction of the hull aluminum skin is welded onto frames, also made of aluminum. The hull supports the gas turbine engine, which usually powers both the lift and propulsion systems. Proportionately far more of the engine's power is used to lift the vehicle than to propel it. For lift, high-speed centrifugal fans are used to drive the air through the jets under the craft. A modified aircraft propeller is used for propulsion. Situated at the rear of the craft, the propeller is often mounted on a pylon that can swivel to give the pilot greater control in manoeuvring. Further directional control is provided by rudderlike fins at the rear of the craft. Control of these vehicles is difficult because of the air cushion, the depth of which is roughly one-tenth of the longest horizontal dimension of the craft. This precludes their use on highways.

Of the principal components, the skirt has perhaps gone through the greatest number of developments since the SR.N1 was launched. Originally the skirt hung like a curtain around the edge of the craft and was made of rubberized material that quickly wore out from friction with the surface (water or land) during high-speed travel. Skirts are now made of highly durable nylon and plastic, and instead of having the appearance of a curtain, the skirts, known as bag skirts, resemble a thick tube around the craft's edge. Air is jetted from holes along the inside of the inflated bag skirt under the craft to form the air cushion. Bag skirts also provide a means of support for the vehicle when it is at rest. Attached to the bottom edge of the bag skirt is a secondary skirt made of fingerlike segments that protect the bag skirt from friction damage.

In the early 1960s it was thought that air-cushion machines would ply the world's oceans at high speeds, or open up the Earth's desert and arctic areas. As the problems of skirt design and engine maintenance (gas turbines are easily clogged and fouled by saltwater spray) arose, the early optimism faded. Although research and development of various craft were being conducted in several nations in the late 20th century, especially for military applications, Britain was the only country in which there was large-scale production. The British built successively larger and faster vehicles and pioneered their commercial use as ferries across the English Channel. The Hovercrafts in use over that route travel at speeds of about 60 knots (about 70 miles per hour) and can carry some 420 passengers and 60 vehicles.

air de cour (French: "court air"), genre of French solo or part-song predominant from the late 16th century through the 17th century. It originated in arrangements, for voice and lute, of popular chansons (secular part-songs) written in a light chordal style. Such arrangements were originally known as *vau-* (or *voix-*) *de-villes,* the name *air de cour* becoming common after its use in 1571 in a collection by Adrian Le Roy and Robert Ballard. Other notable early collections were published by Pierre Attaignant and Pierre Phalèse; Antoine Boesset, Jean de Cambefort, and Michel Lambert were among the composers included.

Early collections drew heavily on chanson arrangements, but new pieces were also composed explicitly as accompanied solo song. Typically, the *air de cour* was a strophic song (the same music for all stanzas) written for one or two voices and lute or harpsichord or for four or five unaccompanied voices. There were two repeated sections, and often a refrain; singers often embellished the melody on the repetitions. The texts were usually love poems in stylized language, sometimes in *vers mesuré* (quantitative verse written in imitation of the poetry of classical antiquity), but they also included drinking songs, religious feats, and other subject matter. *Musique mesurée,* a short-lived musical style that reflected the metre of *vers mesuré* in the duration of the musical notes, left its mark on the *air de cour* in a tendency to use irregular rhythmic patterns. *See also* ayre.

air embolism, also called GAS EMBOLISM, blockage of an artery or vein by an air bubble. Air can be introduced into the blood vessels during surgery or traumatic accidents. One type of traumatic embolization occurs when lung tissue is ruptured; bubbles of air pass from the alveoli (air sacs) of the lungs into nearby capillaries and veins. The air bubbles are then carried into the heart, where, if trapped, they can cause myocardial infarction, the destruction of tissue in the heart muscle; usually, however, the air rises to the brain. The consequent blockage of vessels carrying blood to the brain starves this tissue of its vital blood supply. Nervous tissue becomes irreversibly damaged after about five minutes of oxygen and nutritional starvation; convulsions, unconsciousness, respiratory difficulties, and death may ensue.

Air embolism is one of the most common hazards of underwater diving while breathing compressed air. *See also* mediastinal emphysema; decompression sickness.

air force, one of the armed services of a state analogous to or part of the military and naval services and having the primary missions of gaining control of the air, interdicting the enemy lines of communication and supply, supporting surface forces (as by bombing and strafing), and accomplishing strategic bombing objectives.

A brief treatment of air forces follows. For full treatment, *see* MACROPAEDIA: War, The Theory and Conduct of; War, The Technology of.

The dawn of military aviation occurred at the end of the 18th century when Montgolfier balloons first began to appear and when Sir George Cayley began to achieve some success with model gliders. A balloon school was organized in the first days of the wars of the French Revolution, and the victory of the French at Fleurus in 1794 has been attributed largely to the advantages they enjoyed from balloon reconnaissance. During the siege of 1849 the Austrians employed unmanned balloons to drop bombs on Venice. During the U.S. Civil War, Thaddeus Lowe and others used balloons to provide observation and intelligence of Confederate movements. In 1892 a balloon section was established in the U.S. Signal Corps and a rather feeble attempt was made to use a balloon at San Juan Hill during the Spanish-American War of 1898. In the meantime, however, the British, under the leadership of Col. Robert Baden-Powell, had employed balloons in colonial operations in Bechuanaland and Suakim in 1885 and again during the South African (Boer) War in 1899–1902. The French had also used balloons to take military leaders and messages out of Paris during the siege by the Germans of 1870.

By the end of the 19th century two lines of development were about to bear fruit, owing to the invention of the internal-combustion engine and of the radio. Ferdinand von Zeppelin, the German cavalryman who had observed the American Civil War, was about to fly his rigid airships successfully, and the Wright brothers in the United States were almost ready to make their vital contribution by achieving successful powered flight. Military interest in aviation was stimulated by both the successful Zeppelin flights and those of the Wright brothers and by the aviation meeting at Reims, Fr., in August 1909. Thereafter, developments were fairly rapid, and by World War I, despite the doubts of many older officers, nascent air arms existed in the British, French, German, Russian, and Italian armed forces. The Italians, in fact, had already made use of airships in a tactical role in operations in North Africa.

World War I saw the rapid technological development of the airplane. There were a number of spectacular achievements, such as the German bombing of London, but most of the war in the air was limited to tactical operations over the Western Front. Despite the emphasis placed on fighters and outstanding fighter pilots, much of the really important work was done by reconnaissance machines until late in the war.

By World War II technological developments, together with a greater appreciation of aircraft by military leaders, resulted in large-scale use of aircraft by the major belligerents. Air forces were used in tactical roles in support of the armies, including airborne assaults. Land-based aircraft were used to attack both convoys and submarines, while naval tactical aircraft engaged in both offensive and defensive work. In addition, the air arms undertook a primary role in the gathering of photographic intelligence and in testing the prewar concepts of strategic bombing.

In 1944 the arrival of combat jet aircraft and of ballistic missiles foreshadowed postwar developments which in the next decade of Cold War led directly to the exploration of space as well as to the annihilation of distance as a sufficient form of security from attack. Jet aircraft were used extensively in a continuing series of limited wars from Korea in 1950–53 to Vietnam in the 1960s and '70s. Despite the rapid transition from piston engines, most air forces retained transport and even strike aircraft fitted with the piston-engine type of propulsion, while at the same time devoting considerable research and development funds to helicopters and to vertical (VTOL) or short (STOL) take-off-and-landing types.

Air Force, United States: *see* United States Air Force, The.

air force academy: *see* military, naval, and air academies.

Air France, in full COMPAGNIE NATIONALE AIR FRANCE, French international airline originally formed in 1933 and today serving all parts of the globe. With British Airways, it was the first to fly the supersonic Concorde. Headquarters are in Paris.

On May 17, 1933, four airlines—Société Centrale pour l'Exploitation de Lignes Aériennes (founded 1919), Compagnie Internationale de Navigation (1920), Air Union (1923), and Air Orient (1929)—merged and negotiated with the French government to form a national system. A few months later, on August 30, with the support of the government, the combine merged with another line, Compagnie Générale Aéropostale (founded 1919), to form Air France, which in the years before World War II developed one of the most extensive networks in Europe. Nearly devasted by the war, the company resumed Paris–London service on Oct. 11, 1945. The following year, it reorganized, and on June 16, 1948, a new Compagnie Nationale Air France was incorporated by act of Parliament (70 percent of the new company would be owned by the French government).

The first Air France transatlantic flight, from Paris to New York, was inaugurated on June 25, 1946. Routes expanded in the coming decades so that by the 1980s the airline was servicing more than 150 cities in more than 70 countries. In 1976 it inaugurated Concorde flights, initially from Paris to Rio de Janeiro (January 21); in 1982 that route and others had to be cut owing to their unprofitability, leaving the Paris–New York flight as its sole route.

air gun, weapon based on the principle of the primitive blowgun that shoots bullets, pellets, or darts by expansion of compressed air.

Most modern air guns are inexpensive BB guns (named for the size of the shot fired). The best of these develop about half the muzzle velocity of light firearms, are accurate enough for marksmanship training at ranges up to 100 ft (30 m), and can kill small game. Darts with tranquillizing drugs may be fired to immobilize animals for handling or capture. An air gun projectile seldom carries beyond 300 ft (92 m).

Early weapons had a reservoir of compressed air which, when suddenly released by a trigger, projected a single bullet or charge of shot with limited range and accuracy. During the 16th century a spring was substituted for the reservoir. When the trigger released the spring, the latter actuated a piston that compressed air that in turn drove the missile through the bore or barrel of the gun. This is the principle used in most air "rifles" and it can also be used in air pistols.

Later weapons were constructed on the older principle of a reservoir, but these use cylinders of compressed gas, usually carbon dioxide. A single cylinder will give a number of shots before replacement is necessary; gas guns are comparable in power and accuracy to air guns.

Air-India, airline founded in 1932 (as Tata Airlines) and now an Indian government-owned international airline serving southern and east Asia, the Middle East, Europe, Africa, Australia, and New York. Headquarters are in Bombay.

The first scheduled service was inaugurated in 1932 by J.R.D. Tata, flying mail and passengers between Karāchi, Ahmadābād, Bombay, Bellary, and Madras. By 1939 routes had been extended to Trivandrum, Delhi, Colombo, Lahore, and intermediate points. After World War II, in 1946, Tata Airlines was converted into a public company and renamed Air-India Limited. Two years later, to inaugurate international services between Bombay and Cairo, Geneva, and London, Air-India International Limited was formed.

In 1953 India nationalized all Indian airlines, creating two corporations—one for domestic service called Indian Airlines Corporation (merging Air-India Limited with six lesser lines) and one for international service, Air-India International Corporation. The latter's name was abbreviated to Air-India in 1962. In the following decades, international routes were greatly extended to all continents except South America.

air law, the law governing the use of the airspace and occurrences therein. Airspace is understood as the area stretching from the ground to outer space. Although radio waves, projectiles, and other objects may traverse the airspace, the term air law generally refers only to laws regulating civil aviation and governing airplanes, dirigibles, balloons and other such crafts.

A brief treatment of air law follows. For full treatment, *see* MACROPAEDIA: Transportation Law.

A fundamental principle of international law is that of national sovereignty over airspace, a principle recognized by the Convention Relating to the Regulation of Aerial Navigation (Paris, 1919). That convention was superceded by the Convention of International Civil Aviation (Chicago, 1944), which also recognized that "every state has complete and exclusive sovereignty over the airspace above its territory." The Chicago convention also stated that persons in an aircraft above a state are subject to the laws of that state. The aircraft must also obey the local rules of air and air traffic control, including regulations pertaining to entry, clearance, immigration, passports, customs, health, and documents relating to the aircraft, crew, passengers, and cargo. Furthermore, a state that is a party to the Chicago convention must apply air regulations, including airport and similar fees, to the aircraft of all contracting states without distinction as to nationality. Every state is therefore entitled, by the rules of the Chicago convention, to regulate the transit and traffic of foreign aircraft in its airspace.

Attempts to conclude a similar agreement with respect to traffic rights have been less successful. As a consequence, regulations regarding air traffic are usually determined by bilateral agreements made by states. These agreements regulate the circumstances under which airlines may pick up and set down passengers and cargo in the territory of each nation.

Laws pertaining to airports are also considered a part of air law. In most countries airports are nationally licensed, and unlicensed places can be used for the landing and taking off of aircraft only under restrictive conditions, if at all. In the United States the Civil Aeronautics

Board (CAB) has been charged with the power to make safety regulations, grant licenses, and establish other rules of flight. Parties to the Chicago convention must make airports open to aircraft of other parties on the same basis as they do to their own aircraft.

Laws pertaining to airports also stipulate the mutual responsibilities of nearby landowners and airport operators. Courts have prohibited the establishment or operation of airports where a strong showing of injury to neighbours has been made. The owner of a property adjacent to an airport may be prohibited from using the property to create hazards for air navigation, such as to create structures over a certain height.

Aircraft themselves are subject to the regulations of air law. Aircraft have to be registered in a country, and the Chicago convention stipulated that an aircraft engaged in international navigation is required to have a certificate of airworthiness issued by the state in which it is registered; it also requires that certificates of competency and licenses be issued to pilots and other members of the operating crew.

Air law is also concerned with criminal jurisdiction in airspace. Formerly, when an aircraft flew in the airspace of a foreign nation, the law of that nation was applicable. However, now when outside the airspace of its country, the criminal law of the state of registry is often held to be applicable. This would avoid any problems of determining whose airspace the aircraft was in when the criminal act was committed. An aircraft commander is empowered to protect law and order aboard the aircraft.

Various treaties have also attempted to standardize regulations regarding liability for passengers, cargo, and third parties on the surface. Air law also provides a means to define piracy or acts of violence by the crew, as well as hijacking, known legally as unlawful seizure. It also defines the responsibility of states towards hijacked planes in their territory.

Many international conferences have been convened on various aspects of air law. The chief standing organization regulating air law is the International Civil Aviation Organization, affiliated with the United Nations and headquartered in Montreal.

air lock, device to permit passage between regions of differing atmospheric pressures, most often used between the outside air and working places in which the air is compressed, such as pneumatic caissons and underwater tunnels. The air lock also has been used as a

Air locks for Boston Harbor Tunnel

By courtesy of Robert S. Mayo, C.E. Mayo Tunnel & Mine Equipment, Inc., Lancaster, Pa.

design feature of space vehicles; on March 18, 1965, the Soviet cosmonaut Aleksey Leonov passed through an air lock to become the first man to walk in space.

Sir Thomas Cochrane patented an air lock in 1830 for use in harbour works; its application to bridge foundations was pioneered by Isambard Kingdom Brunel, James Eads, and others; James Henry Greathead used it in tunnelling in the 19th century.

A typical modern air lock consists of a cylinder of steel plate with airtight doors located at both ends, one opening from the outside into the lock, the other from the lock into the compressed-air chamber, together with valves to admit or to exhaust compressed air. One of the doors must always be closed; before the other is opened, the pressure within the air lock must be equalized with that on the opposite side.

Two types of air locks are in general use: the horizontal, for tunnels, in which the doors are hinged on vertical axes; and the vertical, for caissons, in which the door arrangement must make provision for the cable that hoists material from the working chamber to the surface. *Compare* lock.

air mass, large body of air having nearly uniform conditions of temperature and humidity at any given level of altitude. Such a mass has distinct boundaries and may extend hundreds or thousands of miles horizontally and sometimes as high as the stratosphere (about 10 kilometres [6 miles] above the Earth's surface). An air mass forms whenever the atmosphere remains in contact with a large, relatively uniform land or sea surface for a time sufficiently long to acquire the temperature and moisture properties of that surface. The Earth's major air masses all originate in polar or subtropical latitudes. The middle latitudes constitute essentially a zone of modification, interaction, and mixing of the polar and tropical air masses.

Air masses are commonly classified according to four basic source regions. These are continental polar (cold and dry), maritime polar (cool and moist), continental tropical (hot and dry), and maritime tropical (warm and moist).

Continental polar (cP) air usually forms in winter over extensive land areas such as Central Asia, northern Canada, and the Antarctic continent. It is likely to be stable and is characteristically free of condensation forms. When heated or moistened from the ground with strong turbulence, this type of air mass develops limited convective strato-cumulus cloud forms with scattered light snow showers. In summer strong continental heating rapidly modifies the coolness and dryness of the cP air mass as it moves to lower latitudes. Daytime generation of cumulus clouds is the rule, but the upper-level stability of the air mass is usually such as to prevent rain showers.

Maritime polar (mP) air masses develop over the polar areas of both the Northern and the Southern hemispheres. They generally contain considerably more moisture than the cP air masses. As they move inland in middle and high latitudes, heavy precipitation may occur when the air is forced to ascend mountain slopes or is caught up in cyclonic activity (*see* cyclone).

The continental tropical (cT) air mass originates in arid or desert regions in the middle or lower latitudes, principally during the summer season. It is strongly heated in general, but its moisture content is so low that the intense dry convection normally fails to reach the condensation level. Of all the air masses, the cT is most limited in extent and plays the smallest role in world weather.

The maritime tropical (mT) is the most important moisture-bearing and rain-producing air mass throughout the year. In winter it moves poleward and is cooled by the ground surface. Consequently, it is characterized by fog or low stratus or strato-cumulus clouds, with drizzle and poor visibility. A steep lapse rate (*q.v.*) aloft in regions of cyclonic activity ensures the occurrence of heavy frontal and convective rains. In summer the characteristics of the mT air mass over the oceans and in zones of cyclonic activity are basically the same as in winter. Over warm continental areas, however, the air mass is strongly heated so that, instead of fog and low stratus clouds, widely scattered and locally heavy afternoon thunderstorms occur.

Aïr massif, French MASSIF DE L'AÏR, group of granitic mountains rising sharply from the Sahara in central Niger, West Africa. Several of these mountains approach and exceed 6,000 ft (1,800 m), the highest being Mt. Gréboun, 6,378 ft (1,944 m). The mountains are dissected by deep valleys, called *koris*, in which some vegetation permits the pasturage of livestock, owned mainly by Tuaregs. Hot springs are found in the mountains, as are ancient rock carvings. Uranium and other minerals are mined.

air pocket, downdraft encountered by an aircraft in flight. *See* updraft and downdraft.

air power, the extension of military power in the air by means of military aircraft and supporting facilities.

In the 20th century, theories about air power blossomed rapidly as its advocates sought to justify the development of an air force to skeptical officers of the other, older branches of the armed forces. Especially during periods of peace, airmen tended to make claims that, because of technological limitations, they were later unable to substantiate. Thus, air power has generally seemed less effective during wars than the public had been led to believe it would be in prewar years. This was particularly true of strategic bombing before the advent of the atomic bomb in 1945. Tactical air power, however, achieved some notable successes in the German blitzkriegs of 1940 and in the Allied operations in Europe in 1944–45 and the naval operations in the Pacific throughout World War II. By the end of World War II, air power became concentrated in strategic bombing—that is, aerial attack on targets usually well beyond the zones of ground and naval fighting, targets that mainly contain the bases of enemy strength or of his potential military power.

Theories about air power have tended to revolve around the debate over the efficacy of strategic bombing as a method of warfare, particularly the view that bombing can win wars independently of other arms. The classic exponents of this theory were U.S. Brig. Gen. William ("Billy") Mitchell, English Brig. Gen. P.R.C. Groves, and Italian Brig. Gen. Giulio Douhet. With the advent of long-range nuclear missiles a corollary debate has emerged, questioning whether the manned strategic bomber can continue to play an independent role. Apart from the question of strategic air power, however, the tactical role of the air arm—in interdiction (attacks on communication lines), gaining air superiority over the battle zone, attacks on ground installations in support of ground forces, and reconnaissance—has also become a subject of intense debate. Critics have pointed to the wars in Korea and Vietnam as evidence that resolute ground forces can operate effectively even against overwhelming tactical air superiority—as, indeed, German forces did during the greater part of World War II. The brilliant feats of the Israeli air forces in the wars of 1967 and 1973 are cited as evidence on the other side of the argument.

The use of helicopters for close support of U.S. troops in the Korean War and, especially, in the Vietnam War introduced a new aspect of air power: the use of the helicopter as a gun platform as well as for observation and evacuation of wounded. Thereafter, the armed forces of many other countries sought to develop rotor-winged gunships.

air racing, sport of racing airplanes either over a predetermined course or cross-country up to transcontinental limits. Air racing dates back to 1909, when the first international meet was held in at Reims, Fr. Such meets played a large part in the development of airplane design. Various local, national, and international meets have been held since. Formula racing—in imitation of automobile racing as supervised by the Fédération de l'Automobile—in which specific wingspan, undercarriage, airframe weight, stock engine, and brake specifications are predetermined for each class of airplane, with a particular racecourse assigned for each class, originated in the United States in 1969.

Air racing, very popular during the 1920s and 1930s, was largely subsidized by airplane manufacturers interested in demonstrating their wares. Speed and long-distance records were continually being set, and famous trophy races included the Schneider (France), the King's Cup (England), and the Pulitzer, Thompson, and Bendix trophies in the United States. Of these races, only the last two survived after World War II. After World War II, largely because of increased costs, the advent of jets, and the preemption of the best planes by the military, air racing declined in popularity. Formula racing was an attempt to restore air racing to something like its original appeal.

In Formula I racing, the course is as near as possible to 3 miles (4.8 kilometres) in length, with the two longest, or straight sides, a minimum of 1 mi. The course is six-sided, marked by six pylons (30 feet, or 9 metres, high). The winning pilot is the one who finishes first, having completed the required number of laps without penalty by the stewards for not flying outside pylons, flying too low or high, and cutting off or flying too close to other planes.

In racecourse events, each race is normally run by seven or eight planes and two kinds of starts are used: air starts and racehorse starts. In the first, the aircraft take up the race formation while in flight, guided by a pace aircraft. Racehorse starts begin on the ground, the race beginning when the first plane crosses the start line and takes off. Each of the other planes then has 30 seconds to take off or be eliminated. Time trials determine race position in air starts, with the fastest qualifying pilot having choice of position.

In formula racing, pilots must race at least 25 feet (7.5 metres) above the ground, but not higher than 500 ft. *See* Sporting Record: *Air records.*

air sac, any of the air-filled extensions of the breathing apparatus of many animals. Air sacs are found as tiny sacs off the larger breathing tubes (tracheae) of insects, as extensions of the lungs in birds, and as end organs in the lungs of other vertebrates. They serve to increase respiratory efficiency by providing a large surface area for gas exchange. *See also* alveoli, pulmonary.

air–sea interface, boundary between the atmosphere and the ocean waters. The interface is one of the most physically and chemically active of the Earth's environments; consequently, its neighbourhood supports most marine life.

The atmosphere gains much of its heat at the interface in tropical latitudes by back radiation from the heated ocean. In turn, the atmosphere heats the ocean surface in higher latitudes. Atmospheric motion at the interface generates waves and currents. The atmosphere acquires most of its moisture and an additional fund of energy in the form of latent heat from the evaporation of water at the interface. Enormous quantities of oxygen and carbon dioxide are exchanged between the atmosphere and the ocean at the interface; this exchange both aids and benefits from marine life processes.

The impact of climate at the interface controls the salinities and temperatures of surface ocean waters. The density of seawater is determined by these parameters and, in turn, controls to which depths in the ocean the water masses flow. Photosynthesis, the fundamental basis for oceanic life, takes place just below the interface, where the necessary ingredients of solar energy, carbon dioxide, and nutrient seawater salts are all available.

air space, in international law, the space above a particular national territory, treated as belonging to the government controlling the territory. It does not include outer space, which, under the Outer Space Treaty of 1967, is declared to be free and not subject to national appropriation. The treaty, however, did not define the altitude at which outer space begins and air space ends.

air spring, load-carrying component of a suspension system used on machines, automobiles, and buses. A system used on buses consists of an air compressor, an air supply tank, levelling valves, bellows, and connecting piping. Basically, an air spring bellows is a column of air confined within a rubber and fabric container that looks like an automobile tire or two or three tires stacked on top of one another. The levelling valves admit additional air to the bellows to maintain vehicle height when the load is increased or to vent excess air from the bellows when the vehicle rises because of unloading. The vehicle thus remains at a fixed height regardless of load. While an air spring is flexible under normal loads, it becomes progressively stiffer when compressed under an increased load. Air suspension was introduced on some luxury cars in the late 1950s, but it was dropped after several model years. Recently, new levelling systems have been developed for passenger cars, including air-adjustable rear shock absorbers; one new air spring system operates without an air compressor.

air supremacy fighter, also called AIR SUPERIORITY FIGHTER, in military aviation, a fighter aircraft (*q.v.*) specially designed for long range, manoeuvrability, and firepower.

air-traffic control, the supervision of the movements of all aircraft, both in the air and on the ground, in the vicinity of an airport. *See* traffic control.

Airborne Warning and Control System (military technology): *see* AWACS.

aircraft carrier, naval vessel from which airplanes may take off and on which they may land. As early as November 1910, a U.S. civilian pilot, Eugene Ely, flew a plane off a specially built platform on the deck of the U.S. cruiser "Birmingham" at Hampton Roads, Va. On Jan. 18, 1911, in San Francisco Bay, Ely landed on a platform built on the quarter-deck of the battleship "Pennsylvania," using wires attached to sandbags on the platform as arresting gear; he then took off from the same ship.

Aircraft carrier USS "John F. Kennedy"
By courtesy of the U.S. Navy

The British Navy also experimented with the airplane; during World War I it developed the first true carrier with an unobstructed flight deck, the HMS "Argus," built on a converted merchant-ship hull. The war ended before the "Argus" could be put into action, but the U.S. and Japanese navies quickly followed the British example. The first U.S. carrier, a converted collier renamed the USS "Langley," joined the fleet in March 1922. A Japanese carrier, the "Hosyo," which entered service in December 1922, was the first carrier designed as such from the keel up.

Fundamentally, the carrier is an airfield at sea with many special features necessitated by limitations in size and the medium in which it operates. To facilitate short takeoffs and landings, airspeeds over the deck are increased by turning the ship into the wind. Catapults flush with the flight deck assist in launching aircraft; for landing, aircraft are fitted with retractable hooks that engage transverse wires on the deck, braking them to a quick stop.

The control centres of a carrier are situated in the superstructure (the "island"), at one side of the flight deck. Aircraft landings are guided by hand signals from the deck.

Carriers were first used in combat during the early stages of World War II. The Japanese attack on Pearl Harbor by carrier-based planes on Dec. 7, 1941, dramatically demonstrated the potential of the aircraft carrier, which thereafter was the dominant combat vessel of the war. The carrier played leading roles in the major sea battles of the Pacific theatre, such as Midway Island, Coral Sea, and Leyte Gulf.

Carriers built after the war were larger and had armoured flight decks. Jet aircraft posed serious problems because of their greater weight, slower acceleration, higher landing speeds, and greater fuel consumption. Three British innovations contributed toward solution of these problems: a steam-powered catapult, an angled, or canted, flight deck, and a mirror landing-signal system.

On Sept. 24, 1960, the first nuclear-powered carrier, the "Enterprise" (*q.v.*), was launched by the United States. It had no need for the fuel bunkers, smokestacks, and ducts for the elimination of exhaust gases that had occupied space in previous carriers.

Subsequent design modifications produced such variations as the light carrier, equipped with large amounts of electronic gear for the detection of submarines, and the helicopter carrier, for amphibious assault. Another development was the substitution of missile armament for much of the former anti-aircraft firepower. Carriers with combined capabilities are classified as multipurpose carriers.

Airedale terrier, the largest of the terriers, probably descended from the otterhound and an extinct broken-haired dog, the black-and-tan Old English terrier. The Airedale stands about 23 inches (58 centimetres) and usually weighs from 40 to 50 pounds (18 to 23 kilograms). It has a boxy appearance, with a long, squared muzzle; in profile, the line of the forehead extends straight to the nose. Its coat is dense and wiry, with a black saddle and with tan legs, muzzle, and underparts. Intelligent and courageous, powerful and af-

Airedale terrier
Walter Chandoha

fectionate, though reserved with strangers, it has been used as a wartime dispatch carrier, police dog, guard, and big-game hunter. It is nicknamed the "king of the terriers."

airfield: *see* airport.

airfoil, also spelled AEROFOIL, shaped surface, such as an airplane wing, tail, or propeller blade, that produces lift and drag when moved through the air. An airfoil produces a lifting force that acts at right angles to the airstream and a dragging force that acts in the same direction as the airstream.

High-speed aircraft usually employ low-drag, low-lift airfoils that are thin and streamlined. Slow aircraft that carry heavy loads use thicker airfoils with high drag and high lift.

airframe, basic structure of an airplane or spacecraft excluding its power plant and instrumentation; its principal components thus include the wings, fuselage, tail assembly, and landing gear. The airframe is designed to withstand all aerodynamic forces as well as the stresses imposed by the weight of the fuel, crew, and payload.

Most airframes of early airplanes consisted of a fuselage of truss design constructed of narrow hardwood boards or steel tubing and braced with wires. This basic framework supported the wing structure, which was comprised of spars with ribbing. Both the fuselage and wings were covered by a skin of cotton fabric. Airframe construction was radically improved during the 1930s. The aerodynamically contoured fuselage shell characteristic of all modern aircraft was introduced at this time, as was the thin, slightly curved wing structure. Also, high-strength, lightweight metals (chiefly aluminum alloys, magnesium, and some stainless steel and titanium) replaced wood and fabric throughout the airframe.

airglow, faint luminescence of the Earth's upper atmosphere. Most of the airglow emanates from the region about 80 to 120 kilometres (50 to 75 miles) above the surface of the Earth. Unlike the aurora (*q.v.*), airglow does not exhibit structures such as arcs and is emitted from the entire sky at all latitudes at all times. The nocturnal phenomena is called nightglow. Dayglow and twilight glow are analogous terms.

Observations from the Earth's surface and data from rockets and satellites indicate that much of the energy emitted during twilight and nighttime hours results from reactions involving ion–electron recombination (*e.g.,* the reuniting of free electrons with positive oxygen ions in the ionosphere). In the daytime, the processes of chemiluminescence and resonance scattering from sodium, atomic oxygen, nitrogen, and nitric oxide seem to contribute to airglow. Moreover, interactions between highly energetic charged particles from deep space (*i.e.,* primary cosmic rays) and neutral atoms and molecules of the upper atmosphere may play a role in both the nocturnal and daytime phenomena.

Airlangga (Indonesian ruler): *see* Erlangga.

airmail, letters and parcels transported by airplanes. Airmail service was initiated in 1911 in England between Hendon and Windsor, to celebrate the coronation of George V. Service was irregular, however, and only 21 trips were made. Continuous regular air transport of letters between London and Paris was established in 1919 and a similar service for parcels in 1921. The England–India service, which began in 1929, was the first step in extending airmail service from the United Kingdom to the rest of the British Empire. During the 1930s the United Kingdom Post Office introduced the so-called all up system in which first-class mail was sent by air at normal postage rates whenever it would thereby secure earlier delivery.

Airmail service in the United States was begun on May 15, 1918, by the Post Office Department (now the U.S. Postal Service) in cooperation with the War Department, which furnished the planes and the pilots; the mails were first flown between Washington, D.C., and New York City. The first transcontinental, night airmail flight began at San Francisco on Feb. 22, 1921, and ended at Hazelhurst Field on Long Island, N.Y., 33 hours and 21 minutes later. In 1935 transpacific airmail service was inaugurated, with letters being flown from San Francisco to the Philippine Islands by way of Hawaii, Midway, Wake, and Guam. Transatlantic airmail service began on May 20, 1939, from New York City via Bermuda and Portugal to Marseille. In 1953 the Post Office Department initiated on an experimental basis the carrying of regular surface mail by air when space was available between New York City, Chicago, and Washington, D.C., at no extra charge. Since 1975 virtually all first-class mail bound for destinations more than 100 miles (160 kilometres) away has been transported by air. Airmail service for both letters and parcels became available throughout most of the world during the late 1970s.

To make the best use of the Britannica, consult the INDEX *first*

---

airplane, also spelled AEROPLANE, any of a class of fixed-wing aircraft that is heavier than air, propelled by a screw propeller or a high-velocity jet, and supported by the dynamic reaction of the air against its wings. Two kinds of aircraft without fixed wings that are classified as airplanes are the STOL airplane and the VTOL airplane.

A brief treatment of airplanes follows. Articles providing fuller treatment appear in the MACROPAEDIA. For treatment of historical aspects, *see* Transportation; for manufacturing technology, *see* Manufacturing Industries; for military aspects, *see* War, Technology of.

The essential components of an airplane are a wing system to sustain it in flight, tail surfaces to stabilize the wing, movable surfaces (ailerons, elevators, and rudders) to control the attitude of the machine in flight, and a power plant to provide the thrust to push the machine through the air. An enclosed body (fuselage) to house the crew, passengers, and cargo must be provided, as well as controls and instruments for the pilots and navigators. Provision also must be made to support the machine when it is at rest on the ground (or on water) and during takeoff and landing.

Most modern airplanes are monoplanes (*i.e.,* they have only one main supporting surface). They are termed high-wing when the wing is attached at the top of the fuselage, midwing when it extends from or near the centre of fuselage section, and low-wing when the wing structure fastens to the fuselage structure at the bottom. The multiplane with two or more horizontal wing systems, one above the other, connected by a series of struts and wires, has virtually disappeared. The few biplanes still in service are used mainly for sport flying or for agricultural crop dusting.

Monoplanes may be characterized by the planform (top view) of their wings, which may be rectangular, tapered, swept-back, or delta. A so-called variable-geometry concept incorporating adjustable sweepback is a compromise to obtain good high- and low-speed characteristics from the same wing. For takeoff and landing, hinged wing panels are extended at right angles to the fuselage in order to utilize the advantages of long-span and high-aspect ratio. In flight, for maximum speed and manoeuvring, the panels are swung rearward to make (with the tail surfaces) a delta configuration.

The normal location for stabilizers, fins, rudders, and elevators is well behind the wing, mounted on the tapered tail section of the fuselage. The standard arrangement (until the advent of jet engines) was a cruciform assembly, with vertical fins and rudders and horizontal stabilizer and elevators forming a cross, the axis of which was approximately coincident with the fuselage axis. In some large, high-wing airplanes with relatively short, large-diameter fuselages, airflow over the horizontal tail surfaces was disturbed to the extent that control effectiveness under some flight conditions was compromised. Also, in designs in which jet pods were to be mounted at the after end of the fuselage, it was necessary to relocate the horizontal surfaces to keep them clear of the jet blasts. The solution was the so-called T-tail configuration, in which the horizontal surfaces were mounted at the top of the vertical fin structure.

Where three jet engines are used, the fin structure may incorporate the air intake for the centre engine or the entire engine pod. The consequent increase in weight of the tail structure has changed the appearance of many airplanes. To maintain a viable relationship between centre of lift of the wings and centre of gravity of the entire machine, it has been necessary to move the wings aft and to extend the nose section of the fuselage far forward for proper balance.

For small machines, a single engine and propeller combination is usually mounted in the forward end of the fuselage. When two engines are used, they are normally mounted in nacelles joined into leading edges of wings.

In single turbojet trainers or fighters for military use, the engine is usually mounted inside the fuselage behind the pilot's cockpit, with air intakes either in the nose or as scoops along the sides or in the wing roots. The turbine exhausts through an afterburner into a tailpipe, which extends slightly beyond the after end of the fuselage.

For two- or four-engined planes (either piston engine or turbine-propeller combinations or turbojets), the power plants are normally distributed outboard along the wings, either in nacelles projecting from wing and edges or in suspended pods. Jet pods are also attached to the rear of the fuselage, as indicated above. A combination of both systems (wing pods and tail pod) may be employed.

Landing-gear configuration depends on whether the aircraft is designed to operate from land airports or from water surfaces or from both. Pneumatic-tired, wheeled landing gear has been used in most airplanes since the earliest days. Spring-loaded, hydraulically damped shock absorbers take up landing impact loads. Wheel brakes are generally hydraulically operated.

Until the late 1930s the common arrangement called for a pair of wheels well forward of the airplane centre of gravity with a skid, or tail wheel, aft. The airplane rested on the ground in a distinctly nose-up attitude, only becoming parallel to the ground during takeoff and landing. In the late 1930s the undercarriage plan was reversed. For all large aircraft and most small ones, the main wheels were moved aft to a position well behind the aircraft centre of gravity and a nose wheel (steerable) installed well forward. The fuselage remains parallel with the ground at rest, during takeoff run, and on landing.

Airplanes that are designed to operate from water are called either float seaplanes or flying boats, depending on their landing apparatus. In float seaplanes the wheeled landing gear is replaced by two buoyant floats or pontoons. In flying boats the lower part of the fuselage is designed as a boatlike float, and smaller floats are attached to the wings.

For carrier-based planes, landing-gear configurations are similar to those for land-based planes but must be strengthened to take the extra loads imposed by acceleration (from zero to flying speed in some 200 feet [60 metres]) by catapult. Also, fuselages must be modified and reinforced to permit installation of a tail hook to engage arresting gear cables strung crosswise on the deck in the landing area. Another necessary modification for carrier-based airplanes is the folding wing, which makes it possible to accommodate a greater number of machines in limited hangar-deck space and to permit handling on the elevators connecting flight deck and hangar deck.

airport, also called AIR TERMINAL, AERODROME, or AIRFIELD, site and installation for the takeoff and landing of aircraft. Early airports were open, level fields, with adjacent hangars and terminal buildings. Early aircraft, light enough to taxi satisfactorily on ordinary ground, were highly susceptible to wind forces and had to be free to land or take off in any direction. As aircraft grew heavier they needed hardened surfaces for taxiing, but they also were less vulnerable to crosswinds. Modern airports consequently employ runways, long corridors of asphalt or concrete. Originally, three or four were considered necessary, but as the weight of planes continued to increase, this was generally reduced to two, and in at least one major international airport, that of Hong Kong, to one. Length of runways has on the other hand steadily increased; runways of 14,000 feet (4,300 metres) have been built to accommodate four-engined jet aircraft capable of carrying 250 or more passengers. Altitude is a factor in runway length; at a high altitude—for example, at La Paz, Bolivia—the thin air provides less lift for a given speed, so that an aircraft requires a longer run before becoming airborne.

Air-traffic controllers, aided by radar and other electronic navigation devices, direct incoming and outgoing aircraft from airport control towers and control centres located some distance from the airfield. The controllers also direct all aircraft movements on the ground, guiding pilots as they taxi their planes between the loading apron and runway.

Passenger and cargo terminals have grown steadily larger and more complex with the increase in airport size. In some airports special ground transit systems (*e.g.,* monorail) have been installed between parking areas and terminals. Passenger boarding is conducted according to either by the so-called trickle system, in which boarding procedures are stretched out over a period of time, or by the group system, in which all processing is first carried out, and the passengers board in a group. Cargo terminals, where airfreight is loaded, unloaded, and sorted, employ forklift trucks, cargo-cart trains, belt conveyers, and other techniques and machinery.

Lighting is of major importance in an airport, despite development of instrumented landing systems. A revolving green and white beacon has long been the visible mark of an airport. High-intensity approach lights, often running in a straight line beyond the limits of the airport, guide pilots to runways. Amber runway lights are turned on and off as needed by the control tower or by automatic systems. Green threshold lights indicate the ends of the runways, while blue lights mark the taxiways used by aircraft to enter and exit from runways. Red lights are used to mark obstructions, and red flashing lights are used to warn of high obstructions.

Virtually all governments prescribe standards for construction and operation of airports. The International Civil Aviation Organization issues a set of internationally accepted standards covering number, length, and orientation of runways, visual ground aids, and other details.

Airport art, African and Oceanian sculpture and paintings made for sale to tourists. The name was coined by Frank McEwen, founder of the Central African Workshop (*q.v.*) in Salisbury, Rhodesia (now Harare, Zimbabwe). Such objects provide tourists with items that conform to their preconceived notions of African and Oceanian art. Sculptures are smoothly carved and highly polished rather than painted. Usually a wood attractive to Europeans is used—*e.g.,* mahogany and ebony, which traditionally were rarely used. Sometimes traditional forms are used as a basis for Airport art, especially when they are moderately naturalistic; *e.g.,* Ibibio masks of Nigeria have been adapted to hang on a wall. In some parts of Africa, Airport art is characterized by an untraditional "literary" quality. In Tanzania, for example, Maonde refugees from Mozambique founded a flourishing school of sculpture, incorporating some traditional stylistic elements but presenting essentially literary subject matter drawn from traditional folktales. The anonymity of much Airport art is striking: almost identical pieces can be bought at airports and souvenir shops thousands of miles apart. Paintings deriving from the Potopoto school outside Brazzaville, Congo, are available, mass-produced, in most parts of sub-Saharan Africa. Mass production has led to a decline of quality in many parts of Africa.

A Kamba, Mutisya Munge, who served in Tanganyika during World War I, began to carve animals in the manner he had seen among the Zaramo; members of his family copied from him, and they sold their work to settlers. After World War II, which brought foreign soldiers and then a great many tourists, there were hundreds of carvers supplying salad servers or carved antelopes by the thousand. Some of the work is done in the villages and completed by carvers in city workshops. The objects are then exported to curio shops all over the world. Elsewhere, mass production has not brought such a sharp decline in quality. In the 1930s Justus Akeredolu, a Nigerian Yoruba, experimented with carving thorns from the trunk of the silk-cotton tree, using a single thorn, about 3 inches (7.5 centimetres) high, to carve an entire figure with remarkable attention to detail. His former apprentices mass-produce such figures from pre-carved units—legs, arms, heads, trunks—so that complex subjects can be represented on a larger scale. Although the assembled carvings lack the delicacy of the master's work, they present a lively depiction of Yoruba life.

airship, also called DIRIGIBLE, or DIRIGIBLE BALLOON (from French *diriger:* "to steer"), a self-propelled, lighter-than-air craft. The first successful airship was constructed by Henri Giffard of France in 1852. Giffard built a 350-pound (160-kilogram) steam engine capable of developing 3 horsepower, sufficient to turn a large propeller at 110 revolutions per minute. To carry the engine weight he filled a bag 144 feet (44 metres) long with hydrogen and, ascending from the Paris Hippodrome, flew at a speed of 6 miles (10 kilometres) per hour.

The "Hindenburg" landing at Lakehurst, N.J., May 20, 1936

UPI—EB Inc.

In 1872 a German engineer, Paul Haenlein, first used an internal-combustion engine for flight in an airship that used lifting gas from the bag as fuel. Albert and Gaston Tissandier of France successfully powered an airship with an electric motor in 1883. The first rigid airship, with a hull of aluminum sheeting, was built in Germany in 1897. Alberto Santos-Dumont, a Brazilian living in Paris, brought many refinements to airships and set a number of records in the 14 craft he built around the turn of the century. Ferdinand, Graf von Zeppelin, of Germany built large rigid airships, beginning in 1900 and extending through World War I, when a number of zeppelins were used to bomb Paris and London. Airships were also used by the Allies, chiefly for anti-submarine patrol.

In the 1920s and 1930s airship construction continued in Europe and the United States. A British dirigible, the R-34, made a round-trip transatlantic crossing in July 1919. In 1926 an Italian semirigid airship was successfully used by Roald Amundsen, Lincoln Ellsworth, and Gen. Umberto Nobile to explore the North Pole. In 1928 the "Graf Zeppelin" was completed by Zeppelin's successor, Dr. Hugo Eckener, in Germany. Before it was decommissioned nine years later it had made 590 flights, including 144 ocean crossings. In 1936 Germany inaugurated a regular transatlantic passenger service with the dirigible "Hindenburg." Despite these achievements, airships were soon virtually abandoned because of their intrinsic vulnerability to stormy weather. In addition, a succession of disasters—the best known probably being the explosion of the hydrogen-filled "Hindenberg"—coupled with advances in heavier-than-air craft in the 1930s and 1940s made dirigibles commercially obsolete for most applications. Airships, however, can be useful in certain tasks—*e.g.,* transport of very heavy loads, such as rocket launch craft, and oceanographic research.

airspeed indicator, aeronautic instrument that measures the velocity of an aircraft relative to the surrounding air, using the differential in pressure between that of still air (static pressure) and that of moving air displaced by the craft's forward motion (ram pressure); as speed increases, the difference between these pressures increases as well.

Pressures are measured by a pitot tube, a U-shaped apparatus with two openings, one perpendicular to the flow of air past the aircraft and one facing directly into the flow. Mercury or a similar fluid fills the bend in the tube, forming parallel columns balanced by the air pressure on each side. When static and ram pressure are equal, the columns have the same height. As the ram pressure increases, mercury on that side of the tube is pushed back and the columns become imbalanced. The difference between the two columns can be calibrated in appropriate units to indicate the speed; this value, called the indicated airspeed, may be given in knots, miles per hour, or other units.

Since the airspeed indicator is calibrated at standard temperature and pressure, its readings may be in error under conditions of temperature and air density at altitude. Instruments that electronically correct for altitudinal differences and temperature give the true airspeed. In faster aircraft, indicators that measure airspeed relative to the speed of sound, called Machmeters, are sometimes used.

Airy, Sir George Biddell (b. July 27, 1801, Alnwick, Northumberland, Eng.—d. Jan. 2, 1892, Greenwich, London), versatile English scientist and seventh Astronomer Royal (1835–81).

He reorganized the Royal Greenwich Observatory, installing new apparatus and rescuing thousands of observations from oblivion, but his hesitation in acting on the calculations of English astronomer John C. Adams in 1845 somewhat delayed the discovery of Neptune. Airy improved the theory of the orbital motions of Venus and of the Moon, and in 1871 he used a water-filled telescope to test the effect of the Earth's motion on the aberration of light. In 1838 he devised a compass-correction system for the Royal Navy.

Airy in 1827 was the first to attempt to correct astigmatism in the human eye (his own) by use of a cylindrical eyeglass lens. He contributed also, in optics, to the study of interference fringes and to the mathematical theory of rainbows. The Airy disk, the central spot of light in the diffraction pattern of a point light source, is named for him.

In 1854 he measured gravity by swinging the same pendulum at the top and bottom of a deep mine and thus computed the density of the Earth. He was among the first to propose (*c.* 1855) the theory that root structures of lower density must exist under mountains to maintain isostatic equilibrium. Airy was knighted in 1872.

Aisén, also spelled AYSÉN, in full AISÉN DEL GENERAL CARLOS IBÁÑEZ DEL CAMPO, region, southern Chile, bounded on the east by Argentina and on the west by the Pacific Ocean. Created as a province in 1927 and as a region in 1974, Aisén's 43,194-sq-mi- (111,873-sq-km-) territory includes two-thirds of the Chonos Archipelago, the Península de Taitao, and the mainland between the Río Palena and Lago (lake) O'Higgins (formerly Lago San Martín). It is divided into the provinces of Aisén, General Carrera, and Capitán Pratt. In the south and east the Andes Mountains rise from 3,000 to 13,000 ft (1,000 to 4,000 m), appearing as rugged blocks separated by glaciated valleys and fjords. Perennial snowfields cap most elevations above 3,000 ft; glaciers extend into the valleys and, in some cases, to the sea. The rough land at lower elevations is forested, chiefly with broadleaf evergreens. Heavy, all-year rains and uniformly cool temperatures prevail. The rivers of Aisén are among the most turbulent in Chile.

The few Indians who once inhabited this area have all but disappeared, supplanted by emigrants from Chiloé and other parts of Chile who grow potatoes and wheat and raise sheep and cattle. Lumber, lead, zinc, and copper are also produced in the region. Coihaique, the largest town and regional capital, Balmaceda, and Chile Chico are trading centres in the developing interior. The last two have air service to Puerto Montt; the former two are joined by an all-weather road to Puerto Aisén. Pop. (1982 prelim.) 65,478.

ʿĀʾishah, in full ʿĀʾISHAH BINT ABĪ BAKR (b. 614, Mecca, Arabia—d. July 678, Medina), the third and most favoured wife of the Prophet Muḥammad (the founder of Islām), who played a role of some political importance after the Prophet's death. All Muḥammad's marriages had political motivations, and in this case the intention seems to have been to cement ties with ʿĀʾishah's father, Abū Bakr, who was one of Muḥammad's most important supporters. ʿĀʾishah's physical charms, together with the genuine warmth of their relationship, secured her a place in his affections that was not lessened by his subsequent marriages. It is said that in 627 she accompanied the Prophet on an expedition but became separated from the group. When she was later escorted back to Medina by a man who had found her in the desert, Muḥammad's enemies claimed that she had been unfaithful. Muḥammad, who trusted her, had a revelation asserting her innocence and publicly humiliated her accusers. She had no important influence on his political or religious policies while he lived.

When Muḥammad died in 632, ʿĀʾishah was left a childless widow of 18. She remained politically inactive until the time of ʿUthmān (644–656; the third caliph, or titular leader of the Islāmic community), during whose reign she played an important role in fomenting opposition that led to his murder in 656. She led an army against his successor, ʿAlī, but was defeated in the Battle of the Camel. The engagement derived its name from the fierce fighting that centred around the camel upon which ʿĀʾishah was mounted. Captured, she was allowed to live quietly in Medina.

aisle, portion of a church or basilica that parallels or encircles the major sections of the structure, such as the nave, choir, or apse (aisles around the apse are usually called ambulatories). The aisle is often set off by columns or by an arcade.

The name derives from the French for "wing," because in Romanesque architecture the aisles flanked only the nave and were often covered by roofs of lower height, thus forming wings. Although the aisle area may be used for seating, especially in more recent times, it was originally intended as a path to seats or to the front of the church. Today, the word also refers to any passageway that gives access to seating in a church, theatre, or other public structure.

Aisne, *département,* Picardie region, northern France, created from parts of the old provinces of the Île de France, Picardy, and Champagne, and covering an area of 2,845 sq mi (7,369 sq km). Outlying masses of rock, often with steep flanks, occur in much of the region; the Battle of Chemin des Dames (1918) was fought on such terrain. The Aisne River crosses from the east to join the Oise, which has been canalized to include the deep Château-Thierry portion of the Marne Valley.

Soissons on the Aisne River, France
Art Resource—EB Inc.

Well-watered (20–30 in. [500–750 mm] rainfall) and sheltered, Aisne contains rich grainlands in the south and west, with dairying in Thiérache (northeast). World War I battles tore up the forest land. Beet sugar is an important Aisne industry. Gypsum, building stone, and clay are quarried. Saint-Quentin and other towns weave silk, cotton, and wool. Saint-Gobain has made mirrors since the 17th century. The agricultural and industrial centre of northern Aisne is Guise. Laon (the capital), Soissons, Saint-Quentin, and Vervins head *arrondissements* and are, with Château-Thierry and Hirson, the chief towns. The *département* is in the educational division of Douai.

Many architectural monuments were destroyed in World War I, but the medieval churches of Laon, Braine, and Urcel survive, and the basilica of Saint-Quentin was restored. The ruined castle of La Ferté-Milon escaped war damage. Pop. (1982) 533,970.

Aistis, Jonas, also called JONAS KOSSU-ALEKSANDRAVIČIUS, or JONAS KUOSA-ALEKSANDRIŠKIS, pseudonym of JONAS ALEKSANDRAVIČIUS (b. July 7, 1904, Kampiškės, near Kaunas, Lithuania, Russian Empire—d. June 13, 1973, Washington, D.C.), poet whose lyrics are considered among the best in Lithuanian literature and who was the first modern Lithuanian poet to turn to personal expression.

Aistis studied literature at the University of Kaunas and in 1936 went to France on a scholarship to study French literature and philology at the University of Grenoble, receiving his doctorate in 1944. Because of the Soviet occupation, he did not return to Lithuania but went in 1946 to the United States, where, in 1958, he joined the staff of the Library of Congress, Washington, D.C.

Aistis' early collections of verse, written while he was still in Lithuania, contain his finest work; he was awarded the state prize for literature for his fourth collection, *Užgesę chimeros akys* (1937; "The Dead Eyes of the Chimera"). His patriotic verse, written in exile, was not so successful as his earlier work. Three collections of his essays also have been published and he has edited several collections of poetry, among them *Lietuvių poezijos antologija* (1950; "Anthology of Lithuanian Poetry"). *Poezija* (1961; "Poetry") contains his collected poems to that time.

Aitken, John (b. Sept. 18, 1839, Falkirk, Stirlingshire, Scot.—d. Nov. 14, 1919, Falkirk), physicist and meteorologist who, through a series of experiments and observations in which he used apparatus of his own design, elucidated the crucial role that microscopic particles, now called Aitken nuclei, play in the condensation of atmospheric water vapour in clouds and fogs.

Ill health prevented him from holding any official position; he worked instead in the laboratory in his home in Falkirk. The major part of his work was published in the journals of the Royal Society of Edinburgh, of which he was a member.

Aitken, Robert Grant (b. Dec. 31, 1864, Jackson, Calif., U.S.—d. Oct. 29, 1951, Berkeley, Calif.), astronomer who specialized in the study of double stars, of which he discovered more than 3,000.

From 1891 to 1895 Aitken was professor of mathematics and astronomy at the University of the Pacific, Stockton, Calif. In 1895 he joined the staff of Lick Observatory, Mt. Hamilton, Calif., as assistant astronomer, be-

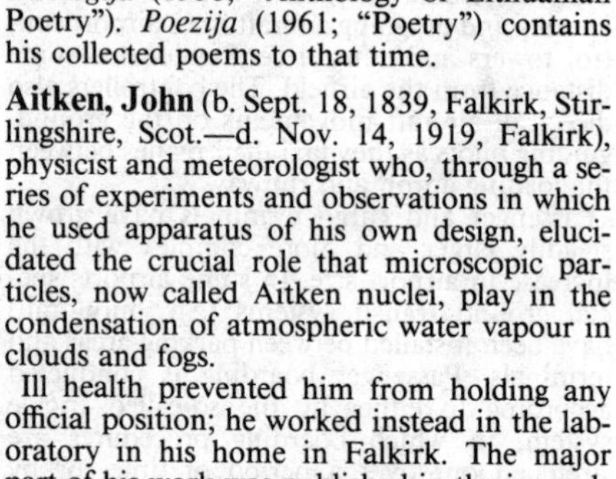

Aitken
By courtesy of the Lick Observatory Archives, Santa Cruz, Calif., and the Niels Bohr Library, Pittsburgh

coming associate director in 1923 and director in 1930; he retired in 1935. For his discoveries he was awarded in 1906 the Lalande Prize by the Académie des Sciences and in 1932 the Gold Medal of the Royal Astronomical Society, London. He published *The Binary Stars* (1918) and *New General Catalogue of Double Stars Within 120° of the North Pole* (1932).

Aitken, William Maxwell: *see* Beaverbrook, (William) Max(well) Aitken, 1st Baron.

Aitmatov, Chingiz (Russian author): *see* Aytmatov, Chingiz.

Aitolia (ancient Greek district): *see* Aetolia.

Aitolía kai Akarnanía (Greece): *see* Aetolia and Acarnania.

AITUC: *see* All-India Trade Union Congress.

Aiun (Western Sahara): *see* El Aaiún.

Aivalli, historically named AIHOLE, town, Belgaum district, Karnātaka (formerly Mysore) state, southwestern India. Aivalli is noted for its Brahmanical cave temples, which contain a series of relief carvings illustrating Purāṇic mythology and legend. Sculptured roofing slabs from Aihole, dating from the early 7th century, are in the Prince of Wales Museum in Bombay.

Aix-en-Provence, city, Bouches-du-Rhône *département,* Provence-Alpes-Côte-d'Azur region, southern France, north of Marseille. Lying on the plain a mile (1.6 km) from the right bank of the Arc River, it is on the crossroads of principal routes to Italy and the Alps. The conquering Roman proconsul, Sextius Calvinus, built a huge entrenched camp called Aquae Sextiae in the valley about 123 BC. In 102 BC, Marius routed the Teutons at the Battle of Aix. The Visigoths, Franks, Lombards, and finally Muslim invaders from Spain successively plundered the town. As the medieval capital of Provence, governed by the counts and dukes of Anjou, Aix flowered as a centre of learning and the arts. Its university, now the Universities of Aix-Marseille, was founded in 1409. In 1486 Provence passed to the French crown, and Aix became the seat of a *parlement.*

North of the tree-lined Cours Mirabeau lies the old town, with Roman ruins and structures of the Middle Ages around the 11th–13th-century archdiocesan Cathédrale Saint-Sauveur; southward is the "new" town, rich in fine 17th- and 18th-century houses, surrounded on all sides by recent urban growth. The hot mineral springs—the most noted is the Thermes Sextius—are still employed medicinally for rheumatic and vascular diseases. Serene, sun-dappled, and fountain-splashed, Aix is an agricultural centre, especially for Provençal olives and almonds from the countryside painted by Cézanne, whose atelier is preserved as one of several city museums. Since the city now functions as a residential suburb of Marseille, industrial development is light but includes food processing and electrical machinery. Pop. (1982) 100,221.

Aix-la-Chapelle (West Germany): *see* Aachen.

Aix-la-Chapelle, Congress of (Oct. 1–Nov. 15, 1818), the first of the four congresses held by Great Britain, Austria, Prussia, Russia, and France to discuss and take common action on European problems following the Napoleonic Wars (1800–15). This congress (held at Aix-la-Chapelle—now Aachen, W.Ger.) was attended by Alexander I of Russia, Francis I of Austria, Frederick William III of Prussia, and their representatives. Great Britain was represented by Viscount Castlereagh and by the Duke of Wellington. Armand-Emmanuel, duc de Richelieu, represented France.

At the first session Richelieu offered to pay most of the war indemnity owed by France to the allies in return for the withdrawal of their armies of occupation by November 30. This offer was accepted. On October 9 a treaty was signed settling the claims against France as a result of the wars. France was admitted to the new Quintuple Alliance as an equal. Although the old Quadruple Alliance of Great Britain, Austria, Prussia, and Russia was secretly renewed in a protocol signed on November 15, this renewal was largely a formality.

The congress also discussed suppression of the slave trade and of the Barbary pirates, but no decision was reached. The status of Jews and many other questions were also considered.

Aix-la-Chapelle, Treaty of (Oct. 18, 1748), treaty negotiated largely by Britain and France, with the other powers following their lead, ending the War of the Austrian Succession (1740–48). The treaty was marked by the mutual restitution of conquests, including the fortress of Louisbourg on Cape Breton Island, Nova Scotia, to France, Madras in India, to England, and the Barrier towns to the Dutch. The right of the Habsburg heiress Maria Theresa to the Austrian lands was guaranteed, but the Habsburgs were seriously weakened by the guarantee to Prussia, not a party to the treaty, of its conquest of Silesia. Both Britain and France were trying to win the friendship of Prussia, now clearly a significant power, for the next war. Maria Theresa gave up to Spain the duchies of Parma, Piacenza, and Guastalla in Italy. The treaty confirmed the right of succession of the House of Hanover both in Great Britain and in Hanover. In the commercial struggle between England and France in the West Indies, Africa, and India, nothing was settled; the treaty was thus no basis for a lasting peace.

Aix-les-Bains, city and Alpine spa, Savoie *département,* Rhône-Alpes region, eastern France, southwest of Geneva. A summer and winter resort with a beach on Lac du Bourget and an aerial cableway up Mt. Revard (5,046 ft [1,538 m]), it is a fashionable Alpine spa maintaining the quiet luxury of the Victorian era. Its sulfur and alkaline springs were exploited by the Romans, to whom they were known as Aquae Gratianae, and are still the basis of modern health resorts. Pop. (1982) 22,331.

Aix-Marseille I, II, and III, Universities of, French UNIVERSITÉS D'AIX-MARSEILLE I, II, ET III, coeducational, state-financed, autonomous institutions of higher learning at Aix-en-Provence and Marseille, founded under France's 1968 Orientation Act, reforming higher education. The institutions developed out of the original University of Provence, founded in 1409 as a *studium generale* by Louis II of Provence and recognized by papal bull in 1413. From the 15th to the 18th century it developed as an institution of classical learning, liberal arts, theology, law, and medicine. It was suppressed during the French Revolution, reestablished in Aix and Marseille, and came to be known as Aix-Marseille.

In 1896 Aix-Marseille became one of 17 self-governing regional universities financed by the state. Under the Orientation Act of 1968, Aix-Marseille was divided into three institutions, each with independent units of teaching and research. The University of Provence (Aix-Marseille I) is the school of languages and letters. It has an observatory and a centre for tele-education. The University of Aix-Marseille (Aix-Marseille II) is the school of medicine and sciences. The University of Law, Economics and Science (Aix-Marseille III) was added in 1973 in a restructuring of Aix-Marseille I and II.

Aiyaíou, Nísoi (Greece): *see* Aegean Islands.

Aiyetoro (Yoruba: Happy City), religious settlement of the Nigerian Holy Apostles' Community established in 1947. The town was founded by a small Yoruba group of the Cherubim and Seraphim society (*see* Aladura) who migrated and built the model settlement on piles on a mudbank in the coastal lagoons 100 miles (160 kilometres) east of Lagos. In the early 1960s up to 2,000 members lived in a communal, non-familial society, under a spiritual leader-ruler, with their own school, nursery, adult education, technical training, post office, electricity, and industries supplying internal needs and soap, shoes, boats, fish, and other products for export.

Though anyone may join, offenders against the strict ethic are sent away. The day opens with worship in the church or the palace courtyard and sometimes ends with a form of communion meal. It is believed by the members that death has been conquered, and those who die will return to the community.

In the last decades of the 20th century the future of Aiyetoro was uncertain. Internal disputes divided the members, and the growth of private enterprise threatened the communal basis of the economy.

Aíyina (Greece): *see* Aegina.

Aizawa Yasushi, also called AIZAWA SEISHISAI (b. 1782, Mito, Hitachi Province, Japan—d. Aug. 27, 1863, Mito), Japanese nationalist thinker whose writings helped provoke the movement that in 1868 overthrew the Tokugawa shogunate and restored power to the emperor.

Aizawa's fief of Mito, one of the branches of the great Tokugawa family, was a center of Confucian learning and loyalty. Thus, the threat to these traditional beliefs posed by growing contact with the West was keenly felt in Mito. Writing in the early 19th century, when Western ships were first beginning to be seen off the Japanese coast, Aizawa argued that the new "barbarians" had to be dealt with firmly and decisively, but that in order to do so Japan had to adopt certain Western military techniques and develop her armaments and defenses. Even so, contact with foreigners should be strictly limited, according to Aizawa, for to encourage trade would undermine the Japanese nation. He realized that the real threat to the country was a weak, apathetic citizenry; strength could be ensured only through promotion of nationalistic sentiment, including loyalty to the emperor as the real sovereign.

According to Aizawa, Japan's natural supremacy and its unique position at the centre of the world resulted from the fact that the Japanese ruling line was directly descended from Amaterasu (the sun goddess), and the basis of morality, which had become confused by the introduction of the false doctrines of Buddhism, was loyalty to the emperor; emperor worship thus provided the basis of later Japanese ultranationalism. Aizawa's book *Shinron* ("New Proposals"), stressing the supremacy of the Japanese nation, remained an influential text of nationalism well into the 20th century.

Aizawl, town, administrative headquarters of Aizawl district, Mizorām union territory, northeastern India. Formerly a subdivisional headquarters, it is at an elevation of about 2,950 ft (900 m) and is the most populous town in the district. In the 1970s Aizawl town was the scene of an armed attack on the government treasury and other offices by members of the Mizo National Front. Aluminum utensils, handloomed textiles, and furniture are manufactured in the town. Electricity is generated by a diesel power station.

Aizawl district, formerly known consecutively as Lushai Hills district and Mizo Hills district, is located in the northern part of the

Mizorām union territory. It has an area of 4,865 sq mi (12,600 sq km) and is bounded by Tripura state on the west, Lunglei district on the south, Assam and Manipur states on the north, and Burma on the east. The region is a part of the Assam–Burma geological province, with north–south aligned, steeply inclined hill ranges. The rapid Dhaleśwarī (Tiwang), Tuivawl, and Sonai (Tuirail) rivers and their tributaries crisscross the region. Timber and bamboo are collected from the dense forests covering the hillsides. The soil cover is generally thin except in the river valleys, where rice, corn (maize), beans, tobacco, cotton, pumpkins, oilseeds, and peanuts (groundnuts) are grown. Poultry raising, hunting, fishing, and animal husbandry supplement agriculture. Handweaving, blacksmithing, carpentry, basketmaking, and hat making are the principal cottage industries. The Mizo Hills tribes inhabiting the region are mostly emigrants from Burma, and most have become Christians. The Border Roads Organization has built many paved roads in the area. Pop. (1981) town, 74,493; district, 340,826.

Aizu-wakamatsu, city, Fukushima Prefecture (*ken*), Honshu, Japan, in the centre of the Aizu basin, surrounded by volcanic mountains. A castle was first built on the site

Tsuruga-jō (14th century, rebuilt in 1965) in Aizu-wakamatsu, Japan
Cosio—Shostal Assoc./EB Inc.

in 1384. Much of the present town dates from 1590, when the castle was rebuilt and named Tsuruga-jō. During the Tokugawa era (1603–1867), Aizu-wakamatsu was an important commercial and manufacturing centre, famous for its lacquer ware. It was held as a fief by a member of the Tokugawa family and was the scene of the last resistance to the Meiji Restoration (1868). During the final battle, the city was razed and the castle destroyed.

In the late 19th century Aizu-wakamatsu became an administrative centre, and its commercial importance was strengthened with the arrival of a railway. Most of its industry continues to be traditional, with small-scale establishments producing lacquer ware, ceramic ware, sake (rice wine), decorative candles, and characteristic little paper oxen (*akabeko*). Larger plants for the production of lacquer ware have been built. Tourists are attracted by the city and the castle (rebuilt in 1965). On Iimori-yama (Mt. Iimori), outside the city, is the cemetery for the samurai of the Byakko-tai (White Tiger Corps), who withstood the Meiji forces. There are also hot springs and maple groves at Higashi-yama (Mt. Higashi), to the southeast. Pop. (1983 est.) 115,894.

Ajaccio, town, capital of Corse-du-Sud *département,* Corse region, France, and Mediterranean port, on the west coast of the island of Corsica. Napoleon's birthplace, Maison Bonaparte, is now a museum, as is a portion of the city hall. The original settlement of Ajax was founded by the Romans 2 mi (3 km) north of the present site, to which the town was removed by the Genoese in 1492. Save for a brief (1553–59) interval, the city did not become French until 1768. From 1793 to 1811, Ajaccio was the capital of Liamone *département* and in 1976 was made capital of Corse-du-Sud *département,* one of the two into which the island was divided. Though its economy is largely supported by tourism, the town also has some light industry and shipping. It is the seat of a prefect and a bishopric. Regular air and steamer services connect Ajaccio to the French mainland. Pop. (1982) 48,324.

Ajaccio, on the Mediterranean coast of western Corsica
Editions "La Cigogne"—Hachette

Ajami language: *see* Mozarabic language.

Ajanta Caves, Buddhist rock-cut cave temples and monasteries, near Ajanta village, Aurangābād district, Mahārāshtra state, western India, celebrated for their wall paintings. The temples are hollowed out of granite cliffs on the inner side of a 70-ft (20-m) ravine in the Wagurna River Valley, 65 mi (105 km) northeast of Aurangābād, at a site of great scenic beauty.

The group of some 30 caves was excavated between the 1st century BC and the 7th century AD and consists of two types, *caityas* (sanctuaries) and *vihāras* (monasteries). Although the sculpture, particularly the rich ornamentation of the *caitya* pillars, is noteworthy, it is the fresco-type paintings that are the chief interest of Ajanta. These paintings depict colourful Buddhist legends and divinities with an exuberance and vitality that is unsurpassed in Indian art.

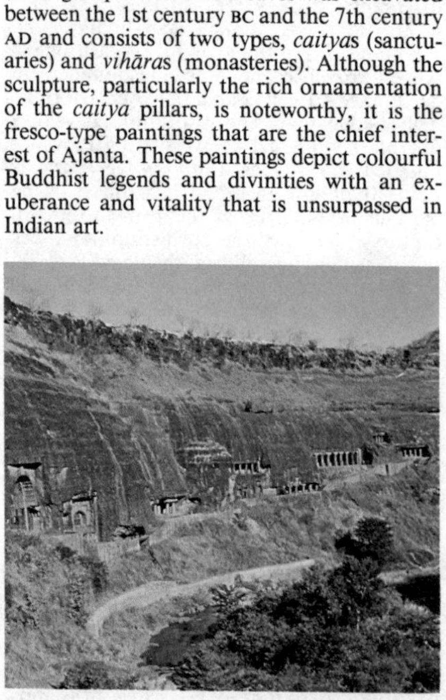

Ajanta Caves in Aurangābād district, Mahārāshtra, India
Art Resource—EB Inc.

Ajax (Latin), Greek AIAS, byname AJAX THE GREATER, in Greek legend, son of Telamon, king of Salamis, described in the *Iliad* as being of great stature and colossal frame, second only to the Greek hero Achilles in strength and bravery. He engaged Hector (the chief Trojan warrior) in single combat and, with the aid of the goddess Athena, rescued the body of Achilles from the hands of the Trojans. He competed with the Greek hero Odysseus for the armour of Achilles but lost, which so enraged him that it caused his death. According to a later story Ajax' disappointment drove him mad. On coming to his senses he slew himself with the sword that he had received as a present from Hector. The legend has it that from his blood sprang a red flower that bore on its leaves the initial letters of his name, AI, letters that are also expressive of lament. Ajax was the tutelary hero of the island of Salamis, where he had a temple and an image and where a festival called Aianteia was celebrated in his honour.

Ajax (Latin), Greek AIAS, byname AJAX THE LESSER, in Greek legend, son of Oileus, king of Locris. In spite of his small stature, he held his own among the other heroes before Troy; but he was also boastful, arrogant, and quarrelsome. For his crime of dragging King Priam's daughter Cassandra from the statue of the goddess Athena and violating her, he barely escaped being stoned to death by his Greek allies. Voyaging homeward, his ship was wrecked, but Ajax was saved. Then, boasting of his escape, he was cast by Poseidon into the sea and drowned.

Ajax was worshipped as a national hero by the Opuntian Locrians (who lived on the Malian Gulf in central Greece and on whose coins he appeared), who always left a vacant place for him in their battle line.

Ajdābiyā, also spelled AGEDABIA, town, northeastern Libya, near the Gulf of Sidra, 95 mi (153 km) south of Banghāzī. The site of Roman and Byzantine colonization (ruins remain), it was a caravan junction during the early Middle Ages. The town was the administrative centre for Sīdī Muḥammad Idrīs al-Mahdī as-Sanūsī, emir of Cyrenaica (later Idris I, King of Libya), from 1919 until its occupation by Fascist Italy in 1923. Used as an Italian military base, during World War II it became the headquarters for the British occupation of the region. Ajdābiyā is on the coastal road and is the junction for the road to the Awjilah (Augila)–Intisar A and D and the Abu Tiffel oil fields, 120 mi south. An oil pipeline also passes through the town to the nearby gulf terminal of az-Zuwaytīnah. Pop. (1979 est.) 37,800.

Ajdukiewicz, Kazimierz (b. Dec. 12, 1890, Ternopol, Pol., Austrian Empire—d. April 12,

1963), Polish logician and semanticist who was the chief contributor to the Warsaw school of philosophy and logic, which analyzed the relationship of language and knowledge. He is credited with developing in 1920 the first deductive theory for the study of logic based on syntax.

Obtaining a doctorate from the University of Lvov, where he studied philosophy, physics, and mathematics, Ajdukiewicz lectured in philosophy at the universities of Lvov, Poznań, and Warsaw (1921–61). His principal works include *Z metodologii nauk dedukcyjnych* (1921; "On the Methodology of the Deductive Sciences"); an essay, "The Axiomatic Systems from the Methodological Point of View" (in *Studia Logica*, vol. 9, 1960), and a collection of his articles from 1920 to 1939 and 1946 to 1964 entitled *Język i poznanie*, 2 vol. (1960–65; "Language and Knowledge").

ajīva, according to the Jaina philosophy of India, "nonliving substance," as opposed to *jīva*, "souls" or "living matter." *Ajīva* is divided into: (1) *ākāśa*, "space"; (2) *dharma*, "that which makes motion possible"; (3) *adharma*, "that which makes rest possible"; and (4) *pudgala*, "matter." *Pudgala* consists of atoms; is eternal yet subject to change and development; is both gross (that which it is possible to see) and subtle (that which cannot be perceived by the senses). The invisible *karman* (causative) matter that adheres to and weighs down the soul is an example of subtle *pudgala*. The first three types of *ajīva* are necessary conditions for the subsistence of both souls and matter.

Some of the above terms are also used in Buddhist philosophy, but with meanings that are quite different.

Ājīvika, an ascetic sect that emerged in India about the same time as Buddhism and Jainism. It was founded by Gośāla Maskarīputra (also called Gosālo Makkhaliputto), a contemporary and early friend of Mahāvīra, the founder of Jainism. His doctrines and those of his followers are known only from Buddhist and Jain sources, which record that he was lowborn and that he died shortly before the Buddha (probably about 484 BC) after a quarrel with Mahāvīra.

The sect professed a total determinism in the transmigration of souls, or series of rebirths. Whereas other groups allowed that man himself can better his lot in the course of his transmigration, the Ājīvikas held that the affairs of the entire universe were ordered by a cosmic force called *niyati* (Sanskrit: "rule, destiny"), which determined all events and thus man's fate to the last detail, and that personal efforts to change or accelerate improvement were doomed to failure. "Just as a ball of string will, when thrown, unwind to its full length, so fool and wise alike will take their course." Despite this melancholy view of man's condition, the Ājīvikas practiced austerities not for any purposeful goal but because their *niyati* had determined them to do so.

After a period of acceptance during the reign of the Maurya dynasty (3rd century BC), the sect apparently dwindled, although followers lived on in what is the modern state of Mysore until the 14th century. In latter-day developments of the sect, the founder Gośāla came to be worshipped as a divinity, and the tenet of *niyati* developed into the doctrine that all change was illusory and that everything was eternally immobile, the last consequence of a consistent determinism.

ʿAjjul, Tall al-, ancient site in southern Palestine, located at the mouth of the Wādī Ghazzah just south of the town of Gaza (modern Ghazzah). The site, often called "ancient Gaza," was excavated between 1930 and 1934 by British archaeologists under the direction of Sir Flinders Petrie. Although the earliest remains on the site date back perhaps as far as 2100 BC, the town seems to have reached its zenith during the Middle Bronze Age (*c.* 2300–*c.* 1550 BC), especially during the 17th and 16th centuries, when it was probably controlled by the Hyksos (15th Dynasty) rulers of Egypt. Included in the remains of that period were a great Hyksos-style fosse (defense ditch), portions of several private dwellings, and a large building covering an area of about a half an acre. If, as seems probable, the building is to be identified as a palace, it is the largest palace of that period yet discovered in Palestine. The palace was succeeded by four other large buildings, the last of which probably dated from *c.* 1200 BC.

Ajka, post-1945 industrial town, Veszprém *megye* (county), west central Hungary, 15 mi (24 km) west of Veszprém in the Csinger Valley in the Bakony Mountains. Ajka developed as a small coal-mining village in the late 19th century, but major growth occurred in the mid-20th century. In 1942 the German occupation forces began bauxite exploitation of a deposit considered to be Europe's largest. Ajka now has an aluminum furnace, an alumina works, a glassworks, food-processing facilities, and a telecommunications parts factory. Major brown-coal-mining centres in the vicinity are Halimba, Szőc, and Nyirád. Manganese is mined at Úrkút. Pop. (1949) 8,307; (1960) 15,657; (1970) 20,263; (1983 est.) 31,000.

Ajman, Arabic ʿAJMĀN, or ʿUJMĀN, constituent emirate of the United Arab Emirates (formerly Trucial States, or Trucial Oman); the smallest state of the country. It is composed of three sections; the principal portion, on the Persian Gulf coast, is completely surrounded by the emirate of Sharjah. This section is the site of Ajman town, the capital and only urban settlement. Ajman also includes two interior exclaves (noncontiguous sections) on the Oman promontory, the horn of the Arabian Peninsula. They are tiny al-Manāmah, 37 mi (60 km) east-southeast of Ajman town, and Maṣfūṭ, 56 mi southeast of Ajman town, in the Wādī Ḥattá, at the promontory's base. Estimated total area is 100 sq mi (250 sq km).

The Shaykh of Ajman signed the British-sponsored General Treaty of Peace, abjuring piracy, in 1820; this was Ajman's first recognition as an autonomous state. It also subscribed to the maritime truce of 1835 and to the Perpetual Maritime Truce in 1853. To forestall Turkish and French expansion along the Trucial Coast, the shaykhs, including Ajman's ruler, signed an Exclusive Agreement (1892), placing their foreign relations in the hands of the British government. In 1968, Britain announced its forthcoming withdrawal from the Persian Gulf area. Negotiations were begun to create a nine-member federation (including Ajman, the six other Trucial States, Bahrain, and Qatar). The latter two states abandoned the proposed federation and became separately independent (August and September 1971). The British left the area in December 1971 and the United Arab Emirates was formed, of which Ajman was an original constituent.

Economically, Ajman is the poorest member of the United Arab Emirates. Shortly after 1900, when the shaykh's influence extended only a few miles from Ajman town, about 40 pearling boats and a date-palm plantation there were the sole economic activites. From 1961 to the early 1970s, one of Ajman's main sources of revenue was from the sale of many varieties of postage stamps, designed to be of interest to Western collectors. These stamps were never shipped to Ajman and served no legitimate postal purpose; most were not recognized by reliable philatelic organizations and catalogs. Some commemorative coins were also issued. In 1972, the United Arab Emirates announced the establishment of a post office department, to take over philatelic emissions from member emirates.

Much of the emirate's revenue is provided by grants from the oil-rich member emirate of Abu Dhabi; Ajman town now boasts a modern ruler's palace and includes other up-to-date structures. The deepening of the creek at Ajman town in order to provide deepwater port facilities was undertaken during the 1970s, and a prefabricated housing factory was built. There is also a ship repair yard. Ajman's interior exclaves have some agriculture; al-Manāmah has a camp of the national defense forces, and Maṣfūṭ has deposits of high-quality marble. The state has little commerce and industry. Foreign aid from Kuwait has helped in the establishment of a few schools. Petroleum concessions have been granted to Western companies, but no oil had been found by the early 1980s. Ajman town is connected by paved road with Dubai town and Ras al-Khaimah town. Pop. (1980 prelim.) 36,101.

Ajmer, also spelled AJMERE, or AJMIR, town, administrative headquarters of Ajmer district, Rājasthān state, northwestern India. The city is on the lower slopes of Tārāgarh Hill, on the summit of which stands a fortress. It was probably founded *c.* 1100 and was the capital of the former state. Architectural monuments include an ancient Jaina temple (converted *c.* 1200 into a mosque); the white marble tomb complex of the Muslim saint Muʿīh-ud-Dīn

The shrine of Khwājah Ṣaḥib at Ajmer, Rājasthān, India

Baldev—Shostal Assoc./EB Inc.

Chishtī (died 1236); and the palace of Akbar (Mughal emperor who ruled from 1556 to 1605), now a museum. The city was a Muslim military base used in operations against the Rājputs (the warrior people who ruled the historic region of Rājputāna). To the north lies Anā Sāgar, a lake created in the 11th century, on the shores of which stand marble pavilions built by Shāh Jahān (Mughal emperor of India from 1628 to 1658). Situated on major road and rail routes, Ajmer is a trade centre for salt, mica, cloth fabrics, and agricultural products. Industries include railway workshops and oilseed mills; cotton and woollen fabrics, as well as hosiery, soap, shoes, saddlery, and pharmaceuticals, are produced there. Ajmer is known for its handicrafts and cloth weaving and dyeing.

Ajmer district (3,274 sq mi [8,479 sq km]) comprises a hilly region, forming a part of the Arāvalli Range and its outliers. It is drained by headstreams of the Lūni River flowing southwestward and by tributaries of the Banās River flowing eastward. Agriculture is the principal occupation; and corn (maize), wheat, millet, gram (chick-pea), barley, cotton, oilseeds, chilies, and onions are the chief crops. The district has cotton, textile, and hosiery mills and cotton ginning and pressing factories. Mica, feldspar, and building-stone deposits are worked.

Ajmer was founded by Ajayadeva, an 11th-century Rājput ruler; it was annexed to the Delhi Slave dynasty in 1193. Upon payment of tribute it was returned to its Rājput rulers, but it was taken by Akbar I in 1556. In 1770 it was annexed by the Marāṭhās, after which it was a continual Rājput-Marāṭhā battleground until it was ceded to the British in 1818. In 1878 Ajmer was constituted as a chief commissioner's province known as Ajmer-Merwara and was divided into two separate tracts. The larger of these comprised Ajmer and Merwara subdivisions; the smaller, to the southeast, comprised Kekri subdivision. It became a part of the state of Rājasthān in 1956. Pop. (1981) town, 375,593; district, 1,440,366.

Ajo, town, Pima County, southwestern Arizona, U.S. Spaniards mined in the area in the 1750s, and the Ajo Copper Company (1854) was the first incorporated mining concern in the Arizona Territory. The mines remained dormant from about 1860 until the 1900s when a townsite was laid out and a railroad built to Gila Bend (40 mi [64 km] north). The town's economy virtually depends on the Phelps Dodge Corporation, which operates the New Cornelia Open Pit Mine (390 ac [158 ha]) and a smelter plant. The community, originally named Muy Vavi (Papago: Warm Water), was renamed Ajo (Spanish: Garlic), for the wild garlic found in the surrounding hills. Nearby are the Papago Indian Reservation (east), the Cabeza Prieta National Wildlife Refuge (west), and the Organ Pipe Cactus National Monument (south). Pop. (1980) 5,189.

AK-47, also called KALASHNIKOV MODEL 1947, Soviet assault rifle that has become one of the most widely used shoulder weapons in the world. The initials AK represent Automat Kalashnikov, Russian for "automatic Kalashnikov," for its designer, Mikhail Kalashnikov. It has both semiautomatic and fully automatic capabilities and fires intermediate-power 7.62-millimetre ammunition. (The bore is the same as that used by the North Atlantic Treaty Organization [NATO], but the cartridge is shorter, lighter, and less powerful. It, therefore, also has a lighter recoil, or "kick.") The AK-47's range is shorter than that of the NATO standard cartridge but greater than the range of submachine gun or pistol cartridges.

The AK-47 is a short and well-designed gun. It has a separate gas return tube above the barrel, a long box magazine that holds 30 rounds, and a cyclic firing rate of 600 rounds per minute. It is manufactured in many countries in two basic designs. One has a wooden stock, the other a folding metal stock. By the early 1980s, the AK-47 was being replaced in the Warsaw Pact countries by the AKM, a modernized version with better sights but the same basic operation. The AK-47 and its AKM version, however, remained the basic shoulder weapons for the Soviet and virtually all Communist armies, as well as of Communist-supported guerrillas and nationalist movements throughout the world. It has been produced in the Soviet Union, Bulgaria, the People's Republic of China, East Germany, Hungary, North Korea, Poland, Romania, and Yugoslavia.

Ak Koyunlu, also spelled AQ QOYUNLU, English WHITE SHEEP, Turkmen tribal federation that ruled northern Iraq, Azerbaijan, and eastern Anatolia from AD 1378 to 1508.

The Ak Koyunlu were present in eastern Anatolia at least from 1340, according to Byzantine chronicles, and most Ak Koyunlu leaders, including the founder of the dynasty, Kara Osman (reigned 1378–1435), married Byzantine princesses.

In 1402 Kara Osman was granted all of Diyār Bakr in northern Iraq by the Turkic ruler Timur. The strong presence of the Kara Koyunlu (*q.v.*; Black Sheep), a rival Turkmen federation, in western Iran and Azerbaijan temporarily checked any expansion, but the rule of Uzun Ḥasan (1452–78) brought the Ak Koyunlu to fresh prominence. With the defeat of Jihān Shāh, the Kara Koyunlu leader, in 1467 and Abū Saʿīd, the Timurid, in 1468, Uzun Ḥasan was able to take Baghdad, the Persian Gulf, and Iran as far east as Khorāsān. The Ottoman Turks were simultaneously (1466–68) moving eastward in Anatolia, threatening Ak Koyunlu domains and forcing Uzun Ḥasan into an alliance with the Qaramānids of central Anatolia. In 1464 the Ak Koyunlu had already turned to the Venetians, enemies of the Ottomans, in an attempt to stave off the inevitable Ottoman attack. Despite promises of military aid, the Venetian arms never were provided, and Uzun Ḥasan was defeated by the Ottomans in Tercan (modern Mamahatun) in 1473.

Yaʿqūb (reigned 1478–90) sustained the dynasty a while longer, but after his death the Ak Koyunlu were torn apart by internal strife and ceased to be a threat to their more powerful neighbours. The Ṣafavids of Iran, members of the Shīʿah sect of Islām, were already undermining the allegiance of some of the Ak Koyunlu, predominantly of the Sunnah sect. The two powers met in battle near Nakhichevan in 1501–02, and the Ak Koyunlu Alwand was defeated by Esmāʿīl I. In his retreat from the Ṣafavid armies, Alwand in his turn destroyed an autonomous Ak Koyunlu state in Mardin, Diyār Bakr (1503). The last Ak Koyunlu ruler, Murād, who had been contending for power with his brothers Alwand and Muḥammad since 1497, was also defeated by Esmāʿīl (1503). Murād established himself briefly in Baghdad (until 1508); but, with his retreat to Diyār Bakr, the dynasty ended.

Akaba (Jordan): *see* ʿAqabah, al-.

Akademgorodok, English ACADEMIC TOWN, scientific research centre located on the northeast corner of the Novosibirsk Reservoir, near the city of Novosibirsk, south central Russian Soviet Federated Socialist Republic. Akademgorodok is the headquarters of the Siberian branch of the Academy of Sciences of the U.S.S.R.

Founded in 1957 by the academicians Mikhail Lavrentyev, Sergey Sobolev, Andrey Trofimuk, and Sergey Khristianovich, Akademgorodok was designed to organize and carry out theoretical and experimental research in the natural and economic sciences and technology, with an eye toward marshalling the productive resources of Siberia and the Soviet Far East. By the early 1980s, Akademgorodok housed more than 20 separate research institutes as well as a university, laboratories, and residential facilities.

Akademiya Nauk Range, also spelled AKADEMIIA NAUK, Russian KHREBET AKADEMI NAUK (Academy of Sciences Range), mountain range, western Pamirs, central Tadzhik Soviet Socialist Republic. The mountains, extending north–south, are approximately 68 mi (110 km) in length and are composed mostly of sedimentary and metamorphic rocks, along with some granite. Glaciation from permanent snowcaps extends over an area of 580 sq mi (1,500 sq km). The highest peak in the Soviet Union, Communism Peak (24,590 ft [7,495 m]), is located in the Khrebet Akademi Nauk; there are 24 peaks above 19,700 ft (6,000 m). The mountains were named in 1927 in honour of the Academy of Sciences of the Soviet Union.

Akaka Falls, waterfall, Hawaii County, northeastern Hawaii Island, Hawaii, U.S., central feature of Akaka Falls State Park (65 ac [26 ha]). Easily reached by foot trail, the falls

Akaka Falls, Hawaii Island
By courtesy of United Air Lines; photograph, James E. McWayne

are located 12 mi (19 km) northwest of Hilo in a canyon 4 mi inland from the village of Honomu on the Hamakua Coast. The falls plunge 420 feet (128 m) through dense tropical overgrowth into a pool of Kolekole Stream.

Akāl Takht (Punjabi: Throne of the Timeless One), the chief centre of religious authority for the Sikh community of India. The Akāl Takht, located at Amritsar, in the state of Punjab, opposite the Harimandir, or principal Sikh house of worship, is also the headquarters of the Shiromanī Akālī Dal (Akālī Religious Party), predominant among the Sikhs. Similar seats of authority are located at Anandpur (Punjab state), Patna (Bihār) and Nanded (Hyderābād).

When in 1708 Gurū Gobind Singh declared that the line of personal Gurūs (religious guides) had come to an end, the authority of the office of Gurū was considered to be embodied in the holy scriptures, the *Ādi Granth.* Disputes in interpretation had to be settled by the entire Sikh community. Decisions were made at annual or semi-annual meetings in Amritsar, when groups would assemble behind their elected leaders in the open area in front of the Akāl Takht. Resolutions had to be carried unanimously; they then became *gurmata*s (decisions of the Gurū) and were binding on all Sikhs. Both political and religious decisions were taken at Akāl Takht meetings up until 1809, when Maharaja Ranjit Singh, the leader of the newly unified Sikh state, abolished political *gurmatas* and began to seek counsel from both Sikhs and non-Sikhs. In the 20th century, resolutions of local congregations on nonpolitical matters relating to the interpretation of Sikh doctrine or rules of conduct can be appealed to the Akāl Takht; decisions taken there are conveyed in the form of *hukamnāmā*s (orders). A *hukamnāmā* issued from the Akāl Takht is considered mandatory for all Sikhs.

Akālī (Punjabi: Timeless One), a movement in Sikhism; also any member of suicide squads in the armies of the Sikhs, a religious group of India. The Akālī suicide squads first appeared about 1690 when the execution of two predecessors and continuing persecution by the Mughals forced the 10th Gurū Gobind Singh to take up arms. The Akālīs were also known as *nihang*s (Persian: "crocodiles"; a name first used by the Mughals for their suicide squads) and wore a distinctive blue uniform. Some present-day Akālīs continue to wear a blue tunic and a conical blue turban and to carry a sword.

The Akālī name was revived in the 1920s during the *gurdwārā* (*q.v.*) reform movement as a semimilitary corps of volunteers raised to oppose the British government. After the Sikhs regained control of their *gurdwārā*s, the Akālīs continued to represent the Sikh community in the Punjab and took the lead in the agitation for an independent Punjabi-speaking, Sikh-majority state. This goal was achieved in 1966 with the establishment of the state of Punjab. A major political party of Punjab state is the Shiromanī Akālī Dal (SAD; Akālī Religious Party). Although it competes in national elections, it is mainly concerned with the status of the Sikhs in Punjab state.

Akan, ethnolinguistic grouping of peoples of the Guinea Coast who speak Akan languages (of the Kwa branch of the Niger-Congo family); they include the speakers of the Akyem, Anyi, Ashanti, Attie, Baule, Brong, Fanti, and Guang languages; some scholars also consider

Akan tribal chief
Jacques Jangoux

Twi to be a distinct Akan language. Most Akan peoples live in Ghana, where they settled in successive waves of migration between the 11th and 18th centuries; others inhabit the eastern part of the Ivory Coast and parts of Togo.

Yams are the staple food crop in the Akan economy, but plantains and taro are also important; cocoa and palm oil are major commercial resources.

Every Akan tribe is grouped into exogamous matrilineal clans, the members of which trace their descent from a common ancestress; these clans are hierarchically organized and are subdivided into localized matrilineages, which form the basic social and political units of Akan society. Most Akan live in compact villages that are divided into wards occupied by the matrilineages and subdivided into compounds of extended multi-generation families. The village is a political unit under a headman, elected from one of the lineages, and a council of elders, each of whom is the elected head of a constituent lineage. The lineage head is the custodian of the lineage's stools, the symbols of unity between the spirits of the ancestors and the living members of the lineage; every lineage also has its own god or gods. There is a strong feeling of corporate responsibility among lineage members. Matrilineal descent also governs inheritance, succession, and land tenure. Paternal descent is also recognized and determines membership in the *ntoro,* a group sharing certain taboos, surnames, forms of etiquette, and ritual purification ceremonies.

The most prominent aspect of Akan religion is an ancestor cult the rites of which serve to enforce tribal unity and morality. Other religious practices are based on belief in a supreme deity who created the universe and in lesser deities and spirits.

Akan states, complex of gold-producing forest states in West Africa lying between the Komoé and Volta rivers (in an area roughly corresponding to the coastal lands of the modern republics of Togo, Ghana, and part of the Ivory Coast); their economic, political, and social systems were transformed from the 16th to the 18th century by their trade with Europeans on the coast.

Of the northern Akan or Bron states the earliest (established *c.* AD 1450) was Bono (*q.v.*); of the southern the most important were Denkyera, Akwamu (*qq.v.*), Fanti (*see* Fanti Confederacy), and Ashanti (*see* Ashanti empire).

Akansa (people): *see* Quapaw.

Akarai Mountains (South America): *see* Acaraí.

Akaroa, community, eastern South Island, New Zealand. It is situated on French Bay, east shore of Akaroa Harbour, a rocky inlet on the Banks Peninsula formed when the sea breached the erosion-enlarged crater of an ancient volcano. In 1838 a French whaler, Capt. Jean Langlois, agreed with the local Maori chiefs to buy 30,000 ac (12,000 ha) of the peninsula. He returned to France to organize the Nanto-Bordelaise Company (1839), which, backed by a warship, dispatched a settlement force. Arriving in 1840, the settlers found that the British had in the interim declared sovereignty over South Island. An agreement reached between the French and the British allowed the company to establish its settlement, which was sold to the New Zealand government in 1849. The settlement serves a fruit- and dairy-farming area. A summer resort and fishing port, Akaroa lies 52 mi (84 km) southeast of Christchurch. The town's name derives from the Maori for "long harbour." Pop. (1982 est.) 710.

Akashi, city, Hyōgo Prefecture (*ken*), Honshu, Japan, adjacent to Kōbe on the Akashi-kaikyō (Akashi Strait) of the Inland Sea. It developed as a castle town, and many relics of the Jōmon and Yayoi eras remain on the nearby hills. Artifacts of the Jōmon era (4500–250 BC; a hunting and gathering society) include pottery with distinctive cord impressions. During the Yayoi era (250 BC–AD 250) immigrants from Korea introduced irrigation techniques and bronze and iron implements. Before World War II it was a thriving city, its economy based on the aircraft industry. During the war, half of the population was lost to air raids in the old part of the city. The heavy steel industry, developed during the Korean War, revived Akashi as an industrial and residential district. The city was formerly a fishing centre, but the yield of marine products has decreased because of overfishing and marine pollution. The Japanese standard-time meridian, 135° E, passes through the city. Pop. (1983 est.) 262,960.

Municipal Astronomical Science Museum and planetarium at Akashi, Japan
World Photo—Shostal Assoc./ EB Inc.

Akashic record, in occultism, a compendium of pictorial records, or "memories," of all events, actions, thoughts, and feelings that have occurred since the beginning of time. They are said to be imprinted on Akasha, the astral light, which is described by spiritualists as a fluid ether existing beyond the range of human senses. The Akashic records are reputedly accessible to certain select individuals—*e.g.,* a spiritualist medium who conducts a séance. Akasha allegedly transmits the waves of human willpower, thought, feeling, and imagination and is a reservoir of occult power, an ocean of unconsciousness to which all are linked, making prophecy and clairvoyance possible.

Akbar, in full ABŪ-UL-FATḤ JALĀL-UD-DĪN MUḤAMMAD AKBAR (b. Oct. 15, 1542, Umarkot, Sind, India—d. 1605, Āgra), greatest of the Mughal emperors of India (reigning 1556–1605), who extended Mughal power over most of the Indian subcontinent. In order to preserve the unity of his empire, Akbar adopted programs that won the loyalty of the non-Muslim populations of his realm, reformed and strengthened his central administration, and also centralized his financial system and reorganized tax collection processes. Although he never renounced Islām, he took an active interest in other religions, persuading Hindus, Parsis, and Christians, as well as Muslims, to engage in religious discussion before him. Illiterate himself, he encouraged scholars, poets, painters, and musicians, making his court a centre of culture.

Early life. Abū-ul-Fatḥ Jalāl-ud-Dīn Muḥammad Akbar was descended from Turks, Mongols, and Iranians—the three peoples who predominated in the political elites of northern India in medieval times. Among his ancestors were Timur (Tamerlane) and Genghis Khan. His father, Humāyūn, driven from his capital of Delhi by the Afghan usurper Shēr Shāh Sūr, was vainly trying to establish his authority in Sind. Soon Humāyūn had to leave India for Afghanistan and Iran, where the Shāh lent him some troops. He regained his throne in 1555, 10 years after Shēr Shāh Sūr's death. Akbar, at the age of 13, was made governor of the Punjab.

Humāyūn had barely established his authority when he died, in 1556. Within a few months his governors lost several important places, including Delhi itself, to Hemū, a Hindu minister who claimed the throne for himself. But a Mughal force defeated Hemū on the historical battlefield of Pānīpat, which commanded the route to Delhi, thus ensuring Akbar's succession.

At Akbar's accession his rule extended over little more than the Punjab and the area around Delhi, but under the guidance of his chief minister, Bayram Khān, his authority was gradually consolidated and extended. The process continued after Akbar forced Bayram Khān to retire in 1560 and began to govern on his own—at first still under household influences but soon as an absolute monarch.

Imperial expansion. Akbar first attacked Mālwa, a state of strategic and economic importance commanding the route through the Vindhya hills to the Deccan and containing rich agricultural land; it fell to him in 1561.

Akbar, miniature portrait from the *Akbar-nāmeh* by Abū-ul-Fazl, *c.* 1600; in the India Office Library, London

By courtesy of the India Office Library, London

Toward the zealously independent Hindu Rājputs, a military race inhabiting rugged, hilly Rājasthān, Akbar adopted a policy of conciliation and conquest. Successive Muslim rulers had found the Rājputs dangerous, however weakened by disunity. But in 1562, when Raja Bihārī Mal of Amber (Jaipur), threatened by a succession dispute, offered Akbar his daughter in marriage, Akbar accepted the offer. The Raja acknowledged Akbar's suzerainty, and his sons prospered in Akbar's service. Akbar followed the same feudal policy toward the other Rājput chiefs. They were allowed to hold their ancestral territories, provided that they acknowledged Akbar as emperor, paid tribute, supplied troops when required, and concluded a marriage alliance with him. The emperor's service was also opened to them and their sons, offering rewards both in honour and in money.

Akbar, however, showed no mercy to those who refused to acknowledge his supremacy. When, after protracted fighting in Mewār, Akbar captured the historic fortress of Chitor in 1568, he massacred its inhabitants. Even though Mewār did not submit, the fall of Chitor prompted other Rājput *raja*s to accept Akbar as emperor in 1570 and to conclude marriage alliances with him, although the state of Mārwār held out until 1583.

One of the notable features of Akbar's government was the extent of Hindu, and particularly Rājput, participation. Rājput princes attained the highest ranks, as generals and as provincial governors, in the Mughal service. Discrimination against non-Muslims was reduced by abolishing the taxation of pilgrims and the tax payable by non-Muslims in lieu of military service. Rājput princes had ruled unhampered in previous centuries, and some Rājputs and many other Hindus had cooperated with previous Muslim governments. Yet Akbar was far more successful than any previous Muslim ruler in winning the cooperation of Hindus at all levels in his administration. The further expansion of his territories gave them fresh opportunities.

In 1573 Akbar conquered Gujarāt, an area with many ports that dominated India's trade with western Asia, and then turned east toward Bengal. A rich country with a distinctive culture, Bengal was difficult to rule from Delhi because of its network of rivers, always apt to flood during the monsoon. Its Afhan ruler, declining to follow his father's example and acknowledge Mughal suzerainty, was forced to submit in 1575. When he rebelled and was defeated and killed in 1576, Akbar annexed Bengal.

Toward the end of his reign, Akbar embarked on a fresh round of conquests. Kashmir was subjugated in 1586, Sind in 1591, and Qandahār in 1595. Mughal troops now moved south of the Vindhya Mountains into the Deccan in peninsular India. By 1601 Khāndesh, Berār, and part of Ahmadnagar were added to Akbar's empire. His last years were troubled by the rebellious behaviour of his son, Prince Salīm, who was eager for power.

Administrative reform. Previous Indian governments had been weakened by the disintegrating tendencies characteristic of pre-modern states—the tendency of armies to split up into the private forces of individual commanders and the tendency of provincial governors to become hereditary local rulers. Akbar combatted this trend by instituting comprehensive reforms that involved two fundamental changes. First, every officer was, at least in principle, appointed and promoted by the emperor, instead of his immediate superior. Second, the traditional distinction between the nobility of the sword and that of the pen was abolished: civil administrators were assigned military ranks, thus becoming as dependent on the emperor as army officers.

These ranks were systematically graded from commanders of 10 to commanders of 5,000, higher ranks being allotted to Mughal princes. Officers were paid either in cash from the emperor's treasury or, more frequently, by the assignment of lands from which they had to collect the revenue, retaining the amount of their salary and remitting the balance to the treasury. Such lands seem to have been transferred frequently from one officer to another: this increased the officers' dependence on the emperor, but it may also have encouraged them to squeeze as much as they could from the peasants with whom their connection might be transitory. Politically, the greatest merit of the system was that it enabled the emperor to offer attractive careers to the able, ambitious, and influential. In this way, Akbar was able to enlist the loyal services of many Rājput princes.

Akbar's reforms required a centralized financial system, and thus by the side of each provincial governor (*sūbadār*, later called nawab) was placed a civil administrator (*dīwān*) who supervised revenue collection, prepared accounts, and reported directly to the emperor. As a further safeguard against abuses, Akbar reorganized the existing network of newswriters, whose duty was to send regular reports of important events to the emperor. Akbar also seems to have instituted more efficient revenue assessment and collection in an effort to safeguard the peasants from excessive demands and the state from loss of money. But such efficiency could only have been enforced in the areas directly administered by the central government. This excluded the lands under tributary rulers such as the Rājputs and also the lands assigned for the maintenance of Mughal officers.

Yet, notwithstanding Akbar's reforms, travellers' accounts indicate that the Indian peasants remained impoverished. The official elite, on the other hand, enjoyed great wealth; liberal patronage was given to painters, poets, musicians, and scholars, and luxury industries flourished. Akbar also supported state workshops for the production of high-quality textiles and ornaments.

Personality and assessment. Akbar maintained a luxurious and brilliant court, at which elaborate ceremonial emphasized his distance from other men, though he was careful to cultivate public opinion outside court circles. Every morning at dawn he stood at an open window to be seen and reverenced by the people. Foreign observers commented on the graceful manner in which he accepted little gifts from the people and showed himself ready to hear the complaint of any man who dared to approach him.

Physically, he was strong and could withstand hardship on campaigns. Although he seems to have been no more than five feet seven inches tall, he impressed observers as a dominating personality. Clearly, although he was illiterate, he had a powerful and original mind. His unprejudiced inquiries into Christian doctrines misled the Jesuit missionaries he invited to his court into thinking that he was on the point of conversion. He persuaded the Muslim theologians at his court to accept him as arbiter on points of Islāmic law in dispute among them. Although this seems to have been little more than an expression of his systematic approach to problems, the orthodox were offended. He gave further offense by the religious discussions he encouraged between Muslims, Hindus, Parsis, and Christians. These discussions were continued by a small group of courtiers who shared with Akbar a taste for mysticism. Although their doctrines and ceremonies, known as the Divine Faith (Dīn-e Ilāhī), assigned a central place to Akbar himself, it would be an oversimplification to ascribe political motives to these developments.

Begun in 1570 and abandoned in 1586, Akbar's capital of Fatehpur Sīkri, near Delhi, was evidence of the resources he could command. Its combination of Hindu and Muslim architectural styles symbolized the contact of cultures that he encouraged. Similarly, he commissioned the translation of Sanskrit classics into Persian, giving illustrated copies to his courtiers. He also received with enthusiasm the European pictures brought by the Jesuits, and his painters incorporated European techniques of realism and perspective in the distinctive Mughal style (characterized by a vivid treatment of the physical world) that began to develop during his reign. Akbar's reign was an example of the stimulating effects of cultural encounter. It has also often been portrayed as a model for future governments—strong, benevolent, tolerant, and enlightened. Effective government in a country geographically as vast and socially as complex as India demands a wide measure of social support: Akbar understood this need and satisfied it.

(K.A.B.)

BIBLIOGRAPHY. Vincent A. Smith, *Akbar the Great Mogul, 1542–1605,* 2nd ed. (1919), is still the standard biography. Ashirbadi Lal Srivastava, *Akbar the Great,* vol. 1, *Political History, 1542–1605,* vol. 2, *Evolution of Administration, 1556–1605* (1962–67), is a reliable account.

Akbar period architecture, building style that developed in India under the patronage of the Mughal emperor Akbar (reigned 1556–1605). The style is best exemplified by the fort at Āgra (built 1565–74) and the magnificent city of Fatehpur Sīkri (1569–74), but fine examples are also found in the gateway to the 'Arab Sarā'ī, Delhi (*c.* 1560), the Ajmer fort (1564–73), the Lahore fort with its outstanding decoration (1586–1618), and the Allahābād fort (1583–84), now largely dismantled.

The architecture of the Akbar period is characterized by a strength made elegant and graceful by the rich decorative work. Many elements from the Hindu tradition were absorbed in the decorative work.

The fortress-palace of Āgra is impressive for the massive enclosure wall, its entire length of $1^1/_2$ miles ($2^1/_2$ kilometres) faced with dressed stone. The main entranceway, which is known as the Delhi gate, is attractively decorated with white marble inlay against the warm red sandstone.

The capital city of Fatehpur Sīkri is one of the most notable achievements of Islāmic architecture in India. The city, which was deserted only a few years after it was built, is a great complex of palaces and lesser residences and religious and official buildings, all erected on top of a rocky ridge 26 miles (42 kilometres) west of Āgra. The so-called Dīvān-e Khāṣṣ (Hall of Private Audience) is arresting in its interior arrangement, which has a single massive column encircled by brackets supporting a stone throne platform, from which radiate four railed balconies. The Jodhā Bāī palace and the residence of the prime minister, Bīrbal, again show—in their niches and brackets—features adopted from the religious and secular architecture of the Hindus.

The most imposing of the buildings at Fatehpur Sīkri is the great mosque, the Jāmiʿ Masjid, which served as a model for later congregational mosques built by the Mughals. The massive gateway, the Buland Darwāzah (Victory Gate), gives a feeling of immense strength

Gateway to the ʿArab Sarāʾī, Delhi, c. AD 1560
P. Chandra

and height, an impression emphasized by the steepness of the flight of steps by which it is approached.

Articles are alphabetized word by word, not letter by letter

Akebia, genus of woody vines comprising two species native to Asia but introduced elsewhere for their ornamental foliage and fast growth. The genus belongs to the family Lardizabalaceae.

Five-leaf akebia, or chocolate vine (*A. quinata*), has five leaflets to each leaf arranged like the fingers on a hand; inconspicuous purplish flowers in small clusters; and oblong purple berries. Three-leaf akebia (*A. trifoliata*) has three leaflets to a leaf. Both species are rampant twining vines often used for shading and screening on arbors and fences and for ground covering on embankments.

akee, also spelled ACKEE (*Blighia sapida*), tree of the soapberry family native to West Africa, widely cultivated throughout tropical and sub-

Akee (*Blighia sapida*)
W.H. Hodge

tropical regions for its edible fruit. The tree grows about 9 metres (30 feet) tall and bears pinnate leaves and fragrant white flowers. Brought to the Caribbean area with slaves from Africa, the akee tree was introduced to science by William Bligh, famous as captain of the ill-fated "Bounty," hence its botanical name.

At maturity, the reddish, woody shell of the fist-sized fruits splits open to reveal three segments of white flesh, each with large shiny black seeds. The soft, bland flesh is eaten as a vegetable. Akee and salt fish is a popular dish in the Caribbean.

Akeley, Carl (Ethan) (b. May 19, 1864, Clarendon, N.Y., U.S.—d. Nov. 17, 1926, Albert National Park, Belgian Congo), U.S. naturalist and explorer who developed the taxidermic method for mounting museum displays to show animals in their natural surroundings. His method of applying skin on a finely molded replica of the body of the animal gave results of unprecedented realism and elevated taxidermy from a craft to an art. His modelling led to sculpture, and he executed notable pieces showing elephants, lions, and lion spearers. Akeley's goal was to create a panorama of Africa and its big game in U.S. museums.

At 19 he became an apprentice at Ward's Natural Science Establishment in Rochester, N.Y., and during his associations with the Field Museum of Natural History in Chicago (1895–1909) and the American Museum of Natural History in New York City (1909–26) he made five trips to Africa to study, hunt, and

Museum display of elephants mounted by Carl Akeley in Stanley Field Hall, the Field Museum of Natural History, Chicago
By courtesy of the Field Museum of Natural History, Chicago

collect big game. In 1923 his book *In Brightest Africa* appeared. He died during his last expedition and was buried on Mt. Mikeno in Albert National Park (now Virunga National Park), in Zaire, the first wildlife sanctuary in central Africa, which he had helped establish. His inventions include the Akeley cement gun, used in mounting animals, and the Akeley camera, a motion-picture camera adapted for use by naturalists, with which Akeley made the first motion pictures of gorillas in their natural habitat.

Akeley's second wife, Mary Lee Jobe Akeley (1886–1966), was well known as an explorer and naturalist before her marriage (1924). Upon her husband's death she remained in Africa in charge of the expedition. She was named his successor as adviser to the American Museum of Natural History, at which the Akeley African Hall was named in their honour.

Aken (West Germany): *see* Aachen.

Aken, Jerome van: *see* Bosch, Hiëronymus.

Akenside, Mark (b. Nov. 9, 1721, Newcastle upon Tyne, Northumberland, Eng.—d. June 23, 1770, London), poet and physician, best known for his poem *The Pleasures of Imagination,* an eclectic philosophical essay that takes as its starting point papers on the same subject written by Joseph Addison for *The Spectator.* Written in blank verse derived from Milton's, it was modelled (as its preface states) on the Roman poets Virgil (the *Georgics*) and Horace (the *Epistles*). A debt to Virgil is certainly apparent in the way in

Akenside, engraving by E. Fisher, 1772, after a painting by A. Pond, 1754
By courtesy of the trustees of the British Museum; photograph, J.R. Freeman & Co. Ltd.

which Akenside invests an essentially unpoetic subject—the abstractions of philosophic thought—with poetic form, through studied elevation of language and with considerable grace. The influence of Horace is clear in the skillfully handled transitions from one theme to another and the tact with which the entire subject is treated.

Later adopting the ode as his favourite poetic form, Akenside was more than willing to consider himself the English Pindar, one of several aspects of his character that was satirized in Tobias Smollett's novel *The Adventures of Peregrine Pickle,* in which Akenside appears as the physician in scenes set on the European continent.

Akenside attended the University of Edinburgh, intending to become a minister but instead studying medicine. His first poem, "The Virtuoso," in imitation of the Elizabethan poet Edmund Spenser, appeared in 1737. *The Pleasures of Imagination* first appeared in three books in 1744. A fourth book was added later, and the whole poem was extensively revised, finally appearing posthumously in *The Poems of Mark Akenside, M.D.* (1772). Also in 1744 Akenside turned to satire in *An Epistle to Curio,* occasioned by the political reversal executed by William Pulteney, who, though opposing the Whig prime minister Sir Robert Walpole, professed Whig sympathies for years but then accepted the earldom of Bath in the Tory ministry that succeeded Walpole's. The following year Akenside published *Odes on Several Subjects.* He had, meanwhile, been unsuccessful in attempts to establish a medical practice either at Northampton or at Hampstead, then a rural suburb of London. In 1747, however, a friend established him in practice in a house in Bloomsbury Square, London. His reputation increased and he was eventually appointed physician to the queen. Later works include "Hymn to the Naiads" and "To the Evening Star" (both 1746).

åkermanite, mineral composed of dicalcium magnesium disilicate, $Ca_2MgSi_2O_7$, one end-member of the melilite mineral series (*see* melilite).

Akershus, *fylke* (county), southeastern Norway. Covering 1,898 sq mi (4,917 sq km), it extends north from Oslofjorden to the southern end of Mjøsa (lake) and east to the Swedish frontier. The Vorma (river) flows through Akershus from Mjøsa into the Glåma (river) and on to Øyeren (lake). The national capital, Oslo, is the county seat, though it is a separate *fylke* and urban municipality (*bykommune*) and thus lies outside the boundaries of Akershus. Embracing numerous suburbs of Oslo, Akershus is one of the most densely populated areas of Norway. It contains the historic village of Eidsvoll, 30 mi (48 km) north of Oslo, in which the National Assembly voted Norway's constitution in 1814. Between Eidsvoll and Oslo is Gardermoen international airport. Shipping, manufacturing, and tourism are the economic mainstays of the *fylke.* Pop. (1983 est.) 376,129.

akh (ancient Egyptian: variously translated as "beneficial," "advantageous," or "glorious"), in Egyptian religion, with *ka* and *ba* (*qq.v.*), a principal aspect of the soul. By enabling it to assume temporarily any form it desired, for the purpose of revisiting the earth or for its own enjoyment, the *akh* characterized the soul of a deceased person as an effective entity in the next world. The *akh*-soul was generally represented as a bird and could appear to the living as a ghost.

Akhaïa (Greece): *see* Achaea.

Akhḍar, al-Jabal al-, also spelled GEBEL EL-ACHDAR, mountain range of northeastern Libya that extends along the Mediterranean coast for about 100 mi (160 km) in an east-northeasterly direction between al-Marj and Darnah. Rising sharply in two steps, the first reaching 985 ft (300 m) and the second 1,640–1,970 ft, the limestone range (about 20 mi wide) then blends into a plateau crowned by hills attaining heights of nearly 3,000 ft. It descends eastward to the barren, stony terrain of al-Buṭnān and southward to the Libyan Sahara. Dissected by river valleys, the chain is covered with sparse low bush, remnants of scrub forest, and scattered cultivation. It has a comparatively high rainfall (15–20 in. [375–500 mm] annually) and high humidity, but periodic drought does occur.

The Akhḍar (Arabic: Green) presented the most promising area of Cyrenaica and was colonized by the Italians in the 1930s. The settlements, interrupted during World War II and later deserted, have now been reoccupied by Libyans. Livestock herding (camels, goats, and sheep) involves a degree of nomadism, and there is limited agriculture, notably in the al-Marj plain and around Darnah, producing grain, olives, grapes, and almonds. A large agricultural project in the area has improved reclamation and irrigation. The chain was a major battleground during World War II.

Akhelóös Potamós (Greece): *see* Achelous River.

Akhenaton, also spelled AKHNATON, or IKHNATON, also called AMENHOTEP IV, or NEFERKHEPERURE AMENHOTEP, Greek AMENOPHIS (fl. 14th century BC, Egypt), king of Egypt (1379–62 BC) of the 18th dynasty, who established a new monotheistic cult of Aton (hence his assumed name, Akhenaton, meaning "one useful to Aton").

Egyptian religion and culture before Akhenaton's reign. The religion of ancient Egypt was static and traditional, urging that the gods had given a good order and that it was necessary for man to hold firmly to the order. When changes did occur, religion tried to incorporate them into the system as though they came from the creation. By the time Akhenaton took the throne as the fourth pharaoh named Amenhotep, the 18th dynasty (1567–1320 BC) had run for nearly 200 years, and there had been a century of imperial conquest and control of foreign lands. Egypt dominated Palestine, Phoenicia, and Nubia. The nation was powerful, rich, and courted by lesser princes. To maintain these gains, a military and political group controlled the culture. Since the Egyptian state had always been theocratic, ruled by a god or gods, according to traditional beliefs, this group interlocked with the priesthood. The richest and most powerful of the gods, such as Amon of Thebes or Re of Heliopolis, it was held, dictated the purpose of the state. The king had to apply to the gods for oracles directing his major activities. In return for wealth, elegance, and the role of the leading actor in a drama of imperial success, the pharaoh had relinquished his religious (and military) authority to others.

Akhenaton, detail of the sandstone pillar statue from the Aton temple at Karnak, c. 1370 BC; in the Egyptian Museum, Cairo

Hirmer Fotoarchiv, Munchen

A century before Akhenaton, the energetic pharaoh Thutmose III had conquered nearby Asia and Africa. His successors continued his vigorous method of life, but, when the conquered territories were firmly held, that vigour turned from warfare to sports. Akhenaton's father, Amenhotep III, was a mighty hunter in his youth, but the son was weak physically and could not follow the pattern of outdoor feats. His activities were intellectual.

The sudden spread of empire had excited the Egyptian culture. Architecture became less firmly planted and soared upward in assertiveness. In the visual arts, the predominant heavy, angular style of rendering became softer and rounder. Egyptian soldiers and officials lived in foreign countries, and foreigners lived in Egypt. The sharp differences between the people of the Nile Valley and the people abroad were blurred. Egyptian gods had temples in other countries, and foreign gods were introduced into Egypt. Gods and goddesses were concerned about Asia and Africa, as well as Egypt. Hymns before Akhenaton's reign show that the spread of empire meant the spread of religion. Gods became universal. Egypt had already combined gods, with Amon and Re (the sun-god) becoming Amon-Re or even Amon-Re-Harakhte. This permitted the Egyptians to think of the gods as unified forces, which was a prelude to monotheism.

There were other breaks in tradition. The royal line, wherever possible, had been kept pure by marriages of the heirs with princesses of the king's own family. Amenhotep III defied this custom by marrying a commoner named Tiy. She apparently enjoyed unusual power in the palace without abandoning her loyalty to her husband. Akhenaton was a child of this marriage.

Empire was held firmly by garrisons abroad, which assured the favourable flow of trade to Egypt. Near the Nile Valley there were rich gold mines, so that the country could dominate both trade and politics. Messengers travelled between Egyptian and foreign cities carrying letters written in Babylonian cuneiform, the international language of the day, on clay tablets. This correspondence shows the imperial power and elegance of Egypt, which seemed to be assured of its unending dominance over all the nearby countries.

Akhenaton's early reign. Scholars disagree whether Amenhotep III associated his son Amenhotep IV on the throne for several years of co-regency or whether the younger king succeeded to rule after the death of his father. It is here assumed that the older king died before the younger pharaoh gained power. The latter still used the family name Amenhotep, and on his ascension he still worshipped the old gods, especially Amon of Thebes and a sun-god, Re-Harakhte. His first buildings near Thebes were started in the older, massive architecture, using huge stone blocks and showing the worship of Re-Harakhte. The art was traditional, even though the figures of men and gods were carved in a softer outline than they had been a century earlier.

Within his first few years as pharaoh there were changes. He abandoned the temple to Re-Harakhte and began to build a place to worship a new form of sun-god—the disk of the sun, called the Aton. It had been a little known deity for two generations before him. The Aton was never shown in human or animal form, except insofar as the extended rays of the sun disk might end in hands to confer blessings upon men. This was the life-giving and life-sustaining power of the sun. He had no image in the hidden sanctuary of a temple but was to be worshipped out in sun-warmed openness. The buildings for the Aton were of a new kind. The massive solidity of the older temples was given up, and walls were run up of much smaller stones and were jammed with excited little scenes in a feverish new art. When artistic inventiveness was encouraged, forms were exaggerated to the point of caricature. Since the young king had a drooping jaw, a scrawny neck, sloping shoulders, a pot belly, and thick thighs, these features were carved in a grotesque way. The shape of the King became the flattering pattern for his followers, so that they also were shown with thin necks and round bellies. The King's wife, Nefertiti, may be beautiful in some of the sculptures made of her, but the new art often showed her as though she were a misshapen hag. Egyptian art changed from a static statement of eternity into a liveliness that is both fascinating and repelling. It came down from eternity to the here and now, with pictures of the King presiding over a specific ceremony, kissing his wife, or gnawing on a bone at the dining table. As long as art had shown the indefinite future, it had had no exact time or place; under the new pharaoh it told stories about what happened to the royal family and their followers.

Life and rule at Akhetaton (*Amarna*). The new temples were built at Karnak, near Thebes, a region dominated by the god Amon and by the families that had run the state for several generations. The new king had to break away sharply from this traditional setting. In the sixth year of his reign he changed his name from Amenhotep (Amon Is Satisfied) to Akhenaton (He Who Serves the Aton), thus formally declaring his new religion; and he moved his capital from Thebes more than 200 miles (300 kilometres) north to a desert bay on the east side of the Nile River, a place now called Tell el-Amarna or Amarna. Here he began to build a new city, which he called Akhetaton (the Place of the Aton's Effective Power). He took an oath that he would never go beyond the bounds of this place, which seems to mean not that he would never leave it but that he would not push the city limits beyond designated boundary stones. He was now free from the hostile forces at Thebes. Akhenaton, Nefertiti, and their six daughters gave themselves over to the new "truth." Their family life was open to the public. They worshipped the Aton in a temple open to the sunlight. The newly made nobles and officials gave their devotion to Akhenaton and Nefertiti.

Although the Egyptian texts always asserted that the king was a god and therefore the source of every benefit for the land, the complexities of a large empire, the activities of the bureaucrats, and the enticements of royal privilege had made Akhenaton's predecessors captives of the state. His political reforms were hence reactionary, inasmuch as he tried to recapture the old authority of the king. If the focus is only on the spectacular new elements that he introduced, the fact that his domination of rule was a restoration of a very old "truth" may be obscured.

The new city at Amarna must have had charm. Officials lived in spacious villas, with trees, pools, and gardens. Indoors the walls were painted in the free flowing new art, with marsh scenes near the floor and floral bouquets near the ceiling. Amarna art ranged from the very gracious, such as the famous bust of Nefertiti, to the grotesque. Everything was lively. Probably the elegant fragility of the portrait of Nefertiti displeased the traditionalists. Instead of presenting a solidity that might last forever, it gave a delicate and fleeting impression. The new "truth" came down to Earth. The Prime Minister was shown running in front of the King's chariot, an exertion that would have been unthinkable in the staid old times. Scenes of the busy market and the soldiers' guardroom, with lively comments of the people, are depicted. The present-day viewer of this ancient art feels as though he were there.

The new religion. The religion of the Aton is not completely understood. Akhenaton and Nefertiti worshipped only this sun-god. For them he was "the sole god." Akhenaton had dropped his older name Amenhotep, and the name "Amon" was also hacked out of the inscriptions throughout Egypt. Here and there the names of other gods and goddesses were removed, and in some texts the words "all gods" were eliminated. The funerary religion dropped Osiris, and Akhenaton became the source of blessings for the people after death. The figure of Nefertiti replaced the figures of protecting goddesses at the corners of a stone sarcophagus. Yet Akhenaton and Nefertiti directed their worship only to the Aton. It was the closest approach to monotheism that the world had ever seen.

The King addressed a beautiful hymn to his god, expressing gratitude for the benefits of life. The Aton, says the hymn, gave these blessings not only to the Egyptians but also to "Syria and Nubia" and to "all distant foreign countries," to "all men, cattle, and wild beasts," to the lion coming from his den, the fish in the river, and the chick within the egg. Men live when the sun has risen, but at night the dark land is as if dead. It has often been pointed out that this hymn has a remarkable similarity to Psalm 104 in the Bible. Both the hymn and the psalm reflect a common family of ideas, according to which God or the god is praised for his bounties.

The Aton religion was a happy nature worship, without an ethical code. Men were asked only to be grateful to the sun for life and warmth. It was unlike the awful austerity of the great gods of former Egypt, who might punish man for disobedience. It was quite unlike the heavy demands that the Hebrew god would lay upon his people. In the Aton religion there was no "Thou shalt . . ." and no "Thou shalt not. . . ."

An aesthetic and intellectual religion, it probably had no deep roots. There is no evidence that the people worshipped the Aton happily; in their tombs they prayed to the Aton but also to Akhenaton and Nefertiti. The people wanted to see a definite force. Akhenaton was the same god-king who had always ruled Egypt, and Nefertiti could substitute for all the former mother goddesses. The King and Queen seem to have accepted this worship as their just due.

The decline and end of Akhenaton's reform movement. The politics of the time must have been troubled. Although the ruling classes had been shorn of their powers, there was still an army. It may have been restless, because the documents show that Akhenaton paid little attention to it. Without a strong army and navy, foreign trade began to fall off, and internal taxes began to disappear into the pockets of local officials, finally causing the discontented priesthood and civil officials to combine with the army to discredit the new movement. Akhenaton was able to withstand these forces, but his weaker successors could not.

The Amarna Letters, discovered in the ruins of Tell el-Amarna from an archive of international correspondence directed by Asian princes to the courts of Amenhotep III and Akhenaton, reflect the new situation. The army commanders and high commissioners in Palestine and Syria were neglected. The local princes, who had seen their advantage in trading with Egypt, became despondent when Egypt did not answer their appeals for support. Hostile forces arose, ambitious princes in Palestine and Syria, invaders from the eastern desert, and the venturesome Hittites to the north. The Amarna Letters, as well as the archives found at the Hittite capital, show the disintegration of the Egyptian Empire in Asia. Loyal princes were forced to flee their cities. Aggressors, aided by the Hittites, captured territory from the Egyptian army. It may be that Egypt lost all of its holdings except the southwest corner of Palestine. Akhenaton's preoccupation with ideas and ideals cost Egypt its proud empire.

Akhenaton may have given in a little in the face of these disasters. In the 12th year of his reign the queen mother Tiy, a practical little woman, made a visit to Amarna. There is some evidence that he modified his extremism after that. The matter is confused, involving Akhenaton's estrangement from Nefertiti and the promotion of his young son-in-law Smenkhkare as a favourite. Since Smenkhkare apparently returned to Thebes, compromise seems to have been in the air.

When Akhenaton died, he was succeeded briefly by Smenkhkare and then by a second son-in-law, Tutankhaton. The latter was forced to change his name to Tutankhamen, dropping the Aton and embracing Amon, to abandon Amarna and move back to Thebes, and to pay penance by giving the old gods new riches and privileges. When the tomb of Tutankhamen was discovered in western Thebes in 1922, it gave a final illustration of the sumptuous glories of Amarna art. A few years after the death of this young king, the army took over the throne in the person of General Horemheb. He instituted counterreforms in order to restore the old system fully.

Assessment. Akhenaton was a strange figure, spiritually and physically. Representations of his peculiar, unmanly body have been studied by pathologists with no unanimous conclusions. Some modern scholars have also questioned his ability to father children, but the presence of six daughters would certainly indicate that he was potent. Despite conflicting statements in the literature, it now seems certain that his mummy has never been found. Anciently and modernly he has been a controversial person, but the very fury of the controversy shows that he was a major figure of ancient history. The strong and changing forces of his day shaped his determined nature, and yet he stood estranged from his day in the strength of his ideas and ideals.

(Jo.A.W.)

BIBLIOGRAPHY. The classic statement about Akhenaton was given by James H. Breasted in *A History of Egypt* (1905); and in the *Cambridge Ancient History,* vol. 2, ch. 6 (1924). Less admiring views are in Sir Alan Gardiner, *Egypt of the Pharaohs,* ch. 9 (1961); and Cyril Aldred, *Akhenaten: Pharaoh of Egypt* (1968). Excavations at Tell el-Amarna are treated in T.E. Peet *et al., The City of Akhenaten,* 3 vol. (1923–51). J.D.S. Pendlebury, *Tell el-Amarna* (1935), was a handy summary up to that date. The art at Amarna is well represented in N. de G. Davies, *The Rock Tombs of El Amarna,* 6 vol. (1903–08); and in J.D. Cooney, *Amarna Reliefs from Hermopolis in American Collections* (1965). The cuneiform correspondence called the Amarna Letters is treated by W.F. Albright and T.O. Lambin in the *Cambridge Ancient History,* 3rd ed., vol. 1, ch. 4 (1966). A brief statement about the new religion is in Jaroslav Cerny, *Ancient Egyptian Religion,* pp. 61–66 (1952). The hymn to the Aton was translated by J.A. Wilson in *Ancient Near Eastern Texts Relating to the Old Testament,* ed. by James B. Pritchard, 3rd ed., pp. 369–371 (1969). An important technical report is R.G. Harrison, "An Anatomical Examination of the Pharaonic Remains Purported To Be Akhenaten," *Journal of Egyptian Archaeology,* 52:95–119 (1966). The first phase of a massive archaeological investigation of the period is treated in *The Akhenaton Temple Project, Vol. 1: Initial Discoveries,* ed. by Ray Winfield Smith and Donald B. Redford (1976).

Akhisar, historically THYATIRA, chief town of Akhisar *ilçe* (district), Manisa *il* (province), western Turkey, in a fertile plain on the Great Zab River (the ancient Lycus). The ancient town, originally called Pelopia, was probably founded by the Lydians. It was made a Macedonian colony *c.* 290 BC and renamed Thyatira. It became part of the kingdom of Pergamum in 190 BC and was an important station on the ancient Roman road from Pergamum (Bergama) to Laodicea (near Denizli). Its early Christian church appears as one of the seven churches in the Revelation to John. Akhisar was incorporated into the Ottoman Empire in the 15th century. The modern town is connected by railway and road to İzmir and Manisa and exports cotton, tobacco, graphite, opium, wool, raisins, and dyes. Pop. (1980) town, 61,491; *ilçe,* 146,444.

Akhlame, also spelled AKHLAMÛ, ancient Semitic nomads of northern Syria and Mesopotamia and traditional enemies of the Assyrians. They are first mentioned *c.* 1375 BC in an Egyptian source (one of the Tell el-Amarna letters), in which they are said to have advanced as far as the Euphrates River; about the same time there was also evidence of them in Assyria, at Nippur, and around the Persian Gulf. During the following century, they interrupted travel between Babylon and Hattusa (Boğazköy), and Tukulti-Ninurta I (1244–08 BC) of Assyria recorded that he conquered "the mountains of the Akhlamû." An inscription of the Assyrian king Tiglath-pileser I (1115–1077), however, refers for the first time to the "Akhlamû-Aramaeans," and soon thereafter the Akhlame disappear from Assyrian annals and are replaced by the Aramaeans. The relationship between the Akhlame and the Aramaeans is still a matter of conjecture.

Akhmadulina, Bella (Akhatovna) (b. April 10, 1937, Moscow), Soviet poet of Tatar and Italian descent, a distinctive voice in post-Stalinist Soviet literature.

Akhmadulina completed her education at the Gorky Literary Institute in 1960, after which she travelled in Central Asia. She was eventually admitted to the Soviet Writers' Union, although her uncompromisingly individualistic work elicited official criticism and met with some difficulty in publication. Like her fellow poet Yevgeny Yevtushenko, to whom she was married during the 1950s, she drew audiences of thousands at readings of her work.

Her first collection, *Struna* ("The Harp String"), appeared in 1962. The long poem *"Moya rodoslovnaya"* (1964; "My Genealogy"), the title of which alludes to a poem by Pushkin from 1830, is marked by ambitious but assured experimentation in both theme and technique. Subsequent volumes include *Uroki muzyki* (1969; "Music Lessons") and *Stikhi* (1975; "Poems"). Akhmadulina has also published translations of poetry from Georgian and other languages.

Akhmatova, Anna, pseudonym of ANNA ANDREYEVNA GORENKO (b. June 23 [June 11, old style], 1889, Bolshoy Fontan, near Odessa, Ukraine, Russian Empire—d. March 5, 1966, Domodedovo, near Moscow), Russian poet recognized at her death as the greatest woman poet in Russian literature.

Anna Akhmatova
Novosti Press Agency

Akhmatova began writing verse at the age of 11 and at 21 became a member of the Acmeist group of poets, whose leader, Nikolay Gumilyov, she married in 1910 but divorced in 1918. The Acmeists, through their periodical *Apollon* ("Apollo"; 1909–17), rejected the esoteric vagueness and affectations of Symbolism and sought to replace them with "beautiful clarity," compactness, simplicity, and perfection of form—all qualities in which Akhmatova excelled from the outset. Her first collections, *Vecher* (1912; "Evening") and *Chyotki* (1914;"Rosary"), especially the latter, brought her fame. While exemplifying the best kind of personal or even confessional poetry, they achieve a universal appeal deriving from their artistic and emotional integrity. Akhmatova's principal motif is love, mainly frustrated and tragic love, expressed with an intensely feminine accent and inflection entirely her own.

Later in her life she added to her main theme some civic, patriotic, and religious motifs but without sacrifice of personal intensity or artistic conscience. Her artistry and increasing control of her medium were particularly prominent in her next collections: *Belaya staya* (1917; "The White Flock"), *Podorozhnik* (1921; "Plantain"), and *Anno Domini MCMXXI* (1922). This amplification of her range, however, did not prevent official Soviet critics from proclaiming her "bourgeois and aristocratic," condemning her poetry for its narrow preoccupation with love and God, and characterizing her as half nun and half harlot. The execution in 1921 of her former husband, Gumilyov, on charges of participation in an anti-Soviet conspiracy (the Tagantsev affair) further complicated her position. In 1923 she entered a period of almost complete poetic silence and literary ostracism, and no volume of her poetry was published in the Soviet Union until 1940. In that year several of her poems were published in the literary monthly *Zvezda* ("The Star"), and a volume of selections from her earlier work appeared under the title *Iz shesti knig* ("From Six Books"). A few months later, however, it was abruptly withdrawn from sale and libraries. Nevertheless, in September 1941, following the German invasion, Akhmatova was permitted to deliver an inspiring radio address to the women of Leningrad. Evacuated to Tashkent soon thereafter, she read her poems to hospitalized soldiers and published a number of war-inspired lyrics; a small volume of selected lyrics appeared in Tashkent in 1943. At the end of the war she returned to Leningrad, where her poems began to appear in local magazines and newspapers. She gave poetic readings, and plans were made for publication of a large edition of her works.

In August 1946, however, she was harshly denounced by the Central Committee of the Communist Party for her "eroticism, mysticism, and political indifference." Her poetry was castigated as "alien to the Soviet people," and she was again described as a "harlot-nun," this time by none other than Andrey Zhdanov, Politburo member and the director of Stalin's program of cultural restriction. She was expelled from the Union of Soviet Writers; an unreleased book of her poems, already in print, was destroyed; and none of her work appeared in print for three years.

Then, in 1950, a number of her poems eulogizing Stalin and Soviet Communism were printed in several issues of the illustrated weekly magazine *Ogonyok* ("The Little Light") under the title *Iz tsikla "Slava miru"* ("From the Cycle 'Glory to Peace' "). This uncharacteristic capitulation to the Soviet dictator—in one of the poems Akhmatova declares: "Where Stalin is, there is Freedom, Peace, and the grandeur of the earth"—was motivated by Akhmatova's desire to propitiate Stalin and win the freedom of her son, Lev Gumilyov, who had been arrested in 1949 and exiled to Siberia. The tone of these poems (those glorifying Stalin were omitted from Soviet editions of Akhmatova's works published after his death) is far different from the moving and universalized lyrical cycle, *Rekviem* ("Requiem"), composed between 1935 and 1940 and occasioned by Akhmatova's grief over an earlier arrest and imprisonment of her son in 1937. This masterpiece—a poetic monument to the sufferings of the Soviet peoples during Stalin's terror—has never been published in the Soviet Union.

In the cultural "thaw" following Stalin's death, Akhmatova was slowly and ambivalently rehabilitated, and a slim volume of her lyrics, including some of her translations, was published in 1958. Since then, a number of editions of her works, including some of her brilliant essays on Pushkin, have been published in the Soviet Union (1961, 1965, two in 1976, 1977); none of these, however, contains the complete corpus of her literary productivity. Akhmatova's longest work, *Poema bez geroya* ("Poem Without a Hero"), on which she worked from 1940 to 1962, was not published in the Soviet Union until 1976. This difficult and complex work is a powerful lyric summation of Akhmatova's philosophy and her own definitive statement on the meaning of her life and poetic achievement. It is widely regarded as one of the great poems of the 20th century. It combines symbolism, allegory, and autobiography, subtly blurring the boundaries between literature and life, and skillfully weaves the themes of time, poetry, suffering, and affirmation around the central tragedy of a young poet's suicide.

Akhmatova executed a number of superb translations of the works of other poets, including Victor Hugo, Rabindranath Tagore, Leopardi, and various Armenian and Korean poets. She also wrote sensitive personal memoirs on Symbolist writer Aleksandr Blok, the artist Amedeo Modigliani, and fellow Acmeist Osip Mandelstam.

Akhmatova's poetry—much of which expresses the various moods of love, reflecting her complicated and unsatisfactory relationships with a number of men, including a second failed marriage—is essentially lyrical and personal, combining classical tact with intense feeling. It is distinguished by a bold and highly individual yet tightly controlled imagery, exquisite verbal music, and a consummate poetic diction wrought of interpenetrating simplicity and subtlety.

In 1964 she was awarded the Etna-Taormina prize, an international poetry prize awarded in Italy, and in 1965 she received an honorary doctoral degree from Oxford University. Her journeys to Sicily and England to receive these honours were her first travel outside her homeland since 1912. Akhmatova's works were widely translated, and her international stature continued to grow after her death.

Akhmīm, also spelled EKHMĪN, town, Sawhāj *muḥāfaẓah* (governorate), Upper Egypt, on the east bank of the Nile, above Sawhāj on the west bank. Extensive necropolises dating from the 6th dynasty (*c.* 2345–*c.* 2181 BC) until the late Coptic period reveal the site's antiquity. In 1981 remains of a temple (Roman period) with Ramesside statues were excavated in the city. The name apparently derives from the pharaonic Khent-min and Coptic Khmin. Its deity was Min, in Hellenistic times identified with Pan, whence the name Panopolis, meaning "city of Pan." Also referred to as Chemmis or Khemmis, it was the capital of the 9th, or Chemmite, nome (department) of Ptolemaic Upper Egypt. Linen weaving is cited as an ancient industry there by the Greek geographer Strabo (born *c.* 63 BC). The 18th-dynasty pharaoh Ay (reigned *c.* 1352–48 BC) and the 5th-century AD Greek poet Nonnus were born at Akhmīm. The Coptic dialect once spoken in the area had an important literature.

In the Islāmic period it became a provincial capital under Faṭīmid caliph al-Mustanṣir (11th century AD); in the 18th century it was incorporated into the former province of Jirjā (Girga), and the town was sacked during the Mamlūk civil wars.

The modern town is a market and processing centre for cereals, sugarcane, dates, and cotton. Manufactures include textiles, clothing, pottery, and bricks; the ancient weaving tradition has been revived as well. An electrical transformer station started operation in 1980.

Akhmīm has a considerable Coptic Christian minority. Pop. (1983) 64,200.

Akhnaton (Egyptian king): *see* Akhenaton.

Akhsĕnāyā: *see* Philoxenus of Mabbug.

Akhṭal, al-, in full GHIYĀTH IBN GHAWTH IBN AṢ-ṢALT AL-AKHṬAL (b. *c.* 640, al-Ḥīrah, Mesopotamia, or the Syrian Desert—d. 710), poet of the Umayyad period (661–750), esteemed for his perfection of Arabic poetic form in the old Bedouin tradition.

Al-Akhṭal (the Loquacious) was a Christian but did not take the duties of his religion seriously, being addicted to drink and women. He was a favourite panegyrist and friend of the caliph Yazīd I and his generals Ziyād ibn Abīhī and al-Ḥajjāj. He continued as court poet to the caliph ʿAbd al-Malik but fell in disfavour under Walīd I.

Together with the poets Jarīr and al-Farazdaq, al-Akhṭal forms a famous trio in early Arabic literary history. Because they closely resembled one another in style and vocabulary, their relative superiority was disputed. The philologist Abū ʿUbaydah, however, placed al-Akhṭal highest of the three because among his poems there were 10 *qaṣīdah*s (formal odes) regarded as flawless and 10 as nearly flawless, and this could not be said of the other poets.

Akhtyrka, also spelled ACHTYRKA, city, Sumy *oblast* (administrative region), Ukrainian Soviet Socialist Republic, on the Vorskla River. It was founded in 1641 as a fortress protecting the southern frontiers of Russia from raids of the Crimean Tatars. It was rebuilt in a different place in 1654 and incorporated in 1703. It has a notable cathedral (1758) designed by the imperial architect Bartolomeo Rastrelli, technical colleges, and a music school. Economic factors include engineering and light industries. Pop. (1970) 41,354.

Akiba ben Joseph (b. *c.* AD 40—d. *c.* 135, Caesarea, Palestine), Jewish sage, a principal founder of rabbinic Judaism, who introduced a new method of interpreting Jewish oral law (Halakha), thereby laying the foundation of what was to become the Mishna, the first post-biblical code of Jewish law.

The subject of numerous popular legends, Akiba is said to have been an illiterate shepherd who began to study after the age of 40. He was martyred at Caesarea. His devoted wife, Rachel, supported him both morally and materially during this arduous period of late learning (12 years according to one account). His principal teachers were the great masters of the Law,. Eliezer ben Hyrcanus and Joshua ben Hananiah, themselves disciples of Johanan ben Zakkai, the illustrious founder of the academy at Jabneh. When, after his long period of study, Akiba returned home and was greeted by his wife, he reputedly said to his pupils: "What I am and what you are comes from her." He established his academy in Bene Beraq (near present-day Tel Aviv–Yafo), and the leading sages of the following generation, especially Meir and Simeon ben Yoḥai, were his disciples. Among his disciples the sources also include an Egyptian proselyte, Minyamin (Benjamin).

Akiba perfected the method of biblical interpretation called "Midrash," whereby legal, sacral, and ethical tenets, sanctioned by tradition, were viewed as being implied in Scripture. Thus, Scripture, in addition to its overt meaning, is understood as replete with implied teaching; it is, in fact, all-encompassing. The "Written Law" of Scripture and the "Oral Law" of tradition are ultimately one. Many midrashic works of the 2nd century originated in Akiba's school. In addition, he collected the oral traditions about the conduct of personal, social, and religious life (Halakha, "law"), and arranged them systematically, thereby laying the foundation of what was to become the Mishna, the first postbiblical code of Jewish law. (Akiba has been called "the father of the Mishna.") His apprehension of Scripture was opposed by the contemporary exegete Rabbi Ishmael ben Elisha, who taught that "the Torah speaks in the language of men" and should not be forced to yield special meanings but be interpreted solely by means of set, logical rules of interpretation.

Akiba's importance lies both in his achievements as a rabbinic scholar and in the impact of his personality on his time. He was strict in matters of law ("No pity in judgment!"—*i.e.,* compassion is irrelevant in establishing what the law is or means), but he opposed the death penalty. Modest in his personal life, he disapproved of parading one's knowledge. He counselled: "Take your place a few seats below your rank until you are asked to take a higher place." He respected the role of the woman in life and attributed the redemption of the Israelites from Egyptian bondage to the meritoriousness of women of that generation. "Man and his wife—the divine presence is between them," he taught. Known for his concern for the poor, he was appointed charity overseer. The term "to do the affairs of heaven" (religious deeds) he interpreted to mean "to scatter one's money among the poor."

As judge he addressed litigating parties: "Know before whom you are standing. You are standing before him whose word created the world, not before Akiba ben Joseph."

His lectures were on legal subjects, scriptural exegesis, and religious thought. For him the central teaching of Judaism resided in the commandment, "love your neighbour as yourself." God's love for man is expressed in that he created man in his image. Man has freedom of will ("Everything is foreseen, yet freedom of choice is given"); his deeds determine his fate, yet his true reward will be granted only in the world to come. In the present life there is much suffering, but "suffering is precious" and man should praise God for it. The people of Israel, who in a special sense are "God's children," have the task to "proclaim the glory of God to all the nations of the world." Akiba interpreted the Song of Solomon as a dialogue of love between Israel and God. For the sake of this love Israel withdraws from the affairs of the world. In these teachings—partly in answer to early Christian tenets—Akiba laid the basis for an ideology of Israel in dispersion among the nations of the world.

About the year 95, Akiba and other sages journeyed to Rome. Arriving at the seaport Puteoli they beheld the power and grandeur of the empire. While his companions wept, remembering the victory of Rome over Judaea some two decades ago, Akiba remained calm. If God is so kind to the wicked Romans, he explained, he will, in the end, be even kinder to Israel. He was equally calm when he visited the ruins of the Jerusalem Temple, destroyed by the Romans in the year 70. The prophecies of doom have come true, he commented; now we may anticipate the fulfillment of the prophecies of reconstruction.

Scholarly opinion is divided on the extent of Akiba's participation in an ill-fated rebellion against Rome (132–135) led by Bar Kokhba (originally Simeon ben Koziba). Some consider Akiba to have been the spiritual force behind the uprising. Others take note of the Talmudic report that Akiba considered Bar Kokhba to be the promised messianic king but see no evidence of further action on his part. Akiba was, it is true, apprehended by the Romans, imprisoned in Caesarea, and finally martyred (*c.* 135), but his offense is recorded as having been his continued public teaching rather than revolutionary activity. He accepted the agony of martyrdom serenely (he was flayed alive, according to tradition), grateful for the opportunity to fulfill the commandment to "love God . . . with all your life," which he always interpreted to mean "even when he takes your life." His last words were, "the Lord is one," the final words of the Jewish confession of faith ("Hear, O Israel! The Lord is our God, the Lord is one"). (N.N.G.)

BIBLIOGRAPHY. Louis Finkelstein, *Akiba: Scholar, Saint and Martyr* (1936), is an extensive biographical narrative, with emphasis on Akiba's intellectual development.

Akimov, Nikolay Pavlovich (b. April 16 [April 3, old style], 1901, Kharkov, Russian Ukraine—d. Sept. 6, 1968, Moscow), scenic designer and producer known for the diversity of his bold experiments in stage design and dramatic interpretation—most especially for

Akimov, self-portrait
Sovfoto

his cynical reinterpretation of *Hamlet* (1932), in which the king's ghost was represented as a fiction cunningly devised by Hamlet, Ophelia was portrayed as intoxicated rather than mad, and her drowning was depicted as the result of a drunken orgy.

Akimov's design career began in 1922. He worked chiefly with Russian dramas, in which he combined cinematic with theatrical methods. His notorious version of *Hamlet*, his first venture as a producer, caused vehement reaction and was eventually withdrawn from distribution. From 1935 to 1949 and after 1955, Akimov was chief producer of the Leningrad Comedy Theatre. He also became professor and head of the faculty for design and production at the Leningrad Theatrical Institute from 1960.

Consult
the
INDEX
first

Akindynos, Gregorios (b. *c.* 1300, Bulgaria—d. *c.* 1349), Byzantine monk and theologian, principal opponent of a Greek monastic movement of contemplative prayer and participant in the resulting turbulent controversy rending the Byzantine imperial dynasty and church that eventually condemned him for heresy.

A student of the monk-theologian Gregory Palamas, Akindynos absorbed from him the Hesychast theory of ascetical contemplation, a method of Eastern mysticism that used repetitive formulas and concentration through specific bodily postures to achieve inner peace and divine union through a vision of God. Theologically conservative and a teacher of logic, Akindynos—who had studied the Aristotelian realism of the Greek monk Barlaam of Calabria and was familiar with scholastic Latin philosophy—at first sided with Palamas but later attempted to convince him of certain errors in the theory.

Abetted by the accession of Emperor John V Palaeologus in 1341 and encouraged by the patriarch of Constantinople, John XII Calecas, Akindynos recorded in 1343 the history of the

Hesychast dispute and by 1344 had composed seven treatises against Palamas' doctrine. Aspiring to be bishop of Thessalonica, Akindynos propagated anti-Palamite views there. In 1347, however, he was condemned by a synod after the pro-Palamas emperor John VI Cantacuzenus came to power and in 1351 was posthumously anathematized (solemnly cursed or banned) by being placed on the official list of heretics.

Akindynos' other writings, largely unedited in manuscript form, include three professions of faith to express the Orthodox tradition to various monarchs, a collection of letters documenting the Palamite controversy, and more than 500 verses in characteristic Byzantine iambic style describing the errors of Hesychasm. Theodore Ouspensky published a Russian version of Akindynos' report to the patriarch Calecas on the controversy (1893). The remaining published writings are his anti-Palamite letters and pieces of poetry to his colleague, the humanist-philosopher Nicephorus Gregoras, contained in *Patrologia Graeca,* edited by J.-P. Migne (1857–66).

Akintola, Samuel Ladake (b. July 10, 1910, Ogbomosho, Southern Nigeria—d. Jan. 14, 1966, Ibadan, Nigeria), administrator and politician, premier of the Western Region of Nigeria and an early victim of the January 1966 military coup.

Like many other African nationalists Akintola was a teacher in the 1930s and early 1940s and a member of the Baptist Teachers' Union and the Nigerian Youth Movement. He left teaching to study public administration and law in England and returned to Nigeria in 1950. He became a legal adviser to the Action Group, the dominant Western Region party, and by 1954 was deputy leader under Oba Femi Awolowo. He was simultaneously active in the federal government; he became minister of labour in 1952 and later held the portfolios of health, communications, and aviation.

In 1959 Akintola became premier of the Western Region, coming to be recognized as a representative of conservative, business-oriented interests, who was content to concentrate party efforts on the region—in diametrical opposition to Awolowo's growing interest in democratic socialism and to his attempt to win minority tribe votes in the North. In mid-1962 Awolowo's supporters repudiated Akintola as a party leader and had him replaced as premier. The Northern-dominated federal government, however, hostile to Awolowo, declared a state of emergency in the region and restored Akintola to his post (1963). He formed the Nigerian National Democratic Party but was never able to win the votes of the majority of the region. His blatantly rigged election in 1965 was undoubtedly an immediate cause of the January 1966 coup in which he was slain.

akiriyāvāda (Buddhist philosophy): *see* akriyāvāda.

Akita, prefecture (*ken*), northwestern Honshu, Japan, on the Sea of Japan coast. Its area of 4,483 sq mi (11,611 sq km) is divided between lowlands (west) and a plateau region (east). The Hachiman-tai (Hachiman Plateau) is dotted with volcanoes such as Komaga-take (5,371 ft [1,637 m]), near the eastern border with Iwate Prefecture. The plateau is covered with white fir trees and alpine plants that grow amid fissures yielding steam, smoke, and boiling mud. In the extreme northeast, on the border with Aomori Prefecture, is Towada-ko (Towada Lake), which is the central feature of Towada-Hachimantai National Park.

Akita Plain, west of the Ōu and Dewa mountain ranges, is crossed by rivers flowing into the Sea of Japan. Chief among them are the Yoneshiro-gawa (Yoneshiro River; north), the Omono-gawa (central), and the Ishizawa-gawa (south). Hachirō-gata (Hachirō Lagoon), on the Oga-hantō (Oga Peninsula), was the second largest body of water in Japan after Lake Biwa, about 50 mi (80 km) in circumference but it was almost totally reclaimed for rice cultivation during the 10-year period after 1958. Because national rice cultivation attained a surplus in the 1970s, part of the area was considered for development as industrial estates.

Lumbering is also important. Mineral wealth includes deposits of copper, sulfur, lead, and manganese. Before and immediately after World War II, oil refineries were operated in Akita, along the Sea of Japan, but as crude oil imports rose sharply, the oil refineries moved to the Pacific coast for convenience of importing. Akita city, the prefecture capital and major city, still produces some petroleum products and chemicals; it is served by the outport of Tsuchizakiminato. Akita University, founded

Young men balancing the *kantō*, bamboo frames hung with paper lanterns, during the Tanabata Matsuri (Tanabata Festival; August 5–7) in Akita, Japan

J. Schmidlin—Bavaria Verlag

in 1949, is located there. Noshiro is known for its wood products. Other important towns are Honjō, Oga, Yokote, and Ōdate. Pop. (1983 est.) city, 293,051; prefecture, 1,255,000.

akita, breed of working dog that originated in the mountains of northern Japan. In 1931 the Japanese government designated the breed as a national treasure. The Akita is a powerful, muscular dog with a broad head, erect, pointed ears (small in relation to head size), and a large curved tail carried over the back or curled against the flank. Akitas are bred in a variety of colours and markings, including all-white, brindle, and pinto. With the exception of the white, all bear a distinct mask (dark area around the muzzle). Akitas were admitted into the show classifications of the American Kennel Club (AKC) in 1973. According to AKC standards males must be 26 to 28 inches (66 to 71 centimetres) high at the withers, females 24 to 26 in. (60 to 66 cm).

'Akkā (Israel): *see* 'Akko.

Akkad, ancient region in what is now the northern part of middle Iraq, home of the ancient Babylonian civilizations. Akkad was located roughly in the area where the Tigris and Euphrates rivers are closest to each other, and its northern limit extended beyond the line of the modern al-Fallūjah and Baghdad; to the south was Sumer, the southern part of middle Iraq. From about 2000 BC, rulers of the whole middle-Iraq region called themselves "kings of Sumer and Akkad."

The name of Akkad was taken from the city of Agade, founded by the Semitic conqueror Sargon I about 2300. At least from that time onward the inhabitants of this northern region were predominantly Semitic, and it is their

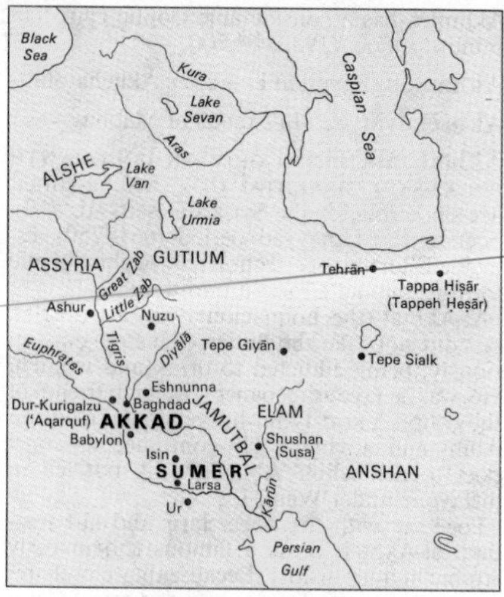

Akkad and Sumer in the 2nd millennium BC

From G. Roux, *Ancient Iraq*

speech (the oldest Semitic dialect preserved, in the cuneiform script) that is called Akkadian.

Akkadian language, also spelled ACCADIAN, also called ASSYRO-BABYLONIAN, extinct Semitic language of the Northern Peripheral group, spoken in Mesopotamia from the 3rd to the 1st millennium BC.

Akkadian spread across an area extending from the Mediterranean Sea to the Persian Gulf during the time of Sargon (Akkadian Sharrum-kin) of the Akkad dynasty, who reigned *c.* 2334–*c.* 2279 BC. By *c.* 2000 Akkadian had supplanted Sumerian as the spoken language of southern Mesopotamia, although Sumerian remained in use as the written language of sacred literature. At about the same time, the language divided into the Assyrian dialect, spoken in northern Mesopotamia, and the Babylonian dialect, spoken in southern Mesopotamia. At first the Assyrian dialect was used more extensively, but Babylonian largely supplanted it and became the lingua franca of the Near East by the 9th century BC. During the 7th and 6th centuries BC, Aramaic gradually began to replace Babylonian as the spoken and written language; after that, Babylonian was still used for writings on mathematics, astronomy, and other learned subjects, but by the 1st century AD it had completely died out. Scholars deciphered the language in the 19th century.

Akkadian, written in a cuneiform script developed from that of the Sumerians, contained about 600 word and syllable signs. The sound system of the language had 20 consonants and 8 vowels (both long and short *a, i, e,* and *u*). Nouns occurred in three cases (nominative, genitive, and accusative), three numbers (singular, dual, and plural), and two genders (masculine and feminine); the feminine was distinguished from the masculine by the addition of the suffix *-t* or *-at* to the stem. The verb had two tenses (past and present-future).

Akkadian writing: *see* cuneiform writing.

Akkerman (Ukrainian S.S.R.): *see* Belgorod-Dnestrovsky.

Akkerman, Convention of (Oct. 7, 1826), agreement signed in Akkerman, Moldavia (now Belgorod-Dnestrovsky, Ukrainian S.S.R.), between the Ottoman Empire and Russia, whereby the Ottomans accepted, under threat of war, Russia's demands concerning Serbia and the Danube principalities of Moldavia and Walachia.

The convention confirmed the signers' earlier (1812) Treaty of Bucharest; recognized the autonomy of Serbia; granted Russia special rights to protect the autonomy of Moldavia and Walachia, including a seven-year term of office for the *hospodars* (princes), who could thenceforth not be dismissed without consent of the Russian ambassador in Istanbul; allowed Russian ships freedom of the Black Sea and the Danube River; and opened the Straits of the Bosporus and the Dardanelles to merchant vessels of any nation sailing to or from Russia. Subsequent Ottoman renunciation of the Akkerman Convention and attempts to regain control of Serbia, Moldavia, and Walachia resulted in a Russian declaration of war against the Ottoman Empire (1828).

ʿAkko, also spelled ACRE, or ʿAKKĀ, city, northwest Israel, on the Mediterranean Sea, at the north end of the Bay of Haifa (formerly Bay of Acre). Its natural harbour was a frequent target for Palestine's many invaders. The earliest mention of ʿAkko is in an Egyptian execration text dating from the 19th century BC. The Bible (Judges 1) states that it did not fall to the Jews under Joshua and his successors; the Canaanites and Phoenicians, Semitic peoples of Palestine and the Levant coast, long held the site. Later it was conquered by Alexander the Great (336 BC) and by the Egyptian king Ptolemy II Philadelphus (reigned 285–246 BC), who renamed the city Ptolemais.

Great Mosque of al-Jazzār, built in 1781, ʿAkko, Israel
Keystone

ʿAkko was a principal base of the Romans when they suppressed the Jewish revolt of AD 66–70. Later conquerors include the Persians (614), the Arabs (638), and the crusaders (1104), who named the city St. Jean d'Acre and made it their last capital. Its capture in 1291 by the Mamlūk sultan al-Ashraf Khalil (reigned 1290–93) marked the end of crusader rule. From 1516 to 1918 ʿAkko was, except for brief intervals, under the Ottoman Turks. In 1918 it was taken by British forces, and subsequently became a part of Palestine under British mandate (1922).

The city's old fortifications and citadel were strengthened by Ahmad Pasha al-Jazzār (Arabic: The Butcher), the Turkish governor (1775–1804), and withstood Napoleon's siege (1799). Though the city had surrendered to the Egyptian viceroy Ibrahīm Pasha in 1832, the citadel itself had never been successfully forced until May 3, 1948, when, as a British prison, it was taken by the Irgun Zva'i Le'umi, a Jewish terrorist group. ʿAkko was occupied by regular Israeli troops on May 17, 1948. Though most of the city's Arab inhabitants fled, about 3,000 remained; the population in the early 1980s was about three-fourths Jewish.

ʿAkko's ancient port has silted up in modern times and has become secondary to Haifa's across the bay. It is used only by small fishing boats. Industries in modern ʿAkko include a steel-rolling mill and match, tile, and plastic plants. Prominent structures, aside from the citadel, include the Great Mosque, built by al-Jazzār and named for him; the Municipal Museum, housed in the Pasha's bathhouse; the Crypt of St. John, actually a crusader refectory; and several churches built on crusader foundations. Just north of the city is the tomb of Bahāʾ Ullāh, Iranian founder of the Bahāʾī faith. To the south is a large industrial zone; paint factories are found in the east. The city remains the major trade centre for Arab settlements in western Galilee and is becoming popular with tourists. ʿAkko is the site of the Nautical College of the Israeli Navy. Pop. (1982 est.) 39,100.

Aklan, province, island of Panay, Philippines. Occupying the northwestern portion of the island, its area of 702 sq mi (1,818 sq km) is bordered by the Sibuyan Sea to the north and east. Its more populated areas—the Aklan River Valley and the coastal lowland—produce rice, sugarcane, and forest products. The principal towns occupy coastal sites. Kalibo, the provincial capital, is a trading centre and transportation junction. New Washington, a port to the east of the capital, has interisland shipping facilities. Other towns include Ibajay, Batan, and Banga. The week-long Ati-atihan festival is held each January; originally coinciding with a Christian feast day and long a mixture of Christian and pagan elements, it celebrates a pact between the Malays and the Negritoes. Pop. (1980) 324,563.

Aklavik, hamlet, northwestern Northwest Territories, Canada, in the Mackenzie Delta near the Yukon border. Its Eskimo name can be translated "where there are bears." Established as a Hudson's Bay Company trading post on the south bank of the river's West Channel in 1912, Aklavik was moved to the north bank in 1920. It is the site of a radio and meteorological station. Fur trapping and the manufacture of fur garments and Eskimo handicrafts are the main sources of income. In 1955 the administrative staff (for the Western Arctic) and some of the population moved to Inuvik (*q.v.*), 33 mi (53 km) east, because shifting permafrost-silt soil hampered building and road and sewer construction. Pop. (1981) 721.

Aklya Kona (Inca religion): *see* Chosen Women.

Akmeist (Russian poet): *see* Acmeist.

Akmolinsk (city, Kazakh S.S.R.): *see* Tselinograd.

Akō, city, Hyōgo Prefecture (*ken*), western Honshu, Japan. During the Heian period (794–1185), it was a seaside resort for courtesans from Kyōto. It became a castle town in the 17th century, when the powerful Ikeda clan took up residence. Since the beginning of the 20th century, the establishment of chemical factories and steel mills has transformed Akō into one of Japan's most polluted industrial cities. Traditional cotton weaving and salt making no longer have much significance. Akō, well known in Japan for its Kabuki theatre productions featuring swordplay, *seppuku*, and samurai, attracts tourists to its annual Akō samurai festival in December. Inc. city, 1951. Pop. (1980) 51,046.

Akola, town, administrative headquarters of Akola district, Mahārāshtra state, western India, on the Mūrna River. An important road and rail junction in the Tāpti River Valley, it is a commercial centre trading chiefly in cotton. There are also textile and vegetable-oil industries. In the past it was incorporated in turn into several local Muslim kingdoms. It is an important educational centre with six colleges affiliated with the University of Nāgpur.

Akola district occupies 4,080 sq mi (10,567 sq km), mainly in the low-lying, undulating plain of Berār. The Tāpti River flows across the northern part of the district from east to west. The district is bounded by outliers of the Sātpura Range (north) and by the Ajanta Hills (south). The Penganga River (tributary of the Godāvari) drains the south. Soils are fertile, and the district is known for its limestone deposits. Chief crops are rice, cotton, wheat, millet, and peanuts (groundnuts). Industries are agriculturally based; cotton ginning, oil processing, and cigarette manufacture are important. There is a thermal power station at Paras. Tourist attractions include the Jaina temple at Sirpur and a Muslim fort at Narnāla. Pop. (1981) town, 225,412; district, 1,826,952.

Akosombo Dam: *see* Volta River Dam.

Akouta (Niger): *see* Arlit and Akouta.

Akow (Taiwan): *see* P'ing-tung.

Akragas (Italy): *see* Agrigento.

Akranes, town, Borgarfjardharsýsla (Borgarfjardhar county), western Iceland, situated on Faxaflói (Faxa Bay), at the tip of a peninsula between Borgarfjördhur and Hvalfjördhur (Borgar and Hval fjords). A fishing port and local market centre, it is connected by road to Reykjavík, 20 mi (32 km) southeast. Akranes is the site of one of Iceland's largest cement plants. Pop. (1982 est.) 5,267.

akriyāvāda (Sanskrit: "doctrine denying the effect of deeds"), Pāli AKIRIYĀVĀDA, set of beliefs held by heretic teachers in India who were contemporaries of the Buddha. The doctrine was a kind of antinomianism that, by denying the orthodox *karman* theory of the efficacy of former deeds on a man's present and future condition, also denied the possibility of man's influencing his own destiny through preferring righteous to bad conduct. The teachers were therefore severely criticized for immorality by their religious opponents, including Buddhists. Their views are known only through uncomplimentary references in Buddhist and Jaina literature. Among the heretic teachers whose names are known are Pūraṇa Kāśyapa, a radical antinomian; Gośāla Maskarīputra, a fatalist; Ajita Keśakambalin, the earliest known materialist in India; and Pakudha Kātyāyana, an atomist. Gośāla's followers formed the Ājīvika sect, which enjoyed some acceptance during the Maurya period (3rd century BC) and then dwindled.

Akron, city, seat (1842) of Summit County, northeastern Ohio, U.S., on the Cuyahoga River, 41 mi (66 km) south-southeast of Cleveland. It is the centre of a metropolitan area that includes the cities of Cuyahoga Falls, Barberton, Tallmadge, and Stow and several villages. At 1,200 ft (370 m) above sea level, it was named for its "high place" (Greek *akros*) on the watershed between the Mississippi River and the Great Lakes. Laid out in 1825 by Gen. Simon Perkins, commissioner of the Ohio Canal Fund, it was assured substantial growth by the completion of the Ohio and Erie Canal, in 1827, and of the Pennsylvania and Ohio Canal, in 1840, linking it with Pittsburgh. Water power and transportation supplied by these canals led to Akron's early development as an industrial centre. The abundant water supply and the arrival of the railroads prompted Benjamin F. Goodrich to move a small rubber factory to the site in 1871. This industry rapidly expanded with the advent of the automobile and the demand for tires. Between 1910 and 1920 the city's population tripled, to more than 200,000, and Akron became known as the "rubber capital of the world," a position it still maintains as the headquarters of the far-flung giants of the rubber industry—Firestone, General Tire, Goodyear, and Goodrich. Manufactures are now well diversified and, apart from a wide variety of rubber and plastic products, include farm machinery, aluminum siding, house fittings, electrical and transportation equipment, fishing tackles, children's books and toys, and chemicals. In the late 1970s, however, some manufacturing plants and downtown stores were closed.

The hangar at the city's airport is the site of the Goodyear Aerospace Corporation Air Dock (for airships [blimps]), one of the world's largest buildings without interior supports. Akron is an important truck terminal and distribution point between the Eastern Seaboard and the Midwest.

More than 4,300 ac (1,700 ha) are occupied by parks; and surrounding lakes and reservoirs and several golf courses afford recreation facilities. The World Series of Golf is an annual professional tournament. Nearby Derby Downs is the site of the annual All-American Soap Box Derby for homemade gravity-powered cars. The city's cultural centres include the Akron Art Institute, American Indian Art Hall of Fame, and the Stan Hywet Hall (with antiques dating from the 16th century). The University of Akron (founded in 1870 as Buchtel College) has an Institute of Polymer Science and an International Rubber Science Hall of Fame gallery. Inc. village, 1836; city, 1865. Pop. (1970) city, 275,425; metropolitan area (SMSA), 679,239; (1980) city, 237,177; metropolitan area (SMSA), 660,328.

Akrotiri, British military enclave in south central Cyprus, retained as a "sovereign base area" by the United Kingdom under the London Agreement of 1959 granting the independence of Cyprus. Located southwest of Limassol, it comprises Akrotiri Peninsula, the southernmost part of the island, and a small coastal area north of Episkopi Bay. It has a hospital, a weather station, and an airfield. Akrotiri and Dhekélia sovereign base to the northeast (together totalling 99 sq mi [256 sq km]) are used as British training facilities and staging areas between Britain and southern Asia and the Far East. They are also support areas for United Nations forces on Cyprus. In 1971 U.S. U-2 reconnaissance planes began monitoring the Near East on flights from Akrotiri's airfield. In the late 1970s controversy arose in Cyprus over the reported use of Akrotiri by the U.S. as a station for monitoring Soviet activities.

aksak (Turkish: "limping"), also called BULGARIAN RHYTHM, variety of musical metre characterized by combinations of unequal units of beats, such as 2 plus 3 or 3 plus 2 and their extensions. Thus 3 + 3 + 2, or 2 + 3 + 3, produces $\frac{8}{8}$ units quite unlike the $\frac{4}{4}$ common to Western music. As non-Western music, as well as eastern European folk music, began to exert influence in the West, *aksak* rhythms found their way into the works of a number of 20th-century composers, Bartók and Stravinsky foremost among them.

The word *aksak* was borrowed from Turkish musical theory to replace the phrase Bulgarian rhythms applied earlier to such rhythms by the Hungarian composer Béla Bartók and the Romanian ethnomusicologist Constantin Brailoiu.

Aksakov, Sergey Timofeyevich (b. Oct. 1 [Sept. 20, old style], 1791, Ufa, Russia—d. May 12 [April 30, O.S.], 1859, Moscow), novelist noted for objective, realistic narrative and for the introduction of a new genre, a cross between memoirs and the novel, into Russian literature.

Brought up in a strongly patriarchal family, he was educated in the pseudo-classical tradition at home, at school, and at the newly founded university in Kazan. He became a translator in the legislative commission of the civil service, served in the militia in the War

Sergey Timofeyevich Aksakov, detail of an oil painting by Ivan Nikolayevich Kramskoy, 1878; in the State Tretyakov Gallery, Moscow
By courtesy of the State Tretyakov Gallery, Moscow

of 1812, married in 1815, and in 1816 retired to the family estate. After a decade as a sporting country squire, he returned to the civil service in Moscow and became literary censor, inspector, and, later, director of the college of land surveying. Inheriting money, he retired in 1839 and lived in and near Moscow, entertaining his friends—mainly writers and Slavophiles.

Before 1834, when his successful *Buran* ("Blizzard") was published, Aksakov's writings reflected outmoded literary tastes: translations of Boileau and Molière, undistinguished verse, and articles on the theatre. Inspired by his love for rural Russia in the days of serfdom, by his Slavophile sons, and by his admiration of the novelist Nikolay Gogol, he set down the story of his grandfather, his parents, and his own childhood, transposed into realistic fiction. This effort resulted in three books that have become classics: *Semeynaya khronika* (1856; *Chronicles of a Russian Family,* 1924), *Vospominaniya* (1856, "Reminiscences"; Eng. trans., *A Russian Schoolboy,* 1917), and *Detskie gody Bagrova-vnuka* (1858; *Years of Childhood,* 1916). Though necessarily introspective, Aksakov unfolds his epic chronicle objectively in an unaffected style and simple language. Its interest lies in the illusion of reality and intimacy created by his vivid remembrance of the continuous past. These works, blending personal reminiscence with the techniques of the novelist, brought Aksakov fame. Also of interest are his books on shooting, fishing, and butterfly collecting and his recollections of Gogol, which are firsthand material on his friend's complex personality.

Akselrod, Pavel Borisovich, also called PAUL AXELROD (b. Aug. 25, 1850?, Chernigov, Ukraine?—d. 1928, Berlin), Marxist theorist, co-founder of the first Russian Social Democratic Party, and Menshevik leader.

Akselrod participated in the *narodnik* (populist) movement during the 1870s and with Georgi Plekhanov formed the antiterrorist group Chorny Peredel (Black Repartition) in 1879. He went to western Europe, became a Marxist, and was a founder of the Osvobozhdeniye Truda (Emancipation of Labour Party; 1883) and a member of the editorial board of the newspaper *Iskra* ("The Spark"; 1900). He adopted Menshevism at the Second Congress of Russian Social Democrats (1903), and after 1905 became the ideologist of "liquidationism," a movement to abandon illegal party activities and to concentrate party efforts on trade union and parliamentary work. During World War I he favoured the defense of Russia; he opposed the Bolshevik Revolution (Oct. 1917) and supported the formation of a non-Communist international (1923). His memoirs *Perezhitoye i Peredumanoye* ("Experiences and Reflections") were published in 1923.

Akshak, ancient city of Mesopotamia on the northern boundary of Akkad, identified by some authorities with Babylonian Upi (Opis). About 2500 BC Akshak was conquered by Eannatum, king of Lagash. About a century later Akshak established its hegemony over Sumer and Akkad. The location of Akshak is uncertain, although the Mari letters (from the royal archives at Mari on the Euphrates River; *c.* 1770) indicate that it lay near Eshnunna in the Diyālā River Valley.

Akṣobhya, in Mahāyāna Buddhism, one of the five "self-born" Buddhas. *See* Dhyāni-Buddha.

Aksum, also spelled AXUM, ancient town in Tigrai province, northern Ethiopia. Once the seat of the Kingdom of Aksum, it is now a tourist town best known for its antiquities. Tall granite obelisks, 126 in all, stand (or lie broken) in the central square. One measuring 110 ft (34 m), now fallen, is said to be the tallest obelisk ever erected. They range from nearly plain slabs to intricately inscribed pillars. The most recent of the obelisks announces the adoption of Christianity by a 4th-century king.

At least 27 carved stone thrones have been unearthed in the overgrown ruins of the ancient palace. According to tradition, the 17th-century Church of St. Mary of Zion contains the original tablets of Moses, brought to Ethiopia by King Menelik I, son of Solomon and Sheba. Emperor Haile Selassie I built the new Church of St. Mary of Zion near the old one in 1965. The monastery museum has a rich display of crosses, crowns, jewels, vestments, and ceremonial swords.

An airport, a hospital, a health centre, and a community centre serve the town. Pop. (1980 est.) 21,595.

Aksum, Kingdom of, also spelled AXUM, a powerful kingdom in northern Ethiopia, in the early Christian era.

Originating from one of the Semitic Sabaean kingdoms that had grown in Southern Arabia during the 1st millennium BC, Aksum at its apogee (3rd–6th century AD) became the greatest market of northeast Africa; its merchants traded as far as Alexandria and beyond the Nile. Aksum continued to dominate the Red Sea coast until the end of the 9th century, exercising its influence from the shores of the Gulf of Aden to Zeila on the northern coast of Somaliland.

During the 2nd and 3rd centuries AD its growth as a trading empire increasingly impinged on the power of the kingdom of Meroe, the fall of which was brought about in the 4th century by an Aksumite invasion.

During the 4th century, the kings of Aksum were Christianized—thus becoming both politically and religiously linked to Byzantine Egypt. At the same time they extended their authority into Southern Arabia. In the 6th century, an Aksumite king reduced the Yemen to a state of vassalage. The subsequent history of Aksum receives a few notices in the works of Arabic writers; thus it is recorded that a war took place between Ethiopia and Nubia *c.* 687 and that *c.* 976 a Jewish queen, Esato (Judith), oppressed the Christian population in the region. Though Esato succeeded in dislodging the Aksumite dynasty, another Christian line—that of the Zague—soon assumed control. In 1270 the reigning prince abdicated in favour of Yekuno Amlak, king of Shewa.

Aksur, el- (Egypt): *see* Luxor.

Aktan (Kazakh S.S.R.): *see* Shevchenko.

Aktiengesellschaft Zoologischer Garten Köln: *see* Cologne Zoo.

Aktyubinsk, also spelled AKTIUBINSK, or AK-T'UBINSK, *oblast* (administrative region), western Kazakh Soviet Socialist Republic, occupying an area of 115,300 sq mi (298,700 sq km), created in 1932. The greater part of the *oblast* is a raised plain broken by river valleys.

In the centre are the Mugodzhar Hills, and in the south the sands of the Aral Kara-Kum and Bolshye and Malye Barsuki. The climate is continental, and precipitation is low, particularly in the south. The river network is scanty, the main rivers being the Emba, the Or and Ilek (both tributaries of the Ural), and the Irgiz, which flows into the Shalkarteniz salt marsh. The Mugodzhar Hills have rich chrome deposits as well as nickel and copper; the chrome is mined near Khromtau, perhaps the largest deposit of high-grade chrome ore in the world, and the nickel at Batamshinsky. There are large phosphorite deposits at Oktyabrsk (formerly Kandagach), but these are not exploited in the local production of fertilizers at Alga, which utilizes phosphorite imported from the Kola Peninsula. Alga is also the major Soviet producer of borax, based on supplies imported from Guryev *oblast*. Otherwise most processing industry is concentrated in the capital, Aktyubinsk city. Crops, chiefly grains, are grown in the northwest, and the remaining dry steppe and desert areas are given over to sheep, horses, and camels. Nearly half of the population is Kazakh, about a quarter Russian, and one sixth Ukrainian; about 50 percent is urban. Pop. (1982 est.) 661,000.

Aktyubinsk, also spelled AKTIUBINSK, or AKT'UBINSK, administrative centre, Aktyubinsk *oblast* (region), Kazakh Soviet Socialist Republic, on the Ilek River. It was founded in 1869 as Aktyube (White Hill), a small Russian fort; the first Russian peasant settlers arrived in 1878. In 1891 it became the capital of an *uyezd* (district) and in 1932 of an *oblast*. During World War II a ferroalloys plant was built to smelt the nickel and chrome ores of the Mugodzhar Hills. Now an important industrial centre, Aktyubinsk also produces chromium compounds, X-ray apparatus, and parts for agricultural machinery and has stockyards and flour mills. Cultural assets include a teacher-training and a medical institute, a theatre, two museums, and a planetarium. Pop. (1983 est.) 218,000.

akund floss, also called CALOTROPIS FLOSS, downy seed fibre obtained from *Calotropis procera* and *C. gigantea,* plants of the Asclepiadaceae family, native to southern Asia and Africa and introduced to South America and the islands of the Caribbean. The yellowish material, made up of thin fibres, 0.75 to 1.12 inches (2 to 3 centimetres) long and 12 to 42 microns (a micron is about 0.00004 inch) in diameter, is harvested by hand.

Akund floss is used primarily as upholstery stuffing, sometimes mixed with the seed fibre kapok. In certain areas it is variously known as ak, mader, or mudar.

Akure, town, capital of Ondo State, southwestern Nigeria, in the southern part of the forested Yoruba Hills (altitude 1,129 ft [344 m]) and at the intersection of roads from Ondo, Ilesha, Ado-Ekiti, and Owo. It is an agricultural trade centre (yams, cassava, corn [maize], bananas, rice, palm oil and kernels, okra, pumpkins) for the Ondo branch of the Yoruba people. Although cocoa is by far the most important local commercial crop, cotton, teak, and palm produce are also cultivated for export. Other local occupations are weaving, hunting, pottery making, tailoring, and bricklaying. Akure is the site of a teacher-training college, an agricultural school, secondary schools, and several hospitals. Pop. (1983 est.) 117,300.

Akureyri, town, Eyjafjardharsýsla (Eyjafjardhar county), north central Iceland, at the southern end of Eyjafjördhur (Eyja Fjord). It is the chief centre of the north and the island's most populous urban centre outside the Reykjavík metropolitan area. While primarily a commercial and distributing centre, Akureyri is also a fishing port, agricultural market, and manufacturing centre for woollen goods, fish

Akureyri, Ice., near the head of Eyjafjördhur (Eyja Fjord)

J. Allan Cash—EB Inc.

oil, shoes, and fish and dairy products. Ironworking, woodworking, and shipbuilding are all significant industries. It has a technical college, an agricultural experimental station, an airport, botanical gardens, and an ultra-modern Lutheran church. Inc. 1876. Pop. (1982 est.) 13,605.

Akutagawa Ryūnosuke, pseudonym CHŌKŌDŌ SHUJIN, or GAKI (b. March 1, 1892, Tokyo—d. July 24, 1927, Tokyo), prolific writer of stories, plays, and poetry, noted for his stylistic virtuosity.

As a boy Akutagawa was sickly and hypersensitive, but he excelled at school and was a voracious reader. He began his literary career while attending Tokyo Imperial University, where he studied English literature from 1913 to 1916.

Akutagawa Ryūnosuke

By courtesy of the International Society for Educational Information, Tokyo

The publication in 1915 of his short story "Rashōmon" (Eng. trans., 1930) led to his introduction to Natsume Sōseki, the outstanding novelist of the day. With Sōseki's encouragement he began to write a series of stories derived largely from 12th- and 13th-century collections of Japanese tales but retold in the light of modern psychology in a highly individual style. He ranged wide in his choice of material, drawing inspiration from such disparate sources as China, Japan's 16th-century Christian community in Nagasaki, and European contacts with 19th-century Japan. Many of his stories have a feverish, unhealthy intensity, well-suited to their often macabre themes.

In 1922 he turned toward autobiographical fiction, but Akutagawa's stories of modern life lack the exotic and sometimes lurid glow of the older tales, perhaps accounting for their comparative unpopularity. His last important work, "Kappa" (1927; Eng. trans., 1947), although a satirical fable about elflike creatures (*kappa*), is written in the mirthless vein of his last period and reflects his depressed state at the time. His suicide came as a shock to the literary world. Akutagawa is probably the most widely translated of all Japanese writers, and a number of his stories have been made into films. The film classic *Rashomon* (1951), directed by Kurosawa Akira, is based on a combination of Akutagawa's story by that title and another story of his, "Yabu no naka" (1921; "In a Grove," 1952).

akvavit (distilled liquor): *see* aquavit.

Akwamu, Akan state (*c.* 1600–1730) of the forest and coastal lands in what is now southern Ghana. At its apogee in the early 18th century, it stretched more than 250 miles (400 kilometres) along the coast from Whydah (now Ouidah) in the east beyond Winneba in the west.

Its founders, an Akan people who are traditionally said to have come from Twifu Heman, northwest of Cape Coast, moved during the late 16th or early 17th century to the region of modern Akim Abuakwa, where they founded the state of Akwamu. As the state grew rich on the sale of gold from the Birim River district, its inhabitants sought to extend their authority. Because they were hemmed in on the north and northwest by the state of Akim and other states in loose alliance with or subject to the powerful Denkyera, they expanded south and southeast toward the Ga and Fanti towns of the coast. These they subdued between 1677 and 1681 under their king (*akwamuhene*), Ansa Sasraku, extending their influence over the state of Ladoku in the east (1679) and, under Ansa's successor, over the Fanti state of Agona in the west (1689). In 1702 they crossed the Volta River to occupy Whydah, a coastal state of Dahomey, and in 1710 subdued the Ewe people of the Ho region. By this time, however, their former satellite, Ashanti, had grown rich and powerful and, though it remained friendly to them, was becoming increasingly hostile to Akim, the ally of Denkyera, Akwamu's rival. Pressured by Ashanti, the Akim peoples retreated upon Akwamu's borders and, after a long war, succeeded in infiltrating them. The *akwamuhene* was forced to flee, and by 1731 the state had ceased to exist. *See also* Akan states.

Akwapim-Togo Ranges, narrow belt of ridges and hills in Ghana, West Africa, extending about 200 mi (320 km) northeast–southwest from the Togo boundary toward the Atlantic coast near the Densu River mouth. Averaging 1,500 ft (460 m) in height, the hills continue eastward to the Niger River as the Togo Mountains in Togo and as the Atacora Mountains in Benin, and they contain isolated peaks near the Togo border (Afadjoto, 2,905 ft [885 m]; Torogbani, 2,861 ft [872 m]; Djebobo, 2,874 ft [876 m]). The Volta River cuts through their complex of closely packed folds at the deep, narrow Ajena Gorge and is harnessed by the great dam at Akosombo one mi downstream.

The fertile area has an annual rainfall of 50–65 in. (1,270–1,650 mm), supporting semideciduous forest. Descent to the surrounding plains is often steep and marked by abrupt cliffs. Communications and roads are sparse and are mainly limited to the south.

Plantain, cassava, and corn (maize) are grown in the south, and yams and rice in the drier north. The central highlands, once important for palm oil and cocoa, have greatly suffered from erosion and disease. The section within the Volta Region is important for the cash crops of cocoa and coffee.

Because of an equable climate, the ranges contain hill resorts such as Aburi, Anum, and Amedzofe.

Akyab (Burma): *see* Sittwe.

AKZO NV, diversified Dutch manufacturer of chemicals and paints, and a leading world manufacturer of synthetic fibres for domestic and industrial use. Headquarters are in Arnhem, The Netherlands.

The company was formed in 1911 as NV Nederlandsche. It assumed its present name in 1969 upon merger with Koninkijke Zout-Organon NV. The company manufactures chemical fibres, plastics, film, industrial chemicals, paint, adhesives, pharmaceuticals, and hospital supplies; synthetic fibres constitute about one-third of the company's business.

In the early 1970s the company expanded rapidly, based on the strength of its synthetic-fibre industry. In the mid-1970s clothes made of synthetic fibre became less fashionable and, at the same time, the price of petroleum-based feedstocks used in making chemicals and fibres rose rapidly. The company found itself faced with an excess of productive capacity and in the midst of a severe financial crisis.

In response, the European Economic Community (EEC) negotiated tighter quotas on textile imports from developing countries, and in 1974 AKZO started a series of plant closings and layoffs. The corporate shrinkage was planned in cooperation with Dutch unions in an attempt to minimize the social impact.

al-, Arabic definite article, meaning "the." It frequently prefixes Arabic proper nouns, especially place-names; an example is al-Jazīrah, Arabic "the island," the name of an interfluvial region in The Sudan. Reference works often alphabetize such forms under the main part of the name (thus, in the example just cited, "Jazīrah, al-"); the *Encyclopædia Britannica* so lists proper nouns, although certain exceptions are listed below. Thirteen Arabic letters—the so-called sun letters, *t, th, d, dh, r, z, s, sh, ṣ, ḍ, ṭ, ẓ,* and *n*—assimilate the *l* of *al-* in pronunciation; thus, ash-Shām (the classical Arabic name of Damascus), not al-Shām.

Care must be taken to avoid confusing the definite article *al-* meaning "the" with the form "Āl," a completely different Arabic construction used to designate a family or tribal name. "Āl" is invariate and does not elide; thus, Āl Sa'ūd, not Ās-Sa'ūd." The form "Āl" is always romanized with a capital letter, irrespective of its position in an English sentence.

al-Azhar University, chief centre of Islāmic and Arabic learning in the world, centred on the mosque of that name in the medieval quarter of Cairo. It was founded by the Fāṭimids in AD 970 and was formally organized by 988. The basic program of studies was, and still is, Islāmic law, theology, and the Arabic language. Late in the Middle Ages philosophy and medicine were added to the curriculum but, because original and independent thinking was suspect in the orthodox scholarly circles of al-Azhar, were soon eliminated. Only in the 19th century, through the efforts of the great educational reformer Jamāl ad-Dīn al-Afghānī, was philosophy reinstated. Twentieth-century efforts at modernization have resulted in the addition of social sciences at its new supplementary campus at Naṣr City.

There are 11 principal institutes affiliated with al-Azhar, attracting students from as far afield as China, Indonesia, Morocco, and Somalia. Women have been admitted since 1962.

Āl Bū Sa'īd DYNASTY, Muslim dynasty of Oman, southeastern Arabia (*c.* 1749 to the present), and Zanzibar, East Africa (*c.* 1749–1964).

Aḥmad ibn Sa'īd, who had been governor of Ṣuḥār, Oman, in the 1740s under the Ya'rubid *imām* of Oman, managed to displace the Ya'rubids by *c.* 1749 and become *imām* of Oman and Zanzibar, Pemba, and Kilwa, in East Africa. His successors—known as *sayyids*, or, later, as sultans—expanded their possessions in the late 18th century to include Bahrain in the Persian Gulf and Bandar 'Abbās, Hormoz, and Kishm (all in Iran). In 1798 the threat of the militant Wahhābīs (a fundamentalist Islāmic sect in central Arabia) decided Sulṭān ibn Aḥmad (reigned 1792–1806) to conclude a treaty with the East India Company, which would assure a British presence in Muscat (Masqaṭ), the Āl Bū Sa'īdī capital, an important port on the trade route to India.

Under Sa'īd ibn Sulṭān (reigned 1806–65) the Bū Sa'īdī family reached the peak of its influence. Sa'īd established commercial relations with the United States (1839) and France (1844), strengthened his ties with Great Britain, and placed the East African Arab and Swahili colonies from Mogadisho to Cabo (cape) Delgado under his suzerainty. The equilibrium of the sultanate was still threatened by Wahhābī attacks and tribal unrest in the mountains, but with British aid Sa'īd kept them in check. In 1854, out of gratitude for such support, the Sayyid gave Great Britain the Kuria Muria Islands.

On Sa'īd's death in 1856, the Āl Bū Sa'īdī dominions were divided by the British between Sa'īd's two sons: Oman came under Thuwaynī's rule (1856–66), while Zanzibar went to Majīd (reigned 1856–70).

In Zanzibar, the Bū Sa'īdīs remained in power even under the British protectorate (1890–1963) but were overthrown in 1964 when Zanzibar was incorporated into the United Republic of Tanzania.

In Oman, an opposition movement, organized in the mountains in 1901 by 'Īsā ibn Ṣāliḥ, threatened the Bū Sa'īds, until a treaty, known as the Treaty of as-Sīb (Sept. 25, 1920), was signed between Imām 'Īsā ibn Ṣāliḥ and Sultan Taymūr ibn Fayṣal (reigned 1913–32), by virtue of which Sultan Taymūr ruled over the coastal provinces and the Imām over the interior. Opposition broke out again in 1954 when the tribes appealed to Saudi Arabia for aid in establishing an independent principality, but Sultan Sa'īd ibn Taymūr (reigned 1932–70) was able to put down the rebellion in 1957 with British aid.

'Alā' od-Dīn 'Aṭā Malek Joveynī (Persian historian): *see* Joveynī, 'Aṭā Malek.

Ala Shan Desert, southernmost portion of the Gobi (desert), occupying about 400,000 sq mi (1,000,000 sq km) in north central China. Covering portions of western Inner Mongolia Autonomous Region and northern Kansu Province, it is bounded by the Huang Ho (river) and Ho-lan Shan (Ala Shan; mountains) on the east; by the Ch'i-lien Shan-mo (mountains) on the south; by the northern reaches of the Hei Ho (river) on the west; and by a tectonic depression and the China–Mongolia border on the north. It extends about 350 mi (550 km) northwest–southeast and has a maximum width of about 170 mi in the northwest, narrowing in the southeast. Physiographically, the desert is a plain, the floor of a great intermontane basin, dissected by low ridges (local relief of 500 to 650 ft [150 to 200 m]) and depressions (called *tsaidams*), the latter often containing saline lakes, swamps, or pans. The plain ranges in elevation from 2,690 ft in the northwest to 5,450 ft in the southeast.

Chinese geographers do not define the Ala Shan Desert as such, but instead divide the region into three smaller deserts, the T'eng-ko-li (Tengri) Sha-mo in the south, the Pa-tan-chi-lin (Badan Zhareng, or Batan Tsalang) in the west, and the Wu-lan-pu-ho (Ulan Buh) in the northeast. The T'eng-ko-li is a sand desert, characterized by barchan dunes (*i.e.,* moving sand dunes, crescent in shape) up to 820 ft high. The other two areas are marked by similar but smaller dune areas interspersed with structural basins containing pebbly desert pavements.

Alabama, constituent state of the United States of America lying in the east south central region of the country.

The following article summarizes the administrative history, geography, demographic patterns, economy, and culture of modern Alabama; for additional treatment of its geography and history, *see* MACROPAEDIA: United States of America: *Alabama.*

Facing the Gulf of Mexico at Mobile Bay in the south, Alabama is also bounded by the states of Florida on the south, Georgia on the east, Tennessee on the north, and Mississippi on the west. The capital is Montgomery. Roughly rectangular in shape, the state extends about 335 mi (540 km) from north to south and 210 mi from east to west.

The earliest inhabitants were Indians, whose occupancy has probably spanned 10,000 years. Visible evidence of pre-Columbian human activity are settlement sites, ceremonial centres, and great twisting burial mounds around Moundville, near Tuscaloosa; and the cavern homesites in the Appalachian ranges of northeastern Alabama. At the time of initial European exploration in the 16th century the main resident Indian groups were the Creeks, Cherokees, Choctaws, and Chickasaws.

Several Spanish treasure seekers, especially Hernando de Soto, made the initial European contact, while the French founded the first permanent settlement at Ft. Louis in 1702. The first blacks arrived in 1719 when a slave ship unloaded its cargo at Dauphin Island. The 17th and 18th centuries were marked by struggles between French, British, and Spanish authorities for control of the region. Although control over most of the territory passed from Britain to the United States in 1783, the Spanish maintained a foothold at Mobile Bay until 1813. The Alabama Territory was created in 1817 and was granted statehood in 1819. Alabama seceded from the Union during the Civil War (1861), joining the Confederate States of America, which had its first capital at Montgomery. Readmission to the Union occurred in 1868. Efforts during Reconstruction to include the black population in the mainstream of government, education, and the economy failed, and by the mid-1870s a rigid policy of racial segregation had developed that rendered blacks virtually powerless until the mid-1960s.

Physiographically Alabama can be divided into two main regions of approximately equal area: the southern extremities of the Appalachian Mountains in the north, and the coastal plain of the Gulf of Mexico in the south. The Cumberland Plateau of the far north drains to the northwest through the Tennessee River, while the rest of the state is drained southward through broad, fertile valleys.

The Alabama climate is temperate with an average annual temperature of some 60° F (17° C) in the north and 67° F (19° C) in the south. Rainfall is fairly evenly distributed throughout the year, with a yearly average of 52 in. (1,320 mm) at Birmingham and 62 in. at Mobile. Under these favourable conditions the growing season ranges from 200 days in the north to 300 days in the south. Soil conditions throughout the state are also well suited for agriculture.

Early rural settlement patterns reflected that fact, and until the 1960s more than one-half of the population was still rural, decreasing only to 40 percent by 1980. Only two cities, Birmingham and Mobile, have populations exceeding 200,000. Almost three-quarters of the population is white and one-quarter black, both groups being characterized by deep genealogical roots in the state. Religious affiliations are primarily Protestant, the vast majority of churches remaining without integrated congregations.

Cotton dominated the economy of Alabama until the boll weevil blight of 1915 forced diversification of crops. Cotton is still a major crop, but Alabama also produces soybeans, corn (maize), peanuts (groundnuts), forest products, poultry, cattle, and hogs. Industrial development centred on the iron and steel industry of Birmingham with its nearby resources of iron ore, coal, and limestone. Hydroelectric plants constructed by the Tennessee Valley Authority (TVA) in the 1930s provided abundant low-cost electricity for the development of such industries as aluminum, textiles, paper, chemicals, fabricated metals, and rubber and plastics. Three nuclear reactor complexes, Browns Ferry, Farley, and Bellefonte, have been providing additional electric power since the mid-1970s.

River-barge traffic on the navigable Tennessee River and the Black Warrior–Tombigbee–Mobile river systems is heavy. New construction at the Alabama State Docks has turned Mobile into a major ocean terminal. Mobile Bay is connected to the Intracoastal Waterway. Highways, airways, and railroads crisscross the state.

Alabamans, often referring to their state as the "Heart of Dixie," have maintained the cultural traditions of the antebellum South as evidenced by the many fine plantation museums and by the rich vein of rural tradition and folklore. Universities include the University of Alabama, Auburn University, and Tuskegee Institute. Important scientific and technological research is conducted at the Alabama Space and Rocket Center at Huntsville. Area 51,609 sq mi (133,667 sq km). Pop. (1980) 3,893,978.

Alabama claims, maritime grievances of the United States against Great Britain, accumulated during and after the U.S. Civil War (1861–65). The claims are significant in international law for furthering the use of arbitration to settle disputes peacefully and for delineating certain responsibilities of neutrals toward belligerents. The dispute centred around the Confederate cruiser "Alabama," built in England and used against the Union as a commerce destroyer, which captured, sank, or burned 68 ships in 22 months before being sunk by the USS "Kearsarge" off Cherbourg, Fr. (June 1864).

Battle between the Confederate blockade runner "Alabama" (foreground) and the Union's "Kearsarge" in the harbour of Cherbourg, Fr.; detail from a painting by Édouard Manet (1832–83)

By courtesy of the John G. Johnson Collection, Philadelphia

At the outset of the war, a Federal blockade of Southern ports and coasts automatically extended belligerent status to the Confederacy. To protect its own interests, Britain took the lead among European countries in proclaiming its neutrality (May 14, 1861). The Confederacy immediately set about building a navy to engage the Union's naval power and to destroy its merchant marine. Along with several other ships, the "Alabama" was built or fitted out privately on British territory and put to sea despite the belated intervention of the British government. Ably commanded by Capt. Raphael Semmes and superbly equipped, the "Alabama," along with other Confederate raiders, virtually drove Union ships from the high seas for almost two years.

Angry feeling developed in the U.S. over the destruction and immobilization of the nation's merchant marine and over the resultant maritime economic advantage accruing to Britain. As early as October 1863, the U.S. minister to Great Britain, Charles Francis Adams, protested that the British must take responsibility for these damages, but he conceded that his government would be willing to submit the matter to arbitration. Amid bombastic U.S. threats of annexing Canada, Anglo-American misunderstanding was exacerbated after the war by unsettled disputes over Canadian fisheries and the northwestern boundary. A proposed settlement in the Johnson-Clarendon Convention was angrily rejected by the U.S. To avoid further deterioration of Anglo-American relations, a joint high commission was set up, and on May 8, 1871, the parties signed the Treaty of Washington, which, by establishing four separate arbitrations, afforded the most ambitious arbitral undertaking the world had experienced up to that time. In addition. Great Britain expressed official regret over the matter.

Certain wartime maritime obligations of neutrals, already agreed to in article 6 of the treaty, were outlined in the principal arbitration of the "Alabama" claims, meeting at Geneva, as follows: that a neutral government must use "due diligence" to prevent the fitting out, arming, or equipping, within its jurisdiction, of any vessel believed to be intended to carry a war against a power with which it was at peace and to prevent the departure of such a vessel (the substance of this clause was included in article 8 of the 1907 Hague Convention) and that a neutral must not permit its ports or waters to be used as a base of naval operations for similar purposes. In addition, on Sept. 14, 1872, the tribunal voted unanimously that Britain was legally liable for direct losses caused by the "Alabama" and other ships and awarded the United States damages of $15,500,000 in gold.

This settlement gave new impetus to the process of arbitration, latent for many years. Differences at first regarded as inviolate questions of national honour were eventually submitted to arbitration as matters of international concern. The unusual procedure of including three arbiters chosen by as many neutral governments contributed to a growing flexibility in the process of arbitration. The consummate diplomacy of members of the joint high commission in planning the labours of a future board of arbitration demonstrated strikingly the importance of prior negotiation as an aid to arbitration. All in all, the arbitration of the "Alabama" claims may be considered a triumph for diplomacy as well as for the forces of international law.

Where the same name may denote a person, place, or thing, the articles will be found in that order

Alabama Platform, Southern political leader William L. Yancey's response (1848) to the anti-slavery Wilmot Proviso (*q.v.*), insisting that the U.S. government protect slavery in territories ceded by Mexico and that no territorial legislature be allowed to prohibit slavery. The Democratic Party declined to adopt Yancey's platform at the national conventions of 1848 and 1860. After the 1860 convention nominated Stephen A. Douglas for the presidency, Southern party members broke away to nominate John C. Breckinridge to run on the Alabama Platform.

Alabama River, river in southern Alabama, U.S., formed by the Coosa and Tallapoosa rivers, 7 mi (11 km) northeast of Montgomery. It winds westward to Selma and then flows southward. Its width is 600–900 ft (180–270 m), and its depth, 3–7 ft; its length is 318 mi. The river drains 22,600 sq mi (58,500 sq km) and is navigable most of the year. It receives its chief tributary, the Cahaba (200 mi long), 17 mi below Selma. The Alabama is joined 44 mi above Mobile by the Tombigbee to form the Mobile and Tensaw rivers, which flow into the Gulf of Mexico. Mobile and Montgomery became major cities largely because they were on this important traffic artery. The Coosa–Alabama river system, with various locks and dams, exerts a dominant influence on economic developments in the state.

alabaster, fine-grained, massive gypsum (*q.v.*) that has been used for centuries for statuary, carvings, and other ornaments. It normally is snow-white and translucent but can be artificially dyed; it may be made opaque and similar in appearance to marble by heat treatment. Florence, Livorno, and Milan, in Italy, and Berlin are important centres of the alabaster trade.

The alabaster of the ancients was a brown or yellow onyx marble.

Alabaster, William (b. 1567, Hadleigh, Suffolk, Eng.—d. early April 1640, Little Shelford, Cambridgeshire), poet, mystic, and scholar in Latin and Hebrew, author of a Latin tragedy, *Roxana* (1597, published 1632), which the 18th-century critic Samuel Johnson thought was the finest Latin writing in England before John Milton's elegies.

Alabaster, detail of an engraving by an unknown artist, 1633

BBC Hulton Picture Library

He was educated at Cambridge University and in 1596 accompanied the Earl of Essex's expedition to Cádiz, Spain, as chaplain but became a Roman Catholic in 1597, consequently suffering intermittent imprisonment. When visiting Rome in 1609, he was denounced to the Inquisition because of his mystical writings. After religious waverings he reverted to Anglicanism and became the king's chaplain in 1618. He also wrote an unfinished Latin epic, *Elisaeis,* glorifying Elizabeth I, as well as occasional poems, spiritual sonnets, mystically inclined prose works, and biblical commentaries.

alabastron, elongated, narrow-necked flask, used as a perfume or unguent container. The Greek alabastron has no handles but often lugs (ear-shaped projections), sometimes pierced with string holes. There are three types of classical alabastron: a basic Corinthian bulbous shape about 3 to 4 inches (8 to 10

Corinthian terra-cotta alabastron, 625–600 BC; in the Metropolitan Museum of Art, New York City

By courtesy of the Metropolitan Museum of Art, New York City, bequest of George D. Pratt, 1935

centimetres) high that appeared from the mid-7th century BC and was common in Greece; a long, pointed version found in eastern Greek, Etruscan, and Italo-Corinthian pottery; and an Attic type, from 4 to 8 inches high, with a rounded base and occasionally two small lugs, common from the late 6th to the early 4th century BC. All three types are found in pottery form. The last two types are justifiably named alabastron, as they were made of alabaster.

Examples of alabastrons in opaque glass exist from 1000 BC in Egypt, 600 BC in Assyria, and the 2nd century BC in Syria and Palestine. The earliest Egyptian alabastron is columnar, with a palm capital and a small plinth as a stand, and is circled with wavy bands of glass thread. Later examples, in dark-blue glass or milk glass, have a funnel-shaped opening or a broad disk-lipped neck; decoration consists of scallops, festoons, or, more commonly, ringed patterns, among which combed zigzags are especially effective.

Alaca Hüyük, ancient Anatolian site northeast of the old Hittite capital of Hattusa at Boğazköy in Çorum *il* (province), Turkey. Its excavation was begun by Makridi Bey in 1907 and resumed in 1935 by the Turkish Historical Society. Inside a sphinx gate, traces of a large Hittite building were discovered. Below the Hittite remains was a royal necropolis of 13 tombs dating from about 2500 BC. Although material from the same period at Alişar Hüyük (*q.v.*) seemed to indicate a relatively primitive community of farmers and traders, the tombs of Alaca Hüyük provide evidence of considerable cultural accomplishment and refinement. While the tomb pottery is comparatively primitive in style, there is ample evidence of the advanced accomplishments of Copper Age metallurgy. Filigree ornaments, jewelry, bowls, jugs, and chalices of gold were found, and sheet gold or gold wire was freely used in ornamentation. Vessels and bands of silver, and bowls and statuettes of copper or bronze are also represented. Included in the tomb finds were female "idols"; these were probably early cult images of the typical Anatolian mother goddess.

Copper finial showing a stag and two steers, from Alaca Hüyük, *c.* 2400–2200 BC; in the Archaeological Museum, Ankara

By courtesy of the Archaeological Museum, Ankara; photograph, Josephine Powell, Rome

Although the ethnic identity of Alaca's preliterate inhabitants is uncertain, it is most plausible to assign them to the non-Indo-European population that preceded the arrival of the people now known as Hittites; archaeological parallels are available among Heinrich Schliemann's Trojan treasures from Troy (level II) and from the Early Bronze Age at Cyprus.

Alacaluf, South American Indian people, very few (about 50) in number, living on the eastern coast of Isla Wellington in southern Chile. Their culture closely resembles that of the extinct Chono (*q.v.*) to the north and the Yámana (*q.v.*) to the south.

The Alacaluf environment is a wild and rugged mountainous region with hundreds of islands. Wind, rain, cold, and almost impenetrable rain forest limit subsistence patterns to food collecting, principally shellfish, sea mammals, and birds. Canoes are essential to the Alacaluf in their exploitation of the ocean resources. The Alacaluf do not establish permanent settlements but move along the beach in search of shellfish, living from day to day. The nuclear family of husband, wife, and unmarried children is the basic social, political, and economic unit; no larger organizational unit is known, although sometimes two or three families travel together. They build huts of skin or tree bark. Their aesthetic and religious ideas are not much developed, although they believe in spirits and practice simple forms of witchcraft.

Aladura (Yoruba: Owners of Prayer), religious movement among the Yoruba peoples of western Nigeria, embracing some of the independent prophet-healing churches of West Africa. The movement, which in the early 1970s had several hundred thousand adherents, began about 1918 among the younger elite in the well-established Christian community. They were dissatisfied with Western religious forms and lack of spiritual power and were influenced by literature from the small U.S. divine-healing Faith Tabernacle Church of Philadelphia. The 1918 world influenza epidemic precipitated the formation of a prayer group of Anglican laymen at Ijebu-Ode, Nigeria; the group emphasized divine healing, prayer protection, and a puritanical moral code. By 1922 divergences from Anglican practice forced the separation of a group that became known as the Faith Tabernacle, with several small congregations. A scandal in the Philadelphia church in 1925 caused the Africans to sever their connection with that institution.

The main expansion occurred when a prophet-healer, Joseph Babalola (1906–59), became the centre of a mass divine-healing movement in 1930. Yoruba religion was rejected, and pentecostal features that had been suppressed under U.S. influence were restored. Opposition from traditional rulers, government, and mission churches led the movement to request help from the pentecostal Apostolic Church in Britain. Missionaries arrived in 1932, and the Aladura movement spread and consolidated as the Apostolic Church. Problems arose over the missionaries' use of Western medicines—clearly contrary to doctrines of divine healing—their exclusion of polygamists, and their assertion of full control over the movement. In 1938–41 the ablest leaders, including Babalola and Isaac B. Akinyele (later Sir), formed their own Christ Apostolic Church, which by the 1960s had 100,000 members and its own schools and had spread to Ghana. The Apostolic Church continued its connection with its British counterpart; other secessions produced further "apostolic" churches.

The Cherubim and Seraphim society is a distinct section of the Aladura founded by Moses Orimolade Tunolase, a Yoruba prophet, and Christiana Abiodun Akinsowon, an Anglican who had experienced visions and trances. In 1925–26 they formed the society, with doctrines of revelation and divine healing replacing traditional charms and medicine. They separated from the Anglican and other churches in 1928. In the same year the founders parted, and further divisions produced more than 10 major and many minor sections, which spread widely in Nigeria and to Benin (formerly Dahomey), Togo, and Ghana.

The Church of the Lord (Aladura) was started by Josiah Olunowo Oshitelu, an Anglican catechist and schoolteacher, whose unusual visions, fastings, and devotions led to his dismissal in 1926. By 1929 he was preaching judgment on idolatry and native charms and medicines, uttering prophecies, and healing through prayer, fasting, and holy water. The Church of the Lord (Aladura), which he founded at Ogere in 1930, spread to north and east Nigeria, Ghana, Liberia, Sierra Leone, and beyond Africa—New York City and London—where several other Aladura congregations also meet. The Aladura movement continues to grow and includes many small secessions, ephemeral groups, prophets with one or two congregations, and healing practitioners who are available on a commercial basis.

Alâeddin Ali Aşik Paşa: *see* Aşık Paşa.

Alagoas, *estado* (state) of northeastern Brazil. It is the second smallest of Brazil's 23 states and is an agricultural region in the early stages of industrialization. Situated on the northern bank of the São Francisco River, it is bounded on the north and west by the state of Pernambuco, on the east by the Atlantic Ocean, on the south by Sergipe, and on the west by Bahia. It has an area of 10,676 sq mi (27,652 sq km). Its coastline is about 138 mi (220 km) long. The name of the state derives from its large number of lakes (*lagôas*). The capital is Maceió.

Pôrto Calvo in the north and Penedo, located on the northern bank of the São Francisco River, were founded during the early years of the Portuguese occupation of Brazil, in the 16th century. In the early part of the 17th century the Dutch obtained a foothold but were soon expelled. At about the same time, *quilombos*—fortified settlements of fugitive slaves, with a distinct culture that had many African characteristics—were established in the forests. Alagoas was a district of Pernambuco until 1817, when it became a captaincy (fief). Following the proclamation of Brazilian independence in 1822, it became a province of the empire, and in 1889 it became a state of the republic.

The climate of Alagoas is hot and humid along the coast and hot and dry in the interior. The terrain slopes downward from a semi-barren plateau to a narrow coastal plain. The principal rivers of the state are the São Francisco and the Mundaú, Paraíba, and Coruripe. Lagoa Mundaú, or Lagoa do Norte (Lake of the North), and Lagoa Manguaba, or Lagoa do Sul (Lake of the South), are the largest of the state's many lakes. Geologically, Alagoas consists mostly of the southern part of the Serra da Borborema (Borborema Mountain Range). The Serra Lisa (Lisa Mountain) is the state's highest point. There are four zones of vegetation: the coastal plain; the Mata, or tropical rain forest; the Agreste, a shrubby savanna parkland; and the Caatinga, an arid region covered with underbrush and cacti. The animal life of the state is rich and varied.

The Alagoans are a mixture of peoples of European, African, and Indian origin. White- and black-skinned peoples predominate in the coastal region of Alagoas, *caboclos*—copper-skinned people of mixed European and Indian descent—in the interior. The language of the state is Portuguese. Roman Catholicism is the principal religion.

In addition to the University of Alagoas there is a state school of medical sciences and a private school of social service. Many institutions provide technical instruction.

Abundant electric power is available from the Paulo Afonso hydroelectric project on the São Francisco River; the towns are supplied with electricity. The water supply, however, remains inadequate. The São Francisco River is being canalized, both for navigation and to supply the hinterland with water for domestic use. Sanitary conditions are poor. Although there are hospitals and other medical establishments in the state, all suffer from shortages of staff and funds.

While Alagoas is still primarily an agricultural state, industrialization is making progress. The main agricultural products are sugarcane, beans, palm, coconuts, cassava (manioc), rice, corn (maize), cotton, and tobacco. Cattle raising is increasing in the Bacia Leitera, a dairying region in the west central part of the state. Sugar refining is the state's most important industry; other industries include textile manufacturing, dairy processing, iron smelting, and the processing of corn, rice, fertilizers, and hides.

Deposits of amianthus, a fine, silky asbestos, are mined. There are a number of oil wells in production, and further drilling and prospecting has taken place. Oil production and exploration are centred on Arapiraca, Maceió, Marechal Deodoro, São Miguel, Coqueiro Sêco, and Piaçabuçu.

The capital, Maceió, is the chief commercial city, has an industrial district, and a modest foreign and coastwise trade is carried on through its port, Jaraguá. Inland water transport is available on the São Francisco River and on several lakes. Flights from Palmares Airport link Maceió to other Brazilian state capitals.

Among the state's cultural institutions are the Historical and Geographic Institute, the Academy of Letters, and a medical society. Pop. (1985 est.) 2,245,000.

Alagoinhas, city, northeastern Bahia state, northeastern Brazil, lying 35 mi (56 km) inland from the Atlantic coast at 607 ft (185 m) above sea level. It was elevated to city rank in 1880, and its municipality is the largest orange-producing region in the state. Bananas, lemons, and cassava (manioc) are also cultivated, and dairying is widespread. Tanning, coal mining, and lumbering are also important. Products are exported by rail and road to Salvador, the state capital, 70 mi south, and to neighbouring communities. Pop. (1980 prelim.) 76,377.

Alain, pseudonym of ÉMILE-AUGUSTE CHARTIER (b. March 3, 1868, Mortagne, Fr.—d. June 2, 1951, Le Vésinet, near Paris), French philosopher whose work profoundly influenced several generations of readers.

Graduating in philosophy, he taught at *lycées* in a number of towns, including Rouen, where he became involved in politics and began contributing a daily short article of 600 words to a Radical newspaper. The high literary quality of these articles soon attracted attention and they were collected and published (1908) in a book that came to be regarded as a classic. Appointed to teach philosophy at the Lycée Henri Quatre, in Paris, Alain became the mentor of most of the teachers of philosophy of the next generation in France. In defiance of public opinion he foretold and denounced World War I; on its outbreak, however, he enlisted in the artillery. Refusing promotion, he spent the whole war in the ranks; and it was in the front line or in battery telephonists' dugouts that he wrote *Mars, ou la guerre jugée* (1921; *Mars; or, The Truth About War,* 1930), *Quatre-vingt-un Chapîtres sur l'esprit et les passions* (1917), and *Système des beaux-arts* (1920). Later he resumed his post at the Lycée Henri Quatre. His most important publications over the ensuing years were *Les Idées et les âges* (1927), *Entretiens au bord de la mer* (1931), *Idées* (1932), *Les Dieux* (1934), *Histoire de mes pensées* (1936), and *Les Aventures de coeur* (1945). When age and painful disease made it impossible for him to teach any longer, he retired to a little house in the neighbourhood of Paris, where his disciples could visit him. In 1951 he was awarded the Grand Prix National de Littérature, of which he was the first recipient; this was the only honour that he accepted.

Alain DE LILLE, Latin ALANUS DE INSULIS (b. *c.* 1128, probably Lille, Flanders—d. 1202, Cîteaux, Fr.), theologian and poet so celebrated for his varied learning that he was known as "the universal doctor." He studied and taught at Paris, lived for some time at Montpellier, and later joined the Cistercians in Cîteaux.

As a theologian, Alain shared in the mystic reaction of the second half of the 12th century against the Scholastic philosophy, adopting an eclectic Scholasticism composed of rationalism and mysticism. In his main theological treatise, *The Art of the Catholic Faith,* he utilized a mathematical demonstration to try to prove the truth of the dogmas defined in the creed. His *Treatise Against Heretics* attempted to refute heterodoxy on rational grounds; and his *Maxims of Theology* assumed that the principles of the faith are self-evident propositions.

Alain is noted in the history of medieval Latin literature for two poems: *Plaint of Nature,* a clever satire on human vices, and *Anticlaudianus,* a lengthy allegory concerning the creation and perfection of the human soul by God and nature, theology and philosophy, the virtues and the arts. M. Baumgartner's *Die Philosophie des Alanus de Insulis* was published in 1896.

Alain-Fournier, pseudonym of HENRI-ALBAN FOURNIER (b. Oct. 3, 1886, La Chapelle-d'Angillon, Cher, Fr.—d. Sept. 22, 1914, in the first Battle of the Marne), French writer whose only completed novel, *Le Grand Meaulnes* (1913; *The Lost Domain,* 1959), is a modern classic. Based on his happy childhood in a remote village in central France, it reflects his longing for a lost world of delight. The hero, an idealistic but forceful schoolboy, runs away and at a children's party in a decrepit country house meets a beautiful girl—whose prototype Alain-Fournier had met in 1905. The rest of the novel describes his search for her and for the house and the mood of wonderment he knew there. Its outstanding quality is evocation of an atmosphere of other-worldly nostalgia, against a realistically observed rural background. Other works, mainly published posthumously, include a correspondence (2 vol., 1948) with the critic Jacques Rivière, his brother-in-law. A biography by R. Gibson, *The Quest of Alain-Fournier,* appeared in 1953.

Alain-Fournier, drawing by André Lhote
J.E. Bulloz

Alajuela, province, northwestern Costa Rica, bounded on the north by Nicaragua. The province, 3,700 sq mi (9,500 sq km) in area, descends northward from the Cordillera Central in the south and the Cordillera Guanacaste in the west to the San Juan River, which drains Lake Nicaragua to the Caribbean Sea and forms part of the international boundary. After San José, Alajuela is the leading province in livestock and the second in industrial and commercial activity. It grows about one-half of the nation's sugarcane and is a significant producer of coffee and fruits. The southern part of the province is traversed by the Pan-American Highway and by the Costa Rica Railway, which pass through Alajuela, the provincial capital. Pop. (1983 est.) 413,765.

Alajuela, capital, Alajuela province, northwestern Costa Rica, on the central plateau at an altitude of 3,141 ft (957 m). Known in colonial days as La Lajuela and Villahermosa, the town was active in support of independence from Spain in 1821; five years later it suffered from a plot to restore Spanish control over Costa Rica. For a brief period in the 1830s Alajuela served as the nation's capital. It was the home of Juan Santamaría, a Costa Rican soldier and hero of the defense against the invasion by the U.S. filibuster (military adventurer) William Walker in 1856. Alajuela was the starting point and centre of much of the construction activity of Costa Rica's coast-to-coast railroad begun in the 1870s. It is now a summer resort, famous for its flowers and markets. The city is on the Pan-American Highway, just northwest of San José, the national capital. Pop. (1983 est.) 42,579.

Alakol, Lake, Russian OZERO ALAKOL, also called OZERO ALA-KUL, salt lake in the Kazakh Soviet Socialist Republic, 110 mi (180 km) east of Lake Balkhash, near the border with Sinkiang Uighur Autonomous Region, China. It has a drainage basin of about 26,500 sq mi (68,700 sq km), an area of 1,025 sq mi, reaches a depth of about 148 ft (45 m), and receives the Urdzhar River (north).

Alalakh, modern TELL AÇANA, also called ʿATSHANAH, ancient Syrian city in the Orontes (Asi) valley, in modern Hatay *il* (province), Turkey. Excavations (1936–49) by Sir Leonard Woolley uncovered numerous impressive buildings, including a massive structure known as the palace of Yarim-Lim, dating from *c.* 1780 BC, when Alalakh was the chief city of the district of Mukish and was incorporated within the kingdom of Yamkhad.

Excavations also revealed a towered palace, occupied by several successive rulers, one of whom, Idrimi, ruled for 30 years and probably died about 1450 BC. The town was raided frequently because of its border location, but it was always rebuilt and remained a rich centre until its final destruction by the Sea Peoples shortly after 1200 BC.

Alamán, Lucas (b. October 1792, Guanajuato, Mex.—d. June 2, 1853, Mexico City), politician and historian, the leader of Mexican conservatives for nearly 30 years and the spokesman for a strong, centralized government that would support industrialization, educational expansion, and agricultural modernization. Living during a corrupt and brutal period of Mexican politics, he stood out as an honest and honourable political figure.

Born in an area of extensive gold and silver mining, Alamán was trained as a mining engineer. He served in 1819 as the Mexican deputy in the Cortes (Spanish Parliament) and sought money and technical assistance for the Mexican mining industry. In Europe he developed a lifelong admiration for the stability of British political institutions.

Returning to an independent Mexico in 1822, Alamán served first as foreign minister under Guadalupe Victoria (1824–29), then as the powerful and influential chief minister of Anastasio Bustamante (1829–32). Alamán's career was marked by his frequent controversies with the United States and his ambitious, but unfulfilled, economic and political plans. He slowed down migration from the U.S. into Texas (at that time part of Mexico) and interfered with the signing of a trade treaty. His economic schemes, which attempted to force Mexico into rapid industrialization, were perhaps utopian for the primitive Mexican economy and remained only as plans on paper.

Alamán, as a historian, was the founder of the National Museum and the Archivo General in Mexico City and is remembered for his historical works *Disertaciones sobre la historia de la república mejicana*, 3 vol (1844–49) and *Historia de México*, 5 vol. (1848–52).

Alamanni (Germanic people): *see* Alemanni.

Alameda, city, Alameda County, California, U.S., on an island (6½ mi [11 km] long by 1 mi wide) in San Francisco Bay, across the Oakland Harbor Channel from Oakland, with which it is connected by tubes and bridges. Originally a peninsula (part of Rancho San Antonio and site of Indian shell mounds), it was settled in the 1850s. Its growth was stimulated by a ferry service to San Francisco and the building of railroad bridges and terminals. The Tidal Canal (1902) changed Alameda (meaning "grove of poplar trees") to an island with an industrialized waterfront dominated by shipbuilding, steel fabrication, and lumber milling. Port facilities attracted fishing and cargo vessels, and in 1940 it became the site of a large naval air station. The College of Alameda opened in 1966. Inc. 1854. Pop. (1980) 63,852.

Alamein, battles of el- (June–July 1942; Oct. 23–Nov. 6, 1942), two engagements between British and Axis forces in Egypt during World War II.

After Italian defeats in North Africa, the German general Erwin Rommel was chosen commander of Axis forces in Libya (February 1941) and in January 1942 started a new drive to seize the Suez Canal. After losing Banghāzī in January, the British held the Germans in check until May. Then a powerful Axis army engulfed most of the British tank force, took Tobruk, and moved into Egypt, reaching el-Alamein (al-ʿAlamayn) on June 30, 1942. By mid-July Rommel was still there, blocked, and had even been thrown on the defensive, thus ending the first engagement.

Gen. Harold Alexander took command of the British troops in this theatre in August; Gen. Bernard L. Montgomery was named field commander. On Oct. 23, 1942, the British 8th Army started a devastating attack from el-Alamein. Rommel's forces—vastly outnumbered, with fewer than 80,000 against the 230,000 British—were routed. By November 6 the British had wound up the second battle and driven the Germans from Egypt. Two days later, "Operation Torch," the Allied landings in northwest Africa, took place, beginning the coordinated attack across North Africa from the west.

ʿĀlamgīr (Mughal emperor): *see* Aurangzeb.

ʿĀlamgīr II, in full ʿAZĪZ-UD-DĪN ʿĀLAMGĪR II (b. June 6, 1699, Multān, India—d. Nov. 29, 1759, Delhi), Mughal emperor of India who disgraced his reign (1754–59) by his weakness and disregard for his subjects' welfare.

A son of the emperor Jahāndār Shāh (ruled 1712–13), ʿĀlamgīr was always the puppet of more powerful men and was placed on the throne by Wazīr ʿImād ul-Mulk Ghāzī-ud-Dīn, who had deposed his predecessor. Provoked by the Wazīr's attempt to reassert control over the Punjab, the Afghan ruler Aḥmad Shāh Durrānī had his agents occupy Delhi in January 1757, at the time "absolutely without a single defender or caretaker." After the city was secured, ʿĀlamgīr was confirmed emperor of Hindustan but was in effect Aḥmad Shāh's puppet.

Threatened in 1759 with another Afghan invasion and the possibility of ʿĀlamgīr's being captured and used against him, Ghāzī-ud-Dīn had the Emperor murdered.

alamiqui (mammal): *see* solenodon.

Alamo (Spanish: Cottonwood), 18th-century Franciscan mission in San Antonio, Texas, site of a historic resistance effort by a small group of determined fighters for Texan independence (1836) from Mexico. The Mexicans,

The Alamo, San Antonio
By courtesy of the Greater San Antonio Chamber of Commerce

having won their own freedom from Spain in 1821, were unable to bridge the cultural gap with the aggressive U.S. settlers in Texas, who by 1836 outnumbered them four to one. Texans, including some of Mexican origin, established a provisional government in November 1835 and appointed Sam Houston commander in chief of their army. There followed a seesaw battle for control of San Antonio, including the ill-advised defense of the Alamo by a force of fewer than 200 Texas volunteers. After a 12-day siege (Feb. 23–March 6, 1836) every fighting man perished under the onslaught of 4,000 Mexican troops under Gen. Antonio López de Santa Anna. Among the fallen defenders were Cols. William B. Travis and James Bowie and the legendary Davy Crockett. Six weeks later, General Houston secured Texan independence with the victory of San Jacinto; during the fighting Col. Sidney Sherman reportedly rallied his company of volunteers with the cry, "Remember the Alamo!"

Alamogordo, city, seat (1899) of Otero County, southern New Mexico, U.S., at the west base of the Sacramento Mountains and east of the Tularosa Basin. Founded by John A. and Charles B. Eddy in 1898, it became a division point on the Southern Pacific Railroad and developed as a lumber town and agricultural-market centre. The Holloman Air Force Base was constructed there during World War II, and the first atomic bomb exploded at the "Trinity Site" (60 mi [97 km] northwest) on July 16, 1945. The base later tested guided missiles, and it now houses aerospace research facilities. Scarcity of water has impeded postwar development, but water is supplied from many wells and the 85-mi Bonito pipeline system. White Sands National Monument, International Space Hall of Fame honouring space pioneers, and the Mescalero (Apache) Reservation are nearby. The city is headquarters for Lincoln National Forest, and its Spanish name means "large cottonwood." It is the site of the New Mexico School for the Blind (1903) and of a branch of New Mexico State University. Inc. 1912. Pop. (1980) 24,024.

Alamosa, city, seat of Alamosa County, southern Colorado, U.S., on the Rio Grande in the San Luis Valley. It was founded and incorporated in 1878 when Garland City, a former terminus of the Denver and Rio Grande Western Railroad, was moved to the site. It developed as a rail and highway centre from which vegetables, including the famous Red McClure potatoes, are shipped. It is the seat of Adams State College (1921) and is the gateway to the Great Sand Dunes National Monument. Segments of the Rio Grande National Forest are nearby. A restored army post where Kit Carson held his last command is at Fort Garland, 25 mi east of Alamosa. Pop. (1980) 6,830.

Alanbrooke (of Brookeborough), Alan Francis Brooke, 1st Viscount, also called (1945–46) BARON ALANBROOKE OF BROOKEBOROUGH (b. July 23, 1883, Bagnères-de-Bigorre, Fr.—d. June 17, 1963, Hartley Wintney, Hampshire, Eng.), British field marshal and chairman of the Imperial General Staff during World War II.

Educated in France and at the Royal Military Academy (Woolwich), he served in World War I. Between wars he distinguished himself in staff duties and was in charge of military training (1936–37). Brooke began service in World War II as commander of a corps in France; after the retreat to Dunkirk, he was responsible for covering the evacuation (May 26–June 4, 1940). In July he took command of the home forces until promoted to chief of staff in December 1941. He established good relations with the U.S. forces and exercised a strong influence on Allied strategy. Alanbrooke's diaries formed the basis for Sir Arthur Bryant's *Turn of the Tide* (1957) and *Triumph in the West* (1959), which provoked controversy because of their criticism of Gen.

Lord Alanbrooke
Karsh of Ottawa—Camera Press

Dwight D. Eisenhower's ability as a military commander and of U.S. strategy in general. For his service Alanbrooke was created a baron in 1945 and viscount in 1946.

Åland Islands, Finnish AHVENANMAA, archipelago comprising Ahvenanmaan *maakunta* (Ahvenanmaa autonomous province), southwestern Finland, at the entrance to the Gulf of Bothnia, 25 mi (40 km) off the Swedish coast at the eastern edge of the Åland Sea. The archipelago has a land area of

572 sq mi (1,481 sq km) and embraces about 80 inhabited islands, 6,000 other, uninhabited islands, and many rocky reefs. The bedrock is primarily granite and covered with a soil that, though mainly clay, is rich in limited areas.

Åland, the largest island in the group, is known locally as "the mainland"; it consists of rugged granite to the north and rich agricultural soil to the southeast. Mariehamn, the administrative capital and chief seaport, is located on Åland, as is Orrdalsklint, the highest point of the archipelago, rising to a height of 423 ft (129 m). The archipelago has the highest crop yields in Finland per unit area because of the mild climate and fertile soil. The Swedish-speaking Ålanders are seamen, fishermen, and farmers. From the 1800s until World War II, Mariehamn served as the centre of a sailing fleet engaged in grain trade with Australia. Few of these ships still operate, though the colourful history of the fleet is reflected in an excellent maritime museum. Economic ties to the sea resulted in the training of expert seamen but poor road development along the coast. Fishing, which originally brought settlement to coastal areas unsuited to agriculture, is a declining source of income. Small, highly mechanized farms produce spring and autumn wheat, oats, barley, rye, cucumbers, and onions. Potatoes are the almost exclusive crop of Kökar Island. The climate also favours apple, plum, and pear orchards. Ayrshire cattle dominate the dairy farms, and sheep are also raised. The islands are linked to Sweden and the Finnish mainland by ferry and steamship services and by air service from Mariehamn airport.

The archipelago shows evidence of Bronze and Iron Age settlement as well as distinctive Viking graveyards and numerous medieval granite churches. The islands were Christianized during the 12th century by Swedish missionaries. In 1714 they were seized by the Russian tsar Peter I the Great after his naval victory over Sweden. When the grand duchy of Finland was ceded to Russia in 1809, the islands were included with the provision that they would not be fortified. Russia began fortification in the 1830s, however, with the building of the Bomarsund garrison. The fortress was destroyed in 1854 during the Crimean War by Anglo-French troops. The Åland Convention between Britain, France, and Russia (1856) stipulated that the islands would never be fortified again. Because of their long history of economic and cultural association with Sweden, the Ålanders claimed the right of self-determination and sought to become part of Sweden when Finland declared its independence in 1917. Finland granted the islands autonomy in 1920 but refused to acknowledge their secession. The League of Nations became mediator of the Åland question, granting the islands a unique autonomy while directing that they remain part of Finland. The Ahvenanmaan *maakunta* (Swedish Åland *landskapet* [province]) has a congress, an elected council, and a land councillor (prime minister); but the provincial governor is appointed by the Finnish government and has the right to veto congressional decisions. Pop. (1983 est.) 23,329.

alang-alang (grass): *see* cogon grass.

Alang language: *see* Halâng language.

Alani, also called ALANS, in ancient times, a nomadic pastoral people that occupied the steppe region northeast of the Black Sea.

The Alani were first mentioned in Roman literature in the 1st century AD and were described later as a warlike people that specialized in horse breeding. They frequently raided the Parthian Empire and the Caucasian provinces of the Roman Empire. About AD 370, however, they were overwhelmed by the Huns, and many fled westward, crossing into Gaul with the Vandals and Suebi (406). Although some of the Alani settled near Orléans and Valence, most went to Africa with the Vandals, causing the official title of the Vandal kings in Africa to be "kings of the Vandals and the Alani." The Alani who remained under the rule of the Huns are said to be ancestors of the modern Ossetes (*q.v.*) of the Caucasus.

alanine, either of two amino acids, one of which (α-alanine) is a constituent of proteins. An especially rich source of α-alanine is silk fibroin, from which the amino acid was first isolated in 1879. It is one of several so-called nonessential amino acids for birds and mammals; *i.e.,* they can synthesize it from pyruvic acid (formed in the breakdown of carbohydrates) and do not require dietary sources.

Beta-alanine is not found in proteins but occurs naturally in two peptides, carnosine and anserine, found in mammalian muscle. It is an important constituent of the vitamin pantothenic acid.

Alanus DE INSULIS (theologian and poet): *see* Alain de Lille.

ālāpa (Sanskrit: "conversation"), in the art music of India and Pakistan, improvised melody structured to reveal a raga (*q.v.*), principally in the introductory section of a performance. There the *ālāpa* is performed without rhythmic accompaniment and is free and rhapsodic in character. With only a drone (sustained-tone) accompaniment, the performer of the *ālāpa* gradually introduces the essential notes and melodic turns of the raga to be performed.

Only when the soloist is satisfied that he has set forth the full range of melodic possibilities of the raga and has established its unique mood and personality will he proceed, without interruption, to the metrically organized section of the piece. If a drummer is present, as is usual in formal concert, his first beats serve as a signal to the listener that the *ālāpa* is concluded.

Alapayevsk, also spelled ALAPAEVSK, city, Sverdlovsk *oblast* (administrative region), west central Russian Soviet Federated Socialist Republic, on the Neyva River. It is one of the oldest centres of the iron and steel industry in the Urals (an ironworks was established there in 1704). It also has machine-tool, timbering, and metalworking industries. Pop. (1983 est.) 50,000.

Alarcón (y Mendoza), Juan Ruiz de (dramatist): *see* Ruiz de Alarcón (y Mendoza), Juan.

Alarcón y Ariza, Pedro Antonio de (b. March 10, 1833, Guadix, Spain—d. July 10, 1891, Valdemoro), writer remembered for his novel *El sombrero de tres picos* (1874; *The Three-Cornered Hat,* 1918, 1935).

Alarcón had achieved a considerable reputation as a journalist and poet when his play *El hijo pródigo* ("The Prodigal Son") was hissed off the stage in 1857. The failure so exasperated him that he enlisted as a volunteer in the Moroccan campaign of 1859–60. The expedition provided the material for his eyewitness account *Diario de un testigo de la guerra de Africa* (1859; "Diary of a Witness of the African War"), a masterpiece in its way as a description of campaigning life. On his return Alarcón became editor of the anticlerical periodical *El Látigo*, but in the years 1868–74 he ruined his political reputation by rapid changes of position. His literary reputation, however, steadily increased. *El sombrero de tres picos,* a short novel inspired by a popular ballad, is notable for its skillful construction and pointed observation and is a masterpiece of the *costumbrismo* literary genre. Manuel de Falla based his ballet of the same title on the story, and Hugo Wolf wrote an opera so titled. Alarcón's other major novels are *El final de Norma* (1855; *The Last Act of Norma,* 1892), *El escándalo* (1875; "The Scandal"), and *El niño de la bola* (1880; "The Lucky Kid").

Alarcos, Battle of (July 18, 1195), celebrated Almohad victory in Muslim Spain over the forces of King Alfonso VIII of Castile. In 1190 the Almohad caliph Abū Yūsuf Yaʿqūb forced an armistice on the Christian kings of Castile and Leon, after repulsing their attacks on Muslim possessions in Spain. At the expiration of the truce (*c.* 1194) Alfonso invaded the province of Seville, prompting Abū Yūsuf to leave his North African capital, Marrakech, with an expedition against the Christians. The Castilians managed to surprise the Muslim advance guard; but, having underestimated the strength of the Almohad army, they were severely beaten by Yaʿqūb, who was joined by the cavalry of the Castilian Pedro Fernández de Castro, a personal enemy of Alfonso. The defeat occurred in a battle fought near the fortress of Alarcos (al-Arak in Arabic). Alfonso and his army fled to Toledo and Alarcos, while Yaʿqūb returned triumphantly to Seville. There he assumed the title al-Manṣūr Billāh (Made Victorious by God). For years afterward, even with the support of the King of Aragon, Alfonso was unwilling to confront the Almohads while they marched through his territories, taking Montánchez, Trujillo, Santa Cruz, and Talavera and destroying the vineyards of Toledo.

Alaric (b. *c.* 370, Peuce Island—d. 410, Cosentia, Bruttium), chief of the Visigoths from 395 and leader of the army that sacked Rome in August 410, an event that symbolized the fall of the Western Roman Empire.

A nobleman by birth, Alaric served for a time as commander of Gothic troops in the Roman Army, but shortly after the death of the emperor Theodosius I in 395, he left the army and was elected chief of the Visigoths. Charging that his tribe had not been given subsidies promised by the Romans, Alaric marched westward toward Constantinople until he was diverted by Roman forces. He then moved southward into Greece, where he sacked Piraeus (the port of Athens) and ravaged Corinth, Megara, Argos, and Sparta. The Eastern emperor Flavius Arcadius finally placated the Visigoths in 397, probably by appointing Alaric *magister militum* ("master of the soldiers") in Illyricum (now part of western Yugoslavia).

In 401 Alaric invaded Italy, but he was defeated by the Roman general Flavius Stilicho at Pollentia (modern Pollenzo) on April 6, 402, and forced to withdraw from the peninsula. A second invasion also ended in defeat, though Alaric eventually compelled the Senate at Rome to pay a large subsidy to the Visigoths. After Stilicho was murdered in August 408, an anti-barbarian party took power in Rome and incited the Roman troops to massacre the wives and children of tribesmen who were serving in the Roman Army. These tribal soldiers thereupon defected to Alaric, substantially increasing his military strength.

Although Alaric was eager for peace, the Western emperor Flavius Honorius refused to recognize his requests for land and supplies. The Visigothic chieftain thereupon laid siege to Rome (408) until the Senate granted him another subsidy and assistance in his negotiations with Honorius. Honorius remained intransigent, however, and in 409 Alaric again surrounded Rome. He lifted his blockade after proclaiming Attalus as Western emperor. Attalus appointed him *magister utriusque militiae* ("master of both services") but refused to allow him to send an army into Africa. Negotiations with Honorius broke down, and Alaric deposed Attalus in the summer of 410, besieging Rome for the third time. Allies within the capital opened the gates for him on August 24, and for three days his troops occupied the city, which had not been captured by a foreign enemy for nearly 800 years. Although the Visigoths plundered Rome, they treated its inhabitants humanely and burned only a few buildings. Having abandoned a plan to occupy Africa. Alaric died as the Visigoths were marching northward.

Alaric II (d. 507), king of the Visigoths, who succeeded his father Euric on Dec. 28, 484. His dominions comprised Spain (except the Kingdom of Galicia), Aquitaine, Languedoc, and western Provence. Alaric, like his father, was an Arian Christian, but he mitigated the persecution of Catholics and authorized the Catholic council at Agde in 506. To provide a law code for his Roman subjects he appointed a commission to prepare an abstract of Roman laws and imperial decrees. This code, issued in 506, is generally known as the *Lex Romana Visigothorum* or *Breviary of Alaric.*

Alaric tried to maintain his father's treaty with the Franks, but Clovis, the Frankish king, made the Visigoths' Arianism a pretext for war. In 507 the Visigoths were defeated in the battle of the Campus Vogladensis (Vouillé or Vouglé, in Poitou). Alaric is said to have been overtaken in flight and killed by Clovis himself.

alarm signal, in zoology, a ritualized means of communicating a danger or threat among the members of an animal group. In many cases the signal is visual or vocal, but some animals—ants, bees, and certain fishes, for example—secrete chemical substances. Alarm communications frequently cross species boundaries. The hawking alarm calls of many small birds are similar and will cause most other birds to take cover. A visual alarm signal, common in mammals, is "flagging," the lifting of the tail to reveal its white undersurface. The white fur shows only in fright situations when the animal raises its tail as it bounds away. Biologists do not agree about the exact meaning of this common mammalian alarm response. While the alarm reaction usually takes the form of a freeze or flight response, it may, if the stimulus is within a critical distance, elicit an attack.

Alas (y Ureña), Leopoldo, byname CLARÍN (Bugle) (b. April 25, 1852, Zamora, Spain—d. June 13, 1901, Oviedo), novelist and the most influential literary critic of Spain in the late 19th century. His biting and often bellicose articles, sometimes called *paliques* ("chit-chat"), and his advocacy of Naturalism and anticlericalism not only made him the nation's most feared critical voice but also created many enemies and greatly obscured his fame.

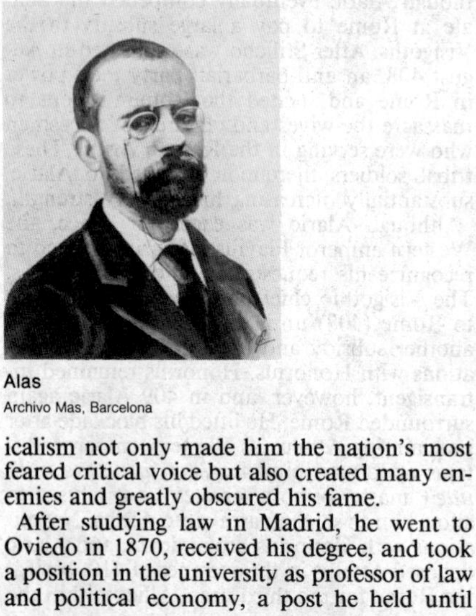

Alas
Archivo Mas, Barcelona

After studying law in Madrid, he went to Oviedo in 1870, received his degree, and took a position in the university as professor of law and political economy, a post he held until his death. His early novels, *La regenta* (1884–85; "The Regent's Wife") and *Su único hijo* (1890; *His Only Son,* 1970), considered two of the greatest Naturalist novels of the century, mercilessly depicted the provincial society of Vetusta, an imaginary town modelled upon Oviedo. Although his short stories, as collected in *Cuentos morales* (1896; "Moral Stories") and *El gallo de Sócrates* (1900; "Socrates' Rooster"), are considered inferior to his novels, they are generally more delightful and humorous and clearly reflect his wide learning and deep sensibility.

Alaşehir, chief town of Alaşehir *ilçe* (district), Manisa *il* (province), western Turkey, in the Kuzu Çay Valley, at the foot of the Boz Dağ (mountain). Founded about 150 BC by a king of Pergamum, it became an important town of the Byzantine Empire. It was not taken by the Ottomans until after all other cities of Asia Minor had surrendered to Ottoman rule. Conquered by Timur (Tamerlane) in 1402, it was recaptured under the Ottoman sultan Murad II (reigned 1421–51). A part of the city was burned down during the Turkish War of Independence (1919–22). Alaşehir is on the Afyon Karahisar–Manisa–İzmir railway. The district's products include tobacco, raisins, and fruits. A mineral spring yields a heavily carbonated water, *eau de vols,* in great demand in İzmir. Pop. (1980) town, 25,611; *ilçe* 74,943.

Alaska, constituent state of the United States of America lying at the extreme northwest of the North American continent along the tectonically active rim of the North Pacific Ocean. The state is the largest in area and the one with the sparsest population.

The following article summarizes the administrative history, geography, demographic patterns, economy, and culture of modern Alaska; for additional treatment of its geography and history, *see* MACROPAEDIA: United States of America: *Alaska.*

Facing Siberia across the Bering Strait and Sea to the west, Alaska is also bounded by the Arctic Ocean on the north and northwest, the Pacific Ocean and Gulf of Alaska on the south, and by the Canadian Yukon Territory and province of British Columbia on the east. The capital is Juneau. Mainland Alaska extends about 900 mi (1,450 km) from north to south and about 800 mi from east to west. When the Aleutian Islands and the southeastern Panhandle are included, the east–west extent is about 3,000 mi.

The Indians of Alaska are thought to be descendents of the first North American immigrants who crossed the Bering Land Bridge probably about 15,000 to 40,000 years ago and went on to people the American continents. The Eskimos (Inuit) and Aleuts appear to be descendants of more sedentary Arctic peoples who arrived in Alaska perhaps 3,000 to 8,000 years ago.

The first European settlement was established in 1784 by Russian fur traders at Three Saints Bay on Kodiak Island. The area was administered by the Russian–American Company from 1799 until 1867, when Secretary of State William H. Seward negotiated its sale to the United States. American settlement was stimulated by significant gold discoveries during the 1880s and 1890s, prompting Congress to establish the Territory of Alaska in 1912. Hostile Japanese activities during World War II necessitated construction of defense facilities as well as the Alaskan (Alcan) Highway. Alaska was admitted to the Union as the 49th state on Jan. 3, 1959. Internal administration of Alaska's land has since been complicated as a result of the retention of vast tracts by the federal government and by the awarding of other vast areas to fulfill the claims of the native peoples.

Physiographically Alaska can be divided into four main regions: (1) the insular and cordilleran south; (2) the interior basins, plains, and tablelands; (3) the Brooks Range; and (4) the tundra-covered northern Arctic Plains. The Alaska Range rises to the highest point on the continent, Mount McKinley, 20,320 ft (6,194 m). The Aleutian mountain system of the southwest and the St. Elias Mountains and Boundary Range of the southeast are characterized by active volcanoes, earthquakes, and glaciers. The marshy interior of central Alaska is drained by the Yukon and Kuskokwim rivers.

The wide-ranging geographical provinces and great physiographic relief provide much climatic diversity. Relatively mild temperatures, high precipitation and fog are the predominant features of the maritime climates of the southern rim. Continental extremes in the interior, intensified by the long summer days and winter nights, give way to high Arctic (polar) desert conditions in the north.

Alaska, despite being the least populous and least densely populated state in the Union, has experienced an extremely high growth rate, the result of large numbers of youthful immigrants who come seeking economic opportunities. The population increased by 454 percent during the period 1940 to 1980. The median age in 1980 was only 26.0 years. Aboriginal peoples constitute about 16 percent of the population. The Eskimos (Inuit) are the largest native American group (34,000), followed by the American Indians (22,000) and the Aleuts (8,000). About 54 percent of Alaskans live in the Anchorage area, about 15 percent around Fairbanks, and about 13 percent in the scattered towns of the southeastern Panhandle region.

The economy of Alaska has become increasingly centred on the oil and natural gas industry. Since the opening of the Trans-Alaska Pipeline in 1977, Alaska is second only to Texas in production of crude oil. Coal, gold, silver, copper, and sand and gravel are important mining products. One-third of the labour force is employed in state and federal government agencies and in defense installations. Traditional fishing and forestry industries continue to operate, but they are under government regulation to prevent over-exploitation. Most cool-weather crops can be raised, but because agricultural land is limited, most food supplies are imported. As a result of increased public awareness and improved transportation facilities, there has been a major upsurge in tourism.

The major transportation links, both internal and external, are by air. The Alaska Marine Highway operates ferry service between most of the coastal communities. The cities of the south-central region are linked by road to the Alaskan Highway, and thus to western Canada and the 48 coterminous states.

The University of Alaska statewide system of higher education has urban centres at Fairbanks, Anchorage, and Auke Lake (Juneau), as well as community colleges at 11 other sites. Schools formerly operated by the U.S. Bureau of Indian Affairs for the native Alaskans have been transferred to the state's public school system.

Alaska's heritage is culturally removed from the U.S. mainstream, centring on the arts and crafts of its native peoples and the remnants of Russian settlement. Much of this vast northern land remains as America's last virgin wilderness, endowed with abundant natural resources, and perceived to have a special beauty and character of people. Area 589,757 sq mi (1,527,464 sq km). Pop. (1980) 401,851.

Alaska, Gulf of, broad inlet of the North Pacific on the south coast of Alaska, U.S. Bounded by the Alaska Peninsula and Kodiak Island (west) and Cape Spencer (east), it has a surface area of 592,000 sq mi (1,533,000 sq km). The coast is deeply indented by fjords and other inlets, including Cook Inlet and

Prince William Sound (on either side of Kenai Peninsula). The gulf receives the Susitna and Copper rivers. Large glaciers cast off huge icebergs, which are taken out to sea by the Alaska Current. Rising from the gulf's shores are the high Chugach, Kenai, Fairweather, and St. Elias mountains. Ports include Anchorage, Seward, and North America's northernmost ice-free harbour, Valdez, which is the trans-Alaskan pipeline terminal. Oil has been found along Cook Inlet and beneath Controller Bay. The British navigator Capt. James Cook entered the gulf in 1778 and proceeded as far north as Prince William Sound.

Alaska blackfish (*Dallia pectoralis*), Arctic freshwater fish, assigned by some authorities to the family Umbridae but by others to the separate family Dalliidae. The fish is about 20 centimetres (8 inches) long, with a dark, streamlined body, protruding lower jaw, and two large opposed fins near the tail. Locally important as a food fish, it lives in shallow streams and ponds of North America and Siberia. Though it is said to withstand being frozen solid, this has never been substantiated.

Alaska Current, surface oceanic current, a branch of the West Wind Drift that forms a counterclockwise gyre in the Gulf of Alaska. In contrast to typical sub-Arctic Pacific water, Alaska Current water is characterized by temperatures above 39° F (4° C) and surface salinities below 32.6 parts per thousand.

Flow velocities at a depth of 16 ft (5 m) have been reported to be as high as 1.9 mi per hour (83 cm per sec) for the southern portion of the current. Volume transport is estimated to be in the range of 350,000,000 to 700,000,000 cu ft (10,000,000 to 20,000,000 cu m) per second.

Alaska Highway, formerly ALCAN HIGHWAY, road (1,523 miles [2,451 kilometres] long) through the Yukon, connecting Dawson Creek, B.C., with Fairbanks, Alaska. It was previously called the Alaskan International Highway, the Alaska Military Highway, and the Alcan (Alaska–Canadian) Highway. It was constructed by U.S. Army engineers (March–November 1942) at a cost of $135,000,000 as an emergency war measure to provide an overland military supply route to Alaska. The Canadian part (1,200 mi, mostly gravel) was turned over to Canada in 1946. A scenic route open all year round, it joins highways to Edmonton and Prince George (in the south) and highways to Valdez, Anchorage, Seward, and Haines (in the north).

Alaska Peninsula, stretch of land extending southwest from mainland Alaska, U.S., for 500 mi (800 km) between the Pacific (southeast) and Bristol Bay, an arm of the Bering Sea. The volcanic Aleutian Range runs along its entire length. It is the site of the Katmai National Park and Preserve, the Aniakchak National Monument and Preserve (*qq.v.*), and the Becharof, Alaska Peninsula and Izembek National Wildlife Refuges.

Alaska Purchase (1867), acquisition by the United States from Russia of 586,412 square miles (1,518,800 square kilometres) of land at the northwestern tip of the North American continent.

William Henry Seward, secretary of state under Pres. Andrew Johnson, had as early as 1860 dreamed of acquiring Alaska. The territory was considered an economic liability by the Russians, and in December 1866 Baron Eduard de Stoeckl, Russian minister to the United States, was instructed to open negotiations with Seward for its sale. On March 29, 1867, Stoeckl and Seward completed the draft of a treaty ceding Russian North America to the United States, and the treaty was signed early the following day. The price—$7,200,000—amounted to about two cents per acre.

Few Americans, however, viewed the purchase as a bargain, and Seward was vilified in the press. "Seward's Icebox" and "Seward's Folly" were the two most popular names for the Alaska Purchase, and ratification by the the Senate and funding by the House seemed in jeopardy as a result of the public outrage. The treaty was submitted for ratification on March 30. Senator Charles Sumner spoke in its favour, and the treaty was passed on April 9. The House passed the necessary appropriation on July 14, 1868. Extensive propaganda campaigns and judicious use of bribes by Stoeckl secured the required votes in each house of Congress.

Alaska Range, segment of the Pacific Coast Ranges that extends generally northward and

The Muldrow Glacier in the Alaska Range
Chas. J. Ott—Photo Researchers

eastward in an arc for about 400 mi (640 km) from the Aleutian Range to the Yukon boundary in southern Alaska, U.S. Mt. McKinley (20,320 ft [6,194 m]), near the centre of the range, in Denali National Park, is the highest point in North America. Many nearby peaks exceed 13,000 ft, including Mts. Silverthrone, Hunter, Hayes, and Foraker. Drained by the Yukon River (north) and the Pacific Ocean (south), the mountains separate the interior tundra prairie from the Pacific coastal region. The peaks present many challenges to climbers, while tourists are attracted by the enormous glaciers and Arctic scenery. The range is crossed at Isabel Pass by the trans-Alaskan oil pipeline en route to its southern terminal at Valdez.

Alaskan brown bear, race or subspecies of grizzly bear (*q.v.*).

Alaskan high: *see* Canadian high.

Alaskan king crab: *see* king crab.

Alaskan Malamute, sled dog developed by the Malemiut, an Eskimo group from which it takes its name. The Alaskan Malamute is a strongly built dog, with a broad head, erect ears, and a plumelike tail carried over its back. Its thick coat is usually gray and white

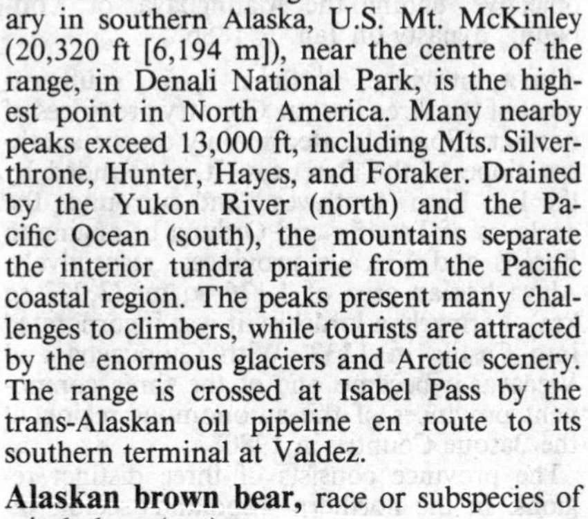

Alaskan Malamute
Sally Anne Thompson—EB Inc.

or black and white, the colours frequently forming a caplike or masklike marking on the head. The Alaskan Malamute stands about 23 to 25 inches (58 to 64 centimetres) high and weighs 75 to 85 pounds (34 to 39 kilograms). Characteristically loyal and friendly, it has been used to haul freight on sleds and has served on expeditions to the Antarctic.

Alaskan Mountains, northwestern continuation of the Rocky Mountains and the Pacific coastal ranges of North America. The Alaskan Mountains cover most of the state of Alaska and encompass the Arctic foothills and the Brooks Range in the north, the mountains of central Alaska and the Seward Peninsula, and the Pacific coastal ranges in the south, including the Alaska Ranges, the Aleutian Range and Islands, and the Talkeetna, Wrangell, Kenai, Chugach, and most of the Saint Elias mountains.

The following article summarizes information about the Alaskan Mountains; for full treatment, *see* MACROPAEDIA: North America.

The Arctic foothills are the northernmost fringe of the Alaskan Mountains and consist of low east–west trending ridges and rolling plateaus with irregular, isolated hills. The Brooks Range rises to the south and extends approximately 600 mi (1,000 km) from the Canadian border to the Chukchi Sea; elevations range from 3,000 ft (900 m) in the west to 6,000 ft in the east. The mountains of central Alaska are lower than the Brooks Range to the north and the Alaska and Aleutian ranges to the south and extend from the Canadian border to the Bering Sea. The Alaska and Aleutian ranges arc northwestward from the Canadian border and then bend southwestward along the Aleutian Islands, an archipelago of volcanic peaks on the crest of an immense submarine ridge. Mt. McKinley, at 20,320 ft (6,194 m) the highest point in North America, dominates the north expanses of the Alaska Ranges and overlooks the Talkeetna Mountains to the southeast. The Talkeetnas are bounded by the coastal Kenai and Chugach mountain ranges to the south and the Wrangell Mountains to the east. The Chugach and Wrangell mountain ranges merge with the Saint Elias Mountains near the Canadian border.

Vegetation above the timberline in the Alaskan Mountains is limited to lichens, grasses, weeds, and dwarf species of willows and alders. White spruce, birch, balsam poplar, and hemlock are found on the lower slopes. Several big game animals are native to the Alaskan Mountains, among them brown, black, and grizzly bears, Dall mountain sheep, mountain goats, moose, caribou, and Sitka deer.

Alatri, town, Frosinone province, Lazio (Latium) region, central Italy, in the Cosa River Valley, at 1,647 ft (502 m) above sea level, just north of Frosinone city. Said to have been founded in 1830 BC as Alatrium (mentioned by the Greek geographer Strabo), it belonged to the confederation of the Hernici, an ancient people of Italy, and later passed under the dominion of Rome (306 BC).

Archaeologically the town is of significance for its great belt of cyclopean walls (6th century BC) that enclose the superb trapezoid Pelasgian (pre-Hellenic) acropolis, the walls of which are almost intact. The outer circle of walls, about 2½ mi (4 km) long, supplemented at intervals by fine medieval towers, is penetrated by three massive gates. Other important buildings are the Palazzo Casagrandi, now the civic museum; the bishop's palace; the episcopal seminary; and the cathedral. Although it is a resort with rail connections to Rome and Naples, Alatri is also an agricultural and manufacturing centre. Pop. (1981 prelim.) mun., 22,657.

Ala'ud'din (d. *c.* 1564, probably Acheh, Sumatra), sultan of the Malay kingdom of Johore from 1528. He is sometimes considered the co-founder of the kingdom with his father, Mahmud Shah, the last sultan of Malacca, who established Johore on the island of Bintang (southeast of Singapore) in 1512–13. Sometime after his father's death (1528), Ala'ud'din moved his capital to Johore Lama. The Achinese sacked Johore Lama in 1564 and took Sultan Ala'ud'din prisoner to die in Acheh (one account, however, gives Johore Lama as the place of death).

Alaudidae (bird family): *see* lark.

Alaungpaya (Burmese: the Victorious), also spelled ALAUNG PHRA, ALOMPRA, or AUNGZEYA (b. 1714, Shwebo, Upper Burma—d. April 13, 1760, Kin-ywa, Martaban province, Burma), king (1752–60) who unified Burma and founded the Alaungpaya, or Konbaung, dynasty, which held power until the British annexed Upper Burma on Jan. 1, 1886. He also conquered the independent kingdom of Pegu (in the Irrawaddy Delta).

Of humble origins, Alaungpaya was a village headman from the small town of Moksobomyo (present-day Shwebo), north of Ava, the Burmese capital, when in April 1752 Binnya Dala (*q.v.*), the Mon king, captured Ava and put an end to the Toungoo dynasty. Refusing to become his vassal, Alaungpaya organized a resistance movement. Proclaiming himself a pretender to the throne, he established a new Burmese capital at Moksobomyo. In 1753 he recaptured Ava and went on the offensive in Lower Burma. In 1757 the city of Pegu was captured, and Binnya Dala was taken prisoner.

Because the French had allied themselves with Pegu, Alaungpaya was eager to gain British support. In 1757 he concluded a treaty with the British East India Company, granting it generous trade concessions. But the company, at war with the French in India, was unwilling to involve itself on a second front in Burma. In October 1759 the King's troops massacred British merchants at Negrais (an island at the mouth of the Bassein River) who were suspected of aiding a local revolt. After that action, relations between Britain and Burma were suspended.

Alaungpaya's last campaign was an invasion of Siam. He led an army through the town of Tavoy southward to Tenasserim and then northward to Ayutthaya (Ayuthia), the Siamese capital, which he surrounded in April 1760. During the siege he was wounded, and he died while his army was in retreat to Burma.

Alaungpaya DYNASTY, also called KONBAUNG, Burma's last ruling dynasty (1752–1885). Its collapse in the face of British imperial might marked the end of Burmese sovereignty for more than 60 years. (Some authorities limit the name Konbaung dynasty to the period beginning with King Bodawpaya in 1782 and continuing to 1885.)

By the 18th century Burma under the Toungoo dynasty (1486–1752) was fragmented: the Shan States to the north and east of Ava were as much Chinese as Burmese; in the southeast, local separatism had been rekindled by 1740. In 1752 Alaungpaya, a *myothugyi* ("township headman") in Shwebo (near Mandalay), organized an army and led a successful attack against the southern rulers. Alaungpaya, who claimed descent from a 15th-century Burmese king, then established the Alaungpaya dynasty. He led his armies southward, crushing all local resistance. Aware that his power rested on his ability to centralize his kingdom, Alaungpaya turned his attention toward the Shan States, forcing the rulers there to accept his suzerainty. Advancing farther eastward, he attacked the Siamese kingdom of Ayutthaya but was forced to withdraw and was mortally wounded (1760) during his retreat.

In 1764, Hsinbyushin, third king of the dynasty, restored order and renewed the conquest of Ayutthaya, which he reduced to ruins in 1767 but which he was unable to hold for long. Hsinbyushin's armies ranged far into the Shan and Lao states and the Manipur kingdom of India and four times defeated invasions by the Chinese. Hsinbyushin, intent upon pacifying the southern areas, was stymied in 1776. Bodawpaya (reigned 1782–1819), sixth king of the dynasty, was committed to the reconquest of Ayutthaya and mounted a number of unsuccessful campaigns against the Siamese. Bodawpaya also moved the capital to nearby Amarapura.

Under Bagyidaw (reigned 1819–37), Bodawpaya's grandson and successor, Burma met with defeat at the hands of the British in the First Anglo-Burmese War (1824–26). During the succeeding years there was a gradual erosion of Burmese territories as well as a weakening of authority. Tharrawaddy (reigned 1837–46) and his son, Pagan (1846–53), both weak kings, accomplished little in foreign or domestic affairs, allowing Great Britain to gain control of all southern Burma in the Second Anglo-Burmese War (1852). Under Mindon, an enlightened ruler (1853–78), Burma tried unsuccessfully to rescue its prestige. Friction developed between Mindon and British Burma, principally because Mandalay (Mindon's new capital) resented the British presumption of suzerainty. Finally, when Mindon's younger son Thibaw ascended the throne in 1878, only an excuse was needed for Britain's total annexation of Burma; the Third Anglo-Burmese War (1885) accomplished this objective, ending the Alaungpaya, or Konbaung, dynasty on Jan. 1, 1886.

Álava, province, northern Spain, southernmost of the three Basque Country provinces of northern Spain, located mainly on the southern slope of the Pyrenees. It is bounded by the Río Ebro (southwest) and surrounds the enclaves of Treviño and Orduña belonging to Burgos and Vizcaya provinces, respectively. Álava has an area of 1,176 sq mi (3,047 sq km). Formerly a lordship, it was incorporated into Castile in 1332. With Guipúzcoa and Vizcaya, it became one of the three component provinces of the autonomous region of the Basque Country in 1980.

The province consists of three distinct regions. In the northern woodlands sector, interspersed with isolated farms, lakes, and the valleys of the Urquiola, Bayas, and Omecillo rivers, the production of corn (maize) is the chief economic activity. The central heartland, as the Basque name Álava (*araiiar,* "set among the mountains") implies, is an intermontane basin (of about 1,500 ft [460 m] elevation) called the Llanada (plain) de Vitoria. Chief crops cultivated on the plains area are wheat, barley, and oats; sugar beets predominate around the provincial capital, Vitoria (*q.v.*). The southern Álavese Rioja, separated from the Llanada de Vitoria by the Cantabrian and Toloño mountains, is known for its vineyards, orchards, and olive groves. Industry (powered by hydroelectric dams on the upper Bayas, Urrunaga, and Zadorra rivers and by the Ebro dam, near Reinosa, in Santander) is concentrated in Vitoria. Pop. (1982 est.) 286,499.

Álava y Esquivel, Miguel Ricardo de (b. 1771, Vitoria, Spain—d. 1843, Barèges, Fr.), soldier in the Napoleonic Wars and statesman. Álava was an aide-de-camp to the Duke of Wellington and the Spanish commissary at the duke's headquarters during the Peninsular War. On the restoration of Ferdinand VII to the throne of Spain, he lost favour because of his liberal ideas but was appointed ambassador to The Netherlands (1815–22). He was president of the Spanish Cortes (parliament) in 1822–23 and later served as ambassador to Great Britain and France.

ālaya-vijñāna (Sanskrit: "store of consciousness"), key concept of the Vijñānavāda (Consciousness-affirming) school of the Mahāyāna Buddhist tradition. Since that school maintains that no external reality exists, while retaining the position that knowledge, and therefore a knowable, exists, it assumes that knowledge itself is the object of consciousness. It therefore postulates a higher storage consciousness, the final basis of the apparent individual. The universe consists in an infinite number of possible ideas that lie inactive in storage. That latent consciousness projects an interrupted sequence of thoughts, while it itself is in restless flux until the *karman,* or accumulated consequences of past deeds, is destroyed. That storage consciousness contains all the impressions of previous experiences (*vāsanās,* "perfumings"), which form the germs (*bīja*) of future karmic action, an illusive force that creates categories that are in fact only fictions of the spirit. That illusive force (*māyā*) determines the world of difference and belongs to man's nature, producing the erroneous notions of an I and a non-I. That duality is conquered only by Enlightenment (*bodhi*), which transforms a person into a Buddha.

alb, liturgical vestment worn in some services by Roman Catholic officiants, some Anglicans, and some Lutherans. A symbol of purity, it is a full-length, long-sleeved, usually white linen tunic secured at the waist by a cord or belt called a cincture. The equivalent vestment in the Eastern churches is the sticharion.

Linen alb from Germany, 13th century; in the Bavarian National Museum (Bayerisches Nationalmuseum), Munich

By courtesy of the Bayerisches Nationalmuseum, Munich

Derived from the long white tunic (*tunica alba* or *linea*) commonly worn in the Greco-Roman world, the alb was retained by the clergy as a vestment after secular styles began changing in the 6th century. In the 10th century the plain alb was decorated with embroidery on the hem and cuff, and it was later decorated with four or five rectangular patches of embroidery called parures, apparels, or orphreys. Apparels became less common in the 16th century and were replaced by lace, which eventually covered most of the garment. In the 20th century, with the Roman Catholic liturgical renewal, the plain white linen alb came back into use.

Alba, the kingdom formed by the union of the Picts and Scots under Kenneth I MacAlpin in 843. Their territory, ranging from modern Argyll and Bute to Caithness, across much of southern and central Scotland, was one of the few areas in the British Isles to withstand the invasions of the Vikings. The ancient link with Ireland (from which the Celtic Scots had emigrated) was broken as a cordon of Scandinavian settlements were established in the Western Isles and Ireland. With southern England also conquered by the Norsemen and Danes, Alba was left isolated. With the withdrawal of the Norsemen, England under the English then launched invasions against Alba but were ultimately repelled by Malcolm II at the Battle of Carham (1016/18). When Malcolm's grandson and successor Duncan I came to the throne in 1034, he united Alba with Strathclyde, Cumbria, and Lothian. Thereafter, the name Alba began to fade away; and every king, at least in retrospect, was normally styled "king of Scots." The first extant recorded use was by Duncan II, the "*Rex Scotie,*" in 1094.

Alba, town, Cuneo province, Piemonte (Piedmont) region, northwestern Italy, on the Tanaro River southwest of Turin (Torino). It occupies the site of the Roman Alba Pompeia, probably founded by Pompeius Strabo (consul, 89 BC) when he constructed the road from Aquae Statiellae (Acqui Terme) to Augusta Taurinorum (Torino). The town became an episcopal see dependent on Milan in the 4th century. The S. Lorenzo cathedral (1486) and the civic museum, with collections of Roman and prehistoric relics, are notable. An agricultural trade centre specializing in wines and white truffles, Alba has a school of viticulture and light industry. Pop. (1981 prelim.) mun., 31,050.

Alba, *județ* (district), western Romania, occupying an area of 2,405 sq mi (6,231 sq km). The Western Carpathians rise above the settled areas in intermontane valleys. The district is drained westward by the Mureș River and its tributaries. Articles from the Neolithic Age (2800–1900 BC), including flint knives, copper axes, gold ornaments, and remains of huts and fireplaces, were found at Alba Iulia (*q.v.;* the district capital), Decea, Pefreşti, Căpîlna, and Sebeș. Teuz town was built on a former Bronze Age settlement. A Celtic community (3rd century BC) was situated at Aiud, and remnants of Daco-Roman villages were found at Aiud, Sebeș, and Alba Iulia. Sebeș was controlled by German Saxons in the 12th century, attacked by Tatars in 1241, and fortified during the 14th century. A citadel with nine towers and an underground wine cellar 500 ft (152 m) long were built at Aiud during the 15th century. There is a Baroque-style 19th-century cathedral with exterior frescoes in Blaj. Vineyards are worked in the Mureș River Valley. Corn (maize) is grown in southern areas, and wheat is cultivated in the north. Mercury, gold, silver, and other nonferrous metals are mined in the western portion of the district, and basalt is quarried. Industries located in the cities and larger towns produce machinery, chemicals, textiles, paper, and leather and wood products. The Rîpu Roșie (Red Ravine), a natural monument, located in the east, dates from the Tertiary Period (about 2,500,000–65,000,000 years ago). Highways and railway lines parallel the district's river courses, extending through Alba Iulia, Cîmpeni, and Aiud. Pop. (1981 est.) 418,431.

alba (Provençal: "dawn"), French AUBE, or AUBADE, in the music of the troubadours (*q.v.*), the 11th- and 12th-century poet-musicians of southern France, a song of lovers' parting at dawn or of a watchman's warning to lovers at dawn. It sometimes takes the form of a dialogue between watchman and lover. Examples for which music also survives include "Reis glorios" by Guiraut de Bornelh and the anonymous "Gaite de la tor." The German counterparts of the troubadours, the minnesingers, also used the form, calling it *Tagelied* ("day song").

Alba, Fernando Álvarez de Toledo y Pimentel, 3er duque de (3rd duke of), Alba also spelled ALVA (b. Oct. 29, 1507, Piedrahita, Old Castile, Spain—d. Dec. 11, 1582, Lisbon), Spanish soldier and statesman famous for his conquest of Portugal (1580) and notorious for his tyranny as governor general of the Netherlands (1567–73). In the Netherlands he instituted the Council of Troubles (nicknamed the Council of Blood), which set aside local laws and condemned thousands.

Alba, oil painting by Sir Antony More, 1549; in the Musées Royaux des Beaux-Arts, Brussels
By courtesy of the Musees Royaux des Beaux-Arts, Brussels

In 1524 Alba joined the Spanish forces fighting the French at Fuenterrabía and so distinguished himself that he was appointed governor of the town after its capture. Subsequent campaigns made him the most thoroughly professional military commander of his age. He insisted on rigorous training and discipline for his troops and developed the tactical use of firearms. He was a master of logistics, and his greatest asset was an unshakable self-confidence that enabled him to resist the rash counsels of his more impetuous officers. He commanded a part of Charles V's army in the successful expedition against Tunis in 1535, and in 1546–47 he commanded the imperial armies against the German Protestant princes of the Schmalkaldic League. By his victory at Mühlberg (April 24, 1547) Alba placed the emperor Charles V at the pinnacle of his power. Alba was made commander in chief of the imperial forces in Italy in 1552 and, after the succession of Philip II of Spain, viceroy of Naples (1556). In the last phase of the Franco-Spanish War in Italy, he outmanoeuvred the Duke of Guise and forced Pope Paul IV to come to terms with Spain (1557).

After the Peace of Cateau-Cambrésis (1559), Alba became one of Philip II's two leading ministers. Charles V, an excellent judge of character, had recommended Alba to his son Philip in a secret testament of 1543 as a reliable adviser in all military matters and in affairs of state but otherwise not to be trusted, for he was enormously ambitious, wished to command everything, and would employ any means, including the use of women, to achieve his ambitions. Philip II therefore never fully trusted Alba. He did, however, summon him regularly to the Council of State, where, in opposition to the other of the King's chief advisers, Ruy Gómez de Silva, he pressed for a vigorous foreign policy.

As early as 1563 Alba advised the King to cut off the heads of the leaders of the aristocratic opposition in the Netherlands. But if this should not be immediately possible, he remarked, the King should dissemble now and execute them at a more opportune moment. In 1565 Philip sent him, together with his queen, Elizabeth of Valois, to meet Elizabeth's mother, Catherine de Médicis, regent of France. Alba managed to hold his own against that virtuoso politician, blocking Catherine's efforts to arrange a Spanish marriage for her son to which Philip II did not wish to commit himself. Understandably, he did not succeed, in his turn, in committing Catherine to a more active anti-Huguenot policy with Spanish assistance. The later Protestant accusation (and Catholic boast) that at Bayonne he and Catherine planned the St. Bartholomew's Day Massacre of Protestants in 1572 has no basis in reality.

Following the popular movements of 1566, Philip sent Alba to the Netherlands with a large army to punish the rebels, root out heresy, and reestablish the King's shaken authority (August 1567). Alba arrested Lamoraal, graaf van Egmond, and Filips van Montmorency, graaf van Hoorne, the rather halfhearted leaders of the opposition, and set up a new court, the Council of Troubles (soon to be known as the Council of Blood). This court set aside all local laws and condemned some 12,000 persons for rebellion, many of whom, however, had fled the country. He allowed himself to be involved in a trade war with England that caused great damage to Netherlands commerce. Worst of all, he mishandled the plan to place his government on a stable financial basis, independent of the estates. He proposed a 10 percent tax on all sales (the "10th penny") and a 1 percent property levy. But the States General would agree only to the property tax and made counter offers, in place of the "10th penny." In the face of the opposition of the lower classes and the clergy, Alba had to modify the tax progressively. In the end it was never collected. While Alba's "10th penny" certainly helped to rouse the country against Spain, it did not cause its economic ruin, as once was thought.

In 1572 the Gueux—Dutch guerrillas—captured most of Holland and Zeeland, and the Prince of Orange and his brother Louis of Nassau invaded the Netherlands from Germany and France, respectively. Alba defeated the land invasions and recaptured part of Holland, where his troops committed terrible atrocities. Short of money and lacking adequate sea power to oppose the fleet of the Gueux, he failed to recapture the remainder of Holland and Zeeland.

Alba's failure and the intrigues of the Gómez party at court induced Philip to recall him (1573). In 1579 Alba was placed under house arrest on his estates after his son had married against the King's wishes. In 1580 Cardinal Granvelle persuaded Philip to let Alba command the invasion of Portugal. Within a few weeks, in one of his most brilliant campaigns, Alba took Lisbon. Yet he never regained Philip's favour.

In Protestant countries Alba's name became a byword for cruelty and religious tyranny. Outside Spain he has never been forgiven for his disregard of legality, for his policy of terror, and for the outrages committed by his troops in the Netherlands and Portugal. Of the responsibility for these acts he cannot be exonerated, nor were they universally accepted even by Catholic opinion in the 16th century. In Spanish history Alba is important as a representative of the old nobility, independent and proud of its rights and privileges yet willing to serve as the champion and defender of an absolute monarchy. (H.G.K.)

BIBLIOGRAPHY. There is no scholarly biography of Alba in any language, although much of the material for such a work is easily accessible, notably in the Duke of Berwick and Alba, *Epistolario del III Duque de Alba,* 3 vol. (1952). The same author's *The Great Duke of Alba As a Public Servant* (1947) is a useful but one-sided corrective to the traditional Protestant view. Alba's financial policy in the Netherlands has received adequate treatment in J. Craeybeckx, "Alva's Tiende Penning, een Myth?," in *Bijdragen en Mededelingen van het Historisch Genootschap te Utrecht*, 76:10–42 (1962).

Alba Fucens, modern ALBE, ancient fortified town at the foot of Monte Velino, Italy. It was originally a town of the ancient Marsi people but was occupied by a Latin colony in *c.* 303 BC. It was situated on a hill with three distinct summits, all of which were enclosed within the walls. Its strong position made it important in the Social War and in the civil wars of the 1st century BC; state prisoners of the Romans were often held there.

Much survives of the main circuit of walls; the gateways, which also remain, were so placed as to expose the right side of an attacking force. The acropolis in the northern corner had a separate line of walls, forming an independent stronghold.

Alba Iulia, German KARLSBURG, Hungarian GYULAFEHÉRVÁR, city, capital of Alba *județ* (district), west central Romania, on the Mureș River, 170 mi (270 km) northwest of Bucharest. One of the oldest settlements in Romania, the site was selected by the Romans for a military camp. The remains of Apulum, an important city in Roman Dacia mentioned by Ptolemy in the 2nd century BC, are 6 mi from Alba Iulia, and the Regional Museum has a rich collection of Roman antiquities. From the 9th to the 11th century the town bore the Slavic name Bălgrad. The Roman name was first documented in 1097, and the use of Alba Iulia in Latin documents ensured the survival of the name.

In the 16th and 17th centuries the town became the capital of the principality of Transylvania. In 1599 Michael the Brave (Mihai Viteazul) proclaimed himself prince of Walachia, Transylvania, and Moldavia at Alba Iulia—achieving for the first time the union of the three great provinces of Romania. The town became a centre of Romanian nationalism and an important Romanian-language printing centre. It was at Alba Iulia that the union of Transylvania with Romania was pronounced on Dec. 1, 1918; King Ferdinand and Queen Marie were crowned in the Orthodox cathedral in 1922.

The city also has a 13th-century Roman Catholic cathedral (Romanesque), an 18th-century fortress, and the Batthyáneum Library, founded in 1794 by Ignatius Batthyány, a Catholic bishop, and containing many incunabula and old manuscripts of great value, notably the *Codex Aureus* from the 8th century. Industries in Alba Iulia include leatherworking and food processing and the production of footwear, construction materials, and wine. Pop. (1981 est.) 52,961.

Alba Longa, ancient city of Latium, Italy, in the Alban Hills about 12 miles (19 kilometres) southeast of Rome, near present Castel Gandolfo. Tradition attributes its founding (*c.* 1152 BC) to Ascanius, the son of the legendary Aeneas, and calls this the oldest Latin city, which in turn founded others, including Rome. It headed a Latin league of uncertain extent until destroyed in *c.* 600 BC by Rome.

Albacete, province in the autonomous community (region) of Murcia, southeast central Spain, that occupies the southeastern end of the Meseta Central (plateau) and has an area of 5,737 sq mi (14,858 sq km). It is the driest interior province of the Iberian Peninsula, with as little as 2 in. (50 mm) annual rainfall in some areas. The south is mountainous or hilly and is crossed by the Júcar and Segura rivers, which are the chief local sources of power and water for irrigation. The Sierra de Alcaraz rises in the west.

Albacete is a stock-raising province, but wheat growing is increasing steadily, with a corresponding decline in livestock. Cheese is sent to all parts of Spain; vines, which have suffered much from phylloxera, and olives are cultivated; the peaches of the Cabriel and Júcar valleys supply canning factories in Valencia. Other products include saffron, esparto grass, and pine lumber.

Industry is concentrated in the provincial capital, Albacete (*q.v.*). Important towns include Almansa, Hellín, and La Roda. A large portion of the province is accessible only by road, although there are good railway connections with Madrid and Alicante. Pop. (1982 est.) 317,498.

Albacete, capital of Albacete province, Murcia, southeast central Spain, in the historic La Mancha region, on the Río de Don Juan at its juncture with the Canal de María Cristina. Of Moorish origin (Arabic, al-Basīṭ), it was the scene of two battles between Christians and Moors, in 1145 and 1146. Refounded in 1365 as Albacete, it played an important part in the War of the Spanish Succession; the Battle of Almansa was won near there by Philip V in 1707. Development came only after the construction in the 19th century of the María Cristina Canal, which drained malarial swamps to the south.

Albacete is divided into the upper town (Alto de Villa), or old quarter, and the lower, modern town. Notable landmarks include the 16th-century San Juan Bautista cathedral (restored after a fire in 1936) and a provincial museum. The city is now a market centre for agricultural produce (fruit and saffron). Industry is primarily based on agriculture. Knives and daggers (now sold chiefly as souvenirs) from Albacete are well known throughout Spain. A provincial museum displaying the work of Benjamin Palencia and other regional and local artists was opened in 1978. Pop. (1982 est.) 110,836.

albacore, also spelled ALBICORE (*Thunnus alalunga*), large oceanic fish noted for its fine flesh. The bluefin tuna (*T. thynnus*) is also sometimes called albacore. *See* tuna.

Albalag, Isaac (fl. 13th century AD, northern Spain or southern France), Jewish philosopher who rendered a Hebrew translation of parts of the *Maqāṣid al-falāsifah* ("Aims of the Philosophers"), a review of doctrines of earlier thinkers by the Arabic philosopher al-Ghazālī, to which Albalag added his own views and comments. In defending philosophy against the accusation that it undermined religion, Albalag espoused the doctrine of the "double truth"—prophetic truth known through revelation and philosophic truth arrived at through reason. He believed philosophy and religion were in fundamental agreement but that religion was for the masses and philosophy for the few. He felt that philosophy need not bow to revelation when the results of its speculations disagree with revelation.

Alban, SAINT (fl. *c.* 3rd century AD, traditionally at Verulamium, Britain; feast day June 22), first British martyr. According to the historian Bede he served in the Roman army and was converted to Christianity by a fugitive priest whom he sheltered, and with whom he exchanged clothes, so that he was martyred in the priest's place (*c.* 304; other dates suggested by scholars are *c.* 254 or *c.* 209). His feast day is commemorated on June 17 in the Church of England, apparently because of misreading of the Roman numerals XXII. His tomb was venerated, and a church had been built on the site as early as 429. Later the Abbey of St. Albans was founded there, and around it grew the town of St. Albans.

Albán, Monte (Mexico): *see* Monte Albán.

Alban Hills, Italian COLLI ALBANI, or MONTI ALBANI, area of extinct volcanoes in the Lazio (Latium) region of central Italy, southeast of Rome. They consist of an outer circle, 6–8 mi (10–13 km) in diameter, rising to 3,113 ft (949 m) at Monte Cavo, and an inner crater rim, about 1.5 mi across, rising to 3,136 ft at Monte Faete. Lakes Albano and Nemi (*qq.v.*) occupy two of the craters. Even before the emergence of Rome as a great power, the Alban Hills were a place sacred to the people of Latium. Roman roads, temples, villas, and theatres are still partly preserved there. Because of their coolness in summer and the absence of malaria, the hills for centuries have been a favourite summer resort of Romans. The Alban vineyards produce the popular wines known as Castelli Romani (after the towns of the district). An electric suburban railway connects Rome with the hill retreats of Frascati, Grottaferrata, Albano, Velletri, Genzano, and Castel Gandolfo (the papal summer residence).

Albani, Francesco, Albani also spelled ALBANO, or L'ABANE (b. March 17, 1578, Bologna, Papal States—d. October 1660, Bologna), painter, one of the 17th-century Bolognese masters trained in the studio of the Carracci. He assisted Guido Reni in a number of major decorative cycles, including that of the chapel of the Annunciation (1609–12) in the Quirinal Palace and the choir (1612–14) of Sta. Maria della Pace.

Albani lived for several years in Rome, where he had his own academy. There he painted, after the designs of Annibale Carracci, the whole of the frescoes in the chapel of S. Diego in the church of S. Giacomo degli Spagnuoli. His best known frescoes are on mythological subjects, such as the "Dance of the Amorini" (*c.* 1625; Brera, Milan). He returned to Bologna in 1616, where he remained except for visits to Mantua in 1621–22 and Florence in 1633.

Albani, Giovanni Francesco (pope): *see* Clement XI.

Albania, officially PEOPLE'S SOCIALIST REPUBLIC OF ALBANIA, Albanian SHQIPËRI, or REPUBLIKA POPULLORE SOCIALISTE E SHQIPËRISË, smallest country of the Balkan Peninsula, located on its western Adriatic coast, covering an area of 11,100 sq mi (28,748 sq km). The capital is Tiranë. The country is bounded roughly by latitudes 42°39′ and 39°38′ N (about 210 mi [340 km] from north to south) and longitudes 19°16′ and 21°04′ E (nearly 95 mi across at its widest extent east to west). Albania is bordered on the north and east by Yugoslavia (296 mi), by Greece on the southeast (159 mi), and its western border consists of a rugged coastline along the Adriatic Sea. The population in 1982 was estimated at 2,858,000.

The article that follows is a summary of significant detail about Albania. Fuller treatment is provided in the following MACROPAEDIA articles. For geography and history, *see* Albania; for information about the country and its history in its regional setting, and about its peoples and their traditional cultures, *see* Balkans.

For current history and for statistics on society and economy, *see* the article "World Affairs" and BRITANNICA WORLD DATA, respectively, in the *Britannica Book of the Year.*

The land. Albania may be divided into two major physiographic regions, a mountainous highland region (north, east, and south) comprising 70 percent of the land area, and a western coastal lowland region which contains nearly all of the country's agricultural lands. The highland region can be divided further into the North Albanian Alps, consisting of rugged limestone peaks reaching heights exceeding 8,800 ft (2,700 m); the central uplands, containing several rugged ranges of mountains along the Yugoslavian border, including Albania's highest peak, Korab (9,025 ft); and the southern highlands, displaying lower and gentler relief than the northern ranges. Albania has an extremely active geologic zone that has suffered at least three severe earthquakes in modern times; it extends southward from the ancient volcanic mountains of the central uplands into the southern highlands. The earthquake of 1851 in Nartë (a village in the southern highlands) was of severe intensity, and 2,000 people were killed.

Albania

Albania's two major river basins, the Drin, sharing half its 6,500-sq-mi basin in the north with Yugoslavia and the Vijosë, sharing one-fourth of its 2,700-sq-mi basin in the south with Greece, characterize the country's general westward drainage into the Adriatic. Albania's hydroelectric power generation expanded threefold during the 1970s to about 3,500,-000,000 kW-hr per year in the early 1980s.

Albania's coastal regions experience a Mediterranean climate, *i.e.*, relatively mild, rainy winters and warm, dry summers; there is an abrupt transition in the mountain regions to a more severe continental climate with hot summers and cold winters. Average annual precipitation is about 55 in. (1,400 mm), greater in the highlands and the interior and less along the coast.

Only about one-fourth of Albania's land is arable, and nearly three-fourths of that is allocated to grains. Another 20 percent is permanent pasture land (supporting substantial herds of sheep, goats, and cattle), and nearly 45 percent is forested. More than half of Albania's cultivated cropland is irrigated. Natural vegetation is greatly affected by the mountainous topography. The drier lowlands have a preponderance of maquis (a Mediterranean bush and scrub complex); the oak is dominant up to about 3,000 ft, where it is replaced by beech and chestnut; coniferous forests predominate at higher elevations.

Albania is estimated to be the world's third largest producer of chromite (the principal ore of chromium) after South Africa and the Soviet Union. Albania also produces significant quantities of low-grade iron ore and soft coal.

The people. Albania's population at mid-year 1982 was 2,858,000. It is estimated to be growing at an annual rate of about 2.1 percent. The birth rate is 27.5 per 1,000 population, among the highest in Europe, and the registered death rate is 6.4 per 1,000. The population density is 257 per sq mi. The ratio of males to females is 100 to 95. The Albanians are descendants of the Illyrians who lived in central Europe and migrated southward to the Gulf of Árta in northern Greece by the beginning of the Iron Age. The two major modern language communities in Albania are the Ghegs in the north and the Tosks in the south. Although under the present government all places of worship have been closed, a large percentage of the population remain Muslims, and the rest are Greek Orthodox or Roman Catholic. There are also a number of Greek immigrants. The state encourages a high birth rate, and good health care services for mother and child are given the highest priority. In 1980 35.3 percent of the population were urban residents. The capital and leading population centre of the country is Tiranë with 190,200 inhabitants (1979). Other important cities include Durrës, 65,900; Shkodër, 64,700; Elbasan, 61,100; Vlorë, 56,400; and Korçë, 52,000.

The economy. Albania has a centrally planned, developing economy based upon agriculture, chromium and nickel mining, and industry. The gross national product (GNP) in 1979 was estimated to be U.S. $2,240,000,-000, about $840 per capita. Annual growth of real GNP was 4.2 percent during the 1970s. The GNP originates in industry and mining, agriculture, and other sources.

Arable agricultural land in Albania amounts to about one-fourth of the total land area. Crops grown include mainly wheat, corn (maize), sorghum, oats, pulses, legumes, sugar beets, cotton, sunflowers, tobacco, potatoes, and fruits. Sheep, goats, cattle, and pigs are the major livestock. Agriculture is organized into state owned collective farms and state managed peasant cooperatives.

Albania's mountainous terrain has rich mineral deposits, and the swiftly flowing rivers provide good hydroelectric energy potential. Energy-related minerals produced include crude petroleum, lignite (brown coal), natural gas, and asphalt. Metallic minerals include chromite ore, nickeliferous iron-ore, copper ore, and smaller quantities of cobalt and nickel. There are deposits of phosphorus, bauxite, precious metals, kaolin clay, asbestos, and titanomagnetite. New oil reserves have been located, ensuring continued petroleum supplies; natural gas reserves have been estimated at 2,140,000,000,000 cu ft (60,600,000,000 cu m). Production of electrical energy totalled 4,350,000,000 kW-hr in 1981, four-fifths from hydroelectric plants and one-fifth from thermal plants.

Manufactures include asphalt, refined petroleum, iron and steel products, refined chrome and copper, petrochemicals, plastics, nitrogenous fertilizers, superphosphates, paper, ceramics, leather goods, cotton and polyester knitwear, raw sugar, beverages, and cigarettes. Albanian development plans now place emphasis on industrial self-sufficiency and on increased production of agricultural staples and consumer goods. Industries are entirely state owned and managed.

Construction projects completed in the late 1970s and early 1980s include the Koman hydroelectric power complex on the Drin River, a metallurgical complex at Elbasan, a new railway, and chrome and copper enrichment plants at Diber, Pukë, and Midrite.

About 60 percent of Albania's economically active population is employed in agriculture, followed by manufacturing, mining and electrical production, construction, and commerce and storage. A shortage of qualified technicians and specialists in mining and manufacturing limits productivity and development.

Budgetary revenue derives mainly from the profits of state-owned and state-operated enterprises and from export income. Expenditure is divided among national economic funding, social and cultural expenditure, defense and security, and administration.

Albania's currency is the lek, which is subdivided into 100 qidarka.

Prior to 1945 Abania had neither a highway network nor a standard-gauge railway, and its transportation system is still developing. Albania has four ports on the Adriatic; of these Durrës is the most important. Air transport remains underdeveloped; there is but one airport for international flights, and there is no internal air transport.

Albania's exports by value are slightly more than imports. Exports include chrome ore and iron ore; iron, steel, and copper products; petroleum products and asphalt; and fruits, vegetables, wool, and tobacco. Major export destinations are Czechoslovakia, Yugoslavia, Italy, and the Peoples Republic of China. Imports consist of machinery, equipment, and spare parts; minerals, metal products, coal, and construction materials; and food products. Import sources are Yugoslavia, Czechoslovakia, the Peoples Republic of China, and Italy.

Administrative and social conditions. Albania is a one-party socialist republic. Members of the party, called the Albanian Party of Labour, occupy all important positions in the government. There is a People's Assembly, a legislature of 250 deputies, but in reality, legislative decisions are made by the Assembly's Presidium, whose president is the head of state. The prime minister acts as chairman of the Council of Ministers. The country's judicial powers rest in the Supreme Court and district and local courts.

Albania has a non-contributory social insurance system and medical treatment is free. Life expectancy in Albania is very high for a developing country, at 68 years for males and 71 years for females (1981).

All education in Albania is free and is compulsory between ages 7 and 15. The government objective for education is to develop a versatile "new man" dedicated to serving the socialist republic. To that end, secondary school students are required to practice a strict yearly regimen of seven months study, two months production or construction work, and one month of physical culture and military training. Higher education in Albania centres on the University of Tiranë.

The government maintains complete control over all news and information media. The most widely circulated newspaper is *Zëri i Popullit*, the organ of the Albanian Party of Labour.

Cultural life. The major cultural institution in the country is the National Library in Tiranë. Important historical museums in the capital include the Albanian Folk Culture Museum and the Museum of the Struggle for National Liberation. By the late 20th century the only writer to have gained international reputation was Ismail Kadare, a novelist and poet. Folk life, expressed in dance, music, and popular literature, is preserved and encouraged. The fine arts are represented by the Albanian Philharmonia (in Tiranë), incorporating the State Choir, and by the Opera and Ballet Theatre.

History. Albanians are descended from the Illyrians, an ancient Indo-European people, and have resided throughout most of their history in the western half of the Balkan peninsula from at least 1000 BC. The southern Albanian tribes were influenced by Greek culture; the modern Albanian cities of Durrës and Lezhë were founded as Greek colonies. The northern Illyrians were united at various times under local kings, the most imporant of whom was Argon (second half of 3rd century BC), whose kingdom extended from Dalmatia in the north to the Vijosë River in the south and whose capital was at Shkodër. After his death, the conquests of his wife, Teuta, aroused the Romans, who by 168 BC conquered all of Illyria. Albania then became part of the Roman province of Illyricum.

Illyricum prospered under the Romans. After 395, the area was connected administratively to Constantinople. In spite of the Visigoth and Hun invasions during the 3rd to 5th century and the Slavic invasions of the 6th and 7th centuries, the Albanians were one of the few peoples who kept their own Illyrian language and customs.

Turkish invasions began in the 14th century. The Ottoman domination was held back by the national hero, George Castriota, whom the Turks had trained, converted to Islām, and called Skanderbeg. In 1443 he reembraced Christianity and successfully resisted Turkish rule in Albania. After his death, the Turks consolidated their rule over Albania, which subsequently declined economically. There was local resistance to Ottoman rule, and an uprising in 1912 created an independent Albania with Ismail Qemal Vlora as its head. The international community, however, gave recognition to Albania only in 1921. Mussolini invaded Albania in 1939 and civil war in 1943–44 resulted in the establishment of Enver Hoxha's Communist state, the People's Republic of Albania (so called until 1976, when the present name and constitution were adopted). Albania was allied with the Soviet Union until 1961. Thereafter relations with China prospered until Mao Tse-tung's death in 1978.

Albanian language, an Indo-European language spoken chiefly in Albania and Yugoslavia. Albanian is the only modern representative of a distinct branch of the Indo-European language family.

A brief treatment of the Albanian language follows. For full treatment, *see* MACROPAEDIA: Languages of the World.

Native speakers of Albanian are found not only in Albania and Yugoslavia but also in southern Italy, Sicily, southern Greece, Bulgaria, Turkish Thrace, and a small section of the Ukraine. There are two principal dialects, Gheg and Tosk, which are mutually intelligible in their most common forms. The Shkumbin River provides a rough dividing line for the dialects, forms of Gheg being common to the north and Tosk to the south. Albanian speakers in Italian and Greek villages speak varieties of Tosk.

The characteristic sound of Albanian resembles that of Hungarian or Greek, with the Gheg dialect having the more unusual sound due to the number of nasal vowels. Grammatically, Albanian retains many archaic traits but bears similarities to modern Greek and the Romance languages. Nouns are declined into three or four cases and show number and gender. An exceptional feature of Albanian grammar is the inflectional attribute of nouns, with changes occurring to specify either definite or general meaning. Nouns, with few exceptions (numerals are one), are followed by their adjectives, and an agreeing particle is required by the adjective; the particle precedes the noun. Verbs are commonly irregular in stem formation. The Albanian vocabulary is heavily affected by contacts with other languages, particularly Latin; since the 16th century major influences are apparent from Italian, Turkish, modern Greek, Serbian, and Macedonian Slav.

The Albanian language is thought to be closely related to the Balto-Slavic group. It appears to be related to such ancient languages as Dacian and Illyrian, although the name Albanian, recorded since the time of Ptolemy, is really of uncertain origin. Some non-Latin influences, shared in common by the Romanian and Albanian languages, indicate early contacts between these peoples. The earliest written records come from the Gheg area in makeshift spellings based on Italian or Greek and sometimes in Turko-Arabic characters. The first recorded evidence of the written language is a baptismal formula from 1462; other documents are dated from the 16th and 17th centuries and indicate the influence of the Roman Catholic missionaries who were active in the area at that time. From the 18th century a literary work by the poet Gjul Variboba is extant. These early documents are very similar in language to examples of the current Albanian language, but they exhibit peculiarities in dialect that make them valuable historically. In 1909 an official, standardized Albanian language was developed, based on the Gheg dialect and employing the Latin alphabet. After World War II the official language changed in that it now adopted the Tosk dialect as its model.

Albanian is of special interest in the study of languages because it stands alone: it is not a part of a larger subgroup of modern languages. It holds its linguistic place along with other principal branches, *e.g.,* Germanic, of the Indo-European language family, despite the fact that the language is spoken by a relatively very small number of the world's people.

Albanian League, in full LEAGUE FOR THE DEFENSE OF THE RIGHTS OF THE ALBANIAN NATION, also called LEAGUE OF PRIZREN, first Albanian nationalist organization. Formed at Prizren, Serbia, on July 1, 1878, the league, initially supported by the Turks, tried to prevent the Congress of Berlin, which was formulating a peace settlement following the Russo-Turkish War of 1877–78, from partitioning Albania (then part of the Ottoman Empire) and transferring some of its districts to Montenegro, Serbia, and Greece. Unsuccessful in its appeals to the congress, the league used military force to prevent Montenegro from annexing the northern Albanian districts assigned to it (February 1879 and April 1880); it also forced the area acquired by Greece to be reduced (1881).

The league, however, was compelled to give up the district of Ulcinj (Dulcigno) to Montenegro (November 1880) and then was crushed by a Turkish army (by May 1881) that had been sent into Albania when the Sultan's government became annoyed with the league's demands for political autonomy. Despite its defeat, the activities of the league between 1878 and 1881 not only demonstrated the existence of a genuine nationalist movement in Albania but also gave impetus to that movement, which in 1912 brought about the declaration of the independence of Albania.

Albano, Francesco (Italian painter): *see* Albani, Francesco.

Albano, Lake, Italian LAGO ALBANO, crater lake in the Alban Hills (Colli Albani), southeast of Rome. Elliptical in shape, formed by the fusion of two ancient volcanic craters, it lies 961 ft (293 m) above sea level and has an area of 2 sq mi (5 sq km) and a maximum depth of 558 ft. It is fed by underground sources and drained by an artificial outlet, reputedly built in 398–397 BC because the oracle at Delphi said that the Etruscan stronghold of Veii could be taken only when the waters of the lake reached the sea. Among the lakeside towns, the best known are the resorts of Albano Laziale and Castel Gandolfo, the papal summer residence.

Albany, southernmost town and seaport of Western Australia, on the northern shore of Princess Royal Harbour, King George Sound. The naturally broad, deep, sheltered harbour was visited and charted by George Vancouver in 1791. In 1826 the first European settlement in the state, a penal colony called Frederickstown (after Frederick, duke of York and Albany), was established there by the British in an effort to prevent French incursions in the area. Known as Albany by 1832, it became an important whaling base during the 1840s and, until its closure in 1978, was the last surviving shore-based whaling enterprise in the Southern Hemisphere.

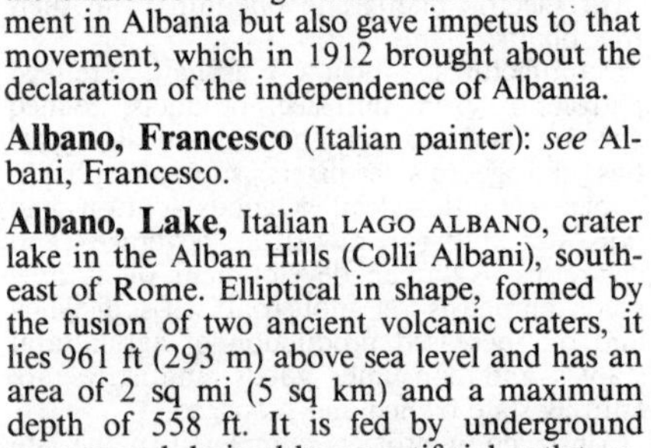

Albany and the Princess Royal Harbour, Western Australia
Photographic Library of Australia

Beginning in 1852, it served as a coaling depot for ships sailing the Indian Ocean. Albany declined temporarily when the newly improved harbour at Fremantle opened in 1900; but with the more recent development of its hinterland, it has revived to become the leading port of the south coastal area. It is an all-weather port, with little trouble from fog, storms, or tides.

On the Great Southern Railway and the South Western and Albany highways to Perth–Fremantle, 240 mi (386 km) northwest, the town serves an area of dairy, beef, lamb, fruit, and potato farming. Its industries include woollen mills, fish and meat canneries, and brick, tile, and superphosphate plants. Albany has a mild summer climate and serves as a resort for Perth and the Wheat Belt (a region traversed by the Perth–Albany Railway). Pop. (1981) 15,222.

Albany, city, seat (1853) of Dougherty County, southwestern Georgia, U.S., on the Flint River at the head of navigation. Founded in 1836 by Col. Nelson Tift, it was named for Albany, N.Y., and was early established as a leading cotton market. In 1857 a railroad connected it with Macon. Later six other lines converged on the point to make it a transportation hub. Cotton growing declined in the Albany area after the boll weevil infestation of 1915. Diversified agriculture followed, with emphasis on papershell pecans, Spanish peanuts, and livestock. Manufactures include aircraft and farm implements. Albany State College was founded in 1903, and Albany Junior College in 1965. Chehaw Indian Monument is located just north of the city. A Marine Corps supply depot is nearby. Radium Springs resort is 4 mi (6 km) south. Inc. 1838. Pop. (1980) city, 73,934; metropolitan area (SMSA), 112,662.

Albany, city, capital (1797) of the state of New York, U.S., seat (1683) of Albany County on the Hudson River, 143 mi (230 km) north of New York City. The heart of a metropolitan area that includes Troy and Schenectady, it is a port of entry, the northern terminus of the deepwater Hudson River Channel, and a natural transshipment point between ocean-going vessels and the New York State Barge Canal routes west to the Great Lakes.

In 1609 Henry Hudson anchored the "Halfmoon" in the shallows near the site while searching for the Northwest Passage. Ft. Nassau, built in 1614 on Castle Island (now part of the Port of Albany), became a trading post for the United Netherlands Company. A group of Walloon families built Ft. Orange near the site in 1624 and began the first permanent settlement, known as Beverwyck. In 1629 the Dutch West India Company granted tracts along both sides of the river (including Beverwyck) to Kiliaen van Rensselaer, an Amsterdam merchant. Renamed Rensselaerswyck, the area attracted a sizable number of colonists, and in 1652 Peter Stuyvesant, colonial governor for the Dutch West India Company, obtained independent status for the village of Beverwyck from the van Rensselaer family. When Ft. Orange surrendered to the British (Sept. 24, 1664), the village was renamed to honour the Duke of York and Albany (later James II). It was granted a city charter by the British governor Thomas Dongan on July 22, 1686. Its strategic location and the construction of Ft. Frederick made it a leading colonial city. Its population of 200 families in 1695 increased to 3,498 people in 1790 (first U.S. census) and to 50,763 by

1850. The Dutch heritage is reflected in many street names and in the annual (May) Tulip Festival held in Washington Park.

In 1689 one of the first intercolonial conventions was held at Albany to discuss a system of mutual defense. A more significant historical gathering took place in 1754, when the Albany Congress adopted Benjamin Franklin's "Plan of Union." This meeting paved the way for the Congress of 1765 and the Continental Congress of 1774. Migrating pioneers began to appear in Albany as early as 1783, and the city, already a thriving fur-trading centre, became a major outfitting point for wagon trains journeying west. The opening of the Erie Canal (1825) and the advent of the railroad (1831) increased the flow of traffic through the city, which became the hub of transportation to Michigan Territory (the upper Great Lakes). Politics remains a prevailing aspect of Albany. Industrial development has been moderate and includes the manufacture of paper, machine tools, felt, and metal products. The city was one of the first in the U.S. to establish a commercial airport (1919), and in 1932 the opening of the Port of Albany to oceangoing shipping made it a maritime centre.

The city has notable examples of Dutch Colonial, Georgian, and French-Gothic Revival architecture, including Ft. Crailo (*c.* 1700, by tradition the place where "Yankee Doodle" was written by Richard Shuckburgh and now a state historic site), the Schuyler Mansion (1762), Historic Cherry Hill (1787; home of the van Rensselaer family), the State Bank of Albany (1803), the Old Dutch Church (1799), City Hall (1883), the state capitol (1871–99) in "French Chateau" style, St. Peter's Episcopal Church (1859), and the Joseph Henry Memorial (originally Albany Academy, completed 1815). The focal point of the city is the Empire State Plaza, facing Capitol Park and embracing a building complex of government, cultural, and conventional facilities, including the New York State Museum.

Institutions of higher learning include the State University of New York at Albany (1844); the professional schools of Union University, which include Albany Medical College (1839), Law School (1851), College of Pharmacy (1881), and Dudley Observatory; and the Roman Catholic colleges of St. Rose (1920) and Maria (1958); and Albany Business College (1857). Pop. (1980) 101,727.

Consult the INDEX *first*

Albany, city, seat of Linn County, western Oregon, U.S., in the Willamette Valley, at the juncture of the Willamette and Calapooya rivers, 26 mi (42 km) south of Salem. Established in 1848 by Walter and Thomas Monteith and named for the New York state capital, it became a shipping point for wool, grain, and cascara bark. The Oregon and California (now Southern Pacific) Railroad arrived in 1870. Wood, leather, metal, and food-processing industries were developed. The U.S. Bureau of Mines maintains the Albany Metallurgy Research Center there. The city is host to the daredevilish World Championship Timber Carnival (July 4). Inc. 1864. Pop. (1980) 26,546.

Albany, DUKES OF, titled Scottish nobility of several creations, grouped below chronologically and indicated by the symbol •.

• Albany, Robert Stewart, 1st duke of (b. *c.* 1340—d. September 1420, Stirling Castle, Stirling, Scot.), regent of Scotland who virtually ruled Scotland from 1388 to 1420, throughout the reign of his weak brother Robert III and during part of the reign of James I, who had been imprisoned in London.

The third son of Robert II of Scotland, he was made high chamberlain of Scotland in 1382 and won a military reputation in campaigns against England. Chosen guardian of Scotland in 1388, he retained the control of affairs after his brother John became king as Robert III in 1390. In April 1398 he was created duke of Albany (of the first creation). In 1399, however, his nephew David, duke of Rothesay, the heir to the crown, succeeded him as governor. Uncle and nephew soon differed, and in March 1402 the latter died in prison at Falkland. While Albany and the Earl of Douglas were certainly responsible for the imprisonment of Rothesay, the cause of his death is unknown, though contemporary suspicion pointed to the uncle's guilt.

Restored to the office of governor, the Duke was chosen regent of the kingdom after the death of Robert III in 1406, because the new king, James I, was a prisoner in London. Albany continued, with no great success, to prosecute the war with England, which had been renewed a few years before. Albany died at Stirling Castle and was buried in Dunfermline Abbey. His son, Murdac (or Murdoch) Stewart, succeeded him as 2nd duke of Albany and regent but was seized in 1425 on the orders of James I on unrecorded charges and tried and executed. The dukedom of the first creation became extinct.

• Albany, Alexander Stewart, duke of, also called (1455–*c.* 1458) EARL OF MARCH (b. *c.* 1454—d. 1485, France), second son of James II of Scotland, created duke of Albany in or before 1458. Both he and John, earl of Mar, quarrelled with their brother James III, who imprisoned them in 1479. Mar died, but Albany escaped to carry on a series of intrigues with the English, who supported his pretensions to the Scottish crown. Although he returned to favour and was lieutenant general of the realm during the winter of 1482–83, he was attainted in 1483 and defeated in another rising in 1484. Escaping to France, he died there the following year.

• Albany, John Stewart, 2nd duke of (b. *c.* 1484—d. June 2, 1536), regent of Scotland during the reign of James V and advocate of close ties between France and Scotland. His father, Alexander Stewart (*c.* 1454–85), the 1st duke of Albany of the second creation, died when he was scarcely more than an infant, and he was raised in France by his mother, Anne de la Tour d'Auvergne.

In 1515, at the request of the Scottish Parliament, he came to Scotland from France. Inaugurated regent in July, he organized resistance to the English influence of Queen Margaret Tudor, whom he took prisoner at Stirling in August. He was declared heir to the throne on Nov. 13, 1516. Returning to France in 1517 he concluded the Treaty of Rouen, which renewed the alliance between France and Scotland and stipulated that a daughter of Francis I of France should marry James V of Scotland.

Returning to Scotland at the close of 1521, he immediately became the object of English attacks. He reconciled himself temporarily with Margaret and was accused by the English government of scheming to marry her himself. This was denied by the Scots, and the English demand for the regent's dismissal was refused. War with England broke out in September 1522, but Albany had little success in the field and retired to France. Returning again in September 1523, he failed once more and finally left Scotland on May 20, 1524. His regency was expressly terminated by the declaration of Parliament later that year.

From 1530 he acted as French ambassador in Rome. In 1533 he conducted Catherine de Médicis, his wife's niece, to France for her marriage to Henry (afterward Henry II of France). Thereafter much of his time was spent in protracted and fruitless negotiations for the marriage of James V. Albany died leaving no legitimate heir.

• Albany, Henry Stewart, duke of: *see* Darnley, Henry Stewart, Lord.

Albany Congress, conference in U.S. colonial history (June 19–July 11, 1754) at Albany, N.Y., which advocated a union of the British colonies in North America for their

"Join, or Die," the first known American cartoon, published by Benjamin Franklin in his *Pennsylvania Gazette*, 1754, to support his plan for colonial union presented at the Albany Congress
The Granger Collection

security and defense against the French, foreshadowing their later unification. The conference was convened by the British Board of Trade to help cement the loyalty of the Iroquois League, wavering between the French and the British in the early phases of the French and Indian War. After receiving presents, provisions, and promises of redress of grievances, 150 representatives of the tribes withdrew without committing themselves to the British cause. In addition, delegates from seven colonies advocated practical measures resulting in closer regulation of Indian affairs and westward migration of pioneers. Except to plant the germ of an important idea, an adopted proposal of Benjamin Franklin to establish a colonial union with broad powers came to naught.

Albany River, river, north central Ontario, Canada, rising in Lake St. Joseph at an elevation of 1,218 ft (371 m) and flowing generally eastward into James Bay. For 250 mi (400 km) of its 610-mi course, the river is navigable, and it served as an important route during the fur-trading days, when boats sailed inland from the Hudson's Bay Company post of Ft. Albany (established 1684) at the mouth. Its largest tributary is the Kenogami River, which is 200 mi long. The flow of the Ogoki River, a former tributary, has been diverted into Lake Nipigon to increase the hydroelectric output at the Nipigon River power sites.

albarello, pottery jar for apothecaries' ointments and dry drugs made in the Near East and in Spain and produced in Italy from the 15th through the 18th century in the form known as maiolica (*q.v.*), or tin-glazed earthenware. Since the jar had to be easy to hold, use, and shelve, its basic form was cylindrical but incurved for grasping and wide-mouthed for access. All albarellos are about 7 inches (18 centimetres) high. A few have close-set handles, but, because they were not designed to hold liquids, they are generally free of spouts, lips, handles, and outcurved forms. A piece of paper or parchment tied around the rim served as a cover for the jar.

Drug jars from Persia, Syria, and Egypt were introduced into Italy sometime before the 15th century, and lustre-decorated pots of Hispano-Moresque origin (influenced by the Moors in Spain) entered the country by way of Sicily. Spanish and Islāmic influence is apparent in the colours used in the decoration of early 15th-century Italian albarellos, which are often blue on white. A conventional oakleaf and floral design frequently occurs, combining handsomely with heraldic shields (bearing the arms of hospitals or families, for example) or with scrollwork and an inscribed label, usually an abbreviation of the name of the jar's contents. Geometric patterns are also common.

Hispano-Moresque albarello from Valencia, Spain, 15th century; in the Victoria and Albert Museum, London

By courtesy of the Victoria and Albert Museum, London

Renaissance craftsmen showed their ingenuity in the sophisticated polychrome albarellos of the 16th century, in which the early decorative motifs gave way to figurative elements: classical grotesques, portraits, historical scenes, allegories, animals, and other themes, varying according to the place of production and the skill of the artist-craftsman. In decoration, no two drug jars are alike, and even in shape there are many subtle variations of proportion and curve. By the end of the 18th century, albarellos had yielded to other containers and lingered only in old-fashioned pharmacies.

Albatenius: *see* Battānī, al-.

albatross, any of more than a dozen species of large seabirds that collectively make up the family Diomedeidae (order Procellariiformes). Because of their tameness on land, many albatrosses are known by the common names mollymawk (from the Dutch for "stupid gull") and gooney. Albatrosses are among the most spectacular gliders of all birds, able to stay aloft in windy weather for hours without ever flapping their extremely long, narrow wings. In calm air an albatross has trouble keeping its stout body airborne and prefers to rest on the water surface. Like other oceanic birds, albatrosses drink seawater. Although they normally live on squid, they are attracted to ships' garbage.

Waved albatross (*Diomedea irrorata*)

Tui De Roy Moore

Albatrosses come ashore only to breed in colonies on islands, where groups and pairs indulge in wing-stretching, bill-fencing displays accompanied by loud groaning sounds. The single large, white egg, laid on the bare ground or in a heaped-up nest, is incubated by the parents in turn. The growth of the young albatross is very slow, especially in the larger species; it attains flight plumage in 3 to 10 months, then spends the next 5 to 10 years at sea, learning navigation and feeding techniques and passing through several pre-adult plumages before coming to land to mate. Albatrosses live long and may be among the few birds to die of old age.

They are sometimes taken on baited hooks by sailors for meat (in spite of the old superstition that killing one brings bad luck) and were formerly slaughtered in large numbers for their feathers, used in the millinery trade and as swansdown.

Some of the best known albatrosses are the following:

Black-footed albatross (*Diomedea nigripes*): one of three North Pacific species; wingspread to about 200 centimetres (6.5 feet); largely sooty brown; nests on tropical Pacific islands; in nonbreeding season wanders widely throughout the North Pacific.

Laysan albatross (*D. immutabilis*): wingspread to about 200 cm (6.5 ft); adult with white body and dark upper wing surfaces; distribution about the same as the black-footed.

Royal albatross (*D. epomophora*): spread to about 315 cm (10.5 ft); adult largely white with black outer wing surfaces; breeds on islands near New Zealand and near the southern tip of South America.

Sooty albatrosses (*Phoebetria,* 2 species): spread to about 215 cm (7 ft); wings and tail longer and more slender than in *Diomedea;* nest on islands in the southern oceans.

Wandering albatross (*D. exulans*): spread to more than 340 cm (11 ft), the largest spread among living birds; adult essentially like royal albatross; nests on islands near the Antarctic Circle and on some islands in the South Atlantic; in the nonbreeding season roams the southern oceans north to about 30° S.

Albatross Cordillera, also called EAST PACIFIC RISE, submarine mountain range on the floor of the south Pacific Ocean, generally paralleling the west coast of South America. It lies generally about 2,000 mi (3,500 km) off the coast and its northernmost outliers extend as far north as the mouth of the Gulf of California and as far south as the continental rise of Antarctica south of New Zealand near the Antarctic Circle. The Albatross Cordillera is a part of the 47,000-mi-long mid-oceanic ridge system extending into the Atlantic and Indian oceans. Its surface is generally smooth and flattish and it drops sharply away at the sides. Its structure is largely of basic igneous crust, overlain or abutted by more or less flat-lying sediments. It rises from 6,000 to 9,000 ft (2,000 to 3,000 m) about the surrounding sea floor and is extensively fractured by faults mostly occurring at intervals of roughly 200 mi. The Albatross Cordillera was discovered in 1929.

Albay, coastal province on the Bicol Peninsula, southeastern Luzon, Philippines, extending between the Burias Pass of the Sibuyan Sea (west) and the Lagonoy and Albay gulfs (east). Basically agricultural (rice, corn [maize], abaca, coconuts, sugarcane, fruits), it has an area of 986 sq mi (2,553 sq km), with fertile soils derived from the active Mayon Volcano (*q.v.*). It includes the offshore islands of San Miguel, Cagraray, Batan, and Rapu-Rapu in Lagonoy Gulf. The area extending from Ligao to Iriga, in Camarines Sur province, and the lower slopes of Mayon Volcano have large abaca plantations; Albay is known for abaca rugs, place mats, slippers, bags, and sinamay cloth. There is some mining in the province. Legaspi, the provincial capital and chief port, is on Albay Gulf. Other towns include Tabaco, Guinobatan, Babacay, and Libog. Most of the people are Bicolanos. Pop. (1980) 809,177.

Albe (Italy): *see* Alba Fucens.

albedo, also called BOND ALBEDO, ratio of the amount of solar radiation reflected by a body to the amount incident upon it, usually expressed as a percentage. Very often only the visible wavelengths of the solar spectrum are considered. For this range, some typical albedos are: concrete, 17–27 percent; green forests, 5–10 percent; moist plowed fields, 14–17 percent; dark soil, 5–15 percent; desert soil, 25–30 percent; snow, 45–90 percent; and clouds, 5–85 percent, depending primarily on their thickness and the size of the cloud droplets.

The albedo of water equals the weighted sum of two components, one associated with radiation coming directly from the Sun and the other with sunlight scattered to the water by the atmosphere. The scattered component averages about 17 percent; the direct-beam component depends strongly on the solar elevation, ranging from 2 percent when the Sun is directly overhead to 58 percent when the Sun is 5° above the horizon.

Earth-orbiting satellites have been used to determine the albedo of the Earth, frequently referred to as the planetary albedo. The most recent values obtained are about 30 percent for both hemispheres. About two-thirds of this reflection occurs from clouds; the remainder is associated with reflection from air molecules, dust, water vapour, and the Earth's surface. The Moon, which has a very tenuous atmosphere and no clouds, has an albedo of only 7 percent. The albedos of cloud-covered planets (Venus, Jupiter, Saturn, Uranus, and Neptune) range from 56 to 73 percent; the value for Mars is about 15 percent.

The association of the name Bond with the albedo commemorates the work of the U.S. astronomer George P. Bond, who in 1860 published a comparison of the brightness of the Sun, the Moon, and Jupiter.

Albee, Edward (Franklin) (b. March 12, 1928, Virginia?, U.S.), U.S. dramatist and theatrical producer, best known for his first full-length play, *Who's Afraid of Virginia Woolf?,* which won virtually every major award of the Broadway season of 1962.

Albee was an adopted child, and his birthplace is uncertain, though it was near Washington, D.C. He grew up in New York City and nearby Westchester County and was educated at Choate School (graduated 1946) and Trinity College, Hartford, Conn. (1946–47). Albee first attempted to write novels and poetry but turned to plays in the late 1950s. His early one-act plays include *The Zoo Story* (first performed 1959), *The Death of Bessie Smith* (1960), and *The Sandbox* (1960). His first three-act play, *Who's Afraid of Virginia Woolf?* (1962), received numerous awards and appeared as a film in 1966. It was followed by *Tiny Alice* (1964), *A Delicate Balance* (1966), *Box* and *Quotations from Chairman Mao Tse-tung* (1968), *Seascape* (1975), *Counting the Ways* (1976), *Listening* (1977), and *The Lady from Du Buque* (1978–79). *A Delicate Balance* and *Seascape* won Pulitzer prizes.

Albee, Edward Franklin (b. Oct. 8, 1857, Machias, Maine, U.S.—d. March 11, 1930, Palm Beach, Fla.), theatrical manager who, as the general manager of the Keith-Albee theatre circuit, was the most influential person in vaudeville (*q.v.*) in the United States. A circus ticket seller when he joined Benjamin Franklin Keith in 1885 to establish the Boston Bijou Theatre, he was responsible for the expansion of the Keith–Albee vaudeville circuit. By the 1920s it controlled nearly 400 theatres in the East and Midwest. Albee was president of the United Bookings Office from its formation in 1900. In 1916 he organized a union, the National Vaudeville Artists, thus gaining a near monopoly on both talent and production in vaudeville in the United States. Albee dominated vaudeville until 1928, when RKO, a film company, absorbed his circuit in order to acquire the theatres.

Albemarle, George Monck, 1st duke of, Monck also spelled MONK: *see* Monck, George.

Albemarle Sound, coastal inlet of northeastern North Carolina, U.S., protected from the Atlantic by the Outer Banks, extends (east–west) for about 50 mi (80 km) and varies in width from 5 to 14 mi. Its average depth is 5–10 ft (1–3 m) and nowhere is it deeper than 25 ft. It receives the Pasquotank, Alligator, Chowan, and Roanoke rivers and discharges this flow at its southeastern end through the Roanoke and Croatan sounds to Pamlico Sound. It is connected with Chesapeake Bay by the Dismal Swamp and Albemarle and Chesapeake Canal and is crossed by the Atlantic Intercoastal Waterway. Elizabeth City is the chief port. Explored by Ralph Lane from the Roanoke Island colony in 1585, it was first called the Sea of Rawnocke (Roanoke Sea) and later Albemarle Bay or River after George Monck, duke of Albemarle. Along its shores were the state's earliest European settlements.

Albéniz, Isaac (Manuel Francisco) (b. May 29, 1860, Camprodón, Spain—d. May 18, 1909, Cambo-les-Bains, Fr.), composer and virtuoso pianist, a leader of the Spanish nationalist school of musicians, known especially for his piano compositions.

Albéniz appeared as a piano prodigy at age 4 and by 13 had run away from home twice. Both times he supported himself by concert tours, eventually gaining his father's consent to his wanderings. He studied at the Leipzig Conservatory at age 14 and, when his money ran out, obtained a royal grant to study in Brussels. In 1883 he settled down to teach in Barcelona and Madrid. He had previously composed facile salon music for piano, but about 1890 he began to take composition seriously. He studied with Felipe Pedrell, father of the nationalist movement in Spanish music, and in 1893 moved to Paris. There he came under the influence of Vincent d'Indy, Paul Dukas, and other French composers and for a time taught piano at the Schola Cantorum. He later developed Bright's disease and was a near invalid for several years before he died.

Albéniz' fame rests chiefly on his piano pieces, which utilize the melodic styles, rhythms, and harmonies of Spanish folk music. The most notable work is *Iberia* (1906–09), a collection of 12 virtuoso piano pieces, considered by many to be a profound evocation of the spirit of Spain, particularly of Andalusia. Also among his best works are the *Suite española,* containing the popular "Sevillana"; the *Cantos de España,* which includes "Córdoba"; *Navarra;* and the *Tango in D Major.* Orchestrated versions of many of his pieces are also frequently played.

Albéniz
By courtesy of the Biblioteca Nacional, Madrid

Alberdi, Juan Bautista (b. Aug. 20, 1810, San Miguel de Tucumán, Río de la Plata—d. June 18, 1884, Paris), perhaps the most important of 19th-century Argentine political thinkers. His writings influenced the assembly that drew up the Argentine constitution of 1853.

Alberdi, portrait by an unknown artist
By courtesy of the Archivo General de la Nacion, Buenos Aires

As an opponent of the dictator Juan Manuel de Rosas, Alberdi went into exile in 1838, studying law in Uruguay and also living in Chile and in Europe. After the overthrow of Rosas in 1852, Alberdi wrote his major book, *Bases y punto de partida para la organización política de la República Argentina.* This work emphasized the need for a central, federal government, urged immigration, and argued for attracting foreign capital.

In the 1850s Alberdi was Argentine plenipotentiary in Paris, Madrid, Washington, and London. He lost official favour in the 1860s, partly because of his opposition to the Paraguayan War (1864–70). He spent his last years in semi-exile in Europe.

Alberoni, Giulio (b. May 21, 1664, Piacenza, Duchy of Parma—d. June 16, 1752, Piacenza), statesman who as de facto premier of Spain (1716–19) played a major role in the revival of that nation after the War of the Spanish Succession (1701–14).

Alberoni, detail of an engraving by Weber
By courtesy of the Bibliotheque Nationale, Paris

The son of a gardener, Alberoni was educated by the Jesuits, took holy orders, and in 1698 was appointed a canon at Parma, in Italy. In 1702 the government of Parma sent him on a diplomatic mission to Louis-Joseph, duc de Vendôme, commander of French forces in Italy during the War of the Spanish Succession. Taken by Vendôme to France as secretary in 1706 and to Spain (1711), he nevertheless continued as an agent of Parma. After Vendôme's death (1712), Alberoni remained in Madrid, becoming the official representative of Parma the following year. He negotiated the marriage of Philip V of Spain to Elizabeth (Isabella) Farnese, daughter of the Duke of Parma. His influence at the Spanish court increased steadily, and by the beginning of 1716 he was exercising the powers of a premier.

Alberoni continued the administrative centralization and fiscal reform begun by the French economist Jean Orry, who exercised considerable influence in the government of Spain during the first years of Bourbon rule there. In addition, Alberoni encouraged the establishment of industry through tariff reform and the importation of foreign craftsmen. His outstanding achievement, however, was the diminution of the royal councils—centres of aristocratic opposition to reform—which he accomplished through a series of decrees in 1717. His foreign policy was designed to drive the Austrians from Italy and to safeguard Spanish trade with its American colonies. The Spanish military expeditions to Sardinia (1717) and Sicily (1718) that led to war with the Quadruple Alliance (Great Britain, France, Austria, and the United Provinces), which he regarded as premature, resulted from a policy imposed on him by the Queen. The defeat of Spanish forces during the Franco-British invasion of Spain resulted in his banishment in December of 1719.

Alberoni went from Spain to Italy, where he was temporarily forced into hiding. But (having been made a cardinal in 1717) he took part in the conclave that elected Pope Innocent XIII in 1721, and he was later acquitted by a papal inquiry into charges brought against him by Spain. He became legate of Ravenna in 1735 and of Bologna in 1740.

Albers, Josef (b. March 19, 1888, Bottrop, Ger.—d. March 25, 1976, New Haven, Conn., U.S.), painter, poet, influential teacher and theoretician of art, important as an innovator of such art styles as Colour Field painting and Op art.

From 1908 to 1920 Albers studied in Berlin, Essen, and Munich and taught elementary school in his native town. In 1920 he became a student at the newly formed Bauhaus, soon to become the most important school of design in Germany. His most important creations of that period were compositions made of coloured glass. After 1923, when he became a teacher at the Bauhaus, Albers created a style of painting characterized by the reiteration of abstract rectilinear patterns and the use of primary colours (red, blue, and yellow) along with white and black.

In 1933, when the Nazi government closed the Bauhaus, Albers left Germany for the U.S. He organized the fine-arts curriculum at

Josef Albers, photograph by Arnold Newman, 1948
© Arnold Newman

Black Mountain College, in North Carolina, where he taught until 1949. The next year he began a 10-year tenure as chairman of the art department of Yale University.

After moving to the U.S., Albers concentrated on several series of works that systematically explored the ambiguous relationships between the physical object of art and its psychological effect. In his series of engraved plastic "Transformations of a Scheme" (1948–52), and in the series of drawings "Structural Constellations" (1953–58), he created complex linear designs, each subject to many possible spatial interpretations. His best known series of paintings, "Homage to the Square," restricts its repertory of forms to superimposed squares of colour carefully calculated so that the colour of each square appears to alter the sizes, hues, and spatial relationships of the other squares. His poems are distinguished by a sense of lyricism and gentle irony. They were collected and published in *Poems and Drawings* (1958).

Albert, name of rulers grouped below by country and indicated by the symbol •.

Foreign-language equivalents:

Czech	Albert, or Albrecht
Dutch	Albert, or Albrecht
French	Albert
German	Albrecht
Hungarian	Albert

AUSTRIA

• **Albert I:** *see* Albert I (Germany/Holy Roman Empire).

• **Albert V:** *see* Albert II (Germany/Holy Roman Empire).

• **Albert VII** (b. Nov. 11, 1559, Wiener Neustadt, Austria—d. July 13, 1621, Brussels), cardinal archduke of Austria who as governor and sovereign prince of the Low Countries (1598–1621) ruled the Spanish Netherlands jointly with his wife, Isabella, infanta of Spain (*see* Isabella Clara Eugenia).

The son of the emperor Maximilian II, Albert was educated for an ecclesiastical career at the court of his uncle, King Philip II of Spain. Although appointed archbishop and cardinal of Toledo (Spain) in 1577, the Archduke served Philip not as a prelate but as a soldier and diplomat; he governed Portugal as Philip's viceroy from 1581 (or 1585) to 1595. After the death of his elder brother, Ernest, governor of the Netherlands, in February 1595, he was appointed governor general by Philip and given the task of subduing the rebellious Protestants in the seven United Provinces of the north. At Philip's insistence, Albert reluctantly obtained a papal release from holy orders and dispensation to marry Philip's daughter, the infanta Isabella. He received joint sovereignty of the Low Countries in 1598 as dowry for his marriage (April 1599) to Isabella. Because Albert could effect neither a military defeat of the United Provinces nor a political reconciliation, he and Isabella controlled only the 10 Catholic provinces of the south. After several years of inconclusive fighting, an armistice was arranged with the Dutch in April 1607, and a 12-year truce began in 1609. During the truce period Albert strengthened the Catholic religion in the Spanish Netherlands and did much to promote the arts.

BELGIUM

• **Albert I** (b. April 8, 1875, Brussels—d. Feb. 17, 1934, Marche-les-Dames, near Namur, Belg.), king of the Belgians (1909–1934), who led the Belgian Army during World War I and guided his country's postwar recovery.

The younger son of Philip, count of Flanders (brother of King Leopold II), Albert succeeded

Albert I
EB Inc.

to the throne in 1909—Leopold's son and Albert's father and older brother having died earlier. Before World War I, Albert worked to strengthen the army, gaining passage in 1913 of a military conscription bill. He reaffirmed Belgian neutrality to France and Germany in the summer of 1914 and rejected the German emperor William II's ultimatum of Aug. 2, 1914, demanding free passage of German troops across Belgian territory. A German invasion followed two days later.

Albert assumed leadership of the Belgian Army at the outset of the war but was forced to retreat beyond the Yser River after the fall of Antwerp in October 1914. German troops then occupied the entire country except for the southwestern districts of Flanders.

Following the Armistice Albert appealed to the Allies to abolish Belgian neutrality, formalized by European treaties in 1839, and gained passage in Parliament of universal male suffrage. For the next 15 years he guided the nation's rebuilding effort, which included public-works construction and redevelopment of industries destroyed by the German occupation. In 1926 he helped introduce a new monetary system. Concerned about Belgium's Congo colony, he presided over the colonial congresses of 1920 and 1926.

BOHEMIA

• **Albert:** *see* Albert II (Germany/Holy Roman Empire).

BRANDENBURG

• **Albert I,** also called ALBERT THE BEAR, German ALBRECHT DER BÄR (b. *c.* 1100—d. Nov. 18, 1170), the first margrave of Brandenburg and founder of the Ascanian dynasties (*q.v.*); he was one of the main leaders of 12th-century German expansion into eastern Europe. In 1123 Albert inherited Saxon estates between the Harz Mountains and the middle reaches of the Elbe River from his father, Otto the Rich. After his mother's death in 1142, he received the central German possessions of the Billung dynasty, but he was unsuccessful in his attempts to win the Saxon duchy.

His greatest achievement was in the east, where, in return for his services to the emperor Lothair II, in Italy (1132), he received the North Mark, east of the junction of the Elbe and Havel rivers (1134). He spent three years campaigning against the Wends and, by an arrangement made with Pribislav, prince of the Havelland, he obtained that district after the Prince's death in 1150.

Taking the title margrave of Brandenburg, Albert pressed the warfare against the Wends, extended the area of his mark, and increased its population and prosperity by introducing Frisian and Saxon settlers.

Albert had the help of the Premonstratensians and Cistercians in forest clearance and drainage of swamps. He coupled colonization with missionary work among the Slavs and revived the bishoprics of Havelberg and Brandenburg.

Lothair's successor, Frederick I Barbarossa, may have made Albert archchamberlain of the empire, an office that later gave the margraves of Brandenburg the rights of an elector.

• **Albert III Achilles** (b. Nov. 24, 1414, Tangermünde, Brandenburg—d. March 11, 1486, Frankfurt am Main), elector of Brandenburg, soldier, and administrative innovator who established the principle by which the mark of Brandenburg was to pass intact to the eldest son, while the younger ones would be granted dynastic holdings.

The third son of Frederick of Hohenzollern, elector of Brandenburg, Albert received his family's Ansbach lands on the death of his

Albert III Achilles, engraving by Peter Rollos, 1628
Archiv fur Kunst und Geschichte, West Berlin

father in 1440. He added Bayreuth at his brother John's death (1464), and when his brother Frederick II abdicated in 1470 he became elector of the mark of Brandenburg.

Throughout much of his life, Albert was engaged in warfare, harbouring a strong antipathy toward the relative autonomy and frequent revolt of cities and towns, especially Nürnberg, which he tried to subdue several times. His administrative policy was more effective than his campaigns, however. On Feb. 24, 1473, he proclaimed the Dispositio Achillea (Disposition of Achilles), which was to preserve Brandenburg as a united whole and keep his dynastic inheritance intact. This settlement gave the mark of Brandenburg to his eldest son and the Hohenzollerns' then more lucrative Franconian possessions to younger sons. While not establishing primogeniture as such, he made a significant step in that direction.

Albert effectively administered his lands, combatting aristocratic banditry, paying his officials salaries, tightening controls over them, and instituting an accounting system in his territories. In the German political sphere, he sided with the Habsburgs for most of his life. At the Frankfurt Reichstag (1486) he supported Maximilian I's election as German king. He also worked for currency and judicial reform and *Landesfrieden* ("peace throughout the land") for all of Germany.

BRANDENBURG-KULMBACH

• **Albert II Alcibiades** (b. March 28, 1522, Ansbach—d. Jan. 8, 1557, Baden), margrave of Brandenburg-Kulmbach, member of the Franconian branch of the Hohenzollern family, and a soldier of fortune in the wars between the Habsburgs and the Valois dynasty of France.

Albert served the Holy Roman emperor Charles V until January 1552, when he joined his friend Maurice, elector of Saxony, in a league with Charles's enemy, Henry II of

Albert II Alcibiades, detail from a portrait by an unknown artist
Archiv fur Kunst und Geschichte, West Berlin

France. The allied forces drove Charles out of Innsbruck, and the Emperor's brother Ferdinand negotiated the Treaty of Passau (August 1552) with Maurice, thereby achieving a truce in the religious disputes within Germany. Albert, however, rejected the treaty and again offered his services to Charles, who was attempting to retake Metz from the French. In return, Charles ratified Albert's seizure of large German territories. By early 1553, however, Charles had handed over control of German affairs to Ferdinand. Maurice, who had allied himself with Ferdinand, then led a coalition against Albert, who was defeated at Sievershausen (July 9, 1553). Not long after, (December 1), the Imperial Chamber at Speyer outlawed Albert, and he sought asylum in France (June 1554). In 1556 Albert returned to Germany with plans of revenge but died before he could carry them out.

GERMANY/HOLY ROMAN EMPIRE

• **Albert I** (b. *c.* 1255—d. May 1, 1308, Brugg, Switz.), duke of Austria and German king from 1298 to 1308 who repressed private war, befriended the serfs, and protected the persecuted Jews.

The eldest son of King Rudolf I of the House of Habsburg, Albert was invested with the duchies of Austria and Styria in 1282. After Rudolf's death (1291), the electors, determined to prevent the German crown from becoming a hereditary possession of the Habsburgs, checked Albert's aspirations by choosing Adolf of Nassau as German king. Albert, however, drew the electors into an alliance and engineered the deposition (June 23, 1298) of Adolf, who was defeated in battle and slain on July 2, 1298, at Göllheim.

Albert I, engraving by an unknown artist
By courtesy of the Bild-Archiv, Osterreichische Nationalbibliothek, Vienna

Albert's election, proclaimed at Mainz before the battle, was repeated at Frankfurt on July 27; he was crowned at Aachen on August 24.

Albert formed an alliance in 1299 with Philip IV of France against Pope Boniface VIII, who had refused to recognize him as king. He tried to increase the power of his house by claiming (unsuccessfully) possession of Holland, Zealand, and Frisia as vacant fiefs. His pro-French policy and his effort to control the mouths of the Rhine were opposed by the four Rhenish electors, who tried to depose him. Albert, aided by the cities of the Rhineland, crushed the coalition in a series of campaigns between 1300 and 1302. He obtained confirmation of his election from Pope Boniface VIII on April 30, 1303, swore an oath of obedience to the pope, and promised that none of his sons should be elected German king without papal consent. His attempt to place his son Rudolf on the vacant throne of Bohemia in 1306 was only momentarily successful, and his claim to Thuringia and Meissen, inherited from Adolf of Nassau, was checked by a defeat near Lucka in 1307. Albert was assassinated by his nephew John of Swabia, later called the "Parricide," from whom the King had unjustly withheld his inheritance.

• **Albert II** (b. Aug. 16, 1397—d. Oct. 27, 1439, Neszmély, Hung.), German king from 1438, king (Albert) of Hungary, king (Albrecht) of Bohemia, and duke (Albrecht) of

Albert II, engraving by Philipp Kilian
By courtesy of the Bild-Archiv, Osterreichische Nationalbibliothek, Vienna

Luxembourg. As a member of the Habsburg dynasty he was archduke (Albert V) of Austria from infancy (1404).

On the death of his father-in-law, the Holy Roman emperor Sigismund, Albert was crowned king of Hungary (Jan. 1, 1438), elected king of Germany (March 18), and, despite opposition, actually crowned king of Bohemia (June 29). Calling a diet at Nürnberg (1438), he ended all feuds based on the right of private warfare and appointed arbiters to settle disputes. He further divided Germany into administrative circles, again with the maintenance of peace in mind. Although he died the following year during a campaign against the Turks, the rule of Albert's successors was stabilized through implementation of his measures.

HUNGARY

• **Albert:** *see* Albert II (Germany/Holy Roman Empire).

LUXEMBOURG

• **Albert:** *see* Albert II (Germany/Holy Roman Empire).

MAINZ

• **Albert,** also called ALBERT OF BRANDENBURG, German ALBRECHT VON BRANDENBURG (b. June 28, 1490—d. Sept. 24, 1545, Mainz, Ger.), margrave of Brandenburg, cardinal, and elector and archbishop of Mainz and Magdeburg, a liberal patron of the arts

Albert of Brandenburg, engraving by Albrecht Dürer, 1523
Archiv fur Kunst und Geschichte, West Berlin

known chiefly as the object of the reformer Martin Luther's attacks concerning the sale of indulgences.

In order to gain the agreement of Pope Leo X to his holding more than one diocese, which was contrary to church law, Albert made a large contribution toward the rebuilding of St. Peter's Basilica in Rome. These funds, borrowed from the banking house of Fugger, were to be repaid through the sale of indulgences, half the proceeds going to Albert, the other half to Leo X. Luther condemned this practice in his Ninety-five Theses.

In 1518 Albert was created cardinal. A religious liberal, he was a friend of the Humanists Ulrich von Hutten and Desiderius Erasmus. Late in life Albert became less tolerant of Protestantism and helped foster the German Counter-Reformation.

MONACO

• **Albert,** in full ALBERT-HONORÉ-CHARLES GRIMALDI (b. Nov. 13, 1848, Paris—d. June 26, 1922, Paris), prince of Monaco (1889–1922), seaman, amateur oceanographer, and patron of the sciences, whose contributions to the development of oceanography included innovations in oceanographic equipment and technique and the founding and endowment of institutions to further basic research.

Albert's love of the sea developed at an early age, and as a young man he served in the Spanish Navy. Later, he conducted his own oceanographic surveys on a series of increasingly large and well-equipped ships. His active involvement in oceanography continued even after he became ruler of Monaco—upon the death of his father, Charles III (1889)—and culminated in his establishment of the Oceanographic Museum of Monaco (1899) and the Oceanographic Institute in Paris (1906).

Albert was succeeded as prince of Monaco by his son, Louis II (1870–1949).

NETHERLANDS

• **Albert:** *see* Albert VII (Austria).

PAPACY

• **Albert,** also called ALERIC (fl. early 12th century), antipope in 1102. He was cardinal bishop of Sabina when elected in February or March 1102 as successor to the antipope Theodoric of Santa Ruffina, who had been set up against the legitimate pope, Paschal II, by an imperial faction supporting the Holy Roman emperor Henry IV in his struggle with Paschal for supremacy. Albert's uncanonical investiture was not accepted and he was soon imprisoned. Later, Paschal ordered him blinded and sent to a monastery, where he remained a monk the rest of his life.

PRUSSIA

• **Albert** (b. May 17, 1490, Ansbach—d. March 20, 1568, Tapiau, East Prussia), last grand master of the Teutonic Knights from 1510 to 1525, first duke of Prussia (from 1525), a Protestant German ruler known chiefly for ending the Teutonic Knights' government of East Prussia and founding a hereditary dukedom in its place.

Albert of Prussia, miniature by Heinrich Königswieser, 1564; in the Kaiser-Friedrichs-Museum, Berlin

By courtesy of the Staatsbibliothek, Berlin

Albert was the third son of Frederick of Hohenzollern, margrave of Ansbach-Bayreuth. In 1510 Albert was named grand master of the Teutonic Order and thus lord of East Prussia, which the order held under Polish suzerainty. A quarrel with the Poles, however, resulted in a war with Poland (1519–21) that caused considerable damage to East Prussia. During the truce that followed, the dispute remained unsettled.

In 1523 the religious reformer Martin Luther advised Albert to dissolve the Teutonic Order and transform his Prussian holdings into a hereditary dukedom under the Polish crown, a solution accepted by King Sigismund I of Poland in 1525. The Holy Roman emperor Charles V in the 1530s placed Albert, now a Protestant, under the ban of the empire and demanded the return of East Prussia to the Teutonic Knights, but the faithful remnant of the latter, with scattered bases in Germany, could do nothing against Albert.

Albert joined anti-imperial coalitions and cultivated Protestant Denmark and Sweden. At home, the East Prussian administration was secularized, but considerable privileges had to be conceded to the nobility before they would confirm his rule and grant him funds to govern.

In his later years, Albert fell under the influence of theological and political adventurers, and his reign became marred by violent disputes. The University of Königsberg, founded on his initiative in 1544, was long troubled by such difficulties. Quiet had once again been restored, orthodox Lutheranism declared binding, the succession finally settled, and the adventurers either expelled or executed, when Albert died.

SAXONY

• **Albert III,** also called ALBERT ANIMOSUS, OR THE COURAGEOUS, German ALBRECHT DER BEHERZTE (b. July 27/31, 1443, Grimma, Saxony—d. Sept. 12, 1500, Emden, East Frisia), duke of Saxony, founder of the Albertine branch of the House of Wettin, and marshal of the Holy Roman Empire.

Albert was the son of Frederick II, elector of Saxony. When he was 12 years of age, he and his brother Ernest were abducted by their father's enemy, the Saxon noble Kunz von Kaufungen, who was quickly thwarted and executed. The incident is known as the *Prinzenraub*, and it became a popular subject for legend and literature, particularly for 16th-century German dramatists. On the death of their father, the brothers ruled their Saxon territories jointly until the Leipzig partition of 1485, when the lands were split between them.

In 1471 Albert's candidature for the Bohemian throne had failed. Governor of the Netherlands for the Holy Roman emperors from 1488 to 1493, he was rewarded for this service in 1498 with the hereditary governorship of Friesland.

• **Albert** (b. April 23, 1828, Dresden, Saxony—d. June 19, 1902, near Öls, Silesia), king of Saxony from Oct. 29, 1873, Catholic king of a Protestant country who was nonetheless popular with his subjects. He also was a capable soldier who fought well in the Seven Weeks' War of 1866 and in the Franco-German War of 1870–71.

He was the eldest son of Prince John, who succeeded to the Saxon throne in 1854. An artillery officer at the age of 15, Albert had one year of university studies at Bonn before serving in the German Schleswig-Holstein campaign of 1849 against the Danes. He married Caroline, granddaughter of King Gustav IV Adolf of Sweden, in 1853. In 1857 he was made general of infantry, and in 1862 he became a member of the upper house of the Saxon parliament.

Commanding the Saxon Army in the Seven Weeks' War, Albert effected an orderly retreat when the Prussians invaded Saxony. After the defeat of Austria and its allies, including Saxony, at Königgrätz (Sadowa) on July 3, 1866, Albert held his position tenaciously. Personally favourable to Prussia, Albert became commander of the XII Corps, formerly the Saxon Army, when his country entered the Prussian-dominated North German Confederation.

In the Franco-German War, Albert's corps played a major part in winning the battles of Gravelotte (August 18) and Sedan (Aug. 31–Sept. 2, 1870). From March 18 to June 8, 1871, he commanded the German army of occupation in France. Soon afterward he was made inspector general of the imperial German Army and was promoted to the rank of field marshal.

As king of Saxony, in succession to his father, Albert was mainly interested in military affairs but approved reforms in local administration, education, and taxation and encouraged industrialization. He left no children and was succeeded by his brother George.

Albert (composer): *see* Halévy, (Jacques-François-)Fromental(-Élie).

Albert, ARCHDUKE, German in full ERZHERZOG ALBRECHT, HERZOG (duke) VON TESCHEN (b. Aug. 3, 1817, Vienna—d. Feb. 18, 1895, Arco, South Tirol, Austria-Hungary), able field marshal who distinguished himself in the suppression of the Italian Revolution of 1848 and in the Austro-Prussian War (1866) and whose reforms turned the Austrian Army into a modern fighting force after its rout by Prussia.

Archduke Albert, detail from a lithograph by Adolph Dauthage, 1856

By courtesy of Bild-Archiv, Osterreichische Nationalbibliothek, Vienna

The son of the archduke Charles, who defeated Napoleon at Aspern-Essling, Albert entered the Austrian Army in 1837. He received a thorough military education from Field Marshal Joseph Radetzky and fought under his mentor in the campaign of 1848–49 in Italy, distinguishing himself as a divisional commander at Novara. In 1851 he became governor of Hungary, retaining the post until 1863. At the outbreak of the war against Prussia, he commanded the Italian front and won the decisive victory at Custoza (June 1866), which so disorganized the Italians that he was able to detach sizable units for the protection of Vienna, which the Prussians threatened after the Austrian defeat at Königgrätz (Sadowa). He was named commander in chief of all Austrian forces on July 10, 1866, but peace intervened before he had a chance to test his plans.

With the end of hostilities, Albert dedicated himself to the reform of the army, becoming inspector general in 1869. Drawing on the lessons learned from Prussia, he concentrated on the development of industries and railways, the creation of short-service conscription to increase the size of the armed forces, and the introduction and improvement of new weapons and the general-staff system. His efforts created as modern a fighting force as the conservative Austro-Hungarian monarchy, with its diverse nationalities and languages, was able to maintain in the latter half of the 19th century.

Albert, PRINCE CONSORT OF GREAT BRITAIN AND IRELAND, original name FRANCIS ALBERT AUGUSTUS CHARLES EMMANUEL, PRINCE OF SAXE-COBURG-GOTHA, German FRANZ ALBRECHT AUGUST KARL EMANUEL, PRINZ VON SACHSEN-COBURG-GOTHA (b. Aug. 26, 1819, Schloss Rosenau, near Coburg, Saxe-Coburg-Gotha—d. Dec. 14, 1861, Windsor, Berkshire, Eng.), the prince consort of Queen Victoria of Great Britain and father of King Edward VII. Although Albert himself was undeservedly unpopular, the domestic happiness of the royal couple was well known and helped to assure the continuation of the monarchy, which was by no means certain on the Queen's accession. On his death from typhoid fever, the British public, which had regarded him almost as an enemy alien, finally recognized his exceptional qualities. Throughout almost 40 years of widowhood, the Queen decided important questions on the

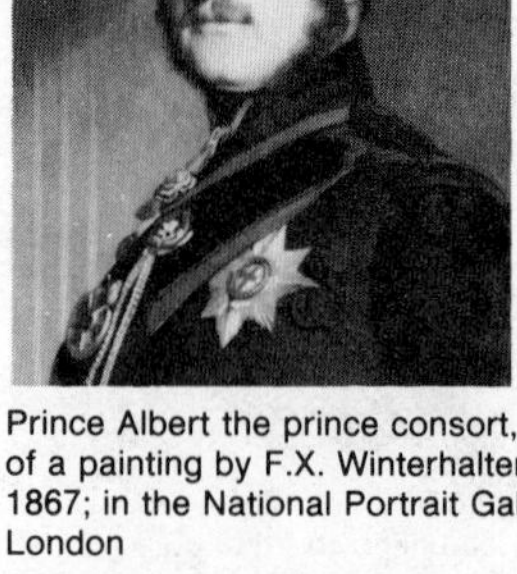
Prince Albert the prince consort, detail of a painting by F.X. Winterhalter, 1867; in the National Portrait Gallery, London

By courtesy of the National Portrait Gallery, London

basis of what she thought Albert would have done.

A member of the Ernestine branch of the Wettin dynasty, he was the second son of Ernest, duke of Saxe-Coburg-Gotha. He was educated in Brussels and at the University of Bonn. The marriage between Victoria and Albert, who were first cousins, was promoted by their uncle Leopold I, king of the Belgians. On Oct. 15, 1839, the young queen proposed to Albert, and they were married on Feb. 10, 1840.

Albert soon became, in effect, Victoria's private secretary and chief confidential adviser. Following his example, the Queen, who had been inclined to indolence, became almost as hardworking as he. At his urging she abandoned her Whig partisanship in favour of political neutrality. Disputes with Prussia in 1856 and the United States in 1861 ended peacefully, in part because Albert suggested rewording Foreign Office dispatches so that they could not be construed as ultimatums.

Albert's vigilance was unwelcome to various government ministers, especially Lord Palmerston. The British aristocracy did not care for the severe moral tone of the royal household, for Albert's professorial manner (although he rode and shot as well as they), or for his artistic versatility. In collaboration with the London contractor Thomas Cubitt, Albert designed Osborne House (1845–51), the royal residence on the Isle of Wight. He was also an accomplished musician. He successfully managed the Great Exhibition of 1851 at the Crystal Palace, London, and was planning the South Kensington Exhibition of 1862 when he became fatally ill.

Lieut. Gen. Charles Grey's *Early Years of His Royal Highness the Prince Consort* (1867) and Sir Theodore Martin's *Life of His Royal Highness the Prince Consort*, 5 vol. (1875–80), were prepared at the Queen's insistence. Excellent, and more recent, biographies include Daphne Bennett's *King Without a Crown* (1978) and Robert Rhodes James's *Albert Prince Consort* (1983).

Albert ANIMOSUS: *see* Albert III *under* Albert (Saxony).

Albert L'OUVRIER (French: Albert the Worker), original name ALEXANDRE MARTIN (b. April 27, 1815, Bury, Fr.—d. May 28, 1895, Mello), workers' representative in the provisional government and National Assembly of 1848; he was the first industrial workingman to enter a government in France.

A Paris mechanic during the 1830s and a member of several secret societies, Albert was imprisoned briefly in 1841. Subsequently, he joined the Christian-Socialist movement, collaborated on *L'Atelier* ("The Workshop"), and by 1846 had become the leader of the Society of the Seasons. When King Louis-Philippe was overthrown in February 1848, Albert was elected to the provisional government, his name appearing on all documents as Albert l'Ouvrier. With Louis Blanc he formed the extreme left contingent, advocating profound socio-economic change and supporting the short-lived Luxembourg Commission of workers and employers that reformed working hours. Elected to the new, moderate, Republican-dominated Constituent Assembly in April, Albert soon played a leading role in the May–June uprising, for which he was arrested and imprisoned. After his amnesty in 1859, he began working for a gas company and remained there for the rest of his life.

Albert OF AIX (fl. 1130), canon of the church of Aachen (Aix-la-Chapelle) and historian of the First Crusade; who gathered oral and written testaments of participants in the crusade and provided an important chronicle on the subject. Little is known about his life; he himself never visited the Holy Land. His work was completed around 1130 and still remains the chief authority on the First Crusade and the history of the Kingdom of Jerusalem until 1120. The sole document on the People's Crusade of 1096, led by Peter the Hermit, Albert's history is a compilation of legends and eyewitness reports.

Albert OF BRANDENBURG: *see* Albert *under* Albert (Mainz).

Albert OF COLOGNE: *see* Albertus Magnus, Saint.

Albert OF LAUINGEN: *see* Albertus Magnus, Saint.

Albert OF SAXONY, also called ALBERT OF RICMESTORP, or OF HALBERSTADT, German ALBERT VON SACHSEN, or VON RICMESTORP, or VON HALBERSTADT (b. *c.* 1316, Helmstedt, Saxony—d. July 8, 1390, Halberstadt), German scholastic philosopher especially noted for his investigations into physics.

He studied at Prague and then at the University of Paris, where he was a master of arts from 1351 to 1362 and rector in 1353. Most probably he is to be identified with the Albert of Ricmestorp, or Rückmersdorf, who was rector of the University of Vienna in 1365 and bishop of Halberstadt from 1366 until his death there in 1390.

Albert based his logic on William Ockham, his physical theory on Jean Buridan, his mathematics on Thomas Bradwardine, and his ethics on Walter Burley (rejecting Buridan's psychological determinism) and was at first respected more for clarity and exactness in exposition than for originality. The later scholastic logicians adopted many of the terminological distinctions first found in his works, and he examined and classified 254 *sophismata* or logical paradoxes. In physics, he wrote at length on place, space, and time; on the impossibility of a plurality of worlds; and, in great detail, on the movement of bodies (Leonardo da Vinci seems to have been indebted to him on this subject). Albert gave particular attention to the problem of gravity, being perhaps the first thinker to distinguish the centre of gravity from the geometrical centre, and to that of the velocity of falling bodies, appreciating that the question was whether velocity was proportional to time or to space. He can also be regarded as a precursor of aerostatics, as he maintained that a light balloon would rise and remain suspended in the air if a particle of fire were enclosed in it. Finally, his search for mathematical formulas to express laws of nature foreshadowed the usage of modern physics.

Albert THE BEAR: *see* Albert I *under* Albert (Brandenburg).

Albert THE COURAGEOUS: *see* Albert III *under* Albert (Saxony).

Albert THE GREAT, SAINT: *see* Albertus Magnus, Saint.

Albert, Eugène (Francis Charles) d' (b. April 10, 1864, Glasgow—d. March 3, 1932, Riga, Latvia), naturalized German composer and piano virtuoso best remembered for his opera *Tiefland* (1903) and his arrangements and transcriptions of the music of J.S. Bach.

After receiving his basic musical training in London, where he enjoyed his first triumphs as a pianist, d'Albert went to Vienna for further study, later becoming a pupil of Franz Liszt. D'Albert toured widely and successfully and taught for many years in Berlin, but his chief interest lay in composition. He wrote 20 operas, two piano concerti, chamber music, songs, piano pieces, and a few orchestral works.

Albert, Heinrich (b. July 8, 1604, Lobenstein, Saxony—d. Oct. 6, 1651, Königsberg, Prussia), composer of a famous and popular collection of songs, the most representative examples of German Baroque solo song.

Albert studied composition with his cousin, Heinrich Schütz, at Leipzig. His musical activities were encouraged by Johann Hermann Schein. In 1631 he became cathedral organist at Königsberg. Albert composed numerous festival pieces for the Brandenburg princes, but he is best known for his *Arien* (1638–50), settings of sacred and secular texts for voice and continuo, some written by himself. He also composed operas, although only two arias from these survive.

Consult the INDEX *first*

Albert, Lake, also called ALBERT NYANZA and (after 1973) LAKE MOBUTU SESE SEKO, northernmost of the lakes in the western Rift Valley system, in east central Africa, on the border between Zaire and Uganda. In 1864 the lake was first visited by a European, Samuel Baker, who was seeking the sources of the Nile; he named it after Queen Victoria's consort and published his experiences in *The Albert N'yanza* (1866). Romolo Gessi, an Italian soldier and explorer, circumnavigated it in 1876. Both Henry Stanley and Mehmed Emin Paşa (Eduard Schnitzer) established forts on its shores.

With an area of about 2,160 sq mi (5,600 sq km), a length of 100 mi (160 km), and an average width of 22 mi, Albert is a shallow body of water, averaging about 80 ft (25 m) in depth; its maximum depth is 190 ft.

In the southwest, the Semliki River brings into the lake the waters of Lake Edward (Lake Idi Amin Dada), of the Congo Escarpment, and of the rain-soaked Ruwenzori Range, building a large alluvial plain in the process. There is a considerable expanse of lowland at the northern end, where the Victoria Nile enters as a sluggish stream in a swampy delta. Almost immediately the lake narrows into the Albert Nile, through which it supplies water to the White Nile. In the west and east, the lake is bordered by forested cliffs and ravines.

Lake Albert lies at an altitude of 2,021 ft in the lowest and hottest part of Uganda. The mean annual temperature is 78° F (26° C), and rainfall averages 34–40 in. (864–1,016 mm). Because of the high rate of evaporation, the waters are somewhat saline, and free phosphate is also present. Game—including elephant, buffalo, hippopotamus, crocodile, and antelope—is abundant, especially in the Semliki Plains and the northern shores near Murchison Falls. Fishing sustains a scanty population, located in lakeshore villages.

Albert Canal, waterway connecting the cities of Antwerp and Liège in Belgium. Completed in 1939, the Albert Canal is about 80 mi (130 km) long, has a minimum bottom width of 80 ft (24 m), and can be navigated by vessels of 2,000 tons having a maximum draft of 9 ft (2.7 m). Traversing a highly industrialized area, the canal has six sets of triple locks and one single lock at Monsin (Liège).

Albert Lea, city, seat of Freeborn County, southern Minnesota, U.S., on Fountain and Albert Lea lakes, in a mixed-farming area. Settled in 1855 and named for the U.S. Army colonel who had surveyed the region in 1835, it became the county seat in 1859 as the result of a race won by a local horse over one backed by the neighbouring town of Itasca (which no longer exists). At the crossroads of a highway and rail complex, it developed as a wholesale distribution and diversified industrial centre with large meat-packing plants. Albert Lea Area Vocational Technical Institute is in the city. Helmer Myre State Park is 2 mi (3.2 km) east. Inc. village, 1878; city, 1927. Pop. (1980) 19,190.

Albert National Park (Zaire): *see* Virunga National Park.

Albert Nile, also called MOBUTU NILE, the Upper Nile River in northwestern Uganda, East Africa, issuing from the north end of Lake Albert (Mobutu), just north of the mouth of the Victoria Nile. It flows 130 mi (210 km) north past Pakwach to the Sudanese border at Nimule, where it becomes the Baḥr al-Jabal, or Mountain Nile. It is navigable throughout its course.

The Albert Nile, near Pakwach, Uganda
Shostal

Albert Nyanza (lake, East Africa): *see* Albert, Lake.

Alberta, westernmost of three Prairie Provinces, southern Canada, 756 mi (1,216 km) in extent from north to south and 404 mi from east to west, covering an area of 255,285 sq mi (661,188 sq km). Alberta is bounded on the east by Saskatchewan, on the west by British Columbia, on the north by the Northwest Territories, and on the south by the United States. The provincial capital is Edmonton.

The following article summarizes the administrative history, geography, demographic patterns, economy, and culture of modern Alberta; for additional treatment of its geography and history, *see* MACROPAEDIA: Canada.

The area now known as Alberta has been inhabited by Indian groups for at least 10,000 years. In the 1750s European fur traders arrived. Two rival trading companies, the Hudson's Bay Company and the Northwest Company, began building trading posts in the last quarter of the 18th century along the Athabasca, North Saskatchewan, and Peace rivers.

The companies merged in 1821. From this time until 1870, when this region was transferred to the Dominion of Canada, the Hudson's Bay Company ruled the area. European settlement increased after 1870, and the Indian population was decimated by European diseases, including alcoholism. The abuses of whiskey traders brought the North West Mounted Police into the area where in 1874 they established Ft. Macleod.

In the late 19th century there was a vigorous and successful effort to increase the population. A railroad was built to Calgary and cheap or free land was provided to newcomers. As a result the population grew from 73,000 in 1901 to 374,000 in 1911. Many of the immigrants were employed in wheat farming.

Alberta was made a district of the Northwest Territories in 1882 and a province of Canada in 1905. The Liberty Party formed the first government. Despite the discovery of oil at Turner Valley in 1914, the growth of both the population and the economy slowed during World War I.

After the war there was a slump in wheat prices that contributed to agrarian political agitation. In 1921 the United Farmers Party of Alberta attained a majority in the government. Alberta began to experience the Great Depression in the 1930s, and in 1935 the Social Credit Party was elected on a platform of monetary reform. It remained in power, growing steadily more orthodox, until its defeat by the Progressive Conservative Party in 1971.

Alberta's southwestern boundary is formed by the Canadian Rockies, with Mt. Columbia (12,294 ft [3,747 m]) the highest of many spectacular peaks. The remainder of the province consists of undulating plateau ranging from above 3,000 ft to less than 1,000 ft. Two river systems dominate Alberta; the Athabasca and its tributaries stretch diagonally across the province, flowing into the Lake Athabasca–Lake Claire complex in the northeast, while the south is drained primarily by the North Saskatchewan. Alberta has a continental climate, with cold, dry winters and warm, wet summers, and more sunshine than any other Canadian province. In the south, Chinook winds originating in the Rockies sometimes raise temperatures dramatically within minutes. Annual precipitation averages 18 in. (727 mm), with half falling in summer months.

The economy began to recover after World War II. Since the discovery of oil at Leduc in 1947 and the ensuing discovery of other major oil and gas deposits, there has been rapid economic expansion in Alberta. Rich natural resources include fossil fuels, timber, hydroelectric power, scenery and wildlife that stimulate tourism, and territory suitable for growing wheat and rasing cattle. These resources are developed by private industry controlled by the Canadian and provincial governments through legislation and regulation. Much of Alberta industry is managed and financed outside Canada.

The British North America Act (1867) and the Alberta Act (1905) provide the constitutional framework for the province. Alberta's parliamentary government consists of a unicameral legislative assembly elected by universal adult (age 18 and older) suffrage to a five-year term. The leader of the majority party becomes premier and chooses 22 members from the assembly to form the executive council. The Canadian governor general appoints the lieutenant governor, who serves as the monarch's representative, for a five-year term. Alberta's supreme court, whose members are appointed by the governor general, is the higest court in the province and has both trial and appellate divisions.

Primary and secondary education (including technical or vocational training) is free in the public schools, and the provincial government subsidizes private religious schools. Schools for Indians are provided by the federal government. The Alberta Institutes of Technology are located in Calgary and Edmonton, and there are universities in Calgary, Lethbridge, and Edmonton. Provincial subsidies are available to all university students. The Banff School of Fine Arts is internationally known.

Alberta's ethnic and cultural character is one of the most varied of the Canadian provinces. The British Isles group is the largest, while other major groups inlude German, Ukrainian, Scandinavian, French, and Dutch. Native Indians, Polish, Austrian, Russian, Chinese, and Japanese inhabitants are also present. These diverse groups have brought to Alberta a rich cultural legacy preserved by an impressive array of museums, art galleries, and libraries. Pop. (1982 est.) 2,320,100.

Alberta Basin, large, petroleum-rich sedimentary basin along the eastern edge of the Rocky Mountains in central Alberta, Canada. The basin was formed when the Earth's crust sank along the continental side of the Rocky Mountains during Devonian time (the Devonian Period began about 395,000,000 years ago and lasted about 50,000,000 years). At that time the region was covered by the sea. Marine sediments gradually accumulated in the deepest parts of the basin and large reefs composed of marine fossils and algae formed along its margins. About 345,000,000 years ago an uplift of the region halted sedimentation and exposed the basin deposits to erosional forces. Over several million years the organic matter buried under layers of sediment and subjected to intense heat and pressure developed into petroleum, which collected in the surrounding porous rock (*e.g.*, limestone reef remnants). Structural traps produced by the folding and faulting of rocks in the basin during the formation of the Rocky Mountains helped promote petroleum accumulation.

Alberti FAMILY, also called ALBERTI DEL GIUDICE, wealthy Florentine merchant banking family that was influential in European politics in the second half of the 14th century and notable for its patronage of the arts and beneficence toward the poor.

The ascendancy of the Alberti family began with Niccolò di Iacopo di Alberti (died 1377), whose immense success at directing a branch of the family's bank at Avignon, then the papal seat, enabled the Alberti to become the almost exclusive banker of the papacy (1362). As co-director of the company (from 1369) and then as its director (from 1372), Niccolò steadily expanded his financial interests and increased his own and his family's wealth and influence. A strong supporter of the pro-papal Guelf party in Florence, he held several important public offices there, including chief magistrate, or prior (1355), and gonfalonier of justice (1363). Later he contributed to Florence's victory over the rival city of Pisa, and in a treaty in 1369 he secured free entry for Florentine ships into the port of Pisa. He built the family's magnificent Villa del Paradiso, where he protected and encouraged men of arts and letters.

Under the leadership of Benedetto (died 1388), the Alberti sought to check the steadily growing ascendancy of the rival Albizzi family. A Guelf leader, Benedetto encouraged and participated in a popular insurrection against the oligarchic Florentine government (July 1378). Although briefly successful, this attempt ultimately failed (1382); Benedetto was exiled several years later.

Engaged also in struggles against the Albizzi was Antonio (1358–1415), who was prior (1384) and a leading patron of the arts. He made the Villa del Paradiso a centre for artists, writers, and intellectuals before being banished in 1401.

In 1402 the Albizzi succeeded in having all male members of the Alberti family banished. Although allowed to return to Florence in 1428, the Alberti did not recover full civic rights until after the fall of the Albizzi in 1434. The most famous of the later Alberti was Leon Battista Alberti.

Alberti, Domenico (b. *c.* 1710, Venice—d. 1740, Formia or Rome), composer whose harpsichord sonatas depend heavily on an accompaniment pattern of broken, or arpeggiated, chords known as the Alberti bass. He studied under the composer Antonio Lotti and was known in Rome as a singer and harpsichordist. Although he probably did not originate the Alberti bass, he consistently used it. This accompaniment pattern sets the melody against a gently moving harmonic background, satisfying the contemporary aesthetic taste for melodic predominance. It was frequently used by Haydn, Beethoven, and Mozart (an example is the first movement of Mozart's *Piano Sonata in C Major*, K. 279) and also appears in 19th-century compositions. Alberti's sonatas were plagiarized by the singer and harpsichordist Giuseppe Jozzi.

Alberti, Leon Battista (b. Feb. 14, 1404, Genoa—d. April 25, 1472, Rome), Italian Humanist, architect, and principal initiator of Renaissance art theory. In his personality, works, and breadth of learning, he is considered the prototype of the Renaissance "universal man."

Childhood and education. The society and class into which Alberti was born endowed him with the intellectual and moral tendencies

Leon Battista Alberti, self-portrait plaque, bronze, *c.* 1435; in the National Gallery of Art, Washington, D.C.

By courtesy of the National Gallery of Art, Washington, D.C., Samuel H. Kress Collection

he was to articulate and develop over a lifetime. He belonged to one of the wealthy merchant-banker families of Florence. At the time of his birth, the Alberti were in exile, expelled from Florence by the oligarchical government then dominated by the Albizzi family. Alberti's father, Lorenzo, was managing the family's concerns in Genoa, where Battista was born. Shortly thereafter he moved to Venice, where he raised Battista (Leo or Leon was a name adopted in later life) and his elder brother, Carlo. Both sons were illegitimate, the natural offspring of Lorenzo and a Bolognese widow, but they were to be Lorenzo's only children and his heirs. An affectionate and responsible father, Lorenzo provided his sons with a Florentine stepmother (whom he married in 1408), and he attended carefully to their education.

It was from his father that Battista received his mathematical training. The useful intellectual tools of the businessman inspired in him a lifelong love for the regular, for rational order, and a lasting delight in the practical application of mathematical principles. "Nothing pleases me so much," Alberti was to have a figure in one of his dialogues remark, "as mathematical investigations and demonstrations, especially when I can turn them to some useful practice as Battista here did, who drew from mathematics the principles of painting [perspective] and also his amazing propositions on the moving of weights." As in Leonardo da Vinci's case, mathematics led Alberti into several seemingly disparate fields of learning and practice. At one stroke, it resolved a diversity of problems and awakened an appreciation of the rational structure and processes of the physical world.

His early formal education was Humanistic. At the age of 10 or 11, Alberti was sent to boarding school in Padua. There he was given the classical Latin training that was to be denied to Leonardo, illegitimate son of a poor notary in a rustic village of Tuscany. The "new learning" was largely literary, and Alberti emerged from the school an accomplished Latinist and literary stylist. Relishing his skill as a classicist, he wrote a Latin comedy at the age of 20 that was acclaimed as the "discovered" work of a Roman playwright—and was still published as a Roman work in 1588 by the famous Venetian press of Aldus Manutius. But it was the content rather than the form of the classical authors that absorbed Alberti as a youth and throughout his life. As for most Humanists, the literature of ancient Rome opened up for him the vision of an urbane, secular, and rational world that seemed remarkably similar to the emerging life of the Italian cities and met its cultural needs. He brought his own emotional and intellectual tendencies to "the ancients," but from them he drew the conceptual substance of his thought.

Alberti completed his formal education at the University of Bologna in an apparently joyless study of law. His father's death and the unexpected seizure of his legacy by certain members of the family brought him grief and impoverishment during his seven-year stay at Bologna, but he persisted in his studies. After receiving his doctorate in canon law in 1428, he chose to accept a "literary" position as a secretary rather than pursue a legal career. By 1432 he was a secretary in the Papal Chancery in Rome (which supported several Humanists), and he had a commission from a highly placed ecclesiastical patron to rewrite the traditional lives of the saints and martyrs in elegant "classical" Latin. From this point on, the church was to provide him with his livelihood. He took holy orders, thus receiving in addition to his stipend as a papal secretary an ecclesiastical benefice, the priory of Gangalandi in the diocese of Florence, and some years later Nicholas V conferred upon him as well the rectory of Borgo San Lorenzo in Mugello. Although he led an exemplary, and apparently a celibate, life, there is almost nothing in his subsequent career to remind one of the fact that Alberti was a churchman. His interests and activities were wholly secular and began to issue in an impressive series of Humanistic and technical writings.

Contribution to philosophy, science, and the arts. The treatise "Della famiglia" ("On the Family"), which he began in Rome in 1432, is the first of several dialogues on moral philosophy upon which his reputation as an ethical thinker and literary stylist largely rests. He wrote these dialogues in the vernacular, expressly for a broad urban public that would not be skilled in Latin: for the *non litteratissimi cittadini,* as he called them. Based upon classical models, chiefly Cicero and Seneca, these works brought to the day-to-day concerns of a bourgeois society the reasonable counsel of the ancients—on the fickleness of fortune, on meeting adversity and prosperity, on husbandry, on friendship and family, on education and obligation to the common good. They are didactic and derivative, yet fresh with the tone and life-style of the Quattrocento (the 1400s). In Alberti's dialogues the ethical ideals of the ancient world are made to foster a distinctively modern outlook: a morality founded upon the idea of work. Virtue has become a matter of action, not of right thinking. It arises not out of serene detachment but out of striving, labouring, producing.

This ethic of achievement, which corresponds to the social reality of his youth, found ready acceptance in the urban society of central and northern Italy in which Alberti moved after 1434. Travelling with the papal court of Eugenius IV to Florence (the ban of exile against his family was lifted with the restoration of Medici influence), Bologna, and Ferrara, Alberti made several congenial and fruitful contacts. The writings, both the Latin and vernacular ones, that he dedicated to his new associates are imbued with his characteristic notions of work, practice, and productive activity; and he took upon himself in turn the technical and practical problems that were absorbing his friends and patrons. In Florence his close associations with the sculptor Donatello and the architect Brunelleschi led to one of his major achievements: the systematization of the painter's perspective. The book *On Painting,* which he wrote in 1435, set forth for the first time the rules for drawing a picture of a three-dimensional scene upon the two-dimensional plane of a panel or wall. It had an immediate and profound effect upon Italian painting and relief work, giving rise to the correct, ample, geometrically ordered space of the perspectival Renaissance style. Later perspectival theorists, such as the painter Piero della Francesca and Leonardo, elaborated upon Alberti's work, but his principles remain as basic to the projective science of perspective as Euclid's do to plane geometry.

His friendship with the Florentine cosmographer Paolo Toscanelli was of comparable practical and scientific importance. It was Toscanelli who provided Columbus with the map that guided him on his first voyage. Alberti seems to have collaborated with him in astronomy rather than geography, but the two sciences were closely bound at the time (and bound to perspective) by the conceptions and methods of geometric mapping rediscovered in the writings of the ancient astronomer and geographer Ptolemy. Alberti's distinctive contribution to this current of thought took the form of a small treatise on geography, the first work of its kind since antiquity. It sets forth the rules for surveying and mapping a land area, in this case the city of Rome, and it was probably as influential as his earlier treatise on painting. Although it is difficult to trace the historical connections, the methods of surveying and mapping and the instruments described by Alberti are precisely those that were responsible for the new scientific accuracy of the depictions of towns and land areas that date from the late 15th and early 16th centuries.

At the Este court in Ferrara, where Alberti was first made a welcome guest in 1438, the Marchese Leonello encouraged (and commissioned) him to direct his talents toward another field of endeavour: architecture. Alberti's earliest effort at reviving classical forms of building still stands in Ferrara, a miniature triumphal arch that supports an equestrian statue of Leonello's father. Leonello inspired a great Humanistic undertaking as well as a mode of artistic practice on Alberti's part by urging him to restore the classic text of Vitruvius, architect and architectural theorist of the age of the Roman emperor Augustus. With customary thoroughness, Alberti embarked upon a study of the architectural and engineering practices of antiquity that he continued when he returned to Rome in 1443 with the papal court. By the time Nicholas V became pope in 1447, Alberti was knowledgeable enough to become the Pope's architectural adviser. The collaboration between Alberti and Nicholas V gave rise to the first grandiose building projects of Renaissance Rome, initiating among other works the reconstruction of St. Peter's and the Vatican Palace. As the Este prince was now dead, it was to Nicholas V that Alberti dedicated in 1452 the monumental theoretical result of his long study of Vitruvius. This was his *De re aedificatoria* (*Ten Books on Architecture*), not a restored text of Vitruvius but a wholly new work, that won him his reputation as the "Florentine Vitruvius." It became a bible of Renaissance architecture, for it incorporated and made advances upon the engineering knowledge of antiquity, and it grounded the stylistic principles of classical art in a fully developed aesthetic theory of proportionality and harmony.

During the final 20 years of his life, Alberti carried out his architectural ideas in several outstanding buildings. The facades of Sta. Maria Novella and the Palazzo Rucellai, both executed in Florence for the merchant Giovanni Rucellai, are noted for their proportionality, their perfect sense of measure. They are worthy successors to the art of Brunelleschi, initiator of the Florentine Quattrocento style of architecture. Other buildings look forward to the 16th century, particularly to Bramante, the architect of St. Peter's. The classical severity of Alberti's Tempio Malatestiano, commissioned by Sigismondo Malatesta, the ruler of Rimini, and the new sense of volume and amplitude of the majestic church of S. Andrea, which he designed for Ludovico Gonzaga, the Humanist marquess of Mantua, announce the fullness of the High Renaissance style. Alberti was not only the foremost theorist of Renaissance architecture: he had become one of its great practitioners as well.

Architecture preoccupied him during the 1450s and 1460s, and he travelled a great deal to the various cities and courts of Renaissance Italy, but Rome and Florence remained his intellectual homes, and he continued to cultivate the interests they had always stimulated. In Rome, where republican life was precluded by the papal government, he was absorbed by technical and scientific matters. His response to certain problems entertained by members of the Papal Chancery led to two highly original works in this category. One is a grammar book, the first Italian grammar, by which he sought to demonstrate that the Tuscan vernacular was as "regular" a language as Latin and hence worthy of literary use. The other is a pioneer work in cryptography: it contains the first known frequency table and the first polyalphabetic system of coding by means of what seems to be Alberti's invention, the cipher wheel. Although he had been dismissed from the Papal Chancery in 1464 because of the retrenchment ordered by Pope Paul II, Alberti undertook this study, of obvious importance to the papacy, at the request of a friend who stayed on as a papal secretary. In this, as in all his projects, his generous disposition, practical attitude, and ethical conviction combined to make him employ his intellectual gifts in some "useful" work—useful to the artistic, cultivated, and courtly circles in which he moved: to painters and builders, map makers and astronomers, Humanists, princes, and popes; and useful to the bourgeois society from which he came, his *non litteratissimi cittadini.* In all of his work, his versatility remained bound to the social outlook that characterized the "civic Humanism" of Florence.

It is fitting that his final and finest dialogue should be set in Florence and be written in the clear Tuscan prose he had helped to regularize and refine. Although the republicanism of Florence was now eclipsed, and Alberti now moved as a familiar in the circle of the princely Lorenzo de' Medici, *De iciarchia* ("On the Man of Excellence and Ruler of His Family") represents in full flower the public-spirited Humanism of the earlier bourgeois age to which he belonged. Alberti is its chief protagonist, and no more appropriate figure is conceivable. For this dialogue, more than any other, celebrates the union of theory and practice Florentine Humanism had attained and the ethic of achievement and public service that he himself had come to exemplify. *De iciarchia* was completed just a few years before his death. He died "content and tranquil," according to the 16th-century biography by Giorgio Vasari.

Assessment. Alberti was in the vanguard of almost every major development in the cultural life of early Renaissance Italy. He has been admired for his many-sided nature, as has Leonardo, who followed him by half a century and resembles him in this respect. Yet in Alberti's case, unity as much as versatility typifies the man and his accomplishments. Leonardo's genius carried him further than Alberti: he saw more and saw more deeply. But Leonardo's vision has a "modern," fragmentary character, whereas Alberti attained a completeness in thought and life that fulfilled the Renaissance ideals of measure and harmony. His intellectual and artistic pursuits were all of a piece and he struck a unique balance between theory and practice, realizing this dominant aspiration of his age at the very moment social and political events had begun to cause it to fade. (J.K.-G.)

MAJOR WORKS. *Architecture.* Palazzo Rucellai, Florence (*c.* 1445–51); S. Francesco, Tempio Malatestiano, Rimini (1447–50); facade, Sta. Maria Novella, Florence (1456–70); S. Sebastiano, Mantua (1460–70); Rucellai Chapel, Florence (1467); S. Andrea, Mantua (*c.* 1470); SS. Annunziata, Florence (designed *c.* 1470).

Writings. Della famiglia (written 1435–44); *De pictura praestantissima* (1435); *Della pittura* (1436; *On Painting,* 1956); *De re aedificatoria* (promulgated in 1452; published in 1485; *Ten Books on Architecture,* 1955); *De iciarchia* (1468).

BIBLIOGRAPHY. For biography, bibliography, and analysis of Alberti's Humanistic, scientific, and artistic work, see Joan Gadol, *Leon Battista Alberti: Universal Man of the Early Renaissance* (1969). Cecil Grayson gives a succinct biography, bibliography, and résumé of Alberti's writings in the *Dizionario biografico degli Italiani,* vol. 1, pp. 702–709 (1960). Among the many special studies of different aspects of Alberti's work, those of most general interest are the articles by Bruno Zevi *et al.,* in the *Encyclopedia of World Art,* vol. 1, col. 188–216 (1959); Sir Kenneth Clark, "Leon Battista Alberti on Painting," *Proceedings of the British Academy,* 30:283–302 (1944); Cecil Grayson, "The Humanism of Alberti," *Italian Studies,* 12:37–56 (1957); and "Universal Man," in Philip Wiener (ed.), *Dictionary of the History of Ideas* (1972). The following studies of some of the fields in which Alberti worked give interesting appraisals of the contributions he made to them: David Kahn, *The Codebreakers: The Story of Secret Writing* (1967); Erwin Panofsky, *Renaissance and Renascences in Western Art* (1960); Rudolf Wittkower, *Architectural Principles in the Age of Humanism,* 3rd ed. rev. (1962); William Harrison Woodward, *Studies in Education During the Age of the Renaissance, 1400–1600* (1906, reprinted 1965).

Alberti, Rafael (b. 1902, Puerto de Santa María, Spain), Spanish poet and playwright of Italian-Irish ancestry, politically active until going into exile at the time of the Civil War in Spain (1936–39).

He studied art in Madrid and enjoyed some success as a painter before 1922 when he began writing and publishing poems in magazines. His first book of poetry, *Marinero en tierra* (1925), recalled the sea of his native Cádiz region, and won a national prize. Alberti helped to celebrate the tercentenary of Luis de Góngora in 1927, and Gongorist influence is apparent in the work published in that period, *El alba del alhelí* (1927) and *Cal y canto* (1928). With his next book, however, the somewhat Surrealist *Sobre los ángeles,* Alberti established himself as a mature and individual voice. In the 1930s he wrote plays, travelled widely, participated in the Communist Party—from which he was later expelled—and founded a review, *Octubre.* He fought for the Republic in the Spanish Civil War and afterward fled to France and then to Argentina, where he worked for the Losado publishing house and resumed both his poetry and his earlier interest—painting. In 1941 he published a collection of poems, *Entre el clavel y la espada,* and in 1942 his autobiography, *La arboleda perdida,* and a book of drama, prose, and poetry about the Civil War, *De un momento a otro.* He published a collection of poems about painting, *A la pintura* (1945), and collections on maritime themes, *Pleamar* (1944) and *Ora marítima* (1953). Anthologies of all of his poems have been issued frequently. After 1961, he lived mostly in Italy.

Albertina Graphics Collection: *see* Graphische Sammlung Albertina.

Albertinelli, Mariotto (b. 1474, Florence—d. 1515, Florence), painter associated with Fra Bartolomeo, an artist whose style upheld the principles of the High Renaissance in Florence a decade after its leading exponents had moved to Rome. Albertinelli and Bartolomeo were fellow pupils and later painted many works together. Albertinelli's chief paintings are in Florence, notably his masterpiece, the "Visitation of the Virgin" (1503; Uffizi). His style, similar to Bartolomeo's, is characterized by simple dignity and monumentality and shows particularly the influence of Leonardo da Vinci in its aristocratic, smiling figures, intimate compositions, and strong contrast of light and dark.

Albertini, Luigi (b. Oct. 19, 1871, Ancona, Italy—d. Dec. 29, 1941, Rome), journalist, an early and outspoken opponent of Fascism, who made the *Corriere della sera* (Milan) one of the most respected and widely read daily newspapers in Europe.

As a young man, Albertini lived in London, where he investigated labour conditions and studied the organization of *The Times.* Becoming business manager (1898) and editor (1900) of the *Corriere della sera,* he installed modern equipment and brought the paper's technical services up to date. Through the *Corriere* he defended individual freedoms and governmental authority, regarding both as necessary. Not a doctrinaire patriot, he favoured Italy's entry into World War I but disapproved of the poet and violent Italian nationalist Gabriele D'Annunzio's freebooting capture of Fiume (now Rijeka, Yugos.) in September 1919 and the Italian annexations in Dalmatia. He supported the agreement of Rapallo (November 1920) between Yugoslavia and Giovanni Giolitti's Italian government. Although Albertini had criticized the earlier postwar governments in Italy for their weakness, he was not reassured by the more forceful regime of Fascism and was one of the few newspaper editors to resist Fascist threats and cajolery. In November 1925, because of his stand against the government, the owners of the *Corriere* dismissed him.

Albertini, detail of an oil painting by Ettore Tito

Microfoto 35

Albertini devoted the rest of his life to historical studies and to land reclamation on his model estate at Torrimpietra, near Rome. He had been a senator since 1914. His major studies, including *Le origini della guerra del 1914,* 3 vol. (1942–43; *The Origins of the War of 1914,* 3 vol., 1952–57), were published posthumously.

Alberto DE MORRA (pope): *see* Gregory VIII.

Albertus MAGNUS, SAINT, English SAINT ALBERT THE GREAT, German SANKT ALBERT DER GROSSE, byname ALBERT OF COLOGNE, or OF LAUINGEN, or DOCTOR UNIVERSALIS (Latin: Universal Doctor) (b. *c.* 1200, Lauingen an der Donau, Swabia—d. Nov. 15,

1280, Cologne; canonized Dec. 16, 1931; feast day November 15), Dominican bishop and philosopher best known as a teacher of St. Thomas Aquinas and as a proponent of Aristotelianism at the University of Paris. By papal decree (1941) he was declared the patron saint of all who cultivate the natural sciences. He was the most prolific writer of his century and was the only scholar of his age to be called "the Great"; this title was used even before his death.

Albertus Magnus, detail of a fresco by Tommaso da Modena, *c.* 1352; in the church of S. Nicolo, Treviso

Alinari—Art Resource/EB Inc.

Albertus was the eldest son of a wealthy German lord. After his early schooling, he went to the University of Padua, where he studied the liberal arts. In the summer of 1223, Jordan of Saxony, master general of the recently founded Dominican order, arrived in Padua hoping to attract new members into the order. Ten students soon sought admission; one of these seems to have been Albertus.

After overcoming the strong opposition of his family, Albertus joined the order. He continued his studies at Padua and Bologna and in Germany and then taught theology at several convents throughout Germany, lastly at Cologne.

Sometime before 1245 he was sent to the Dominican convent of Saint-Jacques at the University of Paris, where he came into contact with the works of Aristotle, newly translated from Greek and Arabic, and with the commentaries on Aristotle's works by Averroës, a 12th-century Spanish-Arabian philosopher. At Saint-Jacques he lectured on the Bible for two years and then for another two years on Peter Lombard's *Sentences,* the theological textbook of the medieval universities. In 1245 he was graduated master in the theological faculty and obtained the Dominican chair "for foreigners."

It was probably at Paris that Albertus began working on a monumental presentation of the entire body of knowledge of his time. He wrote commentaries on the Bible and on the *Sentences;* he alone among medieval scholars made commentaries on all the known works of Aristotle, both genuine and spurious, paraphrasing the original but frequently adding "digressions" in which he expressed his own observations, "experiments," and speculations. The term experiment for Albertus indicates a careful process of observing, describing, and classifying. His speculations gave wide room to Neoplatonic thought. Apparently in response to a request that he explain Aristotle's *Physics,* Albertus undertook—as he states at the beginning of his *Physica*—"to make . . . intelligible to the Latins" all the branches of natural science, logic, rhetoric, mathematics, astronomy, ethics, economics, politics, and metaphysics. While he was working on this project, which took about 20 years to complete, he probably had among his disciples Thomas Aquinas, who arrived at Paris late in 1245.

Albertus distinguished the way to knowledge by revelation and faith from the way of philosophy and of science; the latter follows the authorities of the past according to their competence, but it also makes use of observation and proceeds by means of reason and intellect to the highest degrees of abstraction. For Albertus these two ways are not opposed; there is no "double truth"—one truth for faith and a contradictory truth for reason. All that is really true is joined in harmony. Although there are mysteries accessible only to faith, other points of Christian doctrine are recognizable both by faith and by reason—*e.g.,* the doctrine of the immortality of the individual soul. He defended this doctrine in several works against the teaching of the Averroists (Latin followers of Averroës), who held that only one intellect, which is common to all human beings, remains after the death of man.

Albertus' lectures and publications gained him great renown. He came to be quoted as readily as the Arabian philosophers Avicenna and Averroës and even Aristotle himself. Roger Bacon, a contemporary English scholar who was by no means friendly toward Albertus, spoke of him as "the most noted of Christian scholars."

In the summer of 1248, Albertus was sent to Cologne to organize the first Dominican *studium generale* ("general house of studies") in Germany. He presided over the house until 1254 and devoted himself to a full schedule of studying, teaching, and writing. During this period his chief disciple was Thomas Aquinas, who returned to Paris in 1252. The two men maintained a close relationship even though doctrinal differences began to appear. From 1254 to 1257 Albertus was provincial of "Teutonia," the German province of the Dominicans. Although burdened with added administrative duties, he continued his writing and scientific observation and research.

In 1256 Albertus was ordered by Pope Alexander IV to the papal court at Anagni to join Thomas and Bonaventure, a noted Franciscan scholar, in defending the mendicant orders against the masters of the University of Paris. The mendicant orders had introduced a new form of religious life in which the members renounced all personal and community property and depended upon their work—especially preaching and teaching—to subsist. Because the friars, as the mendicants were called, were not attached to any one monastery or diocese, their superiors had great freedom to send them wherever they were needed.

The Dominicans and the Franciscans, the first models of this kind of religious life, had both established at Paris influential communities that aroused the antagonism of William of Saint-Amour and other university masters who were members of the secular, or diocesan, clergy. The three friars were successful in defending the right of the mendicants to teach at the university.

Albertus resigned the office of provincial in 1257 and resumed teaching in Cologne. In 1259 he was appointed by the Pope to succeed the Bishop of Regensburg, who had been removed from office because of irregularities in the diocese. Despite his own reluctance and the objections of Humbert of Romans, general of the Dominican order, he was installed as bishop in January 1260. After Alexander IV died in 1261, Albertus was able to resign his episcopal see. He then returned to his order and to teaching at Cologne, but, as a bishop, he was in some part exempt from the order's control and could dispose of his time and even of his revenues more as he wished. From 1263 to 1264 he was legate of Pope Urban IV, preaching the crusade throughout Germany and Bohemia; subsequently, he lectured at Würzburg and at Strasbourg. In 1270 he settled definitively at Cologne, where, as he had done in 1252 and in 1258, he made peace between the archbishop and his city.

During his final years he made two long journeys from Cologne. In 1274 he attended the second Council of Lyons, France, and spoke in favour of acknowledging Rudolf of Habsburg as German king. In 1277 he travelled to Paris to uphold the recently condemned good name and writings of Thomas Aquinas, who had died a few years before, and to defend certain Aristotelian doctrines that both he and Thomas held to be true.

BIBLIOGRAPHY. The complete edition of Albert's works, undertaken by the Albertus-Magnus-Institut of Cologne, includes for the first time his *De bono; Super Isaiam; Liber de natura et origine animae, Liber de principiis motus processivi, Quaestiones super de animalibus; De sacramentis, De incarnatione, De resurrectione; Metaphysica; Super Ethica; De anima; De caelo et mundo;* and *De divinis nominibus* (1951–71). For detailed studies see Friedrich Ueberweg and Bernhard Geyer (eds.), *Die patristische und scholastische Philosophie* (1928, reprinted 1951); Thomas M. Schwertner, *St. Albert the Great* (1932); Lynn Thorndike, *A History of Magic and Experimental Science,* vol. 2 (1923); and H.C. Scheeben, *Albertus Magnus* (1955), in German.

Albertville (Zaire): *see* Kalemi.

Albi, city, capital of Tarn *département,* Midi-Pyrénées region, in the Languedoc, south-

Sainte-Cécile cathedral and the Palais de la Berbie (now a museum) overlooking the Tarn River, Albi, Fr.

APA—POUX

ern France, astride the Tarn River where it leaves the Massif Central for the Garonne Plain, northeast of Toulouse. It was capital of the Gallo-Roman Albigenses, later of the viscounty of Albigeois, a fief of the counts of Toulouse. An active centre of Catharism, it gave its name to the Albigensian heresy, which led to the Albigensian Crusade (1209) and later to the development of the Inquisition. The city was captured in 1215, and the bishops subsequently lost their estates to the crown. By a convention (1264) temporal power was granted to the bishops (archbishops after 1678) until the French Revolution.

The town's chief architectural glory is the Gothic Sainte-Cécile cathedral (1277–1512), constructed in brick, without flying buttresses; the austere cliffs of its outer walls have a glowering, fortress aspect, and its interior has no aisles or transepts. Between the cathedral and the river is the red brick Palais de la Berbie, a 13th-century archbishop's palace, now a museum where works of Henri de Toulouse-Lautrec, a native of Albi, are displayed. Below the palace is the 9th-century Old Bridge. The centre of the town is medieval. The church of Saint-Salvi has a splendid cloister (11th–15th centuries). Albi, a base for exploration of the Tarn gorges, has a tourist industry and also manufactures cement, dyes, flour, synthetic textiles, and glass. Pop. (1982) 42,724.

Albian Stage, standard, worldwide division of Lower Cretaceous rocks and time (the Cretaceous Period began about 136,000,000 years ago and lasted about 71,000,000 years). The Albian Stage is uppermost in the Lower Cretaceous Series; Albian rocks overlie rocks of the Aptian Stage and underlie rocks of the Cenomanian Stage. In Britain the Albian is represented by the Upper Greensand–Gault Clay sequence of rocks; elsewhere in northern Europe it consists of the upper portions of the thick Hils Clay. Sandstones and shaly limestones dominate the Albian of the Middle East and North Africa, and sandstones, shales, and basaltic lavas occur in the Far East. The Albian is divided into several zones, smaller divisions of rocks and time, characterized by distinctive fossil ammonite cephalopod (mollusk) genera.

Consult the INDEX *first*

Albigenses, the heretics—and especially the Catharist heretics—of the south of France in the 12th and 13th centuries. The name appears to have been given to them at the end of the 12th century, but the designation is hardly exact, for the centre of the movement was at Toulouse and in the neighbouring districts rather than at Albi (the ancient *Albiga*). The heresy, which had penetrated into these regions probably by trade routes, came originally from eastern Europe. The name of Bulgarians (*Bougres*) was often applied to the Albigenses, and they always kept up intercourse with the Bogomils (*q.v.*) of Thrace.

It is exceedingly difficult to form any very precise idea of the Albigensian doctrines because present knowledge of them is derived from their opponents and from the very rare and uninformative texts which have come down to us, emanating from the Albigenses. What is certain is that, above all, they formed an anti-sacerdotal party in permanent opposition to the Roman Church and raised a continued protest against the corruption of the clergy of their time. The Albigensian theologians and ascetics, known in the south of France as *bons hommes* or *bons chrétiens,* were always few in number.

The first Catharist heretics appeared in Limousin between 1012 and 1020. Protected by William IX, duke of Aquitaine, and soon by a great part of the southern nobility, the movement gained ground in the south, and in 1119 the Council of Toulouse in vain ordered the secular powers to assist the ecclesiastical authority in quelling the heresy. The people were attached to the *bons hommes,* whose asceticism and anti-sacerdotal preaching impressed the masses, and the movement maintained vigorous activity for another 100 years, until Innocent III ascended the papal throne. At first he tried pacific conversion but at last (1209) ordered the Cistercians to preach the crusade against the Albigenses. This implacable war, the Albigensian Crusade, which threw the whole of the nobility of the north of France against that of the south and destroyed the brilliant Provençal civilization, ended, politically, in the Treaty of Paris (1229), which destroyed the independence of the princes of the south but did not extinguish the heresy, in spite of the wholesale massacres of heretics during the war. The Inquisition, however, operating unremittingly in the south at Toulouse, Albi, and other towns during the whole of the 13th century and a great part of the 14th, succeeded in crushing it.

albinism, from the Latin *albus,* meaning "white," the absence of yellow, red, brown, or black pigments in the eyes, skin, scales, feathers, or hair. Albino animals rarely survive in the wild because they lack the pigments that normally screen against light rays and provide protective coloration. An inherited condition in man and other vertebrates, albinism may result from the total absence of pigment cells, interference with the migration of these cells to their intended locations during embryological development, lack of the hormonal stimulus necessary for pigment production, or subcellular abnormalities of the pigment cell. Albinism in the human is caused by the absence of melanin, the dark brown pigment normally present in the skin, hair, and eyes. The complete albino has milk-white skin and hair, the irises of his eyes are pink, and his pupils appear red from light reflected by blood in the unpigmented choroid.

Albino, colour type of horse, characterized by pink skin and a pure white coat. Unlike some other colour types, which develop as the horse matures, the Albino is born white and remains white throughout life. Albinos conform to riding horse type. They are not true biological albinos, however, as they have blue or sometimes brown eyes rather than pink. On White Horse Ranch in Nebraska, Albinos were bred, and the American Albino Horse Club, which registers Albinos on the basis of colour, was organized. The foundation sire of the Thompson Albinos was Old King (1906–28), possibly of Arabian–Morgan ancestry.

Albinoni, Tomaso (b. June 8, 1671, Venice—d. Jan. 17, 1750, Venice), composer whose operas and instrumental works achieved wide popularity and are distinguished by their urbanity and charm.

The son of a wealthy paper merchant, Albinoni enjoyed independent means. Although he was a fully trained musician and held a professional post as chamber musician to the duke of Mantua, he considered himself an amateur. Little is known of his life except for the production of his operas (48 in number), chiefly at Venice (1694–1740). Especially notable among his other works are the *Sinfonie e Concerti a 5* (1707) and the concerti for solo violin and for one and two oboes.

Albinovanus Pedo (fl. early 1st century AD), Roman poet who wrote a *Theseid,* referred to in a letter from his friend the poet Ovid; epigrams that are commended by the Latin poet Martial; and an epic poem on the military exploits of the Roman general Germanicus Caesar, the Emperor Tiberius' adopted son, under whom Pedo probably served. This epic may have been used as a source by the Roman historian Tacitus. All that remains of Pedo's works is a beautiful fragment, preserved in the *Suasoriae* of Seneca the Elder, describing the voyage of Germanicus (AD 16) through the Ems River to the Northern Ocean.

Albinus, Bernard Siegfried (b. Feb. 24, 1697, Frankfurt an der Oder, Brandenburg—d. Sept. 9, 1770, Leiden, Neth.), German anatomist, who was the first to show the connection of the vascular systems of the mother and the fetus. He is best known for the excellent drawings in his *Tabulae sceleti et musculorum corporis humani* (1747). Together with Hermann Boerhaave, he also edited the works of Vesalius and Harvey. From 1718 to his death, Albinus occupied the chair of anatomy, surgery, and medicine at the University of Leiden.

Albinus, Decimus Clodius Septimius (d. 197), Roman general, a candidate for the imperial title in the years 193–197. He represented the aristocracy of the Latin-speaking West, in contrast to Pescennius Niger, candidate of the Greek-speaking East, and to Lucius Septimius Severus, candidate of the army and of the Balkan region.

Originally from Hadrumetum in Roman Africa, Albinus is said to have come from a senatorial family, and he himself was made a senator, evidently in the last years of the reign of the emperor Marcus Aurelius. Soon after 180 Albinus distinguished himself in a campaign somewhere north of Dacia. He was consul in the late 180s and commanded armies on the Rhine and (about 191) in Britain.

Early in 193, after the murder of the emperor Pertinax, the guards in Rome proclaimed M. Didius Salvius Julianus emperor; evidence suggests that Albinus may have encouraged Didius. The armies of the Danube and of Syria, however, proclaimed imperial power for their respective commanders, Severus and Niger. Didius was murdered and Severus, entering Rome as emperor, concluded with Albinus an agreement that acknowledged him as caesar and heir. After Niger was destroyed by Severus, a rupture between the two remaining rivals was inevitable. In 197, Albinus, now proclaimed emperor, entered Gaul and advanced toward Rome with the army of Britain. Severus marched through southern Germany and defeated and killed Albinus in a two-day battle outside modern Lyon, Fr.

Albinus, marble bust by an unknown artist; in the Vatican Museum
Alinari—Art Resource/EB Inc.

Albinus, Decimus Junius Brutus: *see* Brutus Albinus, Decimus Junius.

albite, common feldspar mineral, a sodium aluminosilicate ($NaAlSi_3O_8$) that occurs most commonly in pegmatites and acid igneous rocks such as granites. It may also be found in low-grade metamorphic rocks and as authigenic albite in certain sedimentary varieties. Albite usually forms variously coloured, brittle glassy crystals. It is used in the manufacture of glass and ceramics, but its primary importance is as a rock-forming mineral.

Albite constitutes the sodium end-member of the plagioclase feldspar solid solution series and alkali feldspar series (*see* plagioclase; alkali feldspar). It has a triclinic framework structure with silicon and aluminum in tetrahedral (four-fold) coordination, which forms relatively large void spaces (*i.e.,* crystallographic sites) occupied chiefly by sodium cations. Although all of the silicon and aluminum atoms occupy tetrahedral sites in this structure, the sites differ in detail. At low temperatures the silicon and aluminum atoms are distributed in a highly ordered fashion. At high temperatures (about 1,000° C [1,800° F]), the atoms have a much more random distribution. For detailed physical properties, *see* feldspar (table).

Albizia, also spelled ALBIZZIA, large genus of trees, of the pea family (Fabaceae), native to warm regions of the Old World. The alternate, compound leaves are bipinnate (*i.e.,* the leaflets of the feather-formed leaves, in turn, bear leaflets). The small flowers are borne in

Albizia julibrissin
Grant Heilman—EB Inc.

globular or finger-shaped clusters. The fruit is a large, strap-shaped pod. Several species are grown as ornamentals. *A. julibrissin,* or *julibrizzin* (silk tree, or mimosa tree), native to Asia and the Middle East, grows to about 9 metres (30 feet) tall, has a broad, spreading crown, and bears flat pods about 12 centimetres (5 inches) long. At dusk the leaves fold together. *A. lebbek* (siris, or woman's-tongue tree), native to tropical Asia and Australia, grows about 24 m tall and bears pods 23–30 cm long. *A. lophantha* (plume albizia), native to Australia, grows to about 6 m tall and has pods 7.5 cm long.

Albo, Joseph (b. *c.* 1380—d. *c.* 1444), Jewish philosopher who lived in Spain during one of the most intense periods of anti-Jewish persecution in the Middle Ages. He is remembered for his classic work of Jewish dogmatics, *Sefer ha-ʿiqqarim* (1485; "Book of Principles").

Little is known of Albo's life. If he was indeed born around 1380, he would have been a child of 10 or 11 during the infamous anti-Jewish riots and massacres that occurred in Spain in 1391. His writings acknowledge the philosopher Ḥasdai Crescas as his teacher and give evidence of an education that included Christian and Islāmic theology, as well as mathematics and medicine. Albo is known to have participated in the Disputation of Tortosa (1413–14), a definitive confrontation between Spanish Jews and Christians, in which he distinguished himself by his ability to explain Jewish scriptures. Nonetheless, the Disputation ended in defeat for the Jews and resulted in a papal bull forbidding the study of the Talmud.

The *Sefer ha-ʿiqqarim,* completed in Castile in about 1425 (although not published for some 60 years), was thus conceived in a climate of intense anti-Jewish sentiment and was both Albo's defense and a philosophical exposition of the doctrines of Judaism. *Sefer Haikkarim* (1929–30), by Isaac Husik, was the first translation into English.

Alboin (d. June 28, 572, Verona, Lombardy), king of the Germanic Lombards whose exceptional military and political skills enabled him to conquer northern Italy.

When Alboin succeeded his father, Audoin, in about 565, the Lombards occupied Noricum and Pannonia (now in Austria and western Hungary), while their long-standing enemies the Gepidae bordered them on the east in Dacia (now Hungary). Astutely allying himself with the Avars, the eastern neighbours of the Gepidae, Alboin crushed his foes in a pincer movement, himself killing their king, Cunimund. After the death of his first wife, he forced Cunimund's daughter Rosamund to marry him.

Having absorbed the surviving Gepidae into the Lombard nation, Alboin assembled adventurers from all the other Germanic tribes, including several thousand Saxons, and prepared his combined forces, together with their women and children, for a migration across the Alps into Italy, which was then held by the Byzantines. The severely disorganized Byzantine provinces in Italy offered little resistance to the invading Lombards. Having swept through Venice, Milan, Tuscany, and Benevento, Alboin established Pavia as the capital of the newly created Lombard kingdom in 572. According to tradition, he was assassinated by order of Rosamund after he had forced her to follow the Lombard custom of drinking from the skull of her slain father.

Alboni, Marietta, original name MARIA ANNA MARZIA (b. March 6, 1826, Città di Castello, Papal States—d. June 23, 1894, Ville d'Array, near Paris), operatic contralto known for her classic Italian bel canto.

While a student at Bologna, Alboni captured the attention of Gioacchino Rossini, who later was to instruct her in the main contralto roles in his operas. In 1842 she made her debut as Climene in Giovanni Pacini's *Saffo* at Bologna, and she achieved a notable success in Rossini's *Le siège de Corinthe* at La Scala in Milan. She toured Austria (1843), Russia (1844–45), and Germany and eastern Europe (1846). In 1847 Alboni made sensational English and French debuts at Covent Garden in London and the Théâtre-Italien in Paris in Rossini's *Semiramide.* For the London premiere of Giuseppe Verdi's *Ernani* in 1848 she sang the baritone part of Don Carlos. In 1852–53 Alboni toured Spain and the United States to great acclaim. She married, settled in Paris, sang at Rossini's funeral in 1868, and made her final appearance in 1872 as Fidalma in Domenico Cimarosa's *Il Matrimonio segreto* at the Théâtre-Italien.

Ålborg, also spelled AALBORG, city, port, and seat of Nordjyllands *amtskommune* (county), northern Jutland, Denmark, on the south side of Limfjorden. It has existed since *c.* AD 1000 and is one of the oldest towns in Denmark. Chartered in 1342, it became a bishop's see in 1554. The town recovered slowly from the Count's War (a religious civil war, 1533–36) to become a major commercial centre in the 17th century and was Denmark's second largest city until about 1850. It is the site of the Danish surrender (1629) to Albrecht von Wallenstein (the Catholic commander) during the Thirty Years' War. It has shipbuilding facilities and manufactures cement, tobacco,

The Viking burial ground at Lindholm Høje, near Ålborg, Den.
Inga Aistrup

chemicals, textiles, and spirits, notably *akvavit,* the fiery Danish national drink. Ålborghallen (1953) is Scandinavia's largest conference and concert complex.

Medieval landmarks include the Helligånds-kloster (Holy Ghost Monastery; 1431), the Budolfi Kirke (cathedral; *c.* 1500), and Ålborghus (castle; 1539). The Jens Bang Stonehouse (1624) is a merchant's house in Dutch Renaissance style. The Ålborg art and historical museum houses relics from the Viking ship cemetery at nearby Lindholm Høje (hills). The Rebild Hills National Park (1912), 19 mi (31 km) south, a gift from Danish-Americans, is the site of the Udvandrer-Museum (Emigration Museum). The University Centre of Ålborg opened in 1974. Pop. (1981) city, 114,302; (1982 est.) mun., 154,218.

Albornoz, Gil Álvarez Carrillo de (b. *c.* 1310, Cuenca, Castile—d. Aug. 23/24, 1367, Viterbo, Papal States), Spanish cardinal and jurist, founder of the Spanish college at Bologna.

He was first a soldier, then entered the church and became archbishop of Toledo in 1338. He supported the campaigns of Castile's King Alfonso XI against the Muslims; but, when the King died, his son King Peter I turned against the archbishop, who fled to the papal city of Avignon. Pope Clement VI appointed him cardinal (1350). Under Pope Innocent VI he was made legate and vicar-general of Italy and was ordered to recover the papal estates usurped by others. By 1357 he had succeeded and returned to Avignon.

His book *Liber constitutionum Sanctae Matris Ecclesiae* ("Book of the Constitution of Holy Mother Church") established in detail the rights and duties of secular and ecclesiastical authorities. In 1358 he returned to Italy to disband the Free Companies of mercenaries. He recovered Bologna from the Milanese family of Visconti in 1364, and Pope Urban V appointed him legate there, where he founded the Spanish college that today bears his name. His work in Italy opened the way for Pope Urban V to visit Rome in 1367.

Alborz Mountains, Alborz also spelled ALBOURZ (Iran): *see* Elburz Mountains.

Albrecht (German personal name): *see under* Albert.

Albrechtsberger, Johann Georg (b. Feb. 3, 1736, Klosterneuburg, near Vienna—d. March 7, 1809, Vienna), composer, organist, and music theorist, one of the most learned and skillful contrapuntists of his time; his fame attracted many pupils, including Beethoven.

Albrechtsberger studied organ and thorough bass with Leopold Pittner and from 1755 to 1766 held various posts as organist. In 1772 he became deputy court organist in Vienna, and from 1792 he was chapel-master at St. Stephen's Cathedral. Most of his nearly 250 compositions remain in manuscript.

His works include 26 masses, 42 string quartets, a harp concerto, and other religious and chamber music. His main theoretical work was *Gründliche Anweisung zur Composition* (1790; "Fundamentals of Composition"). A collection of his theoretical writings was edited by his pupil Ignaz Ritter Xaver von Seyfried, 3 vols. (1826). A selection of his compositions was published in *Denkmäler der Tonkunst in Österreich,* vol. xvi, no. 2 (1909; "Monuments of Musical Art in Austria").

Albret FAMILY, Gascon family celebrated in French history. The lords (sires) of Albret included warriors, cardinals, and kings of Navarre, reaching the height of their power in the 14th to 16th centuries. The name derives from Labrit, a small village on the road from Bordeaux to Dax and Bayonne. The family gradually acquired more land through marriages and grants.

Members of the family fought in the First Crusade (1096–99), in the war against the Albigensian heretics in southern France (1209–29), and in the Hundred Years' War (1337–1453). In this conflict Arnaud-Amanieu d'Albret (died 1401) fought for some time for the English but finally changed to the French side and was richly rewarded (1368): King Charles V gave him not only his sister-in-law, Marguerite de Bourbon, but also lands and financial compensation. His son, Charles I d'Albret, constable of France, died at the Battle of Agincourt (1415).

Charles I's grandson, Alain, was known as Alain le Grand (1440–1522). The surname refers not to his deeds but to the vast domains over which he ruled as one of the last feudal lords. A daughter, Charlotte (1480–1514), was married to Cesare Borgia. Alain's son, Jean (died 1516), became king of Navarre through his marriage with Catherine de Foix in 1484. In 1550 the lands of Albret were made a duchy. Jeanne d'Albret (1528–72), Jean's granddaughter, married Antoine de Bourbon and left her titles to her son, Henry III of Navarre, who became king of France as Henry IV. A member of the Miossans branch of the family, César-Phébus d'Albret (1614–76), was made marshal of France in 1654.

Albright, Ivan (Le Lorraine) (b. Feb. 20, 1897, North Harvey, Ill., U.S.—d. Nov. 18, 1983, Woodstock, Vt.), highly individual painter noted particularly for his meticulously detailed, intensely dramatic depictions of decay and corruption.

He was educated at Northwestern University, Evanston, Ill., and the University of Illinois, Urbana, before World War I and, after the war, at the School of the Art Institute of Chicago and, briefly, the Pennsylvania Academy of the Fine Arts and the National Academy of Design, New York City.

In 1927 Albright settled in Warrenville, Ill., near Chicago. Independently wealthy, he devoted himself to painting. In 1930 he completed "Into the World Came a Soul Called Ida," a portrait of an aging, flabby prostitute looking into a mirror. Ultrarealistic, it conveyed the ravages of time with startling surface detail. His first one-man show was held in Chicago the same year.

In 1931 Albright began "That Which I Should Have Done I Did Not Do" (Art Institute of Chicago), showing a scarred, decrepit door on which is hung a funeral wreath; a woman's hand holding a handkerchief provides the only human element. It was completed in 1941 and is considered to be one of his masterpieces. His portrait (1943–44) of the final stage in the dissolute life of the title character in the film *The Picture of Dorian Gray* brought him fame.

Another outstanding and characteristic painting was "Poor Room—There Is No Time, No End, No Today, No Yesterday, No Tomorrow, Only the Forever, and Forever and Forever Without End" (1941–62), in which a debris-filled room is seen through a window.

Albright's identical-twin brother, Malvin Marr Albright (d. Sept. 14, 1983), was a painter and sculptor.

Albright, Tenley (Emma) (b. July 18, 1935, Newton Centre, Mass., U.S.), first U.S. woman to win the world amateur figure skating championship (1953) and an Olympic Games gold medal in figure skating (1956). She was also the first to win the world, North American, and United States titles in a single year (1953).

Albright began to skate seriously at the age of 11 in order to regain her strength following an attack of nonparalytic poliomyelitis. She won five straight U.S. senior women's championships (1952 through 1956) and two consecutive North American titles (1953 and 1955). In 1953 she won her first world championship and in 1955 won again. In the 1952 Olympic Winter Games she won a silver (second-place) medal, and in 1956 she won the Olympic women's figure skating competition.

Educated at Radcliffe College and Harvard (M.D., 1961), Albright was married in 1961 to Tudor Gardiner, an investment broker, and entered medical practice in Boston.

Albright, W(illiam) F(oxwell) (b. May 24, 1891, Coquimbo, Chile—d. Sept. 19, 1971, Baltimore), U.S. biblical archaeologist and Middle Eastern scholar, noted especially for his excavations of biblical sites.

The son of U.S. Methodist missionaries living abroad, he came with his family to the United States in 1903. He obtained his doctorate in Semitic languages at Johns Hopkins University. While there he studied under Paul Haupt, whom he succeeded in 1929 as W.W. Spence professor of Semitic languages, a position he held until his retirement in 1958.

Appointed fellow of the American School of Oriental Research, Jerusalem, in 1919, Albright served as the school's director for 12 years (1920–29, 1933–36). Among his excavations are Gibeah of Saul, Tell Beit Mirsim (Kirjath-Sepher), and, in association with others, Beth-zur and Bethel in Palestine and Baluah, and Petra in Jordan. In 1950–51 he was chief archaeologist of excavations made by the American Foundation for the Study of Man at Wadi Bayhan (Beihan), Hajar Bin Humaid, and Timna in Arabia. Albright was a pioneer in stressing the value of archaeology and of topographical and linguistic studies for biblical history and in making pottery and potsherd identification a reliable scientific tool.

Albright's scientific writings, which considerably influenced the development of biblical and related Middle Eastern scholarship, include, among others, *The Archaeology of Palestine and the Bible* (1932–35), *The Vocalization of the Egyptian Syllabic Orthography* (1934), *The Excavation of Tell Beit Mirsim* (1932–43), *From the Stone Age to Christianity* (1940–46), *Archaeology and the Religion of Israel* (1942–46), and *The Bible and the Ancient Near East* (1961).

Albright-Knox Art Gallery, in Buffalo, N.Y., museum noted for its collections of contemporary painting and sculpture, including American and European art of the 1950s, 1960s, and 1970s. Such schools as Abstract Expressionism, Pop and Op Art, Conceptualism, and Minimalism are strongly represented. The gallery also has a permanent collection containing art objects from many centuries, among them a Cycladic idol dated 3000 BC and paintings by French Impressionists and Postimpressionists of the 19th century. Works by Picasso, Braque, Matisse, Miró, and others represent Cubist, Surrealist, Constructivist, and other trends of the 1920s and 1930s.

Founded in 1862 as the Buffalo Fine Arts Academy, the Albright Art Gallery began to operate in its own building in 1905. In 1962 the gallery opened a major addition, designed by Gordon Bunshaft and donated by the Seymour H. Knox Foundation. The original Albright Art Gallery became at the same time the Albright-Knox Art Gallery.

Albright's syndrome, also called PSEUDOHYPOPARATHYROIDISM, hereditary disease characterized by abnormal bony growths; pigmented skin spots; mental retardation; endocrine disturbances, including precocious puberty in girls; and abnormal calcium metabolism. Calcium is deposited in the skin, the brain, and the lens of the eye and in inappropriate bony sites. Although the symptoms resemble those of hypoparathyroidism (hence the alternative name), parathyroid function is normal; instead, the response to parathyroid hormone is defective. Fractures secondary to bony weakness and bowing of the long bones are common. The syndrome is inherited as a sex-linked dominant trait, occurring twice as frequently in females as in males. The disease is named for the U.S. physician Fuller Albright, who first described it.

Albucasis (physician): *see* Abū al-Qāsim.

Albufera da Valencia, Louis-Gabriel Suchet, duc d' (duke of): *see* Suchet, Louis-Gabriel.

Albula Alps, part of the Rhaetian Alps in eastern Switzerland, lying in Graubünden canton to the north of the resort of Sankt Moritz. The mountains extend northeastward from the Splügen Pass (6,932 ft [2,113 m]) to the Flüela Pass (7,818 ft), and they include the Albula Pass (7,585 ft). Many peaks rise to more than 10,000 ft; the highest is the glacier-covered Piz Kesch (11,214 ft). Winter sports are popular in the region.

album, Latin ALBUS, in ancient Rome, a whitened board on which public notices were inscribed in black. The annals compiled by the *pontifex maximus* (chief priest), the annual edicts of the praetor, the lists of senators and jurors, the *Acta diurna* (an account of daily events), and other notices were placed on *albums.* From this practice is derived the present English word album, meaning a book of blank pages in which autographs, sketches, photographs, or the like are collected.

Albumazar, also spelled ALBUMASAR, or ABŪ MAʿSHAR (b. Aug. 10, 787, Balkh, Khorāsān—d. March 9, 886, al-Wāsit, Iraq), leading astrologer of the Muslim world, who is known primarily for his theory that the world, created when the seven planets were in conjunction in the first degree of Aries, will come to an end at a like conjunction in the last degree of Pisces.

Albumazar's reputation as an astrologer was immense, both among his contemporaries and in later times. He was the archetype of the knavish astrologer in the play *Lo astrologo* by the Italian philosopher and scientist Giovanni Battista della Porta (1606). This play was the basis for *Albumazar* by Thomas Tomkis, performed before James I of England in 1615 and revived by the English poet John Dryden in 1668. Albumazar's principal works include *Kitāb al-Madkhal al-Kabīr ʿalā ʿilm aḥkām al-nujūm* ("Great Introduction to the Science of Astrology"), *Kitāb al-qirānāt* ("Book of Conjunctions"), and *Kitāb taḥāwīl sinī al-ʿālam* ("Book of Revolutions of the World-Years").

albumen paper, albumen also spelled ALBUMIN, light-sensitive paper prepared by coating with albumen, or egg white, and a salt (*e.g.,* ammonium chloride) and sensitized by an aftertreatment with a solution of silver nitrate. The process was introduced by the French photographer Louis-Désiré Blanquart-Evrard in about 1850 and was widely used for about 60 years thereafter. Early employers of the process applied by hand the albumen and the silver solution, but by 1869, paper thus treated could be stored and marketed in bulk.

Albumen was also used during this period as a binder for the light-sensitive crystals on glass-plate negatives. Albumen prints are prized by modern collectors for their subtly graded tones and fine-grained resolution.

albumin, a type of protein that is soluble in water and in water half saturated with a salt such as ammonium sulfate. Serum albumin is a component of blood serum; α-lactalbumin is found in milk. Ovalbumin constitutes about 50 percent of the proteins of egg white; conalbumin is also a component. Seeds contain very small amounts of albumins (0.1–0.5 percent by weight). *See also* proteinuria.

The term albumen was once applied to water-soluble protein systems, such as egg white, containing proteins other than albumins.

albuminuria (medicine): *see* proteinuria.

Albuquerque, largest city of New Mexico, U.S., seat (1852) of Bernalillo County, on the Rio Grande opposite a pass between the Sandia and Manzano mountains to the east. It is encircled by Indian pueblos and sections of the Cibola National Forest (of which it is headquarters). Founded in 1706 by Don Francisco Cuervo y Valdés, governor and captain general of New Mexico, it was named for

The mission church of San Felipe de Neri, Albuquerque, N.M.
W. Hearne—Shostal/EB Inc.

the Duque de Alburquerque, then viceroy of New Spain (the first *r* was later dropped). It became an important trading centre on the Chihuahua Trail from Mexico.

After 1800 growing commerce on the Santa Fe Trail brought an influx of settlers; an army post was established there following U.S. occupation in 1846. During the Civil War the town was captured by the Confederates (1862) but remained loyal to the Union. The original plaza was the town centre until 1880, when the Atchison, Topeka and Santa Fe Railway laid its tracks 1 mi east. The two places were joined by a streetcar line and the settlement grew as a wool centre and food-processing point. The characteristically Spanish "old town" and the mission Church of San Felipe de Neri (1706) have survived.

Since the 1930s more than 100 federal agencies have been established there, and the development of nuclear, aerospace, and solar research industries after World War II (especially at the Sandia Laboratories and Sandia Base, Kirtland Air Force Base [adjacent to the International Airport], and the Defense Atomic Support Agency) caused a large population influx. Manufactures include truck trailers, gypsum products, lumber, clothing, and aerospace components. At an altitude of 5,314 ft (1,620 m) and with a dry, warm climate, Albuquerque became known as a health centre for the treatment of tuberculosis. Tourism is an important adjunct to the economy, and the city is a service centre for ranching, mining, and timber operations. The Sandia Peak Ski Area, with an aerial tramway, is a few miles northeast. The New Mexico State Fair is held annually (in mid-September). The Santa Fe maintains large railroad shops in the city.

The University of New Mexico was founded there in 1889, the University of Albuquerque in 1920, and Albuquerque Academy in 1955. The city is also the site of the Albuquerque Technical-Vocational Institute. Inc. 1890. Pop. (1980) city, 331,767, metropolitan area (SMSA), 454,499.

Albuquerque, Afonso de, THE GREAT (b. 1453, Alhandra, near Lisbon—d. Dec. 15, 1515, at sea, off Goa, India), Portuguese soldier, conqueror of Goa (1510) in India and of Malacca (1511) on the Malay Peninsula. His program to gain control of all the main maritime trade routes of the East and to build permanent fortresses with settled populations laid the foundations of Portuguese hegemony in the Orient.

Albuquerque was the second son of the senhor of Vila Verde. His paternal great-grandfather and grandfather had been confidential secretaries to kings John I and Edward (Duarte); his maternal grandfather had been admiral of Portugal. Albuquerque served 10 years in North Africa, where he gained early military experience crusading against Muslims. He was present at Afonso V's conquest of Arzila and Tangier in 1471. King John II (ruled 1481–95) made him master of the horse, a post Albuquerque held throughout the reign. In 1489 he again served in North Africa at the defense of Graciosa. Under John's successor, Manuel I, Albuquerque was less prominent at court but again served in Morocco.

Although Albuquerque made his mark under the stern John II and gained his experience in Africa, his reputation rests on his service in the East. When Vasco da Gama returned to Portugal in 1499 from his pioneering voyage around the Cape of Good Hope to India, King Manuel straightway sent a second fleet under Pedro Álvares Cabral to open relations and trade with the Indian rulers. The Muslim traders who had monopolized the distribution of spices turned the zamorin, or Hindu prince of Calicut, against the Portuguese. His dependency, Cochin, on the southwestern Indian coast, however, welcomed them. In 1503 Albuquerque arrived with his cousin Francisco to protect the ruler of Cochin, where he built the first Portuguese fortress in Asia and placed a garrison. After setting up a trading post at Quilon, he returned to Lisbon in July 1504, where he was well received by Manuel and participated in the formulation of policy. In 1505 Manuel appointed Dom Francisco de Almeida first governor in India, with the rank of viceroy. Almeida's object was to develop trade and aid the allies of the Portuguese. Albuquerque left Lisbon with Tristão da Cunha in April 1506 to explore the east coast of Africa and build a fortress on the island of Socotra to block the mouth of the Red Sea and cut off Arab trade with India. This done (August 1507), Albuquerque captured Hormuz (Ormuz), an island in the channel between the Persian Gulf and the Gulf of Oman, to open Persian trade with Europe. His project of building a fortress at Hormuz had to be abandoned because of differences with his captains, who departed for India. Albuquerque, though left with only two ships, continued to raid the Persian and Arabian coasts.

King Manuel appointed Albuquerque to succeed Almeida at the end of his term, though without the rank of viceroy. When Albuquerque reached India in December 1508, Almeida had crushed the improvised sea force of Calicut, but a navy from Egypt had defeated and killed his son. Insisting on retaining power until he had avenged his son's death, Almeida, to avoid interference, had Albuquerque imprisoned. Almeida defeated the Muslims off Diu in February 1509, and it was only in the following November, with the arrival of a fleet from Portugal, that he finally turned his office over to Albuquerque.

Albuquerque's plan was to assume active control over all the main maritime trade routes of the East and to establish permanent fortresses with settled populations. His attempt to seize Cochin in January 1510 was unsuccessful. By February Albuquerque had realized that it was better to try to supplant the Muslims; assisted by a powerful corsair named Timoja, he took 23 ships to attack Goa, long ruled by Muslim princes. He occupied it in March 1510, was forced out of the citadel by a Muslim army in May, and was finally able to carry it by assault in November. The Muslim defenders were put to the sword.

After this victory over the Muslims, the Hindu rulers accepted the Portuguese presence in India. Albuquerque planned to use Goa as a naval base against the Muslims, to divert the spice trade to it, and to use it to supply Persian horses to the Hindu princes. By marrying his men to the widows of his victims he would give Goa its own population, and its supplies would be assured by the village communities under a special regime. After providing for the government of Goa, Albuquerque embarked on the conquest of Malacca, on the Malay Peninsula, the immediate point of distribution for the Spice Islands and points east. He took that port in July 1511, garrisoned it, and sent ships in search of spices.

In the meantime Goa was again under heavy attack. He left in January 1512 and relieved Goa. Having established himself there and having gained control over the movement of goods by a licensing system, Albuquerque again turned to the Red Sea, taking a force of Portuguese and Indians. Because Socotra was inadequate as a base, he attempted to take Aden, but his forces proved insufficient. He thereupon explored the Arabian and Abyssinian coasts. Returning to India, he finally subdued Calicut, hitherto the main seat of opposition to the Portuguese.

In February 1515 he again left Goa with 26 ships for Hormuz, gaining control of part of the island. He was taken ill in September and turned back to Goa. On the way he learned that he had been superseded by his personal enemy, Lope Soares; he died embittered on shipboard before reaching his destination.

Albuquerque's plans derived from the crusading spirit of John II and others. He did not allow himself to be diverted from his schemes by considerations of mercantile gain. His boldest concepts, such as turning the Persians against the Turks or ruining Egypt by diverting the course of the Nile, were perhaps superhuman, but so perhaps was his achievement. (H.V.L.)

BIBLIOGRAPHY. Biographies of Albuquerque in English are: H. Morse Stephens, *Albuquerque,* in "Rulers of India Series" (1892); E. Prestage, *Afonso de Albuquerque, Governor of India* (1929), a brief, scholarly account; and E. Sanceau, *Indies Adventure* (1938). Albuquerque's remarkable series of reports and letters have been published by the Lisbon Academy of Sciences, *Cartas,* 7 vol. (1884–1935). They were drawn on by his son Brás (later called Afonso) de Albuquerque for the *Commentarios de Afonso Dalboquerque,* completed in 1557, revised in 1576, and reported in 1774. The Hakluyt Society published an English translation by W. de G. Birch, *The Commentaries of the Great Afonso Dalboquerque,* 4 vol. (1875–84; reprinted 1970).

alburnum (botany): *see* sapwood.

Albury–Wodonga, urban centre comprising twin cities on opposite sides of the Murray River and the New South Wales–Victoria border, Australia. By rail the region is about 398 mi (640 km) southwest of Sydney and nearly 186 mi northeast of Melbourne. In 1973 the Commonwealth and the two state governments agreed to plan and develop the growing cities through the Albury–Wodonga Development Corporation. The area is a focus for agricultural, pastoral, and dairying industries. An important wholesale distributing centre and the largest stock and rail-trucking centre on the Sydney–Melbourne rail line, Albury–Wodonga also has steel plants, automotive and electrical parts factories, concrete and fertilizer works, printing plants, textile mills, and sawmills. Hume Reservoir is used for water sports and irrigation. Pop. (1981) 53,214.

Alburz Mountains (Iran): *see* Elburz Mountains.

Alcaeus (b. *c.* 620 BC, Mytilene, Lesbos—d. *c.* 580 BC), Greek lyric poet and contemporary of Sappho. His work was highly esteemed in the ancient world. A collection of Alcaeus' surviving poems in 10 books (now lost) was made in the 2nd century BC, and he was a favourite model of the Roman lyric poet Horace, who adapted from him his own alcaic stanza.

Only fragments and quotations from Alcaeus' work survive, but they are enough to show the extent of his themes and to reveal his quality as a poet.

His poems may be classed in four groups: hymns in honour of gods and heroes, love poetry, drinking songs, and political poems. Many of the fragments reflect the vigour of the poet's involvement in the life of Mytilene, particularly its political life.

After years of political unrest, some measure of stability had come to Mytilene through the acquisition of power by Pittacus. He had a reputation for mildness and was rated one of the Seven Sages of Greece. Alcaeus fought beside Pittacus against the Athenians, but Pittacus betrayed Alcaeus, whose respect turned into hatred. Several fragments testify to the bitterness of his attack. He derides Pittacus for his splayfeet, his fat belly, his stinginess, and his intemperance. The most serious of the charges brought by this immoderate conservative is made against Pittacus' origin: "They have set up the low-born Pittacus as a tyrant over our gutless and godforsaken city."

Other fragments of Alcaeus' work convey the atmosphere of everyday life in 6th-century Mytilene. He writes of ships and rivers, of wine and banquets, of a girls' beauty contest, of a flock of widgeon in flight, and of the flowers that herald the spring. He managed to convey what can well be believed to have been the spirit and the values of the city-states of the Aegean, as, for example, when he declares where real greatness lies: "Not in well-fashioned houses, nor in walls, canals, and dockyards, but in men who use whatever Fortune sends them."

alcaic, classical Greek poetic stanza composed of four lines of varied metrical feet, with five long syllables in the first two lines, four in the third and fourth lines, and an unaccented syllable at the beginning of the first three lines (anacrusis). The Greek alcaic stanza is scanned:

⏓ | – ⏑ | – ⏓ | – ⏑ ⏑ | – ⏑ | –
⏓ | – ⏑ | – ⏓ | – ⏑ ⏑ | – ⏑ | –
⏓ | – ⏑ | – ⏓ | – ⏑ | – ⏓
– ⏑ ⏑ | – ⏑ ⏑ | – ⏑ | – ⏓.

Named for and perhaps invented by Alcaeus, a poet of the late 7th and early 6th centuries BC, the alcaic became an important Latin verse form, especially in the *Odes* of Horace. Variations on the traditional alcaic include the use of a long initial syllable and of a spondee (– –) in the first complete foot of the first three lines. Alcaics were adapted to English and French verse during the Renaissance and later appeared in works such as Tennyson's "Milton."

Alcalá, Calle de, main thoroughfare of Madrid. It originates at the eastern edge of the Puerta del Sol (the focal point and principal square of the city) and runs northeast approximately 4 mi (6 km) through the Plaza de la Independencia and the Puerta de Alcalá (a gateway originally built in 1599 and rebuilt in 1778). A broad, tree-lined avenue, it contains government offices and banks and is the location of the Real Academia de Bellas Artes de San Fernando (an academy of art and music, founded in 1752).

The Puerta de Alcalá on Calle de Alcalá, Madrid
Archivo Mas, Barcelona

Alcalá de Guadaira, town, Sevilla province, in the autonomous community (region) of Andalusia, southwestern Spain, on the Río Guadaira, just southeast of Seville city. The town is popularly known as Alcalá de los Panaderos (Alcalá of the Bakers) because of its large number of bakeries and flour mills that supply Sevilla with most of its flour. Olives are also exported, and oil is pressed and refined in the town. Tourism, based on the healthful climate of the area, is of growing economic importance. The nearby remains of a Moorish castle, captured by Christian forces in 1246, were declared a national monument in 1925. Pop. (1981) 45,352.

Alcalá de Henares, city, Madrid province, central Spain. Known under the Romans as Complutum, the city was destroyed in 1000 and rebuilt in 1038 by the Moors, who called it al-Qalʿah an-Nahr. It was reconquered in 1088 by Alfonso VI and granted with the surrounding lands to the archbishop of Toledo. The city contains the unique Gothic church of San Justo (built 1136 and called La Magistral), which was badly damaged during the Civil War (1936–39) but later restored, and the former archbishop's palace, now a seminary that houses the General Central Archives of Spain, containing documents of the Inquisitions of Toledo and Valencia. The original University of Alacalá de Henares, founded about the beginning of the 16th century, was moved to Madrid in 1836, and renamed the Complutensian University of Madrid. A new University of Alacalá de Henares was founded in 1977. There is also a university for technical and specialized workers (inaugurated in 1966) and a school of philosophy for Jesuits. The city has an airfield and is the site of military quarters.

Manufactures include chemicals, cotton goods, perfumes, pottery, electrical and domestic appliances, and the famous (iced) almonds of Alcalá. Alcalá de Henares was the birthplace of the author Miguel de Cervantes (who in his great novel *Don Quixote* referred to the city as the Great Complute), the emperor Ferdinand I, and Catherine of Aragon (first wife of the English king Henry VIII). Pop. (1981) 142,862.

Alcalá de Henares, University of: *see* Madrid, Complutensian University of.

Alcalá Zamora, Niceto (b. July 6, 1877, Priego, Spain—d. Feb. 18, 1949, Buenos Aires), Spanish statesman, prime minister, and president of the Second Republic (1931–36), whose attempts to moderate the policies of the various factions led eventually to his deposition and exile.

Elected to the Cortes (parliament) in 1905, Alcalá Zamora became minister of works in 1917 and minister of war in 1922. The Spanish defeat at Anual in Morocco led to an enquiry, as a result of which Gen. Primo de Rivera seized power, dissolved parliament, suppressed the report, and concluded the war. Alcalá Zamora blamed King Alfonso XIII for the dictatorship and became a republican, joining the socialists and Catalan left in the Pact of San Sebastián (August 1930). As leader of the revolutionary committee, he successfully demanded Alfonso's abdication on the basis of the municipal elections of April 1931. Alfonso left Spain, and Alcalá Zamora went from prison to become prime minister. He resigned on Oct. 14, 1931, however, when the Cortes included strongly anticlerical articles in the new constitution. Nevertheless, on December 11 he was elected the first president of the Second Republic.

Although as a Catholic he disagreed with the new constitution, he attempted to use his limited powers to moderate the increasing polarization of parties, curbing the extremists on the left in 1934 and refusing to allow constitutional revisionists to take power. As a result he was attacked by almost all parties; and, after the election of the Popular Front in February 1936, the Cortes voted by 238 to 5 to depose him on a technicality. He went to France and then to Argentina, dying in exile.

alcalde (from Arabic *al-qāḍī*, "judge"), the administrative and judicial head of a town or village in Spain or in areas under Spanish control or influence. The title was applied to local government officials whose functions were various but always included a judicial element. Types of alcaldes were differentiated according to the specialized nature of their judicial functions: the *alcalde de corte* was a judge of the palace court with jurisdiction in and about the residence of the king; the *alcalde mayor* assisted the royally appointed judges (*corregidores*) in the towns. *Alcaldes de crimen* were the ordinary judges in criminal cases in Spanish *audiencias* (courts). From the 19th century the alcalde had the dual character of leader of the local council (*ayuntamiento*) and representative of the central government. His duties became mainly administrative with scarcely any judicial functions. *Alcaldes de hermandad* were minor municipal officials with police and judicial powers.

In the Spanish colonies in the Americas, *alcaldes ordinarios* (magistrates) held seats on *cabildos* (town councils) along with *regidores* (councillors). *Alcaldes mayores* were minor officials sent to small Indian communities (as *corregidores de indios* were sent to larger ones) with practically complete civil and judicial jurisdiction over them; they were usually unsalaried. *Alcaldes de hermandad* (sometimes termed *alcaldes de la Mesta*) were rural police officials. From 1635 in Peru, and probably simultaneously in New Spain, the office of *alcalde provincial* was instituted, which closely paralleled that of the *alcalde de hermandad*. *Alcaldes de indios* were minor officials in the civil *reducciones* (Indian settlements) who answered to the *cacique* (local Indian chief) and the Spanish *corregidor* of the district. *Alcaldes de barrio* were in charge of districts in the larger cities. *Corregidores* and *alcaldes mayo-*

res, often corrupt and rapacious toward their wards, were displaced by 1790 in all of Spanish America by new officials called *intendentes* in Charles III's reform, following a similar policy initiated earlier in Spain and implemented by José de Gálvez, his minister of colonies.

Alcamenes (fl. late 5th century BC, Lemnos, in the Aegean Sea, and Athens), sculptor and younger contemporary of Phidias, noted for the delicacy and finish of his works, among which a Hephaestus and an "Aphrodite of the Gardens" are noteworthy. A copy of the head of his "Hermes Propylaeus" at Pergamum has been identified by an inscription, and he is said by the Greek traveller Pausanias (2nd century AD) to have been the creator of one of the pediments of the Temple of Zeus at Olympia.

Alcamo, town, Trapani province, northwestern Sicily, Italy, west-southwest of Palermo. The name comes from that of the nearby Saracen fortress, Alqamah, on Monte Bonifato. The present town was founded by the emperor Frederick II in 1233. Notable churches include the 17th-century Assunta church, containing frescoes by Guglielmo Borremans and sculptures by Antonello Gagini, and the church of S. Tomaso with an elaborate 14th-century doorway. Alcamo is an agricultural and industrial centre. Pop. (1981 prelim.) mun., 42,059.

Alcan Aluminium Limited, Canadian multinational company incorporated in 1928 (as Aluminum Limited) and now the largest Canadian industrial enterprise, operating in more than 100 countries. It has mining and smelting operations for bauxite ores and chemicals; hydroelectric plants; fabricating plants for a wide variety of aluminum products; and research and development laboratories. Head offices are in Montreal. The current name was adopted in 1966.

The company's history traces to 1902, when the Northern Aluminum Company was incorporated as a Canadian subsidiary of the Aluminum Company of America (Alcoa). In 1925 the name was changed to Aluminium Company of Canada, Ltd., resulting in the Alcan trademark. In 1928 it was renamed Aluminium, reincorporated, and separated from its parent company, Alcoa, which transferred to it almost all of Alcoa's assets then held outside the United States. In return, Alcoa's stockholders received the common stock of Aluminium Limited. Major stockholders of the two companies continued to be identical until 1951, when a U.S. District Court compelled them to sell their stock in one or the other company in order to remove the appearance of collusive action. Shareholders of Alcan are now mainly Canadians.

Alcan Highway: *see* Alaska Highway.

Alcántara, town, Cáceres province, in the provisional autonomous community (region) of Extremadura, western Spain, on a rock above the southern bank of the Tagus River (Río Tajo) just east of the Portuguese frontier. The walled town was named after the six-arched Roman bridge (Arabic al-Qanṭarah, the Bridge), which there spans the Tagus. Built in AD 105–106 in honour of the emperor Trajan, the bridge, 670 ft (204 m) long, was destroyed by the Moors in 1214 but was restored in 1543 and many times since. It has been called "one of the noblest Roman monuments in Spain." In 1218 Alcántara was given to an order of knights who, upon being given the town by Alfonso IX, took its name for their order. Other notable landmarks include the church of Santa María de Almocóbar, dating from the 13th century, and that of San Benito (1576), which belonged to the now ruined convent. The economy is predominantly agricultural. Pop. (1981) 2,317.

Alcántara, Order of, Christian military order in Spain founded in 1156 by Don Suero Fernández Barrientos and recognized in December 1177 by Pope Alexander III in a special papal bull. Its purpose was to defend Christian Spain against the Moors. In 1218 King Alfonso IX of Leon gave the order the town of Alcántara, and during the next two centuries its knights defended the southern borders of Christian Spain. Membership reached 100,000, and the order's annual income was between 40,000 and 50,000 ducats. After Ferdinand II of Aragon and Isabella I of Castile incorporated the military orders into the crown in 1493, the fiefs of the Order of Alcántara formed part of the royal heritage.

Alcântara, Osvaldo, pseudonym of BALTHASAR, or BALTASAR, LOPES DA SILVA (b. April 23, 1907, Vila da Ribeira Brava, São Nicolau, Cape Verde Islands), African poet and novelist who was instrumental in the shaping of modern Cape Verdean literature. Lopes was a high school teacher and later rector of the Liceu Gil Eanes in São Vicente. His dedication to his people was such that he refused more comfortable teaching positions abroad. As a lawyer he frequently worked to help the poor.

His one novel, *Chiquinho* (1947), written in Portuguese under the name Balthasar Lopes, recreates the experiences of a Cape Verdean who grows up to understand that, in his land, life is a prolonged tragedy given meaning by the assertion of human courage, unselfishness, and dignity. *Chiquinho,* marking the beginning of realism in the Cape Verdean novel, is now a classic.

His poems have been published in journals in Cape Verde, Portugal, and Brazil. As a creative writer he was one of the three founders in the 1930s of the journal *Claridade* ("Clarity"), and as a researcher of Cape Verdean culture he wrote *Cabo Verde Visto por Gilberto Freire* (1956). He also organized and edited *A Antologia de Ficção Cabo-Verdiana Contemporânea* (1960).

Alcaraz carpet, floor covering handwoven in 15th- and 16th-century Spain at Alcaraz in

Detail of the border and ground of a late 15th-century Alcaraz carpet; in the Textile Museum, Washington, D.C.

Textile Museum Collection, Washington, D.C.; photograph, Otto E. Nelson—EB Inc.

Murcia. These carpets use the Spanish knot on one warp. A number of 15th-century examples imitate contemporary Turkish types quite closely but differ in their border details and in their colouring.

There are several different forms of carpet, with "wheels" in rectangular compartments, and there is an excellent copy of a Turkish Holbein rug in the Museum of Fine Arts at Boston. Other carpets imitate a wide range of brocade and velvet patterns. A remarkable number of these carpets have survived, either complete or as fragments. The colouring is vivid, with a good, apparently madder, red in the 15th-century examples; but in the 16th century, reds seem suddenly to lighten into coral and salmon shades and then disappear, perhaps due to difficulties in setting the cochineal dye that was being imported in quantity from Mexico. A fashion then arose for carpets in two shades of green, yellow or black-brown, and white. Brocade and velvet patterns continued in use, especially an ogee lattice with crowns at points of intersection. The favourite design, however, was of wreaths of serrated leaves in rows, perhaps a continuation in spirit of the wheel design of the previous century. The border now generally had a broad stripe, sometimes of arabesque dragons, and the narrow guard stripes might display the knotted cord of the Franciscan order. Alcaraz carpets so closely resemble contemporary rugs made at Salamanca and Valencia that it has not been possible to distinguish between them with certainty.

Alcatraz Island, byname THE ROCK, rocky island in San Francisco Bay, California, U.S., occupying an area of 22 ac (9 ha), 1½ mi (2 km) offshore. From 1934 to 1963 the island was the site of a U.S. federal prison housing the most dangerous federal prisoners. Earlier a Spanish fort was located there; it was then called Isla de Alcatraces (Pelican Island). In 1850 the island was reserved by the U.S. government for military purposes, and from 1868 there was a prison for military offenders, in which Indian leaders were later confined. The first lighthouse on the coast of California was erected on Alcatraz in 1854. A group of militant Indians occupied the island (1969–71) in an unsuccessful attempt to gain title from the U.S. government. In 1972 the island became part of the Golden Gate National Recreation Area.

Alcayaga, Lucila Godoy (Chilean poet): *see* Mistral, Gabriela.

alcázar, any of a class of fortified structures built in the 14th and 15th centuries in Spain. (The term is derived from the Arabic word *al-qaṣr,* meaning "castle" or "fortress." As the Spanish efforts to drive out the Moors became more strenuous, the dual need for fortification and an imposing edifice became increasingly apparent. In form, an *alcázar* is generally rectangular with easily defensible walls and massive corner towers.

Inside the *alcázar* was a large open space (patio) surrounded by chapels, salons, hospitals, and sometimes gardens. *Alcázares* were built at Segovia (14th century) and at Toledo (14th

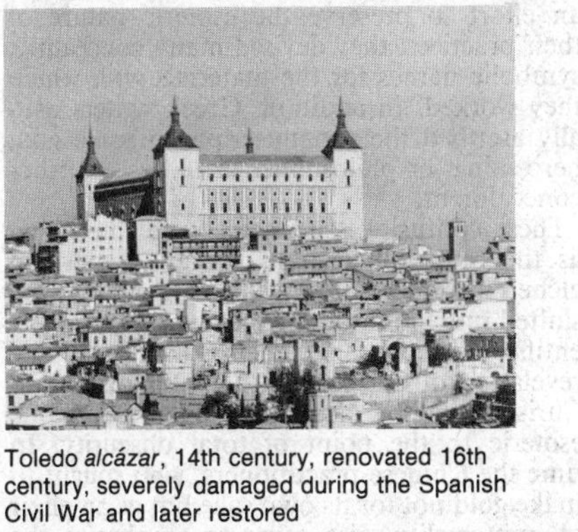

Toledo *alcázar,* 14th century, renovated 16th century, severely damaged during the Spanish Civil War and later restored

Alfonso Gutierrez—Escera

century, renovated 16th century), but the best known is the *alcázar* at Seville; its walls were erected in 1364.

Alcázar de San Juan, town, Ciudad Real province, in the autonomous community (region) of Castile-La Mancha, central Spain, on the high Meseta Central 2,135 ft (650 m) above sea level. Known to the Romans as Alces, the town was renamed al-Qaṣr (the Palace, or the Castle) by the Arabs. Conquered by the Knights of St. John (Spanish San Juan) of Jerusalem (the Hospitallers) in 1186 and captured from them by King Sancho IV of Castile in 1292, it was the centre of the Order of Saint John in the 14th, 15th, and 16th centuries. Historic landmarks include the 14th-century tower of Don Juan of Austria, the Santa María church on the site of a pre-Christian temple of Hercules, and the municipal archaeological museum containing Roman mosaics from the 2nd and 3rd centuries. The town processes wheat, olives, wines, and cheeses, especially a cheese made from sheep's milk. Industry includes soap factories, railway works, and ironworks. Pop. (1981) 25,185.

Alcazarquivir (Morocco): *see* Ksar el-Kebir.

Alcedinidae (bird family): *see* kingfisher.

alchemy, in the strict sense, the pseudoscience that concerns attempts to transform base metals such as lead or copper into silver or gold. At all times, however, such attempts have involved chemical procedures; for most of its early existence the pseudoscience was closely connected with the development of chemistry itself.

A brief treatment of alchemy follows. For full treatment, *see* MACROPAEDIA: Occultism.

The theory that five elements (air, water, earth, fire, space) in various combinations constitute all matter was postulated in almost identical form in ancient China, India, and Greece; further, the world of matter was seen to function by means of antagonistic, opposing "forces"—*e.g.*, hot and cold, wet and dry, positive and negative, male and female. Under their similar astrological heritages, philosophers of these three cultures found correspondences among the elements, planets, and metals.

Astrologers believed that events in the macrocosm of the natural world were reflected in the human microcosm, and vice versa. Thus, under the proper astrological influences, a "perfection" or "healing" of lead into gold might occur, just as the human soul could achieve a perfect state in heaven. The artisan in his laboratory could perhaps hasten this process by careful nurture and long heating, by "killing" the metal and then "reviving" it in a finer form.

While the practical alchemists invented and used many laboratory apparatuses and procedures that in modified form are used today, they were still essentially artisans and did not wish to reveal their trade secrets. In an effort to preserve the esoteric nature of their practices, they devised many concealing, symbolic names for the materials with which they worked. In addition, Greek writers usually ascribed their manuscripts to some god, hero, king, or philosopher of old as a further concealment.

These confusing tendencies were intensified as the mystically minded began to develop alchemical ideas. As Hellenistic philosophy shifted more and more from the technical scientific viewpoint to the emphasis on divine revelation of Gnosticism, Neoplatonism, and Christianity, the alchemical writings became esoteric to the point of total obscurity. In time the Chinese practitioners, who sought to make gold not for its own sake but as an elixir of immortality, also came to emphasize the esoteric aspects at the expense of all practical technique, and the art degenerated into a mass of superstition. Alchemy in India eventually met with a similar fate.

Arabic alchemy is as mysterious in its origins as the other currents. It presumably migrated to Egypt during the Hellenistic period, where it became incorporated into the work of the first alchemist whose identity has been authenticated, Zosimos of Panopolis. Through their contact with China, the Arabs adopted the use of a transmuting "medicine," the mysterious substance that appears later in European alchemy as the philosopher's stone (*q.v.*). Translations of the Arabic works of ar-Rāzī (*c.* 850–923 or 924) by Christian scholars in the 12th century led to a revival of the art in Europe. By 1300 the subject was being discussed by the leading philosophers, scientists, and theologians of the day. Important alchemical discoveries of the period include the mineral acids and alcohol. Medical chemistry or pharmacy emerged from this revival two centuries later under the influence of Paracelsus (1493 or 1494–1541), a Swiss-German alchemist.

Renaissance physicists and chemists began to discount the possibility of transmutation on the basis of a renewed interest in Greek atomism. The chemical facts that had been accumulated by the alchemists were now reinterpreted and made the basis upon which modern chemistry was erected. It was not until the 19th century, however, that the possibility of chemical gold-making was conclusively contradicted by scientific evidence. Sporadic revivals of alchemical philosophies and techniques persisted into the 20th century.

alcheringa (myth): *see* Dreaming, the.

Alchevsk (Ukrainian S.S.R.): *see* Kommunarsk.

Alcibiades (b. *c.* 450 BC, Athens—d. 404, Phrygia), brilliant but unscrupulous Athenian politican and military commander who provoked the sharp political antagonisms at Athens that were the main causes of Athens' defeat by Sparta in the Peloponnesian War (431–404 BC).

Well-born and wealthy, he was only a small boy when his father—in command of the Athenian army—was killed in 447 or 446 BC, at Coronea, Boeotia; and his guardian, the statesman Pericles, a distant relation, was too preoccupied with political leadership to provide the guidance and affection he needed. As he grew up, Alcibiades was strikingly handsome and keen witted, but he was extravagant, irresponsible, and self-centred as well. He was, however, impressed by the moral strength and keen mind of the philosopher Socrates, who, in turn, was strongly attracted by Alcibiades' beauty and intellectual promise. They served together at Potidaea (432) in the Chalcidice region, where Alcibiades was defended by Socrates when he was wounded, a debt repaid when he stayed to protect Socrates in the flight from the Battle of Delium (424), north of Athens. Yet, before he was 30 he had abandoned the intellectual integrity that Socrates demanded, in favour of the rewards of the kind of politics that Socrates despised.

Alcibiades, Roman copy of a Greek sculpture of about the second quarter of the 4th century BC; in the Museo Chiaramonti, Rome

By courtesy of the Direzione Generale dei Monumenti, Musei e Gallerie Pontificie

During the 420s Alcibiades was best known for his personal extravagance and courage in battle, but he had become a recognized speaker in the Assembly (Ecclesia); and, as Athens moved toward peace, he hoped that the ties that had once existed between his family and Sparta would enable him to secure the credit for bringing peace to Athens. According to the historian Thucydides, who knew Alcibiades well and judged him dispassionately, it was the fact that the Spartans chose to negotiate through established political leaders that dictated Alcibiades' choice of policies.

General for the first time in 420, he opposed the aristocratic leader Nicias, who had negotiated peace, and steered Athens into an anti-Spartan alliance with Argos, Elis, and Mantineia, three city-states of the Peloponnese. This alliance was defeated by Sparta at the Battle of Mantineia (418). Alcibiades, however, escaped ostracism, a form of banishment, by joining forces with Nicias against Hyperbolus, the successor of the demagogue politician Cleon as champion of the common people. In 416 he restored his reputation by entering seven chariots at Olympia and taking first, second, and fourth places. This made it easier for him, in 415, to persuade the people to send a major expedition to Sicily against Syracuse. He was appointed to share the command, but shortly before the expedition was due to sail the Hermae (busts of Hermes, messenger of Zeus and patron of all who use the roads, set up in public places throughout the city) were found to have been mutilated. In the ensuing panic Alcibiades was accused of being the originator of the sacrilege as well as of having profaned the Eleusinian Mysteries. He demanded an immediate inquiry, but his enemies, led by Androcles (the successor of Hyperbolus), ensured that he sailed with the charge still hanging over him. Shortly after reaching Sicily, he was recalled; but on the journey home he escaped and, learning that he had been condemned to death in absence, went to Sparta. There he advised the Spartans to send a general to help the Syracusans and to fortify Decelea in Attica, two serious blows to Athens. He also confirmed his reputation with women (which the rich Athenian whom he had married appreciated only too well) by seducing the wife of the Spartan king Agis II, who was at Decelea with his army.

In 412 Alcibiades helped to stir up revolt among Athenian allies in Ionia, on the west coast of Asia Minor; but Sparta now turned against him, and he moved to Sardis to exercise his charm on the Persian governor. When some Athenian officers in the fleet began to plan an oligarchic coup, he held out hopes that if the democracy was overthrown he could secure financial support from Persia. In this he failed and, discarded by the oligarchs who had seized power, he was recalled by the Athenian fleet, which remained loyal to the democracy and needed his abilities. From 411 to 408 he helped Athens to a spectacular recovery, defeating the Spartan fleet in the Hellespont at Abydos (411) and Cyzicus (410) and regaining control over the vital grain route from the Black Sea. These successes encouraged him to return in 407 to Athens, where he was welcomed with enthusiasm and given supreme control of the conduct of the war. In a typically bold gesture he led the procession to the Eleusinian festival by road in spite of the danger from the Spartan force at Decelea; but, in the same year, after a minor naval defeat in his absence, his political enemies persuaded the people to reject him, and he retired to a castle in Thrace. He remained, however, a disturbing influence on Athenian politics and destroyed any hopes of a political consensus. When the Athenians at Aegospotami (405) facing the Spartans in the Hellespont grew increasingly careless, he warned them of their danger. But he was ignored, and, when the Athenians lost their whole fleet in a surprise attack by the Spartan admiral Lysander, Alcibiades was no longer safe in his Thracian castle. He took refuge in Phrygia in northwestern Asia Minor with the Persian governor, who was induced by the Spartans to have him murdered.

Alcibiades was a colourful man, about whom many stories were remembered and many more invented. He was perhaps the most gifted Athenian of his generation; but he lacked self-discipline, and his restless ambition was disastrous to Athens. The radical leaders, Cleon and his successors, carried on a bitter feud with him, which at the critical period undermined Athenian confidence. Alcibiades could not practice his master's virtues, and his example strengthened the charge brought against Socrates in 399 of corrupting the youth of Athens. (Ru.M.)

BIBLIOGRAPHY. Plutarch's life of Alcibiades is a very readable combination of fact and fiction. J. Hatzfeld, *Alcibiade* (1940), is a good critical biography (in French).

Alcidae, bird family, order Charadriiformes, which includes the birds known as auk, auklet, dovekie, guillemot, murre, murrelet, and puffin (*qq.v.*).

Alcindor, Lew (basketball player): *see* Abdul-Jabbar, Kareem.

Alcinous, in Greek mythology, king of the Phaeacians (on the legendary island of Scheria), son of Nausithoüs, and grandson of the god Poseidon. In the *Odyssey* he entertained Odysseus, who had been cast by a storm on the shore of the island. Scheria was identified in very early times with Corcyra, where Alcinous was revered as a hero. In the Argonautic legend, Alcinous lived on the island of Drepane, where he received Jason and Medea in their flight from Colchis.

Alciphron (fl. 2nd or 3rd century AD, Athens), rhetorician who wrote a collection of fictitious letters, a form of literature popular in his day. More than 100 of the letters have survived. The background of them all is the Athens of the 4th century BC, and the imaginary writers are farmers, fishermen, and courtesans. The material of the letters is largely derived from the writers of the so-called New Comedy. They are written in an imitation of the pure Attic dialect and show traces of the influence of Alciphron's contemporary Lucian.

Alcira, city, in the autonomous community (region) of Valencia, eastern Spain, in the Ribera district, south of the city of Valencia. It originated as the Iberian settlement of Algezira Sucro (Island of Sucro, so named because of its insular position between two branches of the Sucro River [Río Júcar]). It became the Saetabicula of the Romans and was called Jazīrat Shuvr by the Moors. United to Christian Spain in 1242, it declined after the expulsion of its large Morisco population in the early 17th century. It has a Renaissance city hall (1540; now a national monument) and a Roman bridge over the Júcar. Ruins of the 14th-century monastery of La Murta are nearby. Alcira exports oranges and by-products, manufactures paper goods, and breeds poultry. Pop. (1981) 37,446.

Alcithoë, in Greek legend, the daughter of Minyas of Orchomenus, in Boeotia. She and her sisters once refused to participate in Dionysiac festivities, remaining at home spinning and weaving. Late in the day Dionysiac music clanged about them, the house was filled with fire and smoke, and the sisters were metamorphosed into bats and birds. According to Plutarch, the sisters, driven mad for their impiety, cast lots to determine which one of their children they would eat. In retribution their female descendants were pursued at the Agrionia (an annual festival) by the priest of Dionysus, who was permitted to kill the one he caught.

alclad, laminated metal produced in sheets composed of a Duralumin (*q.v.*) core and outer layers of aluminum.

Alcmaeon, also spelled ALCMEON, in Greek legend, the son of the seer Amphiaraus and his wife Eriphyle. When Amphiaraus set out with the expedition of the Seven Against Thebes (*q.v.*), which he knew would be fatal to him, he commanded his sons to avenge his death by slaying Eriphyle (who had been bribed to persuade him to fight) and by undertaking a second expedition against Thebes. After leading the Epigoni (the sons of the Seven) in the destruction of Thebes, Alcmaeon killed his mother, but as a punishment he was driven mad and pursued by the Erinyes (goddesses of vengeance) from place to place.

On his arrival at Psophis in Arcadia, he was purified by its king, Phegeus, whose daughter Arsinoë (or Alphesiboea) he married. The land, however, was cursed with barrenness, and an oracle declared that Alcmaeon would not find rest until he reached a spot on which the sun had never shone at the time he slew his mother. Such a spot he found at the mouth of the Achelous River, where an island had recently been formed. There he settled and, forgetting his wife, married Callirrhoë, the daughter of the river god. Phegeus and his sons, however, pursued and killed Alcmaeon. On his death, Callirrhoë prayed that her two young sons might grow to manhood at once and avenge their father. Her prayer was granted, and her sons, Amphoterus and Acarnan, slew Phegeus. After his death Alcmaeon was worshipped at Thebes; his tomb was at Psophis. His story was the subject of the modern parody "A Fragment of a Greek Tragedy," by A.E. Housman.

Alcmaeon, also spelled ALCMEON (fl. 6th century BC), Greek philosopher and physiologist of the academy at Croton (now Crotona, southern Italy), the first person recorded to have practiced dissection of human bodies for research purposes. He may also have been the first to attempt vivisection. He inferred that the brain was the centre of intelligence and that the soul was the source of life. Applying the Pythagorean principle of cosmic harmony between pairs of contraries, he posited that health consists in the isonomy (equilibrium) of the body's component contraries (*e.g.,* dry–humid, warm–cold, sweet–bitter), thus anticipating Hippocrates' similar teaching.

Alcmaeonid FAMILY, a powerful Athenian family, claiming descent from the legendary Alcmaeon, that played a leading part in the politics of the 6th and 5th centuries BC. During the archonship of one of its members, Megacles (632? BC), a certain Cylon failed in an attempt to make himself tyrant, and his followers were slain at an altar sanctuary. Accused of sacrilege and murder, the Alcmaeonids incurred the bloodguilt that was to be used against them in political struggles for more than two centuries. The family was banished but returned during the ascendancy of Solon (early 6th century) to lead a party in Athens, which accepted Solon's reforms.

After Peisistratus became tyrant in 561–560, the Alcmaeonids, allied with the more conservative aristocrats, twice drove him from the city before he managed to have the family exiled. They were recalled later, and one of their members, Cleisthenes, was made archon for 525/524. Upon the murder of Peisistratus' son Hipparchus in 514, they were exiled once more by the tyrant Hippias. In 513 Cleisthenes led the Alcmaeonids in an unsuccessful invasion of Attica from their base in Boeotia. The family was rewarded for rebuilding the fire-damaged temple of Apollo at Delphi when the Spartans, largely at the insistence of the Delphic oracle, finally drove out the Peisistratids in 510. Two years later Cleisthenes introduced a program of constitutional reforms that greatly furthered the development of Athenian democracy.

The policy followed by this opportunistic family during the next generation is obscure. They were suspected of collusion with the Persians at the Battle of Marathon (490), but the direct-line descendants were considerably less prominent after the Persian Wars. Both Alcibiades and Pericles, however, were descended from the family through their mothers. Spartan demands at the beginning of the Peloponnesian War for the expulsion of the Alcmaeonids were provocations directed at Pericles.

Alcman (fl. late 7th century BC, Sparta), Greek poet, the first known writer of Dorian choral lyrics. His work survives in fragments, the longest being a *parthenion* (a choir song for girls) discovered in a 1st-century papyrus in Egypt in 1855. In the *Suda* lexicon (late 10th century AD) Alcman is described as a man "of an extremely amorous disposition and the inventor of love poems." He was clearly a learned man, and his verse is full of geographical detail. One fragment, telling of the sleeping world at the end of the day, imitated by Goethe in his *Wanderers Nachtlied,* is almost unique in Greek poetry for its sympathy with nature.

Alcman's light, gay manner, so different from the later Spartan style, gave rise to the tradition that he was not a native Spartan. He is thought by some to have come from Sardis in Lydia, but this is uncertain.

Alcoa, city, Blount County, eastern Tennessee, U.S., a gateway to Great Smoky Mountains National Park. It was founded in 1913 by the Aluminum Company of America (Alcoa) on a tract of land known as North Maryville. In 1910 the first of a series of power dams was begun on the nearby Little Tennessee River and its tributaries. The purchase of these dams by the company led to the procurement of land north of the city of Maryville (*q.v.*) for plant sites. The community was developed as a planned industrial centre for the production of aluminum pig, ingots, sheet and plate, and aluminum powder and foil. Inc. 1919. Pop. (1980) 6,870.

Alcoa: *see* Aluminum Company of America.

Alcobaça, town and *concelho* (municipality), Leiria district, west central Portugal, at the confluence of the Alcoa and Baça rivers, just south-southwest of the city of Leiria. Alcobaça is notable for its Cistercian monastery

Church of the Cistercian monastery, Alcobaça, Port.
Ernst A. Weber—Photo Researchers

(Mosteiro de Santa Maria), founded in 1152 by King Afonso I in thanksgiving for the reconquest of Santarém from the Moors and rebuilt in the 13th century. During the Middle Ages it rivalled the greatest European abbeys in size and wealth. It now houses the tombs of Portuguese royalty. The vast, austere abbey is early Gothic, with Baroque and later additions. Portions of its library are preserved in the public libraries of Lisbon and Braga. The ec..omy of the town centres on fruit growing (begun in the 12th century by the monks) and preserving, textile milling, and ceramic manufacturing. Pop. (1981 prelim.) town, 5,059; *concelho*, 52,128.

Alcock, John (b. *c.* 1430, Beverley, Yorkshire, Eng.—d. Oct. 1, 1500, Wisbech Castle, Isle of Ely, Cambridgeshire), architect, bishop, and statesman who founded Jesus College, Cambridge, and who was regarded as one of the most eminent pre-Reformation English divines.

Educated at Cambridge, he was made dean of Westminster (1461), and thereafter his promotion was rapid in religious and secular posts. In 1470 he was sent as ambassador to the court of Castile. He became successively bishop of Rochester (1472), Worcester (1476), and Ely (1486). He also held the office of chancellor and conducted negotiations with King James III of Scotland, besides filling other posts under Edward IV and Henry VII.

In addition to founding a charity at Beverley, Yorkshire; a grammar school at Kingston-upon-Hull, Yorkshire; and Jesus College, he worked to restore churches and colleges. His published works, most of which are extremely rare, include *Mons perfectionis* (1497;"The Hill of Perfection") and *Gallicantus Johannis Alcock episcopi Eliensis ad fratres suos curatos in sinodo apud Barnwell* (1498;"Gallicantus [song of the cock] of John Alcock Bishop of Ely to His Brother Clergy in the Synod at Barnwell"). The last is a little treatise written in allusion to his name and decorated with figures of the rooster; it is also a good specimen of early English printing and illustration.

Alcock, Sir John William (b. Nov. 6, 1892, Manchester—d. Dec. 18, 1919, Cottévrard, Fr.), aviator who, with his fellow British aviator Arthur Brown (*see* Whitten-Brown, Sir Arthur), made the first nonstop transatlantic flight.

Alcock received his pilot's certificate in 1912 and joined the Royal Naval Air Service as an instructor in World War I. During his service he performed many daring exploits, including the bombing of Constantinople. In September 1917 enemy anti-aircraft fire forced him down into the sea near Suvla Bay, where he and his companions were taken prisoner by the Turks. He remained a prisoner until the end of the war and left the service in March 1919.

Sir John Alcock, detail of a portrait by Alex McEvoy, 1919; in the National Portrait Gallery, London
By courtesy of the National Portrait Gallery, London

He became a test pilot for Vickers Aircraft, which was preparing an airplane to fly the Atlantic Ocean nonstop for a £10,000 prize offered by the London *Daily Mail.* Alcock and Brown left St. John's, Nfd., at 4:13 PM GMT, on June 14, 1919. They landed the next day in a marshy bog near Clifden, County Galway, Ire., after a flight of 1,890 miles in 16 hours 12 minutes. Alcock was honoured throughout Great Britain and was created Knight Commander, Order of the British Empire. Several months later, while delivering an amphibian aircraft to Paris, he crashed in bad weather and was fatally injured.

alcohol, any of a class of organic compounds characterized by one or more hydroxyl (OH) groups attached to a carbon atom that, in turn, is attached to three other atoms. Alcohols are neither acid nor alkaline. They are, however, quite reactive, and all of them dissolve organic substances.

A brief treatment of alcohols follows. For full treatment, *see* MACROPAEDIA: Chemical Compounds.

Primary alcohols, in which the hydroxyl group is attached to one carbon atom and two hydrogen atoms, can be oxidized to form aldehydes (organic compounds used in making plastics, for example) and acids. Secondary alcohols, in which the hydroxyl group is attached to two carbon atoms and one hydrogen atom, can be oxidized to form ketones (also used in making plastics). In tertiary alcohols, the hydroxyl group is attached to three carbon atoms. When oxidized, these alcohols decompose, breaking the carbon chain.

Alcohols combine with inorganic compounds to form crystalline products similar to common hydrate salts (inorganic compounds combined with water molecules). Alcohols generally react with carboxylic acids to produce esters—neutral organic compounds found in fats and oils. They also can be converted to ethers and to hydrocarbons called olefins.

Most alcohols are colourless liquids or solids. At room temperature, primary alcohols with fewer than 12 carbon atoms are liquid; those with 12 or more carbon atoms are solid. Polyhydric alcohols (those with more than one hydroxyl group) usually have the consistency of syrup. Alcohols with complex arrangements of carbon atoms, such as sterols, are usually solids. With increases in molecular weight, alcohols become less soluble in water and their boiling points, vapour pressures, densities, and viscosities increase.

Adding hydroxyl groups to an alcohol without increasing the number of carbon atoms changes many of its properties. In some cases, it may enhance sweetness, and the resultant alcohols are used as sweeteners. Alcohols with 8 to 12 carbon atoms have a characteristic roselike or lilylike odour and are used in making perfumes. In general, the most important industrial use of alcohols is as chemical intermediates, chiefly because alcohols can readily be converted into a large number of other compounds. This is done by simple chemical reactions to yield products such as fats and waxes—surface active agents used in detergents, plasticizers, emulsifiers, lubricants, emollients, and foaming agents.

Alcohols are among the more abundantly produced organic chemicals in industry. Some, such as ethanol and methanol, are utilized in great quantities. Ethanol, also called ethyl alcohol, or grain alcohol, can be manufactured by fermentation from the carbohydrates found in fruits, molasses, grains, and other agricultural products. It can also be made from ethane, which is derived from natural gas. Ethanol is used in toiletries and pharmaceuticals and to sterilize hospital instruments. It can be used as a fuel. The anesthetic ether is made from ethanol. It is, moreover, the alcohol in alcoholic beverages.

Methanol, also known as methyl alcohol, wood alcohol, or carbinol, can be manufactured from hardwood or from hydrogen and carbon monoxide (CO). It is used as a solvent, as a raw material for manufacture of formaldehyde and special resins, in special fuels, in antifreeze, and for cleaning metals.

Alcoholics Anonymous (AA), voluntary fellowship of alcoholic persons who seek to get sober and remain sober through self-help and the help of other recovered alcoholics. Although general conventions meet periodically and Alcoholics Anonymous World Services, Inc., is headquartered in New York City, all AA groups are essentially local and autonomous. To counteract self-indulgence and promote the group's welfare, members identify themselves only by first name and surname initial. Much of the program has a social and spiritual, but nonsectarian, basis.

AA began in May 1935 in the meeting of two alcoholics attempting to overcome their drinking problems: a New York stockbroker, "Bill W." (William Griffith Wilson [1895–1971]), and a surgeon from Akron, Ohio, "Dr. Bob S." (Robert Holbrook Smith [1879–1950]). Drawing upon their own experiences, they set out to help fellow alcoholics and first recorded their program in *Alcoholics Anonymous* (1939; 3rd ed., 1976). By the late 20th century, Alcoholics Anonymous had some 1,000,000 members forming about 28,000 groups in 92 countries (most of them, however, in the United States and Canada).

alcoholism, repetitive intake of alcoholic beverages to such an extent that repeated or continued harm to the drinker occurs. Conceptions of what constitutes alcoholism vary with the traditional dietary use of alcohol and the social drinking patterns of a community. In the United States, alcoholism may be viewed as a disease, a drug addiction, a learned response to crisis, a symptom of an underlying psychological or physical disorder, or a combination of these factors. The cause of alcoholism is equally uncertain. It has been viewed as a hereditary defect, a physical malfunction, a psychological disorder, a response to economic or social stress, or sin.

Manifestations of alcoholism vary with the individual. Intoxication may be followed by the relatively mild syndrome known as a hangover; extreme symptoms of withdrawal may include delirium tremens, hallucinations, and other acute brain disorders. Polyneuropathy, a degenerative disease of the nervous system, and acute hepatitis are common. Alcoholics also suffer the consequences of a deficient diet. Sudden personality changes may be the result of psychological factors combined with a temporary blood sugar deficiency. Cirrhosis of the liver is associated with chronic alcoholism, as are numerous forms of brain damage. Alcoholics also suffer high accident rates, lowered resistance to infection, loss of employment and family life, and a reduction of life-span of 10 to 12 years.

Most approaches to the treatment of alcoholism require the alcoholic to recognize his illness. Treatment programs then vary according to the accepted definition and theory of cause of alcoholism. They include combinations of inpatient programs; general psychological rehabilitative treatments; organized self-help groups such as Alcoholics Anonymous (AA); the use of abstinence-maintaining drugs, such as Antabuse (disulfiram) and Temposil (citrated calcium cyanamide); injections of vitamins or hormones; and aversion therapy based on behaviour modification.

Alcor, also called 80 URSAE MAJORIS, star with apparent magnitude of 4.03. The name in Arabic means "faint one," and to see Alcor with the unaided eye may have been regarded by the Arabs (and others) as a test of good vision. Alcor makes a visual double with the brighter star Mizar (*q.v.*), in the middle of the handle of the Big Dipper; the pair have also been called the Horse and Rider.

Alcora faience, tin-glazed earthenware produced at a factory established in Valencia, Spain, by the Count of Aranda, and in production from 1727 to the early 19th century. Much of the faience was decorated with highly developed and often beautiful pictorial painting, largely executed by Miguel Soliva. This ware often took the form of large, richly polychromatic plaques and panels depicting biblical or mythological scenes.

Alcott, (Amos) Bronson (b. Nov. 29, 1799, Wolcott, Conn., U.S.—d. March 4, 1888, Concord, Mass.), philosopher, teacher, reformer, and member of the New England Transcendentalist group.

The self-educated son of a poor farmer, he travelled in the South as a peddler before establishing a series of schools for children. His educational theories owed something to J.H. Pestalozzi, the Swiss reformer, but more

Bronson Alcott

Holman's Print Shop, Inc.

to the examples of Socrates and the Gospels. His aim was to stimulate thought and "awaken the soul"; his method was conversational, courteous, and gentle. Questions of discipline were referred to the class as a group and punishment consisted only of requiring the pupil to strike the teacher's hand with a ruler.

These innovations were not widely accepted, and before he was 40 he was forced to close his last school, the famous Temple School in Boston. In 1842 he visited England, where a similar school founded near London was named Alcott House in his honour. He returned from England with a kindred spirit, the mystic Charles Lane, and together they founded a short-lived utopian community, Fruitlands, in Massachusetts.

Alcott was a vegetarian, an Abolitionist, and an advocate of women's rights; his thought was vague, lofty, and intensely spiritual. His life was a deliberate imitation of Christ, whom he did not think divine. Always poor or in debt, he worked as a handyman or lived on the bounty of others until the literary success of his daughter Louisa May Alcott, whom he had educated, brought him financial security.

The best of Alcott's writing is available in *The Journals of Bronson Alcott* (1938), selected and edited by Odell Shepard.

Alcott, Louisa May (b. Nov. 29, 1832, Germantown, Pa., U.S.—d. March 6, 1888, Boston), author known for her children's books, especially *Little Women.* She spent most of her life in Boston and Concord, Mass., where Ralph Waldo Emerson and Henry David Thoreau were her earliest friends, and Nathaniel Hawthorne was her neighbour. From childhood she had been exposed to the conversations of her father, Bronson Alcott, Margaret Fuller, Oliver Wendell Holmes, and other scholars.

Alcott realized early that her father was too impractical to provide for his wife and four daughters; after the failure of Fruitlands, his

Louisa May Alcott, portrait by George Healy; in the Louisa May Alcott Memorial Association collection, Concord, Mass.

By courtesy of Louisa May Alcott Memorial Association

experiment in "consociate" living, her lifelong concern for the welfare of her family began. She taught briefly, worked as a domestic, and finally wrote, potboilers at first, then her more serious works.

Alcott, an ardent Abolitionist, volunteered as a nurse when the Civil War began. She contracted typhoid from unsanitary hospital conditions and was sent home. She was never completely well again, but the publication of her letters in book form, *Hospital Sketches* (1863), brought her the first taste of fame.

Her stories began to appear in *The Atlantic Monthly*, and because family needs were pressing, she wrote the autobiographical *Little Women* (1868–69), which was an immediate success. In 1869 she was able to write in her journal: "Paid up all the debts . . . thank the Lord!"

Other books followed, drawn from her early experiences, including *An Old-Fashioned Girl* (1870); *Aunt Jo's Scrap Bag,* 6 vol. (1872–82); *Little Men* (1871); *Eight Cousins* (1875); and *Jo's Boys* (1886).

Tired and in constant pain, though free from financial worry, the last years of her life were shadowed by the deaths of her sister Elizabeth (the "Beth" of *Little Women*), her mother, and her youngest sister, May, who left behind a little daughter for Alcott to rear.

alcove, recess opening off a room or other space enclosed by walls or hedges. In medieval architecture it was commonly used as a sleeping space off the main body of a drafty hall. The separation of the alcove from the main space was accomplished at first by means of curtains and later by timber partitions to form independent rooms and thus conserve heat. In later centuries bed alcoves and kitchen alcoves reappeared as means of saving space in small living quarters, particularly in apartments.

Alcove also refers to spaces, often semicircular in plan, hollowed out of thick walls and used for displaying statues, as in Roman and Renaissance architecture.

Sleeping alcove in the Villa Mansi, Lucca, Italy, 18th century

SCALA—Art Resource/EB Inc.

Alcoy, town, Alicante province, in the autonomous community (region) of Valencia, southeastern Spain. It lies in the rugged foothills at the confluence of the two headstreams of the Río Serpis, north of Alicante city. The site was settled before Roman times, but the present Alcoy was founded by the Moors, who named it Alcoyll after a city in Tunisia.

The town is a rail terminus and an important centre of the textile industry. A *real fábrica de paños* (royal textile factory) was established there in 1800, and it was the site of the first Spanish industrial school. Manufactures also include paper, especially for cigarettes, and there is also metalworking. Agricultural trade is carried on. A fiesta, held in April on the Festival de San Jorge (St. George), Alcoy's patron, commemorates the 13th-century battle when the Saint supposedly helped the Christians defeat the Moors; it is a great tourist attraction. Pop. (1981) 65,908.

Alcudia, Manuel de Godoy, duque de (duke of): *see* Godoy, Manuel de.

Alcuin (b. *c.* 732, in or near York, Yorkshire, Eng.—d. May 19, 804, Tours, Fr.), Anglo-Latin poet, educator, and cleric who, as head of the Palatine school established by Charlemagne at Aachen, introduced the traditions of Anglo-Saxon Humanism into western Europe. He was the foremost scholar of the revival of learning that is known as the Carolingian Renaissance. He also made important reforms in the Roman Catholic liturgy and left more than 300 Latin letters that have proved to be a valuable source of information on the history of his time.

Alcuin's first 50 years were spent in Yorkshire, where he was first a pupil and, after 778, headmaster of the cathedral school of York, the most renowned of its day. He wrote a long poem, probably shortly before he left York, telling of the renowned men in that city's history. In 781 he met Charlemagne in Italy and

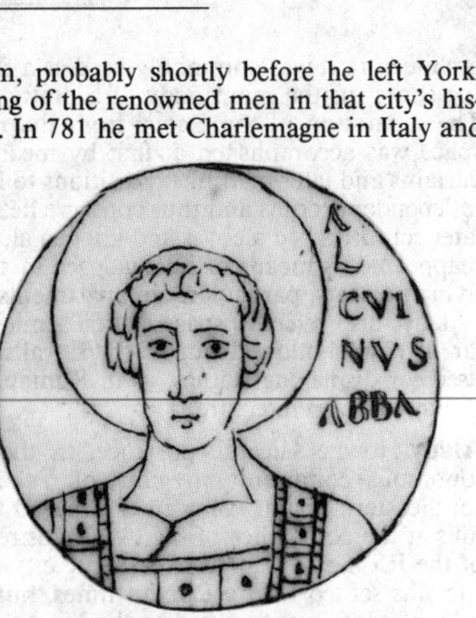

Alcuin, medallion from the Bamberg Bible, 9th century; in the Bibliothèque Nationale, Paris

By courtesy of the Bibliotheque Nationale, Paris

accepted his invitation to Aachen, where the King was gathering the leading Irish, English, and Italian scholars of the age. The school, where Charlemagne himself, his family, his friends, and his friends' sons were taught, became a lively centre of discussion and exchange of knowledge. Alcuin introduced the methods of English learning into the Frankish schools, systematized the curriculum, raised the standards of scholarship, and encouraged the study of liberal arts for the better understanding of spiritual doctrine. In 796 he left the court to become abbot of the Abbey of St. Martin at Tours, where he encouraged the work of his monks on the beautiful Carolingian minuscule script, the ancestor of modern Roman typefaces.

Alcuin's formative influence in the development of Roman Catholicism is ascribed mainly to his revision of the liturgy of the Frankish church. He was responsible for the introduction of the Irish Northumbrian custom of singing the creed. He arranged votive masses for particular days of the week in an order still followed by Catholics, reedited the Latin Vulgate, and wrote works on education, theology, and philosophy.

Alcuin's life embodies contradictions. His leadership in church and state was remembered throughout the Middle Ages, yet he remained only a deacon. Though he was the foremost teacher in a rude age, his writings show no originality. He loved Charlemagne and enjoyed the King's esteem, but his letters reveal that his fear of him was as great as his love. Most of his poetry is mediocre. Toward the end of his life he acquired a great reputation for holiness, but he is not included in the canon of saints.

Aldabra Islands, atoll in the Indian Ocean about 600 mi (1,000 km) southwest of the Seychelles group, and part of the Republic of the Seychelles. The Aldabras, together with Farquhar and Desroches islands and the Chagos Archipelago, formed part of the British Indian Ocean Territory (*q.v.*) from 1965 to 1976. Aldabra Islands were formerly under the hegemony of the Seychelles, to which they were returned on June 28, 1976. They constitute an oval atoll (19 mi long and 8 mi wide) enclosing a large but shallow lagoon. Channels divide the ring into four low islands that rise to about 100 ft (30 m) above the sea and are called South Island (the largest), West Island, Polymnie, and Middle Island. In common with about half of the other islands of Seychelles, the Aldabra Islands are granitic in origin.

In 1955 the islands were leased for the commercial exploitation of mangrove timber and fishing. South Island is used as a fishing station and the Royal Society maintains a research station there for studying the ecology. The island is famous for its giant tortoises, and a nature reserve established in 1965 provides complete protection for them and for all animals on South Island. The Aldabras were once rich in guano, a type of topsoil formed from bird droppings, but it was almost all collected and sold in the early 1950s. Pop. (1982 est.) 180.

Aldan River, river in Eastern Siberia, Russian Soviet Federated Socialist Republic, rising in the Stanovoy Range and flowing northwestward in a huge curve to join the Lena River at Batamay. It is 1,412 mi (2,273 km) long, the second longest tributary of the Lena, and drains more than 281,500 sq mi (729,000 sq km). The annual discharge, averaging 180,000 cu ft/sec (5,000 cu m/sec), varies considerably both seasonally and annually. The river, navigable to Tommot, is frozen from mid-October to mid-May.

Aldan Stage, lowermost stage (or time interval of deposition) of rocks of the Cambrian System of the U.S.S.R. (the Cambrian Period began about 570,000,000 years ago and lasted about 70,000,000 years). The Aldan Stage precedes rocks of the Lena Stage, and, on the Siberian Platform, Aldan rocks consist of continental deposits; marine deposits occur to the east. Aldan marine rocks are characterized by the presence of the trilobite genus *Holmia.* Volcanic deposits are known to occur in Aldan sequences.

A list of the abbreviations used in the MICROPAEDIA *will be found at the end of this volume*

Aldanov, Mark, pseudonym of MARK ALEKSANDROVICH LANDAU (b. Nov. 7 [Oct. 26, old style], 1889, Kiev—d. Feb. 25, 1957, Nice, Fr.), Russian émigré writer best known for work that is bitterly critical of the Soviet system. In 1919 he emigrated to France, which he left for the United States in 1941. He wrote an essay on Lenin (1921), a work comparing the Russian and French revolutions (*Deux Révolutions,* 1921), and a scientific treatise (*Actinochimie,* 1936), as well as many novels. Most of Aldanov's works were translated into English, including a tetralogy on revolutionary France, *Myslitel* (1923–25; *The Thinker,* 1924–28); an anti-Soviet satire, *Nachalo kontsa* (1939; *The Fifth Seal,* 1943); and *Istoki* (1947; *Before the Deluge,* 1948), a picture of Europe in the 1870s.

Aldebaran (Arabic: The Follower), also called ALPHA TAURI, reddish giant star in the constellation Taurus, one of the 15 brightest stars, with an apparent visual magnitude of 0.86. Its diameter is approximately 50 times that of the Sun. It is accompanied by a very faint (13th magnitude) red companion star. Aldebaran lies about 50 light-years from the Earth. The star was once thought to be a member of the Hyades cluster, but in fact Aldebaran is 80 light-years closer to Earth. It was probably named The Follower because it rises after the Pleiades.

Aldeburgh, parish (town), Suffolk Coastal district, county of Suffolk, England. As a result of coastal erosion, most of the old settlement has been submerged, and the 16th-century Moot Hall is now almost on the beach; the Alde Estuary has been diverted sharply, flowing southward for 12 mi (19 km) behind Orford Ness, by a shingle bank. Aldeburgh is chiefly a resort, and since 1947 has been the site of an annual summer festival associated, until his death in 1976, with the composer Benjamin Britten. Pop. (1981 prelim.) 2,911.

Aldecoa, Ignacio (b. July 11, 1925, Vitoria, Spain—d. 1969), Spanish novelist whose work is noted for its local colour and careful composition.

Aldecoa studied at the University of Madrid, became a newspaper writer, and from 1947 to 1956 was a broadcaster for the radio station Voice of the Falange. He published essays on politics, several collections of short stories, and two books of poems, *Todavía la vida* (1947) and *Libro de las algas* (1949), before his first novels, *El fulgor y la sangre* (1954) and *Con el viento solano* (1956). Aldecoa wrote about ordinary workers, their hopes, their fears, and the tendency of their lives toward monotony. He was adept at using the technical terms of different trades for artistic effect, such as sailing in *Gran Sol* (1957) and fishing in *Parte de una historia* (1967).

aldehyde, any of a class of organic compounds characterized by the presence of a carbonyl group, in which a carbon atom is covalently bonded to an oxygen atom. At the two remaining bonds, at least one atom must be hydrogen. Aldehydes are highly reactive, and much of their chemical activity comes from the nature of the carbonyl group.

A brief treatment of aldehydes follows. For full treatment, *see* MACROPAEDIA: Chemical Compounds.

Aldehydes undergo a wide variety of chemical reactions. A major reason is that they can be easily reduced (electrons added) or oxidized. The carbonyl group is also highly polar. That is to say, it exhibits an uneven distribution of electrons, which renders the oxygen electrically negative and the carbon electrically positive. This, too, increases the chemical activities of aldehydes and affects their physical properties as well.

Many aldehydes have characteristic, pleasant odours. They are prepared synthetically by a wide variety of methods. In principle, they are derived from alcohols by dehydrogenation (removal of hydrogen), from which process came the name aldehyde.

Aldehydes are easily oxidized to acids and reduced to alcohols. Many nucleophiles (chemical species rich in electrons) interact with the carbonyl carbon atom. Such reactions form the basis for many important synthetic methods. For example, a hydrogen atom attached to the carbon atom immediately adjacent to the carbonyl group (the so-called alpha carbon atom) can be removed by acids or alkalies. The resulting carbon ion is a nucleophile that causes many useful reactions.

Aldehydes also undergo polymerization. The simpler aldehydes, such as formaldehyde and acetaldehyde, readily link together into chains containing tens of thousands of the molecule. The combination of these aldehydes with other types of molecules produces several familiar plastics. Bakelite, for example, is made from formaldehyde and phenol, and Formica is made from formaldehyde and urea.

Many aldehydes are manufactured on a large scale. They are useful as solvents, polymer components, perfume ingredients, and intermediates in the production of other classes of compounds.

Many aldehydes are involved in physiological processes. Examples are retinene (vitamin A aldehyde), important in human vision, and pyridoxal phosphate, one of the forms of vitamin B_6. Formaldehyde prevents deterioration of substances rich in protein and, thus, is used as a preservative. Glucose and other so-called reducing sugars are aldehydes, as are several natural and synthetic hormones.

Alden, John (b. 1599?, England—d. Sept. 12, 1687, Duxbury, Mass.), one of the Pilgrims who in 1620 emigrated to America in the "Mayflower" and founded the Plymouth colony, the first permanent English colony in New England.

Alden was hired as a cooper by the London merchants who financed the expedition to the New World. He later moved from Plymouth to a farm at nearby Duxbury, where he lived most of his life. From this base he served in a variety of civic capacities: agent for the colony, surveyor of highways, deputy from Duxbury, member of the local council of war, treasurer, and, most important, assistant to the governor of Massachusetts (1623–41 and 1650–86). During this time he twice served as deputy governor.

Two popular myths have combined to perpetuate a romantic aura about the memory of John Alden. One claimed he was the first Pilgrim to set foot on Plymouth Rock. The other was dramatized by Henry Wadsworth Longfellow's poem "The Courtship of Miles Standish," in which Alden presumably won the hand of Priscilla Mullens after first wooing her for his friend Standish. He did wed Priscilla in 1623, and the marriage produced 11 children. When he died, he was the last male survivor of the Mayflower Company.

alder, any of about 30 species of ornamental shrubs and trees constituting the genus *Alnus,* in the birch family (Betulaceae), distributed throughout the Northern Hemisphere and western South America on cool, wet sites at elevations up to 2,500 metres (8,200 feet).

Alder (*Alnus glutinosa*)
Earl L. Kubis—Root Resources

An alder may be distinguished from a birch by its usually stalked winter buds and by cones that remain on the branches after the small, winged nutlets are released. The scaly bark is grayish brown in some species and almost white in others. The oval leaves are alternate, serrate, and often shallowly lobed; sticky on unfolding but glossy when mature, they fall without changing colour. Male and female flowers are borne in separate catkins on the same tree; they form during the summer and usually blossom the following spring before the leaves open.

Familiar North American alders are the red alder (*A. rubra* or *A. oregona*), a tall tree whose leaves have rusty hairs on their lower surfaces; the white, or Sierra, alder (*A. rhombifolia*), an early-flowering tree with orange-red twigs and buds; the speckled alder (*A. rugosa*), a small tree with conspicuous whitish, wartlike, porous markings or lenticels; the aromatic-leaved American green alder (*A. crispa* or *A. mitchelliana*); the closely related but taller Sitka alder (*A. sinuata*); and the mountain, or thinleaf, alder (*A. tenuifolia*), a shrubby tree with yellow or orange-brown midribs on its leaves and a domelike crown of pendulous branches.

The European alder (*A. glutinosa*), sometimes known as black alder for its dark bark and cones, is widespread throughout Eurasia and is cultivated in several varieties in North America. The name black alder is also applied to winterberry, a type of holly (*q.v.*). The green alder (*A. viridis*), a European shrub, has sharply pointed, bright-green leaves. The white alder (*A. incana*) includes several varieties useful as an ornamental.

Alders are practically immune to diseases other than fungal attacks. Usually propagated by seed, they may also be cultivated from cuttings or suckers.

Alder wood, pale yellow to reddish brown, is fine textured and durable, even under water; it is useful for furniture, cabinetry, turnery, and in charcoal manufacture and millwork. Red and European alders are important timber trees. European, Italian, Japanese, Manchurian, speckled, and seaside alders are popular ornamentals. Because of their spreading root systems and tolerance of moist soils, alders are often planted on stream banks for flood control and the prevention of erosion. They are among the first woody plants to appear in denuded areas; although short-lived, they prepare the soil for more enduring trees by increasing its organic matter and nitrogen content.

Alder, Kurt (b. July 10, 1902, Königshütte, Prussia—d. June 20, 1958, Cologne), co-recipient with Otto Diels of the Nobel Prize for Chemistry of 1950 for their development of a widely used method of synthesizing cyclic organic compounds. They gave the first experimental proof of the nature of the reaction and demonstrated its application to the synthesis of a wide range of ring compounds.

Alder studied chemistry at the universities of Berlin and Kiel, where he received his doctorate in 1926. He and Diels wrote their first paper on the reaction of dienes with quinones in 1928. Alder was a professor of chemistry at Kiel from 1934 to 1936. He applied his fundamental research to the development of plastics while working as a research director for I.G. Farbenindustrie AG (1936–40). In 1940 he became professor of chemistry and director of the chemical institute at the University of Cologne.

alder buckthorn, also called ALDER DOGWOOD (*Rhamnus frangula*), woody shrub or small tree, of the buckthorn family (Rhamnaceae), native to western Asia, Europe, and northern Africa. It has been introduced into North America and other regions where it is often cultivated as an ornamental. The plant grows rapidly, reaching a height of 5.5 metres

Alder buckthorn (*Rhamnus frangula*)
Sven Samelius

(about 18 feet); its dark, dense, and lustrous foliage turns yellow in autumn. The alternate, rather oval leaves are 3.75–6 centimetres (1.5–2.5 inches) long. Small white flowers are borne in clusters of 2 to 10. The small fruit turns from red to black. Tallhedge buckthorn (*Rhamnus frangula* 'Columnaris') is a horticultural variety grown for its low maintenance and upright form.

alderfly, any insect of the megalopteran family Sialidae, characterized by long, filamentous antennae and two pairs of large wings (anterior wing length 20 to 50 millimetres [3/4 to 2 inches]), membranous and well-developed, with part of the hind wing folding like a fan. The adult alderfly is dark-coloured, 15 to 30 mm long, sluggish, and a weak flier. It usually inhabits shore vegetation, especially alder trees.

Alderfly (*Sialis*)
N.A. Callow—EB Inc.

The aquatic larvae, which have biting jaws and seven or eight pairs of filamentous abdominal gills, crawl along the bottoms of ponds and streams and feed on small insects. Pupae are found in soil and moss. The life cycle is completed in one year.

alderman, member of a municipal legislative body in England and the United States. In early English law there were up to 11 classes of aldermen. Among the Anglo-Saxons, earls, governors of provinces, and other persons of distinction received the title; later it was used to designate the chief magistrate of a county or group of counties.

English county councils have two types of members—councillors and aldermen. The councillors are elected by the voters; a number of aldermen equal to one-third of the whole number of councillors are then selected by the councillors. In Scotland the bailie corresponds to the alderman.

In the American colonial period, city councils resembled their British prototypes, in which aldermen and common councillors commonly sat together as one body under the chairmanship of the mayor. In most colonial boroughs both the aldermen and the councilmen were chosen by the voters, but in a few cases only councilmen were elected, the aldermen being selected by the councilmen as in England. Following the colonial period, all members of the council, including aldermen, were elected by popular vote. The title alderman came to refer to members of the council in cities governed by mayors and councils; in other forms of city government the term commissioners or councilmen is ordinarily used. Aldermen, as opposed to councilmen and commissioners, are usually elected by wards rather than in city-wide contests.

Alderney, French AURIGNY, one of the Channel Islands (*q.v.*), in the English Channel, with an area of 3 sq mi (8 sq km), separated from the Normandy coast (Cap de la Hague) by the dangerously swift 10-mi (16-km) Race of Alderney. Swinge Race, on the west, separates it from the uninhabited Burhou, Ortac, and smaller islets, beyond which the notorious Casquets, a group of jagged rocks, carry a lighthouse. The nearest English coast is 55 mi (88 km) north.

The island is a tableland that is mostly above 200 ft (60 m) and little dissected. Steep cliffs rise to 275 ft (83 m) on the south and west coasts, while old cliffs rise behind raised beaches on the north and east. The two main inlets are Braye Harbour, protected by a 1,000-yd (914-m) breakwater on the north and Longy Bay (southeast), backed by an almost-filled lagoon.

The earliest known inhabitants were builders of megalithic tombs. The Bronze Age is well represented, and the Romans appear to have built a small fort (the Nunnery) on the island. From the 11th century it was part of the Norman domain and was occupied by the

French from 1338 to 1340. In 1559 it was leased to George Chamberlain and granted (1584) by letters patent to his brother John, who transferred it to the earl of Essex; his descendants held it until the English Civil War. From the Restoration until 1825, the government of Alderney was separated from that of Guernsey, being granted in 1660 to Edward de Carteret, who transferred it in 1661 to Sir George Carteret. Sir George's widow sold it to Edmund Andros of Guernsey (*c.* 1682), from whom it descended to the Le Mesurier family. Alderney is now in the Bailiwick of Guernsey (*q.v.*) but has its own local administration. Under the reformed constitution of 1949, the president and States of Alderney (nine members) are popularly elected; the Court of Alderney administers justice. During the 19th century, the island was heavily fortified by the British, who maintained a garrison there until 1930. Repatriation of the Alderney community, evacuated to England in 1940 prior to German occupation, was carried out after the war. As a result it was necessary to re-create the island's economy, based mainly on dairy farming and tourism. Most inhabitants live in the only town, St. Anne's, overlooking Braye Harbour; Newtown forms an appendage at a lower level. Communications are through Guernsey, to which Alderney is linked by air and shipping services. Pop. (1981) 2,100.

Aldfrith (d. Dec. 14, 704, Driffield, Eng.), king of Northumbria (685–704) and patron of literature. An illegitimate son of Oswiu, he succeeded to the throne when his brother Ecgfrith was killed at the Battle of Nechtansmere. Educated for the priesthood, he stimulated the growth of scholarship in Northumbria during his reign, producing conditions under which the historian Bede flourished.

Aldhelm (*c.* 639–709), West Saxon abbot of Malmesbury, the most learned teacher of 7th-century Wessex, a pioneer in the art of Latin verse among the Saxons, and the author of numerous extant writings in Latin verse and prose. He was trained in Latin and in Celtic-Irish scholarship by Malmesbury's Irish founder and went on to study at the famous School of Canterbury, where he was exposed to continental influences. He read widely in Latin poetry and prose, pagan as well as sacred; he learned Greek; he followed the arithmetic and astronomy of his day; and he experimented with various forms of poetic metre. In about 675 he became abbot of Malmesbury, where he remained, carrying on a threefold work, as monk and priest, as encourager of learning, and as Latin poet. In 705 he was consecrated bishop of Sherborne. He was also a popular vernacular poet, though none of that verse survives.

In addition to his pastoral duties, building churches, and founding monasteries, Aldhelm wrote vigorous letters of encouragement to other scholars, the style of which betrays his Celtic training. In similar prose he also wrote a lengthy treatise on the celibate life for the nuns of Barking. Its flood of learning and its difficult style so delighted the community that he made a second version of it in Latin hexameters.

Metrical science was Aldhelm's special preoccupation, and his most famous work is a treatise on metrics sent to his friend Aldfrith, king of Northumbria (685–704). It includes as examples 100 *aenigmata* (riddles) of Aldhelm's own invention in Latin hexameters, which served as models for such 8th-century Saxon writers as Tatwine, archbishop of Canterbury, and St. Boniface, apostle of Germany.

Aldington, Richard, original name EDWARD GODFREE ALDINGTON, (b. July 8, 1892, Hampshire, Eng.—d. July 27, 1962, Sury-en-Vaus, Fr.), poet, novelist, critic, and biographer who wrote searingly and sometimes irascibly of what he considered to be hypocrisy in modern industrialized civilization.

Educated at Dover College and London University, he early attracted attention through his volumes of Imagist verse (*see* Imagists). In 1913 he married Hilda Doolittle (H.D.), the U.S. Imagist poet. His best and best known novel, *Death of a Hero* (1929), to which *All Men Are Enemies* (1933) was a sequel, reflected the disillusionment of a generation that had fought through World War I. In *The Colonel's Daughter* (1931) he satirized sham gentility and literary preciousness so outspokenly that two lending libraries refused to handle the novel. In his long poems *A Dream in the Luxembourg* (1930) and *A Fool i' the Forest* (1925) he inveighed against the mechanization of modern man more lyrically, with bittersweet romanticism, and his translations from ancient Greek and Latin poets revealed his love for earlier civilizations.

His critical works, uneven in quality, included *Literary Studies* (1924) and *French Studies* (1925) and biographies of Voltaire, D.H. Lawrence, Norman Douglas, and Wellington. *Lawrence of Arabia* (1955), one of his last books, was an uncompromising attack on T.E. Lawrence. Late in life Aldington became a best-seller in the U.S.S.R., where he celebrated his 70th birthday. *A Passionate Pilgrim: Letters to Alan Bird from Richard Aldington, 1949–1962* was published in 1975.

Aldiss, Brian W(ilson) (b. Aug. 18, 1925, East Dereham, Norfolk, Eng.), prolific English author, chiefly of science fiction, whose novels and short stories display considerable range in style and approach.

He served with the British Army (1943–47), part of the time in the Royal Corps of Signals, then was a bookseller until 1956, meanwhile publishing *The Brightfount Diaries* in 1955. Aldiss has also been an influential anthologist of science fiction. Many collections of his stories are available, including *Best Science Fiction Stories of Brian W. Aldiss* (1965) and *A Brian Aldiss Omnibus* (1969 and 1971). Outstanding individual volumes of stories include *Hothouse* (1962) and *The Saliva Tree* (1966). Notable departures from science fiction were his autobiographically based *The Hand-Reared Boy* (1970) and *A Soldier Erect* (1971). Later fiction includes *A Rude Awakening* (1978), *Life in the West* (1980), and *Moreau's Other Island* (1980; also published as *An Island Called Moreau*, 1981).

Aldobrandini, Ippolito (pope): *see* Clement VIII.

aldosterone, a steroid hormone secreted by the adrenal gland. It serves as the principal regulator of the salt and water balance of the body (a mineralocorticoid) and has a small effect on the metabolism of fats, carbohydrates, and proteins.

Aldosterone is synthesized in the body from corticosterone, a steroid derived from cholesterol. Production of aldosterone (in adult humans, about 20–200 micrograms per day) in the zona glomerulosa of the adrenal cortex is apparently regulated by renin angiotensin secreted from the kidney in response to variations in blood pressure and volume, and plasma sodium and potassium levels. It influences salt and water retention by an effect on the proximal tubules of the kidney.

Pure aldosterone was isolated from beef adrenals in 1953 by collaborating groups in England and Switzerland; by 1956 its structure was established and it was synthesized from other steroids. There are several preparative procedures, but the high cost of the hormone and the availability of other mineralocorticoids greatly restrict its use in therapy.

Aldred (Anglo-Saxon archbishop): *see* Ealdred.

Aldrich, Nelson W(ilmarth) (b. Nov. 6, 1841, Foster, R.I., U.S.—d. April 16, 1915, New York City), U.S. senator and financier whose work on the Aldrich–Vreeland Currency Act of 1908 and chairmanship of the National Monetary Commission (1908–12) helped prepare the way for the Federal Reserve Act of 1913.

Aldrich rose from the Providence Common Council through the Rhode Island legislature to the U.S. Congress (representative 1879–81; senator 1881–1911). Meanwhile, he amassed a modest fortune through investments in banking, electricity, gas, rubber, and sugar.

Nelson Aldrich, 1902
By courtesy of the Library of Congress, Washington, D.C.

In Congress, Aldrich was principally associated with the defense of the protective tariff and the gold standard, and opposition to any meaningful regulation of business. He emerged as the leader of the small coterie of Senate Republicans who dominated the party caucus and therefore determined the action of the Senate on most issues between 1895 and 1910. Through his influence the Interstate Commerce Act of 1887 and the Sherman Anti-Trust Act of 1890 were modified in a conservative direction.

The standard biography is N.W. Stephenson's *Nelson W. Aldrich, a Leader in American Politics* (1930).

Aldrich, Thomas Bailey (b. Nov. 11, 1836, Portsmouth, N.H., U.S.—d. March 19, 1907, Boston), poet, short-story writer, and editor whose use of the surprise ending influenced the development of the short story. He drew upon his childhood experiences in New Hampshire in his popular classic *The Story of a Bad Boy* (1870).

Adlrich left school at 13 to work as a merchant's clerk in New York City and soon began to contribute to various newspapers and magazines. After publication of his first book of verse, *The Bells* (1855), he became junior literary critic on the *New York Evening Mirror* and later subeditor of the *Home Journal*. From 1881 to 1890 he was editor of *The Atlantic Monthly*.

His poems, which reflect the cultural atmosphere of New England and his frequent European tours, were published in such volumes as *Cloth of Gold* (1874), *Flower and Thorn* (1877), *Mercedes and Later Lyrics* (1884), and *Windham Towers* (1890).

His best known prose is *Marjorie Daw and Other People* (1873), a collection of short stories.

Aldridge, Ira Frederick (b. 1805, New York City or Belair, Md., U.S.—d. Aug. 10, 1867, Łódź, Pol.), black tragedian, considered one of the greatest interpreters of his day.

Accounts of his life in the United States are conflicting. The great British actor Edmund Kean is believed to have engaged him as a personal attendant while visiting the United States; they returned together to England, where Kean encouraged Aldridge to study for the stage. In 1826 he made a highly successful debut in London as Othello. Billed as

Aldridge, detail from an engraving by T. Hollis, 1833

By courtesy of the Victoria and Albert Museum, London

the "African Roscius," after the great Roman comic actor, he made triumphant tours of Europe in several Shakespearean roles, including Othello, King Lear, and Macbeth. After 1853 he played mostly on the Continent, receiving honours from the Emperor of Austria, in Switzerland, and in Russia, among others.

It is doubtful that Aldridge ever returned to the United States; he became an English citizen in 1863.

aldrin, one of the several isomers (compounds with the same composition but different structures) of hexachlorohexahydrodimethanonaphthalene, a chlorinated hydrocarbon used as an insecticide. Aldrin was first prepared in the late 1940s and is manufactured by the reaction of hexachlorocyclopentadiene with bicycloheptadiene (both derived from hydrocarbons obtained from petroleum). Aldrin stimulates the central nervous system and is toxic to warm-blooded animals; poisoning can result from ingestion, inhalation, or absorption through the skin.

The insecticide dieldrin is made from aldrin by treatment with peroxyacetic acid.

Isodrin, a stereoisomer of aldrin, is made from cyclopentadiene and hexachlorobicycloheptadiene; it has insecticidal properties similar to those of aldrin and can be treated with peroxyacetic acid to form another insecticide, endrin, a stereoisomer of dieldrin. Aldrin, dieldrin, isodrin, and endrin, along with other chlorinated hydrocarbons, are being discontinued as insecticides because of their injurious effects on other animals that become exposed to them.

Aldrin, Edwin Eugene, Jr., byname BUZZ ALDRIN (b. Jan. 20, 1930, Montclair, N.J., U.S.), astronaut who set a record for extravehicular activity and was the second man to set foot on the Moon.

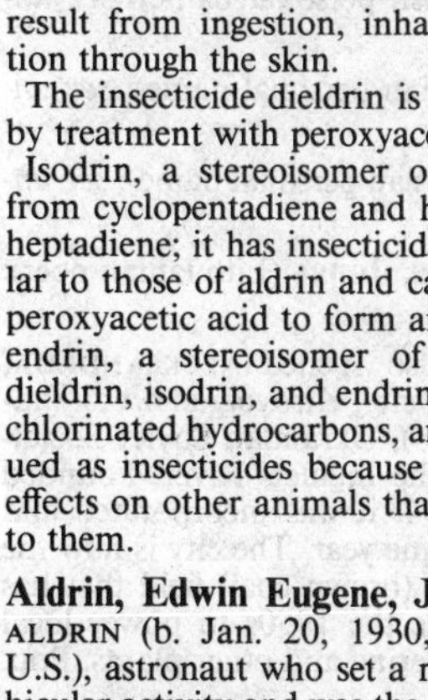

Aldrin, 1969

By courtesy of the National Aeronautics and Space Administration

A graduate of the U.S. Military Academy, West Point, N.Y. (1951), Aldrin became an air force pilot. He flew 66 combat missions in Korea and later served in West Germany. In 1963 he wrote a dissertation on orbital mechanics to earn his Ph.D. from the Massachusetts Institute of Technology, Cambridge. Later that year he was chosen as an astronaut.

On Nov. 11, 1966, he joined James A. Lovell, Jr., on the four-day Gemini 12 flight. Aldrin's 5½-hour walk in space proved that man can function effectively in the vacuum of space.

Apollo 11, manned by Aldrin, Neil A. Armstrong, and Michael Collins, was launched to the Moon on July 16, 1969. Four days later, Armstrong and Aldrin landed near the edge of Mare Tranquillitatis. After spending about two hours in gathering rock samples, taking photographs, and setting up scientific equipment for tests, the astronauts concluded their excursion on the surface. Armstrong and Aldrin later piloted the Lunar Module to a successful rendezvous with Collins and the Command Module in lunar orbit. The mission ended on July 24, with splashdown in the Pacific Ocean.

Aldrin retired from the National Aeronautics and Space Administration in 1971 to become commandant of the Aerospace Research Pilots' School at Edwards Air Force Base, California. In March 1972 he retired from the Air Force to enter private business. He wrote an autobiographical book, *Return to Earth* (1973).

Aldrovandi, Ulisse (b. Sept. 11, 1522, Bologna, Bologna—d. May 4, 1605, Bologna), Renaissance naturalist and physician noted for his systematic and accurate observations of animals, plants, and minerals.

After studying mathematics, Latin, law, and philosophy, Aldrovandi went to Padua in about 1545 to continue his studies. There he began to study medicine, the field in which he eventually earned a degree in 1553. On his return to Bologna in 1549 he was arrested, charged with heresy, and sent to Rome, where he was able to exonerate himself, probably in part because of his noble parentage. Returning to the University of Bologna, he was made a full professor in 1561 as a result of the great interest in his lectures, in which he presented natural history as a systematic study. He founded a botanical garden at Bologna and was named curator. His appointment as inspector of drugs and pharmacies met opposition, but Pope Gregory XIII confirmed the appointment. The official pharmacopoeia that Aldrovandi wrote, *Antidotarii Bononiensis Epitome* (1574), describing the constituents and properties of drugs, became a model for such works.

Pope Gregory XIII gave Aldrovandi financial assistance in publishing his numerous works on natural history, which included detailed observations of the day-to-day changes occurring in the incubation of the chicken embryo. Only four volumes, with detailed copperplate engravings, appeared during his lifetime; the remainder were prepared by his students from only a portion of his manuscripts. He also wrote *Le antichità della città di Roma* (1556), an account of various statues in Rome. His museum of biological specimens, classified according to his own system and left to the city of Bologna at his death, contributed to the later development of animal taxonomy.

ale, fermented malt beverage, full-bodied and somewhat bitter, with strong flavour of hops. Popular in England, where the term is now synonymous with beer, ale was until the late 17th century an unhopped brew of yeast, water, and malt, beer being the same brew with hops added. Modern ale, usually brewed with water rich in calcium sulfate, is made with top-fermenting yeast and processed at higher temperatures than the lager beers popular in the United States. Pale ale has up to 5 percent alcohol content; the darker strong ale contains up to 6.5 percent.

ale cost (herb): *see* costmary.

Aleandro, Girolamo, Dutch HIERONYMUS ALEANDER (b. Feb. 13, 1480, Motta di Treviso, near Venice—d. Feb. 1, 1542, Rome), cardinal and Humanist who was an important opponent of the Lutheran Reformation.

A remarkable scholar, particularly of classical languages, Aleandro was in his youth closely associated with the Dutch Humanist Erasmus. He lectured at Venice, Orléans (France), and Paris, where he was appointed rector of the university.

Aleandro, detail of an engraving by an unknown artist

BBC Hulton Picture Library

In 1520 Pope Leo X sent him to Germany to lead the opposition against Martin Luther at the Diet of Worms, an effort that brought about his break with Erasmus. The edict against Luther, which was adopted by the Diet, was drawn up and proposed by Aleandro, and in Brussels it was Aleandro who was responsible for the death of the first martyrs of the Reformation. In 1523 Clement VII sent him as nuncio to the court of Francis I of France, with whom he was taken prisoner at the Battle of Pavia (1525). He was later employed on various papal missions, especially to Germany, but was unable to check the progress of the new doctrines. He was created cardinal in 1538 by Paul III.

Aleandro's chief work is his unfinished treatise *De habendo Concilio,* setting forth his views on the Council of Trent, of which he was an ardent supporter. This and other documents of Aleandro in the Vatican Library, relating to his opposition to Luther, were used in Sforza Pallavicino's *Istoria del Concilio Tridentino* (1656; "History of the Council of Trent").

Aleardi, Aleardo, Conte (Count), original name GAETANO ALEARDI (b. Nov. 4, 1812, Verona, Austria—d. July 17, 1878, Verona, Italy), poet, patriot, and political figure, an archetype of the 19th-century Italian poet-patriots. His love poems and passionate diatribes against the Austrian government brought him renown.

Brought up in Verona, then controlled by Austria, he studied law at the University of Padua. His love lyrics, *Le lettere a Maria* (1846; "The Letters to Maria"), were eagerly read; but back in Verona and prevented by the Austrian government from practicing law, he wrote a series of bitterly anti-Austrian poems, notably *Le città italiane marinare e commercianti* (1856; "The Maritime and Commercial Italian Cities"), *Il tre fiumi* (1857; "The Three Rivers"), and *I sette soldati* (1861; "The Seven Soldiers"). He also edited, with the poet Giovanni Prati, an outspoken journal, *Il Caffè Pedrocchi.* The Austrians imprisoned him twice (1852 and 1859) and finally sent him into exile.

When the Austrians were expelled in 1866,

Aleardi returned to Verona and became its representative to the Italian parliament after Verona joined the Kingdom of Italy in 1866. He later became a senator and remained in public life until his death.

aleatoric dance, composition made up of steps freely improvised in the course of the dance; or, in a more specialized sense, of choreographed items selected at random, sometimes by a computer. The *Suite by Chance* (1952), by Merce Cunningham (*q.v.*), was the first composition by random choreography.

aleatory music (from Latin *alea,* "dice"), also called CHANCE MUSIC, 20th-century music in which chance or indeterminate elements are left for the performer to realize. The term is a loose one, describing compositions with strictly demarcated areas for improvisation according to specific directions and also unstructured pieces consisting of vague directives, such as "Play for five minutes."

The indeterminate portion of aleatory music commonly occurs in two areas. The performers may be told to arrange the structure of the piece—*e.g.,* by reordering its sections or by playing sections simultaneously as they wish. The musical score may also indicate points where performers are to improvise or even to include quasi-theatrical gestures. Such requirements may give rise to inventive notation, including brackets enclosing a blacked-out space, suggesting pitch area and duration of the improvisation. Among notable aleatoric works are *Music of Changes* (1951) for piano and *Concert for Piano and Orchestra* (1958), by the U.S. composer John Cage, and *Klavierstück XI* (1956; *Keyboard Piece XI*), by Karlheinz Stockhausen, of West Germany.

Alecsandri, Vasile (b. June 14, 1821, Bacău, Moldavia—d. Aug. 22, 1890, Mircesti, Rom.), lyric poet and dramatist, the first collector of Romanian popular songs and a leader of the movement for the union of the Romanian principalities.

He was educated at Iaşi and subsequently in Paris (1834–39). He published his first collection of folk songs in 1844 and was also active in the Romanian revolutionary cause.

His lyrical poems, *Doine şi lăcrimioare,* appeared in Paris in 1853, and during 1852–53 he published at Iaşi two volumes of ballads and songs. In 1868–75 he published his descriptive poems of landscapes entitled *Pasteluri.* As a playwright he created Romanian social comedy, but his most important contributions to the theatre were his poetic dramas: *Despot Vodă* (1879), *Fântâna Blanduziei* (1883; "Blanduzia's Fountain"), and *Ovidiu* (1885; "Ovid").

In later life Alecsandri played an important part in his country's affairs. As minister for foreign affairs (1859–60), he went to London as Prince Alexandru Cuza's special envoy to seek British recognition of the United Romanian Principalities. In 1885 he was appointed Romanian minister in Paris.

Alegre, Caetano da Costa: *see* Costa Alegre, Caetano da.

Alegrete, city, western Rio Grande do Sul state, Brazil, on the Rio Ibirapuitã at 292 ft (89 m) above sea level. It was founded in 1817 and given city status in 1857. The municipality of which Alegrete is the seat supports large cattle herds and substantial numbers of sheep. The city is a meat-processing centre and ships wool and hides. A railroad junction west of Pôrto Alegre, it can also be reached by highway and by air. Pop. (1980 prelim.) 54,786.

Alegría, Ciro (b. Nov. 4, 1909, Saltimbanca, Peru—d. Feb. 17, 1967, Lima), novelist who wrote about the lives of the Peruvian Indians.

Educated at the Colegio Nacional de San Juan, Alegría acquired a firsthand knowledge of Indian life in his native province of Huamachuco; this first appeared in *La serpiente de oro* (1935; *The Golden Serpent,* 1943), portraying the diversified human life along the Marañón River in Peru. *Los perros hambrientos* (1938; "The Hungry Dogs") describes the difficulties faced by the sheepherding Indians of the Peruvian highlands. The novel generally considered Alegría's masterpiece is *El mundo es ancho y ajeno* (1941; *Broad and Alien is the World,* 1941). It depicts in epic manner the struggles of an Indian tribe to survive in the Peruvian highlands against the greed of land-hungry white men. A collection of short fiction, *Duelo de caballeros* (1963) and *Novelas completas* (1963) were his last works.

Alegría, 1941
UPI—EB Inc.

In 1930 Alegría joined the militantly pro-Indian Alianza Popular Revolucionaria Americana, whose members were called Apristas, and became an active agitator for social reform. He was twice jailed, in 1931 and 1933, for illegal political activity, and was exiled to Chile in 1934. From 1941 to 1948 Alegría lived in the United States, but in 1948 he returned to Peru, where he resided until his death.

Aleichem, Sholem: *see* Sholem Aleichem.

Aleijadinho, byname of ANTÓNIO FRANCISCO LISBOA (b. Aug. 9, 1738?, Villa Rica, Brazil—d. Nov. 18, 1814, Mariana), prolific and influential Brazilian sculptor and architect whose Rococo statuary and religious articles complement the dramatic sobriety of his churches. He was of Portuguese and Negro ancestry.

Aleijadinho was born deformed (his sobriquet means "Little Cripple"). He eventually lost the use of his hands and finally became blind, but he worked tirelessly, nonetheless, with tools strapped to his wrists, until the end of his long life. He designed, built, and decorated the sanctuary of Bom Jesus de Matozinhos, Congonhas do Campo (1757–77), and the church of São Francisco, Ouro Prêto (1766–94).

Aleixandre, Vicente (b. April 26, 1898, Seville), Spanish poet, a member of the Generation of 1927, who received the Nobel Prize for Literature in 1977. A member of the Spanish Academy since 1949, he was strongly influenced by the Surrealist technique of poetic composition.

Aleixandre has been considered a master of free verse, the style that appears in his first major book, *La destrucción o el amor* (1935; "Destruction or Love"), which was awarded the National Prize for Literature. In this work the poet explored the theme of human identification with the physical cosmos. Similar themes appear in *Sombra del paraíso* (1944; "Shadow of Paradise"), but in this book his style is less obscure. A greater emphasis upon human life is found in *Historia del corazón* (1954; "History of the Heart") and *En un vasto dominio* (1962; "In a Vast Domain"), works that deal with time, death, and human solidarity.

Aleixandre's later poetry is of a metaphysical nature; he explores death, knowledge, and experience in *Poemas de la consumación* (1968; "Poems of Consummation") and *Diálogos del conocimiento* (1974; "Dialogues of Insight").

In addition to writing poetry of great originality and depth, Aleixandre published the prose work *Los encuentros* (1958; "The Meetings"), a book of fond sketches of his fellow writers.

Alekhine, Alexander, Alekhine also spelled ALEKHIN, or ALJECHIN, original name ALEKSANDR ALEKSANDROVICH ALYOKHIN (b. Nov. 1, 1892, Moscow—d. March 24, 1946, Estoril, Port.), world-champion Chess player from 1927 to 1935 and from 1937 until his death. Noted for using a great variety of attacks, he also won annual world championship tournaments for blindfold chess in 1924, 1925, and 1933.

Alekhine was a precocious Chess player and at the age of 17 had tournament success. He was playing in a tournament in Mannheim, Ger., when World War I broke out and he escaped from internment to serve in the Red Cross division of the Russian army.

After the Russian Revolution of 1917, Alekhine became a naturalized French citizen and studied law at the University of Paris. In 1927, after a contest lasting nearly three months, he won the world championship from José Raúl Capablanca of Cuba. Eight years later he lost the title to Max Euwe of The Netherlands, but he regained it from Euwe in 1937. In World War II he served as an interpreter in the French army.

Aleksandar (Serbo-Croatian personal name): *see under* Alexander.

Aleksander (Polish personal name): *see under* Alexander.

Aleksandr (Russian personal name): *see under* Alexander.

Aleksandra (Russian personal name): *see under* Alexandra.

Aleksandravičius, Jonas (Lithuanian poet): *see* Aistis, Jonas.

Aleksandriya, also spelled ALEKSANDRIJA, or ALEKSANDRIIA, city, Kirovograd *oblast* (administrative region), Ukrainian Soviet Socialist Republic, on the Ingulets River. Founded as Usovka in 1754, it was incorporated and renamed in the same year. The city is now the centre of a lignite (brown coal) field that has been utilized since the 1950s to power local rayon fibre engineering and other plants. Pop. (1982 est.) 87,000.

Aleksandrovka (Russian S.F.S.R.): *see* Belogorsk.

Aleksandrovsk (city, Ukrainian S.S.R.): *see* Zaporozhye.

Aleksandrovsk-Grushevsky (city, Russian S.F.S.R.): *see* Shakhty.

Aleksandrovsk-Sakhalinsky, city, Sakhalin *oblast* (administrative region), far eastern Russian Soviet Federated Socialist Republic, on the western coast of Sakhalin Island. It was founded in 1881 as a centre for penal settlements. In 1890 the writer Anton Chekhov lived there while gathering material about convict life for his book *Ostrov Sakhalin* ("Sakhalin Island"). It became a city in 1926 and from 1932 to 1947 was the centre of an *oblast.* There are coal deposits nearby, and the city is the centre of an agricultural area and the site of a mining college. Pop. (1970) 20,342.

Aleksandŭr (Bulgarian personal name): *see under* Alexander.

Aleksey, also spelled ALEKSEI (Russian personal name): *see under* Alexis.

Alekseyev, Konstantin Sergeyevich (theatre director): *see* Stanislavsky, Konstantin (Sergeyevich).

Alekseyev, Mikhail Vasilyevich, Alekseyev also spelled ALEKSEEV (b. Nov. 15 [Nov. 3, old style], 1857, Tver, Russia—d. Oct. 8, 1918, Yekaterinodar), commander in chief of the Russian Army for two months in World War I and a military and political leader of the White (anti-Bolshevik) forces in the Russian Civil War that followed the Russian Revolution of October 1917.

The son of a private soldier, Alekseyev entered the Russian Army in 1876 and was graduated in 1890 from the staff college. He became a general in 1904. Early in World War I, he planned the successful Russian offensive into Galicia. After a period of command on the northwestern front, he became chief of the general staff (August 1915) and assumed control of all Russian armies in the European theatre.

Alekseyev was handicapped by the growing divergence of Russian public opinion and the wishes of the imperial court. In the fall of 1916 his intention to present the emperor Nicholas II with a peremptory demand for reform became known, and Alekseyev was suspended from duty. In March 1917 when Nicholas abdicated, Alekseyev was appointed commander in chief. He resigned, however, on May 21 in protest against the provisional government's failure to suppress defeatism and anarchy in the army.

Subsequently, Alekseyev tried to arrange a compromise between the conservative Gen. L.G. Kornilov and Aleksandr F. Kerensky, who became prime minister in the Provisional Government (July–October 1917). After the revolution, Alekseyev organized the anti-Bolshevik force (the White Army) in the region of the Don.

Alekseyev, Vasily Ivanovich (b. Jan. 7, 1942, Pokrovo-Shishkino, Russian S.F.S.R.), Soviet super-heavyweight weightlifter (over 110-kilogram [$242\frac{1}{2}$-pound] class) who between 1970 and 1978 set 79 world records.

Akekseyev was the son of a lumberjack; at the age of 12 he was felling trees alongside the men and at the age of 14 was wrestling them on even terms. He was enrolled in a forestry institute in 1961 and was graduated from Novocherkassk Polytechnical Institute in 1971. He was a member of the Communist Party from 1975 and was awarded the Order of Lenin. He became a mining engineer by profession.

Alekseyev began weightlifting competition in 1961, took third place in the 1968 U.S.S.R. meet, and won in 1970. He held this championship through 1976. He was also world champion (1970–71; 1973–75; 1977) and European champion (1970–75; 1977–78). He broke four world records in 1970, including a three-lift record of 200 kg (total 1,323 lb) that he later raised to 231.78 kg. In the 1972 Olympic Games at Munich and the 1976 Olympic Games at Montreal, he won the gold medal in his division. In the 1978 world championship, he withdrew from competition because of an injury, and in the 1980 Olympic Games at Moscow, he did not qualify for the finals. Thereafter he retired from competition.

Articles are alphabetized word by word, not letter by letter

Alekseyevsk (Russian S.F.S.R.): *see* Svobodny.

Aleksin, city, Tula *oblast* (administrative region), western Russian Soviet Federated Socialist Republic, on the Oka River, 40 mi (65 km) northwest of Tula city. Aleksin, first documented in 1236, was at first a fortress, then a river port. The decline of river trade adversely affected the city, but since the October Revolution (1917) it has become a significant industrial centre, with engineering and building-materials industries. Pop. (1982 est.) 69,000.

Alemán, Mateo (baptized Sept. 28, 1547, Seville—d. *c.* 1614, Mexico), novelist, a master stylist best known for his early, highly popular picaresque novel, *Guzmán de Alfarache.*

Descended from Jews who had been forcibly converted to Catholicism, Alemán expressed many aspects of the experiences and feelings of the New Christians in 16th-century Spain. His most important literary work, *Guzmán de Alfarache* (1599; a second part, 1604; Eng. trans., *The Spanish Rogue,* 1622, 1924), which brought him fame throughout Europe but little profit, is one of the earliest picaresque novels. The first part ran through many editions, almost all pirated; even before he could finish the second part, a spurious sequel had appeared. Alemán's life, in many ways like that of his protagonist, Guzmán, was afflicted with severe economic and personal reverses. He was the son of a prison doctor and studied medicine at Salamanca and Alcalá for four years after graduating from the University of Seville in 1564, but he never practiced. In 1580 he was imprisoned for debt. Only after he emigrated to Mexico in 1608 did his fortunes become settled and his life stable.

Alemán, Miguel (b. Sept. 29, 1902, Sayula, Mex.—d. May 14, 1983, Mexico City), president of Mexico from 1946 to 1952.

The son of a village shopkeeper who subsequently became a general in the revolution, Alemán studied law and set up practice in Mexico City, specializing in labour cases. Appointed senator from Veracruz, he became governor of the state in 1936. In 1940 he resigned to manage the successful presidential campaign of Manuel Ávila Camacho, who rewarded him with the powerful post of minister of *gobernación* ("interior"). Alemán became the official candidate for the presidency on the ticket of the Partido Revolucionario Institucional (Revolutionary Institutional Party) in 1946 and easily defeated Ezequiel Padilla. His administration saw a slowdown in Mexico's agrarian reform but greatly accelerated industrial development. Although his regime was charged with extensive graft and corruption, economic progress was marked during his tenure. From the early 1960s he served as president of a national tourist council, a position he held until his death.

Miguel Alemán, c. 1951
By courtesy of the Organization of American States

Alemanni, also spelled ALAMANNI, or ALAMANI, a Germanic people first mentioned in connection with the Roman attack on them in AD 213. In the following decades, their pressure on the Roman provinces became severe; they occupied the Agri Decumates *c.* 260, and late in the 5th century they expanded into Alsace and northern Switzerland, establishing the German language in those regions. In 496 they were conquered by Clovis and incorporated into his Frankish dominions.

The Alemanni were originally composed of fragments of several Germanic peoples, and they remained a loosely knit confederation of tribes in the Suebi group (*see* Suebi). Although several tribes put their military forces under the joint command of two leaders for the duration of a campaign, the different peoples generally found it difficult to combine, and they had nothing that could be called a central government. The French and Spanish words for Germany (Allemagne; Alemania) are derived from their name.

Alembert, Jean Le Rond d' (b. Nov. 17, 1717, Paris—d. Oct. 29, 1783, Paris), French mathematician, philosopher, and writer, who achieved fame as a mathematician and scientist before acquiring a considerable reputation as a contributor to and editor of the famous *Encyclopédie.*

D'Alembert, pastel by Maurice-Quentin de La Tour
By courtesy of the Bibliotheque Nationale, Paris

Early life. The illegitimate son of a famous hostess, Mme de Tencin, and one of her lovers, the chevalier Destouches-Canon, d'Alembert was abandoned on the steps of the Parisian church of Saint-Jean-le-Rond, from which he derived his Christian names. Although Mme de Tencin never recognized her son, Destouches eventually sought out the child and entrusted him to a glazier's wife, whom d'Alembert always treated as his mother. Through his father's influence, he was admitted to a prestigious Jansenist school, enrolling first as Jean-Baptiste Daremberg and subsequently changing his name, perhaps for reasons of euphony, to d'Alembert. Although Destouches never disclosed his identity as father of the child, he left his son an annuity of 1,200 livres. D'Alembert's teachers at first hoped to train him for theology, being perhaps encouraged by a commentary he wrote on St. Paul's Letter to the Romans, but they inspired in him only a lifelong aversion to the subject. He spent two years studying law and became an advocate in 1738, although he never practiced. After taking up medicine for a year, he finally devoted himself to mathematics—"the only occupation," he said later, "which really interested me." Apart from some private lessons, d'Alembert was almost entirely self-taught.

Mathematics. In 1739 he read his first paper to the Academy of Sciences, of which he became a member in 1741. In 1743, at the age of 26, he published his important *Traité de dynamique,* a fundamental treatise on dynamics containing the famous "d'Alembert's principle," which states that Newton's third law of motion (for every action there is an equal and opposite reaction) is true for bodies that are free to move as well as for bodies rigidly fixed. Other mathematical works followed very rapidly; in 1744 he applied his principle to the theory of equilibrium and motion of fluids, in his *Traité de l'équilibre et du mouvement des fluides.* This discovery was followed by the development of partial differential equations, a branch of the theory of calculus, the first papers on which were published in his *Réflexions sur la cause générale des vents* (1747). It won him a prize at the Berlin Academy, to which he was elected the same year. In 1747 he applied his new calculus to the problem of vibrating strings, in his *Recherches sur les cordes vibrantes;* in 1749 he furnished a method of applying his principles to the motion of any body of a given shape; and in 1749 he found an explanation of the precession of the equinoxes (a gradual change in the position of the Earth's orbit), determined its characteristics, and explained the phenomenon of the nutation (nodding) of the Earth's axis, in *Recherches sur la précession des équinoxes et sur la nutation de l'axe de la terre.* In 1752 he published *Essai d'une nouvelle théorie de la résistance des fluides,* an essay containing various original ideas and new observations. In it he considered air as an incompressible elastic fluid composed of small particles and, carrying over from the principles of solid body mechanics the view that resistance is related to loss of momentum on impact of moving bodies, he produced the surprising result that the resistance of the particles was zero. D'Alembert was himself dissatisfied with the result; the conclusion is known as "d'Alembert's paradox" and is not accepted by modern physicists. In the *Memoirs* of the Berlin Academy he published findings of his research on integral calculus—which devises relationships of variables by means of rates of change of their numerical value—a branch of mathematical science that is greatly indebted to him. In his *Recherches sur différents points importants du système du monde* (1754–56) he perfected the solution of the problem of the perturbations (variations of orbit) of the planets that he had presented to the academy some years before. From 1761 to 1780 he published eight volumes of his *Opuscules mathématiques.*

The Encyclopédie. Meanwhile, d'Alembert began an active social life and frequented well-known salons, where he acquired a considerable reputation as a witty conversationalist and mimic. Like his fellow Philosophes—those thinkers, writers, and scientists who believed in the sovereignty of reason and nature (as opposed to authority and revelation) and rebelled against old dogmas and institutions—he turned to the improvement of society. A rationalist thinker in the free-thinking tradition, he opposed religion and stood for tolerance and free discussion; in politics the Philosophes sought a liberal monarchy with an "enlightened" king who would supplant the old aristocracy with a new, intellectual aristocracy. Believing in man's need to rely on his own powers, they promulgated a new social morality to replace Christian ethics. Science, the only real source of knowledge, had to be popularized for the benefit of the people, and it was in this tradition that he became associated with the *Encyclopédie* about 1746. When the original idea of a translation into French of Ephraim Chambers' English *Cyclopædia* was replaced by that of a new work under the general editorship of the Philosophe Denis Diderot, d'Alembert was made editor of the mathematical and scientific articles. In fact, he not only helped with the general editorship and contributed articles on other subjects but also tried to secure support for the enterprise in influential circles. He wrote the *Discours préliminaire* that introduced the first volume of the work in 1751. This was a remarkable attempt to present a unified view of contemporary knowledge, tracing the development and interrelationship of its various branches and showing how they formed coherent parts of a single structure; the second section of the *Discours* was devoted to the intellectual history of Europe from the time of the Renaissance. In 1752 d'Alembert wrote a preface to Volume III, which was a vigorous rejoinder to the *Encyclopédie's* critics, while an *Éloge de Montesquieu,* which served as the preface to Volume V (1755), skillfully but somewhat disingenuously presented Montesquieu as one of the *Encyclopédie's* supporters. Montesquieu had, in fact, refused an invitation to write the articles "Democracy" and "Despotism," and the promised article on "Taste" remained unfinished at his death in 1755.

In 1756 d'Alembert went to stay with Voltaire at Geneva, where he also collected information for an *Encyclopédie* article, "Genève," which praised the doctrines and practices of the Genevan pastors. When it appeared in 1757, it aroused angry protests in Geneva because it affirmed that many of the ministers no longer believed in Christ's divinity and also advocated (probably at Voltaire's instigation) the establishment of a theatre. This article prompted Rousseau, who had contributed the articles on music to the *Encyclopédie,* to argue in his *Lettre à d'Alembert sur les spectacles* (1758) that the theatre is invariably a corrupting influence. D'Alembert himself replied with an incisive but not unfriendly *Lettre à J.-J. Rousseau, citoyen de Genève.* Gradually discouraged by the growing difficulties of the enterprise, d'Alembert gave up his share of the editorship at the beginning of 1758, thereafter limiting his commitment to the production of mathematical and scientific articles.

Later literary, scientific, and philosophical work. His earlier literary and philosophical activity, however, led to the publication of his *Mélanges de littérature, d'histoire et de philosophie* (1753). This work contained the impressive *Essai sur les gens de lettres,* which exhorted writers to pursue "liberty, truth and poverty" and also urged aristocratic patrons to respect the talents and independence of such writers.

Largely as a result of the persistent campaigning of Mme du Deffand, a prominent hostess to writers and scientists, d'Alembert was elected to the French Academy in 1754; he proved himself to be a zealous member, working hard to enhance the dignity of the institution in the eyes of the public and striving steadfastly for the election of members sympathetic to the cause of the Philosophes. His personal position became even more influential in 1772 when he was made permanent secretary. One of his functions was the continuation of the *Histoire des membres de l'Académie;* this involved writing the biographies of all the members who had died between 1700 and 1772. He paid tribute to his predecessors by means of *Éloges* that were delivered at public sessions of the academy. Though of limited literary value, they throw interesting light on his attitude toward many contemporary problems and also reveal his desire to establish a link between the Academy and the public.

From 1752 onward, Frederick II of Prussia repeatedly tried to persuade d'Alembert to become president of the Berlin Academy, but the philosopher contented himself with a brief visit to the King at the Rhine village of Wesel in 1755 and a longer stay at Potsdam in 1763. For many years he gave the King advice on the running of the academy and the appointment of new members. In 1762 another monarch, the empress Catherine II of Russia, invited d'Alembert to become tutor to her son, the grand duke Paul; this offer also was refused. Apart from fearing the harmful effects of foreign residence upon his health and personal position, d'Alembert did not wish to be separated from the intellectual life of Paris.

Although as a skeptic, d'Alembert willingly supported the Philosophes' hostility to Christianity, he was too cautious to become openly aggressive. The expulsion of the Jesuits from France, however, prompted him to publish "by a disinterested author," at first anonymously, and then in his own name, *Sur la destruction des Jésuites en France* (1765; *An Account of the Destruction of the Jesuits in France,* 1766). He there tried to show that the Jesuits, in spite of their qualities as scholars and educators, had destroyed themselves through their inordinate love of power.

During these years d'Alembert's interests included musical theory. His *Éléments de musique* of 1752 was an attempt to expound the principles of the composer Jean-Philippe Rameau (1683–1764), who had consolidated contemporary musical development into a harmonic system that dominated Western music until about 1900. In 1754 d'Alembert published an essay expressing his thoughts on music in general—and French music in particular—entitled *Réflexions sur la musique en général et sur la musique française en particulier.* He also published in his mathematical *opuscules* treatises on acoustics, the physics of sound, and he contributed several articles on music to the *Encyclopédie.* In 1765 a serious illness compelled him to leave his foster-mother's house, and he eventually went to live in the house of Julie de Lespinasse, with whom he fell in love. He was the leading intellectual figure in her salon, which became an important recruiting centre for the French Academy. Although they may have been intimate for a short time, d'Alembert soon had to be satisfied with the role of steadfast friend. He discovered the extent of her passionate involvement with other men only after Julie's death in 1776. He transferred his home to an apartment at the Louvre—to which he was entitled as secretary to the Academy—where he died.

Assessment. Posterity has not confirmed the judgment of those contemporaries who placed d'Alembert's reputation next to Voltaire's. In spite of his original contributions to the mathematical sciences, intellectual timidity prevented his literary and philosophical work from attaining true greatness. Nevertheless, his scientific background enabled him to elaborate a philosophy of science that, inspired by the rationalist ideal of the ultimate unity of all knowledge, established "principles" making possible the interconnection of the various branches of science. Moreover, d'Alembert was a typical 18th-century Philosophe, for in both his life and his work he tried to invest the name with dignity and serious meaning. In his personal life he was simple and frugal, never seeking wealth and dispensing charity whenever possible, always watchful of his integrity and independence, and constantly using his influence, both at home and abroad, to encourage the advance of "enlightenment."

(R.Gr.)

BIBLIOGRAPHY. The main editions of d'Alembert's collected works are: *Oeuvres philosophiques, historiques et littéraires de d'Alembert,* ed. by J.F. Bastien, 18 vol. (1805); and *Oeuvres complètes de d'Alembert,* ed. by Bossange and Belin, 5 vol. (1821, reprinted 1967). These may be supplemented by d'Alembert's *Mélanges de littérature, d'histoire et de philosophie,* 2 vol. (1753), 4 vol. (1759), 5th vol. (1767), which contain a few pieces omitted from the collected editions; and his *Histoire des membres de l'Académie française morts depuis 1700 jusqu'en 1771,* 6 vol. (1785–87, reprinted 1970). General studies are: Joseph Bertrand, *D'Alembert* (1889); and Ronald Grimsley, *Jean d'Alembert, 1717–83* (1963).

Alencar, José (Martiniano) de (b. May 1, 1829, Mecejana, Braz.—d. Dec. 12, 1877, Rio de Janeiro), journalist, novelist, and playwright whose novel *O Guarani* (1857; "The Guarani Indian") initiated the vogue of the Brazilian Indianista novel (romantic tales of indigenous life incorporating vocabulary of Amerindian origin referring to flora, fauna, and tribal customs). *O Guarani,* subsequently utilized as the libretto for an opera in Italian by the Brazilian composer Carlos Gomes, depicts the platonic love affair of Perí, a noble savage, and Ceci, the white daughter of a wealthy landowner.

Alencar's next most popular novel, *Iracema* (1865), deals with the love of a beautiful Indian maiden for a Portuguese soldier. In *O Gaúcho* (1870; "The Gaucho") and *O Sertanejo* (1876; "The Backlander"), Alencar treats life in Brazil's frontier lands. In novels such as *Lucíola* (1862), *Diva* (1864), and *Senhora* (1875), he laid the foundation for Brazilian psychological fiction. Alencar, considered the father of Brazilian fictional writing, also cultivated the historical novel in such works as *As Minas de Prata* (1862; "The Silver Mines"). His Abolitionist stance is revealed in several plays, including *Mãe* (1860; "Mother").

Alencar also was a lawyer, a deputy in the legislature, and minister of justice (1868–70).

Alençon, town and prefecture, Orne *département*, Basse-Normandie region, northwestern France, at the juncture of the Sarthe and Briante rivers. In the centre of a plain ringed by wooded hills, it is known for its tulle and lace (especially *point d'Alençon*), introduced from Venice in the mid-17th century. Incorporated in the duchy of Normandy in 911, it was capital of the county and duchy of Alençon, and passed to the crown in 1549. Parts of its castle, taken by William of Normandy in 1048, remain; law courts have been built into its living quarters. Sainte-Thérèse of Lisieux was born in Alençon in 1873 and was baptized in the church of Notre-Dame (13th–18th centuries). The medieval Maison d'Ozé and the 18th-century town hall survived heavy bombardments in 1944. Recent industrial development includes printing and light manufacturing. Pop. (1982) town, 30,952; *arrondissement,* 101,992.

Alençon, (Hercule-) François, duc d' (duke of): *see* Anjou, (Hercule-) François, duc d'.

Alençon lace, French POINT D'ALENÇON, needle lace made in the French city of Alençon, one of the centres designated by Jean-Baptiste Colbert, minister of finance under Louis XIV, for aid in his effort to make French laces financially and artistically competitive with imported laces. Venetian workers, experts in making *point de Venise,* were brought in to instruct the local needlewomen, who quickly learned the technique and, by the end of the Royal Monopoly (*see* point de France), were evolving a distinctive lace. Alençon lace is characterized by a cordonnet usually made over horsehair, a firm needle mesh of double twisted threads, and many and varied filling stitches within floral and scroll patterns.

Aleni, Giulio (b. 1582, Brescia, Kingdom of Venice—d. Aug. 3, 1649, Foochow, China), Jesuit missionary who was the first Christian missionary in the province of Kiangsi, China.

He entered the Society of Jesus and was sent to the Far East. He landed at Macau in 1610 and went to China three years later. During his more than 30 years in China, he adopted that country's dress and manners. He built several churches in the province of Fukien and wrote the *Life of Christ* (8 vol., 1635–37). Often reprinted, it has been used by Protestant missionaries. He also wrote a six-volume cosmography that was translated into Manchu.

Alentejo, also spelled ALEMTEJO, historical province of south central Portugal, southeast of the Tagus (Tejo) River and bounded on the east by the Spanish frontier and on the southwest by the Atlantic Ocean. It is an almost featureless tableland of less than 650 ft (200 m) in elevation in the south and southwest that ascends to higher elevations in the far south and northeast. Although Alentejo is one of the driest regions in Portugal, irriga-

Stripped cork oak trees in the Alentejo area, Portugal
Josef Muench

tion projects make possible the cultivation of wheat, rye, oats, barley, and sugar beets; construction on the Alqueva hydroelectric project on the Rio Guadiana in Alentejo began in 1976. The region produces two-thirds of the world's output of cork. Cork oak acorns are used locally for pig feed. Some livestock are pastured, and wool textiles, rugs (from Persian designs), and olive oil are manufactured there. The region's quarries yield granite, limestone, basalt, marble, and alabaster; copper and sulfur are mined.

Until the revolution of 1974, Alentejo contained estates of up to 1,000 ac (400 ha), mostly owned by absentee landlords. A part of the forests and cropland has since been divided among the Alentejanos, usually in the form of cooperatives. Contemporary Alentejo comprises all of Beja and Évora districts and most of Setúbal and Portalegre districts.

ʿalenu (Hebrew: "it is our duty"), the opening word of an extremely old Jewish prayer, which has been recited at the end of the three periods of daily prayer since the Middle Ages. The first section of the *ʿalenu* is a prayer of thanks for having set Israel apart for the service of God; the second section, omitted by those who follow the Sefardic (Spanish) rite, expresses a hope for the coming of the messianic age, when "the world will be perfected under the kingdom of the Almighty." The *ʿalenu* is thus both particularistic and universalistic, and ends with the phrase: "And the Lord will become king over all the Earth; on that day the Lord will be one and his name one" (Zechariah 14:9).

Though ancient tradition ascribes the *ʿalenu* to Joshua, it is often credited to Abba Arika, also known as Rav (3rd century AD), the head of a Jewish academy at ʿSura in Babylonia. The *ʿalenu* was originally part of the additional (*musaf*) service for Rosh Hashana (New Year) and was later added to the Yom Kippur (Day of Atonement) liturgy. On the High Holy Days it is included in the *ʿamida,* the main section of the daily prayers, and is repeated in full by the cantor (*ḥazzan*). The version used in the Ashkenazi (German) ritual was censored by Christian Church authorities, who interpreted a sentence as a slighting reference to Jesus and so ordered its deletion. Reform Judaism uses a modified form of the *ʿalenu* that is called Adoration in the ritual. In *Gates of Prayer: The New Union Prayer Book* (1975), however, Reform worshippers were given the option of using the original concept of the *ʿalenu* in their liturgy.

Aleppo, Arabic ḤALAB, Turkish HALEP, principal city of northern Syria and the capital of Ḥalab *muḥāfaẓah* (governorate). It was the chief market of the Middle East under the Ottoman Turks in the 16th century.

Aleppo came successively under Hittite, Mitannian, and Egyptian rule in the 2nd millennium BC. A key point on the ancient caravan route linking the Mediterranean lands to the East, the city was controlled by the Achaemenian Persians (6th–4th century BC) and was absorbed into the Roman province of Syria in the 1st century BC. It prospered under Byzantine rule and in 637 was conquered by the Arabs. It was incorporated into the empire of the Ottoman Turks in 1516 and remained prosperous until the end of the 18th century. In the 20th century the city became an industrial town rivalling Damascus.

Aleppo's principal industries are silk weaving and cotton printing and the preparation of hides, wool, dried fruit, and nuts. Aleppo is also an intellectual centre with a university, an institute of music, and several Muslim *madrasahs*, or theological schools. The National Museum contains material found in northern Syria at the ancient sites of Tall Aḥmar, Tall Ḥalaf, Arslān Ṭāsh, and Ḥamāh, as well as the still active sites of Ugarit (Ras Sham-

Courtyard of the Umayyad Great Mosque, Aleppo, Syria, with the citadel in the background
Sam Abboud—FPG

ra), Māriʿ (Tall Ḥarīrī), and ʿAyn Dārah. Other points of interest include the 13th-century citadel and the Umayyad Great Mosque, built in AD 715. Pop. (1980 est.) 962,954.

aleppo boil (infection): *see* Oriental sore.

alerce (*Fitzroya cupressoides*), coniferous timber tree and only species of the genus *Fitzroya,* of the cypress family (Cupressaceae), native to southern South America. The name alerce also refers to the arartree (*q.v.*) of the eastern Mediterranean region and the whiter alerce of the Chilean Andes.

Alerce often is shrubby in cultivation, but a native forest tree may be over 45 metres (about 150 feet) tall, with a trunk diameter of about 3 m (about 10 ft). The reddish-brown wood is lightweight and durable.

White alerce (*Pilgerodendron uviferum*), also an evergreen timber tree of the cypress family, is the only species in its genus. Its brownish heartwood is used for general construction.

Aleric (antipope): *see* Albert *under* Albert (Papacy).

Alès, town, Gard *département,* Languedoc-Roussillon region, southeastern France, on a bend of the Gardon d'Alès River, at the foot of the Cévennes mountains, north-northwest of Nîmes. The focus of an industrial *arrondissement* (chemicals, coal, metalwork, textiles, cattle feed, and wine), its name meant "industry" in the language of its 10th-century-BC Phoenician founders. Alestium was its Roman name, and until 1926 the French called it Alais. Chartered in 1200, it became part of the kingdom of France in 1243. The Peace of Alais (1629) ended the French Wars of Religion in which the town had been seriously damaged. A fort completed in 1788 to the design of Sébastien Le Prestre de Vauban, the celebrated military engineer, is now a museum and library. Modern urban renewal programs have enlarged the narrow streets of the central section and replaced unhealthful dwellings with modern apartments. New suburbs have developed. Pop. (1982) 38,567.

Alesia, ancient town situated on Mont Auxois, above the present-day village of Alise-Sainte-Reine in the *département* of Côte d'Or, France, famous as the site of the siege of Vercingetorix by Julius Caesar in 52 BC, decisive in his conquest of Gaul. The Gallic town was succeeded on the same site by a Roman town.

Alessandri Palma, Arturo (b. Dec. 20, 1868, Longaví, Chile—d. Aug. 24, 1950, Santiago), Chilean president (1920–25, 1932–38) who early defended workers' groups, especially the nitrate miners of the north, but later became more conservative.

The son of an Italian immigrant, Alessandri was graduated in law from the University of Chile in 1893 and in 1897 was elected to the Chamber of Deputies. He was at various

Alessandri Palma
By courtesy of the Organization of American States

times minister of industry, minister of finance, congressman (six times), senator (twice), and president.

Elected president in 1920 as the candidate of a liberal coalition, he was forced into exile by a military junta on Sept. 15, 1924, but was recalled, returning on March 20, 1925, on condition that the constitution be rewritten to give the president greater power. He became president again in 1932, but as a strict constitutionalist, depending primarily for support on the political right. Although he promoted economic recovery from the depression caused by decreased world demands for Chilean nitrates and copper, he had by then alienated most of his labour and middle class support, who joined the Popular Front. When elected to the Senate in 1946, Alessandri again displayed liberal leanings.

Alessandria, city, capital of Alessandria province, in the Piemonte (Piedmont) region of northwestern Italy, at the confluence of the Bormida and Tanaro rivers, southeast of Turin (Torino). Founded in 1168 by the towns of the Lombard League as an Alpine-valley stronghold against the emperor Frederick I Barbarossa, it was first called Civitas Nova, then Cesaria, until renamed for Pope Alexander III; it became a bishopric in 1175. The town was later ceded to the Emperor, then transferred to the Milanese Visconti family in the 14th century, and passed formally to the House of Savoy in 1713. From 1796 to 1814 it was the capital of the French *département* of Marengo, named for the site of Napoleon's victory outside the city in 1800. Alessandria was a centre of the early 19th-century freedom movement in Piedmont, including the conspiracy of Giuseppe Mazzini in 1833. A strategic stronghold, it was garrisoned by the Austrians after their victory at Novara (1849). Expansion beyond the city's defense works is of comparatively recent date. Notable landmarks include the cathedral, the Romanesque-Gothic church of Sta. Maria di Castello (rebuilt 14th–15th century), the 15th-century episcopal palace and other palaces of the 15th–19th centuries, the town hall (1826), the civic museum, and the picture gallery.

An important rail and road junction, Alessandria is also noted for hat making (notably the Borsalino). It is an important agricultural and wine market and has diversified industries. Pop. (1981 prelim.) mun., 100,518.

Alessandro, in full ALESSANDRO DE' MEDICI (b. 1510/11, Florence—d. Jan. 5–6, 1537, Florence), the first duke of Florence (1532–37).

Alessandro was an illegitimate child, whose paternity is ascribed either to Lorenzo de' Medici (1492–1519), duca di Urbino, or, with more likelihood, to Cardinal Giulio, nephew of Lorenzo the Magnificent. Cardinal Giulio received the lordship of Florence in 1519; but, upon being elected pope in 1523, he made Silvio, Cardinal Passerini, regent in Florence for Alessandro and another bastard heir, Ippolito de' Medici. Alessandro had meanwhile been created duca di Penna by the emperor Charles V (1522).

Republican sentiments and Savonarolan ideas were still strong in Florence, and Cardinal Passerini's regency was unpopular. When imperial forces sacked Rome (May 1527), revolution broke out in Florence, and Passerini and the bastards fled. The Piagnoni family then came to power and restored the old regime of the republic. Pope Clement VII's indignation counted for little so long as he was at variance with Charles V; but in June 1529 Pope and Emperor came to terms. Charles agreed to restore the Medici in Florence and sent an army against the city, which capitulated after a siege of 11 months (October 1529–August 1530). Reprisals were taken against the opponents of the Medici; and Alessandro, whom Charles had nominated head of state for Florence in October 1530, returned in June 1531. Ippolito had been created cardinal (January 1529).

The new Florentine constitution of April 1532 declared Alessandro to be hereditary duke and perpetual gonfalonier of the republic. Though his common sense and his feeling for justice won his subjects' affection, Alessandro was rough and uncultured, a lover of sensual pleasures who enriched himself personally through taxes and duties and was determined to make his authority absolute beyond all question. After Clement VII's death (1534) the exiled opposition sought to oust the Duke from Florence and persuaded Cardinal Ippolito to submit its case to Charles V. Ippolito, however, died suddenly at Itri (Aug. 10, 1535), on his way from Rome to Tunis, where Charles then was; and Charles, returning from Tunis, received Alessandro at Naples and decided to uphold him. Married in 1536 to the Emperor's natural daughter Margaret of Austria, the Duke now felt altogether secure; but in the night of Jan. 5–6, 1537, his distant cousin Lorenzino, or Lorenzaccio, de' Medici (1514–48), the companion and procurer of his licentious amusements, took advantage of his confidence in order to murder him. Disappointed at the Florentines' failure to rise against tyrannical government, Lorenzino fled and was himself murdered in 1548.

Ålesund, fishing port, Møre og Romsdal *fylke* (county), western Norway. At the mouth of Storfjorden, Ålesund is set on two islands, Nørvøya and Aspøy, connected by bridges and overlooked by Aksla (508 ft [155 m]). It dates from the 9th century when Rollo (Rolf) the Ganger built a castle nearby, but township status was not acquired until 1848. After it burned in 1904, the town was rebuilt with stone instead of wood. Ålesund is a regional commercial centre and a point for touring the hills of the Sunnmøre region, the Norang Valley, the Øye glaciers, the island of Runde, and the Viking village of Giske. The site of Norway's largest fishing harbour, it is a base

Ålesund, at the mouth of Storfjorden, Norway
Mittet Foto A/S

for cod and halibut fishing trawlers and the headquarters of the Arctic sealing fleet. Milk and fruit are produced locally. Ålesund has an airport and nationwide road connections, but it is not served by rail. Pop. (1983 est.) mun., 34,909.

alethic modal logic: *see* modal logic.

Aletsch Glacier, the Alps' largest and longest glacier, lying in the Bernese Alps of south central Switzerland. Covering an area of 66 sq mi (171 sq km), it is divided into the Great Aletsch (main) and the Middle and Upper Aletsch (branches). The main glacier is 15 mi (24 km) long and 1 mi (1.6 km) wide. It extends generally southward from the Concordia Platz (where several other glaciers meet) to the Aletschwald (a nature reserve). Descending from the Aletschhorn (peak), the Middle Aletsch reaches the main glacier nearly opposite the Märjelensee, a small lake bordering the Great Aletsch and lying just north of the Eggishorn. The Massa River, a tributary of the Rhône River, issues from the Great Aletsch. The Aletsch Conservation Centre (1976) is at Riederfurka near the glacier. Skiing, mountain climbing, and glacial excursions are popular in the region.

Aleut, a native of the Aleutian Islands and western portion of the Alaska Peninsula. Aleuts speak three mutually intelligible dialects and are closely related to the Eskimo in language, race, and culture. The earliest people, the Paleo-Aleuts, arrived from the Alaskan mainland about 2000 BC.

Aleuts hunted seals, sea otters, whales, sea lions, sometimes walrus, and, in some areas, caribou and bears. Fish, birds, and mollusks were also taken. One-man and two-man skin boats known as bidarkas, or kayaks, and large, open, skin boats (Eskimo umiaks) were used. Aleut women wove fine grass basketry; stone, bone, and ivory were also worked.

Ancient Aleut villages were situated on the seashore near freshwater, with a good landing for boats and in a position safe from surprise attack from other Aleuts or neighbouring tribes. After the arrival of the Russians in the 18th and 19th centuries, internal warfare ceased, and villages were located at river mouths, where salmon were caught in the annual salmon runs. Villages were usually composed of related families. The chieftainship tended to be hereditary, representing prestige and power but not formal authority. A chief might govern several villages or an island, but there was no chief over all Aleuts or even over several islands.

Aleut population declined drastically under Russian domination. When the Russians first arrived, there were about 25,000 Aleuts; in the second half of the 20th century they numbered around 2,500. By the 1830s traditional community life and culture were disrupted.

Only vestiges of the old values, technology, and social forms have survived.

Aleut-Eskimo languages: *see* Eskimo-Aleut languages.

Aleut language, language spoken on the Aleutian, Pribilof, and Commander islands by some native Aleuts; it is classified as a branch of the Eskimo-Aleut languages (*q.v.*). Three mutually intelligible Aleut dialects survive, although one was almost extinct in the late 20th century. The principal dialects are Attuan in the west and Unalaskan in the east.

Aleutian Basin, submarine depression forming the floor of the southwestern section of the Bering Sea in the Pacific Ocean. On the west it rises to meet Siberia and the Kamchatka Peninsula; on the northeast, the continental shelf of North America off southwestern Alaska; and on the south, the Aleutian Islands. The basin extends about 1,100 mi (1,800 km) north–south and 600 mi east–west and lies at a depth of more than 9,800 ft (3,000 m). Its floor is characterized by a thick basaltic crust, which probably belongs to the Paleocene Epoch (from about 54,000,000 to 65,000,000 years ago). The volcanic Aleutian Arc separates it from the floor of the north Pacific Ocean; the Anadyr Current flows southwestward through the basin.

Aleutian Current, also called SUBARCTIC CURRENT, surface oceanic current, an eastward-flowing mixture of the Kuroshio and Oyashio currents, located between the Aleutian Islands and latitude 42° N. Approaching the North American coast, the current divides to become the Alaska and California currents. Another branch of the Aleutian Current enters the Bering Sea, forming a counterclockwise gyre. Near the surface, temperature is reduced by cooling, and salinity by excessive precipitation. Above a depth of 6,600 ft (2,000 m), water transport is estimated at 525,000,000 cu ft (15,000,000 cu m) per second.

Aleutian Islands, chain of small islands, separating the Bering Sea (north) from the main portion of the Pacific Ocean (south) and extending in an arc southwest, then northwest, for about 1,100 mi (1,800 km) from the tip of the Alaska Peninsula to Attu Island, Alaska, U.S. Numbering about 70, the islands occupy a land area of 6,821 sq mi (17,666 sq km) and constitute a census division of the U.S. state of Alaska. The major groups from east to west

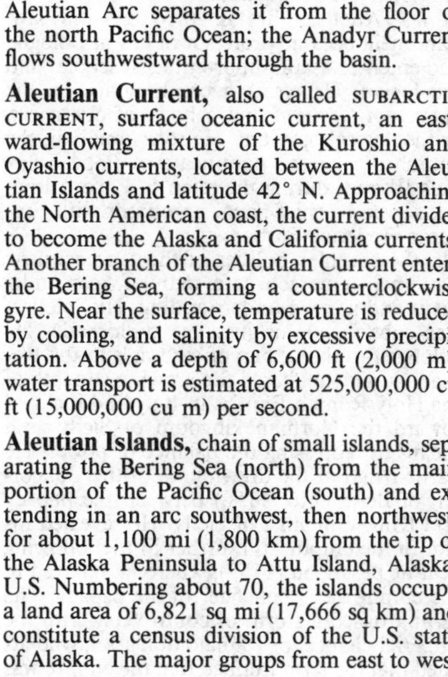

Sweeper Cove of Adak Island, one of the Aleutian Islands, Alaska

Bob and Ira Spring—EB Inc.

are the Fox Islands, the Islands of the Four Mountains, and the Andreanof, Rat, and Near islands. The Commander Islands (Komandorskiye Ostrova) near the Kamchatka Peninsula (Soviet Union) are geographically but not politically part of the Aleutians. The islands form a segment of the circum-Pacific earthquake belt and represent a partially submerged continuation of Alaska's Aleutian Range. Most of them bear marks of volcanic origin, and some remain active. The shores are rocky and worn by the surf, and the approaches are dangerous; the land rises abruptly from the coasts to steep, bold mountains. The main navigational lanes through the chain are the Unimak, Umnak, Amukta, and Seguam passes.

Characterized by fairly uniform temperatures, high winds, heavy rainfall, and persistent fog, the Aleutians are practically devoid of trees but are covered with a luxuriant growth of grasses, sedges, and many flowering plants. The Aleutian Islands unit of the Alaska Maritime National Wildlife Refuge covers 4,250 sq mi and extends between Unimak (east) and Attu (west) islands. By regulating the numbers of wildlife (notably sea otters and seals), the refuge has eliminated the threat of starvation to the native Aleuts, who have always lived by fishing and hunting. The raising of blue foxes has furnished employment for many.

The main settlements are on Unalaska, Adak, and Shemya islands. The oldest, settled 1760–75, is Unalaska, the former headquarters of a large U.S. Coast Guard fleet that patrolled the sealing grounds of the Pribilof Islands to the north. The largest, Adak Station, is the site of a naval station established in 1942. The airport at Shemya Station is an important stopover for flights between the U.S. and the Far East.

In 1741 the Russians sent out Vitus Bering, a Dane, and Aleksey Chirikov, a Russian, on a voyage of discovery. After their ships parted in a storm, Chirikov discovered several of the eastern islands, while Bering discovered several of the western islands. Upon learning of the abundance of fur-bearing animals, Siberian hunters flocked to the Commander Islands and gradually moved eastward across the Aleutians to the mainland. In this manner, Russia gained a foothold in North America but nearly caused the extinction of the Aleuts. The Russians sold the islands, along with the rest of Alaska, to the U.S. in 1867.

During World War II, the strategic importance of the Aleutians became evident. In 1942 the Japanese took over Attu, Agattu, and Kiska islands. A year later, Attu was recaptured by the U.S. after 19 days of heavy fighting. Aleutian military stations are now vital links in the air defense of the North American continent. Amchitka Island has been a site for underground nuclear tests. Pop. (1980) 7,768.

Aleutian low, large atmospheric low-pressure (cyclonic) centre that exists over the Aleutian Islands region in winter; it shifts northward and almost disappears in summer. Although the Aleutian low contains many small eastward-moving low- and high-pressure centres, the region's average pressure is low. It is the source region of the maritime polar air masses that influence the climate of the western U.S. The Northern Hemisphere subpolar low-pressure belt consists of the Aleutian low and the Icelandic low.

Aleutian Range, segment of the Pacific Coast Ranges of western North America, extending southwestward for about 600 mi (970 km) from the west end of the Alaska Range to the head of Cook Inlet of the Gulf of Alaska, U.S. The Aleutian Islands represent a southwest extension of the mountain peaks, which stretch across all of the Alaska Peninsula and include many volcanoes, notably Katmai (6,716 ft [2,047 m]) and Veniaminof. The range embraces the Katmai National Park, the Aniakchak National Monument, and the Valley of Ten Thousand Smokes and was named after the Aleuts, who inhabited the island area.

Aleutian Trench, submarine trench located on the south side of the Aleutian Islands between the Gulf of Alaska and the Commander Islands in the North Pacific Ocean. The Aleutian Trench reaches a maximum depth of 26,604 ft (8,109 m) at about 51° N, 178° W. The average slopes of its northern side range between 3° and 4°, while those of its even shallower southern side are 1° or 2°.

alewife, also called SAWBELLY, GRAYBACK, GASPEREAU, or BRANCH HERRING (*Pomolobus*, or *Alosa, pseudoharengus*), important North American food fish of the herring family, Clupeidae. Deeper bodied than the true herring, the alewife has a pronounced saw-edge on the underside; it grows to about 30 centimetres (1 foot). Except for members of a few lake populations, it spends several years along the

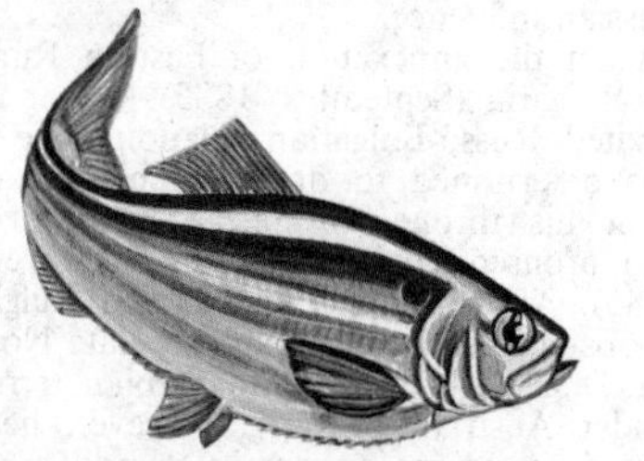

Alewife (*Pomolobus pseudoharengus*)

Painting by Karen Allan

Atlantic coast of North America before ascending freshwater streams (possibly the parent stream) to spawn each spring in ponds or sluggish rivers. Alewives entered the Great Lakes through the St. Lawrence Seaway and the Welland Canal. In the 1960s they multiplied so rapidly that they became a nuisance, threatening the native fishes by competing for the same food sources. Importation of coho and king salmon brought the alewife population into balance in the 1970s.

Alexander, name of rulers grouped below by country or papacy and indicated by the symbol •.

Foreign-language equivalents:

Bulgarian	Aleksandŭr
Greek	Aléxandros
Italian	Alessandro
Latin	Alexander
Polish	Aleksander
Russian	Aleksandr
Serbo-Croatian	Aleksandar

BULGARIA

• **Alexander I** (b. April 5, 1857, Verona, Venice—d. Nov. 17, 1893, Graz, Austria), the first prince of modern autonomous Bulgaria.

The son of Prince Alexander of Hesse (previously created prince of Battenberg upon his morganatic marriage) and a favourite nephew of Alexander II of Russia, Alexander served during 1877 with the Russian forces in the Russo-Turkish War (1877–78) that resulted in the autonomy of Bulgaria. In accordance

Alexander I of Bulgaria

By courtesy of the Bild-Archiv, Osterreichische Nationalbibliothek, Vienna

with the provisions of the Congress of Berlin (1878), Alexander was elected constitutional prince of the newly autonomous Bulgarian state on April 29, 1879, but had to deal with a strong Russian interference in domestic affairs. Saddled with what he regarded as an absurd liberal constitution, however, he set himself to undermining the state's constitutional bases, first dissolving the national assembly (1880) and then suspending the constitution and assuming for himself plenary powers (1881). With the deterioration of his relations with Russia after the accession of Alexander III, however, he restored the constitution (1883) and accepted a new liberal-conservative coalition government to combat Russian influence.

When the annexation of Eastern Rumelia by Bulgaria (September 1885) further exacerbated Russo-Bulgarian relations, the Tsar was determined to drive Prince Alexander from his throne. In Serbia passions were also aroused, and war resulted (November 1885). Alexander successfully led Bulgarian troops against the Serbs and by late November 1885 had pushed into Serbian territory. Under Austrian pressure, however, he was forced to accept an armistice and a peace confirming the status quo (Treaty of Bucharest, March 1886), though he later won the recognition of the Great Powers for Eastern Rumelia's union with Bulgaria (April 1886). Finally, a pro-Russian officers' coup on Aug. 21, 1886, forced him to abdicate, and under heavy guard he was conducted out of the country. He returned shortly to reclaim his crown but, after failing to win the support of Russia, formally abdicated on Sept. 7, 1886. He later assumed the title Graf von Hartenau and served as a general in the Austrian Army.

BYZANTINE EMPIRE

• **Alexander** (b. 870—d. June 6, 913, Constantinople), Byzantine emperor from May 12, 912, third son of the emperor Basil I, who founded the Macedonian dynasty and caused the renewal of warfare between Bulgaria and the Byzantine Empire.

Alexander was crowned co-emperor with his brother Leo VI in 879 after the death of their elder brother, Constantine, but he remained inactive in state affairs until after Leo's death in May 912. Sending Leo VI's fourth wife, Zoe, to a nunnery, he replaced Leo's advisers and reinstated the deposed patriarch, Nicholas Mysticus. Alexander's refusal to pay the annual tribute owed to the Bulgars by the treaty of 896 precipitated war with Symeon, their powerful and aggressive king. Alexander declared his nephew, Leo's young son, later Constantine VII, his heir to the Byzantine throne and was co-regent with him for several months.

FLORENCE

• **Alexander:** *see* Alessandro.

GREECE

• **Alexander** (b. July 20, 1893, Athens—d. Oct. 25, 1920, Tatoi Palace, near Athens), king of Greece from 1917 to 1920.

The second son of King Constantine (ruled 1913–17 and 1920–22) and Queen Sophia, Alexander became king (June 12, 1917) when his father was forced by the Allies of World War I to abdicate and thereby allow his country to join them in the war. Shortly after Alexander's accession to the throne, Eleuthérios Venizélos became premier of Greece, dominating Alexander and the government. Venizélos made Greece a participant in the war and subsequently attained a series of diplomatic triumphs at the peace conference, gaining the territories of Smyrna and eastern and western Thrace from Turkey and Bulgaria (treaties of Sèvres and Neuilly, 1920 and 1919) and presenting Alexander with the prospect of expanding Greece's frontiers farther into Anatolia. Before Alexander was able to pursue that objective, however, he was bitten by a pet monkey and died from blood poisoning.

MACEDONIA

• **Alexander I,** byname ALEXANDER PHILHELLENE, or ALEXANDER THE WEALTHY (d. *c.* 450 BC), 10th king of ancient Macedonia, who succeeded his father, Amyntas I, about 500 BC. More than a decade earlier, Macedonia had become a vassal state of Persia; and in 480 Alexander was obliged to accompany Xerxes I in a campaign through Greece, though he secretly aided the Greek allies. With Xerxes' apparent acquiescence, Alexander seized the Greek colony of Pydna and advanced his frontiers eastward to the Strymon, taking in Crestonia and Bisaltia, with the rich silver deposits of Mt. Dysorus.

It was probably Alexander who organized the mass of his people as a hoplite army called *pezhetairoi* ("foot companions"), with rudimentary political rights, to act as a counterweight to the nobility, the cavalry *hetairoi* ("companions"). His byname, the Philhellene, indicates his efforts to win Greek sympathies; and he obtained admission to the Olympic games. From Persian spoil he erected a golden statue at Delphi, and he entertained the poet Pindar at his court.

• **Alexander III,** byname ALEXANDER THE GREAT, or ALEXANDER OF MACEDONIA (b. 356 BC, Pella, Macedonia—d. June 13, 323, Babylon), king of Macedonia (336–323 BC), son of Philip II. One of the greatest generals in history, he overthrew the Persian empire, carried Macedonian arms to India, and laid the foundations for the Hellenistic world of territorial kingdoms. In the process he became a legendary hero.

A brief account of the life and works of Alexander III follows; for a full biography, *see* MACROPAEDIA: Alexander the Great.

From age 13 to 16, Alexander was taught by the philosopher Aristotle; he came to the Macedonian throne in 336, liquidated potential rivals, and consolidated his political power in Greece. In spring 334 he set off on his celebrated Persian expedition; in the winter of 334–333 he conquered western Asia Minor, and in July 332 stormed the island city of Tyre in his greatest military victory. He then consolidated his hold on the Mediterranean coast and entered and subdued Egypt (332–331). Returning to Tyre (spring 331) he advanced across Mesopotamia and occupied Babylon, city and province. In spring 330 he marched north into Media and occupied its capital, setting out in midsummer on his campaign eastward, to central Asia. Resistance of Scythians and others was strong, and not finally overcome until 328. In early summer 327 Alexander set out to invade India, crossing the Indus in spring 326. He then set about consolidating the empire thus won, dealing with conflicts between Macedonians and Persians, and attempting to solve the problem of wandering mercenaries (summer 324). He died 10 days after being taken ill after a prolonged banquet and drinking bout, and his body, diverted to Egypt, was eventually placed in a golden coffin in Alexandria.

PAPACY

• **Alexander I,** SAINT (d. *c.* 115/119, Rome?; feast day May 3), fifth pope after St. Peter and successor to St. Evaristus. His 10-year rule (105–115 or 109–119) is attested by Pope St. Eusebius (309/310). Some Catholic writers ascribe to him the introduction of holy water and the custom of mixing sacramental wine with water, and he may have made additions to the liturgy. It is believed he suffered martyrdom, possibly by decapitation, under the Roman emperor Trajan or Hadrian. He has sometimes been confused with St. Alexander, one of three Roman martyrs buried along the Via Nomentana. Alexander's jailer, St. Quirinus, and his daughter St. Balbina are said to have been converted by him.

• **Alexander II,** also called (until 1061) ANSELM OF BAGGIO, or OF LUCCA, Italian ANSELMO DA BAGGIO, or DI LUCCA (b. Baggio, near Milan—d. April 21, 1075), pope from 1061 to 1073.

He studied under Lanfranc at Bec. As bishop of Lucca he worked for the abolition of simony and the enforcement of clerical celibacy. Though he was elected pope, the German court nominated Peter Cadalus of Parma as Honorius II, and Alexander was not recognized by the empire until 1064. In 1062 the antipope was dropped by the German regents, and the schism ceased to be important. In cooperation with Hildebrand (later Pope Gregory VII) and St. Peter Damian, Alexander laid the foundations of a reform movement.

• **Alexander III,** original name ROLANDO BANDINELLI (b. *c.* 1105, Siena, Tuscany—d. Aug. 30, 1181, Rome), pope from 1159 to 1181, a vigorous exponent of papal authority, which he defended against challenges by the Holy Roman emperor Frederick Barbarossa and Henry II of England.

Life. After studies in theology and law, Bandinelli became professor of law at Bologna and emerged as an important legal scholar and theologian. He wrote a commentary on the *Decretum Gratiani* and a book of *Sentences,* or theological opinions. He rose rapidly in the church during the pontificate of Pope Eugenius III and, during the reign of Pope Adrian IV, served as chief papal negotiator with Emperor Frederick Barbarossa.

In the complex politics of the 12th century, Bandinelli emerged as a man of keen judgment and shrewd understanding. His intellect was subtle and his instincts diplomatic. He belonged to that group of cardinals in the Roman Curia who feared the growing strength of the Holy Roman Empire in Italy and inclined toward the Norman kingdom of Sicily as a means of redressing the balance of power. He participated in the drawing up of the Concordat of Benevento (1156) between the papacy and King William I of Sicily. He revealed his fear of the empire still further in the following year at Besançon (1157), where he referred to the empire as a "benefice" of the papacy. The term aroused a storm of controversy with the imperial chancellor Rainald of Dassel, who argued that the term implied that the empire was a fief of the church and thus was an insult to the Emperor. Bandinelli and the Pope maintained that it meant only "benefit," but they could hardly have been unaware of the ambiguity of the term. Most likely, they intended its use as a warning to Frederick Barbarossa.

The papal election of 1159, in which the majority of the cardinals chose Bandinelli as pope under the name Alexander III, witnessed a strong effort on the part of Frederick to secure the election of a candidate favourable to his policies. A minority of the cardinals chose Cardinal Octavian (who took the name Victor IV), thus beginning a line of antipopes. Alexander, faced by strong imperial opposition in Italy, fled to France in April 1162. This move prevented a total victory by the Emperor and enabled Alexander to build support in France and England, where he gained the recognition of kings Louis VII and Henry II. During this period Alexander also continued to hold the loyalty of most of the clergy in Italy, especially in the south, and many in Germany. He continued to press forward the program of church reform begun in the previous century under the leadership of Pope Gregory VII. He supported Thomas Becket, archbishop of Canterbury, in his dispute with King Henry II of England on the issue of the legal status of the clergy, despite the risk that he would lose much needed royal support. And he condemned certain propositions of Henry's Constitutions of Clarendon. If Alexander's efforts on Becket's behalf were cautious, he did not compromise the principles on which the Archbishop's case was based. After the murder of Becket, Alexander found Henry easier to deal with and was able to reach some agreement.

Papal relations with the empire in the 12th century revolved around the problems, both theoretical and practical, created by two autonomous powers—one spiritual, the other temporal—vying for authority in the lives of men. The church claimed primary responsibility over moral decisions; secular authorities were attempting to carve out for themselves a sphere of competence over political matters. There was no clear-cut distinction between the two areas, though constant efforts were being made to define them. The important fact is that during the 11th and early 12th centuries medieval society had become increasingly a dualistic society, recognizing two sources of authority and attempting to reconcile them. Alexander found himself playing a large role in the political arena in defense of what he regarded as the legitimate authority of the church. The conflict with Frederick Barbarossa, which consumed most of his efforts in the 1160s and 1170s, was perceived by him as a defense of the papacy, on which the liberty of the church rested.

Following the return of Alexander III to Rome in 1165, which was the result of a more favourable political climate in Italy caused by the temporary absence of Frederick Barbarossa, the conflict entered its critical period. In 1166, Frederick returned to Italy and forced the Pope into exile once more. He entered Rome, where he received the imperial crown from his current antipope, Paschal III. Alexander now turned to the communes of northern Italy for support, finding in many of them a deep concern over the protection of their independence from the empire, a concern that united them with his cause. The result was the formation of the Lombard League, which provided the Pope with the support essential to carry on his conflict with Barbarossa.

Alexander was unwilling, however, to take extreme measures against the Emperor, whom he saw as the legitimate secular leader of Christendom. He rejected the notion proposed by the Byzantine emperor Manuel I Comnenus of a reunification of East and West under Byzantine rule and, instead, placed greater reliance on the Normans of southern Italy and the Lombard cities. It was this policy that was ultimately to prevail and to lay the foundation for the policies followed by the papal Curia in the 13th century. Frederick found himself increasingly isolated in Italy and at odds with powerful elements in Germany. His decisive defeat by the Lombards at Legnano (1176) paved the way for the Peace of Venice (1177), which closed this phase of the struggle.

Assessment. In his rule of the church, Alexander stood in the reform tradition and at the beginning of a line of lawyer-popes that would culminate in Innocent III. His concern for education was typical of his age, which witnessed the early development of the universities, in which he played a role both as teacher and later as pope (by ordering that the license to teach should be conferred on worthy candidates without charge). He presided over important synods at Beauvais (1160) and Tours (1163), as well as over the third Lateran Council (1179). He was among the first popes to express concern over the spread of the Catharist, or Albigensian, heresy in southern France.

With his death, in 1181, the church found itself in a more assured position than at his accession. His policies served as important signposts to his successors. Yet he had succeeded throughout his troubled reign in preserving the image of his moderation and in winning respect even from his enemies. He was not merely one of the abler medieval popes but also one who won greater prestige for his office by his conduct. (J.M.Po.)

BIBLIOGRAPHY. A brief and useful account of the pontificate of Alexander III in English may be found in Marshall Baldwin, *Alexander III and the Twelfth Century* (1966). The standard biography is Marcel Pacaut, *Alexandre III* (1956), in French. Pacaut's views are also available in his study of *Frédéric Barberousse* (1967; Eng. trans. 1970). Of fundamental importance is A. Fliche and V. Martin, *Histoire de l'Église, depuis les origines jusqu'à nos jours,* vol. 9 (1953).

• **Alexander IV,** original name RINALDO DEI SEGNI (b. 1199, Anagni, near Rome—d. May 25, 1261, Viterbo, Papal States), pope from 1254 to 1261.

Alexander was appointed cardinal deacon (1227) and cardinal bishop of Ostia (1231) by his uncle Pope Gregory IX. After becoming pope, Alexander followed the policies of his predecessor Innocent IV: he continued war on Manfred, Emperor Frederick II's bastard son (who was crowned king of Sicily in 1258), by excommunicating him and investing Edmund, son of Henry III of England, with the papal fief of Sicily. He supported the friars at Paris against the secular professors, extended the Inquisition in France, worked for reunion between eastern Christians and Rome, and attempted in vain to organize a crusade against the Tatars.

• **Alexander (V),** byname PETER OF CANDIA, Italian PIETRO DI CANDIA, original Greek name PETROS PHILARGOS (b. *c.* 1339, Candia, Crete—d. May 3, 1410, Bologna, Papal States), antipope from 1409 to 1410.

Alexander became a Franciscan theologian and then archbishop of Milan (1402). Pope Innocent VII appointed him cardinal (1405) and papal legate to Lombardy. Unanimously elected by the invalid Council of Pisa in 1409 when he was 70 years old, Alexander was pope for only 10 months. It was hoped that his election would swiftly terminate the Great Western Schism of 1378–1417, but the council did not persuade Pope Gregory XII and the antipope Benedict XIII to resign. A condominium of three popes resulted. In 1410 Alexander sent to Archbishop Zbynek of Prague a bull which ordered the burning of Wycliffe's heretical works. Alexander died mysteriously, some professing—though without proof—that he was poisoned by his successor, the antipope John XXIII.

• **Alexander VI,** original Spanish name in full RODRIGO DE BORJA Y DOMS, Italian RODRIGO BORGIA (b. 1431, Játiva, Aragon—d. Aug. 18, 1503, Rome), corrupt, worldly, and ambitious pope, whose neglect of the spiritual inheritance of the church contributed to the development of the Protestant Reformation.

Alexander VI, detail of a fresco by Pinturicchio, 1492–94; in the Vatican
Alinari—Art Resource/EB Inc.

Rodrigo was born into the Spanish branch of the prominent and powerful Borgia family. His uncle Alonso de Borgia, bishop of Valencia (later cardinal), supervised his education and endowed him with ecclesiastical benefices while still in his teens. Rodrigo studied law at Bologna, and on Feb. 22, 1456, he was created a cardinal by his uncle, now Pope Calixtus III. As vice chancellor of the Roman Church, Rodrigo amassed enormous wealth and, despite a severe rebuke from Pope Pius II, lived as a Renaissance prince. He patronized the arts and fathered a number of children for whom he provided livings, mainly in Spain. Of a Roman noblewoman, Vanozza Catanei, he had four subsequently legitimized offspring—Juan, Cesare, Jofré, and Lucrezia—whose complicated careers troubled his pontificate.

Despite the shadow of simony that surrounded the disposal of his benefices among the papal electors, Rodrigo emerged from a tumultuous conclave on the night of Aug. 10–11, 1492, as Pope Alexander VI and received the acclaim of the Roman populace. He embarked upon a reform of papal finances and a vigorous pursuit of the war against the Ottoman Turks. His position was menaced by the French king Charles VIII, who invaded Italy in 1494 to vindicate his claim to the Kingdom of Naples. Charles, at the instigation of a rival cardinal of the influential della Rovere family, threatened the Pope with deposition and the convocation of a reform council. Politically isolated, Alexander sought assistance from the Turkish sovereign, Bayezid II. In the course of the Pope's meeting with King Charles in Rome in early 1495, however, he received the traditional obeisance from the French monarch. He still refused to support the King's claim to Naples and, by an alliance with Milan, Venice, and the Holy Roman emperor, eventually forced the French to withdraw from Italy.

In September 1493 Alexander created his teenaged son Cesare a cardinal, along with Alessandro Farnese (the brother of the papal favourite Giulia la Bella and the future pope Paul III). In the course of his pontificate Alexander appointed 47 cardinals to further his complicated dynastic, ecclesiastical, and political policies. His son Juan was made duke of Gandía (Spain) and was married to Maria Enriquez, the cousin of King Ferdinand IV of Castile; Jofré was married to Sancia, the granddaughter of the King of Naples; and Lucrezia was given first to Giovanni Sforza of Milan, and, when that marriage was annulled by papal decree on the grounds of impotence, she was married to Alfonso of Aragon. Upon his assassination Lucrezia received as a third husband Alfonso I d'Este, duke of Ferrara.

Tragedy struck the papal household on June 14, 1497, when Alexander's favourite son, Juan, was murdered. Gravely afflicted, Alexander announced a reform program and called for measures to restrain the luxury of the papal court, reorganize the Apostolic Chancery, and repress simony and concubinage. The Pontiff had shown great forebearance in dealing with the Dominican friar Girolamo Savonarola, who usurped political control in Florence in 1494, condemned the evils of the papal court, and called for the Pope's deposition, and, even before the friar's downfall in May 1498, theologians and men of affairs had expressed support for the papacy. Meanwhile, however, Alexander had returned to a policy of political intrigue.

Cesare resigned the cardinalate in 1498 and married Charlotte d'Albret in order to cement the Borgia alliance with the French king Louis XII, whose request for a marriage annulment was granted by the Pope. By a ruthless policy of siege and assassination, Cesare brought the north of Italy under his control; he conquered the duchies of Romagna, Umbria, and Emilia and earned the admiration of Niccolò Machiavelli, who used Cesare as the model for his classic on politics, *The Prince.* In Rome, Alexander destroyed the power of the Orsini and Colonna families and concluded an alliance with Spain, granting Isabella and Ferdinand the title of Catholic sovereigns. He negotiated the Treaty of Tordesillas (1494), which divided the New World into Portuguese and Spanish zones of exploration and which conferred on the monarchs the *patronato real*—royal control over the church in the mission lands they colonized.

As a patron of the arts, Alexander erected a centre for the University of Rome, restored the Castel Sant'Angelo, built the monumental mansion of the Apostolic Chancery, embellished the Vatican palaces, and persuaded Michelangelo to draw plans for the rebuilding of St. Peter's Basilica. He proclaimed the year 1500 a Holy Year of Jubilee and authorized its celebration with great pomp.

Recent attempts to whitewash Alexander's private conduct have proved abortive. While his religious convictions cannot be challenged, scandal accompanied his activities throughout his career. Even from a Renaissance viewpoint, his relentless pursuit of political goals and unremitting efforts to aggrandize his family were seen as excessive. Neither as corrupt as depicted by Machiavelli and by gossip nor as useful to the church's expansion as apologists would make him, Alexander VI holds a high place on the list of the so-called bad popes. (F.X.M.)

BIBLIOGRAPHY. Ludwig von Pastor, *Geschichte der Päpste seit dem Ausgang des Mittelalters* (*The History of the Popes, from the Close of the Middle Ages,* 2nd ed., vol. 5 and 6, ed. by F.I. Antrobus, 1901), an objective, documented biography based on Vatican sources; Michael de la Bedoyere, *The Meddlesome Friar and the Wayward Pope: The Story of the Conflict Between Savonarola and Alexander VI* (1958), a vigorous, popular account; G. Soranzo, *Il tempo di Alessandro VI papa e di Fra Girolamo Savonarola* (1960), a serious, critical study.

• **Alexander VII,** original name FABIO CHIGI (b. Feb. 13, 1599, Siena, Republic of Florence—d. May 22, 1667, Rome), pope from 1655 to 1667.

Grandnephew of Pope Paul V, Chigi served the church as vice legate at Ferrara and as nuncio at Cologne (1639–51). During the negotiations leading to the Peace of Westphalia (1648), he refused to deliberate with the Protestant heretics and urged the Catholic princes not to sacrifice the rights of the church. The princes, however, were tired of war and, despite his admonition, yielded to France and the Protestants. Secretary of state to Pope Innocent X in 1651 and made cardinal in 1652, Chigi was elected pope on April 7. His pontificate was marked by several disputes.

• **Alexander VIII,** original name PIETRO VITO OTTOBONI (b. April 22, 1610, Venice—d. Feb. 1, 1691, Rome), pope from 1689 to 1691.

Made cardinal in 1652 and bishop of Brescia in 1654, he was elected pope on Oct. 6, 1689. He initiated measures that led eventually to a solution of the disputes between the papacy and Louis XIV of France. Alexander maintained the condemnation of the Gallican Articles of 1682, which restricted papal authority, and opposed Jansenism.

POLAND

• **Alexander,** Polish in full ALEKSANDER JAGIELLOŃCZYK (b. Aug. 5, 1461, Kraków, Pol.—d. Aug. 19, 1506, Vilnius, Lithuania), king of Poland (1501–06) of the Jagiellonian dynasty, successor to his brother John Albert. Alexander carried on the hopeless struggle of the crown against the growing power of the Polish senate and nobles, who deprived him of financial control and curtailed his prerogative. For want of funds, Alexander was unable to assist the Grand Master of the Order of the Sword against Muscovite aggression, or prevent Tsar Ivan III from ravaging Lithuania with the Tatars. The utmost that the King could do was to garrison Smolensk and several other fortresses in his keep and to employ his wife, Helena, the Tsar's daughter, to mediate a truce between his father-in-law and himself. Only the death of Stephen, the great hospodar (ruler) of Moldavia, enabled Poland still to hold her own on the Danube. The liberality of Pope Julius II, who granted Alexander much-needed financial help, enabled the Polish king to restrain somewhat the arrogance of the Teutonic Knights in the Prussian provinces.

RUSSIA

• **Alexander I,** Russian in full ALEKSANDR PAVLOVICH (b. Dec. 23 [Dec. 12, old style], 1777, St. Petersburg, Russia—d. Dec. 1 [Nov. 19, O.S.], 1825, Taganrog), emperor of Russia (1801–25), who alternately fought and befriended Napoleon I during the Napoleonic Wars but who ultimately (1813–15) helped form the coalition that defeated the emperor of the French. He took part in the Congress of Vienna (1814–15), drove for the establishment of the Holy Alliance (1815), and took part in the conferences that followed.

Alexander I, miniature by Jean-Baptiste Isabey, *c.* 1814; in the collection of Mrs. Merriweather Post, Hillwood, Washington, D.C.
By courtesy of Hillwood, Washington, D.C.

Early life. Aleksandr Pavlovich was the first child of Grand Duke Pavel Petrovich (later Paul I) and Grand Duchess Maria Fyodorovna, a princess of Württemberg-Montbéliard. His grandmother, the reigning empress Catherine II (the Great), took him from his parents and raised him herself to prepare him to succeed her. She was determined to disinherit her own son, Pavel, who repelled her by his instability.

A friend and disciple of the philosophers of the French Enlightenment, Catherine invited Denis Diderot, the encyclopaedist, to become Alexander's private tutor. When he declined, she chose Frédéric-César La Harpe, a Swiss citizen, a republican by conviction, and an excellent educator. He inspired deep affection in his pupil and permanently shaped his flexible and open mind.

As an adolescent, Alexander was allowed to visit his father at Gatchina, on the outskirts of St. Petersburg, away from the court. There, Pavel had created a ridiculous little kingdom where he devoted himself to military exercises and parades. Alexander received his military training there under the direction of a tough and rigid officer, Aleksey Arakcheyev, who was faithfully attached to him and whom Alexander loved throughout his life.

Alexander's education was not continued after he was 16, when his grandmother married him to Princess Louise of Baden-Durlach, who was 14, in 1793. The precocious marriage had been arranged to guarantee descendants to the Romanov dynasty, and it was unhappy from the beginning. The sweet and charming girl who became Yelisaveta Alekseyevna was loved by everyone except her husband.

Catherine had already written the manifesto that deprived her son of his rights and designated her grandson as the heir to the throne, when she died suddenly on Nov. 17 (Nov. 6, O.S.), 1796. Alexander, who knew of it, did not dare to disclose the manifesto, and Pavel became emperor.

Ascent to the throne. Paul I's reign was a dark period for Russia. The monarch's tyrannical and bizarre behaviour led to a plot against him by certain nobles and military men, and he was assassinated during the night of March 23 (March 11, O.S.), 1801. Alexander became tsar the next day. The plotters had let him in on the secret, assuring him they would not kill his father but would only demand his abdication. Alexander believed them or, at least, wished to believe that all would go well.

After the darkness into which Paul had plunged Russia, Alexander appeared to his subjects as a radiant dawn. He was handsome, strong, pleasant, humane, and full of enthusiasm. He wanted his reign to be a happy one and dreamed of great and necessary reforms. With four friends, who were of noble families but motivated by liberal ideas—Prince Adam Czartoryski, Count Pavel Stroganov, Count Viktor Kochubey, and Nikolay Novosiltsev—he formed the Private Committee (Neglasny Komitet). Its avowed purpose was to frame "good laws, which are the source of the well-being of the Nation."

Alexander and his close advisers corrected many of the injustices of the preceding reign and made many administrative improvements. Their principal achievement was the initiation of a vast plan for public education, which involved the formation of many schools of different types, institutions for training teachers, and the founding of three new universities. Nevertheless, despite the humanitarian ideas inculcated in him by La Harpe and despite his own wish to make his people happy, Alexander lacked the energy necessary to carry out the most urgent reform, the abolition of serfdom. The institution of serfdom was, in the Tsar's own words, "a degradation" that kept Russia in a disastrously backward state. But to liberate the serfs, who composed three-quarters of the population, would arouse the hostility of their noble masters, who did not want to lose the slaves on whom their wealth and comfort depended. Serfdom was a continuing burden on the Russians. It prevented modernization of the country, which was at least a century behind the rest of Europe.

Out of a sincere desire to innovate, Alexander considered a constitution and "the limitation of the autocracy," but he recoiled before the danger of imposing sudden change on a nobility that rejected it. Moreover, he was a visionary who could not transform his dreams into reality. Because of his unstable personality, he would become intoxicated by the notion of grand projects, while balking at carrying them out. Finally, the "Western" theoretical education of Alexander and his young friends had not prepared them for gaining a clear vision of the realities of Russian life.

Early foreign policy. Displaying an astonishing inconstancy, Alexander abandoned his internal reforms to devote himself to foreign policy, to which he would commit the major portion of his reign. Sensitive to fluctuations in continental politics, he was a "European" who hoped for peace and unity. He felt that he was called to be a mediator, like his grandmother, who had been called the "Arbiter of Europe."

As soon as he came to power, Alexander resealed an alliance with England that had been broken by Paul I. He nonetheless maintained good relations with France in the hope of "moderating" Bonaparte by restraining his spirit of conquest. A feeling of chivalry attached Alexander to the king of Prussia, Frederick William III, and to Queen Louise, and a treaty of friendship was signed with Prussia. Later, he got on good terms with Austria. His idealism persuaded him that these alliances would lead to a European federation.

Napoleon had other ideas. His territorial encroachments, desire for world hegemony, and his coronation in 1804 as emperor forced Alexander to declare war against him. Assuming the role of commander in chief, he relied on the Austrian generals and scorned the counsel of the Russian general Prince Kutuzov, a shrewd strategist. The Russians and Austrians were defeated at Austerlitz, in Moravia, on Dec. 2, 1805, and the emperor Francis II was forced to sign the peace treaty, since his territory was occupied by the enemy. Russia remained intact behind its frontiers. Moreover, Napoleon wanted to spare the Tsar; he hoped to gain his friendship and to divide the world with him. Such a notion did not occur to Alexander, who wanted revenge.

In 1806 Napoleon defeated Prussia at Jena and Auerstädt. Despite the warnings of both his mother and his advisers, the Tsar rushed to the aid of his friend. The battles were fought in east Prussia. After a partial success at Eylau, the Russian Army, under General Bennigsen, was decimated at Friedland, on June 14, 1807. Then occurred the meeting (June 25) of the two emperors on a raft in the middle of the Niemen off Tilsit (now Sovetsk). The sequel of these events demonstrates that, in the course of the Tilsit interview, it was the Tsar of Russia who deceived the Emperor of the French. Seeking to gain time he used his charm to play the admiring friend. He accepted all the victor's conditions, promising to break with England; to adhere to the Continental System set up by Napoleon to isolate and weaken Great Britain; and to recognize the creation of the Grand Duchy of Warsaw, formed from the part of Poland given to Prussia during the Partition of 1795. In "recompense" Napoleon gave Alexander liberty to expand at the expense of Sweden and Turkey.

From Tilsit to the 1812 invasion. Most Russians were angered and humiliated by the Tilsit Alliance; they thought that breaking off trade with England would inevitably create a disastrous economic situation, but Alexander kept his plans secret and bided his time. He reorganized and strengthened his armies with the competent aid of Arakcheyev, the instructor from Gatchina who had become his indispensable colleague. Meanwhile, the monarch's popularity dropped; all levels of the population accused him of having uselessly sacrificed Russian blood and of ruining the country.

Alexander once again turned his attention to internal reforms. He placed responsibility for them on a remarkable legal writer, Mikhail Mikhaylovich Speransky. Of modest origins, Speransky's talent caused him to rise rapidly. He conceived a vast plan for total reorganization of Russian legal structures and authored a complete collection and a systematically coordinated digest of Russian laws. Only a very small part of his great plan was applied, for once again Alexander withdrew from any practical fulfillment, partly because foreign events distracted him from rebuilding his empire on new foundations.

Despite the strong Russian reaction against France, the Tsar again met Napoleon, at Erfurt in Saxony, in 1808, where he showed himself to have become distant from his Tilsit ally. When a new war broke out between France and Austria in 1809, Alexander, despite his commitments, did not intervene in Napoleon's behalf, contenting himself with feigning a military advance. Napoleon reproached the Tsar for trading with England under cover of neutral vessels and for refusing him the hand of his sister, the grand duchess Anna Pavlovna. For his part Alexander tried in vain to obtain from Napoleon a commitment not to create an independent Kingdom of Poland. When Napoleon annexed the German territories on the Baltic, including the Grand Duchy of Oldenburg, a fief of the Tsar's brother-in-law, Alexander protested against what he considered a personal offense.

All of this was a pretext for military preparations on both sides. A violent shift of opinion against Napoleon appeared in Russia. The hostility toward France among the court compelled Alexander to exile his legal adviser, Speransky, an admirer of Napoleon and his Code. Changing his opinions yet again, the Tsar adopted the reactionary ideas of a patriotic group dominated by his favourite sister, the grand duchess Yekaterina Pavlovna. He judged that, under the conditions then prevailing, Russia had best keep its traditional institutions.

The defeat of Napoleon. Napoleon and his Grand Army of 600,000 men invaded Russia on June 24, 1812. The conflict that ensued was justly called the Patriotic War by the Russians; in it, the strong resistance and outstanding endurance of an entire people were displayed. The war transformed Alexander, suffusing him with energy and determination. The French advanced as rapidly as the Russians retreated, drawing them away from their bases. Napoleon thought that, once Moscow was taken, the Tsar would capitulate. But after the bloody Battle of Borodino, Moscow was burned by order of its governor, Count Fyodor Rostopchin, and Alexander did not sue for peace. The conqueror had to camp in a ruined city where he could not remain. The Tsar, meanwhile, under pressure of public opinion, had named Kutuzov, whom he detested, supreme commander. The old warrior, through brilliant strategy and with the aid of heroic partisans, pursued the enemy and drove him from the country. The retreat from Russia, combined with Napoleon's reverses in Spain, precipitated his downfall.

Alexander had declared, "Napoleon or I: from now on we cannot reign together!" He said that the burning of Moscow had "illuminated his soul." He called Europe to arms, to rescue the people who had been enslaved by Napoleon's conquests. His enthusiasm, perseverance, and steadfast determination to triumph aroused the King of Prussia and the Emperor of Austria, and the enheartened allies were victorious at Leipzig in October 1813. This "Battle of Nations" could have been decisive, but Alexander wanted no peace until he reached Paris. He entered Paris triumphantly in March 1814. Napoleon abdicated, and the Tsar reluctantly accepted the restoration of the Bourbons, for whom he had little esteem, and imposed a constitutional charter on the new ruler, Louis XVIII. Alexander showed his generosity toward France, alleviating its condition as a defeated country and protesting that he had made war on Napoleon and not on the French people.

He had become the most powerful sovereign in Europe and the arbiter of its destinies, as he had wished. He inspired the convening of the greatest international congress in history in Vienna, in the autumn of 1814. It was a time of sumptuous feasts and also of diplomatic intrigues and bitter quarrels. The Tsar's allies, whom he had saved, now feared his power and opposed the annexation of Poland to Russia. It was his only claim in reward for what he had done, and he was determined to achieve it.

When Napoleon returned from his exile in Elba and regained the throne, the war resumed, ending with his final defeat by the allies at Waterloo on June 18, 1815. Again the victorious sovereigns met in Paris to frame a peace treaty, and once again Alexander intervened on behalf of France.

The final decade. This period marked a turning point for the Tsar. Since the invasion of his country, he had become religious; he read the Bible daily and prayed often. It was his frequent visits with the pietistic visionary Barbara Juliane Krüdener in Paris that turned him into a mystic. She considered herself a prophetess sent to the Tsar by God, and, if her personal influence was of brief duration, Alexander nevertheless retained his newly found evangelical fervour and came to profess a nondogmatic "universal religion" strongly influenced by Quaker and Moravian beliefs.

Alexander obtained Poland, set it up as a kingdom with himself as king, and gave it a constitution, declaring his attachment to "free institutions" and his desire to "extend them throughout all the countries dependent on him." These words awakened great hopes in Russia, but, when the Tsar returned home after a long absence, he was no longer thinking of reform. He devoted his entire attention to the Russian Bible Society and to an unfortunate innovation, the military colonies, by which he attempted to settle soldiers and their families on the land so that they might enjoy more stable lives. These ill-conceived colonies brought great suffering to Russian soldiers and peasants alike.

After the Second Treaty of Paris, Alexander I, inspired by piety, formed the Holy Alliance, which was supposed to bring about a peace based on Christian love to the monarchs and peoples of Europe. It is possible to see in the alliance the beginnings of a European federation, but it would have been a federation with ecumenical, rather than political, foundations.

The idealistic tsar's vision came to a sad end, for the alliance became a league of monarchs against their peoples. Its members—following up the congress with additional meetings at Aix-la-Chapelle, Troppau, Laibach (Ljubljana), and Verona—revealed themselves as the champions of despotism and the defenders of an order maintained by arms. When a series of uprisings against despotic regimes in Italy and Spain broke out, the "holy allies" responded with bloody repression. Alexander himself was badly shaken by the mutiny of his Semyonovsky regiment and thought he detected the presence of revolutionary radicalism.

This marked the end of his liberal dreams, for, from then on, all revolt appeared to him as a rebellion against God. He shocked Russia by refusing to support the Greeks, his co-religionists, when they rose against Turkish tyranny, maintaining they were rebels like any others. The Austrian chancellor, Prince Metternich, to whom the Tsar abandoned the conduct of European affairs, shamelessly exploited Alexander's state of mind.

After his return to Russia, he left everything in Arakcheyev's hands. For Alexander, it was a period of lassitude, discouragement, and dark thoughts. For Russia, it was a period of reaction, obscurantism, and struggle against real and imagined subversion. Alexander thought he saw "the reign of Satan" everywhere. In opposition, secret societies spread, composed of young men, mostly from the military, who sought to regenerate and liberalize the country. Plots were made. Alexander was warned of them, but he refused to act decisively. His crown weighed heavily on him, and he did not hide from his family and close friends his desire to abdicate.

The Empress was ill, and Alexander decided to take her to Taganrog, on the Azov Sea. This dismal, windy townlet was a strange watering place. The royal pair, however, who had been so long estranged, enjoyed a calm happiness there. Soon after, during a tour of inspection in the Crimea, Alexander contracted pneumonia or malaria and died on his return to Taganrog.

The Tsar's sudden death, his mysticism, and the bewilderment and the blunders of his entourage all went into the creation of the legend of his "departure" to a Siberian retreat. The refusal to open the Tsar's coffin after his death has only served to deepen the mystery.

(D.Ol.)

BIBLIOGRAPHY. N. Schilder, *Imperator Aleksandr Pervy,* 4 vol. (1890–1904), in Russian; Grand-Duke Nicolas Mikhailovitch, *Le Tsar Alexandre Ier,* 2 vol. (1900); and A. Vandal, *Napoléon et Alexandre,* 3 vol. (1891–96), though old, are still the three most important biographies written since the authors—and especially the two first mentioned—had access to many state and family papers. Two good studies in English are Martha E. Almedingen, *The Emperor Alexander I* (1964); and Michael Jenkins, *Arakcheev: Grand Vizier of the Russian Empire* (1969).

• **Alexander II,** Russian in full ALEKSANDR NIKOLAYEVICH (b. April 29 [April 17, old style], 1818, Moscow—d. March 13 [March 1, O.S.], 1881, St. Petersburg, Russia), emperor of Russia (1855–81). His liberal education and distress at the outcome of the Crimean War, which had demonstrated Russia's backwardness, inspired him toward a great program of domestic reforms, the most important being the emancipation (1861) of the serfs. A period of repression after 1866 led to a resurgence of revolutionary terrorism and to Alexander's own assassination.

Alexander II, detail of a portrait by an unknown artist, 19th century; in the collection of Mrs. Merriweather Post, Hillwood, Washington, D.C.
By courtesy of Hillwood, Washington, D.C.

Life. The future Alexander II was the eldest son of the grand duke Nikolay Pavlovich (who, in 1825, became the emperor Nicholas I) and his wife, Alexandra Fyodorovna (who, before her marriage to the Grand Duke and baptism into the Orthodox Church, had been the princess Charlotte of Prussia). Alexander's youth and early manhood were overshadowed by the overpowering personality of his dominating father, from whose authoritarian principles of government he was never to free himself. But at the same time, at the instigation of his mother, responsibility for the boy's moral and intellectual development was entrusted to the poet Vasily Zhukovsky, a humanitarian liberal and romantic. Alexander, a rather lazy boy of average intelligence, retained throughout his life traces of his old tutor's romantic sensibility. The tensions created by the conflicting influences of Nicholas I and Zhukovsky left their mark on the future emperor's personality. Alexander II, like his uncle Alexander I before him (who was educated by a Swiss republican tutor, a follower of Rousseau), was to turn into a "liberalizing," or at any rate humanitarian, autocrat.

Alexander succeeded to the throne at the age of 36, following the death of his father in February 1855, at the height of the Crimean War. The war had revealed Russia's glaring backwardness in comparison with more advanced nations like England and France. Russian defeats, which had set the seal of final discredit on the oppressive regime of Nicholas I, had provoked among Russia's educated elite a general desire for drastic change. It was under the impact of this widespread urge that the Tsar embarked upon a series of reforms designed, through "modernization," to bring Russia into line with the more advanced Western countries.

Among the earliest concerns of the new emperor (once peace had been concluded in Paris in the spring of 1856 on terms considered harsh by the Russian public) was the improvement of communications. Russia at this time had only one railway line of significance, that linking the two capitals of St. Petersburg and Moscow. At Alexander's accession there were fewer than 600 miles (965 kilometres) of track; when he died in 1881, some 14,000 miles (22,525 kilometres) of railway were in operation. In Russia, as elsewhere, railway construction, in its turn, meant a general quickening of economic life in a hitherto predominantly feudal agricultural society. Joint-stock companies developed, as did banking and credit institutions. The movement of grain, Russia's major article of export, was facilitated.

The same effect was achieved by another measure of modernization, the abolition of serfdom. In the face of bitter opposition from landowning interests, Alexander II, overcoming his natural indolence, took an active personal part in the arduous legislative labours that on Feb. 19, 1861, culminated in the Emancipation Act. By a stroke of the autocrat's pen, tens of millions of human chattels were given their personal freedom. By means of a long-drawn-out redemption operation, moreover, they were also endowed with modest allotments of land. Although for a variety of reasons the reform failed in its ultimate object of creating an economically viable class of peasant proprietors, its psychological impact was immense. It has been described as "the greatest social movement since the French Revolution" and constituted a major step in the freeing of labour in Russia. Yet at the same time, it helped to undermine the already shaken economic foundations of Russia's landowning class.

The abolition of serfdom brought in its train a drastic overhaul of some of Russia's archaic administrative institutions. The most crying abuses of the old judicial system were remedied by the judicial statute of 1864. Russia, for the first time, was given a judicial system that in important respects could stand comparison with those of Western countries (in fact, in many particulars it followed that of France). Local government in its turn was remodelled by the statute of 1864, setting up elective local assemblies known as *zemstva.* Their gradual introduction extended the area of self-government, improved local welfare (education, hygiene, medical care, local crafts, agronomy), and brought the first rays of enlightenment to the benighted Russian villages. Before long *zemstvo* village schools powerfully supported the spread of rural literacy. Meanwhile, Dmitry Milyutin, an enlightened minister of war, was carrying out an extensive series of reforms affecting nearly every branch of the Russian military organization. The educative role of military service was underlined by a marked improvement of military schools. The army statute of 1874 introduced conscription for the first time, making young men of all classes liable to military service.

The keynote of these reforms—and there were many lesser ones affecting various aspects of Russian life—was the modernization of Russia, its release from feudalism, and acceptance of Western culture and technology. Their aim and results were the reduction of class privilege, humanitarian progress, and economic development. Moreover, Alexander, from the moment of his accession, had instituted a political "thaw." Political prisoners had been released and Siberian exiles allowed to return. The personally tolerant emperor had removed or mitigated the heavy disabilities weighing on religious minorities, particularly Jews and sectarians. Restrictions on foreign travel had been lifted. Barbarous medieval punishments were abolished. The severity of Russian rule in Poland was relaxed. Yet, notwithstanding these measures, it would be wrong, as is sometimes done, to describe Alexander II as a liberal. He was in fact a firm upholder of autocratic principles, sincerely convinced both of his duty to maintain the God-given autocratic power he had inherited and of Russia's unreadiness for constitutional or representative government.

Practical experience only strengthened these convictions. Thus, the relaxation of Russian rule in Poland led to patriotic street demonstrations, attempted assassinations, and, finally, in 1863, to a national uprising that was only suppressed with some difficulty—and under threat of Western intervention on behalf of the Poles. Even more serious, from the Tsar's point of view, was the spread of nihilistic doctrines among Russian youth, producing radical leaflets, secret societies, and the beginnings of a revolutionary movement. The government, after 1862, had reacted increasingly with repressive police measures. A climax was reached in the spring of 1866, when Dmitry Karakozov, a young revolutionary, attempted to kill the Emperor. Alexander—who bore himself gallantly in the face of great danger—escaped almost by a miracle. The attempt, however, left its mark by completing his conversion to conservatism. For the next eight years, the Tsar's leading minister—maintaining his influence at least in part by frightening his master with real and imaginary dangers—was Pyotr Shuvalov, the head of the secret police.

The period of reaction following Karakozov's attempt coincided with a turning point in Alexander's personal life, the beginning of his liaison with Princess Yekaterina Dolgorukaya, a young girl to whom the aging emperor had become passionately attached. The affair, which it was impossible to conceal, absorbed the Tsar's energies while weakening his authority both in his own family circle (his wife, the former princess Marie of Hesse-Darmstadt, had borne him six sons and two daughters) and in St. Petersburg society. His sense of guilt, moreover, made him vulnerable to the pressures of the Pan-Slav nationalists, who used the ailing and bigoted empress as their advocate when in 1876 Serbia became involved in war with the Ottoman Empire. Although decidedly a man of peace, Alexander became the reluctant champion of the oppressed Slav peoples and in 1877 finally declared war on Turkey. Following initial setbacks, Russian arms eventually triumphed, and, early in 1878, the vanguard of the Russian armies stood encamped on the shores of the Sea of Marmara. The prime reward of Russian victory—seriously reduced by the European powers at the Congress of Berlin—was the independence of Bulgaria from Turkey. Appropriately, that country still honours Alexander II among its "founding fathers" with a statue in the heart of its capital, Sofia.

Comparative military failure in 1877, aggravated by comparative diplomatic failure at the conference table, ushered in a major crisis in the Russian state. Beginning in 1879, there was a resurgence of revolutionary terrorism soon concentrated on the person of the Tsar himself. Following unsuccessful attempts to shoot him, to derail his train, and finally to blow up the Winter Palace in St. Petersburg itself, Alexander, who under personal attack had shown unflinching courage based on a fatalist philosophy, entrusted supreme power to a temporary dictator. The minister of the interior, Count Mikhail Loris-Melikov, was charged with exterminating the terrorist organization (calling itself People's Will) while at the same time conciliating moderate opinion, which had become alienated by the repressive policies pursued since 1866. At the same time, following the death of the Empress in 1880, the Tsar had privately married Yekaterina Dolgorukaya (who had borne him three children) and was planning to proclaim her his consort. To make this step palatable to the Russian public, he intended to couple the announcement with a modest concession to constitutionalist aspirations. There were to be two legislative commissions including indirectly elected representatives. This so-called Loris-Melikov Constitution, if implemented, might possibly have become the germ of constitutional development in Russia. But on the day when, after much hesitation, the Tsar finally signed the proclamation announcing his intentions (March 1, 1881), he was mortally wounded by bombs in a plot sponsored by People's Will.

It can be said that he was a great historical figure without being a great man, that what he did was more important than what he was. His Great Reforms indeed rank in importance with those of Peter the Great and Lenin, yet the impact of his personality was much inferior to theirs. The Tsar's place in history—a substantial one—is due almost entirely to his position as the absolute ruler of a vast empire at a critical stage in its development.

Assessment. The modernization of Russian institutions, though piecemeal, was extensive. In Alexander's reign, Russia built the base needed for emergence into capitalism and industrialization later in the century. At the same time, Russian expansion, especially in Asia, steadily gathered momentum. The sale of Alaska to the U.S. in 1867 was outweighed in importance by the acquisition of the Maritime Province from China (1858 and 1860) and the founding of Vladivostok as Russia's far eastern capital (1860), the definitive subjugation of the Caucasus (in the 1860s), and the conquest of central Asia (Khiva, Bokhara, Turkestan) in the 1870s. The contribution of the reign to the development of what was to be described as Russia's "cotton imperialism" was immense. Here also, the reign of Alexander paved the way for the later phases of Russian imperialism in Asia.

Alexander's importance lies chiefly in his efforts to assist Russia's emergence from the past. To some extent, he was, of course, the representative of forces—intellectual, economic, and political—that were stronger than himself or, indeed, any single individual. After the Crimean War, the modernization of Russia had indeed become imperative if Russia was to retain its position as a major European power. But even within the context of a wider movement, the role of Alexander II, through his position as autocratic ruler, was a highly important one. The Great Reforms, both in what they achieved and in what they failed to do, bear the imprint of his personality. Unfortunately, however, by placing great power in the hands of the influential reactionary minister K.P. Pobedonostsev—whom he appointed minister for church affairs (procurator of the Holy Synod) and entrusted with the education of his son and heir, the future Alexander III—Alexander II, perhaps unwittingly, did much to frustrate his own reforming policies and to set Russia finally on the road to revolution.

(W.E.Mo.)

BIBLIOGRAPHY. S.S. Tatishchev, *Imperator Aleksandr II,* 2 vol. (1903), the standard life of Alexander II, is the prerevolutionary official biography. The fullest modern biography is C. de Grunwald, *Le Tsar Alexandre II et son temps* (1963). A short, concise life of the Emperor is W.E. Mosse, *Alexander II and the Modernization of Russia* (1958). Two popular biographies are S. Graham, *Alexander II: Tsar of Russia* (1935); and Martha E. Almedingen, *The Emperor Alexander II* (1962).

• **Alexander III,** Russian in full ALEKSANDR ALEKSANDROVICH (b. March 10 [Feb. 26, old style], 1845, St. Petersburg, Russia—d. Nov. 1 [Oct. 20, O.S.], 1894, Livadiya, Crimea), emperor of Russia from 1881 to 1894, opponent of representative government, and supporter of Russian nationalism. He adopted programs, based on the concepts of Orthodoxy, autocracy, and *narodnost* (a belief in the Russian people), that included the Russification of national minorities in the Russian Empire as well as persecution of the non-Orthodox religious groups.

Alexander III, detail of a portrait by an unknown artist, 19th century; in the collection of Mrs. Merriweather Post, Hillwood, Washington, D.C.

By courtesy of Hillwood, Washington, D.C.

The future Alexander III was the second son of Alexander II and of Maria Aleksandrovna (Marie of Hesse-Darmstadt). In disposition he bore little resemblance to his softhearted, impressionable father and still less to his refined, chivalrous, yet complex granduncle, Alexander I. He gloried in the idea of being of the same rough texture as the great majority of his subjects. His straightforward manner savoured sometimes of gruffness, while his unadorned method of expressing himself harmonized well with his roughhewn, immobile features. During the first 20 years of his life, Alexander had no prospect of succeeding to the throne. He received only the perfunctory training given to grand dukes of that period, which did not go much beyond primary and secondary instruction, acquaintance with French, English, and German, and military drill. When he became heir apparent on the death of his elder brother Nikolay in 1865, he began to study the principles of law and administration under the jurist and political philosopher K.P. Pobedonostsev, who influenced the character of his reign by instilling into his mind hatred for representative government and the belief that zeal for Orthodoxy ought to be cultivated by every tsar.

The tsesarevich Nikolay, on his deathbed, had expressed a wish that his fiancée, Princess Dagmar of Denmark, thenceforward known as Maria Fyodorovna, should marry his successor. The marriage proved a most happy one. During his years as heir apparent—from 1865 to 1881—Alexander let it be known that certain of his ideas did not coincide with the principles of the existing government. He deprecated undue foreign influence in general and German influence in particular. His father, however, occasionally ridiculed the exaggerations of the Slavophiles and based his foreign policy on the Prussian alliance. The antagonism between father and son first appeared publicly during the Franco-German War, when the Tsar sympathized with Prussia and the tsarevich Alexander with the French. It reappeared in an intermittent fashion during the years 1875–79, when the disintegration of the Ottoman Empire posed serious problems for Europe. At first the Tsarevich was more Slavophile than the government, but he was disabused of his illusions during the Russo-Turkish War of 1877–78, when he commanded the left wing of the invading army. He was a conscientious commander, but he was mortified when most of what Russia had obtained by the Treaty of San Stefano was taken away at the Congress of Berlin under the chairmanship of the German chancellor Otto von Bismarck. To this disappointment, moreover, Bismarck shortly afterward added the German alliance with Austria for the express purpose of counteracting Russian designs in eastern Europe. Although the existence of the Austro-German alliance was not disclosed to the Russians until 1887, the Tsarevich reached the conclusion that for Russia the best thing to do was to prepare for future contingencies by a radical scheme of military and naval reorganization.

On March 13 (March 1, O.S.), 1881, Alexander II was assassinated, and the following day autocratic power passed to his son. In the last years of his reign, Alexander II had been much disturbed by the spread of nihilist conspiracies. On the very day of his death he signed an *ukaz* creating a number of consultative commissions that might have been transformed eventually into a representative assembly. Alexander III cancelled the *ukaz* before it was published and in the manifesto announcing his accession stated that he had no intention of limiting the autocratic power he had inherited. All the internal reforms that he initiated were intended to correct what he considered the too liberal tendencies of the previous reign. In his opinion, Russia was to be saved from anarchical disorders and revolutionary agitation not by the parliamentary institutions and so-called liberalism of western Europe but by the three principles of Orthodoxy, autocracy, and *narodnost.*

Alexander's political ideal was a nation containing only one nationality, one language, one religion, and one form of administration; and he did his utmost to prepare for the realization of this ideal by imposing the Russian language and Russian schools on his German, Polish, and Finnish subjects, by fostering Orthodoxy at the expense of other confessions, by persecuting the Jews, and by destroying the remnants of German, Polish, and Swedish institutions in the outlying provinces. In the other provinces he clipped the feeble wings of the *zemstvo* (an elective local administration resembling the county and parish councils in England) and placed the autonomous administration of the peasant communes under the supervision of landed proprietors appointed by the government. At the same time, he sought to strengthen and centralize the imperial administration and to bring it more under his personal control. In foreign affairs he was emphatically a man of peace but not a partisan of the doctrine of peace at any price. Though indignant at the conduct of Bismarck toward Russia, he avoided an open rupture with Germany and even revived for a time the Alliance of the Three Emperors between the rulers of Germany, Russia, and Austria. It was only in the last years of his reign, especially after the accession of William II as German emperor in 1888, that Alexander adopted a more hostile attitude toward Germany. The termination of the Russo-German alliance in 1890 drove Alexander reluctantly into an alliance with France, a country that he strongly disliked as the breeding place of revolutions. In Central Asian affairs he followed the traditional policy of gradually extending Russian domination without provoking a conflict with Great Britain, and he never allowed the bellicose partisans of a forward policy to get out of hand.

As a whole, Alexander's reign cannot be regarded as one of the eventful periods of Russian history; but it is arguable that under his hard, unsympathetic rule the country made some progress. (M.T.F.)

BIBLIOGRAPHY. Hugh Seton-Watson, *The Russian Empire, 1801–1917* (1967), massive information clearly organized and objectively presented; *The Decline of Imperial Russia, 1855–1914* (1952), good factual record with little attention to personalities; M.T. Florinsky, *Russia: A History and an Interpretation,* vol. 2 (1955), a compact, detailed account, factual and analytical.

SCOTLAND

• **Alexander I** (b. *c.* 1080—d. April 1124, probably Stirling, Stirlingshire, Scot.), king of Scotland from 1107 to 1124.

The son of King Malcom III Canmore (ruled 1058–93), Alexander succeeded to the throne upon the death of his brother King Edgar (ruled 1097–1107). In accordance with Edgar's instructions, Alexander allowed his younger brother and heir, David, to rule southern Scotland.

Alexander probably acknowledged King Henry I of England as his overlord. He married Henry's illegitimate daughter, Sibylla, and in 1114 he led a Scottish contingent in Henry's Welsh campaigns. Nevertheless, Alexander strove to preserve the independence of the Scottish church from the English church and to assert his will over the Scottish bishops. The outcome of these struggles was inconclusive at his death. He was succeeded by David (David I, 1124–53), who ruled over the whole of Scotland.

• **Alexander II** (b. Aug. 24, 1198, Haddington, East Lothian, Scot.—d. July 8, 1249, Kerrera Island, Argyll), king of Scotland from 1214 to 1249; he maintained peace with England and greatly strengthened the Scottish monarchy.

Alexander came to the throne on the death of his father, William I the Lion (ruled 1165–1214). When the English barons rebelled against King John (ruled 1199–1216) in 1215, Alexander sided with the insurgents in the hope of regaining territory he claimed in northern England. After the rebellion collapsed in 1217, he did homage to King Henry III (ruled 1216–72), and in 1221 he married Henry's sister, Joan (d. 1238). In 1237 Henry and Alexander concluded an agreement (Peace of York) by which the Scots king abandoned his claim to land in England but received in exchange several English estates. The boundary of Scotland was fixed approximately at its present location.

Meanwhile, Alexander was suppressing rebellious Scots lords and consolidating his rule over parts of Scotland that had hitherto only nominally acknowledged royal authority. In 1222 he subjugated Argyll. He died as he was preparing to conquer the Norwegian-held islands along Scotland's west coast.

• **Alexander III** (b. Sept. 4, 1241—d. March 18/19, 1286, near Kinghorn, Fife, Scot.), king of Scotland from 1249 to 1286, the last major ruler of the dynasty of kings descended from Malcolm III Canmore (ruled 1058–93), who consolidated royal power in Scotland. Alexander left his kingdom independent, united, and prosperous, and his reign was viewed as a golden age by Scots caught up in the long, bloody conflict with England after his death.

The only son of King Alexander II (ruled 1214–49), Alexander III was seven years old when he came to the throne. In 1251 he was married to Margaret (d. 1275), the 11-year-old daughter of England's King Henry III. Henry immediately began plotting to obtain suzerainty over Scotland. In 1255 a pro-English party in Scotland seized Alexander, but two years later the anti-English party gained the upper hand and controlled the government until Alexander came of age (1262).

In 1263 Alexander repulsed an invasion by the Norwegian king Haakon IV, who ruled the islands along Scotland's west coast. Haakon's son, King Magnus V, in 1266 ceded to Alexander the Hebrides and the Isle of Man. Alexander was killed in 1286 when his horse fell over a cliff. Because his children were all dead, his infant grandchild Margaret "the Maid of Norway" (d. 1290) succeeded to the throne.

SELEUCID EMPIRE

• **Alexander** BALAS, also called ALEXANDER EPIPHANES (d. 145 BC), king of Syria and Pergamum (Greek Asia Minor) and ruler of the remains of the Seleucid Empire (150–145 BC).

The pretended son of Antiochus IV Epiphanes, he won the Seleucid throne with the help of mercenaries, challenging and slaying Demetrius I Soter, the direct Seleucid heir. With the support of the Roman Senate and the Egyptian Ptolemaic dynasty, he ruled the remains of the Seleucid Empire until he was killed in battle against Demetrius II Nicator, son of Demetrius I Soter.

During his reign, Alexander pacified Palestine by naming Jonathan Maccabeus as Jewish governor but alienated the population by his revelry while feigning interest in politics and Stoic philosophy.

SERBIA

• **Alexander,** Serbo-Croatian in full ALEKSANDAR KARAGEORGEVIĆ (b. Oct. 11 [Sept. 29, old style], 1806, Topola, Serbia—d. May 4 [April 22, O.S.], 1885, Temesvár, Binat, Austria-Hungary), prince of Serbia from 1842 to 1858.

The third son of Karageorge, who had led the movement to win Serb autonomy from the Ottoman Turks (1804–13), Alexandar lived in exile until 1842, when the Skupština (Serb parliament) elected him prince of Serbia. Assuming the throne despite Russian challenges to his election and Turkish refusals to make his office hereditary, Alexander allowed his administration to be dominated by an oligarchy consisting of an elite group of senators. In an effort to modernize the Serb bureaucracy, it attempted to improve the principality's educational, legal, and judicial systems, as well as to foster the use of money and credit in Serbia's economy. Although Alexander and his senator-advisers were well intentioned, their innovations, which were quickly undermined by corruption and abuse, stimulated widespread discontent in Serbia's traditional peasant society. In addition, the new intelligentsia, created to provide trained personnel for the reformed bureaucracy, constituted another centre of opposition that encouraged emulation of western European parliamentary government, rather than the simple adoption of bureaucratic reforms.

Alexander responded to a revolt of the Serbs of south Hungary against the Hungarians in 1848 by refusing to support the revolutionary movement but allowing volunteers to cross the border. He later succumbed to Austrian demands that Serbia refrain from aiding Russia and again maintain neutrality during the Crimean War (1853–56). Thus, he lost the support of the many Serbs who advocated pan-Slavism.

Although he overthrew some of the main oligarchs in 1857, the Skupština, which met the following year, insisted that he abdicate. Reluctantly agreeing, Alexander spent the remainder of his life in exile.

Consult the INDEX *first*

• **Alexander,** Serbo-Croatian in full ALEKSANDAR OBRENOVIĆ (b. Aug. 14 [Aug. 2, old style], 1876, Belgrade—d. June 11 [May 29, O.S.], 1903, Belgrade), king of Serbia (1889–1903), whose unpopular authoritarian reign resulted not only in his assassination but also in the end of the Obrenović dynasty.

The only child of Prince, later King, Milan (ruled 1868–89) and his consort, Natalie, Alexander ascended the Serbian throne on March 6 (Feb. 22, O.S.), 1889, after his father had abdicated and named a regency council for the youthful Alexander. On April 13 (April 1, O.S.), 1893, Alexander dismissed the regency council and assumed active control of the government.

Initially well received, Alexander soon alienated a large segment of his supporters by excluding the popular pro-Russian Radical Party from his cabinets, abolishing (1894) the liberal constitution of 1889 in favour of the 1869 constitution (which limited the legislature's powers), frequently changing his Cabinet ministers, and bringing his pro-Austrian father (who had been living abroad since 1889) back to Serbia to become commander in chief of the armed forces (1897). When the press voiced its bitter opposition to Alexander's policies and authoritarian manner, the King, urged by his father, restricted the freedoms of the press and of association. An unsuccessful attempt on Milan's life (1899) brought more repressive measures, which particularly curtailed the activities of the Radicals.

Alexander's prestige reached a low point in 1900, when, despite the strong objections of his father and other political advisers, he declared his intention to marry his mistress, Draga Mašin, *née* Lunjevica, the widow of a Bohemian engineer, a former lady-in-waiting to Alexander's mother, and a woman 10 years his senior with a dubious reputation. Alexander's entire Cabinet resigned in protest.

The scandal forced Alexander to grant a more liberal constitution (1901) and to create a senate as the second house in the legislature. During his reign he also improved his state's economy, reformed the army, and tried to improve Serbia's international position by encouraging the revival of the Balkan alliances that were originally negotiated between 1865 and 1868 by King Michael (Mihailo Obrenović; ruled 1860–68).

But Alexander also made a mockery of constitutional government by suspending the constitution for a few hours when he wanted to make unconstitutional changes (1903). Consequently, with opposition to Alexander mounting, the country generally welcomed the coup d'etat by the military conspirators who invaded the royal palace and murdered Alexander, Draga, and some members of the court.

YUGOSLAVIA

• **Alexander I** (b. Dec. 16 [Dec. 4, old style], 1888, Cetinje, Montenegro—d. Oct. 9, 1934, Marseille), king of the Serbs, Croats, and Slovenes (1921–29) and of Yugoslavia (1929–34), who struggled to create a united state out of his politically and ethnically divided land.

The second son of Peter Karageorgević (king of Serbia 1903–18 and king of the Serbs, Croats, and Slovenes 1918–21) and Zorka of Montenegro, Alexander spent his early youth in Geneva with his father, then in exile from Serbia, and in 1899 went to St. Petersburg, where he entered the Russian imperial corps of pages (1904). In 1909, however, when his elder brother renounced his right of succession, Alexander, having become heir apparent, joined his family in Serbia.

A distinguished commander in the Balkan Wars of 1912–13, Alexander was appointed regent of Serbia by the ailing king Peter (June 24, 1914) and during World War I served as commander in chief of Serbia's armed forces, entering Belgrade in triumph on Oct. 31, 1918. As prince regent, he proclaimed the creation of the Kingdom of the Serbs, Croats, and Slovenes, on Dec. 1, 1918.

The instability of the new state was demonstrated by an attempted assassination on the day (June 28, 1921) that Alexander swore an oath to uphold the constitution. Nevertheless, on August 16 he succeeded his father as king and on June 8, 1922, he married Marie, a daughter of Ferdinand I of Romania. Later Alexander attempted to consolidate the rival nationality groups and political parties into a unified state.

During the 1920s mounting political tensions forced numerous changes in government ministers and culminated in the murder of several Croat deputies by a Montenegrin deputy during a Skupština (parliament) session (June 20, 1928). The Croat members then withdrew from the Skupština; and, because Alexander could neither negotiate a satisfactory compromise for restructuring the body nor form an effective government, he dissolved it, abolished the constitution of 1921, and established a royal dictatorship (Jan. 6, 1929).

Continuing his efforts to unify his subjects, he changed the name of the country to Yugoslavia (Oct. 3, 1929), outlawed all political parties based on ethnic, religious, or regional distinctions, reorganized the state administratively, and standardized legal systems, school curricula, and national holidays. He also tried to relieve the peasantry's financial difficulties, and he eased relations with Bulgaria (1933) and engaged Yugoslavia in the Little Entente (with Czechoslovakia and Romania) and the Balkan Entente, an alliance with Greece, Turkey, and Romania (1934).

In the process Alexander created a police state that required military support for survival. When a new constitution was promulgated (Sept. 3, 1931), the dictatorship was, in effect, given a legal foundation. Although Alexander's acts were at first well received, demands for a return to democratic forms intensified by 1932, when a major economic crisis resulting from the worldwide depression added to political dissatisfaction. As a result, Alexander seriously considered restoring a parliamentary form of government; but before he was able to do so, he was assassinated by an agent of Croatian separatists while making a state visit to France.

Alexander, SAINT: *see* Alexander I *under* Alexander (Papacy).

Alexander AETOLUS (fl. *c.* 280 BC), Greek poet of Pleuron, in Aetolia. He was appointed by Ptolemy II Philadelphus, Macedonian king of Egypt, to arrange and catalog the tragedies in the library at Alexandria. Nothing remains of his own tragic writing except the title of one play, *Astragalistae* ("The Dice Players"). A few fragments of his shorter writings are extant, including a brief appreciation of Euripides. The titles of Alexander's other works are known only because they were quoted by other writers.

Alexander BALAS: *see* Alexander Balas *under* Alexander (Seleucid Empire).

Alexander NEVSKY, SAINT, Russian ALEKSANDR NEVSKY, original name ALEKSANDR YAROSLAVICH (b. *c.* 1220, Vladimir, Grand Principality of Vladimir—d. Nov. 14, 1263, Gorodets; canonized in Russian Church 1547; feast days November 23, August 30), prince of Novgorod (1236–52) and of Kiev (1246–52) and grand prince of Vladimir (1252–63), who halted the eastward drive of the Germans and Swedes but collaborated with the Mongols in imposing their rule on Russia. By defeating a Swedish invasion force at the confluence of the Rivers Izhora and Neva (1240), he won the name Nevsky, "of the Neva."

Alexander was the son of Yaroslav II Vsevolodovich, grand prince of Vladimir, the foremost among the Russian rulers. In 1236 Alexander was elected prince—a figure who functioned as little more than military commander—of the city of Novgorod. In 1239 he married the daughter of the Prince of Polotsk.

When in 1240 the Swedes invaded Russia to punish the Novgorodians for encroaching on Finnish tribes and to bar Russia's access to the sea, Alexander defeated the Swedes at the confluence of the Rivers Izhora and Neva. His standing enhanced by his victory, he apparently began to intervene in the affairs of the city and was expelled a few months later.

When, urged by Pope Gregory IX to "Christianize" the Baltic region, the Teutonic Knights shortly thereafter invaded Russia, Novgorod invited Alexander to return. After a number of battles, Alexander decisively defeated the Germans in the famous "massacre on the ice" in April 1242 on a narrow channel between Lakes Chud (Peipus) and Pskov. Alexander, who continued to fight both the Swedes and Germans and eventually stopped their eastward expansion, also won many victories over the pagan Lithuanians and the Finnic peoples.

In the east, however, Mongol armies were conquering most of the politically fragmented Russian lands. Alexander's father, the grand prince Yaroslav, agreed to serve the new rulers of Russia but died in September 1246 of poisoning after his return from a visit to the Great Khan in Mongolia. When, in the ensuing struggle for the grand princely throne, Alexander and his younger brother Andrew appealed to Khan Batu of the Mongol Golden Horde, he sent them to the Great Khan. Violating Russian customs of seniority, the Great Khan appointed Andrew grand prince of Vladimir and Alexander prince of Kiev—probably because Alexander was Batu's favourite and Batu was in disfavour with the Great Khan. When Andrew began to conspire against the Mongol overlords with other Russian princes and western nations, Alexander went to Saray on the Volga and denounced his brother to Sartak, Batu's son, who sent an army to depose Andrew and installed Alexander as grand prince. Henceforth, for over a century, no northeastern Russian prince challenged the Mongol conquest. Alexander proceeded to restore Russia by building fortifications and churches and promulgating laws. As grand prince, he continued to rule Novgorod through his son Vasily, thus changing the constitutional basis of rule in Novgorod from personal sovereignty by invitation to institutional sovereignty by the principal Russian ruler. When, in 1255, Novgorod, tiring of grand princely rule, expelled Vasily and invited an opponent of Mongol hegemony, Alexander assembled an army and reinstalled his son.

In 1257 the Mongols, in order to levy taxes, took a census in most of Russia. It encountered little opposition, but when news of the impending enumeration reached Novgorod an uprising broke out. In 1258 Alexander, fearing that the Mongols would punish all of Russia for the Novgorodian revolt, helped force Novgorod to submit to the census and to Mongol taxation. This completed the process of imposing the Mongol yoke on northern Russia.

In 1262 uprisings broke out in many towns against the Muslim tax farmers of the Golden Horde, and Alexander made a fourth journey to Saray to avert reprisals. He succeeded in his mission, as well as in obtaining exemption for Russians from a draft of men for a planned invasion of Iran. Returning home, Alexander died on Nov. 14, 1263, in Gorodets on the Volga. After his death Russia once more disintegrated into many feuding principalities. His personal power, based upon support of the princes, boyars, and clergy, as well as the fear of Mongols, could not be transmitted to any other man, including his weak sons.

Whether Alexander was a quisling in his dealings with the Mongol conquerors is a question seldom posed by Russian historians, because some Russian princes had for centuries concluded alliances with Turkic steppe nomads in order to gain advantage in domestic rivalries. Because Alexander was a willing collaborator, he may have reduced the common people's suffering by interceding for them with the Khan. He was supported by the church, which thrived under Mongol protection and tax exemption and feared the anti-Mongol princes who negotiated with the papacy. For these reasons, Alexander by 1381 was elevated to the status of a local saint and was canonized by the Russian Orthodox Church in 1547. Alexander's son Daniel founded the house of Moscow, which subsequently reunited the northern Russian lands and ruled until 1598. Alexander was one of the great military commanders of his time, who protected Russia's western frontier against invasion by Swedes or Germans. This image of him was popular in northwestern Russia and has in succeeding centuries been adduced for propaganda purposes. Thus, after the conclusion of the war with Sweden, the Order of Alexander Nevsky was created in 1725, and during World War II (in July 1942), when Germany had deeply penetrated into the Soviet Union, Stalin pronounced Alexander Nevsky a national hero and established a military order in his name. (R.He.)

BIBLIOGRAPHY. There is no book-length study of Nevsky in English. Information may be found in A.E. Presniakov, *The Formation of the Great Russian State: A Study of Russian History in the Thirteenth to Fifteenth Centuries* (1970; orig. pub. in Russian, 1918); and George Vernadsky, *A History of Russia,* vol. 3, *The Mongols and Russia* (1953).

Alexander OF APHRODISIAS (b. Aphrodisias, Caria, Anatolia; fl. *c.* 200), philosopher who is remembered for his commentaries on Aristotle's works and for his own studies on the soul and the mind.

Toward the end of the 2nd century, Alexander became head of the Lyceum at Athens, an academy then dominated by the syncretistic philosophy of Ammonius Saccas, who blended the doctrines of Plato and Aristotle. Alexander's commentaries were intended to reestablish Aristotle's views in their pure form. Among the extant commentaries are those on Aristotle's *Prior Analytics I,* the *Topics,* the *Meteorology,* the *De sensu,* and the *Metaphysics I–V.* Fragments of lost commentaries are found in later discussions by other writers. In antiquity Alexander's influence was due primarily to the commentaries, which earned him the title "the expositor," but in the Middle Ages he was better known for his original writings. The most important of these are *On Fate,* in which he defends free will against the Stoic doctrine of necessity, or predetermined human action; and *On the Soul,* in which he draws upon Aristotle's doctrine of the soul and the intellect. According to Alexander, the human thought process, which he calls the "mortal intellect," can function only with the help of the "active intellect," which lies in every man and is yet identical with God. This doctrine was frequently and intensely debated in Europe after the beginning of the 13th century. In these disputes, which reflected disagreements over the proper interpretation of Aristotle's attitude toward personal immortality, the Alexandrists accepted Alexander's interpretation that man's intellect does not survive the death of the physical body.

Alexander OF HALES (b. *c.* 1170/85, Hales, Gloucestershire, Eng.—d. 1245, Paris), theologian and philosopher whose doctrines influenced the teachings of such thinkers as St. Bonaventure and John of La Rochelle. The *Summa theologica*, for centuries ascribed to him, is largely the work of followers.

Alexander studied and taught in Paris, receiving the degrees of master of arts (before 1210) and theology (1220). He was archdeacon of Coventry in 1235 and became a Franciscan (*c.* 1236). In Paris he founded the Schola Fratrum Minorum, where he was the first holder, possibly until his death, of the Franciscan chair.

Only the most general features of Alexander's theology and philosophy have been made clear: basically an Augustinian, he had to some extent taken into account the psychological, physical, and metaphysical doctrines of Aristotle, while discarding popular Avicennian tenets of emanations from a Godhead. The "Franciscan" theories of matter and form in spiritual creatures, of the multiplicity of forms, and of illumination combined with experience are probably Alexander's adaptations of similar theories of the Augustinian and other traditions. His original works, apart from sections of the *Summa* and of an *Expositio regulae* ("Exposition of the Rule"), include a commentary on the *Sentences* of Peter Lombard; *Quaestiones disputatae antequam esset frater* ("Questions Before Becoming a Brother . . ."); *Quodlibeta*; sermons; and a treatise on difficult words entitled *Exoticon*. Alexander was known to the Scholastics by the title Doctor Irrefragabilis (Impossible to Refute).

Alexander OF MACEDONIA: *see* Alexander III *under* Alexander (Macedonia).

Alexander OF PHERAE (d. 358 BC), despot of Pherae in Thessaly, Greece, from 369 to 358, whose tyranny caused the intervention of a number of city-states in Thessalian affairs. The other Thessalian cities, refusing to recognize Alexander as *tagos*, or head magistrate, appealed to the Thebans, who sent Pelopidas to their assistance. Alexander imprisoned Pelopidas, and the Thebans had to send a large army to procure his release. In 364 Pelopidas defeated Alexander at Cynoscephalae in Thessaly. Alexander was then compelled by Thebes to acknowledge the freedom of the Thessalian cities, to limit his rule to Pherae, and to join the Boeotian League. He was murdered at his wife's instigation.

Alexander OF TRALLES, Latin ALEXANDER TRALLIANUS (*c.* 525–*c.* 605), Byzantine physician who practiced and taught in Rome, best known for his treatise on pathology and therapy (in 12 books), which served as a basis for instruction long after his death. It was translated into Arabic and Latin (*Libri duodecim de re medica*) and was printed in Greek, Latin, and Greco-Latin editions throughout the 16th century.

Alexander PHILHELLENE: *see* Alexander I *under* Alexander (Macedonia).

Alexander POLYHISTOR, in full LUCIUS CORNELIUS ALEXANDER POLYHISTOR (b. Miletus, in Asia Minor—d. *c.* 35 BC, Laurentum, near Rome), philosopher, geographer, and historian whose fragmentary writings provide valuable information on antiquarian and Jewish subjects.

Imprisoned by the Romans in the war of the Roman general Sulla against King Mithradates of Pontus, Alexander was sold as a slave to a patrician and taken to Rome to educate his master's children. After Alexander's release he continued to live in Italy as a Roman citizen.

Alexander's most important work, of which only fragments exist, consists of 42 books of historical and geographical accounts of nearly all the countries of the ancient world. His other notable treatise is about the Jews; it reproduces in paraphrase relevant excerpts from Jewish, Samaritan, and Gentile writers and is valuable for preserving the substance of Hellenistic Jewish authors of whom otherwise nothing would be known.

Alexander THE GREAT: *see* Alexander III *under* Alexander (Macedonia).

Alexander THE PAPHLAGONIAN (b. Abonouteichos, Paphlagonia; fl. 2nd century AD), celebrated impostor and worker of false oracles. The only account of his career occurs in an exposé by Lucian, whose investigations of Alexander's frauds led to a serious attempt on the writer's life.

Alexander established an oracle of Asclepius (the Greek god of healing) at his native town by staging a "rebirth" of the god in the form of a snake, which he called Glycon. He instituted mystical "rites" from which his particular enemies, the Christians and Epicureans, were excluded. He went so far as to celebrate a marriage between himself and the Moon. Through blackmail and other abuses he was able to amass a fortune.

Alexander THE WEALTHY: *see* Alexander I *under* Alexander (Macedonia).

Alexander, Franz (Gabriel) (b. Jan. 22, 1891, Budapest—d. March 8, 1964, Palm Springs, Calif., U.S.), physician and psychoanalyst sometimes referred to as the father of psychosomatic medicine because of his leading role in identifying emotional tension as a significant cause of physical illness.

Already a physician when he enrolled as the first student at the Berlin Psychoanalytic Institute (1919), Alexander became an assistant there and delivered a lecture series (1924–25) that grew into his first book, *Psychoanalyse der Gesamtpersönlichkeit* (1927; *The Psychoanalysis of the Total Personality,* 1930), a work developing the psychoanalytic theory of the superego and praised by Sigmund Freud. His success in applying psychoanalytic principles to the study and diagnosis of criminal personalities brought him an invitation to the United States (1930), where a professorship in psychoanalysis, the first post of its kind, was created for him at the University of Chicago. A year later, however, he went to Boston to collaborate with William Healy on a psychoanalytic study of delinquency, resulting in their book *Roots of Crime* (1935).

Alexander returned to Chicago in 1932 to establish the Chicago Institute for Psychoanalysis, which he directed until 1956. Under his leadership the institute attracted many analysts and students who conducted extensive research on emotional disturbance and psychosomatic disease, identifying various disorders with particular unconscious conflicts.

From 1938 to 1956 Alexander also served on the faculty of the department of psychiatry at the University of Illinois Medical School, Chicago. In 1956 he embarked on a new research program in psychotherapy and psychosomatic medicine at Mt. Sinai Hospital, Los Angeles. His work there, conducted in cooperation with the University of Southern California and the Southern California Psychoanalytic Institute, particularly explored the effect of the therapist's personality in the treatment process.

A notable authority on Freud, Alexander considered it essential to elaborate Freud's views. Yet he retained a certain independence from Freud, viewing disturbed human relations, rather than disturbed sexuality, as the main cause of neurotic disorder. One of his important works on Freud is *Fundamentals of Psychoanalysis* (1948). His *Western Mind in Transition: An Eyewitness Story* (1960) is partly an autobiographical work, in combination with an analysis of modern civilization.

Alexander, Grover Cleveland (b. Feb. 26, 1887, Elba, Neb., U.S.—d. Nov. 4, 1950, St. Paul, Minn.), professional baseball player, one

Grover Cleveland Alexander, 1929
AP/Wide World Photos

of the finest right-handed pitchers in the history of the game, frequently considered the greatest master of control. From 1911 to 1930 he won 373 or 374 major league games (authorities differ) and lost 208. In his first season he won 28 games. For three consecutive years (1915–17) he won 30 or more games; in 1916, when he achieved 33 victories, 16 were shutouts, a major league record. His career total of 88 or 90 shutouts is second only to Walter Johnson's 110 or 113. Alexander's earned run average of 1.22 in 1915 is one of the lowest in baseball history.

Alexander pitched for three National League teams: the Philadelphia Phillies (1911–17, 1930), the Chicago Cubs (1918–26), and the St. Louis Cardinals (1926–29). His most dramatic performance came in the 1926 World Series when in the seventh and deciding game, he came in as a relief pitcher in the seventh inning with the Cardinals leading 3 to 2 and with the bases loaded. With two out, he struck out Tony Lazzeri. He then pitched scoreless eighth and ninth innings.

After service in World War I, he became an alcoholic and spent his last years in reduced circumstances. He was elected to the Baseball Hall of Fame in 1938.

Alexander (of Tunis), Harold (Rupert Leofric George) Alexander, 1st Earl, also called (1946–52) VISCOUNT ALEXANDER OF TUNIS, or (1942–46) SIR HAROLD ALEXANDER (b. Dec. 10, 1891, London—d. June 16, 1969, Slough, Buckinghamshire, Eng.), prominent

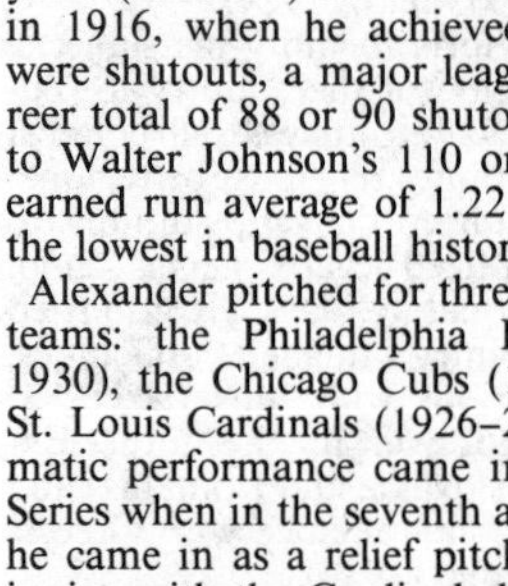

Lord Alexander of Tunis, oil on paper by John Gilroy, 1957; in the National Portrait Gallery, London
By courtesy of the National Portrait Gallery, London

British field marshal in World War II noted for his North African campaigns against Field Marshal Erwin Rommel and for his later roles in Italy and Western Europe.

The third son of the 4th earl of Caledon, Alexander was educated at Harrow and the Royal Military College (Sandhurst) and was commissioned a second lieutenant in the Irish Guards in 1911. He fought with distinction in World War I and led a brigade on the North-West Frontier Province, India. In World War II Alexander commanded British forces at Dunkirk, where he directed the evacuation of 300,000 troops; he was the last man to leave the beaches. In Burma (February 1942) he successfully extricated British and Indian troops before the advancing Japanese.

In the Mediterranean theatre, Alexander reorganized British forces and directed the Allied ground offensives from Egypt and Algeria that resulted in the surrender of the Germans in Tunis in May 1943. He continued to drive the Germans from Sicily and southern Italy. In November 1944 he became commander in chief of all Allied forces in Italy. After the war he was named governor general of Canada (1946–52); as a member of Winston Churchill's Conservative government, he served as minister of defense (1952–54) until his retirement. He was knighted in 1942 and made Viscount Alexander of Tunis in 1946 and an earl in 1952.

Alexander, James W(addell), II (b. Sept. 19, 1888, Sea Bright, N.J., U.S.—d. Sept. 23, 1971, Princeton, N.J.), mathematician and a founder of the branch of mathematics originally known as analysis situs, now called topology.

The son of John Alexander, the American muralist who created works for the Library of Congress, James graduated from Princeton University in 1910. He developed a strong interest in mathematics and physics and remained at Princeton an additional year to obtain his masters degree. In 1912 the mathematics department at Princeton invited him to join the faculty, a position he held until 1933 when he was asked to join the newly created Institute for Advanced Studies, also in Princeton, N.J. Alexander thus became one of the institute's initial members. He remained with the institute until his retirement in 1951.

Alexander's interest in the relationship of geometric figures that undergo transformation led to his developmental work in topology.

Alexander, Marcus Aurelius Severus: *see* Severus Alexander.

Alexander, Samuel (b. Jan. 6, 1859, Sydney—d. Sept. 13, 1938, Manchester), philosopher who developed a metaphysics of emergent evolution involving time, space, matter, mind, and deity.

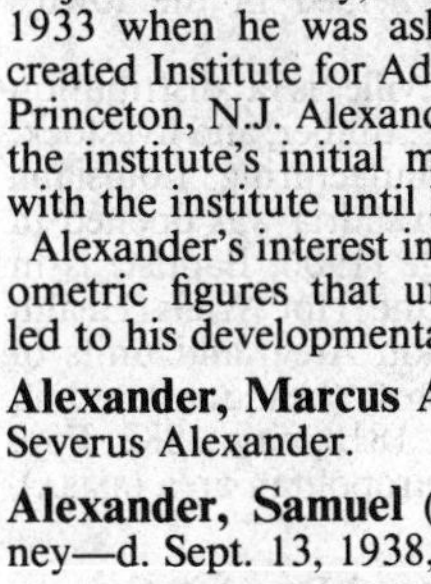

Samuel Alexander, chalk drawing by Francis Dodd, 1932; in the National Portrait Gallery, London

By courtesy of the National Portrait Gallery, London

After studying in Melbourne, Alexander went to Balliol College, Oxford, in 1877 on a scholarship. In 1887 he received the Green Prize for "Moral Order and Progress" (1889), an essay on evolutionary ethics. Alexander's interest in evolution led him to relinquish a fellowship at Lincoln College, Oxford, in order to study (1890–91) experimental psychology under Hugo Münsterberg in Germany. In 1893 he became a professor at Owens College (later Victoria University of Manchester), where he remained until his retirement in 1924. During his tenure there he introduced physiological psychology, still in its infancy in Great Britain. Alexander was awarded the Order of Merit in 1930.

As Gifford lecturer at Glasgow University, Alexander organized his philosophical thought into a comprehensive system published as *Space, Time and Deity* (1920), his only major work. It explains the world as a single cosmic process with space-time as the basic cosmic matrix. "Emergents" (Gestalt-like properties) periodically arise as higher syntheses. Space-time thus produced matter, and matter in turn gave rise to mind (or "awareness") as a further, higher, qualitative synthesis.

"Deity" signifies the upper goal, the next higher level toward which the cosmic order spontaneously tends. In this hierarchy of change, the higher synthesis emerges from below but possesses genuinely new characteristics; hence in each instance the new synthesis is unpredictable. Alexander did not attempt to give an ultimate explanation for the world's existence; he tried merely to explain the world in terms of spontaneous creative tendencies.

Alexander, Sir William: *see* Stirling, William Alexander, 1st earl of.

Alexander Archipelago, group of about 11,000 islands (actually the tops of submerged mountains) off the coast of southeastern Alaska, U.S., lying within the Tongass National Forest and extending southward from Glacier Bay and Cross Sound to the Dixon Entrance. Among the largest islands (north–south) are Chichagof, Admiralty, Baranof, Kupreanof, Kuiu, Mitkof, Wrangell, Prince of Wales, and Revillagigedo. The chief cities are Sitka on Baranof and Ketchikan on Revillagigedo. Lumbering, fishing, fur collecting, and mining are the main economic activities of the area. The irregular shorelines of the islands are separated from the mainland by deep, narrow channels that form part of the Alaska Marine Highway system, or Inside Passage. The name was assigned by the U.S. Coast and Geodetic Survey in 1867 to honour Alexander II, tsar of Russia. Pop. (1980) 32,586.

Alexander City, city, Tallapoosa County, east central Alabama, U.S. Early settlement began in 1836 on the site of a Tuckabatchee Indian village. It was known as Youngville until 1873, when it was incorporated and named for E.P. Alexander, president of the Central of Georgia Railroad. To the south, Martin Dam on the Tallapoosa River provides industrial power, chiefly for textile milling. Production of ornamental ironwork is also important. Lake Martin, formed by the dam (1926), has more than 700 mi (1,125 km) of recreational shoreline. Nearby is Horseshoe Bend National Military Park, where Andrew Jackson's forces defeated the Creek Indians in the War of 1812. Pop. (1980) 13,807.

Alexander Epiphanes: *see* Alexander Balas *under* Alexander (Seleucid Empire).

Alexander Island, also called ALEXANDER LAND, large island in the Bellingshausen Sea, separated from the Antarctica mainland by the George VI Sound. An extremely rugged region with peaks up to 9,800 ft (2,987 m) above sea level, it is 270 mi (435 km) long and up to 125 mi wide and has an area of about 16,700 sq mi (43,250 sq km). The Russian explorers Bellingshausen and Lazarev discovered the land in 1821 and named it after the Russian tsar. It was believed to be part of the mainland until 1940 when a U.S. expedition proved it to be an island, connected to the continent by a 20-mi-wide floating ice shelf. Alexander Island has been claimed by Britain (since 1908), by Chile (1940), and by Argentina (1942). It also has been the site of a British research station.

Alexander romance, any of a body of legends about the career of Alexander the Great, told and retold with varying emphasis and purpose by succeeding ages and civilizations.

The chief source of all Alexander romance literature was a folk epic written in Greek by a Hellenized Egyptian in Alexandria during the 2nd century AD. Surviving translations and copies make its reconstruction possible. It portrayed Alexander as a national messianic hero, the natural son of an Egyptian wizard-king by the wife of Philip II of Macedon. Magic and marvels played a subsidiary part in the epic—in the story of Alexander's birth, for example, and in his meeting with the Amazons in India. In later romances, however, marvels and exotic anecdotes predominated and gradually eclipsed the historical personality. Minor episodes in the original were filled out, often through "letters" supposedly written by or to Alexander, and an independent legend about his capture of the wild peoples of Gog and Magog was incorporated into several texts of many vernacular versions. An account of the Alexander legends was included in a 9th-century Old English translation of Orosius' history of the world. In the 11th century a Middle Irish Alexander romance appeared, and in about 1100, the Middle High German *Annolied.* During the 12th century, Alexander appeared as a pattern of knightly chivalry in a succession of great poems, beginning with the *Roman d'Alexandre* by Albéric de Briançon. This work inspired the *Alexanderlied* by the German poet Lamprecht der Pfaffe. An Anglo-Norman poet, Thomas of Kent, wrote the *Roman de toute chevalerie* toward the end of the 12th century, and *c.* 1275 this was remodelled to become the Middle English romance of *King Alisaunder.* Italian Alexander romances began to appear during the 14th century, closely followed by versions in Swedish, Danish, Scots, and (dating from a little earlier) in the Slavic languages. These last stemmed mainly from a Bulgarian translation of the pseudo-Callisthenes and contained episodes not known elsewhere.

Meanwhile, Latin accounts of Alexander's legendary deeds had continued to appear, including the "letter about marvels" supposedly written by Alexander to his old tutor, Aristotle. New legends also came into being, including one in the 12th century about Alexander's "journey to Paradise."

Eastern accounts of Alexander's fabled career paid a good deal of attention to the Gog and Magog episode, a version of this story being included in the Qur'ān. The Arabs, expanding Syrian versions of the legend, passed them on to the many peoples with whom they came in contact. Through them, the Persian poets, notably Neẓāmī in the 12th century, gave the stories new form.

Alexander romance literature declined in the late 12th century, and, with the revival of classical scholarship during the Renaissance, historical accounts displaced the Alexander romances.

Alexander Severus (Roman emperor): *see* Severus Alexander.

Alexanderson, Ernst F(rederik) W(erner) (b. Jan. 25, 1878, Uppsala, Swed.—d. May, 1975, Schenectady, N.Y., U.S.), electrical engineer and television pioneer who developed a high-frequency alternator (a device that converts direct current into alternating current) capable of producing continuous radio waves and thereby revolutionized radio communication.

In 1901 Alexanderson emigrated to the United States and the following year began working at the General Electric Company in Schenectady, N.Y., under Charles P. Steinmetz.

In 1906 Alexanderson completed his alternator, which in the ensuing years greatly improved transoceanic communication and firmly established the wireless as an important tool in shipping and warfare. He continued to improve the alternator and in addition made important improvements in radio antennas, electric railroads, ship propulsion, and electric motors. In 1916 he patented a selective-tuning device for radio receivers, which became an integral part of modern radio systems.

He also developed the amplidyne, an extremely sophisticated automatic control system first used in factories to automate intricate manufacturing processes and used during World War II in conjunction with anti-aircraft guns.

Alexanderson demonstrated television in his own home as early as 1927 and in 1930 gave the first public exhibition of television with a system that displayed the picture on a seven-foot (two-metre) screen. Alexanderson retired from his full-time position with General Electric in 1948 but continued to act as an engineering consultant. From 1952 he worked at Radio Corporation of America (RCA) as a consultant and was awarded his 321st patent in 1955 for the colour-television receiver that he developed for RCA.

Alexandra, Russian in full ALEKSANDRA FYODOROVNA (b. June 6, 1872, Darmstadt, Ger.—d. July 29/30, 1918, Yekaterinburg, Russia), consort of the Russian emperor Nicholas II. Her misrule while the Emperor was commanding the Russian forces during World War I precipitated the collapse of the imperial government in March 1917.

Alexandra, empress of Russia, *c.* 1913
By courtesy of Hillwood, Washington, D.C.

A granddaughter of Queen Victoria and daughter of Louis IV, duke of Hesse-Darmstadt, Alexandra (German name Alix) married Nicholas in 1894 and soon came to dominate him. She proved to be unpopular at court and turned to mysticism for solace. Through her near fanatical acceptance of Orthodoxy and her belief in autocratic rule, she felt it her sacred duty to help reassert Nicholas' absolute power, which had been limited by reforms in 1905. In 1904 the tsarevich Alexis was born; she had previously given birth to four daughters. The Tsarevich suffered from hemophilia, and Alexandra's overwhelming concern for his life led her to seek the aid of a debauched "holy man" who possessed hypnotic powers, Grigory Yefimovich Rasputin (*q.v.*). She came to venerate Rasputin as a saint sent by God to save the throne and "Holy Russia" and as a voice of the common people who, she believed, remained loyal to the Emperor. Rasputin's influence was a public scandal, but Alexandra silenced all criticism. After Nicholas left for the front in August 1915, she arbitrarily dismissed capable ministers and replaced them with nonentities or dishonest careerists favoured by Rasputin. As a result, the administration became paralyzed and the regime discredited, and Alexandra came to be widely but erroneously believed to be a German agent. Yet she disregarded all warnings of coming changes, even the murder of Rasputin. After the October Revolution, she, Nicholas, and their children were imprisoned by the Bolsheviks and were later shot to death.

Alexandra, borough, south central South Island, New Zealand, at the junction of the Clutha and Manuherikia rivers and surrounded by three mountain ranges. Originally known as Lower Dunstan and Manuherikia, the settlement was named Alexandra South in 1863 to commemorate the marriage of the Danish princess Alexandra to Edward, prince of Wales, later King Edward VII. The name was subsequently shortened to Alexandra, and the town was constituted a borough in 1867.

Alluvial gold deposits in the Alexandra area, found in 1862, were mined until 1963. The surrounding countryside supports sheep pastures and fruit orchards; fruit packing is an important seasonal activity. On rail and road lines to Dunedin (about 120 mi [190 km] southeast), Alexandra is also a holiday resort. Pop. (1982 est.) 4,390.

Alexandretta (Turkey): *see* İskenderun.

Alexandria, Arabic AL-ISKANDARĪYAH, city in Egypt, the country's chief seaport and the centre of a major industrial region. It was the capital of Egypt after its founding by Alexander the Great in 332 BC and in antiquity was a centre of Hellenic scholarship and science.

The following article treats briefly the modern city of Alexandria. Fuller treatment is provided in the following MACROPAEDIA articles. For history and contemporary life, *see* Alexandria; for additional perspective on the city in its national context, *see* Egypt.

Alexandria is located on the Mediterranean Sea at the western edge of the Nile Delta, 129 mi (208 km) northwest of Cairo. It is built on a strip of land separating a low salt lake (Maryūt, or Mareotis) from the sea and on a T-shaped promontory extending into the Mediterranean. The stem of the T was originally a mole leading to the island of Pharos, but over time it was widened by silt to become an isthmus forming two harbours—the old harbour on the east and the modern harbour on the west. Alexandria has a Mediterranean climate with occasional heavy storms in the winter. The city, together with its agricultural hinterland, constitutes a *muḥāfaẓah,* or governorate.

The inhabitants of Alexandria are mostly occupied in the trade of merchandise, harbour work, industries, shipping, and fishing. Industries produce cotton textiles, paper, chocolate, processed foods, asphalt, and oil. Cotton is the most valuable export, followed by cereals and vegetables; imports include tea, coffee, timber, raw wool, and machinery.

At the heart of the city are the ancient quarters: Bruchium (Greek), Rakotis (Egyptian), Regio Judaeorum (Jewish), and Pharos. On the eastern tip of Pharos once stood the great lighthouse, one of the Seven Wonders of the World. Mīdān at-Taḥrīr (Liberation Square; formerly Muḥammad ʿAlī Square) serves as the focal point of the modern city. Though little of the early city remains, Pompey's Pillar and the Hadrianic catacombs of Kawm ash-Shuqāfah are two of the surviving structures. The famed Alexandrian libraries have long been destroyed. Educational institutions include the University of Alexandria (1942) and the Mu'assah Hospital and College of Nursing. Other institutions in the city include the Library of the Greek Orthodox Patriarchate of Alexandria and the Greco-Roman Museum.

A beach-lined road, al-Jaysh (Army) Street, runs for about 15 mi along the coast. Alexandria is headquarters for the development of the Nile Delta and has extensive rail, road, and air service. The port is well developed, with vast networks of breakwaters, quays, and wharves. Area (1979) city, 122 sq mi (314 sq km); *muḥāfaẓah,* 1,034 sq mi (2,679 sq km). Pop. (1979 est.) city, 2,462,000; *muḥāfaẓah,* 2,473,000.

Alexandria, town, capital of Teleorman *judeţ* (district), southern Romania, on the southward-flowing Vedea River in the Danube floodplain. Alexandria is a regional marketing centre for agricultural produce, mostly grain. The town also has flour mills and other food-processing plants. Manufactures include construction materials, chemicals, and rubber products. The town has a historical museum. Highways and railway connections extend throughout the district, from Alexandria to Roşiori de Vede, Videle, and Turnu Măqurele. Pop. (1981 est.) 43,705.

Alexandria, city, seat of Rapides Parish, central Louisiana, U.S., on the Red River, opposite Pineville. It was laid out (1810) at the rapids, which then marked the head of river navigation, and was named after Alexander Fulton, on whose Spanish land grant the first settlement was made in 1785. Prior to the Civil War, the community thrived on river commerce (cotton, sugarcane, and cattle). In May 1863 and again in March 1864 it was occupied by Union forces under Adm. David Porter and Gen. Nathaniel P. Banks. When finally vacated (May 12–13, 1864), Alexandria was burned, and all civic records were lost. Union gunboats, which had passed up the river toward Shreveport at high tide, were caught above the falls at Alexandria; Banks's forces, retreating from defeat at Mansfield, escaped entrapment when wing dams were built to allow passage of the fleet. Railroad expansion and exploitation of the locally dense pine and hardwood forests helped in the town's restoration after the war.

Alexandria with Pineville is a distribution centre for farm products, timber, and livestock. There is also light manufacturing. Louisiana State University at Alexandria was opened in 1960; Louisiana College (1906; Baptist) is in Pineville. Nearby are the Hot Wells Health Resort, Cotile Recreation Area, and units of Kisatchie National Forest (headquartered in Alexandria). Inc. town, 1818; city, 1882. Pop. (1980) city, 51,565; metropolitan area (SMSA), 151,985.

Alexandria, city, seat of Douglas County, western Minnesota, U.S., in a lake-resort and dairy-farm region. Settled in 1858 on land that was once part of Ojibwa and Sioux camping grounds, it was organized as a township in 1866 and named for Alexander Kinkead, an early pioneer. The controversial Kensington Stone, with runic inscriptions describing a visit by Norsemen to the area in 1362, is in the Runestone Museum. A 28-ft (9-m) statue of a Viking and the Kensington Runestone Monument, a gigantic reproduction of the original, promote the belief in early Norse exploration. Diversified farming, light industry, and tourism are the economic mainstays. Lake Carlos State Park is a few miles north. Inc. village, 1877; city, 1908. Pop. (1980) 7,608.

Alexandria, city, adjoining Arlington and Fairfax counties, northern Virginia, U.S., on the Potomac River (there bridged at the Maryland line), south of the District of Columbia. The site was settled in 1695, and a community known as Belhaven was founded in 1731. Organized in 1749, it was renamed for John Alexander, who had originally been granted the land, and was incorporated as a town in 1779. It has the unique distinction

Nineteenth-century town houses in Alexandria, Va.
Milt and Joan Mann from CameraMann

of being an independent city (without county affiliation), designated by an act of Congress (1852). George Washington helped to lay out its streets and drilled troops there during the French and Indian Wars.

From 1791 to 1847, Alexandria was part of the District of Columbia. At the outbreak of the Civil War, it became a Federal operational base and served as the seat of the wartime "restored government of Virginia." Its development as a political and social centre and as a river port for shipping flour and tobacco was overshadowed by the growth of Washington, D.C., and Baltimore. The city, although mainly residential, has large commercial and freight-rail operations and some manufactures (refrigerator cars, fertilizer, chemicals, lumber products).

Many colonial buildings survive—some, associated with George Washington, Gen. Edward Braddock, and Robert E. Lee, include Christ Church, Carlyle House, Gadsby's Tavern, Friendship Fire Engine House, Old Presbyterian Meeting House, Ramsay House, and the home of Henry ("Light-Horse Harry") Lee, father of Robert E. Lee. The Alexandria Academy was established in 1785, and the *Alexandria Gazette* (founded in 1784) is one of the oldest daily newspapers in continuous circulation in the U.S. Washington, who maintained a house (now reconstructed) at Alexandria, served on the town council. The George Washington Masonic Memorial (built in 1922–23) houses mementos of his tenure as the worshipful master of the Masonic Lodge. His estate, Mount Vernon (9 mi [15 km] south), is a national historic landmark and contains his grave and that of his wife, Martha. Pop. (1980) 103,217.

Alexandria, Library of, the most famous library of classical antiquity. The great research institute of the Alexandrian museum and library was founded and maintained by the long succession of the Ptolemies in Egypt from the beginning of the 3rd century BC. The initial organization was the work of Demetrius Phalereus, who was familiar with the achievements of the library at Athens. Both museum and library were organized in faculties, with a president-priest at the head, and the salaries of the staff paid by the king. A subsidiary "daughter library" was established, *c.* 235 BC, by Ptolemy III in the temple of Sarapis, the main museum and library being in the palace precincts, in the district known as the Brucheium. It is not known how far the ideal of an international library—incorporating not only all Greek literature but also translations into Greek from the other languages of the Mediterranean, the Middle East, and India—was realized. Certainly the library was in the main Greek; the only translation recorded was the Septuagint.

The library's editorial program included the establishment of the Alexandrian canon of Greek poets, the division of works into "books" as they are now known (probably to suit the standard length of rolls), and the gradual introduction of systems of punctuation and accentuation. The compilation of a national bibliography was entrusted to Callimachus. Though now lost, it survived into the Byzantine period as a standard reference work of Greek literature. The museum and library survived for many centuries but were destroyed in the civil war that occurred under Aurelian in the late 3rd century AD; the "daughter library" was destroyed by the Christians in AD 391.

Alexandria, School of, the first Christian institution of higher learning, founded in the mid-2nd century AD in Alexandria. Under its earliest known leaders (Pantaenus, Clement, and Origen) it became a leading centre of the allegorical method of biblical interpretation, espoused a rapprochement between Greek culture and Christian faith, and attempted to propound orthodox Christian teachings over against heterodox views in an era of doctrinal flux. Opposing the School of Alexandria was the School of Antioch (*see* Antioch, School of; Antiochene theology), which emphasized the literal interpretation of the Bible.

Alexandria, Synod of (AD 362), a meeting of Christian bishops held in Alexandria, summoned by the bishop of Alexandria, Athanasius. It allowed clergy that were readmitted to communion after making common cause with Arians to return to their former ecclesiastical status, provided they had not themselves subscribed to Arianism. The synod stated explicitly that the Holy Spirit, not a created being, is of the same substance as the Father and the Son, and it clearly defined the Christological terms Person and substance.

Alexandria Municipal Museum, Arabic MATḤIF AL-BALADĪYAH AL-ISKANDARĪ, museum of Greek and Roman antiquities founded in 1892 and housed in Alexandria, Egypt, in a Greek Revival building opened in 1895. The museum contains material found in Alexandria itself as well as Ptolemaic and Roman objects from the Nile Delta, the Fayyūm of Upper Egypt, and Middle Egypt, and antiquities from the Pharaonic period from the Alexandria area and the delta. Among the objects in the collection are a cast of the Rosetta stone (the original was removed to the British Museum) and fine pieces of Hellenistic sculpture, including a large attic funerary stele of the late 4th century BC. There is a colossal porphyry statue representing an emperor or Jesus Christ, found outside the Attarin Mosque, Alexandria, and believed to be the largest example known in that material. Among the many other objects in the collection are terracottas, Tanagra figurines, capitals, pottery, silver objects, and coins.

Alexandrian rite, the system of liturgical practices and discipline found among Egyptians and Ethiopians of both the Eastern rite Catholic and independent Christian churches.

The Alexandrian rite is historically associated with St. Mark the Evangelist, who travelled to Alexandria, the Greek-speaking capital of the diocese of Egypt and the cultural centre of the Eastern Roman Empire.

The liturgy of the modern Coptic Catholic Church (*q.v.*) developed from the Byzantine liturgy attributed to St. John Chrysostom, as modified by Syrian and other influences. The service book is written in Coptic, with the Arabic running in parallel columns, though readings from the Apostles and the Gospels are in Arabic.

The Ethiopian Catholic liturgy (*see* Ethiopian Catholic Church) was derived from the Coptic and is in the classical Ethiopic Geʿez language. The liturgy and Scriptures have been translated into Amharic, the modern official Ethiopic language.

Alexandrina, Lake, estuarine lagoon, southeastern South Australia, 45 mi (72 km) southeast of Adelaide. Together with contiguous Lake Albert and the long, narrow lagoon called The Coorong, it forms the mouth of the Murray River. About 23 mi long and 13 mi wide, the lake has a total surface area of 220 sq mi (570 sq km). Visited by sealers in 1828 and crossed in 1830 by the explorer Charles Sturt, who named the lake after Princess Alexandrina (later Queen Victoria), Lake Alexandrina evoked early interest as a possible maritime outlet for the river. Shallow depths (5 to 15 ft [1.5 to 4.5 m]) and a treacherous sandbar (Younghusband Peninsula) and islands at its seaward approach have precluded such development. Milang, a vegetable and dairy centre on the west shore, did thrive as a river port until the completion of the railroad in 1884. Five barrages built across the lake's exits in 1940 prevent the intrusion of seawater upstream; and, as freshness increases, irrigation is developing along the shores.

alexandrine, verse form, the leading measure in French poetry; it consists of a line of 12 syllables with major stresses on the 6th syllable, preceding the medial caesura (pause), and on the last syllable, and one secondary accent in each half line. Since six syllables is a normal breath group and the secondary stresses are governed by the context of the line, the alexandrine is a flexible form, adaptable to a wide range of subjects. Its structural metrical principle is stress according to sense; the form therefore lends itself to the expression of simple or complex emotions, narrative description, or grandiose patriotic sentiment (it is known as the heroic line in French poetry). The name alexandrine is probably derived from the early use of the verse in the French *Roman d'Alexandre,* a collection of romances compiled in the 12th century about the adventures of Alexander the Great. Revived in the 16th century by the poets of the Pléiade, especially Pierre de Ronsard, the alexandrine became, in the following century, the preeminent French verse form for dramatic and narrative poetry and reached its highest development in the classical tragedies of Corneille and Racine. During the late 19th century, a loosening of structure occurred, notable in the work of Paul Verlaine; poets frequently wrote a modified alexandrine, a three-part line known as *vers romantique,* or *trimètre.*

In English versification, the alexandrine, also called iambic hexameter, contains six primary accents rather than the two major and two secondary accents of the French. Though it was introduced to England in the 16th century, and was adapted to German and Dutch poetry in the 17th century, its success outside France has been limited.

Alexandrinum, opus: *see* opus Alexandrinum.

Alexandrist, Italian ALESSANDRISTÒ, plural ALESSANDRISTI, any of the Italian philosophers of the Renaissance who, in the controversy about personal immortality, followed the explanation of Aristotle's *De anima* (*On the Soul*) given by Alexander of Aphrodisias, who held that it denied individual immortality.

Thomas Aquinas and his followers had maintained that Aristotle, who regarded reason as eternal, also regarded it as a faculty of the individual soul and so should be cited as believing that the individual soul is immortal. The Latin Averroists, on the other hand, had evolved a doctrine of universal (as opposed to individual) immortality, holding that the individual intellect is reabsorbed after death into the eternal intellect, which had been individualized in it. The Alexandrists, however, led by Pietro Pomponazzi, denied that either the Thomist or the Averroist view could justly be attributed to Aristotle. Instead, they held that Aristotle considered the soul as a material and therefore a mortal entity, operating during life only under the authority of universal reason and organically connected with the body, on the dissolution of which it would become extinct.

alexandrite, variety of the gemstone chrysoberyl (*q.v.*).

Alexandropol (Armenian S.S.R.): *see* Leninakan.

Alexandros (Greek mythology): *see* Paris.

Aléxandros (Greek personal name): *see under* Alexander.

Alexandroúpolis, seaport, capital of the *nomós* (department) of Évros, western Thrace (Thráki), Greece, northwest of the Évros (Maritsa) River estuary on the Gulf of Ainos (Enez), an inlet of the Thracian Sea. Founded by the Turks as Dedeağaç in 1860, it began

Alexandroúpolis, Greece
Pierre Streit—Black Star/EB Inc.

to grow with the marketing of its valonia oak after 1871 and further prospered with the arrival of the Istanbul–Thessaloníki railway in 1896. Long a bone of contention between Greece and Bulgaria, it was ceded to the latter in 1913, but the treaties of Neuilly (1919) and Sèvres (1920) granted it to Greece; and the Treaty of Lausanne (1923) confirmed this. In 1941 it was occupied by Bulgaria but was restored to Greece in 1944. It is the seat of the Greek Orthodox metropolitan bishop of Alexandroúpolis–Samothráki. Originally a fishing village, the city has become the burgeoning centre of a fast-developing agricultural hinterland raising grains (wheat, barley), tobacco, cattle, and silk. It has an airport. Pop. (1981) 35,779.

Alexeïeff, Alexandre (b. Aug. 5, 1901, Kazan, Russia—d. Aug. 9, 1982, Paris), French motion-picture animator and an authority on the theory and technique of animation. He invented the pin-screen method of animation with his collaborator, later his wife, the animator Claire Parker.

Alexeïeff spent his childhood near Istanbul, studied painting in Paris, and worked at the Chauve Souris Theatre, where he designed sets and costumes for the Ballets Russes and Ballets Suedois. Alexeïeff's and Parker's first film using the pin screen was *Une Nuit sur le mont chauve* (1933; *Night on a Bare Mountain*). In pin screen animation, a vertical metal surface is perforated by millions of holes into which headless pins are inserted; the pins are depressed to create shadows, and changes in the position of the pins are filmed frame by frame. *Le Nez* (1963;*The Nose*) and the titles to Orson Welles's *Le Procès* (1962; *The Trial*) were other Alexeïeff pin screen productions.

Alexeïeff made greatly admired commercials by photographing swinging pendulums to which a light source was attached. He also made experimental and theatrical cartoons, and, illustrated books, using both wood engravings and still photographs of pin screens.

Alexianus Bassianus, also called GESSIUS BASSIANUS ALEXIANUS (Roman emperor): *see* Severus Alexander.

Alexis, Russian ALEKSEY (b. *c.* 1295, Moscow—d. 1378, Moscow), Metropolitan of Moscow from 1353 to 1378 and the first representative of the Russian Church to take a truly active role in governing Russia.

Alexis became regent during the short reign of Ivan the Fair (1352–59), great-great-grandson of Prince Alexander Nevski, the greatest leader of medieval Russia. Alexis consciously followed the two political principles of Nevski: first, to defer to the powerful Tatars (a branch of the Mongols) who had conquered Russia in the 13th century and who were to dominate Russian affairs for nearly 200 years; and second, to resist the encroachments, military and political, of the Western powers, particularly the Lithuanians, who sought to subjugate Russia.

Alexis wielded the power of his clerical office with cunning political precision. He curried the favour of the Tatars by curing the sick wife of the Khan. He imposed ecclesiastical punishments of excommunication on the princes of Tver and Smolensk because they were conspiring with the Lithuanians. Above all, Alexis strove for political consolidation of the fragmented Russian provincial outposts, and he succeeded. A mere three years after his death, the united Russian army defeated the Mongols at the Battle of Kulikovo Pole (Sept. 8, 1380) signalling the end of Tatar domination.

Alexis, Russian in full ALEKSEY MIKHAYLOVICH (b. March 19 [March 9, old style], 1629, Moscow—d. Feb. 8 [Jan. 29, O.S.], 1676, Moscow), tsar of Russia from 1645 to 1676.

Son of Michael, the first Romanov monarch of Russia (ruled 1613–45), Alexis received a superficial education in reading, writing, and church singing from his tutor Boris Ivanovich Morozov before acceding to the throne at the

Alexis, detail of a portrait by an unknown artist, *c.* 1670; in the State Historical Museum, Moscow
By courtesy of the State Historical Museum, Moscow

age of 16. Morozov, who was also Alexis' brother-in-law, initially took charge of state affairs, but in 1648 a popular uprising in Moscow, caused by a financial crisis and an increase in the salt tax, forced Alexis to send Morozov into exile.

After that, Alexis' government was dominated by a series of advisers: Prince N.I. Odoyevsky, the patriarch Nikon, Afanasy Lavrentyevich Ordyn-Nashchokin, and Artamon Sergeyevich Matveyev. Under their guidance Alexis gave Russia a new code of laws (*Sobornoye Ulozheniye* of 1649) recognizing the legitimacy of serfdom, fought wars with both Poland (1654–67) and Sweden (1656–61), and won possession of the Ukraine east of the Dnepr River and of Kiev (1667). In addition to these acts, Alexis approved Nikon's church reforms that led to a major schism in the Orthodox Church of Russia (1666–67), and suppressed recurrent popular uprisings that culminated in the urban rebellion of 1662 and the peasant rebellion of Stenka Razin (1667–71).

By nature a quiet, kind, and exceedingly devout man, Alexis encouraged the development of foreign trade and promoted the spread of education and western European culture in Russia. He prevented Nikon from transforming the Russian state into a diarchy, in which the church would have held more power than the civil authority.

Alexis, Russian in full ALEKSEY PETROVICH (b. Feb. 28 [Feb. 18, old style], 1690, Moscow—d. July 7 [June 26 O.S.], 1718, St. Petersburg, Russia), heir to the throne of Russia, who was accused of trying to overthrow his father, Peter I the Great, and was condemned to death.

After his mother, Eudoxia, was forced to enter a convent (1698), Alexis was brought up by his aunts and, after 1702, was educated by the tutor Baron Heinrich von Huyssen. Although Alexis dutifully obeyed his father—participating in the siege of Narva (1704) and directing the fortification of Moscow (1707) during the

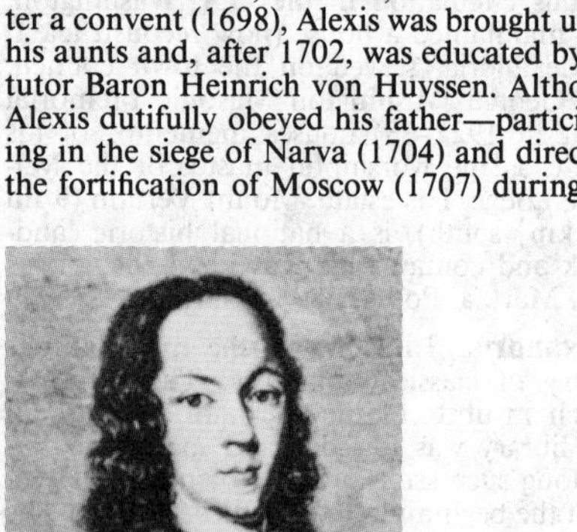

Alexis, detail of an engraving by K. Vortman after a painting by J.P. Lüdden, 1729
Novosti Press Agency

Great Northern War, studying at Dresden in Saxony (1709), and marrying Princess Sophia Charlotte of Brunswick-Wolfenbüttel (October 1711)—he never developed an enthusiasm for Peter's wars and reforms and became increasingly hostile toward his father. After Peter's second wife, Catherine, provided the Tsar with another male heir (Nov. 8 [Oct. 28, O.S.], 1715), Alexis was offered the choice of either renouncing his right of succession or becoming a monk.

When Peter later ordered Alexis to join him and the Russian Army in Denmark (August 1716), Alexis, who not only was in poor health but also had become a heavy drinker, fled to Vienna, where the Holy Roman emperor Charles VI gave him protection. Peter, fearing that his foreign or domestic opponents might take advantage of his son's flight and support Alexis as an alternative ruler, sent envoys to bring Alexis home. Promising him a full pardon, the envoys persuaded Alexis to return to Moscow (Feb. 11 [Jan. 31, O.S.], 1718). Alexis soon discovered, however, that his father's forgiveness was contingent upon his renunciation of his right to the throne and his denunciation of those who had helped him escape.

Although Alexis accepted these terms, Peter, using extraordinarily cruel methods, conducted an investigation of Alexis' supporters, discovered the existence of a potential movement of reaction for which Alexis might become a rallying point, and concluded that his son was involved in a treasonous conspiracy. Alexis was then forced to confess before the Senate, and a special court tried and condemned him to death. Before his execution, however, he died from shock and the effects of torture in the Peter-Paul Fortress.

Alexis, Russian ALEKSEY, original name SERGEI VLADIMIROVICH SIMANSKY (b. 1877, Moscow—d. April 18, 1970, Moscow), Russian Orthodox Patriarch of Moscow and All Russia (1945–70) whose allegiance to the Soviet government helped him strengthen the structure of the church within an officially atheistic country.

Born to an aristocratic family, Alexis received a law degree from the University of Moscow in 1899 before turning to religion. In 1902 he became a monk, receiving his doctoral degree in theology from the Moscow Theological Academy in 1904. By 1913 he had been consecrated bishop of Tivhkin and vicar of Novgorod, positions he was holding at the time of the 1917 Bolshevik Revolution.

During the years 1918–41, while the new Communist government operated under its anti-religious policies, Alexis worked to stabilize church life, gaining prominence within the church as vicar of Petrograd in 1922, metropolitan of Novgorod in 1932, and metropolitan of Leningrad in 1933. Stalin relaxed his opposition to the church in the face of Hitler's 1941 attack, and Alexis was notable for remaining in Leningrad at that time to organize the church's support of the Red Army, an act that earned him the Leningrad Defense Medal.

When the church was officially reestablished in Russia in 1943, Alexis was elected a permanent member of the Holy Synod, and in 1945 he succeeded Patriarch Sergei as patriarch of Moscow, leader of the Russian Church. In that role he actively supported Soviet political policies and attempted to unite Eastern Orthodoxy in the Western Hemisphere. One of his last official acts was to establish an Independent Orthodox Church in the U.S.

Alexis, Russian in full ALEKSEY, or ALEKSEI, NIKOLAYEVICH (b. Aug. 25 [Aug. 12, old style], 1904, Peterhof, near Petrograd, Russia—d. July 29/30 [July 16/17, O.S.], 1918, Ekaterinburg), only son of Nicholas II, the last tsar of Russia, and the tsarina Alexandra. He was the first male heir born to a reigning tsar of the Romanov dynasty since the 17th century.

A hemophiliac, Alexis was often aided by the mystic Grigory Yefimovich Rasputin, whose consequent acquisition of influence at the imperial court caused a decline in confidence in Nicholas II's leadership. When in March 1917 the tsar received at army headquarters a telegram from the president of the Duma informing him of revolutionary events in Petrograd and demanding his abdication, and when emissaries arrived with the act of abdication itself, he submitted with fatalistic composure. At first he favoured giving up the crown to Alexis, with his brother Grand Duke Michael as regent, but he changed his mind, feeling that he could not trust the boy to the danger of a political storm. His abdication was made then in favour of the Grand Duke Michael, who, however, refused to accept the crown unless it were tendered to him by the will of the people. The last chance for a regime of constitutional monarchy was thus cut short.

Alexis was killed with the other members of his immediate family in a cellar where they had been confined by the Bolsheviks at Ekaterinburg. After the October Revolution the imperial family had been placed under arrest first at the palace at Tsarskoe Selo, then had been moved to Tobolsk and finally to Ekaterinburg. With the possibility of a rescue by Admiral A.V. Kolchak's White forces and the Czech Legion as they advanced westward, the executions were ordered by the local Bolshevik Soviet and carried out nine days before the Czech legions reached the village.

Alexis, Willibald, pseudonym of GEORG WILHELM HEINRICH HÄRING (b. June 29, 1798, Breslau, Prussia—d. Dec. 16, 1871, Arnstadt, Ger.), a versatile and prolific writer and critic best known for his German historical novels.

After service as a volunteer in the campaign of 1815, Alexis studied law at Berlin and Breslau but abandoned his legal career for writing

Willibald Alexis, engraving by an unknown artist
Bavaria-Verlag

after the success of his literary hoax *Walladmor* (1824), a parody of Scott published as "freely translated from the English of Walter Scott." The joke, detrimental to Alexis' literary reputation, was repeated in the more ambitious and original novel *Schloss Avalon* (1827). Although his home was in Berlin, where he edited the *Berliner Konversationsblatt* (1827–35) and contributed essays and reviews to literary journals, he travelled widely in Europe and recounted his experiences in travel books, among them *Herbstreise durch Skandinavien* (1828; "Autumn Journey Through Scandinavia").

With *Cabanis* (1832), a story of the age of Frederick the Great, Alexis embarked on a cycle of novels intended to bring to light forgotten but significant periods of Prussian history. He continually experimented with methods of presentation. *Der Roland von Berlin* (1840) portrays the struggle for power in the 15th century between the municipal authorities of Berlin-Kölln and the ruler of Brandenburg; *Der falsche Woldemar* (1842; "The False Woldemas"), recounts the rise and fall of a 14th-century pretender. In the first part of *Die Hosen des Herrn von Bredow* (1846–48; "The Trousers of the Lord of Bredow"), Alexis reveals qualities as a humorist and is unusually successful in organizing his material. The concluding section, describing the elector Joachim's ineffectual opposition to Luther's teaching, strikes a more serious note. In *Ruhe ist die erste Bürgerpflicht* (1852; "Rest Is the Citizen's First Duty") the activities of criminals are presented as symptomatic of Prussian degeneracy in 1806. The sequel *Isegrimm* (1854) foreshadows a rebirth of patriotism.

Alexis was the first writer to reveal the poetic aspects of the Brandenburg landscape. His writing is uneven; passages of effective realistic description alternate with others in which romantic mysticism predominates. His stories, poems, and dramas are largely derivative. From 1842 until 1860 he edited, almost singlehandedly, a remarkable collection of famous lawsuits, *Der neue Pitaval* ("The New Pitaval"). He suffered a stroke in 1856 and later retired permanently to Arnstadt.

Alexius I COMNENUS (b. 1048, Constantinople—d. Aug. 15, 1118), Byzantine emperor (1081–1118) at the time of the First Crusade, who founded the Comnenian dynasty and partially restored the strength of the empire after its defeats by the Normans and Turks in the 11th century.

The third son of John Comnenus and a nephew of Isaac I (emperor 1057–59), Alexius came of a distinguished Byzantine landed family and was one of the military magnates who had long urged more effective defense measures, particularly against the Turks' encroaching on Byzantine provinces in eastern and central Anatolia. From 1068 to 1081 he gave able military service during the short reigns of Romanus IV, Michael VII, and Nicephorus III. Then, with the support of his brother Isaac and his mother, the formidable Anna Dalassena, and with that of the powerful Ducas family, to which his wife, Irene, belonged, he seized the Byzantine throne from Nicephorus III.

Alexius was crowned on April 4, 1081. After more than 50 years of ineffective or short-lived rulers, Alexius, in the words of Anna Comnena, his daughter and biographer, found the empire "at its last gasp," but his military ability and diplomatic gifts enabled him to retrieve the situation. He drove back the south Italian Normans, headed by Robert Guiscard, who were invading western Greece (1081–82). This victory was achieved with Venetian naval help, bought at the cost of granting Venice extensive trading privileges in the Byzantine Empire. In 1091 he defeated the Pechenegs, Turkic nomads who had been continually surging over the Danube into the Balkans, hitherto defying all attempts at placation or subjugation. Alexius halted the further encroachment of the Seljuq Turks, who had already established the Sultanate of Rūm (or Konya) in central Anatolia. He made agreements with Sulaymān ibn Qutalmïsh of Konya (1081) and subsequently with his son Qïlïch Arslan (1093), as well as with other Muslim rulers on Byzantium's eastern border.

At home, Alexius' administrative policy of strengthening the central authority and building up professional military and naval forces resulted in increased Byzantine strength in western and southern Anatolia and in eastern Mediterranean waters. But he was unable or unwilling to make any effective attempt to limit the considerable powers of the landed magnates who had threatened unity of the empire in the past. Indeed, he strengthened their position by further concessions and he had to reward services, military and otherwise, by granting fiscal rights over specified areas. This method, which was to be increasingly employed by his successors, inevitably weakened central revenues and imperial authority. He repressed heresy and maintained the traditional imperial role of protecting the Eastern Orthodox Church, but he did not hesitate to seize ecclesiastical treasure when in financial need. He was subsequently called to account for this by the church.

Alexius I Comnenus, detail of an illumination from a Greek manuscript; in the Vatican Library (Cod. Vat. Gr. 666)
By courtesy of the Biblioteca Apostolica Vaticana

To later generations Alexius appeared as the ruler who pulled the empire together at a crucial time, thus enabling it to survive until 1204, and in part until 1453, but modern scholars tend to regard him, together with his successors John II (reigned 1118–43) and Manuel I (reigned 1143–80), as effecting only stopgap measures. But judgments of Alexius must be tempered by allowing for the extent to which he was handicapped by the inherited internal weaknesses of the Byzantine state, and even more by the series of crises precipitated by the western European crusaders from 1097 onward. The crusading movement, motivated partly by a desire to recapture the holy city of Jerusalem, partly by the hope of acquiring new territory, increasingly encroached on Byzantine preserves and frustrated Alexius' foreign policy, which was primarily directed toward the reestablishment of imperial authority in Anatolia. Alexius had to see his relations with Muslim powers disrupted on occasion and former valued Byzantine possessions, such as Antioch, pass into the hands of arrogant Western princelings, who even introduced Latin Christianity in place of Greek. Thus, it was during Alexius' reign that the last phase of the clash between the Latin West and the Greek East was inaugurated. He did regain some control over western Anatolia; he also advanced into the southeast Taurus region, securing much of the fertile coastal plain around Adana and Tarsus, as well as penetrating further south along the Syrian coast. But neither Alexius nor succeeding Comnenian emperors were able to establish permanent control over the Latin crusader principalities. Nor was the Byzantine Empire immune from further Norman attacks on its western islands and provinces—as in 1107–08, when Alexius successfully repulsed Bohemond I of Antioch's assault on Avlona in western Greece. Continual Latin, particularly Norman, attacks, constant thrusts from Muslim principalities, the rising power of Hungary and the Balkan principalities—all conspired to surround Byzantium with potentially hostile forces. Even Alexius' diplomacy, whatever its apparent success, could not avert the continual erosion that ultimately led to the Ottoman conquest. (J.M.H.)

BIBLIOGRAPHY. F. Chalandon, *Essai sur le règne d'Alexis Ier Comnène, 1081–1118* (1900), still the principal full-length study, in need of some reconsideration; G. Ostrogorsky, *History of the Byzantine State,* 2nd Eng. ed. (1968), a useful brief account with bibliography; J.M. Hussey (ed.), *Cambridge Medieval History,* new ed., vol. 4, pt. 1 (1966), with full bibliography, and *Church and Learning in the Byzantine Empire, 867–1185* (1937, reprinted 1963); S. Runciman, *History of the Crusades,* vol. 1 (1951), a vivid presentation, particularly of the Byzantine point of view; Anna Comnena, *The Alexiad,* trans. by E.R.A. Sewter (1969), a valuable and lively contemporary source by Alexius' daughter.

Alexius II COMNENUS (b. 1169—d. November 1183, Constantinople), Byzantine emperor from 1180 to 1183.

Alexis was the son of Manuel I Comnenus and Mary, daughter of Raymond, prince of Antioch. When his father died on Sept. 24, 1180, he became emperor at the age of 11, with his mother as regent. She, in turn, entrusted the government to her favourite, the unpopular and incapable Alexius (Manuel's nephew). Because Mary was a Latin she was widely opposed, but plotters, who included Alexius II's sister Mary and her husband, Renier of Montferrat, failed to overthrow the regency. Andronicus I Comnenus, Manuel's cousin, eventually succeeded in deposing the regency; he advanced through Asia Minor and was waiting at Chalcedon when anti-Latin riots broke out in the capital (May 1182). The regent Alexius was captured and blinded, and Andronicus entered the capital as the protector of Alexius II. He promptly had his opponents executed, including the dowager empress Mary, whose death warrant her son Alexius had to sign. Crowned co-emperor in September 1183, Andronicus subsequently had Alexius strangled.

Alexius III ANGELUS (d. 1211, Nicaea, Empire of Nicaea), Byzantine emperor from 1195 to 1203. He was the second son of Andronicus Angelus, grandson of Alexius I. In 1195 he was proclaimed emperor by the troops; he captured his brother, the emperor Isaac II, at Stagira in Macedonia and had him blinded and imprisoned. Crowned in April 1195, Alexius III was a weak and greedy emperor, and his coup d'etat had disastrous results. Byzantine prestige declined in the Balkans, where his failure to aid his son-in-law Stephen Nemanja caused the latter to turn to the Bulgars for help. Campaigns against the Bulgars ended in defeat (1195 and 1196), and intrigues and diplomacy were equally unsuccessful because the new Bulgarian ruler, Kalojan, acknowledged the pope's supremacy instead of that of Constantinople.

In 1203 the crusaders restored Isaac II and his son (crowned Alexius IV). Alexius III fled the capital with what treasure he could collect and escaped to Thrace. After an unsuccessful attempt to recover the throne, he wandered about Greece and surrendered to Boniface of Montferrat, then master of a great part of the Balkan Peninsula, but left his protection and sought shelter with Michael I, despot of Epirus. Finally, he went to Asia Minor, where his son-in-law Theodore Lascaris was holding his own against the Latins. Alexius, joined by the Sultan of Iconium (modern Konya, Tur.), demanded Theodore's crown and, when it was refused, marched against him. Taken prisoner by Theodore in 1210, he was sent to a monastery at Nicaea, where he died.

Alexius IV ANGELUS (d. Feb. 8, 1204, Constantinople), Byzantine emperor from 1203 to 1204.

Alexis was the son of Emperor Isaac II. He regained control of his rights to the Byzantine throne with the help of the Fourth Crusade but was deposed soon after by a national revolt. Imprisoned in 1195 with his father, who had also been blinded, by Alexius III, he escaped in 1201 and joined his sister and her husband, Philip of Swabia, in Germany. Promising funds, supplies, and troops to conquer Egypt, the maintenance of 500 Western knights in the Holy Land, and submission of the Byzantine Church to Rome, Alexius convinced Philip of Swabia, Crusade leader Boniface of Montferrat, and their Venetian allies to divert the Fourth Crusade to Constantinople in order to reinstate Alexius and his father as co-emperors; this plan was accomplished in 1203. The new emperors, however, were unable to pay their debts to the West or to unite the two churches. Heavy taxation, as well as wanton behaviour on the part of the crusaders in Constantinople, caused a national revolt led by Alexius Ducas Murtzuphlus, the son-in-law of Alexius III. Alexius Ducas, who was proclaimed emperor in January 1204, as Alexius V, had Alexius IV strangled. Isaac died in prison a few days later.

To make the best use of the Britannica, consult the INDEX *first*

Alexius V DUCAS MURTZUPHLUS (d. 1204, Constantinople), Byzantine emperor in 1204, son-in-law of Alexius III Angelus. He led a Greek revolt against the co-emperors Isaac II and Alexius IV, who had been reinstated by the Latin crusaders, and became the last Greek emperor of a united Byzantium before its overthrow and partition by the crusaders. In January 1204 Alexius began his four-month reign by imprisoning the deposed Alexius IV, whom he later had strangled. The leader of the anti-Latin party in Constantinople, he disavowed Alexius IV's debt to the crusaders and demanded their withdrawal from Constantinople. They instead besieged the city, and three days later (April 12, 1204) Alexius fled to join the fugitive Alexius III. Alexius III, however, blinded him. He was then captured by the crusaders, who put him to death as the murderer of Alexius IV by casting him from the top of a column in Constantinople.

Alf laylah wa laylah: *see* Thousand and One Nights, The.

Alfa Romeo SpA, Italian manufacturer of high-priced sports cars and other vehicles. The company is operated by the Italian government through its state holding company, IRI (Instituto per la Ricostruzione Industriale). Headquarters are in Milan.

The company was formed in 1909 as Anonima Lombarda Fabbrica Automobili (ALFA) when a group of Italian businessmen bought a failing French-owned auto plant located near Milan, hired noted auto designer Giuseppe Merosi, and began making racing and sports cars. In 1915 the company was bought out by industrialist Nicola Romeo and became a limited partnership, which during World War I produced mainly war material.

After the war, Romeo renamed the company Alfa Romeo and began producing prizewinning race cars again. The company held onto its preeminent position in the racing world until 1933, when it was nationalized by the Italian government, which did not provide the financial support needed to continue producing quality cars. After World War II, Alfa Romeo shifted emphasis from custom car production to broader automobile production, though it continued to produce higher priced sports cars.

In addition to automobiles, the company manufactures engines and engine parts, and industrial vehicles. It has subsidiaries in Italy and abroad, and in 1980 formed a partnership with the Japanese Nissan Motor Company, Ltd., to produce cars in Alfa Romeo's Naples plant.

alfalfa, also called LUCERNE, or PURPLE MEDIC (*Medicago sativa*), perennial clover-like plant, of the pea family (Fabaceae), native to Europe. It is widely grown as forage for cattle. The plant grows 30–90 centimetres (1–3 feet) tall and has a long taproot. The alternate leaves have three toothed leaflets. The purplish flowers grow in short terminal clusters.

Alfalfa (*Medicago sativa*)
Dennis E. Anderson

alfalfa weevil, also called CLOVER LEAF WEEVIL (*Hypera postica* or *Phytonomus variabilis*), insect pest of the family Curculionidae (order Coleoptera). The male is dark and tiny (three millimetres long) and has the typical prominent snout used by weevils to bore the small holes in which eggs are deposited. Both sexes hibernate during winter; mating occurs in spring, each female producing 600 to 800 eggs. The plump legless larva is green with a white stripe along the back. Larvae occur in large numbers and strip soft leaf and stem tissues from food plants, usually alfalfa or clover, leaving only the network of veins. In Europe and especially in the U.S. considerable crop damage is caused by generations of alfalfa weevils coming to adulthood in June and August.

Alfarabius (Muslim philosopher): *see* Fārābī, al-.

Alfaro Siqueiros, David (b. Dec. 29, 1896, Chihuahua, Mex.—d. Jan. 6, 1974, Cuernavaca), painter and muralist whose art was informed by his leftist political ideology.

An activist from his youth, Alfaro Siqueiros took part in a student strike while enrolled at the National School of Fine Arts, Mexico City, and in 1913 left his studies to fight in the Army of the Revolution against Pres. Victoriano Huerta. Later he continued his art studies in Europe.

In 1922, after returning to Mexico, Alfaro Siqueiros helped paint the frescoes on the walls of the National Preparatory School. Also at that time, he began organizing and leading unions of artists and workingmen. In 1928 he was a union emissary to the Soviet Union. Union and political activities led to seven jailings over four decades and periods of exile. He taught in Los Angeles and in 1932 organized the Experimental Workshop, New York City, at which the future Abstract Expressionist Jackson Pollock was a student.

Alfaro Siqueiros' murals are distinguished by their sharp delineation, striking colours, massed persons and objects, multi-angular points of interest, and raw emotions of fervour or grief. Realism is mixed with fantasy or phantasmagoria. The subject matter is indicated by such titles as "There Is No Other Road But Ours," "Patricians and Patricides," and "Third World." Despite his past prison terms, many of his murals are in government buildings, and in 1966 his government gave him its national art award.

Alfaro Siqueiros' "From Porfirio's Dictatorship to the Revolution" occupies 4,500 square feet of wall in the National History Museum, Mexico City. His "March of Humanity," which is three times the size of Michelangelo's frescoes in the Sistine Chapel, took more than four years to execute and made use of the help of many hands; it was designed for a hotel in the Parque de la Lama, Mexico City.

Alfasi, Isaac ben Jacob, Alfasi also spelled AL-PHASI, also called RABBI ISAAC FASI, or (by acronym) RIF (b. 1013, near Fès, Morocco—d. 1103, Lucena, Spain), Talmudic scholar who wrote a codification of the Talmud known as *Sefer ha-Halakhot* ("Book of Laws"), which ranks with the great codes of Maimonides and Karo.

Alfasi lived most of his life in Fès (from which his surname was derived) and there wrote his digest of the Talmud, the rabbinical compendium of law, lore, and commentary. In 1088 two of his enemies denounced him to the government on an unknown charge. He fled to Spain, where, in Lucena, he became head of the Jewish community and established a noted Talmudic academy. Alfasi provoked a rebirth of Talmudic study in Spain and was instrumental in changing the centre of such studies from the Eastern to the Western world.

His codification deals with the Talmud's legal aspects, or Halakha (Hebrew Law), including civil, criminal, and religious law. It omits all homiletical passages as well as portions relating to religious duties practicable only in Palestine. He performed a great service by concentrating on the actual text, which had been neglected. His commentaries summarize the thought of the geonim who presided over the two great Jewish academies in Babylonia between the middle of the 7th and the end of the 13th centuries. In addition, his work played a major role in establishing the primacy of the Babylonian Talmud, as edited and revised by three generations of ancient sages, over the Palestinian Talmud, the final compilation of which had been interrupted by external pressures. Alfasi's *Sefer ha-Halakhot* is still important in yeshiva studies.

Alfieri, Vittorio, Conte (Count) (b. Jan. 16, 1749, Asti, Piedmont—d. Oct. 8, 1803, Florence), tragic poet whose predominant theme was the overthrow of tyranny. In his tragedies, he hoped to provide Italy with dramas comparable to those of other European nations. Through his lyrics and dramas he helped to revive the national spirit of Italy and so earned the title of precursor of the Risorgimento.

Educated at the Military Academy of Turin, Alfieri became an ensign. A distaste for military life led him to obtain leave to travel through most of Europe. In England he found the political liberty that became his ideal, and in France the literature that influenced him most profoundly. He studied Voltaire, J.-J. Rousseau, and, above all, Montesquieu.

Alfieri settled in Turin in 1772 and resigned his commission the following year. To divert himself, he composed a play, *Cleopatra*, a tragedy performed with great success in 1775. Thereupon Alfieri decided to devote himself to literature. He began a methodical study of the classics and of the Italian poets, and since he expressed himself mainly in French, the language of the ruling classes in Turin, he went to Tuscany to familiarize himself with pure Italian.

Alfieri, detail of an oil painting by François-Xavier Fabre; in the Museo Civico, Turin, Italy
By courtesy of the Museo Civico, Turin, Italy

By 1782 he had composed 14 tragedies as well as many poems (including four odes in the series *L'America libera*, on American independence, to which a fifth ode was added in 1783) and a political treatise on tyranny, in prose, *Della tirannide* (1777). He also hailed the fall of the Bastille with an ode, "Parigi sbastigliata" (1789). Ten of the tragedies were printed at Siena in 1783.

Meanwhile, in Florence in 1777, Alfieri had met the Countess of Albany, wife of the Stuart pretender to the English throne, Charles Edward. He remained deeply attached to her for the rest of his life.

Alfieri's genius was essentially dramatic. He chose a harsh, bitter style to persuade the oppressed and the resigned to accept his political ideas and to inspire them to heroic deeds. Nearly always, Alfieri's tragedies present the struggle between a champion of liberty and a tyrant. Love has little place in a world so shaken by political passions.

The 19 tragedies that he finally approved for publication in the Paris edition of 1787–89 were *Filippo, Polinice, Antigone, Virginia, Agamennone, Oreste, Rosmunda, Ottavia, Timoleone, Merope, Maria Stuarda, La congiura dei Pazzi, Don Garzia, Saul, Agide, Sofonisba, Bruto primo, Mirra,* and *Bruto secondo*. The best are *Filippo*, in which Philip II of Spain is presented as the tyrant; *Antigone; Oreste;* and, above all, *Mirra* and *Saul*. *Saul*, his masterpiece, is often considered the most powerful drama in the Italian theatre.

Alfieri's autobiography, published posthumously as *Vita di Vittorio Alfieri scritta da esso* (Eng. trans., 1951), is his chief work in prose.

Alfiós Potamós (Greece): *see* Alpheus River.

alfisol, soil type of humid, wooded regions, characterized by a well-developed clay (argillic) horizon. Third in abundance among the 10 orders of soil taxonomy, alfisols occupy between 10 and 15 percent of the world's land surface and occur on all the continents, but especially where broadleaf forests are established. Fairly good fertility and physical properties, combined with occurrence in areas climatically favourable for agriculture, make these soils among the world's most productive. Wheat is a major crop in the three largest areas of alfisols, occupying parts of Canada, the United States, and northern Europe. High moisture content, which distinguishes these soils from the drier mollisols, is responsible for mobilizing clay minerals and ensuring that the chemical bases of calcium, magnesium, and potassium, which are prerequisites for soil fertility, are released by weathering about as rapidly as they are leached out.

Alföld (Hungary): *see* Great Alföld.

Alfonsine Tables, also spelled ALPHONSINE TABLES, set of astronomical tables prepared in Toledo, Spain, for King Alfonso X of León and Castile under the direction of Jehuda ben Moses Cohen and Isaac ben Sid. Completed in 1252, these tables were based on the Ptolemaic theory, which assumed that the Earth was at the centre of the solar system. They enabled astronomers to calculate eclipses and the positions of the planets for any given moment. The original form of the tables was cast into a handier arrangement in Paris around 1320, and manuscript copies of this version rapidly propagated throughout Europe. For more than two centuries they were considered the best astronomical tables available. They were first printed in 1483. The tables were an important source of information for the young Copernicus, but his own work superseded them in the 1550s.

alfonsino, any of the 10 species of exclusively marine fishes constituting the family Berycidae (order Beryciformes). The family contains two genera, *Beryx* and *Centroberyx*. Representatives occur in deep-sea habitats of the Atlantic, Pacific, and Indian oceans.

B. splendens of the African coast is an edible, deepwater species that reaches a length of 60 centimetres (2 feet). It is spectacularly coloured, the lower half being silvery and the upper portions and fins bright scarlet.

Alfonso, name of rulers grouped below by country and indicated by the symbol •.

Foreign-language equivalents:

French	Alphonse
Italian	Alfonso
Portuguese	Afonso
Spanish	Alfonso

FERRARA

• Alfonso I (b. July 21, 1476, Ferrara, Duchy of Ferrara—d. Oct. 31, 1534, Ferrara), duke of Ferrara from 1505, a noted Renaissance prince of the House of Este, an engineer and patron of the arts.

Alfonso succeeded to the duchy at the death of his father, Ercole I. He employed the poet Ludovico Ariosto and the painters Titian and Giovanni Bellini, and made Ferrara's artillery the best in Italy. In the political sphere, Alfonso maintained Ferrara against the expanding power of the papacy by allying himself with France. Lucrezia Borgia, whom he married in 1501, bore him seven children.

KONGO

• Alfonso I: *see* Afonso I *under* Afonso (Kongo).

NAPLES

• Alfonso I: *see* Alfonso V *under* Alfonso (Spain: Aragon).

NAVARRE

• Alfonso: *see* Alfonso I *under* Alfonso (Spain: Aragon).

PORTUGAL

• Alfonso I–VI: *see* Afonso I–VI *under* Afonso (Portugal).

SPAIN: ARAGON

• Alfonso I, byname ALFONSO THE BATTLER, Spanish ALFONSO EL BATALLADOR (b. *c.* 1073—d. September 1134), king of Aragon and of Navarre from 1104 to 1134.

Alfonso was the son of Sancho V Ramírez. He was persuaded by Alfonso VI of Leon and Castile to marry the latter's heiress, Urraca, widow of Raymond of Burgundy. In consequence, when Alfonso VI died (1109) the four Christian kingdoms were nominally united and Alfonso I took his father-in-law's imperial title. The union failed, however, because Leon and Castile felt hostility toward an Aragonese emperor; because Urraca disliked her second husband; and because Bernard, the French Cluniac archbishop of Toledo, wanted to see his protégé, Alfonso Ramírez (infant son of Urraca and her Burgundian first husband), on the imperial throne. At Bernard's prompting, the Pope declared the Aragonese marriage void, but Alfonso continued to be involved in civil strife in the central kingdom until he eventually gave up his claims in favour of his stepson after the death of Urraca (1126). Despite these embroilments, he achieved spectacular victories against the Moors, capturing Saragossa in 1118 and leading a spectacular military raid far into southern Andalusia in 1125. In his campaigns he received much help from the rulers of the counties north of the Pyrenees, resulting in the involvement of Aragon in the affairs of southern France. Alfonso was fatally wounded in battle at Fraga in 1134. Deeply religious, he bequeathed his kingdom to the Templars and the Hospitallers, but his former subjects refused to accept the donation, and the kingdoms eventually came under the control of the counts of Barcelona.

Alfonso II (b. 1152, Barcelona—d. 1196, Perpignan, Roussillon), count of Barcelona from 1162 and king of Aragon from 1164.

The son of Ramón Berenguer IV, Alfonso succeeded his father as count of Barcelona and his mother as ruler of Aragon, thus associating the two countries under the house of Barcelona—a union that was destined to be permanent. Aragonese involvement in France became steadily greater during Alfonso's reign. Nevertheless, the conquest of Teruel (1171) opened the way for the conquest of Valencia; and, in 1179, the pact of Cazorla with his ally, Alfonso VIII of Castile, fixed the future zones of reconquest for the two countries. In his will Alfonso followed the Spanish custom of dividing his kingdom; Provence was thus lost to the Aragonese crown.

• Alfonso III, byname ALFONSO THE LIBERAL, or THE CANDID, Spanish ALFONSO EL LIBERAL, or EL FRANCO (b. 1265—d. June 18, 1291, Barcelona), king of Aragon from 1285 to 1291, son of Peter III. A weak king, he was involved in an unsuccessful constitutional struggle with the Aragonese nobles. In 1287 he was compelled to grant the so-called "Privilegio de la Unión," which handed over a number of important royal prerogatives to baronial control. At Alfonso's death the crown passed to his brother James II, who had been king of Sicily (as James I) since 1285.

• Alfonso IV, byname ALFONSO THE KIND, Spanish ALFONSO EL BENIGNO (b. 1299—d. Jan. 24, 1336, Barcelona), king of Aragon from 1327 to 1336, son of James II. He was well-intentioned but weak. His reign was marked by a serious revolt in Sardinia, which led to war with Genoa, and by the establishment of diplomatic relations with the Moorish kingdoms of North Africa. The failure of the king to resist the efforts of his second wife to further the future of her sons at the expense of Alfonso's heir, Peter, led to serious political disturbances.

• Alfonso V, byname ALFONSO THE MAGNANIMOUS, Spanish ALFONSO EL MAGNÁNIMO (b. 1396—d. June 27, 1458, Naples), king of Aragon (1416–58) and king of Naples (as Alfonso I, 1442–58), whose military campaigns in Italy and elsewhere in the central Mediterranean made him one of the most famous men of his day. After conquering Naples, he transferred his court there.

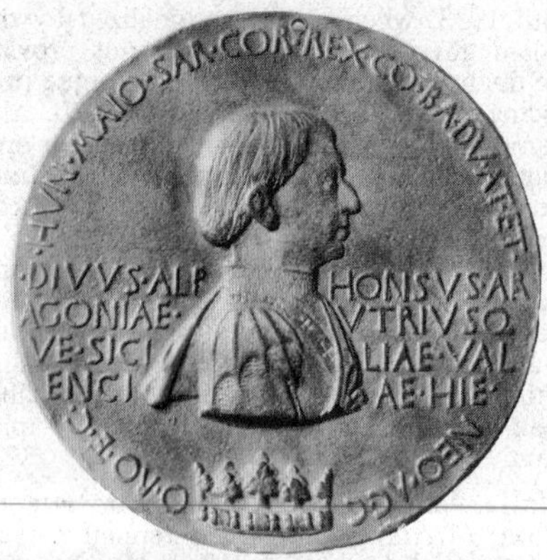

Alfonso V, bronze medal by Pisanello, 1448–49; in the Bargello, Florence

Alinari—Giraudon from Art Resource/EB Inc.

Life. Alfonso was born and brought up in the brilliant Castilian court at Medina del Campo; but when he was 16, his father became king of Aragon, and he himself went to live there. Three years later (1415) he married his cousin María, the daughter of Henry III of Castile, but she produced no children, and they were separated for many years. The marriage was a failure and perhaps helps to explain Alfonso's reluctance to return to his peninsular kingdoms after he had conquered Naples, where he was encouraged to remain by his mistress, Lucrezia de Alagno.

He succeeded his father as king of Aragon in 1416 and, at the beginning of his reign, had political difficulties with both Catalans and Aragonese, because he retained some Castilian counsellors and deprived the *justicia*, the supreme law officer of Aragon, of his position.

From the moment of his accession, Alfonso continued the traditional Aragonese policy of Mediterranean expansion. Thus, in 1420 he set out with a fleet to pacify Sardinia and Sicily and to attack the Genoese possession of Corsica. The queen of Naples, Joan II, then sought his help against Louis III of Anjou and adopted him as her son and heir. Alfonso was received as a liberator in Naples on July 5, 1421; but the volatile character of the Queen, who soon afterward began to make overtures to Louis of Anjou, obliged Alfonso in 1423 to return to Catalonia to seek reinforcements.

After intervening in the internal politics of Castile to defend the interests of his brothers Henry and John in the near civil war that existed during the weak rule of John II, Alfonso set out again for Italy, from where, as it turned out, he was never to return. He was receiving tempting offers (1432) to intervene again in Naples and spent two years in Sicily preparing his fleet and army. His opportunity seemed to come in 1435, after the deaths of Louis III of Anjou and Queen Joan II, but while blockading the port of Gaeta, a key citadel from which to launch an attack on Naples, he was defeated off the island of Ponza by a Genoese squadron. Alfonso was captured, with many others, and sent as a prisoner to Genoa and then to Milan, whose duke, Filippo Maria Visconti, ruled both cities. Alfonso, however, charmed his captor into an alliance and then continued his fight to gain possession of Naples against the opposition of Venice, Florence, and the Pope. He took Naples on June 2, 1442, and transferred his court there permanently in 1443. It became a brilliant centre of art and culture, fed by the fertile interaction of Italian Renaissance and Spanish Gothic influences and forming a cultural bridge between the two peninsulas of the western Mediterranean.

Alfonso engaged in much diplomatic and military activity in Africa, the Balkans, and the eastern Mediterranean in order to protect his commerce with the East and to share in the defense of Christendom against the Turks. He helped the Knights of St. John defend Rhodes; allied himself with Hungary (1444), with Serbia (1447), and with Abyssinia (1450); and fought against Egypt (1453–54). But he was not strong enough to prevent the fall of Constantinople to the Turks in 1453.

Meanwhile, his Spanish dominions were suffering from serious unrest, the result of social and economic tensions to which no solution could be found by his viceroys, his queen, Maria, and his brother John of Navarre. In Catalonia the *remensa*, the peasantry, were vigorously seeking to be freed from feudal dues and received some support from the crown. In Majorca a popular rising, which led to fighting between the capital of the island and the rural population, had to be crushed by troops that Alfonso sent from Naples. And in Barcelona a serious class struggle caused so many disturbances in the city that Alfonso reformed the city government, allowing public offices to be distributed by lot. Meanwhile, the sporadic war with Castile both impoverished the Kingdom of Aragon and deprived Alfonso and his family of their ancestral estates in Castile. Only Valencia, with its flourishing economy, remained unharmed by the general crisis. A restless, energetic ruler to the last, Alfonso was engaged in an assault upon Genoa, which had recently surrendered to the French, when death surprised him in Ovo Castle at Naples in June 1458. In the Kingdom of Naples he was succeeded by his illegitimate son, Ferrante, and in his other states by his brother John (King John II of Aragon), who had been king of Navarre since 1425.

Assessment. Alfonso was praised, respected, and admired by the writers of his own time and also by those of the next generation. The latter were still close enough to him to draw upon a living tradition but were free of the desire to flatter that affected his contemporaries. Among Alfonso's apologists were the Italian Humanist scholars Antonio Beccadelli, Aeneas Sylvius Piccolomini (Pope Pius II), Vespasiano da Bisticci, and Giovanni Pontano. They praised Alfonso for his Humanist education and for his love of books and fine arts, for his delight in hunting, dancing, tournaments, and good clothes, and for his charity, clemency, and deep religious faith. He has been regarded by some scholars as a brilliant Renaissance prince and a great sovereign, but, in general, modern Spanish historians are less enthusiastic about Alfonso and blame him for occupying himself with amorous adventures in Naples while neglecting his duties to his peninsular territories. (E.Sa.)

BIBLIOGRAPHY. The fundamental work on Alfonso V the Magnanimous, although now somewhat outdated, is J. Ametller y Vinyas, *Alfonso V de Aragón en Italia y la crisis religiosa del siglo XV,* rev. ed., 3 vol. (1903–28). Also of value are C. Batlle, "La ideología de la 'Busca,'" *Estudios de Historia Moderna,* 5:167–195 (1955); *Estudios sobre Alfonso el Magnánimo con motivo del quinto centenario de su muerte* (1960); A. Giménez Soler, *Itinerario del rey don Alonso de Aragón el que ganó Nápoles* (1909); J.M. Madurell Marimón (ed.), *Mensajeros barceloneses en la corte de Nápoles de Alfonso V de Aragón* (1963); and A. Soria Ortega, *Los humanistas de la corte de Alfonso el Magnánimo* (1956).

Spain: Asturias and Leon

• **Alfonso I,** byname ALFONSO THE CATHOLIC, Spanish ALFONSO EL CATÓLICO (b. 693?—d. 757, Cangas, Galicia), king of Asturias from 739 to 757, probably the son-in-law of the first Asturian king, Pelayo. The rebellion of the Berber garrisons in Islāmic Spain (741) and the civil strife there that followed gave him the opportunity to incorporate Galicia into his kingdom. He also campaigned far to the south of the Asturian mountains, but lack of manpower made it impossible to exert permanent control on the plains and, in his time, a wide, largely uninhabited no-man's-land came into being between Asturias and the settled territories of the emirate of Córdoba.

• **Alfonso II,** byname ALFONSO THE CHASTE, Spanish ALFONSO EL CASTO (b. 759, Oviedo, Asturias—d. 842, Oviedo), king of Asturias from 791 to 842, the son of Fruela I. He had to face frequent and determined attacks by the armies of the emirate of Córdoba and was often defeated, but his doggedness saved Asturias from extinction. He built a new capital, Oviedo, on a strategic site in the mountains and set about giving the Asturian kingdom a national identity. He tried to enter into relations with Charlemagne, but although he seems to have failed to get Carolingian support, there are some traces of Frankish influence in Asturias. During Alfonso's reign the discovery of the supposed tomb of St. James the Apostle in Galicia made the kingdom the guardian of an important Christian shrine (Santiago de Compostela), and this, too, helped to give it a national identity.

• **Alfonso III,** byname ALFONSO THE GREAT, Spanish ALFONSO EL MAGNO (b. *c.* 838—d. Dec. 20, 910?, Zamora, Leon), king of Asturias from 866 to 910, son of Ordoño I.

Winning a contested succession, he moved his capital forward from Oviedo to the recently restored Roman city of León. Under him, Porto (Oporto) was occupied in 868, and Castile took shape around Burgos, drawing on his Basque allies. He claimed to be reviving the Visigothic monarchy, while making the church of St. James at Santiago de Compostela the shrine of the Christian kingdom. Alfonso's territorial advances were made possible by the convulsion of the Muslim emirate of Córdoba, in which Arab dominion was challenged by the Berber dissidents. For a time Córdoba itself was endangered, and the triumph of Alfonso was thought imminent. This did not occur, but by the end of the reign Alfonso III had occupied Coimbra, Zamora, and Burgos, settling refugees from the south.

• **Alfonso IV,** byname ALFONSO THE MONK, Spanish ALFONSO EL MONJE (d. 933), king of Leon and Asturias from *c.* 926 to *c.* 931, the son of Ordoño II and the successor of his uncle Fruela II. He became a monk, abdicated, and then thought better of it and tried to recover his throne. His short reign was, in consequence, one of political chaos, ending in about 931.

• **Alfonso V,** byname ALFONSO THE NOBLE, Spanish ALFONSO EL NOBLE (b. 994—d. 1028), king of Leon from 999 to 1028, son of Bermudo II. He came to the throne because the devastating campaigns of Almanzor (*see* Manṣūr, Abū ʿAmir al-) had forced his father to accept Almanzor's de facto suzerainty over Leon. The Leonese were forced to take part in the Moorish campaign against the Catalans (1003) and to suffer other indignities and incursions. The political troubles continued until the fall of the caliphate (1031) relieved Leon of Islāmic pressure, but Alfonso was soon faced by the growing power of Sancho III of Pamplona (Navarre). His marriage (1023/24) to Sancho's daughter Urraca ended this threat, and, in the last years of his life, he was able to undertake the reconquest of the Portuguese territories lost during Almanzor's time. He was killed at the siege of Viseu.

Spain: Castile and Leon

• **Alfonso I–V:** *see* Alfonso I–V *under* Alfonso (Spain: Asturias and Leon).

• **Alfonso VI,** byname ALFONSO THE BRAVE, Spanish ALFONSO EL BRAVO (b. before June 1040—d. 1109, Toledo, Castile), king of Leon (1065–70) and king of reunited Castile and Leon (1072–1109), who by 1077 had proclaimed himself "emperor of all Spain" (*imperator totius Hispaniae*). His oppression of his Muslim vassals led to the invasion of Spain by an Almoravid army from North Africa (1086). His name is also associated with the national hero of Spain, Rodrigo Díaz de Vivar (El Cid), who was alternatively his enemy and indifferent supporter.

Alfonso VI, portrait miniature from a manuscript, 12th century; in Santiago cathedral, Spain
Archivo Mas, Barcelona

Alfonso was the second son of King Ferdinand I and his wife Sancha; he was educated by Raimundo, later the bishop of Palencia, and by Pedro Ansúrez, the count of Carrión. On his death in 1065, Ferdinand left to Alfonso the kingdom of Leon together with tribute paid by the Muslim kingdom of Toledo. These possessions aroused the envious hostility of Alfonso's elder brother, Sancho II, who had inherited the kingdom of Castile and the tribute of Saragossa. Alfonso was defeated by his brother in two battles; after the defeat at Llantada (1068) he managed to retain his kingdom, but after that at Golpejera (1072) he was captured and exiled, living for a short while at the court of his vassal Ma'mūn, the Muslim king of Toledo. Soon Alfonso's sister Urraca stirred up a rebellion in Leon, and Sancho besieged her in the walled city of Zamora. During the siege, he was killed, perhaps at Urraca's instigation. She was clearly on Alfonso's side, and some modern historians have even suggested that they had an incestuous relationship.

With Sancho's death, Alfonso recovered his own kingdom of Leon and inherited (1072) that of Castile. He also occupied Galicia, which Sancho had kept from their younger brother García; Alfonso kept García in prison until his death. A late story, in which it is alleged that Alfonso took an oath in St. Gadea's Church, Burgos, that he had had no share in Sancho's murder, probably reflects Castilian reluctance to accept him as king.

Alfonso's reign now entered on a period of success. He seized the Rioja and the Basque provinces and received the feudal homage of Sancho Ramírez for the region of Navarre to the north of the Ebro River. By 1077 he had assumed the title *imperator totius Hispaniae*, in which role other Christian kings accepted him. He then began the conquest of Toledo and, after a long siege, occupied it in May 1085. This was a vital conquest, which recovered for Christian Spain one of the most important historical, strategic, and cultural centres of the peninsula, one that had been in the possession of the Muslims since the early 8th century.

During this period Alfonso regularly exacted *parias*, heavy financial tributes, from the Muslim *ṭā'ifah* kingdoms in return for protection against their other enemies. By thus depriving them of their wealth, he hoped to weaken them so that they would eventually cede their independence without fighting. As a result of his exactions, Christian Spain was flooded with Muslim gold, which was spent on warfare and donations to shrines, churches, and monasteries. The demand for tribute caused the *ṭā'ifah* kings to tax their subjects heavily, producing popular discontent and disturbances and contributing to the weakness that caused the surrender of Toledo. The Muslim ruler al-Muʿtamid of Seville took a desperate decision and called for the help of Yūsuf ibn Tāshufīn, the Almoravid (Berber) *amīr* of North Africa, and his Saharan tribes. The Amīr disembarked in Algeciras at the end of July 1086 and a few months later, on October 23 at Zallāqah, near Badajoz, inflicted a terrible defeat on Alfonso VI. Alfonso appealed for help to the rest of Christendom, and a small crusade was organized as a result; the crusaders did not reach Alfonso's lands but wasted their energies and resources in an unsuccessful siege of the Muslim outpost of Tudela.

The defeat at Zallāqah seriously lessened Alfonso's influence over the *ṭā'ifah* kingdoms. It also led to a reconciliation with Rodrigo Díaz de Vivar, El Cid. Their relationship had been difficult from the start, because El Cid had taken a prominent part in the campaigns of Sancho against Alfonso; although El Cid at first attended Alfonso's court, suspicions deepened, and since 1081 he had been in the service of the Muslim king of Saragossa. Alfonso entrusted El Cid with the occupation and defense of eastern Spain, and Rodrigo carried out this task with great success. Between 1086 and 1109 Alfonso suffered constant defeat by the Almoravids; in the last battle, that of Uclés in 1108, he lost his only son, Sancho. It was characteristic of his indomitable spirit that he at once arranged for his daughter, Urraca, to marry Alfonso I of Aragon so that the war against the Almoravids should be continued after his death, even though it meant that Leon and Castile would be ruled by an Aragonese prince.

Though his reign was politically unsuccessful, Alfonso VI carried out an important cultural task by Europeanizing his dominions. Alfonso married Constance of Burgundy, and influences from across the Pyrenees showed themselves in the introduction of the Romanesque style in art, the adoption of the Roman instead of the Mozarabic liturgy, the replacement of Visigothic by Carolingian script, and the energetic support that Alfonso gave to Cluniac monasticism, as well as in his reconstruction and safeguarding of the pilgrim road to Santiago.

(E.Sa.)

BIBLIOGRAPHY. The most important source for Alfonso VI and his age is Ramón Menéndez Pidal, *La España del Cid*, 7th ed., 2 vol. (1969; Eng. trans. of 1st ed., *The Cid and His Spain*, 1934).

• **Alfonso VII,** byname ALFONSO THE EMPEROR, Spanish ALFONSO EL EMPERADOR (b. 1104?—d. August 1157, Fresneda, Castile), king of Leon and Castile from 1126 to 1157, son of Raymond of Burgundy and the grandson of Alfonso VI, whose imperial title he assumed. Though his reign saw the apogee of the imperial idea in medieval Spain and though he won notable victories against the Moors, he remains a somewhat hazy figure.

His childhood was complicated by the struggle between his mother Urraca and her second husband, Alfonso I of Aragon, for control of Castile and Leon. Only on Urraca's death (1126) did his stepfather finally relinquish his claims. Alfonso was then formally accepted as emperor by the kings of Aragon and Pamplona (Navarre), by the count of Barcelona, and by various Hispano-Moorish rulers. His capture of Almería (1147) from the Moors won him renown, as did other victories, but in the end these led to little expansion of territory. Almería was lost again in 1157 and Córdoba remained in his hands for only three years. In 1146 a new invasion of North African fanatics, the Almohads, began. Alfonso now allied himself with the Almoravids and devoted the rest of his life to a series of campaigns to check Almohad expansion in southern Spain.

Despite the importance of the imperial idea at this time, peninsular fractionalist tendencies were by no means dormant. Alfonso was unable to prevent the establishment of Portugal as an independent kingdom (1140) and, in his will, he himself divided his realm, as was the Spanish custom, between his two sons, Sancho III of Castile and Ferdinand II of Leon. This act finally destroyed the concept of empire in medieval Spain.

• **Alfonso VIII,** byname EL DE LAS NAVAS (Spanish: He of Las Navas) (b. 1155—d. Oct. 6, 1214, Burgos, Castile), king of Castile from 1158, son of Sancho III, whom he succeeded when three years old.

Before Alfonso came of age his reign was troubled by internal strife and the intervention of the kingdom of Navarre in Castilian affairs. Throughout his reign he maintained a close alliance with the kingdom of Aragon, and in 1179 he concluded the Pact of Cazorla, which settled the future line of demarcation between Castile and Aragon when the reconquest of Moorish Spain was completed. From 1172 to 1212 he was engaged in resistance to the Moorish Almohad invaders, who defeated him in 1195. In the same year the kings of Leon and Navarre invaded Castile, but Alfonso defeated them with the aid of King Peter II of Aragon. In 1212 Alfonso secured a great victory at Las Navas de Tolosa over the Almohad sultan and thereby broke Almohad power in Spain.

• **Alfonso IX** (b. 1171, Zamora, Leon—d. Sept. 24, 1230, Villanueva de Sarria, Galicia), king of Leon from 1188 to 1230, son of Ferdinand II of Leon and cousin of Alfonso VIII of Castile (next to whom he is numbered as a junior member of the family). A forceful personality, Alfonso IX was determined to recover Leonese territory lost to Castile; and, despite the fact that he had done homage to Alfonso VIII, he did not hesitate to ally himself with the Almohads to further this end. As a result, his kingdom was placed under papal interdiction, and he was finally compelled to marry the Castilian king's eldest daughter. He refused, however, to join his father-in-law in the crusade against the Almohads in 1212 unless the lost lands were first restored by Castile. This was not done and the Leonese army was, therefore, absent from Las Navas de Tolosa. Nevertheless, operating on his own, Alfonso IX won important victories beyond the southern frontiers of Leon, taking Cáceres (1227) and Mérida and Badajoz (1230) from the Almohads. These victories opened the road for a future reconquest of Seville.

• **Alfonso X,** byname ALFONSO THE WISE, Spanish ALFONSO EL SABIO (b. Nov. 23, 1221, Burgos, Castile—d. April 4, 1284, Seville), king of Castile and Leon from 1252 to 1284.

His father, Ferdinand III, conquered Andalusia and imposed tribute on the remaining Muslim states in Spain—Murcia and Granada. His mother, Beatrice, was granddaughter of the Holy Roman emperor Frederick I. Alfonso, already known as a scholar, became king in 1252. He had many scholars in his travelling court, and he was an active participant in their writing and editing. Some were experts on Roman law, which Alfonso hoped to make the basis of a uniform code for his lands. The court, gifts to friends, and foreign intrigue proved expensive, and Alfonso taxed heavily.

Alfonso crushed a Muslim revolt in 1252, and a revolt by nobles in 1254. Morocco, Granada, and Murcia invaded in 1264, but Alfonso won with Aragonese help, and annexed Murcia. In 1272, a revolt, and withdrawal to Granada, by nobles forced him to confirm local privileges.

In 1273 Alfonso founded, and granted privileges to, the Mesta, a guild of migratory shepherds.

Alfonso claimed many foreign titles, notably that of Holy Roman emperor in 1256. In 1257, bribes won him four electoral votes for emperor to three for Richard of Cornwall, but Richard, unlike Alfonso, could go to Germany. In 1275 Richard died, and Alfonso went to France to appeal to Pope Gregory X, who persuaded him to renounce his claim.

While Alfonso was in France, Morocco and Granada invaded Castile. Ferdinand, Alfonso's eldest son, was killed in the fighting. Sancho, Alfonso's second son, became a hero in defeating the invaders, and proclaimed himself heir, disregarding Ferdinand's sons, who were nephews of the French king. Alfonso recognized Sancho's claim in 1278, but, under French pressure, became ambiguous in 1281. Taking advantage of grievances against Alfonso, Sancho declared himself regent. Towns and nobles rose against Alfonso, who had to take refuge in Seville. Some of Sancho's followers deserted, but, after Alfonso died, Sancho took Seville and became King Sancho IV.

Alfonso's court scholars wrote mostly in Castilian Spanish, which they made a literary language by regularizing the syntax and by borrowing—and defining—words for concepts not previously discussed. In their *Premera crónica general,* they tried to determine historical facts from chronicle, folklore, and Arabic sources. Less factual was their *Gran e general estoria,* a world history, with extensive translations from the Old Testament. The *Tablas Alfonsies* were planetary tables, based on an Arabic source but updated by observations at Toledo 1262–72. *Siete partidas* was the most important law code. It was based on Roman law, and contained discourses on manners and morals, and an idea of the king and his people as a corporation—superior to feudal arrangements—with the king as agent of both God and the people. After Alfonso's death, *Siete partidas* was proclaimed the law of all Castile and Leon in 1348, and the language of Alfonso's court evolved into modern Castilian Spanish.

• **Alfonso XI,** byname ALFONSO THE JUST, Spanish ALFONSO EL JUSTICIERO (b. 1311, Salamanca, Leon—d. March 26, 1350, Gibraltar), king of Castile and Leon from 1312, who succeeded his father, Ferdinand IV, when he was only a year old.

His minority was marked by violent strife between factions of nobles, but when he came of age, in 1325, he restored order with unprecedented vigour. He gave new powers to the municipalities and to the Cortes, in exchange for their support against the nobles, and furthered the power of the crown by choosing officials without aristocratic affiliations. He then turned his attention to the Marinid kings of Morocco, who had seized Gibraltar and routed the Castilian fleet at Algeciras in 1340. With the Portuguese, he defeated the invaders at Río Salado in 1340 and recaptured Algeciras in 1344.

Alfonso XI promulgated important administrative and legal reforms in the ordinances of Alcalá de Henares in 1348. Alfonso was assiduously courted by both France and England, who wished for an alliance that would give them the support of his powerful fleet, but he avoided committing himself to either party.

Spain

• **Alfonso I–XI:** *see* Alfonso I–XI *under* Alfonso (Spain: Castile and Leon).

• **Alfonso XII** (b. Nov. 28, 1857, Madrid—d. Nov. 25, 1885, Madrid), Spanish king whose short reign (1874–85) gave rise to hopes for a constitutional monarchy in Spain.

The eldest surviving son of Queen Isabella II and, presumably, her consort, the Duque de Cádiz, Alfonso accompanied his mother into exile following her deposition by the revolution of September 1868. He received his education at the Theresianum in Vienna and at the Royal Military College, Sandhurst, in England. Isabella abdicated her rights in his favour in June 1870, but it was not until four years later (Dec. 29, 1874) that Alfonso was proclaimed king of Spain. He returned to his country early in January of the following year.

For most of Alfonso's reign Spain enjoyed an unaccustomed tranquillity. The pattern of political life was determined by Antonio Cánovas del Castillo, prime minister from 1875 to 1881 and again from January 1884. The two most urgent problems—ending the civil war unleashed by the Carlists, the partisans of the successors to the Spanish throne in the male line, and drafting the constitution—were both settled in 1876. In addition, the Convention of Zanjón established peace in Cuba. In January 1878 Alfonso married María de las Mercedes, daughter of the Duc de Montpensier. She died six months later and the following year the King married a daughter of the archduke Charles Ferdinand of Austria, María Cristina, by whom he had two daughters and a son, who became Alfonso XIII.

Although politically inexperienced, Alfonso XII demonstrated great natural tact and sound judgment, qualities that gave rise to hope that the monarchy would not suffer if the democratic constitution enacted in 1876 were fully implemented. Attempts on the King's life (October 1878 and December 1879) and a military pronunciamento against the regime (1883) were not indicative of any general discontent with the restored monarchy; on the contrary, Alfonso enjoyed considerable popularity, and his early death from tuberculosis was a great disappointment to those who looked forward to a constitutional monarchy in Spain.

• **Alfonso XIII** (b. May 17, 1886, Madrid—d. Feb. 28, 1941, Rome), Spanish king (1886–1931) who by seeking to enhance the power of the monarchy at the expense of Parliament hastened his own deposition by advocates of the Second Republic.

The posthumous son of Alfonso XII, Alfonso XIII was immediately proclaimed king under the regency of his mother, María Cristina. Though lively and intelligent, he was raised in an ultraclerical and reactionary atmosphere by his doting mother. He reacted early against the boredom of court life and began his lifelong attachment to the Spanish army. In 1902, on his 16th birthday, he assumed full authority as king.

Alfonso relished his position of authority. He continued the system of alternating Conservative and Liberal governments (based on continued elections), but he increasingly intervened in politics in order to rotate governments. Political instability was the result; 33 governments were formed in Spain between 1902 and 1923, and the parliamentary system was steadily discredited. Alfonso's popularity also suffered, and the notorious attempt on his life and that of his bride, Victoria Eugenia of Battenberg, on their wedding day (May 31, 1906) was followed by a constant succession of plots to assassinate him. His great personal courage in the face of these attacks, however, won him considerable admiration.

Alfonso's position worsened after the failure of the government of Antonio Maura (1909); the last hope for the parliamentary regime seemed extinguished. Although his conduct during World War I was irreproachable (he observed a scrupulous neutrality and rendered great service to humanitarian causes), in the postwar period he began to move toward a system of more personal rule, even seeking a means to rid himself of Parliament. He intervened directly in the Moroccan War in 1921 with such disastrous effect that a subsequent commission of inquiry placed the blame squarely on him. A week before the report was to be published, however, Alfonso was rescued from a humiliating situation by a coup d'etat (Sept. 13, 1923) led by Gen. Miguel Primo de Rivera.

By directly associating himself with the overthrow of the parliamentary regime, however, and linking his fortunes to the dictatorship of Primo de Rivera, Alfonso jeopardized the existence of the Spanish monarchy. When Primo de Rivera fell from power in January 1930, a temporary government under Gen. Dámaso Berenguer was called on to save the King. Alfonso tried various methods to bring about a return to a constitutional regime without the risk of elections. Eventually, he agreed to hold municipal elections (April 1931), which, at least in the important towns, resulted in a landslide for the Republican parties. The victors demanded the King's abdication; the army withdrew its support and Alfonso, though refusing to abdicate, was forced to leave Spain (April 14, 1931).

Alfonso never returned. Gen. Francisco Franco reinstated him as a Spanish citizen and restored his property (confiscated in 1932), but he eventually abdicated his rights to his third son, Don Juan.

Alfonso THE AFRICAN: *see* Afonso V *under* Afonso (Portugal).

Alfonso THE BATTLER: *see* Alfonso I *under* Alfonso (Spain: Aragon).

Alfonso THE BRAVE: *see* Alfonso VI *under* Alfonso (Spain: Castile and Leon); Afonso IV *under* Afonso (Portugal).

Alfonso THE CANDID: *see* Alfonso III *under* Alfonso (Spain: Aragon).

Alfonso THE CATHOLIC: *see* Alfonso I *under* Alfonso (Spain: Asturias and Leon).

Alfonso THE CHASTE: *see* Alfonso II *under* Alfonso (Spain: Asturias and Leon).

Alfonso THE CONQUEROR: *see* Afonso I *under* Afonso (Portugal).

Alfonso THE EMPEROR: *see* Alfonso VII *under* Alfonso (Spain: Castile and Leon).

Alfonso THE FAT: *see* Afonso II under Afonso (Portugal).

Alfonso THE GREAT: *see* Alfonso III *under* Alfonso (Spain: Asturias and Leon).

Alfonso THE JUST: *see* Alfonso XI *under* Alfonso (Spain: Castile and Leon).

Alfonso THE KIND: *see* Alfonso IV *under* Alfonso (Spain: Aragon).

Alfonso THE LIBERAL: *see* Alfonso III *under* Alfonso (Spain: Aragon).

Alfonso THE MAGNANIMOUS: *see* Alfonso V *under* Alfonso (Spain: Aragon).

Alfonso THE MONK: *see* Alfonso IV *under* Alfonso (Spain: Asturias and Leon).

Alfonso THE NOBLE: *see* Alfonso V *under* Alfonso (Spain: Asturias and Leon).

Alfonso THE WISE: *see* Alfonso X *under* Alfonso (Spain: Castile and Leon).

Alfred, also spelled AELFRED, byname ALFRED THE GREAT (b. 849—d. 899), king of Wessex (871–899), a Saxon kingdom in southwestern England. He prevented England from falling to the Danes and promoted learning and literacy. Compilation of the Anglo-Saxon Chronicle began during his reign, *c.* 890.

When he was born, it must have seemed unlikely that Alfred would become king, since he had four older brothers; he said that he never desired royal power. Perhaps a scholar's life would have contented him. His mother early aroused his interest in English poetry, and from his boyhood he also hankered after Latin learning, possibly stimulated by visits to Rome in 853 and 855. It is possible also that he was aware of and admired the great Frankish king Charlemagne, who had at the beginning of the century revived learning in his realm. Alfred had no opportunity to acquire the education he sought, however, until much later in life.

Alfred the Great, Anglo-Saxon coin, 9th century; in the British Museum

By courtesy of the trustees of the British Museum; photograph, J.R. Freeman & Co., Ltd.

He probably received the education in military arts normal for a young man of rank. He first appeared on active service in 868, when he and his brother, King Aethelred (Ethelred) I, went to help Burgred of Mercia (the kingdom between the Thames and the Humber) against a great Danish army that had landed in East Anglia in 865 and taken possession of Northumbria in 867. The Danes refused to give battle, and peace was made. In this year Alfred married Ealhswith, descended through her mother from Mercian kings. Late in 871, the Danes invaded Wessex, and Aethelred and Alfred fought several battles with them. Aethelred died in 871 and Alfred succeeded him. After an unsuccessful battle at Wilton he made peace. It was probably the quality of the West Saxon resistance that discouraged Danish attacks for five years.

In 876 the Danes again advanced on Wessex: they retired in 877 having accomplished little, but a surprise attack in January 878 came near to success. The Danes established themselves at Chippenham, and the West Saxons submitted "except King Alfred." He harassed the Danes from a fort in the Somerset marshes, and until seven weeks after Easter he secretly assembled an army, which defeated them at the Battle of Edington. They surrendered, and their king, Guthrum, was baptized, Alfred standing as sponsor; the following year they settled in East Anglia.

Wessex was never again in such danger. Alfred had a respite from fighting until 885, when he repelled an invasion of Kent by a Danish army, supported by the East Anglian

Danes. In 886 he took the offensive and captured London, a success that brought all the English not under Danish rule to accept him as king. The possession of London also made possible the reconquest of the Danish territories in his son's reign, and Alfred may have been preparing for this, though he could make no further advance himself. He had to meet a serious attack by a large Danish force from the Continent in 892, and it was not until 896 that it gave up the struggle.

The failure of the Danes to make any more advances against Alfred was largely a result of the defensive measures he undertook during the war. Old forts were strengthened and new ones built at strategic sites, and permanent arrangements were made for their manning. Alfred reorganized his army and used ships against the invaders as early as 875. Later he had larger ships built to his own design for use against the coastal raids that continued even after 896. Wise diplomacy also helped Alfred's defense. He maintained friendly relations with Mercia and Wales; Welsh rulers sought his support and supplied some troops for his army in 893.

Alfred succeeded in government as well as at war. He was a wise administrator, organizing his finances and the service due from his *thegns* (noble followers). He scrutinized the administration of justice and took steps to insure the protection of the weak from oppression by ignorant or corrupt judges. He promulgated an important code of laws, after studying the principles of lawgiving in the book of Exodus and the codes of Aethelbert of Kent, Ine of Wessex (688–694), and Offa of Mercia (757–796), again with special attention to the protection of the weak and dependent. While avoiding unnecessary changes in custom, he limited the practice of the blood feud and imposed heavy penalties for breach of oath or pledge.

Alfred is most exceptional, however, not for his generalship or his administration but for his attitude to learning. He shared the contemporary view that Viking raids were a divine punishment for the people's sins, and he attributed these to the decline of learning, for only through learning could men acquire wisdom and live in accordance with God's will. Hence, in the lull from attack between 878 and 885, he invited scholars to his court from Mercia, Wales, and the Continent. He learned Latin himself and began to translate Latin books into English in 887. He directed that all young freemen of adequate means must learn to read English, and by his own translations and those of his helpers he made available English versions of "those books most necessary for all men to know," books that would lead them to wisdom and virtue. The *Ecclesiastical History of the English People*, by the English historian Bede, and the *7 Books of Histories Against the Pagans*, by Orosius, a 5th-century theologian—neither of which was translated by Alfred himself, though they have been credited to him—revealed the divine purpose in history. Alfred's translation of the *Pastoral Care* of St. Gregory I, the great 6th-century pope, provided a manual for priests in the instruction of their flocks, and a translation by Bishop Werferth of Gregory's *Dialogues* supplied edifying reading on holy men. Alfred's rendering of the *Soliloquies* of the 5th-century theologian St. Augustine of Hippo, to which he added material from other works of the Fathers of the Church, discussed problems concerning faith and reason and the nature of eternal life. This translation deserves to be studied in its own right, as does his rendering of Boethius' *Consolation of Philosophy*. In considering what is true happiness and the relation of providence to faith and of predestination to free will, Alfred does not fully accept Boethius' position but depends more on the early Fathers. In both works, additions include parallels from contemporary conditions, sometimes revealing his views on the social order and the duties of kingship. Alfred wrote for the benefit of his people, but he was also deeply interested in theological problems for their own sake and commissioned the first of the translations, Gregory's *Dialogues*, "that in the midst of earthly troubles he might sometimes think of heavenly things." He may also have done a translation of the first 50 psalms. Though not Alfred's work, the Anglo-Saxon Chronicle, one of the greatest sources of information about Saxon England, which began to be circulated about 890, may have its origin in the intellectual interests awakened by the revival of learning under him. His reign also saw activity in building and in art, and foreign craftsmen were attracted to his court.

In one of his endeavours, however, Alfred had little success; he tried to revive monasticism, founding a monastery and a nunnery, but there was little enthusiasm in England for the monastic life until after the revivals on the Continent in the next century.

Alfred, alone of Anglo-Saxon kings, inspired a full-length biography, written in 893, by the Welsh scholar Asser. This work contains much valuable information, and it reveals that Alfred laboured throughout under the burden of recurrent, painful illness; and beneath Asser's rhetoric can be seen a man of attractive character, full of compassion, able to inspire affection, and intensely conscious of the responsibilities of kingly office. This picture is confirmed by Alfred's laws and writings.

Alfred was never forgotten: his memory lived on through the Middle Ages and in legend as that of a king who won victory in apparently hopeless circumstances and as a wise lawgiver. Some of his works were copied as late as the 12th century. Modern studies have increased knowledge of him but have not altered in its essentials the medieval conception of a great king. (D.W.)

BIBLIOGRAPHY. On Asser's *Life of King Alfred*, ed. by W.H. Stevenson (1959 reprint with chapter on recent work by D. Whitelock), see D. Whitelock, *The Genuine Asser* (1968). The best modern account is F.M. Stenton, *Anglo-Saxon England*, 3rd ed. (1971); a popular account is E.S. Duckett, *Alfred the Great and His England* (1957). For other sources on the reign, see G.N. Garmonsway, *The Anglo-Saxon Chronicle* (1953); *English Historical Documents*, vol. 1, ed. by D. Whitelock (1955); and F.L. Attenborough, (ed.), *The Laws of the Earliest English Kings* (1922).

Editions of the Alfredian translations: King Alfred's West-Saxon Version of Gregory's Pastoral Care (1871) and *King Alfred's Orosius* (1883), both ed. by H. Sweet; *King Alfred's Old English Version of Boethius*, ed. by W.J. Sedgefield (text 1899; modern English, 1900); *King Alfred's Old English Version of St. Augustine's Soliloquies*, ed. by H.L. Hargrove (text 1902; modern English, 1904); *King Alfred's Version of St. Augustine's Soliloquies*. ed. by T.A. Carnicelli (1969); *The Old English Version of Bede's Ecclesiastical History*, ed. by T. Miller (1890–98); Werferth's translation of Gregory's *Dialogues*, ed. by H. Hecht (1900). See also D. Whitelock, "The Prose of Alfred's Reign," in E.G. Stanley (ed.), *Continuations and Beginnings* (1966), with bibliography; J.M. Bately, "King Alfred and the Old English Translation of Orosius," *Anglia*, 88:433–460 (1970); K. Otten, *König Alfreds Boethius* (1964); and F. Anne Payne, *King Alfred and Boethius* (1968).

Alfred Jewel, elaborate gold ornament consisting of an enamelled plaque with a figure held in place on one side by an engraved design and on the other by a gold fret of Old English words. The inscription reads, "Aelfred mec heht gewyrcan" ("Alfred ordered me to be made").

Alfred Jewel, gold and enamel, Anglo-Saxon, *c.* 9th century; in the Ashmolean Museum, Oxford

By courtesy of the Ashmolean Museum, Oxford

The Alfred Jewel, now in the Ashmolean Museum, Oxford, was found in 1693 near Athelney, Somerset, Eng., the site where Alfred the Great took refuge from the Danes in 878. The ornament shows strong Byzantine influence.

Alfvén, Hannes (Olof Gösta) (b. May 30, 1908, Norrköping, Swed.), astrophysicist and winner, with Louis Néel of France, of the Nobel Prize for Physics in 1970 for his essential contributions in founding plasma physics—the study of plasmas (gaseous aggregates of molecules, electrons, and ions).

Alfvén was educated at Uppsala University and in 1940 joined the staff of the Royal Institute of Technology, Stockholm. During the late 1930s and early 1940s he made remarkable contributions to space physics, including the theorem of frozen-in flux, according to which under certain conditions a plasma is bound to the magnetic lines of flux that pass through it. Alfvén later used the concept to explain the origin of cosmic rays.

In 1939 Alfvén published his theory of magnetic storms and the aurora, which immensely influenced the modern theory of the magnetosphere (the region of the Earth's magnetic field). He discovered a widely used mathematical approximation by which the complex spiral motion of a charged particle in a magnetic field can be easily calculated.

Magnetohydrodynamics (MHD), the study of plasmas in magnetic fields, was largely pioneered by Alfvén, and his work has been acknowledged as fundamental to attempts to control nuclear fusion.

After numerous disagreements with the Swedish government, Alfvén obtained a position (1967) with the University of California, San Diego. Later he divided his teaching time between the Royal Institute in Oslo and the University of California. Much of his early research was included in his *Cosmical Electrodynamics* (1950). He also wrote *On the Origin of the Solar System* (1954), *Worlds-Antiworlds* (1966), and *Cosmic Plasma* (1981).

algae, singular ALGA, primitive plantlike organisms (approximately 25,000 species), ranging in size from one-celled flagellates measuring as little as 3 microns to leafy kelps reaching 62 metres (203 feet). They are capable of photosynthesis but lack true leaves, stems, roots, and vascular systems.

A brief treatment of algae follows. For full treatment, *see* MACROPAEDIA: Protophytes.

There is virtually no part of the Earth's surface that does not support some algal forms, from the forests of the temperate zones to the Arctic tundra. Some varieties live in soil and withstand long periods without water; others live in snow, and a few species thrive in hot springs.

Each of the three major algae groups—Chlorophyta (green algae), Phaeophyta (brown algae), and Rhodophyta (red algae)—include lime-encrusted genera and species, which over millennia have made vast contributions to the geological strata of the Earth's landmasses. Ninety percent of all photosynthesis is carried out by algae, and it is believed that they played an important role in creating the Earth's oxygen-rich atmosphere early in the planet's history.

Planktonic algae are an essential link in

the food chain in the oceans, and all higher aquatic life-forms ultimately depend on it. In addition, algae have been used as feed for livestock and as food for human consumption since prehistoric times. Though its nutritional value is limited, seaweed is important as roughage and adds protein, vitamins, and mineral salts to the diet. It is also believed to be responsible for the low incidence of goitre in areas where it is part of a daily intake.

Algae is used for a wide range of commercial purposes. Among its products is a form of gelose (*e.g.*, agar) that is produced by more than 70 species of red algae. Agar is used to can fish, to transport cooked fish, to size fabric, to make film and high-grade adhesives, and to create soups, sauces, jellies, ice creams, and icings. The uses of carrageenan extracts (a product of Irish moss) parallel those of agar and also include the making of sodium, potassium, or calcium salts. Algenic acids, a constituent of brown algae, produce alkali salts that are spun like silk to make threads.

Algae can reproduce vegetatively (through cell division or fragmentation), asexually (through the release of motile zoospores or the production of other spore forms), or sexually. Sexual reproduction usually occurs at times of stress in the life cycle (*i.e.*, at the end of the growing season or during unfavourable environmental conditions).

Articles are alphabetized word by word, not letter by letter

Algardi, Alessandro (b. 1595, Bologna, Papal States—d. June 10, 1654, Rome), after Bernini, the most important Roman sculptor of the 17th century working in the Baroque style.

Algardi was trained under Lodovico Carracci. After a short period of activity in Mantua (1622), he moved to Rome (1625), where he designed the stucco decorations in S. Silvestro al Quirinale and gained some success as a restorer of classical sculptures. With the monument of Cardinal Millini (died 1629) in Sta. Maria del Popolo, the Frangipani monument in S. Marcello al Corso, and the bust of Cardinal Laudivio Zacchia (Berlin), Algardi emerged as the principal rival of Bernini in the field of portrait sculpture. Lacking Bernini's dynamic vitality and penetrating characterization, Algardi's portraits were appreciated for their sobriety and surface realism.

"Meeting of Attila and Pope Leo," colossal marble relief by Alessandro Algardi, 1646–53; in St. Peter's, Rome

Alinari—Anderson from Art Resource/EB Inc.

After the election of Pope Innocent X (1644) Algardi superseded Bernini in papal favour. Between this date and his death he produced some of his most celebrated works, among them the seated statue of the Pope now in the Palazzo dei Conservatori (1645) and a colossal marble relief of the "Meeting of Attila and Pope Leo" in St. Peter's (1646–53), which influenced the development and popularization of illusionistic reliefs. At this time he also designed the Villa Doria Pamphili and a fountain in the Cortile di S. Damaso of the Vatican.

Algardi's style was less ebullient and pictorial than Bernini's, and, even in such characteristically Baroque works as the tomb of Pope Leo XI in St. Peter's (1634–52) and the high altar of S. Paolo at Bologna (1641), the restraining influence of the antique is strongly felt.

Algarotti, Francesco (b. Dec. 11, 1712, Venice—d. May 3, 1764, Pisa), connoisseur of the arts and sciences esteemed by the philosophers of the Enlightenment for his wide knowledge and elegant presentation of advanced ideas.

Educated at Rome, Bologna, and Florence, Algarotti went to Paris at the age of 20. There his urbanity, his physical beauty, and his versatile intelligence promptly made an impression in intellectual circles. A year later

Algarotti, detail of an engraving by Giuseppe Dala

By courtesy of the Civici Musei, Venice, Italy

he wrote *Il Newtonianismo per le dame* (1737; "Newtonianism for Ladies"), a popular exposition of Newtonian optics. Following a visit to Russia in 1739, he received an invitation to Prussia from Frederick the Great, which led to his staying more than nine years in Germany. Ill health eventually obliged him to return to Italy, first to Venice and then to Pisa. A monument on his tomb was inscribed with "Algarottus non omnis" ("[Here lies] Algarotti [but] not all"). Algarotti's writings include several studies on classical themes and a number of stimulating essays on the subjects of architecture (1753), the opera (1755), and painting (1762).

Algarve, historical province of southern Portugal, corresponding to the modern administrative district of Faro, bounded by the Atlantic Ocean (south and west) and the lower Rio Guadiana (east). Much of the interior upland region is of low productivity and is sparsely populated; the fertile coastal lowland is more densely inhabited.

The Phoenicians established bases in the area, and the Romans later conquered it; Visigoths ruled the region until Muslims took control in the early 8th century. After nearly five centuries of Muslim rule Algarve was taken into the Portuguese kingdom in 1189. Algarve (Arabic al-Gharb, meaning "the west") remains Moorish in appearance.

The economy is based on agriculture (corn [maize], figs, olives, almonds, grapes, pomegranates, and carobs). Fishing (tuna, anchovies, mackerel, and sardines) is also important; industries include the processing of fish, cork, and wine, as well as mining. In recent years tourism in the Algarve region has increased greatly. Prince Henry the Navigator established his school of navigation at Sagres Point *c.* 1418.

Harvesting in the coastal area of Algarve, Portugal

Maurice Landre—APA

After Portugal granted independence to Angola and Mozambique in the 1970s, about 500,000 *retornados* ("returnees") fled to Portugal. The Portuguese government, with assistance from the United States, subsidized housing in Algarve's hotels for the *retornados,* at costs that nearly collapsed the economy. These problems, however, did not hamper development of the tourist industry.

algebra, branch of mathematics in which the procedures of arithmetic are generalized and applied to variable quantities, as well as to specific numbers. To the layman, algebra means elementary algebra, in which one learns to calculate with variables instead of just the numbers of arithmetic and to solve polynomial equations. To the professional mathematician, however, as well as to increasing numbers of scientists in other fields, algebra means rather what is called modern, higher, or abstract algebra—the study of abstract mathematical structures in which there are operations that have the properties of addition and multiplication.

A brief treatment of algebra follows. For full treatment, *see* MACROPAEDIA: Algebra.

Essential to both elementary and higher algebra is the fact that the calculations should always involve only a finite number of quantities and end after a finite number of steps; in other words, processes in which the answers are obtained "in the limit" generally do not belong to algebra. Thus

$$1 + x + x^2 + x^3 + \cdot \cdot \cdot + x^n = \frac{1 - x^{n+1}}{1 - x}$$

is algebra, but

$$1 + x + x^2 + x^3 + \cdot \cdot \cdot + x^n + \cdot \cdot \cdot = \frac{1}{1 - x}$$

is not.

A second characteristic of algebra is its abstractness. Even in elementary algebra calculations are made not with numbers but with letters that represent numbers. In higher algebra the letters may represent much more general objects, and the system of calculation is itself an abstraction of systems having similar properties.

The demands placed on algebra by other branches of mathematics have been the richest and most significant source of new results in algebra, while, at the same time, the axiomatic, abstract algebraic viewpoint has simplified and clarified work in other fields, providing techniques leading both to new results and to unexpected connections between work in widely separated fields. This "algebraization" of mathematics has been one of the most characteristic features of 20th-century mathematics. In this way the influence of algebra has actually been far greater than its results. At the same time, modern algebra has brought a clearer understanding of the processes of elementary algebra and has enabled mathematicians to gain an understanding of the principles that underlie the calculations.

The basic task of elementary algebra is the solution of polynomial, *i.e.*, "algebraic," equations and the stepwise introduction of new types of numbers—negative, real, and complex—to use in solving them. Determinants and matrices are devices for facilitating the solution of simultaneous equations and thus have their place. The quadratic formula is the explicit solution of the quadratic equation, and so also merits attention.

Permutations and combinations (typical problem: in how many ways can six men choose their wives from among six women, assuming no bigamy) are really elementary probability theory, but they use only algebraic arguments and the formulas are occasionally useful—the binomial coefficients, for instance. Exponentials and logarithms, on the other hand, are certainly not algebra, since they involve passage to the limit in their definition. Of course, the emphasis in elementary algebra is not on the precise definition of these functions but rather on the formal rules for operating with them, such calculation with formal rules being universally interpreted as "algebra."

Modern algebra evolved from elementary algebra in a series of jumps beginning essentially with the work of Évariste Galois in 1830. It includes all of elementary algebra and a great deal more, but in an extensively generalized form; each topic of elementary algebra is thus viewable as the starting point of one of the theories of modern algebra. The principle abstract objects of study are groups, rings, fields, vector spaces, and algebras. Groups have one operation (called addition or multiplication); rings have two; fields are commutative rings in which one can divide; vector spaces are additive groups in which there is a scalar multiplication by elements of some field; algebras (sometimes called linear algebras) are vector spaces with a multiplication law defined.

The theory of rings came from study of the formal properties of integers and polynomials. Fields arose from the attempts to provide solutions for algebraic equations. The proof that the equation of fifth degree could not be solved by a formula analogous to the quadratic formula gave rise to group theory. Finally, the solution of simultaneous linear equations in elementary algebra led directly to the theory of vector spaces and matrices; the square $n \times n$ matrices themselves give one of the most important examples of an algebra.

Finally, a word should be said about some of the applications of algebra to sciences other than mathematics. In theoretical physics, the theory of groups and their representations has played an important part in the development of quantum theory, particularly in connection with solid-state physics. The theory of Boolean algebras has been widely used in the design of computing machines. In the social sciences, psychology and economics are finding use for matrices and linear algebra in what is called linear programming. The introduction of algebra into other disciplines has stimulated the further development of algebra itself.

algebraic equation, statement of the equality of two expressions formulated by applying to a set of variables the algebraic operations, namely, addition, subtraction, multiplication, division, raising to a power, and extraction of a root. Equations that involve nonalgebraic operations, such as the evaluation of logarithms or trigonometric functions, are said to be transcendental.

The solution of an algebraic equation is the process of finding a number or set of numbers that, if substituted for the variables in the equation, reduce it to an identity. Such a number is called a root (*q.v.*) of the equation. *See also* Diophantine equation; linear equation; quadratic equation.

algebraic geometry, the study of geometric objects by means of algebra.

A brief treatment of algebraic geometry follows. For full treatment, *see* MACROPAEDIA: Geometry: *Algebraic geometry.*

A Babylonian record of about 1700 BC describes a problem about a rectangle (a geometric object) and involves unknown numbers; it is, thus, an example of algebraic geometry. The Greek mathematicians of classical times had the problem: to construct the edge of a cube that shall have twice the volume of a given cube. Calling the edge of the given cube a and the edge of the sought cube x, we would write $x^3 = 2a^3$. Hippocrates of Chios (*c.* 430 BC) reformulated the problem as one of finding x and y such that $a/x = x/y = y/2a$. Menaechmus (*c.* 350 BC) considered the locus in a rectangular coordinate system of the points (x,y) such that $x^2 = ay$ and similarly of the points (x,y) such that $xy = 2a^2$, recognized the first as a parabola and the second as a hyperbola, and thus found x,y from the intersection of these curves.

The 17th-century French mathematicians René Descartes and Pierre de Fermat studied the conic sections and knew that the points (x,y) of their geometric loci satisfied algebraic equations of degree 2 in x and y. Later, Isaac Newton studied polynomial equations of degree 3 and classified the corresponding loci, cubics, into 72 kinds. Thus, Descartes, Fermat, and Newton can be credited with initiating the study of plane algebraic curves, *i.e.*, loci given by polynomials of arbitrary degree, a basic topic in algebraic geometry.

The scope and generality of modern algebraic geometry are increased by adoption of certain ideas from projective geometry. For example, two (distinct) straight lines should meet in just one point. This is correct except in the case of parallel lines. This exception can be technically circumvented by introducing so-called "points at infinity" and dealing with the images of the lines in the projective plane. Plane geometric curves are represented in the projective plane by homogeneous polynomial equations (a polynomial is homogeneous if all its terms have the same degree). In the projective plane any two (distinct) straight lines, parallel or not, meet in precisely one point. Another difficulty, that of counting the intersections of tangent curves, is overcome by assigning a point of tangency the multiplicity 2.

In these developments some typical phenomena may be noted: in studying the geometry, the understanding of what geometry is changes; and new algebraic methods are devised. A curve in the projective plane over the complex numbers cannot be perceived in the way a real curve in the affine plane is, but geometric terminology, governed by logic, remains valid.

In the plane a point is given by two coordinates (x,y), and in ordinary space by three (x,y,z). One may call, for any positive integer n, a sequence $(x_1, \ldots, x^n)$ of numbers a point of (affine) n-space. In n-space an algebraic variety is defined as the set of points satisfying a system of polynomial equations: $F_1(x_1, \ldots, x_n) = 0$, $f_2(x_1, \ldots, x_n) = 0, \ldots$. These objects and their generalizations are the main objects of study in algebraic geometry.

algebraic number, real number for which there exists a polynomial equation with natural numbers or their negatives as coefficients such that the given real number is a solution. Examples of algebraic numbers are all natural numbers, all rational numbers, and some but not all irrational numbers. Numbers such as that symbolized by the Greek letter pi, π, which are not algebraic, are called transcendental numbers.

algebraic surface, in three-dimensional space, a surface the equation of which is $f(x, y, z) = 0$, with $f(x, y, z)$ a polynomial (*q.v.*) in x, y, z. The order of the surface is the degree of the polynomial equation. If the surface is of the first order, it is a plane. If the surface is of order two, it is called a quadric surface. By rotating the surface, its equation can be put in the form $Ax^2 + By^2 + Cz^2 + Dx + Ey + Fz = G$. If A, B, C are all not zero, the equation can generally be simplified to the form $ax^2 + by^2 + cz^2 = 1$. This surface is called an ellipsoid (*q.v.*) if a, b, and c are positive. If one of the coefficients is negative, the surface is a hyperboloid (*q.v.*) of one sheet; if two of the coefficients are negative, the surface is a hyperboloid of two sheets. A hyperboloid of one sheet has a saddle point (a point on a curved surface at which the curvatures in two mutually perpendicular planes are of opposite signs).

If A, B, C are possibly zero, then cylinders, cones, planes, and elliptic or hyperbolic paraboloids may be produced. Examples of the latter are $z = x^2 + y^2$ and $z = x^2 - y^2$, respectively. Through every point of a quadric pass two straight lines (possibly imaginary) lying on the surface. A cubic surface is one of order three. It has the property that 27 lines lie on it, each one meeting 10 others. In general, a surface of order four or more contains no straight lines.

Algeciras, port town, Cádiz province, in the autonomous community (region) of Andalusia, in extreme southern Spain, across the Bay of Gibraltar from Gibraltar.

The port, at the mouth of the Río de la Miel, was founded in 713 by Moors and is probably on the site of the Roman Portus Albus; its Arabic name, al-Jazīrah al-Khaḍrā', means Green Island, in reference to the offshore Isla Verde. The port was taken by Alfonso XI of Castile in 1344, then recaptured and destroyed in 1368 by the Moors. It was refounded in 1704 by Spanish refugees from Gibraltar and in 1760 was rebuilt by Charles III on its present rectangular plan. The Algeciras Conference (*q.v.*) was held in 1906 in the Casa Consistorial (Town Hall).

The town's main commercial activity is connected with the port, which is a stopping place for transatlantic shipping and handles many passengers, especially from the ferry services to and from Tangier and other ports in Morocco. Tourism, based on the mild winter climate, is growing. Algeciras also has ice-making and preserving plants, and fishing and fish salting are the main occupations. Local agricultural products include cereals, tobacco, hogs, and cattle. Pop. (1981) 86,042.

Algeciras Conference (Jan. 16–April 7, 1906), international conference of the great European powers and the United States, held at Algeciras, Spain, to discuss France's relationship to the government of Morocco. The conference climaxed the First Moroccan Crisis (*see* Moroccan crises).

Two years earlier an Entente Cordiale, signed by Great Britain and France, had provided, among other things, for British support of French special interests in Morocco. France's attempt to implement the agreement by presenting the Moroccan sultan with a program of economic and police "reforms" brought the indignant German emperor William II to Tangier in March 1905. William challenged French intentions by affirming the sovereignty of the Sultan and demanding the retention of the "open door" for commerce.

Tension was relieved as U.S. Pres. Theodore Roosevelt was prevailed upon by the Emperor to help bring about the 1906 conference in Algeciras. Contrary to German expectations, only Austria-Hungary supported Germany's views; Italy, Russia, and, more significantly, Britain and the United States lined up behind France. On the surface, nevertheless, the convention, the Act of Algeciras, signed April 7, 1906, appeared to limit French penetration. It reaffirmed the independence of the Sultan and the economic equality of the powers, and it provided that the French and Spanish police officers were to be under a Swiss inspector general.

The real significance of the conference is to be found in the substantial diplomatic support given France by Britain and the United States, foreshadowing their roles in World War I, of which the Moroccan Crisis was a prelude.

Alger, also called (after 1981) EL-DJAZAIR, English conventional ALGIERS, *wilāyah* (province, or *département*), north central Algeria. Situated in the Sahel Hills of the Tell Atlas range, it fronts the Mediterranean Sea on the north and west and is bounded by the *wilāyāt* of Tizi Ouzou (east), and Bouira and Blida (south). With an area of 303 sq mi (786 sq km) it is the country's smallest *wilāyah.* It receives about 30 in. (750 mm) of rainfall annually, and the local names of suburbs of Algiers city (such as Birmandreis, Birkhadem, and el-Biar) reflect this relative abundance of water (*bir* in Arabic means "water well"). Viticulture and dairy farming are the main agricultural pursuits on the hill slopes, and cereals (including barley and wheat) are grown at higher elevations. Flower growing, first introduced by French settlers, is economically important near the town of Cheraga (Chraga). Algiers city is both the *wilāyah* and national capital. Beach resorts, such as Sidi Ferruch and Zeralda, are found in the western part of the province. Eastern Alger *wilāyah* has a heavy industrial complex that includes an oil refinery, a chemical industry, and metal working and engineering plants. A technical university was established at the town of Boumerdas in 1981. Pop. (1980 est.) 2,091,798.

Alger (city, Algeria): *see* Algiers.

Alger OF LIÈGE, also called ALGER OF CLUNY, or ALGERUS MAGISTER (b. *c.* 1060, Liège, Lower Lorraine—d. *c.* 1131, Cluny, Burgundy), priest widely famed in his day for learning and ecclesiastical writing. He was first a deacon of the Church of Saint-Barthélemy at Liège and was appointed (*c.* 1100) to the cathedral church of St. Lambert. He declined many offers of posts from German bishops and retired to the monastery of Cluny.

His *History of the Church of Liège* and many of his other works are lost. The most important of those remaining are *Liber de misericordia et justitia* ("On Mercy and Justice"), a collection of biblical and patristic extracts with a commentary—an important work for the history of church law and discipline; *De sacramentis corporis et sanguinis Dominici* ("Concerning the Sacraments of the Body and the Blood of the Lord"), a treatise on the Eucharist in opposition to the Berengarian heresy, highly commended by Peter of Cluny and Erasmus; *Libellus de libero arbitrio* ("On Free Will"), in B. Pez's *Anecdota* (vol. 4); and *De sacrificio missae* ("On the Sacrifice of the Mass"), in the *Scriptorum veterum nova collectio* ("New Collection of Ancient Writers") of Angelo Mai (vol. 9).

Alger, Horatio (Jr.) (b. Jan. 13, 1832, Chelsea, Mass., United States—d. July 18, 1899, South Natick, Mass.), most popular author in the U.S. in the last 30 years of the 19th century and perhaps the most socially influential writer of his generation.

Alger was the son of a conservative Unitarian minister, Horatio Alger, Sr., who personally supervised his son's early life and saturated it with prayer, study, and discipline. By the age of nine the boy was reading French, Latin, and Greek, and he early showed an interest in writing. At Harvard he distinguished himself in the classics, graduating in 1852.

Alger had always been intended for the ministry by his family, but after leaving Harvard he tried for several years to make a living as a schoolteacher and a contributor to magazines. In 1857, however, he enrolled in the Harvard Divinity School, from which he took his degree in 1860. After a seven-month tour of Europe with two friends, he returned to the U.S. to find that the Civil War was beginning. Alger made two attempts to enlist, but was rejected because of asthma, and then became junior associate to his father in his pastorate at South Natick. His first novel, *Marie Bertrand: The Felon's Daughter,* an adult book about life in the Paris slums, was serialized in the *New York Weekly* in January–February 1864. His first novel to be published in book form was *Frank's Campaign* (1864), and it was an immediate success.

In 1864 also Alger was ordained and accepted the pulpit of a church in Brewster, Mass. He continued his writing, however, and in 1866 his congregation, feeling that this was accomplished at their expense, voted not to reengage him. In that year he moved to New York City, and with the publication of *Ragged Dick; or, Street Life in New York* (serialized in 1867, published in book form in 1868), a book for boys that was a sensational success, he found the vein that he was to work for the rest of his life.

The success of *Ragged Dick* led to a visit to the Newsboys' Lodging House, a home for foundlings and runaway boys. Alger came to use the home as a base of operations, and for many years he was benefactor and hero to the boys of the institution.

In this atmosphere Alger wrote those stories of poor boys who rose from rags to riches that were to make him famous and contribute the "Alger hero" to the American language. In a steady succession of books, almost alike except for the names of the characters, he preached that by honesty, cheerful perseverance, and hard work, the virtuous lad would have his just reward—though the reward was almost always precipitated by a stroke of good luck. A tour through the West in 1876–77 produced *The Young Miner* (1879) and other books with Western settings.

Alger settled in Brooklyn, N.Y., with his widowed housekeeper, Kate Down, and her two sons, John and Tommy, whom in 1894 he adopted.

A bibliography of his works is given in Ralph D. Gardner, *Horatio Alger* (1964). *Horatio's Boys: The Life and Works of Horatio Alger, Jr.,* by Edwin P. Hoyt was published in 1974.

Algeria, officially DEMOCRATIC AND POPULAR REPUBLIC OF ALGERIA, Arabic AL-JAZĀ'IR, or AL-JUMHŪRĪYAH AL-JAZĀ'IRĪYAH AD-DĪMUQRĀTIYAH ASH-SHA'BIYAH, French ALGÉRIE, or RÉPUBLIQUE ALGÉRIENNE DÉMOCRATIQUE ET POPULAIRE, country of North Africa, located on the Mediterranean coast in the Maghreb (northwestern Africa), covering an area of 896,588 sq mi (2,332,164 sq km). It is the second largest country on the continent (after The Sudan), and its capital is Algiers. It extends about 1,175 mi (1,890 km) from north to south and about 785 mi at its widest from east to west. Algeria is bounded on the east by Tunisia and Libya, on the southeast by Niger, on the southwest by Mali and Mauritania, on the northwest by Morocco, and fronts the Mediterranean Sea on the north. The country's population in 1981 was estimated at 19,590,000.

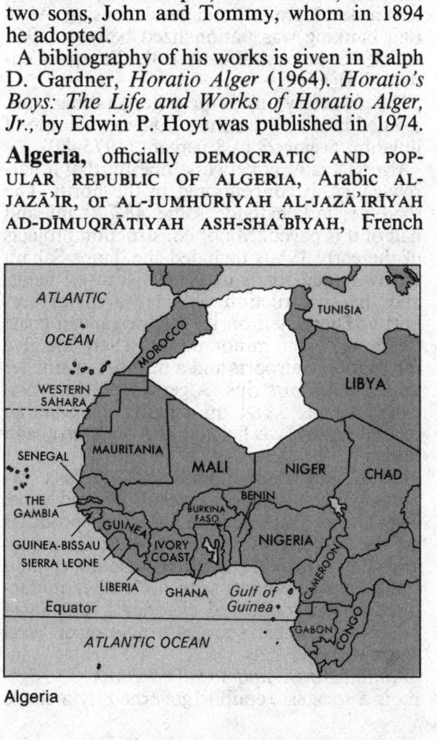

Algeria

The article that follows is a summary of significant detail about Algeria. Fuller treatment is provided in the following MACROPAEDIA articles. For geography and history, *see* North Africa; for information about the country and its major physiographic features in their regional setting, *see* Africa; Mediterranean Sea. For information about regional aspects of Algeria's history, *see* Islāmic World, The; and for information about Algeria's major cultural manifestations, *see* Islām, Muḥammad and the Religion of; Islāmic Arts.

For current history and for statistics on society and economy, *see* the article "World Affairs" and BRITANNICA WORLD DATA, respectively, in the *Britannica Book of the Year.*

The land. Algeria's large Saharan desert in the south occupies slightly more than 85 percent of its total area; a smaller northern region along the Mediterranean coast consists of interspersed plains and mountain ranges of the Atlas system. This system includes, from north to south, the Tell Atlas (Atlas Tellien), a continuation of the Maghreb's Atlas Mountains which extend into Morocco to the west and into Tunisia to the east; to the south lies the high plateaus zone (Hauts Plateaux). The southernmost section is the Saharan Atlas (Atlas Saharien), which separates the Maghreb from the Sahara to the south. The desert is generally more homogeneous in appearance, with its vast areas of stony pavement and sand dunes, but it also provides Algeria with its most striking mountains—the Ahaggar (Hoggar) Massif in the southeast—and its highest peak, Mount Tahat at 9,852 ft (3,003 m). The northern Atlas Tellien, though not as high as the southern mountains (at 3,000 to 7,500 ft), lies in a zone of severe earthquake activity. In 1717 the town of Onan was completely destroyed, and in 1790 Algiers lost about 20,000 people to major earthquakes. In 1954 and 1980 earthquakes killed some 5,200 people at el-Asnam.

Although oases and underground aquifers are scattered across the southern Saharan region, Algeria's major rivers are located in the north. Precipitation (generally less than 32 in. [800 mm] and often less than 16 in. per year) is meagre even in the north. Algeria's rivers tend to be seasonal or intermittent because of uneven seasonal distribution of precipitation, and only the development of reservoirs (primarily in the vicinity of Algiers and westward) allows year-round irrigation. The 23,000-sq-mi river basins of the Cheliff and Hamiz rivers provide about one-third of the country's irrigation needs. Dams in the northeast provide nearly 90 percent of the country's hydroelectric power—but 95 percent of its total electricity comes from thermal plants. The winters (December to March) are rainy, and near drought conditions prevail for the rest of the year. Forests of thugas, a cypress-like tree, are limited and located almost exclusively in the northeast and the Tell Atlas. The steppe-like climate of the Hauts Plateaux, a transition zone, supports only grasses and some shrubs. Among the animals considered endangered are the leopard, the cheetah, and a number of species of gazelle.

Algeria's natural gas fields, located in the north central part of the country, are among the world's largest known reserves, at 131,500,000,000,000 cu ft (3,723,000,000,000 cu m), following only the Soviet Union, Iran, and the U.S. With a petroleum reserve of nearly 1,100,000,000 metric tons, Algeria has one of the largest oil resource bases in Africa, following Libya and Nigeria. As Africa's only producer of mercury, Algeria provides 15 percent of the world's supply. Iron ore reserves are estimated at 4,500,000,000 metric tons (1,000,000,000 of which were in as yet undeveloped deposits in the western desert at Gara Djebilet).

The people. Algeria's population in 1981 was growing at an annual rate of 3.2 percent. The birth rate is extraordinarily high, estimated at 46 per 1,000, and the death rate is 14 per 1,000. The overall population density is only 3 per sq mi because of the large unpopulated areas of the Sahara; densities of more than 200 per sq mi, however, are typical of the more populous areas of the north. Algeria has a very young population; 48 percent are under 15. Life expectancy is low at only 54 years for men and 56 years for women. Most of the people are Arabs; Berbers are the main minority group. The languages are Arabic and Berber, with a few native French speakers. Arabic ethnic groups found in Algeria include the Kabyles and the Mzabites, who are Muslims of the Ibadite sect. Tuaregs are nomadic herders who live mainly on small oases of the Ahaggar and Adrar massifs in the southeastern Algerian Sahara. The Harratin, a Sudanese people of Negroid ancestry, live on small oases scattered throughout the country. The remaining population consists of French, Spanish, and Italian Europeans. The high birth rate has focussed attention on the need for adequate health care services for women and children, and various government measures have received continued funding from the United Nations Fund for Population Activities. According to the 1977 census, 44.3 percent of the population were urban residents. Algiers, the national capital and largest city, has a population of 1,748,000 (1978 est.); Oran had a population of 633,000; Constantine 489,000; Blida 438,000; Sétif 348,000; and Sidi-bel-Abbes 330,000.

The economy. Algeria has a centrally planned developing economy partly private in structure and based primarily on petroleum and natural gas. The gross national product (GNP) in 1980 was $36,410,000,000, about $1,920 per capita. Annual growth of the real GNP was 2.8 percent during the 1970s, relatively low for a petroleum-producing country, partly as a consequence of the high birth rate. The GNP originates primarily from petroleum and natural gas, followed by construction, manufacturing, mining, and services.

Only about three percent of Algeria's land is arable. About two-thirds of that is cultivated but only some 7 percent can be irrigated. Crops grown include wheat, barley, market vegetables, fruit, dates, and smaller quantities of peas, beans, lentils, tobacco, and sugar beets. Pastures consist mostly of arid rangeland, and the livestock raised on them includes sheep, cattle, goats, as well as asses, mules, camels, and horses. Algeria's agricultural sector produces only about 30 percent of national food requirements and the rest must be imported.

Forests, badly devastated during Algeria's war of independence, have been partly restored under reforestation programs. Algeria has large stands of cork oak and ranks among the top three cork producers in the world. Despite its long Mediterranean shoreline, the fisheries remain underdeveloped.

Petroleum and natural gas dominate the mineral sector; other important minerals produced include iron ore, sand, gravel, and crushed stone; phosphate rock; and smaller quantities of gypsum, salt, barite, clays, copper, zinc, lead, mercury, and silver. Algeria cut back its oil production in 1980–81 to extend the life of its reserves. Reserves of uranium, lead, zinc, and tungsten (wolfram) existed in the Ahaggar Mountains. Electrical production in 1980 was 6,200,000,000 kW-hr, 95 percent from thermal plants, the remainder hydroelectric.

Manufacturing is dominated by the hydrocarbon sector, and includes liquefied natural gas (LNG) and refined petroleum products. Other important manufactures are cement, crude steel and pig iron, liquefied petroleum gas (LPG), naphtha, and fertilizers. Light manufacturing includes ceramics, paints, polyester textiles, shoes, flour, edible vegetable oils, wine, and cigarettes. The Algerian government, in its 1980–84 five-year plan, placed increased emphasis on machinery, vehicle assembly, electrical goods, cement, paper, other light manufacturing industries, and home construction. Major construction projects underway in the early 1980s were railway extension (particularly, southward into the Hauts Plateaux zone), road building, and port development.

There are two government agencies to foster tourism, but it remained relatively unimportant in the Algerian economy. Since independence in 1962 Algeria has gradually nationalized the hydrocarbon, mining, heavy industry, transportation, finance, and foreign trade sectors. Light consumer-oriented industries and some housing construction remain in private control, as do retail trade, and ownership of small property holdings.

Nearly half of the economically active population is employed in agriculture followed by services, construction, and manufacturing. The overall trade union organization is the Union Générale des Travailleurs (UGTA), organized in 1956 and closely linked to the government. Farmers are represented by the Union Nationale des Paysans Algériens.

Budgetary revenue originates from oil revenues (more than two-thirds of the total) as well as from corporate and other taxes. Expenditures were mainly for education and research, defense and veterans benefits, and social services and administration. Major expenditures in a development budget provided non-recurrent expenditures, mostly financed by oil revenues for education, community and urban development, and rural housing. Algerian banking was nationalized between 1967 and 1972. Its central bank is the Banque Centrale d'Algérie.

The monetary unit is the Algerian dinar, subdivided into 100 centimes. The annual rate of inflation averaged 11.8 percent (1975–80).

Algeria's railway network, one-third of it narrow-gauge, is concentrated in the north. The road network extends some 48,720 mi and half of it is paved. Major construction projects of the early 1980s included the Trans-Sahara Highway and roads to the Saharan oil fields, and the construction of a tenth major seaport at Djen-Djen on its Mediterranean coast (there are eight minor ports). There are five international airports and a number of smaller airports and airstrips. Algeria's pipeline network extends 5,784 mi, linking the Saharan oil and natural gas fields to the Mediterranean ports.

Crude petroleum dominates Algeria's exports, which also include fertilizers and wine. The largest importers of Algerian products are the United States, France, West Germany, and Italy. Imports include machinery and transport equipment, semi-finished manufactured goods, food, and chemicals. The most important import sources are France, West Germany, and Italy.

Administrative and social conditions. Algeria is a socialist republic governed by a single party, the National Liberation Front (NLF). The constitution, adopted in 1976, concentrates executive power in the president, who also presides over the High Security Council and the Supreme Court, and is commander in chief of the military. The legislative power is vested in the 261-member National People's Assembly; its members are each elected for a five-year term.

The social welfare system in Algeria provides pensions for the old and disabled, allowances for families with children, and free health care for those under 16 years and over 60 years. The country is still plagued by such serious diseases as tuberculosis, venereal infections, malaria, and trachoma. Medical facilities are inadequate in rural areas, which has prompted the government to sponsor disease prevention measures, health education, and expanded health programs for rural areas. High population growth and rural–urban migration have created a severe housing shortage in the cities. To encourage these people to remain in their villages rather than migrating to the overcrowded cities, the government began a "One Thousand Socialist Villages" program in 1972. Each village, when completed, is to have about 1,500 people housed in 200 modern, three-room units.

The literacy rate in Algeria was only 30 percent in the late 1970s, and much of that in French, not Arabic. During the late 1970s, about 80 percent of all school-aged children received some education. Secondary education is still relatively undeveloped. The major centre of higher education is the Université d'Alger.

The government controls all of the printed and electronic news media in Algeria. The most widely circulated newspaper is *el-Moudjahid*, the official organ of the state.

Cultural life. Since independence from France (1962), the government has endeavoured to strengthen the traditional Arabic cultural heritage that was largely repressed during the years of French rule. One of the major traditional and modern art forms is literature. The literary art includes that written in the French language by individuals of French descent born in Algeria, such as Albert Camus, Emmanuel Robles, and René-Jean Clot; literature by native Algerians also written in French, but of Algerian expression, by writers who present a view of the contemporary scene intensely alienated from French Algeria; and poetry and plays written in Arabic or Berber dialects. Rugs, jewelry, and woodwork are also notable, if more traditional, major art forms. The religion of Islām provides a cultural link to the past; the citizenry still celebrates Islāmic festivals such as *Mouboud*, which commemorates the birth of the prophet Muḥammad, and *Aïd es Kebir*, the pilgrimage to Mecca. The country has many ethnographic and archaeological museums, a National School of Fine Arts, and fine examples of early architecture in its many old and beautiful domed mosques.

History. Archaeological excavations in Algeria have revealed human settlements dating back to 200,000 BC. Phoenician traders settled on the Mediterranean coast early in the 1st millennium BC. Carthage, in present-day Tunisia, became Phoenicia's most important city, and later the centre of an empire of its own. Carthage fell to the Romans in 146 BC; by AD 40 Roman control was firmly established at least along the coast, and Algeria became part of what the Romans called Mauretania Caesariensis. The hinterlands, however, remained outside Roman control. The fall of Rome in the 5th century led to invasion by the Vandals and, after them, the Byzantines. During this period Christianity grew in importance and Latin was in general use throughout all of North Africa. The Islāmic invasion began in the 7th century, and by 711, all of North Africa was in the hands of the Ummayads, and the indigenous Berbers were becoming Islāmicized.

In 740, under influence of the Khārijī heresy, the North Africans wrested control from the Ummayads and several Islāmic Berber empires followed, the most famous being the Almoravid (*c.* 1054–1130), which extended its domain to Spain, and the Almohad (*c.* 1130–1269). They are remembered as being the golden age of Islāmic civilization. The decline of the Almohad empire was coupled with an influx of Bedouin immigrants who transformed the basically sedentary population into a nomadic one.

Early 16th-century incursions into North Africa by Spain led the Africans to appeal to the Ottomans who, by 1536, established effective control of the region. The Barbary pirates menaced Mediterranean trade for centuries and gave the French a pretext to enter Algeria in 1830. By 1847 the French had subdued most Algerian resistance though fighting occurred as late as 1884. Movements for national independence resulted in the uprisings of 1954–55 and culminated in 1962 in a plebiscite on independence, which carried. The Algerian government that resulted was overthrown in 1965, and a military regime under Col. Houari Boumedienne took over until his death in 1978. Col. Chadli Benjedid succeeded him. In 1980 there was rioting by Berbers against an announced policy to make Arabic the sole official language.

Algerian Reformist Ulamas, Association of, French ASSOCIATION DES OULEMA RÉFORMISTES ALGÉRIENS, Arabic JAMʿĪYAH AL-ʿULAMĀʾ AL-JAZAʾRĪYAH, a body of Muslim religious scholars (Arabic *ʿulamāʾ*) who, under French rule, advocated the restoration of an Algerian nation rooted in Islāmic and Arabic traditions.

The association, founded in 1931 and formally organized on May 5, 1935, by Shaykh Abd al-Hamid ben Badis, was heavily influenced by the views of the great Muslim reformer Muḥammad ʿAbduh (1849–1905). It adopted his belief that Islām was essentially a flexible faith, capable of adapting to the modern world if freed of its non-Islāmic and vulgar accretions. The Algerian Ulama thus conducted widespread campaigns against the superstition and maraboutism common among the Muslim masses. They also implemented ʿAbduh's belief in the efficacy of modern education by attempting to reform the antiquated educational system that perpetuated a medieval mentality in the country. More than 200 schools were opened, the largest at Constantine with about 300 students, and the possibility of a Muslim university was introduced but never realized. The Algerian Ulama stressed the importance of studying Arabic, the language of Algerian Muslims, and fought for its obligatory instruction in Algerian elementary and secondary schools. In effect, the Association of Algerian Ulama wished to give the Algerian Muslim an identity and tradition rooted in the Islāmic community (*ummah*) and distinct from his French colonizer. Shaykh ben Badis condemned the adoption of European culture by Algerian Muslims, issuing a formal *fatwā* (legal opinion) against it in 1938.

The association met with opposition from two sources. Gallicized Algerian Muslims, known as *évolués,* Arabs by tradition and Frenchmen by education, insisted that Islām and France were not incompatible. They rejected the idea of an Algerian nation and stated that Algeria had for centuries been identified in terms of its economic and cultural relations with France.

Traditional Muslim circles also rejected the Association of Algerian Ulama. The leaders of the Muslim Ṣūfī (mystic) brotherhoods and the marabouts were directly threatened by the purist drive of the Ulama, while the Islāmic functionaries—*imāms* (prayer leaders in the mosques), *qāḍīs* (religious judges), and *muftīs* (religious lawyers)—were affected by their educational reforms and anti-French sentiment.

The popular response to the programs of the association was nonetheless considerable. To counteract the growing influence of the Ulama, the French government issued the *circulaire Michel,* which forbade members of the association from preaching in the mosques. The association, however, did not curtail its activities, even with the arrest of ben Badis in 1938. Shaykh Talib al-Bashir Brahimi succeeded ben Badis on his death in 1940. During the Algerian war against France (1954–62) the association aligned with the Front de Libération Nationale (FLN; 1956), and Tawfiq al-Madani, secretary general of the Algerian Ulama, sat in the provisional government of the Algerian Republic after independence (1962).

Algerus MAGISTER: *see* Alger of Liège.

Alghero, town and episcopal see, Sassari province, northwestern Sardinia, Italy, southwest of Sassari city. It was founded in 1102 by the Doria family of Genoa and became a Catalan colony under Peter IV of Aragon in 1354. Emperor Charles V took up residence there in 1541. It is the only Italian town where the Catalan language can still be heard and where traces of the Aragonese architectural style can be seen (in the 16th-century cathedral). The 14th-century church of S. Francesco is another notable monument. An old fishing port, it has modern beach resort facilities. Coral fishing in season, fruit canning, sawmilling, and olive oil production are the principal industries. Pop. (1981 prelim.) mun., 36,383.

Algiers (province, Algeria): *see* Alger.

Algiers, French ALGER, Arabic AL-JAZAʾIR, capital and chief seaport of Algeria. It is built on the slopes of the Sahel Hills, which parallel the coast, and extends along the Bay of Algiers. The city takes its name (Arabic: The Island), however, from several small islands that formerly existed in the bay, all but one of which have been connected to the shore or obliterated by harbour works.

Algiers was founded by the Phoenicians as one of their numerous North African colonies. It was known to the Carthaginians and the Romans as Icosium. After being destroyed by invasions, the town was revived under a Berber dynasty in the 10th century as a centre of commerce in the Mediterranean. In the 16th century it was held briefly by the Spanish. Under the Turks in the 17th century, it became a flourishing city and the base of pirates who preyed upon commerce in the Mediterranean. The fortress of the Kasbah (Qaṣbah), built on rocky heights overlooking the bay, was the residence of the last two Turkish *deys.* In 1830 the French captured Algiers, making it a military and administrative headquarters for their colonial empire.

Minarets of the mosque of Ketchaoua overlooking the Place des Martyrs, Algiers, Alg.
Shostal Assoc.

Around the old Muslim town with its narrow, winding streets, a new city has grown up squeezed between the hills and the bay. The main thoroughfares run north and south, paralleling the waterfront. A beautiful Ḥanafī mosque remains from the 17th century and a Mālikī mosque from the 11th. West of the main square, a short street leads to the mosque of Ketchaoua (which dates back to Turkish times, and which was consecrated as a cathedral during the French interregnum) and to the ruins of the Jénina (Arabic Jannah), or palace of the *dey.* Also located in the city are the national library, part of which is housed in a Moorish palace of 1798, and the University of Algiers.

During World War II Algiers became the headquarters of Allied forces in North Africa and for a time the provisional capital of France. In the 1950s, when the Algerian rising against France began, the capital city was a focal point in the struggle. After 1962, when Algeria became independent, many far-reaching changes were made to the city as the new government set out to create a modern Socialist society out of a backward colonial one.

Algiers is chiefly a port for the import of raw materials, industrial goods, and general supplies. The main exports are wine, early vegetables and oranges, iron ore, and phosphates. The airport, Dar el-Beïda, lies east of the city. Pop. (1978 est.) 1,998,000.

Consult the INDEX *first*

Algirdas (Lithuanian), Polish OLGIERD (b. *c.* 1296—d. 1377), grand duke of Lithuania from 1345 to 1377, who made Lithuania one of the largest European states of his day. His son Jogaila became Władysław II Jagiełło, king of united Poland and Lithuania.

Algirdas was one of the sons of the country's ruler, Gediminas, and he began his long political career when he married, at his father's request, the daughter of the Prince of Vitebsk and succeeded to the Prince's lands. Together with his father he fought against the Teutonic Knights and attempted to subjugate the Russian territories of Novgorod and Pskov, which had sought Lithuanian protection both from the knights and from the Golden Horde (the Tatar overlords of Russia since the middle of the 13th century). From 1341 to 1345 he was prince of Krevo and Vitebsk and a vassal of his younger brother, Grand Duke Jaunutis, whom he removed in collusion with another brother, Kęstutis, with whose consent he became grand duke.

Defense of Lithuanian Ponemune and Podvine against the knights and their allies, invasion of the Russian and Ukrainian lands subject to the Horde, and the desire to achieve Lithuanian hegemony in the province of Volhynia were the goals of Algirdas' foreign policy. In the pursuit of these aims he relied on dynastic support and especially on his co-ruler Kęstutis. The brothers shared both their losses and their many acquisitions of fortified posts in Russia. They were supported by the princes and boyars who sat in the grand-ducal council and, along with their feudal-dependent peasants, took the field under them.

But though he was the leader of the Lithuanian-Slavic armies against the Teutonic Knights, Algirdas was a stranger to the lower social orders. When, during the anti-German "Uprising of the Night of Yury" in Livonia (1345), one of its leaders, a peasant, told him that he had been chosen king by the rebels and that if Algirdas followed his advice the Germans would be driven out, Algirdas had him decapitated. To the feudal prince, a peasant as king seemed a more terrible threat than the German usurpers.

Observing the ancient courtesies, Algirdas would entertain the lesser nobles at their periodic renewal of their compact with him as their overlord, but he would not tolerate an insult and in 1346 declared war on Novgorod after being scolded by the local governor at a meeting of the municipal assembly. A courageous warrior and man of strong sentiments, Algirdas, when watching his nobles besiege Kaunas but unable to come to their aid, was not above bursting into "great tears and lamentations." Although pagan to the core, he allowed his Orthodox subjects of Vilnius to build a church where formerly the gallows had stood. For political reasons he appointed his many Orthodox viceregents in the Slavic territories of Lithuania, consistently married Orthodox princesses himself, and prevailed on the Patriarch of Constantinople to found a Lithuanian Orthodox metropolitan see in the city of Kiev.

Algirdas saw far beyond the boundaries of his country. When the Polish king Casimir III the Great, Pope Clement VI, and Emperor Charles IV proposed to him that he accept Catholicism, he replied (1358) that he was ready to do so if they returned to him the lands between the Pregolya and Daugava rivers, liquidated the Teutonic Knights, and left him the

> empty lands between the Tatars and the Russians for their protection from the Tatars, leaving the Knights no rights whatever over the Russians but instead granting all Rus [Russia] to the Lithuanians.

But Algirdas' goals were not destined to be realized.

Early in his reign the Teutonic Knights and their allies conducted annual raids from their bases in Prussia and Livonia, ruining Lithuanian lands and subjugating White Russia as far south as Grodno. Aided by their supporters to the east and south, Algirdas and Kęstutis repelled these attacks. Yet, despite the expenditure of so much energy, Algirdas left the resolution of this historic struggle with the Teutonic Knights to his heirs.

The rivalry with Poland over Volhynia was intensified when, in 1349, Casimir tricked Algirdas' brother Lubart out of one of the principal Volhynian cities. By the treaty of 1352 Lithuania took possession of Volhynia, but in 1366, preoccupied with his struggle with the Teutonic Knights, Algirdas had to yield most of Volhynia once again to his ally Casimir. After Casimir's death in 1370, however, he managed to recover part of the province by a treaty (1377) with King Louis of Hungary–Poland.

Algirdas' relations with Russia were characterized by his unsuccessful attempts to claim Pskov and Novgorod. Having met with Muscovite resistance, he concluded peace with Grand Duke Simeon of Moscow (1349). But with the decline of the Golden Horde after the death of the khan Jani Beg (Dzhanibek) in 1357, he extended his influence eastward approximately as far as Mstislavl' and Btyansk. In 1362–63 he campaigned in the territories of the Tatars, defeating three of their governors in the battle at the River Siniye Vody. He secured the principality of Kiev, which he gave to his son Vladimir, and freed little Podolia from the power of the Golden Horde.

In 1349 Algirdas married Yuliana, daughter of the Prince of Tver. Together with Tver and Smolensk he undertook three campaigns against Moscow (1368, 1370, 1372). They were, however, unsuccessful because of an increase in Moscow's prestige among the other Slavic lands.

Algirdas died in the middle of a war with the Knights. He was apparently cremated, along with 18 of his warhorses and other effects. He left his lands to his 12 sons. According to a contemporary chronicle, he

> drank not beer nor mead, nor wine nor fermented kvass. He was temperate and thus found wisdom. And by his cunning he conquered many lands and countries, subjugated many towns and principalities, and achieved great power.

(V.T.P.)

Algol, also called BETA PERSEI, prototype of a class of variable stars called eclipsing binaries, the second brightest star in the northern constellation Perseus. Its apparent visual magnitude changes periodically over the range of (approximately) 2.2 to 3.5; even at its dimmest it remains readily visible to the unaided eye. The name probably derives from an Arabic phrase meaning "demon" or "mischief-maker," and the Arabs may have been aware of the star's variability even before the invention of the telescope.

The first European astronomer to note the light variation was the Italian Geminiano Montanari in 1670; the English astronomer John Goodricke measured the cycle (69 hours) in 1782 and suggested partial eclipses of the star by another body as a cause, a hypothesis proved correct in 1889. The comparatively long duration of the eclipse shows that the dimensions of the two stars are not negligible in comparison with the distance between them. Small fluctuations in the period of the light variation can be explained by assuming that the system contains two other stars, which take no part in the eclipses. The presence of one companion with a period of 1.87 years has been confirmed by spectroscopic observations.

algology, also called PHYCOLOGY, the study of algae, a large heterogeneous group of chiefly aquatic plants ranging in size from microscopic forms to species as large as shrubs or small trees. The discipline is of immediate interest to man because algae play an important role in ecology. Certain algae, particularly planktonic (*i.e.,* floating or drifting) forms, comprise a vital segment of food chains. In coastal regions many large species are used as direct food sources by man. In industry algae are a source of commercially valuable substances such as iodine, agar, carrageenin, alginic acid, and potash. Other algae are used in insulating materials, bricks, scouring powder, and filters. Certain species are used as digestive agents in sewage-oxidation ponds. Some are harmful because of their tendency to suffocate other forms of aquatic life in waters used for fishing and recreation.

Algonkian Languages, also spelled ALGONQUIAN, North American Indian language family whose member languages are or were spoken in Canada, New England, the Atlantic coastal region southward to North Carolina, and the Great Lakes region and surrounding areas westward to the Rocky Mountains. Among the numerous Algonkian languages are Cree, Ojibwa, Blackfoot, Cheyenne, Micmac, Arapaho, and Fox-Sauk-Kickapoo. The term Algonkin (often spelled this way to differentiate it from the family) refers to a dialect of Ojibwa. Algonkian languages have been classified by some scholars as belonging to a larger language group, the Macro-Algonkian phylum. *See also* Macro-Algonkian languages.

Algonkin, any of a number of scattered Algonkian-speaking bands and tribes living in dense forest regions on either side of the upper Ottawa River in Canada. They drew cultural traits from tribes flanking them on east and west, the Montagnais and Naskapi and Ojibwa (*qq.v.*). Primarily hunters, engaging in only marginal maize cultivation, they were always few in number and were decimated by Iroquois raids and European diseases. About 2,000 survived into the 1980s, however, primarily as truck gardeners, hunters' guides, and trappers.

Algonquin, Lake, large glacial lake that once existed in North America and covered most of the area now occupied by the Great Lakes of Superior, Michigan, and Huron. It was present in the Pleistocene Epoch, a geological glacial period when the ice field (called the Laurentide Ice Sheet) was retreating from the Great Lakes region. The body of water, perhaps 100,000 sq mi (250,000 sq km) in area and with depths of up to 1,500 ft (460 m), at various stages drained through channels that included the Trent Valley and the Mattawa, Ottawa, St. Clair, and Mississippi rivers. Remnants of the lake include Lakes Superior, Michigan, Huron, Nipigon, Simcoe, and Nipissing.

Algonquin Provincial Park, wilderness area, southeastern Ontario, Canada, about 140 mi (227 km) northeast of Toronto, covering an area of 2,955 sq mi (7,653 sq km). Established in 1893, the park, once a lumbering area, is a hilly wildlife refuge for bears, beaver, deer, moose, and smaller game. It forms the main part of the watershed between the Ottawa River and Georgian Bay, and its numerous lakes and streams offer canoeing and fishing for bass, lake trout, pickerel, and muskellunge.

algorithm, systematic mathematical procedure that produces—in a finite number of steps—the answer to a question or the solution of a problem. The question or problem, in turn, must belong to a class that has an infinite number of members, such as "Is the integer a prime?" or "What is the greatest common divisor of the integers a and b?" The first of these questions belongs to a class called decidable; an algorithm that produces the answer (yes or no) is called a decision procedure. The second question belongs to a class called computable; an algorithm that leads to the answer (a specific number) is called a computation procedure. For finite classes of questions, trivial algorithms always exist (at least in principle); they consist of tables of values of the answers.

Algorithms exist for many infinite classes of questions; Euclid's *Elements,* published around 300 BC, contained one for finding the greatest common divisor of two integers. Every elementary school student is drilled in long division, which is an algorithm for the question "Upon dividing an integer a by another integer b, what are the quotient and the remainder?" Use of this computational procedure leads to the answer to the decidable question "Does b divide a?" (the answer is yes if the remainder is zero). Repeated application of these algorithms eventually produces the answer to the decidable question "Is a prime?" (the answer is no if a is divisible by any smaller integer besides 1).

For other infinite classes of questions, no algorithms are known. A celebrated question of this kind has occupied mathematicians since about 1637, when Pierre de Fermat claimed to have found a proof that no set of integers n, x, y, z satisfies the equation $x^n + y^n = z^n$ for any n greater than 2. Fermat did not substantiate his claim, and no one since has been able to, but no refutation has been forthcoming either, although a single instance would suffice. Such an instance would also establish an algorithm, because some finite set of calculations would lead to the integers in question, no matter how large they were.

Algren, Nelson, original name NELSON AHLGREN ABRAHAM (b. March 28, 1909, Detroit—d. May 9, 1981, Sag Harbor, N.Y.), writer whose novels of the poor are lifted from routine naturalism by his vision of their pride, humour, and unquenchable yearnings. He also catches with poetic skill the mood of the city's underside: its juke-box pounding, stench, and neon glare.

The son of a machinist, he grew up in Chicago, where his parents moved when he was three. He worked his way through the University of Illinois, graduating in journalism in the depth of the Depression. He went on the road as a door-to-door salesman and migratory worker in the South and Southwest, then returned to Chicago, where he was employed briefly by a WPA (Works Progress Administration) writers' project and a venereal-disease control unit of the Board of Health. In this period, too, he edited with the proletarian novelist Jack Conroy the *Anvil,* a magazine dedicated to the publication of experimental and leftist writing.

Somebody in Boots (1935), his first novel, relates the driftings during the Depression of a young poor-white Texan who ends up among the down-and-outs of Chicago. *Never Come Morning* (1942) tells of a Polish petty criminal who dreams of escaping from his squalid Northwest Side Chicago environment by becoming a prizefighter. Before the appearance of Algren's next book—the short-story collection *The Neon Wilderness* (1947), which contains some of his best writing—he served as a U.S. Army medical corpsman during World War II.

Algren's first popular success was *The Man with the Golden Arm* (1949; filmed 1956), which won the National Book Award. Its hero is Frankie Machine, whose golden arm as a poker dealer is threatened by shakiness connected with his dope addiction. In *A Walk on the Wild Side* (1956; filmed 1962) Algren returned to the 1930s in a picaresque novel of New Orleans bohemian life.

His nonfiction includes the prose poem *Chicago, City on the Make* (1951) and sketches collected as *Who Lost an American?* (1963) and *Notes from a Sea Diary: Hemingway All the Way* (1965).

Alhambra, palace and fortress of the Moorish monarchs of Granada, in the Andalusian region of Spain. The name Alhambra, signifying in Arabic "the red," is probably derived from the colour of the sun-dried *tapia,* or bricks made of fine gravel and clay, of which the outer walls are built.

Constructed on a plateau below which clusters the city of Granada, the palace was built chiefly between 1238 and 1358, in the reigns of Ibn al-Ahmar, founder of the Naṣrid dynasty, and his successors. The splendid decorations of the interior are ascribed to Yūsuf I (died 1354). After the expulsion of the Moors in 1492, much of the interior was effaced and the furniture was ruined, or removed. Charles V, who ruled in Spain 1516–56, rebuilt portions in the Renaissance style and destroyed part of the Alhambra to build an Italianate palace designed by Pedro de Machuca in 1526. In 1812 some of the towers were blown up by the French during the Napoleonic invasion; and in 1821 an earthquake caused further damage to the structure. Restoration of the building was undertaken in 1828 and has continued to the present.

The Moorish portion of the Alhambra includes the Alcazaba, or citadel, which is the oldest part—only its massive outer walls, towers, and ramparts are left. Beyond the Alcazaba is the Alhambra palace, and beyond that the Alhambra Alta (Upper Alhambra), which was originally tenanted by officials and courtiers and was part of a royal city, a seat of government.

The principal courts of the palace are the Patio de los Arrayanes (Court of the Myrtles) and the Patio de los Leones (Court of the Lions), so named because in the centre is the Fountain of the Lions, an alabaster basin supported by the figures of 12 white marble lions, emblems of strength and courage. The most important rooms of the Alhambra are the Sala de los Embajadores (Hall of the Ambassadors), a spatially grand reception room; the Sala de los Abencerrages (the name of this hall was derived from a legend in which Boabdil, the last king of Granada, having invited the Abencerrage chiefs to a banquet in this room, massacred them there); and the Sala de las Dos Hermanas (Hall of the Two Sisters), with its outstanding example of stalactite work (*q.v.*).

Of the outlying buildings, the most important is the Generalife (from the Moorish Jannat al-ʿArīf, or Garden of the Builder). This villa probably dates from the end of the 13th century.

Alhazen, Arabic ABŪ ʿALĪ AL-ḤASAN IBN AL-HAYTHAM (b. *c.* 965, Basra, Iraq—d. 1039, Cairo), mathematician and physicist who made the first significant contributions to optical theory since the time of Ptolemy (flourished 2nd century). In his treatise on optics, translated into Latin in 1270 as *Opticae thesaurus Alhazeni libri vii*, Alhazen published theories on refraction, reflection, binocular vision, focussing with lenses, the rainbow, parabolic and spherical mirrors, spherical aberration, atmospheric refraction, and the apparent increase in size of planetary bodies near the Earth's horizon. He was first to give an accurate account of vision, correctly stating that light comes from the object seen to the eye.

Alhucemas, also called AL-HOCEIMA, or AL-KHUZAMA, Spanish *plaza* (enclave) on the Mediterranean coast of Morocco, comprising a bay, three islets, and a small port. The bay, a semicircular inlet (9 mi wide and 5 mi long [14 km wide and 8 km long]), is protected by Cap Nuevo; its sandy bottom is an extension of the Río Nekor alluvial plain. The islets, administered by Spain since 1673, are uninhabited, although Peñón de Alhucemas was garrisoned until 1961. The Moroccan port of al-Hoceïma (Spanish Villa Sanjurjo), on the mainland opposite, is mainly a fishing port and its fine beaches provide the basis for a bathing resort. Pop. (1970) 63.

Alhucemas (Morocco): *see* Hoceïma, al-.

ʿAlī, in full ʿALĪ IBN ABĪ ṬĀLIB (b. *c.* 600, Mecca—d. January 661, Kūfah, Iraq), son-in-law of Muḥammad, the prophet of Islām, and fourth caliph (successor to Muḥammad), reigning from 656 to 661. The question of his right to the caliphate resulted in the only major split in Islām (into Sunnah and Shiʿah branches). He is revered by the Shiʿah as the only true successor to the Prophet.

ʿAlī was the son of Abū Ṭālib, chief of a local clan. When his father became impoverished, ʿAlī was adopted by Muḥammad, then still a businessman in Mecca, who himself had been cared for by ʿAlī's father as a child. When Muḥammad felt God's call to become his prophet, ʿAlī, though only 10 years old, became one of the first converts to Islām and remained a lifelong devoted follower of Muḥammad. According to legend ʿAlī risked his life by sleeping in the Prophet's bed to impersonate him the night that Muḥammad fled in 622 from Mecca to Medina from enemies who were plotting to assassinate him. In addition, ʿAlī is said to have carried out Muḥammad's request to restore all the properties that had been entrusted to him as a merchant to their owners in Mecca. Only then did ʿAlī himself leave for Medina. There he married Muḥammad's daughter Fāṭimah, who bore him two sons, Ḥasan and Ḥusayn.

ʿAlī is said to have displayed rare courage in battle during the military expeditions Muḥammad conducted to consolidate Islām and always obtained a lion's share of the booty. ʿAlī was also one of Muḥammad's scribes and was chosen to lead several important missions. When the hostile inhabitants of Mecca finally accepted Islām without battle, it was ʿAlī who smashed the pagan idols in the Kaʿbah (holy shrine).

Muḥammad died on June 8, 632. Some say he had unequivocally nominated ʿAlī as his successor while he was returning from his "farewell pilgrimage" to Mecca. Others reject this claim, maintaining that Muḥammad died without naming a successor. ʿAlī, while attending the last rites of the Prophet, was confronted by the fact that Abū Bakr, Muḥammad's closest friend and father of ʿĀʾishah, one of the Prophet's wives, had been chosen caliph. ʿAlī did not submit to Abū Bakr's authority for some time, but neither did he actively assert his own rights, possibly because he did not want to throw the Muslim community into bloody tribal strife. He retired into a quiet life in which religious works became his chief occupation. The first chronologically arranged version of the Qurʾān is attributed to him, and his excellent knowledge of the Qurʾān and Ḥadīth (the sayings and deeds of Muḥammad) aided the caliphs in various legal problems.

Following the murder of ʿUthmān, the third caliph, ʿAlī was invited by the Muslims of Medina to accept the caliphate; reluctant, he agreed only after long hesitation. His brief reign was beset by difficulties due mostly to the corrupt state of affairs he inherited. Acutely aware of the neglect of the Qurʾān and the traditions of Muḥammad that his predecessors had allowed to develop, he based his rule on the Islāmic ideals of social justice and equality. His policy was a blow to the interests of the Quraysh aristocracy of Mecca

The Alhambra, Granada, Spain
C.I.R.I.—EDISTUDIO

who had grown rich in the wake of the Muslim conquests. In order to embarrass ʿAlī they demanded that he bring the murderers of ʿUthmān to trial, and when he rejected their request a rebellion against him was instigated in which two prominent Meccans along with ʿĀʾishah, Muḥammad's widow and daughter of Abū Bakr, the first caliph, took a leading part. This rebellion, known as the Battle of the Camel (the camel ridden by ʿĀʾishah), was quelled. A second rebellion was on the point of being crushed when its leader, Muʿāwiyah, a kinsman of ʿUthmān and the governor of Syria, averted defeat by proposing arbitration. ʿAlī saw through the stratagem but was forced by his army to accept adjudication, which greatly weakened his position. Soon, moreover, he had to fight the very people who had earlier forced him to accept arbitration but now denounced it. Known as Khawārij (Seceders), they were defeated by ʿAlī in the Battle of Nahrawān. Meanwhile, Muʿāwiyah followed an aggressive policy, and by the end of 660 ʿAlī had lost control of Egypt and of the Hejaz. Early one morning while praying in a mosque at Kūfah in Iraq, ʿAlī was struck with a poisoned sword by a Khārijite, intent on avenging the men slain at Nahrawān. Two days later ʿAlī died and was buried near Kūfah.

ʿAlī's political discourses, sermons, letters, and sayings, collected by ash-Sharīf ar-Raḍī (died 1015) in a book entitled *Nahj al-balāghah* ("The Road of Eloquence") and later commented upon by Ibn Abī al-Ḥadīd (died 1258), are well known in Arabic literature.

(I.K.P.)

ʿAlī THE GREAT (West African monarch): *see* Sonni ʿAlī.

Ali, Muhammad: *see* Muhammad Ali.

ʿAlī ar-Riḍā, in full ABŪ AL-ḤASAN IBN MŪSĀ IBN JAʿFAR ʿALĪ AR-RIḌĀ (b. 765/768—d. 818), eighth *imām* of the Twelver Shīʿah, noted for his piety and learning until 817, when the caliph al-Maʾmūn, in an attempt to heal the division between the majority Sunnah and the Shīʿah, appointed him his successor. The appointment aroused varying reactions—few of them, even among the Shīʿah, wholly favourable—and Iraq, already irritated by al-Maʾmūn's transfer of the capital from Baghdad to Merv and by other offenses, rose up in rebellion. Al-Maʾmūn gradually changed his policy. The court party set out from Merv for Baghdad, and on the way ʿAlī ar-Riḍā died, after a brief illness, at Ṭūs. Shīʿī historians attribute his death to poison, possibly administered by the Caliph himself. His shrine (*mashhad*) at Ṭūs became a pilgrimage place and gave its name to the city (Mashhad, or Meshed, in Iran). Many miracles are attributed to ʿAlī ar-Riḍā by the Shīʿī.

A list of the abbreviations used in the MICROPAEDIA *will be found at the end of this volume*

ʿAlī Bey, original Greek name IOSIF, Arabic YUSUF (b. 1728—d. May 8, 1773), Mamluk governor of Egypt under Ottoman suzerainty who attempted to throw off the Ottoman Turkish rule.

The son of a Greek priest, he was kidnapped in 1741 and sold to an Egyptian merchant, who in turn sold him to Ibrāhīm Katthuda, an *amīr*. The *amīr* had him circumcised, gave him a new name (ʿAli), and educated him in the Qurʾān. ʿAli earned the confidence of his master, who later freed him and advanced him to the rank of bey. ʿAli managed to strengthen his position by obtaining slaves and setting them in high positions. His power thus recognized, he was made shaykh al-balad (mayor of Cairo). He was involved in much political manoeuvering and finally succeeded in assuming the title of sultan of Egypt. He seized Syria and the Hejaz, including Mecca. Betrayed by his army commander, he fled to Syria in 1772. He died of wounds suffered in an unsuccessful attempt to reoccupy Egypt.

Ali Gauhar: *see* Shah Alam II.

Ali Haji bin Raja Amhad, Raja (b. *c.* 1809, Penyengat, Riau, East Indies—d. *c.* 1870, Riau), Bugis-Malay prince who, as a scholar and historian, led a renaissance in Malay letters in the mid-19th century.

A grandson of the famed Bugis leader Raja Haji, Raja Ali was born into the Bugis-Malay world of the Riau-Lingga archipelago, last legacy outside the Malay Peninsula of the kingdom of Johore, just before it came under final Dutch domination. As a youth he accompanied his father on a mission to Batavia (now Jakarta) and on a pilgrimage to Mecca, and by the age of 32 he was joint regent of Lingga for its young Malay sultan.

Raja Ali, a man of affairs, was also a religious and literary scholar and did much to establish Riau as the intellectual centre of the Malay world in the mid-19th century. His own writings include several didactic texts, such as *Muqaddimah fi intizām* (1857; "Introduction to Order") on the duties of kings, a Johnsonian dictionary of Malay usage, *Kitab Pengetahuan Bahasa* (*c.* 1869; "Book of Linguistic Knowledge"), and the historical work *Silsilah Melayu dan Bugis* (1865; "Malay and Bugis Genealogy"). His most outstanding contribution to learning, however, is the history begun by his father that he rewrote and expanded as the *Tuhfat al-Nafis* (*c.* 1866; "Precious Gift"), which remains an invaluable source for the history of the Malay Peninsula, Borneo, and Sumatra.

ʿAlī ibn Abī Ṭālib (son-in-law of Muḥammad): *see* ʿAlī.

ʿAlī ibn Būyeh (Būyid founder): *see* ʿImād ad-Dawlah.

ʿAlī ibn Muḥammad al-Jurjānī: *see* Jurjānī, al-.

Ali Khan, Liaquat: *see* Liaquat Ali Khan.

ʿAlī Moḥammad of Shīrāz, Mīrzā: *see* Bāb, the.

Âli Paşa, Mehmed Emin (b. 1815, Constantinople—d. Sept. 7, 1871, Constantinople), Ottoman grand vizier (chief minister) distinguished for his westernizing reform policies, who, together with Mustafa Reşid Paşa and Fuad Paşa, was a main figure of the Tanzimat (Reorganization) period (1839–*c.* 1870) in Ottoman history.

The son of a small shopkeeper, he entered government service as a boy. Without formal education, he acquired some knowledge of French and in 1836 he accompanied a diplomatic mission to Vienna—the first of a series of diplomatic assignments that culminated in his appointment as ambassador to London in 1841. After his return he became foreign minister under Mustafa Reşid Paşa and took part in the congresses of Vienna (1855) and Paris (1856). He served as grand vizier on five occasions (1852, 1855–56, 1858–59, 1861, and 1867–71).

He resisted the sultan's efforts to limit the powers of the grand vizierate; he settled the troubles in Serbia and in Moldavia-Walachia by peaceful means; and, in 1868, he pacified the Cretan revolt by the grant of a measure of local self-government. Ali Paşa was one of the most zealous advocates of friendship with France and Great Britain during the reigns of the sultans Abdülmecid I and Abdülaziz.

Ali Paşa Tepelenë, byname LION OF JANINA (b. 1744, Tepelenë, Albania, Ottoman Empire—d. Feb. 5, 1822, Janja, Bosnia), Albanian brigand who, by murder and intrigue, became pasha of Janina (Ioánnina, Greece) from 1788. He extended his capricious rule within the Ottoman Empire over much of Albania and Macedonia, Epirus, Thessaly, and the Morea.

His father, Veli, bey of Tepelenë, died a poor man when Ali was 14. His mother, Khamco, formed a brigand band to restore the political and material fortunes of the family, and Ali became a notorious brigand leader. After service with the pasha of Negropont (Euboea), he joined the wealthy pasha of Delvino, whose daughter he married in 1768. Becoming lieutenant to the derbend-pasha of Rumelia, he policed the highroads, enriched himself, and sent presents to Constantinople. At length he was rewarded with the pashalik of Trikkala and, after a series of murders and intrigues, obtained that of Janina. His son Veli took over Trikkala and later the Morea, while another son, Mukhtar, became pasha of Lepanto. Though constantly thwarted by the Christian Souliots, whom he finally subdued in 1803, Ali obtained control of the Gulf of Arta and took the ports of Butrinto, Preveza, and Vonitsa. He also gained control of the pashaliks of Elbasan, Delvino, Berat, and Valona (Vlore).

All this time, by murders and extortions, he increased his wealth and, by intriguing with Greeks and Albanians, extended his authority over beys and townships. Though appointed viceroy of Rumelia, he repeatedly failed to carry out the orders of the Sultan, to whom he sent plausible excuses and many presents. Indeed, he acted as an independent sovereign and was treated as such by the British and French, with whom he intrigued, hoping to establish Janina as a sea power. By 1819 the sultan, Mahmud II, who intended to centralize the government of his empire, was determined to remove Ali and sanctioned his assassination. Ali tried to save himself by his old methods of murder, intrigue, and extortion but, deserted by his sons and allies, was finally shot down.

In Ali's time, Janina was the foremost centre of Greek culture, for Ali employed Greeks and founded Greek schools. His court was one of barbarous refinement, and even the liberated Greeks looked back upon him with some respect.

ʿAlī Shāh: *see* Aga Khan II.

Aliákmon River, Modern Greek ALIÁKMON POTAMÓS, river, the longest (185 mi [297 km]) of Greek Macedonia, rising in the Grámmos Óros (mountains) of the eastern Pindus Mountains on the Albanian frontier. It flows southeast through gentle valleys and basins and is joined by a tributary, sometimes also called the Aliákmon, which rises near the Albanian border. After collecting the drainage of Límni (lake) Kastorías, its flow is confined to narrow gorges during much of its middle course along the base of the easternmost Pindus. Near Siátista it receives the Pramorítsa and, further south, the Venétikos. Swinging around the southern end of the Voúrinos Óros (mountains), the Aliákmon is forced into a wide loop toward the northeast by the northeast–southwest-trending Kamvoúnia massif, which forms the watershed between the Aliákmon and the Titanísios Potamós of Thessaly (Thessalía).

Emerging from between the Vérmion and Piéria mountains, the Aliákmon traverses the Thessaloníki (Salonika) plain, through which it apparently was navigable by small ships in the Middle Ages; but today a hydroelectric barrage south of Véroia is a barrier to river traffic. Near Vêroia it is joined by a last tributary, the Moglenítsas, which drains the entire western Thessaloníki plain; together they debouch into the upper Thermaïkós Kólpos (gulf) on the Aegean Sea. Formerly called by its Macedonian name, Vistrítsa (Bistrítsa), the

Aliákmon, throughout history, has formed a natural line of defense against invaders from the north and has often served so, most recently in World War II, when a New Zealand brigade was able to hold it briefly against German forces.

Alībāg, town, administrative headquarters of Raigarh (formerly Kolāba) district, Mahārāshtra state, western India, on the Arabian Sea coast, south of Bombay at the mouth of a tidal creek. Its name, meaning "Ali's garden," was derived in the 17th century from the gardens of a rich Muslim inhabitant. Kolāba fort was built nearby in the same period after Marāṭhā occupation and was used as a headquarters during raids on neighbouring Portuguese towns and on trading ships along the Konkan Coast. The town was ceded to the British in 1890. It is the site of a meteorological observatory. Pop. (1981) 14,051.

Alicante, province, in the autonomous community (region) of Valencia, southeastern Spain, formed (1833) from parts of the historic provinces of Valencia and Murcia, with an area of 2,264 sq mi (5,863 sq km). The barren mountain terrain of the north and northwest contrasts with the densely populated southern fertile coastal plain, which is watered by the Río Segura. Principal products are wines and liquors, fruits, vegetables, and fish; almonds and *turrones* (nougat) have made the names of Alicante (*q.v.*; the provincial capital) and the towns of Alcoy and Jijona well known. The salt industry at Torrevieja is the largest in Spain. The tourist trade has become very important; Denia, Calpe, Altea, Benidorm, and Alicante are well-known summer and winter resorts of the Costa Blanca (part of the Spanish Mediterranean coast). Pop. (1982 est.) 1,217,729.

Alicante, port city, capital of Alicante province, in the autonomous community (region) of Valencia, southeastern Spain, on Bahía (bay) de Alicante of the Mediterranean. Founded as Akra-Leuka ("white summit") by

The port of Alicante, Spain
G. Mairani

Phocaean Greeks (from the west coast of Asia Minor) in 325 BC, the city was captured in 201 BC by the Romans, who called it Lucentum. Under Moorish domination, which lasted from 718 to 1249, it was called al-Akant. Later incorporated into the kingdom of Aragon, it was besieged by the French in 1709 and by the Federalists of Cartagena in 1873. It was under Republican control during the Spanish Civil War of 1936–39. The city is dominated by Benacantil hill (721 ft [220 m]) and the citadel of Santa Bárbara (1,000 ft), the earliest foundations of which date from 230 BC. Arrabal Roig, the old quarter, overlooks the bay from heights known as the Balcón del Mediterráneo. Notable landmarks include the Baroque town hall (1701–60), the church of Santa María (14th century), and the Renaissance collegiate church of San Nicolás de Bari (18th century).

Alicante serves as the commercial port of Madrid and has excellent road, rail, and air transportation facilities. Wine, raisins, vegetables, and esparto grass (all exported), and tomatoes, bricks, cigarettes, aluminum utensils, furniture, and embroideries are its main products. Its mild climate makes it a winter resort, and the beaches of the Costa Blanca (part of the Mediterranean coast) attract tourists. Pop. (1982 est.) 258,465.

Alicante Dam: *see* Tibi Dam.

alicatado, mosaic formed of polygonal, coloured glazed tiles. Made up into geometrical patterns, they have been used mostly for paving Spanish and Moorish patios but also for wall surfaces. The expansion of the lands

Alicatados in the Tower of Comares, the Alhambra, Granada, Spain
Archivo Mas, Barcelona

under Christian control in Spain in the 13th century led to a mixture of Gothic and Islāmic styles (known as the Mudéjar style), in which *alicatado* was much used by Spanish craftsmen. These traditional patterns continue to be used, especially where Spanish or Arabic influences are strong.

Alice, town in the not internationally recognized republic of Ciskei, located on the southwestern bank of the Tyume River, west-northwest of East London, South Africa, at an elevation of 1,720 ft (524 m). Beginning as a mission station established by the Glasgow Missionary Society for the Xhosa people in 1824, was named after Princess Alice (eldest daughter of Queen Victoria) and became the seat of a magistracy in 1847, and a town in 1852. Livestock, citrus fruits, and tobacco are raised on the surrounding undulating coastal plateau. Lovedale Training College and Fort Hare University (1916), South Africa's oldest and most substantial black African university, are located near the town. It has road and rail connections with East London. Pop. (1978 est.) mun., 11,001.

Alice Springs, town, Northern Territory, Australia. It is the main focus of the Centre, a name given to approximately 100,000 sq mi (260,000 sq km) of central Australia that

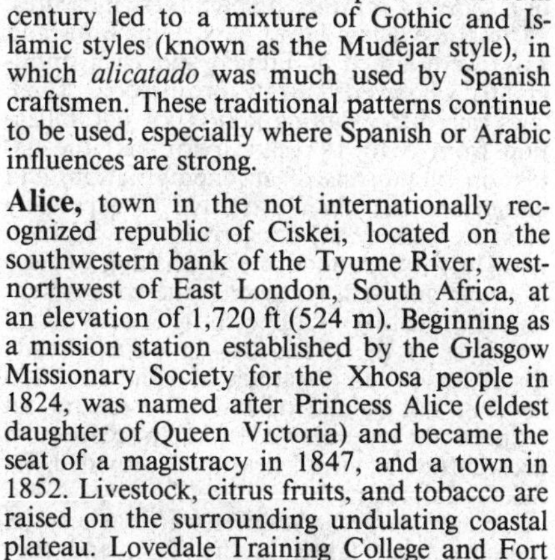

Alice Springs, Northern Territory, Australia
B. Brander—Photo Researchers

includes large areas of desert and rocky ridges. Alice Springs lies on the intermittent Todd River and the Stuart Highway, 1,028 road mi (1,654 km) north of Adelaide and 954 mi south of Darwin. The town originated in 1871 as a station on the Overland Telegraph Line, which crossed the MacDonnell Ranges through Heavitree Gap. The present site was surveyed in 1889, and the town was declared in 1890 under the name Stuart, after the explorer John McDouall Stuart.

Alice Springs is now the northern terminus of the Central Australia Railway, which was extended from Oodnadatta in 1929. The rail line and the cross-continental Stuart Highway have made the town a major shipping point for beef cattle and minerals (gold, copper, wolfram [tungsten], mica). Irrigation allows limited fruit and dairy farming. There are small plants making fibrous plaster, soft drinks, sheet metal, joinery, and bricks.

Tourism is of prime importance; during the mild winter months (May to September) thousands flock to the town, which has become an exploration base for the Centre. They may also attend such celebrations as Henley on the Todd, a "boat race" on the dry riverbed in which the boats are carried by runners. Alice Springs, which was the capital of the short-lived Territory of Central Australia (1926–31), is a regional headquarters for the Royal Flying Doctor Service and the School of the Air (public education by radio). Its original telegraph station has been designated a national park. Pop. (1981) 18,395.

alicyclic compound, in chemistry, any of a large class of organic compounds in which three or more atoms of the element carbon are linked together in a ring. The bonds between pairs of adjacent atoms may all be of the type designated single bonds (involving two electrons), or some of them may be double or triple bonds (with four or six electrons, respectively); six-membered rings for which a system of alternating single and double bonds may be envisioned, however, belong to another important class (aromatic compounds), distinguished from the alicyclic compounds by a characteristically different pattern of chemical reactivity. Those alicyclic compounds in which the ring contains three or four carbon atoms are less stable than the compounds having larger rings, because the angles formed by adjacent covalent bonds are smaller than is necessary for maximum effectiveness. In the larger rings all the bond angles have the preferred value (about 109.5°); consequently, the atoms in the ring do not lie in one plane. Similar restrictions on the angles in double and triple bonds affect the stability of alicyclic compounds containing such bonds.

alien, in national and international law, a foreign-born resident who is not a citizen by virtue of parentage or naturalization and who is still a citizen or subject of another country.

In early times, the tendency was to look upon the alien as an enemy and to treat him as a criminal or outlaw. Aristotle, probably reflecting a common view in the ancient world, saw non-Greeks as barbarous people who were slaves "by nature." The Stoics began to teach the equality of all men, and Plutarch wrote "there should be one Life and one order (*cosmos*), as it were one flock on a common pasture feeding in common under one joint law." The *jus gentium* of the Roman law applied to both citizens and foreigners and tended to favour the idea that aliens had rights; humanity toward aliens was also fostered, in theory at least, by the Christian idea of the unity of all persons in the church. The legal and ideological expression of humanity toward the alien, however, is generally a relatively modern development.

As sovereign national states began to develop in modern times, founders of international law asserted that natural rights were vested in all persons, without regard to citizenship or alienage—rights of which they ought not to be deprived by civilized societies or their governments. There was no general agreement on the content or scope of these natural rights as they affected aliens, but the existence of some minimum standard of civilized treatment was asserted. The minimum standard, it was conceded, did not include the right of the alien to own realty or to engage in gainful professions. To meet this situation, states entered into treaties that provided that each of the contracting states would treat the nationals of the other state on an equal footing with its own nationals in the admission into trades and professions, ownership or possession of property, access to courts, enjoyment of liberty of conscience, and freedom of worship. Some treaties do not purport to extend to aliens, however, rights that are by municipal law reserved exclusively to nationals of the country; thus, municipal law, rather than conventional international law, is actually controlling. In particular, the desire of nations to protect citizens in their jobs, professions, and businesses against both unemployment and competition is a very strong force restricting the latitude of aliens.

Common economic needs of nations, on the other hand, have had some liberalizing effects on the status of aliens. The treaty constituting the European Common Market, for instance, provides that citizens of member states shall be free to reside in any signatory country that offers them employment; wages and working conditions are to be the same for citizens and aliens. This treaty may in time serve as a model to raise the so-called minimum standards in the treatment of aliens.

In the United States, most states by statute accorded aliens the same rights with respect to real property as those enjoyed by citizens, but states on the west coast had laws that radically restricted the rights to own or lease land by aliens who were ineligible for citizenship; those laws affected particularly Chinese and Japanese immigrants. Their legal base was removed by acts of Congress of 1943, 1946, and 1952, which wiped out racial bars on naturalization. Beginning in 1940, all aliens had to register. In 1965 a new law provided for phasing out the immigration quota system based on national origins that had been in effect, with modifications, since 1921. Restrictions continued to be based on considerations of the labour market, and relatives of U.S. citizens and legal resident aliens were given preference.

The Supreme Court in *Truax* v. *Raich* (1915) held that the equal protection clause of the Fourteenth Amendment applies to aliens as well as to citizens and that a state may not deny to aliens the ordinary means of earning a livelihood, though a state may prohibit employment of aliens when such employment is a peril to public welfare. Notwithstanding constitutional limitations, no consistent pattern was followed among the states.

Aliens who are admitted legally to the United States may be so certified and granted "green cards" that entitle them to rights that include employment. But they are still subject to limitations under local laws. The U.S. Supreme Court held, for example, that municipalities may require police officers to be U.S. citizens (1982); "Aliens are by definition those outside the community" of those under self-government, Justice Byron R. White said.

Constitutionally, said Justice Robert H. Jackson in a case decided by the U.S. Supreme Court in 1952, the alien in the United States is afforded a large measure of economic opportunity; he may invoke the writ of habeas corpus; in criminal proceedings he is entitled to the guarantees of the Bill of Rights; and his property cannot be taken without just compensation. But to remain in the country "is not his right, but is a matter of permission and tolerance." As long as the alien is in the United States, the Constitution is his protection; but Congress, not the Constitution, decides whether or not he is to remain.

Illegal aliens, who often become "undocumented" workers and are subject to summary deportation, present special social problems in many U.S. communities. Employers may take advantage of their vulnerable status to exploit them in sweatshops. Such aliens often receive few employment benefits. They may not file tax returns nor be counted in censuses. Communities may be burdened with increased demand for public services, especially public education, without compensating tax support. The U.S. Supreme Court held in 1982 in *Plyer* v. *Doe* that children of illegal aliens come under the equal protection and due process clause of the Fourteenth Amendment and are entitled to tuition-free public education. A Texas law allowing school districts to charge tuition or bar such children was struck down. The court left unanswered questions about illegal aliens' possible rights to other state-supported benefits.

Alien and Sedition Acts (1798), four internal security laws passed by the U.S. Congress, restricting aliens and curtailing the excesses of an unrestrained press, in anticipation of an expected war with France. After the XYZ Affair (1797), war appeared inevitable. Federalists, aware that French military successes in Europe had been greatly facilitated by political dissidents in invaded countries, sought to prevent such subversion in the U.S. and adopted the Alien and Sedition Acts as part of a series of military preparedness measures.

The three alien laws, passed in June and July, were aimed at French and Irish immigrants, who were mostly pro-French. These laws raised the waiting period for naturalization from 5 to 14 years, permitted the detention of subjects of an enemy nation, and authorized the chief executive to expel any alien he considered dangerous. The Sedition Act (July 14) banned the publishing of false or malicious writings against the government and the inciting of opposition to any act of Congress or the president—practices already forbidden by state statutes and the common law but not by federal law. The federal act reduced the oppressiveness of procedures in prosecuting such offenses but provided for federal enforcement.

The acts were the mildest wartime security measures ever taken in the U.S., and they were widely popular. Jeffersonian Republicans vigorously opposed them, however, in the Virginia and Kentucky Resolutions (*q.v.*), which the other state legislatures either ignored or denounced as subversive. Only one alien was deported, and only 25 prosecutions, resulting in 10 convictions, were brought under the Sedition Act. The war threat passing and Republicans winning control of the federal government in 1800, all the Alien and Sedition Acts expired or were repealed during the next two years.

Alien Registration Act of 1940 (U.S.): *see* Smith Act.

alienation, in social sciences, the state of feeling estranged or separated from one's milieu, work, products of work, or self. Despite its popularity in the analysis of contemporary life, the idea of alienation remains an ambiguous concept with elusive meanings, the following variants being most common: (1) *powerlessness,* the feeling that one's destiny is not under one's own control but is determined by external agents, fate, luck, or institutional arrangements; (2) *meaninglessness,* referring either to the lack of comprehensibility or consistent meaning in any domain of action (such as world affairs or interpersonal relations) or to a generalized sense of purposelessness in life; (3) *normlessness,* the lack of commitment to shared social prescriptions for behaviour (hence widespread deviance, distrust, unrestrained individual competition, and the like); (4) *cultural estrangement,* the sense of removal from established values in society (as, for example, in the intellectual or student rebellions against conventional institutions); (5) *social isolation,* the sense of loneliness or exclusion in social relations (as, for example, among minority group members); and (6) *self-estrangement,* perhaps the most difficult to define and in a sense the master theme, the understanding that in one way or another the individual is out of touch with himself.

Recognition of the concept in Western thought has been similarly elusive. Although entries on "alienation" did not appear in major reference books of the social sciences until as late as 1935, the concept had existed implicitly or explicitly in classical sociological works of the 19th and early 20th centuries (by Karl Marx, Émile Durkheim, Ferdinand Tönnies, Max Weber, and Georg Simmel).

Perhaps the most famous use of the term was by Marx, who spoke of alienated labour under capitalism: work was compelled rather than spontaneous and creative; workers had little control over the work process; the product of labour was expropriated by others to be used against the worker; and the worker himself became a commodity in the labour market. Alienation consisted of the fact that man did not fulfill his "species being" in work; the essence of man remained unrealized.

The Marxian tradition, however, represents only one stream of thought concerning alienation. A second stream, considerably less sanguine about the prospects for de-alienation, is embodied in what has come to be called the theory of "mass society." Observing the dislocations brought about by industrialization in the 19th and early 20th centuries, Durkheim and Tönnies—and eventually Weber and Simmel as well—each, in his own way, lamented the passing of traditional society and the consequent loss of the sense of community. Modern man was isolated as he had never been before—anonymous and impersonal in an urbanizing mass, uprooted from old values, yet without faith in the new rational and bureaucratic order. Perhaps the clearest expression of this theme is contained in Durkheim's notion of "anomie" (from Greek *anomia,* "lawlessness"), a social condition characterized by rampant individualism and the disintegration of binding social norms. Both Weber and Simmel carried the Durkheimian theme further. Weber emphasized the fundamental drift toward rationalization and formalization in social organization; personal relations became fewer, and impersonal bureaucracy became larger. Simmel emphasized the tension in social life between the subjective and personal, on the one hand, and the increasingly objective and anonymous, on the other.

The classification of more modern definitions of alienation given in the first paragraph of this article—powerlessness, meaninglessness, normlessness, cultural estrangement, social isolation, and self-estrangement—can serve only as a rough guide because later writers often developed radically different conceptions within any one of the categories. Thus, with respect to self-estrangement, one can be "out of touch" with oneself in several quite different ways. Furthermore, later writers differed not only in their definitions but also in the assumptions that underlie these definitions. Two such contrasting assumptions are the normative and the subjective. First, those who held most closely to the tradition of Marx (Herbert Marcuse and Erich Fromm in the U.S., for example, or Georges Friedmann and Henri Lefebvre in France) treated alienation as a normative concept, as an instrument for criticizing the established state of affairs in the light of some standard based on human nature, "natural law," or moral principle. Marxian theorists, secondly, insisted upon alienation as an objective condition quite independent of individual consciousness—hence, to be a "happy robot" at work is to be alienated irrespective of one's acceptance of the work experience. Alternatively, some writers—most commonly the American empiricists—emphasized that alienation is a social-psychological fact—it is the *experience* of powerlessness, the *sense* of estrangement. Such an assumption is often found in analyses and descriptions of deviant behaviour (and in the work of such theoreticians as Robert K. Merton and Talcott Parsons).

alienation effect, also called A-EFFECT, or DISTANCING EFFECT, German VERFREMDUNGS-EFFEKT, or V-EFFEKT, idea central to the dramatic theory of the German dramatist-director Bertolt Brecht. It involves the use of techniques designed to defamiliarize the audience from the play and to jolt it into realizing that it is watching a theatrical performance.

Examples of such techniques include explanatory captions or illustrations projected on a screen; actors disengaging themselves from the scene to summarize, lecture, or sing songs; and stage designs that do not represent any locality but that, by exposing the lights and ropes, keep the spectators aware of being in a theatre. The audience's degree of identification with characters and events is controlled, therefore, and it can more clearly perceive the "real" world reflected in the drama.

Aliénor D'AQUITAINE: *see* Eleanor of Aquitaine.

Alienus, Aulis Caecina (Roman general): *see* Caecina Alienus, Aulis.

Alīgarh, also called KOIL, or KOL, town, administrative headquarters of Alīgarh district, Uttar Pradesh state, northern India, southeast of Delhi. The town itself is usually called Koil or Kol; Alīgarh is the name of a nearby fort. The town is an agricultural trade centre; the processing of agricultural products and manufacturing are also important. Alīgarh Muslim University (1875) and its affiliated colleges are located there, as are a number of other degree colleges. Another old fort, the Dor fortress (1524), now in ruins, lies at the town's centre; its site is occupied by an 18th-century mosque. The town also contains tombs of Muslim saints.

Alīgarh district is 1,940 sq mi (5,024 sq km) in area. It is a largely level region crossed by the Ganges Canal and several rivers. Wheat, barley, and other crops are grown; butter is exported. There is a glass factory at Sāsni. Major towns are Alīgarh and Hāthras (*q.v.*). Pop. (1981) town, 320,861; district, 2,574,925.

alignment, monument consisting of multiple rows of large upright stones, primarily located in Brittany and built during Neolithic and Early Bronze times. *See* megalith.

Where the same name may denote a person, place, or thing, the articles will be found in that order

---

alignment chart (applied mathematics): *see* nomograph.

alimentary canal, also called DIGESTIVE TRACT, pathway by which food enters an animal and solid wastes are expelled. In lower invertebrates (*e.g.,* flatworms) the digestive tract has only one opening, which serves as both mouth and anus. In higher invertebrates and vertebrates, food enters the alimentary canal through an oral cavity, and wastes are discharged through an anus. In mammals the system includes the mouth, pharynx, esophagus, stomach, small and large intestines, and anus. Variations in detail include the length of the intestines, which are short in carnivores but long in herbivores, whose diet is easier to obtain but requires more time to digest. In many birds the tract has developed a saclike crop to store food and a muscular gizzard in which stones (grit) grind the food before exposing it to absorption in the intestines.

alimentary paste, a shaped and dried dough prepared from semolina, farina, wheat flour, or a mixture of these with water or milk and with or without egg or egg yolk. *See* pasta.

alimony, in divorce law, compensation owed by one spouse to the other for support after divorce. Alimony aims at support of the one spouse, not punishment of the other. In some places, the term means simply a property settlement irrespective of future support. Alimony has traditionally been granted from husbands to wives but has occasionally been granted from wives to husbands.

Alimony obligations were first imposed by the Egyptians, Greeks, and Hebrews. The practice helped to avoid feuds with the divorced wife's relatives. Under the Code of Hammurabi, a Mesopotamian husband divorcing his wife without cause had to forfeit a piece of silver. Similarly, Roman law under Justinian I demanded a forfeiture of gold from the guilty spouse in a divorce.

In England, alimony was purely a creation of statute—probably arising out of the medieval church's belief that divorce could not terminate the obligations of marriage in the eyes of God. Scandinavian countries treat husband and wife as equals in divorce suits, allowing reciprocal claims for injury. Some countries—*e.g.,* the U.S.S.R., Austria, Belgium, and Romania—allow divorce as a normal cancellation of contract, with financial questions being settled by mutual agreement.

Alimony is either temporary—for support and expenses during the lawsuit; or permanent—for support thereafter. Temporary alimony is designed to enable one party to initiate or defend the divorce suit. The granting of temporary or permanent alimony is within the court's discretion, as are the frequency and amounts of payments.

Alinagar, Treaty of (Feb. 9, 1757), pact concluded in India by the British agent Robert Clive after his recovery of Calcutta on January 2, 1757, from the nawab of Bengal, Sirāj-ud-Dawlah. The treaty was the prelude to the British seizure of Bengal. The Nawab had seized Calcutta in June 1756, but he was anxious to secure his rear from the threat of attack by the Afghans, who had just taken and sacked Delhi.

The treaty restored Calcutta to the East India Company with its privileges and permitted the fortification of the town and the coining of money. The treaty was named after the short-lived title given to Calcutta by Sirāj after his capture of the city. Sirāj-ud-Dawlah was defeated and deposed by Clive later the same year.

Alinsky, Saul (David) (b. Jan. 30, 1909, Chicago—d. June 12, 1972, Carmel, Calif., U.S.), U.S. social organizer who stimulated the creation of numerous activist citizen and community groups.

After college training in archaeology and criminology, Alinsky worked as a criminologist in Illinois for eight years. In 1938, he undertook his first community organizing campaign in a working-class area of Chicago; the result was the Back of the Yards Council, which became a prototype for a generation of community organizations. In 1940, Alinsky founded the Industrial Areas Foundation and trained cadres of organizers in his techniques. Following wartime service in several federal agencies, Alinsky and his IAF team carried their techniques to communities throughout the country; the Community Service Organization in California provided early training for César Chavez, who went on to found the United Farm Workers of America.

In his home town of Chicago, Alinsky accomplished one of his most notable successes with The Woodlawn Organization, one of the first successful efforts in the country to organize black inner-city residents.

Alinsky wrote the first of his three books, *Reveille for Radicals* (1946), while serving a term in jail; his others books were *Rules for Radicals* (1971) and a biography of John L. Lewis (1949). He continued his organizing activities up to the time of his death.

aliphatic compound, any chemical compound belonging to the organic class in which the atoms are not linked together to form a ring. One of the major structural groups of organic molecules, the aliphatic compounds include the alkanes, alkenes, and alkynes, and substances derived from them—actually or in principle—by replacing one or more hydrogen atoms by atoms of other elements or groups of atoms.

Alīpore, also spelled ALĪPUR, town, headquarters of Twenty-four Parganas district, West Bengal state, northeastern India. A southern suburb of Calcutta included within the city municipality, it has major industries, including printing and bookbinding, cement manufacture, oilseed milling, and general engineering works. Alīpore is the site of zoological-horticultural gardens and of Belvedere House, one-time residence of the former British lieutenant governor of Bengal and now the location of the National Library. The town has a college affiliated with the University of Calcutta.

Alīpur Duār, town, Jalpaiguri district, West Bengal state, northeastern India, just north of the Kalyāni River. Connected by road with Jalpaiguri, the town is an important market centre for rice, tobacco, and jute; an annual agricultural produce and stock fair is held there. Rice milling is an important industry. Alīpur Duār was declared a municipality in 1951. Pop. (1981) town, 48,605; metropolitan area, 71,573.

Aliquippa, borough, Beaver County, western Pennsylvania, U.S., on the Ohio River, just northwest of Pittsburgh. Settled *c.* 1750 as a post for trade with the Indians, it was first known as Logstown and later renamed for "Queen" Aliquippa, probably a Mohawk Indian. After the French and Indian Wars of 1754–63, the Indians lost their title to the land, and Logstown became a deserted village. White settlement began in the 1770s, and sawmilling and gristmilling were early industries. During the winter of 1793–94, Gen. Anthony ("Mad Anthony") Wayne trained his troops at a site across the river before moving into western Ohio to defeat the Indians at the Battle of Fallen Timbers (Aug. 20, 1794). The borough grew rapidly after expansion of the Pittsburgh steel mills in 1909, and much of the working force is now engaged in steel production. Aliquippa consolidated in 1928 with the adjacent borough of Woodlawn. Inc. 1894. Pop. (1980) 17,094.

Alişar Hüyük, site of an ancient Anatolian town southeast of Boğazköy in Yozgat *il* (province), Turkey. Thorough and extensive excavations there by the Oriental Institute of the University of Chicago (1927–32) were the first systematic stratigraphic investigations on the Anatolian plateau. In the long succession of strata revealed at Alişar—from Chalcolithic (*c.* 4000–*c.* 2600 BC) to Phrygian (*c.* 1200–

c. 700 BC)—the only era that was not represented was the Hittite, from the 17th to the 13th century BC.

The mound consisted of an off-centre top elevation, known as the citadel, and a sloping terrace. The earliest habitation was probably in the Late Chalcolithic Age and Early Copper Age.

Later, in the Bronze Age (*c.* 3000–*c.* 2000 BC), two different cultures appear to have occupied the site; the remains may represent an intrusion of foreign invaders, possibly Indo-European Hittites or related tribes, who were rapidly assimilated. Among the remains of the native Anatolian culture were a number of 19th-century "Cappadocian tablets," the records of Assyrian merchant colonists who lived at Alişar Hüyük.

After the 13th century BC, the mound was the site of a Phrygian fortress, with a walled section on the slope below. The settlement survived perhaps to the 6th century BC and was finally destroyed by fire.

Alismaceae, the water plantain family of freshwater flowering plants, belonging to the order Alismales and including at least 10 genera, the most common of which are *Alisma* and *Sagittaria,* with about 90 species. Most members of the family are native to the Northern Hemisphere, but some species are widely distributed throughout both tropical and temperate regions.

Alismaceae are commonly found in shallow water and swamps or on muddy banks or wet sand. The long, thin leafstalks are clumped together. The flowers have three sepals (modified leaves) and three petals and range in colour from white to rose. *See also* arrowhead; burhead; water plantain.

Alismales, also called ALISMATALES, water-plantain order of flowering plants, belonging to the class called monocotyledon (*q.v.*; characterized by a single seed leaf). Most species are aquatic and grow submerged or partially exposed to the air in freshwater habitats. Many plants belonging to this order are aquatic weeds that hinder irrigation and navigation. Others provide important habitats for fish and help to stabilize shorelines. A few are planted in formal pools.

A brief treatment of Alismales follows. For full treatment, *see* MACROPAEDIA: Angiosperms.

Although of little economic importance, these herbaceous (nonwoody) plants, by forming complex communities with other aquatic and emergent stream-bank plants, bring about vegetational succession; a pond may fill up with plant parts and silt to become a biological landfill, which eventually supports land plants.

Alismales is comprised of three families. The Butomaceae, consisting of a single genus and species (*Butomus umbellatus*), is distributed throughout the North Temperate Zone and is used in landscaped water gardens. The four genera of Limnocharitaceae are tropical and some species grow well in tropical fish aquariums. The Alismaceae, with 14 genera and 90 species, is found in the North Temperate Zone and the tropics. It is notable for developing latex channels (containing milky juice) in its stems and leaves.

Members of Alismales are rather uniform anatomically. Most plants possess short stems and are rooted in mud with only the leaves visible above water level. In some species even the leaves are submerged and fail to differentiate into the familiar lamina (blade) and petiole (leaf stalk) of land plants. Emergent leaf blades are often attractive in form and stance and used in artistic designs. *Alisma,* which gives the order its name, produces heart-shaped leaves noted for contoured venation and delicate cross-veins. The netted venation in leaves of the Alismales is an exception for the monocots, which usually lack connecting veinlets. The blade of *Sagittaria* is shaped like an arrowhead and may be lifted above the surface of the water by the petiole to a height of more than 40 inches (100 centimetres). Leaves lack hairs (except in one species) and produce stomata (small air pores), usually on the upper surface of the blade. Submerged leaves lack stomata.

Succulence is characteristic of Alismales and air spaces may occupy 80 percent of the volume of internal tissues of the leaf and root. The vascular system, which consists of the xylem (water-conducting tissues) and phloem (food-conducting tissues), is rather inconspicuous. Fibres and other thick-walled cells are few in number. The elements of the conducting systems are evolutionarily advanced, but they play a minor role in supporting the plant. Vascular bundles often occur in a circle in stems and in an arc in petioles (when viewed in a slice). In most other monocots the bundles are scattered.

A potential flower cluster (inflorescence) arises as a specialized stem from the flattened vegetative stem at the juncture of a leaf base. As it elongates above water, a succession of flower buds form and develop in the sequence of parts usually observed in many flowering plants. The outermost set (or whorl) consists of three leaflike sepals. The next whorl is composed of three petals, which surround many stamens and several carpels. In the Alismales, the small petals attract flies, which are the main pollinators. Each seed-bearing structure (carpel) possesses the pollen-receptive tip (stigma), often a short stalk (style), and a basal ovary.

Each pistil produces one to several ovules in its swollen, basal ovary. After pollination and fertilization, an ovule becomes the seed. In some species, seeds are shed when the ovary matures into a fruit and eventually ruptures, as in *Butomus.* In other groups, such as the Alismaceae, seeds are liberated only after the ovary wall disintegrates in the water.

Alitalia-Linee Aeree Italiane, Italian international airline founded in 1946 and, by the late 20th century, servicing more than 120 cities in Europe, Africa, Asia, North and South America, and Australia. Headquarters are in Rome.

The company was established in 1946 as Alitalia-Aerolinee Italiane Internazionali and flew its first route, from Turin to Rome, in 1947. In 1957 it merged with the other Italian airline, LAI, or Linee Aeree Italiane, and the current name was adopted. In succeeding decades Alitalia's holdings tended to become conglomerate, with the acquisition or establishment of catering companies, hotel chains, resorts, a property management company, insurance and reinsurance companies, a data processing company, and Alitalia International Holding SA (in Luxembourg), engaged in acquiring holdings in foreign firms.

Alitus (Lithuanian S.S.R.): *see* Alytus.

aliyah, also spelled ʿALIYYA (Hebrew: "going up"), plural ALIYAHS, ALIYOT, ALIYOTH, or ʿALIYYOT, in Judaism, the honour accorded to a worshipper of being called up to read an assigned passage from the Torah (first five books of the Bible). Since the passage assigned for each sabbath-morning service is subdivided into a minimum of seven sections, at least seven different persons are called up for these readings. An additional reader is called up to repeat part of the final reading and to recite the Haftarah (a reading from the prophetical books of the Bible). At certain times throughout the year (*e.g.,* fast days, festivals) there are fewer Torah readings and they may not be subdivided into more than the statutory number.

If a cohen (a direct descendant of Aaron, the first priest) and a Levite (a member of the priestly tribe of Levi) are present, it is their privilege to be called up for the first and second readings, respectively. Normally, therefore, an Israelite (ordinary worshipper) may not be so honoured until the third reading of the Torah.

By the 14th century it had become customary to appoint a trained reader to do the actual reading to avoid embarrassing those whose knowledge of Hebrew was inadequate. The persons who were called up, therefore, merely presided during the reading and recited the appropriate blessings. The practice of selling the *aliyah,* once common, has been discontinued.

In modern times, *aliyah* has also been used to designate the "going up" to Israel of immigrants from other lands, just as in former times it meant going up to the Holy Land.

alizarin, also spelled ALIZARINE, a red dye originally obtained from the root of the common madder plant, *Rubia tinctorum,* in which it occurs combined with the sugars xylose and glucose. Cultivation of madder and use of its ground root for dyeing by the complicated Turkey red process were known in ancient India, Persia, and Egypt; the use spread to Asia Minor about the 10th century and was introduced into Europe in the 16th.

Laboratory methods of preparing alizarin from anthraquinone were discovered in 1868, and, upon commercial introduction of the synthetic dye in 1871, the natural product quickly disappeared from the market. Its application to cotton, wool, or silk requires prior impregnation of the fibre with a metal oxide, or mordant. The shade produced depends upon the metal present: aluminum yields a red; iron, a violet; and chromium, a brownish red.

Aljechin, Alexander: *see* Alekhine, Alexander.

alka, also called ALKAS, in Baltic religion, an open-air religious site, a natural sanctuary—forest, hill, river—that was sacred and inviolate. Trees could not be cut in such forests, sacred fields could not be plowed, and fishing was not allowed in the holy waters. The rituals of various religious cults, involving animal sacrifice and human cremation, took place at the *alka*s. The sense of the ancient *alka* is preserved in the modern Lithuanian word *alkvietė,* meaning any holy place or site of worship.

Alkalai, Judah ben Solomon Hai (b. 1798, Sarajevo, Bosnia, Ottoman Empire—d. 1878, Jerusalem), Sefardic rabbi and an early advocate of Jewish colonization of Palestine.

Alkalai was taken to Jerusalem at an early age, and there he was reared and educated for the rabbinate. At 25 he went to Semlin, in Croatia, as a rabbi and found himself teaching Hebrew to the young men of his congregation, whose native language was Ladino. He wrote two books in that language, the first a text on Hebrew, the second a refutation of heated attacks directed at his proto-Zionist views.

Alkalai argued that a physical "return to Israel" (*i.e.,* to Eretz Yisra'el, the Holy Land in Palestine), was a precondition for redemption (salvation), instead of the symbolic "return to Israel" by means of repentance and resuming the ways of God. This doctrine was unacceptable to Orthodox Jews and generated much controversy. After the Damascus Affair, an anti-Semitic outburst of 1840 reviving old canards about ritual murder, Alkalai took to admonishing Jews that the event was part of a divine design to awaken Jews to the reality of their condition in Diaspora, or dispersion. Believing that Jews should migrate nowhere but to Palestine, he travelled in England and about Europe seeking support for such emigration, founding organizations wherever he went, but these came to naught. Finally in 1874 he left his congregation at Semlin and went to Palestine, where he created a new organization, a society for settlement. It too failed. But Alkalai's writings—he was an inveterate pamphleteer—did have some impact, as did one book—his first in Hebrew—*Goral Ladonai* (1857; "A Lot for the Lord"). These and his personal migration helped pave the way for the coming Zionism of Theodor Herzl and others.

alkali feldspar, any of several common silicate minerals that often occur as variously coloured, glassy crystals. They are used in the manufacture of glass and ceramics; transparent, highly coloured, or iridescent varieties are sometimes used as gemstones. The alkali feldspars are primarily important as constituents of rocks; they are very widespread and abundant in alkali and acidic igneous rocks (particularly syenites, granites, and granodiorites), in pegmatites, and in gneisses.

The alkali feldspars may be regarded as mixtures of sodium aluminosilicate ($NaAlSi_3O_8$) and potassium aluminosilicate ($KAlSi_3O_8$).

Both the sodium and potassium aluminosilicates have several distinct forms, each form with a different structure. The forms stable at high temperatures—high-albite (sodium) and sanidine and high-sanidine (potassium)—have a random distribution of aluminum and silicon atoms in the crystal structure; the low-temperature forms—albite (sodium) and orthoclase and microline (potassium)—have an ordered arrangement. If specimens of the high-temperature varieties are rapidly cooled, the random distribution is preserved. Thus, in the Earth's crust the alkali feldspars display a range of ordering from the fully random distribution of high-sanidine, through sanidine and orthoclase, to the fully ordered distribution of microcline, and probably a similar range of ordering from the random high-albite to the ordered albite.

In natural akali feldspars, there is a continuous variation between the two pure components. At least four distinct series exist. Two are characteristic of relatively high temperatures (above 700° C, or 1,300° F); these are the high-albite–high-sanidine series and the high-albite–sanidine series. Representatives of these series occur infrequently in crustal rocks. Two other series are characteristic of lower temperatures or slow cooling from higher temperatures; these are the low-albite–orthoclase series and the low-albite–microcline-microperthite–microcline series. Representatives of these series are very common. At high temperatures the mixtures are homogeneous; very rapid cooling preserves homogeneity, but slow cooling causes separation into sodium and potassium phases; that is, most alkali feldspars are not homogeneous but are intergrowths, called perthites, of distinct crystals of the pure sodium and potassium compounds.

alkali flat, also called SALINA, or SALT FLAT, a playa, or dried-out desert lake, especially one containing high concentrations of precipitated dry, glistening salts. The term is generally limited to flats in the western United States, the most famous being the Bonneville Salt Flats west of Salt Lake City, where automobile speed records are set.

alkali metal, any of the six chemical elements that make up Group I of the periodic table—namely, lithium (Li), sodium (Na), potassium (K), rubidium (Rb), cesium (Cs), and francium (Fr). The alkali metals are so called because they form alkalies (*i.e.,* strong bases capable of neutralizing acids) when they combine with other elements.

A brief treatment of the alkali metals follows. For full treatment, *see* MACROPAEDIA: Chemical Elements. *See also* MICROPAEDIA for entries on each member of this group.

The only members of the alkali metal family that are relatively abundant in the Earth's crust are potassium and sodium. These two were the first alkali metals to be isolated (1807).

Alkali metals bear little resemblance to the more familiar metals such as iron and copper. They are silver-white in colour, malleable, and soft enough to cut with a knife. The alkali metals are the most chemically active of all metals, readily forming ions with a single positive charge. This property is a consequence of their atoms having only a single, highly mobile electron in the outermost shell. Alkali metals react rapidly, sometimes violently, with both oxygen and water. Because of their reactivity, they always occur in nature in combination with other elements as simple and complex compounds. Pure alkali metals can be extracted from such compounds through the electrolysis of molten salts or hydroxides. Another process known as thermal reduction is also employed to obtain lithium and cesium.

alkaline-earth metal, any of the six chemical elements that comprise Group IIa of the periodic table. The elements are beryllium (Be), magnesium (Mg), calcium (Ca), strontium (Sr), barium (Ba), and radium (Ra).

A brief treatment of the alkaline-earth metals follows. For full treatment, *see* MACROPAEDIA: Chemical Elements. *See also* MICROPAEDIA for entries on each member of this group.

The designation "earth" for these metals derives from the Middle Ages when alchemists referred to substances that were insoluble in water and unchanged by fire as earths. Those earths, such as lime, that bore a resemblance to the alkalines (*e.g.,* soda ash and potash) were called alkaline earths. By the early 1800s it became apparent that the earths, formerly regarded as elements, were in reality compounds of a metal and oxygen—*i.e.,* oxides. The metals whose oxides comprise the alkaline earths subsequently came to be known as the alkaline-earth metals. Magnesium, calcium, strontium, and barium were isolated as impure metals for the first time in 1808 by the English chemist Sir Humphry Davy.

The alkaline-earth metals are basically grayish white in colour. They all are malleable but vary widely in hardness. Beryllium, for example, is hard enough to cut glass; barium, by contrast, is as soft as lead. Like other metals, the alkaline-earth elements are good conductors of electricity. Their melting points and boiling points, though varying in an irregular fashion, are higher than those of the corresponding alkali metals. The atoms of the alkaline-earth elements have a similar electronic structure, which consists of a pair of electrons in the outermost shell. These electrons are removed from their respective atoms relatively easily, and this ionization is the distinguishing chemical property of the alkaline-earth metals. These elements readily combine with most oxides and many nonmetals. Accordingly, they never occur as pure metals in nature.

Magnesium and calcium are the only abundant alkaline-earth elements in the crust of the Earth. They also are the most commercially important members of the family.

alkaline phosphatase, enzyme normally present in high concentrations in growing bone and in bile. It is also present in the blood and is essential for the deposition of minerals in the bones and teeth. Alkaline phosphatase deficiency is a hereditary trait called hypophosphatasia, which results in bone deformities. In severe cases, their deficiency lead to early death from infection.

alkaline rock, any of various rocks in which the chemical content of the alkalies (potassium oxide and sodium oxide) is great enough for alkaline minerals to form. Such minerals may be unusually sodium rich, with a relatively high ratio of alkalies to silica (SiO_2), as in the feldspathoids. Other alkaline minerals have a high ratio of alkalies to alumina (Al_2O_3), as in aegirine pyroxene and the sodic amphibole riebeckite.

English-speaking petrologists have followed Alfred Harker, who divided Tertiary and Recent igneous rocks into calc-alkaline and alkaline suites. Alkaline rocks include many with unusual names, but the more common alkali-basalt, syenite, and phonolite are included in the group. The most common and widely distributed rocks of the world—*e.g.,* granite, granodiorite, andesite, and basalt—do not contain the alkaline minerals. Alkaline rocks are generally considered to be abnormal types, and there have been many intensive studies of their origin, yielding numerous theories, several of which may be valid in specific cases.

alkaloid, any of a class of organic compounds characterized by the presence of carbon, hydrogen, and nitrogen. They have diverse and powerful physiological effects on humans and other animals. Well-known alkaloids include morphine, strychnine, quinine, ephedrine, and nicotine.

A brief treatment of alkaloids follows. For full treatment, *see* MACROPAEDIA: Chemical Compounds.

Alkaloids are a class of chemical compounds that are difficult to categorize precisely. They are found in plants or, much less often, in animals, but they are not widely distributed in either kingdom. They are chemically basic, or alkaline—*i.e.,* they neutralize acids. They have complex molecular structures and are physiologically active. Alkaloids, however, do not always exhibit all these characteristics. For example, colchicine, which is not alkaline, is considered an alkaloid because of its physiological activity.

The molecular structures of alkaloids are extremely complex. Most alkaloids contain at least one nitrogen atom in an amine-type structure. This is a structure derived from ammonia by replacing hydrogen atoms with hydrogen-carbon groups called hydrocarbons. Also, alkaloids generally have this or another nitrogen atom in some type of ring system.

Alkaloids are often grouped according to the characteristic molecular structures they have in common. Thus the simplest ring-structured alkaloids belong to the group designated pyrrolidine alkaloids. They include the five-membered pyrrole ring composed of one nitrogen and four carbon atoms. The indole alkaloids, which include psilocybin, are based on the indole structure, in which a benzene ring (a six-membered ring of carbon atoms) is fused with a pyrrole ring. Other important groups are pyridine, quinoline (*e.g.,* quinine), isoquinoline, imidazole, and pyridine-pyrrolidine (*e.g.,* nicotine).

Alkaloids are also sometimes classified by the biological systems in which they occur. For example, opium alkaloids come from the opium poppy.

The physiological activity of alkaloids is important in medicine. The analgesics are a case in point. Morphine, for example, is derived from the opium poppy, as are its derivatives codeine and morphine. Other medical uses are for cardiac stimulants or respiratory stimulants (*e.g.,* nicotine). Still others are blood vessel constrictors, local anesthetics, or muscle relaxants. Alkaloids such as mescaline, from cacti of the *Anhalonium* species, and psilocybin, from fungi of the *Psilocybe* species, are psychedelics.

A few animals such as the North American beaver and the salamander contain alkaloids. Alkaloids, however, are found primarily in a few species of flowering plants, though certain nonflowering species also produce them. They occur abundantly in dogbane, poppies, lupins, delphiniums, citrus, tobacco, deadly nightshade, tomato, potato, and thorn apple. Scientists are not sure exactly what role alkaloids play in the life of the plants themselves.

Chemists have intensively studied the way alkaloids are synthesized by plants. In general, they seem to be derived from relatively simple precursor compounds, notably amino acids. Radioactive tracer techniques have confirmed that a number of alkaloids are synthesized from amino acids in nature. Alkaloids also have been synthesized from these substances in the laboratory.

Special methods have been developed for isolating commercially useful alkaloids such as morphine. In most cases, plant or animal tissue is processed to obtain aqueous acid solutions of the alkaloids. The alkaloids are then recovered from the solution by a process called extraction. This involves dissolving some components of the mixture with reagents. Different alkaloids must then be separated and purified from the mixture. Chromatography may be used to take advantage of the different degrees of adsorption of the various alkaloids on solid material such as alumina or silica. Alkaloids in crystalline form may be obtained using certain solvents.

alkalosis, abnormally low level of acidity, or high level of alkalinity, in the body fluids, including the blood. Metabolic alkalosis results from any circumstance other than a deviation from the normal in the exchange of oxygen and carbon dioxide in the lungs—a type of alkalosis called respiratory. The underlying causes of metabolic alkalosis include severe vomiting, the taking of diuretics (substances that promote production of urine), and abnormally high secretion of hormones by the cortex (outer substance) of the adrenal glands. *Compare* acidosis.

Alkan, original name CHARLES-HENRI-VALENTIN MORHANGE (b. Nov. 30, 1813, Paris—d. March 29, 1888, Paris), pianist-composer, one of the most enigmatic figures in 19th-century music.

Alkan entered the Paris Conservatoire at the age of six and by 17 had established a reputation as a virtuoso pianist. As a youth, he moved in a circle of friends that included George Sand, Victor Hugo, Chopin, and Franz Liszt, but in his 20s he became a recluse and devoted himself to composition, mostly works for the piano. His music, difficult and often unorthodox, displays considerable ingenuity and imagination in advancing the possibilities of keyboard technique; in this respect Ferruccio Busoni, an Italian composer and pianist, considered him to be excelled only by Liszt and Brahms. His numerous works include preludes and studies in all the major and minor keys; 12 pieces, *Les mois* (*The Months*); the sonata, *Les quatre âges;* and the *Piano Concerto in C Sharp Minor.* César Franck transcribed several of his pieces for organ.

alkane (chemistry): *see* paraffin hydrocarbons.

alkanet, any plant of the 50 or so mostly Mediterranean species of the genus *Anchusa* and the closely related *Pentaglottis sempervirens,* bearing blue, purple, or white forget-me-not–like flower clusters on hairy, herbaceous stems. They belong to the family Boraginaceae. True alkanet (*A. officinalis*) bears purple flowers in coiled sprays, on narrow-leaved plants, 60 centimetres (2 feet) tall. Large blue alkanet (*A. azurea*), popular as a garden species, reaches 120 cm, and has large, bright-blue flowers with a tuft of white hairs in the throats, and narrow leaves. Oval, pointed, evergreen leaves and white-eyed, blue flowers characterize the evergreen alkanet (*Pentaglottis sempervirens*), which reaches 100 cm. All three species grow in fields and roadside waste spaces. True alkanet has become naturalized in some areas of eastern North America.

Alkanet (*Pentaglottis sempervirens*)
M.C.F. Proctor from the Natural History Photographic Agency—EB Inc.

The closely related *Alkanna tinctoria* is dyer's alkanet. Its roots are the source of a water-insoluble red dye used to colour fat, oil, perfume, wood, marble, and pharmaceutical products.

alkaptonuria, rather rare (one in 200,000 births) inherited inability of the body to metabolize the amino acids tyrosine and phenylalanine. In the normal metabolic pathway of tyrosine, homogentisic acid is acted upon in the liver by a specific organic catalyst, or enzyme, called homogentisic acid oxidase. This enzyme is not active in individuals who have alkaptonuria. Except for a blackening of the urine, this disorder has no clinical manifestations until the affected person is in his twenties or thirties, when deposits of ochre pigments begin to appear in various fibrous connective tissues of the body. The pigment, bound to collagen fibres in the deeper layers of joint cartilage and intervertebral disks (the fibrous pads between adjacent bones of the spine), causes these tissues to lose their normal resiliency and become brittle. The erosion of the abnormal cartilage leads to a progressive degenerative disease of the joints, which usually becomes manifest by the fourth decade of life. Usually, the intervertebral disks become thinned and calcified first, and later the knees, shoulders, and hips are affected.

Alkaptonuria is compatible with normal life expectancy. Whether the arteriosclerosis that has been described in some cases is a manifestation of the disease or coincidental is uncertain. No effective treatment is available for the underlying metabolic disorder.

alkene (chemistry): *see* olefin.

Alkmaar, *gemeente* (municipality), Noord-holland *provincie* (province), northwestern Netherlands, on the North Holland Canal, 6 mi (10 km) from the North Sea. The English missionaries Willibrord and Adalbert preached Christianity in the district in the 8th century. A fishing village in the 10th century, Alkmaar (meaning "all marsh," or "all sea") was chartered in 1254 and was the capital of Kennemerland, an early possession of the counts of Holland. Sacked by the Frisians in 1132 and again by a combined force of Frisians and Gelderlanders in 1517, Alkmaar became an important trade centre after 1564, when the surrounding swamps were reclaimed. The town successfully withstood a Spanish siege in 1573 to become a symbol of Dutch resistance (commemorated by a monument in Victorie Park). Under the Convention of Alkmaar (1799), a Russo-British army withdrew from the Netherlands after an unsuccessful campaign to overthrow the Batavian Republic.

A market centre for cattle, dairy products, and vegetables, the town is also a tourist centre noted for its Friday cheese market (Kaasmarkt), held from April to October. Manufactures include furniture, clothing, paper, and church organs. The most notable landmarks are the Weighhouse (1582, rebuilt from a 14th-century chapel), with a carillon tower, and St. Lawrence's Church (1470–1520), with one of the oldest organs in The Netherlands (1511). Other old buildings include the town hall (1520), the 16th-century Sonoy Court, and several alms-houses. Pop. (1982 est.) 77,761.

Cheese market, Alkmaar, Neth.
Malak—Shostal/EB Inc.

alkylation, in petroleum refining, the addition of alkyl groups to olefin molecules; a type of condensation reaction in which a gaseous mixture of olefins is converted to liquid high-octane gasoline by combining chemically with a gaseous paraffin hydrocarbon, which provides the alkyl molecular groups. These small molecules are combined into larger molecules, forming a liquid such as gasoline. The process is the reverse of the cracking operation, which breaks up hydrocarbons. Both thermal and catalytic process conditions are used, and the end products vary, depending on these conditions.

Alkylation, carried out in conjunction with cracking, can increase a refinery's motor-gasoline yield, both because additional gasoline is obtained in the cracking process and because the gases containing three or four carbon atoms are converted by alkylation into desirable gasoline components. *See also* gasoline.

alkyne (chemistry): *see* acetylene.

All-African Trade Union Federation (AATUF), international African trade union federation. A militant supporter of African nationalism, it considers affiliation with world trade union confederations to be incompatible with a pan-African federation. Observers believe that this position is partly in reaction to colonialism and the tendency of international organizations to use their aid to influence African positions in East–West conflicts.

The highly centralized AATUF was founded in 1961 by a nucleus of unions from Ghana, Guinea, Mali, Algeria, Morocco, the United Arab Republic (Egypt), Tanzania, and Nigeria. It views unions as auxiliary arms of African governments rather than independent entities and aims at nonalignment and a uniformity of action among its members.

All-America team, group of a season's outstanding U.S. college football players, first picked by Caspar Whitney in 1889 and publicized in a magazine called *This Week's Sport.* The All-America team is usually associated with Walter C. Camp, who collaborated with Whitney from 1891 to 1896 and then published his own selections from 1897 to 1924, mostly in *Collier's* magazine. Camp's reputation as football player, coach, and rules maker made his selections generally accepted. When Camp died in 1925, *Collier's* engaged Grantland Rice, a prominent football writer, to continue the annual selection.

Even before 1900, other football devotees began making their own All-America choices. The number of these selections increased as the popularity of football grew. Rice and *Collier's* began the practice of compiling their selections from the findings of a countrywide board of the American Football Coaches Association. The major U.S. news services, Associated Press and United Press International, also use the findings of representatives scattered throughout the country to choose All-America teams, as does the Football Writers Association of America.

All-America teams are now also chosen in such sports as baseball, basketball, swimming, and track and field and consist of athletes from colleges, high schools, and prep schools.

all-around (gymnastics): *see* combined exercises.

all-around, track-and-field sports competition held in the United States by the Amateur Athletic Union, similar to the internationally recognized decathlon event. It is a one-day competition consisting of 10 events with no more than a five-minute interval between each. The events are a 100-yard dash, 16-pound shot put, high jump, 880-yard walk, 16-pound hammer throw, pole vault, 120-yard high hurdles, 56-pound weight throw, long jump, and one-mile run. Contestants are scored in each event according to tables published by the AAU. The athlete with the highest total at the end of the competition is the winner.

All-England Championships, byname WIMBLEDON CHAMPIONSHIPS, internationally known lawn tennis championships played annually in London at Wimbledon (*q.v.*).

All Fives (game): *see* Muggins.

All Fools' Day: *see* April Fools' Day.

All-Fours, family of card games dating back to 17th-century England and first mentioned in *The Complete Gamester* of Charles Cotton in 1674. Like Whist, All-Fours was first popular with the lower classes but in the 15th century became accepted into middle-class homes.

Each player is dealt six cards, three at a time. The top card of the remaining pack is then exposed to establish the trump. The player to the dealer's left, called the eldest hand, may dispute the trump, in which case the dealer may agree to "run the cards" (trade three from the pack for three from each hand) and then establish a new trump.

Play is led by the eldest hand, and each player either follows suit or plays trump if he is able; otherwise, he follows with any card of ascending rank, regardless of suit. The highest trump or, if no trumps were played, the highest card in the led suit takes the trick. Each trick is led by the previous trick's winner. Points are awarded at hand's end, and 7 points wins the game.

All-Fours is so named because there are four scoring categories: high (scored by the player who plays the highest trump card); low (scored by the player who plays the lowest trump); jack (knave of trump suit, scored by the dealer if he turns it as trump or by the player winning it in a trick); and game (a plurality of high-card points won in tricks, with each 10 counting 10, jacks 1, queens 2, kings 3, and aces 4). The game is played by two or three players or by two sets of partners.

The game was called Seven-Up, from the 7 winning points, when it first was introduced to North America in the early 1700s. That game was replaced in popularity by Pitch, which introduced bidding: each player has one chance to bid the number of points he thinks he can win, with 4 the high bid. The high bidder pitches (leads first), and the suit of this card becomes trump for the hand. If the pitcher fails to fulfill his contract, he is set back the number of points bid. At times, Pitch is augmented by the rule called smudge, by which the player meeting his bid of 4 wins the game at once. From this comes the variant game Smudge, where collecting all 4 points in one hand, regardless of the bid, wins the game.

All India Muslim League: *see* Muslim League.

All-India Trade Union Congress (AITUC), India's second largest trade union federation after the Indian National Trade Union Congress. The AITUC was formed by the Indian National Congress (the central organ of the independence movement) in 1920 to represent India at the International Labour Organisation of the League of Nations (later United Nations). During the 1920s, British Communists, in their efforts to organize trade unions, gained control of a large portion of the federation; several opposing factions subsequently split away. The Communists gained complete control during World War II, although they lost some popular support when they chose to support the war effort along with Britain after the Soviet Union entered the war. Since that time AITUC leaders have been split into reformist and revolutionary factions. The AITUC is affiliated with the World Federation of Trade Unions.

all-or-none law, a physiological principle that relates response to stimulus in excitable tissues. It was first established for the contraction of heart muscle by the U.S. physiologist Henry P. Bowditch in 1871. Describing the relation of response to stimulus, he stated, "An induction shock produces a contraction or fails to do so according to its strength; if it does so at all, it produces the greatest contraction that can be produced by any strength of stimulus in the condition of the muscle at the time." It was believed that this law was peculiar to the heart and that the other highly specialized and rapidly responding tissues—skeletal muscle and nerve—responded in a different way, the intensity of response being graded according to the intensity of the stimulus. It has been established, however, that the individual fibres of both skeletal muscle and nerve respond to stimulation according to the all-or-none principle. This does not mean that the size of response is immutable, because functional capacity varies with the condition of the tissue, and the response to a stimulus applied during recovery from a previous response is subnormal. The size of response, however, is independent of the strength of stimulus, provided this be adequate. The functional response is essentially alike in these specialized tissues—heart, skeletal muscle, and nerve; its precise nature is not known, but it resembles an explosive reaction in that it depletes for a time the available store of energy on which it depends.

All Saints Bay (Brazil): *see* Todos os Santos, Baía de.

All Saints' Day, in the Christian Church, a day commemorating all the saints of the church, both known and unknown, celebrated on November 1 in the Western churches and on the first Sunday after Pentecost in the Eastern churches. Its origin cannot be traced with certainty, and it has been observed on various days in different places. A feast of all martyrs was kept on May 13 in the Eastern Church according to Ephraem Syrus (died *c.* 373), which may have determined the choice of May 13 by Pope Boniface IV when he dedicated the Pantheon in Rome as a church in honour of the Blessed Virgin and all martyrs in 609. The first evidence for the November 1 date of celebration and of the broadening of the festival to include all saints as well as all martyrs occurred during the reign of Pope Gregory III (731–741), who dedicated a chapel in St. Peter's, Rome, on November 1 in honour of all saints. In 800 All Saints' Day was kept by Alcuin on November 1, and it also appeared in a 9th-century English calendar on that day. In 837 Pope Gregory IV ordered its general observance.

In medieval England, the festival was known as All Hallows, and its eve is still known as Halloween.

All Souls' Day, in the Roman Catholic Church, a day for commemoration of all the faithful departed, those baptized Christians who are believed to be in purgatory because they have died with the guilt of lesser sins on their souls. It is celebrated on November 2, or on November 3 if November 2 is Sunday. Catholic doctrine holds that the prayers of the faithful on earth will help cleanse these souls in order to fit them for the vision of God in heaven.

From antiquity certain days were devoted to intercession for particular groups of the dead. The institution of a day for a general intercession on November 2 is due to Odilo, abbot of Cluny (died 1048). The date, which became practically universal before the end of the 13th century, was chosen to follow All Saints' Day. Having celebrated the feast of all the members of the church who are believed to be in heaven, the church on earth turns, on the next day, to commemorate those souls believed to be suffering in purgatory.

Black vestments are worn, the office of the day is that of the dead, and the Roman liturgy permits every priest to celebrate three requiem masses, one for the intention of the celebrant himself, one for all the faithful departed, and one for the intention of the pope.

The feast was abolished in the Church of England at the Reformation but has been revived in Anglo-Catholic churches.

All-Star Game, in U.S. professional baseball, a game between teams of outstanding players chosen from National and American league teams who oppose each other as league against league. The All-Star Game is held each July; two annual games were played from 1959 to 1962. Most of the gate receipts are donated to the players' pension fund. Arch Ward, a *Chicago Tribune* sports editor, is credited with promoting the first All-Star Game, which was held in Chicago in 1933 in conjunction with the Century of Progress Exposition. Similar contests are conducted in U.S. professional football and basketball, as well as on various amateur levels of these and other sports.

All-Union Council of Evangelical Christians and Baptists, voluntary association in the Soviet Union of Baptist churches organized in 1944 by uniting the Union of Evangelical Christians and the Russian Baptist Union. The Baptists in Russia developed from religious revival movements that began in the 1860s and 1870s. In the Ukraine, groups of Russians influenced by German Mennonite settlers began gathering for Bible study and eventually adopted Baptist beliefs. In Georgia, German Baptists gained converts and developed a Baptist community. These two movements united in 1884 to form the Russian Baptist Union.

Another group that was essentially Baptist in belief preferred to call itself Evangelicals and formed the Union of Evangelical Christians in 1908.

Baptists increased in Russia despite early persecution by the government; but, by 1905, persecution lessened. After the revolution in 1917, religious freedom was declared for all, and Baptist converts increased rapidly. In 1929 the Soviet government began suppressing religion, but, during and after World War II, the government made some concessions to the churches. Educational and social activities, however, have been restricted.

The executive body of the association is elected by delegates from the congregations at meetings that are held at least once every three years.

All-Union Leninist Communist League of Youth: *see* Komsomol.

Allāh (Arabic: God), in Islām, the unique (*wāḥid*) and inherently one (*aḥad*) God, the pivot of Islām, the Muslim faith. Allāh is creator, judge, and rewarder, omnipotent and all-merciful.

A person is introduced into the Muslim community with the *shahādah*, the affirmation that there is no god but God and Muḥammad is the prophet of God. Every obligatory action, including those bringing merit, is opened by an invocation of the divine name (*basmalah*). The formula *inshā'a Allāh,* "if God wills," appears frequently in daily speech as a reminder that every contemplated action and every hope is subject to the divine will. The attitude of a believer, thus, is and must be complete and confiding submission (*islām*) to God, "Whom one does not question."

Muslim piety has collected, in the Qur'ān and in Ḥadīth (the sayings of the Prophet), the 99 "most beautiful names" (*al-asmā' al-ḥusnā*) that are the glory of God, and these have become objects of devoted recitation and meditation. Among the names of Allāh are the One and Only, the Living One, the Subsisting (*al-ḥayy al-qayyūm*), the Real Truth (*al-ḥaqq*), the Sublime (*al-ʿaẓīm*), the Wise (*al-ḥakīm*), the Omnipotent (*al-ʿazīz*), the Hearer (*as-samīʿ*), the Seer (*al-baṣīr*), the Omniscient (*al-ʿalīm*), the Witness (*shāhid*), the Protector (*al-wakīl*), the Benefactor (*ar-raḥmān*), the Merciful (*ar-raḥīm*), the Constant Forgiver (*ghafūr, ghaffār*).

Etymologically, Allāh is probably a contraction of the Arabic *al-ilāh,* "the god." The origin of the name can be traced to the earliest Semitic writings in which the word for god was *Il* or *El,* the latter being an Old Testament synonym for Yahweh. Allāh is the standard Arabic word for God, used by Arab Christians as well as by Muslims.

Allahābād, city, administrative headquarters of Allahābād district, Uttar Pradesh state, northern India, at the confluence of the Ganges and Yamuna (Jumna) rivers. It stands on the site of the ancient holy city of Prayāg. The present city was founded in 1583. Named al-Ilahābād, meaning "city of God," it became a provincial capital in the Mughal Empire. It changed hands often before being ceded to the British in 1801 and was the scene of a massacre during the 1857 mutiny against British rule. From 1901 to 1949 the city was the capital of the United Provinces (now Uttar Pradesh). It was a centre of the independence movement and was the home of the Nehru family, whose estate is now a museum.

Nehru house at Allahābād, Uttar Pradesh, India

Foto Features

Primarily an administrative and educational centre, Allahābād has some industry (food processing and manufacturing) and is a marketplace for agricultural products. The administrative and professional sector and the military cantonment are located north of the city proper. The city is a major road and rail centre and is served by a nearby airport.

The University of Allahābād (1887) has a number of affiliated colleges, and there is an aviation training centre. The city has several museums. Near the city is a fort built in 1583 by the emperor Akbar; it contains a religious monument, the Pillar of Aśoka. Allahābād has a Government House from the British period, Anglican and Roman Catholic cathedrals, and the Jāmiʿ Masjid, or Great Mosque. Each year a religious festival takes place at the rivers' confluence; every 12th year a much larger festival, Kumbha Melā, is attended by millions of Hindus.

Allahābād district is 2,801 sq mi (7,255 sq km) in area. It lies entirely on the Ganges Plain, except where foothills of the Vindhya Range intrude (southeast). Rice, barley, wheat, and gram (chick-pea) are among the district's chief crops. Pop. (1981) city, 616,051; metropolitan area, 650,070; district, 3,797,033.

Allais, Émile (b. Feb. 15, 1912, Megève, Fr.), the first French international ski champion, who in 1937–38 broke the Austrian-Swiss monopoly of the international circuit by winning both the downhill and slalom championships of the Fédération Internationale de Ski (FIS).

Allais helped develop the French technique in slalom racing, involving the *ruade,* in which, after gathering speed before a turn, the skier rolls forward on the tips of the skis while rotating the body in the direction of the turn. After retiring from competition in 1939, Allais taught skiing and founded schools to teach the French technique in North America and Chile. He became director of winter sports at Courchevel, taught water skiing, and held various official sports positions.

Allan, Sir Hugh (b. Sept. 29, 1810, Saltcoats, Ayrshire, Scot.—d. Dec. 9, 1882, Edinburgh), Canadian financier and shipbuilder whose contribution of $300,000 to the Conservative Party campaign in 1872 precipitated the Pacific Scandal that brought down Sir John Macdonald's government.

Allan emigrated to Canada in 1826 and in 1831 began work for a shipbuilding company in Montreal. By 1839 he was a senior partner, and in 1853 he and his brother Andrew owned their own steamship company, the Allan Line, and conducted shipping between Montreal, Glasgow, and Liverpool. His services to Canadian commerce won him a knighthood in 1871.

In 1872 the Canadian government gave Allan the transcontinental railway charter for his Canadian Pacific Railway. It was later revealed, however, that as a member of a Chicago financial syndicate, he had subsidized Macdonald's Conservative Party election campaign. The subsequent scandal not only discredited Macdonald's government but also led to the dissolution of Allan's railway company.

allantois, an extra-embryonic membrane of reptiles, birds, and mammals arising as a pouch, or sac, from the hindgut. In reptiles and birds it expands greatly between two other membranes, the amnion and chorion, to serve as a temporary respiratory organ while its cavity stores fetal excretions. In mammals other than marsupials the allantois is intimately associated with the chorion, contributing blood vessels to that structure as it forms—in conjunction with the endometrium, or mucosal lining, of the uterus—the placenta.

Allbutt, Sir Thomas Clifford (b. July 20, 1836, Dewsbury, Yorkshire, Eng.—d. Feb. 22, 1925, Cambridge), physician, inventor of the short clinical thermometer, whose investigations led to improved treatment of arterial diseases.

Allbutt, detail of a portrait by Sir William Orpen

The Mansell Collection

During a 28-year practice in Leeds Albutt made valuable clinical studies, primarily of arterial and nervous disorders. In 1866 he introduced the modern clinical thermometer, a welcome alternative to the foot-long instrument that required 20 minutes to register a patient's temperature. He also rendered the first description of minute changes in tissue structure caused by syphilitic disease of the cerebral arteries (1868). Three years later he published a monograph outlining use of the ophthalmoscope (used to inspect the interior of the eye) as a diagnostic instrument.

In 1892 Allbutt accepted a chair of physic at Cambridge, where he spent the rest of his life. Continuing his previous work, he postulated that the agonizing heart condition angina pectoris originates in the aorta (1894). He also described the abnormally high blood pressure, hyperpiesia (now called essential hypertension), not connected but concurrent with kidney disease (1895).

Allbutt was not only an authority on the heart but also a noted medical historian. Two of his most important publications were *Diseases of the Arteries, Including Angina Pectoris* (1915) and *Greek Medicine in Rome* (1921). His chief contribution to his field was *Systems of Medicine,* 8 vol. (1896–99). He was knighted in 1907.

allée, feature of the French formal garden that was both a promenade and an extension of the view. It either ended in a terminal feature, such as a garden temple, or extended into apparent infinity at the horizon.

Allée bordered by tall, clipped trees, Schönbrunn Palace, Vienna

Dr. Glauboch—Photo Researchers

The *allée* normally passed through a planted boscage (a small wood); in the 17th century the boscage was square-trimmed at the sides and on top; later the sides were trained so high that the free-branching trees within the wood were invisible. As architectural gardening became unfashionable in the 18th century, the trimming of trees ceased, and the straight *allée* gave way to the meandering walk. Today *allée* can also mean an avenue.

Alleghenian orogeny, a mountain-building event that affected the Appalachian Geosyncline in Late Paleozoic (Late Pennsylvanian and Permian) time, from about 225,000,000 to 300,000,000 years ago. The term Appalachian Revolution formerly was applied to this event. The Alleghenian orogeny is most pronounced in the central and southern Appalachians and produced the compressional folding and faulting of the Ridge and Valley Province, the westward thrusting of the Blue Ridge over Valley and Ridge rocks, and folding and minor metamorphism and igneous intrusion in the Piedmont Province. Evidence of the Alleghenian orogeny is less prominent in the northern Appalachians, but Late Paleozoic folding and igneous intrusions are present along the east coast of New England and parts of the eastern Maritime Provinces of Canada.

The Alleghenian orogeny may have resulted from the collision of the central and southern Appalachian continental margin with that of North Africa in Late Paleozoic time.

Allegheny Airlines, Inc.: *see* USAir.

Allegheny Mountains, also called ALLEGHENIES, mountainous eastern part of the Allegheny Plateau in the Appalachian Mountains, U.S., extending south-southwestward for more than 500 mi (800 km), from north central Pennsylvania to southwestern Virginia. Rising to Mt. Davis (3,213 ft [979 m]; highest point in Pennsylvania) and Spruce Knob (4,862 ft; highest point in West Virginia), the mountains consist of nearly parallel northeast–southwest ridges that are drained mainly through the gorges cut by the North Branch of the Potomac and the New rivers. Parts of the Monongahela, George Washington, and Jefferson national forests encompass the mountains, which are noted for their scenic beauty. Once forming a barrier to western communication, they are now crossed by many railroads and highways. Frequently, the name Alleghenies is also used in reference to the plateau.

Allegheny Plateau, western section of the Appalachian Mountains, U.S., extending southwestward from the Mohawk River Valley in central New York to the Cumberland Plateau in southern West Virginia. Generally sloping toward the northwest, the plateau has been dissected by streams to form the Catskill, Allegheny, and other mountain ranges. Its northern portion is drained by the Allegheny, Delaware, and Susquehanna rivers, while the Ohio River system drains the southern part. The plateau is mainly covered by a hardwood forest, and it embraces the Allegheny and sections of several other national forests.

With the discovery of coal, a large influx of settlers led to an early breakdown of the isolation of this part of the Appalachians. The regional economy depends heavily upon the extraction of bituminous coal, natural gas, and petroleum.

Allegheny River, river rising in the hilly plateau region of Potter County, Pa., U.S., and flowing generally northward for about 80 mi (130 km), looping into New York state where the Allegheny Reservoir is impounded at Allegany State Park; turning southwest it continues for 120 mi, meandering to the southeast and again southwest and eventually joining the Monongahela River at Pittsburgh to form the Ohio River. In its total length (325 mi), it drains an area of 11,700 sq mi (30,300 sq km). Its chief tributaries are the Kiskiminetas, Clarion, and Conemaugh rivers and Red Bank, Oil, and French creeks. The Allegheny was important for keelboat navigation before the beginning of railway competition in the mid-19th century. Several dams were built (1903–38) to make the river navigable from Pittsburgh to East Brady. Flood-control dams have been built on many of its major tributaries.

Allegheny Series, division of Pennsylvanian rocks and time in the U.S. (the Pennsylvanian Period, roughly equivalent to the Upper Carboniferous, began about 325,000,000 years ago and lasted about 45,000,000 years). It was named for exposures studied along the Allegheny River valley in Pennsylvania and also occurs in Ohio, Maryland, West Virginia, and Virginia. The Allegheny Series overlies rocks of the Pottsville Series and underlies those of the Conemaugh Series. In West Virginia, Alleghenian rocks are sandy, whereas shaley beds predominate in Pennsylvania, and marine shales and limestones are characteristic in Ohio. Economically important coal beds occur, including the Freeport and Kittanning coals. In western Pennsylvania, the Allegheny reaches a maximum thickness of about 90 metres (300 feet) but thins to about 30 m (100 ft) eastward and to about 45 m (150 ft) westward. Cyclothems, rhythmically repetitive stratigraphic sequences, occur in the Allegheny Series; about 13 of these have been described in Ohio alone.

allegory, the written, oral, or artistic expression by means of symbolic fictional figures and actions of truths or generalizations about human conduct or experience.

A brief treatment of literary allegory follows. For full treatment, *see* MACROPAEDIA: Literature, The Art of.

Like metaphor, allegory expresses spiritual, psychological, or abstract intellectual concepts in terms of the material and the concrete. In the 13th-century French didactic poem *Roman de la Rose* most of the details of the garden (the obscure wicket gate, the well with its two crystal stones, etc.) have, like the rosebud, a fixed connotation in terms of courtly love; but what may seem the mechanical contrivance of the extended metaphor is redeemed by its imaginative rendering. In *The Faerie Queene* (1589–96), Spenser develops the metaphor of the garden of love with comparable vividness.

In allegorical fictions—especially such medieval morality plays as *Everyman*—many of the characters are personifications. Personification is allegorical insofar as it endows an inanimate object or abstraction with the attributes of a person; it differs from allegory, however, in that the identity of the thing personified is always clearly proclaimed, whether it be Good Deeds, Gluttony, or Riches. Similarly, fable is allegorical in the broadest sense but is distinguished thus: if the principal kind of allegory be defined as "extended metaphor" the commonest kind of fable may be regarded in effect as an "expanded proverb" for which detailed allegorical interpretation is usually neither necessary nor desirable.

Allegory both conceals and reveals. When an author ventures into political allegory, he may protect himself by the element of disguise and, at the same time, make satirical revelations through the implied comparison. Thus, in the prologue of the 14th-century poem *Piers Plowman,* the author, generally considered to have been William Langland, uses the fable of the mice who were afraid to bell the cat to state his views on the House of Commons' unsuccessful attempt to curb John of Gaunt's depredations. In the first part of *Gulliver's Travels* (1726), Swift satirizes political pettiness by causing his hero to visit the imaginary island Lilliput (an "inverted" Utopia), whose inhabitants are diminutive. In *Absalom and Achitophel* (1681), Dryden reveals, under scriptural disguise, the characters (as he sees them) of politicians involved in an attempt to alter the succession. In this series of examples the element of metaphor can be seen to be gradually receding.

Several of these methods (allegorized beast-fable—disguised political satire—"inverted" Utopia) are combined by George Orwell in *Animal Farm* (1945), which, under the guise of a fable about animals who take over a farm from their human oppressor, expresses the author's disillusionment with the Bolshevik Revolution and his horror at the purges under Stalin, showing how one tyranny is merely replaced by another. Perhaps the most original and striking use of allegory in the 20th century is to be found in the works of Franz Kafka, whose enigmatic fantasies about the predicament of the individual in an incomprehensible environment are not susceptible of any single or precise interpretation.

Allegri, Antonio (painter): *see* Correggio.

allele, any one of two or more genes that may occur alternatively at a given site (locus) on a chromosome. Alleles may occur in pairs, or there may be multiple alleles affecting the expression (phenotype) of a particular trait. If the paired alleles are the same, the organism is said to be homozygous for that trait; if they are different, the organism is heterozygous. In some traits, however, alleles may be co-dominant—that is, neither acts as dominant or recessive. An example is the human ABO blood system; persons with type AB blood have one allele for A and one for B. (Persons with neither are type O.) *See also* dominance; recessiveness.

Most traits, however, are affected by more than two alleles; in these cases, multiple forms of the gene exist, although a given chromosomal pair has only two loci at which these alternatives may occur. Furthermore, some traits are controlled by sites on two or more chromosomes, thus multiplying the number of alleles involved. An example of the latter is human hemoglobin, a complex blood protein.

Alleles may mutate into each other or into entirely new forms. Evolution acts by selectively changing the frequency of phenotypes (and therefore their alleles) within a population.

alleluia: *see* hallelujah.

allemande, processional couple dance with stately, flowing steps, fashionable in 16th-century aristocratic circles; also an 18th-

Allemande, detail from the "Court of Love," Tournai tapestry, early 16th century; in the Sotheby and Co. Collection, London

By courtesy of Sotheby and Co., London

century figure dance. The earlier dance apparently originated in Germany but became fashionable both at the French court (whence its name, which in French means "German") and in England, where it was called almain or almand. The French dancing master Thoinot Arbeau, author of *Orchésographie* (1588), a principal source of knowledge of Renaissance dance, regarded it as an extremely old dance. Its popularity waned in the 17th century.

In the allemande the dancers formed a line of couples, extended their paired hands forward, and paraded back and forth the length of the ballroom, walking three steps, then balancing on one foot; a livelier version used three springing steps and a hop. The music was in $\frac{4}{4}$ time. As a 17th-century musical form, the allemande is a stylized version of this dance. In a suite (as in Bach's *English Suites*) it is normally the first movement.

The 18th-century allemande was a figure dance in $\frac{2}{4}$ time for four couples; one of its handholds possibly derived from the earlier allemande. The dancers performed intricate turns called *enchaînements*, or *passés*, with elaborate interlacings of the arms.

allemontite, the mineral arsenic antimonide (AsSb). It commonly occurs in veins, as at Allemont, Isère, Fr.; Valtellina, Italy; and the Comstock Lode, Nevada. It also is present in a lithium pegmatite at Varuträsk, Swed. Polished sections of the vein material show an intergrowth of allemontite with pure arsenic and those of the pegmatite material with nearly pure antimony. Homogenous allemontite has also been found at Varuträsk. For detailed physical properties, *see* native element (table).

Allen, Bog of, Irish MÓIN ALÚINE, group of peat bogs between the Liffey and the Shannon rivers in east central Ireland in Counties Kildare, Offaly, Leix, and Westmeath. Some 370 sq mi (958 sq km) in area, it is developed extensively for fuel for power stations; the cutover land is used for grazing. The bogs are traversed by the Grand and Royal canals, the latter no longer in use. An early monastic site exists within the bog.

Allen, Ethan (b. Jan. 21, 1738, Litchfield, Conn.—d. Feb. 12, 1789, Burlington, Vt., U.S.), soldier and frontiersman, leader of the Green Mountain Boys during the U.S. War of Independence.

After fighting in the French and Indian War (1754–63), Allen settled in what is now Vermont. At the outbreak of the American Revolution he raised his force of Green Mountain Boys (organized in 1770) and Connecticut troops and helped capture the British fort at Ticonderoga, N.Y. (May 10, 1775). Later, as a volunteer in Gen. Philip Schuyler's forces, he conducted a secret mission to take Montreal (September 1775). Allen was captured and held prisoner until May 6, 1778. Congress gave him the brevet rank of colonel with back pay, but he did not serve in the war after his release. Instead, he devoted his time to local affairs in Vermont, especially working for separate statehood from New York. Failing to achieve this, he attempted to negotiate the annexation of Vermont to Canada.

Allen, Fred, original name JOHN FLORENCE SULLIVAN (b. May 31, 1894, Cambridge, Mass., U.S.—d. March 17, 1956, New York City), U.S. humourist whose laconic style, dry wit and superb timing influenced a generation of radio and television performers.

While working as a stack boy in the Boston Public Library, young Sullivan, so Fred Allen later recounted, came across a book on juggling from which he picked up that craft. He began juggling on amateur entertainment circuits and took the stage name Fred St. James (later Fred James). He added ventriloquism to his act, performing in touring amateur shows, and then went on a vaudeville tour that took him in 1915 and 1916 to Australia, New Zealand, and Hawaii. When he returned to the United States it was as a professional. He came back to vaudeville, where he turned increasingly to comedy, and adopted his final stage name, Fred Allen, to honour the American Revolution hero Ethan Allen—who, he noted, was no longer using the name. He married a fellow performer, Portland Hoffa, and during the 1920s he appeared in a number of revues such as *The Passing Show,* the *Little Show,* and *Three's a Crowd.*

Allen was an established entertainer when he entered radio in 1932. He was featured on a variety of programs by the Columbia Broadcasting System (CBS) before the advent of his most remembered work, "Town Hall Tonight" (1937–38), which became "The Fred Allen Show" in 1939 and ran until 1949. Allen and Portland Hoffa took the principal roles, along with the residents of "Allen's Alley," a cast of characters including Falstaff Openshaw, Digger O'Dell, Mrs. Nussbaum, and Senator Claghorn. Allen wrote nearly all of each of the 273 episodes of the program. His movies included *Love Thy Neighbor* (1973), with Jack Benny. His autobiographical book, *Treadmill to Oblivion,* appeared in 1954.

Allen, Gracie: *see* Burns, George; and Allen, Gracie.

Allen, Hervey, original name WILLIAM HARVEY ALLEN, JR. (b. Dec. 8, 1889, Pittsburgh—d. Dec. 28, 1949, Coconut Grove, Fla., U.S.), U.S. poet, biographer, and novelist who had a great impact on popular literature with his historical novel *Anthony Adverse.*

Allen's first published work was a book of poetry, *Ballads of the Border* (1916). During the 1920s he established a reputation as a poet, publishing several more volumes of verse.

Allen was wounded in World War I; the novel *Toward the Flame* (1926) came out of his wartime experience. That same year his authoritative biography *Israfel: The Life and Times of Edgar Allen Poe* was published.

In 1933, after five years of writing, *Anthony Adverse* was published and was a tremendous success. Set in Europe during the Napoleonic ear, *Anthony Adverse* offered a multitude of characters and picturesque settings within a complex plot. The book's undisguised passages about sex and its considerable length introduced a new standard for fiction that Allen would perfect in later novels.

Allen's following novels did not attain the popularity or the critical acclaim of *Anthony Adverse,* although the first three volumes of his planned five-volume series about colonial America (*The Forest and the Fort,* 1943; *Bedford Village,* 1944; *Toward the Morning,* 1948) were widely read. Allen was at work on the fourth volume of the series (*The City in the Dawn;* published posthumously, 1950) at the time of his death.

Consult the INDEX *first*

Allen, Sir Hugh (Percy) (b. Dec. 23, 1869, Reading, Berkshire, Eng.—d. Feb. 20, 1946, Oxford), organist and musical educator who exerted a far-reaching influence on the English musical life of his time. He was an organ scholar at Christ's College, Cambridge, and later held organist's posts at Ely cathedral (1898) and New College, Oxford (1901–18). In 1918 he became director of the Royal College of Music, London, and in the same year professor of music at Oxford. He raised the position of music in the Oxford curriculum and made more adequate provisions for research and teaching, accomplishments that had wide influence elsewhere. He was also noted for his research on Heinrich Schütz and J.S. Bach. He conducted the Bach choirs in Oxford (from 1901) and London (1907–20) and was a leading proponent of contemporary English music.

Sir Hugh Allen, drawing by John Singer Sargent, 1925; in the British Museum

By courtesy of the trustees of the British Museum; photograph, J.R. Freeman & Co. Ltd.

Allen, Sir James (b. Feb. 10, 1855, Adelaide, South Australia—d. July 28, 1942, Dunedin, N.Z.), statesman, leader of the New Zealand Reform Party, and minister of defense (1912–20) who was instrumental in the development of New Zealand's navy and expeditionary military force.

Allen was elected to the New Zealand Parliament in 1887, serving as a leader of the opposition from 1892 to 1912. When the Reform Party took office in 1912, he became minister of finance, defense, and education. He introduced the Naval Defence Act (1913), which established a New Zealand division in the Royal Navy. He guided the development of the New Zealand expeditionary force into an effective fighting unit in World War I and, for these services, was knighted in 1917. Continuing as minister of defense in the Reform–Liberal coalition (1915–19), he was responsible for the War Pensions Act (1915) and the conscription bill of 1916. When the leader of the government, W.F. Massey, attended international conferences (1917–19), Allen served as acting prime minister. He was appointed to the posts of minister of finance and external affairs in 1919.

Allen introduced a repatriation plan for discharged servicemen and guided New Zealand's acquisition of the League of Nations mandate for Western Samoa. He served as high commissioner for New Zealand in London (1920–26) and sat on his country's Legislative Council from 1927 until his retirement in 1938.

Allen, Phog, byname of FORREST C(LARE) ALLEN (b. Nov. 11, 1885, Jamesport, Mo., U.S.—d. Sept. 16, 1974, Lawrence, Kan.), U.S. college basketball coach who was instrumental in making basketball an Olympic sport. He succeeded James Naismith, who created the sport, as coach in 1908 at the University of Kansas, Lawrence, where he coached until 1956. His teams won 771 games and lost 233; his 1951–52 Kansas team won the championship of the National Collegiate Athletic Association (NCAA). His teams won 24 Big Eight Conference championships in his coaching career. In 1936 he secured the addition of basketball to the Olympic Games program, and in 1952 he coached the U.S. team that won the Olympic championship.

Allen, Richard (b. Feb. 14, 1760, Philadelphia—d. March 26, 1831, Philadelphia), founder and first bishop of the African Methodist Episcopal Church, a major U.S. denomination.

Soon after Allen was born, to slave parents, the family was sold to a Delaware farmer. At 17 he became a Methodist convert and at 22 was permitted to preach. Two years later (1784), at the first general conference of the Methodist Episcopal Church at Baltimore,

Allen was considered a talented candidate for the new denomination's ministry. In 1786 he bought his freedom and went to Philadelphia, where he joined St. George's Methodist Episcopal Church. Occasionally he was asked to preach to the congregation. He also conducted prayer meetings for Negroes. Restrictions were placed on the number permitted to attend these meetings and Allen, dissatisfied, withdrew in 1787 to help organize an independent Methodist Church. In 1787 he turned an old blacksmith shop into the first church for Negroes in the United States. His followers were known as Allenites.

In 1799 Allen became the first Negro to be officially ordained in the ministry of the Methodist Episcopal Church. The organization of the Bethel Society led, in 1816, to the founding of the African Methodist Episcopal Church, which elected Allen its first bishop.

Allen, Steve, byname of STEPHEN VALENTINE PATRICK WILLIAM ALLEN (b. Dec. 26, 1921, New York City), pioneer U.S. television entertainer, versatile author, songwriter, and comedian who performed in radio, motion pictures, and theatre, as well as television.

Allen was born into show business: his mother was a comedienne, Belle Montrose, and his father, Billy Allen, a singer and foil for her in their vaudeville act. Steve travelled with them while growing up, attending some 14 elementary and secondary schools, often in the Chicago area where the parents usually had long runs. Young Allen became a radio actor while in high school and studied journalism at two colleges before becoming a radio announcer in Phoenix, Ariz. He moved west as he gained prominence and began working for the Columbia Broadcasting System (CBS) in Hollywood after a stint as a comedian for a regional network. He gained some national network exposure with his own "Steve Allen Show," and in 1953 he created a landmark late-evening talk and variety program "The Tonight Show," over the National Broadcasting Company's (NBC) New York television station. After a year, the program became an NBC network production, continuing until 1957 with Allen as host, providing its creator with a showcase for his diverse talents, and thereafter with a succession of hosts remaining a perennial favorite of late-night viewers. Allen also appeared at various times on other programs.

As a youngster Allen was a prolific songwriter. He composed and wrote lyrics for more than 3,000 songs, among them "Picnic," "This Could Be the Start of Something Big," and "Impossible." In 1977 he created a series called "Meeting of the Minds" in which actors playing noted figures from different periods of history met to discuss subjects of historic or personal interest.

Allen, Viola (Emily) (b. Oct. 27, 1869, Huntsville, Ala., U.S.—d. May 10, 1948, New York City), popular actress, especially famous for her Shakespearean roles and for her roles in Frances Eliza Burnett's *Little Lord Fauntleroy* and Bronson Howard's *Shenandoah,* both extremely popular plays.

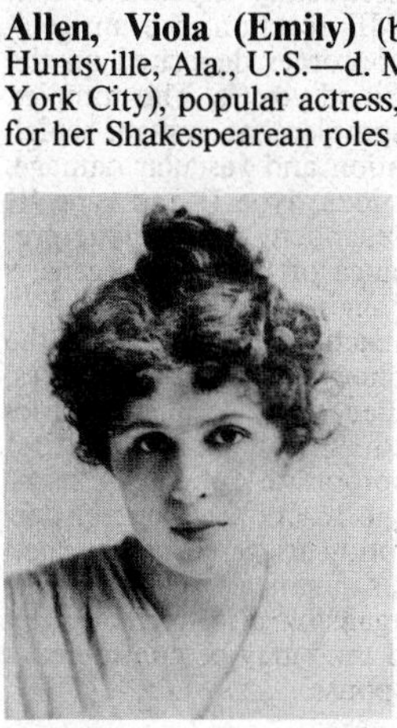

Viola Allen
By courtesy of the Library of Congress, Washington, D.C.

Born into a theatrical family, she made her debut at 14 in New York City in the title role of Frances Eliza Burnett's *Esmeralda.* Between 1884 and 1886, she appeared in a variety of modern and Shakespearean plays with the best known 19th-century actors and in *Little Lord Fauntleroy* and *Shenandoah* (1888–89).

Later she toured in Richard Brinsley Sheridan's *The Rivals* and George Colman the Younger's *The Heir at Law;* starred in Hall Caine's *The Christian* (1898); and formed her own Shakespearean theatre company (1903). In 1915 she made her only motion picture, *The White Sister,* based on a novel by Francis Marion Crawford. Her final professional appearance was in 1918, at a benefit for war relief, but she remained active in support of theatrical and charitable organizations.

Allen, William (b. 1532, Rossall, Lancashire, Eng.—d. Oct. 16, 1594, Rome), English cardinal and scholar who supervised the preparation of the Roman Catholic Reims–Douai translation of the Bible and engaged in intrigues against the Protestant regime of Queen Elizabeth I.

Educated at Oxford University, in 1556 he became principal of St. Mary's Hall there. After the accession of Queen Elizabeth he fell under suspicion for refusing to take an oath acknowledging the Queen as governor of the English Church. Further government pressure caused him to leave England in 1565 for Mechelen in the Spanish Netherlands, where he was ordained priest. In 1568 Allen founded at Douai a seminary for training Englishmen as missionary priests. He was president and lecturer of this seminary until 1585, moving with it to Reims in 1578. The school gave its name to the influential Reims–Douai Version of the Bible, translated by Gregory Martin under Allen's direction.

Allen also helped found the English college in Rome in 1576. In 1580 he organized the first Jesuit missions to England—where Catholic worship was prohibited—but in subsequent years he despaired of restoring Catholicism to his native country by peaceful means. He therefore called upon King Philip II of Spain to conquer England and assume the English throne; as a consequence he was made cardinal at Philip's request in 1587. But England's defeat of the Spanish Armada (1588) ended Allen's political intrigues. In 1584 he wrote a tract defending English Catholics from charges of treason by William Cecil, Lord Burghley. From 1585 until his death the Cardinal lived in Rome, where he helped in the revision of the Catholic version of the Latin Bible, known as the Vulgate.

Allen, Woody, original name ALLEN STEWART KONIGSBERG (b. Dec. 1, 1935, Brooklyn, New York City), U.S. motion-picture director, screenwriter, actor, and author, best known for bittersweet comic films containing elements of parody, slapstick, and the absurd.

Much of Allen's comic material derives from his urban Jewish middle-class background. Intending to be a playwright, Allen began writing stand-up comedy monologues while still in high school. His introduction to show business came a few years later when he was hired to write material for such comedians as Sid Caesar and Art Carney. In the early 1960s, after several false starts, he acquired a following on the night club circuit, performing his own routines. Within a few years he began writing and directing plays and films, also frequently acting in the latter.

Trademarks of Allen's works are a paradoxical blend of comedy and philosophy and a juxtaposition of trivialities with major concerns. His early films, notably *Play It Again, Sam* (1969), *Bananas* (1971), and *Sleeper* (1973), employed a fragmented, joke-oriented style reminiscent of the nightclub sketch form. In *Love and Death* (1975), a parody of 19th-century novels, critics discerned an increased seriousness beneath the comic surface. This observation was borne out in Allen's next film, *Annie Hall* (1977), in which the self-deprecating humour of the protagonist (played by Allen) serves as but one motif in a rich portrayal of a contemporary urban romantic relationship; the film won several Academy Awards, including those for Best Picture and Best Director.

The critical and commercial failure of *Interiors* (1978), a bleak drama of family tensions, was generally attributed to its self-conscious weightiness and slavish imitation of Ingmar Bergman's films. Allen again won acclaim in 1979 for *Manhattan,* which in its depiction of urban life recalled *Annie Hall.* Subsequent films include *Stardust Memories* (1980), *Zelig* (1983), and *Broadway Danny Rose* (1984).

Allenby (of Megiddo and of Felixtowe), Edmund Henry Hynman Allenby, 1st Viscount (b. April 23, 1861, Brackenhurst, near Southwell, Nottinghamshire, Eng.—d. May 14, 1936, London), field marshal, the last great British leader of mounted cavalry, who directed the Palestine campaign in World War I.

Lord Allenby, portrait by Eric Henri Kennington; in the National Portrait Gallery, London
By courtesy of the National Portrait Gallery, London

Educated at the Royal Military Academy, Sandhurst, he joined the Inniskilling Dragoons in 1882 and was active in Bechuanaland (1884–85), Zululand (1888), and in the South African War (1899–1902). During World War I he took the cavalry division to France, where he became commander of the 3rd Army (October 1915) and was prominently engaged at Arras (April 1917).

His service in the Middle East proved more distinguished. In June 1917 Allenby took command of the Egyptian Expeditionary Force. He achieved surprise by improving standard tactical uses of cavalry and mobile forces in position warfare and won a decisive victory over the Turks at Gaza (November 1917), leading to the capture of Jerusalem (Dec. 9, 1917), and a victory at Megiddo (Sept. 19, 1918), which, with the capture of Damascus and Aleppo, ended Ottoman power in Syria.

As high commissioner for Egypt (1919–25) Allenby steered it through political disturbances and saw it recognized as a sovereign state in 1922.

He was created 1st Viscount Allenby of Megiddo and Felixstowe in October 1919. Biographies were published by A.P.W. Wavell (1946) and R.B. Gardner (1965).

Allende (Gossens), Salvador (b. July 26, 1908, Valparaíso, Chile—d. Sept. 11, 1973, Santiago), Chile's first Marxist president.

Allende, born into an upper-middle-class family, received his medical degree in 1932 from the University of Chile, where he was a Marxist activist. He participated in the founding (1933) of Chile's Socialist Party. After election to the Chamber of Deputies in 1937, he served (1939–42) as minister of health in the liberal leftist coalition of President Pedro Aguirre Cerda. Allende won the first of his four elections to the Senate in 1945.

He ran for the presidency for the first time in 1952 but was temporarily expelled from the Socialist Party for accepting the support of the outlawed Communists; he placed last in a four-man race. He ran again in 1958—with Socialist backing, as well as the support of the then-legal Communists—and was a close second to the Conservative-Liberal candidate, Jorge Allesandri. Again with the same support he was decisively defeated (1964) by the Christian Democrat Eduardo Frei. For his successful 1970 campaign Allende ran as the candidate of Popular Unity, a bloc of Socialists, Communists, Radicals, and some dissident Christian Democrats, leading in a three-sided race with 36.3 percent of the vote. Because he lacked a popular majority, however, his election had to be confirmed by Congress, in which there was strong opposition from the right. Nevertheless, it was confirmed on Oct. 24, 1970, after he had guaranteed support to 10 libertarian constitutional amendments demanded by the Christian Democrats.

Inaugurated Nov. 3, 1970, Allende began to restructure Chilean society along Socialist lines. He nationalized several industries and with a constitutional amendment established Chile's right to appropriate its mineral resources, with considerable discretion over compensation. His government took over large estates for peasant cooperatives and favoured large wage increases in industry. Lacking support for outright nationalization, he gained control over banking by purchasing stock with government bonds.

Allende established relations with two Communist governments, the People's Republic of China and Cuba. Relations with the United States were strained by the conflicting interests of U.S. investment and Allende's Socialism. Two years after taking office he faced soaring inflation and opposition from the middle class. His government was overthrown by a military coup on Sept. 11, 1973. He died in the revolt. A four-man military junta took over the government.

Allen's rule, in zoology, a principle that cold-adapted animals have smaller or shorter appendages (ears and legs, tail, and bill) than their warm-adapted relatives, an adaptation that minimizes body-heat loss in cold climates. The rule, a useful generalization despite its many exceptions, was first stated by the U.S. zoologist Joel Asaph Allen.

Allenstein (Poland): *see* Olsztyn.

Allentown, city, seat (1812) of Lehigh County, eastern Pennsylvania, U.S., on the Lehigh River, with Bethlehem and Easton forms an industrial complex. William Allen, mayor of Philadelphia and later chief justice of Pennsylvania, laid out the town (1762), naming it Northampton. It was incorporated as the borough of Northampton in 1811, later (1838) officially renamed Allentown for its founder. Munitions were produced there during the American Revolution.

Construction of a bridge (1812) across the Lehigh and opening of the Lehigh Canal (1829) brought new economic opportunities; an iron industry was started in 1847, a cement plant in 1850, and a rolling mill in 1860. Allentown's location amid rich mineral deposits (iron ore, zinc, limestone) and fertile farmland has enhanced its development as an industrial and market centre.

The city is the seat of five colleges: Muhlenberg (1848), Cedar Crest (1867), Allentown College of St. Francis de Sales (1965), Lehigh Community College (1966), United Wesleyan (1972), and the Allentown campus of Pennsylvania State University, which was opened at nearby Fogelsville in 1912. The Liberty Bell Shrine contains a replica of the original bell, which was brought to Allentown during the Revolution for safekeeping in the Zion Reformed Church. Herds of buffalo, deer, and elk roam the Trexler-Lehigh Game Preserve. Nearby Trout Hall, home of the founder's son, houses the Lehigh County Historical Society. Inc. city, 1867. Pop. (1970) 109,871; (1980) 103,758.

Alleppey, town, administrative headquarters of Alleppey district, Kerala state, southwestern India, on a narrow land spit between the Arabian Sea and Vembanād Lake, south of Cochin. The town's port was opened to foreign trade by the British in the late 18th century to end the commercial supremacy of the Dutch trading post at Porakad, 10 mi (16 km) away. The town's economy is based largely on the coconut. Coconut oil is milled there, and coir ropes, mats, and carpets are manufactured and exported. Black pepper is also produced. The town lies on the main road between Cochin and Trivandrum. No railroad reaches it, but a network of canals connects it to Trichūr to the north and to Trivandrum to the south. The anchorage, about a mile offshore, is protected by a mudbank. Three colleges affiliated with the University of Kerala are located in Alleppey.

Alleppey district has an area of 727 sq mi (1,884 sq km). It was formed in 1968. Pop. (1981) town, 169,940; district, 2,350,145.

Allerdale, district, county of Cumbria, northwestern England, occupying an area of 485 sq mi (1,257 sq km) in the northwestern part of the county. It borders the Irish Sea on the west, Solway Firth on the northwest, and Scotland on the north. Except for its coastal plain on the west and northwest, Allerdale is a scenic mountain and lake-filled valley district forming the northwestern part of the Lake District National Park in the Cumbrian Mountains. The two most populated centres of the district, Workington and Maryport, both on the western coast, have long been associated with the coalfield of Cumbria. Workington, the only deepwater port between Liverpool and Glasgow, has blast furnaces that reduce imported iron ore and metallurgical industries that utilize locally mined anhydrite. Maryport exports footwear, chemicals, and plastics.

The fertile soils of the Solway coast northeast of these ports are used to grow oats and potatoes, except in the low-lying areas that are subject to tidal invasion. Dairy cattle are also raised along the Solway Coast. The local market and footwear-manufacturing centre of Cockermouth was the birthplace of the Romantic poet William Wordsworth. The old stone-built parish of Keswick is a principal tourist centre of the Lake District. The prehistoric stone circles in the mountains and the Roman ruins and Viking graves nearer the seacoast are evidence of ancient settlement in the region. District meetings are held at Wigton. Pop. (1982 est.) 95,600.

allergen, substance that in some persons induces the hypersensitive state of allergy and stimulates the formation of reaginic antibodies; allergens may be naturally occurring or of synthetic origin and include pollen, mold spores, dust, animal dander, insect debris, foods, blood serum, and drugs. Identification of allergens is made by studying both the site of symptoms (*e.g.,* inhalants such as molds, pollens, and dander usually affect the eyes, nose, and bronchi; cosmetics often affect the skin of the face and hands) and the time that symptoms appear (*e.g.,* seasonal allergy to pollen). *See also* antigen; reagin.

allergic rhinitis: *see* hay fever.

allergy, hypersensitive reaction by the body to foreign substances (antigens) that in similar amounts and circumstances are harmless to the bodies of other people. A severe allergic reaction, or anaphylactic shock, is sometimes fatal. (*See also* anaphylaxis.)

A brief treatment of allergies follows. For full treatment, *see* MACROPAEDIA: Immunity.

Antigens that provoke an allergic reaction are called allergens. Typical allergens include pollens, drugs, lints, bacteria, foods, and dyes or chemicals. The immune system contains several mechanisms that normally protect the body against antigens. Prominent among these are the lymphocytes, cells that are specialized to react to specific antigens. There are two kinds of lymphocytes—B-lymphocytes and T-lymphocytes. B-lymphocytes produce antibodies, proteins that bind to and destroy or neutralize antigens. T-lymphocytes do not produce antibodies; instead, they bind directly to an antigen and stimulate an attack on it. Allergic reactions can have immediate or delayed effects, depending on whether the antigen triggers a response by B-lymphocytes or T-lymphocytes.

Allergic reactions with immediate effects are the result of antibody–antigen responses (*i.e.,* they are the products of B-lymphocyte stimulation). These can be divided into three basic types.

Type I reactions, which include hay fever, insect venom allergy, and anaphylactic shock, involve the class of antibodies known as immunoglobulin E (IgE). IgE molecules are bound to mast cells, which are packed with toxic chemicals such as histamine, serotonin, slow-reacting substances (SAS), and bradykinin. When enough IgE antibodies have bound with the antigen, the mast cells release the chemicals. The release of histamine is responsible for visible symptoms of an allergic attack, such as running nose, watery eyes, and tissue swelling. Antihistamine drugs are often used to give temporary relief. The predisposition of a person to type I allergic reactions is genetically determined. The best protection against such allergies is avoidance of the offending substance. Another helpful measure is desensitization, in which increasing amounts of the antigen are injected over a period of time until the sufferer no longer experiences an allergic response.

Type II reactions result when antibodies react with antigens that are found on certain "target" cells. The antigens may be natural components of the cells, or they may be extrinsic components induced by drugs. The resultant antigen–antibody complex activates the complement system, a series of potent enzymes that destroy the target cell.

Type III reactions result when a person who has been strongly sensitized to a particular antigen is subsequently exposed to that antigen. In a type III reaction, the antigen–antibody complex becomes deposited on the walls of the small blood vessels. The complex then triggers the complement system, which produces inflammation and vascular damage. Unlike type I reactions, type II and type III reactions are not dependent on a genetic predisposition. Avoidance of known allergens is the best protection against such reactions.

Delayed allergic reactions are caused by the actions of T-lymphocytes. These responses, which are also called type IV allergic reactions, appear 12 to 24 hours or more after exposure to an appropriate antigen. A common delayed allergic reaction is contact dermatitis, a skin eruption triggered by repeated contact with various chemicals. The rejection of transplanted organs is also mediated by T-lymphocytes and thus may be considered a delayed allergic response.

Allerød, interstadial, or transient, period of glacial retreat that occurred at the close of the Würm Glacial Stage in Alpine Europe. Radiocarbon dating techniques indicate that Allerød time began about 12,000 years ago. The Allerød was followed by a period of renewed cold and glacial advance. During the Allerød, the glacial ice front was situated in southern Finland and the central portions of Sweden. Conditions had moderated sufficiently to allow much of the once-barren tundra regions to become forested again. Tundra conditions still persisted, however, in regions near the still-extant ice sheets. In regions south of the ice, forests dominated by pine and spruce or birch existed in different regions.

Although cooler than modern climatic regimes, Allerød temperatures were significantly warmer than those that had prevailed during the periods of maximum glaciation. During the Allerød in Britain, glaciated regions were restricted to the Highlands of Scotland. Sea levels were higher during the Allerød than during colder times and approached modern sea levels. They were low enough, however, to keep the Strait of Dover and a large area of the North Sea bottom above water.

alley cat: *see* domestic shorthair.

Alleyn, Edward (b. Sept. 1, 1566, London—d. Nov. 25, 1626, London), one of the greatest actors of the Elizabethan stage and founder of Dulwich College, London. Rivalled only by Richard Burbage, Alleyn won the outspoken

Alleyn, oil painting by an unknown artist

By courtesy of the governors of Dulwich College Picture Gallery, London

admiration of such authors as Ben Jonson and Thomas Nashe for his interpretations of Christopher Marlowe's *Tamburlaine, Doctor Faustus,* and *The Jew of Malta* and of Robert Greene's *Orlando Furioso.*

After his marriage (1592) to Joan Woodward, stepdaughter of the theatrical manager Philip Henslowe (*q.v.*), he became part owner in Henslowe's ventures and eventually sole proprietor of several playhouses and other properties in London. Among these were the Rose Theatre at Bankside, the Paris Garden, and the Fortune Theatre in St. Luke's—the last occupied by the Admiral's Men (*q.v.*), with which Alleyn was associated as the leading actor and manager off and on from *c.* 1587. In 1619 Alleyn founded the College of God's Gift at Dulwich, later reorganized as Dulwich College. In 1623 his wife died, and he married Constance, daughter of the poet John Donne.

Allgemeine Enzyklopädie der Wissenschaften und Künste (German: "Universal Encyclopaedia of Sciences and Arts"), monumental uncompleted German encyclopaedia of which 167 volumes were published from 1818 to 1889. Founded by a German bibliographer, Johann Samuel Ersch, who began work on it in 1813, the *Allgemeine Enzyklopädie der Wissenschaften und Künste* is noteworthy for containing the longest known encyclopaedia article—the article about Greece, covering 3,668 pages in volumes 80–87. The signed articles of the work were written by leading German scholars of the 19th century.

Allgemeine Zeitung (German: "General Newspaper"), greatest German newspaper in the 19th century, founded at Tübingen in 1798 by Johann Friedrich Cotta, later Freiherr (baron) von Cottendorf. Censorship and other pressures forced it to move successively to Stuttgart, Ulm, Augsburg, and Munich. The name has been carried on in a sense by the *Frankfurter Allgemeine* and the *Westdeutsche Allgemeine* of Essen; together with the *Süddeutsche Zeitung* of Munich, all leading postwar newspapers of West Germany.

Allgemeines Landrecht: *see* Prussian Civil Code.

Allgood, Sara (b. Oct. 31, 1883, Dublin—d. Sept. 13, 1952, Woodland Hills, Calif., U.S.), Irish character actress whose career included appearances in the original Sean O'Casey plays produced at Dublin's Abbey Theatre and in many American motion pictures of the 1940s. Her early instructors included Frank and W.G. Fay, W.B. Yeats, and John Millington Synge.

In 1903 Allgood joined the Fays' Irish National Theatre as Princess Buan in *The King's Threshold.* In 1904 she played Cathleen in *Riders to the Sea* and late that year made her first appearances in London with the Abbey Theatre Company. During the next 10 years with the Abbey, she also played Mrs. Delane in *Hyacinth Halvey* and Widow Quin in *The Playboy of the Western World.* She joined the Liverpool Repertory Company in 1914, later played with other companies at Manchester and Stratford, and appeared in several plays with her younger sister, Marie O'Neill. She toured Australia in the title role of *Peg O' My Heart* and as Mrs. Geogheghan in *The White-Headed Boy.* For the Abbey Players, she created the original Juno Boyle in *Juno and the Paycock* (1924) and the first Bessie Burgess in *The Plough and the Stars* (1926). The former role was repeated in New York City in 1940 and became the actress's swan song to the legitimate stage. She settled in the the United States and thereafter worked only in motion pictures.

Allgood's film debut took place in the first British talkie, *Blackmail* (1929), and her other English-made films include *The Passing of the Third Floor Back* (1935), *Storm in a Teacup* (1937), and *Kathleen* (1938). Her American films include *How Green was My Valley* (1941), *Roxie Hart* (1942), *Between Two Worlds* (1944), *Jane Eyre* (1944), *The Lodger* (1944), *The Spiral Staircase* (1946), *Mourning Becomes Electra* (1947), *My Wild Irish Rose* (1947), and *Cheaper by the Dozen* (1950).

Alliaceae, family of flowering plants in the order Liliales, with about 30 genera and more than 670 species, distributed throughout most regions of the world, except for the tropics, Australia, and New Zealand. Members of the

Wild garlic (*Allium ursinum*)

A to Z Botanical Collection—EB Inc.

family have corms, bulbs, or underground stems; most have long, thin leaves and clusters of varying numbers of flowers. The genus *Allium* contains the common onion (*A. cepa*), wild onion (*A. cernuum*), garlic (*A. sativum*), wild garlic (*A. ursinum*), leek (*A. porrum*), chives (*A. schoenoprasum*), and shallot (*A. ascallonicum*). Many other onion- or garlic-scented species are cultivated as ornamental border plants, such as *A. moly, A. carinatum,* and *A. pulchellum* of Europe, as well as *A. stellatum* and *A. textile* of North America.

Plants of the genus *Agapanthus* are fast-growing ornamental pot plants with tuberous roots and tall clusters of blue flowers. African lily, or lily of the Nile (*Agapanthus africanus*), has many varieties, some with white or purple flowers and others with patterned leaves. Similar plants of the genus *Tulbaghia* also are popular ornamentals. *Tulbaghia violacea* has a thick stem, garlic-scented leaves, and urn-shaped purple flowers. Ornamental species of the genus *Brodiaea,* known as triplet lilies, have narrow, grasslike leaves and funnel-shaped flowers, usually purple or blue but sometimes white or yellow. Spring starflower (*B. uniflora*) is the most commonly cultivated species.

Alliance, city, Stark County, northeastern Ohio, U.S., on the Mahoning River, 21 mi (34 km) northeast of Canton. In 1854 the villages of Williamsport, Freedom, and Liberty were incorporated as the village of Alliance, so named for the junction and crossing there of the former New York Central and Pennsylvania railroads. The village of Mount Union (settled in 1833) became a part of Alliance in 1854. Now highly industrialized, the city manufactures heavy mill machinery, travelling cranes, bricks and tiles, abrasives, and a variety of steel, machine, and metal products. It is the seat of Mount Union College (1846). Inc. city, 1889. Pop. (1980) 24,315.

alliance, in international relations, a union for joint action of various powers or states, such as the alliance of the European powers and the United States against Germany and its allies during World War II, or of the North Atlantic Treaty Organization (NATO) states against the Soviet Union and its allies.

Alliances in modern times require a joint effort far more integrated than was called for by alliances in earlier times. Thus, for example, in the coalitions of World War II, combined agencies for military and economic planning were a common and conspicuous feature. Even in less tightly knit alliances, such as NATO, great importance is attached to close and cooperative action, both military and political, particularly in the context of the 20th-century strategy of nuclear deterrence.

Alliance for Progress, international economic development program established by the United States and 22 Latin American countries in the Charter of Punta del Este (Uruguay) in August 1961. Objectives stated in the charter centred on the maintenance of democratic government and the achievement of economic and social development; specific goals included a sustained growth in per capita income, more equitable distribution of income, accelerated development in industry and agriculture, agrarian reform, improvement of health and welfare, stabilization of export prices, and domestic price stability.

At the start of the program, it was estimated that $20,000,000,000 of external capital would be needed during the first 10 years; about half was to be obtained from the United States and the rest from international lending agencies and from private sources. The Inter-American Committee on the Alliance for Progress (CIAP) was created in 1963 to serve as the coordinating agent between the international financial community and the countries involved and to review the economic policies and plans of each country to determine the need for and availability of external finance.

Although the program could show some newly built schools, hospitals, and other physical plants, it failed in the judgment of most observers. Massive land reform was not achieved; population more than kept pace with gains in health and welfare. United States aid decreased over the years, and political tensions between the United States and Latin America increased.

Allied Corporation, formerly (until 1958) ALLIED CHEMICAL & DYE CORPORATION, or (1958–81) ALLIED CHEMICAL CORPORATION, U.S. corporation, a leading manufacturer of basic chemicals for industry. Headquarters are in Morristown, N.J.

The corporation was formed in 1920 in the consolidation of the Barrett Company (founded 1903), supplying coal-tar chemicals and roofing; General Chemical Company (founded 1899), specializing in industrial acids; National Aniline & Chemical Company (founded 1917), producing dyes; Semet-Solvay Company (founded 1894), manufacturing coke and its by-products; and Solvay Process Company (founded 1881), producing alkalies and nitrogen materials. In the 1940s these companies were transformed into "divisions" of Allied Chemical. By 1980—after successive reorganizations and the acquisition of additional companies and plants—Allied Chemical consisted of seven divisions: agricultural, fibres, industrial chemicals, Semet-Solvay, specialty chemicals (including plastics), automotive products, and Union Texas Petroleum. In 1982 the company acquired Bendix Corporation, a manufacturer of automotive, aerospace, and other equipment. Allied Chemical International, created in 1966, manages manufacturing enterprises in several countries in Europe, Latin America, and the Far East. Allied Chemical Canada, Ltd., was formed in 1958 in the consolidation of Canadian manufacturing subsidiaries.

Allied Powers, also called ALLIES, those nations allied in opposition to the Central Powers (Germany, Austria-Hungary, and Turkey) in World War I or to the Axis Powers (Germany, Italy, and Japan) in World War II.

The major Allied Powers in World War I were the British Empire, France, and the Russian Empire, formally linked by the Treaty of London of Sept. 5, 1914; other nations that had been, or came to be, allied by treaty to one or more of these powers were also called Allies: Portugal and Japan by treaty with Britain; Italy by the Treaty of London of April 26, 1915, with all three powers. Other nations arrayed against the Central Powers, including the United States after its entry on April 6, 1917, were called "Associated Powers," not Allied Powers; U.S. Pres. Woodrow Wilson emphasized this distinction to preserve America's free hand. The Treaty of Versailles concluding the war listed 27 "Allied and Associated Powers" (Belgium, Bolivia, Brazil, British Empire, China, Cuba, Czechoslovakia, Ecuador, France, Greece, Guatemala, Haiti, the Hejaz, Honduras, Italy, Japan, Liberia, Nicaragua, Panama, Peru, Poland, Portugal, Romania, Serb-Croat-Slovene State, Siam, U.S., and Uruguay).

In World War II the chief Allied Powers were Great Britain, France (except during the German occupation, 1940–44), the U.S.S.R. (after its entry in June 1941), the United States (after its entry on Dec. 8–11, 1941), and China. More generally the Allies included all the wartime members of the United Nations, the signatories to the Declaration of the United Nations. The original signers, of Jan. 1, 1942, were Australia, Belgium, Canada, China, Costa Rica, Cuba, Czechoslovakia, Dominican Republic, Great Britain, Greece, Guatemala, Haiti, Honduras, India, Luxembourg, The Netherlands, New Zealand, Nicaragua, Norway, Panama, Poland, Salvador, South Africa, U.S.S.R., U.S., and Yugoslavia; subsequent wartime signers were the Philippines, Mexico, Ethiopia, Iraq, Free French, and Free Danes.

Allier, *département,* Auvergne region, central France, on the northern rim of the Massif Central; formed from the old province of Bourbonnais, it has an area of 2,829 sq mi (7,327 sq km). Traversed from south to north by the Allier River, it is bounded on the northeast by the Loire River, and the Cher flows parallel to the Allier across the west. Reclamation of heathland, known as the Sologne Bourbonnaise, has expanded stock fattening and pig and poultry breeding. The Limagne Bourbonnaise, in the south central part of the *département*, is fertile and well cultivated. The heights of the Forez region, reaching 3,383 ft (1,031 m; southeast), are wet, with severe winters.

The castle at Bourbon-l'Archambault was the seat of the first Bourbon lords. There are noteworthy medieval buildings at Moulins, Souvigny (Cluniac priory), Saint-Menoux, Èbreuil, Gannat, Veauce, and Ygrande (Romanesque churches), Huriel, and Saint-Pourçain-sur-Sioule.

East of the Cher River are scattered outcrops of coal, especially at Commentry, but the exploitation of the coal basin is declining as industry locates in Montluçon (tires and machinery). Vichy in the south, on the Allier, is the best known spa in France. The *arrondissements* centre on Moulins (the capital), Montluçon, and Lapalisse. Pop. (1982) 369,580.

Allier River, Latin ELAVER, river, central France, joining the Loire, 4 mi west of Nevers, after a course of 255 mi (410 km). Rising in Lozère *département,* it races through deep gorges along structural lines of weakness between the Margeride and Velay mountains. Traversing the basins of Langeac and Brioude, it receives torrents from the mountains of Dore and Puy-de-Dôme and flows, broad and shallow, through the wheat country, the Grande Limagne, north of Clermont-Ferrand, being joined by the Sioule above Moulins, the second largest town on its banks. Its drainage basin covers 5,573 sq mi (14,434 sq km).

Allies: *see* Allied Powers.

alligator (*Alligator*), either of two long-snouted, crocodilian reptiles usually placed with the South American caimans in the family Alligatoridae. Alligators, like other crocodilians, are large, lizard-like animals with

Alligator (*Alligator mississippiensis*)

P. Morris—Woodfin Camp and Associates

powerful tails that are used both in defense and in swimming. Their eyes, ears, and nostrils are placed on top of the long head and project slightly above the water when the reptiles float at the surface, as they often do. Alligators differ from crocodiles in having broader snouts; in crocodiles, moreover, the fourth tooth in each side of the lower jaw projects outside the snout when the mouth is closed. Alligators are carnivorous and live along the edges of relatively large bodies of water, such as lakes, swamps, and rivers. They dig burrows in which they escape from danger and in which they hibernate during cold weather.

The Mississippi, or American, alligator (*Alligator mississippiensis*), the larger of the two species, is found in the southeastern United States. It is black with yellow banding when young and is generally all blackish when adult. The maximum length is about 5.8 m (19 ft), but it more typically ranges from about 1.8 to 3.7 m (6 to 12 ft). The Mississippi alligator has been hunted for its hide and its young have been sold in large numbers as pets. It disappeared from many areas where it was once abundant and was later given legal protection from hunters, until it made an excellent comeback and limited hunting seasons were again established. As an adult, this alligator feeds mainly on fishes, small mammals, and birds, but may sometimes take prey as large as deer or cattle. Members of both sexes hiss, and the males also give loud roars that carry over considerable distances. During the breeding season, the female builds a mound nest of mud and vegetation in which she buries about 20 to 70 hard-shelled eggs. She guards the eggs and may at this time be dangerous. Members of this species usually avoid man.

The Chinese alligator (*A. sinensis*) is a much smaller, little-known reptile found in the Yangtze River region of China. It is similar to the larger form but attains a maximum length of about 1.5 m (5 ft) and is blackish with faint yellowish markings. It is considered endangered (and perhaps extinct) by the International Union for Conservation of Nature and Natural Resources (IUCN).

alligator apple, fruit tree of tropical America valued for its wood. *See* custard apple.

alligator fish: *see* poacher.

alligator pear: *see* avocado.

Alligator Rivers, three perennial rivers, northeastern Northern Territory, Australia, emptying into Van Diemen Gulf, an inlet of the Timor Sea. They were explored in 1818–20 by Capt. Phillip Parker King, who named them in the belief that the crocodiles infesting their lower swampy, jungle-fringed reaches were alligators (actually, Australia has no alligators). The South Alligator rises in the hills near El Sherana, a mining base for uranium, and follows a northerly course for about 100 mi (160 km). The East Alligator rises in Arnhem Land and flows northwesterly for nearly 100 mi; the West Alligator (50 mi) generally parallels the course of the South Alligator. The region includes the Kakadu National Park and is rich in Aboriginal art sites.

Allingham, Margery (Louise) (b. May 20, 1904, London—d. June 30, 1966, Colchester, Essex, Eng.), detective-story writer of unusual subtlety, wit, and imaginative power, who created the bland, bespectacled, keen-witted Albert Campion, one of the most interesting of fictional detectives.

Campion's career was begun with a group of ingenious, popular thrillers: *The Crime at Black Dudley* (1928; U.S. title, *The Black Dudley Murder,* 1929), *Mystery Mile* (1929), *Police at the Funeral* (1931), and *Sweet Danger* (1933). A series of more tightly constructed intellectual problem stories, beginning with *Death of a Ghost* (1934) and including *Flowers for the Judge* (1936), *The Fashion in Shrouds* (1938), and *Traitor's Purse* (1941), gained Allingham critical esteem; and with *Coroner's Pidgin* (1945; U.S. title, *Pearls Before Swine*), *More Work for the Undertaker* (1949), *Tiger in the Smoke* (1952)—a novel that revealed her power to create an atmosphere of pervasive, mindless evil and her psychological insight—and *The China Governess* (1963), she made a valuable contribution to the development of the detective story as a serious literary genre.

Campion's career was continued in *Cargo of Eagles* (1968), left unfinished when Allingham died and completed by her husband, Philip Youngman Carter.

Allison, William B(oyd) (b. March 2, 1829, Ashland, Ohio, U.S.—d. Aug. 4, 1908, Dubuque, Iowa), U.S. representative (1863–71) and senator (1873–1908) from Iowa, best known as cosponsor of the Bland–Allison Act

Allison

By courtesy of the Library of Congress, Washington, D.C.

of 1878, which expanded U.S. Treasury purchase of silver bullion and restored the silver dollar as legal tender. With Nelson W. Aldrich, Orville H. Platt, and John C. Spooner, he made up "the Four" who dominated the Senate in the early 1900s. He was successively a Whig, a Know-Nothing, and a Republican, and twice (1888, 1896) was a contender for the Republican presidential nomination.

Allison practiced law at his birthplace and (from 1857) at Dubuque. In the House of Representatives he was a partisan of railroad interests, but as a senator he helped to pass the Hepburn Act (1906), a railway rate regulation bill, on behalf of Pres. Theodore Roosevelt. Although identified with the silver purchase act, which he cosponsored, he was more important as a member of the powerful House Ways and Means Committee and as chairman of the Senate Committee on Appropriations.

alliteration, in prosody, the repetition of initial consonant sounds in consecutive words or words in close juxtaposition. Sometimes the repetition of initial vowel sounds (head rhyme) is also referred to as alliteration. As a poetic device, it is often combined with assonance (*q.v.*) and consonance (*q.v.*).

Alliteration is found in many common phrases, such as "pretty as a picture," "dead as a doornail," and is a common poetic device in almost all languages. In its simplest form, it reinforces one or two consonantal sounds, as in Shakespeare's line:

When I do *c*ount the *c*lock that *t*ells the *t*ime
(Sonnet XII)

A more complex pattern of alliteration is created when consonants both at the beginning of words and at the beginning of stressed syllables within words are repeated, as in Shelley's line:

The *C*ity's voice it*s*elf is *s*oft like *S*olitude's
("Stanzas Written in Dejection Near Naples")

Though alliteration is now a subsidiary embellishment in both prose and poetry, it was a formal structural principle in ancient Germanic, Celtic, and Welsh verse.

alliterative verse, early verse of the Germanic languages in which alliteration (*q.v.*) is a basic structural principle rather than an occasional embellishment. Although alliteration is a common device in almost all poetry, the only Indo-European languages that used it as a governing principle, along with strict rules of accent and quantity, are Old Norse, Old English, Old Saxon, Old Low German, and Old High German. The Germanic alliterative line consists of two hemistichs (half lines) separated by a caesura (pause). There are one or two alliterating letters in the first half line preceding the medial caesura; these also alliterate with the first stressed syllable in the second half line. Alliteration falls on accented syllables; unaccented syllables are not effective, even if they begin with the alliterating letter.

The introduction of rhyme, derived from medieval Latin hymns, contributed to the decline of alliterative verse. In Low German, pure alliterative verse is not known to have survived after 900; and in Old High German, rhymed verse was by that time already replacing it. In England, alliteration as a strict structural principle is not found after 1066 (the date of the Norman-French conquest of Britain), except in the western part of the country. Although alliteration was still very important, the alliterative line became freer: the second half line often contained more than one alliterating word, and other formalistic restrictions were gradually disregarded. The early 13th-century poetry of Layamon, and later poems such as *Piers Plowman, Sir Gawayne and the Grene Knight*, and *The Pearl* use end rhyme extensively. Sometimes all the verses rhyme; sometimes the succession of alliterative verses is broken by rhymed verses grouped at roughly regular intervals. The last alliterative poem in English is usually held to be "Scottish Fielde," which deals with the Battle of Flodden (1513).

Later Norse poets (after 900) also combined many forms of rhyme and assonance with alliteration in a variety of stanzaic forms. After 1000, Old Norse alliterative verse became practically confined to the Icelanders, among whom it continues to exist.

In Celtic poetry, alliteration was from the earliest times an important, but subordinate, principle. In Welsh poetry it gave rise to the *cynghanedd* (*q.v.*), an intricate bardic verse.

Allobroges, ancient Celtic tribe living in the northeast of Gallia Narbonensis (*i.e.,* in the part of southeastern France bounded by the Rhône and Isère rivers) and in the area around Geneva. The probable meaning of their name, "aliens," suggests that they drove out the original inhabitants. The Allobroges were first mentioned in history when Hannibal passed through their territory in 218 BC. Later, they were attacked by the Romans and finally conquered (121 BC) at the junction of the Rhône and Isère and were thereafter incorporated in Transalpine Gaul.

allocation of resources: *see* resources, allocation of.

allodium, land freely held, without obligation of service to any overlord. Allodial land tenure was of particular significance in Europe during the Middle Ages, when most land was held by feudal tenure.

The anarchy that ensued in France after the decline of the Carolingian monarchy at the end of the 9th century allowed much land to be seized and held free, although a large part of it was eventually brought into a feudal relationship in which the holder owed certain services to his lord. By the 12th and 13th centuries, the only appreciable amount of allodial land remaining was limited to peasant holdings in the southwest. In Germany large allodial estates held by nobles continued to exist, particularly in Saxony. In England there was a considerable amount of allodial land before the Norman conquest, but it disappeared under the new rulers. Allodial land, although free of limitations from above, was not free of restrictions from below if the holder chose to have feudal tenants. He would then owe certain obligations to them, primarily in terms of protection, and could not be considered in absolute control of his holdings.

With the decline of feudalism in France, land that had been under the jurisdiction of a lord came to be under the jurisdiction of the king, who collected certain fees upon its sale or transfer. After the Revolution all land became allodial. In England no land is called allodial, but an estate in fee simple corresponds in practice to absolute ownership.

allomorph, in linguistics, a positional variant of a morpheme (*q.v.*). For example, "am," "art," "is," and "are" are allomorphs of "be," occurring with different grammatical persons.

allophane, clay mineral of the kaolinite group. *See* kaolinite.

allophone, one of the phonetically distinct variants of a phoneme (*q.v.*). The occurrence of one allophone rather than another is usually determined by its position in the word (initial, final, medial, etc.) or by its phonetic environment. Speakers of a language often have difficulty in hearing the phonetic differences between allophones of the same phoneme, because these differences do not serve to distinguish one word from another. In English the *t* sounds in the words "hit," "tip," and "little" are allophones; phonemically they are considered to be the same sound although they are different phonetically in terms of aspiration, voicing, and point of articulation. In Japanese and some dialects of Chinese, the sounds *f* and *h* are allophones.

allopurinol, organic compound used in treating gout. Allopurinol interferes with bodily formation of uric acid, a substance present in abnormally large amounts in the blood of persons suffering from gout; the uric acid forms solid deposits in the joints, the kidneys, and other tissues.

Treatment of gout with allopurinol ordinarily is expected to be continued for many years. The amount of uric acid in the blood serum falls immediately after use, but resorption of the solid deposits requires 6 to 12 months. Allopurinol is preferred when allergic reactions preclude the use of probenecid or sulfinpyrazone, or when renal functions are impaired by disease or affected by other drugs. *See also* uricosuric.

Allosaurus, also called ANTRODEMUS, genus of large carnivorous dinosaurs found as fossils in Late Jurassic to Early Cretaceous rocks of North America (the Jurassic Period preceded the Cretaceous Period and ended 136,000,000 years ago). *Allosaurus* weighed 2 tons and grew to 10.4 metres (34 feet) in length, half of which consisted of a well-developed tail that probably functioned as a counterbalance for the body. *Allosaurus,* a biped, had very strong hind limbs and a massive pelvis with strong anteriorly and posteriorly directed projections. The forelimbs, much smaller than the hind limbs and probably used for grasping, had three fingers ending in sharp claws. The skull was very large in relation to the compact body and was lightened by the presence of several large openings. The powerful jaws had large pointed teeth and were very flexible, allowing the animal to take large bites out of its prey. It is likely that *Allosaurus* preyed upon the medium-sized dinosaurs, especially the duck-billed forms and their relatives. It is possible that *Allosaurus* was also a scavenger, feeding upon carcasses of dead or dying animals. They may have hunted in groups.

allosteric control, in enzymology, inhibition or activation of an enzyme by a small regulatory molecule that interacts at a site (allosteric site) other than the active site (at which catalytic activity occurs). The interaction changes the shape of the enzyme so as to affect the formation at the active site of the usual complex between the enzyme and its substrate (the compound upon which it acts to form a product). As a result, the ability of the enzyme to catalyze a reaction is modified. This is the basis of the so-called induced-fit theory, which states that the binding of a substrate or some other molecule to an enzyme causes a change in the shape of the enzyme so as to enhance or inhibit its activity.

The regulatory molecule may be a product of a synthetic pathway and inhibit an enzyme in that pathway (*see* feedback inhibition), thereby preventing the further formation of itself. Other molecules act as activators; *i.e.,* they interact with an enzyme so as to enhance the binding of the substrate to the enzyme, thus enhancing catalytic activity. The enzyme adenyl cyclase, itself activated by the hormone adrenaline (epinephrine), which is released when a mammal requires energy, catalyzes a reaction that results in the formation of the compound cyclic adenosine monophosphate (cyclic AMP). Cyclic AMP, in turn, activates enzymes that metabolize carbohydrates for energy production. A combination of allosteric activation and inhibition thus provides a way by which the cell can rapidly regulate needed substances.

allotropy, the existence of a chemical element in two or more forms, which may differ in the arrangement of atoms in crystalline solids or in the occurrence of molecules that contain different numbers of atoms. The existence of different crystalline forms of an element is the same phenomenon that in the case of compounds is called polymorphism. Allotropes may be monotropic, in which case one of the forms is the most stable under all conditions, or enantiotropic, in which case different forms are stable under different conditions and undergo reversible transitions from one to another at characteristic temperatures and pressures.

Elements exhibiting allotropy include tin, carbon, sulfur, phosphorus, and oxygen. Tin and sulfur are enantiotropic: the former exists in a gray form, stable below 13.2° C, and a white form, stable at higher temperatures; sulfur forms rhombic crystals, stable below 95.5° C, and monoclinic crystals, stable between 95.5° C and the melting point (119° C). Carbon, phosphorus, and oxygen are monotropic; graphite is more stable than diamond, red phosphorus is more stable than white, and diatomic oxygen, having the formula O_2, is more stable than triatomic oxygen (ozone, O_3) under all ordinary conditions.

Allouez, Claude-Jean (b. June 6, 1622, Saint-Didier, Fr.—d. Aug. 27/28, 1689, near Ft. St. Joseph, New France), Jesuit missionary to New France who has been called the founder of Catholicism in the West.

Allouz entered the Society of Jesus at Toulouse, was ordained priest in 1655, and sailed for Quebec in 1658. He was stationed at settlements along the St. Lawrence River until his appointment (1663) as vicar general of the Northwest. He travelled extensively through that territory, preaching to the Indians and establishing missions—chiefly in present-day Wisconsin, including Chequamegon Bay and Green Bay. His own accounts of his activities are frequently quoted in *The Jesuit Relations,* edited by R.G. Thwaites. Allouez was a predecessor and later a colleague of Jacques Marquette, for whom he wrote a book of prayers. His last years were spent mostly among the Miamis of the St. Joseph River in modern southwestern Michigan.

Allouez Bay (Lake Superior, U.S.): *see* Superior Bay.

Alloway, southern suburb of the town of Ayr, Kyle and Carrick district, Strathclyde region, Scotland, famous as the birthplace, in 1759, of Scotland's national poet, Robert Burns. There is a museum alongside the thatched cottage where he was born and a memorial in the form of a Grecian temple, built in 1820. Brig o' Doon, immortalized in Burns's poem "Tam o' Shanter," is nearby.

alloy, metallic substance composed of two or more elements, as either a compound or a solution. The components of alloys are ordinarily themselves metals, though carbon, a nonmetal, is an essential constituent of steel.

Alloys are usually produced by melting the mixture of ingredients. The value of alloys was discovered in very ancient times; brass (copper and zinc) and bronze (copper and tin) were especially important. Today, the most important are the alloy steels, broadly defined as steels containing significant amounts of elements other than iron and carbon. The principal alloying elements for steel are chromium, nickel, manganese, molybdenum, silicon, tungsten, vanadium, and boron. Alloy steels have a wide range of special properties, such as hardness, toughness, corrosion resistance, magnetizability, and ductility. Nonferrous alloys, mainly copper–nickel, bronze, and aluminum alloys, are much used in coinage. The distinction between an alloying metal and an impurity is sometimes subtle; in aluminum, for example, silicon may be considered an impurity or a valuable component, depending on the application, because silicon adds strength though it reduces corrosion resistance.

The term fusible metals, or fusible alloys, denotes a group of alloys that have melting points below that of tin (232° C, 449° F). Most of these substances are mixtures of metals that by themselves have low melting points, such as tin, bismuth, and lead. Fusible alloys are used as solder, in safety sprinklers that automatically spray out water when the heat of a fire melts the alloy, and in fuses for interrupting an electrical circuit when the current becomes excessive.

Many fusible alloys are formulated to melt at 90–100° C (194–212° F); for example, Darcet's alloy (50 parts bismuth, 25 lead, 25 tin) melts at 98° C. By replacing half the tin in Darcet's alloy with cadmium, the alloy Wood's metal, which melts at 70° C, is obtained. *See also* amalgam; ferroalloy; intermetallic compound.

Allport, Gordon W(illard) (b. Nov. 11, 1897, Montezuma, Ind., U.S.—d. Oct. 9, 1967, Cambridge, Mass.), U.S. psychologist and educator who developed an original theory of personality.

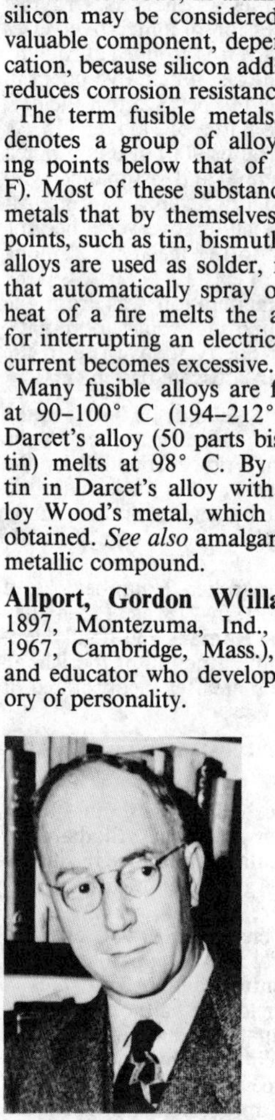

Allport
By courtesy of Harvard University Archives

Appointed a social science instructor at Harvard University in 1924, he became professor of psychology six years later and, in the last year of his life, professor of social ethics. He consistently related his approach to the study of personality to his social interests and was one of a growing number of psychologists who sought to introduce the leavening influence of humanism into psychology. His important introductory work on the theory of personality was *Personality: A Psychological Interpretation* (1937).

Allport is best known for the theory that although adult motives develop from infantile drives, they become independent of them. His approach favoured emphasis on the problems of the adult personality rather than on those of infantile emotions and experiences. In *Becoming* (1955) he stressed the importance of self and the uniqueness of adult personality. The self, he contended, is an identifiable organization within each individual and accounts for the unity of personality, higher motives, and continuity of personal memories. He also made important contributions to the analysis of prejudice in *The Nature of Prejudice* (1954). His last important work was *Pattern and Growth in Personality* (1961).

allspice, tropical evergreen tree (*Pimenta dioica,* formerly *P. officinalis*) of the myrtle family (Myrtaceae), native to the West Indies and Central America and valued for its berries, the source of a highly aromatic spice. Allspice was so named because the flavour of the dried berry resembles a combination of cloves, cinnamon, and nutmeg. It is widely used in baking and is usually present in mincemeat and mixed pickling spice. Early Spanish explorers, mistaking it for a type of pepper, called it

Allspice (*Pimenta diocia*)
J.E. Cruise

pimenta, hence its botanical name and such terms as pimento and Jamaica pepper. The first record of its import to Europe is from 1601.

The allspice tree attains a height of about 9 metres (30 feet). The fruits are picked before they are fully ripe and then dried in the sun. During drying the berries turn from green to a dull reddish brown. The nearly globular fruit, about 5 millimetres (0.2 inch) in diameter, contains two kidney-shaped, dark-brown seeds. Its flavour is aromatic and pungent. The essential oil content is about 4½ percent for Jamaica allspice and about 2½ percent for that of Central America; its principal component is eugenol.

The name allspice is applied to several other aromatic shrubs as well, especially to one of the sweet shrubs, the Carolina allspice (*Calycanthus floridus*), a handsome flowering shrub native to the southeastern United States and often cultivated in England. Other allspices include: the Japanese allspice (*Chimonanthus praecox*), native to eastern Asia and planted as an ornamental in England and the United States; the wild allspice, or spicebush (*Lindera benzoin*), a shrub of eastern North America, with aromatic berries, reputed to have been used as a substitute for true allspice.

Allston, Robert (Francis Withers) (b. April 21, 1801, All Saints Parish, S.C., U.S.—d. April 7, 1864, Georgetown, S.C.), rice planter and governor of South Carolina whose papers, *South Carolina Rice Plantation,* provide important agricultural, political, and social information about the pre-Civil War South. By scientifically draining and reclaiming swamps in his state, he developed one of the last great rice plantations in the Atlantic coast lowlands.

Robert Allston, detail of an oil painting by George Whiting Flagg, 1850s; in a private collection

By courtesy of William F. Allston

He also wrote two authoritative and influential works on crop raising. Allston became president of the state senate (1847–56) and served as governor (1856–58).

Allston, Washington (b. Nov. 5, 1779, Allston plantation, Brook Green Domain on Waccamaw River, S.C.—d. July 9, 1843, Cambridgeport, Mass., U.S.), painter and author, commonly held to be the first important U.S. Romantic painter. Allston is known for his experiments with dramatic subject matter and his use of light and atmospheric colour. Although his production was small, it shaped future American landscape painting by its dramatic portrayals of mood. Allston's work anticipated that of a line of American visionary painters including Albert Pinkham Ryder and Ralph Blakelock.

Allston graduated from Harvard in 1800. He studied in London at the Royal Academy and visited the great museums of Paris (1803–04) and Italy (1804–08). During this period he became friendly with Coleridge and Washington Irving. Allston spent the years from 1808 to 1811 in Boston, then seven productive years in London, and returned to Boston in 1818, finally settling in Cambridgeport, Mass., in 1830.

Before his final return to the United States, Allston's art was dramatic and large in scale. He delighted in the supernatural; *e.g.,* "Belshazzar's Feast" (1817–43; Detroit Institute of Arts). His dramatic landscapes "The Deluge" (1804; Metropolitan Museum of Art, New York City) and "Elijah in the Desert" (1818; Museum of Fine Arts, Boston) are among the first important achievements of American landscape painting.

After his return to Boston in 1818 Allston's art became quieter, striking a new note of reverie and fantasy. "Moonlit Landscape" (1819; Museum of Fine Arts) and "The Flight of Florimel" (1819; Detroit Institute of Arts) are the chief works of the period before he became preoccupied with "Belshazzar's Feast," which he had brought unfinished from London. He worked on this from 1820 to 1828 and from 1839 until his death.

Allston was also a writer whose poems, *The Sylphs of the Seasons with Other Poems*

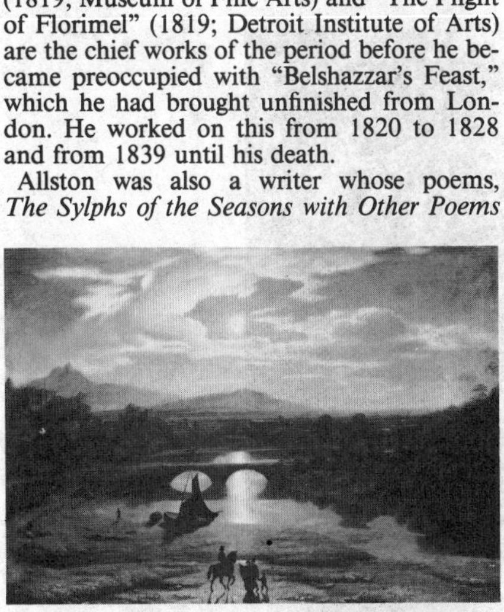

"Moonlit Landscape," oil on canvas by Washington Allston, 1819; in the Museum of Fine Arts, Boston

By courtesy of the Museum of Fine Arts, Boston, gift of William Sturgis Bigelow

(1813) and a Gothic novel, *Monaldi* (1841), were popular in his day. His theory of art was posthumously published as *Lectures on Art, and Poems* (1850).

Allucingoli, Ubaldo (pope): *see* Lucius III.

alluvial fan, unconsolidated sedimentary deposit that accumulates at the mouth of a mountain canyon because of a cessation of sediment transport by the issuing stream. The deposits, which are generally fan shaped in plan view, can develop under a wide range of climatic conditions and have been studied in the Canadian Arctic, Swedish Lappland, Japan, the Alps, the Himalayas, and other areas. They tend to be larger and more prominent in arid and semiarid regions, however, and generally are regarded as characteristic desert landforms. This is particularly true in the basin-and-range type of areas of parts of Iran, Afghanistan, Pakistan, the western United States, Chile and Peru, Sinai and western Arabia, and Central Asia, where the basic landscape configuration consists of mountains set against adjacent basins.

A brief treatment of alluvial fans follows. For full treatment, *see* MACROPAEDIA: Rivers.

Alluvial fans are of practical and economic importance to man, particularly in arid and semiarid areas where they may be the principal groundwater source for irrigation farming and the sustenance of life. In some instances, entire cities, such as Los Angeles, have been built on alluvial fans.

Alluvial fans border the mountain fronts with the apex of each fan just within a canyon mouth that serves as the outlet for a mountain drainage system. Sediment derived by erosion within the mountains is transported by these drainage systems to the adjacent basin; in arid regions this occurs principally during relatively infrequent flash floods that may involve mudflows. The fans, which are the main sites of deposition, are therefore an intrinsic part of an erosional-depositional system in which mountains tend slowly to wear away and basins to fill with sediment through geological time.

Since the rivers that deposit alluvial fans tend to be fast flowing, the first material to be laid down is usually coarse. The composition of fans, however, consists of a wide range of sediment sizes and a high degree of sorting from apex to base. The initial formation of a fan is often furthered by the infiltration of surface water into the early deposit of coarse debris. This infiltration encourages the deposition of finer material. Usually the coarser sedimentary fraction forms towards the apex, with fine sands and silts toward the base. In addition, the braided distributary channels also perform some sorting, laying shallow sheets of sand and silt over the surface of the fan, while coarser sands and gravels are laid down in the main channels where water tends to flow more quickly.

Alluvial fans in desert or semiarid areas may act as groundwater reservoirs when stream water infiltrates the deposit and gradually percolates downwards towards the base. If the water becomes trapped between impermeable layers within the fan, it may be tapped by wells along the base and these may exhibit artesian flow as the groundwater builds up pressure within the fan. The use of desert fans as permanent sources of water is limited, however, because periodic rainfall provides only a very slow rate of recharge.

An alluvial fan can be large and may occupy a wide area, ranging from only a few metres in radius at its base to more than 150 kilometres (95 miles). When a number of rivers discharge onto a plain, their fans may combine to create a piedmont alluvial fan.

Many fans in humid areas are actually fossil features created during earlier periods of intense erosion and deposition. The Plateau de Lannemezan on the northern side of the Pyrenees in France, for example, is a large piedmont alluvial fan that is still being built up by the tributaries of the Garonne and Adour rivers. This fan, though, is much too large to have been constructed by present-day rivers. It was formed during the Late Cenozoic Period and is made up of coarse Pliocene gravels derived from the Pyrenees.

alluvial plain: *see* floodplain.

alluvium, material deposited by rivers. It is usually most extensively developed in the lower part of the course of a river, forming floodplains and deltas, but may be deposited at any point where the river overflows its banks or where the velocity of a river is checked—*e.g.,* where it runs into a lake. Alluvium consists of silt, sand, clay, and gravel and often contains a good deal of organic matter. It therefore yields very fertile soils such as those of the deltas of the Mississippi, the Nile, the Ganges and Brahmaputra, and the Huang rivers. In some regions alluvial deposits contain gold, platinum, or gemstones and the greater part of the world's supply of tin ore (cassiterite).

allyott (plant): *see* jute.

Alma, city, seat of Lac-Saint-Jean-Est regional county (*municipalité régionale de comté*), Saguenay-Lac-Saint-Jean region, south central Quebec province, Canada, on Alma Island and both banks of the Saguenay River, an outlet of Lac-Saint-Jean (Lake St. John) 151 mi (243 km) north of Quebec city. It was mainly an agricultural community until after 1923, when the large Île-Maligne hydroelectric power project was developed. The city's economy now largely depends on aluminum and paper processing and granite quarrying. Founded in 1867 as Saint-Joseph-d'Alma, the settlement was chartered as a village in 1917 and as a town in 1924. In 1954 its name was shortened to Alma. It absorbed the adjacent towns of Naudville, Riverbend, and Isle-Maligne in 1962. In 1976 a new city of Alma was created from the amalgamation of the old city of Alma and the neighbouring Saint-Joseph-d'Alma. The city is near the main entrance to Fundy National Park. Inc. city, 1958. Pop. (1981) 26,322.

Alma, Battle of the (Sept. 20 [Sept. 8, old style], 1854), Crimean War victory by the British and the French that left the Russian naval centre of Sevastopol vulnerable and endangered the entire Russian position in the war. Commanded by Prince Aleksandr Menshikov, the Russians occupied a position on the heights above the Alma River in the southwestern Crimea, thus blocking the road to Sevastopol.

The allies landed in the Crimea (September 14) to capture Sevastopol; commanded by Lord Raglan and Marshal Armand de Saint-Arnaud, they attacked the Russians. Although they repulsed the allies' first assault, the alarmed Russians withdrew their artillery; subsequent allied attacks forced the Russians to retreat toward Sevastopol, which was then poorly fortified. The allies, however, failed to pursue the Russians immediately and lost an opportunity to capture the city easily.

Alma-Ata, *oblast* (administrative region), southeastern Kazakh Soviet Socialist Republic, created in 1932. It extends from Lake Balkhash in the north along both sides of the Ili River to the Chinese frontier in the southeast; its area is 40,400 sq mi (104,700 sq km). In the south the Ketmen, Trans-Alay Alatau, and Kungey-Alatau mountains rise to 16,400 ft (5,000 m), whereas the north is comprised of a plain covered largely by sandy desert. The population is concentrated in the foothills, where the climate is relatively mild and the annual precipitation is about 20–24 in. (500–600 mm). Wheat and other grains, sugar beets, tobacco, pulses, and fodder are

Trans-Alay Alatau mountains, Kazakh S.S.R.
Novosti Press Agency

grown, mainly on irrigated land; fruit growing is also important. Sheep are raised on the desert pastures, and there is fishing in the Ili and Lake Balkhash. Most industry is located in the capital, Alma-Ata. Of the population, about 20 percent of which is urban, Kazakhs and Russians each comprise slightly more than a third, followed by Uighurs, Germans, Azerbaijani, and Ukrainians. Pop. (1982 est.) 1,866,000.

Alma-Ata, formerly (1855–1921) VERNY, city, capital of the Kazakh Soviet Socialist Republic and administrative centre of Alma-Ata

Alma-Ata ballet and opera house, Kazakh S.S.R.
Novosti Press Agency

oblast (region), in the northern foothills of the Trans-Alay Alatau at an altitude of 2,300–3,000 ft (700–900 m), where the Bolshaya and Malaya Almaatinka rivers emerge into the plain. The modern city was founded in 1854 when the Russians established the military fortification of Zailiyskoye (renamed Verny in 1855) on the site of the ancient settlement of Alamaty, which had been destroyed by the Mongols in the 13th century. Cossacks, peasant settlers from European Russia, and Tatar merchants soon established themselves in the vicinity, and in 1867 the fortification became the town of Verny and the administrative centre of newly created Semirechye *oblast* of the governorate general of Turkistan. By 1906 the population had grown to 27,000, two-thirds of whom were Russians and Ukrainians. Soviet rule was established in 1918.

In 1921 the city was renamed Alma-Ata, after its Kazakh name, Almaty, alluding to the many apple trees in the locality. The transfer of the Kazakh capital from Kzyl-Orda to Alma-Ata in 1929 and the completion of the Turk-Sib Railway in 1930 brought rapid growth, and the population rose from 46,000 in 1926 to 221,000 in 1939. A number of food and light industry undertakings were built, and heavy industry, particularly machine building, developed later on the basis of plants evacuated from European Russia during World War II.

The city is located in an area of extensive geological risk, being subject to both earthquakes and mudslides. The city suffered from severe earthquakes in 1887 and 1911, and a mudflow down the Malaya Almaatinka in 1921 caused considerable destruction and loss of life. To reduce risk of future mudslides, an artificial landslide was precipitated by explosives in 1966 to dam nearby Medeo gorge; the 330-ft dam that resulted proved its worth in 1973 by holding back a potentially catastrophic mudslide. Later improvements have raised the dam to 460 ft and further improved the security of the city.

Alma-Ata is now a major industrial centre, with the food industry accounting for about one-third of its industrial output, and light industry one-fourth. There are 15 institutions of higher education, including the Kazakh S.M. Kirov State University (founded 1934), and teacher-training, economics, polytechnic, agricultural, and medical institutes. Alma-Ata also houses the Kazakh S.S.R. Academy of Sciences and its many subordinate research institutes, four museums, an opera house, seven theatres (producing in Russian, Kazakh, and Uighur), and the Pushkin State Public Library of the Kazakh S.S.R. Alma-Ata also has a botanical garden, several stadiums, and the permanent republican Exhibition of Economic Achievements.

Alma-Ata now extends about 12½ mi (20 km) in all directions from its centre and is considered one of the most beautiful cities of the U.S.S.R., with regular planning, wide, tree-lined streets, numerous parks and orchards, and a backdrop of mountains. The former Russian Orthodox cathedral, built in 1907 and the second highest wooden building in the world, survives. Of the population, Russians make up more than two-thirds, with Kazakh, Ukrainian, Tatar, Uighur, and German minorities. Pop. (1982 est.) 1,001,000.

Alma-Tadema, Sir Lawrence (b. Jan. 8, 1836, Dronrijp, Neth.—d. June 25, 1912, Wiesbaden, Ger.), painter of historical idylls and scenes from everyday life who enjoyed an immense popularity in his time.

The son of a Dutch notary who intended him for a medical career, Alma-Tadema studied art at the Antwerp Academy (1852–58) under the historical painter Hendrik Leys, assisting his master in 1859 with frescoes for the Stadhuis, Antwerp. During a visit to Italy in 1863, Alma-Tadema became interested in Greek and Roman antiquity and Egyptian archaeology, afterward depicting subjects almost exclusively from those sources. Moving to England, he became a naturalized British subject in 1873 and was elected a member of the Royal Academy in 1879. He was knighted in 1899.

Almadén, town, Ciudad Real province, in the autonomous community (region) of Castile-La Mancha, west central Spain, in one of the world's richest mercury-producing regions. The town, originally Roman, then a Moorish settlement (Arabic al-Ma'din, "mine"), was captured by Alfonso VII in 1151 and given to the military–religious Knights of the Order of Calatrava, who exploited the mercuric ores. The king of Spain, Charles I (Holy Roman Emperor Charles V), granted the mines to the German Fugger family of merchant-bankers as security for a loan (1525–1645). From 1645 the mines were worked by the royal exchequer but leased to the Rothschild banking family in London. Mining remains the chief economic activity of the town, which is the seat of two mining academies. Cereals and livestock are raised in the surrounding area, and there are flour mills and shoe factories in the town proper. Pop. (1981) 9,521.

Almagest, astronomical and mathematical encyclopaedia compiled *c.* AD 140 by Ptolemy (Claudius Ptolemaeus of Alexandria). It served as the basic guide for Arab and European astronomers until about the beginning of the 17th century. The name, corrupted from the Arabic, means "the greatest"; among other names given to the work were "The Great Treatise," "The Great Astronomer," and "The Mathematical Collection." It was first translated into Arabic in 827 and retranslated from Arabic to Latin in the last half of the 12th century.

The *Almagest* is divided into 13 books. Book One gives, in broad outline, the geocentric, or Ptolemaic, plan of the solar system. Book Two contains the earliest surviving work on trigonometry: a table giving the values of chords of a circle at intervals of ½°, accurate to at least five places; and studies in the solution of spherical triangles. Book Three deals with the motion of the Sun and the length

"The Visit," oil on panel by Sir Lawrence Alma-Tadema, 1868; in the Victoria and Albert Museum, London
By courtesy of the Victoria and Albert Museum, London; photograph, John Webb

of the year; Book Four deals with the Moon and the month, as does Book Five, which also takes up the distances of Sun and Moon and tells how to construct an astrolabe. Eclipses are treated in Book Six, as also are planetary conjunctions and oppositions.

Books Seven and Eight mainly concern the fixed stars, giving ecliptic coordinates and magnitudes for 1,022 of them. This star catalog is based on that of Hipparchus (129 BC); those two books also discuss precession and the construction of celestial globes. The remaining five books, the most original, set forth in detail the Ptolemaic system outlined in Book One.

Almagro, Diego de (b. 1475, Almagro, Castile—d. 1538, Cuzco, Peru), Spanish soldier who played a leading role in the Spanish conquest of Peru.

Following service in the Spanish Navy, Almagro arrived in South America in 1524 and, with his intimate friend Francisco Pizarro, led the expedition that conquered the Inca empire in what is now Peru. Almagro and Pizarro became joint captains general of these conquests, which the Spaniards called New Castile. Bitter enmity soon arose between Almagro and Pizarro, however, leading to much political instability in the new colony.

In 1534 King Charles I of Spain (also Holy Roman emperor as Charles V) sent Almagro to assist in the conquest of what is now Chile, where he is said to have suffered great hardships. During Almagro's absence, Indians in Peru rebelled and even besieged the Spanish fortress of Cuzco. Almagro rushed back to Peru, put down the insurrection, and then imprisoned Pizarro's two brothers Hernando and Alonso for having refused to obey his orders during the fighting. This brought Francisco Pizarro to Cuzco, where he defeated Almagro's army, captured Almagro, and put him to death in the first of several internecine wars between the Spanish captains in the new colony.

Where the same name may denote a person, place, or thing, the articles will be found in that order

Almalyk, city, Tashkent *oblast* (administrative region), Uzbek Soviet Socialist Republic, on the northern slopes of the Kurama Mountains and the left bank of the Akhangaran River. Almalyk was founded in 1951 from several settlements exploiting the rich nonferrous-metal resources of the Kurama Mountains. The city has become an important centre of nonferrous metallurgy, and produces copper, molybdenum, lead, and zinc concentrates. Copper and zinc are also refined. Almalyk (Uzbek: Apple Grove) derives its name from the wild apple trees that grew in the valley. Pop. (1982 est.) 107,000.

almanac, book or table containing a calendar of the days, weeks, and months of the year; a register of ecclesiastical festivals and saints' days; and a record of various astronomical phenomena, often with weather prognostications and seasonal suggestions for the countryman. The term, of medieval Arabic origin, means the place where camels kneel; it later came to mean a campsite or settlement and, finally, the weather at the specific site. In modern Arabic, almanac is the only word for weather. The seasonal nature of weather in Arab countries permitted weather projections to be made from star positions; hence, almanacs were compiled.

Almanacs have appeared in some form since the beginnings of astronomy. The first standard almanacs were issued at Oxford. Scottish observers pioneered astrological almanacs during the 1500s and 1600s.

Most early English almanacs were published by the Stationer's Company; the most famous of them is the *Vox Stellarum* of Francis Moore (1657–1715?), the first number of which was completed in July 1700 and contained predictions for 1701.

The first American almanacs were printed in Cambridge, Mass., under the supervision of Harvard College. Benjamin Franklin's brother James printed *The Rhode Island Almanac* in 1728, and Benjamin Franklin (under the nom de plume of Richard Saunders) began his *Poor Richard's Almanack,* the most famous U.S. almanac, in Philadelphia five years later.

The 18th-century almanac was the forerunner of the modern magazine. Guided by the almanac, the farmer could tell the time of day and estimate the proper season for farm chores. It also furnished much incidental information—instructive and entertaining as well—and was greatly appreciated where reading matter was scarce. *See also* ephemeris.

almandine, either of two semiprecious gemstones: a violet-coloured variety of ruby spinel (*q.v.*) or iron aluminum garnet, most abundant of the garnets. Specimens of the garnet,

Almandite garnet from Southbury, Conn.

By courtesy of the Field Museum of Natural History, Chicago; photograph, John H. Gerard—EB Inc.

frequently crystals, contain up to 25 percent grossular or andradite and are commonly brownish red; gem-quality stone is deep red and slightly purple. Almandine, the so-called precious garnet, is most often faceted for rings. Cabochon-cut (rounded, convex polished surface), deep-red almandine is called carbuncle; its base is often hollowed to lighten its colour. When rutile needles are included in the almandine, the cabochons often show a four-rayed asterism (star-shaped figure).

Almandine is usually found mixed with both pyrope and spessartine. It occurs in metamorphic rocks, where its presence indicates the grade of metamorphism. For detailed chemistry and occurrence, *see* garnet.

Almansa Dam, on the Vega de Belén River, in Albacete Province, Spain, said to be the oldest masonry gravity dam still in use. Probably built in the 16th century, the slender structure has cut-stone facing and a rubble masonry interior. It is 82 feet (25 metres) high, 295 ft long, 7,500 cubic yards (5,700 cubic metres) in volume, and has a reservoir capacity of 1,300 acre-feet (1,600,000 cubic metres).

Almanzor (ruler of Córdoba): *see* Manṣūr, Abu ʿĀmir al-.

Almeida, Francisco de (b. *c.* 1450, Lisbon—d. March 1, 1510, Table Bay, at modern Cape Town), soldier, explorer, and the first Portuguese viceroy of India.

After Almeida had achieved fame in the wars against the Moors, Manuel I made him viceroy of the newly conquered territories of India in March 1505. Setting forth with a powerful fleet of 21 ships, he rounded the Cape of Good Hope, and, sailing up Africa's east coast, took Kilwa (now Kilwa Kisiwani, near Tanzania), where he constructed a fort, and then destroyed Mombasa before reaching India and taking up residence in Cochin. Determined to make Portugal the paramount power in the East and to monopolize the spice trade, he erected a series of fortified posts. Under his forceful administration a commercial treaty was concluded with Malacca (now Melaka, Malaysia) and further explorations were undertaken, especially by his son Lourenço. When the Arabs and their Egyptian allies challenged Portuguese dominance, he burned and pillaged their ports and defeated their combined fleet off Diu, India, in February 1509.

When Afonso de Albuquerque arrived at Cochin to supersede him, Almeida, doubting the legality of his commission, imprisoned him. In November 1509, however, he was forced to recognize Albuquerque's authority and set sail for Portugal the next month. While taking on water at Table Bay, Almeida was killed in a skirmish with the Khoikhoin (Hottentots).

Almeida, José Américo de (b. Jan. 10, 1887, Paraíba, Braz.—d. March 10, 1980, Rio de Janeiro), novelist whose works marked the beginning of an important Brazilian generation of northeastern regional writers; their fiction presents a predominantly socioeconomic interpretation of life in Brazil's most impoverished and drought-stricken region and is filled with local colour and appeals for justice and concern.

Almeida's literary career was paralleled by a career in politics; he served in the first Cabinet of Pres. Getúlio Vargas as minister of public works and transportation (1930–34) and was governor of the state of Paraíba (1951–54).

The problems endemic to the Brazilian northeast, including banditry in the arid backlands and the poverty and ignorance of the sugarcane workers in the more fertile coastal zone, are the focus of Almeida's novels. *A Bagaceira* (1928; "Cane-Trash"), his best known work, deals with a group of *sertanejos* (independent smallholders) forced by drought to leave their own ranches for a life of near-slavery on tropical sugar plantations. Other works in the same vein are *Boqueirão* (1935; "Canyon") and *Coiteiros* (1935; "Bandit-hiders").

Almeida, José Valentim Fialho de (b. 1857, Vila de Frades, Port.—d. March 4, 1911, Alentejo), Portuguese short-story writer and political essayist of the realist-naturalist period. His serial story collection *Os Gatos* (1889–93; "The Cats") is a satiric, caricatural depiction of Lisbon life and customs of the period. In *O País das Uvas* (1893; "Vineyard Country") and other collections, he offers lively, earthy descriptions of rural Portuguese life, which he contrasts favourably with the decadence of the cities. Other collections of short narratives in the satiric vein are *Pasquinadas* (1890; "Lampoons"), *Vida Irônica* (1892; "Ironic Life"), and *Lisboa Galante* (1890; "Courtly Lisbon").

Almeida, Lourenço de (b. *c.* 1450, Portugal—d. 1508, Chaul, India), Portuguese sea captain and leader of a 1505 expedition to Ceylon (now Sri Lanka), probably the first Portuguese voyage to that island.

The son of Francisco de Almeida, the first viceroy of Portuguese India (1505–09), Lourenço de Almeida had been sent by his father to explore the Maldives, to establish alliances, and to form trade relations. Almeida brought Portuguese influence to the region, founding a settlement at Colombo.

In 1508, scouting the positions of an Egyptian fleet at Chaul, off the west coast of India, Almeida found his ship trapped behind a river bar. He fought with bravery, and his exploits were later celebrated by the 16th-century Portuguese poet Camões in his patriotic epic poem *Os Lusíadas* (*The Lusiads,* referring to the ancient Roman territory, Lusitania, that embraced what became Portugal). Almeida died of wounds received in the battle. Two years later the Portuguese scattered a combined Turkish and Muslim fleet near the port of Diu, finally establishing Portuguese power in much of the territory east of Suez.

Almeida, Manuel Antônio de (b. 1831, Magé, Rio de Janeiro—d. Nov. 28, 1861, at sea), author of what is now considered to have been the first great novel in Brazilian literature, *Memórias de um Sargento de Milícias* (anonymously in parts, 1853; as a novel, 1854–55; "Memoirs of a Militia Sergeant"), his only fictional work. Its realism was not only far in advance of the Romanticism of his Brazilian contemporaries but several years in advance of the Naturalist school in Europe. It attracted little critical or popular attention until it was rediscovered by the Modernists in the 20th century.

Almeida studied art and, later, medicine, but his education was frequently interrupted for lack of money, and he supported himself as a translator and journalist. He became minister of the National Printing Establishment, where he befriended a young typographer and aspiring writer, Machado de Assis, who later became the literary giant of Brazil.

The "Memoirs" mirrors the life of Rio de Janeiro in the early 19th century with a sense of everyday reality. Written in an intimate, colloquial style, it offers a vivid glimpse of customs, personalities, and court intrigues, viewed by Leonardo, a young man of slight social standing, who seeks adventure where he finds it—among beggars, society women, priests, or sailors.

Almeida's promising career was cut short when he died at 31 in a shipwreck off the Brazilian coast while on a newspaper assignment.

Almelo, *gemeente* (municipality), Overijssel *provincie* (province), eastern Netherlands, at the junction of the Overijssel Canal and the Almelo-Nordhorn branch of the Twente Canal; it comprises the former municipalities of Ambt-Almelo, Stad-Almelo, and Vriezenveen.

An independent barony belonging to the van Rechteren family, Almelo was acquired through marriage (1350) by the lords of Heeckeren, who also gained the countship of Limburg in 1711. A branch of the family still holds the seat and the Huis te Almelo castle (1662–64).

Almelo shared in the rapid growth of the Twente district in the late 19th century. It is now a textile and metallurgical centre and rail junction. Among its notable buildings are the 17th-century Dutch Reformed Church, the 16th-century town hall (now a tourist office), and the Weighhouse, incorporating an art gallery. Pop. (1983 est.) 63,080.

almemar (Judaism): *see* bimah.

Almendares River, Spanish RÍO ALMENDARES, river of La Habana province, western Cuba, rising at about 740 ft (225 m) in the Alturas (heights) de Bejucal and flowing in a semicircle north and west, then northward across the Cuban coastal plain through the city of Havana to empty into the Straits of Florida after a course of 29 mi (47 km). It is the source of part of Havana's water supply, and its banks are also the site of the much-frequented Parque Almendares.

Almendros, Nestor (b. Oct. 30, 1930, Barcelona), cinematographer and recipient of an Oscar from the U.S. Motion Picture Academy of Arts and Sciences for the best cinematography for his work on *Days of Heaven* (1978).

Emigrating from Spain to Cuba in 1948, Almendros worked there for several years and made amateur films with Tomás Gutiérrez Alea and other young Cuban enthusiasts. He spent a year in Rome at the Centro Sperimentale and then taught for a while in the United States. While there, he became friendly with underground filmmakers Maya Deren and Adolfas and Jonas Mekas. Almendros returned to Cuba after the revolution in 1959 and worked on several documentaries of the early Castro era but found the film industry there too bureaucratic.

Almendros moved to France in 1961, where he did film shorts and television work. His first feature film and his first film in 35-millimetre format was Eric Rohmer's *La Collectionneuse* (1966). He also filmed *Ma nuit chez Maud* (1968; *My Night at Maud's*), *Le Genou de Claire* (1970; *Claire's Knee*), and *L'Amour, l'après-midi* (1972; *Chloe in the Afternoon*) for Rohmer. With François Truffaut he did *L'Enfant sauvage* (1970; *The Wild Child*), *Domicile conjugal* (1970; *Bed and Board*), and *Les Deux Anglaises et le continent* (1971; *Two English Girls*). His later films included the popular *L'Amour en fuite* (1979; *Love on the Run*). Almendros' work is characterized by luminescent lighting, reminiscent of early Swedish films, that heightens the characters' relationship to their physical environment.

Almería, province in the autonomous community (region) of Andalusia, southeastern Spain, bordering the Mediterranean. Formed in 1833, it has an area of 3,388 sq mi (8,774 sq km). Primarily mountainous, it is crossed by sierras in which terminate successive zones of the Penibético Mountain System. The intervening valleys of the Adra, Almanzora, and Andarax rivers provide the only fertile land. Despite a low rainfall, several important irrigation systems have considerably increased cultivation. The infrequency of cloud cover over the province (unusual in Europe) made it the site in 1979 of a major Spanish-West German astronomical observatory at Calar Alto. Fruit growing is the principal agricultural activity, and large quantities of oranges and white grapes are exported. Olive oil, cane and beet sugar, almonds, and esparto are also produced.

Livestock is raised, especially sheep. Mineral resources include iron, lead, and gold, and fine marble is quarried in the Sierra Nevada of the Penibético. There is a flourishing ceramics industry at Níjar. Tourism is of importance because of the year-round resort areas along the Mediterranean coast. The village of Tabernas became in 1980 the site of two 500-kilowatt solar power plants that were to be among the world's most advanced at their completion.

Communications focus on Almería, the provincial capital and seaport. Other chief towns are Adra, Berja, Cuevas del Almanzora, Huércal-Overa, and Garrucha. Pop. (1982 est.) 389,922.

Almería, port city and capital of Almería province, in the autonomous community (region) of Andalusia, southern Spain, on the Mediterranean Golfo de Almería. Known to the Romans as Urci or Portus Magnus and to the Moors as al-Marīyah (Mirror of the Sea), it was captured by the Catholic monarchs Ferdinand and Isabella of Castile in 1489. Historic landmarks include the Gothic cathedral (1524–43), built in the form of a fortress; the bishop's palace and seminary in the Moorish Alcazaba (fortress), built in 773 by the Amīr of Córdoba, ʿAbd ar-Raḥmān I, on the site of a Phoenician settlement; and the ruined Castillo de San Cristóbal, which overlooks the city and harbour.

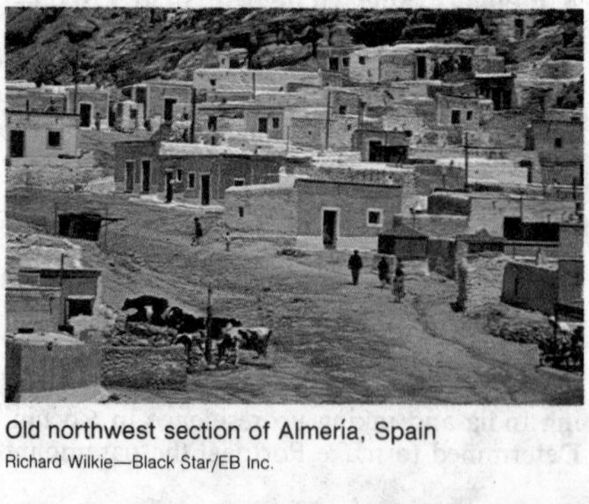

Old northwest section of Almería, Spain
Richard Wilkie—Black Star/EB Inc.

Almería's architecture and dazzling brightness give it a Moroccan rather than a European appearance. The mild and sunny climate, which permits year-round swimming, gives Almería its claim to be the resort centre of the Costa de La Luz (part of the Spanish Mediterranean coast). After 1960 the locale became popular with filmmakers, stimulating the building of hotels and the growth of airport facilities.

Industrial activities include metalworking, canning and salting of fish, refining of oil and sulfur, and manufacture of chemicals. A major cement complex (including quarry, plant, and port) was built in the late 1970s at Carboneras Beach. The port, which is sheltered and equipped with modern facilities, is especially busy from August to December because of the export of oranges and grapes. Pop. (1982 est.) 124,925.

Almetyevsk, also spelled ALMETEVSK, or AL'METJEVSK, city, Tatar Autonomous Soviet Socialist Republic, Russian S.F.S.R., on the left bank of the Stepnoy (Steppe) Zay River. It was founded in 1950 in connection with the discovery of petroleum in the area. Crude oil is sent from Almetyevsk to refineries at Perm and Kstovo (near Gorky) through pipelines completed in 1957. Almetyevsk is also the primary source of crude oil piped to eastern Europe. Local factories produce tires and ferroconcrete materials. Pop. (1983 est.) 118,000.

Almirante Brown, *cabecera* (principal built-up area) and *partido* (political subdivision) of Gran (Greater) Buenos Aires, Argentina, south of the city of Buenos Aires, in Buenos Aires province. The *partido* was founded in 1873 and the *cabecera* is often referred to as Adroqué, the name of its founder, and its railroad station bears that name. Esteban Adroqué petitioned the provincial government to expropriate land from the existing *partidos* of San Vicente and Quilmes to establish the new one. The original settlers were residents of Buenos Aires city who fled the capital during an epidemic of yellow fever. The *partido* covers 47 sq mi (122 sq km) and is bordered by the *partidos* of Lomas de Zamora (north), Quilmes and Florencio Varela (east), San Vicente (south), and Esteban Echeverría (west). Besides the *cabecera,* Almirante Brown, the major localities are Burzaco, Longchamps, Glew, Ministro Rivadavia, Claypole, Rafael Calzada, and José Mármôl. In 1886 Adroqué unveiled a statue in the central plaza honouring Adm. Guillermo Brown (hero of the 1827 naval battle of Juncal, in which Argentine warships defeated a Brazilian fleet). The *cabecera* and *partido* grew slowly in the late 19th and early 20th centuries. By 1947 the region began growing at an accelerated rate as the urbanization of Buenos Aires city started to spill over to surrounding *partidos.* Since then, Almirante Brown has been absorbed into the southern suburban fringe of Gran Buenos Aires. About half of the *partido* is within Gran Buenos Aires urban area, and its density of settlement is lower than in the more urbanized *partidos.* Livestock is raised in the area, and there are textile mills and dairies. Pop. (1980) *partido,* 331,919.

Almohads, Arabic AL-MUWAḤḤIDŪN (Those Who Affirm the Unity of God), a Berber confederation that created an Islāmic empire in North Africa and Spain (1130–1269), founded on the religious teachings of Ibn Tūmart (d. 1130).

A Berber state had arisen in Tinmel in the Atlas Mountains of Morocco *c.* 1120, inspired by Ibn Tūmart and his demands for puritanical moral reform and a strict concept of the unity of God (*tawḥīd*). In 1121 Ibn Tūmart proclaimed himself the *mahdī* (a promised messianic figure), and, as spiritual and military leader, began the wars against the Almoravids. Under his successor, ʿAbd al-Muʾmin, the Almohads brought down the Almoravid state in 1147, subjugating the Maghrib, and captured Marrakech, which became the Almohad capital. Almoravid domains in Andalusia, however, were left virtually intact until the caliph Abū Yaʿqūb Yūsuf (reigned 1163–84) forced the surrender of Seville in 1172; the extension of Almohad rule over the rest of Islāmic Spain followed. During the reign of Abū Yūsuf Yaʿqūb al-Manṣūr (1184–99) serious Arab rebellions devastated the eastern provinces of the empire, whereas in Spain the Christian threat remained constant, despite al-Manṣūr's victory at Alarcos (1195). Then, at the battle of Las Navas de Tolosa (1212), the Almohads were dealt a shattering defeat by a Christian coalition from Leon, Castile, Navarre, and Aragon. They retreated to their North African provinces, where soon afterward the Ḥafṣids seized power at Tunis (1236), the ʿAbd al-Wādids took Tilimsān (Tlemcen) (1239), and, finally, Marrakech fell to the Marīnids (1269).

The empire of the Almohads had kept its original tribal hierarchy as a political and social framework, with the founders and their descendants forming a ruling aristocracy; however, a Spanish form of central government was superimposed on this Berber organization. The original puritanical outlook of Ibn Tūmart was soon lost, and the precedent for building costly Andalusian monuments of rich ornamentation, in the manner of the Almoravids, was set as early as Ibn Tūmart's successor ʿAbd al-Muʾmin. The Booksellers' Mosque (Kutubīya) in Marrakech and the older parts of the mosque of Taza date from his reign. Neither did the movement for a return to traditionalist Islām survive; both the mystical movement of the Ṣūfis and the philosophical schools represented by Ibn Ṭufayl and Averroës (Ibn Rushd) flourished under the Almohad kings.

Rabat, an important cultural centre during the Almohad period, was known particularly for its polychrome pottery. The wares are colourful and gay, usually painted in yellows, greens, and bright blues on a buff background. Almohad pottery wares, however, never reached the artistic level of the work from Syria, Egypt, and Persia, and most are considered products of "folk" rather than "fine" art.

Almon, John (b. Dec. 17, 1737, Liverpool—d. Dec. 12, 1805, Boxmoor, Hertfordshire, Eng.), parliamentary reporter and political writer, who took part in the struggle between press and Parliament for the right to publish reports of debates.

A friend of the political reformer John Wilkes, he became known in the early 1760s as a Whig pamphleteer and as a bookseller from whose London shop political publications were disseminated. His parliamentary reports, published in the *London Evening Post*, precipitated a crisis between printers and Parliament in 1771; others followed the example of the *Post.* Wilkes used his privileged position as alderman of the City of London to prevent the arrest of printers and put an end to Parliament's power to punish journalists who reported its debates. Almon's article in the *Post* (1773) accusing John Montagu, 4th earl of Sandwich, of selling an office of trust cost the *Post*'s printer a £2,000 fine. Almon himself was once imprisoned for libel and once forced to flee the country. In 1774 he began *The Parliamentary Register,* a monthly record of proceedings (continued until 1813). His printed attacks on William Pitt in the 1780s finally brought his imprisonment for 14 months (1792–93), and he was forced to live the rest of his life on bail.

almond (*Prunus dulcis*), tree native to southwestern Asia and its edible seed, or nut. The nuts are of two types, sweet and bitter. Sweet almonds are the familiar edible type consumed as nuts and used in cooking or as a source of almond oil or almond meal.

Almond (*Prunus dulcis*)
Grant Heilman—EB Inc.

The almond tree, growing somewhat larger than the peach and living longer, is strikingly beautiful when in flower. The growing fruit resembles the peach until it approaches maturity; as it ripens, the leathery outer covering, or hull, splits open, curls outward, and discharges the nut.

The sweet almond is cultivated extensively in certain favourable regions between 28° and 48° N and between 20° and 40° S. The tree greatly resembles the related peach, with which it occasionally hybridizes. While dormant, it is nearly as hardy as the peach, although ordinarily flowering earlier, from late January to early April north of the Equator. The nut crops are therefore uncertain wherever frosts are likely to occur during the period of flowering. Sweet almonds mature only occasionally in climates like that of southern England.

The Old World almond cultivation was characterized by small plantings mainly for family use; trees interplanted with other crops; variability in age, condition, and bearing capacity of individual trees; and hand labour, often with crude implements. Modern growers pay more attention than they once did to propagation of approved varieties. Jordan and Valencia almonds come from Spain. Leading exporting countries of shelled almonds during the late 1970s were the U.S., Spain, Italy, Iran, Portugal, and Morocco.

Bitter almonds, as inedible as peach kernels, contain about 50 percent of a fixed oil that also occurs in the sweet almond, together with an enzyme called emulsin, which in the presence of water yields glucose, prussic (hydrocyanic) acid, and the essential oil of bitter almonds called benzaldehyde. When the prussic acid has been removed, the oil of bitter almonds is used in the manufacture of flavouring extracts for foods and liqueurs.

Almonds provide small amounts of protein, iron, calcium, phosphorus, and B vitamins and are high in fat. They may be eaten raw, blanched, or roasted and are commonly used in confectionery baking. In Europe a sweetened paste made from almonds is used in pastries and in marzipan, a traditional candy. The almond is also widely used in meat, poultry, fish, and vegetarian dishes of Asia.

Almond, Gabriel A(braham) (b. Jan. 12, 1911, Rock Island, Ill., U.S.), U.S. political scientist noted for his comparative studies of political systems and his analysis of political development.

Almond received his Ph.D. from the University of Chicago in 1938 and taught at Brooklyn College from 1939 to 1946, except for service in the U.S. Office of War Information in 1942–45. After teaching at Yale University (1947–51 and 1959–63) and at Princeton University (1951–59), he became a professor of political science at Stanford University, Stanford, Calif., in 1963, heading the department there from 1964 to 1968. He was elected president of the American Political Science Association for 1965–66 and was its James Madison lecturer in 1981.

Among Almond's publications are *The Struggle for Democracy in Germany* (1949; written with others and edited by Almond); *The American People and Foreign Policy* (1950); *The Appeals of Communism* (1954); *The Politics of the Developing Areas* (1960; written with others and edited by Almond), in which he presented a functional approach to the study of political systems; *The Civic Culture* (1963, with Sidney Verba), a cross-cultural study of citizen attitudes toward government in five societies; and *Political Development* (1970). He also wrote, with others, *Comparative Politics: System, Process, Policy* (1978), *The Civic Culture Revisted* (1980), and *Progress and Its Discontents* (1982).

almoner, originally, an officer responsible for distributing alms to the poor, usually connected with a religious house or other institution but also a position with some governments. In the 13th century, almoners were attached to the French court to distribute the royal alms, and in 1486 the office of grand almoner of France was established. The grand almoner was a high ecclesiastical dignitary who was in charge of the clergy attached to the court and who supervised charitable works. The office was suppressed in France in 1790, revived by Napoleon I and again by Napoleon III, and finally abolished in 1870.

In England the offices of hereditary grand almoner and high almoner still exist, as part of the Queen's Household. The high almoner, usually a bishop or other prelate, distributes the royal alms on Maundy Thursday.

In modern times the term almoner has also been used in Britain for a trained social worker, usually a woman, qualified to work in a medical setting. In this sense "almoner" was superseded in 1964 by the title medical social worker, the term also used in the United States. Medical social workers are employed by hospitals and public health departments.

almonry school, medieval English monastic charity school supported by a portion of the funds allocated to the almoner (*q.v.*). The practice began in the early 14th century when a form of scholarship was established that provided attendance at the cathedral school, housing, and food for boys at least 10 years old who could sing and read. They sang in the cathedral choir and acted as page boys to the monks. Their teachers were the secular clerks of the monastery. Such schools have now largely disappeared, although a few survived into the 20th century.

Almora, town, administrative headquarters of Almora district, Uttar Pradesh state, northern India, on a ridge of the Himalayan foothills. After the Gurkhas captured Almora in 1790, they built a fort on the ridge's eastern end; another fort stands on the western end. The Gurkhas suffered a defeat by the British near Almora in 1815. An agricultural trade centre, it also has some manufacturing and a college affiliated with Kumaun University. A road links the town with cities to the south.

Almora district has an area of 2,085 sq mi (5,400 sq km). It lies within the Himalayas and borders on Nepal. Much of the district is forested; its irregular topography has confined agriculture largely to the river valleys. Rice, wheat, fruit, millet, and tea are among the crops grown. Minerals include copper and magnetite deposits. Major towns are Almora and Rānīkhet. Pop. (1981) town, 20,758; metropolitan area, 22,705; district, 757,373.

Almoravids, Arabic AL-MURĀBIṬŪN (Those Dwelling in Frontier Fortresses, or Warrior-Monks), confederation of Berber tribes—Lamtūnah, Gudālah, Massūfah—of the Ṣanhājah clan, whose religious zeal and military enterprise built an empire in northwestern Africa and Muslim Spain in the 11th and 12th centuries. These Saharan Berbers were inspired to improve their knowledge of Islāmic doctrine by their leader Yaḥyā ibn Ibrāhīm and the Moroccan theologian ʿAbd Allāh ibn Yasīn. Under Abū Bakr al-Lamtūnī and later Yūsuf ibn Tāshufīn, the Almoravids merged their religious reform fervour with the conquest of Morocco and western Algeria as far as Algiers between 1054 and 1092. They established their capital at Marrakech in 1062. Yūsuf assumed the title of *amīr al-muslimīn* ("commander of the Muslims") but still paid homage to the ʿAbbāsid caliph (*amīr al-muʾminīn,* "commander of the faithful") in Baghdad. He moved into Spain in 1085, as the old caliphal territories of Córdoba were falling before the Christians and Toledo was being taken by Alfonso VI of Castile and Leon. At the Battle of az-Zallāqah, near Badajoz, in 1086 Yūsuf halted an advance by the Castilians but did not regain Toledo.

The whole of Muslim Spain, however, except Valencia, independent under El Cid (Rodrigo Díaz de Vivar), eventually came under Almoravid rule. In the reign (1106–42) of ʿAli ibn Yūsuf the union between Spain and Africa was consolidated, and Andalusian civilization took root: administrative machinery was Spanish in pattern, writers and artists crossed the straits, and the great monuments built by ʿAlī in the Maghrib were models of pure Andalusian art. But the Almoravids were but a Berber minority at the head of the Spanish–Arab empire, and while they tried to hold Spain with Berber troops and the Maghrib with a strong Christian guard, they could not restrain the tide of Christian reconquest that began with the fall of Saragossa in 1118. In 1125 the Almohads began a rebellion in the Atlas Mountains and after 22 years of fighting emerged victorious. Marrakech fell in 1147, and thereafter Almoravid leaders survived only for a time in Spain and the Balearic Isles.

Art of the Almoravid period is most noted for its sobriety and puritanism after the ornamental excesses of the Umayyads. It was only in the "minor," decorative arts of weaving and ivory carving that the Almoravids used ornamentation as an end in itself. Desert dwellers, military monks from the Sahara, the Almoravids shunned the lavish decoration that had characterized the late Umayyad architectural style and built on a practical rather than a monumental scale. Even in the secular sphere, piety and asceticism forbade the building of splendid palaces and monuments. The main architectural motif of the period was the horseshoe arch, which in later times was elaborated and used extensively by the Almohads and the Naṣrids. Minarets, usually placed at the corner of the *miḥrāb* (prayer niche facing Mecca), were square and only sparsely decorated. The most famous work to survive from the Almoravid age is the Great Mosque at Tlemcen, Algeria. Built in 1082, it was restored in 1136 but not in true Almoravid style. The *miḥrāb* is unusually ornate, surrounded by multilobed arches decorated with arabesques. The work is indicative of trends that were to develop in Spain and North Africa under the Almoravids' successors, the Almohads and the Naṣrids.

Almqvist, Carl Jonas Love, Almqvist also spelled ALMQUIST (b. Nov. 28, 1793, Ed, near Stockholm—d. Sept. 26, 1866, Bremen, Bremen), writer whose vast literary output, ranging from bizarre romanticism to bold realism,

Almqvist, detail of an oil painting by C.P. Mazer, 1836, in the Nordiska Museet,Stockholm

By courtesy of the Nordiska Museet, Stockholm

greatly influenced the development of Swedish literature. Although his work is uneven, he is a master of Swedish prose.

After studying at Uppsala, Almqvist entered the Department of Ecclesiastical Affairs in Stockholm. In 1823 he gave up his position and went to western Sweden to lead with a group of friends an idealized peasant existence patterned after the ideas of Rousseau. Two years later he returned to Stockholm, and from 1829 to 1841 was principal of an experimental secondary school. In 1851 he fled to the U.S. after being accused of fraud and the attempted murder of a moneylender. He returned to Europe in 1865.

Almqvist was little known until the mid-1830s when he began to publish a stream of works in prose and verse. Most of these—novels, short stories, poems, and verse dramas—were included in a series called *Törnrosens bok* ("The Book of the Briar Rose"; 13 vol., 1832–40; vol. 14, 1851; 2nd series, 1839–50). Particularly important were *Amorina* (written *c.* 1821; rewritten and published 1839) and *Drottningens juvelsmycke* (1834; "The Queen's Diamond Ornament"), a historical novel whose heroine, the mysterious, hermaphroditic Tintomara, is Almqvist's most fascinating character and a central symbol in his creative writings. *Det går an* (1838; *Sara Videbeck,* 1919) is a brilliant, realistic story pleading for the emancipation of love and marriage. The work foreshadows Strindberg's method of raising problems for debate. He was also a musician and set some of his short lyrics to music.

Almqvist showed an astonishing versatility. He attacked conventional matrimony, satirized the beliefs of the Lutheran Church (although he was ordained in 1837), and as a journalist and in many of his creative writings fought for moral and social reform. But he had strong tendencies toward egocentric aloofness, and the core of his personality remained dominated by Christian mysticism and Swedenborgian otherworldliness.

almshouse, also called POOR HOUSE, or COUNTY HOME, in the United States, a locally administered public institution for homeless, aged persons without means. Such institutions radically declined in number in the second half of the 20th century, to be replaced by other means of subsistence and care.

Dating from colonial days, it was formerly used as a dumping ground for the mentally ill, the epileptic, the feeble-minded, the blind, the deaf and dumb, the crippled, the tuberculous, the destitute aged, homeless unemployed, vagrants, petty criminals, prostitutes, unmarried mothers, and abandoned and neglected children. Operated often in conjunction with a farm, with emphasis on meeting costs through the sale of farm produce, the almshouse, or county home, incurred widespread criticism after the turn of the 20th century for its failure to provide differentiated treatment for the varying problems presented by residents, the minimum character of medical and nursing care offered, the low sanitation and safety standards, and the physical and mental deterioration in residents invited by neglect and the incompetence of the management. These evils were gradually but not altogether eliminated by the shift of the sick, the handicapped, and the young to specialized state institutions, a process that began in the middle of the 19th century, and the transfer out of able-bodied aged who could qualify for old-age assistance under the Social Security Act of 1935. From a peak of probably 135,000 in the early 1930s, the population of county homes dropped to an estimated 88,000 in 1940 and to 72,000 in 1950. Residents in 1950 consisted largely of aged infirm individuals. Closings and consolidations reduced the number of homes from 2,200 in 1923 to approximately 1,200 in 1950.

The prohibition in the Social Security Act against federally aided old-age assistance to residents of public institutions reflected a conviction that almshouses were unnecessary; but experience after 1935, particularly the rapid growth of commercial nursing homes, indicated that many aged persons required sheltered care or at least home-supervised care and that, in the absence of other free facilities, the indigent aged will use some kind of local public institution. Recognition in the 1940s of this need came at a time of increasing public awareness of the lack of adequate facilities for the chronically ill long-term patient. As a result, a number of states passed legislation encouraging the conversion of almshouses to county infirmaries. Social security benefits and, later, Medicaid also substantially lessened reliance on public homes, until they became virtually obsolete.

almucantar, in astronomy, any circle of the celestial sphere parallel to the horizon; when two objects are on the same almucantar, they have the same altitude. The term also refers to instruments of a pattern invented by the U.S. astronomer Seth Carlo Chandler for determining latitude or time by observing the times of transit of stars across a fixed almucantar.

almwirtschaft: *see* alpwirtschaft.

Alness, village, district of Ross and Cromarty, Highland region (until 1975 county of Ross and Cromarty), Scotland, situated on the northern shore of the Cromarty Firth. The village in the early 1970s was destined to accommodate about 16,000 of nearby Invergordon's rapidly increasing population, resulting from the establishment of new industries, in particular an aluminum smelting plant and developments following the discovery and exploitation of North Sea oil. The latter include the construction of the world's largest dry dock and the manufacture of oil rigs. Pop. (1981) 6,289.

alnico, any member of a series of alloys used to make powerful permanent magnets. Primary constituents are aluminum, nickel, and cobalt in various proportions, with small amounts of one or more of the elements copper, iron, and titanium added; the titanium-containing material is sometimes referred to by the trade name Ticonal. These alloys are very hard and difficult to machine; they are usually cast into their final shape and then subjected to a strict regime of heat and magnetic-field treatment.

Alnwick, district, county of Northumberland, northern England, occupying an area of 417 sq mi (1,080 sq km) that borders Scotland on the northwest and the North Sea on the east. The district descends eastward from the peaty moorlands of the Cheviot Hills (elevations above 2,000 ft [610 m]) along the Scottish border and across the valleys of the upper Aln and Coquet rivers and sandstone uplands of the area known as Rothbury Forest (800–1,400 ft) to the fertile coastal plain, meeting the North Sea in low cliffs and shallow bays backed by sand dunes.

Remains of medieval castles and peel towers (small, massive towers for protecting livestock and commoners) in the district bear witness to the former, almost constant border fighting between Scotland and England. The restored Alnwick Castle, in the centre of the coastal plain near the district seat of Alnwick, is an imposing example with its 14th-century gatehouse and barbican (gate tower).

Sheep are grazed throughout the district, with the hardy Cheviot being the significant breed. Lesser numbers of both beef and dairy cattle are raised in the upper Aln and Coquet valleys and on the coastal plain. Crops cultivated on large farms, especially on the coastal plain, include oats, barley, clover, turnips, and cabbage. Manufactures of the district include fishing tackle, canoes, and rock-climbing equipment for local use. The small coastal village of Craster is historically known for its production of kippers (smoked herring). An extension of the Northumberland coalfields in the southeast corner of Alnwick district is of declining importance. Pop. (1982 est.) 28,800.

Alnwick, parish (town), Alnwick district, county of Northumberland, England, on the south bank of the River Aln, between the Cheviot Hills and the sea.

The town is dominated by the Norman castle, since 1309 the principal seat of the Percy family, who later became earls of Northumberland. The house was rehabilitated in the 18th century under the direction of Robert Adam, and the surrounding park was landscaped by Lancelot ("Capability") Brown. Much of Adam's work in the Gothic style was replaced about 1855 by Anthony Salvin, who converted the interior to an Italian Renaissance-style palace.

Alnwick Castle, Northumberland
A.F. Kersting

Hulne Park and North Demesne are remnants of the ancient hunting grounds of the marcher (border) lords. Parts of the medieval town wall (notably the Hotspur Tower), the gatehouse of Alnwick Abbey (1147), and the 15th-century grammar school survive. Pop. (1981 prelim.) 7,191.

Aload, Greek ALOADA, or ALOEIDA, in Greek legend, the name for either Otus or Ephialtes, the twin sons of Iphimedeia, the wife of Aloeus, by the god Poseidon; they were of extraordinary strength and stature. The Aloads made war upon the Olympian gods and endeavoured to storm heaven itself, but Apollo destroyed them before they reached manhood. In a later myth they sought Artemis (goddess of wild animals, vegetation, and childbirth) and Hera (wife of Zeus) in marriage, whereupon Artemis appeared between them in the shape of a stag, which they attempted to kill but instead slew each other.

Aloe, genus of shrubby succulent plants in the lily family (Liliaceae), containing about 200 species native to Africa. Most members of the genus have a rosette of leaves at the base but no stem.

Aloe saponaria
Gerald Cubitt

Several species are cultivated as ornamentals for their sharp-pointed, spiny leaves and colourful clusters of yellow or red flowers. The juice of some species, especially the popular pot plant known as true aloe (*A. vera*), is used as an ingredient in cosmetics and in medicine as a purgative and as a treatment for burns.

aloe (plant): *see* Mauritius hemp.

Alojzy, Fortunat: *see* Żółkowski, Alojzy Fortunat.

Alompra (Burmese king): *see* Alaungpaya.

alopecia: *see* baldness.

Alor Islands, Bahasa Indonesia KEPULAUAN ALOR, group of two major and several lesser islets constituting Alor *kabupaten* (regency), Nusa Tenggara Timur *propinsi* (province), Lesser Sunda Islands, Indonesia, between the Flores and Savu seas. The largest island is Alor (900 sq mi [2,330 sq km]), the two major mountains of which, Kolana (5,791 ft [1,765 m]) and Muna (4,724 ft), are both old volcanoes. Alor is broken up by steep ravines, with only one plateau and some small coastal plains. Pantar Island is high (Mt. Delaki is 4,324 ft), with a rugged coast. The inhabitants speak languages belonging to the Austronesian (Malayo-Polynesian) family. They are animists, except for some Christian communities along the coasts and some Muslims. Festive occasions often involve exchanges of pigs, gongs, and *mokos,* cast-bronze kettle drums of unknown origin. Pop. (1980) 124,948.

Alor Setar, also spelled ALOR STAR, capital of Kedah state, northwestern West Malaysia, on the Sungai (River) Kedah. The town, neatly laid out, is concentrated on the west bank of the river and is the residence of the sultan of Kedah. In addition to its administrative functions, Alor Setar is the major distribution centre for the north Kedah plain, a region in which paddy rice is grown. An intervening swamp forest makes it unapproachable from the sea, 12 mi (19 km) to the west, but road and rail services reach north to Thailand and south to Pinang; there also is an airport at Kepala Batas, 6 mi north-northeast. Pop. (1980) 69,435.

Alost (Belgium): *see* Aalst.

Alotau, port and administrative headquarters (1968) of Milne Bay province, southeast tip of mainland Papua New Guinea. Situated on the northern shore of Milne Bay, the town lies in the forested foothills of an eastward extension of the Owen Stanley Range. Cocoa and vegetables are grown nearby, and coconuts are raised along the coast east of the town. Overseas and coastal wharves, completed in 1975, have made Alotau the province's main port. Copra is brought in for transshipment overseas, and fishing vessels operate out of the port. The Milne Bay Highway connects Alotau with Dogura to the northwest, and an airfield is located at nearby Gurney. Pop. (1980) 4,311.

Aloysius GONZAGA, SAINT (b. March 9, 1568, Castiglione delle Stiviere, Republic of Venice—d. June 21, 1591, Rome; canonized 1726; feast day June 21), patron of Roman Catholic youth, who is one of the most venerated saints.

A son of Ferrante, marquess of Castiglione, Aloysius was educated at the ducal courts of Florence and Mantua and at the royal court of Madrid, where he was page to King Philip II's son Diego. In 1585 he resigned his inheritance and entered the Society of Jesus at Rome, where one of his spiritual directors was the renowned theologian Robert Bellarmine. Shortly before ordination, while nursing victims of the plague, he contracted the disease and died.

He was named patron of youth by Pope Benedict XIII in 1729, an action confirmed by Pope Pius XI in 1926. Among the many lives of Aloysius Gonzaga are those by Virgilio Cepari, S.J. (*c.* 1606, edited by Frederick Schroeder, S.J.; Eng. trans. by F. Goldie, 1891), Maurice Meschler, S.J. (1911), and C.C. Martindale, S.J. (*Saint Aloysius Gonzaga*, 1926).

ALP: *see* Australian Labor Party.

Alp-Arslan, Turkish ALPARSLAN (Courageous Lion), original name ʿAḌUD AL-DAWLA ABŪ SHUJAʿ MUḤAMMAD IBN DĀʾŪD CHAGHRIBEG (b. *c.* 1030—d. November 1072/January 1073), second sultan of the Seljuq Turks (1063–72), who inherited the Seljuq territories of Khorāsān and western Iran and went on to conquer Georgia, Armenia, and much of Asia Minor (won from the Byzantines).

Alp-Arslan was the son of Chaghri Beg, the ruler of Khorāsān in Iran, and the nephew of Toghrïl, the governor of western Iran, the base of Seljuq expansion. In 1061 his father died. When, in 1063, his uncle died without issue, Alp-Arslan became sole heir to all the possessions of the dynasty except Kerman, in southern Iran, which was held by one of his brothers, whom he promptly reduced to vassalage. He likewise easily eliminated the son of one of Toghrïl's widows, as well as Qutlumush, a cousin and rival.

Born outside the traditional Muslim countries that he was later to govern, he left their administration to his vizier, Niẓām al-Mulk, who continued as administrator under Malik-Shāh. While maintaining control of Iraq, Alp-Arslan nevertheless shunned that country in order to avoid such clashes of interests with the caliphate, the seat of which was there, as had complicated Toghrïl's last days.

Alp-Arslan's political activity was based on the ideas that inspired all the three great Seljuq sovereigns. In Central Asia, peace was maintained with the Ghaznavid rulers who were hard to track down in their mountain strongholds in India, whereas against the Qarakhanids of Transoxania, force was used. In the west, where Alp-Arslan was to gain all his glory, he was faced with a more complicated situation. On the one hand, he decided to go to Egypt to crush the Ismāʿīlī Fāṭimid heresy, which the ʿAbbāsid Sunnite caliphate at Baghdad, whose protector he was, would not accept. On the other hand, he was aware of the necessity of keeping his influence over the Turkmens, which was essential to his military strength. The Turkmens were interested above all in the success of the holy war against the infidels and in raids on Christian territory. Against the Byzantines and their Armenian and Georgian neighbours, Alp-Arslan conducted a series of campaigns, which were extended by attacks from autonomous Turkmen bands. In 1064 he seized Ani, the former Armenian capital, and Kars. These operations resulted only in some consolidation of boundaries, which assured the Turkmens control over pastureland on the Aras River. Nevertheless, although the Turkmens returned to Muslim territory to store away their booty, these expeditions upset the Byzantine defense system and prepared the subsequent Turkish conquest of Asia Minor. They resulted in Byzantine reactions in Syria and Armenia, after which the two empires began to negotiate.

Alp-Arslan then judged himself sufficiently protected on the Byzantine side to undertake, at the request of Egyptian rebels, the great anti-Fāṭimid expedition that had been asked for by the orthodox ʿAbbāsid caliphate. As he was about to attack Aleppo, whose prince was too late in siding with the ʿAbbāsids, and was preparing to occupy Syria, Alp-Arslan learned that the Byzantine emperor Romanus IV Diogenes, with a formidable army, was assaulting his rear army in Armenia. Quickly retracing his steps, he faced his adversary near Manzikert in August 1071. The Byzantine army, powerful in numbers but weak in morale, fell before the outnumbered but dedicated Turks. By evening the Byzantine army was defeated, and, for the first time in history, a Byzantine emperor had become the prisoner of a Muslim sovereign. Alp-Arslan's goal was not to destroy the Byzantine Empire: he was content with the rectification of boundaries, the promise of tribute, and an alliance. But the Battle of Manzikert opened Asia Minor to Turkmen conquest. Later, every princely family in Asia Minor was to claim an ancestor who had fought on that prestigious day.

The Sultan's triumph was followed by a commonplace death, permitting moralists to recall that power rests only in God: at the end of 1072, he had returned to the Qarakhanid frontier and, during a quarrel, was mortally wounded by a prisoner. He had designated as his heir his son Malik-Shāh, 13 years old, under the guardianship of Niẓām al-Mulk.

Alp-Arslan's personality, in spite of the glory surrounding his name, is not easy to evaluate. Muslims see in him a great captain, a trainer of men, an honest man, an enemy of all treachery. Christians, contrasting his reputation with that of his son Malik-Shāh, paint him in harsher colours. There is no doubt that conquest seems to have been his favourite pastime. Although an anonymous writer dedicated to him the *Malek-nāmeh*, an attempt to trace the origins of his family and the empire, Alp-Arslan appears to have shown little interest in intellectual matters, leaving them, like the administration of his empire, to his vizier. (C.C.)

BIBLIOGRAPHY. Most works on Alp-Arslan are in Turkish. In English, W. Barthold, *Turkestan Down to the Mongol Invasion*, 2nd ed., translated from the Russian by H.A.R. Gibb (1928; new rev. ed. by C.E. Bosworth, 1968); Claude Cahen, *Pre-Ottoman Turkey* (1968); and the article on Alp-Arslan in the *Encyclopaedia of Islam*, new ed., vol. 1 (1960), may all be recommended.

alpaca (*Lama pacos*), South American member of the camel family, Camelidae (order Artiodactyla), closely related to the llama, guanaco, and vicuña, which are known collectively as lamoids. Unlike the camels, lamoids do not have the characteristic hump; they are slender-bodied animals and they have long legs and necks, short tails, small heads, and large, pointed ears. Lamoids are able to interbreed and to produce fertile offspring. Like the llama, the alpaca is a domestic animal not known to exist in a wild state. Both appear to have been domesticated during or before the Inca Indian civilization.

The alpaca, standing about 90 centimetres (35 inches) at the shoulder, is kept and bred for its wool, which in the breed known as suri grows long enough to touch the ground. The wool is lightweight and high in insulation value, useful in parkas, sleeping bags, and fine coat linings. Robes of alpaca wool were worn by Incan royalty.

The fibre obtained from both huacaya and suri varieties of the alpaca belongs to the group called specialty hair fibres (*q.v.*). The alpaca has been an important source of textile fibre in the Andean region of South America since pre-Columbian times.

The animals are normally sheared every two years, with the suris yielding fine fleeces of about 6.5 pounds (3 kilograms) per animal, and the huacayas giving coarser fleeces weighing about 5.5 pounds. Individual fibres within the fleece range from about 8 to 16 inches (20 to 40 centimetres) in length at the time of shearing. Although the fibre contains some coarse hairs, the animal does not have a protective outer coat. Diameter, often varying throughout the fibre's length, is about 22–30 microns (a micron is about 0.00004 inch). The fibre has indistinct surface scales and a striated cortical layer. The coarser fibres are straight and because they are medullated—*i.e.,* have a hollow core—are lower in density and lighter in weight than wool of similar diameter. Fibres having small diameter, generally the greatest portion of the fleece, are fairly flexible and less likely to be medullated than the coarse.

Colour, often the basis for sorting, includes shades of brown ranging from tan to dark, and gray, black, white, and piebald. Huacaya fibre, accounting for the greatest portion of fleece production, is crimped, forming fluffy fleece, and feels somewhat harsh. Its silvery lustre resembles that of medium wools. Suri fibre, straight or widely waved, forms tight locks, is slippery to the touch, and has lower lustre. Alpaca is stiffer than wool and is stronger than wools of medium diameter, the huacaya type being stronger than suri. Huacaya reacts to chemicals much like wool; suri is more sensitive. Alpaca fibre has felting properties, although the process is slower and produces less compact packing than is found in medium wools. It resembles wool in its ability to absorb and retain moisture.

Alpaca, sometimes combined with other fibres, is made into dress and lightweight suit fabrics and is also woven as a pile fabric used both for coating and as a lining for outerwear. Peru is the leading producer.

Consult the INDEX *first*

Alparslan (Turkish leader): *see* Alp-Arslan.

Alpenrhein River, the part of the Rhine River between the confluence of the Vorder- and Hinterrhein and its entry into Lake Constance. It is 63 mi (102 km) long. From Reichenau to Sargans it flows entirely within Swiss territory; for the next 19 mi it forms the border between Switzerland and Liechtenstein; and the last part separates Switzerland from Austria. The waters are thick with mud.

Alpes (Roman province): *see* Alps.

Alpes-de-Haute-Provence, formerly (until 1970) BASSES-ALPES, *département,* Provence-Alpes-Côte-d'Azur region, southeastern France, created in 1790 out of the northern part of Provence and covering an area of 2,681 sq mi (6,944 sq km), wholly within the Alpes de Provence. It is bounded on the north by Hautes-Alpes *département* and on the east by Italy and Alpes-Maritimes *département.* Alpes-de-Haute-Provence is high and mountainous and is one of the most thinly populated parts of France. Only in the Durance Valley is the altitude below 1,000 ft (300 m), and the mountains near the Italian frontier rise above 10,000 ft. Most of the *département* farther west consists of rugged limestone Pre-Alps. Between mountain-encircled basins, where the Durance River and its tributaries (Ubaye, Bés, Bléone, Asse, and Verdon) open out, are almost impassable gorges dividing the area into separate compartments. Roads that were improved in the 20th century, including the Route Napoléon and the road from Briançon to Nice, much frequented by summer tourists, have helped break down the isolation.

Durance River Valley, Alpes-de-Haute-Provence *département*, France

Almasy, Paris

In the valleys, cereals and vegetables are grown, and fruit orchards and vineyards are cultivated. Sheep are raised in irrigated meadows. In the extreme south of the *département,* the upper Verdon River has been impounded by the Castillon and Chaudanne dams to provide water for irrigation and hydroelectric power, but the middle course is a beautiful gorge frequented by tourists.

Alpes-de-Haute-Provence comprises four *arrondissements,* which centre on Digne (*q.v.*; the departmental capital), Barcelonnette, Castellane, and Forcalquier. The *département* comes under the *académie* (academic district) and court of appeal of Aix. Pop. (1982) 119,068.

Alpes-Maritimes, *département,* in the region of Provence-Alpes-Côte-d'Azur, southeastern France, bounded northeast by Italy, south by the Mediterranean Sea, and west by the *départements* of Var and Alpes-de-Haute-Provence. It has an area of 1,658 sq mi (4,294 sq km) and is divided into the *arrondissements* of Nice (the *département*'s capital) and Grasse. It was formed in 1860 out of the county of Nice (until then a possession of the House of Savoy) with the addition of the districts of Grasse (formerly in Var *département*) and Menton (purchased from the prince of Monaco). Frontier sections ceded by Italy under the terms of the Franco-Italian peace treaty (1947) were also acquired and extended the border northward along the crest of the Maritime Alps. Alpes-Maritimes surrounds the rocky promontory of Monaco, which, with adjoining Monte-Carlo and La Condamine, forms an independent principality.

Most of the *département* consists of limestone mountains (the Maritime Alps east of the Var River and the Provence Alps west of the river), which extend to the coast in rocky headlands, including Cap (cape) Ferrat and Cap d'Antibes. The former shelters the naval base of Villefranche.

The coast, from Cannes in the west to the Italian frontier on the east, has developed as the tourist region known as the French Riviera. Resorts include Nice, Cannes, Menton, Antibes, Monte-Carlo (*qq.v.*), Juan-les-Pins, and many other recently expanded resorts. Grasse, slightly inland, is famous for its perfumes. Agricultural activities, most of which are restricted to the narrow coastal region, include the cultivation of lavender for the perfume industry, vineyards, olive groves, and fruit orchards. Industrialization is poorly developed but includes electronics. Pop. (1982) 881,198.

Alpha and Omega, in Christianity, the first and last letters of the Greek alphabet, used to designate the comprehensiveness of God, implying that God includes all that can be. In the New Testament Revelation to John, the term is used as the self-designation of God and of Christ. The reference in Revelation likely had a Jewish origin, based on such Old Testament passages as Isa. 44:6 ("I am the first and the last"), and Ps. 90:2 ("from everlasting to everlasting thou art God"). In rabbinic literature, the word *emet* ("truth"), composed of the first and last letters of the Hebrew alphabet, is "the seal of God," and in Judaic tradition it carries somewhat the same connotation as Alpha and Omega.

Alpha Aquilae: *see* Altair.

Alpha Aurigae: *see* Capella.

Alpha Boötis: *see* Arcturus.

Alpha Canis Majoris: *see* Sirius.

Alpha Canis Minoris: *see* Procyon.

Alpha Canum Venaticorum: *see* Cor Caroli.

Alpha Centauri, triple star, the faintest component of which, Proxima Centauri, is the closest star to the Sun, at about 4.3 light-years' distance. The two brighter components, about 1/10 light-year farther from the Sun, revolve around each other with a period of about 80 years, while Proxima circles them with a period probably of millions of years. The brightest component star resembles the Sun in spectral type, diameter, and absolute magnitude. Its apparent visual magnitude is 0.1. The second brightest component, of visual magnitude 1.5, is a redder star. The third component, of 11th magnitude, is a red dwarf star.

As seen from Earth, the system is the third brightest star (after Sirius and Canopus); the red dwarf Proxima is invisible to the unaided eye. Alpha Centauri can be seen only from south of about 40° north latitude.

Alpha Crucis, also called ACRUX, 13th brightest star (excluding the Sun) as seen from Earth. It actually is a binary star; its components have apparent magnitudes of 1.58 and 2.09. Alpha Crucis lies about 400 light-years from the Earth in the constellation Crux (The Southern Cross). The alternate name Acrux is probably a contraction of Alpha Crucis.

Alpha Cygni: *see* Deneb.

alpha decay, type of radioactive disintegration in which some unstable atomic nuclei dissipate excess energy by spontaneously ejecting an alpha particle. Because alpha particles have two positive charges and a mass of four units, their emission from nuclei produces daughter nuclei having a positive nuclear charge or atomic number two units less than their parents and a mass of four units less. Thus polonium-210 (mass number 210 and atomic number 84, *i.e.,* a nucleus with 84 protons) decays by alpha emission to lead-206 (atomic number 82).

The speed and hence the energy of an alpha particle ejected from a given nucleus is a specific property of the parent nucleus and determines the characteristic range or distance the alpha particle travels. Not very penetrating, alpha particles, though ejected at speeds of about one-tenth that of light, have ranges in air of only about one to four inches (corresponding to an energy range of about 4 million to 10 million electron volts).

The principal alpha emitters are found among the elements heavier than bismuth (atomic number 83) and also among the rare-earth elements from neodymium (atomic number 60) to lutetium (atomic number 71). Half-lives for alpha decay range from about a microsecond (10^{-6} second) to about 10^{17} seconds.

Alpha Eridani: *see* Achernar.

Alpha Geminorum: *see* Castor.

Alpha Herculis: *see* Ras Algethi.

Alpha Leonis: *see* Regulus.

Alpha Lyrae: *see* Vega.

Alpha Orionis: *see* Betelgeuse.

alpha particle, positively charged particle, identical to the nucleus of the helium-4 atom, spontaneously emitted by some radioactive substances, consisting of two protons and two neutrons bound together, thus having a mass of four units and a positive charge of two. Discovered and named (1899) by Ernest Rutherford, alpha particles were used by him and co-workers in experiments to probe the structure of atoms in thin metallic foils, work that resulted in the first nuclear conception of the atom (1909–11), and to bombard nitrogen, changing it to oxygen, in the first artificially produced nuclear transmutation (1919). Today, alpha particles are produced for use as projectiles in nuclear research by ionization—*i.e.,* by stripping both electrons from helium atoms—and then accelerating the now positively charged particle to high energies.

Alpha Piscis Austrini: *see* Fomalhaut.

Alpha Scorpii: *see* Antares.

Alpha Tauri: *see* Aldebaran.

Alpha Ursae Minoris: *see* Polaris.

Alpha Virginis: *see* Spica.

alphabet, set of symbols or characters used to represent the sounds of a language. Each character in an alphabet usually represents a simple vowel, a diphthong, or a consonant, rather than a syllable or a group of consonants and vowels. The term alphabet, as used by some, however, also includes the concept of syllabaries.

A brief treatment of alphabets follows. For full treatment, *see* MACROPAEDIA: Writing.

An alphabet is a system of representing the sounds of a language by a set of clearly understandable and reproducible symbols. This generally involves assigning to the most common sounds their own individual graphemes, or written forms. Although there are numerous cases of duplication—that is, the same sound being represented by two or more graphemes (*e.g.,* the sound of the *g* in *gentle* and the *j* in *jewel*), or a grapheme having no counterpart in its oral form (*e.g.,* the *c* in the spoken *scissors,* the *g* in the spoken *paradigm*)—these exceptions are, in large part, due to the failure of the users of a language to make the changes in spelling that correspond to the changes that have already occurred in spoken usage.

The origin of the alphabet cannot be given with any precision. It is generally agreed, however, that an alphabet known as the North Semitic, originating somewhere in the area around the eastern shores of the Mediterranean in the period between 1700 and 1500 BC, was the first.

A major development took place toward the end of the 2nd millennium BC. The rising political importance of Israel, Phoenicia, and Aram, the commercial importance of the kingdom of Sheba in southwest Arabia, and the growth of what would become the Greek nation provided four branchings: the Canaanite, the Aramaic, the South Semitic (or Sabaen), and the Greek. From the Canaanite and the Aramaic would eventually spring modern Hebrew and Arabic, while the Western alphabets would come down through the Greek, probably by way of the Phoenician.

The spread of the alphabet is as much in debate as its origins. Among the most widely held opinions are these: (1) conquering armies carried their alphabets with them and imposed them, to one degree or another, on their subjects; (2) the widespread trade originating in and around the Fertile Crescent in the Middle East naturally caused a commingling of alphabets as a result of attempts by traders and merchants to achieve a maximum volume of trade with a minimum of confusion; and (3) various religious groups sent out missionaries or other representatives, spreading alphabets in the form of scriptures, homilies, etc.

The Hebrew alphabet as it is still written today came from a form known as the Square Hebrew alphabet, which was itself the product of an Aramaic alphabet learned during the period of the Babylonian Captivity (586?–538 BC). The Square Hebrew script was standardized sometime around the start of the Christian Era and has remained virtually unchanged to this day. The Hebrew alphabet is read from right to left. It has no vowel graphemes, although 4 of the 22 letters are used to indicate long vowels. The remaining vowel sounds are represented by the use of 16 diacritical marks placed above, below, or to the left of a consonant.

The Arabic alphabet, also a descendant of the Aramaic, developed in two main forms: the Kufic and the Naskhi. The Kufic, virtually nonextant now, was used for stone or metal carvings, coin inscriptions, and the scribing of manuscripts of the Qur'ān (Koran). It was distinguished by its heavy, formal letterforms. The Naskhi, from which modern Arabic descends, was a freer form, more suited to handwriting. Like the Hebrew alphabet, the Arabic is virtually vowelless. Only 3 of its 28 letters are used for long vowels, with 14 diacritical marks supplying not only other vowels but distinguishing between consonants and serving as noun and verb modifiers.

All Indian alphabets have their origins in a script called Brāhmī. It is probable that Brāhmī was also a descendant of Aramaic, if not lineally then by example. Another of the original Indian alphabets, Kharoṣṭī, is almost certainly directly evolved from the Aramaic.

From the Brāhmī was developed the Gupta, which further developed into, among others, the Siddhamatrka script. The Siddhamatrka is significant in that out of it came the script used for the writing of Sanskrit, the Devanāgarī. Another of the long-lived scripts, the Devanāgarī has remained unchanged in essentials since the 9th century AD. A noteworthy aspect of these Indian scripts is that, unlike Hebrew or Arabic, these alphabets contain no consonants that are written by themselves. Where a consonant does appear, it is part of a diphthong or else followed by a short *a*.

The Greek alphabet developed around 1000–900 BC, probably from the Phoenician. It branched into a series of eastern and western subdivisions, more notable for their agreement in structure than their differences in detail. Of these, an eastern variant, the Ionic, gradually came to replace the numerous local alphabets until, in 403 BC, it was adopted as the official Athenian alphabet. In the third century BC one of the last modifications of the alphabet took place: the introduction of three accent marks that were to aid foreigners in the correct pronunciation of Greek. Among the most significant offshoots of Greek were the Cyrillic and Etruscan alphabets. The Cyrillic became the script of the Russian, Ukrainian, Bulgarian, Serbian, and Belorussian peoples, while the Etruscan evolved into the Latin alphabet.

Originally, the Romans borrowed 21 of the 26 Etruscan letters. Two more, the *y* and the *z*, were absorbed following Rome's conquest of Greece in the first century BC. The *j* and the *v*, which had previously been written interchangeably with *i* and *w*, respectively, came into being during the Middle Ages. With the addition of the *w* from a Norman source, the Latin alphabet was brought to its present complement of 26.

There have been several attempts at a perfect alphabet which would ideally use one and only one symbol for each sound of a language. The most notable of these efforts resulted in the International Phonetic Alphabet, invented at the close of the 19th century.

alphabet rhyme, mnemonic verse or song used to help children learn an alphabet; such devices appear in almost every alphabetic language. Some of the early English favourites are about 300 years old and have served as models for countless variations. One is a cumulative rhyme to which there is a printed reference as early as 1671. It often appeared in 18th-century chapbooks under the imposing name *The Tragical Death of A, Apple Pye Who was Cut in Pieces and Eat by Twenty-Five Gentlemen with whom All Little People Ought to be Very well acquainted.* It begins:

A was an apple-pie;
B bit it,
C cut it,
D dealt it, etc.

Another, known as "Tom Thumb's Alphabet," enjoyed continuous popularity. The earliest printed record of it is from *c.* 1712. In its most familiar version, the rhyme begins:

A was an archer, who shot at a frog.
B was a butcher, and had a great dog.

These early rhymes showed little discrimination in subject matter. Lines such as "D was a drunkard, and had a red face," "U was a Usurer took Ten *per* Cent," or "Y was a youth, that did not love school" were later considered to have a harmful effect on children; they were replaced by the widely taught alphabet rhyme of the *New-England Primer,* published by Benjamin Harris (*q.v.*) in the late 17th century, which combined moral messages with the learning of letters:

In Adam's fall
We sinned all.

A simplified version of English alphabet rhyme, popular today, is sung to the tune of "Twinkle, Twinkle, Little Star."

A B C D E F G
H I J K L M N O P
Q and R and S and T
U V W X Y Z
Now I've said my *ABC's*,
Tell me what you think of me.

Alpharabius: *see* Fārābī, al-.

Alphege, SAINT: *see* Aelfheah, Saint.

Alpheus River, also spelled ALPHEIUS, Modern Greek ALFIÓS POTAMÓS, river, the longest of the Peloponnese (Pelopónnisos), Greece, rising near Dhaviá in central Arcadia, with a course of about 70 mi (110 km). Leaving the plain of Megalópolis in a rugged gorge, above which it is known as the Elísson, the Alpheus turns abruptly northwest and eventually empties into the Ionian Sea. Its main tributaries are the Ládhon and Erímanthos. The hydroelectric Ládhon Dam near the village of Trópaia has created a lake 4 sq mi (10 sq km) in area.

The shallow, gravelly stream receives its name from the ancient river god of the Peloponnese, Alpheus, whose waters were said to pass beneath the Ionian Sea and rise again in the fountain of Arethusa near Syracuse, Sicily. The legend may well have been inspired by the fact that the river disappears several times into the limestone Arcadian mountains and reemerges after flowing some distance underground.

Alphonsine Tables: *see* Alfonsine Tables.

Alphonsus, prominent crater on the Moon, named for King Alfonso X of Castile. It was the site in 1958 of the first gaseous eruption on the Moon of which a spectrum was recorded. Alphonsus is about 110 kilometres (70 miles) in diameter and lies at about 14° south latitude, 2° west longitude. In November 1958 the Soviet astronomer Nikolay A. Kozyrev, in a ground-breaking discovery, photographed the spectrum of an eruption near the crater's central peak and detected glows of a type characteristic of carbon compounds. Eruptive activity in the crater had been suspected earlier, though not recorded.

alphorn, long horn played by Alpine herdsmen and villagers, sounded for intercommunication and at daily ceremonies and seasonal festivals. It is carved or bored in wood and overwound with birch bark. Some instruments are straight, reaching 12 feet (4 metres) in length; since the mid-19th century, especially in Switzerland, the bell may be upcurved.

Alphorns being blown at a Swiss Alpine festival
By courtesy of the Swiss National Tourist Office

Others, mainly in the eastern Alps, are trumpet-shaped; S-shapes also occur. The compass and notes are usually those of a natural (unvalved) French horn in F (about three octaves upward from written F below the bass staff). In the 19th century, playing in trios and quartets was introduced.

The alphorn was mentioned by the Roman historian Tacitus (*c.* AD 56–117). Similar instruments occur in Scandinavia, Lithuania, the Carpathians, and the Pyrenees.

Alpine, town, seat (1887) of Brewster County, extreme western Texas, U.S., in a high valley (alt 4,481 ft [1,366 m]), flanked by the Davis Mountains (north) and the Glass Mountains (east), 190 mi (306 km) southeast of El Paso. Founded in 1882 with the arrival of the railroad, it developed as a service centre for a huge ranching area (sheep and Hereford cattle) and later as a mountain resort with dude ranches and ghost mining towns. Davis Mountains State Park, Fort Davis National Historic Site, and McDonald Observatory are a few miles northwest (*see* Davis Mountains), while Big Bend National Park (*q.v.*) is 80 mi south. Alpine's economy was further sustained by the establishment there in 1920 of a normal college, now Sul Ross State University (with Museum of Big Bend on its campus). Brewster County, with an area of 6,204 sq mi (16,068 sq km), greater than that of the state of Connecticut, is the largest county in Texas. Pop. (1980) 5,465.

Alpine lakes, the 11 significant European lakes fringing the great mountainous mass of the Alps. Set in magnificent scenery, they are the focus of considerable settlement and a thriving tourist traffic, as well as of great scientific interest.

Most of the Alpine lakes lie in valleys that were formed during the uplift of the mountain chain of the Alps. During the Ice Age of the geologically recent Pleistocene Epoch, less than 2,000,000 years ago, glaciers flowed through these valleys, deepening and excavating the ground, and leaving moraines (deposits of waste material) when they shrank at the end of the glacial period. Water filled up the excavations or was dammed up by the moraines.

The lakes that originated in mountain valleys are long and narrow and are generally very deep. In some cases the glaciers advanced from the Alps into the adjacent plains where they began to diverge fanwise. In such cases the end of the associated lakes broadens or bifurcates.

The lakes are divided into a northern and a southern group by the Alpine watershed running from west to east. The southern group, which lies in an Alpine environment, is made up of Lake Geneva and the Insubrian lakes (Maggiore, Lugano, Como, and Garda). Parts of the northern lakes (Lakes Neuchâtel, Luzern, Zürich, Constance, Chiemsee, Attersee) are situated in the foothill zone of the Alps or even some distance beyond.

Scientific study of Alpine lakes started in Switzerland with F.A. Forel, who studied the stationary oscillations of the water level (seiches) caused by the wind and also made classic observations on the interrelationship between physical and biological processes in lakes. In his work *Le Léman* (1892–1904) he created the term limnology to characterize the comprehensive study of lakes.

In the lakes of the Eastern Alps the phenomenon of the thermocline (zone of rapid decrease of lake temperature below the warm surface stratum in summer) was first studied in the Wörther See (1891). In the same lake, in 1931, it was discovered that there was an absence of total water circulation during the winter in lakes with wind-sheltered sites. These lakes were henceforth characterized as being of meromictic type. The currents caused by the Rhine's flow through Lake Constance

Alpine lakes

lake	area (sq km)	length (km)	depth (m)	altitude (m)	territory
Geneva	581	72	310	372	Swiss–French
Constance	541	66	252	396	German–Swiss
Garda	370	54	346	65	Italian
Neuchâtel	218	38	153	429	Swiss
Maggiore	212	54	372	194	Italian–Swiss
Como	146	50	410	198	Italian
Luzern	114	38	214	434	Swiss
Zürich	88	29	143	406	Swiss
Chiemsee	82	15	74	518	German
Lugano	51	35	288	271	Italian–Swiss
Attersee	46	20	171	467	Austrian

were investigated in 1926. The increasing pollution of Lake Zürich brought attention to chemical and biological changes, and, by the late 20th century, a number of institutes were studying the pollution of the Alpine lakes.

The water composition of the Alpine lakes is quite uniform. The chief constituent in solution (up to 96 percent) is bicarbonate associated with calcium or, to a lesser degree, with magnesium. Different amounts of brown humic (derived from organic decay) substances cause colour shifts from blue toward green to olive or brown-green.

About 100 years ago almost all the Alpine lakes were poor in plant nutrients, especially in phosphates. During the 20th century, many lakes were manured by the water wastes from households and hotels. The phosphorus content increased causing algae known as phytoplankton to multiply, a process called eutrophication. The extreme growth of phytoplankton under these conditions makes the water turbid and less suitable for bathing. It also intensifies oxygen consumption in the deep layers of the lake as a result of the increased decomposition of dead algae. In extreme cases the spawn of some fish species developing near the bottom can be endangered.

Two methods are used to correct eutrophication. In Switzerland organic substances are removed by mechanical and biological purification and phosphate is eliminated through additional treatment. In Germany pipelines around the lake borders collect the waste water from catchment areas.

Alpine local race, a subgroup, roughly corresponding to a breeding isolate in genetics, of the Caucasoid (European) geographical race, comprising peoples of the Alpine and Balkan regions of Europe and sometimes extended to peoples resembling these in physical type, regardless of genetic relationship. The name Alpine is traditional, having been coined in 1899 by American economist William Zebina Ripley, who classified Europeans into three races or types: Nordic, Alpine, and Mediterranean. The Alpine peoples are physically characterized by rather short stature, round, short head, light skin and brown hair, and heavy body hair. *See also* local race; Caucasoid geographical race.

Alpine orogeny, a mountain-building event that affected a broad segment of southern Europe and the Mediterranean region in Middle Tertiary time (the Tertiary Period began 65,000,000 years ago and ended 2,500,000 years ago). The Alpine orogeny produced intense metamorphism of preexisting rocks, crumpling of rock strata, and uplift accompanied by both normal and thrust faulting. It was responsible for the elevation of the present Alps, from which the name derives, and for the uplifting of plateaus in the Balkan Peninsula and in Corsica and Sardinia. Volcanic activity in England, France, Iceland, and parts of Italy also occurred during the Alpine orogeny.

Alpine skiing, technique that evolved during the late 19th and early 20th century in the mountainous terrain of the Alps in central Europe. The modern Alpine competitive events are the downhill and slalom, the latter on a zigzag course between upright flags. A combination of the results of the two (sometimes the giant slalom as well) is called the Alpine combined.

The Arlberg-Kandahar race, first run in 1928, is the oldest open international competition decided on the results of a downhill and a slalom; it rotates among Mürren, Switz.; St. Anton, Austria; Chamonix, Fr.; Sestriere, Italy; and Garmisch-Partenkirchen, W.Ger. The Fédération Internationale de Ski, world governing body of the sport, first recognized downhill racing in 1930, and the first world downhill and slalom championships were held in 1931. Alpine events were first included in the Olympic Games in 1936.

For world champions, *see* Sporting Record: *Skiing. See also* Olympic Games.

Alpini, Prospero, Alpini also spelled ALPINO (b. Nov. 23, 1553, Marostica, Vicenza—d. Nov. 23, 1616, or Feb. 6, 1617, Padua), physi-

Alpini, engraving
By courtesy of the Ashmolean Museum, Oxford

cian and botanist who is credited with the introduction to Europe of coffee and bananas. While a medical adviser to Giorgio Emo, the Venetian consul in Cairo (1580–83), Alpini made an extensive study of Egyptian and Mediterranean flora. He is reputed to have been the first to fertilize date palms artificially.

Alpini was appointed professor of botany at the University of Padua (1593), where he cultivated several species of oriental plants described in his *De plantis Aegypti liber* (1592; "Book of Egyptian Plants"); included in this work were the first European botanical accounts of coffee, banana, and a genus of the ginger family (Zingiberaceae) that was later named *Alpinia*.

His account of current Egyptian medical practice, *De medicina Aegyptorum* (1591), was a valuable addition to the study of medical history. Alpini's study of Egyptian diseases culminated in his widely acclaimed *De praesagienda vita et morte aegrotontium* (1601; *The Presages of Life and Death in Diseases,* 1746).

Alps, Latin ALPES, in the Roman Empire, small provinces in the western Alps and occupying parts of what is now France, Italy, and Switzerland. The Alpes Maritimae were made a province *c.* 14 BC and included Pedo (Borgo San Dalmazzo in Piedmont) in the Italian foothills as well as Cemenelum (Cimiez, adjoining Nice). They were administered by a prefect, later a procurator, whose main duty was to protect the Via Julia Augusta.

Adjoining the Alpes Maritimae was the province of the Alpes Cottiae, with its capital at Segusio (Susa in Piedmont) and extending west to Eburodunum (Embrun). King Cottius and his son first ruled it early in the 1st century AD, but a procurator was later appointed.

Farther north was a province in Savoy called variously Alpes Graiae, Atrectianae, or Centronicae, with its capital at Forum Claudii Ceutronum (Aime). The entire province was on the transalpine side of the Little St. Bernard (Alpes Graia). All these border areas contained cities that attained Latin rights, a status formally accorded to the whole of the Alpes Maritimae in AD 63.

Alps, great mountain system of south central Europe, extending about 750 mi (1,200 km) in an arc from the Gulf of Genoa of the Mediterranean Sea in the southwest to Vienna in the northeast and covering an area of more than 80,000 sq mi (207,000 sq km).

The following article summarizes information about the Alps. For full treatment, *see* MACROPAEDIA: Europe.

The Alps are divided into western (southeastern France, northwestern Italy), central (north central Italy, southern Switzerland), and eastern (parts of West Germany, Yugoslavia, and Austria) segments, each of which comprises several separate ranges. Geologically belonging to the young folded mountains of the Tertiary Period (2,500,000, to 65,000,000 years ago), much of the Alps' crystalline regions (notably the Matterhorn at 14,691 ft [4,478 m] above sea level) are characterized by high peaks and nearly vertical slopes, while the landscape in limestone regions (the Dolomites of France and Austria) is dominated by huge cliffs and canyons. Elevations average about 6,000 to 8,000 ft, and many peaks rise above 10,000 ft; Mont Blanc (15,771 ft) is the highest. The Alpine relief has been greatly influenced by glacial erosion, which has created great differences in height between mountain summits and adjacent valleys. The Alps, forming a divide between the Atlantic, the Mediterranean, and the Black Sea, give rise to several major European rivers such as the Rhône, the Rhine, and the tributaries of both the Danube and the Po. The mean annual temperature at 6,500 ft is about 32° F (0° C); annual precipitation decreases from 80 in. (2,000 mm) in the outer ranges to about 20 in. in the inner mountains. Glaciers, covering an area of about 1,500 sq mi, are generally found at elevations above 10,000 ft; the largest (more than 50 sq mi) is the Aletsch Glacier in southwestern Switzerland.

Deciduous trees (beech, birch) predominate at lower elevations up to 5,000 ft; coniferous (spruce, pine, fir) in the middle (6,000 ft) zone; and Alpine meadows (grasses, flowers, and shrubs) are found up to 8,000 ft. The higher Alpine zone (above 10,000 ft) is one of rock and permanent snow devoid of vegetation. Several national parks and reserves in the Alps ensure the preservation of native fauna (ibex, chamois, marmot, mountain hare, and golden eagle). The new St. Gotthard Tunnel (1980), at St. Gotthard Pass in southern Switzerland, was the world's longest highway tunnel (10.1 mi [16.3 km]) at its completion. Grenoble, Fr., Innsbruck, Austria, and Bolzano, Italy, are the major Alpine cities.

Alpujarra rug, handwoven floor covering with pile in loops, made in Spain in the Alpujarras district south of Granada. The construction of these rugs makes them more suitable for spreads than for floor use.

The foundation is of linen, and the woollen pile material runs along with the weft, each colour pulled up above the surface in loops

Alpujarra rug from Spain, 1766; in the Hispanic Society of America, New York City

By courtesy of the Hispanic Society of America, New York City; photograph, Margaret E. Jackson and Ann Siebert

as needed in the design. This technique may have been long practiced in the area, but surviving examples probably do not predate the 18th century. The patterns, which can best be described as folk art, are varied, and the colouring is strong.

alpwirtschaft, also called ALMWIRTSCHAFT, type of pastoral nomadism that forms a unique economic system in the Alps and involves the migration of livestock between mountain pastures in warm months, and lower elevations the remainder of the year. In German, *Alp*, or *Alm*, means mountain pasture and *Wirtschaft* means domestic economy. Some scholars consider alpwirtschaft to be a limited type of pastoral nomadism subsumed under a broader form known as transhumance, which includes migration within and between regions.

Alpwirtschaft, often called the old mountain economy, developed because many of the mountain valleys, occupied by villages and cropland, did not provide sufficient land for livestock grazing. The seasonal migration of livestock to different elevations throughout the year was introduced to compensate for the lack of pasture at lower elevations. During the winter the livestock are fed hay and herded between a farmstead in a lower valley and a low mountain farm located at a slightly higher elevation. In the spring, summer, and autumn, the livestock are herded between a lower mountain farm, upland farms, and upland pastures located at the highest elevations. The pastures may be privately owned, shared by neighbours, leased to tenant farmers, or communal. At the lower elevations grazing is supplemented by hay, while pasture at the higher elevations provides ample growth for grazing. At the various elevations of farm and pasture, villages and lodges are located to accommodate the partial or total migration of farmers, herders, and their families.

The location of new industries in many mountain valleys has caused many families to seek industrial employment while retaining their mountain residence. Thus, fewer families participate in the seasonal migration and more pastures have been abandoned; many of the less accessible pastures have been converted into resorts.

Alre (France): *see* Auray.

Als, German ALSEN, island (area 121 sq mi [312 sq km]), in the Little Belt (strait), Sønderjyllands *amtskommune* (county), Denmark, separated from the Sundeved peninsula of southern Jutland by the narrow Als Sund (sound). Fertile clay loams support mixed agriculture, fruit growing, and dairy farming. The earliest known specimen of a northern European boat (*c.* 300 BC) was discovered there in 1921. Als passed with North Schleswig to Germany in 1864 and was returned to Denmark by plebiscite in 1920. Sønderborg is the principal city, dating from the 12th century; other towns are Nordborg and Augustenborg. Nordborg is the site of one of Denmark's premier industrial companies, Danfoss, which produces heating and refrigerating plants. Pop. (1981 est.) 56,821.

Alsace, planning region (French *région de programme*), encompassing the northeastern French *départements* of Haut-Rhin and Bas-Rhin and roughly coextensive with the historic region of Alsace. The capital is Strasbourg. The region has an area of 3,208 sq mi (8,310 sq km) and is bounded by the *départements* of Moselle, Meurthe-et-Moselle, and Vosges to the west. The Territoire de Belfort lies to the southwest, Switzerland to the south, and the Federal Republic of Germany to the east and northeast.

The following article summarizes the political history, geography, demographic patterns, and economy of modern Alsace; for additional treatment of its geography and history, *see* MACROPAEDIA: France.

Occupied by the Romans in the 1st century AD, Alsace became a Frankish duchy in the 5th century. From the 10th to the 17th century, it was part of the Holy Roman Empire. During that period, its territory was divided into a number of secular and ecclesiastical lordships and municipalities, which remained significant until the French Revolution. The medieval period was also marked by the growing importance of its cities; *e.g.*, Strasbourg, Colmar, and Haguenau, which, with the support of the emperors, gradually freed themselves from their feudal overlords.

Protestantism made important gains in Alsace during the Reformation, and Strasbourg, where the reformer Martin Bucer was especially prominent, became a centre of humanistic learning. Catholicism remained strong in areas controlled by the Habsburgs and was later reinforced by France.

French influence, which first gained importance in the 16th century, became dominant in the 17th. The Peace of Westphalia (1648) gave France an informal protectorate over the area, and full control was established during the reign of Louis XIV. In the 18th century, Alsace enjoyed considerable autonomy under the French crown. The administrative incorporation of Alsace into France was completed by the French Revolution, when its existence as a separate province was ended.

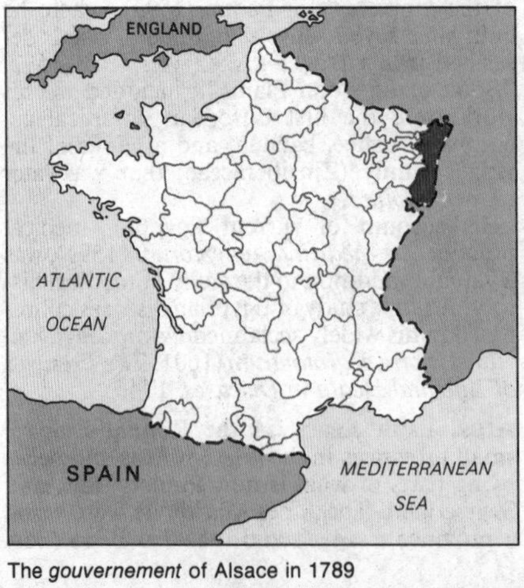

The *gouvernement* of Alsace in 1789

The massif (mountain region) of the Vosges lies in the west and gradually gives way eastward to the plain of Alsace. The region of Sundgau in southern Haut-Rhin belongs to the Jura Mountains. Annual precipitation is relatively low, ranging from 20 to 28 in. (500 to 700 mm).

Alsace is densely populated. Despite a well-developed agricultural and light industrial (textile) economy, the population grew by only 2 percent between 1921 and 1946 (principally because of the consequences of World War II) but subsequently increased at a rate above the French national average. Immigration to this attractive region and a relatively high birth rate have accounted for the increase. Approximately one-half of the population is concentrated in the three main cities, Strasbourg, Colmar, and Mulhouse. Outside the Vosges massif the countryside is densely populated, with the result that farms and other landholdings tend to be small and fragmented.

Viticulture thrives on these small farms; Riesling and Gewürztraminer white wines are internationally known and produced for export. Colmar is the principal centre of the wine-growing region, which is concentrated in the hills ringing the Vosges. Industrial crops are widely cultivated and include sugar beets, hops, and tobacco.

The heavier industries are concentrated in Haut-Rhin. The Grand Canal d'Alsace, which channels the Rhine River for hydroelectric power and transportation, has encouraged the development of industries in the plain of Alsace. Manufactures include textiles, electrical appliances, and chemicals. There is a nuclear power plant at Fessenheim in Haut-Rhin. Pop. (1982) 1,556,048.

Alsace-Lorraine, German ELSASS-LOTHRINGEN, area comprising the present French *départements* of Haut-Rhin, Bas-Rhin, and Moselle.

Between 1871 and 1945, possession of Alsace-Lorraine was disputed by France and Germany. Because of its large German-speaking population, this territory (which included all of the traditional province of Alsace and part of Lorraine) was incorporated into the German Empire after France's defeat in the Franco-German War (1870–71). Its loss was a major cause of anti-German feeling in France in the period 1871–1914.

German rule was initially unpopular in Alsace-Lorraine, and many residents who considered themselves French emigrated. Classified as a *Reichsland* (imperial state), the area was without effective self-government until 1902. Thereafter, especially with the grant of a constitution in 1911, some progress was made toward Germanization.

Alsace-Lorraine was returned to France after World War I in 1919. In the 1920s it developed a strong "home rule" movement, unsuccessfully seeking autonomy within the French Republic, whose anticlerical policies were especially unpopular with Alsatian Catholics. Reannexed by Germany during World War II, it was again returned to France in 1945. Since then many of the prewar government policies that had clashed with the region's particularism have been modified, and the autonomist movement has largely disappeared.

Alsatian (dog): *see* German shepherd.

Alsen (Denmark): *see* Als.

Alster River, tributary of the Elbe River in northern West Germany; it rises 4 mi (6 km) southeast of Kaltenkirchen and flows generally south for 30 mi to Hamburg, where a dam was built in the early Middle Ages. The river then continues to the Elbe in two parallel canals, which mark the division between the newer (since 17th century) part of Hamburg to the west and the older section to the east. A lake formed behind the dam is separated into two parts by fortifications built in the early 17th century to help preserve the city's independence through the Thirty Years' War. The southern portion is called Binnenalster (Inner Alster) and the northern, Aussenalster (Outer Alster).

Alston, Walter (Emmons), byname WALT, or SMOKEY, ALSTON (b. Dec. 1, 1911, Venice, Ohio, U.S.—d. Oct. 1, 1984, Oxford, Ohio), professional National League baseball manager whose career with the Los Angeles (formerly Brooklyn) Dodgers was the third longest for managers after Connie Mack and John McGraw.

Alston learned baseball from his father and earned his nickname Smokey as a pitcher for his high school team. At Miami University (Oxford, Ohio; B.S. 1935), he was a hard hitting infielder. He was signed to a contract by the St. Louis Cardinals as a shortstop, played on their minor league teams (1935–40), and managed in the minor leagues (1940–42). He appeared in one major league game with the Cardinals in 1936, where he made one putout, one error, batted once, and struck out. During the winters he was a basketball coach and teacher at high schools near Darrtown, Ohio. In 1944 Alston moved to the Dodger organization as a minor league player-manager (1944–47) and manager thereafter until 1953, when he became the Dodgers' manager. As a minor league manager he developed such later Dodger stars as Don Newcombe, Roy Campanella, Carl Erskine, and Junior Gilliam. He had managed every player on his first 25-man roster. As a Dodgers manager he won seven pennants and four of the seven World Series they played in. The 1955 World Series victory was the Dodgers' first.

Alston retired after the 1976 season. His *A Year at a Time*, written with Jack Tobin, was published in 1976. The title refers to Alston's one-year contracts with the Dodgers; the manager who preceded him had insisted in vain on a two-year contract. He was elected to the Baseball Hall of Fame in 1983.

alstonite, colourless, transparent to translucent barium, calcium carbonate mineral, $CaBa(CO_3)_2$, with minor amounts of strontium. Its structure is of the aragonite (*q.v.*) type with barium and calcium in nine-fold coordination but ordered within layers; the layers can in turn be arranged in various stacking sequences, resulting in a complex structure. Alstonite is found in association with calcite, barite, and witherite as low-temperature hydrothermal deposits. For detailed physical properties, *see* carbonate mineral (table).

Alta Gracia Island (Nicaragua): *see* Ometepe Island.

Alta Verapaz, department, north central Guatemala, bounded on the west by the Río Salinas. Although much of the territory of 3,354 sq mi (8,686 sq km) lies in the Sierra de Chama and the Sierra de las Minas, it also contains lowlands in the south between the two ranges and in the north.

Highlands in Alta Verapaz department near Panajachel, Guatemala
Carl Frank

In the late 19th century German immigrants were granted land for planting coffee. Though they came to dominate commerce shortly thereafter, when Guatemala entered World War II on the side of the Allies those who had retained German citizenship were expelled and their plantations nationalized. The distinctive Indian-German features resulting from intermarriage are gradually disappearing. Most of the inhabitants live in the highlands, in which there are coffee plantations. Other crops include corn (maize), beans, sugarcane, and cacao; cattle raising is widespread. From the forests of the north come chicle, vanilla, and various woods. Oil has been found near Rubelsanto. The main route to Cobán (*q.v.*), the departmental capital, and to other settlements is via road and rail to the Polochic River and Lake Izabal to Lívingston, on Bahía (bay) de Amatique. The earthquake of 1976 caused much damage to buildings and roads but little loss of life. Pop. (1981 prelim.) 322,132.

Altagracia, La, province, southeastern Dominican Republic, bounded on the northeast by the Atlantic Ocean, on the east by the Mona Passage, and on the south by the Caribbean Sea. Its area of 1,191 sq mi (3,084 sq km) occupies the rolling plains of the extreme eastern Dominican Republic and includes Isla (island) Saona, off the Caribbean coast. It is a leading sugar-producing and cotton-raising centre. Higüey (*q.v.*) is the provincial capital. Pop. (1981) 100,112.

Altai (Russian S.F.S.R.): *see* Altay.

Altai Mountains, Russian ALTAY, complex mountain system of Central Asia extending approximately 1,000 mi (1,600 km) in a southeast–northwest direction from the Gobi (Desert) to the West Siberian Plain, through Chinese, Mongolian, and Soviet territory.

The following article summarizes information about the Altai Mountains; for full treatment, *see* MACROPAEDIA: Asia.

The jagged mountain system, whose name is derived from the Turkish-Mongolian *altan*, meaning "golden," divides the waters of such great rivers as the Ob, flowing northward to the Arctic, from those draining into the vast Central Asian interior basin. There are three main branches of the system (south to north)—the Gobi, Mongol, and Soviet Altai. The highest ridges tower more than 13,000 ft (4,000 m), running latitudinally in the central and eastern portions of the Soviet sector. The Soviet peak Belukha rises to 14,783 ft (4,506 m), the highest point in the range.

The Soviet and Mongol Altai are criss-crossed by a network of turbulent, youthful rivers, fed mainly by melted snow and summer rains; among the largest are the Katun, Bukhtarma, and Biya. Rivers of the Gobi Altai are shorter, shallower, and often frozen in the winter and dry in the summer. There are more than 3,500 lakes throughout the system, most of structural or glacial origin. The regional climate is severely continental with long, bitterly cold winters and, on the lower slopes, very warm summers. Precipitation is high throughout the year on the exposed western mountain ridges but decreases substantially to the east.

There are four fairly distinct vegetation zones in the Altai: mountain subdesert, mountain steppe, mountain forest, and the Alpine regions. About 70 percent of the Soviet Altai territory is covered by mountain forests of conifers, birches, aspens, and larches; forests in the Mongol and Gobi Altai, however, are practically nonexistent. Animal life follows the vegetation patterns. Many species of small rodents populate the mountainous subdeserts and steppes. Siberian animals such as bear, lynx, and musk deer frequent the moist coniferous forests, while mountain goat, snow leopard, and mountain sheep inhabit the Alpine regions.

The Altai are notable for their mining and hydroelectric potential. The mountains contain exploitable deposits of iron, mercury, gold, manganese, and tungsten that have a high commercial value. The development of agriculture and livestock production is resulting in more settled ways of life, especially among the nomadic herders in the dry southern Mongol Altai. An increasing number of health resorts are developing around the region's mineral springs, and the picturesque mountain peaks and lakes are attracting a growing number of tourists.

Altaic languages, grouping of three language families—Turkic, Mongolian, and Manchu-Tungus—that show similarities in vocabulary, grammatical structure, and certain phonological features. They are considered by many linguists to be genetically related. There are more than 40 Altaic languages, with more than 90,000,000 speakers; Turkish is probably the best known language in the group.

A brief treatment of the Altaic languages follows. For full treatment, *see* MACROPAEDIA: Languages of the World.

Altaic languages are native to populations inhabiting areas that cover a huge expanse of the Asian continent (including large sections of such countries as the U.S.S.R., Mongolia, China, Turkey, Iran, and Afghanistan) as well as parts of Europe. There is disagreement regarding the genealogy of some of the languages, and questions remain unanswered as to whether or not they truly constitute a larger family; but, whether genetically or simply historically related, the so-called Altaic languages—named after the Altai Mountains—do include the three basic language families noted above.

Turkic is spoken by the majority of Altaic peoples. Turkish, the major language of the Turkic family—and, indeed, of all the Altaic languages—is spoken in Turkey as well as in parts of the Balkans, Cyprus, the U.S.S.R., and Arab countries, and other countries. Other major languages in this Turkic group include Uzbek, Uighur, Azerbaijani, Tatar, and Kazakh. Turkic languages are recognizably related, though comprehension between speakers of the different languages is at best difficult and, in several cases, impossible.

Mongol, the language spoken by the majority of Mongolian speakers, usually refers to the language itself, whereas Mongolian refers to the family of languages; the terminology is, however, interchangeable. Characteristics of contemporary Mongolian languages such as Mongol, Buryat, and Kalmyk are mutually recognizable; but mutual comprehension in this family is decreasing, particularly in isolated areas and in areas where dialects are nonwritten.

Of the Manchu-Tungus languages and dialects, Manchu was the most important, spoken by some 2,800,000 people. This figure is based on ethnic studies, however, and the Manchu language itself is considered to be almost extinct. Other languages of the Manchu, or Southern group, are spoken in parts of China and the U.S.S.R. The Tungus languages, or Northern group, are spoken by several thousand people, primarily in the U.S.S.R. and China. Differences between the Manchu and Tungus language groups are extreme.

Altaic languages are characterized by a richness in vowels, with only specific combinations of vowels or vowels and consonants occurring. The resulting effect is one of sound harmony and is most noticeable in Turkic and Mongolian. Grammatical characteristics include agglutination, the formation of words by adding suffixes to the roots: rules for governing the order of suffixes added are specific, but the number of suffixes that may be added to a root is not fixed. There are no definite articles, no genders, and no prepositions. There are major differences in syntax between the three Altaic language families, but all share common features. Manchu-Tungus languages show considerable syntactic freedom compared to the Turkic and Mongolian. Of the three language families, vocabulary relationships are most evident between Turkic and Mongolian.

Altaic people probably first inhabited an area between Tibet and China, extending northward into Siberia. They were nomadic, the Turkic and Mongolian peoples evidently travelling much greater distances than the Manchu-Tungus. The first Altaic linguistic records are from the 8th century AD, making any earlier comparative investigation of the languages exceedingly difficult. There is evidence that a variety of writing systems were used, the first-known being that of the Turkic peoples and probably of Semitic origin. The first dated Turkic records, known as the Orkhon Inscriptions, are from Inner Asia. Early Mongolian language records date from 1225, and an important document, the *Secret History of the Mongols,* was written during the same century. The Manchu language is the only one in the Manchu-Tungus family that has linguistic records. The earliest documentation is from the 17th century, reflecting the powerful Manchu rule in China during that time until the early 20th century.

Changes in the Altaic languages have been striking since the period following World War I. New political entities were formed after this war, and their survival made written reforms of the languages essential; in cases where the people were illiterate, new literary languages had to be developed—*e.g.,* Mongolian Buryat was not developed as a literary language until the 1930s. A course of action for linguistic improvement and consolidation was successfully undertaken throughout the Altaic-speaking countries. Changes in Mongolia, the U.S.S.R., and Turkey are particularly evident today, with the latter country showing specific and remarkable reforms: a great emphasis was placed on vocabulary renewal during this period, and this, along with other efforts to modernize the language, resulted in the development of an essentially new literary language based on the previously existing national language.

A list of the abbreviations used in the MICROPAEDIA *will be found at the end of this volume*

Altair, also called ALPHA AQUILAE, one of the 15 brightest stars, the brightest star in the constellation Aquila, with an apparent visual magnitude of 0.77. Its distance from the Earth is about 16 light-years. It is a hot white star somewhat larger and more massive than the Sun and giving out about 10 times as much light. The name probably derives from Arabic words meaning "the eagle," applied to the constellation.

Altaisky Nature Reserve, natural area set aside for research in the natural sciences, in the northern Altai Mountains and bordering Lake Teletsky on the east, south central Russian Soviet Federated Socialist Republic. The reserve, established in 1932, has current boundaries that date from 1963 and an area of 2,134,740 ac (863,900 ha). Its physiographic features include high mountains with glacially produced landforms, high mountain forest, and mountain steppe. The vegetation of the reserve is mostly forest of Siberian silver fir and pine; larch and mixed forests of aspen are also present. The higher elevations have alpine meadows and thickets of rhododendron. Wildlife includes Altai pika, Siberian chipmunk, and Arctic ground squirrel, in the mountain steppe; sable and red deer in the mountain forests; and reindeer and wild sheep in the high mountain regions. Tourism is limited to occasional guided visits.

Altamira, cave famous for its magnificent prehistoric paintings and engravings, situated 30 kilometres (19 miles) west of Santander, in northern Spain. The cave, discovered by a hunter in 1868, was visited in 1875 by Marcelino de Sautuola, a nobleman from Santander, who found animal bones and flint implements there. Sautuola returned in the summer of 1879 and on one visit was accompanied by his little daughter Maria; it was she

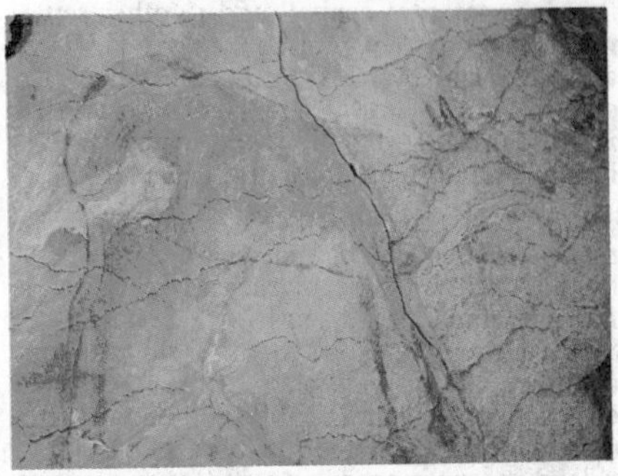

Magdalenian cave painting of a deer, Altamira, Spain
Archivo Mas, Barcelona

who first noticed paintings of bulls (actually bison) on the ceiling. Convinced of the antiquity of the paintings and the objects, Sautuola published descriptions of his finds in 1880. Both Spanish and foreign experts, however, dismissed the paintings as forgeries, and not until the first decade of the 20th century were they accepted as genuine.

The Altamira cave is 270 metres (890 feet) long. In the vestibule numerous archaeological remains belonging to the Aurignacian (Perigordian), upper Solutrean, and lower or middle Magdalenian periods were found, including ceremonial staves and engraved animal shoulder blades. The great lateral chamber that contains most of the paintings measures 18 metres by 9 metres, the height of the vault varying from 1.15 metres to 2.65 metres. The roof of the chamber is covered with paintings, chiefly of bison, executed in a magnificent, vivid polychrome of red, black, and violet tones. There are also two wild boars, some horses, a hind, and some other figures in a simpler style; in addition, there are eight engraved anthropomorphic figures, various handprints, and hand outlines. The other galleries contain numerous black-painted or engraved figures. In many cases, the creator of the designs exploited the natural contours of the rock surface.

Altamsh (Indian sultan): *see* Iltutmish.

Altamura, town, Bari province, Puglia (Apulia) region, southeastern Italy, on the Murge plateau at 1,552 ft (473 m) above sea level, southwest of Bari. It was founded *c.* 1200 by the emperor Frederick II, who created several new towns in Apulia, to which he attracted Saracens and Jews by grants of privileges for their aid in his struggle against the barons. The town is surrounded by the medieval high wall (*alta mura*) from which it takes its name. The Romanesque Cathedral of the Assumption, begun in 1232 by Frederick, has been restored several times. The richly carved portal and central rose window in its facade are notable. The Pulo di Altamura, about 4 mi (6 km) away, is a limestone abyss, 1,640 ft across and 246 ft deep.

Cattle and cereals are the chief products of the district, which also produces almonds and wine. There is a wool market in the town. Pop. (1981 prelim.) mun., 51,328.

Altan, also called ANDA (d. 1583, Mongolia), Mongol khan, or chief, who terrorized China during the 16th century. He converted the Mongols to the reformed, or Dge-lugs-pa (Yellow Hat), sect of Tibetan Buddhism. Altan became chief of the eastern Mongols in 1543 and thereafter posed a constant threat to the northern borders of China under the Ming dynasty (1368–1644). In 1550 he led his forces across the Great Wall, which marked China's northwest border, and raided the outskirts of the capital at Peking. But he was forced to withdraw back into Mongolia a few days later.

Altan soon began his effort to create a stable system of government in his homeland. Using captured Chinese deserters, he set up a bureaucratic administration in the Chinese style, establishing his capital at Kuku-khoto (Blue City), just beyond the Great Wall. He also concluded a peace treaty with the Chinese in 1571, under which Altan was allowed to exchange horses for textiles. The Chinese also honoured him with the title of Shun-i Wang (Obedient and Righteous Prince).

In 1580 Altan was host to the head of the Dge-lugs-pa. Yellow Hat Buddhism was made the official religion of Altan's rule, and the head of the sect was given the title of Dalai Lama, a title implying spiritual primacy. Altan's own grandson became the new Dalai Lama when the head of the Dge-lugs-pa died. With Mongol military aid, later Dalai Lamas crushed the more established Karma-pa (Red or Black Hat) sect in Tibet and became the spiritual and, finally, temporal rulers of that country.

altar, in religion, surface at or on which sacrifice is offered or that is used as a centre for worship or ritual. In primitive religions a natural rock, a stone or heap of stones, or

Israelite horned limestone altar from Megiddo, 10th–9th century BC
By courtesy of the Department of Antiquities, Ministry of Education and Culture, Jerusalem

a mound of earth probably sufficed for this purpose. With the development of the institution of sacrifice in sanctuaries and temples, more elaborate structures were built of stone or brick on which the victim was killed and its blood channelled off or its flesh burned. A trench or pit often was used for offerings to the dead, to divinities, and to the heroes, as, for example, in Greek temples; or an altar might take the form of a table on which food was placed for the deity. In some religions no altars are used; the sacrifice is simply placed on the ground or thrown into the water.

Altar of Augustan Peace: *see* Ara Pacis.

Altare glass, type of Italian glassware produced in the town of Altare, near Genoa. The Altare glass industry was established in the

11th century, by glassmakers from Normandy and developed independently of the much better known glassworks of Venice. During the 15th century the great demand for Venetian glass and, consequently, its profitability led the Venetians to confine glassmakers under pain of death to the island of Murano in an effort to protect their secret techniques. Altare, however, manufactured glassware that was virtually identical to Venetian glass and often sold as such. The rapid spread of Venetian styles and glassmaking techniques can be largely attributed to Altare craftsmen. Unlike their Venetian counterparts, the Altare glassmakers were encouraged to work elsewhere. They, together with a few hundred Venetians who escaped from Murano, helped establish glassworks in many European countries. Their work led to the development of an international style known as *façon de Venise* (*q.v.*) during the 16th and 17th centuries. *See also* Venetian glass.

altarpiece, a structure above the altar table adorned with holy personages, saints, and biblical subjects. The term reredos is used for an ornamental screen, or partition, not directly attached to the altar table but affixed to the wall behind it. A diptych is an altarpiece consisting of two panels, a triptych one of three panels, and a polyptych one of four or more panels. Some of the finest paintings, reliefs, and sculptures in the round have been used in altarpieces. One of the earliest known painted panels, possibly dating to the 11th century, is the triptych of the "Saviour Between the Virgin and St. John" in the cathedral at Tivoli, Italy. One of the most famous is "The Adoration of the Lamb," also known as the "Ghent Altarpiece" (cathedral of Saint-Bavon, Ghent), a polyptych in 12 panels painted by Hubert and Jan van Eyck in 1432. *See also* retable.

Altay, also spelled ALTAI, *kray* (territory), southwestern Siberia, Russian Soviet Federated Socialist Republic, covering 101,050 sq mi (261,700 sq km) in the basin of the upper Ob River and its headstreams, the Biya and Katun. It borders Mongolia and China in the southeast.

Once part of the khanate of Dzungaria, the *kray* was colonized by the Russians from the 18th century. The northern and northwestern parts of the *kray* consist of rolling plain and mountain foreland, with steppe and forest-steppe vegetation. The southern part, which forms the Gorno-Altay autonomous *oblast* (region), consists of forested mountain ranges and high plateaus, with wide intermontane basins and deeply incised valleys. The northern steppes are almost entirely under cultivation, with wheat, oats, and corn (maize) the chief crops, together with sunflowers, flax, hemp, and sugar beets. The mountains provide grazing for large herds of cattle and sheep. Nonferrous ores—copper, zinc, lead, silver, mercury, barium, tungsten, and gold—are mined, chiefly around Zmeinogorsk and Gornyak. Light engineering, chemicals, and timbering are developed in the main cities, notably Barnaul (*q.v.*), the administrative centre. Kamen-na-Obi has been designed as the site for a dam and hydroelectric station to make possible the irrigation of a vast area of the Kulunda Steppe. Pop. (1983 est.) 2,712,000.

Altay Mountains (Central Asia): *see* Altai Mountains.

Altdorf, capital of Uri canton, central Switzerland, near the confluence of the Reuss River and the Schächen torrent, southeast of Luzern. In the centre of the town a bronze statue of William Tell (1895) marks the place at which, according to tradition, he shot, with his crossbow, an apple from his son's head. In 1899 a theatre was opened for the annual performance of Friedrich Schiller's play *Wilhelm Tell.* Tell is said to have been born at nearby Bürglen. Landmarks in Altdorf include a Capuchin monastery from 1581, a medieval tower, and the town church and town hall, both rebuilt after 1799. The town is on the St. Gotthard railway line and has cable and rubber works and a federal ammunition factory. The population is mostly Roman Catholic and German speaking. Pop. (1980) 8,230.

William Tell statue, Altdorf, Switz.
By courtesy of the Swiss National Tourist Office

Altdorfer, Albrecht (b. *c.* 1480—d. 1538, Imperial Free City of Regensburg), German painter and engraver who was one of the founders of landscape painting.

Altdorfer spent most of his life in Regensburg, becoming a citizen in 1505 and in later years official architect of the city and a member of its inner council. As the guiding spirit of the Danube school of painting, he was the first European to paint forests, sunsets, and picturesque ruins, in which he represented man as part of nature, allied with trees, rocks, mountains, and clouds and often resembling them. Several of his altar panels in the church of St. Florian near Linz, completed in 1518, depicting the Passion of Christ and the martyrdom of St. Sebastian, were night scenes in which Altdorfer exploited the possibilities of torch light, star light, or twilight with unusual brilliance. His masterpiece of dramatic illumination was the "Battle of Alexander at Issus" (1529; Alte Pinakothek, Munich). The fantastic element that pervaded his paintings was also prominent in his drawings, most of which were done with black and white lines on brown or blue-gray paper. His engravings and woodcuts, usually miniatures, were distinguished by their playful imaginativeness, the most important being 40 plates entitled "The Fall and Redemption of Man." In 1530 he began using the new medium of etching to produce nine landscapes and a series of fanciful tankards intended as work models for goldsmiths.

"Birth of the Virgin," painting by Albrecht Altdorfer; in the Alte Pinakothek, Munich
By courtesy of the Bayerische Staatsgemaldesammlungen, Munich

Altenburg, city, Leipzig *Bezirk* (district), southern East Germany, on the Pleisse River, at the southern edge of the central German brown-coal deposits, south of Leipzig. Mentioned in 976 as the site of a watchtower near an old Slav fortress, it was a trading centre and royal residence in the 12th century. It passed to the Saxon House of Wettin in 1243 and was the capital of the Duchy of Saxe-Altenburg in 1603–72 and 1826–1918. The city is known as the birthplace of the three-handed card game Skat. There is a playing card museum in the old ducal castle and a fountain with sculptures of Skat players. Notable buildings include the castle church, the town hall (1562–64), and the 15th-century St. Bartholomew Church. The Lindenau Museum has a large art collection.

There are training schools for teachers, papermakers, and railway men. Aside from playing cards, Altenburg makes sewing machines, hats, and cigars and has the only drumskin tannery in East Germany. Pop. (1981 est.) 55,468.

alternating current, abbreviation AC, flow of electric charge that periodically reverses; it starts, say, from zero, grows to a maximum, decreases to zero, reverses, reaches a maximum in the opposite direction, returns again to the original value, and repeats this cycle indefinitely. The interval of time between the attainment of a definite value on two successive cycles is called the period; the number of cycles or periods per second is the frequency, and the maximum value in either direction is the amplitude of the alternating current. Low frequencies, such as 50 and 60 cycles per second (hertz), are used for domestic and commercial power, but alternating currents of frequencies around 100,000,000 cycles per second (100 megahertz) are used in television and of several thousand megahertz in radar or microwave communication. *See also* electric current.

alternation of generations, also called METAGENESIS, or HETEROGENESIS, in biology, the alternation of a sexual phase and an asexual phase in the life cycle of an organism. The two phases, or generations, are often morphologically, and sometimes chromosomally, distinct.

In algae, fungi, mosses, ferns, and seed plants, alternation of generations is common; it is not always easy to observe, however, since one or the other of the generations is often very small, even microscopic. The sexual phase, called the gametophyte, produces gametes, or sex cells; the asexual phase, or sporophyte, produces spores asexually. In terms of chromosomes, the gametophyte has a single (*i.e.,* monoploid, or haploid) set, and the sporophyte has a double (diploid) set.

Among animals, many invertebrates have an alternation of sexual and asexual generations (*e.g.,* protozoans, jellyfish, flatworms), but alternation of haploid and diploid generations is unknown.

Altgeld, John Peter (b. Dec. 30, 1847, Niederselters, Prussia—d. March 12, 1902, Joliet, Ill., U.S.), reformist Democratic governor of Illinois (1893–97) known principally for his

Altgeld

By courtesy of the Chicago Historical Society

pardon (June 26, 1893) of German-American anarchists involved in the Haymarket Riot at a labour protest meeting in which seven Chicago policemen were killed at Haymarket Square on May 4, 1886.

Altgeld's German parents immigrated to Ohio, where he was reared. In the 1870s he moved to Chicago, where he soon accumulated a small fortune in real estate. He early revealed his sympathy for the poor and deprived in a small treatise on crime, *Our Penal Machinery and Its Victims* (1884). He threw himself into Democratic politics and was elected to the superior court of Cook County (1886–91). Associating himself with the public demand for reform legislation, he won his party's nomination for governor (1892) and was elected by the farm and labour vote.

The following year he was petitioned by the noted criminal attorney Clarence Darrow, labour leaders, and others to grant clemency to three of the men convicted of complicity in the Haymarket Riot. Studying the transcript of the case, Altgeld concluded that the prisoners had not been given a fair trial on the grounds that the judge was prejudiced, the jury packed, and that to convict anyone of "constructive" conspiracy to incite to murder was a miscarriage of justice. His reasoning was hailed by labour leaders and has since gained wide credence in judicial circles. At the time, however, his decision evoked an outcry by both business and the conservative press, which branded the governor as a friend to anarchists. A year later, Altgeld's protest to Pres. Grover Cleveland against the use of federal troops in the Pullman Strike produced further vitriolic attacks. The furor over these incidents obscured Altgeld's numerous achievements as governor, such as improvements in the penal system and child labour legislation, and led to his defeat for reelection in 1896. Upon leaving office, he returned to the practice of law in partnership with Clarence Darrow. A standard biography is *Eagle Forgotten; The Life of John Peter Altgeld* (1938) by Harry Barnard.

Althiburos, modern ABBAH QUŞŪR, or EBBA KSOUR, ancient city of Numidia in North Africa, on the road constructed by Hadrian in AD 123, between Carthage and Theveste (Tabassah) in what is now Tunisia. The town, originally an indigenous settlement, obtained municipal rights from Hadrian.

Althiburos enjoyed considerable prosperity in the 2nd and 3rd centuries AD, and was the seat of a bishop from about 400 to 700 AD. Archaeological excavations have uncovered a well-preserved triumphal arch and the ancient forum with its surrounding buildings, including two temples, an arch erected in honour of Hadrian, and a theatre.

althorn: *see* tenor horn.

Althorp, John Charles Spencer, Viscount: *see* Spencer, John Charles Spencer, 3rd Earl.

Althusius, Johannes (Latin), German JOHANNES ALTHAUS (b. 1557, Diedenshausen, Wittgenstein-Berleberg—d. Aug. 12, 1638, Emden, Holland), Dutch Calvinist political theorist who was the intellectual father of modern federalism and an advocate of popular sovereignty.

After philosophic and legal studies in Switzerland, Althusius was a professor at the University of Herborn in Nassau until 1604, when he became syndic of the town of Emden in the Dutch province of Friesland. Author of a noted general treatise on Roman law, as well as other legal essays, his principal work was the *Politica methodice digesta atque exemplis sacris et profanis illustrata* (1603, enlarged 1610 and 1614), a systematized tract on all forms of human association. Seeking to bring the study of politics into line with Calvinist doctrine, he particularly sought to use the Hebrew Bible in the development of political theory.

While reflecting Calvinist puritanism, Althusius stressed that each social group is to be justified by providing a full and happy life to its members.

For several centuries interest in Althusius was slight until he was rediscovered early in the 20th century by Otto von Gierke.

Altichiero (b. *c.* 1330, Zevio, near Verona, March of Verona—d. after 1390, Verona?), early Renaissance painter who was the effective founder of the Veronese school and perhaps the most significant northern Italian artist of the 14th century. He began his career in Verona, where he remained for a number of years, although nothing is known of his work from this period. In 1370 he moved to Padua, perhaps at the invitation of Duke Francesco I Carrara, for whom he painted fresco portraits (since destroyed) of "famous men" in the Sala dei Giganti and the Palazzo del Capitano. His main surviving works are two fresco cycles done in Padua. The first (completed 1379), which includes a Crucifixion and scenes from the life of St. James, is in the chapel of S. Felice in the basilica of S. Antonio; the other (*c.* 1384), with scenes from the lives of St. George and other saints, is in the Cappella di S. Giorgio nearby. The style of these frescoes follows that of the great Florentine painter Giotto in the use of monumental, vital, and dramatically related figures.

Altichiero's figures relate more realistically than do Giotto's to landscape and architecture,

"Decapitation of St. George," fresco by Altichiero, *c.* 1384; in the Cappella di S. Giorgio, Padua, Italy

SCALA—Art Resource/EB Inc.

however, and Altichiero shows greater concern with harmonious composition. He sacrifices some of the drama and plastic validity of his scenes to achieve powerful two-dimensional rhythms. Probably in 1390 Altichiero returned to Verona, where he executed a final fresco series in the church of S. Anastasia.

Altieri, Emilio (pope): *see* Clement X.

altimeter, instrument that measures the altitude of the land surface or any object such as an airplane. The two main types are the pressure altimeter, which is an indicator of atmospheric pressure, and the radio altimeter, which measures the time required for a pulse of radio energy to travel from an object in the atmosphere to the ground and back.

The pressure altimeter contains a thin corrugated metallic bellows (aneroid capsule) from which air has been exhausted and that expands or contracts in response to changes in pressure. Because atmospheric pressure decreases with altitude, a pressure versus altitude relationship exists, and any altitude can be determined by measuring the pressure associated with it. By means of an arrangement of levers and gears, the expansion or contraction of the bellows is converted to a rotation of pointers relative to a dial. Because atmospheric pressure is referred to sea level, a pressure altimeter must be kept in adjustment to compensate for variations in barometric pressure caused by weather changes.

The radio altimeter measures the distance of an aircraft above the ground rather than above sea level. A cathode-ray tube indicates the time that a pulse of radio energy takes to travel from the aircraft to the ground and back to the aircraft. The altitude is equal to one-half the time multiplied by the speed of the pulse. Radio altimeters are used in automatic navigation and blind-landing systems.

Another device for measuring altitude utilizes the effect of atmospheric pressure on the boiling point of a liquid. The instrument, known as a hypsometer, consists of a cylindrical vessel in which the liquid (usually water) is boiled, surrounded by a jacketed column

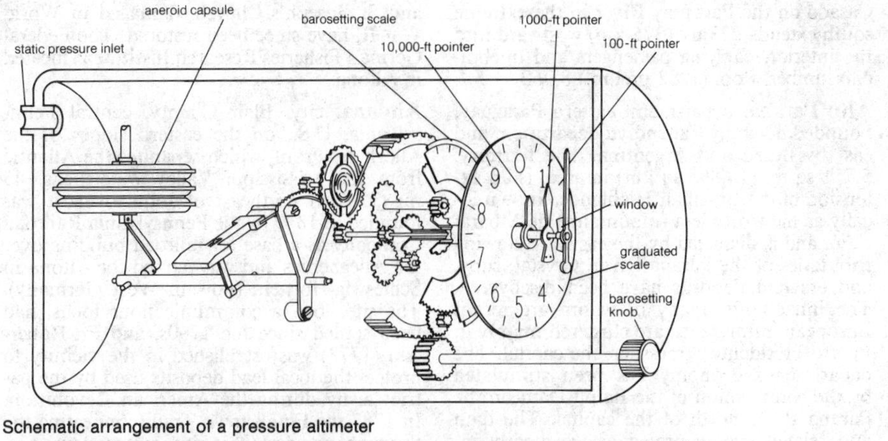

Schematic arrangement of a pressure altimeter

From *McGraw-Hill Encyclopedia of Science and Technology*, Copyright (1971); used with permission of McGraw-Hill Book Co.

through which the vapour circulates around a shielded thermometer; the higher the altitude, the lower the pressure and the lower the temperature at which the liquid boils. The boiling temperature is thus inversely proportional to the altitude.

Altiplano, English HIGH PLAINS, also called PUNA, region of southeastern Peru and western Bolivia, originating northwest of Lake Titicaca in southern Peru and extending about 600 mi

Section of the Altiplano in Potosí department, Bolivia

Reflejo—EB Inc.

(965 km) southeast to the southwestern corner of Bolivia. It is a series of intermontane basins at about 12,000 ft (3,650 m) above sea level, separated by spurs reaching eastward from the Cordillera Occidental. On the eastern side of the Altiplano, however, there is a continuous passageway of gentle gradient extending southward across Bolivia.

The dominant vegetation is low trees or shrubs of the species *Parastrephia lepidophylla* and *Parastrephia phylicaefolia* in the wetter, northeastern areas, and *Psila bolivensis* in the dryer southwest. Wildlife originally included the alpaca and the llama, both now bred by man for wool and serving as pack animals. The southern half of the Altiplano falls within a zone of deficient moisture, while the northern half receives rainfall adequate for the cultivation of crops without irrigation.

Because of the presence of a large body of open water in the Titicaca Basin, temperatures around the shores of Lake Titicaca are more moderate, and corn (maize) and wheat can be grown to an elevation of 12,800 ft. The basin, now the location of urban centres such as Puno and Juliaca, Peru, and La Paz, Bolivia, has been the core of a relatively dense population since ancient times. La Paz, the chief political and commercial city of Bolivia in the Altiplano, is located not far south of Lake Titicaca, at the bottom of a spectacular chasm 1,400 ft below the surface of the Altiplano, but still 11,909 ft above sea level.

The southern half of the Altiplano is much less hospitable to settlement, although its desolate expanses of desert yield important mineral resources including copper, silver, tungsten, and tin. One of Bolivia's main railway lines follows the route provided by the continuous passageway along the eastern edge of the Altiplano, from the southern edge of the Titicaca Basin southward to Oruro, Bolivia, where the line forms two branches, one branch extending to the tin mines of Unicia, Bolivia, in the Cordillera Oriental, and one to the basin of Cochabamba, Bolivia, lower on the eastern slopes.

Altis, in Greek religion, the sacred grove of Zeus, or the sacred precinct in Olympia, Greece. It was an irregular quadrangular area more than 200 yards (183 metres) on each side, and walled except to the north, where it was bounded by the Kronion (hill of Cronus). In it were the temples of Zeus and of Hera, his consort; the principal altars and votive offerings; the small treasuries built by various Dorian states; and the administration buildings for the Olympic Games, which were held nearby. Outside the sacred place were the stadium, hippodrome, baths, and other accommodations for visitors.

altitude and azimuth, in astronomy, gunnery, navigation, and other fields, two coordinates describing the position of an object above the Earth. Altitude in this sense is expressed as angular elevation (up to 90°) above the horizon. Azimuth, in astronomical measurement, is the number of degrees clockwise from due south (usually) to the object's vertical circle (*i.e.,* a great circle through the object and the zenith). For nonastronomical purposes, azimuth (or bearing) is generally measured clockwise from due north.

altitude sickness, also called MOUNTAIN SICKNESS, acute reaction to a change from sea level or other low-altitude environments to altitudes above 8,000 feet. Although most people gradually recover as they adapt to the low atmospheric pressure of high altitude, some persons experience a reaction that can be severe and, unless they return to low altitude, possibly fatal. Much of the reaction is an exaggeration of normal physiological adaptations to the reduced oxygen available at high altitude, such as breathlessness and racing heartbeat. Other manifestations of altitude sickness include giddiness, headache, swelling of the legs and feet, gastrointestinal upsets, and weakness. These usually occur within six hours to four days after arrival at high altitude and may persist for two to five days.

The more serious type of altitude sickness, pulmonary edema, occurs rarely among newcomers to altitude but more often affects those who have already become acclimated to high elevations and are returning after several days at sea level. In pulmonary edema, fluid accumulates in the lungs and prevents the victim from obtaining sufficient oxygen. The symptoms are quickly reversed when oxygen is given and the individual is evacuated to a lower area.

Altitude sickness was not recognized until 1937, but it has become of increasing concern as improved transportation has made it possible for large numbers of tourists to visit previously inaccessible mountain sites high in the Andes, Himalayas, and Rockies. The exact cause of the illness, although presumably related to low atmospheric pressure and lack of oxygen, is not clear; there is evidence that altered hormone secretion may cause some symptoms.

Altizer, Thomas J(onathan) J(ackson) (b. Sept. 28, 1927, Cambridge, Mass., U.S.), radical theologian associated with the Death of God movement (*q.v.*) in the 1960s and 1970s. He insisted "We must recognize that the death of God is a historical event: God has died in our time, in our history, in our existence." His ideas were developed in articles and books, including *Mircea Eliade and the Dialectic of the Sacred* (1963); *The Gospel of Christian Atheism* (1966); and *Radical Theology and the Death of God,* with William Hamilton (1966); *Descent into Hell* (1970), *The Self-Embodiment of God* (1977), and *Total Presence* (1980).

A graduate of the University of Chicago (A.B. 1948, A.M. 1951, Ph.D. 1955), Altizer taught religion first at Wabash College (Crawfordsville, Ind.), from 1954 to 1956, and then at Emory University (Atlanta, Ga.) from 1956 to 1968 before becoming a professor of English at the State University of New York at Stony Brook.

altjira (mythology): *see* Dreaming, the.

Altman, Benjamin (b. July 12, 1840, New York City—d. Oct. 7, 1913, New York City), U.S. merchant, art collector, and philanthropist, who established one of the world's great department stores, B. Altman & Co.

Born on New York's Lower East Side, Altman had little formal schooling, but at the age of 25 he was able to open his first dry-goods store in Manhattan and in 1906 moved it to the uptown section, pioneering the movement of business there. With additions in 1913–14, the store occupied the entire block bounded by Madison and Fifth avenues and 34th and 35th streets. Known for his organizing ability and his promotion of medical service, rest, and other benefits for his employees, he set up a foundation for their welfare and for other philanthropic purposes.

An astute art collector, Altman also built up a valuable art library. He had extensive collections of Chinese porcelains, crystals, rugs, and other objects of art. Among his paintings were 13 Rembrandts and canvasses by Botticelli, Hans Holbein, and Filippo Lippi. The entire collection, appraised at $20,000,000, was bequeathed, with $150,000 for its care, to the Metropolitan Museum of Art.

Altman's estate of $35,000,000 included a substantial gift to the National Academy of Design to encourage American painting.

Altman, Robert (B.) (b. Feb. 20, 1925, Kansas City, Mo., U.S.), unconventional and independent U.S. motion-picture director whose works emphasize character and atmosphere over plot in exploring themes of innocence, corruption, and survival. Perhaps his best known film was his first and biggest commercial success, the anti-war comedy *M*A*S*H* (1970), set in a Mobile Army Surgical Hospital during the Korean War.

Altman served as a U.S. Army pilot from 1943 to 1947, studied at the University of Missouri for three years, and subsequently directed industrial films. During the late 1950s and '60s he directed for such televison series as *Bus Stop* and *Combat*. Altman's first two feature films, *Countdown* (1967) and *That Cold Day in the Park* (1969), met with production difficulties and box office failure. With *M*A*S*H,* however, Altman won critical accolades, including the Grand Prize at the Cannes Film Festival. The directorial innovations that distinguished that film, most notably the disregard for conventional plot and the use of overlapping strains of dialogue and other sound, subsequently became Altman stocks-in-trade. *Brewster McCloud* of later the same year was an eccentric fantasy on human flight, set in the Houston Astrodome. The critically acclaimed *McCabe and Mrs. Miller* (1971) was called an anti-western for its irreverent portrait of life in a frontier boomtown.

While he failed to recapture the commercial success of *M*A*S*H,* Altman stirred both critical and popular debate with the 1976 film *Nashville,* a sprawling, kaleidoscopic view of a political campaign set against the backdrop of the country music industry. Some critics praised the film as a vivid allegory of American life, while others found it overambitious and muddled. Altman's other films include *The Long Goodbye* (1973), an updated rendering of a Raymond Chandler novel; *3 Women* (1977), an enigmatic mood piece derived from a dream; *A Wedding* (1978), which resembled *Nashville* in its use of a huge cast and a festive gathering; and *Popeye* (1980), a musical, live-action version of the classic cartoon. In the early 1980s, Altman began using videotape to record his own theatrical productions.

alto (Italian: "high"), in vocal music the register approximately between the F below middle C to the second D above; the second highest part in four-part music. The word alto originally referred to the highest male voice, singing falsetto (*see* countertenor).

Alto derives from the term *contratenor altus,* which in Renaissance music referred to the part immediately above the tenor part. Female alto voices are often called contralto. The term alto is also used for musical instruments having a more or less comparable range, *e.g.,* alto saxophone, alto clarinet, alto flute. The meaning of *alto* in French is "tenor violin" or "tenor saxhorn"—a pitfall for translators; *contralte* in French for the English "alto."

alto horn: *see* tenor horn.

Alto Paraguay, department, northeastern Paraguay, bounded by Bolivia on the north, by Brazil and the Paraguay River on the east, and by the departments of Presidente Hayes and Boquerón on the south and Nueva Asunción and Chaco on the west. The department's area (17,754 sq mi [45,982 sq km]) is an alluvial tropical lowland adjoining the floodplain of the Paraguay River. The region is part of the Gran Chaco and has much good pastureland suitable for cattle raising, but it also has a climate subject to periodic heavy rains and prolonged drought. The department has extensive forests, with an abundance of Palo Santo palms, and quebracho (Anacardiaceae) trees; forestry and cattle raising are the economic mainstays. Fuerte Olimpo, the departmental capital on the Paraguay River, is the largest city and commercial centre. Fortín Carlos Antonio López, on the eastern bank of Laguna (lake) Pitiantuta, was attacked in 1932 by Bolivian troops, an incident that began the Chaco War. A railway originating at Puerto Casado on the Paraguay River in the extreme south extends 233 mi (375 km) westward into the interior, carrying passengers and quebracho lumber. Pop. (1982 prelim.) 8,960.

Alto Paraná, department, eastern Paraguay, bounded north by Canendiyu department and east by Brazil and Argentina. The territory, 5,751 sq mi (14,895 sq km) in area, is an extension of the Brazilian Highlands, known locally as the Cordillera (mountains) de Mbaracayú, and is dissected by the eastward-flowing tributaries of the Paraná River. Crystal, ruby, and emerald deposits have been discovered. The inhabitants, many of whom are recent European immigrants, are clustered mainly in Puerto Presidente Stroessner, the capital. The department's economy has been stimulated by the construction of the Itaipu Dam on the Paraná River north of the capital. The dam and related energy projects have greatly increased the potential for agricultural modernization, enhanced production, and expanded railway networks for export. The former isolation of Alto Paraná has been alleviated by completion of the highway linking Asunción to Foz do Iguaçu in Brazil and by an airport near Puerto Presidente Stroessner. Pop. (1982 prelim.) 192,518.

Alto Uruguai, Rio (Brazil): *see* Pelotas River.

Alton, parish (town), East Hampshire district, county of Hampshire, England, in the valley of the Wey River, northeast of Winchester. Its church is in Perpendicular style with a Norman tower, and there are many Georgian buildings. William Curtis, the botanist, is commemorated by a museum, which houses a fine collection of rural implements. Alton's biennial fair dates from Edward II's reign (1307–27). Locally grown hops are used for brewing. Pop. (1981 prelim.) 14,646.

Alton, city, Madison County, southwestern Illinois, U.S., part of the St. Louis, Mo., urban–industrial complex, near the confluence of the Mississippi and Missouri rivers. Named for a son of Col. Rufus Easton, a St. Louis lawyer who laid out the townsite in 1817, it became a busy river port by the 1830s and still has considerable river traffic. Its industrial growth was stimulated by the availability of raw materials (iron ore, stone, lead, and zinc) and the establishment of oil refineries. Manufactures include glass, paper, plastic, ammunition, hardware, machine, and steel products. Factories fill the river plain in the lower town, while the residential area lies on the river bluffs, some of which rise to more than 200 ft (60 m). Shurtleff College (Baptist) was established (1827) in Alton (since 1957 part of Southern Illinois University), and at nearby Godfrey, Lewis and Clark Community College was established (1969) on the campus of the former Monticello College (founded 1835). A monument commemorates Abolitionist newspaper editor Elijah P. Lovejoy, who was killed in Alton by a proslavery mob in 1837. The site of the final Lincoln–Douglas debate in 1858 is marked by a tablet. Inc. town, 1821; city, 1837. Pop. (1980) 34,171.

Alton, Charles Talbot, marquess of: *see* Shrewsbury, Charles Talbot, duke and 12th earl of.

Altona, northwest district of the city and *Land* (state) of Hamburg, northwestern West Germany, on cliffs above the right bank of the Elbe River. The name may have come originally from *allzu-nah* ("all too near"), which was the Hamburgers' designation for an inn that lay too close to their territory and was for a long time the only building. As a small fishing village, it was called Altwasser when it fell to the Danes in 1640. Granted trade and customs privileges, it soon became a formidable rival to Hamburg. It was chartered in 1664, passed to Prussia in 1866, and was incorporated into Hamburg in 1937. The cathedral and St. Joseph's Church, damaged in World War II, have since been restored. The Federal German Fisheries Research Institute is located in Altona.

Altoona, city, Blair County, central Pennsylvania, U.S., on the eastern slopes of the Allegheny Front, which separates the Atlantic from the Mississippi Valley watersheds, 45 mi (72 km) northeast of Johnstown. It was founded in 1849 by the Pennsylvania Railroad Company as a base for railroad building over the Alleghenies and was named for Altona in Schleswig-Holstein (now in West Germany). The site, long a communications focus, had been settled since the 1760s, and Ft. Roberdau (1778) was established in the vicinity to protect the local lead deposits used by the patriot army during the American Revolution. In 1787 the Frankstown Trail (connecting the Susquehanna and Ohio river systems) was surveyed through the area; a road was built that shortly after 1800 was extended to Pittsburgh (80 mi west). During the canal-building boom of the 1830s the Portage Railroad, using railroad cars to haul barges up a series of inclined planes and down the western slopes, was developed to span the 36-mi divide between the nearby Juniata and Conemaugh rivers.

Altoona's economy is based on diversified industries and railroad shops. Nearby are 2,375-ft (723-m) Horseshoe (railroad) Curve (with a central curve of 220°), the famous Prince Gallitzin State Park, Wopsononock Mountain (2,580 ft), and Forest Zoo. The Altoona campus of Pennsylvania State University opened in 1939. Inc. borough, 1854; city, 1868. Pop. (1980) 57,058.

Altranstädt, treaties of, agreements made during the Great Northern War (1700–21) by the Swedish king Charles XII with Augustus II the Strong, king of Poland and elector of Saxony (Sept. 24, 1706) and with the Holy Roman emperor Joseph I (Sept. 1, 1707). Shortly after Augustus was crowned king of Poland (Sept. 15, 1697), he formed an alliance with Denmark and Russia against Sweden (autumn 1699) that precipitated the Great Northern War. Charles, however, swiftly defeated the Danish and Russian armies (1700) and then invaded Poland. Insisting that the Poles depose Augustus, he conquered Warsaw and Kraków (1702). In response, some of the gentry in the territory occupied by Sweden formally deposed Augustus and elected Stanisław Leszczyński, the palatine (chief official) of Poznań, king of Poland (July 12, 1704). When Swedish troops subsequently invaded Saxony (autumn 1705), Augustus, who had retreated there, was compelled to accept the first Treaty of Altranstädt, by which he gave up his claim to the Polish throne, acknowledged Stanisław as his successor, withdrew Saxony from the war against Sweden, and renounced his alliance with Russia. Only after Peter I the Great of Russia inflicted a major defeat upon the Swedish army at Poltava (July 8 [June 27, old style], 1709) was Augustus able to declare his agreement with Charles void, return to Poland, and recover the Polish crown from Stanisław.

After Charles's defeat of Augustus in Saxony, the Habsburg emperor Joseph I, who was engaged in a war against France (the War of the Spanish Succession; 1701–14), feared that Sweden would form an alliance with France and successfully attack Vienna. To offset this danger, Joseph signed the second Treaty of Altranstädt with Charles, pledging to grant greater religious freedom to Protestants in Silesia in exchange for Charles's promise not to join France.

altruism, in ethics, a theory of conduct that regards the good of others as the end of moral action. The term (French *altruisme,* derived from Latin *alter,* "other") was coined in the 19th century by Auguste Comte, the founder of Positivism, and adopted generally as a convenient antithesis to egoism. As a theory of conduct, its adequacy depends on an interpretation of "the good." If the term is taken to mean pleasure and the absence of pain, most altruists have agreed that a moral agent has an obligation to further the pleasures and alleviate the pains of other people. The same argument holds if happiness is taken as the end of life. But critics have asked, if no one has a moral obligation to procure his own happiness, why should anyone else have an obligation to procure happiness for him? Other conflicts have arisen between immediate pain and long-range good, especially when the good envisioned by the doer does not coincide with the vision of the beneficiary.

Some British Utilitarians, such as Herbert Spencer and Leslie Stephen, attacked the distinction between self and others that is basic to both altruism and egoism. Such Utilitarians viewed the end of moral activity as the welfare of society, the social organism.

Altun Shan (China): *see* A-erh-chin Shan.

Altus, city, seat (1907) of Jackson County, southwestern Oklahoma, U.S. The original settlement of Frazier (1886), near Bitter Creek (Salt Fork of the Red River), was subject to flooding and was moved 4 mi (6 km) east in 1891 to the present site on higher ground and renamed Altus ("high place"). Demand for agricultural products stimulated the city's growth during World War I, but during the Depression and drought in the 1930s it became part of Oklahoma's "dust bowl." The nearby W.C. Austin Reclamation Project (the state's first large irrigation project, completed in 1948) restored the region's basic agricultural economy (cotton, cattle, and wheat). Altus Reservoir, the project's chief unit, impounded on the North Fork of the Red River by Lugert Dam, lies within Quartz Mountain State Park, 18 mi north. The city is the site of Western Oklahoma State College (1926) and Altus Air Force Base. Inc. town, 1901; city, 1919. Pop. (1980) 23,101.

Altvatergebirge (eastern Europe): *see* Jeseník Mountains.

Altyn Tagh (China): *see* A-erh-chin Shan.

Aluko, T(imothy) M(ofOlorunso) (b. June 14, 1918, Ilesha, Nigeria), writer whose short stories and novels deal with social change and the clash of cultures in modern Africa.

A civil engineer and town planner by profession, Aluko was educated in Ibadan, Lagos, and London and held positions as director of public works for western Nigeria and faculty member at the University of Lagos. He first became known through his short stories, several of which were awarded British prizes and were broadcast by the British Broadcasting Corporation African service.

Four novels followed. *One Man, One Wife* (1959), a satirical novel about the conflict of Christian and Yoruba ethics, relates the disillusionment of a village community with the tenets of missionary Christianity. A second novel, *One Man, One Matchet* (1964), humorously presents the clash of an inexperienced district officer with an unscrupulous politician. *Kinsman and Foreman* (1966) incorporates Aluko's professional experiences into a penetrating study of an idealistic young engineer's battle against the corrupt practices of his highly respected public works foreman, who is also his uncle. *Chief the Honourable Minister* (1970) satirizes the calamity resulting from a schoolmaster's appointment as minister of works in a newly independent country. The novel *His Worshipful Majesty* appeared in 1973. The economy of style, graceful prose, and gentle irony of Aluko's novels have brought him critical acclaim.

alum, any of a group of hydrated double salts, usually consisting of aluminum sulfate, water of hydration, and the sulfate of another element. The alum of greatest commercial importance is aluminum potassium sulfate, also known as potassium alum or potash alum, written as $K_2SO_4 \cdot Al_2(SO_4)_3 \cdot 24H_2O$ or as $KAl(SO_4)_2 \cdot 12H_2O$. It is produced by evaporation of a water solution containing aluminum sulfate and potassium sulfate. Aluminum sulfate can also form alums with the sulfates of sodium, ammonia, cesium, silver, rubidium, thallium, hydrazine, hydroxylamine, many organic amines, and possibly lithium. In addition, sulfates of trivalent iron, chromium, manganese, cobalt, gallium, titanium, vanadium, iridium, rhodium, and indium may take the place of aluminum sulfate.

The alums collectively have many important uses, including the production of medicines, textiles, sugar, paper, paints, matches, and deodorants. They are also used in baking powder, fire extinguishers, as binder (mordant) in dyeing, as a flocculating (aggregating) agent in water purification, and for waterproofing paper.

alum stone: *see* alunite.

Alumbrado (Spanish: Enlightened), Italian ILLUMINATO, plural ILLUMINATI, a follower of a mystical movement in Spain during the 16th and 17th centuries. Its adherents claimed that the human soul, having attained a certain degree of perfection, was permitted a vision of the divine and entered into direct communication with the Holy Spirit. From this state the soul could neither advance nor retrogress. Consequently, participation in the liturgy, good works, and observance of the exterior forms of religious life were unnecessary for those who had received the "light." The Alumbrados came primarily from among the reformed Franciscans and the Jesuits, but their doctrines seem to have influenced all classes of people. The extravagant claims made for their visions and revelations caused them to be relentlessly persecuted. The Inquisition issued edicts against them on three occasions (1568, 1574, and 1623).

alumina, aluminum oxide, a binary compound of oxygen and aluminum that occurs in nature as corundum (*see* aluminum).

aluminum, also spelled ALUMINIUM, (Al), chemical element; lightweight, silvery-white metal of main Group IIIa (boron group) of the periodic table, most abundant metallic element in the Earth's crust and most widely used nonferrous metal. Because of its chemical activity, aluminum never occurs in the metallic form in nature, but its compounds are present to a greater or lesser extent in almost all rocks, vegetation, and animals. Aluminum is concentrated in the outer 10 miles (16 kilometres) of the Earth's crust, of which it constitutes about 8 percent by weight; it is exceeded in amount only by oxygen and silicon.

Occurrence, uses, and properties. Aluminum occurs in igneous rocks chiefly as aluminosilicates in feldspars, feldspathoids, and micas, in the soil derived from them as clay, and upon further weathering as bauxite and iron-rich laterite. Bauxite, a mixture of hydrated aluminum oxides, is the principal aluminum ore. Crystalline aluminum oxide (emery, corundum), occurring in a few igneous rocks, is mined as a natural abrasive or in its finer varieties as rubies and sapphires. Aluminum is present in other gemstones, such as topaz, garnet, and chrysoberyl. Of the many other aluminum minerals, alunite and cryolite have some commercial importance.

Crude aluminum was isolated (1825) by Hans Christian Ørsted by reducing aluminum chloride with potassium amalgam. Sir Humphry Davy had prepared (1809) an iron–aluminum alloy by electrolyzing fused alumina (aluminum oxide) and had already named the element aluminum; the word later was modified to aluminium in England and some other European countries. A German chemist, Friedrich Wöhler, using potassium metal as the reducing agent, produced aluminum powder (1827) and small globules of the metal (1845) from which he was able to determine some of its properties.

The new metal was introduced to the public (1855) at the Paris exposition at about the time aluminum, produced by sodium reduction of the molten chloride, became available in small amounts at great expense. When electric power became relatively plentiful and cheap, almost simultaneously Charles Martin Hall in the U.S. and Paul-Louis-Toussaint Héroult in France discovered (1886) the modern method of commercially producing aluminum: electrolysis of purified alumina (Al_2O_3) dissolved in molten cryolite (Na_3AlF_6). During the 1960s aluminum moved into first place, ahead of copper, in world production of nonferrous metals. For more specific information about the mining, refining, and production of aluminum, *see* MACROPAEDIA: Extraction and Processing of Metals, Petroleum, and Other Minerals.

Aluminum is added in small amounts to certain metals to improve their properties for specific uses as in aluminum bronzes and most magnesium-base alloys; or, for aluminum-base alloys, moderate amounts of other metals and silicon are added to aluminum. The metal and its alloys are used extensively for aircraft construction, building materials, consumer durables (refrigerators, air conditioners, cooking utensils), electrical conductors, and chemical and food-processing equipment.

Pure aluminum (99.996 percent) is quite soft and weak; commercial aluminum (99.0 to 99.6 percent pure) with small amounts of silicon and iron is hard and strong. Ductile and highly malleable, aluminum can be drawn into wire or rolled into thin foil. The metal is only about one-third as dense as iron or copper. Though chemically active, aluminum is nevertheless highly corrosion-resistant because in air a hard, tough oxide film forms on its surface.

It is an excellent conductor of heat and electricity. Its thermal conductivity is about one-half that of copper; its electrical conductivity, about two-thirds. It crystallizes in the face-centred cubic structure. All natural aluminum is the stable isotope aluminum-27. Metallic aluminum and its oxide and hydroxide are nontoxic.

Aluminum is slowly attacked by most dilute acids and rapidly dissolves in concentrated hydrochloric acid. Concentrated nitric acid, however, can be shipped in aluminum tank cars because it renders the metal passive. Even very pure aluminum is vigorously attacked by alkalies such as sodium and potassium hydroxide to yield hydrogen and the aluminate ion. Because of its great affinity for oxygen, finely divided aluminum, if ignited, will burn in carbon monoxide or carbon dioxide with the formation of aluminum oxide and carbide; but at temperatures up to red heat, aluminum is inert to sulfur.

Compounds. Ordinarily, aluminum is trivalent. At elevated temperatures, however, a few gaseous monovalent and bivalent compounds have been prepared (AlCl, Al_2O, AlO).

A number of aluminum compounds have important industrial applications. Alumina, which occurs in nature as corundum, is also prepared commercially in large quantities for use in the production of aluminum metal and the manufacture of insulators, spark plugs, and various other products. Upon heating, alumina develops a porous structure, which enables it to adsorb water vapour. This form of aluminum oxide, commercially known as activated alumina, is used for drying gases and certain liquids. It also serves as a carrier for catalysts of various chemical reactions.

Another major compound is aluminum sulfate, a colourless salt obtained by the action of sulfuric acid on hydrated aluminum oxide. The commercial form is a hydrated crystalline solid with the chemical formula $Al_2(SO_4)_3$. It is used extensively in paper manufacture as a binder for dyes and as a surface filler. Aluminum sulfate combines with the sulfates of univalent metals to form hydrated double sulfates called alums. The most important of such salts is aluminum potassium sulfate, also known as potassium alum or potash alum, $KAl(SO_4) \cdot 12H_2O$. These alums have many applications, especially in the production of medicines, textiles, and paints.

The reaction of gaseous chlorine with molten aluminum metal produces aluminum chloride, $AlCl_3$, the most commonly used catalyst in Friedel-Crafts reactions—*i.e.*, synthetic organic reactions involved in the preparations of a wide variety of compounds, including aromatic ketones and anthroquinone and its derivatives. Hydrated aluminum chloride, commonly known as aluminum chlorohydrate, $AlCl_3 \cdot H_2O$, is used as a topical antiperspirant or body deodorant, which acts by constricting the pores. It is one of several aluminum salts employed by the cosmetics industry.

Aluminum hydroxide, $Al(OH)_3$, is used to waterproof fabrics and to produce a number of other aluminum compounds, including salts called aluminates that contain the AlO_2^- group. With hydrogen, aluminum forms aluminum hydride, AlH_3, a polymeric solid from which are derived the tetrohydroaluminates (important reducing agents). Lithium aluminum hydride ($LiAlH_4$), formed by the reaction of aluminum chloride with lithium hydride, is widely used in organic chemistry—*e.g.*, to reduce aldehydes and ketones to primary and secondary alcohols, respectively.

For statistical data on mine production of ore, refining of metal, reserves (or production capacity), and trade worldwide and for major national industries, *see* mining (table).

atomic number	13
atomic weight	26.9815
melting point	660° C
boiling point	2,467° C
specific gravity	2.70 (20° C)
valence	3
electronic config.	2-8-3 or $1s^2 2s^2 2p^6 3s^2 3p^1$

aluminum bronze, any of a group of strong, corrosion-resistant alloys of copper containing from 4 to 15 percent aluminum and small amounts of other metals, used to make many machine parts and tools. Because of their golden colour and high tarnish resistance, the alloys are also used for jewelry and in architecture. Their resistance to oxidation at high temperatures and to corrosion, particularly by dilute acids, makes them useful for pickling equipment and other service involving exposure to dilute sulfuric, hydrochloric, and hydrofluoric acids. They have strength comparable to that of mild steel and are used for such machinery as papermaking machines, brush holders and clamps for welding machines in the electrical industry, heavy-duty gear wheels, worm wheels, metal-forming dies, machine guides, nonsparking tools, and nonmagnetic chains and anchors. Aluminum bronzes can be welded by the metallic arc process and can be brazed (soldered with certain alloys) with special fluxes.

Alloys with up to about 8 percent of aluminum can be cold-rolled into sheet or drawn into tubes for use in chemical plants and oil refineries for pressure vessels and heat exchangers. Alloys with more than 8 percent of aluminum may also contain iron and manganese; they are capable of limited cold-working but can be hot-rolled, extruded, or forged. The strongest and most corrosion-resistant of the group contains nickel; it has been used for gas-turbine compressor blades. Alloys containing about 10 percent aluminum are fabricated by sand casting and gravity diecasting into strong objects, including ship propellers.

Aluminum Company of America (Alcoa), U.S. corporation founded in 1888 (as the Pittsburgh Reduction Company) and now a leading producer of aluminum. Its operations range from mining bauxite and other ores to smelting and processing aluminum, fabricating aluminum products, and marketing and shipping. It has majority ownership of Alcoa of Australia Limited, a leading producer of aluminum oxide (alumina). It has foreign operations throughout the world. Corporate headquarters are in Pittsburgh.

Pittsburgh Reduction Company was founded by a group of young men that included Charles Martin Hall, who in 1886 had been the first American to succeed in developing a commercially cheap method of smelting aluminum—by electrolysis. In 1891 the company began producing cast products (such as teakettles) and aluminum sheeting, as well as raw aluminum; and in 1899 it acquired its first bauxite mining rights. By 1907, when it reincorporated as the Aluminum Company of America (Alcoa), it had numerous mines, alumina plants, hydroelectric facilities, aluminum smelters and fabricating facilities, and the Alcoa Technical Center (in Pittsburgh) for laboratory research and development.

In 1928 Alcoa created an independent foreign company, Aluminium Limited (*see* Alcan Aluminium Limited), and transferred to it almost all of Alcoa's holdings then outside the United States. In return, Alcoa received the common stock of Aluminium Limited.

Meanwhile, the U.S. government had been turning a critical eye on Alcoa. In 1912, in an antitrust suit, Alcoa agreed to abandon certain monopolistic practices involving restrictive covenants with suppliers. Then, from 1922 to 1930, a Federal Trade Commission investigation brought further accusations of unfair competition and discrimination. Finally, in 1937, the U.S. Department of Justice filed a complaint charging the company with monopolizing interstate commerce in 16 markets and commodities and engaging in conspiracies with foreign producers. The final court decisions in 1951 absolved Alcoa of wrongdoing, but Alcoa's major stockholders were compelled to divest themselves of their common stock in Aluminium Limited.

Alun: *see* Blackwell, John.

alunite, also called ALUM STONE, a widespread rock-forming sulfate mineral that occupies pockets or seams in volcanic rocks such as rhyolites, trachytes, and andesites, where it presumably formed through their chemical reaction with escaping sulfurous vapours. It has been used as a source of potash (during World War I) and as a source of alumina (during World War II); in Europe it was once used extensively to make potash alum, and it has been mined for this purpose since the 15th century. Large deposits exist near Beregovo, Ukrainian S.S.R.; Almería, Spain; and Bullah Delah in New South Wales, Australia. For chemical formula and physical properties, *see* sulfate mineral (table).

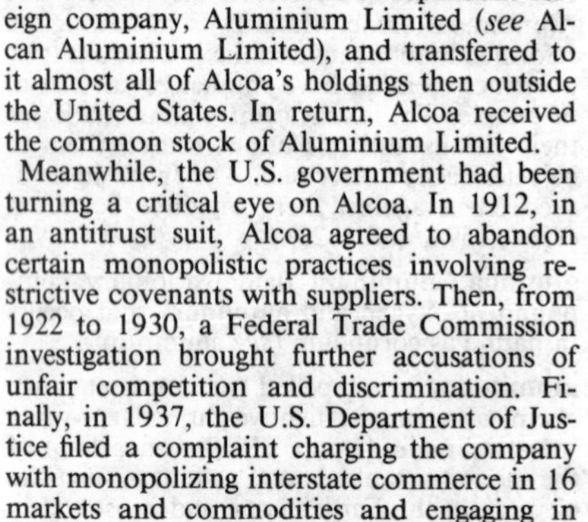

Alunite from Marysvale, Utah

By courtesy of the Field Museum of Natural History, Chicago; photograph, John H. Gerard—EB Inc.

alunogen, a sulfate mineral formed by sulfate solutions that attack aluminous minerals; alunogen is hydrated aluminum sulfate, formulated $Al_2(SO_4)_3 \cdot 18H_2O$. It typically occurs as an efflorescence or crevice filling in pyrite-containing coal formations, shales, or slates, as well as in the gossan (weathered capping) of sulfide ore deposits and in volcanic fumarole deposits. In older literature, alunogen and other hairlike sulfate minerals were called *Haarsalz* ("hair salts"). For detailed physical properties, *see* sulfate mineral (table).

Alushta, also spelled ALUŠTA, tourist resort, Crimea *oblast* (administrative region), Ukrainian Soviet Socialist Republic, on the south coast of the Crimean Peninsula. It is the site of a settlement dating from the 6th century AD; in the 14th century it was a Genoan stronghold. Tourism, based on the fine beach and relatively cool summers, developed in the late 19th century. Pop. (1970) 22,016.

Aluyi (people): *see* Lozi.

Alva, city, seat (1907) of Woods County, northwestern Oklahoma, U.S., on Salt Fork of the Arkansas River near the Kansas border. Established as a land office in 1893 at a Santa Fe Railway stop, it was named for Alva Adams, a railroad attorney. It is a marketing and processing centre for a wheat and livestock area. Manufactures include tractors and furniture; petroleum and natural gas are local resources. It is the seat of Northwestern Oklahoma State University (1897). Two state parks—Alabaster Caverns and Great Salt Plains—are nearby. Pop. (1980) 6,416.

Alva, Fernando Álvarez de Toledo y Pimentel, 3er duque de (3rd duke of): *see* Alba, Fernando Álvarez de Toledo y Pimentel, 3er duque de.

Āḻvār, any of a group of South Indian mystics who in the 7th to 10th century wandered from temple to temple singing ecstatic hymns in adoration of the god Vishnu. Their songs rank among the world's greatest devotional literature. Among the followers of Śiva, the counterpart of the Āḻvārs were the Nāyaṉārs.

The name Āḻvār means, in the Tamil language in which they sang, "man who has intuitive knowledge of God." Of the 12 who are especially remembered as saints, some were of the lowest caste, some were outcastes, and one was a woman; the most famous of them was Nammāḻvār. It has been said that by their singing the Āḻvārs drove the Buddhists and the Jainas out of South India. Their bhakti (religious devotion) was of an intensely passionate kind; they compared the soul to a woman who yearns for her lord's love. The Āḻvārs are described as falling unconscious in rapture before the image of their lord, and the saint Nammāḻvār, in speaking of the "madness" of religious exaltation, exhorted his fellow mystics to "run, jump, cry, laugh and sing, and let every man witness it."

The hymns of the Āḻvārs were gathered in the 10th century by Nāthamuni, a leader of the Śrīvaiṣṇava sect, who introduced the regular singing of the hymns in Vaiṣṇava temples of South India. The collection is called *Nālāyira Prabandham* (book of 4,000 hymns).

Alvarado, Pedro de (b. *c.* 1485, Badajoz, Castile—d. 1541, in or near Guadalajara, New

Spain), a conqueror of Mexico and Central America for Spain.

Alvarado went to Santo Domingo in 1510 and in 1518 commanded one of Juan de Grijalva's ships sent from Cuba to explore the Yucatán Peninsula. In February 1519 he accompanied the army, led from Cuba by Hernán Cortés, that was to conquer Mexico. Alvarado was placed in charge of Tenochtitlán (Mexico City), and in 1522 he became the city's first *alcalde* (mayor or principal magistrate).

In 1523 Alvarado conquered the Quichés and Cakchiquels of Guatemala and in 1524 founded Santiago de los Caballeros de Guatemala (Ciudad Vieja; present Antigua, Guatemala). This town became the first capital of the captaincy general of Guatemala, later including much of Central America, of which Alvarado was governor (1527–31).

In 1534 Alvarado led an unlicensed expedition to Quito, but in 1535 he sold his ships and munitions to Diego de Almagro, one of Francisco Pizarro's captains. He then returned to Guatemala and, in 1537, to Spain, where he was confirmed as governor of Guatemala for seven years and was given a charter to explore Mexico. He arrived in Honduras in 1539 and died while attempting to quell an Indian uprising in central Mexico.

Alvares Pereira, Nuno (Portuguese soldier): *see* Pereira, Nuno Alvares.

Álvarez, Juan (b. 1790, Concepción de Atoyac, Mex.—d. Aug. 21, 1867, Acapulco), revolutionary leader for more than 40 years, before and after the end of Spanish rule, and provisional president of Mexico in 1855.

A landowner of mestizo ancestry, Álvarez in 1811 joined José María Morelos in an unsuccessful campaign for independence from Spain. He was prominent in Antonio López de Santa Anna's revolt of 1822–23, which overthrew the first ruler of independent Mexico, Agustín de Iturbide.

Juan Álvarez, detail of a portrait by L. Garcés, 19th century

By courtesy of the Instituto Nacional de Antropologia e Historia, Mexico City

In 1847 Álvarez fought in the war against the United States. Two years later he became governor of the new state of Guerrero, ostensibly as a liberal. When Santa Anna reestablished his dictatorship in 1853, however, Álvarez accommodated himself to this situation as long as his hegemony in Guerrero was not threatened. In 1854, when Santa Anna tried to secure direct rule over Guerrero, Álvarez started a rebellion at Ayutla. After Santa Anna had gone into exile, Álvarez assumed control of the government and soon resigned in favour of Ignacio Comonfort, his ally against Santa Anna. The work of Álvarez and Comonfort resulted in the liberal trend known as *La Reforma* ("The Reform") and in the constitution of 1857.

Alvarez, Luis W(alter) (b. June 13, 1911, San Francisco), experimental physicist who was awarded the Nobel Prize for Physics in 1968 for work that included the discovery of many resonance particles (subatomic particles having extremely short lifetimes and occurring only in high-energy nuclear collisions).

Alvarez was educated at the University of Chicago (B.S., 1932; M.S., 1934; Ph.D., 1936). He joined the faculty of the University of California, Berkeley, in 1936, becoming professor of physics in 1945 and professor emeritus in 1978. In 1938 Alvarez discovered that some radioactive elements decay by orbital-electron capture; *i.e.*, an orbital electron merges with its nucleus, producing an element with an atomic number smaller by one. In 1939 he and Felix Bloch made the first measurement of the magnetic moment of the neutron, a characteristic of the strength and direction of its magnetic field.

Alvarez worked on microwave radar research at the Massachusetts Institute of Technology, Cambridge (1940–43), and the Los Alamos Scientific Laboratory, Los Alamos, N.M. (1944–45). He participated in the development of microwave beacons, linear radar antennas, the ground-controlled landing approach system, and a method for aerial bombing using radar to locate targets. He also suggested the

Luis Alvarez

By courtesy of the Lawrence Radiation Laboratory, the University of California, Berkeley

technique for detonating the implosion type of atomic bomb. After World War II, Alvarez helped construct the first proton linear accelerator and developed the liquid hydrogen bubble chamber in which subatomic particles and their reactions are detected.

Álvarez Quintero, Serafín and Joaquín (respectively b. March 26, 1871, Utrera, Seville—d. April 12, 1938, Madrid; b. Jan. 20, 1873, Utrera—d. June 14, 1944, Madrid), brothers who collaborated in almost 200 dramas depicting the life, manners, and speech of Andalusia. Their work was among the most popular in Spain during the early 20th century and greatly added to the revival of the Spanish theatre. Their dramas are remarkable for a vivacious and skilled presentation. Among their better known plays are *Los galeotes* (1900; "The Galley Slaves"), *El amor que pasa* (1904; "The Love That Passes"), and *Malvaloca* (1912), a serious drama that received the prize of the Real Academia Española. Several of their plays were translated into English by Helen and Harley Granville-Barker (1927–32); their complete works were published in *Obras completas*, 7 vol. (1953–54).

Alvear, Marcelo T(orcuato) de (b. Oct. 4, 1868, Buenos Aires—d. March 23, 1942, Buenos Aires), statesman and political leader who served as president of Argentina from 1922 until 1928.

Alvear belonged to a distinguished Argentine family. He was educated at the University of Buenos Aires, where he received a doctor of jurisprudence degree. He was a cofounder in 1890 of the Unión Civica Radical (UCR), the political party representing the liberal-democratic viewpoint in Argentina. He took part in revolutions of 1890, 1893, and 1905 that helped to establish liberal democracy in Argentina; he then served as minister of public works in 1911, as a member of Parliament in 1912–17, and as Argentine ambassador to France in 1917–22.

In 1922 Hipólito Irigoyen, the UCR leader and president of Argentina, designated Alvear as his successor. Alvear served as president until

Alvear

By courtesy of the Organization of American States

1928, when he broke with Irigoyen, founded the Unión Anti-Personalista Partida (UAPP), a splinter group of the UCR, and formed an alliance with many conservatives (members of the old oligarchy that opposed the UCR). Despite Alvear's opposition Irigoyen regained the presidency in 1928. Alvear rejoined the UCR after a conservative-oriented military coup overthrew Irigoyen's government in 1930. He ran for the presidency in 1931, but he was declared ineligible because less than a full term had expired since he left office.

Alvear's publications include *Acción democrática* (1938; *Democratic Action*) and numerous state papers and public documents.

Alvensleben-Erxleben, Gustav, Graf von (count of) (b. Sept. 30, 1803, Eichenbarleben, Prussia—d. June 30, 1881, Gernrode, Ger.), Prussian general, adjutant general, and chief personal adviser to King (later Emperor) William I.

As a member of the Prussian general staff (1847–58), Alvensleben participated in the suppression of the revolution of 1849 in Baden and was named chief of staff for the troops that remained in occupation. In 1854 he held a similar position in the military government of the Rhineland. Promoted to major general in 1858 and adjutant general in 1861, he acquired considerable influence in the military cabinets and personal counsels of William I. Dispatched to St. Petersburg (now Leningrad) in 1863, he negotiated a convention that provided for Prussian–Russian cooperation in the suppression of insurrections in their subject Polish lands. Faced with the concerted opposition of the Western powers, however, this agreement—the Alvensleben Convention (1863)—was repudiated by the Prussian government and allowed to pass into oblivion. Subsequently appointed lieutenant general (1863) and general of the infantry (1868), Alvensleben saw service in the Franco-Prussian war as head of the 3rd Army Corps.

alveolar proteinosis, the filling of large groups of alveoli with protein and lipid (fat) particles. The alveoli are air sacs, minute structures in the lungs in which the exchange of respiratory gases occurs. The gas molecules must pass through a cellular wall, the surface of which is generally covered by a thin film of fatty material secreted from the alveolar cells. When too many fat materials are released from the alveolar cells, or when the cells die in large numbers and fragment into the alveolar cavity, gas exchange is greatly hindered and the symptoms of alveolar proteinosis occur.

The disease manifests itself in laboured breathing, often accompanied by pain, coughing, and a yellow sputum (mucus discharge). There may also be general fatigue and weight loss. The skin becomes tinged with blue in the most serious cases, an indication that blood is not being adequately oxygenated or rid of carbon dioxide. X-rays most frequently show swelling and excess fluids in the lungs.

The precipitating cause of the disease is unknown. Persons affected are usually between 20 and 50 years of age. The disease can exist without causing symptoms for considerable periods, and spontaneous improvement has been known to occur; it is sometimes fatal, however. Treatment involves the use of enzymes that dissolve the protein and fat substances, along with rinsing out of the lungs (lavage). One lung at a time is rinsed with a saltwater solution introduced through the windpipe. The fluids drawn back out of the lungs have been found to have a high content of fat. Sometimes the lesions totally clear up after this procedure.

Alver, Amalie: *see* Skram, Amalie.

Alves, Francisco de Paula Rodrigues: *see* Rodrigues Alves, Francisco de Paula.

Alves de Lima e Silva, Luiz: *see* Caxias, Luiz Alves de Lima e Silva, duque de.

Älvsborg, *län* (county), southwestern Sweden, bounded by Lake Vänern, Norway, and the *län* of Göteborg och Bohus, Halland, Jönköping, Skaraborg, and Värmland. Its land area of 4,399 sq mi (11,394 sq km) comprises the traditional *landskap* (province) of Dalsland and part of that of Västergötland. Of the many rivers that drain it, the most important is the Göta älv (Göta River), the falls and rapids of which produce hydroelectric power. Although the *län* has poor soils and remains largely forested, wheat, rye, and oats are grown, and cattle raising and dairying are important. The main base of the economy, however, is industry, centred at Borås. A major hydroelectric power station, locks, and locomotive works are located at Trollhättan. Vänersborg is the capital. Pop. (1983 est.) 425,110.

Locks at Trollhättan in Älvsborg *län*, Sweden
Authenticated News International

Alwar, also spelled ALWUR, town, administrative headquarters of Alwar district, Rājasthān state, northwestern India. The city is surrounded by a wall and moat and dominated by a fort on a conical hill against a backdrop of a range of hills. Alwar was made the capital of Alwar state in 1775; it contains the 14th-century tomb of Tarang Sultān (the brother of Fīrūz Shāh) and several ancient mosques. The palace contains a museum that houses a library of Hindī, Sanskrit, and Persian manuscripts and a collection of Rājasthāni and Mughal miniature paintings. It is an agricultural mart and a communications centre. Major industries include cloth weaving, oilseed and flour milling, and the manufacture of paint, varnish, and pottery. There are several hospitals, and there are colleges affiliated with the University of Rājasthān.

Alwar district has an area of 3,236 sq mi (8,382 sq km). A former princely state, it comprises two distinct regions: the eastern region is flat and cultivated, but the western consists of precipitous parallel hill ridges that are continuations of the Arāvalli Range. The chief crops include gram (chick-pea), barley, and wheat. Beryllium, lead, zinc, silver, barites, marble, and copper deposits are worked.

The palace and *sāgar* (lake) at Alwar, Rājasthān, India
Christine Gascoigne

Alwar princely state was founded in 1771 by a maharaja of the Rājputs (the warrior caste of the historic region of Rājputāna); it came under British paramountcy by a treaty concluded in 1803. In 1948 it joined the Matsya union, which merged with Rājasthān in 1949. Pop. (1981) town, 145,795; district, 1,771,173.

Alwaye, town, Ernākulam district, Kerala state, southwestern India. Lying on the Periyār River north of the town of Ernākulam, it is a major industrial centre. Its products include aluminum, glass, fertilizers, and textiles. Other industries are the milling of rice and other foods and the processing of monazite sand from Kerala's beaches, used as a source of radioactive thorium. From March to May, Alwaye is a popular resort. Pop. (1981) 25,278.

Alyattes (d. *c.* 560 BC), king of Lydia, in west central Anatolia (*c.* 619–*c.* 560 BC), whose conquest created the powerful but short-lived Lydian Empire. Soon after succeeding his father, King Sadyattes, he started five consecutive years of raids that devastated the farmland around the Greek city of Miletus on the southwestern coast of Anatolia. He moved eastward, battling the Medes for five years, until an eclipse of the Sun brought an end to the fighting. Alyattes also fought with the Carians to the south, whom he conquered, and with the nomadic Cimmerians to the east, whom he drove from western Anatolia. He went on to capture and demolish most of the Greek city of Smyrna (on the west coast of Anatolia; now Izmir). He was succeeded by his son Croesus, whose wealth became legendary.

Alyattes' tomb, which was described by Herodotus, can still be seen in west central Anatolia about seven miles north of the ruins of the Lydian capital of Sardis.

Alyn and Deeside, district, Clwyd County, northeastern Wales. It was created in 1974, covers 59 sq mi (154 sq km) of rolling lowlands and hills, and extends from the River Dee south and west toward the Clwydian Hills. Alyn and Deeside district borders the districts of Delyn to the north, Wrexham Manor to the south, Glyndwr to the west, and the English districts of Ellesmere Port and Chester to the east. The region has been an important gateway between England and Wales since the Roman occupation of Britain, when a road was completed from Deva (now Chester) to Segontium (now Caernarvon). During the conquest of Wales (1277–1283) by Edward I of England, the castle at Caergwrle, in what is now southern Alyn and Deeside, was taken over by the king and given to his queen, Eleanor of Castile. The original Hawarden Castle, in central Alyn and Deeside, was an important English stronghold in the Welsh Marches (border country) during the years following the Edwardian conquest and was subjected to numerous Welsh attacks. During the English Civil War in the 1640s it was first garrisoned by Charles I, then betrayed to the parliamentarians, retaken by the royalists, and finally captured by the well-known parliamentary leader and commander General Mytton.

As a result of the exploitation of rich coal deposits in the 19th century, a highly industrialized area developed on the banks of the River Dee. Today the industrial belt centres mainly around the huge Shotton steelworks and is composed of the communities of Conah's Quay, Shotton, Mancot, Queensferry, and Sandycroft. Besides the long established iron-working and shipbuilding industries, engineering, chemical, and synthetic textile industries have been developed. Hawarden is the administrative seat of the district. The residential town of Buckley has long been known for its coarse pottery, although most of its clay is now used to produce bricks for the Shotton steelworks. Alyn and Deeside is traversed by highways from southeast to northwest as well as from north to south, and an airport is located at Broughton. Pop. (1981) 72,088.

Alyokhin, Aleksandr Aleksandrovich (Chess champion): *see* Alekhine, Alexander.

Alypius (fl. 2nd century AD, Alexandria), writer on music whose *Introduction to Music* contains a comprehensive summary of the complex system of Greek scales and their transpositions and includes tables of their method of notation. The treatise was published in 1616 by I. Meursius and in 1652, with the tables of notation, by M. Meibom. The authoritative edition is by K. von Jan in *Musici scriptores Graeci* (1895).

Alyssum (plant): *see* basket-of-gold; sweet alyssum.

Alytus, also spelled ALITUS, German and Polish OLITA, city, southern Lithuanian Soviet Socialist Republic, on the Neman (Lithuanian Nemunas) River 37 mi (60 km) south of Kaunas. The city dates from the 14th century. In the 20th century it developed as an industrial centre, with an iron foundry and factories producing turpentine, linen, and clothing. Alytus is a rail terminus and road junction and has an agricultural college. Pop. (1983 est.) 64,000.

Alzheimer's disease, degenerative disease affecting nerve cells of the frontal and temporal lobes of the cerebrum of the brain. The disease is the major cause of presenile dementia (*i.e.,* the loss of mental faculties not associated with advanced age) and is thought to be the largest single cause of senile dementia as well. Among its effects are speech disturbances and severe memory impairment leading to the progressive loss of the mental faculties. No effective treatment was available by the early 1980s.

The disease was originally described in 1906 by Alois Alzheimer, a German neuropathologist. In the autopsy of a 55-year-old patient who had died with severe dementia, Alzheimer noted the presence in the brain of two abnormalities. The first was neuritic plaque, a structure that had been described previously in the brains of elderly persons. It is now known that neuritic plaque is composed of degenerating nerve terminals, reactive glial cells (non-nervous cells present in nerve tissue), and fibrous material called amyloid. The second abnormality noted by Alzheimer was the neurofibrillary tangle, a fibrous structure within nerve cells, which showed up heavily with the use of a silver stain. The neurofibrillary tangle had not been described before, and it was principally this abnormality that defined a new disease entity. Because of the relatively young age of Alzheimer's patient, the disease was long regarded as a form of presenile dementia. It is now recognized that the same pathological brain atrophy is present in many patients of advanced age, and most authorities no longer restrict the term Alzheimer's disease to presenile cases.

Although the cause remains unknown, the disease is thought to be associated with a deficiency of the neurotransmitter acetylcholine. Some research has suggested the possible existence of a virus-like causative agent; other studies have implicated abnormal concentrations of aluminum in the brain tissue.

In 1984 researchers reported that the neural pathways leading to and from the hippocampus—a small area in the temporal lobe of the brain—are heavily damaged in Alzheimer's victims. Because the hippocampus is necessary for the making and storing of memories, this damage, although confined to a small area of the brain, is thought to be the major cause of the memory impairment that characterizes the disease.

Alzon, Emmanuel(-Marie-Joseph-Maurice) Daudé d' (b. Aug. 30, 1810, Le Vigan, Fr.—d. Nov. 21, 1880, Nîmes), ecclesiastic who founded the order of Augustinians of the Assumption (or Assumptionists). He studied at Saint-Louis and Stanislas colleges in Paris, entered Montpellier Seminary in 1831, and in 1832 continued his studies in Rome, where he was ordained (1834). He was named canon and vicar general of Nîmes and retained this position, under four bishops, until his death.

In 1843 he acquired Assumption College in Nîmes, where he founded (1845) the congregation of the Augustinians of the Assumption, dedicated to education and to missionary and social work; it received papal approval in 1864. To help in this work he also founded a congregation of women, the Oblates of the Assumption. Pope Pius IX sent him to Constantinople to establish an Assumptionist mission there (1863). He attended the Vatican Council of 1869–70 as theologian to his bishop and was active in preparing the definition of papal infallibility. In 1871 he started the Alumniates, apostolic schools for the ecclesiastical education of poor boys.

AM (Judaism): *see* anno mundi.

AM, abbreviation of AMPLITUDE MODULATION, variation of the amplitude of a carrier wave (commonly a radio wave) in accordance with the characteristics of a signal, such as vocal or musical sound composed of audio-frequency waves. *See* modulation.

Amadeus, name of rulers grouped below by country and indicated by the symbol •.

Foreign-language equivalents:

French	Amédée
Italian	Amadeo
Spanish	Amadeo

SAVOY

• Amadeus VI, byname AMADEUS THE GREEN COUNT, Italian AMEDEO IL CONTE VERDE, French AMÉDÉE LE COMTE VERT (b. 1334, Chambéry, Savoy—d. March 1, 1383, Castropignano), count of Savoy (1343–83) who significantly extended Savoy's territory and power.

Son of Aimone the Peaceful, count of Savoy, Amadeus ascended the throne at the age of nine. He crossed the Alps in 1348 to put down a revolt of Piedmontese cities and won his knight's spurs on the field of battle in 1352 in a victory over rebellious inhabitants of the Valais (east of Geneva), subsequently celebrating his 19th birthday with a series of tournaments. In 1355 he married Bonne of Bourbon, sister-in-law of the dauphin Charles (later Charles V of France).

Military victories and purchases in the Alpine region in the 1350s increased his holdings, creating the geographical basis for a unified state comprising nearly the whole of the western Alps. He then acquired lands on the Italian side of the mountains.

In 1365 the Holy Roman emperor Charles IV made him imperial vicar. A year later Amadeus responded to Pope Urban V's call for a crusade against the Turks, whom he fought at Gallipoli. Following a campaign against the Bulgarians in the Black Sea area, he restored his cousin, John V Palaeologus, to the Byzantine throne.

Growing prestige made him the arbiter of many of the quarrels between the Italian powers. He acted as mediator between Pisa and Florence in 1364, between the marquesses of Montferrat and the Visconti family from 1375 to 1379, and between Venice and Milan on the one hand and Genoa on the other, negotiating the Peace of Turin (1381). The following year he brought about an accord between the Genoese and the King of Cyprus and was later invited by the Guelf (pro-papal) nobles of Genoa to become doge and take the city under his protection—an empty offer, since the Guelfs were out of power.

In 1382 Amadeus joined Pope Clement VII and the French prince Louis of Anjou in the project of rescuing Queen Joan I of Naples from the rival pope Urban VI and Charles of Durazzo, pretender to the throne of Naples. Launched in June 1382, the expedition was beset by sickness and hunger and bogged down in southern Italy. The following winter Amadeus was stricken with plague and died.

• Amadeus VII, byname AMADEUS THE RED COUNT, Italian AMEDEO IL CONTE ROSSO, French AMÉDÉE LE COMTE ROUGE (b. 1360, Chambéry, Savoy—d. Nov. 1, 1391, Ripaille), count of Savoy (1383–91), during whose short rule the county of Savoy acquired Nice and other Provençal towns.

Son of Amadeus VI and Bonne of Bourbon, sister-in-law of Charles V of France, Amadeus married (1377) the daughter of Jean, duc de Berry, brother of the King of France. His father, the "Green Count," wore his customary emerald-green livery at the wedding, and the groom earned his own sobriquet by wearing bright red. Invested with the traditional fief of Savoyard heirs apparent, the seigneury of Bresse (west of Geneva), he was soon embroiled in an intermittent six-year war against a vassal, Edward of Beaujeu, who refused him homage. In 1382 he led Savoyard troops against Flemish rebels at the Battle of Rozebeke.

Amadeus died suddenly at the castle of Ripaille, south of Lake Geneva, at the age of 31, apparently as a result of a doctor's blunder.

• Amadeus VIII, byname AMADEUS THE PEACEFUL, Italian AMEDEO IL PACIFICO, French AMÉDÉE LE PAISIBLE, also called POPE FELIX V (b. 1383, Chambéry, Savoy—d. Jan. 7, 1451, Geneva), count (1391–1416) and duke (1416–40) of Savoy, first member of the House of Savoy to assume the title of duke; his 42-year reign saw the extension of his authority from Lake Neuchâtel on the north to the Ligurian coast, and under the title of Felix V he was an antipope for 10 years (1439–49).

The sudden death of Amadeus VII in 1391 left his eight-year-old son under a regency. In 1393 Amadeus married Mary, daughter of Philip the Bold, duke of Burgundy. He increased the territories of Savoy in the early years of his reign, laying claim to Geneva in 1401 and buying other nearby lands in 1402 and 1406. In 1416 the Holy Roman emperor Sigismund visited the Savoyard capital, Chambéry, and elevated the county to the rank of a duchy.

In 1434, after 42 years on the throne, Amadeus retired to a monastery at Ripaille. His retirement was only partial, however, and he continued to exercise power, with his son Louis (Ludovico) acting as his lieutenant. During that period Amadeus' daughter Margherita was betrothed to Louis III of Anjou, pretender to the throne of Naples. Louis III died suddenly in 1434, and Amadeus briefly claimed Naples for Margherita but in the end abandoned the kingdom to Alfonso V of Aragon. In 1440 Amadeus abdicated.

One adventure remained to the aging duke: when Pope Eugenius IV broke off relations with the rebellious Council of Basel in 1439, the mutinous prelates elected Amadeus pope under the name of Felix V. Amadeus-Felix resigned 10 years later, under pressure from the kings of France, England, and Sicily, and became a cardinal for the final two years of his life.

SPAIN

• Amadeus (b. May 30, 1845, Turin, Piedmont—d. Jan. 18, 1890, Turin), king of Spain from Nov. 16, 1870, until his abdication on Feb. 11, 1873, after which the first Spanish republic was proclaimed. The second son of the future King Victor Emmanuel II of Sardinia–Piedmont (later, of Italy), he was originally called Amadeus I, duke of Aosta. His candidacy for the Spanish throne (vacant after the deposition of Isabella II in September 1868) was supported by Juan Prim, the Spanish prime minister, and Francisco Serrano, the regent. It was opposed by adherents of Isabella's son Alfonso de Borbón (later King Alfonso XII) and advocates of a republic. Elected king by the Cortes (parliament), Amadeus arrived in Spain on Dec. 30, 1870, the day on which Prim died from an assassin's attack. Bereft of Prim's help and feebly served by a series of short-lived ministries, Amadeus faced continuous turmoil. Support for Alfonso increased, along with republican agitation, and the Second Carlist War (1872–76) broke out. As soon as circumstances permitted, Amadeus abdicated gracefully and returned to Italy.

Amadeus, Lake, salty mud basin in southwestern Northern Territory, Australia, occupying a shallow trough filled with sediments washed from the MacDonnell (north) and Musgrave (south) ranges. It intermittently contains a few inches of water and at such times may measure as much as 90 mi (145 km) long and 12 mi wide, covering 340 sq mi (880 sq km). When dry, it is a playa, or salt flat. The explorer Ernest Giles visited the lake in 1872 and named it after Amadeus (Amadeo), then king of Spain. Some cattle, sustained by underground water, are raised in the vicinity, and natural gas has been found there. Lake Neale is a similar feature 50 mi west.

Amadi, Elechi (b. 1934, Allura, Nigeria), Nigerian fiction writer whose works depict Nigerian rural life, often that of the Ikwerre people.

Amadi was educated at Government College, Umuahia, and University College, Ibadan, in physics and mathematics, later participating in the Iowa International Writing Program in 1973–74 in the United States. Amadi served in the Nigerian Army, taught, and worked for the Ministry of Information in Rivers State. He was also an active member of the Rivers State Council of Arts and Culture. *Sunset in Biafra* (1973), his only work of nonfiction, describes his personal experiences as a soldier and civilian during the Biafran conflict.

Amadi is best known for his historical trilogy about ordinary people of rural Nigeria presented from an insider's perspective: *The Concubine* (1966), *The Great Ponds* (1969), and *The Slave* (1978). These novels focus on man's fate and the extent to which he can change it; the relationships between people and their gods are central in all of them. Amadi is a keen observer of details of daily life and religious rituals, which he unobtrusively describes in his dramatic stories. Similar emphases are found in his verse play, *Isiburu* (1973), about a champion wrestler who is ultimately defeated by the supernatural power of his enemy. Among his other works are *Pepper Soup and the Road to Ibadan* (1977) and *Dancer of Johannesburg* (1978).

Amadís of Gaul, Spanish AMADÍS DE GAULA, prose romance of chivalry, possibly Portuguese in origin. The first known version of this work, dating from 1508, was written in Spanish by Garci Ordóñez (or Rodríguez) de Montalvo, who claimed to have "corrected and emended" corrupt originals. Internal evidence suggests that the *Amadís* had been in circulation since the early 14th century or even the late 13th.

In Montalvo's version, Amadís was the most handsome, upright, and valiant of knights; the story of his incredible feats of arms, in which he is never defeated, was interwoven with that of his love for Oriana, daughter of Lisuarte, king of England; she was his constant inspiration, and eventually he won her in marriage.

Many characters in the *Amadís* were based on figures from Celtic romance, and the work was, indeed, Arthurian in spirit (*see* Arthurian legend). It differed, however, from the Arthurian cycle in numerous important respects: there was no particular sense of place or time, only a vague unspecified field for the interplay of idealized human relationships; whereas earlier romance had reflected a feudal society, the *Amadís* invested the monarchy with an authority that heralds the advent of absolutism; and Amadís himself was more idealized and therefore less human than such earlier heroes as Lancelot and Tristan. He was also far more chaste: French romance had already put a courtly veneer over the disruptive eroticism of the Celtic tales, but, with the *Amadís,* medieval chivalry achieved complete respectability.

The work and its exaltation of new standards of knightly conduct caught the imagination of polite society all over Europe. In France, especially, it became the textbook of chivalresque deportment and epistolary style. Throughout the 16th century, numerous sequels and feeble imitations appeared, the fashion being given its deathblow by parody early in the 17th century in Miguel de Cervantes' novel *Don Quixote* (though Cervantes held the original in high esteem). The first English adaptation of the *Amadís* appeared in 1567; the best English translation is an abridged version by the poet Robert Southey, first published in 1803.

Amado, Jorge (b. Aug. 10, 1912, Ferradas, near Itabuna, Braz.), novelist whose stories of life in the Brazilian northeast have won international acclaim.

Born and brought up on a cacao plantation, Auricidea, he was educated at the Jesuit college and another school in Salvador, and he published his first novel at the age of 20. Three of his early works deal with the cacao plantations, emphasizing the exploitation and the misery of the migrant Negroes, mulattoes, and poor whites who pick the beans. The best of these, *Terras do Sem-Fin* (1944; *The Violent Land,* 1945), dealing with the struggle of rival planters for some cacao groves, has the primitive grandeur of a folk saga.

Amado became a journalist in 1930, and his literary career parallels a career in radical politics that won him election to the Constituent Assembly as a federal deputy representing the Communist Party of Brazil in 1946. He was imprisoned as early as 1935 and periodically exiled for his leftist activities, and many of his books were banned in Brazil and Portugal. Abroad, he cultivated the friendship of European intellectuals, notably Jean-Paul Sartre. He continued to produce novels with facility, most of them picaresque, ribald tales of Bahian city life, especially that of the racially conglomerate lower classes. *Gabriela, Cravo e Canela* (1958; *Gabriela, Clove and Cinnamon,* 1962) and *Dona Flor e Seus Dois Maridos* (1966; *Dona Flor and Her Two Husbands,* 1969; film, 1978) both preserve Amado's political attitude in their satire. His later works include *Tenda dos Milagres* (1969; *Tent of Miracles,* 1971) and *Tieto do Agreste* (1977; *Tieta, the Goat Girl,* 1979).

Amagasaki, city, industrial suburb of the Ōsaka–Kōbe Metropolitan Area, Hyōgo Prefecture (*ken*), Honshu, Japan. In the feudal period it was a castle town. During the 20th century it attracted large, modern factories, formerly geared to wartime production, to produce iron and steel goods, electrical machinery, transport vehicles, and chemicals. The main industrial belt lies along the coast, where costly protective dikes have been constructed. The city has superb railroad facilities and canals and strong economic ties with Ōsaka. Extensive withdrawal of groundwater for industrial use has led to serious land subsidence, rendering the city vulnerable to high waves during the typhoon season. Preventive measures include landfill and external water supply systems. Pop. (1983 est.) 514,679.

amakihi (*Loxops virens*), perhaps the commonest native songbird in Hawaii, a member of the Hawaiian honeycreeper family, Drepanididae (order Passeriformes). It is 12 centimetres (5 inches) long, with yellow body, black eye-mark, and rather short, slightly curved bill. It feeds on insects and small fruits in brush land and forest, and it has mewing and trilling calls.

Amakihi (*Loxops virens*)
Painting by H. Douglas Pratt

Amakusa-rettō (Japanese: Amakusa Archipelago), archipelago off western Kyushu, Japan, in the Amakusa-nada (Amakusa Sea). Administered by Kumamoto Prefecture, it includes about 100 islands, the largest of which are Kami-shima, Amakusa-shimo-shima, and Ōyano-jima. There is little farming because of the rough, mountainous terrain, but forestry, orange cultivation, offshore fishing, and pearl cultivation are actively pursued. Bituminous coal is mined on the main islands, and pottery-clay deposits are worked.

The islands, linked by five painted bridges, are part of Unzen-Amakusa National Park. They are served by ferry from Misumi on Kyushu proper. The archipelago was long the gateway for Western culture and was an early centre of Christianity. The largest cities are Hondo and Ushibuka, both on Amakusa-shimo-shima.

The Amakusa-rettō, connected by bridges to mainland Kyushu, Japan
Orion Press—FPG/EB Inc.

Amalaric (d. 531), king of the Visigoths, son of Alaric I.

Amalaric was a child when his father fell in battle against Clovis, king of the Franks (507). He was carried for safety into Spain, which country, with southern Languedoc and Provence, was thenceforth ruled by his maternal grandfather Theodoric the Great (*q.v.*) through his vice-regent, an Ostrogothic nobleman named Theudis (*q.v.*). On Theodoric's death in 526, Amalaric assumed full royal power in Spain and a part of Languedoc, relinquishing Provence to his cousin Athalaric. He married Clotilda, daughter of Clovis, but his disputes with her, he being an Arian and she a Catholic, brought on a Frankish invasion, in which he lost his life.

Amalasuntha, also spelled AMALASUENTHA (b. 498—d. 535, Tuscany), daughter of Theodoric the Great, Ostrogothic king of Italy, and queen and regent of the Ostrogoths (526–534).

When her husband died, Amalasuntha was left with a son, Athalaric, and a daughter. At Theodoric's death, in 526, Athalaric was 10 years old, and Amalasuntha assumed the regency. Her pro-Byzantine policy, her patronage of literature and the arts, and her desire to educate her son as a Roman prince were vigorously opposed by a large segment of the Ostrogoth nobility. Hence, she moved even closer to her Byzantine suzerain, arranging with the emperor Justinian that if she were removed from power she would transfer herself and the whole Ostrogothic treasure to Constantinople. After successfully quelling a plot against her in 533, she put to death three suspected Ostrogothic nobles.

Upon Athalaric's death in October 534, Amalasuntha shared the throne with her cousin Theodahad (*q.v.*), hoping to give him the title of king while retaining actual power herself. Theodahad, however, influenced by forces increasingly hostile to Amalasuntha's policies, banished her to an island in the lake of Bolsena, where she was strangled in her bath by relatives of the nobles killed after the plot of 533.

Amalekite, member of an ancient nomadic tribe, or collection of tribes, described in the Old Testament as relentless enemies of Israel, even though they were closely related to Ephraim, one of the 12 tribes of Israel. The district over which they ranged was south of Judah and probably extended into northern Arabia. The Amalekites harassed the Hebrews during their Exodus from Egypt and attacked them at Rephidim near Mt. Sinai, where they were defeated by Joshua. They were among the nomadic raiders defeated by Gideon and were condemned to annihilation by Samuel. Their final defeat occurred in the time of Hezekiah.

Amálfi, town and archiepiscopal see, Salerno province, Campania region, southern Italy, in the ravine of the Valle (valley) dei Mulini, on the Golfo (gulf) di Salerno, southeast of Naples. Although it was known in the 4th century, Amalfi was of little importance until the mid-6th century under the Byzantines.

Cathedral of S. Andrea, Amalfi, Italy
Herbert Fristedt—Ostman Agency

As one of the first Italian maritime republics in the 9th century, it rivalled Pisa, Genoa, Venice, and Gaeta as a naval power in trade with the East. Subdued and annexed by King Roger II of Sicily in 1131, it was sacked by the Pisans in 1135 and 1137 and rapidly declined in importance, although its maritime code, the Tavola Amalfitana (Table of Amalfi), was recognized in the Mediterranean until 1570. The town is dominated by the cathedral of S. Andrea (begun in the 9th century, often restored), which has magnificent bronze doors, executed at Constantinople about 1065, and a campanile (1180–1276). Also notable are the Chiostro del Paradiso (cloister; 1266–68), adjacent to the cathedral, and the former Capuchin convent (founded 1212), which is now a hotel.

Amalfi is now one of the important tourist resorts in Italy, noted for its mild climate and splendid coastal scenery. There are water-driven paper mills in the Valle dei Mulini. The local cultivation of lemons is known throughout Italy. Pop. (1981 prelim.) mun., 6,052.

Amalfi, Ottavio Piccolomini, duca d' (duke of): *see* Piccolomini-Pieri, Ottavio.

amalgam, alloy of mercury and one or more other metals. Amalgams are crystalline in structure, except for those with a high mercury content, which are liquid. They have been known since early times and were mentioned by Pliny the Elder in the 1st century AD. In dentistry, an amalgam of silver and tin, containing minor amounts of copper and zinc, is used to fill teeth.

A sodium amalgam is formed during the manufacture of chlorine and sodium hydroxide by the electrolysis of brine in cells wherein a stream of mercury constitutes the negative electrode. Reaction of the amalgam with water produces a solution of sodium hydroxide and regenerates the mercury for re-use.

Fine particles of silver and gold can be recovered by agitating their ores with mercury and allowing the resultant pasty or liquid amalgam to settle. By distillation of the amalgam, the mercury is reclaimed, and the precious metals are isolated as a residue.

Amalgams of silver, gold, and palladium are known in nature. Moschellandsbergite, silver amalgam, is found at Moschellandsberg, W. Ger.; Sala, Swed.; and Isère, Fr. Gold amalgam occurs in California, Colombia, and Borneo. Potarite, palladium amalgam, is found in diamond washings from the Potaro River in Guyana. For detailed physical properties of naturally occurring amalgams, *see* native element (table).

Amalgamated Clothing and Textile Workers Union, U.S. and Canadian labour union formed in 1976 by the merger of the Amalgamated Clothing Workers of America (ACWA) and the Textile Workers Union of America. The latter was a smaller union, founded in 1939. The ACWA was formed in 1914 as a splinter group from the United Garment Workers. Sidney Hillman (*q.v.*) became president on its founding and held the office until his death in 1946. By the 1930s the ACWA had become the most important and successful of the clothing unions. It provided great improvements and benefits for its members, including cooperative housing, banks, and insurance programs. In 1933 the ACWA was admitted into the American Federation of Labor, but it withdrew to become a founding member of the Congress of Industrial Organizations (CIO) in 1935. At the time of its formation the union had about 500,000 members.

Amalienborg, architectural complex in Copenhagen, built during the reign (1746–66) of King Frederick V, comprising the four interconnected buildings of the Amalienborg royal palace and the octagonal courtyard surrounded by them. The project, as conceived by the Danish architect Niels Eigtved, was originally to have consisted of eight town mansions, separated by streets radiating from the open octagon. After modification to four main buildings by the German-born painter-architect Marcus Tuscher, the plan was executed by Eigtved, who also designed numerous other buildings in the surrounding district. At the centre of the court stands an equestrian statue of Frederick V by the French sculptor J.F.J. Saly.

Amalric I, French AMAURY, or AMAURI (d. July 11, 1174), king of Jerusalem from 1163 to 1174, a strong ruler, noted for his protection of the rights of vassals and for his influence in preventing Muslim unity around the Holy Lands.

Amalric had been count of Jaffa and Ascalon before succeeding his brother Baldwin III on the throne in 1163. He was forced first to annul his marriage to Agnes of Courtenay because she was his third cousin (rights of legitimacy and inheritance, however, were granted to his son and daughter by Agnes). Insisting that a case of an unjustly dismissed vassal be heard, he passed a law giving vassals the right to appeal against treatment by their lords to the High Court.

Because Egypt had never paid the yearly tribute that it had promised Baldwin III in 1160, Amalric, hoping to gain control of Egypt and break Muslim unity, invaded Egypt in 1163. During his unsuccessful attempt, his kingdom was attacked by the Syrian ruler Nureddin. Gradually the war became a contest for control of Egypt. Amalric appealed both to the Byzantine emperor Manuel I Comnenus and to Louis VII of France for help. Manuel agreed to lend his fleet for one of Amalric's campaigns, with the provision that Amalric divide Egypt with Byzantium. The expedition failed, but the Byzantine–Palestinian alliance was maintained. Upon Amalric's death his son Baldwin was crowned king of Jerusalem as Baldwin IV.

Articles are alphabetized word by word, not letter by letter

Amalric II, byname AMALRIC OF LUSIGNAN, French AMAURY, or AMAURI, DE LUSIGNAN (b. *c.* 1155—d. April 1, 1205), king of Cyprus (1194–1205) and of Jerusalem (1198–1205), who ably ruled the two separated kingdoms.

Amalric had been constable of Palestine before he was summoned by the Franks in Cyprus to become king after the death of his brother Guy of Lusignan. Amalric planned a close alliance with Henry of Champagne, uncrowned ruler of Palestine, betrothing his three sons to Henry's three daughters. He also became the vassal of the Holy Roman emperor Henry VI. On Henry of Champagne's accidental death (1197), Amalric, a widower, was induced to marry Henry's widow, Queen Isabella I, because the emperor's German advisers were hoping to get the Latin Kingdom of Jerusalem (then only a thin strip of the Palestinian coast) as a fief like Cyprus. Amalric, however, though he was crowned in 1198, decided to administer Jerusalem separately and to regard himself as merely its regent.

As king of Jerusalem, Amalric was able to make peace with his Muslim neighbours, thanks to the struggle that took place among them after Saladin's death in 1193. Though both sides periodically broke the treaty, it was renewed in September 1204 for six years. On Amalric's death Cyprus was left to his 6-year-old son, Hugh, and the kingdom of Jerusalem remained in Isabella's possession.

Amalthaea, in Greek (originally Cretan) mythology, the foster mother of Zeus, king of the gods. She is sometimes represented as the goat that suckled the infant god in a cave in Crete, sometimes as a nymph who fed him the milk of a goat. This goat having broken off one of its horns, Amalthaea filled the horn with flowers and fruits and presented it to Zeus, who, according to one version, placed it, together with the goat, among the stars. In general, it was regarded as the symbol of inexhaustible riches and plenty and became the attribute of various divinities and of rivers as fertilizers of the land.

Amalthea, small, inner satellite of Jupiter discovered in 1892 by the U.S. astronomer E.E. Barnard. It circles Jupiter once every 11^h59^m at a distance of 181,300 kilometres (112,410 miles) in a nearly circular, uninclined orbit. Photographs transmitted by the U.S. probes Voyagers 1 and 2 in 1979 show that Amalthea is an irregular body measuring 270 × 165 × 150 km (167 × 102 × 93 mi); the long axis always points toward Jupiter. Amalthea has a very red and very dark surface. The red colour might be the result of contamination by sulfur from the nearby satellite Io. The largest crater on Amalthea is Pan, which has a diameter of about 90 km (56 mi).

Amambaí Mountains, Portuguese SERRA DE AMAMBAÍ, Spanish CORDILLERA DE AMAMBAY, highlands in western Mato Grosso do Sul state, Brazil, and eastern Paraguay. Extending south-southwest initially as the Serra de Maracaju for about 200 mi (320 km) from Campo Grande, the capital of Mato Grosso do Sul, they form the western side of the Brazilian Highlands and mark the divide between the tributaries of the Paraguay River and those of the Paraná. Like most of the highlands of the Mato Grosso, the Amambaí Mountains are tabular uplands without sharp peaks. The average elevation is 1,300 ft (400 m) above sea level; the highest elevation is 2,300 ft. The southern end of the highlands forms a part of the border between Brazil and Paraguay. Principal towns of the Amambaí Mountains include Ponta Porã, Brazil, and Pedro Juan Caballero, Paraguay.

Amambay, department, northeastern Paraguay, bounded north and east by Brazil. Between Amambay and Brazil lie the Río Apa and the Cordillera (mountains) de Amambay, the western flanks of which provide Paraguay's highest terrain. Punta Porá is the second highest peak in Paraguay, at a height of 2,296 ft (700 m) above sea level. Exploitation of mountain forests is the main economic activity in the department. Drained by the Paraguay River, the territory comprises 4,993 sq mi (12,933 sq km). The department produces cattle and maté (tea) and practices subsistence agriculture. Route 5 and a railroad link Pedro Juan Caballero, the departmental capital, with communities across the Brazilian frontier and with the river port of Concepción. Pop. (1982 prelim.) 68,534.

Amami-Ō-shima (Japanese: Amami Great Island), Kagoshima Prefecture (*ken*), Japan, largest island in the Amami-guntō group of the northern Ryukyu Islands. Most of the 274-sq-mi (709-sq-km) island is mountainous and forested. A quasi-national park protects landscapes at the higher elevations. Yūwandake (Mount Yūwan) is the highest mountain at 2,276 ft (694 m). The lower, cultivated areas produce timber, sugarcane, and rice. A hydroelectric station operates on the Sumiyō-gawa (Sumiyō River). Naze, the largest city, has a scientific research station and hospitals for senior citizens and retarded children. Naze and Setouchi are domestic shipping ports and Setouchi has a museum. An airport is situated on Kasari-sake (Cape Kasari) and a highway connects Kasari and Setouchi. Pop. (1980 prelim.), incl. adjoining islets, 75,836.

Amana Colonies, settlement in Iowa County, east central Iowa, U.S., near the Iowa River, 20 mi (32 km) west-northwest of Iowa City, comprising a group of seven small villages: Amana, East Amana, Middle Amana, High Amana, West Amana, South Amana, and Homestead.

Amana developed from the Community of True Inspiration, founded in 1714 in Hesse, Ger., by Johann Friedrich Rock and Eberhard Ludwig Gruber, Pietistic mystics reacting against Lutheran orthodoxy. They taught that direct revelation and divine inspiration were current realities. Following Rock's denunciation by the Pietist leader Count von Zinzendorf and then, in 1749, his death, the movement disintegrated. Its remnants were strengthened in 1817, when Christian Metz and Barbara Heinemann reported that they had received the gift of direct inspiration. This group, centred mainly in Württemberg, encountered hostility from the civil authorities because of their opposition to war and other doctrines, and in 1842 they migrated to the United States, purchasing land near Buffalo, N.Y., where they established the communal Ebenezer Society. In 1855 about 800 members moved westward to Iowa, where 18,000 ac (7,280 ha; later expanded to 26,000 ac) had been purchased. This new home, governed by elected elders, was called Amana (a mountain range in Lebanon referred to in Song of Solomon 4:8, and meaning "to remain true" or "believe faithfully") and was incorporated in 1859. Members gave up their property to a common fund and were promised security through life. They held two meetings on Sunday, many on weekdays, and prayer meetings every morning. They celebrated the Lord's Supper, including ceremonial foot washing, once a year. In addition to their opposition to military service, the citizens of Amana also opposed taking oaths, amusement, and a paid ministry.

The community prospered at first but began to decline after the Civil War. Financial disaster caused by the 1930s Depression necessitated reorganization in 1932. Communal property was dissolved and the villages were organized on the basis of a joint stock corporation, called the Amana Society, with the workers as stockholders. Pension benefits and burial were free. In addition to its seven farms, one for each village, the Amana Society operates factories that produce woollens, furniture, wines, bakery goods, and meat specialties. Amana Refrigeration, Inc., formerly a division of the Amana Society, manufactures refrigerators, freezers, and microwave ovens.

The Amana Church Society, separately organized in 1932, continues its Pietistic emphasis and remains the dominating force in the community. Simple worship services, conducted in German in unadorned village churches, include readings from the writings of the sect's founders. The church society, governed by 26 elders, has no ordained clergy. It reported 600 members in four churches in the late 1970s. Pop. (1980 est.) 1,675.

Amanita, genus of about 100 species of mushrooms of the family Amanitaceae, order Agaricales, some of which are poisonous to man. The amanitas typically have white spores, a ring on the stem slightly below the cap, a veil (volva) torn as the cap expands, and a cup from which the stalk arises.

Among the deadliest of all mushrooms are the destroying angels (*A. bispongera, A. ocreata, A. verna,* and *A. virosa*). They develop a large white fruiting body and are found in forests during wet periods in summer and autumn.

Destroying angel (*Amanita verna*)
Mary W. Ferguson

Death cap (*A. phalloides*), also deadly, is found in woods or their borders. It has a green or brown cap and appears in summer or early autumn. Other poisonous species include *A. brunnescens* and *A. pantherina*; common edible species include *A. caesarea, A. rubescens,* and *A. vaginata.*

Fly agaric (*Amanita muscaria*)
Larry C. Moon—Tom Stack & Associates

The fly agaric, or fly amanita (*Amanita muscaria*), is a poisonous mushroom found in pastures and fields in summer. It was once used as a fly poison. *See also* mushroom and mushroom poisoning.

Amānollāh Khān (b. June 1, 1892, Paghmān, Afg.—d. April 25, 1960, Zürich), ruler of Afghanistan (1919–29) who led his country to full independence from British influence.

Amānollāh, 1928
BBC Hulton Picture Library

A favoured son of the Afghan ruler Ḥabībollāh Khān, Amānollāh took possession of the throne immediately after his father's assassination in 1919, at a time when Great Britain exercised an important influence on Afghan affairs. In his coronation address Amānollāh declared total independence from Great Britain. This led to war with the British, but fighting was confined to a series of skirmishes between an ineffective Afghan army and a British Indian army exhausted from the heavy demands of World War I. A peace treaty recognizing the independence of Afghanistan was signed at Rāwalpindi (now in Pakistan) in August 1919.

Although a charming man and a sincere patriot and reformer, Amānollāh was also impulsive and tactless and tended to surround himself with poor advisers. Shortly after ascending the throne, he pushed for reforms, including an education program and road-building projects, but was opposed by reactionaries. In 1928 he returned from a trip to Europe with plans for legislative reform and emancipation of women, proposals that caused his popular support to drop and enraged the mullahs (religious leaders). In 1928 a tribal revolt resulted in a chaotic situation during which a notorious bandit leader, Bachcheh Saqow, seized Kābul, the capital city, and declared himself ruler. Amānollāh attempted to regain the throne but, for reasons that are unclear, failed to do so. He abdicated in January 1929 and left Afghanistan for permanent exile that May.

Amapá, territory, northern Brazil, bounded on the north by a small portion of Suriname and by French Guiana, on the northeast by the Atlantic Ocean, on the south and west by the Brazilian state of Pará, and on the southeast by the Amazon River. Formerly a part of Pará state, Amapá, long claimed by France, was created by a Brazilian territorial decree law in 1943, with its capital at Macapá (*q.v.*). Most of its 54,161 sq mi (140,276 sq km) is tropical rain forest, but there are patches of savanna along the coast, which has long remained scantily populated. The chief products are cabinet woods (mahogany, cedar, pine, eucalyptus, rosewood), medicinal plants, wild-animal skins, rubber, jute, Brazil nuts, fish, crustaceans, and mollusks. Gold is found in the stream gravels. Amapá is known primarily for the large manganese and iron-ore mines inland from Macapá. In the late 1970s factories were built to produce ferromanganese and silicomanganese. Oil was discovered in the continental shelf off Amapá territory, and exploratory wells were drilled. Macapá's port (Pôrto Santana), highways, and railroad link Macapá to the state's interior and to northwestern Brazil. Pop. (1983 est.) 200,000.

Amar Dās (b. 1479, Khadur?, India—d. 1574, Goindwal), third Sikh Gurū, appointed at the advanced age of 73, noted for his division of the Punjab into 22 Sikh dioceses and his dispatch of missionaries to spread the faith. Realizing that periodical meetings of all Sikhs would strengthen the faith, he ordered three great festivals a year. He was much revered for his wisdom and piety, and it was said that even the Mughal emperor Akbar sought his advice and ate in the Sikhs' casteless *laṅgar* (free "kitchen"). Under Amar Dās's direction, the city of Goindwal became a Sikh centre of learning.

Gurū Amar Dās advocated a middle way of life between the extremes of asceticism and sensuous pleasure, and praised the life of the ordinary family man. Thus a man could enjoy prosperity and please God also. Among his social reforms, he further extended the *laṅgar* and made it a rule that anyone wanting to see him must first eat in the kitchen. He purified the Sikh religion of Hindu practices, encouraged intercaste marriage, and allowed widows to remarry. He also strictly enjoined his followers to refrain from the prevailing Hindu practice of suttee (self-immolation of a widow on her husband's funeral pyre).

'Amārah, al-, capital of Maysān *muḥāfaẓah* (governorate), southeastern Iraq. Situated on a low ridge beside the Tigris River, it is Iraq's chief port on that waterway south of Baghdad. It is a trade centre for agricultural produce, livestock, wool, and hides and is known for weaving and silverware. In World War I it was captured by the British during their 1915 Mesopotamia campaign. Before 1958, al-'Amārah was an outstanding example of autocratic rule by *shaykhs*, who owned large estates in this rice-growing area and also maintained large private armies. After the overthrow of the monarchy, land distribution gradually became more democratic. Pop. (1970 est.) 80,078.

Amaral Martins, António Jacinto do: *see* Jacinto, António.

Amaranthaceae, the amaranth family of flowering plants in the order Caryophyllales, with about 60 genera and more than 800 species of herbs, with a few shrubs, trees, and vines, native to tropical America and Africa. The leaves of members of the family usually have nonindented edges. Flowers may be

Love-lies-bleeding (*Amaranthus caudatus*)

A.J. Huxley

male or female or contain both types of reproductive structures; several leaflike bracts are present below each flower; and the fruit may be a capsule, utricle, nutlet, drupe, or berry. Species of globe amaranth (*Gomphrena*) and cockscomb (*Celosia*) are cultivated as ornamentals; the genera *Alternanthera* and *Iresine* each have several species that are cultivated as bedding plants for their attractive and colourful leaves. The genus *Amaranthus* contains the ornamentals love-lies-bleeding, or tassel flower (*A. caudatus*), prince's feather (*A. hybridus erythrostachys*), and Joseph's-coat (*A. tricolor*), and many weedy plants known as pigweed, especially *A. retroflexus*. Prostrate pigweed (*A. graecizans*) and white pigweed (*A. albus*) are common throughout Europe in cultivated and waste areas. Tumbleweed (*A. albus*), a widespread weed in the western U.S., has been introduced elsewhere in the world.

Some *Amaranthus* species are potential high-protein grain crops; strains are being bred for high yield and seedhead stability.

Amarapura, town, Mandalay Division (*taing*), Upper Burma, on the left bank of the Irrawaddy River. A suburb of Mandalay, it is also known as Taung-myo (Southern Town) or Myohaung (Old City). Founded by King Bodawpaya in 1783 as his new capital, it supplanted Ava, 6 mi (10 km) southwest. Its population in 1810 was estimated at 170,000, but a fire in that year and the return of the court to Ava in 1823 caused a decline to about 30,000 by 1827. King Tharrawaddy (reigned 1837–46) restored Amarapura as the capital, but an earthquake in 1839 destroyed much of the city, which was finally abandoned for Mandalay by King Mindon Min in the late 1850s. Ruined walls indicate that Amarapura, called the "City of Immortals," was laid out as a square with sides 3/4 mi long. A solid brick pagoda, 100 ft (30 m) high, stood at each corner; a celebrated temple with 250 pillars of gilt wood contained a colossal bronze statue of Buddha. The tombs of Bodawpaya and his successor, Bagyidaw, are in the city.

Long known for its silk weaving, Amarapura is the site of a weaving school. Colourful *longyis* (skirts worn by both sexes) are produced in a distinctive heavy silk. The long-established bronze industry is famous for Buddha figures, bells, and gongs. Tile, pottery, and baskets are also manufactured. On the Rangoon–Mandalay railway, Amarapura serves as the junction for Lashio and Myitkyinā. Near the city, one of a chain of lakes is crossed by U Bein's Bridge; built of teak from the palaces of Ava more 200 years ago, it leads to the Taungthaman Kyauktawgyi pagoda. Pop. (latest census) 10,519.

Amaravalli (India): *see* Amreli.

Amarāvati, also spelled AMARAVATHI, town, Guntūr district, Andhra Pradesh state, southern India. Situated on the Krishna River, it was an ancient Buddhist centre in the region. Its monasteries and university attracted students from throughout India and the Far East. Amarāvati is known for the relief sculptures that were a part of its great Buddhist shrine, although most of these are now in museums, including a museum in Amarāvati.

Amarāvatī sculpture, Indian sculpture that flourished in the Andhra region of southeastern India from about the 2nd century BC to the end of the 3rd century AD, during the rule of the Sātavāhana dynasty. It is known for its superb reliefs, which are among the world's finest examples of narrative sculpture.

In addition to the ruins of the great *stūpa,* or relic mound, at Amarāvatī, the style is also seen in the *stūpa* remains at Jaggayyapeta, Nāgārjunīkoṇḍa, and Goli, in Andhra Pradesh, and as far west as Ter, Mahārāshtra state. The style also spread to Ceylon (now Sri Lanka), as seen at Anurādhapura, and to much of Southeast Asia.

Dream of Māyā presaging the Buddha's birth, marble relief from Nāgārjunīkoṇḍa, Andhra Pradesh, India, Amarāvatī school, *c.* 3rd century AD; in the Indian Museum, Calcutta

P. Chandra

The Amarāvatī *stūpa* was begun about 200 BC and underwent several renovations and additions. One of the largest *stūpa*s built in Buddhist India, it was about 160 feet (50 metres) in diameter and 90 to 100 feet (about 30 metres) high, but it has been largely destroyed, much of the stone having been used by local contractors during the 19th century to make lime mortar. Many of the surviving narrative reliefs and decorative plaques are in the Government Museum, Madras, and the British Museum. A depiction of the monument on a railing slab gives an indication of the appearance of the *stūpa* at the end of the 2nd century AD. The slab shows a low drum with a hemispherical dome, the railings and drum covered with carvings, and the whole surrounded by an elaborate and richly carved railing. The four cardinal points are marked by groups of five pillars, while free-standing columns topped by lions are set up at the four entrances, replacing the *toraṇa* (ceremonial gateway) of earlier *stūpas*.

The reliefs, carved on the greenish-white limestone characteristic of the region, mostly depict events of the Buddha's life and his previous births (*Jātaka* stories). The crowded yet unified compositions of the later period are filled with dynamic movement, a keen awareness of the dramatic, and a delight in the sensuous world. Overlapping figures and the use of diagonals suggest depth. There is an abundance of rounded forms and a richness so overwhelming that the frame is barely able to contain the sculpture. The four centuries over which the style developed were also a period of change from aniconic to iconic representation of the Buddha, and at Amarāvatī both methods of depiction appear together on one slab—the iconic being represented by images of the seated and standing Buddha, and the aniconic by an empty throne symbolizing his presence.

Amargosa Range, group of mountains in eastern California and southern Nevada, U.S., separating Death Valley from the Amargosa Desert. Part of the Basin Ranges of eastern California, the Amargosa Range extends 110 mi (180 km) from Grapevine Peak (8,705 ft [2,653 m]), south-southeastward to the Amargosa River. It is composed of three distinct mountain groups: the Grapevine, Funeral, and Black. Dante's View, in the Black mountains, rises to 5,475 ft (1,669 m) and provides a clear view of Death Valley and the Panamint Range, which lies beyond it.

Amarillo, city, seat (1887) of Potter County (and partly in Randall County), on the High Plains of northern Texas, U.S., 122 mi (196 km) north of Lubbock. Now the chief city of the Texas Panhandle, it originated in 1887 as a railroad construction camp and grew after 1900 when wheat cultivation and ranching became important in the region. The discovery of petroleum and natural gas deposits in the 1920s further promoted the community's development as a regional and industrial centre, though in the 1930s general economic depression and prolonged drought restricted growth. After 1940, however, extensive irrigation from underground water increased agricultural output. In addition to oil, farming, and ranching, the city has a large copper refinery and ordnance and helicopter factories. Helium is found in large quantities in the area, and Amarillo is the site of a major helium plant and an unusual monument (a six-story stainless steel column built in 1968 to commemorate the element).

Amarillo College, with the Amarillo Art Center on its campus, was founded in 1929. The city has a notable medical centre, holds a huge livestock auction, and is the headquarters of the American Quarter Horse Association. West Texas State University (1910) is at nearby Canyon. Palo Duro Canyon State Park is 16 mi southeast, and Buffalo Lake National Wildlife Refuge is southwest. The name Amarillo probably comes from the Spanish word for yellow, the colour of local clay deposits. Inc. 1892. Pop. (1980) city, 149,230; metropolitan area (SMSA), 173,699.

Amarinya language: *see* Amharic language.

Amarna, Tell el-, also spelled TALL AL-AMARNA, or TEL EL-AMARNA, site of the ruins and tombs of the city of Akhetaton (Horizon of Aton) in Upper Egypt, 44 miles (71 kilometres) north of modern Asyūt in al-Minyā *muḥāfaẓah* (governorate). On a virgin site on the east bank of the Nile, Akhenaton (Amenhotep IV) built the city *c.* 1375 BC as the new capital of his kingdom when he abandoned the worship of Amon and devoted himself to that of Aton. About four years after Akhenaton's death (*c.* 1360) the court returned to Thebes, and the city was abandoned.

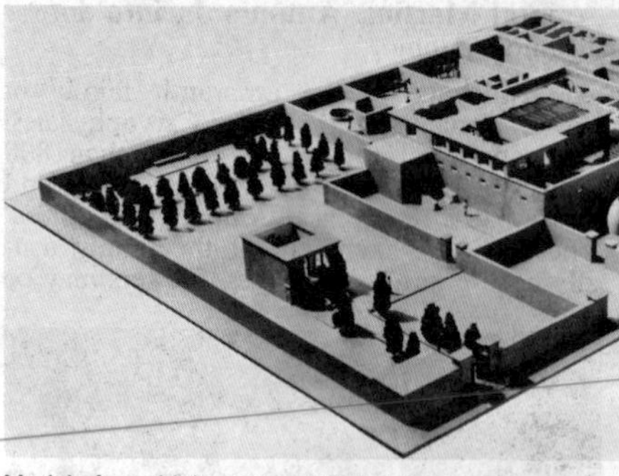

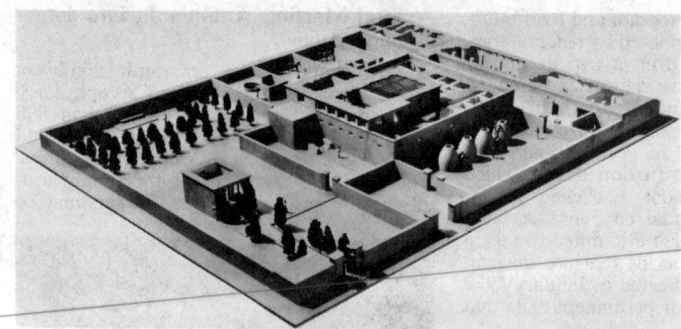

Model of a noble's estate at Tell el-Amarna
By courtesy of the Oriental Institute, the University of Chicago

Though it had a brief existence, Akhetaton is one of the few ancient Egyptian cities that has been carefully excavated. Because Akhenaton chose a virgin site for his capital and because of the relatively short duration of its occupancy, the excavators could reconstruct an unusually accurate picture of the layout of the city.

The principal buildings of Akhetaton lay on either side of the Royal Road, the largest of them being the Great Temple of the Aton, primarily a series of walled courts leading to the completely open-air main sanctuary. Near the Great Temple were the palace and the commodious residence of the royal family. Most of the dwellings at Tell el-Amarna were of baked mud brick, and the walls, floors, and ceilings of many of the rooms were painted in a lively naturalistic style; each house had a shrine with a stela including scenes depicting the intimate family life of Akhenaton.

Among other major archaeological finds were portrait busts of Queen Nefertiti in the house of the sculptor Thutmose, and the 300 cuneiform tablets accidentally discovered in 1887 by a peasant woman. From them it was possible to trace the decline of the Egyptian Empire in the late 18th dynasty.

Unlike those of Thebes, the nobles' villas at Akhetaton had only one floor; the roof of the central living room, however, was usually higher than the rest of the house, thus permitting clerestory lighting and ventilation. The workers lived in simple row-houses.

Officials' tombs, resembling those at Thebes, were hewn into the desert hills to the east. Although the painted reliefs in the tomb chapels often appear to have been hastily carried out, they have been a major source of information on the daily life and religion of Akhenaton. Also, the drawings on the tomb walls depicting various buildings of the city helped the excavators to interpret the often meagre architectural remains. The reliefs, in an unconventional, often exaggerated style, tend to reflect a momentary and emotional aspect rather than the static mood that had characterized earlier Egyptian art.

The tomb of Akhenaton and his family, situated in the side of a dry watercourse east of the city, contained an unprecedented scene of the royal family in mourning over the death of the princess Meketaton, who was buried there. Excavations in the 1890s and late 1970s yielded fragments of Akhenaton's deliberately smashed sarcophagus and numerous broken ushabti.

When Tutankhamen transferred the residence back to Thebes, he moved the royal burials to the Theban necropolis where Smenkhkare, Queen Tiy, and, from the latest research, Akhenaton himself were found in a cache of royal mummies.

After its abandonment, Horemheb razed the city and Ramses II reused the stone blocks of its temples for his work at nearby Hermopolis.

Amarna style, also called TELL EL-AMARNA STYLE, revolutionary style of Egyptian art created by Amenhotep IV, who took the name Akhenaton during his reign (1379–62 BC) in the 18th dynasty. Often referred to as the Amarna heresy, Akhenaton's alteration of the artistic and religious life of Egypt was drastic. He returned to the ancient concept of the pharaoh as the greatest god, an incarnation, as his new name indicated, of the god he designated the supreme and only deity, Aton, the sun disk. This sun cult, also an archaic revival, was practiced to the exclusion of worship of the entire Egyptian pantheon, including Amon-Re, formerly considered king of the gods and patronized liberally by Akhenaton's father. Not content to erect temples to Aton merely in Thebes, the capital, Akhenaton moved to the edge of the desert, near the present Tell el-Amarna, and named his new capital Akhetaton (Horizon of Aton).

After the banishment of all Egyptian gods except Aton, Akhenaton limited artistic subject matter mainly to depictions of himself and his family, both in casual domestic scenes, which were his favourite, and in concert with Aton, who was shown as a golden orb radiating beams of light that ended in little hands proffering the sign of life, the *ankh*, to Akhenaton and his queen, Nefertiti. It was in the method of portraying the Pharaoh and his family that the most remarkable aspect of Amarna art lies, for the old stiff canon was abandoned in favour of a "naturalistic" depiction, which showed them more as actual human beings. Essentially it was a secularization of art that took place; the royal family was now shown in the same casual poses and settings as servants and commoners had been depicted in the past. Some experts see the depictions of Akhenaton himself—with an elongated head, slender neck and limbs, and protruding belly—as artistic overstatements of basically real physical attributes, possibly the result of a rare disease that deformed his head and hips. Whatever the reason, the expressionistic physical type eventually became canonized and was used to some degree in most depictions of human form throughout the Amarna period.

Painted wall reliefs found in the tombs of Akhetaton officials reveal much about everyday life there, as opposed to the life-after-death scenes usually found in tombs. Painted scenes spread from wall to wall, ignoring the tradi-

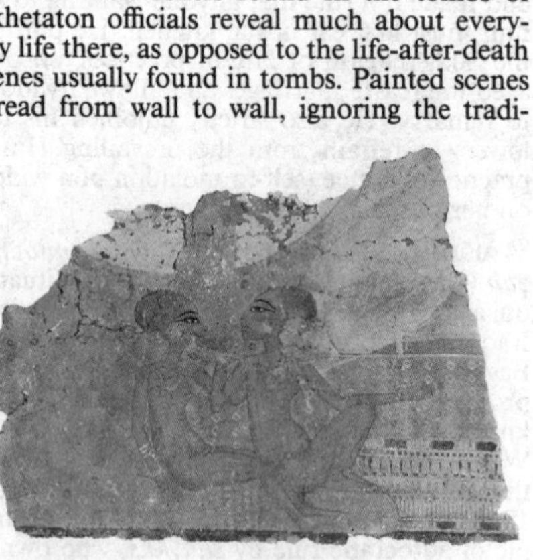

"Daughters of Akhenaton," fragment of a wall painting from the tomb of Akhenaton, Tell el-Amarna, *c.* 1372–55 BC, New Kingdom, 18th dynasty; in the Ashmolean Museum, Oxford
Holle Bildarchiv, Baden-Baden

tional practice of dividing pictorial space into registers, or horizontal bands. A love of natural form developed, and pure landscape came into its own as subject matter. Portraits, in the form of busts and masks, were done for their own sake for the first time in history.

Neither the artistic revolution nor the worship of Aton survived Akhenaton. The great temple was razed to the ground by opponents of the Aton cult, and Akhenaton's name was deleted from official king lists, being referred to thereafter as "that criminal of Akhetaton." His successor, the young Tutankhamen, attempted to return to more traditional artistic ideas, but Amarna influence is still evident in the art of this period. Throughout the remainder of the 18th dynasty, a steady purge of unorthodox artistic elements continued, and, by the reign of Horemheb, rigid formality had returned.

Articles are alphabetized word by word, not letter by letter

Amaryllidaceae, family of perennial herbs in the flowering plant order Liliales, containing about 65 genera and at least 835 species, distributed primarily in tropical and subtropical areas of the world. Members of the family have bulbs or underground stems; several strap- or lance-shaped leaves grouped at the base of the stem or arranged alternately along the stem; flowers usually with three petals and three sepals; and dry, capsule-shaped, and fleshy or berrylike fruits.

Many species are cultivated as garden ornamentals, especially belladonna lily (*Amaryllis belladonna*), tuberose (*Polianthes*), snowdrop (*Galanthus*), snowflake (*Leucojum*), and daffodil (*Narcissus*). Many tropical lilylike plants also belong to the family, such as those of the genera *Haemanthus* (Cape tulip, or blood lily), *Alstroemeria* (Peruvian lily), and *Hippeastrum.* An ornamental Eurasian plant known as winter daffodil (*Sternbergia lutea*) is often cultivated in borders or rock gardens. *Clivia miniata,* a South African perennial, is cultivated as a houseplant for its scarlet flowers lined with yellow.

Amasis (kings of Egypt): *see* Ahmose I; Ahmose II.

Amasis Painter (fl. *c.* 555–525 BC), Greek vase painter who, with Exekias, was among the most accomplished of Archaic vase painters. He was responsible for the decoration of several of the black-figure amphorae (two-handled jars), *cenochoae* (wine pitchers), and lekythoi (oil flasks) of the Amasis Potter.

"Dionysus and the Maenads," amphora by the Amasis Painter, *c.* 530 BC; in the Cabinet des Médailles, Paris

Hirmer Fotoarchiv, Munchen

Signatures of the Amasis Painter have been recognized on eight vessels. Among those thought to have been decorated by him are a Dionysus and the Maenads now in the Bibliothèque Nationale at Paris; an "Apollo and Heracles" in the Boston Museum of Fine Arts; and a wedding procession in the Metropolitan Museum of Art, New York City.

Amasya, historical name AMASEIA, or AMASIA, city, capital of Amasya *il* (province), northern Turkey, on Yeşil Irmak (Green River), also called the Iris River. Capital of the kings of Pontus until about 183 BC, it was made a free city and the administrative centre of a large territory by Pompey in 65 BC. In the 2nd century AD, it received the titles "metropolis" and "first city" under the Romans. It was the capital of the Turkmen Dānişmend *amīrs* until annexed by the Seljuq ruler Qïlïc Arslan a century later. It became a major centre of learning in Anatolia after being incorporated into the Ottoman Empire by Sultan Bayezid I (reigned 1389–1402).

Amasya, Tur., on the Yeşil Irmak (river), flanked by a gorge (right)

Maynard Williams—Shostal/EB Inc.

Beautifully situated in a narrow gorge with renowned orchards, it was much favoured by the early Ottomans; crown princes often served as governors. A castle mentioned by the ancient geographer Strabo, who was born there, now lies in ruins on the summit of a rock, though it was restored during Byzantine and Ottoman periods. Notable medieval buildings include several mosques and a library. Old buildings are concentrated on the heavily populated southern side of the river, connected to the north by five bridges. Many monuments were damaged by earthquakes in 1734, 1825, and 1939.

Amasya *il,* 2,212 sq mi (5,730 sq km) in area, between the Black Sea and inner Anatolia, contains fertile plains crossed by the Yeşil, Çekerek, and Tersakan rivers. Economic activities include agriculture, mining, textiles, and cement production. Pop. (1980) city, 48,066; (1982 est.) *il,* 347,716.

Amaterasu, in full AMATERASU ŌMIKAMI (Japanese: Great Divinity Illuminating Heaven), the celestial sun goddess from whom the Japanese Imperial family claims descent, and an important Shintō deity. She was born from the left eye of her father, Izanagi, who bestowed upon her a necklace of jewels and placed her in charge of *Takamagahara* (High Celestial Plain), the abode of all the *kami.* One of her brothers, the storm god Susanoo, was sent to rule the sea plain. Before going, Susanoo went to take leave of his sister. As an act of good faith, they produced children together, she by chewing and spitting out pieces of the sword he gave her, and he by doing the same with her jewels. Susanoo then began to behave very rudely—he broke down the divisions in the rice fields, defiled his sister's dwelling place, and finally threw a flayed horse into her weaving hall. Indignant, Amaterasu withdrew in protest into a cave, and darkness fell upon the world.

The other 800 myriads of gods conferred on how to lure the sun goddess out. They collected cocks, whose crowing precedes the dawn, and hung a mirror and jewels on a *sakaki* tree in front of the cave. The goddess Amenouzume (*q.v.*) began a dance on an upturned tub, partially disrobing herself, which so delighted the assembled gods that they roared with laughter. Amaterasu became curious how the gods could make merry while the world was plunged into darkness and was told that outside the cave there was a deity more illustrious than she. She peeped out, saw her reflection in the mirror, heard the cocks crow, and was thus drawn out from the cave. The *kami* then quickly threw a *shimenawa,* or sacred rope of rice straw, before the entrance to prevent her return to hiding.

Amaterasu's chief place of worship is the Grand Shrine of Ise, the foremost Shintō shrine in Japan. She is manifested there in a mirror that is one of the three Imperial Treasures of Japan (the other two being a jewelled necklace and a sword). The genders of Amaterasu and her brother the moon god Tsukiyomi no Mikato are remarkable exceptions in worldwide mythology of the sun and the moon. *See also* Uke-mochi-no-kami.

Amateur Athletic Association (AAA), English national governing organization for the sport of track and field (athletics). Founded in 1880, it took over as the governing power from the Amateur Athletic Club, founded in 1866. The association was the first such organization in the world. The AAA was one of the first groups to reject the requirement of upper-class background that had previously been necessary to achieve amateur athletic status.

The AAA promotes, organizes, and regulates athletic competition, coaching, and training and holds annual national and junior national championships. Association headquarters is in London.

Amateur Athletic Union of the United States (AAU), alliance of national and district associations, amateur athletic groups, and educational institutions formed in the United States in 1888 for the purpose of certifying athletes as amateurs in various sports. By 1980 the AAU had 330,000 individual members and 7,500 local groups and served as the governing body of numerous sports, including basketball, boxing, gymnastics, handball, swimming, diving, water polo, wrestling, weight lifting, track and field, bobsledding, luge, horseshoe pitching, judo, baton twirling, and karate. It also supervised tryouts for Olympic competitors and played an important role in raising funds for U.S. Olympic athletes. The James E. Sullivan Memorial Trophy, named for an early AAU official, is awarded annually to the nation's outstanding amateur athlete. Publications include *Amateur Athlete* (monthly) and sports guides and rule books. Its headquarters is in Indianapolis, Ind.

amateur radio, noncommercial, two-way radio communications. Messages are sent either by voice or in International Morse Code.

Interest in amateur radio arose around the turn of the century, shortly after the Italian inventor Guglielmo Marconi successfully sent the first transatlantic wireless signal in 1901. The interference of amateur broadcasts with commercial and military transmissions led to the institution of government control in 1911. After World War I, amateurs became active in radio experimentation, contributing to developments in long-distance broadcasting and becoming the first radio operators successfully to exploit the upper medium-frequency and lower high-frequency radio bands. Over the years, amateur radio operators have also provided emergency communications during forest fires, floods, hurricanes, and other disasters. They serve as an important link between stricken communities and the outside world until normal communications are reestablished.

Amateur radio operators in the United States are subject to international and federal regulations. There are five classes of licenses. Competence in the use of the International Morse Code and a knowledge of radio theory and regulation are required to obtain the advanced-level licenses. Amateur radio is allocated frequencies at the extreme high-frequency end of the medium-wave band, five groups of frequencies in the shortwave band, two groups in the very-high-frequency band, three in the ultrahigh-frequency band, and seven in the superhigh-frequency band for telegraphic and telephonic communication using amplitude and frequency modulation. There are restrictions on the power of the transmitters, and certain of the frequencies must be shared with due regard for the needs of other users.

Amathus, ancient city located near Limassol, Cyprus, among sandy hills and sand dunes, which may explain its name (Greek *amathos,* "sand"). Founded by the Phoenicians (*c.* 1500 BC), Amathus maintained strong sympathies with the Phoenician mainland and refused to join various Cypriot revolts against Persia. When the rest of Cyprus was annexed to Egypt after the death of Alexander the Great, Amathus resisted annexation. It derived its wealth from grain and from copper mines. Its temple of Adonis and Aphrodite was famous in Roman times, hence the Latin epithet Amathusia applied to Venus. The city still flourished in the 7th century AD but was almost deserted by the 12th century.

Amati FAMILY, a family of celebrated Italian violin makers in Cremona in the 16th and 17th centuries.

Andrea (*c.* 1520–*c.* 1578), the founder of the Cremona school of violin making, was perhaps originally influenced by the work of slightly earlier makers from Brescia. His earliest known violins are dated about 1564. In essentials, they set the style for all the models made by later members of the family and, with the modifications introduced by Antonio Stradivari, for the modern violin.

His two sons Antonio (*c.* 1550–1638) and Girolamo (Hieronymus) (1551–1635) worked together until the latter's death and are known as the brothers Amati.

Nicolò (1596–1684) was the son of Girolamo. The most famous of the family, he produced instruments notable for beauty of workmanship and tone and was the master from whom Stradivari and Andrea Guarneri, among others, learned their craft. He was succeeded by his son Girolamo (1649–1740). Although the instruments made by Girolamo are as fine as those of his father and grandfather, they suffered in comparison with those made by Stradivari.

Amatique Bay, Spanish BAHÍA DE AMATIQUE, inlet of the Gulf of Honduras in the Caribbean Sea, indenting northeastern Guatemala and southeastern Belize (formerly British Honduras). Extending northwestward for approximately 40 mi (64 km) from Santo Tomás de Castilla, Guatemala, it is approximately 15 mi from northeast to southwest. Amatique Bay receives the Rió Dulce, which drains Lago (lake) de Izabal; the Sarstoon (Sarstún), which forms the Belize–Guatemala border; and, in the northwest, the Moho River. The principal ports are Puerto Barrios (*q.v.*), Santo Tomás de Castilla, and Livingston (at the mouth of the Dulce), in Guatemala; and Punta Gorda, in Belize.

Amatitlán, Lake, Spanish LAGO DE AMATITLÁN, Guatemala department, south central Guatemala, in the central highlands at 4,085 ft (1,248 m) above sea level. The volcanic lake, 130 ft deep, is 7 mi (11 km) long and 2 mi wide and has an area of about 6 sq mi (15 sq km). It is fed by the Río Villalobos and drained by the Río Michatoya. A popular tourist area, the lake and the town of Amatitlán, at the head of the Michatoya, are situated by highway south-southwest of Guatemala City. The waters have become polluted, and, because most of the shore is privately owned, the lake can be approached by tourists at only a few places. In the vicinity are a United Nations Park, thermal springs, and coffee plantations.

Amaury, also spelled AMAURI (kings of Jerusalem): *see under* Amalric.

Amazon, in Greek mythology, member of a race of women warriors. The story of the Amazons probably originated as a variant of a tale recurrent in many cultures, that of a distant land organized oppositely from one's own. The ascribed habitat of the Amazons necessarily became more remote as Greek geographical knowledge developed. When the Black Sea was colonized by Greeks, it was first said to be the Amazon district; but when no Amazons were found there, it was necessary to explain what became of them. Traditionally, one of the labours required of the Greek hero Heracles was leading an expedition to get the girdle of the Amazons' queen (Hippolyte), during which he was said to have conquered and expelled them from their district.

The Mattei Amazon, Roman copy after an original attributed to Phidias, *c.* 440 BC; in the Vatican Museum
Alinari—Art Resource/EB Inc.

Subsidiary tales grew up to explain why, if the whole nation consisted of women, it did not die out in a generation. In one of these, Theseus attacked the Amazons either with Heracles or independently. The Amazons in turn invaded Attica but were finally defeated, and at some point Theseus married one of them, Antiope. In Hellenistic times the Amazons were associated with Dionysus (the god of wine), either as his allies or, more commonly, as his opponents.

In works of art combats between Amazons and Greeks were placed on the same level as and often associated with combats of Greeks and centaurs. They were similar in model to Athena (goddess of war, handicrafts, and practical reason), and their arms were the bow, spear, light double ax, a half shield, and, in early art, a helmet. In later art they were more like Artemis (goddess of wild animals, vegetation, chastity, and childbirth), wearing a thin dress, girded high for speed; on the later painted vases their dress is often peculiarly Persian.

According to some accounts, the Amazon River was named by the 16th-century Spanish explorer Francisco de Orellana for the fighting women he claimed to have encountered on what was previously known as the Marañon.

Amazon Rain Forest, large, tropical rain forest occupying the drainage basin of the Amazon River and its tributaries, covering an area of 2,700,000 sq mi (7,000,000 sq km). Comprising 40 percent of Brazil's total area, it is bounded by the Guiana Highlands to the north, the Andes Mountain Ranges to the west, the Brazilian central plateau to the south, and the Atlantic Ocean to the east.

The following article summarizes information about the Amazon Rain Forest; for full details, *see* MACROPAEDIA: South America.

The forest stretches from the swampy mangroves in the east near the Atlantic Ocean to the tree line on the Andes. High in the Andean region, there are large and small meadows of grass, sometimes with gigantic cacti, and on lower levels, swamps with arborescent calla-like Araceae (Montrichardia) are common. The Andean forest gradually turns into tropical rain forest to the east. On the Brazilian central plateau, the forest proper is limited by a parklike vegetation of grasses and small to medium trees and bushes, characterized by twisted trunks, thick bark, and leathery leaves. Nearer the streams, the trees grow taller, and pampas (open plains) sometimes occur suddenly.

The Amazon Valley is like an immense canyon opening into the Atlantic Ocean with a mouth more than 250 mi (400 km) wide. With more than 1,000 tributaries, it is the largest basin area in the world. Characterized by luxuriant vegetation, the Amazonian rain forest has a wide variety of trees including myrtle, acacia, rosewood, Brazil nut, rubber tree, and palm. Excellent timber is furnished by the mahogany and the Amazonian cedar. Major wildlife includes jaguar, matee, tapir, red deer, capybara, and several types of monkeys. Parrots, toucans, haugnests, perdizes, cormorants, and scarlet ibises belong to the rich bird life of the forest. A major oil field lies southward from Manaus, and tin mining is important in the region.

Amazon River, Portuguese RIO AMAZONAS, Spanish RÍO AMAZONAS, greatest river of South America and the largest in the world in volume and area of its drainage basin.

The following article summarizes information about the Amazon River; for full details, *see* MACROPAEDIA: South America.

Lying within 100 mi (160 km) of the Pacific Ocean at its westernmost source high in the Peruvian Andes, the Amazon flows almost 4,000 mi across northern Brazil to its mouth in the Atlantic Ocean on the northeastern coast of Brazil. Its length is second only to that of the Nile. It is estimated that from 20 to 25 percent of all the water that runs off the Earth's surface is carried by the Amazon. The annual average discharge of 6,350,000 cu ft per sec (180,000 cu m per sec) at its 150-mi-wide mouth is roughly 10 times that of North America's Mississippi River and about four times that of the Congo (Zaire) River in Africa, the world's second greatest river. The discharge is so great that it turns the ocean's water from salty to brackish for more than 100 mi offshore. There are more than 1,000 known tributaries of the Amazon that rise in the Guiana Highlands, the Brazilian Highlands, and (principally) in the Andes. Seven of these are longer than 1,000 mi; one, the Madeira, flowing northeastward from Bolivia, is more than 2,000 mi long. Navigable throughout the year, the Amazon can accommodate large freighters as far inland as Manaus, 1,000 mi upriver from the Atlantic. Flowing over a gently sloping terrain, the Amazon is characterized by oxbow lakes, abandoned channels, and other marks of a meandering river. Floods (*várzeas*), by depositing fertile silt as they recede, annually rejuvenate an area of some 25,000 sq mi (65,000 sq km), or nearly double that of The Netherlands, and the river's total drainage basin, about 2,722,000 sq mi, is nearly twice as large as the area drained by any other river in the world. The Amazon, its tributaries, swamps, and oxbow lakes may be described as a vast sea of fresh water, supporting millions of fish, including catfish, electric eels, and piranhas.

Amazonas, largest *estado* (state) of Brazil, situated in the northwestern part of the country. It is bounded to the northwest by Colombia, to the north by Venezuela and the Brazilian territory of Roraima, to the east and southeast by the states of Pará and Mato Grosso, to the south by the Brazilian state of Rondônia, to the southwest by the Brazilian state of Acre, and to the west by Peru. It has an area of 601,928 sq mi (1,558,987 sq km). Despite its size, it is the most thinly populated Brazilian state.

Amazonas occupies the greater part of the Hiléia (Hylea), the tropical forest zone of the Amazon Basin, and has its northernmost tracts north of the Equator. The capital, Manaus, is located in the eastern part of the state at the confluence of the Rio Negro with the mainstream of the Amazon. The state takes its name from the Amazon River—Rio Amazonas in Portuguese.

The Spanish explorer Francisco de Orellana passed through this region in 1541–42 during a voyage down the Amazon from the Coca, one of its Andean headwaters, to its Atlantic estuary. In 1669 a Portuguese captain, Francisco da Mota Falcão, founded the fort of São José do Rio Negrinho on the site of the present Manaus; and in 1755 the Capitania de São José do Rio Negro was established, with its seat of administration at Mariuá, now Barcelos, farther up the Rio Negro.

After Brazilian independence Rio Negro remained dependent on the state of Pará until 1850, when it gained autonomy, becoming the province of Amazonas in 1852. After the overthrow of the imperial regime in 1889, the province became a federal state, adopting a constitution in 1891.

From 1880 until its decline in 1910, the rubber trade brought prosperity to Amazonas, for which a modern port was constructed at Manaus by 1900. In 1946 the Brazilian government launched a plan for the economic development of Amazonia that has been continued to the present.

Except on the northern borders, where Pico da Neblina (Neblina Peak) reaches 9,888 ft (3,014 m), the highest point in Brazil, the state's mean elevation is not more than 300 ft above sea level. The mainstream of the great Amazon river (known as the Rio Solimões from the Peruvian frontier to the Rio Negro confluence) traverses the state from west to east; its major tributaries are the Içá, the Japurá, and the Negro from the north and the Javari, the Juruá, the Purus, and the Madeira from the south.

With an annual average temperature of 79° F (26° C) and an annual rainfall of 80 in. (2,000 mm), the climate is warm and extremely humid. Apart from small areas of savanna (grassy parkland) on the northern borders, the equatorial rain forest of the Hiléia covers the country.

The native animal life is numerous and varied. Mammals are represented by monkeys, bats, and rodents; birds by ant thrushes, parrots, toucans, and various marsh birds; reptiles by caymans (crocodilians, related to alligators), turtles, boas, anacondas, and iguanas.

Most of the people of the areas remote from the Amazon mainstream live in settlements on the banks of the other rivers. Nearly all of the rural population consists of caboclos—persons of mixed European and Indian descent. There is also a large group descended from immigrants from northeastern Brazil who arrived during the rubber boom. The Indian population in the late 20th century was estimated at 60,000, or one-fifth of the total Indian population in Brazil. The Indian groups, of which about 30 may be distinguished, have been progressively reduced in numbers by imported disease and by economic misery. Large areas of the state's territory are uninhabited. About two-fifths of the population is concentrated in Manaus.

The language of Amazonas is Portuguese, but the local vocabulary also incorporates many words from the Indian languages. Roman Catholicism is the dominant religion, but other Christian persuasions are also represented. The Indians have preserved elements of their original religions. A constant struggle against disease is carried on in scores of hospitals. Yellow fever, malaria, leprosy, and other tropical diseases occur sporadically; the average life span is only 54 years.

The Universidade do Amazonas, at Manaus, was founded in 1965. The Instituto Nacional de Pesquisas da Amazônia (National Research Institute for Amazonia), with its headquarters in Manaus, conducts research on Amazonian ecology.

The products of the state's vegetation—rubber, Brazil nuts, timber, guarana (a climbing shrub containing tannin and caffeine), vegetable oils, and fibres—form the basis of the economy. There are a few mineral deposits and a small iron foundry in operation. Cassava (manioc), jute, sugarcane, bananas, and sweet potatoes are grown on the belts of land fertilized annually by the rivers. Cattle have been introduced to the higher lands through government assistance programs that promote large-scale cattle ranching. Brazilian industry absorbs most of the raw materials produced by Amazonas, but rubber, timber, jute, vegetable oils, nuts, resins, aquarium fishes, and skins are exported to foreign countries.

Transport is mainly by water; the rivers accommodate both large ships and canoes. The Transamazônica highway, however, runs from east to west and connects the Atlantic coast, near Recife, with the Peruvian border. Pop. (1980 prelim.) 1,444,135.

Amazonas, commissariat, southeastern Colombia, located in the warm, humid Amazon Basin. It is bounded northwest by the Río Caquetá, northeast by the Río Apaporis, east by Brazil, and south by Peru and the Río Putumayo. Colombia's only direct contact with the Amazon River is through the commissariat. It is the largest political division in Colombia—occupying an area of 42,342 sq mi (109,665 sq km)—but also is one of the least densely populated. Principal economic activities are forestry (mahogany, rubber, ipecac, and many other species), fishing, and agriculture (peanuts [groundnuts]; bananas, pineapples, and other fruits; rice; and sugarcane). Most of the population lives in and around Leticia (*q.v.*), the capital and major trade centre. No good roads penetrate the rain forest; travel is entirely by river or by air. Pop. (1981 est.) 18,471.

Amazonas, department (formed 1832), northern Peru, bounded on the north by Ecuador. It occupies an area of 15,945 sq mi (41,297 sq km) with rain forest mostly in the north; in the south, the Marañón River and its tributaries dissect the Cordillera Central. The Marañón forms part of the western boundary with Cajamarca department before flowing northeastward into the Amazon Basin. The density of the largely rural population is low, with most settlements in the south. Chachapoyas (*q.v.*), the capital, at 7,657 ft (2,334 m) above sea level, is accessible by air and by road. Paved highways connect Amazonas with San Martín department to the east and Cajamarca to the west. Agricultural products, grown mainly in the south, include sugarcane, corn (maize), rice, potatoes, cotton, and cereals. There are some mineral deposits in the department. Pop. (1984 est.) 289,800.

Amazonas, territory, southern Venezuela, bounded north by the state of Bolívar, east and south by Brazil, and west by Colombia. The large (67,857 sq mi [175,750 sq km]) but sparsely populated territory lies within the drainage basins of the Orinoco River, which rises near the Brazilian border, and the Río Negro, a northern tributary of the Amazon. Near the centre of the territory is a maze of intricate natural channels. One stretch of 204 mi (328 km), the Casiquiare, flows south from the Orinoco; it is usually navigable by small boats for half the year and links the Orinoco with the Negro, and thus the Amazon. Amazonas also includes the western outliers of the Guiana Highlands. Largely unexplored, the territory consists mainly of hot, humid rain forest, with much tropical savanna. About two-thirds of the inhabitants are forest-dwelling Indians who hunt and fish for food, mainly on a subsistence basis; they include several linguistic groups. There are no large cities; Puerto Ayacucho (*q.v.*), the territorial capital, lies on the Orinoco, just below rapids that block continuous navigation of the river. The economy is based principally on the gathering of rubber, balata, vanilla, and chicle. Only a small area is under cultivation, the chief crops being rice, bananas, plantains, beans, wheat, and cassava. Transportation is mainly by boat, airplane, and dugout canoe, although there are some local roads. Pop. (1983 est.) 30,222.

amazonstone, also called AMAZONITE, a gemstone variety of green microcline (*q.v.*), a feldspar mineral. Its colour varies from yellow-green to blue-green and may be pale to very deep. It is usually opaque and therefore is cut *en cabochon* (with a rounded and convex polished surface) or is used for beads and ornaments. Principal localities include Ontario and Quebec, Can.; Minas Gerais, Braz.; the Urals, U.S.S.R.; Tanzania; Madagascar; and Virginia and Colorado, U.S. Transparent amazonstone has been reported from Baffin Island, in the eastern Canadian Arctic.

Amb, small frontier state that acceded (1947) to Pakistan. It lies on the west bank of the Indus River, 15 mi (24 km) north of the Tarbela Dam, in Peshāwar Division, North-West Frontier Province, Pakistan, northwest of Abbottābād. Formerly included in Upper Tanāwal across the Indus, it now (apart from Amb, the principal township) consists of only three villages covering an area of 27 sq mi (70 sq km). The residence of the ruler (nawab), formerly at Amb, is at Darband, the administrative headquarters. The state is mainly agricultural, with wheat, barley, and corn (maize) as the chief crops. Amb township has a small arms factory. Pop. (1972) 8,605.

Ambāla, also called UMBALA, city, administrative headquarters of Ambāla district, Haryāna state, northwestern India, just east of the Ghaggar River. A major grain, cotton, and sugar trade centre, it is connected by road and rail with Delhi and Amritsar (Punjab state). Other rail lines run northward to Simla and Kālka and southeastward to Sahāranpur. The city is also served by Ambāla Airport. One of India's largest military cantonments, which also houses a commercial centre and an airfield, lies 4 mi (6.5 km) southeast. Major industries include cotton ginning, flour milling, food processing, and various manufactures. Cloth weaving and bamboo furniture making are important handicrafts. Constituted a municipality in 1867, the city and cantonment have a hospital, a government metalworks institute, and several colleges affiliated with Kurukshetra University.

Ambāla district, with an area of 1,480 sq mi (3,833 sq km), is composed chiefly of a fertile alluvial plain sloping gradually from the Siwālik Range in the northeast between the Sutlej and Ganges rivers. There is some canal irrigation. Grains, gram (chick-pea), cotton, sugarcane, peanuts (groundnuts), and mangoes are the chief crops. Pop. (1981) city, 104,565; metropolitan area, 121,203; district, 1,409,463.

Ambaniandro (people): *see* Merina.

Ambartsumian, Viktor Amazaspovich (b. Sept. 18 [Sept. 5, old style], 1908, Tbilisi, Georgia, Russian Empire), Soviet astronomer and astrophysicist best known for his theories concerning the origin and evolution of stars and stellar systems. He was also the founder of the school of theoretical astrophysics in the Soviet Union.

Ambartsumian was born of Armenian parents. His father, a teacher of literature, encouraged the development of his outstanding

Ambartsumian, 1970
Tass—Sovfoto

aptitude for mathematics and physics. In 1925 he entered the University of Leningrad with the intention of devoting his life to research in astrophysics and in the following year published a paper on solar activity, the first of 10 papers he published while an undergraduate. After graduating in 1928, Ambartsumian became a graduate student in astrophysics under the direction of A.A. Belopolskii at Pulkovo Observatory near Leningrad.

From 1931 to 1943 he lectured at the University of Leningrad, where he headed the Astrophysical Department. In 1932 he advanced his theory of the interaction of ultraviolet radiation from hot stars with the surrounding gas, a theory that led to a series of papers on the physics of gaseous clouds. His statistical analysis of stellar systems in 1934–36, in which for the first time their physical properties were taken into account, was found to be applicable to many related problems, such as the evolution of double stars and star clusters. These accomplishments were recognized with his election as a corresponding member of the Academy of Sciences of the U.S.S.R. in 1939 and his appointment as deputy rector of the University of Leningrad in 1941–43. His theory of the behaviour of light in a scattering medium of cosmic space, put forward in 1941–43, became an important tool in geophysics, space research, and particularly astrophysics, such as in studies of interstellar matter.

In 1943 Ambartsumian joined the Armenian Academy of Sciences in Yerevan, the capital of Soviet Armenia, and began teaching at Yerevan State University. In 1946 he organized the construction near Yerevan of the Byurakan Astronomical Observatory, now one of the most important observatories in the U.S.S.R., where he began another successful period of activity. In 1947 he discovered a new type of comparatively recent stellar system, which he named stellar association. The most important result of his study is the conclusion that the process of star formation in the galaxy containing our solar system still continues and, specifically, that most stars have their origin in changing systems of groups of stars.

Later, Ambartsumian studied the phenomena in the atmosphere of stars that are changing in physical characteristics, such as luminosity, mass, or density. He saw these changes as being connected with the direct release of interstellar energy in the outer layers of the stars. He also investigated nonstationary processes in galaxies. These investigations are of great importance, both for the problem of the evolution of galaxies and for the study of still unknown properties of matter.

His textbook, *Theoretical Astrophysics* (1958), went through many editions and translations. It contains examples of his unique and fruitful approaches to stubborn astronomical problems. In addition, he studied radio signals coming from outside our galactic system of stars. He was led to conclude that these radio signals represent not colliding systems of stars, according to a widely accepted interpretation, but the subatomic process of fission within galaxies. Therefore, according to his view, "radio galaxies" may represent systems of stars, interacting in close proximity, that were formed from superdense formations of stellar material. In support of this view, he pointed out the presence of jets, condensations, and streamers that are bluish in colour; found around certain galaxies, which are characteristics of an early stage in stellar development. Ambartsumian's later works include *Problemy sovremennoi kosmogonii* (1969; "Problems of Modern Cosmogony") and *Filosofskie voprosy nauki o Vselennoi* (1973; "Philosophical Problems of the Study of the Universe").

Ambartsumian's thought-provoking manner of presentation drew large audiences to his lectures at international symposia where he enlivened even his most abstrusely mathematical lectures with quotations from classic and contemporary poets.

Many governmental decorations and awards were presented to Ambartsumian. In 1947 he was elected president of the Armenian S.S.R. Academy of Sciences and member of the Parliament of Soviet Armenia and from 1950 has served in the Supreme Soviet of the U.S.S.R. In 1953 he was elected to full membership in the Academy of Sciences of the U.S.S.R. In 1948–56 he was vice president, and in 1961–63 president, of the International Astronomical Union. In 1968 he became president of the International Council of Scientific Unions, and he participated in activities of many foreign academies and scientific societies. For his many contributions to Soviet science, his country awarded him two Stalin prizes and five Orders of Lenin, among many other honours.

Ambartsumian, a popular figure among Soviet Armenians, was honoured in 1968, when his 60th birthday was celebrated as a national event. His two daughters and two sons all embarked on scientific careers in mathematics and physics. (A.G.Ma.)

BIBLIOGRAPHY. For further information, see A. Massevitch, "Viktor Amazaspovich Ambartsumian: A Portrait," *ICSU Rev.*, 5:29–33 (1963).

ambassador, highest rank of diplomatic representative sent by one government to another. The Vienna Convention on Diplomatic Relations (1961) divided diplomatic representatives into three categories: (1) ambassadors and other heads of mission of equivalent rank accredited to host heads of state; (2) envoys, ministers, and other representatives accredited to host heads of state; and (3) chargés d'affaires, who are accredited to the foreign minister of the host country.

Ambassadors were originally accredited only to monarchies but later were sent to republics regarded as being of equal rank. There was a general exchange of ambassadors among the great powers—Austria-Hungary, France, Germany, Great Britain, Italy, Japan, Russia, and the United States—along with Spain and Turkey. Since 1945, in accordance with the doctrine of the formal, legal equality of all states, most governments have sent representatives of ambassadorial rank to all countries to which they have extended diplomatic recognition.

Prior to the development of modern communications, ambassadors were frequently entrusted with extensive, even plenary powers. They have since tended, however, to become spokesmen of their foreign offices, and rarely does an ambassador enjoy extensive discretion. An ambassador's personality and prestige, on the other hand, may play an important part in making the views of his government understood, and his firsthand knowledge of the country to which he is accredited may enable him to influence his government's policy decisively. For the immunities enjoyed by ambassadors, *see* diplomatic immunity.

Ambato, capital of Tungurahua province, central Ecuador, on the Río Ambato in an intermontane basin near the northeastern foot of Mt. Chimborazo, at an elevation of about 8,500 ft (2,600 m). It was the scene of a decisive victory in 1821 by Antonio José de Sucre, lieutenant of the liberator Simón Bolívar, against the Spanish during the wars for Latin-American independence. Frequently damaged by volcanic eruptions and earthquakes, much of the city was destroyed in the earthquake of August 1949. Remaining landmarks include a Renaissance cathedral and the mausoleum of Juan Montalvo, a noted Ecuadorian writer and freedom fighter, who was born in Ambato in 1832.

The cathedral (built mid-20th century), Ambato, Ecuador
Shostal—EB Inc.

The city is an agricultural trade centre; the Ambato Basin is renowned for fresh fruits. There are also sugarcane plantations and grain farms in the locality. Industrial activity includes tanneries, leatherworks, food processing, and textile milling.

An important communications centre, Ambato is located on the Guayaquil–Quito railway line and on the Pan-American Highway. A road from the city leads over the eastern cordillera of the Andes via Baños to El Oriente region, the sparsely settled lowland jungle area of eastern Ecuador. Ambato's lush suburb of Miraflores is a favourite resort for the upper classes of Guayaquil. Pop. (1983 est.) 111,505.

Ambedkar, Bhimrao Ramji (b. April 14, 1893, Mhow, India—d. Dec. 6, 1956, New Delhi), leader of the Harijans (untouchables or low-caste Hindus) and law minister of the government of India (1947–51).

Born of an untouchable Mahar family of western India, he was as a boy humiliated by his high-caste schoolfellows. His father was an officer in the Indian Army. Awarded a scholarship by the Gaekwar (the ruler) of Baroda, he studied at universities in the United States, Britain, and Germany. He entered the Baroda Public Service at the Gaekwar's request, but, again ill-treated by his high-caste colleagues, he turned to legal practice and teaching. He soon established his leadership among Harijans, founded several journals on their behalf, and succeeded in obtaining special representation for them in the legislative councils of the government. Contesting Mahatma Gandhi's claim to speak for Harijans, he wrote *What Congress and Gandhi Have Done to the Untouchables* (1945).

In 1947 Ambedkar became the law minister of the government of India. He took a leading part in the framing of the Indian constitution, outlawing discrimination against untouchables, and skillfully helped to steer it through the assembly. He resigned in 1951, disappointed at his lack of influence in the government. In October 1956, finally in despair because of the perpetuation of untouchability in Hindu doctrine, he renounced Hinduism and became a Buddhist, together with about 200,000 fellow untouchables, at a ceremony in Nāgpur, India.

Amber (India): *see* Āmer.

amber, fossil tree resin that has achieved a stable state through loss of volatile constituents and chemical change after burial in the ground. Amber has been found throughout the world, but the largest and most significant deposits occur along the shores of the Baltic Sea in sands 40,000,000 to 60,000,000 years old.

Amber occurs as irregular nodules, rods, or droplike shapes in all shades of yellow with nuances of orange, brown, and, rarely, red. Milky-white opaque varieties are called bone amber. The turbidity of some amber is caused by inclusions of many minute air bubbles. Many hundreds of species of fossil insects and plants are found as inclusions. Deeply coloured translucent to transparent amber is prized as gem material.

Modern investigative techniques are directed toward isolating and identifying as many as possible of the individual resin components and, ultimately, to establishing a genetic relationship between fossil resins and modern resin-producing trees. By means of infrared spectroscopy, Mexican (Chiapas) amber has been shown to be related to a modern leguminous tree, *Hymenaea.* Though in the past amber was believed to be completely amorphous, subsequent X-ray diffraction studies have revealed crystalline components in some fossil resins.

Ornamental carved objects, beads, rosaries, cigarette holders, and pipe mouthpieces are made from amber. Amberoid, or "pressed amber," is produced by fusing together small pieces of amber under pressure. Parallel bands, or flow structure, in amberoid help to distinguish it from natural amber. Despite the introduction of numerous synthetic substitutes, the beauty of the real material has remained unexcelled.

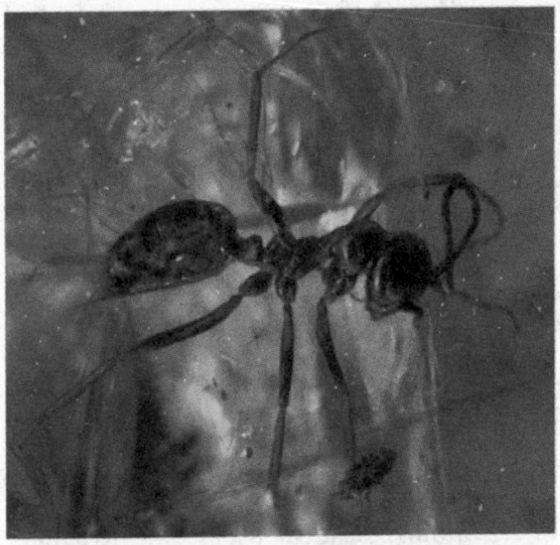

Sphecomyrma freyi, primitive wasp-like ant in amber from New Jersey, Cretaceous Period, *c.* 100,000,000 years old; in the Museum of Comparative Zoology, Harvard University

Frank M. Carpenter, Museum of Comparative Zoology, Harvard University, Cambridge, Mass.

Amber Valley, district, county of Derbyshire, England, to the north of Derby. With an area of 102 sq mi (265 sq km), it comprises the former urban districts of Alfreton, Belper, Heanor, and Ripley and Belper rural district. It takes its name from the River Amber, which joins the Derwent at Ambergate. The industrial eastern half of the district contrasts with the still rural western portion. Traditionally coal mining and ironworking were the staple industries, but from the late 1950s industrial diversification has taken place as mining declined in importance. Some of the derelict mining land has been reclaimed for new industrial estates, notably near Alfreton. Engineering is important at Ripley and Belper, which is also a centre of the cotton and hosiery industry. Jedediah Strutt, inventor of a stocking ribbing machine, built the town's first cotton mill in 1776. Among buildings of interest are the picturesque remains of Wingfield Manor House, begun in 1440 and dismantled in 1646. Pop. (1982 est.) 109,100.

Amberes, Gil de: *see* Siloé, Gil de.

Amberg, city, Bayern *Land* (Bavaria state), southeastern West Germany, on the Vils River, in the foothills of the Franconian Jura and Bayernwald (Bavarian Forest), southeast of Nürnberg. First mentioned in 1034, it was a court town with considerable trade (in iron and tinplate) and industry in the 14th–16th century. The ducal residence (until 1621) and the capital (until 1810) of the Upper Palatinate, it had many trading and shipping privileges and was considered one of the strongest fortified towns in medieval Germany. The old walls and town gates still stand. In 1796 the Austrians under Archduke Charles decisively defeated the French under Gen. (later Marshal) Jean-Baptiste Jourdan there; the battle is recorded on the Arc de Triomphe in Paris. The 15th-century town hall, the ducal castle, and the electoral palace are among many surviving medieval and Baroque buildings. St. Martin's Church (1421), St. George's (14th century, transformed into Baroque in the 18th century), and the pilgrimage church (1697–1702) on the Mariahilfberg are also notable. The state archives for the Upper Palatinate as well as the municipal archives are in Amberg, and there is a fine provincial library (founded 1730). Amberg's diversified industries include iron-ore mining and working, glass grinding, enamelling, porcelain and brick works and breweries. Pop. (1983 est.) 43,840.

ambergris, solid substance formed in the intestine of the sperm whale (*Physeter catodon*). It is used chiefly as a spice in the East, and in the West it is used to fix the scent of fine perfumes. Ambergris is thought to form as a collection of feces around the indigestible parts of squid and other prey of the sperm whale. It is not definitely known whether the process is normal or pathological. Ambergris, when fresh, is soft and black and has a disagreeable odour. When exposed to sun, air, and sea water, it hardens, fades, and develops a pleasant scent. It has been washed ashore in many countries, especially the Bahamas, and has also been found in the bodies of captured whales or floating free on the sea. Pieces are usually small, but one find weighed about 418 kilograms (922 pounds).

amberina glass, blended colour glass in which the lower part, a yellowish amber, merges into a ruby-red colour higher in the vessel. It was patented in 1883 for the New England Glass Company at East Cambridge, Mass., and was produced extensively there and by the successor company, the Libbey Glass Company at Toledo, Ohio, into the 1890s. The base metal was an amber glass containing some gold, and the tinges were developed by applied reheating. The glass was sometimes blown in molds. A wide range of table and ornamental wares, with diamond or ogival designs, or swirled ribbing, were produced by the New England Glass Company, and amberina glass was also produced at New Bedford, Mass., under the name rose amber.

amberjack, any of several popular sport fishes. *See* jack.

Part of the medieval town wall spanning the Vils River at Amberg, W.Ger.

Emil Bauer—Bavaria Verlag

ambiguity, use of words that allow alternative interpretations. In factual, explanatory prose, ambiguity is considered an error in reasoning or diction; in literary prose or poetry, it often functions to increase the richness and subtlety of language and to imbue it with a complexity that expands the literal meaning of the original statement. William Empson's *Seven Types of Ambiguity* (1935; rev. ed., 1947) remains a full and useful treatment of the subject.

Ambikāpur (India): *see* Surguja.

Ambler, Eric (b. June 28, 1909, London), author widely regarded as one of the most distinguished writers of stories of espionage and of crime.

After studying engineering at London University, Ambler turned to literature and established his reputation with *The Dark Frontier* (1936), *Uncommon Danger* (1937; U.S. title, *Background to Danger,* 1937), *Epitaph for a Spy* and *Cause for Alarm* (1938), *The Mask of Dimitrios* (U.S. title, *A Coffin for Dimitrios,* both 1939), and *Journey into Fear* (1940).

Following service in World War II as a film director for the British Army, Ambler wrote screenplays. With Charles Roda he wrote a series of novels under the joint pseudonym Eliot Reed. In his first postwar book under his own name, *Judgment on Deltchev* (1951), set in the Balkans, Ambler used his wide knowledge of Europe to provide factual detail in his treatment of a more overtly political theme. *The Night-Comers* (1956; U.S. title, *State of Siege,* 1956) describes the fear engendered by a revolution in the Far East. In a two-novel series, *The Light of Day* (1962) and *Dirty Story* (1967), he chronicles the life of a battered soldier of fortune who has been involved in shady deals in Istanbul, Athens, and Central Africa. Later works include *The Levanter* (1972), *Dr. Frigo* (1974), *Send No More Roses* (1977; U.S. title, *The Siege of the Villa Lipp,* 1977), and *The Care of Time* (1981). Several of Ambler's novels have been made into motion pictures.

amblygonite, phosphate mineral composed of lithium, sodium, and aluminum phosphate [$(Li,Na)AlPO_4(F,OH)$], that is an ore of lithium. It occurs in lithium- and phosphate-rich granitic pegmatites, often in very large, white, translucent masses. It has been mined at Keystone, S.D., and in South Africa, Zimbabwe, and several other countries. Clear material from Hebron, Maine, has been faceted as a gemstone. For detailed physical properties, *see* phosphate mineral (table).

Montebrasite, a similar mineral, contains more hydroxide than fluoride ion; in nature there is a continuous chemical variation, called a solid-solution series, between montebrasite and amblygonite.

amblyopia, dimness of vision that may be gradual or sudden in onset and may affect both eyes or one. It may be transient or permanent and can develop into blindness. The disorder may be caused by hysteria or by poisoning with ethyl or methyl (wood) alcohol, lead, arsenic, thallium, quinine, ergot, male fern, carbon disulfide, stramonium, or *Cannabis sativa* (Indian hemp, the plant from which marihuana and hashish are derived).

One form of amblyopia, known as lazy eye, develops in 2 to 3 percent of the population before the age of 5 years. It is related to the suppression of vision in the macula (the centre of the retina) of one eye in order to avoid double vision due to impaired ability to fuse the images of both eyes into one image in the brain. *See also* strabismus; visual-field defect.

Ambo, also called OVAMBO, ethnolinguistic group located in the dry grassland country of northern South West Africa/Namibia and southern Angola. They are usually called Ovambo in South West Africa/Namibia and Ambo in Angola and speak Kwanyama, a Bantu language. The Ambo were originally ruled by hereditary kings who performed priestly functions.

The Ambo economy rests almost equally on agriculture and animal husbandry, supplemented by fishing, hunting, and gathering. Millet and sorghum are the most extensively cultivated crops; cattle, sheep, and goats are owned by all of the groups, cattle being of particular importance for marriage payments, as well as for milk and butter.

Despite their small size, traditional Ambo groups exhibited typical characteristics of African centralized states: the above-mentioned priest-king, official tax collectors, a queen mother of great prestige, a hereditary aristocracy, and slaves.

Descent is matrilineal, and polygyny is practiced. The first wife enjoys seniority, but each has her own hut, a circular structure of wattle and daub with a thatched, conical roof. Family compounds, which contain only a nuclear family (parents and dependent children), are grouped around a central meeting place, in which is found a chief's hut or a council house containing a sacred fire tended by the principal wife or daughter of the local chief. It cannot be used for cooking (except for the meal of a departing warrior) or for warmth; it is a symbol of the community, and its extinction is regarded as an omen of impending destruction. Local chiefs and headmen light their sacred fires from those of their superiors.

ambo, in the Christian liturgy, a raised stand formerly used for reading the Gospel or the Epistle, first used in early basilicas. Originally, the ambo took the form of a portable lectern. By the 6th century it had evolved into a stationary church furnishing, which reflected the development and codification of the Christian liturgy. By the Byzantine and early Romanesque periods, it had become an essential part of the church plan. In the 12th century, however, the ambo was gradually superseded by the pulpit, and it passed out of liturgical use.

The ambo had either a single or a double construction, and its position in the Latin-cross church plan was not absolutely uniform. Its position varied in the plan of Eastern religious buildings. In Russian Orthodox churches, for instance, the ambo took the form of steps leading to a platform in front of the iconostasis (*q.v.*). In the Greek Orthodox Church it retained its earlier movable form and was placed at one side. The Byzantine rite of the Catholic Church merely used a table set before the doors of the iconostasis.

The normal single ambo consisted of raised platforms on three levels reached by steps and protected by railings. Each level was consecrated to a special part of the service.

By at least the 11th century, double ambos appeared and were normally placed on either side of the choir, with the north ambo used for the reading of the Epistle and the south for the Gospel. A double ambo of this type is represented by those in S. Clemente at Rome, which was rebuilt during the 11th and 12th centuries. Ambos in richly decorated churches were often made of marble and sometimes decorated with mosaics or carving.

Amboina (Indonesia): *see* Ambon.

Amboina Massacre, execution that took place in Amboina (now Ambon, Indonesia) in 1623, when 10 Englishmen, 10 Japanese, and one Portuguese were put to death by local Dutch authorities. The incident ended any hope of Anglo-Dutch cooperation in the area, a goal that both governments had been pursuing for several years, and marked the beginning of Dutch ascendancy in the Indies.

During the first quarter of the 17th century the Dutch East India Company had already established itself in Amboina, one of the Spice Islands (Maluku, formerly Moluccas). A Dutch garrison was stationed in Ft. Victoria and a local Dutch governor was appointed. The English merchants associated with the British East India Company, however, were also attracted to the island, and their interests eventually came into conflict with those of the Dutch. Early in 1623 the Dutch local governor, Herman van Speult, believed that the English merchants, helped by Japanese mercenaries, planned to kill him and overwhelm the Dutch garrison as soon as an English ship arrived to support them. He then ordered the arrest of the alleged plotters. Under torture they admitted their guilt and were found guilty by the court of Amboina and executed in February 1623. The term massacre was applied to this incident by the English.

Amboise, town, Indre-et-Loire *département,* Centre region, central France, on both banks of the Loire, east of Tours. It is the site of a late Gothic château (with Renaissance additions), one of a great company of castles in the rich, rolling Loire country.

The town was first mentioned in 504 as Ambatia, when on the isle of Saint-Jean (now Île d'Or), Clovis, king of the Franks, met Alaric II, king of the Visigoths, to make a short-lived pact. In the 11th century Fulk III Nerra, count of Anjou, took the town from the Count of Blois and built a high, square stone keep, from which the present château emerged. Thrusting up from a rock above the river, the château has a three-story facade flanked by two enormous squat towers (Minimes and Hurtault) each containing a spiral

The château at Amboise, Fr., on the Loire River

By courtesy of the Commissariat General au Tourisme (France); photograph, Knecht

ramp. It was a favourite residence of French monarchs from the mid-15th century to the 17th. Charles VIII, who was born and died there, brought artists and artisans from Italy to embellish the place, as did Francis I.

Huguenot efforts to remove Francis II from the influence of the House of Guise were exposed in 1560 as the Conspiracy of Amboise, and subsequently Protestant corpses hung from the balcony of the King's house, a Gothic portion of the château. Nevertheless, the Édict d'Amboise (1563) granted freedom of worship to Protestant nobility and gentry. From the time of Henry IV, the château was often used as a prison, and Abdelkader, the Algerian national leader, was confined there (1848–52). In 1872, after private owners had razed portions of the château, the National Assembly voted its return to the Orléans family.

In the town itself the 16th-century town hall is a museum. The Porte de l'Horloge is a 15th-century gateway with a carillon. To the southeast is Le Clos-Lucé, formerly the castle of Cloux, where Leonardo da Vinci died; it is now a museum. Immediately south is the seven-tiered Pagoda of Chanteloup, a piece of 18th-century chinoiserie. Industrial development has extended there from Paris and includes the manufacture of machine tools, chemical products, and shoes. Pop. (1982) 10,823.

Amboise, Conspiracy of, abortive plot of young French Huguenot aristocrats in 1560 against the Catholic House of Guise.

On the accession of the 14-year-old Francis II in 1559, the Guise family gained ascendancy in the government, creating enmity among the smaller nobility. A conspiracy to overturn their government was formed at Nantes, with a needy Périgord nobleman named La Renaudie as its nominal head, though the agitation had in the first instance been fostered by the agents of Louis I de Bourbon, prince de Condé. The Guises were warned of the conspiracy while the court was at Blois, and for greater security they removed the King to Amboise. La Renaudie, however, merely postponed his plans, and the conspirators assembled in small parties in the woods around Amboise. They had, however, been again betrayed, and many of them were surrounded and captured before the coup could be delivered; on March 19, 1560, La Renaudie and the rest of the conspirators openly attacked the château of Amboise. They were repelled, La Renaudie was killed, and a large number were taken prisoners.

The Guises exercised merciless vengeance. For a week the torturings, quarterings, and hangings went on, the bodies being cast into the Loire. The Guises further convened a special commission to try Condé, who was condemned to death; but the affair was postponed by the chancellor, and the death of Francis II in December saved Condé.

Amboise, Georges d' (b. 1460, Chaumont-sur-Loire, Fr.—d. May 25, 1510, Lyon), cardinal and chief minister of the French state under King Louis XII, known for his domestic reforms and his role in Louis's Italian campaigns.

Son of Pierre d'Amboise, who was chamberlain to Charles VII and Louis XI and ambassador to Rome, Georges received the bishopric of Montauban when only 14, and was appointed an almoner of Louis XI. Later, under Charles VIII, he was imprisoned as a follower of the Duc d'Orléans, the future Louis XII. When the Duc d'Orléans was restored to favour, d'Amboise received the archbishoprics of Narbonne (1492) and Rouen (1493) and was made lieutenant general of Normandy. When Orléans became king in 1498, d'Amboise became a cardinal and first minister of the crown.

D'Amboise reduced administrative spending and thus was able to reduce taxes; he also instituted important judicial reforms. He did much for the organization of Louis XII's expedition against Milan (begun 1499). When Pope Alexander VI died in 1503, d'Amboise hoped to become pope but refused to use French troops to force his election. An Italian was chosen as Pius III, and, on his death a month later, another Italian was chosen as Julius II. As compensation, Cardinal d'Amboise was made legate for life to France and to the Comtat-Venaissin. Remaining active in the French government, he was one of the negotiators of the Treaty of Blois (1504) with the emperor Maximilian I, and of the League of Cambrai against Venice. His death occurred on his return from another venture into Italy with Louis XII.

D'Amboise, detail of an engraving by an unknown artist
By courtesy of the Bibliotheque Nationale, Paris

Amboise, Jacques (Joseph) d': *see* d'Amboise, Jacques (Joseph).

Ambon, formerly AMBOINA or AMBOYNA, island and *kotamadya* (city) in Maluku Tengah *kabupaten* (Central Moluccas regency) of Maluku *propinsi* (province), Indonesia. Ambon island is located 7 mi (11 km) off the southwestern coast of the island of Seram. Its 294 sq mi (761 sq km) are generally hilly, with Mt. Salhatu rising to 3,405 ft (1,038 m). Although subject to earthquakes, Ambon has no active volcanoes, but it does have some hot springs and hot-gas vents, or solfataras. It has a tropical climate with an abundant rainfall. The hard and knotty Ambon wood, of great value for ornamental woodwork, is obtained from Seram. There are few mammals indigenous to Ambon, but birds include a racquet-tailed kingfisher, a crimson lory, and a vivid crimson brush-tongued parrot. Many varieties of fish live in Teluk (bay) Ambon, whose eastern end contains some marine gardens.

Zebras in the Amboseli National Park, Kenya
John Lewis Stage—Photo Researchers

Ambon's clove trade first attracted the Portuguese, who named the island and founded a settlement in 1521. The Dutch captured the Portuguese fort in 1605, took over the spice trade, and in 1623 destroyed a British settlement in the Amboina Massacre. The British took it in 1796, and after it had exchanged hands twice between the British and Dutch, it was restored finally to the latter in 1814. An important naval base, Ambon was occupied by Japan during World War II. In 1950, after Indonesian independence, the Ambonese—many of whom had been educated in Christian schools and served in the Dutch administration and army—found their new social and economic prospects unpromising; they refused to join the unitary Republic of Indonesia and proclaimed an independent South Moluccan Republic. The movement was suppressed by military action, though guerrilla warfare continued in Seram for over a decade, and many Ambonese fled to The Netherlands.

The Ambonese are mainly Melanesian, commonly with dark skin, curly to frizzy hair, flat noses, and thick lips; they also live in the Uliasers and on the nearby Seram coast. The Muslims generally live in the north, and the Christians, in the majority, the south. The language, related to Timorese, serves as a regional lingua franca: it is of the Indonesian family, with many Portuguese and Dutch loanwords.

Agricultural production, generally insignificant, includes corn (maize), coffee, root crops, sago, and cloves. Copra, sugar, and fish are exported, and palm wine is made. Ambon's port is the chief centre for shipment of produce and for distribution of imports. The island has adequate local roads, a government radio station, a telephone system, and Pattimura airport (on the western side of the harbour). Cultural amenities include Universitas Pattimura Ambon (1956), a religious college, and a museum.

The port city of Ambon, on Laitimor Peninsula on the eastern side of the bay, is about 8 mi from the harbour's outer entrance. The capital of Maluku province, it was known under the Dutch for its wide, tree-lined streets; stone houses; and imposing public buildings, including a hospital, a church dating from earliest settlement, and Ft. Victoria, built in the early 17th century and later restored. Much of this, including government buildings and barracks, was destroyed in World War II and the following years. Pop. (1980) island, 650,927; city, 208,898.

Amboseli National Park, formerly MASAI AMBOSELI GAME RESERVE, national park, southern Kenya, East Africa. Amboseli was originally established as a game reserve in 1948 and covered 1,259 sq mi (3,261 sq km), northwest of Kilimanjaro in Tanzania. Within it were distinguished seven habitats: open plains, acacia woodland, lava-strewn thorn-bush country, swamp, marshland, the Amboseli lake bed, and the slopes of Oldoinyo Orok. The reserve was also occupied by the Masai and their herds.

In 1974 a little more than 10 percent of the Reserve was established as the Amboseli National Park, with an area of 151 sq mi (392 sq km). Centred on Lake Amboseli, normally dry with a flat basin of alkaline soils, the park encompasses three of the original seven habitats: open plains, thorn-bush country, and acacia woodland. A great variety of wildlife inhabits the park. Important fauna include the baboon, lion, cheetah, elephant, black rhinoceros, hippopotamus, Masai giraffe, buffalo, oryx, wildebeest, gerenuk, impala, and gazelle.

Ambridge, borough, Beaver County, western Pennsylvania, U.S., on the Ohio River, just northwest of Pittsburgh. Within its boundaries is the former village of Economy (1825–1906) established by the communal Harmony Society, led by George Rapp. The Harmonists (Rappites) were religious immigrants from Württemberg, Ger., who had previously settled at Harmony, Pa., and New Harmony, Ind. The community prospered for about 50 years but declined because of the practice of celibacy and the lack of converts. In 1901 the American Bridge Company purchased 2,500 ac (1,012 ha) and established a town, which was incorporated as a borough in 1905 and renamed Ambridge in 1906. The state of Pennsylvania purchased (1919) many of the original Rappite buildings, which have been restored as the historical village of Old Economy. In addition to the bridge works, manufactures include wrought iron, pipe, electrical equipment, and building materials. Pop. (1980) 9,575.

Ambrim (Vanuatu): *see* Ambrym.

Ambrogini, Angelo (Renaissance scholar): *see* Politian.

Ambros, August Wilhelm (b. Nov. 17, 1816, Vysoké Mýto, near Prague—d. June 28, 1876, Vienna), musicologist, author of *Geschichte der Musik,* a comprehensive history of music.

Ambros studied law, entered the civil service in 1840, and became public prosecutor in Prague in 1850. A keen, well-trained musician and composer of a Czech opera, *Bretislaw a Jitka,* he also established himself as a brilliant writer on music. His pamphlet *Über die Grenzen der Poesie und Musik* (1856) contributed to a heated aesthetic controversy. In 1869 he became professor of music at Prague and, in 1872, of music history at Vienna. His *Geschichte der Musik*, incomplete at his death, covered antiquity, the Middle Ages, and the Renaissance. Scholars completed the work from his notes.

Ambrose, SAINT, Latin AMBROSIUS (b. *c.* AD 339, Augusta Treverorum, Belgica, Gaul—d. 397, Milan; feast day December 7), bishop of Milan, biblical critic, and initiator of ideas that provided a model for medieval conceptions of church–state relations. His literary works have been acclaimed as masterpieces of Latin eloquence, and his musical accomplishments are

St. Ambrose, detail of a fresco by Pinturicchio, 1480s; in Sta. Maria del Popolo, Rome
Alinari—Art Resource/EB Inc.

remembered in his hymns. Ambrose is also remembered as the teacher who converted and baptized St. Augustine of Hippo, the great Christian theologian, and as a model bishop who viewed the church as rising above the ruins of the Roman Empire.

Early career. Though Ambrose, the second son of the prefect (imperial viceroy) of Gaul, was born in the official residence at Augusta Treverorum (Trier), his father died soon afterward, and Ambrose was reared in Rome, in a palace frequented by the clergy, by his widowed mother and his elder sister Marcellina, a nun. Duly promoted to the governorship of Aemilia-Liguria in *c.* 370, he lived at Milan and was unexpectedly acclaimed as their bishop by the people of the city in 374.

Ambrose, a popular outsider, chosen as a compromise candidate to avoid a disputed election, changed from an unbaptized layman to a bishop in eight days. Coming from a well-connected but obscure senatorial family, Ambrose could be ignored as a provincial governor; as bishop of Milan he was able to dominate the cultural and political life of his age.

Ecclesiastical administrative accomplishments. An imperial court frequently sat in Milan. In confrontations with this court, Ambrose showed a directness that combined the republican ideal of the prerogatives of a Roman senator with a sinister vein of demagoguery. In 384 he secured the rejection of an appeal for tolerance by pagan members of the Roman senate, whose spokesman, Quintus Aurelius Symmachus, was his relative (Letters 17, 18). In 385–386 he refused to surrender a church for the use of Arian heretics. In 388 he rebuked the emperor Theodosius for having punished a bishop who had burnt a Jewish synagogue. In 390 he imposed public penance on Theodosius for having punished a riot in Thessalonica by a massacre of its citizens. These unprecedented interventions were palliated by Ambrose's loyalty and resourcefulness as a diplomat, notably in 383 and 386 by his official visits to the usurper Maximus at Trier. In his letters and in his funeral orations on the emperors Valentinian II and Theodosius—*De obitu Valentiniani consolatio* (392) and *De obitu Theodosii* (395)—Ambrose established the medieval concept of a Christian emperor as a dutiful son of the church "serving under orders from Christ," and so subject to the advice and strictures of his bishop.

Literary and musical accomplishments. Ambrose's relations with the emperors formed only part of his commanding position among the lay governing class of Italy. He rapidly absorbed the most up-to-date Greek learning, Christian and pagan alike—notably the works of Philo, Origen, and St. Basil of Caesarea and of the pagan Neoplatonist Plotinus. This learning he used in sermons expounding the Bible and, especially, in defending the "spiritual" meaning of the Old Testament by erudite philosophical allegory—notably in the *Hexaëmeron* ("On the Six Days of Creation") and in sermons on the patriarchs (of which *De Isaac et anima* ["On Isaac and the Soul"] and *De bono mortis* ["On the Goodness of Death"] betray a deep acquaintance with Neoplatonic mystical language). Sermons, the dating of which unfortunately remains uncertain, were Ambrose's main literary output. They were acclaimed as masterpieces of Latin eloquence, and they remain a quarry for students of the transmission of Greek philosophy and theology in the West. By such sermons Ambrose gained his most notable convert, Augustine, afterward bishop of Hippo in North Africa and destined, like Ambrose, to be revered as a doctor (teacher) of the church. Augustine went to Milan as a skeptical professor of rhetoric in 384; when he left, in 388, he had been baptized by Ambrose and was indebted to Ambrose's Catholic Neoplatonism, which provided a philosophical base that eventually transformed Christian theology.

Ambrose provided educated Latins with an impeccably classical version of Christianity. His work on the moral obligations of the clergy, *De officiis ministrorum* (386), is skillfully modelled on Cicero's *De officiis.* He sought to replace the heroes of Rome with Old Testament saints as models of behaviour for a Christianized aristocracy. By letters, visitations, and nominations he strengthened this aristocratic Christianity in the northern Italian towns that he had once ruled as a Roman governor.

In Milan, Ambrose "bewitched" the populace by introducing new Eastern melodies and by composing beautiful hymns, notably "Aeterne rerum Conditor" ("Framer of the earth and sky") and "Deus Creator omnium" ("Maker of all things, God most high"). He spared no pains in instructing candidates for Baptism. He denounced social abuses (notably in the sermons *De Nabuthe* ["On Naboth"]) and frequently secured pardon for condemned men. He advocated the most austere asceticism: noble families were reluctant to let their marriageable daughters attend the sermons in which he urged upon them the crowning virtue of virginity.

Evaluations and interpretations. Ambrose's reputation after his death was unchallenged. For Augustine, he was the model bishop: a biography was written in 412 by Paulinus, deacon of Milan, at Augustine's instigation. To Augustine's opponent, Pelagius, Ambrose was "the flower of Latin eloquence." Of his sermons, the *Expositio evangelii secundum Lucam* (390; "Exposition of the Gospel According to Luke") was widely circulated.

Yet, Ambrose is a Janus-like figure. He imposed his will on emperors. But he never considered himself as a precursor of a polity in which the church dominated the state: for he acted from a traditional fear that Christianity might yet be eclipsed by a pagan nobility and Catholicism uprooted in Milan by Arian courtiers. His attitude to the learning he used was similarly old-fashioned. Pagans and heretics, he said, "dyed their impieties in the vats of philosophy"; yet his sermons betray the pagan mysticism of Plotinus in its most unmuted tints. In a near-contemporary mosaic in the chapel of S. Satiro in the church of S. Ambrogio, Milan, Ambrose appears as he wished to be seen: a simple Christian bishop clasping the book of Gospels. Yet the manner in which he set about his duties as a bishop ensured that, to use his own image, the Catholic Church would rise "like a growing moon" above the ruins of the Roman Empire. (P.R.L.B.)

BIBLIOGRAPHY. *Collected editions.* The edition of the complete works given in J.P. Migne (ed.), *Patrologia Latina*, vol. 14–17 (1845), is gradually being superseded by that of the "Corpus Christianorum Series," *Sancti Ambrosii Mediolanensis Opera* (1957–). English translations of Ambrose's letters and various works are given in vol. 26, 42, and 44 (1954–63; reprinted with corrections, 1967), in the series "The Fathers of the Church."

Life. The contemporary biography, written by Ambrose's former secretary, Paulinus of Milan, was edited by Michele Pellegrino as Paolina de Milano, *Vita di S. Ambrogio* (1961). The most comprehensive biography is F. Homes-Dudden, *The Life and Times of St. Ambrose*, 2 vol. (1935). A shorter account is Angelo Paredi, *S. Ambrogio e la sua età*, 2nd ed. (1960; *Saint Ambrose: His Life and Times*, 1964). Ambrose's current position is dealt with in J.R. Palanque, *Saint Ambroise et l'Empire romain* (1933); his relation to Neoplatonism is considered in Pierre Courcelle, *Les Lettres grecques en Occident, de Macrobe à Cassiodore*, rev. ed. (1948; *Late Latin Writers and Their Greek Sources*, 1969).

Ambrose OF CAMALDOLI, Italian AMBROGIO CAMALDOLESE, original name AMBROGIO TRAVERSARI (b. Sept. 16, 1386, Portico, Republic of Florence—d. Oct. 20, 1439, Florence), Humanist, ecclesiastic, and patristic translator who helped effect the brief reunion of the Eastern and Western churches in the 15th century. He entered the Camaldolese Order in 1400 at Florence, where, over a period of 30 years, he mastered Latin and particularly Greek, which enabled him to translate Greek patristic works into Latin, including those of SS. Athanasius the Great of Alexandria, Basil the Great of Caesarea, and John Chrysostom of Constantinople. His reputation in Humanist circles won him the patronage of Cosimo de' Medici.

Pope Eugenius IV appointed him minister

general of the Camaldolese Order in 1431 and papal emissary to the Council of Basel in 1435. He served a prime role at the Council of Ferrara–Florence when, in 1438, as papal representative, he received at the council the Byzantine emperor John VIII and Patriarch Joseph of Constantinople. His expertise in Greek and Eastern theology made him a chief negotiator for the decree of union between the Latin and Greek churches promulgated shortly before his death. Although never formally beatified, he is commemorated at Florence and by the Camaldolese on November 20.

Consult the INDEX *first*

Ambrosian chant, monophonic, or unison, chant that accompanies the Latin mass and canonical hours of the Ambrosian rite. The word Ambrosian is derived from St. Ambrose, bishop of Milan (374–397), from which comes the occasional designation of this rite as Milanese. Despite legends to the contrary, no Ambrosian-chant melodies can be attributed to Ambrose.

The Ambrosian Ordinary (chants of the mass having texts that do not change from day to day) has some relationship to the Roman Gregorian Ordinary (the standard Roman Catholic liturgy and chant): they each have a Kyrie and Gloria, except that the Kyrie is appended to the Ambrosian Gloria (in the Roman Ordinary it precedes the Gloria); each has a Credo (called Symbolum in the Ambrosian rite) and a Sanctus. For the breaking of the Communion breads, the Ambrosian rite uses the Confractorium, a Proper chant (one having a text that varies during the church year), whereas the Gregorian has the Agnus Dei, an Ordinary chant. The Ambrosian Ordinary chants are generally but not always syllabic (one note per syllable). The festive Gloria has expressive melismas (many notes per syllable) at the conclusion of syllabic phrases. Compared to the Gregorian rite, the Ambrosian has few Ordinary chants.

The late date of the Ambrosian-chant manuscripts (12th century) raises doubt concerning the time of the origin of this chant. It is thought that the Ambrosian chant was established and differed stylistically from Gregorian chant in the era of Charlemagne (d. 814), who unsuccessfully endeavoured to replace the Ambrosian with the Gregorian liturgy. Gregorian melodies and texts from this time and later are found integrated within the Ambrosian repertory. Ambrosian chants, however, also include a primitive body of less uniform and theoretically unorganized chants that remained apparently uninfluenced by the polished and systematized Gregorian repertory.

There are several traits native to the Ambrosian chants and not typically Gregorian. Unlike the Gregorian chants, the Ambrosian are not stylistically uniform for any liturgical category; *e.g.,* Gregorian Tracts (a category of chant) have certain musical traits in common with each other, but no such consistencies appear among Ambrosian chants. The Ambrosian chants are not written in any mode (theoretical melodic and scale pattern), whereas a given Gregorian chant is in one of the eight church modes. The Ambrosian psalm tones (formulas for intoning psalms) differ from the Gregorian psalm tones in that the former have no middle cadence (stopping point) and have a greater choice of reciting tones and terminations. Representative of Oriental influence are the Ambrosian *melodiae* (freely interchangeable melismatic fragments) found in the responsories (a type of chant) for Matins (a service of the canonical hours).

Ambrosiaster, the name given to the author of a commentary on St. Paul's letters in the New Testament, long attributed to St. Ambrose (died 397), bishop of Milan. The work is valuable for the criticism of the Latin text of the New Testament.

In 1527 Erasmus expressed doubts that the work was written by Ambrose. His judgment was eventually accepted by scholars, and the author is generally called Ambrosiaster or Pseudo-Ambrosius. Since Augustine in the 4th century attributed some parts of the commentary on Romans to Sanctus Hilarius, the work has been ascribed by various scholars to almost every known Hilary.

Ambrym, also spelled AMBRIM, island of Vanuatu, southwestern Pacific Ocean. It has an area of 257 sq mi (665 sq km) and is known for its two active volcanoes: Mt. Marum, 4,167 ft (1,270 m), which last erupted in 1973; and Mt. Benbow, 3,720 ft, which had major eruptions in 1894, 1913, 1929, 1942, 1950, 1972 and 1973. The 1950 eruption was serious enough to warrant the evacuation of several hundred persons for resettlement on Éfaté. The island produces copra. Pop. (1979) 6,311.

ambulatory, in architecture, continuation of the aisled spaces on either side of the nave (central part of the church) around the apse (semicircular projection at the east end of the church) or chancel (east end of the church where the main altar stands) to form a continuous processional way. The ambulatory often provided improved sites for the numerous altars for saints, which formerly were located along a crowded corridor behind the high altar; the altars are reached through circular arches piercing the curved outer wall of the ambulatory.

Ambulatory, Saint-Benoît-sur-Loire, Fr., 11th century
Jean Roubier

The first ambulatory was developed during the rebuilding of Saint-Martin at Tours in France (begun *c.* 1050, now destroyed). By the beginning of the 13th century the Benedictines had introduced the ambulatory to England, and many English cathedrals were extended eastward in this manner.

ambush bug, any member of the insect family Phymatidae (order Heteroptera), which contains about 200 species, generally in the tropical Americas and Asia. As its common name indicates, the ambush bug hides on a flower or plant; when prey approaches closely enough, the ambush bug grasps it with its front legs. The upper section (tibia) of each foreleg has teethlike structures that mesh into similar structures on the lower, greatly thickened leg section (femur). Holding its victim in these pincers, the ambush bug inserts its short beak and sucks out the body fluids. Even though the ambush bug is small (usually less than 12 millimetres, or 0.5 inch), its prey may be as large, comparatively, as a bumblebee, wasp, or butterfly.

The ambush bug has an odd shape, with lateral extensions and rounded projections. The Asian genus *Carcinocoris* is covered with spines. *Phymata erosa,* one of the most common North American representatives, is yellowish green and is usually found on goldenrod plants.

Ambush bug (Phymatidae)
Earl L. Kubis from Root Resources—EB Inc.

AMC: *see* American Motors Corporation.

Amda Tseyon (Amharic: Pillar of Zion) (d. 1344?), ruler of Ethiopia from 1314 to 1344, best known in the chronicles as a heroic fighter against the Muslims; he is sometimes considered to have been the founder of the Ethiopian state.

The earliest Ethiopian chronicle, which is more than simply a king list, tends to support this hypothesis, for it concerns Amda Tseyon's reign, and the earliest known examples of the written Amharic language are hymns praising him. His image is reminiscent of that of Henry V of England in his transformation from a youthful carouser to an audacious warrior and ruler. Most of his wars were against the Muslim kingdoms to the southeast, which he was able to fight and generally defeat one by one, despite their plans to unite against him. Hence, he substantially enlarged his kingdom by gradually incorporating a number of smaller states.

ameba, amebic, ameboid, etc.: *see under* amoeba, amoebic, amoeboid, etc.

Amédée (French personal name): *see under* Amadeus.

Amedeo (Italian personal name): *see under* Amadeus.

Ameghino, Florentino (b. Sept. 19, 1853, Moneglia, Kingdom of Sardinia—d. Aug. 6, 1911, La Plata, Arg.), paleontologist, anthropologist, and geologist, whose fossil discoveries on the Argentine Pampas rank with those made in the western United States during the late 19th century.

Ameghino's family immigrated to Argentina when he was a small child. He began collecting fossils as a youth and soon developed an interest in fossil classification. His first contributions were largely ignored by South American journals, but correspondence with French paleontologist and zoologist Paul Gervais, director of the *Journal de Zoologie,* led to international recognition. Altogether, he discovered more than 6,000 fossil species of extinct fauna. He was appointed professor of zoology at the University of Córdoba (1884) and professor of geology and mineralogy at La Plata National University (1887).

Although he spent three years in Europe, Ameghino remained isolated from the mainstream of scientific thought, which led him to misinterpret some of his fossil finds and to advance radical anthropological theories that drew severe criticism. He stated, in effect, that all mammals, including man, originated on the Argentine pampas. He was dismissed from his teaching posts, and so clouded was his reputation that only near the end of his life did other paleontologists begin to realize the value of his work. He served as director of the Museum of Natural History, Buenos Aires (1902–11), and was reappointed professor of geology at La Plata National University (1906). Nearly 200 monographs and memoirs are contained in *Obras completas y correspondencia científica de Florentino Ameghino*, 24 vol. (1913–36; "Complete Works and Scientific Correspondence of Florentino Ameghino").

Amelanchier, genus of flowering shrubs and small trees, of the rose family (Rosaceae), several species of which are useful as ornamental plants. Most species are North American; exceptions include the shrubby *A. ovalis,* which ranges over Europe, and *A. asiatica*, a small tree of eastern Asia. A number of amelanchiers are variously called juneberry, sugarplum, serviceberry, or sarvistree. The name shadbush, or shadblow, refers to the tendency of certain species to produce their profuse small blossoms (before the leaves) when the shad swim upriver to spawn, in early spring in eastern North America. The terminal white flower clusters are followed by reddish to purple-black fruit resembling tiny apples. The fruits are eaten by birds. Some species bear fruit that is used in making jellies.

The popular ornamental amelanchiers include juneberry (*A. alnifolia*), a shrub that grows up to about 3 metres (10 feet); shadblow serviceberry (*A. canadensis*), up to about 8 m; and Allegheny serviceberry (*A. laevis*), like *A. canadensis* but taller and with more nodding flower clusters. Downy serviceberry (*A. arborea*) is also similar to *A. canadensis* but is more vigorous and has larger hanging flower clusters. Apple serviceberry (*A. grandiflora*), a natural hybrid of *A. arborea* and *A. laevis*, grows up to 9 m and has larger individual blossoms, pinkish on some trees. Running serviceberry (*A. stolonifera*) is a spreading shrub about 1 m tall, useful in semiwild plantings and for stabilizing soil, especially on embankments.

Shadblow serviceberry (*Amelanchier canadensis*)
A to Z Botanical Collection—EB Inc.

The wild amelanchiers appear to hybridize freely. Their differences are slight and often puzzling to both gardeners and horticulturists.

Amelung glass, American glass produced from 1784 to about 1795 by John Frederick Amelung, a native of Bremen in Germany. Financed by German and U.S. promoters, Amelung founded the New Bremen Glassmanufactory near Frederick, Md., and attempted to establish a self-sufficient community, importing glassworkers and other craftsmen, schoolmasters, music teachers, and a physician from Germany. The enterprise was encouraged by such men as Washington, Jefferson, and Franklin, and in 1789 a duty on window and other glass, the first protective tariff passed under the new U.S. Constitution, was proposed. Amelung's ambitious project failed to prosper, however, and in 1790 he petitioned Congress for help. After debating whether such a loan was within its constitutional powers and whether it was advisable to set such a precedent, Congress defeated the measure. The New Bremen industry subsequently failed.

Covered tumbler of Amelung glass, New Bremen Glassmanufactory of John Frederick Amelung, New Bremen, Md., 1788; in the Corning Museum of Glass, Corning, N.Y.
By courtesy of the Corning Museum of Glass, Corning, N.Y.

Only a few authenticated pieces of Amelung glass survive, most of them presentation pieces decorated with restrained engraving. Among them are a service given to George Washington and the Bremen pokal, a covered goblet sent to Amelung's German backers.

Amen (Egyptian god): *see* Amon.

amen, expression of agreement, confirmation, or desire used in worship by Jews, Christians, and Muslims. The basic meaning of the Semitic root from which it is derived is "firm," "fixed," or "sure," and the related Hebrew verb also means "to be reliable" and "to be trusted." The Greek Old Testament usually translates amen as "so be it"; in the English Bible it has frequently been rendered as "verily" or "truly."

In its earliest use in the Bible, the amen occurred initially and referred back to the words of another speaker with whom there was agreement. It usually introduced an affirmative statement. For emphasis, as in solemn oaths, the amen was sometimes repeated. The use of the initial amen, single or double in form, to introduce solemn statements of Jesus in the Gospels (52 times in the Synoptic Gospels—Matthew, Mark, and Luke—and 25 times in the Gospel According to John) had no parallel in Jewish practice. Such amens expressed the certainty and truthfulness of the statement that followed.

Use of the amen in Jewish Temple liturgy as a response by the people at the close of a doxology or other prayer uttered by a priest seems to have been common as early as the time of the Chronicler (probably the 4th century BC). This Jewish liturgical use of amen was adopted by the Christians. Justin Martyr (2nd century AD) indicated that amen was used in the liturgy of the Eucharist and was later introduced into the baptismal service.

A final amen, added by a speaker who offered thanksgiving or prayers, public or private, to sum up and confirm what he himself had said, developed naturally from the earlier usage in which others responded with the amen. Use of the final amen is found in the Psalms and is common in the New Testament. Jews used amen to conclude prayers in ancient times, and Christians closed every prayer with it. As hymns became more popular, the use of the final amen was extended.

Although Muslims make little use of amen, it is stated after every recital of the first *sūrah*.

Amendola, Giovanni (b. April 15, 1882, Rome—d. April 7, 1926, Cannes, Fr.), journalist, politician, and in the early 1920s, foremost opponent of the Italian Fascists.

As a journalist, Amendola expressed his philosophical and ideological views in articles appearing first in *La Voce* ("The Voice") and then in the newspapers *Resto di Carlino* and *Corriere della sera.* He urged Italy's entry into World War I in 1915 and fought as a volunteer, reaching the rank of captain and winning a medal of valour.

After the war, Amendola devoted himself entirely to politics as a Democratic Liberal in favour of a policy of rapprochement with the Slavs. First elected to Parliament in 1919, he was in 1922 minister for the colonies in Luigi Facta's cabinet. With Mussolini's advent to power he became a leader of the opposition and attacked the new regime through the columns of his newspaper *Il Mondo.* After the murder of Giacomo Matteotti he was one of the deputies who withdrew from the chamber. In spite of threats against his life during the election campaign of 1924, he declared the Fascist electoral law to be unconstitutional. He died as a result of injuries received when a gang of Fascists attacked him in the Italian spa of Montecatini.

Amendola, 1922
Microfoto 35

Amenemhet, also spelled AMENEMHAT, name of kings of Egypt grouped below chronologically and indicated by the symbol •.

• **Amenemhet I,** king of Egypt (reigned 1991–62 BC), founder of the 12th dynasty who, with a number of powerful nomarchs (provincial governors), restored unity to Egypt after the civil war that followed the death of his predecessor, under whom he had served as vizier.

Amenemhet, an experienced administrator, moved the capital from Thebes to a more central location at Itj-towy (near modern al-Lisht), to the south of Memphis, and appointed his supporters to various posts within the administration. Levying troops from one of the nomarchies, Amenemhet sailed up the Nile, destroying what resistance remained to his rule. To safeguard the Delta he built fortresses along the eastern and western frontiers. Amenemhet also added to the Temple of Amon at Thebes and built at various other sites in Upper Egypt.

In the 20th year of his reign, 1971 BC, Amenemhet made Sesostris I, his son, co-regent. The younger ruler assumed the task of extending Egyptian control into Nubia to the south, advancing as far as the Second Cataract of the Nile and building fortifications at strategic points. Under Amenemhet, the copper mines at Sinai were worked and punitive raids were made against the local Bedouin tribes. In the 30th year of his father's reign, on returning from a raid against the Libyans in the Wādī an-Naṭrūn (a large dry watercourse, extending into Egypt, near Cairo, from Libya), Sesostris received news of Amenemhet's assassination and hastened back to the capital to assume the kingship. *The Instructions of Amenemhet,* a political piece, couched in the old king's words, described the assassination attempt, confirmed the new king, and gave him advice concerning government. Another politically motivated work, *The Story of Sinuhe,* described Sesostris' receipt of the news, his reaction, and the glory of his reign.

• **Amenemhet II,** king of Egypt (reigned 1929–1895 BC), grandson of Amenemhet I (founder of the 12th dynasty); he furthered Egypt's trade relations and internal development.

While he was still co-regent with his father, Sesostris I, Amenemhet led a gold-mining expedition to Nubia. Later, during his own reign, additional expeditions were made to Nubia and Sinai for gold and copper, a new mine shaft was opened at Sinai, and a trade venture was made to Punt, a land on the African coast near modern Somalia. Statues of Amenemhet have been found at several Syrian cities; and treasure of his reign discovered in a temple at Ṭawd, a town in Upper Egypt, reveals Cretan and Syrian stylistic patterns, verifying the foreign contacts.

Within Egypt the provincial governors continued to play administrative key roles, and fine tombs were provided them near their hometowns. Amenemhet's pyramid tomb, built at Dahshūr, close to al-Fayyūm, an oasis-like depression southwest of Cairo, was patterned after his father's, with a fine limestone casing built over retaining walls and a rubble core. Near it was found the jewelry belonging to a daughter of Amenemhet, revealing the artistic heights of his reign.

• **Amenemhet III,** king of Egypt (reigned 1842–1797 BC) of the 12th dynasty, who brought Middle Kingdom Egypt (comprising the 11th and 12th dynasties) to a peak of economic prosperity by completing a system to regulate the inflow of water into Lake Moeris, in the al-Fayyūm depression southwest of Cairo. To celebrate the reclamation of 153,600 acres (62,200 hectares) of land for agricultural use, he erected two colossuses of himself nearby, later described by the Greek historian Herodotus.

Amenemhet also excavated an outflow canal from the lake, thereby utilizing its water for irrigation. The resulting stabilization of the water level also drained some of the marshes that had surrounded the old lake. As part of this great work, the labyrinth described by Herodotus was probably built nearby. It was probably a multifunctional building—palace, temple, town, and administrative centre; ruins of the structure exist south of Amenemhet's pyramid at Hawara, in al-Fayyūm.

Amenemhet also worked the copper mines at Sinai with unprecedented intensity. Permanent quarters were erected for the miners, with wells nearby and fortifications to repel Bedouin raiders. Quarries throughout Egypt and Nubia, to the south, likewise were the site of much activity to support the King's building enterprises. Except for minor punitive raids, his reign was peaceful.

Amenemhet III, granite statue from Bubastis; in the British Museum

Reproduced by courtesy of the trustees of the British Museum

In Nubia Amenemhet retained the empire won by his predecessors. Artifacts of his reign have been found from beyond the Third Cataract of the Nile to Byblos, an important seaport in Lebanon, an indication of Egypt's primacy as a commercial power. His was the last long and successful reign of the 12th dynasty.

Amenemope, ancient Egyptian author of "The Instruction of Amenemope," probably composed during the late New Kingdom (1567–1085 BC). Amenemope's text, similar in content to most of the instruction or wisdom literature written earlier, was a collection of maxims and admonitions setting forth practical injunctions for living. Although the work was first believed to have been derived from the Hebrew Book of Proverbs, most scholars now view the text as the culmination of a long history of Egyptian wisdom literature.

Amenhotep, also called AMENOPHIS, name of Egyptian kings grouped below chronologically and indicated by the symbol •.

• **Amenhotep I,** king of Egypt (reigned 1546–26 BC), son of Ahmose I, the founder of the 18th dynasty; he effectively extended Egypt's boundaries in Nubia (the modern Sudan).

The biographies of two soldiers confirm Amenhotep's wars in Nubia. As shown by a graffito from the seventh year of his reign, he reached the frontier at the Second Cataract

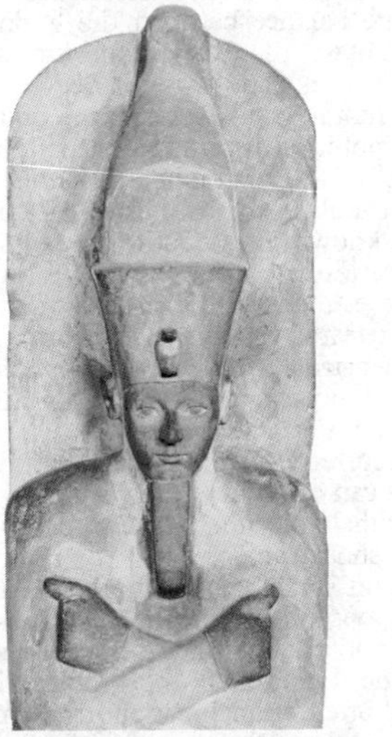

Amenhotep I, limestone sculpture from Dayr al-Baḥrī, *c.* 1550 BC; in the British Museum

Reproduced by courtesy of the trustees of the British Museum

of the Nile. Amenhotep also raided Libya, but no details of the operation are recorded. His only confirmed activities in Asia are the reopening of the copper mines at Sinai and the reoccupation of the fortress erected there during the Middle Kingdom.

Little is known about Amenhotep's building activity, because ancient Egyptian buildings were often demolished for stone. A fine, small limestone chapel of the King has been recovered, and the King's official in charge of construction credits another temple to Amenhotep. His tomb was probably a rock-cut structure separated from its temple, a departure from earlier royal practice. He founded the cemetery workers' village at Dayr al-Madīnah in western Thebes, and in later periods the King and his mother were worshipped there.

• **Amenhotep II,** king of Egypt (reigned 1450–25 BC), son of Thutmose III. Ruling at the height of Egypt's imperial era, he strove to maintain his father's conquests by physical prowess and military skills.

Amenhotep II's upbringing was carefully guided by his warrior father, with great emphasis on physical strength, skills of warfare,

Amenhotep II offering sacrifices, statue, 15th century BC; in the Egyptian Museum, Cairo

By courtesy of the Egyptian Museum; photograph, Hirmer Fotoarchiv, Munchen

and sportsmanship. Amenhotep never tired of boasting of his feats in these skills, and he was even buried with his great bow.

Amenhotep's first campaign was against uprisings in north Syria, during which he extracted loyalty oaths from other Asiatic princes. Returning from Asia, he forwarded the body of a rebel Asiatic chief to the Nubian capital, where it was hung on the town wall as an example; the gesture was sufficient to maintain peace in Nubia. His second campaign was smaller, reaching only to the Sea of Galilee, but after it Amenhotep received gifts from Mitanni, Babylon, and the Hittites. No further northern wars occurred, which suggests that a balance of power had been achieved.

Within Egypt, many of his father's administrators continued to serve Amenhotep, and the King completed some buildings begun by Thutmose III. He also built new sanctuaries in Lower Egypt and added his mortuary temple in western Thebes. Amenhotep's mummy was discovered in the Valley of the Tombs of the Kings at Thebes, in his fine, well-preserved tomb.

• **Amenhotep III,** byname AMENHOTEP THE MAGNIFICENT, king of Egypt (reigned 1417–1379 BC) in a period of peaceful prosperity, who devoted himself to expanding diplomatic contacts and to extensive building in Egypt and Nubia.

After a revolt in Nubia (the modern Sudan) erupted in the fifth year of his reign, Amenhotep dispatched two punitive expeditions, possibly leading one himself, against the rebels. Thereafter his reign was peaceful, except for some disturbances in the Nile Delta, which Amenhotep, son of Hapu, the King's most prominent official, quelled by carefully regulating access into Egypt by land and sea.

Amenhotep III, in his early years, enjoyed hunting, in the tradition of his father, Thutmose IV, and grandfather, Amenhotep II, and on two occasions issued large commemorative scarabs to proclaim his feats. Early in his reign he married Tiy, who, though a commoner, was a shrewd and able woman. She became the chief queen and the mother of the reforming King Akhenaton. In the 11th year of his reign, Amenhotep ordered the excavation of a large artificial lake near her native city, Akhmim, 100 miles (160 kilometres) north of Luxor.

Utilizing the talents of Amenhotep, son of Hapu, the King engaged in a great construction program, which included the mortuary temple in western Thebes, of which only the Colossi of Memnon survive, and a major temple in Nubia. The King also built the main portions of the temple of Luxor and a pylon in the temple of Karnak, both in ancient Thebes.

Amenhotep carried on lively diplomatic exchanges with the other great contemporary powers, as confirmed by the Amarna Letters (diplomatic archive of Amenhotep III and Akhenaton), which reveal that Egyptian gold was exchanged for horses, copper, and lapis lazuli from Asia. He contracted political marriages with the sisters and daughters of the kings of Mitanni (a powerful empire on the Euphrates River in northern Syria) and Babylon, to consolidate alliances, and sought to marry a Hittite princess as well. Diplomatic correspondence was also sent to Assyria, Cyprus, and a number of Egypt's Syrian vassals. Late in Amenhotep's reign, Tushratta, the ruler of Mitanni, forwarded a divine image to Egypt, to cure the ailing king. Queen Tiy played a great role in his last days, and Tushratta even corresponded with her after her husband's death.

Amenhotep III, head of a statue from western Thebes, *c.* 1420 BC

Reproduced by courtesy of the trustees of the British Museum

• Amenhotep IV: *see* Akhenaton.

Amenhotep, SON OF HAPU (b. *c.* 1460 BC, Athribis, Lower Egypt—d. *c.* 1380 BC), high official of the reign of Amenhotep III of Egypt, who was greatly honoured by the King within his lifetime and was deified more than 1,000 years later in the Ptolemaic era.

Coming from a noble family of the Nile Delta, Amenhotep rose through the ranks of the government service, becoming scribe of the recruits, a military office, under Amenhotep III. Still serving in the Delta, Amenhotep was charged with positioning troops at checkpoints on the branches of the Nile to regulate entry into Egypt by sea; he also checked upon the infiltration of Bedouin tribesmen by land. On one of his statues, he is called a general of the army.

Some time later, when he was placed in charge of all royal works, he probably supervised the construction of Amenhotep III's mortuary temple at Thebes near modern Luxor, the construction of another temple in Nubia (the modern Sudan), and the transport of building material and erection of other works. Two statues from Thebes indicate that Amenhotep also served as an intercessor in Amon's temple and that he supervised the celebration of one of Amenhotep III's Sed festivals (a renewal rite celebrated by the pharaoh after the first 30 years of his reign and periodically thereafter). The King honoured him by embellishing Athribis, his native city. Amenhotep III even ordered the building of a small funerary chapel for him, next to his own temple, a singularly rare honour for a nonroyal person in Egypt.

Amenhotep, son of Hapu, black stone statue, *c.* 1400 BC; in the Egyptian Museum, Cairo

By courtesy of the Egyptian Museum, Cairo; photograph, Hirmer Fotoarchiv, Munchen

Amenophis (Egyptian king): *see* Akhenaton.

Amenophis (kings of Egypt): *see under* Amenhotep.

amenorrhea, also spelled AMENORRHOEA, failure to menstruate. Menstruation is the normal cyclic bleeding from the uterus in the female reproductive tract. Primary amenorrhea is the delay or failure to start menstruating upon reaching adulthood, while secondary amenorrhea is the abnormal cessation of cycles once they have started. Amenorrhea is not itself a disease. It reflects some failure in the intricate balance between the hypothalamus, the pituitary, the ovaries, and the uterus. The pituitary is a gland situated deep between the two cerebral hemispheres of the brain, next to the hypothalamus, and is partially under the control of this area of brain tissue. The pituitary stimulates the ovaries by means of a hormone known as gonadotropin, which causes the ovaries to produce the reproductive hormones estrogen and progesterone. Estrogen, when released to the uterus (womb), regulates the menstrual (monthly reproductive) cycle and produces periods of bleeding if fertilization of the egg released from the ovary has not occurred. Any disturbance in this chain of events can cause amenorrhea.

Hypothalamic amenorrhea is caused by emotional shock, anxiety, fear, or injuries to the midbrain. Fractures to the base of the skull or nervous system infections such as meningitis or encephalitis may disrupt hypothalamic function, but usually the problem is psychological or emotional. Amenorrhea may be the main or the only symptom in these disturbances.

Disorders that disrupt secretion by the pituitary include tumours, systemic diseases, and dietary deficiencies. When amenorrhea is primary, the reproductive organs remain infantile, the breasts do not develop, there is no pubic hair, there is dwarfism, and muscle development is deficient. When amenorrhea is secondarily caused by tumours, destructive lesions, or hemorrhagic shock, the genitals atrophy; pubic hair diminishes; there may be lethargy, weight loss, or obesity; and masculine traits may develop. Treatment is directed toward the underlying cause.

The ovarian disturbances causing amenorrhea include cysts, tumours, and excessive or deficient secretion of hormones. Most of the same genital symptoms occur as with the pituitary, but the growth pattern is different.

Other causes of amenorrhea include general obesity, obstructions of the vagina, and the normal bodily states of pregnancy, lactation, and menopause.

Amenorrhea, if not resulting from organic disease, and infrequent menstruation do no harm to the body.

Amenouzume, in full AMENOUZUME NO MIKOTO, in Japanese mythology, the celestial goddess who performed a spontaneous dance enticing the sun goddess Amaterasu out of the cave in which she had secluded herself, thus depriving the world of light.

Amenouzume decorated herself with club moss and leaves of the *sakaki* tree, lit bonfires, and made a platform of an upturned tub. Her inspired cries and divine dancing, in the course of which she exposed herself, so delighted the assembled gods that they roared in laughter, thus awakening the curiosity of the sun goddess.

Amenouzume is the patron goddess of dancers. The classical music and dancing used in Shintō religious ceremonies, *kagura,* is said to have originated with her performance. In popular mythology, as the embodiment of the female principle, she is often associated with Sarudahiko (*q.v.*), who represents male sexuality and who offered himself as a guide to the divine grandchild Ninigi when he descended to earth. Amenouzume and Sarudahiko are sometimes pictured as husband and wife.

amensalism, association between organisms of two different species in which one is inhibited or destroyed and the other is unaffected. There are two basic modes: competition (*q.v.*), in which a larger or stronger organism excludes a smaller or weaker one from living space or deprives it of food; and antibiosis, in which one organism is unaffected but the other is damaged or killed by a chemical secretion.

The classic demonstration of antibiosis is the destructive effect that the bread mold *Penicillium* has upon certain bacteria; the secretion, known as penicillin, has become a potent medicine in combatting bacterial infections. Some higher plants secrete substances that inhibit the growth of—or kill outright—nearby competing plants. An example is the black walnut (*Juglans nigra*), which secretes juglone, a substance that destroys many herbaceous plants within its root zone.

The composition of chaparral and desert in the western United States is largely dependent on such antibiotic associations between species, which results in stable communities that have been freed of competition for the scarce water.

Āmer, also called AMBER, town, Jaipur district, Rājasthān state, northwestern India, part of the Jaipur urban agglomeration. It is entirely surrounded by hills and stands at the foot of a rocky gorge. Āmer was made the capital of the state of the Kachwāhā Rājputs (warrior rulers of the historic region of Rājputāna) in the 12th century and for 600 years continued to be a political centre. Its name is derived from Ambarisha, the king of Ayodhyā; its full name was Ambarikhanera, but this was later contracted to Ambiner or Amber. The official name, however, is Āmer. The palace, an example of Rājput architecture, was begun *c.* 1600 and was completed in the 18th century, but the capital was transferred to Jaipur in 1728. Jaigarh fort stands on a hill summit overlooking the town. The area is the alleged location of fabled buried treasure, but a 1977 government excavation, based on supposedly authentic maps, failed to find it. Pop. (1981) 16,054.

Amerada Hess Corporation, integrated U.S. petroleum company involved in exploration and development of oil and natural gas resources, and the transportation, production, marketing, and sale of petroleum products. Headquarters are in New York City.

The company was incorporated in 1920 as Amerada Corporation. It assumed the name Amerada Petroleum Corporation in 1941 upon merging with a subsidiary of that name, and adopted its present name in 1969 by merging with Hess Oil and Chemical Corporation.

The company operates the chain of Hess brand gas stations along the East and Gulf coasts. This chain was one of the first to sell discount gasoline. These stations offer only gas and perform no repair services. Amerada Hess also owns the world's largest oil refinery, located in St. Croix, Virgin Islands. The company also owns two smaller refineries in New Jersey and Mississippi, the East Coast's most extensive oil storage facilities, and a large fleet of oil tankers. Amerada Hess has invested heavily in several oil and natural gas exploration projects both in the United States and abroad.

amercement, in English law, an arbitrary financial penalty, formerly imposed on an offender by his peers or at the discretion of the court or the lord. Although the word has become practically synonymous with fine, there is a distinction in that fines are fixed by statute, whereas amercements are decided by the court. Originally, an amercement represented a commutation of a sentence that required the forfeiture of goods, while a fine was an arrangement agreed upon between the judge and the prisoner to avoid imprisonment. The Magna Carta attempted to regulate the assessment of amercements.

America (Western Hemisphere): *see* Americas.

America, Reformed Church in: *see* Reformed Church in America.

America, Volunteers of, religious social welfare organization in the U.S. that offers spiritual and material aid to those in need. It was founded in New York City in 1896 by Ballington and Maud Booth as a result of a schism in the Salvation Army and is organized along quasi-military lines. The Grand Field Council, made up of all officers of the rank of lieutenant major or higher, is the chief governing body. It elects the commander in chief and other administrative officers.

Through more than 800 service centres the organization offers a broad variety of welfare services, including day nurseries, homes and clubs for the aged, summer camps for children and adults, maternity homes for unwed mothers, aid to convicts and former convicts and their families, salvage and rehabilitation programs for the physically and mentally handicapped, residences for girls, emergency shelters for women and children, and family centres. Its spiritual services include mission churches and Sunday schools, in which a conservative interpretation of the Christian faith is presented.

Local administration is performed by a resident officer aided by an advisory board of local citizens. Funds are provided by direct public contribution and through the local federated fund. Headquarters are in New York City.

America First Committee, influential political pressure group in the United States (1940–41), opposing aid to the Allies in World War II. Fearing direct national military involvement, the committee claimed a membership of 800,000 and attracted such leaders as Gen. Robert E. Wood, Charles A. Lindbergh, and Sen. Gerald P. Nye. Though failing in its campaigns to block the Lend-Lease Act, the use of the Navy for convoys, and the repeal of the Neutrality Act, its public pressure undoubtedly discouraged greater direct military aid to a Great Britain beleaguered by Nazi Germany. After the Japanese attack on Pearl Harbor (Dec. 7, 1941), the committee dissolved and urged its members to support the war effort.

American Airlines, Inc., U.S. international airline controlled by the holding company AMR Corporation (*q.v.*) since 1982.

American Anti-Slavery Society (1833–70), promoter, with its state and local auxiliaries, of the cause of immediate abolition of slavery in the United States. As the main activist arm of the Abolition Movement (*q.v.*), the society was founded in 1833 under the leadership of William Lloyd Garrison.

By 1840 its auxiliary societies numbered 2,000, with a total membership ranging from 150,000 to 200,000. The societies sponsored meetings, adopted resolutions, signed anti-slavery petitions to be sent to Congress, published journals and enlisted subscriptions, printed and distributed propaganda in vast quantities, and sent out agents and lecturers (70 in 1836 alone) to carry the impassioned anti-slavery message to Northern audiences.

Participants in the societies were drawn mainly from religious circles (*e.g.*, Theodore Dwight Weld) and philanthropic backgrounds (*e.g.*, businessmen Arthur and Lewis Tappan and lawyer Wendell Phillips), as well as from the free black community, with six blacks serving on the first Board of Managers. In addition, public meetings were most effective when featuring the eloquent testimony of former slaves like Frederick Douglass or William Wells Brown. Anti-slavery activities frequently met with violent public opposition, with mobs invading meetings, attacking speakers, and burning presses.

In 1839 the national organization split over basic differences of approach: Garrison and his followers were more radical than other members; they denounced the U.S. Constitution as supportive of slavery and insisted on sharing organizational responsibility with women. The less radical wing, led by the Tappan brothers, formed the American and Foreign Anti-Slavery Society, which advocated moral suasion and political action and led directly to the birth of the Liberty Party (*q.v.*) in 1840. Because of this cleavage in national leadership, the bulk of the activity in the 1840s and 1850s was carried on by state and local societies. The anti-slavery issue entered the mainstream of American politics through the Free Soil Party (1848–54) and subsequently the Republican Party (founded in 1854). The American Anti-Slavery Society was formally dissolved in 1870, after the Civil War and Emancipation.

American arborvitae, also called EASTERN ARBORVITAE, or NORTHERN WHITE CEDAR (*Thuja occidentalis*), ornamental and timber evergreen conifer of the cypress family (Cupressaceae), native to eastern North America. In the lumber trade it is called, among other names, white cedar, eastern white cedar, and New Brunswick cedar.

American arborvitae (*Thuja occidentalis*)
G.J. Chafaris—EB Inc.

Often 20 metres (about 65 feet) tall, the tree is the most common and probably the hardiest of the arborvitae. Its trunk sometimes is forked near the ground into several main stems covered with reddish-brown bark. The cones have 8 to 10 scales, of which only four are usually fertile. Most cultivated varieties are narrow, densely pyramidal shrubs, and many have interesting variations in foliage colour. *See also* arborvitae.

American Association for the Advancement of Science, society of American scientists founded in 1848 in Boston at a meeting of geologists and naturalists. It includes all major fields of science and, in the 1980s, had 130,000 individual members and as formal affiliates nearly 300 national and regional scientific societies and academies. Its headquarters are in Washington, D.C., and its major publication is the weekly *Science*.

American Ballet, company founded in conjunction with the School of American Ballet in 1934 by Lincoln Kirstein and Edward Warburg, with George Balanchine as artistic director. Its initial performances were held in 1934 in Hartford, Conn. In 1935 it became the resident ballet company for the Metropolitan Opera, whose disapproval of Balanchine's unconventional choreography caused the ballet company to disband temporarily in 1938.

Ballet Caravan, founded by Kirstein in 1936 to produce works by young U.S. choreographers, presented many American Ballet dancers in the early works of Eugene Loring, Lew Christensen, and William Dollar. The company toured the United States in 1938. Its dancers rejoined the American Ballet, renamed the American Ballet Caravan, in 1941 for a government-sponsored tour of South America. After the tour the companies were disbanded, but they formed the nucleus for the founding of the New York City Ballet (*q.v.*) in 1946 (then called Ballet Society). The School of American Ballet continued to be a creative centre of U.S. ballet as a part of the latter company.

American Ballet Theatre, ballet company based in New York City and with an affiliated school, founded in 1939 by Lucia Chase and Richard Pleasant and first called Ballet Theatre. The company made its first international tour, sponsored by the U.S. State Department, in 1950. Ten years later it became the first U.S. ballet company to dance in the Soviet Union.

Works were created for the company by such choreographers as Antony Tudor, Agnes deMille, Jerome Robbins, Michael Kidd, Eliot Feld, Twyla Tharp, Glen Tetley, and Mikhail Baryshnikov; Michel Fokine revived many of his masterpieces for the company and created *Bluebeard* (1941) and *Russian Soldier* (1942). Such dancers as Alicia Alonso, Baryshnikov, Erik Bruhn, Anton Dolin, André Eglevsky, Cynthia Gregory, Rosella Hightower, Nora Kaye, John Kriza, Hugh Laing, Natalia Makarova, Alicia Markova, Ivan Nagy, Janet Reed, Violette Verdy, and Igor Youskevitch were members of the company.

American Baptist Association, fellowship of autonomous Baptist churches, organized in 1905 by Baptists who withdrew from the Southern Baptist Convention. Originally known as the Baptist General Association, the fellowship adopted its present name in 1924. It was a development of the Landmarker (or Landmarkist) teaching of some Southern Baptists in the mid-19th century. They believed that early Christians were Baptists who baptized only adult believers by immersion and who were organized in local autonomous congregations. The Landmarkers wished to retain what they considered the "old landmarks" of early Christianity, and, therefore, they refused to cooperate or associate with non-Baptist churches and other Baptists with whom they disagreed. As the Southern Baptist Convention adopted a more centralized denominational church government, the Landmarkers believed the local church was losing its autonomy, and eventually they withdrew to form their own fellowship.

The American Baptist Association believes in the absolute autonomy of the local congregation. Local churches originate and support foreign and home missions. Church doctrine is Fundamentalist; the literal interpretation of the Bible is accepted, and the Second Coming of Christ is expected.

An annual meeting of the association is held, and meetings for ministers and youth are arranged. An active publications program is carried out. Headquarters are in Texarkana, Texas.

American Baptist Churches in the U.S.A., association of Baptist churches, organized in 1907 as the Northern Baptist Convention, which became the American Baptist Convention in 1950 and adopted its present name in 1973. It developed out of the various Baptist associations and mission and publication societies organized by Baptist churches in the United States in the 18th and the 19th centuries.

Through the missionary activity of the Philadelphia Baptist Association, organized in 1707 by five Baptist churches in Pennsylvania, Delaware, and New Jersey, many other Baptist churches were organized. Additional associations of local churches were formed, and by 1800 there were about 48 such associations in the United States. In the 19th century the Baptists began cooperating in national organizations formed to carry out particular duties. The Board of International Ministries, also known as American Baptist Foreign Mission Society, was organized in 1814 as the General Missionary Convention of the Baptist Denomination in the United States for Foreign Missions, also known as the Triennial Convention; its name was changed to the American Baptist Missionary Union in 1845 and the American Baptist Foreign Mission Society in 1910. In 1824 the American Baptist Publication Society was organized, followed in 1832 by the American Baptist Home Mission Society (since 1973 called the Board of National Ministries).

Disagreements among Southern and Northern Baptists concerning slavery led the Southern Baptists to form an independent organization in 1845, the Southern Baptist Convention. The mission and publication societies continued to operate independently in the North and West until they became part of the Northern Baptist Convention in 1907.

Generally considered more liberal than the Southern Baptist Convention, the American Baptist Churches in the U.S.A. is a member of the National Council of Churches of Christ in the U.S.A. and of the World Council of Churches. It has taken an active part in ecumenical affairs and has worked for closer union among the various Baptist groups.

The denomination meets annually and carries out its work through various divisions and societies. The basic units are the autonomous local churches, which are grouped into state conventions. Headquarters are in Valley Forge, Pa.

American Basketball Association (ABA), professional basketball league formed in the United States in 1967 to rival the older National Basketball Association (NBA). George Mikan, a former star player in the NBA, was the ABA's first commissioner. The ABA fielded 11 teams in its first season.

At a proposed merger between the ABA and the NBA, a class action was instituted by ABA players alleging violations of the antitrust laws. The settlement in 1976 resulted in the dissolution of the ABA, with four ABA teams absorbed into the NBA, a dispersal draft of certain ABA players by NBA teams, and the remaining players granted permission to act as free agents. *See also* Sporting Record: *Basketball: Professional champions.*

American bear: *see* black bear.

American Bible Society (ABS), international agency under lay control formed in New York in 1816 as a union of 28 local Bible societies "to encourage the wider circulation of the Holy Scriptures throughout the world, without note or comment, through translation, publication, distribution, and stimulation of use." Early in its history it set as its goal the placing of a Bible in every home, including the frontier. The ABS is supported by more than 80 Protestant denominations. The ABS has on occasion divided territory with the British and Foreign Bible Society.

American Board of Commissioners for Foreign Missions, first U.S. foreign missionary society, established in 1810 by New England Congregationalists. Missionaries were sent to numerous countries and to American possessions, but the work in Hawaii was especially outstanding. From 1820 to 1855 more than 150 missionaries (ministers, teachers, doctors, printers, businessmen, and farmers) worked in Hawaii and introduced Christianity, education, and the press.

When the United Church of Christ was formed in 1961 by merger of the Evangelical and Reformed Church and the Congregational Christian Churches, the American Board of Commissioners was absorbed into the new church's mission organization, the United Board for World Ministries.

American Brands, Inc., U.S. industrial conglomerate with major interests in the tobacco industry in the United States and the United Kingdom. It was formed in 1969 as the parent company for the American Tobacco Company (founded 1890) and several associated companies engaged in a wide range of goods and services from food products and distilled beverages to engineering products, life insurance, office supplies, and retailing and wholesaling. Corporate headquarters are in New York City.

The history of the American Tobacco Company traces to the post-Civil War period in North Carolina, when a Confederate veteran, Washington Duke (1820–1905), began trading in tobacco. In 1874 he and his sons, Benjamin N. Duke (1855–1929) and James B. Duke (1856–1925), built a factory and in 1878 formed the firm of W. Duke, Sons & Co., one of the first to introduce cigarette machines. Entering the "cigarette war," the Dukes eventually established the American Tobacco Company in 1890, with James as president. Through mergers and purchases, the Duke brothers eventually acquired corporate control of virtually the entire U.S. tobacco industry—some 150 factories in all. In 1911, however, after five years of litigation, a U.S. Court of Appeals judged this tobacco trust in violation of the Sherman Anti-Trust Act and ordered it dissolved. The principal manufacturers to emerge, in addition to American, were R.J. Reynolds, Liggett & Myers, and Lorillard.

In 1916 American introduced one of its most famous cigarettes, Lucky Strike. In 1939 it introduced a king-size cigarette, Pall Mall (an old name reapplied to a new cigarette).

American Broadcasting Companies, Inc. (ABC), U.S. corporation formed on Feb. 9, 1953, in the merger of American Broadcasting Company, Inc., and United Paramount Theatres, Inc. Called American Broadcasting-Paramount Theatres, Inc., upon merger, it adopted the present name in 1965. Headquarters are in New York City.

The company's history traces to 1927, when the Radio Corporation of America (RCA), finding itself with an excess of affiliates in the same cities, formed a second NBC network and called its two networks the Red and the Blue. In 1943 Edward J. Noble (1882–1958), the millionaire maker of Life Savers candy, formed the American Broadcasting System and purchased the Blue Network; the following year he changed the parent company's name to American Broadcasting Company, Inc. (ABC), and merged the Blue Network into it.

On Dec. 30, 1949, under a consent decree in a U.S. antitrust suit seeking to separate motion-picture production from theatre ownership, United Paramount Theatres was divorced from Paramount Pictures. In 1953 United Paramount Theatres merged with ABC, and ABC thus became owner of several hundred movie houses across the country (123 in the Midwest and Far West were sold in 1974). In 1955 ABC entered the phonograph record business with the purchase of a subsidiary and, over the years, under the consolidated ABC Records Division, developed several labels, such as ABC, Westminster, Dot, and Impulse. In 1979 the record division was sold and a video division begun. In further diversification, ABC purchased or developed subsidiaries in such industries as publishing, amusement and wildlife parks, and film production.

From the early 1960s ABC television network has been a major broadcaster of sports; instant replay was developed by ABC engineers in 1961.

American Can Company, diversified U.S. corporation that produces paper, metal, and plastic packaging and such consumer products as disposable cups, containers, towels, and tissues; manufactures chemicals and pharmaceuticals; and is involved in waste recycling, financial services, insurance, and publishing. Headquarters are in Greenwich, Conn.

The company was founded in 1901 through the consolidation of several producers of metal cans that primarily supplied the food-canning industry. That year American Can monopolized 90 percent of the nation's can-making capacity; by 1913 the percentage had dropped to about 30 percent, and an antitrust suit brought by the U.S. government to dismember the firm failed in the courts (1916). Another antitrust decision in 1950 did restrict the company's selling and leasing procedures.

The company is notable for its pioneering research in tin-plating, container sterilization, and the use of aluminum in cans. It operates a number of plants, subsidiaries, and affiliates located in North and South America, Europe, and Asia.

American Civil Liberties Union (ACLU), organization founded by Roger Baldwin and others in New York City in 1920 to champion constitutional liberties in the United States. The ACLU has frequently defended unpopular causes and people hostile to its objectives in various legal actions in which the issue of civil liberties was central. From its founding the ACLU has initiated test cases as well as intervened in cases already in the courts. One of its most famous test cases was the Scopes trial (1925), in which it supported the decision of a Tennessee science teacher, John T. Scopes, to defy a Tennessee law forbidding the teaching of Darwin's theory of evolution. It has been active in overturning censorship laws, often through test cases resulting from the deliberate purchase of banned material and consequent arrest and trial. The ACLU has not always succeeded in these trials, but the public airing of the issues has often led to success on appeal or in legislative reconsideration later. As a result of its efforts against censorship, such books as James Joyce's *Ulysses,* among others, could be imported into the United States. One of the ACLU's most significant freedom of religion cases involved the defense of Jehovah's Witnesses who refused, on biblical grounds, to allow their children to salute the flag in their public classrooms. The ACLU lost the case in 1936, but the verdict was reversed in 1943.

American Civil War, also called WAR BETWEEN THE STATES, in U.S. history, a four-year war (1861–65) between the federal government of the United States and 11 states that asserted their right to secede from the Union.

A brief treatment of the American Civil War follows. For full treatment, *see* MACROPAEDIA: United States of America.

The secession of the Southern states (in chronological order, South Carolina, Mississippi, Florida, Alabama, Georgia, Louisiana, Texas, Virginia, Arkansas, Tennessee, and North Carolina) and the outbreak of armed hostilities were the culmination of decades of growing sectional friction over the issues of trade and tariffs, slavery, and the doctrine of states' rights. Organized as the Confederate States of America, the Southern states, under Pres. Jefferson Davis, counted on patriotic fervour, the strategic advantage of interior lines of communication, and the international importance of their chief cash crop, cotton, to win a short war of independence. The federal Union, under Pres. Abraham Lincoln, commanded more than twice the population and even greater advantages in manufacturing and transportation capacity.

War began in Charleston, S.C., with the firing of Confederate artillery on Ft. Sumter on April 12, 1861. Both sides quickly began raising and organizing armies. On July 21 some 30,000 Union troops marching toward the Confederate capital of Richmond, Va., were stopped at Bull Run (Manassas) and then driven back to Washington, D.C., by Confederates under Gen. Thomas J. "Stonewall" Jackson and Gen. P.G.T. Beauregard. The shock of defeat galvanized the Union, which called for 500,000 more recruits. Gen. George B. McClellan was given the job of training the Army of the Potomac.

The first major campaign of the war began in February 1862, when Gen. Ulysses S. Grant captured the Confederate strongholds of Ft. Henry and Ft. Donelson in western Tennessee; this action was followed by Gen. John Pope's capture of New Madrid, Mo., a bloody but inconclusive battle at Shiloh (Pittsburgh Landing), Tenn., on April 6–7, and the occupation of Corinth and Memphis, Tenn., in June. Also in April, Commo. David G. Farragut ran his Gulf Squadron past Confederate batteries and gained control of New Orleans. In the East, McClellan launched a long-awaited offensive by landing 100,000 men at Ft. Monroe, Va., in another attempt to capture Richmond. Opposed by Gen. Robert E. Lee and his able lieutenants Jackson and J.E. Johnston, McClellan moved cautiously and in the Seven Days' Battles (June 26–July 2) was turned back, his Peninsular Campaign a failure. At the Second Battle of Bull Run (August 29–30), Lee drove another Union army, under Pope, out of Virginia and followed up by invading Maryland. McClellan came into possession of a copy of Lee's orders, however, and was able to check him at Antietam (or Sharpsburg, September 17). Lee withdrew, regrouped, and dealt McClellan's successor, A.E. Burnside, a heavy defeat at Fredericksburg, Va., on December 13.

Burnside was in turn replaced by Gen. Joseph Hooker, who took the offensive in April 1863. He attempted to outflank Lee's position at Chancellorsville, Va., but was completely outmanoeuvred (May 1–4) and forced to retreat. Lee then undertook a second invasion of the North. He skillfully avoided Hooker in Maryland and entered Pennsylvania. A chance encounter of small units developed into a climactic battle at Gettysburg (July 1–3), where the new Union commander, Gen. George G. Meade, commanded defensive positions. The battle of Gettysburg, marked in legend by Pickett's famous charge, came to be known as the "high tide of the Confederacy." Lee fell back into Virginia. At almost precisely the same time a turning point was also reached in the West. After two months of masterly manoeuvring, Grant captured Vicksburg, Miss., on July 4; with the relatively easy elimination of a few remaining Confederate posts, the Mississippi River was entirely under Union control. In October, after a Union army under Gen. W.S. Rosecrans had been defeated at Chickamauga, Ga. (September 19–20), Grant was called to take command in that theatre. Ably assisted by Gen. William T. Sherman, Grant drove Confederate general Braxton Bragg out of Chattanooga (November 23–25) and out of Tennessee; Sherman subsequently secured Knoxville.

In March 1864 Lincoln gave Grant supreme command of the Union armies. Grant took personal command of the Army of the Potomac in the east and soon formulated a strategy of attrition based upon the Union's overwhelming superiority in numbers and supplies. He began to move in May, suffering extremely heavy casualties in the battles of the Wilderness, Spotsylvania, and Cold Harbor, and by mid-June he had Lee pinned down in fortifications before Petersburg, Va. For nearly 10 months the seige of Petersburg continued, while Grant slowly closed around Lee's positions. Meanwhile, Sherman faced the only other Confederate force of consequence in Georgia. Sherman captured Atlanta early in September, and in November he set out on his 300-mi (480-km) march through Georgia, leaving a swath of devastation behind him. He reached Savannah on December 10.

By March 1865 Lee's army was thinned by casualties and desertions and was desperately short of supplies. Grant began his final advance on April 1 at Five Forks, captured Richmond on April 3, and accepted Lee's surrender at Appomattox Court House on April 9. Sherman had moved north into North Carolina, and on April 26 he received the surrender of J.E. Johnston. The war was over.

Naval operations in the Civil War were secondary to the war on land, but there were nonetheless some celebrated exploits. Gunboat operations helped immeasurably in opening the Mississippi; Farragut was justly hailed for his actions at New Orleans and at Mobile Bay (Aug. 5, 1864); the battle of the ironclads "Monitor" and "Merrimack" (March 9, 1862) is often held to have opened the modern era of naval warfare; and the adventures of the Confederate raiders "Alabama" and "Florida" were long recounted. For the most part, however, the naval war was one of blockade as the Union attempted, largely successfully, to stop the Confederacy's commerce with Europe.

American Colonization Society, U.S. organization founded in 1817 to transport free-born blacks and emancipated slaves to Africa. It was supported by local branches, churches, and the legislatures of border states.

The society's program focussed on purchasing and freeing slaves, paying their passage to the west coast of Africa, and assisting them after their arrival there. In 1821, after protracted negotiations with local chiefs, the society acquired the Cape Mesurado area, subsequently the site of Monrovia, Liberia. An attempt in 1827 to secure federal financial backing was frustrated by the opposition of the Deep South cotton states. The society received another setback in 1832, when the anti-slavery leader William Lloyd Garrison denounced it because it drained off the best of the free Negro population while still preserving slavery. Reviled by extremists on both sides of the slavery dispute and suffering from a shortage of money, the society declined after 1840. In 1847 Liberia, until then virtually an overseas branch of the society, declared its independence. Between 1821 and 1867 about 6,000 Negroes were resettled by the group, which was dissolved in 1912 after years of peripheral involvement in Liberian affairs.

American Coloured local race, also called AMERICAN NEGRO, a population of mixed heritage, deriving its genes from the populations of West Africa (Forest Negro local race, Negroid [African] geographical race) and about 20–30 percent from European populations. Physical characteristics of the American Negroes include medium to tall stature, moderate to heavy skin pigmentation, curly to frizzy hair ranging in colour from blond to black, and facial features more frequently aquiline than in the Forest Negro local race. As many as 5 percent of American Negroes carry the gene for sickle-cell anemia. *See also* local race; Negro, American; Negroid geographical race; sickle-cell trait and sickle-cell anemia.

American Crisis, The (Thomas Paine): *see* Crisis, The.

American Dictionary of the English Language, An (1828), two-volume dictionary by the American lexicographer Noah Webster. He began work on it in 1807 and completed it in France and England in 1824–25, producing a two-volume lexicon containing 12,000 words and 30,000 to 40,000 definitions that had not appeared in any earlier dictionary. Based on the principle that word usage should evolve from the spoken language, the work was attacked for its "Americanism," or unconventional preferences in spelling and usage, as well as for its inclusion of nonliterary words, especially technical terms in the arts and sciences. Despite harsh criticism, the work sold out, 2,500 copies in the United States and 3,000 in England, in little over a year. It was relatively unpopular thereafter, however, despite the appearance of the second, corrected edition in 1840; and the rights were sold in 1843 by the Webster estate to George and Charles Merriam.

American Evangelical Lutheran Church, church established by Danish immigrants who in 1874 took the name Danish Evangelical Lutheran Church in America and formally organized as a synod in Neenah, Wis., in 1878. A constitution was accepted in 1879, and the present name was adopted in 1954.

Immigration of Danes to the United States increased after the 1850s. A Danish pastor, Claus L. Clausen (1820–92), had begun working among both the Norwegians and Danes in 1843, and, in response to his urging, the Lutheran Church in Denmark sent additional pastors to serve the immigrants. The church spread throughout the United States but was concentrated in the Middle West.

Theological disagreements caused a schism in the church in 1893–94. Those who interpreted Scripture conservatively and were Pietists—*i.e.,* influenced by the Lutheran-based movement that emphasized personal religious experience and reform—left the church and organized the United Danish Evangelical Lutheran Church in America (subsequently named United Evangelical Lutheran Church). Those who remained in the church were primarily Grundtvigians, followers of N.F.S. Grundtvig (*q.v.*), the Lutheran church leader, poet, and organizer of folk schools in Denmark.

In 1962 the American Evangelical Lutheran Church (with about 24,000 members), the

United Lutheran Church in America, the Augustana Evangelical Lutheran Church, and the Suomi Synod merged into the Lutheran Church in America.

American Express Company, U.S. company founded on March 18, 1850, as an express transportation company, but today operating as a worldwide organization providing primarily travel-related and insurance services and international finance operations and banking. Headquarters are in New York City.

The original company resulted from the consolidation of three companies active in the express transport of goods, valuables, and specie between New York City and Buffalo and points in the Midwest: (1) Livingston, Fargo & Company (formerly Western Express), founded in 1845 by Henry Wells (1805–78) and William G. Fargo (1818–81), later of Wells Fargo fame; (2) Wells & Co. (formerly Livingston, Wells & Co.), cofounded by Wells in 1846 and under his ownership at the time of the merger; and (3) Butterfield & Wasson, founded by John Butterfield (1801–69) and James D. Wasson. American Express was at first an unincorporated association of investors headed by Wells as president and Fargo as secretary. By the end of the Civil War, its business had so flourished, with some 900 offices in 10 states, that it attracted competition in 1866 in the formation of Merchants Union Express Company. For two years the two companies engaged in cutthroat competition and, on the verge of financial exhaustion, finally merged on Nov. 25, 1868, to form the American Merchants Union Express Company, with Fargo succeeding as president. The company was renamed American Express Company in 1873.

On Fargo's death in 1881, his younger brother, James Congdell Fargo (1829–1915), became president and ruled for 33 years, introducing the American Express Money Order (1882) and the American Express Travelers Cheque (1891) and opening the first European office in Paris (1895), where various touring and banking activities were soon handled along with the company's traditional freight business. The first separate Travel Department was established in 1915 in New York City.

On July 1, 1918, the U.S. federal government nationalized the express industry, consolidating all domestic express operations in the American Railway Express Company (reorganized and denationalized in 1929). Deprived of its express business, American Express turned almost wholly to its travel and banking operations (though it continued its international freight business until its sale in 1970).

Today, American Express Company (newly incorporated in 1965) operates primarily in four areas: travel, insurance, banking, and investment services. In travel, it provides travellers checks, credit cards, travel agencies, tour packages, and agencies for motel and car-rental reservations. In insurance, it has owned since 1968 the Fireman's Fund American Insurance Companies group, which offers a wide range of insurance policies for individuals or groups. In banking, its American Express International Banking Corp., with subsidiaries, conducts commercial banking in Europe, the Middle East, Asia, and elsewhere and provides banking services for U.S. military personnel overseas. In investment services, the company built a large network of operations through acquisitions made in the 1980s. The company purchased Shearson Loeb Rhoades, Inc. in 1981, making it a subsidiary under the name of Shearson/American Express Inc., which in 1984 merged with Lehman Brothers Kuhn Loeb Inc. The resulting American Express subsidiary, Shearson Lehman/American Express Inc., became one of the largest investment services firms in the United States, with operations in securities underwriting, and distribution, investment management, options and commodities brokerage, real estate financing, corporate finance, and money markets trading. American Express also has diversified holdings in such areas as education, publishing, research, geophysical exploration, and cable television. In 1984 American Express acquired Investors Diversified Services Inc., a large Minneapolis-based insurance, mutual fund, and financial advisory concern.

American Federation of Labor–Congress of Industrial Organizations (AFL–CIO), U.S. federation of autonomous labour unions formed in 1955 by the merger of the AFL (founded 1886), which was originally based on the principle of organizing workers in craft unions, and the CIO (founded 1935, as the Committee for Industrial Organization), which organized workers by industries.

The organization that appeared in 1886 as the American Federation of Labor (AF of L) had as its precursor the Federation of Organized Trades and Labor Unions, begun in 1881. The Knights of Labor (*q.v.*), the most powerful industrial union of the era, sought to absorb the existing craft unions, to subject them to the loss of autonomy, and to involve them in industrial disputes in which their own direct interests were apparently not at stake. Against this tendency craft unions revolted under the leadership of Samuel Gompers, organizing themselves in 1886 in the loose federation which remained for a half century the sole unifying agency of the American labour movement.

In its beginnings, the American Federation of Labor was dedicated to the principles of craft unionism and autonomy and of collective bargaining to win recognition of organized labour and advances in working conditions. To this plan the federation consistently adhered. Its undeviating policy made it a loose federation of about 100 national and international unions, each retaining full autonomy over all the affairs of a labour organization. In return, each union received from the federation protection of its charter or of the workers and industrial territory over which it claimed jurisdiction. Out of this policy grew bitter jurisdictional disputes among unions affiliated with the federation, but union membership grew.

The 1920s were the first period of economic prosperity which did not witness an expansion of unionism. During the Great Depression that followed the stock market collapse of 1929 and assumed catastrophic proportions in 1932 and early 1933, labour was too benumbed to do more than engage in a few desultory desperate strikes. With the new administration of Franklin D. Roosevelt came a new dawn for labour.

The new political climate, with its ascendancy of government over business and the former's patronage of unionism as a major stabilizer of the economy, gave the U.S. labour movement unprecedented opportunities to expand its numbers. To facilitate this, the AF of L chartered federal (plant-wide) locals. This new opportunity, however, soon brought a characteristic difficulty. A federation minority, with the support of most of these new federal locals, demanded an aggressive organizing drive and the chartering of industrial unions in the mass production industries. The craft unionists, representing a majority of the federation's membership, argued for a more cautious policy and for the preservation of established jurisdictional rights. These "old" unionists tended to look upon industrial unions in the mass-production industries as dual unions and hence disruptive of the labour movement. They held this view because the craft unions theoretically had the right to organize certain workers in these industries.

The issue came to a head in the 1935 convention of the American Federation of Labor. The industrial unionist resolution stating that "in the great mass production industries . . . industrial organization is the only solution" was voted down.

As a result of the convention's defeat of the industrial union resolution, representatives of eight international unions announced on Nov. 9, 1935, the formation of the Committee for Industrial Organization (CIO). Its purpose was "to encourage and promote (industrial union) organizations of the workers in the mass-production industries of the nation, and affiliation with the American Federation of Labor."

Still refusing to compromise, the executive council of the AF of L in January 1936, ordered the immediate dissolution of the CIO movement as a dual unionism move. When the CIO unions refused to dissolve their organization, the council in August 1936 suspended all 10 of them (two others had subsequently joined). But the CIO proceeded to organize such key industries as steel, rubber, and motor cars and reached agreements with such large corporations as U.S. Steel and General Motors. In the following years the CIO and the AF of L engaged in a bitter struggle for leadership of U.S. labour.

The CIO held its first convention at Pittsburgh on Nov. 14–18, 1938, at which it adopted a new name (Congress of Industrial Organizations) and a constitution and elected John L. Lewis president.

Lewis pledged to resign as president if Franklin D. Roosevelt, whom he had previously supported, was reelected in 1940. He kept his promise and was succeeded in that year by Philip Murray, who had served under Lewis in the United Mine Workers' union. In the following year the CIO organized the employees of the Ford Motor Company, the "little steel" companies (Bethlehem, Republic, Inland, and Youngstown), and other big industrial corporations that previously had refused to enter into signed agreements with it.

In 1943 the CIO established the Political Action Committee (PAC), which supported Roosevelt in his successful campaign for reelection in 1944. In 1946, however, the candidates it supported were generally defeated. The passage of the Taft-Hartley Act in 1947 and the changes in national labour policies implicit in the statute aroused unions to renewed political activity. The CIO joined the AF of L in uncompromising opposition to the new law, but political unity was not translated into union unity. The CIO proposed that the AF of L join with them in mobilizing the political strength of organized labour but the AF of L opposed any joint action short of a complete merger of the two organizations. After the death of Philip Murray late in 1952, Walter P. Reuther, head of the CIO's United Automobile Workers, became president; and three years later, in 1955, the merger occurred, with George Meany, former head of the AF of L, becoming president of the new federation.

The primary governing body of the AFL–CIO is the biennial convention, with national unions being represented in proportion to their membership. The executive council, usually meeting three times a year, consists of the president, secretary-treasurer, and 27 vice presidents, each of whom is a president of a national union. An executive committee consisting of six vice presidents selected by the council meets more often with the president and secretary-treasurer to discuss policy matters. In addition, a general board, consisting of the executive council and a principal officer of each affiliated union, meets at least once a year to decide policy questions referred to it.

The federation is supported by a per capita tax on affiliated unions and organizing committees. The federation engages in organizing efforts, educational campaigns on behalf of the labour movement, the settlement of jurisdictional disputes among its affiliates, and political support of legislation deemed beneficial. Internationally, it maintains training schools in foreign countries and offers courses for foreign unionists visiting the United States.

A list of the abbreviations used in the MICROPAEDIA *will be found at the end of this volume*

American Football League (AFL), U.S. professional football organization, formed in 1959 to rival the older National Football League (NFL). Three earlier organizations of the same name did not fare well, each surviving only one or two years (1926, 1936–37, and 1940–41). AFL teams in 1960, the first season of play, were the Boston Patriots (later the New England Patriots), Buffalo Bills, Denver Broncos, Houston Oilers, New York Titans (later Jets), Oakland Raiders, Dallas Texans, and Los Angeles Chargers. The Los Angeles team moved to San Diego in 1961, and the team in Dallas became the Kansas City Chiefs in 1963. The Miami Dolphins were added to the league in 1966.

At first the NFL refused to recognize the new league. The two competed in bidding for players, but plans for merger were announced in 1966. In 1967 the first world-championship game, the Super Bowl, was played between the two league champions—Green Bay (NFL) defeated Kansas City (AFL), 35–10. That year the leagues engaged in a common draft of players, and in 1968 preseason interleague play was begun. In 1970 the old AFL teams, with Cleveland, Baltimore, and Pittsburgh of the NFL, became the American Conference of a new 26-team National Football League. *See* Sporting Record: *Football: U.S. professional football.*

American Friends Service Committee (AFSC), organization to promote peace and reconciliation through programs of social service and public information, founded by U.S. and Canadian Friends (Quakers) in 1917. In World War I it helped conscientious objectors to find work in relief projects and ambulance units as an alternative to military service. In World War II it broadened the scope of alternative service possibilities to include duty in mental hospitals and other humanitarian work. In peacetime it continued to administer such national and international programs as community development, racial reconciliation in the United States, aid to migrant workers, relief to civilians in war-torn areas, and refugee work. Its program of Voluntary International Service Assignments (VISA) served as a model for the U.S. Peace Corps. In 1947 the AFSC was awarded the Nobel Peace Prize jointly with the Friends Service Council, its British counterpart.

AFSC is financed by contributions from individuals, foundations, and, in some cases, governments of countries where its programs are carried out. Headquarters of the organization are in Philadelphia.

American frontier, in U.S. history, the advancing border between civilization and wilderness from the original Atlantic coast settlements (17th century) to those of the Far West (19th century). It is usually defined as an area having no fewer than two but no more than six European inhabitants per square mile, which means that the frontier was territory that had progressed beyond the era of explorers, missionaries, and trappers, for example. The frontier was the dividing line between settled farms and virgin land.

While often romanticized, life on the frontier was brutally hard and frequently fatal. Back-breaking labour, disease, malnourishment, hostile Indians, and antisocial whites were accepted as inescapable aspects of frontier life. Most frontier families lived a subsistence existence at best; one sign of the transition out of frontier status was the capacity of farmers to produce surplus crops for a market economy. On the other hand, land was cheap on the frontier and there were few obstacles for the ambitious to overcome in a quest for wealth.

When the U.S. census in 1890 declared an official end to the frontier, historian Frederick Jackson Turner put forward a seminal thesis on the dominant influence of the frontier in shaping American life. In a paper on "The Significance of the Frontier in American History" (1893), Turner focussed on the impact of the pioneer environment in transforming white European civilization into one distinctively American. To Turner the frontier was not so much a region or even a way of life as it was a process for change.

Particularly arresting were his observations concerning the role of the frontier in molding a distinctively American character. The fresh opportunities afforded by abundant cheap and arable land put a premium on individualism, energy, self-confidence and self-reliance, coarseness and strength, ingenuity, and pragmatism. Social status, class hierarchy, and vested interests that had prevailed in the Old World quickly succumbed to the rugged conditions of frontier living. Egalitarianism and social mobility were not just ideals but facts of life on the frontier, and American political institutions were almost necessarily democratic due to frontier influences.

Turner was always quite tentative about his "frontier thesis," but his ideas came to form a major school in American historiography. Following his death in 1932, however, the thesis came under attack from historians who argued that Turner had underplayed the role of European precedents and ignored slavery and race in explaining the origins of American institutions and character. *See also* Westward Movement.

American Fur Company, enterprise incorporated in New York State (April 6, 1808) by John Jacob Astor, which dominated the fur trade of the central and western United States during the first third of the 19th century. The company absorbed or crushed its rivals during the colourful course of its search for furs in the Great Lakes region, Missouri River Valley, Rocky Mountains, and Oregon. Explorations by the firm's traders and trappers, directed chiefly from its office in St. Louis, did much to prepare the frontier for settlement.

In 1810 Astor organized the Pacific Fur Company as a subsidiary to exploit the fur trade with China by way of the Pacific Northwest. The subsidiary company's major post, Astoria, located at the mouth of the Columbia River in the Oregon Territory, was lost during the War of 1812, thus ending the enterprise. By 1834, when Astor sold his interest, the company with its subsidiaries had become the largest commercial organization in the United States.

American Hebrew Congregations, Union of, oldest U.S. federation of Jewish congregations, which, since its founding (1873) in Cincinnati, Ohio, has sponsored a great variety of programs to strengthen Jewish congregations and promote Jewish education on every level.

The union was organized by Rabbi Isaac Mayer Wise for the immediate purpose of establishing and supporting a seminary for the training of American-born rabbis, who, Wise felt, were the key to the future of Judaism in the United States. Two years later the union established Hebrew Union College, the first successful rabbinic seminary in the United States. In 1950 it merged with the Jewish Institute of Religion of New York, founded in 1922 by Rabbi Stephen S. Wise. Both institutions were long-time centres of Reform Judaism and are still supported by the union.

Within 10 years of its founding, the union included within its membership virtually every important synagogue in the United States, many seeing in it an effective instrument to serve all American Judaism. Objections to "extreme" Reform attitudes, however, soon caused many members to sever their affiliation.

When the union absorbed the Board of Delegates of American Israelites in the 1870s, it assumed the responsibility to press for the rights of oppressed Jews everywhere. Because one of its urgent concerns was the plight of Jewish immigrants to America, it undertook the first census (1880) of Jews in the United States. Throughout the years the union has strenuously fought anti-Semitism in Europe and America.

To facilitate the carrying out of its aims, the union organized five auxiliary groups: the National Federation of Temple Sisterhoods (1913), of Temple Brotherhoods (1923), of Temple Youth (1939), of Temple Secretaries (1943), and the National Association of Temple Educators (1955). Each group operates independently within the union and promotes those activities for which it is best suited.

The union at one time or another has sponsored or co-sponsored religious schools, teacher seminars, a correspondence school, student study groups, and leadership training courses, often in cooperation with other groups. It has supported the publication of school textbooks, literature for youth, guidelines on recreational and social service, and a large number of books on Jewish history, Hebrew, and religion. It has organized regional meetings for Jewish congregations, has helped to furnish synagogues, has fostered liturgy, and in 1917 inaugurated a pension plan for rabbis. Many of its programs were implemented by local groups. Though the education of rabbis has always been a paramount concern, the union has never ceased to provide for the Jewish education of the common people.

The union, now numbering some 600 Reform congregations (including several in Canada), is affiliated with the World Union for Progressive (Reform) Judaism and maintains headquarters in New York City.

American Highland, interior plateau region of eastern Antarctica, extending from Enderby Land (west) to Wilkes Land (east) and inland from Ingrid Christensen Coast and Amery Ice Shelf. The ice-capped upland, which averages 7,000–10,000 ft (2,000–3,000 m) above sea level, was discovered and named in 1939 by the U.S. explorer Lincoln Ellsworth. It is the central part of a large area of eastern Antarctica claimed by Australia.

American Indian, also called AMERINDIAN, or AMERIND, a member of any of the aboriginal peoples of the Western Hemisphere, with the exception of the Eskimos and Aleuts.

A brief treatment of the American Indians follows. For a full treatment, *see* MACROPAEDIA: American Indians.

The ancestors of the American Indians were nomadic hunters of Asian Mongoloid stock who migrated over ice bridges into North America during the last glacial period (about 20,000 to 35,000 years ago); and they shared certain cultural traits with their Asian contemporaries, including the use of fire, the domesticated dog, and particular rites and healing practices. Other traits of Old World culture (*e.g.,* animal husbandry, cultivation of certain plants, and the wheel and the plow) were absent in the Americas.

North America. The prehistoric settlers of North America belonged to a number of separate traditions. The Paleo-Indian hunting societies of the West, the Great Plains, and eastern North America had similar economies despite environmental differences. Their major food source was meat, and their clothing was made from animal hides. Archaeological remains of this tradition have been discovered on kill sites, areas that were used for slaughtering Pleistocene mammals. One of the most distinctive artifact types is the Clovis fluted projectile point, first discovered on a kill site near Clovis, N.M., and dated at approximately 9000 BC. The lance shaped point was used for killing mammoths.

Desert culture groups were dispersed throughout what is now the western United States—from Oregon to northern Mexico and from the Pacific Coast to the eastern Rockies. Many desert peoples were nomadic hunters and gatherers who dwelt in caves and rock shelters. Artifacts such as the milling stone, which was used for grinding seeds, have indicated the development of primitive agricultural techniques.

The Eastern Archaic period lasted from 8000 to 1500 BC. The cool, moist climate of the Great Plains and the Great Basin became hot and dry, resulting in the eventual extinction of Pleistocene animals. Societal patterns shifted to hunting and collecting economies, and by 6000 BC, coastal and riverine living was common. The Late Archaic was characterized by such technological developments as grooved stone axes, pestles, gouges and plummets; and systems of trade between tribes of different geographical areas evolved. The hunting economy during the Archaic period (8000–3000 BC) was distinguished by Plano projectile points, which were no longer fluted, and the primary game animal was bison. A moderation of climate between 3000 and 2000 BC (Late Plano) caused some groups to follow grazing game animals into Saskatchewan and Alberta and further north to the Arctic tundra zone.

Several societies in the southwestern United States began cultivating corn (maize) around 2000 BC, but it wasn't until after AD 1 that primitive agriculture had a substantial impact on Indian culture. In the Ohio and Illinois river valleys, corn cultivation played a crucial role in the sophisticated Hopewell economy (200 BC–AD 200). Surplus resources designated wealth for a particular, privileged group, and they were also used in elaborate burial rituals. A cold phase between AD 200 and 700 thwarted agricultural progress and resulted in cultural regression. In the Mississippi River Valley area, a village-based culture developed between 700 and 1200, distinguished by improved agricultural methods and intricate religious rituals. The latter involved ceremonial ornaments, which were produced in specialized centres, and an organized priesthood.

The Anasazi, Mogollon, and Hohokam were pre-Pueblo societies interspersed throughout the Southwest between 700 and 1200. Mogollon agricultural techniques—particularly the use of rainfall and stream division for watering crops—were improved by the Anasazi. The Hohokam culture of southern Arizona depended on irrigation to maintain an agricultural economy. A period of aridity from 1100 to 1300 inhibited cultural development and substantially depleted the size of these groups.

Pueblo culture began in the first millennium AD, when the techniques for building apartment houses of stone masonry and adobe were developed. Crops included several varieties of corn as well as long-staple cotton. The Classic Pueblo period (1050–1300) was characterized by significant advances in architecture and pottery. The great cliff houses had from 20 to 1,000 rooms and one to four stories, and polychrome pottery in specialized regional styles was created. The Regressive Pueblo period occurred between 1300 and 1700. Many apartment houses were abandoned during this time of southward and eastward migration. The Modern Pueblo period began with the permanent settlements of the Spanish in the late 1600s. Some aspects of Pueblo culture and agricultural methods still survive.

In colonial times, European nations adopted different formal policies concerning the North American Indians. The Spaniards tried to Christianize native Americans and relocate them to designated areas, but the French were primarily interested in establishing trade relations with the Indians. Early English legislation prohibited unauthorized confiscation of Indian land, and the Proclamation of 1763 appropriated the entire area west of the Appalachians to native Americans. The latter policy held to the end of British rule and was adopted by the United States. The British North America Act of 1867, which created modern Canada, gave the new country exclusive legislative rights regarding the Indians and their lands.

The Indian Removal Act of 1830 marked the beginning of a long series of coercive policies. The discovery of gold in California in 1848 resulted in massive westward migration of the white man, and a number of treaties nullified Indian claims to land along the westward paths. Many gruesome wars ensued, including the Custer massacre by the Sioux and Cheyenne in 1876.

By 1887 most Indian peoples had been moved onto reservations. The Dawes General Allotment Act of that year caused them to lose approximately 134,400 square miles (348,100 square kilometres) of land. The Indian Reorganization Act of 1934 established programs for the advancement of native American peoples. Since the 1950s, new policies and social emphasis on civil rights resulted in the formation of Indian organizations and heightened national awareness of their problems.

Middle America. Indians entered Middle America, the area from Nicaragua to northern Mexico, more than 10,000 years ago. The development of farming techniques can be traced to around 4500 BC, and steady advances in the domestication of such staples as corn and beans led to the establishment of agricultural communities by 2000 BC. During the following centuries an increasingly stable food supply facilitated an evolution from minor settlements to large towns and inspired a growth in ceramics and many other arts.

During the first millennium AD, known as the Classic period, there arose such civilizations as the Maya, the people of which were unified by their ritual practices and ruled by a class of priests whose functions were thought to influence cycles of agricultural fertility. Among their most important divinities was the fertility god Tlaloc, whose symbol, the jaguar, is a recurrent motif on extant carvings. The jaguar was supplanted in later cultures by the traditionally more warlike eagle, and human sacrifice became a common religious practice. These religion-based societies were superseded, beginning around AD 1000 by the empires of the Toltecs and Aztecs, which flourished and expanded until the Spanish invasion of the 16th century. At its apex, the military strength of the Aztec Empire had brought nearly all of Middle America under its dominion.

From the initial race of immigrants several cultural subgroups evolved that can be classified according to the geophysical regions they inhabited. The coastal, desert, and mountainous terrain of the northwestern part of what is now Mexico supported one of these subgroups; another subgroup, the Tarascans, settled in the mountains of Michoacán. The Maya occupied parts of Guatemala, the Yucatan Peninsula, and Mexican Chiapas; the Aztecs were concentrated in the highlands of central Mexico and the site of present-day Mexico City; and a fifth subgroup developed on the coasts and highlands of southern Mexico.

Characteristically, Middle American Indian cultures have settled in small communities, of which the basic units are individual families. Male members and elders are dominant, and inheritance is channelled through the line of paternal descent, though lineage is acknowledged through both paternal and maternal relations. Communal activities are centred in the markets, where agricultural and crafted products are exchanged, and in the political bureaus, whose members also serve in a religious capacity. Each community is also represented by leaders on the national level. Though the primary form of worship is the Roman Catholicism introduced by the Spanish, remnants of earlier ritual practices persist in the devotion of cults to individual Christian saints and in a widespread adherence to animism, superstition, and divination.

Along with Catholicism, the Spanish conquest brought the tools and techniques of European industry and signalled a permanent reorganization of earlier social structures. During the first period of colonization, Jesuits set up religious reservations in northwest areas, and other sectors were settled in *encomiendas,* plots of land developed under Spanish supervision. Later, when the *encomiendas* were dissolved and the reservations removed from the auspices of the church, plantations, cattle herds, and mines became the economic centres of colonial society.

A revolution in 1821 achieved independence from European control for native-born Spaniards and others of mixed extraction in Mexico and Guatemala, who organized the policies of the new republics. During the following periods of industrialization and commercialization, Indian communities became increasingly isolationist in order to preserve their cultural integrity, despite the resulting economic deprivation. A subsequent revolution in Mexico in 1910 effected the removal of exclusionary social and economic policies and marked the beginning of the assimilation of Indian political, cultural, and economic contributions. Major programs were established for the solution of specifically Indian problems, and national attention was given to native Mexican art and tradition. Similar policies were adopted by Guatemala but were soon overthrown. By the late 20th century it appeared that a more complete integration of Indians into both urban and rural communities had occurred in Mexico than in Guatemala, though the native population of Guatemala continued to increase more rapidly.

South America. The civilizations of South America began, according to archaeological records, with the first migrations from North and Middle America at some point after 10,000 BC.

Among the first immigrants, the hunters and gatherers settled in what are now known as Tierra del Fuego, Argentina, southern Chile, the south-central plains of the Gran Chaco region, and portions of the central Andes, where they were later supplanted by more highly developed agricultural societies. The nomadic hunters organized themselves into small groups, which facilitated their frequent movement to areas of more plentiful game or more favourable climatic conditions. Like the agricultural inhabitants of the tropical forests, hunters formed groups based on kinship ties, and stratification within each group was determined by age and sex. Farming societies, located on the coasts of Brazil and Arawak, in the Greater Antilles, and in inland forest regions, however, were able to sustain larger and more stable social units through the successful cultivation of corn, beans and other indigenous crops, supplemented by hunting. Both the nomadic and the forested agricultural societies practiced the ritual magic, designed to attain control over their environment, that is characteristic of many preliterate cultures.

Other agrarian peoples, situated in the regions

bordering the Caribbean and in the northern Andes, developed more complex modes of social organization based on military and ritual leadership and supported by more technologically sophisticated farming practices. Warfare was important among these nations as a vehicle for social advancement within the tribe and as a means of supplying slaves and victims for ritual sacrifices. Rudimentary forms of centralized rule and an eventual transition from magic and ritual to the early stages of religion further distinguish these societies from the forested agricultural communities.

The most advanced of the native South American civilizations took root in the central Andes in approximately 2300 BC and evolved, culturally and technologically, for several thousand years. Beginning around AD 1000 they were organized into a number of kingdoms—the Chimú, the Tiahuanoco, and later, the Inca—that flourished until the Spanish invasion of the early 16th century. Occupying a region that extends from Peru through northern Chile, the Inca developed efficient irrigation works and a sophisticated, state-controlled system of food production, storage, and distribution that at the empire's apex supported a population of nearly 3,500,000. Its social hierarchy descended from a hereditary royal class, through strata of nobles and craftsmen, to the agricultural commons. Among the most conspicuous innovations of Incan civilization are the replacement of social regimentation by custom with a system of laws and the attainment of a high standard of artistic production, particularly in metalworking.

These four sociocultural patterns correspond to stages in the historical development of the native South American nations. Several thousand years after the initial influx of a uniformly nomadic hunting population, advances in animal domestication, agriculture, and other technology—achieved without the benefit of foreign models—gave rise to increasingly complex social structures and fostered the emergence of centralized government and rigid class systems. The central Andean empires of the 11th century AD were the culmination of earlier regional prototypes whose origins can be traced to around 500 BC.

The effects of the 16th-century European conquest range from near extinction of some of the southern populations, through degrees of cultural depredation, to full absorption into colonial society. The native civilizations most severely depleted were those dwelling along major navigational routes, while some of the more remote Andean tribes have retained their culture up to the present and have even experienced a steady growth in population. The agricultural and political practices of the Incan Empire, however, were completely replaced by those of the Spaniards, and Incan religion was subjugated to Roman Catholicism. While the Incan aristocratic and artisan classes were to some extent absorbed into the colonial hierarchy, the native farming population was relegated to menial servitude. In less exploited regions, remnants of the Incan nation have preserved some of their cultural heritage and participated in economic exchanges with modern industrial centres. Other South American Indians, such as the Araucanians, successfully resisted Spanish domination until late into the 19th century but have since been suppressed and assimilated or assigned to reservations.

American Indian geographical race, a group of human populations (local races and microraces) of North and South America and the Caribbean islands. Because of European migration to North and South America since 1500, the American Indian race has been greatly reduced in numbers and largely displaced. In Central and South America a large percentage of the modern population is of mixed Indian and European ancestry, and in the Caribbean and parts of South America, a portion of the population is of mixed Indian and African descent.

Characteristics include medium skin pigmentation; straight, coarse black hair; high frequency of shovel-shaped incisors; sparse body hair and a very low frequency of male pattern balding; absence of blood type B (ABO system) and Rh-negative blood type (Rh blood group system); very low levels of blood type N (MNSs blood group system); and a very high incidence of the Diego-positive blood type. In all these blood features the American Indians are markedly different from the Mongoloid peoples, with whom they were sometimes classed in the past. *See also* Andean civilization, history of; Andean cultures; Californian Indians; Central American and northern Andean cultures; Eastern Woodlands Indians; Eskimo–Aleut languages; Meso-American civilization, history of; Middle American peoples and cultures; North American Great Basin Indians; North American Indian languages; North American peoples and cultures; North American Plains Indians; North American Plateau Indians; North Mexican Indian cultures; Northwest Coast Indians; South American Indian languages; South American nomad cultures; South American peoples and cultures; South American tropical forest cultures; Southeast American Indians; Southwest American Indians; Western Arctic cultures.

American Indian languages, languages spoken by the original inhabitants of the Western Hemisphere and their modern descendants. The American Indian languages do not form a single historically interrelated stock (as do the Indo-European languages), nor are there any structural features (in phonetics, grammar, or vocabulary) whereby American Indian languages can be distinguished as a whole from languages spoken elsewhere.

A brief treatment of American Indian languages follows. For full treatment, *see* MACROPAEDIA: Languages of the World.

In the pre-Columbian era, the American Indian languages covered both continents and the islands of the West Indies. There were, however, considerable differences in the distribution of the languages and language groups and in the size of the populations that spoke these languages.

In America north of Mexico, where the Indian population was thinly spread, there were a number of language groups, *e.g.,* the Eskimo-Aleut, Algonkian, Athabascan, and Siouan, which covered large territories and included some 20 or more closely related idioms. Other language groups, however, were smaller and the areas containing them correspondingly more diverse in language. In California, for example, more than 20 distinct language groups were represented. These, according to Edward Sapir, exhibited greater and more numerous linguistic extremes than may be found in all of Europe. America north of Mexico, taken as a whole, had about 300 distinct languages, spoken by a population estimated at about 1,500,000.

Meso-America (Mexico and northern Central America) had a much larger Indian population—estimated at about 20,000,000—which spoke at least 80 languages. Some of these languages, *e.g.,* of the Aztecs of central Mexico and the Maya of Yucatan and Guatemala, belonged to large and complexly organized empires and probably accounted for most of the native population. Others were far more restricted in area and numbers of speakers. The area of greatest linguistic diversity appears to have been in southern Mexico and the region now occupied by the northern Central American republics.

South America had an aboriginal population of between 10,000,000 and 20,000,000 and the greatest diversity of languages—more than 500 languages. The bulk of the population was in the Andean region, where there was also a powerful Indian empire, that of the Incas. Their Quechuan languages have spread beyond their original homeland in the southern Peruvian highlands and have resulted in the extinction or reduction of many other Indian tongues.

European conquest and colonization ultimately led to the disappearance of many American Indian language groups and to radical changes in the lives of the groups that survived. A number of languages have become extinct: in the West Indies the aboriginal languages have almost entirely disappeared, and in America north of Mexico one-third of the aboriginal languages have become extinct. The situation is somewhat different in Meso-America and South America. Although there are no precise figures, a greater number of languages are still spoken, some of them by large populations.

Of the American Indian languages still spoken, many have only a bare handful of speakers. In America north of Mexico, more than 50 percent of the surviving languages have fewer than 1,000 speakers each. In communities as small as these, most people are bilingual, and the younger people, educated in English, often have little more than a superficial command of the native idiom. In short, even though the Indian population north of Mexico is actually increasing, most of the aboriginal languages are slowly dying out. Only a few languages are flourishing: Navaho, spoken in New Mexico and Arizona; Ojibwa, in the northern United States and southern Canada; Cherokee, in Oklahoma and North Carolina; and Dakota-Assiniboin, in the northern portions of the midwestern United States. Even in these groups, however, there was a high proportion of bilingualism.

In parts of South America and Meso-America there are still a number of widespread and flourishing language groups. Quechuan is one of these: it is estimated that this group of closely related dialects has several million speakers in Ecuador, Peru, and parts of Bolivia and Argentina. One of these extant languages, the dialect of Cuzco, Peru, was the principal language of the Inca Empire. The Indians of Mexico and Central America also still speak languages that date to the time of the Spanish conquest; Uto-Aztecan, a group of languages in central and parts of southern Mexico; the Mayan languages, spoken in Yucatan, Guatemala, and adjacent territories; and Oto-Manguean, of central Mexico. All three of these were languages of Indian empires before 1500, and both the Maya and Aztec peoples had writing systems.

The Tupí-Guarani languages, spoken in eastern Brazil and in Paraguay, constitute a major Pre-Colombian language group that has survived into modern times. Before the arrival of the Europeans, languages of this group were spoken by a large and widespread population. Tupí of Brazil became, after the conquest, the basis of a lingua geral, the medium of communication for Europeans and Indians throughout the Amazonian region. Guarani similarly became a general language for much of Paraguay. Tupí was, by the late 20th century, gradually being replaced by Portuguese, but Guarani remained an important second language of modern Paraguay, and an extensive folk literature has been created.

American Indian Movement (AIM), militant American Indian civil rights organization, founded in Minneapolis, Minn., in 1968 by Dennis Banks, Clyde Bellecourt, Eddie Benton Banai, and George Mitchell. Later, Russell Means became a prominent spokesman for the group. Its original purpose was to help Indians in urban ghettos who had been displaced by government programs that had the effect of forcing them from the reservations. Its goals eventually encompassed the entire spectrum of Indian demands—economic independence, revitalization of traditional culture, protection of legal rights, and, most especially, autonomy over tribal areas and the restoration of lands that they believed had been illegally seized.

AIM was involved in many highly publicized protests. It was one of the Indian groups involved in the occupation (1969–71) of Alcatraz Island, the march (1972) on Washington, D.C., to protest violation of treaties (in which AIM members occupied the office of the Bureau of Indian Affairs), and the takeover (1973) of a site at Wounded Knee (*q.v.*) to protest the government's Indian policy. In the mid-1970s AIM's efforts were centred on the prevention of resource exploitation of Indian lands by the federal government. With many of its leaders in prison, and torn by internal dissension, the national leadership disbanded in 1978, although local groups continued to function. Since 1981 an AIM group has occupied part of the Black Hills (South Dakota) to press its demands for return of the area to Indian jurisdiction.

American Institute of Electrical Engineers: *see* Electrical and Electronics Engineers, Institute of.

American ivy: *see* Virginia creeper.

American League, one of the two associations in the United States and Canada of professional baseball teams designated as major leagues. The American League of Professional Baseball Clubs was founded in 1900, and in 1903 it was granted equal status by the older National League. In the 1980s the league had two divisions: the East, comprising the Baltimore Orioles, Boston Red Sox, Cleveland Indians, Detroit Tigers, Milwaukee Brewers, New York Yankees, and Toronto Blue Jays; and the West, comprising the California Angels, Chicago White Sox, Kansas City Royals, Minnesota Twins, Oakland Athletics, Texas Rangers, and Seattle Mariners. *See* Sporting Record: *Baseball.*

American lion: *see* puma.

American literature, the body of written works produced in the English language in the United States or by citizens of the United States.

A brief treatment of the literature of the United States follows. For full treatment, *see* MACROPAEDIA: American Literature.

The origins of American literature lie in the 17th century, in the earliest colonial days of America. It was only after the American Revolution, when the United States had gained its independence and was preoccupied with its newly emerging institutions, that writers consciously sought to create a characteristically American literature. As the country developed its own distinctive national character and institutions, a literary tradition that would reflect those unique characteristics—social, economic, geographic, and artistic—began to evolve. Some of the themes that emerged derived from the vast size of the country, its diversity of people, its frontier, and its great unspoiled wilderness.

The earliest American writings were based on European models and included not only fiction and poetry but treatises on political and religious subjects. Of the poets, Anne Bradstreet and Edward Taylor wrote verse of high literary quality, and both were strongly influenced by English poets in form and in content.

The two leading literary figures of the middle part of the 18th century, both of whom wrote nonfiction on subjects of political importance, were Benjamin Franklin and Thomas Paine. Franklin began his career as a journalist, and his popular series entitled *Poor Richard's Almanac,* with its epigrams displaying both wit and common sense, spoke meaningfully to the colonial society and examined the conflict between the colonies and Great Britain. Paine's pamphlet *Common Sense* (1776) encouraged readers to declare independence, and his writings continued to inspire Americans throughout the Revolutionary period.

After the Revolution, the quest for a characteristic American literature began. Important writers of the early part of the 19th century included Washington Irving, James Fenimore Cooper, and Edgar Allan Poe. Cooper's fiction explored native American life, particularly that of the frontier; Irving was a satirist; while Poe was one of the inventors of the horror and detective story genres.

The first great period of American literature came between about 1830 and the beginning of the Civil War, when many writers were inspired by the mood of expansion and democracy that characterized the presidency of Andrew Jackson, when a new spirit of hope and adventure had pervaded the country. They took as their subject the common man instead of the aristocratic figures found in English literature. The greatest of this group were the novelist Herman Melville, whose major work was the epic moral tale *Moby Dick* (1851), and the poet Walt Whitman, whose progressive and unconventional poetic autobiography was entitled *Leaves of Grass* (1855). Other writers of the period included the poet Emily Dickenson and a group known as the Transcendentalists, including Ralph Waldo Emerson, a liberal philosopher, the individualist Henry David Thoreau, whose well-known book *Walden* (1854) described his experience of learning self-reliance, and Nathaniel Hawthorne, author of such novels as *The Scarlet Letter* (1850).

The Civil War marked a watershed in American history; from then until World War I, the country continued to expand and develop, resulting in the creation of much regional and humorous literature. The most important was that of Samuel L. Clemens, better known as Mark Twain, whose *The Adventures of Tom Sawyer* (1876) and *The Adventures of Huckleberry Finn* (1884) described life along the Mississippi River. Toward the end of the 19th century a group of writers known as Naturalists emerged. They saw man as a victim of his fate and treated everyday subjects in a completely unromantic way, sometimes in horrifyingly explicit detail. Among the greatest of this group was Stephen Crane, whose masterpiece of the horrors of war was *The Red Badge of Courage* (1895). Others included Theodore Dreiser and Frank Norris. Upton Sinclair's *The Jungle* (1906), describing the evils of the meat-packing industry, continued this tradition but with a definite social purpose and a reforming zeal. Henry James's novels of the same period were quite different, dealing with the psychological processes of upper middle-class characters.

After World War I an important group of novelists and poets, collectively known as the "Lost Generation," reflecting their disillusionment with postwar society, won acclaim. It included the novelists F. Scott Fitzgerald and Ernest Hemingway and the poets Ezra Pound, T.S. Eliot, and William Carlos Williams. Dissatisfaction and protest in the 1920s gave way in many American writers to patriotic enthusiasm and concern with social inequalities.

The work of William Faulkner, a pioneer in the stream-of-consciousness technique, was a high-water mark in American prose. In such novels as *The Sound and the Fury* (1929) and *As I Lay Dying* (1930), Faulkner dealt with a rural Mississippi county. After World War II a number of distinguished writers came to prominence, including Saul Bellow, Norman Mailer, James Baldwin, and John Updike.

American poets of the mid-20th century were pioneers of new techniques and styles of expression. Of these, Wallace Stevens, Robert Frost, e.e. cummings, Robert Lowell, and Allen Ginsberg were prominent. In drama an important American tradition emerged in the 20th century with the work of Eugene O'Neill, Tennessee Williams, Thornton Wilder, and Arthur Miller.

American Lutheran Church (ALC), the first Lutheran church to be formed in the 20th century that cut across ethnic lines. The present American Lutheran Church was created in 1961 by merger of three Lutheran churches: the American Lutheran Church, the Evangelical Lutheran Church (*q.v.*), and the United Evangelical Lutheran Church (*q.v.*). On Feb. 1, 1963, the ALC was joined by the Lutheran Free Church (organized in 1897 by a group that left the United Norwegian Lutheran Church).

The former American Lutheran Church (1930–60) had been organized in Toledo, Ohio, by merger of three Lutheran synods comprised primarily of members of German descent. These were (1) the Evangelical Lutheran Joint Synod of Ohio and Other States, organized in 1818; (2) the Lutheran Synod of Buffalo, organized in 1845 in Milwaukee, Wis., by German immigrants settled primarily around Buffalo, N.Y., and Milwaukee, who began leaving Prussia in 1838 because they refused to take part in a union of Lutheran and Reformed churches ordered by the King of Prussia in 1817; schism split this synod in 1866, with J.A.A. Grabau and his followers continuing the Buffalo Synod; and (3) the Evangelical Lutheran Synod of Iowa and Other States, organized in 1854 in Iowa by Lutheran missionary pastors from Germany who wished to serve the German immigrants in the Middle West.

The church was essentially conservative in its teachings concerning the Bible and the Lutheran confessions. After years of discussions with the United Lutheran Church in America and the Lutheran Church–Missouri Synod, the American Lutheran Church merged with the Evangelical Lutheran Church and the United Evangelical Lutheran Church to form the present American Lutheran Church.

The ALC is governed by the General Convention, which meets biennially, and the church council, which meets annually; the president and other officers are elected. Headquarters are in Minneapolis, Minn. It cooperates with the Lutheran Church in America, generally considered more liberal theologically, and the more conservative Lutheran Church–Missouri Synod in the Lutheran Council in the United States of America.

American Mercury, U.S. monthly literary magazine known for its often satiric commentary on American life, politics, and customs. It was founded in 1924 by H.L. Mencken and George Jean Nathan.

The periodical, under the editorship of Mencken, fast gained a reputation for Mencken's vitriolic articles directed at the American public (the "booboisie") and for Nathan's excellent theatrical criticism. Its fiction and other articles were the work of the most distinguished U.S. authors and often the sharpest satiric minds of the day. Under Mencken's successor as editor, Eugene Lyons, the *American Mercury* was responsible for generating much of the pressure exerted on the U.S. Congress to vote for funding of air power at the beginning of World War II. Later, the magazine passed through the hands of several publishers and over a period of time developed a militant anti-Communist stand and a strident right-wing tone.

American mole shrew: *see* short-tailed shrew.

American Motors Corporation (AMC), U.S. company primarily engaged in the manufacture of automobiles and other automotive products. It produces AMC compact cars (*e.g.*, Hornet, Gremlin, Pacer), Jeeps, AM General trucks and buses, garden tractors and mowers, and various molded plastic parts for cars, appliances, and other products. From 1936 until the sale of the division in 1968, Kelvinator appliances were a major product line. The headquarters of American Motors are in Southfield, Mich.

American Motors descends from two pioneering automobile manufacturers—Nash Motors Company, incorporated in 1916, and Hudson Motor Car Company, founded in 1909. Nash Motors in 1916 had taken over the automotive business of the Thomas B. Jeffery Company, which had produced its first Rambler automobile in 1902; from 1916 to 1950 almost all the company's cars and trucks bore the Nash name. In 1937 the Nash company merged with Kelvinator Corporation, resulting in the Nash-Kelvinator Corporation, which produced both automotive vehicles and appliances. In 1950 Nash-Kelvinator produced the first modern American compact car, the Rambler.

The Hudson company produced three major makes of automobiles over the years: the Hudson, the Essex (produced from 1919 to 1932), and the terraplane (1932–38). On May 1, 1954, the company merged with Nash-Kelvinator, and the American Motors Corporation was created. From the year of merger until 1970, the Rambler compact car was the company's best known automobile.

In 1970 American Motors purchased the Jeep Corporation (then known as Kaiser-Jeep Corporation), a company dating to 1903. In its early years, as Willys-Overland Company (1908–53), it had produced Overland and Willys cars and in 1940 had introduced the first military Jeep (registered trademark). In 1953 the company had been taken over by the Henry J. Kaiser interests.

In 1978 American Motors became the official American and Canadian distributor of Renault cars, and Renault became the international distributor of Jeeps. The following year Renault became the principal stockholder in the financially troubled auto maker, and by 1982 American Motors began producing Renault-designed cars in the United States, sharply cutting back on production of its own models. In 1983 American Motors entered into a joint venture with China to produce four-wheel-drive vehicles in Peking.

To make the best use of the Britannica, consult the INDEX *first*

American Museum of Natural History, institute established in New York City in 1869. It includes a 350,000-volume library on natural history, research laboratories, and collections with more than 1,800,000 specimens. The Hayden Planetarium forms part of the museum, and its zoo, in Bronx Park, is under the control of the New York Zoological Society. It has a 10,000-volume library on astronomy and a 75-foot-diameter Sky Theatre.

American Muslim Mission, formerly NATION OF ISLAM, or WORLD COMMUNITY OF AL-ISLAM IN THE WEST, also called BLACK MUSLIM MOVEMENT, religious and cultural community that evolved in the 20th century in the United States out of various quasi-religious black nationalist organizations. Prominent among these precursor groups was the Moorish Science Temple, founded in Newark, N.J., in 1913 by Prophet Drew Ali, born Timothy Drew, who posited the Moorish, and thus Muslim, origins of all blacks and advocated a return to Islām as the only means of redemption from racial oppression. The secular Universal Negro Improvement Association, founded in 1914 by Marcus Garvey, also espoused principles later adopted by the black Muslims.

The movement proper, however, was founded by Wallace Fard Muhammad (also called W.D. Fard, or Wali Farad), believed to have been an orthodox Muslim born in Mecca around 1877. He migrated to the United States in 1930 and established a temple (or mosque) in Detroit a year later.

Most of Fard's initial followers were black migrants from the southern United States who, because of prevailing racial policies and economic conditions, were clustered together in the black ghettos of the great northern industrial cities. They believed Fard to be an incarnation of Allāh who had come to liberate what he called the "Lost-Found Nation of Islam in the West." Fard promised that if they would heed his teachings and learn the truth about themselves, they would overcome their white "slave masters" and be restored to a position of dignity and primacy among the peoples of the world.

The chief developer of the movement was Elijah Muhammad (*q.v.*; born Elijah Poole), who succeeded Fard as leader of what had come to be called the Nation of Islam after the latter's mysterious disappearance in 1934. Shortly thereafter he founded the movement's second temple in Chicago. The movement spread slowly at first. By the end of World War II, however, American blacks had caught the spirit of protest and black nationalism that was sweeping Africa. The Nation of Islam benefitted directly from the pent-up frustrations of the black masses and offered those frustrations a militant, if avowedly nonviolent, expression. Soon there were mosques in all larger cities with sizable black populations.

Under Muhammad's leadership, the Nation of Islam professed the moral and cultural superiority of "black men," who were seen as destined by Allāh to assume cultural and political leadership of the Earth. Blacks were enjoined to give up Christianity, which was regarded as the white man's chief stratagem for the enslavement of nonwhite people. The white race was conceived of as a race of devils whose time to reign was coming to an end. Meanwhile black people were urged to work together to reclaim their fallen (criminals, drug addicts, etc.), learn their true history, strive for economic independence, and prepare for the Battle of Armageddon, the final struggle between good and evil.

During the 1960s the movement achieved national prominence through the personality of Malcolm X, Elijah Muhammad's spokesman, whose forceful articulations of racial pride and Muslim principles made him a cultural hero, especially among black youth. The publication of a book by C. Eric Lincoln entitled *The Black Muslims in America* (1961) established during this period what became the standard, though never official, name for the movement in the public mind. Disagreements among the sect hierarchy eventually led to Malcolm's suspension and to the establishment of a rival group, the Muslim Mosque, Inc., under his leadership. Violent disputes between the two organizations were suspected by some as a contributing factor to Malcolm's assassination in 1965.

A series of changes in the social, intellectual, and spiritual direction and development of the Nation of Islam were effected in the late 1970s under the leadership of Elijah Muhammad's successor, his son Warith Deen (or Wallace D.) Muhammad. During this period all precepts of colour-consciousness, racism, and the deification of Fard were repudiated, and a new name for the organization was adopted.

In the organization of the American Muslim Mission, the Qur'ān and the example of the Prophet Muḥammad serve as authorities on all aspects of community life. The mosque functions as a place of prayer and worship and as a centre of community activities. Mosques have been established throughout the United States and in the Caribbean region. Each mosque is overseen by an imam (a leader of prayer), who is chosen by the mosque's members.

The primary concerns of the mosque membership are religious propagation, education, and family, community, and economic development. In most large cities, certified elementary and secondary schools—called the Sister Clara Muhammad Elementary and Secondary schools—are affilated with the mosques; their courses of instruction include Islāmic studies, Arabic, English, and history as well as reading, writing, and mathematics. Mosque meetings take place on Fridays and Sundays. Attendance and membership are now open to all.

In the fall of 1981, the American Muslim Mission Library was dedicated in Chicago, and the following year the American Muslim Teachers' College was established in Sedalia, N.C.

A splinter group based in New York City and under the leadership of Louis Farrakhan retained both the name and the founding principles of the Nation of Islam.

American Negro: *see* American Coloured local race; Negro, American.

American organ (musical instrument): *see* melodeon.

American Party: *see* Know-Nothing Party.

American plum weevil: *see* plum curculio.

American Protective Association (APA), an anti-Catholic, anti-immigrant group, which briefly acquired a membership greater than 2,000,000 during the 1890s. A successor in spirit and outlook to the pre-Civil War Know-Nothing Party, the American Protective Association was founded by Henry F. Bowers at Clinton, Iowa, in 1887. It was a secret society that played upon the fears of rural Americans about the growth and political power of immigrant-populated cities.

At first the APA grew slowly, but the economic depression in 1893 sent its membership soaring. Its anti-immigrant stance appealed to native-born Americans who blamed their unemployment and economic stress on the influx of foreigners. The APA successfully transformed such resentment into voting strength, capturing a number of Republican organizations and local elections in the Midwest.

Prior to the presidential election in 1896 the APA split, many members deserting Republican William McKinley in their enthusiasm for Democrat William Jennings Bryan and the free silver issue. Following McKinley's election and the restoration of agricultural prosperity in the Midwest, membership dwindled further. By 1900 the APA no longer exerted any noticeable political power, and it had disappeared entirely by 1911.

American quarter horse, breed of horse developed for racing a quarter-mile. Originating in the American colonies as fast, quarter-mile racers, it was overshadowed by the Thoroughbred but eventually found acceptance in the western and southwestern United States as a stock horse. It was bred for performance and had considerable Thoroughbred blood as well as traits of other lines. Important sires include Janus, an English Thoroughbred imported to Virginia in 1756; Steel Dust (b. 1843), who was so popular that his descendants and similar quarter-horse types were called Steel Dusts for many years; and Peter McCue (b. 1895), called the most influential sire in improving the breed.

Modern American quarter horses are short and stocky, with a heavy muscular development and deep, broad chests. Since these horses are used to cut cattle from herds, fast starting, turning, and stopping ability and speed for short distances are essential qualities. Colours are variable; height varies from 14.2 to 16 hands (about 58 to 64 inches, or 147 to 163 centimetres) and weight from 900 to 1,250 pounds (410 to 570 kilograms). They have a calm, cooperative temperament.

For many years little attempt was made to develop a distinct breed. In 1940 the American Quarter Horse Association was organized, and in 1950 it was reorganized to include other quarter-horse organizations. It controls the *American Quarter Horse Stud Book and Registry.*

American Railway Express Company: *see* REA Express, Inc.

American Renaissance, also called NEW ENGLAND RENAISSANCE, period from the 1830s until the end of the Civil War in which American literature, in the wake of the Romantic movement, came of age as an expression of a national spirit.

The literary scene of the period was dominated by a group of New England writers, the Brahmins, notably Henry Wadsworth Longfellow, Oliver Wendell Holmes, and James Russell Lowell. They were aristocrats, steeped in foreign culture, active as professors at Harvard, and interested in creating a genteel American literature based on foreign models. Longfellow adapted European methods of storytelling and versifying to narrative poems dealing with American history; Holmes, in his occasional poems and his "Breakfast Table" series (1858–91), brought touches of urbanity and jocosity to polite literature; and Lowell put much of his homeland into verse, especially in his *Biglow Papers* (1848–67), but adhered to European critical standards.

One of the most important influences in the period was that of the Transcendentalists (*see* Transcendentalism), centred in the village of Concord, Mass., and including Ralph Waldo Emerson, Henry David Thoreau, Bronson Alcott, George Ripley, and Margaret Fuller. The Transcendentalists advocated reforms in church, state, and society, contributing to the rise of Free Religion, the Abolition Movement, and to the formation of various utopian communities (*see* Brook Farm). The Abolition Movement was also bolstered by other New England writers, including the Quaker poet John Greenleaf Whittier and the novelist Harriet Beecher Stowe, whose *Uncle Tom's Cabin* (1852) effectively dramatized the plight of the Negro slave.

Apart from the Transcendentalists, there emerged during this period great imaginative writers—Hawthorne, Melville, and Whitman—whose novels and poetry left a permanent imprint on American literature. Contemporary with these writers but outside the New England circle was the Southern genius Edgar Allan Poe, who later in the century had a strong impact on European literature.

American Revolution: *see* United States War of Independence.

American Round, in archery, a target shooting event consisting of five ends (six arrows each), shot from distances of 60, 50, and 40 yards (55, 46, and 37 metres). Two American Rounds and two York Rounds, consisting of 12 ends of 6 arrows each, constituted the U.S. men's championship until 1968, when other combinations of rounds were introduced. In the junior American Round for boys and girls, 30 arrows each are shot from distances of 50, 40, and 30 yards.

American saddle horse, breed of riding horse possessing several easy riding gaits and great vigour and style. It is the prevailing riding horse of U.S. horse shows. The Thoroughbred, Morgan, Standardbred, Arabian, pacers, and easy riding horses of a mixed background contributed various qualities to this American breed. Selection for an easy riding gait, style, and beauty, accompanied by line breeding, helped shape them into a breed.

Average height and weight for the breed are 15 to 16 hands (about 60 to 64 inches, or 152 to 163 centimetres) and 1,000 to 1,200 pounds (about 450 to 540 kilograms). The American saddle horse is characterized by a short, strong back; the barrel is rounder than in most light breeds. The neck is long, slender, and well arched; it blends smoothly into a well-shaped shoulder. The croup is long and almost level. American saddle horses have most of the solid colours with limited white markings and are shown under flat saddles as either three- or five-gaited horses. The three gaits are the walk, trot, and canter. The five-gaited horse has these three gaits plus the rack and one slow gait. The slow gait is usually the stepping pace but may be the running walk or foxtrot. Three-gaited horses are shown with a roached (clipped, standing) mane and a clipped tail. Five-gaited horses are shown with a full mane and tail. They are also used as pleasure horses, driving horses, and quite often as hunters and jumpers.

American saddle horses were recognized as a distinct breed in 1891, when the American Saddle Horse Breeders' Association was organized. It publishes the *American Saddle Horse Register.*

American Samoa, unincorporated territory of the United States in the southwestern Pacific Ocean, comprising the eastern Samoan islands of Tutuila, Aunuu (Aunu'u) and Rose; three islands (Tau [Ta'u], Olosega, and Ofu)

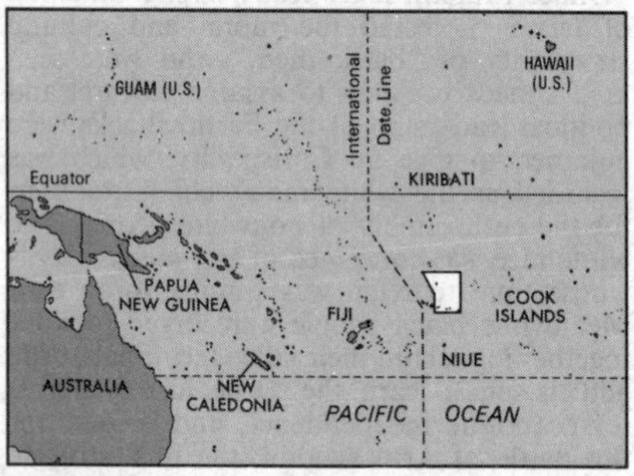

American Samoa

of the Manua (Manu'a) group; and Swains Island. Their total land area is 77 sq mi (199 sq km). The territorial capital is Pago Pago, located on Tutuila. The population was estimated at 33,000 in 1982.

The article that follows is a summary of significant detail about American Samoa. For information about regional aspects of American Samoa, *see* MACROPAEDIA: Pacific Islands. For current history and for statistics on society and economy, *see* the article "World Affairs" and BRITANNICA WORLD DATA, respectively, in the *Britannica Book of the Year.*

The land. Tutuila, accounting for more than two-thirds of the total land area, is the largest island of American Samoa and is located in the westernmost region of the island group, less than 100 mi (33 km) from the Western Samoan island of Upolu. The Manua island group, situated about 60 mi east of Tutuila, constitutes the second largest land area; Tau is the largest of the three islands in the group. The remaining islands are quite small; Aunuu is located off the southeastern tip of Tutuila, and Rose Island is an uninhabited coral atoll about 250 mi east of Tutuila. Swains Island is a privately owned coral atoll some 280 mi north of Tutuila.

Except for the atolls of Swains and Rose, the islands were formed from the remains of extinct volcanoes. Central mountain ranges dominate the landscapes of Tutuila and the islands of Manua. The highest peak of Tutuila is Mt. Matafao (2,142 ft [653 m]), but the most noted is Mt. Pioa (1,847 ft), known as the "Rainmaker" because of its frequent cloud cover. Tau is a cone-shaped island, rising to Lata Mountain (3,179 ft), the highest peak in the territory. The highest points on Olosega and Ofu are 2,094 and 1,588 ft, respectively, and low-lying Swains Island rises to about 20 ft above sea level.

Coral reefs are common to the extremities of the islands, particularly Tutuila; some of the reefs form barriers that enclose lagoons. The mountain ranges and the coral reefs tend to limit the width of the coastal plains in most areas. Most streams carry greater volumes of water in the highlands than near the sea and do not reach the ocean; rather they filter into the porous basalt rocks.

The tropical climate is moderated by oceanic trade winds and frequent rains. Pago Pago receives about 200 in. (5,080 mm) of rain annually, the majority of which falls between December and March. The average temperatures range between 74° F (21° C) and 90° F (32° C), and the average relative humidity is about 80 percent.

About 70 percent of the land area is forested by tall ferns and trees such as the *Barringtonia asiatica*, the pandanus, and abundant coconut trees. Animals include the Polynesian rat, fruit bat, and pigs in small numbers. More than 30 species of birds have been observed, including parrots, doves, wild ducks, and the toothbilled pigeon, unique to Samoa.

The people. About 95 percent of the total population is concentrated on Tutuila, and more than half of Tutuila's population resides on the eastern part of the island, including the largest settlement, Pago Pago. Virtually all of the remaining population lives on the islands of Manua; a few people reside on Swains Island. Since the mid-19th century, Tutuila has been the focus of population growth, increasing from about 19,000 persons in 1950 to 30,538 persons in 1980. The Manua island group, on the other hand, has maintained a fairly stable population of about 2,000, reaching a population zenith of 2,819 in 1950 but declining to 1,732 in 1980.

Since the mid-20th century the birthrate of American Samoa has declined gradually, dropping to about 32 births per 1,000 persons in 1980. The death rate has remained fairly stable with about 4 deaths per 1,000 (1980). Prior to 1951 most immigration to and emigration from islands was confined to neighbouring Western Samoa. Since then thousands of American Samoa residents have migrated to Hawaii and the continental United States. Since 1960 more people from Western Samoa have settled in American Samoa than have left the territory to live in Western Samoa.

The population of American Samoa is quite homogeneous, with Samoan or part-Samoan individuals constituting the overwhelming majority of the population. The Samoans are a Polynesian people, closely related to the native peoples of Hawaii, Tahiti, Tonga, and New Zealand. The Samoan language belongs to the Austronesian (Malayo-Polynesian) language family; most of the American Samoans also speak English. Citizens of American Samoa are considered U.S. nationals. The Congregational Church has the largest following among religious institutions; most of the remaining population is either Roman Catholic or Methodist.

The economy. A thriving fishing industry is the foundation of American Samoa's economy; its gross national product (GNP) was estimated at U.S. $140,000,000 in 1981, with a GNP per capita of $4,170, which was one of the highest among the Pacific islands. In 1980 more than 270 tons of fish were caught for processing and canning in factories. Canned tuna accounts for more than 90 percent of

American Samoa's export income, and the export of tuna is the principal reason the islands have maintained a balance of trade surplus for many years.

Only about 30 sq mi of the total land area is arable, and about half of the arable land is under permanent cultivation. Agricultural production is primarily used for domestic consumption. The principal crops are coconuts, roots and tubers, bananas, papayas, pineapples, and breadfruit. Many food products must be imported, accounting for about one-sixth of the total value of imports.

Local commerce caters to the needs of the islanders and to the tourist trade, which accommodated more than 85,000 visitors in 1978. The American Samoan government makes the second major economic contribution, employing more than 40 percent of the labour force. The government is financed by local revenues, funding from the U.S Department of the Interior, and special-purpose grants from the U.S. government.

The United States is the source of the vast majority of imports, but items are also imported from Japan, Australia, and New Zealand. The major imports are food, machinery and spare parts, petroleum products, and clothing. Most of the paved and unpaved roads are located on Tutuila. An international airport is located on Tutuila and a smaller airport operates from Tau. Pago Pago is the major port, but the volume of trade declined in the late 1970s as other port facilities were developed.

Administrative and social conditions. The structure of the American Samoan government closely resembles that of the United States, with executive, legislative, and judicial branches. The executive is headed by an elected governor, who until 1977 was appointed by the U.S. Department of the Interior. The legislature, or Fono, has a Senate and a House of Representatives. The Senate is composed of members serving four-year terms, chosen by traditional Samoan custom from each of the 15 counties. The House of Representatives consists of members popularly elected from 17 distics, excluding Swains Island, which has one nonvoting member; each representative serves a two-year term.

The judicial branch consists of the High Court and the district courts. The chief justice and associate justice of the High Court are appointed by the U.S. secretary of the interior. District court judges are appointed by the governor and preside over misdemeanor criminal cases, civil suits, small claims cases, and traffic offenses.

Education in American Samoa is patterned on the U.S. system of eight years of elementary schooling and four years of high school. The American Samoan Community College offers a wide range of vocational training, including a nursing program. College and university education is obtained in Hawaii or on the U.S. mainland, aided by a government scholarship program for Samoan students.

In 1972 the government instituted a social security program for its workers; the fishing industry followed suit and in the late 1970s more than 60 percent of all employees were covered by some form of social security or retirement system. The unemployment rate for American Samoa has been consistently high for a number of years. The Samoan culture, with its subsistence family and village orientation, however, has ameliorated many of the adverse effects of high unemployment.

The principal hospital for the islands is the Lyndon B. Johnson Tropical Medical Centre, with units for tuberculosis, leprosy, and obstetrics. The Department of Health operates clinics throughout the islands. The major diseases are venereal disease, particularly gonorrhea, hepatitis, infantile diarrhea, and influenza. Tuberculosis and filariasis are no longer major health problems.

History. According to archaeological evidence, the islands that are now American Samoa were probably inhabited by Polynesians more than 2,500 years ago. Prior to European contact and exploration, Tutuila was a subordinate district of the island of Upolu (now part of Western Samoa), and the Manua Islands were ruled by their own powerful chief. The Dutch navigator Jacob Roggeveen sighted the Manua Islands in 1722 and made contact with the islanders. French explorers arrived in 1768, and in 1787, 11 members of a French expedition were massacred. For the next 40 years European explorers avoided the islands, during which time the islands became a haven for runaway sailors and escaped convicts. The first missionaries of the London Missionary Society arrived on the islands in the 1830s, and more Christian missionaries followed as Tutuila and later the Manua Islands were brought under missionary influence.

In January 1878, the United States signed a treaty with the Kingdom of Samoa obtaining rights to establish a naval station at Pago Pago. In 1889, the United States, Britain, and Germany agreed to Samoan neutrality and created a tripartite protectorate over the islands. A convention in 1899 recognized the paramount interests of the United States in the islands east of longitude 171° W and of the Germans in the islands west of the meridian. By deeds of the high chiefs, the eastern group was ceded to the United States in 1904 but was not accepted by the U.S. Congress until 1929 (Swains had been granted to the United States by Britain in 1925). The islands were placed under the Jurisdiction of the U.S. Navy until 1951, when their administration was transferred to the U.S. Department of the Interior. In 1960, a constitutional convention of American Samoans approved the first constitution of the territory. In 1978, the territory's first elected governor took office.

American spikenard (plant): *see* spikenard.

American Standardbred (horse): *see* Standardbred.

American States, Organization of (OAS), organization including almost all of the independent states of the Western Hemisphere, with the notable exception of Canada. Cuba was a member but had been excluded from participation since 1962.

The OAS Charter was signed on April 30, 1948, at the conclusion of the Ninth Pan-American Conference held in Bogotá. The aims of the organization are to strengthen the peace and security of the Western Hemisphere, to promote peaceful settlement of disputes among member states, to provide for collective security, and to encourage cooperation in economic, social, and cultural matters. The OAS is largely anti-Communist in its orientation.

Among the organs of the organization, the most important is the General Assembly, meeting annually. Supplementing the Assembly, the Meeting of Consultation of Foreign Ministers serves as the executive body in the event of an attack or an act of aggression within member states. A third organ, in permanent session, is the Permanent Council, composed of an ambassador from each member state; it acts as the executive committee of the OAS. In addition, specialized committees deal with technical matters. The General Secretariat is in Washington, D.C.

The founding of the OAS was based on the general acceptance of the principles of the U.S. Monroe Doctrine by the countries of the Western Hemisphere, especially the principle that an attack upon one American state would be considered as an attack upon all. The OAS attempted to "continentalize" the Monroe Doctrine, creating obligations for the other states without restricting the right of the United States to take immediate action in self-defense.

Important decisions on regional security taken by the OAS include the support extended to Pres. John F. Kennedy in 1962 in the quarantine against the shipment of Soviet missiles to Cuba, and, in 1965, the support of U.S. intervention in the Dominican Republic. In the economic and social field, the most notable achievement was the adoption by the OAS of the Charter of Punta del Este (1961), establishing the Alliance for Progress. The Inter-American Court of Human Rights was established at San José, Costa Rica, in 1979.

American Stock Exchange (AMEX), second largest stock exchange in the United States. Originally known as "the Curb" because its transactions took place outdoors during much of its existence, the marketplace is believed to have begun around 1849. By 1908 it was known officially as the New York Curb Agency. From 1929–53 it was known as the New York Curb Exchange, when its name became changed to its present title. The market first moved indoors in 1921, at a location it still occupies in New York's Wall Street area. For many years it was a marketplace for securities not considered reputable enough for listing on the New York Stock Exchange, but it is now considered an equally respectable exchange with its own listing requirements for securities and admissions requirements for members.

American Telephone & Telegraph Company (AT&T), world's largest corporation in assets (in 1978 it became the first corporation in history to exceed $100,000,000,000 in assets); it provides about 98 percent of all long-distance service for itself and some 1,700 independent U.S. telephone companies. The system governed by AT&T includes manufacturing, research, telecommunications, information systems, and an international unit. Twenty-two regional "operating companies" that had previously been wholly owned by AT&T were divested by Jan. 1, 1984, as part of a 1982 antitrust settlement. Corporate headquarters of AT&T are located in New York City.

The company's origins trace to 1875, when Alexander Graham Bell signed an agreement with two investors, Gardiner C. Hubbard and Thomas Sanders. A year later, Bell secured a patent for a yet undeveloped device, but within a week his experimental telephone gave history's first wire transmission of intelligible speech. In 1877 the three members of the patent agreement formed the Bell Telephone Company, which then began a race with the giant Western Union Company for the development of telephone service—Western Union by this time having acquired its own telephone devices and its own patents. Bell interests were represented by Theodore N. Vail, who became general manager in 1878 and led the patent fight against Western Union. Western Union—itself involved in a war of control between the Vanderbilts and Jay Gould—finally capitulated on Nov. 10, 1879, and in an out-of-court settlement gave up all its patents, claims, and facilities in the telephone business.

The Bell company underwent a series of reorganizations and renamings in the years 1878 to 1900. The American Telephone and Telegraph Company, incorporated in 1885, was at first a subsidiary, responsible for building long lines; in 1900 it was made the central organization of the Bell System. (Western Electric, founded in 1869, had come under Bell control in 1881. The Mechanical Department, forerunner of Bell Telephone Laboratories, had been formed in 1883; the laboratories would be incorporated as a separate company in 1925.)

During the period 1907–19, Vail, as president of AT&T, molded the Bell System into virtually the organization that lasted until 1984, consolidating the Bell associated companies into state and regional organizations and assimilating many previously independent companies.

Pursuant to an act of Congress, AT&T was nationalized under the U.S. Post Office Department in 1918 but was returned to private ownership in 1919. In a commitment first enunciated in 1913 but affirmed by the Graham-Willis Act of 1921, AT&T, as a "natural monopoly," agreed to provide long-distance service to all independent telephone companies and to buy out independent telephone companies only on approval of the Interstate Commerce Commission.

In 1934 a new Federal Communications Commission replaced the ICC as the agency with jurisdiction over telephones, and from 1935 to 1939 it made exacting investigations of Bell corporate practices. As an outcome of these investigations, the Justice Department in 1949 brought suit against AT&T under the Sherman Anti-Trust Act, seeking, among other things, to divorce Western Electric from the Bell System; the suit ended in 1956 in a consent decree that kept Western Electric in the system but restricted monopolistic practices. In 1974 the United States instituted a second antitrust suit for the more extensive dismemberment of the Bell System. In 1982 AT&T agreed to divest itself of its 22 local operating companies. The agreement would allow the company to enter such previously prohibited fields as data processing, computer communications, and equipment sales. In the ultimate agreement, however, AT&T was forced to severely restrict its use of the Bell name, which was reserved for the use of the local operating companies that had separated from AT&T.

The 22 operating companies, after divestiture, were reorganized and converted into seven regional phone companies: Nynex (serving Connecticut, Maine, Massachusetts, New Hampshire, New York, Rhode Island, and Vermont), Bell Atlantic (serving Delaware, Maryland, New Jersey, Pennsylvania, Virginia, West Virginia, and the District of Columbia), Ameritech, or American Information Technologies, Inc. (serving Illinois, Indiana, Michigan, Ohio, and Wisconsin), BellSouth (serving Alabama, Florida, Georgia, Kentucky, Louisiana, Mississippi, North Carolina, South Carolina, and Tennessee), Southwestern Bell Corporation (serving Arkansas, Kansas, Missouri, Oklahoma, and Texas), US West (serving Arizona, Colorado, Idaho, Iowa, Minnesota, Montana, Nebraska, North Dakota, South Dakota, Oregon, Utah, Washington, and Wyoming), and Pacific Telesis Group (serving California and Nevada).

American trypanosomiasis: *see* Chagas' disease.

American yew, also called CANADA YEW, DWARF YEW, GROUND HEMLOCK, or CREEPING HEMLOCK (*Taxus canadensis*), a prostrate, straggling evergreen shrub of the family Taxaceae that is found in northeastern North America. American yew also is a lumber trade name for the western yew. The American yew is the hardiest of the yew (*q.v.*) species and provides excellent ground cover in forested regions. Usually growing about one metre (about three feet) high, it has small yellowish-green leaves that taper abruptly to a tiny point.

Americana, city, in the highlands of east central São Paulo state, Brazil, near the Rio Piracicaba at 1,732 ft (528 m) above sea level. Settled in 1868 by immigrants from the former Confederate States of America, it was known as Vila Americana until 1938. The settlement was made a seat of a municipality in 1924. Agriculture is the main local source of income, and foodstuffs are processed in the city. Highways and railroads link Americana to São Paulo, the state capital, 68 mi (109 km) to the southeast. Pop. (1980 prelim.) 121,794.

Americanism, in Roman Catholic Church history, a certain set of doctrinal proposals concerning the adaptation of the church to modern civilization that was reprobated by Pope Leo XIII in his apostolic letter *Testem Benevolentiae* of Jan. 22, 1899. The letter was written in response to a controversy in France following the publication there in 1897 of a translation of a biography of Isaac Thomas Hecker, founder of the missionary Paulist Fathers. The views attributed to Hecker included minimizing certain traditional doctrines likely to be obstacles to conversion.

Americanization, those activities designed to prepare foreign-born residents of the United States for full participation in citizenship. It aims not only at the achievement of naturalization but also at an understanding of and commitment to principles of American life.

Before the outbreak of World War I in 1914, the American public generally took it for granted that the constant flow of newcomers from abroad brought strength and prosperity to the country. The metaphor of the "melting pot" had been introduced to symbolize the mystical potency of the great democracy, whereby people from every corner of the earth were fused into a harmonious and admirable blend. After the war began, however, American reactions to European hostilities produced an intense awareness of the aliens and "foreigners" in their midst. Assimilation, it was believed, must be achieved by deliberate, purposeful means.

The Americanization movement that came into being was primarily a program of education, in schools, voluntary associations, and various public programs. The teaching of foreigners became a favourite form of patriotic service, particularly after the entry of the United States into the war.

In its earliest days the program was directed toward the correction of the most obvious deficiencies. The core of the curriculum was the English language, American history, and the governmental structure of the United States, understanding of which was necessary for naturalization. Those who were interested in teaching other subjects began to capitalize on the popularity of the movement. Soon the offering included courses in millinery, cooking, social amenities, and the care of children, all presented, of course, as essential elements of American culture.

Enthusiasm for Americanization persisted throughout World War I and was prolonged into the postwar period. Gradually, however, popular interest diminished. Wartime apprehensions subsided, and new legislation severely limited the influx of immigrants. Before long Americanization became no more than a fairly obscure but continuing effort to prepare people for naturalization by teaching them English, civics and history, or even English alone.

Meanwhile, there had developed a thorough reexamination of the concept of Americanization. The idea of the melting pot and the early belief that all foreigners should be transformed into typical Americans began to appear naive. Who is the typical American? Are American cultural habits (as defined in any particular curriculum) necessarily better than the way of life with which the foreign resident is familiar? The United States was built by people who came from many backgrounds; is not the effort to impose conformity itself un-American? These and other questions proved hard to answer in the 1920s. So deeply did the disillusionment penetrate that within less than a decade after the Armistice "Americanization" was a term to be shunned, not used. In the years that followed, it never regained its earlier lustre.

In place of the old idea of supplanting all foreign traits by a standard pattern there grew up the idea of cultural "pluralism." It was argued by some that assimilation in its accepted sense was not a desirable goal but that U.S. civilization would benefit by preserving many separate cultures side by side. Still others contended that this pluralism would gradually disappear over the years, that the American character was still in the process of formation, and that, as it gradually emerged, it would be enriched by the blending of the admirable features of the various foreign nationalities.

Americas, also called AMERICA, the two continents, North and South America, of the Western Hemisphere. The climatic zones of the two continents are quite different. In North America, sub-Arctic climate prevails in the north, gradually warming southward and finally becoming tropical near the southern isthmus. In South America, the climate in the north is tropical, becoming cooler southward, and finally becoming a cold, marine climate at Cape Horn.

The Americas can be roughly divided into two cultural regions: Latin America, which includes North America south of the Rio Grande, most of the West Indies, and all of South America; and Anglo-America, which includes Canada and the United States. The term Middle America (or Meso-America) is sometimes used to designate Mexico, Central America, and the West Indies collectively.

The name America was first used by the German geographer Martin Waldseemüller in his *Cosmographiae introductio* (1507; *Introduction to Cosmography*); he suggested the name (apparently unaware of the discoveries of Columbus) in recognition of the voyages of the Italian explorer Amerigo Vespucci. The book was widely read, and Waldseemüller's appellation was eventually universally accepted. The term Mundus Novus, or New World, commonly used in reference to land in the Western Hemisphere, first appeared in one of Vespucci's letters, published in 1504.

Americas, pony of the, riding-pony breed used as a child's mount, developed in the United States in the 1950s by crossing ponies with Appaloosa horses. To qualify for registration with the Pony of the Americas Club, a pony must have the dappled Appaloosa (*q.v.*) patterning and measure from 11.2 to 13.2 hands (46 to 54 inches, or 117 to 137 centimetres) tall at maturity.

America's Cup, one of the oldest and best known trophies in international sailing yacht competition. It was first offered as the Hundred Guinea Cup in 1851 by the Royal Yacht Squadron of Great Britain for a race around the Isle of Wight. The cup was won by the "America," a 100-foot (30-metre) schooner from New York, and subsequently became

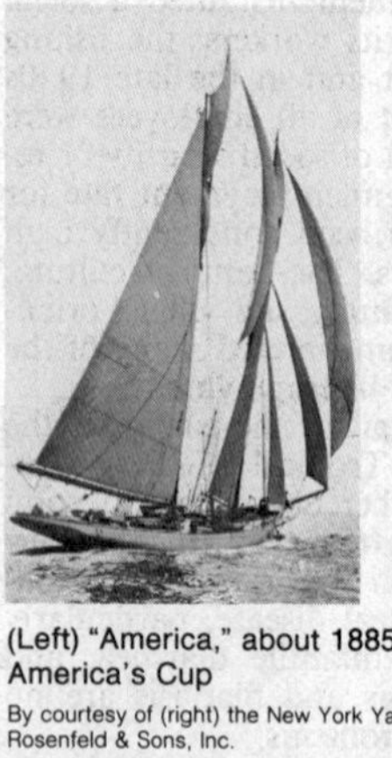

(Left) "America," about 1885, and (right) the America's Cup

By courtesy of (right) the New York Yacht Club; photograph (left), Morris Rosenfeld & Sons, Inc.

known as the America's Cup. It was donated to the New York Yacht Club in 1857 for a perpetual international challenge competition.

The original terms of donation imposed many disadvantages on challenging yachts. Not until 1956 was a clause eliminated that required a challenger to sail on its own bottom to the scene of the contest, forcing a heavier style of construction than that of the defender. Also, since 1956, smaller yachts have been permitted, effectively eliminating the much larger and more costly J-Class and other yachts previously used. Since the 1958 challenge, the competition has been a best four of seven races, with each race run over a triangular 24-mile (39-kilometre) course by yachts of the 12-metre class. In 1983, after American yachts had successfully defended the cup 24 times without a loss since the first defense in 1870, the Australian yacht "Australia II" won the cup. *See* Sporting Record: *Yachting: America's Cup races.*

americium (Am), synthetic chemical element (atomic number 95) of the actinide series in Group IIIb of the periodic table. Undetected in nature, americium (as the isotope americium-241) was artificially produced from plutonium-239 (atomic number 94) in 1944 by Glenn T. Seaborg, Ralph A. James, Leon O. Morgan, and Albert Ghiorso in a nuclear reactor. It was the fourth transuranium element to be discovered (curium, atomic number 96, was discovered a few months previously). The metal is silvery white and tarnishes slowly in dry air at room temperature. The most important isotope is americium-241 because of its availability; it has been prepared in kilogram amounts from plutonium and has been used industrially in fluid-density gauges, thickness gauges, aircraft fuel gauges, and distance-sensing devices, all of which utilize its gamma radiation. All isotopes of americium are radioactive; the stablest isotope, americium-243, has proved more convenient for chemical investigations in view of its longer half-life (7,370 years as compared with 458 years for americium-241).

Americium reacts with oxygen to form the dioxide AmO_2 and with hydrogen to form the hydride AmH_2. There is some evidence that the ion Am^{2+} has been prepared in trace amounts, its existence suggesting that americium is similar to its lanthanide homologue, europium, which can be reduced to its divalent state. Americium has four oxidation states, from +3 to +6, in acidic aqueous solution with the following ionic species: Am^{3+}, pink; Am^{4+}, rose (very unstable); AmO_2^+, yellow; and $AmO2_2^{2+}$, light tan. In the common tripositive state, americium is very similar to the other actinide and lanthanide elements.

atomic number	95
stablest isotope	243
melting point	above 850° C (1,550° F)
specific gravity	13.67 (20° C)
valence	2,3,4,5,6
electronic config.	2-8-18-32-25-8-2 or (Rn)$5f^7 7s^2$

Americus, city, seat (1831) of Sumter County, southwest central Georgia, U.S., on Muckalee Creek. Founded in 1830, it was named for Amerigo (Americus) Vespucci or, legend says, for the "merry cusses" who were its first settlers. It is a trade and processing centre for agriculture, livestock, and timber, with some light industry, and kaolin and bauxite are mined nearby. To the northeast is Andersonville National Historic Site, where many Federal soldiers died during the Civil War. Charles A. Lindbergh made his first solo flight at Souther Field. Americus is the seat of Georgia Southwestern College (1906). Plains, the hometown of Jimmy Carter, former president of the United States, is 10 mi (16 km) west-southwest. Inc. 1855. Pop. (1980) 16,120.

Amerindian, also called AMERIND: *see* American Indian.

Amersfoort, *gemeente* (municipality), in Utrecht *provincie* (province), central Netherlands, on the Eem (formerly Amer) River. The site (the name means "ford on the Amer") was fortified in the 12th century. Its medieval street pattern and some old walls remain, as does the Koppelpoort (a water gate dating

The Koppelpoort across the Eem River, Amersfoort, Neth.

Van Phillips—Shostal/EB Inc.

from around 1400 and spanning the Eem). Landmarks include the 13th–16th-century St. George's Church and the Gothic Tower of Our Lady (the bell tower of a church destroyed in 1787). There is a regional museum, a government archaeological research station, a school for bell ringers, and a Jansenist college.

Amersfoort is now a centre for poultry raising and market gardening, and since World War II there has been rapid development of light industry, chiefly the manufacture of metals and chemicals.

Johan van Oldenbarnevelt, the Dutch statesman, was born in the town. Pop. (1983 est.) 87,461.

Amersham, parish, Chiltern district, county of Buckinghamshire, England, in the Misbourn Valley. The wide High Street of the old town is flanked by half-timbered coaching inns, Georgian houses, and a 17th-century town hall. The parish Church of St. Mary dates from the 14th century. Amersham lies on a main rail line from London (26 mi [42 km] southeast) and has attracted commuters. Pop. (1971) 17,254.

Amery, L(eopold Charles Maurice) S(tennett) (b. Nov. 22, 1873, Gorakhpur, India—d. Sept. 16, 1955, London), British politician who was a persistent advocate of imperial preference and tariff reform and did much for colonial territories. He is also remembered for his part in bringing about the fall of the government of Neville Chamberlain in 1940.

The son of a colonial administrator in the North-Western Provinces in India, Amery was educated at Harrow and Balliol College, Oxford. In 1899–1900 he was chief correspondent of the *Times* from the South African War and remained on the staff of that paper until 1909, editing *The Times History of the South African War,* 7 vol. (1900–09). He entered Parliament in 1911. During World War I, Amery served abroad with the British army in 1914–16, but from 1917 he was on the staff of the War Cabinet in London and of the inter-Allied war council at Versailles. He became undersecretary of state for the colonies in 1919 and was moved to a junior post at the admiralty in 1921.

Amery was made a privy councillor in 1922; and thereafter, apart from a term as first lord of the admiralty (1922–24), he spent the rest of his career as a minister in imperial departments. He created in 1925 the Dominions Office which later became the Commonwealth Relations Office. He was excluded from office by the national government (1931–40) and was a sharp critic of the Munich Agreement with Hitler and Mussolini. Despite his industry and passionate advocacy of his own causes, Amery never dominated the House of Commons, but in 1940 his voice was influential in breaking the Chamberlain government to which he applied Cromwell's injunction to the Long Parliament: "In the name of God, go!" From 1940 to 1945 he was secretary of state for India and Burma.

Amery Ice Shelf, large body of floating ice, in an indentation in the Indian Ocean coastline of Antarctica, east of the American Highland. Though its exact dimensions are unknown, it extends inland from Prydz and MacKenzie bays more than 200 mi (320 km) to the foot of Lambert Glacier. The region in which the ice shelf is located was claimed by Australia in 1933.

Ames, city, Story County, central Iowa, U.S., on the Skunk River, 30 mi (48 km) north of Des Moines. It was laid out in 1865 by the John I. Blair Land Company near the right-of-way of the Cedar Rapids and Missouri Railroad (now the Chicago and North Western) and was named for Oakes Ames, a railroad financier and Massachusetts congressman. Its development was assured when it became the seat of Iowa State University of Science and Technology, established in 1858 as a "state agricultural college and model farm" and formally opened in 1869. The university's College of Veterinary Medicine (1879) is the oldest in the United States. The National Animal Disease Center, the Institute for Atomic Research (1945), and other federal and state institutions are in the city. There is some light industry. Inc. town, 1870; city, 1893. Pop. (1980) 45,775.

Ames, Fisher (b. April 9, 1758, Dedham, Mass.—d. July 4, 1808, Dedham, Mass., U.S.), essayist and Federalist politician of the 1790s, who was an arch-opponent of Jeffersonian democracy.

After graduating from Harvard in 1774, he taught school for five years while also studying Greek, Latin, and English classics. In 1779 he turned from classics to law, and in 1781 was admitted to the bar.

Advocating repression of Shays's Rebellion, a farmers' uprising in western Massachusetts (1786–87), and supporting the drive for a new, more powerful federal government, Ames became known for uncompromising conservatism, trenchant writing, and commanding speech. He argued for ratification of the Constitution at the Massachusetts convention, and in 1788 Ames defeated Samuel Adams for a seat in the first session of the U.S. House of Representatives. Ames was reelected in 1790, 1792, and 1794.

Certain that the country could survive only with a strong central government, Ames supported Alexander Hamilton's financial measures. He argued against retaliation for British violations of American rights during 1793 and 1794 when American vessels were seized and American sailors impressed into British service. He gave the greatest speech of his life in favour of the Jay Treaty (1794), which preserved peace with Great Britain, when he swayed the House to pass an enabling appropriation.

Ames declined to run for reelection in 1796 and returned to Dedham the following year. Citing failing health, he refused the presidency of Harvard College. He wanted war with France (1797–98), to cleanse the United States of "Jacobinism," and he approved the Sedition Act of 1798.

Following Thomas Jefferson's election in 1800, Ames was sure the republic would sink into anarchy and mob rule. He urged Federalists to gain control of state governments, and—in the years just prior to his death—he became a leader in creating a New England sectional consciousness.

Ames, Oakes (b. Jan. 10, 1804, Easton, Mass., U.S.—d. May 8, 1873, Easton), leading figure in the Credit Mobilier scandal following the U.S. Civil War.

Ames left school at age 16 to enter his father's shovel company, Oliver Ames & Sons. Assuming progressively more responsible positions in the firm, he eventually took over management of the company (along with his brother Oliver [1807–77]) upon his father's retirement in 1844.

The gold rushes in California and Australia, along with agricultural development of the Mississippi Valley, created enormous demand for Ames's shovels. By the outbreak of the Civil War, the business was worth $4,000,000. Drawn to the Republican Party by his ardent beliefs in free soil and free enterprise, Ames ran for a Massachusetts congressional seat in 1862. He won—and then won reelection four times. He was, however, an inconspicuous member of the House.

In 1865, along with brother Oliver and railroad executive T.C. Durant, Ames helped create the Credit Mobilier—a company formed to build the Union Pacific Railroad. The Credit Mobilier allowed a small number of individuals to reap vast fortunes from the construction of the line. By early 1868, Congress seemed certain to investigate charges of improper use of government grants to the railroad. But Ames, through shrewd sale of Credit Mobilier stock at bargain prices to appropriate members of Congress, induced his colleagues to abandon the investigation.

A quarrel between Ames and Credit Mobilier investors led, in 1872, to the publication of documents detailing Ames's misuse of company stock to derail the congressional investigation of 1868. An immediate congressional investigation ensued, concluding with a vote of 182–36 in favour of censuring Ames. He returned to Easton in 1873, a disgraced and broken figure.

Ames, William (b. 1576, Ipswich, Suffolk, Eng.—d. Nov. 14, 1633, Rotterdam), English Puritan theologian remembered for his writings on ethics and for debating and writing in favour of strict Calvinism in opposition to Arminianism.

As a student at Cambridge, Ames viewed cardplaying as an offense to Christian living—no less serious than profanity. In 1609 his dispute with the Church of England's customs of conduct came to a head in his sermon attacking what he saw as the debauchery attending the feast of St. Thomas. Obliged to leave England, he sailed in 1610 to Rotterdam. There, in the fisherman's habit donned for the passage, he debated Nicolaas Grevinckhoven (Grevinchovius), minister to the local Arminian Church, on the doctrines of atonement and predestination. The Calvinists emphasized that salvation is limited to those who are foreordained by God to receive it and are not capable of falling out of his grace. The Arminians, on the other hand, believed that all men are capable of receiving God's grace if they are believers and if they fulfill certain other conditions.

Ames, considered triumphant in the debates, became widely known throughout the Low Countries. Subsequently, he entered into written disputes with Grevinckhoven on universal redemption and related questions. He served as an observer at the Synod of Dort (1618–19), at which Arminianism was firmly denounced, and as professor of theology at Franeker, in Friesland (1622–33). Among his more important works are *Medulla Theologiae* (1623; *The Marrow of Sacred Divinity,* 1642) and *De Conscientia et Ejus Jure vel Casibus* (1632; *Conscience,* 1639). The latter text was considered for many years by the Dutch Reformed Church to be a standard treatise on Christian ethics and the variety of ethical situations faced by believers.

Ames, Winthrop (b. Nov. 25, 1870, North Easton, Mass., U.S.—d. Nov. 3, 1937, Boston), theatrical producer, manager, director, and occasional playwright known for some of the finest productions of plays in the United States during the first three decades of the 20th century.

Though his interests lay in the theatre, to please his family Ames entered the publishing business for a few years after completing his education in 1896. He travelled to Europe in 1904, however, to study the management of 60 opera and theatrical companies and returned to Boston to manage the Castle Square Theatre with Loren F. Deland. He became known for his experiments with the stock company there, though they were not a financial success.

In 1908 he became managing director of the New Theatre, largest in New York and intended to house a repertory company producing the very finest in drama, free from commercial pressures. Opening on Nov. 6, 1909, with *Antony and Cleopatra,* Ames went on to produce *The Blue Bird* by Maurice Maeterlinck, John Galsworthy's *Strife,* and others—*Twelfth Night, The Winter's Tale,* and *The School for Scandal*—over a two-year period. The plays received much praise, but costs of production were too high and the theatre closed.

Ames then bought the Little Theatre in New York and the Booth Theatre. Productions in the two theatres, which he managed into the 1930s, included *The Philanderer* (1913), by George Bernard Shaw, Galsworthy's *Old English* (1924), George S. Kaufman and Marc Connelly's *Beggar on Horseback* (1924), an extremely successful series of Gilbert and Sullivan revivals at the Booth (1926–29), and *Snow White and the Seven Dwarfs* (1913), the first play designed especially for children and which Ames himself wrote under a pseudonym. Ames also directed the plays he produced. He retired in 1932 because of ill health.

Amesbury, parish, Salisbury district, county of Wiltshire, England, in the valley of the River Avon. It is rich in prehistoric remains, including Stonehenge, 1.5 mi (2.5 km) west, the greatest surviving megalithic structure in the British Isles. At Amesbury (Ambresbyrig, or Ambresbery) a Witan, or Witenagemot, the Anglo-Saxon kings' council of wise men, was held in 932. Now a small market town, Amesbury also caters to the needs of tourists visiting Stonehenge and serves such neighbouring army camps as Larkhill. Pop. (1971) 5,684.

Amesbury, urban town (township), Essex County, northeastern corner of Massachusetts, U.S., on the Merrimack River, at the New Hampshire border. Settled in 1642 as part of Salisbury, it was named for Amesbury, Eng., became a separate precinct in 1654, and was incorporated as a township in 1666. In 1693 the town was a focus of witchcraft hysteria. Amesbury thrived as a shipbuilding port and was an early manufacturing centre (iron, nails, hats, carriages). Textile production flourished after 1812 but declined in the 1920s. The town's economy is now based on light manufacturing. John Greenleaf Whittier lived in Amesbury from 1836 to 1876, and many of his poems describe the surrounding country and life of the community; his house is preserved and his grave is in Union Cemetery. Pop. (1980) 13,971.

amesha spenta (Avestan: "beneficent immortal"), Pahlavi AMSHASPEND, in Zoroastrianism, any of the six divine beings or archangels created by Ahura Mazdā, the Wise Lord, to help govern creation. Three are male, three female. Ministers of his power against the evil spirit, Ahriman, they are depicted clustered about Ahura Mazdā on golden thrones attended by angels. They are the everlasting bestowers of good. They are worshipped separately and are said to descend to service on paths of light. Each has a special month, festival, and flower and presides over an element in the world order. In later Zoroastrianism each is opposed by a specific archfiend.

Of the six, Asha Vahishta and Vohu Manah are by far the most important. Asha Vahishta (Avestan: Excellent Order, or Truth) is the lawful order of the cosmos according to which all things happen. He presides over fire, sacred to the Zoroastrians as the inner nature of reality. To the devotee he holds out the path of justice and spiritual knowledge. Vohu Manah (Avestan: Good Mind) is the spirit of divine wisdom, illumination, and love. He guided Zoroaster's soul before the throne of heaven. He welcomes the souls of the blessed in paradise. Believers are enjoined to "bring down Vohu Manah in your lives on Earth" through profound love in marriage and toward one's fellowman. He presides over domestic animals. Khshathra Vairya (Desirable Dominion), who presides over metal, is the power of Ahura Mazdā's kingdom. The believer can realize this power in action guided by Excellent Order and Good Mind. Spenta Armaiti (Beneficent Devotion), the spirit of devotion and faith, guides and protects the believer. She presides over Earth. Haurvatāt (Wholeness or Perfection) and Ameretāt (Immortality) are often mentioned together as sisters. They preside over water and plants and may come to the believer as a reward for participation in the natures of the other *amesha spentas.*

amethyst, a transparent, coarse-grained variety of the silica mineral quartz (*q.v.*) that is valued as a semiprecious gem for its violet colour. It contains more iron oxide (Fe_2O_3) than any other variety of quartz, and experts

White-tipped amethyst from Guerrero, Mexico
Lee Boltin

believe that its colour arises from its iron content. Other theories attribute the colour to contained manganese or hydrocarbons. Heating removes the colour from amethyst or changes it to the yellow of citrine; most commercial citrine is made in this manner. Notable occurrences include Brazil, Uruguay, Ontario, and North Carolina.

The name, derived from the Greek *amethystos,* "not intoxicated," expresses the ancient folk belief that the stone protects its owner against drunkenness. In ancient writings the Latin name *amethystus* was used for amethyst, purple corundum, and purple garnet. Amethyst, the birthstone for February, is usually facetted with step cuts or emerald cuts, but has been used for carved intaglios since ancient times. Amethyst is mentioned in the Bible (Ex. 28:19; 39:12) as one of the 12 stones adorning the breastplate (*ḥoshen*) of the high priests of Yahweh. Its physical properties are those of quartz. *See* silica mineral (table).

Ameura, genus of trilobites (extinct arthropods) found as fossils in North America in Pennsylvanian to Permian rocks (between 225,000,000 and 325,000,000 years old). *Ameura* is characterized by a well-developed cephalon (head) and a long pygidium (tail region) that includes many segments of the central axial lobe. Specimens are frequently found rolled up in a defensive position, as if the animals were attempting to shield their vulnerable undersides.

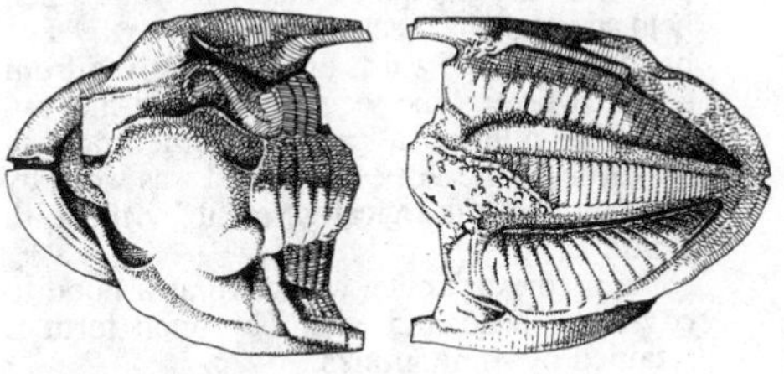

Ameura

After a photograph by J.M. Weller in H. Shimer and R. Shrock, *Index Fossils of North America*, by permission of the M.I.T. Press, Cambridge, Mass., copyright 1944 by the Massachusetts Institute of Technology, copyright renewed 1972 by the Massachusetts Institute of Technology

AMEX: *see* American Stock Exchange.

Ámfissa (Greece): *see* Amphissa.

Amga Stage, lowermost stage (or time interval of deposition) of the Middle Cambrian Series of rocks of the Soviet Union (the Cambrian Period began about 570,000,000 years ago and lasted about 70,000,000 years). The Amga Stage follows the Lena Stage and precedes the Maya Stage. On the Siberian Platform, several fossil zones (representing shorter spans of time) have been recognized, the zone of the trilobite genus *Paradoxides* being especially notable. In the Tamir region, dolomites and other calcareous facies predominate. The Amga is well represented in many regions of the Soviet Union.

Amhara and Tigre, also called ABYSSINIANS, peoples of the Ethiopian central highlands who together compose over one-quarter of the population of Ethiopia and who for centuries were known to the world as "Abyssinians." (The Tigre in this grouping are southern Tigre, who speak Tigrinya; for a discussion of the northern, culturally distinct groups who speak Tigré, *see* Tigre, northern.)

Although the Amharic and Tigrinya languages are different, they are both related to Geʿez, the sacred literary language of the Ethiopian Orthodox (Coptic) Church, an ancient religion preserved virtually intact from the Monophysite Christianity of the Byzantine Church of the 5th century.

The Amhara have managed to dominate the history of their country; their language is the official language of Ethiopia. The Amhara and Tigre are the descendants of Semitic conquerors who crossed the Red Sea from southern Arabia between the 6th century BC and the 1st century AD and who mingled with the already-present Cushitic population, established political and cultural dominance, and founded the kingdom of Aksum (Axum) in the 2nd to the 9th century AD. The Tigre inhabit this area still, in the provinces of Tigre and Eritrea in northern Ethiopia. The Amhara, participants in a southward movement that continues today, inhabit the huge provinces of Begemdir and Simen, Gojam, Welo, and Shewa (Shoa). All except one of the emperors from 1270 to 1974 were Amhara. Despite competitive quarrels, the Amhara and Tigre maintain a consciousness of their common identity, rooted in a sacred past.

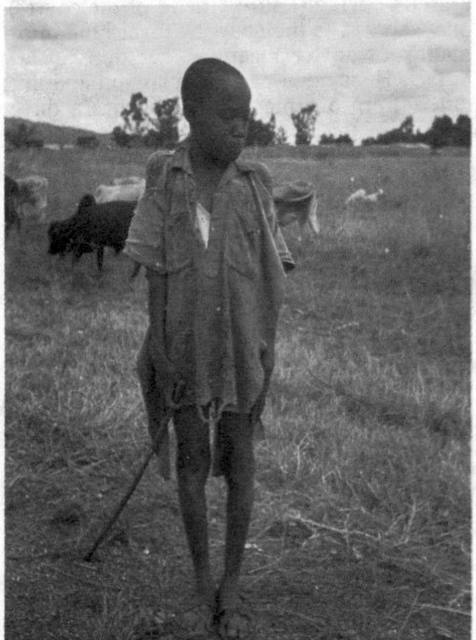

Amhara boy guarding cattle

Harrison Forman

The Amhara and Tigre peoples are agriculturalists, producing corn (maize), wheat, barley, sorghum, and teff, a cereal grass (*Eragrostis abyssinica*) that is grown for its grain and is a staple of the region. Amhara social structure is dominated by strong personalized ties between patrons and clients, superiors and inferiors. Generally, a man's importance is in direct proportion to the amount of land he owns. A man of wealth who owns no land, such as a merchant, has little influence. The largest landowners, or landed gentry, continue the feudal warrior class of the ancient Amhara and Tigre peoples. Land was granted to titled nobles in return for military service to the emperor. The land is farmed by tenant clients. Even in family life all privilege and authority devolve from the patriarch.

Descent is reckoned patrilineally, and married couples usually reside near the husband's home. The Amhara and Tigre know three types of marriage: *qurban,* the church marriage; *semyana,* or civil contract, by far the commonest; and *damoz,* or temporary wage marriage. All first marriages are arranged by the parents. Sixty to 90 percent of all *semyana* marriages end in divorce. *Qurban* marriages are sacred before God and cannot be dissolved, even after the death of one partner, except in extraordinary circumstances.

Amhara Plateau, montane region of northern and central Ethiopia, the historical home of the Amhara and Tigrai peoples. Itself a portion of the larger Ethiopian Plateau, it is composed, north to south, of the Tigrai Plateau, centred on the city of Aksum; the Semien Mountains, northeast of Gonder; the Gojam Massif, east of Lake Tana; and the Shewa Plateau, north of Addis Ababa. Its average elevation is 8,200 to 9,200 ft (2,500 to 2,600 m). The highest point is Ras Dashen (15,158 ft [4,620 m]), the highest peak in Ethiopia, situated within the Semien National Park. The plateau is drained westward by the Tekeze and Blue Nile (Abbay) rivers and their tributaries.

Amharic language, also called AMARINYA, AMHARINYA, or KUCHUMBA, official language of Ethiopia, spoken in the central and southern highlands of the country. It is a Semitic language of the Southern Peripheral group, to which also belong Geʿez, or Ethiopic, the liturgical language of the Ethiopian church; Tigre; Tigrinya; and the South Arabic dialects.

Although the oldest extant records in Amharic are songs and poems dating from the 14th century, significant literature in any quantity did not begin until the 19th century.

Amharic is written in a slightly modified form of the alphabet used for writing the Geʿez language. There are 33 basic characters, each of which has seven forms depending on which vowel is to be pronounced in the syllable. The language has been strongly influenced by the Cushitic languages, especially Gallinya. The dialects of Amharic are not strongly differentiated from one another.

Amherst, town, seat of Cumberland County, northern Nova Scotia, Canada, near the Cumberland Basin, an arm of Chignecto Bay, just south of the New Brunswick border and Ft. Beauséjour National Historic Park, 38 mi (61 km) southeast of Moncton, N.B. Standing on rising ground above the Tantramar Marshes, it was called La Planche by the original French settlers; but it was renamed in 1759 after repopulation by New England colonists to honour Jeffrey (later Baron) Amherst, who captured Louisbourg (on Cape Breton Island) from the French in 1758. Historic structures include the ruined Ft. Lawrence, built by the British in 1750, and the town's first Presbyterian church (1788). Amherst lies in a timber, farming, and coal-mining region; its manufactures include iron and structural steel, boilers, clothing, chemicals, salt, luggage, and aircraft components. Inc. 1889. Pop. (1981) 9,684.

Amherst, town (township), Hampshire County, west central Massachusetts, U.S., in the Connecticut River Valley just northeast of Northampton. Settled as part of Hadley in the 1730s, it was recognized in 1759 as a separate district and named for Jeffrey (later Baron) Amherst, British commander in North America in the French and Indian Wars. It was incorporated as a town in 1776. Early industries (textiles, bricks, carriages) gave way to farming in the 19th century, but the town has developed principally as an educational centre.

Noah Webster lived there (1812–22) while working on his dictionary and was one of the founders of Amherst College, which was established in 1821 to train youths for the ministry. The college's facilities include the Robert Frost Library, the Mead Art Museum, the Kirby Theatre, and the Pratt Geology Museum. The University of Massachusetts (1947) was founded at Amherst in 1863 as an agricultural land-grant college; its central campus covers 1,100 ac (445 ha) and contains more than 160 buildings. Hampshire College, south of the town, opened in 1970 to join the county's academic community, which also includes Smith and Mt. Holyoke colleges, both within 10 mi (16 km) of Amherst.

A number of homes of literary interest are in the town. Those of the poet Emily Dickinson (born in Amherst, 1830) and of the poet-novelist Helen Hunt Jackson are owned by Amherst College. Others include those of Robert Frost, Ray Stannard Baker (David Grayson), and Eugene Field. A plaque across from the town hall marks the site of Noah Webster's farm. Pop. (1980) 33,229.

Amherst (Burma): *see* Kyaikkami.

Amherst, Jeffrey Amherst, lst Baron, also called (1761–87) SIR JEFFREY AMHERST (b. Jan. 29, 1717, Sevenoaks, Kent, Eng.—

d. Aug. 3, 1797, Sevenoaks), army commander who captured Canada for Great Britain (1758–60) and for whom Amherst, Mass., and several other American towns were named.

He received a commission in the foot guards in 1731 and was selected as aide-de-camp first by Lord Ligonier and then by the Duke of Cumberland. William Pitt and Ligonier selected him for the Canadian command in 1758. With a force of 14,000 men he besieged and captured Louisburg (Nova Scotia) and was promoted to chief command in America. He then drew up a plan for a concentric advance on Montreal by three columns, one moving westward up the St. Lawrence River and capturing Quebec, the second northward from Albany by Ticonderoga and Crown Point, and the third westward from Fort Niagara. The first column, under the command of James Wolfe, captured Quebec late in 1759, and the final offensive was launched in 1760, when Montreal surrendered and Canada passed into British hands.

Amherst remained in Canada as governor general until 1763, quelling the Indian rising under Pontiac in 1761. He acted as commander in chief of the British army almost continuously from 1772 to 1795, but, though

Baron Amherst, detail of a portrait by Thomas Gainsborough; in the National Portrait Gallery, London
By courtesy of the National Portrait Gallery, London

he suppressed the Gordon riots in 1780, his tenure of office was not a successful one, being marred by failure in the war with the American colonies and by the growth of serious abuses in the army.

He was created a baron in 1776 and a field marshal in 1796.

Articles are alphabetized word by word, not letter by letter

Amherst (of Arracan), William Pitt Amherst, lst Earl, also called (1797–1826) 2ND BARON AMHERST (b. Jan. 14, 1773, Bath, Somerset, Eng.—d. March 13, 1857, Knole, Kent), diplomat who, as British governor general of India (1823–28), played a central role in the acquisition of Asian territory for the British Empire after the First Burmese War (1824–26).

He inherited in 1797 the baronial title of his uncle Jeffrey Amherst. After serving as British envoy at the court of Naples (1809–11), he was sent to China (1816) to negotiate commercial matters. At the Imperial court, however, he declined to perform the kowtow (to strike his forehead on the ground nine times in obeisance), and his mission failed.

In India he was confronted by a demand from the ruler of Bengal to surrender the whole of eastern Bengal. That demand precipitated the First Burmese War, which Amherst brought to a conclusion with the annexation (1826) of the jungle coastal strips of Arakan and Tenasserim (both in modern Burma) and

Earl Amherst, detail of an oil painting after A. Devis; in the National Portrait Gallery, London
By courtesy of the National Portrait Gallery, London

Assam (a state of modern India). He was created earl in 1826.

Amherst College, private, independent liberal arts college for men and women in Amherst, Mass., established in 1821 and chartered in 1825. Noah Webster was one of the founders of the college, originally intended to train men for the ministry. In 1914 Amherst president Alexander Meiklejohn instituted the first college survey course, "Social and Economic Institutions." Meiklejohn sought to incorporate in the college curriculum his belief that knowledge should be pursued not for itself but for its contribution to life. It offers flexible programs of study, including one free of formal courses in the third and fourth years. Originally a men's college, Amherst admitted women as transfer students in 1975 and as first-year students in 1976.

Amhurst, Nicholas (b. Oct. 16, 1697, Marden, Kent, Eng.—d. April 12, 1742, Twickenham, Middlesex), satirical poet, political pamphleteer on behalf of the Whigs, and editor of *The Craftsman,* a political journal of unprecedented popularity that was hostile to the Whig government of Sir Robert Walpole.

Expelled from Oxford in 1719 (probably because of his outspoken views and his satirizing the university in verse), Amhurst settled in London and began a series of satirical papers, *Terrae Filius* ("Son of the Land"). *The Craftsman,* founded in 1726, published articles by Tories as well as by Whigs. In 1737 Amhurst published in it a letter purporting to come from Colley Cibber, then poet laureate, attacking the new (censorship) act for licensing plays; for this "suspected libel," Amhurst and the printer of the journal were imprisoned. After release he was forgotten and passed the rest of his life in obscurity and poverty.

Ami, most numerous indigenous ethnic group on the island of Taiwan, numbering 89,802 in 1964 and located in the fertile but relatively inaccessible southeastern hilly region and along the eastern coastal plain. Of Malay stock, they speak three dialects of an Indonesian-related language, also called Ami. The Ami traditionally practice slash-and-burn agriculture, growing dry rice, millet, sweet potatoes, tobacco, and betel nut. Today, wet rice cultivation is also important. Composed of extended family units, Ami society revolves around villages (each headed by a chief) containing up to 1,000 people. Men and women have equal rights and responsibilities, but clan organization is actually matrilineal; women own property and the eldest daughter receives the family inheritance. Daily life is closely bound to religious beliefs; each family group has a hereditary priestess and a shaman, who practices dream divination. The Ami honour both ancestral and divine spirits; their most important ceremony is held annually after the millet harvest. The Ami have undergone pronounced acculturation, primarily through trading contacts with the Chinese.

amice (derived from Latin *amictus,* "wrapped around"), liturgical vestment worn under the alb. It is a rectangular piece of white linen held around the neck and shoulders by two bands tied at the waist. Probably derived from a scarf worn by the secular classes, it first appeared as a liturgical garment in the Frankish kingdom in the 9th century and was worn by all clergy as a liturgical garment by the 12th century.

The medieval amice was worn as a hood to cover the head and ears. The hood form is retained by some monks.

The Eastern Church has no comparable vestment.

Amici, Giovanni Battista (b. March 25, 1786, Modena, Duchy of Modena—d. April 10, 1863, Florence), astronomer and optician who made important improvements in the mirrors of reflecting telescopes and also developed prisms for use in refracting spectroscopes (instruments used to separate light into its spectral components).

Amici served as professor of mathematics at the University of Modena from 1815 to 1825 and then became astronomer to the Grand Duke of Tuscany and director of the observatory at the Royal Museum in Florence, where he also lectured at the museum of natural history. He made major advancements in compound-microscope design and introduced (1840) the oil-immersion technique, in which the objective lens is immersed in a drop of oil placed atop the specimen under observation in order to minimize light aberrations.

His name is most often associated with improvements in the microscope and reflecting telescope, but he also put his instruments to good use. His observations of Jupiter's satellites and certain double stars were highly esteemed. Using an improved micrometer of his own design, he made accurate measurements of the polar and equatorial diameters of the Sun. With his improved compound microscope he made revealing studies of the circulation of sap in plants as well as important discoveries about the processes of plant reproduction.

Amicis, Edmondo De: *see* De Amicis, Edmondo.

amicus curiae (Latin: "friend of the court"), one who assists the court by furnishing information or advice regarding questions of law or fact. He is not a party to a lawsuit and thus differs from an intervenor, who has a direct interest in the outcome of the lawsuit and is therefore permitted to participate as a party to the suit.

An amicus curiae normally may not participate except by leave of the court, and most courts seldom permit persons to appear in such a capacity. The Supreme Court of the United States, however, permits federal, state, and local governments to submit their views in any case that concerns them without obtaining the consent of either the court or the parties. Private persons may appear as amici curiae in the Supreme Court, either if both parties consent or if the court grants permission.

Amida (in Buddhism): *see* Amitābha.

Amida (Turkey): *see* Diyarbakır.

ʿamida, also spelled AMIDAH (Hebrew: "standing"), plural AMIDOT, or AMIDOTH, in Judaism, the main section of morning, afternoon, and evening prayers, recited while standing up. On weekdays the *ʿamida* consists of 19 benedictions. These include 3 paragraphs of praise,

13 of petition, and another 3 of thanksgiving. Some call this section of the daily prayer by the ancient name, *shemone 'esre* (Hebrew: "eighteen"), although the 19th benediction was added around 100 CE.

On sabbaths, festivals, and New Moon services, the *'amida* consists of the first three praises and the last three thanksgivings, but one special paragraph for the appropriate day replaces the usual 13 benedictions in the middle. Thus the *'amida* at these services has only seven sections and is known as *bircath sheva.* The 13 petitions are omitted because it is forbidden to speak of need and sadness at these joyous services.

During the worship service, the *'amida* is first recited by each individual as a silent prayer, giving any sinner a chance to atone without embarrassment. The prayer is then repeated aloud by the reader. There is never a Jewish service without an *'amida.*

amide, any member of either of two classes of nitrogen-containing compounds related to ammonia and amines. The covalent amides are neutral or very weakly acidic substances formed by replacement of the hydroxyl group (OH) of an acid by an amino group (NR_2, in which R may represent a hydrogen atom or an organic combining group such as methyl, CH_3). The carboxamides ($R'CONR_2$), which are derived from carboxylic acids ($R'COOH$), are the most important group. Sulfonamides (RSO_2NR_2) are similarly related to the sulfonic acids (RSO_3H).

Ionic, or saltlike, amides are strongly alkaline compounds ordinarily made by treating ammonia, an amine, or a covalent amide with a reactive metal such as sodium.

Covalent amides derived from ammonia are solids, except formamide, which is liquid; those containing fewer than five carbon atoms are soluble in water. They are nonconductors of electricity and solvents for both organic and inorganic substances. Covalent amides, even those of low molecular weight, have high boiling points.

There are no practical natural sources of simple covalent amides, although polyamides (amides linked together to form large molecules called polymers) occur in great abundance as the protein of living systems. Simple amides ordinarily are prepared by reaction of acids or acid halides with ammonia or amines. They can also be produced by the reaction of water with nitriles.

The characteristic reaction of covalent amides is hydrolysis (a chemical reaction with water), by which they are converted to acids and amines; this reaction ordinarily is slow unless it is catalyzed by a strong acid, an alkali, or an enzyme. Amides also can be dehydrated to nitriles. Amides are not readily oxidized nor reduced, although hydrogenation (addition of hydrogen at high temperatures and pressures) in the presence of a catalyst will convert most amides of carboxylic acids to amines. The powerful reducing agent lithium aluminum hydride transforms amides into amines. Reaction of amides with acid chlorides or anhydrides produces imides, which are compounds with two carbonyl (CO) groups attached to the same nitrogen atom.

Among the amides of commercial importance are acetamide, also called ethanamide (CH_3CONH_2) and dimethylformamide $HCON(CH_3)_2$, which are used as solvents, the sulfa drugs, and the nylons. Urea or carbamide $[CO(NH_2)_2]$ is a crystalline compound that is formed as the end product of the metabolism of protein and excreted in the urine of mammals. It is synthesized in large quantities from ammonia and carbon dioxide for use in fertilizers, in animal feed, and in manufacturing a class of polymers known as urea-formaldehyde resins, used in making plastics.

Amidism, sect of Mahāyāna Buddhism centring on worship of Amida (in Japanese; Sanskrit Amitābha; Chinese O-mi-t'o-fo), Buddha (Buddha of Infinite Light), whose merits can be transferred to a believer. Amidism holds that the faithful—by believing in Amida, hearing or saying his name, or desiring to share in his Western Paradise—can be reborn in the Pure Land (*see* Pure Land Buddhism). Originating in India, Amidism emerged in China in the 4th century and by the 9th century was brought to Japan, where, in the 20th century, the Pure Land sects compose one of the two largest Buddhist groups. *See also* Amitābha.

Amiel, Henri Frédéric (b. Sept. 27, 1821, Geneva—d. May 11, 1881, Geneva), Swiss writer known for his *Journal intime,* a masterpiece of self-analysis. Despite apparent success (as professor of aesthetics, then of philosophy, at Geneva), he felt himself a failure. Driven in on himself, he lived in his *Journal,* kept from 1847 until his death and first published in

Amiel, detail of a heliograph by an unknown artist
J.P. Ziolo

part as *Fragments d'un journal intime* (1883–84; later enlarged editions; definitive ed. by L. Bopp, 1939–48). It reveals a sensitive man of great intellectual ability, struggling for values against the skepticism of the age. Widely translated, it gained Amiel lasting fame.

Amiens, city, capital of Somme *département,* Picardie region, principal city and ancient capital of Picardy, northern France, in the Somme Valley, north of Paris. Famed since the Middle Ages are its textile industry and its great Gothic cathedral of Notre-Dame, one of the finest in France. Known as Samarobriva in pre-Roman times and capital of the Ambiani (whence the modern name), Amiens became a Roman city, Christianized in the 4th century by St. Firmin, its first bishop. Its territory became the medieval countship of Amiénois, and its citizens profited from rivalry between bishop and count to gain a charter early in the 12th century. The Peace of Amiens (1802) marked a short pause in the Napoleonic Wars. In 1914, after a brief incursion into the city, the invading Germans dug in 18 mi (29 km) east; their final drive in 1918 was stopped 8 mi (13 km) from the city. In World War II, Amiens was occupied by the Germans. After serious damage in both wars, the city centre was rebuilt.

The old part of Amiens, including the reconstructed 17th-century city hall, the 15th-century church of Saint-Germain, and the ancient theatre with the Louis XVI facade, is latticed with seven branches of the river.

The cathedral was begun in 1220 on the plans of Robert de Luzarches and was finished about 50 years later (there were subsequent additions). Its galleried and rose-windowed facade, pierced by three portals and topped by twin towers, is splendid. It has a remarkable interior with a soaring nave and bold supporting columns, employing the logic of Romanesque while imposing the open and dramatic qualities of Gothic.

Apart from textiles, there is some manufacturing, including machinery, chemicals, and tires. Truck farmers from the adjacent heavily watered bottom lands (*hortillons*) hold market in the city from small boats. Longeau, near Amiens, is an important railroad junction. Pop. (1982) 130,302.

Amiens, Treaty of (March 27, 1802), an agreement signed at Amiens, Fr., by Britain, France, Spain, and the Batavian Republic (the Netherlands), achieving a peace in Europe for 14 months during the Napoleonic Wars. It ignored some questions that divided Britain and France, such as the fate of the Belgian provinces, Savoy, and Switzerland and the trade relations between Britain and the French-controlled Continent. Notwithstanding military reverses overseas, France and its allies recovered most of their colonies, though Britain retained Trinidad (taken from Spain) and Ceylon (taken from the Dutch). France recognized the Republic of the Seven Ionian Islands and agreed to evacuate Naples and the Papal States. The British were to restore Egypt (evacuated by the French) to the Ottoman Empire and Malta to the Knights of St. John within three months. The rights and territories of the Ottoman Empire and of Portugal were to be respected, with the exception that France would keep Portuguese Guinea.

'Āmilī, Muḥammad ibn Ḥusayn Bahā' ad-Dīn, al-, also called SHAYKH BAHĀ'Ī (b. March 20, 1546, Baalbek, Syria—d. Aug. 20, 1622, Iran), theologian, mathematician, jurist, and astronomer who was a major figure in the cultural revival of Ṣafavid Iran.

Al-'Āmilī was educated by his father, Shaykh Ḥusayn, a Shī'ah theologian, and by excellent teachers of mathematics and medicine. After his family left Syria in 1559 to escape persecution by the Ottoman Turks, al-'Āmilī lived in Herāt (now in Afghanistan) and Isfahan, Iran. He attached himself to the court of 'Abbās I the Great, serving for many years as the *shaykh al-Islām* (chief judge of the Muslim court of law) of Isfahan, and writing during that time a treatise on Shī'ah jurisprudence and its application in Iran (*Jāmi'e Abbāsī*). He made a pilgrimage to Mecca and visited with many scholars, doctors, and mystics on a homeward journey that took him to Iraq, Egypt, the Hejaz, and Palestine.

In his poetry al-'Āmilī expounded complex mystical doctrines in simple and unadorned verse. His best known poem, *Nān o-ḥalvā* ("Bread and Sweets"), describes the experiences of an itinerant holy man who may well be al-'Āmilī himself on the Mecca pilgrimage. *Kashkūl* ("The Beggar's Bowl"), containing both stories and verses, was translated widely. His major work of astronomy is *Tashrīhu'l-aflāk* ("Anatomy of the Heavens").

Al-'Āmilī was responsible for the revival of mathematical sciences in Iran, the study of which had been neglected for more than 100 years. His *Khulāṣah fi al-ḥisāb* ("The Essentials of Arithmetic"), written in Arabic, was translated several times into Persian and German. The work was a standard textbook until the beginning of the 20th century.

Amīn, (Muḥammad) al- (b. April 787—d. Sept. 24/25, 813, Iraq), sixth caliph of the 'Abbāsid dynasty.

As the son of Hārūn ar-Rashīd, the fifth caliph, and Zubayda, a niece of al-Manṣūr, the second caliph, al-Amīn took precedence in the succession over his elder half brother, al-Ma'mūn, whose mother was a Persian slave. In 809, al-Amīn succeeded to the caliphate, and al-Ma'mūn was vested with the administration of the eastern Khorāsān region. Relations between the brothers soon broke down, and in 810 al-Amīn declared his own son as his direct heir. Open hostilities began in 811, and by 812 al-Amīn was besieged in Baghdad, the defense of which lasted more than a year. Al-

Amīn was captured and executed, apparently against the wishes of his brother.

Amin, Idi, in full IDI AMIN DADA OUMEE (b. 1924/25, Koboko, Uganda), military officer and president (1971–79) of Uganda.

A member of the small Kakwa tribe of northwestern Uganda, he had little formal education and joined the King's African Rifles of the British colonial army in 1943. He served in the Allied forces' Burma campaign during World War II and in the British action against the Mau Mau revolt in Kenya (1952–56). He was the heavyweight boxing champion of Uganda (1951–60) and a noted rugby player.

Amin was one of the few Ugandan soldiers elevated to officer rank before Ugandan independence in 1962, and he became closely associated with the new nation's prime minister and president, Milton Obote. Amin's activities on behalf of the rebels in the Congo (now Zaire) in 1965 led to scandal, but he emerged as chief of the army and air force (1966–70). Conflict with Obote arose, however, and on Jan. 25, 1971, Amin staged a successful military coup. He became president and chief of the armed forces in 1971, field marshal in 1975, and life president in 1976.

Amin ruled directly, shunning the delegation of power. He was noted for his abrupt changes of mood, from buffoonery to shrewdness, from gentleness to tyranny. He was often extreme in his nationalism. He expelled all Asians from Uganda in 1972, an action that led to the breakdown of Uganda's economy, and publicly insulted Great Britain and the United States. A Muslim, he reversed Uganda's amicable relations with Israel and befriended Libya and the Palestinians; in July 1976 he was personally involved in the Palestinian hijacking of a French airliner to Entebbe, involving Israeli and other Jewish passengers. Border skirmishes with Tanzania and Kenya weakened the East African Community.

Amin also took tribalism, a long-standing problem in Uganda, to its extreme by allegedly ordering the persecution of Acholi, Lango, and other tribes. Amidst reports of the torture and murder of 100,000 to 300,000 Ugandans during Amin's presidency, Uganda was invaded by Ugandan nationalist and Tanzanian troops in October 1978. When the invasion forces reached Kampala, Uganda's capital, on April 13, 1979, Amin had fled. Escaping first to Libya, he finally settled in Saudi Arabia.

A French documentary film, *General Idi Amin Dada,* was produced with Amin's cooperation in 1974. A good journalistic biography, *General Amin,* by David Martin, appeared in 1974 and *A State of Blood: The Inside Story of Idi Amin* by Henry Kyemba (a former Cabinet minister under Amin) in 1977.

amine, any member of a family of nitrogen-containing organic compounds derived, either in principle or in practice, from ammonia. Amines are classified as primary, secondary, or tertiary depending on whether one, two, or three of the hydrogen atoms of ammonia have been replaced by organic groups. Diamines, triamines, and polyamines contain two, three, or more nitrogen groupings of the types mentioned above. Amines are alkaline, although the intensity of this property varies considerably.

Naturally occurring amines include the alkaloids, present in certain plants, and the amino acids, the units that compose proteins.

Several amines are major industrial commodities used in making rubber, dyes, pharmaceuticals, synthetic resins and fibres, and in a host of other applications. Most of the numerous methods for the preparation of amines may be broadly divided into two groups: (1) chemical reduction (replacement of oxygen with hydrogen atoms in the molecule) of members of several other classes of organic nitrogen compounds and (2) reactions of ammonia or amines with organic compounds.

Amines form salts with acids; with many organic acids or acid anhydrides, primary and secondary amines undergo further reaction to form amides.

amino acid, any organic compound incorporating both acidic groups and one or more amino groups. The 20 or so most important amino acids, the *α*-amino acids (so called because of the position within the molecule of a primary amino [$-NH_2$] group relative to the carboxyl group [$-COOH$]), are obtainable from proteins and polypeptides. The only exceptions to this basic structure are proline and hydroxyproline, in which the primary amino group is replaced by a secondary amino group ($>NH$) present in a cyclic structure.

In the diagram, *R* represents an organic radical called the side chain, which varies greatly in composition and structure. Differences in the number and sequences of amino acids combined in proteins are responsible for the species- and organ-specificity of those substances (*see also* protein).

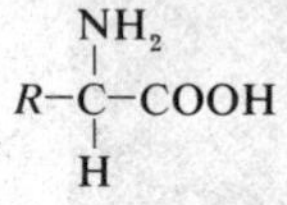

α-amino acid

aminosalicylic acid: *see* para-aminosalicylic acid.

Amiot, Jean-Joseph-Marie, Amiot also spelled AMYOT (b. Feb. 8, 1718, Toulon, Fr.—d. Oct. 9, 1793, Peking), Jesuit missionary who provided a key to the thought and life of the Far East. Amiot entered the Society of Jesus in 1737 and was sent (1750) as a missionary to China. He soon won the confidence of the emperor Ch'ien Lung and spent the remainder of his life at Peking. His Tatar–Manchu grammar and dictionary in French provided Europeans with their first key to that Oriental language. His other writings are to be found chiefly in the *Mémoires concernant l'histoire, les sciences et les arts des Chinois* (1776–91) and the *Vie de Koung-Tsée,* of which the 12th volume is complete.

amīr, also spelled EMIR (Arabic: "commander," or "prince"), in the Muslim Middle East, a military commander, governor of a province, or a high military official. Under the Umayyads, the *amīr* exercised administrative and financial powers, somewhat diminished under the ʿAbbāsids, who introduced a separate financial officer. Sometimes, as in the cases of the Aghlabids and Ṭāhirids, the *amīr*s ruled virtually independently in their provinces with but token allegiance to the caliph. In other cases the province was first taken by force, then the *amīr*s applied for legitimacy to the caliph.

The title *amīr al-muʾminīn,* sometimes used of leaders of Muslim military campaigns, was assumed by ʿUmar, the second caliph, probably on the basis of the Qurʾānic "Obey God and obey the Apostle and those invested with command (*ūlī al-amr*) among you" (iv, 59); it was used by all his successors until the abolition of the caliphate in 1924.

In the 10th century the commander of the caliph's armies at Baghdad was styled *amīr al-umarāʾ* ("commander in chief"). *Amīr* could also denote office, as in *amīr al-ḥājj,* "leader of the pilgrimage" to Mecca, held by the caliph or his delegate, a precedent set by Abū Bakr and Muḥammad himself (630 and 631).

The title *amīr* was later adopted by the rulers of several independent states in central Asia, notably those of Bukhara and Afghanistan. In the modern United Arab Emirates, however, none of the rulers of the constituent states are called emirs, or *amīr*s; all are *shaykhs* (sheikhs). The word Emirates was included in the name of the federation by default, because *mashyakhah* (sheikhdom) was already in use for the smallest of Arab administrative units, comparable to a parish or township.

Amir Ali, Sayyid (b. April 6, 1849, Cuttack, India—d. Aug. 3, 1928, Sussex, Eng.), jurist, writer, and Muslim leader who favoured British rule in India as an alternative to possible Hindu domination of an independent India. Founder of the National Mohammedan Association (1877), created to provide Muslims with experience in Western political techniques and to protect their interests, he helped secure in 1909 the first communal electorates for his people.

Amir Ali, who traced his ancestry to the prophet Muḥammad's daughter Fāṭimah, took his law degree at the University of Calcutta, was called to the bar of the Inner Temple (1873) in England, and returned to practice in Calcutta, becoming a judge of the High Court in 1890. A permanent resident of England from 1904, he was appointed to the judicial committee of the Privy Council in 1909.

Amir Ali founded the British Red Crescent Society for aiding Muslims in need, and he furthered Western understanding of Islām by writing the first presentation of Islām by a Muslim in the English language, *The Critical Examination of the Life and Teachings of Mohammed* (1873). His *Spirit of Islam* (1891) remains a Muslim classic.

Amīr Kabīr (Iranian prime minister): *see* Mīrzā Taqī Khān.

Amīr Khosrow (b. 1253, Patiāla, Punjab, India—d. 1325, Delhi), poet and historian, considered one of India's greatest Persian-language poets.

Amīr Khosrow was the son of a Turkish officer in the service of Iltutmish, sultan of Delhi, and for his entire life enjoyed the patronage of the Muslim rulers of Delhi, especially Sultan Ghīyās-ud-Dīn Balban and his son Muḥammad Khān of Multān. During his youth he became a dedicated follower of the saint of Delhi, Muḥammad Niẓām-ud-Dīn Awliyā, of the Chishtī dervish order; eventually he was buried next to the saint's tomb.

Sometimes known as "the parrot of India," Amīr Khosrow wrote numerous works, among them five divans, which were compiled at different periods in his life, and his *Khamsah* ("Pentology"), a group of five long idylls in emulation of the *Khamseh* of the celebrated Persian poet Neẓāmī (1141–*c.* 1203). Amīr Khosrow's Pentology deals with general themes famous in Islāmic literature. In addition to his poetry, he is known for a number of prose works, including the *Khazāʾin al-futūḥ* ("The Treasure-Chambers of the Victories"), also known by the title *Tārīkh-e ʿAlāʾī* ("The History of Ala"). Two historical poems for which he is well known are *Nuh Sipihr* ("The Nine Heavens") and the *Tughluq-nāmah* ("The Book of Tughluq").

Amirante Isles, group of coral islands in the western Indian Ocean about 200 mi (320 km) southwest of the Seychelles group and which, with the Seychelles and other islands, form the Republic of Seychelles. The Amirante Isles were known to Persian Gulf traders centuries ago and were sighted by Vasco da Gama on his second voyage to India in 1502, but they are still virtually uninhabited. Individual islands are frequently leased by the Seychelles government to private companies to exploit, usually by growing and harvesting coconut. Tern eggs are also collected, and guano-enriched topsoil was once collected but little remains. Pop. (1982 est.) 109.

ʿĀmirīyah, al-, formerly MARYŪṬ, industrial district of al-Iskandarīyah (Alexandria) *muḥāfaẓah* (governorate), northern Egypt. The centre of the 913-sq-mi (2,365-sq-km) district, which adjoins Buḥayrat Maryūṭ (Lake Mareotis) on the southwest, is the town of al-ʿĀmirīyah. Originally a small gypsum-mining centre on the desert roads leading south to Cairo and west along the coast to Maṭrūḥ, the town's modern development began in the late 1970s, when construction started on major industrial plants in the district, including an oil refinery and textile, steel, and chemical plastics plants operated with energy from the natural gas field at Abū Qīr Bay. The city is served by the newly expanded port at ad-Dikheila to the north, by Alexandria's airport at al-Hawafiah, and by the railroad linking Alexandria and Maṭrūḥ. It also is situated beside the Fu'ād al-Auwa highway. Pop. (1976) 47,063.

Amis, Kingsley (b. April 16, 1922, London), novelist, poet, critic, and teacher who created in his first novel, *Lucky Jim* (1954; filmed 1957), a comic figure who became a household word in Great Britain in the 1950s. His disgruntled anti-hero, Jim Dixon, epitomized a newly important social group risen by dint of scholarships from lower middle-class and working-class backgrounds only to find the more comfortable perches still occupied by the well-born. Amis was generally grouped among the Angry Young Men (*q.v.*), who expressed similar social discontent. As a poet, Amis is a representative member of a group sometimes called "The Movement" who, appearing in 1956 in the anthology *New Lines,* wrote a reasonable and unemphatic verse that purposely avoided experimentation and grandiose themes.

Amis was educated at the City of London School and St. John's College, Oxford (B.A., 1949). His education was interrupted during World War II by his service as a lieutenant in the Royal Corps of Signals. From 1949 to 1961 he taught at universities in Wales, England, and the United States.

Amis's next novel, *That Uncertain Feeling* (1955; filmed as *Only Two Can Play,* 1962), had a similar anti-hero. A visit to Portugal resulted in the novel *I Like It Here* (1958), while observations garnered from a teaching stint in the United States were expressed in the novel *One Fat Englishman* (1963).

Moral quandaries usually involving sex occur with more or less prominence in his later novels, including *Take a Girl Like You* (1960); *The Anti-Death League* (1966); *I Want It Now* (1968); *The Green Man* (1969); *Girl, 20* (1971); and *Jake's Thing* (1979).

Amis and Amiles, chief characters in an Old French metrical romance, based on an older and widespread legend of friendship and sacrifice. In its simplest form the story tells of the knights Amis and Amiles and of their lifelong devotion to one another.

The tale, probably of Oriental origin, was introduced to the West by way of Byzantium and found its way into French literature through Latin (hence the characters' names: "Amicus" and "Amelius" in Latin). It became attached to the web of Charlemagne legends in the late 12th-century chanson de geste of *Amis et Amiles,* a poem that contains passages of great beauty, and later versions appeared in most European languages. The first version of the story in English was *Amis and Amiloun,* composed in the Midlands dialect late in the 13th century.

Amish, also called AMISH MENNONITE, member of a conservative Christian group in North America, primarily members of the Old Order Amish Mennonite Church. They originated in Europe as followers of Jakob Ammann, a 17th-century Mennonite elder whose teachings caused controversy and schism during the years 1693–97 among the Mennonites in Switzerland, Alsace (now in France), and south Germany. Ammann insisted that any Mennonite who had been excommunicated should be shunned or avoided by all other Mennonites and that anyone who told a falsehood should be excommunicated. He introduced washing of feet into the worship service and taught that church members should dress in a uniform manner, that beards should not be trimmed, and that it was wrong to attend services in a state church. Although Ammann subsequently sought reconciliation with the Mennonites who disagreed with him, he continued to insist that all who had been excommunicated should be avoided, and reconciliation attempts failed. Amish settlements and congregations existed in Switzerland, Alsace, Germany, Russia, and Holland, but migration to North America in the 19th and 20th centuries and assimilation with Mennonite groups gradually eliminated the Amish in Europe.

The Amish began migrating to North America around 1720 and first settled in eastern Pennsylvania, where a large settlement is still found. In the 20th century, Amish groups could be found in western Pennsylvania, Ohio, Indiana, central Illinois, Iowa, Nebraska, Kansas, and Ontario. Schisms and disruptions occurred after 1850 because of tensions between the "old order," or traditional Amish, and those who wished to adopt "new order" or progressive methods and organizations. During the next 50 years about two-thirds of the Amish either formed separate, small churches of their own or joined either the Mennonite Church or the General Conference Mennonite Church. *See* Mennonite.

Those who continued the characteristic life style of the Amish (see below) are primarily members of the Old Order Amish Mennonite Church. In the mid-1950s there were about 50 Old Order Amish settlements in the United States and Canada; the largest were located in Ohio, Pennsylvania, Indiana, Iowa, Illinois, and Kansas. Settlements are divided into church districts that are autonomous congregations composed of about 75 baptized members. If the district becomes much larger it is again divided because the members meet in each other's homes. There are no church buildings. Each district has a bishop, two to four preachers, and an elder; but there are no general conferences, mission groups, or cooperative agencies. The Amish differ little from the Mennonites in formal doctrine. Holy Communion is celebrated twice each year, and washing of feet is practiced by both groups. Adults are baptized when they are admitted to formal membership in the church at about age 17 to 20. Services are conducted in Palatine German with a mixture of English, commonly known as Pennsylvania Dutch.

The Amish are best known for their severely plain clothing and their nonconformed way of life. The men wear broadbrimmed black hats, beards—but not moustaches—and homemade plain clothes fastened with hooks and eyes instead of buttons. The women wear bonnets, long full dresses with capes over the shoulders, shawls, and black shoes and stockings. No jewelry of any kind is worn. This cultural nonconformity is thought by the Amish to be obedience to biblical strictures, but it is primarily the continuance of 17th-century European rural costume. The Amish also shun telephones and electric lights and drive horses and buggies rather than automobiles. They are generally considered excellent farmers, but they often refuse to use modern farm machinery. Children attend public elementary schools and are not sent to high schools. This practice has caused the Amish some difficulty because of compulsory school attendance laws, and some Amish parents have gone to jail rather than allow their children to go to high school.

Amisus (Turkey): *see* Samsun.

Amitābha (Sanskrit: Infinite Light), Japanese AMIDA, Chinese O-MI-T'O, in Buddhism, the great saviour deity worshipped principally by members of the Pure Land sect in Japan. As related in the *Sukhāvatī-vyūha-sūtra* (the fundamental scripture of the Pure Land sects), many ages ago a monk named Dharmākara made a number of vows, the 18th of which promised that, on his obtaining Buddhahood,

Great bronze Amida (Daibutsu) at Kamakura, Japan, 1252
Asuka-en

all those who believed in him and who called upon his name would be born into his paradise and would reside there in bliss until such time as they had obtained Nirvāṇa. Having accomplished his vows, the monk reigned as the Buddha Amitābha in the Western Paradise, called Sukhāvatī, the Pure Land.

The cult of Amitābha, which emphasizes faith above all else, came to the fore in China in about AD 650 and from there spread to Japan, where it led in the 12th and 13th centuries to the formation of the Pure Land school and the True Pure Land school, both of which continue to have large followings today. Depictions of the Western Paradise and of Amitābha descending to welcome the newly dead are beautifully expressed in the Raigō paintings of Japan's Late Heian Period (AD 897–1185).

Amitābha as a saviour figure was never as popular in Tibet and Nepal as he was in the Far East, but he is highly regarded in those countries as one of the five "self-born" Buddhas who have existed eternally (*see* Dhyāni-Buddha). According to this concept he manifested himself as the earthly Buddha Gautama and as the *bodhisattva* ("Buddha-to-be") Avalokiteśvara. His colour is red, his posture one of meditation (*dhyāna-mudrā*), his symbol the begging bowl, his mount the peacock, his consort Pāṇḍarā, his family Rāga, his element water, his sacred syllable "ba" or "āh," his *skandha* (element of existence) *saṇjnā* (perceptions of sense objects), his direction the west, his sense perception taste, his sense organ the tongue, his location in the human body the mouth.

As a bestower of longevity, Amitābha is called Amitāyus (Sanskrit: Infinite Life). In China and Japan the two names are often used interchangeably, but in Tibet the two forms are never confounded, and Amitāyus is worshipped in a special Lamaist ceremony for obtaining long life. He is depicted wearing ornaments and a crown and holding the ambrosia vase from which spill the jewels of eternal life. *See also* Amidism; Pure Land Buddhism.

Amitāyur-dhyāna-sūtra (Sanskrit: "Discourse Concerning Meditation on Amitāyus"), one of three texts basic to Pure Land Buddhism. Together with the larger and smaller *Sukhāvatī-vyūha-sūtras* (Sanskrit: "Description of the Western Paradise Sūtras"), this text envisions rebirth in the celestial Pure Land of Amitāyus, the Buddha of Infinite Life (virtually identical with Amitābha, "Infinite Light"; called Amida in Japan).

This *sūtra* presents 16 forms of meditation as means of reaching the Pure Land and concludes that even the most wicked can attain this paradise by invoking the name of Amitāyus. It contains many references to *bodhisattva*s, or Buddhas postponing final bliss in order to accomplish the salvation of men.

The *Amitāyur-dhyāna-sūtra* was translated into Chinese under the title *Kuan-wu liang-shou ching* in AD 424 and has inspired many Chinese commentaries. The Japanese version is entitled *Kammuryōju-kyō*. The Sanskrit original has since been lost.

Amiternum, in ancient Italy, a Sabine town five miles (eight kilometres) north of present L'Aquila in the Aterno Valley. It was stormed by the Romans in 293 BC, but the fertility of its fields helped it to regain its prosperity under the empire (after 27 BC). The Roman historian Sallust was born there in 86 BC.

Amiternum was located at the junction of four roads—the Via Caecilia, the Via Claudia Nova, and two branches of the Via Salaria. Archaeological remains include an aqueduct, an amphitheatre, and a theatre, all of the imperial period, and several Christian catacombs.

ʿAmm (Arabian god): *see* Ilumquh.

Amman, Arabic ʿAMMĀN, biblical Hebrew RABBAH, or RABBAT BENE ʿAMMON (the Great [or Capital] City of the Sons of Ammon), Greek PHILADELPHIA, capital of the Hashemite Kingdom of Jordan and of ʿAmmān *muḥāfaẓah* (governorate). By far the largest city of Jordan, it is the only one with a modern urban infrastructure. Amman is built on rolling hills at the eastern boundary of the Jabal ʿAjlūn mountains, on the small, partly perennial Wādī ʿAmmān and its tributaries.

As-Salṭ Street, a main thoroughfare, Amman, Jordan
Shostal/EB Inc.

Its focus of settlement throughout history has been the small, high triangular plateau (modern Jabal al-Qalʿah) just north of the wadi. Fortified settlements have existed there from remote antiquity; the earliest remains are of the Chalcolithic period (*c.* 4000–*c.* 3000 BC). Later, the city became capital of the Ammonites, a Semitic people frequently mentioned in the Bible; the biblical and modern names both trace back to "Ammon." The "royal city" taken by King David's general Joab (II Samuel 12:26) was probably the acropolis atop the plateau. King David sent Uriah the Hittite to his death in battle before the walls of the city so that he might marry his wife Bathsheba (II Sam. 11); the incident is also a part of Muslim folklore.

Rabbah declined in later centuries; conquered by Egypt's King Ptolemy II Philadelphus (ruled 285–246 BC), he renamed it Philadelphia after himself; the name was retained through Byzantine and Roman times. Philadelphia was a city of the Decapolis (Greek: Ten Cities), a Hellenistic league of the 1st century BC–2nd century AD. It was rebuilt by the Romans and some fine ruins of their rule remain.

At the rise of Islām, Amman was taken by the Arab general Yazīd ibn Abī Sufyān in AD 635; by about 1300 it had entirely disappeared from causes unknown to historians. In 1878 the Ottoman Turks resettled the site with Circassian refugees from Russia; it remained a small village until after World War I.

After the war Transjordan became part of the Palestine mandate, but the British government, as mandatory, effectively severed it from western Palestine (1921), and established a protected emirate of Transjordan, under the rule of Abdullah, son of Husayn ibn ʿAlī, then king of the Hejaz and *sharīf* of Mecca. Amman soon became capital of this new state; its modern development began in this period, and was accelerated by Jordanian independence (1946). The city grew rapidly; the urban area received a large influx of Palestinian Arab refugees after the Arab–Israeli War of 1948–49. The refugee problem became even more serious after the Six-Day War of 1967, when Jordan lost all its territories west of the Jordan River to Israel. Political conflict between the Jordanian government and rebellious Palestinian guerrillas erupted into open civil war in 1970 in the streets of Amman; although the government forces finally prevailed, the city was severely damaged.

Amman is Jordan's chief commercial, financial, and international trade centre. The royal palaces are to the east; the Parliament is in the western section. The University of Jordan (1962) is at Amman. Chief industries include food and tobacco processing, and manufacture of textiles, paper products, plastics, and aluminum utensils. On the city's outskirts are factories making electrical batteries and related products and cement. Amman is Jordan's chief transportation centre: two highways lead west toward Jerusalem, one of the city's main thoroughfares becomes the road to as-Salṭ, to the northwest. Jordan's main north–south highway, with its southern terminus at al-ʿAqabah port, runs through the city. Just east is Amman International Airport, near the tracks of the old Hejaz Railway. Sites of interest include the remains of the ancient citadel, the adjoining archaeological museum, and a large finely preserved Roman amphitheatre. Pop. (1979 prelim.) city, 623,925; (1981 est.) *muḥāfaẓah,* 1,281,900.

Amman, Jost (b. June 13, 1539, Zürich—d. March 17, 1591, Nürnberg), painter and printmaker, one of the most prolific and skilled book illustrators of the 16th century. His engraving of the poet-dramatist Hans Sachs testifies to his craftsmanship. In numerous drawings, such as "Entry of Maximilian II into Nürnberg in 1570," he revealed himself as a brilliant and witty recorder of contemporary events. His engravings include historical portraits, such as those of the kings of France; heraldic designs; title pages; and scenes of warfare, hunting, and pageantry. He also produced thousands of woodcuts for various works. One of the most notable was a book on the arts and crafts with poems by Hans Sachs entitled *Eygentliche Beschreibung aller Stände auff Erden* (1568; "Actual Description of All the Professions in the World").

Ammanford, industrial town, southern Dinefwr district, Dyfed County, Wales. Situated on an anthracite coalfield in close proximity to the major centres of industrial activity in South Wales, Ammanford grew rapidly as a mining centre in the late 19th century. Although the town is now the industrial centre of Dinefwr district, with hosiery, furniture, and precision-tool manufacturing, as well as coal mining, it is surrounded by agricultural land and unspoiled scenery rather than by industrial wasteland. The town's chapel was once a renowned school that educated many prominent men; it was run by the Rev. John Jenkins, who later became Archdruid of Wales. Pop. (1981 prelim.) 5,711.

Ammann, Othmar Herman (b. March 26, 1879, Schaffhausen, Switz.—d. Sept. 22, 1965, Rye, N.Y., U.S.), engineer and designer of numerous long suspension bridges, including the Verrazano-Narrows Bridge over New York harbour, at its completion (1965) the longest single span in the world.

In 1904 Ammann emigrated to the United States, where he helped design railroad bridges. Joining the Pennsylvania Steel Company the following year, he worked on the Queensboro Bridge, New York City. During his term (1912–23) as chief assistant to the noted bridge engineer Gustav Lindenthal, he helped design and build the Hell Gate (steel arch) Bridge, New York City, and the Ohio River Bridge, Sciotoville, Ohio.

In 1923 Ammann set up his own engineering firm in New York City, and the following year the Port of New York Authority agreed to finance his proposed bridge across the Hudson River between New Jersey and upper Manhattan. When finished in 1931, the George Washington Bridge was the longest in the world, almost double the length of the previous record holder.

Ammann was chief engineer of the Port of New York Authority from 1930 to 1937 and director of engineering from 1937 to 1939. In the former capacity he was in charge of building the Bayonne Bridge over the Kill van Kull, N.J., the Outerbridge Crossing and Goethals Bridge across Arthur Kill, and the Lincoln Tunnel under the Hudson River. In the latter capacity he directed the building of the Bronx-Whitestone Bridge and the Triborough Bridge, New York City. He also sat on the Board of Engineers in charge of San Francisco's Golden Gate Bridge, which opened in 1937.

In 1939 Ammann returned to private practice, designing bridges and highways in New Jersey and New York. He served on the three-man board that investigated the Tacoma Narrows Bridge aerodynamic failure in 1941. In partnership with Charles S. Whitney from 1946, Ammann designed the Throgs Neck Bridge, New York City, the Dulles International Airport, outside Washington, D.C., and three buildings for New York City's Lincoln Center for the Performing Arts.

Ammannati, Bartolommeo (b. June 18, 1511, Settignano, near Florence—d. April 22, 1592, Florence), sculptor and architect, a principal participant in the final flowering of Florentine culture under the Medicis.

Ammannati began his career as a sculptor; he was responsible for the Neptune fountain in the Piazza della Signoria, Florence. He trained as an architect under Jacopo Sansovino in Venice, working with him on the Libreria Sansoviana.

He was called to Rome in 1550 by Pope Julius III on the advice of Giorgio Vasari, an architect who was the chief historian and biographer of the Renaissance. Ammannati's most important work there was in collaboration with Vasari and Giacomo da Vignola on the villa of Pope Julius, the Villa Giulia (begun 1551). The rusticated stonework of the villa, unusual in Roman domestic architecture, prefigured Ammannati's later works.

Cosimo de' Medici (Cosimo I) brought Ammannati back to Florence in 1555; he was to spend almost all of his remaining career in service to the Medicis. His first commission was to finish the Laurentian Library, begun by Michelangelo. Ammannati interpreted a clay model sent him by Michelangelo in 1558 to produce the especially impressive staircase, leading from the *ricetto,* or vestibule, into the library proper.

"Doris," detail from the "Fountain of Neptune," executed from Bartolommeo Ammannati's model by Andrea Calamech, 1563–75; in Piazza della Signoria, Florence

Alinari—Art Resource/EB Inc.

Ammannati's masterpiece in Florence is the Palazzo Pitti, where, beginning in 1560, he enlarged the basic structure by Filippo Brunelleschi, designing a courtyard and facade opening onto the Boboli Gardens, which Ammannati had a part in designing. The entirely rusticated facade of the palace is very unusual, in that the crudely dressed surface—meant to suggest the naturalness of rough-hewn stone—was usually confined to the lowest story of a building. At the Palazzo Pitti it provides an appropriately rural yet impressive backdrop for the gardens.

The Ponte a Santa Trinità (1567–69), Ammannati's other major work in Florence, is noted for its three graceful arches. In a famous letter of 1582, Ammannati, under Jesuit influence, addressed the Academy of Design, repudiating the "freedom" shown in his earlier works. This document signalled a constriction of artistic activity under the Counter-Reformation and prefigured the end of the humanistic Renaissance spirit.

Ammassalik, also spelled ANGMAGSSALIK, town, southeastern Greenland, on the south coast of Ammassalik Island. The island is 25 mi (40 km) long and 12–20 mi wide, with a high point of 4,336 ft (1,322 m). Although Europeans landed as early as 1472, the region was not explored until 1884, when Gustav Holm, a Dane, mapped the coast. A trading and mission station was established in 1895 to help sustain the Greenlandic (Eskimo) population, which had been declining, with imported food and firearms for hunting. It was named for a fish called *angmagssat* (capelin) found in coastal waters. A weather and radio station is located there. Pop. (1982) 1,228.

Cotton grass flowering at the foot of the mountains near Ammassalik, Greenland

Art Resource—EB Inc.

Ammers-Küller, Jo(hanna) van (b. Aug. 13, 1884, Noordeloos, Neth.—d. Jan. 23, 1966, Bakel), Dutch writer best known for her historical novels.

Van Ammers-Küller began her writing career as a playwright. Her first successful novels, *Het huis der vreugden* (1922; *The House of Joy,* 1924) and *Jenny Huysten* (1923; *Jenny Huysten's Career,* 1930), deal with life in and around the theatre and draw on her experiences as a dramatist in London (1912–21). In 1925 *De opstandigen* (*The Rebel Generation,* 1928), her most successful novel, was published. It presents the struggle of three generations of women in the Coornvelt family for equality with men and against the strictures of their Calvinist environment.

With the publication and translation of *De opstandigen,* van Ammers-Küller's reputation grew, and she was invited to lecture in London and Hamburg. The family saga was a form that particularly suited her, and she wrote several more historical novels, including the trilogy *Heren, knechten, en vrouwen* (1934–38, retitled *De Tavelincks; The House of Tavelinck,* 1938), the story of an aristocratic family of Amsterdam set from 1778 to 1815; *Elzelina* (1940), the fictionalized biography of a Dutch woman set from 1776 to 1845; and *Ma* (1943), a family chronicle set from 1871 to 1901.

Van Ammers-Küller continued to write throughout the 1940s and '50s, but her pro-German stand during World War II contributed to the waning of her popularity and she never regained her literary reputation.

ammeter, instrument for measuring either direct or alternating electric currents. Ammeters can measure a wide range of current values because at high values only a small portion of the current is directed through the meter mechanism; a shunt in parallel with the meter carries the major portion.

Ammeters vary in their operating principles and accuracies. The D'Arsonval movement ammeter measures direct current with accuracies of from 0.1 to 2.0 percent. The electrodynamic ammeter uses a moving coil rotating in the field produced by a fixed coil. It measures direct and alternating current with accuracies of from 0.1 to 0.25 percent. In the thermal ammeter, used primarily to measure alternating current with accuracies of from 0.5 to 3 percent, the measured current heats a thermoconverter (thermocouple); the small voltage thus generated is used to power a millivoltmeter. Digital ammeters, with no moving parts, use a circuit such as the dual slope integrator to convert a measured analogue (continuous) current to its digital equivalent. Many digital ammeters have accuracies better than 0.1 percent.

Ammianus Marcellinus (b. *c.* 330, Antioch, Syria—d. 395, Rome), last major Roman historian, whose work continued the history of the later Roman Empire to 378.

Born of a noble Greek family, Ammianus served in the army of Constantius II in Gaul and Persia. He fought against the Persians under Julian the Apostate and took part in the retreat of his successor, Jovian. Leaving the army at Antioch, he travelled to Egypt and Greece, eventually settling in Rome. There he wrote his Latin history of the Roman Empire from the accession of Nerva to the death of Valens, thus continuing the work of Tacitus.

This history, *Rerum gestarum libri* ("The Chronicles of Events"), consisted of 31 books, of which only the last 18, covering the years 353–378, survive. It is a clear, comprehensive account of events by a writer of soldierly qualities, independent judgment, and wide reading. Roman history no longer turned on the city of Rome but was played out in the various theatres of imperial policy from west to east. Drawing upon his own experience, Ammianus gives vivid pictures of the empire's economic and social problems.

A pagan who was religiously tolerant, he took a detached view of the intellectual trends of the day. His judgment in political affairs was limited only by his own straightforward attitude. He used the regular techniques of later Roman historiography: rhetoric in his speeches, ethnographical digressions in descriptions, such as that of the culture of the Huns, and biographical conventions in character sketches along with fondness for literary allusion, overabundant metaphor, and much ornament. In conscious imitation of Tacitus, he wrote with vivid and striking dramatic power.

Ammókhostos (Cyprus): *see* Famagusta.

Ammon (Egyptian god): *see* Amon.

ammonia (NH_3), colourless, pungent gas composed of nitrogen and hydrogen. It is the simplest stable compound of these elements and serves as a starting material for the production of many commercially important nitrogen compounds.

Ammonia is highly soluble in water, forming an alkaline solution called ammonium hydroxide. Moreover, it becomes highly reactive when dissolved in water and readily combines with many chemicals. Ammonia is easily liquefied by compression or by cooling to about −33° C (−27.4° F). In returning to the gaseous state, it absorbs substantial amounts of heat from its surroundings (*i.e.,* one gram of ammonia absorbs more than 325 calories of heat). Because of this property, it is frequently employed as a coolant in refrigerating and air-conditioning equipment.

Large quantities of ammonia are produced commercially by the Haber process (*q.v.*), which involves the direct synthesis of the compound from its constituent elements. Ammonia from the Haber process is supplemented by ammonia obtained as a by-product of coke ovens—about three kilograms are released per ton of coal.

Appreciable amounts of ammonia are used in agriculture. Some of it is applied directly to the soil from tanks containing the liquefied gas. Additional quantities are converted into ammonium nitrate, ammonium phosphate, and other salts that also are utilized primarily in commercial fertilizers. In the textile industry ammonia is used in the manufacture of synthetic fibres such as nylon and rayon. In addition, it is employed in the dyeing and scouring of cotton, wool, and silk. Ammonia serves as a catalyst in the production of Bakelite and some other synthetic resins. More importantly, it neutralizes acidic by-products of petroleum refining, and in the rubber industry it prevents the coagulation of raw latex during transportation from plantation to factory.

Ammonia also finds application in a widely used method for producing soda ash known as the Solvay, or ammonia–soda, process. Large quantities are utilized in various metallurgical processes, including the nitriding of alloy sheets to harden their surfaces. Because ammonia can be decomposed easily to yield hydrogen, it is a convenient portable source of atomic hydrogen for welding. Finally, among its minor uses is inclusion in certain household cleansing agents.

ammonia–soda process, also called SOLVAY PROCESS, modern method of manufacturing the industrial alkali sodium carbonate, also known as soda ash, devised and first put to commercial use by Ernest Solvay, who built a plant in 1865 in Couillet, Belg. The process was improved in the 1870s by the German-born British chemist Ludwig Mond.

In the ammonia–soda process, common salt, sodium chloride, is treated with ammonia and then carbon dioxide, under carefully controlled conditions, to form sodium bicarbonate and ammonium chloride. When heated, the bicarbonate yields sodium carbonate, the desired product; the ammonium chloride is treated with lime to produce ammonia for reuse and calcium chloride.

For some years after its introduction, the ammonia–soda process encountered stiff competition from the older Leblanc process (*q.v.*), but it ultimately prevailed because it produced soda ash more cheaply.

Ammonite, member of an ancient Semitic people whose principal city was Rabbath Ammon, in Palestine. The "sons of Ammon" were in perennial, though sporadic, conflict with the Israelites. After a long period of semi-nomadic existence, the Ammonites established a kingdom north of Moab in the 13th century BC. With difficulty, their fortress capital was captured by David. An Ammonite woman, one of many foreigners taken into Solomon's harem, was responsible for inducing the King to worship the Ammonite god Malcom.

During the reign of Jehoiakim (6th century BC), the Ammonites allied themselves with the Chaldeans, Syrians, and others in an attack on Judah and also harassed the Israelites when they attempted to rebuild the Temple of Jerusalem after the Babylonian Exile. In the 2nd century BC they were defeated by Judas Maccabeus.

ammonium chloride (NH_4Cl), also called SAL AMMONIAC, the salt of ammonia and hydrogen chloride. Its principal use is as an electrolyte in dry cells, and it is also extensively employed as a constituent of galvanizing, tinning, and soldering fluxes to remove oxide coatings from metals and thereby improve the adhesion of the solders. It is a component of many proprietary cold medicines and cough remedies.

Ammonium chloride is a colourless, crystalline substance. It is highly soluble in water, readily forming a slightly acidic solution. It vaporizes without melting at 340° C (644° F) to form equal volumes of ammonia and hydrogen chloride. Ammonium chloride is yielded as a by-product in the ammonia–soda process for making sodium carbonate. It also is produced by reaction of ammonium sulfate and sodium chloride solutions.

ammonium hydroxide, also called AQUA AMMONIA, solution of ammonia gas in water, a common commercial form of ammonia. It is a colourless liquid with a strong characteristic odour. In concentrated form, it can cause burns on contact with the skin; ordinary household ammonia, used as a cleanser, is dilute ammonium hydroxide.

The water solution is generally represented by the formula NH_4OH. Actually, no appreciable amount of the molecular species NH_4OH is present: the solution consists primarily of large quantities of water and ammonia (NH_3) and smaller quantities of ammonium ion, NH_4^+, and hydroxide ion, OH^-.

ammonium nitrate (NH_4NO_3), a salt of ammonia and nitric acid, used widely in fertilizers and explosives. The commercial grade contains about 33.5 percent nitrogen, all of which is in forms utilizable by plants; it is the most common nitrogenous component of artificial fertilizers. It is employed to modify the detonation rate of other explosives, such as nitroglycerin in the so-called ammonia dynamites, or as an oxidizing agent in the ammonals, which are mixtures of ammonium nitrate and powdered aluminum.

Ammonium nitrate is a colourless, crystalline substance (melting point 169.6° C [337.3° F]). It is highly soluble in water; heating of the water solution decomposes the salt to nitrous oxide (laughing gas). Solid ammonium nitrate can undergo explosive decomposition when heated in a confined space. Government regulations have been imposed on the shipment and storage of ammonium nitrate to minimize the likelihood of disastrous explosions such as those that occurred at Oppau, now in W.Ger. (1921), and Texas City, Texas (1947).

Ammonius HERMIAE (fl. *c.* 550), Greek philosopher whose thinking was primarily oriented toward logic and the sciences; he spent a good part of his intellectual life in writing critical works on Aristotle. As a student, he worked closely with Proclus, and later in life was appointed the head of the Alexandrian school. His major commentaries, on the *Categoriae* and *Analytica priora* of Aristotle's *Organon,* were well respected and closely studied down to the time of the Renaissance. He also wrote on some of the physical treatises of Aristotle.

ammonoid, any of a group of extinct cephalopods, forms related to the modern pearly nautilus, that are frequently found as fossils in marine rocks of Devonian to Cretaceous age (between 65,000,000 and 395,000,000 years old). The ammonoids were shelled forms, many predacious in habit. Ammonoid shells, which are either straight or coiled, served as protective and supportive structures as well as hydrostatic devices, enabling the animal to compensate for varying water depths. Ammonoids are characterized and distinguished from nautiloids by the highly crenulated and complex suture that occurs where internal partitioning walls come in contact with the outer shell wall. Ammonoids are important index fossils because of their wide geographic distribution in shallow marine waters, rapid evolution, and easily recognizable features. Three groups of ammonoids succeeded one another through time, each group having a more complex suture pattern. Ammonoids with a simple suture pattern, called goniatite, flourished during the Paleozoic Era (about 225,000,000 to 570,000,000 years ago). Ammonoids characterized by a more highly folded suture, called ceratite, replaced the goniatites, and were most abundant in the Triassic Period (about 190,000,000 to 225,000,000 years ago). Most ammonoid genera became extinct at the end of that period, but a few survived and evolved into many diverse forms during the Cretaceous Period (about 65,000,000 to 136,000,000 years ago). These forms are characterized by a complex interwoven suture called the ammonite pattern.

Polished cross section of a Middle Jurassic ammonoid from southern France; in the Eichstätt Museum, Eichstätt, W. Ger.

Lilly Stunzi-Zurich-New York

ammunition, the projectiles and their propelling charges for small arms, artillery, and other guns. Rockets and guided missiles are sometimes classified as artillery ammunition, although they are not ordinarily launched from cannon.

A brief treatment of ammunition follows. For full treatment, *see* MACROPAEDIA: War, The Technology of.

In general, cartridges whose projectile elements are less than 25 millimetres (one inch) in diameter are classified as small arms ammunition, whereas the larger calibres are classified as artillery ammunition. In the first category, all components of a single round are commonly assembled into a compact unit which includes a metal or metal-and-cardboard case housing the powder, a projectile (affixed to one end of this case), and a primer (inserted in the other end). Artillery ammunition is likewise so assembled in the lesser calibres and is then known as fixed ammunition, as contrasted with semifixed which, though loaded into the gun as a unit, embodies a missile which may, in order to adjust the propelling charge, be detached from the case and its contents. A third and final type, as commonly employed in pieces of medium and large bore, is separate-loading ammunition wherein powder, primer, and missile are not brought together until placed in the gun from which fired, the propellant being supplied in one or more cloth bags or some other container. Here the naked projectile is first rammed into the chamber, to be followed by the bag or bags of powder, after which the primer is separately inserted into its seat in the breechblock. (Or the bags may be assembled into a preprimed case, in which instance the cartridge thereupon assumes characteristics approaching those of the semifixed type.) The combination—in no matter what form (fixed, semifixed, or separate-loading) of one full set of elements (powder, projectile, primer) necessary for a single firing of a piece to which adapted—is known as a complete round.

The introduction of instruments employing gunpowder to project missiles dates from early in the 14th century, and Berthold Schwartz, a monk of Freiburg, Ger., is credited with their invention. The necessary propellant (black powder) had been described a full half century earlier by another cleric, the English friar Roger Bacon, but he apparently remained unaware of its manifold military applications. The first ordnance projectiles were obviously adaptations of those already used in contemporary weapons (crossbow and longbow), being nothing more nor less than iron darts feathered with brass, their shafts wrapped with stuffings of leather to lessen leakage of powder gases.

The next weapons were primitive cannon that fired such ammunition as balls of stone or metal or sometimes several projectiles at once. By the 16th century, explosive ammunition was used in the form of hollow balls filled with gunpowder. Linked balls joined by a length of chain or a bar were used to damage the rigging of ships: they were called grapeshot.

In the mid-18th century rifled ammunition was developed, with helical grooves cut into the inside of a gun barrel to give a spin to the projectile. This greatly improved its accuracy. In the early 19th century, percussion ignition for hand-held weapons came into use, a great improvement over the flintlock musket. Breech-loading cannon and small arms came into use not long after, with all components of the ammunition carried in one cartridge case, which was simply shoved into the breech before firing.

The development of smokeless powder was a major milestone in the history of ammunition in the late 19th century. Not only did it have three times the energy of gunpowder but it reduced telltale flash and smoke and proved to have greater stability in storage over extended periods of time.

Ammunition for modern weapons has many complexities. Different levels of energy and different rates of burning may be achieved with modern explosives.

Specialized forms of ammunition include tracer bullets, which leave a visible light trail on their way to the target; incendiary ammunition, used for setting fires; and armour-piercing shells (used against tanks or other armoured vehicles), which have a specially shaped charge to aid in burning through armour and then exploding inside.

amnesia, loss of memory as a result of brain injury or deterioration, shock, fatigue, senility, drug use, alcoholism, anesthesia, illness, or psychoneurotic reaction. Amnesia may be anterograde, in which events following causative trauma or disease are forgotten; or retrograde, in which events preceding the causative event are forgotten.

The condition can often be traced to some severe emotional shock, in which case personal memories (*e.g.,* identity), rather than less personal material (*e.g.,* language skills), are affected. Such amnesia seems to represent a psychoneurotic escape from or denial of memories that might cause anxiety, an example of repression or motivated forgetting. These memories are not actually lost, since they can generally be recovered under hypnosis or after the amnesic state has ended.

Occasionally amnesia may last for weeks, months, or even years, during which time the person may begin an entirely new life pattern. Such protracted reactions are called fugue states. When recovered, the person is usually able to remember events that occurred prior to onset, but events of the fugue period are forgotten. Posthypnotic amnesia, the forgetting of most or all events that occur while under hypnosis in response to a suggestion by the hypnotist, has long been regarded as a sign of deep hypnosis.

The common difficulty of remembering childhood experiences is sometimes referred to as childhood amnesia.

amnesty, in criminal law, sovereign act of oblivion or forgetfulness (Greek *amnēsia*) for past acts, granted by a government to persons who have been guilty of crimes. It is often conditional upon their return to obedience and duty within a prescribed period. Amnesty is granted usually for political crimes against the state, such as treason, sedition, or rebellion. It is addressed generally to classes or communities and takes the form of a legislative act or other constitutional or statutory act of the supreme power of the state. Thus in 1865 Pres. Andrew Johnson issued a proclamation granting full pardon to all former Confederates (except certain leaders) who would take an unqualified oath of allegiance to the United States. Technically, however, an amnesty differs from a general pardon in that the latter simply relieves from punishment whereas the former declares innocence or abolishes the crime.

Amnesty International (AI), international organization headquartered in London which seeks to inform public opinion about violations of human rights, especially the abridgements of freedom of speech and of religion and the imprisonment and torture of political dissidents, and which actively seeks the release of political prisoners and the relief, when necessary, of their families. In 1977 Amnesty International was awarded the Nobel Prize for Peace.

The organization was founded in London on May 28, 1961, through the principal efforts of Peter Benenson, who had been a defense lawyer for political prisoners in Hungary, South Africa, and Spain and who sought to establish a collective agency for the advancement of human rights. From 1961 to 1975 the chairman of AI's International Executive Committee was Seán MacBride (recipient of the 1974 Nobel Prize for Peace). Five years after its birth, AI was operating on an annual budget of only £25,000 and a staff of eight full-time workers. Twenty years later it had a budget of more than £2,000,000, an international secretariat of 150 persons, national "sections," or offices, in more than 40 countries, and about 200,000 individual members in some 100 countries.

Aside from generally publicizing governmental wrongdoing in newsletters, annual reports, and background papers, AI relies strongly on the worldwide distribution of "adoption groups," each of which, manned by three to eight persons, takes on a limited number of cases of "prisoners of conscience" and barrages the offending government with letters of protest until the prisoners are released. The research department at London headquarters, in contact with human-rights activists and other interested parties around the world, provides the network of information for all the organization's activities.

Amnesty International's logo is a burning candle wrapped in barbed wire.

amnion, in reptiles, birds, and mammals, a membrane forming a fluid-filled cavity (the amniotic sac) that encloses the embryo. The amniotic sac and the fluid it contains are sometimes referred to as the bag of waters.

In development, the amnion arises by a folding of a mass of extra-embryonic tissue called the somatopleure. Lined with ectoderm and covered with mesoderm (both are germ layers), the amnion contains a thin, transparent fluid in which the embryo is suspended, thus providing a cushion against mechanical injury. The amnion also provides protection against fluid loss from the embryo itself and against tissue adhesions.

Amnok-kang (China): *see* Yalu River.

amodiaquin, also called CAMOQUIN, synthetic antimalarial drug introduced into medicine in the 1940s. A derivative of quinoline, amodiaquin is administered orally as its hydrochloride. It inhibits the development of the malarial parasites *Plasmodium vivax* and *P. falciparum* in the erythrocytic stage, in which they circulate in the bloodstream inside the red blood cells of the host. Possible side effects include nausea, vomiting, and diarrhea.

Consult the INDEX *first*

amoeba, also spelled AMEBA, plural AMOEBAS, or AMOEBAE, any of the microscopic unicellular protozoans of the rhizopodan order Amoebida. The well-known type species, *Amoeba proteus,* is found on decaying bottom vegetation of freshwater streams and ponds. There are numerous parasitic amoebas. Of six species found in the human alimentary tract, *Entamoeba histolytica* causes amebic dysentery (*see* Entamoeba). Two related free-living genera of increasing biomedical importance are *Acanthamoeba* and *Naegleria,* strains of which have been recognized as disease-causing parasites in several vertebrates, including humans.

Amoebas are identified by their ability to form temporary cytoplasmic extensions called pseudopodia, or false feet, by means of which they move about. This type of movement, called amoeboid movement, is considered to be the most primitive form of animal locomotion.

Amoebas are used extensively in cell research for determining the relative functions and interactions of the nucleus and the cytoplasm. Each amoeba contains a small mass of jellylike cytoplasm, which is differentiated into a thin outer plasma membrane, a layer of stiff, clear ectoplasm just within the plasma membrane, and a central granular endoplasm. The endoplasm contains food vacuoles, a granular nucleus, and a clear contractile vacuole. The amoeba has no mouth or anus; food is taken in and material excreted at any point on the cell surface. During feeding, extensions of cytoplasm flow around food particles, surrounding them and forming a vacuole into which enzymes are secreted to digest the particles. Oxygen diffuses into the cell from the surrounding water, and metabolic wastes diffuse from the amoeba into the surrounding water. A contractile vacuole, which removes excess water from the amoeba, is absent in most marine and parasitic species. Reproduction is asexual (binary fission).

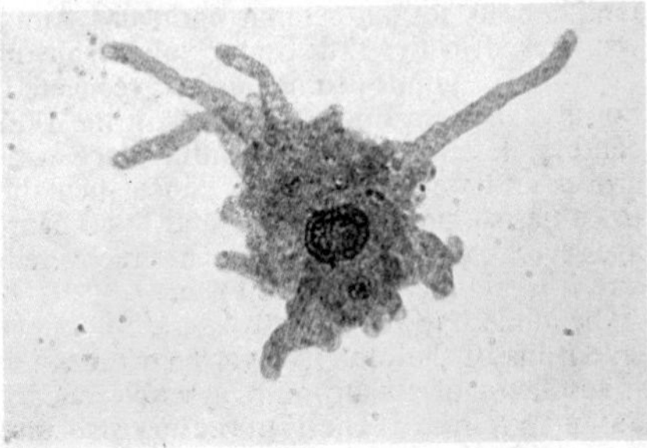

Amoeba (magnified)
Russ Kinne—Photo Researchers

During adverse environmental periods many amoebas survive by encystment: the amoeba becomes circular, loses most of its water, and secretes a cyst membrane that serves as a protective covering. When the environment is again suitable, the envelope ruptures, and the amoeba emerges.

amoebean verse, a device used in classical Greek and Latin bucolic or pastoral poetry in which couplets or stanzas are sung alternately by two characters. Usually, this takes the form of a contest, in which each singer attempts to surpass the other. The device was developed by Theocritus (*q.v.*) in some of his *Idylls* and by Virgil in the third and seventh *Eclogues* and was widely used thereafter—*e.g.,* by Horace in Book III, number 9, of the *Odes.*

Amoghasiddhi (Sanskrit: Unfailing Success), in Mahāyāna Buddhism, one of the five "self-born" Buddhas. *See* Dhyāni-Buddha.

Āmol, also spelled AMUL, town, central Māzandarān *ostān* (province), northern Iran, on the Harhāz River. The exact date of the founding of the town is unknown and enshrouded in legend, but it is certain that there has been a town on the site since Sāsānian times. During the Sāsānian period, the district of Āmol, together with the neighbouring district of Gīlān, formed a Nestorian Christian

Mausoleum of Buaurjmihr, Āmol, Iran
Colin Wyatt—Photo Researchers

episcopate. After the Arab conquest in the 8th century, the town became an important trading and scholarly centre, and it was the capital of the ʿAbbāsid province of Ṭabaristān, famous for its ceramic industry. Āmol was sacked in the 11th century and again in the 14th by Timur (Tamerlane). It recovered, however, and an English traveller in the 17th century described it as a fruitful place with groves and well-built houses. Since then the town has suffered earthquake and flood damage several times but each time has recovered, and it is still a considerable town.

The modern town is slightly east of the extensive ruins of the old city, which includes the mausoleum of Buzurjmihr, a semilegendary Sāsānian minister. The 17th-century structure is built on the foundations of a 10th-century one, which was destroyed by Timur. Oranges and rice are grown in the area, and there are nearby deposits of coal and iron. Pop. (1976) 68,782.

Amon, also spelled AMUN, AMEN, or AMMON, Egyptian deity revered as king of the gods. Amon was originally a local deity at Khmun in Middle Egypt; his cult reached Thebes, where he became the patron of the pharaohs in the reign of Amenemhet I (1991–1961 BC). At about that time he also became identified with the sun god Re of Heliopolis and, as

Amon, bronze statue, *c.* 750–*c.* 550 BC; in the Brooklyn Museum
By courtesy of the Brooklyn Museum

Amon-Re, was received as a national god. Represented in human form, sometimes with a ram's head, or as a ram, Amon-Re was worshipped as part of the Theban triad including a wife, Mut, and adopted son, Khons.

Amon's name meant The Hidden One, and his image was painted blue to denote invisibility. This attribute of invisibility led to a popular belief during the New Kingdom (1567–1085 BC) in the omniscience and impartiality of Amon, making him a god for the poor and oppressed.

Nevertheless, Amon's influence was also closely linked to the political well-being of Egypt; during the Hyksos domination (1674–1567 BC) the princes of Thebes sustained his worship. Following their victory over the Hyksos and the creation of an empire, Amon's stature and the wealth of his temples grew. In the late 18th dynasty the pharaoh Akhenaton directed his religious reform primarily against the cult of Amon, but he failed to convert the common people from their belief in Amon and the other gods, and under Tutankhamen, Ay, and Horemheb (*c.* 1361–1320 BC) Amon was gradually restored as the god of the empire and patron of the pharaoh.

In the 19th dynasty (1320–1200 BC) the speculations of the theologians among Amon's priests led to the concept of Amon as part of a trinity (with Ptah and Re), and as a single god in whom all the other gods, even Ptah and Re, were manifested. Under the sacerdotal state ruled by the priests of Amon at Thebes (1085–945 BC), Amon evolved into a universal god whose authority extended beyond Egypt.

The emergence of a Libyan dynasty (the 22nd), the invasion of Egypt by Assyria (671–663 BC), and the sack of Thebes (664/63 BC) did not reduce the stature of the cult in Egypt, for it had become a focus for Egyptian nationalism. Moreover, the worship of Amon had become established among the Cushites of Nubia who were hailed as heroes by Egyptian worshippers of Amon when they invaded Egypt and ruled as the 25th dynasty (712–671 BC). From this period onward resistance to foreign occupation of Egypt was strongest in Thebes, and Amon's cult spread to the oases, especially Siwa in Egypt's western desert, where Amon was linked with Jupiter. Alexander the Great won acceptance as pharaoh by consulting the oracle at Siwa, and he also embellished Amon's temple at Luxor. The early Ptolemaic rulers contained Egyptian nationalism by supporting the temples, but starting with Ptolemy IV Philopator in 217 BC nationalistic rebellions in Upper Egypt erupted. After suppressing one of these revolts, Ptolemy IX Soter II sacked Thebes during the revolt of 88–85 BC, dealing Amon's cult a severe blow. In 27 BC a strong earthquake devastated the Theban temples, and in the Greco-Roman world, the cult of Isis and Osiris gradually displaced Amon.

Amontons, Guillaume (b. Aug. 31, 1663, Paris—d. Oct. 11, 1705, Paris), physicist and inventor of scientific instruments, best known for his work on friction and temperature measurement.

Amontons is often credited with having discovered the laws of friction (1699), though in fact his work dealt solely with static friction—*i.e.,* the friction of objects at rest. It was only after Isaac Newton formulated his laws of motion that the friction of moving bodies was analyzed.

Amontons also developed an air-pressure thermometer (1702) and published two notable papers on thermometry (1702–03). He devised a method of measuring a change in temperature in terms of a proportional change in pressure of a constant mass and volume of air. This method eventually led to the concept of the absolute zero of temperature in the 19th century.

amora (Hebrew and Aramaic: "interpreter, speaker, reciter"), plural AMORAIM, in ancient times, a Jewish scholar attached to one of several academies in Palestine (Tiberias, Sepphoris, Caesarea) or in Babylonia (Nehardea, Sura, Pumbedita). The *amoraim* collaborated in writing the Gemara, collected interpretations of and commentaries on the Mishna (the authoritative code of Jewish oral laws) and on its critical marginal notes, called Tosefta (Addition). The *amoraim* were thus the successors of earlier Jewish scholars (*tannaim*), who produced the Mishna and were themselves the creators of the Talmud (the Mishna accompanied by the Gemara). Writing in various Aramaic dialects interspersed with Hebrew, the two groups of *amoraim* began work about AD 200 on the Gemara section of the Talmud. Because the Babylonian *amoraim* worked about a century longer than their counterparts in Palestine, completing their work about AD 500, the *Talmud Bavli* (Babylonian Talmud) was more comprehensive and, consequently, more authoritative than the *Talmud Yerushalmi* (Palestinian Talmud), which lacks the Babylonian interpretations. In Palestine an ordained *amora* was called a rabbi; in Babylonia, a *rav*, or *mar*. *See also* Gemara.

Amorbach, city, Bayern *Land* (Bavaria state), southwestern West Germany, in the Odenwald (wooded upland), southwest of Würzburg. It originated around a Benedictine monastery in the 8th century and came under the jurisdiction of the electors of Mainz in 1272. It became the residence of the princes of Leiningen in 1803 and passed to Bavaria in 1816. Its most notable buildings are 18th-century Baroque and Rococo in style, including the palace of the princes (the former abbey), the abbey church, and the parish church of St. Gangolf. Amorbach is a health resort and has woodworking and textile industries. Pop. (1983 est.) 4,299.

Amorgós Island, modern Greek NÍSOS AMORGÓS, island trending northeast–southwest in the Cyclades (Kikládhes) group of the Greek Aegean Islands. For the most part mountainous and narrow, it has an area of about 47 sq mi (121 sq km). Prosperous in the early Bronze Age, in classical times it had three cities, Arcesine, Minoa, and Aegiale. The island produced *amorgina,* fine transparent fabrics made from locally grown flax or cotton. It was used by the Romans as a place for exiles. Today it supports a dwindling agricultural community, chiefly in the Katápola Plain, which has the only good anchorage for visitors. The principal village is Amorgós (Chora) on the southern coast. There are also two ports on the north coast, Katápola and Aiyiáli (Hagios Nicolaos). The latter is situated near the ruins of ancient Amorgós, about 9 mi (14 km) from modern Amorgós. Pop. (1981) 1,718.

Amorite, member of an ancient Semitic-speaking people who dominated the history of Mesopotamia, Syria, and Palestine from *c.* 2000 to *c.* 1600 BC. In the oldest cuneiform sources (*c.* 2400–*c.* 2000 BC), the Amorites were equated with the West, though their true place of origin was most likely Arabia, not Syria. They were troublesome nomads and were believed to be one of the causes of the downfall of the 3rd dynasty of Ur (*c.* 2112–*c.* 2004 BC).

During the 2nd millennium BC the Akkadian term Amurru referred not only to an ethnic group but also to a language and to a geographical and political unit in Syria and Palestine. At the beginning of the millennium, a large-scale migration of great tribal federations from Arabia resulted in the occupation of Babylonia proper, the mid-Euphrates region, and Syria–Palestine. They set up a mosaic of small kingdoms and rapidly assimilated the Sumero-Akkadian culture. It is possible that this group was connected with the Amorites mentioned in earlier sources; some scholars, however, prefer to call this second group Eastern Canaanites, or Canaanites.

Almost all of the local kings in Babylonia (such as Hammurabi of Babylon) belonged to this stock. One capital was at Mari (modern Tall al-Ḥarīrī, Syria). Farther west, the political centre was Ḥalab (Aleppo); in that area, as well as in Palestine, the newcomers were thoroughly mixed with the Hurrians. The region then called Amurru was northern Palestine, with its centre at Hazor, and the neighbouring Syrian desert.

In the dark age between *c.* 1600 and *c.* 1100 BC, the language of the Amorites disappeared from Babylonia and the mid-Euphrates; in Syria and Palestine, however, it became dominant. In Assyrian inscriptions from *c.* 1100 BC on, the term Amurru designated part of Syria and the whole of Phoenicia and Palestine but no longer referred to any specific kingdom, language, or population.

Amorite language, one of the most ancient of the archaic Semitic languages, distributed in an area that is now northern Syria. Amorite is known almost exclusively from glosses and names, and the only known grammar is the grammar of names. Despite the unknown linguistic characteristics, Amorite is dated from the known chronology of proper names of the period in the last century of the 3rd millennium BC. It was probably the language of the semi-nomads of the West Semitic area and is sometimes called East Canaanite. As a Northern Central Semitic language, Amorite is affiliated with the Hamito-Semitic family of languages.

Amoroso Lima, Alceu, pseudonym TRISTÃO DE ATAÍDE (b. Dec. 11, 1893, Rio de Janeiro), essayist, philosopher, and literary critic, a leading force in the Neo-Catholic intellectual movement in Brazil. He was also an enthusiastic supporter of the Modernist cultural movement of the 1920s.

Amoroso Lima's multifaceted career included positions as professor of sociology, law, and literature, university president, literary critic for the *Jornal do Brasil* and numerous other periodicals, and director of the Cultural Division of the Pan American Union in Washington, D.C. (1951–53). He was a founder of the Agir Publishing House (1944), received an honorary doctorate from Catholic University, Washington, D.C., and was elected to the Brazilian Academy of Letters (1935). In 1957 he co-founded the Latin American Christian Democrat Movement.

Examples of his varied publications are *Contra-revolução espiritual* (1932; "The Spiritual Counter-Revolution"), *Problema da burguesia* (1932; "The Problem of the Bourgeoisie"), *Mitos de nosso tempo* (1943; "Myths of Our Time"), *Humanismo pedagógico* (1944; "Pedagogical Humanism"), an exposition of Christian humanism, and *Revolução, reação ou reforma* (1964; "Revolution, Reaction, or Reform").

amortization, in finance, the systematic repayment of a debt; in accounting, the systematic writing off of some account over a period of years.

An example of the first meaning is a mortgage on a home that may be repaid in monthly installments that include interest and a gradual reduction of the principal obligation. Such systematic annual reduction increases the safety factor for the investor by imposing a small annual burden rather than a single, large, final obligation.

In the second sense, the amortization of an asset, such as a building, a machine, or a mine, over its estimated life has the effect of reducing its balance-sheet valuation and charging its cost into the expenses of operation. Such expense is called depreciation or, for exhaustible natural resources, depletion. Some assets, such as property that is abandoned or lost in a catastrophe, may continue to be carried among the firm's assets until their extinction is achieved by gradual amortization.

Accelerated amortization was permitted in the United States during World War II and extended after the war to encourage business to expand productive facilities that would serve the national defense. In the 1950s, accelerated amortization encouraged the expansion of export and new product industries and stimulated modernization in Canada, western European nations, and Japan. Other countries have also shown interest in it as a means of encouraging industrial development, but the current revenue lost by the government is a more serious consideration for them.

The advantage of accelerated amortization for tax purposes lies in the deferment of taxes rather than in their reduction. When amortization is accelerated, the drain of income taxes is reduced for the business during the years immediately after the purchase, thus releasing more funds for the repayment of any obligations incurred in financing the property. A financial problem may result later from the absence of any deduction in the normal income taxes for depreciation. Income-tax expenses can be equalized, however, by treating taxes not paid in the early years as a deferred tax liability.

Amory, Thomas (b. 1691?—d. Nov. 25, 1788, London?), British writer of Irish descent, best known for his extravagant "autobiography," *The Life of John Buncle*, 2 vol. (1756 and 1766), in which the hero marries seven wives in succession, each wife embodying one of Amory's ideals of womanhood. Rich, racy, and eccentric, his works contain something of the spirit of both Dickens and Rabelais.

Amory, detail of an engraving by Hopwood after a drawing by G. Baxter
Mary Evans Picture Library, London

A staunch Unitarian and a student of medicine, geology, and antiquities, he filled his writings with a variety of information on these and other subjects. He is thought to have lived in Dublin (where he knew the satirist Jonathan Swift) and later at Westminster.

Amos (fl. 8th century BC), the first Hebrew prophet to have a biblical book named for him. He accurately foretold the destruction of the northern kingdom of Israel (although he did not specify Assyria as the cause) and, as a prophet of doom, anticipated later Old Testament prophets.

The little that is known about Amos' life has been gleaned from his book, which was, in all likelihood, partly or wholly compiled by other hands. A native of Tekoa, an ancient desert town (now a ruin) 12 miles (19 kilometres) south of Jerusalem, Amos flourished during the reigns of King Uzziah (*c.* 783–742 BC) of Judah (the southern kingdom) and King Jeroboam II (*c.* 786–746 BC) of Israel. By occupation, he was a shepherd; whether he was merely that or a man of some means is not certain. He actually preached for only a short time.

Under the impact of powerful visions of divine destruction of the Hebrews in such natural disasters as a swarm of locusts and fire, Amos travelled from Judah to the neighbouring richer, more powerful kingdom of Israel, where he began to preach. The time is uncertain, but the Book of Amos puts the date as two years before an earthquake that may have occurred in 750 BC. He fiercely castigated corruption and social injustice among Israel's pagan neighbours, Israel itself, and Judah; asserted God's absolute sovereignty over man; and predicted the imminent destruction of Israel and Judah. After preaching at Bethel, a famous shrine under the special protection of Jeroboam II, Amos was ordered to leave the country by Jeroboam's priest Amaziah. Thereafter his fate is unknown.

From his book, Amos emerges as a thoughtful, probably well-travelled man of fierce integrity, who possessed a poet's gift for homely but forceful imagery and rhythmic language. So distinctive is his style of expression that in many instances the reader can distinguish those portions genuinely by Amos from parts probably invented by others, such as the concluding, optimistic section foretelling the restoration of the Davidic kingdom.

As a theologian, Amos believed that God's absolute sovereignty over man compelled social justice for all men, rich and poor alike. Not even God's chosen people were exempt from this fiat, and even they had to pay the penalty for breaking it; hence, Amos also believed in a moral order transcending nationalistic interests.

Amos, Book of, the third of 12 Old Testament books that bear the names of the Minor Prophets, collected in one book under the Jewish canon titled The Twelve. Amos, a Judaean prophet from the village of Tekoa, was active in the northern kingdom of Israel during the reign of Jeroboam II (*c.* 786–746 BC). Amos was neither a prophet nor the son of a prophet; his only credential to prophesy to Israel was a summons by Yahweh.

The book is a collection of individual sayings and reports of visions. Whether Amos himself committed any of his sayings to writing is not certain; his words may have been recorded by a scribe from Amos' dictation or by a later writer who knew the sayings from oral tradition. The present arrangement of the sayings reflects the activity of someone other than the prophet.

Amos' message is primarily one of doom. Although Israel's neighbours do not escape his attention, his threats are directed primarily against Israel, who, he contends, has defected from the worship of Yahweh to the worship of Canaanite gods. This belief prompts his polemic against the feasts and solemn assemblies observed by Israel. He also pronounces judgment on the rich for self-indulgence and oppression of the poor, on those who pervert justice, and on those who desire the day of Yahweh on which God will reveal his power, punish the wicked, and renew the righteous. That day, Amos warned, will be a day of darkness for Israel because of its defection from Yahweh.

The book ends unexpectedly (9:8–15) with a promise of restoration for Israel. Because these verses so radically differ from the threatening nature of the rest of the book, many scholars believe them to be a later addition.

amosite, a variety of the silicate mineral cummingtonite, which is a source of asbestos (*see* cummingtonite).

amour courtois: *see* courtly love.

Amoy, Wade–Giles romanization HSIA-MEN, Pinyin XIAMEN, city and port on the coast of southern Fukien Province (*sheng*), China. Amoy is a prefecture-level municipality (*shih*), the territory of which also includes the county (*hsien*) of T'ung-an, to the north. Amoy is situated on the southwest coast of Hsia-men Tao (island) at the mouth of the Chiu-lung Chiang (river). Known as the "garden on the sea," it has an excellent harbour, sheltered by a number of offshore islands, the most important of which, Quemoy (Chin-men Tao), in the mouth of the estuary, has remained a fortress in the hands of the Chinese Nationalist government on Taiwan.

During the Sung (960–1279) and Yüan (1279–1368) dynasties, Amoy was known as Chia-shu Island and formed a part of T'ung-an County. It was notable chiefly as a lair of pirates and a centre of contraband trade. The name Hsia-men first appeared when the island was fortified as one of a series of measures taken against piracy in 1394. During the 1600s it was under the control of Cheng Ch'eng-kung, or Koxinga (1624–62), the ruler of Taiwan, at which time it was called Ssu-ming Prefecture. In 1680 it was taken by the forces of the Ch'ing dynasty (1644–1911), after which it became the headquarters of the Ch'üan-chou naval defense force. Foreign trade there began with the arrival of the Portuguese in 1544, but they were expelled shortly thereafter. Under Cheng Ch'eng-kung's rule, English and Dutch ships had called at Amoy; and British traders continued occasionally to visit Amoy until 1757, when trade was restricted to Canton. After this only a few Spanish ships were allowed to visit Amoy. After the Opium War of 1839–42 between Britain and China, Amoy was one of the first five ports to be opened to foreign trade and to residence by foreigners. A foreign settlement grew up on Ku-lang Hsü (island), in the harbour. Amoy in the 19th century was preeminently a tea port, exporting teas from southeastern Fukien. The peak of this trade was reached in the 1870s but then declined, after which Amoy became the chief market and shipping port for Taiwanese tea produced by local growers who had emigrated to that island.

In the later 19th century, Amoy was the base from which Taiwan was settled and exploited; and the port retained a close link with the island even after the Japanese conquest of Taiwan in 1895; it also was one of the chief ports of departure for Chinese emigrants settling elsewhere in Southeast Asia. With the decline of the tea trade in the early 20th century, Amoy continued to export canned fruits, canned fish, paper, sugar, and timber. Before World War II, Amoy prospered not only because of its own trade but also because of family remittances received from overseas Chinese. From 1938 to 1945 Amoy was occupied by the Japanese.

After 1949 considerable development took place. A causeway was built in 1956, linking the island to the mainland, and a railway line was constructed from Amoy to the border of Chekiang Province, with a branch to Fu-chou. The railway was completed in 1956. Industrial development since 1949 has consisted chiefly of light industry. The canning of fruit and fish, the production of cod-liver oil, fish meal, and other fish products, and sisal processing, sugar refining, tanning, and tobacco curing are important industries. There is also a sizable ship-repairing and engineering industry. In the late 1970s, more than half of the population of Amoy consisted of returned emigrants and their families. The city has a university that was founded in 1921. Pop. (1948) 158,000; (1953) 224,000; (1958) 308,000; (1980 UN est.) 588,000.

Amparai, town, eastern Sri Lanka, near the Gal Oya (river). A large multipurpose project on the Gal Oya is important for irrigation and hydroelectric power. Amparai is also the site of the Hardy Technical School, which provides courses in commerce and crafts. Pop. (1981 prelim.) 16,531.

ampere, unit of electric current in the metre–kilogram–second–ampere (mksa) system of physical units, used by both scientists and technologists. Since 1948 the ampere has been defined as the constant current which, if maintained in two straight parallel conductors of infinite length of negligible circular cross section and placed one metre apart in a vacuum, would produce between these conductors a force equal to 2×10^{-7} newton per metre of length. Named for the 19th-century French physicist André-Marie Ampère, it represents a flow of one coulomb of electricity per second. A flow of one ampere is produced in a resistance of one ohm by a potential difference of one volt. *See* current, electric.

Ampère, André-Marie (b. Jan. 20, 1775, Lyon—d. June 10, 1836, Marseille), French physicist who founded and named the science of electrodynamics, now known as electromagnetism.

Ampère was a prodigy who mastered all mathematics then extant by the time he was 12 years old. He became a professor of physics and chemistry at Bourg in 1801 and a professor of mathematics at the École Polytechnique in Paris in 1809.

Ampère was not a methodical experimenter; he was subject to brilliant flashes of inspiration, which he would then pursue to their conclusion. Upon hearing of the discovery of the Danish physicist Hans Christian Ørsted

André-Marie Ampère, detail of an oil painting by an unknown artist
The Mansell Collection

in 1820 that a magnetic needle is deflected when placed near a current-carrying wire, thus establishing a relationship between electricity and magnetism, Ampère prepared within a week the first of several papers in which he fully expounded the theory of this new phenomenon. He formulated a law of electromagnetism (commonly called Ampère's law) that describes mathematically the magnetic force between two electric currents. He also performed many experiments, the results of which served to develop a mathematical theory that not only explained electromagnetic phenomena already reported but predicted new ones as well. The first man to develop measuring techniques for electricity, Ampère built an instrument utilizing a free-moving needle to measure the flow of electricity. Its later refinement was known as the galvanometer. His chief published work appeared in 1827 as *Mémoire sur la théorie mathématique des phénomènes électrodynamique, uniquement déduite de l'expérience.*

Ampère, Jean-Jacques (-Antoine) (b. Aug. 12, 1800, Lyon—d. March 27, 1864, Pau, Fr.), French historian and philologist who initiated important studies of the diverse cultural origins of western European languages and mythology. A world traveller, he wrote both scholarly works and Romantic poetry.

The son of the distinguished scientist André-Marie Ampère, Jean-Jacques Ampère made his first journey to Germany in 1826, where his work greatly impressed Goethe. On the basis of his study of Scandinavian mythology, he was named to a chair in the history of foreign literature at the Sorbonne in 1830; three years later he became a professor at the Collège de France, where he did the research for his major philological works, *Histoire littéraire de la France avant le douzième siècle* (3 vol., 1839–40; "History of French Literature before the 12th Century") and *Histoire de la formation de la langue française* (1841; "History of the Development of the French Language"). In his theories of environmental influences on history, he was a precursor of the French critic and historian Hippolyte Taine. Enamoured much of his adult life of the famous beauty and hostess Mme Récamier, who was much older than he, Ampère was a habitué of her salon. In 1848 he was elected to the Académie Française. In the company of the writer Prosper Mérimée, he visited the Near East and, later, the United States and Mexico. Ampère's major historical work is *L'Histoire romaine à Rome* (4 vol., 1861–64; "Roman History in Rome"); his other diverse works include *De l'histoire de la poésie* (1830; "On the History of Poetry") and *Promenade en Amérique: États-Unis, Cuba et Mexique* (1855; "Travels in America: The United States, Cuba, and Mexico").

Ampère's law, one of the basic relations between electricity and magnetism, stating quantitatively the relation of a magnetic field to the electric current or changing electric field that produces it. The law is named in honour of André-Marie Ampère, who by 1825 had laid the foundation of electromagnetic theory. An alternative expression of the Biot–Savart law (*q.v.*), which also relates the magnetic field and the current that produces it, Ampère's law is generally stated formally in the language of calculus: the line integral of the magnetic field around an arbitrarily chosen path is proportional to the net electric current enclosed by the path. James Clerk Maxwell is responsible for this mathematical formulation and for the extension of the law to include magnetic fields that arise without electric current, as between the plates of a capacitor, or condenser, in which the electric field changes with the periodic charging and discharging of the plates but in which no passage of electric charge occurs. Maxwell also showed that even in empty space a varying electric field is accompanied by a changing magnetic field. The complete Ampère's law describes all these effects.

amphetamine, prototype of a series of synthetic drugs, all called amphetamines, that have pronounced stimulatory actions on the central nervous system. Amphetamine itself is a colourless liquid with an acrid taste and a faint odour; the most widely used preparation of the drug is amphetamine sulfate, marketed under the name Benzedrine, a white powder with a slightly bitter, numbing taste. Dextroamphetamine, marketed under the name Dexedrine, is the more active of the two optically isomeric forms in which amphetamine exists. Other members of the amphetamine series include methamphetamine (*q.v.*) and benzphetamine.

These drugs partially reverse the depressing effects of anesthetics, narcotics, hypnotics, and alcohol. All cause profound psychic effects, including wakefulness, mental alertness, increased initiative and confidence, euphoria, lessened sense of fatigue, talkativeness, and increased ability to concentrate.

Amphetamine is useful for the symptomatic treatment of certain mild nervous depressions and, to a lesser extent, of the more severe depressions accompanying some forms of mental disorder. In chronic alcoholism, the drug is of value as an aid to psychological suggestion in helping patients abstain. It effectively dulls the appetite when taken before meals, so it is widely used as an adjunct to dietary restriction in weight reduction.

Amphetamines can produce undesirable effects, the commonest of which is overstimulation, with restlessness, insomnia, tremor, tenseness, irritability, and toxic psychosis. Abdominal cramping with nausea, vomiting, and diarrhea also may occur. Large doses can produce loss of consciousness, collapse, and death. Amphetamine addiction frequently is associated with similar abuse of barbiturates and alcohol.

amphibian, class name AMPHIBIA, vertebrate animal that is midway in evolutionary development between the fish and reptile. Included in the approximately 2,400 living species are the frogs and toads, salamanders and sirens, and caecilians.

A brief treatment of amphibians follows. For full treatment, *see* MACROPAEDIA: Amphibians.

Amphibians (Greek *amphi,* "both"; *bios,* "life") were the first vertebrates to move from an aquatic environment to land, and they are the ancestors of all reptiles, birds, and mammals. Although a few species spend their lives in water, most live at least part of the time on land. They are distributed worldwide, but the majority are found in the tropics.

Most amphibians have an aquatic larval, or tadpole, stage that metamorphoses into a terrestrial adult. In caecilians and salamanders, fertilization is usually internal. The male caecilian introduces sperm into the female by means of a protrusible portion of the cloaca, the lower end of the digestive track. The male salamander deposits sperm on a gelatinous structure, which the female manoeuvres into her cloaca. Fertilization is external in most frogs and toads, with the male clasping the female and releasing sperm over the eggs as the female extrudes them. The eggs of amphibians do not have shells and must be deposited in water or in a moist place, such as damp soil or on a female's back.

There are three living groups of amphibians, all of which differ markedly in structure. The caecilians (order Gymnophiona) resemble worms and have no limbs, practically no tail, a simple intestine, and minute eyes buried in a smooth skin. The compact skull facilitates burrowing. The segmented body consists of circular folds separated by grooves. Sensory tentacles are buried in pits near each eye, and several series of teeth are found on bones around the jaws.

The sirens and salamanders (order Urodela) belong to a second group, which is prevalent in the southeastern United States and in Mexico. The sirens are elongated aquatic animals without hindlimbs but with anterior pectoral girdles to which the front legs are attached. They breathe through gills or gulp air at the surface. The eyes are buried in the smooth skin, and teeth are attached to the roof of the mouth. Tail fins assist locomotion. Salamanders have forelegs, hindlegs, a tail, smooth skin, and a neck. Teeth are found on the jaws and roof of the mouth. Some species remain in the water as permanent larvae with gills.

Frogs and toads (order Anura) constitute the largest group of amphibians. These animals are distinguished by a segment in the hindleg, formed by two elongated tarsal bones, that is used for hopping and swimming. Teeth are usually found in the upper jaw. The glandular skin, usually smooth and soft, is occasionally dry and rough in terrestrial species.

Amphibians evolved from lobe-finned fishes (Crossopterygii) of the Upper Devonian period (about 370,000,000 years ago). These fishes had lungs, muscular fins supported by bones, and in some species, passages from nasal sacs to internal openings in the roof of the mouth. In time of drought, these creatures probably propelled themselves out of the drying pools on their muscular fins to search for other water. They then perhaps added insects and other small arthropods to their diet and became less dependent on water. Caecilian fossils are unknown, but fossils of sirens have been found in Cretaceous rocks and salamanders in those of the Jurassic Period (136,000,000 to 190,000,000 years ago). Both apparently evolved in the Northern Hemisphere, but the earliest frogs, dating from the Lower Triassic, evolved below the Equator.

amphibious vehicle, device for transporting men and equipment, usually military, that can operate as a wheeled vehicle on land or as a boat in water. Two principal types appeared during World War II: the LVT, a tractor developed for the U.S. Marine Corps, and the "duck" (DUKW), an army-sponsored vehicle. The LVT resembled a tank, whereas the duck moved on rubber tires ashore and was propeller-driven when afloat. An air-cushion machine, such as the British Hovercraft, is not considered an amphibious vehicle.

amphibious warfare, military operations characterized by attacks launched from the sea by naval and landing forces against hostile shores. The principal form is the amphibious assault, which may be conducted for any of several purposes: as a prelude to further combat operations ashore; to seize a site required as an advanced naval or air base; or to deny the use of the site or area to the enemy. Landing of expeditionary forces on a shore or at a port already secured by friendly forces is not ordinarily included in the concept.

Amphibious warfare has been conducted since ancient times, although specialized landing vessels are a modern development. The Greeks attacking Troy (1200 BC) had to gain a lodgment on the shore, as did the Persian invaders of Greece in the Bay of Marathon (490 BC). After the decline of Rome and during the Middle Ages, the most successful practitioners of amphibious warfare, although on a small scale, were the Norse raiders on the coasts of northern, western, and Mediterranean Europe. During the Napoleonic Wars, Napoleon's failure to control the English Channel and invade England is frequently cited as a classic example of the inability of a strong continental force lacking in sea power to project its strength over even the narrowest of seas. Similarly, Germany was disadvantaged during World War II by its lack of adequate amphibious capability.

Modern amphibious warfare integrates virtually all forms of land, sea, and air operations. Its greatest advantage lies in its mobility and flexibility; its greatest limitation is that the attacker must build up his strength ashore from an initial zero.

After World War II, new debarkation methods and capabilities were developed to overcome the previously slow and ponderous off-loading process. Helicopters were used for resupply and medical evacuation, as well as for landing troops. Petroleum products were pumped ashore from tanker ships through temporary pipelines for storage in collapsible bags. To improve tactical air support in the battle area, airfields were developed that in a matter of days provided substantially the same capabilities ashore as an attack aircraft carrier.

In the late 1940s military opinion had recognized that the great concentrations of shipping and the congested beachheads of World War II would be futile against a nuclear-equipped enemy. To eliminate such congestion, helicopters and other vertical-rising or short-takeoff aircraft were to converge on the objective area from high-speed assault transports located many miles out at sea. Though the new concepts were not put to the test by a nuclear-equipped enemy, they did add a new dimension to amphibious operations against conventionally armed enemies, as was demonstrated in landings such as those conducted during the Vietnam War in the 1960s.

amphibole, any of a group of common rock-forming silicate minerals. Amphiboles occur in most igneous rocks as minor and major constituents and form the major component in many metamorphic gneisses and schists. (See table, page 352.)

A brief treatment of amphiboles follows. For full treatment, *see* MACROPAEDIA: Minerals and Rocks.

The amphiboles are inosilicates. They are characterized by two planes of well-developed prismatic cleavages that intersect at angles of about 124° and 56°. Many of the amphiboles develop elongate crystals, some becoming needlelike and fibrous. Several of these fibrous forms, riebeckite, cummingtonite, anthophyllite, and tremolite, are known collectively as asbestos. In general, amphiboles crystallize in either the orthorhombic or monoclinic system.

The amphiboles show considerable variation in composition. Besides silicon (Si) and oxygen (O), their components include sodium (Na), calcium (Ca), magnesium (Mg), iron (Fe), aluminum (Al), hydrogen (H), and fluorine (F). The general chemical formula of the amphibole group may be expressed as:

$$(Na,Ca)_{2-3}(Mg,Fe^{3+},Al)_5(Si,Al)_3O_{22}(OH,O,F)_2$$
$$\text{or}\quad (Mg,Fe^{2+},Fe^{3+},Al)_7(Si,Al)_8O_{22}(OH,O,F)_3.$$

The amphibole structure consists of double chains of silicon-oxygen tetrahedrons in which alternate tetrahedrons link two single chains by sharing an oxygen atom. The double-chain groups are bonded to parallel adjacent double chains by the Na, Ca and Mg, Fe^{2+}, Fe^{3+}, Al ions of the crystal. There are only small differences between the ionic sizes of Mg, Fe^{2+}, Fe^{3+}, and Al, so that the positions in the crystal that are occupied by Mg can also be occupied by these similarly sized ions (*i.e.,* they can substitute for each other). The ionic sizes of Ca and Na are similar enough that they can substitute for each other. Moreover, the ionic size of Al is close enough to the size of Si that a limited Al substitution for Si occurs.

amphibole asbestos, a variety of the silicate mineral actinolite (*q.v.*).

amphibolite, a rock composed largely or dominantly of minerals of the amphibole group; the term has been applied to rocks of either igneous or metamorphic origin. In igneous rocks, the term hornblendite is more common and restrictive; hornblende is the most common amphibole and is typical of such rocks. Hornblendite is an ultramafic rock (dominantly dark minerals) and is also ultrabasic (low in silica content). True hornblendites contain little other than amphibole and are probably derived from the alteration of pyroxene and olivine.

Metamorphic amphibolites are a more widespread and variable group of rocks formed through metamorphism. Typically, they are medium- to coarse-grained and are composed of hornblende and plagioclase. These are the diagnostic rocks of the amphibolite facies of regional metamorphism and may be derived from pre-metamorphic rocks of various types. Basic igneous rocks (*e.g.,* basalts and gabbros) and sedimentary dolomite can be the parent rocks of amphibolite.

amphibolite facies, one of the major divisions of the mineral facies classification of metamorphic rocks, the rocks of which formed under conditions of moderate to high temperatures (500° C, or about 950° F, maximum) and pressures. Less intense temperatures and pressures form rocks of the epidote-amphibolite facies, and more intense temperatures and pressures form rocks of the granulite facies. Amphibole, diopside, epidote, plagioclase, almandite and grossularite garnet, and wollastonite are minerals typically found in rocks of the amphibolite facies. The disappearance of epidote and increase in calcium in plagioclase are characteristic chemical changes as metamorphic intensity increases through this facies. Water is usually lost from the parent rock as these changes take place. Amphibolite facies rocks are widely distributed in Precambrian gneisses; they are interpreted as having formed in the deeper parts of folded mountain belts.

amphictyony, also spelled AMPHICTIONY (from Greek *amphiktyones,* "dwellers around"), in ancient Greece, association of neighbouring states formed around a religious centre. The most important was the Amphictyonic League (Delphic Amphictyony). Originally composed of 12 tribes dwelling around Thermopylae, the league was centred first around the shrine of Demeter and later became associated with the Temple of Apollo at Delphi. Member states sent two kinds of deputies (*pylagorai* and *hieromnēmones*) to a council (*pylaia*) that met twice a year and administered the temporal affairs of the shrines and their properties, supervised the treasury, and conducted the Pythian Games. In the 4th century BC the league rebuilt the Delphic temple. Although primarily religious, the league exercised a political influence through its membership oath, forbidding destruction of member cities or the cutting off of water supplies; the *hieromnēmones* could punish offenders and even proclaim a sacred war against them. Other important amphictyonies were the Delian and, in the Archaic period, the Calaurian (composed of states around the Saronic Gulf).

Amphion and Zethus, in Greek mythology, the twin sons of Zeus by Antiope (*q.v.*). When children, they were left to die on Mt. Cithaeron but were found and brought up by a shepherd. Amphion became a great singer and musician, Zethus a hunter and herdsman. After rejoining their mother, they built and fortified Thebes, huge blocks of stone forming themselves into walls at the sound of Amphion's lyre. Amphion later married Niobe (*q.v.*) and killed himself after the loss of his wife and children.

amphioxus, plural AMPHIOXI, or AMPHIOXUSES, also called LANCELET, or CEPHALOCHORDATE, any member of the invertebrate subphylum Cephalochordata of the phylum Chordata. They are small marine animals found widely in the coastal waters of the warmer parts of the world and less commonly in temperate waters.

A brief treatment of amphioxi follows. For full treatment, *see* MACROPAEDIA: Chordates.

Amphioxi are seldom more than eight centimetres (three inches) long, and in appearance they resemble small, slender fishes without eyes or definite heads. They are grouped in two genera, each constituting a family, with about two dozen species. The chordate features—the notochord (or stiffening rod), gill slits, and dorsal nerve cord—appear in both the larval and adult forms.

Amphioxi spend much of their time buried in gravel or mud on the ocean bottom, although they are able to swim. When feeding, they let the anterior part of the body project from the surface of the gravel so that they can filter food particles from water passing through their gill slits. At night they often swim about near the bottom. Burrowing is done by rapid movements of the body, which is tapered at both ends and is covered by a coarse sheath called the cuticle.

The animals swim by contracting the muscle blocks, or myotomes, that run from end to end on each side of the body. The blocks on each side are staggered, and movement is in fits and starts. Amphioxi are not buoyant, and they sink quickly when they stop swimming. A fin runs along the entire back, rounds the tip of the tail, and then continues part of the way as a ventral fin. Some species have a distinct tail fin.

The notochord runs through the body from tip to tip, providing a central support. A slight bulge distinguishes the anterior end of the nerve cord, but there is no brain. The blood flows forward along the ventral side and backward along the dorsal side, but there is no distinct heart.

The buccal cavity of amphioxi is furnished with a hood whose edges are lined with buccal cirri, fringe-like structures that form a coarse filter to screen out particles too large to be consumed. Water is directed through the small mouth into the pharynx by the action of cilia on the gill slits. Food particles in the passing water are caught by the mucus lining of the gill basket and passed into the gut, where they are exposed to the action of enzymes. Unlike other chordates, amphioxi are capable of a digestive process called phagocytosis, in which food particles are enveloped by individual cells.

Above the pharynx is the excretory system made up of the nephridia, which opens into an excretory canal leading to the atrium. The endostyle corresponds to the thyroid in vertebrates, since it seems to produce iodinated, tyrosine molecules, which may function as regulatory substances, much like hormones, in amphioxi.

Male and female amphioxi are identical in outward appearance and differ internally only in the nature of the gonads, or reproductive

Amphiboles

name formula	colour	lustre	Mohs hardness	specific gravity	habit or form	fracture or cleavage	refractive indices	crystal system space group	remarks
actinolite $Ca_2(Mg, Fe)_5[Si_8O_{22}]$ $(OH, F)_2$	colourless to gray; darkens with increased Fe through green to black	silky; oily	5–6	2.9–3.2	fibrous massive	one perfect cleavage of 56°	tremo ferro α=1.600–1.672 β=1.614–1.686 γ=1.627–1.693	monoclinic $C\frac{2}{m}$	tremolite is Mg end-member Mg:Fe>4:1; ferrotremolite is Fe end-member, Mg:Fe<1:4; actinolite is intermediate, 4:1>Mg:Fe>1:4
anthophyllite $(Mg, Fe)_7[Si_8O_{22}](OH, F)_2$	white, gray, green, or various shades of brown	vitreous	5½–6	2.9–3.2	fibrous or lamellar masses; bladed and prismatic crystal aggregates	one perfect cleavage of 54°	antho gedr α=1.587–1.642 β=1.602–1.655 γ=1.613–1.661	orthorhombic Pnma	forms solid solution series with gedrite in which Al partially replaces both Mg and Si
arfvedsonite $Na_{2.5}Ca_{0.5}$ $(Fe^{+2}, Mg, Fe^{+3}Al)_5$ $[Si_{7.5}Al_{0.5}O_{22}](OH, F)_2$	dark bluish green to greenish black or black	vitreous	5–6	3–3.5	long prisms; prismatic aggregates	one perfect cleavage of 56°	ecker arfv α=1.612–1.700 β=1.625–1.709 γ=1.630–1.710	monoclinic $C\frac{2}{m}$	forms solid solution series with eckermannite in which Mg replaces Fe and which contains Li
basaltic hornblende $Ca_2(Na, K)_{0.5-1.0}$ $(Mg, Fe^{+2})_{3-2}(Fe^{+3}, Al)_{2-3}$ $[Si_6Al_2O_{22}](O, OH, F)_2$	brown to black	glassy	5–6	3.2–3.3	massive	one perfect cleavage of 56°	α=1.622–1.690 β=1.672–1.730 γ=1.680–1.760	monoclinic $C\frac{2}{m}$	
common hornblende $(Ca, Na, K)_{2-3}$ $(Mg, Fe^{+2}, Fe^{+3}, Al)_5$ $[Si_6(Si, Al)_2O_{22}](OH, F)_2$	pale to dark green	glassy	5–6	3–3.4	massive	one good cleavage of 56°	α=1.615–1.705 β=1.618–1.714 γ=1.632–1.730	monoclinic $C\frac{2}{m}$	
cummingtonite $(Mg, Fe)_7[Si_8O_{22}](OH)_2$	dark green; brown	silky	5–6	3.1–3.6	fibrous or lamellar massive	one good cleavage of 55°	cumm grun α=1.643–1.688 β=1.658–1.711 γ=1.663–1.731	monoclinic $C\frac{2}{m}$	forms solid solution series with grunerite in which Fe:Mg<7:3; natural cummingtonite contains at least 30% Fe
glaucophane $Na_2Mg_3Al_2[Si_8O_{22}]$ $(OH, F)_2$	gray or lavender-blue	vitreous	6	3.1–3.3	fibrous or columnar massive	one good cleavage of 58°	α=1.606–1.661 β=1.622–1.667 γ=1.627–1.670	monoclinic $C\frac{2}{m}$	forms solid solution series with riebeckite and magnesioriebeckite (see below), the intermediate members having physical properties between glaucophane and riebeckite
richterite $Ca_3Na_2(Mg, Mn)_{10}$ $Si_{16}O_{44}(OH)_4$	brown, yellow, brownish red, pale to dark green	vitreous	5–6	3–3.4	elongated crystals	one perfect cleavage of 56°	α=1.605–1.685 β=1.618–1.700 γ=1.627–1.712	monoclinic $C\frac{2}{m}$	related to tremolite, but has Na replacing Ca
riebeckite $Na_3Fe^{+2}{}_3Fe^{+3}{}_2$ $[Si_8O_{22}](OH, F)_2$	dark blue or black	vitreous	5	3–3.4	longitudinally striated prismatic crystals; fibrous massive	one good cleavage of 56°	magnes rieb α=1.645–1.701 β=1.662–1.711 γ=1.668–1.717	monoclinic $C\frac{2}{m}$	forms solid solution series with magnesioriebeckite, in which Mg replaces Fe^{+2}, and with glaucophane, in which Mg replaces Fe^{+2} and Al replaces Fe^{+3} (see above)

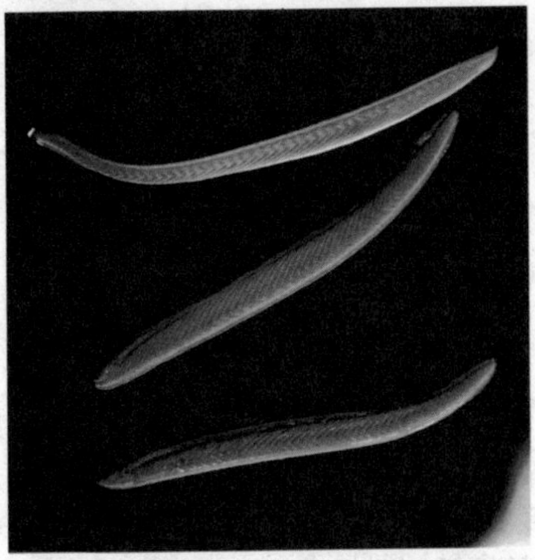

Amphioxus (*Branchiostoma*)
Walter Dawn

glands, which form in rows on the wall of the atrial cavity. Breeding takes place several times a year in tropical regions but only once in temperate areas. Sacs containing eggs or sperm burst and discharge their contents into the water through the atriopore, an opening on the underside of the body. Fertilization takes place in the water, and after about two days, larvae develope from the fertilized eggs. The larvae drift with ocean currents until they reach a certain size and metamorphose into adults. The animals then sink to the bottom, to live in the gravel, most commonly at depths of not more than 50 fathoms.

Amphioxi are useful in filtering the water, and in areas where they abound the water is usually clean. Along parts of the coast of China, they are so numerous that they constitute the basis of a fishing industry. Their unmistakable resemblance to vertebrates sheds light on vertebrate origins. No fossil has been found that can be definitely classified as an amphioxus, however, and classification is based wholly on study of living forms.

amphipod, any member of the invertebrate order Amphipoda (class Crustacea) inhabiting all parts of the sea, lakes, rivers, sand beaches, caves, and moist (warm) habitats on many tropical islands. Marine amphipods have been found at depths of more than 30,000 feet. Freshwater and marine beach species are commonly known as scuds; those that occupy sand beaches are called sand hoppers or sand fleas (*see* sand flea). About 4,600 species have been described. Extraordinarily abundant in the rocky coastal regions of all seas and often exceeding densities of 10,000 per square metre (9,000 per square yard), amphipods are often mistaken for tiny shrimp, which they resemble. They are important food for many fishes, invertebrates, penguins, shore birds, small cetaceans, and pinnipeds. Amphipods are also important as scavengers of carrion.

Body length varies from 1–140 millimetres (0.04–5.5 inches), but the amphipod of mid-latitude regions is about 4–10 millimetres long (0.16–0.4 inch). Many amphipods are brightly coloured—red, pink, yellow, green, or blue. The body is usually compressed from side to side (*i.e.,* height is greater than width), thus in part facilitating rapid sliding movement through algal fronds (leaflike structures). Most amphipods are active swimmers, being propelled by three pairs of abdominal appendages. That they are also strong jumpers is best seen in beach hoppers.

The antennae are long and hairy. As in the shrimp, the head and tail ends are often curved downward. The eyes are sessile (without a stalk). Some species with piercing and sucking mouthparts are rather strictly confined to sedentary positions on large, mostly nonmoving invertebrates, such as cnidarians and sponges. One marine family (Cheluridae) chews wood and is obligatorily associated with the isopod *Limnoria,* another wood borer. Few gammarideans (suborder Gammaridea) are predatory; they are mostly scavengers and herbivores, many species burrowing into the soft mud of the sea bottom. Amphipod gills are partially protected by long coxae, which are ventral extensions of the basal leg segments.

The sexes are separate, males often being characterized by enlarged gnathopods (claws on the second thoracic segment) used to grasp females during copulation. The male presumably emits sperm, or spermatophores (balls of sperm), to fertilize the eggs of the female externally.

The number of eggs in a clutch varies from one to more than 250. The arrangement of gills (described above) provides a chamber for fertilized eggs, which are carried externally by the female and held in a cluster near the gills. The gammaridean egg cluster is probably kept fresh with water currents created by beating appendages called pleopods. Eggs hatch in 2–59 days, and the young may remain in the brood pouch for from 2 to 35 days. After six to nine molts over an interval of one to four months, sexual maturity is attained. A few cold-water species live at least a year, perhaps far longer.

The generic diversity of amphipods is apparently higher in cool waters than in warm ones. One enigma is the enormous diversity of species, more than 290 in the Siberian Lake Baikal. Fossilization of amphipods is

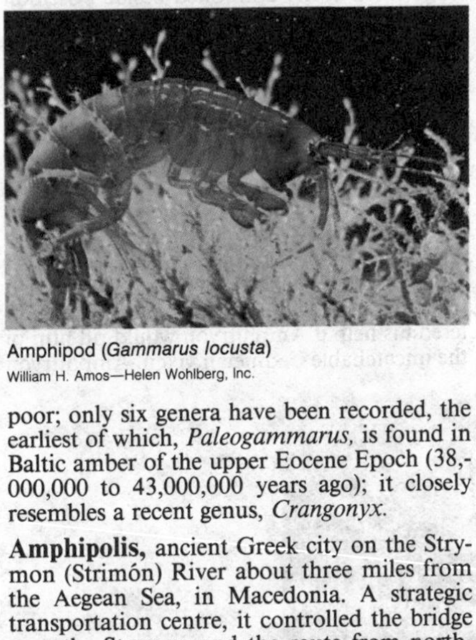

Amphipod (*Gammarus locusta*)
William H. Amos—Helen Wohlberg, Inc.

poor; only six genera have been recorded, the earliest of which, *Paleogammarus,* is found in Baltic amber of the upper Eocene Epoch (38,000,000 to 43,000,000 years ago); it closely resembles a recent genus, *Crangonyx.*

Amphipolis, ancient Greek city on the Strymon (Strimón) River about three miles from the Aegean Sea, in Macedonia. A strategic transportation centre, it controlled the bridge over the Strymon and the route from northern Greece to the Hellespont, including the western approach to the timber, gold, and silver of Mt. Pangaeum in Thrace. Originally a Thracian town (Ennea Hodoi, Nine Roads), it was colonized by Athens in 436 BC. The Spartan Brasidas seized it in 424 and defeated the Athenian Cleon, who tried to recapture it in 422. It was officially returned to Athens by the Peace of Nicias (421) but actually remained independent, despite Athenian attempts to regain control (416 and 368–365). Philip II of Macedonia occupied it in 357, and it remained under Macedonian control until 168, when Rome made it a free city and also the headquarters of the Roman governor of Macedonia. Traces of ancient fortifications and a Roman aqueduct are on the city's site, which is occupied by the modern town of Amfipolis.

Amphissa, Modern Greek ÁMFISSA, agricultural centre, chief town of the *eparkhía* (province) of Parnassus (Parnassós), capital of the *nomós* (department) of Fokís (Phocis), central Greece, at the northwestern limit of the fertile, Krissaean plain between the Gióna Oros (mountains) and the Parnassus massif. The economy includes trade in wheat, livestock, and particularly olives grown on the Crisaean plain. Bauxite is mined southeast of Amphissa and trucked to an aluminum-reduction plant at neighbouring Antikyra on an inlet of the Gulf of Corinth.

During the Middle Ages, Itéa, the ancient Chaleion, supplanted the 6th-century-BC port of Cyrrha (Kírra), situated just southeast of Itéa. On Amphissa's acropolis sits a ruined Franco-Catalan fortress supported by ancient foundations. The town is the seat of a metropolitan bishop of the Orthodox Church of Greece.

Close to Delphi, ancient Amphissa was the capital of Ozolian (western) Locris. The ruined acropolis of the modern tiered town dates apparently from about the 5th century BC, or late Archaic period. The city provoked the Third Sacred War when it was denounced (339 BC) for the impiety of cultivating the sacred wooded plain of Crisa, still drained by the stream Pleistus. The following year it was destroyed by Philip II of Macedonia, who undertook the punitive mission on behalf of the Council of the Delphic Amphictyony (a league of Greek states), a task that also gave him an excuse to tighten his control on other Greek cities, leading to their permanent loss of independence after the Battle of Cheronaea (338 BC). The rebuilt city joined the Aetolian League, remaining a member until 167 BC, when it was forced to secede by Roman conquest. The 2nd-century-AD Greek traveller Pausanias reported that Amphissa had a temple to Athena with a very early statue of the goddess. Inscriptions concerning repairs on the city's aqueduct indicate that it remained active through the late Roman period.

Destroyed by the Bulgars about the 10th century, Amphissa was rebuilt by the Franks and became known as Sálona. It was held by the Catalans (1311–35), passing then to Count Alphonse Frederick of Aragon, whose family held it until its fall to the Turks in 1394. Amphissa became part of Greece when it won its independence from Turkey in 1829. Pop. (1981) 7,233.

amphitheatre, freestanding building of round or, more often, oval shape with a central area, the arena, and seats concentrically placed around it. The word is Greek meaning "theatre with seats on all sides," but as an architectural form the amphitheatre is of Italic or Etrusco-Campanian origin and reflects the requirements of the specific forms of entertainment these people cherished; *i.e.,* gladiatorial games and *venationes,* contests of beasts with one another, or men with beasts. Originally such games took place in the forum, and wooden stands were erected from time to time to accommodate the spectators. The earliest permanent extant amphitheatre is one at Pompeii (*c.* 80 BC), in which the arena is sunk below the natural level of the surrounding ground. It is built of stone 445 by 341 feet (136 by 104 metres) and seated approximately 20,000 spectators.

The great Flavian Amphitheatre, or Colosseum, in Rome was erected by the emperors Vespasian and Titus (*c.* AD 70–82) on the site of the Golden House of Nero. The name Colosseum was applied to this structure some time after the 8th century because of its immense size and capacity, accommodating nearly 50,000 people.

Great Roman amphitheatres were also built at Verona and at ancient Capua (modern Santa Maria Capua Vetere), where the amphitheatre, built in the 1st century, is second in size to the Colosseum, measuring 560 by 460 feet, and 95 feet high. Outside Italy, Roman amphitheatres were built at Nîmes and

Arles in France, Pola in Istria (Yugoslavia), and Thysdrus (El Djem) in Africa. The arenas were about 200 to 300 feet (60 to 90 metres) long and about 115 to 200 feet (35 to 60 metres) wide. Fragmentary remains of more than 75 Roman amphitheatres have been found in widely scattered areas throughout the provinces of the Roman Empire. The best preserved in Britain is the Roman amphitheatre at Caerleon in Gwent.

In most of the Roman amphitheatres, an elaborate labyrinth was constructed below the arena. The passages, including the *media via* for scenery, spaces for elevators and machinery that lifted the animals and stage sets, and rooms for the gladiators, were ingeniously arranged to connect, by means of many trap-doors, with the arena above. Around this arena, and separated from it by a high wall topped by a metal screen, rose the spectator seats. These were divided, by passageways running around the amphitheatre, into several sections (*maeniana*). In the lowest section, or podium, the emperor and his retinue had a special box; on the opposite side of the amphitheatre, but still in the podium, the vestal virgins, consuls, praetors, ambassadors, priests, and other distinguished guests were seated; the rest of the first gallery contained senators and those of the equestrian rank. The second gallery was reserved for patricians, the third for plebeians, and the fourth, uppermost, gallery for women, who were seated in boxes. An awning (*velum,* or *velarium*) was manipulated by sailors to shelter the spectators from the sun. Each of these galleries was divided into wedge-shaped sections (*cunei*) by radial walks that led to the many exits (*vomitoria*).

In modern usage the word amphitheatre is sometimes used for a theatre or concert hall whose seats surround the central area, as, for example, the Albert Hall, London, and both the new and the old Madison Square Garden in New York City, or may refer to a stadium where athletic competitions are held.

Outdoor amphitheatres, both ancient and relatively recent (*e.g.,* Chicago's Soldier Field), continue to be used for sports events and many other kinds of entertainment, although in the mid-20th century, the structure took the form of a vast, roofed stadium (*q.v.*).

Amphitherium, extinct genus of early mammals known as fossils from Middle Jurassic deposits (the Jurassic Period began 190,000,000 years ago and lasted 54,000,000 years). *Amphitherium* is the earliest representative of the pantotheres (*see* Theria), a group of early mammals that, it is believed, represents the stock that gave rise to all the higher mammals of later times. *Amphitherium* is known from a lower jaw found in Europe and is characterized by the large number and distinctive structure of its teeth.

Roman amphitheatre, Verona, Italy

Anderson–Alinari from Art Resource/EB Inc.

Amphitrite, in Greek mythology, the goddess of the sea, wife of the god Poseidon, and one of the 50 (or 100) daughters (the Nereids) of Nereus and Doris (the daughter of Oceanus). Poseidon chose Amphitrite from among her sisters as the Nereids performed a dance on the isle of Naxos. Refusing his offer of marriage, she fled to Atlas, from whom she was retrieved by a dolphin sent by Poseidon. Amphitrite then returned, becoming Poseidon's wife; he rewarded the dolphin by making it a constellation. In works of art Amphitrite was represented either enthroned beside Poseidon or driving with him in a chariot drawn by sea horses or other fabulous sea creatures.

Amphitrite and Poseidon in a chariot, drawn by Tritons, detail of a frieze from an altar in the Temple of Neptune, Rome, 40 BC

Giraudon—Art Resource/EB Inc.

Amphitryon, in Greek mythology, son of Alcaeus, king of Tiryns. Having accidentally killed his uncle Electryon, king of Mycenae, Amphitryon fled with Alcmene, Electryon's daughter, to Thebes, where he was cleansed from the guilt by Creon, his maternal uncle, king of Thebes. Alcmene refused to marry Amphitryon until he had avenged the death of her brothers, all of whom except one had fallen in battle against the Taphians. Creon offered his help if Amphitryon would rid him of the uncatchable Cadmeian vixen. Amphitryon borrowed Cephalus' invincible Creton hound Laelaps, and Zeus changed both Laelaps and the vixen to stone. The Taphians, however, remained invincible until Comaetho, the king's daughter, out of love for Amphitryon, cut off her father's golden hair, the possession of which rendered him immortal. On Amphitryon's return to Thebes he married Alcmene.

The more famous portion of the myth concerns Amphitryon's wife. When Amphitryon was once absent at war, Alcmene became pregnant by Zeus, who, disguised as her husband, visited her; she became pregnant again by her real husband upon his return. Of these unions were born twin boys, of whom Iphicles was the son of Amphitryon, Heracles the son of Zeus. A number of ancient dramatists presented the theme, notably Plautus, whose comedy *Amphitruo* still survives.

amphiuma, also called CONGO EEL, or CONGO SNAKE (*Amphiuma*), any of three species of North American salamanders belonging to the family Amphiumidae (order Urodela). Because they are long and slender and have inconspicuous legs, they are often mistaken for eels or snakes. The body is gray or brown and paler on the lower side. The usual habitat is swamps and drainage ditches.

Although there are both three-toed and one-toed species, the most widely distributed (Virginia to Louisiana) is *Amphiuma means,* which usually grows to 60–75 centimetres (24–30 inches) in length and has two toes on each foot. Amphiumas have strong jaws and sharp teeth and, unlike most salamanders, can bite viciously. Their diet consists chiefly of crayfish, clams, snails, and other small animals. The female is fertilized internally and lays from 40 to 150 eggs in a single clutch.

amphora, one of the principal vessel shapes in Greek pottery, a two-handled pot with a

Attic red-figure amphora by Euthymides showing revellers, *c.* 510 BC; in the Staatliche Antikensammlungen und Glyptothek, Munich

By courtesy of the Staatliche Antikensammlungen und Glyptothek, Munich

neck narrower than the body. There are two types of amphora: the neck amphora, in which the neck meets the body at a sharp angle; and the one-piece amphora, in which the neck and body form a continuous curve. The first is common from the Geometric period (*c.* 900 BC) to the decline of Greek pottery; the second appeared in the 7th century BC. The height of amphorae varies from large Geometric vases of 5 feet (1.5 metres) to examples of 12 inches (30 centimetres) or even smaller (the smallest are called *amphoriskoi*). The average normal height is about 18 inches (45 centimetres). Amphorae, which survive in great numbers, were used as storage and transport vessels for olives, cereal, oil, and wine (the wine amphora was a standard Attic measure of about 41 quarts [39 litres]) and, in outsize form, for funerals and as grave markers. Wide-mouthed, painted amphorae were used as decanters and were given as prizes.

The neck amphora, prefigured in Mycenean (14th-century-BC) pottery and remodelled as a main shape in the Protogeometric style (1000–*c.* 900 BC), has about 12 distinct shape variations, determined as much by utilitarian as by aesthetic considerations. Noteworthy are the Nolan type (from Nola, Italy), some of which had triple handles popular in red-figure pottery; the Panathenaic amphora, painted in black-figure and presented as a prize (filled with olive oil and having the inscription "I am one of the prizes from Athens") at the Panathenaic Festivals from the 6th to the 2nd centuries BC; and the *loutrophoros,* slender-bodied, with a tall neck and flaring mouth, used from the 6th century for ritual purposes at weddings and funerals. The one-piece amphora maintained a more consistent shape, with cylindrical handles, flaring lip, echinus foot, and amply curved belly. Amphorae, such as wine containers, continued to be made in profusion during the Roman Empire; although most examples are crude and unadorned, some attractive versions survive.

amphora, ancient Roman unit of capacity equal to 48 *sextarii* and equivalent to 6.7 U.S. gallons (25.36 litres). The term amphora was borrowed from the Greeks, who used it to designate a measure equal to about 9 gallons.

amphoterism, in chemistry, reactivity of a substance with both acids and bases, acting as an acid (proton donor or electron pair acceptor) in the presence of a base and as a base (proton acceptor or electron pair donor) in the presence of an acid. Water is an example of an amphoteric substance. The dissolution of ammonia (a base) and hydrogen chloride (an acid) in water may be represented by the equations:

$$H_2O + HCl \rightleftharpoons H_3O^+ + Cl^-$$
$$H_2O + NH_3 \rightleftharpoons NH_4^+ + OH^-$$

With hydrogen chloride, water accepts a proton to form a hydronium ion (H_3O^+), while, with ammonia, water acts as a proton donor and is converted to a hydroxide ion (OH^-). Other amphoteric substances include ammonia and the hydroxides of zinc, aluminum, chromium, lead, and tin.

amplifier, in electronics, device that responds to a small input signal (voltage, current, or power) and delivers a larger output signal that contains the essential waveform features of the input signal. Amplifiers of various types are widely used in such electronic equipment as radio and television receivers, high-fidelity audio equipment, and computers. Amplifying action can be provided by electromechanical devices such as transformers and generators, feedback circuits, vacuum tubes, and transistors.

The ratio of the output (current, voltage, or power) to the input, both expressed in the same units, is a measure of the amplification and is termed the gain. The term amplification factor, inherent where vacuum tube amplifiers are concerned and usually applied to a single tube, is defined as the ratio of a change in the plate voltage to a change in grid voltage that will produce no change in plate current. Both the gain and the amplification factor are pure numbers since they express ratios of similar quantities.

A single amplifier may be insufficient to raise the output to the desired level. In such cases the output of the first amplifier is fed into a second, whose output is fed to a third, and so on, until the output level is satisfactory. The result is cascade, or multistage amplification. Long-distance telephone, radio, television, electronic control and measuring instruments, radar, and countless other devices all depend on this basic process of amplification. The overall amplification of a multistage amplifier is the product of the gains of the individual stages.

There are various schemes for the coupling of cascading electronic amplifiers, depending upon the nature of the signal involved in the amplification process. The method of coupling employed is one scheme of amplifier classification.

An important property of an electronic amplifier is its ability to produce a magnified output signal, identical in every respect to the input signal. This is linear operation. If the output is altered in shape after passing through the amplifier, amplitude distortion exists. If the amplifier does not amplify equally at all frequencies, frequency distortion or discrimination results. When the phases of some frequencies are shifted more than those of other frequencies, phase distortion exists. Frequency distortion usually results in phase distortion.

When the power required from the output of the amplifier is so large as to preclude the use of electronic devices, dynamo-electric and magnetic amplifiers find wide application.

amplitude, in physics, the maximum displacement or distance moved by a point on a vibrating body or wave measured from its equilibrium position. It is equal to one-half the length of the vibration path. The amplitude of a pendulum is thus one-half the distance that the bob traverses in moving from one side to the other. Waves are generated by vibrating sources, their amplitude being proportional to the amplitude of the source.

For a transverse wave (*q.v.*), such as the wave on a plucked string, amplitude is measured by the maximum displacement of any point on the string from its position when the string is at rest. For a longitudinal wave, such as a sound wave, amplitude is measured by the maximum displacement of a particle from its position of equilibrium. When the amplitude of a wave steadily decreases because its energy is being lost, it is said to be damped.

amplitude modulation (AM), variation of the amplitude of a carrier wave (commonly a radio wave) in accordance with the characteristics of a signal, such as a vocal or musical sound composed of audio-frequency waves. *See* modulation.

amputation, removal of any part of the body; commonly the term is restricted to mean surgical removal of a part of or an entire limb, either upper or lower extremity. The reasons for surgical amputation in general are injury, infection, tumour, diabetes, or insufficient blood supply; occasionally surgical amputation is performed on nonfunctioning or grotesquely deformed limbs. Persons born without a limb or limbs are said to have suffered congenital amputation. Surgical amputation may be a lifesaving measure for injured persons suffering from both loss of blood and infection; for persons with diabetic or arteriosclerotic gangrene, in whom amputation may be the only method of preventing spread of the gangrene; and for persons suffering from malignant tumours of soft tissue or bone.

Modern reconstructive surgery makes possible the rehabilitation of many badly damaged limbs without amputation, and experience gained in World War II of early and thorough treatment of the severely injured, particularly through the use of blood and plasma, has saved many extremities. Furthermore, modern prostheses (artificial parts), particularly for amputations in the lower extremity, have reduced the handicap for the amputee. The congenital amputee seldom requires any corrective surgery but is benefitted by prosthetic replacement. There is no definitely known causative factor for congenital amputation, but it probably is not a hereditary deformity.

AMR Corp., holding company for the U.S. international airline American Airlines, Inc. The airline derives from a holding company founded in 1929 and called The Aviation Corporation, which was reorganized as an operating company and renamed American Airways, Inc., in 1930 and reorganized and incorporated as American Airlines, Inc., in 1934. In 1930, in the amalgamation of several airlines, it had routes extending from Boston and New York City to San Diego and Los Angeles, via Cleveland and Kansas City. By 1982 it was serving cities in several states of the continental United States and in Canada, Hawaii, Mexico, South America, and various points in the Caribbean (having acquired, through merger, Trans Caribbean Airways, Inc., in 1971). The holding company AMR Corp. was established in 1982. Company headquarters is in Dallas, Texas.

American Airlines developed over the years out of the union or merger of some 85 companies. Two nucleate companies of the early days of mail carriers were Robertson Aircraft Corporation and Colonial Air Transport. Robertson, first organized in 1921 in Missouri as a general flying service and manufacturer, flew its first mail route on April 15, 1926, between Chicago and St. Louis, Mo.; the pilot on the first flight was Charles A. Lindbergh. Colonial—developed out of a charter service called The Bee Line, formed in 1923—flew mail between New York City and Boston, beginning June 18, 1926.

In 1934, when most U.S. airlines were compelled to reorganize owing to new congressional guidelines and the loss of mail contracts, American thoroughly reworked its routes into an integrated system. Cyrus Rowlett Smith was elected president in that year and, as president or chairman of the board, guided the company's fortunes until 1968, when he became U.S. secretary of commerce. Returning briefly as chief executive officer in 1973, he retired in 1974.

An American Airlines subsidiary, Sky Chefs, formed in 1942, is primarily engaged in catering in-flight food for various airlines; it also operates coffee shops and gift shops in several airports. Another subsidiary, Americana Hotels, formed in 1963, operates or participates in the operation of hotels and inns in the United States, the Caribbean, Mexico, and other countries. Another subsidiary, Security '76, Inc., formed in 1972, provides ground transportation, airport baggage handling, and maintenance services for airports and other businesses.

ʿAmr ibn al-ʿĀṣ (d. 663, al-Fusṭāṭ, Egypt), the Arab conqueror of Egypt. A wealthy member of the Banū Sahm clan of the important tribe of Quraysh, he accepted Islām in 629–630. Sent to Oman, in southeastern Arabia, by the Prophet Muḥammad, he successfully completed his first mission by converting its rulers to Islām. As the leader of one of the three military forces sent to Palestine by the caliph Abū Bakr, he took part in the battles of Ajnādayn (634) and the Yarmūk River (636) and was responsible for the Muslim conquest of southwestern Palestine. He achieved lasting fame, however, for his conquest of Egypt—a campaign, according to some sources, he undertook on his own initiative. After defeating large Byzantine forces at Heliopolis (now a suburb of Cairo) in 640 and Babylon (a Byzantine town on the site of the present quarter called Old Cairo) in 641, he entered the capital, Alexandria, in 642.

A successful general, ʿAmr was also a capable government administrator and an astute politician. In Egypt he organized the system of taxation and the administration of justice and founded the garrison city of al-Fusṭāṭ adjacent to Babylon, where he built a mosque bearing his name. It still stands. At the Battle of Ṣiffīn (657), fought to decide the succession to the caliphate, he sided with Muʿāwiyah I, governor of Syria, against ʿAlī, the fourth caliph of Islām. In the ensuing arbitration, he faithfully represented Muʿāwiyah, who rewarded him with the governorship of Egypt at the advent of the Umayyad caliphate (named for the Banū Umayyah clan of Muʿāwiyah) in 661.

ʿAmr ibn al-ʿĀṣ, Mosque of, earliest Islāmic building in Egypt, erected in 641 by ʿAmr ibn al-ʿĀṣ, the leader of an invading Arab army. The mosque was built in al-Fusṭāṭ, a city that grew out of an Arab army encampment on the site of present-day Cairo.

Though originally a modest structure, it was destroyed and restored so often that it is impossible to know the appearance of the first building. The Umayyad 'Abd al-'Azīz demolished the mosque and rebuilt it, probably keeping much the same dimensions, in 698. In 827 the 'Abbāsids rebuilt it, doubling its size. The mosque was restored by Saladin in 1172 after the city of al-Fusṭāṭ was burned by crusaders. After periodic cycles of ruin and restoration, the mosque was left to decay with the coming of Napoleon Bonaparte's troops to Cairo in 1798. The present mosque is a 19th-century reconstruction that still preserves elements and ornamental work from various periods of the building's history.

'Amr ibn Kulthūm (fl. 6th century), pre-Islāmic Arab poet whose *qaṣīdah* ("ode") is one of the seven that comprise the celebrated anthology of pre-Islāmic verse *al-Mu'allaqāt.*

Little is known of his life; he became chief of the tribe of Taghlib in Mesopotamia at an early age and according to tradition killed 'Amr ibn Hind, the Arab king of al-Ḥīrah, *c.* 568.

'Amr ibn Kulthūm lived to a very advanced age, highly respected for his noble character, for a poem, allegedly his, praising a Taghlib victory over the Bakr tribe, and for his successfully independent stance against the Lakhmid kings of al-Ḥīrah. 'Amr's *qaṣīdah,* as it appears in *al-Mu'allaqāt,* was probably altered by a later poet. It violently attacks 'Amr ibn Hind for an insult addressed to the poet's mother.

Amram bar Sheshna (d. 875?), head of the Talmudic academy at Sura, Babylonia, traditionally regarded as the first Jewish authority to write a complete domestic and synagogal liturgy for the year, the *Siddur Rav Amram* ("Order of Prayers of Rabbi Amram"). Amram's work, forerunner in this field of those of Sa'adia ben Joseph and Maimonides, laid the foundations for the liturgies of both the Sephardim (Spanish Jews) and Ashkenazim (Germanic Jews). In addition to the prayers, his liturgy included a related Talmudic commentary. Surviving in manuscript form, it was first published (in two parts) in Warsaw in 1865. Neither the first part, composed of the main body of prayers, nor the second, consisting of propitiatory prayers and liturgical poems for the month of Elul (August–September), the New Year, and the Day of Atonement, can be definitely attributed to Amram, and it is obvious that many of the devotions and interpolations are by other hands.

Amram also composed numerous responsa (replies to inquiries about Jewish Law), which, touching upon such subjects as dietary restrictions and regulations for sabbaths and holidays, reveal much of the Jewish Law and custom of his time.

Amratian culture, also called NAQĀDAH I CULTURE, Egyptian predynastic cultural phase, centred in Upper Egypt, its type-site being al-'Āmirah near Abydos in Qinā *muḥāfaẓah* (governorate). Numerous sites, dating to about 3600 BC, have been excavated and reveal an agricultural way of life similar to that of the preceding Badarian culture, but with advanced skills and techniques, including mud-brick structures in fair-sized towns. Pottery characteristic of this period includes black-topped red ware and a dark-red burnished ware, occasionally decorated in white paint with bold linear designs—human or animal figures; on an Amratian shard excavated at Naqādah the earliest known representation of the pharaonic red crown is drawn. Other important remains include disk-shaped maceheads, slate cosmetic palettes, well-made stone vases and ivory carvings, and numerous figurines of various materials.

Amratian tools and utensils
By courtesy of the Royal Scottish Museum, Edinburgh

Amrāvati, also called AMRAOTI, town, administrative headquarters of Amrāvati district, Mahārāshtra state, western India, in the Berār region. Its name means "city of the immortals." The town occupies an important position near passes through the hills that separate the cotton-growing regions of the Pūrna Basin (west) and the Wardha Basin (east). A growing industrial centre, it is expanding toward nearby Badnera; its cotton mills supply Bombay, Calcutta, and Ahmadābād. The town houses seven colleges affiliated with the University of Nāgpur.

Amrāvati district occupies an area of 4,714 sq mi (12,210 sq km). The Melghāt Range forms the northern boundary with Madhya Pradesh state and contains the popular resort town of Chikalda (3,900 ft [1,200 m]). The broad alluvial basin of the Pūrna River in the south is one of India's principal cotton-growing areas. The district's towns are primarily agricultural markets, and its industry is mainly cotton ginning and pressing. The chief industrial centres are Amrāvati town and Badnera. Pop. (1981) town, 261,404; district, 1,861,410.

Amreli, formerly AMARAVALLI, town, administrative headquarters of Amreli district, southwestern Gujarāt state, west central India, on the Kāthiāwār Peninsula, southwest of Ahmadābād. Primarily a commercial centre, its industries include *khādī* (coarse cotton cloth) manufacture, tanning, silverworking, and cotton ginning. Amreli is served by a railway and an airfield.

Amreli district occupies an area of 2,610 sq mi (6,760 sq km). Organized in 1959, it is composed of the Kāthiāwār possessions of former Baroda princely state (acceded to India in 1949); Gogho *mahāl* (subdivision), formerly in Ahmadābād district; and *mahāls* from adjacent districts. Chief crops of the district are millet, peanuts (groundnuts), cotton, wheat, and pulses. Pop. (1981) town, 56,598; metropolitan area, 58,241; district, 1,079,097.

'Amri (Israelite general): *see* Omri.

Amritsar, city, administrative headquarters of Amritsar district, Punjab state, northwestern India, on the Pakistani border, the largest city in the state. A major commercial, cultural, and transportation centre, it lies approximately 30 mi (50 km) from the border. Amritsar was founded in 1577 by Rām Dās, fourth guru (religious preceptor) of the Sikhs, around a sacred tank, or pool, called Amrita Saras, from which the city's name is derived. A temple stands on an island in the tank's centre; after its copper dome was covered with goldfoil, it was named the Golden Temple. Amritsar became the centre of the Sikh faith. As the centre of growing Sikh power, it experienced a corresponding increase in trade. It was annexed to British India in 1849. The Amritsar Massacre, in which government troops fired on a political gathering and killed or wounded hundreds, occurred at a park, Jalliānwālla Bāgh, in the city in 1919; the site is now a national monument. Another violent political clash took place in Amritsar in 1984, when troops of the Indian army attacked hundreds of Sikh separatists who had taken up positions in and heavily fortified the Golden Temple.

Headquarters of the Organization for the Management of the Sikh Temples at Amritsar, Punjab, India
Milt and Joan Mann—CAMERAMANN INTERNATIONAL

Amritsar's varied industries include textiles, food milling and processing, silk weaving, tanning, canning, and manufacturing. The city lies on the main highway from Delhi to Lahore, Pak., and is a major rail hub. An airport is nearby. Besides the Medical College, dental, arts, and technical colleges are located in Amritsar; and Khalsa College (established 1899) is just outside.

Amritsar district, 1,964 sq mi (5,088 sq km) in area, is an almost level plain drained by the Rāvi and Beās rivers. Because of the fairly dry climate the district's agriculture depends on irrigation, chiefly from the Upper Bāri Doāb Canal system; wheat, cotton, pulses, and corn (maize) are the biggest crops. Pop. (1981) city, 594,844; district, 2,188,490.

Amritsar, Massacre of (April 13, 1919), incident in which British troops fired on a crowd of Indian protesters, killing a large number. It left a permanent scar on Indo-British relations and was the prelude to Mahatma Gandhi's Non-cooperation Movement of 1920–22.

In 1919 the British government of India enacted the Rowlatt Acts, extending its World War I emergency powers to combat subversive activities. At Amritsar, Punjab (Pañjāb) district, about 10,000 demonstrators unlawfully protesting these measures confronted troops commanded by Brig. Gen. Reginald Dyer in an open space known as the Jallianwalla Bāgh, which had only one exit. The troops fired on the crowd, killing an estimated 379 and wounding about 1,200, according to one official report. The shooting was followed by the proclamation of martial law, public floggings, and other humiliations. The Hunter Commission condemned General Dyer (1920), but the House of Lords praised his action, and a fund was raised in his honour.

Amritsar, Treaty of (April 25, 1809), pact concluded between Charles T. Metcalfe, representing the British East India Company, and Ranjit Singh, head of the Sikh kingdom of

Punjab (Pañjāb); it settled Indo-Sikh relations for a generation. The immediate occasion was the French threat to northwestern India, following Napoleon's Treaty of Tilsit with Russia (1807) and Ranjit's attempt to bring the Cis-Sutlej states under his control. The British wanted a defensive treaty against the French and control of Punjab to the Sutlej River. Although this was not a defensive treaty, it did fix the frontier with Ranjit broadly along the line of the Sutlej River.

Metcalfe's mission gave Ranjit much respect for the company's disciplined troops and determination never to cross swords with them. His further conquests were to the west and north.

Amroha, town, Morādābād district, Uttar Pradesh state, northern India, west-northwest of Morādābād town, on the Sot River. A marketplace for agricultural produce, its chief industries are handloom weaving, pottery making, and sugar milling. Colleges of Āgra University are located there, as is the shrine of Sheikh Saddu, a Muslim saint. Amroha is connected by rail with Morādābād and Delhi. Pop. (1981) 112,682.

Amrouche, Jean (b. 1906, Ighil Ali, Alg.—d. April 16, 1962, Paris), foremost poet of the earliest generation of Francophonic, Maghribian writers.

Amrouche was born into one of the few Roman Catholic families in the Kabyle mountains but immigrated with his family to Tunisia when still quite young. He completed his studies in Tunis and in Paris.

As a young man, Amrouche published *Cendres* (1934) and *Étoile secrète* (1937), the most significant volumes of Algerian poetry ever written in French. Taking inspiration from his Berber roots as well as from modern European post-Symbolism, Amrouche testifies to the purity of his origins, evoking the quest for a lost homeland and the sense of ancestral nobility. A lyricist of the first order, he clothed his verse, written in the borrowed language of the colonial rulers, in an eloquent and fluid beauty. Later works included a collection of Berber lyrics and an essay, "L'Éternel Jugurtha" (1943), that stands as the definitive statement on the Maghribian identity torn by the complexes of acculturation and alienation. Amrouche was a teacher and devoted time in his later years to speaking on radio for the Algerian cause to the French people.

Where the same name may denote a person, place, or thing, the articles will be found in that order

---

Amrouche, Marguerite Taos, original name MARIE-LOUISE AMROUCHE, also called MARY-LOUISE TAOS (b. March 4, 1913, Tunis), Kabyle singer and writer.

Amrouche was the daughter of Fadhma Aïth Mansour Amrouche (*Histoire de ma vie,* 1968), the only sister in a family of six sons, and was born after the family had moved to Tunisia to escape persecution after their conversion to Catholicism. Despite this exile, both she and her brother Jean returned to Algeria for extended visits. Through her mother's influence she became interested in the rich oral traditions of the Kabyle Berber people. In 1934 she obtained her *brevet supérieur* in Tunis, and in the following year she went to France for studies at the École Normale at Sèvres. She worked briefly as an assistant at a boarding school in Radès. Starting in 1936, in collaboration with Jean and her mother, Amrouche collected and began to interpret Kabyle songs. In 1937–38 she presented her repertoire in Paris and in Munich. At the Congrès de Chant de Fès in 1939 she received a scholarship to study at the Casa Velasquez in Spain, where she researched the ties between Berber and Spanish popular songs.

Amrouche's first novel, *Jacinthe noire* (1947), recounts the story of an "uncivilized" young Tunisian girl who is sent to a French pension for studies. Differences in life-style, attitudes, and experiences set her apart, and exile, prejudice, and rupture are themes of the novel, which is one of the earliest ever published in French by a North African woman writer. A second novel, *Rue des tambourins* (1960), describes a sense of marginality and owes a great deal to its author's recollections of her childhood in Tunis. A third novel, *Solitude ma mère,* was also well received.

Le Grain magique (1966)—a collection of legends, short stories, songs, poems, and proverbs from the Kabyle, translated by her from Berber into French—is perhaps her best known work. She recorded several phonograph albums, and, as a producer for French radio and television, produced such programs as *Chants sauvés de l'oubli* and *Hommage au chant profond.*

Amsdorf, Nikolaus von (b. Dec. 3, 1483, Torgau, Saxony—d. May 14, 1565, Eisenach), Protestant Reformer and major supporter of Martin Luther.

Educated at Leipzig and then at Wittenberg, where he became a theology professor in 1511, Amsdorf attended the Leipzig Debate with Luther in 1519 and the Diet of Worms two years later, where he participated in the plan to protect Luther from his detractors by pretending to kidnap him while actually lodging him secretly in Wartburg, near Eisenach.

Amsdorf, lithograph 1820, after a 16th-century engraving
Kester Lichtbild-Archiv

Amsdorf subsequently aided the Reformation at Magdeburg (1524), Goslar (1531), Einbeck (1534), and Schmalkalden (1537). When Luther, in 1539, supported the intended bigamous marriage of Philip, landgrave of Hesse, Amsdorf temporarily opposed him but was made bishop of Naumburg by Luther and by John Frederick I, elector of Saxony, in 1541.

As an Evangelical holding a bishopric, Amsdorf found his position difficult but remained under Luther's persuasion until it was necessary to yield to the Roman Catholic bishop Julius von Pflug in 1547. Exiled to Magdeburg, Amsdorf superintended the Jena edition of Luther's works. Continuing to fight for the purity of Luther's doctrine, he opposed the more liberal views of Philipp Melanchthon and other Reformers. In particular he emphasized that salvation could come only to men of faith and that their efforts to perform good works might even be self-defeating. Among Amsdorf's extant writings are numerous letters and varied short works.

BIBLIOGRAPHY. H. Stille, *Nikolaus von Amsdorf, 1483–1542* (1937); P. Brunner, *N. von Amsdorf als Bischof von Naumburg* (1961).

Amstelveen, *gemeente* (municipality), in Noordholland *provincie* (province), western Netherlands, near the Amstel River. Amstelveen (meaning "peat bog on the Amstel") was formerly a village in the municipality of Nieuwer-Amstel. A residential suburb of Amsterdam, it is a water-sports centre with some agriculture and light industry. Schipol international airport is nearby to the west. Pop. (1983 est.) 68,894.

Amsterdam, city and port, western Netherlands, located at the head of the IJsselmeer, an inlet of the North Sea. Amsterdam occupies some 90 islands connected by about 600 bridges and is the nominal capital of The Netherlands, but not its seat of government (which is The Hague).

The following article treats briefly the modern city of Amsterdam. Fuller treatment is provided in the following MACROPAEDIA articles. For history and contemporary life, *see* Amsterdam. For additional perspective on the city in its regional context, *see* Low Countries, The.

Amsterdam is situated on the IJ, an inland arm of the former Zuiderzee, now IJsselmeer, and is connected by canal with the North Sea. It is divided by the canalized Amstel River into two main sections. To protect themselves from floods, the early inhabitants built dikes on both sides of the Amstel River, and in 1270 they built a dam between these dikes, the Amstel-dam. By the mid-17th century Amsterdam had become the financial centre of the world and remains today the main wholesale and industrial centre of The Netherlands.

The medieval portion of Amsterdam, enclosed by the semicircular Singel gracht (canal), lies on both sides of the Amstel at the city's centre. There are many reminders of the city's glorious past—the gabled houses, the almshouses, the richly decorated cornices, the towers and churches, and the music of carillons and barrel organs. Among the ancient buildings still preserved are the 13th-century Oude Kerk (Old Church), and the Nieuwe Kerk (New Church, 1468). Other notable buildings include the Royal Palace, in classical Palladian style; the Munttower (Mint Tower); and the Westerkerk (West Church, 1631), where Rembrandt van Rijn is buried. The former Jewish quarter, in the east of the old town, is the site of the Portuguese Synagogue (1670) and the Rembrandthuis (Rembrandt's house), now a museum. The old town's three main squares are the Dam, the Leidseplein, and the Rembrandtsplein. Buildings constructed in the late 19th century include the Rijksmuseum (State Museum; 1876–85), known for its collection of 17th-century art; the Concertgebouw (Concert Hall); and the Olympic Stadium (1928).

Since 1935 city development plans have been undertaken to improve housing, recreation areas, traffic, schools, other public buildings, and public transportation. New cities constructed on the polders (land reclaimed from the sea) of the former Zuiderzee, east of the city, are designed to absorb some of Amsterdam's growth. Although Amsterdam's urban area has doubled since 1945, the population has not significantly increased.

Amsterdam has been an important economic centre since the 17th century, when the Amsterdam Exchange Bank was founded to correct the chaotic monetary situation of the time. It soon developed into the largest clearinghouse in Europe and made the city an international financial centre. The Dutch East India Company was also founded there during the 17th century and laid the basis for modern dealings in stocks; the Amsterdam Stock Exchange is considered to be the oldest in the world.

Amsterdam has played an important role in wholesale trade since the 14th century. By 1968 the harbour mouth at IJmuiden (about 15 miles northwest of the city) had been modernized. There is a major international airport at Schiphol, about 5 mi from the city.

Area city, 65 sq mi (167 sq km); metropolitan area, 177 sq mi (458 sq km). Pop. (1983 est.) city, 687,397; metropolitan area, 936,410.

Amsterdam, city, Montgomery County, eastern New York, U.S., on the Mohawk River, 16 mi (26 km) northwest of Schenectady. Settled by Albert Veeder in 1783, it was known as Veedersburg until renamed for Amsterdam, Neth., in 1804. Its location on the Mohawk Trail, the completion of the Erie Canal in 1825 (improved as the New York State Barge Canal), and the arrival of the railroad (1836) stimulated its development. By 1838 textile mills were established along Chuctanunda Creek, a tributary of the Mohawk. The once dominant carpet and textile industries have to some extent given way to diversified manufactures, notably electronic equipment and toys. The Guy Park Manor, built in 1766 by Sir William Johnson and now a state historic site, and the nearby old Ft. Johnson (1749) are maintained as museums. The National Shrine of the North American Martyrs (René Goupil, Fr. Isaac Jogues, Jean Lalande, and five priests who were massacred by Mohawk Indians) is at Auriesville, 6 mi (10 km) west. The Schoharie Crossing State Historic Site, 5 mi west, includes locks and a remarkable nine-arched aqueduct (1841) built across transverse streams to control the passage of the Erie Canal. Inc. village, 1830; city, 1885. Pop. (1920) 33,524; (1970) 25,524; (1980) 21,872.

Amsterdam Cabinet, Master of the (late Gothic painter and engraver): *see* Housebook, Master of the.

Amsterdam–Rhine Canal, Dutch AMSTERDAM-RIJNKANAAL, waterway connecting the port of Amsterdam with the Lek River (via Utrecht) and the Waal River (at Tiel). Inaugurated in 1952, it has a total length of 45 mi (72 km) and four locks. Considered to be the most heavily used canal in western Europe, it handles vessels of up to 4,300 tons' displacement; minimum depth is 13.8 ft (4.2 m).

Amsterdam Zoo, Dutch STICHTING KONINKLIJK ZOOLOGISCH GENOOTSCHAP NATURA ARTIS MAGISTRA, also called ARTIS, zoological garden founded in 1838 by the Royal Zoological Society of Holland. It occupies a 10-hectare (25-acre) site in Amsterdam and houses nearly 5,600 specimens of some 1,350 species. Heavily oriented toward scientific research, the zoo has its own animal behaviour laboratory and is closely affiliated with a library and natural history museum.

Amstetten, town, *Bundesland* Niederösterreich (federal province of Lower Austria), northeastern Austria, near the Ybbs River, northeast of Steyr. Recorded in 996 as a possession of the bishops of Passau, it was fortified and granted market rights when it passed to the Habsburgs in 1276. It achieved town status in 1897. The 14th-century parish church incorporates an earlier Romanesque basilica. Amstetten has metal, wood, and construction industries and manufactures baked goods, glass, clothing, and chemicals. Pop. (1981) 22,015.

Amtrak, formally NATIONAL RAILROAD PASSENGER CORPORATION, federally supported corporation that operates nearly all intercity passenger trains in the United States. It was established by Congress in 1970 and assumed control of passenger service from the nation's private rail companies the following year. Virtually all railways, with the exception of a small handful, signed contracts with Amtrak. The corporation pays the railroads to run their passenger trains and also compensates them for the use of certain facilities, including tracks and terminals. It bears all administrative costs, such as those incurred for the purchase of new equipment, and manages scheduling, route planning, and the sale of tickets.

Amtrak was founded to relieve U.S. railroads of the financial burden of providing passenger service and to improve the quality of that service. Since about the early 1960s the railroads had lost millions of dollars annually on their passenger lines as a result of a steady decline in ridership and increase in operating costs. To avert further losses, many of the companies dropped their unprofitable routes. In 1950 there were approximately 9,000 passenger trains in service, which carried just under 50 percent of all intercity traffic. By 1970, however, there were only about 450 trains still in operation with a total share of the passenger traffic amounting to a mere seven percent.

The creation of Amtrak marked the first time that rail passenger service received any form of direct financial assistance from the U.S. government (although land grants and other assistance had been given railroads to spur completion of a transcontinental line some 109 years earlier). Congress provided Amtrak with an initial grant of $40,000,000 and authorized an additional $100,000,000 in government-guaranteed loans. Moreover, Amtrak receives several million dollars in federal funds annually to cover operating losses. Although the corporation derives income from ticket sales and from its mail carrying service, revenues are not enough to offset expenditures.

Amu Darya (River), Russian AMUDARYA, also spelled AMUDARJA, the OXUS RIVER of the ancient West, longest river of Soviet Central Asia, formed by the confluence of the Vakhsh and Pyandzh rivers, flowing west-northwest to its mouth on the southern shore of the Aral Sea, forming part of the border between the Tadzhik Soviet Socialist Republic and Afghanistan. It has a length of 879 mi (1,415 km); but its length is 1,578 mi (2,540 km), if measured from the remotest sources of its longest headstream, the Daryā-ye Vākhjīr in the Eastern Pamirs. Called Jayḥūn by the Arabs, its present name allegedly derives from the city of Āmul, which is said to have occupied the site of modern Chardzhou.

The Amu Darya Basin extends for 600 mi from north to south and for over 900 mi from east to west. It borders on the Syrdarya Basin in the north, on the Tarim Basin in the east, and on the Indus and Helmand basins in the south. Of its total area of 179,700 sq mi (465,500 sq km), only 88,000 sq mi belong to the regions whence the river is fed; that is to say, to the mountain ranges or to the Zeravshan and Kashkadarya reservoir zones. The mountainous part of the basin lies among the drifting, permanent snows and glaciers of the Pamirs (with the adjacent Alay Range [Alaysky Khrebet] to the northwest) and of the Hindu Kush, where heights average from 16,400 to 18,000 ft and in some places reach 19,000 and even 23,000 ft. Its plains form part of the Turan Lowland (Turanskaya Nizmennost) within which the desert of Kyzylkum and part of the Kara-Kum Desert also lie. Below its conventional source the river is joined by only three tributaries: from the left by the Surkhob, and from the right by the Kafirnigan and Surkhandarya. Thenceforth, the river continues to its mouth without receiving a single tributary, losing much of its water in evaporation and drainage or to irrigation on the way.

The Amu Darya may be divided into five parts: (1) from the confluence of the Pyandzh and Vakhsh rivers to the city of Kerki; (2) thence to the Ilchik Ravine; (3) from there to the Tyuyamuyun Ravine; (4) to the village of Takhiyatas; and (5) to the Delta. In its first section the river spreads lakelike to wind through a valley crisscrossed by channels and with many lakes and marshes. In its second section the valley varies from 2.5 to 16 mi wide, with the river branching around many islands. From the Ilchik to the Tyuyamuyun Ravine the river valley narrows to widths of from one to 2.5 mi, and within it the river branches and bends very much less. In its fourth section the river widens into an area of marked erosion, while in its final section—from the village of Takhiyatas to the Delta—many distributaries, characterized by temporary flooding, begin to form.

Junipers and poplars grow down to the river's edge in the mountain regions where bushes of sweetbrier and blackberries also abound. Willows, buckthorn, and oleasters predominate lower down, while on the river's middle course the *tugai*, or dense flood-meadow forest, made up of different varieties of willow and poplar, proliferates. Willows, oleasters, and poplars continue along the river's lowest reaches to form an impenetrable tangle at the river's reed-covered delta. Fish found in the Amu Darya include varieties of sturgeon, carp, barbel, and trout, while riverain animals include boar, wildcat, jackal, fox, and hare. There are also 211 species of birds.

Well known as it was in antiquity and to the Arabian geographers of the 2nd and 3rd century, the Amu Darya, nevertheless, received but little attention until the reign of Peter I. Though the first relatively authentic map was made in 1734, systematic research of the river was begun only at the end of the 19th century. At the end of the 1920s a map of the entire Amu Darya Basin was published in Tashkent. Detailed studies by Soviet scientists are still going on.

The Amu Darya is largely dependent on the waters of its tributaries, the Pyandzh and the Vakhsh, the greater part of the flow of which derives from melting snow and ice. Increasing from March to May, when snow melts on the plains and rainfall increases, the river's flow is further augmented in June, July, and August as the ice and snow of the mountain ranges thaw. It gradually abates from September to February. Ice forms along the banks of the upper reaches, as do sludge and drifting ice. Lower down near the delta, however, Nukus is icebound for from two to two and a half months. Beginning to disperse at the beginning of February in the middle reaches and elsewhere toward the end of March, ice floes jam the river downstream. In its upper course the river's flow is stable; in its lower course it is much less so. The amount of matter suspended in the water is very high. Near Kerki, for example, it has averaged 210,000,000 tons per year since 1960 and, near Nukus, 130,000,000 tons. At the same places ratios of alluvium of 0.25 lbs and 0.17 lbs, respectively, per cu ft have been recorded. The water also contains hydrocarbonate.

The diversion to irrigation of water from the main stream and from its tributaries is desirable—particularly in summer—for, though more than 100 canals water the cultivated lands that border its lower course, and more are being built, water supplies elsewhere remain inadequate.

The unstable river bed and shoals so hamper navigation that though the Amu Darya is navigable from its mouth to Termez little transport is conveyed by it. A complex system of dams has been erected, mainly on the lower course, to protect the cultivated fields from floods. Further dams, reservoirs, and barrages are at the planning stage or are already under construction. Two giant hydroelectric stations, the Nurek and the Rogun, were under construction during the 1970s and early 1980s on the Vakhsh River. At 984 ft (300 m) and 1,098 ft, respectively, they would be the two highest dams in the world at their completion.

Amud remains, skeletal remains of two adults and two children estimated to have lived about 50,000–60,000 years ago, found in 1961 in a cave near Tiberias, Israel, by Hisashi Suzuki on a Tokyo University scientific expedition to western Asia. The remains are held in the Rockefeller Archaeological Museum, Jerusalem. They consist of a skeleton of an adult male about 25 years old, a fragment of an adult jaw, and skull fragments of infants.

The skull and some bones of the skeleton were crushed but have been largely reconstructed. The palate and central part of the face are still missing but the dentition and jaw are complete. The cranial capacity (volume of the skull) is the largest of all the fossils so far found, indicating a large brain, but one probably not as developed as that of *Homo sapiens sapiens*. Though the bones are incomplete, an estimate for the height of the skeleton is given as from 172 to 177 centimetres (68 to 70 inches). The long bones are slender and long, the hand is large with large joints, and the pelvis is narrow. The skull has the features of Neanderthal man with a receding forehead, divided brow, and prominent mastoid processes.

The remains suggest that they are part of a group known as Near Eastern Neanderthal man with a mixture of West Asian features similar to those of fossils found in 1957 in Iraq that were estimated to have lived about 46,000 years ago and those of the Upper Paleolithic people who lived in southwestern France and the Middle East from about 10,000 to 35,000 years ago. The stone tools found with the Amud remains are classified as Mousterian, dating about 50,000 years ago. The evidence provides more proof that Neanderthal man was a highly varied species, the last of archaic man, who lived in much of the Northern Hemisphere, except the New World.

Amul (Iran): *see* Āmol.

amulet, an object, either natural or man-made, believed to be endowed with special powers to protect or bring good fortune. Amulets are carried on the person or kept in the place that is the desired sphere of influence—*e.g.*, on a roof or in a field.

Natural amulets are of many kinds: precious stones, metals, teeth and claws of animals, plants, etc. Man-made amulets, equally varied, include small models of animals or of objects, medallions bearing religious images or inscriptions, and lockets containing such inscriptions on paper or metal. Amulets are thought to derive power from their connection with natural forces, from religious associations, or from being made in a ritual manner at a favourable time.

The use of amulets has a long history. The MacGregor papyrus lists 75 amulets employed by the ancient Egyptians. One of the commonest was the scarab beetle, worn by the living and dead alike. The scarab (*q.v.*) symbolized life—perhaps because it swarmed in great quantities at flood time, perhaps because its hieroglyph was pronounced the same as that for life—and was thought to restore the dead person's heart in the next world. In Egypt the magic formulas originally recited over amulets to give them their power were eventually inscribed and worn themselves.

In the Middle Ages the use of amulets incurred the disapproval of the Christian church, but, among Jews, the later Kabbalists seemed to sanction their use. Indeed, the preparation of amulets became a rabbinic function. Among Oriental Jews, amulets against Lilith are commonly suspended in the birth chamber.

Amun (Egyptian god): *see* Amon.

Amundsen, Roald (b. July 16, 1872, Borge, near Oslo—d. June 18, 1928?, Arctic Ocean), polar explorer who was the first to reach the South Pole and was one of the first to cross the Arctic by air.

Amundsen studied medicine before he sailed as first mate on a Belgian expedition (1897) that was the first to winter in the Antarctic. He next sailed the Northwest Passage, east to west, in the 47-ton sloop "Gjöa" (1903–06).

While planning a drift across the North Pole in 1909, he learned that Robert E. Peary had reached it in April of that year. Amundsen continued preparations and set sail from Norway in June 1910, but for the South Pole. Based 60 miles closer to the pole than was the English explorer Robert Falcon Scott, Amundsen set out by sledge with four companions and 52 dogs on Oct. 19, 1911, and arrived at the pole on December 14.

With funds resulting from his Antarctic adventure, Amundsen established a successful shipping business. After the failure of an Arctic voyage in 1918, he sought to reach the North Pole by air and in 1925, with the U.S. explorer Lincoln Ellsworth, flew within 170 miles of it. In 1926, with Ellsworth and the Italian aeronautical engineer Umberto Nobile, he passed over the pole in a dirigible, crossing from Spitsbergen (now Svalbard), north of Norway, to Alaska. Disputes over the credit for the flight embittered his final years. In 1928 Amundsen lost his life in flying to rescue Nobile from a dirigible crash near Spitsbergen. Amundsen's books include *The South Pole* (1912) and, with Ellsworth, *First Crossing of the Polar Sea* (1927).

Amundsen Gulf, southeastern extension of the Beaufort Sea of the Arctic Ocean, extending for 250 mi (400 km) and separating Banks Island (north) from the Canadian mainland (south). It lies between Mackenzie and Franklin districts in the Northwest Territories, Canada. The first expedition to traverse the Northwest Passage, led by the British explorer Robert McClure, entered Amundsen Gulf, the passage's westernmost section, in 1850 but had to use another route because of ice in the Prince of Wales Strait, a northeasterly extension of the gulf. The gulf is named for the Norwegian explorer Roald Amundsen, who first navigated the Northwest Passage.

ʿAmūq, Turkish AMİK, triangular plain of southern Turkey, bordering Syria, about 190 sq mi (500 sq km) in area, defined by the cities of Antioch, Kırıkhan, and Reyhanlı; it centres on Amik Gölü (lake), with an elevation of only 266 ft (81 m), though surrounded by mountains. The plain is the site of some 180 Neolithic and later settlements, not all of which have been excavated. The name ʿAmūq is given to a series of 12 chronological stages, identified by letters from A (earliest; about 6000 BC) through L (latest; about 1600 BC).

Amur, *oblast* (administrative region), eastern Russian Soviet Federated Socialist Republic, created in 1932. Its 140,425 sq mi (363,700 sq km), lying in the basins of the middle Amur and its tributary the Zeya, extend up to the crest of the Stanovoy Range. The southern part, the fertile, black-earth lowland of the Zeya-Bureya Plain, is now largely under cultivation. The higher north and east are almost entirely forested. Most of the population is Russian or Ukrainian; the largest of the 16 indigenous groups are the Yakuts and Evenks of the north. The chief city and administrative centre is Blagoveshchensk (*q.v.*). Grain, chiefly spring wheat, is the dominant crop of the lowland. Soybeans, sunflowers, and flax are the main industrial crops. Open-pit coal mining is carried on at Raychikhinsk, and gold is found in the north. There is some timber production. The Zeya dam and hydroelectric station on the Zeya River, with a design capacity of nearly 1,300 megawatts, was to be surpassed by the Bureya dam and hydroelectric station, scheduled to begin operation in the mid-1980s with an expected capacity of 2,000 megawatts. A major new railroad, the BAM (Baikal–Amur Magistral), was under construction in the early 1980s. Pop. (1983 est.) 1,007,000.

Amur River, Wade–Giles romanization HEI-LUNG CHIANG, Pinyin HEILONG JIANG, Mongol KHARAMUREN, river of East Asia, forming part of the frontier between the Soviet Union and the People's Republic of China.

The following article summarizes information about the Amur River; for full details, *see* MACROPAEDIA: Asia.

The headwaters of the Amur rise along the northern borders of northeast China and the Inner Mongolian Autonomous Region of China and form the Amur proper at the confluence of the Shilka and Argun rivers. Downriver the Amur, with a total length of 1,755 mi (2,824 km), flows generally east and southeast along the Soviet–Chinese border to Khabarovsk, Siberia. There it turns northeastward and flows across Soviet territory to empty into the Tatar Strait of the Pacific Ocean, a narrow channel connecting the Sea of Japan (south) and the Sea of Okhotsk (north).

The Amur's drainage basin covers an area of 716,200 sq mi (1,855,000 sq km), and among the river's major tributaries are the Zeya, Bureya, Sungari, Ussuri, and Amgun rivers. The Upper and Middle Amur sections flow alternately through mountain valleys and open plateau country. Much of the Lower Amur runs between low, often overflowing banks into a vast marsh, the surface of which is broken by channels and dotted with lakes and ponds; the riverbed branches often, and the channel becomes very wide. The Amur Basin has a monsoon climate—a seasonal alternation of winds from the mainland and the ocean. In winter the dry, cold air from Siberia brings clear, dry weather with strong frost, while in summer the moist ocean winds predominate. The river, with an average annual discharge of 380,000 cu ft/sec (10,900 cu m/sec), is fed primarily by monsoon rains that fall in summer and autumn. During the high-water season from May to October, regions of the Lower Amur Basin often become enormous lakes.

The Amur is rich in fish; more than 25 species are of commercial value. The river basin was originally populated by hunting and cattle-breeding nomadic tribes. From the 18th century onward the area north of the Amur was settled by Russians along with Ukrainians, Belorussians, Tatars, Latvians, and other internal deportees from European Russia. South of the Amur live Chinese, Mongols, Manchus, and many other peoples. The Amur is navigable throughout its entire course for about half the year. The potential for hydroelectric power production in the Amur River Basin is high, but only limited development has taken place to date.

Amurath (Ottoman sultan): *see* Murad.

Amursk, city, Khabarovsk *kray* (territory), Russian Soviet Federated Socialist Republic, on the left bank of the Amur River, 25 mi (40 km) south of Komsomolsk-na-Amure. Founded in 1958, Amursk became one of the fastest growing towns in the far eastern Soviet Union. A wood-processing complex, opened in 1967, is one of the largest in the Soviet Union, producing wood pulp, container board, and fibreboard. The industry is expected to expand as more of the goods shipped by the Trans-Siberian Railroad are containerized. Pop. (1970) 24,010.

Amursky, Nikolay Nikolayevich Muravyov, Graf (Count): *see* Muravyov, Nikolay Nikolayevich, Graf.

Amuzgo, also spelled AMUSGO, ethnolinguistic Indian group of eastern Guerrero and western Oaxaca, Mexico. Their language is related to that of the Mixtec, their neighbours to the north and west. Although many Amuzgo can speak Spanish, the majority (about 65 percent) speak only Amuzgo.

The people are agricultural, using the plow or digging stick to plant the Middle American staples of corn, beans, and squash, as well as some chilies and tomatoes, and sugarcane as a cash crop. Wild game and seafood are eaten, and farm animals are also kept. Houses are traditionally round thatched huts, two or more for each household. Settlements may be in towns or villages or dispersed. Weaving and pottery are the major crafts practiced, though hammocks, ropes, and nets are also made. For clothing, men wear cotton shirts and pants and straw hats and may carry a small bag; women wear a calf-length underskirt and a *huipil,* a long cotton overblouse.

The *compadrazgo,* or godparent relationship, is widely practiced, godparents being chosen at baptism and marriage. Children owe great respect to godparents, and parents and godparents participate in various rituals of kinship. Nominally Roman Catholic, the Amuzgo celebrate their community's patron saint's day and practice baptism and marriage in the church; however, several non-Christian rituals are also observed, and the mythology of the community is non-Christian.

Amvrakikós Kólpos (Greece): *see* Árta, Gulf of.

amygdule, secondary deposit of minerals found in a rounded, elongated, or almond-shaped cavity in igneous rock. The cavities (vesicles) were created by the expansion of gas bubbles or steam within lava. Some amygdules consist partially of lava, which indicates their formation during solidification of the rock. Since gas bubbles tend to rise through the lava, amygdules are most common near the tops of flows. The secondary minerals may form after the solidification of the lava; the gases may help to form the filling minerals. A great variety of minerals have been found as amygdules, including some of the spectacular museum specimens of zeolites.

amyl alcohol, also called PENTYL ALCOHOL, any of eight organic compounds having the same molecular formula, $C_5H_{11}OH$, but different structures; the term is commonly applied to mixtures of these compounds, used as solvents for resins and oily materials and for the manufacture of other chemicals, especially amyl acetate, a solvent for nitrocellulose lacquers. Commercial amyl alcohols are colourless liquids, slightly soluble in water, and having a characteristic penetrating odour.

Before the 1920s, the only economical source of amyl alcohol was fusel oil, formed as a minor product in fermentation of carbohydrates to make ethyl alcohol. More abundant and dependable production results from two industrial syntheses that employ hydrocarbons available from petroleum. In the first of these methods, introduced in 1926, chlorination of pentane gives mixed amyl chlorides that are converted to the desired alcohols by reaction with water and caustic alkali. A second process, introduced in 1953, is based on the reaction of carbon monoxide and hydrogen with butene.

amylase, any member of a class of enzymes that catalyze the fragmentation of molecules of starch, which are built up by plants from thousands of molecules of glucose, into molecules of maltose, which are composed of just two bonded glucose molecules. Two categories of amylases, denoted alpha and beta, are recognized; they differ in the way they attack the bonds of the starch molecules.

Alpha-amylase is widespread among living organisms. In the digestive systems of man and many other mammals, an alpha-amylase called ptyalin is produced by the salivary glands; another, called amylopsin, is secreted by the pancreas into the small intestine. Human ptyalin and human amylopsin have been isolated and found indistinguishable.

Ptyalin is mixed with food in the mouth, where it acts upon starches. Although the food remains in the mouth for only a short time, the action of ptyalin continues for up to several hours in the stomach—until the food is mixed with the stomach secretions, the high acidity of which inactivates ptyalin. Ptyalin's digestive action depends upon how much acid is in the stomach, how rapidly the stomach contents empty, and how thoroughly the food has mixed with the acid. Under optimal conditions as much as 50 percent of ingested starches can be broken down to maltose by ptyalin during digestion in the stomach.

When food passes to the small intestine, the remainder of the starch molecules are catalyzed to maltose by amylopsin. Most of starch digestion occurs in the first section of the small intestine (the duodenum) because the pancreatic juices empty into this region. Starches first reduced to maltose are ultimately broken down into molecules of glucose, which are rapidly absorbed through the intestinal wall. When maltose molecules are attracted to the duodenum's membrane cells, enzymes secreted by these cells split the maltose and absorb the glucose products. This group of intestinal enzymes, sometimes called an amylase, is better regarded as a maltase.

Beta-amylases are present in yeasts, molds, bacteria, and plants, particularly in the seeds. They are the principal components of a mixture called diastase used in removal of starchy sizing agents from textiles and in the conversion of cereal grains to fermentable sugars.

amyloidosis, disease characterized by the deposition of amyloid in the connective tissues. Amyloid is a fibrous protein–carbohydrate complex that is derived from immunoglobulins, a group of proteins that have antibody activity. The disease may affect the whole system or may be localized in tumourlike masses, particularly in the larynx (voice box) or in some other portion of the upper respiratory tract. The localized form is primary—unassociated with any other disease. The systemic form may be primary or associated with some chronic infection such as tuberculosis or syphilis or with a lasting inflammation such as rheumatoid arthritis. No successful treatment of primary systemic amyloidosis has been devised; some improvement in secondary systemic amyloidosis has been achieved occasionally by successful management of the underlying disease. Localized amyloidosis is treated by surgical removal.

Amyntas III (or II) (d. 370/369 BC), king of Macedonia from *c.* 393 to 370/369. His skillful diplomacy created a minor role for Macedonia in Greek affairs and prepared the way for its emergence as a great power under his son Philip II (ruled 359–336). Amyntas came to the throne during the disorders that plagued Macedonia after the death of the powerful king Archelaus (ruled *c.* 413–399). Amyntas soon had to fight off attacks by the Illyrians (of present-day Albania) and by the Chalcidian League, a confederation of cities of the Chalcidic peninsula, east of Macedonia. The threat from the latter was removed when intervention by Sparta led to the dissolution of the league in 379. Amyntas continued to maintain his independence by siding with the powers ascendant in Greece, including first Athens and then Thessaly, under its tyrant Jason of Pherae (ruled *c.* 385–370).

Amyot, Jacques (b. Oct. 30, 1513, Melun, near Paris—d. Feb. 6, 1593, Auxerre, Fr.), bishop and classical scholar famous for his translation of Plutarch's *Lives* (*Les Vies des hommes illustres Grecs et Romains*), which became a major influence in shaping the Renaissance concept of the tragic hero. Amyot was educated at Paris University and at Bourges, where he became professor of Latin and Greek and translated Heliodorus' *Aethiopica.* For this Francis I gave him the abbey of Bellozane and commissioned him to complete his translation of Plutarch's *Lives,* on which he had been engaged for some time. He went to Rome to study the Vatican text of Plutarch's *Bioi paralleloi* ("Parallel Lives"). On his return to France he was appointed tutor to the sons of Henry II. Both favoured him on accession, making him grand almoner and, in 1570, bishop of Auxerre, where he spent the rest of his life. Amyot translated seven books of the *Bibliotheca historica* of Diodorus Siculus in 1554, the *Daphnis et Chloé* of Longus (Greek originator of pastoral romance, 2nd–3rd century AD) in 1559, and the *Opera moralia* of Plutarch in 1572, as well as the *Lives.*

Amyot's *Vies* was an important contribution to the development of Renaissance Humanism in France and England, and Plutarch was an ideal choice because he presented the moral hero as an individual rather than in abstract, didactic terms. Moreover, Amyot supplied his readers with a sense of identification with the past and the writers of many generations with characters and situations to build upon. He also gave the French an example of simple and pure style; Montaigne observed that without Amyot's *Vies,* no one would have known how to write. His reasons were not solely stylistic: Amyot added many new words to the French language, enabling philosophical writers to express thoughts for which only Latin had been adequate previously. The *Lives* was translated into English by Sir Thomas North (1579) and was the source for Shakespeare's Roman plays.

Amyot, Jean-Joseph-Marie: *see* Amiot, Jean-Joseph-Marie.

amyotrophic lateral sclerosis (ALS), also called LOU GEHRIG'S DISEASE, degenerative nervous-system disorder of unknown cause. The disease usually occurs after age 40, more often in men than in women; prognosis is grave—almost always negative—and victims usually die within two to five years.

ALS affects the motor neurons—*i.e.,* those neurons that control muscular movements. The muscles innervated by the degenerating neurons become weak and eventually atrophy. The disease has an insidious onset. The early signs are usually weakness of the hands, along with muscle atrophy. The muscular weakness and atrophy slowly creep up the forearms to the shoulders. The lower limbs also become weak and spastic. Fibrillation (rapid twitching) is almost always present. Weakness and spasticity may be present for months before actual atrophy is evident. Death generally results from atrophy of the respiratory muscles.

A variety of ALS in which the neuron degeneration is most pronounced in the spinal cord is termed progressive muscular atrophy. Its symptoms are similar to the above, except that, instead of spasticity in the feet and legs, atrophy and weakness may be present. Victims of progressive muscular atrophy generally survive longer than those suffering from classic ALS.

In progressive bulbar palsy—a variety of ALS in which the degeneration is centred on the neurons of the cranial nerves and brainstem—chewing, talking, and swallowing are difficult. Often there are involuntary outbursts of laughing and crying; tongue fibrillation and atrophy are common. The prognosis is especially bleak in this form of ALS, with death commonly occurring within one to three years of onset.

These diseases must be differentiated from similar diseases.

Amyrtaeus OF SAIS, Egyptian king (reigned 404–399 BC) whose reign constituted the entire 28th dynasty. He was possibly a relative of the Amyrtaeus who had earlier aided Inaros, a Libyan prince who had attempted to oust the Achaemenians from the Delta (Lower Egypt). In 404 Amyrtaeus of Sais successfully led a revolt against Achaemenian control of the Delta and finally gained control of all of Upper Egypt in 400. Although his rule was plagued by insurrections, the Achaemenians were unable to regain power. Amyrtaeus left no monuments, and very little detailed information is known about his reign; according to a late Egyptian tradition, he in some way transgressed the law, and thus his son was not allowed to succeed him.

An (Mesopotamian god): *see* Anu.

An Abhainn Mhór (Northern Ireland): *see* Blackwater, River.

An Aird (Northern Ireland): *see* Ards.

An Baile Meanách (Northern Ireland): *see* Ballymena.

An Bhanna (Northern Ireland): *see* Bann, River.

An Caisleán Nua (Northern Ireland): *see* Newcastle.

An Caisleán Riabhach (Northern Ireland): *see* Castlereagh.

An-ch'ing, formerly (1911–49) HUAI-NING, Pinyin ANQING, or HUAINING, conventional ANKING, city situated on the north bank of the Yangtze River (Ch'ang Chiang) in southwestern Anhwei Province (*sheng*), China. It is a county-level municipality (*shih*) and administrative centre of An-ch'ing Prefecture (*ti-ch'ü*). Situated at a crossing place on the Yangtze, it commands the narrow section of the floodplain between the Ta-pieh Shan (mountains) to the north and the Huang Shan on the south bank, at the west end of the Lower Yangtze Plain. An-ch'ing is the terminus of a highway running northward through Ho-fei, to Pang-pu in northern Anhwei, and on to Shang-ch'iu in southern Honan Province; the road joins another, which follows the northern edge of the Yangtze floodplain on its way upstream to Wu-han (Hupeh Province), just south of An-ch'ing.

A county (*hsien*) was founded at this place under the Han dynasty (206 BC–AD 220) in the 2nd century BC and was named Wan. In the 4th century AD it was called Huai-ning—a name it retained until the 20th century. It became the seat of a commandery (*chün*) called T'ung-an under the Sui dynasty (581–618). Under the T'ang (618–907) and Sung (960–1126) dynasties the town was known as the Shu Prefecture (*chou*). The name An-ch'ing was first given to a military prefecture set up in the late 12th century; this was subsequently transformed into a civil superior prefecture (*fu*) called An-ch'ing. At the beginning of the Ch'ing dynasty (1644–1911), it became the capital of the new province of Anhwei and the administrative seat of its governor general. It remained the provincial capital until 1949, when it was replaced by Ho-fei; from 1911–49 it was officially known as Huai-ning Hsien.

An-ch'ing played an important role during the Taiping Rebellion in the mid-19th century. Taken by the rebel forces in 1853, it remained one of their most important bases until 1861, when it was lost by them after a desperate defense. It was in the vicinity of An-ch'ing that Taiping reforms were most in evidence.

After its recapture the Chinese commander, Tseng Kuo-fan (1811–72), ordered the establishment there of flour mills, granaries, and munition factories for his armies. From 1861 onward these works were under Chinese management, but, because of the lack of skilled technicians, the products of the arsenal were of little practical use, and after a few years it was shut down.

It became a port of call for foreign shipping under the Chefoo Convention (1876) between China and the United Kingdom, and under the Sino-British trade agreement of 1902 it was to be opened to foreign trade. Little trade resulted, however, as it had no large or rich hinterland and its communications were relatively poor; later, when railways to the interior of Anhwei reached the Yangtze further east, its importance declined even more. It has remained a medium-sized provincial city, an important commercial centre for the plain north of the Yangtze, and a market for tea produced in the mountains both north and south of the river. While also a local cultural centre, it has remained comparatively stagnant after losing its status as provincial capital. Modern industrial development includes a petrochemical works, producing fuel oils and synthetic ammonia, an oil refinery, and construction of a new port. Pop. (1953) 105,300; (1980 UN est.) 295,000.

An Chorr Chríochach (Northern Ireland): *see* Cookstown.

An Chung-sik, also called SHIMJON (Korean: Spirit Field) (b. 1861, Seoul—d. 1919, Seoul), the last gentleman painter of the great Korean Yi dynasty (1392–1910).

As a promising young painter, An Chung-sik was sent to China for training by the Korean court. Upon his return he became a master of the popular Southern style, with its emphasis on fingertip technique. He was also a noted calligrapher who mastered all the writing styles. Interested in new trends, especially those from the West, he experimented with ideas of perspective and depth, grafting them to the traditional style. His work furnished the starting point for many younger painters. Toward the end of his life he was the central figure in the establishment (1918) of the Sohwa Hyobhoi (Association of Painters and Calligraphers).

An Dún (Northern Ireland): *see* Down.

An Giang, *tinh* (province), Mekong delta region, southwestern Vietnam. The 1,348-sq-mi (3,493-sq-km) province is bounded to the north by Kampuchea (Cambodia) and to the east by the Song (river) Tien Giang of the Mekong delta and by Dong Thap province. It is traversed northwest–southeast by the Song Hau Giang, a channel of the Mekong, on whose right bank is located Long Xuyen, the provincial seat. Forested mountains are found to the northwest.

The province was part of the Khmer Empire of Cambodia until occupied in the 18th century by the Vietnamese, who made it part of southern Vietnam. After numerous boundary changes, the former provinces of Chau Doc to the north and An Giang to the south were merged in 1976. Crisscrossed by canals and waterways, An Giang province is a major producer of paddy rice, which is adapted to the deep flooding of the summer southwest monsoon. Double-cropping of rice has been extended. Corn (maize), soybeans, potatoes, sugarcane, cotton, and tobacco are grown, and cattle are raised. Provincial industries include the processing of ricefield fish and making of a fish sauce; brick, tile, and ceramic making; and bamboo and woodworking. Sandstone, granite, and molybdenum are found within the province. Linked by highway north to Takêv, Kampuchea, and east to Ho Chi Minh City, the province is connected by the Kinh (canal) Vinh Te river channel (forming the Vietnamese–Kampuchean border) to the port of Ha Tien on the Gulf of Thailand. The population consists of the predominant Vietnamese together with Khmer, Cham, and the militant Hoa Hao Buddhist sect. Pop. (1979) 1,532,352.

An-k'ang, also called HSING-AN, Pinyin ANKANG, or XINGAN, city in southeastern Shensi Province (*sheng*), China. It is a county (*hsien*) seat and the administrative centre of An-k'ang Prefecture (*ti-ch'ü*). Situated in the narrow valley of the Han Shui (river) between the Tsinling Shan (mountains) and Ta-pa Shan, it has been an important trade centre since antiquity, being situated at the junction of the east–west route via the Han Valley and the route to the north over the mountains to Hsi-an (Ch'ang-an). A rail line, completed in 1978, links An-k'ang with Ch'ung-ch'ing (Chungking; Szechwan) and Hsiang-fan (Hupeh) via the Han Shui Valley. It is also in an important strategic area near the borders of Szechwan, Shensi, and Hupeh provinces.

It first emerged as an independent administrative centre in the 3rd century AD, under the name Liang-chou. Later, in the 5th century, it took the name Chin-chou, the county town bearing the name Hsi-ch'eng. In 1583 the prefecture was renamed Hsing-an. The county town was renamed An-k'ang in the early 18th century. In 1912 the superior prefecture of Hsing-an was abolished, and it reverted to county status once more. It comprised two separate walled towns and was a flourishing centre of trade, having been intimately linked since the 18th century with Han-k'ou. The city became the collecting centre for the agricultural produce of the surrounding area, which had been extensively colonized only since the 17th century. The main products of the area are grains, various types of oilseeds, sesame, hides, and forest products (notably lacquer). Pop. (1953) 50,000; (mid-1970s est.) 10,000–50,000.

An Lu-shan, Pinyin AN LUSHAN, original name (Wade-Giles romanization) K'ANG, imperial name HSIUNG WU, canonized name YEN LA WANG (b. 703—d. 757, Lo Yang, China), Chinese general of Iranian and Turkish descent who, as leader of a rebellion in AD 755, proclaimed himself emperor and unsuccessfully attempted to found a dynasty to replace the T'ang dynasty. Despite its failure, the rebellion precipitated far-reaching social and economic change.

Early life and career. The family name An was derived from the Chinese name for Bukhara in Sogdiana (present Uzbekistan). The given name Lu-shan is a Sinicized form of the Iranian *rowshān*, "light." An Lu-shan's ancestors belonged to a group of Sogdians who had been incorporated into the Eastern Turks, and his mother was from a noble Turkish clan.

The Eastern Turks, whose ascendancy in Mongolia dated from the 6th century, had been conquered by the Chinese emperor T'ai-tsung at the beginning of the T'ang dynasty but had made themselves independent and were enjoying renewed prosperity at the time of An Lu-shan's birth. The death of their ruler, Qapaghan Qaghan, in 716, however, led to disorder and strife, and the Ans sought refuge in China. Just at that period the frontier policies of the emperor Hsüan Tsung (reigned 712–756) were providing opportunities for men such as An Lu-shan, his cousin An Ssu-shun, and other soldiers of non-Chinese origin to serve in the Chinese armies. Their rise to positions of command was further aided after 736 by the dictatorial rule of China's chief minister, Li Lin-fu, who was unwilling to appoint native Chinese as generals for fear that they would gain prestige that would enable them to rival his own position at court.

An Lu-shan's military career took place on the northeastern frontier in what is now southern Manchuria. The first occurrence of his name in the T'ang annals is under the year 736, when, as a reconnaissance officer, he lost his force through rash conduct and was condemned to death. He was pardoned and, thereafter, rose rapidly in rank, receiving his first independent command in 742. As a military governor he became a political figure, made frequent visits to the capital, and became a personal favourite of the Emperor and his consort, the celebrated beauty Yang Kuei-fei. An Lu-shan, an enormously fat man, was adept at playing the buffoon in order to ingratiate himself. Such was his favour at court that once, three days after his birthday, he was taken into the women's quarters of the palace (wrapped in an enormous baby diaper) and put through a mock ceremony of adoption by Yang Kuei-fei. Indecorous conduct of this kind led to rumours of improper relations between him and Yang Kuei-fei, which have added spice to the later legend, but his position at court depended at least as much on the Emperor himself as on his consort.

An Lu-shan's rebellion. By the time of Minister Li Lin-fu's death in 752, An Lu-shan had accumulated three frontier provinces under his command and was the most powerful general in the empire. After the dictator's demise an intense struggle developed between An Lu-shan and Yang Kuo-chung, the cousin of Yang Kuei-fei, who attempted to take over Li Lin-fu's position. Though Yang Kuo-chung could attack and destroy An Lu-shan's supporters at court, he was unsuccessful in his attempts to establish a countervailing military base in the provinces or to undermine An Lu-shan's position in the northeast, and he only succeeded in exacerbating An Lu-shan's suspicions and frustrations. Finally, toward the end of 755, alleging that he had received a secret command from the Emperor to get rid of Yang Kuo-chung, An Lu-shan turned his large, war-hardened army inward and marched on the capital.

Within a month the rebels had taken the eastern capital, Lo-yang, and at the beginning of the lunar year corresponding to 756 An Lu-shan proclaimed himself emperor of the Great Yen dynasty.

Meanwhile, loyal T'ang forces had been mobilized and had taken up defensive positions in the narrow pass up the Huang Ho leading into Shensi. For six months the rebels were unable to advance. There was great suspicion and rivalry between Yang Kuo-chung and Ko shu-han, the general in charge of the defense of the eastern approaches to Ch'ang-an, capital of China. Fearing a coup against himself, Yang Kuo-chung goaded Ko shu-han into abandoning his defensive posture and moving eastward against the rebels. The T'ang army was routed, and the way to Ch'ang-an was left open. The Emperor hastily abandoned the city and fled westward. At Ma-wei, a small village west of the capital, his guard mutinied, assassinated Yang Kuo-chung, and demanded the death of the Emperor's favourite, Yang Kuei-fei. The Emperor reluctantly consented, and her assassination became the theme of the great poet Po Chü-i's "Everlasting Remorse" and of countless other works of art.

Although An Lu-shan's forces occupied Ch'ang-an, he himself remained behind in Lo-yang. By this time he was seriously ailing, perhaps with diabetes. He was nearly blind and suffered from extreme irascibility, which made his attendants go in constant fear of their lives. At the beginning of 757 he was murdered by a eunuch slave with the connivance of his own eldest son, An Ch'ing-hsü, and others. The rebellion dragged on for several years, first under An Ch'ing-hsü, then under a former subordinate, Shih Ssu-ming, then under Shih Ssu-ming's son, Shih Ch'ao-i. Finally in 763 it officially came to an end with the defeat and death of Shih Ch'ao-i. A major role in the defeat of the rebels was played by contingents sent by the Uighurs, who had replaced the Eastern Turks as masters of the eastern steppes and who were traditional allies of T'ang. By this time the T'ang government was too exhausted to undertake a thorough pacification of the rebel territory, and the surviving rebel generals were allowed to surrender and remain in command of the regions they occupied in return for a nominal submission to T'ang. Other parts of the country fell under the control of T'ang generals who were almost as insubordinate as the former rebels. The second half of the T'ang dynasty and the following Five Dynasties period were troubled by a chronic warlordism that only came to an end with the rise of the Sung dynasty in 960.

After his death, An Lu-shan became the object of a cult on the northeastern frontier among the non-Chinese soldiers who constituted the bulk of the army and whose aspirations he symbolized. Conversely, the non-Chinese, "barbarian" character of the rebellion was influential in stirring up the xenophobic sentiments of the Chinese that increasingly characterized the second half of the T'ang dynasty, in marked contrast to the receptive, cosmopolitan attitudes of the first half.

(E.G.P.)

BIBLIOGRAPHY. E.G. Pulleyblank, *The Background of the Rebellion of An Lu-shan* (1955), places the man and his rebellion in historical context. Howard S. Levy, *Biography of An Lu-Shan* (1960), is a translation of the official biography of An Lu-shan; and R. des Rotours, *Histoire de Ngan Lou-chan* (1962), is a scholarly and thoroughly annotated translation from a large collection of source material on An Lu-shan.

An Ómaigh (Northern Ireland): *see* Omagh.

An-p'ing, *chen* (town), seaport, and district of T'ai-nan *shih* (municipality), southwestern Taiwan, the traditional outport for T'ai-nan. It is the oldest Chinese settlement in southern Taiwan, dating from the late 16th century. It is connected to T'ai-nan proper by canal and by light railway. Until the late 19th century, An-p'ing was a busy port, with strong commercial connections with Foochow and Amoy and other ports on the Chinese mainland. The harbour, however, was always shallow and subject to silting, and by the early 1970s it was largely reduced to use as a fishing harbour. The growth of nearby Kao-hsiung to the south and the construction of the railway system, giving T'ai-nan access both to Kao-hsiung and Chi-lung at the northern end of Taiwan, led to An-p'ing's rapid decline. Pop. (1982 est.) 19,376.

An-shan, Pinyin ANSHAN, industrial city in central Liaoning Province (*sheng*), China, about 50 mi (80 km) southwest of Shen-yang (Mukden). It is a prefecture-level municipality (*shih*), the territory of which also includes the counties (*hsien*) of Hai-ch'eng and T'ai-an. Originally a post station on the road from China proper to Liao-yang, 15 mi to the northeast, An-shan was established in 1387 and was fortified in 1587 as part of the defenses set up by the Ming dynasty (1368–1644) against the rising power of the Manchus. Under the Ch'ing (Manchu) dynasty (1644–1911), however, its walls fell into decay, and during the Boxer Rebellion (an anti-foreign uprising in 1900) the town was destroyed by fire; further destruction followed during the Russo-Japanese War (1904–05), which reduced it to little more than an impoverished village.

Steelworks in An-shan, Liaoning Province, China
Jorgen Bitsch—Black Star/EB Inc.

Modern An-shan grew up some 6 mi north of the old town and was entirely industrial in its origins. In 1909 extensive iron-ore deposits were found in the area. There are further iron deposits in a belt around An-shan at the towns of Ta-ku-shan, Ying-t'ao-yüan, and Kung-ch'ang-ling. The South Manchurian Railway established an ironworks at An-shan in 1918, but production was low until initial difficulties, caused by the low grade of the iron ore, were overcome by new techniques. Under the Japanese occupation after 1931, An-shan was at first a producer of pig iron for use in the Japanese steel industry, but a local steelworks was established, and production began in 1935. In 1937 An-shan was taken over by the Manchurian Heavy Industry Company, a company partly backed by the Manchukuo government, the Japanese puppet regime in Manchuria. The industry concentrated on the production of steel for armaments, and the city expanded rapidly. In addition to the steelworks, various heavy engineering plants were built, and a shortage of coking coal ended with the development of coal mining at Fu-hsin and elsewhere.

After World War II, An-shan suffered from looting by Soviet forces, who removed most of the advanced equipment. The plant had been heavily bombed toward the end of the war and was further damaged during civil warfare that followed the Soviet withdrawal. By 1948 the population had fallen, and steel production had virtually ceased. After 1949 the rehabilitation of heavy industry at An-shan and elsewhere became a major goal of the Communist government. Under the First Five-Year Plan (1953–57) An-shan was built up again into the major iron and steel complex in China and was reequipped with the latest equipment, much of it from the Soviet Union. By 1957 it was producing a wide variety of steel products (such as heavy rails, steel plates, seamless tubes, and alloy steels). An-shan also produced equipment for other major iron and steel complexes elsewhere in China. By the late 1950s it was producing more than 40 percent of the total Chinese production of iron and steel. As the chief centre for industrial development, numbers of technicians and workers were sent to An-shan from other parts of the country for training. An-shan suffered from the withdrawal of Soviet aid in 1960 and the industrial cutbacks that followed, but the city recovered. By the early 1980s it was producing one-fourth of China's steel.

In the 1960s the attempt simply to increase productive capacity was replaced by efforts to make specialized products, which had previously been imported. In the late 1970s An-shan was China's chief centre for metallurgical research and technological innovation in the steel industry. It was also a centre of the engineering industry. Industrial products include tractors, chemicals, cement, and paper.

An-shan is part of a well-integrated industrial complex in the southern section of the Northeast (Manchuria). It is supplied with coal from Fu-hsin, Fu-shun, and Pen-ch'i, magnesium from Ta-shih-ch'iao, and obtains food largely through Liao-yang. Its steel production is supplied to the engineering and machine building industry in other large cities in the Northeast. It also has an oil refinery. It ranks as the fourth industrial city in China by capacity, being exceeded only by Shanghai, Tientsin, and Wu-han. An-shan is connected by railway with Shen-yang and Lü-ta. Pop. (1935) 33,000; (1940) 214,000; (1948) 166,000; (1953) 549,000; (1958 est.) 833,000; (1983 est.) 1,210,000.

An-shun, Pinyin ANSHUN, city, west central Kweichow Province (*sheng*), China. An-shun is a county-level municipality (*shih*) and the administrative centre of An-shun Prefecture (*ti-ch'ü*). It first became a city in 1958, later lost its municipal status, but was made a city again in 1966. An-shun is situated at the centre of various radiating highways covering the entire western part of the province, some 60 mi (100 km) west-southwest of Kuei-yang, on the main highway and railway routes between Kuei-yang and K'un-ming in Yunnan Province. It is the chief market and commercial centre for the district, acting as a collecting centre for agricultural produce and as a distribution point for manufactures from Kuei-yang. An-shun has various small-scale food-processing, oil-extracting, and agricultural-implement factories. There are considerable coal reserves in the area, supplying a large power plant at Hsüan-wei to the west in Yunnan. A small steel plant was established at An-shun in 1959–60, being supplied with iron ore from Weng-an and Ch'ing-chen. Pop. (1958 est.) 80,000; (mid-1970s est.) 50,000–100,000.

An-ski, S. (Jewish writer): *see* Ansky, S.

An Srath Bán (Northern Ireland): *see* Strabane.

An tlúr (Northern Ireland): *see* Newry.

An-tung (China): *see* Tan-tung.

An-yang, city in Honan Province, northeastern China, on the An-yang Ho (An-yang River), a tributary of the Wei Ho. It was important in history as the site of the ancient city of Yin, the capital of the Shang dynasty from 1384 to 1111 BC; the Shang palace stood about 10 mi (16 km) west of the present city. An-yang declined when the succeeding Chou capital arose at Lo-yang.

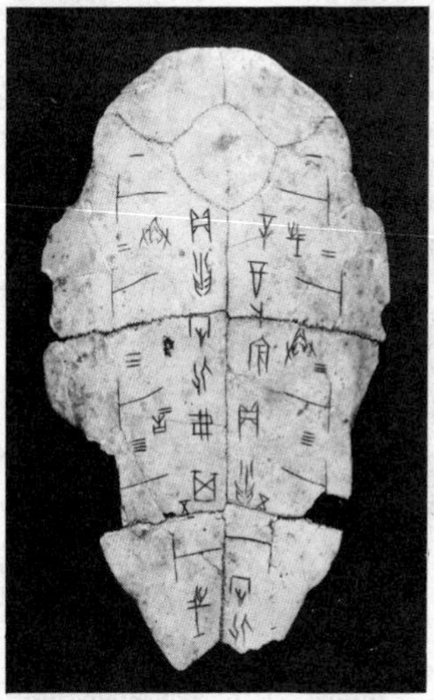

Oracle bone inscription on tortoise shell from An-yang; in the Institute of History and Philology, Academia Sinica, Taipei

By courtesy of Li Chi, Institute of History and Philology, Academia Sinica, Taipei, Taiwan, Republic of China

Modern excavations have revealed historical remains of the Shang, fully illustrating the splendour and advanced stage of a civilization that developed more than half a millennium before the beginning of authentic Chinese history in 776 BC. This discovery has provided the most authentic evidence to date of the ancient civilization of China.

The site of the Shang capital at An-yang had been known to scholars since the beginning of the 20th century through the accidental discovery of inscribed oracle bones, the earliest Chinese written records. It was not until 1928, however, that the first organized scientific expedition started systematic excavation of these remains under the auspices of Academia Sinica, organized by the Nationalist government of the Republic of China. Field work was carried out by the archaeologist Li Chi from 1928 until the Japanese invasion in 1937. The finds include building foundations, bronzes, chariots, pottery, stone and jade, and thousands of oracle bones. Several other excavations were conducted after 1950.

An-yang has been a regional agricultural and trade centre for centuries. In modern times, it became a station on the main north-south rail line from Peking to Wu-han. Coal mining is important. An-yang's textile mills and food-processing plants have been supplemented by heavier manufactures since the Communists came to power in 1949. Pop. (1970 est.) 100,000–300,000.

Ana, Wādī (Europe): *see* Guadiana River.

Anabaena, genus of nitrogen-fixing blue-green algae with beadlike or barrellike

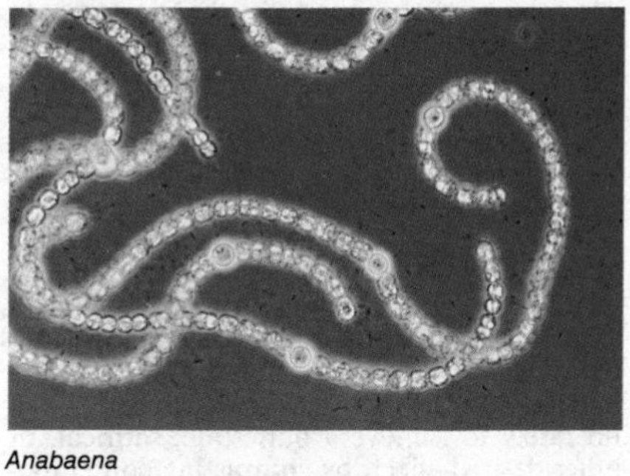

Anabaena

J.R. Waaland

cells and occasionally an enlarged cell (heterocyst), found as plankton in shallow water and on moist soil. There are both solitary and colonial forms, the latter resembling a closely related genus, *Nostoc.* In northern latitudes during the summer months *Anabaena* may form water blooms that remain suspended instead of forming a surface scum. A toxic substance produced by *Anabaena* is fatal to cattle and other animals if present in drinking water in sufficient concentration.

Anabaptist, also called REBAPTIZER, member of radical, or left-wing, movement of the 16th-century Protestant Reformation. Its most distinctive tenet was adult Baptism. In the first generation of the movement, converts submitted to a second Baptism, which was a crime punishable by death under the legal codes of the time. The Anabaptists, of course, denied that they were rebaptizers, for they repudiated their own infant Baptism as a blasphemous formality. They considered the public confession of sin and faith, sealed by adult Baptism, as the only proper Baptism. Following the Swiss Reformer Huldrych Zwingli, they held that infants were not punishable for sin until an awareness of good and evil emerged within them, and that then they could exercise their own free will, repent, and accept Baptism.

The Anabaptists also believed that the church, which to them was the community of the redeemed, should be separated from the state, which for them existed only for the punishment of sinners. Most Anabaptists opposed the use of the sword by Christians in the maintenance of social order and in the conduct of a just war. They also refused to swear civil oaths. For their beliefs thousands of Anabaptists were put to death.

The Anabaptists did not aim to reform the medieval church. They were determined instead to restore the institutions and the spirit of the primitive church and were quite confident that they were living at the end of all ages. They readily recognized in their leaders divinely summoned prophets and apostles, and all converts stood ready to give a full account of their faith before the magistrates. They often identified their suffering with that of the martyrs of the first three Christian centuries.

The Anabaptist movement originated in Zürich among a group of young intellectuals who rebelled against Zwingli's apparent subservience to the magistrates and his reluctance to proceed swiftly with a complete reform of the church. One of their leaders was Konrad Grebel, a highly educated Humanist from a patrician family. The first adult baptisms took place at Zollikon, outside Zürich, at the beginning of 1525, and soon a mass movement was in progress. Some of the more distinctive convictions of the Swiss movement were set forth in the seven articles of the Schleitheim Confession (1527), prepared under the leadership of Michael Sattler.

The vehemence and intransigence of the Anabaptist leaders and the revolutionary implications of their teaching led to their expulsion from one city after another. This simply increased the momentum of an essentially missionary movement. Soon civil magistrates took sterner measures, and most of the early Anabaptist leaders died in prison or were executed.

Thomas Müntzer was among those (sometimes called "spirituals") who emphasized that the Anabaptists were living at the end of all ages. He was executed after leading Thuringian peasants in the revolt of 1525. His disciple Hans Hut (died in prison in Augsburg in 1527) was the principal radical Reformer in southern Germany.

Balthasar Hubmaier (executed in Vienna in 1528) was a leader in Nicholsburg, Moravia. Also in Moravia, where the ruling lords desired colonists and where many Anabaptists settled, a type of Anabaptism developed that stressed the community of goods modelled on the primitive church in Jerusalem. Under the leadership of Jakob Hutter the growing communistic colonies assumed his name. Hutterite groups survived and are now primarily located in the western United States and Canada.

Melchior Hofmann was the Anabaptist apostle in the Netherlands, where he developed a very large following. He taught that the world would soon end and that the new age would begin in Strasbourg, where he was imprisoned in 1533 and died *c.* 1543.

Some of Hofmann's followers came under the influence of the Dutchman Jan Mathijs (died 1534) and of John of Leiden (Jan Beuckelson; died 1535). The two leaders and many refugees settled in 1534 in Münster, Westphalia, where they gained control of the city, established a communistic theocracy, and practiced polygamy. The city was captured in 1535 by an army raised by German princes, and the Anabaptist leaders were tortured and killed.

Modern historians have come to see the episode at Münster as an aberration of the Anabaptist movement. In the years following the episode, however, classical Protestants and Catholics increased the persecution of Anabaptists throughout Europe without discrimination between the belligerent minority and the pacifist majority. The pacifist Anabaptists in the Netherlands and north Germany rallied under the leadership of the former priest Menno Simons and his lieutenant, Dirk Philips. Their followers survived and were eventually accepted as the Mennonite (*q.v.*) religious group. *See also* Hutterite.

Anabasis, in full ANABASIS KYROU (Greek: "Upcountry March"), prose narrative account, now in seven books, by Xenophon, of the story of the Greek mercenary soldiers who fought for Cyrus in his attempt to seize the Persian throne from his brother, Artaxerxes II. It contains a famous account of the mercenaries' long trek ("the march of the 10,000") from near Babylon to the Euxine (Black Sea) after Cyrus' disastrous defeat at the Battle of Cunaxa (401 BC). Xenophon, who had accompanied the force in a private capacity, was largely responsible for their successful retreat through his resourcefulness and courage.

The first part, written at Scillus in the Greek Peloponnese soon after 386 BC, is a lively, detailed, and vivid narrative. It was first published under a pseudonym, Themistocles of Syracuse. The second part, written *c.* 377 BC, is marred by a self-justifying tone and was probably composed in reply to a rival public account that Xenophon considered unfair.

anabatic wind, also called UPSLOPE WIND, local air current that blows up a hill or mountain slope facing the Sun. During the day, the Sun heats such a slope (and the air over it) faster than it does the adjacent lowland because the slope's surface is more nearly perpendicular to the Sun's rays. This warming decreases the density of the air, causing it to rise. More air rises from below to replace it, producing a wind. An anabatic wind may attain a velocity of 6 metres per second (about 13 miles per hour).

anabolism, also called BIOSYNTHESIS, the sequences of enzyme-catalyzed reactions by which relatively complex molecules are formed in living cells from nutrients with relatively simple structures. Anabolic processes, which include the synthesis of such cell components as carbohydrates, proteins, and lipids, require energy in the form of energy-rich compounds (*e.g.*, adenosine triphosphate) that are produced during breakdown processes (*see* catabolism). In growing cells, anabolic processes dominate over catabolic ones; in nongrowing cells, a balance exists between the two.

Anacardiaceae, the cashew or mango family of flowering plants in the order Rutales, with about 73 genera and 600 species of evergreen or deciduous trees. It is native to tropical areas of the world, but a few species occur in temperate regions. Members of the family have resin ducts in the bark, leaves usually composed of leaflets in various arrangements, flowers often with only male or female parts, and usually fleshy fruits. The pistachio (*Pistacia vera*) and cashew (*Anacardium occidentale*) produce edible nuts, and mango (*Mangifera indica*), mombin (*Spondias*), and Kaffir plum (*Harpephyllum caffrum*) have edible fruits. The mastic tree (*Pistacia lentiscus*) and the varnish tree (*Ioxicodendron vernicifera*) contain useful oils, resins, and lacquers. The reddish-brown wood of quebracho (trees of the genus *Schinopsis,* especially *S. lorentzii*) yields commercial tannin. Pepper tree (*Schinus molle*), *Cotinus* species, and several species of sumac (*Rhus*) are cultivated as ornamentals. Poison ivy, poison oak, and poison sumac (all *Rhus*, or, according to some authorities, *Toxicodendron*) are irritating to the skin.

Poison oak (*Rhus diversiloba*)

Barry Lopez—Photo Researchers

anachronism (from Greek *ana,* "back" and *chronos,* "time"), neglect or falsification, intentional or not, of chronological relation. It is most frequently found in works of imagination that rest on a historical basis, in which appear details borrowed from a later age; *e.g.*, a clock in Shakespeare's *Julius Caesar,* an attendant to the Pharaoh shod in tennis shoes in Cecil B. deMille's *The Ten Commandments.* Anachronisms originate in disregard of the different modes of life and thought that characterize different periods, or in ignorance of the facts of history.

Anachronisms abound in the painting of Raphael and the plays of Shakespeare. Artists tended to represent characters in terms of their own nationality and time. The Virgin has been pictured both as an Italian peasant and as a Flemish housewife; Alexander the Great appeared on the French stage down to the time of Voltaire in the full costume of Louis XIV. Modern realism, the progress of archaeological research, and the scientific approach to history came to make an unconscious anachronism an offense. On the other hand, anachronisms may be introduced deliberately to achieve a burlesque, satirical, or other desired effect; by contrasting contemporary customs or morals with an alien age, the writer or artist reevaluates the past or present, or both. Thus Mark Twain wrote of a Connecticut Yankee visiting King Arthur's court, and the Belgian James Ensor painted Christ entering Brussels (1888).

Anacletus, SAINT, also called CLETUS, or ANENCLETUS (fl. 1st century AD; feast day April 26), second pope (76–88 or 79–91) after St. Peter. According to St. Epiphanius and the priest Tyrannius Rufinus, he directed the Roman Church with St. Linus, successor to St. Peter, during Peter's lifetime. He died, probably a martyr, during the reign of Domitian.

Anacletus (II), original name PIETRO PIERLEONI (b. Rome—d. Jan. 25, 1138, Rome), antipope from 1130 to 1138 whose claims to the papacy against Pope Innocent II are still supported by some scholars. After study in Paris, he became a monk at Cluny and was made cardinal at Rome in 1116 by Pope Paschal II. In 1118 he accompanied Pope Gelasius II, who fled to France from the persecuting Frangipani, an influential Roman family.

After the death of Pope Honorius II in 1130, a majority of cardinals elected Pietro as successor with the name of Anacletus II. Concurrently, a minority elected Cardinal Gregorio Papareschi (Innocent II) as successor. The claimants were both consecrated on February 23, precipitating a serious schism. Anacletus, backed by most Romans and by the Frangipani, forced Innocent to flee from Rome to France, where he was supported by Abbot St. Bernard of Clairvaux, who attacked Anacletus' Jewish ancestry. Although Anacletus was allied with the ambitious and powerful Roger II after investing him as king of Sicily (1130), Innocent's supporters, including the Holy Roman emperor Lothair II and the Byzantine emperor John II Comnenus, were overwhelming.

The Council (1130) of Étampes, Fr., convoked by King Louis VI the Fat of France to decide the legitimacy of the papal succession, chose Innocent. In 1132 Lothair, accompanied by Innocent and Bernard, led a German army into Italy and, by early summer, occupied all Rome except that section held by the Anacletans, who, upon Lothair's departure, again forced Innocent out of Rome. He fled to Pisa, where in 1134 he held a council that excommunicated Anacletus. Lothair's second expedition (1136–37) expelled Roger from southern Italy. Anacletus, with little remaining support, died amid the aftermath of this crisis. In 1139 the second Lateran Council convoked by Innocent ended the schism, though opinion remained divided.

Anaconda, city, former seat (1883) of Deer Lodge County, southwestern Montana, U.S., 23 mi (37 km) northwest of Butte. Laid out in 1883 as Copperopolis by Marcus Daly, founder of Montana's copper industry, the settlement grew rapidly after 1884 when Daly built a copper smelter on nearby Warm Springs Creek. The plant became one of the world's largest nonferrous and reduction works, and its 585-ft (178-m) smokestack dominates the landscape. The city was incorporated in 1888 and was renamed Anaconda, after Daly's mining camp in Butte, to avoid confusion with Copperopolis in Meagher County. Daly, who had hoped to make it the state capital, built there Hotel Marcus Daly, then one of the most ornate in the nation. His newspaper, the *Anaconda Standard,* had a plant as modern as any in New York City at the time, though it had a readership of only a few thousand. In 1977, the governments of Anaconda and Deer Lodge County were consolidated to form the city of Anaconda-Deer Lodge County.

Copper smelting and the manufacture of phosphate products remained the city's economic mainstay until 1980, when Atlantic Richfield Company, the owner of the Anaconda Company, permanently closed the copper smelter, putting some 25 percent of Anaconda's workforce out of work.

Recreation areas include nearby Deerlodge National Forest, Lost Creek State Park, and Georgetown Lake. Pop. (1980) 12,518.

anaconda (*Eunectes*), either of two South American snakes belonging to the family Boidae. The giant anaconda, or great water boa (*Eunectes murinus*), is a heavily built snake usually not more than about 5 metres (16 feet) long, but a 7.6-m (25-ft) specimen is known, and even longer specimens have been reported. If reports in excess of 9 m or more are accepted, the giant anaconda rivals the largest pythons in length. The yellow anaconda (*E. noteus*) is much smaller.

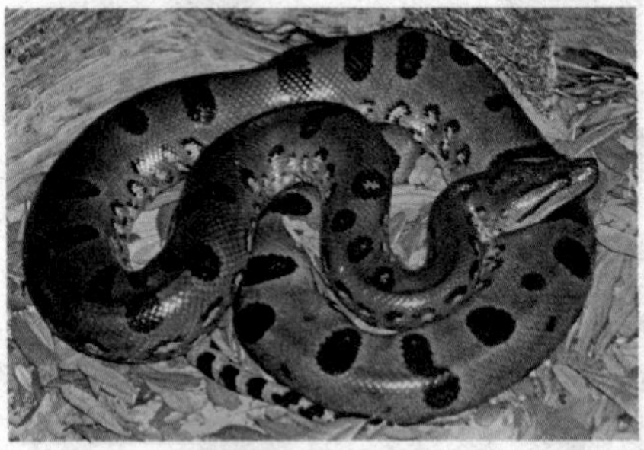

Giant anaconda (*Eunectes murinus*)

The giant anaconda is typically dark green with alternating oval black spots. It occurs along tropical rivers east of the Andes and in Trinidad. At night it lies in the water waiting to kill, by constriction, creatures as large as young pigs and caimans that come to drink; occasionally, it forages in trees for birds. This species bears about 75 live young at a time.

Anaconda Company, one of the largest U.S. mining companies, producing copper, aluminum, silver, and uranium. Since 1977 it has been a subsidiary of Atlantic Richfield Company. Headquarters are in Denver, Colo.

In 1882 Marcus Daly, an Irish immigrant, and George Hearst, father of publisher William Randolph Hearst, built Anaconda's first copper mine and smelter in Montana. Anaconda grew to become the world's largest copper producer, and in 1899 the company was purchased by the Standard Oil Trust. The deal created a national scandal when it was discovered that officers of the trust had made huge profits by selling public stock in the new company before the old owners had been paid.

In 1914 Anaconda started buying into foreign mining companies. By 1929 the company owned all of Chile Copper Company, whose Chuquicamata mine was the world's most productive. In 1971 Chile's newly elected Socialist president, Salvador Allende, expropriated Anaconda's Chilean copper mines under powers granted by an amendment to Chile's constitution. The Allende government was toppled in 1973, and the new government agreed to pay Anaconda over $250,000,000 for its expropriated mines.

Losses from the Chilean takeover, however, had seriously weakened the company's financial position, and in 1977 the company was sold to Atlantic Richfield Company (ARCO), a diversified energy corporation. This action led to an antitrust suit against ARCO, and in 1979 it was ordered to divest itself of some assets of Anaconda.

Anaconda plan, early federal military strategy proposed by Gen. Winfield Scott in the U.S. Civil War. The plan called for a naval blockade of the Confederate littoral, a thrust down the Mississippi, and the strangulation of the South by Union land and naval forces.

Anacreon (b. *c.* 582 BC, Teos, Ionia—d. *c.* 485), last great lyric poet of Asian Greece. Only fragments of his poetry have survived. He spent much of his life at the court of Polycrates of Samos; later he lived at Athens, writing under the patronage of the tyrant Hipparchus, and his popularity there continued even after Hipparchus' assassination in 514.

Though Anacreon may well have written serious poems, those that were quoted by later writers are chiefly in praise of love and wine. He disliked the excessive and the unrefined, however, and his treatment of these subjects is unusually formal. His sentiments and style were widely imitated, and the Anacreontic metre in poety was named for him.

Later writers influenced by Anacreon include the 16th-century French poet Ronsard and the 19th-century Italian Leopardi.

Anadarko, city, seat (1907) of Caddo County, southwest central Oklahoma, U.S., on the Washita River. Founded in 1901 when the site was opened to white settlement, its name is a corruption of Nadako, a Caddo Indian tribe. Rich in artifacts of the Indian culture, Anadarko is the site of the Southern Plains Indian Museum and Crafts Center, the National Hall of Fame for Famous American Indians, an area office of the Bureau of Indian Affairs, and the Riverside Indian School (1871). Indian City—U.S.A. (a reconstruction of tribal villages) is nearby. The annual American Indian Exposition is held there. Anadarko is an agricultural trading and processing centre with some light industry, notably carpet milling. Oil and natural gas wells are in the vicinity. Pop. (1980) 6,378.

Anadyr, formerly (until 1920) NOVO-MARIINSK, town and administrative centre, Chukchi autonomous *okrug* (area), far northeastern Russian Soviet Federated Socialist Republic, on the southern shore of the estuary of the Anadyr River. Incorporated as a town in 1965, it is a port on the Northern Sea Route and has a meteorological station and a fishery factory. Small amounts of lignite (brown coal) for local requirements are mined near the town. Pop. (latest est.) 12,000.

Anadyr, Gulf of, also called ANADYR BAY, Russian ANADYRSKY ZALIV, gulf in the eastern Russian Soviet Federated Socialist Republic, in the northwestern part of the Bering Sea. The width of the gulf at its entrance is about 250 mi (400 km), and it runs inland for some 200 mi, extending into the Bay of Krest and the Anadyr River estuary. The Gulf of Anadyr is closed by floating ice for 10 months of the year, being freed only in August and September. On the estuary of the Anadyr lies the port of Anadyr, serving the Chukchi Peninsula.

anaemia: *see* anemia.

anaesthetic: *see* anesthetic.

Anagni, town, Frosinone province, Lazio (Latium) region, central Italy, on a hill above the Sacco Valley, southeast of Rome. The ancient Anagnia, capital of the Hernici people, lost its independence to Rome in 306 BC. A bishopric from the 5th century AD, it was besieged by the Saracens in 877. Its leading medieval families were the Conti and Caetani. It was a papal residence in the Middle Ages and the birthplace of four popes: Innocent III, Gregory IX, Alexander IV, and Boniface VIII, who was imprisoned there by the French for three days in 1303. Notable landmarks include the cathedral (begun 1074) with a fine triple apse, the 14th-century Casa Barnekow, and the Palazzo Comunale (begun 1163). The ancient city walls still stand.

Anagni is an agricultural centre and has distilling, gas, and rubber industries. Pop. (1981 prelim.) mun., 18,469.

anagnorisis (Greek: "recognition"), in a literary work, the startling discovery that produces a change from ignorance to knowledge. It is discussed by Aristotle in the *Poetics* as an essential part of the plot of a tragedy, although anagnorisis occurs in comedy, epic, and, at a later date, in the novel as well. Anagnorisis usually involves revelation of the true identity of persons previously unknown, as when a father recognizes a stranger as his son, or vice versa. One of the finest occurs in Sophocles' *Oedipus Rex* when a messenger reveals to Oedipus his true birth, and Oedipus recognizes his wife Jocasta as his mother, the man he slew at the crossroads as his father, and himself as the unnatural sinner who brought misfortune on Thebes. This recognition is the more artistically satisfying because it is accompanied by a peripeteia ("reversal"), the shift in fortune from good to bad that moves on to the tragic catastrophe. An anagnorisis is not always accompanied by a peripeteia, as in the *Odyssey,* when Alcinous, ruler of Phaeacia, has his minstrel entertain a shipwrecked stranger with songs of the Trojan War, and the stranger begins to weep and reveals himself as none other than Odysseus. Aristotle discusses several kinds of anagnorisis employed by dramatists. The simplest kind, used, as he says, "from poverty of wit," is recognition by scars, birthmarks, or tokens. More interesting are those that arise naturally from incidents of the plot.

anagram, transposing letters of a word or group of words to produce other words that possess meaning, preferably bearing some logical relation to the original. The construction of anagrams is of great antiquity. Their invention is often ascribed without authority to the Jews, probably because the later Hebrew writers, particularly the Kabbalists, were fond of them, asserting that "secret mysteries are woven in the numbers of letters." Anagrams were known to the Greeks and Romans, although known Latin examples of words of more than one syllable are nearly all imperfect. They were popular throughout Europe during the Middle Ages and later, particularly in France, where a certain Thomas Billon was appointed "anagrammatist to the king."

The making of anagrams was an exercise of many religious orders in the 16th and 17th centuries, and the angelical salutation "Ave Maria, gratia plena, Dominus tecum" ("Hail Mary, full of grace, the Lord is with thee") was a favourite base; it was transposed to hundreds of variations, as, for example, "Virgo serena, pia, munda et immaculata" ("Virgin serene, holy, pure, and immaculate"). Some scientists of the 17th century—for example, Galileo, Christiaan Huygens, and Robert Hooke—embodied their discoveries in anagrams, while they were engaged in further verification, to keep others from claiming the credit.

The pseudonyms adopted by authors are often anagrams. In the 20th century, anagrams frequently have been used in crossword puzzles, in both the clues and the solutions.

Consult the INDEX *first*

ʿĀnah, town, al-Anbār *muḥāfaẓah* (governorate), western Iraq. Located on the Euphrates River and on a main road connecting Iraq and Syria, it is a local trade centre for crops grown in the fertile strip along the river below the cliffs of the desert. A town with a similar name has existed on or near the present site at least since the beginning of the 2nd millennium BC. By the 14th century AD the town was on an island in the river; on it, ruins can still be seen. In the 17th century it occupied both riverbanks, and *amīr*s of the powerful al-Mwali tribe lived there. The Persians sacked ʿĀnah during this period, and the town suffered frequent raids from desert peoples, leading to its decline. It remained a staging post on the route to the Mediterranean Sea until the advent of motor transport, which follows a more southerly route. ʿĀnah is now confined to the river's south bank. Pop. (1970 est.) 8,295.

Anaheim, city, Orange County, California, U.S., on the Santa Ana River. Founded by German immigrants in 1857 as a cooperative community, its name corresponds to "home on the Ana." After 1950 citrus groves and vineyards had all but disappeared with the Los Angeles–Orange County urban-industrial expansion. Disneyland amusement park (1955), Anaheim Stadium (1966; home of the California Angels baseball team and [since 1979] the Los Angeles Rams football team), and Anaheim Convention Center all have become major economic assets. Anaheim forms a metropolitan complex with the cities of Santa Ana, and Garden Grove. Inc. 1915. Pop. (1980) city, 221,847; metropolitan area (SMSA), 1,931,570.

Anahita, ancient Iranian goddess of waters, fertility, and procreation. Possibly of Mesopotamian origin, her cult was made prominent by Artaxerxes II, and statues and temples were set up in her honour throughout the Persian Empire. A common cult of the various peoples of the empire at that time, it persisted in Asia Minor long afterward. In Greece Anahita was identified with Athena and Artemis.

Anáhuac, historical and geographical region of Mexico. The heartland of Aztec Mexico, Anáhuac (Nahuatl, meaning "land by the water") designated that part of New Spain that became independent Mexico in 1821. The original Anáhuac of the Aztecs was the central plateau valley of Mexico, an area about 50 mi (80 km) long by 30 mi wide, with an average elevation of 7,500 ft (2,300 m). When the Spaniards arrived in 1519, the valley contained five interlocking lakes (Zumpango,

Xaltocan, Texcoco, Xochimilco, and Chalco), in the midst of which stood Tenochtitlán (now Mexico City), the Aztec capital, linked to the mainland by three long causeways. In 1607–08 much of the water was drained off to the Pánuco River system by a ditch and tunnel, and in the 20th century, Lake Texcoco was further emptied. Its salt marshes remain, as do Xochimilco's floating gardens, but the vast water area is gone. Saline deposits make the reclaimed land unfit for agriculture, and the lake beds give Mexico City a very unstable subsoil.

Anai Mudi, peak in Kottayam district, eastern Kerala state, southwestern India. Located in the Western Ghāts range, it rises to 8,842 ft (2,695 m) and is peninsular India's highest peak. From this point radiate three ranges—the Anaimalai to the north, the Palni to the northeast, and the Cardamom Hills to the south. Several rivers, including the Periyār and Amarāvati, rise in the surrounding ranges.

Anaimalai Hills, also called ELEPHANT MOUNTAINS, mountain range in the Western Ghāts, Tamil Nādu state, southern India. Bounded by Malabar and Cochin districts on the west, Travancore district on the south, and Madurai district on the east, the Anaimalai Hills are a junction of the Eastern Ghāts and Western Ghāts and have a general northwest–southeast trend. Anai Mudi peak, rising to 8,842 ft (2,695 m), is situated at the extreme southwestern end of the range and is the highest peak in southern India. Formed by fault-block movements in the Recent epoch, the Anaimalai Hills descend to form a series of terraces about 3,300 ft high. Dense monsoon forests including rosewood, sandalwood, teak, and sago palm cover most of the region. The soils are mottled red and brown containing oxides of aluminum and iron and are used as building material mixed with mortar and in road construction. The Kadar, Maravar, and Pooliyar peoples inhabit the sparsely populated hills; their economy is based on hunting and gathering and on shifting cultivation. There are tea, coffee, and rubber plantations where the hills have been cleared of forests. Industries are mainly household and comprise basket weaving and the making of coir and coir mat, metal articles, and *bidi* (cigarettes). Srīvilliputtūr, Uttamapālaiyam, and Mānūr are the important towns.

anal canal, the terminal portion of the digestive tract in most animals, distinguished from the rectum because of the transition of its internal surface from a mucus membrane layer (endodermal) to one of skinlike tissue (ectodermal). In man the anal canal is 1 to 1½ inches (2.5 to 4 centimetres) in length; its diameter is narrower than that of the rectum to which it connects. The canal is divided into three areas: the upper part, with longitudinal folds called rectal columns; the lower portion, with internal and external constrictive muscles (sphincters) to control evacuation of feces; and the anal opening itself.

The anal canal connects with the rectum at the point where it passes through a muscular pelvic diaphragm. The upper region has 5 to 10 vertical folds in the mucus membrane lining, called the anal or rectal columns; each column contains a small artery and vein. These are the terminal portions of the blood vessels that furnish the rectal and anal areas; they are susceptible to enlargement, commonly known as hemorrhoids. The mucus membrane of the upper portion is similar to that in the rest of the large intestine; it contains mucus-producing and absorptive cells.

The lower portions of the anal columns are joined by small concentric circular folds of the mucus membrane known as anal valves. Between the valves are small anal sinuses that open to lymph ducts and glands; these sometimes become abscessed and infected. The internal wall of the anal canal is first lined by moist, soft skin that lacks hair or glands; it then becomes a tough (keratinized) layer of skin containing hair and glands. The keratinized layer is continuous with the skin of the anal opening and external body. Both the upper and lower portions of the anal canal have circular and longitudinal muscle layers that allow expansion and contraction of the canal. The anal opening is keratinized skin that has several folds while contracted. When open, the folds allow the skin to stretch without tearing. In the skin around the anal opening but not immediately adjacent to it are glands that function as sweat glands, giving off perspiration.

The lower anal canal and the anal opening are composed of two muscular constrictions that regulate fecal passage. The internal sphincter is part of the inner surface of the canal; it is composed of concentric layers of circular muscle tissue and is not under voluntary control. The external sphincter is a layer of voluntary (striated) muscle encircling the outside wall of the anal canal and anal opening. One can cause it to expand and contract at will, except during the early years of life when it is not yet fully developed.

Waste products pass to the anal canal from the rectum. Nerve responses from the rectum cause the internal sphincter to relax while the external one contracts; shortly thereafter the external sphincter also relaxes and allows fecal discharge. The pelvic diaphragm and longitudinal muscles draw the anus and rectum up over the passing feces so that they are not extruded (prolapsed) out of the anal opening with the feces.

Nerves in the anal canal cause sphincter response and the sensation of pain. The lower part of the canal is very sensitive to heat, cold, cutting and abrasion. *See also* anus; rectum.

anal stage, in Freudian psychoanalytic theory, the period in a child's psychosexual development during which the child's main concerns are with the processes of defecation. The anal stage, generally the second and third years of life, is held to be significant for the child's later development because his responses to parental demands for bowel control may have far-reaching effects on his personality. Should a person become fixated, or locked, in the anal stage, he may develop what has been termed an anal character—orderly, frugal, and obstinate.

analbite, the form of the feldspar mineral albite (*q.v.*) that is stable only at temperatures above 700° C (1,300° F).

analcime, also called ANALCITE, common feldspathoid mineral, a hydrated sodium aluminosilicate ($NaAlSi_2O_6 \cdot H_2O$) that occurs in seams and cavities in basalt, diabase, granite, or gneiss. It also occurs in extensive beds thought to have formed by precipitation from alkaline lakes. Analcime is found in Trentino, Italy; New Zealand; and Wyoming and Utah in the United States. Although a feldspathoid, analcime is closely related to the zeolite minerals with which it is sometimes classed. Its name is derived from the Greek *analkis,* "weak," which refers to the weak electrical charge generated by heating or rubbing it. For detailed physical properties, *see* feldspathoid (table).

Analects: *see* Lun yü.

analgesia, loss of sensation of pain that results from an interruption in the nervous pathway between sense organ and brain. Different forms of sensation (*e.g.,* touch, temperature, and pain) from one area of skin travel to the spinal cord by different nerve fibres in the same nerve bundle. Hence, any injury or disease affecting such a nerve would abolish all forms of sensation in the area supplied by it. When the sensory nerves reach the spinal cord, however, their fibres separate and pursue different courses on their way upward to the brain. Thus, it is possible for certain forms of sensation to be lost, while others are preserved, in diseases that affect only certain areas in the spinal cord. Because some of the sensations of pain and temperature travel the same path, they may be lost together. Diseases of the cord that may cause analgesia without loss of the sensation of touch are tabes dorsalis, syringomyelia, and tumours of the cord. Analgesia may also be a manifestation of hysteria. The term is also used for pain relief induced by the action of such drugs as aspirin, codeine, and morphine.

analgesic, drug that relieves pain without blocking the conduction of nerve impulses or markedly altering the function of the sensory apparatus.

A brief treatment of analgesics follows. For full treatment, *see* MACROPAEDIA: Drugs and Drug Action.

All the commonly used analgesics are derived from one or another of three compounds, all first discovered in the 19th century: salicylic acid, pyrazolone derivatives, and phenacetin (or acetophenetidin). The most commonly used analgesic is aspirin, or acetylsalicylic acid, which acts by bringing down temperature and relieving inflammation, as well as killing pain. It also stimulates and then depresses respiration and causes a change in electrolyte balance. Taken in overdose aspirin can cause deafness, ringing in the ears, diarrhea, nausea, and headache, which disappear when the dose is reduced or stopped. Continual use of aspirin often causes irritation to the stomach wall with associated pain, nausea, vomiting, and bleeding.

Acetaminophen is another popular mild analgesic. Chemically it is a phenacetin derivative and is a suitable alternative to aspirin for patients who develop severe symptoms of stomach irritation, because it is not as harmful to the gastrointestinal tract. It does not possess, however, equal anti-inflammatory activity and so is ineffective in treating rheumatoid arthritis. Acetaminophen and similar drugs can cause kidney and liver damage if taken in even slightly more than the recommended doses.

The pyrazolone analgesics have similar effects to aspirin. An occasional harmful side effect is the development of blood abnormalities, particularly agranulocytosis. Phenylbutazone is a pyrazolone derivative that is valuable in treating rheumatoid arthritis because of its anti-inflammatory activity, but it is effective for a short period only. It, too, affects blood-cell formation.

Indomethacin and mefenamic acid are sometimes used as alternatives to aspirin to treat rheumatoid arthritis by reducing inflammation and pain. Side effects include headache, dizziness, gastrointestinal disturbances, and mental confusion.

analogous structure (biology): *see* analogy.

analogue computer, any of a class of devices in which variable physical quantities such as electrical potential, fluid pressure, or mechanical motion are represented in a way analogous to the corresponding quantities in the problem to be solved. The analogue system is set up according to initial conditions and then allowed to change freely. Answers to the problem are obtained by measuring the variables in the analogue model. *See also* digital computer.

The earliest analogue computers were special-purpose machines, as for example the tide predictor developed in 1876 by William Thomson (later known as Lord Kelvin). Along the same lines, A.A. Michelson and S.W.

Stratton built in 1898 a harmonic analyzer (*q.v.*) having 80 components. Each of these was capable of generating a sinusoidal motion, which could be multiplied by constant factors by adjustment of a fulcrum on levers. The components were added by means of springs to produce a resultant. Another milestone in the development of the modern analogue computer was the invention of the so-called differential analyzer in the early 1930s by Vannevar Bush, a U.S. electrical engineer. This machine, which used mechanical integrators (gears of variable speed) to solve differential equations, was the first practical and reliable device of its kind.

Most present-day analogue computers operate by manipulating potential differences (voltages). Their basic component is an operational amplifier, a device whose output current is proportional to its input potential difference. By causing this output current to flow through appropriate components, further potential differences are obtained and a wide variety of mathematical operations, including inversion, summation, differentiation, and integration, can be carried out on them. A typical electronic analogue computer consists of numerous types of amplifiers, which can be connected so as to build up a mathematical expression, sometimes of great complexity and with a multitude of variables.

Analogue computers are especially well suited to simulating dynamic systems; such simulations may be conducted in real time or at greatly accelerated rates, thereby allowing experimentation by repeated runs with altered variables. They have been widely used in simulations of aircraft, nuclear power plants, and industrial chemical processes. Other major uses include analysis of hydraulic networks (*e.g.*, flow of liquids through a sewer system) and electronics networks (*e.g.*, performance of long-distance circuits).

analogy (from Greek *ana logon,* "according to a ratio"), originally, a similarity in proportional relationships. It may be a similarity between two figures (*e.g.*, triangles) that differ in scale or between two quantities, one of which, though unknown, can be calculated if its relation to the other is known to be similar to that in which two other known quantities stand. Thus, if $2{:}4{::}4{:}x$, it can be seen that $x = 8$. Another form of analogy noted by the Greeks is that of inferring similarity of function, known as "educing the correlate." Aristotle (*Topics,* i, 17) stated the formulas of these two kinds of analogy: "As *A* is to *B,* so *C* is to *D*"; and "As *A* is in *B,* so *C* is in *D.*"

Plato employed a functional analogy when he argued that the Idea of the Good makes knowledge possible in the intelligible world just as the Sun makes vision possible in the perceptual world. Here a relationship not yet understood is analogous to one already familiar.

In the Middle Ages it was believed that the universe forms an ordered structure such that the macrocosmic pattern of the whole is reproduced in the microcosmic pattern of the parts so that it is possible to draw inferences by analogy from the one to the other. Thus, the law of nature conceived in the juridical sense, which prescribes the fitting order of human relationships, could be assimilated to the physical sense of law, which describes the order obtaining in the natural world. Because the natural world exhibits hierarchical degrees of subordination, it was argued, human relationships should also exhibit such subordination. Such parallels were held to constitute arguments and not merely allegorical illustrations; it was contended, for instance, that, as there were two luminaries to light the world and two authorities set over man (the papacy and the empire), then, as the Moon's light is reflected from the Sun, so the imperial authority must be derived from the papal. Dante, in his *De monarchia* (*c.* 1313), while claiming that it is light and not authority that the empire derives from the papacy, nevertheless accepted the principles on which such arguments are built.

In scientific thinking analogies or resemblances may be used to suggest hypotheses or the existence of some law or principle, especially if a comparison can be made between the functions of elements in two systems, as when observation of the moons of Jupiter suggested by analogy the modern conception of the solar system. The argument of Thomas Robert Malthus, the English economist, that populations tend to increase in numbers beyond the means of their subsistence suggested to Charles Darwin the evolutionary hypothesis of natural selection. The fruitfulness of such analogies depends on whether any testable consequences can be deduced from them, which is likely to depend on whether the resemblance is of a fundamental or a merely superficial kind. Functional resemblances are more likely to be fundamental than qualitative ones (such as colour). It would not be legitimate, for instance, to conclude from the model of the atomic nucleus as a miniature solar system that the process of nuclear fission is similar to that by which new planetary systems may be formed or disrupted.

In social and political discussion analogies may elucidate some unfamiliar point in terms of what is more familiar. Thus, biological analogies may suggest that a community has an "organic" relationship. Such analogies are misleading, however, insofar as they overlook the fact that individual members of the community also have purposes, rights, and responsibilities of their own. In employing the method of analogy, it should always be possible to show that the resemblances noted bear relevantly on the point to be established, whereas the differences are irrelevant. In many cases it is difficult to be sure of this distinction, and arguments from analogy are therefore precarious unless supported by considerations that can be established independently.

analogy, in biology, similarity of function and superficial resemblance of structures that have different origins. For example, the wings of a fly, a moth, and a bird are analogous because they developed independently as adaptations to a common function—flying. The presence of the analogous structure, in this case the wing, does not reflect evolutionary closeness among the organisms that possess it. Analogy is one aspect of evolutionary biology and is distinct from homology (*q.v.*), the similarity of structures as a result of similar embryonic origin and development, considered strong evidence of common descent.

In many cases analogous structures, or analogs, tend to become similar in appearance by a process termed convergence. An example is the convergence of the streamlined form in the bodies of squid, shark, seal, porpoise, penguin, and ichthyosaur, animals of diverse ancestry. Physiological processes and behaviour patterns may also exhibit analogous convergence. Egg-guarding behaviour in the cobra, the stickleback, the octopus, and the spider is thought to have evolved independently among those animals, which are quite distant in their biological relationships.

Many New World cacti and African euphorbias are similar in appearance, being succulent, spiny, water-storing, and adapted to desert conditions generally. They are classified, however, in two separate and distinct families, sharing characteristics that have evolved independently in response to similar environmental challenges.

analysis, in mathematics, the extended sequence of mathematical developments that flow out of the discovery, by Sir Isaac Newton and Gottfried Wilhelm Leibniz in the late 17th century, of the differential and integral calculus. Since that time, several more or less distinct fields of analysis have evolved, including infinite series, the calculus of variations, differential equations, Fourier analysis, complex analysis, vector and tensor analysis, and functional analysis. Other branches of mathematics have been profoundly affected by ideas originating in analysis, notably differential geometry, set theory, and topology.

A brief treatment of analysis follows. For full treatment, *see* MACROPAEDIA: Analysis (in Mathematics).

The development of the calculus introduced several ideas fateful for the subsequent history of mathematics. New techniques for calculating properties of functions—in particular their maxima and minima and the areas and volumes of plane and three-dimensional regions—made it possible for many previously difficult results to be derived routinely. Important notions of indefinitely close approximation (limits) and related techniques for arbitrarily close approximation of solutions to general equations also were introduced. Another significant idea was that of the infinite series—the expression of a quantity or function as the sum of an unending series of smaller and smaller increments. Newton and his immediate followers realized that this procedure made it possible to adapt older techniques, developed for calculations with finite polynomials, to the investigation of more general mathematical relationships.

The immediate successors of Newton and Leibniz, including the Bernoulli family and Leonhard Euler, extended the techniques of the calculus, defining the subject matter and approach that have subsequently remained standard. Euler, in particular, investigated the properties of the trigonometric, logarithmic, and exponential functions, establishing many relationships between them by manipulation of their representations as infinite series. He and the Bernoullis also extended Newton's techniques to quantities dependent upon the entire shape of a curve or surface, thereby inventing the so-called calculus of variations. These studies and Newton's use of the differential calculus to study physical motions led to an interest in differential equations, that is, relationships between functions of one or more variables and their derivatives.

Early mathematical analysts sought explicit integrals or solutions of differential equations, in terms of finite combinations of known classical functions, or, at worst, by infinite series of such terms. By the latter part of the 18th century, however, it was realized that many important problems had no explicit solutions of this type. Investigations in analysis then became more qualitative, emphasizing the derivation of useful general properties of classes of functions, rather than requiring specific formulas for them.

The calculus of functions of several variables proved useful in the study of curves and curved surfaces in space, an application pursued by Carl Friedrich Gauss, who, by applying the methods of the differential calculus to the study of geometric questions, founded differential geometry.

Early in the 19th century, J.-B.-J. Fourier showed that arbitrary functions can be represented by infinite series of sines and cosines. These series are analogous to the representation of a vector in three-dimensional space. This analogy served in the 20th century to spur the rise of functional analysis.

A.-L. Cauchy and others extended the calculus to complex functions. Cauchy showed that if a function of a complex variable has a derivative, then its value at a given point can be expressed as an integral (Cauchy integral) of its values at other points. Cauchy's work eventually related analysis to topology, as emphasized in the work of Bernhard Riemann, which opened themes that were adequately explored only a century later.

During the 19th century, increasing concern for logical rigour and a series of critical studies of the foundations of analysis—among which the works of Cauchy, Richard Dedekind, and Georg Cantor are particularly important—resulted in a stringent decomposition of the concept of continuity into more primitive set-theoretic notions and in the recognition that the whole structure of analysis built during the two preceding centuries could be based firmly on a handful of such principles.

The exploitation of analogies between the geometry of vectors and the properties of collections of functions has been a major theme of 20th-century analysis. David Hilbert emphasized the close relationship between certain types of equations involving integrals and linear systems of algebraic equations in several variables. Hermann Weyl showed that Hilbert's methods allowed important classes of series expansions to be derived through the study of simple differential equations. John von Neumann and Stefan Banach systematically developed this new field, called functional analysis, giving polished abstract formulations to many of its principles and techniques.

Functional analysis has led to deeper understanding of the solutions of partial differential equations important in physics and engineering. It also has revealed relationships between algebra, analysis, and topology.

analysis, in physics and chemistry, determination of the physical properties or chemical composition of samples of matter or, particularly in modern physics, of the energy and other properties of subatomic particles produced in nuclear interactions. A large body of systematic procedures intended for these purposes has been continuously evolving in close association with the development of other branches of the physical sciences since their beginnings.

A brief treatment of analysis follows. For full treatment, *see* MACROPAEDIA: Analysis and Measurement, Physical and Chemical.

Chemical analysis, in particular, has developed into a highly diversified discipline, with distinct branches oriented toward the solution of specific kinds of problems. A sample of a single compound may be analyzed to establish its elemental composition or its molecular structure; composition is most commonly found by procedures involving chemical reactions, which destroy the sample, but structure is more often studied by nondestructive measurements of physical properties. Many such measurements entail spectroscopic techniques that pinpoint the wavelengths at which electromagnetic radiation is absorbed or emitted by the substance.

Mixtures of substances are ordinarily analyzed by separating, detecting, and identifying their components by methods that depend on differences in their physical properties, such as volatility, mobility in an electric or a gravitational field, or distribution between two immiscible substances.

analytic geometry, also called COORDINATE GEOMETRY, the mathematical subject in which algebraic symbolism and methods are used to represent and solve problems in geometry. The importance of analytic geometry is that it establishes a correspondence between geometric curves and algebraic equations. This correspondence makes it possible to reformulate problems in geometry as equivalent problems in algebra, and vice versa; the methods of either subject can then be used to solve problems in the other.

A brief treatment of analytic geometry follows. For full treatment, *see* MACROPAEDIA: Geometry: *Analytic geometry.*

Many mathematicians of ancient times were aware that the geometry of figures was related to the algebra of numbers. Even the Greeks were limited, however, by the primitive state of algebraic symbolism and procedures and by their view of mathematics as being tied to and representative of the physical world. For example, the Greeks thought of ordinary numbers in terms of line segments, the product of two numbers in terms of areas, and the product of three numbers in terms of volumes. Since lengths, areas, and volumes are the only three types of geometric measurements inherent in the physical world, the Greeks were unable to consider the geometric equivalents of other types of algebraic relationships such as $y = x^4$. It was only when algebra had become a more complete and useful subject in its own right, and mathematics had moved away from a complete dependence on and relationship to the physical world, that the possibility of establishing a fruitful correspondence between geometry and algebra became evident.

Analytic geometry was established in France in the 17th century by René Descartes and Pierre de Fermat, who independently pointed out the correspondence between ordered pairs of real numbers and the distances of a point from two intersecting lines in the plane, called the axes, or coordinate axes. Once the axes are selected, every geometric point has a unique representation by an ordered pair of real numbers (x,y) and, conversely, every ordered pair of real numbers represents a unique geometric point. Modern analytic geometry employs axes that are perpendicular to each other; this type of coordinate system, and the coordinates (x,y) themselves, are called Cartesian, after René Descartes.

The correspondence established between points in a plane and ordered pairs of real numbers can easily be extended to a correspondence between points in three-dimensional space and ordered triples of real numbers (x,y,z) by using a three-dimensional Cartesian coordinate system. It is perfectly reasonable to consider and work with ordered sets of as many real numbers as is desired. Therefore, the methods of analytic geometry allow mathematicians to study the theoretical properties of spaces with dimensions greater than three, even though such spaces cannot exist in the real world. The coordinate systems developed by Descartes and Fermat are not the only ones possible; one of the most useful alternatives is the polar coordinate system developed by Sir Isaac Newton. In this system any point A in the plane can be represented by its distance r from a reference point O and by the angle θ between the half-line from O through A and a reference direction; the ordered pair (r,θ) specifies the polar coordinates of the point. Certain geometric curves have much simpler algebraic equivalents when expressed in polar coordinates than when expressed in Cartesian coordinates: an example is the logarithmic spiral. In Cartesian coordinates the equation for this curve would be

$$\frac{1}{2}\log(x^2+y^2) = \left[\text{arc cos}\left(\frac{x}{\sqrt{x^2+y^2}}\right)\right]\log a,$$

with a an arbitrary constant. In polar coordinates the equation is the much simpler

$$r = a^\theta.$$

analytic language, any language that uses specific grammatical words, or particles, rather than inflection (*q.v.*), to express syntactic relations within sentences. An analytic language is commonly identified with an isolating language (*q.v.*), since the two classes of language tend to coincide. Typical examples are Vietnamese and Classical Chinese, which are analytic and isolating. Analytic language is to be contrasted with synthetic language (*q.v.*).

Analytic philosophy, also called LINGUISTIC PHILOSOPHY, a movement, dominant in Anglo–U.S. philosophy in the mid-20th century, distinguished by its method, which has focussed upon language and the analysis of the concepts expressed in it. Representatives of the Analytic school have tended to hold that the purpose of philosophy is therapeutic—to clarify obscurities and confusions, in the expectation that many of the traditional problems of philosophy will thus dissolve.

A brief treatment of Analytic and Linguistic philosophy follows. For full treatment, *see* MACROPAEDIA: Philosophical Schools and Doctrines.

Analytic and Linguistic philosophers have advanced a variety of divergent views. The Austrian Ludwig Wittgenstein (1889–1951), for example, in a career perhaps unique in the history of philosophy, wrote two major works central to the development of Analytic philosophy—*Tractatus Logico-Philosophicus* and *Philosophical Investigations*—the second of which refuted the first.

Analytic philosophy, flourishing between 1945 and 1960, was the successor of the Logical Positivism of the 1930s, which in its turn derived to some extent from the Realism and Pluralism of the British thinkers Bertrand Russell and G.E. Moore, worked out in the decade before 1914. Russell was an inspirer of Positivism (the insistence on a knowledge based on facts verifiable by the methods of empirical sciences); Moore, with his determination to avoid unintelligibility in philosophical discourse and his resistance to beliefs at odds with common sense, was the chief anticipator of the Analytic and Linguistic philosophy of 1945 to 1960.

The leading exponents of the movement were Wittgenstein and the British thinkers Gilbert Ryle (1900–76) and J.L. Austin (1911–60). Its explicit formulation began with Wittgenstein's return, after a period of withdrawal, to philosophy and Cambridge in 1929. While the brightest young philosophers were becoming committed to the Positivism of the Vienna Circle, in the British form given to it in 1936 in the *Language, Truth and Logic* of A.J. Ayer, Wittgenstein's new ideas were confined, with a few exceptions, to a close circle of personal disciples in Cambridge.

The conquest of philosophically more populous Oxford was signalled in 1946 by a celebrated symposium paper of Austin's on the topic of other minds. Ryle's *The Concept of Mind* (1949) was the first important book in the new mode. Wittgenstein's earlier, and in many ways different, views were not generally available until his *Philosophical Investigations* was published posthumously in 1953, to be followed by a long sequence of other writings. In the U.S. his influence was rapidly diffused after 1945 by former pupils teaching at Cornell.

The school's decline clearly began in 1960—the year of Austin's death and of the publication of *Word and Object* by the U.S. thinker W.V. Quine, a constructive and highly original development of the Positivism of the 1930s. That was also the epoch of the emergence of the U.S. linguist Noam Chomsky's radical renovation of linguistic science, which must have indirectly helped to undermine the classically based amateurism of the British Analytic philosophers.

The starting point of Analytic philosophy is not simply the belief that language is the proper or immediate object of philosophical inquiry. That is the conviction of many philosophers of the past, particularly when they have been academic or professionalized. It is also accepted by those who, taking thought and knowledge to be the prime business of philosophy, realize that all but the most primitive thoughts require linguistic articulation. The distinguishing mark of Analytic philosophy is the thesis that traditional philosophical problems can be solved, or dissolved, by close attention to the manner in which the words employed in stating and discussing them are actually used.

The Analytic philosophers agreed in rejecting as arbitrary and absurd the verification principle of their Positivist predecessors, which implied that only utterances affirming matters of empirical or conceptual fact are meaningful. Both its branding as senseless of utterances not in the indicative mood and judgments of value, and the curious accounts it gave of utterances about material things, the minds of others, and the past so as to bring them under the principle by main force, were to Analytic philosophers outrages on common sense.

In its place, they argued that language is a social and functional phenomenon, part of the natural life of the human species. It is not an abstract calculus whose essence has been revealed once and for all by modern mathematical logic. It is used in many different ways and for many different purposes. There is no single basis of, or paradigm for, significant speech to which everything must be forcibly reduced if it is not to be ruled out as senseless. Echoing Moore's attachment to the convictions of common sense, the Analytic philosophers took conflict with such convictions to be a sign of conceptual confusion, a misunderstanding of the rules that actually govern the use of words in normal everyday life, and which can be followed perfectly well in practice, but which one is led to ignore in reflective moods by mistaken but seductive analogies (according to Wittgenstein) or mere oversimplification, a "one-sided diet of examples" (in the words of Austin). From this it follows that the right way to deal with philosophical problems is to bring to light the mistakes about the meaning of words that give rise to them. True philosophy, therefore, is a kind of therapy for conceptually confused intellects.

Wittgenstein applied his new conception of language to a large extent to the problem of explaining discourse about mental processes—understanding, suffering, pain, and intentionality. Ryle's *Concept of Mind* offered a simplified, perhaps simplistic, version of Wittgenstein's ideas on this subject, which arrived in the end at something close to the behaviourism of most Positivists, but by way of a mass of interesting detail. Austin wrote brilliantly but inconclusively about perception, truth, promising, and responsibility. By his inconclusiveness he succeeded in avoiding Wittgenstein's paradox of propounding the philosophical theory that philosophy should propound no theories.

Where Wittgenstein philosophized about language only so far as needed for the therapeutic purpose in hand, the Analytic philosophers of Oxford were well disposed to the study of language for its own sake. Ryle's view of philosophy as conceptual geography suggested the possibility of a comprehensive atlas. Austin, in his last book, *How to Do Things with Words* (1962), sketched the outlines of a systematic theory of the uses of language. Although Ryle and Austin have passed into history as influences, Wittgenstein remains a living force in contemporary philosophy.

analytic proposition, in logic, a statement or judgment that is necessarily true on purely logical grounds and serves only to elucidate meanings already implicit in the subject; its truth is thus guaranteed by the principle of contradiction. Such propositions are distinguished from synthetic propositions, the meanings of which include information imported from nonlogical (usually empirical) sources and which are therefore contingent. Thus the proposition that all bodies are extended is analytic, because the notion of extension is implicit in the notion of body; whereas the proposition that all bodies are heavy is synthetic, since the notion of weight supposes in addition to the notion of body that of bodies in relation to one another. In the 19th century Bernard Bolzano, a Prague logician and epistemologist, added a third category, the analytically false.

Gottfried Wilhelm Leibniz, a 17th-century German Rationalist, had made a parallel distinction between "truths of reason" and "truths of fact," and David Hume, a Scottish Skeptic, had distinguished between "relations of ideas" and "matters of fact." The first definition of an analytical statement approaching logical adequacy was that of Bolzano, who held that a sentence is analytically true if either (1) its propositional form is true for all values of its variables or (2) it can be reduced to such a sentence.

Most contemporary logicians hold that the most fundamental domain to which analyticity pertains is not that of judgments (which are too psychological), nor of sentences (which belong to a specific language), nor of definitions (which are about words instead of objects); it is, instead, that of statements (which refer to meanings of sentences). To this reference to meanings Gottlob Frege, one of the founders of contemporary logic, added a reference to "general logical laws," these two references being the only requirements for the proof of an analytic statement.

The distinction between analytic and synthetic statements aroused extensive debate in the mid-20th century, particularly in view of objections raised by the U.S. logician Willard Van Orman Quine.

analytic psychology, the psychoanalytic method of the Swiss psychiatrist Carl Jung as he distinguished it from that of Sigmund Freud. He attached less importance than did Freud to the role of sexuality in the neuroses, and he stressed the analysis of the patient's immediate conflicts as being more useful in understanding his problems than the uncovering of the conflicts of childhood. He defined the unconscious as including both the individual's own unconscious and that which he inherited from his ancestors (the "collective unconscious"). He classified people into introverted and extroverted types and further distinguished them according to four primary functions of the mind—thinking, feeling, sensation, and intuition—one or more of which predominated in any given person.

Anambra, state, east central Nigeria, created in 1976 from the northern half of former East-Central State, that was part of the former Eastern Region prior to 1967. With an area of 6,892 sq mi (17,850 sq km), the state is bounded by the states of Benue on the north, Imo on the south, Bendel on the west, and Cross River on the east. It is divided by the southern extension of the Udi-Nsukka Plateau that rises to more than 1,000 ft (300 m). Most of the plateau is covered by open grassland with occasional clusters of woodlands and oil palm trees. The western part of the state includes a tropical rain forest along the eastern bank of the Niger River, which runs parallel to the western boundary. The Ibos comprise the majority of the population; English is widely spoken.

Agriculture plays an important role in the economy; cocoa, yams, oil palm products, corn (maize), rice, cassava, avocadoes, and citrus fruit are the main crops. Enugu, the state capital, is an important centre for coal mining. Iron ore, lead, zinc, salt, and lignite are mined; deposits of limestone, fine clay, marble, and silica sand are worked. Petroleum and natural gas are extracted. An industrial estate, located 7 mi (11 km) east of Enugu, produces steel rods, asbestos, cement products, and oxygen and acetylene gases. Other industries include textile manufacturing, food processing, tire re-treading, lumbering, soft-drink bottling, brewing, publishing, furniture manufacturing, and the production of phonograph records. A large modern market is located in Onitsha, the hub of the state's commerce and industry. There is a network of roads that connect Enugu with Onitsha, Awgu, Ezzangbo, and Nsukka. Enugu is also linked by the eastern branch of the Nigerian Railways with Port Harcourt, and it also has an international airport. The University of Nigeria (founded 1960) at Enugu is the site of the University of Nigeria's Teaching Hospital. Pop. (1983 est.) 5,880,600.

anamorphosis, in the visual arts, an ingenious perspective technique used to give a distorted image of the subject represented in a picture when seen from the usual viewpoint, but so executed that if seen from a particular angle, or reflected in a curved mirror, the distortion disappears, and the image in the picture appears normal. Derived from the Greek word meaning "to transform," the term

"Edward VI," anamorphic oil portrait, 1546; in the National Portrait Gallery, London

By courtesy of the National Portrait Gallery, London

anamorphosis was first used in the 17th century, although this technique had been one of the more curious by-products of the discovery of perspective (*q.v.*) in the 14th and 15th centuries. The first examples appear in Leonardo da Vinci's notebooks. It was regarded as a display of technical virtuosity, and it was included in most 16th- and 17th-century drawing manuals. Two important examples of anamorphosis are a portrait of the young Edward VI (1546; National Portrait Gallery, London) that has been attributed to Cornelis Anthonisz, and a skull in the foreground of Hans Holbein the Younger's painting "Jean de Dinteville and Georges de Selve" ("The Ambassadors," 1533; National Gallery, London). Many examples are provided with special peepholes through which the viewer can obtain the rectified view that first eluded him.

A modern equivalent of anamorphosis is the so-called Ames Room, in which the appearance of people and objects is distorted by manipulation of the contours of the room in which they are seen. This and other aspects of anamorphosis have received a good deal of attention in the 20th century from psychologists interested in perception.

Anan, city, Tokushima Prefecture (*ken*), Shikoku, Japan, on the Naka-gawa (Naka River), facing the Kii-suidō (Kii Channel) between the Inland Sea and the Pacific Ocean. It was created in 1958 by the merger of the former castle town of Tomioka and the fishing village of Tachibana. A market centre for the agricultural hinterland, its industry produces lime, timber, ships, and wooden goods. During the late 1970s construction of a harbour, thermal power station, and industrial site began. Pop. (1980) 61,253.

Anan ben David (fl. 2nd half of the 8th century), Persian Jew, founder of the Ananites, a heretical and antirabbinical order from which the still existing Karaite sect developed.

Anan seems to have become prominent in the 760s, when he competed with his younger brother for the office of exilarch, head of the Jews of the Babylonian Exile. The office was a hereditary one, needing the confirmation of the ruling caliph, which Anan failed to obtain. He therefore declared himself antiexilarch, an action that caused him to be jailed by the civil authorities. At his trial Anan pleaded that the caliph had confirmed his brother as head of one religion but that he, Anan, had founded a new religion, one with similarities to Islām. As a result, he was released and given government protection.

In 770 Anan wrote the definitive code of his order, the *Sefer ha-mitzwot* ("Book of Precepts"). Its unifying principle is its rejection of much of the Talmud and of the rabbinate, which based its authority on the Talmud. Only the Bible is held to be valid, but it is interpreted with a strange mixture of freedom and literalism.

After Anan's death, his followers settled in Jerusalem. Eventually his sect developed into the order known as Karaism, which also was ascetically oriented and rejected Talmudic authority. When the State of Israel was founded in 1948, several thousand Karaites settled there.

Anand, Mulk Raj (b. Dec. 12, 1905, Peshāwar, India), prominent Indian author of novels, short stories, and critical essays in English who is known for his realistic and sympathetic portrayal of the poor in India.

The son of a coppersmith, Anand graduated with honours in 1924 from Punjab University, Lahore, and pursued additional studies at Cambridge University and at University College, London. While in Europe, he became politically active in India's struggle for independence and shortly thereafter wrote a series of diverse books, including *Persian Painting* (1930), *Curries and Other Indian Dishes* (1932), and *The Hindu View of Art* (1933).

A prolific writer, Anand first gained wide recognition for his novels *Untouchables* (1935) and *Coolie* (1936), both of which examined the problems of poverty in Indian society, and in 1945 he returned to Bombay to campaign for national reforms. Among his other major works are *The Village* (1939), *The Sword and the Sickle* (1942), and *The Private Life of an Indian Prince* (1953). Anand also edited numerous magazines and journals, including *Marg*, an art quarterly that he founded in 1946, and continued to work on his seven-volume autobiographical novel entitled *Seven Ages of Man*.

Ānanda (fl. 6th century BC, India), first cousin of the Buddha and one of his principal disciples, known as his "beloved disciple" and devoted companion.

He entered the order of monks in the second year of the Buddha's ministry and in the 25th year was appointed his personal attendant. According to the *Vinaya Piṭaka* texts, he persuaded the Buddha, much against the Buddha's own inclination, to allow women to become nuns. Of the Buddha's intimate disciples, Ānanda alone had not attained Enlightenment when the Buddha died. He attained it, however, just before the first council (*c.* 544 or 480 BC), at which he repeated the "Basket of Discourse" (*Sutta Piṭaka*). He is represented as being interlocutor in many discourses and the actual author of several. A collection of verses is ascribed to him in the *Theragāthā*. According to tradition, he lived to the age of 120 years.

ānanda (Sanskrit: "joy, bliss"), in Indian philosophy of the *Upaniṣads* and the school of Vedānta, an important attribute of the supreme being Brahman. Bliss is characteristically used in the *Taittirīya Upaniṣad* (*c.* 6th century BC) to define Brahman and, simultaneously, the highest state of the individual self. This bliss is identified with the bliss that is brought to the self by its release from the shackles of the body. In this sense *ānanda* continues to play an important role in the orthodox school of Hindu philosophy, the Vedānta, though the nature of this bliss is differently interpreted according to the views held about Brahman itself.

Ananda Bazar Patrika, morning daily newspaper published in Calcutta, India's largest Indian-language newspaper in terms of circulation. Published in the Bengali language, *Ananda Bazar Patrika* was founded in 1922 and is something of a rarity among newspapers in Indian languages, most of which do not attain circulations of more than a few thousand. The newspaper, which also publishes an Allahabad edition, rivals the country's most widely circulated daily, the English-language *Indian Express*. *Ananda Bazar Patrika*'s circulation far outstrips that of the country's most influential papers, the *Times of India*, the *Statesman*, and the *Hindu*.

Ananda Mahidol, also called RAMA VIII (b. Sept. 20, 1925, Heidelberg, Ger.—d. June 9, 1946, Bangkok), eighth king of the Chakkri dynasty of Siam, whose mysterious death was one of the most traumatic events in the history of modern Thailand.

Ananda was only 10 years old and a schoolboy in Switzerland when he succeeded his uncle, King Prajadhipok, in 1935. World War II prevented his return to Thailand to assume his constitutional duties until 1946. Shortly thereafter, early in the morning of June 9, he was found dead in his bed of a gunshot wound. The case was never fully explained, and the controversy over it contributed to the weakening of civilian constitutional government and help precipitate the return of military government in Thailand.

Ānandatīrtha (Hindu philosopher): *see* Madhva.

Ananke, in Greek literature, necessity or fate personified. In Homer the personification has not yet occurred, although even the gods admit they are limited in their freedom of action. Ananke is rather prominent in post-Homeric literature and theological speculation, particularly in the mystic cult of Orphism, but is definitely known to emerge into a cult only at Corinth, where she was worshipped with Bia (Might, or Force). Because of her unalterable nature it was pointless to render to her offerings or sacrifice—"Nothing is stronger than dread Necessity" was a Greek byword.

In literature she is associated with the nymph Adrasteia, the Moirai or Fates (of whom she was the mother, according to Plato in *The Republic*), and similar deities. In Italy she does not appear to have been worshipped at all; the description of Necessitas (Ananke) in Horace's *Carmina* is purely literary.

Anantapur, town, administrative headquarters of Anantapur district, southern Andhra Pradesh state, southern India. The town is located 120 mi (190 km) north of Bangalore (Karnātaka state) on the Hyderābād–Bangalore main road. The town's name is derived from Ananda, the name of the wife of a dewan (official) of the medieval kingdom of Vijayanagar, who built the town. Colleges of science and arts and engineering are located there.

The district (7,384 sq mi [19,125 sq km]) is part of the great Deccan Plateau and has a varied terrain of hills, plains, and basins and is well forested. Because of a high amount of rainfall between June and September, cotton, peanuts (groundnuts), pulses, and jowar (sorghum) are grown commercially. The bulk of the steatite (soapstone) of India is mined in Anantapur; it is used in fertilizers and also exported to Europe. Peanut and castor-bean milling is the mainstay of the economy. Pop. (1981) town, 119,531; district, 2,548,012.

ānantarika-karma (Sanskrit: "the deed bringing immediately successive retribution"), Pāli ĀNANTARIKA-KAMMA, in the Theravāda (Way of the Elders) tradition of Buddhism, a heinous sin that causes the agent to be reborn in hell immediately after death and never to attain the Enlightenment. The sin is incurable and its retribution unavoidable. There are five sins of this kind: killing one's mother, killing one's father, killing an *arhat* (saint), injuring the body of a Buddha, and causing a division in the Buddhist community.

Anantnāg, formerly ISLĀMĀBĀD, town, administrative headquarters of Anantnāg district, in the Indian-held sector of Jammu and Kashmir state, southeast of Srīnagar, on the Jhelum River. Located north of the Pīr Panjāl Range, it is an agricultural trade centre and the southern headquarters for navigation by large boats in the Vale of Kashmir. Many springs issue from the land around the town, including the slightly sulfurous Anant Nāg. Anantnāg was formerly the chief town of the valley and contains a summer palace, mosque, and shrine.

Anantnāg district (2,078 sq mi [5,382 sq km]) is an agricultural region (rice, corn [maize], oilseeds, and wheat) whose main population centres include Anantnāg and Pāmpur. Pop. (1981) town, 33,978; district, 656,351.

anapest, metrical foot consisting of two short (in classical verse) or unstressed (in English verse) syllables followed by one long or stressed syllable, as in the word introduce. First found in early Spartan marching songs, anapestic metres were widely used in Greek and Latin dramatic verse, especially for the entrance and exit of the chorus. Lines composed primarily of anapestic feet, often with an additional unstressed syllable at the end of the first line, are much rarer in English verse. Because of its jog-trot rhythm, pure anapestic metre was originally used only in light or popular English verse, but after the 18th century it appeared in serious poetry. Byron used it effectively to convey a sense of excitement and galloping in "The Destruction of Sennacherib":

∪ ∪′ ∪ ∪ ′ ∪ ∪ ′ ∪ ∪ ′
The Assyr|ian came down|like a wolf|on the fold.
∪ ∪′ ∪ ∪ ′ ∪ ∪ ′ ∪ ∪ ′
And his co|horts were gleam|ing in pur|ple and gold.

In Swinburne's "By the North Sea," however, anapestic trimeter conveys a more subdued effect:

∪ ∪ ′ ∪ ∪ ′ ∪ ∪ ′ ∪
And his hand|is not wea|ry of giv|ing.
∪ ∪ ′ ∪ ∪ ′ ∪ ∪ ′
And the thirst|of her heart|is not fed.

anaphora (Greek: "a carrying up or back"), a literary or oratorical device involving the repetition of a word or phrase at the beginning of several sentences or clauses, as in the well-known passage from Ecclesiastes 3:1–2, that begins:

For everything there is a season, and a time
for every matter under heaven:
a time to be born, and a time to die;
a time to plant, and a time to pluck up
what is planted; . . .

Anaphora (sometimes called epanaphora) is used most effectively for emphasis in argumentative prose and sermons and in poetry, as in these lines from Shakespeare's *Hamlet:* "to die, to sleep / To sleep—perchance to dream."

anaphylaxis, severe, immediate, often fatal reaction to contact with an antigen to which the individual is sensitized. The condition has been extensively studied in guinea pigs, a species very liable to anaphylactic shock. The first injection of an antigen, such as egg albumin, into this animal is generally harmless. A similar injection two or three weeks later leads within seconds to severe respiratory symptoms that are usually quickly fatal.

Anaphylaxis occurs, with varying severity, in many animals. Rats are resistant, rabbits moderately so. In man it occurs rarely, after such events as injection of antiserum or antibiotic or after bee or wasp stings. Symptoms in man include itching of the scalp and tongue, skin flush of the whole body, difficulty in breathing because of swelling or spasm of the bronchi, an abrupt fall in blood pressure, and unconsciousness. In milder cases, hives may spread over the whole body, and often there is a severe headache. Treatment, which must begin within a few minutes of attack, involves the injection of epinephrine (adrenaline), followed by the administration of antihistamines, cortisone, or similar drugs.

The mechanism of anaphylaxis is not fully understood but apparently results from antigen–antibody reactions taking place on the surface of certain cells, thus damaging them and causing them to suddenly release a combination of chemicals including histamine, serotonin, bradykinin, or "slow-reacting substance" (SRS-A). These in turn produce the symptoms of anaphylactic shock. Anaphylaxis may occur after contact with extremely small amounts of antigen and is more common in persons with a history of atopic dermatitis.

Anápolis, town, south central Goiás state, south central Brazil, on the Rio Corumbá, 3,182 ft (970 m) above sea level. It was given city status in 1907. Today it is a rapidly growing frontier town serving a zone of pioneer settlement near an "island" of forest, the Mato Grosso de Goiás. Anápolis is a busy commercial centre with attractive squares, such as

Praça Bom Jesus, the main square of Anápolis, Braz.
Dilson Martins

Praça Bom Jesus, and is the northwestern terminus of railroads leading inland from coastal Rio de Janeiro and São Paulo. It has an airport and is also strategically situated on the highway linking Brasília, the national capital, with Goiânia, the state capital, and São Paulo. The region's livestock, *xarque* (jerked beef), coffee, rubber, corn (maize), wheat, and minerals (rock crystals, nickel, copper, manganese, phosphate, tin, titanium, gold, and diamonds) are sent to Brazil's largest urban markets. Pop. (1980 prelim.) 160,520.

anarchism, a social philosophy whose central tenet is that human beings can live justly and harmoniously without government and that the imposition of government upon human beings is in fact harmful and evil. Anarchists are distinguished from Marxists and other socialists in that the latter believe that the state must first be taken over before it can "wither away"; anarchists are too suspicious of the corruptions of power to believe that this is desirable or even possible.

A brief treatment of anarchism follows. For full treatment, *see* MACROPAEDIA: Socioeconomic Doctrines and Reform Movements, Modern.

The word anarchism derives from *an archos* (Greek: "without a rule"). When the word first appeared it was used as a pejorative term; the Levellers of the English Civil War and the Enragés of the French Revolution were labelled anarchists by their opponents. In 1793 William Godwin anticipated many later anarchist views in his *Enquiry concerning Political Justice*, although he did not use the word. Godwin not only supplied an outline of a decentralized society but also made explicit many of the theoretical assumptions involved. He insisted on the natural benevolence of individual human beings apart from governmental institutions and on the natural harmony of such individuals in their interactions. He therefore advocated the progressive breaking down of all institutions that contributed to coercion and inequality—eventually to include even marriage. Future organizations would be loose and voluntary associations.

The French writer Pierre-Joseph Proudhon adopted the word anarchism as a positive term for the first time in *Qu'est ce que la propriété?* ("What Is Property?") in 1840. Proudhon's book laid much of the theoretical groundwork for later anarchist movements, of which he is generally considered to be the father. First praised and later viciously attacked by Karl Marx, Proudhon denounced property ("property is theft") but rejected Communism in advocating the relative autonomy of local communities, and even, to a certain extent, of individuals.

The various heresies which Marxism faced during the last half of the 19th century consisted chiefly of different forms of anarchism that grew out of the work of Proudhon. The earliest of these, and Marx's chief obstacle in the First International, was that of Mikhail Bakunin. Bakunin's brand of anarchism came to be called collectivism. He and his followers agreed with Marx in stressing the role of workers' associations and the need for violent revolutionary action but protested what Bakunin called Marx's German authoritarianism in favour of a looser confederation of associations. When the International disbanded in 1872 Bakunin and his followers retained control of workers' organizations in Latin countries such as Spain and Italy. It was in those countries that anarchist movements attained their greatest strength, and they were finally and decisively crushed only by the victories of fascism just before the onset of World War II. Bakunin's emphasis on violence and revolutionary action inspired later anarchists, such as the Italian Errico Malatesta, to stress the value of violent acts as means of revealing the vulnerability of the state. A string of assassinations by anarchists took a heavy toll on world leaders around the turn of the century, including President Carnot of France (1894), Empress Elizabeth of Austria (1898), King Umberto of Italy (1900), and President McKinley of the United States (1901).

Not all anarchist movements were associated with violence. Many forms, such as that developed by Proudhon and known as Mutualism, rejected revolutionary activity; certain of Proudhon's followers even rejected strikes as a tactic, since they represented a form of coercion. Leo Tolstoy advocated a form of pacifist anarchism that denounced property and the state and sought a moral revolution whose tactic was disobedience. Max Stirner developed an extremely individualistic brand of anarchism. The form of anarchism to attract the largest following was known as anarchosyndicalism, which developed in the late 1880s after the crushing of the Paris Commune. Anarchosyndicalism combined the anarchists' distrust of political action with the tactics of the trade union movement; the labour *syndicats* were to become the basis for direct action by the working class, to culminate in a general strike that would paralyze the economy and the state. Anarchosyndicalism generated a mystique of the working class instead of the mystique of the individual that was characteristic of other forms of anarchism.

Owing to their repudiation of political action and to their vision of a just and harmonious society of individuals linked only by voluntary associations, many anarchist thinkers tended to take a high moral tone; notable among them was Peter Kropotkin. Anarchism as a social movement did not survive World War II. Nevertheless, some of its tenets, such as that human beings can be naturally moral and complete without governments, continue to attract followers.

Anarcho-Syndicalism: *see* Syndicalism.

Anasazi culture, a North American civilization that developed from about AD 100 to modern times, centring generally on the area where the boundaries of Arizona, New Mexico, Colorado, and Utah intersect. (Anasazi is Navajo for Ancient Ones.) It is customarily divided into these developmental periods: Basket Maker period, 100–500; Modified Basket Maker period, 500–700; Developmental Pueblo period (formerly designated Pueblo I and II), 700–1050; Classic Pueblo (formerly designated Pueblo III), 1050–1300; Regressive Pueblo (formerly designated Pueblo IV), 1300–1700; and Modern Pueblo (formerly designated Pueblo V), 1700 to date.

The origin of the Basket Maker Indians is not known, but it is evident that when they first settled in the area, they were already excellent basket weavers, and that they were supplementing hunting and wild-seed gathering with the cultivation of maize and pumpkins. They lived either in caves or out in the open in shelters constructed of a masonry of poles and adobe mud. Both caves and houses contained special pits, often roofed over, that were used for food storage.

This basic pattern continued into the period of the Modified Basket Makers, when agriculture occupied major interest (bean crops were added and turkeys were domesticated) and hunting and gathering were reduced to supplementary roles. Villages remained either in caves or out in the open; but those in caves consisted of an array of semi-subterranean houses, and those in the open consisted of chambers both aboveground and belowground, all often contiguously joined in straight lines or crescents. Aboveground chambers probably served as storage places and the pit houses as domiciles and ceremonial rooms. These pit houses were actually elaborations of the old storage pits. Pottery, sun-dried, was introduced during this period.

During the Developmental Pueblo period, the same type of straight-line or crescent-shaped multiple house was built, but gradually enlarged. Stone masonry, too, began to replace the earlier pole-and-mud construction. The pit houses became kivas, the underground circular chambers used henceforth primarily for ceremonial purposes. Aboveground chambers were used wholly as domiciles. Agriculture may have been augmented at this time by the cultivation of cotton. Pottery assumed a greater variety of shapes, finishes, and decorations. Basketry was less common. Throughout the period the area of occupation continued to expand.

The Classic Pueblo period was the time of the great cliff houses, the villages built in sheltered recesses in the faces of cliffs but otherwise differing little from the masonry or adobe houses and villages built elsewhere. This was also the time of the large, freestanding, apartment-like structures built along canyons or mesa walls. In either locale, many dwellings consisted of two, three, or even four stories, often built in stepped-back fashion so that the roofs of the lower rooms served as porches for the rooms above. These community structures had from 20 to as many as 1,000 rooms. An actual shrinking of the inhabited areas took place as people of the outer fringes moved in to build the large units (the appearance of hostile strangers on the fringes may have been the motivation). Craftsmanship in pottery reached a high level, and cotton and yucca fibre were skillfully woven into such articles as clothing, blankets, and mats.

Abandonment of the cliff houses and large community dwellings marked the close of the Classic Pueblo period. In part this may have resulted from the incursion of nomadic Navajo and Apache from the north and a prolonged drought that occurred from 1276 to 1299.

The Regressive Pueblo period was characterized by movement of the people south and east, some to the Rio Grande valley or the White Mountains of Arizona. New villages, some larger than those of Classic Pueblo, were built but were generally poorer and cruder in layout and construction (sometimes walls consisted wholly of adobe). Fine pottery making still flourished, however, though changed in design, and weaving continued as before.

The Modern Pueblo period is usually dated from about 1700, when Spanish influences first began to be pervasive. Official Spanish occupancy of the area had begun in 1598, and missionaries and some colonists had followed, but the Spaniards' attempts at forced religious conversions and tribute caused hostility among the Indians, leading in 1680 to open revolt and the killing or expulsion of the Spaniards. Not until around 1694 was Spanish authority reimposed. A century of unsettled conditions, however, had reduced the number of Pueblo settlements from about 70 or 80 to 25 or 30. Much of the culture and many of the skills in agriculture and crafts, nevertheless, have continued down to modern times.

Anastasia, Russian in full ANASTASIYA NIKOLAYEVNA (b. June 18 [June 5, old style], 1901, Peterhof, near St. Petersburg, Russia—d. July 29/30 [July 16/17, O.S.], 1918, Ekaterinburg), grand duchess of Russia and the youngest daughter of Tsar Nicholas II, last emperor of Russia, and Aleksandra Fyodorovna.

Anastasia was probably killed with the other members of her immediate family in a cellar where they had been confined by the Bolsheviks following the October Revolution. After the executions several women outside Russia claimed her identity, making her the subject of periodic popular conjecture and publicity. Each claimed to have survived the firing squad and escaped from Russia, and some claimed to be heir to the Romanov fortune held in Swiss banks. The facts of Anastasia's death seem as certain as such things can be, however. The best available accounts report that she received numerous bayonet wounds after having been shot and that the bodies of all the victims were destroyed.

The story of a surviving Anastasia provided the germ of a French play, *Anastasia*, written by Marcelle-Maurette (1903–72) and first produced in 1954. An American film version appeared in 1956, with Ingrid Bergman winning an Academy Award for her title role.

Anastasia, Albert, original name UMBERTO ANASTASIO (b. 1902/3, Tropea, Italy—d. Oct. 25, 1957, New York City), major U.S. gangster.

He immigrated to New York City from Italy in 1917 and, in the 1920s, rose through Giuseppe Masseria's gang. He was one of Masseria's executioners in 1931, at Lucky Luciano's command. In the late 1930s he became active head of Murder, Inc., a notorious murder-for-hire outfit, and in the late 1940s became boss of one of the so-called Five Families of organized crime in New York City. He was murdered by two gunmen (hired by rival Vito Genovese) as he sat in a barber chair in the Park Sheraton Hotel.

Anastasius, Greek ANASTASIOS, name of rulers grouped below by country or papacy and indicated by the symbol •.

Byzantine Empire

• **Anastasius I** (b. 430?, Dyrrachium, Epirus Vetus—d. July 9, 518, Constantinople), Byzantine emperor from 491 who perfected the empire's monetary system, increased its treasury, and proved himself an able administrator of domestic and foreign affairs; his heretical Monophysite religious policies, however, caused periodic rebellions.

After serving as an administrator in the department of finance and as a personal bodyguard to the emperor Zeno, Anastasius was chosen at the age of 61 to be emperor by his predecessor's widow, Ariadne, who married him shortly thereafter. He began his rule by abolishing the sale of offices, reforming taxation, and refusing rewards to informers. His replacement of a tax on trade goods with a land tax to support the army placed more demands on farmers, who periodically rebelled.

Among the first actions of Anastasius was the expulsion of Zeno's rebellious and powerful countrymen, the Isaurians, from Constantinople and their later resettlement in Thrace. To protect Constantinople against the raiding Bulgarians and Slavs, Anastasius built a wall (512) from the Black Sea to the Sea of Marmara. In foreign affairs he recognized Theodoric's Ostrogoth rule in Italy (497), but the two rulers were soon in opposition, Anastasius sending a fleet to ravage the Italian coast (508). Meanwhile, war with Persia erupted in 502, when Anastasius refused to pay a share for the defense of the Caucasian Gates, a pass through which nomadic tribes often raided Persia and Byzantium. After the Persians attacked, Anastasius built forts to secure his eastern frontier (in defiance of a treaty of 442). The status quo was restored when peace was concluded in 505, with Anastasius agreeing to payments to the Persian king.

At first professing orthodoxy, Anastasius gradually adhered more to Monophysite doctrine, which held that Christ had one, divine nature. Although this stand caused great unrest in Constantinople and in the European provinces, it did buy peace with Egypt and Syria. In Thrace, however, it inspired rebellion by the military commander Vitalianus, who revolted twice, withdrawing each time after being promised satisfaction; when he attacked a third time, he was defeated (515).

Anastasius, who had planned for his nephews to be his heirs, was instead succeeded by the 70-year-old Justin I, commander of the guard and uncle of his illustrious successor, Justinian.

• **Anastasius II,** original name ARTEMIS (d. 721), Byzantine emperor from 713 to 715, who was chosen to take the throne after an army coup deposed Philippicus, under whom he had served as secretary. He reversed the ecclesiastical policies of Philippicus and tried to reform the army before he, too, was deposed. Assuring Pope Constantine of his orthodoxy, Anastasius withdrew Philippicus' Monothelite decrees, which had imposed the heretical doctrine of a single, divine will of Christ. Militarily he fortified Constantinople, selected the island of Rhodes as a Byzantine naval base, and sent the Isaurian Leo, the future Leo III, to defend Syria against the Arabs. In the meantime, however, troops in the Opsikian province rebelled and proclaimed as emperor Theodosius, a local tax collector, who was seated (715) in Constantinople after a six-month civil war. Anastasius fled and became a monk in Thessalonica in 716. Failing in an attempt to regain his throne in 720, he was executed by Theodosius' successor, Leo III.

Papacy

• **Anastasius I,** SAINT (b. Rome?—d. Dec. 19, 401, Rome; feast day December 19), pope from Nov. 27, 399, to 401, succeeding Pope Siricius. He earned the praise of St. Jerome (Letter 127) for censuring (*c.* 400) the works of Origen, one of the most influential theologians of the early Greek Church. In papal letters Anastasius condemned several Origenist writings and disapproved the spreading of Origen's teaching. Anastasius' virtues were praised by his admirers SS. Augustine of Hippo, Jerome, and Paulinus of Nola.

• **Anastasius II** (b. Rome—d. Nov. 19, 498, Rome), pope from Nov. 24, 496, to 498. In notifying the Byzantine emperor Anastasius I of his accession, the Pope expressed a conciliatory attitude toward the late patriarch Acacius of Constantinople, who had been deposed and excommunicated in 484 by Pope St. Felix III. The Acacian Schism resulted from that act. The Pope's reception of the Byzantine deacon Photinus, sent to Rome by a supporter of Acacius, was followed by a schism at Rome and the charge that the Pope desired to rehabilitate Acacius. Anastasius died in the midst of the controversy.

A confused tradition blamed Anastasius for being led by Photinus into heretical opinions concerning the divinity of Jesus Christ. Dante (*Inferno* XI, 8) placed him among the heretics in the sixth circle of hell.

• **Anastasius III** (b. Rome—d. June or August 913, Rome), pope from April or June 911 to 913. Because his pontificate came during a period when Rome was under the control of the house of Theophylactus, he had little authority or freedom of action.

• **Anastasius IV,** original name CORRADO DI SUBURRA (b. *c.* 1073, Rome—d. Dec. 3, 1154), pope from July 1153 to December 1154. As cardinal bishop of Sabina, he had staunchly supported Pope Innocent II in 1130, serving as his vicar in Rome during the contest with the antipope Anacletus II. During his brief pontificate he was a peacemaker noted especially for settling two long-standing problems: one regarding Emperor Frederick I Barbarossa and the see of Magdeburg, the other regarding St. William of York and his see.

Anastasius SINAITA, SAINT (fl. 7th century; feast day April 21), theologian and abbot of the Monastery of St. Catherine, on Mt. Sinai, whose writings, public disputes with various heretical movements in Egypt and Syria, and polemics against the Jews made him in his day a foremost advocate of orthodox Christian doctrine, specifically on the person and work of Christ, and provided key documents for the history of early Christian thought. By his leadership and eloquence he won the title "the New Moses."

Of unknown origin and sometimes confused with others of the same name, including the early-7th-century Orthodox patriarch of Antioch, Anastasius periodically descended from his Mt. Sinai community to refute the ideas of theological dissidents. In his principal work, *Ho dēgos* (*c.* 685; "The Guide"), he marshalled arguments against the Monophysites, a heretical sect believing that Christ comprised a single, divine nature that subsumed his humanity. The faulty transmission of the original text caused it to be attributed to other Syrian authors, and only through later research has its true source been determined. Drawn up in the desert, "The Guide" is flawed by unverified citations and paraphrased references to texts from the early Church Fathers, formulas from church councils, and Aristotelian concepts applied to the analysis of the Christological problem, all quoted from memory. In this work Anastasius cites himself in other writings now lost: a comprehensive "Essay on Christian Dogma"; an "Apology for Christianity"; and a treatise "Against Nestorius," the 5th-century heretical theologian who proposed that Christ's humanity subsisted autonomously from his divinity.

Anastasius' other notable extant writings include a survey of heresies prominent in his time, "Exposition on Faith," and "Questions and Answers," reedited by a later author and largely devoted to the relation of monastic life to secular culture. Anastasius' "Commentary on the Six Days of Creation" shows a tendency toward Alexandrian allegorical biblical exegesis and interprets the book of Genesis as directly signifying Christ and the church. Two tracts on the creation of man in the intellectual and spiritual image of God show the same tendency. In them is the earliest recorded reference to the doctrinal controversy on Monothelitism, the condemned teaching that only a divine volition was operative in Christ. Shorter works on worship, the communion of the Lord's Supper, and mystical prayer exhibit the Aristotelian method in depicting the psychology of learning and the spiritual nature of the mind and its orientation toward ultimate truth and beauty.

Some scholars credit Anastasius with contributing to the collection of texts known as "The Doctrine of the Fathers on the Incarnation of the Word (Son of God)."

Anastasius THE LIBRARIAN, Latin ANASTASIUS BIBLIOTHECARIUS (b. *c.* 810, probably Rome—d. *c.* 878), language scholar, Roman cardinal, and influential political counsellor to 9th-century popes.

Related to an Italian bishop, Anastasius became cardinal priest of the church of St. Marcellus, Rome, *c.* 848, after gaining prominence as a Greek scholar. Deposed in 853 because of political activity, he stood for a short time as antipope to Benedict III (855–858). After a reconciliation Anastasius became papal librarian and disputed with the Greek Orthodox theologian Photius, patriarch of Constantinople (858–867; 878–886), over the question of the Holy Spirit's relationship within the Christian Trinity, a controversy crucial to Eastern and Western doctrinal differences leading to open schism.

Exhibiting thorough efficiency in expressing the ideas of the papacy, Anastasius maintained the post of librarian of the Holy Roman Church under Popes Adrian II (867–872) and John VIII (872–882). On the visit of SS. Cyril and Methodius to Rome, he supported their Christianizing mission among the Slavic peoples and their development of a native liturgy. Representing the Holy Roman emperor, the Frank Louis II (*c.* 824–875), Anastasius undertook a diplomatic mission to the Byzantine emperor Basil I (867–886) in an unsuccessful attempt to arrange a marriage between the two dynasties. He remained in Constantinople nevertheless to assist at the eighth general council of 869–870, a convocation that achieved final doctrinal formulations concerning the Trinity, emphasizing the divinity of the Holy Spirit and condemning Photian teaching. Anastasius' Latin translations of the council's proceedings and compilation of other documents relating to the Monothelite controversy (*see* Monothelite) contributed to the history of Western theology. A later Latin collection also incorporated his "Threepart Chronicle" of Byzantine history from the 6th to the 9th century.

Included in Anastasius' major writings are commentaries on the influential 6th-century Neoplatonic philosopher Pseudo-Dionysius the Areopagite and probably the accounts of Popes Nicholas I and Adrian II in the *Liber pontificalis* (Latin: "The Book of the Popes"), an essential source for the history of primitive Christianity.

anastatic printing, also called RELIEF ETCHING, a technique of printmaking from a plate on which all but the design to be printed is etched away, leaving the design in relief. In zinc etching, the most popular anastatic process, the design is painted on a zinc plate in asphalt varnish and the uncoated portions of the plate are bitten away by a solution. The process is best known as that in which the English poet and artist William Blake (1757–1827) executed the text and illustrations of many of his books.

"The Tyger," anastatic print by William Blake, 1794, from *Songs of Innocence and of Experience, Showing the Two Contrary States of the Human Soul*

By courtesy of the Metropolitan Museum of Art, New York City, Rogers Fund, 1917

Anat (goddess): *see* Anath.

anatase, one of three minerals composed of titanium dioxide (TiO_2), the other two being rutile and brookite (*qq.v.*). It is found as hard, brilliant crystals of tetragonal symmetry and various colours in veins in igneous and metamorphic rocks and commonly in placer deposits of detritus. Notable vein deposits exist in many regions of the Alps; placer deposits are common in Minas Gerais and Bahia, Braz. Much anatase is formed by weathering of titanite, and it is itself altered to rutile; rutile paramorphs (replacements having the same outward shape) after anatase are common in the detrital deposits of Brazil and the Sanarka region of the Urals. For detailed physical properties, *see* oxide mineral (table).

anatexis, in geology, the differential, or partial, melting of rocks. Each mineral in a rock has its own melting temperature, which is decreased to varying degrees by its close association with other minerals. In addition to the melting temperature of each individual mineral, pressure, temperature, and the presence of volatiles all influence the melting temperature of a mineral assemblage; a rock has a melting range dependent upon these parameters. In the process of anatexis, it is assumed that rocks are buried to such great depths that an increase of pressure and temperature causes partial melting; as the temperature is increased, an increasing percentage of the rock becomes liquid. The rock fraction with the lowest melting range typically has a granitic composition, and the unmelted residuum is more basic (silica-poor). The layers of granite in migmatites, and perhaps larger granitic bodies, may have formed through anatexis.

Consult the INDEX *first*

Anath, also spelled ANAT, chief West Semitic goddess of love and war; sister and helpmate of the god Baal. Considered a beautiful young girl, she was often designated "the Virgin" in ancient texts. Probably one of the best known of the Canaanite deities, she was famous for her youthful vigour and ferocity in battle; in that respect she was adopted as a special favourite by the Egyptian king Ramses II (reigned *c.* 1304–*c.* 1237 BC). Although Anath was often associated with the god Resheph in ritual texts, she was primarily known for her role in the myth of Baal's death and resurrection, in which she mourned and searched for him and finally helped to retrieve him from the netherworld.

Egyptian representations of Anath show a nude goddess, often standing on a lion and holding flowers. During the Hellenistic Age, the goddesses Anath and Astarte (*q.v.*) were blended into one deity, called Atargatis (*q.v.*).

anathema (from Greek *anatithenai:* "to set up" or "to dedicate"), in the Old Testament, a creature or object set apart for sacrificial offering. Its return to profane use was strictly banned, and such objects, destined for destruction, thus became effectively accursed as well as consecrated. Old Testament descriptions of religious wars call both the enemy and their besieged city anathema inasmuch as they were destined for destruction.

In New Testament usage a different meaning developed. St. Paul used the word anathema to signify a curse and the forced expulsion of one from the community of Christians. In AD 431 St. Cyril of Alexandria pronounced his 12 anathemas against the heretic Nestorius. In the 6th century anathema came to mean the severest form of excommunication that formally separated a heretic completely from the Christian Church and condemned his doctrines; minor excommunications, while prohibiting free reception of the sacraments, obliged (and permitted) the sinner to rectify his sinful state through the sacrament of penance.

Anatidae, bird family that includes ducks, geese, and swans; it constitutes the suborder Anseres—by far the larger part of the order Anseriformes.

A widely accepted system of classification divides the Anatidae into 3 subfamilies and 8 to 12 tribes, as follows:

Anseranatinae—tribe Anseranatini (*see* magpie goose).

Anserinae—tribes Dendrocygnini (*see* whistling duck, or tree duck) and Anserini (*see* goose; swan). A third tribe, Stictonettini, has been proposed (*see* freckled duck).

Anatinae—tribes Tadornini (*see* sheldgoose; shelduck), Anatini (*see* dabbling duck), Cairinini (*see* perching duck), Aythyini (*see* pochard), Somateriini and Mergini (*see* diving duck), and Oxyurini (*see* stifftail). Some authorities include the eiders (Somateriini) in the Mergini; some separate a tribe Tachyerini (*see* steamer duck) from the Tadornini; and some recognize a tribe Merganettini (*see* torrent duck) aside from the Anatini. The Aythyini, Somateriini, Mergini, and (from one standpoint) the Oxyurini (pochard, diving duck, and stifftail) are often considered together in popular usage.

An older division of the family appeared in several field books in wide use in the U.S. and Europe in the late 1960s. It assigned the Anatidae into the following main subfamilies (without tribes): Cygninae, swans; Anserinae, true geese; Dendrocygninae, whistling ducks; Anatinae, dabbling ducks, including shelducks and perching ducks; Nyrocinae (or Aythyinae), diving ducks other than mergansers; Erismaturinae (or Oxyurinae), stifftails; and Merginae, mergansers.

anātman (Indian philosophy): *see* anattā.

Anatolia, also called ASIA MINOR, the peninsula of land that today constitutes the Asiatic portion of Turkey. Because of its location at the point where the continents of Asia and Europe meet, Anatolia was, from the beginnings of civilization, a crossroads for numerous peoples migrating or conquering from either continent.

A brief treatment of the history of Anatolia follows. For full treatment, *see* MACROPAEDIA: Turkey and Ancient Anatolia.

Anatolia has been known from the earliest period as a battleground between the East and the West. The central plateau, with no navigable rivers and few natural approaches, its monotonous scenery, and severe climate, is a continuation of Central Asia. The western coast, with its fertile valleys and fine climate, is almost a part of Europe. These conditions are unfavourable to permanence, and the history of Anatolia is that of the march of nomad tribes and colonists and of the rise and fall of small states.

About 1950 BC western Anatolia appears to have been held by the 1st dynasty of Hittites, with their capital at Kushara (?). Two centuries later, Aryan races seem to have invaded the country and imposed at least their language on the Hittites, who in the 17th century BC emerged suddenly as a powerful empire at Hattusa (modern Boğazköy), ruling over Anatolia and fighting the Egyptian pharaohs for the mastery of Syria, and Assyria for the mastery of Mittani (Jerablus).

This Hittite Empire was overthrown by Indo-European races, possibly Greeks, who, crossing the Hellespont from Europe to Asia, with their iron weapons defeated the Hittites, who possessed only bronze weapons. These Indo-European races established many colonies all along the Aegean coast and in the hinterland, from which arose the Phrygian kingdom. Traces of this kingdom remain in various rock tombs, forts, and towns and in legends preserved by the Greeks. In the 8th century BC the Cimmerians coming from Armenia overran the Phrygian kingdom, and on its decline rose the kingdom of Lydia, with its centre at Sardis. A second Cimmerian invasion, followed later by Cyaxares, almost destroyed the rising kingdom, but the invaders were stopped by Alyattes (*c.* 617–560 BC). The last king, Croesus (560–546 BC), carried his boundaries to the Halys and subdued the Greek colonies on the coast. These flourishing Greek colonies formed a chain of settlements extending from Trebizond to Rhodes. Too jealous of each other to combine and too demoralized by luxury to resist, they fell an easy prey to Lydia. After the capture of Sardis by the Persian Cyrus II the Great (*c.* 546 BC), these colonies passed to Persia without resistance. Under Persian rule, Anatolia was divided into four satrapies, but the Greek cities were governed by Greeks, and the tribes in the interior retained their native princes and priest-dynasts. Beginning with Darius' attempt to conquer the European, as well as the Asiatic, Greeks, the Greco-Persian Wars ended in 334 BC, when Anatolia was invaded by Alexander the Great.

After the death of Alexander, various *diadochoi* (succession rulers) established their rule over various parts of the peninsula. Rhodes became a great maritime republic. The Ptolemies of Egypt ruled over the Mediterranean coast of Anatolia. A small independent kingdom was founded at Pergamum in 283 BC and lasted a century and a half. Bithynia became an independent monarchy, Cappadocia and Paphlagonia tributary provinces under native princes. In the south, the Seleucids founded Antioch, Apamea, Attalia, the Laodiceas, and other cities as centres of commerce, some of which afterwards played an important part in the Hellenization of the country and in the spread of Christianity. During the 3rd century BC, certain Celtic tribes crossed the Bosporus and established their power in districts between the Sangarius and Halys, called Galatia. Its capital was at Ancyra—the modern Ankara, the capital of republican Turkey.

The defeat of Antiochus the Great at Magnesia (190 BC) placed Anatolia at the mercy of Rome, but it was only in 133 BC that the first Roman province, Asia, was formed to include western Anatolia. Under Mithradates the Great, Pontus rose into a formidable power; but he was driven from his country by Pompey the Great and died in 63 BC. The Romans organized the peninsula into various provinces, leagues, and almost independent principalities, and under their dominion Anatolia, or Asia Minor, developed and became prosperous. At the end of the 3rd century AD, in reorganizing the empire, Diocletian broke the great military commands and united the provinces into groups called dioceses. A great change followed the introduction of Christianity, which gradually spread over the region. The seven Christian Churches of Asia Minor were built up in this period.

When the Roman Empire was divided in two in 395, Anatolia fell to the Eastern Roman Empire with its capital at Constantinople; the native languages and old religions partly disappeared, and the country was thoroughly Hellenized. At the close of the 6th century, Anatolia had become wealthy and prosperous, but centuries of peace and overcentralization produced a state of affairs that is embodied in the term Byzantine. The vigorous Persian monarch Khrosrow II invaded Anatolia from 616 to 626 and pitched his camp on the Bosporus. The emperor Heraclius, however, restored the Byzantine power by marching his army to Kurdistan; but soon after, the Arabs entered Anatolia and in AD 668 laid siege to Constantinople. For the following three centuries, Byzantium and the caliphs of Baghdad waged occasional warfare for the mastery of the bridgeheads of the Euphrates and the Cilician gates. But a more dangerous enemy was soon to appear from the East. In 1067 the Seljuq Turks ravaged Cilicia and Cappadocia; in 1071 they defeated and captured the emperor Romanus Diogenes; in 1080 they took Nicaea. One branch of the Seljuqs founded the empire of Rum with its capital at Iconium. During the 12th century, a number of Seljuq Atabeks ruled in different districts of Anatolia; the Mamlūks of Egypt in Syria and farther east; Greeks in Pontus; Armenians in Cilicia; Danishmends (an Armenian family) at Sivas; Bayandurs (a Greek family) at Erzerum; etc. The Mongols swept the whole region and in 1243 subdued the Seljuq sultan of Rum. In the ensuing struggle for power among the Turkish tribes, the Ottoman Turks eventually assumed supremacy and established their state at Brusa. In 1400 Sultan Bayezid I held almost all Anatolia west of the Euphrates. But he was defeated and imprisoned by Timur, who swept through the country to the shores of the Aegean. On the death of Timur, the Ottoman power was reestablished after a prolonged struggle that ended with the annexation by Mehmed II (1451–81) of Karamania and Pontus. The later history of Anatolia is that of the Ottoman Empire. The Turks dominated Anatolia until their supreme power was challenged in 1832 by an Egyptian army under Ibrahim Pasha, and their rule shattered in World War I.

The Seljuq hordes who devastated Anatolia in the 11th century, were followed by a long succession of nomad Turkish tribes. The latter did not ill-treat the native people, but they left the country bare and desolate. Whole provinces passed out of cultivation, and the natives, taking to the mountains or to towns, abandoned their lands to these nomads. The native peasants were thus forced to become nomads themselves. The Mongols, as they advanced, sacked towns and razed to the ground "all that might serve as a place of armed resistance." Nearly all traces of Hellenic civilization disappeared with the enforced use of the Turkish language and the wholesale conversions to Islām under the early Ottoman sultans.

In modern times, Anatolia slowly recovered, but the construction of railways and the consequent growth of trade and local industries were seriously interrupted by World War I. When the Turks signed the Armistice on Oct. 30, 1918, British armies had captured all the Arab-speaking lands of Anatolia. In May 1919 a Greek army seized Smyrna and most of the Ionian coast and gradually extended its occupation to Eski-Shehir (the ancient Dorylaeum) and Afiun-Karahissar.

The Treaty of Sèvres, signed by the Turks in August 1920, reduced Anatolia to the geographical and ethnic boundaries established by five centuries of Turkish domination. Great Britain assumed the mandates of Palestine and Iraq, and France that of Syria. Meanwhile, Great Britain, France, and Italy had signed a tripartite agreement by which they divided south and southeastern Anatolia into spheres of influence. The Turkish nationalist movement, however, led by Mustafa Kemal (afterwards Atatürk) soon reasserted itself. The Turks drove the French from Cilicia and the Greeks from Smyrna. The Treaty of Sèvres was not ratified and was superseded by the Treaty of Lausanne (July 1923), which left Turkey sovereign in Anatolia in the narrow sense. After the suppression of the sultanate in November 1923, soon followed by that of the Caliphate, Turkey declared itself a republic with its capital at Ankara.

Under the auspices of the Allied Powers and in conjunction with the Treaty of Lausanne, a convention for the exchange of populations was signed between Turkey and Greece by which about 1,000,000 Greeks, were transferred from western Anatolia to Greece and Macedonia.

Anatolian languages, the extinct Indo-European and non-Indo-European languages spoken in Anatolia from sometime in the 3rd millennium BC until the early centuries of the present era, when they were gradually supplanted by Greek. They include the Indo-European languages Hittite, Palaic, Luwian, Hieroglyphic Luwian, Lydian, Lycian, and Phrygian and the non-Indo-European languages Hattic, Hurrian, and Urartian. Two other Anatolian languages, Carian and Sidetic, are so poorly attested that whether or not they are Indo-European is unknown. Anatolian is also used in a narrow sense to refer to the languages that belong to the Anatolian branch of Indo-European. This branch includes all of the Indo-European languages listed above with the exception of Phrygian. The non-Indo-European languages of Anatolia are sometimes called Asianic.

A brief treatment of the Anatolian languages follows. For full treatment, *see* MACROPAEDIA: Languages of the World.

Hittite is the best attested of the Anatolian languages. It is known chiefly from approximately 25,000 clay tablets or fragments of tablets that were excavated at Boğazköy-Hattusa, the Hittite capital, in Central Anatolia. It was written in a cuneiform script that closely resembles that used in the 17th century BC in Alalakh. The language was first shown to be Indo-European in 1902 by a Norwegian Assyriologist, Jørgen Alexander Knudtzon, who based his study on two Hittite letters that had been found in the Amarna archive. Hittite was first interpreted in 1915 by a Czech Orientalist, Bedřich Hrozný, who worked with the tablets excavated at Boğazköy. The majority of the Hittite texts are concerned with religious subjects (oracle texts, hymns, prayers, myths, rituals, and festival texts), but there are also many of historical, political, administrative, literary, and legal character.

Palaic was used as a ritual language in a few Hittite cuneiform texts. It was spoken in Pala (probably Blaëne in the Greek period) in northwest Anatolia. It is closely related to Hittite and Luwian, but very little else is known about it because it is so poorly attested.

Luwian was spoken in southern Anatolia and northern Syria. It is known from texts stemming from three major periods: the Hittite New Empire (*c.* 1400–*c.* 1190 BC) found at Boğazköy-Hattusa; the period of the Neo-Hittite states (*c.* 1190–*c.* 700 BC); and monumental inscriptions of *c.* 400–*c.* 200 BC. Hieroglyphic Luwian is the daughter language of the East Luwian dialect, while Lycian is a later descendant of a West Luwian dialect.

The Anatolian hieroglyphic system begins as early as the Hittite stamp seals of the 18th and 17th centuries BC; the youngest texts date from approximately the last quarter of the 8th century BC. Geographically they are attested across southern Anatolia well into northern Syria and as far north as the Hittite capital, Boğazköy-Hattusa. The decipherment of Hieroglyphic Luwian was accomplished during the 1930s and 1940s. Significant contributions were made by the British archaeologist Archibald H. Sayce, the German-born Orientalist Hans G. Güterbock, and the German archaeologist Helmuth T. Bossert.

Lydian is attested in sepulchral inscriptions, votive texts, and many graffiti, the majority of which were excavated at the Lydian capital, Sardis. Most stem from the 4th century BC. The Lydian alphabet was derived from an East Greek prototype. The study of Lydian is hampered by many lexicological uncertainties, but the grammar indicates that it belongs to the Anatolian subgroup of Indo-European.

The Anatolian branch of Indo-European is characterized by a number of grammatical archaisms combined with the absence of several typical Indo-European categories such as the dual number, the feminine gender, and the perfect tense. Another peculiarity is a strong preference for the linking together of particles and enclitic pronouns to form "chains" that are placed at the beginning of a sentence or a clause. A striking phonological trait is the presence of certain guttural sounds (laryngeals) which are not found in the other Indo-European languages.

Phrygian is the one Indo-European language of Anatolia that does not belong to the Anatolian subgroup. The Phrygian inscriptions and graffiti may be separated into two groups: Old Phrygian texts in a typical Phrygian alphabet dating from *c.* 730–450 BC, and New Phrygian inscriptions (sepulchral texts in the Greek alphabet) from the 1st and 2nd centuries AD.

Hattic is known from its ritual use in the Hittite cuneiform texts. It was the linguistic substratum of northern Anatolia before the invasion of the Indo-European speakers. Hattic has no known relatives.

Hurrian texts have been found in Urkish (*c.* 2300 BC), Mari (18th century BC), Amarna (*c.* 1400 BC), Boğazköy-Hattusa (*c.* 1400–*c.* 1190 BC), and Ugarit (14th century BC). All of these texts are in cuneiform, with the exception of several that are in the Ugaritic alphabetic script. The many Hurrian personal names found at Boğazköy-Hattusa, Alalakh, Ugarit, and especially Nuzu constitute a second important source of information about this language.

Urartian was used in northeastern Anatolia during the 9th through 6th centuries BC as the official language of Urartu. The Urartian texts are written in a variant of the Neo-Assyrian cuneiform script. There is also an indigenous hieroglyphic script that is poorly attested and remains undeciphered. Hurrian and Urartian are descended from a common parent language. They are agglutinative and chiefly suffixing.

Carian is attested mainly by graffiti found in Egypt that were written in an alphabetic script by Carian mercenaries, but it is also attested by monumental inscriptions and clay tablets found in Caria itself. The assumption that Carian belongs to the Anatolian branch of Indo-European is still unproved.

Sidetic was spoken in the city of Side on the Pamphylian coast. It is attested by legends on coins of the 5th(?) through the 3rd(?) century BC and by five inscriptions from the 3rd and 2nd centuries BC, two of which are bilingual. The script is only partly deciphered, so nothing is known about the contents of the texts or the classification of the language.

Anatom, also spelled ANEITYUM, southernmost island of Vanuatu, in the southwestern Pacific Ocean. Volcanic in origin, it has a circumference of 35 mi and an area of 25 sq mi (65 sq km) and rises from a fertile coastal plain and valleys to a height of 2,795 ft (852 m). Anatom was a centre of sandalwooders, whalers, and missionaries in the New Hebrides in the 19th century; its valuable stands of kauri pine were once exploited. Anelgauhat is a good harbour on the south coast, with an airstrip on nearby Inyeug Island. Pop. (1979) 463.

anatomy, a branch of biology dealing with the shape and structure of organisms. One method commonly used to study the details of gross internal structures is dissection. The microscope is used to study the composition of tissues, cells, and subcellular organelles. Comparative anatomy deals with the structures of related organisms and was used extensively by Darwin in advancing the theory of evolution. The science of anatomy is of basic interest because the life activities of organisms are to some extent both shaped and limited by their structure.

Anatosaurus, formerly TRACHODON, genus of bipedal duck-billed dinosaurs common as fossils in Late Cretaceous rocks of North America (the Cretaceous Period began 136,000,000 years ago and lasted 71,000,000 years); closely related forms have a worldwide distribution. *Anatosaurus,* a very large reptile, grew to a length of between 9 and 12 metres (30 to 40 feet) and was heavily built. The hind limbs and pelvic girdle were very well developed. The skull was long and the jaws broad and flat, much like a duck's bill. As many as 2,000 rather blunt teeth were present in the jaws at any one time; not all were functional simultaneously, but, as teeth were worn or lost, they were replaced by new ones. It is probable that the anatosaurs were aquatic to a certain degree; their tails were compressed laterally, much like the tails of crocodiles.

Anatosaurus in Wyoming landscape during the Cretaceous Period, reconstruction painting by Charles R. Knight, 1909

By courtesy of the American Museum of Natural History, New York

Some anatosaur specimens have been found remarkably well preserved as desiccated mummies; in these, skin and internal structures remain. The anatosaurs had webbing between the toes, a further indication of their partially aquatic habit. The outer hide was very leathery and rough. At least some anatosaurs fed mostly on twigs, seeds, fruits, and pine needles; no remains of aquatic plants have been found in the stomachs. It seems likely that the aquatic habit of the anatosaurs was a means of escaping predators and that they fed on land rather than in the water.

anattā (Pāli: "non-self," or "substanceless"), Sanskrit ANĀTMAN, in Buddhism, the doctrine that there is in man no permanent, underlying substance that can be called the soul. Instead, the individual is compounded of five factors of consciousness (Pāli *khandha,* Sanskrit *skandha*) that are constantly changing. The concept of *anattā,* or *anātman,* is a departure from the Hindu belief in *ātman* ("the self"). The absence of a self, *anicca* (the impermanence of all being), and *dukkha* ("suffering") are the three characteristics of all existence (*ti-lakkhaṇa*). Recognition of these three doctrines —*anattā, anicca,* and *dukkha*—constitutes the "right understanding," which is the first stage in the Buddhist system of spiritual discipline leading to Enlightenment, known as the Eightfold Path.

anauxite, mineral, an interstratified mixture of kaolinite and free silica. *See* kaolinite.

Anawrahta, also spelled ANIRUDDHA (fl. 11th century AD), the first king of all of Burma (reigned 1044–77), who introduced his people to Theravāda Buddhism. His capital at Pagan on the Irrawaddy River became a prominent city of pagodas and temples.

During his reign he united the northern homeland of the Burmese people with the Mon kingdoms of the South. He extended his dominion as far north as the kingdom of Nanchao, west to Arakan, south to the Gulf of Martaban (near what is now Rangoon), and as far east as what is now northern Thailand.

In 1057 Anawrahta captured the Mon city of Thaton, a centre of Indian civilization. Its fall led the other Mon rulers to submit to Anawrahta; for the first time, a Burmese ruler dominated the Irrawaddy Delta. Contact with the Mons enriched Burmese civilization. The Mons gave them an artistic and literary tradition and a system of writing. The earliest Burmese inscription, written in Mon characters, appeared in 1058.

Anawrahta was converted to Theravāda Buddhism by a Mon monk, Shin Arahan. As king he strove to convert his people from the influence of the Ari, a Mahāyāna Tantric sect that was at that time predominant in Upper Burma. Largely through his efforts, Theravāda Buddhism became the dominant religion of Burma and the inspiration for its culture and civilization. He maintained diplomatic relations with King Vijayabāhu of Ceylon, who in 1071 requested the assistance of Burmese monks to help revive the Buddhist faith. The Ceylonese king sent Anawrahta a replica of the Buddha's tooth relic, which was placed in the Shwezigon pagoda at Pagan.

Anaxagoras (b. *c.* 500 BC, Clazomenae, Anatolia—d. *c.* 428, Lampsacus), Greek philosopher of nature remembered for his cosmology and for his discovery of the true cause of eclipses. He was associated with the Athenian statesman Pericles.

About 480 Anaxagoras moved to Athens, then becoming the centre of Greek culture, and brought from Ionia the new practice of philosophy and the spirit of scientific inquiry. After 30 years' residence in Athens, he was prosecuted on a charge of impiety for asserting that the Sun is an incandescent stone somewhat larger than the region of the Peloponnese. The attack on him was intended as an indirect blow at Pericles, and, although Pericles managed to save him, Anaxagoras was compelled to leave Athens. He spent his last years in retirement at Lampsacus.

Only a few fragments of Anaxagoras' writings have been preserved, and several different interpretations of his work have been made. The basic features, however, are clear. His cosmology grows out of the efforts of earlier Greek thinkers who had tried to explain the physical universe by an assumption of a single fundamental element. Parmenides, however, asserted that such an assumption could not account for movement and change, and, whereas Empedocles sought to resolve this difficulty by positing four basic ingredients, Anaxagoras posited an infinite number. Unlike his predecessors, who had chosen such elements as heat or water as the basic substance, Anaxagoras included those found in living bodies, such as flesh, bone, bark, and leaf. Otherwise, he asked, how could flesh come from what is not flesh? He also accounted for biological changes, in which substances appear under new manifestations: as men eat and drink, flesh, bone, and hair grow. In order to explain the great amount and diversity of change, he said that "there is a portion of every thing, *i.e.,* of every elemental stuff, in every thing," but "each is and was most manifestly those things of which there is most in it."

The most original aspect of Anaxagoras' system was his doctrine of *nous* ("mind," or "reason"). The cosmos was formed by Mind in two stages: first, by a revolving and mixing process that still continues; and, second, by the development of living things. In the first, all of "the dark" came together to form the night, "the fluid" came together to form the oceans, and so on with other elements. The same process of attraction of "like to like" occurred in the second stage, when flesh and other elements were brought together by Mind in large amounts. This stage took place by means of animal and plant seeds inherent in the original mixture. The growth of living things, according to Anaxagoras, depends on the power of Mind within the organisms that enables them to extract nourishment from surrounding substances. For this concept of Mind, Anaxagoras was commended by Aristotle. Both Plato and Aristotle, however, objected that his notion of Mind did not include a view that Mind acts ethically—*i.e.,* acts for the "best interests" of the universe.

Works on Anaxagoras include J. Zafiropulo's *Anaxagore de Clazomène* (1948) and F.M. Cleve's *Philosophy of Anaxagoras* (1949).

Anaximander (b. 610 BC, Miletus—d. 546/545 BC), Greek philosopher often called the founder of astronomy, the first thinker to develop a cosmology, or systematic philosophical view of the world.

He is thought to have been a pupil of Thales of Miletus. There is evidence that he wrote

Anaximander, represented with a sundial, mosaic, 3rd century AD; in the Rheinisches Landesmuseum, Trier, W.Ger.

By courtesy of the Landesmuseum, Trier, W.Ger.

treatises on geography, astronomy, and cosmology that survived for several centuries, and that he made a map of the known world. As a rationalist he prized symmetry and introduced geometry and mathematical proportions into his efforts to map the heavens. Thus, his theories departed from earlier, more mystical conceptions of the universe and prefigured the achievements of subsequent astronomers.

Only one sentence of Anaximander's writings survives, however, so that reports from later writers form the primary record of his discoveries. That sentence describes the emergence of particular substances such as water or fire in metaphors drawn from human society, in which injustices are penalized. For example, neither hot nor cold prevails permanently, but each "pays reparations" in order to keep a balance between them.

Anaximander derived the world from a nonperceptible substance called the *apeiron* ("unlimited"). This state preceded the "separation" into contrasting qualities, such as hot and cold, wet and dry, and thus represents the primitive unity of all phenomena. Anaximander subscribed to the philosophical view that unity could definitely be found behind all multiplicity. A novel element in Anaximander's theory was his rejection of the older notion that the Earth was somehow suspended or supported from elsewhere in the heavens; instead, he asserted that the Earth remained in its unsupported position at the centre of the universe because it had no reason to move in any direction and therefore was at rest.

BIBLIOGRAPHY. G.S. Kirk and J.E. Raven, *The Presocratic Philosophers* (1957); Charles H. Kahn, *Anaximander and the Origins of Greek Cosmology* (1960); Paul Seligman, *The Apeiron of Anaximander* (1962).

Anaximenes OF MILETUS (fl. *c.* 545 BC), Greek philosopher of nature and one of three thinkers of Miletus traditionally considered to be the first philosophers in the Western world. Of the other two, Thales held that water is the basic building block of all matter, whereas Anaximander chose to call the essential substance "the unlimited."

Anaximenes substituted *aer* ("mist," "vapour," "air") for his predecessors' choices. His writings, which survived into the Hellenistic Age, no longer exist except in passages in the works of later authors. Consequently, interpretations of his beliefs are frequently in conflict. It is clear, however, that he believed in degrees of condensation of moisture that corresponded to the densities of various types of matter. When "most evenly distributed," *aer* is the common, invisible air of the atmosphere. By condensation it becomes visible, first as mist or cloud, then as water, and finally as solid matter such as earth or stones. If further rarefied, it turns to fire. Thus hotness and dryness typify rarity, whereas coldness and wetness are related to denser matter.

Anaximenes' assumption that *aer* is everlastingly in motion suggests that he thought it also possessed life. Because it was eternally alive, *aer* took on qualities of the divine and became the cause of other gods as well as of all matter. The same motion accounts for the shift from one physical state of the *aer* to another. There is evidence that he made the common analogy between the divine air that sustains the universe and the human "air," or soul, that animates people. Such a comparison between a macrocosm and a microcosm would also permit him to maintain a unity behind diversity as well as to reinforce the view of his contemporaries that there is an overarching principle regulating all life and behaviour.

A practical man and a talented observer with a vivid imagination, Anaximenes occasionally noted the rainbows seen in moonlight and described the phosphorescent glow given off by an oar blade breaking the water. His thought is typical of the transition from mythology to science; its rationality is evident from his discussion of the rainbow not as a goddess but as the effect of sun rays on compacted air. Yet his thought is not completely liberated from earlier mythological or mystical tendencies, as seen from his belief that the universe is hemispherical. Thus, his permanent contribution lies not in his cosmology but in his suggestion that condensation and rarefaction play a part in the making of a world. This suggestion, together with Anaximenes' reduction of apparent qualitative differences in substances to mere differences of quantity, was highly influential in the development of scientific thought.

Anazarbus, in full CAESAREA AD ANAZARBUS, modern AĞAÇLI, formerly ÇEÇENA-NAVARZA, city of the ancient province of Cilicia in Anatolia. Important in the Roman and Byzantine periods, it was located in what is now Adana *il* (province), Turkey. Founded by the Romans in 19 BC, it rivalled Tarsus, the Cilician capital, in the 3rd century AD, and later became the seat of the separate province of Cilicia Secunda. Anazarbus was an archbishopric under the Byzantine Empire. Devastated by earthquakes in the 6th century, it was rebuilt, first as Justinopolis, later as Justinianopolis.

Under Muslim occupation it was renamed 'Ayn Zarbah and retained its strategic importance. Regained for Byzantium by Nicephorus Phocas about 962 and subsequently devastated during the Crusades, it became, as Anavarza, the capital of Cilician Little Armenia early in the 12th century. The Mamlūks of Egypt finally destroyed the city in 1374.

A Byzantine-Armenian castle—the finest medieval monument in Cilicia—stands on the ruins of the site. Remnants of several Byzantine churches, a triumphal arch, a theatre, stadium, amphitheatre, and aqueducts are also preserved. Pop. (1975) 281.

Anbar, also called MASSICE, or FAIRUZ SAPUR, ancient Mesopotamian town located on the left bank of the Euphrates River, downstream from modern ar-Ramādī in al-Anbār *muḥāfaẓah* (governorate), Iraq. Originally called Massice and Fairuz Sapur, it was destroyed by the Roman emperor Julian in AD 363. The town was rebuilt and became known from at least the 6th century as Anbar (Stores). Jews from the academy of Pumbedita took refuge there from Sāsānian persecution in 588, and it became a Jewish centre. Anbar was the capital of the 'Abbāsid caliphs from the beginning of that caliphate (750) until the founding of Baghdad (762).

Anbār, al-, formerly AR-RAMĀDĪ, *muḥāfaẓah* (governorate), formerly a *liwā'* (province), in western Iraq. With an area of 32,332 sq mi (83,740 sq km), it stretches from the divide between the Tigris and Euphrates rivers to the Syrian and Jordanian borders and contains large expanses of desert. Most of the streams, other than the Euphrates, are intermittent. The Euphrates floodplain is under irrigation and produces cotton, wheat, and vegetables. A dam on the Euphrates near ar-Ramādī was planned for the 1980s to increase both irrigation and hydroelectric power. The *muḥāfaẓah* is traversed by roads from Syria and Jordan. The capital is ar-Ramādī (*q.v.*). Pop. (1977) 466,059.

ANC (South African political party): *see* African National Congress.

Ancaeus, in Greek mythology, the son of Zeus or Poseidon and king of the Leleges of Samos. In the Argonautic expedition, after the death of Tiphys, helmsman of the "Argo," Ancaeus took his place. Traditionally, while planting a vineyard, he was told by a seer that he would never drink of its wine. When the grapes were ripe, he squeezed the juice into a cup and, raising it to his lips, mocked the seer, who retorted with the words "There is many a slip between cup and the lip." At that moment it was announced that a wild boar was ravaging the land. Ancaeus set down the cup, leaving the wine untasted, hurried out, and was killed by the boar.

Ancash, also spelled ANCACHS, department (formed 1836), west central Peru, between the arid Pacific coast on the west and the deep valley of the Marañón River on the northeast. Its area of 14,158 sq mi (36,669 sq km) is extremely rugged terrain. The Santa River flows northwest from its Andean source through the Callejón de Huaylas (*see* Huaylas,

Río Santa in the Cañón de Pato, Ancash department, Peru
Reflejo—EB Inc.

Callejón de), a scenic valley surrounded by snowcapped peaks, and then turns abruptly, plunging seaward. The valley is the site of Huaraz (*q.v.*), the capital, at 10,011 ft (3,052 m), and is the most densely populated part of Ancash. There is subsistence farming, but the department's economic mainstay is mining (including coal, silver, lead, and copper) and industry. At Chimbote, a rapidly growing coastal city, a modern steel plant is operated by electric power from the Río Santa development. The Pan-American Highway runs along the coast; roads and a railroad lead into the Callejón de Huaylas. In much of Ancash cities, hamlets, and roads were rebuilt or relocated after the widespread destruction caused by the earthquake and landslides on May 31, 1970. Pop. (1984 est.) 922,900.

ancestor worship, any of a variety of religious beliefs and practices concerned with the spirits of dead persons regarded as relatives, some of whom may be mythical. Ancestor worship, though not so nearly universal as tendance and fear of spirits of the dead, occurs in widely distributed cultures. It is prevalent in preliterate societies of Africa, Asia, and the Pacific area; existed among the ancient Mediterranean peoples and the peoples of ancient Europe; and is manifest in Asian cultures, particularly in India, China, and Japan.

A brief treatment of ancestor worship follows. For full treatment, *see* MACROPAEDIA: Religious and Spiritual Belief, Systems of.

In cultures that practice ancestor worship the living and the dead are as much related as any other two classes of a given community, for death does not make a person cease to belong to his social unit (family, clan, tribe, village, nation). The dead may be regarded as friendly, as kindred beings with whom kindly relations are possible; they may be for a time displeased and angry with their people, but such displeasure may be dispelled when proper respect, reverence, and worship are manifest. The dead, particularly the spirits of deceased strangers, also may be regarded as unfriendly to the living persons of a given community, as malevolent spirits capable of rendering harm to individuals or to the entire community.

Worship directed toward ancestors, believed to possess such powers as those suggested above, is of several types. The dead may be worshipped by an entire group—family, clan, tribe, or nation—of which they were members while living. Such communal worship was manifest in the Roman cult of the *manes* or the cult of the *parentum*, which involved the tendance of all the dead of a particular line. The dead individual as such was not the object of worship, but the life-force or *genius*.

More prevalent is the worship of individual ancestors, which may be combined in various ways with communal worship, as in the Roman emperor cult, Egyptian worship of ancestral rulers, and Japanese worship of members of the imperial household.

Not all ancestors are equally worthy of worship, for some are regarded as being more powerful than others. Ordinary members of a group, when dead, are tended only by their immediate relatives or perhaps not at all or not for very long, while the spirits of great personages become the focus for more elaborate cultic expression by an entire community. Seniority as well as prominence may have brought about the emergence of a dead person to the rank of a worshipful ancestor. The founder of a family, for example, may be worshipped by that family for an indeterminate number of generations.

Some one ancestor may so combine in his image all the worshipful qualities desired in a worthy ancestor, or show such preeminence in some one quality, that he is no longer treated as a departed spirit but is given the status of a god. An apparent example is Asclepius, worshipped in many parts of Greece as a god but also spoken of as a hero, with a cultic clan (known as the Asclepiadae, a guild of physicians) committed to revere him.

Ancestral spirits may be called upon to assist the community of the living in many ways: to assure the continuation of the line; to avert illness or plague; to assist in the obtaining of good crops (in many cultures ancestors are viewed as living in the ground); to intercede with gods, since they are associated with gods and often are viewed as living in the sky or in the abode of the deities. There is almost nothing that an ancestral spirit may not be called upon to grant or to avert. Generally, the relation of ancestral spirits to gods is that of inferior to superior, but they are commonly viewed as having a larger share of divine favour than the living.

Anchieta, José de (b. March 19, 1534, Canary Islands—d. June 9, 1597, Espírito Santo, Braz.), Portuguese Jesuit acclaimed as a poet, dramatist, and scholar who is considered one of the founders of the national literature of Brazil and is credited with converting more than a million Indians.

Anchieta came from a prominent Portuguese family and was even thought to be related to the founder of the Jesuit order, St. Ignatius Loyola. He was educated in Portugal and entered the Society of Jesus in 1551. He first arrived in Brazil on July 13, 1553, in what is now the province of Bahia. In 1554 he went to São Paulo, a new Jesuit settlement in the interior, where he played a major role in Jesuit efforts to convert the Indians. For the rest of his life he was influential in converting and helping the Indians, especially in trying to protect them from the institution of slavery, which was developing in the growing plantation economy of the Portuguese colony.

Anchieta's most famous literary work was the Latin mystic poem *De beata virgine dei matre Maria* ("The Blessed Virgin Mary"). He also wrote and staged several religious plays in the Brazilian wilderness, many of which have been lost. In addition, he wrote the first grammar of the Indian language Tupí and many letters describing the Indians' way of life, customs, folklore, and diseases, as well as the flora and fauna of Brazil. His other accomplishments include playing a role in the founding of Brazil's two largest cities, São Paulo and Rio de Janeiro, the founding of three colleges (at Pernambuco, Bahia, and Rio de Janeiro), and becoming provincial of the Jesuit order in Brazil in 1577.

Anchises, in Greek legend, member of the junior branch of the royal family of Troy; he was king of Dardanus on Mt. Ida. There the goddess Aphrodite met him and, enamoured of his beauty, bore him Aeneas. For revealing the name of the child's mother, Anchises was killed or struck blind by lightning. In later legend and in Virgil's *Aeneid*, he was conveyed out of Troy on the shoulders of his son Aeneas, whose descendants founded Rome, and died in Sicily.

anchor, device, usually of metal, attached to a ship or boat by a cable or chain and lowered to the seabed to hold the vessel in a particular place by means of a fluke or pointed projection that digs into the bottom.

Ancient anchors consisted of large stones, basketfuls of stones, sacks filled with sand, or logs of wood loaded with lead; these held the vessel merely by their weight and by friction along the bottom. When iron was introduced for their construction, an improvement was made by forming them with teeth or flukes.

Until the beginning of the 19th century, anchors were of imperfect manufacture, the means of effecting good and efficient welding

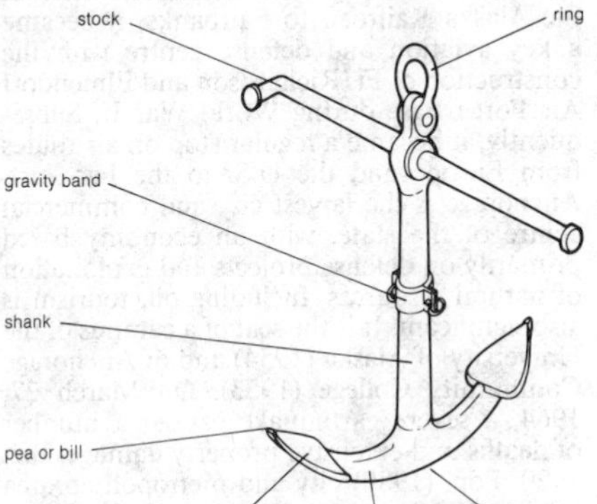

Figure 1: Admiralty pattern anchor
Used with the permission of the Controller of Her Britannic Majesty's Stationery Office

being absent and the iron being poor, while the arms, being straight, generally parted at the crown when weighing (being raised) from good holding ground. Curved arms were introduced in 1813, however, and after 1852 the admiralty anchor was supplied to ships of the British Navy. The present form of the admiralty anchor, still used for light work and for boats, is shown in Figure 1. By removing the keep pin, the anchor can be unstocked for stowing; *i.e.,* the stock or horizontal crosspiece at the top can be folded down so the anchor can be stowed in the side of the ship. The anchor must be stocked (the stock must be folded up again) before letting go, to ensure that one of the flukes takes the ground.

The patent or stockless anchor (Figure 2), patented in England in 1821, became widely used principally because of the ease in handling and stowing in the hawsepipe. Stockless anchors have replaced the older admiralty anchor on most of the large ships of the world.

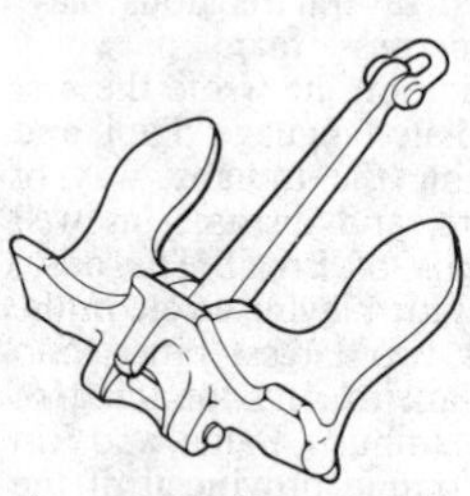

Figure 2: Stockless anchor
By courtesy of U.S. Navy

Several other types of anchors are in common use on ships and boats. These include the mushroom anchor, shaped like an upside-down mushroom and used widely as a permanent mooring for lightships, dredges, and lighters; the sea anchor, a floating device usually made of spars and canvas to keep the bow of the ship headed into the wind and sea and also used to reduce leeway and for riding heavy seas in greater safety; the drogue, a sea anchor used by small boats when landing through a surf to prevent being thrown broadside; the grapnel, a lightweight, stockless anchor with four or five curved, clawlike arms, used for dragging to recover objects on the bottom and for anchoring small boats; and the kedge, a small anchor of the stock or stockless type, used to move a ship short distances by carrying the anchor out in a boat, letting it go, and then hauling the ship up to it, and also to change the heading of a ship by moving the bow or stern around.

anchor bend (knot): *see* fisherman's bend.

Anchorage, city, southern Alaska, U.S., port at the head of Cook Inlet (a bay of the Pacific). Founded in 1914 as the headquarters of the Alaska Railroad to Fairbanks, it became a key aviation and defense centre with the construction of Ft. Richardson and Elmendorf Air Force Base during World War II. Subsequently, it became a regular stop on air routes from Europe and the U.S. to the Far East. Anchorage is the largest city and commercial centre of the state, with an economy based primarily on defense projects and exploitation of natural resources, including oil; tourism is also significant. It is the seat of a campus of the University of Alaska (1954) and of Anchorage Community College (1953). On March 27, 1964, a severe earthquake caused a number of deaths and extensive property damage. Inc. 1920. Pop. (1980) city and metropolitan area (SMSA), 173,017.

anchovy, any of numerous schooling saltwater fishes of the family Engraulidae (order Clupeiformes) related to the herring and distinguished by the large mouth, almost always extending behind the eye, and by the pointed snout. Most of the more than 100 species live in shallow tropical or warm temperate seas, often entering brackish water around river mouths. A few tropical anchovies inhabit fresh water.

Anchovies (*Engraulis mordax*)
Tom McHugh—Photo Researchers

Anchovies lay large numbers of elongate, transparent, floating eggs in spring and summer. The eggs hatch in about two days, and the larvae sink to the bottom. Young and adults feed on plankton, and growth is rapid. Adult anchovies are 10–25 centimetres (4–10 inches) long. Temperate-water types such as the northern anchovy (*Engraulis mordax*) and the European anchovy (*E. encrasicholus*) are important food fishes; tropical ones such as the tropical anchovy or anchoveta (*Cetengraulis mysticetus*) are important bait, especially in the tuna fishery. Large numbers of anchovies of the genus *Coilia,* with long anal fins and tapered bodies, are dried and eaten in China. Many species of anchovies are easily injured and are killed by contact with a net or other solid object.

anchovy pear (*Grias cauliflora*), evergreen tree, of the family Lecythidaceae, native to the West Indies. The name is also applied to its edible fruit, for which the tree is cultivated.

The plant grows to about 15 metres (about 50 feet) tall and bears spear-shaped, glossy leaves about 90 centimetres (3 feet) long that are produced in palmlike tufts. The fragrant yellow flowers are about 5 cm (2 in.) across. The fruit, which contains one seed, is pear-shaped, russet brown, and 5–7 cm long.

Anchura, genus of extinct marine gastropods (snails) found as fossils only in marine deposits of Cretaceous age (between 136,000,000 and 65,000,000 years old). It is thus a useful guide or index fossil because it is quite distinctive and easily recognizable. The shell whorls are globular and ornamented with raised crenulations; the spire is sharply pointed; the body whorl, the final and largest whorl, has a prominently extended outer lip.

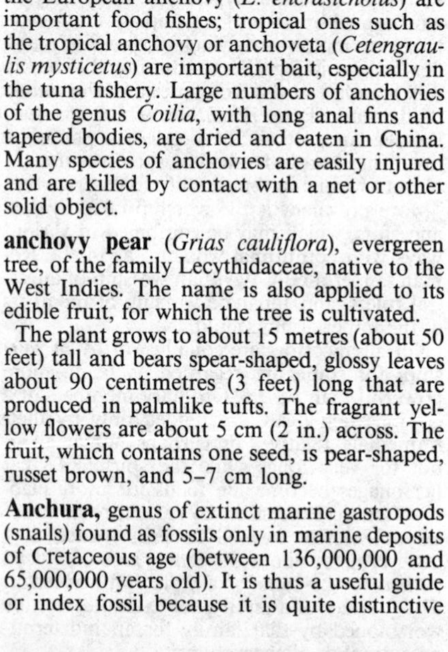

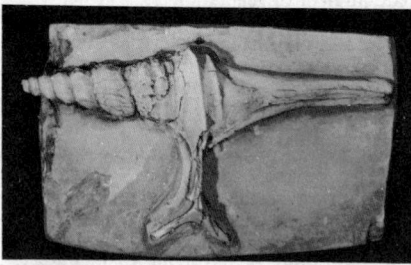

Anchura
By courtesy of the trustees of the British Museum (Natural History); photograph, Imitor

ancient lights, in English property law, the right of a building or house owner to the light received from and through his windows. Windows used for light by an owner for 20 years or more could not be obstructed by the erection of an edifice or by any other act by an adjacent landowner. This rule of law originated in England in 1663, based on the theory that a landowner acquired an easement to the light by virtue of his use of the windows for that purpose for the statutory length of time. It did not acquire wide acceptance by U.S. courts.

ancients and moderns, subject of a celebrated literary dispute that raged in France and England in the 17th century. The "ancients" maintained that classical literature of Greece and Rome offered the only models for literary excellence; the "moderns" challenged the supremacy of the classical writers. The rise of modern science tempted some French intellectuals to assume that, if Descartes had surpassed ancient science, it might be possible to surpass other ancient arts. The first attacks on the ancients came from Cartesian circles in defense of some heroic poems by Desmarets de Saint-Sorlin that were based on Christian rather than classical mythology. The dispute broke into a storm with the publication of Nicolas Boileau's *L'Art poétique* (1674), defining the case for the ancients and upholding the classical traditions of poetry. From then on, the quarrel became personal and vehement. Among the chief supporters of the moderns were Charles Perrault and Bernard de Fontenelle. Supporters of the ancients were La Fontaine and La Bruyère.

In England the quarrel continued until well into the first decade of the 18th century. In 1690 Sir William Temple's *Essay upon Ancient and Modern Learning* attacked the members of the Royal Society by rejecting the doctrine of progress and supporting the virtuosity and excellence of ancient learning. William Wotton responded to Temple's charges in his *Reflections upon Ancient and Modern Learning* (1694). It praised the moderns in most but not all branches of learning, conceding the superiority of the ancients in poetry, art, and oratory. The primary points of contention were then quickly clouded and confused, but eventually two main issues emerged: whether literature progressed from antiquity to the present as science did, and whether, if there was progress, it was linear or cyclical. These matters were seriously and vehemently discussed. Jonathan Swift, defending his patron Temple, satirized the conflict in his *Tale of a Tub* (1704) and, more importantly, in *The Battle of the Books* (1704). At a later date Swift was to make an even more devastating attack on the Royal Society in *Gulliver's Travels,* Book III, "The Voyage to Laputa."

Ancillon, Charles (b. July 28, 1659, Metz, Fr.—d. July 5, 1715, Berlin), lawyer, educator, historian, and the leader of the French Protestant refugees in Germany who played an important role in advancing the intellectual and educational interests of that community.

Born of a distinguished family of French Protestants, Ancillon studied law at Marburg, Geneva, and Paris. He pleaded the cause of the Huguenots—the French Protestants—of Metz at the court of Louis XIV, urging that an exception be made for them in the revocation of the Edict of Nantes (1685, forbidding the exercise of the Protestant religion); his *Réflexions politiques* (1686; "Political Reflections") outlined the arguments against the persecutions. Ancillon's efforts were unsuccessful, however, and he moved to Berlin, where he was appointed by Frederick III, the elector of Brandenburg, as judge of the French refugees in that state. Made director in 1687 of the Academy of Nobles, the principal educational establishment of the state, he cooperated with the German philosopher Gottfried Wilhelm Leibniz in the founding of the Academy of Berlin, a society of arts and sciences.

Appointed historiographer to the Elector in 1699, Ancillon replaced, in the same year, his uncle, Joseph Ancillon, as judge of all the French refugees. As councillor of embassy at the Imperial court, he was involved in the negotiations that resulted in the election of

Frederick the Elector to be king in 1701 as Frederick I. His works include the *Histoire de l'établissement des français réfugiés dans les états de S.A.E. Brandenbourg* (1690; "The History of the Establishment of the French Refugees in Brandenburg State") and *L'Irrévocabilité de l'édit de Nantes* (1688; "The Irrevocability of the Edict of Nantes").

Ancillon, Johann Peter Friedrich, French JEAN-PIERRE-FRÉDÉRIC ANCILLON (b. April 30, 1767, Berlin—d. April 19, 1837, Berlin),

Johann Peter Friedrich Ancillon, detail from a lithograph by Friedrich Jentzen after a drawing by Franz Krüger

By courtesy of the Staatsbibliothek, Berlin

Prussian statesman, foreign minister, historian, and political philosopher who worked with the Austrian statesman Metternich to preserve the reactionary European political settlement of 1815.

Educated in Geneva, Ancillon acquired a chair in history at the Berlin Military Academy in 1792. After the publication of *Tableau des révolutions du système politique de l'Europe depuis le XVe siècle,* 4 vol. (1803–05; "View of European Political Revolutions Since the Fifteenth Century"), he was admitted to the Berlin Academy and became tutor to the future Frederick William IV, in whom he instilled a profound antipathy toward revolution.

During his service with the ministry of foreign affairs, which he headed from 1832 until his death, Ancillon, a Prussian nationalist and romantic, worked closely with Austria and Russia in combatting liberalism.

Anckarsvärd, Carl Henrik, Greve (Count) (b. April 22, 1782, Stockholm—d. Jan. 25, 1865, Stockholm), a leader of the 1809 coup d'etat that deposed the absolutist Swedish king Gustav IV, and a champion of liberal political, economic, and social causes in the first half of the 19th century.

Unlike many other "men of 1809," Anckarsvärd did not retreat from his liberal principles when a democratization of society became a practical possibility. Although a member of the largely conservative noble estate in the Riksdag (estates general), he fought for free trade, open government fiscal policy, a modern parliament, and mass public education. While the experience of the 1848 revolutions caused him to doubt the benefit of universal suffrage, which he had formerly favoured, his efforts were vital to the achievement in 1865 of a modern parliamentary system.

Ancón, city, Panamá province, central Panama, just northeast of Balboa city. It is a residential and medical centre. As Balboa and Panama City have grown, Ancón has become virtually a suburb of the latter. It is noted for the Gorgas hospital for tropical diseases, named after Col. William Crawford Gorgas (*q.v.*), the yellow fever pioneer. Ancón is on the Transisthmian Railway. Pop. (1983 est.) 28,113.

Ancona, capital of Ancona province and of Marche region, in central Italy, on the Adriatic Sea on the farthest branch of the promontory that descends from the Conero massif. Founded by Syracusan colonists *c.* 390 BC, it was taken by Rome in the 2nd century BC and became a flourishing port, particularly favoured by the Roman emperor Trajan, who enlarged the harbour. Attacked by Goths, Lombards, and Saracens, Ancona declined but recovered its importance in the Middle Ages; it was one of the five cities of the Maritime Pentapolis under the Byzantine exarchate of Ravenna. The seat of a Carolingian march (frontier borderland), it eventually became a semi-independent republic under papal control; direct papal rule was established in 1532 and, with the exception of a period of French domination (1797–1816), was maintained until Ancona became part of Italy in 1860. The city was bombarded by the Austrian fleet (1915) during World War I and suffered severe damage from Allied bombings (1943–44) during World War II.

Notable landmarks, restored since the war, include the marble Arch of Trajan (AD 115); the 11th- to 12th-century church of Sta. Maria della Piazza, with an ornate facade of 1210 and remains of 5th- and 7th-century mosaics; and the 12th- to 13th-century cathedral of S. Ciriaco, which is supposed to occupy the site of a Roman temple of Venus and incorporates the remains of a basilica of the 5th–6th centuries. The city has many fine Gothic buildings and is the site of the National Museum of Marche, with a valuable archaeological collection and art gallery, although some local monuments suffered earthquake damage during the 1970s. Ancona is the seat of an archbishop.

The harbour, originally protected only by the elbow-shaped promontory from which the city takes its name (Greek *angkon,* "elbow"), has modern installations built since World War II, including an oil refinery. Although Ancona's importance as a port has diminished, it is a busy market centre, with ships plying between

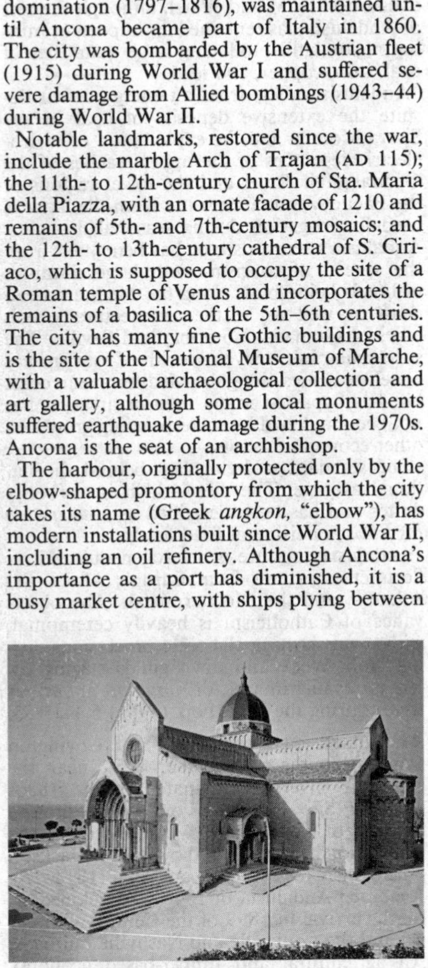

Cathedral of S. Ciriaco, Ancona, Italy

SCALA—Art Resource/EB Inc.

Italian and Yugoslav ports on the Adriatic. Ancona is on the main east coast rail line from Milan and Bologna to Brindisi and Foggia; it is also connected to Rome by a main line. Industries include shipbuilding and the manufacture of machinery, chemicals, medicines, foodstuffs, textiles, furniture, and bricks. Pop. (1981 prelim.) mun., 106,421.

Ancre, Concino Concini, marquis d': *see* Concini, Concino.

Ancud, town and commune in Los Lagos region, southern Chile. It lies on the northern coast of Chiloé Island, across the Straits of Chacao from the mainland. Founded in 1769 as San Carlos de Ancud, it was one of the last strongholds of royalist forces during Chile's struggle for independence from Spain in the first quarter of the 19th century. It was the provincial capital of Chiloé province from 1937 to 1974. Ancud is a port, resort, and commercial centre for its hinterland, which yields potatoes, wheat, livestock, and lumber. Timber is its principal export. The town is linked by road and ferry to Puerto Montt and by road to Castro, the provincial capital and oldest settlement on Chiloé Island. Pop. (1982 prelim.) com., 29,324; (1970) town 4,462.

Ancus Marcius (fl. 7th century BC), traditionally the fourth king of Rome, from 642 to 617 BC. The details of his reign, provided by Roman historians such as Livy (64 or 59 BC–AD 17), must be regarded as largely legendary; *e.g.,* the settlement of the Aventine Hill outside Rome, the first extension of Rome beyond the Tiber River to the Janiculum Hill, and the founding of the port of Ostia at the mouth of the Tiber.

ancylostomiasis: *see* hookworm disease.

Ancylus Stage, early span of post-glacial time in northern Europe marked by an impounding and freshening of the Baltic Sea Basin. The Ancylus Stage, characterized by the common fossil snail genus *Ancylus,* lasted about 2,000 years—from about 8,500 to 6,500 years ago. The Ancylus Lake was formed as a result of crustal uplift along the southwestern margin of the Baltic Basin, which was produced by the withdrawal of the thick continental ice sheet from the land. It probably attained its greatest size (larger than that of the present Baltic Sea, more than 160,000 sq mi [414,000 sq km]) about 6500 BC, and then once again became a saline, ocean-connected body before 4500 BC, when the rising level of the sea, resulting from increased melting of the ice sheet, finally overflowed the land and once again made the Baltic an arm of the sea. At its maximum extent, the Ancylus Lake covered a large area of present Sweden and Finland. A rich fossil record, including pollen information, has provided a full history of the Ancylus Lake.

Andalusia, Spanish ANDALUCIA, autonomous region (*junta de la communidad autónoma*) of Spain, a governmental entity encompassing the southernmost Spanish provinces of Huelva, Cádiz, Sevilla, Málaga, Córdoba, Jaén, Granada, and Almería and ratified by a regional referendum on December 30, 1981.

The following article summarizes the administrative status and history, geography, demographic patterns, economy, and culture of modern Andalusia; for fuller treatment of its geography and history, *see* MACROPAEDIA: Spain.

Andalusia corresponds roughly to the ancient Roman province of Baetica. The Arabic name al-Andalus was originally applied by the Muslims (Moors), who occupied Spain in the 8th century, to the whole Iberian Peninsula. It probably means the country of the Vandals—a Germanic people who had invaded Spain in the 5th century. In the 11th century, when the Christians began to reconquer the peninsula, al-Andalus, or Andalusia, came to mean only the area still under Muslim control and thus became permanently attached to the region defined above. After the breakup of the unified Spanish Muslim state in the early 11th century, Andalusia was divided into a number of small kingdoms, which had a strong cultural and artistic influence on the North Africans, who in turn reinvigorated Spanish Islām. North African influence was finally excluded in the 14th century, and by the end of the 15th century all of Andalusia had been incorporated into the Christian kingdom of Castile. The present-day provinces were created in 1833. The regional government established in 1981 is the *Junta,* consisting of an executive council (headed by a president) and a unicameral parliament.

Andalusia faces both the Atlantic and the Mediterranean to the southeast, with the provinces of Huelva and Cádiz bordering the Gulf of Cádiz on the west and the provinces of Málaga, Granada, and Almería opening on the Mediterranean. These two distinctive marine zones display sharp variations in terrain and climate, working against a strong sense of regionalism in the populace. The topography of Andalusia is divided by mountain ranges into several distinct zones, each running southwest to northeast. The Sierra Morena is the northernmost range, comprising parts of the provinces of Huelva, which borders Portugal, and Sevilla and Córdoba, which adjoin the Castilian provinces of Badajoz and Ciudad Real. The Sierra Morena presents a relief of desolate ridges punctuated by narrow valleys that sheltered bandits well into the 18th century. The Sierra Morena is terminated to the south by the Guadalquivir, or Baetic, Basin, a triangular plain drained southwestward by the Guadalquivir River and partitioned by human occupance into large estates, or latifundios. The Penibético, or Baetic, Mountains rise abruptly to the south, forming an alpine range with the highest elevations in the Iberian Peninsula south of the Pyrenees. The Baetic Mountains extend southward from the province of Jaén into Granada and Almería, which border the Castilian provinces of Ciudad Real and Albacete, and give way to the Andalusian steppes in the southeast corner of the peninsula. The steppes descend from the border of the province of Murcia (east) and cover much of Granada and Almería provinces. The Baetic Mountains effectively block precipitation from reaching the steppes, creating a region of badlands with scorched tablelands and sharp gorges. Mediterranean Andalusia stretches southwestward from the city of Almería to the western limits of Málaga province. The region is one of Spain's most popular tourist rivieras (the Costa del Sol being the westernmost part of this coast), with mountains commonly extending down to the sea. Geological uplift and erosion of the mountains have enlarged the coastal deltas since antiquity. A Mediterranean climate prevails in most of Andalusia, with mild and rainy winters; colder climate marks the Baetic Mountains, where heavy snows and low temperatures leave the upper reaches snowbound between November and May. Annual precipitation ranges from 40 in. (1,000 mm) in the Sierra Nevada to as little as 4 in. in the desertic Andalusian steppes.

The population of western Andalusia has traditionally been concentrated in large rural towns from which agricultural labourers commute daily to work on the surrounding estates, or *cortijos,* but in modern times it has increasingly concentrated in the provincial capitals. From the Baetic Mountains eastward, small villages predominate, located wherever water is available. Cities have been growing at the expense of rural settlements, but emigration to the industrialized regions of Spain and western Europe has resulted in a levelling off of population growth despite the region's high birthrate. However, emigration declined in the early 1980s as the demand for imported labour diminished in the countries of the European Economic Community.

Andalusia is underdeveloped, accounting for a disproportionately small percentage of Spain's gross national product and for a disproportionately high percentage of agricultural output. Latifundios have dominated Andalusian agriculture since the reconquest (completed 1492), producing the traditional Mediterranean crops of wheat, grapes, and olives by dry farming. The large farms have increased the mechanization of agriculture, but the region continues to lag behind the national average in the use of tractors, irrigation, and fertilizers. Though absentee landowners continue to dominate rural Andalusia, a middle class is emerging in the farming towns.

The region's industrial sector is poorly developed and is dominated by the processing of agricultural products and mining; manufacturing is of relatively little importance. Wine and brandy are produced in Jerez (where sherry originated), Niebla, Montilla, and Málaga, while the provinces of Sevilla, Córdoba, and Jaén process large quantities of olive oil. Andalusia's mining, though still substantial, is in decline, having reached its peak toward the late 19th century when Spain led Europe in the exploitation of minerals. Virtually all of Andalusia's production of copper and lead was then exported to Great Britain and Germany, although the region benefitted relatively little from the boom because of extensive foreign ownership of the mines. Mining districts in Almería, Córdoba, and Málaga approached exhaustion by World War I, although the rest of Andalusia has remained an important mining region, still producing large quantities of coal, iron, copper, and lead.

Andalusia suffers from an energy deficit despite the extensive deposits of coal in the Sierra Morena and the exploitation of hydroelectric resources of the upper reaches of the Guadalquivir River and the lower regions of the Baetic Mountains; water from the latter is used for irrigation during seasonal droughts. Andalusia's service sector has benefitted from the spread of tourism, with large numbers of hotels being built along the Mediterranean coast as well as in the architecturally rich cities of Granada, Córdoba, and Seville. The spectacular but uneven growth of tourism has benefitted cities along the Mediterranean coast but has bypassed many interior areas; it has not been matched by corresponding growth in other economic sectors.

The standard of living lags behind the national average. The diet is high in carbohydrates and has been described as a *cocina de los fritos,* a cuisine of fried foods.

Andalusian culture is heterogeneous and reflects crosscurrents from Europe, Africa, the Atlantic, and the Mediterranean. The observance of Catholicism is heavily ceremonial, with towns hosting elaborate processions during Holy Week and town guilds staging ostentatious pilgrimages, or *romerías,* at various times during the year. Pop. (1981) 6,441,755.

Andalusia, city, seat (1841) of Covington County, southern Alabama, U.S., near the Conecuh River. It originated in the 1830s as New Site (relocated on higher ground because of floods) and was crossed by the Three-Notched Trail, used by Andrew Jackson during his Creek Indian campaign (1813–14). Renamed Andalusia in 1846, it developed after the arrival in 1899 of the Central of Georgia and the Louisville and Nashville railroads. An agricultural and timber-based economy prevails, supplemented by light manufacturing. Lurleen B. Wallace State Junior College was opened in 1969. Conecuh National Forest is 10 mi (16 km) south. Inc. 1901. Pop. (1980) 10,415.

Consult the INDEX *first*

andalusite, aluminum silicate mineral, formulated Al_2SiO_5, that occurs in small amounts in many contact metamorphic rocks, particularly in altered sediments. It occurs in commercial quantities at White Mountain, Calif., and in Oreana, Nev., in the U.S.; Kazakh S.S.R.; and the Transvaal, South Africa. Such deposits are mined as a raw material for refractories and porcelain used in spark plugs and other products. For detailed physical properties, *see* silicate mineral (table).

The unaltered mineral occurs as greenish or reddish pebbles in the gem gravels of Minas Gerais, Brazil, and in Sri Lanka. The variety chiastolite (also called cross-stone or macle), characteristic of clay slates near a granite contact, forms elongated prismatic crystals enclosing symmetrically arranged wedges of carbonaceous material. In cross section, it shows a black cross on a grayish ground; when polished, cross sections are worn as charms.

Andalusite from Tirol, Austria

By courtesy of the Field Museum of Natural History, Chicago; photograph, John H. Gerard—EB Inc.

Andaman, island group and district, Andaman and Nicobar union territory, India, in the southeastern part of the Bay of Bengal. The Andamans constitute one of the two major groups of islands in the union territory. The Andaman district includes 204 islands, extending over an area of 3,200 sq mi (8,300 sq km), within which lie North Andaman, Middle Andaman, South Andaman, Baratang, Little Andaman, and Rutland Island. Of the original inhabitants, only the Jarawa and Onge, living on the lesser islands of South Andaman, Rutland, and Little Andaman, retain their traditional hunting-and-gathering way of life.

The Andamans, situated on the ancient India–Burma trade route, were visited by Lieut. Archibald Blair of the Indian Navy in 1789. The first European settlement on the islands was at Port Blair, situated along the eastern coast of South Andaman and now the district and union territory headquarters.

The islands are a succession of dome-shaped, forest-covered hill ranges running parallel to each other from north to south. The highest peak is Saddle, at 2,461 ft (750 m), on North Andaman. Flat land is scarce and confined to a few valleys, such as the Bitampur and Diglipur. The islands are formed of Tertiary sandstone, limestone, and shale and are highly dissected. Their surface is covered with dense forest, and large mangrove swamps occur in the northern part of North Andaman. Perennial rivers are few, and adequate water supply is a continuing problem.

Agriculture is the principal occupation; crops include cereals, pulse (legumes), coconuts, betel nuts, fruits, cassava, chilies, and turmeric. A government five-year plan introduced a match factory and a marine-engineering, boat-building, and repair shop at Port Blair. Only South Andaman has roads; an interisland steamer service connects Port Blair with North, Middle, South, and Little Andaman. Vinayak Damodar (Vir) Savarkar, the great Indian revolutionary, was imprisoned for life (1911–37) in the Cellular Jail (declared a national monument in 1979) in Port Blair. Pop. (1981) district, 158,287.

Andaman and Nicobar Islands, union territory of India, consisting of two island groups in the Bay of Bengal. Comprising 3,200 sq mi (8,300 sq km), the Andamans are separated from the Nicobars to the south by the Ten Degree Channel, which is 90 mi (145 km) wide. The Andaman group includes 204 islands and islets with three chief islands in the main group—North, Middle, and South Andaman—so closely adjoining that they have been known collectively as Great Andaman. The Nicobars are a group of 12 inhabited and 7 uninhabited islands; they include Great Nicobar (largest and southernmost), Kamorta and Nancowry (central group), and Car Nicobar (northern group). The principal harbours are Port Blair, the territorial capital, Diglipur, Rangat, Neil, and Mayabandar in the Andamans, and Car Nicobar and Kamorta in the Nicobars.

Because of their position on the India–Burma trade routes, their existence has been known from earliest times. After the mid-18th century the islands were associated with the British, who established penal colonies there. They were occupied by the Japanese (1942–45) and passed to India on the establishment of Indian independence (1947). In the 1950s the Andamans were colonized with displaced persons from East Pakistan (now Bangladesh), evacuees from Burma, and Indian emigrants from British Guiana (now Guyana).

Exports from the territory include timber, especially Andaman redwood, gurjan for plywood, and softwoods, coconuts, and copra. Pop. (1981) 188,741.

Andaman Sea, sea, part of the northeastern Indian Ocean, with an area of 308,000 sq mi (798,000 sq km). Through such ports as Bassein, Moulmein, Tavoy, and Mergui—as well as Rangoon itself—it forms Burma's most important sea link with other nations; it also forms part of a shipping route between India and China, via the Strait of Malacca. It is bounded to the north by the Irrawaddy Delta of Burma; to the east by peninsular Burma, Thailand, and Malaysia; to the west by the Andaman and Nicobar Islands, which are under Indian administration; and to the south by the island of Sumatra (part of Indonesia) and by the Strait of Malacca. The sea takes its name from the Andaman Islands. It is 750 mi (469 km) long, from north to south, and 400 mi wide. Less than 5 percent of the sea is deeper than 10,000 ft (3,000 m), but in a system of submarine valleys east of the Andaman–Nicobar Ridge, depths exceed 14,500 ft.

Trading vessels have plied the Andaman Sea since ancient times. It formed part of the early coastal trade route between India and China and from the 8th century onward formed a link in a thriving trade between India and Sri Lanka (Ceylon) to the west and the Burmese ports of Thaton, Martaban, and Tavoy to the east.

The sea's northern and eastern third is less than 600 ft deep. The Irrawaddy River is continually forming a delta shelf of silty clay, incised by a shallow channel system that merges into the submarine Martaban Canyon to the south. During the Tertiary Period (70,000,000 to 10,000,000 years ago), a continental shelf was formed adjacent to the Malay Peninsula. Subsequent faulting and folding molded parts of this shelf into two submarine terraces and a shelf basin north of Sumatra. A discontinuous veneer of shelly quartz sands covers the continental margin, while the shelf basin has accumulated over 3,000 feet of silty clays. The continental slope is 500 mi long with a relief variation of 6,000 ft.

The Andaman–Nicobar Ridge has a core of serpentinite (primarily hydrous magnesium silicate) and associated rocks, overlain by at least 10,000 ft of folded and faulted sandstone and shale. The western and central half of the sea, between the ridge and the Malay Continental Slope, is 3,000 to 10,000 ft deep, and consists of a broad central trough, two seamounts, a system of smaller seamounts and rift valleys, and the volcanic Narcondam and Barren islands. This basin's basaltic rock is partially and thinly covered by Irrawaddy clays. This silt blanket is thin because most Tertiary sediment was probably shed into an adjacent trough that was then molded into the Andaman–Nicobar Ridge. The basin was produced approximately 10,000,000 years ago when the Andaman–Nicobar Ridge was rifted from the shelf in a movement that continues today.

Southeast Asia's monsoonal regime governs the sea's climate and waters. In the winter, light northeasterly winds cause south to southeasterly Andaman currents to flow into the Bay of Bengal. Humidity is low, the sea receives little rainfall or runoff, and surface salinities are high. In May southwest monsoon winds cause westerly currents. Huge volumes of runoff water from Burma flow into the sea during the summer monsoon, forming a marked pattern of low surface salinity in its northern third.

Andaman water—categorized as Equatorial India Water—is stratified in three layers. A surface layer 200 to 300 ft thick, with temperatures between 75° and 84° F (24°–29° C) and seasonally variable salinities, is separated by a strong thermocline (layer of water in which temperatures drop more than 1° C per metre of depth) from a 1,500-ft-thick intermediate layer, with a maximum salinity of 35 parts of salt per 1,000 parts of seawater. Down to 4,000 ft the temperature potential is 40.5° F (4.7° C), and salinity is 34.86 parts of salt per 1,000 parts of seawater. Deeper waters, replenished by waters from the Bay of Bengal, maintain these temperatures and salinity levels down to the bottom.

The plankton biomass in the surface waters is relatively low. Bottom fauna is extremely poor, while coral reefs occur only along the Andaman and Nicobar Islands. The Malay Shelf waters, however, favour molluscan growth, and there are about 250 edible species of fish—20 of which are common—in the intensively fished coastal waters.

Mineral resources are limited. Southern extensions of the Burmese oil fields may underlie the Irrawaddy Shelf, and petroleum may also occur in the shelf-basin off Sumatra. Submerged extensions of the tin and ilmenite deposits of the Malayan coastal plains are intensively sought after, while tin dredging has begun off the coast of Thailand.

The two largest ports are Pinang (Malaysia) to the southeast and Rangoon (in Burma) to the north, and most maritime traffic is along the coast of the Malay Peninsula. Westbound shipping enters the sea through the Strait of Malacca and exits through the Great Passage to Colombo or the Ten Degree Channel to Madras.

BIBLIOGRAPHY. On the physiography, submarine morphology, geology, and geologic history, see K.S. Rodolfo, "Bathymetry and Marine Geology of the Andaman Basin, and Tectonic Implications for Southeast Asia," *Bull. Geol. Soc. Am.*, 80:1203–1230 (1969); on bottom deposits, "Sediments of the Andaman Basin, Northeastern Indian Ocean," *Mar. Geol.*, 7:371–402 (1969).

Andamanese, aboriginal inhabitants of the Andaman and Nicobar Islands in the Bay of Bengal. They belong to Negrito stock, which is represented also by the Semang of Malaysia and the Pygmies of the Philippines. Most have been detribalized and absorbed into modern Indian life, especially on the three chief islands known collectively as the Great Andaman; but traditional culture survives among such tribes as the Jarawa and Onge of the lesser islands of South Andaman, Rutland Island, and Little Andaman. Speakers of Andamanese number about 1,000.

Until the mid-19th century, the remoteness of the Andamanese and their practice of killing all foreigners preserved them from any considerable physical or cultural modification. The remnant tribes still live by hunting and collecting, cultivation being unknown. The only indigenous weapon is the bow, used for both fishing and hunting wild pigs; they have no traps or fishhooks. Turtle, dugong, and fish are caught with nets and harpoons; the last are used from single-outrigger canoes. Pottery is made; and iron, obtained from wrecks, has been used for arrowheads, knives, and adzes from at least the 18th century. It is shaped by breaking and grinding, a technique derived from the working of shell. The Andamanese were unique in knowing no method of making fire.

Andamanese language, language spoken by the indigenous people of the Andaman Islands; the number of speakers of the language has been steadily decreasing. Andamanese dialects are usually classified into northern, central, and southern groups, with the southern dialects being the most archaic. The dialect of Little Andaman island is the southernmost of the Andamanese dialects and diverges greatly from the others.

One of the chief characteristics of Andamanese grammar is the use of affixes (especially prefixes) to specify the functions of the words of a sentence. The language has no number system; the two number words in the language mean "one" and "more than one."

Andamanese is not known to be related to any other language.

Andania Mysteries, ancient Greek mystery cult, held in honour of the earth goddess Demeter and her daughter Kore (Persephone) at the town of Andania in Messenia. A long inscription of 92 BC gives elaborate directions for the conduct of the rites, although it relates no details of the initiation ceremonies. The ritual was performed by certain "holy ones" of both sexes, who were chosen from the various tribes, presumably the same number from each tribe. Supervising the whole procedure was a committee of 10 persons of mature age (not less than 40 years old).

Initiation seems to have been open to men, women, and children, bonded and free, and some details have survived as to the costumes to be worn by each class of initiates: all were to be severely plain and of inexpensive material. An exception was made for those who were to be "costumed into the likeness of deities," from which many scholars have assumed that a pageant of drama was performed. There was a procession, precedence in which was strictly regulated, and the main ceremonial was preceded by sacrifices to a number of deities.

Andean bear: *see* spectacled bear.

Andean Geosyncline, a linear trough in the Earth's crust in which rocks of Mesozoic and Cenozoic age were deposited in South America (the Mesozoic Era began 225,000,000 years ago and ended 65,000,000 years ago; it was followed by the Cenozoic Era, the last 65,000,000 years of Earth history). An intense orogenic (mountain-building) event affected the older sediments in the geosyncline in Late Cretaceous time (about 75,000,000 years ago) and, combined with later deformational episodes, produced a pattern of scattered marine deposition in basins along the western margin of the geosyncline. The total area of deposition was great enough for some geosynclinal segments to be separately named; *e.g.,* the Venezuelan–Peruvian Geosyncline. The rising highland belts provided much coarse sediment, and thicknesses as great as 6,080 metres (20,000 feet) are known from Early Cenozoic sequences. During Middle Cenozoic time, another orogenic phase occurred, accompanied by widespread volcanism. A complex history of intermittent uplift, block faulting, and erosion in Late Cenozoic time led to a series of extensive uplifted erosion surfaces in Peru, Bolivia, and elsewhere. Uplift continued through the late Pleistocene (the Pleistocene Epoch began about 2,500,000 years ago and ended 10,000 years ago), giving rise to the present configuration of the Andes. Elevations of 4,600 metres (15,200 feet) are widespread, and many peaks attain 6,000 metres (19,800 feet) or more. Some of the latter are volcanic cones that rest upon one of the uplifted erosion surfaces mentioned above.

Andean Group, Spanish GRUPO ANDINO, South American organization founded to encourage industrial, agricultural, social, and trade cooperation among members. Formed in 1969 by the Cartagena Agreement, the group originally consisted of Bolivia, Colombia, Ecuador, Peru, and Chile; Venezuela joined in 1973, and Chile withdrew in 1977. Several subgroups include the Andean Group Commission, the Andean Reserve Fund, the Andean Development Corporation, and various councils dealing with trade, monetary exchange, economic planning, tourism, social affairs, etc.

One of the most significant acts of the Andean Group has been plans for new industries, especially one for motor vehicles. Members tend to rely on high regional tariff policies to encourage preferential trade agreements, but with limited success. Several businesses have been adversely affected, prompting Chile's withdrawal in January 1977.

Anderlecht, municipality, Brabant province, central Belgium, on the Charleroi-Brussels Canal, just southwest of Brussels; it is one of the 19 communes comprising the Greater Brussels area. A natural clearing in the primitive forest where foundations of a Roman villa and Frankish cemeteries have been found, it is believed to be the original site of what is now Brussels. A residential and manufacturing suburb, its industries include textiles, leather, chemicals, lumber, paper, and glassware. Medieval remains include the Church of SS. Peter and Guidon, containing an 11th-century crypt of St. Guidon (the patron saint of farm animals), and a *béguinage* (retreat for secular nuns) dating from 1252. The visit in 1521 of the Dutch Humanist Erasmus is commemorated by a museum in the house where he stayed. In Anderlecht is a university hospital attached to the Free University of Brussels. Pop. (1983 est.) mun., 92,912.

Andernach, city, Rheinland-Pfalz *Land* (Rhineland-Palatinate state), eastern West Germany, on the left bank of the Rhine, just northwest of Koblenz. It originated in 12 BC as the Roman garrison town of Antunnacum, and became a member of the Hanseatic League in 1253. A 12th-century watchtower and a medieval Romanesque church survive. Andernach was occupied by the French from 1795 until it was ceded in 1815 to Prussia. The city is now a manufacturing centre (notably textiles, pottery, chemicals) and a rail junction. Pop. (1983 est.) 27,092.

Anders, William A(lison) (b. Oct. 17, 1933, Hong Kong), U.S. astronaut who participated in the Apollo 8 flight (Dec. 21–27, 1968), in which the first manned voyage around the Moon was made. The astronauts, including

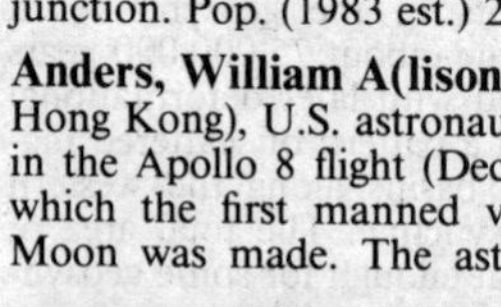

William A. Anders, 1964
By courtesy of the National Aeronautics and Space Administration

Anders, Frank Borman, and James Lovell, remained in an orbit about 70 miles (112 kilometres) above the surface of the Moon for about 20 hours, transmitting television pictures back to Earth and verifying that lunar landmarks could be used for navigation to lunar landing sites.

Anders resigned from the National Aeronautics and Space Administration and the Air Force in 1969 to become executive secretary of the National Aeronautics and Space Council. He served as a member of the Atomic Energy Commission (1973–74) and of the Nuclear Regulatory Commission (1974–76); as U.S. ambassador to Norway (1976–77); and as general manager of the Nuclear Products Division of General Electric Company (from 1977).

Anders, Władysław (b. Aug. 11, 1892, Błonie, Pol.—d. May 12, 1970, London), army officer who commanded the Polish forces in the Middle East and Italy during World War II and became a leading figure among the anti-Communist Poles who refused to return to their homeland after the war.

After service in the Russian Army during World War I, Anders entered the armed forces of the newly reconstituted Polish state and fought the Red Army in the Russo-Polish War of 1919–20. Campaigning against both Germany and the Soviet Union at the outbreak of World War II (September 1939), he was captured by the U.S.S.R. and imprisoned until the Polish-Soviet agreement of August 1941. Allowed to form a Polish fighting force on Russian soil from former prisoners of war and deportees, Anders soon had 80,000 men, but he realized that he had no chance of liberating Poland from the East with an army now under Soviet control. As a result of both Polish and British pressure, Stalin allowed Anders to march into Iran and Iraq (1942). The Poles subsequently distinguished themselves in the Italian campaign, capturing Monte Cassino. A staunch anti-Communist, Anders remained in Great Britain after World War II; the new Communist Polish government deprived him of his citizenship in 1946. Thereafter he became a prominent leader of Polish exiles in the West.

Andersen, Hans Christian (b. April 2, 1805, Odense, near Copenhagen, Den.—d. Aug. 4, 1875, Copenhagen), unique master of the fairy tale whose stories are famous throughout the world; he is also the author of plays, novels, poems, travel books, and several autobiographies. While many of these works are almost unknown outside Denmark, his fairy tales are among the most frequently translated works in all literary history.

Andersen was born in a slum and had a difficult battle breaking through the rigid class structure of his time. The first significant help came from Jonas Collin, one of the directors of the Royal Theatre in Copenhagen, to which Andersen had gone as a youth in vain hopes of winning fame as an actor. Collin raised money to send him to school. Although school was an unhappy experience for Andersen because of an unpleasant headmaster, it allowed him to be admitted to the University of Copenhagen in 1828.

The next year he produced what is considered his first important literary work, *Fodrejse fra Holmens Kanal til Østpynten af Amager i aarene 1828 og 1829* (1829; "A Walk from Holmen's Canal to the East Point of the Island of Amager in the Years 1828 and 1829"), a fantastic tale in the style of the German writer E.T.A. Hoffmann. This work was an immediate success. He then turned to playwriting. After two unsuccessful attempts, he achieved recognition for *Mulatten* (1840; "The Mulatto"), a play portraying the evils of slavery, but the theatre was not to become his field, and for a long time Andersen was regarded primarily as a novelist. Most of his novels

Hans Christian Andersen
The Bettmann Archive

are autobiographical; among the best known are *Improvisatoren* (1835; *The Improvisators,* 1845), *O.T.* (1836; Eng. trans., 1845), and *Kun en spillemand* (1837; *Only a Fiddler,* 1845). He also published numerous accounts of his travels abroad.

The first *Eventyr, fortalte for børn* ("Tales, Told for Children"), including such stories as "The Tinderbox," "Little Claus and Big Claus," "The Princess and the Pea," and "Little Ida's Flowers," was published in 1835, but it was not until some eight years later that Andersen's tales won real acclaim. Although often based on folk legend, the tales were informed by moral realism rather than wish fulfillment. New collections appeared in 1843, 1847, and 1852. The genre was expanded in *Nye eventyr og historier* (1858–72). While some tales reveal an optimistic belief in the victory of goodness and beauty (*e.g.,* "The Snow Queen"), others are deeply pessimistic and end unhappily. A strong autobiographical element runs through these sadder tales. Never satisfied that he was completely accepted, Andersen suffered in his closest personal relationships. He never married, although he was deeply in love several times, notably with the famed Swedish singer Jenny Lind.

Because Andersen rarely destroyed anything he wrote, his diaries and thousands of his letters are available to posterity, as well as his literary production. The picture that these reveal is one of an ambitious, high-strung and neurotic man, vain, sensitive, quick-witted, and with remarkable powers of observation.

A real innovator in his method of telling tales, he used the idioms and constructions of the spoken language, thus breaking with the literary tradition of his time.

Elias Bredsdorff's, *Hans Christian Andersen: The Story of His Life and Work* was published in 1975.

Andersen, Tryggve (b. Sept. 27, 1866, Ringsaker, Nor.—d. April 10, 1920, Gran), novelist and short-story writer of the Neoromantic movement in Norway who depicted the conflict between the bureaucratic and peasant cultures.

Born on a farm and educated at the University of Kristiania, Andersen was an office worker. The young Andersen was fascinated with German Romanticists, especially the fantastic tales of E.T.A. Hoffmann, but Gotthold E. Lessing developed his interest in literature and style. In his main work, *I cancelliraadens dage* (1897; *In the Days of the Counsellor,* 1969), short stories tied together by their central figure, Andersen portrayed the world of the rural civil servants in Norway. His other novel *Mot kvæld* (1900; "Toward Evening"), dealt with the cultural gulf between the intellectual and the people. He also published four volumes of short stories. His diary of a sea voyage after the death of his wife and a son in 1902, *Dagbog fra en sjoreise,* appeared in 1923.

Andersen's disease, also called GLYCOGENOSIS TYPE IV, rare hereditary disease produced by absence of the enzyme amylo-1:4,1:6-

transglucosidase, an essential mediator of the synthesis of glycogen. An abnormal form of glycogen is produced and accumulates in body tissues, particularly in the liver. Affected children appear normal at birth but fail to thrive and later lose muscle tone, becoming lethargic. The liver and spleen become enlarged, and progressive liver failure occurs prior to death, usually before age two, caused by heart failure or bleeding from the esophagus. Because Andersen's disease is so rare, the pattern of inheritance is not certain; it is believed to be an autosomal recessive trait, as are most similar enzyme defects.

A list of the abbreviations used in the MICROPAEDIA *will be found at the end of this volume*

Anderson, city, seat (1828) of Madison County, east central Indiana, U.S., on the West Fork of White River, in a corn- and wheat-producing region, 38 mi (61 km) northeast of Indianapolis. Founded in 1823 on the site of a Delaware Indian village, it was named Andersontown for a subchief, Koktowhanund, also known as William Anderson. In 1886 the town's industrial growth was assured with the discovery of natural gas. Manufactures now include automobile parts and fire trucks. Anderson College was established in 1917 as the Anderson Bible Training School by the Church of God whose world headquarters it is. Mounds State Park, 3 mi east, contains the largest known single earthwork in Indiana as well as several other prehistoric mounds. Inc. 1838, again in 1865. Pop. (1980) 64,695.

Anderson, city, seat (1826) of Anderson County, in northwestern South Carolina, U.S., in the foothills of the Blue Ridge Mountains. It was founded in 1826 on what had been Cherokee Indian land, and its original settlers were mostly descendants of Scots-Irish migrants from Virginia and Pennsylvania. Named for a local Revolutionary War hero, Gen. Robert Anderson, it has been called the "electric city" because of early (1898) long-distance power transmission from the Seneca River.

Anderson is a manufacturing centre, with a long-established textile industry; newer industries include the production of glass fibre, metals, and electrical machinery and parts. Cotton growing, once preeminent, has yielded to the cultivation of wheat, soybeans, and market vegetables. Tree farming to supply paper mills and livestock (beef and dairy cattle) raising are also significant. Anderson College (1911; Baptist) began in 1848 as the Johnson Female Seminary. Clemson University (1889) is 18 mi (29 km) northwest of Anderson. Forrest College, a business training school, opened in 1946. The Hartwell Dam and Reservoir (1962), on the Savannah River, provides power and recreation facilities. Inc. 1882. Pop. (1980) city, 27,313; metropolitan area (SMSA), 133,235.

Anderson, Carl David (b. Sept. 3, 1905, New York City), physicist who shared the Nobel Prize for Physics in 1936 for his discovery of the positron, or anti-electron, the first known particle of antimatter.

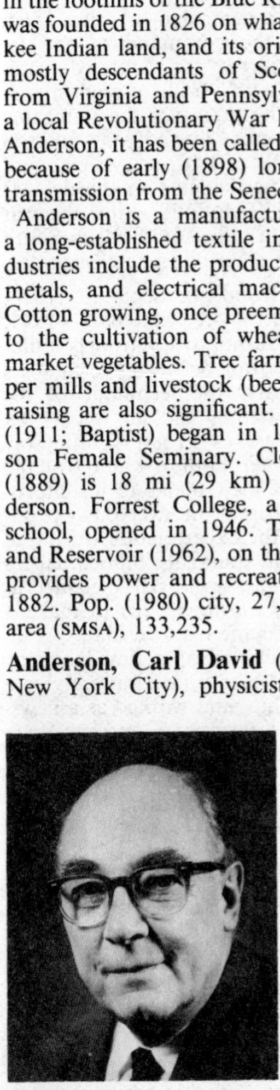

Carl David Anderson
Harvey of Pasadena

He received his Ph.D. in 1930 from the California Institute of Technology, Pasadena, where he spent his entire career, becoming professor emeritus in 1976. Having studied X-ray photoelectrons (electrons ejected from atoms by interaction with high-energy photons) since 1927, he began research in 1930 on gamma rays and cosmic rays, utilizing the magnetic cloud chamber. In 1932 Anderson discovered the positron in the course of cosmic-ray interaction studies and one year later succeeded in producing positrons by gamma irradiation. In 1936 he participated in the discovery of the muon, an elementary particle about 207 times as massive as the electron.

Anderson, Elizabeth Garrett (b. June 9, 1836, Aldeburgh, Suffolk, Eng.—d. Dec. 17, 1917, Aldeburgh), physician who sought admission of women to professional education, especially in medicine.

Refused admission to medical schools, she began, in 1860, to study privately with accredited physicians and in London hospitals and was licensed to practice in 1865 by the Society of Apothecaries. She was appointed (1866) general medical attendant to St. Mary's Dispensary, later the New Hospital for Women, where she worked to create a medical school for women. In 1918 the hospital was renamed Elizabeth Garrett Anderson Hospital in her honour.

Anderson received the M.D. degree from the University of Paris in 1870, and in 1908 she became the first woman mayor of Aldeburgh.

Anderson, John Henry (b. July 14, 1814, Craigmyle, Aberdeen, Scot.—d. Feb. 5, 1874, Darlington, Durham, Eng.), conjurer and actor, the first magician to demonstrate and exploit the value of advertising. Described on playbills as "Professor Anderson, the Wizard of the North," he first performed in 1831. Seasons at Edinburgh (1837) and Glasgow (1838–39) followed. In London (1840) he fascinated audiences with the most elaborate collection of magical apparatus ever seen there. During a tour in the United States (1851–53) Anderson first demonstrated his famous "gun trick," by which he appeared to catch a bullet fired by someone in the audience. Returning to Great Britain he performed before Queen Victoria, then took the title role in the melodrama *Rob Roy* at the Lyceum and Covent Garden theatres (1855–56). The three-day "Grand Carnival" with which the Covent Garden seasons were concluded ended in disaster in 1857 when Anderson attempted to dispel drunken revellers by lowering the gaslights. The ceiling caught fire, and the theatre was burned down. This only added to his fame, and he continued to tour widely, his style of presentation gradually becoming less flamboyant.

Anderson, Dame Judith, original name FRANCES MARGARET ANDERSON (b. Feb. 10, 1898, Adelaide, S.Aus., Australia), stage and motion-picture actress.

She was only 17 years of age when she first made her stage debut in 1915 in Sydney and 20 when she first appeared in New York City. Her portrayal of Lavinia in the 1932 *Mourning Becomes Electra* led to her first starring role in motion pictures in *Blood Money* (1933). Her interpretation of Gertrude in John Gielgud's 1936 *Hamlet* and her starring performance in the title role of *Medea* in 1947 are considered the pinnacles of her stage career.

Anderson specialized in character portrayals and was at her best in roles that hinted of evil. She is most remembered for her role as Mrs. Danvers in *Rebecca* (1940) and Ann Treadwell in *Laura* (1944). She made a memorable television performance in 1960, when she played Lady Macbeth opposite Maurice Evans in *Macbeth,* and, in the same year, Queen Elizabeth II named her Dame Commander of the British Empire. In 1965 she retired temporarily but returned in 1970 to play the title role of *Hamlet* on the stage and to film one of her most difficult roles, that of Buffalo Cow Head in *A Man Called Horse,* in which her dialogue was entirely in Sioux. One of her later films, *Inn of the Damned* (1974), was made in her native Australia.

Anderson, Lindsay (Gordon) (b. April 17, 1923, Bangalore, India), English writer, critic, and motion-picture director whose artistic talents helped shape the renewal of vitality in British stage and motion-picture productions during the Free Cinema movement that began in the 1950s.

Anderson received a degree in English from Oxford and in 1947 became a founding editor of the anti-establishment film magazine *Sequence,* which lasted until 1951. Subsequently he wrote for *Sight and Sound,* published by the British Film Institute, and various other journals. As a director, Anderson began his career making short documentaries for an industrial firm. In 1955 he won an Academy Award for his short documentary *Thursday's Children,* and in 1955–56 he directed the first five episodes of a British television series, *The Adventures of Robin Hood.* The term Free Cinema, coined by Anderson in 1956, drew greater attention to his ongoing criticism of the British cinema. This movement was part of a larger ferment signalled by John Osborne's play *Look Back in Anger* (1959). Members of the Free Cinema movement allied themselves with the emerging new left in politics and took their themes from contemporary working-class life.

The motion picture *This Sporting Life* (1963), adapted by David Storey from his novel about a miner who becomes a success as a professional rugby player, was Anderson's first feature film and won the International Critics Award. *If. . .* (1968), which won the Cannes Film Festival's Golden Palm award, is the story of three English public-school students who rebel against rigid authority and discipline, plot an armed rebellion, and on Speech Day massacre the parents, teachers, and other students.

For the stage Anderson directed the *Diary of a Madman* at the Royal Court Theatre (1963), *Julius Caesar* at the British National Theatre (1964), *The Cherry Orchard* (1966), and the first Polish production of John Osborne's *Nit Do Obrony* (1966; *Inadmissible Evidence*) in Warsaw. At the Royal Court Theatre, where Anderson was coartistic director, he directed *In Celebration* and *The Contractor* in 1969 and *Home* in 1970. Other stage productions include *What the Butler Saw* (1975), *The Bed Before Yesterday, The Kingfisher* (1977), *Alice's Boys* (1978), *Early Days* (1980), and *Hamlet* (1981).

Anderson's subsequent films, *O Lucky Man!* (1973), *In Celebration* (1975), and *Britannia Hospital* (1982) were praised by the critics for their impressive virtuosity. Anderson served as governor of the British Film Institute and as a juror at many of the world's major film festivals.

Anderson, Marian (b. Feb. 17, 1902, Philadelphia), singer, one of the finest contraltos of her time.

Born of poor black parents, she received her earliest musical training in the choir of the Union Baptist Church, which she joined when she was six, already having displayed a remarkable voice. Her church raised enough money for her to take private voice lessons.

In 1925 her teacher entered her in a contest for an appearance at Lewisohn Stadium in New York City with the New York Philharmonic Orchestra. She was placed first among

300 competitors. She had already made several concert tours and, despite struggles against poverty and racial discrimination, was beginning to make a name for herself. Real success came after several trips to Europe between 1925 and 1935, during which time she expanded and deepened her experience as a performer. After her return to New York City in 1935 she achieved even greater success.

In 1939 she was prohibited, because of her race, from singing at Constitution Hall in Washington, D.C. As a demonstration of protest, a group of citizens including Eleanor Roosevelt arranged a concert at the Lincoln Memorial that drew an audience of 75,000. She was asked to sing at the White House and was the first black to sing at the Metropolitan Opera in New York City, making her debut in 1955 as Ulrica in Verdi's *Un ballo in maschera* (*A Masked Ball*).

Marian Anderson
By courtesy of RCA Records

She is acclaimed for her work in behalf of black people and for her warmth of personality as well as for her vocal and interpretative powers. As a singer, her outstanding characteristics are wide range, richness and purity of tone, and mastery of a variety of styles. She wrote an autobiography, *My Lord, What a Morning* (1957), and retired in 1965. In 1978 U.S. Pres. Jimmy Carter presented her with a Congressional gold medal bearing her profile.

Anderson, Mary (b. July 28, 1859, Sacramento, Calif., U.S.—d. May 29, 1940, Broadway, Worcestershire, Eng.), actress who achieved great popularity because of her great beauty and highly successful publicity.

Acclaimed by the public from the time of her debut in Louisville, Ky., at the age of 16, she remained popular throughout her career despite critics' complaints that she lacked feeling. Among her most famous roles were Galatea in W.S. Gilbert's *Pygmalion and Galatea;* Clarice in his *Comedy and Tragedy,* written especially for her; Hermione and Perdita in her own arrangement of Shakespeare's *Winter's Tale;* Lady Macbeth in *Macbeth;* and Ion in Sir Thomas Noon Talfourd's *Ion.* In 1889 she suffered a nervous breakdown and temporarily retired, settling in England in 1890. She returned to the stage in 1903 and remained active in the theatre until after World War I. She wrote *A Few Memories* (1896) and *A Few More Memories* (1936).

Anderson, Maxie, byname of MAX LEROY ANDERSON (b. Sept. 10, 1934, Sayre, Okla., U.S.—d. June 27, 1983, near Bad Brückenau, W.Ger.), balloonist who, with Ben Abruzzo and Larry Newman, made the first transatlantic balloon flight and, with his son Kristian, made the first nonstop trans-North American balloon flight.

Anderson entered the Missouri Military Academy, Mexico, Mo., at the age of eight and throughout his schooling (B.S. in industrial engineering, 1956, University of North Dakota, Grand Forks) worked summers with his father, a pipeline builder. The son held a pilot's license at the age of 15, having lied about his age. By the age of 29 he owned his own mining company in Albuquerque, N.M. He began flying hot-air balloons in New Mexico, alone and with his friend Ben Abruzzo, a fellow Albuquerquan and real-estate developer, who was also a light-aircraft flyer (planes, gliders, and helicopters). In 1977 they decided to attempt the transatlantic flight in honour of the 50th anniversary of Charles Lindbergh's flight to Le Bourget field near Paris. Ed Yost, balloonist and balloon builder, whose transatlantic flight had failed in 1958, built the "Double Eagle," a helium balloon, for them and trained them to fly it. They launched the "Double Eagle" from near Marshfield, Mass., on Sept. 9, 1977, but had to set down off the coast of Iceland on September 13. In 1978 a third crew member was added, Larry Newman, head of the Electra Flyer Corporation, a maker of hang gliders, who applied his expertise to the building of the "Double Eagle II." On August 11 it was launched from Presque Isle, Maine, and landed near Miserey, Fr., on August 17. Charles McCarry's *Double Eagle: Ben Abruzzo, Maxie Anderson, Larry Newman* was published in 1979.

On May 8, 1980, Anderson and his son Kristian launched the helium balloon "Kitty Hawk" from Fort Baker, Calif., and landed, on May 12, at Ste. Félicité, Que., Can., the first trans-North American nonstop balloon flight.

Anderson was killed in an accident during a balloon race.

Anderson, Maxwell (b. Dec. 15, 1888, Atlantic, Pa., U.S.—d. Feb. 28, 1959, Stamford, Conn.), prolific playwright noted for his efforts to make verse tragedy a popular form.

Anderson was educated at the University of North Dakota and Stanford University. He collaborated with Laurence Stallings in the World War I comedy *What Price Glory?* (1924), his first hit, a realistically ribald and profane view of World War I. Anderson's prestige was increased by two ambitious historical dramas in verse—*Elizabeth the Queen* (1930) and *Mary of Scotland* (1933)—and by a success of a very different nature, his humorous Pulitzer Prize winning prose satire, *Both Your Houses* (1933), an attack on venality in the U.S. Congress. He reached the peak of his career with *Winterset* (1935), a poetic drama set in his own times. A tragedy inspired by the Sacco and Vanzetti case of the 1920s and set in the urban slums, it deals with the son of a man who has been unjustly condemned to death, who seeks revenge and vindication of his father's name. *High Tor* (1936), a romantic comedy in verse, expressed the author's displeasure with modern materialism. Collaborating with the German refugee composer Kurt Weill (1900–50), Anderson also wrote for the musical theatre a play based on early New York history, *Knickerbocker Holiday* (1938), and *Lost in the Stars* (1949), a dramatization of Alan Paton's South African novel *Cry, the Beloved Country.* His last play, *The Bad Seed* (1954), was a dramatization of William March's novel about an evil child.

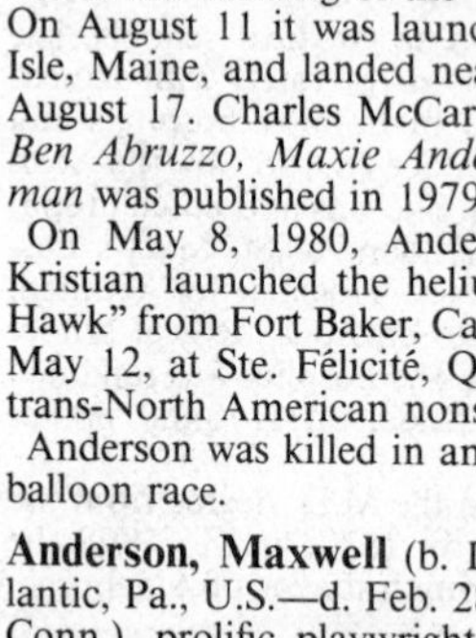

Maxwell Anderson
Brown Brothers

Anderson, Philip W(arren) (b. Dec. 13, 1923, Indianapolis, Ind., U.S.), physicist who won a Nobel Prize for his part in the development of advanced electronic circuitry.

Educated at Harvard University, where he received his doctorate in 1949, Anderson that year joined Bell Telephone Laboratories in Murray Hill, N.J. From 1975 he divided his time between Bell and Princeton University, where he was professor of physics. For his research in solid state physics, which made possible the development of inexpensive electronic switching and memory devices in computers, he was awarded jointly with John H. Van Vleck and Sir Nevill F. Mott the 1977 Nobel Prize for Physics. His writings include *Absence of Diffusion in Certain Random Lattices* (1958) and *Concepts of Solids* (1963). Anderson was a certified first degree-master of the Japanese board game Go.

Anderson, Richard Heron (b. Oct. 7, 1821, Statesburg, S.C., U.S.—d. June 26, 1879, Beaufort, S.C.), Confederate general in the American Civil War.

He graduated from the U.S. Military Academy at West Point in 1842 and won the brevet of first lieutenant in the Mexican War, becoming first lieutenant in 1848 and captain in 1855; he took part in the following year in the Kansas troubles. At the outbreak of the Civil War in 1861 he resigned from the U.S. Army and entered the Confederate service as a brigadier general, being promoted major general on July 14, 1862. Except for a few months spent with the army under Braxton Bragg in 1862, Anderson's service was wholly in the Army of Northern Virginia under Gen. Robert E. Lee.

In the Wilderness campaign, in May 1864, he succeeded to the command of the 1st Corps when Longstreet was wounded. After saving Spotsylvania by a brilliant night march on May 7–8, at the outset of the punishing Battle of Spotsylvania Courthouse, Anderson was given the rank of temporary lieutenant general. He later participated in the defense of Petersburg and Richmond. After the war Anderson became a railroad official in South Carolina and then state phosphate inspector.

Anderson, Sherwood (b. Sept. 13, 1876, Camden, Ohio, U.S.—d. March 8, 1941, Colon, Panama), author who strongly influenced American writing between World Wars I and II, particularly the technique of the short story. His writing had an impact on such notable writers as Ernest Hemingway and William Faulkner, both of whom owe the first publication of their books to his efforts. His prose style, based on everyday speech and derived from the experimental writing of Gertrude Stein, was markedly influential on the early Hemingway—who parodied it cruelly in *Torrents of Spring* (1926) to make a clean break and become his own man.

One of seven children of a day labourer, Anderson attended school intermittently as a youth in Clyde, Ohio, and worked as a newsboy, house painter, farmhand, and racetrack helper. After a year at Wittenberg Academy, a preparatory school in Springfield, Ohio, he worked as an advertising writer in Chicago until 1906, when he went back to Ohio and for the next six years sought—without success—to prosper as a businessman while writing fiction in his spare time. A paint manufacturer in Elyria, Ohio, one day in 1912 he left his office abruptly and wandered off, turning up four days later in Cleveland, dishevelled and mentally distraught. He later said he deliberately staged this episode in order to get away from the business world and devote himself to literature.

Anderson went back to his advertising job in Chicago and remained there until he began to earn enough from his published work to quit. Encouraged by Dreiser, Floyd Dell, Carl Sandburg, and Ben Hecht—leaders of the Chicago literary movement—he began to contribute experimental verse and short fiction to *The Little Review, The Masses,* the *Seven Arts,* and *Poetry.* Dell and Dreiser arranged the publication of his first two novels, *Windy McPherson's Son* (1916; rev. 1921) and *Marching Men* (1917), both written while he was still a manufacturer.

Winesburg, Ohio was his first mature book and made his reputation as an author. Its interrelated short sketches and tales are told by a newspaper reporter-narrator who is as emotionally stunted in some ways as the people he describes. Anderson saw the prime cause of the stultification of village life in the rise of industrialization, a process he studied in his novel *Poor White* (1920).

His novels include *Many Marriages* (1923), which stresses the need for sexual fulfillment; *Dark Laughter* (1925), which values the "primitive" over the civilized; and *Beyond Desire* (1932), a novel of Southern textile mill labour struggles.

His best work is generally thought to be in his short stories, collected in *Winesburg, Ohio, The Triumph of the Egg* (1921), *Horses and Men* (1923), and *Death in the Woods* (1933) and including such frequently anthologized tales as "I Want to Know Why," "I'm a Fool," and "Brother Death." Also valued are the autobiographical sketches *A Story Teller's Story* (1924), *Tar: A Midwest Childhood* (1926), and the posthumous *Memoirs* (1942; critical edition 1969). A selection of his *Letters* appeared in 1953.

Andersonville, village, Sumter County, southwest central Georgia, U.S., best known as the site of a Confederate military prison from February 1864 until May 1865. Inadequate conditions at the prison leading to the death of nearly 13,000 Union prisoners evoked bitter controversy on both sides and resulted in the post-Civil War trial and hanging of Capt. Henry Wirz, prison commander. Preserved as the Andersonville National Historic Site, the area contains Providence Spring, which erupted after a prayer vigil by the prisoners during the drought of August 1864; the Andersonville National Cemetery, with the graves of more than 14,000 Civil War and other veterans; and the Sundial Monument honouring Clara Barton, who led a campaign to mark the graves of Federal soldiers. Pop. (1980) 267.

Anderssen, Adolf (b. July 6, 1818, Breslau, Prussia—d. March 13, 1879, Breslau), Chess master considered the world's strongest player from his victory in the first modern international tournament (London, 1851) until his defeat (1858) by Paul Morphy in match play; and again, after Morphy's retirement (*c.* 1861) until his defeat by Wilhelm Steinitz (1866). Anderssen was noted for his ability to discover combination plays calculated to force an immediate decision. One of his famous games was dubbed the Immortal Game. Anderssen studied mathematics and philosophy and taught mathematics and German at the Friedrichs Gymnasium in Breslau.

Andersson, Dan(iel) (b. April 6, 1888, Skattlösbergett, Swed.—d. Sept. 20, 1920, Stockholm), poet and prose writer, an early practitioner of working class literature who became one of the few Swedish poets really loved by the common people.

Born to a very poor family, he was a woodsman and charcoal burner before he became a temperance lecturer. His first two published volumes, which made the charcoal burners and, incidentally, himself famous, were *Kolarhistorier* (1914; "Charcoal Burner's Tales") and *Kolvaktarens visor* (1915; "Charcoal Watcher's Songs"; a selection was translated into English in *Charcoal Burner's Ballad & Other Poems,* 1943). He published one more book of poems during his lifetime, *Svarta ballader* (1917; "Black Ballads"), and two autobiographical novels, *De tre hemlösa* (1918; "The Three Homeless Ones") and *David Ramms arv* (1919; "David Ramm's Heritage"). A considerable part of his verse and prose was published after his death in *Efterskörd* (1929; "Late Harvest") and *Tryck och Otrycke* (1942; "Printed and Unprinted").

Andersson, Johan Gunnar (b. July 3, 1874, Knista, Swed.—d. Oct. 29, 1960, Stockholm), geologist and archaeologist whose work laid the foundation for the study of prehistoric China. In 1921, at a cave near Chou-k'ou-tien in the vicinity of Peking, on the basis of bits of quartz that he found in a limestone region, he predicted that a fossil man would be discovered. Six years later the first evidence of the fossil hominid *Sinanthropus* (Peking man) was found there.

He first went to China in 1914 as a technical adviser on oil and coal resources. He immediately became interested in fossil remains and eventually devoted himself to archaeological exploration. In 1921, at Yang-shao-ts'un, Honan Province, he found elegant painted pottery that provided the first evidence of Neolithic culture in China. Within a year he discovered many other comparable sites across the vast stretch of the Yellow River Valley of northern China and published a preliminary account of his findings, *An Early Chinese Culture* (1923). His study helped to define what is now termed Yang-shao culture, which he related to the cultures of southwest Asia and dated at about 3000–1500 BC. Of his bronze findings, none could be dated earlier than about 1300 BC, during the period of the Shang dynasty. He described his progress as an archaeologist in *Children of the Yellow Earth: Studies in Prehistoric China* (1934).

Andes, Army of the, military force of 3,500 soldiers organized by the South American independence leader José de San Martín, who led it from Argentina across the Andes mountains (1817) to liberate Chile from Spanish colonial rule. San Martín's strategic problem was to coordinate the difficult passage across the Andes of four columns, two major ones, the first under Generals Miguel Soler and Bernardo O'Higgins, and the second under Juan Las Heras; and two smaller wing divisions. All four columns had to execute the month-long march by different routes and appear in Chilean territory between Feb. 6 and 8, 1817.

The success of this operation established San Martín as a great general. On February 12 the rebels met a Spanish army under Gen. Raphael Maroto at Chacabuco. San Martín divided his forces into two wings under Soler and O'Higgins, respectively. O'Higgins attacked prematurely, narrowly averting defeat. When Soler appeared, O'Higgins was able to regroup and mount a two-battalion bayonet charge which left the Spaniards surrounded. The victorious San Martín entered Santiago, Chile, on February 14.

Andes Mountain Ranges, also called ANDES, Spanish CORDILLERA DE LOS ANDES, or LOS ANDES, great mountain system of South America and one of the great natural features of the globe, stretching the length of the South American continent from Lago (Lake) de Maracaibo in the north to the Tierra del Fuego archipelago in the south.

The following article summarizes information about the Andes Mountain Ranges; for full details, *see* MACROPAEDIA: South America.

Occupying significant portions of seven countries, the Andes may be separated, from north to south, into six major subdivisions: the Venezuelan Cordillera, the Colombian cordilleras, the Ecuadorian Andes, the Peruvian Andes, the Central Andes, and the Patagonian Andes. The Venezuelan Cordillera separates the Orinoco Basin from Lago de Maracaibo and the Caribbean Sea as it extends southwestward to join the eastern segment of the Colombian ranges (Cordillera Oriental). The Colombian cordilleras, consisting of three or four ranges, extend finger-like northeastward from Nudo de los Pastos (a mountain knot) at the Ecuadorian border to dominate the Colombian landscape. The Ecuadorian Andes is composed of a large plateau (often called the Avenida de los Volcanes) that runs from north to south and extends between two chains of high volcanic peaks (the Cordilleras Occidental and Central). A third, low-lying range, the Cordillera Oriental, does not exceed 7,900 ft (2,400 m) and was only recently discovered within the Ecuadorian rain forests. The cordilleras of the Peruvian Andes turn generally southeastward along three distinctive ranges, dominated for the most part by the western Cordillera Occidental. The Peruvian and the Central Andes merge and widen at the Altiplano (among the world's largest interior basins, extending south and southeastward some 500 mi (800 km) across the Peruvian and Bolivian frontier) which contains the 110-mi-long Lake Titicaca, the highest navigable lake in the world. Before narrowing again southward, the Andes enter northern Argentina, occupying its northwestern provinces. The Patagonian Andes, forming some of the most rugged terrain of the entire South American cordilleras, provide the boundary between Chile and Argentina from Bolivia south through Tierra del Fuego. The highest peak of the Andes, Mt. Aconcagua, rises to 22,834 ft (6,960 m) above sea level within these southern ranges.

andesine, variety of the feldspar mineral plagioclase (*q.v.*).

andesite, any member of a large family of rocks that occur in most of the world's volcanic areas. Andesites occur mainly as surface deposits and, to a lesser extent, as dikes and small plugs. Many of the deposits are not normal lava flows but rather flow breccias, mudflows, tuffs, and other fragmental rocks; the peperino near Rome and the trass of the Eifel district in West Germany are examples. Not only the Andes, where the name was first applied to a series of lavas, but most of the cordillera (parallel mountain chains) of Central and North America consist largely of andesites. The same rock type occurs in abundance in volcanoes along practically the entire margin of the Pacific Basin. The volcanoes Montagne Pelée, the Soufrière of St. Vincent, Krakatoa, Bandai-san, Popocatépetl, Fuji, Ngauruhoe, Shasta, Hood, and Adams have emitted great quantities of andesitic rock.

Andesite most commonly denotes fine-grained, usually porphyritic rocks; in composition these correspond roughly to the intrusive igneous rock diorite and consist essentially of andesine (a plagioclase feldspar) and one or more ferromagnesian minerals, such as pyroxene or biotite. Smaller amounts of sanidine, a potassium-rich feldspar, may be present. The larger crystals of feldspar and ferromagnesian minerals are often visible to the naked eye; they lie in a finer groundmass, usually crystalline, but sometimes glassy.

There are three subdivisions of this rock family: the quartz-bearing andesites, or dacites, sometimes considered to be a separate family; the hornblende- and biotite-andesites; and the pyroxene-andesites. The dacites (*q.v.*) contain primary quartz, which may appear in small blebs or crystals or only as minute interstitial grains in the groundmass. The hornblende- and biotite-andesites are comparatively rich in feldspar and are usually pale pink, yellow, or gray. Pyroxene-andesites are the commonest type of andesite and occur in amounts comparable to basalt. They are darker, denser, more basic rocks.

The geographic line that separates the andesite–dacite–rhyolite rock association of the Pacific margin from the olivine basalt–trachyte rock association of the Pacific Basin islands is known as the andesite line. This line, mainly determined petrographically, runs on the western side of the Pacific from Alaska to east of New Zealand via Japan, the Marianas, the Palau Islands, the Bismarck Archipelago, the Fiji Islands, and the Tonga Islands. East of the Pacific the line is less well defined but probably follows the west coasts of North and South America; the line's position in the South Pacific has not been determined.

Andfjorden, fjord, in the Norwegian Sea, indenting northwestern Norway, between the islands of Andøya (west) and Senja (east). The fjord, divided between Nordland and Troms *fylker* (counties), penetrates into the offshore island of Hinnøya in the south, where it is called Gullesfjorden. Its total length is about 55 mi (90 km) from its broad opening into the Norwegian Sea at the Andenes lighthouse on Andøya to its head in the interior of Hinnøya (*q.v.*), the largest Norwegian island except Svalbard (Spitsbergen).

Andhra (India): *see* Telingāna.

Andhra Pradesh, constituent state of the Republic of India, located in the southeastern part of the Indian subcontinent. It is bounded by the states of Tamil Nādu to the south; Karnātaka to the west; and Mahārāshtra, Madhya Pradesh, and Orissa to the north. The Bay of Bengal bounds the state to the east. Its name derives from the Andhra people who have long inhabited the area and have their own language, Telugu.

The following article summarizes the administrative history, geography, demographic patterns, economy, and culture of modern Andhra Pradesh; for additional treatment of its geography and history, *see* MACROPAEDIA: India.

A number of dynasties ruled in the area, dating back to the 3rd century BC, and Buddhism prospered there. Rulers during the 12th and 13th centuries expanded Andhra power, which reached its peak in the 16th century. The Andhras came under British influence in the 17th century, then played a decisive role in the rise of Indian nationalism in the 19th. Pride in their historical and linguistic achievements led them to demand a separate state, and the state in its present form dates from 1956.

Three main physiographic regions characterize Andhra Pradesh: a coastal plain to the east, running from the Bay of Bengal to the mountain ranges; the Eastern Ghāts, the mountains; and a plateau to the west of the Ghāts. Summer lasts from March to June; a period of tropical rains follows from July to September; and winter begins in October and concludes in February. Andhra Pradesh thus has three seasons. Maximum and minimum temperatures range from 74° to 82° F (23° to 28° C) and from 50° to 53° F (10° to 12° C), with summers cooler and winters colder on the plateau. The southwest monsoon causes the most rainfall, which ranges from a maximum of 55 in. (1,400 mm) to 20 in. annually. Rainfall is heavy in the coastal area.

The state's cultural pattern is revealed by the distribution of its languages and religions. Eighty-six percent of the people speak Telugu, and about 7 percent speak Urdū, largely the language of the Muslim population. The remaining groups consist of people speaking border-area languages, including Tamil, Kannaḍa, and such tribal languages as Lambadi.

Some 70 percent of the Andhra Pradesh population is engaged in agriculture, which accounts for 50 percent of the state's income. About a third of the agricultural area is devoted to producing food grains, yielding some 5,000,000 tons of rice alone each year. Andhra Pradesh produces 95 percent of the total Virginia tobacco of the country and is the second largest rice-producing state in India. Other crops include castor seed and sugarcane, along with chilies, oilseeds, peas, beans, and lentils. The deltas of the Godāvari and Krishna rivers in the central part of the alluvial coastal plains contain especially fertile soil. Forested areas yield timber and forest products.

Andhra Pradesh contains such minerals as asbestos, mica, manganese, barite, coal, and low-grade iron ore but is industrially underdeveloped, manufacturing accounting for no more than 10 percent of its income. Government-run industries include shipbuilding, aeronautics, electrical equipment, machine tools, cement, and drugs; private-sector activities include chemical and textile production. As a means of stimulating industry, Andhra Pradesh has in recent years increased its hydroelectric and thermoelectric generating capacity by 1,600,000 kW. The state's rail system amounts to more than 5,000 mi (12,700 km) of track, and Andhra Pradesh has four airports—at Hyderābād (the capital), Vijayawāda, Tirupati, and Vishākhapatnam.

The Andhra people have made major contributions to India's culture in the realms of art, architecture, music, dance, and literature, and the arts and literature of Andhra Pradesh thrive under both state and private sponsorship. The *kuchipudy* dance style is unique in the Indian tradition, and Telugu—one of the four literary languages of the Dravidian family—occupies a prestigious position among Indian languages. Folk culture predominates in rural areas, through such forms as minstrel-ballad performances, puppet shows, and mythological storytelling. These forms also appear frequently in social and political communication. Radio broadcasting from such cities as Hyderābād and Cuddapah has effected a rural-urban cultural exchange—rural residents becoming acquainted with the classical culture, city dwellers learning about folkways.

Andhra Pradesh has universities at Hyderābād, Waltair, Warangal, Guntur, Anantpur, and Tirupati. An agricultural university is at Hyderābād. Colleges affiliated with those universities total more than 200. Various industrial-training institutes provide vocational education. Area 106,204 sq mi (275,068 sq km). Pop. (1981 prelim.) 53,549,673.

Andizhan, also spelled ANDIŽAN, *oblast* (administrative region), Uzbek Soviet Socialist Republic, with an area of 1,600 sq mi (4,200 sq km). Located in eastern Fergana Valley, it consists of a plain in the west and the foothills of the Fergana and Alay mountains in the east. The chief river is the Karadarya (*darya*, river), a tributary of the Syrdarya. The *oblast* is also traversed by the Bolshoy (Great) and Yuzhny (Southern) Fergana and Bolshoy Andizhan trunk irrigation canals. The climate is continental, with hot summers and relatively cold winters; precipitation is about 8–12 in. (about 200–300 mm) a year. More than half the territory is irrigated; cotton, grapes, and fruit are major crops, and silkworms are raised there. The *oblast* is the main oil-producing area of Uzbekistan, and natural gas is extracted at Khodzhaabad. Other industry is largely concerned with processing raw cotton and other agricultural products and with producing irrigation equipment. The population of Andizhan *oblast* was more than 30 percent urban in 1983. It is the most densely settled region in the Soviet Union. Uzbeks account for over four-fifths of the number. Major cities are Andizhan (*q.v.*), the administrative centre, and Leninsk. Pop. (1983 est.) 1,481,000.

Andizhan, also spelled ANDIŽAN, city and administrative centre, Andizhan *oblast* (region), Uzbek Soviet Socialist Republic, southeastern Fergana Valley. The city, which stands on ancient deposits of the Andizhan-Say River, dates back at least to the 9th century. In the 15th century it became the capital of the Fergana Valley and, being on the caravan route to China, its chief centre of trade and handicrafts. In the 18th century it became part of the khanate of Kokand, and in 1876 it was captured by the Russians. In 1898 it was the scene of an abortive native uprising against tsarist rule. Subject to frequent earth tremors, Andizhan was destroyed by a quake in 1902 that took more than 4,000 lives.

Today Andizhan is a road and rail junction and has engineering, electrotechnical, textile, and food-processing industries. Cultural assets include teacher-training, medical, and cotton-growing institutes, an Uzbek theatre of musical drama and comedy, a puppet theatre, and a museum. Pop. (1983 est.) 247,000.

Andō Hiroshige (Japanese artist): *see* Hiroshige.

Andō Kichijirō, also called ANDŌ KATSUSABURŌ (Japanese painter): *see* Shiba Kōkan.

Andō Shōeki (fl. *c.* 1750), Japanese philosopher considered to be one of the forerunners of the 19th-century movement to restore power to the emperor. He was also one of the first Japanese to begin to study European thought.

Andō was a native of Akita. He practiced medicine at Hachino-he, in the present Aomori Prefecture, but became prominent as a social thinker in the 1750s. Andō was critical of the feudal society of the Tokugawa shogunate. In his work the *Jinen shin'ei dō* ("The True Way of Administering [the society] According to Nature"), he called for the abolition of the warrior class and a return to agrarian egalitarian society, which was to be administered directly by the national government.

Andocides (b. *c.* 440 BC—d. after 391), Athenian orator and politician. Born into one of the most prominent Athenian families, he was imprisoned on suspicion of having taken part in the mutilation of the sacred busts called herms shortly before the departure of Athens' expedition to Sicily in 415. These mutilations caused a general panic, and Andocides was induced to turn informer on the guilty persons. Although the historian Thucydides was not convinced that Andocides' testimony was genuine, it was accepted, and those whom he implicated were condemned to death. Andocides went into exile and returned under the general amnesty of 403, when the democracy was restored. In 400 he was tried for impiety, but he had powerful support and was acquitted. In 392, during the Corinthian War, he went with three colleagues to negotiate peace with Sparta, but Athens rejected the terms and exiled the ambassadors. Although an unsuccessful politician, Andocides had a gift for vivid narrative. Three of his speeches survive: "On His Return"; "On the Mysteries," his defense in 400; and "On the Peace" (392).

Andong, city, Kyŏngsang-pukto (North Kyŏngsang Province), east central South Korea. It is 215 mi (345 km) from the mouth of the Naktong River, at the terminus of its navigable section, near a multipurpose dam. The city has been in existence since the Three Kingdoms period (beginning *c.* 57 BC) under various names and since the Koryŏ period (935–1392) has been known by its present name. Until the end of the Yi dynasty (1392–1910), it was the local administrative centre, producing a number of great scholars and political leaders. Traditional domestic products are alcoholic spirits (Andong-Soju), hemp cloth (Andong-Po), and silk. Pop. (1980 prelim.) 102,024.

Andong (China): *see* Tan-tung.

Andorra (Catalan and Spanish), French ANDORRE, small autonomous European principality lying within the Pyrenees Mountains and bounded by Spain (south and west) and by France (north and east).

A brief discussion of Andorra follows. For a full discussion of Andorra in its regional setting, *see* MACROPAEDIA: Europe.

Andorra's independence is traditionally ascribed to Charlemagne (who recovered the region from the Muslims in AD 803) and to his son Louis I the Pious, who in 819 granted a part of his empire to the Spanish bishop of Urgel. Dual allegiance to co-princes, one in Spain and one in France, originated in the late 13th century, and, with interruption only during the French Revolution, Andorra has been governed jointly by the bishop of Urgel and the French head of state, each of whom receives an annual payment of a token tribute.

Historic, traditional, and geographic factors lend the principality a strong affinity with the region of Catalonia in northern Spain. Andorra's official language is Catalan. Its institutions are based in Catalonian law, and a large proportion of the Spanish immigrants are Catalan. Most Andorrans are Roman Catholic,

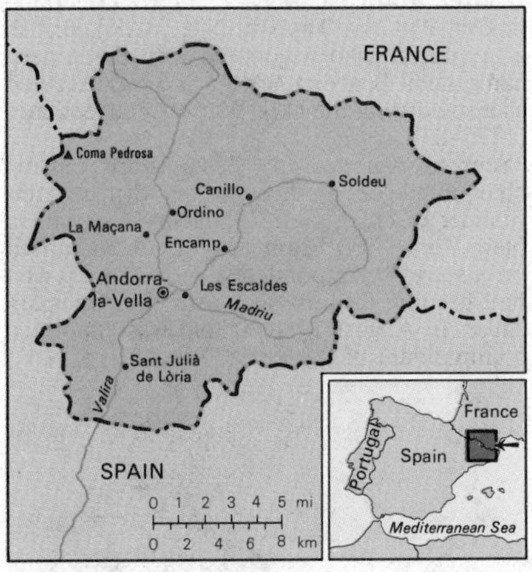

Andorra

and the principality is part of the diocese of Seo de Urgel (See of Urgel).

With only about 4 percent of the land cultivable, the traditional economy revolved about the pasturing of sheep and the harvesting of timber and tobacco. Industry is limited to processing the latter two products and to exploiting the considerable hydroelectric resources. Since the 1950s, however, commerce has risen in importance, and Andorra has become an international marketplace. Tourism also has grown through the attraction of the mountains, the marketplace, and the excellent facilities for winter sports. There is no national monetary unit, and both French and Spanish currencies are used.

The physical geography of Andorra prohibits air transportation. No railway system exists, but good roads link Andorra with France and Spain.

The co-princes represent Andorra internationally and exercise jointly all legislative, executive, and judicial powers. These powers are, in actuality, granted to permanent delegates and judges, or *veguers.* The elected Council General of the Valleys is the supreme administrative body but has no legislative power. Such public services as education, postal services, and telegraph are provided by the Spanish and French governments. Others—*e.g.,* telephone service, fire brigade, and social security—are the responsibility of the Council General.

Andorra's social and legal traditions are recorded in the *Manual Digest* (1748) of usages and the *Politar andorrà* (1763), which serve as references in legal proceedings and for cultural history.

Splendid samples of pre-Romanesque and Romanesque religious architecture remain, notably in the Lombardian style. There are also remarkable Romanesque paintings attributed to the Master of Santa Coloma and the Master of Andorra (12th and 13th centuries). Altarpieces and altar decorations known as retables and triptychs remain from the Gothic era. Popular music and dances are usually connected with the celebration of village feasts and religious ceremonies. Pop. (1982) 38,050.

Andorra-la-Vella (Catalan: Andorra the Old), French ANDORRE-LA-VIEILLE, Spanish ANDORRA-LA-VIEJA, *comun* (municipality) and capital of the autonomous co-principality of Andorra. It is located near the confluence of the Riu (river) Valira and the Riu Valira del Norte in the narrow Gran Valira Valley on the southern slopes of the Pyrenees.

After the establishment in the 13th century of joint governorship of Andorra by the Bishop of Urgel and the French head of state, Andorra-la-Vella remained relatively isolated from the outside world. Modernization began in the 1930s with the construction of carriage roads, and population increased after World War II as a result of the growth of the tourist industry. In the 1960s and '70s local banks investing in a building boom and real estate speculation helped transform Andorra-la-Vella from a rustic town into a busy commercial centre catering to shoppers and tourists. Winter sports areas are nearby. Because of Andorra's duty-free status, the town is now primarily a marketing centre for goods imported from elsewhere in Europe and from Asia. The Council General of the Valleys (Andorra's highest administrative body) meets at the House of the Valley, built in the 16th century. The town is connected by road to the Spanish and French frontiers and shares in both cultures. The *comun* has an area of 23 sq mi (59 sq km) and includes the valley of the Riu Madriu and the noted spa of Les Escaldes. Pop. (1982) *comun,* 14,928.

Andover, town (township), Essex County, northeastern Massachusetts, U.S., on the Merrimack River, just south of Lawrence. Originally known as Cochicewick (an Indian word meaning "great cascade"), it was settled in 1642, incorporated in 1646, and named for Andover, Eng. Textile mills were established there in 1813, and woollen and worsted goods are still important products. Manufactures now also include electronic parts, rubber and canvas footwear, and chemicals. Shawsheen Village, a model community, was planned and built in Andover by the American Woolen Company. The town's two noted educational institutions, Phillips Academy (founded in 1778 and one of the nation's oldest boarding schools for boys) and Abbot Academy for girls (1829), merged in 1973. The Addison Gallery of American Art on the grounds of Phillips Academy contains a notable collection of paintings, ship models, and prehistoric arts and crafts. North Andover, seat of Merrimack College (1947), was separated from Andover in 1855. Pop. (1980) 26,370.

Andover Academy: *see* Phillips Academy.

Andrada e Silva, José Bonifácio de (b. *c.* 1763, Santos, Braz.—d. April 6, 1838, Niterói, Braz.), Brazilian statesman called the "Patriarch of Independence" who was also a naturalist and geologist of international reputation.

Andrada went to Portugal as a student and remained there until he was 56, becoming a professor at the University of Coimbra and the permanent secretary of the Lisbon Academy. Returning to Brazil in 1819, he devoted himself to politics. He headed the ministry formed in January 1822 by the regent, Dom Pedro (later the emperor Pedro I), and supported Pedro in his determination that Brazil should be independent. After Pedro proclaimed independence (Sept. 7, 1822), Andrada became prime minister of the new empire.

In the constituent assembly of 1823, Andrada led the opposition to Pedro's Portuguese ad-

Andrada e Silva, portrait by an unknown artist

By courtesy of the Arquivo Nacional do Brasil

visers and was exiled until 1829. Once more coming to the aid of Pedro I, he worked for the imperial cause even after Pedro's abdication (April 7, 1831) and became tutor to the young Dom Pedro II. After being arrested in 1833 for political intrigue, Andrada retired from public life.

Andrade, Jorge (b. April 21, 1922, Barretos, Braz.), one of the most powerful playwrights within the wave of theatrical renewal that began in Brazil just after 1950. After staging *O faqueiro de prata* ("The Silver Cutlery") and *O telescópio* ("The Telescope") in 1954, he came even more forcefully to public attention in 1955 with *A moratória* ("The Moratorium"). Among his later plays, *Pedreira das almas* (1958; "Quarry of the Souls") and *Rasto atrás* (1967; "The Road Back") are the strongest in terms of dramatic effect.

Andrade exhibits an intense preoccupation with social issues, combined with a profound sense of the differences between generations, a feeling for economic reality, and psychological finesse in the creation and development of his characters. His works reflect the rural–urban population shift in southern Brazil, the rise and fall of the one-crop coffee economy, and the drama of individuals trying to come to terms with themselves, their backgrounds, and their changing environment. In *Vereda da salvação* (1965; "The Path of Salvation") he vividly depicts the delirium and destruction of a group of religious mystics at the hands of the authorities; the play was made into a film later the same year.

In 1970 Andrade won the Molière Prize for the three-play cycle *Marta, A árvore* ("The Tree"), and *O relógio* ("The Watch"). Among his favourite staging techniques is the use of a two-level stage to depict two time periods within the lives of the same group of protagonists.

Andrade, Mário (Raul) de (Morais) (b. Oct. 9, 1893, São Paulo, Braz.—d. Feb. 25, 1945, São Paulo) writer whose chief importance was his introduction of a highly individual prose style that attempted to reflect colloquial Brazilian speech rather than "correct" Portuguese. He was also important in the Modernist movement (*see* modernismo, Brazilian). He was a brother of Oswald Andrade.

Educated at the conservatory in São Paulo, Andrade helped organize what proved to be a key event in the future artistic life of Brazil, the Semana de Arte Moderna (Week of Modern Art), held in São Paulo in February 1922. His own contribution to the event, a reading of poems from his *Paulicéia Desvairada* (1922; *Hallucinated City,* 1969), was greeted by catcalls, but it has since been recognized as the single most significant influence on modern Brazilian poetry.

Andrade's diverse interests and wide knowledge ranged among all the arts and found expression in several. As director of the Departamento de Cultura of São Paulo from 1935 until his death, he organized research into Brazilian folklore and folk music. His own novels reflect his concern for folk themes; *Macunaíma* (1928) is written in his highly idiomatic style in an attempt to recreate actual Brazilian speech.

Andrade's complete poems were collected and published posthumously (*Poesias Completas,* 1955). These, together with his critical writings, continue to influence the arts in Brazil.

Andrade, (José) Oswald de (Sousa) (b. Jan. 11, 1890, São Paulo, Braz.—d. Oct. 22, 1954, São Paulo), poet, playwright, and novelist, social agitator and revolutionary, one of the leaders of the Modernist (*see* modernismo, Brazilian) movement in the arts in Brazil.

Born into a wealthy and aristocratic family, Andrade travelled extensively in Europe during his youth and there became aware of avant-garde literary trends in Paris and Italy. After his return to São Paulo, where he received his degree in law in 1919, he, with his brother Mário, helped organize the Semana de Arte Moderna (Week of Modern Art) at São Paulo in 1922, to introduce the Modernist movement to the public.

Focussing specifically on the nationalistic aspects of Modernism, Andrade, in his literary manifesto *Pau-Brasil* (1925; "Brazil Wood"), called for a rejection of Portuguese social and literary artifice and a return to what he saw as the primitive spontaneity of expression of the indigenous Brazilians, emphasizing the need for modern Brazil to become aware of its own heritage. To this end, he founded the literary movement known as Antropofagia (Cannibalism), a splinter group of Modernism, which, although short-lived, proved influential in its emphasis on folklore and native themes.

Intent on bringing about social as well as literary reform in Brazil, Andrade joined the Communist Party in 1931 but left it, disillusioned, in 1945. He remained a controversial figure for his radical political views and his often belligerent outspokenness.

In the years after his death, his novels, especially *Memórias Sentimentais de João Miramar* (1924; "Sentimental Memoirs of João Miramar"), came to be appreciated for their originality of style, rather than solely for their ideological or historical significance.

andradite, calcium iron garnet, perhaps the most spectacular garnet because of its high dispersion (separation of light into colours), even greater than that of diamond, and refractive index. It is found in various colours, some of the most beautiful being yellowish (termed topazolite, because of its resemblance to topaz) and yellowish green or emerald green (Uralian emeralds, or demantoid). Titanium may extensively replace both the iron and the silicon, as in schorlomite, or may simply produce a black colour, as in melanite. Andradite is typically found with grossular in metamorphic limestone. For details of chemistry and occurrence, *see* garnet.

Andradite garnet from the Banat region, Romania

By courtesy of the Field Museum of Natural History, Chicago; photograph, John H. Gerard—EB Inc.

András (Hungarian personal name): *see under* Andrew.

Andrássy, Gyula, Gróf (Count), German in full JULIUS, GRAF (Count) ANDRÁSSY VON CSIKSZENTKIRÁLY UND KRASZNAHORKA (b. March 3, 1823, Kassa, Hung., Austrian Empire—d. Feb. 18, 1890, Volosco, Istria, Austria-Hungary), Hungarian prime minister and Austro-Hungarian foreign minister (1871–79), who helped create the Austro-Hungarian dualist form of government. As a firm supporter of Germany, he created, with the imperial German chancellor Otto von Bismarck, the Austro-German alliance of 1879, which became the cornerstone of Austria's foreign policy until the monarchy's eventual collapse in 1918.

Andrássy; detail of a lithograph by Katzler, 1872

By courtesy of the Bild-Archiv, Osterreichische Nationalbibliothek, Vienna

A member of the radical Hungarian reform party under Lajos Kossuth, Andrássy entered the Hungarian Diet in 1847. He commanded a battalion in the revolt against Austria of 1848–49. Fleeing into exile on Hungary's surrender, he was condemned to death in absentia and was hanged in effigy, but he obtained an amnesty in 1857 and returned. Andrássy thereafter supported Ferenc Deák in the negotiations leading to the dualist compromise of 1867. Appointed Hungarian prime minister and defense minister (Feb. 17, 1867), he was largely responsible for the final constitutional negotiations between Austria and Hungary.

Viewing the Slavs as a threat to his country, Andrássy became a staunch supporter of dualism and opposed Karl Siegmund von Hohenwart's scheme (1871) to raise the constitutional status of the lands of the Bohemian crown. He further cultivated relations with Germany as a counterweight to Russia and opposed the destruction of Turkey, which would have resulted in tremendous gains for the Slavic powers. On his insistence, Austria remained neutral during the Franco-German War of 1870–71.

When Emperor Francis Joseph abandoned his policy of revenge against Prussia, Andrássy became Austro-Hungarian foreign minister (Nov. 14, 1871). During his tenure Austria-Hungary's international position was strengthened considerably. He tried to avoid an increase in the monarchy's Slavic population, but to prevent Russia from profiting alone from the Balkan crisis beginning in 1875, he agreed at the Congress of Berlin (1878) to Austria's occupation of Bosnia and Hercegovina. This act, highly unpopular in both Austria and Hungary, contributed to his decision to resign (Oct. 8, 1879). The previous day, however, he signed the fateful Austro-German alliance that was to link these two great powers until the end of World War I.

After his retirement, Andrássy remained in public life as a member of Hungary's upper house. His younger son and namesake also became a distinguished Austro-Hungarian political leader.

André (French personal name): *see under* Andrew, except as below.

André LE CHAPELAIN, Latin ANDREAS CAPELLANUS (fl. 12th century), French writer on the art of courtly love (*q.v.*), best known for his three-volume treatise *Liber de arte honeste amandi et reprobatione inhonesti amoris* (*c.* 1185; "Book of the Art of Loving Nobly and the Reprobation of Dishonourable Love"). He is thought to have been a chaplain at the court of Marie, countess of Champagne, daughter of Eleanor of Aquitaine. At Marie's request André wrote the *Liber.* It was translated into French twice during the 13th century; Guillaume de Lorris drew upon it for the *Roman de la rose.* The *Liber* codifies the whole doctrine of courtly love, containing practically all the elements of the cult.

André, John (b. May 2, 1750, London—d. Oct. 2, 1780, Tappan, N.Y., U.S.), British army officer who negotiated with the American general Benedict Arnold and was executed as a spy during the U.S. War of Independence (1775–83).

Sent to America in 1774, André became chief intelligence officer to the British commander in chief, Gen. Sir Henry Clinton, in New York City. From May 1779 he carried on a secret correspondence with Arnold, who had become disillusioned with the American cause. In August 1780 Arnold was appointed commandant of the fort at West Point, N.Y., which, at a meeting with André on September 21, he agreed to surrender for £20,000.

André, ink on paper, self-portrait, 1780; in the Yale University Art Gallery

By courtesy of the Yale University Art Gallery, gift of Ebenezer Baldwin

While returning to New York City, André was captured by three American militiamen; he failed to use the pass that Arnold had given him, and papers concerning West Point were found in one of his boots. A board of officers designated by Gen. George Washington found him guilty of spying and condemned him to death. When General Clinton refused to exchange him for Arnold, who had escaped to British territory, André was hanged. He was mourned on both sides because of his personal charm and literary talent.

Andrea DA BARBERINO (b. *c.* 1370, Barberino di Val d'Elsa, near Florence—d. *c.* 1432, Florence), ballad singer, prose writer, and compiler of epic tales.

The material for his prose compilation of Charlemagne legends (*q.v.*), *I reali di Francia* (1491; modern edition by G. Vandelli, 1892–1900) was drawn mostly from earlier Italian versions, though the author added much pseudo-historical material and invented many exciting amplifications. His epic tale *Guerin meschino* (1473), although told also by other writers, is largely of Andrea's own creation. It follows the fortunes of the slave-born hero Guerrino, who emerges strong and unshaken from a multitude of fantastic adventures and dangers to discover his royal parentage, secure his parents' release from prison, marry a Persian princess, and live happily until his death.

Andrea also compiled (and himself recited) such romances as *Aspromonte, Le storie Narbonesi* (published 1873–82) and *La storia di Ugone* and *La discesa di Guerino all'inferno* (both 1882).

Andrea DA FIRENZE, also called ANDREA DI BONAIUTI (fl. *c.* 1337–77), Florentine fresco painter whose considerable ability is demonstrated by his works in the church of Sta. Maria Novella in Florence.

"St. Thomas Aquinas Enthroned Between the Doctors of the Old and New Testaments, with Personifications of the Virtues, Sciences, and Liberal Arts," fresco by Andrea da Firenze, *c.* 1365; in the Spanish Chapel of the church of Sta. Maria Novella, Florence

SCALA—Art Resource/EB Inc.

Andrea studied at the Arte dei Medici e degli Speziali in Florence. At the end of 1365 he was commissioned to decorate the chapter house of the church of Sta. Maria Novella. Also attributed to him are the decorations in the Spanish chapel and the cartoon (full-scale drawing) for the stained-glass window of the facade. Although he was acquainted with Giotto's innovations in modelling and spatial depth, he was strongly influenced by the linear, hieratic art of his Florentine contemporary Andrea Orcagna, and most of his works display the rigid compositions and immobile faces associated with the Byzantine tradition.

Also attributed to Andrea are the three upper panels of a mural showing the life of St. Ranieri in the Campo Santo (cemetery) at Pisa.

Andrea DEL GOBBO: *see* Solari, Andrea.

Andrea DEL SARTO, original name ANDREA D'AGNOLO (b. July 16, 1486, Florence—d. Sept. 28, 1530, Florence), Italian painter and draftsman whose works of exquisite composition and craftsmanship were instrumental in the development of the Florentine-Roman school in the first half of the 16th century. His most striking among other well-known works is the series of frescoes on the life of St. John the Baptist about 1511 and completed in 1526.

Life. Sarto's family name was probably Lanfranchi, and his father was a tailor (hence "del Sarto"; Italian *sarto*, "tailor"). Little of real interest is known about his life, probably because it was for the most part uneventful. He was notably short in stature and known to his friends as Andreino. With two brief exceptions, his working life was spent in Florence. It is possible that Sarto was apprenticed to a goldsmith and a wood-carver before settling with the painter Raffaellino del Garbo soon after 1500. Raffaellino was a respectable and, in these years, still competitive representative of the traditions of late 15th-century painting, but his influence not unnaturally disappeared rather quickly as Sarto looked about him at the works of Leonardo, Michelangelo, and Fra Bartolommeo. He began to produce independent work about 1506—not precociously. Almost immediately he began a long association with a new church and convent of SS. Annunziata (for which he did frescoes in 1509–14 and 1525), and he moved to a workshop near it in or about 1511. There, for five or six years, he shared the experiences and sometimes commissions of a major sculptor, Jacopo Sansovino, which led him to an increasingly and, in the end, exceptionally solidly structured style. These were the years in which Il Rosso and Pontormo were his pupils, and it may fairly be said that around 1513–14 the leadership in Florentine painting passed from Fra Bartolommeo's workshop to his.

In 1517 or 1518 Sarto married Lucrezia del Fede, a widow whom he had, according to her testimony, used as a model for several years; she brought him property and a useful dowry. In 1518 he was summoned by the king of France, Francis I, to Fontainebleau, where he was preceded by a reputation based upon pictures made for export. It is unlikely that he found the life of a court artist congenial, and he remained for a year or less without beginning any major commission. Soon after his return, his connections with the Medici family (powerful since their return to Florence from exile in 1512) led to the most significant contract of his career—for part of the decoration of the Villa Medici at Poggio a Caiano, near Florence. The patron was in fact the pope, Leo X, whom Sarto almost certainly visited in Rome in 1519–20; but the project, the only one that ever offered Florentine artists the scope that Raphael had in the Vatican Palace, collapsed when the Pope died in December 1521. Sarto's fresco "Tribute to Caesar" is a fragment now incorporated into a much later scheme of decoration.

In 1520 Sarto began to build himself a house in Florence, which was later inhabited and modified by several other painters; it was a substantial property without being a palace. By 1523 he had a manservant as well as apprentices. Throughout his life he was content to work, when it suited him, for nominal fees, for no remuneration at all, or for only part of a fee offered to him, probably because he was in comfortable circumstances. He would paint for a carpenter or a king. A plague in 1523–24 drove Sarto and his wife to seek security in the Mugello, a valley north of Florence, but the interruption was brief. After the expulsion of the Medici, once more, in 1527, he worked for the republican government of Florence. His "Sacrifice of Isaac," intended as a political present to Francis I, was painted in this period. After the siege of Florence by imperial and papal forces, he succumbed to a new wave of plague and died in his house. He was buried in SS. Annunziata.

Andrea del Sarto's most striking monument is the grisaille (gray monochrome) series of frescoes on the life of St. John the Baptist in the Chiostro dello Scalzo, Florence. Begun about 1511, the work was not completed until 1526, and almost all of it was painted by his own hand, so that it reads like an artistic autobiography covering the greater part of his career. His portraits of his wife, Lucrezia (*c.* 1513–14, Prado, Madrid; and *c.* 1522, Staatliche Museen Preussischer Kulturbesitz, Berlin), can be supplemented by many others disguised as Madonnas (*e.g.,* the celebrated "Madonna of the Harpies"), just as his self-portraits in the Uffizi and in the National Gallery of Scotland at Edinburgh (both *c.* 1528) can be extended by several others, more or less hidden in his paintings from 1511 onward. A badly damaged pair of circular portraits of Andrea and Lucrezia at the Art Institute of Chicago appear to be signed (completed about 1530).

Sarto's style is marked throughout his career by an interest, exceptional among Florentines, in effects of colour and atmosphere and by sophisticated informality and natural expression of emotion. In his early works such as the "Marriage of St. Catherine," the search for the expression of animation and emotion led to an ecstatic and nonidealistic style that proved immensely attractive to a younger generation of painters. Restraint increasing with maturity did not inhibit the achievement of such passionate later works as the "Pietà" (*c.* 1520), but the mood is always intimate and never rhetorical. In the 1520s his style, as a result of the influence of Michelangelo or of artistic events in Rome, became perceptibly more ideal, more polished, and approximates what may properly be called a grand manner in the last of the Scalzo frescoes, the "Birth of the Baptist" (1526). From first to last, Sarto's integrity as a craftsman, his sheer professionalism, is impressively consistent; and it is characteristic of him that he refused to have his works engraved. His real quality is most vividly revealed, however, where there were no rewards of publicity, in his drawings.

Assessment. The reputation of Sarto has not yet recovered from the discovery, made in the 19th century, that the conventional characterization of his works—"faultless"—could be used as a term of reproach. His drawings are eloquent witness to only one ambition: to make each picture more perfect in terms of composition and craftsmanship than the last. Until the patient pursuit of perfection is thought, once more, to be a proper ideal for a naturally gifted artist, his importance is best presented as that of a great teacher. Among his pupils and followers were most of the significant Florentine painters of the first half of the 16th century—Rosso Fiorentino, Pontormo, Francesco Salviati, and Giorgio Vasari, for example—and it is largely through his example that the tradition of Florentine art was transmitted (but transformed) through to the end of the Renaissance and was able to embrace the stylistic innovations made around 1500 by Leonardo da Vinci and Michelangelo.

The suspicion that, while he was worthy and sound, Sarto nevertheless lacked some essential creative fire can be traced back to malicious accounts written by Giorgio Vasari, a 16th-century biographer and artist for whom Sarto was a disgrace to the profession. Vasari's specific complaint was that Sarto lacked ambition, and in Vasari's terms the complaint was probably true, for the opportunities for worldly success that Raphael enjoyed could have been his, too, but he did not take them. (J.K.Sh.)

MAJOR WORKS. "Madonna" (*c.* 1508; Galleria Nazionale, Rome); "Five Episodes from the Life of S. Filippo Benizzi" (1509–10; SS. Annunziata, Florence); "Noli Me Tangere" (1510; Uffizi, Florence); "The History of St. John the Baptist" (fresco series; *c.* 1511–26; Chiostro dello Scalzo, Florence); "Baptism of Christ" (*c.* 1511; Chiostro dello Scalzo); "The Archangel Raphael, Tobias, St. Leonard, and a Donor" (1511; Kunsthistorisches Museum, Vienna); "Procession of the Magi" (1511; SS. Annunziata); "Annunciation" (1512; Pitti Palace, Florence); "Marriage of St. Catherine" (1512–13; Gemäldegalerie, Dresden, E.Ger.); "Holy Family" (*c.* 1513; Hermitage, Leningrad); "Birth of the Virgin" (1513–14; SS. Annunziata); "Portrait of a Young Woman" ("Lucrezia del Fede"; 1513–14; Prado, Madrid); "Christ the Redeemer" (*c.* 1515; SS. Annunziata); "Holy Family" (1515; Louvre, Paris); "The Stories of Joseph the Jew" (1515–16; Pitti Palace); "Madonna with Child and St. John" (1516; Borghese Gallery, Rome); "The Virgin and Child with St. John the Baptist and Two Angels" (*c.* 1517; Wallace Collection, London); "Madonna of the Harpies" (1517; Uffizi); "Portrait of a Young Man" (1517–18; National Gallery, London); "Disputation on the Trinity" (1517–18; Pitti Palace); "Holy Family" (1517–18; Louvre); "Charity" (1518; Louvre); "Pietà" (*c.* 1520; Kunsthistorisches Museum); "Madonna della Scala" (1522; Prado); "Assumption of the Virgin" (1522–23; Pitti Palace); "Pietà" (1524; Pitti Palace); "The Last Supper" (completed 1527; S. Salvi, Florence); "Sacrifice of Abraham" (*c.* 1527; Cleveland Museum of Art); "Holy Family with the Infant St. John" (*c.* 1527; Metropolitan Museum of Art, New York City); "Madonna with Six Saints" (1528; Pitti Palace); "Charity" (1528; National Gallery of Art, Washington, D.C.); "Abraham's Offering" (1528; Gemäldegalerie); "Self-Portrait" (*c.* 1528; National Gallery of Scotland, Edinburgh); "The Sacrifice of Isaac, Prisoner of an Angel" (*c.* 1529; Prado); "Portraits of the Artist and His Wife, Lucrezia" (*c.* 1530; Art Institute of Chicago).

BIBLIOGRAPHY. Sydney J. Freedberg, *Andrea del Sarto*, 2 vol. (1963); and John K. Shearman, *Andrea del Sarto*, 2 vol. (1965), are well-illustrated monographs containing references to earlier writings; the selected bibliography in the former is especially useful. Each contains a catalogue raisonné of paintings, the second has in addition a separate catalog of drawings and register of documents. There are significant differences of opinion as to attributions, chronology, and general assessment, but at present it seems to be generally believed that the truth lies somewhere between them.

Andrea DEL VERROCCHIO, also called ANDREA DI MICHELE DI FRANCESCO CIONI (sculptor): *see* Verrocchio, Andrea del.

Andrea DI CIONE (*c.* 1308–*c.* 1368): *see* Orcagna, Andrea.

Andrea PISANO (Italian sculptor): *see* Pisano, Andrea.

Andreani, Andrea (fl. *c.* 1580–*c.* 1625, Italy), Italian printmaker known especially for his chiaroscuro printing, a technique developed in the early 16th century to facilitate shading; several wood blocks are used for the same print, each block engraved to produce a different tone of the same colour.

Andreani was active in Florence (1584–85), in Siena (1586–93), and in Mantua (1599). Between 1602 and 1610 he appears in contemporary documents as a publisher of prints that were not of his own design. All of Andreani's known woodcuts, in fact, are after the paintings of other artists, especially the 15th-century Mannerists Giambologna and Domenico Beccafumi, and the Venetian early Baroque painter Jacopo Ligozzi. The best known of Andreani's works are 12 large woodcuts representing the "Trionfo di Giulio Cesare" ("Triumph of Julius Caesar") and a series of prints reproducing nine sequential canvases by Andrea Mantegna. The several sections of Andreani's work were intended to be pasted together or mounted as a single frieze; each print has an individual character yet fits into its place in the unified whole.

Andreanof Islands, group of the Aleutian Islands, southwestern Alaska, U.S., between the Pacific Ocean (south) and the Bering Sea (north) and extending east–west for about 270 mi (430 km) between the Fox and Rat islands. They were strategically important in World War II, and there are U.S. military installations on Adak and Shemya islands. Pop. (1980) 3,408.

Andreas (German personal name): *see under* Andrew.

Andreas CAPELLANUS (12th century): *see* André le Chapelain.

Andreas-Salomé, Lou (b. Feb. 12, 1861, St. Petersburg, Russia—d. Feb. 5, 1937, Göttingen, Ger.), German writer remembered for her friendships with the great men of her day. Beloved of Nietzsche in 1882, she rejected his proposal of marriage and later married an Orientalist, F.C. Andreas. In 1897 she met the poet Rainer Maria Rilke, who was 14 years younger than she and who also fell in love with her; she became one of the formative influences on his life. In 1911 she became associated with the Vienna circle of psychoanalysts and was a friend and disciple of Sigmund Freud.

Besides novels, her works include *Friedrich Nietzsche in seinen Werken* (1894; "Friedrich Nietzsche in His Works"), *Rainer Maria Rilke* (1928), and *Mein Dank an Freud* (1931; "My Thanks to Freud"). Her correspondence with Rilke was published in 1952.

Andreev, Leonid Nikolayevich (Russian novelist): *see* Andreyev, Leonid Nikolayevich.

Andreini, Francesco (b. 1548, Pistoia, Italy—d. Aug. 20, 1624, Mantua), actor of commedia dell'arte (*q.v.*) who, with his wife, Isabella (*see* Andreini, Isabella), was a founder and star performer of the Compagnia dei Gelosi (*q.v.*), one of the earliest and most famous of commedia dell'arte troupes.

Andreini began his career as a soldier but was captured by the Turks and held in slavery by them for several years. Upon his return to Italy, he joined the company of the producer-director Flaminio Scala, playing lovers. He is identified with the character of Capitano Spavento, the braggart Spanish soldier, and in 1607 published descriptions of that role, including dialogue and stage business, as *Le bravure del Capitano Spavento* ("The Bravery of Captain Spavento"). The Gelosi troupe visited the French court intermittently and travelled all over Europe. Isabella's death in 1604 led to Andreini's retirement from the stage and to the dissolution of the Gelosi.

Andreini, Giovambattista (b. Feb. 9, 1579?, Florence—d. June 7/8, 1654, Reggio nell'Emilia, Sicily), actor of commedia dell'arte and author of the play *Adamo* ("Adam"), which, it has been claimed, suggested the idea of *Paradise Lost* to John Milton.

Andreini began his stage career with the Compagnia dei Gelosi (*q.v.*) of his parents, Francesco and Isabella Andreini (*qq.v.*), but about 1601 he formed his own troupe, the Compagnia dei Fedeli, and toured Italy until 1613, when the company was invited to Paris by Marie de Médicis, to whom he dedicated his play *Adamo* (1613). In 1618 he returned to Italy for three years, then travelled back to Paris in 1621, again at the invitation of Marie, where he played at the Hôtel de Bourgogne until 1624 and again in 1625. He acted throughout Europe nearly until he died. His writings include several ecclesiastical dramas, some religious poems, and a number of comedies.

Andreini, Isabella, *née* ISABELLA CANALI (b. 1562, Padua—d. July 10, 1604, Lyons, Republic of Venice), celebrated leading lady of the Compagnia dei Gelosi (*q.v.*), most famous of the early commedia dell'arte companies.

In 1578 Flaminio Scala, a theatrical manager and scenario writer, engaged Isabella Canali to play female lovers in his company. There she met Francesco Andreini and married him the same year. They helped form the Gelosi troupe, with which she toured Italy and France until her death. A brilliant and beautiful woman, she was the subject of adoring verse by both French and Italian poets. At a Roman festival, given by her admirer Cardinal Cinzio Aldobrandini, her portrait was hung, crowned with laurels, between those of Tasso and Plutarch. Isabella was herself a minor poet and author of a pastoral play, *Mirtilla;* a book of songs, sonnets, letters, and other verse was published after her death by her husband and Scala. Her death prompted her husband's retirement from the stage and was the inspiration of numerous elegies. Her son Giovambattista was a commedia dell'arte actor and a prolific author.

Andreis, (Andrew James) Felix (Bartholomew) de (b. Dec. 13, 1778, Demonte, Piedmont—d. Oct. 15, 1820, St. Louis, Missouri territory), Vincentian priest and pioneer missionary to the American West.

Ordained at Piacenza, Italy, in 1802, Andreis was transferred (1806) to Rome, where he served as preacher, professor of theology, and apostle to the poor. William Du Bourg, bishop of Louisiana, on a visit to Rome in 1815 arranged for Andreis to serve his diocese. Andreis was appointed temporary vicar general and superior of a band of missionaries who embarked for the American missions. After a long delay at the Seminary of St. Thomas in Kentucky, where he taught theology, Andreis arrived in St. Louis in 1817 and was appointed vicar general. He was professor and administrator of two colleges, one for seminarians and one for laymen, and supervised the erection of a novitiate at the Barrens, 80 miles (130 kilometres) south of St. Louis. During his lifetime he gained a reputation for sanctity, and several miracles were attributed to his intercession after his death. J. Rosati's *Life of the Very Reverend Felix de Andreis, C.M.* appeared in 1900.

Andreotti, Giulio (b. Jan. 14, 1919, Rome), a leader of Italy's Christian Democrat Party, prime minister twice in 1972 and from 1976 to early 1979. His government's stability depended upon the tacit support of the Communists.

The young Andreotti took a degree in law at the University of Rome and was president of the Catholic students' federation. A member of the Constituent Assembly elected in June 1946, he was given an appointment as under secretary by Premier Alcide De Gasperi and retained that post until 1953. He chose to be left out when Giuseppe Pella formed a centre-right government with the Liberal Party in 1953, but was interior minister in Amintore Fanfani's first government the following year. He was later in charge of finances (1955–58), treasury (1958–59), defense (1959–66), and industry and commerce (1966–68). His first government, a one-party attempt in 1972, lasted only four months. The crisis that followed ended after 21 days when Andreotti himself was able to form his second government, this time in a coalition with the Liberals and Social Democrats. His third government, formed in 1976, was a one-party minority government voted in by the Chamber of Deputies and the Senate only by virtue of the abstention of the Communist Party. Andreotti survived longer than most Italian premiers because there seemed no suitable alternative to his leadership.

Long active in journalism, Andreotti was a co-founder of his party's daily newspaper, *Il Popolo.* He was a writer of repute and author of, among other works, *De Gasperi e il suo tempo* (1956; "De Gasperi and His Time").

Andretti, Mario (Gabriel) (b. Feb. 28, 1940, Montona, Italy), automobile racing driver who drove stock cars, U.S. championship cars, and Formula I cars.

Mario and his twin brother Aldo studied automobile mechanics, frequented racing car garages, and participated in a race-driving training program in Italy. In 1955 the Andretti family came to the United States and settled in Nazareth, Pa. By 1958 the brothers were racing stock cars and in 1959 became U.S. citizens. Aldo was severely injured in an accident and gave up racing after 1959. In the early 1960s Mario drove sprint and midget cars in races, and in 1964 he began racing in the championship-car division of the United States Automobile Club (USAC). He won USAC championships (1965–66, and 1969). He also won the Daytona Beach (Fla.) 500-mile stock-car race (1967) and the sports-car Grand Prix of Endurance race at Sebring, Fla. (1967, 1970).

He won the Indianapolis 500 race in 1969 with a then record speed of 156.867 mph (252.11 kph), later broken. An apparent victory in the 1981 race was ultimately given to Bobby Unser (*q.v.*). Andretti was the second U.S. driver to win the Formula I world driving championship in 1978. (Phil Hill was the first in 1961).

To make the best use of the Britannica, consult the INDEX *first*

Andrew I, Russian in full ANDREY YURYEVICH BOGOLYUBSKY (b. *c.* 1111—d. June 1174, Bogolyubovo, near Vladimir, Russia), prince of Rostov-Suzdal (1157) and grand prince of Vladimir (1169), who increased the importance of the northeastern Russian lands and contributed to the development of government in that forest region.

Having accompanied his father, Yury Dolgoruky, on his conquest of Kiev, Andrew refused to remain in the ancient southern Russian capital and returned to Vladimir, a town in his father's principality of Rostov-Suzdal in northeastern Russia. When his father died (1157), the cities of Rostov and Suzdal elected Andrew their prince and he transferred the capital of the entire principality to Vladimir. Subsequently, he encouraged colonists to settle in his principality, fortified and enlarged Vladimir, and built many churches.

In addition to strengthening his own lands, Andrew strove to extend his authority over other Russian principalities. In 1169 he and his allies sacked Kiev, and Andrew acquired the title grand prince. But rather than move his seat to Kiev, as his father had done, Andrew made Vladimir the centre of the grand principality and placed a series of his relatives on the now secondary princely throne of Kiev. Later he also compelled Novgorod to accept a prince of his choice. In governing his realm, Andrew not only demanded that the subordinate princes obey him but also tried to reduce the traditional political powers of the boyars (*i.e.,* the upper nobility) within his hereditary lands. In response, his embittered courtiers formed a conspiracy and killed him.

Andrew II, Hungarian ENDRE, or ANDRAS (b. 1175—d. Oct. 26, 1235), king of Hungary (1205–35) whose reign was marked by controversy with barons and the great feudatories and by the issuance of the Golden Bull of 1222 (*q.v.*), which has been called the Hungarian Magna Carta.

Son of Béla III, Andrew succeeded László III, his elder brother's son, on the throne in 1205. Powerful landed interests forced Andrew to spend royal funds so recklessly that the crown was soon impoverished and dependent on the feudatories, who soon reduced Hungary to a state of near anarchy. Objecting to the prodigality of the German followers of Andrew's first wife, Gertrude of Meran, rebellious nobles murdered her in 1213. Four years later, with an army of 15,000 men, Andrew set off on an ill-fated crusade to the Holy Land. After his return the barons forced him to agree to the Golden Bull, which became an important source of the Hungarian constitution. It limited royal rights and prerogatives, confirmed basic rights of smallholders and nobles, guaranteed justice for all, and promised to improve the coinage. Under it, nobles had the right to resist by force any royal decree.

During Andrew's reign the Teutonic Knights, who had occupied parts of Transylvania for 14 years, came into conflict with both royal and ecclesiastical authority, and the order was expelled from Hungary in 1225. Andrew's daughter by Gertrude was canonized as St. Elizabeth of Hungary.

Andrew, SAINT (d. traditionally 60/70, Patras, Achaia; feast day November 30), one of the Twelve Apostles and brother of St. Peter; patron saint of Scotland and of Russia. In the Synoptic Gospels (Matthew, Mark, and Luke), Peter and Andrew—whose Greek name means "Manly"—were called from their fishing by Jesus to follow him, promising that he would make them fishers of men. With SS. Peter, James, and John, Andrew asked Jesus on the Mount of Olives for signs of the earth's end, which inspired the eschatological discourse in Mark 13. In John's Gospel he is the first Apostle named, and he was a disciple of St. John the Baptist before Jesus' call.

Early Byzantine tradition (dependent on John 1:40) calls Andrew *protokletos,* "first called." Early church legends recount his missionary activity in the area about the Black Sea. Apocryphal writings centred on him include the *Acts of Andrew, Acts of Andrew and Matthias,* and *Acts of Peter and Andrew.* A 4th-century account reports his death by crucifixion, and late medieval accretions describe the cross as X-shaped. He is iconographically represented with an X-shaped cross (*e.g.,* the Scottish flag).

St. Jerome records that Andrew's relics were taken from Patras (modern Pátrai) to Constantinople by command of the emperor Constantius II in 357. From there the body was taken to Amalfi, Italy (church of S. Andrea), in 1208, and in the 15th century the head was taken to Rome (St. Peter's, Vatican City). In September 1964 Pope Paul VI returned Andrew's head to Pátrai as a gesture of goodwill toward the separated Christians of Greece. Peter M. Peterson's *Andrew, Brother of Simon Peter: His History and His Legends* and F. Dvornik's *Idea of Apostolicity in Byzantium and the Legend of the Apostle Andrew* appeared in 1958.

Andrew OF CAESAREA (fl. 6th–7th century), bishop of Caesarea, author of possibly the most significant Greek commentary on the book of Revelation (Apocalypse) from the era of the Church Fathers. His annotations seem to have influenced the Greek version of the biblical text.

Andrew's interpretation apparently was influenced largely by the celebrated 4th-century Greek theologian Gregory of Nazianzus and by the 6th-century Neoplatonist Dionysius the Areopagite. His exposition of the text is marked by a specific Christian interpretation of history that views the book of Revelation as expressing the actual divine government of the world. Andrew concluded that history and mystery are not to be understood univocally or synonymously. He submitted that, although the biblical text comprises at least three levels of meanings, viz., historical (literal), tropological (metaphorical), and anagogical (mystical), its figurative and symbolic senses are not to be taken as simply imaginative. Rather, these "mystical" forms are to be seen as expressions of realities and experiences that transcend the capacity of human language. Interested in facts, Andrew admitted the limits of the biblical expositor and cautioned restraint in the elucidation of prophecy. He emphasized, nevertheless, the mystical or spiritual sense of Sacred Scripture. He stressed the transitoriness of all earthly things and the yearning for the glories of the future life (eschatology). Presenting a selection of biblical interpretations from early Christian writers, he provided a choice of views. These and quotations from his own writings often provide the only surviving fragments of the works cited.

Critical scholarship has suggested that Andrew's glosses frequently became part of the book of Revelation's text, resulting in some of its enigmatic passages. This commentary, in more than 70 manuscripts that have been used as sources by subsequent commentators, is contained in the series by J.P. Migne (ed.), *Patrologia Graeca* (vol. 106, 1866).

Andrew OF CARNIOLA, also called ANDREW OF KRAINA (d. Nov. 13, 1484, Basel, Switz.), archbishop, advocate of conciliar rule in the Western Church—*i.e.,* the supremacy of a general council of bishops over the papacy. Because of his personal animosity and eccentric conduct toward Pope Sixtus IV, church historians generally do not consider Andrew a precursor of reform.

From the scant data available on Andrew's life, it appears that he was of Slavic origin and a member of the quasi-monastic Dominicans at the order's convent in Udine, Italy. Supported by the German emperor Frederick III, he was named archbishop of Carniola, now in Yugoslavia, in January 1476, while continuing to live elsewhere. He arrived in Rome *c.* 1478 to represent Emperor Frederick at the court of Pope Sixtus IV. After an unsuccessful attempt to be named a cardinal of the church, he denounced the Pope and was imprisoned. Freed by Frederick's intervention, Andrew travelled to Florence and Milan, seeking support from Sixtus' foes. Arriving at Basel, he announced a general council, principally to depose Sixtus, and nailed a formal indictment of the Pope to the doors of the cathedral. This action apparently was an appeal to reconvene the Council of Basel (1431–37), which had vainly attempted to subject the pope to its authority by decreeing that the assembly of bishops governed directly by divine right.

Lacking the support of the bishops, Andrew met with antipapal agents from Florence and Milan to devise strategy. In September 1482 Pope Sixtus placed Basel under interdict (prohibiting the clergy to exercise any sacramental ministry) for extending protection to the excommunicated Andrew. Papal ambassadors then obtained from Frederick a decree placing Andrew in the custody of Basel's governing council, but he later was consigned to papal authorities. Condemned to life imprisonment in Basel, Andrew is said to have hanged himself in his cell.

Andrew OF CRETE, SAINT (b. *c.* 660, Damascus, Syria—d. July 4, 740; feast day July

4), archbishop of Gortyna, Crete, regarded by the Greek Church as one of its greatest hymn writers.

From his monastery in Jerusalem he was sent to Constantinople (modern Istanbul), where he became deacon of the Hagia Sophia. During the reign of the Byzantine emperor Philippicus Bardanes he was made archbishop of Gortyna and took part in the Synod of Constantinople (712), where he subscribed to Monothelitism (*see* Monothelites). He recanted his Monothelitic views in 713.

In developing the Byzantine liturgy, he is credited with inventing the canon, a new genre of hymnography that consists of nine odes in stanzaic form, each sung to a different melody. His canon replaced the kontakion, a homiletic hymn of which all stanzas were sung to the same melody. Andrew was the author of many hymns and canons still used in Greek liturgical books.

Andrew OF LONJUMEL, Lonjumel also spelled LONGJUMEAU, or LONGUMEAU (fl. 1238–53), French Dominican friar who, as an ambassador of Louis IX (St. Louis) of France, led a diplomatic mission destined for the court of the Mongol khan Güyük. His report of the journey across Central Asia and back (1249 to 1251/52), though a mixture of fact and fiction, contains noteworthy observations.

On his first diplomatic mission, to Constantinople (1238), he brought back the relic revered as Christ's crown of thorns, for which Louis built Sainte-Chapelle at Paris as a repository. In 1247 he accompanied a mission sent by Pope Innocent IV to the Mongols at Kars, Armenia (now in Turkey), and returned to Louis with a Mongol proposal for a joint attack upon Islām for the conquest of Syria. Louis then sent Andrew on a diplomatic mission to Güyük to continue negotiations. Departing from Cyprus with several companions early in 1249, he travelled around the southern and eastern shores of the Caspian Sea and, continuing through Turkistan north of Tashkent, went on to Karakorum in central Mongolia. Upon reaching the court, Andrew found that Güyük was dead, and was sent back to Louis with an insolent letter from the regent mother, Ogul-Gaimish. Andrew's account of the journey, though known only from references in the travel writings of the Franciscan friar William of Rubruquis, describes Tatar customs with fair accuracy.

Andrew OF WYNTOUN: *see* Wyntoun, Andrew of.

Andrew, John Albion (b. May 31, 1818, Windham, Maine, U.S.—d. Oct. 30, 1867, Boston), U.S. antislavery leader who, as governor of Massachusetts during the Civil War, was one of the most energetic of the Northern "war governors."

Andrew entered political life as a Whig opposed to the Mexican War (1846–48). In 1848

John Albion Andrew, photograph by Mathew Brady

By courtesy of the Library of Congress, Washington, D.C.

he joined the Free-Soil movement against the spread of slavery. After the passage of the Kansas–Nebraska Act (1854), which permitted those territories to choose between slavery and freedom, he helped organize the Republican Party in Massachusetts. In 1859 he defended the abolitionist John Brown so vigorously that he was summoned to Washington to appear before an investigating committee of the Senate. In 1860 he led the Massachusetts delegation at the Republican convention at Chicago, which nominated Lincoln for the presidency; from 1861 to January 1866 he was governor of Massachusetts.

Andrewes, Lancelot (b. 1555, London—d. Sept. 26, 1626, London), theologian and court preacher who sought to defend and advance Anglican doctrines during a period of great strife in the English church.

Lancelot Andrewes, detail of an oil painting by an unknown artist

By courtesy of the curators of the Bodleian Library, Oxford

Andrewes was elected a fellow of Pembroke College, Cambridge, in 1575 and was ordained a deacon in 1580. His service to several parishes from 1589 was followed by consecration as bishop of Chichester in 1605 and his transfer to Ely in 1609 and to Winchester in 1619; he had earlier refused the sees of Salisbury and Ely because Elizabeth I had insisted that he cooperate with the crown in reducing the power of the church. Under James I and Charles I he was lord almoner (1605–19) and dean of the chapels royal (1619–26). A master of rhetoric, he earned a reputation as an eloquent and learned court preacher.

Despite his exposure to Puritan influence at Cambridge, Andrewes was a critic, consistent, if cautious, of both Calvinist dogmas and Puritan reform platforms. His major writings, however, were apologetic works directed against the Roman Church, in which he combined a critique of distinctly Roman Catholic dogmas with a positive statement of Anglican teachings.

Among his sermons are those he preached on several successive anniversaries of the thwarted Gunpowder Plot of 1605, in which an attempt was made to blow up Parliament and the royal family by Catholics angry over anti-Catholic legislation; the sermons stress the deliverance by God of both the nation and the church. A bibliography of his sermons and other writings is included in the biography by P.A. Welsby, *Lancelot Andrewes, 1555–1626* (1958).

Andrews, Augustus George (English actor): *see* Arliss, George.

Andrews, Charles McLean (b. Feb. 22, 1863, Wethersfield, Conn., U.S.—d. Sept. 9, 1943, New Haven, Conn.), U.S. teacher and historian whose *Colonial Period of American History*, vol. 1 of 4, won him a Pulitzer Prize in 1935.

After teaching at various American universities, Andrews was professor of American history at Yale University from 1910 to 1931. Well started on his important guides to colonial materials in English archives before he went to Yale, he became a leader in colonial historiography. His own history belongs to the "imperial school," which places the emphasis on the American colonies as dependent parts of the British system so that the centre of the colonial story belongs in Great Britain. This interpretation runs through his widely accepted books and those of historians he trained.

Among his writings are *Colonial Self-Government, 1652–89,* vol. 5 of *The American Nation, a History* (1904), and *The Colonial Period* (1912).

Andrews, Frank M(axwell) (b. Feb. 3, 1884, Nashville, Tenn., U.S.—d. May 3, 1943, Iceland), U.S. soldier and air force officer who contributed signally to the evolution of U.S. bombardment aviation during his command (1935–39) of the General Headquarters Air Force, first U.S. independent air striking force.

Graduating from the U.S. Military Academy at West Point, N.Y., in 1906, Andrews was commissioned in the cavalry, serving in the Philippines and Hawaii, but in 1917 he transferred to the new air service, rising to lieutenant colonel by the end of World War I. After holding a number of routine service assignments, he was named commander of the newly created General Headquarters Air Force in 1935.

A determined though moderate advocate of strategic air power, Andrews is credited with development of the Boeing B-17 bomber; his command became the model for the powerful army air forces of World War II. During the war Andrews, as air commander in the Caribbean and later as head of the Caribbean defense command, was the first U.S. airman to command an entire theatre. He was promoted to lieutenant general in 1941. In February 1943, three months before his death in an air crash, he assumed command of all U.S. forces in Europe, succeeding Gen. Dwight D. Eisenhower when the latter was named Allied

Frank Andrews

By courtesy of the U.S. Army

Commander of the North African theatre of operations.

Andrews, Roy Chapman (b. Jan. 26, 1884, Beloit, Wis., U.S.—d. March 11, 1960, Carmel, Calif.), naturalist, explorer, and author, who led many important scientific expeditions for which he obtained financial support through his public lectures and books, particularly on central Asia and eastern Asia.

After graduating from Beloit (Wis.) College in 1906, he took a position at the American Museum of Natural History in New York City. In 1908 he went on his first expedition, to Alaska, and on that trip and until 1914 he specialized in the study of whales and other aquatic mammals; through his efforts the museum's collection of cetaceans became one of the best in the world. In 1909–10 he was a naturalist on the USS "Albatross" on its voyage to the Dutch East Indies; in 1911–12 he explored northern Korea and in 1913 participated in the Borden Alaska expedition.

While serving as chief of the division of Asiatic exploration of the American Museum of Natural History, he led three expeditions, to

Roy Chapman Andrews

By courtesy of the American Museum of Natural History, New York

Tibet, southwest China, and Burma (1916–17); northern China and Outer Mongolia (1919); and central Asia (1921–22 and 1925). Numerous important discoveries were made on the third Asian expedition: the first known dinosaur eggs; a skull and other parts of *Baluchitherium,* the largest known land mammal; extensive deposits of fossil mammals and reptiles previously unknown; evidence of prehistoric human life; and geological strata previously unexplored in that region.

Andrews was the director of the American Museum of Natural History from 1935 to 1942, when he resigned in order to write. His books include *Whale Hunting with Gun and Camera* (1916), *Camps and Trails in China* (1918), *Across Mongolian Plains* (1921; with Yvette Borup Andrews), *On the Trail of Ancient Man* (1926), *Ends of the Earth* (1929), *The New Conquest of Central Asia* (1933), *This Business of Exploring* (1935), *This Amazing Planet* (1940), the autobiographical *Under a Lucky Star* (1943) and *An Explorer Comes Home* (1947), and *Beyond Adventure* (1954).

Andrews, Thomas (b. Dec. 19, 1813, Belfast, Ire.—d. Nov. 26, 1885, Belfast), chemist and physicist who established the concepts of critical temperature and pressure and showed that a gas will pass into the liquid state, and vice versa, without any discontinuity, or abrupt change in physical properties. He also proved that ozone is a form of oxygen.

Following studies in Britain and Paris, he received a medical degree from the University of Edinburgh (1835). He was appointed vice president of Northern College in Belfast in 1845 and helped to prepare it for its reorganization as Queen's College, Belfast (1849). He was professor of chemistry there from 1849 to 1879.

Andrey (Russian personal name): *see under* Andrew.

Andreyev, Leonid Nikolayevich, Andreyev also spelled ANDREEV (b. Aug. 21 [Aug. 9, old style], 1871, Oryol, Russia—d. Sept. 12, 1919, Kuokkala, Fin.), novelist whose best work has a place in Russian literature for its evocation of a mood of despair and absolute pessimism.

At the age of 20 Andreyev entered St. Petersburg University but lived restlessly for some time. In 1894, after several attempts at suicide, he transferred to the University of Moscow, where he studied law. He became a barrister and then a law and crime reporter, publishing his first stories in newspapers and periodicals. Encouraged by Maksim Gorky, who became a close friend, he was at first regarded as Gorky's successor as a Realist. His "Zhili-byli" ("Once There Lived . . .") attracted attention and was included in his first collection of short stories (1901). Two stories of 1902, *Bezdna* ("The Abyss") and *V tumane* ("In the Fog"), caused a storm by their candid and audacious treatment of sex. Andreyev's work became widely discussed, and he acquired fame and wealth with a series of novels and short stories that, at their best, resemble Tolstoy in their powerful themes and ironic sympathy for suffering humanity. Among his best tales are *Gubernator* (1905; *His Excellency the Governor,* 1921) and *Rasskaz o semi poveshennykh* (1908; *The Seven That Were Hanged,* 1909).

Andreyev's fame as a novelist declined rapidly as his works became increasingly bizarre and sensational. He began a career as a dramatist in 1905. His most successful plays—*Zhizn cheloveka* (1907; *The Life of Man,* 1915) and *Tot, kto poluchayet poshchyochiny* (1916; *He Who Gets Slapped,* 1921)—were allegorical dramas, but he also attempted Realist comedy.

During World War I, Andreyev became editor of a government-inspired newspaper, and his writing became predominantly patriotic. A fervent antirevolutionary, he moved to Finland after the Bolsheviks came to power; his last work, *S.O.S.* (1919), was an appeal to the Allies to save Russia.

Andria, city, Bari province, Puglia (Apulia) region, southeastern Italy, on the eastern slopes of the Murge plateau, just south of Barletta. Andria was perhaps the Netium mentioned by the 1st-century BC Greek geographer Strabo, but its recorded history began with the arrival of the Normans in the 11th century AD, when Pietro I, Norman count of nearby Trani, enlarged and fortified the minor settlement of Locum Andre. It later became a favourite hunting residence of the emperor Frederick II, who in 1240 built the Castel del Monte (11 mi [17 km] south), a massive octagonal Gothic structure. Eventually the city passed to the Angevin dynasty, Otto IV (Otto of Brunswick), and the Orsini, Acquaviva, and Carafa families. The city has some Roman remains, and the restored 10th-century cathedral contains the tombs of Isabella (Yolande) of Brienne and Isabella of England, the second and third wives of Frederick II. There are several other notable churches and palaces.

Castel del Monte, near Andria, Italy

Bohnacker—L. Palnic

Andria is on the railway from Bari to Foggia. Agriculture, especially the cultivation of vines, olives, and almonds, is the chief industry; there is also wine production, oil refining, and the manufacture of textiles. Pop. (1981 prelim.) mun., 83,319.

Andrić, Ivo (b. Oct. 10, 1892, Dolac, near Travnik, Bosnia—d. March 13, 1975, Belgrade), writer of Serbo-Croatian novels and short stories who was awarded the Nobel Prize for Literature in 1961.

Andrić, 1961

By courtesy of Information Service, Yugoslavia

Andrić studied at Zagreb, Kraków, Vienna, and Graz. His potentialities as a writer of both prose and verse were recognized early, and his reputation was established with *Ex Ponto* (1918), a contemplative, lyrical prose work written during his internment by Austro-Hungarian authorities for nationalistic political activities during World War I. Collections of his short stories were published at intervals from 1920 onward.

Following World War I, he entered the Yugoslavian diplomatic service. Although his career took him to Rome, Bucharest, Madrid, Geneva, and Berlin, it was his native province, with its wealth of ethnic types, that provided the themes and psychological studies to be found in his works. Of his three novels, written during the second World War, two—*Travnička hronika* (1945; *Bosnian Story,* 1959) and *Na Drini ćuprija* (1945; *The Bridge on the Drina,* 1959)—are concerned with the history of Bosnia.

Andrić's works reveal his deterministic philosophy and his sense of compassion and are written objectively and soberly, in language of great beauty and purity. The Nobel Prize committee commented particularly on the "epic force" with which he handled his material, especially in *The Bridge on the Drina.*

Androcles, also spelled ANDROCLUS, Roman slave who allegedly lived about the time of the emperor Tiberius or Caligula and who became the hero of a story by Aulus Gellius. The story, taken originally from Apion's *Aiguptiaka* and also found in Aelian's *De natura animalium,* tells that Androcles had taken refuge from the cruelties of his master in a cave in Africa, when a lion entered the cave and showed him his swollen paw, from which Androcles extracted a large thorn. Later, the grateful animal recognized him when Androcles had been captured and thrown to the wild beasts in the circus and, instead of attacking him, began to caress him; he was then set free. The story is the subject of the play *Androcles and the Lion* by George Bernard Shaw.

androgen, any of a group of hormones that primarily influence the growth and development of the male reproductive system.

Production. The predominant and most active androgen is testosterone (*q.v.*), which is produced by the male testes. The other androgens, which support the functions of testosterone, are produced mainly by the adrenal cortex—the outer substance of the adrenal glands—and only in relatively small quantities. Trace quantities of androgens are found in the female blood plasma. It is believed that the adrenal glands produce most of these small amounts. The ovaries, which normally secrete the female hormones known as estrogens, also produce minute amounts of androgens.

In the male, the interstitial cells of Leydig, located in the connective tissue surrounding the sperm-producing tubules of the testes, are responsible for the production and secretion of androgens. In male animals that breed only seasonally, such as migratory birds and sheep, Leydig cells are prevalent in the testes during the breeding season but diminish considerably in number during the nonbreeding season. The actual secretion of androgens by these cells is controlled by luteinizing hormone (LH) from the pituitary gland.

Effects. Androgens are needed for the development of the male reproductive system. Without injections of testosterone, males that have been castrated prior to adolescence and sexual maturity do not develop functioning adult reproductive organs. Androgens given to normal males tend to increase the size of the reproductive organs; castration performed on males that have already reached maturity causes the organs to shrink and to stop functioning. Androgens are also necessary for the formation of sperm cells (spermatogenesis) and for the maintenance of sexual interest and behaviour.

Other effects of androgens upon the male body are diversified. The growth of pubic hair and of facial and chest hair and the regression of scalp hair, or baldness, are influenced by androgens. During adolescence, androgens lengthen and thicken the male vocal cords, causing voice deepening; they also enhance bone growth and increase the number and thickness of muscle fibres in the male body. Other growth patterns that androgens stimulate are kidney weight and size, the increase of protein in bone tissue, the regeneration of red blood cells, the presence of pigments in the skin, and the increased activity of sweat and sebaceous (oil-producing) glands.

androgyny, condition in which characteristics of both sexes are clearly expressed in a single individual. In biology, androgyny refers to individuals with fully developed sexual organs of both sexes, also called hermaphrodites. Body build and other physical characteristics of these individuals are a blend of normal male and female features.

In psychology, androgyny refers to individuals with strong personality traits associated with both sexes, combining toughness and gentleness, assertiveness and nurturing behaviour, as called for by the situation. Androgynous individuals are more likely to engage in cross-sexual behaviour than those who maintain traditional sex roles. The rise of feminism and the influence of the women's rights movement made certain aspects of androgynous behaviour more socially attractive than in the past. Androgynous figures occurred frequently in Greek mythology, often embodying a blend of desirable male and female characteristics. The blind seer Tiresias, a figure of great wisdom, was sometimes depicted as a hermaphrodite.

Andromache, in Greek legend, the daughter of Eëtion (prince of Thebe in Mysia) and wife of Hector (son of King Priam of Troy). All Andromache's relations perished in or shortly after the taking of Troy by the Greek warrior Neoptolemus (Pyrrhus). When the captives were allotted, Andromache fell to Neoptolemus, the son of Achilles, whom she accompanied to Epirus and to whom she bore three sons. Neoptolemus was slain at Delphi, and he left Andromache and the kingdom as well to Helenus, the brother of Hector. After the death of Helenus, Andromache returned to Asia Minor with her youngest son, Pergamus, who there founded a town named after himself.

Andromeda, in Greek mythology, beautiful daughter of King Cepheus and Queen Cassiope of Joppa in Palestine (called Ethiopia) and wife of Perseus. Cassiope offended the Nereids by boasting that Andromeda was more beautiful than they, so Poseidon sent a sea monster in revenge. Since only Andromeda's sacrifice would appease the gods, she was chained to a rock and left for the monster. Perseus flew by on the winged horse Pegasus, fell in love with Andromeda, and asked Cepheus for her hand. Cepheus agreed, and Perseus slew the monster. At their marriage feast, however, Andromeda's uncle, Phineus, to whom she had originally been promised, tried to claim her. Perseus turned him to stone with Medusa's head. Andromeda bore Perseus six sons and a daughter.

Andromeda, in astronomy, constellation of the northern sky at about one hour right ascension (the coordinate on the celestial sphere analogous to longitude on the Earth) and 40° north declination (angular distance north of the celestial equator), named for Andromeda of Greek legend. Its most notable feature is the great Andromeda Galaxy.

Andromeda Galaxy (catalog numbers NGC 224 and M 31), great spiral galaxy in the constellation Andromeda, the nearest external galaxy (except for the Magellanic Clouds, which are companions of the galaxy in which Earth is located). The Andromeda Galaxy is one of the few visible to the unaided eye, appearing as a milky blur. It is located about 2,000,000 light-years from the Earth; its diameter is approximately 200,000 light-years; and it seems at least roughly similar to the Milky Way Galaxy. It was mentioned as early as AD 964, in the *Book of the Fixed Stars,* by the Arab astronomer aṣ-Ṣūfī, and rediscovered in 1612, shortly after the invention of the telescope, by the German astronomer Simon Marius, who said it resembled the light of a candle seen through horn. Many individual stars, star clusters, nebulae, and novae (exploding stars) have been observed in it with modern instruments. Andromeda Galaxy was the first galaxy proved to be located beyond the Milky Way Galaxy.

Andromeda Galaxy (NGC 224, M 31)
By courtesy of Hale Observatories

Andronicus, name of Byzantine emperors grouped below and indicated by the symbol •.

• Andronicus I Comnenus (b. 1118, Constantinople—d. Aug. 12, 1185, Constantinople), Byzantine emperor from 1183 to 1185, the last of the Comnenus dynasty, who attempted to reform the government but whose bitter opposition to Western Christianity precipitated a Norman invasion.

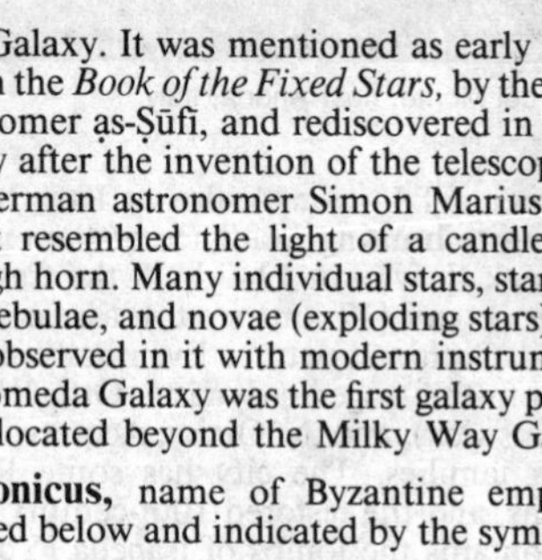

Andronicus I (left), effigy on a gold solidus, 1183–85; in the British Museum
Peter Clayton

A cousin of the emperor Manuel I Comnenus (reigned 1143–80), Andronicus opposed the unpopular regency of the dowager empress Mary of Antioch after Manuel's death. In the spring of 1182 he raised an army and entered Constantinople posing as the protector of the young emperor Alexius II; one of the results of his seizure of power was a massacre of the Westerners living in the city, mostly Venetians and Genoese. Soon after, he contrived the death of the Dowager Empress. In September 1183 he was crowned co-emperor to Alexius and two months later had him strangled. To legitimize his usurpation, the 65-year-old Andronicus married Alexius' 13-year-old widow.

Although Andronicus caused a bloodbath in the capital, he attempted to improve life in the provinces by reforming the decaying political system, prohibiting the sale of offices, punishing corrupt officials, and, above all, checking the power of the great feudal nobles and landowners whose privileges undermined the unity of the empire. He repudiated the pro-Western policy of Manuel I, asserting the independence of the Eastern Church, thus arousing the hostility of Western Christians. In 1183 Béla III of Hungary, claiming to be the avenger of the Dowager Empress (a Westerner), invaded the empire and sacked several cities. Sicilian Normans led by William II in August 1185 marched through Greece, occupying Thessalonica (modern Thessaloníki), the second city of the empire. At the news of the approaching Normans, a revolt broke out in the capital, Isaac II Angelus was proclaimed emperor, and Andronicus was put to death by a street mob.

• Andronicus II Palaeologus (b. 1260, Constantinople—d. 1332, Constantinople), Byzantine emperor, the son of Michael VIII Palaeologus, who liberated Constantinople from the Latins in 1261. During Andronicus' reign (1282–1328) the Byzantine Empire declined to the status of a minor state, confined by the Ottoman Turks in Anatolia and the Serbs in the Balkans.

An intellectual and a theologian rather than a statesman or soldier, Andronicus weakened Byzantium by reducing its land forces to a few thousand cavalry and infantry and eliminating the navy altogether, relying solely on a Genoese mercenary fleet. His lack of military initiative enabled the Ottoman Turks to gain control of nearly all of Anatolia by 1300, and his employment of Catalan mercenaries in 1304 ended disastrously, because the Catalans proved more inclined to pillage Byzantine cities than to fight the Turks. In the war between the Italian city-states of Venice and Genoa, he unwisely took sides, favouring Genoa, and suffered the wrath of the greatly superior Venetian navy.

Internally, Andronicus' reign was marked by a steady disintegration of centralized authority and increasing economic difficulties, but he did sponsor a revival of Byzantine art and culture and championed the independence of the Eastern Orthodox Church. During his reign the great monastery complex at Mt. Athos in Greece enjoyed its golden age.

In 1328 Andronicus, after quarrelling with his grandson Andronicus III and excluding him from the succession, was deposed by him and entered a monastery.

• Andronicus III Palaeologus (b. 1296, Constantinople—d. June 15, 1341, Constantinople), Byzantine emperor who sought to strengthen the empire during its final period of decline.

Andronicus was the grandson of the emperor Andronicus II Palaeologus, but his youthful excesses cost him the favour of his grandfather, and, after he accidentally caused the death of his brother in 1320, the Emperor excluded him from the succession. A civil war ensued, with the younger Andronicus enlisting the support of the powerful Byzantine nobility, particularly the wealthy John VI Cantacuzenus; in 1325 Andronicus compelled the old emperor to recognize him as co-emperor, with control over the provinces of Thrace and Macedonia. In May 1328 he forced his grandfather to abdicate and enter a monastery, and Adronicus became sole ruler.

As emperor, Andronicus relied heavily on the guidance of Cantacuzenus, who encouraged reform of the law courts and initiated the rebuilding of the imperial navy, which had been neglected in the reign of Andronicus' predecessor. Cantacuzenus himself became emperor in 1347. Also under Andronicus, the orthodox monasteries took an increasingly active part in both ecclesiastical and civil affairs.

In foreign policy Andronicus was forced to recognize Serbian suzerainty over Macedonia (August 1334) and suffered losses to the Ottoman Turks in Anatolia; but he managed to regain the islands of Chios, Phocaea, and Lesbos from the Genoese with the aid of the navy provided by Cantacuzenus and reasserted imperial control over the separatist Greek states of Epirus and Thessaly.

• **Andronicus IV** PALAEOLOGUS (b. 1348?, Constantinople—d. June 28, 1385), Byzantine emperor from 1376 to 1379. Conspiring against his father, John V Palaeologus, he was imprisoned and deprived of his rights to the succession. John's rivals, the Genoese, however, helped Andronicus to escape, and he entered Constantinople on Aug. 12, 1376, and took his father prisoner; he was crowned the following year (Oct. 18, 1377). In 1379, however, it was his father's turn to escape—with Venetian and Turkish aid—and be restored to the throne, on the condition that he recognize Andronicus as his rightful heir and swear allegiance as the vassal of the sultan. Andronicus predeceased his father, and his own son became emperor as John VII Palaeologus.

Andronicus OF CYRRHUS, also called ANDRONICUS CYRRHESTES (fl. *c.* 100 BC), Greek astronomer best known as the architect of the horologium at Athens called the Tower of the Winds, known during the Middle Ages as the Lantern of Demosthenes. A considerable portion of the tower still exists. It was octagonal, with figures carved on each side to represent the eight principal winds. In addition, there were eight sundials, visible in all directions from a great distance. Inside the tower was a water clock for use when there was no sunlight. A brazen statue of Triton, rod in hand, atop the horologium turned with the wind to indicate its direction. From this device is derived the custom of placing weathervanes on steeples. Andronicus also built a multiple-faced sundial in the sanctuary of Poseidon on the Island of Tenos.

Andronicus OF RHODES (fl. 1st century BC), Greek philosopher noted for his meticulous editing and commentary of Aristotle's works, which had been passed from one generation to the next in such a way that the purity and clarity of the original texts had been lost and much superfluous material had been added to many of the important treatises. Andronicus studied the original texts to sift out the extraneous material and arranged them in an order that he thought reflected the workings of Aristotle's mind. After completing the editing, he wrote a treatise that covered four topics: a defense of his procedure, a biography of Aristotle, an exploration into the question of authenticity, and an examination of the Aristotelian system of thought.

Andronicus, Lucius Livius: *see* Livius Andronicus, Lucius.

Andropov, formerly (until 1946 and 1957–84) RYBINSK and (1946–57) SHCHERBAKOV, city, Yaroslavl *oblast* (administrative region), northwestern Russian Soviet Federated Socialist Republic, on the Volga River. The 12th-century village of Rybnaya *sloboda* became the town of Rybinsk in 1777. Its river port flourished with the opening (1810) of the Mariinsk Waterway, linking the Volga to the Baltic, and again with its reconstruction as the deep Volga–Baltic Waterway in 1964. A wide range of engineering and other products are made. In 1941 a large barrage and a hydroelectric station were completed on the Volga immediately above Rybinsk. The city's first name change occurred in 1946, when it was renamed for A.S. Shcherbakov, an associate of Stalin; Nikita Khrushchev restored the city's original name in a de-Stalinization program in 1957. The present name was adopted in 1984 to commemorate Yury V. Andropov, chairman of the Supreme Soviet, upon his death. Pop. (1983 est.) 247,000.

Andropov, Yury Vladimirovich (b. June 15 [June 2, old style], 1914, Nagutskoye, Russia—d. Feb 9, 1984, Moscow), head of the Soviet Union's KGB (State Security Committee) from 1967 to 1982 and his country's leader as general secretary of the Communist Party's Central Committee from November 1982 until his death 15 months later.

The son of a railway worker, Andropov worked as a telegraph operator, film projectionist, and boatman on the Volga River before attending a technical college and, later, Petrozavodsk University. He became an organizer for the Young Communist League (Komsomol) in the Yaroslav region. His abilities attracted the notice of his superiors, and he was appointed head of the Komsomol in the newly created Karelo-Finnish Autonomous Republic (1939–40). When the Germans invaded, Andropov organized guerrilla groups in this area behind the enemy lines. After the war this dangerous part of his career was rewarded with the party leadership of Petrozavodsk.

The turning point in Andropov's career was his transfer to Moscow (1951), where he was assigned to the party's Secretariat staff, considered a training ground for promising young officials. As ambassador to Hungary (July 1954–March 1957) he played a major role in coordinating the Soviet invasion of that country. Andropov then returned to Moscow, rising rapidly through the Communist hierarchy. In May 1967 party leader Leonid Brezhnev moved Andropov from the 10-member Secretariat to become head of the KGB, a reassignment calculated to tighten political control over the too-independent security system. While serving as head of the KGB, Andropov was elected to the Politburo (the inner cabinet of the Central Committee) as an alternate member in 1967 and then as a full voting member in 1973; in 1976 he rose to the rank of army general. Andropov's policies as head of the KGB were repressive; his tenure was noted for its suppression of political dissidents, he was one of those who planned the 1968 invasion of Czechoslovakia, and in 1981 he, with others, pressured the Polish regime to impose martial law.

As Brezhnev's health declined, Andropov began to position himself for succession. On May 24, 1982, Andropov resigned his KGB post, considered a political liability, and moved back to his former position on the Secretariat. Andropov was chosen by the Communist Party Central Committee to succeed Brezhnev on November 12, scarcely two days after Brezhnev's death.

In his short tenure he sought to institute reforms in the nation's ponderous economic system, to crack down on corruption and on vested interests, and to pursue a hard line in foreign relations. But ill health overtook him by August 1983, and thereafter he was never seen again in public. He accomplished little and was succeeded by a former rival, Konstantin Chernenko, a friend of old-line officials wedded to the status quo.

Ándros, island, most northerly and second largest of the Cyclades group of Greek Aegean Islands, 145 sq mi (380 sq km) in area. Wooded, well watered, and mountainous, it is an *eparkhía* (province), with its capital at Ándros, on the east coast, which has many Albanian inhabitants. South of the capital is the port of Kórthion; to the north, the Palaiókastron (2,050 ft [625 m]), with ruins of a Venetian castle and medieval town. The ruins of Palaeopolis, the ancient capital, support a hamlet, Palaiópolis, on the western coast.

The ancient population was mainly Ionian. Originally dependent upon Eretria, the second city of ancient Euboea, it sent colonies to Chalcidice, the great peninsula of northeastern Greece, in the 7th century BC. It submitted to Persia in 490 BC and was harried by the Athenian fleet for supplying ships to the Persian king Xerxes in 480. The Athenian leader Pericles forced Ándros to admit Athenian settlers, but it revolted in 411 or 410. During the 4th century it was again a member of the revived anti-Spartan Delian League. In 200 it was captured by a combined Roman, Pergamese, and Rhodian fleet. It remained with Pergamum until 133 BC, when it became part of the Roman province of Asia. From AD 1207 to 1566 it was under the protection of Venice, falling to Turkey in the latter year. It became part of Greece in 1829. Pop. (1981) island, 9,020; town, 1,631.

Andros, Sir Edmund (b. Dec. 6, 1637, London—d. Feb. 24, 1714, London), English administrator in America, best known for his part in an abortive attempt to stem growing colonial independence by imposing a kind of supercolony (the Dominion of New England) on the New World.

Andros grew up as a page in the royal household, and his fidelity to the Crown during its exile after the English Civil War was rewarded in 1674 by his appointment as governor of New York and New Jersey. (He was also knighted in 1678.) Although the mother country regarded him as an able and conscientious administrator, the colonists considered him both arrogant and arbitrary, and he was recalled in 1681.

Andros returned to America in 1686 as governor of the Dominion of New England, including jurisdiction of all the New England colonies and later of New York and New Jersey as well. Andros' imposition of Episcopalian worship in the Old South Meetinghouse in Boston, his vigorous enforcement of the Navigation Acts, his requirement that landholders take out new land patents, and his limitations upon town meetings and rights of local taxations all aroused sharp resentment in colonial America. When news of the overthrow of James II (1688) reached Boston, the colonists revolted, deposing Andros and imprisoning him. Returned to England, he was tried and immediately released. He later served as governor of Virginia (1692), Maryland (1693–94), and the island of Guernsey (1704–06).

Androscoggin River, river in northeastern New Hampshire and southern Maine, U.S. It flows south from Umbabog Lake to Gorham, N.H., east to Jay, Maine, and then south again to the Atlantic Ocean. In its 175-mi (280-km) course, the river descends over 1,245 ft (379 m), the two steepest drops occurring at Berlin, N.H., and at Rumford, Maine. The major products of the communities within its drainage basin are pulp and paper (because of the abundance of waterpower, process water, and spruce-fir forests), textiles (in Auburn and Lewiston, Maine), and shoes. The Androscoggin (an Algonkian Indian word meaning "fish-curing place") is renowned for its fishing, hunting, and boating facilities.

Androuet du Cerceau FAMILY: *see* Cerceau, du, family.

Andrusovo, Truce of, Polish ANDRUSZOW (Feb. 9 [Jan. 30, old style], 1667), long-lasting treaty that ended the Thirteen Years' War between Russia and Poland for control of the Ukraine (1654–67). In 1654 the Russian government accepted the Pereyaslav Agreement (*q.v.*), a proposal to annex the Ukraine made by the hetman (military leader) of the Zaporozhian Cossacks, Bohdan Khmelnytsky, who had led a revolt in the Ukraine against Polish rule (1648–54).

That agreement precipitated war between Poland and Russia. During the war, control of the Ukraine shifted back and forth many times; and the allegiances of the inhabitants became sharply divided, some preferring Russian rule, others Polish.

In 1664 peace negotiations began. Although Polish military achievements and Russian exhaustion gave Poland a negotiating advantage, the outbreak of a new rebellion forced the Poles to accept terms favourable to Russia. According to the truce, the Ukraine was divided along the Dnepr River; Russia received the eastern portion of the Ukraine, the city of Kiev, and the provinces of Smolensk and Seversk. The truce was confirmed by a treaty concluded in 1686.

Andrzejewski, Jerzy (b. Aug. 19, 1909, Warsaw—d. April 20, 1983, Warsaw), Polish novelist, short-story writer, and political dissident.

In 1936 he published *Drogi nieuniknione* ("Unavoidable Ways"), followed by *Ład serca* (1938; "Heart's Harmony"), in which he tried to find in Roman Catholic teachings solutions to the problems of contemporary life. During the German occupation of World War II he worked in the Polish underground.

After World War II he wrote *Noc* (1945; "Night"), a collection of wartime stories, and *Swięto Winkelrieda* (1946; "Winkelried's Feast"), in which he revealed not only his predilection for historic themes but also his satirical inclinations. Both trends are prominent in *Popiół i diament* (1948; Ashes and Diamonds, 1962), generally considered his finest novel, in which he presented the tragic situation of young Polish nationalists in conflict with idealistic Communists in the time immediately after World War II. This story was used in the production of a film (1961) directed by the author and Andrzej Wajda, of the Polish cinema.

Andrzejewski rejected the Socialist Realism forced on Polish literature during 1949–54 by the nation's Stalinist rulers. He was one of the first to criticize the imposition of narrow political strictures on creative writing. For several years he was forbidden to publish his works. He appeared, in the eyes of Communist Party bosses, as a more serious "transgressor" when in 1976 he became one of the co-founders of the Workers' Defense Committee (KOR), from which grew a brief but powerful renewal movement that ended with the Polish government's imposition of martial law in 1981.

Andújar, city, Jaén province, in the autonomous community (region) of Andalusia, southern Spain, northwest of Jaén city, on the Río Guadalquivir. Called Isturgi or Ilurgia by the Celto-Iberians, it was besieged and captured by the Roman general Scipio Africanus (206 BC) during the Second Punic War. Ferdinand III of Castile united the city to Christian Spain in AD 1224. Andújar contains a number of fine old mansions and the Gothic church of Santa María la Mayor, with a 13th-century tower. Uranium mining and processing are also significant. The area also has lead and copper mines, cattle ranches, and poultry farms. Its traditional industry is the manufacture of porous jars (*alcarrazas*) from a local clay. Pop. (1981) 34,946.

anechoic chamber, also called FREE-FIELD ROOM, or FREE-SPACE ROOM, sound laboratory so designed as to minimize sound reflections as well as external noise. External sound is excluded by physical isolation of the structure, by elaborate acoustical filters in the ventilating ducts, and by thick masonry walls. Interior surfaces are covered with absorptive

Auditory localization experiment in an anechoic chamber

By courtesy of Bell Laboratories, Murray Hill, N.J.

material, such as glass fibre or mineral wool in blankets or in horizontal and vertical wedges (*see* illustration). Ceiling and floor are similarly padded; a thin steel mesh just above the floor provides a surface for walking. Sound reflection can be reduced to one part in 1,000 in such a room, thus simulating the acoustical conditions of unobstructed free space.

Anegada Island, one of the British Virgin Islands and the northernmost of the Lesser Antilles, a chain separating the Atlantic Ocean and Caribbean Sea, lying about 80 mi (130 km) northeast of Puerto Rico. The island has an area of 15 sq mi (39 sq km). Annual rainfall averages a moderate 50 in. (1,275 mm). Unlike the other Virgin Islands, Anegada (Spanish: Inundated) is fairly flat, being made of coral and limestone with very little subsoil and no water. There are dangerous reefs, and Anegada's waters contain many still unexplored shipwrecks. Pop. (1980 prelim.) 169.

Anegada Passage, channel in the West Indies, connecting the Atlantic Ocean with the Caribbean Sea; it is 40 mi (65 km) wide and separates the British Virgin Islands (west) from the Leeward Islands (southeast). It has the greatest depth (more than 7,550 ft [2,300 m]) of any channel in the eastern Caribbean. The passage is one of the two through which subsurface water enters the Caribbean (the other being the Windward Passage).

Anécho, formerly ANÉCHO, town, Lacs *préfecture* in Maritime economic *région*, southern Togo, West Africa, lying on the Gulf of Guinea, near the border of Benin. Founded in the late 17th century by Ane peoples fleeing from Ashanti attacks in Elmina (now in Ghana), Anécho developed as a slave port and commercial centre. It was the capital of German Togoland from 1885 to 1887 and of the French occupation from 1914 to 1920. Anécho remains an important intellectual centre for Togo, through it has not grown as rapidly as Togo's other major cities. Pop. (1977 est.) 13,300.

Aneirin (fl. 6th century AD), one of five poets renowned among the Welsh in the 6th century, according to Nennius in his *Historia Britonum* (written *c.* 800); the others are Taliesin (*q.v.*) and Talhaearn Tad Awen, Blwchbardd, and Cian, whose works are unknown. Aneirin's reputation rests on a single work, *Y Gododdin* (O'Grady, Desmond, ed., 1980) considered the earliest extant Welsh work, though preserved only in a manuscript known as *The Book of Aneirin,* which dates from about 1250. The language of the poem is direct for the most part, although simile and metaphor are skillfully used, and alliteration and internal rhyme abound. The poem praises the strength, courage, and military prowess of Aneirin's contemporaries in the army of Mynyddawg Mwynfawr (Mynyddawg the Wealthy) of Caereidyn (near Edinburgh) and consists of a series of sharp characterizations of each hero who participated in the ill-starred expedition of the war band of 300 men sent by their lord Mynyddawg Mwynfawr to recapture the old Roman stronghold of Catraeth (Catterick in Yorkshire) from the Saxons of Deira.

Aneityum (Vanuatu): *see* Anatom.

anemia, also spelled ANAEMIA, condition in which the red cells of the blood (erythrocytes) are reduced in number or volume or are deficient in hemoglobin, their oxygen-carrying pigment. There are close to 100 different varieties of anemia, depending on the cause, the size and hemoglobin content of the abnormal cells, and the symptoms. Causally, anemia may result from (1) chronic or acute blood loss; (2) increased destruction of the red cells (hemolysis), which may be caused by hereditary cell defects, as in sickle-cell anemia, hereditary spherocytosis, or glucose-6-phosphate dehydrogenase deficiency; exposure to hemolytic chemicals (substances causing the release of hemoglobin from the red cells) such as sulfanilamide, primaquine, or naphthalene (mothballs); development of antibodies against the red blood cells, as in erythroblastosis fetalis; or (3) reduced production of red cells, which may be caused by disorders of the bone marrow, as in leukemia and aplastic anemia; deficiency of one or more of the nutrients, notably vitamin B_{12}, folic acid, and iron, that are necessary for the synthesis of red blood cells; deficiency of certain hormones; inhibition of the red-cell-forming processes by certain drugs or by toxins produced by disease, particularly chronic infection, widespread cancer, and kidney failure.

Structurally, the anemias generally fall into the following types: (1) macrocytic, characterized by larger than normal red cells (*e.g.,* pernicious anemia); (2) normocytic, characterized by a decrease in the number of red cells, which are otherwise relatively normal (*e.g.,* anemia caused by sudden blood loss, as in bleeding peptic ulcer, most cases of hemophilia, and purpura); (3) simple microcytic, characterized by smaller than normal red cells (encountered in cases of chronic inflammatory conditions and in renal disease); and (4) microcytic hypochromic, characterized by a reduction in red-cell size and hemoglobin concentration (frequently associated with iron-deficiency anemia, but also seen in thalassemia).

The most noticeable outward symptom of anemia is usually pallor of the skin, mucous membranes, and nail beds. Symptoms of tissue oxygen deficiency include pulsating noises in the ear, dizziness, fainting, and shortness of breath. Compensatory action of the heart may lead to its enlargement and to a rapid pulse rate. The treatment of anemia varies greatly, depending on the diagnosis. It includes supplying the missing nutrients in the deficiency anemias, detecting and removing toxic factors, improving the underlying disorder with drug and other forms of therapy, decreasing the extent of blood destruction by methods that include surgery (*e.g.,* splenectomy), or restoring blood volume with transfusion.

anemia, equine infectious: *see* equine infectious anemia.

anemia, pernicious: *see* pernicious anemia.

anemia, sickle-cell: *see* sickle-cell trait and sickle-cell anemia.

anemia of bone-marrow failure: *see* aplastic anemia.

anemometer, device for measuring the speed of airflow in the atmosphere, in wind tun-

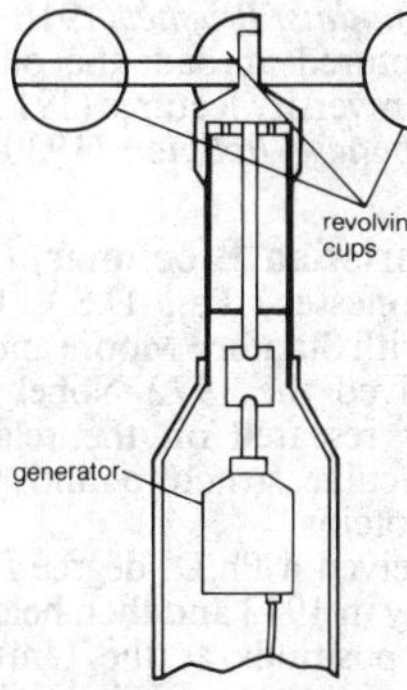

Revolving-cup electric anemometer

From D.M. Considine, ed., *Process Instruments and Controls Handbook.* Copyright (1957). Used with permission of McGraw-Hill Book Company

nels, and in other gas-flow applications. Most widely used for wind-speed measurements is the revolving-cup electric anemometer, in which the revolving cups drive an electric generator. The output of the generator operates an electric meter that is calibrated in terms of wind speed. The useful range of this device is approximately from 5 to 100 miles (8 to 160 kilometres) per hour. A propeller may also be used to drive the electric generator, as in the propeller anemometer. In another type of wind-driven unit, revolving vanes operate a counter, the revolutions being timed by a stopwatch and converted to airspeed. This device is especially suited for low airspeeds, around 1 to 25 miles (1.6 to 40 kilometres) per hour.

The fact that a stream of air will cool a heated object (the rate of cooling being determined by the speed of the airflow) is reflected in the use of the hot-wire anemometer. An electrically heated fine wire is placed in the airflow. As the airflow increases, the wire cools. In the most common type of hot-wire anemometer, the constant-temperature type, power is increased to maintain a constant wire temperature. The input power to the hot wire is then a measure of airspeed, and a meter in the electrical circuit of the hot wire can be calibrated to indicate airspeed. This device is useful for very low airspeeds, below about five miles per hour. The kata thermometer is a heated-alcohol thermometer; the time it takes to cool is measured and used to determine air current. It is useful for measuring low speeds in studies of air circulation.

A stream of air striking the open end of a tube closed at the other end will build up pressure within the tube. The difference in pressure between the interior of this tube (called a pitot tube) and the surrounding air can be measured and the pressure converted to airspeed. Pitot tubes are also used to measure the flow of liquids, particularly in the course of flume studies in fluid mechanics. This anemometer is most useful, however, in strong, steady air streams, such as in wind tunnels and aboard aircraft in flight. With modifications, it can be used to measure supersonic air flow. Another type of pressure anemometer is the Venturi tube, which is open at both ends and of larger diameter at the ends than at the middle. Airspeed is determined by measuring the pressure at the constriction in the tube. Venturi tubes have some applications in industry. A bridled pressure plate, which measures pressure on a plate balanced by a spring, is useful in measuring the velocity of gusts of air.

anemone, also called PASQUEFLOWER, or WINDFLOWER, any of about 120 species of perennial plants constituting the genus *Anemone* of the buttercup family (Ranunculaceae). Many colourful varieties of the tuberous poppylike anemone, *A. coronaria,* are grown for the garden and florist's trade. Popular spring-flowering anemones, especially for naturalizing, are *A. apennina, A. blanda,* and *A. pavonina.* Other species, such as the Japanese anemone (*A. hupehensis,* or *A. japonica*) are favourite border plants for autumn flowering. Some species whose fruits differ in structure are placed in a separate section, *Pulsatilla,* often given the rank of genus. Anemones are distributed throughout the world but occur most commonly in woodlands and meadows of the North Temperate Zone. Many varieties are cultivated in gardens for their colourful flowers.

The wood anemone of Europe, *A. nemorosa,* which bears white flowers, causes blistering of the skin and was formerly used as an ingredient in medicines. In North America, wood anemone refers to *A. quinquefolia,* a delicate plant with deeply cut leaves. "Windflower," the English version of the Greek-derived

(Top) Anemone (*Anemone patens*); (bottom) wood anemone (*Anemone quinquefolia*)

(Top) John Kohout from Root Resources—EB Inc., (bottom) Grant Heilman—EB Inc.

"anemone," refers to the fact that the flowers seem to be blown open by the wind. The term pasqueflower (from Old French *pasque,* Easter) refers to such floral emblems of Easter as *A. patens, A. pratensis,* and *A. pulsatilla.*

anemone fish, any of about 12 species of Indo-Pacific fishes constituting the genus *Amphiprion* of the family Pomacentridae (order

Clown fish (*Amphiprion percula*), one of the anemone fishes

A. Bernhaut—Bavaria-Verlag

Perciformes), noted for their association with large sea anemones. Anemone fishes live and shelter among the tentacles of the anemones, swimming in and out unharmed by the stinging cells (nematocysts) that are present on the tentacles and that can be fatal to other fishes. A representative species, common in the Indo-Australian archipelago, is *Amphiprion percula,* also called the clown fish. Bright orange, with three wide, blue-white bands circling the body, it grows to a length of about five centimetres (two inches).

Anencletus, SAINT (pope): *see* Anacletus, Saint.

Anerio, Felice (b. *c.* 1560, Rome—d. Sept. 27, 1614, Rome), one of the leading Roman composers of his time, who succeeded his master, Palestrina, as composer to the Papal Chapel in 1594. Most of Anerio's early works are secular, but he began to concentrate on sacred music after his appointment as papal composer.

In general, he modelled his style on that of Palestrina, and several of his pieces were for a long time mistaken for those of the celebrated master. His later compositions, however, do not slavishly imitate the Palestrina style but contain many passages of personal expression. Anerio's works include madrigals, both sacred and secular, canzonets, masses, motets, and other sacred music.

anesthetic, also spelled ANAESTHETIC, agent which produces a local or general loss of sensation, including pain. General anesthesia involves loss of consciousness, usually for the purpose of relieving the pain of surgery. Local anesthesia involves loss of sensation in one area of the body by the blockage of conduction in nerves. Anesthesia may also result from disease or injury to the brain, spinal cord, or peripheral nerves.

A brief treatment of anesthetics follows. For full treatment, *see* MACROPAEDIA: Drugs and Drug Action.

Drugs of various kinds have been used for many centuries to reduce the distress of surgical operations. Homer wrote of nepenthe, which was probably cannabis or opium. Arabian physicians used opium and henbane. More recently powerful rum was administered freely to British sailors before emergency amputations were carried out on board ship in the aftermath of battle.

In 1799 Sir Humphry Davy, British chemist and inventor, tried inhaling nitrous oxide (laughing gas) and discovered its anesthetic properties, but the implications of his findings for surgery were ignored.

By the early 1840s the equivalent of "pot parties" had become fashionable in Britain and the United States, at which nitrous oxide, contained in bladders, was passed round and inhaled for its soporific effect. It was soon found that ether, which could be carried much more conveniently in small bottles, was equally potent. In the United States several young dentists and doctors experimented independently with the use of nitrous oxide or ether to dull the pain of tooth extractions and other minor operations. In 1845, Horace Wells, a U.S. dentist, attempted to publicly demonstrate the use of nitrous oxide anesthesia for dental extractions. Unfortunately, the demonstration was unsuccessful.

Historians argue about who should get the credit for the first use of true surgical anesthesia, but it fell to William Morton, a U.S. dentist, to convince the medical world that general anesthesia was a practical proposition. He administered ether to a patient having a neck tumour removed at the Massachusetts General Hospital, Boston, in October 1846. Crawford Long, a U.S. surgeon, had used ether in his practice since 1842 but did not make his findings public until 1849.

A few weeks after Morton's demonstration, ether was used during a leg amputation performed by Robert Liston at University College Hospital, London. In Britain, official royal sanction was put on anesthetics by Queen Victoria, who accepted chloroform from her physician, John Snow, when giving birth to her eighth child, Prince Leopold, in 1853.

Early anesthetics had unpleasant side effects (often causing vomiting on recovery) and were somewhat hazardous, since the dose needed to produce unconsciousness and full muscle relaxation (so that the surgeon could work unimpeded) was not far short of that which would paralyze the breathing centre of the brain. In addition, the early anesthetics were administered by simple devices consisting of glass or metal containers for sponges soaked in ether or chloroform (which was introduced as an anesthetic in 1847) and allowed no control of dosage.

Modern inhalation anesthetics such as trichlorethylene and halothane have a much wider safety margin, and are administered from an anesthetic machine mixed with oxygen and nitrous oxide. The anesthetist can control the flow and composition of the gas mixture precisely, and, with the use of a tube placed down the trachea (windpipe) after the patient is unconscious, can, if necessary, maintain respiration by mechanical means. Delivering the gas mixture to the lungs through a close-fitting, endotracheal tube also prevents the accidental inhalation of mucus, saliva, and vomit.

With respiration artificially maintained it is possible to paralyze the muscles with drugs like curare, the neuromuscular blocking agent, and so procedures which require full muscle relaxation, such as chest and abdominal surgery, can be carried out under light anesthesia.

Many short operations can be carried out under anesthesia produced by injecting an agent such as the barbiturate thiopental sodium (Pentothal) into a vein, either as a single dose or intermittently through a saline drip. Patients are also commonly put to sleep by this method before the administration of an inhalation anesthetic is begun, since it is a distress-free procedure, and unconsciousness occurs smoothly within 10 or 15 seconds of starting the injection.

Local anesthetics work by blocking the passage of impulses along nerves. Cocaine was thus used for eye operations in 1884 by a Viennese surgeon, Carl Koller, acting on the suggestion of Sigmund Freud. A solution of the drug was applied directly to the part to be operated on. Soon it was being injected under the skin to facilitate small, local operations, and was later successfully used for larger procedures by injecting it into the trunks of nerves supplying a part. Now synthetic cocaine substitutes are widely employed in the same manner.

Major operations on the lower half of the body can be carried out after injecting a suitable local anesthetic into the fluid-filled space between the spinal cord and its outer membrane coverings (spinal anesthesia). Painless childbirth can be achieved by an epidural block, which involves injecting the anesthetic agent through a fine tube threaded into the space surrounding the tough membrane covering the lower end of the spinal cord, thus bathing the emerging nerves which supply the pelvic organs.

In recent years much interest has been shown in acupuncture anesthesia, whereby apparently painless major operations are carried out after the insertion of acupuncture needles into specified points on the skin. Often an electric current is passed through the needle used. The results of some research into the efficacy of acupuncture have suggested that the stimulation of the peripheral nerves by the needles triggers the release of endorphins, a group of neurochemicals that have pain-killing effects.

aneuploidy (biology): *see* ploidy.

aneurysm, bulging and thinning of some point in the wall of a blood vessel (usually an artery) or of the heart because of arteriosclerosis ("hardening of the arteries"), embolism, infection, or physical injury. A false aneurysm is a collection of blood in the tissues that pulsates because there is a passage to it from a ruptured artery. An arteriovenous aneurysm (*see* arteriovenous fistula) is the direct flow from an artery to a vein due to injury, a connecting sac (varicose aneurysm), or congenital defect. In a dissecting aneurysm a vessel wall bulges because of blood that has penetrated the wall and has split the media, or middle layer.

A popliteal artery aneurysm is easily detected by the affected person because it causes a noticeable, pulsating bulge behind the knee. The bulge brings discomfort and interferes with crossing the legs. Pressure on nearby nerves may be painful, and there may be intermittent lameness of the calf muscles (intermittent claudication). An aneurysm in this location may also cause formation of a blood clot and cutting off of circulation to the lower leg with danger of gangrene unless an emergency operation restores the circulation.

The symptoms of aortic aneurysm vary with the size of the defect and its location. If it presses against the windpipe and the bronchi, for example, it may interfere with breathing and lead to coughing. An aneurysm caused by syphilis may erode the breastbone and cause severe chest pain.

The element common to all true aneurysms is injury to the media. After the aneurysm has developed it tends to grow, with danger that the vessel wall will rupture. The treatment of aneurysm involves surgical removal of the diseased section of artery and its replacement with a plastic graft.

Anezaki Masaharu, also called ANEZAKI CHŌFŪ (b. 1873, Kyōto—d. 1949), Japanese scholar who did pioneer work in various fields of the history of religions. After graduating from Tokyo Imperial University, he went to India and Europe for further studies (1900–03). Returning to Japan, he was appointed to the chair of science of religion at Tokyo Imperial University.

He started his academic career as a student of Indian religions and Buddhism in particular. Before him, studies in Buddhist scriptures had been conducted mostly from an apologetic point of view; he was one of the first to apply the modern objective, historical method to the study of Buddhism. Working from the conviction that the true spirit of Buddhism must be sought in its initial stage, he attempted text criticism of Pāli and Chinese canons in "Original Buddhism" (1910). He also initiated research in the history of Kirishitan, the specifically Japanese form of Catholic Christianity, during the period it was banned, from the 17th through the 19th century. He became increasingly interested in the 15th-century monk Nichiren and published *Nichiren the Buddhist Prophet* (1916). Anezaki taught and lectured abroad; the outcome of his Harvard University lectures (1913–15) was *History of Japanese Religion* (1930), a standard work.

Anfinsen, Christian B(oehmer) (b. March 26, 1916, Monessen, Pa., U.S.), U.S. biochemist who with Stanford Moore and William H. Stein received the 1972 Nobel Prize for Chemistry for research on the relationships between molecular structure and biological function of proteins.

Anfinsen received a Ph.D. degree from Harvard University in 1943 and then held research and teaching positions at the University of Pennsylvania, Harvard, and the Nobel Medical Institute in Stockholm. He joined the staff of the National Institutes of Health (Bethesda, Md.) in 1950. His research has centred on the adaptation of the structure of enzymes and other proteins to their physiological activities. His writings include *The Molecular Basis of Evolution* (1959).

Consult
the
INDEX
first

Ang, Khmer word denoting a person of royal blood, usually translated "prince" or "princess." For articles on such persons, see the personal name; *e.g.,* for Ang Duong, *see* Duong.

Ang Thong, also spelled ANGTONG, town and *changwat* (province) in the Central region of Thailand, north of Bangkok. Ang Thong town, the provincial capital, and Pa Mok, both lie on the left bank of the Mae Nam (river) Chao Phraya and are linked by road to Phra Nakhon Si Ayutthaya. The provinces area of 374 sq mi (968 sq km) is well irrigated by the Mae Nam Chao Phraya, and its rich alluvium supports rice, corn (maize), and oilseed production. Pop. (1980) town, 9,520; province, 256,706.

aṅgā (Pāli and Sanskrit: "limb," or "division"), any of several categories into which Buddhist canonical writings were divided in early times, beginning before the *Abhidhamma* (scholastic) works were added to the canon. The system, based on a combination of form and content, originally categorized types of material within the various texts; later, it was used to classify the texts themselves. The Theravāda and Mahāsaṅghika schools used an ancient ninefold division; a system of 12 categories was the commonest division in other schools, especially Mahāyāna.

The nine *aṅgā*s in Pāli, with their Sanskrit counterparts where different, are:

1. *Sutta,* or *sūtra* ("discourse"), sermons or discourses of the Buddha in prose. This category was said to include the *vinaya* (monastic discipline) material. Apart from the *aṅgā* system, *sutta* is distinguished from *vinaya* (and the prose limitation is dropped).

2. *Geyya,* or *geya* (a technical term meaning mixed prose and verse), *sutta* that incorporates *gāthā* ("verse").
3. *Veyyākaraṇa* ("explanation," or "prophecy"), a category into which the whole Pāli *Abhidhamma Piṭaka* ("Basket of Special Doctrine") has been placed, together with miscellaneous works. For the Sarvāstivāda (Doctrine That All Is Real) school, the Sanskrit category *vyākaraṇa* meant the Buddha's prophecies concerning his disciples.
4. *Gāthā* ("verse"), works in poetic form.
5. *Udāna* ("inspired utterance"), special sayings of the Buddha in prose or verse (also the name of a work in the Pāli *Khuddaka Nikāya* ["Short Collection"]).
6. *Itivuttaka* ("thus it is said"), sayings of the Buddha introduced by these words; many of them comprise a *Khuddaka Nikāya* work with this title. The Sanskrit category *itivṛttaka* comprises stories about past lives of disciples.
7. *Jātaka* ("birth"; *see* Jātaka), tales of former lives of the Buddha.
8. *Abbhutadhamma,* or *adbhutadharma* ("wondrous phenomena"), stories of miracles and supernatural events.
9. *Vedalla* (perhaps meaning "subtle analysis"), teachings in catechetical form, according to the Pāli system. The Sanskrit tradition places here, as *vaipulya,* a number of important Mahāyāna works, including the *Lotus Sūtra, Aṣṭasāhasrikā-prajñāpāramitā,* and *Laṅkāvatāra-sūtra.*

The 12-fold Sanskrit system adds these categories:

Nidāna ("cause"), a classification for introductory material and historical narratives.

Avadāna ("Noble Deeds"), Buddha's stories of the good deeds in people's former lives and their present results (*see* Apadāna).

Upadeśa ("instruction"), discussions of doctrine—sometimes esoteric doctrine—often in question-and-answer form. The term has also been used for *Abhidhamma* (scholastic section of the canon), for philosophical treatises, for Tantric works, and for commentaries.

Aṅgad, also called LEHNA, or LAHINA (b. 1504, Matte di Sarai, India—d. 1552, Khadur), second Sikh Gurū and originator of the Punjabi script, Gurmukhi, in which many parts of the *Ādi Granth,* the sacred book of the Sikhs, are written.

While on a pilgrimage to the shrine of a Hindu goddess, Aṅgad met the founder of the Sikh religion, Gurū Nānak, whom he resolved to follow. Aṅgad was able to give form and a definitive character to the somewhat vague ideals propounded by Gurū Nānak. He was appointed Gurū in 1539 and set up schools to teach youth the regional language, Punjabi, instead of the classical Sanskrit. He was a firm believer in the importance of physical education and emphasized the ideal of a sound mind and a healthy body.

Gurū Aṅgad also promoted an important Sikh institution, the *Gurū ka laṅgar* ("kitchen of the Gurū"), which, with its insistence on commensality, broke down the traditional Hindu caste system.

Angara River, river in southeast central Russian Soviet Federated Socialist Republic. It is the outlet for Lake Baikal and a major tributary of the Yenisey, which it joins near Yeniseysk. The river flows for 1,105 mi (1,779 km) across the southern part of the Central Siberian Plateau and drains over 400,000 sq mi (1,040,000 sq km). It cuts across basalt flows, which cause many rapids and provide great potential for the generation of hydroelectric power. Dams and power stations were completed at Irkutsk (1958) and Bratsk (1966), the latter creating a reservoir of 2,125 sq mi; a third station at Ust-Ilimsk was completed in 1980; and another hydroelectric station and dam at Boguchany, downstream from Ust-Ilimsk, were under construction in the early 1980s. Power is used in the Irkutsk-Cheremkhovo industrial area along the river.

The Angara River at Irkutsk, Russian S.F.S.R.
Alexander M. Chabe

angaria, Roman imperial postal system modelled on that of Achaemenidian Persia, probably originally established in the 6th century BC by Cyrus the Great. The name was derived from the Greek form of a Babylonian word meaning a mounted courier, the means used to carry royal dispatches by night and day in all weather.

The angaria presumably survived in Hellenistic times and passed down to the Romans. In the Roman system, the supply and maintenance of post horses was a compulsory duty from which the emperor alone could grant exemption; thus, the word came to mean compulsory service.

Angarsk, city, Irkutsk *oblast* (administrative region), southeast central Russian Soviet Federated Socialist Republic, on the Trans-Siberian Railroad. Founded in 1948, Angarsk has grown rapidly as a major centre of oil refining and petrochemicals. The city's industrial products include such goods as synthetic fibres, artificial fertilizers, plastics, boilers, and cement; there are also electro-engineering works and brewing facilities. Petroleum is piped from West Siberian fields to Angarsk's refinery and petrochemical complex. Pop. (1983 est.) 251,000.

angary, in international law, the right of belligerents to requisition for their use neutral merchant vessels, aircraft, and other means of transport that are within their territorial jurisdiction. Generally, the right of angary should be applied only in case of pressing need in time of war, and compensation is due to the neutral owner. The right of angary has, in effect, come to be extended to cover not only land and sea transport but also any kind of neutral property under the jurisdiction of a belligerent.

The right of angary was applied on several occasions during World Wars I and II. Thus, by proclamation of March 20, 1918, the President of the United States took over merchant vessels of Dutch registry lying in U.S. waters. Similar action was taken by Great Britain, France, and Italy. The United States in 1941, though formally still neutral, took over foreign vessels lying idle in its territorial waters but did so under a special right conferred by statute.

It has come to be recognized, however, that the peacetime powers of expropriation grant adequate authority to seize and requisition property under the territorial jurisdiction of a belligerent state without having recourse to the right of angary.

Ängby Stone, 11th-century memorial stone found in Uppland, Swed., bearing a runic inscription carved by Asmund Kareson (Osmundus), earliest known professional rune carver in Uppland. The stone is inscribed with a Maltese cross surrounded by two intertwining serpents and bears the message: "Ragnfrid had this stone erected in memory of Björn, her and Kättilmund's son. God and God's Mother help his soul. He fell in Virland [in Estonia]. But Asmund engraved [the stone]." A replica of the inscription was found on another stone at Frösunda, Swed.

Ängby Stone
By courtesy of Kungl. Vitterhets Historie Och Antikvitets Akademien, Stockholm

angel, primarily in Western religions (*i.e.,* Zoroastrianism, Judaism, Christianity, and Islām), any of numerous benevolent spiritual beings, powers, or principles that mediate between the realm of the sacred (*i.e.,* the transcendent realm) and the profane realm of time, space, and cause and effect. Comparable beings in Eastern religions include the Hindu *avatāras* and the Buddhist *bodhisattvas.*

A brief treatment of angels follows. For full treatment, *see* MACROPAEDIA: Doctrines and Dogmas, Religious.

Functioning as messengers or servants of the deity (the term angel derives from the Greek word for "messenger") or as guardians of individuals or nations, angels have been classified into ranks or hierarchies by theologians or philosophical thinkers of the major Western religions, of sects that have become religions in their own right (*e.g.,* the Druzes, a religion that developed from Islām), and of syncretistic movements (*e.g.,* Gnosticism, a religious dualistic-belief system that incorporated Jewish, Christian, Iranian, and Hellenistic religious concepts and that viewed matter as evil, the spirit as good, and salvation as being achieved through esoteric knowledge, or gnosis).

The number of such celestial beings in the rankings—often 4, 7, or 12—was generally based on the theory of planetary spheres in Hellenistic or Iranian astrology or on the hierarchy derived from Oriental monarchical government. In Zoroastrianism, a religion founded by the 6th-century-BC Persian reformer Zoroaster, the *amesha spentas,* or bounteous immortals, of Ahura Mazdā, the Good Lord, are arranged in a hierarchy of seven: Spenta Mainyu (the Holy Spirit), Vohu Manah (Good Mind), Asha (Truth), Armaiti (Right Mindedness), Khshathra Vairya (Kingdom), Haurvatāt (Wholeness), and Ameretāt (Immortality).

In Judaism, the hierarchy of angels—often called in the Old Testament the "hosts of heaven" or the "company of divine beings"—is not strictly defined. In postbiblical Judaism—especially in apocalyptic literature, which describes God's dramatic intervention in history—seven angels, sometimes called archangels (*q.v.*), lead the heavenly hosts that in the Talmud (an authoritative compendium of Jewish law, lore, and commentary) are viewed as countless. These seven, noted in the noncanonical *First Book of Enoch* (chapter 20), are: Uriel (leader of the heavenly hosts and guardian of *sheol,* the underworld); Raphael (guardian of human spirits); Raguel (avenger of God against the world of lights); Michael (guardian of Israel); Sariel (avenger of the spirits, "who sin in the spirit"); Gabriel (ruler of paradise, the seraphim, and the cherubim); and Remiel, also called Jeremiel (guardian of the souls in *sheol*). Of these, two (Michael and Gabriel) are mentioned in the Old Testament and two others (Raphael and Uriel) in the Apocrypha, a collection of noncanonical works. In rabbinic literature, angels are classified into two basic groupings: higher and lower. Included among the higher group are the cherubim and seraphim, winged guardians of God's throne or chariot, and the *ofannim* (Hebrew: "wheels"), all of which are noted in the Old Testament. Among the sectarians associated with the Dead Sea Scrolls, the higher angels include the angels of light, darkness, destruction, and holiness.

Christianity developed a hierarchy of angels based on the Judaic tradition. In addition to angels, archangels, seraphim, and cherubim, five other spiritual angelic groups—named in the letters of Paul in the New Testament—were accepted in the church by the 4th century: virtues, powers, principalities, dominions, and thrones. Together they made up a hierarchy or choir of angels. As objects of devotion, special attention has been given to the archangels Michael, Gabriel, and Raphael in the Roman Catholic and Eastern Orthodox churches.

Inheriting concepts of angelology from Judaism and Christianity, Islām also developed a hierarchy of angels. In a descending order of importance are: the four throne bearers of Allāh (*ḥamalat al-ʿarsh*), symbolized by a man, a bull, an eagle, and a lion in Islāmic legend (which drew from the imagery of the Revelation to John in the New Testament); the cherubim (*karūbiyūn*), who praise Allāh; four archangels (Jibrīl, or Gabriel, the revealer; Mīkāl, or Michael, the provider; ʿIzrāʾīl, the angel of death; and Isrāfīl, the angel of the Last Judgment); and lesser angels, such as the *ḥafaẓah,* or guardian angels.

Hierarchies of celestial or spiritual beings also were developed among various religions that arose out of the major Western religions, such as the Druzes, and among syncretistic religions, such as Gnosticism, which combined elements of Jewish, Greek, and Christian traditions, and Manichaeism, a dualistic religion that was founded by the 3rd-century-AD Persian reformer Mani. Such religions usually incorporated into their hierarchical concepts aspects of emanation theories, such as aeons or Archons (*qq.v.*), or of astrology, such as the signs of the zodiac.

angel dust (drug): *see* PCP.

Articles are alphabetized word by word, not letter by letter

Angel Falls, Spanish SALTO ÁNGEL, also called SALTO CHURÚN MERÚ, waterfall in the Guiana Highlands in Bolívar state, southeastern Venezuela, on the Río Churún, a tributary of the Caroní, 160 mi (260 km) southeast of Ciudad Bolívar. The highest waterfall in the world, the cataract drops 3,212 ft (979 m) and is 500 ft wide at the base. It leaps from a flat-topped plateau, Auyán-Tepuí (Devils Mountain), barely making contact with the sheer face. The falls, discovered in 1935, were named for James Angel, a U.S. adventurer who crash-landed his plane on a nearby mesa in 1937. Because of the dense jungle surrounding the falls they are best seen from the air.

Angel Falls (Salto Ángel), La Gran Sabana region of Bolívar State, Venezuela
G. De Steinheil—Shostal Assoc./EB Inc.

Angel of Death: *see* Mengele, Josef.

Angela MERICI, SAINT (b. March 21, 1470/74, Desenzano, Republic of Venice—d. Jan. 27, 1540, Brescia; canonized 1807; feast day January 27), founder of the Ursulines (*q.v.*), the oldest order of women in the Roman Catholic Church dedicated to teaching.

Orphaned young, she went to Salo to live in the home of an uncle. Later she joined the Third Order of St. Francis. At the age of 20 she returned to Desenzano, where she gathered about her a group of girls who taught the catechism to the children of the village.

In 1506, while praying in the fields of Brudazzo, Angela had a vision in which she was told that she would found a society of virgins at Brescia. During the ensuing years the citizens of Brescia came to regard her as a prophet and a saint.

On Nov. 25, 1535, at Brescia, Angela and 27 companions consecrated themselves to God by a vow of virginity, and the Company of St. Ursula was born. Angela drew up her rule in 1536, which provided for the Christian education of girls in order to restore the family and, through the family, the whole of Christian society. She was unanimously elected superior of the company in 1537. Before her death she dictated her *Testament and Souvenirs,* which contain her counsels to her nuns; they insist on interest in the individual, gentleness, and the efficacy of persuasion over force.

Angela is often celebrated as a woman of foresight and courage who founded an entirely new form of religious life in the church and who enjoined her successors to make changes according to the needs of the time.

Angeles, chartered city, Pampanga province, central Luzon, Philippines. Situated in the north of Pampanga province, Angeles lies on the principal north–south highway and railway lines 50 mi (82 km) north of Manila. Clark Air Base (U.S.) is located there and has been responsible for the rapid growth of the city by providing substantial employment, housing, and business opportunities. Known as the "city of the dollar," Angeles is also the site of Angeles University (founded 1962), a Roman Catholic seminary, and several other colleges. Inc. city, 1963. Pop. (1980) 188,834.

Angeles, Victoria de los, original name VICTORIA LÓPEZ CIMA (b. Nov. 1, 1923, Barcelona), Spanish soprano known for her interpretations of Spanish songs and operatic parts and for the beauty and timbre of her voice.

Of a musical family, she sang and played guitar before studying piano and voice at the Conservatorio del Liceo in Barcelona. There she performed in concert and in 1945 made her opera debut as the Countess in Wolfgang Amadeus Mozart's *Le nozze di Figaro.* In 1947, after winning first prize in an international competition in Geneva, she gave concert and opera performances throughout Europe. In 1950 she had highly successful debuts at Covent Garden, London, as Mimi in Giacomo Puccini's *La Bohème;* at La Scala, Milan, in the title role of Richard Strauss's *Ariadne auf Naxos;* and at Carnegie Hall, New York City, in recital. Her debut at the Metropolitan Opera the following year was as Marguerite in Charles Gounod's *Faust.* An exceptionally versatile artist, she made many recital tours and performed extensively in such roles as Manon, Melisande, Eva, Agatha, Rosina, and Desdemona.

angelfish, any of various unrelated fishes of the order Perciformes. The angelfishes, or scalares, popular in home aquariums are members of the genus *Pterophyllum* and the cichlid (*q.v.*) family. They are thin, deep-bodied fishes with elongated dorsal, anal, and pelvic fins. Depending on the authority, one to three species may be recognized: *P. scalare, P. eimekei,* and *P. altum.* Angelfishes are native to the freshwaters of South America and may grow to a length of about 15 centimetres (6 inches). They are commonly silvery with vertical dark markings but may be solid or partially black. They are carnivorous and take care of their eggs and young.

An aquarium angelfish (*Pterophyllum*)
Jane Burton—Bruce Coleman Ltd.

The brightly coloured marine angelfishes seen among tropical reefs are members of the family Pomacanthidae. Sometimes placed with the similar butterfly fishes in the family Chaetodontidae, they are compressed, deep-bodied fishes with small mouths and rather rough scales; the largest grows about 46 centimetres (18 inches) long. They are distinguished from the butterfly fishes by a sharp

Emperor angelfish (*Pomacanthus imperator*)
E.R. Degginger—EB Inc.

spine on each cheek. These angelfishes feed on algae and various marine invertebrates. The family, which includes fewer than 100 species, is represented in both the Atlantic and the Indo-Pacific. In many species, colouring of the young differs greatly from that of adults.

Among the better known species are the black and gold angelfish (*Centropyge bicolor*) of the Indo-Pacific; the French angelfish, *Pomacanthus paru* (or *P. arcuatus*), a black and yellow species of the Atlantic; and the queen angelfish (*Holacanthus ciliaris*), a blue and yellow fish of the Atlantic.

angelica, large genus of aromatic herbs of the family Apiaceae (Umbelliferae). The roots and fruit of the Eurasian species, *Angelica*

Angelica (*Angelica archangelica*)
Ingmar Holmasen

archangelica, yield angelica oil used to flavour liqueurs and in perfumery, while the tender shoots are used in making certain kinds of aromatic sweetmeats; tea made from the roots and leaves is a traditional medicine for respiratory ailments. In the Faeroe Islands and in Iceland, where the plant grows abundantly, it is considered a vegetable. The British species, *A. sylvestris,* is a tall perennial herb with large bipinnate leaves and large compound umbels of white or purple flowers. The common name alexanders is applied to *A. atropurpurea* in the United States.

angelica, sweet, fortified dessert wine said to have originated near Los Angeles, for which it is named. Angelica is one of the oldest California wines; it was probably originally made from the mission grape, a European variety brought to California in the 18th century by Spanish padres. Early versions of angelica were occasionally extraordinary; some that survived from the 1870s remained superb more than a century later.

angelica tree, also called DEVIL'S WALKING STICK, HERCULES' CLUB, or PRICKLY ASH (*Aralia spinosa*), prickly-stemmed shrub or tree,

Angelica tree (*Aralia spinosa*)
Walter Dawn

of the ginseng family (Ara-liaceae), that can reach a height of 15 metres (about 50 feet). Its leaves are large, with leaflets arranged feather-fashion and often prickly. The angelica tree is native to low-lying areas from Delaware to Indiana, south to Florida, and as far west as Texas.

Angelico, FRA (Brother), original name GUIDO DI PIETRO, also called GIOVANNI DA FIESOLE (b. *c.* 1400, Vicchio, Republic of Florence—d. Feb. 18, 1455, Rome), Italian painter whose works, within the framework of the early Renaissance Florentine style, embody a serene religious attitude and reflect a strong classical influence. Most of his early work consists of murals that he painted for the monastery of S. Marco in Florence while he was in residence there. Around 1450, near the end of his life, he produced a cycle of 35 paintings for the doors of a silver chest in the sanctuary of the church of SS. Annunziata, also in Florence.

S. Domenico period. Baptized Guido di Pietro, he gained a reputation as a painter under this name by 1417. In that year he became associated with a miniaturist of the late Gothic tradition, Battista Sanguigni, who was later his assistant.

Sometime between the years 1420 and 1422, he became a Dominican monk and resided in the monastery of S. Domenico at Fiesole, there taking the name of Fra Giovanni da Fiesole. At Fiesole, he was probably influenced by the teachings of Giovanni Dominici, the militant leader of the reformed Dominicans; the writings of Dominici defended traditional spirituality against the onslaught of Humanism. Angelico was also influenced by his fellow monk St. Antoninus Pierozzi, who became the archbishop of Florence when Fra Angelico refused the post and who may have consolidated Angelico's faith and inspired some of his compositions.

Angelico was probably trained by the greatest painter and miniaturist of the Gothic tradition, Lorenzo Monaco, whose influence may be seen in the clear, painstaking delicacy of execution and the vibrant luminosity that seem to spiritualize the figures in Angelico's paintings. These qualities are apparent in two small altarpieces in the Museo di San Marco (or dell'Angelico) in Florence: one with the "Madonna of the Star" and the other with "The Annunciation."

Angelico's "Deposition" for Sta. Trinita in Florence was once attributed to Lorenzo Monaco, who had begun it before he died in 1425. Monaco had divided it into a triptych and executed the pinnacles. Angelico, however, made it a unified altarpiece with a vast landscape dominated by a varicoloured hill town. It is perhaps an imaginative evocation of Cortona, where Fra Angelico spent some time and where important works of his are to be found. Against that background are sharply outlined human figures in interconnected groups; their features are so delicately traced that attempts have been made to identify them as portraits. These arrangements of figures attest to Angelico's deep knowledge of the formalism that characterized the art of the early Renaissance.

Two strands were interwoven in Angelico's life at Fiesole: the pious life of a monk and continuous activity as a painter. Vasari described him as "saintly and excellent," and, not long after his death, he was called *angelico* ("angelic") because of his moral virtues. This subsequently became the name by which he is best known, often preceded by the word *beato* ("blessed").

Angelico did not remain absorbed in prayer in his monastery, however; he knew and followed closely the new artistic trends of his time, above all the representation of space by means of perspective. In works such as the large "Last Judgment" and "The Coronation of the Virgin" in the Uffizi, for example, the human figures receding toward the rear themselves create a feeling of space similar to that in the paintings of Angelico's great Florentine contemporary Masaccio. The earliest work by Angelico that can be dated with certainty is a triptych of huge dimensions that he painted for the linen merchants' guild (or Arte dei Linaiuoli; hence its name, the "Linaiuoli Altarpiece"); it is dated July 11, 1433. Enclosed in a marble shrine designed by the Florentine sculptor Lorenzo Ghiberti, this altarpiece represents the Virgin and Son facing forward, monumentally, and, surrounding them in a minor key, charming angels, developing the motif of the "Madonna of the Star." The group has affinities with the Florentine Maestàs (*i.e.,* Madonna and child entoned in majesty) of the 14th century, but the influence of Masaccio may be seen in the formalism of the construction, extending in a somewhat strained manner to the four saints painted on the two folding shutters. Angelico finished the work with a predella, or narrow strip of paintings at the bottom: these include "The Adoration of the Magi" and "The Martyrdom of St. Mark," which are lucid and compact in their narrative and have a strictly defined perspective, a technique that is even more effective in the small painting depicting the naming of John the Baptist.

"The Annunciation," fresco by Fra Angelico, 1438–45; in the Museo di San Marco, Florence
Alinari—Art Resource/EB Inc.

In 1436, Angelico was commissioned to paint an altarpiece for the Brotherhood of Sta. Maria della Croce al Tempio, which he completed by December of that year. In the serene "Lamentation," he executed figures in silent contemplation surrounding the dead Christ. Angelico was inspired by a famous painting by the 14th-century master Giottino (now in the Uffizi), but he expanded the subject to include more figures in a more complex arrangement, and he set them within a melancholy landscape, extending across the long walls of Jerusalem, with a leaden overhanging sky. In this painting Angelico included figures from sacred tradition and persons who had existed historically, probably to point up the historical continuity of devotion to the Redeemer.

Also in the 1430s, Angelico painted one of the most inspired works of the Florentine Renaissance, "The Annunciation," now in the Museo Diocesano of Cortona, an altarpiece significantly superior to his two other paintings on the same subject. It shows the Garden of Eden with Adam and Eve being driven out by the Angel, yet also under the sway of the radiant messenger and pure maiden who are portrayed in the space of a Renaissance-style portico. The predella is skillfully divided into stories of the Virgin Mary, naturalistically portrayed, especially the Visitation, which has a realistic panorama. Angelico always followed reality closely, even when he used a miniaturist technique. Occasionally, he resorted to medieval techniques, such as a gold background, in deference to the taste of those who commissioned the work, but his figures still emerge quite distinctly from the panels, in the Renaissance manner, revealing the painter's increasingly sure and harmonious pictorial idiom. Angelico's "Annalena Altarpiece," also of the 1430s, is, so far as is known, the first *sacra conversazione* (*i.e.,* "sacred conversation," a representation of the Holy Family) of the Renaissance.

Years at the monastery of S. Marco. Angelico remained in the Fiesole monastery until 1439, when he entered the monastery of S. Marco in Florence. There he did most of his work as a mural painter. S. Marco had been transferred from the Sylvestrine monks to the Dominicans in 1436, and the rebuilding of the church and its spacious monastery began around 1438, from designs by the Florentine architect and sculptor Michelozzo. The construction was generously subsidized by the Medici family. Angelico was commissioned around 1438 by Cosimo de' Medici the Elder to execute the altarpiece, for which he again painted a *sacra conversazione.* When the church was consecrated at Epiphany in 1443, the altarpiece must have dominated the place of worship. Angelico portrayed the Virgin and child raised high on a throne, with saints on either side receding into space; among them are the two patron saints of the Medici, Cosmas and Damian. This work, one of the most compelling Fra Angelico ever created, ends in a dense grove of cypresses, palms, and pines against a deep but toneless sky. His figures seem cleansed of any human passion and to have supreme serenity of spirit. A predella, showing eight little legends of the two Medicean saints separated by a Pietà (Virgin Mary holding the body of Christ), completed the work. Unfortunately, these paintings are now scattered among various museums. The narrative in all the scenes is more organized and simplified than in his previous work, with creative touches that he was later to carry forward in his mural painting.

On the walls of the monastery of S. Marco in Florence are the paintings that mark the high point of Angelico's career. In the chapter hall, he executed a large "Crucifixion" that seems akin to the "Moralities" of the 14th century, which urged detachment from worldly vanities and salvation through Christ alone. In addition to the three crucified figures against the sky, Angelico painted groups of ritual figures, rhythmically arranged, with a chorus of martyrs, founders of religious orders, hermits, and defenders of the Dominican order (whose genealogical tree is depicted beneath this striking scene), as well as the two Medicean saints. Thus, in the comprehensiveness of this work, Fra Angelico developed a concept that was barely suggested in his earlier altarpieces.

He portrayed the exaltation of the Redeemer in many other paintings in the monastery's first cloister and in its cells. In one corridor he executed an Annunciation that broadened the pattern of his earlier one in Cortona and, beyond it, a *sacra conversazione,* bathed in lucid light. In the cells, he proclaimed devotion to Christ crucified in at least 20 examples, all related to monastic life. The pictorial work in these narrow spaces is intricate, probably the work of numerous hands directed by the master, including Benozzo Gozzoli, the greatest of Fra Angelico's disciples, and Zanobi Strozzi, another pupil better known as a miniaturist, as well as his earliest collaborator, Battista Sanguigni. The hand of Fra Angelico himself is identifiable in the first 10 cells on the eastern side. Three subjects merit particular attention: a Resurrection, a coronation of the Virgin, and, especially, a gentle Annunciation, presented on a bare white gallery, with St. Peter Martyr in prayer, timidly facing the group, his coloured habit contrasting with the delicate two tones of pink in the garments of the Virgin and the Angel. The cells, originally hidden from public view because of monastic vows of reclusion, reveal the secret joy of the painter-monk in creating figures of purity to move his fellow monks to meditation and prayer. The images in these paintings are the lyrical expressions of a painter who was also their prior.

Roman period. At the end of 1445 Fra Angelico was called to Rome by Pope Eugene IV, and he remained there until about 1450. In the summer of 1447, however, he had undertaken to decorate the chapel of S. Brizio in the cathedral of Orvieto. Angelico's assistants, above all, Gozzoli, worked closely with him on two canvases, crowded with figures, in this chapel. These canvases of Christ the Judge, amid the hierarchy of angels, and the chorus of the prophets, respectively, were only partially executed by Angelico; they were continued more than 50 years later by Luca Signorelli.

In Rome, the frescoes that Angelico executed in a chapel of St. Peter's (*c.* 1446–47), in the chapel of the Sacrament in the Vatican (not before 1447), and in the studio of Pope Nicholas V (1449) have all been destroyed. But the Vatican still possesses his decorative painting for the Cappella di Niccolò V. There, he painted scenes from the lives of SS. Stephen and Lawrence, along with figures of the Evangelists and saints, repeating some of the patterns of the predella on his altarpiece of S. Marco. The consecration scene of St. Stephen and that of St. Lawrence are both set in solemn cathedral interiors, and the almsgiving of St. Lawrence is set against the background of a temple. In this scene particularly, Angelico imbued the poor and afflicted who surround the deacon-saint with a serenity that purifies them and illuminates them with an inner light, rendering them equals of the blessed figures on the altarpieces. At the same time, the organization of these works and the rendering of architecture in them mark the culmination of his development as a Renaissance artist.

Around 1450 Fra Angelico returned to Florence, where, still a monk, he became prior of the monastery of S. Domenico in Fiesole (1450–*c.* June 1452). His most notable work of this time was the cycle of 35 paintings of scenes from the life of Christ and other subjects, for the doors of a silver chest in the sanctuary of the church of SS. Annunziata in Florence. These works, which have been extensively repainted, are probably distant echoes of the destroyed paintings in the Cappella di Niccolò V. Although the authenticity of these works is disputed, the "Massacre of the Innocents," "Flight into Egypt," and "Presentation in the Temple" seem to be Angelico's because of the bright spontaneity of the slender figures, as well as the spatiality of the surroundings and the landscape. Such traits derived from the artist's vast experience in mural painting. In most of these little pictures, however, there is a kind of disconnectedness and weariness, indicating the hand of pupils whose art was a far cry from Fra Angelico's ineffable poetry. There is still a certain monumental tone in the late altarpiece he executed in the monastery of Bosco ai Frati in the Mugello (now in the Museo di San Marco, Florence). With the completion of this altarpiece and several other minor works, Fra Angelico's fertile artistic labours drew to a close.

In 1453 or the following year, Fra Angelico again went to Rome, where he died in the Dominican monastery in which he had stayed during his first visit to Rome. It was close by the church of Sta. Maria della Minerva, where his tomb remains an object of veneration.

Assessment. In addition to the influence he had on his followers, Fra Angelico exerted a significant influence in Florence, especially between 1440 and 1450, even on such an accomplished master as Fra Filippo Lippi. As a monk, Fra Angelico was lauded in writings of the 15th century and later, some of which bestowed a legendary halo on him. As a painter, he was acclaimed as early as 1438 by the contemporary painter Domenico Veneziano. Vasari, in his section on Angelico in *Lives of the Most Eminent Italian Painters, Sculptors and Architects,* was inaccurate in his biographical data but correctly situated Fra Angelico in the framework of the Renaissance. Vasari characterized him in terms that remained standard until the end of the 18th century, when writers of the Neoclassical period, using judgments of a philosophical and didactic nature, placed him out of his time and even in the 14th century, thus making him an artist of transition. Almost all modern art critics, however, place him again within the framework of the Renaissance. With classical measure, Fra Angelico embodied a deeply religious attitude. (M.Sal.)

MAJOR WORKS. "The Dead Christ with Saints" (1425–28; Courtauld Institute Galleries, London); "Madonna of the Star" ("Madonna della Stella," 1425–30; Museo di San Marco, Florence); "Madonna with Child and Two Angels" (1425–30; van Beuningen Collection, Vierhouten, Neth.); "The Coronation of the Virgin" (1428; Uffizi, Florence); "Madonna and Child" (1428–30; S. Domenico, Fiesole, Italy); "The Martyrdom of St. Peter" (1429; Museo di San Marco); "The Madonna of Humility" (1430–33; National Gallery of Art, Washington, D.C.); "The Last Judgment" (*c.* 1430–33; Museo di San Marco); "The Coronation of the Virgin" (1430–35; Louvre, Paris); "Linaiuoli Altarpiece" (1433; Museo di San Marco); "Sta. Trinita Altarpiece" (*c.* 1433; Museo di San Marco); "The Death and Assumption of the Virgin" (*c.* 1434; Isabella Stewart Gardner Museum, Boston); "Virgin and Child with Angels, Saints and Donor" (*c.* 1435; Museum of Fine Arts, Boston); "The Annunciation" (*c.* 1436; Prado, Madrid); "Lamentation" (1436; Museo di San Marco); "The Annunciation" (*c.* 1436; Museo Diocesano, Cortona, Italy); triptych (*c.* 1436; Museo Diocesano, Cortona); "Triptych: Madonna and Child with Saints and Angels" (*c.* 1437; Galleria Nazionale dell'Umbria, Perugia, Italy); "Madonna and Child Enthroned Between SS. Cosmas and Damian, Peter Martyr, John the Evangelist, Lawrence, and Francis" ("Annalena Altarpiece," begun 1437; Museo di San Marco); "Virgin and Child Enthroned with Angels Between SS. Lawrence, John the Evangelist, Mark, Cosmas,

Damian, Dominic, Francis and Peter Martyr" (1438–40; Museo di San Marco); frescoes at San Marco, Florence (1438–50); frescoes, Cappella di Niccolò V (1448–50; Vatican, Rome); 35 paintings for the doors of a silver chest in SS. Annunziata, Florence, Museo di San Marco.

BIBLIOGRAPHY. John Pope-Hennessy, *Fra Angelico* (1952); *Mostra delle opere del Beato Angelico nel V Centenario della morte* (1955), exhibition of Fra Angelico's works on the 500th anniversary of his death; Mario Salmi, *Il Beato Angelico* (1958), with a critical bibliography; Stefano Orlandi, *Beato Angelico* (1964), in Italian; Elsa Morante and Umberto Baldini, *L'opera completa dell'Angelico* (1970), an important catalog.

Angell, Sir Norman, original name RALPH NORMAN ANGELL-LANE (b. Dec. 26, 1873, Holbeach, Lincolnshire, Eng.—d. Oct. 7, 1967, Croydon, Surrey), English economist and worker for international peace who was awarded the Nobel Peace Prize for 1933.

After an education in France, London, and Geneva, he spent several years (1890–98) in the United States, working as a cowboy, a prospector, and finally a journalist for the *St. Louis Globe-Democrat* and *San Francisco Chronicle.* Upon his return to Europe, other editorial posts followed, notably editorship of *Galignani's Messenger* (1899–1903) and *Foreign Affairs* (1928–31).

Angell's most famous work, *The Great Illusion* (1910), translated into more than a score of languages, tried to establish the fallacy of the idea that conquest and war brought a nation great economic advantage and insured its living space and access to markets, trade, and raw materials. *The Great Illusion, 1933* (1933) explored the economic developments and ideas of the 23 years since publication of the first edition. Angell's literary output was great, producing sometimes more than one book a year. He also invented the Money Game, a series of card games using paper money to teach the fundamentals of currency and credit.

Angell, Robert Cooley (b. April 29, 1899, Detroit), U.S. sociologist known for his studies of individuals interacting in social groups such as government units, the church, the family, business enterprises, clubs, cooperatives, and other associations.

He received his education at the University of Michigan, obtaining his Ph.D. in 1924. He then taught at the University of Michigan in Ann Arbor, becoming professor of sociology in 1935, a position he held until 1969, when he became professor emeritus. He served as department chairman from 1940–52. He was the director of the Tensions Project for UNESCO in Paris from 1949 to 1950 and a member of the U.S. National Commission for UNESCO from 1950 to 1956. He was Deiches Lecturer at Johns Hopkins University (1957), co-director of the Center for Research on Conflict Resolution (1961–65), and executive director of Sociological Resources for Secondary Schools (1966–71).

Angell wrote numerous publications containing his sociological investigations. Among his many works are *The Campus* (1928), which studies the undergraduate life of American universities; *Sociological Theory and Social Research* (1930); *A Study of Undergraduate Adjustment* (1930); *The Family Encounters the Depression* (1936); *The Integration of American Society* (1941); *Readings in American Social Classes* (1945); *The Moral Integration of American Cities* (1951); *Free Society and Moral Crisis* (1958); *A Study in the Value of Soviet and American Elites* (1963); *Peace on the March* (1969); and *The Quest for World Order* (1979).

Angelus FAMILY, family that produced three Byzantine emperors. The Angelus family was of no particular significance until the 12th century, when Theodora, youngest daughter of the emperor Alexius I Comnenus, married Constantine Angelus of Philadelphia (Asia Minor). Numerous members of the family then held high positions under Manuel I Comnenus and were involved in an aristocratic revolution that in 1185 overthrew Andronicus I Comnenus and placed Isaac II Angelus on the throne. Isaac and his brother Alexius III, who deposed and blinded Isaac in 1195, were among the least competent of all Byzantine rulers.

The despots of Epirus and Thessaly, who saved much of northern Greece from Western conquest after 1204, and whose dynasty survived until 1318, were direct descendants of Constantine Angelus and Theodora. One of the last prominent members of the family was John Angelus, who was appointed governor of Thessaly in 1342.

Angelus SILESIUS, original name JOHANN SCHEFFLER (b. December 1624, Breslau, Silesia—d. July 9, 1677, Breslau), religious poet remembered primarily as the author of *Der Cherubinischer Wandersmann* (*The Cherubic Wanderer*), a major work of Catholic mysticism.

The son of a Lutheran Polish nobleman, Scheffler was court physician to the duke of Oels in his native Silesia when readings in the mystics, especially Jakob Böhme, and in the Church Fathers led him to the Roman Catholic Church, into which he was received in 1653. After six years as physician to the Holy Roman emperor Ferdinand III, at Vienna, he returned to Breslau and was ordained to the priesthood in 1661. Fanatical in his opposition to Protestantism, he contributed some 55 polemical pieces to a Lutheran–Catholic controversy, notable even in that day for asperity and insults on both sides.

The first of his poetic works, published in 1657, was *Geistreiche Sinn- und Schlussreime* ("Epigrammatic Verses on the Spiritual Life"), a collection of couplets on various religious truths. It became better known under the title of its second edition, *Der Cherubinischer Wandersmann* (1674; "The Cherubic Wanderer"). Another collection, *Heilige Seelenlust* ("Holy Pleasure of the Soul"), contains his religious songs celebrating the nuptials of the soul with God, many of which survive to the present day in both Protestant and Catholic hymnals.

Angelus, Isaac (Byzantine emperor): *see* Isaac II Angelus.

Ångermanälven, English ANGERMAN RIVER, river in the *län* (counties) of Västerbotten and Västernorrland, northern Sweden. It rises in Swedish Lapland near the Norwegian border and flows in a winding course for 280 mi (450 km) southeast past Vilhelmina, Åsele, Sollefteå, and Kramfors, emptying into the Gulf of Bothnia a few miles northeast of Härnösand. Fjällsjöälven and Faxälven, both on its right bank, are its main tributaries. In the plateau region are Vojmsjön (31 sq mi [80 sq km]; 1,355 ft [413 m] above sea level) and Flåsjön (43 sq mi; 873 ft above sea level), lakes valuable in regulating the river flow. Because of the many falls along its route, hydroelectric power stations are numerous. Lumber and pulp mills are found along the 20-mi navigable estuary.

Ångermanland, *landskap* (province) in northeastern Sweden, bounded on the east by the Gulf of Bothnia, on the south and west by the *landskap* (provinces) of Medelpad and Jämtland, and on the north by those of Lappland and Västerbotten. The northeastern corner of its land area of 7,681 sq mi (19,894 sq km) is included for administrative purposes in the *län* (county) of Västerbotten, and all the remainder in those of Jämtland and Västernorrland. One of the traditional *landskap* comprising the region of Norrland (*q.v.*), it consists of vast forests and large rivers, such as Faxälven and Ångermanälven.

Archaeological finds indicate that Ångermanland was inhabited as early as the Stone Age. During the Middle Ages, settlements increased along the coast and in the river valleys, where the people engaged in agriculture, hunting, and fishing. Iron mining was important from the 17th century to the end of the 19th. Forestry flourished throughout the 19th century, particularly after 1850. The principal towns are Härnösand (*q.v.*), Sollefteå, and Örnsköldsvik. Pop. (1983 est.) 159,938.

Angers, city, capital of Maine-et-Loire *département,* Pays de la Loire region, western France, former capital of Anjou, on the Maine River 5 mi (8 km) above its junction with the Loire, northeast of Nantes. The old city is on the river's left bank, with three bridges crossing to Doutre. Capital of the Andecavi, a Gallic tribe of the state of Andes, it became Juliomagus under the Romans. The succession of counts of Anjou began in the 9th century, and the rule of the Plantagenets was marked by construction of magnificent monuments, of which the French Hôpital Saint-Jean, which now houses an archaeological museum, is the most striking. The massive, moated château, whose 17 towers are from 130 to 190 ft (40 to 58 m) high, was built in 1230 on the site of earlier castles; it houses the late 14th-century Apocalypse series of tapestries (woven by

Angers, Fr., and the château on the Maine River
Photo Spirale—Diapofilm

Nicholas Bataille). Despite the damage of past wars, particularly World War II, the city is still rich in medieval architecture. The 12th–13th-century cathedral of Saint-Maurice retains its original stained glass. The 15th-century Logis Barrault (Barrault House) houses the public library, an art museum, and the complete works of the sculptor Pierre-Jean-David d'Angers, born in the city. The prefecture is in the former Saint-Aubin abbey (11th century), with Roman arcades. The medieval Universitas Andegavensis was refounded in 1875 as the Facultés Catholiques de l'Ouest. Traditional industries such as slate quarrying, distilling, rope and cable manufacture, and weaving have been supplemented by electronics, photographic equipment, and elevators. Pop. (1982) 135,293.

Angevin DYNASTY: *see* Plantagenet, House of.

Angevin Empire, the territories, extending in the latter part of the 12th century from Scotland to the Pyrenees, which were ruled by the English king Henry II and his immediate successors, Richard I and John; they were called the Angevin kings because Henry's father was count of Anjou. Henry acquired most of his continental possessions before becoming king of England. By inheritance through his mother (King Henry I's daughter, Matilda), he became duke of Normandy in 1150; he succeeded his father as count of Anjou, Maine, and Touraine in 1151; and in 1152, by marrying Eleanor of Aquitaine, he acquired that duchy, together with Gascony, Poitou, and Auvergne. Brittany, first conquered by Henry I in 1113, was finally brought into the Angevin "empire" when Henry II's son Geoffrey, who had married the heiress of Duke Conan IV, succeeded as duke of Brittany in 1171. Although all these lands were fiefs, held of the king of France, their concentration in one man's hands was a serious threat to the French monarchy, which had direct control of a much smaller area of land. As king of England from 1154, Henry had direct rule over all England and southern Wales, and suzerainty over the principality of Gwynedd in northern Wales. In 1171 he annexed Ireland and obtained direct control of the eastern part of the island and nominal control of the remainder. Finally, from 1174 to 1189, William I the Lion, king of Scotland, captured in a skirmish in 1174, was obliged to accept Henry as his overlord.

Henry's plans to divide his "empire" among his sons led to many quarrels and wars, which the French king eagerly fostered. Only Richard and John survived their father's death (1189), and although John was confirmed as lord of Ireland, which he had held since 1177, he was subject to Richard, who otherwise held all his father's possessions. Early in John's reign (1199–1216) the French king Philip II Augustus wrested from him Normandy, Anjou, Maine, and Touraine. By the Treaty of Paris (1259) the English retained only the duchy of Guyenne (a much-reduced vestige of Aquitaine, with Gascony). Its confiscation in 1337, together with an English claim to the French throne, led to the outbreak of the Hundred Years' War, by the end of which England retained in France only Calais, which was finally lost in 1558.

Anghiera, Peter Martyr d': *see* Peter Martyr d'Anghiera.

Angilbert (b. *c.* 740, Aachen, Kingdom of the Franks—d. Feb. 18, 814, Centula, Picardy), Frankish poet and prelate at the court of Charlemagne. Of noble parentage, he was educated at the palace school at Aachen under Alcuin and was closely connected with the court and the imperial family. In 800 he accompanied Charlemagne to Rome and was one of the witnesses to his will. He was made abbot of Centula (Saint-Riquier), Picardy, in 794.

Angilbert's Latin poems show the culture and tastes of a man of the world. A fragment of an epic, probably by him, describes life at the palace and the meeting between Charlemagne and Pope Leo III and earned him the nickname of "Homer" from Alcuin. Shorter poems show skill in versification and are interesting for their picture of the imperial circle.

angina pectoris, spasms of deep, aching pain felt beneath the breastbone and over the heart and stomach, and sometimes radiating into the left shoulder and down the inner side of the left arm. The attacks are precipitated by exercise or emotional stress and are caused by inability of diseased coronary arteries to deliver sufficient oxygen-laden blood to the heart muscle. They are relieved by rest or by taking nitroglycerin or other drugs that relax the blood vessels. Frequency of attacks is lessened by avoidance of emotional stress and by shifting to exercise that is less vigorous.

angiocardiography, method of following the passage of blood through the heart and great vessels, by intravenous injection of a radiopaque fluid, followed by serialized X-ray pictures. A thin plastic tube (catheter) is positioned into a heart chamber by inserting it into an artery, usually in the arm, threading it through the vessel around the shoulder, across the chest, and into the aorta (*see* cardiac catheterization). The radiopaque dye is then injected through the catheter. With the use of X-ray, the dye can be seen to flow easily through the healthy sections but narrows to a trickle or becomes completely pinched off where lesions, such as fatty deposits, line and obstruct the lumen of blood vessels (characteristic of atherosclerosis). The most frequently used angiocardiographic methods are biplane angiocardiography and cineangiocardiography. In the first method, large X-ray films are exposed at the rate of 10 to 12 per second in two planes at right angles to each other, thus permitting the simultaneous recording of two different views.

In cineangiocardiography, the X-ray images are brightened several thousandfold with photoamplifiers and photographed on motion-picture films at speeds of up to 64 frames per second. When projected at 16 to 20 frames per second, the passage of the opacified blood may be viewed in slow motion. Angiocardiography is used to evaluate patients for cardiovascular surgery. Although it is a valuable tool in assessing some of the more complicated aspects of heart function, it is also one of the most hazardous of all diagnostic procedures; serious reactions to the iodine-containing compounds used, including radiopaque media, are not infrequent, despite continued efforts to develop less harmful materials. *See also* contrast medium; diagnostic radiology.

angioedema, also called ANGIONEUROTIC EDEMA, or GIANT URTICARIA, allergic disorder in which large, localized, painless swellings similar to hives appear under the skin. Swelling is caused by massive accumulation of fluid (edema) following exposure to an allergen (a substance to which the person has been sensitized) or, in cases with a hereditary disposition, after infection or injury. The reaction appears suddenly and persists for a few hours or days, occurring most often on the face, hands, feet, genitals, and mucous membranes.

A number of foods and drugs can precipitate allergic angioedema. The condition can usually be controlled with antihistamines or epinephrine and seldom poses serious danger to the affected person. In hereditary angioedema, caused by a defect in the immune system, swellings in the intestinal tract may produce pain, vomiting, or diarrhea, and edema of the larynx may cause death by asphyxiation. Hereditary angioedema usually first appears in late adolescence or early adulthood. It cannot be controlled by the same methods as allergic angioedema; however, drugs to treat this form have also been developed.

angiography, radiographic examination of arteries and veins, one of the procedures of diagnostic radiology (*q.v.*). These structures cannot be differentiated from the surrounding organs in conventional radiography. It is therefore necessary to inject into the lumen of the vessels a substance that will distinguish them from the surrounding tissues. The contrast medium used is a water-soluble substance containing iodine. On the radiograph, iodine-containing structures cast a denser shadow than do other body tissues. The technique now in use was perfected in 1953.

A needle is used to puncture the main artery in the groin, armpit, or crook of the arm and to place a coiled wire in the artery. The needle is withdrawn, and a small, flexible hollow tube (catheter) is passed over the wire and into the artery. The wire is removed, and contrast medium is injected through the catheter. Both the arteries and the structures they supply with blood can be visualized. All organs of the body can be examined in this way. Radiographic evaluations of diseased arteries supplying the legs, the brain, and the heart are necessary before corrective surgical procedures are undertaken. *See also* angiocardiography; cerebral angiography.

angiohemophilia: *see* von Willebrand's disease.

angiokeratoma corpus diffusum: *see* Fabry's disease.

Angiolieri, Cecco (b. *c.* 1260, Siena, Italy—d. *c.* 1312), poet who is considered by some the first master of Italian comic verse.

Of Angiolieri's life it is known that he married, had children, did military service, was exiled for a time, sometimes had trouble with the law, and was a lover of women, drink, and gambling. Apparently an irascible man, Angiolieri pours contempt in various sonnets upon his parents, his wife, his former mistress, and such contemporary poets as Dante and Guido Cavalcanti. Some critics, however, attribute his subject matter and attitude to the medieval goliard tradition, whose followers were writers of ribald and disrespectful verse, rather than to his own meanness of temper. In any event, poetic skill, vivid language, and a keen sense of the incongruities of life enliven his poems.

Angiolieri's works have been collected in *Sonetti burleschi e realistici dei primi due secoli* (1920; "Comic and Realistic Sonnets of the First Two Centuries") and in *Il canzoniere* (1946; "The Collection of Sonnets"), the latter a gathering of 150 poems. *The Sonnets of a Handsome and Well-Mannered Rogue,* translated by Thomas Chubb, appeared in 1970.

Angiolini, Gasparo, Gasparo also spelled GASPARE, pseudonym ANGELO GASPARINI (b. Feb. 9, 1731, Florence—d. Feb. 6, 1803, Milan), choreographer and composer who was among the first to integrate dance, music, and plot in dramatic ballets.

In 1757 he became ballet master of the Vienna court opera house, where his first ballet dramas frequently relied upon gesture to convey plot. In 1761, however, Angiolini collaborated with the composer Cristoph Gluck to produce *Don Juan, ou le festin de pierre,* based on Molière's play of the same name; in this ballet much of the action was expressed through dance itself. In 1765 he choreographed the ballet *Sémiramis* to music by Gluck and in 1762 staged the ballet sequences in the original production of Gluck's *Orfeo ed Euridice,* which is significant in the history of opera for its dramatic unity and its increased emphasis on dance. In 1765 Angiolini became ballet master at the Imperial Theatre in St. Petersburg (now Leningrad), where he choreographed several ballets to music of his own composition.

Angiolini's reforms were similar in basic intent to those of Gluck and Hilverding; they also paralleled those of his rival, the choreographer Jean-Georges Noverre. In spite of their differences, both Angiolini and Noverre were instrumental in transforming ballet from its customarily disjointed, unemotional plots and emphasis on displays of technique to more expressive themes in which all elements were integrated.

Angiolo DI COSIMO: *see* Bronzino, Il.

angioma, congenital mass of blood vessels intruding into bone or other tissues, causing loss of tissue and, in the case of bone, weakening. Angiomas may occur in any bone and are often associated with angiomas of the skin or muscles. Most angiomas remain symptomless throughout life, but they may cause collapse of the vertebrae if they occur in the vertebral bodies, and hemorrhage is a danger in some positions that expose them to stress. Treatment is usually by irradiation, which is supposed to cause clot formation within the mass of vascular tissue; it is believed the clot will then gradually calcify. Surgery is also done but involves a risk of hemorrhage.

angioneurotic edema: *see* angioedema.

angiosperm, any member of the more than 250,000 species of flowering plants (division Magnoliophyta) having roots, stems, leaves, and well-developed conductive tissues (xylem and phloem). Angiosperms are often differentiated from gymnosperms by their production of seeds within a closed chamber (the ovary), but this distinction is not always clear-cut. *Compare* gymnosperm.

A brief treatment of angiosperms follows. For full treatment, *see* MACROPAEDIA: Angiosperms.

The Magnoliophyta division is composed of two classes, the Liliopsida, or monocotyledons, and the Magnoliospsida, or dicotyledons. The embryo of monocots possesses one seed leaf (cotyledon) and the dicot embryo develops two. Other developmental differences that are used to distinguish the monocots include flower parts in threes, scattered conducting strands in the stem, and the absence of a cambium (the cell layer responsible for secondary growth). Dicots have flower parts in fours or fives, conducting strands arranged in a cylinder, and a cambium. Less reliable traits include the prominent parallel veins in a monocot leaf and the net-veined pattern of the dicot leaf.

Angiosperms reflect an immense diversity in habit, size, and form. Species of angiosperms have been assigned to more than 300 families growing on every continent, including Antarctica. Some survive up to 1,000 years, while others live only a few weeks. They range in size from the floating duckweed, about 0.02 inch (0.5 millimetre), to *Eucalyptus regnans,* which grows to 300 feet (90 metres).

Angiosperms have also adapted to an almost infinite variety of habitats—from freshwater lakes to brackish coastal waters; from rich, well-drained soils to arid desert regions and rocky ledges; from below sea level to high mountains.

Some angiosperms propagate vegetatively; *i.e.,* roots or stems (or sometimes other parts, or buds) can be separated from the main body and be planted. The great majority of angiosperms, however, reproduce chiefly by cross-pollination, *i.e.,* sexually. This reproduction by seeds involves the specialized reproductive organs (stamens or carpels or both) that are present in all flowers. After pollination and fertilization occur, the seed-bearing ovary matures and becomes the fruit, which may be dry (as in a grain of wheat) or fleshy (as in a watermelon, tomato, or grape).

Angkor, archaeological site in what is now northwestern Kampuchea (Cambodia), just 4 mi (6 km) north of the modern town of Siĕmréab. It was the capital of the Khmer (Cambodian) Empire from the 9th to the 15th century. Its most imposing monuments are Angkor Wat, a temple complex built in the 12th century by King Suryavarman II (reigned 113–*c.* 1150), and Angkor Thom, a temple complex built *c.* 1200 by King Jayavarman VII.

The city of Angkor served as the royal centre from which a dynasty of Khmer kings ruled one of the largest, most prosperous, and most sophisticated kingdoms in the history of Southeast Asia. From the last decade of the 9th century AD, when King Yaśovarman I moved his capital to Angkor, until the early years of the 13th century (excluding one short period when the capital was moved to another site, and occasional crises created by foreign invasions), the kings of Angkor ruled over a territory that extended from the tip of the Indochinese peninsula northward to Yunnan and from Vietnam westward to the Bay of Bengal. During this entire period, these rulers utilized the vast resources of labour and wealth at their disposal to carry through a series of prodigious construction projects designed to glorify both themselves and their capital city. After the reign of King Jayavarman VII (1181–*c.* 1215), the power and vitality of the kingdom gradually waned until finally, after Thai armies captured and sacked Angkor in 1431, the city was abandoned.

During the period of great construction and building at Angkor, which lasted more than 300 years, many changes in architecture and artistic style can be discerned, and there was a religious movement from the Hindu cult of the god Śiva to that of Vishnu to a Mahāyāna Buddhist cult devoted to the *bodhisattva* Avalokiteśvara.

Like many other premodern cities in Southeast Asia, Angkor was preeminently a centre for administration and for the worship of a divine monarch; it was planned, constructed, and often reconstructed on the basis of religious and political conceptions imported from India and adapted to local traditions. From the time of Yaśovarman I, who gave the city its original name of Yaśodharapura, Angkor was conceived as a symbolic universe structured according to the model provided by the traditional Indian cosmology. Thus, the city was oriented around a central mountain or pyramid temple, which was identified with Mt. Meru, the central mountain of the Indian cosmic system, and was, at the same time, believed to concentrate the potency of the soil upon which the prosperity of the kingdom depended. In the case of the original Yaśodharapura, the central mountain temple was an architectural adaptation and completion of the one natural hill in the area, the Phnom Bakheng; in the later history of the city, the central temples were completely architectural creations (*i.e.,* pyramid temples), such as the Phimeanakas of Jayavarman V (reigned 968–1001); the Baphuon of Udayadityavarman II (reigned 1050–66); and the Buddhist temple of Bayon, which was the central temple built by Jayavarman VII when he gave the city, which by then had become known as Angkor Thom, its more or less final form. Moreover, the vast system of reservoirs, canals, and moats that constituted one of the primary characteristics of Angkor served not only as a means of water control and irrigation but also as symbols of the great ocean that, according to the Indian conception, surrounded the central cosmic mountain.

The relationships between the cosmological conceptions and the city itself had their counterparts in the relationships between its leading inhabitants and the gods. In the central mountain, or pyramid, temples, a cult of the *devarāja,* or god-king, was maintained, through which the king became identified with one of the great sovereign deities, an identification that was finalized when, at the king's death, the central temple became his personal funerary temple or mausoleum. Many of the other great temples at Angkor, all of which gave expression to Indian cosmological and mythic themes, were built in order to provide a locus for cults through which the kings who did not construct a new central temple, members of the royal family who were not actual rulers, and, in some cases, certain members of the aristocracy could be assured of immortality through becoming identified with Śiva or one of the other preeminent gods of the realm. For example, Angkor Wat, which is perhaps the greatest and certainly the most famous of all the temples in the Angkor complex, was built by King Suryavarman II as a vast architectural microcosm within which his remains were to be deposited and his permanent identity with Vishnu symbolically and cultically confirmed.

In the late 13th century, according to the vivid account of the Chinese commercial envoy Chou Ta-kuan, Angkor was still a large and thriving metropolis and one of the most magnificent capitals in all of Asia. Nevertheless, by this time the great building frenzy that had culminated during the reign of Jayavarman VII had clearly come to an end, the new and more restrained religious orientation represented by Theravāda Buddhism was on the rise, and the armies of the Thai kingdoms established in the western sections of the empire were already beginning to encroach on the Khmer heartland. By the 16th century, when the next available firsthand description was written, these trends had long since culminated in the abandonment of the city; and all that remained were the jungle-covered remnants of the ancient temples and the ruins of the once-magnificent system of reservoirs and waterways.

During the more than four centuries between the demise of the ancient city and the beginning of the modern period (*i.e.,* from the early 15th century to the late 19th century), interest in Angkor was largely focussed on Angkor Wat, which, having been taken over and kept largely intact by Theravāda monks, became one of the most important pilgrimage sites in Southeast Asia. Even during this period, however, a number of early European visitors to Cambodia showed a strong curiosity concerning the "lost city," and when the French colonial regime was established (1863), the entire site became the focus of an intense scholarly interest and concern. Working at first independently and then under the aegis of the government-sponsored École Française d'Extrême-Orient, a talented and dedicated group of French archaeologists and philologists initiated a comprehensive program of research, which has gradually yielded the knowledge now possessed about the history of the city and the fascinating religious and political system that informed and guided its life. Archaeologists also carried through an arduous and painstaking program of reconstruction, through which the ancient complex of temples, reservoirs, and canals was restored to something of its original grandeur.

During the political and miltary upheavals of the 1960s, '70s, and early 1980s in Kampuchea, there was some war damage and thievery among the temples at Angkor, but the major problem was one of neglect. Without adequate caretaking, the buildings became the prey of engulfing vegetation and eroding water and elements. (F.E.R.)

BIBLIOGRAPHY. The classic work on Angkor, including both the city and the "Angkor region," remains George Coedes, *Pour mieux comprendre Angkor,* 2nd rev. ed. (1947), which is available in slightly abbreviated form under the title *Angkor: An Introduction,* ed. and trans. by Emily F. Gardiner (1963). For an excellent visual presentation, see Bernard Groslier and Jacques Arthaud, *Angkor: hommes et pierres,* rev. ed. (1968; Eng. trans. by Eric E. Shaw, *Ankor: Art and Civilization,* rev. ed., 1966). For a colourful 13th-century description, see Paul Pelliot's translation of the famous memoirs of Chou Ta-kuan, published in the *Bulletin de l'École Française d'Extrême-Orient devarāja,* 2:123–177 (1902). An English rendering of Pelliot's translation has been published in Bangkok by J. Gilman D'Arcy Paul, entitled *Notes on the Customs of Cambodia* (1967).

anglaise (in calligraphy): *see* copperplate script.

Angle, member of a Germanic people, which, together with the Jutes and Saxons, invaded England in the 5th century AD. The Angles gave their name to England, as well as to the word Englisc, used even by Saxon writers to denote their vernacular tongue. The Angles are first mentioned by Tacitus (1st century AD) as worshippers of the deity Nerthus. According to the Venerable Bede in the *Ecclesiastical History of the English People,* their continental homeland was centred in Angulus, traditionally identified as the Angeln district in Schleswig between the Schlei inlet and the Flensburger Förde, which they appear to have abandoned at the time of their invasion of Britain. They settled in large numbers during the 5th and 6th centuries in the kingdoms of Mercia, Northumbria, and East and Middle Anglia.

anglerfish, any of about 210 species of marine fishes of the order Lophiiformes. Anglers are named for their method of "fishing" for their prey. The foremost spine of the dorsal fin is located on the head and is modified into a "fishing rod" tipped with a fleshy "bait." Often bizarre in form, anglerfishes are also characterized by small gill openings and by limblike pectoral and (in some species) pelvic fins. Most species of anglerfishes inhabit the sea bottom. They are divided into four groups: batfish, goosefish, frogfish (*qq.v.*), and deep-sea angler.

The deep-sea anglers comprise about 10 families of the suborder Ceratioidei. Unlike other anglers, they lack pelvic fins, and they swim about, though feebly, rather than live on the bottom. They may be up to 1.2 metres (4 feet) long, but most are much smaller. Only the females have a "fishing rod." This ranges from short to long, and the "bait"—almost always luminous—from simple to ornate. In some species there are also other luminous organs.

Deep-sea anglers prey on various fishes and invertebrates. Some have been known to swallow prey larger than themselves. Four families are notable for the fact that the males are very small in comparison with the females and, further, live as permanent parasites on their mates. In these species, the male attaches himself, by biting, to the body of the female. His mouth fuses with her skin, and the bloodstreams of the two fishes become connected, the male thereafter remaining totally dependent on the female for nourishment.

Anglesey, Isle of, Welsh YNYS MÔN, Latin MONA, largest island in England or Wales (261 sq mi [676 sq km]), separated from the North Wales mainland by the Menai Strait. With adjoining Holy Island (main town Holyhead), it forms the Ynys Môn district of Gwynedd county, Wales (district area 276 sq mi). It has low relief, with a series of low ridges and valleys running from northeast to southwest; the highest point is Parys Mountain (418 ft [127 m]) in the north.

Anglesey is known for its ancient history and its prehistoric and Celtic remains. Low and fertile, in contrast to the mountainous North Wales mainland, it was an early grain-growing and stock-raising centre. Seafaring and fishing were also significant; the island established early trading contacts with Ireland and lay on a prehistoric sea route linking the Mediterranean with northern countries. Megalithic burial chambers and standing stones indicate late Neolithic and early Bronze Age habitation. By 100 BC the Celts had colonized the island. It became a famous Druid centre and a stronghold of resistance to the Romans; Suetonius Paulinus invaded in AD 61, slaying Druid priests and destroying sacred groves, and Agricola completed the conquest in 78. Early Celtic Christian churches and monasteries include Penmon Priory, founded by St. Seiriol in the 6th century. Aberffraw on the southwest coast was the capital of the Gwynedd princes from the 7th to the 13th century. Highly exposed to invasion from the sea, the island was attacked by Irish, Saxon, Viking, and Norman venturers. It was finally subdued by Edward I, who built the castle in Beaumaris (begun 1295).

Anglesey remains predominantly agricultural. Copper was mined on a large scale at Parys Mountain between 1775 and 1844. Tourism has become important. The market town of Llangefni serves as the administrative seat for Ynys Môn district. Pop. (1982 est.) district, 68,500.

anglesite, naturally occurring lead sulfate ($PbSO_4$). A common secondary mineral that is a minor ore of lead, it is usually formed by the oxidation of galena and often forms a concentrically banded mass surrounding a core of unaltered galena. The formation of cerussite (lead carbonate) often accompanies or follows the formation of anglesite. For detailed physical properties, *see* sulfate mineral (table).

Angleterre, in full POINT D'ANGLETERRE (French: "English lace"), bobbin lace comparable to fine Brussels lace in thread, technique, and design; but whether it was made in England or Brussels or both is debatable. To encourage home industries, both England and France had laws in the 1660s prohibiting the importation of Brussels lace, which was much in demand. To circumvent these laws, merchants bought Brussels lace and took it, often by smuggling, to England and to France (which had no restrictions against English lace) for sale as point d'Angleterre.

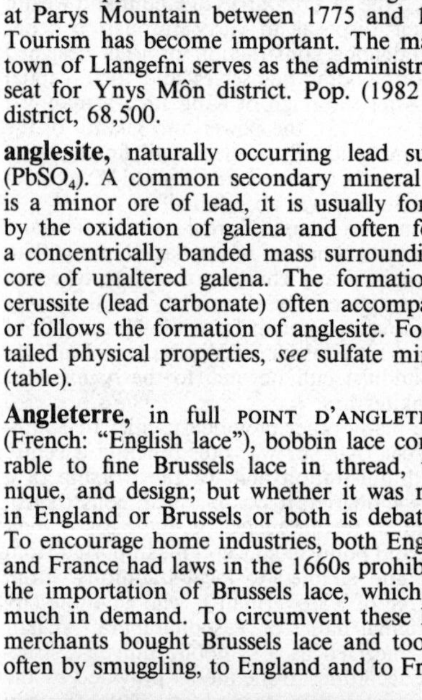

Angleterre lace from Belgium, late 19th century; in the Institut Royal du Patrimoine Artistique, Brussels

By courtesy of the Institut Royal du Patrimoine Artistique, Brussels; photograph, © A.C.L., Brussels

angleworm: *see* earthworm.

Anglia, Middle: *see* Middle Anglia.

Anglican chant, simple harmonized setting of a melodic formula devised for singing prose versions of the psalms and canticles in the Anglican Church. The formula is made up of a reciting tone with middle and final cadences (meditation and termination), much like the Gregorian-chant psalm tones from which Anglican chant derives. When John Marbeck published *The Booke of Common Praier Noted* (1550), he used the first seven psalm tones for the canticles and tone eight for the psalms. Like Marbeck, various English composers used the psalm tones in their polyphonic (multipart) psalm settings, placing them in the tenor part "measured," *i.e.,* with a regular metrical pattern. The harmonic style of these polyphonic settings was probably derived from the continental *falsobordone* style, which also employed the plainsong psalm tones but in the topmost voice. The double chant (two successive verses set to different melodic formulas) traditionally dates from about 1700, but Robert Crowley's psalter (1549) contains what is virtually the same thing. Triple and even quadruple forms also exist.

When the Restoration of the monarchy was effected in 1660 and choirs and organists returned to their posts, a great need was felt for cathedral choral service settings. Thus, plainsong harmonizations again appeared, as in James Clifford's *Divine Services and Anthems Usually Sung in Cathedral and Collegiate Choires in the Church of England* (1663). By the end of the 17th century composers began to write their own melodies, using the recitation note and the cadences of the psalm tone as a framework but omitting intonation. In the 18th century the psalm tone melody was placed in the upper part if it was used at all.

After the Oxford Movement (promoting a reorientation toward Roman Catholic liturgy) began in 1833, parish churches turned to choral services, formerly confined to cathedrals. To facilitate better singing by lesser trained choirs, a method of pointing the psalms first appeared in printed form in 1837—a system of signs that pointed out how a text was to be fitted to a given chant.

A renewed interest in Gregorian chant sung in the vernacular was promoted by the Plainsong and Mediaeval Music Society (founded 1888). Francis Burgess in England and C. Winfred Douglas in the U.S. had great influence in the movement. In 1912 the English poet Robert Bridges pointed out that the chant must be fitted to the words and not the other way around. He gained the support of Dr. Hugh Allen at Oxford, and in 1925 the *Psalter Newly Printed* was published.

Anglican Church of Australia, formerly (until 1981) CHURCH OF ENGLAND IN AUSTRALIA, independent church within the Anglican Communion. It developed from the churches established by the English settlers in the 18th century. The first settlers, convicts sent from England to settle the country in 1788, were accompanied by one chaplain. Subsequently, more settlers and priests went to Australia. For many years the bishop of London was officially responsible for all British subjects outside Britain, but in 1814 Australia was included in the area of the new bishop of Calcutta. In 1836 the diocese of Australia was founded, and William Grant Broughton, who went to Australia in 1829, was consecrated as the first bishop. A period of expansion and church building then occurred, and in 1847 Broughton became bishop of Sydney when the dioceses of Melbourne, Adelaide, and Newcastle were established with their own bishops.

Over the years the church continued to grow as the population of Australia increased and expanded into new territories. Additional dioceses were established, and eventually five provinces of the church were organized, each composed of several dioceses. General Synods of the entire church were held every five years, with the primate of Australia, elected from the diocesan bishops, as president. For many years, however, the Australian church did not attain complete independence from the Church of England, because it lacked a constitution that clearly defined the legislative powers of the General Assembly. Dioceses and provinces experienced considerable independence. After many years of discussion and several unsuccessful attempts, a constitution was accepted in 1959, and the Church of England in Australia became autonomous in 1962.

Anglican Communion, religious body of national, independent, and autonomous churches throughout the world that evolved from the Church of England. The Anglican Communion is united by a common loyalty to the archbishop of Canterbury in England as its senior bishop and titular leader and by a general agreement with the doctrines and practices defined in the 16th-century *Book of Common Prayer.*

A brief treatment of the Anglican Communion follows. For full treatment, *see* MACROPAEDIA: Protestantism: *Anglican Communion.* For further information on the history of Anglicanism, *see* MICROPAEDIA articles on individual Anglican churches (*e.g.,* England, Church of; Protestant Episcopal Church).

From the time of the Reformation, the Church of England followed explorers, traders, colonists, and missionaries into the far reaches of the known world. The colonial churches generally exercised administrative autonomy within the historical and creedal context of the mother church. It was probably not until the first meeting of the Lambeth Conference (*q.v.*) in 1867 that there emerged among the various churches and councils a mutual consciousness of an Anglican Communion. Since its inception, the Lambeth Conference has constituted the principal cohesive factor in Anglicanism.

While population differences and other factors account for some variation in the basic structure among the churches, several elements do predominate. The diocese, under the administration of a bishop, is the basic administrative unit throughout the Communion. The diocese is made up of parishes, or local church communities, each under the care of a pastor. In many of the national churches, dioceses are grouped into provinces. In some, parishes may be grouped also below the diocesan level into rural deaneries and archdeaconries.

In the 20th century the Anglican Communion has played a prominent role in the ecumenical movement. A milestone in Anglican–Roman Catholic relations was reached in 1982 when Pope John Paul II met with Robert Runcie, the archbishop of Canterbury, at Canterbury to discuss prospects for reconciliation between the two churches.

Anglican Evangelical, one who emphasizes biblical faith, personal conversion, piety, and, in general, the Protestant rather than the Catholic heritage of the Anglican Communion. Such persons have also been referred to as low churchmen because they give a "low" place to the importance of the episcopal form of church government, the sacraments, and liturgical worship. The term Low Church was used by about the end of the 17th century, although this emphasis within Anglicanism was evident since the time of King Edward VI (1537–53).

The movement that became known as the Evangelical movement began within the Church of England in the 18th century, although it had many points in common with earlier Low Church attitudes and with 16th- and 17th-century Puritanism. The followers of John Wesley, the founder of Methodism, eventually left the Church of England, but many with very similar beliefs remained within the established church. They emphasized evangelism, social welfare, and missions, and they established the Church Missionary Society (1799) and the Colonial and Continental Church Society (1838). Included among the Evangelicals' many leaders were the influential Clapham Sect, a group of wealthy lay persons prominent in England from about 1790 to 1830. Many of them were members of Parliament, and they were responsible for ending the slave trade.

In the 19th century the Evangelicals opposed the Oxford Movement, which emphasized the Catholic heritage of Anglicanism. In the 20th century they were influenced by liberalism and the new, scientific methods of studying the Bible. (*See* Broad Church.) Some continued to stress the verbal inspiration and accuracy of the Bible and became known as conservative Evangelicals. Others, a much larger group, accepted the new learning and became known as liberal Evangelicals. In general, they continued as the Low Church party within the Anglican Communion.

Anglican religious community, any of various religious communities for men and for women that first began developing within the Anglican Communion in the 19th century. Although monastic communities were numerous in the pre-Reformation English Church, they were suppressed in the 16th century by Henry VIII when he broke with the Roman Catholic Church. Their revival almost 300 years later was due primarily to the interest and encouragement of some of the leaders of the Oxford Movement, who emphasized the Catholic rather than the Protestant heritage of Anglicanism.

The first community, the Sisterhood of the Holy Cross, was founded in London at Park Village, in 1845. In the following 10 years the Society of the Holy Trinity at Devonport (1845); the Community of St. Mary the Virgin at Wantage, Berkshire (1848); the Community of St. John the Baptist at Clewer, near Windsor (1851); the Community of All Saints, London Colney, Hertfordshire (1851); and the Society of St. Margaret at East Grinstead, Sussex (1855) were founded. Notable among later 19th-century foundations were the Community of the Holy Name, Malvern Link, Worcestershire (1865); the Sisters of Bethany, London (1866); the Sisters of the Church, London (1870); and the Community of the Epiphany, Truro (1883).

Almost all the sisterhoods combined an active life (teaching, nursing, helping in parishes, etc.) with a life of prayer and worship. Anglican sisters were among those who accompanied Florence Nightingale to the Crimea and took part in the work of raising the standards and status of the nursing profession. In various forms of social and educational work the Anglican sisterhoods offered opportunities of service not readily available to women in mid-19th-century England, but the religious motive predominated in the revival.

Many English sisterhoods opened branch houses abroad, and independent communities were founded in other provinces of the Anglican Communion. In the United States the oldest surviving sisterhood is the Community of St. Mary at Peekskill, N.Y. (1865); in Canada there is the Sisterhood of St. John the Divine (1884), at Willowdale, Ontario, and in Australia the Community of the Holy Name (1886), at Melbourne.

During the 20th century the foundation of new communities continued, though at a slower rate. A number of enclosed communities of contemplative nuns were established both in England and in the United States. A flourishing active community, the Order of the Holy Paraclete, was founded at Whitby, Yorkshire, in 1917.

The first Anglican religious community for men was the Society of St. John the Evangelist (the Cowley Fathers), founded in 1866 at Oxford. Since then numerous other communities or brotherhoods have been founded in England. The largest men's communities are the Community of the Resurrection (Mirfield Fathers) founded in 1892 at Mirfield, Yorkshire; the Society of the Sacred Mission (Kelham Fathers), at Kelham, Nottinghamshire, founded in 1892; and the Society of St. Francis, Cerne Abbas, Dorset, founded in 1921. An Anglican Benedictine community was established at Pershore in 1914 and moved to Nashdom Abbey, Burnham, Buckinghamshire, in 1926. It has a branch house in the United States. The only indigenous men's community of any size in the Protestant Episcopal Church in the U.S. is the Community of the Holy Cross, West Park, N.Y. (1881).

In the late 20th century more than 50 Anglican religious communities for men and for women, many with several houses or branches, were in existence. Several English communities have branch houses overseas. In general the communities are not large.

The Anglican Communion has never made provision for religious communities in canonical legislation, and the relations of the communities with the ecclesiastical authorities were at first vague and undefined. Since 1935 it has been possible for those in England to obtain formal recognition from the advisory council on religious communities established for the provinces of Canterbury and York.

Anglin, Margaret (Mary) (b. April 3, 1876, Ottawa—d. Jan. 7, 1958, Toronto), one of the most brilliant actresses of her day, equally effective in Greek tragedies, Shakespearean plays, and contemporary dramas.

After a brief study of acting in New York City, she made her debut (1894) in Bronson C. Howard's *Shenandoah.* She achieved stardom in 1898 as Roxane in Edmond Rostand's *Cyrano de Bergerac.* She was also a great success in William Vaughn Moody's *Great Divide,* which ran for almost three years (1906–08) in New York City. By her own estimate, she appeared in more than 80 plays. Her last appearance was in 1943 with a touring company of Lillian Hellman's *Watch on the Rhine.*

angling: *see* fishing.

Anglo-Afghan Wars, also called AFGHAN WARS (1839–42; 1878–80; 1919), three conflicts in which Great Britain, from its base in India, sought to extend its control over neighbouring Afghanistan and to oppose Russian influence there. The first war demonstrated the ease of overrunning Afghanistan and the difficulty of holding it. The second war proved to be a Pyrrhic victory for the British.

Though unable to occupy Afghanistan permanently, the British controlled its foreign affairs until the last war established full Afghan independence.

Anglo-America, cultural entity of North America whose common spoken language is English and whose folkways and customs historically have been those of northern Europe. It comprises most of the United States and Canada, with French-speaking Canada a notable exception. The term also designates a geographical area on the North American continent as apart from Latin, Spanish, or Ibero-America (comprising Middle and South America) with strong Hispanic traditions and heritage. The expression Anglo has come to signify a white, English-speaking North American as distinct from one of Latin-American descent.

Anglo-American law: *see* common law.

Anglo-Boer War: *see* South African War.

Anglo-Burmese Wars (1824–26, 1852, 1885), three conflicts that collectively forced the Burmese into a vulnerable position from which they had to concede British hegemony in the region of the Bay of Bengal. The First Anglo-Burmese War arose from friction between Arakan in western Burma and British-held Chittagong to the north. After Burma's defeat of the kingdom of Arakan in 1784–85, Arakanese refugees went north into British territory and from their sanctuaries in Bengal formed armed contingents and recrossed the border, attacking Burmese garrisons in Arakan. At one point, Arakanese patriots recaptured the provincial capital of Mrohaung. In retaliation, Burmese forces crossed into Bengal, withdrawing only when challenged by Bengal authorities.

In 1823 Burmese forces again crossed the frontier; and the British responded in force, with a large seaborne expedition that took Rangoon (1824) without a fight. The British hope of making the Burmese submit by holding the delta region and threatening the capital failed as Burmese resistance stiffened. In 1825 the British Indian forces advanced northward. In a skirmish south of Ava, the Burmese general Bandula was killed and his armies routed. The Treaty of Yandabo (*see* Yandabo, Treaty of; February 1826) formally ended the First Anglo-Burmese War. The British victory had been achieved mainly because India's superior resources had made possible a sustained campaign running through two rainy seasons. But in the fighting the British-led Indian troops had suffered more than 15,000 fatalities.

After 25 years of peace, the British Indian government sent a naval officer, Commodore Lambert, to Rangoon to investigate British merchants' complaints of extortion. When Lambert seized a ship that belonged to the Burmese king, another war began.

By July 1852 the British had captured the ports of Lower Burma and had begun a march on the capital. Slowly but steadily the British–Indian forces occupied the central teak forests of Burma. The new king Mindon Min (ruled 1853–78) requested the dispersal of British forces. The British were unreceptive but were hesitant to advance farther northward; with both sides at an impasse, the fighting simply ceased. The British now occupied all Lower Burma but without formal recognition of the Burmese court.

Mindon tried to readjust to the thrust of imperialism. He enacted administrative reforms and made Burma more receptive to foreign interests. To offset the British, he entertained envoys from France and sent his own emissaries there. Those moves aroused British suspicions, and Anglo-Burmese relations once again worsened. During the reign of Thibaw (1878–85), the British were willing to ignore Upper Burma and to concentrate on French moves in Laos, Vietnam, and Yunnan.

The ensuing Anglo-French tension was the result not so much of French design as of Burmese initiative. A letter to the French premier from the Hlutdaw (ministerial council) suggesting a bilateral treaty posed a direct threat to British teak monopolies in Lower Burma. Meanwhile, the Hlutdaw fined the Bombay Burmah Trading Corporation for underreporting its extractions of teak from Toungoo. That action provoked British forces to strike. The annexation of Upper Burma was announced on Jan. 1, 1886, ending the Konbaung dynasty and Burmese independence. The Third Anglo-Burmese War formally ended before it had even developed, but resistance to British rule continued for another four years.

Anglo-Catholicism, movement that emphasizes the Catholic rather than the Protestant heritage of the Anglican Communion. It was an outgrowth of the 19th-century Oxford Movement (*q.v.*), which sought to renew Catholic thought and practice in the Church of England. The term Anglo-Catholic was first used in some of the writings of leaders of the Oxford Movement who wished to demonstrate the historical continuity of the English (Anglican) Church with Catholic Christianity.

In addition to stressing Catholic elements in worship and theology, Anglo-Catholics have worked among the poor and unchurched and have attempted to renew the church. Although their beliefs and activities have often been opposed by Anglican Evangelicals, who stress the Protestant heritage of Anglicanism, Anglo-Catholics have continued to be an important force within the Anglican Communion.

Anglo-Catholics are sometimes called high churchmen, in that they give a "high" place to the importance of the episcopal form of church government, the sacraments, and liturgical worship. The term High Church was first used about the end of the 17th century to express this particular emphasis within the Church of England. Historically, however, High Church attitudes, like Low Church (Evangelical) attitudes, were evident within the Church of England from the time of Elizabeth I (1533–1603). The Oxford Movement and Anglo-Catholicism renewed this emphasis within Anglicanism. *See also* Broad Church.

Anglo-Dutch Wars, also called DUTCH WARS, Dutch ENGELSE OORLOGEN (English Wars), the four 17th- and 18th-century naval conflicts between England and the Dutch Republic. The first three wars, stemming from commercial rivalry, established England's naval might, and the last, arising from Dutch interference in the American Revolution, spelled the end of the republic's position as a world power.

The First Anglo-Dutch War (1652–54) began during a tense period following England's institution of the 1651 Navigation Act, which was aimed at barring the Dutch from involvement in English sea trade. An incident in May 1652 resulting in the defeat of a Dutch force under Adm. Maarten Tromp led England to declare war on July 8 (June 28, old style). The Dutch under Tromp won a clear victory off Dungeness in December, but most of the major engagements of the following year were won by the larger and better armed men-of-war of England. In the summer of 1653 off Texel (Terheide), in the last battle of the war, the Dutch were defeated and Tromp killed, with both sides suffering heavy losses. The war was ended by the Treaty of Westminster (April 1654).

The commercial rivalry of the two nations again led to war in 1665 (the Second Anglo-Dutch War of 1665–67), after hostilities had begun the previous year and the English had already captured New Amsterdam (New York). England declared war in March 1665 and won a victory over the Dutch off Lowestoft in June. Most subsequent battles (which occurred in the following year), however, were won by the Dutch. England's ally, the principality of Münster, sent troops into Dutch territory in 1665 but was forced out of the war in the following year by France, which took the Dutch side in January 1666. A plague epidemic in 1665 and the Great Fire of London in 1666 contributed to England's difficulties, which culminated in the destruction of its docked fleet by the Dutch at Chatham in June 1667. The war was ended the following month by the Treaty of Breda.

The Third Anglo-Dutch War (1672–74) formed a part of the general European war of 1672–78 (*see* Dutch War).

England and the Dutch Republic had been allied for a century when they again went to war (the Fourth Anglo-Dutch War of 1780–84) over secret Dutch trade and negotiations with the American colonies, then in revolt against England. The English declared war on Dec. 20, 1780, and, in the following year, quickly took key Dutch possessions in the West and East Indies while imposing a powerful blockade of the Dutch coast. In the only significant engagement of the war, a small Dutch force won a victory off Dogger Bank in August 1781. The republic was never able to assemble a proper fleet for combat, however, and when the war ended in May 1784, the Dutch were at the nadir of their power and prestige.

Anglo-Egyptian Condominium, the joint British and Egyptian government that ruled the eastern Sudan from 1899 to 1955. It was established by the Anglo-Egyptian Condominium Agreements of Jan. 19 and July 10, 1899, and, with some later modifications, lasted until the formation of the sovereign, independent Republic of The Sudan on Jan. 1, 1956. (The Anglo-Egyptian Agreement of 1953 had outlined the steps to be taken for Sudanese self-rule and self-determination.)

The Condominium agreements established an office of governor-general, to be appointed, on British recommendation, by the khedive of Egypt and vested with supreme civil and military command. In theory, Egypt shared a governing role; but in practice the structure of the Condominium ensured full British control over the Sudan. The governors and inspectors were customarily British officers, though technically serving in the Egyptian Army; and key figures in the government and civil service always remained graduates of British universities and military schools.

Anglo-Egyptian Treaty (Aug. 26, 1936), treaty, signed at Montreux, Switz., in May 1937, establishing Egypt as a sovereign state after 50 years of British occupation. The 20-year military alliance allowed Great Britain to impose martial law and censorship in Egypt in the event of international emergency; provided for the stationing of up to 10,000 British troops and 400 Royal Air Force pilots in the Suez Canal Zone until the Egyptians should be capable of protecting the area; and permitted Great Britain to retain its naval base at Alexandria for a maximum of eight years. Further, a British ambassador to Egypt replaced the former high commissioner. After a transitional period, the Capitulations (*q.v.*) were to be abolished, and, with the additional extinction of the Mixed Courts, foreigners would be subject to Egyptian law.

Anglo-Japanese Alliance (1902–23), alliance that bound Britain and Japan to assist one another in safeguarding their respective interests in China and Korea. Directed against Russian expansionism in the Far East, it was a cornerstone of British and Japanese policy in Asia until after World War I.

The alliance served Japan in the Russo-Japanese War (1904–05) by discouraging France, Russia's European ally, from entering the war on the Russian side. It was renewed in 1905 and again in 1911 after Japan's annexation of Korea. On the basis of its tie with Britain, Japan participated in World War I on the side of the Allies.

After the war the British no longer feared Russian encroachment in China and wished to maintain close ties with the United States, which tended to view Japan as its rival in the Pacific. Following an unsuccessful attempt to bring the U.S. into the alliance at the Washington Conference of 1921–22, Britain allowed it to lapse. It was specifically terminated by the Four-Power Pacific Treaty (1921), a vaguely worded agreement that left the Japanese without allies until the conclusion of their Tripartite Pact with Germany and Italy in September 1940.

Anglo-Norman literature, also called NORMAN-FRENCH LITERATURE, or ANGLO-FRENCH LITERATURE, body of writings in the French dialect of medieval England. Though this dialect had been introduced to English court circles in Edward the Confessor's time, its history really began with the Norman Conquest in 1066, when it became the vernacular of the court, the law, the church, schools, universities, parliament, and later of municipalities and of trade. For the aristocracy, Anglo-Norman became an acquired tongue and its use a test of gentility, and the more widely it was known the more it was corrupted. It was introduced into Wales and Ireland and used to a limited extent in Scotland before and during the wars of independence. The earliest extant literary texts belonged to the reign of Henry I, the latest to that of Henry IV. The alienation toward France during the Hundred Years' War started an increasing use of English, the last strongholds of a French dialect being Parliament and the law, in both of which it still survives in a few formulas.

Most types of literary works were represented in Anglo-Norman as in French, with a slight difference of emphasis. The chanson de geste was an exception. The type was not unknown in England (*e.g.,* the only surviving manuscript of the assonanced version of the *Chanson de Roland* is Anglo-Norman), but there seem to be no original works of the kind. Conversely, Anglo-Norman works were known, copied, or imitated on the Continent. One important difference between continental and Anglo-Norman literature is that the Fourth Lateran Council of 1215 led to an outpouring of doctrinal and devotional works for the laity in England not paralleled in France, which perhaps explains the fact that in the early periods England was often in advance of the Continent in the development of new literary forms. History was popular both in Normandy and in the rest of the Continent; and although, after the Norman Conquest, Latin replaced English in documents and chronicles, examples of both are found in Anglo-Norman. Religious houses caused lives of native saints to be written, and the nobility had a taste for romances about imaginary English ancestors. Thus social and political differences prevented Anglo-Norman literature from being a mere imitation of French.

Religious and didactic writings. In the 12th century the oldest substantial Anglo-Norman prose work, "The Book of Kings," was written in England, as were many versions of the Psalter. Sanson de Nanteuil translated into verse the proverbs of Solomon, with commentary; and in the 13th century Robert of Greatham wrote the "Sunday Gospels" for a noble lady. The same century saw the beginning of the magnificent series of Anglo-Norman apocalypses, best known for their superb illustrations, which served as a model for a series of tapestries at Angers, France. In the 14th century an Anglo-Norman Bible was begun, though never completed. Anglo-Norman was rich in literature of legends of saints, of which Benedeit's "Voyage of St. Brendan" was perhaps the oldest purely narrative French poem in the octosyllabic couplet. Wace led the way in writing a saint's life in standard form but was followed by Anglo-Norman writers in the 12th century who wrote numerous lives, many connecting religious houses with their patron saints.

The oldest play in French, the *Mystère d'Adam,* is Anglo-Norman. The resurrection play *La Seinte Resureccion* was probably 12th century but was rewritten more than once in the 13th century. There were a few religious allegories, the most important, the "Castle of Love," being the oldest in French.

The Fourth Lateran Council of 1215 led to the compilation of instructive works, the oldest and most attractive being the *Merure de seinte église* ("Mirror of Holy Church") by St. Edmund of Abingdon. In the 13th–14th century countless treatises appeared on technical subjects—manuals for confession, agriculture, law, medicine, grammar, and science, together with works dealing with manners, hunting, hawking, and chess. Spelling treatises produced in the late 13th, 14th, and 15th centuries are valuable for the light they shed on continental French as well as Anglo-Norman.

Romances. Anglo-Norman literature was well provided with romances. In the 12th century one Thomas wrote a courtly version of the Tristan story, which survived in scattered fragments and was used by Gottfried von Strassburg in *Tristan und Isolde* as well as being the source of the Old Norse, Italian, and Middle English versions of the story. Béroul's *Tristan,* also 12th century, was probably written in England, but by a Norman; *Waldef,* a long, confused story of an imaginary king of East Anglia and his sons, has passages of remarkable originality. In the 12th century some romances were composed in the form of the chanson de geste; for example, *Horn,* by Master Thomas, which is connected with the Middle English *Horn Childe and Maiden Rimnild.* Yet another Thomas wrote the *Roman de toute chevalerie* ("Romance of All Chivalry"), an independent version of the Alexander romance and the source of the Middle English romance *King Alisaunder.* In the 13th century the more courtly type of romance reappeared in *Amadas et Idoine* and in *Amis et Amiloun,* perhaps derived from the same source as the Middle English poem *Amis and Amiloun.*

Lais and fabliaux. Marie de France, earliest named French woman poet, wrote fables based on an English source and 12 narrative lays (dedicated, probably, to Henry II of England) in octosyllabic rhymed couplets. She claimed that they had Breton lays as their originals. The lais combined realistic and fairy-tale elements, and their author was skillful in the analysis of love problems and often showed a keen interest in contemporary life. A few fabliaux have been found copied in manuscripts from religious houses, probably for exemplary purposes.

Political and historical writings. Anglo-Norman lyrics were few in number and unoriginal in form, but numerous political satires and songs were written. Fragments of political songs are found in Peter Langtoft's *Chronicle,* which begins as a *Brut*—a complete chronicle of British history—but became a source for the times of Edward I. The Dominican Nicholas Trevet wrote a prose chronicle of European history from which Chaucer derived his "Man of Law's Tale." Earlier than these was an Anglo-Norman verse, *Estoire des Engleis,* by Geffrei Gaimar (*c.* 1140), the earliest chronicle in French. Two magnificent biographies of the 1st earl of Pembroke (William Marshal) and of Edward, the Black Prince, were written for English patrons by foreigners. Official documents were often in Anglo-Norman, and the *Yearbooks,* unofficial reports of cases in the common pleas, ran from the reign of Edward I to that of Henry VIII. English began to be used in Parliament alongside French in the late 14th century.

Natural history and science. One of the earliest writers in Anglo-Norman, Philippe de Thaon, or Thaün, wrote *Li Cumpoz* (*The Computus*), the first French bestiary, and a work on precious stones. Simund de Freine based his *Roman de philosophie* on Boethius, to whom the 13th-century *Petite Philosophie* also owes much. (D.Le.)

BIBLIOGRAPHY. Mary D. Legge, *Anglo-Norman Literature and Its Background* (1963, reprinted 1978).

Anglo-Normandes, Îles (Great Britain): *see* Channel Islands.

Anglo-Saxon, member of the Germanic peoples inhabiting and ruling England from the 5th century AD to the time of the Norman Conquest (1066). The term seems to have been used first by continental writers in the late 8th century to distinguish the Saxons of Britain from those of the Continent, whom the Venerable Bede had called Antiqui Saxones (Old Saxons).

After the Norman Conquest, chroniclers in England used the term to mean "the English." The name formed part of a title, *rex Angul-Saxonum* ("king of the Anglo-Saxons"), sometimes used by King Alfred (died 899) and his immediate successors and revived by 11th-century kings.

Anglo-Saxon art, manuscript illumination and architecture produced in Britain from about the 7th century to the Norman Conquest of 1066. Anglo-Saxon art may be divided into two distinct periods, one before and one after the Danish invasions of England in the 9th century.

Page of interlaced designs from the Book of Durrow, Hiberno-Saxon, 7th century; in Trinity College Library, Dublin

By courtesy of the Board of the Trinity College, Dublin; photograph, The Green Studio Ltd., Dublin

Before the 9th century, manuscript illumination was the major art in Britain. There were two schools of illumination: a somewhat limited one at Canterbury, which produced works influenced by the Roman missionaries who began the Christian conversion of southern England and ensured that models within the classical tradition were used through the 8th century; and a more widely influential school that flourished in Northumbria. Manuscript illumination in northern England received its impetus from a revival of learning initiated in the 7th century by the establishment of monasteries on the island of Lindisfarne and at Wearmouth and Jarrow in Northumbria, institutions that were largely an extension of the Irish monastic system. The Irish monks carried with them an ancient Celtic decorative tradition of curvilinear forms—scrolls, spirals, and a double curve, or shield, motif known as a pelta—that were integrated with the abstract ornamentation of the native pagan Anglo-Saxon metalwork tradition, characterized particularly by bright colouring and zoomorphic interlace patterns. The additional influence, from southern England, of Mediterranean art introduced the representation of the human figure. The characteristics of Hiberno-Saxon art, however, remained basically those of pagan art: concern for geometric design rather than naturalistic representation, love of flat areas of colour, and the use of complicated interlace patterns. All of these elements appear in the great manuscripts produced by the Hiberno-Saxon school: the Lindisfarne Gospels (early 8th century), the Book of Durrow (7th century), and the Book of Kells (*c.* 700). The Hiberno-Saxon style (*q.v.*), eventually imported to the Continent, exercised great influence on the art of the Carolingian Empire.

The Danish invasions had a disastrous effect on Anglo-Saxon art that was felt until mid-10th century, when the monasteries were revived and interest in architecture grew strong. Some idea of the architecture of the period can be deduced from contemporary descriptions and the excavation of remains. Many of the early stone churches seem to have depended upon the contribution of foreign masons, and Anglo-Saxon building, which consisted mainly of extremely small churches attached to monasteries, continued to be heavily influenced by continental types. By the 11th century, ties with continental architecture, especially that of Norman France, were strong; King Edward the Confessor's Romanesque Westminster Abbey (begun *c.* 1045–50, replaced in 1245 by the present Gothic church), for example, was similar in plan to French models, being cruciform with one central and two western towers. Certain features, however, distinguish Anglo-Saxon architecture: the frequent use of timber for construction; a square, eastern termination (a feature revived in English Gothic churches) instead of the almost universal apse, or semicircular projection behind the altar; and certain distinctive masonry techniques.

The monastic revival resulted in a vast production of books and the flowering, by the second half of the 10th century, of the so-called Winchester school of illumination. The new style was based on the classical naturalism of Carolingian art, but it was highly individual and unusually vivacious, characterized especially by a nervous, highly expressive line. Masterpieces in both painting and drawing have survived; for example, the Benedictional of St. Aethelwold, produced at Winchester in the 10th century, and a copy of the Utrecht Psalter begun at Canterbury in *c.* 1000. The Winchester style influenced French illumination to the extent that Norman art was reasonably acceptable to English illuminators after the conquest of 1066. *See also* Winchester school.

Anglo-Saxon language: *see* Old English language.

Anglo-Saxon law, the body of legal principles that prevailed in England from the 6th century until the Norman Conquest (1066) and after. In conjunction with Scandinavian law and the so-called barbarian laws (*leges barbarorum*) of continental Europe, it made up the body of law called Germanic law. Anglo-Saxon law was written in the vernacular and was relatively free of the Roman influence found in continental laws that were written in Latin. Roman influence on Anglo-Saxon law was indirect and exerted primarily through the church. There was a definite Scandinavian influence upon Anglo-Saxon law as a result of the Viking invasions of the 8th and 9th centuries. Only with the Norman Conquest did Roman law, as embodied in Frankish law, make its influence felt on the laws of England.

Anglo-Saxon law was made up of three components: the laws and collections promulgated by the king, authoritative statements of custom such as those found in the Norman-instituted Domesday Book, and private compilations of legal rules and enactments. The major emphasis was on criminal rather than private law, although certain material dealt with problems of public administration, with public order, and with ecclesiastical matters.

Before the 10th century, the codes often merely presented lists of compositions—money paid to an injured party or his family—but by the 10th century a new penal system had evolved, based on outlawry (declaring a criminal an outlaw), confiscation, and corporal and capital punishment. By this time there had also been an increased development of the law relating to administrative and police functions.

The Anglo-Saxon legal system rested on the fundamental opposition between folkright and privilege. Folkright is the aggregate of rules, whether formulated or not, that can be appealed to as an expression of the juridical consciousness of the people at large or of the communities of which it is composed. It is tribal in its origin, and it is differentiated on highly localized bases. Thus there was a folkright of East and West Saxons, of Mercians, Northumbrians, Danes, and Welshmen, and these main folkright divisions persisted even after the tribal kingdoms disappeared in the 8th and 9th centuries. The responsibility for the formulation and application of the folkright rested, in the 10th and 11th centuries, with the local shire moots (assemblies); the national council of the realm (*see* witan) only occasionally used folkright ideas. The older laws of real property, succession, contracts, and compositions were mainly regulated by folkright; the law had to be declared and applied by the people themselves in their communities.

Folkright could, however, be broken or modified by special enactment or grant, and the foundation of such privileges was royal power. In this manner a privileged land tenure was created; the rules pertaining to the succession of kinsmen were replaced by concessions of testamentary power and confirmations of grants and wills; and special privileges as to levying fines were conferred. In time the rights originating in the royal grants of privilege came to outweigh folkright in many respects and were the starting point for the feudal system.

Before the 10th century a man's actions were considered not as exertions of his individual will but as acts of his kinship group. Personal protection and revenge, oaths, marriage, wardship, and succession were all regulated by the law of kinship. What began as a natural alliance later became a means of enforcing responsibility and keeping lawless individuals in order. As the associations proved insufficient, other collective bodies, such as guilds and townships, assumed their responsibilities. In the period before the Norman Conquest, much regulation was formalized by the king's legislation in order to protect the individual. In the area of property, for example, witnesses were required at cattle sales, not to validate the sale but as protection against later claims on the cattle. Some ordinances required the presence of witnesses for all sales outside of the town gate, and others simply prohibited sales except in town, again for the buyer's protection.

The preservation of peace was an important feature of Anglo-Saxon law. Peace was thought of as the rule of an authority within a specific region. Because the ultimate authority was the king, there was a gradual evolution of stringent rules and regulations against violating the king's peace.

Anglo-Saxon poetry: *see* Old English poetry.

Angmagssalik (Greenland): *see* Ammassalik.

Ango, Jean (b. *c.* 1480, Dieppe, Fr.—d. 1551, Dieppe), shipowner who, succeeding to his father's import–export business, eventually controlled, by himself or in association with others, a fleet of 70 ships. Thus he was able, in Francis I's reign, to ensure representation for France in maritime exploration. In 1524 he equipped the "Dauphine," in which Giovanni da Verrazano explored the east coast of North America, discovering the site of the future New York City. Jean and Raoul Parmentier in 1529 reached the coast of Sumatra in two of Ango's ships, the "Pensée" and the "Sacre."

Ango also sponsored privateering. One of his captains, Jean Fleury, seized three ships carrying Aztec treasures from Mexico to Spain in 1523. Francis I, who generally upheld Ango, borrowed his ships for use against Spain and England. In 1530 Francis authorized Ango to raid Portuguese shipping to compensate for losses sustained at Portuguese hands. Alarmed, the Portuguese came to terms with Francis.

On the King's death, Ango became a victim of rivals and was imprisoned for a time in 1549 on a charge of official misconduct.

Angol, capital of Malleco province, Araucania region, southern Chile, on the Río Rehue near its confluence with the Río Malleco, in the southern portion of the fertile Central Valley. It was founded in 1862 on the site of a former Araucanian Indian outpost. The valley produces fruits (especially apples and wine grapes), wheat, oats, and cattle. Angol's industries include flour milling, brewing, tanning, and lumbering. Pop. (1982 prelim.) 30,662.

Consult the INDEX *first*

Angola, officially PEOPLE'S REPUBLIC OF ANGOLA, Portuguese REPÚBLICA POPULAR DE ANGOLA, coastal country of southwestern Africa, covering an area of 481,350 sq mi (1,246,700 sq km). The capital is Luanda. The country extends about 800 mi (nearly 1,300 km) from north to south and about 675 mi from east to west. Angola's northernmost coastal province, Cabinda, is separated from Angola proper by a narrow corridor of Zairian territory and is bordered on the north by the Congo. Angola proper is bordered on the north and east by Zaire, on the southeast by Zambia, and on the south by South West Africa/Namibia. The Atlantic Ocean comprises the entire western

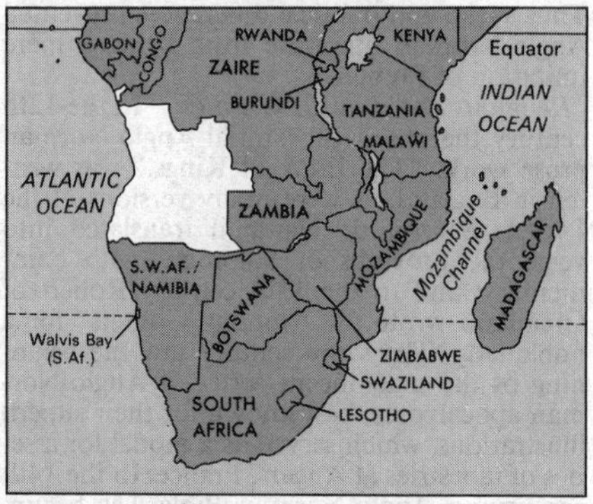

Angola

boundary. The population in 1981 was estimated at 6,851,000.

The article that follows is a summary of significant detail about Angola. Fuller treatment is provided in the following MACROPAEDIA articles. For geography and history, *see* Southern Africa; for information about the country in its continental setting, *see* Africa.

For current history and for statistics on society and economy, *see* the article "World Affairs" and BRITANNICA WORLD DATA, respectively, in the *Britannica Book of the Year.*

The land. Angola may be divided into four major physiographic regions; the largest, representing 60 percent of the country's area, is the *planalto* (plateau) *central*, a continuation of the great southwest African plateau, and ranges in elevation from 3,500 to 4,500 ft (1,100 to 1,400 m). It occupies the south and east-central portions of the country. Rising above the *planalto central* to the north, to elevations greater than 8,000 ft, is a highland plateau region containing the Malanje, Benguela, Bié, Huíla, and Lunda Divide plateaus. These plateaus dominate the country's mid-section, determining many of Angola's east–west and north–south streamflow patterns. There a few peaks reach more than 8,500 ft, and the country's highest point, Mount Moco, rises 8,596 ft. Two further regions, also defined primarily by elevation, are a western coastal desert, a narrow lowland rarely exceeding 50 mi in width (75 mi at its widest, near Luanda); and, in the east, a region of upland escarpments, sloping downward toward the coastal lowlands in the west and toward the Zaire and Zambezi drainage systems in the northeast.

The highland plateaus separate Angola into three distinct drainage systems: the Lunda Divide separates two of these, one in the northeast, which drains northward into the great Congo River basin of Zaire, from another in the southeastern sector that drains eastward into the Zambezi system and southeastward into the interior drainage system of the Okavango River basin culminating in the Okavango Swamp in northern Botswana. The remaining drainage, westward into the Atlantic, provides most of Angola's hydroelectric power. The Cambambe dam on the Kwanza River, northwest of Luanda, provides more than one-third of the country's hydroelectric power. Irrigation is poorly developed.

Angola's rainfall patterns vary dramatically from southwest to northeast. Annual precipitation increases from negligible along the southwestern coastal desert (a continuation of South West Africa/Namibia's Namib Desert), where the cool Benguela current adversely affects rainfall along much of the southern African coastline, to more than 40 in. (1,000 mm) through much of the northeastern third of the country (averaging more than 70 in. in the extreme northeast and in Cabinda). The seven-month summer rainy season in the north (October to May) is often as much as two months longer than it is in the south. Temperatures vary little by season, and the variation by altitude is slight—from a cool 60° F (16° C) in the highlands to 80° F in Soyo in the north.

Of Angola's total land area, nearly 40 percent is estimated to be forests and woodlands, the densest forests lying in the northwest (especially in Cabinda province); all other areas, other than the desert southwest, have at least some scattered woodlands. Only about three percent of the land area is arable, and it lies mostly in the south and west. Food crops grown include corn (maize), tuberous crops (cassava and sweet potatoes), and pulses (primarily dry beans). Most remaining cropland is devoted to cash crops such as palm products, sugarcane, coffee, tobacco, and sisal. Wildlife is abundant through much of Angola, but many species are endangered by human encroachment; among these are the African elephant, the black rhinoceros, the cheetah, and the leopard.

Angola has huge petroleum and natural gas reserves (more than two percent of African reserves) and is also a major producer of diamonds. Other mineral reserves include iron ore, manganese, copper, and cobalt.

The people. Angola's population (1981) was 6,851,000 with an annual growth rate of 2.5 percent. The birth rate (1970–75) was estimated at a very high 48 per 1,000 population and the death rate at 25 per 1,000. The population density is 13 per sq mi (5 per sq km). The ratio of males to females is 104 to 100. The main ethnic groups are the Ovimbundu, who speak Umbundu, and the Mbundu who speak Kimbundu. Other major groups are the Kongo, the Lunda-Chokwe, the Nganguela, the Nyaneka and Humbe, and the Ambo. The Khoisan-speaking San (Bushmen) are largely found scattered in isolated, densely forested refuge areas. Although Portuguese is the official language of Angola, many indigenous dialects are spoken. Most of the population practice traditional religions, and the rest are Roman Catholics and Protestants.

Luanda, the capital and largest city in Angola, had a population of 480,613 (1970); other major towns are Huambo 61,885; Lobito 59,258; Benguela 40,996; Lubango (Sá da Bandeira) 31,674; and Malanje 31,559. With the Portuguese withdrawal in 1975, a large proportion of Angola's white population fled the country. More than 300,000 Portuguese nationals returned to Portugal; the civil war that persisted after that time led to large scale relocations of the population. There was also general movement from the cities to rural areas. Strife, famine, and disease were responsible for the deaths of more than 150,000 people after 1975. By early 1981, 500,000 internal refugees had been relocated in settlements once occupied by the Portuguese.

The economy. Angola has a mixed economy based largely upon petroleum and other mineral resources. The gross national product (GNP) was estimated in 1980 at U.S. $3,900,-000,000, about $520 per capita. Angola experienced an average annual decline of −9.6 percent in real GNP (1970–79). Beginning in 1977, the GNP resumed slow growth, and by 1979 had surpassed the 1976 level. The minerals sector produces most of the GNP; petroleum and diamonds are the two chief products. Manufacturing, followed by the construction, administration, and social services sectors, rank next. Commerce, transportation, and agriculture and fishing are lowest.

Pastures occupy 23 percent of Angola's total land area. The principal livestock raised in 1981 included cattle, goats, pigs, and sheep. Angola is also one of the largest producers of honey.

Forests occupy more than 40 percent of Angola's total land area, and forest produce includes roundwood, all of it broadleaf. Most of the roundwood produced is used for fuel. Angola's long coastline has good fishing banks, and the catch comprises mackerel and sardines.

The mineral sector is the only part of the economy that experienced growth in the late 1970s and early 1980s, primarily because of petroleum extraction. Two-thirds of Angola's petroleum originates from the Cabinda enclave. Diamonds are next in importance, followed by natural gas. Other important minerals included salt, gypsum, and phosphates. Iron ore production resumed in 1982. Angola has proven reserves of more than 30 different minerals, including cobalt, chromium, manganese, vanadium, and uranium, all unexploited. Electricity production (1980) was 1,500,000,000 kW-hr, of which 27 percent was hydroelectric energy and the remainder from thermal plants. Industrial production includes refined petroleum products, cement, iron and steel, raw sugar, palm oil, sawn lumber, plywood, wood pulp, radio receivers, cotton fabric, beer, and cigarettes.

Construction in the late 1970s to the early '80s was hindered by shortages in materials, poor transportation, and the ongoing guerrilla warfare. Luanda's oil refinery was sabotaged in 1981. The influx of large numbers of refugees into the northern areas of Angola created severe housing shortages. Construction activity was centred on reactivating iron ore and phosphate mining operations.

The government, committed to centralized economic planning, nationalized the larger industries but had to slow down due to the void resulting from Portuguese withdrawal, and encouraged private enterprise. A new foreign investment code was adopted in 1979 to encourage joint Angolan–foreign ventures. The oil industry is state owned, while the diamond industry has a share of foreign investment. In agriculture collectivization failed, and in the early 1980s the government began reintroducing private ownership of farms, and peasant cooperatives were organized. Likewise in the business, commerce, and transportation sectors, some enterprises nationalized in 1975–76 have been returned to private control; however, 80 percent of heavy industry remains under government ownership.

The labour force, estimated at 1,904,000 in 1981, comprises 27 percent of the total population. About 57 percent of the labour force is engaged in agriculture, and 2 percent in construction. No employment data are available for the remaining sectors of the economy. There are two trade unions in Angola, the União Nacional dos Trabalhadores Angolanos and the Syndicat National des Employés de l'Angola. Both are closely controlled by the government. Workers, except military and public service employees, have the right to strike, restricted by an anti-economic sabotage provision that effectively bans unofficial strikes. Farmers belong to cooperatives which are grouped under the Associações de Camponeses.

The national currency unit is the Angolan *kwanza* (AK), subdivided into 100 *lwei*. Since the early 1980s Angola has begun to borrow funds from western European and other international financial sources to spur its economic development. Revenues from petroleum and diamond exports enabled the country to balance its budget and foreign trade accounts. Still, the costly border wars hindered its economic development.

Angola's budgetary revenue (1978) was AK 38,866,000,000. It was derived from petroleum taxes, state enterprises and rents, non-petroleum taxes, outstanding balances of dissolved bodies, and other sources. Expenditures amounted to AK 41,331,000,000; the items included general expenditures received; economic and social development; defense and security; education, health, culture, and sports; and publio debt service and other. Banks were nationalized in 1975. The central bank is the Banco Nacional de Angola, with 46 branches. The Banco Popular de Angola is the country's centralized commercial bank, with branches throughout the country. Insurance also is nationalized under a single company, the Empresa Nacional de Seguros e Resseguros de Angola.

Angola is a member of the United Nations and its agencies; it also has membership in the Organization of African Unity and the Non-Aligned Movement.

The country's railway network extends for 1,982 mi, in three principal east–west lines. The road network includes 45,875 mi (73,828 km) of roads. The warfare of 1975–76 and the ongoing strife in the early 1980s prevented further development of railways and new roads. Angola has one international airport and a number of smaller domestic airfields. Linhas Aeras de Angola is the national airline, and it provides both internal and international service. There are three principal ports (Luanda, Lobito, and Namibe) as well as five minor ones. Angola's merchant fleet (1981) had 44 cargo vessels (of more than 100 gross tons each), displacing 79,889 gross tons. There is a total of 111 mi of oil pipelines, most running from the oil fields to the Malongo terminal in the Cabinda enclave.

Angola's exports (1980) had an estimated value of U.S. $1,900,000,000, while imports were set at $1,350,000,000, yielding a positive trade balance. Exports (1979) were crude oil and refined petroleum products, coffee, diamonds, sisal, cement, and fishmeal (1 percent). Principal importers of Angolan goods were The Bahamas, the United States, the United Kingdom, and Algeria and Japan. Imports consisted of machinery and equipment, foodstuffs, raw materials, textiles and footwear, and consumer goods and tools. Major sources for imports were South Africa, Portugal, the Soviet Union, the United States, West Germany, Brazil, and the United Kingdom.

Administrative and social conditions. Angola is a Marxist-oriented state dominated by the Popular Liberation Movement of Angola (MPLA). The party's Central Committee elects a chairman, who also serves as the country's president. Legislative authority vests in the People's Assembly. Angola's 18 provinces are administered by commissioners appointed by the national government. The MPLA has encountered stiff opposition from the National Union for the Total Independence of Angola (UNITA) and the National Front for the Liberation of Angola (FNLA). South Africa, meanwhile, undertook military incursions into Angola to interdict guerrillas from the South West Africa People's Organization (SWAPO), who were allegedly operating from Angolan bases. The MPLA opposed these military challenges with about 33,000 Angolan troops, more than 30,000 Cuban and East German troops, and many Soviet military advisers and technicians.

The MPLA established free medical care and a National Health Service in 1975. Its implementation, however, is made difficult by civil war and a shortage of trained medical personnel. There is widespread malnutrition and lack of sanitary education, causing disease in both town and country. Mass immunization campaigns have been undertaken against endemic tropical and other common diseases. Infant mortality, despite governmental measures, is high. Life expectancy in Angola stands at only 40 years for men and 43 years for women.

Most rural Angolans live in traditional wattle and clay or timber houses. In the towns the modern, often Portuguese-built, villas and apartment and office buildings stand in sharp contrast with the sprawling peripheral shanty towns, or *musseques*, "cities of sand." A national housing program, with priority for rural areas, involves government construction of low-cost housing and a government-run self-help program, with building plans and materials.

Free education is guaranteed to all citizens under the constitution, though compulsory education extends only to primary schoolchildren. The number of primary school pupils increased from 300,000 in 1973 to about 1,400,000 in 1978. The number of secondary school students rose from 4,000 to about 150,000 in the same period. The MPLA has also taken steps to eradicate illiteracy.

All communication media are owned by the state. The country's only daily newspaper is *O Jornal de Angola*; many people gain their news from wall newspapers. Angola's broadcasting services reach about 120,000 radio and 2,000 television receivers.

Cultural life. A National Council for Culture is working to revive and rediscover indigenous Angolan culture while encouraging new creative forms it considers proper to the revolutionary post-independence era. The National Museum Directorate has set up an Anthropology Museum, a Slavery Museum, and a War Museum. Greater emphasis is placed on anthropology and Angolan history and culture. In 1978 the Luanda and Lobito *carnaval* was revived and taken to many other parts of the country. It was from Angola that the *carnaval* was originally taken to Brazil, on slave ships. Cinemas exist in all Angolan towns, and a mobile cinema unit tours the provinces.

History. Angolan history extends into great antiquity, though little is known of that history. The original inhabitants of what is now Angola were probably Khoisan-speaking hunters and gatherers. During the first millennium AD, large-scale Bantu-speaking migrations (possibly originating in central Africa) into southern Africa absorbed the older population and introduced, or at least expanded, iron technology and cereal cultivation in the area. Eventually, they became the dominant ethnolinguistic group of southern Africa. Their occupation of what is now Angola was complete by 1600.

The most important of the Bantu kingdoms in Angola was the Kongo, with its capital at Mbanza Kongo, called by the Portuguese São Salvador do Congo. This kingdom was a highly centralized and complex state that was divided into six provinces. South of the Kongo was the Ndongo kingdom of the Mbundu people. It was equally centralized and gave Angola its name from the title for its king, the *ngola*.

In 1483 Portuguese explorers reached Angola, Christianized the ruling family of the Kongo, and gave aid in education and technology. However, increasing Portuguese involvement in the slave trade eventually turned the Kongo against Portugal, which in turn led to Portugal's destruction of the Ndongo kingdom to the south. Colonization of the area was slow, but the slave trade flourished, so much so that by the early 17th century some 5,000 to 10,000 slaves were being exported annually from Luanda.

The boundaries of Angola were not firmly fixed until 1926, when a dispute with South West Africa was settled. Other boundaries had been fixed in the 1890s. Armed resistance against the Portuguese continued until 1930. Under Portuguese rule economic opportunities for Africans were minimal. Forced labour practices continued into the 20th century, and all economic development was directed toward Portugal's benefit.

Nationalist movements began in earnest in the 1950s. The MPLA, a Marxist-oriented party, became a dominant force in the Angolan fight for independence, but other groups developed, based on regional, class, and ideological lines. Fighting intensified in the 1960s and 1970s and the Portuguese finally withdrew from Angola in 1975. Inter-party struggles within Angola, however, resulted in civil war after Portugal's departure. The MPLA, with Soviet and Cuban assistance, seized control of Angola, but sporadic fighting continued with dissident groups. The fighting along the Angola–South West Africa/Namibia border was particularly intense.

Angoulême, Fr., with the 19th-century town hall and its two medieval towers in the foreground

Editions "La Cigogne"—Hachette

Angola, city, seat (1837) of Steuben County, northeastern Indiana, U.S, 42 mi (68 km) north-northeast of Fort Wayne. Settled in 1836, and named for Angola, N.Y., it is the centre of a resort region that boasts more than 100 lakes. Angola is also the seat of Tri-State University, which was established in 1884. Most popular of the nearby lakes (which have facilities for fishing and boating in the summer and ice skating in the winter) are Silver, Otter, Crooked, James, and Hamilton. Pokagon State Park is 6 mi north. Inc. 1906. Pop. (1980) 5,486.

Angoni (people): *see* Ngoni.

Angora (city, Turkey): *see* Ankara.

Angora, Battle of (1402): *see* Ankara, Battle of.

Angora goat, breed of domestic goat originating in ancient times in the district of Angora in Asia Minor; its silky coat yields the mohair of commerce. The Angora had been widely but unsuccessfully imported into Europe by the mid-18th century; not until the animal was established in South Africa a century later did the Western mohair industry develop. Importation to the United States followed shortly, with development centring in Texas and the Southwest.

The Angora is generally smaller than other domestic goats and sheep. Both sexes are horned, and the ears are long and drooping. The strong elastic fibre of the coat differs from wool primarily in its smoothness and lustre. *See* mohair.

Angostura, Battle of (Feb. 22–23, 1847): *see* Buena Vista, Battle of.

Angoulême, city, capital of Charente *département*, Poitou-Charente region, former capital of Angoumois, southwestern France, on a high plateau above the junction of the Charente and Anguienne rivers, southwest of Limoges. Taken from the Visigoths by Clovis in 507, it was the seat of the counts of Angoulême from the 9th century. Fought over by the French and English in the Hundred Years' War, it also suffered in the religious wars of the late 16th century. The 19th-century town hall occupies the site of the counts' château (birthplace of Marguérite d'Angoulême) of which two towers, the Valois (15th century) and the Lusignan (13th century), remain. The cathedral of Saint-Pierre (1105–28; restored 19th century) is a domed Romanesque-Byzantine structure; its elaborate facade, enriched with Romanesque sculpture, contrasts sharply with the stark, aisleless interior. The old city ramparts have been razed to make boulevards with extensive views. The Land of Angoulême was the name given to New York in 1524 by Giovanni da Verrazano, who discovered the harbour while serving Francis I, who was also count of Angoulême. Diversified manufacturing, mostly located in the surrounding suburbs, includes papermaking and the manufacture of felt, iron, jewelry, bricks, and refrigerators. Pop. (1982) 45,495.

Angoulême DYNASTY (reigned 1515–74), a branch of the Valois dynasty (*q.v.*) in France.

Angoulême, Charles, duc d' (duke of): *see* Orléans, Charles, duc d'.

Angoulême, Charles de Valois, duc d' (duke of) (b. April 28, 1573, Fayet, Fr.—d. Sept. 24, 1650, Paris), illegitimate son of King Charles IX of France and Marie Touchet, chiefly remembered for his intrigues against King Henry IV and for his later military exploits, particularly as commander at the siege of La Rochelle in 1627.

Received favourably at the French court as a youth because of his ready wit and good looks, Charles was granted the title of comte d'Auvergne and was made colonel general of the cavalry. He served Henry IV during the religious strife of the period in his campaigns against the Catholic League, but after Queen Margaret successfully contested his right to Auvergne, he took part in a series of conspiracies against the crown.

Pardoned for his part in the Marshal de Biron's conspiracy of 1601, he began to engage in more treasonable plots with Spain (1604) in concert with his half sister, Henriette d'Entragues, mistress of Henry IV. Soon he went into open rebellion; after his capture in 1605 he was condemned to life imprisonment. Released in 1616 to serve the Marshal d'Ancre, he was created duc d'Angoulême in 1619. The Cardinal de Richelieu gave him military commands against the Protestants at the sieges of Montauban (1621) and of La Rochelle (1627) and in Lorraine (1635). Cardinal Mazarin gave him a command in the north in 1643. Angoulême's *Mémoires*, first published in 1667, were reprinted in the Michaud-Poujoulat collection (1836).

Angoulême, Diane de France, duchessede Montmorency et: *see* Diane de France.

Angoulême, Louis-Antoine de Bourbon, duc d' (duke of) (b. Aug. 6, 1775, Versailles, Fr.—d. June 3, 1844, Gorizia, Venetia, Austrian Empire), last dauphin of France and prominent figure in the restoration of the Bourbon line after the defeat of Napoleon in 1814.

When revolution broke out in 1789, the Duc d'Angoulême left France with his father, the comte d'Artois (afterward Charles X of France), and his younger brother, the duc de Berry. After living in Poland and England, Angoulême returned to France in 1814 and with British help raised the royal standard again at Bordeaux. As chief of the royalist army in the southern Rhône Valley, he was unable to prevent Napoleon's return to Paris. After Waterloo and the second restoration of Louis XVIII, Angoulême served Louis loyally. During the reign of his father, Charles X, he worked to rid the army of former imperial officers and commanded the French expedition that helped quell an anti-Bourbon revolt in Spain (1823). In 1830, when Charles was compelled to abdicate, Angoulême renounced his claim to the throne and went into exile.

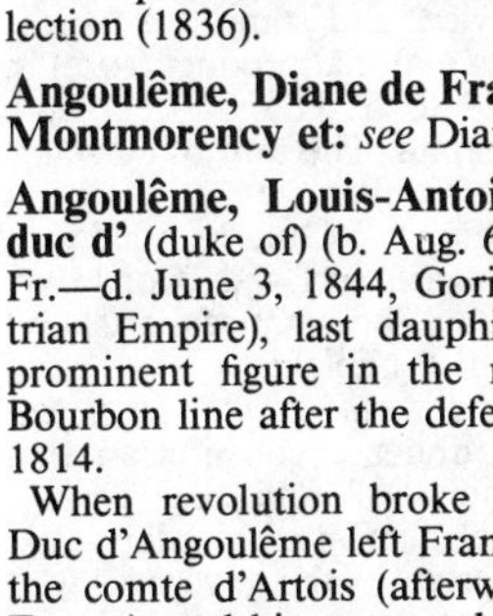

Louis, duc d'Angoulême, lithograph by François-Séraphin Delpech after a portrait by Pierre-Louis-Henri-Grévedon, 1824

By courtesy of the Bibliotheque Nationale, Paris

Angoumois, former province of France, nearly corresponding to the modern *département* of Charente, that represented the possessions of the counts of Angoulême from the 10th to the 12th century. Long part of Aquitaine, it was recovered by France from the English in 1373. In the 17th century it was made part of a joint *gouvernement* of Saintonge and Angoumois.

The province of Angoumois

Angra do Heroísmo, also called ANGRA, capital, Angra do Heroísmo district, on the south coast of Terceira, an island of the Portuguese Azores archipelago in the North Atlantic. It lies at the base of Monte Brasil. Angra became a city in 1534. The words *do heroísmo* commemorate the island's resistance to invading Spaniards in 1580–82. The capital of the Azores from 1766 to 1832, it is the see of the Azorean diocese. Fortresses include the 17th-century São João Baptista (on Monte Brasil), São Sebastião, and a 17th-century citadel. Angra increased in importance after the establishment of a North Atlantic Treaty Organization (NATO) military air base at nearby Lajes.

Angra do Heroísmo, Terceira Island, Azores

Walter Imber

The district, consisting of the islands of Terceira, Graciosa, and São Jorge, has an area of 271 sq mi (703 sq km). The islands export dairy products, meat, and other agricultural produce. Kaolin, quarried in the area, is used to make pottery. A major earthquake in 1980 severely damaged many structures on Terceira and São Jorge but left the military base at Lajes relatively unscathed. Pop. (1981 prelim.) town, 12,156; district, 71,180.

Angra dos Reis, city, southwestern Rio de Janeiro state, eastern Brazil, on the Baía (bay) da Ilha Grande, an inlet of the Atlantic. The city's income derives from its port operations, a sizable fishing industry, and cultivation of bananas in the agricultural hinterland. A railway running from Barra Mansa transports sugar, coffee, *feijão* (beans), steel, and coal from Angra dos Reis for export. Since the development of the city of Volta Redonda, 35 mi (56 km) inland, with its huge steel-mill complex, the shipbuilding and port facilities of Angra dos Reis have gained added importance. West Germany agreed to help build three nuclear reactors in Angra dos Reis beginning in 1981. The city is on the Rio de Janeiro–Santos highway. Surviving colonial buildings include the 17th-century Church of Our Lady of Mount Carmel. Pop. (1980 prelim.) 24,894.

Angra Mainyu (in Zoroastrianism): *see* Ahriman.

Angra Pequena (South West Africa/Namibia): *see* Lüderitz.

Angren, city, Tashkent *oblast* (administrative region), Uzbek Soviet Socialist Republic, on the left bank of the Akhangaran River, 70 mi (115 km) east of Tashken city. The centre of the Uzbekistan coal industry, it was created in 1946 from mining settlements that had grown up in the rich Angren coal basin during World War II; it still consists of disconnected settlements. Angren has a large power station and a large construction-materials industry. There is also a rubber-fabricating plant. A teacher-training institute and a museum are located in the city. Pop. (1983 est.) 117,000.

Angrezābād (India): *see* English Bāzār.

Angry Young Men, British literary generation that emerged in the 1950s as a distinctly new breed of intellectuals. Most were of working class or of lower middle-class origin; some had been educated at the postwar red-brick universities at the state's expense, though a few were from Oxford. They were not all personally known to one another. They shared an outspoken irreverence for the traditional British establishment of pedigreed families, the Church of England, and the elitist Oxford and Cambridge universities and an equally uninhibited disdain for the drabness of the postwar welfare state.

The trend that was evident in John Wain's novel *Hurry on Down* (1953) and in *Lucky Jim* (1954) by Kingsley Amis (*q.v.*) was crystallized in 1956 in the play *Look Back in Anger*, which became the representative work of the movement. When the Royal Court Theatre's press agent described the play's 26-year-old author John Osborne (*q.v.*) as an "angry young man," the name was extended to all his contemporaries who expressed a rage at the persistence of class distinctions, a pride in their lower-class mannerisms, and a dislike for anything highbrow or "phoney." When Sir Laurence Olivier played the leading role in Osborne's second play, *The Entertainer* (1957), the Angry Young Men were acknowledged as the dominant literary force of the decade, and they enjoyed outstanding commercial success.

Among the other writers embraced in the term are the novelists John Braine (*Room at the Top,* 1957) and Alan Sillitoe (*Saturday Night and Sunday Morning,* 1958) and the playwrights Bernard Kops (*The Hamlet of Stepney Green,* 1956) and Arnold Wesker (*Chicken Soup with Barley,* 1958). Like that of the Beat movement in the U.S., the impetus of the movement was exhausted in the early 1960s.

angstrom, unit of length used chiefly in measuring wavelengths of light, equal to 10^{-10} metre. It is named for the 19th-century Swedish physicist Anders Jonas Ångström. The symbol is Å. The angstrom and multiples of it, the micron and the millimicron, are also used to measure such quantities as molecular diameters and the thickness of films on liquids.

Ångström, Anders Jonas (b. Aug. 13, 1814, Lögdö, Swed.—d. June 21, 1874, Uppsala), physicist, a founder of spectroscopy for whom the angstrom, a unit of length equal to 10^{-10} metre, was named.

Ångström's most important work concerned heat conduction and spectroscopy. He devised a method of measuring thermal conductivity, showing it to be proportional to electrical conductivity. In 1853 he pointed out that the electric spark yields two superposed spectra, one from the metal of the electrode and the other from the gas through which it passes. From Euler's resonance theory Ångström deduced a principle of spectrum analysis: that an incandescent gas emits rays of the same refrangibility as those it can absorb.

Ångström's studies of the solar spectrum led to his discovery, announced in 1862, that hydrogen is present in the Sun's atmosphere. In 1868 was published his great map of the normal solar spectrum, which long remained authoritative. He was first, in 1867, to examine the spectrum of the Aurora Borealis and to detect and measure the characteristic bright line in its yellow-green region, but he was mistaken in supposing that this same line is also to be seen in the zodiacal light.

Educated at the University of Uppsala, Ångström became *Privatdozent* in 1839 and succeeded to the chairmanship of the physics department in 1858. In 1843 he became observer at Uppsala Observatory.

His son Knut Johan Ångström (1857–1910) became professor of physics at Uppsala in 1896. He investigated the radiation of heat from the Sun and its absorption by the Earth's atmosphere. Various delicate methods and instruments of his invention include his electric compensation pyrheliometer (1893) and apparatus for obtaining a photographic representation of the infrared spectrum (1895).

Anders Jonas Ångström, *c.* 1865

By courtesy of the Kungl. Biblioteket, Stockholm

Anguier, François and Michel-André (respectively, b. *c.* 1604, Eu, Fr.—d. Aug. 9, 1669, Paris; b. *c.* 1613, Eu—d. July 11, 1686, Paris), sculptors who produced decorations for tombs, churches, palaces, and public monuments.

Beginning their training in France, they went in about 1641 to Rome, where they studied in the workshop of the Baroque sculptor Alessandro Algardi (François until 1643 and Michel-André until 1651). The brothers collaborated between 1648 and 1652 on a tomb for Henri II, duc de Montmorency, at Moulins.

François's most characteristic work is the funerary statue of Gasparde de la Châtre, second wife of the historian Jacques de Thou, in the Louvre, Paris. Michel-André was employed in the decoration of Anne of Austria's apartments in the Louvre, modelled on Pietro da Cortona's decorations in the Pitti Palace in Florence. Michel-André worked at Vaux-le-Vicomte—the château of Louis XIV's minister Nicolas Fouquet, near Melun—with Charles Le Brun and André Le Nôtre. His most important commission, completed in 1667, was the decoration of the church of Val-de-Grâce in Paris, founded by Anne of Austria, to which he contributed reliefs and a marble nativity group for the high altar (1665), now in the church of Saint-Roch in Paris. His reliefs for the triumphal arch of the Porte Saint-Denis, executed in a severely classical style, were completed in 1674.

Anguilla, island, a British dependency, in the eastern Caribbean Sea, until 1980 officially a part of the associated state of St. Christopher-(St. Kitts-) Nevis-Anguilla, although administered as a separate entity since 1971. The most northerly of the Leeward Islands, its territory includes Scrub, Seal, and Dog islands and Prickly Pear Cays. Saint-Martin lies 5 mi (8 km) to the south and St. Christopher about 60 mi to the southeast. The land area of Anguilla covers about 35 sq mi (91 sq km). The chief town, near the centre of the island, is The Valley. The population in 1983 was estimated to be 7,000.

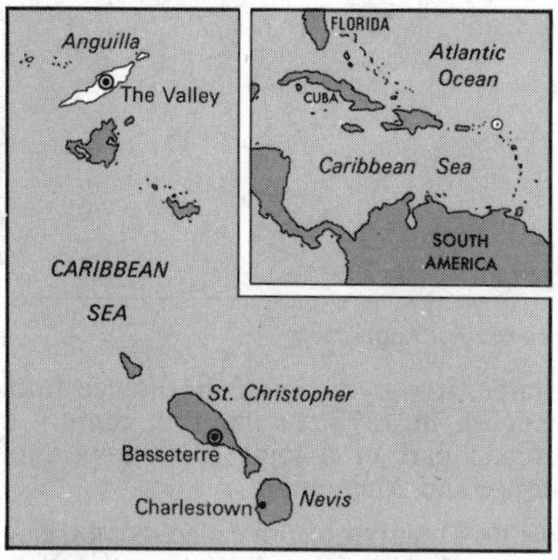

Anguilla

The article that follows is a summary of significant detail about Anguilla. For information about regional aspects of Anguilla, *see* MACROPAEDIA: West Indies.

For current history and for statistics on society and economy, *see* the article "World Affairs" and BRITANNICA WORLD DATA, respectively, in the *Britannica Book of the Year.*

The land. Anguilla is a relatively flat, coral and limestone island covered with sparse, dry woodlands and fringed by white sand beaches. Numerous bays and inlets indent the shoreline. Its shape is long (16 mi) and narrow (3.5 mi), giving rise to its name (French *anguille,* "eel"). The highest elevation is about 213 ft (65 m), at Crocus Hill. There are some stretches of fertile soil on the island, but most of the land is suitable only for grazing. Anguilla has no rivers. There are a few salt ponds, however, which provide some commercial quantities of salt. The tropical climate is sunny and dry most of the year. Temperatures average about 80° F (26.7° C) throughout the year, and rainfall amounts to about 35 in. (900 mm) annually. The wettest period is usually from September to January. Hurricanes, which usually occur from July to October, sometimes strike with damaging force.

Harbour and new road, Anguilla

Bradley Smith, New York

The people. Most of the people of Anguilla are blacks and mulattoes, the descendants of African slaves; the few white inhabitants are mostly of European descent. The chief language is English, and the largest religious memberships are in the Protestant denominations. The island's population density is about 200 people per sq mi (76.9 per sq km). The population is young, more than half of the people being less than 16 years of age. The Anguillan birth rate in 1983 was estimated to be 26.5 per 1,000 population and the death rate 11.1 per 1,000. The average annual growth rate was 0.83 percent from 1960 to 1974 but was estimated to have dropped slightly by 1984.

The economy. Anguilla's dry climate and its unsuitable soil limit the role of agriculture; the island's economy is more dependent upon fishing as a source of revenue. The richly nutrient offshore reefs abound with fish and lobster, providing one of the island's main sources of foreign exchange. Lobster is exported to nearby islands and to the United States. Salt, obtained by natural evaporation from Anguilla's salt ponds, is also produced in exportable quantities. The island's marine life and white sand beaches, considered to be among the finest in the Caribbean, are the basis of a growing tourist industry. The development of hotels and other tourist facilities is important in Anguilla's economic planning. Some foreign exchange also comes from islanders who work abroad and send money back to their families on Anguilla. The chief crops are pigeon peas, maize, and sweet potatoes. Domestic animals raised include sheep, goats, pigs, cattle, and poultry. There is a government-run cattle-breeding service, and some livestock is exported. The gross national product (GNP) in 1983 was estimated to be U.S. $17,600,000, about $2,700 per capita. The unit of currency is the East Caribbean dollar.

The island has about 57 mi of roads, of which some 32 mi are surfaced. Road Bay and Blowing Point are the main seaports, and there is an airport at Wallblake.

Administrative and social conditions. Anguilla is governed under a constitution that became effective in 1982 and that gave it considerable control over internal affairs. Executive power is vested in the governor, who is appointed by the monarch of the United Kingdom. The governor is advised in the execution of his duties by an executive council made up of a chief minister, three other ministers, and two ex-officio members. The legislative branch is the House of Assembly, some of whose members are elected.

Anguillans live under rather poor conditions, and employment is unsteady. Nevertheless, housing conditions are good compared with the general standard of Caribbean islands. Most houses are built of concrete and are relatively spacious in design. The general health of the islanders is good; they are served by a cottage hospital and have access to a limited range of health services. Preventative medicine has been emphasized. In 1981, 2,000 students attended the government's six elementary schools and its single secondary school. Advanced training and education is available at schools elsewhere in the Caribbean region. A government-owned radiobroadcasting station operates for about 10 hours a day, and a modern internal telephone system connects all parts of the island. Fresh water supply is rather limited on Anguilla, although plans have been made to make it more readily available throughout the island. Electrical service reaches all parts of the island.

History. Anguilla does not seem to have been a stronghold of the Carib Indians for any length of time, and it is uncertain whether or not the island was visited by Columbus. It was first colonized in 1650 by English settlers coming from St. Christopher and has remained a British territory ever since. The island was attacked in 1688 by a party of Irishmen who eventually settled there and whose surnames are still in evidence. Anguilla was attacked twice by the French in the 18th century (1745 and 1796), but they were repelled. The territory was administered as part of the Leeward Islands after colonization, and from 1825 it was closely associated with St. Christopher, a situation it protested. In 1875 Anguilla petitioned for separate status but was rejected. St. Christopher, Nevis, and Anguilla were united as a single colony in 1882. From 1958 until 1962 the islands were a unit of the Federation of the West Indies. Opposition to rule from St. Christopher continued into the 1960s, reaching a climax in 1967, when the associated state of St. Christopher-Nevis-Anguilla was formed. In reaction, Anguilla ejected the St. Christopher police, set up its own council, and subsequently proclaimed its independence. After negotiations failed, the British intervened in March 1969 to restore legal government with troops and a temporary British commissioner. The troops were withdrawn in September 1969, and the Anguilla Act (July 1971) placed the island directly under British control. A new constitution in 1976 provided a large measure of internal autonomy under the crown, while formally retaining Anguilla as part of the associated state. On Dec. 19, 1980, Anguilla was formally separated from St. Christopher and Nevis, and in 1982 a new Anguillan constitution became operative.

Anguilliformes, order of bony fishes that contains more than 500 species of eel (*q.v.*).

angular harp, musical instrument in which the neck forms a clear angle with the resonator, or belly; it is one of the principal

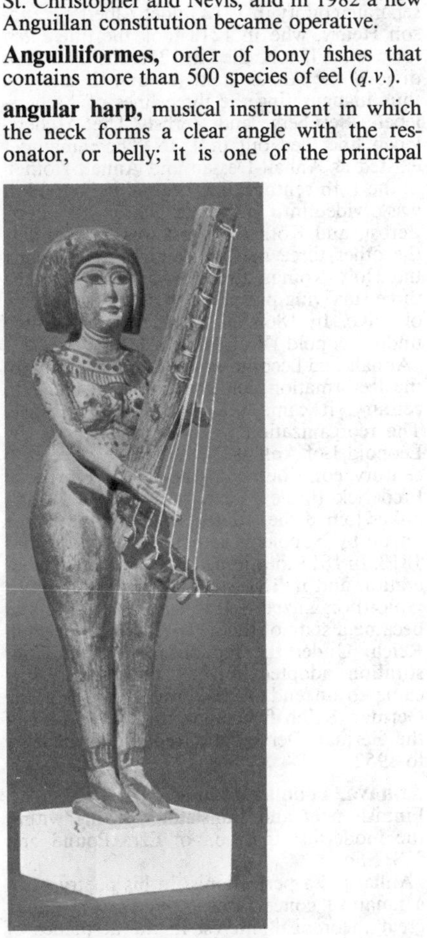

Egyptian statuette with angular harp, painted wood, Late Period (1085–525 BC); in the British Museum, London

By courtesy of the trustees of the British Museum, London; photograph, J.R. Freeman & Co. Ltd.

varieties of the harp. The earliest known depictions of angular harps are from Mesopotamia from *c.* 2000 BC. In Egypt, especially, and in Mesopotamia, this harp was played vertically, held with the neck at the lower end, and plucked with the fingers of both hands. In Mesopotamia it was sometimes also placed horizontally across the player's lap, strings toward him, the strings swept with a plectrum as the left hand damped unnecessary strings.

The pre-Islāmic Persian reliefs at Ṭāq-e Bostān (*c.* AD 600) contain both the latest known depiction of a horizontal angular harp and the earliest representation of the medieval angular harp of Persia (*chang*) and Arabic-speaking countries (*junk*). Placed with the neck near the floor and played by a kneeling musician, it survived until the 16th century in Egypt, the 17th century in Turkey, and the 19th century in Persia.

angular momentum, property characterizing the rotary inertia of an object or system of objects in motion about an axis that may or may not pass through the object or system. The Earth has orbital angular momentum by reason of its annual revolution about the Sun and spin angular momentum because of its daily rotation about its axis. Angular momentum is a vector quantity, requiring the specification of both a magnitude and a direction for its complete description. The magnitude of the angular momentum of an orbiting object is equal to its linear momentum (product of its mass m and linear velocity v) times the perpendicular distance r from the centre of rotation to a line drawn in the direction of its instantaneous motion and passing through the object's centre of gravity, or simply mvr. For a spinning object, on the other hand, the angular momentum must be considered as the summation of the quantity mvr for all the particles composing the object. Angular momentum may be formulated equivalently as the product of I, the moment of inertia (*q.v.*), and ω, the angular velocity (*q.v.*), of a rotating body or system, or simply $I\omega$. The direction of the angular momentum vector is that of the axis of rotation of the given object and is designated as positive in the direction that a right-hand screw would advance if turned similarly. Appropriate MKS or SI units for angular momentum are kilogram metres squared per second (kg-m^2/sec).

For a given object or system isolated from external forces the total angular momentum is a constant, a fact that is known as the law of conservation of angular momentum. A rigid spinning object, for example, continues to spin at a constant rate and with a fixed orientation unless influenced by the application of an external torque. (The rate of change of the angular momentum is, in fact, equal to the applied torque.) A figure skater spins faster, or has a greater angular velocity ω, when the arms are drawn inward because this action reduces the moment of inertia I while the product $I\omega$, the skater's angular momentum, remains constant. Because of the conservation of direction as well as magnitude, a spinning gyrocompass in an airplane remains fixed in its orientation, independent of the motion of the airplane.

For the extension of the conception of orbital and spin angular momentum to analogous properties of subatomic particles such as electrons, *see* spin. *See also* momentum.

angular velocity, time rate at which an object rotates or revolves about an axis, or at which the angular displacement between two bodies changes. In the Figure, this displacement is represented by the angle θ between a line on one body and a line on the other.

In engineering, angles or angular displacements are commonly expressed in degrees or revolutions (of 360°), and angular velocities in revolutions per minute (rpm). In mathematics and physics, angles are usually expressed in radians (*see* radian measure) and angular velocities in radians per second. These measures are related through the following conversion factors: 1 degree equals $\pi/180$ (about 0.0175) radian; 1 rpm equals $\pi/30$ (about 0.105) radian per second.

In many situations, an angular velocity—usually symbolized by the Greek letter omega (ω)—is equally well regarded as a frequency (*q.v.*), and the choice of terms depends upon the particular aspect of a system being considered. Thus, in electrical engineering, the rotational speed of a generator might be ex-

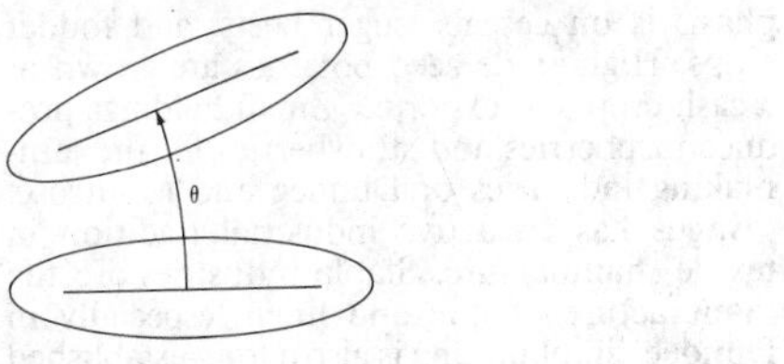

Angular displacement

pressed in revolutions per minute, whereas the alternating electric current produced by the generator would be described in terms of its frequency.

The angular acceleration is the time rate of change of the angular velocity and is usually designated by a and expressed in radians per second per second. For the case in which the angular velocity is uniform (non-varying), $\theta = \omega t$ and $a = 0$. If a is uniform but not zero, $\omega = at$ and $\theta = \frac{1}{2}at^2$.

Angus, formerly FORFARSHIRE, until the reorganization of 1975 a county in eastern Scotland, bounded on the east by the North Sea and on the south by the Firth of Tay. It is now largely in the district of Angus (*q.v.*).

Angus, district, Tayside region, eastern Scotland; created by the reorganization of 1975, it covers most of the former county of Angus. The district has an area of 785 sq mi (2,033 sq km); Forfar, a textile manufacturing town, is the seat of the district authority.

Angus is bisected roughly by the Highland Boundary Fault running northeast–southwest from Edzell to Lintrathen. The Highland area is composed of plateaus of 2,000–3,000 ft (600–900 m) dissected by three broad glens (Glen Isla, Glen Clova, and Glen Esk). The uplands were little eroded by glaciation except in the main valleys, in which glaciers excavated ribbon lochs (lakes)—*e.g.,* Loch Lee in Glen Esk, now used as a reservoir. South of the impressive Highland edge lies the rich Vale of Strathmore (the Howe [hollow] of Angus), where the underlying Old Red Sandstone is overlain by fertile glacial deposits. The Sidlaw Hills form the southeastern boundary of the Vale of Strathmore, and their scarp face looks southeastward over the coastal lowlands covered with till, unstratified rock material deposited by a glacier. Sand dunes and postglacial raised beaches fringe the shore.

The climate is generally dry, with cool, dry springs and frequent sea mists. Late summer and early autumn are typically warm and dry, and there are long hours of sunshine, dictating a late harvest. Upland soils are thin and poor, with peat bogs in flatter areas. Light, well-drained soils occur on the fluvio-glacial and raised beach sands, and fertile riverine clays surround the Montrose Basin. The lowlands are predominantly agricultural, except for the moorland crest of the Sidlaws and some woodland on the gravel soils.

In Roman times the area was occupied by the Picts. Underground houses (weems) and several hill forts remain. Traces of Roman camps and roads are common. During the 12th century, colonies of Flemings established the wool and linen industries, and the county enjoyed a prosperity little affected by the Scottish Wars of Independence. It suffered more during the English Civil War in the 17th century, when both Dundee and Brechin were sacked.

The economy ranges from remote upland farms to complex industrial and port activities in Dundee to the tourist industry. The upland areas support extensive sheep farms, and beef cattle are intensively raised in the glens. About half of the land area is cultivated; emphasis is on cereals, sugar beets, and fodder crops. High-grade seed potatoes are grown as a cash crop and exported. Small holdings produce raspberries and strawberries for the jam-making industries of Dundee and Montrose.

Angus has an active industrial tradition in textile manufacture. Staple industries are the manufacture of jute and linen, especially in Dundee. Shipbuilding is also a long-established industry in Dundee and engineering in Arbroath. Diversification of industry in Dundee, the industrial and commercial centre, is reflected in its large, modern industrial estate. In other towns, alternative industries have been developed, as in the golfing and holiday resort of Carnoustie and in Brechin, where engineering industries have been established. There is a thriving whitefish industry at Arbroath, with associated establishments for curing and preserving the catch; and throughout the region are facilities for canning locally grown produce. Pop. (1982 est.) 93,086.

Angus, breed of black, polled beef cattle, for many years known as Aberdeen Angus, originating in northeastern Scotland. Its ancestry is obscure, though the breed appears closely related to the curly-coated Galloway, sometimes called the oldest breed in Britain. The breed was improved and the present type of the cattle fixed early in the 19th century by a number of constructive breeders among whom Hugh Watson and William McCombie were the most famous.

The characteristic features of the breed are black colour, polled head, compact and low set body, fine quality of flesh, and high dressing percentage. The Angus is a beef breed of the highest rank, and for years purebred or crossbred Angus steers have held high places of honour at the leading fat-stock shows in Great Britain and the United States. This breed was introduced into the U.S. in 1873, and after that date its influence spread widely there and in other countries.

Within the breed, a strain known as Red Angus was gaining in popularity in the late 20th century, particularly for purposes of outcrossing and crossbreeding. The Brangus, a separate breed developed from Brahman and Angus stocks, is notable for its resistance to heat.

Angus, EARLS OF, titled Scottish nobility of several creations, notably in the family Douglas, grouped below chronologically and indicated by the symbol •.

• Angus, Archibald Douglas, 6th earl of (b. *c.* 1489—d. January 1557, Tantallon Castle, East Lothian, Scot.), powerful Scottish lord during the reigns of King James V and Mary, Queen of Scots. He was the grandson of the 5th earl, Archibald Douglas (*c.* 1449–*c.* 1514).

By his second marriage in 1514 to the queen dowager Margaret Tudor, he aroused the jealousy of the nobles. Margaret was supplanted in 1515 as regent and guardian of the infant James V by the Duke of Albany and fled to England. On her return she found that Angus had formed a liaison with a daughter of the laird of Traquair, and she therefore allied with Albany against her husband. He was charged with high treason in 1522 and sent to France. But he returned two years later with the support of Henry VIII of England, entered Edinburgh in 1525, and called a parliament. He and the Douglases then wielded supreme power until Margaret obtained a divorce and James V escaped from his stepfather's tutelage (1528), issuing a decree of forfeiture against him. Angus took refuge in England, and James took vengeance on his relations, burning at the stake (July 17, 1537) Angus' sister Janet, Lady Glamis.

After the death of James V in 1542, Angus returned to Scotland, and the act of forfeiture was annulled. He was commissioned to arrange a marriage between Mary Stuart and Prince Edward (afterward Edward VI of England), but his English sympathies were disappearing. He was appointed lieutenant of southern Scotland, defeated the English at Ancrum moor on Feb. 27, 1545, and led the van when the Scots were defeated at Pinkie in 1547.

His was a career in which national interests were completely subordinated to those of his family. His only surviving legitimate child, by Margaret Tudor, was Margaret, who married Matthew, 4th earl of Lennox, and became the mother of Lord Darnley, husband of Mary, Queen of Scots. He was succeeded by his nephew David Douglas (*c.* 1515–57).

• Angus, Archibald Douglas, 8th earl of, EARL OF MORTON (b. 1555—d. Aug. 4, 1588, Smeaton, near Dalkeith, Midlothian, Scot.), Scottish rebel during the reign of James VI, a strong advocate of Presbyterian government. He was son of the 7th earl, who was nephew of the 6th, and succeeded to the earldom at the age of two. The earldom of Morton came to him in 1586.

During the regency of his uncle, the earl of Morton, he rose rapidly to power. He became privy councillor and sheriff of Berwick (1573), lieutenant general of south Scotland (1574), warden of the west marches and steward of Fife (1577), and lieutenant general of the whole realm (1578). But when Morton fell in 1581 Angus was declared guilty of high treason for supporting him and fled to London. After a brief reconciliation with James VI he joined the rebellion of the Earl of Mar and the master of Glamis, and sentence of attainder was pronounced against all three. The rebels fled to Newcastle, which became a centre of Presbyterianism and of projects against the Scottish government encouraged by Elizabeth I of England. They returned to Scotland in October 1584 and secured from James the restoration of their estates and a share in the government. Angus was appointed warden of the marches and lieutenant general on the border, but his support of Presbyterianism prevented his gaining real favour with the King.

• Angus, William Douglas, 10th earl of (b. 1554—d. March 3, 1611, Paris), Scottish rebel and conspirator, convert to Roman Catholicism during the reign of James VI.

He joined the household of the Earl of Morton and then, while visiting the French court, became a Roman Catholic; in consequence, on his return, he was disinherited and placed under restraint. Nevertheless, he succeeded to his father's titles and estates in 1591, and though in 1592 he was disgraced for his complicity in the Earl of Bothwell's plot, he was soon liberated and performed useful services as the king's lieutenant in the north of Scotland. In July 1592, however, he was asking for help from Elizabeth I of England in a plot against Sir John Maitland, the chancellor, and began intriguing also with Spain; and thus he was imprisoned (on the discovery of the treason) in Edinburgh Castle in January 1593. He succeeded on January 13 in escaping by the help of his countess, joining the earls of Huntly and Erroll in the north. They were offered an act of "oblivion" or "abolition" provided they renounced their religion or quitted Scotland. Declining these conditions they were declared traitors and "forfeited." Huntly and Erroll were subdued by James VI himself in the north, and Angus failed in an attempt upon Edinburgh in concert with the Earl of Bothwell. Subsequently in 1597 they all renounced their religion, declared themselves Presbyterians, and were restored to their estates and honours.

Not long afterwards, however, Angus recanted and was again excommunicated in 1608. In 1609 he withdrew to France, and died in Paris. He was succeeded by his son William, as 11th earl of Angus, afterward 1st marquess of Douglas (1589–1660).

Anhalt, former German state, which was a duchy from 1863 to 1918 and a *Land* (state) until 1945, when it was merged in Saxony-Anhalt. Saxony-Anhalt was a *Land* of the German Democratic Republic from 1949 to 1952, when it was broken up into *Bezirke* (districts), the former territories of Anhalt being divided between the *Bezirke* of Magdeburg and of Halle.

Territorially the duchy of Anhalt was divided into two major parts (the eastern one comprising Zerbst, Dessau, Köthen [Cöthen], and Bernberg, the western one being centred on Ballenstedt) and five smaller ones, all of them enclaves within the geographical boundaries of the Prussian province of Saxony.

The level country around the upper Elbe River from which Anhalt was constituted was in the 11th century still part of the duchy of Saxony. It was united in the 12th century in the possession of Albert I the Bear, margrave of Brandenburg, and was made a separate county in 1212 under Albert's grandson Henry, who in 1218 took the title *Fürst* (prince). When he died in 1252, his three sons divided the Anhalt lands among themselves, thus inaugurating the three lines of Aschersleben, Bernberg, and Zerbst. The Aschersleben line died out in 1315. The remainder existed as Anhalt-Dessau and Anhalt-Köthen in the 16th century, but, beginning in 1603, it was divided into four parts: Dessau, Bernberg, Zerbst, and Köthen. Zerbst was absorbed by the other three in 1793, and in 1806, when the Holy Roman Empire was dissolved, the three surviving princes each assumed the title of duke. In 1863 all of Anhalt was united under Leopold IV of Anhalt-Dessau.

Anhalt had become Protestant at the time of the Reformation, and, beginning in the 17th century, it came under Prussian influence. The reorganization of the Prussian army by Leopold I of Anhalt-Dessau in the early 18th century contributed to the later victories of Frederick II the Great. In 1807 the Anhalt dukes joined the Confederation of the Rhine set up by Napoleon and supported him until 1813. In 1815 they joined the German Confederation and in 1828 the Zollverein (Customs Union) organized by Prussia. In 1871 Anhalt became a state of the newly founded German Reich. Under the republican Weimar Constitution, adopted in 1919, the ducal regime came to an end. Anhalt was a *Land* of the German Reich from then until 1945 and of the German Democratic Republic from 1949 to 1952.

Anhava, Tuomas (b. June 5, 1927, Helsinki), Finnish poet and translator working within the modernist tradition of Ezra Pound and T.S. Eliot.

Anhava is a perfectionist in his poetry, with a fanatical concern for *le mot propre* and a great theoretical interest in the aesthetics of modern poetry. His *Runoja* (1955; "Poems") has as its central theme alienation and a search for a transcendence of everyday reality. These motifs are developed in the technically difficult poems of *36 runoa* (1958; "36 Poems"). The images in these poems are strongly reminiscent of the Japanese and Chinese poetry Anhava translated during the same period. The simplification and compression of Oriental epigrams is employed in *Runoja 1961* and *Kuudes kirja* (1966; "The Sixth Book").

Even though Anhava never achieved great popularity, he had a great influence on many young Finnish poets through his uncompromising search for aesthetic perfection.

anhinga (water bird): *see* snakebird.

Anhwei, Wade-Giles romanization AN-HUI, Pinyin ANHUI, *sheng* (province) in the People's Republic of China. Anhwei, one of the smallest of the 21 provinces, is landlocked, bounded by the provinces of Kiangsu to the northeast, Chekiang to the southeast, Kiangsi to the south, and Hupeh and Honan to the west.

The article that follows is a brief summary of the significant detail about Anhwei. For additional information about its geography, history, economy, and culture, *see* MACROPAEDIA: China.

The history of Anhwei, the first part of southern China to be settled by the Chinese people dates to 481 BC. The province was the hub of the early water transportation system developed to carry grain. In the early 1850s the Huang Ho, or Yellow River, made one of its great changes in course. The loss of water resulted in great distress for the farmers of northern Anhwei. Subsequent peasant uprisings led to prolonged unrest in the province resulting in widespread devastation. In 1938 flooding of an enormous area caused serious loss of life. During World War II, most of Anhwei was occupied by Japanese forces. Between 1946 and 1949 the province was controlled by the Kuomintang (Nationalist) forces. Up until this time, Anhwei had been regarded as the most backward province of eastern China. In 1954 it became a province of the People's Republic of China. The capital is Ho-fei.

The northern portion of Anhwei is occupied by the North China Plain—an immense level surface that has periodically been flooded by its dominant rivers. The southern section of the province, the Yangtze Valley, is separated from the northern plain by a series of mountains that stretch roughly from west to east. The northern plain is drained by the Huai Ho, which flows across the level plain and drains into the Hungtse Hu Lake. The river basin is subject to widespread and disastrous floods. Vast irrigation schemes on the major rivers have alleviated severe periodic flooding and have also provided increased agricultural land and electric power. The Yangtze plain is crisscrossed by canals that are used for irrigation, drainage, and transport. Anhwei shares with the rest of China the seasonal monsoon climate characterized by hot, wet summers and cooler, dry winters.

Anhwei's regions of densest population are the tributaries and banks of the Huai Ho above Pang-fou and the diked areas along the right bank of the Yangtze. In both these areas the average density exceeds 1,000 persons per sq mi. There are four large towns: Hofei, the capital; Huai-nan; Pang-fou; and Wu-hu. The population is almost totally Chinese.

In the Huai Basin to the north wheat is the predominant crop. Rice is grown in the Yangtze Basin to the south. Most of the land produces two crops a year. Summer crops include rice, sweet potatoes, *kaoliang* (sorghum), soybeans, peanuts (groundnuts), and sesame. Winter crops are wheat, barley, rape (an herb of the mustard family), peas, and green manure crops which are plowed in as fertilizer. The main industrial crops are vegetable oilseeds, cotton, tea, fibres, and tobacco. Anhwei has also been famous for its tea since the 7th century, when rare teas from the province were exported to the rest of China, as well as abroad. Sericulture, the raising of silkworms for the production of raw silk, has also been revived since the 1950s. Both the mulberry-feeding moth and the tussah silkworm are reared, providing the raw material for Nanking brocades and Wuhan silk fabrics.

Pigs are the main source of meat, and sheep are raised in increasing numbers in northern Anhwei. Aquaculture flourishes all along the Yangtze. Coal, iron ore, and iron and steel are all produced in Anhwei. Secondary in importance are textiles and machine accessories. Local handicrafts include the making of wrought iron silhouettes for wall decoration.

Waterways are the main means of transport. Railways and highways criss-cross the province. Area 54,000 sq mi (139,900 sq km). Pop. (1983 est.) 50,160,000.

anhydride, any chemical compound obtained, either in practice or in principle, by the elimination of water from another compound. Examples of inorganic anhydrides are sulfur trioxide, SO_3, which is derived from sulfuric acid, and calcium oxide, CaO, derived from calcium hydroxide. Sulfur trioxide and other oxides formed by the removal of water from an acid are often called acid anhydrides, whereas those such as calcium oxide that are produced by a base upon the loss of water are designated basic anhydrides. For certain metals that have several oxidation states, the oxides in which the metal has the lower oxidation values are basic anhydrides and those in which the metal has higher values are of the acid variety—*e.g.*, chromous oxide, CrO, is a basic anhydride, whereas chromium trioxide, CrO_3, is an acid anhydride.

The most important of the organic anhydrides is acetic anhydride, $(CH_3CO)_2O$. It is prepared industrially in either of two ways: (1) by atmospheric oxidation of acetaldehyde in the presence of a metal acetate; and (2) from acetic acid by reaction with acetylene or ketene. Other organic anhydrides can be prepared from carboxylic acids by reaction with acetic anhydride, ketene, methoxyacetylene, or isopropenyl acetate. Anhydrides also are produced when acyl halides react with acetic anhydride or with carboxylic acid and pyridine.

The organic anhydrides are used to introduce the acyl group (RCO) in organic synthesis. They react with water to give carboxylic acids, with alcohols or phenols to give esters, and with ammonia and amines to give amides. Acetic anhydride is employed in the manufacture of cellulose triacetate, which is widely used as a base for magnetic tape and in the manufacture of textile fibres. Also, it is heated with salicylic acid to produce acetylsalicylic acid, commonly known as aspirin.

anhydrite, an important rock-forming mineral, anhydrous calcium sulfate ($CaSO_4$). It differs chemically from gypsum, to which it alters in humid conditions, by having no water of crystallization. It forms masses appearing to have orthogonal cleavage, fibrous masses, or contorted concretions (tripestone); it also forms fine or scaly granular masses, as the variety vulpinite from Vulpino, Lombardy,

Anhydrite from Lockport, N.Y.

By courtesy of the Field Museum of Natural History, Chicago; photograph, John H. Gerard—EB Inc.

Italy. Anhydrite is one of the most important minerals in evaporite deposits; it also is present in dolomites and limestones, and as a gangue mineral in ore veins. It is used in plasters and cement. Vulpinite is cut and polished for ornamental use. Anhydrite crystals possess orthorhombic symmetry. For physical properties, *see* sulfate mineral (table).

ani, any of three species of big-billed, glossy black birds of the genus *Crotophaga* of the cuckoo family (Cuculidae), of tropical America. These insect eaters forage on the ground in close and noisy flocks, often in fields with cattle. The bill is high arched, bladelike, and hook tipped; the tail is long and broad; the wings are short; and the plumage is floppy, so

Ani (*Crotophaga*)

J. Foott—Bruce Coleman Inc.

that the bird looks disheveled. Anis fly poorly and utter whining cries. They build a communal tree nest of twigs, in which several females may lay a total of 25 chalky-blue eggs (usually 10 to 15) and share duties of incubation and chick raising.

The common, or smooth-billed, ani (*C. ani*), found from southern Florida to Argentina, is a bird 36 centimetres (14 inches) long that looks like a huge-beaked grackle. The great ani (*C. major*) is common in swamplands of South America, chiefly east of the Andes. The groove-billed ani (*C. sulcirostris*), found from southern Texas to western Peru and northern Brazil, has several grooves in the upper mandible.

Aniakchak National Monument and Preserve, formerly ANIAKCHAK NATIONAL MONUMENT, national monument and preserve in southwestern Alaska, U.S., on the southern shore of the Alaska Peninsula. Proclaimed a monument in 1978, the area underwent boundary and title changes in 1980. A great dry caldera in the volcanically active Aleutian Mountains, Aniakchak last erupted in 1933. The crater, with an average diameter of about 6 mi (10 km), includes lava fields and cinder cones; pioneer plant life; brown and grizzly bears, moose, and caribou; sea lions, seals, and other marine mammals; and geese, swans, and other waterfowl. Surprise Lake, which cascades through a rift in the crater wall, forms the Aniakchak River. The monument and preserve cover an area of 514,000 ac (208,097 ha).

anicca (Pāli), Sanskrit ANITYA, in Buddhism, the doctrine of impermanence, one of the basic characteristics of all existence. *Anicca, anattā* (the absence of a self), and *dukkha* ("suffering") together make up the *ti-lakkhaṇa,* or three characteristics of all phenomenal existence. That the human body is subject to change is empirically observable in the universal states of childhood, youth, maturity, and old age. Similarly, mental events come into being and dissolve. Recognition of the doctrine of impermanence is one of the first steps in the Buddhist's spiritual progress toward Enlightenment.

Anicetus, SAINT (fl. 2nd century; b. Syria?—d. Rome; feast day April 17), pope from *c.* 155 to *c.* 166. Possibly a Syrian, he worked to combat the errors of the heresies of Valentine and Marcion and to prevent heresies, working particularly against the Marcionites and Gnostics. Although he suffered tribulations, it is questionable whether or not he was actually martyred. During his pontificate St. Polycarp, bishop of Smyrna, visited Rome (*c.* 154/155) to confer with him about the controversy over the date of Easter. He allowed Polycarp to celebrate the Eucharist in his church on the Eastern date.

aniconism, in religion, opposition to the use of icons or visual images to depict living creatures or religious figures. Such opposition is particularly relevant to the Jewish, Islāmic, and Byzantine artistic traditions. The Second Commandment (part of the First to Roman Catholics and Lutherans), "You shall not make yourself a graven image, or any likeness of anything . . . ." meant as a protection against idol worship, came to have a restricting effect on the production of Jewish art, though this effect varied in strength in different periods and was strongest on sculpture. Figural representations were absolutely prohibited in the early period of Islām and under the Berber dynasties of Africa and the Mamlūks of Egypt and Syria, though under the ʿAbbāsids and most of the Shīʿī and Turkish dynasties it was excluded only from public buildings. In the Byzantine Empire, during the Iconoclastic Controversy (725–843), a ban was imposed on representations of saintly or divine personages.

Anielewicz, Mordecai, also spelled MORDECHAI ANILOWITZ (b. 1919, Wyszków, Pol.—d. May 10, 1943, Warsaw), hero and principal leader of armed Jewish resistance in the Warsaw Ghetto during World War II.

Anielewicz was born into a working-class family and attended Hebrew gymnasium. As a boy he joined Betar, a Zionist youth organization that among other things advocated self-defense for Jews. By 1940 he had gone to Warsaw and become active in the branch there of a pro-Soviet group of young Zionists, Hashomer Hatzair. When Germany invaded Poland, he escaped to Wilno, which the Soviet Union had annexed with Lithuania. He eventually made his way back to the Warsaw Ghetto where he set up an underground newspaper (*Neged Hazerem* [Against the Stream]) and cultural and educational activities. He was out of Warsaw, spreading his educational and political ideas underground in western Poland when the population of the Warsaw Ghetto was decimated by deportation and execution in the late summer of 1942. Anielewicz had become convinced that Jews in Hitler's Europe should protect themselves with arms, and he rushed back to Warsaw to urge armed resistance on his elders, most of whom feared that resistance would fuel intolerable retaliation by the Nazis. With strong support from other young activists, notably Itzhak Zuckerman (*q.v.*), his view prevailed and the Jewish Combat Organization (Żydowska Organizacja Bojowa, ŻOB) was formed. Anielewicz was the obvious choice to command the ŻOB. He stressed discipline, the construction of bunkers, and the acquisition of arms in the Ghetto.

On January 18, 1943, the Germans entered the Ghetto to select Jews for a new shipment to the death camp at Treblinka, and the ŻOB met them with force, mainly pistols and grenades, starting a fight in the streets that lasted four days and killed about 50 Germans—and all of the ŻOB defenders except Anielewicz himself. The Germans withdrew and for two months tried various deceptions to persuade the Ghetto's remaining Jews to go peacefully to the boxcars. Anielewicz had effectively become the commander of the Ghetto as well as the ŻOB, and he pushed defensive preparations until the Germans returned with 2,000 troops and tanks on April 19. The ŻOB held them off at first, then gave ground slowly until on May 8 the Germans found its headquarters bunker and gassed it. Civilian occupants surrendered but Anielewicz and about a hundred comrades died, those not killed in the fighting taking their own and each other's lives to avoid falling alive into Nazi hands. He is commemorated in Israel by a kibbutz, Yad Mordecai. *See also* Warsaw Ghetto Resistance.

Aniello, Tomasso: *see* Masaniello.

Aniene River, also called TEVERONE, Latin ANIO, major tributary of the Tiber (Tevere) River in central Italy. It rises from two springs in the Monti (mountains) Simbruini near Subiaco, southeast of Rome, flows through a narrow valley past Tivoli, and meanders through the Campagna di Roma (territory) to join the Tiber north of Rome. It is 67 mi (108 km) long and has a drainage basin of 569 sq mi (1,474 sq km). The Roman emperor Nero created a group of artificial lakes in the upper course of the river above Subiaco and built a villa there, the remains of which survive. In Roman times, two huge aqueducts, the Anio Vetus and the Anio Novus, supplied Rome with water. The series of falls at Tivoli (*q.v.*), where the Aniene descends from the mountains to the plain, were once a main scenic attraction of the Roman countryside; but the heavy use of the river's waters by hydroelectric plants and by aqueducts has reduced the once famous cascades to a trickle. The middle valley of the Aniene is followed by the Rome–Pescara railway and motor road.

Ponte Nomentano on the Aniene River, Italy
Anderson—Alinari from Art Resource/EB Inc.

Aniliidae, family of harmless burrowing snakes, composed of three genera and more than 10 species with primitive features such as a vestigial pelvic girdle, an external claw on each side of the anal opening, and two lungs. One genus, the false coral snake (*Anilius*), is South American. Its commonest species, *A. scytale,* has red and black rings, grows to 75 centimetres (30 inches), and eats other snakes and lizards.

The second genus, *Anomalochilus,* is restricted to Sumatra and Malaya. The third, *Cylindrophis,* the dark coloured pipe snake, is found in rice paddies throughout southeast Asia; it lives on other snakes and eels. When disturbed it coils its tail up to expose its bright red underside.

aniline, an organic base used to make dyes, drugs, explosives, plastics, and photographic and rubber chemicals.

Aniline was first obtained in 1826 by destructive distillation of indigo. Its name is taken from the specific name of the indigo-yielding plant *Indigofera anil* (*Indigofera suffruticosa*); its chemical formula is $C_6H_5NH_2$.

Aniline is prepared commercially by the catalytic hydrogenation of nitrobenzene or by the action of ammonia on chlorobenzene. The reduction of nitrobenzene can also be carried out with iron borings in aqueous acid.

A primary aromatic amine, aniline is a weak base and forms salts with mineral acids. In acidic solution, nitrous acid converts aniline into a diazonium salt that is an intermediate in the preparation of dyes and other organic compounds of commercial interest. When aniline is heated with organic acids it gives amides, called anilides, such as acetanilide from aniline and acetic acid. Monomethylaniline and dimethylaniline can be prepared from aniline and methyl alcohol. Catalytic reduction of aniline yields cyclohexylamine. Various oxidizing agents convert aniline to quinone, azobenzene, nitrosobenzene, *p*-aminophenol, and the phenazine dye aniline black.

Pure aniline is a highly poisonous, oily, colourless substance, with a pleasant odour.

aniline green (dye): *see* malachite green.

aniline printing: *see* flexography.

animal, in biology, any member of a group of living organisms distinguishable from plants on the basis of certain somewhat arbitrary differences in morphology and physiology.

The actual boundaries between animals and plants are somewhat artificial. The most obvious distinction is that the animal cell wall is either absent or composed of a nitrogenous material, whereas the plant cell wall is composed of a carbohydrate material—cellulose. The animal body, if composed of many cells, also follows a different architectural plan; the compact nature of its food and the relative elasticity of its cell walls result in a structure, of more or less limited growth, consisting essentially of tubular or spherical masses of cells arranged concentrically around the food cavity.

The animal and the plant both require food; but although both animals and plants take their water and inorganic salts directly as such, the animal cell can absorb its carbohydrate and protein food only in the form of complex organic substances; it is dependent, in fact, on the pre-existence of these organic substances, themselves the products of living matter, and in this respect the animal is essentially a parasite on existing animal and plant life.

In general, an animal is a living organism that is incapable of synthesizing carbohydrates and proteins from inorganic or simple organic substances but must ingest them in complex form as food. In general, also, animals are distinguished from plants by freedom of spatial movement.

Animals are treated in a number of articles in the MACROPAEDIA. For descriptions of various classes and orders of animals, *see* Sponges; Cnidarians; Aschelminths; Moss Animals; Lamp Shells; Mollusks; Annelids; Arthropods; Arachnids; Crustaceans; Insects; Echinoderms; Chordates; Fishes; Amphibians; Reptiles; Birds; Mammals; Evolution, Human. *See also* Pets; Horses and Horsemanship. For discussions of animals in relation to the biosphere, *see* Biosphere; Growth and Development of Living Organisms; Soil Organisms. For special characteristics of animals, *see* Behaviour, Animal; Learning, Animal. For the study of animals, *see* Biological Sciences. *See also* Animals and Plants in Myth and Legend.

For a description of the place of animals in the circle of learning and for a list of both MACROPAEDIA and MICROPAEDIA articles on the subject, *see* PROPAEDIA: Part Three.

animal behaviour, any observable activity of a whole living animal. The ways in which animals solve their common problems—*e.g.,* eating, drinking, protecting themselves from predators, reproducing, and grooming—are all the concerns of an ethologist, a scientist who studies animal behaviour.

A brief treatment of animal behaviour follows. For full treatment, *see* MACROPAEDIA: Behaviour, Animal.

Animal behaviour is largely dictated by innate programming. Depending on external factors such as the season or the cycle of the Moon, an animal's body may secrete hormones that regulate its metabolism or behaviour. Hormones, for example, will decrease a bear's metabolic rate until the animal falls into a torpid state that lasts throughout the winter, and other hormones encourage the bear throughout its active months to consume enough food so that it will survive hibernation. None of this is under the bear's conscious control—no more than a woman can control her menstrual cycle.

Animals solve their problems in a variety of ways. In the winter, birds remedy their reduced food supply by migrating toward the Equator or Southern Hemisphere where the seasons are reversed. It is not fully known whether birds navigate over long distances by the stars and Sun or by a compass sense. Nor can the behaviour of salmon, which find their way back to the same freshwater where they were born after years in the ocean, be explained. Some hormones are produced at particular times; *e.g.,* sex hormones, which prepare the body for parenthood. Other hormones may be triggered by a particular occurrence, such as the sight of a predator.

Many animals also secrete chemical substances called pheromones, which send messages to other animals. When a female fly is ready to produce eggs, she releases a pheromone into the air. A male that smells this substance will immediately approach and inseminate the female or any object that a scientist may have dabbed with the pheromone. Pheromones can also serve as a message between males, as when a dog marks with urine what it would like to claim as its territory. Still other pheromones transmit information to the entire group, as in an ant trail that leads to a food source.

Animals that live in communities demonstrate a variety of social behaviour. Some perform actions that benefit others without receiving any direct benefit themselves. Animal altruism helps to preserve a species, as when parents gather food for their young and protect them against predators. Similarly, rats and monkeys in laboratory experiments will sacrifice food rather than allow others of their species to receive an electrical shock.

Complex animal societies tend to build shelters (*e.g.,* an ant hill), while others establish and guard territories. A pattern of leaders and followers within an animal society indicates some social organization, as in herds of sheep or schools of fish, but does not always indicate that the group has a leader. Among many species of birds, for example, different members lead the flock during a single flight.

A dominance hierarchy, in which one animal bullies another into submitting to its wishes, is present in almost all animal interactions and does not indicate social organization. Ethologists argue that the more advanced animal societies do not have dominance hierarchies. Other factors of social behaviour in animals include migration patterns and labour division.

Social behaviour should not be correlated with intelligence or with evolutionary development. The simplest organisms form colonies, and the most complex colonies are formed by the relatively simple ant and bee. Man, the highest animal on the evolutionary scale, can be relatively solitary. Social behaviour is not a key to evolutionary development but rather is the adaptation of animals to the world around them.

animal breeding, the controlled propagation of domestic animals with the purpose of improving inherent qualities considered desirable by man. Animals are bred for utility (*e.g.,* food, fur), sport, pleasure, and research.

A brief treatment of animal breeding follows. For full treatment, *see* MACROPAEDIA: Farming and Agricultural Technology.

Improvement or favourable change in animals is brought about by changing the inheritance or the environment. Hereditary characteristics are those that arise from gene differences and account for common differences in animals as, for example, the white-face characteristic of Hereford cattle. Nonhereditary differences are mainly environmental; *e.g.,* animals poorly fed and managed will not develop to their maximum capacity. Environment, if markedly improved, can bring forth changes in animals with dramatic swiftness, but the changes continue only while the improved environment prevails. Changes in the hereditary makeup of a population are made slowly, but usually are fairly permanent. Some characteristics, however, revert to the original level when man withdraws his attention to selection.

Origin of breeds. Breeds were formed usually from small localized groups thought to be superior to the prevailing stock. Man began to isolate such groups to get a more desirable stock. Certain hereditary traits became characteristic of animals within an area, which tended to distinguish them from others of the same species. The English began to develop the purebred idea for breeding stock late in the 18th century. As breeds were formed and recognized, herdbooks were started to maintain pedigree records of selected animals.

The animal breeder had in mind a type or ideal animal, representing particular desirable characteristics, these being determined by the purpose for which the animal was intended. Thus there are two common types of sheep—mutton and wool; two main types of cattle—dairy and beef; and analogous designations for other kinds of livestock. The breeder of pet or fancy stock had mainly the human appeal to consider.

A breeding program, to be effective, must include measurements of the individual for comparison with the ideal. The measuring of milk production in terms of quantity and butterfat content was one of the first attempts at production evaluation. However, since production typically varies from year to year, and certain other features do not lend themselves to objective measurement, over-all merit is generally not based on a few characteristics, but on several of them and on their interaction.

Systems of selection and mating. With an ideal and methods of evaluation established, the next step in animal breeding is to choose the breeding stock. Several types of selection are commonly distinguished. Mass selection is the choosing of animals for producing the next generation wholly upon their own individual merit; it is sometimes referred to as phenotypic selection, as it is based on what an animal is and does. Pedigree selection is based upon the merit of the individual's ancestors. Family selection refers to selection based mainly upon collateral, or nonlineal, relatives or those descended from the same stock but from a different line. Progeny testing is a means of estimating an animal's breeding worth and is based on the performance of offspring or lineal or direct descendants.

After the breeding stock has been chosen, the next step is to decide how they should be mated. Systems of mating range from the mating of closely related individuals, or inbreeding, to line breeding, which combines mild inbreeding with selection, to the mating of unrelated individuals, as in crossbreeding. Mating systems may also be assortative, that is, based upon similarity of characteristics. In outbreeding, it is not uncommon for the progeny to surpass the parent stock in vigour and vitality. The main use of cross-breeding has been in commercial livestock production, in which the method results in faster and more economical gains. The mule is an outstanding example of a hybrid resulting from a cross between species or an extremely wide outcross; in some such crosses fertility is impaired.

The development of artificial insemination techniques has permitted the extensive use of selected males, since more females can be bred to one male by this method than by natural service. The practice has proved extremely successful with horses and with dairy cattle. Increased understanding of the principles of population genetics has greatly enhanced the efficacy of modern breeding programs. *See also* cat; dog; horse.

animal communication, the sending of a message through a medium to a receiver so as to change the status or behaviour of the receiver. Information can be transmitted among animals by sight, taste or odour, electrical impulse, or touch, and many animals have more than one system.

A brief treatment of animal communication follows. For full treatment, *see* MACROPAEDIA: Behaviour, Animal.

Sound has several advantages in animal communication. It fades quickly, leaving no trace of the communicator's location, and it can vary in pitch, duration, loudness, and repetition, thus permitting the creation of special codes. Sound is also best used where other means are unsuccessful, as in a forest or across great distances under water. Most communication is vocal, but there are many exceptions. Male gorillas beat their chests, the ground, or any suitable object, while beavers slap the surface of the water with their tails, sending signals through the underwater tunnels leading to their lodges. Some male spiders cautiously announce their presence by strumming on a female's web, indicating that they are to be taken as mate and not prey. Hyenas, which hunt in packs of up to 30, have a rich repertory of grunts, snorts, and giggles. Their complex tracking strategy is guided by their sounds, and once the prey is taken, other sounds, including their well-known laugh, calls the rest of the pack to join in the feast. In contrast, a small bird squawking at the sight of a falcon serves to warn other birds that appropriate actions must be taken to avoid imminent danger.

Visual communication may be conducted through the use of badges (*i.e.,* special characteristics such as a patch of bright colour or horns), which give some indication of the communicator's identity (*e.g.,* species, sex, and age). A juvenile baboon, for example, can be distinguished by hair colour, which permits it to act in an immature manner forbidden to adults. Information can also be conveyed visually by the assumption of various poses or motions. Males of many species adopt characteristic attitudes to attract females for mating, and females have evolved various ways of indicating readiness for copulation. Some species set aside a display arena or build a structure that is itself intended as a form of communication, such as the elaborate bower built by the bowerbird. Other visible signs include special dung heaps left by rabbits and the scars left on tree trunks by bears.

The use of chemical signals, called pheromones, which are produced by the animal's endocrine system, is yet another form of communication. Ants exude an unpleasant aroma designed to convince a predator of their bad taste. Some pheromones are deposited with urine or feces to mark territorial boundaries, as demonstrated by the familiar habit of dogs. Other chemical signs may be produced by a female in heat to signify sexual readiness or laid down as a trail along the ground, signalling the direction of a food source. There are even pheromones that dictate the hierarchy within a group, but these are the least understood.

Touch is less prevalent as a mode of communication than sound, sight, or smell. The dance of the honeybee, which is performed in a dark hive, conveys primarily through touch the direction and distance to a food source; this activity also includes an element of taste, because the honeybee usually has some of the nectar on its body.

Eels and a number of other fishes that live in muddy waters generally use electrical impulses to send messages to one another as well as to ward off enemies.

animal domestication: *see* domestication, plant and animal.

animal feed: *see* feed.

animal interlace, in calligraphy, rich, fanciful decorative motif characteristic of work by the Hiberno-Saxon book artists of the early Middle Ages. Its intertwined, fantastic animal and bird forms are often densely and minutely detailed—an example in the Book of Kells (*c.* 700) contains 158 interlacements in a space of one-fourth square inch (1.61 square centimetre). Another work of comparable stylistic maturity is the Lindisfarne Gospels, written in Northumbria in honour of St. Cuthbert soon after his death in 687.

Interlace patterns of the initial page of the Gospel According to St. John from the Lindisfarne Gospels, Hiberno-Saxon, 8th century (British Library, Cotton Nero D. IV, fol. 211)

By courtesy of the trustees of the British Library

animal magnetism, term used with various significations to refer to some intangible or mysterious force that influences human beings. The term was applied by Franz Mesmer to the hypnotism that he used in the treatment of patients. He believed that it was an occult force or invisible fluid emanating from his body and that, more generally, the force permeated the universe, deriving especially from the stars.

animal worship, veneration of an animal, usually because of its connection with a particular deity. The term was used by Western religionists in a pejorative manner and by ancient Greek and Roman polemicists against theriomorphic religions—those whose gods are represented in animal form. Most examples given for animal worship in primitive religions, however, are not instances of worship of an animal itself. Instead, the sacred power of a deity was believed to be manifested in an appropriate animal that was regarded as an epiphany or incarnation of the deity (*e.g.,* fertility deities frequently were represented as manifesting themselves in the form of a bull).

The universal practice among hunting peoples of respect for and ceremonial behaviour toward animals stems from the religious customs attendant on the conducting of the hunt and not from worship of the animal itself. Another phenomenon that has been confused with animal worship is totemism, in which animal or plant categories fulfill a social classificatory system that does not imply worship of the animal.

Animal symbolism in religious iconography and allegory has been used in associating certain qualities with certain animal species (*e.g.,* wisdom with the owl—hence, Athena, the Greek goddess of wisdom, is frequently represented as an owl). This associative factor does not imply, as polemicists have strongly suggested, a more primitive style in which an animal itself was worshipped and then later rationalized into an anthropomorphic figure or abstract quality.

In contemporary scholarship, the term animal worship seldom occurs, because it has been rejected as a misleading interpretive category.

animals, cruelty to, the willful or wanton infliction of pain, suffering, or death upon an animal, or the intentional or malicious neglect of an animal. It is illegal in virtually every country in the world, and in the mid-20th century, interest in endangered species gave further impetus to the anticruelty movement. Reflecting such interest, many laws have been passed, although they are seldom enforced without active and vocal public pressure being brought to bear upon the appropriate enforcement officials.

The movement against cruelty to animals is rooted in antiquity. Pythagoras taught kindness toward all subhuman creations as a duty, and the poet Bion put it in its simplest terms: "Boys stone a frog in sport, but the frog dies in earnest." Even the Romans, despite the barbarities of the circus, had feelings about proper treatment of animals; when Pompey the Great organized a particularly revolting slaughter of elephants, the populace rose up and cursed him for his ruthlessness.

If St. Francis of Assisi was the greatest friend of animals, René Descartes, the French philosopher, was perhaps their greatest enemy. He believed that animals had no souls and that, as thinking and feeling processes in his view were part of the soul, animals could feel no pain. Further, Descartes concluded that animals were mere machines. He and his followers marvelled that these "mechanical robots," as they called them, "could give such a realistic illusion of agony." The issue produced a century of controversy.

It was an Englishman, Jeremy Bentham, who first phrased the matter so as to move the argument into reality. "The question is not," he wrote, "can they reason, nor can they talk, but can they suffer?" It was also England that moved the subject from theorizing about the "animal question" to the field of political action. In 1809 the Scottish Lord Erskine presented a bill in Parliament to prevent malicious and wanton cruelty to such animals as horses, pigs, oxen, and sheep. The bill passed the House of Lords in the face of sarcasm, but failed in the House of Commons. In 1822, however, Richard "Humanity Dick" Martin was responsible for the actual passing of the Martin Act, which represented the world's first anticruelty law. Although it applied only to large domestic animals, thus excluding dogs, cats, and birds, it was a landmark. Before the Martin Act, cruelty to an animal had, as a necessary legal component, to include malice toward the owner of the animal, not the animal itself. The Martin Act made cruelty per se an offense.

Two years later in England, in 1824, came the world's first animal welfare society—the Society for the Prevention of Cruelty to Animals (which in 1840 added the prefix Royal to its name at Queen Victoria's behest). France was not far behind. In 1845 Gen. Jacques Delmas de Grammont founded the Société Protectrice des Animaux; in 1850 he also pushed through an act similar to the English statute, known as the Loi Grammont. Other countries that soon followed suit and initiated both laws and animal welfare societies included Ireland, Germany, Austria, Belgium, and The Netherlands. In the United States, both laws and a society did not come until much later, and, when they did, they were almost the sole creation of one man—Henry Bergh, Abraham Lincoln's minister to Russia. In St. Petersburg, Bergh had seen a Russian droshky driver beating a horse, and from the moment of that incident to the end of his life he campaigned for animals in every issue from bullfighting to vivisection.

By the late 20th century, animal welfare societies and laws against cruelty to animals had come to exist in almost every country in the world. Associations ranged from the Japan Animal Welfare Society to Spain's Sociedad de Animales y Plantes, the latter being particularly notable because, though located in one of the few countries still tolerating the bullfight, it undertakes to protect plants as well as animals. International anticruelty societies also developed; among these are the World Federation for the Protection of Animals, with headquarters in Zürich; the International Society for the Protection of Animals, with headquarters in London; and the Fund for Animals, Inc., with headquarters in New York. The late 20th century also witnessed the burgeoning of special interest groups concerned with the preservation of certain endangered animals—whales, dolphins, seals, tigers—and groups that protested against particularly painful or brutal methods of trapping and killing.

A list of the abbreviations used in the MICROPAEDIA *will be found at the end of this volume*

animals, master of the, supernatural figure regarded as the protector of game in the traditions of early hunting peoples. The name was actually devised by scholars who have studied such hunting societies. In some traditions, the master of the animals is believed to be the ruler of the forest and guardian of all animals; in others, he is the ruler of only one species, usually a large animal of economic or social importance to the tribe. Thus, among Eurasian peoples the animal most frequently is the bear; among the reindeer cultures of the tundra, the reindeer; among the northern coastal peoples of Eurasia and America, the whale, the seal, or the walrus; among the North American Indians, the bear, the beaver, or the caribou; and among Meso-American and South American Indians, the wild pig, jaguar, deer, or tapir. In some traditions he is pictured in human form, at times having animal attributes or riding an animal; in other traditions he is a giant animal or can assume animal form at will.

A complex system of customs governs the relationship between the master of the animals, the game animal, and the hunter. The master controls the game animals or their spirits (in many myths, by penning them). He releases a certain number to man as food. Only the allotted number may be killed, and the slain animal must be treated with respect. The master of the animals, if properly invoked, will also guide the hunter to the kill. The souls of the animals, when slain, return to the master's pens and give him a report of their treatment. If this system is violated, the master will avenge an animal improperly slain, usually by withholding game. A ceremony then must be held to remove the offense or a shaman (a religious personage with healing and psychic transformation powers) sent to placate the master.

animation, the process of giving the illusion of movement or life to cinematographic drawings, models, or inanimate objects. Animated drawings predate the cinema proper. From the 1830s onward, optical toys—such as the phenakistoscope (a revolving disk with figures arranged around the centre), zoetrope (where figures on the inside of a revolving cylinder are seen through slits in its circumference), and the French inventor Emile Reynaud's Praxinoscope (which used reflections of objects)—were designed to demonstrate or exploit the physical phenomenon of "persistence of vision." Such instruments used a technique comparable to the modern cartoon film: drawings of successive stages of an action were presented so rapidly that they produced an illusion of movement.

A brief treatment of animation follows. For full treatment, *see* MACROPAEDIA: Motion Picture.

Before the turn of the century the French conjurer and filmmaker George Méliès had indicated the possibilities of the frame-by-frame technique by which animated films have generally been produced. By 1907 J. Stuart Blackton in the United States had made an animated film, *Humorous Phases of Funny Faces*; and a year later, in Paris, Émile Cohl embarked on a series of witty cartoon films. Cohl's successors in the silent period included such distinguished animation artists as Robert Lortac, Benjamin Rabier, and Joseph Hémard.

The earliest U.S. cartoon films were derived from newspaper comic strips, where characters such as "Mutt and Jeff," "Happy Hooligan," and "The Katzenjammer Kids" originated. The first American artist to draw for film was Winsor McKay, with his *Gertie the Dinosaur* and a series called *Dreams of a Rarebit Fiend.* The most famous cartoon personality before Walt Disney's *Mickey Mouse*, however, was *Felix the Cat,* created by the Australian cartoonist Pat Sullivan and animated by Otto Mesmer. Meanwhile, the Russian Ladislav Starevich used other silent animation methods, such as stop-action techniques, to animate his exquisite little puppets as early as 1911. Lotte Reiniger, a German artist who adapted the ancient techniques of the shadow show, completed the world's first full-length animated film, *Die Abenteuer des Prinz Achmets* (*The Adventures of Prince Achmed*) in 1926.

With the arrival of sound, Walt Disney rapidly achieved preeminence through imaginative use of sound and colour, the vitality of his characters (mostly anthropomorphized animals), and the inventiveness of his gags (largely inspired by early slapstick films). Disney's *The Three Little Pigs* (1933), with the optimism of its theme song ("Who's Afraid of the Big Bad Wolf?"), came to be a symbol of the New Deal era. In 1937 Disney made his first full-length cartoon, *Snow White and the Seven Dwarfs.* Subsequently, although no studio surpassed his technical achievement, the individuality of the early productions was sacrificed to mass production.

Simultaneously there were experiments abroad in new techniques. In the Soviet Union Aleksandr Ptushko's *The New Gulliver* (1935) combined live actors and cartoon figures in the same scenes.

The 1940s and '50s saw violent reactions against the Disney style. Such artists as Bill Hanna and Joe Barbera, Tex Avery, Paul Terry, Walter Lantz, and Charles Jones continued in the same style of animation but added a new anarchic and surreal comedy. The artists of United Productions of America (UPA)—most of whom, including Art Babbitt and John Hubley, had broken away from Disney—reacted against the detail and naturalism of the Disney style with spare, non-naturalistic drawing inspired by contemporary art and such practitioners as the Romanian-born Saul Steinberg.

In Canada the Scots animator Norman McLaren, who had joined the National Film Board in 1941, experimented with stereoscopy (two-dimensional depictions that through perspective give the impression of being in three dimensions), synthetic sound, and other techniques, many of which were further developed by the school of animators he built up. Among McLaren's colleagues and disciples was George Dunning, who subsequently worked in Great Britain, where the animated cinema was vigorous after 1950. Other notable animators working in Britain include John Halas and Joy Batchelor, already established there during World War II; Peter Földes; Bob Godfrey, an inspired exponent of low comedy; and Richard Williams, a Canadian whose studio constantly sought to emulate the Disney craft traditions.

In eastern Europe the most notable animated films have come from Czechoslovakia, where Jiří Trnka developed a singular tradition of animation work with puppets, and Yugoslavia, where the Zagreb Studios produced such distinguished practitioners as Vatroslav Mimica, Dušan Vukotić, and Nikola Kostelac.

By the 1970s the animated film had become a remarkably varied and supple medium, ranging in its possibilities from the lyrical documentary visions of Hubley's *Of Stars and Men* to the Rabelaisian farces of the Japanese Yoji Kuri. The late 1970s and early '80s opened up vast new possibilities in the use of computers and electronic video equipment.

Animikie Series, division of Precambrian rocks and time in North America (the Precambrian began about 4,600,000,000 years ago and ended 570,000,000 years ago). The Animikie Series, the uppermost division of the Huronian System, overlies rocks of the Cobalt Series. The Animikie Series was named for exposures along the north shore of Lake Superior, in the Thunder Bay area (animiki is the Chippewa word for thunder); Animikian rocks occur in Ontario, northern Michigan, northern Wisconsin, and northeastern Minnesota. In the Port Arthur area, Animikian rocks overlie pre-Huronian metamorphic (altered) rocks; rocks of the Cobalt Series are absent. The Animikie Series begins with a basal conglomerate, which is succeeded by very thick sequences of sandstones, shales, and limestones. Animikie rocks are rich in iron ores and provide many important sources for mining. The Mesabi, Gunflint, and Cuyuna ranges are Animikian in age and provide rich deposits of taconite, a mineral assemblage consisting of the iron-containing minerals hematite, siderite, pyrite, and magnetite, and others. Algal structures known as stromatolites, concentric and finely laminated, are common in Animikian limestones. Animikian rocks are commonly intruded by igneous masses but are not strongly folded or faulted.

animism, belief in spiritual beings concerned with human affairs and capable of intervening in them—a belief pervasive among most tribal or primitive peoples. Animistic beliefs were first competently surveyed by Sir Edward Burnett Tylor in the late 19th century.

A brief treatment of animism follows. For full treatment, *see* MACROPAEDIA: Religious and Spiritual Belief, Systems of.

Tylor's theory. Tylor wrote his great work, *Primitive Culture* (1871), in order to prove that religion began in animism. In his view, animism is the attribution of a soul or spirit to living things and inanimate objects. In full-blown animism nothing is really inanimate; everything is alive with spirit, active or not. Further, Tylor observed, every individual is regarded as being endowed not only with a life-spirit but also with a phantom, such as appears to others in dreams or visions. Both life and phantom are perceived to be separable from the body: the life as able to go away and leave it insensible or dead; and the phantom as appearing to people at a distance. The second step taken by Tylor's "ancient savage philosophers" was to combine the life and the phantom and thus arrive at "that well-known conception which may be described as an apparitional soul, a ghost-soul." Tylor argued that in further steps of reasoning it was thought that the ghost-soul was able to enter into, possess, and act in animals, plants, and objects (*e.g.*, weapons, clothing, food).

Tylor felt that religion had its origin in early man's attribution of a soul like his own to every sort of living being and physical object around him. Religion is man's establishment of a relationship between himself and the spirits which he felt "possessed, pervaded, crowded" all nature.

Even though Tylor's theory has impressed anthropologists with its plausibility, his notion of "ancient savage philosophers" who developed theories to explain death and dreams has been widely criticized as too intellectualistic. It also began to be felt that the facts are misinterpreted when it is said that the primitive man considers all objects to be alive. Later scholars, responding to evidence of simpler beliefs that yet entailed a properly religious awe toward the sacred, began to debate the possibilities of a "pre-animistic stage" of theological evolution. British anthropologist R.R. Marett, notably in his book *The Threshold of Religion* (1914), limited the conception of aliveness to objects that attracted special attention, either by their appearance or by their "behaviour." In addition, he asserted that the potency or aliveness attributed to such objects did not necessarily correspond to soul or spirit. Marett found confirmation of his theory in the Melanesian conception of mana (*q.v.*), a kind of "communicable energy."

Émile Durkheim, a French sociologist, in his *Elementary Forms of Religious Life* (1915), held that religion originated in totemism, which in turn derived from man's expectation of security in the bosom of society. Durkheim has been criticized for not seeing totemism as one animistic cult among many. Still other theorists of this period, notably Sir James G. Frazer in his *The Golden Bough* (1890–1915), argued that religion sprang from man's frustrated attempt to control nature by means of his own crude magical science.

The term animism, as it survives in contemporary anthropology, denotes not a single creed or doctrine but a view of the world consistent with a certain range of religious beliefs and practices, many of which may survive in more complex and hierarchical religions.

Anio (river, Italy): *see* Aniene River.

anion, atom or group of atoms carrying a negative electric charge. *See* ion.

Aniruddha (king of Burma): *see* Anawrahta.

anise, annual herb, *Pimpinella anisum*, of the parsley family (Apiaceae, or Umbelliferae), cultivated chiefly for its fruits, called aniseed, the flavour of which resembles that of licorice. The plant, up to 2.5 feet (0.75 metre) tall, has long-stalked basal leaves and shorter, stalked stem leaves. Its small, yellowish-white flowers form loose umbels. The fruit, or seed, is nearly ovoid in shape, about 0.12 inch (3.5 millimetres) long, and has five longitudinal dorsal ridges. Native to Egypt and the eastern Mediterranean region, anise is cultivated in southern Europe, southern Soviet Union, the Near East, North Africa, Pakistan, China, Chile, Mexico, and the United States.

Aniseed is widely used to flavour pastries; it is the characteristic ingredient of a German bread called *Anisbrod.* In the Mediterranean region and in Asia aniseed is commonly used in meat and vegetable dishes. It makes a soothing herbal tea and has been used medicinally from prehistoric times. The essential oil content is about 2.5 percent, and its principal component is anethole. The essential oil is used to flavour absinthe, anisette, and pernod liqueurs.

Star anise is the dried fruit of the *Illicium verum,* an evergreen tree of the Magnoliaceae

Anise (*Pimpinella anisum*)

A–Z Botanical Collection—EB Inc.

family, indigenous to the southeastern part of China and to Vietnam. Its flavour and uses are similar to those of anise. The fruit takes its name from the starlike arrangement of its carpels around a central axis. The dried fruit is about 0.1 to 0.2 in. in diameter; individual carpels are usually about 0.4 in. in length and contain a single seed. Dried carpels are hard, rough, and reddish brown; the seeds are smooth, lustrous, and light brown in colour. Essential oil content is about 3 percent, and its principal component is anethole.

Anisian Stage, standard, worldwide division of Triassic rocks and time (the Triassic Period began about 225,000,000 years ago and lasted about 35,000,000 years). It was first recognized in the Austrian Alps and is composed of a thick sequence of rocks that were deposited in a deep marine environment. Rocks of the Anisian Stage, the lowermost stage of the Middle Triassic Series, underlie those of the Ladinian and overlie rocks of the Spathian Stage. A characteristic fossil fauna occurs in the Anisian, dominated by distinctive ammonoid cephalopods that allow widespread correlations to be made between various stratigraphic sequences.

anisotropy, in physics, the quality of exhibiting properties with different values when measured along axes in different directions. Anisotropy is most easily observed in single crystals of solid elements or compounds, in which atoms, ions, or molecules are arranged in regular lattices. In contrast, the random distribution of particles in liquids, and especially in gases, causes them rarely, if ever, to be anisotropic.

A familiar example of anisotropy is the difference in the refractive index of light along different axes of crystals of the mineral calcite. Another example is the electrical resistivity of selenium, which is high in one direction but low in the other; when an alternating current is applied to this material, it is transmitted in only one direction (rectified), thus becoming a direct current.

anitya (Buddhism): *see* anicca.

Anius, in Greek mythology, the son of the god Apollo and of Rhoeo, a descendant of the god Dionysus. His mother, when pregnant, had been placed in a chest and cast into the sea by her father; floating to the island of Delos, she gave birth to Anius, who became a seer and a priest of Apollo. Anius' three daughters, Oeno, Spermo, and Elais—that is, Wine, Grain Seed, and Oil—were granted by Dionysus the gift of bringing these three crops to fruition. They supplied both the Greek expedition on its way to Troy and Aeneas in his flight from Troy to Italy.

Anjala League (1788–89), a conspiracy of Swedish and Finnish army officers that undermined the Swedish war effort in the Russo-Swedish War of 1788–90. Shortly after the outbreak of war, 113 officers in the Finnish town of Anjala dispatched a letter to Empress Catherine II the Great of Russia calling for peace on the basis of the pre-1743 status quo—one favourable to Sweden. Although this condition made Catherine's acceptance unlikely, it did not lessen the letter's treasonable nature. When King Gustav III of Sweden learned of the letter, he called upon the officers to repudiate it in return for a full pardon. The officers, however, answered that the war was unjust and therefore Swedes could not be inspired to fight to victory; they denied that their act had been treasonable, noting that they would consider a refusal by Catherine to negotiate as a personal attack on them. Unmoved by this explanation, Gustav III, after first dealing successfully with an attack in the west by Denmark, punished the Anjala group in 1789: one officer was executed and many were imprisoned.

Anjō, city, Aichi Prefecture (*ken*), Honshu, Japan, in the middle of the Hekkai Terrace. Irrigation was introduced into the area in the late 19th century, permitting cultivation of two crops of rice and wheat annually. In 1891 the Anjō station on the railroad between Tokyo and Kōbe was opened, and the new town developed around it. With far-sighted planning and the early establishment of agricultural cooperatives, Anjō became a model farm community. Its diversified farming of rice, wheat, poultry, and cattle lent it the name Little Denmark of Japan. After 1960 industrialization increased rapidly, and farming became secondary to the large textile factory and several smaller plants making machinery and metal products. Pop. (1983 est.) 129,246.

Anjou, historic and cultural region encompassing the western French *département* of Maine-et-Loire and coextensive with the former province of Anjou.

The following article summarizes the political history, geography, and modern culture of Anjou; for additional treatment of its geography and history, *see* MACROPAEDIA: France.

The former province of Anjou encompassed the modern *département* of Maine-et-Loire, with the regions of La Flèche and Château-Gontier. Organized in the Gallo-Roman period as the Civitas Andegavensis, it later became the countship of Anjou and (from 1360) the duchy of Anjou.

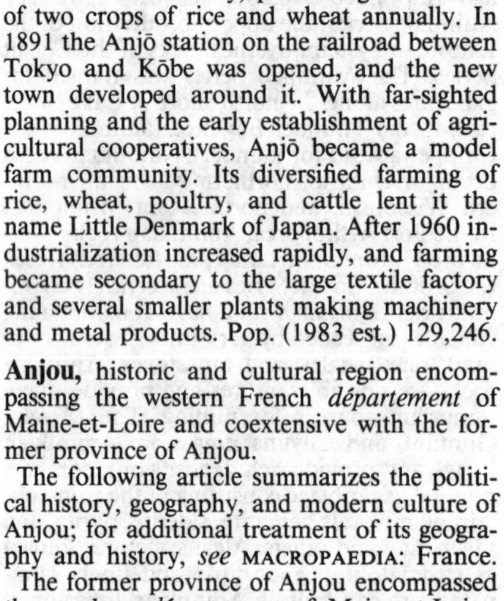

The *gouvernement* of Anjou in 1789

Under the Carolingians, Anjou was nominally administered by a count representing the French king, but the region became vulnerable to attack by marauding Vikings, or Northmen, in the 9th century.

First dynasty of counts. Under one of the sons of Robert the Strong, Anjou was entrusted to a certain Ingelger, who became the founder of the first Angevin dynasty. Ingelger's son Fulk I the Red rid the country of the Normans and enlarged his domains by taking part of Touraine. He died in 942, and under his successor, Fulk II the Good, the destruction caused by the preceding wars was repaired. Geoffrey I Grisegonelle, who succeeded Fulk II *c.* 960, began the policy of expansion which was to characterize this first feudal dynasty. He helped Hugh Capet to seize the French crown but died some months after the new king's accession (987).

Geoffrey's successor Fulk III Nerra (*q.v.*), one of the most remarkable figures of his period and the most powerful member of the dynasty, ruled from 987 to 1040. He finally drove his encroaching neighbours back beyond the frontiers of Anjou and built strongly fortified castles of stone (instead of wood) along the border of his territory. Fulk's son Geoffrey II Martel (1040–60) pursued the policy of expansion begun by his father and annexed the Vendômois and a part of Maine to Anjou. Because he left no sons, his two nephews, Geoffrey III the Bearded and Fulk IV le Réchin, shared the succession. However, they soon came into armed conflict and Fulk defeated Geoffrey in 1068. Nevertheless, he had to give up most of the lands that Fulk Nerra had acquired and to defend his fief against the claims of the Duke of Normandy. After the death of Fulk IV in 1109 his son Fulk V the Young endeavoured to make good the losses caused by the various wars. He married his son Geoffrey Plantagenet to Matilda, the daughter of Henry I of England and widow of the emperor Henry V.

By his marriage to Matilda, Geoffrey Plantagenet acquired a claim to Normandy and England. Forced to spend his whole life fighting his rivals and the Angevin castellans, he nevertheless succeeded in pacifying Anjou, which in 1151 he left to his son Henry (later Henry II of England), count of Anjou and Maine and duke of Normandy, who married Eleanor of Aquitaine after the annulment of her marriage to Louis VII of France. Thus the Anglo-Angevin empire of the Plantagenet dynasty was founded, extending from England to the Pyrenees.

Philip II Augustus of France, however, conquered Anjou from John of England at the beginning of the 13th century. An attempt by the English to retake Anjou failed when they were defeated at La Roche-aux-Moines in 1214. Anjou was definitively ceded to France by the Treaty of Paris (1259).

Second dynasty. In 1246 Louis IX of France gave Anjou as an appanage to his brother Charles, the future king of Naples and Sicily. Charles was succeeded by his son Charles II and the latter by his son-in-law Charles of Valois, under whose rule the economic and social conditions of the people of Anjou saw much improvement.

The son of Charles of Valois became king of France, as Philip VI, in 1328. From that year until 1351 Anjou was once more united to the crown and benefitted from royal attention.

Third dynasty. John II of France gave the countship of Anjou to his son Louis in 1351. Thus began the third Angevin dynasty, which was raised to ducal rank in 1360. At this period bands of English soldiers under the command of Sir Robert Knollys were wandering through Anjou, causing great destruction. The later Angevin princes were more interested in the conquest of the kingdom of Naples than in the defense of their duchy, and Louis II, as his father, Louis I, spent most of his life away from Anjou. After his death his widow, Yolande of Aragon, strove to protect Anjou against attacks by the English.

The last of the rulers of Anjou was René I (*q.v.*). After his death (1480) Anjou was for the last time returned to the crown of France and its fate was thenceforth linked with that of the French kingdom.

During the French Revolution, Anjou was one of the centres of the counterrevolutionary Wars of the Vendée (1793–96). Its legal existence ended with the establishment of the departmental system (1790).

The modern region is strongly rural and farms are ordinarily owned by families; the large estates which historically incorporated several farms have largely disappeared. The rich lowlands along the Loire River produce wines, fruits, and flowers for the markets of Paris. They centre on the city of Angers and are fringed by poorer highland and plateau regions of the Massif Armoricain to the north and the Mauges to the south.

Notable wines from vineyards along the Loire are Savennières, La Possonière, Epiré, Saint-Georges-sur-Loire, Roche-aux-Moines, Mûrs, Soulaines, and Saint-Florent-le-Vieil. The *vin d'Anjou* is ordinarily white, with a fruity taste. The white wines of Saumur are dry.

In the countryside Roman Catholicism predominates, but relatively few Catholics outside the regions of Choletais (in the environs of the city of Cholet in the Mauges) and Segréen (in the northwest) attend Mass on a regular basis. The number of priests per inhabitant has remained relatively constant during the 20th century, although candidates for the priesthood are recruited vigorously. Protestant parishes were established in Angers, Saumur, and Cholet after 1850. The langue d'oïl is the dominant language; older peasants continue to speak an archaic French. *Les Rimiaux d'Anjou* (1913–48), a folkloric collection by Marc Leclerc, is representative of efforts by contemporary authors to revive a regional patois.

Anjou, DUKES OF, titled French nobility, comprising royal princes of the blood, grouped below chronologically and indicated by the symbol •.

• Anjou, (Hercule-)François, duc d' (duke of), also called (1566–76) DUC D'ALENÇON (b. March 18, 1554, Saint-Germain-en-Laye, Fr.—d. June 10, 1584, Château-Thierry), fourth and youngest son of Henry II of France and Catherine de Médicis; his three brothers—Francis II, Charles IX, and Henry III—were kings of France. But for his early death at age 30, he too would have been king.

Catherine de Médicis gave him Alençon in 1566, and he bore the title of duc d'Alençon until 1576. Small and swarthy, ambitious and devious, but a leader of the moderate Catholic faction called the *Politiques,* he secured in the general Treaty of Beaulieu (May 6, 1576) a group of territories that made him duke of Anjou. He also courted Elizabeth I of England and even succeeded in negotiating with her a marriage contract (1579), which, however, was never concluded, even after two wooing visits to London (1579, 1581–82). Seeking also to exploit the unsettled conditions in the Netherlands during the Dutch revolt against Spanish rule, he had himself proclaimed duke of Brabant and count of Flanders (1581), but the titles remained fictitious.

Anjou's death in 1584, during the reign of the childless Henry III, made his distant cousin, the Protestant Henry of Bourbon-Navarre (the future Henry IV), heir presumptive to the crown of France.

• Anjou, Gaston-Jean-Baptiste, duc d' (duke of): *see* Orléans, Gaston-Jean-Baptiste, duc d'.

• Anjou, Philippe de France, duc d' (duke of): *see* Orléans, Philippe I de France, duc d'.

• Anjou, Philippe, duc d' (duke of): *see* Philip V *under* Philip (Spain).

Anjou, HOUSE OF: *see* Plantagenet, House of.

Ankara, *il* (province) in Turkey, the second largest of the country, bordered on the north by the Köroğlu Mountains, on the south by the Tuz Gölü (lake), and drained by the Delice, Çubuk, Aladağ, and Ankara rivers. Ankara (*q.v.*) city, the capital of Turkey as well as of the *il,* is situated with other towns on the green belt that encircles the steppe of central Anatolia and is linked by corridors with the eight adjoining *il*s. The present *il,* 12,236 sq mi (31,692 sq km) in area, was once part of the Hittite domain and includes most of ancient Galatia within its boundaries. Ruins of the ancient Phrygian town of Gordium have been excavated 13 mi (21 km) northwest of Polatlı. The region was long famous for its Angora (Ankara) goat, bred for the long silk hair that provides mohair, and the Angora cat. Its agricultural products include wheat, barley, fruits, and sugar beets. Industries of the province include the manufacture of textiles, carpets, medicines, beer, cement, leather goods, iron, and steel. Pop. (1982 est.) 2,951,114.

Ankara, formerly Europeanized as ANGORA, capital of Turkey and of Ankara *il* (province), in the northwestern part of the country. It lies about 125 mi (200 km) south of the Black Sea, near the confluence of the Hatip, İnce Su, and Çubek streams.

While the date of the city's foundation is uncertain, archaeological evidence indicates habitation at least since the Stone Age, and a thriving Phrygian town was located in the area at the end of the 2nd millennium BC. Alexander the Great conquered Ankara in 334 BC, and in the 3rd century BC the town served as the capital of the Tectosages, a tribe of Galatia (the ancient name for the region around Ankara). In 25 BC Ankara was incorporated into the Roman Empire by the emperor Augustus.

As a city of the Byzantine Empire, Ankara was attacked by both the Persians and the Arabs. In about 1073 Ankara fell to the Seljuq Turks, but the crusader Raymond IV of Toulouse drove them out again in 1101. The Byzantines, however, were unable to maintain their control, and Ankara became a bone of contention between the Seljuqs and their rivals among the Turkish frontier lords. After 1143 Seljuq princes fought among themselves for possession of the city. With the establishment of the Seljuq Empire, Ankara declined.

In 1356 the city was captured by Orhan (Orkhan), the second sultan of the Ottoman dynasty, and it became a part of the Ottoman domains in 1360. Ankara was besieged during the Anatolian campaign of Timur (Tamerlane). In 1403 it again became subject to Ottoman rule and, in subsequent centuries, regained its importance as a commercial and urban centre because of its location on the caravan route to the East.

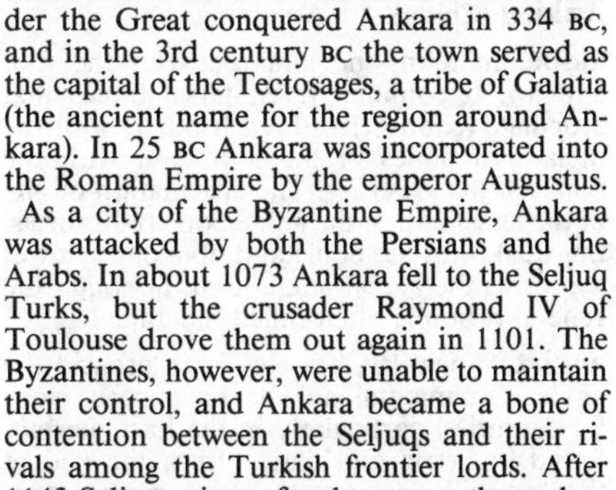

The Atatürk Mausoleum, Ankara, Tur.
Robert Harding Picture Library, London

After World War I, Mustafa Kemal Atatürk, the Turkish nationalist leader, made Ankara the centre of the resistance movement against both the government of the Ottoman sultan and the invading Greek forces; he established his headquarters there in 1919. Ankara was declared the capital of Turkey in 1923.

The architecture of the city reflects its varied history. Remains from the Roman era include a bath, the Column of Julian, and the Temple of Roma and Augustus. Byzantine remnants include the citadel and a cemetery. The square Alâeddin Mosque, with one minaret, is located near the walled citadel and dates from the Seljuq era. Ottoman buildings are numerous and include the Hacı Bayram Cami (1429), the Mahmud Pasa market (1464), and a 15th-century bazaar and caravansary that has been converted to house the Museum of Anatolian Civilizations. The modern city contains the huge Atatürk Mausoleum complex.

Government is the main business in the city, but Ankara is also Turkey's second most important industrial city after Istanbul. Factories for the production of wine and beer, flour, sugar, macaroni products, biscuits, milk, cement, terrazzo (mosaic paving), construction materials, and tractors are well established. Service and tourist industries are expanding rapidly.

Ankara is an important crossroads for trade and forms a major junction in the road network of both Turkey and the *il* of Ankara. The city lies on the main east–west rail line across Anatolia. Esenboğa Airport, to the northeast, provides international services.

The city is the seat of the University of Ankara (established 1946), Hacettepe University (1206), and the Middle East Technical University (1956). The National Library is also located there, as are the state theatre and the Presidential Symphony Orchestra.

Several of Ankara's museums, which present a panorama of Anatolian history, are housed in renovated Ottoman buildings. The most important of these are the Museum of Anatolian Civilizations (with its world-renowned Hittite collection) and the Ethnographic Museum (with its holdings related to Turkish history, folklore, and art). The Atatürk Mausoleum contains the Atatürk Museum, which displays many of Atatürk's personal effects. Pop. (1980) 1,877,755.

Ankara, Battle of, Ankara also spelled ANGORA (July 20, 1402), military confrontation in which forces of the Ottoman sultan Bayezid I were defeated by those of the Central Asian ruler Timur (Tamerlane) and which resulted in the collapse of Bayezid's hastily founded empire.

While challenging the Christian world in the West, Bayezid had annexed the Anatolian Turkmen principalities and posed as heir to the Seljuqs of Anatolia. Meanwhile, Timur claimed suzerainty over these same principalities and gave refuge to the Turkmen princes defeated by Bayezid. The Sultan, on his part, protected Timur's enemies, the Kara Koyunlu (Black Sheep) and Jalāyirid rulers. Exasperated, Timur seized Sivas in central Anatolia (August 1400); Bayezid retaliated by capturing Timur's protégé, the ruler of Erzincan in eastern Anatolia. Finally the two rivals met at Çubukovasi, near Ankara, where Bayezid's Turkmen vassals deserted to Timur and the Ottomans were overwhelmed. The Sultan himself was captured; he died in captivity in 1403.

Ankara, Treaty of, also called FRANKLIN-BOUILLON AGREEMENT (Oct. 20, 1921), pact between the government of France and the Grand National Assembly of Turkey at Ankara, signed by the French diplomat Henri Franklin-Bouillon and Yusuf Kemal Bey, the

Turkish nationalist foreign minister. It formalized the de facto recognition by France of the Grand National Assembly, rather than the government of the Ottoman sultan Mehmed VI, as the sovereign power in Turkey.

The Turkish government in Ankara had refused to ratify the Treaty of Sèvres (Aug. 10, 1920), which had been signed by the Sultan and which had awarded parts of western Turkey to Greece; reaction to the treaty brought about a Turkish nationalist revival. After defeats by Turkish nationalists in southeastern Anatolia (Cilicia) in 1920–21, the French decided to withdraw southward and strengthen their forces in Syria and Lebanon. Under the terms of the Treaty of Ankara, the French agreed to evacuate Cilicia. A "special administrative regime" was established in Hatay (Alexandretta), and the Turkish-Syrian boundary was fixed.

The agreement assisted the Turkish nationalist cause by revealing differences between France and Great Britain, which continued to recognize the Sultan's government in Istanbul, and by releasing Turkish nationalist forces from the southeastern front for fighting on the western front against the Greeks.

ankaramite, extrusive igneous rock that occurs near the bottoms of thick flows and sills, where large crystals (phenocrysts) of augite and olivine settle and accumulate. Ankaramite consists of about 50 percent augite both as phenocrysts and smaller grains, with olivine phenocrysts, plagioclase laths, and biotite, magnetite, apatite, and carbonates. The rock was named for its occurrence near Ankaratra, in Madagascar.

Ankaratra, volcanic mountainous region in Antananarivo province, central Madagascar, covering an area of about 2,000 sq mi (5,200 sq km) and rising to 8,671 ft (2,643 m) in Mt. Tsiafajavona, the nation's second highest peak. The main range runs south-southwest from Antananarivo. Antsirabe (*q.v.*), on the slopes of Mt. Tsiafajavona, is the major town.

ankerite, a carbonate mineral containing calcium and iron. Pure ankerite is not known; in the natural species considerable magnesium or manganese has replaced the iron. It is one end-member in a chemical substitution series with dolomite (*q.v.*), in which magnesium has completely replaced iron in the crystal structure. Its physical and chemical properties are the same as those of dolomite (*see* carbonate mineral [table]); its chemical formula is $Ca(Fe,Mg)(CO_3)_2$.

ankh, ancient Egyptian hieroglyph signifying "life," a cross surmounted by a loop and known as a *crux ansata* (ansate, or handle-shaped, cross). It is found in ancient tomb inscriptions, including those of Tutankhamen, and gods and pharaohs are often depicted holding it. The *ankh* forms part of words for such concepts as health and happiness. The form of the symbol suggests a sandal strap as its original meaning, though it has been seen as representing a magical knot. As a cross, it has been extensively used in the symbolism of the Coptic Christian Church.

Ankhesenamen, original name ANKHESENPAATEN, queen of Egypt (reigned 1362–*c.* 1351 BC), who attempted a diplomatic coup after her husband Tutankhamen's death.

The third daughter of Akhenaton and Nefertiti, the rulers of the Amarna revolution, Ankhesenamen probably was married to her father around the 16th year of his reign, after her elder sister became queen of Akhenaton's coregent. Although the marriage was primarily political, to secure Akhenaton's throne, a daughter was evidently born to Ankhesenamen.

At Tutankhamen's accession, Ankhesenamen was married to him to secure his kingship. As his queen, she appears prominently in his tomb—on a shrine, a throne, and on other objects. Based upon the presence of two fetuses of seven and five months in the tomb, she bore him two daughters who were stillborn. When the King's name was altered to include Amon's name, so was hers. She also originally appeared on a stela restoring the old order.

At Tutankhamen's unexpected death Ankhesenamen became the royal heiress because no son had been born to the couple. Whomever she married would become pharaoh. According to Hittite archives, unwilling to associate herself with either of the likeliest Egyptian candidates, she sent a secret letter to the Hittite king, asking him for a son whom she would make pharaoh. Because the Hittites had just completed a season's campaign against Egyptian forces in Syria, their ruler was astounded. Suspecting treachery, he sent an ambassador to learn the Queen's true intent. In the spring of 1351 BC, his envoy and an Egyptian emissary arrived in the Hittite capital with Ankhesenamen's assurances and another more urgent plea. The Hittite ruler dispatched a son to Egypt, but the prince was intercepted and murdered, perhaps by Horemheb, Egypt's commander of armies and an aspirant to the throne.

According to an inscribed ring seen in Cairo in 1932, Ankhesenamen was perhaps married to Ay, her husband's former vizier and close adviser, who succeeded Tutankhamen. On Tutankhamen's stela of restoration Ankhesenamen's figure was thoroughly erased by King Horemheb, who usurped the monument.

Anking (China): *see* An-ch'ing.

ankle, in man, the joint between the foot and leg. It contains seven tarsal bones that articulate (connect) with each other, with the metatarsal bones of the foot, and with the bones of the lower leg. The articulation of one of the tarsal bones, the ankle bone (talus or astragalus), with the fibula and tibia of the lower leg forms the actual ankle joint, although the general region is often called the ankle.

anklet, in jewelry, bracelet worn around the ankle. Ornamental anklets have been worn for centuries, particularly in the East. Jewelry found in Persia and dating from the end of the 2nd millennium to the 7th century BC includes anklets, some decorated with animals such as an ibex with curving horns.

Anklets are still common in India, where they are sometimes adorned with jewels and bells and often hollowed and filled with shot, so as to jangle rhythmically when worn by dancers. Anklets worn in the West are usually thin gold chains, sometimes with small, engraved plaques.

Ankobra, river in southern Ghana, West Africa, almost totally confined to the Western Region. Rising northeast of Wiawso, it flows about 120 mi (190 km) south to the Gulf of Guinea (Atlantic) just west of Axim, commercial centre of the river basin. Its chief tributaries are the Mansi and the Bonsa, and much of its basin is shared with the Tano River to the west. There are rapids in the upper reaches, but the Ankobra is navigable for 50 mi (80 km) from its mouth and is tidal as far as Tomento, with a 2-ft (0.6-m) low- to high-tide difference. The relatively underdeveloped Ankobra Basin is important for its gold, manganese, and diamond deposits and timber resources. Until construction of the railroad (1911), the Ankobra was the chief means of access to the Prestea gold mines.

Ankole, also spelled ANKORE (people): *see* Nkole.

ankyloglossia (congenital malformation): *see* tongue-tie.

Ankylosaurus, also called EUOPLOCEPHALUS, armoured herbivorous dinosaur of the Late Cretaceous of North America (the Cretaceous Period began 136,000,000 years ago and lasted 71,000,000 years). *Ankylosaurus,* moderately large, was about 5 metres (15 feet) long. The

Ankylosaurus
By courtesy of the American Museum of Natural History, New York

hind limbs were larger than the forelimbs, indicating that *Ankylosaurus,* though it had evolved from bipedal ancestors, had reverted to a quadrupedal pose. The back of the low, flat body was covered by bony plates that were pointed at the flanks of the animal; at the end of the rather long tail was a thick knob of bone that could have been used as a club. Close relatives of *Ankylosaurus* varied the armour theme somewhat, but all were formidable. In place of a bony club at the end of the tail, some forms had long, pointed bony spikes; in others, spikes of bone were present in the shoulder region.

ankylosing spondylitis, also called MARIE-STRÜMPELL ARTHRITIS, a progressive disease of the spine and larger joints mainly affecting adolescent and young adult males. Ankylosing spondylitis is self-limiting but may be in an active phase for several years and if untreated may result in complete fusion (ankylosis) of the spinal column. Morning backache is an early symptom; later, swollen joints, progressive deformity, and anemia develop. Irradiation and corticosteroids are used to control symptoms; orthopedic care may lessen deformity. Histologically similar to rheumatoid arthritis, ankylosing spondylitis shows distinctive traits, and it is usually considered a separate entity.

Anlaf GUTHFRITHSON (Danish king in England): *see* Olaf Guthfrithson.

Anlaf SIHTRICSON (Danish king in England): *see* Olaf Sihtricson.

Ann, Cape (Massachusetts, U.S.): *see* Cape Ann.

Ann, Mother (Shaker leader): *see* Lee, Ann.

Ann Arbor, city, seat (1827) of Washtenaw County, southeastern Michigan, U.S., on the Huron River. John Allen and Elisha W. Rumsey founded the community in 1824, which they named for their wives (both called Ann) and the local natural groves, or arbors. The settlement developed as an agricultural trading centre after the arrival in 1839 of the Michigan Central Railroad, which connected it with Detroit (38 mi [61 km] east). The University of Michigan (moved there in 1837 from Detroit, where it was founded in 1817) has played a major role in Ann Arbor's growth.

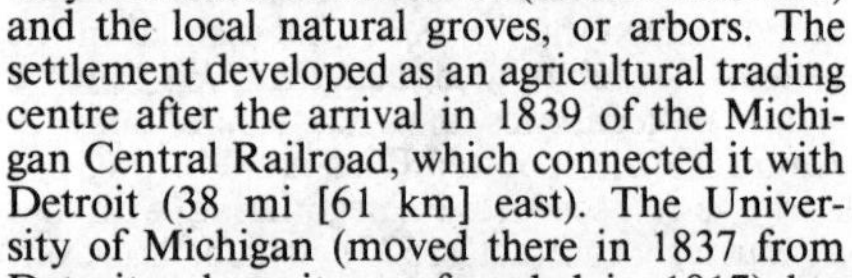

Law quadrangle, University of Michigan, Ann Arbor, Mich.
Milt and Joan Mann from CameraMann

Events of student interest dominate the life of the city, while a complex of hospitals and the university's medical school have made Ann Arbor a leading medical centre. Private industrial research and development joined by the university's Institute of Science and Technology have raised Ann Arbor to rank as a major Midwest centre for aeronautical, space, nuclear, chemical, and metallurgical research. Diversified manufactures include ball bearings, scientific instruments, and precision machinery. Washtenaw Community College (1966) and Concordia (Lutheran) College (1963) are in the city. Inc. village, 1833; city, 1851. Pop. (1980) 107,316.

Anna (mother of Samuel): *see* Hannah.

Anna (personal name): *see under* Anne, except as below.

Anna, in full ANNA IVANOVNA (b. Feb. 7 [Jan. 28, old style], 1693, Moscow—d. Oct. 28 [Oct. 17, O.S.], 1740, St. Petersburg), empress of Russia from 1730 to 1740.

Anna Ivanovna, enamelled miniature by an unknown artist, 18th century; in the collection of Mrs. Merriweather Post, Hillwood, Washington, D.C.
By courtesy of Hillwood, Washington, D.C.

Daughter of Ivan V (ruled 1682–96) and niece of Peter I the Great (ruled 1682–1725), Anna was married to Frederick William, ruler of the Baltic seacoast duchy of Courland, on Nov. 11 (Oct. 31, O.S.), 1710. Although her husband died on the journey to Courland after their wedding in St. Petersburg, Anna remained at Mitau (Jelgava), the capital of Courland, until 1730, when Peter II died and the Supreme Privy Council, the actual ruling body in Russia (1726–30), offered her the Russian throne.

Having accepted the council's proposal as well as its stipulation that she agree to certain "conditions" placing the real power of the state in the council's hands and effectively creating a limited monarchy in Russia, Anna proceeded to Moscow (February 1730, O.S.). But when she arrived and found widespread opposition to the council's conditions among the gentry and officers of the guard, she tore up the conditions (Feb. 25, 1730, O.S.), abolished the Supreme Privy Council, and reestablished the autocracy.

Anna, however, had little interest in government affairs and relied heavily on her lover, Ernst Johann Biron, and a small group of German advisers, including the head of Russia's foreign affairs, Andrey Osterman, and the chief of the army, Burkhard Münnich, to manage the state. While the Empress concerned herself primarily with extravagant entertainments and crude amusements in the court at St. Petersburg, her favourites engaged Russia in the War of the Polish Succession (1733–35), which placed a pro-Russian king on the Polish throne, and in the Russo-Turkish War of 1736–39. In addition, Anna's ruling clique, which employed excessively brutal and repressive practices against its opponents, alienated the gentry, which resented domination by German officials.

Shortly before her death Anna named as her successor Ivan, the son of her niece Anna Leopoldovna, and Biron as the infant's regent (August 1740).

Anna, in full ANNA LEOPOLDOVNA (b. Dec. 18 [Dec. 7, old style], 1718, Rostock, Mecklenburg—d. March 18 [March 7, O.S.], 1746, Kholmogory, Russia), regent of Russia (November 1740–November 1741) for her son, the emperor Ivan VI.

Anna Leopoldovna, detail of an engraving by J. Wagner after a portrait by N.A. Venetus, 18th century
Novosti Press Agency

A niece of Empress Anna (ruled 1730–40), Anna Leopoldovna married a nephew of the Holy Roman emperor Charles VI in 1739 and gave birth to a son, Ivan (Aug. 13 [Aug. 2, O.S.], 1740), who was named heir to the Russian throne by Empress Anna in 1740, on the day before she died.

A few weeks later, however, the Empress' appointed regent, Ernst Johann Biron, was arrested by certain members of the ruling German clique in Russia, led by Burkhard Münnich and Andrey Osterman. Münnich and Osterman appointed Anna Leopoldovna regent and assumed dominant positions in her government. But they were unpopular among the Russians, and when they weakened the administration by quarrelling with each other, Anna's major rival, Elizabeth, the daughter of Peter I the Great (ruled 1682–1725), staged a palace revolution (Dec. 6 [Nov. 25, O.S.], 1741). Elizabeth imprisoned Anna and her family in 1742 and in 1744 exiled them to Kholmogory, where Anna died.

Anna COMNENA (b. Dec. 1, 1083—d. after 1148), Byzantine historian and daughter of the emperor Alexius I Comnenus, is remembered for her *Alexiad,* a history of the life and reign of her father, which became a valuable source as a pro-Byzantine account of the early Crusades.

Anna received a good education, studying among other subjects literature, philosophy, history, and geography. She married the leader of Bryennium, Nicephorus Bryennius (1097), and joined her mother, the empress Irene, in a vain effort to persuade her father, during his last illness, to disinherit his son, John II Comnenus, in favour of Nicephorus. Later conspiring to depose her brother after his accession to the throne (1118), Anna was, however, unable to obtain the support of her husband; the plot was discovered, and she forfeited her property, retiring to a convent, where she wrote the *Alexiad.* This work, in Greek, provides a picture of religious and intellectual activities within the empire, reflecting the Byzantine conception of the imperial office. It suffers from a defective chronology and excessive adulation of Alexius I.

Annaba, *wilāyah* (province, or *département*), northeastern Algeria, established in 1974. The name Annaba is derived from a local word for jujube trees. The *wilāyah* is fronted by the Mediterranean Sea (north), and bordered by Tunisia (east), and the *wilāyāt* (provinces) of Guelma (south) and Skikda (west). The Oued (river) Seybouse passes through the middle of the province, creating a valley among the highlands. To the west, the slopes of the coastal Djebel (ridge) Edough are covered with cork and oak trees. Annaba *wilāyah* has an area of 1,347 sq mi (3,489 sq km). The huge bay to the north has served as a port since Phoenician times. It was in Annaba that Saint Augustine of Hippo wrote his famous work "City of God." In the western and eastern interior, marshy plains, lakes, and lagoons provide rich pasture; the area has the largest herds of cattle in Algeria. Crops grown intensively include grapes, olives, and citrus fruits. The main towns include Annaba city, the provincial capital, el-Hadjar (site of Algeria's giant iron and steel works that opened in 1968), Besbes, and Drean (or Deraân; birthplace of Albert Camus, the 20th-century moralist and novelist). Pop. (1980 est.) 596,675.

Annaba, formerly BÔNE, or BONA, town, Mediterranean port, and capital of Annaba *wilāyah* (province, or *département*), Algeria, near the mouth of the Oued (stream) Seybouse, close to the Tunisian border. Its location on a natural harbour (Golfe d'Annaba) between Caps (capes) Garde and Rosa attracted the Phoenicians probably in the 12th century BC. It passed to the Romans as Hippo Regius, residence of the Numidian kings, and achieved independence after the Punic Wars.

Hippo Regius later became a centre of Christian thought, housing the Council of Hippo (AD 393) and comprising the bishopric of St. Augustine (396–430). Destroyed by the Vandals in 431, Hippo Regius passed to the Byzantine emperor Justinian in 533, and about two centuries later (697) it was overcome by Arabs. An early centre of piracy, it remained one of the small cities of North Africa under a succession of rulers until the French captured it in 1832. In 1848 it was created a *commune* administered from Paris.

Annaba rises from the shore up the cork-tree-covered slopes of the Edough foothills. The old town with its narrow streets dominates the centre of the city and is grouped around La Place du 19-Août and its early French houses and the mosque of Salah Bey (1787). The 11th-century mosque of Sīdī Bou Merouan was built with columns taken from Roman ruins. The new town, built since 1870 along both sides of the Cours de la Révolution, contains the cathedral (1850) and basilica (1881) of Saint-Augustine, the chief public buildings, schools, the Hippo Museum, and public gardens. Annaba also has an international airport.

Annaba is Algeria's chief exporter of minerals, mainly iron ore and phosphates from the Tébessa deposits to the southeast. Surrounded by fertile farms (where wheat is grown), forests, and mines, it also serves as a trading and fishing port and port of call. Major industries include an iron and steel complex, a fertilizer plant, automobile and railway shops, and aluminum works. Pop. (1977 prelim.) mun., 255,938.

Annaberg-Buchholz, town, Karl-Marx-Stadt *Bezirk* (district), southern East Germany, high in the Erzgebirge (Ore Mountains), near the Czechoslovak border, south of Karl-Marx-Stadt (Chemnitz). It was formed in 1949 by the union of Annaberg (chartered 1497) and Buchholz (chartered 1501), both of which were founded as silver-mining settlements. With the decline of mining and smelting in the 16th century, the pillow lace industry was introduced in 1561 and became, with related manufactures, the principal industry. The town has grown considerably since a Soviet organization began mining uranium after World War II. Historic buildings, which survived fires in the 17th and 18th centuries, include the Gothic Church of St. Anne (1499–1525) and the Baroque Bergkirche (1665).

In addition to mining and textiles, the town has factories producing cardboard, paper, and electrical equipment. Pop. (1981 est.) 26,618.

annabergite, hydrated nickel arsenate mineral very similar to erythrite (*q.v.*).

Annam (Chinese: Pacified South), French-governed Vietnam or, more strictly, its central region, known in precolonial times as Trung Ky (Central Administrative Division). The term Annam was never officially used by the Vietnamese to describe their country, even during the French colonial period.

The central section of Vietnam known to the French as Annam is largely a highland region extending between the Song (river) Ma and Mui (cape) Ba Kiem (47 miles [76 kilometres] east-southeast of Ho Chi Minh City [formerly Saigon]). The former imperial capital Hue (*q.v.*) has remained the chief cultural centre in the region.

Much of central Vietnam was under the control of the Cham empire until the expanding Vietnamese state defeated the Cham rulers in 1471, opening the way for slow but steady Vietnamese movement toward the Mekong Delta. With the de facto division of Vietnam under the seigneurial Nguyen and Trinh families in the 16th century, Hue became the seat of the Nguyen. When Nguyen Anh, as the emperor Gia Long, united the whole of Vietnam in 1802, Hue became the imperial capital.

Central Vietnam came under French "protection" in 1883–85, leaving the court at Hue with only nominal power. In the confused, immediate post-World War II period, Vietnam was temporarily divided at the 16th parallel of latitude, leaving parts of central Vietnam under different occupying authorities. Following the end of the First Indochina War in 1954, the temporary dividing line determined at the Geneva Conference again ran through central Vietnam, this time at the 17th parallel.

The predominant hills and plateaus of central Vietnam are occupied by a variety of hill peoples, some speaking variants of the Cham language, others using Mon-Khmer languages. The narrow, fertile coastal plain of central Vietnam is occupied by the majority Vietnamese and is devoted largely to rice culture. The largest city in central Vietnam is Da Nang (*q.v.*) and its best anchorage is Vinh (bay) Cam Ranh. There is as little as 30 inches (760 millimetres) of rainfall annually because the northeast winter monsoon tends to blow parallel to the coast.

Annamitique, Chaîne, Vietnamese TRUONG-SON, English ANNAMITE, or ANNAMESE, CORDILLERA, principal mountain range of Indochina and the watershed between the Mekong River and the South China Sea. It extends parallel to the coast in a gentle curve generally northwest–southeast, forming the boundary between Laos and Vietnam. A fairly continuous range for about 700 mi (1,100 km), its rather precipitous eastern slopes leave a narrow coastal plain. Although its highest peak, Ngoc Linh, is only 8,524 ft (2,598 m) high, the range has few substantial passes, the most important being the Deo (pass) Keo Nua in northern Vietnam, part of a route between Thakhek, Laos, and Vinh, Vietnam, and the Deo Mu Gia (*see* Mugia, Deo).

The geologically complex range is constituted mainly of limestones, sandstones, granites, and gneisses in the north and in the south an exposed, folded crystalline basement overlain in several places by basaltic lava flows. Among the plateaus created by these flows are the Plateau des Bolovens (*see* Bolovens, Plateau des) in southern Laos and the Kontum and Dac Lac plateaus in southern Vietnam. To their south, the Chaîne Annamitique begins to reverse itself, reaching 7,500 ft or higher in peaks west of Nha Trang before terminating in the Saigon plain of southern Vietnam.

Annandale and Eskdale, district, Dumfries and Galloway region, southwestern Scotland; created by the reorganization of 1975, it is the eastern part of the former county of Dumfries. The district, area 600 sq mi (1,554 sq km), is crossed by the River Annan, rising in the Southern Uplands above Moffat to flow south to the Solway Firth. Sheep are raised in the hills, which rise to 2,600 ft (800 m), and in the valleys; on the plain by the firth grain crops and root vegetables are grown and lambs raised. Annan (*q.v.*) is the seat of the district authority. Pop. (1982 est.) 35,701.

Annapolis, capital of Maryland, U.S., and seat of Anne Arundel County, home of the U.S. Naval Academy, on the Severn River near its mouth on Chesapeake Bay, 27 mi (43 km) southeast of Baltimore. Settled in 1649 as Providence by Virginian Puritans, it was later known as Town of Proctor's, Town at the Severn, and Anne Arundel Town. In 1694, the same year the provincial capital was removed from St. Mary's City, it was renamed to honour Princess Anne who, as queen, gave it a charter (1708). Annapolis patriots, like those of Boston, had a "tea party," Oct. 19, 1774, forcing the owner of the ship "Peggy Stewart" to burn his cargo of taxed tea. George Washington resigned as commander in chief of the Continental Army (Dec. 23, 1783) while the U.S. Congress was in session there (Nov. 26, 1783, to June 3, 1784). The city escaped the battle scars of the Revolution, the War of 1812, and the Civil War, though many Civil War wounded were hospitalized there. The Annapolis Convention (1786) considered measures for the regulation of commerce.

A port of entry, Annapolis is a trade and shipping centre for agricultural and seafood products and has boatyards and small diversified manufactures. The old waterfront area with its city slip is home port for the declining Chesapeake oyster fleet. Nearby is an oceanographic laboratory maintained by Johns Hopkins University. City life, however, focusses largely on state government and the naval academy. Graduation of the midshipmen in June is preceded by parades, concerts, and other events.

The U.S. Naval Academy (1845), occupying the site of old Ft. Severn, has a 309-ac campus built on the river, and John Paul Jones (*q.v.*) is buried in its chapel crypt. The Naval Academy Museum displays relics of American naval history and has a large collection of ship models. St. John's College was chartered (1784) as a continuation of King William's School (1696). The city's colonial heritage is preserved in its Registered National Historic Landmark District, which contains the State House (1772–80), oldest state capitol still in legislative use, where the Congress ratified the Treaty of Paris ending the Revolution; the Old Treasury (1735); St. Anne's Episcopal Church (founded 1692); and more than 60 pre-Revolutionary houses, including the homes of three signers of the Declaration of Independence—William Paca, Samuel Chase, and Charles Carroll. Inc. 1796. Pop. (1980) 31,740.

Annapolis Academy: *see* United States Naval Academy.

Annapolis Convention, in U.S. history, regional meeting at Annapolis, Md., in September 1786; it was an important rallying point in the movement toward a federal convention to revise the inadequate Articles of Confederation. Growing out of an earlier meeting of representatives of Maryland and Virginia to discuss ways of improving navigation on the Potomac River, the convention of delegates from five states found that it could not deal effectively with national commercial problems without changes in the Articles. Realizing that they could not recommend the needed revisions, the delegates stretched their authority by issuing a new call to all the states for a meeting eight months later in Philadelphia, where the present federal Constitution was drafted.

Annapolis Royal, formerly (until 1713) PORT ROYAL, town, seat of Annapolis county, southwestern Nova Scotia, Canada, at the mouth of the Annapolis River where it enters Annapolis Basin (an arm of the Bay of Fundy), 126 mi (203 km) west of Halifax. Founded in 1605 as Port Royal by the explorers Samuel de Champlain and Pierre du Gua, the sieur de Monts, it was the first French colony in North America and is Canada's oldest settlement. Destroyed by the British in 1613, it was later reconstructed and resettled by Scottish colonists, only to be turned over to the French in 1632 by the Treaty of Sainte-Germain-en-Laye. It was abandoned soon after, when the fort was moved to its present site about 6 mi (10 km) to the east.

The new settlement, repeatedly under British attack, was finally captured in 1710, formally ceded to the British by the Treaty of Utrecht (1713), and renamed Annapolis Royal in honour of Queen Anne. From then until the founding of Halifax in 1749 it served as the capital of Nova Scotia. Once an important lumbering, shipbuilding, and administrative centre, it is now a quiet market town and tourist resort with apple growing, dairying, and sawmilling interests. The old Ft. Anne (built 1687–1705), on the site of an older French fort built in 1636, is preserved within a national historic park, as is a reconstruction of the Port Royal Habitation (settlement) of 1605. Pop. (1981) 631.

To make the best use of the Britannica, consult the INDEX *first*

Annapūrna, mountain massif of the Himalayas in north central Nepal, forms a ridge 30 mi (48 km) long between the basins of the Kāli Gandak and Marsyandi rivers. It contains four main summits, two of which, Annapūrna I (26,545 ft [8,091 m]) and II (26,040 ft [7,937 m]), stand at the western and eastern ends of the range, respectively; III (24,786 ft [7,555 m]) and IV (24,688 ft [7,525 m]) lie between them. Annapūrna I is one of the world's highest peaks. Although climbers had

Annapūrna seen from Gorapani, Nepal, in the Kāli Valley

Syndication International, London

reached 28,150 ft (8,580 m) on Mt. Everest in 1924, Annapūrna I became famous in 1950 as the first peak more than 26,000 ft (8,000 m) to be ascended to the summit. The feat was achieved by a French expedition led by Maurice Herzog, who with Louis Lachenal reached the top on June 3. Annapūrna IV was climbed on May 30, 1955, by H. Biller, H. Steinmetz, and J. Wellenkamp, and Annapūrna II on May 17, 1960, by R.H. Grant and C.J. Bonington in an expedition led by James O.M. Roberts. In 1970 an all-woman Japanese climbing team scaled Annapūrna III.

annates, a tax on the first year's income (first fruits) from an ecclesiastical benefice given by a new incumbent either to the bishop or to the pope. The first mention of the practice appears in the time of Pope Honorius III (died 1227). The earliest records show that the annates were sometimes a privilege conceded to the bishop for a term of years and sometimes a right based on immemorial precedent. Eventually popes claimed the privilege for themselves, at first only on a temporary basis to meet particular financial needs. Thus, in 1305 Clement V claimed the first fruits of all vacant benefices in England, and in 1319 John XXII claimed those of all of Christendom vacated within the next two years. The system was never applied uniformly or effectively throughout the church's territories and was the cause of much protest. Under the Annates Statute of 1534, Henry VIII claimed the English annates for the crown. Papal annates fell into disuse with the transformation of the system of benefices after the Council of Trent (1545–63).

From the time of Pope Benedict XIV (1740–58) the term has referred to the half portion (Latin *media annata*) of the first year's income from parochial benefices, which in Italy and the adjacent islands was to be contributed toward the restoration of the cathedral and collegiate churches of the respective dioceses.

annatto (*Bixa orellana*), tree native to the New World tropics and the only species of the family Bixaceae. Annatto grows up to 9 metres (30 feet) tall and has rose-pink flowers about 5 centimetres (2 inches) wide and oval-

Annatto or lipstick tree (*Bixa orellana*)
Walter Dawn

ish leaves about 8 to 18 cm long. The brown seed pods, about 5 cm long, yield a reddish or yellowish powder used in a dye for butter, cheese, and oleomargarine. The plant is cultivated in tropical and subtropical areas of the world.

Anne (personal name): *see under* Anna, except as below.

Anne (b. Feb. 6, 1665, London—d. Aug. 1, 1714, London), queen of Great Britain from 1702 to 1714. The last Stuart monarch, she wished to rule independently, but her intellectual limitations and chronic ill health caused her to rely heavily on her ministers, who directed England's efforts against France and Spain in the War of the Spanish Succession (1701–14). The bitter rivalries between Whigs and Tories that characterized her reign were intensified by uncertainty over the succession to her throne.

Anne was the second daughter of James, duke of York (King James II, 1685–88), and Anne Hyde. Although her father was a Roman Catholic, she was reared a Protestant at the insistence of her uncle, King Charles II. In 1683 the Princess was married to the handsome, if uninspiring, Prince George of Denmark (1653–1708), who became her devoted companion. Of greater political consequence was Anne's intimate relationship with her childhood friend Sarah Jennings Churchill, wife of John Churchill (later 1st duke of Marlborough). The beautiful, intelligent Sarah became Anne's lady of the bedchamber and soon had the Princess in her power.

It was Sarah who persuaded Anne to side with the Protestant ruler William III of Orange, stadholder of the Netherlands, when William overthrew James II in 1688. By the Bill of Rights (1689), William and his wife Mary, Anne's elder sister, were made king and queen of England, and Anne was placed in line for the succession to the throne. Anne and Mary had a bitter falling-out, and after Mary's death in 1694 William cultivated Anne's goodwill, but he refused to appoint her regent during his absences from England.

Although Anne was pregnant 18 times between 1683 and 1700, only five children were born alive, and of these, only one, a son, survived infancy. His death in 1700 ended Anne's hopes of providing herself with a successor. Hence, she acquiesced to the Act of Settlement of 1701, which designated as her successors the Hanoverian descendants of King James I of England.

Anne became queen upon William's death in March 1702. From the first she was motivated largely by an intense devotion to the Anglican Church. She detested Catholics and Dissenters and sympathized with High Church Tories. At the same time, she sought to be free from the domination of the political parties. Her first ministry, though predominantly Tory, was headed by two neutrals, Sidney Godolphin and the Duke of Marlborough. The influence of Sarah Churchill (now duchess of Marlborough) over Anne was slight after 1703, though the Duke remained commander of the British forces.

Anne soon discovered that she disagreed with the Tories on strategy for the war; the Queen, Marlborough, and the Whigs wanted to commit English troops to continental campaigns, while the Tories believed England should engage the enemy only at sea. Consequently, as Marlborough accumulated impressive victories on the Continent, pressure was exerted on Anne to admit Whigs to the ministry. She resisted obstinately and even grew cold toward the Duchess, who adopted the cause of the Whig politicians. By 1707 the Duchess had been supplanted in the Queen's affections by Abigail Masham, the tool of the leading Tory, Robert Harley (later 1st earl of Oxford). Nevertheless, the schemes of Harley and Masham caused Anne so much embarrassment that in 1708 she was forced to dismiss Harley and admit the most prominent Whigs into her administration. As the war dragged on, the nation turned against the Whigs. In 1710 Anne was able to expel them and appoint a Tory ministry. She dismissed both Marlboroughs from her service in 1711.

The Queen's advancing age and her infirmities made the succession a crucial issue. Leading Tories were in constant communication with Anne's exiled Catholic brother, James, the Old Pretender, who had been excluded by law from the succession. Nevertheless, the suddenness of Anne's final illness and death frustrated any plans the Tories might have had for capturing the throne for the Pretender. Her last act was to secure the Protestant succession by placing the lord treasurer's staff in the hands of a capable moderate, Charles Talbot, duke of Shrewsbury, who presided over the peaceful accession of the Hanoverian prince George Louis (King George I, 1714–27). A biography, *Queen Anne*, by David Green, was published in 1970.

Anne BOLEYN, Boleyn also spelled BULLEN (b. 1507?—d. May 19, 1536, London), second wife of King Henry VIII of England

Anne Boleyn, drawing by Hans Holbein, *c.* 1534–35; in the collection of the Earl of Bradford
By courtesy of the Earl of Bradford; photograph, Courtauld Institute of Art

and mother of Queen Elizabeth I. The events surrounding the annulment of Henry's marriage to his first wife, Catherine of Aragon, and his marriage to Anne led him to break with the Roman Catholic Church and brought about the English Reformation.

Anne's father was Sir Thomas Boleyn, later earl of Wiltshire and Ormonde. After spending part of her childhood in France, she returned to England in 1522 and lived at Henry's court and drew many admirers. A desired marriage with Lord Henry Percy was prevented on Henry's order by Cardinal Wolsey, and at some undetermined point the King himself fell in love with her.

In 1527 Henry initiated secret proceedings to obtain an annulment from his wife, the aging Catherine of Aragon; his ultimate aim was to father a legitimate male heir to the throne. For six years Pope Clement VII, under pressure from Henry's rival Charles V, refused to grant the annulment, but all the while Henry's passion for Anne was strengthening his determination to rid himself of his queen. About Jan. 25, 1533, Henry and Anne were secretly married. The union was made public on Easter of that year, and on May 23 Henry had the archbishop of Canterbury, Thomas Cranmer, pronounce the marriage to Catherine null and void. In September Anne gave birth to a daughter, the future queen Elizabeth I.

Anne's arrogant behaviour soon made her unpopular at court. Although Henry lost interest in her and began liaisons with other women, the birth of a son might have saved the marriage. Anne had a miscarriage in 1534, and in January 1536 she gave birth to a stillborn male child. On May 2, 1536, Henry had her committed to the Tower of London on a charge of adultery with various men and even incest with her own brother. She was tried by a court of peers, unanimously convicted, and beheaded on May 19. On May 30 Henry married Jane Seymour. That Anne was guilty as charged is unlikely; she was the apparent victim of a temporary court faction supported by

Thomas Cromwell. A full biography is *Anne Boleyn* by Marie Louise Bruce (1972).

Anne DE PISSELEU: *see* Étampes, Anne de Pisseleu, duchesse d' (duchess of).

Anne OF AUSTRIA, French ANNE D'AUTRICHE (b. Sept. 22, 1601, Valladolid, Spain—d. Jan. 20, 1666, Paris), queen consort of King Louis XIII of France (reigned 1610–43) and regent during the opening years of the reign of her son King Louis XIV (from 1643).

The eldest daughter of King Philip III of Spain and Margaret of Austria, Anne was married to the 14-year-old Louis XIII in November 1615. Throughout his life Louis treated her with a cool reserve. In 1625 the English George Villiers, 1st duke of Buckingham, created a scandal at the French court by revealing his passion for the Queen. Her plight worsened as the powerful Cardinal de Richelieu, Louis XIII's chief minister from 1624 to 1642, sought to prevent her from exercising any influence over her husband. Anne took as her confidante the scheming Marie de Rohan-Montbazon, duchesse de Chevreuse. Anne and the queen mother, Marie de Médicis, failed in their attempt to persuade Louis to dismiss the Cardinal (the Day of Dupes, 1630).

After Richelieu declared war on Anne's brother, King Philip IV of Spain, in 1635, she remained sympathetic to the Spanish cause. Richelieu's spies kept her under surveillance, and in 1637 the Cardinal humiliated her by proving that she had been visiting the nunnery of Val-de-Grâce in order to conduct treasonable correspondence with Philip. Her status at court was enhanced, however, by the birth of her two sons, the dauphin Louis (the future Louis XIV) in 1638, and Philippe (later duc d'Orléans) in 1640. Through the provisions of his will, Louis XIII attempted to deprive her of her right to be sole regent for Louis XIV. Louis XIII died in May 1643, and shortly thereafter Anne had the will annulled by the Parlement of Paris.

As soon as she was declared sole regent, the leading nobles demanded the restoration of the privileges they had lost under Richelieu. Determined that her son should succeed to the absolute power that Richelieu had won for Louis XIII, she resisted these demands and took as her first minister the Italian-born Cardinal Jules Mazarin, one of Richelieu's most able associates. Anne and Mazarin were devoted to one another, and some historians have concluded that they were secretly married. Together they faced the series of revolts known as the Fronde (1648–53). The rebels forced Anne to dismiss Mazarin in February 1651, but, by faithfully following the Cardinal's instructions, she was able to divide her enemies. The rebellion virtually collapsed in October 1652, and Mazarin returned to Paris.

Anne's regency officially ended in 1651, when Louis XIV was proclaimed of age to rule. In 1659 France finally made peace with Spain, and the following year Louis XIV was married to Anne's niece, Marie-Thérèse, the daughter of Philip IV.

Anne of Austria, detail of a portrait by Peter Paul Rubens, in the Rijksmuseum, Amsterdam

By courtesy of the Rijksmuseum, Amsterdam

Anne OF BEAUJEU: *see* Anne of France.

Anne OF BRITTANY, French ANNE DE BRETAGNE (b. Jan. 25, 1477, Nantes, Fr.—d. Jan. 9, 1514, Blois), duchess of Brittany and twice queen consort of France, who devoted her life to safeguarding the autonomy of Brittany within the kingdom of France.

Daughter of Duke Francis II of Brittany and Margaret of Foix, Anne succeeded to her father's duchy on Sept. 9, 1488. The future of the duchy depended on her marriage. In desperation Anne allied herself with Maximilian of Austria, who married her by proxy on Dec. 19, 1490. King Charles VIII of France, fearful that Brittany might pass into the hands of a foreign power, attacked it, and Anne was forced in the end to break with Maximilian and marry Charles (Dec. 6, 1491); the process of the union of Brittany with the French crown was thus begun.

Anne of Brittany, portrait attributed to Jean (Jehan) Bourdichon; in a private collection

Giraudon—Art Resource/EB Inc.

Charles died in 1498 without issue, and Anne, in accordance with an agreement made at the time of their marriage, was married to his successor, Louis XII, on Jan. 8, 1499. The marriage contract declared that Brittany should eventually fall to the second son or to the eldest daughter of the marriage or, failing issue, to Anne's natural heirs; the special rights and privileges of the duchy were to be maintained.

For the remainder of her life, Anne, a woman of great intelligence, devoted herself to the administration of her duchy and jealously guarded its autonomy, but in the end her daughter Claude was betrothed (1506) to Francis of Angoulême, the future Francis I of France.

A patron of artists and poets, Anne commissioned a *Book of Hours* that is one of the most beautiful of French manuscripts. She also instituted the queen's maids of honour at the French court.

Anne OF CLEVES (b. Sept. 22, 1515—d. July 16, 1557, London), fourth wife of King Henry VIII of England. Henry married Anne because he believed that he needed to form a political alliance with her brother William, duke of Cleves, who was a leader of the Protestants of western Germany. He thought the alliance was necessary because in 1539 it appeared that the two major Roman Catholic powers, France and the Holy Roman Empire, were about to join together to attack Protestant England. That threat prompted Henry's chief minister, Thomas Cromwell, to arrange the marriage to establish ties between England and the Lutheran enemies of the Holy Roman emperor, Charles V.

On Jan. 1, 1540, Anne arrived in England to meet her fiancé for the first time. Five days later the wedding took place. Henry was keenly disappointed, Anne being less attractive than he had been led to expect, and he soon came to resent her lack of sophistication and limited command of the English language.

When the alliance between the Catholic powers failed to materialize, the marriage became a political embarrassment and was annulled by an Anglican convocation (July 9, 1540). Anne acquiesced and was rewarded with a large income, on the condition that she remain in England. She lived at Richmond or Bletchingley, with occasional visits to court, until her death.

Anne OF DENMARK (b. Dec. 12, 1574—d. March 2, 1619), queen consort of King James I of Great Britain (James VI of Scotland); although she had little direct political influence, her extravagant expenditures contributed to the financial difficulties that plagued James's regime.

The daughter of King Frederick II of Denmark and Norway, Anne was married to James in 1589. Her Lutheran upbringing and frivolous nature cost her the affection of James's Scottish Presbyterian subjects, and James alienated Anne by entrusting the upbringing of their first son, Prince Henry (1594–1612), to John Erskine, 2nd earl of Mar. Nevertheless, after James ascended the British throne in 1603, he and Anne lived in harmony, although they had separate quarters during the last few years of her life. Most of the Queen's time and energy were devoted to lavish court entertainments, and her patronage contributed to the development of the arts, particularly of the masque. She embarrassed James, however, by displaying sympathy for Roman Catholicism. Their second son succeeded James as King Charles I (ruled 1625–49). A biography, *Anne of Denmark*, by E.C. Williams, was published in 1970.

Anne of Denmark, detail of an oil painting after Paul van Somer, 1617; in the National Portrait Gallery, London

By courtesy of the National Portrait Gallery, London

Anne OF FRANCE, also called ANNE OF BEAUJEU (b. 1461—d. Nov. 14, 1522, Chantelle, Fr.), eldest daughter of Louis XI of France and Charlotte of Savoy, who exercised, with her husband, Pierre de Bourbon, seigneur de Beaujeu, a virtual regency in France from 1483 to 1491, during the early years of the reign of King Charles VIII.

Anne's energy, strength of will, cunning, and political sense enabled her to overcome the difficulties threatening the kingdom, the most important of which was unrest among the magnates, who had suffered under Louis XI's callous oppressions. Concessions were made: many of Louis's favourites were sacrificed; lands were restored to hostile nobles, among whom was the Duc d'Orléans, the future Louis XII of France; and the States General were convened (1484). When the Beaujeus ignored that assembly's demand to control taxation and hold regular meetings, the "Mad War" broke out between, on the one side, the crown

Anne of France, detail from a portrait by an unknown artist, *c.* 1498; in the cathedral of Moulins, Fr.

Giraudon—Art Resource/EB Inc.

and, on the other, the Duc d'Orléans and Francis II of Brittany, which ended in a royal victory.

In 1491, despite Austrian and English opposition, the Beaujeus concluded the marriage of Charles VIII with Anne of Brittany, which had the effect of joining the domains of Brittany with the crown. When Charles freed himself from tutelage, however, his former guardians were exposed to the wrath of the new queen, whose duchy's independence had been compromised.

Anne of France had been the dominant party in the Beaujeu marriage and was a competent administrator. When Pierre died in 1503, Anne remained administrator of his Bourbon lands, protecting them from royal encroachment.

Anne and Joachim, SAINTS (fl. 1st century BC, Palestine; Western feast day July 26, Eastern feast day July 25), according to tradition derived from certain apocryphal writings, the parents of the Virgin Mary. Information concerning their lives and names is found in the 2nd-century-AD *Protevangelium of James* ("First Gospel of James") and the 3rd-century-AD *Evangelium de nativitate Mariae* ("Gospel of the Nativity of Mary"). According to these, Anne (Hebrew: Ḥannah) was born in Bethlehem, Judaea. She married Joachim, and, although they shared a wealthy and devout life at Nazareth, they eventually lamented their childlessness. Joachim, reproached at the Temple for his sterility, retreated into the countryside to pray, while Anne, grieved by his disappearance and by her barrenness, solemnly promised God that, if given a child, she would dedicate it to the Lord's service. Both received the vision of an angel, who announced that Anne would conceive and bear a most wondrous child. Messengers announced Joachim's return, and Anne happily met him at the city gate.

They rejoiced at the birth of their daughter, whom Anne named Mary. When the child was three years old, Joachim and Anne, in fulfillment of her divine promise, brought Mary to the Temple at Jerusalem, where they left her to be brought up. This event became so important in Church doctrine that by 1585 Pope Sixtus V included in the Western Church calendar the liturgical feast of the Presentation of the Virgin Mary (November 21). Although this festival originated early in the East, probably at Jerusalem in 543, its first Western observance was recorded in England in the 11th century.

The account of their lives startlingly parallels the Old Testament story of the barren Hannah and her conception of Samuel (I Sam. 1). According to later legends, Joachim died shortly after Mary's birth, and Anne, encouraged by the Holy Spirit, remarried. Anne's cult was fervent in the Eastern Church as early as the 4th century, and in the early 8th century Pope Constantine probably introduced her devotion to Rome. Joachim's cult was introduced to the West in the 15th century.

The effect of the aforementioned apocryphal writings and the spread of Anne's veneration have had a colourful history. The *Protevangelium* became the foundation for establishing the liturgical feasts of the Nativity of the Virgin Mary (September 8) and the Immaculate Conception of the Blessed Virgin Mary (December 8); many churches, the first dating from the 6th century, were built in Anne's honour. Anne's cult became extremely popular in the Middle Ages and influenced such theologians as Jean de Gerson, Konrad Wimpinar, and Johann Eck (who endorsed the interpolation that Anne in her alleged subsequent marriages became the grandmother of the Apostles John and James [sons of Zebedee], Simon, Jude [Judas], James, son of Alphaeus, and also of James ["the Lord's brother"]). Martin Luther and others vehemently attacked the cult of Anne, which was then promoted by post-Reformation popes. Eastern literature on Anne, going back to the 4th century, does not follow the fantastic legends of medieval Western tradition. Anne is the patron saint of Brittany and Canada and of women in labour.

BIBLIOGRAPHY. P.V. Charland, *Madame Saincte Anne et son culte au moyen age* (2 vol., 1911–13); M.V. Ronan, *St. Anne: Her Cult and Her Shrines,* 1927; B. Kleinschmidt, *Die heilige Anna: Ihre Verehrung in Geschichte, Kunst und Volkstum* (1930).

annealing, treatment of a metal or alloy by heating to a predetermined temperature, holding for a certain time, and then cooling to room temperature to improve ductility and reduce brittleness. Process annealing is carried out intermittently during the working of a piece of metal to restore ductility lost through repeated hammering or other working. Full annealing is done in order to give workability to such parts as forged blanks destined for use in the machine tool industry. Annealing is also done for relief of internal stresses. Annealing temperatures vary with metals and alloys and with properties desired but must be within a range that prevents the growth of crystals.

Annecy, city, capital of Haute-Savoie *département,* Rhône-Alpes region, southeastern France, on the Lac d'Annecy at the entrance to one of the cluses (transverse gorges) of the Savoy Pre-Alps, south of Geneva. Traces of the Gallo-Roman Boutae have been found nearby. Seat of the counts of Genevois from the 10th century and attached to the dukedom of Savoy from 1401, Annecy became important during the Reformation when the bishop's seat was transferred there from Geneva in 1535 along with monastic institutions expelled from Switzerland. St. Francis de Sales was bishop (1602–22) and, with St. Jane Frances Chantal, founded the first Couvent de la Visitation de la Vierge. In 1728 the 16-year-old Jean-Jacques Rousseau took refuge there. The city was reattached to France again in 1860. The château, now a refuge for homeless families, stands above the old part of the town, whose arcaded streets are interlaced with canals. Tourism is an economic mainstay; industry includes electronics, confectionary, and precision instruments. Pop. (1982) 49,753.

Canal in the old quarter of Annecy, Fr.

Yves Dejardin—Rapho/Photo Researchers

annelid, phylum name ANNELIDA, also called SEGMENTED WORM, any member of a phylum of invertebrate animals that are characterized by the possession of a body cavity (or coelom), movable bristles (or setae), and a body divided into segments by transverse rings, or annulations. Comprising over 9,000 species, the annelids are divided into three classes: Polychaeta (marine worms), Oligochaeta (earthworms), and Hirudinea (leeches).

A brief treatment of annelids follows. For full treatment, *see* MACROPAEDIA: Annelids.

The polychaetes, or annelids of the class Polychaeta, number more than 5,400 species and are worldwide in distribution. They are most often found in marine environments, although a few species are known to inhabit certain rivers and lakes in the United States. They are evenly divided between free-living and sedentary (tube-dwelling) forms. They range in length from less than an inch to over 20 feet (6 metres). Free-living polychaetes have bodies made up of a head (or prostomium), a segmented trunk, and a tail (or pygidium); sedentary polychaetes have a prostomium (which may be distinct or indistinct), gills (in most species), thoracic and abdominal regions, and a pygidium. Respiration occurs either through gills or the body wall, and the digestive system of most polychaetes consists of a mouth, an esophagus, an intestine, and an anus.

Parasitism is rare in polychaetes, although commensalism (a beneficial relationship between two organisms) is common among the scale worms (order Aphroditamorpha). The polychaetes exhibit a rudimentary ability to learn, as well as occasional aggressive behaviour, and some species are capable of producing light (bioluminescence), a trait often related to sexual maturity.

Polychaetes reproduce sexually, though a few sedentary species are known to reproduce asexually, and hermaphroditism is rare. Reproduction is generally accomplished by the shedding of gametes (sperm and eggs) directly into the water. Fertilized eggs develop into diamond-shaped, free-swimming larvae called trochophores, which gradually come to resemble adults once they settle on a suitable surface. Most species are capable of regenerating lost body parts, particularly tails, though in the species *Ctenodrilus* and *Dodecaceria* regeneration from only one segment is possible.

The oligochaetes, of the class Oligochaeta, number approximately 3,250 species and are generally found dwelling in the soil, although a few species live in aquatic environments. The range of their length compares with that of the polychaetes; their bodies are made up of a head and a cylindrical trunk, which is divided into as many as 600 segments. Setae project from the bottom, or ventral, side of the body. Respiration occurs through the body wall in most oligochaetes, and their digestive systems usually consist of a mouth, a muscular pharynx, an esophagus, a muscular gizzard, a long intestine, and an anus. At sexual maturity, a saddle-shaped thickening in the centre of the body, called a clitellum, is present.

Parasitism is also rare in oligochaetes, although the family Branchiobdellidae is wholly parasitic. Some species are capable of rudimentary learning and bioluminescence, and nearly all oligochaetes are thigmotactic (attracted to surfaces). In addition, they can probably sense tactile stimuli, heat, and pain. Oligochaete locomotion involves extension of the anterior (front) end of the body, anchoring the extended part with setae, and contraction of the posterior end of the body. Because both oligochaetes and polychaetes possess setae (and leeches do not), they are sometimes classified as subclasses within a larger class called the Chaetopoda.

Oligochaetes are primarily hermaphroditic, and copulation usually takes place with a pair of worms in a head-to-tail position, simultaneously exchanging sperm and eggs. Eggs are laid in a cocoon secreted by the clitellum, and the entire development of the young worm takes place inside this cocoon. There is no stage in oligochaetes (or leeches) similar to that of the larval trochophore in polychaetes. Aquatic species are often capable of a form of asexual reproduction, in which the body of the worm fragments into segments that then grow into new worms, and some species can lay self-fertilized eggs or reproduce by parthenogenesis. Regeneration is common in oligochaetes, though lower forms possess this ability to a greater extent than higher forms.

The leeches, of the class Miradinea, number about 300 species and are generally found in freshwater or humid environments. They are elliptical in shape, with 34 segments each and a sucker at both ends of the body (the larger sucker on the posterior end). They can reach lengths of up to 16 inches. Unlike polychaetes or oligochaetes, leeches have no setae; however, they do exhibit a clitellum during the reproductive period as in oligochaetes. Respiration occurs through the skin, and leech digestive systems usually consist of a mouth surrounded by the front sucker, an esophagus, a crop, an intestine, a rectum, and an anus.

All leeches feed on blood. All are uniformly hermaphroditic and their reproduction is always sexual. Eggs are deposited in cocoons secreted by the clitellum, and the entire development of the young leech takes place inside this cocoon, the same as with young oligochaetes. Because leeches and oligochaetes possess a clitellum (and polychaetes do not), they are sometimes classified as subclasses with a larger class called the Clitellata. Bioluminescence and regeneration are unknown in leeches. The mode of locomotion consists in anchoring of a sucker, contraction of muscles, and then attachment of the other sucker.

The annelids are important to mankind in several ways. Polychaetes turn over sediment on the bottom of the ocean, while oligochaetes such as the earthworm (*Lumbricus terrestris*) turn over terrestrial soil. The bloodworm (*Glycera dibranchiata*), a polychaete, is used as saltwater fish bait, and the palolo worm (*Leodice viridis*), another polychaete, is used for food in the Samoan Islands. The sludge worm *Tubifex,* which is an oligochaete, grows near sewer outlets and is used as an idicator of water pollution, as well as food for tropical fish. Earthworms are used as freshwater fish bait and as humus builders in gardens. Leeches have a long history of medical use, and even today, Hirudin, an extract made from leeches, is used as a blood anticoagulant.

annexation, a formal act whereby a state proclaims its sovereignty over territory hitherto outside its domain. Unlike cession, whereby territory is given or sold through treaty, annexation is a unilateral act made effective by actual possession and legitimized by general recognition.

Annexation is frequently preceded by conquest and military occupation of the conquered territory. Conceivably, as in the German annexation of Austria in 1938, a conquest may be accomplished by the threat of force without active hostilities. Military occupation does not constitute or necessarily lead to annexation. Thus, for instance, the Allied military occupation of Germany after the cessation of hostilities in World War II was not followed by annexation; on the contrary, the Allies, by proclamation, expressly denied any intention to annex. When military occupation results in annexation, an official announcement is normal, to the effect that the sovereign authority of the annexing state has been established and will be maintained in the future. Subsequent recognition of annexation by other states may be explicit or implied. Annexation based on the illegal use of force is condemned in the Charter of the United Nations. *See also* conquest.

Annia Galeria Faustina: *see* Faustina, Annia Galeria.

Anniceris (fl. 4th and 3rd centuries BC), Greek philosopher who was drawn to the ideas of the Cyrenaic school of philosophy, founded by Aristippus, and to its basically hedonistic outlook. Anniceris dedicated himself to reviving some of the original principles of the school. During his lifetime the Cyrenaic school was undergoing a transformation, and two key figures responsible for this change were Theodorus and Hegesias. Anniceris differed from Theodorus in believing that pleasure had to be understood as embracing much more than sensual enjoyment and from Hegesias, a pessimist, in believing that there are qualities of pleasure, in and of themselves, that are good, apart from their ability to assuage pain.

annihilation, in physics, reaction in which a particle and its antiparticle collide and disappear, releasing energy. The most common annihilation on Earth occurs between an electron and its antiparticle, a positron. A positron, which may originate in radioactive decay, usually combines briefly with an electron to form a quasi-atom, called positronium, composed of the two particles spinning around each other before they collide. After annihilation, two or three gamma rays (similar to X-rays) radiate from the point of collision.

The amount of energy (E) produced by annihilation is equal to the mass (m) that disappears multiplied by the square of the speed of light in a vacuum (c)—*i.e.,* $E = mc^2$. Thus annihilation is an example of the equivalence of mass and energy and a confirmation of the special theory of relativity, which predicts this equivalence.

Other annihilation reactions also occur. Nucleons (protons and neutrons), for example, annihilate antinucleons (antiprotons and antineutrons), and the energy is carried away as pions and kaons, particles in the class of mesons. Annihilation of matter and antimatter has been invoked by some cosmologists to explain the enormous energy of quasars (quasi-stellar sources) and to explain the apparent expansion of the universe.

Anniston, city, seat (1898) of Calhoun County, northeastern Alabama, U.S., in the foothills of the Appalachian Mountains. Founded in 1872 by Samuel Noble and Daniel Tyler as a private industrial community (opened to the public in 1883), it was originally named for the Woodstock Iron Company; to avoid confusion with another Woodstock in Alabama, it was renamed Anniston (Annie's Town) after the wife of Alfred Tyler, the company president. Cast-iron pipe, textiles, and chemicals are major products. The Regar Memorial Museum of Natural History, with a notable collection of bird groups (900 specimens), is in the city. Nearby Ft. McClellan was headquarters for the Women's Army Corps until it was abolished in 1978. Inc. 1879. Pop. (1980) 29,523.

Anno, SAINT, Anno also spelled HANNO (b. *c.* 1010, Swabia—d. Dec. 4, 1075; feast day December 4), archbishop of Cologne who was prominent in the political struggles of the Holy Roman Empire.

Educated at Bamberg, Anno became confessor to the Holy Roman emperor Henry III, who appointed him archbishop in 1056. He was the leader of the party that abducted the young king Henry IV from his mother, Agnes of Poitou. Anno then seized the regency but was compelled to share it with Adalbert, the powerful archbishop of Hamburg–Bremen. In 1064 he left the court but recovered some of his former influence over Henry when Adalbert fell from favour in 1066.

Anno's most important service was his action at the Council of Mantua (May 1064), when he succeeded in having Alexander II recognized as pope against the antipope Honorius II, who was originally a nominee of the German court. Anno retired to a life of strict penance at the Abbey of Siegburg, which he had founded in 1064.

anno mundi (Latin: "in the year of the world"), abbreviation AM, present form of Jewish chronology based on rabbinic calculations; since the 9th century AD, the year 3760 BC has been generally accepted as the beginning of the era; however, critical dates that underlie the calculations are uncertain. Rabbis used the genealogy in Genesis to calculate the date of the creation and then added to their calculations the time that had elapsed since the time of Genesis. Despite the uncertainties, Jews use this dating system as a sign of attachment to tradition. The Jewish year is a lunar one with a periodic leap year to harmonize the lunar cycle with the solar cycle.

Annobón, formerly (until 1981) PAGALU, volcanic island in the South Atlantic Ocean near the Equator. Located about 350 mi (565 km) southwest of continental Equatorial Guinea, it occupies an area of 6.5 sq mi (17 sq km) and rises to an altitude of 2,200 ft (671 m). A part of Equatorial Guinea (formerly Spanish Guinea), the island constitutes one of the three provinces of the country. Fishing and lumbering activities are centred in San Antonio, the chief settlement. Pop. (latest census) 1,436.

Annonaceae, the custard apple, or annona, family, the largest family of the magnolia order (Magnoliales). According to some authorities, it contains 122 genera and 1,100 species, many valuable for their large, pulpy fruits, some useful for their timber, and others prized as ornamentals. The family consists of trees, shrubs, and woody climbers, found mainly in the tropics although a few species extend into temperate regions.

Leaves and wood are often fragrant. Leaves are simple, with smooth margins, and alternately arranged in two rows along the stems. The radially symmetrical flowers are usually bisexual. In most species the three sepals are united at the base. There are six brown or yellow petals, many stamens in a spiral and many pistils, each with a one-chambered ovary containing many ovules. The fruit is a berry. Flowers in some species are borne directly on large branches or on the trunk.

Bark, leaves, and roots of many species are important in folk medicine, and others bear edible fruits or are important sources of perfume and spice.

A handsome ornamental of the family is the weeping form of the mast tree (*Polyalthia longifolia pendula*), of Sri Lanka. Its shining, brilliant green, willowy, wavy-edged leaves hang from pendant branches that almost clasp the tall, straight trunk. The leaves are used as temple decorations in India.

A South American tree, *Porcelia saffordiana*, bears immense fruits sometimes weighing 18 kilograms (40 pounds) or more.

The alligator apple (*Annona glabra*) of tropical America and western Africa, also known as pond apple and corkwood, is a 12-metre (40-foot) evergreen with 18-centimetre- (7-inch-) long oval leaves and fragrant yellowish flowers. It bears smooth, gnarled, yellowish fruits, 5–10 cm long, which are edible but of poor flavour. Its roots are used to make bottle corks and fishing floats and as rootstock for grafting less hardy species of *Annona*.

The custard apple (*A. reticulata*), a small, tropical American tree, gives the family one of its common names. Also known as bullock's-heart for its globose shape, it has fruits with creamy white, sweetish, custard-like flesh.

annual aster: *see* China aster.

annuity, in the simplest sense, a payment made yearly, as, for example, under a contract to provide retirement income. The term is also applied to any series of periodic payments made at regular, fixed intervals; the length of the interval is called the annuity period.

There are two main classes of annuities: annuities certain and contingent annuities. Under an annuity certain, the payments are to continue for a specified number of payments, and calculations are based on the assumption that each payment is certain to be made when due. With a contingent annuity, each payment is contingent on the continuance of a given status, as with a life annuity under which each payment is contingent on the survival of one or more specified persons.

A special case of the annuity certain is the perpetuity, which is an annuity that continues forever. Perhaps the best known example of a perpetuity is the interest payment on the British government bonds known as consols. Because these obligations have no maturity date, it is intended that the interest payments will be continued indefinitely.

The contingent annuity used in life insurance and pension plans is based upon the risk-sharing principle. The price of an annuity paying a given sum for life is based upon the life expectancy of the annuitant at the time the annuity is to begin. In effect, the annuitant joins with a large number of other persons of the same age in establishing a fund that is calculated, on the basis of mortality tables, to be sufficient to pay each person the life income agreed upon. Some will live longer than others and receive more in payments than they have put into the fund, whereas others will not live long enough to receive all that they have put in. This risk-sharing principle makes it possible to purchase an annuity that guarantees much higher payments than could be obtained if the same sum of money were invested at interest. It has the disadvantage that upon the death of the annuitant nothing is left for his heirs. *See also* pension.

annulment, legal invalidation of a marriage. Annulment announces the invalidity of a marriage that was void from its inception. It is to be distinguished from dissolution, which ends a valid marriage for special reasons; *e.g.,* insanity of one partner after marrying. The annulment decree attempts to leave the parties *in statu quo ante* (as they were before the marriage), unless doing so would adversely affect a third person.

In secular law, only the government, through its courts, can invalidate a marriage; and generally only a party to the marriage can seek annulment. The canon law of Christian churches also has procedures for invalidating marriages.

To justify annulment, there must be a defect in the marriage contract—*e.g.,* incompetence of one party because of age, insanity, or a pre-existing marriage. Continued absence of one party also justifies annulment. Thus, in some places, one party may get an annulment if the other is sentenced to a long prison term. Generally, annulment is easier if the marriage is unconsummated.

In annulment lawsuits, the validity of the marriage must be clearly disproved. The so-called clean hands doctrine figures heavily in such cases, meaning that the conduct of the person seeking the annulment must be fair and above suspicion if he is to prevail. Thus, a party who knew the partner was underage but proceeded with the marriage would probably be denied annulment.

Annunciation, the announcement by the angel Gabriel to the Virgin Mary that she would conceive a Son of the Holy Spirit to be called Jesus (Luke 1:26–38). In the Christian Church the Feast of the Annunciation is celebrated on March 25 (Lady Day). The first authentic allusions to the feast (apart from the Gelasian and Gregorian sacramentaries, in both of which it is mentioned) are in acts of the Council of Toledo (656) and of the Trullan Council (692). Because its significance is much more than narrative, the Annunciation had a particularly important place in the arts and church decoration of the early Christian and medieval periods and in the devotional art of the Renaissance and Baroque. It represents one of the principal feasts of the church and was thus one of the few narrative scenes selected for illustration in Byzantine churches; moreover, because the event coincides with the Incarnation of Christ, it also represents a prelude to the redemption of the world.

"The Annunciation," centre panel of the "Mérode Altarpiece" by Robert Campin, *c.* 1428; in The Cloisters, Metropolitan Museum of Art, New York

By courtesy of the Metropolitan Museum of Art, New York, The Cloisters Collection, Purchase

anoa: *see* buffalo.

anode, the terminal or electrode from which electrons leave a system. In a battery or other source of direct current the anode is the negative terminal, but in a passive load it is the positive terminal. For example, in an electron tube electrons from the cathode travel across the tube toward the anode, and in an electroplating cell negative ions are deposited at the anode. In electrochemistry oxidation occurs at the anode. *Compare* cathode.

anodizing, method of plating metal for such purposes as corrosion inhibition, electrical insulation, thermal control, sealing and joining, wear and abrasion resistance, and decorative finishing. Anodizing consists of electrically depositing a metal substance, most often aluminum, from an aqueous solution in an electrolytic cell of which the object to be plated is the anode, to create a hard, nonporous film on the surface of a metal object. In the most common type of anodizing, which uses a 15 percent sulfuric acid bath, the substance to be deposited can be mixed with a dye to achieve a coloured surface. Aluminum that has been anodized and coloured in this way is used widely in giftware, home appliances, and architectural decoration.

anointment, ritual application of oil or fat to the head or body of a person or to an object; an almost universal practice in the history of religions, although both the cultic practice followed and the sacred substance employed vary from one religion to another. It is possible to recognize three distinct, though not separate, meanings ascribed to ritual anointments by the devotees of various religions.

Anointment as healing. The medicine man of a tribe may be both its priest and its physician; "salvation" literally means "healing" or restoration to soundness. In the practice of ritual anointing, this conjunction of religion and medicine is clear. Anointment seems intended to apply the power of natural and supernatural forces to the sick and thus to ward off the baneful influences of diseases and of demons.

Anointment as consecration. In preparation for battle, in danger from wild animals, in the hour of death, and at other special times, anointment is used to endow an ordinary person with special holiness. He is "set aside" for a particular relation to that which is regarded as holy and good. Anointment as consecration is frequently applied not only to persons but also to objects. Altars, sacred vessels, temples, and sometimes even weapons and items of clothing are anointed to dedicate them to the service of the divine and to assure and symbolize the presence and pleasure of the divine in the holy place. In the Roman Catholic and Eastern Orthodox churches, the ritual anointing of the seriously ill and the elderly has been practiced as a sacrament since early times. In the Roman Catholic Church, unction was long regarded as a last rite, usually postponed until death was imminent and the dying Christian was *in extremis*; thus, the name extreme unction developed. In modern times, a more lenient interpretation permitted anointing of the less seriously ill. In the Eastern Orthodox churches the name extreme unction was never used, and the healing aspects of the sacrament have been considered most important. In the Greek Orthodox Church the sacrament is sometimes administered to well persons to prevent illness.

Anointment as ordination. Over and above the consecration applied to ordinary men, anointment has a place in the particular rituals by which certain men receive positions of eminence. In many religions priests are inducted into their sacred office with a holy chrism (*q.v.*). In ancient Israel and in various Christian cultures, the king was anointed in the rite of coronation as the one chosen by God to rule over the people.

anole, any of about 250 species of lizards in the large arboreal (tree-dwelling) genus *Anolis* (family Iguanidae). They occur throughout the warmer regions of North and South America and are abundant in the West Indies. Like the gecko (*q.v.*), all anoles have enlarged finger and toe pads that are covered with microscopic hooks. These clinging pads, together with sharp claws, enable them to climb, even over the smoothest surface, with great speed and agility. Anoles attain 12 to 45 centimetres (5 to 18 inches) in length and can change colour from brown or yellow to several shades of green. The male often has a large red or yellow expansible dewlap (fold of skin in the neck region).

The most familiar anole (*A. carolinensis,* or green anole, commonly but erroneously called chameleon) is native to the southern United States and islands in the Caribbean; it is the false "chameleon" sold in pet shops. Its colour varies at times from green to brown or mottled, but its colour-changing ability is poor compared to that of the true chameleons of the Old World. Green anoles reach a maximum length of 18 centimetres and have a pink dewlap.

Green anole (*Anolis carolinensis*)

Robert J. Erwin—The National Audubon Society Collection/Photo Researchers

anomalous water, also called ORTHOWATER, or POLYWATER, liquid water generally formed by condensation of water vapour in tiny glass or fused-quartz capillaries and with properties very different from those well established for ordinary water; *e.g.,* lower vapour pressure, lower freezing temperature, higher density and viscosity, higher thermal stability, and different infrared and Raman spectra. For a few years after the announcement of the discovery of the substance (1968) by a group of Soviet scientists, many investigators held the view that the substance was a new form of water, possibly a polymer. In the 1970s thorough study established that anomalous water is ordinary water containing ionic contaminants that cause it to have the unusual properties.

anomaly, in astronomy, originally the nonuniform (anomalous) apparent motions of the planets. In present usage, three kinds of anomaly are distinguished to describe the position in the orbit of a planet, a satellite, or a star (in a binary system) around the centre of mass. The following text relates to the orbit of a planet. True anomaly is the angle, V, between lines drawn from the centre of mass (near the centre of the Sun, S), to a planet P, and to the perihelion point B, where the planet comes closest to the Sun. The mean anomaly is the angle between lines drawn from the Sun to the perihelion B and to a point (not shown) moving in the orbit at a uniform rate corresponding to the period of revolution of the planet. The eccentric anomaly is the angle E, between the perihelion B, the centre of the ellipse at C, and the point P′, which is located by drawing a perpendicular to AB passing through the planet and intersecting a circle of diameter AB.

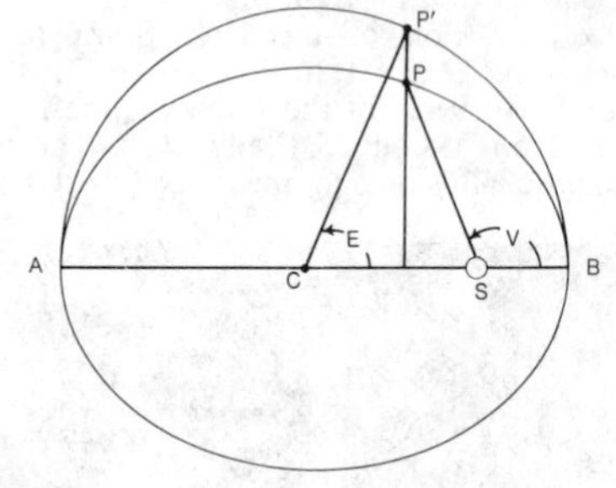

Anomaly

A-aphelion; B-perihelion; C-centre of the orbit; E-eccentric anomaly; P-planet; S-Sun; V-true anomaly

From *Dictionary of Astronomical Terms* by Ake Wallenquist, translated and edited by Sune Engelbrektson. Copyright © 1966 by Sune Engelbrektson. Reproduced by permission of Doubleday & Company, Inc.

anomie, also spelled ANOMY, in societies or individuals, a condition of instability resulting from a breakdown of standards and values or from a lack of purpose or ideals.

The term was introduced by the French sociologist Émile Durkheim in his study of suicide. He believed that one type of suicide (anomic) resulted from the breakdown of social standards that people need to regulate their behaviour. When a social system is in a state of anomie, common values and common meanings are no longer understood or accepted, and new values and meanings have not developed. Such a society produces, in many of its members, psychological states characterized by a sense of futility, lack of purpose, and emotional emptiness and despair. Striving is considered useless, because there is no accepted definition of what is desirable.

Robert K. Merton, in the United States, studied the causes of anomie, or normlessness, finding it severest in persons who do not have acceptable means of achieving their cultural goals. Goals may become so important that, if institutionalized means—*i.e.,* those means acceptable according to the standards of the society—fail, illegitimate means may be used. Greater emphasis on ends rather than means results in a stress that leads to a breakdown in the regulatory structure—*i.e.,* anomie. If, for example, a society impelled its members to acquire wealth, yet offered inadequate means for them to do so, the strain would cause many people to violate norms. The only regulating agencies would be the desire for personal advantage and the fear of punishment. Social behaviour thus becomes unpredictable. Delinquency, crime, and suicide are often reactions to anomie.

Although Durkheim's concept of anomie referred to a condition of relative normlessness of a society or social group, other writers have used it to refer to conditions of individuals. In this psychological usage, anomie means the state of mind of a person who has no standards or sense of continuity or obligation and who has rejected all social bonds. Individuals may feel that community leaders are indifferent to their needs, that society is basically unpredictable and lacking order, and that goals are not being realized. They may have a sense of futility and a conviction that associates are not dependable sources of support.

Anomoean (from Greek *anomoios,* "unlike"), any member of a religious group of the 4th century that represented an extreme form of Arianism (*q.v.*), a Christian heresy that held that the essential difference between God and Christ was that God had always existed, while Christ was created by God. Aëtius, the founder of the Anomoeans, reasoned that the doctrine carried to its logical conclusion must mean that God and Christ could not be alike. Because *agennēsia* ("self-existence") is a part of the essence of God, Christ could not be like God because he lacked this necessary quality. Aëtius' chief convert and the second leader of the movement was Eunomius, after whose death (*c.* 394) the Anomoeans soon disappeared.

anomy (sociology): *see* anomie.

anorexia, persistent lack of appetite not caused by repletion. It may spring from psychoneurotic causes, as in anorexia nervosa (*q.v.*), a lack of appetite, primarily in young women, that may lead to extreme emaciation and even to death. Anorexia, like nausea and vomiting, may be brought about by shock, pain, or an inadequate supply of oxygen to a centre in the medulla oblongata (the part of the brain immediately above the spinal cord). An increase in pressure within the skull may cause anorexia, nausea, or vomiting, as may infections in the mouth or badly fitting dentures. Obstruction at some point in the gastrointestinal system, chronic disease of the kidneys, liver disease, allergic reactions to foods, and the taking of certain drugs (*e.g.,* amphetamines) are among the many other causes of the disorder.

anorexia nervosa, extreme body emaciation caused by emotional or psychological aversion to foods and to eating. The condition occurs predominantly in young women. Emotional manifestations may range from a neurotic overreaction to a weight-reduction diet to full-blown schizophrenic delusions resulting in the abhorrence of food.

Body weight may drop to half of normal. Associated symptoms usually consist of variable digestive disturbances, with vomiting that may be spontaneous or self-induced, and of amenorrhea (failure to menstruate). There seem to be no causative organic defects. In contrast to famine victims, sufferers from anorexia nervosa are often able to maintain their strength and daily activities at approximately normal levels; they appear characteristically unconcerned with their undernourished state and do not feel hungry.

The treatment of anorexia nervosa is seldom straightforward and requires full cooperation among the patient, attending physician, and a psychiatrist. Some cases do not respond to treatment, and a small percentage result in death.

anorthite, a feldspar mineral, calcium aluminosilicate ($CaAl_2Si_2O_8$), that occurs as white or grayish, brittle, glassy crystals. Primarily a rock-forming mineral, it is used in the manufacture of glass and ceramics. Anorthite occurs in basic igneous rocks, as at Trentino, Italy; Södermanland, Swed.; Tamil Nadu, India; Miyake, Japan; and Franklin, N.J. For detailed physical properties, *see* feldspar (table).

The feldspar minerals are mixtures of sodium,

potassium, and calcium aluminosilicates; they belong to a ternary system in which any mineral may be classed by its percentage of each of three pure compounds, called end-members: sodium aluminosilicate, potassium aluminosilicate, and calcium aluminosilicate. Anorthite is the calcium-bearing end-member of the system; its symbol is *An.*

Anorthite and the sodium-bearing end-member of the system, albite ($NaAlSi_3O_8$), form a solid-solution series in which the two intermingle; thus, in nature there is a continuous chemical variation between the two compounds. The members of this series are called plagioclase (*q.v.*).

anorthoclase, any member of a continuous series of feldspar minerals related to sanidine (*q.v.*).

anorthosite, intrusive igneous rock that consists largely or entirely of plagioclase feldspar. The plagioclase of anorthosite in layered complexes is ordinarily labradorite or bytownite; in the absence of layering, however, plagioclase that is more silica-poor (basic) than calcium-rich andesine is uncommon.

Anorthosite is considerably less abundant than either basalt or granite, but the complexes in which it occurs are, nevertheless, often of immense size. For instance, about 155,000 square kilometres (60,000 square miles) of eastern Canada is underlain by anorthosite, the Saguenay Mass alone accounting for a tenth of this. The Morin Anorthosite in the same area occupies 2,600 sq km (1,040 sq mi), and the Adirondack Anorthosite is exposed over an area of about 3,900 sq km (1,560 sq mi). The Bushveld Complex underlies an area of about 50,000 sq km (20,000 sq mi); and the Great Dyke of Zimbabwe, another layered complex, has been traced for more than 480 km (300 mi).

Although these large masses are generally supposed to provide the best sample of the deep lithosphere (the solid part of the Earth), they often appear to be floored over most of their outcrop area. They are usually laccoliths (inserted between sedimentary beds), lopoliths (laccoliths with basin-shaped bases), or sills (tabular bodies inserted while molten between other rocks); the Canadian anorthosites are thought to be laccolithic, the Adirondack Anorthosite a floored sheet. The thickness of the Sudbury Lopolith is estimated at three km (1.8 mi), that of the Bushveld at five km (3 mi). Anorthosite dikes (tabular bodies inserted in fissures) are very rare, and effusive equivalents of anorthosite are unknown. The massive anorthosites, such as the layered ones, are thought to be crystal accumulates.

Anouilh, Jean(-Marie-Lucien-Pierre) (b. June 23, 1910, Bordeaux, Fr.), playwright who became one of the strongest personalities of the French theatre and achieved an international reputation after World War II. His plays are intensely personal messages; often they express his love of the theatre as well as his grudges against actors, wives, mistresses, critics, academicians, bureaucrats, and others.

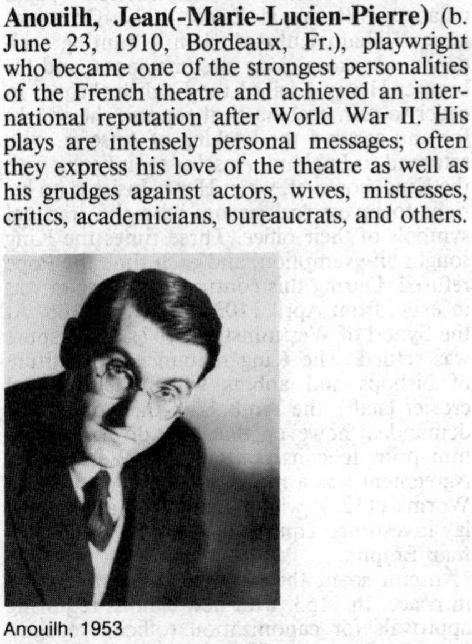

Anouilh, 1953
H. Roger-Viollet

Anouilh's characteristic techniques include the play within the play, flashbacks and flash forwards, and the exchange of roles.

The sparse autobiographical details revealed by Anouilh provide few keys to his works. He studied law and worked briefly in advertising. At 18, however, he saw Jean Giraudoux's drama *Siegfried,* in which he discovered a theatrical and poetic language that determined his career. He worked briefly as the secretary to the great actor-director Louis Jouvet.

L'Hermine (performed 1932; *The Ermine,* 1955) was Anouilh's first play to be produced, and success came in 1937 with *Le Voyageur sans bagage* (*Traveller Without Luggage,* 1959), which was soon followed by *La Sauvage* (1938).

Anouilh rejected both Naturalism and Realism in favour of what has been called "theatricalism," the return of poetry and imagination to the stage. Technically he evidenced a great versatility, from the stylized use of Greek myth, to the rewriting of history, to the *comédie-ballet,* to the modern comedy of character. Although not a systematic ideologist like the Existentialist Jean-Paul Sartre, Anouilh developed his own view of life focussing on the contradictions within human reality, for example, or the ambiguous relationships between good and evil. He called two major collections of his plays *Pièces roses* ("Rose-coloured Plays") and *Pièces noires* ("Black Plays"), in which similar subjects are treated more or less lightly. His dramatic vision of the world poses the question of how far the individual must compromise with truth to obtain happiness. His plays show men or women facing the loss of the privileged world of childhood. Some of his characters accept the inevitable; some, such as the light-headed creatures of *Le Bal des voleurs* (1938; *Thieves' Carnival,* 1952), live lies; and others, such as *Antigone* (1944; Eng. trans., 1946), reject any tampering with ideals.

With *L'Invitation au château* (1947; *Ring Around the Moon,* 1950), the mood of Anouilh's plays became more sombre. His aging couples seem to perform a dance of death in *La Valse des toréadors* (1952; *The Waltz of the Toreadors,* 1956). *L'Alouette* (1953; *The Lark,* 1955) is the spiritual adventure of Joan of Arc, who, like Antigone and Thérèse Tarde (*La Sauvage*), is another of Anouilh's rebels who rejects the world, its order, and its trite happiness. In another historical play, *Becket ou l'honneur de Dieu* (1959; *Becket, or, The Honour of God,* 1962), friendship is crushed between spiritual integrity and political power.

In the 1950s Anouilh introduced into his vision of the world the novelty of political ferment: *Pauvre Bitos, ou le Dîner de têtes* (1956; *Poor Bitos,* 1964). In the 1960s his plays were considered by many to be dated compared with the Absurdist dramatists Eugène Ionesco or Samuel Beckett. *Le Boulanger, la boulangère et le petit mitron* (1968; "The Baker, the Baker's Wife, and the Baker's Boy") was coolly received, but in the following decade other new plays appeared to confirm his place as a master entertainer: *Cher Antoine; ou, l'amour raté* (1969; *Dear Antoine; or, The Love That Failed,* 1971), *Les Poissons rouges; ou, Mon père, ce héros* (1970; "The Goldfish; or, My Father, This Hero"), *Ne réveillez pas madame* (1970; "Do Not Awaken the Lady"), *Le Directeur de l'opéra* (1972: "The Director of the Opera"), *L'Arrestation* (1975; "The Arrest"), *Le Scénario* (1976; "The Scenario"), *Vive Henry IV* (1977; "Long Live Henry IV"), and *La Culotte* (1978; "The Trousers").

Anouilh also wrote several successful film scenarios, including *Monsieur Vincent* (1947).

Anpu (Egyptian god): *see* Anubis.

Anqing (China): *see* An-ch'ing.

Anquetil-Duperron, A(braham)-H(yacinthe) (b. Dec. 7, 1731, Paris—d. Jan. 17, 1805, Paris), scholar and linguist who was generally credited with the first translation of the Avesta (Zoroastrian scripture) into a modern European language and with awakening interest in the study of Eastern languages and thought.

At the University of Paris, Anquetil mastered Hebrew as his first Eastern language; later, he added Persian and Arabic to his linguistic stock. At the Royal Library in Paris he found some ancient works in Avestan, an Iranian language of the time of the 6th-century-BC religious prophet Zoroaster. The largest remaining group of Zoroastrians, the Parsis, had fled to India to escape Muslim persecution. In search of the ancient Zoroastrian texts, Anquetil travelled to India, where he acquired and translated nearly 200 such manuscripts. He also wrote numerous papers and treatises on Oriental languages, laws, and systems of government.

In 1771 his *Zend-Avesta* appeared. Despite its many discrepancies and inaccuracies, it remains a pioneer work. Among his other works are his *Législation orientale* (1778), *Historical and Geographical Research on India* (1786), and *The Dignity of Commerce and the Commercial State* (1789). His *India in Rapport with Europe* appeared in 1798, and his last major work was *Upanishada* (1804; "Secrets Never To Be Revealed").

Ansar, also spelled AL-ANṢĀR (Sudanese faction): *see* Mahdist.

Ansbach, formerly ANSPACH, city, Bayern *Land* (Bavaria state), southern West Germany, on the Rezat River, southwest of Nürnberg. It originated around the Benedictine monastery of Onolzbach (founded 748) and was sold to a Franconian branch of the Hohenzollern line (later margraves of Brandenburg-Ansbach-Bayreuth) in 1331. It passed to Prussia in 1791 and to Bavaria in 1806. Queen Caroline, consort of George II of Great Britain, was born there in 1683, and there is a memorial to Kaspar Hauser (a mysterious youth reputed to be the hereditary prince of Baden), who died there in 1833.

Notable buildings in Ansbach are the 12th-century Romanesque Church of St. Gumbertus (restored in the Baroque style) and the palace of the margraves (1713–32), with a fine park. The International Bach Festival is held at Ansbach annually.

A rail and road junction, Ansbach has printing, metal, textile, plastic, cardboard, and leather industries. Pop. (1983 est.) 38,023.

Anschar, SAINT (patron saint of Scandinavia): *see* Ansgar, Saint.

Anschluss (German: Union), political union of Austria with Germany, achieved through annexation by Adolf Hitler in 1938. Mooted in 1919 by Austria, *Anschluss* with Germany remained a hope (chiefly with Austrian Social Democrats) during 1919–33, after which Hitler's rise made it unattractive.

In July 1934 Austrian and German Nazis attempted a concerted takeover but were prevented from doing so. An authoritarian right-wing government took power in Austria and prevented perhaps half the population from voicing legitimate dissent; that cleavage prevented concerted resistance to developments in 1938. In February of that year Hitler invited the Austrian chancellor Kurt von Schuschnigg to Germany and forced him to agree to give the Austrian Nazis virtually a free hand. Schuschnigg later repudiated the agreement and announced a plebiscite on the *Anschluss* question. Nazis then bullied Schuschnigg into cancelling the plebiscite; Schuschnigg obediently resigned, ordering the Austrian Army not to resist the Germans. Pres. Wilhelm Miklas of Austria refused to appoint the Austrian Nazi leader Arthur Seyss-Inquart as chancellor. The German Nazi minister Hermann Göring ordered Seyss-Inquart to send a telegram requesting German military aid, but he refused, and the telegram was sent by a German agent in Vienna. On March 12 Germany invaded, and the enthusiasm that followed persuaded Hitler to annex Austria outright on March 13. A controlled plebiscite of April 10 gave a 99.7 percent approval.

Anselm OF BAGGIO: *see* Alexander II *under* Alexander (Papacy).

Anselm OF CANTERBURY, SAINT (b. 1033/34, Aosta, Lombardy—d. April 21, 1109, possibly at Canterbury, Kent, Eng., canonized 1163?; feast day April 21), founder of Scholasticism, a philosophical school of thought that dominated the Middle Ages; he was recognized in modern times as the originator of the

St. Anselm (centre), terra-cotta altarpiece by Luca della Robbia; in the Museo Diocesano, Empoli, Italy
Alinari—Art Resource/EB Inc.

ontological argument for the existence of God (based on the idea of an absolutely perfect being, the fact of the idea being in itself a demonstration of existence) and the satisfaction theory of the atonement or redemption (based on the feudal theory of making satisfaction or recompense according to the status of a person against whom an offense has been committed, the infinite God being the offended party and man the offender). Incomplete evidence suggests that he was canonized in 1163.

Early life and career. Anselm was born in the Piedmont region of northwestern Italy. His birthplace, Aosta, was a town of strategic importance in Roman imperial and in medieval times, because it stood at the juncture of the Great and Little St. Bernard routes. His mother, Ermenberga, belonged to a noble Burgundian family and possessed considerable property. His father, Gondolfo, was a Lombard nobleman who intended that Anselm would make a career of politics and did not approve of his early decision to enter the monastic life. Anselm received an excellent classical education and was considered one of the better Latinists of his day. His early education impressed on him the need to be precise in his use of words, and his writings became known for their clarity.

In 1057 Anselm left Aosta to enter the Benedictine monastery at Bec (located between Rouen and Lisieux in Normandy, France), because he wanted to study under the monastery's renowned prior, Lanfranc. While on his way to Bec, he learned that Lanfranc was in Rome, so he spent some time at Lyon, Cluny, and Avranches before entering the monastery in 1060. In 1060 or 1061 he took his monastic vows. Because of Anselm's reputation for great intellectual ability and sincere piety, he was elected prior of the monastery after Lanfranc became abbot of Caen in 1063. In 1078 he became abbot of Bec.

In the previous year (1077), Anselm had written the *Monologium* ("Monologue") at the request of some of his fellow monks. A theological treatise, the *Monologium* was both apologetic and religious in intent. It attempted to demonstrate the existence and attributes of God by an appeal to reason alone rather than by the customary appeal to authorities favoured by earlier medieval thinkers. Moving from an analysis of the inequalities of various aspects of perfection, such as justice, wisdom, and power, Anselm argued for an absolute norm that is everywhere at all times, above both time and space, a norm that can be comprehended by the mind of man. Anselm asserted that that norm is God, the absolute, ultimate, and integrating standard of perfection.

Under Anselm, Bec became a centre of monastic learning and some theological questioning. Lanfranc had been a renowned theologian, but Anselm surpassed him. He continued his efforts to answer satisfactorily questions concerning the nature and existence of God. His *Proslogium* ("Address," or "Allocution"), originally titled *Fides quaerens intellectum* ("Faith Seeking Understanding"), established the ontological argument for the existence of God. In it he argued that even a fool has an idea of a being greater than which no other being can be conceived to exist; that such a being must really exist, for the very idea of such a being implies its existence.

Anselm's ontological argument was challenged by a contemporary monk, Gaunilo of Marmoutier, in the *Liber pro insipiente*, or "Book in Behalf of the Fool Who Says in His Heart There Is No God." Gaunilo denied that an idea of a being includes existence in the objective order and that a direct intuition of God necessarily includes God's existence. Anselm wrote in reply his *Liber apologeticus contra Gaunilonem* ("Book [of] Defense Against Gaunilo"), which was a repetition of the ontological argument of the *Proslogium*.

Appointment as archbishop of Canterbury. William the Conqueror, who had established Norman overlordship of England in 1066, was a benefactor of the monastery at Bec, and lands in both England and Normandy were granted to Bec. Anselm made three visits to England to view these lands. During one of those visits, while Anselm was founding a priory at Chester, William II Rufus, the son and successor of William the Conqueror, named him archbishop of Canterbury (March 1093). The see had been kept vacant since the death of Lanfranc in 1089, during which period the King had confiscated its revenues and pillaged its lands.

Anselm accepted the position somewhat reluctantly but with an intention of reforming the English Church. He refused to be consecrated as archbishop until William restored the lands to Canterbury and acknowledged Urban II as the rightful pope against the antipope Clement III. In fear of death from an illness, William agreed to the conditions, and Anselm was consecrated Dec. 4, 1093. When William recovered, however, he demanded from the new archbishop a sum of money, which Anselm refused to pay lest it look like simony (payment for an ecclesiastical position). In response to Anselm's refusal, William refused to allow Anselm to go to Rome to receive the pallium—a mantle, the symbol of papal approval of his archiepiscopal appointment—from Urban II, lest this be taken as an implied royal recognition of Urban. In claiming that the king had no right to interfere in what was essentially an ecclesiastical matter, Anselm became a major figure in the investiture controversy; *i.e.*, over the question as to whether a secular ruler (*e.g.*, emperor or king) or the pope had the primary right to invest an ecclesiastical authority, such as a bishop, with the symbols of his office.

The controversy continued for two years. On March 11, 1095, the English bishops, at the Synod of Rockingham, sided with the King against Anselm. When the papal legate brought the pallium from Rome, Anselm refused to accept it from William, since it would then appear that he owed his spiritual and ecclesiastical authority to the king. William permitted Anselm to leave for Rome, but on his departure he seized the lands of Canterbury.

Anselm attended the Council of Bari (Italy) in 1098 and presented his grievances against the King to Urban II. He took an active part in the sessions, defending the doctrine of the *Filioque* ("and from the Son") clause in the Nicene-Constantinopolitan Creed against the Greek Church, which had been in schism with the Western Church since 1054. The *Filioque* clause, added to the Western version of the Creed, indicated that the Holy Spirit proceeded from the Father and Son. The Greek Church rejected the *Filioque* clause as a later addition. The Council also reapproved earlier decrees against investiture of ecclesiastics by lay officials.

The satisfaction theory of redemption. When Anselm left England, he had taken with him an incomplete manuscript of his work *Cur Deus homo?* ("Why Did God Become Man?"). After the Council of Bari, he withdrew to the village of Liberi, near Capua, and completed the manuscript in 1099. This work became the classic treatment of the satisfaction theory of redemption. According to this theory, which is based upon the feudal structure of society, finite man has committed a crime (sin) against infinite God. In feudal society, àn offender was required to make recompense, or satisfaction, to the one offended according to that person's status. Thus, a crime against a king would require more satisfaction than a crime against a baron or a serf. According to this way of thinking, finite man, since he could never make satisfaction to the infinite God, could expect only eternal death. The instrument for bringing man back into a right relationship with God, therefore, had to be the God-man (Christ), by whose infinite merits man is purified in an act of cooperative recreation. Anselm rejected the view that man, through his sin, owes a debt to the devil, and placed the essence of redemption in individual union with Christ in the Eucharist (Lord's Supper), to which the sacrament of Baptism (by which a person is incorporated into the church) opens the way.

After completing *Cur Deus homo?* Anselm attended a council at the Lateran (papal palace) in Rome at Easter 1099. One year later, William Rufus died in a hunting accident under suspicious circumstances, and his brother Henry I seized the English throne. In order to gain ecclesiastical support, he sought for and secured the backing of Anselm, who returned to England. Anselm soon broke with the King, however, when Henry insisted on his right to invest ecclesiastics with the spiritual symbols of their office. Three times the King sought an exemption, and each time the Pope refused. During this controversy, Anselm was in exile, from April 1103 to August 1106. At the Synod of Westminster (1107), the dispute was settled. The King renounced investiture of bishops and abbots with the ring and crosier (staff), the symbols of their office. He demanded, however, that they do homage to him prior to consecration. The Westminster Agreement was a model for the Concordat of Worms (1122), which settled for a time the lay-investiture controversy in the Holy Roman Empire.

Anselm spent the last two years of his life in peace. In 1163, with new canons requiring approvals for canonization (official recognition of persons as saints), Archbishop Thomas

Becket of Canterbury (1118?–1170) referred Anselm's cause to Rome. Anselm was probably canonized at this time, for the Canterbury records for 1170 make frequent mention of the pilgrimages to his new shrine in the cathedral. For several centuries he was venerated locally. Clement XI (pope from 1700 to 1721) declared Anselm a doctor (teacher) of the church in 1720. (J.A.Ke.)

BIBLIOGRAPHY. Major bibliographies are U. Chevalier, *Répertoire des sources historiques du moyen âge*, vol. 1, pp. 256–259 (1905); for more recent periodical literature in English, French, German, and Italian, see F. van Steenberghen, *Philosophie des Mittelalters* (1950); and George Watson (ed.), *The New Cambridge Bibliography of English Literature*, vol. 1, pp. 752–754 (1974).

For Anselm's life and thought, see M. Rule, *Life and Times of St. Anselm*, 2 vol. (1883), and Rule's edition of Eadmer's *Vita Anselmi*, "Rolls Series" (1884); R.W. Church, *St. Anselm* (1870, many reprints); J. Clayton, *St. Anselm: A Critical Biography* (1933); J. McIntyre, *St. Anselm and His Critics: A Re-interpretation of the Cur Deus Homo* (1954); W.R.W. Stephens, "Saint Anselm," in *Dictionary of National Biography*, vol. 1, pp. 482–503 (1908); E. Gilson, *History of Christian Philosophy in the Middle Ages* (1955); F. Copleston, *History of Philosophy*, vol. 2 (1950); F. Cayré, *Manual of Patrology and History of Theology* (1940); Z.N. Brooke, *The English Church and the Papacy* (1931, reprinted 1968); R. Fairweather (ed. and trans.), *A Scholastic Miscellany: Anselm to Ockham* (1956); R.W. Southern, *St. Anselm and His Biographer* (1963).

Anselm OF LAON, French ANSELME DE LAON (b. first half of the 11th century, Laon, Archbishopric of Laon—d. July 15, 1117, Laon), theologian who became eminent in early Scholasticism.

Anselm apparently studied at Bec, Fr., under St. Anselm of Canterbury. In the final quarter of the 11th century, he taught with distinction at Paris, where with William of Champeaux he supported realism. About 1100 he returned to Laon, where his theological and exegetical school became famous. Peter Abelard attended Anselm's school (*c.* 1114), and John of Salisbury referred to Anselm and Anselm's brother Rudolph as "those most brilliant lights of the Gauls."

Anselm was influenced by the Platonic and the Neoplatonic ideas transmitted by Bishop St. Augustine of Hippo. Anselm's principal work was *Interlinear Glosses*, a commentary on the entire Vulgate Bible; it became a leading medieval authority. Some of his scriptural commentaries were ascribed to other writers, notably St. Anselm. His known works were published by J.-P. Migne in *Patrologia Latina* (vol. 162).

Anselm OF LUCCA: *see* Alexander II *under* Alexander (Papacy).

Anselm OF SAINT MARY, also called FATHER ANSELM, French ANSELME DE SAINTE-MARIE, OR PÈRE ANSELME, original name PIERRE DE GUIBOURS (b. 1625, Paris—d. Jan. 17, 1694, Paris), genealogist and friar whose history of the French royal family and nobility is a valuable source of detailed and unusual information.

Anselm of Saint Mary, engraving by François Huret
J.E. Bulloz

Anselm entered the order of the Discalced Hermits of St. Augustine in 1644 and, remaining in their monastery (Couvent des Petits Pères), devoted his entire life to genealogical studies. Among his early works are *Le Palais de l'honneur* (1663–1668; "The Palace of Honour"), concerning the genealogy of the houses of Lorraine and Savoy; *Le Palais de la gloire* (1664; "The Palace of Glory"), dealing with the genealogy of various illustrious French and European families; and *La Science héraldique* (1675; "The Science of Heraldry").

His most important work is the *Histoire généalogique et chronologique de la maison royale de France, des pairs, des grands officiers de la couronne, et de la maison du roy et des anciens barons du royaume* (2 vol., 1674; "Genealogical and Chronological History of the Royal House of France, the Peers, the Grand Officers of the Crown, and of the Royal House and the Ancient Barons of the Realm"). After his death this history of French nobility was continued by Honoré Caille, seigneur du Fourny, who had encouraged its publication, and by two other friars at the monastery. The third and most complete edition is that of 1726–33. A valuable source, it contains in its notes exact references to many original documents.

Anselme, Nicolas (French actor): *see* Baptiste.

Anser, bird genus of the family Anatidae (order Anseriformes). For a general discussion of the genus, *see* goose; for *A. Albifrons, see* white-fronted goose; for *A. anser, see* greylag; for *A. caerulescens, see* snow goose.

Articles are alphabetized word by word, not letter by letter

anseriform, any member of the bird order Anseriformes, which contains the waterfowl, or wildfowl, family Anatidae (ducks, geese, and swans) and the screamers (family Anhimidae).

A brief treatment of anseriforms follows. For full treatment, *see* MACROPAEDIA: Birds.

Waterfowl are typically stocky birds with medium to long necks. The bill is generally of medium length, somewhat flattened, and often has a hooked nail on the tip. There is no characteristic wing shape among the waterfowl, but all of these birds are capable of flight, and many undertake extensive migrations. The screamers are long-legged, and their very large toes are webbed only at the base. Their bill is more chickenlike than ducklike and has a pronounced downward hook.

The anseriforms, along with the ratites, curassows, and tinamous, possess an intromittent male organ. While this is not homologous to the mammalian penis, it serves the same reproductive function. Its presence, and the concomitant ability to mate while swimming, undoubtedly helped the anseriforms as they diversified into their aquatic niches.

Several species of waterfowl have been domesticated. The mallard (*Anas platyrhynchos*) has been domesticated for at least 2,000 years. The muscovy duck (*Cairina moschata*) was domesticated in pre-Columbian South America. The greylag goose (*Anser anser*) and swan goose (*A. cygnoides*) are the basis of the several varieties of domestic geese. Wild waterfowl were important to early man as a source of meat, feathers, fat, and down. In some parts of the modern world, sport hunting of waterfowl is a major leisure activity.

There are three main feeding styles within the waterfowl: dabbling, diving, and grazing. Dabbling ducks feed on or just below the surface and are known for upending to reach food (mostly vegetation) on the bottom of shallow waters. Among the diving waterfowl the freshwater forms generally inhabit fairly shallow waters and feed mostly on the seeds, leaves, and roots of aquatic plants. The marine ducks inhabit deeper sea waters and live on fish and invertebrates.

Waterfowl are typically social birds and have a well-developed set of formal displays and group cohesion signals; for instance, in many species a head-shaking or chin-lifting display is used to coordinate group takeoff. Swans and geese use vocalizations to maintain contact while in flight. Preening and maintenance of plumage is a major individual activity.

Most waterfowl have highly developed, innate pair-forming and bonding displays which differ from species to species. Among the ducks, which generally take a new mate each season, various bows and poses such as the "head-up-tail-up" display exhibit plumage markings that are otherwise not usually seen. In species that mate for life, such as the swans and geese, displays serve to reinforce the pair bond. The "triumph ceremony" of geese, for example, in which both birds call and wave their heads, is commonly performed after the male has driven off a rival.

Almost all waterfowl breed in water, which provides safety and isolation. Territoriality plays a part in mating. Nest site selection and nest building are usually done by the female who pulls together any vegetation within reach. The eggs are usually laid one per day, in the morning. The shells may be white, green, or brown and clutches of the various species average from 3 to 12 eggs. The incubation period ranges from 22 to 39 days and incubation is almost always the job of the female. Shortly after hatching the young waterfowl imprint on their mother. Imprinting is an instinctive response to attach to and follow the nearest large moving object. The down-covered waterfowl follow the mother from the nest within 24 to 48 hours and are soon swimming and feeding. Young ducks may fledge as early as five weeks and are then on their own. Larger species, however, may not fledge for up to five months and geese and swans complete their first migration in the company of the parents. All of these birds are fairly long-lived; in captivity ducks may live 20 years, geese and swans for more than 30.

Migration is a characteristic of many anseriform species, increasing the ecological flexibility of waterfowl. However, as their habitats are being destroyed, many species are facing extreme population pressures.

Ansermet, Ernest (b. Nov. 11, 1883, Vevey, Switz.—d. Feb. 20, 1969, Geneva), conductor known for his authoritative interpretations of the works of Stravinsky and other 20th-century composers and for his keen intellectual approach to problems of contemporary musical aesthetics. He studied at Lausanne and from 1906 to 1910 taught mathematics there. Later he studied composition under the Swiss-born composer Ernest Bloch and conducted under two outstanding figures, Felix Mottl and Arthur Nikisch. About 1914 he met Stravinsky and in 1915 he became conductor of Diaghilev's Ballets Russes. In 1918 he formed the renowned Orchestra de la Suisse Romande, which he led until 1967. He frequently toured Europe and the U.S. and introduced many works by contemporary composers. Late in life he turned against 12-tone music (*e.g.*, in his book *The Fundamentals of Music in the Human Consciousness*, 1961), although he continued to espouse other contemporary music.

His own works include a symphonic poem, settings of poems by Baudelaire, and the orchestration of Debussy's *Épigraphes antiques*.

Ansett Transport Industries Limited, Australian conglomerate founded in 1936 (as

Ansett Airways Proprietary Ltd.) by Reginald Ansett. Head offices are in Melbourne.

Ansett (Sir Reginald since 1969) began in 1931 with a motorcar passenger service in the Western District of the state of Victoria. In 1936 he founded the airline company for service between Melbourne and Hamilton. After World War II the company began new inter-state services and manufacturing and in 1946 changed its name to Ansett Transport Industries Limited. By 1951 the company had extended its activities into hotels and was operating some 200 motor coaches. In 1957 it purchased Australia's largest privately owned airline, Australian National Airways (renamed Ansett Airlines of Australia), and later acquired other regional airlines in Australia and New Guinea. The company secured a license for a television station in Melbourne in 1963 and another one in Brisbane in 1964. Further diversification extended into motels, resorts, freight services, industrial equipment manufacturing, automotive sales, aircraft sales, etc. In 1979 Rupert Murdoch, the newspaper baron, gained control through majority interest in Ansett.

Ansgar, SAINT, Ansgar also spelled ANSKAR, or ANSCHAR (b. probably 801, near Corbie, Austrasia—d. Feb. 3, 865, Bremen, Saxony; canonized 865; feast day February 3), missionary of medieval Europe, first archbishop of Hamburg, and the patron saint of Scandinavia.

Of noble birth, Ansgar entered the Benedictine abbey of Corbie in Picardy, where he was educated. After 823 he taught in the monastic school at Corvey ("New Corbie"), Westphalia, where he also began his pastoral work. When Harald, an exiled Danish king, appealed to the Carolingian emperor Louis I the Pious for support, Louis dispatched Ansgar to accompany and assist the King in evangelizing Denmark. Ansgar in 826 began short-lived missionary work in Schleswig. Harald's downfall in 827 and the death of his assistant, Autbert, were blows to the mission, and in 829 Ansgar returned to the Franks. With the help of Witmar, a monk from Corvey, Ansgar began his evangelization of Sweden. The first to preach the gospel in Sweden, he was cordially received by King Björn.

Louis recalled Ansgar in 831, making him abbot of Corvey and bishop of the newly established diocese of Hamburg. Consecrated in 832, he initiated a mission to all the Scandinavian peoples and went to Rome, where Pope Gregory IV made him archbishop and papal legate to the Scandinavians and Slavs, thereby earning him the title of "the Apostle of the North." At Hamburg, Ansgar founded a monastery and a school, and in 834 Louis endowed him with Turholt Abbey, to be used as the centre of his activities.

When Denmark had become united under King Haarik (Horec) I, he allowed the revival of Ansgar's work in Schleswig. Ansgar lost Turholt after Louis I's death (840); and in 845 Northmen destroyed Hamburg, and the Swedish missions were extinguished by the expulsion of Bishop Gautbert. Returning to paganism, Sweden and Denmark rejected Christianity.

In 847 Louis the German, king of the East Franks, made Ansgar bishop of Bremen, from where he revived and redirected his northern evangelization. He dispatched a missionary to Sweden in 851 and converted the succeeding Danish king Haarik II. He then went to Sweden (853–854), where the King (himself destined for conversion) allowed the Christian missionaries to preach. Ansgar succeeded in thwarting a pagan rebellion before returning to Bremen. He was canonized shortly after his death by Pope St. Nicholas I the Great.

A biography by his successor as bishop of Bremen, St. Rembert, is important as a historical document and portrait. C.H. Robinson's English translation of Rembert's *Anskar* appeared in 1921, followed by É. de Moreau's *Saint Anschaire* in 1930.

Anshan, also spelled ANZAN, city and territory of ancient Elam, north of modern Shīrāz, in southwestern Iran. The city's ruins, covering 350 acres, have yielded important archaeological discoveries, including examples of early Elamite writing. Anshan came into prominence about 2350 BC as an enemy of the Mesopotamian dynasty of Akkad. Its most important period, however, was during the 13th and 12th centuries BC, when, as "kings of Anshan and Susa," Elamite rulers periodically raided Babylonian cities. About 675 BC the country appears to have come under the control of Achaemenian Persians, who bore the title "kings of Anshan" down to the accession of Darius I (522 BC).

Anshar and Kishar, in Mesopotamian mythology, the male and female principles, the twin horizons of sky and earth. Their parents were either Apsu (the watery deep beneath the earth) and Tiamat (the personification of salt water) or Lahmu and Lahamu, the first set of twins born to Apsu and Tiamat. Anshar and Kishar, in turn, were the parents of Anu (An), the supreme heaven god. *See also* Anu.

Anshe Kneset ha-Gedola (religious assembly): *see* Kneset ha-Gedola.

Anskar, SAINT: *see* Ansgar, Saint.

Ansky, S., Ansky also spelled AN-SKI, pseudonym of SOLOMON ZANVEL RAPPOPORT (b. 1863, Chashnik, Russia—d. Nov. 8, 1920, Warsaw), Russian Jewish writer and folklorist best known for his play *The Dybbuk.*

Ansky was educated in a Ḥasidic environment and as a young man was attracted to the Jewish Enlightenment and to the populist doctrines of the Narodniki, a group of socialist revolutionaries. For a time he worked among the peasants and contributed articles to the Narodnik journal. His first novel, written in Yiddish, was published in 1884.

Compelled to leave Russia in 1892, he settled in Paris. Working as a factory hand, Ansky studied French folklore and Socialist doctrine and became secretary to the revolutionary émigré Pyotr Lavrov. He also wrote articles and popular poems, many of them for the Jewish Workers' Party, the Bund. In 1905 he was permitted to return to St. Petersburg. He joined the Socialist Revolutionary Party, ideological heir of the Narodniki, and continued to write articles, folktales, and short stories on Jewish life.

In 1911 Ansky organized a large-scale ethnographic expedition to gather Jewish folklore, songs, melodies, manuscripts, and books. His fieldwork was interrupted by the outbreak of World War I, during which he did relief work and wrote about the destruction of the Jewish communities in Poland, Galicia, and Bukovina. Also during this period he produced his most famous work, the classic Yiddish drama *Der Dybbuk* (*The Dybbuk,* 1926). The play, which drew on Jewish mystical folklore, was widely translated and performed, most notably in the celebrated Moscow production of the Hebrew company Habima. It was also set to music and was filmed in Polish and Hebrew.

After the Russian Revolution Ansky was elected to the All-Russia Constituent Assembly, but in 1918 he left for Vilna. The following year he settled near Warsaw and devoted himself to preparing his collected works and to organizing a Jewish ethnographic society. His Yiddish works, in 15 volumes, were published between 1920 and 1925.

Anson, Cap, byname of ADRIAN CONSTANTINE ANSON (b. April 11/17, 1851, Marshalltown, Iowa, U.S.—d. April 14, 1922, Chicago), professional baseball player and manager, known later as Pop, played professionally for 27 years and was still in his team's regular lineup at the age of 46.

Anson played in the National Association, the first professional baseball league, with the Forest City team of Rockford, Ill., in 1871 and with the Philadelphia Athletics (1872–75). He is believed to have batted .352 during the five years. In 1876, when the Chicago National Association team switched to the newly formed National League, Anson joined this club. In 1879 he became manager. He retired as a player and resigned as Chicago manager after the 1897 season and then was nonplaying manager of the New York team in the National League in 1898.

Anson, who played first base for most of his career, was credited with batting championships in 1879, 1881, 1887, and 1888. He hit .399 in 1881 and is thought to have batted over .400 in 1879 and 1887. His total of hits in the National League is given as 2,995 or 3,081 (authorities differ); his National League career batting average is .329 or .339.

As a manager Anson led Chicago to five National League championships. He was elected to the Baseball Hall of Fame in 1939.

Anson, George Anson, Baron (b. April 23, 1697, Shugborough, Staffordshire, Eng.—d. June 6, 1762, Moor Park, Hertfordshire), British admiral whose four-year voyage around the world is one of the great tales of naval heroism. The reforms he instituted as a naval administrator increased the efficiency of the British fleet and contributed to its success in the Seven Years' War (1756–63) against France.

Anson entered the navy in 1712 and became a captain 11 years later. In September 1740 Commodore Anson set off across the Atlantic with six poorly manned, ill-equipped vessels to capture Spanish treasure ships in the Pacific. He lost three ships rounding Cape Horn but went on to raid Spanish mining settlements on the coast of Chile. Although he and his crew suffered incredible hardships while crossing the Pacific in their one remaining ship, the "Centurion," Anson managed to capture a Spanish treasure galleon near the Philippines. He sold this prize for £400,000 in Canton, China, the "Centurion" being the first British warship to enter Chinese waters. By the time he reached England in June 1744, more than half the original crew of nearly 2,000 men had died, chiefly of scurvy.

Baron Anson, detail of an oil painting by an unknown artist, *c.* 1745–46; in the National Maritime Museum, Greenwich, Eng.

By courtesy of the National Maritime Museum, Greenwich, Eng.

Because of the support of the Duke of Newcastle, Anson was first lord of the Admiralty from 1751 to 1756. Although sacked by William Pitt, Anson returned as first lord from 1757 to 1762. His reforms included a reorganization of the fleet, a revision of the articles of war, and the creation of a permanent marine corps. A biography, *Admiral Lord Anson,* by S.W.C. Pack, was published in 1960.

Ansongo, town, Gao *région,* southeastern Mali, West Africa, on the Niger River. It is a mining (antimony) and agricultural (grains, livestock) marketing centre. Prospecting for uranium began in the late 1970s. The Niger is navigable for about 1,000 mi (1,600 km) above Ansongo. Directly east is the Ansongo-Ménaka animal reserve, covering an area of more than 4,300,000 ac (1,750,000 ha). Pop. (1976) 3,483.

Ansonia, city, coextensive with the town (township) Ansonia of New Haven County, southwestern Connecticut, U.S., on the Naugatuck River. From 1651 a part of the township of Derby, it was incorporated as a separate township in 1889 and chartered as a city in 1893. Its separate identity was established in 1843 when Anson Greene Phelps of New York City refused to pay an exorbitant price for land in Derby and established his copper and brass mills at the settlement that took his given name. Heavy machinery was manufactured there as early as 1848. Ansonia and the neighbouring cities of Derby and Shelton form one of the important groups of industrial communities of the state. Pop. (1980) 19,039.

Anspach (West Germany): *see* Ansbach.

Anstey, Christopher (b. Oct. 31, 1724, Brinkley, Cambridgeshire, Eng.—d. Aug. 3, 1805, Bath, Somerset), poet whose epistolary novel in verse, *The New Bath Guide,* went through more than 30 editions between 1766 and 1830. After an education at Eton and at King's College, Cambridge, Anstey in 1754 inherited an independent income; and in 1770 he settled permanently at Bath, fashionable spa of the 18th century. *The New Bath Guide; or, Memoirs of the B—R—D Family* (1766) is a satire on various aspects of Bath life.

Anstey, detail of an engraving by F. Engleheart after a drawing by J. Thurston

Mary Evans Picture Library, London

Much of the poem's charm arises from Anstey's mastery of versification, but the element of parody, together with the simple caricature and occasional accurate delineation of scenes well-known to 18th-century readers, helps to explain the poem's popularity.

ant, any member of the approximately 8,000 species of the insect family Formicidae (order Hymenoptera). Ants occur worldwide but are especially common in hot climates. All ants are social in habit; *i.e.,* they live together in organized colonies, and they range in size from 2 to about 25 millimetres (about 0.08 to 1 inch). Their colour is usually yellow, brown, red, or black. A few genera (*e.g., Pheidole* of North America) have a metallic lustre.

Typically, an ant has a large head and a slender, oval abdomen joined to the thorax, or midsection, by a small waist. The antennae are elbowed. The mouth has two sets of jaws: the outer pair is used for carrying objects such as food and for digging, and the inner pair is used for chewing. Some species have a powerful sting at the tip of the abdomen.

There are generally three castes, or classes: queens, males, and workers. Some species live in the nests of other species as parasites; *i.e.,* the larvae are given food and nourishment by the host workers. *Wheeleriella santschii* is a parasite in the nests of *Monomorium salomonis,* the most common ant of northern Africa.

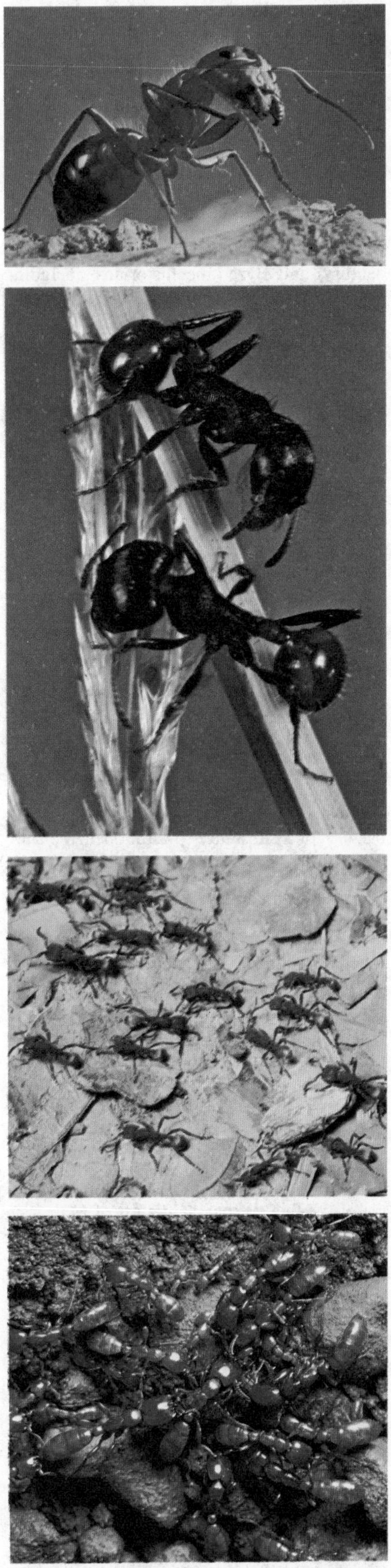

(Top to bottom) The carpenter ant (*Camponotus*) may be a household pest; when some of the seeds stored by harvester ants (*Pogonomyrmex*) germinate, the young plants are carried from the nest and may grow around the nest opening; army ants (*Eciton*) do not build nests but form a clustered mass with their bodies; driver ants (*Dorylus*), like army ants, have enormous wingless queens, who lay up to about 25,000 eggs at a time

(Top two) Grace Thompson—The National Aubudon Society Collection/ Photo Researchers (bottom two) E.S. Ross

Most ants live in nests, which may be located in the ground or under a rock or built aboveground and made of twigs, sand, or gravel. Carpenter ants (*Camponotus*)—large, black ants common in North America—live in old logs and timbers. Some species live in trees or in the hollow stems of weeds. Tailor, or weaver, ants, found in the tropics of Africa (*e.g., Tetramorium*), make nests of leaves and similar materials held together with silk secreted by the larvae. *Dolichoderus,* a South American genus, glues together bits of animal feces for its nest. The widely distributed pharaoh ant (*Monomarium pharaonis*), a small yellowish insect living in houses, builds its nest outdoors only in warm climates. Army ants, of the subfamily Dorylinae, are nomadic and notorious for the destruction of plant and animal life in their path. The army ants of tropical America (*Eciton*), for example, travel in columns, eating insects and other invertebrates along the way. Periodically the colony rests for several days while the queen lays her eggs. As the colony travels, the growing larvae are carried along. Habits of the African driver ant (*Dorylus*) are similar. The fire ant (*Solenopsis saevissima*), introduced into Alabama from South America, had spread throughout the southern United States by the mid-1970s. It inflicts a painful sting and is considered a pest because it builds large mounds as nests. Effective, ecologically acceptable methods to control it are being sought.

The life cycle of the ant has four stages—egg, larva, pupa, and adult—and spans a period of 8 to 10 weeks. The queen spends her life laying eggs. The workers are females and do the work of the nest; the larger ones, the soldiers, defend the colony. At certain times of the year, many species produce winged males and queens. They fly into the air, where they mate. The male dies soon afterward, and the fertilized queen establishes a new nest.

The food of ants consists of both plant and animal substances. Certain species, including those of the genus *Formica,* often eat the eggs and larvae of other ants or those of their own species; other species eat the liquid secretions of plants. The honey ants (Camponotinae, Dolichoderinae) eat the so-called honeydew, a by-product of digestion secreted by certain aphids. The ant usually obtains the liquid by gently stroking the aphid's abdomen with its antennae. Some genera (*Leptothorax*) eat the honeydew that has fallen onto the surface of a leaf. The so-called Argentine ant (*Iridomyrmex humilis*) and the fire ant also eat honeydew. Harvester ants (*Messor, Pogonomyrmex*) store grass, seeds, or berries in the nest; whereas ants of the genus *Trachymyrmex* of South America eat only fungi, which they cultivate in their nests. The Tes leaf-cutting ant (*Atta texana*) is a pest that often strips the leaves from plants to provide nourishment for its fungus beds.

The social behaviour of the ants, along with that of the honeybees, is the most complex in the insect world. Slave-making ants, which include many species, have a variety of methods for "enslaving" the ants of other species. The queen *Bothriomyrmex decapitans* of Africa, for example, allows herself to be dragged by *Tapinoma* ants into their nest. She then bites off the head of the *Tapinoma* queen and begins laying her own eggs, which are cared for by the "enslaved" *Tapinoma* workers.

ant bear, common name sometimes used for the giant anteater and for the aardvark. *See* anteater; aardvark.

ant cow (insect): *see* aphid.

anta, in architecture, slightly projecting column at the end of a wall, produced either by a thickening of the wall or by attachment of a separate strip. The former type, commonly flanking porches of Greek and Roman temples, is a masonry vestige of the wooden structural posts used to reinforce the brick walls of such early antique temples as the Heraeum of Olympia (*c.* 600 BC).

The bases and capitals of these antas were not required to conform to the style, or order, of the temple column. The attached strip anta is commonly found in Renaissance and post-Renaissance styles of architecture influenced by classical antiquity. As a decorative feature, the anta is considered to be the forerunner of the pilaster (*q.v.*).

Columns set in the space between antas, such as those in the temple of Ramses III at Madīnat Habu, Egypt, are termed "in antis."

antacid, also spelled ANTIACID, any substance, such as sodium bicarbonate, magnesium hydroxide, or aluminum hydroxide, used to counteract or neutralize gastric acids and relieve the discomfort caused by gastric acidity. Indigestion, gastritus, and several forms of ulcers are alleviated by the use of antacids.

Numerous nonpresciption liquid antacids reduce the acidity of indigestion or gastritus for up to three hours after a single dose. Of the many liquid antacids available, those consisting of either magnesium or aluminum alkalinizing agents are preferable to antacids containing calcium salts, which have been shown to lead to a secondary increase in gastric acidity. The timing of antacid ingestion is important; they should be taken when gastric acidity is most likely to be increasing, namely, one hour and three hours after each meal and at bedtime. Although they are more convenient, antacid tablets are not nearly so effective as liquid forms. The usual dose of concentrated antacids is one tablespoon and of regular antacids twice that amount. Because magnesium-containing antacids tend to have a laxative effect if used regularly and aluminum-containing antacids tend to constipate, many patients prefer to alternate doses of the two types.

Acid secretion itself can be reduced by the use of agents that block the action of histamine on the acid-secreting cells of the stomach. Two such agents, cimetidine (Tagamet) and ranitidine (Zantac), are quite effective and generally well tolerated in full doses for at least two months and for longer periods at reduced dosage.

In the treatment of ulcers, antacids may be used to neutralize hydrochloric acid and pepsin, to control pain, and even, in some cases, to promote healing. Not all antacids, however, are equally beneficial in ulcer treatment. Those that contain calcium may have undesirable side effects. Sodium bicarbonate should not be taken over long periods of time. Doctors should evaluate the antacids that they prescribe in order to be certain that the drugs do not contain excessive sodium for patients with high blood pressure or heart disorders. Patients with kidney disease should not take antacids that contain magnesium.

A special group of drugs known as anticholinergics have been used for years to delay the emptying of the stomach. By doing so, they also diminish acid secretion and help to reduce the frequency and severity of ulcer pain. These drugs should also be carefully evaluated before they are prescribed. Patients who have a tendency to develop glaucoma, who are markedly debilitated, who have an enlargement of the prostate gland, or who have difficulty urinating should not take anticholinergics.

Antae, also spelled ANTES, federation of eastern Slavic nomadic tribes known by the 3rd century AD, dwelling in southern Russia between the Dnepr and Dnestr rivers. A powerful people with highly developed agriculture, handicrafts, and ironwork, the Antae fought the Goths, who were fleeing westward from the Huns in the 4th century. In the early 6th century they joined in Slavic raids against the Byzantine Empire but were nearly annihilated by the Avars, who passed through their lands *c.* 560. Information about the Antae was recorded by the Gothic historian Jordanes (6th century) and Byzantine historians, including Procopius of Caesarea (6th century).

Antaeus, in Greek mythology, a giant of Libya, the son of the sea god Poseidon and the Earth goddess Gaea. He compelled all strangers who were passing through the country to wrestle with him. Whenever Antaeus touched the Earth (his mother), his strength was renewed, so that even if thrown to the ground, he was invincible. Heracles, in combat with him, discovered the source of his strength and, lifting him up from Earth, crushed him to death.

antagonism, in chemotherapy, any action by which one drug opposes, resists, or counteracts the effects of another. Antagonism may result from changes in the distribution, biotransformation, or excretion of the drugs or may occur because the two drugs act at the same specific cell component (receptor antagonism). A drug that combines with receptors and initiates action has both affinity (*i.e.*, the drug is localized at the receptor) and intrinsic activity (efficacy); such drugs are called agonists.

Sulfonamides, for example, are agonists; they act by preventing the incorporation by certain bacteria of a substance (p-aminobenzoic acid, PABA) necessary for their growth. Substances closely related to PABA (*e.g.*, procaine) have an action similar to it and counteract (*i.e.*, antagonize) sulfonamide action.

In some instances, drug antagonists are deliberately combined, as when digitalis, a stimulant, and quinidine, a depressant, are used to treat congestive heart failure (physiological antagonism). In other instances, antagonism is not advantageous, as when aspirin and probenecid are used to treat gout; either is effective alone, but the action of probenecid is prevented by aspirin when the two are used together.

Antaimoro, also spelled ANTIMORONA, a Malagasy people living on and near the southeastern coast of Madagascar. Antaimoro (People of the Banks) speak a dialect of Malagasy, the West Indonesian language that is common to all Malagasy peoples. Traditionally they were ruled by five families of Arabic origin who probably came to Madagascar at different times during the 16th century. Several Antaimoro clans claim Indian origins, while others consider themselves indigenous. After the final French conquest of the island in 1895, Antaimoro political organization was brought into the colonial structure.

The Antaimoro live in dense concentration along river valleys, their villages often adjoining one another and running up and over the tops of the rolling hills characteristic of their land. Others live in a narrow band of coastal swamp and are renowned fishermen. Antaimoro are known for their large canoes rigged with square sails. Women fish in streams or from shore, while men go to open waters. Antaimoro grow rice and other crops in the rich alluvial soils and keep cattle in areas away from the coast. In the past they refined salt for use in trade, and they were celebrated healers and purveyors of magical medicines. Other than the immigrants from Pakistan and the Comoros who have come only in relatively recent times, the Antaimoro are among a small minority of Malagasy people who actively practice Islām. For many years Antaimoro were the only indigenous literate recorders of local history and culture, although the Arabic texts left by early Antaimoro authors have yet to be examined systematically.

Antakya (Turkey): *see* Antioch.

Antalya, Ancient Greek ATTALIA, city and Mediterranean port, capital of Antalya *il* (province), southwestern Turkey, on the Gulf of Antalya. Attalia was founded as a seaport in the 2nd century BC by Attalus II, a king of Pergamum. It was bequeathed to the Romans by his successor, Attalus III. St. Paul and St. Barnabas embarked from the seaport on their evangelical mission to Antioch. The "Hadrian Gate," a marble portal of three identical arches, was built to commemorate a visit by Hadrian in AD 130.

The Yivli Minare (centre) at Antalya, Tur.
Peter Fraenkel—Ostman Agency

During the Middle Ages the city was a Byzantine stronghold and an important embarkation point for troops going to Palestine during the Crusades. It was captured by the Turkish Seljuq ruler Kay-Khusraw in 1207 and soon became the most important town and port of the region. Although it was first occupied by the Ottoman sultan Bayezid I in 1391, its incorporation into the Ottoman Empire was delayed until the late 15th century because of the disruption caused by the invasion of Timur (Tamerlane). In the tripartite agreement of 1917 for the postwar division of the Ottoman Empire among Italy, France, and the United Kingdom, Italy claimed Antalya and its hinterland. Italian troops occupied the district in 1919 but were driven out in July 1921 by Turkish nationalist forces.

With a subtropical warm climate and an abundance of ancient sites nearby, Antalya is the chief tourist resort on the Turkish Riviera. The old town, surrounded by fortified walls restored during Roman, Byzantine, and Seljuq periods, occupies the summit of a low cliff overlooking the harbour. Notable monuments include an ancient tower, probably once used as a lighthouse, and a Seljuq religious college and mosque dating from 1250. Yivli Minare, a former Byzantine church converted into a Seljuq mosque, now houses the local archaeological museum with Hittite, Greco-Roman, Byzantine, and Turkish collections unearthed from surrounding areas.

Antalya *il,* 8,595 sq mi (22,260 sq km) in area, lies in a crescent-shaped coastal plain hemmed in by the Elmalı and Taurus mountains and drained by the Köprü and Aksu rivers. Occupying the areas known in classical times as Lycia and Pamphylia, it contains the historical sites of Alanya, Aspendus, Perga, and Side. Economic activities include mining (chiefly quartz, chromium, and lignite), agriculture (citrus fruits), and tourism. Pop. (1980) city, 173,501; (1982 est.) *il*, 777,348.

Antampatrana (people): *see* Antandroy.

Antanala (people): *see* Tanala.

Antananarivo, formerly TANANARIVE, town and province (*faritany*), central Madagascar. The town is the capital of Madagascar. It was founded in the 17th century and was the capital of the Hova chiefs. It stands on a high hill. Avenues and flights of steps lead up to a rocky ridge (4,694 ft [1,431 m]) on which stands the Royal Estate, with towered palaces built by the Imerina kings, who captured the town in 1794 and ruled until the end of the 19th century. Below are banks and administrative buildings and lower still the commercial quarter. Public buildings include the French Residency and the Anglican and Roman Catholic cathedrals; and there are research institutes, an observatory, and the Bibliothèque Nationale. The University of Madagascar was founded there in 1961. Industries include tobacco and food processing and the manufacture of leather goods and clothing. Air transport is widely used, and the international airport at Ivato is 11 mi (17 km) north of the city. A railway connects the capital with Toamasina, the island's chief port, to the east, as well as with Antsirabe to the south and Lake Alaotra to the north. Main roads from the north, south, east, and west converge at Antananarivo.

The province, with an area of 22,503 sq mi (58,283 sq km), is Madagascar's only landlocked province. The Ankaratra (*q.v.*) highland acts as a watershed, and streams flow from the area to both the east and west coasts. It is a region of hills, lakes, and hot springs (*see* Antsirabe). Livestock (cattle, pigs, sheep, and poultry) is important, and Tsiroanomandidy, west of the capital, is a major zebu cattle trading centre. There are large rice fields, vegetable farms, orchards, and vineyards. Pop. (1982 est.) city, 600,000; (1977) province, 2,322,019.

Antandroy, also called ANTAMPATRANA, a Malagasy people living in southernmost Madagascar. Antandroy (People of the Thorn Bush) speak a dialect of Malagasy, the West Indonesian language that is common to all Malagasy peoples; their chiefs claim Indian origins. The Antandroy maintained their independence from interior or western Malagasy kingdoms (*e.g.*, Merina and Sakalava), and at the time of the French conquest in 1895 they were divided among five small states that observed the four-tiered social stratification common to Madagascar. The French quickly dissolved all kingdoms and incorporated the Antandroy into their colony.

The Antandroy live in densely populated areas separated by virtually empty expanses of swamp and forest. Coastal Antandroy are fishermen, but they are not as renowned for this as are some of their neighbours. Cattle are kept by Antandroy living away from the coast. As for all Malagasy peoples, rice is the staple crop, while cassava, yams, and bananas are also important.

ʿAntar, Romance of, tales of chivalry centred on the black Arab desert poet and warrior ʿAntarah ibn Shaddād, one of the poets of the celebrated pre-Islāmic collection *al-Muʿallaqāt*. It was composed anonymously between the 8th and 12th centuries, though the *Romance* itself credits the 9th-century philologist al-Aṣmaʿī with its authorship. Written in rhymed prose (*sajʿ*) interspersed with 10,000 poetic verses, it is commonly divided into 32 books, each leaving the conclusion of a tale in suspense.

The *Romance* relates the fabulous childhood of ʿAntar, son of an Arab king by a black slave girl, hence regarded as a bastard by his people, and the adventures he undertakes to attain the hand of his cousin ʿAblah in marriage. These take him beyond Arabia and his own time period to Iraq, Iran, Syria, Spain, North Africa, Egypt, Constantinople, Rome, and the Sudan; they bring him in contact with a Byzantine emperor and with Frankish, Spanish, and Roman kings. Though childless by ʿAblah, ʿAntar fathers several children, including two crusaders, Ghadanfar (by the sister of the King of Rome) and Jufrān (Godfrey, by a Frankish princess).

The *Romance of ʿAntar* evolved out of a Bedouin tradition that stressed nobility of character and desert chivalry and of which ʿAntar was made the epitome. With the advent of Islām, it assumed a new outlook that reinterpreted ʿAntar as a precursor of the new religion. A strong Persian hand in the later authorship of the *Romance*—evidenced by the detailed knowledge of Persian history and court life—then shows ʿAntar in Iran. The *Romance* finally incorporated elements encountered among the crusaders, displaying a finer understanding of the West than European writers of the period had of the Muslim East.

Antarctic anticyclone, large atmospheric high-pressure centre that exists continuously over Antarctica. The Antarctic anticyclone contains the world's coldest surface air because of the Antarctic's polar location, large land area, and high altitude. A semipermanent front, where violent storms frequently occur, separates the Antarctic anticyclone from the maritime polar air masses to the north.

Antarctic Archipelago (Antarctica): *see* Palmer Archipelago.

Antarctic Circle, parallel, or line of latitude around the Earth, at 66°30′ S. Because the Earth's axis is inclined about 23½° from the vertical, this parallel marks the northern limit of the area within which, for one day or more each year, at the summer and winter solstices, the Sun does not set (about December 22) or rise (about June 21). The length of continuous day or night increases southward from one day at the Antarctic Circle to six months at the South Pole. The South Pole is located on the central ice-covered plateau of the large continental mass, the Antarctic, which almost fills the area within the Antarctic Circle. On any particular date, the length of day and night at the Antarctic Circle is the converse of those at the Arctic Circle. The Antarctic circle, which separates the South Frigid Zone from the South Temperate Zone, was first crossed by Capt. James Cook on January 17, 1773.

Antarctic Circumpolar Current, also called WEST WIND DRIFT, surface oceanic current encircling Antarctica and flowing from west to east. Affected by adjacent land masses, submarine topography, and prevailing winds, the Antarctic Circumpolar Current is irregular in width and course. Its motion is further complicated by continuous exchange with other water masses at all depths. The volume of transport south of latitude 40° S is thought to be at least 25,000,000 cu m (880,000,000 cu ft) per second. The term West Wind Drift is also a proper term for a large-scale system of oceanic currents in the Atlantic and Pacific oceans.

Antarctic Convergence, also called SOUTHERN HEMISPHERE POLAR FRONT, major boundary zone of the world's oceans that separates the waters surrounding Antarctica into Antarctic and sub-Antarctic regions. South of the convergence cold, dense surface waters sink and flow northward, thus creating a major meridional circulation system. This zone of convergence forms a significant biological boundary. There are many species of plants and of birds, fish, and other animals that are typical of Antarctic water and rare on the other side of the convergence.

Antarctic Intermediate Water, ocean water mass found in all the southern oceans at depths of about 1,650 to 4,000 ft (500 to 1,200 m), characterized by temperatures of 37° to 45° F (3° to 7° C) and salinities of 33.8 to about 34.5 parts per thousand. This water mass forms at the Antarctic Convergence in the latitudinal belt between 50° and 60° S, where water with the relatively low salinity of 33.8 parts per thousand is cooled to about 40.7° F. The resulting density, 1.02702, causes the water to sink beneath the surface before it slowly flows laterally northward. It becomes modified by mixing with other waters, but it is still discernible as minima in temperature and salinity profiles obtained at hydrographic stations as far north as latitude 35° N in the Atlantic Ocean and latitude 20° S in the Indian and Pacific oceans.

Antarctic Ocean, also called SOUTHERN OCEAN, the southern portions of the Pacific, Atlantic, and Indian oceans and their tributary seas surrounding Antarctica. Unbroken by any other continental land mass, the Antarctic Ocean's narrowest constriction is the Drake Passage, 690 mi (1,112 km) wide, between South America and the tip of the Antarctic Peninsula. The structure of the ocean floor includes a continental shelf usually less than 160 mi wide that attains its maximum width of more than 1,600 mi in the vicinity of the Weddell and Ross seas. There are oceanic basins farther north that are as much as 14,765 ft (4,500 m) deep, defined by oceanic rises and often marked by ranges of abyssal hills. There are also narrow oceanic trenches with high relief marking the sides of the trenches, such as the South Sandwich Trench on the eastern side of the South Sandwich Islands. Other relief features include oceanic plateaus, rising from the oceanic basins to depths of less than 6,560 ft below sea level, and forming rather flat regions which are often covered by relatively thick sedimentary deposits. The most extensive such plateau is the Campbell, or New Zealand, Plateau, which rises southeast of New Zealand and extends southward beyond the Campbell Islands.

The flow of currents in the Antarctic is complex. Water cooled by the coastal ice masses of the Antarctic continent sinks and flows northward along the ocean bottom, and is replaced at the surface by an equal volume of warmer water flowing south from the Indian, Pacific, and Atlantic oceans. The meeting point of the two is the Antarctic convergence, where conditions favour the development of phytoplankton, consisting of diatoms and other single-celled plants. The ocean's most important organism in the higher food chain is the small, shrimp-like krill. Animals on the sea bottom of the near-shore zone include the sessile hydrozoans, corals, sponges, and bryozoans, as well as the foraging, crablike pycnogonids and isopods, the annelid worm polychaete, echinoids, starfish, and a variety of crustaceans and mollusks. At sea bottom there are also eelpouts (Zoarcidae), sea snails (Liparidae), rat-tailed fishes (Macrouridae), and codlike fishes (Gadidae). Rare nonbony types of fish in the Antarctic zone include hagfish and skates. Many species of deep-sea fish are known south of the Antarctic Convergence, but only three, a barracuda and two lantern fishes, seem to be confined to this zone.

Antarctic Peninsula, also called PALMER PENINSULA, GRAHAM LAND, or TIERRA DE O'HIGGINS, peninsula claimed by Britain as part of the British Antarctic Territory (*q.v.*) and also claimed by Chile and Argentina. It forms an 800-mi (1,300-km) northward extension of Antarctica toward the southern tip of South America. The peninsula is ice-covered and mountainous, the highest point being Mt. Jackson (rising more than 10,000 ft [3,050 m]). Marguerite Bay indents the west coast, and Bransfield Strait separates the peninsula from the South Shetland Islands to the north. Many other islands and floating ice shelves lie off the coast. One of the first recorded sightings of Antarctica occurred on Jan. 30, 1820, when William Smith, a sealer, and Edward Bransfield, of the Royal Navy, sailed through what is now Bransfield Strait and saw the Antarctic Peninsula to the south. Countries operating Antarctic Survey stations on the peninsula or adjacent islands in 1979 were Argentina, Great Britain, Chile, Poland, the United States, and the Soviet Union.

Antarctic Treaty (Dec. 1, 1959), an agreement signed by 12 nations, in which the Antarctic continent was made a demilitarized zone to be preserved for scientific research. The treaty was the result of a conference in Washington, D.C., attended by representatives of Argentina, Australia, Belgium, Britain, Chile, France, Japan, New Zealand, Norway, South Africa, the United States, and the U.S.S.R. Later other nations acceded to the treaty.

The treaty did not deny or support national claims to territorial sovereignty in Antarctica, but it did forbid all contracting parties from establishing military bases, carrying on military manoeuvres, testing any weapons (including nuclear weapons), or disposing of radioactive wastes in the area. The treaty encouraged the freedom of scientific investigation and the exchange of scientific information and personnel in Antarctica. The treaty bound its members for a period of 30 years.

Antares, also called ALPHA SCORPII, red, semiregular variable star, with apparent visual magnitude about 0.9, the brightest star in the zodiacal constellation Scorpius and one of the largest known stars, having several hundred times the diameter of the Sun and several thousand times the Sun's luminosity. It has a fifth-magnitude blue companion. Antares lies about 400 light-years from the Earth. The name seems to come from a Greek phrase meaning "rival of Ares" (*i.e.,* rival of the planet Mars) and was probably given because of the star's colour and brightness.

antbird, family name FORMICARIIDAE, any of numerous birds of the American tropics (order Passeriformes). There are about 230 species in more than 50 genera. Like their near relatives the Furnariidae, antbirds are highly diverse; all are of small to medium size (9.5 to 37 centimetres [4 to 14 inches]), with drab, fluffy plumage (sexes usually unlike); short, rounded wings; variable but often rather stout bill with

Barred antshrike (*Thamnophilus doliatus*)
Paul Schwartz

a hooked (sometimes also notched) tip; strong legs; and front toes partly joined at the base. Most make cup-shaped nests. All have loud, usually unmusical voices that may be heard in echo duets. Antbirds are insectivorous, and many species habitually follow columns of marching ants. Beyond these few generalizations, subgroups are vaguely characterized by popular names likening them to birds of other families—antwren, antpitta, antshrike, ant-vireo, antthrush (the former name of the group); still other antbirds are called bare eyes, fire eyes, and bush bird.

The gnateaters, or antpipits, of the genus *Conopophaga*, eight or nine species of moderately long-legged, short-tailed ground birds, were formerly grouped with the genus *Corythopis* (*see* antpipit) in a separate family, but an increasing number of authorities include them in the Formicariidae.

anteater, any of four species of toothless, insect-eating mammals, family Myrmecophagidae, placed with the armadillos and sloths in the order Edentata. Anteaters are found in tropical savannas and forests from Mexico to northern Argentina and Uruguay. They are densely furred, long-tailed animals, with long skulls and tubular muzzles. The mouth opening is small and the tongue long and wormlike. The salivary glands are large and secrete sticky saliva.

Anteaters live alone or in pairs and feed mainly on ants and termites. They obtain their prey by inserting their long, sticky tongues into insect nests torn open by the long, sharp, curved claws of their forefeet.

The giant anteater (*Myrmecophaga tridactyla*), sometimes called ant bear, is the largest of the anteaters. Gray with a diagonal, white-bordered black stripe on each shoulder, it attains a length of about 1.8 metres (6 feet), including the long, bushy tail, and weighs up to 25 kilograms (55 pounds). It is primarily diurnal, except in inhabited areas, where it is most active at night. It walks with a shuffle, bearing its weight on the knuckles of its forelimbs. When harried, it is capable of a galloping run. Like the other anteaters, it grasps and claws when forced to fight. The female bears a single young after a gestation period of about 190 days.

Unlike the giant anteater, the lesser anteater, or tamandua (*Tamandua*), and the two-toed anteater (*Cyclopes didactylus*) are arboreal and mainly nocturnal. Members of both genera have prehensile tails, which they use in climbing.

Depending on the authority, there are one or two species of lesser anteaters. These animals are often tan with a blackish "vest" around the shoulders and on the body; some are entirely tan or entirely blackish. Lesser anteaters are about 1.2 m long including the tail. They have shorter fur and shorter muzzles than the giant anteater.

The two-toed, silky, or dwarf anteater is the smallest and least known member of the family. It attains an overall length of about 37 centimetres (15 inches), about one-half of which is tail. It has a silky, yellowish coat and has two clawed toes on each forefoot (the giant and lesser anteaters have four).

Lesser anteater (*Tamandua tetradactyla*)
Robert C. Hermes—Annan Photo Features

Animals known as anteaters but not of the family Myrmecophagidae include the aardvark (*q.v.*), or Cape anteater; the pangolin (*q.v.*), or scaly anteater; the numbat (*q.v.*), or banded anteater; and the echidna (*q.v.*), or spiny anteater.

Antelami, Benedetto (b. *c.* 1150—d. *c.* 1230, Parma, Italy), foremost Italian architect and sculptor of his time. He is known to have done the sculptures in the magnificent baptistery of Parma cathedral. His last work was the decoration of the church of S. Andrea at Vercelli, the individual style of which helped him win his place as the leading Italian Romanesque sculptor.

"Deposition," marble relief by Benedetto Antelami; in the cathedral of Parma, Italy
Anderson—Alinari from Art Resource/EB Inc.

antelope, any of numerous Old World grazing or browsing mammals belonging to the family Bovidae (order Artiodactyla), which also includes sheep, goats, and cattle. The pronghorn of North America, though a member of the family Antilocapridae, is also sometimes referred to as an antelope. The term has no precise zoological definition.

Antelopes are even-toed, hoofed mammals that typically are swift, slender, and graceful plains dwellers. Most are African; the others, except for the North American pronghorn, are Eurasian. Antelopes range in shoulder height from 25 centimetres (10 inches) in the royal antelope (*Neotragus pygmaeus*) of Africa to 175 cm in the giant eland (*Taurotragus derbianus*), also of Africa. The male antelope, and sometimes the female, bears distinctive, backwardly curved horns. The horns vary in form, some being short and spikelike, as in the duikers (*Cephalophus* and *Sylvicapra*); some spirally twisted, as in the kudus (*Tragelaphus*); and some long and lyre shaped, as in the impala (*Aepyceros*).

The horns of certain species are valued as trophies and may be the principal goal of a hunter. Hides and meat—the latter often coarse and rather dry—are also sought. A number of antelopes are listed in the *Red Data Book* of rare and endangered animals. The Arabian oryx (*Oryx leucoryx*), the giant sable antelope (*Hippotragus niger variani*), and others are almost extinct.

For information on related animals, *see* duiker; eland; impala; kudu; oryx; pronghorn; royal antelope; sable antelope.

antenna, a component of electronic systems designed to produce radio waves from electrical impulses (transmitting antenna), or, conversely, to intercept radio waves and convert them back into electrical impulses (receiving antenna). It is an integral part of virtually all electronic communications networks.

A brief treatment of antennas follows. For full treatment, *see* MACROPAEDIA: Electronics.

The size and shape of an antenna depends upon the particular purpose for which it is used; for instance, whether it is a transmitting or receiving antenna, what frequencies it must handle, and the desired pattern of radiation. Antennas can range in size from short metal rods used on transistor radios to dish-shaped antennas thousands of feet in diameter used in radio telescopes to detect radio waves from deep space.

The waves transmitted and received by antennas are electromagnetic waves, caused by the interplay of electric and magnetic fields. Electromagnetic waves are generated by alternating electric currents. A transmitting antenna is essentially an electrical conductor designed to radiate patterns of electromagnetic waves (radio signals) corresponding to an impressed signal current. The electromagnetic waves radiated from the transmitting antenna (at a radio or television broadcasting station, for instance) move outward like an expanding soap bubble. When this expanding electromagnetic wave front intercepts a receiving antenna, it sets up an alternating electric current in the antenna that accurately matches the one supplied to the transmitting antenna. This electric signal is then decoded by the receiving station (a radio or television set, for instance), and converted back into sound or visual images.

Many different types of antennas have been developed for different purposes. An antenna may be designed specifically to transmit or to receive, although these functions may be performed by the same antenna. A transmitting antenna, in general, must be able to handle much more electrical energy than a receiving antenna. An antenna may also be designed for the specific frequencies it is intended to handle. In the United States, amplitude modulation (AM) radio broadcasting, for instance, is done at frequencies between 535 and 1,605 kHz; at these frequencies, a wavelength is hundreds of yards long, and the size of the antenna is therefore not critical. Frequency modulation (FM) radios, on the other hand, operate from 88 to 108 MHz. At these frequencies a typical wavelength is about 3 metres (10 feet) long, and the antenna must be adjusted more precisely to the electromagnetic wave, both in transmitting and receiving. Antennas may consist of single lengths of wire or rods in various shapes (dipole, loop, and helical antennas), or of more elaborate arrangements of elements (linear, planar, or electronically steerable arrays). Reflectors and lens antennas use a parabolic dish to collect and focus the energy of electromagnetic waves, in much the same way that a parabolic mirror in a reflecting telescope collects light rays. Directional antennas are designed to be aimed directly at the broadcasting source and are used in direction-finding.

The Scottish physicist James Clerk Maxwell first predicted the existence of electromagnetic waves, of which he claimed light was one variety, in his 1873 work *A Treatise on Electricity and Magnetism.* The German physicist Heinrich Hertz confirmed Maxwell's predictions in a series of experiments conducted in 1885–89. During the course of these experiments, Hertz set up the first rudimentary antenna to generate and receive electromagnetic waves. Hertz's first antenna consisted simply of two flat, square metal plates. Later on he added cylindrical reflectors to improve reception.

In the next decade the Italian physicist Guglielmo Marconi introduced important improvements into the antenna and other pieces of radio equipment. In early radio experiments the size and shape of the antenna generally determined the frequency of the electromagnetic waves used. One of the major breakthroughs in antenna development occurred after the development of the electronic oscillator, which took over the task of determining the operating frequency of radio transmission and reception. This revolutionized antenna design, for the shape of an antenna could now be determined by the requirements of transmission and reception rather than by frequency control. The development of communications systems using different parts of the electromagnetic spectrum brought about new features in antenna design. The use of microwaves in the 1930's, for instance, called for antennas shaped like a bullhorn (*see* wave guide), while the discovery of radio signals originating in deep space led to the development of huge parabolic radio telescopes.

antenna array, system of two or more antennas or antenna elements joined to obtain directional effects.

A broadside antenna array is arranged so that the intensity of electromagnetic radiation is maximized in the direction perpendicular to the line or plane of the array. In the end-fire array, the direction of maximum radiation is parallel to the long axis of the array. A Yagi antenna is a closely spaced array consisting of a driven element (the element connected to the transmission line) and a number of parallel parasitic elements, or reflectors (passive devices that affect the direction of maximum signal pickup and the amount of signal picked up), arranged along a line to obtain the maximum signal from a given direction with a minimum of size. There are many other types of specialized antenna arrays.

Antenor (fl. *c.* 540–500 BC), Athenian sculptor of the late Archaic period who carved the first group of statues of the tyrannicides Harmodius and Aristogiton for the Athenian agora and a kore (a freestanding figure of a maiden) for the Acropolis (now in the Acropolis Museum in Athens).

Antenor's sculpture of the tyrannicides probably dates from shortly after 510. In 480, when Xerxes I captured Athens, the sculpture was carried off to Susa, and no copies of it have been found. Antenor's kore, which probably dates from *c.* 530 to 520, is one of the finest examples of late Archaic sculpture. The greater part of this figure was found in 1886, northwest of the Erechtheum, on the Acropolis. It is of marble, larger than life, and traces of its painted colour remain.

Antequera, city, Málaga province, in the autonomous community (region) of Andalusia, southern Spain, northwest of Málaga, at the foot of the Sierra del Torcal. Neolithic dolmens (Menga, Viera, and El Romeral) attest to prehistoric occupation of the site. The city, known to the Romans as Anticaria and to the Moors as Madīnah Antakira, was reconquered for Christian Spain by the infante Don Fernando (Ferdinand, regent of Castile) in 1410, after which it served as a religious and seignorial centre. Examples of its 16th-century architecture include the churches of Santa María la Mayor of San Francisco and of San Sebastián, which houses works of the great Spanish painter Murillo.

Agriculturally based, Antequera produces olives, cereals, fertilizers, sugar, ice cream, Christmas candles, woollen blankets, and cotton goods. Pop. (1981) 35,171.

Antequera, El de (Spanish: He of Antequera), also called EL INFANTE DE ANTEQUERA: *see* Ferdinand I *under* Ferdinand (Spain: Aragon).

Anterus, SAINT (b. Greece—d. Jan. 3, 236, Rome; feast day January 3), pope for several weeks at the end of 235 and the beginning of 236. He was elected (possibly Nov. 21, 235) while St. Pontian, his successor, was condemned to the Sardinian mines. Anterus was soon prosecuted and sentenced to death. According to the *Liber pontificalis*, he was martyred for having ordered a collection of the acts of the martyrs to be made and included in the archives of the church. The site of his burial in the catacombs was discovered by the Italian archaeologist Giovanni Battista de Rossi in 1854.

Antes (Slavic nomads): *see* Antae.

Antheil, George (b. July 8, 1900, Trenton, N.J., U.S.—d. Feb. 12, 1959, New York City), U.S. composer known for his ultramodern music in the 1920s.

Antheil studied with Ernest Bloch in New York. In 1922 he went to Europe, gave piano recitals, and became prominent in the literary and artistic circles of the Parisian avant-garde. Ezra Pound wrote *Antheil and the Treatise on Harmony* (1924; with supplementary notes, 1927).

His most celebrated work, *Le Ballet mécanique,* scored for player pianos, automobile horns, electric bells, and airplane propellers, produced a hostile outcry in Paris (1926) and New York (1927); on its revival in 1954 it was considered fairly tame. In 1936 Antheil moved to Hollywood and subsequently produced many film scores, among them *Tokyo Joe* (1949), *Angels over Broadway* (1940), and *Fighting Kentuckians* (1950). After about 1939 he abandoned the avant-garde style for a mixture of Classicism, Romanticism, and Impressionism. His other works include six symphonies; the ballet *Capital of the World* (1953); chamber music; and the operas *Transatlantic* (1930), *Helen Retires* (1934), *Volpone* (1953), and *The Wish* (1955). He wrote an autobiography, *Bad Boy of Music* (1945).

anthelmintic, any drug that acts against helminthic infections, *i.e.,* those caused by parasitic worms. The term vermifuge is often applied to remedies used to remove intestinal worms; only rarely do the agents directly kill the parasites. No anthelmintic is completely effective, completely without toxic effect upon the host, or equally active against all worms.

Most of the anthelmintics used in human medicine before World War II were replaced by more efficacious and less toxic drugs after the war. Anthelmintics have been developed to improve livestock production. Hygromycin is an antibiotic used as a feed additive to eliminate or reduce the large roundworms (*Ascaris*), nodular worms (*Oesophagostomum*), and whipworms (*Trichuris*) of swine, and the large roundworms (*Ascaridia*) and cecal worms (*Heterakis*) of poultry.

Intestinal worm infections in general are more easily treated than those in other locations in the body. Because the worms need not be killed by the drug and the drug need not be absorbed when given by mouth, there is usually a wider margin of safety than with drugs for worm infections in other sites. Piperazine, introduced into human medicine about 1950 and shortly thereafter into veterinary medicine, relaxes the large intestinal roundworms (ascarids) and pinworms (oxyurids) of man and domesticated animals so that they are eliminated with the feces. Piperazine, still extensively used for infections of domesticated animals, including poultry, was superseded by the more active pyrvinium pamoate for the treatment of human pinworm infection.

Other anthelmintics include dithiazanine, used for the treatment of the *Strongyloides* and whipworm of man and dog; thiabendazole, used primarily for the treatment of several nematodes of cattle, horses, and sheep but also used for treatment of whipworms and *Strongyloides* of man; tetramisole, used in some European countries, being, unlike most anthelmintics, apparently almost as effective against larval stages of intestinal nematodes as against adult worms in cattle, sheep, and poultry.

Tetrachlorethylene, introduced in 1925 for the treatment of hookworms of man and dogs, is still used for the so-called American hookworm (*Necator americanus*) of man but was superseded by bephenium hydroxynaphthoate for the treatment of the European hookworm (*Ancylostoma duodenale*) of man and by disophenol for the treatment of canine hookworm (*Ancylostoma caninum*). Phenothiazine, introduced in the 1930s, is still used against the wireworm (*Haemonchus contortus*) of sheep and cattle. Quinacrine, an early synthetic World War II antimalarial later superseded, is now often used as an anthelmintic for the removal of the large tapeworms of man; it is also useful in the treatment of tapeworm infection of dogs.

Other compounds used for intestinal worms of domesticated animals, but rarely of man, include arecoline hydrobromide, *n*-butyl chloride, carbon disulfide, copper sulfate, dichlorophen, lead arsenate, phthalofyne, and toluene. Dibutyltin dilaurate is used for tapeworm infections in poultry.

anthem (Greek *antiphōna:* "against voice"; Old English *antefn:* "antiphon"), choral composition with English words, used in Anglican and other English-speaking church services. It developed in the mid-16th century in the Anglican Church as a musical form analogous to the Roman Catholic motet (*q.v.*), a choral composition with a sacred Latin text.

The musical resources needed for performing an anthem are not standardized. At first, unaccompanied choral writing (full anthem) was the norm. In the 16th century the growth of the verse anthem (which used a solo vocal part and eventually many soloists as well as a choir) encouraged the use of instrumental accompaniment, either by the organ or by instrumental groups, such as wind instruments or viols. Shortly after the restoration of the monarchy in 1660 it was common, at least in the royal chapel, to perform anthems with orchestral accompaniment. In the 1700s the full anthem ousted to some extent the verse anthem, although solo passages were occasionally used for special effect.

Both full and verse anthems frequently utilized antiphony, the alternation of two half choirs. These were usually referred to as decani (the dean's side) and cantoris (the precentor's, or choirmaster's, side). The contrast of the half choirs and, in elaborate verse anthems, of subsections for soloists, instruments, or choir, provided a subtle effect of fluctuating tone colour and sonority that often reflected the mood or sense of the text. Verse anthems alternating soloists, instrumental passages, and choir often resembled the cantatas used in Lutheran worship. Among notable composers of anthems are Thomas Tomkins (1572–1656), Henry Purcell (*c.* 1659–95), Handel (1685–1759), Samuel Sebastian Wesley (1810–76), and Ralph Vaughan Williams (1872–1958).

anthemion, design consisting of a number of radiating petals, developed by the ancient Greeks from the Egyptian and Asiatic form known as the honeysuckle or lotus palmette. The anthemion was used widely by the Greeks and Romans to embellish various parts of ancient buildings. The Greeks originally decorated only pottery with the motif, but they soon adapted it to ornament architecture. The single-palmette form appears on acroteria (decorative pedestals), antefixes (roof or cornice elements), and the tops of vertical stelae. The continuous pattern of alternating lotus and palmette springing from connecting spirals decorates especially the cyma recta molding of the cornice.

Anthemion molding on the Erechtheum, the Acropolis, Athens, designed by Mnesicles, 5th century BC
Alison Frantz

Anthemius (d. 472), Western Roman emperor who reigned from April 12, 467, until July 11, 472.

The son-in-law of the Eastern emperor Marcian, Anthemius was appointed to his office by Marcian's successor, Leo I, who wanted help in attacking the Vandals in North Africa. The powerful patrician Ricimer, kingmaker of the Western Empire, accepted Anthemius with the stipulation that his daughter, Alypia, marry Ricimer. Anthemius' popularity in Italy suffered, however, because as a Greek and a philosopher he was suspected of wanting to restore paganism. The vast expedition against the Vandals ended in utter defeat for the Romans. Ricimer and Anthemius quarrelled, and, in 472, the patrician besieged the Emperor in Rome. Anthemius' forces were defeated; he was found disguised as a beggar and beheaded. The 5th-century Christian poet Sidonius Apollinaris wrote a panegyric on him.

antheridium, the male reproductive organ in ferns and mosses. It develops from a single cell into a structure that is frequently club-shaped. The outer layer of the mature antheridium consists of so-called jacket cells; the interior is filled with sperm-producing cells. The corresponding female organ is called the archegonium.

Anthesteria, one of the several Athenian festivals in honour of Dionysus, the wine god, held annually for three days in the month of Anthesterion (February–March) to celebrate the beginning of spring and the maturing of the wine stored at the previous vintage. On the first day libations were offered to Dionysus from the newly opened casks.

The second day was a time of popular merrymaking, but the state performed a secret ceremony in a sanctuary of Dionysus in the Lenaeum, in which the wife of the king archon went through a ceremony of marriage to Dionysus. On these days, it was believed, the souls of the dead came up from the underworld and walked abroad; people chewed leaves of whitethorn and smeared their doors with tar to protect themselves from evil. The third day was a festival of the dead; in fact, the entire festival may have originally been a great annual ceremony for the exorcism of the spirits of the dead.

Anthim OF TREBIZOND: *see* Anthimus I.

Anthimus I, also called ANTHIM OF TREBIZOND (fl. 6th century), Greek Orthodox patriarch of Constantinople (reigned 535–536), the last notable Byzantine churchman explicitly to advocate Monophysitism (*see* Monophysite).

As bishop of Trebizond Anthimus participated in discussions at Constantinople in 532, to effect religious and political unity between East and West. Although avowing support for the orthodox party, Anthimus harboured Monophysite sentiments and corresponded with the chief theoreticians of that doctrine, the patriarchs Severus of Antioch and Theodosius of Alexandria.

On the death of Patriarch Epiphanius in June 535, the empress Theodora, who was sympathetic toward the Monophysites, had Anthimus appointed patriarch of Constantinople. While promising to promote orthodoxy in alliance with Pope Agapetus I, Anthimus secretly furthered the Monophysite cause. Discovering Anthimus' real beliefs on a visit to Constantinople in early March 536, Pope Agapetus convened a synod, broke off ecclesiastical communion with the patriarch, deposed him, and nullified his ministerial power. He was condemned by the council of Constantinople.

Until his death *c.* 548, Anthimus remained in monastic seclusion under the protection of Empress Theodora. The remains of his writings include his Monophysite tracts and anathemas against orthodox Christological doctrine (on the nature and person of Christ), which have been preserved in the *Thesaurus of Orthodoxy,* by the 12th-century Byzantine historian Nicetas Choniates.

Anthimus VI, original name JOANNIDES (b. *c.* 1790, Kutali Island, Aegean Sea—d. 1878, Kandilli, near present Istanbul), Eastern Orthodox patriarch of Constantinople who attempted to maintain his ecclesiastical authority over the rebellious Bulgarian Orthodox Church, and, with others, wrote an Orthodox encyclical letter repudiating Roman Catholic overtures toward reunion.

In about 1840 Anthimus, a monk of a monastery on Mt. Athos, in Greece, was chosen metropolitan of Ephesus, near modern Selçuk, Tur. He later became patriarch of Constantinople, reigning for three intervals: 1845–48, 1853–55, and 1871–73. The successive dismissals and reappointments of Anthimus to the patriarchate reflected the policy of the Turkish rulers of reacting sensitively to political events and of preventing the patriarchate from acquiring political strength.

Together with the patriarchs of Alexandria, Jerusalem, and Antioch, Anthimus wrote the *Encyclical of the Patriarchs* (1848), an open letter to the Orthodox world criticizing papal ambitions to exercise authority over the universal Catholic Church as represented in Pope Pius IX's encyclical letter of Jan. 6, 1848, *In Suprema Petri Apostoli Sede* ("On the Supreme Throne of Peter the Apostle"), which invited the Orthodox Church to reunite with the church of Rome.

Anthimus VII TSATSOS (b. *c.* 1835, possibly Janina, Yugos.—d. December 1913, Halki, Tur.), Eastern Orthodox patriarch of Constantinople (1895–96), theologian, orator, and a leading critic of the Roman Catholic Church.

Like Anthimus VI, his predecessor of a half-century earlier, Anthimus VII is known for his encyclical letter to the Orthodox world refuting a papal encyclical, *Praeclara Gratulationis* ("Splendid Rejoicing") of Pope Leo XIII (June 20, 1894), which proposed grounds for the reunion of the Orthodox and Roman churches. Besides citing the traditional Eastern arguments attacking Western corruption of early Christian doctrine, Anthimus made new charges occasioned by Roman Catholic teaching formulated during the 19th century. He accused the Latin Church of introducing novel approaches to Christian faith, viz., Pope Pius IX's solemn pronouncement in 1854 of the dogma of the Virgin Mary's Immaculate Conception (*i.e.,* the divine act exempting her from original sin) and the first Vatican Council's (1869–70) decree on papal infallibility, which held as necessary for salvation belief in the pope's exemption from error when treating of doctrine and morality.

Anthimus OF IBERIA, Romanian ANTIM IVIREANUL (d. 1716, probably Rumelia), metropolitan of Walachia (now part of Romania), linguist, typographer, and ecclesiastical writer who contributed greatly to the development of the Romanian language and literature by his translation and printing of biblical and liturgical texts and by his own writings in ethics and asceticism. He is also honoured as one of the earliest Romanian nationalist leaders.

The superior of the Walachian monastery of Snagov, he was later chosen bishop of Ramnic and in 1708 became metropolitan of all of Walachia. Famed for his precise typography and artistic frontispieces, usually with floral designs, Anthimus produced a wealth of material in Romanian and Greek, including the New Testament Gospels (1693), which he also translated in a Romanian version in 1697. Desiring to give his people a guide for a Christian life, he compiled the *Margaritare* ("Pearls"), an anthology of the moral and ascetic letters of the 4th-century Greek church father St. John Chrysostom. A proponent of traditional Orthodoxy, he edited in 1699 the *Orthodoxa Confessio Fidei* ("The Orthodox Confession of Faith") by the 17th-century Ukrainian theologian Peter Moghila.

In addition to his own sermons, Anthimus also wrote in Romanian the *Didahii* ("Teachings"), a two-volume collection of moral exhortations containing historically important descriptions critical of the luxurious life of the Walachian boyars (aristocracy). The *Didahii* also is a unique source document on 18th-century Balkan social life.

As an advocate of Walachian nationalism, Anthimus urged his ruler, Prince Constantin, Brâncoveanu, to assist the Russian tsar Peter I the Great in his unsuccessful campaign of 1711 against the Turks. When war broke out between Austria and Turkey in 1716, the Greek administrator for the Turkish regime of Walachia, Nikolaos Mavrokordatos, ordered Anthimus returned to Constantinople under guard. During the journey he was executed by drowning, probably in the Tundzha River. The Antim monastery was erected in Bucharest as a memorial to Anthimus.

anthocorid bug (insect): *see* flower bug.

anthology, literary collection of short pieces or extracts from different authors. The term anthology denoted a garland of flowers (Greek *anthologia*) and, hence, a selection of choice pieces tastefully arranged. The first of these was the *Garland* of Meleager, compiled in the early part of the 1st century BC, followed by the *Garland* of later poets compiled by Philippus of Thessalonica (1st century AD) and a third, which for the first time was called an anthology, by Diogenianus (2nd century). The poems in each of these collections were arranged alphabetically by the initial letter of the opening line. The first collection in which the poems were arranged by subject was the *Circle* of Agathias (late 6th century). All of these anthologies were incorporated into a larger collection by Constantinus Cephalas (late 9th century). This version, revised and augmented in the 10th century, constitutes the *Greek Anthology* (*q.v.*), perhaps the best known collection of its kind in the world.

Other works of the nature of anthologies existed in antiquity; the *Eklogai* ("Selections") of Stobaeus (5th century AD) groups extracts in prose and verse under topics. Anthologies similar to Stobaeus' were common throughout the Middle Ages and furnished the medieval author with the greater part of his learning.

The Renaissance was a great age for anthologies of lyric poetry. Among the best known collections in English are the *Songes and Sonnetes* published by Richard Tottel in 1557, usually referred to as *Tottel's Miscellany*, and *England's Helicon* (1600), containing poems by Spenser, Sidney, Robert Greene, Thomas Lodge, and Shakespeare. A later example, in French, is the famous *Le Parnasse contemporain* (1866–76). Such anthologies of a contemporary school of poets are quite common.

In the 19th century the anthology in English began to be arranged on chronological principles, showing the historical scope and development of a literature, and the works often included essays of a critical or historical nature, for example, Thomas Campbell's *Specimens of the British Poets* (1819). *Des Knaben Wunderhorn* (1805–08; "The Boy's Wonderhorn") was a very influential anthology of German folk songs. Arthur Waley published notable collections of Chinese (1917) and Japanese (1919) poems. The standard anthology of lyric poetry in the Victorian period, Francis Turner Palgrave's *Golden Treasury* (1861), fixed the educated taste for the lyric for several generations. It was superseded in general favour by Sir Arthur Quiller-Couch's *Oxford Book of English Verse* (1900 and 1939); a companion volume, *The Oxford Book of American Verse,* edited by F.O. Matthiessen (1950), is considered an excellent collection of American poetry. Oxford anthologies proliferated with light verse, children's verse, carols, madrigals, and verse compiled by centuries and by other countries. Among other 20th-century anthologies of poetry, *The New Poetry* (1917; rev. and enlarged, 1932), edited by Harriet Monroe and A.C. Henderson, may be mentioned for its historical importance, and Robert Bridges' *Spirit of Man* (1916) for the excellence of its selection of prose and verse. There are similar anthologies in nearly every language. The term anthology is used for a collection of almost every form of writing, *e.g.,* plays, speeches, jokes, and anecdotes.

anthomyiid fly, a common insect of the family Anthomyiidae (order Diptera) resembling the housefly in appearance. The lesser housefly (*Fannia canicularis*) and the latrine fly (*F. scalaris*) are important anthomyiid flies. They breed in filth, can carry diseases, and are often found in the home. Some larvae feed on plants and are serious pests, many are scavengers and live in excrement and decaying material, and others are aquatic. Among the larvae the cabbage maggot (*Hylemya brassicae*), an important pest of Canada and the northern United States, attacks the underground parts of cabbage, cauliflower, broccoli, radishes, and turnips. It was introduced from Europe early in the second half of the 19th century. The best control is treatment of the soil with insecticides.

The onion maggot (*H. antiqua*), found in North America, injures onions by feeding on the underground bulb and stem. The adult is a bristly, gray fly about 6 or 7 millimetres (0.2 to 0.3 inch) long with large wings. It is best controlled by chemical applications before planting. The seed-corn maggot (*H. cilicrura*) feeds in corn, pea, and bean seeds, which consequently either develop into weak plants or fail to sprout. This species has a short life cycle and produces from three to five generations each year. Damage caused by the seed-corn maggot can be reduced by delayed planting.

Another important pest is the spinach leaf miner (*Pegomyia hyoscyomi*). It produces blotches or linear mines (internal passages) on spinach leaves.

Anthoniszoon, Jeroen: *see* Bosch, Hiëronymus.

Anthony (personal name): *see under* Antony, except as below.

Anthony MELISSA (fl. 11th century), Byzantine monk, author whose collection of teachings and maxims taken from Sacred Scripture, early Christian writers, and secular authors promoted a popular Greek Orthodox tradition of moral–ascetical practice.

Anthony, whose surname is derived from the title of his chief work, *Melissa* (Greek: "The Bee"), compiled an anthology based largely on two leading sources for Eastern Orthodox spirituality: the *Hiera Parallēla* ("Sacred Parallels"), commonly credited to the early-8th-century Greek church father John of Damascus, and the *Eklogai* ("Selections"), incorrectly ascribed to the 7th-century Greek master of ascetical theology, St. Maximus the Confessor.

Composed of two books, *Melissa* provides comprehensive extracts from a broad spectrum of early Christian and non-Christian literature, chosen for their relevance to contemplative spirituality and liturgical piety. *Melissa* appears in a turgid 16th-century Latin translation, accompanying the Greek text, in the series by J.-P. Migne (ed.), *Patrologia Graeca,* (vol. 136, 1866). Anthony possibly also wrote an informal work, *Christoithia* ("Good Manners"), designed for the social and moral edification of Greek youth, which gained popularity in Byzantine society. Some historians claim the work is actually that of an 18th-century Greek scholar, Anthony the Byzantine, headmaster of the Greek school in Istanbul, who supposedly in 1720 rendered into literary Greek the *De civilitate morum puerilium* ("On the Civility of Adolescent Manners") by the early-16th-century Humanist Erasmus.

Anthony OF BOURBON, also called ANTHONY OF NAVARRE, French ANTOINE DE BOURBON, or DE NAVARRE, Spanish ANTONIO DE BORBÓN, or DE NAVARRA (b. April 22, 1518—d. Nov. 17, 1562, Andelys, Fr.), king of Navarre, duke of Vendôme, and father of Henry IV of France.

Son of Charles of Bourbon, duke of Vendôme, he married (1548) Jeanne d'Albret, daughter of Henry II, king of Navarre; as sole heir, she brought her husband the title of king of Navarre. Anthony was involved with his brother, Louis I de Bourbon, prince de Condé (*q.v.*), in the Huguenot conspiracy of Amboise, but, nevertheless, he survived to be later named lieutenant general of the French armies (1560), having turned Roman Catholic. He commanded the army that besieged Rouen and there received a mortal wound.

Anthony OF EGYPT, SAINT, Anthony also spelled ANTONY, or ANTONIOS (b. *c.* 251, Koma, near al-Minyā, Heptanomis [Middle Egypt], Egypt—d. Jan. 17?, 355, Dayr Mārī Antonios hermitage, near the Red Sea; feast day January 17), religious hermit and one of the earliest monks, considered the founder and father of organized Christian monasticism. His rule represented one of the first attempts to codify guidelines for monastic living.

A disciple of Paul of Thebes, Anthony began to practice an ascetic life at the age of 20 and after 15 years withdrew for absolute solitude to a mountain by the Nile called Pispir (now Dayr al-Maymūn), where he lived from about 286 to 305. During the course of this retreat, he began his legendary combat against the devil, withstanding a series of temptations famous in Christian theology and iconography. In about 305 he emerged from his retreat to instruct and organize the monastic life of the hermits who imitated him and who had established themselves nearby. When Christian persecution ended after the Edict of Milan (313), he moved to a mountain in the Eastern Desert, between the Nile and the Red Sea, where the monastery Dayr Mārī Antonios still stands. Here he remained, receiving visitors and, on occasion, crossing the desert to Pispir. He ventured twice to Alexandria, the last time (*c.* 350) to preach against Arianism, a heretical doctrine teaching that Christ the Son is not of the same substance as God the Father.

The early monks who followed Anthony into the desert considered themselves the vanguard of God's army, and, by fasting and performing other ascetic practices, they attempted to engage the hosts of demons who often appeared as temptresses in various sensual guises. Rejecting the visual or auditory temptations, the monks believed that they were helping to defeat the forces of evil.

Anthony's spiritual combats with the hosts of evil made his life one long struggle against the devil. St. Athanasius, the bishop of Alexandria, says that Anthony was first tempted by thoughts of family joys and duties and of the difficulty of his chosen life but that the devil, finally finding argument useless and hoping to arouse in Anthony the pride of success, appeared as a cringing black boy admitting that he had been defeated by the saint. At other times, the devil appeared in the guise of a monk bringing bread during his fasts, or in the form of wild beasts, women, or soldiers, sometimes beating the saint and leaving him in a deathly state. Anthony endured many such attacks, and those who witnessed them were convinced they were real. Every vision conjured up by Satan was repelled by Anthony's fervid prayer and penitential acts. So exotic were the visions and so steadfast was Anthony's endurance that the subject of his temptations has often been used in literature and art, notably in the paintings of Hiëronymus Bosch, Matthias Grünewald, and Max Ernst.

From these psychic struggles Anthony emerged as the sane and sensible father of Christian monasticism. The rule that bears his name was compiled from writings and discourses attributed to him in the *Life of St. Antony* (by Athanasius) and the *Apophthegmata patrum* and is still observed by a number of Coptic and Armenian monks.

Anthony's popularity as a saint reached its height in the Middle Ages. The Order of Hospitallers of St. Anthony was founded at La Motte (*c.* 1100), and this institution became a pilgrimage centre for persons suffering from the disease known as St. Anthony's fire (or ergotism; *see* ergot). The black-robed hospitallers, ringing small bells as they collected alms, were a common sight in many parts of western Europe. The bells of the hospitallers, as well as their pigs—allowed by special privilege to run free in medieval streets—became part of the later iconography associated with St. Anthony.

BIBLIOGRAPHY. John Henry Newman, *Church of the Fathers* (1931); Alban Butler Herbert and Donald Attwater Thurston, *Lives of the Saints* (1956); Edward Cuthbert Butler, *Lausiac History of Palladius* (1898–1904); Johannes Quastan, *Patrology*, vol. 3 (1960).

Anthony OF KIEV, also called ANTHONY OF PECHERSK (b. Ukraine—d. 1073, Kiev), founder of Russian monasticism through the institution of the Greek Orthodox ideal of the contemplative life.

Seeking a solitary life, Anthony became a monk in about 1028 at the Greek Orthodox monastery of Esphigmenon on Mt. Athos, in Greece. According to an account contained in the 12th-century *Russian Primary Chronicle* (*Povest vremennykh let*), Anthony was counselled by his abbot to carry the Athonite monastic tradition to Russia. He consequently returned to Kiev, where he settled in a cave on the side of Mt. Berestov, overlooking the Dnieper (Dnepr) River. His fame as a holy hermit and wonder worker spread throughout the region, and by the mid-11th century the number of disciples warranted a larger cave on the same site to house them. When the community of hermits had grown to 15, requiring the construction of a church and refectory, Anthony resigned as spiritual leader and retired to another grotto. Soon the prince of Kiev, Izyaslav, ceded Mt. Beretsov to the monks, and Anthony laid the foundation for the Pecherskaya Lavra (Monastery of the Caves), an institution that later acquired reputation as the cradle of Russian monasticism. Reverting to his Athonite training, he sent to Constantinople for architects to construct the new monastery complex.

By such a foundation Anthony established the basis for the Russian assimilation of the three elements of Byzantine monasticism: the writings of the early Egyptian and Palestinian monks, the eremitical practices of Mt. Athos, and the communal spirituality in the rule of Constantinople's Stoudion monastery. As described by the *Russian Primary Chronicle,* he favoured the solitary life, marked by superhuman efforts to suppress human passions in a demon-haunted world. Reflecting the Byzantine ascetical tradition, Anthony expressed the basic tension, never fully resolved, between the contemplative's search for God through asceticism and the social responsibilities of the hermit. He realized the moral and psychological pitfalls of solitude and consequently provided hermitages near the monastery. Anthony's institution exerted a wide influence on the Russian Orthodox Church and later evolved into the cenobitical (community life) ideal out of which some 50 monks became bishops by the year 1250.

The latter part of Anthony's life was marked by a strained relationship with Izyaslav, who suspected him of conspiring with a rival lord during the stormy years following the death, in 1054, of the forceful grand prince of Kiev, Yaroslav I the Wise.

The Russian Primary Chronicle, Laurentian Text was translated and edited by S. H. Cross and O. Sherbowitz-Wetzor in 1953.

Anthony OF NOVGOROD, original name DOBRYNIA JADREJKOVIČ (fl. 13th century), monk and archbishop of Novgorod, Russia (1211–*c.* 1231), noted for his political and commercial diplomacy with the West and for the earliest cultural and architectural chronicle of Constantinople and a résumé of the Greek Orthodox liturgy at the basilica of Hagia Sophia (Holy Wisdom).

Anthony's importance derives principally from his *Pilgrim's Book,* written during a visit to Constantinople in about 1200. The *Pilgrim's Book* is unique for information on late 12th-century Constantinople and as the most comprehensive source for knowledge of its archaeology and religious culture before the French and Venetian pillage (1204) during the Fourth Crusade.

Anthony OF PADUA, SAINT, Anthony also spelled ANTONY, Italian SAN ANTONIO DI PADOVA, original name FERNANDO (b. 1195, Lisbon—d. June 13, 1231, Arcella, Verona; canonized 1232; feast day June 13), Franciscan friar, doctor of the church, and patron of the poor. Baptized Ferdinand, he joined the Augustinian canons (1210) and probably became a priest. He joined the Franciscan order in 1220, hoping to preach to the Saracens and be martyred. Instead, he taught theology at Bologna, Montpellier, Toulouse, and Puy-en-Velay, winning great admiration as a preacher in southern France and Italy. After an attack of dropsy, he died en route to Padua, Italy, where he is buried.

Anthony was the most celebrated of St. Francis of Assisi's followers and had the reputation of a miracle worker. On Jan. 16, 1946, Pope Pius XII declared him a doctor of the church. Padua and Portugal claim him as their patron saint, and he is invoked for the return of lost property. In art he is shown with a book, a heart, a flame, a lily, or the child Jesus. Among his authentic writings are sermons for Sundays and feast days, published at Padua, 1895–1913.

BIBLIOGRAPHY. R.M. Huber, *St. Anthony of Padua: A Critical Study* (1948); M. Farnum, *St. Anthony of Padua: His Life and Miracles* (1948); Sophronius Clasen, *St. Anthony, Doctor of the Gospel* (1961).

Anthony OF TAGRIT (fl. 9th century), Syrian Orthodox theologian and writer, a principal contributor to the development of Syriac literature and poetry.

Originally from Tagrit, near Latakia, Syria, Anthony belonged to the part of the Eastern Syriac Church called the Jacobites, which had separated from the authority of the Eastern Orthodox patriarch of Constantinople in the 6th century. Anthony sympathized with the Monophysite view of Christological doctrine (*see* Monophysite).

Known also as "The Orator," Anthony wrote a treatise on rhetoric (*c.* 825) that remains the only original Syriac example of its kind. Influenced by Arab poets, he was the first to use rhyme in Syriac verse. He also wrote a tract on sacramental theology, *Misron* ("Anointing").

Anthony, Earl (Roderick), byname THE ICEMAN (b. April 27, 1938, Tacoma, Wash., U.S.), professional bowler who was the first to win $100,000 in a single season (1975) and to win more than $1,000,000 in total prize money (1982).

Anthony began bowling only at the relatively late age of 21. After bowling in three Professional Bowlers Association (PBA) tournaments in 1970, he became a regular on the tour in 1971, bowling a record of 42 games with scores in the 200s. He led the tour in number of tournaments won and prize money in 1974–76 and 1981–82. Anthony's left-handed precision and consistent accuracy won him the Bowler of the Decade award in 1980. By the early 1980s he had won more than 35 PBA tournaments. He was three times named bowler of the year (1980–83), before retiring from the tour in 1983. His *Winning Bowling,* an instructional book written with Dawson Taylor, was published in 1977.

Anthony, Katharine (Susan) (b. Nov. 27, 1877, Roseville, Ark., U.S.—d. Nov. 20, 1965, New York City), U.S. biographer best known for *The Lambs* (1945), a controversial study of the British writers Charles and Mary Lamb. The greater portion of her work examined the lives of notable women, particularly Americans.

A college teacher of geometry, Anthony was deeply interested in psychiatry. Eventually this interest came to shape her approach to biography, and her books centred increasingly on the psychological development and motivation of her subjects. Some of these works include *Margaret Fuller, A Psychological Biography* (1920); *Catherine the Great* (1925); *Louisa May Alcott* (1938); *Dolly Madison, Her Life and Times* (1949); and *Susan B. Anthony, Her Personal History and Her Era* (1954). Anthony's readers were scandalized by *The Lambs,* subtitled *A Story of Pre-Victorian England,* in which she theorized that incestuous feelings within the Lamb family were reflected in the lives and literary collaborations of Charles Lamb and his sister, Mary. As with her previous biographies, *The Lambs* brought a mixed response from critics, many of whom objected to her unscholarly approach to biography and her unprofessional application of psychoanalytic theory.

Anthony, Susan B(rownell) (b. Feb. 15, 1820, Adams, Mass., U.S.—d. March 13, 1906, Rochester, N.Y.), pioneer crusader for the woman suffrage movement in the United States and president (1892–1900) of the National American Woman Suffrage Association. Her work helped pave the way for the Nineteenth Amendment (1920) to the Constitution, giving women the right to vote.

A tone of independence and moral zeal pervaded her childhood home, dominated by

Susan B. Anthony

By courtesy of the Library of Congress, Washington, D.C.

her father, Daniel Anthony, a Quaker Abolitionist. As an adult, Susan Anthony taught school, organized temperance societies, and, after 1854, devoted herself with vigour and determination to the anti-slavery movement and women's rights. From 1856 to the outbreak of the Civil War (1861), she served as an agent for the American Anti-Slavery Society. Later, collaborating with Elizabeth Cady Stanton, she published the New York liberal weekly *The Revolution* (1868–70). In 1872, demanding for women the same civil and political rights extended to male Negroes under the Fourteenth and Fifteenth amendments, she led a group of women to the polls in Rochester to test the right of women to vote. She was arrested, tried, and convicted but refused to pay the fine. From then on she campaigned relentlessly for a federal woman suffrage amendment through the National Woman Suffrage Association (1869–90) and the National American Woman Suffrage Association (1890–1906) and by lecturing throughout the country.

With her close associates Stanton and Matilda Joslyn Gage she compiled and published *The History of Woman Suffrage,* 4 vol. (1881–1902). In 1888 she organized the International Council of Women and in 1904 the International Woman Suffrage Alliance. At meetings in London (1899) and Berlin (1904) she was acclaimed by worldwide audiences for her pioneer contribution to women's rights.

Anthony, William Arnold (b. Nov. 17, 1835, Coventry, R.I., U.S.—d. May 29, 1908, New York City), physicist and pioneer in the teaching of electrical engineering in the United States.

After studying at Brown (Providence, R.I.) and Yale universities, Anthony taught physics and chemistry at Antioch College, Yellow Springs, Ohio (1865–69); Iowa State University, Ames (1869–72); Cornell University, Ithaca, N.Y. (1872–87); and Cooper Union, New York City (1894–1908). While at Cornell he originated and developed one of the first courses in electrical engineering in the United States (1883).

Anthony also designed and built improved dynamos, including the one used for the first underground distributing system for electrical energy and for the first outdoor-lighting system in the United States. He also contributed to the development of the gas-filled electric lamp.

Anthony Lagoon, settlement, east central Northern Territory, Australia, on the Barkly Tableland. Named after a permanent water hole in the course of Creswell Creek, sighted in 1878 by Ernest Favenc, it became an important watering point on a cattle route from Western Australia to Queensland. Anthony Lagoon has an airfield and is an important station on the "beef road," which carries linked cattle trucks to Alroy Downs, Brunette Downs, and eventually to the Barkly Highway. Pop. (1981) fewer than 200.

anthophyllite, an amphibole mineral, a magnesium and iron silicate that occurs in altered rocks, such as the crystalline schists of Kongsberg, Nor., southern Greenland, and Pennsylvania. Anthophyllite is commonly produced by regional metamorphism of ultrabasic rocks. Because its fibres have a low tensile strength, anthophyllite asbestos is not as important as crocidolite or amosite and much less so than chrysotile. For chemical formula and detailed physical properties, *see* amphibole (table).

Anthophyta (botany): *see* Magnoliophyta.

anthracene, a tricyclic aromatic hydrocarbon found in coal tar and used as a starting material for the manufacture of dyestuffs and in scintillation counters.

Crude anthracene crystallizes from a high-boiling coal-tar fraction. It is purified by recrystallization and sublimation. Oxidation gives 9,10-anthraquinone (*q.v.*), an intermediate in the production of dyes and pigments.

Pure anthracene crystallizes in colourless monoclinic plates, which show a blue fluorescence.

anthracite, also called HARD COAL, most highly metamorphosed variety of coal. It contains more fixed carbon (about 90 to 98 percent) than any other form of coal and the lowest amount of volatile matter (less than 8 percent), giving it the greatest calorific, or heat, value. Because of this, anthracite is the most valuable of the coals. It is, however, also the least plentiful. Anthracite makes up less than 1 percent of all coal found in North America. Most of the known deposits occur in the eastern part of the United States.

Anthracites are black and have a brilliant, almost metallic lustre. They can be polished and used for decorative purposes. Hard and brittle, anthracites break with conchoidal fractures into sharp fragments that are clean to the touch. Anthracites burn with a pale-blue flame and require little attention to sustain combustion. They are particularly adaptable for domestic use because they produce little dust upon handling and burn slowly while emitting relatively little smoke. They are sometimes mixed with bituminous coal (*q.v.*) for heating factories and other commercial buildings to reduce the amount of smoke produced but are seldom used alone for this purpose because of their high cost.

anthracnose, plant disease of warm humid areas that infects a variety of plants from trees to grasses. It is caused by certain fungi (usually *Colletotrichum* or *Gloeosporium*) producing spores in tiny, sunken, saucer-shaped fruiting bodies (acervuli). Symptoms include sunken spots of various colours in leaves, stems, fruits, or flowers. The spots often enlarge, leading to wilting, withering, and dying of tissues.

Anthracnose can be avoided by destroying diseased parts, using disease-free seed and disease-resistant varieties, applying fungicides, and controlling insects and mites that spread anthracnose fungi from plant to plant.

Consult the INDEX *first*

anthracosis, also called BLACK LUNG, or BLACK LUNG DISEASE, respiratory disorder, a type of pneumoconiosis caused by repeated inhalation of coal dust over several years, common in coal miners. The disease gets its common name from a distinctive blue-black marbling of the lung caused by accumulation of the dust. Georgius Agricola, a German mineralogist, first described lung disease in coal miners in the 16th century, and it is now widely recognized. It may be the best known occupational illness in the United States, where more than 50 percent of miners in some regions develop anthracosis after 30 or more years in the mines.

The disease is most common among miners of hard coal (anthracite) but also occurs in soft-coal miners and graphite workers. Onset is gradual; the symptoms usually appear only after 10–20 years of exposure, and the extent of disease is clearly related to the total dust exposure. It is not clear, however, whether coal itself is solely responsible for the disease, as coal dust is often contaminated with silica, which causes similar symptoms. Much evidence also indicates that tobacco smoking aggravates the condition. Although uncomplicated anthracosis may have no symptoms, more advanced disease is frequently associated with pulmonary emphysema or chronic bronchitis and can be disabling; tuberculosis is also more common in victims of anthracosis.

anthraquinone, also called 9,10-ANTHRAQUINONE, the most important quinone derivative of anthracene and the parent substance of a large class of dyes and pigments. It is prepared commercially by oxidation of anthracene or condensation of benzene and

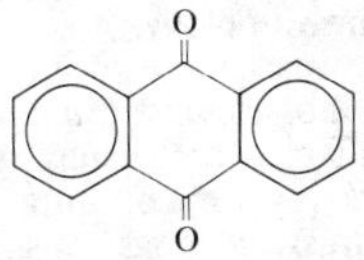

Anthraquinone

phthalic anhydride, followed by dehydration of the condensation product.

Alizarin and many other vegetable pigments are anthraquinone derivatives. Anthraquinone can be converted to alizarin and to a number of synthetic dyestuffs, including a large family of vat dyes.

Although extremely stable toward oxidation, anthraquinone can be easily reduced to a variety of products. In alkaline solution, sodium dithionite reduces it to anthrahydroquinone, the alkali metal salts of which are water-soluble. The use of anthraquinones as vat dyes depends on this chemical reaction.

anthraquinone dye, any of a group of organic dyes having molecular structures based upon that of anthraquinone. The group is subdivided according to the methods best suited to their application to various fibres.

Anthraquinone acid dyes contain sulfonic acid groups that render them soluble in water and substantive for wool and silk; that is, they have an affinity for these fibres without the aid of auxiliary binding agents (mordants).

Anthraquinone disperse dyes lack the water-solubilizing groups of the acid dyes, but they are adsorbed by hydrophobic fibres such as nylon or acetate rayon with the aid of soap or other agents that keep the dye suspended in the application bath.

In several mordant dyes, the anthraquinone structure contains hydroxyl groups that participate in binding the dye to fibres such as cotton, wool, or silk that have been previously impregnated with the oxide of a metal such as aluminum, iron, tin, or chromium.

The anthraquinone vat dyes, valued for their brilliant colours and fastness to light and washing, are insoluble in water but become soluble upon treatment with a reducing agent, usually sodium hydrosulfite. The soluble vat or leuco form is adsorbed by the fibre and is then converted back to the insoluble form.

anthrax, also called SPLENIC FEVER, MALIGNANT PUSTULE, or WOOLSORTERS' DISEASE, acute, specific, infectious, febrile disease of animals, including humans, caused by *Bacillus anthracis,* an organism that under certain conditions forms highly resistant spores capable of persisting and retaining their virulence in contaminated soil or other material for many years. A disease chiefly of herbivores (grass eaters), the infection may be acquired by persons handling wool, hair, hides, bones, or the carcasses of affected animals.

Anthrax is one of the oldest recorded diseases of animals, being mentioned by Moses in Exodus 9:9 and, among the classical authors of Greek and Roman antiquity, by Homer, Hippocrates, Ovid, Galen, Virgil, and Pliny. Devastating epidemics of the disease are recorded by many medieval and modern writers. In the 18th and 19th centuries it sometimes spread like a plague over the southern part of Europe, taking a heavy toll of human and animal life. Anthrax was the first disease of man and animals in which the causative agent was definitely demonstrated as a specific microorganism—by the French biologist Casimir-Joseph Davaine in 1863 and in 1876 by the German bacteriologist Robert Koch, who isolated the organism in pure culture. It was also the first infectious disease against which a bacterial vaccine was found to be effective, by Louis Pasteur in 1881. These discoveries led to the origin and development of the modern sciences of bacteriology and immunology.

Practically all animals are susceptible to anthrax. Cattle, sheep, goats, horses, and mules are the most commonly affected and usually acquire the disease by grazing on contaminated pastures. Outbreaks in swine, dogs, cats, and wild animals held in captivity generally result from consumption of contaminated food. The disease may occur in a peracute (extremely acute), acute, or subacute form (internal anthrax) or in a chronic or localized form (external anthrax). In the acute forms there is excitement and a rise in body temperature followed by depression, spasms, respiratory or cardiac distress, trembling, staggering, convulsions, and death. Bloody discharges sometimes come from the natural body openings, and edematous (serous fluid) swellings may appear on different parts of the body. The peracute and acute forms usually terminate in death within a day or two; the subacute form may lead to death in three to five days or longer or to complete recovery after several days. Chronic anthrax occurs mostly in swine and dogs and is characterized by marked swelling of the throat, difficult breathing, and a blood-stained frothy discharge from the mouth. Affected animals sometimes die of suffocation. Prophylactic vaccination is extensively used in preventing anthrax in livestock. During outbreaks, strict quarantine measures, disposal of diseased carcasses by burning, fly control, and good sanitation are essential in controlling the disease.

Anthrax in humans occurs as a cutaneous, pulmonary, or intestinal infection; the most common type occurs as a primary localized infection of the skin in the form of a carbuncle. It usually results from handling infected material, lesions occurring mostly on the hands, arms, or neck as a small pimple that develops rapidly into a large vesicle with black necrotic centre (the malignant pustule). Should this condition become generalized, a fatal septicemia (blood poisoning) may ensue. The pulmonary form (woolsorters' disease) affects principally the lungs and pleura and results from inhaling anthrax spores in areas where hair and wool are processed. This form of the disease usually runs a rapid course and terminates fatally. The intestinal form of the disease, which sometimes follows the consumption of contaminated meat, is characterized by an acute inflammation of the intestinal tract, vomiting, and severe diarrhea. Anthrax is occasionally transmitted to humans by spore-contaminated brushes or by wearing apparel such as furs and leather goods. Prompt diagnosis and early treatment are of great importance. Antianthrax serum, arsenicals, and antibiotics are used with excellent results. The hazard of infection to industrial workers can be reduced by sterilization of potentially contaminated material before handling, protective clothing, use of respirators, and good sanitary facilities and in agricultural workers by avoiding the skinning or opening of animals that died of the disease.

Anthropoidea, suborder of primates including the families Callitrichidae (marmoset, *q.v.*), Cebidae (*q.v.;* New World monkeys), Cercopithecidae (*q.v.;* Old World monkeys), Hylobatidae (gibbon and siamang, *qq.v.*), Pongidae (gorilla, chimpanzee, and orangutan, *qq.v.*), Hominidae (man and fossil relatives), and the fossil group Parapithecidae.

anthropological linguistics, study of the relationship between language and culture; usually refers to work on languages that have no written records. In the United States a close relationship between anthropology and linguistics developed as a result of research by anthropologists into the American Indian cultures and languages. Early students in this field discovered what they felt to be significant relationships between the languages, thought, and cultures of the Indian groups (*see* Whorfian hypothesis). The issue of the relatedness of language and culture is still a controversial one, and it is now thought by many that the relationship is not as close as was first suspected. Anthropologists currently draw on linguistic techniques mainly for the analysis of such areas as kinship systems, botanical taxonomies, and colour terms, and many anthropologists are engaged in fieldwork and language description.

anthropology, a science, literally the "study of man" but practically one of several disciplines concerned with human beings; it is often further subdivided into physical anthropology and cultural anthropology. It can be characterized as the naturalistic description and interpretation of the diverse peoples of the world, but neither its subject matter nor its methods of study are unique to it. Anthropology differs from history, as commonly understood, not by excluding historical studies of peoples, institutions, beliefs, or customs, but by using as far as possible direct observation of human beings, their activities and their products rather than documentary accounts; and also by viewing the results of any such study as part of the total human record and as a contribution to the better understanding of the complex processes involved in the biological and cultural development of mankind. Similarly, it differs in approach from physiology or psychology in concerning itself with variations and collective differences in human physique and mentality. Thus, anthropologists seek to study and interpret the special characteristics of any particular population or activity in terms of its time and place in the total history of mankind.

A brief treatment of anthropology follows. For full treatment, *see* MACROPAEDIA: Social Sciences, The.

Modern anthropology as a field of research has its roots in the great Age of Discovery, when technologically advanced European cultures came into extended contact with various "traditional" cultures, which for the most part they grouped indiscriminately under the general rubrics "savage" or "primitive." By the mid-19th century, a decline in religious control over intellectual endeavour produced a new interest in such subjects as the origins of man, the classification of human races, comparative anatomy, and the languages of the world.

The concept of evolution, as formally proposed by Charles Darwin with the publication in 1859 of *The Origin of Species,* lent considerable impetus to research into the development of societies and cultures over time, as well as to further study of the development of the human species. Anthropology was dominated throughout the latter part of the 19th century by a linear conception of history, in which all human groups were said to pass through specified stages of cultural evolution, from a state of "savagery" or "barbarism" to that of "civilized man," (*i.e.,* western European man).

At about the same time, Karl Marx and his disciples proposed an alternate theory of social evolution, according to which the mode of economic production in a society determined a set of governing principles that characteristically lingered after the mode had changed; resultant conflict gave rise to a new social order. This unified theoretical framework gained considerable intellectual ground over the years, in distinct contrast to a more diffuse body of miscellaneous information gathered by travellers, traders, and missionaries, which were collected in such popular works as Sir James Frazer's *The Golden Bough* (1890).

At the onset of the 20th century, the strong cultural biases of the early western European and North American anthropologists were gradually discarded in favour of a more pluralistic, relativistic outlook on the wide variety of societies and cultures, in which each culture was viewed as a unique product of physical environment, cultural contacts, and other divergent factors. Out of this orientation came a new emphasis on empirical data, fieldwork, and hard evidence of human behaviour within a given cultural and natural environment. The prime exemplar of this approach was a German-born American, Franz Boas, known as the founder of the culture history school of anthropology.

Boas and his followers—notably, Ruth Benedict, Margaret Mead, and Edward Sapir—dominated American anthropology throughout much of the 20th century. The culture history school was rooted in a functionalist approach to cultural material, which sought an expression of unity between various patterns, traits, and customs within a culture. Meanwhile, in France, Marcel Mauss, founder of the Institute of Ethnology of the University of Paris, studied human societies as total systems, self-regulating and adaptive to changing circumstances in ways designed to preserve the integrity of the cultural system.

Mauss exerted considerable influence over such disparate figures as Claude Lévi-Strauss in France and Bronislaw Malinowski and A.R. Radcliffe-Brown in England. While Malinowski went on to pursue a strictly functionalist approach, Radcliffe-Brown and Lévi-Strauss developed the principles of structuralism. The two schools agreed in rejecting social history as a basis for social theory. The functionalists asserted that the only valid method of analyzing social phenomena was to define the function they performed in a society. The structuralists, by contrast, sought to identify facts or objects that suggest the character of a system or structure underlying the broad spectrum of phenomena, a system of which the members of a society maintain only a dim awareness through the use of myths and symbols.

Studies of Southwest American Indian groups in the 1930s by Ruth Benedict, marked the emergence of the sub-discipline of cultural anthropology known as cultural psychology. Benedict proposed that cultures in their slow development imposed a unique "psychological set" on their members, who interpreted reality along lines oriented by the culture, regardless of environmental factors. The interrelation of culture and personality, as exemplified in the cultural "configurations" or value-systems of modern societies as well as so-called traditional ones, became the subject of extensive research.

While cultural anthropology continued to evolve independently into a full-fledged social science, physical anthropology continued to concern itself with defining man's place in the natural environment, with determining the differences between man and other primates, and with classifying the physical differences between the various races of man. With Darwin's theories of evolution achieving a general acceptance by the latter half of the 19th century, physical anthropologists began to draw on the findings of archaeologists and paleontologists in tracing the considerable antiquity of man.

By the turn of the century, the races had been reliably classified and the differences among the higher primates extensively inventoried. In 1900, the rediscovery of Gregor Mendel's general genetic principles and the identification of the ABO blood groups lent new meaning to the concept of evolutionary change within a species. By the late 20th century, physical anthropologists had charted approximately half a million years of human evolution on the basis of evidence provided by fossil skeletons.

The interests and techniques of contemporary anthropology spill over into a wide spectrum of specialties in the physical, biological, behavioural, and social sciences. Atomic physics, for example, has contributed such techniques as radiocarbon dating for estimating the relative ages of archaeological finds. Efforts to establish the geographic origins of the different peoples have been supported with methods developed by biological scientists, particularly those concerned with the study of human heredity. In applying the techniques of genetics to the inheritance of blood types, for example, it has been possible to verify the conclusion that European gypsies originally came from India. Psychological principles, especially those from psychoanalytic theory, have been employed by anthropologists in an effort to understand family relationships, taboos such as those regarding incest, and religious and legal practices among different peoples.

anthropometry, systematic collection and correlation of measurements of the human body. Now one of the principal techniques of physical anthropology, the discipline originated in the 19th century, when early studies of human biological and cultural evolution stimulated an interest in the systematic description of populations both living and extinct. In the later part of the 19th century, anthropometrical data were applied, often subjectively, by social scientists attempting to support theories associating biological race with levels of cultural and intellectual development. The Italian psychiatrist and sociologist Cesare Lombroso, seeking physical evidence of the so-called criminal type, used the methods of anthropometry to examine and categorize prison inmates.

In the 20th century the application of anthropometry to the study of racial types was replaced by more sophisticated techniques for evaluating racial differences. Anthropometry continued to be a valuable technique, however, gaining an important role in paleoanthropology, the study of human origins and evolution through fossil remains. Craniometry, the measurement of the skull and facial structure, also a development of the 19th century, assumed new importance with the discoveries in the 1970s and '80s of human and prehuman fossils greatly predating any such previous finds. Craniometric studies of prehistoric skull and face bones have enabled anthropologists to trace the gradual changes that occurred in the size and shape of the human head as it enlarged to accommodate increased brain volume; as a result, craniometry and other anthropometric techniques led to a major reevaluation of prevailing theories that the adoption of an erect posture and the enlargement of the brain occurred simultaneously in human development.

In addition to its scholarly functions, anthropometry also has commercial applications. Anthropometric data have been used by industrial researchers in the design of clothing, especially military uniforms, and in the engineering of, *e.g.*, automobile seats, airplane cockpits, and space capsules.

anthropomorphism, in religion, any view about God or the gods that tends to speak of him or them as being like man. The word means literally "in the form of man" (derived from the Greek words *anthrōpos*, "man," and *morphē*, "form").

Any reference to the divine as having a human body or a part of a human body is an anthropomorphism; *e.g.*, the hand of God, the eye of God, or the mouth of God. References to manlike mental aspects are also regarded as anthropomorphisms; *e.g.*, the will of God, the mind of God, the compassion of God, and even the love of God.

References to the nature of God as anthropomorphic are often intended negatively. Some anthropomorphic terms, however, such as the hand of God or the mouth of God, are used figuratively and are thus regarded as legitimate ways of referring to God.

Further, many religionists believe that such phrases as the love of God and the compassion of God, though anthropomorphic, are meaningful descriptive terms when applied to God.

anthropophagy: *see* cannibalism.

anthroposophy, philosophy based on the premise that the human intellect has the ability to contact spiritual worlds. It was formulated by Rudolf Steiner (*q.v.*), an Austrian philosopher, scientist, and artist, who described it as "spiritual science." Steiner postulated the existence of a spiritual world comprehensible to pure thought but fully accessible only to the faculties of knowledge latent in all humans. He regarded man as having originally participated in the spiritual processes of the world through a dreamlike consciousness. Because Steiner claimed that an enhanced consciousness can again perceive spiritual worlds, he attempted to develop a faculty for spiritual perception independent of the senses. Toward this end, he founded the Anthroposophical Society in 1912. The society, now based in Dornach, Switz., has branches around the world and is known for its cultural, social, and educational activities.

anthroposphere, that part of the biosphere (world of living things) inhabited and controlled by man and physically affected by human activity. Man disrupts natural geochemical cycles by mining for minerals or petroleum, by producing synthetic compounds or metals (such as aluminum and magnesium) that do not exist in nature, by generating waste products of industry, and by continually encroaching upon natural areas through construction. The anthroposphere is regarded by some theoretical biologists as replacing the biosphere.

Anthurium, genus of tropical American herbaceous plants, comprising about 600 species in the arum family (Araceae), many of which are popular foliage plants. A few species are widely grown for the florist trade for their showy, long-lasting blossoms, which consist of colourful leathery, shiny spathes surrounding or subtending a central rodlike spadix that bears numerous tiny bisexual flowers.

Flamingo lily (*A. andraeanum*), with stems up to 60 centimetres (2 feet) tall, has a salmon-red, heart-shaped spathe about 5–8 cm (2–3 in.) long; its hybrids produce white, pink, salmon, red, and black-red spathes. Flamingo flower, or pigtail plant (*A. scherzeranum*), is a shorter plant with a scarlet spathe and a loosely coiled orange-red spadix; one variety has a 13-cm long spathe and another has a white-spotted red spathe.

Because anthuriums require warm temperatures and high humidity, they are usually grown under greenhouse conditions.

anti-: *see below* and *see also* unhyphenated words with this prefix.

Anti-Atlas, also called LESSER ATLAS, mountain range in Morocco running parallel to and southward of the central range of the Atlas Mountains of North Africa. Although it has a mean altitude of 5,000 ft (1,500 m), some peaks and passes exceed 6,000 ft. This rugged, arid region, which encloses the Sous lowland and reaches the Atlantic coast at Sidi Ifni, is linked to the Haut (High) Atlas by Jebel Siroua, a volcanic peak rising to 10,840 ft.

Anti-Comintern Pact, agreement concluded first between Germany and Japan (Nov. 25, 1936) and then between Italy, Germany, and Japan (Nov. 6, 1937), ostensibly directed against the Communist International (Comintern) but, by implication, specifically against the Soviet Union.

The treaties were sought by Adolf Hitler, who at the time was publicly inveighing against Bolshevism and who was interested in the Japanese successes in the opening war against China. The Japanese were angered by a Soviet–Chinese nonaggression treaty of August 1936 and the subsequent sale of Soviet military aircraft and munitions to China. For propaganda purposes, Hitler and Benito Mussolini were able to present themselves as defenders of Western values against Russian Communism.

On Aug. 23, 1939, Japan, outraged by the German-Soviet Nonaggression Pact, renounced the Anti-Comintern Pact but later acceded to the Tripartite Pact (Sept. 27, 1940), which pledged Germany, Italy, and Japan "to assist one another with all political, economic and military means" when any one of them was attacked by "a Power at present not involved in the European War or in the Sino-Japanese Conflict" (*i.e.*, the Soviet Union or the United States).

Anti-Fascist Council of National Liberation of Yugoslavia, Serbo-Croatian ANTIFAŠISTIČKO VEĆE NARODNOG OSLOBOĐENJA JUGOSLAVIJE (AVNOJ), administrative body of the National Assembly, convoked during World War II by Tito's Partisans and representing both occupied and liberated areas, which met at Bihać (Nov. 26–27, 1942). Under the presidency of Ivo Ribar (speaker of the Yugoslav Constituent Assembly of 1919–20), AVNOJ assumed control of the local governing organs—the national liberation committees. At its second session at Jajce (Nov. 29–30, 1943), AVNOJ assumed greater legislative and executive functions and elected a central National Liberation Committee, which virtually became a provisional government. The AVNOJ congresses, by demonstrating the national scope and strength of the Partisans and by setting goals limited to liberation of the country and reestablishment of a federal Yugoslav state, won for the Partisans increased support within the country and from the Allies. After its third session at Belgrade (Aug. 7–10, 1945), AVNOJ yielded its authority to a new Constituent Assembly, which met in November 1945.

Anti-Federalists, in early U.S. history, a loose political coalition of popular politicians such as Patrick Henry, who unsuccessfully opposed the strong central government envisioned in the U.S. Constitution of 1787 and whose agitations led to the addition of a Bill of Rights. The first in the long line of states'-rights advocates, they feared the authority of a single national government, upper-class dominance, inadequate separation of powers, and loss of immediate control over local affairs. Stilling their opposition in order to support the first administration of Pres. George Washington, the Anti-Federalists in 1791 became the nucleus of the Jeffersonian Republican Party (subsequently Democratic-Republican, finally Democratic) as strict constructionists of the new Constitution and in opposition to a strong national fiscal policy.

Anti-Lebanon Mountains, Arabic AL-JABAL ASH-SHARQĪ, or LUBNĀN ASH-SHARQĪ, French ANTI-LIBAN, Middle Eastern mountain range running northeast–southwest along the Syrian–Lebanese border parallel to the Lebanon Mountains, from which they are separated by the al-Biqāʿ Valley. The range averages 6,500 ft (2,000 m) above sea level, with several peaks exceeding 8,000 ft. Rising from the Syrian plain in the north, they are separated in the south by a broad shoulder (the Zabadani Saddle) from the ridge of Mt. Hermon, 9,232 ft (2,814 m) high, sometimes considered to be the southernmost extension of the Anti-Lebanon Mountains. Because of thin soils, limestone sinks, steep slopes, and aridity, the range is sparsely populated and economically useful only for nomadic herding.

Anti-Masonic Movement, in U.S. history, popular movement based on public indignation at and suspicion of secret fraternal orders in the Era of the Common Man. Opponents of Andrew Jackson (a Freemason), U.S. president 1829–37, seized upon the emotional uproar to create the Anti-Masonic Party. It was the first U.S. third party, the first political party to hold a national nominating convention, and the first to offer the electorate a platform of party principles.

The movement was ignited in 1826 by the mysterious disappearance of William Morgan, a bricklayer in western New York who supposedly had broken his vow of secrecy as a Freemason by preparing a book revealing the organization's secrets. When no trace of Morgan could be discovered, rumours of his murder at the hands of Masons swept through New York and then into New England and the Mid-Atlantic states.

As Anti-Masonic candidates proved successful in state and local elections, anti-Jackson politicians recognized the vote-catching possibilities that the issue offered. Anti-Masonic newspapers flourished in the heated political atmosphere. In September 1831, the Anti-Masonic Party held a national convention in Baltimore, nominated William Wirt for president, and announced a party platform condemning Masonry for its secrecy, exclusivity, and undemocratic character.

Wirt won only the state of Vermont (seven electoral votes) in the 1832 election, and the party went into decline after that. By the late 1830s much of its reform impulse had been taken over by antislavery agitation, and its anti-Jackson politicians had joined the newly formed Whig Party.

Although short-lived, the Anti-Masonic movement demonstrated Americans' deep belief in egalitarianism. The Anti-Masonic Party made a lasting contribution to the American political process by opening up the nominating procedure for national candidates to broader public participation than the preceding caucus system had allowed.

Anti-Saloon League, leading organization lobbying for prohibition in the United States in the early 20th century. It was founded as a state society in Ohio in 1893, but its influence spread rapidly and in 1895 it became a national organization. It drew most of its support from Protestant evangelical churches, and it lobbied at all levels of government for legislation to prohibit the manufacture and sale of intoxicating beverages. After the adoption of the Eighteenth (prohibition) Amendment in 1919, the league sought strict enforcement of the prohibition laws, but after the repeal of that amendment in 1933, it ceased to be a force in U.S. politics. In 1950 it merged with other groups to form the National Temperance League.

anti-Semitism, hostility toward Jews ranging from mild antipathy to a violently expressed hatred; it has existed to some degree wherever Jews have settled outside of Palestine (*see* Diaspora). In the classical world, religious differences were the primary basis for anti-Semitism. Judaism's rejection of idol worship was little understood, and the refusal of Jews to participate in emperor worship was seen as lack of patriotism. To the early Christians the Jews were the crucifiers of Christ, an allegation that for centuries was the justification for anti-Semitism. The ritual murder canard, or blood libel—*i.e.,* the alleged sacrifice of Christian children at Passover—was first made in the 12th century. The legend was revived sporadically in eastern Europe and Poland and, in the 1930s, became part of Nazi anti-Semitic propaganda, as did another instrument of 12th-century anti-Semitism—the compulsory yellow badge, which identified the wearer as a Jew.

There were periodic persecutions, massacres, and expulsions of Jews until the 18th century, when the Enlightenment brought Europe a new religious freedom. When the nationalism of the 19th century swept Europe, however, the basis of anti-Semitism shifted from religion to racial pride and gained a new respectability and much popular support. In Germany in the late 19th century, anti-Semitism became an organized movement. Concerted efforts were made to disenfranchise the Jews, and to this end a petition with 225,000 signatures was presented to Chancellor Otto von Bismarck.

In France the Dreyfus affair (*q.v.*) became a focal point for anti-Semitism. In 1894 Alfred Dreyfus (*q.v.*), a highly placed Jewish army officer, was falsely accused of treason. His vindication was hampered by the bitterly anti-Semitic French press, and the controversy that ensued destroyed the cohesion of French political life.

In tsarist Russia a medieval form of anti-Semitism continued as an integral part of imperial policy. Since the late 18th century, Jews had been confined to a huge territory in the western provinces known as the Pale of Settlement (*see* pale). In 1882 there was widespread anti-Semitic rioting followed by legislation that confiscated the rural holdings of Jews and restricted them to towns within the Pale. The result was a mass emigration of Jews into western countries where anti-Semitic agitators exploited xenophobic sentiments.

During the first decade of the 20th century, there was a period of moderate decline in anti-Semitic tensions, but the many Jewish leaders in the Russian Revolution of 1917 gave anti-Semites a new focus for their prejudices in the name of "Jewish Bolshevism."

The storm of anti-Semitic violence let loose by the triumph of Adolf Hitler in 1933 not only reached a terrifying degree in Germany but inspired a worldwide anti-Jewish movement unequalled in modern history. Anti-Semitism was spread in France by the Cagoulards (French: Hooded Men), in Hungary by the Arrow Cross, in England by the British Union of Fascists, and in the United States by the German-American Bund and the Silver Shirts.

The novelty of the Nazi brand of anti-Semitism was that it crossed class barriers. The idea of Aryan racial superiority appealed both to the masses and to economic and hereditary elites. In Germany anti-Semitism became official government policy—taught in the schools and elaborated in "scientific" journals, research institutes, and by a huge, highly effective organization for international propaganda. In 1941 the liquidation of European Jewry became official party policy. An estimated 6,000,000 Jews were exterminated in the large death installations of Auschwitz, Chełmno, Belzec, Bergen-Belsen, Buchenwald, Dachau, Majdanek, and Treblinka.

After the Nazi defeat in 1945, anti-Semitism lost ground in western Europe and the United States, but developments in the Soviet Union, eastern Europe, and the Middle East gave it new significance in those areas. Because the Arabs are Semitic, their hostility to the new state of Israel has been primarily political (or anti-Zionist) rather than racial. Whatever the designation, however, the result has been the adoption of many anti-Jewish measures throughout the Middle East. *See also* ghetto; pogrom.

antiacid: *see* antacid.

antiaircraft gun, artillery piece fired from the ground or shipboard in defense against aerial attack. Antiaircraft weapon development began in World War I, when the airplane became an effective weapon. At first, ground machine-gun fire was directed at strafing airplanes. Field artillery pieces up to about 90 millimetres (3.5 inches) were converted to antiaircraft use by mountings that enabled them to fire nearly vertically, but aiming methods were inadequate. Between World Wars I and II great progress was made in development of range finders, searchlights, time fuses, and gunlaying mechanisms. Muzzle velocities were also increased, improving both range and accuracy.

In World War II, rapid-firing automatic antiaircraft guns were introduced. A 40-mm gun, produced first by the Bofors firm in Sweden, was used more than any other antiaircraft gun by British and U.S. forces. It fired 2-pound (0.9-kilogram) projectiles to a height of 2 miles (3.2 kilometres) at 120 rounds per minute.

Heavier guns were loaded and fired manually. By the later years of World War II, there had evolved such types as the U.S. 120-mm stratosphere gun, which fired a 50-lb projectile to a height of 50,000 feet (15.2 km). In 1953 the U.S. Army introduced the Skysweeper, a 75-mm automatic cannon firing 45 shells per minute, aimed and fired by its own radar-computer system. In succeeding years, ground-to-air rockets and missiles augmented guns in the main task of antiaircraft defense.

antiarch, any of an order of extinct, mainly freshwater, jawed fishes, class Placodermi, abundant during Middle and Late Devonian times. Members of such genera as *Bothriolepis* and *Pterichthys* were representative. Antiarchs were small and weak-jawed and had closely set eyes on top of the head. Armour shields covered the front part of the body and armoured, jointed appendages extended from the shoulder regions. The hind part of the body was naked in *Bothriolepis* and covered with scales in *Pterichthys.*

Antiarchs may have been bottom dwellers that fed upon small animals and on plants and pulled themselves about with the pectoral appendages. The presence of paired sacs in these primitive fishes suggests that lungs were evolved earlier than was once thought.

Antibes, port town, Alpes-Maritimes *département,* Provence-Alpes-Côte-d'Azur region, France, on the eastern side of the Garoupe Peninsula across the Baie des Anges (Bay of the Angels) from Nice. Originally Antipolis, a Greek trading post established by Phocaeans from Marseille, it became a Roman town and eventually a fief of the coast-ruling Grimaldi family from 1384 to 1608. The Grimaldi château, much rebuilt over the ages, is now a museum featuring works of Pablo Picasso, who painted there in 1946. There is

The ramparts, old city, and port of Antibes, Fr.
Editions "La Cigogne"—Hachette

also an archaeological museum displaying the Grimaldi fossils, remains of prehistoric man discovered locally. Juan-les-Pins, with its parasol pines and sand beach, is part of the Antibes *commune,* which also includes the luxury resort of Cap d'Antibes. An important part of the economy, in addition to tourism, is the production of flowers, many under glass. In the early 1980s, the French national scientific research organization, CNRS, planned to establish laboratories there. Pop. (1982) 62,427.

antibiotic, chemical substance produced by a living organism, generally a microorganism, that is detrimental to other microorganisms.

A brief treatment of antibiotics follows. For full treatment, *see* MACROPAEDIA: Drugs and Drug Action.

Although antibiotics are released naturally into the soil by bacteria and fungi, they did not come into worldwide prominence until the introduction of penicillin in 1941. Selman Waksman, the discoverer of streptomycin, introduced the term antibiotic in 1941. Since then they have revolutionized the treatment of bacterial infections in humans and other animals.

Sir Alexander Fleming drew attention in 1928 to the phenomena that led to the development of penicillin. He noticed that colonies of bacteria growing on a nutrient medium had been affected by a mold, *Penicillium notatum,* which had contaminated the culture. A decade later Ernst Chain, Howard Florey, and others isolated the ingredient responsible, penicillin, and showed that it was highly effective against many serious bacterial infections. Toward the end of the 1950s scientists then added various chemical groupings to the core of the penicillin molecule to generate semi-synthetic versions. A range of penicillins is thus now available to treat diseases caused by gram-positive bacteria (so-called because they retain a special stain) such as staphylococci, streptococci, pneumococci, gonococci, and the spirochaetes of syphilis.

Conspicuously unaffected by penicillin is the tubercle bacillus, but this organism proved to be highly sensitive to streptomycin, isolated from *Streptomyces griseus* in 1943. As well as being dramatically effective against tuberculosis, streptomycin also vanquishes many gram-negative bacteria, including the typhoid fever bacillus. Unlike penicillins, however, which are extraordinarily nontoxic (except to the small percentage of people who are allergic to them), it can cause vertigo and deafness and must be used with great care.

Two other early discoveries were gramicidin and tyrocidin, made by bacteria of the genus *Bacillus.* Discovered in 1939 by René Dubos, they have proved to be valuable in treating surface infections, but are too toxic for internal use. Other, more recently isolated, drugs are the cephalosporins. Related to penicillins, they are produced by the mold *Cephalosporium acremonium.*

The principle governing the use of antibiotics is to ensure that the patient receives one to which the bacterium concerned is sensitive, at a high enough concentration to be effective (but not cause side effects), and for a sufficient length of time to ensure that the infection is totally eradicated. This usually means testing organisms on a swab from the infected area against several antibiotics in order to select the most potent. Administration of an antibiotic depends on its characteristics and on the site of infection. Thus some semi-synthetic penicillins can be taken orally because, unlike the original version, they are not destroyed by acid in the stomach. Many antibiotics have to be given by intramuscular injection.

Antibiotics vary in their range of action. Some are highly specific. Others, such as the tetracyclines, act against a broad spectrum of different bacteria. These are particularly useful in combatting mixed infections and in circumstances where there is no time to conduct sensitivity tests.

A problem that has plagued antibiotic therapy from the earliest days is the resistance which bacteria can develop to the drugs. Different antibiotics work in different ways, either by killing bacteria outright or by inhibiting their growth. Occasionally, however, the organisms become invulnerable to such action. Some bacteria produce an enzyme, penicillinase, which destroys certain penicillins. In other cases, particularly among bacteria causing gastrointestinal infections, resistance spreads via tiny, transmissable pieces of genetic material. This results in the proliferation of strains resistant to, and thus unaffected by, several different drugs. Faced with such an otherwise untreatable infection, doctors sometimes need to use substances that may have significant side effects. One such drug is chloramphenicol (classified as an antibiotic though it is made synthetically), which can cause a serious form of anemia but is particularly active against typhoid fever bacilli.

Indiscriminate use of antibiotics encourages the spread of resistance. Factors contributing to this problem include the administration of antibiotics in inadequate dosages and for trivial conditions, particularly in countries where they are too easily available. Their agricultural use, to promote the growth of livestock and poultry, also seems to have contributed to the growth of drug-resistant bacteria.

There are also antibiotics to combat fungal diseases. They include griseofulvin for ringworm and nystatin for Candida infections. Others are active against some forms of cancer. Antibiotics can also be employed to combat bacterial diseases of plants, but have now been largely replaced by synthetic organic compounds. Virus infections cannot be treated by antibiotics, although a few chemical compounds have limited value against some of them.

antibody, protective substance formed in the spleen, liver, lymph nodes, thymus gland, or bone marrow in response to stimulation by a foreign antigen. The antibody combines with the inductive antigen and thereby renders it inactive and noninfective. Antibodies are soluble and occur in the globulin fraction of blood serum protein and in other body fluids, such as lymph, milk, saliva, tears, and mucous secretions. First exposure of the adult body to an antigen induces certain cells to elaborate, synthesize, and release a specific antibody. For example, the initial response in a rabbit that has received an injection of red blood cells of sheep is characterized by a latent period of several days, a rapid rise of antibody to peak strength (peak titre), and a subsequent slow decline. Second and succeeding injections of the same antigen lead to an immune response characterized by a more rapid rise, usually in increased amount, of the same antibody. Some antibodies, termed natural, are found in low titre in normal animals—most are probably formed in response to antigens from inapparent infections or food, but others are formed without known exposure to antigen (*e.g.,* some blood groups). Natural antibodies play a significant role in innate immunity.

Antibodies are divided into a number of classes on the basis of molecular size, electrophoretic mobility, and other characteristics. They are collectively designated Ig's (immunoglobulins) and are further differentiated by the addition of a letter. IgA, for example, designates a class of antibodies that occur, among other places, in the secretions of the upper respiratory tract and the small bowel to provide local immunity to infections in those areas. Antibodies are also classified by their observed actions (*e.g.,* agglutinins cause the antigen–antibody complex to be agglutinated; opsonins make the antigen–antibody complex more susceptible to ingestion by phagocytes). Reagins (designated IgE), also called atopic or homocytotropic antibodies, are associated with hypersensitivity reactions; they are common in the skin of allergic persons and are apparently responsible for many of the harmful effects of allergy.

An auto-antibody is one formed in an individual against one of his own tissues. Certain auto-antibodies are common and without harmful effects; others are characteristic of certain diseases, such as systemic lupus erythematosus or idiopathic thrombocytopenic purpura. Most antibodies act at body temperature and are termed warm; certain cold antibodies combine with antigen only at temperatures below normal body heat and appear during the course of some diseases (*e.g.,* paroxysmal cold hemoglobinuria, viral pneumonia). *See also* antigen; antigen–antibody reaction; auto-antibody.

anticathode, target within an X-ray tube onto which high-speed electrons (cathode rays) are directed and from which X-rays characteristic of the target element are emitted. The anticathode is the anode (*q.v.*), or positive electrode; usually it is hollow to permit the flow of a coolant so that heat generated by bombarding electrons is dissipated.

anticholinesterase, any of several substances that interfere with the enzyme-catalyzed reaction by which certain nerve impulses (*e.g.,* between a voluntary muscle and a nerve) are transmitted. Destruction of the transmitter substance (acetylcholine) by the action of the enzyme acetylcholinesterase allows the stimulated nerve cell, muscle, or gland to rest preparatory to another stimulation. An anticholinesterase (*e.g.,* the drug edrophonium) inhibits acetylcholinesterase, thus preventing the breakdown of the transmitter and prolonging its effects. Certain organic phosphorus compounds, the so-called nerve gases, are very powerful anticholinesterases; their action can be reversed by hydrolysis, though very slowly. When hydroxylamine or certain oximes are used instead of water, the regeneration of cholinesterase is more rapid.

Anticholinesterases are used as insecticides and drugs (*see* cholinergic drug). Physostigmine (an alkaloid) and neostigmine (a synthetic compound) are used to treat myasthenia gravis.

Antichrist, the chief enemy of Christ. The earliest mention of the name Antichrist, which was probably first coined in Christian eschatological literature (concerned with the end of time), is in the letters of St. John (I John 2: 18, 22; II John 7), although the figure does appear in the earlier II Thessalonians as "the lawless one." Yet the conception of a mighty ruler who will appear at the end of time and whose essence will be enmity of God is older and was taken over by Christianity from Judaism.

Jewish eschatology had been influenced by Iranian and Babylonian myths of the battle of God and the devil at the end of time. In the Old Testament the Jewish conception of the struggle is found in the prophecy of Daniel, written at the beginning of the Maccabean period (*c.* 168 BC). The historical figure who served as a model for the Antichrist was Antiochus IV Epiphanes, the persecutor of the Jews, and he left a lasting impression upon the conception. Since then, ever-recurring characterizations of this figure are that he would appear as a mighty ruler at the head of gigantic armies, destroy three rulers (the three horns, Dan. 7:8,24), persecute the saints (7:25), and devastate the Temple of God. In later times, the tyrant who was God's enemy became a figure of prophecy, applied to various situations of crisis. Also, Jewish and Christian writers of apocalypses saw in the emperor Nero (died AD 68) the Antichrist.

A Christian view of the Antichrist is given in II Thess. 2. Here Antichrist appears as a tempter who works by signs and wonders and seeks to obtain divine honours; it is further signified that this "man of lawlessness" will obtain credence, especially among the Jews because they have not accepted the truth. This version of the figure of Antichrist, who may now really for the first time be described by this name, appears to have been at once widely accepted in Christendom. The idea that the Jews would believe in Antichrist as punishment for not having believed in the true Christ seems to be expressed by the author of the Fourth Gospel (John 5:43). The conception of Antichrist as a perverter of men led naturally to his connection with false doctrine (I John 2:18, 22, 4:3; II John 7). In the Book of Revelation the Antichrist is seen as a worker of wonders and a seducer.

In the Middle Ages the idea of the Antichrist developed into a powerful historical and political factor, especially in times of crisis. Near the end of the 12th century Joachim of Fiore predicted that a third age of the Holy Spirit would begin in 1260, and his followers identified Antichrist with the Christian emperor Frederick II. Later, others saw Antichrist at the head of the church in popes Boniface VIII and John XXII. It became common for opponents, including popes and emperors, to call each other the Antichrist.

Immense interest continued to be focussed on the person and date of the coming of Antichrist and "the signs of the times" preceding it: upheavals in nature, wars, pestilence, famine, and other disasters. Preachers spread warnings of the coming of Antichrist in order to call the people to repentance throughout the 14th and 15th centuries.

During the Reformation, the Reformers, especially Martin Luther, did not attack individual popes but the papacy itself as Antichrist. This idea that evil was embodied in the head of the church itself, with the clergy as the "body of the Antichrist," became the most powerful weapon to discredit and denigrate the papacy.

After the Reformation, emphasis on the Antichrist figure gradually diminished. Among some modern Protestant theologians the Antichrist can be interpreted as whatever resists or denies the lordship of Christ and tends to deify a political power—within either the church or the state. In dispensational and premillennial theology the expectancy of a personal Antichrist at the end of time remains strong.

anticlericalism, opposition to the clergy for its real or alleged influence in political and social affairs, for its doctrinairism, for its privileges or property, or for any other reason. Although the term has been used in Europe since the 12th and 13th centuries, it is associated in more recent history with the French Revolution and its aftermath and with the Russian Revolution.

Three principal forms can be identified. The first, developed during the 18th century, was based on opposition to clerical privilege, often corrupt, as established by feudalism. The second is associated with the rise of liberalism, which in general accused the clergy of servility to the monarchy or of ignorance in terms of scientific thought. The third, endorsed by totalitarian systems of both the right and the left, considered religion, as Marx did, the "opiate of the people," administered by a clergy chronically opposed to the "race," the "nation," or "democracy." Protestant or Anglican state churches were often criticized for undue conservatism or subservience, but the chief objects of hostility have been the Roman Catholic Church in the West and the Russian Orthodox Church and other churches in the East.

France. In the 18th century such skeptics as Voltaire and the Encyclopaedists chafed under royal censorship and the clergy's influence on the monarchy. The culmination of such anticlericalism was the French Revolutionaries' assault on the Catholic Church, abolishing its privileges and confiscating property. In 1801 Napoleon Bonaparte ended the Revolution, signed a concordat with the papacy, and "established" the church as a religious agency supported by and subservient to the French state. With modifications, this system lasted for a century, during monarchist, republican, and Bonapartist regimes.

The creation of the Third Republic in 1871, however, intensified the old-time conflict between clericals and anticlericals. In the struggle between 1871 and 1879, royalist-clerical parties opposed republican-anticlerical parties. Léon Gambetta phrased the slogan, *le cléricalisme, voilà l'ennemi* ("clericalism is the enemy"). The victorious republicans enacted a good deal of anticlerical legislation. The Jesuits were suppressed (1880); and the Ferry laws (1881–82) established free, secular education, compulsory civil marriage, and the opportunity for divorce. The second conflict took place as a result of the bid of Georges Boulanger for dictatorial powers, and ended with a republican, anticlerical triumph. The third took place during the Alfred Dreyfus affair (1894–1906), when an anticlerical republican bloc was formed, consisting of all republican groups in the Chamber of Deputies, determined to oust royalists, militarists, and clericals from public life. Further anticlerical legislation resulted. The Law of Associations (1901) suppressed nearly all of the religious orders in France and confiscated their property, and the separation law (1905) sundered church and state.

Italy. Spreading from France, anticlerical ideas and methods were adopted, in varying ways, in other Latin countries. In Italy anticlericalism was fused with nationalism and liberalism. Pope Pius IX, defending his position as temporal ruler of the Papal States, opposed Italian unity. When Camillo Cavour embarked on his career as architect of a united Italy, he put through the Piedmontese Parliament a series of anticlerical laws, abolishing the civil jurisdiction of canonical courts and suppressing many monasteries. Cavour's slogan, "a free church in a free state," was adopted by the anticlerical liberals of Italy.

After the unification of Italy, the struggle between clericals and anticlericals continued. When Rome became the capital, the temporal power of the popes was ended. Anticlerical legislation decreased the number of monastic establishments, suppressed university theological faculties, and sanctioned civil marriage. But no divorce law was enacted, nor was religious instruction banned from the schools. The Law of Guarantees accorded the pope full power to exercise his spiritual function. Pius IX did not, however, recognize the Italian government and in 1874 forbade Catholics to participate in political activities. This caveat was not ended until 1919. The advent to power of Benito Mussolini in 1922 for a time intensified anticlericalism, since Fascism claimed absolute control by the state. Yet no serious conflict occurred, despite continuing papal opposition to some curtailments of religious liberty. In 1929 the Lateran Treaty was signed, ending the dispute over the temporal power by making the pope ruler of the small state of Vatican City.

Spain. The Napoleonic invasion (1808) started an anticlerical movement in Spain. The Constitution of 1812 abolished the Inquisition and restricted the number of religious orders but recognized Catholicism as the established church. This constitution was in turn abrogated when Ferdinand VII was restored to the throne in 1814. Anticlericals reacted bitterly, and from that time until 1939 the struggle between the right and left in Spain was far more a conflict between clericals and anticlericals than elsewhere in Latin Europe. The conflict became especially intense after 1870. Barcelona, traditionally a centre of anti-Catholic feeling, witnessed the formation of powerful syndicalist and anarchist groups. The first Spanish Republic (1873) enacted some anticlerical laws, but these were repealed or disregarded when the monarchy was restored in 1875. During an anticlerical outbreak in 1909, mobs burned churches and attacked priests. As a pacification measure, religious orders were restricted in number and taxes were levied on their industrial enterprises. Civil marriage was made compulsory. The revolution of 1931 that established the Second Republic brought to power an anticlerical government. The legislation adopted resembled that of France. The government was, however, unable to curb mob attacks on churches and monasteries, during which priests and nuns were slain. Catholics mustered their forces in opposition. Counterrevolutionaries led by Gen. Francisco Franco declared war on the republic, and the Falangist dictatorship that was subsequently established repealed or ignored the anticlerical laws, though conflict between church and state did not cease, even after the death of Franco in 1975.

Central and South America. The struggle for independence from Spain and Portugal, which characterized the history of Central and South America during the 19th century, was often strongly influenced by ideas associated with the French Revolution, among them anticlericalism. But it is difficult, in view of turbulent political events that led almost everywhere to a succession of dictators, to determine whether recurring patterns of anticlerical activity—the suppression of religious orders, primarily the Jesuits; the confiscation of ecclesiastical property; the fostering of secular education, sometimes with a caveat against religious instruction; and the introduction of civil marriage and divorce—were due to an intellectual ferment caused by the French Revolution or whether they were primarily incidents in the constant tussle between factions for political control. The situation varied considerably from country to country. Although Colombia, for example, witnessed the enactment of anticlerical legislation and its enforcement during more than three decades (1849–84), it soon restored "full liberty and independence from the civil power" to the Catholic Church (1888). In Venezuela, on the other hand, the government of Antonio Guzmán Blanco (1870–88) virtually crushed the institutional life of the church, even attempting to legalize the marriage of priests. Some of the restrictions were later relaxed, but on the whole anticlericalism remained dominant. Elsewhere, upon occasion, there were strong outbursts of anticlerical resentment, one of the most noteworthy being that which took place in Mexico (1924–38). Suppressive anticlerical legislation accompanied social reform in Mexico.

Germany. Anticlericalism was not novel in Germany, but it was strengthened intellectually by ideas generally accepted during the French Revolution. Free thought, with its principle of the "lay state," made headway particularly in southern Germany, and played a part in the revolutionary incidents of 1848. The rise of Marxian Socialism likewise brought large segments of the working population into the anticlerical camp. But Catholics in the populous Rhenish areas were prevailingly constitutionalists, in sympathy with some tenets of liberalism and vigorous in support of social and electoral reform. Their political program, which led to the formation of the Centre Party, included the defense of the right of all religious minorities.

Shortly after the unification of Germany in 1871, Chancellor Otto von Bismarck, adopting part of the liberal program, began the series of attacks on the Catholic Church known as the *Kulturkampf.* Anticlerical legislation was enacted, applicable in part to the empire as a whole and in part to the Kingdom of Prussia. The number of religious orders was restricted, the Jesuits were banned, civil marriage was sanctioned, uncooperative priests were removed from their parishes, and a variety of measures were adopted to curb the freedom of the clergy. Resistance was punished, and some bishops were deposed. But by 1878 a desire to end the *Kulturkampf* was manifest, and during the next decade most of the anticlerical legislation was removed from the statute books. The prohibition of the Jesuits remained in force, however, until 1917. The period of the Weimar Republic (1919–33) was characterized by the grant of complete freedom to Catholics, though as a result of the activity of the Centre Party some anticlerical comment was engendered.

The Nazi dictatorship (1933–45) enforced its own anticlerical program on Catholics and Protestants alike. Hitler acceded to a concordat with the Vatican in 1933, but this was honoured in the breach rather than in the observance. Hundreds of clergymen, both Catholic and Lutheran, were brought to trial, imprisoned, or executed. A decade after the close of World War II the Nazi ideology seemed to have lost all but vestiges of its influence. Anticlericalism in Germany became a normal ingredient of opposition to the Christian Democratic Party, membership in which was predominantly Catholic.

The Communist bloc. Russian anticlericalism under Communism has been characterized by unrelenting hostility to religion in any form save that of complete subservience to the Kremlin. The initial administrative measures taken by the Soviet government against the church in 1917–18, which included the nationalization of all ecclesiastical lands and the separation of church and state, were followed by brutal persecution, instanced in the arrest of bishops and in the trial and execution of Veniamin, metropolitan of St. Petersburg (1922.) Thereafter the church remained under constant pressure, and antireligious propaganda continued to alternate with active persecution.

After the Soviet seizure of the Baltic states and of eastern Poland in 1939, repression also fell heavily on the Catholic and Protestant churches of Estonia, Latvia, Lithuania, and Poland. Occupation and eventual subjection of the satellite countries and East Germany after the war were followed by usually less violent but nonetheless implacable actions in the area of religious activity. At the conclusion of notorious trials, the foremost prelates of Yugoslavia, Czechoslovakia, Hungary, Poland, and Romania were imprisoned. Many thousands of bishops, clergymen, and faithful layfolk were sent to prisons or slave labour camps. Religious education and publishing were forbidden, only a handful of convents and monasteries were suffered to remain, and hospitals were secularized. The Catholic clergy in Albania was decimated, and the Uniate churches in Romania and Bulgaria were destroyed.

anticoagulant, any substance that prevents clotting of blood. Anticoagulants used in medicine include heparin, a complex carbohydrate found in various animal tissues, and a group of agents including bishydroxycoumarin and warfarin that are effective upon oral administration. These drugs inhibit the action of one or more of the clotting factors normally present in the blood, but their exact mode of action is not fully understood. Salts of citric acid or edetic acid inhibit the clotting of blood by sequestering calcium ion, which is involved in one of the steps of the clotting process.

Anticona (Peru): *see* Ticlio.

anticorona: *see* Brocken bow.

Anticosti Island, French ÎLE-D'ANTICOSTI, island in the Gulf of St. Lawrence at the mouth of the St. Lawrence River, part of the Côte-Nord (North Shore) region, southeastern Quebec province, Canada. Covering 3,059 sq mi (7,923 sq km), the island is 135 mi (217 km) long, and its greatest width is 30 mi. A hazard to shipping, Anticosti rises to 625 ft (191 m) in hills along its north coast; it is well forested with spruce, balsam, and pine.

The island was discovered by the French navigator Jacques Cartier in 1534 and named Assomption. Since the 17th century, it has been called Anticosti, probably derived from the Indian word *naticousti,* meaning "where bears are hunted."

Granted to the French explorer Louis Jolliet in 1680, it was ceded by France to Great Britain in 1763 and was annexed to Newfoundland. It became part of Quebec province in 1774. After attempts to settle Anticosti failed, it was leased in 1895 by Henri Menier, a French chocolate manufacturer, who developed its resources. He built a château at Port-Menier, near the island's west end, and founded a village at Baie-Sainte-Claire. Retaining only fishing rights to Anticosti's salmon-filled Jupiter River, Menier's brother Gaston transferred ownership in 1926 to a Canadian paper corporation, which conducted lumbering operations and shipped pulpwood to plants near Trois-Rivières on the St. Lawrence River. There are good hunting facilities with permission of the corporation. Lighthouses built by the Canadian government have reduced the number of shipwrecks that formerly plagued the island. Pop. (1981) 275.

anticyclone, any large wind system occurring in regions outside the equatorial belt and rotating about a centre of high atmospheric pressure clockwise in the Northern Hemisphere and counterclockwise in the Southern. Its flow is roughly the reverse of that of a cyclone (*q.v.*).

antidepressant drug, also called PSYCHIC ENERGIZER, any member of a class of drugs used in medicine to combat depression. Such a drug commonly belongs to one of two chemical types of stimulant—a tricyclic stimulant, whose molecules are composed of three rings, or a monoamine-oxidase inhibitor. Introduced in the late 1950s, antidepressant drugs have been used widely as adjuncts in therapy of chronically ill and mentally depressed patients. The tricyclic antidepressant drugs include imipramine, amitriptyline, desmethylimipramine (desipramine), and nortriptyline. Monoamine-oxidase inhibitor drugs include isocarboxazid, nialamide, phenelzine, tranylcypromine, and pargyline.

antiderivative, also called PRIMITIVE, of a real mathematical function f, a differentiable real function the derivative of which is f. If an antiderivative exists, it is unique up to an additive constant on any interval. *See* integral.

antideuteron, composite antiparticle consisting of an antiproton and an antineutron, produced and detected in 1965 at Brookhaven National Laboratory, Long Island, N.Y. Having a charge of negative one unit and an atomic mass of two units, it may be considered as the antinucleus of the hydrogen isotope deuterium.

Antietam, Battle of, also called BATTLE OF SHARPSBURG (Sept. 17, 1862), a decisive engagement in the U.S. Civil War (1861–65) that halted the Confederate attempt to "liberate" Maryland and gain military supplies; the advance was also regarded as one of the greatest Confederate threats to Washington, D.C. The battle took its name from Antietam Creek, which flows south from Gettysburg, Pa., to the Potomac River near Harpers Ferry, W.Va.

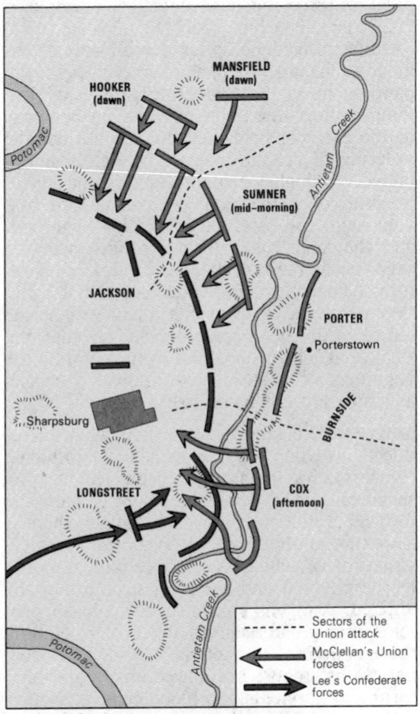

The Battle of Antietam, Sept. 17, 1862

Following the Union defeat at the Second Battle of Bull Run, Confederate Gen. Robert E. Lee advanced into Maryland with some hope of capturing the Federal Capitol to the southeast. On Sept. 17, 1862, his forces were met at Antietam by the reorganized Federal Army under Gen. George B. McClellan, who blocked Lee's advances but allowed him to retire to Virginia. Most military historians have strongly criticized McClellan's conduct of the battle, which proved to be one of the bloodiest of the war. The South lost between 9,000 and 10,000 men killed or wounded and the North suffered casualties of about 12,000.

In addition to protecting the Capitol, the engagement is sometimes cited as having influenced Great Britain not to recognize the Confederacy. Pres. Abraham Lincoln used the occasion of the Antietam victory to issue his preliminary Emancipation Proclamation (Sept. 22, 1862), announcing that unless the Confederates laid down their arms by Jan. 1, 1863, he would free their slaves.

antiferromagnetism, type of magnetism in solids such as manganese oxide (MnO) in which adjacent ions that behave as tiny magnets (in this case manganese ions, Mn^{2+}) spontaneously align themselves at relatively low temperatures into opposite, or antiparallel, arrangement throughout the material so that it exhibits almost no gross external magnetism. In antiferromagnetic materials, which include certain metals and alloys in addition to some ionic solids, the magnetism from magnetic atoms or ions oriented in one direction is cancelled out by the set of magnetic atoms or ions that are aligned in the reverse direction.

This spontaneous antiparallel coupling of atomic magnets is disrupted by heating and disappears entirely above a certain temperature, called the Néel temperature, characteristic of each antiferromagnetic material. (The Néel temperature is named for Louis Néel, French physicist, who in 1936 gave one of the first explanations of antiferromagnetism.) Some antiferromagnetic materials have Néel temperatures at, or even several hundred degrees above, room temperature, but usually these temperatures are lower. The Néel temperature for manganese oxide, for example, is 122 K (−151° C, or −240° F).

Antiferromagnetic solids exhibit special behaviour in an applied magnetic field depending upon the temperature. At very low temperatures, the solid exhibits no response to the external field, because the antiparallel ordering of atomic magnets is rigidly maintained. At higher temperatures, some atoms break free of the orderly arrangement and align with the external field. This alignment and the weak magnetism it produces in the solid reach their peak at the Néel temperature. Above this temperature, thermal agitation progressively prevents alignment of the atoms with the magnetic field, so that the weak magnetism produced in the solid by the alignment of its atoms continuously decreases as temperature is increased.

antigen, foreign substance that, when introduced into the body, is capable of inducing the formation of antibodies and of reacting specifically in a detectable manner with the induced antibodies. For each antigen there is a specific antibody the physical and chemical structure of which is produced in response to the physical and chemical structure of the antigen. Antigens comprise virtually all proteins that are foreign to the host, including those contained in bacteria, viruses, protozoa, helminths, foods, snake venoms, egg white, serum components, red blood cells, and other cells and tissues of various species, including man. Polysaccharides and lipids may also act as antigens when coupled to proteins. A functional antigen consists of a relatively large protein molecule and smaller parts, called haptens, that determine its antigenic specificity. The amount of antibody formed in response to stimulation depends on the kind and amount of antigen involved, the route of entry to the body, and individual characteristics of the host. *See also* antibody; hapten; immunization.

Antigone, in Greek legend, the daughter born of the unwittingly incestuous union of Oedipus (*q.v.*) and his mother, Jocasta. After her father blinded himself upon discovering that Jocasta was his mother and that, also unwittingly, he had slain his father, Antigone and her sister Ismene served as Oedipus' guides, following him from Thebes into exile until his death near Athens. Returning to Thebes, they attempted to reconcile their quarrelling brothers—Eteocles, who was defending the city and his crown, and Polyneices, who was attacking Thebes. Both brothers, however, were killed, and their uncle Creon became king. After performing an elaborate funeral service for Eteocles, he forbade the removal of the corpse of Polyneices, condemning it to lie unburied, declaring him to have been a traitor. Antigone, moved by love of her brother and convinced of the injustice of the command, buried Polyneices secretly. For that she was ordered to be executed by Creon and was immured in a cave, where she hanged herself. Her beloved, Haemon, son of Creon, committed suicide. According to Euripides, however, Antigone escaped and lived happily with Haemon.

Antigonid DYNASTY, ruling house of ancient Macedonia from 306 to 168 BC. The Antigonid dynasty was established when Demetrius I Poliorcetes, the son of Antigonus I Monophthalmus, ousted Cassander's governor of Athens, Demetrius of Phaleron, and conquered the island of Cyprus, thereby giving his father control of the Aegean, the eastern Mediterranean, and all of the Middle East except Babylonia. Antigonus I was proclaimed king in 306 by the assembled army of these areas.

Demetrius succeeded Antigonus I to the throne and his son, Antigonus II Gonatas, strengthened the Macedonian kingdom by routing a band of Galatian invaders from Macedonia. In about 240 Gonatas died, his resilience and solid work having given to Macedonia a sound and durable government. Gonatas' son Demetrius II (reigned 239–229 BC) at once became involved in a war with the Greek Achaean and Aetolian leagues, which lasted until his death. Macedonia was weakened, and Demetrius' heir, Philip V, was a child. Conditions became so unsettled that the child's guardian, Antigonus Doson, took the throne as Antigonus III. He marched into Greece, and, after defeating the Spartan king Cleomenes III at Sellasia (222), he reestablished the Hellenic Alliance as a confederacy of leagues, with himself as president. Doson died in 221, having restored internal stability and reestablished Macedonia in a stronger position in Greece than it had enjoyed since the reign of Gonatas.

Under Philip V (*see* Philip V *under* Philip [Macedonia]), Macedonia first clashed with Rome (215), but Philip seriously miscalculated Rome's strength, and his defeat at Cynoscephalae (197) led to a peace that confined him to Macedonia. The Hellenic alliance, which had fallen apart, was replaced by a series of leagues in former Macedonian areas. Above all, the old balance of power was upset and Rome became the decisive power in the eastern Mediterranean.

Philip's successor, Perseus (reigned 179–168 BC), was recognized as a champion of Greek freedom against Rome. But Perseus' failure to deploy his full resources brought about his defeat (168) at Pydna in Macedonia and signalled the end of the dynasty.

Antigonish, town, seat of Antigonish county, northeastern Nova Scotia, Canada, at the head of Antigonish Bay, an inlet of Georges Bay, 31 mi (50 km) east of New Glasgow. Encircling the town are conelike hills; the highest, Sugarloaf (750 ft [229 m]), affords a view of Cape Breton Island.

The site was originally settled by the French in 1762; the first British immigrants (soldiers and Scottish Highlanders) did not arrive until after 1785. The earlier name, Dorchester, was replaced by Antigonish, a word that is of Micmac Indian origin and has a disputed meaning—either "broken branches" or "river of fish."

Antigonish is now chiefly residential; but lumber, farm products, and fish are exported, and gypsum and limestone are quarried nearby. It is the seat of a Roman Catholic diocese; and St. Ninian's Cathedral, a granite and blue-limestone structure, dates from about 1875. The town is the seat of Mount St. Bernard's College (1883) and of St. Francis Xavier University (1853), where the Antigonish Movement, a cooperative, self-help program, was instituted in 1930. The Highland Games, patterned after the Braemar Games of Scotland, are held there annually in mid-July. Inc. 1888. Pop. (1981) 5,205.

Antigonus I MONOPHTHALMUS (One-Eyed), also called ANTIGONUS I CYCLOPS (b. 382 BC—d. 301, Ipsus, Phrygia, Asia Minor), Macedonian general under Alexander the Great who founded the Macedonian dynasty of the Antigonids (306–168 BC), becoming king in 306. An exceptional strategist and combat leader, he was also an astute ruler who cultivated the friendship of Athens and other Greek city-states.

Military campaigns. In 333 Alexander had appointed Antigonus satrap of Phrygia, and upon Alexander's death he also received the governorship of Pamphylia and Lycia from the regent Perdiccas. He then formed an alliance against Perdiccas with Antipater, the governor of Macedonia, Ptolemy of Egypt, and Lysimachus of Thrace and Craterus (all of whom had served under Alexander). Perdiccas was murdered, and Antipater became regent. In 321 Antipater appointed Antigonus commander in chief of his army in Asia and sent him against Eumenes, the satrap of Cappadocia and an adherent of Perdiccas. Antigonus defeated Eumenes and then besieged him unsuccessfully in the mountain fortress Nora. Polyperchon succeeded Antipater as regent, and Antigonus joined forces against him with Cassander (Antipater's son), Ptolemy, Lysimachus, and Eumenes in 319. When Eumenes, his rival in Asia Minor (Anatolia), went over to Polyperchon, he defeated him with the aid of Seleucus and Peithon, the satraps of Babylonia and Media, at Gabiene. Then, wishing to eliminate all possible rivals, he had both Eumenes and Peithon executed; Seleucus managed to escape to Egypt.

Antigonus was now in complete control of Asia Minor, but Ptolemy, Lysimachus, Cassander, and Seleucus allied themselves against him in the first coalition war (315–311) in an attempt to thwart his plan of reuniting Alexander's empire. Antigonus occupied Syria and proclaimed himself regent. In order to win the support of the Greek city-states, whose resistance to subjugation presented the chief stumbling block to the formation of a Hellenistic monarchy, he announced to his assembled army that all the Greeks should be free, autonomous, and ungarrisoned. This political slogan was to be sounded again and again—almost immediately by Ptolemy and for a final time by the Romans in 196. With the aid of his officers in Greece, Antigonus drove out Cassander's Macedonian forces of occupation there and formed the island cities in the Aegean into the League of the Islanders, preparatory to his invasion of Greece. His ally, the city of Rhodes, furnished him with the necessary fleet.

While he was engaged in conquering Caria, his son, Demetrius Poliorcetes, was defeated at Gaza by Ptolemy and Seleucus (312). Seleucus returned to his former province, Babylonia. In view of this new threat from the East, Antigonus decided to make peace with all of his adversaries except Seleucus. All of the *diadochoi* (Alexander's successors) confirmed the existing boundaries and the freedom of the Greek cities. Antigonus, no longer regent but merely *stratēgos* (officer in charge) of the whole of Asia, was to rule in Syria and from the Hellespont to the Euphrates.

Activities in Greece. Then Ptolemy attacked Cilicia, and the second coalition war (310–301) against Antigonus broke out. In Greece in 307, Antigonus' son Demetrius ousted Demetrius of Phaleron, Cassander's governor of Athens, and reestablished the old Athenian constitution. The grateful Athenians honoured Antigonus and Demetrius as divine saviours (*theoi sōtēres*). Cassander's influence in Greece was now broken, and in 306 Demetrius defeated Ptolemy's fleet near Salamis on the island of Cyprus and conquered the island. This victory gave Antigonus control of the Aegean, of the eastern Mediterranean, and of all of the Near East except Babylonia. The assembled army proclaimed him king, and his friends adorned him with the diadem. For his part, he appointed Demetrius king and coregent and sent him the diadem. This was to become a traditional ceremony in the Hellenistic monarchy.

In 305, after Antigonus had vainly attacked Egypt, Ptolemy also assumed the title of king, and Cassander, Lysimachus, and Seleucus followed suit. The partition of Alexander's empire into five states had now been formally established. In 305 Antigonus sent Demetrius to conquer Rhodes, which had refused him armed support against Ptolemy. After a year's unsuccessful siege he concluded a peace treaty and an alliance with the island state, guaranteeing it autonomy and neutrality in his conflicts with Ptolemy. This concession was necessary because in the meantime Cassander had invaded Attica and was besieging Athens. Demetrius drove him out of central Greece, and the Athenians bestowed on him a new religious honour, *synnaos* ("having the same temple") of the temple of the goddess Athena.

In 303 he occupied Corinth, Sicyon, and Argos in the Peloponnese, and Achaea, Elis, and almost all of Arcadia joined his side. In 302 Antigonus and Demetrius crowned their success by renewing the pan-Hellenic league, which Philip II of Macedonia had formed in 337. Ambassadors from all the Hellenic states—with the exception of Sparta, Messenia, and Thessaly—elected Antigonus and Demetrius protectors of the new league at Corinth. It was to be an "eternal" treaty, extending to the descendants of the kings. Each member state furnished a contingent of troops for a league army that was commanded by the kings or their deputies. The league was to ensure a general peace in Hellas, but first and foremost it was to aid Antigonus against Cassander.

Final campaigns. Now at the zenith of his power, Antigonus demanded Cassander's unconditional submission. He wanted possession of Macedonia, the native land of his dynasty, and to establish his dominion over Alexander's former empire. The other *diadochoi*, however, warned by Cassander's fate, now joined forces to attack the omnivorous old man. From Babylonia, Seleucus invaded Asia Minor, Ptolemy attacked Syria, and Lysimachus moved into the western part of Asia Minor. Docimus, the regent of Phrygia, and Phoenix, the *stratēgos* of Lycia, deserted Antigonus. He, in turn, recalled Demetrius, left his capital city, Antigoneia (which he had founded on the Orontes in 306), and crossed the Taurus Mountains. Lysimachus, who was waiting for Seleucus, avoided an engagement. In vain Antigonus sent a corps of raiders into Babylonia in order to divide his enemies' forces. In 301 the united armies of Lysimachus and Seleucus engaged the forces of Antigonus and Demetrius at Ipsus in Phrygia. Demetrius made the error of pursuing the enemy's cavalry too far, and as a result Antigonus, age 80, lost the battle and his life.

Antigonus had been an excellent strategist who, until then, had never lost a battle. He had a genuine admiration for Greek civilization. He founded several cities, especially in Asia Minor, and united several small communities into unitary, large centres: Lebedus (Lebedos) and Teos, for example. Several Greek artists graced his court; Apelles painted his portrait in profile because of his missing eye (the cause of which is unknown). (H.V.)

BIBLIOGRAPHY. C. Wehrli, *Antigone et Demetrios* (1968), a comprehensive biography with a discussion of sources and literature; H.H. Schmitt, *Die Verträge der griechisch-römischen Welt von 338 bis 200 v. Chr.* (1969), treats the foundation of the Hellenic union.

Antigonus II GONATAS (b. *c.* 319 BC—d. 239), king of Macedonia from 276 BC who rebuilt his kingdom's power and established its hegemony over Greece.

Antigonus II was the son of Demetrius I Poliorcetes and grandson of Antigonus I. While his father, Demetrius, was busy fighting in Macedonia and Asia Minor against Lysimachus of Thrace, Ptolemy I of Egypt, Pyrrhus of Epirus, and Seleucus I, Antigonus, as his regent, was engaged in maintaining Macedonian hegemony in Greece, which had been achieved in 287 BC. Demetrius was taken prisoner in 285 by Seleucus, who then claimed the Macedonian kingship. This contested title was assumed by Antigonus himself on the death of his father two years later; however, he did not count the beginning of his reign until 276. Although he had only a few bases in Greece, Antigonus laid claim to Macedonia when Seleucus was murdered in 281. His claim was disputed by Seleucus' successor, Antiochus I. Antigonus took part in the defense of Greece against the invading Celts (279). In the following year he concluded a peace with Antiochus. This surrendered his claim to Macedonia. Thereafter Antigonus' foreign policy was marked by friendship with the Seleucids.

In 277 he crossed the Hellespont and defeated the Celts near Lysimacheia. After this success he was acknowledged king by the Macedonians in 276. Pyrrhus, returning in 274 after the failure of his campaign in Italy, drove Antigonus out of Upper Macedonia and Thessaly. Although he retained only a few Macedonian cities, Antigonus followed Pyrrhus when the latter marched into the Peloponnese; and when Pyrrhus died in Argos in 272, Antigonus' control over Macedonia was assured. He was now also the chief of the Thessalian League and on good terms with neighbouring Illyria and Thrace. He secured his position in Greece by keeping Macedonian occupation forces in the cities of Corinth, Chalcis on Euboea, and Demetrias in Thessaly, the three "shackles" of Hellas.

Beyond that he supported the pro-Macedonian faction in various cities in the Peloponnese and the rise to power of tyrants in Sicyon, Argos, Elis, and Megalopolis. In order to keep Greece in a state of complete dependency by controlling the straits and the supply of grain from the southern Russian region, Macedonia—its vigour restored—needed only to gain mastery over the Aegean Sea. To avert this danger, King Areus of Sparta and the city of Athens—urged on by Ptolemy II of Egypt—declared a war for the liberation of Greece (the Chremonidean War, 267–261). Although the Egyptian fleet had blockaded the Saronic Gulf, Antigonus defeated the King of Sparta near Corinth in 265 and then besieged Athens. In 263–262 the city capitulated. Athenian officials were replaced by Antigonus' appointees, and Athens became no more than a Macedonian provincial city.

Immediately after the Chremonidean War, Antigonus joined forces with the Seleucid Antiochus II against their common enemy, Ptolemy II. Whether his naval victory of Cos, which secured Antigonus the Aegean Sea and the League of the Islanders, belongs to this (255) or to the Chremonidean War (261) is uncertain. In 255 a peace was concluded with Ptolemy, and by marrying his stepbrother Demetrius the Fair to Berenice of Cyrene, Antigonus established Macedonian influence in this neighbour country of Egypt.

But his position in Greece was now shaken by a number of reversals. In 253 Alexander, Antigonus' nephew and regent, revolted in Corinth with Ptolemy's help and declared himself an independent monarch. Antigonus lost Corinth and Chalcis, the two bases from which he dominated southern Greece. As the Aetolians had occupied Thermopylae, he was cut off from Athens and the Peloponnese. After Alexander's death, however, Antigonus gave Nicaea, Alexander's widow, to his son Demetrius in marriage and by means of a stratagem regained Corinth in 244. In the meantime the Achaean League was becoming a dangerous opponent. Since 251 it had been under the leadership of Aratus of Sicyon and was receiving financial aid from Ptolemy II. In vain, Antigonus sent gifts to win over Aratus. In 243, without a declaration of hostilities, Aratus made a surprise attack on Corinth and forced the withdrawal of the Macedonian occupation troops. Megara, Troezen, and Epidaurus also deserted Antigonus. He made no attempt to regain these territories but instead formed an alliance with the Aetolian League, which made unsuccessful raids of pillage into the Peloponnese. Nevertheless, by defeating the Egyptian fleet at Andros *c.* 244 Antigonus was able to maintain his hegemony in the Aegean. After a life of endless warfare he died in 239 at 80 years of age.

Personally, Antigonus was unassuming, short of stature, and snub-nosed. In Macedonia the cult of the ruler, so usual in the other Hellenistic states, was unknown. He chose his friends not because of their noble ancestry but for their personal abilities. He conceived his monarchic rule in philosophical terms—*i.e.*, by the strict observance of his duties as a ruler. Once, when his son treated some subjects arbitrarily, he said to him: "Do you not understand that our kingship is a noble servitude [*endoxos douleia*]?" This paradoxical concept of monarchy envisaged the ruler as bearing the burden of his office, serving the people and the law. In his youth Antigonus had been a student of Zeno, the founder of Stoicism. He had been taught by him in Athens and in 276 invited him to his court in Pella in Macedonia. The philosopher, however, did not come and instead sent two of his students, Persaeus and the Theban Philonides. Persaeus wrote a treatise on kingship, was the mentor of Halcyoneus, the son of Antigonus, and became commandant of Corinth in 244. When Zeno died in 263 the King lamented that he had lost the only man whose judgment of his public actions he valued, and he prevailed upon the Athenians to bury him in state. Among the literati at his court was the historian Hieronymus of Cardia, who recorded the war with Pyrrhus, and the poet Aratus, a native of Cilicia, author of the much read didactic poem on astronomy, *Phaenomena.*

(H.V.)

BIBLIOGRAPHY. W.W. Tarn, *Antigonos Gonatas* (1913, reprinted 1969), a comprehensive biography; M. Chambers, "The First Regnal Year of

Antigonus," *Am. J. Philology,* 75:385–394 (1954), provides the dating for his reign; H. Volkmann, *Historia,* 16:155–161 (1967), comments upon the notion of noble servitude (in German).

Antigonus III Doson (b. *c.* 263 BC—d. *c.* 220 BC), king of Macedonia (from 227 BC) who, in defeating Cleomenes of Sparta, ended that city's long independence. His surname may have signified "one who is about to give but never does."

Antigonus, a descendant of Antigonus I, was the son of Demetrius (a half brother of Antigonus II) of Cyrene and Olympias of Larissa. On the death of Demetrius II (229 BC), Antigonus was made guardian of his son Philip. After two years, Antigonus married Demetrius' widow, Phthia, and assumed the crown.

His first military task was to secure Macedonia against barbarians on its borders. He then became involved in Greek affairs, in which he displayed exceptional statesmanship. Reviving a policy of Alexander III the Great, he created a Hellenic league of free alliances, incorporating Aratus and the Achaean League, to oppose Cleomenes, king of Sparta, and the Aetolians.

After a long war, Cleomenes was defeated (222 BC), and Antigonus occupied Sparta. He soon had to return to Macedonia to face an invasion by Illyrians, whom he defeated. Polybius mentions Antigonus as being a wise and moderate ruler. He was succeeded by his stepson, Philip V.

antigorite, mineral, a polymorph of serpentine (*q.v.*).

Antigua and Barbuda, island nation of the Lesser Antilles in the eastern Caribbean Sea, lying at the southern end of the Leeward Islands. It is composed of three islands, including uninhabited Redonda, and covers an area of 171 sq mi (442 sq km). Formerly British colonies, the islands had free-association status with the United Kingdom from 1967 and achieved independence in 1981. The capital is St. John's on Antigua. The nation's nearby Leeward Island neighbours include Anguilla to the northwest, St. Christopher-Nevis to the west, and Montserrat to the southwest. The Atlantic Ocean washes Antigua's northeastern shore. The population in 1983 was estimated to be 78,000.

The article that follows is a summary of significant detail about Antigua and Barbuda. For information about regional aspects of Antigua and Barbuda, *see* MACROPAEDIA: West

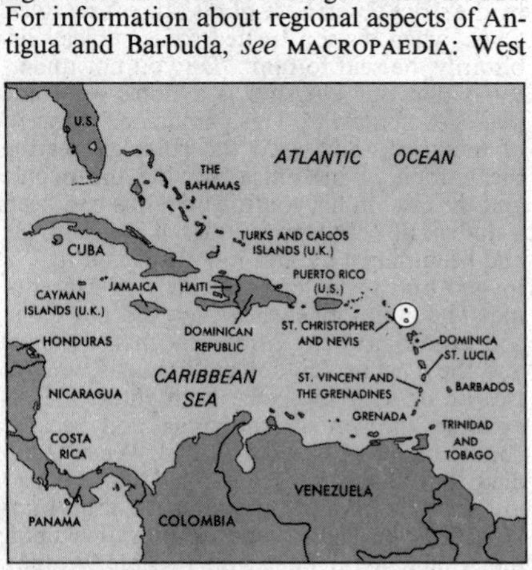

Antigua and Barbuda

Indies. For current history and for statistics on society and economy, *see* the article "World Affairs" and BRITANNICA WORLD DATA, respectively, in the *Britannica Book of the Year.*

The land. The largest of the islands, Antigua, covers a total area of 108 sq mi. Unlike the other Leeward Islands, it lacks forests, mountains, and rivers and is subject to droughts. Though mostly low and undulating and underlain by limestone, the terrain rises westward in volcanic rocks that reach 1,330 ft (405 m) at Boggy Peak. The intricate coastline has bays and headlands fringed by reefs and shoals. Anchorages include the deepwater harbour of St. John's and the shallower harbours of Parham and English. The mean

Nelsons Dockyard in English Harbour, Antigua and Barbuda
Harrison Forman

average temperature of this tropical island is about 81° F (27° C), and the annual rainfall averages about 44 in. (1,118 mm), which is relatively sparse compared with other islands of the Lesser Antilles. Antigua and the nation's other islands lie in the path of the seasonal hurricanes that occur in the West Indies.

Barbuda, formerly Dulcina, lies 25 mi (40 km) north of Antigua and covers 62 sq mi. It is a coral island, flat and well-wooded, with highlands rising to 207 ft at Lindsay Hill in the northeast. A game reserve, Barbuda is inhabited by a variety of wildlife, including duck, guinea fowl, plover, pigeon, wild deer, and wild pig. The only settlement is Codrington, situated on a lagoon on the west side of the island. Barbuda was colonized in 1628 and granted to the Codrington family in 1680, but it reverted to the British crown in the late 19th century. Although planned as a slave-breeding colony, it never became one; the slaves became self-reliant sailors, hunters, fishermen, and skilled workers. They came to regard all the land as communally owned, a position that was the basis of strenuous opposition from Barbudans when Antigua showed signs of interest in taking over the land for commercial development.

Redonda, an uninhabited rock covering 0.5 sq mi and rising sheer to 1,000 ft, lies 25 mi southwest of Antigua proper. Phosphate deposits are located there.

The people. Most of the population of Antigua and Barbuda is made up of the descendants of African slaves who had been brought there during colonial times to work on sugar plantations. Today the people are largely engaged in agricultural pursuits and in tourism. The main settlements are the capital of St. John's, with about 25,000 residents (1979 est.), and Codrington on Barbuda. The language is English, and the vast majority of the population are Christians, with the Anglican Church being predominant. The birth rate in 1980 was about 16 per 1,000 and the death rate about 6 per 1,000. Annual population growth in 1970–80 was 1.3 percent. The people live to an average of about 68 years of age.

The economy. After a slowdown caused by a recession in its traditional markets of the United States, Canada, and the United Kingdom, Antigua and Barbuda experienced a slow but steady growth in its economy between 1977 and 1981. The gross national product (GNP) was estimated (1981) at U.S. $120,000,000, about $1,550 per capita. The real GNP per capita decreased by 1.7 percent per year, on the average, during the period from 1970 to 1980. In 1981, however, the GNP per capita was one of the highest in the eastern Caribbean. Tourism is the mainstay of the economy, accounting for about 60 percent of the gross domestic product (GDP) in 1981, when related services are taken into account. In that year some 208,000 tourists contributed about $42,500,000 to the economy.

Since the 1950s agriculture's contribution to the GDP dropped dramatically, from about 40 percent during that decade to less than 10 percent in 1979. Over the same period the number of agricultural workers fell from about 8,000 to 2,100. A severe blow to the agricultural sector came in 1972 when the sugar industry closed down. Attempts were being made in the early 1980s to replant some of the sugarcane fields and to restore the refinery. Cotton has traditionally been a major crop, with export potential, and fruits, vegetables, and livestock are also raised. The fishing industry has grown in importance, especially after the government established a corporation for catching and processing fish. Part of the lobster catch is exported.

Manufacturing is in the development stage in Antigua and Barbuda. Most of the industries are involved with the processing of agricultural products, and the chief items produced include foods, clothing and textiles, paints, optical lenses, and wood and paper products. There is some production of metal products, and petroleum products made up a significant export until the oil refinery was shut down during the oil crisis of the mid-1970s. The refinery, however, was refurbished in 1982. The country's imports include food, clothes, timber, and nonedible oils. Antigua and Barbuda's main trading partners are the United States and the United Kingdom.

Transportation on the islands is mainly provided by motor vehicles. There are about 150 mi of main roads and about 88 mi of secondary roads. The main airfield, which handles international flights, is at Coolidge on Antigua; there is another, smaller field on Barbuda. The main port is St. John's, with its deepwater harbour.

Administrative and social conditions. Antigua and Barbuda is an independent member of the Commonwealth. The constitution provides for a two-house parliamentary type of government. Members of the House of Representatives are elected every five years, and members of the Senate are appointed by the governor general, who represents the British monarch as the country's head of state. The governor general is advised in his Senate selections by the prime minister and the leader of the minority party.

Two welfare plans administered by the government are available to the islanders. One is a medical plan, which covers most expenses for medical treatment and hospitalization. The other is a social security plan, which provides old-age pensions and a number of other benefits. Hygiene and sanitation are under the direction of the Central Board of Health. The groundwater supply is augmented by distillation of seawater.

Basic education is compulsory, and in 1980 students attended more than 60 primary and secondary schools. The country also has a teachers' college and a technical and vocational school. The literacy rate is high and has been estimated at about 88 percent of the total population.

Radio and television broadcasting is controlled by a government agency. The country has two newspapers, both under private ownership. Telephone service is operated by the government.

Points of interest to visitors on Antigua include the colourful public market, the old Court House (1748–50) in which the parliament meets, and St. John's Cathedral (1847), all in St. John's. The annual Midsummer Carnival, second only to Trinidad's in size, includes calypso contests, processions, and other celebrations.

Antigua Guatemala, capital, Sacatepéquez department, southwestern Guatemala, at an altitude of 5,029 ft (1,533 m). Capital of the former captaincy general, Antigua Guatemala was once the most important seat of Spanish colonial government between Mexico City and Lima, Peru. Founded as Santiago de los Caballeros de Guatemala in 1527, it was destroyed by an eruption that swept down from the slopes of Volcán de Agua. The village

The colonial church of La Merced, Antigua Guatemala

Harrison Forman

that became reestablished on the site came to be called Ciudad Vieja ("old city"). Another capital city with the name Santiago was constructed in 1542 near the site of Ciudad Vieja, and it became a thriving political, economic, and cultural centre of some 60,000 persons. When Santiago was demolished by an earthquake in 1773, the capital was moved 15 mi (24 km) to the site of Nueva Guatemala ("new Guatemala"), the modern Guatemala City, and Santiago became known as Antigua Guatemala ("Guatemala of old"), or Antigua.

Antigua Guatemala is noted chiefly for the ruins of colonial edifices that make it a museum of Spanish colonial history. On or near the central plaza, several of the principal buildings of the colonial capital still serve public functions; and scattered throughout the city are numerous ruins of religious structures and rebuilt private dwellings. Antigua Guatemala has several modern hotels situated in quiet, picturesque surroundings. The grandeur of its setting at the base of towering volcanoes and its benign climate make the city a favourite resort and residential site. The annual Holy Week festival is one of the best known in the country. A paved highway connects the town with Guatemala City. Pop. (1981 prelim.) mun., 27,014.

antihistamine, any of a group of synthetic drugs that selectively counteract the pharmacological effects of histamine (*q.v.*), following its release from certain large cells (mast cells). Antihistamines replace histamine at one or the other of the two sites at which it becomes bound to various susceptible tissues, thereby preventing histamine-triggered reactions under such conditions as stress, inflammation, and allergy.

The antihistamines first introduced are bound at the so-called H_1 sites; they are therefore designated H_1-blocking agents and oppose selectively all the pharmacological effects of histamine except those on gastric secretion. Development of antihistamines dates from about 1937, when French workers discovered compounds that protected animals against both the lethal effects of histamine and those of anaphylactic shock. The first antihistamines were derivatives of ethylamine; aniline-type compounds, tested later and found to be more potent, were too toxic for clinical use. In 1942, the forerunner of most modern antihistamines (an aniline derivative called Antergan) was discovered; subsequently, compounds that were more potent, more specific, and less toxic were prepared. More than 100 antihistaminic compounds soon became available for treating patients.

Since histamine is involved in the production of some symptoms of allergy and anaphylaxis, antihistamines can control certain allergic conditions, among them hay fever and vasomotor rhinitis; the nasal irritation and watery discharge are most readily relieved. Persons with urticaria, edema, itching, and certain sensitivity reactions respond well. Antihistamines are not usually beneficial in treating the common cold and asthma. Antihistamines with powerful antiemetic properties are used in the treatment of motion sickness and vomiting. Used in sufficiently large doses, nearly all antihistamines produce undesirable side effects; the incidence and severity of the side effects depend both on the patient and on the properties of the specific drug. The most common side effect in adults is drowsiness; cerebral stimulation may occur in infants. Other side effects include gastrointestinal irritation, headache, blurred vision, and dryness of the mouth. If a patient's condition does not improve after three days of treatment with antihistamines, it is unlikely that he will benefit from them. Antihistamines are readily absorbed from the alimentary tract, and most are rendered inactive by monoamine oxidase enzymes in the liver.

During the 1970s an H_2-blocking agent, cimetidine (Tagamet) was introduced. Compounds of this class suppress histamine-induced gastric secretion and have proved useful in treating ulcers.

antiknock rating: *see* octane number.

Antilles, group of islands comprising all of the West Indies (*q.v.*) except the Bahamas. They are divided into two major groups: the Greater Antilles (*q.v.*), including Cuba, Hispaniola (Haiti and Dominican Republic), Jamaica, and Puerto Rico; and the Lesser Antilles, comprising all the rest of the islands.

The term Antilles dates traditionally from before Europeans discovered the New World, when Antilia referred to semimythical lands located somewhere west of Europe across the Atlantic. On medieval charts it was sometimes indicated as a continent or large island and sometimes as an archipelago. After discovery of the West Indies by Columbus, the Spanish term Antillas was commonly assigned to the new lands, and "Sea of the Antilles" in various European languages is used as an alternate designation for the Caribbean Sea.

Antilles Current, branch of the Atlantic North Equatorial Current, forming part of the clockwise-setting ocean-current system in the North Atlantic Ocean. It flows northwestward along the north side of the Greater Antilles islands and merges with the Florida Current, which issues from the Gulf of Mexico through the Straits of Florida to form the initial portion of the Gulf Stream system.

A list of the abbreviations used in the MICROPAEDIA *will be found at the end of this volume*

Antilochus, in Greek legend, son of Nestor, king of Pylos. One of the suitors of Helen, whose abduction caused the Trojan War, he accompanied his father to the war and distinguished himself as acting commander of the Pylians. When Nestor was attacked by Memnon (king of the Ethiopians), Antilochus saved his father's life at the sacrifice of his own, thus fulfilling the oracle that had bidden him "beware of an Ethiopian." According to later accounts, he was slain by Hector or by Paris (both sons of King Priam of Troy) in the temple of the Thymbraean Apollo together with his friend Achilles.

Antim IVIREANUL: *see* Anthimus of Iberia.

antimacassar, protective covering thrown over the back of a chair or the head or cushions of a sofa, named after Macassar, a hair-oil in general use in the 19th century. The original antimacassars were made of stiff

Chairs with antimacassars, Palmer House, Chicago, 1875

By courtesy of the Library of Congress, Washington, D.C.

white crochet-work, but later soft, coloured materials, such as embroidered wools or silks, were used. In the 20th century the use of antimacassars largely died out.

Antimachus OF COLOPHON (fl. *c.* 410 BC), a Greek poet and scholar who wrote a lengthy epic entitled *Thebais,* an account of the expedition of the Seven Against Thebes. His work was greatly admired in antiquity, and his pedantic style made him the model of the learned Alexandrian epic poets. The emperor Hadrian rated Antimachus above Homer, a judgment that did something to rescue him from obscurity. His work survives chiefly in the quotations cited by later writers to illustrate obscure words and out-of-the-way mythological detail.

antimatter, substance composed of atoms made up of elementary particles that have the mass and charge of electrons, protons, or neutrons, their counterparts in ordinary matter, but for which the charge is opposite in sign. Such particles are called positrons (e^+), antiprotons ($\bar{p}$), and antineutrons ($\bar{n}$), or, collectively, antiparticles. Matter and antimatter cannot coexist at close range for more than a small fraction of a second because they annihilate each other with release of large quantities of energy. It has been suggested that some distant galaxies may be composed entirely of antimatter.

The concept of antimatter first arose in analysis of the duality between positive and negative charge. The work of P.A.M. Dirac on the energy states of the electron led to the prediction and, finally, to laboratory production of a particle identical in every respect but one to the electron, that is, with positive instead of negative charge. Such a particle, called the positron (e^+), is not found in ordinary matter. The life expectancy or duration of the positron in ordinary matter is very short. Unless the positron is moving extremely fast, it will be drawn close to an ordinary electron by the attraction between opposite charges. A collision between the positron and electron results in their simultaneous disappearance, their masses being converted into energy in accordance with the Einstein relation $E = mc^2$, where c is the velocity of light. This process is called annihilation, and the resultant energy is emitted in the form of high-energy quanta of electromagnetic radiation or gamma rays. The inverse reaction $\gamma \rightarrow e^+ + e^-$ can also proceed under appropriate conditions, and the process is called electron-positron creation. This last process is the one commonly used to produce positrons in the laboratory.

The antimatter counterparts of the proton and neutron, the antiproton ($\bar{p}$) and the antineutron ($\bar{n}$), were discovered in the mid-1950s after many years of speculation on the possibility of their existence. Antideuterons, the antiparticles corresponding to the nucleus of deuterium, have been produced in very high energy collisions, at the 30 GeV (giga-electron volt) synchrotron of the Brookhaven (N.Y.) National Laboratory.

The electrical properties of antimatter are opposite to those of ordinary matter; thus, for example, the $\bar{p}$ has a negative charge, and the $\bar{n}$, although electrically neutral, has a magnetic moment opposite in sign to that of the neutron.

The Dirac theory of electrons and positrons predicts that an electron and a positron, because of Coulomb attraction, will bind together into an atom just as an electron and a proton form a hydrogen atom. The e^+e^- bound system is called positronium; its annihilation into gamma rays has been observed. Its lifetime is of the order of 10^{-7} second or 10^{-10} second, depending on the orientation of the two particles. These lifetimes agree well with those computed from Dirac's theory.

Both protons and neutrons are described by the Dirac equation. Antiprotons can be produced by bombarding protons with protons. If enough energy is available, that is, if the incident proton has a kinetic energy of at least 5.6 GeV (5.6×10^9 electron volts) extra particles of proton mass appear according to the formula $E = mc^2$. Such energies became available in the 1950s at the Berkeley (Calif.) Bevatron. In 1955 a team of physicists led by Owen Chamberlain and Emilio Segrè observed that antiprotons are produced by high-energy collisions. Antineutrons also were discovered at the Berkeley Bevatron by observing their annihilation in matter with a consequent release of high energies.

By the time the antiproton was discovered, a host of new subatomic particles had also been discovered; all of these particles are now known to have corresponding antiparticles. Thus, there are positive and negative muons, positive and negative pions, the K-meson and the anti-K-meson, plus a long list of baryons and antibaryons. Most of these newly discovered particles have too short a lifetime for them to be able to combine with electrons. The exception is the positive muon that together with an electron has been observed to form a muonium atom.

Many attempts have been made to investigate the importance of antimatter in cosmological problems; theoretical and experimental knowledge of matter and antimatter is relevant to the understanding of the creation and constitution of the universe. Obviously no star can contain a close mixture of matter and antimatter; otherwise it would instantaneously explode with more violence than a supernova. Interstellar gas, and even intergalactic gas, cannot be a mixture, either. This is because among the annihilation products of proton plus antiproton into pions there is a certain amount of neutral pion (π^0) mesons, which in turn decay into two energetic gamma rays. Satellite experiments have not detected enough of such gamma rays to suggest a significant amount of antimatter annihilation. One could resort to the hypothesis that matter and antimatter are separated on the scale of clusters of galaxies. The creation of baryon-antibaryon pairs, however, is very localized, the particle and antiparticle being created at distances of approximately 10^{-13} centimetre. No present understanding of the evolution of the universe can explain the unmixing of matter and antimatter if they had been originally created together.

It has been repeatedly proposed that the existence of antimatter might offer a natural explanation of the quasar phenomenon. Quasars, or quasi-stellar objects, if at distances comparable to those of the external galaxies as one hypothesis suggests, are pouring out energy at an enormous rate from a small volume of space; the rate is so high that ordinary processes of physics do not suffice to explain it. Annihilation of matter and antimatter is the most efficient energy-producing process and would easily provide the tremendous energy output observed for these objects. Some scientists feel that a more conventional explanation of such objects is possible without the assumption of matter-antimatter annihilation. No such assumptions are needed to explain cosmic rays and astronomical sources of X-rays.

Nevertheless, the presence of large amounts of antimatter in the universe cannot at present be ruled out completely, nor can the possibility that some cosmic sources of intense radiation might be due to the interpenetration of matter and antimatter. But it can be shown that the total relative amount of antimatter in the Galaxy must be less than one part in 10^7.

Soon after the discovery of the antiproton the question was raised as to whether antimatter would be subject to gravitational attraction or repulsion from ordinary matter. This question is of extreme importance because gravitational repulsion between matter and antimatter is inconsistent with the theory of general relativity. The answers to such questions can be obtained experimentally because of the properties of K^0 and $\bar{K}^0$ mesons. Observation of the interference phenomena between $K^0{}_1$, and $\bar{K}^0{}_2$ led to the conclusion, by M.L. Good, that the gravitational interaction between matter and antimatter is identical to that between matter and matter.

Where the same name may denote a person, place, or thing, the articles will be found in that order

---

antimer (chemistry): *see* enantiomorph.

Antimerina (people): *see* Merina.

antimetabolite, a specific antagonist of a chemical change essential in the utilization or formation of a substance required by a living cell. Either of these types of processes, which comprise individual reactions that are catalyzed by enzymes, are interrupted by an antimetabolite that is similar in structure to a substrate (a substance acted upon by an enzyme to form a product) and that exerts its effect by combining with the enzyme, thereby preventing the interaction of the enzyme with its substrate. An antimetabolite produced by a living organism (*e.g.*, a fungus) is called an antibiotic (*q.v.*). Many compounds have been synthesized in attempts to discover new antimetabolites for possible use in chemotherapy of cancers and other diseases. *See also* antagonist, drug; inhibition (in enzymology).

antimicrobial agent, any of a large variety of chemical compounds and physical agents that are used to destroy microorganisms or to prevent their development.

Antiseptics and germicides. Antiseptics and germicides may be applied either directly or as gases or vapours on living and nonliving objects. These agents are used in hospitals, in eating and drinking establishments, and in homes.

Although antiseptic literally means against putrefaction or prevention of sepsis (spread of bacteria), the term usually is used to refer to agents applied to the living tissues of animals (including man) and plants in order to destroy or inhibit the growth of infectious microorganisms. In low concentrations, an antiseptic may inhibit microbial growth; in high concentrations, it may kill them. Substances (*e.g.*, salves, ointments, and dressings) that are in contact with external tissues, such as skin, for long periods of time are considered antiseptics if they inhibit microbial growth. On the other hand, substances (*e.g.*, mouthwashes, douches, gargles) that have only brief contact with internal tissues such as mucous membranes are considered antiseptics only if recommended amounts destroy microorganisms. The term asepsis is used to describe a process by which microorganisms are prevented from entering some object; surgical asepsis, for example, refers to preventing the introduction of disease-causing bacteria into wounds of animals, including man.

Germicides (disinfectants) destroy harmful microorganisms and also may inactivate viruses and protozoans but ordinarily do not affect bacterial or fungal spores, which are walled, usually dormant, reproductive bodies. Disinfection has been officially defined as the killing of disease-causing (pathogenic) agents by direct application of chemical or physical methods. The term disinfectant is usually used to refer to the substances that destroy microorganisms on inanimate surfaces; *e.g.*, surgical instruments, floors, walls, linens (*see* disinfectant).

Many antiseptics and germicides are specific regarding destruction of certain microorganisms and not others. An ideal compound that will destroy all microorganisms, without causing any residual toxic effect in high concentrations, has not yet been developed.

Sterilization. Sterilization, any process, physical or chemical, that destroys all forms of life, is used especially to destroy microorganisms, spores, and viruses. Precisely defined, sterilization is the complete destruction of all microorganisms by a suitable chemical agent or by heat, either wet steam under pressure at 120° C (250° F) or more for at least 15 minutes, or dry heat at 160° to 180° C (320° to 360° F) for three hours. Objects that are to be sterilized must withstand treatment without suffering deleterious effects.

Sanitization. A sanitizer is an agent, usually chemical in nature, that is used to reduce the number of microorganisms to a level that has been officially approved as safe. Sanitizers are commonly used to control bacterial levels in equipment and utensils found in dairies, other food-processing plants, eating and drinking establishments, and other places in which no specific pathogenic microorganisms are known to be present and destruction of all microorganisms may not be necessary.

Chemical preservatives, antibiotics, and other antimicrobials. Preservatives, usually chemical agents, are added to certain foods and medicines to prevent the growth of microorganisms that may cause spoilage or disease. Prophylactics also are agents used to prevent infections and diseases. Although antibiotics usually are used to treat infectious diseases already in progress in man and other animals, they also have been used as antiseptics, especially on the skin or on mucous surfaces, to prevent the entry of pathogenic microorganisms. Vaccination is the administration of harmless amounts of disease-causing microorganisms into animals, including man, to prevent diseases. (*See* antibiotic; vaccination.)

Sterile filtration usually removes large microorganisms (*e.g.*, bacteria, fungi, and their spores) from heat-sensitive solutions, but this physical method does not effectively remove small infectious microorganisms (*e.g.*, filterable viruses and rickettsiae). Surface-active quaternary ammonium germicides, effective against most bacteria, are not effective against bacterial spores, the tubercle bacillus, and

Examples of chemical and physical agents with antimicrobial properties

Acids
hydrochloric acid
nitric acid
sulfuric acid
phosphoric acid
acetic acid
boric acid
benzoic acid
salicylic acid

Alkalies
calcium hydroxide
sodium hydroxide
potassium hyroxide
trisodium phosphate
sodium borate
sodium carbonate

Aldehydes
acetaldehyde
formaldehyde
glyceraldehyde
glycoaldehyde
methoxybenzaldehyde
isovaleraldehyde

Aromatic oils
camphor oil
peppermint oil
pine oil
cinnamon oil
eucalyptus oil

Dyes
acridine
brilliant green
gentian violet
malachite green

Sulfonamides
sulfanilamide
sulfathiazole
sulfapyridine
sulfaguanidine
sulfadiazine
sulfamerazine
sulfasuxidine

Antibiotics
penicillin
streptomycin
chloramphenicol
polymyxin
neomycin
terramycin
tyrothricin (Gramicidin)

Alcohols
methyl alcohol
ethyl alcohol
propyl alcolhol
isopropyl alcohol
benzyl alchohol
amyl alcohol

Coal-tar derivatives
phenol (carbolic acid)
cresols
phenol bismuth
phenol diiodide
para-nitrophenol

Reducing agents
carbon monoxide
hydrogen
sodium thiosulfate
sodium thioglycollate

Oxidizing agents
bromine
chlorine
fluorine
iodine
oxygen
ozone
perchloric acid
sodium bromate
sodium permanganate
sodium peroxide

Surface-active agents
anionics (true soaps, synthetic soaps, sulfonates)
cationics (quaternary ammonium salts)
non-ionics (alkylated aryl polyether alcohol; polyethylene oxide derivative of sorbitan mono-oleate)

Metals (as salts)
aluminum
cobalt
copper
iron
mercury
silver
zinc

Physical agents
heat
radiation
sterile filtration

some viruses. Although both X-rays and certain radioactive isotopes emit similar rays (gamma rays), X-rays usually are used to combat fungal infections of the skin; radioactive isotopes seldom are used in this way because they are difficult to confine to one area. Sulfonamides and antibiotic drugs are chemotherapeutic agents; *i.e.,* drugs that combat infectious diseases already in progress. The specificity of chemicals, even in a single class of antimicrobial agents, is often difficult to determine; one may affect some organisms more than others.

Modes of action. Some antimicrobial compounds act directly on microbial cells to dissolve them. Surface-active agents may not dissolve the microorganisms; instead, they may penetrate the cells and cause the release of amino acids, nuclear material, and other important chemical constituents. Some compounds penetrate microbial cell walls and inactivate essential membrane transport systems, so that the cells can no longer obtain the nutrients necessary for them to survive and to reproduce. Others coagulate certain vital materials in cells, thereby destroying the microorganisms. A few agents disrupt the metabolism of the cells, so that they can no longer assimilate nutrients; as a result, the cells starve and die. The antimicrobial effects of some of these compounds can be seen with an ordinary light microscope. The effects of many chemical agents on disease-causing microorganisms (*e.g.,* viruses, rickettsiae, mycoplasma), however, must be studied with more elaborate techniques. (C.A.L./Ed.)

BIBLIOGRAPHY. C.A. Lawrence and S.S. Block (eds.), *Disinfection, Sterilization, and Preservation,* pp. 109–233 (1968). Other information may be obtained from the United States Department of Agriculture, Disinfectants Evaluation Department, Pesticides Regulation Division, Washington, D.C.

antimonide, any member of a rare mineral group consisting of compounds of one or more metals with antimony (Sb). The coordination of the metal is virtually always octahedral or tetrahedral—*i.e.,* in the former each metal ion occupies a position within an octahedron comprised of six oppositely charged antimony ions, while in the latter the metal ion is surrounded by six oppositely charged neighbours that are arranged tetrahedrally. The crystal structure of octahedral coordination is identical to that of the sulfide mineral galena; that of tetrahedral coordination corresponds to the structure of another member of the same mineral group, argentite.

Two common antimonides are dyscrasite (Ag_3Sb) and stibiopalladinite (Pd_3Sb). Dyscrasite exhibits a distinct orthorhombic symmetry. It is an important silver ore that occurs in deposits of hydrothermal origin associated with intrusive igneous rocks; significant amounts are found at Cobalt, Ontario, Can. and Kongsberg, Nor. Stibiopalladinite also manifests orthorhombic symmetry. It is a principal palladium mineral that occurs in nickel-ferrous deposits associated with platinum, pyrrhotite, and chalcopyrite. It has been found in the Bushveld Complex, South Africa, and Choco, Col. Other antimonides include:

horfordite	Cu_6Sb(?)
aurostibite	$AuSb_2$
seversite	$PtSb_2$
breithauptite	NiSb

All antimonides have a metallic lustre, are opaque, and have high specific gravity and intermediate to low hardness.

antimony (Sb, from Latin *stibium*), a metallic element belonging to the nitrogen family (Group Va of the periodic table), existing in many allotropic forms (physically distinct conditions that result from different arrangements of the same atoms in molecules or crystals, as in diamond and graphite). A bright silvery-white metal having a hard, brittle, crystalline structure, antimony occurs chiefly as the gray sulfide mineral stibnite (Sb_2S_3).

One method of obtaining antimony from stibnite is by roasting the ore to form the oxide Sb_2O_4, which is then reduced to the element by heating it with carbon. Another is to melt the ore with scrap iron in a furnace; as the iron combines with the sulfur to form a liquid layer of molten iron sulfide, the heavier liquid antimony settles to the bottom and is drawn off.

Antimony from Prince William, New Brunswick, Can.
By courtesy of the Field Museum of Natural History, Chicago; photograph, Mary A. Root—EB Inc.

A poor conductor of heat and electricity, antimony does not tarnish in dry air but it is slowly converted to an oxide if the air is moist. When heated in air it burns with a brilliant blue flame and gives off white fumes of the trioxide Sb_2O_3. The trioxide of antimony is amphoteric; that is, it is soluble in either acids or alkalies.

In its pure state antimony has no important uses, but when combined physically or chemically with other substances, it is an extremely useful metal. Because it expands on solidifying (a rare characteristic that it shares with water), antimony is a particularly valuable ingredient of alloys used for castings and type metal; the expansion of the alloy forces the metal to fill the small crevices of casting molds. Moreover, the presence of antimony in type metal, which also includes lead and small amounts of tin, increases the hardness of the type and gives it a sharp definition. Even when added in minor quantities, antimony imparts strength and hardness to other metals, particularly lead, with which it forms alloys used in plates of automobile storage batteries, in bullets, and in coverings for telephone cables. Combined with tin, lead, and copper, antimony forms antifriction alloys called babbitt metals that are used as components of machine bearings.

Among the many applications of antimony compounds, the sulfide is used in ammunition and friction matches, the trioxide and the trichloride in flameproofing fabrics, and the trioxide in paints and plastics both as a pigment and as a fire-retarding agent. Several other antimony compounds are used as paint pigments; tartar emetic (an organic salt of antimony) is used in the textile industry to aid in binding certain dyes to fabrics and in medicine as an expectorant and a nauseant.

atomic number	51
atomic weight	121.75
melting point	630.5° C (1,166.9° F)
boiling point	1,380° C (2,516° F)
density	6.691 g/cc at 20° C (68° F)
oxidation states	−3, +3, +5
electron config.	2-8-18-18-5 or $1s^2 2s^2 2p^6 3s^2 3p^6 3d^{10} 4s^2 4p^6 4d^{10} 5s^2 5p^3$

antimony poisoning, harmful effects upon body tissues and functions of ingesting or inhaling certain compounds of antimony. Such poisoning resembles arsenic poisoning.

Antimony poisoning has resulted from drinking acidic fruit juices containing antimony oxide dissolved from the glaze of cheap enamelware containers. Toxicity can also result from repeated exposure to antimony in medications, such as tartar emetic (antimony and potassium tartrate), used to induce vomiting and in treatment of helminthic and fungal infestations. The industrial use of antimony has not appeared to be associated with serious occupational poisoning. It is believed that the toxicity of antimony and of arsenic is due to the fact that in combination with enzymes (the organic catalysts of the cell) they interfere with cellular metabolism.

Antimorona (people): *see* Antaimoro.

antimycotic: *see* fungicide.

Antin, Mary (b. 1881, Polotsk, Russia—d. May 15, 1949, Suffern, N.Y., U.S.), author of the autobiographical *Promised Land* and other books on immigrant life in the United States.

Antin emigrated to the United States in 1894 and attended Teachers College of Columbia University and Barnard College, New York City, 1901–04. She wrote (in Yiddish) about her voyage to the United States in her first book, *From Polotsk to Boston* (Eng. trans., 1899). *The Promised Land* (1912), which first appeared as a serial in *The Atlantic Monthly* and won wide acclaim, narrates the experiences of European Jews and the contrast with life in the United States. After its publication she toured the United States as a lecturer. Her third book on immigrants, *They Who Knock at Our Gates,* was published in 1914.

antineutrino, subatomic particle that is the antimatter counterpart of the neutrino (*q.v.*).

antineutron, antiparticle of the ordinary neutron, first produced in 1956 at the University of California (Berkeley) by passing an antiproton beam through matter. Antineutrons were detected along with neutrons after antiprotons in the beam exchanged their negative charge with nearby protons, which have a positive charge. Antineutrons are quickly annihilated by neutrons or protons.

antinomianism (Greek *anti,* "against"; *nomos,* "law"), doctrine according to which Christians are freed by grace from the necessity of obeying the Mosaic Law. The antinomians rejected the very notion of obedience as legalistic; to them the good life flowed from the inner working of the Holy Spirit. In this circumstance they appealed not only to Martin Luther but also to Paul and Augustine.

The ideas of antinomianism had been present in the early church, and some Gnostic heretics believed that freedom from law meant freedom for license. The doctrine of antinomianism, however, grew out of the Protestant controversies on the law and the gospel and was first attributed to Luther's collaborator, Johann Agricola. It also appeared in the Reformed branch of Protestantism. The left-wing Anabaptists were accused of antinomianism, both for theological reasons and also because they opposed the cooperation of church and state, which was considered necessary for law and order. For similar reasons, in the 17th century, Separatists, Familists, Ranters, and Independents in England were called antinomians by the established churches. In New England, Anne Hutchinson was accused of the doctrine when she said that the churches were preaching "the covenant of works." The Evangelical movement at the end of the 18th century produced its own antinomians who claimed an inner experience and a "new life," which they considered the true source of good works.

antinomy, in philosophy, contradiction, real or apparent, between two principles or conclusions, both of which seem equally justified; it is nearly synonymous with the term paradox. Immanuel Kant, the father of critical philosophy, in order to show the inadequacy of pure reason in the field of metaphysics, employed the word antinomies in elaborating his doctrine that pure reason generates contradictions in seeking to grasp the unconditioned. He offered alleged proofs of the two propositions that the universe had a beginning and is of finite extent (the thesis) and also of a contrary proposition (the antithesis). Similarly, he offered proofs both for and against the three propositions: (1) that every complex substance consists of simple parts; (2) that not every phenomenon has a sufficient "natural" cause (*i.e.,* that there is freedom in the universe); and (3) that there exists a necessary being, either within or outside the universe. Kant used the first two antinomies to infer that space and time constitute a framework imposed, in a sense, by the mind. Kant's "Copernican Revolution" was that things revolve around the knower, rather than the knower around things. He resolved the four antinomies by drawing a distinction between phenomena (things as they are known or experienced by the senses) and noumena (things in themselves; *see* noumenon). Kant insisted that we can never know the noumena, for we can never get beyond phenomena.

In the 20th century more specific suggestions for resolving the antinomies arose. Because the philosophical significance of these possible resolutions continues to be debated, however, the force of Kant's case against pure reason is yet to be assessed.

Antinoöpolis, modern SHEIKH ABADE, Roman city in ancient Egypt, on the east bank of the Nile, 24 miles (37 kilometres) south of modern al-Minyā in al-Minyā *muḥāfaẓah* (governorate). On the site of a Ramesside temple, the Roman emperor Hadrian officially founded the city Oct. 30, AD 130, naming it after his companion Antinoüs, who had drowned in the Nile near the site earlier that year. The Via Hadriana, which led to the Red Sea, began at Antinoöpolis. Papyri found there have provided information about its constitution, based on that of Naukratis. The citizens were considered Greeks, though they could marry Egyptian women. The city survived at least to the 8th century AD.

Antinoüs (b. *c.* 110, Bithynium, Bithynia—d. 130, near Besa, Egypt), favourite of the Roman emperor Hadrian, who was deified by the Emperor after his death. Antinoüs, with whom Hadrian had a homosexual relationship, accompanied him on his many journeys throughout the Mediterranean world. While the two were visiting Egypt, Antinoüs drowned in the Nile. Hadrian erected temples to him all over the empire and founded a city, named Antinoöpolis in his honour, near the place of his death. Many sculptures, gems, and coins survive depicting Antinoüs as a model of youthful beauty.

antinovel, also called NOUVEAU ROMAN (French: "new novel"), avant-garde novel of the mid-20th century marking a radical departure from the conventions of the traditional novel. Starting from the premise that everything in the novel had been done—that whole societies had been portrayed in panorama and individual psychologies probed minutely—the antinovelists sought new avenues of fictional exploration. In their efforts to overcome literary habits and to challenge the expectations of their readers, they deliberately frustrated conventional literary expectations, avoiding any expression of the author's personality, preferences, or values. They rejected the traditional elements of character, entertainment, dramatic progress, and dialogue that reveal character or further plot.

The term antinovel was first used by Jean-Paul Sartre in an introduction to Nathalie Sarraute's *Portrait d'un inconnu* (1948; *Portrait of a Man Unknown,* 1958). It is usually associated with the French *nouveau roman* of the 1950s and '60s, but works of other writers, such as the German novelist Uwe Johnson's *Mutmassungen über Jakob* (1959; *Speculations About Jacob,* 1963), also reveal vaguely identified characters, casual arrangement of events, and uncertainty of meaning.

Antioch, also called ANTIOCH PISIDIAN, Greek ANTIOCHEIA PISIDIAS, ancient city in Phrygia, near the Pisidian border, close to modern Yalvaç, in Isparta *il* (province), Turkey. Founded by Seleucus I (*c.* 358–281 BC), it was made a free city in 189 BC by the Romans, who took direct control in *c.* 25 BC; soon thereafter the emperor Augustus made it a colony with the name Caesarea Antiochia. It became the centre of civil and military administration in southern Galatia, and in the time of the emperor Claudius I (reigned AD 41–54), St. Paul made it one of the centres of his mission in that province. Antioch was finally assigned to Pisidia under Diocletian's provincial reorganization. Its ruins include a large rock cutting which may have held the temple of Men Ascaënus, the local Phrygian deity.

Antioch, Turkish ANTAKYA, populous city of ancient Syria, since 1939 the chief town of the *il* (province) of Hatay in southern Turkey, near the mouth of the Orontes River (Turkish Asi Nehri). It was founded in 300 BC by the Greeks and was the centre of the Seleucid Kingdom until 64 BC, when the Romans made it the capital of their province of Syria. The city was one of the earliest centres of Christianity, serving as the headquarters of the missionary St. Paul in about AD 47–55. Antioch prospered in the 4th and 5th centuries

The Four Seasons (corner panels) and mythological scenes, mosaic floor of the House of the Red Pavement, Antioch, *c.* 5th century AD

By courtesy of the Department of Art and Archaeology, Princeton University from nearby olive plantations and in the 6th century developed a silk industry. That century also brought a series of earthquakes and fires. Antioch was captured temporarily by the Persians in 540 and 611 and was absorbed into the Arab caliphate in 637. Under the Arabs, it shrank to the status of a small town. The Byzantines recaptured the city in 969, and it served as a frontier fortification until taken by the Seljuq Turks in 1084. In 1098 it was captured by the crusaders and was taken by the Mamlūks in 1268. It finally fell to the Ottoman Turks in 1517 and remained under Ottoman control until World War I.

The activities of the modern town are based mainly on the agricultural produce of the adjacent area, including the intensively cultivated Amik plain. The chief crops are wheat, cotton, grapes, rice, olives, vegetables, and fruit. The town has soap and olive-oil factories and cotton ginning and other processing industries. Silk, shoes, and knives are also manufactured. Important archaeological discoveries have been made there. Pop. (1980) 94,942.

Antioch, Council of (AD 341), a non-ecumenical Christian Church council held at Antioch (modern Antakya in southeastern Turkey) on the occasion of the consecration of Constantine's Golden Church there. It was first of several 4th-century councils that attempted to replace orthodox Nicene theology with a modified Arianism (*q.v.*). Attended by the Eastern emperor Constantius II and about 100 Eastern bishops, the council developed four creeds as substitutes for the Nicene, all of them to some degree unorthodox and omitting or rejecting the Nicene statement that Christ was "of one substance" (*homoousios*) with the Father. The disciplinary 25 canons of Antioch are generally thought to have come from this council, but some scholars believe they were the work of an earlier council (330) at Antioch.

Antioch, Orthodox Church of: *see* Greek Orthodox Patriarchate of Antioch and All the East.

Antioch, Principality of, a state centred on the city of Antioch, founded by European Christians in territory taken from the Muslims in 1098, during the First Crusade. It survived as a European outpost in the East for nearly two centuries.

Antioch's territory included the well-fortified, predominantly Christian city, the leading commercial centre of the Latin East, and an area that stretched north into Cilicia, east to the frontiers of Edessa and Aleppo, and south into central Syria. Its first prince, Bohemond I (ruled 1098–1111), and regents, Tancred (1104–12) and Roger, prince of Antioch (regent from 1112 to 1119), were successful in their attempts to expand the state, but the Muslims thwarted their campaigns to conquer Aleppo. Antioch's princes often died in battle, leaving heirs too young to rule; succession disputes were frequent, and the king of Jerusalem, the princes' feudal overlord, often intervened to restore order.

The state prospered economically despite domestic unrest and Muslim onslaughts. Because trade was vital to Christian and Muslim alike, agreements were reached that enabled trade to continue despite religious differences. Spices, dyes, silk, and porcelain came on caravans from the East and were shipped to European markets. Nearby orchards and olive groves supplied sweet lemons and olive oil for export, and wood from the forests of Lebanon was traded to the Egyptians in return for fine cloth.

In 1187 Bohemond III (reigned 1163–1201) of Antioch obtained guarantees for the principality from the Muslim leader Saladin (reigned 1169–93), after Saladin had conquered a large part of the kingdom of Jerusalem. After Bohemond's death, Antioch was torn by wars over the succession, and, though peace was restored, these disputes gave the Muslims time to gather their forces. By 1268 Antioch's territory had been severely diminished, and the city itself surrendered to the attacking army of Baybars I (1260–77), Mamlūk sultan of Egypt and Syria.

Antioch, School of, Christian theological institution in Syria, traditionally founded *c.* AD 200, that stressed the literal interpretation of the Bible and the completeness of Christ's humanity, in opposition to the School of Alexandria (*see* Alexandria, School of), which emphasized the allegorical interpretation of the Bible and stressed Christ's divinity. Flourishing in the 4th–6th century, the School of Antioch produced several significant theologians, including Diodore of Tarsus, Theodore of Mopsuestia, St. John Chrysostom, and Theodoret of Cyrrhus.

Antioch College, private coeducational institution of higher learning founded in 1852 in Yellow Springs, Ohio, noted for its experimental curriculum and work-study program. Horace Mann was its first president from 1852 until his death in 1859.

Although the college from its outset was coeducational, nonsectarian, and committed to equal opportunity for blacks, its real innovations began in 1921 when its president, Arthur E. Morgan, undertook what has been called the first progressive venture of consequence in higher education, an attempt to combine "a liberal college education, vocational training, and apprenticeship for life." Students were required to alternate their time between traditional subjects and full-time jobs, to give them experience of "actual living in actual society." Antioch conducts cooperative and work-experience programs in many U.S. states and in foreign countries, maintaining centres in France, Germany, Switzerland, and England.

Its Graduate School of Education, with campuses in several U.S. cities, conducts experimental educational programs. A campus in the Washington, D.C.–Baltimore area offers interdisciplinary programs combining academic courses, environmental study, and social research. Antioch Law School was established in Washington, D.C., in 1972.

Antiochene rite, also called WEST SYRIAN RITE, the system of liturgical practices and discipline observed by Syrian Monophysites (Jacobites), the Malabar Christians of Kerala, India (Jacobites), and three Eastern rite communities of the Roman Catholic Church: Catholic Syrians, Maronites, and Malankarese Christians of Kerala. The Antiochene rite is sometimes called the West Syrian rite to distinguish it from the Chaldean, or East Syrian, rite.

The Antiochene rite, which served as the earliest model for almost all Eastern rites, originated in the patriarchate of Antioch and later generated the Byzantine and Alexandrian rites. The Liturgy of St. James evolved from the Jerusalem–Antioch liturgy and is currently used in modified form by both Catholic and Jacobite Syrians and Maronites.

Antiochus, name of kings of the Seleucid kingdom of Syria, grouped below chronologically and indicated by the symbol •.

• **Antiochus I** SOTER (b. 324 BC—d. 262/261), king of the Seleucid kingdom of Syria, who ruled *c.* 292–281 BC in the east and 281–261 over the whole kingdom. Under great external pressures, he consolidated his kingdom and encouraged the founding of cities.

Antiochus was the son of Seleucus I, founder of the Seleucid kingdom, and his Sogdian queen, Apama. When an invasion of nomads threatened the eastern possessions (between the Caspian and Aral seas and the Indian Ocean) of his father's realm, Antiochus was appointed king (292). He restored some of the damage caused by the invaders and rebuilt three cities. As his father still had interest in expanding the eastern trade, Antiochus dispatched a noted geographer and general to explore the environs of the Caspian Sea.

After his father's assassination in 281, Antiochus succeeded to the entire realm, but he was immediately beset by revolts in Syria, probably instigated by Egypt, by independence movements in northern Anatolia, and by a war led by Antigonus II Gonatas, ruler of the Greek cities and Macedonia. In 279, after the Gauls invaded Greece and almost ruined Antigonus, he and Antiochus signed a pact promising not to interfere with each other's territory. The next year, however, 20,000 Gauls crossed into Asia Minor, and the independent states in the northern part recruited them to harass Antiochus. The King was preoccupied with the pacification of Syria until 275, when, utilizing Indian elephants brought from the east, he defeated the Gauls, who were afterward settled by their allies in Phrygia to make it a buffer state. The Ionian city-states that Antiochus had spared from the Gauls' ravages hailed him as a god and named him Soter (Saviour). In 275 the alliance with Antigonus, now fully in possession of Macedonia, was cemented by marriage to Antiochus' half sister.

Following the Gallic incursions in Greece, Antiochus encouraged Greek immigration to his realm and established many new cities in Asia Minor to serve as counterweights to the Gauls. He built other cities in Iran to forestall the Parthian threat to his eastern frontier, and he probably fostered a revival of Babylonian culture and religion to counteract Persian influence. At Babylon he rebuilt the ancient Esagila shrine, although he moved the city's populace to a great Seleucid city a short distance away on the Tigris River.

The aggressions of Ptolemy II of Egypt caused continuous friction with Antiochus. In 279 he lost Miletus, in southwestern Asia Minor, and in 276 the Egyptians invaded northern Syria. Antiochus, however, defeated his opponent and repelled him and secured an alliance with the Egyptian ruler's half brother who ruled Cyrene. After Ptolemy married the energetic Arsinoe II, however, the war turned against the Seleucids; and around 273–272, Phoenicia and the coast of Asia Minor were lost to Egypt.

The continuous troubles in the west caused Seleucid control in the far eastern part of the empire to weaken. In 280 Antiochus made his eldest son king in the east, but he proved incompetent. Between 266 and 261 Antiochus was drawn into a war with Pergamum, and in 262 he suffered a defeat and lost additional territory. Soon afterward he died, leaving his son Antiochus II as successor.

The primary source in English of knowledge about the members of the Seleucid dynasty is Edwin Robert Beran's *The House of Seleucus*, 2 vol. (1902; reprinted 1966).

• **Antiochus II** THEOS (b. *c.* 287 BC—d. 246), king of the Seleucid dominions in the Middle East, who succeeded his father, Antiochus I, in 261 and spent much of his reign at war with Egypt, recovering much territory in Anatolia.

Finding a willing ally in Antigonus, ruler of Macedonia, who had suffered at the hands of Ptolemy II of Egypt, Antiochus waged the Second Syrian War (259–255) against Ptolemy to avenge his father's losses. While Antigonus defeated the Egyptian fleet at sea, Antiochus reconquered much of Anatolia, including the cities of Miletus and Ephesus, and also the Phoenician coast.

In Miletus, Antiochus overthrew a tyrant after he recaptured the city, and the citizens worshipped him as a god in thanksgiving. He later organized an empire-wide cult, as suggested by his epithet, Theos (God). He also established the freedom of the other Ionian cities. Further, he continued his predecessors' policies of encouraging the foundation of cities in his realm.

For unknown reasons, around 253, Antiochus dismissed his first queen, Laodice, and married Ptolemy's daughter Berenice. At his death in 246, a civil war erupted between the two queens. He was succeeded by his son Seleucus II, while another son, Antiochus Hierax, established himself in western Anatolia.

The primary source in English of knowledge about the members of the Seleucid dynast is Edwin Robert Bevan's *The House of Seleucus*, 2 vol. (1902; reprinted 1966).

• **Antiochus III,** byname ANTIOCHUS THE GREAT, Greek ANTIOCHUS MEGAS (b. 242 BC—d. 187, near Susa, Iran), Seleucid king of the Hellenistic Syrian Empire from 223 BC to 187, who rebuilt the empire in the East but failed in his attempt to challenge Roman ascendancy in Europe and Asia Minor. He reformed the empire administratively by reducing the provinces in size, established a ruler cult (with himself and his consort Laodice as divine), and improved relations with neighbouring countries by giving his daughters in marriage to their princes.

Antiochus III, coin, late 3rd–early 2nd century BC; in the British Museum

By courtesy of the trustees of the British Museum; photograph, J.R. Freeman & Co. Ltd.

The son of Seleucus II, Antiochus succeeded his brother Seleucus III as king. He retained from the previous administration Hermias as chief minister, Achaeus as governor of Asia Minor, and Molon and his brother Alexander as governors of the eastern provinces, Media and Persis. In the following year, when Molon rebelled and assumed the title of king, Antiochus abandoned a campaign against Egypt for the conquest of southern Syria, on the advice of Hermias, and marched against Molon, defeating him in 220 BC on the far bank of the Tigris and also conquering Atropatene, the northwestern part of Media. Shortly thereafter he had Hermias killed and was thus rid of most of the influences from the previous administration. In the same year, Achaeus set himself up as king in Asia Minor, but a mutiny in his army kept him from attacking Antiochus.

Antiochus was now free to conduct what has been called the Fourth Syrian War (219–216), during which he gained control of the important eastern Mediterranean sea ports of Seleucia-in-Pieria, Tyre, and Ptolemais. In 218 he held Coele Syria (Lebanon), Palestine, and Phoenicia. In 217 he engaged an army (numbering 75,000) of Ptolemy IV Philopator, a pharaoh of the Hellenistic dynasty ruling Egypt, at Raphia, the southernmost city in Syria. His own troops numbered 68,000. Though he succeeded in routing the left wing of the Egyptian army, his phalanx (heavily armed infantry in close ranks) in the centre was defeated by a newly formed Egyptian phalanx. In the subsequent peace settlement, Antiochus gave up all his conquests except the city of Seleucia-in-Pieria.

After the Syrian war, he proceeded against the rebel Achaeus. In alliance with Attalus I of Pergamum, Antiochus captured Achaeus in 213 in his capital, Sardis, and had him executed in a barbaric manner. After the pacification of Asia Minor he entered upon his later to be famous eastward campaign (212–205), pressing forward as far as India. In 212 he gave his sister Antiochis in marriage to King Xerxes of Armenia, who acknowledged his suzerainty and paid him tribute. He occupied Hecatompylos (southeast of the Caspian Sea), the capital of the Parthian king Arsaces III, and forced him to enter into an alliance in 209 and the following year defeated Euthydemus of Bactria, though he allowed him to continue to rule and retain his royal title. In 206 he marched across the Hindu Kush into the Kābul Valley and renewed a friendship with the Indian king Sophagasenos.

Returning westward via the Iranian provinces of Arachosia, Drangiana, and Carmania, he arrived in Persis in 205 and received tribute of 500 talents of silver from the citizens of Gerrha, a mercantile state on the east coast of the Persian Gulf. Having established a magnificent system of vassal states in the East, Antiochus now adopted the ancient Achaemenid title of "great king," and the Greeks, comparing him to Alexander the Great, surnamed him also "the Great."

After the death of Ptolemy IV, Antiochus concluded a secret treaty with Philip V, ruler of the Hellenistic kingdom of Macedonia, in which the two plotted the division of the Ptolemaic empire outside Egypt. Antiochus' share was to be southern Syria, Lycia, Cilicia, and Cyprus; Philip was to have western Asia Minor and the Cyclades. Antiochus invaded Coele Syria, defeated the Ptolemaic general Scopas at Panion near the source of the Jordan River in the year 200, gained control of Palestine, and granted special rights to the Jewish temple state. But Philip, marching along the Dardanelles, became involved in a war with Rhodes and Pergamum, both of whom appealed to Rome for help against Macedonia, informing Rome of the alliance between the two Hellenistic kings. Rome intervened decisively in the system of Hellenistic states. Philip was defeated by the Romans in the Second Macedonian War (200–196), and Antiochus refused to help him. Instead, taking advantage of the Romans' involvement with Philip, Antiochus marched against Egypt. Though the Romans had sent ambassadors to Ptolemy V, they could not lend him any serious assistance. When peace was concluded in 195, Antiochus came permanently into possession of southern Syria—which had been fought over for 100 years by the Ptolemies and Seleucids—and of the Egyptian territories in Asia Minor. He also gave his daughter Cleopatra in marriage to Ptolemy V. Egypt practically became a Seleucid protectorate.

In his insatiable expansionist drive, Antiochus occupied parts of the kingdom of Pergamum in 198 and in 197 Greek cities in Asia Minor. In 196 BC he crossed the Hellespont into Thrace, where he claimed sovereignty over territory that had been won by Seleucus I in the year 281 BC. A war of harassment and diplomacy with Rome ensued. A number of times the Romans sent ambassadors demanding that Antiochus stay out of Europe and set free all the autonomous communities in Asia Minor. To meet these demands would have meant the actual dissolution of the western part of the Seleucid Empire, and Antiochus thus refused. Tensions with Rome increased further when the great Carthaginian general Hannibal, who had fled from Carthage in the aftermath of defeat by the Romans in the Second Punic War, found refuge with Antiochus in 195 BC and became his adviser.

Antiochus offered an alliance to Philip of Macedonia, whom he had previously forsaken, but was rebuffed. Philip, Rhodes, Pergamum, and the Achaean League joined Rome. Only the Aetolians, discontent with Rome's growing influence in Greece, called upon Antiochus to be their liberator and appointed him commander in chief of their league. Relying on them Antiochus landed in Demetrias in the autumn of 192 with only 10,500 men and occupied Euboea. But he found little support in central Greece. In 191 the Romans, numbering more than 20,000, cut him off from his reinforcements in Thrace and outflanked his position at the pass of Thermopylae (in Greece). With the remainder of his troops Antiochus fled to Chalcis on Euboea and from there by sea to Ephesus; his fleet was wiped out by the combined naval forces of Rome, Rhodes, and Pergamum. Meeting no resistance, the Roman army crossed the Hellespont in 190. Antiochus was now eager to negotiate on the basis of Rome's previous demands, but the Romans insisted that he first evacuate the region west of the Taurus Mountains. When Antiochus refused, he was decisively defeated in the Battle of Magnesia near Mt. Sipylus, where he fought with a heterogeneous army of 70,000 men against an army of 30,000 Romans and their allies. Although he could have continued the war in the eastern provinces, he renounced all claim to his conquests in Europe and in Asia Minor west of the Taurus at the peace treaty of Apamea. He also was obliged to pay an indemnity of 15,000 talents over a period of 12 years, surrender his elephants and his fleet, and furnish hostages, including his son Antiochus IV. His kingdom was now reduced to Syria, Mesopotamia, and western Iran. In 187 Antiochus was murdered in a Baal temple near Susa, where he was exacting tribute in order to obtain much needed revenue. (H.V.)

BIBLIOGRAPHY. Edwin Robert Bevan, *The House of Seleucus*, 2 vol. (1902; reprinted 1966), is the primary source in English; W.W. Tarn, *The Cambridge Ancient History*, 7:723–726 (1928); E. Will, *Histoire politique du monde hellénistique*, vol. 2 (1967), short biographical sketches; J. Seibert, *Historia-Einzelschrift*, 10:60 (1967), explains Antiochus' politics in marriage; H.H. Schmitt, *Untersuchungen zur Geschichte Antiochos des Grossen und seiner Zeit* (1964), treats the first 25 years of his reign and his policies; E. Badian, "Rome and Antiochus the Great: A Study in Cold War," *Classical Philology*, 54:81–99 (1959), describes the negotiations between Rome and Antiochus before the war of 192–188 BC; H. Bengtson, *Die Strategie in der hellenistischen Zeit*, vol. 2 (1944), delineates his administrative reforms; G.M.A. Richter, *The Portraits of the Greeks*, vol. 3 (1965), discusses the preserved portrait of Antiochus.

• **Antiochus IV** EPIPHANES (God Manifest), also called ANTIOCHUS EPIMANES (the Mad) (b. *c.* 215 BC—d. 164, Tabae, Iran), Seleucid king of the Hellenistic Syrian kingdom who reigned from 175 to 164 BC. As a ruler he was best known for his encouragement of Greek culture and institutions. His attempts to suppress Judaism brought on the Wars of the Maccabees.

Early career. Antiochus was the third son of Antiochus III the Great. After his father's defeat by the Romans in 190–189, he served as hostage for his father in Rome from 189 to 175, where he learned to admire Roman institutions and policies. His brother, King Seleucus IV, exchanged him for Demetrius, the son of Seleucus; and after Seleucus was murdered by Heliodorus, a usurper, Antiochus in turn ousted him. During this period of uncertainty in Syria, the guardians of Ptolemy VI, the Egyptian ruler, laid claim to Coele Syria, Palestine, and Phoenicia, which Antiochus III had conquered. Both the Syrian and Egyptian parties appealed to Rome for help, but the Senate refused to take sides. In 173 Antiochus paid the remainder of the war indemnity that had been imposed by the Romans on Antiochus III at the Treaty of Apamea (188).

Antiochus forestalled an Egyptian expedition to Palestine by invading Egypt. He defeated the Egyptians between Pelusium and Mount Kasion, conquered Pelusium, and in 169 occupied Egypt with the exception of Alexandria, the capital. Ptolemy VI was Antiochus' nephew—Antiochus' sister, Cleopatra I, had married Ptolemy V—and Antiochus contented himself with ruling Egypt as Ptolemy's guardian, giving Rome no excuse for intervention. The citizens of Alexandria, however, appealed to Ptolemy VIII, the brother of Ptolemy VI, and to his sister Cleopatra II to form a rival government. Disturbances in Palestine forced Antiochus to return to Syria, but he safeguarded his access to Egypt with a strong garrison in Pelusium.

In the winter of 169/168 Perseus of Macedonia in vain begged Antiochus to join forces with him against the danger that Rome presented to all of the Hellenistic monarchs. In Egypt, Ptolemy VI made common cause with his brother and sister and sent a renewed request to Rome for aid, and Antiochus prepared for battle. The fleet of Antiochus won a victory at Cyprus, whose governor surrendered the island to him. Antiochus invaded Egypt again in 168, demanded that Cyprus and Pelusium be ceded to him, occupied Lower Egypt, and camped outside Alexandria. The cause of the Ptolemaeans seemed lost. But on June 22, 168, the Romans defeated Perseus and his Macedonians at Pydna, and there deprived Antiochus of the benefits of his victory. In Eleusis, a suburb of Alexandria, the Roman ambassador, Gaius Popillius Laenas, presented Antiochus with the ultimatum that he evacuate Egypt and Cyprus immediately. Antiochus, taken by surprise, asked for time to consider. Popillius, however, drew a circle in the earth around the king with his walking stick and demanded an unequivocal answer before Antiochus left the circle. Dismayed by this public humiliation, the king quickly agreed to comply. Roman intervention had reestablished the status quo. By being allowed to retain southern Syria, to which Egypt had laid claim, Antiochus was able to preserve the territorial integrity of his realm.

Efforts to hellenize the kingdom. Both economically and socially he made efforts to strengthen his kingdom—inhabited in the main by Orientals (non-Greeks of Asia Minor and Persia)—by founding and fostering Greek cities. Even before he had begun his reign he had contributed to the building of the temple of Zeus in Athens and to the adornment of the theatre. He enlarged Antioch on the Orontes by adding a section to the city (named Epiphania after him). There he built an aqueduct, a council hall, a marketplace, and a temple to Jupiter Capitolinus. Babylon, which revered him as Soter (Liberator, or Saviour) of Asia, was given a Greek colony that was granted freedom of the city. Another Epiphania was founded in Armenia. Ecbatana (in Persia) was also named Epiphania and became a Greek city. Many of these cities were granted the right to coin their own municipal currency. The mint of Antioch on the Persian Gulf served the trade along the sea route between India and the district at the mouth of the great Mesopotamian rivers.

Antiochus' hellenizing policies brought him into conflict with the prosperous Oriental temple organizations, and particularly with the Jews. Since Antiochus III's reign the Jews had enjoyed extensive autonomy under their high priest. They were divided into two parties, the orthodox Hasideans (Pious Ones) and a reform party that favoured Hellenism. For financial reasons Antiochus supported the reform party and, in return for a considerable sum, permitted the high priest, Jason, to build a gymnasium in Jerusalem and to introduce the Greek mode of educating young people. In 172, for an even bigger tribute, he appointed Menelaus in place of Jason. In 169, however, while Antiochus was campaigning in Egypt, Jason conquered Jerusalem—with the exception of the citadel—and murdered many adherents of his rival Menelaus. When Antiochus returned from Egypt in 167 he took Jerusalem by storm and enforced its Hellenization. The city forfeited its privileges and was permanently garrisoned by Syrian soldiers.

The revolt of Judas Maccabeus. The Greeks and those friendly toward them were united into the community of Antiochians; the worship of Yahweh and all of the Jewish rites were forbidden on pain of death. In the Temple an altar to Zeus Olympios was erected, and sacrifices were to be made at the feet of an idol in the image of the King. Against that desecration Judas Maccabeus, leader of the anti-Greek Jews, led the aroused Hasideans in a guerrilla war and several times defeated the generals Antiochus had commissioned to deal with the uprising. Judas refused a partial amnesty, conquered Judaea with the exception of the Acra in Jerusalem, and in December 164 was able to tear down the altar of Zeus and reconsecrate the Temple. Antiochus apparently had underestimated the strength of the Hasidean movement, which was behind the success in maintaining an independent Judaean state for about a century. The fighting spirit of the Jews was all the more impressive because at the beginning of their rebellion in 166 Antiochus had just demonstrated his might to the world at Daphne, near Antioch, with a grand review of his army: 46,000 foot soldiers were on parade, among them a Macedonian phalanx of 20,000 men and 500 mercenaries equipped with Roman arms, followed by 8,500 horsemen and 306 armoured elephants.

Antiochus then mounted a campaign against the Parthians who were threatening the empire in the east, recovered the income from that area, forced Artaxias of Armenia—who had defected—to recognize his suzerainty, founded the city of Antioch on the Persian Gulf, set out on an expedition to the Arabian coast, and, at the end of 164, died of an illness at Tabae (or Gabae, probably present Isfahan) in Persis. Many believers saw his death as a punishment for his attempt to loot the shrine of Nanaia in Elam (in modern Iran).

(H.V.)

BIBLIOGRAPHY. Edwin Robert Bevan, *The House of Seleucus*, 2 vol. (1902; reprinted 1966), is the primary source in English; O. Morkolm, *Antiochus IV of Syria* (1966), a comprehensive biography with extensive literature; E. Bickermann, *Der Gott der Makkabäer* (1937); and S.K. Eddy, *The King Is Dead: Studies in the Near Eastern Resistance to Hellenism 334–31 B.C.* (1961), discuss the response of the Jews toward Antiochus' demand of Hellenization.

• **Antiochus VII** SIDETES (b. *c.* 159 BC—d. 129), who, after reuniting his country, ruled as king of the Seleucid state of Syria in 139/138–129 BC and successfully recovered much of his forefathers' territory before he was slain by the Parthians.

The son of Demetrius I and brother of Demetrius II, both Seleucid kings, Antiochus spent his youth in the Greek islands. In 141 his brother was captured while fighting the Parthians. Cleopatra Thea, Demetrius II's queen, meanwhile was regent; but a usurper, Tryphon, had risen and threatened to seize full power. At this point, Antiochus VII, an energetic prince, arrived in Syria (139), married Cleopatra Thea, and put Tryphon to flight. A passage in the Bible (I Maccabees 14:1–14) suggests that he first assured himself of the neutrality of possible opponents, such as Judah. By 138, Antiochus had ended Tryphon's career, and he delivered an ultimatum to the Jews to acknowledge him as overlord. When they refused, he sent one army against them, which was defeated, and, later, in 135/134, himself led a siege, which captured Jerusalem. Internal dissension among the leaders of Judah aided him.

Antiochus razed Jerusalem's walls and made John Hyrcanus, who had recently assumed leadership, his vassal. Rejecting suggestions to exterminate the Jews, he appointed Hyrcanus high priest and allowed religious autonomy.

With Palestine secured, Antiochus set out to restore his forefathers' eastern realm. With enthusiastic support from the Hellenized cities he drove the Parthians from Mesopotamia and invaded Media. The Parthians, perhaps hopeful of stirring up civil war behind him, released Antiochus' brother, who had been a prisoner since 141.

In early 129 the Parthians made a surprise attack on the Seleucid winter quarters and slew Antiochus, who left five children by his queen. Syria lapsed into civil war, with all hopes of empire gone.

The primary source in English of knowledge about the members of the Seleucid dynasty is Edwin Robert Bevan's *The House of Seleucus*, 2 vol. (1902; reprinted 1966).

• **Antiochus** HIERAX (fl. *c.* 263–226 BC), younger brother of Seleucus II, heir to the Seleucid dominions in the Middle East. During his brother's war with Egypt, he declared independence in Anatolia and attempted to take over the throne.

Antiochus Hierax and Seleucus II, were the sons of Antiochus II's former wife, Laodice. While his brother was involved in the Third Syrian War (246–241) with Egypt, which had erupted over the death of his father's second wife (daughter of Ptolemy II), Antiochus was sent as ruler to Seleucid Anatolia, where Laodice was living. Perhaps in league with his mother, late in the war he sent an army into Syria ostensibly to assist Seleucus but actually to seize the rest of the empire. The appearance of Hierax' troops, however, brought peace between Egypt and his brother, and Seleucus promptly invaded Anatolia and began the War of the Brothers (239–236). Antiochus Hierax fared badly until he allied himself to the Galatians (Celts) and two other states that were traditional foes of the Seleucid kingdom. With the aid of these forces, he inflicted a crushing defeat on his brother's army at Ancyra (236). His alliance with the Galatians, however, provoked the ruler of Pergamum (another Hellenistic state), who, in a war in 236–228, expelled Hierax from Anatolia.

Back in Syria, Antiochus tried to raise revolts against his brother in Syria and the East. Consequently, he was exiled to Thrace in 227, where he lived as a virtual prisoner. The following year he managed to escape and fled to the mountains to raise an army, but he was killed by a band of Galatians.

The primary source in English of knowledge about the members of the Seleucid dynasty is Ernest Robert Bevan's *The House of Seleucus*, 2 vol. (1902; reprinted 1966).

• **Antiochus** OF ASCALON (b. *c.* 120 BC—d. 68 BC), Greek philosopher who followed Philo of Larissa as the head of the Academy, charting a new course for Platonism. He built up his philosophical system on a foundation of three schools: Platonism, Peripateticism, and Stoicism. Stoic ideas played the most important role in his thinking. He rebelled against two Skeptics, Arcesilaus and Carneades, both of whom had a strong influence on the direction of Platonism, and broke the ground for a more positive direction.

Antiope, in Greek legend, the mother, by the god Zeus, of the twins Amphion and Zethus. According to one account, her beauty attracted Zeus, who, assuming the form of a satyr, took her by force. Pregnant, she escaped the threats of her father by running away and marrying Epopeus, king of Sicyon; she was later brought back and imprisoned by her uncle Lycus. On the way back from Sicyon, or after escaping from prison, Antiope bore Amphion and Zethus, who were brought up by herdsmen. Later she joined them; they recognized her and killed Lycus and Dirce, his wife. Because of Dirce's murder, Dionysus, to whose worship she had been devoted, caused Antiope to go mad. She wandered restlessly over all of Greece until she was cured and married by Phocus of Tithorea, on Mt. Parnassus.

Antiope was also the name of a daughter of Ares, the god of war, and a queen of the Amazons, a race of warrior women. The Greek hero Theseus stole her for his wife.

Antioquia, department, northwestern Colombia, occupying the northern extreme of the Cordilleras (mountains) Occidental and Central of the Andes. It is bounded northwest by the Caribbean Sea and east by the Río Magdalena. The 24,274 sq mi (62,870 sq km)

Cattle ranch in Antioquia department, Colombia
Carl Frank

area is bisected by the deep gorge of the Río Cauca. The Antioquia highland is diagonally pierced by the canyon of the Río Porce, a Cauca tributary, which widens out into the lovely, mile-high valley where the departmental capital of Medellín is situated.

The colonial economy of Antioquia was based on mining and the department still produces almost all Colombian gold and silver. Antioquia also has large asbestos and copper deposits and is the country's largest coffee producer. Other agricultural products of the region include beans, sugarcane, plantain, rice, bananas, and African palm. Antioquia is supported not only by agriculture and cattle raising, but ranks among the most heavily industrialized regions of Colombia. The department is a major textile area, especially around Medellín, which is also an important transportation centre and the seat of the department's academic and cultural institutions. Pop. (1981 est.) 3,936,493.

antioxidant, any of various chemical compounds added to certain foods, natural and synthetic rubbers, gasolines, and other substances to retard autoxidation, the process by which these substances combine with oxygen in the air at room temperature. Retarding autoxidation delays the appearance of such undesirable qualities as rancidity in foods, loss of elasticity in rubbers, and formation of gums in gasolines. Antioxidants most commonly used are such organic compounds as aromatic amines, phenols, and aminophenols.

Autoxidation has been found to proceed by a chain reaction; that is, a reaction consisting of a series of successive steps occurring in repetitive cycles, in each of which intermediate products called chain carriers are regenerated. Such a reaction will continue as long as the chain carriers persist. In autoxidation the chain carriers are free radicals, electrically neutral molecular fragments containing unpaired electrons. The chain can be initiated by thermally excited molecules, free radicals, metal catalysts, or light. Antioxidants, by reacting with chain carriers, terminate the oxidative chain reaction.

An example of autoxidation that is of great commercial concern is the one leading to the rancidity of fats, oils, and fatty foods. Rancidity is caused by the degradation of the fat molecule, by reaction with oxygen, to a mixture of volatile aldehydes, ketones, and acids. The reaction can be initiated by exposure to light or by the presence of trace amounts of metals that serve as catalysts. To retard the development of rancidity, organic antioxidants, commonly tocopherol, propyl gallate, butylated hydroxytoluene (BHT), or butylated hydroxyanisole (BHA), are used. These compounds react with chain carriers by donating hydrogen atoms. The use of antioxidants for food is closely regulated in most countries. Specific limitations are normally imposed on the type and quantity of antioxidants that may be used.

antiparticle, subatomic particle having the same mass as one of the particles of ordinary matter but opposite electric charge and magnetic moment. Thus the positron (positive electron) is the antiparticle of the negative electron (negatron). The spinning antineutron with net charge zero, like the ordinary neutron, has its magnetic polarity opposite to that of a similarly spinning neutron. The neutrino, a massless, uncharged particle that travels at the speed of light, spins counterclockwise as viewed from behind, whereas the antineutrino spins clockwise as viewed from behind. A particle and its antiparticle mutually react to produce energy by annihilation.

antipasto, in Italian cuisine, a first course or appetizer (*q.v.*). In the home, cured or smoked meats and sausages, olives, salted anchovies, sardines, fresh or pickled vegetables, shellfish, peppers, and cheeses are favoured, while restaurant presentations add to these elaborate prepared dishes such as seafood salads, stuffed mushrooms, vitello tonnato (cold braised veal in tuna mayonnaise), and the like.

Antipater (b. *c.* 397 BC—d. 319), Macedonian general, regent of Macedonia (334–23) and of the Macedonian Empire (321–319) whose death signalled the end of centralized authority in the empire. One of the leading men in Macedonia at the death of Philip II in 336, he helped to secure the succession to the Macedonian throne for Philip's son, Alexander the Great, who upon departure for the conquest of Asia (334) appointed Antipater regent in Macedonia with the title of general in Europe. Antipater's main task was to hold the northern frontiers against hostile tribes and to keep order among the Greek states. He ruled Greece by cooperating with the League of Corinth but was unpopular because he supported oligarchic governments. The settlement of the satrapies (provinces) of the Macedonian Empire by the new regent, Perdiccas, at Babylon in 323, immediately after Alexander's death, left Antipater in control of Macedonia and Greece, though as former regent his status in relation to Perdiccas was not clearly defined. Antipater then took the side of the Macedonian generals Antigonus, Seleucus, and Ptolemy, who were opposed to the claims of Perdiccas. By the settlement at Triparadisus, Syria (321), after Perdiccas' death, Antipater became regent of the Macedonian Empire for the two kings: the intellectually retarded Philip III Arrhidaeus and the infant Alexander IV.

Antipater (d. 43 BC), Idumaean founder of the Herodian dynasty in Palestine. Antipater gained power in Judaea by making himself useful to the Romans. In return for Antipater's support, Caesar appointed him procurator of Judaea in 47 BC. Although Antipater was assassinated by a political rival four years later, his son, Herod I the Great, was later made king of Judaea by the Romans.

Antipater (d. 4 BC), son of Herod the Great, who conspired against his half brothers Aristobulus and Alexander for the succession to the throne of Judaea and secured their execution (7 or 6 BC). The following year he was tried for plotting against Herod and Pheroras, Herod's brother, and was executed five days before his father's death.

Antiphanes (fl. early 4th century BC, Athens), together with Alexis, the principal representative of the writers of the Middle Comedy at Athens. In this genre, which succeeded the Old Comedy of Aristophanes, scurrility gave place to parody and to criticism of literature and philosophy. Only fragments of Antiphanes' writing survive, though the titles of 134 plays by him are known.

Consult
the
INDEX
first

Antiphon (fl *c.* 480—411 BC, Athens), orator and statesman, the earliest Athenian known to have taken up rhetoric as a profession. He was a *logographos*; *i.e.,* a writer of speeches for other men to deliver in their defense in court, a function that was particularly useful in the climate of accusation and counter-accusation that prevailed in Athens at the conclusion of the Peloponnesian War, between Athens and Sparta.

As a politician Antiphon was the prime mover in the anti-democratic revolution of the Four Hundred, an oligarchic council set up in 411 BC in an attempt to seize the Athenian government in the midst of war. Others may have been more conspicuous in the forefront of the political struggle, but Thucydides' judgment in his *History*, when describing the revolution of the Four Hundred, is that it was Antiphon "who conceived the whole matter and the means by which it was brought to pass." He was reluctant to put himself forward in public debate because, says Thucydides, he realized that his reputation for cleverness made him unpopular with the people. But when the regime of the Four Hundred fell, he defended himself in a speech Thucydides describes as the greatest ever made by a man on trial for his life. Nevertheless, the defense was unsuccessful and Antiphon was executed for treason.

Fifteen of Antiphon's compositions survive, of which three, "On the murder of Herodes," "On the Choreutes," and "Against a Stepmother," were actually delivered in court. The remaining 12 speeches are arranged in three sets of four known as tetralogies, which were composed as exercises for the instruction of students. Each tetralogy consists of two speeches each for the defense and the prosecution in a homicide case.

The 1st-century-BC teacher of rhetoric Dionysius of Halicarnassus selected Antiphon's work as an example of the austere in oratory. His language is dignified and he nowhere indulges in the personal abuse that characterizes many of the later orators. Even when he is dealing with actual events, however, he seems remote from the realities of the situation, and he makes no attempt to suit his speeches to the differing personalities of those who were to deliver them. An edition by K.J. Maidment in *Minor Attic Orators*, volume 1, is in the Loeb Classical Library with Greek text and English translation.

antiphon, in Roman Catholic liturgical music, chant melody and text sung before and after a psalm verse, originally by alternating choirs (antiphonal singing). Antiphonal psalm singing was adopted from Hebrew worship by the early Christian churches, notably that of Syria, and was introduced into the West in the 4th century by St. Ambrose. The two choirs either both sang the psalm text or one choir sang a short refrain between the psalm verses (V) sung by the other choir. The refrain was called an antiphon (A). The resulting musical form was A V_1 A V_2 . . . A. Actually, most of the presentations of the antiphon were in abbreviated form. The antiphon text normally referred to the meaning of the feast day or the psalm. Canticles from the New or Old Testament might also be sung in this way.

Antiphons are now found principally in the canonical hours, or divine office. In the mass the Introit, Offertory, and Communion originally consisted of antiphons and psalm verses. During the late Middle Ages the psalm verses were dropped from the Offertory and Communion, which now consist only of an antiphon. The Introit was shortened to one psalm verse and an antiphon (A V A). Musically, the several thousand extant antiphons can be reduced to a small number of melodic types of simple structure. The old antiphonal method of performance was eventually abandoned, and antiphonal chants are now frequently sung responsorially; *i.e.,* by soloist(s) and choir.

The four Marian antiphons are long hymns, not true antiphons but independent compositions especially noted for their beauty: the "Salve Regina" ("Hail, Holy Queen"), "Ave Regina caelorum" ("Hail, Queen of Heaven"), "Regina caeli, laetare" ("Queen of Heaven, Rejoice"), and "Alma Redemptoris Mater" ("Kindly Mother of the Redeemer"). They were frequently set polyphonically (in part music) by composers from about 1400 onward. There are also special "antiphons" used for processionals at certain high feasts.

antiphonal singing, alternate singing by two choirs or singers. Antiphonal singing is of great antiquity and occurs in the folk and liturgical music of many cultures. Descriptions of it occur in the Old Testament. The antiphonal singing of psalms occurred both in ancient Hebrew and early Christian liturgies; alternating choirs would sing—*e.g.,* half lines of psalms verses.

Similar instances of alternating singing occur in the folk music of modern Yemenite Jews, in African and Afro-American folk music, and in eastern European folk music. The principle is also used in large compositions for double choir by such composers as J.S. Bach. *Compare* responsorial singing.

Antipodes Islands, outlying island group of New Zealand in the South Pacific Ocean, 350 mi (560 km) southeast of South Island, comprising a central island (5 mi by 3 mi) and several islets; total land area is 24 sq mi (62 sq km). Coastal cliffs flank an interior that rises to 1,320 ft (402 m) at Mt. Galloway. The terrain is poorly drained and the climate cool and humid. Discovered in 1800 by the crew of the British ship "Reliance," the Antipodes were once the home of large herds of fur seals, which have been drastically reduced by uncontrolled hunting. The islands are uninhabited.

Antipolo, municipality, south Rizal province, central Luzon, Philippines. Located 12 mi (19 km) east of Manila in the foothills of the Sierra Madre, it was founded in 1578. Antipolo is noted as the home of the icon of Nuestra Señora de la Paz y Buen Viaje (Our Lady of Peace and Safe Voyage). The icon, after repeated safe journeys between New Spain (Mexico) and the Philippines early in the 17th century, came to be acknowledged as the heavenly protector of Spain's galleons. After Franciscan priests first enshrined it, Jesuits moved the icon to its present location, a hillside shrine near Antipolo, in 1632. It is the focus of pilgrimages each May.

Government-sponsored housing has been built near Antipolo as the first phase of a decongestion plan for crowded metropolitan Manila. A highway leading to Quezon City was under construction in the early 1980s. Pop. (1980) 68,912.

antipope, in the Roman Catholic Church, one who opposes the legitimately elected bishop of Rome, endeavours to secure the papal throne, and to some degree succeeds materially in the attempt. The elections of several antipopes are greatly obscured by incomplete or biased records, and at times even their contemporaries could not decide who was the true pope. It is impossible, therefore, to establish an absolutely definitive list of antipopes. Historically, antipopes have arisen as a result of a variety of causes; the following are some examples:

1. Doctrinal disagreement. The spread of Monarchianism (a Trinitarian heresy) led a Roman priest, Hippolytus, to try to replace Pope Calixtus I in the 3rd century. Hippolytus was later reconciled to Pope Pontianus during the persecution of Maximinus and died a martyr's death (235).

2. Deportation of the pope. The Arian emperor Constantius II exiled Pope Liberius for his orthodoxy (355) and imposed the archdeacon Felix on the Roman clergy as Pope Felix II. Eventually, Liberius was allowed to return, and Felix lived in retirement until his death.

3. Double elections arbitrated by the secular authority. In 418 the archdeacon Eulalius was elected by a faction partial to him, and he was supported by the imperial prefect and the Byzantine court. The rest of the clergy, however, chose the priest Boniface I, who was eventually given official recognition by the Emperor.

4. Double elections and subsequent recourse to a third candidate. In the 7th century Paschal and Theodore were rivals for the papacy, and both were unwilling to renounce their claims. Finally, a part of the community more inclined to moderation gained the papacy for Sergius I.

Somewhat similarly, in the 14th century the official residence of the papacy was moved to Avignon, Fr. This led to a schism (the Great Western Schism) beginning in 1378 that resulted in a papacy in Rome (regarded as canonical), a papacy in Avignon (regarded as antipopes), and eventually a third papacy established by the Council of Pisa (also regarded as antipopes). Unity was finally achieved by the election of Martin V on Nov. 11, 1417.

5. Change in the manner of choosing the pope. In 1059 a new procedure for electing popes, proclaimed by Pope Nicholas II, deprived the German emperors of the leading role they had played in earlier papal elections and also limited the influence of the Roman nobility. This led to the election of the antipope Honorius II in opposition to the canonically elected Alexander II, who was eventually recognized by the Emperor. *See also* papacy (table).

antiproton, subatomic particle of the same mass as a proton but having a negative electric charge and oppositely directed magnetic moment. It is the proton's antiparticle. Antiprotons were produced and identified in 1955 by Emilio Segrè, Owen Chamberlain (for which they received the Nobel Prize for Physics in 1959), and coworkers by bombarding a copper target with high energy protons from the proton synchrotron at the University of California (Berkeley). Antiprotons were predicted in the early 1930s, but their discovery had to wait for the technology of high-energy particle accelerators to reach the 6,000,000,000 electron-volt range. A collision of an antiproton with a proton results in mutual annihilation, but a near miss may produce by charge exchange an antineutron–neutron pair.

antipyrine, analgesic now little used, though the oldest and least toxic of the synthetic drugs that relieve pain, reduce fever, and combat inflammation. It is longer acting and more potent than aspirin in treating severe rheumatic disorders. Antipyrine causes fewer side effects than aspirin, though it may cause skin eruptions and vascular collapse. Unlike aminopyrine, it rarely has been associated with agranulocytosis. In combination with glycerin and benzocaine, antipyrine is used as a topical agent to relieve earache. The use of antipyrine in the United States has been greatly reduced since its undesirable side effects have been recognized.

Antique, province, island of Panay, Philippines. It has an area of 974 sq mi (2,522 sq km). The province lies along the western coast of the island and includes a number of islands in Cuyo East Pass, a channel of the Sulu Sea (west). A rugged mountain range forms its eastern boundary. The coast does not have good harbours, but fishing is a major industry. Rice and sugarcane are among the major food and cash crops. The largest lowland is in the south on the Sibalom River delta and floodplain, the site of San Jose de Buenavista, the provincial capital and an interisland port. A coastal road runs from Libertad in the north to Anini-y in the south, connecting the larger coastal towns. Two-thirds of the people are Roman Catholic; many of the rest are Protestants. Pop. (1980) 344,879.

antique, a relic or old object having aesthetic, historic, and financial value. Formerly, it referred only to the remains of the classical cultures of Greece and Rome; gradually, decorative arts—courtly, bourgeois, and peasant—of all past eras and places came to be considered antique.

Antiques have been variously defined by law for tariff purposes. The U.S. Tariff Act of 1930 exempted from duty specified antiquities and objects of art produced prior to 1830, and that year became more or less internationally accepted as an appropriate terminal date in defining "antique." In 1952 the Florence Agreement, sponsored by UNESCO and signed by 17 countries, agreed to "facilitate the free flow of educational, scientific and cultural materials by the removal of barriers that impede the international movement of such materials," and antiques were affected by subsequent legislation adopted in the participating countries to implement the agreement. The United States, for instance, passed a new tariff act in 1966 permitting the duty-free importation of "antiques made prior to 100 years before their date of entry"; comparable regulations had already gone into effect in other participating countries. In general usage, antiques frequently are now defined as objects of artistic and historical significance that are at least 100 years old.

The collecting of antiques goes back almost as far as history, beginning with the preservation of temple treasures. In England, concern for the historical as well as aesthetic significance of antiques led, as early as the 16th century, to collections illustrating the national past. In 1857 the museum now called the Victoria and Albert opened in London as a repository for decorative arts, intended to stimulate designers as well as collectors. It was followed in 1863 by a great public collection in Vienna, in 1882 by the Musée des Arts Décoratifs in Paris, and in 1897 by the Museum of the Arts of Decoration at Cooper Union School of Art and Architecture in New York City. Collecting antiques became a truly popular pursuit in the 20th century.

Antiquities of the Jews, The, Latin ANTIQUITATES JUDAICAE, an account of Jewish history from its early beginnings to the revolt against Rome in AD 66, written in Greek in about AD 93 by Flavius Josephus, a general in the Jewish army who defected to Rome. His writings are not always accepted as totally reliable.

Antirent War (1839–46), in U.S. history, civil unrest and rioting in upper New York state arising from the dissatisfaction of leaseholding farmers over the patroon system then prevailing on the great hereditary estates, originally established by the Dutch. In addition to rent, a farmer had to provide certain services to the landowner; the farmer's position was similar to that of a copyholder or villein under European feudalism. On the sale of the lease, a New York farmer had to pay the proprietor an alienation fine of from one-tenth to one-third of the sale price.

While this system had long been considered unjust, no direct action was taken until 1839, when the heirs of Stephen Van Rensselaer tried to collect back rent from leaseholders in Albany County. The farmers rose in active opposition and refused to pay. Violence broke out and Gov. William H. Seward called out the militia. But acts of resistance spread, especially against rent and tax collectors, and Gov. Silas Wright declared martial law in August 1845. Thereafter, the disturbances lessened, and they finally ceased when a new state constitution in 1846 abolished the leasehold system of land tenure and instituted fee-simple ownership.

antiseptic, any of several substances used to inhibit the growth of or destroy infectious microorganisms. *See* antimicrobial agent.

antiserum, blood serum that contains specific antibodies against an infective organism or poisonous substance. Antiserums are produced in animals (*e.g.,* horse, sheep, ox, rabbit) and man in response to infection, intoxication, or vaccination and may be used in another individual to confer immunity to a specific disease or to treat bites or stings of venomous animals. Antiserums from animals are most often used, but in persons allergic to animals, human antiserums have proved valuable. *See also* antibody; antitoxin; immunization; vaccine.

Antisthenes (b. *c.* 445 BC—d. *c.* 365), Greek philosopher, of Athens, who was a disciple of Socrates and is considered the founder of the Cynic school of philosophy, though Diogenes of Sinope often is given that credit.

Antisthenes was born into a wealthy family, and the philosophical ideas that he developed had their roots in the contradictions and injustices that he found embedded in society. He sought to build a foundation of ideas that

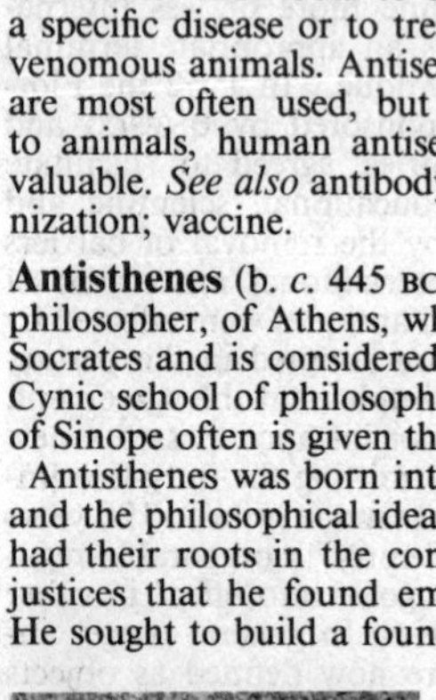

Antisthenes, herm; in the Sala delle Muse, Vatican

By courtesy of the Direzione Generale dei Monumenti, Musei e Gallerie Pontificie

would serve as a guiding principle toward a happier, more thoughtful way of life. Antisthenes believed that happiness was dependent on moral virtue and that virtue could be instilled through teaching.

In teaching people how to be virtuous, Antisthenes demarcated two categories of objects: (1) external goods, embracing such elements as personal property, sensual pleasure, and other luxuries; and (2) internal goods, including the truth and knowledge of the soul. He advocated great restraint on the part of an individual tempted to take pleasure in external goods, and he encouraged his students to accept the burden of physical and mental pain that accompanies the soul's search for its own inner wealth. To dramatize his method of teaching, Antisthenes, after the myth of Hercules, would stand on his platform of ideas and beliefs and "bark" at the folly and injustices of his society. The Cynic (Greek: Canine, or Doglike) school of philosophy long survived him.

antitank weapon, any of several guns, missiles, and mines intended for use against tanks. The first response to the introduction of tanks during World War I was a variety of projectiles designed to penetrate their relatively thin armour. Land mines and ordinary artillery were also used effectively. By the beginning of World War II a family of antitank guns, mostly of 37-millimetre (1.46-inch) calibre, had emerged, firing special ammunition. During the war increasingly larger calibres were used, and a variety of ammunition types—including shells tipped with harder alloys, improved propellants to give higher velocities, and more powerful explosives—were developed. Especially effective was the shaped or hollow charge shell, designed to explode on impact and channel the explosive energy forward, enhancing penetrating force.

World War II also produced a variety of antitank missiles and launching devices, of which the American bazooka (*q.v.*) and its counterparts in other armies were the best known; these were small, short-range rocket launchers carried and aimed by a single operator. After World War II the technology of antitank weaponry advanced in several directions. Most important was a new family of electronically guided missiles, employing either beam- or wire-guidance systems. By the early 1970s these had attained a high degree of refinement in accuracy, range, and versatility, as was dramatically demonstrated in the Yom Kippur War of October 1973, in which the effectiveness of the Soviet-supplied Arab weapons against Israeli tanks seemed to portend a new era of defensive supremacy in land warfare. Antitank guns also developed rapidly in this period, with further improvements in propellants, explosives, projectiles, and the design of gun tubes. Some antitank guns were smooth-bored instead of rifled in order to fire both missiles and projectiles.

antithesis (from Greek *antitheton,* "opposition"), a figure of speech in which irreconcilable opposites or strongly contrasting ideas are placed in sharp juxtaposition and sustained tension, as in the saying "Art is long, and Time is fleeting."

The opposing clauses, phrases, or sentences are roughly equal in length and balanced in contiguous grammatical structures.

> The world will little note nor long remember what we say here, but it can never forget what they did here.
>
> (Abraham Lincoln, "Gettysburg Address")

In poetry, the effect of antithesis is often one of tragic irony or reversal.

> Saddled and bridled
> And booted rade he;
> A plume in his helmet,
> A sword at his knee;
> But toom [empty] cam' his saddle
> A' bloody to see,
> O hame cam' his gude horse
> But never cam' he!
> ("Bonnie George Campbell," anonymous)

antitoxin, antibody, formed in the body by the introduction of a bacterial poison, or toxin, and capable of neutralizing the toxin. People who have recovered from bacterial illnesses often develop specific antitoxins that confer immunity against recurrence.

For medical use in treating human infectious diseases, antitoxins are produced by injecting an animal with toxin; the animal, most commonly a horse, is given repeated small doses of toxin until a high concentration of the antitoxin builds up in the blood. The resulting highly concentrated preparation of antitoxins is called an antiserum.

The first antitoxin, to diphtheria, was discovered in 1890 by Emil von Behring and Shibasaburo Kitasato, for which Behring received the 1901 Nobel Prize for Physiology or Medicine. Today, antitoxins are used in the treatment of botulism, diphtheria, dysentery, gas gangrene, and tetanus. If the toxin is a venom, the antitoxin formed, or the antiserum containing it, is called an antivenin. *See also* antiserum.

antitrade wind, steady wind that blows poleward and eastward between latitudes 30° N and 30° S, at altitudes of 2 to 12 kilometres (about 1 to 7 miles). Such winds overlie the westward-blowing trade winds and descend poleward, where they merge with the mid-latitude westerly winds. The subtropical high-pressure belts at 30°–35° N and 30°–35° S result partially from the descent of the antitrades to the surface. *See also* atmospheric circulation.

antitrust law, any law restricting business practices considered unfair or monopolistic. The United States has the longest standing policy of maintaining competition among business enterprises through a variety of laws. The best known is the Sherman Antitrust Act of 1890, which declared illegal "every contract, combination . . . or conspiracy in restraint of trade or commerce." Another important U.S. antitrust law, the Clayton Antitrust Act of 1914, as amended in 1936 by the Robinson–Patman Act, prohibits discrimination among customers through prices or other means; it also prohibits mergers of firms, or acquisitions of one firm by another, whenever the effect may be "to substantially lessen competition."

In Europe, antitrust legislation received much attention after World War II, when provisions against restraint of competition were embodied in a number of national laws and international agreements. The Commission of the European Communities in Brussels regularly passes upon cases involving practices of companies trading in the Common Market; its decisions are based upon Articles 85 and 86 of the Treaty of Rome (1957), which deal with rules of fair competition.

Antium (Italy): *see* Anzio.

Antler orogeny, a mountain-building event in Late Devonian and Mississippian time (about 340,000,000 to 350,000,000 years ago) that affected a linear belt in the Cordilleran Geosyncline, extending from the California–Nevada border northward through the central part of Nevada into Idaho. The term Antler Orogenic Belt, and formerly Manhattan Geanticline, is applied to the deformed rocks produced by this orogeny.

Evidence for the Antler orogeny consists of the widespread extent of coarse clastic sediments of Mississippian and Early Pennsylvanian age east and west of the belt and the development of a very prominent eastward-moving thrust fault in Early Mississippian time, the Roberts Mountain Thrust.

antlerite, a copper sulfate mineral, $Cu_3(SO_4)(OH)_4$, that is found in the oxidized zone of copper deposits, particularly in arid regions. At Bisbee, Ariz; Kennicott, Alaska; Sierra Mojada, Coahuila, Mex.; and Chuquicamata, Chile, it is the principal copper ore mineral.

Antlerite from Puerto de Gomez, Chihuahua, Mex.

By courtesy of the Field Museum of Natural History, Chicago; photograph, John H. Gerard—EB Inc.

For detailed physical properties, *see* sulfate mineral (table).

antlike flower beetle, any of the approximately 1,000 species of the insect family Anthicidae (order Coleoptera). They are usually seen around flowers, foliage, refuse, or dead wood.

These voracious beetles resemble ants and range from 2 to 12 millimetres (up to 1/2 inch) in length. Some can be found in debris and under stones and logs.

antlion, any insect larva of the neuropteran family Myrmeleontidae. The oval, sandy-gray abdomen of the larva is covered with bristles; the prothorax forms a mobile neck; and the large square head has powerful, sickle-like jaws. The antlion digs a funnel-shaped pit (from 2.5 to 5 centimetres deep and 2.5 to 7.5 centimetres wide at the edge) by using its abdomen as a plow, heaping the loosened particles on its head and throwing them clear of the pit. When the pit is completed the larva buries itself so that only its jaws project. Any small insect that ventures over the edge of the sandy pit slips to the bottom and is seized by the antlion. After sucking the contents of its victim, the antlion throws the empty skin out of the pit. The larvae of certain species (*e.g.*, the spotted-winged antlion, *Dendroleon obsoletus*) do not make a pitfall but seize passing prey from a hiding place.

After a period of feeding and growth the larva prepares a cocoon of sand and spun silk; it emerges as a sexually mature adult. The adult antlion, a weak flier, has relatively short, clubbed antennae and four narrow, delicate, densely net-veined wings that may be marked with brown or black. Since the adult does not feed, the larva must consume sufficient food to sustain the adult.

Antlion

William E. Ferguson

Myrmeleon formicarius, the best known of the 65 described species, occurs in both North America and Europe but not in England; it matures in late summer. In the United States the antlion is frequently known as a doodlebug.

Antofagasta, region, in an extremely arid part of northern Chile, bounded on the east by Bolivia and Argentina and on the west by the Pacific Ocean. Antofagasta (area 48,642 sq mi [125,981 sq km]) is the second largest of Chile's regions; about 90 percent of its population lives in urban areas, chiefly the capital city of Antofagasta (*q.v.*), and in Tocopilla, Calama, and Chuquicamata. Occupied in 1879 by Chilean forces early in the War of the Pacific, it was ceded by Bolivia in 1884 and created a Chilean province in 1888 and a region in 1974. It includes the provinces of Tocopilla, Antofagasta, and El Loa. The population grew greatly after the discovery of nitrate deposits in 1866, mainly in the Pampa del Tamarugal, lying between the coastal range and the volcanic Andes. After World War I, nitrate prices fell, and the population declined. From the region now comes more than 50 percent of Chile's copper production, especially from Chuquicamata. Borax, sulfur, and iodine are also important mineral resources. It is the leading region in road and railroad mileage and is linked with the rest of Chile and with Oruro, Bolivia, and Salta, Arg. Pop. (1982 prelim.) 341,203.

Antofagasta, capital of Antofagasta province and Antofagasta region, northern Chile, and a Pacific port on Bahía (bay) Moreno. A Bolivian city before 1879, it occupies a terrace at the base of bleak, arid coastal mountains. Its early growth resulted from the nitrate boom that began in 1866 and from the Caracoles

The cathedral on Plaza San Martín, Antofagasta, Chile

Art Resource—EB Inc.

silver discovery of 1870, at which time Antofagasta's name became official. Supplying the mines and exporting copper and sulfur continue as its major functions. Besides foundries and refineries, ore-concentration and sulfuric acid manufacturing facilities, there are local food and beverage processing and fish-meal production industries. There is also a shipyard for trawlers. The largest city in northern Chile, Antofagasta is the site of the University of the North (founded in 1956). It is also a communications centre on the Pan-American Highway, is linked by rail to the mines, to Oruro, Bolivia, and to Salta, Arg., as well as to urban areas to the north and south, and has an international airport. Pop. (1982 prelim.) 183,365.

Antoine (French personal name): *see under* Anthony.

Antoine, André (b. Jan. 31, 1858, Limoges, Fr.—d. Oct. 19, 1943, Pouliguen), actor, theatrical manager, critic, and film director, a pioneer of naturalistic drama who founded the Théâtre-Libre in Paris. His contributions to the development of realism in modern films was only beginning to gain appreciation in the second half of the 20th century.

Largely self-educated, Antoine was working as a clerk for the Paris Gas Company and acting part-time when in 1887 he founded the Théâtre-Libre as a showcase for the work of contemporary naturalistic playwrights. Despite an initially unenthusiastic reception he soon won wide acceptance and began financing his productions through private subscription.

In its heyday (1887–93), the Théâtre-Libre introduced to French audiences the work of Brieux, Ibsen, Hauptmann, Strindberg, and others. It greatly influenced the modern French theatre and spawned a host of imitators around the world, among them the Freie Bühne in Berlin, the Moscow Art Theatre, the Theatre Guild in New York City, and the Independent Theatre in London. In 1896 financial losses forced him to close the theatre, but a year later, after serving briefly as co-director of the Théâtre de Odéon, he founded the Théâtre-Antoine, offering productions similar to those of his original company. In 1906 he was appointed sole director of the Odéon; he resigned after eight years to become a drama critic and an extremely innovative film director (1914–24). He directed such films as *Les Frères corses* (1915), *Mademoiselle de la Seiglière* (1920), and *L'Arlésienne* (1921).

Antoku, in full ANTOKU TENNŌ, personal name TOKIHITO (b. Dec. 22, 1178, Kyōto—d. April 25, 1185, Nagato Dannoura, Japan), 81st emperor of Japan; his death in the famous naval Battle of Dannoura (1185) on the Inland Sea in western Japan resulted in the loss of the great sword that was one of the Three Imperial Regalia, the symbols of Imperial authority, supposedly brought to earth when the first Japanese emperor descended from heaven.

He was placed on the throne in 1180, at the age of two, by the Taira clan, and assumed the reign name Antoku. Because of his youth, real power resided in the hands of the former emperor Shirakawa and Antoku's grandfather, the renowned warrior Taira Kiyomori. In 1181 the Taira clan was driven from Kyōto, the capital city, by forces under the control of Minamoto Yoshinaka. The Tairas fled westward, taking Antoku with them. The Minamotos pursued the Tairas, finally annihilating them four years later at the Battle of Dannoura, during which, in an attempt to escape capture, Antoku and his attendants jumped into the sea and drowned.

Anton (Czech, Danish, Dutch, Romanian, etc., personal name): *see under* Anthony.

Antonelli, Giacomo (b. April 2, 1806, Sonnino, Papal States—d. Nov. 6, 1876, Vatican City), cardinal and secretary of state to Pope Pius IX.

Though never ordained priest, Antonelli was created cardinal by Pius in 1847 and became premier (1848) of the Papal States, which were then governed for the first time by a democratic constitution. After his own and succeeding governments had fallen and the revolutionary situation at Rome had led to the assassination of the papal premier Count Pellegrino Rossi in 1848, he courageously remained with Pius at the Quirinal and planned the Pope's flight to Gaeta, Italy, where Antonelli was made acting secretary of state.

After the Pope's return to Rome in 1850, Antonelli was officially appointed secretary of state, which he remained until his death. He was in general control of the government of the Papal States until their elimination in 1870 and was in charge of the Pope's relations with other governments until 1876. His policy was to avoid further attempts to introduce constitutional government into the Papal States because he felt it was impossible either to distinguish the pope's spiritual from his temporal power or to subject him to a lay assembly. As a diplomatic opportunist, Antonelli knew that his only hope of preserving the Pope's temporal sovereignty over central Italy during the growing movement for Italian unity was to retain the goodwill of the French government of Napoleon III, which had maintained a garrison in Rome after 1850. He was therefore opposed to the raising of a papal army, which took place in 1860, and to all quarrels with Paris. When the Piedmontese forces entered Rome (1870), he requested them to preserve order by extending occupation around the Vatican, and the papal army was disbanded. Despite his faithful service to the Pope, Antonelli died little mourned by him because of frequent reports of the impurity of his life and of the wealth he accumulated while in office.

Antonello DA MESSINA (b. *c.* 1430, Messina, Sicily—d. *c.* Feb. 19, 1479, Messina), painter who probably introduced oil painting and Flemish pictorial techniques into mid-15th-century Venetian art. His practice of building form with colour rather than line and

"Portrait of a Man," panel painting by Antonello da Messina, *c.* 1472; in the National Gallery, London

By courtesy of the trustees of the National Gallery, London

shade greatly influenced the subsequent development of Venetian painting.

Little is known of Antonello's early life, but it is clear that he was trained in Naples, then a cosmopolitan art centre, where he studied the work of Provençal and Flemish artists, especially that of Jan van Eyck. His earliest known works, a "Crucifixion" (*c.* 1455; Museum of Art, Sibiu, Rom.) and "St. Jerome in His Study" (*c.* 1460; National Gallery, London), already show Antonello's characteristic combination of Flemish technique and realism with typically Italian modelling of forms and clarity of spatial arrangement.

In 1457 Antonello returned to Messina, where he worked until 1474. The chief works of this period, the polyptych of 1473 and the "Annunciation" of 1474 (both in the Museo Nazionale, Messina), are relatively conservative altarpieces commissioned by the church, but the "Salvator Mundi" (1465; National Gallery, London), intended for private devotions, is bold and simple, showing a thorough understanding of the human form and the depiction of personality. It was but a short step from the "Salvator Mundi" to such incisive characterizations of human psychology as seen in "Portrait of a Man" (*c.* 1472; National Gallery, London), a work that presaged the uncanny vitality and meticulous realism of such panels as "Portrait of a Condottiere" (1475; Louvre, Paris), which established his reputation in northern Italy.

From 1475 to 1476 Antonello was in Venice and possibly Milan. Within a short time of his arrival in Venice, his work attracted so much favourable attention that he was supported by the Venetian state, and local painters enthusiastically adopted his oil technique and compositonal style. In "St. Sebastian" (*c.* 1476; Gemäldegalerie, Dresden, E.Ger.), his most mature work, Antonello achieved a synthesis of clearly defined space, monumental, sculpture-like form, and luminous colour, which was one of the most decisive influences on the evolution of Venetian painting down to Giorgione's day. In 1476 he was again in Messina, where he completed his final masterpiece, "The Virgin Annunciate" (*c.* 1476; Galleria Nazionale, Palermo).

Antonescu, Ion (b. June 15, 1882, Pitești, Rom.—d. June 1, 1946, near Jilava), Romanian general and statesman who became dictator of the pro-German government during World War II.

After World War I, Antonescu served as military attaché in Paris and in London and, in 1934, as chief of the Romanian general staff. Named minister of defense in 1937, he retained office with the establishment of King Carol II's corporatist dictatorship (1938), only to be dismissed after a few weeks as a sympathizer of the principal Romanian Fascist group, the Iron Guard.

Appointed prime minister Sept. 4, 1940, after Romania had lost one third of its territory partitioned among the Axis powers and the U.S.S.R. (June–September 1940), Antonescu established a Fascist dictatorship and openly embraced the Axis powers. His "National Legionary State" briefly brought the Iron Guard to power; but, after a period of Guardist revolutionary and criminal excesses, he suppressed the organization (1941). He at first secured widespread popular support for his domestic reform program and, as Germany's ally, for his declaration of war against the U.S.S.R. (1941). His administration also permitted a certain latitude to opposition critics, and some historians believe it may have been the least servile among the German satellite governments. His popular support gradually eroded, however, as manpower losses mounted on the Russian front. His regime was finally toppled by a coup d'etat in August 1944 led by King Michael; Antonescu subsequently was sentenced to death by the Romanian Communist people's court and was executed as a war criminal.

Antonin (French chef): *see* Carême, Marie-Antoine.

Antonina, port, eastern Paraná state, southeastern Brazil, at the head of the Baía (bay) de Paranaguá, an inlet of the Atlantic Ocean, northwest of the port of Paranaguá and east of Curitiba, the state capital. Wood and maté (tea), from Ponta Grossa, 100 mi (160 km) inland, and bananas and iron ore are exported. There is some iron smelting, based on nearby magnetite deposits. Other industries include rice processing, wood veneer production, sugar and flour milling, and the manufacture of rope and soap. Pop. (1980 prelim.) 11,950.

Antonine, either of the Roman emperors Antoninus Pius (reigned AD 138–161) and his adopted heir Marcus Aurelius (161–180). The term Antonines also usually includes Lucius Verus (161–169), another adopted heir of Antoninus Pius and co-emperor with Marcus Aurelius, as well as Commodus (176–192), son of Marcus Aurelius and co-emperor and then sole emperor. The Antonine period 138–180 was one of great internal peace and prosperity, when the sense of unity, the reconciliation of peoples, was greatest throughout the Roman Empire. *See* Five Good Emperors.

Antonine Wall, Roman frontier barrier in Britain, extending about $36\frac{1}{2}$ miles (58.5 kilometres) across Scotland between the Clyde River and the Firth of Forth. Ordered by the Roman emperor Antoninus Pius, the wall was built in AD 142 by Lollius Urbicus, governor of Britain. The wall was 14 to 16 feet ($4\frac{1}{2}$ metres) wide and probably 10 feet (3 metres) high; a ditch 40 feet (12 metres) wide and 12 feet (4 metres) deep ran in front of the wall, and a military road ran behind it. A series of 19 forts, separated by intervals of 2 miles (3 kilometres), controlled the wall.

Construction of the wall extended the northern boundary of Roman Britain farther into Scotland and provided defense beyond Hadrian's Wall (*q.v.*), which had been completed some 100 miles (160 kilometres) to the south in about 136. Occupation of the Antonine Wall was interrupted during the northern revolt (AD 155–158), and the garrison withdrew to Hadrian's Wall not later than the year 196. Traces of the wall still remain.

Antoninus, SAINT, original name ANTONINO PIEROZZI, or DE' FORCIGLIONI, Antonino also spelled ANTONIO (b. March 1, 1389, Florence—d. May 2, 1459, Florence; canonized 1523; feast day May 10), archbishop of Florence who is regarded as one of the founders of modern moral theology and Christian social ethics.

In Florence Antoninus joined the Dominican order (1405); he became an active leader of the order's Observant movement, especially at Fiesole, near Florence. As vicar of the Observants he founded the convent of San Marco, Florence, in 1436. There he served as prior (1439–44) and attended the Council of Florence (1439–45).

He became archbishop of Florence (1446), where he was greatly beloved for his charity and particularly for his indefatigable aid during the plague of 1448 and the earthquake 1453. He was canonized by Pope Adrian VI. Antoninus' principal works are his *Summa moralis* (Venice, 1477) and *Summa confessionum* (Mondovì, 1472).

Antoninus Pius, in full CAESAR TITUS AELIUS HADRIANUS ANTONINUS AUGUSTUS PIUS, original name TITUS AURELIUS FULVIUS BOIONIUS ARRIUS ANTONINUS (b. Sept. 19, 86, Lanuvium, Latium—d. March 7, 161, Lorium, Etruria), Roman emperor from AD 138

Antoninus Pius, marble bust; in the British Museum

Reproduced by courtesy of the trustees of the British Museum

to 161. Mild-mannered and capable, he was the fourth of the "five good emperors" who guided the empire through an 84-year period (96–180) of internal peace and prosperity. His family originated in Gaul, and his father and grandfathers had all been consuls.

After serving as consul in 120, Antoninus was assigned by the emperor Hadrian (ruled 117–138) to assist with judicial administration in Italy. He governed the province of Asia (*c.* 134) and then became an adviser to the Emperor.

In 138 Antoninus was adopted by Hadrian and designated as his successor. Hadrian specified that two men—the future emperors Marcus Aurelius and Lucius Verus—were to succeed Antoninus. Upon acceding to power, Antoninus persuaded a reluctant Senate to offer the customary divine honours to Hadrian. For this, and possibly other such dutiful acts, he was given the surname Pius by the Senate. When his wife, Faustina, died in late 140 or early 141 he founded in her memory the Puellae Faustinianae, a charitable institution for the daughters of the poor.

References to Antoninus in 2nd-century literature are exceptionally scanty; it is certain that few striking events occurred during his 23-year reign. A rebellion in Roman Britain was suppressed, and in 142 a 36-mile (58-kilometre) garrisoned barrier—called the Antonine Wall—was built to extend the Roman frontier some 100 miles north of Hadrian's Wall (*q.v.*). Antoninus' armies contained revolts in Mauretania, Germany, Dacia, and Egypt.

The feeling of well-being that pervaded the empire under Antoninus is reflected in the celebrated panegyric by the orator Aelius Aristides in 143–144. After Antoninus' death, however, the empire suffered invasion by hostile tribes, followed by severe civil strife.

Antonio (Italian, Spanish, etc., personal name): *see under* Anthony, except as below.

António, PRIOR OF CRATO, Portuguese PRIOR DO CRATO, byname DOM ANTÓNIO (b. 1531, Lisbon—d. Aug. 26, 1595, Paris), ecclesiastic and claimant to the throne of Portugal who never gained the crown despite armed assistance from France and England.

António was the illegitimate son of Luís, duke of Beja, brother of King John III of Portugal. He became head of the Order of St. John in Portugal and was endowed (1555) with the wealthy priory of Crato. He accompanied King Sebastian (reigned 1557–78), John III's grandson, to North Africa, where, in the Battle of the Three Kings (1578), Sebastian was killed and António captured. On his return to Portugal, António's claim to the throne was rejected by Sebastian's successor Henry, the last surviving brother of John III, and later by the council that governed Portugal for some months after Henry's death (January 1580). In June 1580 he was acclaimed king as António I at Santarém by his supporters. His possession of the crown, however, was contested by Philip II of Spain, whose army, under the Duke of Alba, defeated António outside Lisbon two months later. The Spanish king then became Philip I of Portugal, and António sought refuge in Paris.

With French help, António sent two naval expeditions (1582 and 1583) to the Azores, where he was still recognized as king. Both of his forces were defeated by Spanish squadrons. He next went to England, where he enlisted the assistance of Elizabeth I. An English fleet under Sir Francis Drake and Sir John Norris effected a landing near Lisbon in support of António in 1589, but the expedition proved a costly failure. Impoverished and in ill health, António returned to Paris, where he planned further expeditions until his death.

António, Mário, original name MÁRIO ANTÓNIO FERNANDES DE OLIVEIRO (b. April 5, 1934, Maquela do Zombo, Angola), scholar, short-story writer, and poet whose works focus alternately on Angolan and Portuguese cultures. A poet of personal love and social protest in his early years, António in his later poems frequently presents verbal portraits of moods, places, and experiences.

He completed his primary and secondary studies in Luanda. After spending 11 years as a public civil servant in the Angolan capital, he moved to Lisbon in 1963. He visited and lectured in the United States in 1979.

António argued in his essays that Portuguese colonialism produced a creole, or mixed, culture in Angola in which European and African attitudes, values, and perspectives were shared by whites and blacks, as well as mulattos. He is a prolific contributor to journals and magazines in Angola and Portugal. His principal volumes of poetry include *Amor: poesias* (1960; "Love: Poems"), *100 Poemas* (1963), and *Rosto de Europa* (1968; "Face of Europe"). By the mid-1980s he was the author of more than 20 works in Portuguese, including the poems, several collections of stories, cultural and literary essays on 19th- and 20th-century Angola, and translations.

Antonio, Nicolás (b. July 28/31, 1617, Seville—d. April 13, 1684, Madrid), first systematic historian of Spanish literature. His *Bibliotheca Hispana* appeared in two parts (*Nova*, 1672; *Vetus*, 1696). The first is a vast bibliography of Peninsular and Spanish colonial writers after 1500, with critical evaluations. The second, a history of Peninsular literature from the reign of Augustus to 1500, marks the emergence of modern bibliography and the transformation of literary history into a scholarly discipline. A second edition (1788; vol. 1 of the *Nova* dated 1783), with additions from Antonio's manuscripts, is still consulted.

Antonioni, Michelangelo (b. Sept. 29, 1912, Ferrara, Italy), Italian film director, cinematographer, and producer, noted for his avoidance of "realistic" narrative in favour of character study and a vaguely metaphorical series of incidents. Among his major films are *Le amiche* (1955), *L'avventura* (1959), *L'eclisse* (1962), and *Blow-up* (1966).

Life. Antonioni is recognizably the product of the mild, uneventful plains of northern Italy that form the background for several of

Antonioni

his films. Reserved and unexpansive in manner, he has said that the experience most important to his development as a filmmaker and as a man was his upbringing in a settled, bourgeois, provincial home, with a sufficiency of money; a traditional education; a code of reserve and self-discipline; and the leisure and ease necessary for a detached view of people and of life. He attended school in Ferrara and went to the university at Bologna, though he continued to live at home and commuted daily to his studies. As a child his consuming interests were architecture and painting; at the university he studied classics, then economics and commerce. He also began haunting the cinemas and writing film criticism for a newspaper in the neighbouring city of Padua. In 1939 he decided to make the cinema his career.

The obvious place to do this was Rome, where Antonioni soon became a staff member of the magazine *Cinema*; he also spent some months studying at a film school. What else he did in his 20s (apart from becoming an amateur tennis champion for northern Italy) remains obscure; his first credited film work dates from his 30th year, when he collaborated on the scripts of some major feature films, one of them Roberto Rossellini's *Pilota ritorna*, and went to France to assist the director Marcel Carné on his wartime production *Les Visiteurs du soir.* In 1943 he began to direct his own first film, a short documentary called *Gente del Po*, but its completion was interrupted by the chaos of Italy's defeat in World War II. For a while Antonioni made his living by translating from the French, then became film critic of the underground paper *Italia libera*, and wrote some unproduced scripts. *Gente del Po* finally appeared in 1947; it was followed by six more shorts and then, in 1950, by his first feature, *Cronaca di un amore*, a rather bitter romance that immediately established him as a talent to be watched.

After that time, Antonioni's life, to the outside world at least, consisted of little more than the production of films. The landmarks are his first great film, *Le amiche* (based on a story by the Italian writer Cesare Pavese), in 1955; his first big international success, *L'avventura*, in 1959; his first film in colour, *Deserto rosso*, in 1964; his first full-length English-language film, *Blow-up*, in 1966; and his first American film, *Zabriskie Point*, in 1970. He was responsible for shaping the career of the actress Monica Vitti, whose exquisite, mysterious presence provided the warming touch of human interest that assured *L'avventura*, despite its puzzling narrative structure and obscurity of motive, its breakthrough to a large international audience. Some mediation of this sort is necessary in Antonioni's films since without it his approach remains too cold and abstract to reach more than a select, esoteric audience. Human beings for him are depicted as moving parts in a pictorially exquisite pattern of moods and atmospheres; they wander around unable to engage in meaningful action, uncommunicative, lost in their dreams, while the outside world mirrors the feelings they never express, their alienation from one another and from the life around them.

Antonioni's critical reputation stood at its highest when the impact of his new, personal vision was most immediate, between *L'avventura* in 1959 and *L'eclisse* in 1962, in both of which a young woman, portrayed by Monica Vitti, unsuccessfully seeks in romance a means of coping with the emptiness of her life. His later films—including *Chung Kuo-China* (1972), *The Passenger* (1974), and *The Mystery of Oberwald* (1980)—did not receive as much acclaim. Antonioni's place in the history of the cinema and in the development of 20th-century sensibility, however, remains secure.

Assessment. One of the cinema's leading aesthetes, Antonioni spearheaded a critical and commercial reaction against the overwhelming acceptance, during post-World War II years, of unvarnished reality as a cinematic ideal. Under his direction the film became a metaphor for human experience, rather than a record of it.

He never structured his films around a traditional plot or a character analysis; it was rather the visual image that became his fundamental vehicle of expression, most noticeably, the modern industrial landscape. After Antonioni, few people saw a water tower or a plastics dump with quite the same unappreciative eyes; in his films a new kind of beauty was revealed in the mechanical jungle of 20th-century urban society. (J.R.T.)

BIBLIOGRAPHY. Pierre Leprohon, *Michelangelo Antonioni* (1963), a critical study, with documents and extracts from Antonioni's writings and interviews; John Russell Taylor, *Cinema Eye, Cinema Ear* (1964), includes a critical study of Antonioni, with filmography and bibliography; Ian Cameron and Robin Wood, *Antonioni* (1969), a film-by-film analysis; Michelangelo Antonioni, *Screenplays: Il Grido, L'Avventura, La Notte, L'Eclisse* (Eng. trans. 1963), reading texts of four major works, with an introduction by Antonioni.

Antonius (Latin personal name): *see under* Anthony.

Antony (personal name): *see under* Anthony, except as below.

Antony, Mark, also spelled MARC ANTHONY, Latin MARCUS ANTONIUS (b. 82/81 BC—d. August, 30 BC, Alexandria), Roman general under Julius Caesar and later triumvir (43–30 BC), who, with Cleopatra, queen of Egypt, was defeated by Octavian (the future emperor Augustus) in the last of the civil wars that destroyed the Roman Republic.

Mark Antony, detail of a marble bust; in the Vatican Museum
Alinari—Art Resource/EB Inc.

Early life and career. Mark Antony was the son and grandson of men of the same name. His father was called Creticus because of his military operations in Crete, and his grandfather, one of the leading orators of his day, was vividly portrayed as a speaker in Cicero's *De oratore*. After a somewhat dissipated youth, the future triumvir served with distinction in 57–54 as a cavalry commander under Aulus Gabinius in Judaea and Egypt. He then joined the staff of Julius Caesar, to whom he was related on his mother's side, and served with him for much of the concluding phase of Caesar's conquest of central and northern Gaul and its aftermath (54–53, 52–50). In 51 Antony held the minor office of quaestor, an office of financial administration that gave him a place in the Senate, and he was subsequently elected to the politically influential priesthood of the augurs.

Civil war and triumvirate. In 49, the year in which the Civil War broke out between Pompey and Caesar, Antony became tribune of the people (an official with the traditional function of protecting the plebeians from arbitrary actions of the magistrates) and vigorously supported Caesar in the Senate. He fled from Rome to his patron's headquarters after receiving threats of violence. After Antony had fought in the brief Italian campaign in which Pompey was forced to evacuate the Italian peninsula, Caesar left him in charge of Italy, a post he again occupied in 48–47 as Master of the Horse (the dictator's assistant) after the decisive battle at Pharsalus (in Thessaly) in which he had commanded Caesar's left wing. Thereafter, because his methods as regent of Italy had displeased Caesar, he was removed from the post and was without employment until 44 when he became consul as the dictator's colleague. After Caesar's murder, he used a variety of methods, including the falsification of the dead man's papers, to control events and to arouse the people against Caesar's assassins, Marcus Brutus and Cassius. In June, Antony was granted a five-year governorship of northern and central Transalpine Gaul (Gallia Comata) and Cisalpine Gaul (northern Italy). Despite his growing power and popularity among the people, the orator Cicero attacked him fiercely in a series of speeches from September 44 to April 43 BC (he never tired of saying that Antony should have been murdered also), and the 19-year-old Octavian, Caesar's great-nephew and adopted son, gradually emerged as a rival. In April 43 a coalition of Octavian, the two consuls of the year, and Decimus Brutus (another of the former conspirators against Caesar) defeated Antony at Mutina (Modena) and compelled him to withdraw into the southern part (Narbonensis) of Transalpine Gaul. There, however, he was joined by a number of leading commanders including Marcus Aemilius Lepidus, who, after Antony, had been Caesar's Master of the Horse. In early November Octavian met Antony and Lepidus in Bononia (Bologna), and the three entered into an official five-year autocratic pact, the second triumvirate (November 43). The enemies of the triumvirs, including the orator Cicero, were proscribed and executed, and in the following year Marcus Brutus and Cassius killed themselves after their defeat at the Battle of Philippi, in which Antony greatly distinguished himself as a commander. The republican cause was now dead.

The triumvirs had agreed to divide the empire; so Antony proceeded to take up the administration of the eastern provinces. He first summoned Cleopatra, the queen of Egypt, to Tarsus (southeastern Asia Minor) to answer reports that she had assisted their enemies. She successfully exonerated herself, and Antony spent the winter of 41–40 as her lover at Alexandria. In spite of the romantic accounts of ancient authors, however, she did not at this stage establish a permanent dominance over him, since he made no move to see her again for more than three years.

Early in 40 he received two pieces of bad news: that his brother Lucius Antonius and his third wife, Fulvia, on their own initiative and without success, had revolted against Octavian, thus setting off the Perusine War (after the central point of the rising, Perusia, the modern Perugia); and that the Parthians, the eastern neighbours of the empire, had invaded Roman Syria. In spite of the latter information, Antony first proceeded to Italy, where he became reconciled to Octavian at Brundusium (Brindisi), and, since Fulvia had died in the meantime, he married Octavian's sister Octavia. The two triumvirs agreed that Herod, who had fled from Judaea to escape the Parthians and their Jewish allies, should be encouraged to retake the country and become its king. In the following year they concluded the short-lived Treaty of Misenum with Pompey's son Sextus Pompeius, who because of his control of wide areas of the Mediterranean had been pirating Roman ships.

Accompanied by Octavia, Antony then proceeded to Athens, where he was enthusiastically greeted and hailed as the New Dionysus, mystic god not only of wine but also of happiness and immortality. In 38 Antony's lieutenant Publius Ventidius won a decisive victory over the Parthians, and, in the following year, Herod was able to reestablish himself at Jerusalem. Meanwhile, however, further differences had arisen between Antony and Octavian, and, although these were ostensibly settled by the Treaty of Tarentum, which prolonged the triumvirate for a further five years, Antony sent Octavia back to Italy from Corcyra (modern Corfu, or Kérkira) when he left again for the east and arranged for Cleopatra to join him in Syria. Henceforward, apart from his absences on land campaigns, they lived together for the remaining seven years of their lives.

Alliance with Cleopatra. Religious propaganda declared Cleopatra the New Isis, or Aphrodite, to his New Dionysus, and it is possible (but unlikely) that they contracted an Egyptian marriage: it would not have been valid in Roman law since Romans could not marry foreigners. Apart from their undoubted mutual affection, Cleopatra needed Antony in order to revive the old boundaries of the Ptolemaic kingdom (though her efforts to convince him to give her Herod's Judaea failed), and Antony needed Egypt as a source of supplies and funds for his planned attack on Parthia. His invasion, however, of Parthia's ally Media Atropatene (southwest of the Caspian) in 36 BC ended in a retreat involving heavy losses. On his return to Syria, Cleopatra met him with money and supplies. Octavian, exploiting the occasion and the contrast of Antony's failure with the decisive victory he himself—or rather his admiral Agrippa—had won against Sextus Pompeius, sent Octavia to Antony along with troops and provisions. But the soldiers fell far short of the numbers Antony expected (and were owed by his fellow-triumvir), and he then made a future breach between the two leaders almost inevitable by ordering Octavia to return to Rome.

The break was accelerated in 34, when he celebrated a successful expedition to Armenia by appearing in a triumphal procession through the streets of Alexandria, a proceeding regarded by Romans as an impious parody of their traditional Triumph. A few days later he staged a ceremony at which Cleopatra was pronounced Queen of Kings, her son and joint monarch Ptolemy XV Caesar, or Caesarion (for Cleopatra, and now Antony, claimed that Julius Caesar had fathered the boy), was declared King of Kings, and the two sons and a daughter that Cleopatra had borne to Antony were also given imposing royal titles. The exact significance and substantiality of these Donations are disputable, but critics interpreted them as involving the transfer of Roman territories into alien, Greek, hands. In the next year, 33, the Roman leaders launched unprecedented, savage propaganda attacks upon one another, including the production by Octavian of a document (of dubious though possible authenticity) that purported to be a will of Antony favouring the children of Cleopatra and providing for his own burial at Alexandria. In 32 the triumvirate had officially ended, although Antony continued to call himself triumvir on his coins. Both consuls at Rome, however, happened to support Antony, and now, threatened by Octavian, they left for his headquarters, bringing numerous, probably more than 200, Roman senators with them. After Antony had officially divorced Octavia, her brother formally broke off the ties of personal friendship with him and declared war, not against him but against Cleopatra. Antony successively established his headquarters at Ephesus (Selçuk), Athens, and Patras (Pátrai) and marshalled his principal fleet in the gulf of Ambracia (northwestern Greece). More naval detachments occupied a long line of posts along the west coast of Greece. But Octavian's admiral Agrippa, and then Octavian himself, succeeded in sailing from Italy across the Ionian Sea and effecting landings, and Agrippa captured decisive points all along the line.

As Antony lost more ground, the morale of his advisers and fighting forces deteriorated, a process aided by Cleopatra's insistence on being present at his headquarters against the wishes of many of his leading Roman supporters, thus providing Octavian with fresh propaganda fuel. Because of this lack of unity and the inexperience of Antony's crews, the decisive battle was lost before it ever began. It took place off Actium, outside the Ambracian Gulf, on Sept. 2, 31 BC. Antony suffered the inevitable defeat, but Cleopatra, by prearranged plan rather than treachery, broke through the enemy line with her 60 ships (carrying her and Antony's treasury) and, joined by her lover, made for Egypt. It was nearly a year before Octavian reached them there, but soon after his arrival, when resistance proved impossible, first Antony and then Cleopatra committed suicide (August 30 BC).

Personality. Antony was a man of considerable ability and impressive appearance, far more genial than his adversary but not quite equal to Octavian's exceptional efficiency and energy and, in particular, unfit or unwilling to grasp the moment for action. Nevertheless, he was an outstanding leader of men and a competent general, though, in the end, not such a successful admiral as the experienced Agrippa. As a politician, he was astute enough—aided by a talent for florid oratory—but gradually lost touch with Roman feeling and fatally lacked the cold deliberateness of Octavian. Since the latter proved victorious in his struggle for power, it is his interpretation of events, rather than Antony's, that has remained lodged in the history books. Cicero had earlier depicted Antony as a drunken, lustful debauchee—though his adulteries may have been less extensive than Octavian's. More significantly for history, the outcome of the battle off Actium made certain that Octavian's Roman-Italian policy prevailed throughout the empire, and the Antonian theme of Greco-Roman collaboration was not given a trial until the emperor Constantine captured Byzantium three centuries later.

(M.Gr.)

BIBLIOGRAPHY. Plutarch, *Life of Antony*; Appian, *Civil Wars*, I–V; Cassius Dio, XLI–LIII; Cicero, *Philippics, Letters to Atticus, and Letters to Friends;* Josephus, *Jewish War* and *Jewish Antiquities,* the basic ancient literary sources, all available in translation, but none of first-class reliability or sufficiently comprehensive; H.H. Scullard, *From the Gracchi to Nero,* 3rd ed. (1970), with a bibliography of recent additions to the extensive periodical literature; J.M. Carter, *The Battle of Actium* (1970), an account of the events from 44 to 30 BC, with bibliography; W.W. Tarn and M.P. Charlesworth, *Octavian, Antony and Cleopatra,* reprint of *Cambridge Ancient History,* vol. 10, ch. 1–4 (1965), sympathetic description, first published in 1934 and superseded in detail, of Antony's regime in the eastern provinces.

Antony Khrapovitshy, original name ALEKSEY PAVLOVICH KHRAPOVITSKY (b. March 17, 1863, Novgorod, Russia—d. Aug. 10, 1936, Sremski Karlovci, Yugos.), Russian Orthodox metropolitan of Kiev, anti-papal polemicist, and controversialist in theological and political affairs who attempted an exclusively ethical interpretation of Christian doctrine.

After graduating from St. Petersburg Theological Academy, Antony entered a neighbouring monastery and in 1885 was ordained an Orthodox priest. Consecrated bishop in 1897, Antony was given the jurisdiction of Volhynia, in the Ukraine, in 1902, where he suppressed remnants of the Ukrainian Uniate Church (Roman Catholic) and quelled national aspirations within the Ukrainian Orthodox Church. In 1912 he was selected a member of the Holy Synod, the ruling council of the Russian Orthodox Church, served as archbishop of Kharkov from 1914 to 1917, and became metropolitan of Kiev in 1918.

With the outbreak of the Russian Revolution, Antony participated in the 1917–18 Pan-Russian Orthodox Council and was named one of the three candidates for the Russian patriarchate. After the Ukraine declared its independence from the tsarist regime, Antony was exiled to Buchach, southwest Ukraine, because of his efforts to prevent Ukrainian autonomy. The Bolshevik occupation of the Ukraine forced him to flee to Sremski Karlovci, Yugos., where in 1920 he assumed the leadership of the Russian Orthodox Church in exile.

With a reputation for polemics, Antony vigorously protested papal claims to supremacy over the universal church. According to some of his co-religionists who charged him with heresy, he was influenced by the anti-intellectual moralism of the Russian novelist Fyodor Dostoyevsky. He compiled a *Dictionary of the Works of Dostoyevsky* in 1921 to better integrate Dostoyevsky's ideas with his own.

In his principal ascetical–moral writings, *Concerning the Dogma of Redemption* (the English version appearing in *The Constructive Quarterly,* 1919) and "Essay on the Orthodox Christian Catechism" (1924), he relegated Christ's work to the level of ethical symbolism that would inspire Christian dedication to a moral life.

antpipit, either of two species of South American birds of the genus *Corythopis* that resemble pipits in size, shape, and coloration. The name is sometimes applied to the gnateaters (*Conopophaga*), with which *Corythopis* was formerly grouped in the family Conopophagidae (*q.v.*); *Corythopis* is now usually classified with the tyrant flycatchers in the family Tyrannidae (*q.v.;* order Passeriformes).

Antratsit, also spelled ANTRACIT, city, Voroshilovgrad *oblast* (administrative region), Ukrainian Soviet Socialist Republic. Incorporated in 1938, it is an anthracite-mining town, from which product it takes its name. It is a typical industrial centre on the Donets Coal Basin whose rise was due to the Soviet five-year plans for economic growth. Pop. (1983 est.) 65,000.

Antrim, former (until 1973) county, northeastern Northern Ireland, occupying an area of 1,176 sq mi (3,046 sq km), across the 13-mi-(21-km-) wide North Channel from the Mull of Kintyre in Scotland.

Antrim was bounded by the Atlantic Ocean (north), the North Channel and the Irish Sea (east), Belfast Lough (inlet of the sea) and the River Lagan (south), and by Lough (lake) Neagh and the lower River Bann (west).

Its northern and eastern parts were composed of the Antrim Mountains, an ancient basalt plateau of moorland and peat bogs cut by deep glens, ending at its northeastern corner in Fair Head (635 ft [194 m]), a perpendicular cliff. Collapse of the basalt caused the depression holding Lough Neagh, the largest inland lake in the British Isles. Prominent peaks in Antrim included Trostan (1,817 ft), Knocklayd (1,695 ft), and Slieveanorra (1,676 ft); Divis (1,574 ft) is the highest of the Belfast hills. The basalt reaches the north coast as steep cliffs and, at the Giant's Causeway, forms perpendicular hexagonal columns.

Man probably first came to Ireland through Antrim from western Scotland. Quantities of flint implements, or tools, dating from about 6000 BC occur in the Lough Neagh district. Migrations between Ireland and Scotland were common, especially in the 6th century. Scandinavian invaders reached Lough Neagh but made no permanent settlements. Antrim was partially penetrated by Anglo-Norman adventurers during the 12th century and formed part of the earldom of Ulster. Disorders in the late Middle Ages and the invasion by Edward Bruce (later king of Ireland) and his army from Scotland in 1315 caused the decline of English power. Only Carrickfergus remained in English hands until the Tudor period (1485–1603), when attempts were made to colonize the county and many Scots settled there. Although Antrim was not part of the territory involved in the scheme for the plantation of Ulster, it continued to attract many English immigrants.

At one time Carrickfergus was the county town (seat); but, when Belfast became the site of a new county courthouse in 1847, the grand jury also moved there. In 1898, however, Belfast became a county borough, and for a time the county lacked a county town. Until 1973 Ballymena filled that role. In the 1973 administrative reorganization of Northern Ireland, the county was divided into the districts of Moyle, Ballymoney, Ballymena, Larne, Antrim, Carrickfergus, Newtownabbey, and Belfast, and portions of Coleraire, Lisburn, Castlereagh, and Craigavon districts.

Antrim, Irish AONTROIM, town, seat, and district (established 1973), formerly in County Antrim, Northern Ireland. Antrim town is located in the valley of the Six Mile Water stream, at the northeastern corner of Lough (lake) Neagh. In 1798, the town was the scene of a battle in which several thousand nationalist (essentially Presbyterian) insurgents, led by the United Irishmen rebel Henry Joy McCracken, were defeated by the British military. Just north is one of the finest examples of the Irish round (watch) towers, dating from the 10th century; it is 93 ft (28 m) high and 17 ft in diameter. Antrim Castle, built in the 17th century, is evidence of the town's earlier strategic importance. A busy market centre and road junction, Antrim town was formerly an important locale for the linen industry.

Antrim district covers 217 sq mi (562 sq km) of high, rolling moorlands gradually descending to the Bann Valley and the lowlands along the shoreline of Lough Neagh,

The Antrim Mountains, Northern Ireland

G.E. Brown—Shostal/EB Inc.

the largest inland lake in the United Kingdom. Antrim borders the districts of Ballymena to the north, Newtownabbey to the east, and Belfast and Lisburn to the south, encompassing the villages of Crumlin, Randalstown, Toomebridge, Templepatrick, and Parkgate in addition to the town of Antrim, and supports considerable farming activity, mostly in livestock. Important synthetic fibre companies were established in the district in the 1970s, and service industries are scattered throughout. Antrim district is traversed by a national highway that extends from Belfast to Randalstown. Belfast's international airport is located within the district at Aldergrove, 7 mi (11 km) south of Antrim town. Pop. (1971) town, 8,351; (1981) district, 44,384.

Antrim, Randal MacDonnell, 1st marquess of (b. June 9, 1609—d. Feb. 3, 1683, Ballymagarry, County Antrim, Ire.), prominent Roman Catholic Royalist during the English Civil War who later turned against King Charles I and was employed in various capacities by Oliver Cromwell.

A grandson of the noted Irish chieftain (of Scottish ancestry) Sorley Boy MacDonnell, he married (1635) the widow of the 1st Duke of Buckingham, a close friend of Charles I. On the outbreak of the Bishops' Wars in 1639, MacDonnell planned an attack on Argyll in Scotland; this project was abortive, as were numerous later schemes by which he hoped to assist the King against Parliament. In May 1643 MacDonnell was captured in County Down by Parliamentary forces and was found to be carrying papers that concerned a planned rising in Scotland by the 5th Earl of Montrose with support from Ireland. MacDonnell escaped after several months' captivity and, on Jan. 26, 1644, was created marquess of Antrim.

Wanting the lord lieutenancy of Ireland for himself, Antrim was angered when the 12th Earl of Ormonde was reappointed to the post in 1648. The following year Antrim offered his services to Cromwell and later served with Parliamentary forces in the sieges of Ross (now New Ross, County Wexford) and Carlow. On going to England in December 1650, he was given a pension.

At the Restoration (1660), Antrim was imprisoned in the Tower of London but was pardoned by Charles II in 1663.

Antrodemus (dinosaur): *see* Allosaurus.

Antropología, Museo Nacional de: *see* Museo Nacional de Antropología.

Antschel, Paul: *see* Celan, Paul.

Antsirabe, town, Antananarivo province, central Madagascar, on the slopes of the nation's second highest peak, Tsiafajavona, in the Ankaratra mountains. Thermal springs, associated with ancient volcanism, together with an altitude of 4,000 ft encouraged the development of a health resort there in 1923. The terminus of a rail line from Antananarivo, the national capital (70 mi [110 km] northeast), Antsirabe serves a district supporting fruit (apples, grapes), dairy, pig, and poultry farms. Industries in the town include spinning and weaving, cigarette making, and food processing. A military academy opened there in 1965. Pop. (1982 est.) 90,816.

Antsiranana, also spelled ANTSERANANA, formerly DIÉGO-SUAREZ, town and province (*faritany*), at the northern tip of Madagascar. The town, on a promontory at the south end of a bay, developed from a French naval base. The local economy depends on the naval yards and on transshipment of cargoes between coasters and larger vessels. The main industry is ship construction and repair. Other industrial products include soap, salt, chemicals, and processed foods. The town is a regional centre (1977) of the University of Madagascar. The airport of Anamakia (6½ mi [10½ km] southwest) is served by internal air services.

The bay and port at Antsiranana, Madagascar
A. Picou—De Wys Inc.

The province, with its capital at Antsiranana, covers an area of 16,620 sq mi (43,046 sq km) at the northern extreme of the island. At the heart of the province is the forested Tsaratanana Massif, which includes the highest mountain in the country, Maromokotra (9,436 ft [2,876 m]). Most of the people live in the lowlands along the east and west coasts, and a road runs along each coast. Notable features of the province include the Ankara caves south of Antsiranana, once a hiding place for royal treasures, and the island of Nosy Be (*q.v.*) off the west coast. Major crops include rice, manioc, sweet potatoes, peanuts (groundnuts), and sugarcane. Vanilla is grown on a large scale in the southeast and is processed at Antalaha. Pop. (1982 est.) town, 49,000; (1977) province, 620,228.

Antwerp, Flemish ANTWERPEN, French ANVERS, province, northern Belgium, adjoining the Dutch frontier (north). It has an area of 1,104 sq mi (2,859 sq km) and is drained by the Scheldt, Dijle, Nete, and Rupel rivers. Formerly part of the old Duchy of Brabant, and part of the French province of Deux-Nèthes after the French occupation of 1795, its present boundaries were established in 1815, although subsequently modified. It is divided into three *arrondissements,* Antwerp, Mechelen, and Turnhout, with the capital at Antwerp.

The Kempen (Campine) heathlands, covering most of the northern and central area, are characterized by sand dunes, areas of broom, and poor pasture. There are extensive blocks of coniferous plantations. Around the scattered towns and villages the soil has been fertilized to produce oats, potatoes, vegetables, and fodder for cattle raising. Much of the industry in the province is concentrated in the port area around Antwerp; it includes oil refining, petrochemical and chemical works, shipbuilding and naval repair, automobile assembly, steel, and nonferrous metallurgy. In the Kempen area the opening of the Albert Canal (1930–39) linking Antwerp with Liège has favoured the expansion of the zinc, copper, and nuclear energy industries. The Zuiderkempen development area is part of a long-range plan for industrial expansion. The Kempen is served by four rail lines.

The southern and western parts of the province are hilly, and the soil, although sandy, is more fertile and supports market gardening, sugar beet cultivation, and dairy farming. Baarle-Hertog (Baerle-Duc), a small enclave in The Netherlands, is administered by Antwerp province, the Dutch part being called Baarle-Nassau.

The chief provincial cities are Antwerp, Mechelen, Turnhout, Lier (*qq.v.*), Herentals, and Mol (the site of the Belgian Nuclear Energy Study Centre). There are many medieval castles in the Kempen and in the "green belt" around Antwerp. At Tongerlo is the most notable of many old monasteries in the Kempen; the Abbey of Prémontré, founded in 1133, has a modern aspect reflecting its reconstruction in the 17th century. The Natural Reserve of Kalmthout (1968; 2,000 ac [810 ha]) preserves the old Kempen countryside and has a bird sanctuary. Pop. (1983 est.) 1,577,246.

Antwerp, Flemish ANTWERPEN, French ANVERS, capital of Antwerp province, Belgium, located 55 mi (88 km) southeast of the North Sea on the estuary formed by the Schelde, Meuse, and Rhine rivers. It is often identified as the unofficial capital of Flanders, the Dutch- (Flemish-) speaking portion of Belgium. Inhabited since the 2nd century AD, it is one of the world's major seaports.

The following article treats briefly the modern city of Antwerp. Fuller treatment is provided in the following MACROPAEDIA articles: for history and contempory life, *see* Antwerp; for additional perspective on the city in its national context, *see* Low Countries.

The original site of Antwerp on the right bank of the Schelde is a vast alluvial plain; since 1923, however, the city's territory has also included land on the left bank. Antwerp's contemporary economic life reflects its long history as a seaport and world trade centre. In addition to shipping and port-related activities, major manufactures include automobiles, petrochemicals, and electronics. The city is also a centre for diamond cutting.

Antwerp can be divided into three major sections: the old city, with narrow, winding streets, which lies within the confines of the 16th-century fortifications; the 19th-century city, which stretches beyond and merges with some of the suburban extensions; and the newer neighbourhoods, which lie still farther from the old city and blend into adjacent municipalities.

The Cathedral of the Holy Virgin, begun in the 14th century, is a fine example of Gothic architecture and the largest church in the country. Other examples of Antwerp's rich cultural heritage are preserved in several museums, notably the Rubens' House, the Museum Plantin–Moretus, and the Royal (State) Museum of Fine Arts. The city has both state and private institutions of higher learning and is the site of the Academy for Fine Arts (1663) and the Royal Conservatory.

The shipping complex of docks, locks, and canals handles heavy ship and barge traffic. Antwerp is a domestic and international railway centre, and its Deurne airfield (1928) handles both freight and passenger flights.

The city almost tripled its population on Jan. 1, 1983, with the annexation of six neighbouring municipalities (Berchem, Borgerhout, Deurne, Hoboken, Merksem, and Wilrijk) and part of a seventh (Ekeren). Area city (excluding part from Ekeren), 75 sq mi (195 sq km); metropolitan area, 121 sq mi. Pop. (1983 est.) city, 490,524; (1982 est.) metropolitan area, 627,967.

Antwerp Mannerists, the unidentified creators of a group of works having a similar appearance that were painted in the years around 1520, principally in Antwerp but also in other Flemish centres. The paintings are instructive records of an unavailing attempt to combine Gothic and Renaissance styles and to incorporate disparate Flemish and Italian traditions into the same composition. Frequently painted subjects by the exponents of the style include the Adoration of the Magi and the Nativity, both of which are generally represented as night scenes, crowded with figures, and illuminated with flickering, often irrational lighting. The Adoration scenes were especially popular with the Antwerp Mannerists, who took delight in the patterns of the elaborate clothes worn by the Magi and the ornamentation of the architectural ruins in which the dramatic confrontation was staged.

Although attempts have been made to iden-

"Adoration of the Magi," centre panel of a triptych by the Antwerp Mannerist painter Jan de Beer, *c.* 1520(?); in the Brera, Milan

SCALA—Art Resource/EB Inc.

tify the individuals responsible for the several stylistic groups, most of the paintings remain attributed to anonymous masters. Characteristic of Antwerp Mannerism are works attributed to Jan de Beer (died *c.* 1535), those of the Master of 1518 (Jan van Dornicke), and, to a lesser degree, certain early paintings of Jan Mabuse (died *c.* 1532) and Adriaen Ysenbrandt (died 1551).

Antwerp Zoo, Dutch ZOO ANTWERPEN, zoological garden with one of the largest and most diversified animal collections in Europe. It houses more than 6,000 specimens, including about 300 reptiles and 1,700 fish, which represent more than 1,160 different species. Among the most notable specimens of the mammal collection are the rare Père David's deer and white rhinoceroses. The Antwerp Zoo is perhaps best known for its development of a special display technique for reptile exhibits. This technique involves the use of a cold barrier (*i.e.,* a refrigerated zone), rather than iron bars or glass panels, as a means of containing reptiles in their enclosures.

The Antwerp Zoo was first opened to the public in 1843. It occupies a 10-hectare (25-acre) site in the centre of the city and is administered by the Royal Zoological Society of Antwerp. During the 1920s the zoo gained prominence for breeding the then newly discovered okapi and Congo peafowl. In 1936 the zoo acquired 36 hectares (90 acres) in Planckendael on which it later developed a breeding station for endangered species such as the bongo antelope and Indian rhinoceros.

Where the same name may denote a person, place, or thing, the articles will be found in that order

antyeṣṭi, Hindu funeral rites, varying according to the caste and religious sect of the deceased but generally involving cremation followed by disposal of the ashes in a sacred river. *Antyeṣṭi* rites are the final sacraments (*saṃskāras*) in a series that ideally begins at the moment of conception and is performed at each important stage of a man's life.

At the approach of death, relatives and Brahmins (priests) are summoned, mantras (sacred formulas) and sacred texts are recited, and ceremonial gifts are prepared. The body is removed as soon as possible to the cremation grounds, located usually on the banks of a river. The eldest son of the deceased and the officiating priest perform the final cremation rites. For 10 days thereafter, the mourners—the immediate family members—are considered impure and are subject to certain taboos. During this period they perform rites intended to provide the naked soul of the deceased with a new spiritual body with which it may pass on to the next life. Ceremonies include the setting out of milk and water, and the offering of rice balls. At a prescribed date, the bones are collected and disposed of by burial or by immersion in a river. Rites honouring the dead, called *śrāddha* (*q.v.*), continue to be performed by the survivors at specified times.

Anu (Akkadian), Sumerian AN, Mesopotamian sky god and a member of the triad of deities completed by Bel (Sumerian Enlil) and Ea (Enki). Like most sky gods, Anu, although theoretically the highest god, played only a small role in the mythology, hymns, and cults of Mesopotamia. He was the father not only of all the gods but also of evil spirits and demons; Anu was also the god of kings and of the yearly calendar. He was typically depicted in a headdress with horns, a sign of strength.

His Sumerian counterpart, An, dates from the oldest Sumerian period, at least 3000 BC. Originally he seems to have been envisaged as a great bull, a form later disassociated from the god as a separate mythological entity, the Bull of Heaven, which was owned by An. His holy city was Erech, in the southern herding region, and the bovine imagery suggests that he belonged originally to the herders' pantheon. In Akkadian myth Anu was assigned a consort, Antum (Sumerian Antu), but she seems often to have been confused with Ishtar (Sumerian Inanna), the celebrated goddess of love.

Anu (Celtic goddess): *see* Danu.

Anu, Chao, also called ANOU, ANOUVONG, or ANURUTTHARAT (b. 1767—d. Jan. 1829, Bangkok, Siam), ruler of the Lao kingdom of Vientiane who tried unsuccessfully to secure independence for central and southern Laos from its Siamese overlords.

In his youth Anu, along with his brother Inthavong, fought with the Siamese against the Burmese. His military ability and bravery won him the respect and trust of the Siamese, who chose him to succeed Inthavong as king of Vientiane in 1804. In the early years of his reign he strengthened his internal administration and undertook major public works and the enlargement of his capital city. He cultivated good relations with neighbouring Vietnam, to which he sent tribute every three years (as opposed to annual tribute to Siam).

When the southern Lao principality of Champassak succumbed to internal collapse, Anu persuaded the Siamese to name his son, Chao Yo, to rule there from 1819. Anu now controlled both central and southern Laos, on both banks of the Mekong River, and constructed fortifications throughout the region. He further sought from the northern Lao kingdom of Luang Prabang its neutrality in the conflict that was building with Siam. After an unpleasant stay in Bangkok for the funeral of King Rama III in 1825, Anu returned to Vientiane and organized for rebellion. Believing a false rumour that the British were preparing to attack Siam, he led his armies toward Bangkok, and he managed to get within three days of the Siamese capital by pretending to be rushing to the defense of Siam against the British. His plans for Lao independence leaked out, however, and the Siamese, in a counterattack, captured and sacked Vientiane. By 1828 the rebellion had been quelled.

After receiving inadequate assistance from the Vietnamese, Anu was forced to flee into the forests, but he was captured by a second Siamese expedition and brought to Bangkok, where he was displayed in an iron cage and punished before he succumbed. The Siamese razed Vientiane and transported most of the population of the central Mekong region across the river into what was later to become northeastern Thailand. With the collapse of Anu's rebellion, the independence of Vientiane came to an end.

Anuak, also spelled ANYWAK, a riverain Nilotic people of the northern Luo language group. About one-fourth of the Anuak live in southeastern Sudan, the remainder in Ethiopia. The Anuak are believed to have migrated from lands east of the African great lakes several centuries ago.

The Sudanese Anuak occupy high ground in savanna grasslands along riverbanks that are flooded annually; separate wet- and dry-season villages are maintained. The Ethiopian Anuak live in forested savanna. Because more dry ground is available to the eastern (Ethiopian) Anuak—resulting in more closely connected villages—they have a wider political organization than that afforded by the autonomous villages of the western Anuak. Unlike most Nilotic peoples, the eastern Anuak keep no cattle; instead they fish, hunt, and maintain gardens.

Through the turbulent 19th and early 20th centuries, the Anuak fought with neighbouring Nuer and resisted colonial occupation. From 1930 the Anuak, represented by chiefs, have participated in the Sudanese administration. They were active participants, however, in the civil war (1954–72) to create an independent black state for the southern Sudanese.

Anuak clans are patrilineal. Lineage members live in the same village, but each village, of 50 to 2,000 people, comprises several nonrelated clans. Eastern Anuak traditionally have had a royal clan and a king, while western village headmen have had autonomy. Most Anuak are monogamous.

Anubis, also called ANPU, ancient Egyptian god of the dead, represented by the figure of a man with the head of a jackal. In the early dynasties of the Old Kingdom he enjoyed a preeminent (though not exclusive) position as lord of the dead but was later overshadowed by Osiris.

His particular concern was with the funeral cult and the care of the dead: hence he was reputed to be the inventor of embalming, an art he first employed on the corpse of Osiris. In his later role as the "conductor of souls,"

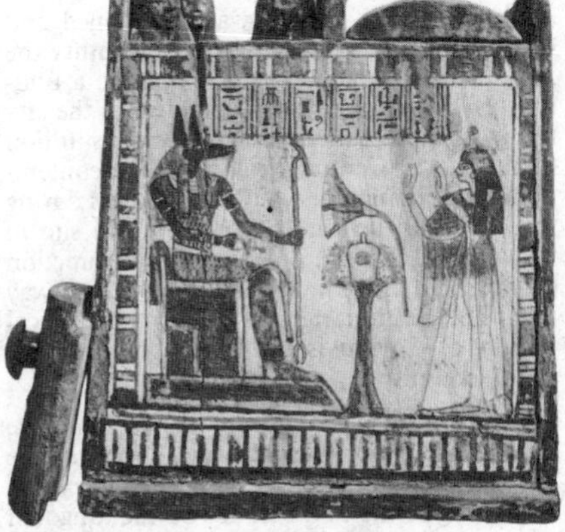

Anubis (left), painted on a funeral case, 19th dynasty; in the Museo Archeologico, Florence

Alinari—Art Resource/EB Inc.

he was sometimes identified by the Greco-Roman world with the Greek Hermes in the composite divinity Hermanubis.

anumāna (Sanskrit: "measuring along some other thing," or "inference"), in Indian philosophy, the second of the five means of knowledge (*pramāṇa*) that enable man to have accurate cognitions. Inference occupies a central place in the Hindu school of logic (Nyāya). This school worked out a syllogism that has the form of an argument rather than a formula and that goes through five stages: (1) the proposition (*pratijñā*, literally "promise"), (2) the ground (*hetu*), (3) the illustration (*udāharaṇa*), (4) the application (*upanaya*), and (5) the conclusion (*nigamana*). A syllogism is vitiated by a fallacious ground; this is called *hetvābhāsa* ("the mere appearance of a ground"). A number of types of invalid grounds are distinguished: simple error, contradiction, tautology, lack of proof for the ground, and inopportunity. *See also* pramāṇa.

Anura, also called SALIENTIA, order of about 2,660 species of tailless amphibians including the frog and toad (*qq.v.*).

Anuradhapura, capital of North Central Province, Sri Lanka (Ceylon), on the Aruvi Aru River. The old section of Anuradhapura (Anurādhapura), now preserved as an archaeological park, is the best known for its architectural distinction of Sri Lanka's ancient ruined cities; in the immediate vicinity are temples, sculptures, palaces, and other ruins as well as ancient irrigation reservoirs. Its location in the dry zone of Sri Lanka (50–70 in [1,270–1,778 mm] of rain per year) may account for the flourishing of ancient civilization here. Anuradhapura was founded in the 5th century BC and was the Sinhalese capital of Sri Lanka from the 4th century BC until AD 760, when Tamil invasions forced the shifting

Thūpārāma *dāgaba* (Buddhist religious building), Anuradhapura, Sri Lanka

Harrison Forman

of the capital. The city was abandoned and overrun by the jungle; in the 19th century the British rediscovered it, and it became a Buddhist pilgrimage centre. The revival of the city began in earnest in 1872 with the constitution of the North Central Province. The contemporary city, much of which was moved during the mid-20th century to preserve the site of the ancient capital, is a major road junction of northern Sri Lanka and is on a railway line. The headquarters of the Archaeological Survey of Ceylon is in Anuradhapura. Pop. (1981 prelim.) 36,248.

Anurādhapura, kingdom of, a Sinhalese state centred at Anurādhapura from *c.* the 3rd century BC to the early 10th century AD. Beginning in the 2nd century BC the kingdom of Anurādhapura was plagued by invasions from South India, which increased in later centuries. The South Indians gained actual control of the kingdom several times—in the 2nd century BC, in the 5th century AD, and most notably in the late 10th century, when Anurādhapura was finally abandoned as capital in favour of the city of Polonnaruva. In addition to the South Indian invasions, the kingdom was often beset with internal strife among warring Sinhalese clans, each wishing to establish its own dynastic line. In these struggles the insurgent clan frequently sought alliance with a South Indian kingdom or hired South Indian mercenaries. The most prominent dynasties were the Vijayan (3rd century BC–1st century AD) and the Lamakaṇṇa (1st–4th century AD and 7th–10th century).

During the more than 1,000 years of its existence, the kingdom of Anurādhapura developed a high degree of culture, especially manifest in its art and architecture. Because of its geographic situation in the northern dry zone of Ceylon, it developed a remarkably complex system of irrigation, considered by many scholars to be its major achievement.

anus, terminal portion and opening of the alimentary canal of vertebrates and many invertebrates. In humans it comprises the anal canal and opening, the end of the large intestine. Its function is to excrete fecal material from the body. Numerous blood vessels surround the anal canal and may be subject to enlargement and rupture; this condition, commonly called hemorrhoids (*q.v.*), or piles, may cause pain, bleeding, and projection of the vessels from the anal opening. *See also* anal canal; rectum.

Other animals have different arrangements and specializations of the anus. The bird's anus forms a saclike cavity, or cloaca, that absorbs water, excretes urine, and removes fecal contents. Frogs and reptiles have a cloaca that functions like that of birds, except that the reproductive systems of birds also excrete into the cloaca. The crayfish has a tubelike hindgut and anus. When this animal sheds its outer protective skin, the internal wall of the gut is also pulled out of the body and shed through the anal opening. The anus of the squid is located near its mouth. When frightened by an enemy, it expels an inky black substance from a gland connected to the anus; the ink obscures its whereabouts and interferes with the enemy's sense of smell. Likewise, skunks have a special anal gland that gives off an offensive odour when the animal is excited or approached.

Anūshīrvan (Persian ruler): *see* Khosrow I of Persia.

Anvarī, pseudonym of AWḤAD AD-DĪN ʿALĪ IBN VĀḤID AD-DĪN MUḤAMMAD KHĀVARĀNĪ, also called AWḤAD AD-DĪN MUḤAMMAD IBN MUḤAMMAD or AWḤAD AD-DĪN ʿALĪ IBN MAḤMŪD (b. *c.* 1126, Abivard, Turkistan—d. *c.* 1189, Balkh, Khorāsān), poet considered one of the greatest panegyrists of Persian literature. He wrote with great technical skill, erudition, and a strong satirical wit.

Like many Persian poets, Anvarī was not only well versed in Persian and Arabic literature but was skilled in such other fields as geometry, astronomy, astrology, logic, music, metaphysics, and natural science, as well as being a skilled chess and backgammon player. His work is replete with complicated, often obscure allusions.

Anvarī was a prolific writer who especially excelled in the art of the *qaṣīdah* (ode) and *ghazal* (lyric). In his divan, or collected poems, are 632 pages of *qaṣīdah*s and *ghazal*s, *robāʿīs* (quatrains), *qiṭʿah*s (shorter poems), and *maṣnavīs* (couplets). Of his life relatively little is known. Rather early in his career he certainly served as court poet of Sultan Sanjar of the great Seljuq dynasty. Later he composed biting and satirical works sharply criticizing all aspects of the social order.

His life was characterized by contradictions: he did not consider poetry the loftiest skill and was not fond of the life of a court poet. Recognizing the fundamental paradoxes and tensions between artistic freedom and creativity and the need to curry favour with political authorities, he noted resentfully and sarcastically that patronage was the only means of acquiring adequate wealth. Thus he remained a court poet until later in life, when circumstances forced him to follow the more independent and probably much preferred course of the scholar, and he ended his life in quiet seclusion.

Anvers (Belgium): *see* Antwerp.

anvil, iron block on which metal is placed to be shaped, originally by hand with a hammer. The blacksmith's anvil is usually of wrought iron, but sometimes of cast iron, with a smooth working surface of hardened steel. A projecting conical beak, or horn, at one end is used for hammering curved pieces of metal. Sometimes the other end has a beak with a rectangular section. Tools such as the anvil cutter or

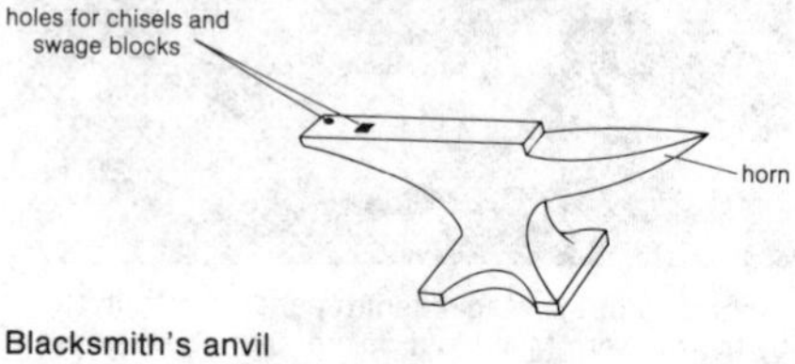

Blacksmith's anvil

chisel can be placed cutting edge uppermost into a holder consisting of a square hole in the anvil's surface. When power hammers are used, the anvil is supported on a heavy block, which in turn rests on a strong foundation of timber and masonry or concrete.

Anville, Jean-Baptiste Bourguignon d' (b. July 11, 1697, Paris—d. Jan. 28, 1782, Paris), geographer, cartographer, and classical scholar who greatly improved the standards of mapmaking. Distinguished by their accuracy and clarity, his maps were sometimes accompanied by valuable source materials. Much of his output related to ancient and medieval geography and revealed a judicious choice and use of authorities. Whenever possible, he adjusted measurements to astronomically determined positions. His preeminence was recognized by his appointment as first geographer to the king of France (1773).

His first important maps of China (1735) were based on Jesuit surveys. His representation of Italy (1743) corrected many errors of earlier maps. Later he produced important maps of Africa (1749), Asia (1751), India (1752), and the world in hemispheres (1761). His delineation of Africa removed many fictitious features of the interior and remained authoritative until the explorations of the 19th century. His extensive geographical collection is in the Bibliothèque Nationale.

anxiety, a feeling of strong fear or apprehension, often with no clear justification.

Anxiety is subjectively experienced as dread or tension and may arise in any situation in which the integrity of the personality is threatened. It frequently arises when there is a failure of repression of forbidden sexual impulses or aggressive urges, usually in association with major shifts in vocational, interpersonal, sexual, or marital adaptations. Some amount of anxiety is considered normal and can be handled by an array of cognitive or behavioral operations known as defense mechanisms, which minimize the discomfort. Research on the relationship between stress and anxiety has identified two classes of stress that appear to have different implications for the initiation of anxiety states. One class involves the threat to an individual's ego or self-esteem, as may arise due to inadequate sexual or job performance. The other type of stress is characterized by physical danger, such as the fear for one's health or safety.

An anxiety disorder may develop where anxiety is insufficiently managed, characterized by a continuing or periodic state of anxiety or diffuse fear that is not restricted to definite situations or objects, and is generally classed as one of the psychoneuroses (neuroses). The tension is frequently expressed in the form of insomnia, outbursts of irritability, agitation, palpitations of the heart, and fears of death or insanity. Fatigue is often experienced as a result of excessive effort expended in managing the distressing fear. Occasionally the anxiety is expressed in a more acute form and results in physiological concomitants such as nausea, diarrhea, urinary frequency, suffocating sensations, dilated pupils, perspiration, and rapid breathing. Similar symptoms occur in several physiological disorders and in normal situations of stress or fear, but they may be considered neurotic when they occur in the absence of any organic defect or pathology and in situations that most people handle with ease.

Other types of anxiety-related disorders include hypochondriasis, hysteria, obsessive-compulsive disorders, phobias, and schizophrenia.

Anyang, city, Kyŏnggi-do (Kyŏnggi Province), northwestern South Korea, 19 mi (31 km) southwest of Seoul. Given the status of a municipality in 1973, it has become the largest industrial satellite of Seoul. Industries include brewing and the manufacture of textiles, pottery, paper, and bricks. The country's largest motion-picture studio is located there. Among the city's historical remains are two temples, Yŏmbul-am and Jŭngcho-sa, both built in the 9th century. Pop. (1983 est.) 274,093.

Anyi, also spelled AGNI, African people who inhabit the tropical forest of the eastern Ivory Coast and Ghana and speak a language of the Kwa branch of the Niger-Congo family. About the middle of the 18th century most of the Anyi were expelled from Ghana by the Ashanti and migrated westward.

The Anyi, living in neighbourhoods of dispersed homesteads, are shifting cultivators, producing food crops (yams, manioc, and plantains), as well as the cash crops (coffee and cacao) from which they derive most of their income.

The traditional organization consisted of small states, with a social hierarchy comprising four strata: a prince and others of royal blood, village chieftains, freemen, and (formerly) slaves and their descendants. The village chief is chosen from the family that holds the hereditary, ceremonial stool; he is elected by that family and the village notables.

The traditional systems of inheritance and succession are based on matrilineal descent, though a married couple resides in the vicinity of the husband's family. This system produces considerable tension, increased by the development of cash-crop plantations, because, although a young man usually works with his father, he generally will not inherit the plantation on which he works. Fear of sorcery is commonly a result of this tension.

Although the Anyi have accepted much of European material culture, the traditional elements of their social structure remain effective as a basis for everyday political organization.

Anyte (fl. early 3rd century BC, Tegea, Arcadia), Greek poet of the Peloponnesus who was so highly esteemed in antiquity that in the well-known *Stephanos* ("Garland"), a collection compiled by Meleager (early 1st century), the "lilies of Anyte" are the first poems to be entwined in the "wreath of poets." Anyte's fame persisted, and Antipater of Thessalonica, writing during the reign of Augustus (27 BC–AD 14), called her "a woman Homer" and placed her in a list of nine lyric poetesses. Of 24 extant epigrams assigned to her, 20 are believed to be genuine. In her dedicatory epigrams her verse is akin to that of Theocritus and Leonidas, her contemporaries. Her dedications for fountains and to the nymphs of the springs show the Greek feeling for a quiet landscape that is so often illustrated in the Greek Anthology. She wrote epitaphs, perhaps literary rather than for actual use, on various animals. She gives no suggestion of herself in her poems and never employs the theme of love. Her love of nature and interest in animals mark her as typical of the early years of the Hellenistic period.

Anywak (people): *see* Anuak.

ANZAC, abbreviation of AUSTRALIAN AND NEW ZEALAND ARMY CORPS, combined corps that served with distinction in World War I. The corps is best known for its heroic service in the ill-fated 1915 Gallipoli Peninsula campaign, an attempt to capture the Dardanelles from Turkey. In 1916 ANZAC infantry units were sent to France, where they took part in some of the bloodiest actions of the war. The cavalry units were assigned to the Middle East. ANZAC ceased to be an official designation after the separation of the Australian and New Zealand forces in 1917. In Australia and New Zealand, ANZAC Day—April 25 (the date of the Gallipoli landing)—has been a major occasion for expressing national sentiment.

Anzalī, Bandar-e, formerly ENZELI, BANDAR-E PAHLAVĪ, or PAHLAVĪ, principal port and a resort, Gīlān *ostān* (province), Iran, on the Caspian Sea, connected with Māzandarān, Azerbaijan, and Tehrān by road. The population includes Russians, Armenians, Caucasians, and Turkmens.

Founded in the early 19th century, the town lies on both sides of the entrance to Mordāb Lagoon. It was occupied by the Russians in 1920; they declared a Soviet Republic of

Wharf at Bandar-e Anzalī, Iran
Fred J. Maroon—Photo Researchers

Gīlān, but that entity collapsed in 1921. The port lies in the channel between two sandy peninsulas; Ghāzīān Peninsula, to the east, has an airfield. The channel is quite irregular in depth. The entrance is protected by two breakwaters, and dredging is necessary. Port installations are mainly on the eastern side. There is a small wharf, an oil depot, and a fishery station. During World War II the port was modernized, and traffic greatly increased as a consequence of the U.S. lend-lease program for the Soviet Union. Pop. (1976) 55,-978.

Anzan (ancient city, Iran): *see* Anshan.

Anzengruber, Ludwig (b. Nov. 29, 1839, Vienna—d. Dec. 10, 1889, Vienna), playwright and novelist who won acclaim for his realistic plays of peasant life. After working as an actor he published an anti-clerical drama, *Der Pfarrer von Kirchfeld* (1870; "The Pastor of Kirchfeld"), which was a great success. Except for the melancholy *Der Meineidbauer* (1872; "The Farmer Forsworn"), most of his plays were gay and witty comedies set among the people of small towns; they include *Die Kreuzelschreiber* (1872; "The Cross Makers"), *Der G'wissenswurm* (1874; "The Worm of Conscience"), and *Doppelselbstmord* (1876; "Double Suicide"). He wrote a problem play, *Das vierte Gebot* (1878; "The Fourth Commandment"), and also novels: *Der Schandfleck* (1877, revised 1884; "The Stain"), *Der*

Anzengruber
By courtesy of the Bild-Archiv, Osterreichische Nationalbibliothek, Vienna

Sternsteinhof (1884; "The Sternstein Farm"), and other tales of village life.

Anzhero-Sudzhensk, city, Kemerovo *oblast* (administrative region), Russian Soviet Federated Socialist Republic, on the Trans-Siberian Railroad at the northern limit of the Kuznetsk Coal Basin. Coal mining, begun early in the 20th century, expanded rapidly after 1928, when the townships of Anzherka and Sudzhenka were amalgamated, to be given city status in 1931. Other industries produce pharmaceutical goods, mining machinery, and window glass. Anzhero-Sudzhensk has chemical and medical institutes and a teachers college. Pop. (1983 est.) 109,000.

Anziku, Kingdom of, also called KINGDOM OF TEKE, or KINGDOM OF TYO, historic African state on and north of the Congo (Zaire) River in the vicinity of Malebo Pool. The Teke people lived on the plateaus of the region from early times. It is not known when they organized as a kingdom, but by 1600 their state was a rival of the Kongo kingdom south of the river. Controlling the lower Congo River and extending northwest to the upper Kouilou-Niari basin, Anziku was situated to dominate inland trade, especially trade in slaves. Traditional crafts were gradually abandoned in favour of cloth, pottery, and metal products imported from Europe in exchange for slaves. In 1882 King Iloo signed a treaty with the French colonialist Pierre Savorgnan de Brazza, making Anziku a French protectorate. Nine years later (1891) it became the French (Middle) Congo. Anziku's historic territory is now the central part of the People's Republic of the Congo and includes the site of Brazzaville, the national capital.

Anzilotti, Dionisio (b. Feb. 20, 1867, Pescia, Italy—d. Aug. 23, 1950, Pescia), jurist who was one of the main founders of the so-called positive school of international law, a legal philosophy advocating a sharp distinction between the legal and the political and moral aspects of international relations.

In 1906 Anzilotti was cofounder of the *Rivista di diritto internazionale* ("International Law Review"). He was professor of law at the universities of Palermo, Bologna, and Rome (1911–37). In 1921 he was appointed a judge of the Permanent Court of International Justice of The Hague, where he presided from 1928 to 1930.

Anzio, Latin ANTIUM, town, Roma province, Lazio (Latium) region, Italy, on a peninsula jutting into the Tyrrhenian Sea. Of uncertain origin, it was founded, according to legend, by Anteias, son of the Greek chieftain Odysseus, and the enchantress Circe. It was a stronghold of the Volsci, an ancient people prominent the 5th century BC, and was older than Rome, which conquered it in 338 BC. Antium became an all-season resort where many wealthy Romans owned villas; Augustus, the first Roman emperor, was proclaimed "father of the Roman nation" there, and the emperors Caligula and Nero were born there. A key commercial centre under the Volsci, its importance increased after AD 59, when Nero built a port there. Destroyed by the Saracens in the early Middle Ages, it was virtually deserted until a new port to the east of the old one was built by Pope Innocent XII in 1698. Anzio became part of Italy in 1860.

Anzio was the scene of extremely heavy fighting late in World War II. On Jan. 22, 1944, the Allies achieved what probably was the most complete tactical surprise of the war by landing in excess of 36,000 troops and 3,000 vehicles before midnight, securing a beachhead only 37 miles from Rome. However, the Allied force took so long—most of a week—to consolidate its position that German Field Marshall Albert Kesselring was able to surround the beachhead, keeping its eventual force of six Allied divisions penned there while he mounted a succession of massive attacks on them during February. Only in late May, when Kesselring withdrew most of his troops, were the Allies able to break out of the beachhead (May 25); then the Allied force greatly facilitated the advance on Rome and its capture. Casualties during the four-month operation approximated 25,000 for the Allies and 30,000 for the Axis forces.

Extensive Roman remains include the ruins of the port, a theatre, and Nero's villa, where valuable works, including the famous Greek statue of Apollo Belvedere, were found.

A seaside resort with long sandy beaches and a small port for yachts and fishing boats, Anzio is connected with the main Rome–Naples railway by a branch line from Campoleone. Fishing is the chief industry; there is also a frozen fish-processing plant and a soap and detergent factory. Pop. (1981 prelim.) mun., 27,094.

Anzoátegui, state, northeastern Venezuela, bounded north by the Caribbean Sea, east by Monagas, south by the Orinoco River, and west by Guárico. Most of the territory of 16,718 sq mi (43,300 sq km) lies in the Llanos (plains). The coastal range tapers off to form the Barcelona Gap near the state capital, Barcelona (*q.v.*), a cattle- and coffee-shipping centre on the Río Neverí. Cattle raising has been important for generations, but agriculture, mostly confined to the highland valleys, is relatively insignificant. Petroleum was discovered about 1930, and by the late 1970s Anzoátegui produced about one-tenth of Venezuela's oil. The Orinoco Heavy Oil Belt is the site of extensive oil exploration. Pipelines transport natural gas to Caracas, Maracay, Valencia, and Puerto La Cruz, and coal is mined at Naricual. Manufacturing has become important in the Barcelona–Guanta–Puerto La Cruz complex. The highway network is extensive. Pop. (1983) 707,639.

ANZUS Pact, formally PACIFIC SECURITY TREATY, security treaty between Australia, New Zealand, and the United States, signed Sept. 1, 1951, for the purpose of providing mutual aid in the event of aggression and of settling disputes by peaceful means. The ANZUS Council, consisting of the foreign ministers of the member states, meets annually.

Aoba, also spelled OBA, volcanic island of Vanuatu, in the southwestern Pacific Ocean, 30 mi (50 km) east of Espiritu Santo. Its 154-sq-mi (399-sq-km) area is dominated by a more than 4,500-ft (1,400-m) peak with a lake in its crater, which was last active about 1870. The headquarters of the Melanesian Church is located at Lolowai, a good harbour on the east coast. The island has a hospital and airstrips and exports copra. Pop. (1979) 7,819.

Aod (Old Testament hero): *see* Ehud.

AOF (Afrique Occidentale Française): *see* French West Africa.

Aomori, northernmost prefecture (*ken*), Honshu, Japan, bordered by the Pacific Ocean (east), the Tsugaru-kaikyō (Tsugaru Strait; north), and the Sea of Japan (west). The peninsulas of Tsugaru and Shimokita enclose Mutsu-wan (Mutsu Bay). The prefecture occupies an area of 3,713 sq mi (9,616 sq km). Aomori has a relatively poor, unstable agricultural economy that is handicapped by long, cold, snowy winters and poor drainage. Rice and Japan's largest apple crop are grown in the west, while the east specializes in dry grains and potatoes. Horse breeding for military use has long given way to beef cattle and dairy farming. Most large-scale manufacturing is found in Hachinohe, in the southeast. In the mountainous interior are some of Japan's finest timber (cryptomeria and cypress) stands, mostly in national forests not yet developed for public use. Coastal and deep-sea fishing operations centre on Hachinohe, the leading fishing port, and Aomori.

The city of Aomori, located on Aomori-wan (Aomori Bay), is the capital and largest city of the prefecture. One of Japan's most important transportation centres, it is the terminus of both northern Honshu rail lines and railroad ferry services across the Tsugaru-kaikyō to Hakodate, Hokkaido. The Tohoku Highway and Seikan Tunnel, a submarine tunnel beneath the Tsugaru-kaikyō, 22 mi (36 km) long, under construction during the early 1980s, will facilitate communication between Hokkaido and Honshu. Strong winter winds make extensive breakwaters necessary in its artificial harbour, which ships lumber and fish and is noted for coastal trade. The city of Hirosaki is a major commercial centre of the interior. Pop. (1983 est.) city, 292,860; prefecture, 1,531,000.

Aontroim (Northern Ireland): *see* Antrim.

Aornos, Siege of (327 BC), during the invasion of Asia by Alexander the Great, conflict in which he seized a nearly impregnable natural stronghold blocking his route to India. Aornos is evidently modern Pīr Sarāi, a steep ridge a few miles west of the Indus and north of the Buner rivers in modern Pakistan. The name is a corruption of the Sanskrit *āvaraṇa,* which means "enclosure" or "fortress"; the Macedonians interpreted this word to mean "the place to which no bird can rise." Unable to storm the rock, Alexander seized the hill opposite and threatened the Indians' encampment with his catapults. They retreated but were caught, and many were slaughtered. Another natural fortress called Aornos referred to in the histories of Alexander's campaigns has been identified as the town of Tashkurghan (modern Savnob) in ancient Bactria.

aorta, blood vessel found in vertebrates and in certain invertebrates. In invertebrates, such as spiders, for example, the large vessel carrying blood from the heart is called the aorta. In vertebrates, the aorta is the trunk for oxygenated blood from the left ventricle (left lower chamber) of the heart to all the organs and structures of the body.

For a depiction of the aorta in human anatomy, shown in relation to other parts of the body, *see* the colour Trans-Vision in the PROPAEDIA: Part Four, Section 421.

At the opening from the ventricle into the artery is a three-part valve that prevents backflow of blood from the aorta into the heart (*see* heart valves). The aorta emerges from the heart as the ascending aorta, turns to the left and arches over the heart (the aortic arch), and passes downward as the descending aorta. The left and right coronary arteries branch from the ascending aorta to supply the heart muscle. The three main arteries branch from the aortic arch and give rise to further branches that supply oxygenated blood to the head, neck, upper limbs, and upper part of the body. The descending aorta runs down through the posterior centre of the trunk past the heart, lungs, and esophagus, through an opening in the diaphragm, and into the abdominal cavity.

In the chest the aorta, as it descends, gives off branches to the pericardium, the sac that encloses the heart; the connective tissues of the lungs; the bronchi, which carry air from the windpipe into the lungs; the esophagus; part of the diaphragm; and the chest wall.

In the abdominal cavity the aorta gives off a number of branches, which form an extensive network supplying blood to the stomach, liver, pancreas, spleen, small and large intestines, kidneys, reproductive glands, and other organs. At the level of the fourth lumbar vertebra, which is about even with the top of the hip bones, the aorta divides into the right and left common iliac arteries, the principal arteries to the legs.

aorta, coarctation of the, congenital condition involving constriction, or narrowing, of a short section of that portion of the aorta that arches over the heart. The aorta is the principal artery conducting blood from the heart into the systemic circulation. The partial obstruction of the aorta's channel causes a characteristic murmur and causes abnormally high blood pressure in the arms. The left ventricle (lower left chamber of the heart) is usually enlarged. Blood flow to the abdomen, pelvis, and legs is reduced. Intercostal (between-the-ribs) branches from the aorta enlarge and cause characteristic notching of the ribs. Treatment of the defect is surgical and varies with the age of the person affected. In children and adolescents the narrow section of the aorta is removed, and the two free ends are sewn together. In older persons, either the constricted section of artery is replaced with a section of Dacron tubing, or the defect is left but is bypassed by a Dacron tube opening into the aorta on either side of the defect—a sort of permanent bypass for the blood flow. Surgery for this condition is most effective in the young and is rarely performed on patients over 50.

aortic arch syndrome, group of disorders that cause blockage of the vessels that branch off from the aorta in the area in which the aorta arches over the heart. The aorta is the principal vessel through which the heart pumps oxygen-rich blood into the systemic circulation. The aortic branches that may be affected supply blood to the head, the neck, the arms, and part of the body wall. Most often the condition occurs in middle-aged or elderly persons and is caused by atherosclerosis, in which fatty plaques form in the artery lining.

A rare form of the aortic arch syndrome that affects Oriental women primarily is called Takayasu's disease or nonspecific arteritis (also called pulseless disease). The progressive blockage causes impaired cerebral circulation, which can lead to blindness and paralysis. Most deaths from the disease result from damage to the heart muscle and to the brain. Treatment involves bypass grafting.

Congenital defects of the aortic arch include patent ductus arteriosus, in which the channel connecting the aorta and the left pulmonary artery in the fetus does not close after birth and must be closed surgically, and coarctation (narrowing) of the aorta, which causes an increased work load on the left ventricle.

aortic insufficiency, failure of the valve at the mouth of the aorta—the principal artery that distributes blood from the heart to the tissues of the body—to prevent backflow of blood from the aorta into the left lower chamber (ventricle) of the heart, from which it has been pumped. The defect causes characteristic heart sounds, audible through a stethoscope. Affected persons may experience difficulty in breathing after mild physical exertion and may suffer spasms of difficult breathing while resting in bed. Congestive heart failure—the effects of the heart's inability to function adequately as a pump—may develop. Aortic insufficiency may result from a congenitally defective valve, from rheumatic heart disease, or from syphilis. Medical treatment is directed toward management of the congestive heart failure; prevention of the recurrence of rheumatic heart disease; and prevention of bacterial endocarditis, bacterial invasion of the heart lining. Surgical treatment consists in replacing the diseased valve with a synthetic substitute or a transplant.

aortic stenosis, narrowing of the passage between the left lower chamber (ventricle) of the heart and the aorta, the principal artery of the systemic circulation. The defect is most often in the valve at the mouth of the aorta but may be just above or below the valve (supravalvular and subvalvular aortic stenosis, respectively). Aortic stenosis in a person younger than 20 years of age is usually congenital in origin. If it appears during middle age, it is most often the result of rheumatic heart disease. Aortic stenosis in elderly persons may be the result of degeneration of the valve with age. Most patients are male.

Aortic stenosis causes characteristic heart sounds, audible through a stethoscope. Affected persons may faint after exertion or may experience the chest pain known as angina pectoris. The stenosis may bring about congestive heart failure—the effects of the heart's inability to function adequately as a pump. Medical treatment is directed toward the angina pectoris and heart failure and toward prevention of bacterial invasion of the heart lining (endocarditis). Surgical treatment consists in repairing the aortic valve or replacing it with a synthetic substitute or a transplant.

Aosta, city, capital of Valle d'Aosta region, northwestern Italy, at the confluence of the Buthier and Dora Baltea rivers and commanding the Great and Little St. Bernard pass roads, north-northwest of Turin. It was a stronghold of the Salassi, a Celtic tribe that was subdued by the Romans in 25 BC, and a Roman town (Augusta Praetoria) was founded there by Augustus in 24 BC. A bishopric from the 5th century, the town was always the most important centre of the Valle d'Aosta; it became the regional capital in 1945. It was the birthplace of St. Anselm (1033/34–1109), archbishop of Canterbury.

Ruins of Roman theatre, Aosta, Italy
Marzari—SCALA from Art Resource/EB Inc.

Aosta retains the walls, two gates, and the street plan of its Roman predecessor, as well as a triumphal arch in honour of Augustus and remains of the theatre, the amphitheatre, and the road from Eporedia (modern Ivrea). The rectangular street plan, laid out in equal blocks (*insulae*), is an outstanding example of Roman formal city planning. Of later monuments, the cathedral is notable for its treasury and 12th-century floor mosaics, and the collegiate church of S. Orso for its Romanesque cloisters and Gothic choir stalls. Aosta is a commercial centre and has a metallurgical industry. Pop. (1981 prelim.) mun., 37,682.

aoudad, also called BARBARY SHEEP (*Ammotragus lervia*), north African sheep, family Bovidae (order Artiodactyla). The only wild sheep in Africa, the aoudad stands about 102 centimetres (40 inches) at the shoulder. It has a fringe of long, soft hair hanging from its throat and forequarters and has semicircular horns that curve outward, back, and then inward over the neck. Both fringe and horns are more pronounced in the male. The aoudad lives in dry, mountainous or broken country and associates in small family groups. It can go without water for about five days. When threatened, the aoudad stands motionless and is concealed by its tawny brown coat, which blends with the surrounding rocks.

Aoudad, or Barbary sheep (*Ammotragus lervia*)
William McKinney—The National Audubon Society Collection/Photo Researchers

Aouelloul Crater, large crater located 28 mi (45 km) southwest of Chinguetti, Mauritania, and thought to be of meteoritic origin. Discovered by air in 1951, it is 833 ft (250 m) in diameter and 33 ft in depth. A large amount of fused silica glass has been found in the area, but only one small meteorite fragment has been recovered from the crater.

Aozou, also spelled AOUZOU, town and military post in Tibesti, northern Chad. Military conflict plagued the town and the surrounding region after Chad became independent in 1960. As in the rest of Tibesti, the Muslim Teda nomads of the area resisted the rule of N'Djamena (then called Fort Lamy), the capital of Chad, and French troops remained to govern northern Chad until 1965. Aozou was one of the French bases. After 1965 the central government of Chad continued to maintain a garrison at Aozou. In 1968 a group of Teda rebels attacked and killed most of the soldiers stationed there. Four years later Libyan troops captured the post and began a long-term occupation. Interest in Aozou intensified in the 1970s with the discovery that the surrounding region might be rich in uranium.

Apa Tani, tribal people of Arunāchal Pradesh (former North East Frontier Agency), a mountainous state in the extreme northeast of India. They speak a Tibeto-Burman language of the Sino-Tibetan family and numbered about 13,100 in the 1970s.

Unlike other tribes in the area, the Apa Tani practice a settled wet rice (paddy) agriculture. The typical household consists of a husband and wife and their unmarried children. Their society is formed of clans, of which there are two classes, ruling and plebeian. Representatives of the clans compose the village council. They believe in spirits associated with nature.

Apabhraṃśa language, literary, primarily poetic language that reflects a late stage of Middle Indo-Aryan, immediately prior to Modern Indo-Aryan (*c.* 12th century). Apabhraṃśa literature includes major Jaina works. Though a literary language, Apabhraṃśa shows developments that must have taken place in spoken dialects. In early times, the term Apabhraṃśa referred to usage considered corrupt, including Middle Indo-Aryan usage (Apabhraṃśa is Sanskrit for "departure from correct speech"). Some authorities class Apabhraṃśa as a Prākrit language (*q.v.*). Moreover, as has been recognized by various authorities, including the prosodist Rudraṭa (*c.* 800), Apabhraṃśa showed dialectal differences.

Apache, farmer-raider Indians of the North American Southwest who, under such leaders as Cochise, Mangas Coloradas, Geronimo, and Victorio, figured largely in the history of the region during the latter half of the 19th century. Their domain extended over what is now east central and southeastern Arizona, southeastern Colorado, southwestern and eastern New Mexico, western Texas, and, in Mexico, northern Chihuahua and Sonora states. This distribution is a recent one. The ancestors of the Apache (and the Navajo) apparently were from the far north, for the Apachean languages are distantly related to other Athabascan languages spoken in Canada. These ancestors probably did not reach the Southwest until AD 1000 or later. Some Apachean peoples are known to have been in the Southwest prior to the 15th century, but as late as 1700 Plains Apache farmers were still living along the Dismal River in Kansas. With the introduction of the horse, these and other Plains Apache were severely pressed south and west by the Comanche and Ute.

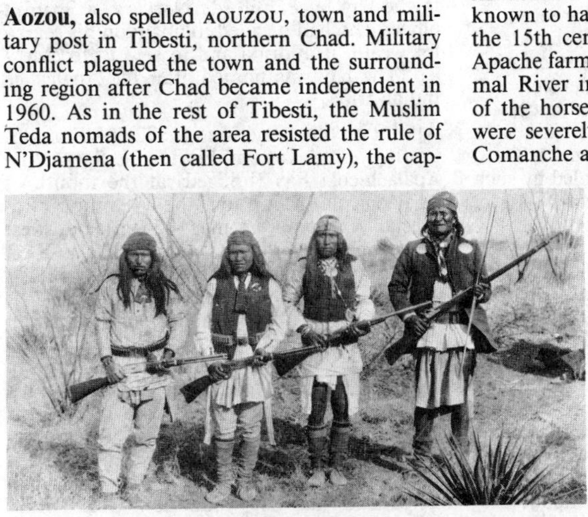

Geronimo (right) and three of his warriors, photographed in their camp by C.S. Fly in 1886
By courtesy of the Smithsonian Institution National Anthropological Archives, Bureau of American Ethnology Collection

Culturally, the Apache are divided into Eastern Apache, which include the Mescalero, Jicarilla, Chiricahua, Lipan, and Kiowa Apache, and Western Apache, which include the Cibecue, Mimbreño, Coyotero, and Northern and Southern Tonto or Mogollon Apache. Characteristic of both Eastern and Western Apache, with the exception of the Kiowa Apache (*see* Kiowa), was the lack of a centralized tribal organization. The band, an autonomous collection of small local groups within a given locality, was the primary political unit as well as the primary warring and raiding unit. The strongest headman of the local groups was recognized as an informal chief, and several bands might be united under one leader. Chieftainship was thus not generally hereditary.

The Apache subsistence pattern was based partly on hunting and on gathering wild plant foods, partly on farming, and partly on raiding; but the proportion of each varied greatly from tribe to tribe. The Jicarilla (*q.v.*) farmed fairly extensively, growing maize and other vegetables, but also had adopted part of the Plains Indians reliance on bison hunting. The Lipan of Texas, who were probably originally a band of Jicarilla, had largely given up farming and were, therefore, more mobile than the Jicarilla. The Mescalero (*q.v.*) were influenced by the Plains Indians, but their chief food staple was the mescal plant (hence the name Mescalero). The Chiricahua (*q.v.*) were perhaps the most nomadic and aggressive of the Apache west of the Rio Grande, raiding into northern Mexico, Arizona, and New Mexico from their strongholds in the Dragoon Mountains. The Western Apache appear to have been more settled than their Eastern relatives, with considerably more emphasis on farming, though they did raid, frequently with various Yuman tribes.

Although the Apache wars were among the fiercest fought on the frontier, the Apache had attempted to be friends of the Spanish, the Mexicans, and, later, the Americans. As early as the 17th century, however, Apache were raiding Spanish missions, and the Apache may have been partial instigators of the Pueblo Revolt of 1680 (*see* Pueblo Indians). In 1858 a meeting between Americans and Chiricahua Apache took place at Apache Pass in the Dragoon Mountains, resulting in a peace that lasted until 1861, when Cochise went on the warpath. This marked the beginning of the Apache and Navajo wars, a quarter-century confrontation between U.S. military forces and the Indians of the Southwest.

Despite their adept use of swift horses and their knowledge of the terrain, the Indians were outmatched by the superior arms of the federal troops. The Navajo surrendered in 1865 and agreed to settle on a reservation in New Mexico. The Apache ostensibly followed suit in 1871–73, but large numbers of warriors refused to yield their nomadic ways and to accept permanent confinement. Thus, intermittent raids continued to be led by such Apache leaders as Geronimo and Victorio, evoking federal action once more.

The last of the Apache wars ended in 1886 with the surrender of Geronimo and his few remaining followers. The Chiricahua tribe was evacuated from the West and held as prisoners of war successively in Florida, in Alabama, and at Ft. Sill, Okla., for a total of 27 years. In 1913 the members of the tribe were allowed either to take allotments of land in Oklahoma or to live in New Mexico on the Mescalero Reservation. About one-third chose the former and two-thirds the latter.

The Apache population totalled about 11,000 in the late 20th century. The Western Apache live on the Fort Apache and San Carlos reservations in east central Arizona. The Chiricahua (except those still living near Apache, Okla.), the Mescalero, and the Lipan live on the Mescalero Reservation in southern New Mexico. The Jicarilla have a reservation in north central New Mexico.

Apache Canyon, Battle of: *see* La Glorieta Pass, Battle of.

Apadāna (Pāli: "Stories"), collection of legends about Buddhist saints, one of the latest books in the latest section (the *Khuddaka Nikāya*) of the *Sutta Piṭaka* ("Basket of Discourse") of the Pāli canon. This work, which is entirely in verse, presents stories about 547 monks and 40 nuns. For each personage there are tales about one or more previous lives as well as about his or her present existence, all of the tales presented as the words of the Buddha. The deeds these stories commend are meritorious acts of formal piety and charitable service. The Sanskrit cognate of the term is *Avadāna* (*q.v.*).

Apaiang (Kiribati): *see* Abaiang Atoll.

Apalachee, extinct tribe of North American Indians who spoke a Muskogean language and inhabited the area in northwestern Florida between the Aucilla and Apalachicola rivers above Apalachee Bay. They became known in the 16th century when the Spanish explorers Pánfilo de Narváez (in 1528) and Hernando de Soto (in 1539) led expeditions to Apalachee territory. The tribe was divided into clans that traced descent through the maternal line; chieftainship and office were hereditary, probably in the lineage within the clan.

An agricultural people who cultivated corn (maize), squash, and orange groves, the Apalachee were also noted warriors. They were ultimately subdued about 1600 and missionized by Spanish Franciscans. They continued to prosper (in 1655, 6,000–8,000 Apalachee occupied eight towns, each with a Franciscan mission) until early in the 18th century when Creek (*q.v.*) tribes to the north, incited by the British, began a series of raids on Apalachee settlements. These attacks culminated in 1703 when an army made up of a few hundred Englishmen and several thousand Creek warriors defeated the combined Spanish and Apalachee. The tribe was almost totally destroyed, and 1,400 Apalachee were removed to Carolina where some of them merged with the Creek. The remnants of the Florida tribe sought the protection of the French at Mobile and in Louisiana.

Apalachee Bay, arm of the Gulf of Mexico indenting northwestern Florida, U.S., 25 mi (40 km) south of Tallahassee. It receives the Ochlockonee, St. Mark, and Aucilla rivers, and its marshy coast forms St. Marks National Wildlife Refuge. In 1528, five boats were built in the bay by Pánfilo de Narváez, a Spanish officer who had decided to abandon his search for wealth in Florida and to set out for Mexico. The bay was named after the Apalachee Indian tribe.

Apalachicola, city, seat (1832) of Franklin County, northwestern Florida, U.S., on the Apalachicola Bay (bridged) at the mouth of Apalachicola River, on the Atlantic Intracoastal Waterway, 65 mi (105 km) southwest of Tallahassee. Founded about 1820 as West Point (renamed Apalachicola, Hitchiti Indian for "people on the other side," in 1831), it was an important cotton shipping port from 1830 until the U.S. Civil War blockade ended this activity. In the 1840s John W. Gorrie of Apalachicola invented a refrigerant apparatus to cool the rooms of yellow-fever patients (commemorated by a state historic memorial). An important fishing (oysters, shrimp) centre, the city also exports lumber and naval stores and has fish canneries. Old Trinity Church (1839), a notable landmark with Ionic columns, was shipped in wooden sections from New York. Nearby are St. George Island (bridged) and Apalachicola National Forest. Inc. town, 1827; city, 1838. Pop. (1980) 2,565.

Apamama (Kiribati): *see* Abemama Atoll.

Apamea Cibotus, also called APAMEA AD MAEANDRUM, Apamea also spelled APAMEIA, city in Hellenistic Phrygia, partly covered by the modern town of Dinar, Tur. Founded by Antiochus I Soter in the 3rd century BC, it superseded the ancient Celaenae and placed it in a commanding position on the great east–west trade route of the Seleucid Empire. In the 2nd century BC Apamea passed to Roman rule and became a great centre for Italian and Jewish traders. Disorganization in the 3rd century AD and the diversion of trade to Constantinople led to its decline. It was captured by the Turks in 1070 and finally destroyed by an earthquake.

Apanás, Lake, Spanish LAGO DE APANÁS, reservoir in Jinotega department, northern Nicaragua. Formed by damming the Río Tuma just north of Jinotega city, it has an area of 20 sq mi (51 sq km). It supplies the Asturias hydroelectric station, largest in the country and the focus of a power grid serving much of the more densely settled Pacific zone of Nicaragua.

apapane (*Himatione sanguinea*), Hawaiian songbird, common on larger islands, a nectar-feeding member of the Hawaiian honeycreeper family, Drepanididae (order Passeriformes). About 13 centimetres (5 inches) long, it is red, except for its dark wings and tail and its white vent. Its bill is fairly short and slightly curved. The apapane lives chiefly in upland forests and is especially fond of ohia flowers.

Apapane (*Himatione sanguinea*)
Drawing by John P. O'Neill

Apapocuva, also called NANDEVA, a Guarani-speaking South American Indian people living in small, scattered villages throughout the Mato Grosso, Paraná, and São Paulo states of southeastern Brazil. In the second half of the 20th century, the Apapocuva probably numbered fewer than 500 individuals.

Traditionally, the Apapocuva were swidden agriculturalists who supplemented their crops of corn (maize), bitter and sweet cassava, beans, tubers, and other vegetables with gathered fruits and other forest products. The nominal leader of each village was usually a successful shaman who advised his group according to the revelations of his dreams. In 1879, an entire village followed its shaman in an eastward trek, in search of the Land-Without-Evil, which was believed to be somewhere over the Atlantic Ocean. In 1910, another Apapocuva group attempted to reach the Land-Without-Evil by dancing feverishly for days, in the hope of becoming light enough to fly over the Atlantic Ocean. The present-day wide dispersal of Apapocuva over southeastern Brazil reflects their numerous and far-flung religious migrations of the past hundred years.

Aparanta (India): *see* Konkan.

Aparni (Parthian tribe): *see* Parni.

Aparri, town, Cagayan province, northeastern Luzon, Philippines, on the Babuyan Channel of the Philippine Sea, near the mouth of the Cagayan River. It is the interisland port for much of northeastern Luzon. Anti-Spanish insurgents landed there in 1898 under Col. Daniel Tirona. Civil government was restored in 1901 under the United States. Aparri was occupied by the Japanese on Dec. 10, 1941, and regained by U.S. forces in June 1945. The principal exports are rice, corn (maize), copra, logs, and fish products. Fishing, cattle raising, and the manufacture of fish paste are primary local industries. The population is mainly Christian Ilocanos and Ibanags. The town of Lal-lo (Nueva Segovia), 8 mi (13 km) upriver, was the Spanish provincial capital, and in its early history Aparri served as Lal-lo's outport. The town has an airport. Pop. (1980) mun., 45,070.

apartheid (Afrikaans: "apartness"), policy governing relations between South Africa's white minority and nonwhite majority; it sanctions racial segregation and political and economic discrimination against nonwhites. The implementation of apartheid, often called "separate development" since the 1960s, has been made possible through the Population Registration Act of 1950, which classifies the people as Bantu (the designation for all black Africans), Coloured (those of mixed race), Indian (Asian), or white.

Racial segregation, sanctioned by law, was widely practiced in South Africa before 1948, but the National Party, which gained office that year, extended the policy and give it the name apartheid. The Group Areas Act of 1950 established residential and business sections in urban areas for each race, and the government strengthened existing "pass" laws (requiring nonwhites to carry documents authorizing their presence in restricted areas). Other laws forbade most social contacts between the races, authorized segregated public facilities, established separate educational standards, restricted each race to certain types of jobs, curtailed nonwhite labour unions, and denied nonwhite participation (through white representatives) in the national government.

Under the Bantu Authorities Act of 1951 the government reestablished tribal organizations for black Africans, and the Promotion of Bantu Self-Government Act of 1959 created 10 African homelands. The Bantu Homelands Citizenship Act of 1970 made every black African, irrespective of actual residence, a citizen of one of the homelands, thereby excluding blacks from the South African body politic. By the early 1980s four of the homelands had been granted independence as republics, and the remaining, called Black States, had varying degrees of self-government; but all remained dependent, both politically and economically, on South Africa. The dependence of the South African economy on nonwhite labour has, in turn, made it difficult for the government to carry out this policy of separate development.

Although the government has the power to suppress virtually all criticism of its policies, there has been opposition to apartheid within South Africa. Black African groups, with the support of some whites, have held demonstrations and strikes, and there have been many instances of violent protest and of sabotage. An attempt to enforce Afrikaans language requirements for black African students led to the Soweto riots in 1976. Some white politicians have called for the relaxation of minor restrictions, referred to as "petty apartheid," or for the establishment of racial equality.

Apartheid has also received international censure. South Africa was forced to withdraw from the Commonwealth in 1961 when it became apparent that other member countries would not accept its racial policies. Members of the United Nations have called, with little success, for sanctions against South Africa.

apartment house, also called APARTMENT BLOCK, or BLOCK OF FLATS, building containing more than one dwelling unit, most of which are designed for housekeeping, but sometimes including shops and other nonres-

Unité d'Habitation, apartment house, Marseille, designed by Le Corbusier, 1946–52
Wayne Andrews

idential features. The residential units may be grouped in many ways and vary in size, appointments, and facilities, providing a wide variety of living accommodations capable of satisfying the requirements of many different types of families and individuals.

Communal dwellings and apartment buildings have existed for centuries. In the great cities of the Roman Empire, because of urban congestion, the individual house, or domus, had given way in early imperial times to the communal dwelling, or insula (*q.v.*), except for the residences of the very wealthy. Four stories were common, and six-, seven-, or eight-story buildings were occasionally constructed. Among the North American Indians the most noted multiple dwellings were the long houses of the Iroquois. These buildings ranged in width from about 18 to 20 feet (5.5 to 6 metres) and in length from 60 to 100 feet (18 to 30 metres) and were divided into separate bays, one for each family.

In the American Southwest the prehistoric Indians constructed apartment buildings that were in fact single-room houses forming a continuous structure. Because they were built on heights or in narrow gorges, for ease of defense, they could be extended only upward. New houses rose above the old, tier on tier, until heights of several stories were reached, each story of dwellings stepped back to give a terrace at every floor.

In Europe, tall blocks of flats appeared in Edinburgh and Paris as early as the 16th century, but real development of the apartment building did not begin in England until the 1850s, after upper middle-class homes had been converted first to boardinghouses and later to small flats.

In the middle of the 19th century, a new building type arose that was designed to house the increasing urban populations, swollen by the influx of workers to newly industrialized centres. The typical New York City apartment—or tenement, as they were sometimes disparagingly called—conceived and built under municipal codes, probably holds a record for intensive use of space in the worst possible way. First constructed in the 1830s, this type of dwelling consisted of apartments popularly known as railroad flats because the narrow rooms were arranged end-to-end in a row like boxcars. It is perhaps significant that sections of the cities that contained apartments for the rich were almost as densely populated and as poorly planned as those in the sections characterized by poverty. Much so-called model housing of this period was only slightly better. Few low-cost apartment buildings erected in Europe or America before 1918 show any signs of good design according to 20th-century standards. In many European cities, however, particularly in Paris and Vienna, the second half of the 19th century witnessed great progress in the design of apartments for the upper middle class and the rich.

From 1919 to about 1934, many large housing projects were constructed in Europe, a majority of them built either by the government or by public-utility societies with government aid. In the United States a subsidized public-housing program was started under the National Housing Act of 1937, by which the federal government made loans and subsidy grants to cities and other local governments to provide housing for low-income families. Much of this housing was in the form of apartment buildings.

The demand for rental housing after World War II was greater than ever before as the result of increased building costs, shifts in population, and large concentrations of workers in the cities. One of the most interesting examples of a multifamily dwelling is the Unité d'Habitation (1946–52) in Marseille designed by Le Corbusier to provide individual apartments, each occupying a story and a half, as well as numerous community facilities such as a swimming pool, child-care centre, and shops. Suburban housing developments also increased in the postwar period, a result primarily of the lack of adequate urban sites at economically feasible prices.

The commonest form of occupancy of apartment houses has been on a rental basis. However, multiple ownership of units on a single site was established in English common law by the early 18th century, and in recent times it has been authorized by law in a number of European countries. Cooperative ownership of apartment buildings enjoyed an upsurge of interest in the United States after World War I but fell into disfavour after many such projects failed during the Depression. The increasing popularity of condominiums, first authorized in the U.S. by Puerto Rico in 1958, is based largely on the fact that, unlike members of a cooperative, condominium owners are not financially interdependent and can mortgage their property.

apathy, in Stoic philosophy, condition of being totally free from the *pathē,* which roughly are the emotions and passions, notably pain, fear, desire, and pleasure. Although remote origins of the doctrine can probably be found in the Cynics (second half of 4th century BC), it was Zeno of Citium (4th–3rd century BC) who explicitly taught that the *pathē* were to be extirpated entirely.

Attacks on the Stoics suggesting either that they were insensitive to the human condition or merely stupid invoked rejoinders from the later Stoics, some of whom compromised by distinguishing between good and evil *pathē.* Early Stoics, however, rejected the *pathē* altogether, breaking with the Aristotelians, who sought a mean between them, and with the Epicureans, who proclaimed pleasure, rightly chosen, to be the only criterion by which to judge an action. One of the greatest men of the Middle Stoics (2nd–1st century BC), however, Panaetius, rejected the idea of apathy altogether and reintroduced the Aristotelian doctrine of the golden mean (or of virtue as a mean between two extremes), and argued (as did Seneca, the 1st-century-AD Roman Stoic philosopher) that some of the goods of this world might be worth pursuing for their own sake.

apatite, any member of a series of phosphate minerals, the world's major source of phosphorus, found as variously coloured, glassy crystals, masses, or nodules. Except for its softness (Mohs hardness 5, compared with the 7 to 9 of most gems), apatite would be a popular gemstone; much of the material found is clear, but it is fragile and difficult to cut and polish. Asparagus stone is a clear, asparagus-green gem variety of apatite; moroxite, a clear blue.

The series includes fluorapatite (the most important mineral commercially), chlorapatite, hydroxylapatite, and carbonate-apatite. These minerals are all calcium phosphates, differing from one another chemically only in that fluorapatite contains fluorine; chlorapatite, chlorine; hydroxylapatite, a hydroxyl (OH) group; and carbonate-apatite, a carbonate (CO_3) group. The fluorine, chlorine, hydroxyl, and carbonate substitute for one another, so that in nature most apatite is a mixture of several of the compounds. Chlorapatite and carbonate-apatite are comparatively rare. For properties, *see* phosphate mineral (table).

Apatite is a member of a group of structurally related minerals having compositions symbolized $A_5(BO_4)_3X$, in which A is a metal, commonly calcium or lead; B is phosphorus, vanadium, or arsenic; and X is chlorine, fluorine, or hydroxyl. The group contains three series: the apatite series, the pyromorphite series, and the svabite series (intermediate between the other two).

Apatosaurus, formerly BRONTOSAURUS, genus of giant herbivorous dinosaurs, one of the largest land animals of all time, found in Late Jurassic deposits of North America and Europe (the Jurassic Period began 190,000,000 years ago and lasted 54,000,000 years). *Apatosaurus* weighed as much as 30 tons and

Apatosaurus drawn with (top) blunt skull incorrectly assigned *c.* 1879 and (bottom) slender skull assigned in 1978

By courtesy of the Carnegie Museum of Natural History, Pittsburgh

was as much as 21 metres (70 feet) long, including its long neck and tail. It had four massive and pillar-like legs.

The size, shape, and features of the *Apatosaurus* head were disputed for more than a century after its remains were first uncovered, certainty clouded in part by incomplete fossil finds and by a suspected mixup of fossils during shipment from an excavation site. The head was represented in models as a massive, snub-nosed skull with spoonlike teeth until 1978, when scientists rejected that representation in favour of a slender, elongated skull containing long, sharp teeth.

Much discussion has centred on whether *Apatosaurus* and related forms were able to support their great bulk on the land or whether they were forced to adopt aquatic habits. It seems probable that *Apatosaurus* was able to move about on land with efficiency, but it is likely that it represents the maximum size and bulk attainable in a land animal. Animals related to *Apatosaurus* appear to have been at least partially aquatic; for example, *Brachiosaurus* had nostrils located high on the skull and was the most massive of the brontosaur-like forms, attaining weights of as much as 85 tons.

It is likely that the long and powerful tail of *Apatosaurus* was its main defense and that it sought refuge from pursuers by retreating to the water. *See also* Diplodocus.

Apaturia, Greek religious festival that was held annually in nearly all the Ionian towns. At Athens it took place in the month of Pyanopsion (October–November) and lasted three days, on which occasion the various phratries (clans) of Attica met to discuss their affairs. The name probably means the festival of "common relationship." The most important day was probably the third, Koureotis, when children born since the last festival were presented by their fathers or guardians; after an oath had been taken as to their legitimacy, their names were inscribed in the register.

Apatzingán, in full APATZINGÁN DE LA CONSTITUCIÓN, city, west central Michoacán state, west central Mexico. It lies on the Río Apatzingán (Acahuato), approximately 1,650 ft (500 m) above sea level and 176 mi (283 km) southwest of Morelia, the state capital. Its name commemorates the signing there, in 1814, of the Constitution of Apatzingán by the congress that was called by the revolutionary leader José María Morelos to declare the independence of Mexico. Apatzingán serves as a link between the sparsely inhabited southern and densely populated central portions of Michoacán. Although the climate is hot and semi-arid, the agricultural and pastoral hinterland is rich. Corn (maize), beans, sesame, rice, cotton, and fruits are the principal crops. Deposits of silver and gypsum are found in the vicinity. The city is accessible by highway and railroad, and it has an airfield. Pop. (1979 est.) 80,000.

apavarga (Indian philosophy): *see* mokṣa.

Ape (pseudonym): *see* Pellegrini, Carlo.

ape, any of the tailless, manlike primates of the families Hylobatidae (gibbon and siamang) and Pongidae (the great apes—chimpanzee, orangutan, and gorilla). Apes live in the tropical forests of Africa and Southeastern Asia. The gibbon, siamang, and orangutan (*qq.v.*) are arboreal, while the gorilla and chimpanzee (*qq.v.*) spend some or much of their time on the ground. Destruction of their forest habitats and hunting by man have resulted in severe population declines among the apes, all species of which have been classified as endangered by the U.S. Department of the Interior.

The evolutionary history of the apes includes numerous extinct forms, many of which are known only from fragmentary remains. The earliest known fossils date from the Oligocene (beginning about 38,000,000 years ago) in Egypt and include such forms as *Aeolopithecus*, a possible ancestor of the gibbon, and *Aegyptopithecus*, a possible ancestor of the great apes. Later deposits have yielded such fossils as the gibbon-like *Pliopithecus* and *Limnopithecus*, and the great-ape-like *Dryopithecus* (including *Proconsul*).

Apes are intelligent animals and are more closely related to man than any other living primates. They are popular zoo and circus animals and are widely used in biomedical and psychological studies. They also have figured widely in the legends and folktales of many countries.

The term ape is used in a less restricted sense to refer to certain large monkeys, such as the Celebes black ape (*q.v.*).

Apeldoorn, *gemeente* (municipality), Gelderland *provincie* (province), east central Netherlands, east of the sandy and wooded Veluwe Hills, on the edge of the Soeren (Suren) Forest. Noted for its many gardens, Apeldoorn is a residential and industrial town, manufacturing paper products, pharmaceuticals, chemicals, and refrigeration machinery. There are many sanitariums in the district, and the Hoge Veluwe National Park is 8 mi (13 km) southwest. On the northern outskirts is Het Loo, a royal palace built for William III in 1686 around a smaller castle; it was the home of the queen mother Wilhelmina after her abdication in 1948. The city is a junction for roads and railways and is connected by canal to Zwolle. Pop. (1983 est.) 143,178.

apella, ancient Spartan assembly, corresponding to the *ekklēsia* of other Greek states. Its monthly meetings, probably restricted to full citizens over 30, were presided over at first by the kings, later by ephors (magistrates). Not empowered to initiate proposals, the body considered subjects forwarded by the ephors or *gerousia* (council of elders). Only kings, elders, ephors, and perhaps other magistrates could engage in debate, and voting was conducted by shouts. Foreign policy, including treaties and issues of peace and war, as well as questions of succession to the throne, were within the province of the *apella.* It also appointed military commanders, elected the elders and ephors, and voted on proposed changes in the laws.

Apelles (fl. 4th century BC), early Hellenistic Greek painter whose work was held in such high esteem by ancient writers on art that he continues to be regarded, despite the fact that none of his work survives, as the greatest painter of antiquity. Almost as little is known of his life as of his art. He was of Ionian origin but became a student at the celebrated Dorian school of Sicyon in southern Greece, where he worked under the painter Pamphilus. His works are said to have combined Dorian thoroughness with Ionic grace.

He became the recognized court painter of Philip II of Macedonia and his son Alexander III the Great. His picture of Alexander holding a thunderbolt ranked among his outstanding works. Other notable works of Apelles include portraits and a great allegorical picture representing Calumny and a painting representing Aphrodite rising out of the sea. Of these works no copies survive; descriptions of his works, however, inspired later artists to emulate them, especially during the Italian Renaissance.

It is said that he attached great value to the drawing of outlines, practicing every day. The tale is well known of his visit to Protogenes and the rivalry of the two masters as to which could draw the finest and steadiest line. He probably used only a small variety of colours and avoided elaborate perspective. Simplicity of design, beauty of line, and charm of expression were supposedly his chief merits.

Apelles was also noted for improvements in technique. He used a dark glaze, called *atramentum,* that served both to preserve his paintings and to soften their colour. There is little doubt that he was one of the boldest and most progressive of artists of his time.

Apellicon OF TEOS (d. *c.* 84 BC), a wealthy Greek book collector, who became an Athenian citizen. He had bought from the descendants of Neleus of Scepsis in the Troad the libraries of Aristotle and Theophrastus, which were in a damaged condition but might have contained the only copies of the Aristotelian treatises to survive. Apellicon is said to have published them with corrections and supplements. After his death, when Sulla captured Athens, the books were carried off to Rome where eventually they formed the basis of a famous edition by Andronicus of Rhodes.

Apennine Range, also called THE APENNINES, Italian APPENNINO, arc of mountains forming the backbone of peninsular Italy that have had considerable influence on the human geography of the nation.

The following article summarizes information about the Apennine Range. For full treatment, *see* MACROPAEDIA: Europe.

The Apennines extend from the Colle di Cadibona, close to the maritime Alps in the northwest, as far as the Isole (islands) Egadi to the west of Sicily. Their total length is approximately 870 mi (1,400 km), and their width ranges from 25 to 125 mi. Monte Corno at 9,560 ft (2,914 m) is the highest point. The range follows a northwest to southeast orientation as far as Calabria, at the southern tip of Italy; the regional trend then changes direction, first toward the south and then westward. The Apennines are among the younger ranges of the Alpine system and, geologically speaking, are related to the coastal range of the Atlas mountains of North Africa. Geographically, the Apennines differ strikingly from the Alps. They have lower elevations and lack glaciers, and the maritime influence on the valleys and exposed slopes is much greater. The geological youth of the Apennines and a great variety of rock types are responsible for the rugged appearance of the range. Rock types include sandstones, marls, greenstones, and clays. Earthquakes are frequent, especially within the central and southern Apennines and Sicily, and are caused by structural settling of the young mountain chain, movements along the abundant faults, and by volcanic activity.

Apepi, also called APEP, APOPHIS, OR REREK, ancient Egyptian god of chaos, who took the form of a serpent and, as the foe of the sun god, Re, represented all that was evil. Although the serpent generally symbolized divinity and royalty, Apepi inhabited the underworld and personified death and chaos. Each day Apepi encountered Re at an appointed hour in the sun god's ritual journey through the night in his divine bark. The voice of Apepi betrayed him, and Seth (*q.v.*), who rode as guardian in the front of Re's bark, attacked him with daggers, slaying him. The ancient Egyptians believed that they could help Re by reciting prayers against Apepi.

apéritif, any of several types of alcoholic drinks taken before meals, as appetizers. The term is most commonly applied to certain proprietary brands, such as Campari, Dubonnet, and Lillet, dry or sweet vermouth, and other wine-based fortified drinks. But champagne, sherry, white table wine, and cocktails or other mixed drinks may also be considered apéritifs.

Pineau des Charentes from the Cognac region of France is an apéritif made by mixing fresh grape juice with cognac. Kir, an apéritif that originated in Burgundy in the 20th century and took its name from that of a city official in Dijon, consists of dry white wine sweetened with a few drops of *cassis* (black currant syrup or liqueur).

Apert's syndrome (congenital malformation): *see* acrocephalosyndactyly.

aperture, in optics, the maximum diameter of a light beam that can pass through an optical system. The size of an aperture is limited by the size of the mount holding the optical component, or the size of the diaphragm placed in the bundle of light rays. The hole in the mount or diaphragm that limits the size of the aperture is called an aperture stop. Thus, an aperture stop determines the amount of light that traverses an optical system and hence determines the image illumination.

Closely related to the aperture stop is its image, called the entrance pupil of the optical system. The angle that the diameter of the entrance pupil subtends at an object point is called the angular aperture, which can be taken as a measure of the light-gathering power of the instrument. *See also* pupil; relative aperture.

Apet (Egyptian goddess): *see* Taurt.

Aphanomyces, genus of parasitic fungi (division Mycota) of the order Saprolegniales (class Oomycetes) that forms two successive asexual, motile spores (zoospores). The first one is produced in a spore sac (sporangium) but soon forms a cyst from which the second zoospore arises. The latter, on contact, infects a susceptible host plant. A thick-walled structure (oospore) forms after sexual union. *A. euteiches* causes root rot of English pea.

aphasia, also called DYSPHASIA, brain-generated defect in sounding words. Symptoms are associated with the location and extent of involved brain tissues. An afflicted person, for example, although able to move his mouth parts and utter sounds and able to understand spoken words, may be totally unable to form words himself. Another aphasic person may be able to say the word hopper but be unable to say the word hop.

The term aphasia is extended to a group of related disturbances. In agraphia (dysgraphia) the patient may be totally or partially unable to write words, although he is perfectly competent in speaking, reading, and drawing pictures.

Perceptual aphasias are called agnosias; *e.g.*, a person can see perfectly but be unable to recognize what he sees, even though he may be able to recognize it by feeling, hearing, or smelling it. A specific form of visual agnosia seen as a reading difficulty (alexia, dyslexia) may be found in otherwise normal, intelligent people. Also known are agnosias of smell, touch, and taste.

All of the aphasias are of importance in psychology and psychiatry because they show that the apparent unity of what is commonly called "mind" rests on the interaction of functionally independent parts of the brain, each of which may be damaged without interfering with the function of other parts. Thus, there seems to be no such unitary power as memory, because visual memories may be abolished without affecting auditory, olfactory, tactile, or any other memory functions.

Aphek, Canaanite royal city near the present-day Israeli city of Petaḥ Tiqwa (*q.v.*). Conquered by Joshua (Josh. 12:18), it became a Philistine stronghold in the period of the Judges. Its importance is attested by its mention among the cities conquered by the pharaohs Thutmose III and Amenhotep II.

aphid, also called PLANT LOUSE, GREENFLY, OR ANT COW, any of several species of sap-sucking, soft-bodied insects (order Homoptera) about the size of a pinhead, with tubelike projections (cornicles) on the abdomen. It is a serious plant pest. Aphids not only stunt plant growth, produce plant galls, and transmit plant virus diseases but also deform leaves, buds, and flowers. The life cycle of the aphid is complicated. Wingless females, called stem mothers, produce living young without fertilization (*i.e.*, by parthenogenesis) throughout the summer. Eventually the plant containing the stem mother and her offspring becomes overcrowded; when this occurs, some aphids develop two pairs of large membranous wings and seek new plants. In late summer, both males and females are produced; after they mate, the female lays eggs that survive the winter. In warm climates there may be no egg stage. The white, woolly-ball appearance of many aphids is the result of wax-gland secretion. Aphids are controlled by chemical sprays and natural enemies—*e.g.*, ladybird beetles, aphid lions, and lacewings.

Rose aphids (*Macrosiphum rosae*)
Anthony Bannister—EB Inc.

Ants may take care of aphids, protecting them from weather and natural enemies and transferring them from wilted to healthy plants. In this way they ensure their source of honeydew, a sweet excretory product of aphids. Ants obtain honeydew by stroking, or "milking," the aphids. Common types of aphids include:

Apple aphid (*Aphis pomi*), yellow-green adults with dark head and legs; cornicles; overwinters as black eggs on its only host, the apple tree; curls leaves and deforms apples; produces honeydew that supports growth of a sooty mold.

Cabbage aphid (*Brevicoryne brassicae*), small gray-green adults with a powdery, waxy covering; found in clusters on the underside of leaves; common in North America on cabbage, cauliflower, Brussels sprouts, and radishes; overwinters as black eggs in old cabbage in the North; no sexual stage in the South; up to 30 generations per year; controlled by dusts or sprays.

Cooley spruce gall aphid (*Chermes cooleyi*) causes formation of conelike galls about seven centimetres long on the tips of spruce twigs; in midsummer when the galls open, adults migrate to Douglas firs to lay eggs; the life cycle may proceed on either spruce or Douglas fir; control is by spraying with insecticide, removing galls before aphids emerge, and planting spruce and Douglas fir apart from each other.

Corn root aphid (*Anuraphis maidi-radicis*), a serious pest dependent on the cornfield ant; the ants store aphid eggs in their nests during the winter; in spring the aphids are carried by the ants to weed roots and then transferred to corn roots; the aphid stops growth of corn and causes plants to turn yellow and wilt; also infests other plants.

Eastern spruce gall aphid (*Chermes abietis*) produces pineapple-shaped galls 1 to 2.5 cm long composed of many cells, each containing about 12 aphid nymphs; galls open in midsummer, releasing mature aphids that infect the same or another spruce; new galls are green with red or purple lines, old galls are brown; infested branches often die; individual trees vary in susceptibility; best control is by poisonous spray.

Greenbug (*Toxoptera graminum*), one of the most destructive pests of wheat, oats, and other small grains; appears as patches of yellow on the plant and may wipe out an entire field; pale-green adults have a dark-green stripe down the back; each female produces between 50 and 60 young per generation, and there are 20 generations annually; controlled by parasites and chemical sprays.

Green peach aphid (*Myzus persicae*), also called spinach aphid; pale yellow-green adults with three dark lines on back; life cycle involves two hosts; female reproduces parthenogenetically during summer, produces sexual males and females in autumn; a serious pest, transmitting many plant mosaics and potato leaf roll.

Melon, or cotton, aphid (*Aphis gossypii*); green to black in colour; live young are produced all year in warm climates, while in cooler areas there is an egg stage; among the dozens of possible hosts are melon, cotton, and cucumber; destructive to crops, causing leaves to curl and die; usually controlled by parasites and natural predators.

Pea aphid (*Macrosiphum pisi*), pale-green adults; kills pea plants and carries yellow bean mosaic; overwinters on clover and alfalfa, migrating to peas in spring; each female produces 50 to 100 young in each of 7 to 20 generations a year; controlled by sprays and weather conditions.

Potato aphid (*Macrosiphum euphorbiae*), black eggs on rose plants hatch into pink and green young that feed on rosebuds and leaves; in early spring they migrate to the summer host (potato plant); one generation occurs every two to three weeks; carrier of tomato and potato mosaic virus diseases; feeding curls potato leaves, kills vines and blossoms.

Rose aphid (*Macrosiphum rosae*), large green adults with black appendages and pink markings; common on its only host, the cultivated rose; natural predators are ladybird larvae and aphid lions.

Rosy apple aphid (*Anuraphis roseus*), important apple pest; deforms fruit, producing "aphis apples"; causes leaves to curl about it, forming a protection from poisonous sprays; life cycle involves an alternate host, plantain; returns to the apple tree to deposit eggs in the fall; also attacks pear, hawthorn, and mountain ash; controlled by sprays and by natural enemies, chiefly syrphid flies, lady beetles, lacewings, and parasitic wasps.

Woolly apple aphid (*Eriosoma lanigerum*), worldwide distribution wherever apple trees exist; native to North America; reproduces solely by parthenogenesis in Europe because its alternate host, the American elm, is absent; lives on roots; may stunt or kill the tree; white cottony masses enclose the young aphids; controlled by parasites. *See also* grape phylloxera.

Consult the INDEX *first*

aphorism, a concise expression of doctrine or principle or any generally accepted truth conveyed in a pithy, memorable statement. Aphorisms have been especially used in dealing with subjects that were late in developing their own principles or methodology, for example, art, agriculture, medicine, jurisprudence, and politics. The term was first used in the *Aphorisms* of Hippocrates, a long series of propositions concerning the symptoms and diagnosis of disease and the art of healing and medicine. The first aphorism, which serves as a kind of introduction to the book, runs as follows: "Life is Short, Art long, Occasion sudden and dangerous, Experience deceitful, and Judgment difficult. Neither is it sufficient that the Physician be ready to act what is necessary to be done by him, but the Sick, and the Attendants and all outward necessaries must be lightly prepared and fitted for the business."

A well-known medieval collection of aphorisms is that formulated *c.* 1066 in Latin verse by the celebrated doctor Joannes de Meditano, giving the precepts of the medical school of Salerno. Another collection of aphorisms, also medical and also in Latin, is that of the Dutchman Hermann Boerhaave, published at Leiden in the year 1709; it gives a terse summary of the medical knowledge prevailing at the time and is of great interest to the student of the history of medicine.

The term was gradually applied to the principles of other fields and finally to any statement generally accepted as true, so that it is now roughly synonymous with maxim.

Aphraates, Syriac AFRAHAT (fl. 4th century), Syrian ascetic and the earliest known Christian writer of the Syriac Church in Persia.

Aphraates became a convert to Christianity during the reign of the anti-Christian Persian king Shāpūr II (309–379), after which he led a monastic life, possibly at the monastery of St. Matthew (Syriac: Mar Mattay) near Mosul, Iraq. Later he may have become a bishop when he assumed the name James. Termed "the Persian Sage," Aphraates between the years 336 and 345 composed Syriac biblical commentaries, 23 of which have been preserved, for his monastic colleagues. They are inaccurately known as his "Homilies," and they survey the Christian faith predominantly in theological, ascetical, and disciplinary matters, at times marked by a sharp polemical nature. Nine treatises against the Jews, who were numerous in Mesopotamia and had established outstanding schools, are particularly acrimonious; they treat of Easter, circumcision, dietary laws, the supplanting of Israel by Gentiles as the new chosen people, and Jesus' divine sonship.

Aphraates' writings are distinguished by their primitive biblical–theological tradition, as yet unaffected by the doctrinal controversies and linguistic complexity growing out of the Trinitarian (nature of God) and Christological (nature of Christ) controversies prior and subsequent to the Council of Nicaea in 325. Insulated from the intellectual currents traversing the Greco-Roman ecclesiastical world, the "Homilies" manifest a teaching indigenous to early Assyrian Judeo-Christianity, with a simplicity bordering on the ambiguous and thereby suspect by orthodox standards.

Aphraates articulated the pivotal concepts of Christian experience, accentuating salvation through the indwelling Spirit of the Christ-God who invaded the lower regions (Semitic: *sheol*) and conquered the devil in his own domain. His frequent biblical quotations derive from an old Syriac text antedating even the 2nd-century version (*Diatesseron*) and exhibit an esteem for the Old Testament, which he regarded as intimately linked to the New. Included in the treatises are expositions on faith in the three divine persons, the unity of the person of Christ in the duality of human and divine natures, and, reflecting a psychology characteristic of the East, the tripartite distinction in man of body, soul, and spirit. Aphraates, moreover, combatted the magical cults practiced among the Mesopotamian Chaldeans.

Aphrem SYRUS, SAINT: *see* Ephraem Syrus, Saint.

aphrodisiac, any of various forms of stimulation thought to arouse sexual excitement. Aphrodisiacs may be classified in two principal groups: (1) psychophysiological (visual, tactile, olfactory, aural) and (2) internal (food, alcoholic drinks, drugs, love potions, medical preparations).

Despite long-standing literary and popular interest in internal aphrodisiacs, almost no scientific studies of them have been made. Scientific research is limited to occasional tests of drugs or hormones for the cure of male impotence. Most writings on the subject are little more than unscientific compilations of traditional or folkloric material. Of the various foods to which aphrodisiacal powers are traditionally attributed, fish, vegetables, and spices have been the most popular throughout history. In none of these foods, however, have any chemical agents been identified that could effect a direct physiological reaction upon the genitourinary tract, and it must be concluded that the reputation of various supposedly erotic foods is based not upon fact but upon folklore.

It has been suggested that man's universal attribution of libidinous effects to certain foods originated in the ancient belief in the therapeutic efficacy of signatures: if an object resembled the genitalia, it possessed, so it was reasoned, sexual powers. Thus the legendary aphrodisiacal powers of ginseng root and powdered rhinoceros horn.

With the exception of certain drugs such as alcohol or marijuana, which may lead to sexual excitation through disinhibition, modern medical science recognizes a very limited number of aphrodisiacs. These are, principally, cantharides and yohimbine, both of which stimulate sexual arousal by irritating the urinary tract when excreted. Cantharides, or cantharidin, consists of the broken dried remains of the blister beetle (*q.v.*) *Lytta vesicatoria.* It has been a traditional sexual stimulant fed to male livestock to facilitate breeding. In humans the substance produces skin blisters on contact, and attempts to ingest it as an aphrodisiac are considered extremely hazardous. Yohimbine is a crystalline alkaloid substance derived from the bark of the yohimbé tree (*Corynanthe yohimbe*) found in Central Africa, where it has been used for centuries to increase sexual powers. Although it has been promoted as an aphrodisiac, most investigators feel that any clinical change in sexual powers after its use is probably due to suggestion, because stimulatory effects are elicited only with toxic doses.

Aphrodite, ancient Greek goddess of sexual love and beauty, identified by the Romans with Venus (*q.v.*). Because the Greek word *aphros* means "foam," the legend arose that Aphrodite was born from the white foam produced by the severed genitals of Uranus (Heaven), after his son Cronus threw them into the sea. Aphrodite was, in fact, widely worshipped as a goddess of the sea and of seafaring; she was also honoured as a goddess

Aphrodite and Eros, gilt bronze mirror with incised design, Greek, 4th century BC; in the Louvre, Paris
Giraudon—Art Resource/EB Inc.

of war, especially at Sparta, Thebes, Cyprus, and elsewhere. Aphrodite was, however, primarily a goddess of love and fertility and even occasionally presided over marriage. Although prostitutes considered Aphrodite their patron, her public cult was generally solemn and even austere.

Many scholars believe Aphrodite's worship came to Greece from the East, and many of her characteristics must be considered Semitic. Although Homer called her "Cyprian" after the island chiefly famed for her worship, she was already Hellenized by the time of Homer, and, according to him, she was the daughter of Zeus and Dione, his consort at Dodona. In the *Odyssey,* Aphrodite was mismatched with Hephaestus, the lame smith god, and spent her time philandering with the handsome god of war, Ares (by whom she became the mother of Harmonia).

Of Aphrodite's mortal lovers, the most important were the Trojan shepherd Anchises, by whom she became the mother of Aeneas, and the handsome youth Adonis (in origin a Semitic nature deity and the consort of Ishtar-Astarte), who was killed by a boar while hunting and was lamented by women at the festival of Adonia. The cult of Adonis had underworld features, and Aphrodite was also connected with the dead at Delphi.

Aphrodite's main centres of worship were at Paphos and Amathus on Cyprus, and on the island of Cythera, a Minoan colony, where her cult probably originated in prehistoric times. On the Greek mainland Corinth was the chief centre of her worship. Her close association with Eros, the Graces (Charites), and the Horae (Seasons) emphasized her role as a promoter of fertility. She was universally honoured as Genetrix, the creative element in the world. Her epithets Urania (Heavenly Dweller) and Pandemos (Of All the People) were incorrectly taken by the philosopher Plato to refer to intellectual and common love; rather, the title Urania was honorific and applied to certain Oriental deities, while Pandemos referred to her standing within the city-state. Among her symbols were the dove, pomegranate, swan, and myrtle.

Early Greek art represented Aphrodite either as the Oriental, nude-goddess type, or as a standing or seated figure similar to all other goddesses. Aphrodite first attained individuality at the hands of the great 5th-century-BC Greek sculptors. Perhaps the most famous of all statues of Aphrodite was carved by Praxiteles for the Cnidians; it later became the model for such Hellenistic masterpieces as the Venus de Milo.

Aphthartodocetism (Greek *aphthartos,* "incorruptible"), a Christian heresy of the 6th century that carried Monophysitism ("Christ had but one nature and that divine") to a new extreme; it was proclaimed by Julian, bishop of Halicarnassus, who asserted that the body of Christ was divine and therefore naturally incorruptible and impassible; Christ, however, was free to will his sufferings and death voluntarily. Severus, patriarch of Antioch, himself a condemned Monophysite, vigorously challenged Julian on the ground that the doctrine of salvation was meaningless unless Christ's body was truly human. The Byzantine emperor Justinian I proclaimed the new heresy in an edict of 564 and would have imposed it on the Eastern Church but for his death the following year.

Apia (Kiribati): *see* Abaiang Atoll.

Apia, city, port, and capital (since 1959) of Western Samoa, South Pacific Ocean, on the north coast of Upolu Island. Commercial activities centre on export of copra, bananas, cocoa, and coffee; staples, including taro and other root crops, are shipped to American Samoa. Vailima, former home of Robert Louis Stevenson, is now the residence of the head of state. Stevenson is buried at Mt. Vaea (1,500 ft [460 m]) on the town's southern outskirts. The Apia Observatory, the legislative council chambers, and the broadcasting station are on the Mulinuu Peninsula, a promontory dividing Apia Harbour from Vaiusu Bay. The government holds title to the town land.

Vailima, former home of the Scottish writer Robert Louis Stevenson in Apia, Western Samoa

Morton Beebe—Photo Researchers

During the period of colonial tensions a severe typhoon on March 16, 1889, destroyed six warships (three German, three U.S.) in the Apia roadstead; only the British "Calliope" escaped. U.S. Marines were garrisoned in Apia during World War II. Pop. (1981 prelim.) 33,170.

Apiaceae, also called UMBELLIFERAE, the parsley family, in the dogwood order (Cornales), comprising about 250 genera of plants distributed throughout a wide variety of habitats, principally in the north temperate regions of the world. Most members are aromatic herbs with alternate, feather-divided leaves that are sheathed at the base. The flowers are arranged in a conspicuous umbel (a flat-topped cluster of flowers). Each small individual flower is usually bisexual, with five sepals, five petals, and an enlarged disk at the base of the style. The fruits are ridged and are composed of two parts that split open at maturity.

(Top) Masterwort (*Astrantia*) and (bottom) sea holly (*Eryngium maritimum*)

(Top) G.E. Hyde from the Natural History Photographic Agency—EB Inc., (bottom) Klaus Fiedler—Bruce Coleman Ltd.

Many species of the Apiaceae are poisonous, including poison hemlock (*Conium maculatum*), water hemlock (*Cicuta maculata*), and fool's parsley (*Aethusa cynapium*). Other species, however, are widely used vegetables, including parsley (*Petroselinum crispum*), carrot (*Daucus carota*), celery (*Apium graveolens*), parsnip (*Pastinaca sativa*), and fennel (*Foeniculum vulgare*). Species used as herbs and spices include anise (*Pimpinella anisum*), dill (*Anethum graveolens*), coriander (*Coriandrum sativum*), caraway (*Carum carvi*), and cumin (*Cuminum cyminum*). Several species have long been used as herbal and folk remedies; *e.g.,* gum ammoniac (*Dorema ammoniacum*) and goutweed (*Aegopodium podagraria*). Some species are grown for their ornamental value; *e.g.,* masterwort (*Astrantia major*), blue lace flower (*Trachymene caerulea*), and sea holly (*Eryngium maritimum*).

apiculture: *see* beekeeping.

Apion, Ptolemy: *see* Ptolemy Apion.

Apis (Greek), Egyptian HAP, HEP, or HAPI, in ancient Egyptian religion, sacred bull deity worshipped at Memphis. Apis was originally a form of the Nile god Hapi and, like other bull deities in Egypt, Apis was probably at first a fertility god concerned with the propagation of flocks and herds; but he became associated with Ptah, the paramount deity of the Memphite locality, and also with Osiris (as User-Hapi) and Sokaris, gods of the dead and of the underworld. As Apis-Atum he was associated with the solar cult and was often represented with the sun-disk between his horns.

Much of what is known about Apis came from Greco-Roman writers. He was black and white and distinguished by special markings. Some ancient writers said that he was begotten by a ray of light from heaven, and others, that he was sired by an Apis bull. When a sacred bull died, the calf that was to be his successor was sought and installed in the Apieion at Memphis. His priests drew omens from his behaviour, and his oracle had a wide reputation. When an Apis bull died, it was buried

Apis, bull deity, painted on the bottom of a wooden coffin, *c.* 700 BC; in the Roemer und Pelizaeus Museum, Hildesheim, W.Ger.

Bavaria Verlag

with great pomp at Ṣaqqārah, in underground galleries known in the classical world as the Sarapeum. It was probably at the Sarapeum that the worship of Sarapis (after the Greek form Osorapis, a combination of Osiris and Apis in the image of an Anatolian god) arose under Ptolemy I. Transplanted to Alexandria, it spread among the Greeks and Romans to become one of the most universally popular oriental cults.

Apizaco, city, central Tlaxcala state, east central Mexico. It lies at 7,900 ft (2,400 m) above sea level in the cool Apizaco Valley of the Sierra Madre Oriental. Formerly known as Barrón Escandón, the city is a commercial, manufacturing, and transportation centre. Corn (maize), beans, barley, and wheat, the principal crops of the agricultural hinterland, are processed there. Tanneries, pulque distilleries, textile mills, and railroad repair yards are also located in the city. The main Mexico City–Veracruz railroad line passes through it, and highways from highland and coastal communities, including Mexico City, 84 mi (135 km) to the west, converge upon the city. It also has an airfield. Pop. (1970) 21,189.

aplastic anemia, also called ANEMIA OF BONE-MARROW FAILURE, disease in which bone marrow fails to produce an adequate number of blood cells. There may be lack of all cell types (white blood cells, red blood cells, and platelets; this form is called pancytopenia) or of one or more cell types. Rarely, the disease may be congenital (Fanconi syndrome); more commonly it is acquired by exposure to certain drugs (*e.g.*, chloramphenicol) or non-pharmaceutical chemicals (*e.g.*, benzene) or to ionizing radiation. About half of all cases are idiopathic (cause unknown). Aplastic anemia is most common in youth (ages 15 to 30), though it may occur at any age. Onset may be abrupt, the disease arising suddenly with great severity, with early death; more commonly it is insidious, running a chronic course of several years. Symptoms of chronic aplastic anemia include weakness and fatigue in the early stages, followed by shortness of breath, headache, fever, and pounding heart. There is usually a waxy pallor, and hemorrhages occur in the mucous membranes, skin, and other organs. If white blood cells (specifically, neutrophils) are lacking, resistance to infection is much lowered, and infection becomes the major cause of death. When platelets are very low, bleeding may be severe.

The treatment of choice for severe aplastic anemia is bone marrow transplantation, provided a compatible donor can be found. If transplantation is not practical, treatment involves avoidance of the toxic agent if known, supportive care (administration of fluids, glucose, and proteins, often intravenously), transfusions of blood components, and administration of antibotics. Spontaneous recovery occurs occasionally.

aplite, also spelled HAPLITE, any intrusive igneous rock of simple composition, such as granite composed only of alkali feldspar, muscovite mica, and quartz; in a more restricted sense, uniformly fine-grained (less than 2 millimetres [0.08 inch]), light-coloured, intrusive igneous rocks that have a characteristic sugary texture. Unlike pegmatite, which is similar but coarser grained, aplite occurs in small bodies that rarely contain zones of different minerals. The two rocks often occur together, cutting across or forming lenses (thin-edged strata) within each other, and are assumed to have formed at the same time from similar magmas (molten materials), the aplite magma containing fewer mineralizers and volatiles. *See* pegmatite.

Apo, Mount, active volcano, south central Mindanao, 20 mi (32 km) west of Davao City; it is the highest point in the Philippines, rising to 9,690 ft (2,954 m). Part of the Cordillera Central, it is covered by a forest of tall, tropical hardwoods; two subsidiary peaks nearly match its height. Mt. Apo National Park, established in 1936, has an area of 199,819 ac (80,864 ha); it is the home of the monkey-eating eagle and features numerous peaks and valleys, as well as Malasita Falls, Sibulao Lake, and the Kisinte Hot Springs.

Apocalypse of John: *see* Revelation to John.

apocalyptic literature, literary genre that flourished from about 200 BC to about AD 200, especially in Judaism and Christianity. Written primarily to give hope to religious groups undergoing persecution or the stress of cultural upheavals, apocalypses (from the Greek *apokalypsis:* "revelation") describe in cryptic language understood by believers the sudden, dramatic intervention of God in history on behalf of the faithful elect. Accompanying or heralding God's dramatic intervention in human affairs will be cataclysmic events of cosmic proportions, such as a temporary rule of the world by Satan, signs in the heavens, persecutions, wars, famines, plagues, and earthquakes.

Though presenting current afflictions as verifications of past apocalyptic prophecies, apocalyptic writers generally concentrated on themes such as the future overthrow of evil, the coming of a messianic figure, and the establishment of the Kingdom of God and of eternal peace and righteousness. The wicked are described as consigned to hell and the righteous or elect as reigning with God or a messiah in a renewed earth or heaven.

The Book of Daniel in the Old Testament and the Revelation to John in the New Testament represent apocalyptic writing, and several intertestamental books contain apocalyptic themes.

Apocalyptic themes have been revived in modern literature and frequently appear in science fiction.

apocalypticism, eschatological (end-time) views and movements that focus on cryptic revelations about a sudden, dramatic, and cataclysmic intervention of God in history; the judgment of all men; the salvation of the faithful elect; and the eventual rule of the elect with God in a renewed heaven and earth. Arising in Zoroastrianism, an Iranian religion founded by the 6th-century-BC prophet Zoroaster, apocalypticism was developed more fully in Judaic, Christian, and Islāmic eschatological speculation and movements. *See also* eschatology.

Apocrita, one of two suborders of the insect order Hymenoptera, the other being Symphyta. Included in the group are the ants, bees, wasps, braconids, ichneumons, chalcids, nearly all parasitic hymenopterans, and a few other forms. The suborder includes the most highly evolved members of the order and is represented by several thousand species distributed worldwide.

Among most species, the grublike larvae are sedentary forms. They may feed as parasites on other arthropods or within plant structures, or they may be fed by adults within a nest. The base of the adult's abdomen is constricted, a diagnostic feature of the group. The adults feed mainly on plants, although some species are parasites and others are hyperparasites (that is, they feed on insects that are parasitic on other insects).

Although the suborder includes some species that are destructive to crops—for example, the seed chalcids (Eurytomidae)—the majority of species are beneficial to man. Beneficial members include the bee (*q.v.*), which pollinates a great variety of economically important plants; the honeybee (*q.v.*; *Apis*) is also important for the honey it produces; and many species are important as parasites of insect pests. Such parasites include ichneumon, chalcid (*qq.v.*), pteromalid, figitid, ensign wasp (*q.v.*), and bethylid.

apocrypha (from Greek *apokryptein*, "to hide away"), in biblical literature, works outside an accepted canon of scripture. In its broadest sense apocrypha refers to any writings of dubious authorship. The word came into use early in the Christian Church to refer to writings of questionable authenticity that were not to be read to the congregation.

A brief treatment of apocrypha follows. For full treatment, *see* MACROPAEDIA: Biblical Literature and Its Interpretation.

There are several levels of dubiety within the general concept of apocryphal works in Judeo-Christian biblical writings. Apocrypha per se are outside the canon, not considered divinely inspired but regarded as worthy of study by the faithful. Pseudepigrapha are spurious works ostensibly written by a biblical figure. Deuterocanonical works are those that are accepted in one canon but not in all.

At the time when Greek was the common spoken language in the Mediterranean region, the Old Testament—the Hebrew Bible—was incomprehensible to most of the population. For this reason, Jewish scholars produced the Septuagint, a translation of the Old Testament books from various Hebrew texts, along with fragments in Aramaic, into Greek. That version incorporated a number of works identified by later Jewish scholarship as outside the authentic Hebrew canon. The Talmud separates these works as *Sefarim Hizonim* (Extraneous Books).

The Septuagint was an important basis for St. Jerome's translation of the Old Testament into Latin for the Vulgate Bible; and, although he had doubts about the authenticity of some of the apocryphal works that it contained, he was overruled and most of them were included in the Vulgate; the Council of Trent declared the canonicity of nearly the entire Vulgate, excluding only the Third and Fourth Books of Maccabees, the Prayer of Manasseh, Psalm 151, and the First and Second Books of Esdras. Eastern Christendom, meanwhile, had accepted some of the Old Testament apocrypha—Tobit, Judith, the Wisdom of Solomon, and Ecclesiasticus (Wisdom of Jesus the Son of Sirach)—but rejected the rest.

The other apocryphal writings, canonical only to Roman Catholicism, with an exception or two, include the Book of Baruch (a prophet) and the Letter of Jeremiah (often the sixth chapter of Baruch); the First and Second Books of Maccabees; several stories from Daniel, namely, the Song of the Three, Daniel and Susanna, and Bel and the Dragon; and extensive portions of the Book of Esther. The works accepted by the Roman Catholic Church but not by Jews or Protestants are called deuterocanonical (*i.e.*, from a second canon).

Old Testament pseudepigrapha are extremely numerous and offer accounts of patriarchs and events, attributed to various biblical personages from Adam to Zechariah. Some of the most significant of these works are the Ascension of Isaiah, the Assumption of Moses, the Life of Adam and Eve, the First and Second Books of Enoch, the Book of Jubilees, the Letter of Aristeas, and the Testaments of the Twelve Patriarchs.

All the New Testament apocrypha are pseudepigraphal, and most of them fall into the categories of acts, gospels, and epistles, though there are a number of apocalypses and some can be characterized as wisdom books. The apocryphal acts purport to relate the lives or careers of various biblical figures, including most of the apostles; the epistles, gospels, and others are ascribed to such figures. Some relate encounters and events in mystical language and describe arcane rituals. Most of these works arose from sects that had been or would be declared heretical, such as, importantly, the Gnostics. Some of them argued against various heresies, and a few appear to have been neutral efforts to popularize the life of some saint or other early leader of the church, including a number of women. In the early decades of Christianity no orthodoxy had been established, and various parties or factions were vying for ascendancy and regularity in the young church. All sought through their writings, as through their preaching and missions, to win believers. In this setting virtually all works advocating beliefs that later became heretical were destined to denunciation and destruction.

In addition to apocryphal works per se, the New Testament includes a number of works and fragments that are described by a second meaning of the term deuterocanonical: "added later." The Letter to the Hebrews attributed to Paul, who died before it was written, is one of these; others are the letters of James, Peter (II), John (II and III), and Jude, and the Revelation to John. Fragments include Mark 16:9–20, Luke 22:43–44, and John 7:53 and 8:1–11. All are included in the Roman canon and are accepted by the Eastern Church and most Protestant churches.

Heretical movements such as Gnosticism and Montanism spawned a great body of New Testament pseudepigrapha. The existence of such purported scriptures lent great impetus to the process of canonization in the young and orthodox Christian Church. *See also* various apocryphal works cited above.

Apocynaceae, the dogbane family of flowering plants of the gentian order (Gentianales), including more than 150 genera and about

Golden-trumpet (*Allamanda cathartica*)
Walter Chandoha

1,000 species of trees, shrubs, woody vines, and herbs, distributed primarily in tropical and subtropical areas of the world. Members of the family have milky, often poisonous juice; smooth-margined leaves; and flowers in clusters (rarely solitary). The fruit may be berrylike or fleshy but usually is a dry pod (follicle) that splits open at maturity, releasing many winged or tufted seeds.

Garden ornamentals belonging to the family include periwinkle (*Vinca*), oleander (*Nerium*), yellow oleander (*Thevetia*), frangipani (*Plumeria*), Natal plum (*Carissa*), and crepe jasmine (*Tabernaemontana coronaria*). Several species of the genera *Trachelospermum* (especially star jasmine, *T. jasminoides*), *Mandevilla,* and *Allamanda* are attractive woody vines. Dogbane (*Apocynum*) and *Amsonia* sometimes are grown as ornamentals. The genera *Adenium* and *Pachypodium* are African succulents with alternate leaves and strangely shaped trunks. The impala lily (*Adenium multiflorum*) is an ornamental shrub with star-shaped flowers and large underground tubers. Arrow poisons are obtained from many plants in the dogbane family, and the poisonous alkaloids of species belonging to the genera *Strophanthus* and *Rauwolfia* (*qq.v.*) also are used in medicines.

Periwinkle (*Vinca minor*)
Walter Chandoha

apodiform, order of birds (Apodiformes) that comprises the swifts and hummingbirds.

A brief treatment of apodiforms follows. For full treatment, *see* MACROPAEDIA: Birds.

The common characteristic that has swifts and hummingbirds classified together is their mastery of aerial locomotion; they are superb fliers and share some wing modifications that differentiate them from most other birds. The hummingbirds are classed in one suborder, the Trochili, and the approximately 320 species are members of the family Trochilidae. The suborder Apodi, which contains the swifts, is divided into two families, the Apodidae for the true swifts and the Hemiprocnidae for the tree, or crested, swifts.

Hummingbirds are native only to the Western Hemisphere and most species are found in the tropics of northwestern South America. Several species, including the North American ruby-throated hummingbird (*Archilochus colubris*), have adapted to temperate zones, and one, the rufous hummingbird (*Selasphorus rufus*), even ranges into Alaska. The tree swifts are limited in range, inhabiting an area from India through southeast Asia and into the East Indies. The true swifts are the most widespread members of the order, being found throughout the Old and New World wherever the land can support a large enough number of flying insects.

Hummingbird shape is much the same throughout the family. The bee hummingbird of Cuba (*Mellisuga helenae*) is the smallest known species of bird; it is only 2.5 inches (6.4 centimetres) in length. The largest of the family is the giant hummingbird (*Patagona gigas*), which reaches all of 8 in. Variation occurs in the shape and size of the bill and in the ornamental plumage. The bill may be quite short, as in the bearded helmetcrest (*Oxypogon guerinii*), or longer than the rest of the body, as in the sword-billed hummingbird (*Ensifera ensifera*). It is often straight but may be downcurved, as in the sicklebills (*Eutoxeres*), or less frequently, upcurved. The shape of the bill is related to the flowers on which each species of hummingbird preferentially feeds. The legs and feet are small, suitable only for perching, not walking. Bright iridescent plumage, especially on the throat, is characteristic of most hummingbirds. The tails of most species are short and simple, but in a few, such as the marvelous spatuletail (*Loddigesia mirabilis*), they are elongated and ornate.

The swifts show a much greater range in size than the hummingbirds, and members of the Old World genus *Apus* can weigh 30 times as much as the 0.2-ounce (5.7-gram) pygmy swiftlet (*Collocalia troglodytes*). The structure which shows the most variation is the tail. In the spine-tailed swifts, including the American chimney swift (*Chaetura pelagica*), the central shafts of the tail feathers extend beyond the flattened vane as pointed spikes. Other swifts have tails that are either squared off, slightly forked, or deeply forked (swallow-tailed). The feet of the true swifts are too weak to use for perching, and they rest by clinging to vertical surfaces with their sharp claws. In the tree swifts the feet are stronger and larger and these birds perch regularly. Adaptations to their exclusive diet of flying insects are the short weak bill and the large mouth.

The swifts are limited in habitat only by the availability of flying insects. Swifts drink by dipping their bills as they fly low over a body of water. Hummingbirds, being highly specialized to subsist basically on nectar, are restricted to areas where flowering plants are available. This explains the predominant number of species in the seasonless tropics, where different plants are in flower all year. When feeding, a hummingbird hovers over a flower and extends its long tubular tongue to suck up the nectar. In addition to hovering, these birds can fly backwards and occasionally upside down. Many will also eat some insects and spiders, which they capture with their bills.

Hummingbirds and swifts are both able to enter torpor, in which the metabolism slows down and the body temperature drops. This allows the hummingbirds to roost at night without exhausting their energy reserves, supporting their otherwise very high metabolism. It enables the swifts to survive long periods of fasting when aerial foraging is not possible.

Courtship among swifts is completely aerial and copulation takes place while in flight. Nests of tree swifts are frequently simple cups placed on a tree limb. The palm swifts (*Cypsiurus parvus*) glue their nests to the underside of palm leaves with a sticky secretion produced by the salivary glands, and some species glue the eggs into the nest so the wind cannot bounce them out. The nest of one species, the edible-nest swiftlet (*Collocalia fuciphaga*), is constructed almost entirely of this salivary cement; these nests are the basis of the Orient's famous bird's-nest soup. Clutches range from one to six white eggs, with species from the northern regions laying the higher numbers. The Indian house swift, *Apus affinus*, is one of the few birds known to have two distinct breeding seasons per year; it breeds in January and again from late May to June. Incubation in the swifts is shared by both sexes. The naked young are left unattended for longer periods than are most birds as the parents forage for many small insects; however, the young swifts are basically cold-blooded (poikilothermic) during their first few weeks.

Hummingbirds, unlike swifts, are usually polygamous. Territoriality is absent in some species while others may vigorously defend nesting or feeding sites. These birds are typically aggressive and take advantage of their great manoeuvrability in the air to drive off hawks and other large predators. Most courtship displays are aerial, although in those of the drably coloured hermits (*Phaethornis*) singing is important. In some species, leks—areas of communal male display—occur. Hummingbird nests are typically situated on a branch and composed of vegetable fibre, lichens, bark fragments, and spider webs. The female incubates her clutch of two white eggs and cares for the young alone. To feed the hatchlings she thrusts her bill deeply into a young bird's throat and regurgitates.

Apollinaire, Guillaume, pseudonym of WILHELM APOLLINARIS DE KOSTROWITZKI (b. Aug. 26, 1880, Rome?—d. Nov. 9, 1918, Paris), poet who in his short life took part in all the avant-garde movements that flourished in French literary and artistic circles at the beginning of the 20th century and who helped to direct poetry into unexplored channels.

The son of a Polish *émigrée* and an Italian officer, he kept his origins secret. Left more or less to himself, he went at the age of 20 to Paris, where he led a bohemian life. Several months spent in Germany in 1901 had a profound effect on him and helped to awaken him to his poetic vocation. He fell under the spell of the Rhineland and later recaptured the beauty of its forests and its legends in his poetry. More important, he fell in love with a young Englishwoman, Annie Playden, whom he pursued, unsuccessfully, as far as London;

his romantic disappointment inspired him to write his famous "Chanson du mal-aimé" ("Song of the Poorly Loved").

Apollinaire, drawing by Pablo Picasso from the frontispiece to *Calligrammes*, 1918

H. Roger-Viollet

After his return to Paris, Apollinaire became well known as a writer and a habitué of the cafes patronized by literary men. He also made friends with some young painters who were to become famous—Maurice de Vlaminck, André Derain, Raoul Dufy, and Pablo Picasso; he introduced his contemporaries to Henri Rousseau's paintings and to African sculpture; and with Picasso, he applied himself to the task of defining the principles of a Cubist aesthetic in literature as well as painting. His *Peintures cubistes* appeared in 1913 (*Cubist Painters*, 1944).

His first volume, *L'Enchanteur pourrissant* (1909), is a strange dialogue in poetic prose between the magician Merlin and the nymph Viviane. In the following year a collection of vivid stories, some whimsical and some wildly fantastic, appeared under the title *L'Hérésiarque et Cie* (1910). Then came *Le Bestiaire* (1911), in mannered quatrains. But his poetic masterpiece was *Alcools* (1913; Eng. trans., 1964). In these poems he relived all his experiences and expressed them sometimes in alexandrines and regular stanzas, sometimes in short unrhymed lines, and always without punctuation.

In 1914 Apollinaire enlisted, became a second lieutenant in the infantry, and received a head wound in 1916. Discharged, he returned to Paris and published a symbolic story, *Le Poète assassiné* (1916; *The Poet Assassinated*, 1923), and more significantly, a new collection of poems, *Calligrammes* (1918), dominated by images of war and his obsession with a new love affair. Weakened by war wounds, he died of Spanish influenza.

His play *Les Mamelles de Tirésias* was staged the year before he died (1917). He called it surrealist, believed to be the first use of the term. Francis Poulenc turned the play into a light opera (first produced in 1947).

In his poetry Apollinaire made daring, even outrageous, technical experiments; his *calligrammes*, thanks to an ingenious typographical arrangement, are designs as well as poems. More generally, Apollinaire set out to create an effect of surprise or even astonishment by means of unusual verbal associations and, because of this, could be called the herald of Surrealism.

Apollinaris THE YOUNGER, Latin APOLLINARIUS (b. *c.* 310—d. *c.* 390), bishop of Laodicea who developed the heretical position concerning the nature of Christ called Apollinarianism. With his father, Apollinaris the Elder, he reproduced the Old Testament in the form of Homeric and Pindaric poetry and the New Testament in the style of Platonic dialogues after the Roman emperor Julian had forbidden Christians to teach the classics.

Apollinaris denied the existence in Christ of a rational human soul, a position he took to combat Arianism (*see* Arius). Excommunicated from the church for his views, Apollinaris was readmitted but in 346 excommunicated a second time. Nevertheless the Nicene congregation at Laodicea chose him as bishop (*c.* 361). Skilled in logic and Hebrew and a teacher of rhetoric, Apollinaris also lectured at Antioch *c.* 374.

Apollinopolis (Egypt): *see* Idfū.

Apollo, byname PHOEBUS, in Greek religion, a deity of manifold function and meaning, the most widely revered and influential of all the Greek gods. Though his original nature is obscure, from the time of Homer onward he was the god of divine distance, who sent or threatened from afar; the god who made men aware of their own guilt and purified them of it; who presided over religious law and the constitutions of cities; who communicated to man through prophets and oracles his knowledge of the future and the will of his father, Zeus. Even the gods feared him, and only his father and his mother, Leto, could endure his presence. Distance, death, terror, and awe were summed up in his symbolic bow; a gentler side of his nature, however, was shown in his other attribute, the lyre, which proclaimed the joy of communion with Olympus (the home of the gods) through music, poetry, and dance. In humbler circles he was also a god of crops and herds, primarily as a divine bulwark against wild animals and disease, as his epithet Alexikakos (Averter of Evil) indicates. His forename Phoebus means "bright" or "pure," and the view became current that he was connected with the sun. *See* Helios.

Apollo Belvedere, restored Roman copy of the Greek original attributed to Leochares, 4th century BC; in the Vatican Museum, Rome

Alinari—Art Resource/EB Inc.

Among Apollo's other epithets was Nomios (Herdsman), and he is said to have served King Admetus of Pherae in the lowly capacities of groom and herdsman as penance for slaying Zeus's armourers, the Cyclopes. He was also called Lyceius, presumably because he protected the flocks from wolves (*lykoi*); because herdsmen and shepherds beguiled the hours with music, scholars have argued that this was Apollo's original role.

Though the most Hellenic of all gods, Apollo apparently was of foreign origin, coming either from somewhere north of Greece or from Asia. Traditionally, Apollo and his twin, Artemis, were born on the isle of Delos. From there Apollo went to Pytho (Delphi), where he slew Python, the female dragon that guarded the area. He established his oracle by taking on the guise of a dolphin, leaping aboard a Cretan ship, and forcing the crew to serve him. Thus Pytho was renamed Delphi after the dolphin (*delphis*), and the Cretan cult of Apollo Delphinius superseded that previously established there by Earth (Gaea). During the Archaic period (8th to 6th century BC), the fame of the Delphic oracle spread as far as Lydia in Anatolia and achieved pan-Hellenic status. The god's medium was the Pythia, a local woman over fifty years old, who, under his inspiration, delivered oracles in the main temple of Apollo. The oracles were subsequently interpreted and versified by priests. Other oracles of Apollo existed on the Greek mainland, Delos, and in Anatolia, but none rivalled Delphi in importance.

Of the Greek festivals in honour of Apollo, the most curious was the octennial Delphic Stepterion, in which a boy reenacted the slaying of the Python and was temporarily banished to the Vale of Tempe.

Although Apollo had many love affairs, they were mostly unfortunate: Daphne, in her efforts to escape him, was changed into a laurel, his sacred shrub; Coronis (mother of Asclepius) was shot by Apollo's twin, Artemis, when Coronis proved unfaithful; and Cassandra (daughter of King Priam of Troy) rejected his advances and was punished by being made to utter true prophecies that no one believed.

In Italy Apollo was introduced at an early date and was primarily concerned, as in Greece, with healing and prophecy; he was highly revered by the emperor Augustus because the Battle of Actium (31 BC) was fought near one of his temples. In art Apollo was represented as a beardless youth, either naked or robed, and often holding either a bow or a lyre.

Apollo program, Moon-landing project executed by the United States National Aeronautics and Space Administration in the 1960s and 1970s. The Apollo program was announced in May 1961, but the choice among competing techniques for achieving a Moon landing and return was not resolved until considerable further study. The method ultimately employed was that of lunar-orbit rendezvous, by which a powerful launch vehicle (Saturn V) placed a 50-ton spacecraft in a lunar trajectory. Several launch vehicles, essentially large rockets, and accompanying spacecraft, were built. The Apollo spacecraft were supplied with a relatively slight rocket power of their own, capable of permitting them to brake on approach to the Moon and go into a lunar orbit. They also possessed the capability of releasing a component of the spacecraft, the Lunar Module (LM), carrying its own rocket power, to land persons on the Moon and bring them back to the lunar orbiting Apollo craft.

The first manned Apollo flight was delayed by a tragic accident, a fire that broke out in the spacecraft during a launch rehearsal, killing three astronauts. On Oct. 11, 1968, following several unmanned Earth-orbit flights, Apollo 7 made a 163-orbit flight carrying a full crew of three astronauts. Apollo 8 carried out the first step of manned lunar exploration; from Earth orbit it was injected into a lunar trajectory, completed lunar orbit, and returned safely to Earth. Apollo 9 carried out a prolonged mission in Earth orbit to check out the Lunar Module. Apollo 10 journeyed to lunar orbit and tested the LM to within 9½ miles (15 kilometres) of the Moon's surface. Apollo 11, in July 1969, climaxed the step-by-step procedure with a lunar landing; the astronaut Neil Armstrong became the first human to set foot on the Moon's surface.

Apollo 13, launched in April 1970, suffered an accident caused by an explosion in an oxygen tank but returned safely to Earth. Remaining Apollo missions carried out extensive exploration of the lunar surface, collecting large numbers of samples of Moon rocks and installing many instruments for scientific research, such as the solar wind experiment, and the seismographic measurements of the lunar surface. Apollo 17, the final flight of the program, took place in December 1972.

Apollodorus (fl. 5th century BC), Athenian painter thought to have been the first to gradate light and colour, that is, to shade his paintings. For this reason he was known, in his own day, as "Sciagraphos," or "Shadow Painter." Pliny called him the "first to give his figures the appearance of reality."

Apollodorus' paintings are now all lost, though ancient sources mention several of his works. Among them, all in Athens, were: "Odysseus," "A Priest at Prayer," and "Ajax Struck by Lightning."

Apollodorus OF ATHENS (fl. 140 BC), Greek scholar of wide interests who is best known for his *Chronicle* of Greek history. A pupil of the scholar Aristarchus, he left Alexandria about 146 for Pergamum and eventually settled at Athens. The *Chronicle,* written in iambic trimeter, commonly used in Greek comedy, covers the period from the fall of Troy (1184 BC) to 144 BC and was later continued to 119 BC. Apollodorus' other works include a treatise *On the Gods;* one on the Homeric catalogue of ships, used by Strabo in his *Geography;* and critical and grammatical writings. A compendium to Greek mythology, called *The Library,* extant under his name, is, in fact, not by him.

Apollodorus OF DAMASCUS (fl. early 2nd century AD), Greek engineer and architect who worked primarily for the Roman emperor Trajan (reigned 98–117). He was banished by the emperor Hadrian and executed *c.* AD 130. The most famous works associated with him are the designs for Trajan's Forum in Rome and for Trajan's Column.

Apollonius DYSCOLUS (Greek: the Crabbed) (fl. 2nd century AD), Greek grammarian who was reputedly the founder of the systematic study of grammar. His life was passed at Alexandria during the reigns of the Roman emperors Hadrian and Antoninus Pius. Priscian, the Latin grammarian, styled him *grammaticorum princeps* ("prince of grammarians") and used his work as the basis for his own. Four of Apollonius' works are extant: *On Syntax* and three smaller treatises, *On Pronouns, On Conjunctions,* and *On Adverbs.*

Apollonius OF PERGA (b. *c.* 262 BC, Perga, Pamphylia, Anatolia—d. *c.* 190, Alexandria), mathematician, known by his contemporaries as "The Great Geometer," whose treatise *Conics* is one of the greatest scientific works from the ancient world. Most of his other treatises were lost, although their titles and a general indication of their contents were passed on by later writers, especially Pappus of Alexandria (fl. *c.* AD 320).

As a youth Apollonius studied in Alexandria (under the pupils of Euclid, according to Pappus) and subsequently taught at the university there. He visited Pergamum, capital of a Hellenistic kingdom in western Anatolia, where a university and library similar to those in Alexandria had recently been built. While at Pergamum he met Eudemus and Attalus, and he wrote the first edition of *Conics.* He addressed the prefaces of the first three books of the final edition to Eudemus and the remaining volumes to Attalus, whom some scholars identify as King Attalus I of Pergamum.

It is clear from Apollonius' allusions to Euclid (fl. *c.* 295 BC), Conon of Samos (fl. *c.* 250 BC), and Nicoteles of Cyrene (fl. *c.* 250 BC) that he made the fullest use of his predecessors' works. Books 1–4 contain a systematic account of the essential principles of conics, which for the most part had been previously set forth by Euclid, Aristaeus (fl. *c.* 320 BC), and Menaechmus (fl. *c.* 350 BC). A number of theorems in Book 3 and the greater part of Book 4 are new, however, and he introduced the terms parabola, ellipse, and hyperbola. Books 5–7 are clearly original. His genius takes its highest flight in Book 5, in which he considers normals as minimum and maximum straight lines drawn from given points to the curve (independently of tangent properties), discusses how many normals can be drawn from particular points, finds their feet by construction, and gives propositions determining the centre of curvature at any point and leading at once to the Cartesian equation of the evolute of any conic.

The first four books of the *Conics* survive in the original Greek and the next three in Arabic translation. Book 8 is lost. The only other extant work of Apollonius is *Cutting Off of a Ratio* (or *On Proportional Section*), in an Arabic translation. Pappus mentions five additional works, *Cutting Off of an Area* (or *On Spatial Section*), *On Determinate Section, Tangencies, Vergings* (or *Inclinations*), and *Plane Loci.*

Tangencies embraced the following general problem: given three things, each of which may be a point, straight line, or circle, construct a circle tangent to the three. Sometimes known as the problem of Apollonius, the most difficult case arises when the three given things are circles.

Of the other works of Apollonius referred to by ancient writers, one, *On the Burning Mirror,* concerned optics. Apollonius demonstrated that parallel light rays striking a spherical mirror would not be reflected to the centre of sphericity, as was previously believed. The focal properties of the parabolic mirror were also discussed. A work entitled *On the Cylindrical Helix* is mentioned by Proclus (*c.* AD 410–485). Apollonius also wrote *Comparison of the Dodecahedron and the Icosahedron,* considering the case in which they are inscribed in the same sphere. According to Eutocius (fl. *c.* AD 500), in Apollonius' work *Quick Delivery,* closer limits for the value of π (pi) than the $3\frac{1}{7}$ and $3\frac{10}{71}$ of Archimedes were calculated. In a work of unknown title Apollonius developed his system of tetrads, a method for expressing and multiplying large numbers. His *On Unordered Irrationals* extended the theory of irrationals originally advanced by Eudoxus of Cnidus and found in Book 10 of Euclid's *Elements.*

Lastly, from references in Ptolemy's *Almagest,* it is known that Apollonius introduced the systems of eccentric and epicyclic motion to explain planetary motion. Of particular interest was his determination of the points where a planet appears stationary.

Apollonius OF RHODES (b. *c.* 295 BC), Greek poet and grammarian who was the author of the *Argonautica.*

The two lives contained in the Laurentian manuscript of the *Argonautica* say that Apollonius was a pupil of Callimachus; that he gave a recitation of the *Argonautica* at Alexandria; and that when this proved a failure he retired to Rhodes. The first life adds the detail that the poet was still an adolescent when this happened, though it had previously said that he turned late to writing poetry. Both lives say that the *Argonautica* was well received in Rhodes, and the second cites a report that Apollonius returned to Alexandria and was appointed chief librarian. Another work has him succeed Eratosthenes in this post. But in a list of Alexandrian librarians on a late 2nd-century AD papyrus (Oxyrhynchus Papyrus 1241), Apollonius succeeds Zenodotus and precedes Eratosthenes. If this evidence is accepted it may be conjectured that Apollonius became librarian *c.* 260 BC and continued as such until *c.* 247, when he fell out of favour under the new king, Ptolemy Euergetes, and retired to Rhodes.

Apollonius of Rhodes, bronze bust by an unknown artist, in the Museo Archeologico, Florence

By courtesy of the Museo Archeologico, Florence

In the *Argonautica*, an epic in four books on the voyage of the Argonauts, Apollonius adapted the language of Homer to the needs of a romantic epic with considerable success; in recounting Medea's love for Jason, he shows a capacity for sympathetic analysis not found in earlier Greek literature. Apollonius often holds the reader by his fresh handling of old episodes, his suggestive similes, and his admirable descriptions of nature. Besides the *Argonautica*, Apollonius wrote epigrams and poems on the foundations (*Ktiseis*) of cities, most of which are lost. As a grammarian, Apollonius is credited with a work "against Zenodotus" and commentaries on several Greek poets.

Apollonius OF TRALLES (fl. 2nd century BC), Greek sculptor from the province of Caria, in Asia Minor, known for his execution in collaboration with his brother Tauriscus of a marble group known as the "Farnese Bull." The work represented Zethus and Amphion, the twin builders of Thebes, tying their stepmother, Dirce, to the horns of a wild bull in punishment for her torment of their mother, Antiope.

Apollonius OF TYANA (fl. 1st century AD, Tyana, Cappadocia), a Neo-Pythagorean who became a mythical hero during the time of the Roman Empire. Empress Julia Domna instructed the writer Philostratus to write a biography of Apollonius, and it is speculated that her motive for doing so stemmed from her desire to counteract the influence of Christianity on Roman civilization. The biography portrays a figure much like Christ in temperament and power and claims that Apollonius performed certain miracles. It is believed that most of the biography is based more on fiction than fact. Many of the pagans in the Roman Empire believed what was said in this work, and it kindled religious feeling in many of them. To honour and worship Apollonius, they erected shrines and other memorials.

Apollonius OF TYRE, chief personage in a medieval Latin romance of unknown authorship, which may be assumed to derive from a lost Greek original. The story enjoyed long and widespread popularity in European literature, and versions of it exist in almost every European language. The story tells of the separation of Apollonius from his wife and daughter (whom he thinks dead) and his ultimate reunion with them after many travels.

The Greek original on which this story is thought to be based probably dates from the 3rd century AD. The Latin version is first mentioned in the second half of the 6th century by Venantius Fortunatus, a Christian poet and bishop. The survival of numerous Latin manuscripts (the earliest dating from the 9th or 10th century) testifies to its popularity in the Middle Ages. The most widespread versions in the Middle Ages include one by Godfrey of Viterbo in his *Pantheon,* a late

12th-century verse rendering that treated the story as authentic history, and one contained in the *Gesta Romanorum,* a 14th-century collection of folktales. An Anglo-Saxon translation (the first English vernacular version) was made in the 11th century, and the poet John Gower used the tale as an example of the seventh deadly sin (Sloth) in his late 14th-century poem *Confessio amantis.* Shakespeare (although changing his hero's name) used the story as the basis of his play *Pericles.*

Apollonius THE ATHENIAN (fl. 1st century BC), sculptor known only by his signatures on the marble "Belvedere Torso," now in the Vatican, and the bronze "Boxer," now in the Museo Nazionale Romano of Rome. At one time these sculptures were thought to be 1st-

"The Boxer," Roman bronze copy of Greek sculpture by Apollonius the Athenian, 1st century BC; in the Museo Nazionale Romano, Rome

Alinari—Art Resource/EB Inc.

century originals. Now it is believed they are fine 1st-century copies of original 2nd-century works; although the inscriptions are datable to the 1st century, the style of the sculptures is similar to that of the great altar at Pergamum, a key monument of the 2nd century. Thus, Apollonius appears to have been one of the most talented copyists of his time.

apologetics, in Christianity, the intellectual defense of the truth of the Christian religion, usually considered a branch of theology. In Protestant usage, apologetics can be distinguished from polemics, in which the beliefs of a particular Christian sect are defended. Roman Catholics, however, use the term to mean defense of Catholic teaching as a whole and identify apologetics with fundamental theology.

Apologetics has traditionally been positive in its direct argument for Christianity and negative in its criticism of opposing beliefs. Its function is both to fortify the believer against his personal doubts and to remove the intellectual stumbling blocks that inhibit the conversion of unbelievers. Apologetics has steered a difficult course between dogmatism, which fails to take seriously the objections of non-Christians, and the temptation to undermine the strength of defense by granting too much to the skeptic. Apologetics has rarely been taken as providing a conclusive proof of Christianity; many apologists believe that to insist on such proof is to sacrifice the supernatural element to purely rational considerations. Some theologians have been skeptical about the value of apologetics to a religion based on faith.

In the New Testament, the thrust of apologetics was defense of Christianity as the culmination of the Jewish religion and its prophecies concerning a messiah. In the early church, the Apologists, such as Justin Martyr and Tertullian, defended the moral superiority of Christianity over paganism and pointed out Christianity's fulfillment of Old Testament prophecies. Origen, a 2nd–3rd-century Alexandrian philosophical theologian, stressed the supernatural witness of the Holy Spirit in Christian belief. The Platonic theologian Augustine, around the turn of the 4th century, presented Christianity as God's answer to the fall of the Roman Empire, which the sin of man was effecting.

In the later Middle Ages, apologists focussed on Christianity's superiority over the rival religions of Judaism and Islām. In the 13th century, however, Thomas Aquinas developed a still-influential defense of belief in God based on Aristotelian theories of a first cause of the universe.

During the Protestant Reformation apologetics was substantially replaced by polemics, in which many sects sought to defend their particular beliefs rather than Christianity as a whole. In the 18th century, Joseph Butler, an English bishop, met the rising challenge of Deism in the wake of advancing science by arguing that a supernatural Christianity was at least as reasonable and probable as any scientific doctrine could be. A later Englishman, William Paley, argued that a universe exhibiting design must have a Designer, much as a watch implies a watchmaker.

In the 19th century the historical reliability of the Gospels came under attack, and apologists stressed the difficulty of accounting for the Resurrection of Jesus and the rapid spread of Christianity if supernaturalism were denied. Moral arguments for Christianity based on the philosophy of religion of the German philosopher Immanuel Kant also gained prominence as attacks on traditional historical and metaphysical apologetics increased. Further objections to Christianity based on the theory of evolution, the views of the German philosopher Friedrich Nietzsche, Marxism, and psychoanalysis have been met by apologists either by attempts to refute the fundamentals on which they are based, or by turning some aspects of the criticisms into new arguments favourable to Christianity.

In the 20th century such Protestant theologians as the Germans Rudolf Bultmann and Paul Tillich abandoned the attempt to preserve the literal historical truth of the Gospels and focussed on presenting Christianity as the best answer to the existential needs and questions of man. Other Protestants stress the need to make the ancient stories and symbols of Christianity meaningful to modern man in a "post-Christian" era dominated by Materialistic ideologies. The German scholar Karl Barth, however, one of the century's most influential theologians, expressed skepticism about the whole task of the apologetical system, insisting that Christianity must be rooted exclusively in faith. The Roman Catholic apologetical system, that of Thomas Aquinas and his intellectual successors, has been profoundly influenced in the 20th century by the second Vatican Council (*see* Vatican Council, second). Some apologetical functions have been absorbed by "fundamental theology." Contemporary apologetics in the Roman communion focusses principally on the community of believers, whose faith is under constant challenge by numerous competing views and value systems.

Apologist, any of the Christian writers, primarily in the 2nd century, who attempted to provide a defense of Christianity and criticisms of Greco-Roman culture. Many of their writings were addressed to Roman emperors, and it is probable that the writings were actually sent to government secretaries who were empowered to accept or reject them. Under these circumstances, some of the apologies assumed the form of briefs written to defend Christians against the accusations current in the 2nd century, especially the charges that their religion was novel or godless or that they engaged in immoral cultic practices.

The Apologists usually tried to prove the antiquity of their religion by emphasizing it as the fulfillment of Old Testament prophecy; they argued that their opponents were really godless because they worshipped the gods of mythology; and they insisted on the philosophical nature of their own faith as well as its high ethical teaching. Their works did not present a complete picture of Christianity because they were arguing primarily in response to charges by their opponents.

The Greek Apologists include Quadratus, Aristides, Justin Martyr, Tatian, Apollinaris (bishop of Hierapolis), Melito, Athenagoras, Theophilus, and Clement of Alexandria. Latin Apologists in the 2nd century included Marcus Minucius Felix and Tertullian.

The few early manuscripts of the works of the early Apologists that have survived owe their existence primarily to Byzantine scholars. In 914 Arethas, bishop of Caesarea Cappadociae, had a collection of early apologies copied for his library. Many of the later manuscripts were copied in the 16th century, when the Council of Trent was discussing the nature of tradition. The genuine writings of the Apologists were virtually unknown, however, until the 16th century.

apology, autobiographical form in which a defense is the framework for a discussion by the author of his personal beliefs and viewpoints. An early example dating from the 4th century BC is Plato's *Apology,* a philosophical dialogue dealing with the trial of Socrates, in which Socrates answers the charges of his accusers by giving a brief history of his life and his moral commitment. Such an apology is usually a self-justification. Among the famous apologies of Western literature are *Apologie de Raimond Sebond* (1580), an essay by Montaigne, who uses a defense of the beliefs of a 15th-century Spaniard as a pretext for presenting his own skeptical views on the futility of reason; *An Apology for the Life of Mr. Colley Cibber (Comedian)* (1740), in which the 18th-century English actor-manager answers his critic Alexander Pope with a summary of the achievements of his long career that is also one of the best theatrical histories of the period; and *Apologia pro Vita Sua* (1864; later retitled *History of My Religious Opinions*), by Cardinal Newman, a spiritual autobiography in which the general religious principles that inspired Newman's conversion to the Roman Catholic Church are examined.

Apology of the Augsburg Confession, one of the confessions of Lutheranism, a defense and elaboration of the Augsburg Confession, written by the Reformer Philipp Melanchthon in 1531. The first version of the Apology was hastily written and presented to Emperor Charles V on Sept. 22, 1530, at the Diet of Augsburg, after the Emperor had declared that the Confutation (Aug. 3, 1530), prepared by Catholic theologians to refute the Augsburg Confession (June 25, 1530), properly presented his Catholic faith. The Emperor demanded that the Reformers return to the Catholic Church, and he refused to accept the Apology when it was presented to him.

After Melanchthon returned to Wittenberg, he obtained a copy of the Confutation and decided that a more complete reply to the arguments of the Catholic theologians was necessary. He rewrote and expanded the Apology to more clearly and completely explain the faith of the Reformers. The Latin edition was completed in April or May and a German translation by Justus Jonas was published in the autumn of 1531. Luther and others soon recognized the Apology as an excellent exposition of the Lutheran faith. It was cited at various meetings and conferences and was finally included in the *Book of Concord* (1580), a collection of doctrinal standards of Lutheranism.

Seven times longer than the Augsburg Confession, the Apology is considered one of the most brilliant of the Reformation theological works. Melanchthon's knowledge of Scripture, theology, history, and linguistics is evident. About one-third of the work is concerned with the problem of justification, while other subjects treated include the church, human tradition, the invocation of saints, marriage of priests, the mass, monastic vows, penitence, and original sin.

apomixis, reproduction without fertilization by special generative tissues. It includes parthenogenesis in animals, in which the new individual develops from the unfertilized egg, and apogamy in certain plants, in which the generative tissue may be the sporophyte or the gametophyte. Apomixis provides for the perpetuation of traits favourable to individual survival but eliminates the longer term evolutionary advantage of biparental inheritance.

apomorphine, drug prepared from morphine. The primary action of apomorphine, which lacks the characteristic narcotic properties of morphine, is exerted on the vomiting centre in the brain. Used in medicine as an emetic, apomorphine is administered hypodermically as a solution of its hydrochloride salt. Its use should be controlled carefully since therapeutic doses have been known to exert a profound depressant effect.

Apomorphine hydrochloride occurs as white crystals or powder and is soluble in water or alcohol.

aponeurosis, a flat sheet or ribbonlike piece of tendonlike material that anchors a muscle or connects it with the part that the muscle moves. The aponeurosis is composed of dense fibrous connective tissue containing fibroblasts (collagen-secreting spindle-shaped cells) and bundles of collagenous fibres in ordered arrays. Aponeuroses are structurally similar to tendons and ligaments.

Apophis (Egyptian god): *see* Apepi.

apophyllite, potassium-calcium fluoride-silicate mineral that is related structurally to the zeolite family of aluminosilicates. Like the zeolites, it has a high water content, although apophyllite has no aluminum in its chemical composition, which is approximately represented by the formula $Ca_4KFSi_8O_{20} \cdot 8H_2O$. In many respects it is more similar to the micas. It is most commonly found as glassy, white to grayish crystals with zeolite minerals in basalt, granite, and gneiss, as in Trentino, Italy; Belfast, County Down; the Faeroe Islands; Kimberley, S.Af.; and Guanajuato, Mex. For detailed physical properties, *see* silicate mineral (table).

Apopis I, Apopis also spelled APOPHIS, or APOPI, last great Hyksos king of Egypt (reigned *c.* 1607–*c.* 1566 BC) who began in control of most of Egypt and was driven back to the vicinity of his capital by the successive attacks of the Theban pharaohs.

Apopis is attested in Upper Egypt by stone fragments from Gebelein that show his name surrounded by the sun disks of the solar god, Re. He also was the king in whose reign a great mathematical papyrus was copied.

A story concerning Apopis and the Theban king Seqenenre shows that the Thebans were vassals of the Hyksos ruler. Egyptians and Hyksos peacefully coexisted for some time, as the Thebans grazed their cattle in the Delta, ruled by the Hyksos.

Apopis quarrelled with Seqenenre, and war may have erupted between them. The Theban's mummy displays terrible head wounds. His successor, Kamose, declared a Middle Egyptian town as his frontier. He carried on the war, as is shown by two monuments from Thebes, and drove the Hyksos to the vicinity of Memphis (near Cairo). A Theban fleet also sailed by Avaris, Apopis' Delta capital.

Apopis reacted by calling on his ally to the south, the Cushite prince, to attack the Thebans in their rear. His messenger, however, was intercepted, and his plan was thwarted by Kamose. Some time soon after this raid, but before the final Hyksos expulsion, Apopis died. Contrary to later Egyptian propaganda, he honoured the solar god, Re, and had many Egyptian collaborators in Middle and Lower Egypt.

apoplexy (medicine): *see* stroke syndrome.

aposematic mechanism, biological means by which a dangerous, or noxious, organism advertises its dangerous nature. Aposematic, or warning, mechanisms have evolved along with protective systems; it is advantageous for the protected organism not to risk the injury that is likely to occur in even a successfully repelled attack.

The most common aposematic mechanism is the possession of bright, contrasting colours, such as the black and yellow of many wasps and the red of ladybird beetles. Other organisms, such as the North American rattlesnakes, employ acoustic warning systems.

aposiopesis (Greek: "becoming silent"), a speaker's deliberate failure to complete a sentence. Aposiopesis usually indicates speechless rage or exasperation and sometimes implies vague threats as in, "Why, I'll . . . ." The listener is expected to complete the sentence in his mind. In ancient Greek rhetoric, the aposiopesis is occasionally a pause before a change of subject or a digression.

apostasy, traditional term denoting the total rejection of Christianity by a baptized person who, having at one time professed the faith, publicly rejects it. It is distinguished from heresy, which is limited to the rejection of one or more Christian doctrines by one who maintains an overall adherence to Jesus Christ. A celebrated controversy in the early church concerned the question of sanctions against those who had fallen away from the church during persecution and had then returned when Christians were no longer being persecuted.

Some early Christian emperors added civil sanctions to ecclesiastical laws regarding apostates. Certain church theologians of the 4th and 5th centuries considered apostasy to be as serious a sin as adultery and murder. In the 20th century, the Roman Catholic Code of Canon Law still imposed the sanction of excommunication reserved to the Holy See for those whose rejection of the faith fitted the technical definition of apostasy. The absence of civil sanctions, increasing tolerance of divergent viewpoints, and the various changes affecting the cultural context of religious practice have tended increasingly to mitigate the reaction of believers to those who reject Christianity.

The term has also been used to refer to those who have abandoned the monastic and clerical states without permission.

Apostle (from Greek *apostolos,* "person sent"), any of the 12 disciples chosen by Jesus Christ; the term is sometimes also applied to others. In Luke 6:13 it is stated that Jesus chose 12 from his disciples "whom he named apostles," and in Mark 6:30 the Twelve are called Apostles when mention is made of their return from the mission of preaching and healing on which Jesus had sent them. The full list of the Twelve is given with some variation in Mark 3, Matt. 10, and Luke 6: Peter; James and John, the sons of Zebedee; Andrew; Philip; Bartholomew; Matthew; Thomas; James, the son of Alphaeus; Thaddaeus or Judas, the son of James; Simon the Cananaean, or the Zealot; and Judas Iscariot.

The privileges of the Twelve were to be in continual attendance on their master and to be the recipients of his special teaching and training. At least once they were sent on a special mission, two by two, to announce the imminence of the messianic Kingdom (Mark 6: *cf.* Matt. 10; Luke 9). Three of them, Peter, James, and John, formed an inner circle who alone were permitted to witness such events as the raising of Jairus' daughter (Mark 5:37; Luke 8:51), the Transfiguration (Mark 9; Matt. 17; Luke 9), and the agony of Jesus in the Garden of Gethsemane (Mark 14:33; Matt. 26:37).

Special importance seems to have been attached to the number 12, which some scholars interpret as a reference to the 12 tribes of Israel. When a gap had been left by the defection and death of the traitor Judas Iscariot, immediate steps were taken to fill it by the election of Matthias (Acts 1). It is to members of this band of 12 that the word Apostle is usually applied in Acts.

Paul himself regularly claimed the title of Apostle, apparently on the ground that he had seen the Lord and received a commission directly from him. This appears to agree with the condition in Acts that a newly appointed Apostle should be capable of giving eyewitness testimony to the Lord's Resurrection. According to the works of some early Christian writers, however, some were called apostles after the period covered by the New Testament. The word also has been used to designate a high administrative or ecclesiastical officer.

Apostle Islands National Lakeshore, national lakeshore in northwestern Wisconsin, U.S., at the southwestern end of Lake Superior. Established in 1970, it consists of 20 islands and an 11-mi (18-km) strip of the adjacent Bayfield Peninsula, covering a total area of 42,009 ac (17,008 ha). The islands are noted for high cliffs of sandstone, most from 10 to 30 ft (3 to 9 m) in height but reaching extremes of 60 ft, with many wave-formed arches and caverns.

Apostle of the North: *see* Gilpin, Bernard.

apostle spoon, spoon for personal use at table, the handle of which is surmounted by a small figure of an apostle, a saint, or Jesus Christ. English silver examples, dating from at least mid-15th century to the end of the 17th century, were sometimes made in sets of 13, consisting of the Twelve Apostles and Christ.

Apostle spoon, 1504; in the Ashmolean Museum, Oxford
Ashmolean Museum, Oxford

In the 16th and 17th centuries apostle spoons seem to have been popular as christening presents. In the 20th century, silver-plated versions of the spoons were manufactured for use as demitasse spoons.

Apostles' Creed, also called APOSTOLICUM, a statement of faith used in the Roman Catholic, Anglican, and many Protestant churches. It is not officially recognized in the Eastern Orthodox churches. According to tradition, it was composed by the 12 Apostles, but it actually developed from early interrogations of catechumens (persons receiving instructions in order to be baptized) by the bishop. An example of such interrogations used in Rome *c.* 200 has been preserved in the *Apostolic Tradition* of Hippolytus. The bishop would ask, "Dost thou believe in God the Father almighty?" and so forth through the major Christian beliefs. Stated affirmatively, these statements became a creed; such creeds were known as baptismal creeds.

The present text of the Apostles' Creed is similar to the baptismal creed used in the church in Rome in the 3rd and 4th centuries. It reached its final form in southwestern France in the late 6th or early 7th century. Gradually it replaced other baptismal creeds and was acknowledged as the official statement of faith of the entire Catholic Church in the West by the time that Innocent III was pope (1198–1216).

The accepted Latin version reads as follows:

Credo in Deum Patrem omnipotentem; Creatorem caeli et terrae. Et in Jesum Christum, Filium ejus unicum, Dominum nostrum; qui conceptus est de Spiritu Sancto, natus ex Maria virgine; passus sub Pontio Pilato, crucifixus, mortuus, et sepultus; descendit ad inferna; tertia die resurrexit a mortuis; ascendit ad caelos; sedet ad dexteram Dei Patris omnipotentis; inde venturus (est) judicare vivos et mortuos. Credo in Spiritum Sanctum; sanctam ecclesiam catholicam; sanctorum communionem; remissionem peccatorum; carnis resurrectionem; vitam aeternam. Amen.

A modern English version (as used in the Roman Catholic Church) is the following:

I [We] believe in God, the Father almighty,
creator of heaven and earth.
I [We] believe in Jesus Christ, his only Son,
our Lord.
He was conceived by the power
of the Holy Spirit
and born of the Virgin Mary.
He suffered under Pontius Pilate,
was crucified, died, and was buried.
He descended to the dead.
On the third day he rose again.
He ascended into heaven,
and is seated at the right hand of the Father.
He will come again to judge the living and the dead.
I [We] believe in the Holy spirit,
the holy catholic Church,
the communion of saints,
the forgiveness of sins,
the resurrection of the body,
and the life everlasting. Amen.

Apostolic, Latin APOSTOLICUS, plural APOSTOLICI, member of any of the various Christian sects that sought to reestablish the life and discipline of the primitive church by a literal observance of the precepts of continence and poverty.

The earliest Apostolics (known also as Apotactici, meaning Abstinents) appeared in Asia Minor about the 3rd century. Extremely austere, they renounced property and marriage. In the 12th century certain groups of heretical itinerant preachers called Apostolics were found in various centres of France, Flanders, and the Rhineland. This movement seems to have developed from a dualistic heretical current that entered Italy and France from the East during the 11th century. The wealth and worldliness of the Western Church at that time encouraged its growth. These groups condemned marriage, the eating of meat, and infant Baptism; and they harshly criticized the church and denied priestly power.

About 1260 a religious sect known as the Apostolic Brethren was founded at Parma, Italy, by Gerard Segarelli, an uncultured workman, to restore what he considered the apostolic way of life. His emphasis on repentance and poverty reflected ideas propagated by Joachim of Fiore, a 12th-century mystic. In 1286 Pope Honorius IV ordered the eccentric sect to conform to an approved rule of life, and in 1290 Pope Nicholas IV issued a bull of condemnation; but the sect continued to spread. In 1294 four of the Apostolics were burned at the stake, and Segarelli met a similar fate in 1300. Thereafter, under the leadership of Fra Dolcino, the sect became openly heterodox and anticlerical. Its power was finally broken when Dolcino was burned as a heretic in 1307.

During the Protestant Reformation many of the doctrines of the various Apostolics were espoused by the Anabaptists.

Consult
the
INDEX
first

Apostolic Constitutions, formally ORDINANCES OF THE HOLY APOSTLES THROUGH CLEMENT, largest collection of ecclesiastical law that has survived from early Christianity. The full title indicates that these regulations were drawn up by the Apostles and transmitted to the church by Clement of Rome. In modern times it is generally accepted that the constitutions were actually written in Syria about AD 380 and that they were the work of one compiler, probably an Arian (one who believes that Christ, the Son of God, is not divine, but a created being).

The work consists of eight books. The first six are an adaptation of the *Didascalia Apostolorum,* written in Syria *c.* AD 250. They deal with Christian ethics, the duties of the clergy, the eucharistic liturgy, and various church problems and rituals.

Book 7 contains a paraphrase and enlargement of the *Didachē* (*Teaching of the Twelve Apostles*) and a Jewish collection of prayers and liturgical material, which includes the *Gloria in excelsis* as the liturgical morning prayer.

In book 8, the first two chapters seem to be based on a lost work of Hippolytus of Rome, *Concerning Spiritual Gifts.* Chapters 3–22 apparently are based on Hippolytus' *Apostolic Tradition* (formerly called *Egyptian Church Order*) and contain an elaborate description of the Antiochene liturgy, including the so-called Clementine liturgy. This is a valuable source for the history of the mass.

Chapters 28–46 of book 8 contain a series of canons, and chapter 47 comprises the so-called *Apostolic Canons,* a collection of 85 canons derived in part from the preceding constitutions and in part from the canons of the councils of Antioch (341) and Laodicaea (*c.* 360). It includes a list of biblical books that omits the Revelation to John but places the *Apostolic Constitutions* and the two letters of Clement in the canon of Scripture.

apostolic delegate, Vatican representative with no diplomatic status and hence no power to deal with civil governments. His relations are with the ecclesiastical hierarchy of a country that maintains no diplomatic relations with the Holy See. An apostolic delegate is not allowed to interfere with the exercise of the local bishops' authority in their own jurisdictions. He concerns himself with church conditions in a region, gathering and channelling all relevant information to and from the Holy See.

Apostolic Father, any of the Greek Christian writers, several unknown, who were authors of early Christian works dating primarily from the late 1st and early 2nd centuries. Their works are the principal source for information about Christianity during the two or three generations following the Apostles. They were originally called apostolic men (Apostolici). The name Apostolic Fathers was first applied in the 6th century, after the conception of the authority of the Fathers had been developed. The name did not come into common use, however, until the 17th century.

These writers include Clement of Rome, Ignatius, Polycarp, Hermas, Barnabas, Papias, and the authors of the *Didachē* (*Teaching of the Twelve Apostles*), *Letter to Diognetus, Letter of Barnabas,* and the *Martyrdom of Polycarp.* Not everything written by them is considered to be equally valuable theologically, but taken as a whole the writings of the Apostolic Fathers are more valuable historically than any other Christian literature outside the New Testament. They provide a bridge between it and the more fully developed Christianity of the late 2nd century.

Apostolic Overcoming Holy Church of God, black Pentecostal church founded in 1919 as the Ethiopian Overcoming Holy Church of God by Bishop W.T. Phillips in Mobile, Ala. The name was changed in 1927. The founder left the Methodist Episcopal Church, which he served as a minister, after becoming concerned about the doctrine of holiness and the process of sanctification.

Worship services are spontaneous and emotional and include foot washing, divine healing, ecstatic dancing, and speaking in tongues. Headquarters of the church are in Mobile.

apostolic succession, in Christianity, the doctrine that bishops represent a direct, uninterrupted line of descent from the Apostles of Jesus Christ. According to this doctrine, bishops possess certain special powers handed down to them from the Apostles; these consist primarily of the right to confirm church members, to ordain priests, to consecrate other bishops, and to rule over the clergy and church members in their diocese (an area made up of several congregations).

The origins of the doctrine are obscure, and the New Testament records are variously interpreted. Those who accept apostolic succession as necessary for a valid ministry argue that it was necessary for Christ to establish a ministry to carry out his work and that he commissioned his Apostles to do this (Matt. 28:19–20). The Apostles in turn consecrated others to assist them and to carry on the work. Supporters of the doctrine also argue that evidence indicates that the doctrine was accepted in the very early church. About AD 95 Clement, bishop of Rome, in his letter to the church in Corinth (*First Letter of Clement*), expressed the view that bishops succeeded the Apostles.

A number of Christian churches believe that the apostolic succession and church government based on bishops are unnecessary for a valid ministry. They argue that the New Testament gives no clear direction concerning the ministry, that various types of ministers existed in the early church, that the apostolic succession cannot be established historically, and that true succession is spiritual and doctrinal rather than ritualistic.

Roman Catholic, Eastern Orthodox, Old Catholic, Swedish Lutheran, and some other Christian churches accept the doctrine of apostolic succession and believe that the only valid ministry is based on bishops whose office has descended from the Apostles. This does not mean, however, that each of these groups necessarily accepts the ministries of the other groups as valid. Roman Catholics, for example, generally regard the ministry of the Eastern Orthodox churches as valid but do not accept the Anglican ministry. The Anglicans, on the other hand, consider episcopacy necessary to the "well-being" but not to the "being" of the church; therefore, they not only accept the ministries of the other groups as valid but also have entered into close associations with Protestant groups that do not accept apostolic succession.

Apostolicum: *see* Apostles' Creed.

apostome, any protozoan of the small, holotrichous order Apostomatida (fewer than 50 species). These organisms have minute hairlike projections (cilia) and are parasitic on marine crustaceans. The life cycle is complex. Members of the genus *Foettingeria* multiply by fission, after which immature swimming forms called larvae, or tomites, develop, attach to crustaceans, form cysts, and develop within them. Apostomes have a small, rosette-like cytostome (mouth).

apothecaries' weight, traditional European system of weight used for the measuring and dispensing of drugs and based on the grain, scruple (20 grains), dram (3 scruples), ounce (8 drams), and pound (12 ounces). The apothecaries' grain is equal to the troy and avoirdupois grains and represents $\frac{1}{5,760}$ part of the troy and apothecaries' pound and $\frac{1}{7,000}$ part of the avoirdupois pound. One apothecaries' pound equals approximately 0.82 avoirdupois pound and 0.37 kilogram.

Apothecaries' weight was used officially in both the United States and Great Britain until 1858. In that year, under the authority of the Medical Act, Great Britain adopted the avoirdupois system for dispensing medicines. Apothecaries' weight is still common in the United States. In recent years, however, the metric system has gained in use for dispensing medicines.

apothecium (fungi): *see* ascocarp.

apotheosis, elevation to the status of a god. The term (from Greek *apotheoun,* "to make a god," "to deify") implies a polytheistic conception of gods while it recognizes that some individuals cross the dividing line between gods and men.

The ancient Greek religion was especially disposed to belief in heroes and demigods. Worship after death of historical persons or worship of the living as true deities occurred sporadically even before the conquests of Alexander the Great brought Greek life into contact with Oriental traditions. Ancient monarchies often enlisted polytheistic conceptions of divine or semidivine individuals in support of the dynasties. Ancestor worship, or reverence for the dead, was another factor, as was also mere flattery.

The corresponding Latin term is *consecratio.* The Romans, up to the end of the republic, had accepted only one official apotheosis, the god Quirinus having been identified with Romulus. The emperor Augustus, however, broke this tradition and had Julius Caesar recognized as a god; Julius Caesar thus became the first of a new class of deities proper. The tradition established by Augustus was steadily followed and was extended to some women of the imperial family and even to imperial favourites. Worship of an emperor during his lifetime, except as the worship of his genius, was in general confined to the provinces. Apotheosis, after his death, being in the hands of the Senate, did not at once cease, even when Christianity was officially adopted. The most significant part of the ceremonies attendant on an imperial apotheosis was the liberation of an eagle, which was supposed to bear the emperor's soul to heaven.

apotropaic eye, a painting of an eye or eyes used as a symbol to ward off evil, appearing most commonly on Greek black-figured drinking vessels called kylikes ("eye cups"), from the 6th century BC; the exaggeratedly large eye on these cups may have been thought to prevent dangerous spirits from entering the mouth with the wine.

Chalcidian black-figured kylix decorated with apotropaic eyes, attributed to the Phineus Painter, *c.* 520 BC; in the Metropolitan Museum of Art, New York City
By courtesy of the Metropolitan Museum of Art, New York City, gift of F.W. Rhinelander, 1898

Appalachian Geosyncline, a linear trough in the Earth's crust in which rocks of Late Precambrian and Paleozoic age (from about 225,000,000 to 650,000,000 years ago) were deposited along the eastern coast of North America from Newfoundland in the north to Alabama in the south. The geosynclinal concept was first applied to this area. Originally, the Appalachian Geosyncline was believed to consist of the thick sequence of folded and faulted Paleozoic sedimentary rocks occupying what is today the Ridge and Valley Province of Alabama northward to New York, but it is now extended eastward to include the metamorphic and intrusive igneous complexes, also predominantly of Paleozoic age, to the east and southeast of the sedimentary belt. These complexes represent a deepwater portion of the whole, a eugeosyncline. The northern end of the Appalachian Geosyncline may have been continuous with the southwestern end of the Caledonian Geosyncline in the British Isles; the southern end of the Appalachian Geosyncline either intersects, crosscuts, or overrides the southeastern end of the Ouachita Geosyncline beneath the undisturbed Cretaceous and Cenozoic sediments (younger than 136,000,000 years) of the Mississippi Embayment. Numerous orogenic (mountain-building) episodes are recorded by the rocks of the geosyncline, the most prominent being the Avalonian, Taconic, Acadian, and Alleghenian. Final deformation of the geosyncline occurred during the Alleghenian orogeny, although several of the earlier orogenies (Taconic and Acadian) had a more profound effect in the interior parts of the Appalachian Geosyncline.

Appalachian Highlands, the regions of the Appalachian Plateau, Ridge and Valley, Blue Ridge, and Piedmont (*qq.v.*) in the eastern United States.

Appalachian Mountains, great highland system of eastern North America, extending for more than 1,200 mi (1,900 km) from the Gaspé Peninsula in the Canadian province of Quebec through the eastern United States southward to central Alabama. They form a natural barrier between the eastern seaboard and the vast lowlands of the continental interior. As a result, they have played a vital role in the settlement and development of the entire continent.

The following article summarizes information about the Appalachian Mountains; for full details, *see* MACROPAEDIA: North America.

The system may be divided into three large regions: northern, central, and southern Appalachia. In the northern area these include such mountains as the Shickshocks and the Notre Dame ranges in Quebec; the Long Range in Newfoundland; Katahdin in Maine; the White Mountains of New Hampshire; and Vermont's Green Mountains, which become the Berkshires in Massachusetts, Connecticut, and eastern New York. New York's Catskills and the beginnings of the Blue Ridge range in southern Pennsylvania and the Alleghenies of western Pennsylvania and Maryland and eastern Ohio are in central Appalachia. The southern region includes portions of the Alleghenies of West Virginia and Virginia, the Blue Ridge range of Virginia and western North Carolina, the Unakas (of which the Great Smoky Mountains are a part) near the Tennessee–North Carolina border, and the Cumberland Mountains, extending from eastern Kentucky south to northern Alabama. The highest altitudes in the Appalachians are found in the northern division in the White Mountains and in the southern region, where peaks of the North Carolina Black Mountains and the Great Smoky Mountains rise above 6,000 ft (1,800 m) and where the entire system reaches its highest summit on Mt. Mitchell (6,684 ft [2,037 m]). A distinctive feature of the mountain system is the Great Appalachian Valley. It includes the St. Lawrence Valley in Canada and the Kittatinny, Cumberland, Shenandoah, and Tennessee valleys. A non-commercial motor route stretches 469 mi from the Shenandoah Valley in Virginia to the Great Smoky Mountains National Park, and the Appalachian Trail is a 2,000-mi footpath.

The Appalachians are among the oldest mountains on Earth, consisting mostly of crystalline rocks and Paleozoic sediments. The entire Appalachian system is laced with an intricate network of springs, streams, waterfalls, and rivers, especially in the southern Appalachians. Generally, northeast of the New River in Virginia, the major Appalachian rivers flow into the Atlantic Ocean, while southwest of the New the rivers drain into the Ohio Valley. The most extensive broad-leaved deciduous forests in the world flourish particularly in southern Appalachia, and a mix of conifers and northern hardwoods predominate in the north. The western slopes of the Great Smokies receive an annual rainfall as high as 90 in., producing trees that have reached record maximum heights and diameters.

Important lumber and pulp industries, coal, iron, salt, granite, and marble industries operate in the region but have had some deleterious effects on the environment. Despite the early arrival of the lumber industry and coal mining, some areas remained isolated until early in the 20th century, notably those mountain areas of southern Appalachia where rough terrain hindered road construction. Consequently, Southern highlanders developed a distinctive culture characterized by handicrafts, ballads, and folklore. The Appalachians combine a heritage of natural beauty and a distinctive regional culture with contemporary problems of economic deprivation and environmental deterioration.

Appalachian Plateau, plateau in the northeastern U.S., extending from the Adirondacks in the north through New York, Pennsylvania, West Virginia, Ohio, Kentucky, Tennessee, and the Gulf Coastal Plain to Alabama in the south. Forming part of the Southwest Appalachians, it stretches into the Central Lowlands in the west and the Ridge and Valley region in the east. Rock layers in the plateau are nearly horizontal, and both anthracite and bituminous coal are extracted by drift mining. The Appalachian coalfields are the largest in the country and supply the steel industries in the northeast, including Pittsburgh. Other important minerals are iron ore, limestone, petroleum, and natural gas. The scenic landscape includes several national parks and forests. The Great Smoky Mountains National Park and other recreation areas attract several thousand visitors every year.

Appalachian Trail, mountain footpath for hikers extending from northeast to southwest over 2,034 mi (3,254 km), from Mt. Katahdin, Maine, U.S., to Springer Mountain, Georgia, along the crest of the Appalachian Mountains. The trail passes through 14 states, 8 national forests, and 2 national parks. Hikers are responsible for the upkeep of the primitive shelters and trail-side campsites, located 7 to 8 mi apart. The Appalachian Trail Conference (Harper's Ferry, W.Va.) coordinates group activities.

Appaloosa, colour breed of horse popular in the United States. The breed is said to have descended in the Nez Percé Indian territory of North America from wild mustangs, which in turn descended from Spanish horses brought in by explorers. The name derives from the Palouse River of Idaho and Washington. The Appaloosa has several distinctive colour patterns and all of the regular coat colours. Some Appaloosas have a solid colour except for a white patch over the hips, interspersed with small, round spots of the same colour as the body. Others have a basic solid colour with white dots over the entire body, or are white with coloured dots. They are 15 to 15.3 hands (about 60 to 63 inches, or 152 to 160 centimetres) tall and weigh from 1,000 to 1,100 pounds (450 to 500 kilograms). Appaloosas are of light but sturdy conformation and useful for many purposes. The Appaloosa Horse Club was organized in 1938.

Appaloosa
Sally Anne Thompson

appanage, in France, primarily before the Revolution, the provision of lands within the royal domain, or in some cases of pensions, to the children of the royal family so that they might live in a style corresponding to their position in society. Appanages were established to provide for the younger brothers and sisters of the king but were also given to an heir to the throne before his succession, at which time the land was reannexed to the crown. Appanages were most prevalent from the 13th to the 16th century.

Appanages raised certain problems for the crown, largely because of the personal relationship that existed between the holder and the king. At the same time, however, they afforded an opportunity for the growth and development of royal administration within the areas held by appanage, facilitating their ultimate reunion with the crown. After the 14th century, except in a few special instances, women ceased to receive land appanage but received pensions instead.

In 1566 the Ordinance of Moulins established the principle of the inalienability of the domain, although during the Wars of Religion of the next 30 years it was not always strictly adhered to. With the growth of the absolute power of the monarch during the 17th century, appanages ceased to be much of a problem. Early in the French Revolution (1790), appanages were reduced to pensions or rents and then completely abolished. They were reestablished in 1810 according to the provisions of 1790 and finally abolished in 1832.

äppäräs, in Lapp belief, the ghost of a dead child, haunting the place of its death because it had not received proper burial rites. The *äppäräs,* which is called *äpärä* in Finnish, is only one of several of the anomalous dead figures in Finno-Ugric mythology who serve as warnings for the living that they should observe the norms of the society or expect supernatural intervention. The *äppäräs* was most often thought of as the restless soul of an illegitimate child murdered by its mother. Other placeless or wandering dead, such as the Finnish *ihtiriekko* and the Ostyak *vylep* or *patshak,* often manifest themselves in apparitions or auditory experiences indicating the uneasiness of the people about the proper fate of their dead. The Lapp *rawga,* Finnish *raukka* or *meriraukka,* most likely from old Scandinavian *draugr,* are similar ghosts, in this case of people who perished at sea and thus received no proper burial.

apparel industry: *see* clothing and footwear industry.

apparition, in occultism, the perception of a disembodied person, living or dead, or, more rarely, perception of a phantomlike animal or inanimate object. Sometimes all, sometimes only one or more, of those present see the apparition. Apparitions are most often associated with an urgent message, sometimes veiled, of impending danger or death. The degree to which apparitions are merely subjective experiences is still disputed, and modern researchers tend to classify them as hallucinations. Although the term is generally thought of as referring to visual images, apparitions may also take the form of sounds, odours, or tactile sensations.

appeal, the resort to a higher court to review the decision of a lower court, or to any court to review the order of an administrative agency. Every legal system provides, at least in form, for some type of appeal.

The concept of appeal requires the existence of a judicial hierarchy, although it is possible for a court to review its own judgments. A typical hierarchy will include trial courts of limited or special jurisdiction, often called magistrates' courts, justices of the peace, small-claims courts, municipal courts, police courts; trial courts of general jurisdiction that usually carry the name of district court, circuit court, or superior court; and a court of appellate jurisdiction, which may be the ultimate supreme court of a system. Some countries introduce an intermediate appellate court, called the court of appeals, between the trial court level and the court of ultimate appeal.

Usually, each court in the hierarchy is subject to review only by the court immediately above it. Frequently, however, an intermediate step may be omitted because the importance or immediacy of the problem calls for direct review of the trial court by the highest appellate tribunal.

In some countries different courts serve as the highest appeals court according to the types of cases and judicial problems. In France the Cour de Cassation (*q.v.*; the supreme court) hears appeals on the interpretation of the law, whereas the court of appeal retries cases on the issue of fact. The Conseil d'État (*q.v.*), on the other hand, hears appeals both on facts and on the interpretation of law from a separate system of administrative courts. Constitutional questions, when dealt with at all, are handled by a constitutional council that is both legislative and judicial.

In West Germany the Bundesgerichtshof (Federal Court of Justice) is concerned primarily with a unified interpretation of the law, and there is a separate constitutional court (Bundesverfassungsgericht) to deal with constitutional questions. The court of appeals (Oberlandesgericht) retries cases both on issues of law and of fact in civil matters, and on issues of law only in criminal matters. The Supreme Court of the United States (*q.v.*) hears appeals on fact, interpretation, and constitutional cases, but except for cases that have an important effect on the public interest, appeal stops with the Federal Circuit Court of Appeals. In England appeals on matters of fact in some instances go to different courts than do those on matters of law. In some cases, appeals to the House of Lords, the final court of appeal, are prohibited. The Supreme Court of Japan (*q.v.*) serves as final-appeals court on questions of fact and law and on constitutional compatibility.

As a practical as well as a legal matter, only the party aggrieved by an order or judgment is entitled to seek a review of it in the appellate court. Neither an outsider nor the party who had prevailed in the case is permitted to seek a review of the decision by a higher court. When, however, persons not originally parties to the action have been permitted to intervene or have been represented by others, as in class actions, they generally have the same rights of appeal as have the original parties. There are few jurisdictions in which an appeal on a verdict of acquittal is allowed.

Orders and judgments of trial courts may be divided into two categories for the purposes of appeal: final and interlocutory. A final judgment is one that brings an end to litigation and leaves nothing but the execution of the judgment. In the course of a trial, however, a court is required to enter decisions that settle only subsidiary questions or some but not all of the ultimate issues. These decisions are regarded as interlocutory decrees. Although all jurisdictions sanction appeals from final judgments, appeals from interlocutory decrees are far less widespread.

Basically, the appeal serves two functions. Its first and primary function is to assure the litigants that justice under law has been done in the resolution of a specific controversy. The second function is the promulgation of rules of decision that will be binding on all lower courts within a judicial system, thus assuring uniformity of treatment and some measure of certainty and guidance to those whose actions bring them within the ambit of the rule.

Appeal, Court of, in England and Wales, the highest court below the House of Lords, which sits as the final court of appeal in both criminal and civil matters.

The court is divided into two divisions: the Civil Division and the Criminal Division. The Civil Division takes cases on appeal from the High Court of Justice and the county courts. Four members of its judiciary are considered ex officio: the lord chancellor (who is head of the Chancery Division of the High Court), the lord chief justice (who presides over the Queen's [or King's] Bench Division of the High Court), the president of the Family Divison of the High Court, and the master of rolls. There are also 14 regular members who are called the lord justices of appeal.

The Criminal Division consists of a president (either the lord chief justice or a lord justice of appeal) and other High Court judges hearing the cases as "ordinary" members. Appeals may come from the High Court immediately below or from the Crown Court.

Appeals against a sentence of conviction may be brought on a point of law. Occasionally, with the permission of either the trial judge or the Court of Appeal, a question of fact may be entered, or a question of *both* fact and law may be permitted as the basis for an appeal.

The Court of Appeal may uphold the decision of the lower court; it may reverse it; or it may change the sentence. (However, the new sentence may not be more severe than the original.) Although the court rarely orders a retrial, it may do so in the interests of justice. The Court of Appeal may also act as an advisory body for the attorney general.

If the House of Lords refuses to hear an appeal from a decision of the Court of Appeal, that decision is final.

appearance, in philosophy, what seems to be (*i.e.,* things as they are for human experience), without necessarily implying any opposition between the appearance of a thing and objective reality.

Numerous philosophical systems, in one way or another, have posited that the world as it appears is not the world of reality. The cosmologies that predominated in Asia Minor in the 6th century BC, for example, distinguished between sensible appearance and a reality accessible only to reason. In the Advaita Vedānta school of Indian philosophy, particularly as expounded by Śaṅkara (700?–750?), the finite phenomenal world is regarded as an illusory appearance (*maya*) of the one eternal unchanging reality (Brahman). In the modern West, Immanuel Kant created the term noumenon (*q.v.*) to signify unknowable reality, which he distinguished from phenomenon (*q.v.*), the appearance of reality.

By contrast, for the Empiricists, whose philosophical tradition extends back to the Sophists of ancient Greece, data apprehensible by the senses not only partake of the truth but constitute the sole measure by which the validity of any belief or concept may be judged.

Appel, Karel (b. April 25, 1921, Amsterdam), Dutch painter of turbulent, colourful, semi-abstract compositions, a cofounder (1948–49) of the Cobra group of northern European Expressionists. He attended the Royal Academy of Fine Arts, Amsterdam (1940–43), and helped found the "Reflex" group, the Dutch precursor of Cobra, in 1948. He moved to Paris in 1950 and, finally, by the 1960s, had settled in New York City.

Partly in reaction against what they perceived as the sterile academicism of the de Stijl movement, the Cobra artists assimilated a variety of more impulsive influences, including folk art, children's art, and *l'art brut* ("raw art") of Jean Dubuffet. They exploited the spontaneity and intensity of the contemporary American Action painting while maintaining a degree of representation. Appel's style is characterized by thick layering of pigment, violent brushwork, and a crude, reductive figuration.

He first visited the United States in 1957, where he painted portraits of prominent jazz musicians, including Miles Davis and Dizzy Gillespie. His public works include a mural in the UNESCO building in Paris. His figurative sculptures in wood and metal share with the paintings a brutal, imaginative expressionism.

appendicitis, inflammation of the vermiform appendix. The appendix is a tube of which one end is closed and the other opens into the cecum, the pouchlike beginning of the large intestine. The appendix has muscular walls, ordinarily capable of expelling into the cecum the mucous secretions of the appendiceal walls or any of the intestinal contents that have worked their way into the structure. If anything blocks the opening—the most common obstruction is a fecalith, a stone that has formed from digestive wastes—the continued secretion and the work of bacteria within the organ build up pressure. Fluid collects in the walls of the appendix. Pressure on the blood vessels may close them off, causing necrosis (death) of appendiceal tissue. The walls of the appendix, weakened by the distension and the necrosis, may burst, spilling their contents into the abdominal cavity and infecting and inflaming the membranes that line the cavity and cover the abdominal organs (*see* peritonitis).

A person experiencing an attack of appendicitis may feel abdominal pain and tenderness, particularly around the navel and, later, in the right lower region of the abdomen; he may feel nauseated and vomit or have diarrhea. Fever is usually slight unless the appendix has burst. Appendicitis is treated by prompt surgical removal of the appendix.

appendicularian, also called LARVACEAN, any member of the class Larvacea—tiny transparent pelagic (living in the open sea) forms of the invertebrate subphylum Urochordata, or Tunicata. They occur in all oceans and are most common to depths of 100 metres (about 300 feet). The U-shaped body consists of a trunk and tail. The body covering secretes a structure larger than the body, and the animal can move freely within it.

appendix (anatomy): *see* vermiform appendix.

Appendix on the Papacy (1537): *see* Treatise on the Power and Primacy of the Pope.

Appenzell, canton, northeastern Switzerland, consisting of two autonomous half cantons. Appenzell is entirely surrounded by present-day Sankt Gallen canton. It was first mentioned by name in 1071 as Abbatis Cella, in reference to its rulers, the abbots (later prince abbots) of Sankt Gallen. As early as 1377, however, this portion of the abbots' domains formed an alliance with the Swabian free imperial cities and adopted a constitution of its own. The region defended itself against the abbots in the Appenzell War of 1403–10 and in 1411 was placed under the "protection" of the Swiss Confederation, of which it became a member in 1513. Religious differences after the Counter-Reformation led to the division of the canton in 1597 into the independent half cantons of Appenzell Inner-Rhoden (predominantly Roman Catholic) and Appenzell Ausser-Rhoden (predominantly Protestant). These names refer simply to the inner or outer portions, or districts, of Appenzell itself; *Rhoden* in its singular form is said originally to have meant a clearing.

Appenzell, capital of the half canton of Appenzell Inner-Rhoden, northeastern Switzerland, in the Sitter Valley, south of Sankt Gallen. Originally a possession of the abbey of Sankt Gallen, it was the traditional capital of the Appenzell region and became the capital of Inner-Rhoden after the canton was divided in 1597. Notable landmarks include an ancient chapel of the abbots of Sankt Gallen, whose summer residence was in the town; a modern church with a late Gothic choir; the town hall (1561–63); the 16th-century castle housing a historical museum; and two Capuchin convents, one for men (founded 1588) and one for women (founded 1613). Two important annual events are the Corpus Christi procession and the meeting of the Landsgemeinde (or open-air cantonal "parliament"—actually a cantonal legislative meeting of all concerned citizens, a nearly unique manifestation of "pure democracy"). Pastoral occupations, embroidery, and the manufacture of textiles and furniture are the principal economic activities. The population is German speaking and Roman Catholic. Pop. (1980) 4,781.

Appenzell Ausser-Rhoden (German), French APPENZELL RHODES-EXTÉRIEURES, English APPENZELL OUTER RHODES, half canton, comprising the northern and western parts of former Appenzell canton, northeastern Switzerland. It has an area of 94 sq mi (243 sq km) and was divided for religious reasons from Appenzell Inner-Rhoden half canton in 1597. Its constitution dates from 1908, and its capital and largest town is Herisau (*q.v.*), although the Landsgemeinde (open-air general legislative meeting) meets alternately at nearby Hundwil and at Trogen. Cotton goods, muslins, and embroideries are manufactured. The population is German speaking and predominantly Protestant. Pop. (1983 est.) 48,364.

Appenzell Inner-Rhoden (German), French APPENZELL RHODES-INTÉRIEURES, English APPENZELL INNER RHODES, half canton, comprising the southern part of former Appenzell canton, northeastern Switzerland, at the north foot of the Säntis Peak. It has an area of 67 sq mi (172 sq km) and was divided from Appenzell Ausser-Rhoden half canton in 1597 for religious reasons. Its constitution dates from 1872, and its capital is Appenzell (*q.v.*). Although mountainous, the canton is largely pastoral with extensive cattle breeding and dairying. Hand embroidery is also important. The population is German speaking and almost entirely Roman Catholic. Pop. (1983 est.) 12,940.

Appert, Nicolas (-François) (b. *c.* 1750, Châlons-sur-Marne, Fr.—d. June 3, 1841, Massy, near Paris), French chef, confectioner, and distiller who invented the method of preserving food by enclosing it in hermetically sealed containers. Inspired by the French Directory's offer of a prize for a way to conserve food for transport, Appert began a 14-year period of experimentation in 1795. Using

Appert, lithograph by Guffanli
H. Roger-Viollet

corked-glass containers reinforced with wire and sealing wax and kept in boiling water for varying lengths of time, he preserved soups, fruits, vegetables, juices, dairy products, marmalades, jellies, and syrups. A 12,000-franc award in 1810 specified that he publish his findings, which appeared that year as *L'Art de conserver, pendant plusieurs années, toutes les substances animales et végétales* (*The Art of Preserving All Kinds of Animal and Vegetable Substances for Several Years,* 1811). He used the money to establish the first commercial cannery, the House of Appert, at Massy, which operated from 1812 until 1933. Appert also developed the bouillon tablet, devised a nonacid gelatin extraction method, and perfected an autoclave.

appetite, a person's cultural preference for food, which may or may not be associated with hunger. The desire to eat steak and potatoes, for example, rather than fish and rice depends on habits of eating and on cultural indoctrinations. Foods having the same nutritional value and equally satisfying the desire to eat are commonly selected for their smell, flavour, appearance, and appeal. A person may be totally filled with food from a meal and still have an appetite for dessert. The appetite may be increased or diminished depending on pleasant or unpleasant experiences associated with certain foods.

"Specific hunger," on the other hand, is the choice of food to satisfy bodily deficiencies. Animals deprived of calcium, for example, select foods containing a high calcium content over those with a lesser amount, when given several choices. Animals whose adrenal glands have been surgically removed and who therefore suffer from a lack of sodium will drink water containing salt, in preference to plain water, to replenish deficient sodium. The taste receptors in the tongue may be important in regulating the urge for a specific hunger. If these receptors are destroyed, an animal lacking sodium ceases to prefer salty water.

appetizer, food eaten to pique the appetite or to moderate the hunger stimulated by drink. Cocktails, especially apéritifs, the characteristic "dryness" of which stimulates the appetite, are customarily served with appetizers. Hors d'oeuvres, small portions of savoury foods, often highly seasoned, and canapés, small pieces of bread, crackers, or croutons with various toppings, are the classic appetizer categories.

The Scandinavian smorgasbord, Spanish *tapas*, Greek *meze*, Egyptian *mazza*, and Russian *zakuska* are all elaborate appetizer displays offering many dishes, with traditional beverage counterpoints, *e.g.*, vodka or sherry. Many cuisines offer a mixed hors d'oeuvre, of which the Italian antipasto may be the best known, made up of such foods as olives, nuts, cheese, sausage, peppers, fish, raw vegetables, and eggs. *Crudités* are raw or barely cooked vegetables, often served with a dip or sauce.

Because appetizers are intended to be provocative, they enable the diner to enjoy foods that are too pronounced in taste or too rich to be eaten in larger quantities.

Apphus: *see* Maccabeus, Jonathan.

Appia, Adolphe (b. Sept. 1, 1862, Geneva—d. Feb. 29, 1928, Nyon, Switz.), stage designer whose theories, especially on the interpretive use of lighting, opened the way internationally for a new realism and creativity in 20th-century theatre.

Although his early training was in music, Appia studied theatre in Dresden and Vienna from the age of 26. In 1891 he propounded his revolutionary theories of theatrical production. Four years later he published *La Mise en scène du drame Wagnérien* (1895; "The Staging of the Wagnerian Drama"), a collection of stage and lighting plans for 18 of Wagner's operas that clarified the function of stage lighting and enumerated in detail practical suggestions for the application of his theories. In *Die Musik und die Inszenierung* (1899; "Music and Staging"), Appia established a hierarchy of ideas for achieving his aims: (1) a three-dimensional setting rather than a flat, dead, painted backdrop as a proper background to display the movement of the living actors; (2) lighting that unifies actors and setting into an artistic whole, evoking an emotional response from the audience; (3) the interpretive value of mobile and colourful lighting, as a visual counterpart of the music; and (4) lighting that spotlights the actors and highlights areas of action. He expanded his theories in a second book, *L'Oeuvre d'art vivant* (1921; "The Living Work of Art").

Appia designed sets in Germany, France, Italy, and Switzerland. He collaborated with Émile Jaques-Dalcroze on numerous experimental theatre and dance productions. He also designed sets for La Scala opera house in Milan and for the opera house at Basel.

A topical profile of Appia's work, Walther Volbach's *Adolphe Appia, Prophet of the Modern Theatre* (1968), also gives a clear account of the designer's life.

Appian OF ALEXANDRIA (fl. 2nd century AD), Greek historian of the conquests by Rome from the republican period into the 2nd century AD. He held public office in Alexandria, where he witnessed the Jewish insurrection in AD 116. After gaining Roman citizenship he went to Rome, practiced as a lawyer, and at an advanced age became a procurator.

In addition to a lost autobiography, Appian wrote in Greek a *Romaica,* or history of Rome, in 24 books, arranged ethnographically according to the peoples (and their rulers) conquered by the Romans. The books that survive in complete form deal with Spain, Carthage, Illyria, Syria, Hannibal, Mithradates, and the civil wars from the Gracchi onward. Extracts from other books survive in Byzantine compilations and elsewhere.

Appian wrote in a Greek that was no longer classical. Not himself an able historian, he nevertheless preserved much information of value by his transmission of earlier sources. His first book on the civil wars, dealing with the period from Tiberius Gracchus (tribune 133 BC) to Sulla (died 78 BC), is a major historical source.

Appius (ancient Roman personal name, or praenomen): *see under* gens or family name or honorific (*e.g.,* under Claudius for Appius Claudius Caecus).

apple, fruit of the genus *Malus* (about 25 species) belonging to the family Rosaceae, the most widely cultivated tree fruit. The apple is one of the pome (fleshy) fruits, in which the ripened ovary and surrounding tissue both become fleshy and edible. The apple flower of most varieties requires cross-pollination for fertilization and a desirable fruit set by 2 to 4 percent of the bloom. Apples at harvest, though varying widely in size, shape, colour, and acidity, depending upon cultures (variety) and environmental character, are, nevertheless, usually roundish, 50–100 millimetres (2–4 inches) in diameter, and some shade of red or yellow in colour.

Apples (*Malus*)
Grant Heilman—EB Inc.

Apple varieties, of which there are thousands, fall into three broad classes: (1) cider varieties; (2) cooking varieties; and (3) dessert varieties, which differ widely but tend to emphasize colour, size, aroma, smoothness, and perhaps crispness and tang. Many are relatively high in sugar, only mildly acidic, and very low in tannin. The apple is eaten fresh and cooked in a variety of ways. It is frequently used as a pastry filling, the apple pie being perhaps the archetypal American dessert. Especially in Europe, fried apples characteristically accompany certain dishes of sausage or pork.

Malus species are native to the temperate zones of both hemispheres. Apples were eaten by the earliest Europeans; improved selections had been made and varieties were recognized more than 2,000 years ago. Hundreds of varieties were recognized in Europe before the settlement of the Americas. As the wave of settlement moved across North America, it was accompanied by the distribution of seedling apple varieties, perhaps by Indians and trappers, certainly by itinerants who became local legendary figures, the most prominent being Johnny Appleseed (John Chapman), a professional nurseryman who planted extensively in Ohio and Indiana.

Since the apple requires a considerable period of dormancy, it thrives in areas having a distinct winter period, generally from latitude 30° to 60°, both north and south. Northward, culture is limited by low winter temperatures and a short growing season.

Soils must be well drained; fertilizers can be used if fertility is not high enough. Rolling hilltops or the sloping sides of hills are preferred because they provide "air drainage," allowing the colder, heavier air to drain away to the valley below during frosty spring nights, when blossoms or young fruit would be destroyed by much exposure to cold.

Scions of desired varieties are commonly grafted to hardy nursery seedlings of about 18 months of age; orchard planting follows one or two years later. Management during the six to eight years before appreciable production is reached may consist of little more than protection from competing vegetation and pests. Careful attention to pruning is required, however, especially during the first five years, so that the main scaffold branches will be well distributed along the trunk and so that weak crotches will not develop to break under heavy fruit loads. With mature trees, a rigorous spraying regime must be followed to protect against insect pests and possibly to delay spring development, to thin young fruit, and to hold the autumn drop of ripening fruit to a minimum.

Apple varieties that ripen during late summer are generally of poor quality for storage. Varieties that ripen in late autumn may be stored for as long as one year for the best keeping sorts handled by the best methods. For long holding, temperatures only slightly above the freezing point of the fruit are generally desirable. Apples may also be stored in inert gases or in controlled atmospheres.

The world crop of apples averages about 16,000,000 metric tons a year. Of the U.S. crop, more than half is normally used as fresh fruit. About one-fifth is used for vinegar, juice, jelly, and apple butter. About one-sixth is canned as pie stock and applesauce. In Europe a larger fraction of the crop goes for cider, wine, and brandy. Of the total world production, one-fourth goes for cider.

The U.S. produces more than 3,250,000 tons per year. Italy produces about 2,000,000 tons; France and West Germany about 1,650,000. Central Europe, including Switzerland and the northern Balkan countries, is an area of heavy production. Japan and North and South Korea are big producers but not exporters. Australia, New Zealand, Argentina, and Chile are also important producers of apples.

Apples provide vitamins A and C, are high in carbohydrates, and are an excellent source of dietary fibre.

apple moss (*Bartramia pomiformis*), member of the order Bryales that has apple-shaped capsules (spore cases) and forms wide, deep cushions in moist, rocky woods throughout the Northern Hemisphere. It is one of more than 100 species in the genus *Bartramia;* more than 10 are found in North America. An apple moss is usually erect, with a two-forked caulid (stem) about 6 centimetres (about 2¼ inches) tall, with rust-coloured, feltlike hairs on its lower part. The top half of each phyllid (leaf) is serrated.

Appleseed, Johnny: *see* Chapman, John.

Appleton, city, seat (1851) of Outagamie County, east central Wisconsin, U.S., on the Fox River near its outflow from Lake Winnebago, 31 mi (48 km) southwest of Green Bay. Settlement of the area was encouraged by the presence of Lawrence College (chartered 1847, now a university), founded by Amos A. Lawrence of Boston, and of abundant waterpower. First called Grand Chute, it was later renamed for Samuel Appleton, Lawrence's father-in-law. Milling dominated Appleton's early economy. In 1882 America's first hydroelectric power station was opened there. Foremost among the city's diversified manufactures are paper and paper-mill machinery and equipment. The Institute of Paper Chemistry (1929), affiliated with the university, has a notable library on pulp and paper as well as the Dard Hunter Paper Museum. Fox Valley Technical Institute (1967) is in Appleton. Inc. 1857. Pop. (1980) city, 59,032; metropolitan area (SMSA) 291,325.

Appleton, Sir Edward Victor (b. Sept. 6, 1892, Bradford, Yorkshire, Eng.—d. April 21, 1965, Edinburgh), winner of the Nobel Prize for Physics in 1947 for his discovery of the so-called Appleton layer of the ionosphere, which is a dependable reflector of radio waves and as such is useful in communication. Other ionospheric layers reflect radio waves sporadically, depending upon temperature and time of day.

Educated at St. John's College, Cambridge, Appleton worked at the Cavendish Laboratory from 1920 until he was appointed Wheatstone professor of physics at King's College, University of London, in 1924. There Appleton attained an international reputation with his research into the propagation of electromagnetic waves and the characteristics of the ionosphere. He showed that radio waves of wavelength sufficiently short to penetrate the lower region of the ionosphere are reflected by an upper region (now known as the Appleton layer, or F region). This discovery made possible more reliable long-range radio communication and aided in the development of radar.

In 1936 Appleton returned to Cambridge as Jacksonian Professor of Natural Philosophy and in 1939 became secretary of the government's Department of Scientific and Industrial Research, where he worked on radar and the atomic bomb during World War II. He was knighted in 1941 and became principal and vice chancellor of Edinburgh University in 1949.

Appleton layer, upper layer (called F_2) of the F region (*q.v.*) of the ionosphere.

appliance, home: *see* home appliance.

application lace, French POINT APPLIQUÉ, lace in which motifs (flowers and the like) are worked individually and then joined to a net background (whether made by machine or hand), in contrast to the method in which the net is worked round the solid parts of the design and the whole lace worked as a single piece without joins. In the 19th century it was made especially at Brussels and, in England, at Honiton. The method shortened the time required for production by employing a team of women, each a specialist in a certain procedure, simultaneously on the same piece of lace.

Application lace from Brussels, 1880; in the Institut Royal du Patrimoine Artistique, Brussels

By courtesy of the Institut Royal du Patrimoine Artistique, Brussels; photograph, © A.C.L., Brussels

applied psychology, the use of the findings and methods of scientific psychology in solving practical problems of human and animal behaviour and experience. A more precise definition is impossible because the activities of applied psychology range from laboratory experimentation through field studies of specific utility to direct services to troubled persons.

The same intellectual streams whose confluence produced psychology as an independent subject in the latter part of the 19th century led to the later development of an applied psychology. Francis Galton's publication in 1883 of *Inquiries Into Human Faculty* foreshadowed the measurement of individual differences. In 1896 Lightner Witmer established at the University of Pennsylvania, Philadelphia, a clinic that was a forerunner of clinical psychology. Intelligence testing began with the work of Alfred Binet and Théodore Simon in the Paris schools. Also in France, in 1905, M. Lahy was studying the abilities required for typewriting and streetcar driving. Group testing, legal problems, industrial efficiency, motivation, and delinquency were among other early areas of application. At the Carnegie Institute of Technology, Pittsburgh, a division of applied psychology was established as a teaching and research department in 1915. The *Journal of Applied Psychology* appeared in 1917 along with the first applied psychology text, by H.L. Hollingsworth and A.T. Poffenberger. World Wars I and II fostered work on vocational testing, teaching methods, evaluation of attitudes and morale, performance under stress, propaganda and psychological warfare, rehabilitation, and counselling.

After World War II many of the trends in applied psychology were accentuated by the demands of the space age. Educational psychologists applied themselves to the task of early identification and discovery of talented persons as it was recognized that trained intelligence is an important national resource. Such activities were linked with the work of counselling psychologists, who sought to help persons clarify and attain educational, vocational, and personal goals. Counselling services sponsored by government agencies, social service organizations, schools, and colleges and those offered by private practitioners became available. Concern for the optimum utilization of human resources also increased the importance of industrial and personnel psychology in business and industrial organizations. The aviation industry and the various space agencies and organizations were important in the rapid development of the field of engineering psychology; as machines and engineering systems grew in complexity it was necessary to study man-machine relationships. In response to society's concern for treatment of the mentally ill and for preventive measures against mental illness, clinical psychology showed the greatest absolute growth rate within psychology; it also produced some of applied psychology's major professional problems, involving relations with older medical specialties. The application of automation was studied by psychologists, and in the developing countries psychologists were used to help with the problems of rapid industrialization and manpower planning.

Regardless of the applied psychologist's professional focus, his job description is likely to overlap with those of other areas. The applied psychologist may or may not engage in original research and/or teach. In addition to drawing on experimental findings gleaned from psychological research, the applied psychologist utilizes information from many disciplines. The scope of the field is continually broadening as new types of problems (*e.g.*, technological) arise. Other branches of applied psychology include consumer, school, and community psychology. Prevention and treatment of emotional problems in naturalistic settings (*i.e.*, the community) have received a great deal of attention, as have medically related questions (*e.g.*, sports psychology and the psychology of chronic illness).

Psychometrics, or the measurement and evaluation of psychological variables such as personality, aptitude, or performance, is an integral part of applied psychology fields. For example, the clinical psychologist may be interested in measuring the traits of aggressiveness or obsessiveness; the counselling psychologist, areas of career interest or aptitude; the industrial psychologist, work effectiveness under certain conditions of lighting or office design; or the community psychologist, psychological effects of living near a nuclear power plant or radioactive waste disposal site. *See also* clinical psychology; counselling; educational psychology; industrial psychology.

appoggiatura (from Italian *appoggiare,* "to lean"), in music, an ornamental note of long or short duration that temporarily displaces, and subsequently resolves into, a main note, usually by stepwise motion. During the Renaissance and early Baroque, the appoggiatura was of moderate length, averaging one-third of the main note, and was more in the nature of a melodic than a harmonic ornament. By the time of J.S. Bach (1685–1750), appoggiaturas were divided into two species: the short, which borrows an inconsiderable length from its main note and therefore has little effect on the harmony, and the long, which takes half or more of the length of its main note and therefore substantially affects the harmony, creating a dissonance that then resolves, on the main note, to a consonance. Because its purpose was mainly expressive, whether in purely melodic or harmonic terms, the typical appoggiatura in 17th- and 18th-century music occurred on the beat, rather than before it, "leaning" on the principal note, as suggested by the term's derivation.

The most common sign for the appoggiatura was a small note indicating the precise pitch of the ornament but only implying by relative size its duration, which depended largely upon the context and was governed by broadly acknowledged conventions. Convention also accounts for the fact that appoggiaturas were not always written out in Baroque music, even where their performance was taken for granted, as in the final cadences of operatic recitatives. In such instances, their omission by modern performers violates the composer's original intent.

The 19th-century tendency to notate the long appoggiatura in regular, rather than small, print foreshadowed the gradual abandonment of most embellishments, including the traditional symbol for the short appoggiatura, a small note with a slashed stem. The latter had in fact led to some confusion with the acciaccatura, a dissonant ornamental note played simultaneously with the main note but quickly released. Moreover, in 19th-century practice, grace notes, including the appoggiatura, were increasingly performed before the beat, and it was to take several generations of pioneering in the history of performance practice before the stylistic significance of the appoggiatura in pre-19th-century music was once again appreciated and understood.

Appomattox Court House, in the U.S. Civil War, site in Virginia of the surrender of the Confederate forces to those of the North on April 9, 1865. After an engagement with Federal cavalry, the Confederate Army of northern Virginia was surrounded at Appomattox, seat of Appomattox County, Va., 25 miles east of Lynchburg. Three miles to the northeast, at the former county seat, known as Appomattox Court House, Gen. Robert E. Lee surrendered to Gen. Ulysses S. Grant, thus effectively ending the Civil War. This location was virtually deserted after removal of the county seat to the new town of Appomattox in 1892 but was made a national historical monument in 1940; its buildings, including the McLean House, in which the actual surrender took place, were restored to their 1865 condition. In 1954 the entire 968-acre area was designated a historical park.

Apponyi, Albert, Gróf (Count) (b. May 29, 1846, Vienna—d. Feb. 7, 1933, Geneva), Hungarian statesman whose political philosophy blended the conservative traditions of his background with Hungarian nationalism.

Born into an ancient and famous family, he was the son of Count György Apponyi, who

Apponyi, detail from a lithograph by an unknown artist

By courtesy of the Bild-Archiv, Osterreichische Nationalbibliothek, Vienna

was leader of the Progressive Conservatives and chancellor from 1846 to 1848. Entering the Hungarian Parliament in 1872, Apponyi remained a member of it, with one short exception, until 1918. From the late 1880s, he was the leader of the "united opposition," which consisted of all parties hostile to the Austro-Hungarian "compromise" (*Ausgleich*) of 1867.

As minister of education (1906–10) in the coalition government, Apponyi introduced changes in the school curricula that were greatly resented by the non-Magyars for their Magyarizing tendencies. After the breakdown of the coalition he returned to the opposition as a member of the Party of Independence, of which he became president after Ferenc Kossuth's death (1914). He was again minister of education in 1917–18.

Apponyi returned to Parliament after World War I and headed the Hungarian peace delegation at Paris. He also represented Hungary several times at the League of Nations. When he died in 1933 he was serving as Hungarian delegate to the disarmament conference. His published works include several versions of his memoirs (Eng. trans., 1935) and many studies on Hungarian constitutional problems. Apponyi was one of the most brilliant orators in Hungarian public life.

apport, in occultism, a material object that arrives suddenly and mysteriously through the powers of a medium. Often the arrival of an apport may require its passage through other material objects. Apports usually occur during a séance (*q.v.*) and may involve living or inanimate objects. The apporting of human beings is sometimes called transportation. Spiritualists explain apport as a process involving dematerialization and subsequent reintegration of the objects. Although numerous instances of apport have been reported, many have been proven to be fraudulent.

apprenticeship, training in an art, trade, or craft, under a legal agreement defining the relationship between master and learner and the duration and conditions of their relationship.

Early history. From the earliest times, in Egypt and Babylon, training in craft skills was organized to maintain craftsmen in adequate numbers. The laws of Hammurabi of Babylon, which date from the 18th century BC, required artisans to teach their crafts to the young. In some ancient societies, Rome for example, many craftsmen were slaves, but in the later years of the Roman Empire, craftsmen began to organize themselves into *collegia* to maintain the standards of their trades.

By the 13th century a similar practice reappeared in western Europe with the emergence of the craft guilds, which supervised quality and methods of production and regulated conditions of employment for each occupational group in a town. The guilds were controlled by the master craftsmen, and the recruit entered after a period of training as an apprentice, commonly lasting seven years. It was a system suited to domestic industry. The master operated on his own premises, where his assistants resided as well as worked. An artificial family relationship was thus created, with the articles of apprenticeship taking the place of kinship.

As time went on, however, governments had to contend with the exclusiveness of the guilds, who, controlled by their wealthiest members and frequently abusing their privileges, monopolized their trades in each town. Outsiders were prevented from entering by heavy fees, and apprenticeship was restricted to sons of guild members or of their wealthy neighbours. The English government tried to define conditions of apprenticeship by the Statute of Artificers of 1563, which attempted to arrest these undesirable practices and to ensure adequate labour for industrial and agricultural production. Under its terms, no one might exercise a craft unless he had been apprenticed, and the nature of employment was determined by the boy's parentage. The act also established a ratio between the number of journeymen and the number of apprentices; each master with three apprentices was compelled to keep at least one journeyman. Justices of the peace were required to administer the statute, which also gave them authority to assess wages.

The notion of individual training extended beyond the craft guilds in the Middle Ages. The university accepted the same principle with its master's degree, and the religious orders insisted on the newcomer's passing through a novitiate. In medicine, the guild system applied to the surgeon, who also performed the function of barber and was regarded as a craftsman, with less prestige than the physician. The lawyer served an apprenticeship by working in close association with a master of the profession. This has persisted in England, with the articles of clerkship that bind pupils to a solicitor or barrister, but in the United States and in most European countries, the law degree is now the main avenue to the profession.

The coming of the Industrial Revolution. The Industrial Revolution altered attitudes toward training. Machines created a need for unskilled labour for which formal training was unnecessary, and employees who showed aptitude moved on to semiskilled jobs. Yet craftsmen remained an essential feature of industrial society, both to build machines and to keep them running and to maintain trades still dependent on individual skill, and so apprenticeship continued, and, indeed, a new development strengthened its position. The trade unions became directly interested in maintaining standards and in controlling recruitment to protect skilled workers. As the factory system replaced domestic industry, a new kind of apprenticeship developed in which the employer was the factory owner, and, after his training, the apprentice became a factory worker.

In France there was an early reaction against free admission to all trades; legislation concerning apprenticeship was reintroduced in 1803, to be greatly strengthened in 1851. In the reconstruction of Prussia, which began during the Napoleonic Wars, apprenticeship became an important feature of industrial training. In England apprenticeship was maintained by the craft industries and even extended to analogous fields. In education, for example, there were various schemes for pupil teachers, which were in effect a kind of apprenticeship, and there was a comparable system of pupil training for young farmers.

In the United States apprenticeship existed in colonial times. Indentured apprentices were brought there from England in the 17th century. Benjamin Franklin served as apprentice to his brother in the printing trade. But apprenticeship was less important than in Europe because of the high proportion of skilled workers among immigrants.

The development of large-scale machine production increased the demand for semiskilled workers whose skills were confined to a particular specialty, created by an ever-increasing division of labour. The more ambitious among them sought to increase their effectiveness and potential for advancement by voluntary study. To meet this need, mechanics' institutes were established, such as the one founded in London in 1823 by George Birkbeck, which still exists in modernized form as Birkbeck College, and Cooper Union for the Advancement of Science and Art in New York City, established in 1859. In France, technical education on a national scale dates from 1880.

Preparation for clerical work has been more closely associated with the regular educational structure. In the late 19th century evening schools were established to prepare students for employment as clerks, cashiers, and bookkeepers, but, apart from the secretarial schools made necessary by the invention of the typewriter and the widespread use of shorthand, training for office work, after recruitment, has been a relatively recent development.

The new technology also demanded more theoretical understanding and skills, for which the universities made no provision, and the earliest attempt to meet this requirement was inspired by the French Revolution, although it is commonly associated with Napoleon. This was the École Polytechnique (Polytechnic) established in 1794, which soon came to be a great scientific and technological institution. It was the first of the great professional schools (*grandes écoles*), peculiar to France. Each profession has its school; for example, the School of Mines, the School of Roads and Bridges, the National School of Agriculture and, among more recent creations, the School of Aeronautics and the National School of Administration. Admission to each is by a nationwide entrance examination, which requires special preparation.

Modern apprenticeship. Apprenticeship in Europe has maintained remarkable continuity from medieval times, but early in the

20th century assembly-line methods created repetitive work of an unskilled or semiskilled character, which made the long period of apprenticeship unattractive. This led many countries to attempt planned organization of the labour market, designed to help juveniles and unskilled and semiskilled workers to find suitable employment.

The need for apprenticeship has remained in craft industries, in spite of the fact that mechanization has progressively increased the number of jobs for which little formal instruction is necessary. After World War I a new pattern of recruitment emerged. Apprenticeship on traditional lines was maintained for skilled craftsmanship; for less skilled work learnership became a common practice—the newcomer was given facilities to learn by working with others. Some industries introduced a system of upgrading; labourers and unskilled workers were allowed to undertake skilled work after having served as assistants to other skilled workers. These training schemes were supplemented by pupil apprenticeship, whereby the recruit learned working skills with the intention of qualifying for a responsible position in the industry, and student apprenticeship, offering entrants with a university or technical education working experience to qualify for staff appointments.

Trade unions emerged, like the medieval guilds, as guardians of the principle of restricting entry to skilled trades by means of rigorous apprenticeship, but with the opportunity for semiskilled labour to move gradually into skilled jobs, the craft unions themselves began to change. From the 1920s they began to accept for membership workers who had not entered as apprentices. The ratio of apprentices to journeymen ceased then to be an issue.

After World War II the situation changed, with considerable variations between different countries. Perhaps the most radical changes took place in West Germany, which had the advantage of a practically new start. There, a distinction is made between skilled trades needing apprentices, semiskilled trades needing trainees, and handicrafts employing artisans. Trades are grouped under local chambers of industry, handicrafts under chambers of handicrafts. The apprentice's contract is registered with the appropriate chamber. He keeps a workbook, which its officials inspect from time to time, and there are regular tests at monthly or three-monthly intervals. The school-leaving age is 14, but part-time attendance at a vocational school, included in the hours of employment, is compulsory until 18. The apprentice can apply to take his school-leaving examination when he is ready, sometimes resulting in a training period of as little as three years.

In France, vocational training is supervised by the Directorate of Technical and Vocational Education of the Ministry of Education. There are 24 national professional consultative commissions on which employers, government, and trade unions are represented, and since 1930 the government has developed technical colleges, which train about one-third of all skilled workers, about one-third of them girls. There are also a number of works schools, such as the noted Renault School. Apprenticeship may be by contract with a private employer, by attendance at school beyond the normal leaving age of 16 (called the complementary course), or by apprenticeship to an artisan trade. There is always a passing-out examination; those at the colleges and schools supervised by the Directorate and those for apprentices by the local chambers of crafts.

In Britain, the Employment and Training Act of 1948 created a Central Youth Employment Executive and led to proposals for a National Joint Apprenticeship and Training Council to be set up in each industry. The printing trade, usually conservative in these matters, introduced selection by objective testing of suitability and aptitude. The motor-vehicle-repair industry developed an apprenticeship scheme with a final passing-out test, an examination for a national craftsman's certificate. The Post Office Engineering Department, which never accepted the traditional pattern of apprenticeship in the training of its telephone and telegraph technicians, has a three-year course for recruits, accepted between the ages of 16 and 20, with the first two years spent in general training and the third year in one of several fields of specialization. But the most significant break with the past is the module system in the engineering industry. This provides a year's training in a wide selection of skills, followed by selected training in specialized skills. There are performance tests and appropriate further education. Apprentices are allowed to qualify as quickly as possible; the traditional five-year period has disappeared. Because some small firms are unwilling to take apprentices and to afford them part-time day release, it is the large corporations who have in fact made the best use of apprenticeship.

In the United States conditions of apprenticeship are more flexible than in Europe. The lowest age for entry is 16, but in many trades the requirement of a high school diploma makes the effective entry age 18. The upper limit normally is 24 years of age and in some trades it is higher. The period varies from two to five years but is usually three or four, and much of the training is at technical and vocational schools. The Bureau of Apprenticeship was set up in 1937 in the U.S. Department of Labor, and the National Apprenticeship and Training Council promotes schemes for individual industries. Apprenticeship normally is phased in periods of 1,000 credit hours, each equivalent to six months and including 144 hours as the minimum of related classroom instruction. The trainee advances from phase to phase after passing qualifying examinations. Pay, varying from 60 to 90 percent of the journeyman's rate, increases at each phase. Apprentices can be indentured to the Local Apprenticeship Committee of the craft, and thus, in effect, to the industry not to an employer. This has been particularly successful in the building industry.

In Japan, apprenticeship and employee training often have a personal orientation rarely found in other industrial nations. The Japanese concept of apprenticeship differs from elsewhere because of a difference in the relationship between employer and employee. Employment with a Japanese firm tends to become a lifetime relationship. Social obligations require the employer to provide work for his employee and require the employee to continue with the same employer until death or retirement in any capacity to which he may be assigned. The apprenticeship is thus oriented toward employment with a particular company, in which the employee is likely to spend his whole working life, expecting permanent employment even if his specific assignment may vary from time to time. The close relationship between the apprenticeship and a specific trade, common elsewhere, is thus missing in Japan.

apprenticeship novel, biographical novel that concentrates on an individual's youth and his social and moral initiation into adulthood. The class derives from Goethe's *Wilhelm Meisters Lehrjahre* (1795–96; *Wilhelm Meister's Apprenticeship*, 1824). It became a traditional novel form in German literature, where it is called Bildungsroman ("novel of educational formation"). An English example is Dickens' *David Copperfield* (1850). In the 20th century Thomas Wolfe's *Look Homeward, Angel* (1929) is an American example. *See also* Bildungsroman; Künstlerroman.

approximant, in phonetics, a sound that is produced by bringing one articulator in the vocal tract close to another without, however, causing audible friction (*see* fricative). Approximants include semivowels, such as the *y* sound in "yes" or the *w* sound in "war."

Apra Harbor, also called PORT APRA, port on the west coast of Guam, Mariana Islands, western Pacific, the best anchorage on the island, located just west of Agana. It is the port of entry and site of a U.S. naval base. With 2,400 ft (730 m) of frontage for deepwater docking, it is the transshipment point for the U.S. Trust Territory of the Pacific Islands. The harbour, which is protected (south) by Orote Peninsula and (north) by Cabras Island and reefs, was the point of the Allied seaborne invasion of Guam (July 21, 1944) during World War II. It attained renewed importance as a base with the escalation of the war in Vietnam in the 1960s. A commercial port with facilities for handling containerized cargo was opened in the harbour in 1969. Pop. (1980) 5,633.

apraxia, disturbance, caused by cerebral lesion, in the ability to carry out useful or skilled acts; motor power and mental capacity remain intact. Kinetic, or motor, apraxia results in one upper extremity's being affected so that the individual, even though there is no muscle weakness, cannot carry out fine motor acts, such as turning a key in a lock.

Ideational apraxia is the ultimate in absent-mindedness, the loss of capability to formulate a plan of action. The plan is never wholly organized, and even that part that is organized cannot be maintained sufficiently long to be carried out. Portions of the act may be completed but not in proper sequence. The individual may strike a match, for example, to light a campfire, but then hold the match until it burns his fingers. This type of apraxia is usually caused by diffuse lesions or toxemia in the cerebral cortex.

Ideokinetic apraxia is a condition brought about by an interruption of the association tracts, in which there is no coordination between ideation and motor activity. An affected individual will complain, for example, that he cannot use his hand, but then he will slap a mosquito with it. He is unable to perform certain acts (*e.g.*, whistling or making a fist) upon command but is able to do so automatically. The cortical lesion responsible for ideokinetic apraxia is usually in the supramarginal gyrus and may be on one or both sides.

Constructional apraxia, caused more often by a lesion in the right cerebral hemisphere than in the left, is the inability to put together elements in the correct fashion to form a meaningful whole; for example, building a structure with blocks or copying a design.

Aprey faience, tin-glazed earthenware produced by the factory of Jacques Lallemant

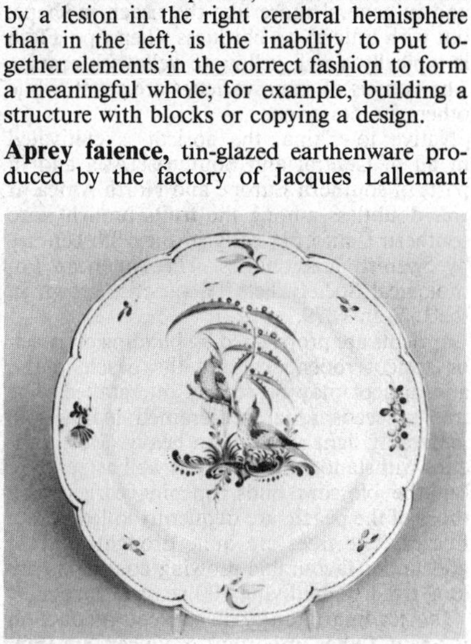

Aprey faience plate decorated with exotic birds and flowers, second half of the 18th century; in the Victoria and Albert Museum, London

By courtesy of the Victoria and Albert Museum, London; photograph, EB Inc.

de Villehaut, Baron d'Aprey, established in 1744 on his estate at Aprey, near Dijon, Fr. The early pieces, which are heavy and rather crude, recall blue-and-white earthenware in the Rouen style or have Rococo forms decorated with chinoiseries (motifs influenced by the Chinese), flowers, and birds. From about 1772 to 1781 the activity of the painters Jacques Jarry and Antoine Mège established the factory's reputation for brilliant, exotically styled bird and flower decoration, with such devices as miniature landscapes on Rococo scrolls. Aprey continued to produce until the mid-19th century, but without distinction, copying earlier ware from its own molds.

apricot (*Prunus armeniaca*), stone fruit of the family Rosaceae, cultivated generally throughout the temperate regions of the world and used fresh for dessert, cooked in a variety of pastries, or preserved by canning or drying. Trees are large and spreading with broad,

Apricot (*Prunus armeniaca*)
Stephen Dalton—EB Inc.

heart-shaped leaves, dark green in colour and held erect on the twigs. The flowers are white in full bloom and borne singly or doubly at a node on very short stems. The apricot sets fruit after self-pollination of its blossoms. The pit is smooth, somewhat like that of the plum but broader, somewhat flatter, and more winged. The fruit is nearly smooth, round to oblong in some varieties, somewhat flattened, and in general more like the peach in shape, but with little to no hairiness when ripe. Flesh is typically a rich yellow to yellowish orange. The kernels of some varieties are sweet, while others are poisonous.

Native to China, the apricot is cultivated in all of Central and Southeast Asia and in parts of southern Europe and North Africa. It was doubtless among the fruits brought into southern California early in the 18th century by Spanish missionaries. The American Pomological Society lists 11 varieties grown in the U.S. in 1879.

Apricots are propagated by budding on peach or apricot rootstocks, and the peach, plum, and apricot may be readily intergrafted. The tree succeeds in a well-drained loamy soil, preferably light rather than heavy. Most varieties withstand winter cold as well as peaches, but the blossom buds, opening earlier than those of the peach, are frequently killed by late freezes. The trees are quite drought-resistant and under favourable growing conditions are long-lived, some living 100 years or longer.

The leading country in apricot production is Spain. Other important producers are Iran, Syria, the U.S., France, Italy, and Yugoslavia.

Apricots are a good source of vitamin A and are high in natural-sugar content. Dried apricots are an excellent source of iron.

Apries, also spelled OUAPHRIS, Egyptian HAAIBRA WAHIBRA, Hebrew HOPHRA (d. 567 BC), fourth king (reigned 589–570 BC) of the 26th dynasty of Egypt; he succeeded his father, Psamtik II.

Apries failed to help his ally King Zedekiah of Judah against Babylon, but after the fall of Jerusalem he received many Jewish refugees into Egypt. Later he took the Phoenician port of Sidon, but, because of his subsequent failure in an attack on Cyrene in Libya, the Egyptian army mutinied and elected their general Ahmose as king instead (570). Apries was imprisoned but escaped; he met his death during a second battle.

April, fourth month of the Gregorian calendar. *See* month.

April Fools' Day, also called ALL FOOLS' DAY, first day of April, named from the custom of playing practical jokes or sending friends on fools' errands on that date. Although it has been observed for centuries in several countries, the origin of the custom is unknown. It resembles other festivals, such as the Hilaria of ancient Rome (March 25) and the Holī festival of India (ending March 31). Its timing seems related to the vernal equinox (March 21), when nature "fools" mankind with sudden changes in the weather.

On April Fools' Day all people are given an excuse to play the fool. In France the fooled person is called *poisson d'avril* ("April fish"), but the origin of the name is unknown. In April the cuckoo, emblem of simpletons, comes, so in Scotland the victim is called gowk (cuckoo). The custom of playing April Fools' jokes was taken to America by the British. It has continued to be observed by children and adults and sometimes involves rather elaborate hoaxes as well as merely simple jokes.

April Laws (Hungarian Revolution of 1848): *see* March Laws.

April Theses, Russian APRELSKIYE TEZISY, in Russian history, program developed by Lenin during the Russian Revolution of 1917, calling for Soviet control of state power; the theses, published in April 1917, contributed to the July Days uprising and also to the Bolshevik coup d'etat in October 1917.

During the February Revolution two disparate bodies had replaced the imperial government—the Provisional Government and the Petrograd Soviet of Workers' and Soldiers' Deputies. The Socialists who dominated the Soviet interpreted the February Revolution as a bourgeois revolution and considered it appropriate for the bourgeoisie to hold power. They therefore submitted to the rule of the Provisional Government, formed by liberals from the Duma. The Soviet agreed to cooperate with the government and to advise it in the interests of workers and soldiers.

Lenin, however, viewed the two bodies as institutions representing social classes locked in the class struggle. He felt that, as one class gained dominance over the other, its governing body would crush the rival institution; thus the two could not indefinitely coexist. On the basis of this interpretation he developed his theses, in which he urged the Bolsheviks to withdraw their support from the Provisional Government and to call for immediate withdrawal from World War I and for the distribution of land among the peasantry. The Bolshevik Party was to organize workers, soldiers, and peasants and to strengthen the Soviets so that they could eventually seize power from the Provisional Government. The theses also called for the nationalization of banks and for Soviet control of the production and distribution of manufactured goods. Lenin first presented his theses to a gathering of Social Democrats and later (April 17 [April 4, old style], 1917) to a Bolshevik committee, both of which immediately rejected them. The Bolshevik newspaper *Pravda* published them but carefully noted that they were Lenin's personal ideas.

Nevertheless, within a few weeks the party's seventh all-Russian conference (May 7–12 [April 24–29, old style]) adopted the theses as its program, along with the slogan "All Power to the Soviets." Although some Bolsheviks still had reservations about the program, the concepts contained in the theses became very popular among the workers and soldiers of Petrograd, who, using Bolshevik slogans, unsuccessfully tried to force the Soviet to take power in July. It was not until October, however, that Lenin's party was able to begin implementation of its program and seize power from the Provisional Government in the name of the Soviets.

Consult the INDEX first

apse, in architecture, a semicircular or polygonal termination to the choir, chancel, or aisle of a secular or ecclesiastical building. First used in pre-Christian Roman architecture, the apse often functioned as an enlarged niche to hold the statue of a deity in a temple. It was also used in the thermae of ancient baths and in basilicas such as the imperial basilica in the Palace of Domitian on the Palatine Hill.

During the Early Christian era (*c.* 4th–mid-8th century), the domed apse became a standard part of the church plan, and from the time of Constantine I, it was placed at the west end of the basilica (*e.g.,* Old St. Peter's). Between the 6th and 7th centuries the Roman branch of the Catholic Church changed the orientation of the apse to the east, as the

Apse, basilica of S. Vitale, Ravenna, 526–547
Alinari—Art Resource/EB Inc.

Byzantine churches had done earlier. The apse was the most elaborately decorated part of the church, with the walls sheathed in marble and the vault ornamented with mosaic that depicted an embodiment of the godhead.

At the beginning of the 7th century, changing liturgical practices resulted in the addition of apses at the end of either the side aisles or the transept. In addition, the clergy moved its seating from the apse to the choir, and the altar, which had previously been placed between the clergy and the main part of the church, was pushed into the apse. By the Renaissance the altar was often placed against the back wall. This arrangement removed the sacrifice of the mass from the congregation, an adjustment that eventually led, during the 17th century, to increased preaching in the nave of the church with mass said at the distant altar.

Variations to the apse also developed during the Romanesque period. Although the form of the apse remained simple in Italian architecture—gaining its exterior ornamentation from wall arcading, cornices, and buttressing—outside of Italy, particularly in France, an ambulatory (*q.v.*) and apse chapels were added to the main structure to form the complex chevet.

The apse has remained a standard part of ecclesiastic architecture through the 20th century, especially in churches that are designed from the traditional Latin cross or from centralized plans. *See also* church.

apse, also spelled APSIS, plural APSIDES, in astronomy, either of the two points on an elliptical orbit that are nearest to, and farthest from, the focus, or centre of attraction. The line of apsides, connecting the two points, is the major axis of the orbit. The point nearest the focus is the pericentre, or periapsis, and that farthest from it is the apocentre, or apoapsis. Specific terms can be used for individual bodies: if the Sun is the centre, the specific terms perihelion and aphelion are generally used; if the Earth, perigee and apogee. Periastron and apastron refer to an orbit around a star, and perijove and apojove refer to an orbit around Jupiter.

Apsheron Peninsula, also spelled ABŠERON, Russian APSHERONSKY POLUOSTROV, peninsula, in the Azerbaijan Soviet Socialist Republic, extending 37 mi (60 km) into the Caspian Sea and reaching a maximum width of 19 mi. An eastern extension of the Caucasus Mountains, the Apsheron Peninsula consists of a gently undulating plain, in part dissected by ravines and characterized by frequent salt lakes and saltings (land often flooded by tides). The climate is basically semidesert but is modified by maritime influences; vegetation includes such drought-resisting plants as feather grasses. Vineyards and tea plantations are features of the regional economy. The peninsula is especially noted for its oil-bearing strata, and the workings extend into the sea.

apteran: *see* dipluran.

apterygote, broadly, any of several types of small, primitive, wingless insects or insect-like creatures. Recent taxonomic revisions have raised three groups formerly classed among the apterygotes to the status of class, parallel to the class Insecta. Thus the strict sense of apterygote no longer includes them but refers only to a subclass of Insecta that includes the silverfish, firebrats, and bristletails (order Thysanura).

A brief treatment of apterygotes follows. For full treatment, *see* MACROPAEDIA: Insects.

The reclassified groups no longer considered strictly apterygotes are the Collembola, commonly known as springtails, the Diplura, or forktails, and the Protura. True apterygotes, which are thought to be the evolutionary progenitors of winged insects, include the orders Thysanura, Microcoryphia, and the extinct Monura. These two groups are distinguished from one another by the positioning of their mouth apparatus, either externally (ectognathous) as in the Thysanura, Microcoryphia, and Monura, or internally (entognathous) as in the Collembola, Diplura, and Protura. Other taxonomically significant distinctions are based on the position of eyes, the number of body segments, and the structure of legs and antennae. All of these organisms may be referred to simply as hexapods.

The extant hexapods range in size from the Protura, which attain a maximum length of 2 millimetres (0.08 inch), to some Diplura that may reach 50 mm; most are under 10 mm. Most are yellow or white in colour, and all but Protura and Collembola have single or double tail filaments. Collembola are the most various and widely distributed, with over 3,500 known species. Antennae and optical structures also differ among these varieties. All of the hexapods inhabit soil, leaf litter, and other forms of organic debris. Since the epidermal layers of the hexapods are thin and allow free passage of air and water vapour, the presence of moisture is essential to their survival. The food of these organisms generally consists of fungi, decayed vegetation, algae, and spores, but the silverfish also consume carrion and even paper products. Apterygotes are preyed upon by certain species of flies, beetles, and ants, and occasionally by fish and reptiles.

The bodies of all hexapods are comprised of three sections (except those of the extinct Monuran group, which contained 14 segments): the abdomen, thorax, and head. The thorax is in turn divided into three segments, each bearing one pair of legs that terminate in claws. Most breathe through their outer layer (cutaneous respiration), though some varieties have developed breathing systems with tracheae and thoracic orifices (spiracles). On the abdomen of the Collembola, appendages that were once limbs have developed into a spring-like leaping mechanism called a furcula and a tenaculum that controls the furcula. The Diplura, Microcoryphia, and Thysanura have sensory appendages (cerci) on the abdomen that are also modified limbs. The sensory apparatus of the hexapod head varies widely: Diplura have none at all, while Collembola frequently have simple eyes called ocelli in addition to their other sensory organs, and Microcoryphia have both ocelli and compound eyes.

Sexual reproduction is characteristic of the hexapods, although eggs can sometimes develop without fertilization (a process called parthenogenesis). Typically, sperm is dropped in packets at random by males and retrieved by females, which retain the packets until they are needed for fertilization or until they are lost during a succeeding molt. Apterygote young, sometimes called nymphs, molt periodically with little physical change. Molting sometimes continues throughout their life cycle. Collembola may go through up to 50 instars (stages between molts) with little actual growth between them. Microcoryphia generally molt six times during a life span, while the total for Thysanura is often over 40.

Populations of Collembola, the most common apterygote, are highly sensitive to the condition of microscopic vegetative growth in the soil. Often existing in densities of 100,000 or more per cubic metre of soil, Collembola are susceptible to some insecticides and are normally unaffected by herbicides. Different species of Collembola and members of the same species at different stages of growth tend to inhabit different strata of the soil. Like most soil-dwelling insects, apterygotes may serve a valuable function in soil aeration and enriching processes.

Aptian Stage, standard, worldwide division of Lower Cretaceous rocks and time (the Cretaceous Period began about 136,000,000 years ago and lasted about 71,000,000 years). Rocks of the Aptian Stage overlie those of the Barremian Stage and underlie rocks of the Albian Stage. In Great Britain the Aptian is represented by the Lower Greensand; elsewhere in northern Europe it consists of portions of the thick Hils Clay. Limestones, shales, and sandstones dominate the Aptian record of the Middle East, North Africa, India, Australia, and Japan. The Aptian of the U.S. is well developed in the western interior region. Several zones, representing smaller divisions of rocks and time, have been recognized in the Aptian and are characterized by distinctive fossil ammonite cephalopods (mollusks).

aptitude test, examination that attempts to determine and measure those characteristics of a person that are regarded as indices of his capability to acquire, through future training, some specific set of responses (intellectual, motor, etc.). The tests assume that people differ in their special abilities and that these differences are related in a predictable manner to their later achievements. General, or multiple, aptitude tests are similar to intelligence tests in that they measure a broad spectrum of abilities (*e.g.,* verbal comprehension, general reasoning, numerical operations, perceptual speed, mechanical knowledge). They yield a profile of scores rather than a single IQ and are widely used in educational and vocational counselling. Aptitude tests have also been developed to measure professional potential and capabilities (*e.g.,* legal, medical) and special abilities (*e.g.,* clerical, mechanical).

Apu-Punchau (Inca religion): *see* Inti.

Apuleius, Lucius (b. *c.* 124, Madaura, Byzacium—d. probably after 170), Platonic philosopher, rhetorician, and author remembered for *The Golden Ass,* a prose narrative that proved influential long after his death. The work, called *Metamorphoses* by its author, narrates the adventures of a young man changed by magic into an ass.

Apuleius, who was educated at Carthage and Athens, travelled in the Mediterranean region and became interested in contemporary religious initiation rites, among them the ceremonies associated with worship of the Egyptian goddess Isis. Intellectually versatile and acquainted with works of both Latin and Greek writers, he taught rhetoric in Rome before returning to Africa to marry a rich widow, Aemilia Pudentilla. To meet her family's charge that he had practiced magic to win her affection, he wrote the *Apologia* ("Defense"), the major source for his biography.

For *The Golden Ass* it is likely that he used material from the lost *Metamorphoses* by Lucius of Patrae, which is cited by some as the source for the brief extant Greek work on a similar theme, *Lucius, or the Ass,* attributed to the Greek rhetorician Lucian. Though Apuleius' novel is fiction, it contains a few definitely autobiographical details, and its hero has been seen as a partial portrait of its author. It is particularly valuable for its description of the ancient religious mysteries, and Lucius' restoration from animal to human shape, with the aid of Isis, and his acceptance into her priesthood suggests that Apuleius himself had been initiated into that cult. Considered a revelation of ancient manners, the work has been praised for its entertaining and at times bawdy episodes that alternate between the dignified, the ludicrous, the voluptuous, and the horrible. Its "Cupid and Psyche" tale (Books 4 through 6) has been frequently imitated by later writers, including the English poets Shakerley Marmion in 1637, Mary Tighe in 1805, William Morris in *The Earthly Paradise* (1868–70), and Robert Bridges in 1885 and 1894, and C.S. Lewis in the novel *Till We Have Faces: A Myth Retold* (1956). Some of Lucius' adventures reappear in *The Decameron* by Giovanni Boccaccio, in *Don Quixote* by Miguel de Cervantes, and in *Gil Blas* by Alain Le Sage. Of Apuleius' other literary works his *Florida* is, like *The Golden Ass,* stylistically affected.

More influential than this collection of the author's declamations on various subjects are his philosophical treatises. He wrote three books on Plato (the third is lost): *De Platone et ejus dogmate* ("On Plato and His Teaching") and *De Deo Socratis* ("On the God of Socrates"), which expounds the Platonic notion of demons, beneficent creatures intermediate between gods and men. His *De mundo* ("On the World") adapts a treatise incorrectly attributed to Aristotle. Apuleius' claim that he was also the author of numerous poems and works on natural history has not been proved, and the noted *Asclepius,* a Latin version of a Greek dialogue, has been wrongly attributed to him. His collected works were first edited by Joannes Andreas (1469); later editions include one by R. Helm and P. Thomas (1907–31) and the *Index Apuleianus* by W.A. Oldfather, H.V. Canter, and B.E. Perry (1935).

Apulia (Italy): *see* Puglia.

Apure, state, southwestern Venezuela, bounded north by Táchira, Barinas, and Guárico states, south and west by Colombia, and east by the Orinoco River. The state has an area of 29,537 sq mi (76,500 sq km); cattle raising dominates the economy. The terrain consists of Llanos (plains); drainage is poor, and annual floods are extensive and prolonged. During the dry season the savanna grasses become virtually inedible, and many cattle are driven to wetter areas as far south as the Orinoco. During the flood season, they are often driven northward to Calabozo or to low mesas that stand above the floodwaters. San Fernando de Apure (*q.v.*), the state capital, has a large meat-packing industry, from which fresh beef is flown to Caracas and other large cities. Several dry-season highways run deep into the state from the north and west. Since 1969 the state has been part of a government regional development corporation. Pop. (1983 est.) 226,079.

Apure River, Spanish RÍO APURE, river in western Venezuela. The major navigable tributary of the Orinoco River, it arises in the Cordillera de Mérida and flows for 510 mi (820 km) northeast and east through the heart of the Llanos (plains), Venezuela's most important cattle-raising area. The river's principal tributaries, including the Portuguesa and the Guárico, flow mainly from the north. During the rainy season (May to November), the Apure is navigable for small steamers from Ciudad Bolívar up to San Fernando de Apure and Puerto de Nutrias. Since 1957 the highway connecting San Fernando de Apure with Calabozo and the densely populated north has reduced river traffic drastically.

Apurímac, department (formed 1873) in the Andean interior of southern Peru. It has an area of 7,934 sq mi (20,550 sq km). Most of the land is at a high elevation, dissected with deep canyons cut by the Río Apurímac and its tributaries. The inhabitants are mainly subsistence farmers and herders. The chief products are wool, corn (maize), wheat, and potatoes. At lower elevations sugarcane and fruit are grown. Gold, copper, lead, and salt are mined. The capital, Abancay (*q.v.*), is in the centre of the largest area of settlement, located in an intermontane basin that lies between 7,000 and 8,000 ft (2,100 and 2,400 m) above sea level. Pop. (1984 est.) 370,700.

Apurímac River, Spanish RÍO APURÍMAC, river in southern Peru, one of the headwaters of the Amazon River. Arising from glacial meltwaters of the Altura de Pampahuasi, about 16,500 ft (5,000 m) high, in Arequipa department, Peru, it flows northwest through the Andes, descending to less than 860 ft to join the Urubamba and form the Río Ucayali. For most of its 430-mi (700-km) length it flows through narrow canyons, and its torrential course is frequently interrupted by falls and rapids. It is known as the Apurímac only to the junction of the Río Mantaro. From there to the Perené it is known as the Ene, and from the Perené to the Urubamba it is known as the Tambo.

Apuseni Mountains, Romanian MUNŢII APUSENI, large mountain chain, a subgroup of the Western Carpathians, lying north of the Mureş River, northwestern Romania. The Apuseni (Western) Mountains are not high—reaching a maximum of only 6,063 ft (1,848 m)—but as a uniform, imposing group they dominate the low surrounding area. Central to the group, and the highest, is the Bihor Massif (*q.v.*), from which radiate six lower mountain groups. To the west the Criş (Hungarian Körös) River system drains the massif onto the Great Hungarian Plain; to the east stretches the Transylvanian Tableland. The streams off the southern groups flow into the Mureş River. The rounded crests contrast sharply with deep river valleys, and extensive limestone formations give rise to some spectacularly eroded scenery. Pastureland and settlements are scattered, and the Metaliferi (Metal) Mountains in the south, with volcanic conical crests, are rich in mineral ores.

Aq Qoyunlu (Turkmen tribal federation): *see* Ak Koyunlu.

Āqā Khān: *see* Aga Khan.

Āqā Mīrak, also spelled ĀGHĀ MĪRAK, in full SAYYID ĀQĀ JALĀL AD-DĪN MĪRAK AL-ḤASANĪ (fl. 16th century), Persian painter, an admired portraitist and an excellent colourist who painted in a sumptuous style. A descendant of the Prophet and a native of Isfahan, he worked mostly in the city of Tabrīz, the capital of the Ṣafavid empire. He knew Behzād, the most highly admired of Persian painters, who was director of the royal library. Mīrak, one of the senior court artists, painted as a colleague of Sulṭān Muḥammad, the most remarkable painter of the 16th century at Tabrīz. Mīrak also was the teacher of Shāh Qūlī, a Persian painter later active at the court of the Ottoman sultan Süleyman the Magnificent.

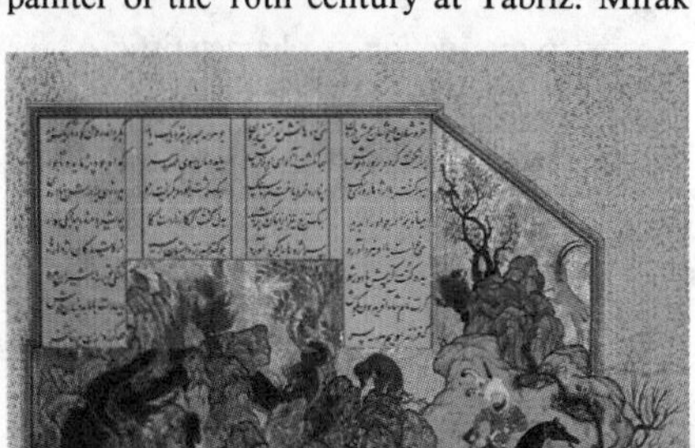

"Faridun Tests His Sons in the Guise of a Dragon," miniature by Āqā Mīrak, *c.* 1527–28, from the *Shāh-nāmeh* ("Book of Kings") by Ferdowsi; in the Metropolitan Museum of Art, New York City

By courtesy of the Metropolitan Museum of Art, New York; Collection of Arthur A. Houghton

A bon vivant and poet, Mīrak became a boon companion of the Ṣafavid Shāh Ṭahmāsp I, who was a committed patron of the arts.

Āqā Rezā: *see* Rezā.

Aqaba, Gulf of, Arabic KHALĪJ AL-ʿAQABAH, northeastern arm of the Red Sea, penetrating between Saudi Arabia and the Sinai Peninsula. Varying in width from 12 to 17 mi (19 to 27 km) it is 100 mi long, lying in a pronounced cleft with hills rising abruptly to about 2,000 ft (600 m). Navigation is difficult because of the narrow entrance and its islands, coral reefs, and sudden squalls. Part of the complex East African Rift System, the gulf's head touches the Egyptian, Israeli, Jordanian, and Saudi Arabian boundaries. Although Dahab is the only sheltered harbour, Jordan and Israel created the ports of al-ʿAqabah and Elat, respectively, as outlets to the Red Sea and the Indian Ocean.

Beach on the Gulf of Aqaba

Photo Research International

ʿAqabah, al-, also spelled AQABA, or AKABA, Latin AELANA, port town, Maʿān *muḥāfaẓah* (governorate), extreme southwest Jordan, on the Gulf of Aqaba, an inlet of the Red Sea. Jordan's only outlet to the sea, it is just east of the Jordan–Israel frontier on the gulf. Because of freshwater springs in the vicinity, it has been settled for millennia; King Solomon's port and foundry of Ezion-geber lay nearby. Excavations at Tallal-Khalīfa west of the town have revealed foundry workings.

In Roman times it was, under Trajan's rule (AD 98–117), garrisoned by the powerful Legio X (10th Legion) Fretensis and was the southern terminus of a trade route leading from Syria. Under Byzantine rule it became the seat of a bishopric in the early 4th century. Conquered by Muḥammad in 630/631, it became an important way-station for Egyptian Muslims making the obligatory pilgrimage to Mecca. The town was taken by the crusaders (12th century) and finally returned to Muslim rule in 1183. Originally called Ayla by the Arabs, the present name is an abbreviation of ʿAqabat Ayla, the "pass of Ayla" through the mountains to the north (now occupied by the highway to Maʿān), which was improved for traffic as early as the 9th century AD. Al-ʿAqabah declined under Ottoman rule; at the beginning of the 20th century it was only a small village. Its pilgrim traffic had largely disappeared following the opening of the Suez Canal (1869) and the completion of the Hejaz Railway (1908).

A strategic fortified Turkish outpost in World War I, al-ʿAqabah was bombarded by the British and French navies and captured by Arab irregulars led by T.E. Lawrence in July 1917. After the war the status of al-ʿAqabah was in dispute; Britain claimed an outlet on the Gulf of Aqaba for its newly created protectorate of Transjordan (technically part of the Palestine mandate), while the Kingdom of Hejaz based a counterclaim to the town and regions to the north on the former political subdivisions of the Ottoman Empire. When King Ibn Saʿūd conquered the Hejaz (1925), the British placed al-ʿAqabah and the Maʿān district under Transjordanian authority; this de facto situation continued when Jordan became fully independent (1946). Saudi Arabia had never agreed to these frontiers, which were a matter of dispute until 1965. Then, a boundary agreement between the two states was signed, giving Saudi Arabia desert territories in the interior that were formerly part of Jordan; in return, the Saudis officially recognized al-ʿAqabah as part of Jordan and gave

Jordan an additional frontage on the Gulf of Aqaba of about 10 mi (16 km).

Al-ʿAqabah's harbour, somewhat improved by the British in World War II, was greatly modernized under independent Jordan; deep-water facilities were opened in 1961. It is not only Jordan's sole port but is also the only outlet to the Red Sea and Indian Ocean for Syria and Lebanon. The port's principal export is Jordanian bulk phosphates; imports are chiefly manufactured goods. The reopening of the Suez Canal in 1975 and the Iraq–Iran war in the early 1980s created new business for the port. Pop. (1979 prelim.) 26,999.

ʿAqarqūf (Iraq): *see* Dur-Kurigalzu.

Aqhat Epic, ancient West Semitic legend concerned with the cause of the annual summer drought. The epic records that Danel, a sage and king of the Haranamites, had no son until the god El, in response to Danel's many prayers and offerings, finally granted him a child, whom Danel named Aqhat. Some time later Danel offered hospitality to the divine craftsman Kothar who in return gave Aqhat one of his marvelous bows. That bow, however, had been intended for the goddess Anath, who became outraged that it had been given to a mortal. Anath made Aqhat a variety of tempting offers, including herself, in exchange for the bow, but Aqhat rejected all of them. Anath then plotted to kill Aqhat, luring him to a hunting party where she, disguised as a falcon, carried her henchman, Yatpan, in a sack and dropped him on Aqhat. Yatpan killed Aqhat and snatched the bow, which he later carelessly dropped into the sea.

Meanwhile, because of the blood shed in violence, a strange famine came over the land, leading Aqhat's sister and father to discover the crime and to set about avenging it. The conclusion is not known, however, because the legend's main text breaks off at that point.

The legend appears to have been a seasonal myth designed to account for the earth's bareness during the dry summer months. Presumably the rest of the text related how fertility returned to the earth, either through the resurrection of Aqhat or through the fathering of a new family by Danel.

ʿāqil (Arabic: "knowledgeable"), in Islāmic law, one who is in full possession of his mental faculties. Such a person is legally responsible for his actions and punishable for any deviation from religious commandments. *ʿĀqil* is often used with the adjective *bāligh* ("grown-up," or "of age") in contrast to *qāṣir* ("juvenile"). In Islāmic law, a *qāṣir* cannot qualify as a witness in court without consideration of his mental capabilities. For this reason many Muslim scholars directly relate *ʿāqil* to a person's age. Though there is no uniform opinion on the exact age at which an individual becomes an *ʿāqil,* the years 13 to 15 are often mentioned.

ʿAqqād, ʿAbbās Maḥmūd al- (b. June 28, 1889, Aswān, Egypt—d. March 12, 1964, Cairo), journalist, poet, and literary critic who was a prolific writer and an innovator of 20th-century Arabic poetry and criticism. Born in modest circumstances, al-ʿAqqād continued his education through reading when his formal schooling was cut short. He supported himself throughout most of his career by writing. An outspoken political commentator, he was imprisoned for some months in 1930–31 for remarks opposing the government. In 1942, with the advance of German troops, al-ʿAqqād sought refuge in the Sudan as a precaution against German reprisals for his attacks on Hitler.

Al-ʿAqqād's literary works included poems; a novel, *Sarāh* (1938), based on one of his own romances; and critiques of classical and modern Arabic authors. His essays show the influence of 19th-century English practitioners of the form, particularly Thomas Carlyle. Al-ʿAqqād devoted much thought to religion and politics, and his works include studies of the philosophy of the Qur'ān, of political and social philosophy, and biographies of such early Muslims as the 7th-century military commander Khālid ibn al-Walīd and of the 20th-century leader of the Egyptian Nationalist Party, Saʿd Zaghlūl.

aqua ammonia: *see* ammonium hydroxide.

aqua regia, mixture of concentrated nitric and hydrochloric acids, usually one part of the former to three parts of the latter by volume. This mixture was given its name (literally, "royal water") by the alchemists because of its ability to dissolve gold and other so-called noble metals.

Aqua regia and other mixtures similar to it are used in analytical procedures for the solution of certain iron ores, phosphate rocks, slags, nickel–chromium alloys, antimony, selenium, and some of the less soluble sulfides, such as those of mercury, arsenic, cobalt, and lead.

aquaculture, also called FISH FARMING, FISH CULTURE, or MARICULTURE, an approximate equivalent in fishing to agriculture, that is, the rearing of fish, shellfish, and some aquatic plants to supplement the natural supply. Fish are reared under controlled conditions all over the world.

Fish may be confined in earth ponds, concrete pools, cages suspended in the open sea, or in barricaded coastal waters. In these enclosures, the fish can be supplied with adequate food and protected from many natural predators.

While most fish farming is devoted to the commercial food market, many governmental agencies engage in it to stock lakes and rivers for sport fishing; there is, in addition, a steady commercial market for goldfish and other decorative fish for home aquariums. Aquaculturists also raise bait fish for both sport and commercial fishing.

Ocean ranching by governments is intended to restock lakes and oceans. The young fish are bred in the controlled environment and when sufficiently mature are released into the open sea. Oysters (as a source of both food and pearls), scallops, and mussels are raised throughout most of the world, as are carp and trout. In the United States and Europe experiments with ocean ranching of lobster are under way. Through aquaculture sturgeon is raised in the Soviet Union and salmon in the United States and Scotland.

aquaculture (plants): *see* hydroponics.

aquamarine, pale blue-green variety of beryl (*q.v.*) that is valued as a gemstone. The commonest variety of gem beryl, it occurs in pegmatite, in which it forms much larger and clearer crystals than emerald (one completely transparent crystal from Brazil weighed 110 kilograms [243 pounds]). Aquamarine occurs in Brazil, the chief source; the Urals, Soviet Union; Madagascar; Sri Lanka; India; and Maine, New Hampshire, Connecticut, North Carolina, and Colorado in the United States. Heat treatment improves the colour of many gem beryls; green beryl turns blue between 300° and 450° C (570° and 840° F).

aquarelle, technique of painting in transparent, rather than opaque, watercolours. Although aquarelle was known to the ancient Egyptians, it did not achieve popularity until the 18th and 19th centuries. It was used especially in France and England by landscape painters. *See* watercolour.

aquarium, receptacle for maintaining aquatic organisms, either freshwater or marine, or a facility in which a collection of aquatic organisms is displayed or studied.

Historical background. The earliest known aquarists were the Sumerians, who kept fishes in artificial ponds at least 4,500 years ago; records of fish keeping also date from ancient Egypt and Assyria. The Chinese, who raised carp for food as early as 1000 BC, were probably the first to breed fish with any degree of success. Their selective breeding of ornamental goldfish was later introduced to Japan, where the breeding of ornamental carp was perfected. The ancient Romans, who kept fish for food and entertainment, were the first known marine aquarists; they constructed ponds that were supplied with fresh seawater from the ocean. Although goldfish were successfully kept in glass vessels in England during the middle 1700s, aquarium keeping did not become well established until the relationship between oxygen, animals, and plants became known a century later.

By 1850 the keeping of fishes, amphibians, and reptiles had become useful in the study of nature. It was in the works of Philip Gosse, a British ornithologist, that the term aquarium first appeared. His work and the work of others aroused increased public interest in aquatic life. The first display aquarium was opened to the public in 1853 at Regent's Park in England. It was followed by aquariums in Berlin, Naples, and Paris. P.T. Barnum, the circus entrepreneur, recognized the commercial possibilities of living aquatic animals and, in 1856, opened the first display aquarium at the American Museum in New York City as a private enterprise. By 1928 there were 45 public or commercial aquariums throughout the world, but growth then slowed and few new large aquariums appeared until after World War II.

Many of the world's principal cities now have public aquariums as well as commercial ones. Another category encompasses those aquariums that serve chiefly as research institutions. Among the best known of the latter are those at Naples; L'Institut Oceanographique, Monaco; Plymouth Aquarium, Marine Biological Station, Plymouth, Eng.; and Scripps Institution of Oceanography, La Jolla, Calif. Still another category includes temporary aquariums that have served as exhibits at world's fairs and expositions.

The first oceanarium, or large marine aquarium, Marineland of Florida, was built in 1956 as a private enterprise; it featured a giant community fish tank and trained dolphins. Marineland of the Pacific, at Palos Verdes, Calif., and the Seaquarium, Miami, are similar. The emphasis in this type of aquarium is on very large tanks, up to 1,000,000 gallons each, in which a great variety of fishes is placed with no attempt to separate them. In the formal aquarium (*e.g.,* the John G. Shedd Aquarium, Chicago) the kinds and types of fishes are separated.

Function and purpose. Early aquariums were considered to be special museums, but their recreational appeal was soon recognized and developed. Publicly owned aquariums are primarily educational institutions. Privately owned ones, varying in size from small one-keeper operations to huge oceanariums, however, also frequently provide educational programs and exhibits; for example, the oceanariums pioneering in the capture, care, and training of dolphins and whales have increased public awareness of their importance.

Closely related to aquarium management is the raising of fishes and invertebrates to provide food or stock for sport fishing. This is now usually termed aquaculture or aquiculture. The maintenance of ornamental ponds may also serve a useful purpose, particularly since filtration and water treatment are sometimes used to improve pond-water quality. Such ponds may be small garden pools, primarily for water lilies, or larger ponds on farms for the culture of food fishes.

Design and architecture. The first containers specifically designed for aquatic specimens were the strictly functional open-air tanks used by the Romans to preserve and fatten fish for market. It was not until the 18th century that the importation of goldfish into France from the Orient for aesthetic enjoyment created the demand for small aquariums; ceramic bowls, occasionally fitted with transparent sections, were produced. In the large public aquariums built in many European cities between 1850 and 1880, efforts were made to create the illusion that the spectator was entering into the underwater world. More recently, the trend has been to emphasize the natural beauty of the specimens and to make a sharp distinction between the water and the viewing space.

Regardless of size—whether a small jar with a capacity of less than one gallon or a huge tank with a capacity of more than 1,000,000 gallons—aquariums must be constructed with care; many substances, especially plastics and adhesives, nontoxic to humans, are toxic to water-breathing animals.

Glass is probably the safest basic material, although polyethylene, polypropylene, acrylic plastics (Plexiglas), and fluorocarbon plastics are normally nontoxic. Fibre glass has been widely used and is nontoxic if properly prepared. Adhesives for sealing include epoxy resins, polyvinyl chloride, silicone rubber (except for certain coloured preparations), and neoprene. Metals are not usually used, especially in seawater, which is highly corrosive. Stainless steel, however, has a low toxicity, and is often used, especially in freshwater systems.

A small aquarium can be constructed entirely of glass and without supporting frames by using silicone rubber as an adhesive. Fibre glass is probably the most practical supporting material for all but the largest tanks since it is lightweight, strong, does not deteriorate, and is easily fabricated into any shape. Wood, though widely used, is subject to rot and boring organisms and thus must be protected. Reinforced concrete, including special mixes for seawater, is the principal supporting material used in the construction of large aquariums.

In modern aquariums tanks of a variety of sizes and shapes are often grouped together in order to avoid the "boxes of fish" look that characterizes some of the older, formal aquariums. Dry dioramas at the rear of the tank create the illusion of distance; the tank habitat can be a natural one or one in which fibre glass has been impregnated or painted to duplicate almost any environment. Modern aquariums attempt to illustrate the natural environment of the specimens displayed.

Polished plate glass, fully tempered polished plate glass, and Plexiglas are the most commonly used glazing materials. Polished plate glass is usually used only in small aquariums because it breaks into large pieces when it fails. One generally accepted practice is to glaze large tanks with two or three layers of tempered glass so that if breakage occurs it is confined to one layer. Although Plexiglas is easily scratched, it can be repolished.

Accessories for individual tanks normally include filters, air pumps, lights, and electric thermostatically controlled immersion heaters, or perhaps alternately, some means of chilling the water. In aquarium buildings the tanks are usually grouped so that they have a common filter and method of temperature control. Water sterilizers may be included. Plumbing in large aquariums with multiple systems is sometimes complex, involving a variety of automatic controls and water-quality monitoring systems. Because of its cost and fragility, glass plumbing (*e.g.,* for aeration or circulation of water within an aquarium) is used only in cases in which low toxicity is essential. Unplasticized polyvinyl chloride pipe is widely used. Fibre-glass pipe and epoxy-lined asbestos pipe are sometimes used, but lead and hard rubber pipe are obsolete. In seawater systems the growth of fouling organisms such as mussels and barnacles is avoided by providing the system with duplicate pipes and alternating their use on a weekly basis. When a line is dry, the few organisms present die and are flushed out when the line is again put into service.

Nonmetallic or plastic-lined pumps are better than metal ones in terms of toxicity, but stainless steel is often satisfactory. Airlift pumps (such as those used in home aquarium subsand filters) move large volumes of water when the lift pipes are of sufficient diameter.

Generally, the most effective illumination is by incandescent lamps placed above the front glass. Fluorescent lights provide even illumination but may overilluminate the tank walls; coloured lights accentuate natural colours; and mercury-vapour lamps encourage maximum growth of marine plants.

The introduction of some form of aquatic plant life is of practical value in an aquarium, although the presence of plants can cause complications. Aquatic plants consume dissolved oxygen and give off carbon dioxide; under the influence of bright light, plants also consume carbon dioxide and give off oxygen while engaged in photosynthesis. In turn, the waste products of the fishes form fertilizer or food for the plants and are consumed by them. This operates very well so long as light of a certain intensity falls on the plants—the animals thus give off what the plants can use and vice versa. Aquariums in which the plants and animals are believed to balance each other in the respiratory process are generally referred to as balanced aquariums.

Maintenance problems. The design of a large aquarium must take into account the requirements of the specimens, especially since exhibits at modern aquariums include all types of aquatic organisms: mammals, birds, reptiles, amphibians, and invertebrates as well as fishes. Among the many factors that must be considered are traffic flow patterns of visitors, reflections off glass, acoustics, and tank-maintenance problems such as water clarity, dissolved wastes, temperature, tank decor, disease treatment, and nutrition.

The primary requirement for maintaining aquatic organisms is water quality. The water supply must be free of pollutants, including sewage and industrial wastes, and it should be in gaseous equilibrium with the atmosphere to ensure adequate oxygen and to avoid supersaturation with nitrogen. In recirculating systems, water treatment must not only ensure clarity of the water but also purification of metabolic wastes. The source of fresh water is usually water supplies from which chlorine and other additives have been removed, either by carbon filtration or by the addition of a chemical. Marine organisms can be maintained in either natural or artificial seawater; the latter has the advantage of being initially free from disease-causing organisms and pollutants but may not be as suitable for some organisms.

There are three basic types of water systems: open, closed, and semiclosed. In open systems the water flows through the aquarium once and is discarded. This provides water quality comparable to that of the natural environment and there is no buildup of toxic metabolic wastes; however, temperature control and pumping are usually costly, and filtration often is necessary.

Water is continuously recirculated in closed systems and is only renewed periodically. Metabolic wastes must be treated since they are not continuously flushed from the system. An important problem is that ammonia must be rapidly removed or transformed because it is harmful even at very low concentrations. In the aquarium the bacteria that convert ammonia to nitrite reside primarily in the filter material, and a slow sand filter with a large surface area is usually provided to ensure their abundance. Plant growth in the aquarium, especially in marine systems, is not usually sufficient to utilize all the nitrate produced by bacteria from nitrite. Although some aquariums have operated many years with a minimum of water renewal, it is normally necessary to replace from 1 to 10 percent of the water per month to maintain a low level of nitrates. The use of charcoal in both fresh water and seawater systems helps to slow the accumulation of nitrogenous wastes. Metabolic wastes also cause an increase in the acidity of the water. Carbonate compounds are commonly used to maintain an optimal level of acidity, particularly when water renewal is infrequent.

Semiclosed systems are essentially the same as closed except that there is a constant connection to the water supply, and the problem of dissolved wastes is controlled by the regular addition of new water; this system is less costly than the open one with regard to temperature control and pumping.

Filters vary from simple flow-through systems to completely automated recirculating systems, with special provisions for monitoring and controlling the physical and chemical characteristics of the water.

The turnover rate, or rate of water replacement, of individual aquariums is important and should be no more than two hours. In addition, aeration by means of air stones (diffusers) should be provided to guard against asphyxia in the event of an unexpected water-supply failure.

Fishes and invertebrates can also be maintained without filtration or aeration in aquariums that are "balanced" with plants; however, the balance between plants and animals is very difficult to attain on a large scale or even in a normally stocked aquarium, especially a seawater aquarium.

Freshwater pools for mammals and birds present special problems. They generally require a higher filtration rate and greater filter capacity because they accumulate large amounts of fecal wastes. Air-breathing animals, however, are not highly sensitive to water quality; thus, chemical treatments, such as chlorination, which would kill fishes, can be used to control bacteria and to improve water clarity. Seawater formulas are simpler; for example, a 2 percent sodium chloride solution will satisfactorily maintain whales and dolphins. Seals and sea lions have been kept in fresh water, but this may increase their eye problems because of the osmotic effect of the fresh water on the eye tissues.

Aquarius (Latin: Water Bearer), in astronomy, zodiacal constellation lying between

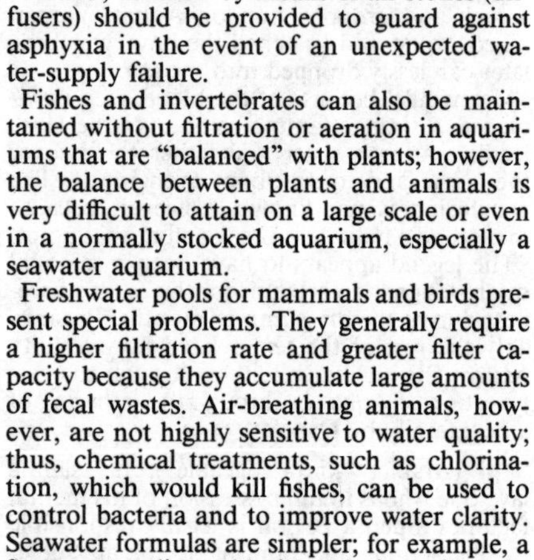

Aquarius, illumination from a Book of Hours, Italian, *c.* 1475; in the Pierpont Morgan Library, New York City (MS. G.14)

Capricornus and Pisces, at about 23 hours right ascension (the coordinate on the celestial sphere analogous to longitude on the Earth) and 10° south declination (angular distance south of the celestial equator). It lacks striking features, the brightest stars being only of the third magnitude.

In astrology, Aquarius is the 11th sign of the zodiac, considered as governing the period *c.* January 20–*c.* February 18. Its representation as a man pouring a stream of water out of a jug came about, it has been suggested, because in ancient times the rising of Aquarius coincided in the Middle East with a period of floods and rain. In the conceptual scheme of the "Great Year"—the more than 25,000 years it takes the Earth to pass in turn through the influence of each of the signs of the zodiac—the Earth is said to have passed into the age of Aquarius early in the 19th century.

aquatic locomotion, in animals, movement through water either by swimming or by progression in contact with the substrate (*i.e.,* the bottom or other surfaces).

Free-swimming locomotion is found in animals ranging from protozoans to whales. For effective swimming the animal controls its buoyancy and has a propulsion system able to compete with the resistance of water movements. Many invertebrates, especially mollusks, propel themselves by water jets; others use undulatory movements of their soft parts. The most widespread mechanism, however, is some means (*e.g.,* a paddle) of physically pressing against the water. This may take the form of anguilliform (undulatory) movements in eellike fishes; using the forelimbs as in turtles and penguins, hind limbs as in frogs and many diving birds, or all four limbs as in bears and most other terrestrial mammals. Highly evolved swimmers, such as whales and bony fishes, have the thrust concentrated in the tail and have reduced limbs, which are folded against the body in fast swimming.

Many animals, principally invertebrates and certain fishes, achieve locomotion by contact with the substrate. In fast-moving or turbulent water the animal usually has one or more adhesive disks for attachment to the substrate. In calmer water animals such as lobsters usually walk on the bottom.

aquatint, a variety of etching widely used by printmakers to achieve a broad range of tonal values. The process is called aquatint because finished prints often resemble watercolour drawings or wash drawings. The technique consists of exposing a copperplate to acid through a layer of granulated resin or sugar. The acid bites away the plate only in the interstices between the resin or sugar grains, leaving an evenly pitted surface that yields broad areas of tone when the grains are removed and the plate is printed. An infinite number of tones can be achieved by exposing various parts of the plate to acid baths of different strengths for different periods of time. Etched or engraved lines are often used with aquatint to achieve greater definition of form.

In the 17th century a number of attempts were made at producing what later became known as aquatint prints. None of the efforts was successful, however, until 1768, when the French printmaker Jean-Baptiste Le Prince discovered that granulated resin gave satisfactory results. Aquatint became the most popular method of producing toned prints in the late 18th century, especially among illustrators. Its textural subtleties, however, remained largely unexplored by well-known artists except for Francisco de Goya. Most of his prints are aquatints, and he is considered the greatest master of the technique.

After Goya's death aquatint was largely ignored until Edgar Degas (1834–1917) and Camille Pissarro (1830–1903) began to experiment with it. After a century of neglect, sugar aquatint, sometimes called sugar lift, was revived by 20th-century artists such as Pablo Picasso and Georges Rouault. Many contemporary printmakers also use pressurized plastic sprays in place of resin.

"Por que fue sensible," aquatint by Francisco de Goya from "Los Caprichos," 1799

By courtesy of Mrs. Geoffrey Wilson and Courtauld Institute of Art, London

aquavit, also spelled AQUAVITE, or AKVAVIT, also called SNAPS, flavoured, distilled liquor, clear to pale yellow in colour, dry in flavour, and ranging in alcohol content from about 42 to 45 percent by volume. It is distilled from a fermented potato or grain mash, redistilled in the presence of flavouring agents, filtered with charcoal, and usually bottled without aging. Various aromatic flavourings are employed, usually including caraway or cumin seed; lemon or orange peel, cardamom, aniseed, and fennel also may be used.

The beverage, produced in the Scandinavian countries, derives its name from *aqua vitae* (Latin: "water of life"), applied originally to liquor distilled from wine, and was made from imported wine; the product therefore was highly expensive until Swedish soldiers learned to make aquavit from grain. In the 18th century the potato became an important raw material.

Swedish and Norwegian aquavits are sweet and spicy and of straw colour. Sweden is the largest producer, manufacturing about 20 brands. Norway's production, comparatively low, includes Linie Aquavit, so called because it is shipped to Australia and back (across the Equator, or Line) in oak containers to produce mellow flavour. Finnish aquavit has a cinnamon flavour. The Danish product, also called *snaps,* is colourless, with a pronounced caraway flavour. One of the best known Danish types is Ålborg akvavit, named for a small town in Jutland, on Denmark's northern coast. The only brand exported from Denmark, it is produced by Danish Distilleries, a private organization granted the sole right to produce alcohol and yeast since 1927 under a monopoly of the Danish government.

In both the Scandinavian countries and northern Germany, aquavit is usually served chilled and unmixed, in small glasses, and is usually accompanied by appetizers or sandwiches; it is the traditional accompaniment to a smorgasbord.

Aquaviva, Claudio, Aquaviva also spelled ACQUAVIVA (b. Sept. 14, 1543, Atri, Kingdom of Naples—d. Jan. 31, 1615, Rome), fifth and youngest general of the Society of Jesus, considered by many to have been the order's greatest leader. The youngest son of the Duke of Atri, he joined the order in 1567. Shortly after completing his studies he was appointed provincial superior of Naples and then of Rome.

He was elected general in 1581, and his major political achievement occurred at the Jesuits' fifth General Congregation (1593–94). He succeeded in overcoming the efforts of some Spanish Jesuits—supported at first by King Philip II of Spain—to introduce modifications in the Institute of the Society of Jesus and to obtain a privileged status for the Spanish provinces.

Aquaviva's rule was marked by the rapid growth of the order from about 5,000 to more than 13,000 members and from 21 to 32 provinces, with the number of colleges reaching 372. His practical legislation strengthened the society and made it more efficient in its numerous foreign missions and colleges. He promoted the use of the *Spiritual Exercises* of St. Ignatius Loyola for the clergy and laymen. He encouraged the order's theologians and spiritual writers to more profound investigation and to publication. He organized the first scholarly writing of the history of the order and the compilation of annual reports of all the provinces (*Litterae Annuae*).

In the Constitutions of the order, Ignatius had indicated only in outline the Jesuit system of education. The fourth General Congregation, which had elected Aquaviva general, entrusted him with the task of drawing up a practical code of education for its schools. This work, *Ratio atque institutio studiorum* ("The Reason and Establishment of Studies"), was first published in 1586, at which time it was distributed to Jesuit schools for criticism and revision. The definitive text (1599) unified Jesuit teaching throughout the world, yet allowed for adaptation to local needs. His work strengthened the order internally and guided its external relations. He successfully furthered the apostolate of the Roman Catholic Church under eight popes, from Gregory XIII to Paul V.

Consult
the
INDEX
first

aqueduct, man-made conduit for carrying water (Latin *aqua,* "water," and *ducere,* "to lead"). In a more restricted sense, aqueducts are structures used to conduct a water stream across a hollow or valley. In modern engineering "aqueduct" refers to a system of pipes, ditches, canals, tunnels, and supporting structures used to convey water from its source to its main distribution point.

A brief treatment of aqueducts follows. For full treatment, *see* MACROPAEDIA: Public Works.

Although the Romans are considered the greatest aqueduct builders of the ancient world, *qanāt* systems were in use in ancient Persia, India, Egypt, and other Middle Eastern countries hundreds of years earlier. These systems utilized tunnels tapped into hillsides that brought water for irrigation to the plains below. Somewhat closer in appearance to the classic Roman structure was a limestone aqueduct built by the Assyrians around 691 BC to bring fresh water to the city of Nineveh. Approximately 2,000,000 large blocks were used to make a water channel 30 feet (10 metres) high and 900 feet long across a valley.

The elaborate system that served the capital of the Roman Empire, however, remains a major engineering achievement. Over a period of 500 years—from 312 BC to AD 226—11 aqueducts were built to bring water to Rome from as far away as 57 miles (92 kilometres). Some of these aqueducts are still in use. Only a portion of Rome's aqueduct system actually crossed over valleys on stone arches (30 mi out of a total of about 260 mi); the rest consisted of underground conduits made mostly of stone and terra cotta pipe but also of wood, leather, lead, and bronze. Water flowed to the city by the force of gravity alone and usually went through a series of distribution tanks within the city. Generally water was not stored, and the excess was used to flush out sewers. Rome's famous fountains were also supplied in this way.

Roman aqueducts were built throughout the empire, and their arches may still be seen in Greece, Italy, France, Spain, North Africa, and Asia Minor. As central authority fell apart in the 4th and 5th centuries, the systems also deteriorated. For most of the Middle Ages aqueducts were not used in western Europe, and people returned to getting their water from wells and local rivers. Modest systems sprang up around monasteries, and, by the 14th century, Bruges, with a large population for the time (40,000), had developed a system utilizing one large collecting cistern from which water was pumped, using a wheel with buckets on a chain, through underground conduits to public sites.

Major advances in public-water systems since the Renaissance have involved the refinement of pumps and of pipe materials. By the late 16th century London had a system that used five waterwheel pumps fastened under the London Bridge to supply the city, and Paris had a similar device at Pont Neuf that was capable of delivering 120 gallons (454 litres) per minute. Both cities were compelled to bring water from greater distances in the next century. A private company built an aqueduct to London from the river Chadwell, some 38 mi distant, that utilized more than 200 small bridges built of timber. A French counterpart combined pumps and aqueducts to bring water from Marly over a ridge and into an aqueduct some 525 ft above the Seine.

One of the major innovations during the 18th and 19th centuries was the introduction of steam pumps and the improvement of pressurized systems. One benefit of pumping water under pressure was that a system could be built that followed the contours of the land; the earlier free-flowing systems had had to maintain certain gradients over varied terrain. Pressurization also created the need for better pipe material. Wood pipes banded with metal and protected with asphalt coating were patented in the United States in 1855 and could withstand pressures up to 172 pounds per square inch (12 kilograms per square centimetre). Before long, however, wood was replaced first by cast iron and then by steel. For large siphons (conduits that draw water from elevated sources under the pressure of siphoning), reinforced concrete became the preferred construction material early in the 20th century.

Modern aqueducts, although lacking the arched grandeur of those built by the Romans, greatly surpass the earlier ones in length and in the amount of water that they can carry. Aqueduct systems hundreds of miles long have been built to supply growing urban areas and crop-irrigation projects. The water supply of New York City comes from three main aqueduct systems that can deliver from 1,800,000,000 gal of water a day from sources up to 120 mi away. The aqueduct system in the state of California, however, is by far the largest in the world. One major project, which has been under construction since 1960, will eventually bring water from the northern part of the state some 600 mi south to the Mexican border and is designed to yield 4,230,000 acre-feet (one acre-foot equals 325,851 gallons) per year.

Aquem-os-Montes (Portugal): *see* Minho.

Aquen, Jerome van: *see* Bosch, Hiëronymus.

aqueous humour, watery, alkaline liquid that occupies the anterior and posterior chambers of the eye—the space in front of the iris and lens and the ringlike space encircling the lens. The aqueous humour resembles blood plasma in composition, but contains much less protein, less glucose, more lactic acid, and much more ascorbic acid. Aqueous humour is formed from the blood by filtration through the surface of the back of the iris and of the ciliary body, the muscular structure that controls the curvature of the lens. It leaves the eye through a porous tissue into Schlemm's canal, a ringlike passageway around the outer angle of the anterior chamber. From the canal the liquid enters the veins.

When the aqueous humour does not adequately drain from the eye, pressure builds up and glaucoma can result.

Aquidneck Island (Rhode Island, U.S.): *see* Rhode Island.

aquifer, in hydrology, rock layer that contains water and releases it in appreciable amounts. The rock contains water-filled pore spaces, and, when the spaces are connected, the water is able to flow through the matrix of the rock. An aquifer also may be called a water-bearing stratum, lens, or zone.

A confined aquifer is a water-bearing stratum that is confined or overlain by a rock layer that does not transmit water in any appreciable amount or that is impermeable. There probably are few truly confined aquifers, because tests have shown that the confining strata, or layers, although they do not readily transmit water, over a period of time contribute large quantities of water by slow leakage to supplement production from the principal aquifer.

A groundwater aquifer is said to be unconfined when its upper surface (water table) is open to the atmosphere through permeable material. As opposed to a confined aquifer, the water table in an unconfined aquifer system has no overlying impervious rock layer to separate it from the atmosphere.

Aquifoliaceae, the holly family, in the order Celastrales, found worldwide, comprising two genera and about 400 species of shrubs and trees, best known for the genus *Ilex* (*see* holly). Four species of *Byronia* are in the Polynesian and Australian area, and only one species of mountain holly (*Nemopanthus mucronatus*) is native to northeastern North America.

The Aquifoliaceae differ from other members of the order Celastrales in lacking a nectar-secreting disk in the flowers.

Aquila, also called AKILAS (fl. 2nd century AD), scholar who in about AD 140 completed a literal translation into Greek of the Old Testament; it replaced the Septuagint (*q.v.*) among Jews and was used by the Church Fathers Origen in the 3rd century and St. Jerome in the 4th and 5th centuries. St. Epiphanius (*c.* 315—403) preserved in his writings the popular Christian tradition that Aquila was a relative of the Roman emperor Hadrian, who employed him in rebuilding Jerusalem. There he was converted to Christianity, but, on being reproved for practicing pagan astrology, he returned to Judaism.

The Talmud, the rabbinic compendium of law, lore, and commentary, states that Aquila was influenced in his translation by the great martyred scholar Rabbi Akiba ben Joseph (*q.v.*).

Aquila's version survives only in fragments, chiefly in extant portions of Origen's *Hexapla* and in manuscripts found in the *geniza* (synagogue storeroom for books) at the Ezra synagogue in Cairo. Aquila's exacting translation is important for what it reveals of the original Hebrew text of the Bible and also for what it demonstrates about the state of Hebrew learning in his time.

Aquila, L' (Italy): *see* L'Aquila.

Aquileia, formerly a city of the Roman Empire and a patriarchate of the Roman Catholic Church; it is now a village in Udine province of the Friuli-Venezia Giulia region in northeastern Italy, on the Natisone River near the Adriatic coast, northwest of Trieste.

Founded as a Roman colony in 181 BC to prevent barbarian incursions, Aquileia's position at the junction of the Via Postumia with roads north and east to the Roman provinces of Illyria, Pannonia, and Noricum encouraged its rapid growth as a commercial as well as military centre. By the 4th century it had become capital of the administrative regions of Venetia and Istria. Although the city had been unsuccessfully besieged by the Marcomanni and the Quadi (Germanic tribes) in 167, it fell to the Huns and was sacked in 452. The Lombards' invasion of Italy in 568 and their conquest of the Venetian mainland marked the final eclipse of Aquileia's political and economic importance; it became part of the Lombard duchy of Friuli.

The Basilica Teodoriana, Aquileia, Italy
Shostal—EB Inc.

An episcopal see (according to tradition, founded by St. Mark) from about the middle of the 3rd century, Aquileia became in the 5th century the metropolitan see for Venetia and Istria as well as for the outlying region north and east. After the condemnation in 533 by Pope Vigilius of the Three Chapters (heretical writings based on the emperor Justinian's ecclesiastical policies), Aquileia seceded from Rome, its bishop Macedonius adopting the title of patriarch in defiance of the Pope. The see remained schismatic when the patriarch Paolino I fled to Grado (the earlier foreport of Aquileia) after the Lombard invasion. When Candianus, who was loyal to Rome, was elected metropolitan at Grado in 607, the suffragan bishops of the Lombard mainland elected an abbot, John, at Aquileia, and he continued the schismatic policy of his predecessors.

The schism was finally ended under the pontificate of Sergius I (687–701) at a council at Pavia. Henceforth, Aquileia and Grado were recognized as separate sees and patriarchates. The residence of the patriarch of Aquileia had been transferred to Cormons in 627 for reasons of safety and to Cividale in 730. Aquileia's ecclesiastical importance was much enhanced by the mission of Bishop Paolino II (died 802) to the Avars and Slovenes, and in the 11th century Aquileia acquired extensive political privileges and feudal dominions, largely from the German kings. Bishop Poppone, who built Aquileia's Basilica Teodoriana (1021–31), was granted the right to coin money, and the see was invested with the county of Friuli and the marches (frontier territories) of Carniola (1077) and Istria (1209).

It remained a feudal principality until the conquest of Friuli by Venice in 1419–20. By the treaty of 1445, the patriarch finally acquiesced in the Venetian conquest and retained only Aquileia itself, San Vito, and San Daniele del Friuli. From the 15th century onward, the patriarchs were always Venetians. In 1751 Pope Benedict XIV suppressed the patriarchate and created the archbishoprics of Udine and Gorizia in its place. Aquileia, with its cathedral, was placed under papal jurisdiction. Pop. (1981 prelim.) mun., 3,281.

Aquino, Latin AQUINUM, town, Frosinone province, Lazio (Latium) region, south central Italy, southeast of Frosinone city. The ancient town (site nearby) prospered from its position on the Roman road, Via Latina, until it was laid waste by Totila, a Gothic king, at mid-6th century and abandoned for the more fertile present site. During the feudal struggles Riccardo, count of Acerra, uncle of St. Thomas Aquinas, was an important figure. His son captured Roccasecca Castle (4 mi [7 km] north of Aquino), the birthplace of St. Thomas, from the Holy Roman emperor Frederick II in the 13th century. Natives of the town are said to include the 1st–2nd-century Latin poet Juvenal and the 2nd-century emperor Pescennius Niger.

Impressive Roman ruins include a temple, an amphitheatre, and a triumphal arch supposed to honour the general and triumvir Mark Antony. The Benedictine church of Sta. Maria della Libera (1125), built on the ruins of a Roman temple, is roofless but has a fine doorway and beautiful mosaics.

Aquino is on the railway between Rome and Naples, and agriculture is the chief occupation. There is a sulfur and iron spring. Pop. (1981 prelim.) mun., 4,815.

Aquino, Benigno Simeon, Jr., byname NINOY (b. Nov. 27, 1932, Tarlac, Phil.—d. Aug. 21, 1983, Manila), the chief opposition leader during the era of martial law in the Philippines (1972–81) under Pres. Ferdinand E. Marcos. Returning from exile in 1983, he was assassinated on arrival at Manila airport.

The grandson of a Philippine general and the son of a well-known politician and landowner, Aquino began his career as a journalist at age 17 and four years later, as a journalist, facilitated the surrender of the Huk leader Luis Taruc. Aquino became mayor of Concepción in 1955, vice governor of Tarlac province in 1959, governor of Tarlac province in 1961, Philippine senator in 1967, and national leader of the Liberal party in 1968. Meanwhile, he had become wealthy through his marriage (1963) to the daughter of one of the largest landowners and manufacturers in the country.

Ostensibly planning to run for president in 1973, he was thwarted in 1972 when President Marcos declared martial law; he spent the next eight years in prison, being sentenced to death in November 1977, allegedly for giving aid to Communists and plotting the death of a village elder in 1967. In 1980 Marcos commuted the death sentence and allowed Aquino to go to the United States for heart-bypass surgery. Aquino remained there, with his family, for three years, receiving research grants from Harvard University and the Massachusetts Institute of Technology. Two years after martial law was lifted in the Philippines, he flew home, intending to campaign in promised elections. He was shot in the head while leaving the airplane at Manila Airport under security guard.

Aquitaine, planning region (French *région de programme*), encompassing the southwestern French *départements* of Dordogne, Gironde, Landes, Lot-et-Garonne, and Pyrénées-Atlantiques; it is roughly coextensive with the western half of the historic region of Aquitaine. The capital is Bordeaux. The region has an area of 15,987 sq mi (41,407 sq km) and is bounded by the *départements* of Charente-Maritime, Charente, and Haute-Vienne to the north and Corrèze, Lot, Tarn-et-Garonne, Gers, and Hautes-Pyrénées to the east. Pyrénées-Atlantiques, which is bordered by Spain to the south, and Landes and Gironde face the Bay of Biscay to the west.

The following article summarizes the political history, geography, demographic patterns, and economy of modern Aquitaine; for additional treatment of its geography and history, *see* MACROPAEDIA: France.

In Julius Caesar's description of Gaul, "Aquitania" was an area extending from the Pyrenees to the Garonne River. The Roman emperor Augustus (reigned 27 BC–AD 14) made it a Roman administrative district, and its borders were extended as far north as the Loire and east to the Massif Central.

A Visigothic province in the 5th century, Aquitaine came under Frankish rule in the 6th century, although it retained a measure of provincial identity exploited by local rulers. Long resistant in the 8th century, it was finally subdued by Charlemagne, who bestowed it (less Gascony) as a kingdom upon his son Louis (the future emperor Louis I). It remained a kingdom under Louis's son Pepin I and under the latter's son Pepin II, its chief towns being Toulouse, Limoges, and Poitiers. Devastation by the Normans in the 9th century, however, led to political and social upheavals during which various feudal domains were established.

The title of duke of Aquitaine, which had already been used by various little-known persons in the 7th century, was assumed at the end of the 9th by William I the Pious, count of Auvergne, the founder of the abbey of

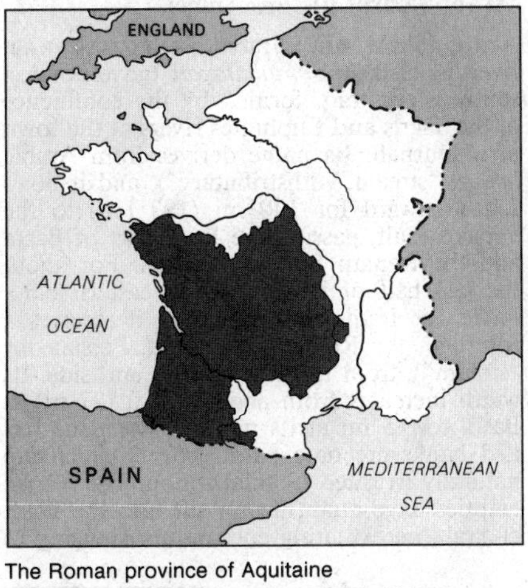

The Roman province of Aquitaine

Adapted from *Westermann Grosser Atlas zur Weltgeschichte*; Georg Westermann Verlag, Braunschweig

Cluny. In the first half of the 10th century the counts of Auvergne, of Toulouse, and of Poitiers each claimed this ducal title, but it was eventually secured by William I, count of Poitiers (William III of Aquitaine). The powerful house of the counts of Poitiers retained Aquitaine during the 10th and 11th centuries, endeavouring from time to time to restore to the name its former significance by extending the boundaries of the duchy to include Gascony and Toulouse. Then on the death without heirs of the last duke, William X (William VIII of Poitiers), in 1137, his daughter Eleanor united Aquitaine to the kingdom of France by her marriage with Louis VII. When Louis divorced her, however, Eleanor of Aquitaine married in 1152 the count of Anjou, Henry Plantagenet, who two years later became king of England as Henry II. The duchy thus passed to her new husband, who, having suppressed a revolt there, gave it to his son, Richard the Lion-Heart, who spent most of his life there, often subduing rebellious vassals. When Richard died in 1199, it reverted to Eleanor, and on her death five years later, it was united to the English crown and henceforward followed the fortunes of the English possessions in France.

Aquitaine, as it came to the English kings, stretched as of old from the Loire to the Pyrenees, but its extent was curtailed on the southeast by the wide lands of the counts of Toulouse. The name Guyenne (or Guienne), a corruption of Aquitaine, seems to have come into use about the 10th century, and the subsequent history of Aquitaine is merged in that of Gascony and Guyenne (*qq.v.*), which were completely reunited to France by the end of the Hundred Years' War.

Lowlands predominate outside the Pyrenees mountains themselves, which rise in the south. The highest point in the region is the peak of Midi d'Ossau (9,465 ft [2,885 m]); most land, however, lies below 1,600 ft. Annual precipitation exceeds 30 in. (800 mm) outside Lot-et-Garonne and southern Dordogne and increases toward the Pyrenees. An oceanic climate prevails.

The depopulation that characterized much of rural France in the 19th and early 20th centuries was very pronounced in Aquitaine. The regional population declined by fully 10 percent between 1886 and 1921, and has shown only modest growth since 1946. Immigrants from North Africa attracted by industrial jobs in the Bordeaux and Lacq regions have accounted for much of the postwar increase. The population is increasingly urban. Small towns are generally in decline, though Libourne, Bergerac, and Sarlat-la-Canéda continue to show vitality.

Corn (maize) was introduced in the late 16th century and has become the leading cereal. Viticulture is widespread. Cash crops were introduced in the late 19th century and include tobacco, apples, pears, peaches, French beans, and peas. Forests cover much of the land. The industrial sector is of little importance outside Bordeaux. Approximately one-half of the natural gas produced at Lacq (*q.v.*) is exported to other French regions. The separatist Socialist Party of the Basque Country (Basque *Euskal Herriko Alderdi Sozialista*) is particularly active in Bayonne. Pop. (1982) 2,656,544.

Aquitaine, John of Gaunt, duc d' (duke of): *see* John of Gaunt, duke of Lancaster.

Aquitanian Stage, major worldwide division of lower Miocene rocks and time (the Miocene Epoch began about 26,000,000 years ago and lasted about 19,000,000 years). The Aquitanian Stage is the lowermost stage of the Miocene Epoch (although early studies included the Aquitanian in the preceding Oligocene Epoch) and precedes the Burdigalian Stage. The Aquitanian was named for exposures studied in the region of Aquitaine in southwestern France. In Europe, Aquitanian rocks are widespread and include both marine and continental deposits. Important limestone deposits are found in the Paris Basin region and in Brittany. In the Middle East the Middle Asmari Limestone is representative; the upper Nari Series of India and Pakistan is also Aquitanian. The Aquitanian is characterized by a distinctive fossil fauna frequently represented by molluscan forms related to the pectinoid clams.

Ar (Scotland): *see* Ayr.

AR-15 (U.S. rifle): *see* M16 rifle.

ar-Ruhā (Turkey): *see* Urfa.

Ara (India): *see* Arrah.

Ara Pacis, also called ARA PACIS AUGUSTAE (Altar of the Augustan Peace), shrine consisting of a marble altar in a walled enclosure erected in Rome's Campus Martius by the emperor Augustus and dedicated on Jan. 30, 9 BC. The sculptures on the walls and the altar representing the shrine's dedication ceremonies, scenes from Roman legend, and floral motifs are considered to be among the finest examples of Roman art.

Arab, Arabic singular masculine ʿARABĪ, singular feminine ʿARABĪYAH, plural ʿARAB, one whose native language is Arabic. (*See* Arabic language.) Before the spread of Islām and, with it, the Arabic language, "Arab" referred to any of the largely nomadic Semitic inhabitants of the Arabian Peninsula. In modern usage, it embraces any of the Arabic-speaking peoples living in the vast region from Mauritania, on the Atlantic coast of Africa, to southwestern Iran, including the entire Maghrib of North Africa, the Arabian Peninsula, and the Middle East.

This diverse assortment of peoples defies physical stereotyping. Most Arabic-speaking peoples are of Mediterranean physical type, but there is considerable regional variation, with admixtures of Negroid, Caucasoid, and Mongoloid peoples of Africa, Europe, and Asia.

The early Arabs of the Arabian Peninsula were mainly nomadic pastoralists, who herded their sheep, goats, and camels through the harsh desert environment. Settled Arabs practiced date and cereal agriculture in the oases, which also served as trade centres for the caravans transporting the spices, ivory, and gold of southern Arabia and the horn of Africa to the civilizations farther north. The distinction between the desert nomads, on the one hand, and town-dwellers and agriculturalists, on the other, still pervades much of the Arabic-speaking world.

Islām (*q.v.*), which developed in the west central Arabian Peninsula in the late 7th century AD, was the religious force that unified the desert subsistence nomads—the Bedouins—with the town-dwellers of the oases. Within a century, Islām spread throughout most of the present-day Arabic-speaking world, and beyond, into Central Asia and the Iberian Peninsula. Elements of Arab culture, including the veneration of the desert nomad's life, were integrated with local Persian, Jewish, Greek, and Indian traditions. Arabs of the 20th century, however, are not exclusively Muslim; approximately 5 percent of the native speakers of Arabic worldwide are Christians, Druzes, Jews, or animists.

The original caliphate, or empire of Muḥammad, was supplanted by the Umayyad dynasty of Syria in the 7th and 8th centuries. The Ummayyads established a system of local autonomy, but used the Arabic language and the Qurʾān (Koran), the sacred text of Islām, as unifying forces. The ʿAbbāsid dynasty governed the Islāmic world from Baghdad between the 8th and 13th centuries, the period of greatest Arab intellectual achievement in chemistry, mathematics, historiography, and architecture and in the preservation of classical Greek philosophy. From the 13th century onward, Arab power and cultural achievement declined with the erosion of Arab rule in Europe and Central Asia. By the 16th century, the Ottoman Turks had gained hegemony over most of the Arabic-speaking world, and they retained political control until World War I, when the British replaced them. Only after World War II did most of the Arabic-speaking world achieve self-rule and face the problems raised by modernization and technological advancement.

In the 20th-century Arab world, traditional values have been modified by the pressures of urbanization, industrialization, detribalization, and Western influence. About 40 percent of the Muslim Arabs live in cities and towns, where family and tribal ties tend to break down, where women, as well as men, have greater educational and employment opportunities, and where the newly emerging middle class of technical and professional people, bureaucrats, and industrialists gained influence as typically urban economic goals were pursued. Urban Arabs tended to identify themselves more by occupation or nationality than by tribe.

The majority of Arabs continue to live in small, isolated farming villages, where traditional values and occupations prevail. Village farmers venerate the pastoral nomad's way of life and claim kinship ties with the great desert tribes of the past and present. Nationalism and the change in standards of living made possible by the expanded oil industry, however, have altered the nomadic life.

The pastoral desert nomad, the traditional ideal of Arab culture, makes up barely 5 percent of the modern Arab population. Many of the remaining nomads have given up full-time subsistence pastoralism to become full- or part-time stock breeders. Others have specialized in carrying goods from the remote countryside to the towns or in bringing manufactured goods, luxury items, and processed foods from the cities to the villages. Those who leave the nomadic life become village agriculturalists or find employment with oil companies or other employers in the towns and cities.

The strategic location of the Arab countries between the world's major political powers, and the social, political, and technological problems created by the West's demand for Arab oil all presage great social and cultural changes.

ʿArab, Jazīrat al-: *see* Arabia.

Arab, Shatt al-, Arabic SHAṬṬ AL-ʿARAB, river in al-Baṣrah *muḥāfaẓah* (governorate), southeastern Iraq, formed by the confluence of the Tigris and Euphrates rivers at the town of al-Qurnah. Its name derives from Arabic (*shaṭṭ*, "stream," "distributary"), and it flows southeastward for 120 mi (193 km) to the Persian Gulf, passing the Iraqi port of Basra and the Iranian port of Abadan. For about the last half of its course the eastern bank forms the Iraqi–Iranian border; it receives a tributary, the Rūd-e Kārūn (*rūd*, Persian for "stream"), from the eastern (Iranian) side. Its width increases from about 120 ft (37 m) at Basra to 0.5 mi at its mouth. Along the settled banks are date palm groves, which are naturally irrigated by tidal action. The Kārūn empties large quantities of silt into the Shatt al-Arab, necessitating continuous dredging to keep the channel navigable for shallow-draft oceangoing vessels. The present river pattern probably is relatively recent, but its mode of formation is uncertain. The Tigris and Euphrates possibly once flowed to the Persian Gulf by a more westerly channel, while the Shatt al-Arab's present lower course may have been part of the Rūd-e Kārūn.

Dhows moored in the Shatt al-Arab, Iraq
Diane Rawson—Photo Researchers

Arab Bank for Economic Development in Africa, French BANQUE ARABE POUR LE DÉVELOPPEMENT ÉCONOMIQUE EN AFRIQUE (BADEA), Arabic AL-BANK AL-ʿARABĪ LIL-TAṬAWŪR AL-IQTIṢĀDĪ FĪ AFRIQĪYĀ, bank created by the Arab League summit conference in Algiers, in November 1973, to finance development projects. In 1975, BADEA began operating by supplying African countries with technical assistance. All members of the Organization of African Unity (OAU) are eligible as recipients, except those countries belonging to the Arab League. BADEA includes all members of the Arab League except Djibouti, Somalia, Yemen (Aden), and Yemen (Ṣanʿāʾ). BADEA's objectives are twofold: to assist African countries with large balance-of-payment deficits by providing aid and to sponsor Arab investments in Africa through investment guarantees. The headquarters are in Khartoum, The Sudan.

Consult the INDEX *first*

Arab Economic Unity, Council of, Arabic AL-JAMʿĪYAH AL-ʿARABĪYAH LIL-WIḤDAH AL-IQTISĀDĪYAH, Arab organization established in June 1957 by a resolution of the Arab Economic Council of the Arab League. The first meeting of the council was held in 1964. Membership is composed of Iraq, Jordan, Kuwait, Libya, Mauritania, the Palestine Liberation Organization, Somalia, Sudan, Syria, United Arab Emirates, Yemen (Aden), and Yemen (Ṣanʿāʾ).

The council's focus is regional, devoted to achieving economic integration through the framework of economic and social development. An agreement within the council between Iraq, Jordan, Libya, Mauritania, and Syria established the Arab Common Market, oriented toward facilitating the international movement of capital, goods, and people.

Arab Fund for Economic and Social Development, Arabic AL-ṢANDŪQ AL-ʿARABĪ LIL-ISTITHMĀR WA AL-TANMĪYAH AL-IJTIMĀʿIYAH, fund designed to promote economic and social development of Arab countries. Established in May 1968, the fund commenced operations in 1972 and serves 21 Arab countries and the Palestine Liberation Organization.

By financing development projects, promoting investments, and providing technical assistance, the fund encourages investment of public and private capital in the development of the Arab economies. It grants loans on easy terms to governments and to both private and public institutions for projects of specific interest to Arabs. The fund also provides assistance and technical expertise in various economic fields.

Arab–Israeli wars, major encounters between Israeli and various Arab forces, most notably in 1948–49, 1956, 1967, 1973, and 1982.

The first war immediately followed the proclamation of the State of Israel, May 14, 1948. Arab forces from Egypt, Transjordan, Iraq, Syria, and Lebanon occupied the areas in southern and eastern Palestine not apportioned to the Jews, then captured the small Jewish quarter of the Old City of Jerusalem. The Israelis, meanwhile, won control of the main road to Jerusalem through the Judaean Hills and successfully beat off Arab attacks. By early 1949 the Israelis managed to occupy all of the Negev up to the former Egypt–Palestine frontier, except for the Gaza Strip. Between February and July 1949, as a result of separate armistice agreements between Israel and the Arab states, a temporary frontier was fixed where the line had been at the beginning of the negotiations.

Tensions mounted again with the rise to power of the strongly nationalist Egyptian president Gamal Abdel Nasser; in October 1956, in the midst of the international crisis caused by Nasser's seizure of the European-owned Suez Canal, Israel invaded the Sinai Desert peninsula to destroy hostile Arab bases there. In five days the Israeli Army captured Gaza, Rafa, and al-ʿArīsh—taking thousands of prisoners—and occupied most of the peninsula east of the Suez Canal. The Israelis were then in a position to open sea communications through the Gulf of Aqaba, an added threat to the Egyptians. In December, after a joint Anglo-French intervention, a United Nations Emergency Force was stationed in the area, and Israeli forces finally withdrew in March 1957.

Arab–Israeli forces clashed for the third time June 5–10, 1967, in what came to be called the Six-Day War. In early 1967 Syrian bombardments of Israeli villages had been intensified. When the Israeli Air Force shot down six Syrian MiG planes in reprisal, Nasser mobilized his forces near the Sinai border. During this war Israel eliminated the Egyptian Air Force and established air superiority. The war cost the Arabs the Old City of Jerusalem, the Sinai and the Gaza Strip, the Jordanian territory west of the Jordan River, known as the West Bank, and the Golan Heights, on the Israeli–Syrian border.

The sporadic fighting that followed the Six-Day War again developed into full-scale war in 1973. On October 6, the Jewish holy day of Yom Kippur (thus "Yom Kippur War"), Israel was attacked by Egypt across the Suez Canal and by Syria on the Golan Heights. The Arab armies showed greater aggressiveness and fighting ability than in the previous wars, and the Israeli forces suffered heavy casualties. The Israeli Army, however, pushed its way into Syrian territory and encircled the Egyptian Army by crossing the Suez Canal and establishing forces on the Canal's west bank.

Israel and Egypt signed a cease-fire agreement in November and, on Jan. 18, 1974, peace agreements. The accords provided for Israeli withdrawal into the Sinai west of the Mitla and Gidi passes, while Egypt was to reduce the size of its forces on the east bank of the canal. A UN peace-keeping force was established between the two armies. This agreement was supplemented by another signed on Sept. 4, 1975. On May 31, 1974, Israel and Syria signed a cease-fire agreement that also covered separation of their forces by a UN buffer zone and exchange of prisoners of war.

On June 5, 1982, less than six weeks after Israel's complete withdrawal from the Sinai, increased tensions between Israelis and Palestinians resulted in the Israeli jet bombings of Beirut and southern Lebanon, where the Palestine Liberation Oranization (PLO) had a number of strongholds. By June 14 Israel's land forces had invaded Lebanon as far as the outskirts of Beirut, which was encircled; but the Israeli government agreed to halt advancement and begin negotiations with the PLO. After much delay and massive Israeli shelling of West Beirut, the PLO evacuated the city under the supervision of a multinational force, and Palestinians were assigned to refugee camps. Eventually, Israeli troops also withdrew from West Beirut. On September 14, however, when Lebanese president Bashir Gemayel was assassinated, the Israelis reentered the city reportedly to protect the Palestinian refugees, who might suffer reprisals from Gemayel's Lebanese Christian supporters. Nevertheless, on September 16, Lebanese Christians gained access to two refugee camps and killed hundreds of Palestinians.

The incident received international condemnation, and several top Israeli defense officials were forced to resign after they were found indirectly responsible for the tragedy by an independent commission of inquiry.

Arab League, Arabic AL-JĀMIʿA AL-ʿARABĪYAH, also called LEAGUE OF ARAB STATES, Arabic AL-JĀMIʿA AL-DUWAL AL-ʿARABĪYAH, regional organization of Arab states in the Middle East, formed in Cairo on March 22, 1945. The founding member states were Egypt, Syria, Lebanon, Iraq, Transjordan (now Jordan), Saudi Arabia, and Yemen (now Yemen [Ṣanʿāʾ]). Other members are Libya (1953); The Sudan (1956); Tunisia and Morocco (1958); Kuwait (1961); Algeria (1962); Yemen ([Aden]; 1967); Bahrain, Oman, Qatar, and the United Arab Emirates (1971); Mauritania (1973); Somalia (1974); the Palestine Liberation Organization (PLO; 1976); and Djibouti (1977). Each member has one vote on the League Council, decisions being binding only on those states that have voted for them.

The aims of the league in 1945 were to strengthen and coordinate the political, cultural, economic, and social programs of its members and to mediate disputes among them or between them and third parties. The signing on April 13, 1950, of an agreement on joint defense and economic cooperation also committed the signatories to coordination of military defense measures.

In its early years, the Arab League concentrated mainly on economic, cultural, and social programs. In 1959 it held the first Arab petroleum congress and in 1964 established the Arab League Educational, Cultural, and Scientific Organization (ALECSO). Also in 1964, despite objections by Jordan, the league admitted the PLO as the representative of all Palestinians. Under the leadership of Mahmoud Riad, the third secretary general (1972–79), political activity increased. The league, however, was weakened by internal dissension on political issues, especially those concerning Israel and the Palestinians. After Egypt signed a peace treaty with Israel on March 26, 1979, other Arab League members met in Baghdad and, in protest of what they considered to be a separate peace, voted to suspend Egypt's membership and to transfer the league's headquarters from Cairo to Tunis.

Arab Legion, Arabic AL-JAISH AL-ARABĪ, police force raised in 1921 by British Lieut. Col. Frederick Gerard Peake in Transjordan, a British protectorate, to keep order among Transjordanian tribes and to safeguard Transjordanian villagers from Bedouins. In 1939 Maj. (later Gen.) John Bagot Glubb, called Glubb Pasha, became the Legion's commander and transformed it into the most effective military force in the Arab world. At the end of the Palestine War in 1948, the Arab legion, 6,000 strong, was the only Arab army that had been able to retain any Palestinian territory. King Abdullah of Transjordan annexed those portions, which included Jerusalem, Hebron, and Nablus, and proclaimed his country the Arab Hashemite Kingdom of Jordan.

Even after Jordan proclaimed its independence from Britain, the Arab Legion remained under Glubb's command, but nationalist sentiments in the country grew until King Hussein, who came into power in 1953, was forced to dismiss Glubb on March 1, 1956. The legion was then nationalized under the command of Ali Abu Nawwar, Hussein's personal adjutant. In that same year the Arab Legion, which was a volunteer army, merged with the Jordanian National Guard, a conscripted force, to form a unified Jordanian army.

Arab Monetary Fund, Arabic AL-ṢANDŪQ AL-MĀLĪ AL-ʿARABĪ, fund that aims to assist its participants, all 21 members of the Arab League, by developing their capital markets, balancing payment difficulties, and helping with foreign exchange rates. Established in April 1976, the agreement entered into force in February 1977. During its annual meeting, the Board of Governors of the fund formulates policy aimed at integrating and liberalizing trade. Specifically, the fund issues guarantees meant to fortify borrowing capacities, provides technical assistance to monetary institutions, and provides short- and medium-term loans. The headquarters are in Abu Dhabi, United Arab Emirates.

Arab Petroleum Exporting Countries, Organization of (OAPEC), Arabic MUNAẒAMAT AL-DŪWAL AL-ʿARABĪYAH AL-MUṢADDARAH LIL-BITRŪL, Arab organization formed in January 1968 to promote international economic cooperation within the petroleum industry. Chairmanship rotates annually; meetings occur four times yearly. Member countries include Algeria, Bahrain, Iraq, Kuwait, Libya, Qatar, Saudi Arabia, Syria, and United Arab Emirates. The headquarters are in Kuwait.

OAPEC seeks to achieve four basic goals. These include realizing close national ties, determining ways and means of safeguarding member interests, unifying efforts to maintain a flow of petroleum to markets on profitable terms, and creating a suitable climate for industry investment in member countries.

The secretariat of OAPEC is divided into seven departments—administrative and financial, legal, economic, information and public relations, oil projects, library and documentation, and exploration and production. Joint national undertakings have centred on the transportation of crude oil, gas, and refined products and increased Arab participation in the transport industry and the construction of vessels and of petrochemical plants.

Arab Socialist Renaissance Party: *see* Baʿth Party.

ʿArabah, Wādī al-, Hebrew HA-ʿARAVA, topographical depression in southern Palestine extending about 100 mi (160 km) south from the Dead Sea to the Gulf of Aqaba; it is part of the East African Rift Valley. Largely sandy desert, it is divided between Israel and Jordan. In the Old Testament, except in Deuteronomy 2:8, ʿArabah refers to the Jordan Valley, but eventually the name came to be applied exclusively to the southern area. As the site of important trade routes and the only iron and copper mines in Canaan, the ʿArabah was frequently fought over in biblical times by the kings of Judah and Edom.

ʿArabat al-Madfuna, al- (Egyptian city): *see* Abydos.

arabesque, style of decoration characterized by intertwining plants and abstract curvilinear motifs. Derived from the work of Hellenistic craftsmen working in Asia Minor, the arabesque originally included birds in a highly naturalistic setting. As adapted by Muslim artisans about AD 1000, it became highly formalized; for religious reasons, no birds, beasts, or human figures were included. The arabesque became an essential part of the decorative tradition of Islāmic cultures.

In Europe from the Renaissance until the early 19th century, arabesques were used for the decoration of illuminated manuscripts, walls, furniture, metalwork, and pottery. These designs usually were composed of either twining or sinuous scrolls of branches and leaves or ornate lines abstracted from such natural forms. Human figures often were integral to Western arabesque designs. Though the word had meant simply "Arabian" in 16th-century France, it was defined in a dictionary of 1611 as "rebesque work, a small and curious flourishing."

The earliest Western models inspiring the work of early Renaissance Italian artists were actually ancient Roman stucchi, plaster models found in Roman tombs. Arabesque stonework was designed by the mid-15th century, and painting in the style executed by Giulio Romano and the pupils of Raphael

Arabesque decoration on the dome of the Madar-i-Shāh *madrasah* ("school") built by Ḥusayn I, early 18th century, at Isfahan, Iran

Ray Manley—Shostal Assoc./EB Inc.

decorated the open galleries, or loggie, of the Vatican in the following century. Delicate silverwork of northern Italy and, later, Spain also used the motifs, and they began to appear in the decoration of majolica at Urbino, armour at Milan, tapestry at Florence, and illuminated manuscripts at Mantua.

Renaissance arabesques maintained the classical tradition of median symmetry, freedom in detail, and heterogeneity of ornament. The arabesque of this period also allowed the inclusion of a broad range of elements—human beings, beasts, birds, fishes, flowers—in imaginative or fantasy scenes, usually with copious inter-lacings of vines, ribbons, or the like.

With the coming of the Baroque, the use of arabesque decoration fell into disfavour until the middle of the 18th century, when a new series of Roman arabesques was discovered at Herculaneum. In 1757 the Comte de Caylus published his *Recueil de peintures antiques* ("Collection of Ancient Paintings"), and by 1770, engraved models for arabesques again were being published in Paris. The late French reliefs and paintings are among the most beautiful arabesques ever produced, but the formality of Directoire and Empire design after the Revolution gradually ended the fashion.

'Arabestān (Iran): *see* Khūzestān.

Arabi (Egyptian nationalist): *see* 'Urābī Pasha.

'Arabī, Ibn al- (Muslim mystic–philosopher): *see* Ibn al-'Arabī.

Arabia, also called ARABIAN PENINSULA, Arabic SHIBH AL-JAZĪRAH AL-'ARABIYAH, or JAZĪRAT AL-'ARAB, peninsula of southwestern Asia, bounded by the Red Sea (southwest), the Gulf of Aden and the Arabian Sea (south), the Gulf of Oman and the Persian (or Arabian) Gulf (east), and by Iraq, Jordan, and the Gulf of Aqaba (north). Its area is about 1,000,000 sq mi (2,600,000 sq km).

The article that follows is a summary of the significant detail about Arabia. Fuller treatment is provided in the MACROPAEDIA articles named below. For geography, economy, demography, administrative and social conditions, and history, *see* Arabia; for information about the region in its continental setting and about associated physical features, *see* Asia. For additional information about its major cultural manifestations, *see* Islām, Muḥammad and the Religion of; Middle Eastern Religions, Ancient; Islāmic Arts. For further information about regional aspects of Arabia's history, *see* Islāmic World, The. For information about its major cities, *see* Mecca and Medina.

Politically, Arabia comprises the territory of eight sovereign countries: Saudi Arabia; the two Yemens, the Yemen Arab Republic (or Yemen [Ṣan'ā']) and the People's Democratic Republic of Yemen (or Yemen [Aden]); Oman; and the Persian Gulf states of the United Arab Emirates, Qatar, Bahrain, and Kuwait. There is also a small, nonsovereign Neutral Zone, shared by Saudi Arabia and Iraq. The population of the peninsula in the early 1980s was approximately 20,000,000.

The land. Geographically, the Arabian Peninsula is a basin-shaped plateau, separated from the sea on three sides by mountains and sloping gently downward toward the fourth side, the eastern lowland areas adjoining the Persian Gulf. Geologically, the mountains on the western side of the peninsula constitute a single province with those across the Red Sea, to which they were once joined and from which they have been separated by the geological action of the East African Rift System in opening the Red Sea some 50,000,000 years ago. This geological activity is apparent in the incidence of damaging earthquakes. The southern wall of mountains also slopes gently inward toward the centre of the geologically stable Arabian Shield. The interior of the plateau is marked by a succession of desert regions from the Great Nafud in the northwest to the Rub' al-Khāli (or Empty Quarter) in the south. Sandy coastal lowlands surround the Persian Gulf in the northeast. None of the mountain regions is particularly high, with the maximum elevation on the peninsula at Ḥādur Shu'ayb in Yemen (Ṣan'ā'), 12,336 ft (3,760 m) above sea level. The narrow coastal plain that separates the plateau from the sea on three sides contains much of the cultivated land and most of the trading cities that for 3,000 years have connected the region with the rest of Asia and Africa.

The wall of mountains keeps most of the peninsula very dry (usually less than 4 in. [100 mm] of rainfall annually), except for a few eastern areas under the influence of the Indian Ocean monsoon and for western coastal areas, which benefit from the mountain rain barrier. The most congenial areas for human habitation are those of the Yemens, where rainfall may reach 20 to 40 in. annually. Elsewhere, temperatures are often terribly hot (reaching 130° F [54° C]) in the summer, and, although the climate may be pleasant in spring and fall, it is still usually too dry to permit much cultivation. There are seasonal winds, such as the *shamal* from the north and (less frequently) the *kaus* from the southeast. Geological evidence indicates that in the past the peninsula has been much more hospitable to human settlement and habitation, even during comparatively recent times. The wadis, seasonal watercourses, once were year-round streams.

Arabia is largely devoid of trees, except for the date palm, which grows everywhere and was for centuries a staple of domestic economy. Some other trees, such as acacia, tamarisk, and mimosa, are used as windbreaks to stabilize dunes. Alfalfa is often planted as a fodder crop, and such crops as cotton, wheat, and millet can be cultivated in the drier areas. Salt scrub is the only natural vegetation in much of the desert and highland areas. In the better watered Yemen and 'Asir regions, cactus-like euphorbia, eucalyptus, buddleia scrub, aloe, and other vegetation grow naturally, but overgrazing by livestock and terracing for agriculture have reduced natural vegetation to useless patches.

Animal life includes mammals such as wolf, hyena, fox, honey badger, and mongoose, widely distributed but small in numbers. Bird life is more extensive, but many are seasonal migrants; included are eagles, hawks, and falcons (long used for sport and hunting); owls; flamingos; and others. The status of nature protection is precarious; many species have been hunted to virtual extinction. Marine life in the surrounding seas is rich and varied, particularly among the reef areas of the Red Sea.

The only important mineral resource in the peninsula is petroleum; Arabia has more than two-fifths of the world's reserves. Most of these deposits are on or off the shore of the Persian Gulf, and their exploitation also leads to extraction of associated sulfur. Gypsum and marble are quarried, but copper and phosphate deposits are not exploited, although they are being explored.

The people. The population of Arabia in the early 1980s was estimated to be growing at an annual rate of some 3 percent, one of the highest rates in the world. The people are mostly ethnic Arabs whose geographical distribution generally follows patterns of rainfall and arable soil: the Najd, or central region of settlement on the plateau, has the Riyadh metropolitan area, nearing 1,000,000 in the early 1980s, as well as many smaller agricultural towns; similarly, the 'Asir of the well watered southwestern highlands; the Persian Gulf littoral, more populous than ever because of the oil industry; and the highlands of Yemen (Ṣan'ā'), one of the most populous sections of the peninsula. There is also a small Bedouin community.

The birth rate almost everywhere exceeds 40 births per 1,000 population, while death rates typically are estimated at about 15 per 1,000. Throughout most of Arabia, therefore, the population is very young; in many regions more than 45 percent of the population is under 15 years of age. Linguistically, most of the population are speakers of Arabic, though in many regional dialects. The great majority are Sunnī Muslims; Arabia believes itself heir to the great tradition of Muslim proselytism that carried Islām as far as Spain and China, and today, 2,000,000 pilgrims annually are attracted to Mecca, the great historical centre of Islām.

More than two-thirds of the population is urban in most of Arabia. Oman and Yemen (Ṣan'ā') are about 10 percent urban, principally because of their tradition of small agricultural towns. Most of the smaller countries have a single primate city (Kuwait, Manama, Abu Dhabi, Doha) that contains half or more of the national population. Only Saudi Arabia supports four major agglomerations: Riyadh, Jidda, Mecca, and Medina, the first two being almost 1,000,000 in population. Most government planning for regional and urban development is predicated on the creation of new urban centres (for better provision of services), rather than on maintaining existing rural populations in an improved environment.

The economy. With the exception of Yemen (Aden), which has a Socialist government, most of Arabia can be characterized as free-enterprise in nature, though most of the enterprise is strictly controlled by either the royal family or planning authorities of the countries themselves. In the early 1980s, the aggregate gross national product (GNP) of the eight countries constituting Arabia was some $175,000,000,000—about one-fifteenth that of the United States—and originated largely from extracting and refining petroleum. The GNP per capita was overall about $9,000, but this was very unevenly distributed within any single country, varying from $420 per capita in Yemen (Aden) to $30,000 per capita in the United Arab Emirates. The high oil prices of the 1970s, however, were showing signs of decline in the 1980s. Only the two Yemens, both oil-poor, had an agriculture sector that exceeded 20 percent of the GNP. Manufacturing seldom amounts to as much as 7 percent of the GNP. The service sector typically contributes about half of the GNP in the non-oil-producing countries and about one-fifth in the producing countries.

Agricultural land usually amounts to little more than 1 percent of land area. Three-fifths of the population, however, is still employed in agriculture in most of Arabia. The region is not self-sufficient in food production and is very dependent on good weather, although as much as 30 percent of agricultural land is watered or irrigated from subsurface water supplies. Crops range from cereal grains (where the climate permits) to melons and fruits (at the better watered oases) to aromatic essences and spices, coffee, and the narcotic qāt (in the terraced fields of Yemen [Ṣan'ā']). Principal livestock includes, cattle, asses, and camels (Yemen [Ṣan'ā'] and Saudi Arabia), and sheep and goats (which are omnipresent and probably responsible for much of the degradation of the vegetation of Arabia during historic times). Fisheries are insignificant, although most coastal towns have a small fishing fleet.

Most national development plans in the region have provided heavy investment in the expansion of the manufacturing sector to prepare for the end of the century, when oil reserves will be exhausted and jobs needed for these countries' burgeoning populations to replace income no longer provided by oil. In the early 1980s, the principal industry was still the refining of oil. The construction sector, outside the two Yemens, is very active, providing the infrastructure, new cities, pipelines, and other facilities that will be required for the self-sustaining economy it is hoped will replace the oil windfalls. The service sector is dominated by financial services and technical services to the oil industry.

The principal labour problems are those associated with the massive adjustment of Arabia's traditional economies to oil income and with the modernization of those like the Yemens, where there is no such income. Especially in the smaller producing countries, a major problem is the great numbers of guest workers attracted to the region after 1970 both by jobs and by the entrepreneurial opportunities of such great wealth. These workers and their dependents represent a strain on existing services and a potential social and political problem after the boom.

Arabian banking—private, commercial, and development—was among the fastest growing in the world in the early 1980s, largely owing to the prosperity of the oil industry. Economic and political relations among the countries of Arabia are arranged through such organizations as the Arab League, the Organization of Arab Petroleum Exporting Countries, the Arab Fund for Economic and Social Development, and the Arab Monetary Fund.

Internal transportation in the Arabian Peninsula is very poorly developed, except around the Persian Gulf, the Saudi Arabian heartland, the 'Asir, and the main coastal commercial routes connecting the peninsula with neighbouring countries. And, except in the gulf area, roads seldom connect any country with another. The Hejaz Railway, connecting Riyadh with Damascus, Syria, was completed by the Ottoman Turks in 1908 but was severely damaged during World War I. Its reopening remains a goal of Arabian planners. A second, 360-mi railroad connects the port of ad-Dammān with Riyadh. Air travel, particularly since the 1960s, substituted for the inadequate road system, and by the early 1980s, Gulf Air (serving four countries), Kuwait Airways, and Saudia, over a network of airports, especially in Saudi Arabia, were capable of transporting almost any equipment. Although the peoples of Arabia have a long seafaring tradition, in the early 1980s only Saudi Arabia and Kuwait had sizable fleets of merchant vessels, primarily oil tankers. Ports and harbours, however, are numerous and, in the Persian Gulf, among the largest and most technologically modern in the world, handling extremely large crude-petroleum carriers of more than 500,000 tons displacement. A vast network of oil, gas, and petroleum-product pipelines carries these goods from fields and refineries to the gulf ports from which they are then transported.

In international trade the export of oil dominates all, and even the enormously increased import levels of the 1970s and early 1980s could be financed without difficulty. Financial commitments by oil-producing countries, both for purchase of consumer goods and for capital-development projects, however, were so high by the early 1980s that threatened drops in oil prices raised the spectre of foreign exchange and repayment problems. Principal imports included machinery and equipment, especially construction equipment; transportation equipment, particularly trucks; complete structures such as turnkey plants; textiles and clothing; and food. The major export customers were the industrialized countries of western Europe and North America. The major import suppliers were the United States, Japan, and West Germany.

Administrative and social conditions. The governmental forms of the countries of Arabia range from the socialist People's Democratic Republic of Yemen to the more republican forms of the Yemen Arab Republic and the partially (until 1976 and 1975) constitutional monarchies of the Bahrain and Kuwait to the more unrestricted monarchies of the remaining countries. Constitutional forms are not traditional to the region and are poorly developed.

Whether Marxist–Leninist or monarchical in form, the governments of the Arabian Peninsula generally have not adopted the political party as a form of public discourse. No country in the peninsula finds it expedient to permit public expression of opposition views.

Throughout most of Arabia, traditional Islāmic law, or Shari'ah, is the basis of civil and criminal sanctions; the Shari'ah is administered by local qadis, or judges. Only in Kuwait is a modern legal code in force.

The states of the peninsula tend to be nonaligned or Western in orientation, although Yemen (Aden) has treaty arrangements with several countries of the Soviet-organized Council for Mutual Economic Assistance (Comecon). Those countries that were dependencies or protectorates of the United Kingdom continue to maintain a strong connection with the U.K. for military advice, training, and materiel; the U.S. is also a principal supplier.

Standards of living until the early 1970s were often unsatisfactory because the countries of the region were so poor. The surge of oil wealth begun in the 1970s permitted the creation of so much new social infrastructure that by the early 1980s life expectancy had risen to near the 70-year mark in the most developed countries, like Kuwait, although it remained nearer 50 years for the larger, less developed parts of Arabia. Infant mortality and nutritional standards followed a similar pattern. Health manpower was difficult to train and recruit; most modern services were available only in the largest cities. The main health problems are those associated with supply and improvement of potable water (though the increasing use in the peninsula of desalinated water is alleviating this), sewage disposal, and vector (insects or animals carrying communicable diseases) control. The major diseases in the rural areas were malaria, trachoma, gastroenteritis, and influenza; in the cities the urban problems of automobile accidents, cardiovascular disease, and mental illness were of growing significance.

Housing, though susceptible of improvement during the 1970s through the infusion of oil money and the creation by the oil industry of a work force skilled in construction techniques, remained insufficient to supply the rapidly growing population. In many of the older cities, the building of the new has advanced so far that traditional housing types can no longer be seen.

Education is recognized as a development tool by all of the countries of the Arabian Peninsula, but the traditional separation of the sexes has often meant much lower enrollment ratios for women than for men. Literacy is still low in the least developed regions but is somewhat higher in the larger oil-exporting countries, like Saudi Arabia (25 percent), and reaches more than 60 percent in the small oil-producing countries where large numbers can be reached by literacy programs in the cities. University education usually is pursued outside the region, although higher vocational and teacher-training institutions were established, especially during the 1970s, for maintenance of traditional religious and cultural values within the framework of development.

Social security programs are not as comprehensive as in more developed regions, and although Saudi Arabia, Kuwait, and Bahrain had such programs, by the early 1980s most of the population was not covered.

The press and broadcast media are a relatively recent development in Arabia, the first newspaper having been published only in 1908 in Mecca. Most press is government owned or influenced, and the broadcast media are more tightly controlled; they have a strong role in education and national development. A number of countries have official or semi-official news agencies.

The period before the revelation of Islām in the early 7th century AD is referred to as *jāhilīyah* (time of ignorance) by the Arabs. In turn, the word Arab means "desert," or its inhabitants; in the Qur'ān the word is used to designate the Bedouin. A popular saying, "Poetry is the public register of the Arabs," sums up the importance of poetry in *jāhilīyah* and since. In nomadic encampments, music and poetry commemorated every event in life. In the markets of the Arabs, competitions of poetry and musical performances were held periodically, attracting the most distinguished poet-musicians. The advent of the Qur'ān, in the 7th century, was considered a miracle and Muḥammad a great poet. Arabic poetry appeared in AD 500 in the oral tradition and remained oral for about 150 years, preserved by the *rawī* (reciter) tradition. The *qaṣisdah* (ode) was thought to be the highest form of poetry. It is believed to have been originated by Muhalhil ibn Rabi'a. The best of the classical pre-Islāmic poetry is found in *al-Mu'allaqat* ("Suspended"), known also as *al-Mudhahhabāt* ("Golden Odes"), which used to be hung in al-Ka'bah in Mecca. The introduction of *nasīb* (a sentimental opening for the *qaṣīdah*) has been attributed to Imru'al-Qays (Hundj ibn Hujr).

According to the Qur'ān, however, poets rove about without any ethical purpose, and for some Muslims, pious poetry was suspect because it sang mostly of forbidden wine and free love. It was believed that Muḥammad tolerated only functional music such as war songs, pilgrimage chants, and festival songs—and the *adhān* ("call to prayer"), chanted by the *mu'adhdhin*, which he himself instituted in 622. But in time the poetical tradition revived, and 8th- and 9th-century poets flourished and produced important poetry.

While Islām inhibited the visual arts by prohibiting the representation of beings, calligraphy and geometric designs might be encouraged. The pervasive influence of the Wahhabīs (particularly their opposition to ornamentation) kept Arabian architecture in the 18th century to simple mud-brick construction. Their influence extended to music and dance. Music and poetry, linked in Arab folk music, remain important, nevertheless. The classical *qaṣīdah* form is widely sung and is the most ancient form created by Bedouins in the Arabian Peninsula. Another genre is the *ḥudā'* (caravan song). The *naham* genre was performed by a *naham* (singer) hired onto a boat to encourage pearl fishers, especially in Kuwait and Bahrain. In the Hadhramaut there is a category of songs called *dana dana* that include a refrain to be repeated by the audience after each improvised stanza. Later, through Islāmic conquests, the Arabs came into contact with other cultures that led them to further improve instruments and elaborate musical forms already developed.

In South Arabia the domestication of the camel (*c.* 400 BC) and increasing demand by northern civilizations for incense and myrrh led to prosperity for the south (Yemen and Oman). By 330 BC a network of roads linked the southern highlands of the peninsula. In the north the Nabataeans controlled the trade route up the Red Sea coast to Egypt and Syria.

The national hero of South Arabian legend is Tubba' Asad Kamil, called Abū Karīb in folk poetry, which tells about his adventures in Medina and Mecca and the establishment of Judaism in the Yemen. A Historical and Archeological Society has been formed in Saudi Arabia to investigate the past of the Arabian Peninsula, and there is an archeological journal, *Atlal*, on the subject. There are regional museums that act as research centres. Arabia remains, however, the most culturally conservative region of the Middle East, adhering strictly to Islāmic and traditional values.

History. Although archaeological work in the Arabian Peninsula is still in its infancy, there is evidence that Arabia was the home of Paleolithic hunters. Finds on the Persian Gulf attest Arabian connections with Sumer cultures as early as the 3rd millennium BC.

South Arabia was the location of the peninsula's greatest pre-Islāmic kingdoms. The Ma'īn, Saba' (the Biblical Sheba), Qatabān, and Haḍramawt kingdoms flourished in the southwestern corner, growing wealthy from the lucrative trade in frankincense and spices. The Sabaens built a dam at Ma'rib and an elaborate irrigation system from it. Their kingdom gave way to that of the Ḥimyarītes (*c.* 100 BC), who ruled South Arabia until AD 525, when they were destroyed by the Christian Abyssinians.

Ethnically, the people of Arabia have been related to different groups whose homelands lie in almost all directions outside Arabia proper. Important tribes of the interior of the peninsula were the Thamūd, located in the northern Hejaz near the Red Sea, and the Liḥyānites, located in and around Dedan.

Arabic peoples not located in Arabia itself influenced and controlled much of the peninsula in early times. The Nabataens and the Palmyrenes, on the outskirts of Arabia, extended their authority to the regions of Northern and Central Arabia, through which their trade routes passed. When Palmyra fell in AD 273, power shifted to the Lakhmids of Transjordan, who were the first to adopt Arabic as their official language. In 528 Northern Arabia passed to the Ghassānids, Christians who spoke Syriac.

The Prophet Muḥammad's flight to Medina (622) marks the beginning of the Muslim era. Within a generation, all of Arabia was converted to Islām, but the struggle among Muḥammad's successors led to the establishment of the Umayyad caliphate, headquartered in Damascus. The political centre of Islām never returned to the Arabian Peninsula, and it was characterized thereafter by petty kingdoms, intertribal warfare, and incursions from non-Arab Islāmic powers.

The Ottomans attempted to exert control over all of Arabia in the 16th century, but their penetration was short-lived in South Arabia and nonexistent in parts of the interior and the Persian Gulf. The Persians tried to take Bahrain (17th and 18th centuries) and the Portuguese Oman (16th and 17th centuries), but both were repulsed by native leaders.

As the Sa'ūdi family, under Wahhābī influence, was spreading over Central Arabia, the British were establishing protectorates in the Persian Gulf: Muscat (later Oman) in 1798, the Trucial States (later the United Arab Emirates) and Bahrain in 1820, Aden in 1839, Kuwait in 1899, and finally Saudi Arabia itself in 1915. Yemen (Ṣan'ā') was never under British protection and received recognition of its independence in 1934. The Saudis achieved independence in 1927. As for the rest of the peninsula, Kuwait became independent in 1961, Yemen (Aden) achieved independence in 1967, and Oman became independent in 1970. With the evacuation of the British from the Arabian peninsula, Bahrain, Qatar, and the United Arab Emirates (composed of Abu Dhabi, Dubai, Ajman, Sharjah, Umm al-Qaiwain, Ras al-Khaimah, and Fujairah) gained independence in 1971.

Arabia, Roman province created out of the former kingdom of the Nabataeans and the adjacent Syrian cities of Gerasa and Philadelphia (modern Jarash and 'Ammān, Jordan, respectively), after the formal annexation of the Nabataean kingdom by the Roman emperor Trajan in AD 105. The province was bounded by the western coast of the Sinai Peninsula, the present Syrian-Lebanese border to a line south of Damascus, and the eastern coast of the Red Sea as far as Egra (Madā'in Ṣāliḥ in the Hejaz). It prospered economically in the 2nd century, and it became a source of customs revenue to the Romans because of the South Arabian caravan and maritime trade in incense and other Far Eastern commodities that passed through the area. Under the Romans, Bostra (Bozrah; now Buṣrā ash-Shām, Syria) in the extreme north became the capital and legionary camp, but the old royal capital of Petra remained the religious centre. By constructing a road linking Damascus, via Bostra, Gerasa, Philadelphia, and Petra, to Aelana on the Gulf of Aqaba, the Romans further strengthened the province's communications and secured control over restless Bedouin tribes to the east.

At the end of the 3rd century, the Roman emperor Diocletian divided Arabia into a northern province, enlarged by the Palestinian regions of Auranitis and Trachonitis, with Bozrah as the capital, and a southern province, with Petra as capital. The southern province, united to Palestine by the emperor Constantine I the Great, became known as Palaestina Salutaris (or Tertia) when detached again in AD 357–358. The cities of both provinces enjoyed a marked revival of prosperity in the 5th and 6th centuries and fell into decay only after the Arab conquest in 632–636.

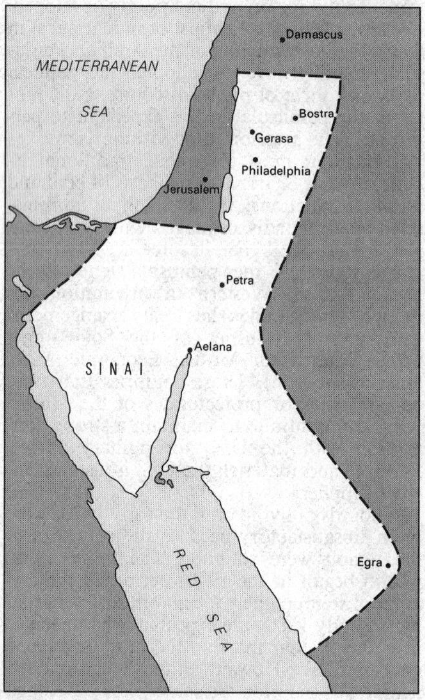

The Roman province of Arabia, *c.* AD 200

Where the same name may denote a person, place, or thing, the articles will be found in that order

Arabia Felix (Latin: Happy, or Flourishing, Arabia), in ancient geography, the comparatively fertile region in southwestern and southern Arabia (in present-day Asir and the Yemens), a region that contrasted with Arabia Deserta in barren central and northern Arabia and with Arabia Petraea (Stony Arabia) in northwestern Arabia, which came under the suzerainty of imperial Rome. The Greeks and Romans chose the name because of the area's pleasant climate and reputed riches in agricultural products and in spices. The emperor Augustus (reigned 27 BC–AD 14) sent an expedition under Gaius Aelius Gallus to Arabia Felix, with disastrous results. Partly because of a native guide's treachery, the troops travelled by a circuitous way through waterless regions, so that they reached southern Arabia weakened by disease, heat, and want of water, unable to accomplish much commercially or politically. But the expedition did bring back a considerable knowledge of the country and its products. *See also* Saba'.

Arabian Basin, submarine basin of the southern Arabian Sea, rising to meet the submerged Carlsberg Ridge to the south, the Maldive Island chain to the southeast, India and Pakistan to the northeast, Iran to the north, and the Arabian Peninsula to the west. It has a maximum depth of 19,275 ft (5,875 m) and is separated by the Carlsberg Ridge from the deeper Somali Basin to the south and west. The sill depth between the Arabian and Somali basins is about 9,800 ft. The floor of the basin is covered by sediment deposited by the Indus River in the form of a great alluvial fan whose thickness diminishes to the south.

Arabian Desert, great desert region occupying nearly all of the Arabian Peninsula in Southwest Asia, an area of about 900,000 sq mi (2,331,000 sq km).

The following article summarizes information about the Arabian Desert; for full details, *see* MACROPAEDIA: Asia.

The Arabian Desert is bordered by the Syrian Desert to the north; the Persian Gulf, Gulf of Oman, and Arabian Sea to the east; the Arabian Sea and Gulf of Aden to the south; and the Red Sea to the west. A large part of the desert lies within Saudi Arabia; it also extends into Jordan, Iraq, Kuwait, Qatar, the United Arab Emirates, Oman, Yemen (Aden), and Yemen (Ṣan'ā').

Two major regions comprise the desert: the ancient Afro-Arabian Shield of igneous and metamorphic rocks in the west, and the younger sedimentary rocks that pitch gently away from the shield toward the Persian Gulf Basin to the east. Mountainous highlands rise in the northwest, southwest, and southeast corners of the desert; steep cliffs and canyons descend from the highlands into adjacent seas to the south and west. To the north and east elevations decrease more gradually to the moderate relief of the interior plateaus and broad plains or steppes. A number of lesser highland ranges have been uncovered by erosion in the interior.

Sand covers at least a third of the Arabian Desert, occurring as dunes or ridges of varying size and complexity or as a thin film on surfaces of low relief. The two largest sand bodies are an-Nafūd in the northwest and the Rub'al-Khali (ar-Ramlah) in the southeast. Between them are two almost parallel arcs of more or less continuous dunes, separated by the great Jabal at-Tuwayq cuesta. Twice a year *shamāl* winds blow at velocities averaging 30 mph (50 kmh) from the north and northwest for 30 to 50 days, transporting huge loads of sand and dust, and altering the shapes of sand dunes. Summer heat in the desert is intense, reaching a maximum temperature of about 124° F (51° C). In the interior the heat is dry and tolerable, but coastal regions and some highlands suffer from high summer humidity.

Rainfall averages less than 4 inches (100 mm) a year, but can range from 0 to 20 in. Most drainage channels in the desert are either dry or intermittent, the latter flowing only when rains are heavy. Two systems flow perennially in the region—the Tigris–Euphrates river system in the northeast and the Wādī Ḥajar in the southern Ḥaḍramawt of Yemen (Aden).

Plants of the Arabian Desert are primarily xerophytic or halophytic types, structurally adapted to dry and saline conditions, respectively.

Man has inhabited the desert since Pleistocene times (ending about 10,000 years ago). The nomadic Bedouin adapted to desert life by migrating seasonally with their herds of camels, Arabian horses, and sheep into the desert during the rainy winter season, and moving back toward the cultivated lands in the dry summer months. Date palms are grown in many oases, the dates providing food for humans and livestock, and the palm supplying wood for building. Many fruits and vegetables such as rice, alfalfa, henna, citrus, melons, onions, tomatoes, barley, and wheat are also grown in the oases, and—in the higher regions—peaches, grapes, and prickly pears. The Arabian people, Muslim from the 7th century AD, remained practically unaffected by Western cultural influences until the discovery of petroleum in 1936. Their desert, once crossed only by camel trails, is now laced by networks of roads; about 80 percent of the territory is accessible by motor vehicles.

Arabian Gulf (Asia): *see* Persian Gulf.

Arabian horse, earliest improved breed of horse, valued for its speed, stamina, beauty, intelligence, and gentleness. The Arabian breed is first mentioned in 400 BC and is said to have stemmed from five mares given to Muḥammad by his followers, but the Arabs undoubtedly had horses earlier. The breed has contributed its qualities to most of the modern breeds of light horses.

Arabian horse
Sally Anne Thompson—EB Inc.

The Arabian is a compact, relatively small horse with a small head, protruding eyes, wide nostrils, marked withers, and a short back. It usually has only 23 vertebrae, while 24 is the usual number for other breeds. Average height is about 15 hands (60 inches, or 152 centimetres) and average weight ranges from 800 to 1,000 pounds (360 to 450 kilograms). Its legs are strong with fine hooves. The coat, tail, and mane are of fine silky hair. While many colours are possible in the breed, gray prevails. The most famous stud farm is in the region of Najd, Saudi Arabia, but many fine Arabian horses are now bred in the United States. The Arabian Horse Registry of America and its predecessor organizations date from 1908.

Arabian-Indian Ridge (Arabian Sea): *see* Carlsberg Ridge.

Arabian Nights' Entertainment, The: *see* Thousand and One Nights, The.

Arabian Peninsula: *see* Arabia.

Arabian Sea, northwestern part of the Indian Ocean covering a total area of about 1,490,000 sq mi (3,860,000 sq km).

The following article summarizes information about the Arabian Sea; for full details *see* MACROPAEDIA: Asia.

The Arabian Sea is bounded to the east by India, to the north by Pakistan and Iran, and to the west by the Arabian Peninsula and the Horn of Africa. It is located north of an imaginary line connecting Cape Comorin at the southern tip of India to Ras Hafun, a peninsula on the eastern coast of Somalia. To the north, the Gulf of Oman connects the Arabian Sea with the Persian Gulf via the Strait of Hormuz. To the west, the Gulf of Aden connects it with the Red Sea via the Strait of Bāb el-Mandeb. Political units bordering the sea include India, Pakistan, Iran, Oman, Yemen (Aden), and Somalia. Islands in the sea include Socotra (a part of Yemen [Aden]), off the Horn of Africa; the Kuria Muria Islands, off the coast of Oman; and the Laccadive Islands (a part of India), off the southwest (Malabar) coast of India. Among the chief ports are Bombay in India, Karāchi in Pakistan, and Aden in Yemen (Aden). The Indus is the principal river draining into the sea.

Most of the Arabian Sea has depths that exceed 9,600 ft (2,900 m), and deep water reaches close to the bordering coastlines except in the northeast, off Pakistan and India. The Carlsberg Ridge, a submarine belt of elevated sea floor characterized by high seismic activity, divides the Arabian Sea into two major basins—the Arabian Basin to the east and the Somali Basin to the west. The mean depth of the sea is 8,750 ft (2,734 m); the deepest soundings, 15,900 ft, have been recorded in the Somali Basin.

High levels of inorganic nutrients, such as phosphate concentrations, which support a rich fish life, occur off the southeastern coast of the Arabian Peninsula. The chief fish include tuna, sardine, billfish, wahoo, shark, lancet fish, and moonfish, but fishing operations have yet to be fully developed. The sea lies within the trade wind latitudes and was part of the principal sea route between Europe and India for centuries.

Arabic alphabet, second most widely used alphabetic writing system in the world (the Latin alphabet is the most widespread). Originally developed for writing the Arabic language and carried across much of the Eastern Hemisphere by the spread of Islām, the Arabic script has been adapted to such diverse languages as Persian, Turkish, Spanish, and Swahili. Although it probably developed in the 4th century AD as a direct descendant of the Nabataean alphabet (*q.v.*), its origins and early history are vague. The earliest extant example of Arabic writing is a trilingual inscription in Greek, Syriac, and Arabic dating from AD 512.

The Arabic alphabet has 28 letters, all representing consonants, and is written from right to left. Twenty-two of the letters are those of the Semitic alphabet from which it descended, modified only in letter form, and the remaining six letters represent sounds not used in the languages written in the earlier alphabet. The shape of many letters depends on their position in a word—initial, medial, and final. The letters *alif, waw,* and *ya* (standing for glottal stop, *w,* and *y,* respectively) are used to represent the long vowels *a, u,* and *i.* A set of diacritical marks developed in the 8th century AD are sometimes used to represent short vowels and certain grammatical endings otherwise left unmarked.

Two major types of Arabic script exist. Kūfic, a thick, bold monumental style, was developed in Kūfah, a city in Mesopotamia, toward the end of the 7th century AD. It was chiefly used for inscriptions in stone and metal but was also sometimes employed to write manuscripts of the Qur'ān. A very handsome monumental script, it has passed out of use, except in cases in which more cursive scripts cannot be used. *Naskhī,* a cursive script well adapted to writing on papyrus or paper, is the direct ancestor of modern Arabic writing. It originated in Mecca and Medina at an early date and exists in many complex and decorative variant forms.

Arabic language, South Central Semitic language spoken in a large area including North Africa, most of the Arabian Peninsula, and parts of the Middle East. Arabic is the language of the Qur'ān (or Koran, the sacred book of Islām) and is the religious language of all Muslims. Literary Arabic, usually called Classical Arabic, is essentially the form of the language found in the Qur'ān, with some modifications necessary for its use in modern times; it is uniform throughout the Arab world.

Colloquial Arabic includes numerous spoken dialects, some of which are mutually unintelligible. The chief dialect groups are those of Arabia, Iraq, Syria, Egypt, and North Africa. With the exception of the dialect of Algeria, all Arabic dialects have been strongly influenced by the literary language. The earliest known written Arabic is a royal funerary inscription dating from AD 328.

The sound system of Arabic is very different from that of English and the other languages of Europe. It includes a number of distinctive guttural sounds (pharyngeal and uvular fricatives) and a series of velarized consonants (pronounced with accompanying constriction of the pharynx and raising of the back of the tongue). There are three short and three long vowels (*a, i, u; ā, ī, ū*). Words always start with a single consonant followed by a vowel, and long vowels are rarely followed by more than a single consonant; clusters containing more than two consonants do not occur.

Arabic shows the fullest development of typical Semitic word structure. An Arabic word is composed of two parts: (1) the root, which generally consists of three consonants and provides the basic lexical meaning of the word, and (2) the pattern, which consists of vowels and gives grammatical meaning to the word. Thus, the root *ktb* combined with the pattern *-i-ā-* gives *kitāb* ("book") whereas the same root combined with the pattern *-ā-i-* gives *kātib* ("one who writes, clerk"). The language also makes use of prefixes and suffixes, which act as subject markers, pronouns, prepositions, and the definite article.

Verbs in Arabic are regular in conjugation. There are two tenses: the perfect, formed by the addition of suffixes, which is often used to express past time; and the imperfect, formed by the addition of prefixes and sometimes containing suffixes indicating number and gender, which is often used for expressing present or future time. In addition to the two tenses there are imperative forms, an active participle, a passive participle, and a verbal noun. Verbs are inflected for three persons, three numbers (singular, dual, plural), and two genders. In Classical Arabic there is no dual form and no gender differentiation in the 1st person, and the modern dialects have lost all dual forms. The classical language also has forms for the passive voice.

There are three cases (nominative, genitive, and accusative) in the declensional system of Classical Arabic nouns; nouns are no longer declined in the modern dialects. Pronouns occur both as suffixes and as independent words.

With the spread of literacy and the increase in higher education in the Arab world, the influence of Classical Arabic on the colloquial dialects has become greater.

Arabic language, South: *see* South Arabic language.

Arabic literary renaissance, Arabic AN-NAHDAH AL-ADABĪYAH, 19th-century movement aimed at the creation of a modern Arabic literature, inspired by contacts with the West and a renewed interest in the great classical literature.

After the Napoleonic invasion of Egypt (1798) and the subsequent establishment of an autonomous and Western-minded ruling dynasty there, many Syrian and Lebanese writers sought out the freer environment of Egypt, making it the centre of the renaissance. Under the impact of the dismemberment of the Ottoman Empire after World War I and the coming of independence after World War II, the revival spread to other Arab countries.

The novel and drama, literary forms new to Arabic literature, were developed largely under the influence of the European works that became available in the 19th century in Arabic translation. Other forms owed much to Western models but had roots in classical Arabic literature, such as the short story, new verse forms, and the essay.

That the renaissance succeeded in altering the direction of Arabic literature is probably attributable to two factors. The emergence of an Arabic press made writing a realistic livelihood and forced writers to abandon the traditional, ornate style of past centuries in favour of a simpler and more direct style that would appeal to a wider reading public. The spread and modernization of education further served to provide a body of readers receptive to new styles and ideas.

Arabic literature, writings in the Arabic language, composed or written by non-Arabs as well as Arabs. In the golden age of Arabic literature following the advent of Islām in 622, Arabic writers included Persians, Iranians, Indians, Spanish Muslims, Egyptians, Syrians, and many others of mixed descent.

Arabic literature is divided into two main periods. The classical, beginning with the proverbs and poetry of the nomadic northern Arabs of the desert, was preserved by oral transmission from the early 6th century or before and first recorded in the 7th and 8th centuries; it continued into the 16th century. The conquest of most of the Arabic-speaking world in the 17th and 18th centuries essentially eradicated Arabic literature in that time. The modern period, beginning with the 19th-century literary renaissance in Syria, Egypt, Lebanon, and Iraq, extends to the present.

ʿArabīyah, Shibh al-Jazīrah al-: *see* Arabia.

Aracaju, port city and capital, Sergipe state, northeastern Brazil, lying on the Rio Continguiba at the base of a ridge of sand hills 6 mi (10 km) from the coast. The city, which was founded in 1855 as a new state capital, is laid out in an unusual grid pattern. It is a regional commercial and industrial centre, processing leather, bananas, cassava, *feijão* (beans), mangoes, cashews, salt, cotton, and sugar. Chemicals are also produced in Aracaju, and limestone is quarried in the vicinity. Anchorage at the port is good, but a dangerous bar at the river's mouth prevents the entrance of vessels drawing more than 12 ft (4 m). Small-scale offshore petroleum drilling was begun in the late 1970s. Aracaju is linked by air, coastal shipping, and paved roads to Salvador, Maceió, and Recife. The Universidade Federal de Sergipe was founded there in 1967. Pop. (1980 prelim.) 288,106.

aracari, any of certain toucan species. *See* toucan.

Araçatuba, city, western São Paulo state, Brazil, near the Tietê River, which is dammed for power and irrigation. The city was founded in 1908 and was given town rank in 1917. In 1921 it was separated administratively from Pentapolis (to the southeast) and was designated the seat of a municipality. It serves an agricultural area (cotton, coffee, rice, corn [maize], and *feijão* [beans]). Araçatuba processes cotton and foodstuffs and produces tannin, ceramics, shoes, and other items. Goods are shipped by highway to São Paulo and to other cities in the state. Araçatuba also has an airfield. Pop. (1980 prelim) 113,486.

Arachne (Greek: Spider), in Greek mythology, the daughter of Idmon of Colophon in Lydia, a dyer in purple.

Arachne was a weaver who acquired such skill in her art that she ventured to challenge Athena. The goddess wove a tapestry depicting the gods in majesty, while that of Arachne showed their amorous adventures. Enraged at the perfection of her rival's work, Athena tore it to pieces, and in despair Arachne hanged herself. But the goddess out of pity loosened the rope, which became a cobweb; Arachne herself was changed into a spider, whence the name of the zoological class to which spiders belong, Arachnida.

arachnid, class name ARACHNIDA, any member of a group of arthropods that is composed of primarily carnivorous terrestrial invertebrates, including the spiders, scorpions, mites, and ticks.

A brief treatment of arachnids follows. For full treatment, *see* MACROPAEDIA: Arachnids.

Arachnid bodies are segmented, with well-developed heads and hard external skeletons. They range in size from the tiny mite 0.1 millimetre (0.004 inch) long to the 18-centimetre (7-inch) black scorpion of Africa. The body is divided into two parts: the cephalothorax (joint head and thorax), with six pairs of appendages, and the abdomen, or opisthosoma. The first two pairs of appendages, the chelicerae and the pedipalps, are used to hold or grasp prey. The remaining pairs are walking legs. Arachnids have no antennae but rely on tactile hair, simple eyes, and slit sense organs for sensory information.

Courtship among arachnids is necessary, with the male giving off a chemical or visual key. The male arachnid usually deposits the sperm on the ground or web and then transfers it into the female. Most arachnids lay eggs, but some species (*e.g.*, scorpions) bear living young. Maternal care is negligible, although the scorpion young are carried on the female's back. Arachnids molt, or shed their skins, several times before reaching maturity.

Many arachnid forms are distributed worldwide, inhabiting nearly every region from deserts to rain forests. Most arachnid groups are free-living, but many species of mites and ticks are parasitic. The latter also are carriers of serious human and animal diseases. Certain venomous spiders and scorpions pose a danger to humans, but most are harmless and are important economically as they prey on insect pests.

arachnodactyly: *see* Marfan's syndrome.

Arachosia, Persian HARAUVATISH, or HARAHUVATISH, in ancient times a province of the Achaemenian, Seleucid, and Parthian empires. It occupied what is now southern Afghanistan and was bounded on the south by Gedrosia (Baluchistan). The capital city, Alexandria-of-the-Arachosians, was founded in the 4th century BC by Alexander the Great; the city of Qandahār now stands on its site. Arachosia was famous for its ivory and elephants.

ʿArad, town, southern Israel, in the northeast Negev, named for the biblical Arad, the ruins of which are visible at Tel ʿArad, about 5½ mi (9 km) east-northeast. The book of Numbers (21:1–3) tells how the Canaanite king of Arad fought the Israelites during the exodus from Egypt, but his cities were "utterly destroyed" by Israel's armies. The city's name appears on the Temple of Amon, al-Karnak, Egypt, in the triumphal inscription of Pharaoh Sheshonk I (biblical Shishak), first ruler of the 22nd dynasty (reigned *c.* 935–914 BC).

Modern housing with memorial to town's dead in the Arab-Israeli War of 1967, ʿArad, Israel

Ehud Locker—Shostal/EB Inc.

The first modern attempt to settle the site was made in 1921 by veterans of the Zion Mule Corps, a Jewish unit of the British Army in World War I. It failed because of the lack of fresh water. ʿArad is now supplied with water by a branch of the Yarqon-Negev pipeline. The present settlement is a residential community for the employees of the Dead Sea Works at nearby Sedom (*q.v.*). The hinterland of ʿArad has valuable mineral resources—in addition to the minerals of the Dead Sea, there are phosphate deposits at Zefaʿ, 10 mi south, and important gas fields at Rosh Zohar, 3 mi southeast on the Dead Sea highway. ʿArad became the first town in Israel to have a piped gas supply. Chemical processing and textile manufacturing are principal industries. Pop. (1982 est.) 11,900.

Arad, *judeţ* (district), western Romania, occupying an area of 91,699 sq mi (237,500 sq km), bounded on the west by Hungary. The Mureş and Crişul Alb rivers drain westward through the district. The Western Carpathians, including the Zărand and Codru-Moma ranges, lie in the eastern portion of the district. Settlements are found in the lowlands and intermontane valleys. Arad city, a district capital since 1919, was originally a Neolithic settlement and subsequently passed through Roman, Tatar, Turkish, and Hungarian hands. Şiria town, built on a Roman settlement, has a museum devoted to Ioan Slavici (1848–1925), the writer; and Pecica town was a Geto-Dacian walled city during Burebistas' rule (*c.* 60–44 BC). The centre of a feudal domain during the Middle Ages, Lipova town experienced several peasant rebellions. The town has a 14th-century building that was converted into a mosque during the Turkish occupation (1552–1718), and mineral springs are found nearby. A 15th-century castle and a nature reserve are located at Savîrşin town. Pauliş town underwent severe damage by German troops in 1944. Cereal growing, livestock raising, and vineyards and fruit cultivation are the main agricultural activities. Clover, alfalfa, and onions are other crops. Quarries in Arad district produce road ballast, granite, and limestone. Factories in Arad city produce railroad cars, machinery, furniture, and chemicals. Handicrafts include embroidered, leather, and fur products and ceramics. Highway and railway lines extend through Arad. A highway and a railway line that parallel the Mureş River were based on a former Roman road. A domestic airport is located near Arad city. Pop. (1982 est.) 509,168.

Arad, city, capital of Arad *judeţ* (district), western Romania. It is in the lower Mureş Valley close to the Hungarian border, 30 mi (50 km) north-northeast of Timişoara. There is a large Magyar population. The site of a small Neolithic settlement, it later became a Roman outpost south of the river at Aradu Nou (New Arad), now part of Arad. The first documented mention of Arad dates from 1156.

Arad was in Turkish hands, with brief interruptions, from 1552 until 1685, when it came under the control of Austria. During the Hungarian rebellion of 1848–49, it was captured by the Hungarians (on July 1, 1849) and was their headquarters during the latter part of the insurrection. After the rebellion was put down, with the assistance of Russia, 13 Hungarian generals, "the martyrs of Arad," were executed there on Oct. 6, 1849. Arad became part of Romania after World War I.

Arad is a railway junction and commercial and industrial centre. Its manufactures include machine tools, railway cars, and textiles. Milling, distilling, and woodworking are also important. The city has a state theatre (with departments in Romanian and Hungarian), a puppet theatre, an orchestra, and a cultural centre with a library and museum. Pop. (1982 est.) 184,517.

Arados (Syria): *see* Arwād, Jazīrat.

ʿArafāt, Yāsir, byname of RAḤMĀN ʿABD AR-RAʾŪF AL-QUDWAH (b. 1929, Jerusalem), chairman of the Palestine Liberation Organization (PLO) since 1969 and leader of al-Fatah (largest of the constituent PLO groups).

The young ʿArafāt was one of seven children of a well-to-do merchant whose wife was related to the anti-Zionist grand *muftī* of Jerusalem, Amīn al-Ḥusaynī (d. 1974). After schooling in Gaza, ʿArafāt went to the University of Cairo, where he was graduated as a civil engineer. While in Egypt he joined the Muslim Brotherhood and the Union of Palestinian Students, of which he was president during 1952–56. He was also commissioned into the Egyptian Army and in 1956 served in the Suez campaign.

After Suez, ʿArafāt went to Kuwait, where he worked as an engineer for the government and set up his own contracting firm. While there, he was a co-founder of al-Fatah, which was to become the leading military component of the PLO. After assuming the PLO chairmanship in 1969, he became commander in chief of the Palestinian Revolutionary Forces in 1971 and, two years later, head of the PLO's political department. Subsequently, he directed his efforts increasingly toward political persuasion rather than military confrontation and terrorism.

In November 1974 ʿArafāt became the first representative of a nongovernmental organization—the PLO—to address a plenary session of the UN General Assembly. He paid official visits to a number of Eastern bloc countries, but his contacts with Western leaders were generally more informal because of the latters' need not to appear to grant political recognition to the PLO.

Beginning in 1982, ʿArafāt became less secure as leader of the Palestinians' nationalist cause. He became the target of criticism and military attack from various factions within the PLO and from the Syrians (Syria having been a mainstay of Arab support for the PLO). The criticisms from these and other sources escalated after the Israeli invasion of Lebanon forced ʿArafāt to abandon his Beirut headquarters at the end of August 1982 and set up a new base in Tunisia. Returning to Lebanon in 1983, he was forced to flee again later the same year after he and his followers were attacked by rebels in the PLO.

Arafura Sea, shallow sea of the western Pacific Ocean, occupying an area of 250,000 sq mi (650,000 sq km) between the north coast of Australia and the Gulf of Carpentaria and the south coast of New Guinea. It merges with the Timor Sea on the west and the Banda and Ceram seas on the northwest. The Torres Strait connects it with the Coral Sea on the east. Most of the Arafura Sea is underlain by the Arafura Shelf, part of the more extensive Sahul Shelf. It is generally shallow, with depths of 165 to 260 ft (50 to 80 m), deepening at its western edge, on which coral growths rise from 2,000-ft depths. The Arafura Shelf appears to have been a low-relief land surface that had an arid climate before it became inundated by the post-glacial rise of the sea. The Aru Islands in the north, formed by localized uplift, border the Aru Trough, a curving trench that reaches a maximum depth of 12,000 ft. The trough is part of a chain of depressions that underlie the Ceram, Arafura, and Timor seas, extending west as the Java Trench in the Indian Ocean. Surface currents in the sea are not evident north of latitude 8° S. South of that line, currents run west during the winter but lose any specific pattern during the summer.

Torres Strait is a notoriously dangerous ship passage, and the Arafura Sea itself contains numerous uncharted shoals that are hazards to navigation. The Arafura Shelf is a prospective petroleum area. The protected and clear waters around the Aru Islands have yielded a small but continuous harvest of pearls.

Aragats, Mount, Russian GORA ARAGATS, also spelled GORA ARAGAC, mountain, in the Armenian Soviet Socialist Republic, northwest of Yerevan and north of the Ararat Plain. The highest point in both the Armenian S.S.R. and the Little Caucasus range (13,418 ft [4,090 m]), Aragats is a circular, shieldlike mountain composed of both lavas and tufas. A volcanic cone of recent geologic periods lies atop far older rocks. The crater of the volcano has developed into the steep-walled basin, or cirque, of a glacier, and there are several other minor glaciers. Near the jagged summit are high mountain meadows and rockfalls. On the slopes can be found steppe vegetation and xerophytes (dry and arid climate vegetation). On the southern slope are the ruins of the medieval Armenian fortress Anberd.

Aragh (Vanuatu): *see* Pentecôte.

Arago, (Dominique-) François (-Jean) (b. Feb. 26, 1786, Estagel, Roussillon, Fr.—d. Oct. 2, 1853, Paris), physicist who discovered the principle of the production of magnetism by rotation of a nonmagnetic conductor and devised an experiment that proved the wave theory of light. Further, he engaged with others in research that led to the discovery of the laws of light polarization.

In 1820, elaborating on the work of H.C. Ørsted of Denmark, Arago showed that passage of an electric current through a cylindrical spiral of copper wire caused it to attract iron filings as if it were a magnet and that the filings fell off when the current ceased. In 1824 he demonstrated that a rotating copper disk produced rotation in a magnetic needle suspended above it. Michael Faraday later proved these to be induction phenomena.

Arago supported A.-J. Fresnel's wave theory of light against the emission theory favoured by P.-S. Laplace, J.-B. Biot, and S.-D. Poisson. According to the wave theory, light should be retarded as it passes from a rarer to a denser medium; according to the emission theory, it should be accelerated. Arago's test for comparing the velocity of light in air and in water or glass was described in 1838, but the experiment required such elaborate preparation that Arago was not ready to perform it until 1850, when his sight failed. Before his death, however, the retardation of light in denser media was demonstrated by A.-H.-L. Fizeau and Léon Foucault, who used his method with improvements in detail.

In astronomy, Arago is best known for his part in the dispute between U.-J.-J. Le Verrier, who was his protégé, and the English astronomer J.C. Adams over priority in discovering the planet Neptune and over the name to be given to the planet. Arago had suggested in 1845 that Le Verrier investigate anomalies in the motion of Uranus. When the investigation resulted in Le Verrier's discovery of Neptune, Arago proposed that the newly found planet be named for Le Verrier.

Arago was educated in Perpignan and at the École Polytechnique, Paris, where, at the age of 23, he succeeded J.-J.-L. de Lalande in the chair of analytical geometry. Subsequently he was director of the Paris Observatory and permanent secretary of the Académie des Sciences. He was also active as a Republican in French politics. As minister of war and marine in the provisional government formed after the Revolution of 1848, he introduced many reforms.

Arago remains, fossils of early *Homo sapiens* found in southern France by Henry and Marie-Antoinette de Lumley in a cave near the town of Tautavel in 1971. While there is no absolute date given to these finds, it is estimated that they are between 200,000 and 300,000 years old, based on the animal fossils, particularly rodents, found with them. Stone tools also found at the site belong to the Late Acheulian industry. They suggest that this species existed just prior to the European Neanderthals, in the Late Middle Pleistocene Period.

The Arago man, estimated to be about 20 years old, had a forward-jutting face, heavy brow ridges, a slanting forehead, and a braincase somewhat smaller than the average modern human. The two jaws also found were massive, indicating his powerful chewing ability.

Aragon, Spanish ARAGÓN, region of Spain, an autonomous governmental entity (*comunidad autónoma*) encompassing the northeastern Spanish provinces of Huesca, Zaragoza, and Teruel.

The following article summarizes the administrative status and history, geography, demographic patterns, economy, and culture of modern Aragon; for fuller treatment of its geography and history, *see* MACROPAEDIA: Spain.

The modern region of Aragon is roughly coextensive with the historic Kingdom of Aragon, whose reconquest from the Muslims was complete by the late 12th century. The Kingdom of Aragon belonged to the Crown of Aragon, which also encompassed Catalonia,

Valencia, and various French and overseas Mediterranean territories.

In 1035 Sancho III the Great of Navarre left to his third son, Ramiro I, the small Pyrenean county of Aragon and established it as an independent kingdom. To this mountain domain Ramiro added the counties of Sobrarbe and Ribagorza to the east.

The union of Aragon and Catalonia in 1140 principally benefitted the Catalans, who could then devote themselves to commerce and maritime expansion, knowing that the financial and military responsibility of defending them from Castile would fall largely on the inhabitants of the Aragonese hinterland. By the 15th century the nobles of Aragon proper had come to favour union with Castile to counterbalance the power of the mercantile Catalans. In 1479 the two kingdoms were united, but the Aragonese lands retained autonomous parliamentary and administrative institutions until the early 18th century, when their constitutional privileges were abrogated by Philip V.

The old Kingdom of Aragon survived as an administrative unit until 1833, when it was divided into the three existing provinces.

Mountains dominate the relief north and south of the cultivated Ebro River basin. The central Pyrenees extend southward from France into the northernmost province of Huesca and into the northwest corner of Zaragoza province. Huesca is bounded by the provinces of Navarre to the northwest and Lérida to the east. The pre-Pyrenees decline in height southward into the Ebro basin, which links Zaragoza with the provinces of Lérida and Tarragona to the southeast and Navarre and Logroño to the northwest. The Ebro drains most of Aragon, with the exception of the southernmost zone of the province of Teruel, which is linked to the Tagus River (locally Tejo) basin and the Mediterranean. The Iberian range (Sierra de Súdar) rises in the southwestern corner of Zaragoza and marks its border with the provinces of Soria and Guadalajara. The Iberian range occupies all but the northernmost corner of the province of Teruel, which is bounded by the provinces of Guadalajara to the west, Cuenca to the southwest, Valencia to the south, and Castellón and Tarragona to the east. Annual precipitation is low outside the central Pyrenees, rarely exceeding 12 in. (300 mm). Precipitation is also highly variable, ranging from 8 to 24 in., with the result that dry farming is extremely precarious. A Mediterranean climate prevails outside the central Pyrenees, with precipitation concentrated in the autumn and spring; the climate of the Iberian range is modified by continental influences.

The population tends to be concentrated in the irrigated zones of the Ebro basin and is much sparser in the adjoining mountains. In the central Pyrenees it is scattered among the valleys, where the custom of undivided inheritance has led to the emigration of propertyless descendants, leaving behind an aging and dwindling population. In Huesca and Teruel the population has been steadily declining since the early 20th century, when phylloxera destroyed numerous vineyards in the pre-Pyrenees and Iberian range. Towns become larger as they approach the Ebro, with the population of the province and city of Zaragoza growing at the expense of the provinces of Huesca and Teruel. Fully one-half of Aragon's population lives in Zaragoza city; other centres have shown little or no growth since 1900.

Most of the land under cultivation is dry-farmed, producing traditional Mediterranean crops of wheat, olives, and grapes. The land under irrigation, however, is far more productive and accounts for the better part of Aragon's agricultural output. The government has sponsored various projects to expand the land under irrigation, beginning with the Imperial Canal, which was completed in 1783. By 1904 the Canal of Aragon and Catalonia had brought wide stretches of land in the province of Huesca under irrigation, while the Plan Bardenas and the Plan Monegros, both initiated after 1945, are expected to bring close to 2,000,000 ac (800,000 ha) under irrigation by the end of the century. The Plan Bardenas channels the Arba and Aragon rivers and centres around the town of Ejea de los Caballeros, while the Plan Monegros draws on the Flumen and Ebro rivers. The principal crops of the irrigated zones are fodder, cotton, sugar beets, and fruit.

Aragon's industrial sector is heavily concentrated in greater Zaragoza. The introduction of sugar beets in the late 19th century hastened the industrialization of the city; seven sugar refineries were established between 1900 and 1905. Metalworking has become Zaragoza's leading industry, with electric appliances, machinery, industrial vehicles, and automobiles being the leading manufactures.

Aragon produces approximately one-half of Spain's lignite, some three-quarters of which is used in Aragon to generate electricity. Aragon's primary source of energy, however, is hydroelectricity, generated by the damming of the Ebro and its affluents in the province of Huesca. Electricity is exported to the industrial cities of Bilbao and Barcelona. Zaragoza was linked by railroad to Madrid, Barcelona, Pamplona, and Bilbao in 1864 and to Calatayud and Valencia by 1901. Highways connect Zaragoza with Spain's major industrial centres, among them Madrid, Barcelona, Bilbao, and Valencia.

Tiles and ceramics made in Teruel, Muel, Calatayud, and Villafeliche feature Morisco (Moorish) designs. The traditional costume worn by men includes a black velvet jacket with slashed sleeves and ornamental buttons, a *faja,* or scarlet waistband, breeches made of black velvet, and *alpargatus,* or hemp espadrilles. Aragonese cuisine is frugal; specialties include codfish cooked with garlic, eggs and salmon, and ham and tomatoes. Lécera is noted for its liqueurs. Irrigated plots and grainfields are privately owned, while pastures tend to be common lands; villages in the central Pyrenees may use the pastures of adjoining villages by the right of *alera floral* or *faceria.* Pop. (1981) 1,213,099.

Aragon, Louis (b. Oct. 3, 1897, Paris—d. Dec. 24, 1982, Paris), poet, novelist, and essayist who was a political activist and spokesman for Communism.

Through the Surrealist poet André Breton, Aragon was introduced to avant-garde movements such as Dadaism; and together with Philippe Soupault, he and Breton founded the Surrealist review *Littérature* (1919). Aragon's first poems, *Feu de joie* (1920) and *Le Mouvement perpétuel* (1925), were followed by a novel, *Le Paysan de Paris* (1926; *The Night-Walker,* 1950). In 1927 his search for an ideology led him to the Communist Party, with which he was identified thereafter, as he came to exercise a continuing authority over its literary and artistic expression. In 1928 he met Elsa Triolet (the Russian-born sister-in-law of the poet Mayakovsky), who became his wife and his inspiration (she died in 1970). In 1930 he visited the Soviet Union, and in 1933 his political commitment resulted in a break with the Surrealists. The four volumes of his long novel series, *Le Monde réel* (1933–44), describe in some historical perspective the class struggle of the proletariat marching toward social revolution. Aragon continued to employ a traditional Social Realism in another long novel, *Les Communistes* (6 vol., 1949–51), a bleak chronicle of the party from 1939 to 1940. His next three novels—*La Semaine sainte* (1958; *Holy Week,* 1961), *La Mise à mort* (1965), and *Blanche ou l'oubli* (1967)—became a veiled autobiography, laced with pleas for the Communist Party. They reflected the newer novelistic techniques of the day.

The poems of *Le Crève-Coeur* (1941) and *La Diane française* (1945) express Aragon's ardent patriotism, and those of *Les Yeux d'Elsa* (1942) and *Il n'est Paris que d'Elsa* (1964) sing his love for his wife, in whose face he sees the face of France. From 1953 to 1972 Aragon was editor of the Communist weekly of arts and literature *Les Lettres Françaises.* Still militant at the age of 71, Aragon joined the students demonstrating in the streets of Paris in 1968. He was made a member of the French Legion of Honour in 1981.

aragonite, widespread mineral, the stable form of calcium carbonate ($CaCO_3$) at high pressures. It may be distinguished from calcite, the commoner form of calcium carbonate, by its greater hardness and specific gravity. Aragonite is always found in deposits formed at low temperatures near the surface of the Earth, as in caves as stalactites, in the oxidized zone of ore minerals (with lead substituting for calcium), in serpentine and other basic rocks, in sediments, and in iron-ore deposits. Aragonite is the mineral normally found in pearls. It is polymorphous (same chemical formula but different crystal structure) with calcite and vaterite, and, with geologic time, probably inverts to calcite even under normal conditions. For detailed physical properties, *see* carbonate mineral (table).

Aragonite is an important element in the shells and tests of many marine invertebrates. These animals can secrete the mineral from waters that would ordinarily yield only calcite; they do so by physiological mechanisms that are not fully understood.

Aragua, state, northern Venezuela, bounded north by the Caribbean Sea, east by the Distrito Federal and Miranda, south by Guárico, and west by Carabobo. The territory of 2,708 sq mi (7,014 sq km) is comprised largely of two Andean ranges separated by an intermontane basin, in which lies Lake Valencia. The 222,390-ac (90,000-ha) Henri Pittier National

Sugarcane plantation, Aragua Valley, Venezuela
Georges de Steinheil

Park, with its exceptionally rich and varied flora, occupies the entire northern half of Aragua. The climate is tropical, and, though there is considerable rain inland, the coast is dry. The Aragua Valley produces a variety of agricultural products. Although sugarcane has ranked first for many years, potatoes have attained high commercial value. Other important crops include beans, coffee, cotton, corn (maize), rice, and tobacco. Aragua still ranks high in cattle, but herds have diminished as rangelands are converted to farmlands. The state lies in what has traditionally been Venezuela's most important political, industrial, urban, and population region. Its industrial development has been notable, particularly in and around the state capital, Maracay (*q.v.*). The state has a good system of hard-surface roads. Pop. (1983 est.) 786,125.

Araguaia River, Portuguese RIO ARAGUAIA, river, central Brazil, rising on the Brazilian Highlands near Alto Araguaia town in Mato Grosso state and flowing north-northeast for 1,632 mi (2,627 km) to its junction with the Tocantins River, at São João do Araguaia. Its upper course forms part of the boundary between Mato Grosso and Goiás states. In mid-course the river divides into two channels on either side of Bananal Island, which is about 200 mi long and the site of the Parque Nacional de Araguaia. The major, western arm is interrupted by many falls and rapids; the smaller, eastern channel can be navigated by small boats. Although the Araguaia drains a vast area of interior Brazil, it offers poor transportation, for it is frequently interrupted by falls. Hydroelectric projects were built on the river during the late 1970s to provide power for the extraction of mahogany. The area around the Araguaia's upper course has unexploited minerals, including uranium, copper, cobalt, zinc, and diamonds.

Araguari, city, western Minas Gerais state, Brazil, on the Rio Jordão, a tributary of the Rio Paranaíba, at 3,051 ft (930 m) above sea level. Formerly called Freguesia do Brejo Alegre, the settlement was made the seat of a municipality in 1882 and was elevated to city rank in 1888. Araguari's main source of income is from the large herds of cattle raised in the hinterlands, where rice, corn (maize), *feijão* (beans), and cassava are also cultivated. The city has an airport and is accessible by railroad and highway from other urban centres in Minas Gerais and Goiás states. Pop. (1980 prelim.) 73,302.

arahant (Buddhism): *see* arhat.

Arai Hakuseki (b. March 24, 1657, Edo, Japan—d. June 29, 1725, Edo), statesman and scholar who was a chief adviser to the Tokugawa shoguns in the early years of the 18th century.

Born into an impoverished samurai, or warrior, family, Arai declined several offers of marriage to the daughters of wealthy, socially ambitious merchant families because he felt that such matches were beneath his dignity as a samurai. After educating himself under conditions of extreme hardship, he found employment in 1682 under Hotta Masatoshi (1634–84), a top government official. When Hotta died two years later, Arai became tutor to Tokugawa Ienobu (reigned 1709–12), the heir apparent to the shogun, or hereditary military dictator of Japan. Ienobu became shogun in 1709, and Arai became the leading architect of governmental policy.

The Tokugawa government had grown lax, and bureaucratic rigidity had come to hamper efficiency. Arai attempted to make the laws of the country more practical; he reformed the currency and instituted a rigid system of budgeting and accounting. To stop the drain of precious metals from the country, he further tightened governmental control over foreign trade. Despite his hostility to foreigners, Arai was conscious of foreign relations, and he attempted to institute a policy by which it would be clear to foreign powers that the emperor was merely symbolic and real sovereignty resided with the shogun. To this end, he attempted to get the shogun to marry daughters of the Imperial line and to increase the ceremony at the shogun's court.

Although Ienobu died in 1712, Arai remained in the government throughout the reign of his successor, Tokugawa Ietsugu. But when the strong-minded Tokugawa Yoshimune came to power in 1716, Arai was forced to retire. He then devoted the rest of his life to writing.

Arai's works (more than 160 books) encompass almost the entire range of human knowledge. He wrote pioneering studies in Japanese geography, philosophy, and legal institutions and is considered one of the greatest historians of Japan. Among his best known works are *Dokushi yoron* ("A Reading of Political History"), a study of Japanese history from the 9th to the 16th century; *Koshi tsū* ("The Understanding of Ancient History"), a critical study of the earliest documentary sources; and his autobiography, *Oritaku shiba no ki*.

Arainn (Ireland): *see* Aran Islands.

Arakan State, coastal state in Lower Burma, facing India across the Bay of Bengal. Its coast extends for about 300 mi (480 km) south along the bay's northeastern shore, from the Nāf estuary on the border with Bangladesh to a point south of Gwa. (The Arakan coastal region extends 100 mi farther south into Irrawaddy Division; and the northern Arakan Hill Tracts, before Burmese independence in 1948 a part of Arakan, are now a part of Chin State.) Arakan reaches its greatest width (90 mi) in the north and includes many offshore islands, including Cheduba and Ramree. The Arakan Yoma range (*q.v.*) is the eastern boundary. Watered by the Nāf estuary and the Mayu, Kaladan, and Lemro rivers, the state has an area of 14,200 sq mi (36,778 sq km).

Only one-tenth of the land is cultivated. Rice is the dominant crop in the delta areas, where most of the population is concentrated. Other crops include fruits, chilies, *dhani* (thatch), and tobacco. The natural hillside vegetation of evergreen forest has been destroyed over wide areas by shifting cultivation (slashing and burning to clear land for cultivation) and has been replaced by a tangle of bamboo. There has been exploration for oil along the coast.

The main towns are coastal and include Akyab, the state's capital, Sandoway, Kyaukpyu, and Taungup. Long accessible only by sea, Arakan is now linked by air and road with the rest of the country. An all-weather road connects Taungup with Pyè in Pegu Division.

The Arakanese are Buddhists of Burmese stock with a dialect and customs of their own. Separated from the parent group in central Burma by the mountain's of the Arakan Yoma, they trace their history to 2666 BC, have a lineal succession of as many as 227 princes, and claim that their empire once extended across Burma into China and Bengal. History does not corroborate these claims, but the Arakans' most sacred image of the Buddha, the Mahamuni (now in Mandalay), is said to predate the Pagan kingdom (1044–1287) by a millennium. Engravings indicate that a dynasty existed in Arakan in the 4th century. The Mongols, Pegus, and Portuguese invaded Arakan at different times. It became part of the Burmese kingdom in 1785, and, as a province, it was ceded to the British in 1826 by the Treaty of Yandabo. The former capital, Arakan (now called Myohaung, [Mrohaung in Arakanese] or Old City), is on a branch of the Kaladan, 50 mi northwest of Akyab. *See also* Mrohaung, Arakanese Kingdom of. Arakan State has a large minority of Bengali Muslims.

In concession to separatist ethnic feelings, the Burmese constitution of 1947 established Arakan Division. This became Arakan State, with limited local autonomy, under the 1974 constitution. Pop. (1973) 1,711,000.

Arakan Yoma (Burmese: Arakan Mountain Range), mountain arc in western Burma, between the Arakan Coast and the Irrawaddy Valley. The arc extends northward for about 600 mi (950 km) from Cape Negrais (Burma) to Manipur (India) and includes the Nāga, Chin, Lushai, and Pātkai hills. Arakan Yoma itself is about 250 mi long. Called Arakan Roma in Arakanese, its highest point is Mt. Victoria (10,150 ft [3,094 m]). Dividing Arakan State from the rest of Burma, the range historically has been a barrier between Burma and the Indian subcontinent. It functions as a climatic barrier, cutting off the southwestern monsoon rains from central Burma. Arakan Yoma is crossed by the An route to Ngape and Minbu and by an all-weather road from Taungup to Pyè on the Irrawaddy.

Arakcheyev, Aleksey Andreyevich, Graf (Count) (b. Oct. 4 [Sept. 23, old style], 1769, near Bezhetsk, Tver province, Russia—d. May 3 [April 21, O.S.], 1834, Gruzino), military officer and statesman whose domination of the internal affairs of Russia during the last decade of Alexander I's reign (ruled 1801–25) caused that period to be known as Arakcheyevshchina.

An artillery officer in the Russian Army, Arakcheyev became a close associate and adviser to the tsarevich Paul, who, when he became emperor in 1796, gave Arakcheyev the task of reorganizing the entire army. When his harsh disciplinary measures alienated the officers' corps, however, he was dismissed (1798) and was recalled to active duty only after Alexander I ascended the throne. Made an inspector general of the artillery in 1803, Arakcheyev reorganized that branch of the army; he then became minister of war (1808), and in 1809, during the Russo-Swedish War of 1808–09, he personally compelled the reluctant Russian forces to cross the frozen Gulf of Finland and make the attack on the Åland Islands that ultimately resulted in Sweden's cession of Finland to Russia (September 1809).

Arakcheyev, detail of an engraving by N.I. Utkin after a portrait by G. Wagner, 1818

Novosti Press Agency

Arakcheyev generally opposed the liberal administrative and constitutional reforms considered by Alexander, and when Alexander created the advisory Council of State (1810), Arakcheyev resigned as minister of war. He later accepted a post as head of the council's military department; and, as one of Alexander's most trusted military advisers, he handled all of the Emperor's military correspondence and dispatches during the War of 1812. Afterward, when Alexander became almost exclusively involved in foreign affairs, Arakcheyev was made responsible for supervising the Council of Ministers' management of domestic matters (1815).

For the next decade Arakcheyev dominated the administration of Russia's internal affairs. Despite his basic conservatism, he took part in the emancipation of serfs in Russia's Baltic provinces (1816–19) and also developed a plan for gradually emancipating all of Russia's serfs (1818). In addition, he supervised the system of military–agricultural colonies, which between 1816 and 1821 housed nearly one-third of Russia's standing army. After Nicholas I succeeded Alexander (1825), Arakcheyev resigned all of his offices (April 1826) and went into retirement.

Araki Sadao (b. May 26, 1877, Tokyo—d. Nov. 2, 1966, Nara, Japan), Japanese Army general, statesman, and a leader of the Kōdōha (Imperial Way) faction, an ultranationalistic group of the 1930s. He strongly advocated the importance of character building through rigid mental and physical discipline, whereas the dominant Tōsei-ha (Control) faction emphasized the importance of modernization along with self-discipline.

Araki, a graduate of the Army War College, served in the Russo-Japanese War in 1904 and with Japanese forces in Siberia in 1918. He was promoted to lieutenant general in 1927. He was the choice of zealous young officers to head a new cabinet to be created when they executed a planned coup d'etat against the government (October 1931); the coup, however, was not implemented. Meanwhile, the Japanese Army invaded Manchuria in September 1931, against orders from Tokyo, and on Feb. 26, 1936, a group of young militant officers attempted a coup and assassinated Prime Minister Saito Minoru and several cabinet members. Though Araki, who had been appointed minister of war in the Inukai Tsuyoki Cabinet, and other high officers were not connected with the group, Araki was relieved from active duty and placed on the reserve list. In 1938 the prime minister, Prince Konoye, appointed him minister of education in an effort to balance the growing domination by the Tōsei-ha. Araki vigorously promoted ultranationalism and militarism with profound effects. He remained active in the government throughout World War II. After the war, the International Military Tribunal convicted him of first-class war crimes and sentenced him to life imprisonment. He was released in June 1955.

Araks River (Asia Minor): *see* Aras River.

Aral Sea, Russian ARALSKOYE MORE, also spelled ARALSKOJE MORE, oval-shaped sea 25,659 sq mi (66,458 sq km) in area. The shallow Aral Sea is the world's fourth largest body of inland water. It nestles in the climatically inhospitable heart of Soviet Central Asia, to the east of the Caspian Sea, and about equidistant from Moscow, Baghdad, and Karāchi. Of great interest to scientists because of the remarkable changes in area and volume it has experienced in geologically recent times, the sea is also notable for the changes introduced by modern man, who has diverted some of the waters of the Syrdarya and Amu Darya (*darya,* "river"), which discharge into it, for purposes of irrigation.

The Aral Sea lies 174 ft (53 m) above sea level, straddling the boundary between the Kazakh S.S.R. to the north and the westernmost dependency of the Uzbek S.S.R. Its greatest north to south extent is almost 270 mi (435 km), while that from east to west is just over 180 mi. Although the average depth is a shallow 70 ft or so, it descends to a maximum of 226 ft off the western shore. The total volume has been calculated at 255 cu mi (1,060 cu km). The Aral Sea derives its name from the Kirgiz Aral-denghiz, "Sea of Islands"—an apt designation, as there are no fewer than 1,130 islands of a size of 2.5 ac (1 ha) or more strewn across its waters.

The sea's northern shore—high in some places, low in others—is indented from west to east by the bays of Chernyshev, Tushchibas, Shevchenko, Butakov, and Saryshiganak. The low-lying and irregular eastern shores are interrupted in the north by the huge delta of the Syrdarya and in the south are bordered by a wide tract of shallow water. The equally vast Amu Darya Delta lies on the southern shore, and along the sea's western periphery extends the almost unbroken eastern edge of the 820-ft-high Ustyurt Plateau. The largest islands are, from west to north, Vozrozhdeniye, Barsakelmes, and Kokaral.

The shoreline region is made up of marine and continental deposits laid down from the Cretaceous Period (65,000,000–136,000,000 years ago) onward. Cretaceous outcrops in the coastal areas have produced mainly limestone, sandstone, and sand and clay deposits in the northern, southern, and western parts of the sea. Tertiary (2,500,000–65,000,000 years ago) deposits are composed mainly of marl, limestone, compact clay, and clayey sand. Quaternary deposits (sediments younger than 2,500,000 years) of various origins are widely distributed along the shores, especially in the east and south: the marine and eolian deposits consist mainly of sandy sediments, the alluvial ones mainly of sand and clay. The seabed is mainly smooth and unbroken and descends from east to west. Bottom deposits, comprising quartz and limestone sands and clays, and clay–limestone silts are the products of the rivers' powerful flow and the erosion of the shores by wind and ice. Stony sediments from rock deposits occur only in the coastal areas.

The Aral Sea depression was formed toward the beginning of the Pleistocene Epoch (2,500,000 years ago), when the Earth's crust subsided and the hollow was filled with water—some of which came from the Syrdarya. In the early and middle Pleistocene, the depression was subject largely to eolian processes, and in the late Pleistocene Epoch (until about 10,000 years ago) it was inundated for a second time by the Syrdarya and for the first time by the Amu Darya, which had temporarily changed its course from the Caspian to the Aral Sea. At the turn of the 3rd and 2nd centuries BC and at the beginning of the 1st century BC the Aral depression was again inundated by both rivers. Between these inundations dry periods with water occurring only in the western hollow resulted largely from changes in the behaviour of the Syrdarya. But from the Pleistocene Epoch onward, the rivers' combined flow maintained a high water level, which was almost unaffected by climatic changes.

The Aral Sea area is characterized by a desert-continental climate of which the typical features are wide-ranging air temperatures, cold winters, hot summers, and sparse rainfall. Average monthly air temperatures from January to February vary from 10.4° F (−12° C) in the north to 21° F (−6° C) in the south and in July from 73.9° F (23.3° C) to 79° F (26.1° C), respectively. The rate of precipitation—an average of four in. (100 mm) in all, occurring mainly in spring and autumn—equals one-twelfth the rate of evaporation. The average water temperature for July is 73°–77° F (23°–25° C), and, when ice forms in November and December, the mercury falls to 30.8° F (−0.7° C). Northeasterly winds prevail in autumn and winter and westerly and southwesterly winds in spring and summer.

Factors affecting the water balance of the Aral Sea are precipitation, river flow (accounting for about 90 percent of inflow), and evaporation, which takes out each year about the same amount of water that the rivers bring in. Climate may quite considerably influence the long-term variation in water level. Over the centuries, variations have exceeded 20 ft, while annual and seasonal variations of between 10 ft and less than a foot have been recorded. In the short term, similar variations have been caused by oscillations of barometric pressure and by a combination of condensation and distillation. From 1960 onward the water level has been systematically reduced by climatic changes and by the diversion of water from the Amu Darya and Syrdarya to agricultural irrigation. The mean salt level of the sea is from 10 to 11 parts per thousand rising to 14 parts per thousand on the southeastern shores and from 80 to 150 parts per thousand in the shallow bays.

Aralsk in the northeast and Muynak in the south are important economic centres and ports between which ships steam for seven months of the year. Fishing villages are scattered along the northern and eastern shores in the Aralsk region, to which catches of such freshwater fish as sturgeon, carp, barbel, zander, rapfen (*Aspius aspius*), bream, and roach are conveyed. Newly introduced strains of Atlantic herring, striped mullet, and goby are also caught in coastal waters. The inhabitants of the settlements near Muynak are similarly engaged in fishing but also—though to a lesser extent—in stock raising, muskrat breeding, and the cultivation of melons. In many of the shallow bays and coves—particularly in the east—there are large accumulations of sodium sulfate and sodium chloride.

Consult the INDEX *first*

Arales, order of monocotyledonous flowering plants comprising the families Araceae and Lemnaceae, of herbs, climbing shrubs, marsh plants, and floating aquatic forms, the majority of which live in the tropics.

The Arales may share common evolutionary ancestors with the palm order (Arecales) and the Panama hat palm order (Cyclanthales) from the immediate ancestors of the lily order (Liliales). The order is rich in horticulturally popular ornamentals and foliage plants, all in the arum or aroid family (Araceae). The duckweed family (Lemnaceae) is remarkable for containing the smallest known flowering plants.

The species may be terrestrial, aquatic, or epiphytic. Some are herbaceous and stemless, with few arrow-shaped leaves arising from a rootstock. Others are climbers, clinging by aerial roots to tree trunks and other upright supports and unfurling very large, sometimes dissected, leaves alternately along the stem, with each leaf bearing a temporary, almost colourless sheath at the base of the leaf stalk (petiole). The inflorescence, adapted to insect pollination, is formed of a single spike, or spadix, on which few to many minute to small flowers are variously arranged, the entire structure being enveloped by a sometimes colourful floral leaf, or spathe. The spadix often emits a fetid odour that attracts flies, which are trapped for a time and then escape to pollinate other plants. The fruit may be a brightly coloured berry (sometimes many, clustered on the spadix); rarely it is dry and leathery, rupturing to release seed. The sap often contains calcium oxalate crystals, which upon ingestion can numb the tongue and throat.

The Araceae has about 115 genera and 2,000 species, native primarily to the tropics and subtropics. The few temperate zone species are widely distributed, especially in wet habitats. The family is known for several wildings and many greenhouse and foliage ornamentals. The largest genera in the family Araceae are *Anthurium* (*q.v.*; 600 species); *Philodendron* (275 species); *Arisaema* (150 species), which is believed to be pollinated by snails; *Homalomena* (140 species); *Rhaphidophora* (100 species); *Amorphophallus* (100 species), some species of which produce inflorescences up to one metre (about 40 inches) tall; *Pothos* (75 species); and *Alocasia* (70 species).

The genera *Philodendron* and *Monstera* are grown for their vinelike habit and large, green leaves. The elephant's ear (*Colocasia esculenta*) is a variable species that includes the dasheen, taro, and eddo of the tropics; these plants are grown for their large edible corms, or bulblike underground stems. The florist's calla lily is *Zantedeschia aethiopica*, and the genus *Calla* includes the water arum (*C. palustris*); both are grown ornamentally. Species of dumb cane (*Dieffenbachia*) are popular indoor foliage plants that can cause inflammation and swelling of the throat if a piece of stem is chewed. Jack-in-the-pulpit (*Arisaema triphyllum*) is a well-known woodland plant. The golden club (*Orontium aquaticum*) is occasionally cultivated in ponds or greenhouse pools for its bright yellow spadices. Water

(Top left) *Dieffenbachia amoena;* (top right) Jack-in-the-pulpit (*Arisaema triphyllum*); (centre left) skunk cabbage (*Symplocarpus foetidus*); (centre right top) *Anthurium;* (centre right bottom) water lettuce (*Pistia stratiotes*); (bottom left) *Caladium;* (bottom right) duckweed (*Lemna minor*)

(Top left) John H. Gerard—EB Inc., (top right) Dr. G.J. Chafaris—EB Inc., (centre left) Grant Heilman—EB Inc., (centre right top) Joan F. Falk, (centre right bottom) Phil Clark, (bottom left) Derek Fell, (bottom right) Dr. Wm.M. Harlow—Photo Researchers

lettuce or water cabbage (*Pistia stratiotes*) is an edible and attractive floating ornamental. *Amorphophallus* includes several curiosities grown for their large and ill-smelling inflorescences. Sweet flag rhizome, or calamus root (*Acorus calamus*), contains a spicy, aromatic oil often used in medicines and flavourings. Eastern skunk cabbage (*Symplocarpus foetidus*) is a well-known marsh plant with a fetid odour. The lords-and-ladies, or cuckoopint (*Arum maculatum*), is one of the few arums found as far north as Europe. Several species of *Spathiphyllum* are grown as indoor potted plants. Another beautiful foliage plant is *Caladium*, available in many horticultural varieties with large, colourful leaves.

The Lemnaceae, with 6 genera and 30 species of minute floating aquatic forms, is widespread in the temperate and tropic zones. The family is remarkable for the smallest known flowering plants, the duckweeds (*Lemna* species) and watermeals (*Wolffia* species). Certain of these green, leaflike, flattened species, with or without rootlets and only a few millimetres across, are used in aquariums and pools as ornamentals or as food for waterfowl and fish.

Flowers, rarely produced, bear only the essential organs, no sepals or petals: the male flower has one or two stamens and the female a single pistil. The plants reproduce primarily by basal division.

Araliaceae, the ginseng family of flowering plants, in the dogwood order (Cornales), comprising about 85 genera centred in Southeast Asia and tropical America. Most members are shrubs or trees, though there are a number of climbers and a few herbs. The family has large, usually alternate, compound leaves,

Wild sarsaparilla (*Aralia nudicaulis*)

Stephen Collins

five-parted flowers arranged in compound umbels (flat-topped clusters), and a berry or (rarely) a drupe (a one-seeded fruit). Several members of the family are economically important. Ivies (*Hedera* species) are grown as ornamental plants and houseplants. The rice-paper plant (*Tetrapanax papyriferum*) is the source of rice paper, and the wood of several species provides timber, especially that of *Dendropanax arboreum* and several members of the genus *Didymopanax*.

Wild sarsaparilla (*Aralia nudicaulis*) has an aromatic root that is used as a substitute for sarsaparilla. Ginseng root, from *Panax schinseng,* has long been used by the Chinese in the treatment of various diseases; its American relative, *Panax quinquefolium,* is used in the United States as a stimulant. *Hari-giri,* or castor aralia (*Acanthopanax ricinifolius*), is used in Japan in building and in furniture making.

Aram, Eugene (b. *c.* September 1704, Ramsgill, Yorkshire, Eng.—d. Aug. 6, 1759, York, Yorkshire), noted English scholar and murderer, whose notoriety was romanticized in a ballad by Thomas Hood and in the novel *Eugene Aram*, by Bulwer-Lytton.

In 1745, when Aram was schoolmaster at Knaresborough, a man named Daniel Clark, his intimate friend, after obtaining a considerable quantity of goods from tradesmen, disappeared. Suspicions of being concerned in this swindling transaction fell upon Aram. His garden was searched, and some of the goods were found there. However, because there was insufficient evidence to convict him of any crime, he was discharged. For several years he travelled through parts of England, acting as usher in a number of schools, and settled finally at Lynn, in Norfolk. During his travels he had amassed considerable material for a projected comparative lexicon of the English, Latin, Greek, Hebrew, and Celtic languages. He was undoubtedly an original philologist, who recognized what was then not yet admitted by scholars, that the Celtic language was related to the other languages of Europe and that Latin was not derived from Greek. But he was not destined to live in history as the pioneer of a new philology.

In February 1758 a skeleton was dug up at Knaresborough, and some suspicion arose that it might be Clark's. Aram's wife had often hinted that her husband and a man named Houseman knew the secret of Clark's disappearance. Houseman was at once arrested and confronted with the bones that had been found. After denials, he confessed that he had been present at the murder of Clark by Aram and another man, Terry, of whom nothing further was heard. He also gave information as to the place where Clark's body had been buried. A skeleton was dug up, and Aram was immediately arrested and sent to York for trial. He was found guilty and condemned to be executed. While in his cell he confessed his guilt and asserted that he had discovered an intimacy between Clark and his own wife.

Aramaean, one of a confederacy of tribes that spoke a North Semitic language (Aramaic) and, between the 11th and 8th centuries BC, occupied Aram, a large region in northern Syria. In the same period some of these tribes seized large tracts of Mesopotamia.

In the Old Testament the Aramaeans are represented as being closely akin to the Hebrews and living in northern Syria around Harran from about the 16th century BC. The Aramaeans also are mentioned often in Assyrian records as freebooters jointly with another people called Akhlame. The first mention of the Aramaeans occurs in inscriptions of the Assyrian Tiglath-pileser I (1115–1077). By the end of the 11th century BC, the Aramaeans had formed the state of Bit-Adini on both sides of the Euphrates below Carchemish and held areas in Anatolia, northern Syria, and the Anti-Lebanon area, including Damascus. About 1030 BC a coalition of the southern Aramaeans, led by Hadadezer, king of Zobah, in league with the Ammonites, Edomites, and the Aramaeans of Mesopotamia, attacked Israel but was defeated by King David.

To the east, however, the Aramaean tribes spread into Babylonia, where an Aramaean usurper was crowned king of Babylon under the name of Adad-apal-iddin. By the 9th century the whole area from Babylon to the sea was in the hands of the Aramaean tribes known collectively as Kaldu (or Kashdu)—the biblical Chaldeans. Assyria, nearly encircled, took the offensive, and, in 853, Shalmaneser III fought a battle at Karkar against the armies of Hamath, Aram, Phoenicia, and Israel. This battle was indecisive, but, in 838, Shalmaneser was able to annex the area held by the tribes on the middle Euphrates.

Between Israel and Damascus, intermittent wars continued until Tiglath-pileser III of Assyria captured Arpad, the centre of Aramaean resistance in northern Syria, in 740 BC. He overthrew Samaria in 734 and Damascus in 732. Finally, the destruction of Hamath by Sargon II of Assyria in 720 marked the end of the Aramaean kingdoms of the west.

Aramaeans on the lower Tigris maintained their independence longer. In 626 a Chaldean general, Nabopolassar, proclaimed himself king of Babylon and joined with the Medes and Scythians to overthrow Assyria. In the New Babylonian, or Chaldean, Empire, Chaldeans, Aramaeans, and Babylonians became largely indistinguishable.

Few specifically Aramaic objects have been uncovered by archaeologists. The Aramaean princes in Syria apparently patronized a provincial form of Syrian art under strong Hittite or Mitannian influence.

In religion, though their pantheon included Canaanite, Babylonian, and Assyrian gods, the Aramaeans had deities of their own. Their chief god was Hadad, or Ramman (Old Testament Rimmon), equated with the Hurrian storm god, Teshub; their chief goddess was Atargatis (Atar'ate), a fusion of two deities corresponding to the Phoenician Astarte and Anath. A. Dupont-Sommer's *Les Araméens* was published in 1949.

Aramaic alphabet, major writing system in the Near East in the latter half of the 1st millennium BC. Derived from the North Semitic script, the Aramaic alphabet was developed in the 10th and 9th centuries BC and came into prominence after the conquest of the Aramaean states by Assyria in the 9th and 8th centuries BC.

The Aramaic language and script were used as a lingua franca over all of the Near East, and documents and inscriptions in the Aramaic alphabet have been found in Greece, Afghanistan, India, northern Arabia, and Egypt. The oldest inscription in Aramaic script yet discovered dates from approximately 850 BC.

The Aramaic alphabet consists of 22 letters, all indicating consonants, and it is written from right to left. It is ancestral to Square Hebrew and the modern Hebrew alphabet, the Nabataean and modern Arabic scripts, the Palmyrene alphabet, and the Syriac, as well as hundreds of other writing systems used at some time in Asia east of Syria. Aramaic also has been influential in the development of such alphabets as the Georgian, Armenian, and Glagolitic.

Aramaic language, Semitic language of the Northern Central or Northwestern group; in the 7th and 6th centuries BC, it gradually supplanted Akkadian as the lingua franca of the Near East and later became the official language of the Persian Empire. Aramaic replaced Hebrew as the language of the Jews; portions of the Old Testament books of Daniel and Ezra are written in Aramaic, as are the Babylonian and Jerusalem Talmuds. Jesus and the Apostles are believed to have spoken this language. Its period of greatest influence extended from *c.* 300 BC until *c.* AD 650; it was supplanted by Arabic.

In the early centuries AD, Aramaic divided into East and West varieties. West Aramaic dialects include Nabataean (formerly spoken in parts of Arabia), Palmyrene (spoken in Palmyra, which was northeast of Damascus), Palestinian-Christian, and Judeo-Aramaic. West Aramaic is still spoken in a small number of villages in Lebanon.

East Aramaic includes Syriac, Mandaean, Eastern Neo-Assyrian, and the Aramaic of the Babylonian Talmud. One of the most important of these is Syriac, which was the language of an extensive literature between the 3rd and 7th centuries. Mandaean was the dialect of a Gnostic sect centred in lower Mesopotamia. East Aramaic is still spoken by a few small groups of Jacobite and Nestorian Christians in the Middle East. *See also* Syriac language.

aramina (plant): *see* urena.

Aran Islands, Irish ARAINN, three limestone islands—Inishmore, Inishmaan, and Inisheer—comprising 18 sq mi (47 sq km) and lying across the mouth of Galway Bay on the west coast of Ireland. The islands, whose sheer cliffs face the Atlantic, are generally bleak. Steamers call at Kilronan on Inishmore, the largest island; the other two are accessible only by currach, a primitive type of boat. The people, who speak Irish, farm and fish under very difficult conditions. Aspects of their life formed the basis of the play *Riders to the Sea* (1904) and the book of impressions *The Aran Islands* (1907) by John Millington Synge; *Man of Aran*, a documentary film (1934) by Robert Flaherty also depicted the island life. The islands contain impressive prehistoric and early Christian hill forts and other remains. Author Liam O'Flaherty is a native of Gortnagapul, Inishmore. Pop. (1981) 803.

The beach on Inishmaan, Aran Islands, Ireland
Peter Carmichael—Aspect Picture Library

Aranda, also spelled ARUNTA, Aboriginal tribe that originally occupied a region of 25,000 square miles (65,000 square kilometres) in central Australia, along the upper Finke River and its tributaries.

The Aranda were divided into five subtribes, which were thought to have originated as food-gathering groups that remained separated for months each year and for longer periods during droughts. The subtribes were marked by differences in dialect and in some cases also by variations in social organization, ritual practices, and doctrinal emphasis. Each subtribe was divided into eight (or, in one instance, four) sections, or categories; and questions of who might marry whom, what rules of descent and kinship applied in various situations, and so on were correlated with membership in the respective sections.

Belief in preexistence and reincarnation was fundamental in Aranda religion, which also held that ancestors were in totemic relationship with natural species and phenomena. Severe initiation training and ordeals, including circumcision and subincision (incision in the urethra), were prescribed for males. Sorcery was believed to be a cause of illness and death, and "doctor men," who had passed through special revelatory rites and training, could cure, protect, and exert psychological influence in general.

Aranda art, mainly geometrical and symbolic, was mostly temporary, being expressed on ritual paraphernalia discarded after the ceremony and in blood and ochre body painting. (A modern group of Aranda, however, has become successful as watercolour artists, specializing in landscapes.)

In common with other Aborigines, the Aranda were greatly reduced in number during the first 70 years of contact with whites, but by the late 20th century they showed signs of holding their own and even of increasing, as a result of readaptation, medical services, and greatly improved living conditions. In 1982 the Aranda people at Hermannsburg in the Northern Territory were given freehold title to their land.

Aranda, Pedro Pablo Abarca de Bolea, conde de (count of) (b. Dec. 18, 1718, Siétamo, Spain—d. Jan. 9, 1798, Épila), Spanish general and minister, one of the most prominent reformers in the government of King Charles III (1759–88).

Aranda came from the Aragonese nobility and entered the army, in which he became director of the artillery, introduced the Prussian system of drill in the Seven Years' War, and commanded in the short campaign against Portugal (1762). In 1764 he became captain general of Valencia.

In 1766, after riots in Madrid, Charles III dismissed his Italian minister Leopoldo de Gregorio Squillace and called Aranda to be president of the Council of Castile. He convinced Charles that the riots had been instigated by the Jesuits and prepared the decree for their expulsion from Spain and Spanish America in April 1767.

Aranda held strong regalist views, but his authoritarian character caused him difficulty. He was dismissed in 1773 and made ambassador to France, where he remained until 1787 and absorbed "French ideas," becoming an admirer of Voltaire. His friends worked for his return against his rival, the Conde de Floridablanca, but Charles III died and Charles IV made no change. When Floridablanca attempted to silence news of the French Revolution and failed to intervene to save Louis XVI, Charles IV was persuaded to dismiss him and recall Aranda, who relaxed the censorship and tried without success to placate the French. In November 1792 he was dismissed and returned to his command. After the French regicide, he opposed Godoy's policy of war with France and was ejected from the royal council and exiled to Jaén. In 1795 Charles allowed him to retire to his estate in Aragon, where he died.

Araneida (arachnid order): *see* spider.

Arango, Doroteo: *see* Villa, Pancho.

Aranguren, José Luis (b. June 9, 1909, Avila, Spain), Spanish philosopher.

Aranguren developed his own philosophy, based on deep Christian faith, in *El catolicismo y el protestantismo como formas de existencia* (1945), considered by many critics to be his best work. In 1945 he published *La filosofía de Eugenio d'Ors,* an ambitious analysis of every aspect of d'Ors's thought. In 1955, he published *Catolicismo días tras días.* He was professor of ethics at the University of Madrid from 1955 to 1965. In *Crítica y meditación* (1957) he held that poets have a role in reconciling the world to God's will. In 1958 he published *La ética de Ortega.* He discussed the major problems of the day in *Ética y política* (1963) and *Moral y política* (1966). His ideas have had considerable influence on Spanish youth and Catholic philosophers.

Aranha, José Pereira da Graça: *see* Graça Aranha, José Pereira da.

Aranjuez, town, Madrid province, central Spain, on the southern bank of the Tagus River near its confluence with the Jarama. Inhabited in Roman times, it was called Ara Jovis. The town was the headquarters of the Knights of Santiago (1387–1409) and became the seat of a royal summer residence and hunting lodge in the 17th century. It was rebuilt *c.* 1750 by Ferdinand VI. The royal palace (completed in 1778 after being damaged several times by fire) has a large collection of treasures, and the Casita del Labrador, built by Charles IV, who abdicated at Aranjuez in 1808, recalls the Trianons (châteaux) at Versailles, Fr. Aranjuez is on the main railway from Madrid city (29 mi [47 km] north) and serves a rich agricultural district in which asparagus and strawberries are especially important and horses are bred. Industries include the manufacture of chemicals, metal products, and textiles, and the preservation of fruits. Pop. (1981) 35,936.

Arany, János (b. March 2, 1817, Nagyszalonta, Hung.—d. Oct. 22, 1882, Budapest), the greatest Hungarian epic poet.

Born of an impecunious farming family, he went to school in Debrecen but abandoned his studies to join for a short time a group of strolling players. Arany made his real advent on the literary scene in 1847 with his popular epic *Toldi,* which was received with enthusiasm by a public craving for a national literature of quality in a language all could grasp. Sándor Petőfi wrote a poem in its praise, and this was the beginning of a lifelong friendship.

In 1848 Arany took part in the Hungarian revolution and for a short period edited a government newspaper for peasants. With the crushing of the revolution he took up teaching. In 1858 he was elected a member of the Hungarian Academy. He moved then from Nagykőrös to Pest, where he edited a literary periodical, the *Szépirodalmi Figyelő* (later the *Koszorú*), and was elected first secretary and in 1870 secretary-general of the academy.

Arany's main epic work is the trilogy *Toldi* (1847), *Toldi szerelme* (1848–79; "Toldi's Love") and *Toldi estéje* (1854; "Toldi's Evening"). Its hero, a youth of great physical strength, is taken from a verse chronicle written by Péter Ilosvai Selymes in the 16th century. Set in the 14th century, the first part of the trilogy relates the adventures of Toldi in reaching the royal court; the second part tells of his tragic love; and the third, of his conflicts with the king and his death. Though only a fragment, another epic poem, *Bolond Istók* (1850; "Stephen the Fool"), a strange mixture of humour and bitterness, is valuable for Arany's rare moments of self-revelation. Arany started work on a Hun trilogy, connected with Hungarian prehistory, but finished only the first part of it, *Buda halála* (1864; *The Death of King Buda,* 1936).

Arany, engraved frontispiece to *Toldi,* 1858

By courtesy of the trustees of the British Museum; photograph, J.R. Freeman & Co. Ltd.

The poems of his two great lyrical periods are fraught with melancholy. The earlier poems, written in the 1850s, are overshadowed by the loss of Petőfi and by his despair for the Hungarian nation and for himself. The *Őszikék,* his beautiful swan songs, written just before his death, poignantly reflect Arany's sense of unfulfillment and solitude.

The best edition of Arany's collected works is by Géza Voinovich, six volumes (1951–52).

Āraṇyakas (Sanskrit: "Books of the Forest"), a later development of the *Brāhmaṇa*s, or expositions of the Vedas, which were composed in India *c.* 700 BC. The *Āraṇyakas* are distinguished from the *Brāhmaṇa*s in that they may contain information on secret rites to be carried out only by certain persons, and more philosophic speculation. Thus they were intended to be studied only by the initiated, by which might have been meant either hermits who had withdrawn into the forest and no longer took part in ritual sacrifices, or by pupils who were given instruction by their teachers in the seclusion of the forest, away from the village. The *Āraṇyakas* are given over to secret explanations of the allegorical meaning of the ritual and to discussion of the internal, meditative meaning of the sacrifice, as contrasted to its actual, outward performance. The philosophic portions, more speculative in content, are sometimes called *Upaniṣads* (*see* Upaniṣad).

Arányi, Jelly d' (b. May 30, 1895, Budapest—d. March 30, 1966, Florence), violinist known for her performances of contemporary music. Béla Bartók's two sonatas for violin and piano were written for her; Maurice Ravel's *Tzigane for Violin and Orchestra* and Ralph Vaughan Williams' *Violin Concerto* were dedicated to her.

The grandniece of the celebrated violinist Joseph Joachim, she made her debut in Vienna in 1909. She settled in London in 1913. Her playing was considered fiery and temperamental, and she was esteemed as a performer of Romantic music. Arányi frequently gave joint recitals with pianist Dame Myra Hess. She was also known for performances, with her sister Adila Fachiri (1888–1962), of Bach's double concertos.

Arao, city, Kumamoto Prefecture (*ken*), Kyushu, Japan, facing Ariake-wan (Ariake Bay). It was a poor village until the opening of the Miike coal mine and the arrival of a major railway in the early 20th century. A military munitions factory was established in the city in 1940. After World War II, however, the mine and the factory were closed. Arao now serves as a residential suburb of Ōmuta to the north. Pop. (1980) 61,485.

Arapaho, North American Plains Indian people of Algonkian linguistic stock who lived along the Platte and Arkansas rivers during the 19th century. Their early tradition suggests that they once had permanent villages in the eastern woodlands, where they engaged in agriculture. After a gradual westward movement, they split into northern and southern groups after 1830, the southern group settling in the region of the Arkansas River. Remnants of two or three other divisions have also been recognized.

Like other Plains tribes, the Arapaho led a nomadic life, living in tepees and depending on the buffalo for existence. They traded with the Mandan and Arikara (*qq.v.*) and with Spanish settlements in the Southwest. They were a highly religious people for whom everyday actions and objects (*e.g.,* beadwork designs) had symbolic meanings. Their chief object of veneration was a flat pipe that was kept in a sacred bundle with a hoop or wheel. In common with many other Plains tribes, they practiced the sun dance. Their social organization included age-graded military societies as well as men's shamanistic societies and other groups.

From early times the Arapaho were continually at war with the Shoshoni, the Ute, and the Pawnee. The southern Arapaho were for a long period closely associated with the southern Cheyenne; some Arapaho fought with the Cheyenne against Lieut. Col. George Armstrong Custer at Little Bighorn in 1876. In the Treaty of Medicine Lodge in 1867, the southern Arapaho were assigned a reservation in Oklahoma together with the Cheyenne, while the northern Arapaho were assigned a reservation in Wyoming with the Shoshoni. In the late 20th century there were about 2,000 Arapaho living on a reservation in Wyoming and more than 3,000 intermingled Arapaho and Cheyenne in Oklahoma.

arapaima (fish): *see* pirarucu.

ʿArʿar, town and capital of al-Ḥudūd ash-Shamālīyah *minṭaqah* (province), northern Saudi Arabia, situated in the Northern region at an elevation of 1,854 ft (565 m). ʿArʿar was developed in the early 1950s by seminomadic people who were attracted by water made available around the Trans Arabian Pipeline (Tapline). Agriculture and livestock raising are the main economic activities. Crops include alfalfa, dates, fruits, and vegetables. ʿArʿar has a technical institute, a hospital, and an airport.

Araraquara, city, in the highlands of central São Paulo state, Brazil, at 2,119 ft (646 m) above sea level on a tributary of the Rio Jacaré-Guaçu. Formerly known as Freguesia de São Bento de Araraquara, it was given town status in 1817 and was made the seat of a municipality in 1832. Araraquara's industries process sugarcane and coffee from the hinterland. Textiles, liquor, and furniture are also produced there. The city is accessible by railway, highway, and air from São Paulo, the state capital, 155 mi (250 km) southeast. Highways extend to other cities in São Paulo and Minas Gerais states. Pop. (1980 prelim.) 77,202.

Ararat, city, southwestern Victoria, Australia, on the northern flanks of the Pyrenees Range, near the Hopkins River. The community and a nearby peak (2,020 ft [616 m]) were named in 1840 by a sheep farmer who likened his settling there to the legendary resting of Noah's Ark on Mt. Ararat in Turkey after the Flood. Although gold was discovered in 1854, the rush of miners was delayed until 1857. Declared a borough in 1858 and a town in 1934, Ararat was made a city in 1950. It is now a commercial centre for a region of wheat and grape cultivation and livestock farming and lies on the main Adelaide–Melbourne rail line. It is connected to the harbours of Portland and Warrnambool by rail and is also the junction of the Pyrenees and Western highways. Industries include textile and timber mills, light engineering and rail workshops, cordial and butter plants, and a large postal relay facility. Notable annual events are a Highlands sports competition (New Year) and a nationally attended chess tournament (Queen's Birthday). Pop. (1981) 8,336.

Ararat, Mount, Turkish AGRI DAGI, extinct volcanic massif in extreme eastern Turkey overlooking the point at which the frontiers of Turkey, Iran, and the Armenian S.S.R. converge. Its northern and eastern slopes rise from the broad alluvial plain of the Aras River, about 3,300 ft (1,000 m) above sea level; its southwestern slopes rise from a plain about 5,000 ft above sea level; and on the west a low pass separates it from a long range of other volcanic ridges extending westward toward the eastern Taurus ranges. The Ararat Massif is about 25 mi (40 km) in diameter.

Ararat consists of two peaks, their summits about 7 mi apart. Great Ararat, or Büyük Ağrı Dağı, which reaches an elevation of 16,854 ft above sea level, is the highest peak in Turkey. Little Ararat, or Küçük Ağrı Dağı, rises in a smooth, steep, nearly perfect cone to 12,782 ft. Both Great and Little Ararat are the product of eruptive volcanic activity. Neither retains any evidence of a crater, but well-formed cones and fissures exist on their flanks. Towering 14,000 ft above the adjoining plains, the snowcapped conical peak of the Great Ararat offers a majestic sight. The snowline varies with the season, retreating to 14,000 ft above sea level by the end of the summer. The only true glacier is found on the northern side of the Great Ararat, near its summit. The middle zone of Ararat, from 5,000 to 11,500 ft, is covered with good pasture grass and some juniper; there the local Kurdish population graze their sheep. Most of the Great Ararat is treeless, but Little Ararat has a few birch groves. Despite the abundant cover of snow, the Ararat area suffers from scarcity of water.

Ararat traditionally is associated with the mountain on which Noah's Ark came to rest at the end of the Flood. The name Ararat, as it appears in the Bible, is the Hebrew equivalent of Urardhu, or Urartu, the Assyro-Babylonian name of a kingdom that flourished between the Aras and the Upper Tigris rivers from the 9th to the 7th century BC. Ararat is sacred to the Armenians, who believe themselves to be the first race of humans to appear in the world after the Deluge. A Persian legend refers to the Ararat as the cradle of the human race. There was formerly a village on the slopes of the Ararat high above the Aras plain, at the spot where, according to local tradition, Noah built an altar and planted the first vineyard. Above the village Armenians built a monastery to commemorate St. Jacob, who is said to have tried repeatedly but failed to reach the summit of Great Ararat in search of the Ark. The village, the monastery of St. Jacob, and a nearby chapel of St. James were all totally destroyed by an earthquake and avalanche in 1840.

Local tradition maintained that the Ark still lay on the summit but that God had declared that no one should see it. In September 1829, Johann Jacob von Parrot, a German, made the first recorded successful ascent. Since then Ararat has been scaled by several explorers, some of whom claim to have sighted the remains of the Ark.

Mount Ararat from the Doğubayazıt plains, Turkey
Josephine Powell, Rome

arartree, also called ALERCE, or EVERGREEN TIMBER CONIFER (*Tetraclinis articulata*), only species of the genus *Tetraclinis* of the cypress family (Cupressaceae), found in hot, dry areas of southeastern Spain, Malta, and North Africa.

A pyramidal tree 12 to 15 metres (about 40 to 50 feet) tall, the arartree has fragrant, brown or reddish-brown wood that has long been popular for furniture and cabinetmaking. The tree also yields large quantities of sandarac, a fragrant resin.

Aras River, Russian ARAKS, Persian RUD-E ARAS, Turkish ARAS NEHRİ, Greek ARAXES, river rising south of Erzurum in the Bingöl Dağları (mountains) of Turkish Armenia; it flows eastward, forming for approximately 274 mi (441 km) the international boundary between the U.S.S.R. on the north and Turkey and Iran on the south. Below Jolfā, a rail and road crossing in Iran, the stream emerges into a broad valley in which it crosses the Mugan Steppe. About 666 mi long, it joins the Kura River in the Azerbaijan Soviet Socialist Republic, 75 mi from its mouth on the Caspian Sea. Since a flood in 1897 a separate distributory (canalized since 1909) of the Aras also empties into the Caspian. The swift-flowing unnavigable Aras accounts for most of the sediment composing the Kura-Aras Delta. Principal tributaries of the Aras are the Razdan, draining Lake Sevan and the Qareh Sū, flowing off the Kūhhā-ye Sabalān in northeastern Iranian Azerbaijan. On an island in the river stood Artaxata, capital of Armenia from 180 BC to AD 50. Some have held that the Aras Valley was the legendary Garden of Eden.

Arason, Jón (b. 1484, Eyjafjördur, Ice.—d. Nov. 7, 1550, Skálholt), poet and last Roman Catholic bishop in Iceland, remembered as a national as well as a religious hero.

The son of poor parents, he rose quickly to eminence in the church and was consecrated bishop of Hólar, the northern diocese of Iceland, in 1522. He administered his diocese prosperously until Christian III of Denmark began to impose Lutheranism on all his subjects. The two Icelandic bishops, Jón in the north and Ögmundr in the south, protested (1537). Ögmundr was deported by the Danes in 1541, but Jón continued his resistance. He captured the Lutheran bishop Marteinn and seized his see (1549–50) but was soon afterward taken by the King's agents and beheaded with two of his sons. Jón was the author of splendid religious and satirical poetry; he brought the first printing press to Iceland. His life was the subject of novels and plays by later Icelandic writers.

ārātrika (religious rite): *see* ārtī.

Aratus (fl. *c.* 315–*c.* 245 BC, Macedonia), Greek poet of Soli in Cilicia, best remembered for his poem on astronomy, *Phaenomena.*

He resided at the courts of Antigonus II Gonatas, king of Macedonia, and Antiochus I of Syria. The *Phaenomena,* a didactic poem in hexameters, is his only completely extant work. Lines 1–757 versify a prose work on astronomy by Eudoxus of Cnidus (*c.* 390–*c.* 340), while lines 758–1154 treat of weather signs and show much likeness to Pseudo-Theophrastus' *De signis tempestatum.* The poem became immediately popular and provoked many commentaries, the most important of which is by Hipparchus (*c.* 150 BC) and is still extant. In form, the *Phaenomena* belongs to the Alexandrian school, but the author's Stoicism adds a strong note of seriousness. It enjoyed a high reputation among the Romans. Cicero, Caesar Germanicus, and Avienus translated it; the two last versions and fragments of Cicero's survive. One verse from the opening invocation to Zeus has become famous because it was quoted by St. Paul (Acts 17:28).

Aratus OF SICYON (b. 271 BC—d. 213), Greek statesman of the Hellenistic Period, a skilled diplomatist and guerrilla fighter who for many years was the leading spirit of the Achaean League.

After liberating Sicyon in 251, he established a democracy there and united it with the Achaean League for defense against Macedonia. As general of the league (a post he normally held each alternate year after 245), he captured Acrocorinth (243), defeated the Aetolians at Pellene (241), and pursued a policy of establishing democracies in the Peloponnese. With Aetolia as ally from 239, Sicyon repeatedly attacked Athens and Argos. Aratus brought Megalopolis (235) and Argos (229) into the league and helped liberate Athens from Macedonian rule (229). The hostility of Sparta, however, threatened these gains.

After being defeated twice by the Spartans under Cleomenes III, Aratus' League was saved by timely support from Antigonus Doson (king of Macedonia, 227–221) in 224. A combined force of Achaeans and Macedonians defeated and dethroned Cleomenes in 222.

On the accession of Philip V of Macedonia in 221, Aratus countered Aetolian aggression by obtaining the assistance of the Hellenic League. The resulting social war ended in 217, and Aratus then began to resist Philip's anti-Roman policy and his interference in Messene. Although Philip was popularly believed to have had Aratus murdered, the Greek leader probably died of tuberculosis. His memoirs, no longer extant, provided an important source for Polybius' *History*.

Arauca, intendency, eastern Colombia, located in the Río Orinoco basin and bounded north by Venezuela and south by the Río Casanare and the Río Meta. Given intendency status in 1955, the territory, 9,196 sq mi (23,818 sq km), consists of llanos (plains), except in the extreme west, where it rises abruptly into the Cordillera (mountains) Oriental of the Andes. It is drained by several tributaries of the Río Orinoco, which are navigable only part of the year.

Cattle raising is the dominant economic activity; agricultural products include corn (maize), cacao, sugarcane, and rice. Furs, hides, rubber, and resins are shipped by river to Venezuela. A bridge over the Río Arauca gives Arauca town, the intendency capital, all-weather connections to the paved highway leading northwest to San Cristóbal, Venezuela. Another road runs south to the Río Meta from Arauca, which contains an airport and a customs house. Pop. (1984 est.) town, 21,970; (1981 est.) intendency, 82,165.

Arauca River, Spanish RÍO ARAUCA, western tributary of the Orinoco, flowing through Venezuela and Colombia. It rises in the Cordillera Oriental of the Andes mountains, near the Venezuelan–Colombian border. Its easterly course is about 500 mi (800 km) long and forms part of the Venezuela–Colombia boundary. The Arauca flows nearly parallel to the Apure and the Meta rivers to join the Orinoco about 60 mi southeast of San Fernando de Apure, Venezuela.

The level nature of the vast surrounding plains, combined with seasonal rainfall, results in widespread flooding during the rainy season (April to November). The Arauca has few tributaries. It is navigable by small craft as far as El Amparo, on the Colombian border, but is little used.

Araucanía, region, southern Chile, between the Bío-Bío and Toltén rivers, bordered by Argentina on the east and by the Pacific Ocean on the west. The region, composed of Cautín and Malleco provinces (both created in 1887), took its present form in 1974. Its 12,263 sq mi (31,760 sq km) embrace the coastal mountain range, the fertile Central Valley, and the Andean cordillera.

It is the home of the Araucanian, or Mapuche, Indians (also living in Arauco and Bío-Bío provinces (Bío-Bío region), who maintained independence under Spanish and Chilean authority until the late 19th century despite periodic methodical campaigns to subdue them. Settlement of the conquered area by Chileans and Europeans, beginning with German colonists in the 1850s, has been encouraged by the national government. Land was reserved for the Indians, whose process of incorporation into national life continues.

Two partially navigable rivers, the Imperial and the Toltén, traverse southern Araucanía region from east to west. The cordilleran ridges and volcanoes at Tolguaca, Lonquimay, and Llaima and the forests, lakes, and hot springs at Tolguaca, Río Blanco, and Manzanares are prime scenic attractions. Tourism, however, in economic importance ranks below farming (especially wheat), cattle raising, and lumbering; the region is heavily forested. The Pan-American Highway and the main north–south railway pass through Temuco (*q.v.*), the regional capital. Pop. (1982 prelim.) 692,924.

The Toltén River with the Llaima Volcano in the background. Araucanía region, Chile

Fenno Jacobs—Photo Researchers

Araucanian, group of South American Indians living in the temperate climate of the fertile valleys and basins of central Chile, from the Coquimbo Valley in the north to the Seno (bay) Reloncaví in the south. At the time of the Spanish arrival in Chile, most of central Chile was settled by scattered populations of Araucanian farmers who grew corn (maize), beans, squash, potatoes, and other vegetables. They hunted, fished, and kept guinea pigs for meat; llamas were both pack animals and sources of wool for weaving fine fabrics that were traded with the Inca to the north. They had established and well-known metalsmithing and pottery-making traditions.

Although the pre-Spanish Araucanians did not themselves recognize political or cultural unity above the village level, the Spanish distinguished three Araucanian populations geographically: the Picunche in the north, the Mapuche in the middle valleys, and the Huillche in the south. The first Araucanians encountered by the Spanish (*c.* 1536) were the Picunche, who had lived under Inca cultural influence or political domination for centuries. The Picunche were accustomed to outside rule and put up very little resistance to the Spanish. By the end of the 17th century, the Picunche had been assimilated into Spanish society and had vanished into the peasant population. The southernmost people, the Huillche, were too few and too scattered to resist the Spanish for long. They, like the Picunche, vanished into the rural population of Chile.

The Mapuche (*q.v.*) of the central valleys were more numerous and less tolerant of foreign domination than the Picunche. In the face of the Spanish threat, the Mapuche formed widespread alliances above the village level, adopted the strategic use of horses in battle, and, in a series of conflicts called the Araucanian wars, successfully resisted Spanish and Chilean control for 350 years.

When Pedro de Valdivia's expedition occupied central Chile and founded Santiago in 1541, it met with strong resistance from the Mapuche. In 1550 Valdivia pressed southward and founded Concepción at the mouth of the Río Bío Bío, but in 1553 he and his followers were defeated by the Mapuche under Lautaro, a chief who had spent about two years in Valdivia's service. After Valdivia's disaster the Mapuche nearly captured Santiago, but the death of Lautaro on the battlefield and a smallpox epidemic among the Indians saved the colony. Another chief, Caupolicán, continued the fight until his capture by treachery and subsequent execution by the Spaniards in 1558. Thereafter the Spaniards pushed the Mapuche into the forest region south of the Bío Bío, which remained the boundary between the two peoples for the next three centuries.

After the Chileans had annexed slices of Peruvian and Bolivian territory in the War of the Pacific (1879–84), they subdued the remaining Mapuche in the south; they had begun to raid German-speaking settlements there in the late 1840s and had thus prevented further expansion of the white man into the Araucanian homeland. After their defeat at the hands of the Chilean Army, the Mapuche signed treaties with the Chilean government and were settled on reservations farther to the south. The Mapuche survive in great numbers today—on reservations in Chile and in the towns and cities of Chile and Argentina; in contemporary usage, "Araucanian" is synonymous with "Mapuche."

Araucaria, a genus of pinelike coniferous plants in the family Araucariaceae. For *A. bidwillii, see* bunya pine; *A. araucana, see* monkey puzzle tree; *A. cunninghamii, see* Moreton Bay pine; *A. heterophylla* (or *A. excelsa*), *see* Norfolk Island pine; and for *A. angustifolia, see* Paraná pine.

Araucariaceae, the monkey puzzle family of conifers, consisting of two genera native to the Southern Hemisphere. The genus *Agathis* includes about 20 species of the Australasian area, several reaching heights of 60 metres (200 feet) or more; the most important commercially is the kauri pine (*q.v.*), or dammar pine. The genus *Araucaria* contains about 18 species ranging from Australasia through South America; the bunya pine, monkey puzzle tree, Moreton Bay pine, Norfolk Island pine, and Paraná pine (*qq.v.*) are of commercial importance. Most members of the family are used for timber and the manufacture of paper pulp; some are the source of resins such as kauri gum, or kauri copal.

Arausio, Battle of (Oct. 6, 105 BC), the defeat of a Roman army by Germanic tribes near Arausio (now Orange in southern France). The Cimbri and the Teutoni had invaded the Roman province of Transalpine Gaul *c.* 110 BC. The consul Gnaeus Mallius Maximus was sent from Italy in 105 with an army to reinforce that of the proconsul Quintus Servilius Caepio and began negotiations with the invaders; while these were going on, Caepio attacked the Cimbri. He was overwhelmed, and the consul's army, drawn into the fighting, was also destroyed. Although the Cimbri and the Teutoni did not advance into Italy, the disaster and the need to raise new forces led to the multiple consulships of Marius and to his army reforms.

'Arava, Ha- (Palestine): *see* 'Arabah, Wadi al-.

Arāvalli Range, hill system of northern India, running northeasterly for 350 mi (560 km) through Rājasthān state from Sirohi district to Khetri in Jaipur district. Isolated rocky offshoots continue to just south of Delhi. The series of peaks and ridges, with breadths varying from 6 to 60 mi, are generally between 1,000 and 3,000 ft (300 and 900 m) in elevation. The system is divided into two sections—the Sāmbhar–Sirohi ranges, taller and broader and including Guru Sikhar on Mt. Abu, the highest peak in the Arāvalli Range (5,650 ft); and the Sāmbhar to Khetri ranges, consisting of three ridges that are discontinuous. The Arāvalli Range is rich in natural resources (including minerals) and serves as a check to the growth of the western desert. It gives rise to several rivers, including the Banās, Lūni, Sakhi, and Sābarmati. Though heavily forested in the south, it is generally bare and thinly populated, consisting of large areas of sand and stone and of masses of rose-coloured quartzite.

Āravīḍu DYNASTY, fourth and last dynasty of the Hindu empire of Vijayanagar in South India. Its founder was Tirumala, whose brother Rāma Rāya had been the masterful regent of the last ruler of the previous dynasty. Rāma Rāya's death at the Battle of Rakasa-Tangadi (also known as Tālikota) in 1565 and the subsequent destruction of Vijayanagar by the combined forces of the Muslim states of Bijāpur, Ahmadnagar, and Golconda was a deadly blow to the empire.

Tirumala, who became emperor in 1570, fixed his capital at Penugonda. But, beset by the Muslim powers, family disputes, and revolts of Hindu chiefs in the south, the Vijayanagar empire gradually dissolved by the first half of the 17th century. It was from one of the last of the Āravīḍu rulers that the English East India Company obtained its fortified factory at Madras.

Aravinda, Śrī (Indian philosopher): *see* Aurobindo, Śrī.

Arawa, town and administrative headquarters of North Solomons province, on the southeast coast of Bougainville Island, Papua New Guinea. Situated on what was once a large coconut plantation, Arawa is a planned suburban town on flatland near Arawa Bay. It was built to house the employees of Bougainville Copper Ltd., whose open-pit mine is located 16 mi (26 km) to the southwest at Panguna. The initial stage of the town was completed in 1972, at which time it also became the provincial headquarters. The towns of Panguna, Arawa, Kieta, and Toniva, as well as the Aropa airport, are essentially one commercial and industrial entity involved in copper mining and the shipment of ore. Arawa is a retail centre, and boating is popular in the area. Pop. (1984 est.) 14,900.

Arawak, American Indians of the Greater Antilles and South America who spoke languages of the Arawakan linguistic group.

The Antillean Arawak, or Taino, were agriculturists who lived in villages, some with as many as 3,000 inhabitants, and practiced slash-and-burn cultivation of cassava and corn (maize). The people were arranged in social ranks and gave great deference to theocratic chiefs. Religious belief centred on a hierarchy of nature spirits and ancestors, paralleling somewhat the hierarchies of chiefs. Despite the complex social organization, the Antillean Arawak were not given to warfare. They were driven out of the Lesser Antilles by the Carib shortly before the appearance of the Spanish.

The South American Arawak inhabited northern and western areas of the Amazon basin, where they shared the means of livelihood and social organization of other tribes of the tropical forest. They were sedentary farmers who hunted and fished, lived in small autonomous settlements, and had little hierarchical organization. The Arawak were found as far west as the foothills of the Andes. These Campa Arawak, however, remained isolated from influences of the Andean civilizations.

Arawakan languages, most widespread of all South American Indian language groups. Before the Spanish conquest, Arawakan languages were spoken in a number of disconnected areas from what is now Cuba and the Bahamas southward to the present Gran Chaco and the sources of the Xingu River in southern Brazil, and from the mouth of the Amazon River to the eastern foothills of the Andes. A great many communities still speak Arawakan languages in Brazil, and other groups of speakers are found in Peru, Colombia, Venezuela, Guyana, French Guiana, and Suriname. Taino, a now extinct Arawakan language, once predominated in the Antilles and was the first Indian language to be encountered by Europeans. Spoken languages of importance are Goajiro in Colombia, Campa and Machiguenga in Peru, and Mojo and Bauré in Bolivia.

arawana (*Osteoglossum bicirrosum*), species of freshwater fish of tropical South America in the family Osteoglossidae (order Osteoglossiformes). Arawanas seldom reach lengths of more than 60 centimetres (2 feet) but are regarded as superb sports fish and highly edible. In appearance they have large scales and long flowing dorsal and anal fins that almost join with the tail fin. The mouth angles upward to a point above the eyes and has two long, filamentous barbels that extend forward. Arawanas are believed to be mouth breeders, the female carrying the eggs in her mouth until they hatch.

Araxes (river, Asia): *see* Aras River.

arbaʿ kanfot, also spelled ARBAʿ KANFOTH (Hebrew: "four corners"), also called ṬALLIT QAṬAN, or TALLITH KATAN ("small shawl"), Jewish religious garment that apparently came into use during times of persecution as a substitute for the larger and more conspicuous prayer shawl (*ṭallit*). Both garments have fringes (*tzitzit*) on the four corners, increasing the likelihood that one was a conscious imitation of the other. The *ṭallit,* however, generally falls across the head, neck, and shoulders, while the *arbaʿ kanfot* has an opening for the head (like a poncho), so that it can be worn beneath the upper garments. Orthodox male Jews, including children, wear the *arbaʿ kanfot* during the day to fulfill the requirement of wearing fringes (Numbers 15:37–41) as reminders of God's commandments.

Arbe (Yugoslavia): *see* Rab.

Arbeau, Thoinot, original name JEHAN TABOUROT (b. 1519, Dijon, Fr.—d. 1595, Langres), theoretician and historian of the dance, whose *Orchésographie* (1588) contains carefully detailed, step-by-step descriptions of 16th-century and earlier dance forms. Ordained a priest in 1530, he became a canon at Langres (1571), where he was encouraged to pursue his studies by the Jesuits, who considered dance to be educationally important.

Orchésographie is written in the form of a dialogue between the author and a student. Such dances as the pavane, gavotte, and allemande are not only exactly described but also usually illustrated and directly associated with their musical forms. The book also outlines principles that, more than a century later, formed the basis of the five fundamental feet positions of classical ballet. In addition to its wealth of technical information, it is an interesting account of social behaviour and manners.

ARBED SA, in full ACIÉRIES RÉUNIES DE BURBACH-EICH-DUDELANGE, integrated steel-producing company that is the largest industrial concern in Luxembourg.

The company was formed in 1911 through the merger of Les Forges d'Eich, Le Gallais, Metz et Cie. (established in 1838 under a different name); La Société Anonyme des Mines du Luxembourg et Forges de Sarrebruck (1856), and La Société Anonyme des Hauts Forneaux et Forges de Dudelange (1882). Since then the company has formed subsidiaries in Europe and South America.

Through its subsidiary and affiliate companies, the company engages in every step of steel production and processing, from the extraction of coal and iron ore (from its own mines), to the fabrication of highly specialized steel products, including the whole range of rolled steel products and some finished products, especially wire. In 1980 it entered into a joint venture with Bethlehem, a U.S. steel company, to produce Galvalume, a sheet steel product patented by Bethlehem, for distribution to Europe and abroad.

Arbela (Iraq): *see* Irbīl.

Arbela, Battle of (Oct. 1, 331 BC): *see* Gaugamela, Battle of.

Arbenz (Guzmán), Jacobo (b. Sept. 14, 1913, Quezaltenango, Guatemala—d. Jan. 27, 1971, Mexico City), soldier, politician, and president of Guatemala (1950–54) whose nationalistic economic and social reforms gained him the support of Communists but led to his overthrow by the military.

The son of a Swiss pharmacist who had emigrated to Guatemala, Arbenz was educated at the National Military Academy of Guatemala. He joined a group of army officers that overthrew the Guatemalan dictator Jorge Ubico in 1944, and in 1949 he was the minister of war in Juan José Arévalo's government. In November 1950 he succeeded to the presidency, supported by the army and the left-wing political parties, especially the Guatemalan Communist Party, which enthusiastically supported his policies of increasing

Arbenz, 1950
By courtesy of the Organization of American States

the influence of labour organizations and of distributing large parcels of land to landless Indians.

Arbenz' radical policies—particularly his promotion of legislation to expropriate a substantial part of the holdings of the United Fruit Company (*q.v.*) in Guatemala without compensation—resulted in a U.S.-led condemnation of him as a Communist at the 10th Inter-American Conference, held in Caracas in March 1954. Three months later his government was overthrown by Col. Carlos Castillo Armas, and he was forced to flee to Mexico. In 1957 he moved to Uruguay and then to Cuba and later returned to Mexico.

Arber, Agnes, *née* ROBERTSON (b. Feb. 23, 1879, London—d. March 22, 1960, Cambridge, Cambridgeshire, Eng.), botanist noted chiefly for her studies in comparative anatomy of plants, especially monocotyledons.

She attended the universities of London (B.Sc., 1899; D.Sc., 1905) and Cambridge (M.A.) and in 1909 married Edward Alexander Newell Arber, a paleobotanist who had been her teacher at Cambridge. In 1946 she became the first woman botanist to be named a fellow of the Royal Society.

Her first and perhaps most widely read work is *Herbals, Their Origin and Evolution* (1912), an account of herbals published between 1470 and 1670. Her studies in comparative anatomy include *Water Plants: A Study of Aquatic Angiosperms* (1920), *Monocotyledons: A Morphological Study* (1925), and *The Gramineae: A Study of Cereal, Bamboo and Grass* (1934). Later works reflect her interest in philosophy: *The Natural Philosophy of Plant Form* (1950), *The Mind and the Eye: A Study of the Biologist's Standpoint* (1954), and *The Manifold and the One* (1957).

Arber, Edward (b. Dec. 4, 1836, London—d. Nov. 23, 1912, London), scholar whose editing, and publication at reasonable prices, of Elizabethan and Restoration texts first made detailed study of them possible to the ordinary student.

An Admiralty clerk, he studied literature and entered academic life, serving as professor of English at Birmingham from 1881 to 1894. His editions of many texts remain the only ones easily accessible. His *English Reprints*, 30 vol. (1868–71), began with a sixpenny edition of Milton's *Areopagitica*. Later series include the important *English Garner*, 8 vol. (1877–96), and *The English Scholar's Library of Old and Modern Works*, 16 vol. (1878–84). Also valuable are his *Transcript of the Registers of the Company of Stationers of London, 1554–1640 A.D.* (*The Stationers' Register*, 5 vol., 1875–94) and *The Term Catalogues, 1668–1709 A.D.*, 3 vol. (1903–06), edited from booksellers' quarterly lists.

Arber, Werner (b. June 3, 1929, Gränichen, Switz.), Swiss microbiologist, co-recipient with Daniel Nathans and Hamilton Othanel Smith (*qq.v.*) of the United States of the Nobel Prize for Physiology or Medicine for 1978. All three were cited for their work in molecular genetics, specifically the discovery and application of enzymes that break the giant molecules of dioxyribonucleic acid (DNA) into manageable pieces, small enough to be separated for individual study but large enough to retain bits of the genetic information inherent in the sequence of units that make up the original substance.

Arber studied at the Swiss Federal Institute of Technology in Zürich, the University of Geneva, and the University of Southern California. He served on the faculty at Geneva from 1960 to 1970, when he became professor of microbiology at the University of Basel.

During the late 1950s and early 1960s Arber and several others extended the work of an earlier Nobel laureate, Salvador Luria (*q.v.*), who had observed that bacteriophages (viruses that infect bacteria) not only induce hereditary mutations in their bacterial hosts but at the same time undergo hereditary mutations themselves. Arber's research was concentrated on the action of protective enzymes present in the bacteria, which modify the DNA of the infecting virus; *e.g.*, the restriction enzyme, so-called for its ability to restrict the growth of the bacteriophage by cutting the molecule of its DNA to pieces.

Arbil (Iraq): *see* Irbīl.

arbitrage, business operation involving the purchase of foreign exchange, gold, financial securities, or commodities in one market and their almost simultaneous sale in another market, in order to profit from price differentials existing between the markets. Opportunities for arbitrage may keep recurring because of the working of market forces. Arbitrage generally tends to eliminate price differentials between markets. Whereas in less developed countries arbitrage can consist of the buying and selling of commodities in different villages within the country, in highly developed countries the term is generally used to refer to international operations involving foreign-exchange rates, short-term interest rates, prices of gold, and prices of securities.

Foreign-exchange arbitrage, confined to spot-exchange markets—in which exchange is bought and sold for immediate delivery—may involve two or more exchange centres (two-point arbitrage or multiple-point arbitrage). For example, assume that Country A's sovereign is exchanging at two to the dollar in New York City, while Country B's franc is valued at five to the dollar. Logically, Country A's sovereign should exchange at two sovereigns to five francs. But for some reason banks in Country B are paying four francs for two sovereigns. A New York City operator with $100,000 at his disposal may then make three moves: (1) buy 500,000 francs in New York City in the form of a cable transfer to his account in Country B; (2) instruct his correspondent in Country B to use a similar amount of francs to buy 250,000 of Country A's sovereigns at the going rate of four francs for two sovereigns, in the form of a cable transfer to his account in Country A; and (3) sell the same amount of sovereigns in New York City at two to the dollar for a total of $125,000, or a profit of $25,000. Foreign exchange operators will continue to do this until the heavy demand for francs in New York City has raised their price and eliminated the profit.

Opportunities for interest arbitrage arise when the money rates differ among countries. Gold arbitrage and securities arbitrage operate in principle very much like commodity arbitrage in the domestic market, except that in the two former cases exchange rates are important, either because funds must be remitted abroad for the operation or because the proceeds must be brought home at the end of the operation.

arbitration, a legal method of settling disputes between parties outside ordinary court procedures by deferring to a mutually agreed-upon third party who has the authority to determine an "award," a legally binding decision.

A brief treatment of arbitration follows. For full treatment, *see* MACROPAEDIA: Judicial and Arbitrational Systems.

Arbitration is most commonly resorted to in cases involving commercial disputes, but it is also practiced in resolving disputes between labour unions and management and in international controversies between sovereign states where diplomatic channels are not sufficient.

The third party or arbitrator may be a single individual or a body known as a tribunal chosen by the parties and knowledgeable in the area of dispute. In general, awards are based on the existing laws related to the contracts or issues in dispute as they are understood and agreed upon in advance by the parties concerned and by the arbitrator.

Commercial arbitration. Commercial arbitration began in medieval Europe as a means for settling disputes between individual merchants and became an increasingly favoured method as courts of law were given the power to enforce arbitration agreements and awards. Today, in most parts of the world, parties engaged in arbitration must agree in advance to accept a decision as irrevocable, and the courts provide a means for securing awards from recalcitrants.

Arbitration is often resorted to as a substitute for lengthy court procedures because it has the advantage of avoiding costly litigation, resolving disputes faster, and allowing privacy for the disputants. The disadvantage is that it is difficult to set guidelines; therefore the outcome is often less predictable than a court decision.

Selection of arbitrators may be made at the time that the conflict arises or after basic arbitration agreements have been made, or they may be appointed in advance of disputes by such administrative agencies as trade associations and produce exchanges, which have preestablished procedural rules and often maintain a panel of arbitrators. Arbitrators have the responsibility for determining procedures for the arbitration process if they do not already exist or if those that exist are not sufficient for the particular case.

Since implicit within the arbitration process is an agreement to abide by the decision, appeal of an award to the courts can be justified only under certain conditions, which are also usually stipulated in the arbitration agreement. These conditions include misconduct by the arbitrator in denying a party full presentation of arguments and in rendering awards that may be in conflict with public policy.

Labour-management arbitration. Unlike commercial arbitration, labour arbitration is not a method practiced in lieu of court procedures, but rather it is a technique for settling or avoiding strikes. It has two aspects, arbitration of rights and arbitration of interests.

Arbitration of rights concerns a dispute over the application of a current contract between labour and management and is a more prevalent practice in the United States than in other countries. The arbitrator may be chosen at the time of dispute or named "umpire" as part of the collective-bargaining agreement for the duration of the contract. The arbitrator's decision is legally binding. Further, the procedures used in arbitration do not have to comply with court procedures, especially in the areas related to burden of proof and presentation of evidence. The courts are rarely called upon to review an arbitrator's decision. However, when they are, their review is limited to determining if the issues are covered by, and the awards are based on, the collective-bargaining agreements.

Arbitration of interests refers to the process of settling disputes in the formation of a new contract when labour and management have been unable to come to an agreement by any other method. It is seldom used, but it is becoming a more favoured method in industries and services that involve such essential public interests as transportation and medical services.

International arbitration. International arbitration has a long history dating back to the civil wars between the ancient Greek city-states. Its modern development begins with the Jay Treaty of 1794 between Great Britain and the United States to settle claims stemming from the American Revolution. In the Hague Conference of 1899, a basis for peaceful settlement of disputes by international arbitration was established in a convention that was revised in a conference in 1907. Since that time there have been several multilateral international treaties that provide for arbitration in disputes in which all other avenues of reconciliation have failed. Most notably among these treaties are provisions adopted by the General Assembly of the United Nations in 1949.

There are still great difficulties in international arbitration because sovereign states prefer to maintain great flexibility in determining their actions, thus precluding a definite body of rules that can be universally applied. A general international treaty, therefore, does not deal with the selection of arbitrators, procedures, limits of subject matter or issues, site of arbitration, presentation of evidence, and determination of applicable laws or timetables for rendering awards. The parties involved in a dispute usually formulate a "compris"—an agreement that defines the procedures and elements of arbitration relevant to a case (such as what laws will govern the decision-making). In most cases in which no laws are circumscribed, international law will prevail.

The greatest impediment to resolving disputes peacefully through international arbitration is the infrequency of its practice. The custom of most nations is to reject arbitration as a method if there is no assurance of a favourable outcome or if either party is unwilling to comply with an unfavourable decision.

Arbogast (d. Sept. 8, 394), barbarian general of the Roman Empire, the first to establish a Roman nominee of his own as a puppet emperor.

Probably of Frankish descent, he rose to the rank of *magister equitum* ("master of the cavalry") in the Western Roman army and was sent by the emperor Gratian, in 380, to assist the Eastern ruler Theodosius against the Goths in Thrace. He remained in the service of Theodosius. In 388, after the defeat in Italy of the usurper Magnus Maximus by Theodosius, Arbogast recovered Gaul for the Western emperor Valentinian II from Maximus' son, Flavius Victor. The following year Arbogast pacified the Rhine frontier, imposing a treaty on the Frankish leaders Marcomer and Sunne, who had invaded Gaul in 384.

By 391 the general was all-powerful in Gaul as *comes* ("count") and regent. When Valentinian attempted to dismiss him, Arbogast declared that only Theodosius had the power to do so. On May 15, 392, Valentinian died at Vienna (modern Vienne, Fr.) in circumstances suggestive of murder instigated by Arbogast. Proclaiming Eugenius, a professor of rhetoric, as emperor in the West, Arbogast set about restoring paganism. In the winter of 393–394, he conducted a successful campaign against the Ripuarian Franks, the Chamavi, and along the Rhine, but the following May, Theodosius marched west to suppress the pagan revolution. A two-day battle ended in victory for Theodosius. Eugenius was beheaded; Arbogast committed suicide.

Considered a great general and an energetic statesman, Arbogast attempted to revive pagan ways because of his admiration for the Roman Republic and his contempt for the quarrels between Catholic and Arian Christians.

arbor, garden shelter providing privacy and partial protection from the weather. The name is used for a modest garden building of any material; it has been applied to examples as varied as a wrought-iron shelter at Melbourne Hall, Derbyshire, Eng., and houses constructed

Arbor, Moffat-Ladd Garden, Portsmouth, N.H.
Douglas Armsden

of pebbles, brick, or masonry. It is more correctly limited to rustic garden houses that are made up entirely of interlaced branches of growing trees and shrubs or of greenery trained over a light framework of wood or metal.

If there is a distinction between an arbor and a bower, it is that the bower is an entirely natural recess whereas an arbor is only partially natural. Both are archaic words, lending a sentimental, poetic air to the shelters. Because true arbors are ephemeral, few genuine examples—even those made in the early 20th century—survive.

arboriculture, cultivation of trees, shrubs, and woody plants for shading and decorating. Arboriculture includes propagating, transplanting, pruning, applying fertilizer, spraying to control insects and diseases, cabling and bracing, treating cavities, identifying plants, diagnosing and treating tree damage and ailments, arranging plantings for their ornamental values, and removing trees. The well-being of individual plants is the major concern of arboriculture, in contrast to such related fields as silviculture and agriculture, in which the major concern is the welfare of a large group of plants as a whole.

The basic principles and objectives of arboriculture are of ancient origin. Early Egyptians transplanted trees with a ball of earth and originated the practice of shaping the soil around a newly planted tree to form a saucer to retain water, both still practiced. About 300 BC the Greek philosopher Theophrastus wrote *Peri phytōn historia* ("Inquiry into Plants"), in which he discussed transplanting of trees and the treatment of tree wounds. Virgil's *Georgics* portrays Roman knowledge of tree culture. The English horticulturist John Evelyn, in his *Sylva, or a Discourse of Forest-trees, and the Propagation of Timber* (1664), offered advice on pruning, insect control, wound treatment, and transplanting.

Trees or plants may be propagated by seeding, grafting, layering, or cutting. In seeding, seeds are usually planted in either a commercial or home nursery in which intensive care can be given for several years until the plants are of a size suitable for transplanting on the desired site. In soil layering, the shoots, or lower branches of the parent plant, are bent to the ground and covered with moist soil of good quality. When roots have developed, which may require a year or more, the branch is severed from the parent and transplanted. In an alternative technique, air layering, the branch is deeply slit and the wound covered by a ball of earth, moss, or similar material. The ball, enclosed in a divided pot supported from underneath, or in a sturdy paper cone, is kept moist. As in soil layering, the branch is severed and transplanted after roots have developed. Root cuttings can be used for propagating trees that do not normally produce roots from stems. Tree species such as willow and poplar that sucker, or send up shoots readily, are usually propagated from stem cuttings. Cuttings are made from deciduous plants during dormancy, preferably from the terminal growing shoots of the current season. Pieces 6 to 10 inches (15 to 25 centimetres) long with two or more buds are tied in bundles and stored in damp sand or moss for callus formation before planting in prepared beds. Root formation may be stimulated by application of growth-promoting chemicals or growth hormones.

In treating tree-trunk wounds in which large areas of bark are torn away, the bark around the wound is trimmed back to sound tissue and, at the top and bottom of the injury, trimmed to form a pointed ellipse of the wound area. The exposed wood is covered with wound dressing material, protecting it from wood decay fungi.

Flexible cables (guys) or rigid braces are used to support recently transplanted trees until the roots become established, or to lessen the danger that a tree with a weakened root system will be blown over by the wind; bracing is also used to support unduly long or heavy branches, to prevent splits developing at branch forks, or to permit healing of splits already developed.

Cavities in trunks, caused by decay-inducing fungi, weaken trees and make them susceptible to wind damage. To hold the cavity walls in position and to help compensate for the tissue loss, some arborists favour treating the inside of the cavity with antiseptic dressing and leaving it open, with drains installed at the bottom; others fill the cavity with concrete or other material after removing the decayed wood. *See also* graft; pruning; transplant.

arborvitae (Latin: "tree of life"), any of six species of the genus *Thuja*, resinous, evergreen ornamental and timber conifers of the cypress family (Cupressaceae), native to North America and eastern Asia. A closely related genus is false arborvitae (*q.v.*).

Arborvitae are trees or shrubs, usually pyramidal in habit, with thin, scaling outer bark and fibrous inner bark, horizontal or ascending branches, and characteristically flattened, spraylike branchlet systems. Each branchlet has four rows of tiny, scalelike leaves. Juvenile leaves are much longer and needlelike and in some species may persist along with the mature foliage.

Male and female reproductive structures (cones) are borne at the tips of different branchlets of the same tree, the male cones rounded and reddish or yellowish, the female very small and green or tinged with purple. Mature cones are solitary, egg shaped or oblong, 8 to 16 millimetres (about 1/2 inch) long, with 4 to 6 (but sometimes 3 or as many as 10) pairs of thin, flexible scales that terminate in thickened ridges or processes.

The oriental, or Chinese, arborvitae (*T. orientalis*), a popular ornamental native to Asia, is a gracefully symmetrical shrub about 10 metres (33 feet) tall. Some authorities have assigned it to a separate genus (*Biota*) because of distinctions such as its erect branches, vertically arranged, fanlike branchlet systems, and six to eight hook-tipped cone scales.

Other Asian species of *Thuja* include the Japanese arborvitae (*T. standishii*), a pyramidal tree 15 m tall in its native region, with reddish brown bark and bright green foliage; and the Korean arborvitae (*T. koraiensis*), a spreading bush, or small tree, less than 10 m tall, with leaves that are dark green on the upper surface and silvery beneath.

Yellowish or reddish-brown arborvitae wood is soft, light in weight but very durable, fragrant, and easily worked. The giant arborvitae (*q.v.; T. plicata*) is the most important timber-producing species, but the wood of the American arborvitae (*q.v.; T. occidentalis*) is also frequently used.

arbovirus, acronym derived from *ar*thropod-*bo*rne *virus*, a group of viruses that develop in arthropods (chiefly blood-sucking mosquitoes and ticks), in which they cause no apparent harm, and are subsequently transmitted by bites to vertebrate hosts, in which they establish infections and complete their growth cycle. The group includes the agents responsible for yellow fever, equine encephalitis, dengue, and louping ill (*qq.v.*). The spheroidal virus particle is enveloped in a fatty membrane, varies in size from 30 to 100 nanometres (nm; 1 nm = 10^{-9} metre) across, and contains ribonucleic acid (RNA). Some regions of the tropics, locally rich in arboviruses, present a complicated picture of the ecological net of arthropod carrier, vertebrate host, and the environment.

The arbovirus group is a diverse assemblage, the members of which are often assigned to viral families as they become better known, *e.g.*, as togavirus (family Togaviridae) and rhabdovirus (family Rhabdoviridae).

Arbroath, also called ABERBROTHOCK, royal burgh, North Sea fishing port, and holiday resort, district of Angus, Tayside region, Scotland. Arbroath Abbey, once the richest in Scotland, was founded in 1178 by William I the Lion, king of Scotland, who is buried there. It was in the abbey in 1320 that the Declaration of Arbroath, asserting the independence of Scotland, following Robert I the Bruce's victory over the English at Bannockburn (1314), was composed by the Scottish Parliament and sent to the Pope at Avignon, Fr. Engineering, iron founding, textile manufacturing, and boat building are the town's main industries. Pop. (1981) 24,120.

Arbuckle, Fatty, byname of ROSCOE CONKLING ARBUCKLE (b. March 24, 1887, Smith Center, Kan., U.S.—d. June 30, 1933, New York City), early star of silent comedy motion pictures, who was the central figure in notorious trials for manslaughter.

A veteran of vaudeville and carnivals, Arbuckle became a screen extra for the Selig Polyscope Company in 1908 and performed in many one-reel comedies. He was an agile comedian in spite of his 320-pound weight and soon rose to star status in Mack Sennett's studio. He was for a time a member of Sennett's Keystone Kops and appeared with Chester Conklin, Charlie Chaplin, and other silent-film stars.

By 1917 Arbuckle had formed his own production company and was instrumental in the development of the career of Buster Keaton. At the peak of popularity his career ended in scandal. A starlet, Virginia Rappe, died of a ruptured bladder following an alleged sexual assault by Arbuckle at a drinking party in a San Francisco hotel. He was tried three times for manslaughter, two ending in hung juries and the final one in an acquittal. He was forced by the negative publicity into retirement, and his films were banned. Through the aid of friends he was able to reenter the film industry as a director under the pseudonym of William B. Goodrich. One result of the case was the institution of the Hays Office, designed to regulate and censor the movie industry.

Arbuckle orogeny, period of high-angle block faulting, some thrusting and tilting of strata, and deposition of coarse clastic sediments in adjacent basins in the Wichita-Arbuckle System of western Oklahoma and the Texas panhandle. The faulting began in the Middle Pennsylvanian, culminated in the Late Pennsylvanian, and continued locally into the Permian (the Pennsylvanian began 325,000,000 years ago and ended 280,000,000 years ago, at which time the Permian Period began).

Rocks deformed by the Ouachita orogeny appear to override subsurface rocks deformed by the Arbuckle orogeny. Hence the Ouachita orogeny may be somewhat later in time.

Arbuthnot, John (b. April 1667, Inverbervie, Kincardine, Scot.—d. Feb. 27, 1735, London),

Arbuthnot, detail of an oil painting by W. Robinson; in the Scottish National Portrait Gallery, Edinburgh
By courtesy of the Scottish National Portrait Gallery, Edinburgh

Scottish mathematician, physician, and occasional writer, remembered as the close friend of Jonathan Swift, Alexander Pope, and John Gay and as a founding member of their famous Scriblerus Club, which aimed to ridicule bad literature and false learning.

After taking a medical degree in 1696 at St. Andrews, Arbuthnot became a Fellow of the Royal Society in 1704 and was one of Queen Anne's physicians from 1705 until her death. Though he published mathematical and other scientific works, his fame rests on his reputation as a wit and on his satirical writings. The most important of the latter fall into two groups. The first consists of a political allegory dealing with the political jockeying of the British, French, Spanish, and Dutch that led up to the Treaty of Utrecht (1713). Published in five pamphlets, the earliest appearing in 1712, it was collected in 1727 under the composite title *The History of John Bull,* and it established and popularized for the first time the character who was to become the permanent symbol of England in cartoon and literature. An edition by A.W. Bower and R.A. Erickson was published in 1976.

The other satire in which Arbuthnot had an important share was the *Memoirs of Martinus Scriblerus,* a mocking exposure of pedantry, first published in the 1741 edition of Pope's works, but largely written as early as 1713–14 by the members of the Scriblerus Club. The other members of the club acknowledged Arbuthnot as the chief contributor and guiding spirit of the work. Arbuthnot was indifferent to literary fame, and many of his witticisms and ideas for satires were later developed by and credited to his more famous literary friends. *See also* Scriblerus Club.

Arbutus, genus of about 14 species of broad-leaved evergreen shrubs or trees, of

Strawberry tree (*Arbutus unedo*)
A to Z Botanical Collection—EB Inc.

the heath family (Ericaceae), characterized by white or pink flowers in loose, terminal clusters and many-seeded, fleshy, red or orange berries; the leaves are alternate and stalked. The plants are native to southern Europe and western North America. Two species, *A. menziesii* and *A. unedo,* are cultivated as ornamentals in warm regions.

Arbutus menziesii, the madrona, Pacific madrona, laurelwood, and Oregon laurel, occurs in western North America from British Columbia to California. It grows about 23 metres (75 feet) tall. The dark, oblong, glossy leaves are from 5 to 15 centimetres (2 to 6 inches) long and coloured grayish green beneath. The whitish flowers grow in pyramidal clusters 7–23 cm tall. As the tree grows, the old bark peels off, revealing reddish or cinnamon-coloured bark beneath.

Arbutus unedo is the strawberry tree, native to southwestern Europe but introduced into warm regions of western North America. It grows from 3 to 9 m tall, with one to several trunks, and has lustrous elliptic or oblong leaves about 9 cm long. The branches are sticky and hairy. The white or pinkish flowers droop in clusters, and the fruit, edible but tasteless, resembles a strawberry in size and colour.

arc, electric: *see* electric arc.

arc furnace, type of electric furnace (*q.v.*) in which heat is generated by an arc between carbon electrodes above the surface of the material (commonly a metal) being heated.

arc lamp, device for producing light by maintaining an electric arc across a gap between two conductors; light comes from the heated ends of the conductors (usually carbon rods) as well as from the arc itself. Arc lamps are used in applications requiring great brightness, as in searchlights, large film projectors, and floodlights. The term arc lamp is usually restricted to lamps with an air gap between consumable carbon electrodes, but fluorescent and other electric discharge lamps generate light from arcs in gas-filled tubes. Some ultraviolet lamps are of the arc type.

Sir Humphry Davy constructed the first arc lamp (1807), using a battery of 2,000 cells to create a 4-inch (100-millimetre) arc between two charcoal sticks. When suitable electric generators became available in the late 1870s, practical use of arc lamps began. The Yablochkov candle, an arc lamp invented by the Russian engineer Paul Yablochkov, was used for street lighting in Paris and other European cities from 1878.

arc welding, use of a sustained luminous electrical discharge (arc) as a source of heat for melting the filler metal (welding rod) and the metals being welded. *See* welding.

arcade, in architecture, series of arches carried by columns or piers, a passageway between arches and a solid wall, or a covered walkway that provides access to adjacent shops. An arcade that supports a wall, a roof, or an entablature gains enough strength from lateral thrusts that each individual arch exerts against the next to carry tremendous weight loads and to stretch for great distances.

Ancient aqueducts show an early use of the arcade. Later Roman builders used the pattern to construct large wall surfaces: the Colosseum, with 80 arcaded openings on each of its three stories, is one of the finest examples of this architectural form.

An arcade with pilasters, or engaged columns attached to piers carrying an entablature, is known as a Roman arcade. During the late empire this was replaced by arches that rested on the capitals of a row of columns, a style that was standard in the Romanesque and Gothic periods and that was revived and widely used during the Renaissance (*e.g.,* Brunelleschi's Ospedale degli Innocenti in Florence). In Byzantine arcades, spreading blocks called impost blocks were often placed between the capitals and arches, a style used widely throughout the East.

As a purely decorative element, arcades are

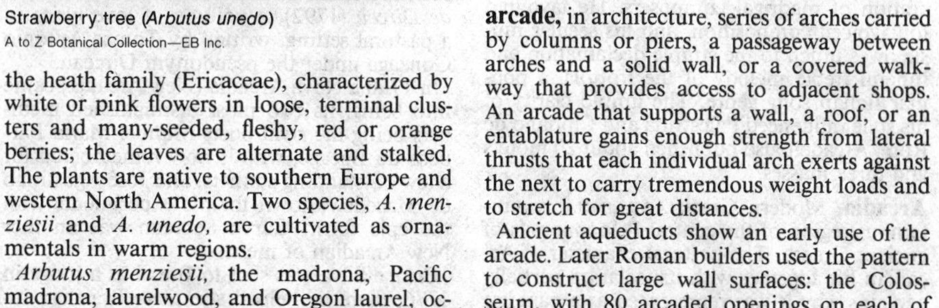

Arcade, Ospedale degli Innocenti, Florence (1419–26), by Filippo Brunelleschi
Alinari—Art Resource/EB Inc.

used in Gothic churches to divide the nave wall into three horizontal parts—the arcade at floor level, the triforium above, and the clerestory at the top—as well as to frame sculpture on the facade (as can be seen, with excellent effect, on Amiens cathedral). To a lesser extent, Baroque architects made use of this form of the arcade, and it remained a significant element in Europe and America throughout the 19th century.

As a covered passageway the arcade has been in use since Roman times. Medieval cloisters often featured arcades, and most Islāmic mosques include arcaded courtyards. In Renaissance towns such as Bologna, arcades line shops and other buildings. Eastern bazaars are often arcaded rows of shops, and the design of modern enclosed or partially enclosed shopping centres has made the use of the label, if not the original form, common in America.

Arcadelt, Jacob, Arcadelt also spelled ARCADEL, ARCHADELT, ARCHADENTE, ARCHADET, or HARCHADELT, Jacob also spelled JACQUES, or JAKOB (b. *c.* 1500, Liège?, Bishopric of Liège—d. Oct. 14, 1568, Paris?), composer who helped establish the musical form of the madrigal.

Arcadelt was a singer and later choirmaster in the papal chapel in Rome (1539–49) and later spent time in France and Italy. He entered the service of Charles, duke of Guise, in 1555 and in 1557 was a member of the French royal chapel.

His reputation rests on about 120 chansons and more than 200 Italian madrigals. With two contemporary composers, Costanzo Festa and Philippe Verdelot, he set the style for a generation of madrigal composers. He favoured four-voiced composition, and his secular music owes much to the simple declamation and tuneful treble melody of the frottola, a popular Italian song genre. The limpid clarity of his style influenced Palestrina and Cipriano de Rore. Arcadelt also published about 20 motets and three masses.

Arcadia, Modern Greek ARKADHÍA, mountainous region of the central Peloponnesus of ancient Greece. The pastoral character of Arcadian life together with its isolation partially explains why it was represented as a paradise in Greek and Roman bucolic poetry and in the literature of the Renaissance. A region of erratic rainfall, Arcadia has a few vineyards but no olive trees. There are patches of oak forest, but the eastern reaches are drier and less verdant. The region is not exactly coextensive with the present-day *nomós* (department), Arkadhía, which has an area of 1,706 sq mi (4,419 sq km) and extends on the east to the gulf known as Argolikós Kólpos; its capital is Trípolis.

The plateau of Arcadia, with basins at altitudes of 1,650 to 3,300 ft (500 to 1,000 m), is bounded on the north by the Erímanthos and Killíni mountains and is itself divided by numerous subsidiary ranges. In eastern Arcadia they enclose a series of plains drained only by underground channels. The western plateau is more open, with isolated mountains through which wind the Alpheus River and its tributaries. One of those, the Ládhon, provides hydroelectric power at a dam and reservoir.

Isolated topographically from the remainder of mainland Greece, Arcadia was not occupied by the Dorians during their invasion of Greece (1100–1000 BC) and retained a dialect that still resembles that of the Greeks who settled in Cyprus (the Arcado-Cypriot dialects). During the many centuries of warfare among the regions and city-states of ancient Greece, the allegiances and the welfare of Arcadians were unstable. In Roman times Arcadia fell into decay, but in the 8th century AD an influx of Slavic settlers checked depopulation. Later Arcadia suffered much from the quarrels of its Frankish barons (1205–60), but Turkish rule and Albanian immigration restored some prosperity. Arcadia was a scene of conflict during the War of Greek Independence (1821–29). Pop. (1981) *nomós,* 107,932.

Arcadia, city, Los Angeles County, California, U.S., at the base of the San Gabriel Mountains. Laid out in 1888 on lands of Rancho Santa Anita and developed by E.J. ("Lucky") Baldwin, it was named for the district in ancient Greece said to symbolize pastoral beauty. An early agricultural centre, it was promoted as a residential community. Freeway connections to Los Angeles, 15 mi (24 km) southwest, aided its growth. It is the site of the Los Angeles Arboretum and the Santa Anita Race Track. Inc. 1903. Pop. (1980) 45,994.

arcádia, any of the 18th-century Portuguese literary societies that attempted to revive poetry in that country by urging a return to classicism. They were modelled after the Accademia dell'Arcadia, established in Rome in 1690 as an arbiter of Italian literary taste.

In 1756 Antônio Dinis da Cruz e Silva established with others the Arcádia Lusitana, its first aim being the uprooting of Gongorism, a style studded with Baroque conceits, and Spanish influence in general. Cruz e Silva's mock-heroic poem *O Hissope* (1768), inspired by the French poet Nicolas Boileau's mock epic *Le Lutrin* (1674), was a telling satirical document. Pedro Antônio Correia Garção, the most prominent Arcadian, was an accomplished devotee of the Latin classical poet Horace. The bucolic verse of Dómingos dos Reis Quita signified a return to the native tradition of two centuries earlier. Sincerity and suffering spoke in the better known *Marília de Dirceu* (1792), a volume of love lyrics in a pastoral setting, written by Tomás Antônio Gonzaga under the pseudonym Dirceau.

In 1790 a Nova Arcádia (New Arcadia) came into being, its two most distinguished members being the rival poets Manuel Maria Barbosa du Bocage, who is now remembered for a few outstanding sonnets, and José Agostinho de Macedo, known for his experiments with the epic form. Curvo Semedo was another New Arcadian of merit.

Cruz e Silva was sent to Brazil as a judge in 1776; there he helped stimulate Brazilian interest in the Arcadian movement, which gave rise to the so-called Minas school of epic and Neoclassical poets, which includes Basílio da Gama and José de Santa Rita Durão.

A list of the abbreviations used in the MICROPAEDIA *will be found at the end of this volume*

Accademia dell'Arcadia, Italian literary academy founded in Rome in 1690 to combat Marinism (*q.v.*), the dominant Italian poetic style of the 17th century, named after Giambattista Marino. The Arcadians sought a more natural, simple poetic style based on the classics and particularly on Greek and Roman pastoral poetry.

The Accademia dell'Arcadia was inspired by Queen Christina of Sweden, who, having given up her throne, gathered a literary circle in Rome. After Christina's death in 1689, her friends founded the academy to give their meetings permanence and "to exterminate bad taste, and to see to it that it shall not rise again . . . . " They named the academy for Arcadia, a pastoral region of ancient Greece, and assumed Greek names themselves; they chose the pipe of Pan for their emblem and the baby Jesus, whose first visitors had been shepherds, for their patron.

Among the founding members of the Accademia dell'Arcadia were the classicist and critic Gian Vincenzo Gravina, Giovan Mario Crescimbeni, Giovan Battista Zappi, Alessandro Guidi, and Carlo Innocenzo Frugoni. Although most Arcadian poetry was rather pale and imitative, the academy had two outstanding writers in the 17th and 18th centuries: Paolo Rolli, who was particularly skilled in *canzonetti;* and Pietro Metastasio, one of the greatest lyricists and librettists in Italian literature. Gabriello Chiabrera, who experimented with metrical forms, was also an Arcadian, as were Gabriele Rossetti (the father of the English poets Dante Gabriel and Christina Rossetti) and Pope Leo XIII, an accomplished poet who wrote a poem for the academy's 200th anniversary.

The Accademia dell'Arcadia was an important influence in achieving a simplification of Italian poetry and inspired the establishment in Italy of many Arcadian colonies that sought a return to a pastoral existence rather than having a specifically literary purpose. The 18th-century reformer of Italian comedy, Carlo Goldoni, was a member of one such colony at Pisa before he began his career.

In 1925 the academy was made an academic and historical institute and was renamed Accademia Letteraria Italiana.

Arcadius (*c.* 377–408), Eastern Roman emperor conjointly with his father, Theodosius I, from 383 to 395, then solely till 402, when he associated his son Theodosius II with his own rule. Frail and ineffectual, he was dominated by his ministers, Rufinus, Eutropius, and Anthemius. His empire was a prey to the Goths, and his consort Eudoxia abetted the persecution of the patriarch St. John Chrysostom.

arcanist (from Latin *arcanum:* "secret"), in the 18th century, a European who knew or claimed to know the secret of making certain kinds of pottery (especially true porcelain), which until 1707 was known only by the Chinese. The secret was discovered in Saxony by Ehrenfried Walter von Tschirnhaus and Johann Friedrich Böttger and was carefully guarded from potential rivals. A factory was established at Meissen about 1710, giving opportunities for gain to defecting workmen, who could sell the secret to other pottery factories. There were many arcanists (and pseudoarcanists) itinerant in Europe in the 18th century, including Joseph Jakob Ringler, Robert Dubois, and Paul-Antoine Hannong and his sons Joseph-Adam and Pierre-Antoine.

Arcaro, Eddie, byname of GEORGE EDWARD ARCARO (b. Feb. 19, 1916, Cincinnati, Ohio, U.S.), jockey who was the first to ride five Kentucky Derby winners and two U.S. Triple Crown champions (winners of the Kentucky Derby, the Preakness Stakes, and the Belmont Stakes). In 31 years of riding Thoroughbreds (1931–61), he won 549 stakes events, a total of 4,779 races, and more than $30,000,000 in purses. On Feb. 20, 1958, at Santa Anita Race Track in California, he became the third jockey (after Sir Gordon Richards and Johnny Longden) to achieve 4,000 victories.

Arcaro won 17 Triple Crown races: the Kentucky Derby five times (1938, 1941, 1945, 1948, 1952), the Preakness six times (1941, 1948, 1950–51, 1954, 1956), and the Belmont six times (1941–42, 1945, 1948, 1952, 1955). He rode Whirlaway to Triple Crown honours in 1941, and Citation in 1948. He established a record of $645,145 earned by one horse (Citation) in a single season. In 1960–61, at the end of his career, Arcaro teamed with the horse Kelso to win several major stakes.

After his retirement, he became a television sports commentator.

Arce, Louis-Armand de Lom d': *see* La Hontan, Louis-Armand de Lom d'Arce, baron de.

Arcellinida, protozoan order, formerly called Testacida, the members of which are commonly known as testaceans. *See* testacean.

Arcesilaus (b. 316/315 BC, Pitane, Aeolis—d. *c.* 241), philosopher who succeeded Crates as head of the Greek Academy; he introduced a skepticism derived either from Socrates or from Pyrrhon and Timon. Refusing to accept or deny the possibility of certainty in knowing, Arcesilaus advocated a skeptical "suspension of judgment" (*epochē*). The Stoics (who held a theory of "irresistible impressions") attacked him for thus paralyzing man and vitiating the goal of philosophy, which they believed was to make man happy and vigorous. Arcesilaus replied that a wise man need know only that his actions are "reasonable" (*eulogon*).

arch, structural member in building construction and civil engineering, used to span an opening and to support loads from above. The arch formed the basis for the evolution of the vault.

Early builders in masonry spanned wide openings with small, easily carried blocks of

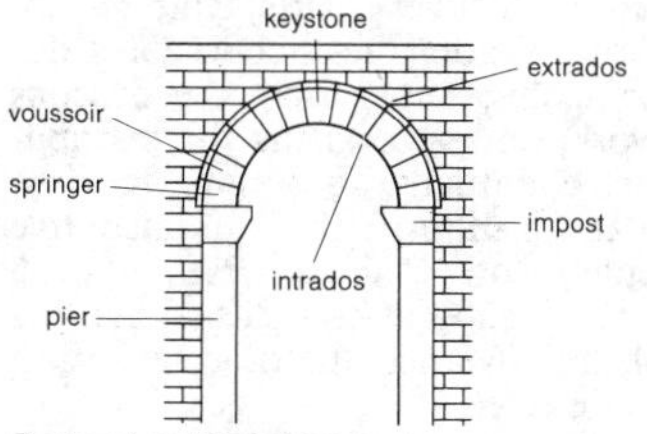

Parts of a circular arch

From *Webster's Third New International Dictionary* (1971); reproduced by permission from G. & C. Merriam Co.

brick or stone, forming a circular arch; because the upper edge has a greater circumference than the lower edge, each block must be cut as a wedge (voussoir) so that it presses firmly against the surface of neighbouring blocks and conducts loads uniformly. The central voussoir is called the keystone. The point from which the arch rises from its vertical supports is known as the spring or springing.

The stresses in this arch tend to squeeze the blocks outward radially, and loads divert these outward forces downward to exert a diagonal force, called thrust, which can cause the arch to collapse if it is not buttressed. An arch cannot replace a lintel on two freestanding posts unless the posts are massive enough to buttress the thrust and to conduct it into the foundations.

The arch was known in Egypt and Greece but was considered unsuitable for monumental architecture and was little exploited. The Romans, in contrast, used the semicircular arch in bridges, aqueducts, and large-scale architecture. In most cases they did not use mortar, relying simply on the precision of their stone dressing. In the Mayan ceremonial structures of pre-Columbian America, the corbel arch was characteristic.

Medieval builders developed the pointed arch, which constituted a basic element in Gothic architecture. In the late Middle Ages the segmental arch was introduced, in which the arc was less than one half of a circle. This form and the elliptical arch had great value in bridge engineering because they permitted mutual support by a row of arches, carrying the lateral thrust to the abutments at either end of the bridge.

Modern arches of steel, concrete, or laminated wood are highly rigid and light in weight, so that the horizontal thrust against the supports is small; this thrust can be further reduced by stretching a tie between the ends of the arch. Stresses within the arch or at the abutments can be decreased by using hinges at the two abutments, at the crown of the arch, or at all three places.

Arch, Joseph (b. Nov. 10, 1826, Barford, Warwickshire, Eng.—d. Feb. 12, 1919, Barford), organizer and leader of English agricultural labourers.

The son and grandson of farm labourers, Arch used his training as a Primitive Methodist preacher to good effect in the early 1870s when farm labourers in the south and central areas of England began to protest against low wages and harsh living conditions. Arch was elected president of the National Agricultural Labourers' Union when it was formed in 1872 and remained as president until it was dissolved in 1896.

A strong-willed, self-confident man, Arch elicited more respect than affection in his career as leader of English farm workers. When membership in the union began to decline after 1874, Arch began to turn his attention to politics and in 1885 served the first of two terms as a member of Parliament (1885–86, 1892–1900). He also served on the Warwickshire County Council from 1889 to 1892. His political skills were put to use on behalf of farm workers, for Arch is credited with having played an instrumental part in obtaining the vote for them in 1884.

archaeocyathid, any member of an extinct phylum (Archaeocyatha) of marine organisms of uncertain relationships found as fossils in marine limestones of Early and Middle Cambrian age (the Cambrian Period began 570,000,000 years ago and lasted 70,000,000 years). The archaeocyathid fossils represent the calcareous supporting structure built by what is presumed to be an animal, but of the creature itself little is known. Indeed, it has been considered possible that the archaeocyathid organism was some sort of calcareous algae, although this seems unlikely.

Archaeocyathid structures are conical or tubular in shape and superficially resemble horn corals. The archaeocyathid skeleton consists of thin inner and outer walls, supported by vertical partitions. The entire structure is porous. Variations are evident in the form and structure of the walls, in the number and arrangement of the pores, and in the general overall shape; these distinctions have been employed to differentiate different forms of archaeocyathids, but their real significance is uncertain. It is thought that the archaeocyathids most closely resemble the calcareous sponges. The archaeocyathids probably fed much as sponges do—by drawing in water and separating food material from it before discharging the strained water. Archaeocyathids lived upon the sea bottom in shallow water and formed large, reeflike masses. Archaeocyathid reefs have a worldwide distribution and have been found in Australia (in much the same region currently occupied by the Great Barrier Reef), Antarctica, Spain, Sardinia, Siberia, Newfoundland, Quebec, Labrador, New York, and California. It is possible that the Early and Middle Cambrian archaeocyathids filled much the same role as the later true corals and, like them, inhabited warm, shallow marine environments.

archaeological time scale, the chronological subdivisions of human prehistory, first developed by the Danish archaeologist C.J. Thomsen (1788–1865) as the Stone Age, Bronze Age (*q.v.*), and Iron Age (*q.v.*). The early portion of this scale has since been refined into more complex subdivisions. *See* Paleolithic Period; Mesolithic Period; Neolithic Period.

archaeology, also spelled ARCHEOLOGY, the branch of learning concerned with study of the material remains of man's past. The discipline has many branches and may be divided by geographical areas (such as the archaeology of ancient Greece and Rome) or by periods (such as medieval archaeology or industrial archaeology). Archaeological investigations are the principal sources of knowledge of prehistoric cultures.

A brief treatment of the discipline of archaeology follows. For full treatment, *see* MACROPAEDIA: History, The Study of: *Archaeology*. For references to specific archaeological data, *see* INDEX under names of sites and cultures.

For a description of the place of archaeology in the circle of learning, *see* PROPAEDIA: Part Ten, Division IV.

The materials of archaeology are both the things made by man and the things used by man. The things made by man are the settlements, buildings, utensils, tools, weapons, objects of ornament or pure artistic expression—the sum total of things fashioned in some way for human purposes. A general term for any one of the things made by man is artifact. The nonartifactual materials which were used—but not made or fashioned—by man are the unworked bones of the animals that he ate, the traces of the plants either grown or collected for food, the charcoal from ancient hearths—all the things utilized by man as given by nature.

Both the artifactual and the nonartifactual materials have their important roles in archaeological interpretation.

Strictly speaking, archaeology is not concerned with the analysis and interpretation of the bones of ancient man himself—whether fossilized or not. The study of the skulls and skeletons of ancient man is the concern of the physical anthropologist or human paleontologist. Neither is the archaeologist normally prepared to decipher or interpret the writings of ancient man—this is the specialty of the epigraphist and philologist.

The principal activities of the archaeologist include preliminary fieldwork (*i.e.,* the discovery and recording of sites and their superficial examination), excavation, and classification, dating, and interpretation of materials. Archaeological reconnaissance techniques range from simple exploration by walking or motoring to aerial photography, the use of ground probes, and electromagnetic detection.

Excavations may be classified, from the point of view of their purpose, as planned, rescue, or accidental. Most important excavations are conducted only after careful planning, although many important sites have been discovered and excavated in the course of preparation for construction projects and even as a result of exposure by bombing. Underwater reconnaissance and excavation have become important in the 20th century.

Analysis of artifacts entails numerous aspects, including precise description and classification of objects by form and use, determination of the materials from which they were made, placing of the objects in environmental and cultural contexts, relative or absolute dating, and historical interpretation. For many years, dating was based on historical records (in the case of Classical archaeology), stratigraphy (the study of the relative chronology of the Earth's strata), and dendochronology (analysis of tree rings). In 1948, however, the development of radioactive carbon dating permitted absolute dating of materials up to 40,000 years old; subsequent techniques have extended this time-scale considerably further. *See* carbon-14 dating.

Archaeopteris, fossil genus of plants originally—and sometimes still—considered early tree ferns in the order Protopteridales but now generally and tentatively assigned to a transitional fern group ancestral to both seed ferns and conifers. It was common in the Late Devonian Period (ending 345,000,000 years ago).

Callixylon, a genus reserved for fossil stem fragments of a plant in the order Cordaitales, is now also known to contain many stem fragments associated closely with the fronds of *Archaeopteris* and is judged to belong to that genus.

Archaeopteryx, fossil with both birdlike and reptile-like features, fossil birds, which flourished during the Late Jurassic age (the Jurassic Period began 190,000,000 years ago and lasted

Archaeopteryx skeleton, cast made from a fossil found in matrix

By courtesy of the American Museum of Natural History, New York

54,000,000 years). The known specimens were found in the Solenhofen Limestone Formation in Bavaria, a very fine grained Jurassic limestone formed in a shallow, tropical marine environment, probably in a coral lagoon, where lime-rich muds slowly accumulated and permitted fossil material to be exceptionally well preserved.

Archaeopteryx was reptile-like in appearance. Small in size (about as large as a crow), it shared many anatomical characters with some of the smaller bipedal dinosaurs. The skull, like those of birds, possessed an expanded braincase, large eye sockets, and a pronounced beak. Unlike modern birds, however, well-developed teeth were present in the jaws. The head was balanced upon a long, thin, and probably very flexible neck. The spinal column was simple in character. A long, well-developed tail was present, similar to the tail structure in the smaller dinosaurs, but it had feathers in a row on either side. The hind legs possessed three claws at their extremities and were birdlike. The forelimbs retained many primitive reptilian characteristics and had not completed their transformation into wings. *Archaeopteryx* may have been capable of flight, but it certainly was not efficient if it did fly. The prominent keel, or sternum, found in modern birds, which provides attachment for the powerful flight muscles, was weakly developed in *Archaeopteryx,* a further indication of its incapacity for sustained flight. It is largely because of the presence of well-developed, essentially modern feathers that *Archaeopteryx* is classified by some scholars as a bird rather than as a reptile. Their excellent insulating properties also indicate that *Archaeopteryx* may have been warm-blooded.

Archaic culture, any of the ancient woodlands cultures of North America, in what is now the northeastern United States, dating from about 8000 BC to 1000 BC. Variants of these cultures persisted much later to the west and to the north. The people subsisted on small-game hunting, fishing, and collecting and characteristically made such tools as large, broad, chipped-stone projectile points, milling and grinding stones, and bone implements and ornaments; by about 5000 BC they had developed such ground and polished stone objects as axes, spear-thrower weights, and bowls. From the 5th to the 2nd millennium BC, there appeared a related Old Copper culture in the upper Great Lakes region, which used copper for tools and weapons.

Archaic period, in history and archaeology, the earliest phases of a culture; the term is most frequently used by art historians to denote the period of artistic development in Greece from *c.* 750 to 480 BC, the date of the Persian sack of Athens.

During the Archaic period, art became more humanistic and naturalistic. Paintings on vases evolved from geometric designs to representations of human figures, often illustrating epic tales. Sculpture became less stiff and stylized; faces were animated with the characteristic "Archaic smile," and bodies were rendered with a growing attention to human proportion and anatomy. The development of the Doric and Ionic orders of architecture in the Archaic period also reflected this concern with true proportions.

Archaic smile, the smile that characteristically appears on the faces of Greek statues of the Archaic period (*c.* 750–*c.* 500 BC), especially the second quarter of the 6th century BC. The meaning of the convention is not known, although it is often assumed that for the Greeks this kind of smile reflected a state of ideal health and well-being. It has also

Archaic smile, detail of a kouros (statue of a young man) from Tenea, Greece, *c.* 575–550 BC; in the Antikensammlung, Munich

Hirmer Fotoarchiv, Munchen

been suggested that it is simply the result of a technical difficulty in fitting the curved shape of the mouth to the somewhat blocklike head typical of Archaic sculpture.

archangel, any of several chiefs, rulers, or princes of angels in the hierarchy of angels of the major Western religions, especially Judaism, Christianity, and Islām, and of certain syncretic religions, such as Gnosticism. *See* angel.

Archangel (city, Russian S.F.S.R.): *see* Arkhangelsk.

archbishop, in the Christian Church, the title of a bishop who, in addition to his ordinary episcopal authority in his own diocese, usually has jurisdiction (but no superiority of order) over the other bishops of a province. The functions of an archbishop developed out of those of the metropolitan, a bishop presiding over a number of dioceses in a province, though the title of archbishop, when it first appeared, implied no metropolitan jurisdiction. It seems to have been introduced in the Eastern Church in the 4th century as an honorary title of certain bishops. In the Western Church it was little known before the 7th century, and it did not become common until the Carolingian emperors revived the right of metropolitans to summon provincial synods. The metropolitans then commonly assumed the title of archbishop to mark their preeminence over the other bishops. The Council of Trent (1545–63) reduced the powers of the archbishop, which had been quite extensive in the Middle Ages. In the modern Roman Catholic Church the title is also used occasionally as an honorary title for certain bishops who are not metropolitans.

In the Orthodox and other churches of the East, the title is far more common than in the West, and it is less consistently associated with metropolitan functions. In the Orthodox Church there are autocephalous archbishops who rank between bishops and metropolitans.

In the Protestant churches of continental Europe the title of archbishop is rarely used. It has been retained by the Lutheran bishop of Uppsala, who is metropolitan of Sweden, and by the Lutheran bishop of Turku in Finland.

In the Church of England the ecclesiastical government is divided between two archbishops: the archbishop of Canterbury, who is called the "primate of all England" and metropolitan of the province of Canterbury, and the archbishop of York, who is called the "primate of England" and metropolitan of York. *See also* metropolitan.

archdeacon, in the Christian Church, originally the chief deacon at the bishop's church; during the Middle Ages, a chief official of the diocese; an honorary title in the modern Roman Catholic Church. The name was first used in the 4th century, although a similar office existed in the very early church. Appointed by the bishop, the archdeacon's duties were preaching, supervising the deacons and their work, and supervising the distribution of alms. Eventually he became the first assistant to the bishop in the administrative and disciplinary work of the diocese and even represented the bishop at councils. When the bishop died, he governed the diocese until a successor was elected.

From the 10th to the 13th century the archdeacon (usually an ordained priest) became more powerful. He was given jurisdiction over a defined territory, and dioceses were divided into several archdeaconries. The office was conferred irrevocably by the cathedral chapter rather than by the bishop. Thus, archdeacons became rivals of the bishop and exercised in their territories all the rights of a bishop except the power of ordaining.

During the 13th century a reaction began by the bishops, and the power and authority of archdeacons declined rapidly during the 14th and 15th centuries. The Council of Trent took away most of their powers.

The office developed similarly in the Eastern Church and is now primarily an honorary title.

In the Anglican Church, archdeacons have administrative authority, delegated by a bishop, over an entire diocese or part of one. Their duties vary.

archduke, feminine ARCHDUCHESS, a title, proper in modern times for members of the House of Habsburg. The title of archduke Palatine (*Pfalz-Erzherzog*) was first assumed by Rudolf IV, duke of Austria, on the strength of a forged privilege, in the hope of gaining for the dukes of Austria an equal status with the electors of the Holy Roman Empire. The emperor Charles IV refused to recognize the title, and it was not juridically held by the Habsburgs until 1453, when the emperor Frederick III, a Habsburg, confirmed Rudolf's privilege

Archduke, archduchess
foreign language equivalents

	masculine	feminine
Czech	arcivévoda	arcivévodkyně
Danish	ărkehertug	ărkehertuginde
Dutch	aartshertog	aartshertogin
French	archduc	archduchesse
German	Erzherzog	Erzherzogin
Hungarian	főherceg	főhercegnő
Italian	arciduca	arciduchessa
Latin	archidux	archiducissa
Norwegian	erkehertug	erkehertuginne
Polish	arcyksiążę	arcyksiężna
Portuguese	arquiduque	arquiduquesa
Romanian	arhiduce	arhiducesa
Russian	zrtsgertsog	zrtsgertsogynya
Serbo-Croatian	nadvojvoda	nadvoyvotkinja
Spanish	archiduque	archiduquesa
Swedish	erkehertig	erkehertiginna

and granted the title of archduke of Austria to his son Maximilian and his heirs. All males of the House of Habsburg bore this title; their daughters and wives were archduchesses. The title of archduke, or archduchess, of Austria also occurred in the royal style of the Bourbon kings and queens of Spain, though they were not descended in the male line from their Habsburg predecessors.

arche-, archeo- (combining form): *see under* archae-, archaeo-.

arched harp, musical instrument in which the neck extends from and forms a bow-shaped curve with the body. One of the principal forms of harp, it is apparently also the most ancient: depictions of arched harps survive from Sumer and Egypt from *c.* 3000 BC. Both areas had harps played in vertical position, plucked with the fingers of both hands, often by a kneeling musician. Sumer also had horizontal arched harps—*i.e.,* laid across the lap, strings toward the player, and sounded by a plectrum swept across the strings, the left-hand fingers damping unneeded strings. The arched harp disappeared from Sumer and subsequent Mesopotamian civilizations but continued in use in Egypt—as a large harp with kneeling player, as a small harp the neck of which lay pointed back across the player's shoulder, and in other sizes.

From ancient civilizations the arched harp apparently diffused southward in Africa, where it is still played (*e.g.,* the *ennanga* of Uganda), and eastward across India (where it is pictured being played both horizontally and vertically) to Southeast Asia, where it survives as the Burmese harp, *saung gauk.* Modern African harps often have cloth rings on the neck that produce a buzzing tone colour as the strings vibrate against them.

Uganda musician playing the *ennanga* arched harp
Gerhard Kubik

Arched harps were prominent in ancient Central Asia, and 1st-century frescoes (Gandhāra culture, in modern Pakistan) show a seemingly archaic variety that survives almost unchanged in the *vaji,* or Kafir harp, of Nūrestān (formerly Kāfiristān, Hindu Kush mountains, Afghanistan). Its neck pierces and then emerges from the skin belly; the strings run from the neck to the protruding end (in most harps they pass through the belly). Such a form lends weight to the speculation that harps developed from the musical bow. Arched harps survive also among the Abchas, a people of the Caucasus, and the Vogul, a Siberian people.

archegonium, the female reproductive organ in ferns and mosses. An archegonium also occurs in some gymnosperms, *e.g.,* cycads and conifers. A flask-shaped structure, it consists of a neck, with one or more layers of cells, and a swollen base—the venter—which contains the egg. Neck canal cells, located above the egg, disappear as the archegonium matures, thus producing a passage for entry of the sperm. The sperm are produced in the corresponding male reproductive organ, the antheridium.

Archelaus (d. 399 BC), king of Macedonia from 413 to 399. Although he acceded to power illegally, Archelaus was a capable and beneficent ruler. His father was King Perdiccas II (ruled *c.* 450–413) and his mother a slave. Archelaus seized the throne after murdering his uncle, his cousin, and his half brother, the legitimate heir. He then set about strengthening Macedonia by fortifying cities, constructing roads, and reorganizing the army. In an effort to spread the refinements of Greek civilization among his people, Archelaus invited many renowned artists, among them the tragedian Euripides, to his new capital at Pella. The King also celebrated Greek-style games at Dium, in Macedonia.

During Archelaus' reign the Macedonian economy was strengthened through the development of trade and adoption of the Persian coin standard. His relations with other states were generally peaceful. In 410 he seized Pydna, immediately to the east, and 10 years later helped establish a pro-Macedonian oligarchy at Larissa in Thessaly. Archelaus was assassinated by one of his favourites while hunting.

Archelaus, in full ARCHELAUS SISINES (d. AD 17), last king of Cappadocia (reigned 36 BC–*c.* AD 14), a Roman client during the late republic and the early empire. Although granted the kingdom by Mark Antony, Archelaus retained his crown by making peace with Octavian (later Augustus) after Antony's defeat at the Battle of Actium (31 BC).

In 20 BC Cilicia Trachea, eastern Lycaonia, and Armenia Minor were added to his domain, and his marriage to King Polemo's widow gave him indirect control of most of Pontus. When Tiberius succeeded Augustus (AD 14), Archelaus was summoned to Rome, accused in the Senate, and soon deprived of his throne. He died soon after. In AD 17 Cappadocia was made a Roman province.

Archelon, extinct giant sea turtle known from fossilized remains found in Late Cretaceous rocks in North America (the Cretaceous Period began about 136,000,000 years ago and lasted about 71,000,000 years). *Archelon,* protected by its formidable bony armour, reached a length of about 3.5 metres (12 feet). The front feet developed into powerful structures that could efficiently propel the great bulk of *Archelon* through the water.

archeology: *see* archaeology.

Archer (constellation): *see* Sagittarius.

Archer, Frederick Scott (b. 1813, Bishop's Stortford, Hertfordshire, Eng.—d. May 2, 1857, London), English inventor of the first practical photographic process by which more than one copy of a picture could be made.

Archer, a butcher's son, began his professional career as an apprentice silversmith in London, then turned to portrait sculpture. To assist him in this work, he began experimenting with the calotype photographic process of William Henry Fox Talbot. In 1851 he described his wet collodion process, by which finely detailed glass negatives were produced; from these, paper positives could be printed. The plates had to be developed before the sensitized collodion dried after exposure, so that a darkroom tent and portable laboratory were needed for outdoor photography, but the new process produced such good results that it dominated photography for a generation. A lawsuit by Talbot claiming that the wet collodion was merely a variant of his own process was dismissed.

Archer also invented the ambrotype, a cheap form of portraiture, in collaboration with another photographer, but, having devoted all his funds to research, he died in poverty.

Archer, Thomas (b. *c.* 1668—d. May 23, 1743, London), architect and practitioner of what was, for England, an extraordinarily extravagant Baroque style, marked by lavish curves, large scale, and bold detail.

Archer, the son of a Warwickshire squire, was educated at Trinity College, Oxford, and then spent four years abroad. The recipient of some lucrative royal appointments, he bought the manor of Hale, Hampshire, in 1715 and rebuilt the house and church.

The Church of St. John, Smith Square, Westminster, London, by Thomas Archer, 1714
A.F. Kersting

Archer's work, essentially dynamic, borrowed much from the 17th-century Italian architects Gian Lorenzo Bernini and Francesco Borromini; although he was not as original as some of the prominent English architects of his time, he was considered an important architect. Most of his designs were executed from 1705 to 1715, including the north front of Chatsworth House, Derbyshire (1705); Heythorpe Hall, Oxfordshire (*c.* 1705); a garden pavilion at Wrest Park, Bedfordshire (1711); Roehampton House, Surrey (1712); and the churches of St. Philip, Birmingham (1710), St. Paul, Deptford (1712), and St. John, Westminster (1714). The last two resulted from his appointment in 1711 as a commissioner for the building of 50 new churches.

A biography by Marcus Whiffen was published in 1973.

Archer, William (b. Sept. 23, 1856, Perth, Perth, Scot.—d. Dec. 27, 1924, London), drama critic whose translation introduced Henrik Ibsen to the British public. While studying law at Edinburgh he began his journalistic career on the *Edinburgh Evening News.* After a world tour (1876–77), in 1878 he moved to London and in 1879 became drama critic on the *London Figaro.* In 1884 he joined the *World;* his reviews for it and other periodicals were collected in *The Theatrical "World,"* 5 vol. (1893–97). He was later drama critic on the *Nation,* the *Tribune,* and the *Manchester Guardian.*

The translations of Ibsen that were to make him famous began with *Pillars of Society* (1880), the first of the plays produced in England. Later translations included *A Doll's House* (1889), *Ibsen's Prose Dramas,* 5 vol. (1890–91), *Peer Gynt* (1892), *The Master Builder* (1893), and the *Collected Works,* 12 vol. (1906–12). Despite faults, these had great influence and remain popular. His support for a national theatre prompted *A National*

Theatre: Scheme and Estimates (1907), with Harley Granville-Barker.

Of his plays, four were posthumously published; *The Green Goddess* (New York, 1921; London, 1923) was extremely successful and often revived. Archer also wrote polemical essays for the Rationalist press (collected by J.M. Robertson in *William Archer as Rationalist,* 1925).

archer fish, any of five species of Indo-Pacific fishes of the family Toxotidae (order Perciformes) noted for their ability to knock their insect prey off overhanging vegetation by "shooting" it with drops of water expelled from their mouths. Archer fishes are elongated, with relatively deep bodies that are almost flat from the dorsal fin forward. The head is pointed, the mouth is large, and the dorsal and anal fins are placed toward the back of the body. Depending on the species, the fishes are spotted or vertically banded with black.

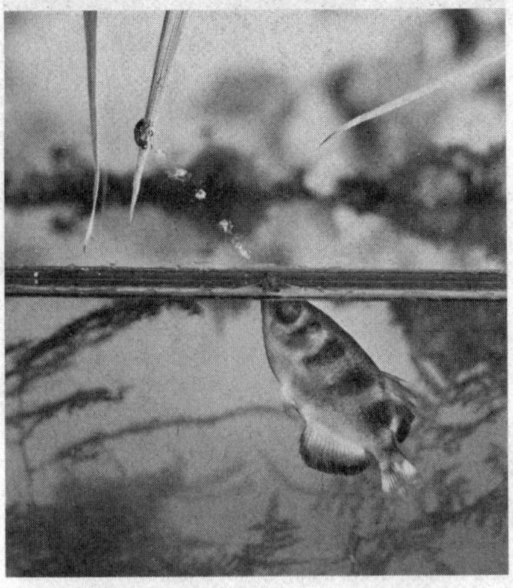

Archer fish (*Toxotes jaculator*)
Roy Pinney

Archer fishes live in both fresh water and salt water, usually remaining near the surface. One of the best known species is *Toxotes jaculator* (or *T. jaculatrix*), which grows about 18 centimetres (7 inches) long.

archery, sport involving shooting arrows with a bow, either at an inanimate target or in hunting (*q.v.*). This article is restricted to target archery. For an account of the use of bows and arrows as a military missile system, *see* bow and arrow. *See also* crossbow.

From prehistoric times the bow was a principal weapon of war and of the hunt throughout the world except in Australia. Recreational archery was also practiced, along with military, among the ancient Egyptians and Greeks, one instance of the latter being the competition in which Odysseus won the hand of Penelope. Otherwise, though, the sport sprang up as the military use waned.

History. As the bow was displaced by firearms as a military weapon, the general use of it in practice prevailed, and the seeds of the sport in England and Scotland were sown. The displacement also was a long one. Although the glorious military victories achieved mainly by the bow belonged to the Hundred Years' War (1357–1453), at the time of the Armada in 1588 a county levy consisted of one-third bowmen to two-thirds soldiers with guns; and not until near the end of the century was the bow abandoned as a weapon. In a period extending from the 13th century, English monarchs had made sure that bows and arrows were available for practice, and practice was compulsory. Other sports such as bowls, golf, and football were from time to time banned lest they encroach on archery practice. Most English monarchs were themselves archers, a practice that continued intermittently to Queen Victoria in the 19th century.

Roger Ascham in *Toxophilus, the Schole of Shooting* (1545), the first book in English on archery, in his dedication to Henry VIII recommended archery as a recreation and for exercise.

Early British societies. In 1537 Henry VIII had granted a patent to the Fraternity of St. George, or Honourable Artillery Company, whose members used longbows, crossbows, and handguns, and the company's practice ground was confirmed or reinstated in 1603 and 1633 as Finbury Fields in London. On the Fields archers set up many marks for roving, a competition in which archers shot from one mark to the next, the object being, as in golf, to use the fewest shots in going around the course. A plan in 1628 showed 164 marks, which by 1737 had dwindled to 21, but several butts had been provided for target shooting.

After the bow was discarded as a military weapon, the Finsbury Archers began to flourish, holding annual competitions until about 1761. The last of the Finsbury Archers joined the Toxophilite Society when it was founded in 1780. The Prince of Wales, later George IV, became the society's patron in 1787, thus creating the Royal Toxophilite Society. His activity involved setting the prince's lengths of 100 yd (91 m), 80 yd (73 m), and 60 yd (55 m), distances still used in the British men's championship York Round (six dozen, four dozen, and two dozen arrows shot at each of the three distances), and the method for scoring hits called the prince's reckoning. An earlier society was the Royal Company of Archers, the queen's bodyguard in Scotland, founded in 1676. The Grand National Archery Society, the governing body of archery in the United Kingdom, was founded in 1841.

England exported archery to Canada and Australia in the mid-19th century, but the sport really flourished only in the period after 1930.

North America. The bow was the chief war and hunting weapon of the Indians, but the European colonizers brought firearms, and the Indians soon adopted them for hunting and war. The first archery organization was the United Bowmen of Philadelphia, founded in 1828 and active until 1859, later revived in 1932. In the early days archery materials were imported from England, and the sport was, as there, a popular upper- and middle-class recreation. (For long the sexual division of archers was made as gentlemen and ladies.) In the 1870s many archery clubs sprang up, and in 1879 eight of them formed the National Archery Association of the United States, which held its first tournament in that year. The revival of hunting with the bow and arrow and field archery (*q.v.*) was greatly furthered by Maurice Thompson's *The Witchery of Archery* (1878; 2nd ed., 1879). U.S. manufacture of bows and arrows began to displace English ones. In 1939 a group of California archers organized the National Field Archery Association of the United States, to promote hunting, roving, and field archery, and thereafter held annual tournaments.

International archery. Archery events for men were held in the Olympic Games from 1900 through 1920 (except in 1912) and for women in 1904 and 1908. They were then suspended until the 1972 Games, when they were reintroduced for both men and women and continued thereafter. In the early period such events as shooting fixed and moving bird targets showed an aspect of archery outside of the English–American tradition. In the 1900 Games at Paris, the sole English-speaking winner was an Australian in game shooting. In the 1904 Games at St. Louis, all contestants

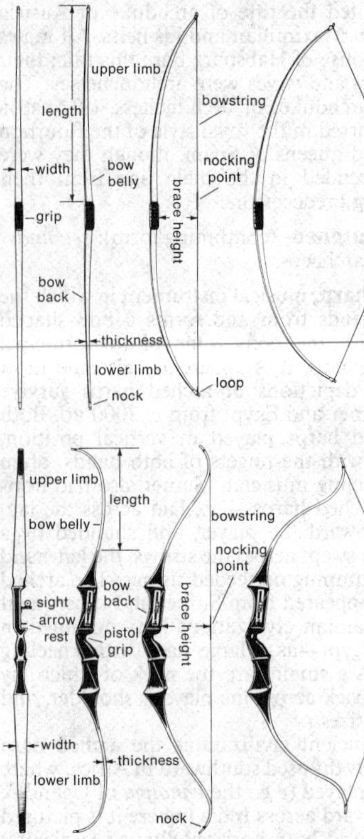

Front and side views of (top) longbow and (bottom) modern composite bow relaxed, braced, and full drawn

were from the United States competing in American versions of English events. At the 1908 Games in London, the British won the British-type events, but there was a sop to the non-English with an event called "Continental style," which was won by the French. Again in the 1920 Games at Antwerp, the events and the winners were continental.

Small wonder then that the formation of the international governing body, the Fédération Internationale de Tir à l'Arc (FITA), in 1931, was made by Belgium, France, Poland, and Sweden. (Great Britain joined in 1932, and the United States in 1933.) FITA events (including 1972 and later Olympic Games) are shot at metric distances, and since 1957 in double FITA rounds (*see* FITA Round). World championships were held biennially from 1933 except during World War II.

The new bow. Up to about 1930 the history of archery as a sport was the history of the longbow. Made traditionally of a single piece of yew, it had, however, disadvantages. It was subject to differing conditions of temperature and humidity, and it needed to be left unstrung when not in use. Using the longbow was an art. The bow that replaced it was composite, laminating plastic and fibre glass, and little affected by changes of temperature and humidity. Archers of equal skill scored on an average 30 to 40 percent higher with the new bow than with the longbow.

The new bow shoots farther than the longbow: more than 850 yd for the new to about 300 yd for the longbow. The efficiency (the percentage of energy in a full drawn bow that is transferred to the arrow at the moment of loose) of the new bow doubles that of the longbow, the velocity of the arrow with the new bow reaching 212 ft (65 m) per second as opposed to 150 ft per second. In design the modern composite archery bow has resemblances to the Turkish bow.

Similarly, arrows came to be made from aluminum-alloy or fibre glass tubing, and plastic fins replaced feathers. Points are of steel and nylon is used for the bowstring. For a comparison of the design of the longbow and the modern composite bow, see Figure.

Equipment. The modern target bow varies in length according to the height of the archer but is usually about 5 ft 6 in. (The longbow was originally the height of the archer.) Similarly, arrows vary from 25 to 30 in. The longbow arrow was called the cloth-yard shaft, the cloth yard ultimately becoming the British statute yard (a little less than one metre). The drawing force of a bow (the number of pounds of energy needed to draw back an arrow to the fullest) varies from 30 to 50 lb (14 to 23 kg) for men and from 20 to 40 lb for women. The archer usually carries arrows in a quiver, a container slung out of the way at the waist. A glove or finger protector shields the fingers used to draw the bowstring back, and a bracer is fitted to the inside forearm of the bow arm, that holding the bow, to protect against the released bowstring. For the method of pulling back the bowstring, *see* Mediterranean draw.

An archery range is most desirably laid out on level turf north to south, with shooting done to the north. A target is a boss of tightly coiled straw rope about 4 in. thick and about 4 ft in diameter on which is stretched a canvas face with concentric scoring rings (British, 5 rings; FITA, 10), scored 9, 7, 5, 1 outward from the centre (British) and 10 through 1 (FITA). Target sizes vary at different distances.

Competition. A round is a specified number of arrows shot at a specified distance and scoring is done after the round (or rounds, as in the FITA double rounds). *See also* American Round, Hereford Round, National Round, York Round.) FITA distances are 90, 70, 50 and 30 m (295, 230, 164, and 98 ft) for men and 70, 60, 50, and 30 m for women, three dozen arrows per round being shot by both men and women at each distance. Distances and other conditions may vary with local clubs, but the increased popularity of international archery from the 1930s makes FITA specifications most widely used.

Other forms of sport archery. Clout shooting (*q.v.*) originated at least as early as the late 16th century and is mainly British. Flight shooting (*q.v.*) was practiced in England at the end of the 16th century and was popular in Turkey with a composite bow at the end of the 18th century.

Popinjay shooting, mainly European, originally involved a live tethered parrot atop a pole and dates to the late 16th century. Latterday popinjay shooting uses a frame of cylinders with feathers attached, a cock, hens, and chicks, set atop a mast at which archers shoot vertically from the base of the mast.

E.G. Heath's *The Grey Goose Wing* (1971) is an illustrated history of the bow and arrow in military and hunting use as well as for target shooting.

For world records and world championships, individual and team, *see* Sporting Record: *Archery. See also* Olympic Games.

(P.E.K./Ed.)

Arches National Park, a desert area of rock pinnacles, windows, and arches, in eastern Utah, U.S., on the Colorado River, just north of Moab. It was established as a national monument in 1929 and as a national park in 1971 and is 115 sq mi (297 sq km) in area.

The area's red limestone has been eroded into unusual shapes, including Courthouse Towers (with spires that resemble skyscrapers), The Windows Section, Delicate Arch, Fiery Furnace (which glows in the setting sun), and Devils Garden (the site of Landscape Arch, at 291 ft [89 m] the longest such span in the world). There are several kinds of animal life, and during the summer months colourful wild flowers grow in the Salt Valley section.

archetype (from Greek *archetypos,* "beginning pattern"), in literary criticism, a primordial image, character, or pattern that recurs throughout literature and thought consistently enough to be considered a universal concept or situation. The term was adopted by literary critics from the writings of the psychologist Carl Jung, who formulated a theory of a "collective unconscious." For Jung, the varieties of human experience have somehow been genetically coded and transferred to successive generations. Originating in pre-logical thought, these primordial image patterns and situations evoke startlingly similar feelings in both reader and author.

Archidamus II (d. 427 BC), king of Sparta from about 469. A member of the Eurypontid house (one of the two royal families of Sparta), he succeeded to the throne of his grandfather, Leotychides. When the Messenian helots (serfs) revolted against their Spartan masters following a severe earthquake about 464, Archidamus organized the defense of Sparta. Nevertheless, for the next 30 years all known operations of the Spartan army were commanded by members of the other royal house (the Agiads), and there is no further record of Archidamus' activities until 432, when, according to the Greek historian Thucydides, the King attempted without success to prevent the outbreak of war with Athens (Peloponnesian War, 431–404).

Archidamus led the Spartan invasions of Attica in 431, 430, and 428 and a campaign against Plataea in 429. The first 10 years of the conflict are known as the Archidamian War. His two sons became the Spartan rulers Agis II and Agesilaus II.

Archidamus III (d. 338 BC, Manduria, Calabria), king of Sparta, 360–338, succeeding his father, Agesilaus II. Archidamus headed the force sent to aid the Spartan Army after its defeat by the Thebans at Leuctra in 371 and was commander later during the confused fighting in the Peloponnese. He scored a victory over the Arcadians in 367 but was in turn defeated by them in 364 at Cromnus. In 362 he showed great courage in the defense of Sparta against the Theban commander Epaminondas.

As king, Archidamus supported the Phocians against Thebes in the Sacred War of 355–346. Leading a mercenary army to help Tarentum (modern Tarento, Italy) against the Lucanians, he fell with most of his troops at nearby Manduria.

archil (dye): *see* orchil.

Archilochus (fl. 7th century BC; b. Paros), a writer of the first Greek poetry extant that can properly be described as personal.

Archilochus was the son of a free father and a slave mother, but he was a citizen of Paros because his father acknowledged him. His half-servile status, however, denied him the right to succeed to his father's possessions. He therefore chose to seek his fortune as a soldier.

Remaining on Paros, he entered into a contract of marriage with Neoboule, but the match was broken off by her father, Lycambes, probably because of Archilochus' origin. Archilochus responded to this treatment in a series of bitter poems. Fragments remain of a poem written in the form of a fable in which the eagle and the fox, like Lycambes and Archilochus, have made a treaty of friendship. But the eagle breaks his word and destroys the fox's cubs. So the fox calls upon Zeus for vengeance, and the result is that the eagle's young are destroyed as well. There are also poems about Neoboule in which she is depicted in future time as a repulsive old woman. Such was the bitterness of Archilochus' rejected love.

Perhaps as a consequence of his rejection, Archilochus left Paros and set off on a colonizing expedition to Thasos, a rocky island off the coast of Thrace. Here he became involved in war with the Thracians. It is noteworthy that, unlike the writers who came before him, Archilochus saw no glory in war. In one poem, which Horace was later to imitate, he speaks of his inglorious action in throwing away his shield in order to save his life: "no matter," he says, "I can always find another."

There is a tradition that Archilochus died in a battle between the Thasians and the men of Naxos. Even in the fragments of his poetry that remain he seems to have been a man of spirit. He is a pioneer of the cult of individualism in literature in which the poetry of heroism gives way to that of feeling and reflection.

Archimedes (b. *c.* 290–280 BC, Syracuse, Sicily—d. 212/211 BC, Syracuse), the most famous mathematician and inventor of ancient Greece, especially important for the discovery of the relation between the surface and volume of a sphere and its circumscribing cylinder. He is also known for Archimedes' principle in hydrostatics and the Archimedes screw (a device for raising water).

Following is a brief treatment of the life of Archimedes. For fuller treatment, *see* MACROPAEDIA: Archimedes.

Except for a brief period early in his career in the intellectual centre of Alexandria, Archimedes spent most of his life in the Greek city-state of Syracuse. War machines of his construction greatly delayed the capture of the city by Roman forces in 212 or 211 BC, when Archimedes was killed by a Roman soldier.

Archimedes was accorded much contemporary popularity because of his inventions, such as the Archimedes screw and two astronomical globes, and there are several anecdotes about his life, although the veracity of their details is uncertain. For example, although his war machines were long successful against the Romans, it is doubtful that he constructed an array of mirrors to burn their ships.

Archimedes' theoretical work that could be simply expressed—such as the formulas for the surface area and volume of a sphere—became mathematical commonplaces, and one of the bounds that he established for pi, $\frac{22}{7}$, was adopted as the usual approximation into the Middle Ages. But his influence on the development of mathematics was unimportant until it was revived by the Arabs in the 8th or 9th century and the Europeans in the 16th and 17th centuries.

There are nine known extant treatises in Greek by Archimedes, and the references of later authors indicate that he had written a number of other works that are now lost. Of the known works, five are of particular interest.

On the Sphere and Cylinder contains his discovery that the volume of a sphere is two-thirds that of the cylinder in which it is inscribed and that the surface area of a sphere is four times that of its greatest circle. A short work, *Measurement of the Circle,* contains his accurate and rational approximations of the value of pi and of the square roots of several numbers.

On Floating Bodies, which survives only partly in Greek, is the first known work in hydrostatics, of which Archimedes is the recognized founder. It contains the work leading to Archimedes' principle—that a solid denser than a fluid will, when immersed in that fluid, be lighter by the weight of the fluid it displaces.

The Sand-Reckoner remedies the inadequacies of the Greek numerical notational system by creating a place-value system of notation.

Method Concerning Mechanical Theorems describes the "mechanical" technique used by Archimedes to arrive at the values proved mathematically in *On the Sphere and Cylinder.* The author's hope that this treatise would lead other mathematicians to new discoveries was unfulfilled because the work was lost until the 19th century.

Archimedes screw, machine for raising water, said to have been invented by the 3rd-century-BC Greek scientist Archimedes for removing water from the hold of a large ship. One form consists of a circular pipe enclosing a helix and inclined at an angle of about 45

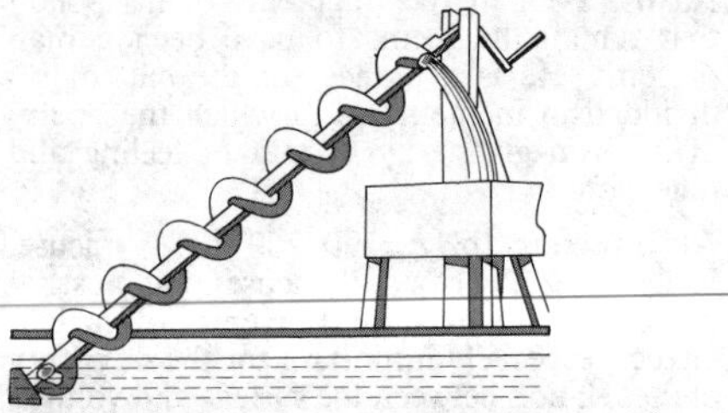

Archimedes screw, invention attributed to the Greek scientist Archimedes

degrees to the horizontal with its lower end dipped in the water; rotation of the device causes the water to rise in the pipe. Other forms consist of a helix revolving in a fixed cylinder or a helical tube wound around a shaft.

Modern screw pumps, consisting of helices rotating in open inclined troughs, are effective for pumping sewage in waste-water-treatment plants. The open troughs and the design of the screws permit the passage of debris without clogging.

Archimedes' principle, physical law of buoyancy, discovered in the 3rd century BC by the Greek mathematician and inventor Archimedes, stating that any body completely or partially submerged in a fluid (gas or liquid) at rest is acted upon by an upward, or buoyant, force the magnitude of which is equal to the weight of the fluid displaced by the body. The volume of displaced fluid is equivalent to the volume of an object fully immersed in a fluid or to that fraction of the volume below the surface for an object partially submerged in a liquid. The weight of the displaced portion of the fluid is equivalent to the magnitude of the buoyant force. The buoyant force on a body floating in a liquid or gas is also equivalent in magnitude to the weight of the floating object and is opposite in direction; the object neither rises nor sinks. A ship that is launched sinks into the ocean until the weight of the water it displaces is just equal to its own weight. As the ship is loaded, it sinks deeper, displacing more water, and so the magnitude of the buoyant force continuously matches the weight of the ship and its cargo.

If the weight of an object is less than that of the displaced fluid, the object rises, as in the case of a block of wood released beneath the surface of water or a helium-filled balloon let loose in air. An object heavier than the amount of the fluid it displaces, though it sinks when released, has an apparent weight loss equal to the weight of the fluid displaced. In fact, in some accurate weighings, a correction must be made to compensate for the buoyancy effect of the surrounding air.

Buoyancy is caused by the increase in fluid pressure at increasingly greater depths. The pressure on a submerged object, therefore, is greater on the parts more deeply submerged, and the buoyant force is always upward, or opposite to the gravitational force; it is the net effect of all the forces exerted on the object by the fluid pressure.

archinephric duct: *see* Wolffian duct.

archinephros, ancestral vertebrate kidney, retained by larvae of hagfish and of some caecilians and occurring in the embryos of higher animals. Two tubes, the archinephric, or Wolffian, ducts, extend between the body cavity and the back and lead to the exterior. A series of tubules, one pair for each body segment, connects the body cavity with the Wolffian ducts. Each tubule is ciliated where it opens into the body cavity, and a knot of capillaries occurs at each of these openings, which are called nephrostomes.

The three types of adult vertebrate kidneys develop from the embryonic archinephros: the pronephros from the anterior section, the mesonephros from the middle section, and the metanephros from the hindsection.

archipallium, a portion of the pallium, in the forebrain. The pallium is the mantle, or covering, over the lateral ventricles, or cavities, of the brain. The archipallium is first distinguishable as a part of the pallium in amphibians. In humans and other mammals this portion of the brain is overshadowed by the neopallium, or cerebral cortex. The part of the brain evolved from the archipallium forms the upper, inner wall of each lateral ventricle and, among other functions, serves as an olfactory centre.

archipelagic apron, layers of volcanic rock that form a fanlike slope around groups of ancient or recent islands, most commonly in the central and southern Pacific. The aprons typically have a slope of 1° to 2°, with the slope decreasing nearer the shore; the upper parts may be indented by deep-sea channels. Although some aprons are rough, they are typically smooth because a veneer of Recent sediments masks any volcanic relief present. Turbidity currents may play an important role in transporting debris over the aprons and enhancing their smoothness.

Archipelagic aprons occur around such island groups as the Marquesas, Marshall, Hawaiian, Samoan, and the Gilbert. These aprons seem to be a topographic expression of what geophysicists term the second layer, a layer of rock that transmits seismic waves with velocities between four and six kilometres (two and four miles) per second; this second layer thickens near volcanic islands to form the archipelagic aprons. Formation of the thick layer seems to be caused by very fluid lava pouring out of fissures near the bases of volcanic islands.

Archipenko, Alexander (b. May 30, 1887, Kiev—d. Feb. 25, 1964, New York City), Russian-born U.S. sculptor and painter who originated a new style in which the representation of the human figure was subordinated to the formal composition of voids and solids.

After studying in Russia, Archipenko attended the École des Beaux-Arts in Paris (1908), where he was active in the Cubist movement. He taught art briefly in Berlin (1921–23) and for the rest of his life in New York City (1923–64), except for a short time (1937–39) when he was connected with the New Bauhaus in Chicago.

Archipenko's abstract shapes have a primitive vitality and rhythmic movement. In his "Walking Woman" (1912), holes were punched in the face and torso and concavities substituted for the convexities of the lower legs. This opening up of the form revolutionized modern sculpture. "Boxing Match" (1913) attempted to convey the brutal energy of the sport in nonrepresentational, machine-like cubic and ovoid forms. In 1912 he executed the first collage in sculpture in his famous "Medranos," circus figures in multicoloured glass, wood, and metal, defying traditional use of materials. His later works were less revolutionary in form and conception.

Architects' Collaborative, The (TAC), association of architects specializing in school buildings that was founded in 1946 in Cambridge, Mass., by Walter Gropius. The original partners included Norman Fletcher, John Harkness, Sarah Harkness, Robert McMillan, Louis McMillen, and Benjamin Thompson.

Among the works that were cooperatively designed through TAC teamwork were the Harvard University Graduate Center (1949–50); the U.S. Embassy in Athens (1956); the Arts and Communications Center and the Evans Science Building (both 1959) at Phillips Academy in Andover, Mass.; and the University of Baghdad (design accepted 1960). Gropius remained active with TAC until his death in 1969.

architectural rendering, branch of the pictorial arts and of architectural design whose special aim is to show, before buildings have been built, how they will look when completed. Modern renderings fall into two main categories: the quick perspective "design-study," by which an architect records or develops his initial concept of a proposed building; and the carefully executed "presentation rendering," which is a final design made for exhibition and publication.

Vitruvius, a Roman architect-engineer of the 1st century BC, referred to the use of architectural renderings in antiquity, although no examples have survived. Some architectural sketches in perspective do remain from the Middle Ages; *e.g.,* the famous sketchbook of Villard de Honnecourt, a French master mason of the 13th century. But architectural rendering as it is known today did not begin until the Renaissance with such Italian architects as Brunelleschi, Alberti, Peruzzi, Bramante, the Sangallos, Leonardo da Vinci, and Michelangelo. In the 19th century the École des Beaux-Arts in Paris led in perfecting an academic type of rendering which involved the addition to carefully drawn plans and elevations of washes in monotone or colour, so applied as to elucidate and enhance the presentation.

architecture, the art and technique of building, as distinguished from the skills associated with construction. As with other arts, the practice of architecture embraces both aesthetic and utilitarian ends that may be distinguished but not separated, and the relative weight given to each can vary widely from work to work. Thus, at one end of the scale are purely functional structures (that may nonetheless possess certain aesthetic qualities, intended or not), while at the other are purely decorative ones with no genuine practical function at all.

All but the simplest cultures have evolved characteristic forms of architecture, and the more complex societies command a great variety of styles, techniques, and purposes that shape their buildings.

Architecture is treated in a number of articles in the MACROPAEDIA. For a general discussion of architecture and its history, *see* Architecture, The Art of; Architecture, The History of Western. For a discussion of the place of architecture and architectural theory in the realm of the arts, *see* Aesthetics; Arts, Classification of the. For related forms of artistic expression, *see* Cities: *Urban Planning;* Folk Arts; Furniture and Accessory Furnishings; Interior Design; Landscape Architecture. For information on the particular styles and forms of architecture practiced by non-European peoples, *see* African Arts; American Indians; Central Asian Arts; East Asian Arts; Egyptian Arts and Architecture, Ancient; Islāmic Arts; Oceanic Arts; Prehistoric Peoples and Cultures; South Asian Arts; Southeastern Asian Arts.

For a description of the place of architecture in the circle of learning and for a list of both MACROPAEDIA and MICROPAEDIA articles on the subject, *see* PROPAEDIA: Part Six.

architrave, in Classical architecture, the lowest section of the entablature (horizontal member), immediately above the capital of a column. *See* entablature.

archives, also called RECORDS, or RECORD OFFICE, repository for an organized body of records produced or received by a public, semipublic, institutional, or business entity in the transaction of its affairs and preserved by it or its successors. The term archives, which also designates the body of records themselves, derives from the French, and it, or a cognate, is used in most continental European countries and in the Americas. The terms records and record office are used in the United Kingdom and in some parts of the British Commonwealth.

Although the institution of archives and something of archival administration may be traced from antiquity, archives and archival administration as they are understood today date from the French Revolution. With the establishment of the Archives Nationales in 1789 and of the Archives Départementales in 1796, there was for the first time a unified administration of archives that embraced all extant repositories and record-producing public agencies. The second result was the implicit acknowledgment that the state was responsible for the care of its documentary heritage. The third result was the principle of accessibility of archives to the public.

Practice and principle have varied somewhat from country to country, but the pattern has generally been a central repository and, if conditions warrant them, provincial repositories. France has kept in the departmental archives not only the modern archives relating to the area but also those from the prerevolutionary period. The Netherlands has a central state archives and the provincial archives. The schism following World War II gave the Federal Republic of Germany a Bundesarchiv at Koblenz and the German Democratic Republic a central archives at Potsdam; but there are also repositories in the several *Länder*, or states. Italy has no single, central institution for state archives but has a series of important repositories, united under the ministry of the interior, which reflect the earlier divisions of the country. In the United States the National Archives was established in 1934 to house the retired records of the national government; the Federal Records Act of 1950 authorized the establishment also of "intermediate" records repositories in the several regions into which the country has been divided by the General Services Administration. Under the federal system of government each of the states of the United States independently has its own archival agency. In Canada, similarly, both the federal Ottawa government and the several provinces maintain their own archives. The Australian Archives has headquarters in Canberra and branches in all the state capitals and in Darwin and Townsville; the states have their own archives, usually under the management of state libraries.

The English Public Record Act of 1838 brought all separate collections together and placed them under the Master of the Rolls. England, therefore, is the outstanding example of centralization, whereas the more usual practice, as already suggested, is decentralization of archives to the domestic areas in which they originated. New Zealand's National Archives is similarly centralized, as are the archives of India and Pakistan. Japan has no national archives; its records still remain in the custody of ministries.

The United Nations and the several international organizations maintain archives. The International Council on Archives was founded in 1948 by professional archivists meeting in Paris under the auspices of UNESCO. Membership is open to all professional archivists and to representatives of (1) central archival directorates or administrations, (2) national or international regional associations of archivists, and (3) all archival institutions.

The science of records control has had to face at least three central issues: (1) the determination of types of records to be removed from agencies of origin, (2) the time of disposition, and (3) the manner of disposition. Practice has varied, but elimination usually has occurred before records have been transferred from the agency of origin. Some countries, especially those whose history reaches back many centuries, have prohibited the elimination of records made before a specified date.

In the 20th century archivists have been faced with handling new kinds of records, such as photographic records, motion pictures, sound recordings, and computer-kept records. Microcopy, or microfilm, the legal status of which as record copy usually has had to be determined by special legislation, is a practical medium for making additional copies of records as security against risk through acts of warfare; as preservation against normal deterioration or damage; for use in international exchange; in lieu of loan or as a convenience to scholars; for reducing costs of repair, binding, and storage; as a means of supplementing by collateral materials the main bodies of records; and as a form of publication. Practice as well as belief has varied from country to country. As the concepts of social, economic, and cultural history developed, as industrialization played an increasingly prominent role in national and international affairs, as democratization spread over the surface of the globe, so there was an increasing awareness of the significance of business archives, institutional archives, and the papers of persons not necessarily distinguished. Germany was the first to recognize the value of business archives; Belgium, Switzerland, and The Netherlands followed shortly; France, England, Denmark, and the United States are examples, in varying degree and nature, of later recognition.

archivolt, molding running around the face of an arch immediately above the opening. The architectural term is applied especially to medieval and Renaissance buildings, where

Romanesque archivolts over the arches of the nave of Southwell Minster, Nottinghamshire, England, mid-12th century

By courtesy of the Courtauld Institute of Art, London

the archivolts are often decorated with sculpture, as in the archivolts on the west facade of Chartres cathedral (1140–50).

archlute, large 16th-century bass lute provided with additional bass strings, or diapasons, and producing a deeper sound that could be used in orchestral basso continuo parts. The diapasons were tuned according to individual preference, usually in a descending scale from the lowest principal string.

There were three main varieties of archlute: the chitarrone, theorbo (*qq.v.*), and theorbolute, or French lute. The angelica, or angel lute, of the 17th and 18th centuries, was related but had diatonically tuned strings and no frets.

archon, Greek ARCHŌN, in ancient Greece, the chief magistrate or magistrates in many city-states. The office became prominent in the Archaic period, when the kings (*basileis*) were being superseded by aristocrats.

At Athens the list of annual archons begins with 682 BC. By the middle of the 7th century BC, executive power was in the hands of nine archons, who shared the religious, military, and judicial functions once discharged by the king alone. The archon proper was the principal civil and judicial officer and may have presided over both Boule (Greek *boulē*, council) and Ecclesia (Greek *ekklēsia,* assembly); as eponymous archon, he gave his name to his year of office.

Next came the polemarch, commander in war and judge in litigation involving foreigners. Third, the kingship survived in the *basileus,* who, as chief religious officer, presided over the Areopagus (aristocratic council) when it sat as a homicide court. Lastly there were six *thesmotetai* ("determiners of custom"), who dealt with miscellaneous judicial problems.

The potential power of the archons placed them under a variety of restrictions. Before entering office they had to undergo an examination (*dokimasia*) by the Boule and the law courts of birth qualifications, physical fitness, treatment of parents, and military activity; at the end of their term, they underwent an examination (*euthyna*) of their conduct, especially financial, while in office. Membership was originally open only to nobles by birth (*eupatrids* or *eupatridai*), who served as archons for life. The term of office was eventually reduced to 10 years, then to a single year, after which, since they could not be reelected, the archons became life members of the Areopagus. The eupatrid monopoly was broken *c.* 594 BC, when Solon made the top or top two property classes eligible for office.

Under the Cleisthenic constitution (508–*c.* 487), archons were elected directly by the Ecclesia; later they were chosen by lot from 500 previously elected candidates. Until 457 the office was still restricted to the top two classes. Then eligibility was first extended to the third property class; finally the fourth class was admitted in fact, though theoretically ineligible.

In the 5th century the authority of the archons declined. The polemarch lost his army command to 10 tribal commanders (*stratēgoi*), who also replaced the archons in the administrative sphere. The archons thus became primarily judicial officers. By the mid-5th century they no longer gave their own judgments but merely conducted preliminary inquiries (*anakrisis*), then brought the case before a jury, presiding over the hearing, but with no responsibility for directing the jury on matters of law.

Archons were also found at Delphi, Plataea, Phocis, and eastern and western Locris. During the 5th century the institution spread widely in the Aegean islands, mainly under Athenian influence, and then in the Hellenistic period to Anatolia.

Archon, in Gnosticism, any of a number of world-governing powers that were created with the material world by a subordinate deity called the Demiurge (Creator). The Gnostics were religious dualists who held that matter is evil and the spirit good and that salvation is attained by esoteric knowledge, or gnosis.

Because the Gnostics of the 2nd and 3rd centuries, who generally originated within Christianity, regarded the material world as outright evil or as the product of error, Archons were viewed as maleficent forces. They numbered 7 or 12 and were identified with the seven planets of antiquity or with the signs of the zodiac. Sometimes the Demiurge and the Archons were identified with the God, the angels, and the law of the Old Testament and hence received Hebrew names. The recurring image of Archons is that of jailers imprisoning the divine spark in human souls held captive in material creation. The purpose of the gnosis sent from the realms of divine light beyond the universe through the divine emanation (aeon) Christ was to enable Gnostic initiates to pass through the spheres of the Archons into the realms of light.

To make the best use of the Britannica, consult the INDEX *first*

Archosaurus, early genus of reptiles found as fossils in Late Permian deposits of Europe (the Permian Period began 280,000,000 years ago and lasted 55,000,000 years). *Archosaurus* typifies the progressive changes occurring in reptilian structure that eventually led to their dominance as the major vertebrates. A clear trend was in the modification of the limbs and the pelvis.

Archytas OF TARENTUM (fl. 400–350 BC, Tarentum, Magna Graecia), Greek scientist, philosopher, and major Pythagorean mathematician, who is sometimes called the founder of mathematical mechanics. Plato, a close friend, made use of his work in mathematics, and there is evidence that Euclid borrowed from him for Book viii of his *Elements.* Also an influential figure in public affairs, Archytas served for seven years as commander in chief of his city.

A member of the second generation of followers of Pythagoras, the Greek philosopher who stressed the significance of numbers in explaining all phenomena, Archytas sought to combine empirical observation with Pythagorean theory. In geometry, he solved the problem of doubling the cube by constructing a three-dimensional model. The conclusions that he then drew concerning continued proportions, expressed as $a:b = b:c = c:d$, he applied to musical harmony. Thus, he was able to discern intervals of pitch in the enharmonic scale in addition to those already known in the chromatic and the diatonic scales. Rejecting earlier views that the pitch of notes sounded on a stringed instrument is related to the length or tension of the strings, he proposed instead that pitch is related to the movement of vibrating air. Incorrectly, however, he asserted that the speed at which the vibrations travel to the ear is a factor in determining pitch.

Archytas' reputation as a scientist and mathematician rests on his achievements in geometry, acoustics, and music theory, rather than on his extremely idealistic explanations of human relations and the nature of society according to Pythagorean number theory. Nonmathematical writings usually attributed to him, including a fragment on legal justice, are most likely the work of other authors.

Arcila (Morocco): *see* Asilah.

Arcimboldo, Giuseppe, Arcimboldo also spelled ARCIMBOLDI (b. *c.* 1527, Milan—d. 1593, Milan), Italian painter of social satire whose grotesque compositions of fruits, vegetables, animals, books, and other objects were arranged to resemble human portraits. In the 20th century these double images were greatly admired by Salvador Dali and other Surrealist painters.

Beginning his career as a designer of stained-glass windows for the Milan cathedral, Arcimboldo moved to Prague, where he became one of the favourite court painters to the Habsburg rulers Maximilian II and Rudolph II. He also painted settings for the court theatre there and developed an expertise for illusionistic trickery. His paintings con-

"Summer," painting on canvas by Giuseppe Arcimboldo, 1563; in the Kunsthistorisches Museum, Vienna

By courtesy of the Kunsthistorisches Museum, Vienna; photograph, Erwin Meyer

tained allegorical meanings, puns, and jokes that were appreciated by his contemporaries but lost upon audiences of a later date. His eccentric vision is epitomized in his portraits "Summer" and "Winter" (Kunsthistorisches Museum, Vienna).

Arciniegas, Germán (b. Dec. 6, 1900, Bogotá), Colombian historian, essayist, diplomat, and statesman, one of the most eminent men of letters in modern Spanish America. His long and distinguished career at home in journalism and public service strongly influenced the cultural development of his country in the 20th century, and his contributions abroad as an educator and a diplomat played an important role in introducing North Americans and Europeans to Spanish-American history and contemporary culture.

Arciniegas became a prominent figure in public life soon after his graduation from the law school of the Universidad Nacional, Bogotá, in 1924. He contributed essays to several newspapers and magazines, founding the review *Universidad* ("University") in Bogotá in 1928 and becoming editor of the newspaper *El tiempo* ("The Times") there in 1939. Also active in education, he served as Colombian minister of education (1941–42 and 1945–46) and taught at several universities in the U.S., including Chicago (1944) and Columbia (1947–57).

Arciniegas was concerned with understanding and interpreting Latin America, publishing numerous volumes on diverse aspects of its culture and history that reveal his original perceptions as well as his encyclopaedic knowledge. Such works as *Biografía del Caribe* (1945; *Caribbean, Sea of the New World,* 1946) and *El continente de siete colores* (1965; *Latin America: A Cultural History,* 1966) introduced an international audience to Arciniegas' panoramic view of his continent.

In his 50s, Arciniegas turned to a diplomatic career. In 1959 he was appointed Colombian ambassador to Italy; later he also served in Israel, Venezuela, and Vatican City. He became dean of the faculty of philosophy and letters at the Universidad de los Andes, Bogotá, in 1979.

Arco, city, seat (1917) of Butte County, south central Idaho, U.S. After its founding in 1879 as Junction, the town was moved twice and is now on the Big Lost River. The origin of the place-name is uncertain; it has been attributed to a Count Arco, who supposedly visited the site, and to Arco Smith, a stagecoach operator. The U.S. Department of Energy's Idaho National Engineering Laboratory (nuclear reactor testing and energy research) occupies 894 sq mi (2,315 sq km) just to the east of Arco; it was established in 1949 by the former U.S. Atomic Energy Commission and became the first station in the country to produce electricity from atomic energy (1951). Craters of the Moon National Monument (*q.v.*) is 20 mi (32 km) southwest. Pop. (1980) 1,241.

Arcos de la Frontera, city, Cádiz province, in the autonomous community (region) of Andalusia, southern Spain. It is located on a high rock bounded on three sides by the Río Guadalete. Rich in Moorish architecture, the city also contains the Gothic churches of Santa María de la Asunción and San Pedro, with additions dating from the 16th to the 18th century. Called Colonia Arcensium by the Romans and Medina Arkosh by the Moors, Arcos was taken for the Christians by Alfonso X of Castile in 1264 and was made a city in 1472. In medieval times it was on the border between Christian and Muslim Spain. It is now an agricultural centre and manufactures cork and esparto products. Pop. (1981) 24,902.

Arcot, town, North Arcot district, Tamil Nādu state, southeastern India, on the Pālār River. Located at the point where the Pālār Valley meets the Coromandel Coast, it commands the inland route from Madras to Bangalore, between the Mysore Ghāt and the Javādi Hills. A fortified capital of the Muslim nawabs, it was the scene of numerous battles between the Muslims, Marāṭhās, French, and British in the 17th and 18th centuries. In the second half of the 20th century, it has been superseded by Vellore, the administrative headquarters of North Arcot district. Pop. (1981) town, 38,826; metropolitan area, 94,363.

Arctic, northernmost region of the Earth, centred on the North Pole and characterized by distinctively polar conditions of plant life, climate, etc.

The article that follows is a summary of significant detail about the Arctic; for fuller treatment of its geography, history, and peoples, *see* MACROPAEDIA: Arctic, The.

Unlike the Antarctic continent, which is surrounded by ocean, the Arctic is composed largely of an ocean basin almost completely surrounded by continents. Included in the Arctic region are the northern reaches of Canada, Alaska, the U.S.S.R., Norway, the Atlantic Ocean, Svalbard, most of Iceland, Greenland, and the Bering Sea. The region is not coextensive with the area enclosed by the Arctic Circle—a line drawn at about 66° 30′ N, marking the southern limit of the zone in which there is at least one annual 24-hour period during which the Sun does not set and one during which it does not rise. A more useful line to mark the Arctic's southern boundary might be the northernmost tree line on the continents, but no universally agreed boundary exists.

The land. The Arctic land areas surrounding the Arctic Ocean are generally flat and low-lying. Greenland and the eastern Canadian Arctic have distinctive highlands, where mountains and plateaus exceed 6,600 ft (2,000 m) in altitude over wide areas; much of the Greenland ice sheet rises above an altitude of 8,200 ft. Less continuous uplands occur in the Lena delta and the peninsula of northeastern Siberia in the U.S.S.R., while a narrower but higher belt of mountains is found in Alaska, where Mt. McKinley reaches an altitude of 20,269 ft.

Three shields—the Canadian-Greenland, the Baltic, and the Angara—comprise the main structural features of the Arctic. The shield rocks are generally covered by flat-lying Paleozoic sedimentary rocks and fringed by orogenic belts of sedimentary rocks of Paleozoic and younger age, which include the fold mountains of the Urals and Novaya Zemlya in the U.S.S.R. The shields contain rich mineral reserves of iron, nickel, copper, and zinc, while the sediments flanking them contain reserves of coal and oil. Early oil discoveries in the folded sequences of north Alaska have been followed by exploration eastward along the line of the folded structures in Arctic Canada and northern Greenland and into equivalent structures of the Barents Sea and Svalbard. The rich oil and gas reserves associated with the sediments in western Siberia are immensely important on a world scale. Active earthquake regions with associated volcanic activity are located in the Cordillera of southern Alaska. Three of the world's largest rivers, the Ob, the Yenisey, and the Lena, flow northward through the Soviet Arctic and empty into the Arctic Sea.

More then three-fifths of the Arctic is ice-free, and the glaciation limit varies considerably with local conditions. The climate in much of the ice-free area is moderately continental with long, cold, and relatively dark winters, although the darkness is far from absolute. The length and darkness of the winter increases toward the pole because of the low angle of the sun in relation to the ground surface. The snow cover is patchy and thin, and during spring and early summer the ground becomes saturated and boggy with melted snow. The coastal areas experience warmer winters and cooler summers. The lowest temperatures are recorded at the southern edge of the Arctic. Summer temperatures over the Arctic Ocean approximate 32° F (0° C), while the surrounding land areas are warmer, often exceeding 60° F (15° C), as in northeast Siberia. These temperature patterns and contrasts reflect the interaction of topography and atmospheric circulation. Arctic topography generally favours a northward movement of warm air in winter over the Atlantic sector, which explains the sharp longitudinal temperature gradients in the Arctic. The pole is kept warm in comparison to surrounding land by the existence of Arctic Ocean water below a relatively thin layer of ice. Precipitation is light and most of the zone is arid. Annual precipitation is generally less than 5 in. (130 mm) inland, while the coasts may receive close to 10 in. annually. This variance in precipitation is more pronounced in the case of the North American Arctic than in the Soviet Arctic. Cyclones and blizzards are common, as the generally tree-less land areas and the relatively smooth ice surfaces over the sea provide no friction against the wind.

Apart from the Greenland ice sheet, the glaciers in the continent are restricted to the eastern uplands of the Canadian Arctic and the maritime islands and peninsulas off northwestern Eurasia. Glaciers are generally characterized by extensive layers of ice built up on a flat land area and superimposing a roughly radial outflow of ice over the area. The Greenland glacier, covering an area of approximately 700,000 sq mi (1,800,000 sq km), is the largest glacier in the Northern Hemisphere. It is contained within a saucer-shaped depression, and in the centre the base of the ice is more than 1,000 ft below sea level. Iceland has five major glaciers, the largest of which, Vatnajö Kull, covers about 3,400 sq mi. Clique glaciers, occupying armchair-shaped hollows, are found in northeastern Siberia and the Brooks Mountain Range in Alaska. Glaciomarine deposits suggest that glaciers were active in the mountains facing the Gulf of Alaska 10,000,000–13,000,000 years ago, and glaciers probably existed in mountains bordering the Arctic 4,000,000–6,000,000 years ago. The North American and Eurasian ice sheets are in retreat, and the continued existence of the Greenland ice sheet is largely due to the fact that its depressed centre is essentially land-bound and thus shielded from sapping by sea.

The extensive area immediately surrounding the glaciers in the Arctic is characterized by the presence of permafrost. Permafrost is permanently frozen earth where the temperature is constantly below 0° C. In North America most of the Arctic area north of the tree line lies in a zone of continuous permafrost; in the Soviet Arctic the permafrost is continuous north of the tree line and east of the Ural Mountains. Near the northern coast of each continent, permafrost extends to depths of 1,640 to 1,970 ft, and nearly four-fifths of its volume is ice.

Three broadly concentric vegetation zones could be noted in the Arctic: low Arctic tundra, high Arctic tundra, and polar desert. Low Arctic tundra vegetation, the furthest from the pole, consists of dwarf shrubs, mosses, sedges, grasses, and lichens; it occurs in northern Alaska, southern Baffin Island, the southern coastal areas of Greenland, and a strip in the Soviet Arctic. The vegetation varies with soil moisture, and on well-drained sites it may include willow, birch, Arctic heather, and a carpet of moss; full of colourful flowers in summer, it changes to vivid tints of red and yellow at the onset of autumn. Toward the pole, plant cover becomes less complete and plant height decreases, thus high Arctic tundra vegetation consists largely of a more or less continuous cover of herbs and moss with occasional prostrate species. Polar desert vegetation is found on the northernmost tips of the continents reaching closest to the pole. It consists mainly of scattered cushion plants covering less than 10 percent of the ground surface.

Animal life is influenced both by vegetation characteristics and the climate. The zonal decrease in vegetation northward is mirrored by decreasing animal populations. The caribou occurs on the North American and Asian continents, and musk-ox roam most of the Arctic tundra. A huge population of geese inhabits eastern Greenland. Carnivores include the Arctic wolf, Arctic fox, and snowy owl. There are no reptiles in the Arctic, owing to the absence of frost-free winter refuges. The dominant feature of Arctic rivers is their intense seasonality of flow. Discharge during the summer is generally low but very sensitive to rainstorms, because permafrost and scanty vegetation provide little interception to rainwater. In the summer, water temperatures rise as high as 60° F (19° C), and thermal erosion causes riverbanks to collapse. Rivers whose basins lie wholly within the Arctic, such as the Colville in Alaska, hold hardly any water in winter. Rivers like the Ob and Mackenzie, however, whose headwaters lie in lower latitudes, maintain flow throughout the year.

The people. Though many nations participated in the exploration of the Arctic, only the Russians, Norwegians, Swedes, and Finns settled; Russians predominate numerically in the Arctic. The region is the most sparsely populated in the world. The settlement pattern is varied. Several cities in the Soviet Arctic have populations of more than 100,000, while in Greenland and Svalbard, towns have populations of less than 10,000. The chief native population groups are the Lapps of Europe, the Samoyeds of the western U.S.S.R., the Inuit (Eskimos) of North America, the Nordic Caucasians of Iceland, the Greenlanders (also Inuit in heritage) of Greenland, and the Yakuts, Tungus, Yukaghirs, and Chukchis of the eastern U.S.S.R. There has been considerable immigration since the 1930s, and in the late 1970s immigrants (defined as peoples arriving from a relatively developed southern culture who continue to draw support from that culture) outnumbered natives 7 to 1.

The economy. The inability to plant crops has been a fundamental constraint to economic activity, and yet almost all indigenous populations are self-sufficient, drawing almost entirely on resources from the sea. The waves of economic exploitation that have intruded into the Arctic from the rest of the world, however, are gradually transforming its economic landscape. Oil and other minerals are extracted from the Arctic by North American, European, Soviet, and Japanese companies. The coastal Arctic is exploited for seals and whales, and inland areas are exploited for furs.

Contrasts are visible in the Arctic development plans of the Soviet Union, Denmark and North America. The Soviet system is based on long-term planning, supported by massive investment over decades, for large-scale development. In the North American system, planning has tended to follow economic exploitation, and infrastructure investments take place only when necessitated by economic demands. The Danes, by artificially protecting Greenland from the rest of the world, have reduced economic exploitation and enabled themselves to carry out significant infrastructural development. Limited economic and strategic exploration is closely linked with lines of communication, which run inland from the more populated coastline to areas where one or more resources are exploited.

High labour and transport costs and tremendous capital investment are typical of all areas of the Arctic. Transient labour makes creation of a settled community difficult. The construction of transport arteries to link the Arctic with the main land masses is vital to long-term development. Indigenous populations of the Arctic generally have a low level of participation in development, and many have suffered the loss of land or resources essential to their traditional ways of life.

Administrative and social conditions. The Soviet Arctic, constituting by far the largest national unit within the Arctic region, is administered by the U.S.S.R., the Alaskan Arctic by the U.S., and the Canadian Arctic by Canada. The Norwegian Arctic of the Svalbard archipelago and the northern mainland is subject to the constitutional monarchy of Norway. Iceland is a parliamentary democracy with an elected president as head of state; Greenland is a self-governing part of the Danish realm.

Although the provision of health services is difficult in such terrain, standards in all countries are good. Health services on the North American continent in the early 1980s involved a vigorous attack on tuberculosis, which had become widespread. Nutritional intake is very high, because of the extreme climate; average food supplies per capita in the Arctic region range from 110 percent of the United Nation's recommended requirements in Iceland to as much as 158 percent on the Soviet mainland. Average life expectancy in the Arctic ranges from 62 years in Greenland to 75 years in Norway.

The encroachment of the cultural modes and standards of the nations that claim portions of the Arctic has tended to destroy the traditional cultures of the indigenous peoples of the region. Modern Arctic settlements range from isolated scientific research stations to sizable mining towns and local administrative centres with schools and churches.

History. The earliest inhabitants of the Arctic were probably the Paleo-Siberians, who lived in the unglaciated lowland of northeastern Siberia around 5000 BC. The first of two waves of hunting and gathering cultures emerged about 2000 BC, originating in Siberia and sweeping across Arctic Canada to northern Greenland. The second wave originated in the Bering straits about AD 10, and extended along the Canadian straits as far as Greenland. These large-scale migrations were probably due to environmental changes and availability of game. Hunting and gathering came to be gradually replaced by farming. In some areas the development of reindeer herding, which involved following the reindeer into the tundra in summer and retreating to the forests in winter, necessitated a nomadic existence.

The Russians were the first to explore the Arctic region with an expedition to Russia's northeastern lands in 1733 that lasted more than 10 years. Other smaller expeditions were directed principally toward geographic exploration of coastal lands. By the latter part of the 19th century most of the Arctic region's coastline had been charted. The 1879 expedition of G.W. DeLong in search of possible new lands north of Siberia ended when his ship sank, crushed by an ice pack. During 1893–96 the Norwegian explorer Fridtjof Nansen successfully navigated the ocean passage from the New Siberian Islands to Spitsbergen. In 1937 the Soviet Union landed an airplane equipped with skis on Arctic ice and established a scientific station.

The years following World War II (1939–45) led to the establishment and maintenance of Arctic weather and scientific observatories that accumulated an enormous body of data. In 1958 the USS "Nautilus" and "Skate" voyaged beneath the ice cap, and in 1978 the Soviet nuclear ice-breaker "Sibir" opened a southern passage across the coast of northern Siberia.

Arctic Circle, parallel, or line of latitude around the Earth, at approximately 66°30′ N. Because of the Earth's inclination of about 23½° to the vertical, it marks the southern limit of the area within which, for one day or more each year, the Sun does not set (about June 21) or rise (about December 21). The length of continuous day or night increases northward from one day on the Arctic Circle to six months at the North Pole. The Antarctic Circle is the southern counterpart of the Arctic Circle, where on any given date conditions of daylight or darkness are exactly opposite.

Arctic fox, also called WHITE FOX, or POLAR FOX (*Alopex lagopus*), northern fox of the family Canidae, found throughout the Arctic, usually on tundra or mountains near the sea. In adaptation to the climate, it has short, rounded ears, a short muzzle, and fur-

"White" phase of Arctic fox changing to its summer coat
Russ Kinne—Photo Researchers

covered soles. Length is about 50–60 centimetres (20–24 inches), exclusive of the 30-cm tail; and weight is about 3–8 kilograms (6.6–17 pounds). Coloration depends on whether the animal is of the "white" or the "blue" colour phase. Individuals of the white phase are grayish brown in summer and white in winter, while those of the blue phase (blue foxes of the fur trade) are grayish in summer and gray-blue in winter.

The Arctic fox is a burrow dweller and may be active at any time of day. It feeds on whatever animal or vegetable material is available and often follows polar bears to feed on the remains of their kills. It usually breeds once yearly, a litter of up to 14 dark-furred pups being born between April and June; gestation is about 52 days. Both the white and blue phases are valuable fur bearers.

Arctic Ocean, smallest of the world's oceans, centring approximately on the North Pole.

The article that follows is a summary of significant detail about the Arctic Ocean; for full treatment, *see* MACROPAEDIA: Arctic, The.

It is divided into four principal basins by three parallel submarine ridges. The Nansen Basin (due north of the Siberian mainland) lies between the Nansen cordillera and the Eurasian continental margin. The Fram Basin is situated farther north, between the Nansen cordillera and the Lomonosov Ridge. The Makarov Basin lies beyond, between the Lomonosov Ridge and the Alpha cordillera. The largest basin, the Canada, extends from the Beaufort Sea Shelf of North America to the Alpha cordillera. The ocean is almost completely surrounded by the landmasses of Eurasia, North America, and Greenland. The dream of a Northwest Passage attracted many explorers from the 16th century on, even though little was known of the region.

For tens of thousands of years inhabited mainly by Eskimo and Aleut, the Arctic Ocean basin began to attract western scientific inquiry in the 18th century. The Russian Second Kamchatka (or Great Northern) Expedition explored the Russian shores of the Arctic for 10 years, beginning in 1733. Fridtjof Nansen spent three years (1893–95) drifting across the Arctic in the "Fram," a ship specially designed to stay afloat in heavy ice. In the late 19th and early 20th centuries the U.S. explorer Robert E. Peary made several expeditions across parts of the Arctic, reportedly reaching the North Pole by sledge. The ocean was the focus of many cooperative scientific explorations such as the First and Second International Polar Years (1882–83, 1932–33) and the International Geophysical Year (1957–58). In 1958 the submarines USS "Nautilus" and "Skate" sailed beneath the Arctic ice cap. A southern passage through the ocean off the coast of Siberia was established in 1969 and 1970 by the ice-breaking tanker "Manhattan" and by a Soviet nuclear-powered icebreaker. Petroleum and mineral exploration are bringing more visitors and scientific study of the Arctic.

Large sea mammals are the most conspicuous form of polar wildlife, and the most important fish is the Arctic char, a member of the salmon family.

The Arctic peoples inhabiting the ocean-basin region are divided into the Eurasian and Western Arctic cultures. Eskimos inhabit the coastal areas of the western Arctic and are named for the regions that they inhabit, such as Siberian, North Alaskan, Mackenzie, Labrador, Polar, and Caribou. Most Eskimo groups are engaged in hunting and fishing activities, while the traditional economy of the Eurasian Arctic peoples is characterized by domestic reindeer herding. Eurasian peoples differ more among themselves on ethnic grounds than do the Eskimos and include peoples such as the Lapp, the Komi, the Mani, the Khant, and others. Area 4,732,000 sq mi (12,257,000 sq km); maximum depth 18,050 ft (5,502 m).

Arctolepis, extinct genus of Early Devonian fishlike animals, considered to be an early and primitive member of a group known as the arthrodires, or jointed-neck fishes (the Devonian Period began 395,000,000 years ago and lasted 50,000,000 years). *Arctolepis* had a bony head and trunk shield but was unarmoured behind the trunk region; the body tapered to a pointed tail; a tail fin was developed only on the lower margin of the tail. *Arctolepis* was a small animal, less than 30 centimetres (12 inches) in length but with enormously developed pectoral spines that must have been some aid to swimming but could hardly have been very efficient.

Arctolepis, of Early Devonian Period
By courtesy of the American Museum of Natural History, New York

Arcturus, also called ALPHA BOÖTIS, one of the five brightest stars in the night sky, and the brightest star in the northern constellation Boötes, with an apparent visual magnitude of 0.00. It is an orange-coloured giant star about 40 light-years from the Earth. It lies in an almost direct line with the tail of Ursa Major (the Great Bear); hence its name, derived from the Greek words for "bear guard."

Arculf (fl. late 7th century, Germany), bishop who was the earliest Western Christian traveller and observer of importance in the Near East after the rise of Islām. Although he most likely was connected with a monastery, some believe he was the bishop of Périgueux, Aquitaine.

On his return from a pilgrimage to the Holy Land (*c.* 680), he was driven by storm to Scotland and so arrived at the Hebridean island of Iona, where he related his experiences to his host, Abbot St. Adamnan. Adamnan's narrative of Arculf's journey, *De locis sanctis*, came to the attention of the Venerable Bede, who inserted a brief summary of it in his *Ecclesiastical History of the English People.* Bede also wrote a separate and longer digest that endured throughout the Middle Ages as a popular guidebook to the Eastern holy places.

Among the places Arculf visited were the sacred sites of Judaea, Samaria, and Galilee; Damascus and Tyre; and the Nile and the volcanic islands of Aeolia (modern Eolie Islands). He drew plans of the churches of the Holy Sepulchre and of Mt. Zion in Jerusalem, of the Ascension on Olivet, and of Jacob's Well at Shechem. His records also include the first form of the story of St. George, patron saint of England.

Ard Mhacha (Northern Ireland): *see* Armagh.

Arda River, Greek ÁRDHAS, river in Bulgaria, rising in the central Rhodope Mountains near the town of Smolyan, and following a 180-mi (290-km) course eastward past Kŭrdzhali and Ivaylovgrad to enter the Maritsa just west of Edirne, Tur., after a 23-mi course in Greece. The Bulgarian section has three hydroelectric and irrigation dams, among the largest in Bulgaria. In the upper valley are the mining towns of Rudozem, Madan, and Smolyan on the tributary Cherna River. The Arda Valley is known for its tobacco growing.

Ardaban (Persian statesman): *see* Artabanus.

Ardabīl, Turkish ERDEBIL, chief town of a district, Āzārbāijan-e Sharqī *ostān* (province), Iran, 38 mi (61 km) from the Caspian Sea. It stands on an open plain 4,500 ft (1,400 m) above sea level, just east of Mt. Sabalān (15,784 ft [4,811 m]), where cold spells occur until late spring. Persian historians have ascribed a founding date to the town in the Sāsānian period, but its known history does not begin until the Islāmic period. The town was taken by treaty by ʿAlī (*c.* 600–661), the fourth caliph. It was at that time the residence of the Sāsānian governor. The Umayyad governor made Ardabīl his capital, but the Arab hold on the region did not last. Local rulers fought continuously in the area until the Mongol conquest in 1220, when the town was destroyed. It lost all importance until Shaykh Ṣafī od-Dīn made it the centre of his Ṣūfī order in the 13th century, at the beginning of the rise of the Ṣafavid dynasty. Ardabīl became a Ṣafavid shrine, especially enriched by gifts from Ṣafavid rulers. Much of the library of the shrine, once the greatest in Iran, and many of the treasures were looted by the Russians after their sack of Ardabīl in 1827.

The town once shared in trade with Russia via the Caspian, but such activity has stagnated; industry consists of a cement factory and the making of carpets and rugs. Local warm mineral springs are frequented. The population speaks Azeri, a Turkic dialect. Pop. (1976) 147,404.

Ardabīl Carpet, Persian floor covering, among the most famous examples of early classical Persian workmanship. Measuring 34 feet by 17½ feet (10.4 by 5.3 metres), the carpet has a silk warp and wool pile. Woven at the behest of Shāh Esmāʿīl I (1501–24), the carpet was originally laid in the mosque of Ardabīl in the Iranian province of Azerbaijan. The carpet has a rich, exquisitely detailed and organized design, in which a deep-indigo field is covered with delicate, intricate floral tracery and a central medallion of pale yellow terminates in 16 minaret-shaped points with almond pendants.

The Ardabīl Carpet bears the inscription: "I have no refuge in the world other than thy threshold; My head has no protection other than this porch way; The work of the slave of the Holy Place, Maksoud of Kashan, in the year 942 [AD 1539–40]." It is now in the Victoria and Albert Museum, London.

Ardagh Chalice, large, two-handled silver cup, decorated with gold, gilt bronze, and enamel, that is one of the best known examples of Irish ecclesiastical metalwork. It was discovered in 1868, together with a small bronze cup and four brooches, in a potato field in Ardagh, County Limerick, Ire. The decoration consists

Ardagh Chalice, chased silver with gold inlay, gilt bronze, and enamel, Irish, *c.* 720; in the National Museum of Ireland, Dublin

By courtesy of the National Museum of Ireland, Dublin

principally of panels of fine gold and silver filigree applied to the otherwise plain body of the vessel. Studs set with coloured enamels are arranged at intervals amid the filigree decoration, which combines interlaced animal forms and spirals with repeating abstract patterns. The outside of the bowl is engraved with the Latin names of some of the Apostles. There are similarities between the letters of this inscription and some of the large initials in the celebrated Lindisfarne Gospels, which probably dates from about AD 710–720. Thus, the Ardagh Chalice is thought to date from the first half of the 8th century.

It has so far proved impossible to attribute its manufacture to any particular workshop, but affinities do exist between the filigree decoration on the chalice and the decoration of the celebrated Tara brooch. Another well-known example of Irish ecclesiastical metalwork, the Moylough belt-reliquary is also decorated in a similar manner. It is likely that the Ardagh Chalice formed part of the treasury of some early Irish church or monastery, until it was disestablished and the cup was concealed for safekeeping. It is now housed in the National Museum of Ireland at Dublin.

Ardashīr, Old Persian ARTAKHSHATHRA, name of Sāsānian kings, grouped below chronologically and indicated by the symbol •.

• **Ardashīr I** (fl. mid-3rd century), the founder of the Sāsānian Empire in ancient Persia (reigned AD 224–241). He was the son of Bābak, the son or descendant of Sāsān, and a vassal of the chief petty king in Persis, Gochihr. After Bābak got Ardashīr the military post of *argabad* in the town of Dārābgerd (near mod-

Ardashīr I, coin, 3rd century; in the British Museum

By courtesy of the trustees of the British Museum; photograph, J.R. Freeman & Co. Ltd.

ern Darab, Iran), Ardashīr extended control over several neighbouring cities. Meanwhile, Bābak had slain Gochihr and taken the title of king. Although Bābak's request that the Parthian king Artabanus V allow him to transmit the crown to his eldest son, Shāpūr, was refused, Shāpūr nevertheless succeeded him. In the ensuing struggle between him and Ardashīr, Shāpūr was killed, and Ardashīr was crowned king of Persis in 208. Having suppressed a revolt in Dārābgerd, he gradually conquered the neighbouring province of Kermān and the coastal Persian Gulf lands. He made his capital at Gūr (modern Fīrūzābād), which he renamed Ardashīr-Kwarrah.

Ardashīr then moved against western Iran, taking Isfahan, Kerman, Elymais, and Mesene. Withdrawing again to Persis, in AD 224 he met the Parthian army at Hormizdagān (site unknown) and won a decisive victory, slaying Artabanus. Soon after, Ardashīr entered the Parthian capital of Ctesiphon, in Mesopotamia, in triumph and was crowned "king of kings of Iran."

With his son and successor, Shāpūr I, Ardashīr established the Sāsānian Empire. Nothing is known of Ardashīr's personal life; his deeds, however, indicate that he was ruthless, a great soldier, and a capable king. He founded or rebuilt many cities and is credited with digging canals and building bridges. Several great rock carvings commemorate his reign.

Ardashīr made Zoroastrianism the state religion, and he and his priest Tosar are credited with collecting the holy texts and establishing a unified doctrine. Two treatises, *The Testament of Ardashīr* and *The Letter of Tosar,* are attributed to them. As patron of the church, Ardashīr appears in Zoroastrian tradition as a sage. As founder of the dynasty, he is celebrated in a 5th-century book in Pahlavi, the *Karnamag-i Ardashīr.*

• **Ardashīr II** (fl. late 4th century), king of the Sāsānian Empire in ancient Persia (reigned AD 379–383). During the reign of his brother Shāpūr II, he had been king of Adiabene (now a region of northeast Iraq), where he took part in the persecution of the Christians. After Shāpūr's death, he was set on the throne by the nobles, presumably at an advanced age. His investiture is commemorated in a rock carving at Ṭāq-e Bostān. His attempts to assert himself were futile, and he was soon deposed.

Ardea, ancient town of the Rutuli, now a modern village in the Italian region of Lazio, 23 miles (37 kilometres) south of Rome. In ancient times it was an important centre of Danaë and Juno cults.

Originally Ardea was an Early Iron Age settlement (early 8th century BC) that developed into one of the most important Latin cities, a member of the Latin leagues of the 6th and 5th centuries BC. In 444 the town signed a treaty with the Romans, who, according to Livy, colonized it as a barrier against the Volsci. The decline of Ardea, from the 4th century onward, was hastened by malaria and the wars under Marius and Sulla in the 1st century BC. Pop. (1971) 1,598.

Ardèche, *département,* Rhône-Alpes region, southern France, formed in 1790 from the Vivarais district of Languedoc. On the Cévennes edge of the Massif Central, it is a highland region (area 2,132 sq mi [5,523 sq km]), deeply scored by torrents feeding the Ardèche River flowing to the Rhône, which forms its eastern boundary. North of the Ardèche Valley, the volcanic hills of the Coirons jut out southeast toward the Rhône Valley, and in the west Mount Mézenc, part of the Velay volcanic plateau, rises to 5,755 ft (1,754 m). The upper Allier River forms part of the western boundary. The sheltered valleys near the Rhône are warm, but winter is severe on the higher ground.

Fruit trees, vines, even olives are grown in the lower valleys, and some meadows are irrigated to bring in more than one hay crop each summer. Cereals, potatoes, and fodder crops grow in the bottom lands, and chestnuts are harvested as high as 2,500 ft. Mulberry cultivation (for silkworms) on the hillside terraces has greatly declined. However, several textile mills remain active, using local hydropower. There are still high summer pastures for sheep and cattle but the heights are almost denuded of woodlands. The *département* has large cement plants along the Rhône Valley, but neither the minor exploitation of small ore deposits nor thermal springs adds much to the departmental economy.

The main road from Le Puy to the Rhône Valley traverses the region by the Ardèche Valley. Privas, the capital, heads an *arrondissement,* as do Largentière and Tournon. The court of appeal is outside the *département* at Nîmes. The countryside, especially in the west, has become depopulated during the last century; Annonay is the largest town in a region of small settlements. Pop. (1982) 267,970.

Arden, John (b. Oct. 26, 1930, Barnsley, Yorkshire, Eng.), one of the most important of the British playwrights to emerge in the mid-20th century; his plays mix poetry and songs with colloquial speech in a boldly theatrical manner and involve strong conflicts purposely left unresolved.

Arden grew up in the industrial town of Barnsley, the personality of which he captured in his play *The Workhouse Donkey* (1963). He studied architecture at the University of Cambridge and at Edinburgh College of Art, where fellow students performed his comedy *All Fall Down* (1955), about the construction of a railway. He continued to write plays while working as an architectural assistant from 1955 to 1957. His first play to be produced professionally was a radio drama, *The Life of Man* (1956), about the fatal voyage of a boat captained by a madman. *Waters of Babylon* (1957), a play with a roguish but unjudged central character, revealed the moral ambiguity that troubled critics and audiences in later dramas. His next two plays, *Live Like Pigs* (1958) and *Serjeant Musgrave's Dance* (1959), also caused controversy.

In 1957 Arden married Margaretta D'Arcy, actress and playwright, with whom he wrote a number of stage pieces and improvisational works for amateur and student players. *The Happy Haven,* produced in 1960 in London, is a sardonic farce about an old people's home. *The Workhouse Donkey* is a crowded, exuberant, and comic drama of municipal politics. *Armstrong's Last Goodnight* (1964), written in lowland Scots vernacular, is a drama of struggle between a courtier and a freebooter, pointing to resemblances between 16th-century Scotland, its setting, and the contemporary Congo. *Left-Handed Liberty* (1965), written on the occasion of the 750th anniversary of the signing of Magna Carta, characteristically dwells on the failure of the document to achieve liberty. *The True History of Squire Jonathan and His Unfortunate Treasure* (1968) is an erotic "duologue" adapted to the then current fad of nudity on stage, and *The Island of the Mighty* (1972), written in collaboration with Margaretta D'Arcy, is a non-Romantic ballet-drama about King Arthur. Later plays include *The Non-Stop Connolly Cycle* (1975), *Vandaleur's Folly* (1978), and *The Little Gray Home in the West* (1978).

Ardennes, also spelled ARDENNE, wooded plateau covering part of the ancient Forest of Ardennes, occupying most of the Belgian provinces of Luxembourg, Namur, and Liège; part of the Grand Duchy of Luxembourg; and the French *département* of Ardennes. It is an

The wooded hills of the Ardennes in Belgium
Thomas B. Hollyman—Photo Researchers

old plateau comprising the western extension of the Middle Rhine Highlands, stretching in a northeast-southwest direction and covering more than 3,860 sq mi (10,000 sq km). Its geological history is complex; as a result of intense folding, faulting, uplifts, and denudations, some older strata of rock have been thrust over younger strata.

The name Ardennes used in a strict sense refers to the southern half of the area, where the elevations range from 1,150 to 1,640 ft [350 to 500 m], though the high point at Botrange, south of Liège, is 2,277 ft. This part consists of sandstone, quartzite, and some slate and limestone. Its rounded summits are separated by shallow depressions containing peat bogs, from which rise many rivers that cut narrow and sinuous valleys. These High Ardennes form the watershed between rivers flowing north and west to the Meuse River and south and east to the Moselle River. Heavy precipitation, combined with low clouds, fog, and frost, make the uplands distinctly bleak. Although one-half of the area is covered by forest, the thin, acid, and waterlogged soil is generally infertile, supporting only heath.

The northern part is much lower, between 655 and 985 ft. Most of the small farmland is under permanent grass for pasture, but there is some cultivation of oats, rye, potatoes, and clover in the valleys. Cattle are raised mainly for dairy production, pigs for the ham that has long been a local specialty of the Ardennes, and sheep for a small wool industry. Cattle hides are processed with the abundant local supplies of tannin from the oak trees. Stone quarrying is widespread, but mining and manufacturing are limited.

Despite a certain raw inhospitality of the area, its economy increasingly depends upon the development of tourism. The Ardennes has one of the lowest population densities of Europe, but it is located in the middle of the heavily populated triangle of Paris-Brussels-Cologne. Mineral springs at Spa, Belg. (whence the English word spa), have made it a favourite health resort since the 16th century. The lonely forests offer respites for central Europeans from the pressures of the surrounding urbanization.

During World Wars I and II, the Ardennes became a battleground, the scene of bitter fighting in 1914, 1918, and 1944 (Battle of the Bulge; *q.v.*).

Ardennes, *département,* Champagne-Ardennes region, northeastern France, bordering on Belgium, covering an area of 2,015 sq mi (5,219 sq km) and including the southwest margin of the Ardennes highland and the adjacent lowlands in the Meuse and Aisne valleys, which are connected by the Ardennes Canal. The Meuse turns northwest after leaving Lorraine, and from Charleville-Mézières to Givet on the frontier it flows in deeply entrenched meanders, some of which provide defensive points marked by castle towns. The rugged Argonne Massif pushes north into the southeastern part of the *département,* drained by the Aisne River. The Aisne Valley and the flanking chalk country are well cultivated (grains and sugar beets), but there are heavy forests in the Argonne and Ardennes.

Although unfavourable terrain for manoeuvre, the region has been the scene of battles since the French Revolution, including the campaign of 1794, the Franco-German War (with Napoleon III's surrender at Sedan, 1870), the Battle of the Ardennes in World War I and the bitter U.S.-German fighting in the Argonne in 1918, the German breakthrough near Sedan in 1940 that marked the Battle of France, and the final offensive action in France by the Germans in December 1944 (Battle of the Bulge; *q.v.*).

Sedan on the Meuse and Rethel on the Aisne have long-established woollen mills. Charleville-Mézières has wood-working and iron industries. There is a nuclear power plant at Chooz (270 mW; operational since 1967). Charleville-Mézières (the capital), Sedan, Rethel, and Vouziers head *arrondissements.* The appeal court is at Nancy, and education is directed from Reims. Pop. (1982) 302,338.

Ardennes, Battle of the (1944–45): *see* Bulge, Battle of the.

Ardhanārīśvara (Sanskrit: Lord Who Is Half Woman), composite male-female figure of the Hindu god Śiva, together with his consort Pārvatī. As seen in many beautiful Indian and Southeast Asian sculptures, the right (male) half of the figure is adorned with the traditional ornaments of Śiva. Half of the hair is piled in a hairdress of matted locks, half of a third eye is visible on the forehead, a tiger skin covers the loins, and serpents are used as ornaments. The left (female) half shows hair well combed and knotted, half of a *tilaka* (a round dot) on the forehead, the eye outlined in black, one well-developed breast, a silk garment caught with girdles, an anklet, and the foot tinted red with henna.

The symbolic intent of the figure accord-

Ardhanārīśvara, stone sculpture, Cōḷa period; in the Nāgeśvarasvāmin temple, Kumbakonam, India
By courtesy of the Archaeological Survey of India, New Delhi

ing to most authorities is to signify that the male and female principles are inseparable. A popular explanation, as given in a collection of legends known as the *Śiva-Purāṇa,* is that Brahmā created male beings and instructed them in turn to create others, but they were unable to do so. When Śiva appeared before him in an androgynous form, Brahmā realized his omission and created females. Yet another legend has it that the sage (*ṛṣi*) Bhṛṅgi had vowed to worship only one deity and so failed to circumambulate and to prostrate himself before Pārvatī. Pārvatī tried to force him to do so by asking to be united with her lord, but the sage assumed the form of a beetle and continued to circumambulate only the male half, whereupon Pārvatī became reconciled and blessed Bhṛṅgi.

Árdhas (Europe): *see* Arda River.

Ardmore, city, seat (1907) of Carter County, southern Oklahoma, U.S., north of the Red River, near Lake Texoma and the Texas state line. Founded in 1887 in Chickasaw Indian Territory after the arrival of the Santa Fe Railway, the town was named for the Philadelphia, Pa., suburb that was the home of a Santa Fe official. It developed as the business centre of a large cattle and farming region and grew rapidly after the discovery of oil nearby in 1905.

Oil refining, manufacturing, ranching, tourism, and wholesaling are the major economic activities of the city. Ardmore is the site of Carter Seminary for Chickasaw Indian Girls (formerly Hargrove College; Methodist, founded 1895). Lake Murray State Park and the Chickasaw National Recreation Area (embracing Arbuckle Mountains) are nearby. Inc. 1898. Pop. (1980) 23,689.

Articles are alphabetized word by word, not letter by letter

Ards, Irish AN AIRD, district, Northern Ireland. Formerly within County Down, in 1973 Ards was established as a district with an area of 139 sq mi (361 sq km). It extends northward from just south of the village of Killinchy along the western shoreline of Strangford Lough (inlet of the sea) to the town of Newtownards and encompasses the peninsula of land east of Strangford Lough. Bordered by North Down and Castlereagh districts to the northwest and Down district to the southwest, Ards is composed of relatively dry, rolling lowlands in the west; the peninsula is characterized by clusters of drumlins (oval mounds of glacial till). Newtownards, settled *c.* 1608 by Scots of the Montgomery clan at the site of a Dominican friary (now in ruins), is the district's administrative seat and manufacturing centre with textile, metal, and engineering industries. Much of the district's land is devoted to crops (potatoes and barley) and pastureland. Donaghadee, at the northeastern end of the peninsula, is a popular resort town, and bird sanctuaries are found along the lough-side. Roads extending throughout the district merge with a national highway at Newtownards, then run westward to Belfast. Pop. (1981) 57,626.

Arduino, Giovanni (b. Oct. 16, 1714, Caprino Veronese, Veneto, Republic of Venice—d. March 21, 1795, Venice), the father of Italian geology, who established bases for stratigraphic chronology by classifying the four main layers of the Earth's crust as Primary, Secondary, Tertiary, and Quaternary.

From an early age, Arduino showed an interest in mining, establishing a reputation throughout northern Italy as a mining expert, and in 1769 the Republic of Venice named him director of agriculture and industry. With occasional help from his brother Pietro (1728–1805), a botanist at the University of Padua, Arduino supervised such enterprises as land reclamation, livestock raising, and the construction of improved agricultural equipment. He also did research in mining, metallurgy, and chemistry for the republic.

In the early 1760s Arduino indentified four distinct major geological strata composed of numerous fossil-filled minor strata. He also recognized the significance of the fossil layers and pioneered the use of fossils and chemical methods to determine the age of rock formations.

are, basic metric unit of area measure, equal to 100 square metres. Its multiple, the hectare (*q.v.*), has become the principal unit of land measurement in common use.

area, culture: *see* culture area.

areca nut: *see* betel.

Arecales, order of flowering plants that contains only one family, the palms (Palmae). About 2,600 species are known. *See* palm.

Arecibo, town and municipality, northern Puerto Rico, on a small inlet near the mouth of the Arecibo River. One of the oldest municipalities in the commonwealth, it was authorized in 1537 by the Spanish crown and settled in 1556. In 1616 it was chartered as a town and in 1778 received the royal title *villa.* An official U.S. port of entry, the town has Puerto Rico's largest rum distilleries and produces agricultural machinery, clothing, paper, plastics, and sporting goods; it is linked by rail to San Juan. The town has a regional college of the University of Puerto Rico.

The municipality, with an area of 127 sq mi (329 sq km), is the island's largest. It is crossed by the Arecibo River. The alluvial lowlands produce sugarcane, pineapples, and coffee. Two major dams, the Dos Bocas and the Caonillas, harness the lower Arecibo River system. South of Arecibo town is one of the world's most powerful radar-radio telescopes, a 1,000-ft (300-m) installation used for space research. The Arecibo municipality has produced several noted writers, including Manuel Zeno Gandia (1855–1930), author of *La Charca.* Pop. (1980) town, 48,779; mun., 86,766.

Arecibo Observatory, astronomical observatory located 16 kilometres (10 miles) south of the city of Arecibo, P.R.; it is the site of the world's largest single-unit radio telescope. This instrument, built in the early 1960s, employs a 300-metre (1,000-foot) spherical reflector consisting of perforated aluminum panels that focus incoming radio waves on movable antenna structures positioned about 168 m (550 ft) above the reflector surface. The antenna structures can be moved in any direction, making it possible to track a celestial object in different regions of the sky. The observatory also has an auxiliary 30-m (100-ft) telescope that serves as a radio interferometer (*q.v.*) and a high-power transmitting facility used to heat and study the Earth's atmosphere.

The Arecibo Observatory conducts radar studies of the Earth's ionosphere, the asteroids, and the planets. Such work has yielded detailed radar maps of the surface of Venus and precise information about the planet's rotation. The observatory also has made such significant contributions to radio astronomy as the detection of neutron star matter in pulsars.

Arecibo River, Spanish in full RÍO GRANDE DE ARECIBO, river in west central Puerto Rico, rising in the Cordillera Central just east of Mt. Guilarte, at 3,949 ft (1,204 m) above sea level. It flows north-northeast about 40 mi (65 km) through the Utuado municipality, a coffee region, and descends across the humid northern coastal plain to empty into the Atlantic Ocean just east of the port of Arecibo. At the northern edge of the cordilleran foothills, the river is impounded by the Dos Bocas hydroelectric dam and reservoir system (1943), which is linked to the even larger Caonillas hydroelectric dam and reservoir upstream on the Caonillas, a tributary.

Aremorica (area, ancient Gaul): *see* Armorica.

arena, central area of an amphitheatre (*q.v.*).

Arena Chapel, also called SCROVEGNI CHAPEL (consecrated March 25, 1305), small chapel built in the first years of the 14th century in Padua, Italy, by Enrico Scrovegni and containing frescoes by the Florentine painter Giotto. A "Last Judgment" covers the entire west wall. The rest of the chapel is covered with frescoes in three tiers representing scenes from the lives of SS. Joachim and Anna, the life of the Virgin, the Annunciation, and the Life and Passion of Christ, concluding with the Pentecost. Below the three narrative bands is a fourth containing monochrome personifications of the virtues and vices. The frescoes were completed in or before 1309, and they are generally dated *c.* 1305–06.

arena stage: *see* theatre-in-the-round.

Arend-Roland, Comet, comet remarkable for its anomalous second tail, which projects toward rather than away from the Sun. It was discovered on the night of Nov. 8–9, 1956, by S. Arend and P. Roland in Belgium. Its perihelion passage (*i.e.,* its closest approach to the Sun) occurred on April 20, 1957. Because it was discovered months before perihelion, lengthy observations could be carried out. The anomalous tail appeared for a few nights late in April, changing direction from night to night and appearing as a sharp spike aimed at the Sun. This appearance was an effect of perspective, of viewing edgewise a fan of debris from the comet, scattered ahead of it along its orbit.

Arendal, town, port, and seat of Aust-Agder *fylke* (county), southern Norway. Its excellent harbour is on Tromøysundet, a protected sound sheltered by the offshore island of Tromøy. A port since the 14th century, Arendal had the largest fleet in Norway before the steamship era. From the 16th century it prospered from timber exports. Some timber is still floated down the Nidelva (river), emptying into the Skagerrak (strait between Norway and Denmark), at Arendal. Besides sawmilling, chief industries include metal processing and fabricating (particularly electrical appliances) and food and tobacco processing. Poultry hatcheries are of regional importance.

Arendal is one of the most important coastal shipping centres of Norway and the terminus of a branch of the Oslo–Kristiansand rail line and of a car ferry crossing the Skagerrak to Hirtshals, Den. Its four-story town hall is one of the largest wooden buildings in Norway. The historic battery, overlooking the harbour, was used during the war that forced Denmark to cede Norway to Sweden (1814). Pop. (1983 est.) 11,743.

Arendt, Hannah (b. Oct. 14, 1906, Hannover, Ger.—d. Dec. 4, 1975, New York City), German-born U.S. political scientist and philosopher known for her critical writing on Jewish affairs and her study of totalitarianism.

Arendt was educated at the universities of Marburg, Freiburg, and Heidelberg, where she received her Ph.D. in 1928. When the Nazis came to power in Germany in 1933, she fled to Paris, where she served as a social worker and in 1940 married Heinrich Bluecher, a philosophy professor. She again became a fugitive from the Nazis the following year.

In New York City she served as research director of the Conference on Jewish Relations (1944–46), chief editor of Schocken Books (1946–48), and executive director (1949–52) of Jewish Cultural Reconstruction, Inc., which sought to salvage Jewish writings dispersed by the Nazis. She became a U.S. citizen in 1951.

In her monumental *Origins of Totalitarianism* (1951) Arendt related the development of totalitarianism to 19th-century anti-Semitism and imperialism and saw its growth as the outcome of the disintegration of the traditional nation-state. Totalitarian regimes, she argued, because of their pursuit of raw political power and neglect of material or utilitarian considerations, have revolutionized the social structure and made contemporary politics nearly unpredictable. That work established her as a major political thinker. She was invited to lecture at major U.S. universities and served on the faculty of the University of Chicago (1963–67) and thereafter at the New School for Social Research, New York City.

Eichmann in Jerusalem (1963), in which she emphasized what she viewed as the cooperative role of Jewish community leaders in facilitating Nazi extermination of the Jews during World War II, stimulated much debate. Among her other works are *The Human Condition* (1958), *Between Past and Future* (1961), *On Revolution* (1963), *Men in Dark Times* (1968), *On Violence* (1970), and *Crises of the Republic* (1972).

Arenig Series, post-Tremadoc division of Ordovician rocks (the Ordovician Period began about 500,000,000 years ago and lasted about 70,000,000 years). The Arenig was first studied in northern Wales, where the series attains a thickness of about 1,200 metres (4,000 feet). Rocks correlated with the Arenig have a worldwide distribution, but different series names are applied in different regions. Two graptolite fossil zones, shorter spans of time, are generally recognized in the Arenig: a lower zone of the species *Didymograptus extensus* and an upper zone of *D. hirundo.* In some regions, especially the Baltic–Scandinavian area, the Arenig is characterized by the dominance of trilobites, of which the genus *Asaphus* is prominent. As in Great Britain, the Arenig of Scandinavia coincides with the first phase of the Caledonian orogeny.

Elsewhere in the world, equivalents of the Arenig are prominent in the Soviet Union, southern China, and especially Australia. In the Australian Tasman Geosyncline, numerous graptolite zones are recognized. In South America the Arenig has been recognized in western Argentina.

arenite, any sedimentary rock that consists of sand-sized particles (0.06–2 millimetres

[0.0024–0.08 inch] in diameter), irrespective of composition. More formal nomenclature of such rocks is based on composition, particle size, and mode of origin; *e.g.*, sandstone, arkose, quartzite, graywacke, and subgraywacke.

Arensky, Anton (Stepanovich) (b. Aug. 11 [July 30, old style], 1861, Novgorod, Russia—d. Feb. 25 [Feb. 12, O.S.], 1906, Terijoki, Finland, Russian Empire), Russian composer known especially for his chamber music and his songs. Though a composition student of Rimsky-Korsakov, he was more akin to Tchaikovsky; the predominant moods of his music are lyrical and elegiac. Of his three operas only the first, *A Dream on the Volga* (Moscow, 1892), was successful. His *Piano Trio in D Minor* and *String Quartet in A Minor* show him at his best. His piano pieces, which exceed 100 in number, include four suites for two pianos. Besides conducting in Moscow, he held teaching posts at the Moscow Conservatory (1882–95) and the directorship of the imperial chapel at St. Petersburg (1895–1901).

Arensky
Novosti Press Agency

Areopagus, low hill northwest of the Acropolis in ancient Athens, noted as the meeting place of the earliest aristocratic council of the city, the name being extended to denote the council itself.

The Areopagite Council probably began as the king's advisers. Early in the Archaic period it exercised a general and ill-defined authority until the publication of Draco's Code of Law (*c.* 621). Membership continued for life and was secured by having served as archon, an office limited to the eupatrids (Greek *eupatridai,* "nobles by birth"). Under Solon (archon 594 BC), the composition and authority of the council were materially altered when the archonship was opened to all with certain property qualifications, and a Boule, a rival council of 400, was set up. The Areopagus nevertheless retained "guardianship of the laws" (perhaps a legislative veto); it tried prosecutions under the law of *eisangelia* ("impeachment") for unconstitutional acts. As a court under the presidency of the *archōn basileus,* it also decided cases of murder.

For about 200 years, from the middle of the 6th century BC, the prestige of the Areopagus fluctuated. The fall of the Peisistratids, who during their tyranny (546–510) had filled the archonships with their adherents, left the Areopagus full of their nominees and thus in low esteem; its reputation was restored by its patriotic posture during the Persian invasion. In 462 the reformer Ephialtes deprived the Areopagus of virtually all its powers save jurisdiction on homicide (*c.* 462). From the middle of the 4th century BC, its prestige revived once again, and by the period of Roman domination in Greece it was again discharging significant administrative, religious, and educational functions.

Arequipa, department (formed 1822), southern Peru, bounded on the southwest by the Pacific. Its area of 24,528 sq mi (63,528 sq km) comprises an arid but irrigated coastal region, cut intermittently by streams flowing from a mountainous, partly volcanic, upland zone. Coastal crops include cotton, rice, sugarcane, and olives. Corn (maize), potatoes, and cereals are cultivated in the uplands, which are also important for livestock grazing, mainly sheep. Large quantities of alpaca wool are exported. Mining is also important, with gold, silver, copper, and lead among the leading mineral products. Matarani and Mollendo are major coastal ports; the city of Arequipa (*q.v.*), the capital, is in the mountains. In the southeast, Mollendo is connected by rail, via the capital, with Cuzco and Puno departments. The Pan-American Highway provides access to Chile. Pop. (1984 est.) 798,200.

Arequipa, city, southern Peru, capital of Arequipa province and department, standing at more than 7,550 ft (2,300 m) above sea level, in the Río Chili Valley. In the Inca Empire it was an important point on the route from Cuzco to the seacoast. Refounded in 1540 on orders from the conquistador Francisco Pizarro to establish a stronghold in the region, its original name was Nuestra Señora de la Asunción del Valle Hermoso (Our Lady of the Assumption of the Beautiful Valley). Arequipa lies at the foot of snowcapped Misti Volcano, which has an elevation of 19,101 ft (5,822 m). Several other snowcapped mountains add to its scenic backdrop. Earthquakes, usually associated with volcanic activity, have damaged the city several times; there was a severe earthquake in the 1960s. The air is dry, and the climate is pleasant, with a yearly rainfall of about 4 in. (100 mm) and an annual average temperature of 58° F (14° C).

The cathedral at Arequipa city, Peru, with Misti Volcano in the background
Walter Aguiar—EB Inc.

The fertile soils of the surrounding district produce a variety of crops, notably cereals and pasturage. Arequipa is the nation's wool-processing centre and has diversified industries. It is the commercial, political, and military centre of southern Peru, easily accessible by air, rail, and highway.

The city is one of the most picturesque in the country, with many buildings constructed of sillar, a local white volcanic stone. The seat of an archbishopric, Arequipa has a cathedral (founded 1612) and several churches dating from the Spanish colonial period. The National University of San Agustín was founded there in 1828 and the Catholic University of Santa María in 1961. It is also a popular tourist centre, with bathing resorts, hot springs, and Inca remains in the vicinity. Pop. (1981 prelim.) city, 447,431; province, 498,347.

Arequipa, Volcán de (Peru): *see* Misti Volcano.

Ares, in Greek religion, god of war or, more properly, the spirit of battle. Unlike his Roman counterpart, Mars (*q.v.*), he was never very popular, and his worship was not extensive in Greece. He represented the distasteful aspects of brutal warfare and slaughter. From at least the time of Homer, who established him as the son of the chief god, Zeus, and Hera, his consort, Ares was one of the Olympian deities; his fellow gods and even his parents, however, were not fond of him (*Iliad* v, 889 ff.). Nonetheless, he was accompanied in battle, by his sister Eris (Strife) and his sons (by Aphrodite) Phobos and Deimos (Panic and Rout). Also associated with him were two lesser war deities: Enyalius, who is virtually identical with Ares himself, and Enyo, a female counterpart.

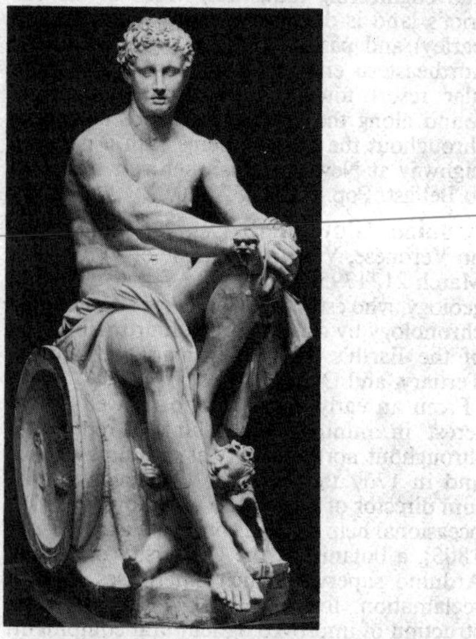
Ares, classical sculpture; in the Museo Nazionale Romano, Rome
Anderson—Alinari from Art Resource/EB Inc.

Ares' worship was largely in the northern areas of Greece, and, although devoid of the social, moral, and theological associations usual with major deities, his cult had many interesting local features. At Sparta, in early times, at least, human sacrifices were made to him from among the prisoners of war. At Sparta also a nocturnal offering of dogs—an unusual sacrificial victim, which might indicate a chthonic (infernal) deity—was made to him as Enyalius. During his festival at Geronthrae in Laconia, no women were allowed in the sacred grove, but at Tegea he was honoured in a special women's sacrifice as Gynaikothoinas (Entertainer of Women). At Athens he had a temple at the foot of the Areopagus (Ares' Hill).

The mythology surrounding the figure of Ares is not extensive. He was associated with Aphrodite from earliest times; in fact, Aphrodite was known locally (*e.g.*, at Sparta) as a war goddess, apparently an early facet of her character. Occasionally, Aphrodite was Ares' legitimate wife, and by her he fathered Deimos, Phobos, and Harmonia. By Aglauros, the daughter of Cecrops, he was the father of Alcippe. He was the sire of at least two of Heracles' adversaries: Cycnus and Diomedes of Thrace. On vases, Ares is usually the typical armed warrior. The Parthenon frieze contains a group of Olympians, among whom Ares, in unwarlike garb, has been tentatively identified. He also appears on the great frieze of the altar at Pergamum.

Aretaeus OF CAPPADOCIA (fl. 2nd century AD), Greek physician from Cappadocia who practiced in Rome and Alexandria, led a revival of Hippocrates' teachings, and is thought to have ranked second only to the father of medicine himself in the application of keen observation and ethics to the art. In principle he adhered to the pneumatic school of medicine, which believed that health was maintained by "vital air," or *pneuma.* Pneumatists felt that an imbalance of the four humours—blood, phlegm, choler (yellow bile), and melancholy (black bile)—disturbed the *pneuma,* a condition indicated by an abnormal pulse. In practice, however, Aretaeus was an eclectic physician, since he utilized the methods of several different schools.

After his death he was entirely forgotten until 1554, when two of his manuscripts, *On the Causes and Indications of Acute and Chronic Diseases* (4 vol.) and *On the Treatment of Acute and Chronic Diseases* (4 vol.), both written in the Ionic dialect, were discovered. These works not only include model descriptions of pleurisy, diphtheria, tetanus, pneumonia, asthma, and epilepsy but also show that he was first to distinguish between spinal and cerebral paralyses. He gave diabetes its name (from the Greek word for siphon, indicative of the diabetic's intense thirst and excessive emission of fluids) and rendered the earliest clear account of the disease now known.

arête (French: "ridge"), sharp-crested serrate ridge separating the heads of opposing valleys (cirques) that formerly were occupied by Alpine glaciers. It has steep sides formed by the collapse of unsupported rock, undercut by continual freezing and thawing (glacial sapping; *see* cirque). Two opposing glaciers meeting at an arête will carve a low, smooth gap, or col. An arête may culminate in a high triangular peak or horn (such as the Matterhorn) formed by three or more glaciers eroding toward each other.

Arethusa, in Greek mythology, a nymph who gave her name to a spring in Elis and to another on the island of Ortygia, near Syracuse.

The river god Alpheus fell in love with Arethusa, who was in the retinue of Artemis; Arethusa fled to Ortygia, where she was

Arethusa on a silver coin from the workshop of Euainetos, *c.* 413 BC; in the Museo Archeologico Nazionale, Syracuse, Sicily

Konrad Helbig

changed into a spring. Alpheus, however, made his way beneath the sea and united his waters with those of the spring. According to Ovid's *Metamorphoses,* Arethusa, while bathing in the Alpheius River, was seen and pursued by the river god in human form. Artemis changed her into a spring that, flowing underground, emerged at Ortygia.

In an earlier form of the legend, it was Artemis, not Arethusa, who was the object of the god's affections and who escaped by smearing her face with mire, so that he failed to recognize her. The story probably originated from the fact that Artemis Alpheiaia was worshipped in both Elis and Ortygia and also that the Alpheius in its upper part runs underground.

Aretino, Leonardo: *see* Bruni, Leonardo.

Aretino, Pietro (b. April 20, 1492, Arezzo, Republic of Florence—d. Oct. 21, 1556, Venice), poet, prose writer, and dramatist celebrated throughout Europe in his time for his bold and insolent literary attacks on the powerful. His fiery letters and dialogues are of great biographical and topical interest, and his

Aretino, detail of an oil painting by Titian, in the Frick Collection, New York

tragedy, *Orazia,* and his five comedies have been judged by some as the best of his period.

Although Aretino was the son of an Arezzo shoemaker, he later pretended to be the bastard son of a nobleman and derived his adopted name ("the Aretine") from that of his native city (his real name is unknown). While still very young, he went to Perugia and painted for a time and then moved on to Rome in 1517, where he wrote a series of viciously satirical lampoons supporting the candidacy of Giulio de' Medici for the papacy (Giulio became Pope Clement VII in 1523). Despite the support of the Pope and another patron, Aretino was finally forced to leave Rome because of his general notoriety and his 1524 collection of *Sonetti lussuriosi* ("Lewd Sonnets"). From Rome he went to Venice (1527), where he was the object of great adulation and lived in a grand and dissolute style for the rest of his life.

One of Aretino's closest friends in Venice was the painter Titian, for whom he sold many paintings to Francis I, king of France; a great gold chain that Aretino wears in Titian's portrait (*c.* 1545; Pitti Palace, Florence) was a gift from the King.

Among Aretino's many works, the most characteristic are his satirical attacks, often amounting to blackmail, on the powerful. His six volumes of letters (published 1537–57, modern edition, *Il I e il II libro delle lettere di Pietro Aretino,* 1913–16; Eng. trans. included *Works,* 2 vol., 1926 by Samuel Putnam; selected letters by T. Chubb, 1967, and by G. Bull, 1976) show his power and cynicism and give ample justification for the name he gave himself, "*flagello dei principe*" ("scourge of princes"). Aretino was particularly vicious in his attacks on Romans because they had forced him to fly to Venice. In *Ragionamenti* (1534–36, modern edition, 1914; "Discussions"), Roman prostitutes reveal to each other the moral failings of many important men of their city, and in *I dialoghi* and other dialogues (Eng. trans. by Raymond Rosenthal, 1971) he continues the examination of carnality and corruption among Romans.

Only Aretino's dramas were relatively free of such venomous assaults. His five comedies are vigorous and acutely perceived pictures of lower-class life, free from the conventions that burdened other contemporary dramas. Of the five comedies, written between 1525 and 1544 (modern collection, *Commedie,* 1914), the best known is *Cortigiana* (published 1534, first performed 1537, "The Courtesan"), a lively and amusing panorama of the life of the lower classes in papal Rome. Aretino also wrote a tragedy, *Orazia* (published 1546; "The Horatii"), which has been judged by some the best Italian tragedy written in the 16th century. Biographies in English include T. Chubb's (1940) and J. Cleugh's (1966).

Arevaci, a Celtiberian tribe, formed by the mingling of Iberians and migrating Celts in the 6th century BC, who inhabited an area near Numantia and Uxama in what is now Spain. The Celtiberians excelled at horsemanship, fighting, and metalworking. They wore sewn garments made of woven and dyed cloth.

The Arevaci and the Belli rose up against the Romans in the Celtiberian War, which lasted from 153 to 133 BC. After such victories as that of 137 BC, in which 20,000 Romans surrendered to between 4,000 and 8,000 Celtiberians at Numantia, the tribes' resistance was broken by the Roman siege and destruction of Numantia in 133 BC.

Arévalo, Juan José (b. 1904, Guatemala), president of Guatemala (1945–1951), who pursued a strongly nationalistic foreign policy while internally encouraging the labour movement and instituting vast social reforms.

Arévalo was educated at the University of Guatemala and the University of La Plata (1928–34) in Argentina, where he received a doctorate. After serving as Guatemalan minister of education in 1936, he returned to Argentina, where he held a variety of academic positions. After a coup d'etat (Oct. 20, 1944), Arévalo was elected president in an election in which, for the first time in Guatemalan history, organized labour played an important part. He received 85 percent of the vote. His policies increasingly favoured urban and agricultural workers. During his administration a social security system was established, a labour code enacted, and important programs in education, health, and road building begun. He allowed freedom of speech and of the press and, in accord with his revolutionary nationalist policy, re-opened the dispute over Belize with the British. He was appointed ambassador at large in 1951. During his term in office he refused to recognize Somoza's Nicaragua, Franco's Spain, and Trujillo's Dominican Republic. In 1963 he was prevented from running for president after Col. Enrique Peralta seized the government.

Arévalo is the author of a widely circulated book, *The Shark and the Sardines* (1961), which denounces U.S. domination of Latin America. He served as ambassador to France from 1970 to 1972.

Arévalo Martínez, Rafael (b. July 25, 1884, Quezaltenango, Guatemala—d. 1975), Guatemalan novelist and short-story writer whose work is considered one of the most important precursors of modern Spanish-American fiction.

He was appointed director of the Guatemalan National Library in 1926, a post he held until 1946, at which time he served for a year as the Guatemalan ambassador to the Organization of American States. A short-story writer of marked ability, he introduced a new form known as the "psycho-zoological" tale, the most famous of which, "El hombre que parecía un caballo" (1914; "The Man Who Looked Like a Horse"), deals with the conflict between man's spiritual and animal natures. As a novelist, he attempted to explore social problems and problems of the human personality without resorting to realism; he became one of the foremost writers of what has been called fictional magical realism, a form that eventually led to the novel of the absurd. His most famous novels are *Oficina de paz en Orolandia* (1938; "Office of Peace in Orolandia"), *El mundo de los Maharachías* (1938; "The World of the Maharachias"), and *Viaje a Ipanda* (1939; "Voyage to Ipanda"). *Hondura* (1947) is an autobiographical novel.

Arezzo, Latin ARRETIUM, city, capital of Arezzo province, Toscana (Tuscany) region of north central Italy, in a fertile plain near the confluence of the Chiana and Arno rivers southeast of Florence. An important Etruscan

S. Domenico church, Arezzo, Italy
John Ross—Photo Researchers

city, it was known to the Romans as Arretium and was noted for its red-clay Arretine ware (*see* terra sigillata ware). A flourishing commune in the Middle Ages, it fell to Florence in 1384 and later became part of the grand duchy of Tuscany. After a short period of French rule during the Napoleonic Wars, the Habsburg grand dukes were restored until Arezzo became part of Italy in 1861. It was severely damaged in World War II.

A bishopric, Arezzo's churches include the cathedral, begun in 1286 and finally completed in 1914; the Romanesque Sta. Maria della Pieve; S. Domenico (begun 1275), with a crucifix by Cimabue; the Renaissance Sta. Maria delle Grazie, with an altar by Andrea della Robbia; and S. Francesco, with a series of frescoes, the "Legend of the True Cross," by Piero della Francesca. There are numerous 14th-century palaces and houses around the former city centre, notably the Palazzo della Fraternità. A collection of Arretine vases is housed in the remains of a Roman amphitheatre, and the Etruscan museum and the picture gallery contain fine collections. Arezzo was the birthplace of the writers Petrarch and Pietro Aretino; the artist Spinello Aretino; Guido d'Arezzo, the inventor of the musical scale; and the painter, architect, and writer Giorgio Vasari.

A centre of road communications, Arezzo has a basic agricultural economy augmented by railroad construction shops and clothing and footwear factories; goldware and lace are exported. Pop. (1981 prelim.) mun., 91,535.

Arfersiorfik Fjord, fjord in western Greenland, extending east from Davis Strait to the inland icecap. It is 95 mi (152 km) long with a maximum width of 15 mi. Its arms receive several glaciers, including the Nordenskiölds. Niaqornaarsuk, a settlement on the northern shore near the fjord's mouth, was the starting point of an expedition in 1883 led by Adolf Erik Nordenskiöld.

Arfon, district, Gwynedd County, northwest Wales. It was created in 1974, covers an area of 178 sq mi (460 sq km), and extends southward from just north of the village of Aber along the coast of the Menai Strait of the Irish Sea to a point just south of Llandwrog village and eastward to the Snowdonian range. Mt. Snowdon, 3,560 ft (1,085 m) above sea level, the highest mountain in England and Wales lies on the southeastern border. Arfon borders the districts of Aberconwy to the east and Dwyfor to the south and southwest with the Menai Strait comprising the western border. The town of Bangor, at the northern entrance to the Meani Strait, became a centre for Celtic Christianity as early as AD 550, when a church, subsequently enlarged to become the town's present cathedral, was founded by St. Deniniol. Many monks fled here in the early 600s after the massacre at Bangor Is-coed, near Wrexham. Caernavon, located farther south of Bangor on the Menai Strait, is the site of an enormous castle built by Edward I of England in 1283 to symbolize the strength and splendour of England and as a base from which to subjugate the Welsh. Although the original wooden castle was burned in a revolt, the castle was rebuilt in stone and withstood numerous attacks from Welsh forces led by Owen Glendower, in 1403 and 1404; today it is one of the most well-known castles in Britain, having been the scene of royal investitures in 1911 and 1969.

Arfon district provides access for tourists to both the Isle of Anglesey and Snowdonia National Park. The town of Llanberis, situated between two lakes at the entrance to Llanberis pass, is a tourist centre for Snowdonia National Park as well as the site of a large hydroelectric facility (under construction in the 1980s). The vast Dinorwic slate quarries face Llanberis across the valley, while the once thriving Bethesda quarries are located to the northwest. The slate industry experienced a rapid decline following the introduction of manufactured roof tile, and some light industries have since been established in the area. The town of Bangor is both the administrative seat of the district and a regional cultural centre with the University College of North Wales (1884), a group of denominational theological colleges, and a museum of Welsh antiquities. Caernavon is the seat of Gwynedd County. Arfon district is traversed by highways, and railway service from Chester extends through Bangor to Holyhead on the Isle of Anglesey to provide a rail-ferry sea link between Dublin and London. Pop. (1982 est.) 54,900.

Arfons, Art, byname of ARTHUR EUGENE ARFONS (b. Feb. 3, 1926, Akron, Ohio, U.S.), three-time holder of the world's land-speed record for wheeled vehicles.

Arfons worked in his father's feed-mill business in Akron, Ohio, before and after service in the U.S. Navy (1943–46), which trained him in diesel mechanics. He began his career as a drag racer in the early 1950s with his brother Walter, with whom he built a series of racing cars, each called the "Green Monster"; and by 1959 he was involved in car racing full time. In the early 1960s he designed the ultimate "Green Monster," powered by a J-79 jet aircraft engine, which he drove at the Bonneville Salt Flats, Utah. He reached speeds of 434.02 mph (698.34 kph), Oct. 5, 1964; 536.71 mph, Oct. 27, 1964; and 576.533 mph, Nov. 7, 1965. The last of these records was broken eight days later by Craig Breedlove's 600.601 mph performance.

Arfons also designed speedboats, using the name "Green Monster Cyclops."

arfvedsonite, amphibole mineral, an iron-rich sodium silicate. Lithium and magnesium replace iron in the structure to form eckermannite. Both minerals characteristically occur as dark-green crystals in alkali igneous rocks and their associated pegmatites. For chemical formula and detailed physical properties, *see* amphibole (table).

argali (*Ovis ammon*), the largest living wild sheep, found in the highlands of eastern Central Asia. It may stand 1.3 metres (4 feet) high at the shoulders and weigh more than 140 kilograms (300 pounds). Large horns, present in the rams, are especially massive in the Pamir argali, or Marco Polo sheep, in which they may be 1.8 m or more in length.

Argall, Sir Samuel (b. *c.* 1572, Bristol, Gloucestershire, Eng.—d. *c.* 1626), English sailor and adventurer who defended British colonists in North America against the French.

Employed by the Virginia Company of London, Argall was commissioned in 1609 to discover a shorter route to Virginia and to fish for sturgeon. In 1610 he was named admiral of Virginia and commissioned to expel the French from all territory granted to the English by James I. In 1613 he sailed up the Potomac River, searching for corn for the colonists, and abducted the Powhatan Indian princess Pocahontas, whom he held hostage for the return of seven English prisoners. On venturing farther northward along the coast, Argall discovered a new French settlement at St. Sauveur. He destroyed the settlement and took some French prisoners and goods to Jamestown. The council of the Virginia Company then commissioned him to destroy all French settlements south of the 46th parallel, including Port Royal (now Annapolis Royal, Nova Scotia), which he captured in 1614. He returned in that year to England, where he was cleared of charges of wrongdoing in his actions against the French.

Still in the service of the Virginia Company, Argall was elected deputy governor of the province in 1616 and ruled the colony in 1616–19 during the governor's absence. The harshness of his administration led to another inquiry and exoneration. In 1620 he was made captain of a 24-gun merchant vessel in an expedition against Algiers. He became a member of the Council for New England and was knighted in 1622. In 1625, as a member of the King's War Council, Argall commanded a fleet of 28 vessels and conducted an unsuccessful offensive against Cádiz. He died the following year, possibly at sea, but more likely in retirement.

Argand burner, first scientifically constructed oil lamp, patented in 1784 in England by a Swiss, Aimé Argand. The first basic change in lamps in thousands of years, it applied a principle that was later adapted to gas burners. The Argand burner consisted of a cylindrical wick housed between two concentric metal tubes. The inner tube provided a passage through which air rose into the centre to support combustion on the inner surface of the cylindrical flame in addition to that on the outer surface. A glass chimney increased the draft, allowing more complete burning of the oil; an Argand lamp gave about 10 times the light of an earlier lamp of the same size, as well as a cleaner flame, but its oil consumption was greater.

Argand diagram, graphic portrayal of complex numbers, those of the form $a+bi$, in which a and b are real numbers and i is the square root of -1; it was devised by the Swiss mathematician Jean Robert Argand around 1806. One axis represents the pure imaginary numbers (those consisting of the bi portion only); the second represents the real numbers (a values only). This permits the complex numbers to be plotted as points in the field defined by the two axes.

Argead DYNASTY, ruling house of ancient Macedonia from *c.* 700 to *c.* 311 BC; under their leadership the Macedonian kingdom was created and gradually gained a predominant position throughout the whole of Greece. From about 700 onward the founder of the dynasty, Perdiccas I, led the people who called themselves Macedonians eastward from their home on the Haliacmon (modern Aliákmon) River. Aegae (Edessa) became the capital, and by the reign of Amyntas I (6th century BC) Macedonian power extended eastward beyond the Axius (Axiós) River to dominate the neighbouring Thracian tribes. Amyntas' successor, Alexander I (reigned before 492–*c.* 450), advanced his frontiers eastward to the Strymon (Struma) River. His byname, "the Philhellene," indicates his efforts to win Greek sympathies. He spread the legend deriving his Argead house from the Temenids of Argos and thus obtained admission to the Olympic Games.

Alexander's son Perdiccas II (reigned *c.* 450–*c.* 413) asserted his succession against various brothers and united the Greek cities of Chalcidice in a federation centring on the city of Olynthus. Perdiccas' son Archelaus (reigned *c.* 413–399) adopted a strongly philhellenic policy, introducing Greek artists to his new capital at Pella. He strengthened Macedonia by building roads and fortresses, improving army equipment, and encouraging city life, and his assassination in 399 was followed by seven years of murder and anarchy.

Finally, a great-grandson of Alexander I, Amyntas III, took the throne in 393/392. Although his reign was filled with anarchy and intrigue, he successfully brought unity to Macedonia. His death in 370/369 left three lawful sons, of whom the first two, Alexander II and Perdiccas III, ruled only briefly. In 359 Amyntas' third son, Philip II, assumed control in the name of Perdiccas' infant heir; having restored order he made himself king (reigned 359–336) and raised Macedonia to a predominant position throughout the whole of Greece. Philip's son Alexander III the Great (reigned 336–323) overthrew the Achaemenian Empire and carried Macedonian arms to the Nile and Indus rivers. On Alexander III's death at Babylon his generals divided up the satrapies of his empire. Although Alexander's two successors, his half-brother Philip III Arrhidaeus and his son Alexander IV, furnished a nominal focus for loyalty until about 311, the real power in the empire lay in other hands.

Argelander, Friedrich Wilhelm August (b. March 22, 1799, Memel, East Prussia—d. Feb. 17, 1875, Bonn), German astronomer who established the study of variable stars as an independent branch of astronomy and is

Argelander, detail from an engraving

By courtesy of the Staatsbibliothek, West Berlin

renowned for his great catalog listing the positions and magnitudes of 324,188 stars. He studied at the University of Königsberg, Prussia, where he was a pupil and later the successor of Friedrich Wilhelm Bessel. Argelander was appointed director of the Åbo (Turku) Observatory in Finland in 1823 and of the Helsinki Observatory in 1832. In 1837 he published the first major investigation of the Sun's motion through space and in the same year was appointed director of the new observatory in Bonn. In 1844 he began studies of variable stars.

His greatest achievement was the publication of the *Bonner Durchmusterung* (1859–62), which cataloged stars from the north celestial pole to 2° south of the celestial equator. The result of 25 years' labour, the catalog included all stars down to about the ninth magnitude. This work was reissued in 1950.

Argelander founded the Astronomische Gesellschaft (Astronomical Society), whose object was to expand his work in collaboration with many observatories.

Argens, Jean-Baptiste de Boyer, marquis d' (marquess of) (b. June 27, 1703, Aix-en-Provence, Fr.—d. Jan. 12, 1771, Toulon), French writer who helped disseminate the skeptical ideas of the Enlightenment by addressing his polemical writings on philosophy, religion, and history to a popular readership. Argens's writings simplified the unortho-

Marquis d'Argens, detail of an engraving by E.-J. Desrochers after a painting by van Pee

Giraudon—Art Resource/EB Inc.

dox empirical reasoning of such Philosophes as Pierre Bayle, Bernard de Fontenelle, and Voltaire; the latter considered him an ally.

Of an aristocratic Catholic family, he led a life of dissipation in his youth. He joined the army and then eloped to Spain; at one time he attempted suicide. He spent 25 years in the court of Frederick the Great as chamberlain, producing 18 volumes of letters, *Correspondance philosophique.* As a freethinker, he challenged authoritarian religion and scholasticism, relying on empirical reason and personal ethics. His *Lettres juives* (1738; "Jewish Letters"), *Lettres cabalistiques* (1741; "Cabalistic Letters"), and *Lettres chinoises* (1739–40; "Chinese Letters") are patterned after Montesquieu's *Lettres persanes.*

Argenson, René-Louis de Voyer de Paulmy, marquis d' (b. Oct. 18, 1694, Paris—d. Jan. 26, 1757, Paris), French minister of foreign affairs under King Louis XV

René-Louis, marquis d'Argenson, engraving, 18th century

By courtesy of the Bibliotheque Nationale, Paris

from 1744 to 1747. The son of a lawyer, he received legal training and, from 1720 to 1724, served as intendant (royal agent) in Hainaut. As patron of the Club de l'Entresol in Paris, he discussed the political concepts of the Enlightenment with Voltaire and other *philosophes.* In November 1744, several months after France had officially entered the War of the Austrian Succession (1740–48) on the side of Prussia, Argenson was appointed Louis XV's foreign minister. Aspiring to reestablish French hegemony in Europe, he tried unsuccessfully to implement his own doctrinaire schemes for international arbitration. His plans were directed against Spain, Austria, and Russia; but his program was undermined by Louis's own secret diplomacy—about which the minister was not informed—and by court intrigues. By failing to press the diplomatic advantage that resulted from the victory over the Austrians at Fontenoy (May 1745), he left himself open to criticism. In January 1747 he was compelled to resign. As president of the Académie des Inscriptions et Belles-Lettres, Argenson spent the rest of his life in literary pursuits. His *Journal et mémoires* (published 1859–67) forms one of the major sources for the literary and political history of Louis XV's reign.

Argenta, town, Ferrara province, Emilia-Romagna region, northeastern Italy, on the Fiume (river) Reno, southeast of Ferrara city. It has some fine medieval and Renaissance buildings, including the churches of S. Domenico and S. Francesco, and a notable picture gallery. The town was flooded by the German forces during World War II. It is now mainly an agricultural centre. Pop. (1981 prelim.) mun., 24,232.

argentaffin cell, one of the round or partly flattened cells occurring in the lining tissue of the digestive tract and containing granules thought to be of secretory function. These epithelial cells, though common throughout the digestive tract, are most concentrated in the small intestine and appendix. The cells locate randomly within the mucous membrane lining of the intestine and in tubelike depressions in that lining known as the Lieberkühn glands. Their granules contain a chemical called serotonin, which stimulates smooth muscle contractions. Functionally, it is believed that serotonin diffuses out of the argentaffin cells into the walls of the digestive tract, where neurons leading to the muscles are stimulated to produce the wavelike contractions of peristalsis. Peristaltic movements encourage the passage of food substances through the intestinal tract.

Argentan lace, French POINT D'ARGENTAN, lace made at the French town of Argentan from the 17th century, when Louis XIV's minister Jean-Baptiste Colbert founded the lace industry. Characteristic of this lace is a net background consisting of a large hexagonal mesh, the six sides of which are worked over with buttonhole stitching. Flower patterns are similar to those of Alençon, 25 miles away, but are more solid-looking than their Alençon

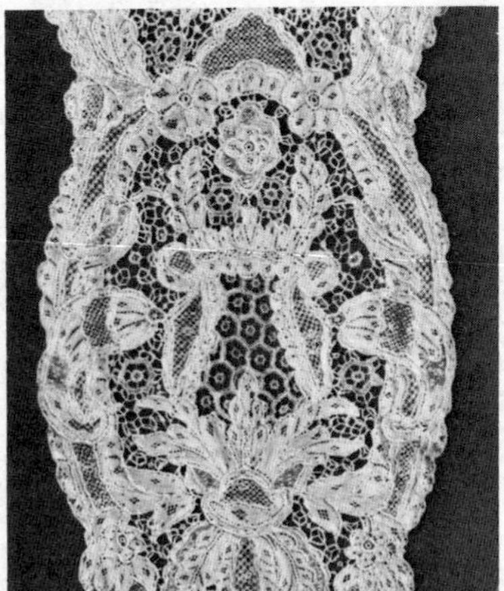

Argentan lace from Argentan, Fr., mid-18th century; in the Institut Royal du Patrimoine Artistique, Brussels

By courtesy of the Institut Royal du Patrimoine Artistique, Brussels; photograph, © A.C.L., Brussels

counterparts. Argentan lace making declined after the Revolution but was revived briefly in the 1870s.

Argenteau, Florimund Mercy d': *see* Mercy d'Argenteau, Florimund, Graf von.

Argentera (France–Italy): *see* Maddalena Pass.

Argenteuil, town, Val-d'Oise *département,* Paris region, on the north bank of the Seine, northwest of Paris. The town's name comes from silver (*argent*) deposits exploited by the Gauls. A convent was founded there in the 7th century, and Charlemagne's daughter Théorade may have been an early abbess. Héloïse, of the tragic Héloïse–Abelard romance, became prioress in about 1118; she was expelled in 1129, and the establishment was made a monastery. On its site the basilica of Saint-Denis enshrines the putative seamless robe of Christ, a gift from Charlemagne, who received it from the Byzantine empress Irene. Heavy industry (machinery, aluminum, and aeronautical engineering) and suburban housing have almost completely obliterated the vineyards and asparagus fields that once surrounded Argenteuil. Pop. (1982) 94,826.

Consult the INDEX *first*

Argentia, village, southeastern Newfoundland, Can., on the western coast of Avalon Peninsula just north of Placentia town and overlooking Placentia Bay. It was formerly a herring and salmon fishing port called Little Placentia, which was renamed Argentia (derived from *argentum,* Latin for "silver") when silver was discovered in the vicinity. Most of its inhabitants moved to the nearby community of Freshwater in 1941, when Argentia became the site of the first U.S. lend-lease military base acquired from Great Britain. In August 1941 the Atlantic Charter on sovereign rights of nations was signed by Franklin D. Roosevelt and Sir Winston Churchill aboard warships anchored offshore; a memorial chapel on the base commemorates the event. The village is a coastal-boat terminus, connected by highway and railroad to St. John's, 81 mi (131 km) east-northeast. Pop. (1981) 93.

Argentière, L' (France–Italy): *see* Maddalena Pass.

Argentina, officially ARGENTINE REPUBLIC, Spanish REPUBLICA ARGENTINA, large country occupying much of the southern tip of South America, covering a triangular area of 1,068,301 sq mi (2,776,888 sq km). The capital is Buenos Aires. The country lies between latitudes 22° and 52° S (about 2,170 mi [3,500 km] from north to south) and between longitudes 54° and 74° W (about 870 mi, at its widest extent, from east to west). Argentina is bordered on the south and west by Chile, on the north by Bolivia and Paraguay, on the northeast by Brazil and Uruguay. To the southeast, Argentina is bounded by the Atlantic Ocean (with a coastline of more than 2,500 mi) and by the Andes Mountain Ranges to the west and southwest. About 320 mi northeast of the southern tip of the country lie the Falkland Islands (Islas Malvinas), which remain under British control despite Argentine claims to sovereignty, which date to 1820, and a short-lived occupation by Argentine military forces in 1982. The population of Argentina in 1983 was estimated at 29,627,000.

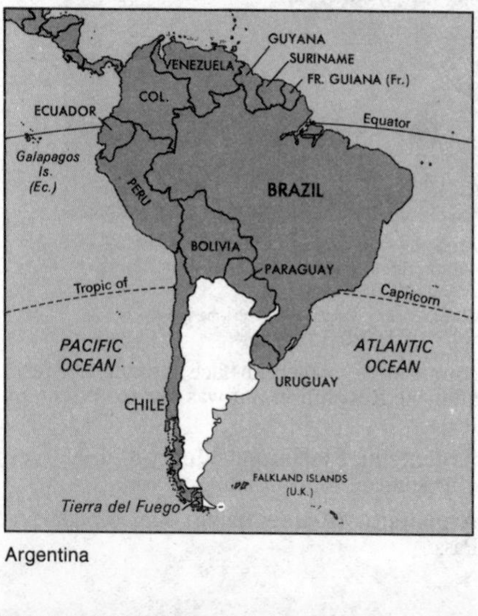

Argentina

The article that follows is a summary of significant detail about Argentina. Fuller treatment is provided in the MACROPAEDIA articles named below. For geography and history, *see* Argentina; for information about the country in its regional setting, *see* South America. For information about regional aspects of Argentina's history and traditional cultures, *see* American Indians; Pre-Columbian Civilizations; Latin America. For information about its capital city, *see* Buenos Aires.

For current history and for statistics on society and economy, *see* the article "World Affairs" and BRITANNICA WORLD DATA, respectively, in the *Britannica Book of the Year.*

The land. Argentina can be divided into at least four general regions. The subtropical plains in the northeast are divided by the Paraná River into Mesopotamia to the east and Argentina's share of South America's Gran Chaco region to the west and north. Much of Argentina's wooded areas lie in the northeastern plains, including some rainforests in Mesopotamia. The Pampa, the most densely populated region, supporting more than three-fourths of the country's population, lie south and west of the Paraná River and extend to the Atlantic coast between the Río de la Plata in the north and the Río Colorado in the south; the region, previously a sparsely settled prairie, has become one of the world's most productive agricultural areas. Patagonia, primarily a barren semidesert, lies south of the Río Colorado, includes most of the country's southern extent, and provides pastureland for huge herds of sheep. Much of Argentina's extensive reserves of coal, petroleum, and natural gas lie in Patagonia's southern provinces, and the only developed iron-ore deposits are in the northern part of the region. The Andean highlands along the entire western border contain extensive mineral resources and some of the world's most rugged mountain terrain (including the country's highest peak, Mount Aconcagua at 22,835 ft [6,960 m]). In 1944 there was a severe earthquake that killed more than 5,000 people in the Andean province of San Juan (a geologically active area); there was a similar earthquake in 1977.

Argentina's hydrology is dominated by the rivers that drain into the Río de la Plata that covers a total of nearly 2,000,000 sq mi; about one-third of the basin lies within the boundaries of Argentina, and the rest lies in Brazil, Paraguay, Bolivia, and Uruguay. Rivers that contribute to the discharge of the Río de la Plata include the Paraná, Uruguay, and Pilcomayo. During the 1970s Argentina expanded its hydroelectric generating capacity more than sixfold; thermal plants produce the bulk of the country's electricity.

The northeastern plains has a humid subtropical climate with warm to hot summers and cool winters. To the west and south, the climate of the Andean highlands and northern Patagonia is much drier, like that of continental steppes. This gives way to desert and semidesert climates in the interior southern lowlands and to a moderate subpolar climate in the Andes. Rainfall (other than the heavy precipitation in the Andes) is scanty in the south and southwest, but in Mesopotamia it reaches 80 in. (2,000 mm) or more annually.

In the early 1980s, Argentina had large reserves of copper ore that were estimated to have a metal content of about 9,000,000 metric tons. Other minerals include lead, zinc, gold, silver, and manganese. Among the more extensively developed resources were iron ore, natural gas, petroleum, and coal.

The people. Argentina's population at midyear 1981 was 28,085,000 and was growing at an annual rate of 1.6 percent. The birth rate is quite low for a developing country, at 25 per 1,000, and the death rate is 9 per 1,000. The country's population density is 26 per sq mi (10 per sq km); however, much of the Gran Chaco, Andes, and Patagonia regions have fewer than 5 persons per sq mi. The ratio of males to females is 97 to 100. In 1980 about 28 percent of the population was less than 15 years of age, while about 9 percent was 65 years or more. Life expectancy for men is 66 years and 73 years for women. The people of Argentina are predominantly white and of European ancestry. The inhabitants of Buenos Aires city are largely of Spanish, French, English, Italian, and German descent. The Indians and mestizos (mixture of Indian and white) have been mostly absorbed and now constitute only 3 percent of the population. It is estimated that 250,000 persons of German descent presently live in Argentina, most of whom speak both Spanish and German. There are about 500,000 Jews, of whom about three-fourths live in Buenos Aires. Spanish is the national language, but numerous foreign languages and dialects are spoken, from Basque and Sicilian to Welsh and Ukrainian. Most of the people are Roman Catholics, members of the official religion of the country; there are also some Protestants. In 1980, about 86 percent of the population lived in urban areas. Buenos Aires, the largest city, had a metropolitan population of 9,766,030 in 1980; other major urban centres were Córdoba 982,018; Rosario 954,606; and La Plata 560,341.

The economy. Argentina has a free market structure in a well developed economy based largely upon industrial production and agriculture. The gross national product (GNP) was projected (1980) at U.S. $66,430,000,000, about $2,390 per capita. Between 1970 and 1979 the real GNP grew at an average annual rate of only 1 percent, a figure kept low by severe inflation and political instability. One-fourth of the GNP originates from manufacturing; smaller contributions are made by trade, agriculture, forestry, hunting, fishing, transport, and communications.

Arable land in Argentina amounts to about 13 percent of the total land area, more than three-fourths of which is cultivated. Cereals (primarily wheat, corn [maize], and sorghum) are grown on about two-thirds of the cultivated land. Soybeans, sunflower seeds, fruits (apples, oranges, and grapes), linseed, sugar cane, and vegetables and melons are also economically important. Pastures amount to more than half of the total land area. Argentina produces the world's third largest output of beef; sheep, pigs, horses, and goats are also raised.

Forests cover about two-fifths of the total land area. Forest produce includes roundwood, two-thirds of which is broadleaf and the rest coniferous, mainly for industrial use. A noted Argentine forest product is quebracho tannin.

Argentina's coast is one of the longest in South America, but the fish catch is much less than that of Chile, Peru, Brazil, or Ecuador.

Argentina is almost self-sufficient in mineral output with the exceptions of iron ore, manganese, bauxite, chromite, and coal. In petroleum and natural gas Argentina is about 95 percent self-sufficient. The most important minerals produced are crude petroleum, natural gas, and iron ore, as well as smaller amounts of lead, zinc, gold, silver, and uranium. Nonmetallic minerals include sand, limestone, granite, and tufa. Argentina's total electric production (1980) was 40,000,000 kW-hr, comprising thermal (51 percent), hydroelectric (42 percent), and nuclear (7 percent).

Manufacturing is well diversified; the principal products include refined petroleum products, portland cement, crude steel, pig and sponge iron, steel tubes, wine, beer, cigarettes, refined sugar, cattle hides, wood pulp, particle board, ovens, automobiles, motorcycles, sewing machines, refrigerators, washing machines, railway carriages, and ships.

Construction (about 8 percent of GNP in 1980) was mainly concentrated on energy related and industrial projects. Among the electric complexes under construction in the early 1980s were the Yacreta project, jointly with Paraguay on the Paraná River; Salto Grande, jointly with Uruguay on the Uruguay River; and the Chocon-Cerros Colorados, in southern Argentina. Two nuclear power plants were also under construction in the early 1980s, and a plutonium reprocessing plant was being built at Ezeiza. Factories for the aluminum, cement, and petrochemical industries, natural gas pipelines, and several large manganese and copper mining complexes were also being built.

The Argentine monetary unit is the peso (new peso introduced in 1970), subdivided into 100 centavos. The economy suffered from runaway inflation in the late 1970s and early '80s. The military government introduced drastic reforms that reduced the rate of inflation to 140 percent annually in 1979 from a high of 348 percent in 1976, but the Falklands (Malvinas) war of 1982 again caused a sharp rise in the inflation rate.

Budgetary revenue, about 10 percent less than expenditures, originates from sales taxes (30 percent) and social security taxes (28 percent) followed by non-tax revenue, customs duties, and income tax. Expenditures are mainly for social security, health, and welfare (38 percent); and public services and administration; defense; and education.

Transportation includes about 15,350 mi of railroad track and about 80,350 mi of roads, about one-fourth of which are paved. Buenos Aires has a subway system 12 mi in length. Argentina has 7 principal and 21 minor seaports. There are about 6,800 mi of internal waterways on the Paraná, Plata, Paraguay, and Uruguay rivers. The country's fleet of merchant ships (of more than 100 gross tons each) numbers about 520. Argentina has 10 international airports and about 100 permanent-surface airfields. Pipelines in operation include those for crude petroleum (about 2,540 mi); refined petroleum products (about 1,400 mi); and natural gas (about 5,100 mi).

Argentina's principal exports, exceeding imports in value by about one-seventh, consist of fresh fruits and vegetables (more than one-third of the total); live animals, meat, and meat products; wine, beer, and tobacco products; and skins, hides, and leather goods. The principal importers of Argentine products are Brazil, The Netherlands, Italy, and the United States. Principal imports consist of machinery and equipment, including electrical (about one-fifth of the total); minerals and mineral ores, excluding petroleum and natural gas; chemicals; transport equipment; and metals and metal manufactured goods. The principal sources for imports are the U.S., Brazil, West Germany, and Italy.

Administrative and social conditions. Argentina is a federal republic governed by a military junta consisting of the three commanders-in-chief of the armed forces. The president, appointed by the junta, serves a three-year term. The junta is advised on legislative matters by the Legislative Advisory Commission, a body of high ranking military officers. Governors appointed by the junta administer the nation's provinces. According to a 1976 amendment to the country's constitution of 1853, Argentina's highest judicial power is vested in the Supreme Court, whose members are appointed and dismissed by the junta. The military junta's rule was opposed by insurgent organizations and members of suspended political parties in the late 1970s and the early 1980s. As a conciliatory gesture, the junta promised to install a civilian democratic regime as soon as reconstruction of the nation's social and political systems was completed.

Argentina's social welfare system covers retirement, disability, and survivors' pensions; family allowances; and health insurance. Many of the country's health indicators such as the numbers of doctors per 1,000 population are favourable. The country's daily per capita food supply in 1977 was 3,346 calories, the highest of any South American country. The country's rate of infant mortality is, however, high (40.8 per 1,000 live births in 1978). Argentinian cities suffer from a severe housing shortage, caused mostly by the large influx of migrants from the rural areas.

Education in Argentina is free from pre-school to the university level. Primary education is compulsory for children between the ages of 6 and 14. Universidad de Buenos Aires, a national university, provides higher education.

The press in Argentina is one of the largest and most sophisticated in Latin America. Freedom of the press, however, has been under considerable restraint since the establishment of military rule in 1976. The nation's television stations are privately owned, but under military regulation, and the number of radio and television receivers in the country is very high.

Cultural life. The traditions of Argentina's various nationalities remain strong, being kept alive in fairs, fiestas, and regional folklore. Buenos Aires, the national capital, serves as Argentina's most important cultural centre, with about 100 art galleries and numerous theatres, museums, and concert halls. One of the most prominent cultural institutions in Buenos Aires is the Teatro Colón, a large and beautiful opera house featuring artists from Argentina and abroad.

History. Little is known of the precolonial history of Argentina. In the south the indigenous Indians were mostly nomadic hunters and fishers, but in the northwest, where the empire of the Incas had penetrated, they were agriculturalists. The Incas had built a highway as far south as what is now Mendoza.

The first Europeans to arrive were the Spanish and their settlement in Argentina was slow. Buenos Aires, founded in 1536, was abandoned a year later because of attacks from Indians and a lack of fresh water. Subsequent Spanish settlements in Argentina originated from other parts of Spanish South America, and intermarriage with the Indians was widespread.

Until 1776 Argentina was part of the viceroyalty of Peru; after 1776 it became part of the newly created Viceroyalty of the Río de la Plata, with Buenos Aires as the capital. This new status, and the exposure to European intellectual and social ideas that resulted, gave Buenos Aires a position of regional leadership.

In 1816 a congress meeting at Tucumán declared the United Provinces of the Río de la Plata to be independent. In 1829 Juan Manuel de Rosas firmly established himself in the province of Buenos Aires and by 1835 had extended his control over the rest of the country. His dictatorship fell in 1852. A constitutional convention was held at Santa Fe, and the new constitution was adopted in 1853. The province of Buenos Aires refused at first to join the union but did so in 1860 after its defeat by the armed forces of other provinces.

In 1880 a period of conservative oligarchical rule began and was followed by a radical, socially oriented one. A military coup in 1930 replaced the civilian rule. A troubled decade followed, and Juan Perón emerged as the new popular leader in the early 1940s and was elected president in 1946. Under military pressure, he fled the country in 1955. The next 20 years witnessed runaway inflation, strikes, high unemployment, and frequent changes in government.

In 1973 Perón returned from exile and was reelected president. On his death in 1974, he was succeeded by his wife, who was deposed by military officers in 1976. Amid continuing economic distress and political instability, a military junta appointed the next four presidents: Lieut. Gen. Jorge Rafaél Videla (March 1976), Gen. Roberto Eduardo Viola (March 1981), Lieut. Gen. Leopoldo Galtieri (December 1981), and Maj. Gen. Reynaldo Bignone (July 1982). In April 1982 the Argentines invaded and took possession of the Falkland Islands, which they had claimed for more than a century. When a British force recaptured the islands in June, Galtieri resigned. During Bignone's brief term, the first general election since 1973 was held; a lawyer, Raúl Alfonsín, won the presidency and began a program designed to correct the abuses committed by the military governments.

Argentina, La, byname of ANTONIA MERCÉ (b. Sept. 4, 1890, Buenos Aires—d. July 18, 1936, Bayonne, Fr.), dancer who originated the Neoclassical style of Spanish dancing and helped establish the Spanish dance as a theatrical art.

La Argentina
Dance News

She studied ballet with her parents, both of whom were professional dancers of Spanish birth. At the age of 11 she became premiere danseuse at the Madrid Opera, but she resigned at 14 to study the native dances of Spain. For many years her style was not accepted for concert performance, and her dancing was limited mainly to cafés and music halls. After World War I she was acclaimed in Paris, where she danced at the Moulin Rouge, among other places.

Her first successful solo concert was in 1927 at the Théâtre des Champs-Élysées in Paris, and from that time until her death she gave concerts and recitals in Europe, America, and the East, acclaimed as the finest Spanish dancer of the era. Her interpretation of *El amor brujo* (by Manuel de Falla), with its "Ritual Fire Dance" and "Dance of Terror," was one of her most famous creations. Her choreography, derived rather than copied from traditional Hispanic dances, displayed the creative possibilities of Spanish dance. Although she eventually formed a small company, she is remembered primarily as a master of the solo. Her technique, particularly on the castanets, was outstanding.

argentine, any fish of the family Argentinidae, small, outwardly smeltlike fishes found in deeper waters of the Atlantic and Pacific oceans. The family is usually placed in the order Salmoniformes. Argentines of the species *Argentina silus* are silvery fishes about 45 centimetres (18 inches) long; they live about 145–545 metres (480–1,800 feet) below the surface and are sometimes caught by fishermen.

The true smelts (family Osmeridae) were formerly considered part of the Argentinidae.

Argentine Basin, submarine basin in the floor of the Atlantic Ocean, lying directly east of Argentina. Its deepest sections, the western and southwestern margins, are called the Argentine Abyssal Plain and reach a maximum depth of 20,381 ft (6,212 m). The basin is bounded by the Rio Grande Rise (north), the Mid-Atlantic Ridge (east), the Falkland Rise (south), and the South American continental shelf (west).

Argentine Museum of Natural Sciences, Spanish MUSEO ARGENTINO DE CIENCIAS NATURALES "BERNARDINO RIVADAVIA," national museum (founded 1823) in Buenos Aires. It has zoological, botanical, and geological departments.

The museum has about 2,000,000 exhibits and a library of more than 500,000 volumes. Areas of expertise include archaeology, botany, ecology, entomology, hydrobiology, mineralogy, paleontology, and zoology.

argentite, a silver sulfide mineral (Ag_2S) that is the most important ore of silver. It is abundant, with other silver minerals, in the sulfide mineral deposits of Kongsberg, Nor.; Kremnica, Czech.; Zacatecas, Mex.; and the Comstock Lode, Nev.

Argentite, like several other sulfides, selenides, and tellurides of silver and copper, forms isometric crystals at high temperatures, but upon cooling the crystals invert from isometric (cubic) to nonisometric structures while remaining unchanged in external appearance. For example, argentite gives an X-ray pattern identical to that of acanthite, its orthorhombic modification (stable below 91° C, or 196° F). This shows that despite its isometric appearance argentite consists of lamellae of orthorhombic crystals, formed after the overall crystal shape was determined. For detailed physical properties, *see* sulfide mineral (table).

Arges, *judeţ* (district), southern Romania, occupying an area of 2,625 sq mi (6,801 sq km). The Transylvanian Alps (Southern Carpathians) and the sub-Carpathians rise above the settlement areas that are found in intermontane valleys. The district is drained westward by the Argeş, Cotmeana, and Teleorman rivers. It was formerly included in feudal Walachia. Agricultural activities consist of vineyard and orchard cultivation and livestock raising. Piteşti (*q.v.*), an oil-processing centre, is the district capital. Manufactures of Piteşti and other towns in the district include machinery, textiles, and paper. Coal and lignite are mined north of Mihăieşti, and salt mines, located near Apa Sărăta, were worked from the Roman occupation until the 12th century. A hydroelectric dam, measuring 541 ft (165 m) high and 1,007 ft (307 m) long impounds Lake Vidraru. Curtea de Argeş town has a 16th-century church that according to legend, contained the body of the church architect's wife inhumed in the walls. Cîmpulung, a former Roman fortified settlement, has a 13th-century monastery; and Goleşti town is known for a 17th-century manor that was owned by the Goleseu family. A 16th-century sandstone church and hermitage and the house of the poet Gheorge Topisceanu (1886–1937) are found in Namaeşti. Topoloveni town has a craft cooperative that makes traditional costumes and wood carvings. The 15th-century fortress of Poenari was constructed, overlooking the Argeş River Valley, by Vlad Tepes, or Vlad the Impaler, a prince known for executing his enemies by impalement, who was the prototype for Count Dracula in Bram Stoker's novel (1897). The fortress has a stairway of 1,400 steps. An arboretum, a forestry experimental station, and a roe deer reserve are found in Mihaeieşti; and ancient limestone quarries, designated a natural monument, are located near Albeşti. The road between Piteşti and Cîmpulung was a former Roman–Dacian route. Most of the district's railway lines and highways parallel river courses. Pop. (1982 est.) 659,289.

Argeş River, river, that rises in the Southern Carpathians, on the southern faces of Moldoveanu and Negoiu peaks in the Făgăraş Range, southern Romania. The river's principal tributaries from the mountains include the Vîlsan, Doamnei, and Tîrgului rivers. It flows southward through Curtea de Argeş and Piteşti, in the sub-Carpathians, and then southeastward across the Danube Plain to enter the Danube near Olteniţa. Its length is 203 mi (327 km), and the area of its basin is 4,850 sq mi (12,550 sq km). Its major tributary is the Dîmboviţa, which flows through Bucharest on a parallel course. A dam on the Argeş at Căpăţîneni creates Lake Vidraru, which is a reservoir for the Gheorghe Gheorghiu-Dej hydroelectric power station.

Arghūn (b. *c.* 1258—d. March 10, 1291, Bāghcha, Arrān, Iran), fourth Mongol Il-Khan (subordinate *khan*) of Iran (reigned 1284–91). He was the father of the great Maḥmūd Ghāzān (*q.v.*).

Upon the death of his father, Il-Khan Abagha (reigned 1265–82), Prince Arghūn was a candidate for the throne but was forced to yield to a stronger rival, his uncle Tegüder. Arghūn thereafter accused Tegüder's followers of having poisoned his father, protested Tegüder's conversion to Islām, and, by the beginning of 1284, was at the head of a rebellion. After some reverses, he succeeded in overthrowing Tegüder and having him executed (Aug. 10, 1284); Arghūn was formally enthroned the following day and, as an ardent Buddhist, countermanded the Islāmic policies of his predecessor.

In 1289 Arghūn appointed an anti-Islāmic Jew, Saʿd ad-Dawlah, first as his minister of finance and then (in June) as vizier of his entire empire. The predominantly Muslim population may have resented the rule of a Buddhist and a Jew, but their administration proved lawful and just and restored order and prosperity.

In hopes of renewing the war against the Egyptian Mamlūks, Arghūn sought alliances with the Christian West—first, in 1285, writing Pope Honorius IV and then, in 1287, sending emissaries to such leaders as Pope Nicholas IV, Edward I of England, and Philip IV of France. Except for an exchange of letters, however, nothing came of this diplomacy, and the war was not resumed. Arghūn also showed interest in sciences and such pseudosciences as alchemy.

While he was dying, fevered and bedridden, in the winter of 1290–91, those factions opposed to Saʿd ad-Dawlah and Arghūn's other favourites rose up and put them to death. After Arghūn's own death, he was succeeded by his brother Gaykhatu (1291–95), his cousin Baydū (1295), and his son Ghāzān (1295–1304).

arginine, an amino acid obtainable by hydrolysis of many common proteins but particularly abundant in protamines and histones, proteins associated with nucleic acids. First isolated from animal horn (1895), arginine plays an important role in mammals in the synthesis of urea, the principal form in which these species excrete nitrogen. Arginine is one of several so-called nonessential amino acids for adult mammals; *i.e.,* they can synthesize it from glutamic acid and do not require dietary sources.

Argirocastro (Albania): *see* Gjirokastër.

Argolís, *nomós* (department), northeastern Peloponnese, southern Greece. It is a narrow, mountainous peninsula projecting eastward into the Aegean Sea between the Saronic Gulf, (to the northeast) and the Gulf of Argolis (to the southwest). Bordered on the north by Kórinths and on the west by the mountains of Arcadia, it embraces 855 sq mi (2,214 sq km) and has been inhabited since Neolithic times. A limestone plateau comprises the highland areas of Argolís, while its lowland plain is alluvial and fertile, though too dry to cultivate without irrigation. The main natural vegetation is macchie, but with cultivation the land supports vegetables, olives, citrus, and grapes. On the coast trees are cultivated for resin. Goats and sheep are raised, especially for milk, which is used in the production of cheese.

The Argolid is an archaeological treasure house and thus a tourist trade centre: Mycenae was the home of Agamemnon, Tirins the birthplace of Heracles, Epidaurus the home of an ancient healing cult. In ancient times the Gulf of Argolis gave Greece access to trade and exchange of ideas from Crete and Egypt. The city of Argos gave its name to the plain; Nauplia, the chief town of the *nomós,* is a seaport and seaside resort. It was also the first capital of an independent Greece in the 19th century. Pop. (1981) 93,020.

Argolis, Gulf of, Modern Greek ARGOLIKÓS KÓLPOS, deep inlet of the Mirtóön Pélagos (sea), a western arm of the Aegean, eastern Peloponnese, Greece; it is separated from the Saronikós Kólpos (gulf) by the Argolís peninsula. Some 30 mi (50 km) long and 20 mi wide, it includes some small islands off the eastern shore, notably Psilí and Platiá. At the head of the gulf are its principal port, Návplion, and

The Greek Gulf of Argolis from the Palomedes fort
C.J. Coulson—Photo Trends

the mouth of the Ínakhos Potamós (river). Just north of the head of the gulf is Árgos (*q.v.*), an important Mycenaean and Dorian centre continuously occupied since the Early Bronze Age (*c.* 3500 BC). At the entrance to the gulf is Nísos (island) Spétsai, an Athenian summer resort.

argon (Ar), chemical element, inert gas of Group 0 (noble gases) of the periodic table, terrestrially the most abundant and industrially the most frequently used of the noble gases. Colourless, odourless, and tasteless, argon gas was isolated (1894) from air by the British scientists Lord Rayleigh and Sir William Ramsay. Henry Cavendish, while investigating atmospheric nitrogen ("phlogisticated air"), had concluded in 1785 that not more than 1/120 part of air might be some inert constituent. His work was forgotten until Lord Rayleigh, more than a century later, found that nitrogen prepared by removing oxygen from air is always about 0.5 percent more dense than nitrogen derived from chemical sources such as ammonia. The heavier gas remaining after both oxygen and nitrogen had been removed from air was the first of the noble gases to be discovered on Earth and was named argon because of its chemical inertness. (Helium had been spectroscopically detected in the Sun in 1868.)

Argon constitutes 1.3 percent of the atmosphere by weight and 0.94 percent by volume and is found occluded in rocks. A major portion of terrestrial argon has been produced, since the Earth's formation, in potassium-containing minerals by decay of the rare, naturally radioactive isotope potassium-40. The gas slowly leaks into the atmosphere from the rocks where it is still being formed. The production of argon-40 from potassium-40 decay is utilized as a means of determining the Earth's age (potassium-argon dating). On Earth naturally occurring argon is a mixture of three stable isotopes: argon-36 (0.34 percent), argon-38 (0.06 percent), and argon-40 (99.60 percent).

Argon is isolated on a large scale by fractional distillation of liquid air. It is used in gas-filled electric light bulbs, radio tubes, and Geiger counters. It also is widely utilized as an inert atmosphere for arc-welding metals, such as aluminum and stainless steel; for production and fabrication of metals, such as titanium, zirconium, and uranium; and for growing crystals of semiconductors, such as silicon and germanium.

Argon gas condenses to a colourless liquid at −185.8° C (−302.4° F) and to a crystalline solid at −189.4° C (−308.9° F). The gas cannot be liquefied by pressure above a temperature of −122.3° C (−188.1° F), and at this point a pressure of at least 48 atmospheres is required to make it liquefy. At 12° C (53.6° F), 3.94 volumes of argon gas dissolve in 100 volumes of water. An electric discharge through argon at low pressure appears pale red and at high pressure, steely blue.

The outermost (valence) shell of argon has eight electrons, making it exceedingly stable and, thus, chemically inert. Argon atoms do not combine with one another; nor have they been observed to combine chemically with atoms of any other element. Argon atoms have been trapped mechanically in cagelike cavities among molecules of other substances, as in crystals of ice or the organic compound hydroquinone (called argon clathrates).

atomic number	18
atomic weight	39.948
melting point	−189.2° C (−308.6° F)
boiling point	−185.7° C (−302.3° F)
density (1 atm, 0° C)	1.784 g/litre
valence	0
electronic configuration	2-8-8 or $1s^22s^22p^63s^23p^6$

Argonaut, in Greek legend, any of a band of 50 heroes who went with Jason (*q.v.*) in the ship "Argo" to fetch the Golden Fleece. That task had been imposed on Jason by his uncle Pelias, who had usurped the throne of Iolcos in Thessaly, which rightfully belonged to Jason's father, Aeson.

According to the legend, Jason's uncle Athamas had two children, Phrixus and Helle, by his first wife, Nephele, the cloud goddess. Ino, his second wife, hated the children of Nephele and persuaded Athamas to sacrifice Phrixus as the only means of alleviating a famine. But before the sacrifice, the shade of Nephele appeared to Phrixus, bringing a ram with a golden fleece on which he and his sister Helle tried to escape over the sea. Helle fell off and was drowned in the strait that after her was called the Hellespont. Phrixus safely reached the other side, and, proceeding to Colchis on the farther shore of the Euxine (Black) Sea, he sacrificed the ram and hung up its fleece in the grove of Ares, where it was guarded by a sleepless dragon.

The Argonauts, detail of a painting by Lorenzo Costa in the Museo Civico, Padua, Italy

SCALA—Art Resource/EB Inc.

Jason, having undertaken the quest of the fleece, called upon the noblest heroes of Greece to take part in the expedition. According to the original story, the crew consisted of the chief members of Jason's own race, the Minyans; later, other and better known heroes were added to their number.

The Argonauts arrived at Lemnos, which was occupied only by women, and remained there several months. Proceeding up the Hellespont, they sailed to the country of the Doliones, by whose king, Cyzicus, they were hospitably received. After their departure, however, they were driven back to the same place by a storm and were attacked by the Doliones, who did not recognize them. In the ensuing battle Jason killed Cyzicus. On reaching the country of the Bebryces, the Argonauts were challenged to a boxing contest by the king Amycus; Polydeuces accepted the challenge and slew him. At the entrance to the Euxine they met Phineus, the blind and aged king whose food was constantly polluted by the Harpies. After being freed by the winged sons of Boreas, Phineus told them the course to Colchis and how to pass through the Symplegades, or Cyanean rocks—two cliffs that moved on their bases and crushed whatever sought to pass. Following his advice, Jason sent ahead a dove that was damaged between the rocks, but the "Argo" slipped through while the rocks were rebounding. From that time the rocks became fixed and never closed again.

When the Argonauts finally reached Colchis, they found that the king, Aeetes, would not give up the fleece until Jason yoked the King's fire-snorting bulls to a plow and plowed the field of Ares. That accomplished, the field was to be sown with the dragon's teeth from which armed men were to spring. Aeetes' daughter, the sorceress Medea, who had fallen in love with Jason, gave him a salve that protected him from fire and advised him to cast a stone at the newborn warriors to cause them to fight to the death among themselves. After these tasks were accomplished, Aeetes still refused to give over the fleece. Medea, however, put the dragon to sleep, and Jason was able to abscond with the fleece and Medea. Various accounts are given of the homeward course; eventually the "Argo" reached Iolcos and was placed in a grove sacred to Poseidon in the Isthmus of Corinth.

The story of the expedition of the Argonauts was known at least as early as Homer, and the wandering of Odysseus may have been partly founded on it. In ancient times the expedition was regarded as a historical fact, an incident in the opening up of the Euxine to Greek commerce and colonization.

Argonaut, first submarine to navigate extensively in the open sea, built in 1897 by the U.S. engineer and naval architect Simon Lake. Designed to send out divers rather than to sink ships, the "Argonaut" was fitted with wheels for travel on the bottom of the sea and had an airtight chamber with a hatch that could be opened to the sea when the air pressure of the chamber and of the water outside were made equal. In 1898 the "Argonaut" travelled from Norfolk, Va., to New York through heavy storms, proving the seaworthiness of this type of submarine construction.

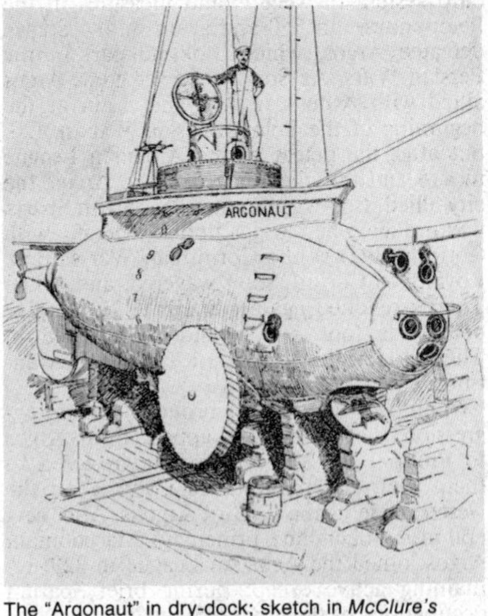

The "Argonaut" in dry-dock; sketch in *McClure's Magazine*, 1899, from original photographs by Simon Lake, inventor and builder of the boat

Culver Pictures

Argonne, wooded, hilly region, eastern France, the natural barrier between Champagne and Lorraine, about 40 mi long and 10 mi wide (65 km by 15 km). The massif rarely exceeds 650 ft (200 m) in elevation but is slashed with numerous deep valleys formed by watercourses associated with the Aire and Aisne rivers, which constitute a barrier to communication. Strategically important, it was here the Prussians were repulsed in 1792 by the French at Valmy, and where U.S. forces swept over the Germans (Meuse-Argonne Offensive) in 1918.

Argonne National Laboratory, located in Argonne, Ill., U.S., one of several national laboratories of the United States Department of Energy, operated by the University of Chicago and the Argonne Universities Association. Founded in 1946 to conduct basic atomic research and to develop peaceful uses of nuclear energy, Argonne National Laboratory now carries on work with other alternative sources of energy, such as synthetic fuels and solar energy. Its research also includes investigations of subatomic particles, atmospheric pollutants, and the effects of nuclear radiation on living organisms.

Argos, Modern Greek ÁRGOS, city, *nomós* (department) of Argolis, northeastern Peloponnese, Greece, just north of the head of the Argolikós Kólpos (gulf). The name Argos (adjectival form Argive), apparently signifying an agricultural plain, was applied to several districts in ancient Greece. Historically, the Argolis was all the eastern Peloponnesian peninsula. The present town lies about 4 mi (6.5 km) from the gulf below Kástro hill (ancient Larissa), a site probably occupied since the Early Bronze Age and very prominent in Mycenaean times (*c.* 1300–1200 BC). A small market town on the Corinth–Návplion rail line, it is built over much of the site of the classical city.

Possibly the base of Dorian operations in the Peloponnese (*c.* 1100–1000 BC), Argos was challenged by Sparta in the middle of the 7th century, but the Argive king Pheidon seized Olympia and held the Olympic Games there, according to the historian Herodotus. The Argives, who defeated the Spartans at Hysiae (669), established a long-lasting standard system of weights and measures in the Peloponnese. In 550 and again in 494 Sparta defeated Argos, which took no part in the Persian Wars. As Spartan power grew, Argos allied with Athens in 461 and again at the beginning of the Peloponnesian War in 420, but after the defeat of the Athenian League in 418 and the oligarchic rising in Argos, the city allied itself with Sparta. Peace with Sparta was broken when Argos united federally with Corinth (392) as the Corinthian War started. Loyalty to Corinth soon wavered, and, when Thebes revolted against Sparta (379), Argive democrats took power and participated in Theban victories at Leuctra (371) and Mantineia (362).

Waning Theban power brought Spartan aggression that forced an appeal from Argos to Philip II of Macedonia, who restored to them their old province of Cynuria on the western side of the Gulf of Argolis. After several more incursions, principally Macedonian, Argos joined the Achaean League in 229, remaining active except during brief Spartan occupations of the city (225 and 196).

Roman conquest and the destruction of Corinth (146) increased the importance of Argos, which became the centre of the Achaean League. The city was held briefly by the Goths in AD 267 and 305, but it flourished in Byzantine times. The Frankish principality of Achaea was established (1204) after the Fourth Crusade, and Argos declined. In 1397 the Turks captured it, and again in 1500, massacring the inhabitants and replacing them with Albanians. During the War of Greek Independence (1821–29) the first free Greek Parliament was convened at Argos (1821 and 1829).

Archaeological excavations began on the site—just northeast of the present town, on a rocky spur of Mt. Euboea near the ruins of Mycenae—in 1854, concentrating on the second temple, and the American School of Classical Studies at Athens began excavations on the Argive Heraeum (Heraion) in 1892 and 1895. The temple had been the centre of the worship of the mother-goddess Hera and the natural sanctuary of the Argolis long before the Dorians came (*c.* 1100–1000 BC). The prehistoric settlement on the upper terrace excavated by an American expedition (1925–28) was tentatively identified with the legendary Prosymna.

After the Dorian invasion a more substantial temple was erected, probably in the late 7th century BC, but nothing survives of this except the limestone platform and a part of the column-supporting pavement, or stylobate. The Greek geographer Pausanias records its burning (423 BC) through its priestess' negligence. An even more splendid temple was begun by the local architect Eupolemus, designed in limestone with Doric columns. In this temple King Pheidon dedicated offerings of the ingot currency that was used before the first issue of Aeginetan silver money.

The French School at Athens conducted various excavations at Argos before and after World War II, uncovering part of the prehistoric city of Aspis and the remains of a temple of Apollo of the Saddle, on the neck dividing Aspis hill from the summit of Larissa. On the lower ground their researches uncovered another temple site, as well as the site of what was in all probability the *Bouleuterion* (council house) of the Greek city, city baths and a *Heroon* (hero-cult shrine) of Roman date, and a cemetery with graves extending from the middle Helladic period (*c.* 2000–*c.* 1600 BC) to late Roman times.

In the early Classical period, prominent Argive sculptors included Ageladas and his student Polyclitus the Elder, who executed the colossal gold and ivory cult statue of Hera at the Heraeum, since lost—though some idea of the head may be gained from certain Argive coins of this period. Today, Argos is a prosperous agricultural and commercial centre for vegetables and fruits grown in the plain and food-processing industries based on them. Pop. (1981) 20,702.

Argostólion, also spelled ARGOSTÓLI, chief port and capital, *nomós* (department) of Cephalonia, which is the largest of the Ionian Islands of Greece, and a seat of a bishop of the Greek Orthodox Church. It was founded in 1757 by the Venetians when an earthquake destroyed the former capital. The well-protected harbour is situated on the eastern prong of a large inlet. The island produces olive oil, wine, currants, and vegetables. Argostólion and its sister port, Sámi, on the east coast were completely devastated by an earthquake in 1953 and since rebuilt. Pop. (1981 prelim.) 7,294.

Argovie (Switzerland): *see* Aargau.

Arguedas, Alcides (b. July 15, 1879, La Paz, Bolivia—d. May 8, 1946, Chulumani), novelist, journalist, sociologist, historian, and diplomat whose sociological and historical studies and critically acclaimed realistic novels were among the first to focus attention on the social and economic problems of the South American Indian.

Arguedas studied sociology in Paris and pursued an active career in government. He represented Bolivia in London, Paris, Colombia, and Venezuela and was a leader of Bolivia's Liberal Party, serving as a national deputy and a senator and becoming minister of agriculture in 1940. Throughout his public career he explored in his own works the plight of the Indians, sympathetically portraying their manners and customs and documenting the social and economic forces that had brought about their exploitation and decline.

Noted for such sociological studies as *Pueblo enfermo* (1909; "Dying Pueblo") and for his *Historia general de Bolivia* (1922; "General History of Bolivia"), Arguedas is best remembered for his novels about the Indians, especially *Raza de bronce* (1919; "Race of Bronze"), an epic portrayal of the travels of a group of Bolivian Indians, ending with their extermination by white men. His exploration of the Indian problem foreshadowed the *Indianista* novel of the 1930s and '40s in Latin America.

Arguedas, José María (b. Jan. 18, 1911, Andahuaylas, Peru—d. Nov. 28, 1969, Lima), Peruvian novelist, short-story writer, and ethnologist whose writings capture the contrasts between the white and Indian cultures.

Arguedas was the son of a white travelling judge and a Quechuan Indian. Though his mother died when he was only three years old, Arguedas learned to speak Quechua before he learned Spanish while accompanying his father on his journeys. As a youth he also studied Quechua music and customs as well as familiarized himself with the dominant Spanish culture. All of his works reflect the tensions that underlie Peruvian society, in which the Indians, who comprise the majority of the population, are still often considered marginal beings.

He attended the University of San Marcos in Lima, worked in the post office (1932–37), and taught at the National University in Sicuani (1939–41).

After holding a series of administrative positions, in 1959 he began teaching Peruvian regional cultures at the University of San Marco, also serving as the director of the House of Culture (1963–64) and later of the National Museum of History (1964–69).

Agua (1935; "Water"), a collection of three stories, depicts the violent injustices and disorder he saw in the white world as opposed to the peaceful and orderly existence he found in the lives of the exploited but passive Indians. *Yawar Fiesta* (1941; "Bloody Feast") treats in detail the ritual of the primitive bullfight symbolizing the social struggle of the Indians and the whites. Arguedas' masterpiece is the novel *Los ríos profundos* (1958; *Deep Rivers,* 1978), an autobiographical work that reiterates themes previously treated. The novel *El sexto* (1961; "The Sixth One") is based on Arguedas' imprisonment, 1937–38, during Oscar Benavides' dictatorship. *Todas las sangres* ("All the Races") appeared in 1964 and was followed by an unfinished novel, *El zorro de arriba y el zorro de abajo* (1971; "The Fox from Above and the Fox from Below"), the writing of which was prescribed to him by his psychiatrist. It relates the agony of a man completely shattered and disillusioned by life. Arguedas methodically and passionately discusses the events leading to his final day—he committed suicide in a deserted classroom in Lima. In addition to his novels, Arguedas published a number of scholarly works and translations from Quechua.

Argüello, Leonardo (b. 1873—d. Dec. 15, 1947, Mexico City), president of Nicaragua for only 25 days under the Somoza regime.

An intellectual, Argüello served as minister of education. In fact, it was at a fête convened to honour him (1925) that one of the more comic attempted coups in Latin American history took place, led by the somewhat inebriated Gabry Rivas. Argüello was elected president with Gen. Anastasio Somoza's support and inaugurated May 1, 1947. He soon alienated Somoza by proving to be less than docile and dismissing some of Somoza's relatives from government posts. Somoza accused him of plotting to remove him from his position as head of the National Guard and ousted him on May 25. Argüello took refuge in the Mexican embassy for six months and was finally permitted to enter Mexico on November 30. He was replaced in office by provisional president Benjamin Lacayo Sacasa.

Arguin Island, island off the coast of Mauritania, West Africa, about 50 mi (80 km) southeast of Cap Blanc, in a sheltered Atlantic inlet (Arguin Bay). The island (4 mi by 2½ mi) was incorporated into the newly independent Mauritania in 1960. Aridity and poor anchorage have prevented the establishment of permanent settlements, but the coastal reefs, known as the Arguin Banks, are major fishing grounds. The island is also an important site for turtle fishing and produces gum arabic.

argument, in logic, reasons that support a conclusion, sometimes formulated so that the conclusion is deduced from premises. Erroneous arguments are called fallacies in logic (*see* fallacy). In mathematics, an argument is a variable in the domain of a function and usually appears symbolically in parentheses following the functional symbol.

Argun River, Russian ARGUN, Wade–Giles romanization O-ERH-KU-NA HO, Pinyin ER-

GUN HE, river rising in Heilungkiang Province, China, on the western slope of the Greater Khingan Range, where it is known as the Hai-la-erh Ho. Its length is 1,007 mi (1,620 km), of which about 600 mi form the boundary between China and the Soviet Union. The confluence of the Argun with the Shilka is regarded as the beginning of the Amur River. The Argun flows for the most part through a wide valley; it has a drainage basin of 63,000 sq mi (163,000 sq km). In years of abundant rainfall, the Argun overflows into the basin of Hu-lun Hu (lake; Mongol Dalay Nor) in Heilungkiang. Navigation is irregular.

Argungu, town and traditional emirate, Sokoto State, northwestern Nigeria. The town is on the Sokoto (Kebbi) River and lies at the intersection of roads from Birnin Kebbi, Gwandu, Sokoto town, Augi, and Kaingiwa. A settlement of the Kebbawa people, a subgroup of the Hausa, it was formerly called Birnin Lelaba dan Badau and was ruled from *c.* 1700 to 1805 by the Hausa kings of Kebbi, one of the Banza Bakwai (the seven illegitimate Hausa states), the capital of which was at Birnin Kebbi to the southwest. Although the *sarkin* ("king of") *Kebbi,* Muhammadu Hodi, was forced to submit to Fulani rule *c.* 1813, many of the Kebbawa continued to defy the Fulani *jihād* ("holy war") led by Usman dan Fodio. In 1827 Samaila (Karari), a *sarkin Kebbi* who refused to submit, established Argungu (from *a yi gungu,* "let us gather in one place") as the new Kebbi capital. After Samaila was defeated in 1831 by the combined forces of the Fulani emirates of Sokoto and Gwandu, Argungu, as the kingdom was then called, was ruled by Fulani *amīrs* until Yakubu Nabame, Samaila's son, proclaimed himself *sarkin Kebbi* in 1849 and defeated the Fulani forces.

Although the *sarkin musulmi* of Sokoto recognized Argungu as an independent kingdom under the Lafiyar Toga (a treaty signed in 1866 by Abdullahi Toga, then *sarkin Kebbi*), frequent Kebbawa–Fulani warfare continued until the arrival in 1902 of the British, who recognized Samaila (Sama) as the *amīr* of Argungu but ceded the considerable western part of the kingdom to France in 1907. Argungu *amīr*ate became a separate division of the province in 1906; it constituted the Argungu division of 3,356 sq mi (8,692 sq km). Most of its Muslim inhabitants are Kebbawas, but there are clusters of Fulani, Arewa (Ariwa), and Tienga (Kengawa) peoples. The traditional ruling family, the Lekawa, selected the *amīr*, the *sarkin Kebbi.*

The town is a collecting point for tobacco, grown in the surrounding riverine floodplains, and peanuts (groundnuts) and a major local market centre for rice, millet, sorghum, fish, cotton, cattle, goats, and sheep.

Argungu is noted for its Fashin Ruwa, an annual fishing festival usually held in February, and for its Kanta Museum, which houses 16th-century artifacts. The ruins of the walled town of Surame, the 16th- and 17th-century capital of Kebbi, are 35 mi (56 km) east-northeast. In addition to the government school (1919) and Kanta College (1970), Argungu has a health office and a medical centre. Pop. (1972 est.) town, 26,268.

Argus, the first true aircraft carrier. Construction of the Argus began in 1914, and initially it was an Italian liner; it was purchased in 1916 by the Royal Navy and converted, work being completed in September 1918. Argus had an unobstructed flight deck about 560 feet (170.7 metres) long and a hangar that could accommodate 20 aircraft. It was armed with six four-inch guns and could reach a speed of 20.2 knots.

Argus PANOPTES (Greek: All Seeing), figure in Greek legend described variously as the son of Inachus, Agenor, or Arestor or as an aboriginal hero (autochthon); his surname derives from the hundred eyes in his head or all over his body. Argus was appointed by the goddess Hera to watch the cow into which Io (Hera's priestess) had been transformed, but he was slain by Hermes. His eyes were transferred by Hera to the tail of the peacock. This Argus was often confused with the son of Niobe who gave his name to the city of Argos.

Argyll, also called ARGYLLSHIRE, Gaelic EARRAGHAIDHEAL (Coastland of the Gael), former county, western Scotland, since the reorganization of 1975 largely in Argyll and Bute (*q.v.*) district, of Strathclyde (*q.v.*) region.

Argyll, EARLS, MARQUESSES, AND DUKES OF, titled Scottish nobility, in the families Campbell of Lochow and Campbell of Mamore, grouped below chronologically and indicated by the symbol •.

• Argyll, Archibald Campbell, 5th earl of (b. 1530—d. Sept. 12, 1573), Scottish Protestant who supported Mary, Queen of Scots.

Campbell succeeded his father, Archibald, the 4th earl, in 1558. He was an adherent of John Knox and assisted Lord James Stewart (afterward the regent Moray) in the warfare of the lords of the congregation against the regent Mary of Lorraine, the mother of Mary Stuart. Argyll's support of Mary Stuart after her return to Scotland (1561) gradually separated him from John Knox's party. When Mary escaped from Lochleven Castle in 1568, he commanded her forces during the few days that preceded her flight to England. He then made his peace with Moray, although he may have connived at Moray's murder in 1570. He became lord high chancellor of Scotland in 1572. His first wife was an illegitimate daughter of James V, and he was thus half brother-in-law to Mary and Moray.

• Argyll, Archibald Campbell, 1st marquess and 8th earl of (b. 1607—d. May 27, 1661, Edinburgh), leader of Scotland's anti-Royalist party during the English Civil Wars between King Charles I and Parliament. He guided his country to a brief period of independence from political and religious domination by England.

Entering politics as a privy councillor in 1626, Campbell fell out of royal favour in 1637–38 by calling for the abolition of episcopacy in Scotland and by signing the National Covenant pledging to defend Scottish Presbyterianism against Charles I's attempts to impose Anglican forms of worship. As he gained political ascendancy he earned the bitter enmity of James Graham, earl of Montrose, leader of the Scottish Royalists, whom Campbell consistently managed to outmanoeuvre. Campbell inherited the earldom of Argyll from his father in 1638, and, as part of Charles I's concession to the Covenanters in 1641, he was created a marquess. He then set about forging an alliance with the English Parliament, at that time dominated by Presbyterians.

1st Marquess and 8th Earl of Argyll, detail of a portrait after D. Scougall; in the National Portrait Gallery, London

By courtesy of the National Portrait Gallery, London

While his army was occupying northern England for Parliament in 1644, Argyll remained in Scotland to hold Montrose in check. Montrose defeated him at Inverlochy in February 1645 and at Kilsyth in August, but Argyll helped rout the Royalist general in a decisive battle at Philiphaugh on September 13.

In 1648, after the Scottish Royalists had met defeat in their invasion of England, Argyll established a new government at Edinburgh and allied himself with the Parliamentarian commander Oliver Cromwell. But the execution of Charles I (Jan. 30, 1649) by Cromwell's Independents horrified the Scots and ruined the alliance. In desperation, Argyll allowed the Covenanters to invite Charles I's son to Scotland, and on Jan. 1, 1651, crowned him King Charles II. The defeat of Charles II in England in September 1651 caused Argyll to submit to Cromwell.

When Charles finally came to power in England in 1660, following Cromwell's death, he at once arrested Argyll for collaborating with the Commonwealth and had him beheaded at Edinburgh the following year. Argyll's career is recounted in John Willcock's *The Great Marquess* (1903).

• Argyll, Archibald Campbell, 9th earl of (b. Feb. 26, 1629, Dalkeith, Midlothian, Scot.—d. June 30, 1685, Edinburgh), Scottish Protestant leader who was executed for his opposition to the Catholic James II of Great Britain.

In his youth he studied abroad but returned to Scotland in 1649. He fought at Dunbar (Sept. 3, 1650) and, after the Battle of Worcester, joined the Royalist leader Glencairn in the Highlands. Ultimately he fell foul of both the Royalists and their opponents; he was imprisoned in 1657 during the Commonwealth for refusing to renounce allegiance to the Stuarts and again in 1661 for incautious criticisms of the government of Charles II. He was released in 1663 and his father's earldom and lands were restored to him. However, his staunch Protestantism and great territorial influence made him suspect to James, duke of York (the future James II), who became high commissioner in Scotland in 1680. He was sentenced to death on a dubious charge of high treason in 1681 but escaped to Holland and there joined the conspiracy to procure the succession of the Duke of Monmouth. He led an unsuccessful invasion of Scotland in 1685, was captured at Inchinnan on the River Clyde on June 18, and was beheaded at Edinburgh on June 30.

• Argyll, Archibald Campbell, 10th earl and 1st duke of (b. 1651?—d. Sept. 25, 1703, Cherton House, near Newcastle-upon-Tyne, Northumberland, Eng.), one of the Scottish leaders of the Revolution of 1688.

Campbell was the eldest son of the 9th Earl, and he tried to get his father's attainder reversed by seeking the favour of King James II. Being unsuccessful, however, he went over to The Hague and joined William of Orange as an active promoter of the Revolution of 1688. In spite of the attainder, he was admitted in 1689 to the convention of the Scottish estates as earl of Argyll, and he was deputed, with Sir James Montgomery and Sir John Dalrymple, to present the crown to William III in its name and to tender him the coronation oath.

In 1690, after the Revolution, an act was passed restoring his title and estates, and it was in connection with the refusal of the Macdonalds of Glencoe to join in the submission to him that he organized the terrible massacre that made his name notorious. In 1696 he was made a lord of the treasury, and his political services were rewarded in 1701 by his being created duke of Argyll. He had two sons by his wife Elizabeth: John (the 2nd duke) and Archibald (the 3rd duke).

•Argyll, John Campbell, 2nd duke of, DUKE OF GREENWICH, also called (1705–19) EARL OF GREENWICH, BARON OF CHATHAM (b. Oct. 10, 1678, Petersham, Surrey, Eng.—d. Oct. 4, 1743, Petersham), Scottish supporter of the union with England and commander of the British forces in the Jacobite rebellion of 1715.

The son of the 1st Duke of Argyll (in the Scottish peerage), he actively furthered the union of England and Scotland and was created a peer of England (1705), with the titles earl of Greenwich and baron of Chatham. He served under the Duke of Marlborough from 1706 in the War of the Spanish Succession, gaining particular distinction at the Battle of Malplaquet in 1709. He acted as commander in chief in Spain and as ambassador to the archduke Charles in 1711. Argyll's intervention at Queen Anne's last council meeting helped to ensure the Hanoverian succession (August 1714), and during the early years of George I's reign he stood in high favour at court.

As commander in chief of the forces in north Britain during the Jacobite rebellion of 1715, he managed with very little bloodshed to suppress the rising in Scotland. After a temporary eclipse, caused by disagreement with the ministry rather than the disfavour of the King, he regained his influence and was created duke of Greenwich (1719). He held various offices and in 1736 was made a field marshal. He strenuously opposed in 1737 the bill to penalize the city of Edinburgh over the Porteous riots, and a violent speech against the government in April 1740 led again to his dismissal from office. Apart from one further short period of power, he spent the remainder of his life in retirement.

•Argyll, Archibald Campbell, 3rd duke of, also called (1707–43) EARL OF ISLAY (b. June 1682, Ham House, Petersham, Surrey, Eng.—d. April 15, 1761, London), brother of the 2nd Duke of Argyll, and a prominent politician during the early Hanoverian period in Britain.

He served in the army for a short time under the Duke of Marlborough, but he was appointed treasurer of Scotland in 1705 and the following year was one of the commissioners for negotiating the union of the two kingdoms, Scotland and Ireland. Raised to the peerage of Scotland as earl of Islay, he was among the 16th Scottish peers chosen to sit in the first Parliament of Great Britain. He became a privy councillor in 1711, keeper of the privy seal of Scotland in 1721, and keeper of the Great Seal of Scotland in 1733. He played an important part in the movement led by Duncan Forbes of Culloden to promote Scottish loyalty to the Hanoverians by raising Highland regiments from among the Whig clans.

Succeeding his brother as duke in 1743, he rebuilt Iveraray castle and collected one of the most valuable private libraries in Great Britain. He died without legitimate issue, and the title descended to his cousin John Campbell, son of John Campbell of Mamore, second son of the 9th Earl of Argyll.

Argyll and Bute, district, Strathclyde region, southwestern Scotland. Created by the reorganization of 1975, it embraces most of the former county of Argyll and part of the former county of Bute. The district, area 2,609 sq mi (6,757 sq km), in the southwestern Grampians, reaches the Irish Sea in ragged peninsulas trenched by deepwater lochs (sea inlets and lakes). It includes many islands of the Inner Hebrides (notably Mull, Islay, and Jura).

The area is approximately one-third of the wet, deeply dissected North-West Highlands, whose short, vigorous rivers drain westward to the Atlantic Ocean. There is a marked southwest–northeast trend in the structure of the landscape. The mountains, ranging from 1,000 to 3,000 ft (300 to 900 m), have been eroded by ice and water, forming spectacular scenery. Glacial action is responsible for the formation of corries, or hillside hollows, and deeply eroded lochs (Loch Awe), sea lochs (Lochs Fyne and Long), and deposits of coarse moraines and boulder clay on lower land. The deeply indented complex coastline of peninsulas and sea lochs is the result of postglacial drowning. Coastal Argyll has a cool, damp climate, while inland conditions are much wetter and less equable.

Recorded history begins in the 2nd century AD, when Argyll was invaded by the Scots from Ireland who eventually established the independent kingdom of Dalriada, which in 843 or 844 was united by Kenneth I MacAlpin with the Pictish kingdom of central Scotland. Invading Norsemen subsequently gained control and held sway until their defeat in the Battle of Largs (1263). Semi-independent chiefs of mixed Celtic and Norse descent (the lords of the Isles) controlled Argyll and the Isles until the late 15th century. During the 18th and 19th centuries, the clearance of Highland villages and farms to accommodate extensive sheep farming caused the displacement of thousands of crofters, or tenant farmers.

Farming, including sheep and cattle raising, remains the main occupation. Less than 5 percent of the total area is under cultivation, mainly oats and hay for fodder. Crofting is widespread in the north. Whisky distilling is important at a number of places, especially Campbeltown and Fort William and on Islay. The extensive estates of the Forestry Commission continue to expand. Silver, copper, and lead previously were mined; there are still slate quarries at Ballachulish, but these, too, are declining. Industries such as the manufacture of clipboard, paper pulp, pit props, and fence posts from local timber, in addition to the thriving tourist trade, are Argyll's hopes for future expansion. The once-important herring fisheries have declined and have been replaced to some extent by whitefish fishing. Lochgilphead, the seat of the district authority, Tobermory, Oban, Campbeltown, and Rothesay are among the widely dispersed local and tourist centres. Pop. (1982 est.) 64,701.

argyrodite, heavy, dark sulfosalt mineral, a silver and germanium sulfide (Ag_8GeS_6), in which the element germanium was discovered (1886). It is a relatively scarce mineral found in sulfide veins in East Germany and in Bolivia. It forms a solid solution series with canfieldite in which tin replaces germanium in the crystal structure, which belongs to the isometric system. For detailed physical properties, *see* sulfosalt (table).

Argyrókastron (Albania): *see* Gjirokastër.

arhat (Sanskrit), Pāli ARAHANT (one who is "fit" or "worthy"), in Buddhism, a perfected person, one who has gained insight into the true nature of existence and has achieved Nirvāṇa (spiritual Enlightenment). The *arhat,* having freed himself from the bonds of desire, will not be reborn again.

The state of an *arhat* is considered in the Theravāda tradition to be the proper goal of a Buddhist. Four stages of attainment are described in Pāli texts: (1) the state of the "stream-enterer"—*i.e.,* a convert (*sotāpanna*)—achieved by overcoming false beliefs and doubts regarding the Buddha, the teaching (*dhamma*), and the order (*saṅgha*); (2) the "once-returner" (*sakadāgāmin*), who will be reborn only once again, a state attained by diminishing lust, hatred, and illusion; (3) the "non-returner" (*anāgāmin*), who, after death, will be reborn in a higher heaven, where he will become an *arhat*, a state attained by overcoming sensuous desire and ill will, in addition to the attainments of the first two stages; and (4) the *arhat.* Except under extraordinary circumstances, a man or woman can become an *arhat* only while living in a monastery.

Mahāyāna Buddhists criticize the *arhat* ideal on the grounds that the *bodhisattva* (*q.v.*) is a higher goal of perfection, for the *bodhisattva* vows to remain within the cycle of rebirths, even though capable of Enlightenment, in order to work for the good of others. This divergence of opinion continues to be one of the fundamental differences between the Theravāda and Mahāyāna traditions.

In China, as well as in Korea, Japan, and Tibet, *arhats* (Chinese *lohan;* Japanese *rakan*) were often depicted on the walls of temples in groups of 16 (later enlarged to 18, or even 500). They represent 16 close disciples of the Buddha who were entrusted by him to remain in the world and not to enter Nirvāṇa until the coming of the next Buddha, in order to provide people with objects of worship.

Arhuaco, any of various Chibchan-speaking Indian peoples of the Sierra Nevada de Santa Marta in northern Colombia. The term does not include the highly civilized extinct pre-Conquest peoples of the area but only peoples of fairly simple culture: the Ica, Cágaba (or Koghi), Sanha, and Buntigwa. In the late 20th century several thousand Arhuaco lived in the Sierra Nevada. Of these the most numerous are the Cágaba (about 3,000) and the Ica (about 4,000). It is not known whether any Sanha remain.

The Arhuaco are primarily agricultural; crops are sweet manioc (cassava), corn (maize), potatoes, *arracacha* (a parsnip-like edible root), plantain, and sugarcane. The Ica and Buntigwa also keep domestic animals, including chickens, turkeys, pigs, and sheep. Oxen are kept as pack animals. Houses are round or rectangular, built of mud and thatched with grass. Settlements are groups of villages, each of which has a temple, also used as a men's house, and a Catholic church. Villages are often fenced completely or partially, with gated entrances. Clothing is of cotton: men wear a long, loose robe or tunic over tight pants, a hat, and a shoulder bag; women wear a dress fastened over one shoulder, leaving the other bare, and a wide sash. Shoes are not worn. The major craft is weaving.

Puberty rites are observed for both sexes, and formerly both boys and girls were initiated sexually by older persons at the conclusion of such rites. Now only boys are so initiated. Married couples also observe a taboo against sexual intercourse indoors. Some Arhuaco are Roman Catholic, but the indigenous religion, with its own priests and temples, flourishes. It is likely that the Arhuaco religion is similar to that of the Tairona (*q.v.*), whose civilization once flourished in the same region.

A list of the abbreviations used in the MICROPAEDIA *will be found at the end of this volume*

Århus, also spelled AARHUS, city, seat of Århus *amtskommune* (county), eastern Jutland, Denmark, on Århus Bugt (bay). Its origin is unknown, although traces of a Viking settlement have been found near the outflow of the now-covered Århus stream. The oldest existing charter (1441) refers to an earlier one. It became a bishopric in 948 and prospered during the Middle Ages but declined after the Reformation. Industrialization, extension of the Danish railway system, and construction of the harbour in the 19th century stimulated growth. Århus has become Jutland's foremost city (the second largest in Denmark) and the centre of commerce and industry there. Man-

Section of the open-air museum "Den Gamle By," Århus, Den.
Toni Schneiders

ufactures include metals, chemicals, machinery, beer, and tobacco products, and there are shipbuilding facilities. Medieval landmarks include the 11th-century crypt of St. Nicholas under Vor Frue Kirke (Church of Our Lady) and the 13th-century Århus cathedral dedicated to St. Clement, the longest church (305 ft [93 m]) in Denmark. The town hall (1938–42) and the university buildings (1933–46) are examples of modern Danish architecture. The Århus Kunstmuseum (1858) includes a display of runic stones, and Den Gamle By is a unique open-air museum (1909) of an old Danish town. In addition to Århus University (opened 1928), there are four specialized colleges and an academy of music.

Århus *amtskommune* (area 1,764 sq mi [4,569 sq km]), created in 1970 from the former counties of Århus, Randers, and part of Skanderborg, extends along Jutland's eastern coast between Mariager and Horsens fjords. The northern part of the county is dominated by the Djursland Peninsula, an area of castles and estates, including Rosenholm Castle (home of the Rosenkrantz nobles) and Gammel Estrup, an early 17th-century manor house converted into the Jyllands Herregårdsmuseum (Museum of the Jutland Estates). In the southwest, between Silkeborg and Skanderborg, lie the Silkeborg Lake district and Himmelbjerget (Hill of Heaven). Most of the county is fertile lowland country forming a prosperous agricultural region. Pop. (1981) city, 181,830; (1982 est.) mun., 246,679; (1982 est.) *amtskommune*, 576,705.

Ari THORGILSSON THE LEARNED (b. *c.* 1067—d. Nov. 9, 1148), Icelandic chieftain, priest, and historian whose *Íslendingabók* (*Libellus Islandorum;* trans. by H. Hermannssen, *The Book of the Icelanders,* 1930) is the first history of Iceland written in the vernacular. Composed before 1133 and covering the period from the settlement of Iceland up to 1120, it includes information on the founding of the Althing (Parliament) and on the settlement of Greenland and Vinland. Ari is also believed to have written much of the original version of *Landnámabók* ("Book of Settlements"), a work listing the genealogies and histories of noble Icelandic settlers. It served as a source for many of the 12th-century "Icelander," or family sagas.

Ari, ha-: *see* Luria, Isaac ben Solomon.

aria, solo song with instrumental accompaniment, an important element of opera, but also found extensively in cantatas and oratorios; also, a lyrical instrumental piece. The term originated in Italy in the 16th century and first gained currency after 1602, when Giulio Caccini published *Le nuove musiche* (*The New Music*), a collection of solo songs with continuo (usually cello and harpsichord) accompaniment. Caccini called his strophic, or stanza-form, songs *arie* (singular *aria*). Most such songs published in Italy after 1602 were called arias; and in 1607 the form made its way into opera, in *Orfeo* by Claudio Monteverdi (1567–1643).

Instead of using the same music for every stanza, some composers placed variations of a melody over a repeated, steadily moving bass line. Arias of a popular or frivolous cast were often called canzonetta or arietta. After about 1620, arias were nearly always composed in triple time (*e.g.,* $\frac{3}{4}$) and also were longer and in new musical forms, often suggested by the texts. By the mid-17th century the leading form had become the da capo aria, in which the initial melody and text were repeated after an intervening melody and text had been sung, *i.e.,* ABA. Often the inner B section was set in duple time (*e.g.,* $\frac{2}{4}$), the outer A sections in triple time (*e.g.,* $\frac{3}{4}$).

For more than a century the da capo aria, found mainly in Italian operas and cantatas, was the dominant musical form. Aria texts became shorter, a few lines to each section. The central B section was usually terse and often in a related key, with contrasting mood and tempo. The story of an opera was advanced through recitative (dialogue sung in quick, speech-like rhythms); in contrast, arias were dramatically static, allowing individual characters to reflect the immediately preceding action, after which they left the stage.

Arias might assume different moods and were classified as *aria cantabile* (lyric aria), *aria di bravura* (virtuoso aria), *aria parlante* (speech-like aria), and so on. These were supposed to be carefully distributed throughout an opera, although such composers as Handel and Alessandro Scarlatti did not observe this convention rigidly. The acclaimed singers of the age decorated the reprise of the A section with brilliant improvised embellishments, culminating in an unaccompanied cadenza. The da capo aria also appeared in cantatas and oratorios.

By the late 18th century, reaction set in against the da capo form, and it went into sharp decline. Such influential persons as the philosopher Jean-Jacques Rousseau (1712–78) and composer Christoph Willibald Gluck (1714–87) protested the da capo aria, objecting to its excessive coloratura (or florid singing), to the dramatic impropriety of returning to the mood of section A after the contrasting mood of section B, and to the absurdity often resulting from the repeated section of text.

The aria continued to be prominent in opera after about 1770, but in many different, less stereotyped musical forms, ranging from simple strophic songs to long elaborate scenes. The operas of Gluck were the first important ones to utilize such a variety of arias. The aria also enjoyed a vogue as a concert piece. Operatic arias (*e.g.,* Leporello's "Catalogue Aria" in Mozart's *Don Giovanni*) were often written in two parts, one dramatic and one lyrical.

In Italian opera up to *Aida* (1871), the aria was cultivated over a longer period than in German opera. Wagner in his operatic reforms utilized a continuous musical texture in place of separate numbers, using arias only in special instances, *e.g.,* the "Prize Song" in *Die Meistersinger.* In the 20th century, arias occur largely in operas by composers uninfluenced by or hostile to Wagner (*e.g.,* Stravinsky's *Rake's Progress* and the operas of Benjamin Britten). The word aria is occasionally used for instrumental pieces of a songlike nature, as the two middle movements of Stravinsky's *Violin Concerto.*

Ariadne, in Greek mythology, daughter of Pasiphae and the Cretan king Minos. She fell in love with the Athenian hero Theseus, and with a thread or glittering jewels she helped him escape the Labyrinth after he slew the Minotaur, a beast half bull and half man that Minos kept in the Labyrinth. Here the legends diverge: she was abandoned and hanged herself; she was carried to Naxos and left there to die or to marry the wine god Dionysus; or she died in childbirth on Cyprus.

Ariadne with Dionysus and a satyr, antique bas-relief; in the Vatican Museum
Anderson—Alinari from Art Resource/EB Inc.

Ariadne was once a vegetation goddess of pre-Greek Minoan Crete, Cyprus, Naxos, and perhaps elsewhere. The Naxians, who alone preserved her divinity, honoured the elder Ariadne, wife of Dionysus, with a joyous festival and the younger with gloomy sacrificial rites. Originally there must have been but one Ariadne, and these rituals reflected the death and revival of the vegetation she personified. In this role she was definitely an original product of Minoan religious thought, since in comparable religions the dying vegetation is ordinarily personified as male.

Arianism, a Christian heresy first proposed early in the 4th century by the Alexandrian presbyter Arius. It affirmed that Christ is not truly divine but a created being. The fundamental premise of Arius was the uniqueness of God, who is alone self-existent and immutable; the Son, who is not self-existent, cannot be God. Because the Godhead is unique, it cannot be shared or communicated so that the Son cannot be God. Because the Godhead is immutable, the Son, who is mutable, being represented in the Gospels as subject to growth and change, cannot be God. The Son must, therefore, be deemed a creature who has been called into existence out of nothing and has had a beginning. Moreover, the Son can have no direct knowledge of the Father since the Son is finite and of a different order of existence.

According to its opponents, especially Athanasius, Arius' teaching reduced the Son to a demigod, reintroduced polytheism (since worship of the Son was not abandoned), and undermined the Christian concept of redemption since only he who was truly God could be deemed to have reconciled man to the Godhead.

The controversy seemed to have been brought to an end by the Council of Nicaea (AD 325), which condemned Arius and his teaching and issued a creed to safeguard orthodox Christian belief. This creed states that the Son is *homoousion tō Patri* ("of one substance with the Father"), thus declaring him to be all that the Father is: he is completely divine. In fact, however, this was only the beginning of a long-protracted dispute.

From 325 to 337, when Constantine died, the Arian leaders, exiled after the Council of Nicaea, tried by intrigue to return to their churches and sees and to banish their enemies. They were partly successful.

From 337 to 350 Constans, sympathetic to the orthodox Christians, was emperor in the West, and Constantius II, sympathetic to the Arians, was emperor in the East. At a council held at Antioch (341), an affirmation of faith that omitted the *homoousion* clause was issued. Another council was held at Sardica (modern Sofia) in 342, but little was achieved by either council.

In 350 Constantius became sole ruler of the empire, and under his leadership the Nicene party (orthodox Christians) was largely crushed. The extreme Arians then declared that the Son was "unlike" (*anomoios*) the Father. These Anomoeans succeeded in having their views endorsed at Sirmium in 357, but their extremism stimulated the moderates, who asserted that the Son was "of similar substance" (*homoiousios*) with the Father. Constantius at first supported these Homoiousians but soon transferred his support to the Homoeans, led by Acacius, who affirmed that the Son was "like" (*homoios*) the Father. Their views were approved in 360 at Constantinople, where all previous creeds were rejected, the term *ousia* ("substance" or "stuff") was repudiated, and a statement of faith was issued stating that the Son was "like the Father who begot him."

After Constantius' death (361), the orthodox Christian majority in the West consolidated its position. The Arian persecution conducted by Emperor Valens (364–378) in the East and the success of the teaching of Basil the Great of Caesarea, Gregory of Nyssa, and Gregory of Nazianzus led the Homoiousian majority in the East to realize its fundamental agreement with the Nicene party. When the emperors Gratian (367–383) and Theodosius I (379–395) took up the defense of orthodoxy, Arianism collapsed. In 381 the second ecumenical council met at Constantinople. Arianism was proscribed, and a statement of faith, the Nicene Creed, was approved.

Although this ended the heresy in the empire, Arianism continued among some of the Germanic tribes to the end of the 7th century. In modern times some Unitarians are virtually Arians in that they are unwilling either to reduce Christ to a mere human being or to attribute to him a divine nature identical with that of the Father. The Christology of Jehovah's Witnesses, also, is a form of Arianism; they regard Arius as a forerunner of Charles Taze Russell, the founder of their movement.

Arianism, Semi-: *see* Semi-Arianism.

Ariano Irpino, town, Avellino province, Campania region, southern Italy, on a rocky eminence in the Apennines, east of Benevento, in a fertile district that has often been devastated by earthquakes. It supposedly occupies the site of Aequum Tuticum, an ancient Samnite town that was regarded as a Roman post station on the Via Traiana; but this was probably at San Eleuterio, 5.5 mi (nearly 9 km) north. There is a castle of Norman origin in Ariano Irpino and a 16th-century cathedral, which suffered earthquake damage in 1980. Cave dwellings can still be seen in the vicinity. Cement, pottery, and textiles are manufactured locally, and gypsum mines are nearby. Pop. (1981 prelim.) mun., 21,631.

Ariaramnes, also spelled ARIYARAMNA (fl. late 7th century BC), early Achaemenid king of Persia (ruled *c.* 640–*c.* 615). The son of the previous king, Teispes, Ariaramnes ruled over Persis (modern Fārs, in southwestern Iran); his brother Cyrus I was given control of Anshan in Elam, north of the Persian Gulf. A campaign by the Medes, however, broke the power of Ariaramnes, and he and his son Arsames, who succeeded him, became vassals of Media (in modern northwest Iran). Dating to the reign of Ariaramnes is an important gold tablet written in cuneiform—the first historical inscription in Old Persian from Achaemenid times. The tablet, found at Ecbatana (Hamadan, Iran), where it had probably been carried by the Medes, not only traces the royal line of Ariaramnes but also provides the first Persian mention of Ahura Mazdā, the supreme god.

Arias (Madrid), Arnulfo (b. Aug. 15, 1901, Penonomé, Panama), three times president of Panama (June 1940–October 1941, November 1949–May 1951, and Oct. 1–12, 1968) and three times deposed.

The younger brother of Harmodio Arias (Panamanian president, 1932–36), Arias was educated at the University of Chicago and Harvard Medical School (to become a surgeon) and served as minister of agriculture and public works in the 1930s. During his first term, he forced foreign businessmen to transfer their companies to Panamanian ownership and divested black West Indians of their citizenship. He sympathized with the Axis powers during World War II and opposed U.S. requests for defense installations. After the coup which deposed him (probably supported by the United States), he went into exile until 1945. During his dictatorial and corrupt second term, he replaced the constitution, dissolved the National Assembly and the Supreme Court, and was finally deposed by the police. Denied political rights from 1951 to 1960, Arias ran unsuccessfully for president in 1964, was elected in 1968, and then deposed by the military 11 days after taking office.

Arias Dávila, Pedro, also called PEDRARIAS DÁVILA (b. 1440?, Segovia, Castile—d. March 6, 1531, Léon, New Spain), Spanish soldier and colonial administrator who led the first Spanish expedition to found permanent colonies in the New World.

As a soldier in his youth, Arias Dávila earned such titles as "the gallant" and "the jouster." He served with distinction in wars against the Moors in Granada in the 1490s and in North Africa in 1508–11. It is believed that he owed his appointment as captain general of the Spanish lands in the New World, which he received in 1513, to the Bishop of Burgos. Arias Dávila sailed for the New World in 1514 with 19 ships and about 1,500 men.

Arias Dávila's accomplishments include establishing colonies in what are now Panama (1514) and Nicaragua (1522), serving as governor of Panama (1514–26) and Nicaragua (1527–31), and founding Panama City (1519). He also sent out expeditions of conquest, such as that led by Hernán Ponce and Bartolomé Hurtado to what are now Costa Rica and Nicaragua in 1516 and that led by Francisco Pizarro and Diego de Almagro, which conquered the Inca empire in what is now Peru in 1524.

Arias Dávila, however, has been described both as being too old and as lacking the intellectual and moral capacity needed by a captain general. He seems to have deliberately promoted discord among the captains placed under his command, and he was held responsible for the trial and execution of the explorer Vasco Núñez de Balboa in 1519.

Arias de Saavedra, Hernando, byname HERNANDARIAS (b. 1561?, Asunción, Río de la Plata—d. 1634, Santa Fe, Río de la Plata), Spanish-American explorer and soldier, served as lieutenant governor (1597–1602) and governor (1602–09, 1614–18) of the Spanish district of Río de la Plata in South America.

Hernandarias was known for his protection of the Indian population, for establishment of closer ties between the Church and the civil authorities, and for encouraging the establishment of Jesuit and Franciscan missions. An efficient and incorruptible official, he inadvertently caused economic setbacks to the area by rigidly enforcing the laws against smuggling, an activity which had become virtually institutionalized under more lenient governors. Hernandarias founded the city of Corrientes (Argentina) and helped develop Buenos Aires, Santa Fe, and Asunción. After his second terms, Río de la Plata was divided into two administrative units, each with its own governor.

Aribau, Buenaventura Carles (b. Nov. 4, 1798, Barcelona—d. Sept. 17, 1862, Barcelona), economist and man of letters whose poem *Oda a la patria* (1832; "Ode to the Fatherland") marked the beginning of the renaissance of Catalan literature in the 19th century in Spain.

After working in Madrid at the banking establishment of Gaspar Remisa (1830–41), Aribau became the director of the treasury and financial secretary to the royal household.

Aribau, oil painting by J.E. Rull; in the Real Academia de Bellas Artes de San Jorge de Barcelona
Archivo Mas, Barcelona

Animated by a deep patriotism, Aribau's work is marked by the early Romanticist concern with history. He was one of the editors of *El Europeo* and *El vapor,* two of the most important periodicals of the Romantic movement, the latter heavily reflecting the medievalist influence of the British novelist Sir Walter Scott. His *Oda a la patria,* upon which his fame rests, was a defense of regional feeling, written in the vernacular of Catalan, which attempted to unite contemporary intellectual trends with native tradition. Aribau also edited, along with Manuel de Rivadeneyra, the first four volumes of the famous *Biblioteca de autores españoles,* a monumental attempt to bring together all the important literature of Spain. (It filled 71 volumes upon completion in 1880.)

Ariböx (Mongol ruler): *see* Arigböge.

Arica, capital of Arica province, Tarapacá region, Chile, on the Pacific coast, at the foot of El Morro (a precipitous headland), fringed by sand dunes of the rainless Atacama Desert. Arica is situated near the Peruvian border and

The harbour at Arica, Chile
Jacques Jangoux—Photo Researchers

is the northernmost Chilean seaport. Founded as San Marcos de Arica in 1570 on the site of a pre-Columbian settlement, it belonged to Peru until 1879, when it was captured by the Chileans, who gained control under the Treaty of Ancón (1883). The question of Chile's legal possession was not finally resolved until 1929.

Until the mid-20th century, Arica served as a free port and handled considerable Bolivian transit trade. It is still a free port for Bolivia, a commercial centre for Peru and northern Chile, and industries, chiefly fish meal processing and automobile assembly, have developed. It is the terminus of an oil pipeline from Oruro, Bolivia. The irrigated Azapa and Río Lluta valleys yield farm produce for Arica and olives and citrus fruit for export. With its seaport, international jet airport, railways to Tacna, Peru (39 mi [63 km] north), and La Paz, Bolivia (285 mi [459 mi] northeast), and location on the Pan-American Highway, Arica is also a transportation hub. Pop. (1982 prelim.) 138,989.

aridisol, the dominant soil type of deserts and other relatively arid regions. First in abundance among the 10 orders of soil taxonomy, the aridisols cover almost one-fifth of the total area of the world's soils. Supporting far less vegetation than the soils of humid regions, they have a low organic matter content. Winds play a major role in their development by blowing away fine particles, leaving a concentration of gravel or producing a desert pavement.

In areas where aridisols form, little water is available for leaching soluble salts or moving clay minerals. Most aridisols, at a certain depth, display a calcic horizon—a layer of calcium carbonate deposited by what little water manages to percolate downward from the surface. Many aridisols have well-developed clay (argillic) horizons, evidence of considerable movement of clay minerals at some time in the distant past, presumably when the climate was more humid than today. Aridisols that contain these horizons are grouped in the argid suborder; others are classified as orthids. Although aridisols are unsuitable for cultivation in their natural state, they become highly productive when they are irrigated (as in the valleys of the western United States).

Ariège, *département,* Midi-Pyrénées region, southern France, bordering Andorra and Spain. Its 1,888 sq mi (4,890 sq km) embrace the widest and highest of the Pyrenees, including many peaks over 9,000 ft (2,700 m), notably Montcalm (10,098 ft), and passes above 6,000 ft, which remain snow-blocked for many months of the year. The outermost ridge, the Montagne du Plantaurel, intersected by the Ariège River, drops steeply to the lowlands of Aquitaine. The outer limestone ranges have picturesque gorges, river tunnels, and caves. Controlling the Ariège gateway into the mountains and the approach to the Col de Puymorens, the countship of Foix (approximately the modern *département* in extent) retained its distinctness from the 11th century to the French Revolution. This ancient county now forms the nucleus of the *département,* which also includes parts of Languedoc and Gascony. Although it largely comprises the upper basin of the river Ariège, the *département* extends westward into that of the Salat headstream of the Garonne.

A pastoral economy prevails in the high mountains, and as use of the summer pastures from the French side has decreased, more use has been made of them by Spanish shepherds. There are only limited forests, because within the forest zone farming has made extensive encroachments. Corn (maize), haricot beans, potatoes, and deciduous fruits are grown in the lower valleys, and the mixed farming (wheat and corn) that is so typical of the lowlands of Aquitaine is practiced in the lower country in the north of the *département.* Although high-grade iron ore has been depleted, lead and zinc deposits are still exploited. Gypsum and anhydrite mining is important at Tarascon, and talc at Luzenac. Hydroelectric power is an increasingly important economic factor, supporting aluminum refining at Sabart.

The Col (pass) de Puymorens, Ariège, Fr.
Club Iris

A growing tourist industry has revived old spas such as Ax-les-Thermes. The grottoes of Le Mas-d'Azil and Niaux are rich in Paleolithic archaeological remains.

Foix (the capital), Pamiers, and Saint-Girons head *arrondissements.* Pamiers is the seat of the bishopric that is coextensive with the *département.* The court of appeal and the educational headquarters are outside the *département* at Toulouse. Pop. (1982) 135,725.

Ariel, one of the five known satellites of Uranus. It was discovered in 1851 by William Lassell, an English astronomer, but was probably seen four years earlier by the Russian-born astronomer Otto Struve.

Ariel is the second most distant satellite from Uranus, orbiting at a distance of 192,000 kilometres (119,040 miles) from the centre of the planet. It has a period of 2.52 days. No direct measurements of Ariel's diameter or mass have yet been made, but the discovery in 1980 of frozen water on its surface has led investigators to surmise that it has a high surface reflectance. Its interior is probably composed primarily of ices of water and methane in addition to a small amount of rocky material. Ariel's estimated diameter is 800 km (500 mi), and its mass is thought to be about 4×10^{-6} that of Uranus (*q.v.*).

Ariel, the first international cooperative Earth satellite, launched April 26, 1962, as a joint project of the United States and the United Kingdom. Design, construction, telemetry, and launching of the 14.5-kilogram (32-lb) satellite was handled in the United States by the National Aeronautics and Space Administration. Design of the equipment and of experiments to measure electron density and temperature and composition of positive ions, intensity of solar radiation in ultraviolet Lyman-alpha line, and cosmic rays was done by the United Kingdom.

Aries (Latin: Ram), in astronomy, zodiacal constellation lying between Pisces and Taurus, at about 3 hours right ascension (the coordinate on the celestial sphere analogous to longitude on the Earth) and 20° north declination (angular distance from the celestial equator).

Aries contains no very bright stars. The first point of Aries, or vernal equinox, is an intersection of the celestial equator with the apparent annual pathway of the Sun and the point in the sky from which celestial longitude and right ascension are measured. It no longer lies in Aries but has been moved into Pisces by the precession of the equinoxes.

In astrology, Aries is the first sign of the zodiac, considered as governing the period *c.* March 21–*c.* April 19. Its representation as a ram is identified with the Egyptian god Amon and, in Greek mythology, with the ram with the golden fleece, on the back of which

Phrixus, the son of King Athamas, safely fled Thessaly to Colchis, where he sacrificed the

Aries, illumination from a Book of Hours, Italian, *c.* 1475; in the Pierpont Morgan Library, New York City (MS. G.14)

By courtesy of the Pierpont Morgan Library, New York, the Glazier Collection

ram to Zeus, who placed it in the heavens as the constellation. The ram's golden fleece was recovered by Jason, leader of the Argonauts.

Arigböge, also spelled ARIKBÖGE, or ARIBÖX (d. 1266), brother of the great Mongol leader Kublai Khan and the Mongol chief most disposed toward Christianity. As commander of the Mongol homeland when the great khan Mangu died in 1259, Arigböge had himself proclaimed the chief Mongol leader. Meanwhile, his elder brother, Kublai, returned from his campaigns in China and also assumed the title. A series of battles ensued, and Arigböge was finally defeated in 1264. Kublai held him prisoner until his death.

Arīḥā (Jordan): *see* Jericho.

Arikara, American Plains Indian people of the Caddoan linguistic family who lived along the Missouri River between the Cheyenne River in South Dakota and Ft. Berthold in North Dakota. The cultural roots of Caddoan-speaking peoples lay in the prehistoric mound-building societies of the lower Mississippi Valley. The Arikara were culturally related to the Pawnee, from whom they broke away and moved gradually northward, becoming the northernmost Caddoan tribe.

"Bear's Belly—Arikara," photograph by Edward S. Curtis, 1908; from *The North American Indian*

Courtesy of the Edward E. Ayer Collection, The Newberry Library, Chicago

The Arikara were expert in raising corn, which they traded with other tribes for meat and robes. In addition, they also raised beans, squash, tobacco, and sunflowers. The women did the farming; the men hunted deer, elk, and some buffalo. They lived in semipermanent villages of earth-covered lodges. Village activities were controlled by reference to a sacred bundle in the hands of a priest. This office and the posts of chiefs tended to be the hereditary prerogative of a few leading families. Lower posts were associated with organized military, dancing, and curing societies. They shared with other Plains tribes the practice of self-torture in tribal sun dance ceremonies.

The Arikara became an obstacle to white trading parties moving up the Missouri River; a battle with traders in 1823 resulted in the first U.S. Army campaign against a Plains tribe. Although they had numbered between 3,000 and 4,000 near the end of the 1700s, wars and smallpox epidemics had severely reduced their numbers by the 19th century. In the 1860s they banded together with the Mandan and Hidatsa tribes at Ft. Berthold, and a reservation was created for them there. By 1885 they had taken up farming on scattered family farmsteads. In the 1950s construction of Garrison Dam and the discovery of oil in the Williston Basin forced another removal to new homes.

Arikböge (Mongol ruler): *see* Arigböge.

aril, special covering of certain seeds that commonly develops from the seed stalk. It is often a bright-coloured fleshy envelope, as in such woody plants as the yews and nutmeg and in members of the arrowroot family, the genus *Oxalis,* and the castor bean. Animals are attracted to arils and eat the seeds, dispersing them in their wastes. In the castor bean, the aril is spongy and absorbs water during germination. The aril of nutmeg is the source of the spice known as mace.

Ariminum, Council of, also called COUNCIL OF RIMINI (AD 359), one of the several 4th-century church councils concerned with Arianism, called by the pro-Arian emperor Constantius II. It was attended by the Western bishops, the Eastern bishops simultaneously meeting at Seleucia. Although the majority of bishops at Ariminum were orthodox and accepted the faith of Nicaea, the Arian minority included skilled diplomats who succeeded in undoing the orthodox decision of the majority when it reached the Emperor. The remaining bishops at Ariminum were forced to recant and subscribe to an Arian creed drawn up at Nice in Thracia. Pope Liberius repudiated this creed, declaring the council without authority.

Arinnitti, Hattian WURUSEMU, Hittite sun goddess, the principal deity and patron of the Hittite empire and monarchy. Her consort, the weather god Taru, was second to Arinnitti in importance, indicating that she probably originated in matriarchal times. Arinnitti's precursor seems to have been a mother-goddess of Anatolia, symbolic of earth and fertility. Arinnitti's attributes were righteous judgment, mercy, and royal authority. The powerful Hittite queen, Puduhepa, adopted Arinnitti as her protectress; the queen's seal showed her in the goddess' embrace.

Arinos River, Portuguese RIO ARINOS, river, west central Brazil, rising in the Serra de Araporé northeast of Diamantino and flowing west for a short distance and then north-northwest across the Planalto (plateau) do Mato Grosso to its junction with the Juruena River, a major headstream of the Rio Tapajós.

Ariobarzanes (d. *c.* 360 BC), Persian satrap (provincial governor) of Phrygia after *c.* 387. The son of a nobleman, he cultivated the friendship of Athens and Sparta and, *c.* 366, led the unsuccessful revolt of the satraps of western Anatolia against the Persian king Artaxerxes II (ruled 404–359/358 BC).

Arion, semilegendary poet and musician of Methymna in Lesbos. He is said to have invented the dithyramb (choral poem or chant performed at the festival of Dionysus); that is, he gave it literary form. His father's name, Cycleus, indicates the connection of the son with the cyclic or circular chorus of the dithyramb. None of his works survives, and only one story about his life is known.

After a successful performing tour of Sicily and Magna Graecia, Arion sailed for home. The sight of the treasure he carried roused the cupidity of the sailors, who resolved to kill him and seize his wealth. Arion, as a last favour, begged permission to sing a song. The sailors consented, and the poet, standing on the deck of the ship, sang a dirge accompanied by his lyre. He then threw himself overboard; but he was miraculously borne up in safety by a dolphin, which had been charmed by the music. Thus he proceeded to Corinth, arriving before the ship. There Arion's friend Periander, tyrant of Corinth, eventually learned the truth by a stratagem. Summoning the sailors, he demanded what had become of the poet. Upon affirming that he had remained behind, they were suddenly confronted by Arion himself. The sailors confessed and were punished, and Arion's lyre and the dolphin became the constellations Lyra and Delphinus.

Ariosto, Ludovico (b. Sept. 8, 1474, Reggio Emilia, Duchy of Modena—d. July 6, 1533, Ferrara), Italian poet remembered primarily for his epic poem *Orlando furioso*, generally regarded as the most perfect expression of the artistic tendencies and spiritual attitudes of the Italian Renaissance. As a playwright, he also contributed to the development of the drama: his plays, which are themselves minor works, were the first of those imitations of Latin comedy in the vernacular that have characterized European domestic comedy.

Ariosto, woodcut after a drawing by Titian from the third edition of *Orlando furioso*, 1532

By courtesy of the trustees of the British Museum; photograph, J.R. Freeman & Co. Ltd.

Ariosto's father, Count Niccolò, was commander of the citadel at Reggio Emilia. When Ludovico was 10, the family moved to his father's native Ferrara, and the poet always considered himself a Ferrarese. He showed an inclination toward poetry from an early age, but his father intended him for a legal career, and so he studied law, unwillingly, at Ferrara from 1489 to 1494. Afterward he devoted himself to literary studies until 1499. Count Niccolò died in 1500, and Ludovico, as the eldest son, had to give up his dream of a peaceful life devoted to humanistic studies in order to provide for his four brothers and five sisters. In 1502 he became commander of the citadel of Canossa and in 1503 entered the service of Cardinal Ippolito d'Este, son of Duke Ercole I.

Ariosto's duties as a courtier were sharply at odds with his own simple tastes. He was expected to be in constant attendance on the Cardinal and to accompany him on dangerous expeditions as well as travel on diplomatic missions. In 1509 he followed the Cardinal in Ferrara's campaign against Venice. In 1512 he went to Rome with the Cardinal's brother Alfonso, who had succeeded Ercole as duke in 1505 and had sided with France in the Holy League war in an attempt to placate Pope Julius II. In this they were totally unsuccessful and were forced to flee over the Apennines to avoid the Pope's wrath. In the following year, after the election of Leo X, hoping to find a situation that would allow him more time to pursue his literary ambitions, Ariosto again went to the Roman court. But his journey was in vain, and he returned to Ferrara.

So far he had produced a number of Latin verses inspired by the Roman poets Tibullus and Horace. They do not compare in technical skill with those by Pietro Bembo, a contemporary poet and outstanding scholar, but they are much more genuine in feeling. Since about 1505, however, Ariosto had been working on *Orlando furioso,* and, indeed, he continued to revise and refine it for the rest of his life. The first edition was published in Venice in 1516. This version and the second (Ferrara, 1521) consisted of 40 cantos written in the metrical form of the ottava rima (an eight-line stanza, keeping to a tradition that had been followed since Boccaccio in the 14th century through such 15th-century poets as Politian and Matteo Maria Boiardo). The second edition shows signs of Bembo's influence in matters of language and style that is still more evident in the third edition.

Orlando furioso is an original continuation of Boiardo's *Orlando innamorato.* Its hero is Orlando, the Italian form of Roland, hero in the so-called Charlemagne epics. In the poem there are three principal nuclei around which a variety of episodes and themes, mostly taken from the literature of the Middle Ages, is grouped: Orlando's passion for Angelica, the war between Christians and pagans near Paris, and the secondary love story of Ruggiero and Bradamante. The first is the most important, particularly in the first part of the poem; the second represents the epic background of the whole narrative; the third is introduced partly as a literary courtesy to the Este family, who are supposed to owe their origin to the union of the two lovers.

In 1517, one year after the first publication of *Orlando furioso,* the Cardinal was created bishop of Buda. Ariosto refused to follow him to Hungary, however, and in the following year he entered the personal service of Duke Alfonso, the Cardinal's brother. He was thus able to remain in Ferrara near his mistress, Alessandra Benucci, whom he had met in 1513. But, in 1522, financial necessity compelled him to accept the post of governor of the Garfagnana, a province in the wildest part of the Apennines. It was torn by rival political factions and overrun by brigands, but Ariosto showed great administrative ability in maintaining order there.

During this period, from 1517 to 1525, he composed his seven satires (titled *Satire*), modelled after the *Sermones* (satires) of Horace. The first (written in 1517 when he had refused to follow the Cardinal to Buda) is a noble assertion of the dignity and independence of the writer; the second criticizes ecclesiastical corruption; the third moralizes on the need to refrain from ambition; the fourth deals with marriage; the fifth and sixth describe his personal feelings at being kept away from his family by his masters' selfishness; the seventh (addressed to Pietro Bembo) points out the vices of humanists and reveals his sorrow at not having been allowed to complete his literary education in his youth.

By 1525 Ariosto had managed to save enough money to return to Ferrara, where he bought a little house with a garden. Probably between 1528 and 1530 he married Alessandra Benucci (though secretly, so as not to forego certain ecclesiastical benefices to which he was entitled). Thus his dreams of a peaceful life devoted to study and poetry came true, and he spent the last years of his life with his wife, his crippled brother Gabriele, and his son Virginio, cultivating his garden and revising the *Orlando furioso.* The third edition of his masterpiece (Ferrara, 1532) contained 46 cantos (a *giunta,* or appendix, known as the *Cinque canti,* or "Five Cantos," was published posthumously in 1545). In this final version the poet's style and poetic personality, which confer on his characters a refined spirituality, at last achieved perfection. It was published a few months before his death. (G.A.)

MAJOR WORKS. *Poetry. Orlando furioso* (1st ed. 1516; 2nd rev. ed. 1521; 3rd rev. ed. 1532); *Satire* (1517–25).

Plays. Cassaria (1508); *I suppositi* (1509); *Il negromante* (1520); *La lena* (1529); *I studenti* (completed by Gabriele Ariosto, published posthumously as *La scholastica*).

BIBLIOGRAPHY. Modern editions of Ariosto's works are: Lanfranco Caretti, *Orlando furioso* (1954); Cesare Serge, *Orlando furioso* (1964), a critical edition; and *Opere minori* (1954); Antonio Cappelli, *Lettere,* 3rd ed. (1887); Angelo Stella, *Lettere* (1965); A. Salza, *Gli Studenti, con le continuazioni di Gabriele e Virginio Ariosto* (1915). See also Giuseppi Agnelli and Giuseppi Ravegnani, *Annali delle editione ariostee* (1933), a detailed catalog of editions of Ariosto's work; Giuseppe Fatini, *Bibliografia della critica ariostea, 1510–1956* (1958), a fundamental bibliographical list; Pio Rajna, *Le fonti dell'Orlando furioso,* 2nd ed. (1900), on the sources of the poem; Michele Catalano, *Vita di Ludovico Ariosto riconstruita su nuovi documenti,* 2 vol. (1930–31), the standard biography of the poet; Benedetto Croce, *Ariosto, Shakespeare, e Corneille* (1920; *Ariosto, Shakespeare, and Corneille,* 1966); and Attilio Momigliano, *Saggio su l' "Orlando furioso,"* 5th ed. (1959), both fundamental for an aesthetic appreciation of the poem.

Arisaema, genus of stemless, tuberous-rooted herbs, comprising about 190 species in the arum family (Araceae), native mostly to the Old World but including a few notable wildings of North America.

Of the hardy species often planted in the shady wild garden, two are especially familiar. Jack-in-the-pulpit, or Indian turnip (*A. triphyllum*), native to eastern North America, usually has two leaves, each about 25 centimetres (10 inches) long, three-parted, and on a leaf stalk up to 60 cm tall. The blossom consists of a greenish to purple tubelike spathe (the "pulpit"), 10 to 18 cm long, surrounding and covering with a drooping hood the green to purple rodlike spadix ("Jack"), which bears the small unisexual flowers. Varieties have colourful white to bronzy spathe markings and variant leaf shapes and sizes.

Green dragon, or dragonroot (*A. dracontium*), with leaves up to 25 cm long on petioles up to 90 cm long, has an 8-cm-long greenish spathe, with an erect hood, surrounding a spadix that extends beyond the spathe by several times its length.

The rootstocks of both species are acrid, but those of *A. triphyllum* when cooked provided an Indian food. The red berries formed on the spadix are poisonous to humans but are eaten by many wild animals.

The curious cobra lily (*A. speciosum*), from Nepal and Sikkim state of India, has a slightly dropping spathe and a spadix decorated by a long threadlike extension. *A. fimbriatum,* from the Malay Peninsula, has a tasselled spadix.

ʿArīsh, al-, also spelled EL-ARISH, town and largest settlement of the Sinai Peninsula in the northeastern section, on the Mediterranean coast, the capital of Egypt's Sīnāʾ ash-Shamālīyah (Northern Sinai) *muḥāfaẓah* (governorate). It was under Israeli military administration from 1967 to 1979, when it returned to Egyptian rule. It is near the mouth of the Wādī al-ʿArīsh, the longest seasonal watercourse of the Sinai, usually identified with the biblical Brook of Egypt (Hebrew Naḥal Mizrayim), the southwestern border of the Holy Land according to the Old Testament.

Known as Rhinocorura to classical authors, the town is mentioned from at least the 2nd century BC. The Roman general Titus prepared his invasion of Judaea there (1st century AD). Later, Baldwin I, crusader king of Jerusalem, died there while returning from an Egyptian expedition (1118). It was prosperous as a Muslim trade centre in the Middle Ages. Taken by Napoleon during his unsuccessful Palestine campaign (1799), al-ʿArīsh was the site of the signing of an abortive treaty providing for French evacuation of Egypt.

In the early 20th century al-ʿArīsh and environs were proposed as a site for Zionist colonization near, but not in, Palestine; the scheme was vetoed by Lord Cromer, British administrator of Egypt (1902). In 1906, when the administrative boundary between Egypt and Ottoman dominions proper was demarcated from the Mediterranean to the Gulf of Aqaba, al-ʿArīsh was placed definitively in Egypt. The town was formerly a station on the trans-Sinai railway, built by Britain in World War I; after 1967, however, Israel destroyed the line from al-ʿArīsh to the Suez Canal for security reasons.

The local economy is based on agriculture (date palms, castor beans), fishing, and quail trapping; there is a small castor-oil producing plant. Commercial fishing in Sabkhat (lake) al-Bardawīl began in the late 1970s. Coal deposits just to the south of the town are used to fuel an electric power plant that was started in the early 1980s. The governorate's offices are headquartered there, and the town has become a transfer point for materials passing between Egypt and Israel overland. Tourist facilities were opened in 1980 as well. Al-ʿArīsh is linked by highway to the Suez Canal zone and Israel. It also has an airfield. Pop. (1983 est.) 56,200.

Arishima Takeo (b. March 4, 1878, Tokyo—d. June 9, 1923, Karuizawa, Japan), novelist known in his country as "the man of love" for his humanitarian idealism.

Arishima was the eldest son of a talented and aristocratic family; his younger brothers included the painter Arishima Ikuma and the novelist Satomi Ton. He went to the Peers School, where he was chosen as a companion to the Crown Prince. He went on to Sapporo Agricultural School (now Hokkaido University), noted in the late 19th century as a centre of modern thought. There he was awakened to the plight of the lower classes. Arishima had studied English from childhood, and, after graduating in 1896, he went to the United States, where he spent three years at Harvard University.

After returning to Japan, he taught school in Sapporo and Kyōto; but in 1910 he joined his brothers and their friends Shiga Naoya and Mushanokōji Saneatsu in publishing the journal *Shirakaba* ("White Birch"), which was dedicated to disseminating the humanistic and benevolent ideals shared by the young men. Arishima seems to have struggled most deeply with the social contradictions inherent in his position as a wealthy aristocrat that conflicted with his ideal of universal love. His novel *Kain no matsuei* (1917; *Descendants of Cain,* 1955), dealing with the miserable condition of tenant farmers, attracted little attention, but he soon received recognition with the novel *Aru onna* (1919; *A Certain Woman,* 1978). In 1922 he published *Sengen hitotsu* ("A Manifesto"), in which he expressed his despairing conviction that only the labouring classes could help themselves and that there was nothing he as a bourgeois ideologist could do for them. That year he distributed his land and farms in Hokkaido among the tenants; the following year he committed suicide with his mistress at a mountain retreat.

Aristaeus, Greek divinity whose worship was widespread but concerning whom myths are somewhat obscure. The name is derived from the Greek *aristos,* "best." According to the generally accepted account, Aristaeus, son of Apollo and the nymph Cyrene, was born in Libya but later went to Thebes, where he received instruction from the Muses in the arts of healing and prophecy and became the son-in-law of Cadmus and the father of Actaeon. After travelling extensively, Aristaeus reached Thrace, where he finally disappeared near Mt. Haemus.

Aristaeus was essentially a benevolent deity; he introduced the cultivation of bees and the vine and olive and was the protector of herdsmen and hunters. He was often identified with Zeus, Apollo, and Dionysus. He was represented as a young man dressed like a shepherd and sometimes carrying a sheep.

Ariṣṭanemi, also called NEMINĀTHA, 22nd of the 24 Tīrthaṅkaras, or saviours, of Jainism, a religion of India.

Though the last two saints (the 23rd and 24th) may be considered historical personages, the details of Ariṣṭanemi's life are obscured in legend. He is said to have lived 84,000 years before the coming of the next saint, Pārśvanātha; he is also said to have been a contemporary of the Hindu god Krishna, who was his cousin. On his marriage day, Ariṣṭanemi heard the cries of the animals that were to be slaughtered for the marriage feast and immediately renounced the world. The name Ariṣṭanemi is attributed to his mother's dream before he was born in which she saw a wheel of black jewels (Ariṣṭanemi, "the rim [*nemi*] of whose wheel is unhurt [*ariṣṭa*]"). In paintings he is always shown black in colour (in paintings of the Digambara sect, blue), and his symbol is the conch. He attained *mokṣa* (release from earthly existence) on the Girnār Hills in Kāthiāwār (western India), which has become a place of pilgrimage for the Jainas.

Aristarchus OF SAMOS (*c.* 310–230 BC), Greek astronomer, first to maintain that the Earth rotates and revolves around the Sun. On this ground, Cleanthes the Stoic declared that he ought to be indicted for impiety.

Aristarchus' advanced ideas on the movement of the Earth are known from Archimedes and Plutarch; his only extant work is a short treatise, "On the Sizes and Distances of the Sun and Moon." The values he obtained, by using geometry, are inaccurate, because of faulty observations.

Aristarchus found a more precise value for the length of the solar year. A lunar crater is named for him; a peak in its centre is the brightest formation on the Moon.

Aristarchus OF SAMOTHRACE (b. *c.* 217 BC—d. 145 BC, Cyprus), Greek critic and grammarian, noted for his contribution to Homeric studies.

Aristarchus in Alexandria, where he was a pupil of Aristophanes of Byzantium, and, *c.* 153 BC, became chief librarian there. Later he withdrew to Cyprus. He founded a school of philologists, called after him Aristarcheans, which long flourished in Alexandria and afterward at Rome. Cicero and Horace regarded him as the supreme critic. His works fall into three categories: (1) two editions of the text of Homer and editions of Hesiod, Pindar, Archilochus, Alcaeus, and Anacreon; (2) numerous commentaries on these poets and on Aeschylus, Sophocles, Aristophanes, and Herodotus; (3) critical brochures, especially on Homeric problems.

Aristeas, Letter of, pseudepigraphal work of pseudo-history produced in Alexandria, probably in the mid-2nd century BC, to promote the cause of Judaism. Though the size and prestige of the Jewish community had already secured for itself a definite place in Alexandrian society and serious anti-Semitism had not yet gained currency, the Jewish community was in conflict. While some Jews embraced Greek culture and philosophy, others refused any rapprochement with Hellenistic culture. The author's purpose was to present Judaism in a favourable light to pagans and make strict observance of religious laws attractive to Hellenistic Jews. The author assumed the name of a 2nd-century-BC writer and purported to give a contemporary account of the translation of the Hebrew Pentateuch, the first five books of the Bible, into Greek. He presented himself as a pagan admirer of Judaism who held a high position in the court of Ptolemy II Philadelphus (285–246 BC) in Alexandria. The writer used current Hellenistic literary conventions and the technical language of the Alexandrian court, but his Greek style and several historical inaccuracies indicate that he was a deliberate archaist. His concern for the welfare of Jewish slaves, his romantic picture of Palestinian Jewry, and his efforts to explain the theory behind Jewish dietary laws mark him as a Jew rather than a pagan.

Modern scholars call this work a "letter" because it was addressed by Aristeas to his brother Philocrates. The narrative draws upon a wide variety of sources: a report on Egyptian Jews from official archives, texts of Ptolemaic legal decrees, administrative memoranda preserved in royal files or in the Alexandria library, accounts of pilgrimages to Jerusalem, a treatise on the ideals of kingship, and an apology for Jewish law. The first writer to quote directly from the *Letter* was the Jewish historian Josephus (1st century AD). Several early Christians also used the book, ignoring its Jewish apologetic features.

Aristeides THE JUST: *see* Aristides.

Aristides (fl. 2nd century), Athenian philosopher, one of the earliest Christian Apologists, his *Apology for the Christian Faith* being one of the oldest extant Apologist documents. Known primarily through a reference by the 4th-century historian Eusebius of Caesarea, Aristides addressed his *Apology* either to the Roman emperor Hadrian (reigned 117–138) or to his successor Antoninus Pius (reigned 138–161). A primitive, general apology, Aristides' simple argument was the forerunner of the more personal and literary apologies in the late 2nd and early 3rd centuries, such as those produced by Athenagoras and Tertullian.

In the perspective of a pagan philosopher, Aristides' *Apology* begins with a discussion of the harmony in creation and, in the manner of the Stoic philosophers, establishes a correlation with the Divine Being responsible for the creation and preservation of the universe. Aristides reasons that such a Being would need to be eternal, perfect, immortal, all-knowing, the Father of mankind, and sufficient to himself. He then divides the pre-Christian human race into three categories according to their idea of deity and religious practices. In his judgment, all were inadequate: the barbarians, including the Babylonians (Chaldeans) and the Egyptians, with their cults of the elements of the universe and animals; the Greeks with their worship of anthropomorphic gods whose infamies made them anything but divine; and the Jewish monotheistic ideal, deserving respect because of its faith in the Creator, genuine prophets, superior standards of morality, and social conscience, but excessive in devotion to angels and external ceremonies. Only the "new nation," as Aristides called the Christians, has a true idea of God, who creates all things through his Son and the Holy Spirit. Christian worship of God is manifested by a highly moral life based upon the commandments of Christ, to whom they look for the resurrection of the dead and life in the world to come. Profoundly impressed by the lofty mission of the new religion, Aristides stressed the charity of the Christian community and insisted that, although few in number, Christians were justifying the continued existence and salvation of the world by their intercession before God.

Long considered lost, Aristides' *Apology* was discovered in the late 19th century in fragmentary Armenian and Syriac versions. With the subsequent identification of a complete Greek version contained in the medieval Christian legend of Barlaam and Josaphat, the reconstruction of Aristides' original text finally was achieved. English translations were done by J.R. Harris (1893) and by D.M. Kay in *The Ante-Nicene Fathers* (1924).

Aristides QUINTILIANUS (fl. 2nd or 3rd century AD), Greek author of a treatise on music (*Perì musikês*), one of the principal sources of modern knowledge of ancient Greek music. The work deals with scales, metres, and the composition of melodies, as well as with the educational value of music and the relation of music, through mathematics, to phenomena in nature. It was regarded by Byzantine and Arab scholars as a basic work, and its importance is generally accepted by modern scholars. It was published in 1652, edited by Marcus Meibom; in 1882 in a critical edition by Albert Jahn; and in 1937, in German translation with commentary, by Rudolf Schäfke.

Aristides THE JUST, Aristides also spelled ARISTEIDES (fl. 5th century BC), Athenian statesman and general and founder of the Delian League, which developed into the Athenian Empire.

Little is known of Aristides' early life. He appears to have been prominent within the party that favoured resistance to Persia, but in 482 he was ostracized, probably because he opposed Themistocles' plan to use the silver from a new vein of the mines at Laurium to build a large fleet. Recalled in 480, Aristides distinguished himself in the decisive victory over the Persians near the island of Salamis (480) and commanded the Athenian army at the Battle of Plataea (479) when the Persians were driven from Greece.

The following year Aristides commanded the Athenian contingent of 30 ships in the fleet that the Spartan Pausanias led to free the Greek cities of Cyprus and capture Byzantium. Toward the end of the year the eastern Greek allies revolted from Spartan control and at Delos offered their allegiance, through Aristides, to Athens. The Delian League, based on Athenian naval power and the trust Aristides inspired, was his greatest achievement. Entrusted with the assessment of the members' contributions, Aristides carried out his task to general satisfaction, using as his basis the assessment imposed by the Persians on the Ionians in 493.

The military command of the league's forces passed to Cimon, and there is no reliable information about Aristides' later career or the date of his death. The view that Aristides was a democratic reformer is contradicted by the fact that his main associations were with Miltiades and Cimon, the enemies of the democratic leaders Xanthippus and Ephialtes.

Aristippus (b. *c.* 435 BC, Cyrene, Libya—d. 366, Athens), philosopher who was one of Socrates' disciples and the founder of the

Cyrenaic school of hedonism, the ethic of pleasure (*see* Cyrenaics). The first of Socrates' disciples to demand a salary for teaching philosophy, Aristippus believed that the good life rests upon the belief that among human values pleasure is the highest and pain the lowest (and one that should be avoided). He also warned his students to avoid inflicting as well as suffering pain. Like Socrates, he took great interest in practical ethics. While he believed that men should dedicate their lives to the pursuit and enjoyment of pleasure, he also believed that they should use good judgment and exercise self-control to temper powerful human desires. His motto was, "I possess, I am not possessed." None of his writings survives.

Aristo (philosopher): *see* Ariston of Chios.

Aristobulus I, also called JUDAS ARISTOBULUS (d. 103 BC), Hasmonean (Maccabean) king of Judaea who seized the throne from his mother in 104 BC. According to the 1st-century-AD historian Josephus, Aristobulus conquered the Ituraeans of Lebanon and forcibly converted them to Judaism. He was the first of his house to adopt the title of king (*basileus*).

Aristobulus II (d. 49 BC), last of the Hasmonean (Maccabean) kings of Judaea. On the death (67 BC) of his mother, Salome Alexandra, he succeeded to the throne, defeating his brother and rival, John Hyrcanus II (*q.v.*). When Hyrcanus sought help from the Nabataeans, the Romans under Pompey intervened and subjected Judaea to their rule (63 BC). After an unsuccessful attempt to regain power in 56, Aristobulus was sent to Rome as a prisoner and remained there until his death.

aristocracy, government by a relatively small privileged class or by a minority consisting of those felt to be best qualified to rule.

Politically, as conceived by Plato and Aristotle, aristocracy means the rule of the best few, the morally and intellectually superior, governing in the interest of the people. Such a form of government differs from the rule of one (monarchy or tyranny), of many (democracy or mob-rule), or of the selfish or militarily ambitious few (oligarchy or timocracy). Unfortunately, since "the best" is an evaluative and somewhat subjective notion, it is difficult objectively to distinguish aristocratic from oligarchic or timocratic governments. Because monarchy has its own aristocracy and because, in democracies, the people try to elect the best as their rulers, the aristocratic element is also present in these regimes. For these reasons aristocracy, in a more objective sense, means the upper layer of a stratified group. Thus, the upper ranks of the government form the political aristocracy of the state. The stratum of the highest dignitaries comprises the aristocracy of the church. The richest captains of industry and finance constitute an aristocracy of wealth in an economic group. The eminent leaders of arts and sciences represent the aristocracy of scientific, artistic, and philosophical groups. The ruling stratum of labour unions is the aristocracy of labour. The Brahman caste in the caste society of India, the Spartiates in Sparta, the *eupatridai* in Athens, the patricians or optimates in Rome, and the medieval nobility in Europe are examples of the social aristocracy or nobility in these groups and societies. Moreover, most such social aristocracies have been—both legally and factually—hereditary aristocracies (*i.e.*, those by reason of birth). Other aristocracies have been nonhereditary, recruited from different strata of the population, such as the upper stratum of the Roman Catholic Church, the ruling aristocracy of elective republics and monarchies, the leaders of scientific and artistic organizations, certain aristocracies of wealth, and even some emperors like the emperors of the Roman Empire, of whom about 43 percent were "upstarts." The distinction between aristocracy of birth and nonhereditary aristocracy is relative, however, because even in a caste society some lowborn persons climb into the higher castes and some of the highborn members slide down into the lower castes. On the other hand, even in open aristocracies there is always a tendency for the upper stratum to become a hereditary group filled mainly by the offspring of the aristocratic parents. In the United States, for example, among the living multimillionaires—the aristocracy of wealth—the percentage of those born of wealthy parents is notably higher than among the American multimillionaires of the middle of the 19th century.

Aristogiton: *see* Harmodius and Aristogiton.

Aristolochiales, the birthwort order of flowering plants, containing one family, Aristolochiaceae, which consists of 10 genera and about 600 species. *See* birthwort.

Aristomenes, traditional hero of an unsuccessful revolt against the Spartans by the Messenians, who had been enslaved by Sparta in the 8th century BC. Although Aristomenes is probably a historical figure, his career has been heavily overlaid with legend; the standard version makes him a leader of a rebellion about 650 BC—the so-called Second Messenian War. After several victories he was betrayed by King Aristocrates of Arcadia at the battle of "the Great Trench." For about 11 years he was besieged in Eira, Messenia. When the Spartans finally conquered that stronghold, Aristomenes escaped to live in exile on the island of Rhodes.

This tradition can probably be traced to the Greek historian Callisthenes of the 4th century BC. Rhianus, a Cretan poet of the 3rd century BC, wrote an epic in six books, placing Aristomenes in a revolt of 490 BC. In the 2nd century BC the historian Myron of Priene connected him with the original 8th-century Spartan conquest of Messenia. From these and other sources the Greek geographer Pausanias in the 2nd century AD compiled the longest surviving account, a story of the 7th-century rebellion with romantic embellishments drawn largely from Rhianus.

Ariston OF **CHIOS,** Ariston also spelled ARISTO (fl. mid-3rd century BC), Greek philosopher who studied under Zeno, the founder of the Stoic school of philosophy; he combined Stoic and Cynic ideas in shaping his own beliefs. Ariston believed that the only topic of genuine value in philosophy is the study of ethics and went even further in claiming that only general and theoretical issues are worth discussing in ethics and that there is only one true virtue in life—an intelligent, healthy state of mind.

Aristophanes (b. *c.* 450 BC—d. *c.* 388 BC), the greatest representative of ancient Greek comedy.

A brief account of the life and works of Aristophanes follows; for a full biography, *see* MACROPAEDIA: Greek Dramatists, The Classical.

The little that is known of his life is derived mainly from Aristophanes' own words in the plays themselves, though a little outside information is to be had from the various hypotheses or arguments appended to these plays and stemming probably from a commentary or edition by the grammarian Symmachus (fl. *c.* AD 100). Aristophanes, son of Philippus, was an Athenian citizen belonging to the tribe named Pandionis, though he, or his father, seems to have owned some property on the island of Aegina, and it may be this which gave rise to certain unlikely, not to say absurd, accusations of foreign birth which seem to have been brought against him.

Only 11 of about 40 plays by the Athenian playwright survive virtually intact: *The Acharnians, The Knights, The Clouds, The Wasps, The Peace, The Birds, Lysistrata, The Thesmophoriazusae, The Frogs, Women in Parliament,* and *The Plutus.* Two posthumous comedies, *Aeolosicon* (probably a skit on Euripides' *Aeolus*) and *Kokalos* (also, presumably, a mythological burlesque), were produced in or about the year of his death by his son, Araros. Aristophanes' dramatic activity covered the end of the period of Old and the start of that of the so-called Middle Comedy; and though the line of demarcation between these two is shadowy, it is not unreasonable to say that the first 10 of Aristophanes' 11 surviving plays belong to the Old and the last to the Middle. (One of the indications of the change from Old to Middle Comedy is the dwindling importance of the chorus.) His creative life was spent mainly in satirizing society, the fashionable philosophies and literature, and the aggressive foreign policy of Athens during the Peloponnesian War.

Aristophanes OF **BYZANTIUM** (b. *c.* 257 BC—d. 180 BC, Alexandria), Greek literary critic and grammarian who, after early study under leading scholars in Alexandria, was chief librarian there *c.* 195 BC.

Aristophanes was the producer of a text of Homer and also edited Hesiod's *Theogony,* Alcaeus, Pindar, Euripides, Aristophanes, and perhaps Anacreon. Many of the *Arguments* prefixed in the manuscripts to Greek tragedies and comedies are ascribed to Aristophanes, and his study of Greek comedy led to separate works on Athenian courtesans and on character types. He revised and continued the *Pinakes* of Callimachus, a biographical history of Greek literature. As a lexicographer he compiled collections of archaic and unusual words, technical terms, and proverbs.

As a grammarian Aristophanes founded a school and wrote a treatise, *About Analogy,* which laid down rules for declension, etc. In editing the work of lyric and dramatic poets he introduced innovations in metrical analysis and textual criticism that were widely adopted by later scholars. He was responsible for arranging Plato's dialogues in trilogies and is generally credited with the foundation of the so-called Alexandrian Canon, a selection in each genre of literary work that contemporaries considered to be models of excellence.

Aristotelian criticism, system of critical investigation of literature that takes as its foundation the writings of Aristotle, especially the *Poetics.* The Aristotelian approach is an empirical and descriptive analysis of the subject; it focusses on the work and attempts to deal with its constituent parts and their relation to the whole without reference to its historical genesis or extrinsic moral values. It is opposed to the social and ethical approach inherent in Platonic criticism (*q.v.*).

Aristotle, Greek ARISTOTELES (b. 384 BC, Stagirus, Macedonia—d. 322, Chalcis, Euboea, Greece), ancient Greek philosopher, scientist, and organizer of research, one of the two greatest intellectual figures produced by the Greeks (the other being Plato). He surveyed the whole field of human knowledge as it was known in his day; and his encyclopaedic writings dominated Western and Muslim thought in many fields for nearly 2,000 years.

A brief account of the life and works of Aristotle follows; for a full biography, *see* MACROPAEDIA: Aristotle and Aristotelianism.

The son of the court physician to the King of Macedonia, Aristotle was introduced to Greek medicine and biology at an early age. Following the death of his father, he was sent to the Athenian Academy of Plato (367) and there engaged in dialogue for 20 years. On Plato's death in 348/347, he left Athens and travelled for 12 years, establishing new academies at

Assus (where he married Pythias, the King's adopted daughter or niece, and, after her death, Herpyllis) and at Mytilene. He lived at Pella, the capital of Macedonia, for three years, tutoring the future Alexander the Great, and retired to his paternal property at Stagirus *c.* 339. In 335 he returned to Athens, devoting himself to purely scientific work, and in that year opened the Lyceum, an institution to rival the Academy. For the next 12 years he organized it as a centre for speculation and research in every department of inquiry; the chief contributions of the Lyceum lay in biology and history. On the death of Alexander in 323, an anti-Macedonian agitation broke out in Athens, and Aristotle withdrew to Chalcis, north of Athens, where he died the following year.

Of Aristotle's many works, 47 remain. They comprise mostly, it seems, notes used in giving Lyceum courses and are of a concentrated, academic nature. The form, titles, and order of the extant texts were given to them by an editor almost three centuries after the philosopher's death.

Aristoxenus (fl. late 4th century BC), Greek peripatetic philosopher, the first authority for musical theory in the classical world.

Aristoxenus was born at Tarentum (now Taranto) in southern Italy and studied in Athens under Aristotle and Theophrastus (371/370–288/287 BC). He was interested in ethics as well as in music and wrote much, but most of his work is lost. Apart from his musical treatises, fragments remain of his reconstruction of the old Pythagorean ethics as well as of his biographies of Pythagoras, Archytas, Socrates, and Plato. His theory that the soul is related to the body as harmony is to the parts of a musical instrument seems to follow early Pythagorean doctrine. In musical theory, Aristoxenus held that the notes of the scale should not be judged by mathematical ratio but by the ear. His remaining musical treatises include parts of his *Elements of Harmonics* (edited by P. Marquard, 1868, and by H. Macran, 1902) and of his *Elements of Rhythm* (edited by R. Westphal, 1861 and 1893) that are extant. The fragments of his other works were edited by F. Wehrli in *Aristoxenos*, being part 2 of Wehrli's *Die Schule des Aristoteles; Texte und Kommentar* (1945; "The School of Aristotle; Text and Commentary").

Arita ware: *see* Imari ware.

Aritan Stage, major division of Cretaceous rocks and time in Japan (the Cretaceous Period began about 136,000,000 years ago and lasted about 71,000,000 years). Rocks of the Aritan Stage overlie those of the Kochian Stage and underlie those of the Lower Miyakoan Stage. The Aritan is correlated with the upper part of the Neocomian Stage, the lowermost standard worldwide division of the Cretaceous. The Aritan is characterized by distinctive ammonite cephalopods (mollusks).

arithmetic, branch of mathematics in which numbers, relations among numbers, and operations on numbers are studied and used to solve problems.

A brief treatment of arithmetic follows. For full treatment, *see* MACROPAEDIA: Arithmetic.

The numbers under consideration may be the natural numbers (1,2,3, . . .), the whole numbers or integers (. . . −3,−2,−1,0,1,2,3, . . .), the rational numbers (positive and negative fractional or decimal numbers, such as $1/3$, 0.68, $2\frac{2}{3}$, 3.7, $-7/9$, along with the integers), the real numbers (irrational numbers, such as $\sqrt{3}$, π, sin 32°, along with the rational numbers), or various more exotic number systems. The choice of number system depends on the physical situation that is to be dealt with by the arithmetic.

Virtually every known society has had some method of dealing with numbers. In some very primitive societies the system may be as simple as having a name for "one" and a name for "more than one." On the other hand, the Sumerians of Mesopotamia could do quite respectable arithmetic more than 5,000 years ago, and other societies in various parts of the world independently developed sophisticated systems of arithmetic.

The numeration system (or system for writing number symbols) widely used throughout the world today is a place-value system based on the number 10 and usually called the Arabic, or Hindu-Arabic, numeration system. In this system the position a symbol occupies helps determine the value of the symbol. For example, in 333, the 3 on the right means three, but the 3 in the middle means three tens and the 3 on the left means three hundreds. In Roman numerals, on the other hand, CCC means 300—each C stands for one hundred, and the relative position of the C's is of no importance. There are rules regarding the order of symbols in the Roman numeral system, and variations in that order may indicate subtraction (for example, IX means 9, while XI means 11), but generally position is not important.

For many centuries, Roman numerals exclusively were used in Europe, and computations were generally done on an abacus. Arabic numerals were introduced into western Europe by the Moors in the 8th century AD, but the Europeans were slow to accept this way of writing numerals and the accompanying methods of calculation. As late as 1542, in *The Ground of Arts,* Robert Recorde explained methods of doing calculations with Arabic numerals while assuming that the reader was familiar with Roman numerals.

A place-value system, such as the Arabic numeral system, has clear advantages in economy of symbolism and in efficiency of computation. Only the 10 symbols 0,1,2,3,4,5,6,7,8, and 9 and the decimal point are needed to write numbers of any size.

Arithmetic includes such esoteric subjects as the arithmetic of complex numbers and of quaternions, and number theory; but for most practical purposes, the arithmetic of whole numbers and of rational numbers and the relation of these to the real world is sufficient.

arithmetic function, any mathematical function defined for integers, and dependent upon those properties of the integer itself as a number, in contrast to the algebraic functions or functions of analysis, which depend upon algebraic or limiting operations done with numbers. Examples of arithmetic functions are given by the following functions that associate with each integer *n* either of the following numbers: (1) the number of divisors of *n;* (2) the number of ways *n* can be represented as a sum or product of a specified number of integers; (3) the number of primes (integers not divisible by any number greater than one, except themselves) dividing *n* (including *n* itself). Arithmetic functions have applications in number theory, combinatorial analysis, counting, probability, and mathematical analysis, in which they arise as the coefficients of power series.

n	$f(n)$
1	0
2	1
3	1
4	1
5	1
6	2
7	1
8	1
9	1
10	2
11	1
12	2

An arithmetic function; $f(n)$ equals the number of primes dividing n

Arius (b. *c.* 250, Libya—d. 336, Constantinople), Christian priest of Alexandria, Egypt, whose teachings gave rise to a theological doctrine known as Arianism (*q.v.*), which, in affirming the created, finite nature of Christ, was denounced by the early church as a major heresy challenging its orthodoxy.

An ascetical, moral leader of a Christian community in the area of Alexandria, Arius attracted a large following through a message integrating Neoplatonism, which accented the absolute oneness of the divinity as the highest perfection, with a literal, rationalist approach to the New Testament texts. This point of view was publicized *c.* 323 through the poetic verse of his major work, *Thalia* ("Banquet"), and was widely spread by popular songs written for labourers and travellers.

The Council of Nicaea, in May 325, declared Arius a heretic after he refused to sign the formula of faith stating that Christ was of the same divine nature as God. Influential support from colleagues in Asia Minor and from Constantia, the Emperor's daughter, succeeded in effecting Arius' return from exile and his readmission into the church after consenting to a compromise formula. Shortly before he was to be reconciled, however, Arius collapsed and died while walking through the streets of Constantinople.

Arius (river, Afghanistan): *see* Harīrūd.

ariya-puggala (Pāli: "noble person"), abbreviation ARIYA, Sanskrit ARYA-PUDGALA, in Theravāda Buddhism, a person who has attained one of the four levels of holiness. A first type of holy person, called a *sotāpanna-puggala* ("stream-winner"), is one who will attain *Nibbāna* (Sanskrit *Nirvāṇa,* the supreme goal of Buddhist thought and practice) after no more than seven rebirths. Another type of holy person is termed a *sakadāgamin* ("once-returner"), or one who is destined to be reborn in the human world only once more before reaching *Nibbāna.* A third type of *ariya-puggala* is the *anāgamin* ("never-returner"), or one who will not be reborn in the human realm and will enter the realm of the gods at the time of death. The never-returner, however, is still not considered to have reached *Nibbāna.*

The Theravāda Buddhist at the highest level of holiness is the *arahant* (Sanskrit *arhat*), one who has reached final and absolute emancipation from all rebirths in any human or superhuman realm. The *arahant*—a model person for Theravāda Buddhists—is to be distinguished from the personal ideal of the Mahāyāna Buddhist schools, the *bodhisattva* (*q.v.;* Sanskrit: "Buddha-to-be"). The latter is a holy person who has reached enlightenment but refuses to enter *Nirvāṇa,* choosing rather to teach his insights until all creatures have similarly been liberated.

ʿārīyah (Arabic: "gratuitous loan"), in Islāmic law, a contract by which a person loans something to another for a specific period of time and later recovers it according to the specifications of the contract; *ʿārīyah* never involves money. The recipient is required under law to restore the object after use and accept responsibility for any damages that may have occurred. Under an *ʿārīyah* contract a Muslim may pay a debt by allowing his debtor to use, for example, his house or his land for a certain period of time while maintaining full ownership of the premises. *ʿĀrīyah* also enables an individual to loan possessions to another at a time when he would not be able to take care of them himself. In this case, the lender cannot demand payment from the recipient if the latter uses those possessions while the owner is away.

Ariyaramna (king of Persia): *see* Ariaramnes.

Arizona, constituent state of the United States of America lying in the southwestern mountain region of the country.

The following article summarizes the administrative history, geography, demographic patterns, economy, and culture of modern Arizona; for additional treatment of its geography and history, *see* MACROPAEDIA: United States of America: *Arizona.*

Facing the Mexican state of Sonora to the south, Arizona is also bounded by the U.S. states of New Mexico to the east, Colorado to the northeast, Utah to the north, and Nevada and California to the west. The capital is Phoenix. Roughly rectangular in shape, the state extends about 400 mi (650 km) from north to south and 340 mi from east to west.

Human settlement in the area has probably spanned 25,000 years. The nomadic Apache and Navaho Indians arrived after the collapse of the Anazazi and Hohokam civilizations and only a few centuries before the Spanish.

Spanish treasure seekers from Mexico, most notably Francisco Coronado, made the initial European contact in the region early in the 16th century, thus establishing Mexico's claim to the area. In 1692 Father Eusebio Kino founded the first of many missions, and in 1776 the army built the first *presidio* (fort) at Tucson. After the Mexican War, Arizona was ceded to the United States as part of New Mexico in 1848, and the Gadsden Purchase, an area south of the Gila River, was added in 1853. Arizona was organized as a territory in 1863 and became the 48th state in 1912.

Physiographically Arizona can be divided into two main regions: the Colorado Plateau of the north, containing large and often spectacular canyons, mesas, and remnants of volcanic mountains; and the Basin and Range Province of the south, where isolated mountains rise from the desert plain. The north drains into the Grand Canyon of the Colorado River, and the south drains westward through the Gila River.

The climate of Arizona is mostly semiarid or arid. The southern Basin and Range Province, receiving over 85 percent of the possible sunshine, has an average annual temperature of about 70° F (21° C) with annual rainfall in the west of about 3 in. (75 mm) increasing to 12 in. in the east. Temperatures in the northern Colorado Plateau average 10 to 15 degrees cooler, with rainfall varying between 10 and 20 in. Summer thunderstorms are the main source of precipitation throughout most of the state, which depends increasingly on fossil water or on underground aquifers.

Between 1970 and 1980 Arizona experienced a higher percentage population increase (53 percent) than any other state except neighbouring Nevada. There was a 444 percent gain between 1940 and 1980. In spite of the tremendous growth, Arizona remains one of the 10 least densely populated states. About 16 percent of the population is Spanish-speaking, most identifying themselves as Mexican. Another 6 percent (152,000) are Indians, the largest population of any state except California and Oklahoma. The largest Indian tribal groups are the Navaho, Hopi, Apache, Papago, and Pima. Recent waves of immigrants seeking climatic amenities and economic opportunities have produced a relatively homogenous white population usually not identifying with particular ethnic groups so much as with "home states."

The well-diversified economy contains elements of primary, secondary, and tertiary industries. Agriculture is based primarily on citrus fruits, cotton, and livestock. The main mining product is copper ore, obtained from large open-pit mines; and copper smelting is one of the largest industries. Lighter industries such as aerospace, electronics, and communications have developed rapidly. Large tourist expenditures in the state are a result of the warm winter climate and the scenery afforded by the natural landscape. One-half of Arizona's land is owned by the federal government, including Grand Canyon and Petrified Forest National Parks, seven national forests, and 20 national monuments, recreation areas, and historic sites. In addition to that role in Arizona's economy, the federal government also holds another one-quarter of Arizona's land in trust as Indian reservations and operates numerous military facilities.

Using traditional Indian folk arts and crafts and having not too distant memories of the Old West, Arizonans have begun to develop their own special brand of urbanized desert culture. Emphasis has so far been placed on art forms, architecture, and technology designed to enhance and preserve the openness and cleanliness of the natural desert environment. Major universities include the University of Arizona and Arizona State University. Art museums and symphony orchestras are located in both Tucson and Phoenix. The Arizona–Sonora Desert Museum near Tucson demonstrates the implications of the occupancy of the desert by man. Area 113,909 sq mi (295,023 sq km). Pop. (1980) 2,718,425.

Arizona Meteor Crater (Arizona): *see* Meteor Crater.

Arizona–Sonora Desert Museum, one of the finest zoos in the United States, located about 15 miles west of Tucson, Ariz. Opened in 1952, this 79-ac (32-ha) zoo is a private nonprofit organization that specializes in the unique fauna of the Sonora Desert. Its collection contains more than 850 specimens of approximately 200 species indigenous to the area. The zoo offers exhibits featuring various habitats, including—in addition to the desert—subtropical swamps, alpine meadows, and cold-water pools. These displays, noted the world over for their imaginativeness, are constructed with excellently simulated cast-concrete rockwork and are adorned with native flora. Among the most popular exhibits are the grottoes for small cats and the "Tunnel in the Desert," an underground display that enables visitors to observe nocturnal and burrowing animals such as skunks, rattlesnakes, and ants under reversed lighting. A new walk-through aviary exhibits desert birds in four different habitat groupings. Museum-type displays are used throughout the zoo grounds to acquaint visitors with many other aspects of local natural history, including geological features. Serving in part as an educational facility, the museum maintains many mobile classrooms that travel to schools throughout Arizona and Sonora, Mex. It also sponsors various research projects on the natural history of the region and is involved in local conservation efforts.

To make the best use of the Britannica, consult the INDEX *first*

Arjun (b. 1563, Goindwal, Punjab, India—d. 1606, Delhi), the Sikh religion's fifth Gurū and its first martyr. He compiled the *Ādi Granth* or *Granth Sāhib* (Lord Book), the sacred scripture of the Sikhs, a book revered almost as a god. One of the greatest of the Sikh Gurūs, he immediately completed the Harimandir, or the Golden Temple, at Amritsar, where all could worship as they pleased. He expanded that great Sikh centre commercially and thus was the first Gurū to serve both as temporal and spiritual head of the Sikhs. The social reform and missionary efforts undertaken by earlier Gurūs were extended under him.

Gurū Arjun prospered until the Mughal emperor Akbar died and his successor Jahāngīr began to oppress the Sikhs. Rumours against the Gurū were spread by persons jealous of Arjun's popularity, and he was brought before Jahāngīr, who fined him 200,000 rupees and ordered the elimination of all sections of the *Ādi Granth* that gave offense to either Vedānta (Hinduism) or Islām. Gurū Arjun refused and was boiled alive. From that time on, the Sikhs, realizing they would be subject to further persecution by Mughal rulers, became more militaristic.

Arjuna, one of the five Pāṇḍava brothers, heroes of the Indian epic the *Mahābhārata* ("Great Epic of the Bharata Dynasty"). Arjuna's hesitation before a battle became the occasion for his friend and charioteer, the god Krishna, to deliver a discourse on duty, or the right course of human action. These verses, which are in the form of a quasi-dialogue between Krishna and Arjuna, are collectively known as the *Bhagavadgītā*, the most celebrated religious text of India. *See also* Mahābhārata.

ark, also called ARK OF THE LAW, Hebrew ARON, or ARON HA-QODESH ("holy ark"), in Jewish synagogues, an ornate cabinet that enshrines the sacred Torah scrolls used for public worship. Because it symbolizes the Holy of Holies of the ancient Temple of Jerusalem, it is the holiest place in the synagogue and the focal point of prayer. The ark is reached by steps and is commonly placed so that the worshipper facing it also "faces Jerusalem." When the scrolls are removed for religious services, the congregation stands, and a solemn ceremony accompanies the opening and closing of the ark doors.

Ashkenazi (German-rite) Jews cover the doors of the ark with a richly embroidered cloth (*parokhet*), while Sephardic (Spanish-rite) Jews place the cloth inside. Before or near the cabinet hangs the eternal light (*ner tamid*), and generally an inscription of the Ten Commandments (often in abbreviated form) or some relevant sacred text is placed above the doors.

Ark of the Covenant, Hebrew ARON HA-BERIT, ornate, gold-plated, wooden chest that in biblical times housed the two tablets of the Law given to Moses by God. The Ark rested in the Holy of Holies inside the Tabernacle and was seen only by the high priest on Yom Kippur, the Day of Atonement. The Levites (priestly functionaries) carried the Ark with them during their wanderings in the wilderness. Following the conquest of Canaan, the Promised Land, the Ark resided at Shiloh, but from time to time it was carried into battle by the Israelites. Taken to Jerusalem by King David, it was eventually placed in the Temple by King Solomon. The final fate of the Ark is unknown.

ark shell, any of the species of marine bivalve mollusks of the family Arcidae. Such clams are characterized by boat-shaped shells with long straight hinge lines bearing many small interlocking teeth. The shells are usually coated with a thick, sometimes hairy periostracum (outer organic shell layer). Many of these clams have rows of simple eyes along the mantle margins. Most of the 200 or so known species are found in tropical seas, with relatively few occurring in temperate areas. Ark shells are slow-moving or sedentary. Many species, especially those of the genera *Arca* and *Barbatia*, live attached by a byssus (a tuft of horny threads) in rock and coral crevices. Other species, particularly of the genus *Anadara*, live shallowly buried in sands and silts. Some species, such as the West African *Anadara senilis* and the Southeast Asian *Anadara granosa*, have provided a major source of food for humans since prehistoric times.

Arkadelphia, city, seat (1842) of Clark County, south central Arkansas, U.S., on the Ouachita River, south of its confluence with the Caddo. The site was settled *c.* 1811 by John Hemphill, operator of nearby salt licks. It was known as Blakelytown until 1838, when the settlement adopted its present name, a combination of the name Arkansas and of *adelphia* (Greek: "brother-place"). Incorporated in 1857, it became a city of the second class in 1874 and of the first class in 1962. An agricultural and light manufacturing economy prevails. Power is supplied by DeGray Dam on the Caddo. Arkadelphia is the home of Henderson State University (1890) and Ouachita Baptist University (1886). Pop. (1980) 10,005.

Arkadhía (Greece): *see* Arcadia.

Arkalyk, city and administrative centre of Turgay *oblast* (region), Kazakh Soviet Socialist Republic. Settlement began in 1956 in connection with the exploitation of the Turgay bauxite deposits, and it became a city in 1965 and the administrative centre of the new *oblast* in 1970. Arkalyk is linked to the Tselinograd–Tobol railway by a branch line from Yesil. In the early 1970s a major construction program was under way to provide the city with the amenities appropriate to an *oblast* administrative centre. Pop. (1983 est.) 62,000.

arkān al-Islām: *see* Islām, Pillars of.

Arkansas (people): *see* Quapaw.

Arkansas, constituent state of the United States of America lying on the west bank of the Mississippi River, in the west south central region of the country. The capital is Little Rock.

The following article summarizes the administrative history, geography, demographic patterns, economy, and culture of modern Arkansas; for additional treatment of its geography and history, *see* MACROPAEDIA: United States of America: *Arkansas.*

Facing the states of Tennessee and Mississippi across the Mississippi River, Arkansas is also bounded by Missouri on the north, Oklahoma on the west, Texas on the southwest, and Louisiana on the south. The state is roughly square in shape and extends about 250 mi (400 km) in each direction.

The earliest inhabitants were bluff dwellers along the banks of the Mississippi River, whose farming and hunting culture flourished *c.* AD 500. Later mound-building cultures left sepulchral mounds and other remains along the Mississippi. At the time of initial European exploration the main Indian groups in the area were the Caddo, Osage, and Quapaw.

In the 16th and 17th centuries Spanish and French explorers, the most notable being De Soto, Marquette and Jolliet, and La Salle, traversed the region. The first permanent European settlement was founded at Arkansas Post in 1686 by the Frenchman Henry de Tonty. Arkansas was acquired by the United States as part of the Louisiana Purchase from France in 1803. Arkansas Territory was formed in 1819, and Arkansas entered the Union as the 25th state in 1836.

Arkansas seceded from the Union in 1861, and during the Civil War was a member of the Confederate States of America. It was readmitted to the Union in 1868. Following Reconstruction a rigid policy of racial segregation evolved that ended in 1957 when federal troops entered Little Rock to maintain order after the state militia had been ordered to prevent the court-ordered desegregation of a public high school.

Physiographically Arkansas can be divided into two main regions roughly equal in size. A line drawn diagonally from the southwest corner to the northeast corner approximates the division between the forest-covered Ozark Plateau and Ouachita Mountains of the north and west and the fertile Gulf Coastal Plain and Mississippi River alluvial plain of the south and east. The state drains generally southeastward through the Arkansas and Mississippi rivers. Several large lakes have been created by damming streams in the Ozark and Ouachita mountains.

The Arkansas climate is temperate with mild winters and hot summers. Average temperatures at Little Rock, in the centre of the state at the border between the highlands and lowlands, are 42° F (6° C) in January and 82° F (28° C) in July. Annual precipitation of about 48 in. (1,220 mm) is distributed about equally during the year.

Settlement of the Mississippi lowlands was primarily by slave-holding cotton planters from more easterly southern states. The black population in 1860 was about 110,000, or 25 percent of the total; in 1980 it was nearly 374,000 but only about 16 percent. Three counties, all touching the Mississippi, are more than half black. Settlement of the uplands, where plantation agriculture was not practicable, was by whites who until recently lived in relative isolation. Statewide, barely more than half of the population lives in areas classified as urban. Little Rock, the largest city, numbers only 159,000. In recent years numerous "retirement villages" in the Ozarks have attracted visitors and buyers from across the country.

The Arkansas economy is no longer primarily agricultural, and cotton no longer dominates agriculture. Rice, soybeans, corn (maize), and poultry are the major farm products. Reserves of bauxite (aluminum ore), obtained by stripmining in the central region, represent more than 95 percent of the U.S. supply. More than one-half of the state is covered by forests, notably extensive stands of white pine and white oak. Hydroelectric power is produced at most dams, but steam-generated power plants produce most of the energy. Two nuclear generating stations are in operation near Dardanelle. Manufacturing is chiefly of consumer-goods, mostly food processing and the manufacture of wearing apparel, furniture, and electrical and non-electrical machinery.

The entire lengths of the Arkansas and Mississippi rivers within Arkansas are navigable. Highways, railways, and airways crisscross the state.

Tourism is important to the economy; the most popular destinations are the mineral springs at Hot Springs National Park and the lakeside resorts in the Ozarks.

Eastern Arkansas is typically Southern in speech pattern and customs. Black spirituals and "soul music" flourished in Arkansas long before they became popular nationally. The rural areas of the Ozarks and Ouachitas have retained to the fullest degree their traditional folk arts and culture. The major higher education institution is the University of Arkansas at Fayetteville. Area 53,104 sq mi (137,539 sq km). Pop. (1980) 2,286,419.

Arkansas City, city, Cowley County, southern Kansas, U.S., near the confluence of the Arkansas and Walnut rivers. Founded in 1870, it was successively named Walnut City, Adelphi, and Creswell; the present name was adopted at the city's incorporation (1872). It was a starting place for the 1893 settlement of the Cherokee Strip in Indian Territory (now Oklahoma), and the Cherokee Strip Living Museum is 2 mi (3 km) south. Oil was discovered nearby in 1914. Arkansas City is a shipping centre and a railroad junction with repair shops. Oil refining, tile manufacturing, flour milling, meat-packing, and food processing are important industries. Cowley County Community College was founded there in 1922. Cowley State Fishing Lake is nearby. Pop. (1980) 13,201.

Arkansas Post, historic village, Arkansas County, southeastern Arkansas, U.S., on the Arkansas River. A fort, the first permanent white settlement in the lower Mississippi Valley, was built there in 1686 by Henri de Tonty, a lieutenant of Robert Cavelier, sieur de la Salle. It became the residence of the French and Spanish governors and was an important trading post. John Law's "Mississippi Bubble" (a development plan that ran afoul of speculative complications and political intrigue) attracted settlers (1717), but most left after it "burst" in 1720. With the Louisiana Purchase, Arkansas Post was the first capital of the Arkansas Territory (1819–21). During the Civil War it fell to Federal troops and subsequently declined when bypassed by the railroads. Arkansas Post National Memorial (305 ac [123 ha]) was created in 1960. White River National Wildlife Refuge is to the east.

Arkansas River, large tributary of the Mississippi River, rising in the Sawatch Range of the Rocky Mountains near Leadville in central Colorado, U.S., and flowing generally east-southeastward for 1,450 mi (2,330 km) through Kansas, Oklahoma, and Arkansas before entering the Mississippi 40 mi northeast of Arkansas City, Ark. It has a total fall of 11,400 ft (3,475 m), and its drainage basin covers 160,600 sq mi (416,000 sq km).

From Leadville the Arkansas River flows southeast for about 100 mi to Canon City,

Arkansas River near Leadville, Colo.
S. Voynick—Shostal/EB Inc.

Colo., falling 6,750 ft. It leaves the mountains near Canon City through the Royal Gorge, a narrow canyon cut into solid granite with vertical walls more than 1,000 ft high. The Purgatoire River enters just above the John Martin Reservoir (1948), near Las Animas, Colo. Between Canon City and Great Bend, Kan., the channel is wide and shallow and meanders through a dry area that is extensively irrigated. Heavy rainfalls upstream will occasionally cause floods. Southeastward from Great Bend the river flows through a more humid area and is frequently more than ½ mi wide with a deep channel. The river receives its main tributaries in the Oklahoma portion: the Salt Fork, Cimarron, Verdigris, Grand, and Canadian rivers. The Arkansas River Navigation System enters the river 5 mi northeast of Muskogee, Okla., at the mouth of the Verdigris River, and continues through Arkansas to the Mississippi. Many water-control projects have been established in the basin, including a multiple-purpose reservoir at Eufaula on the Canadian River near McAlester, Okla. Principal riparian cities are Pueblo, Colo.; Wichita, Kan.; Tulsa, Okla.; and Fort Smith and Little Rock, Ark.

The Arkansas is believed to have been crossed by the Spanish explorer Francisco Vázquez de Coronado in 1541 near the site of Dodge City, Kan., and in 1806 the American explorer Zebulon Pike travelled through the upper reaches.

Arkansas River Navigation System, official name McCLELLAN-KERR ARKANSAS RIVER NAVIGATION SYSTEMS, improved portion of the Verdigris and Arkansas rivers, extending southeastward for 439 mi (767 km) from Catoosa (near Tulsa) in northeastern Oklahoma, U.S., through Arkansas to the Mississippi River 25 mi north of Arkansas City, Ark. Approved by the U.S. Congress in 1946 and completed in January 1971, the project controls the Arkansas River's regular flooding and provides a navigable waterway for year-round shipment of the river basin's resources—agricultural products, lumber, petroleum, and coal. Seventeen dams and locks along the waterway, which is 250 ft (75 m) wide and 9 ft deep, create a large supply of hydroelectric power.

Arkatag, also spelled ARKHA TAGH, also called PRZHEVALSKY RANGE, one of the complex mountain chains that form the Kunlun Mountains in western China. The Arkatag is the highest range of the Kunluns with the peaks of Ulugh Muz Tagh at its western end and Shapka Monomakha (also known as Chong Karlik Tagh) at the eastern end, both more than 25,300 ft (7,700 m).

Arkell, Anthony John (b. July 29, 1898, Hinxhill, Kent, Eng.—d. Feb. 26, 1980, Chelmsford, Essex), historian and Egyptologist, an outstanding colonial administrator who combined a passion for the past with a humanitarian concern for the peoples of modern Africa.

After serving with the Royal Flying Corps and the Royal Air Force, Arkell joined the Sudan Political Service in 1920 and set about abolishing the slave trade between the Sudan and Ethiopia, establishing villages for the freed slaves, who called themselves "the Sons of Arkell." He was appointed commissioner for archaeology and anthropology in 1938 and undertook several digs that opened up the previously unknown field of Sudanese prehistory. He returned to England in 1948 and was appointed curator of the Flinders Petrie Collection of Egyptian Antiquities at University College, University of London; he reorganized and cataloged this collection while writing his authoritative *History of the Sudan* (1955). He was professor of Egyptology at University College until his retirement in 1963, when he was ordained.

Arkell, William Joscelyn (b. June 9, 1904, Highworth, Wiltshire, Eng.—d. April 18, 1958, Cambridge, Cambridgeshire), paleontologist, an authority on Jurassic fossils (from 136,000,000 to 190,000,000 years in age). Arkell taught at Trinity College, Cambridge University. His work includes the classification of Jurassic ammonites and an interpretation of the environments of that period. He wrote *Jurassic Geology of the World* (1956), which stimulated further development of a stratigraphical classification applicable to all geological systems and periods.

Arkhangelsk, *oblast* (administrative region), Russian Soviet Federated Socialist Republic, with an area of 226,800 sq mi (587,400 sq km), along the northern coast of European Russia, from the Gulf of Onega to the Yugorsky Peninsula. Centred in Arkhangelsk city, it encompasses the Nenets autonomous *okrug* (area) in the east and a number of islands, including the Solovets, Novaya Zemlya, and Franz Josef Land archipelagoes. The low morainic hills and broad valleys are covered by tundra in the north and dense taiga (swampy forests) of spruce, pine, and birch in the south. Timber working dominates the economy. There is some fishing on the coasts and rivers and reindeer herding among the Nenets people. Pop. (1983 est.) 1,504,000.

Arkhangelsk, English ARCHANGEL, city and administrative centre of Arkhangelsk *oblast* (administrative region), Russian Soviet Federated Socialist Republic, on the Northern Dvina River, 30 mi (50 km) from the White Sea. With its suburbs, Solombala and Ekonomiya, the city extends for 10 mi along the river. Founded in 1584 as the fortified monastery of the archangel Michael, it was the first port of the Russian Empire to conduct trade with England and later with other countries. The

Docks at Arkhangelsk, Russian S.F.S.R.

Novosti Press Agency

port reached the height of its prosperity in the 17th century but subsequently declined with the founding of St. Petersburg (1703) and the exhorbitant customs dues introduced by Peter I the Great to divert trade to his new town. Arkhangelsk later revived with the building of a railway from Moscow in 1898. It is now the largest timber-exporting port of the U.S.S.R. It has large-scale timber-processing industries, including sawmilling and pulp making and papermaking. Shipbuilding and repair are important. Arkhangelsk is the base for a fishing fleet and the western terminus of the Northern Sea Route. There are institutes of epidemiology and of forestry and a teachers college. Pop. (1983 est.) 399,000.

Arklow, Irish AN TINBHEAR MÓR, port, seaside resort and urban district on the Irish Sea coast, in County Wicklow, southeast Ireland. In 431 St. Palladius, the Christian missionary, landed at the present site of Arklow. The Vikings had a settlement there, and the town was granted by John of England in 1189 to Theobald Fitz-Walter, Lord Butler of Ireland. It was an English stronghold during the late medieval period, and there are remains of a 13th-century Dominican friary and fragments of the Butler castle. Small boats, pottery, and fertilizers are manufactured there. Pop. (1981) 8,646.

Arkona, West Slavic citadel-temple of the god Svantovit, dating from the 9th–10th century AD and destroyed in 1168/69 by Christian Danes when they stormed the island of Rügen in the southwestern Baltic. From a description by Saxo Grammaticus, the 12th-century Danish historian, it is known that the Arkona was a wooden structure of consummate workmanship; around the temple extended a yard, and around this was a wooden fence, splendidly carved and bearing various symbols painted in heathen style. The temple itself was log-built and was topped by a red roof; the inner chamber had partitions of heavy tapestry. In this inner sanctum loomed the statue of Svantovit, larger than life size, awe-inspiring with its four heads and throats joined together facing in opposite directions. Saxo mentions that not only the whole land of Wends but also Scandinavian neighbours paid tribute to Svantovit. When the statue was cut and removed, the Danes carried away seven boxes of treasures (gifts to the god). O. Schuchhardt's excavation in 1921 proved the actual existence of the temple. Repeated excavations in 1969–70 revealed an earlier layer of the sanctuary dated to the 10th and possibly 9th century AD.

arkose, coarse sandstone (sedimentary rock composed of cemented grains 0.06–2 millimetres [0.0024–0.08 inch] in diameter) presumed to have formed by the disintegration of a granite without appreciable decomposition. Arkose thus consists primarily of quartz and feldspar grains together with small amounts of mica, all moderately well sorted, slightly worn, and loosely cemented with calcite or, less commonly, iron oxides or silica. Arkoses are distinguished from the normal quartzose sandstones (orthoquartzites) by their high feldspar content (more than 25 percent of the sand grains) and from the graywackes by their lighter colour. The feldspar content of subarkoses is 5–25 percent of the sand grains; it is diminished by more extensive weathering or by dilution from nonigneous source rocks. In the absence of stratification, arkose may bear superficial resemblance to granite, and it aptly has been described as reconstituted granite, or granite wash. Like the granites from which they were formed, arkoses are pink or gray.

The geological significance of arkose has been much debated. Under normal conditions most of the feldspar decomposes and is converted to clay minerals during weathering of the source rocks, whereas under conditions of extreme dryness or low temperatures, decomposition of the feldspar is inhibited or greatly retarded. Arkoses were, therefore, presumed to be derived from the erosion of a granitic terrane characterized by an arid or glacial climate. Now, however, it is known that the feldspar may escape destruction and thus be transported and deposited with quartz sands if rates of uplift, erosion, and deposition are great enough. Under such conditions, irrespective of the climate, weathering processes are incomplete and the sands derived from such terrane are high in feldspar content. Arkoses, therefore, may be said to indicate either a climatic extreme or high relief. Most ancient arkose deposits seem to be the product of high relief.

Arkwright, Sir Richard (b. Dec. 23, 1732, Preston, Lancashire, Eng.—d. Aug. 3, 1792, Cromford, Derbyshire), textile industrialist and inventor whose use of power-driven machinery and employment of a factory system

Arkwright, detail of an engraving by J. Jenkins after a portrait by Joseph Wright

By courtesy of the Science Museum, London

of production were perhaps more important than his inventions.

In his early career as a wig-maker, Arkwright travelled widely in Great Britain and began his lifelong practice of self-education. He became interested in spinning machinery at least by 1764, when he began construction of his first machine (patented in 1769). Arkwright's water frame (so called because it operated by waterpower) produced a cotton yarn suitable for warp. The thread made on James Hargreaves' spinning jenny (invented about 1767), lacked the strength of Arkwright's cotton yarn and was suitable only for weft. With several partners, Arkwright opened factories at Nottingham and Cromford. Within a few years he was operating a number of factories equipped with machinery for carrying out all phases of textile manufacturing from carding to spinning. In 1773 he began to manufacture an all-cotton calico (previously linen had been used for warp), thus establishing cotton-cloth manufacture as the leading industry in northern England.

He maintained a dominant position in the textile industry despite the rescinding of his comprehensive patent of 1775. He may have borrowed the ideas of others for his machines, but he was able to make the machines and make them work successfully. By 1782 Arkwright had a capital of £200,000 and employed 5,000 workers. In 1786 he was knighted.

Arlberg, mountain pass (5,882 ft [1,793 m]) and tunnel, at the northern end of the Rhaetian Alps, in western Austria. The pass forms a divide between the Danube and Rhine river systems. The region is a noted winter sports area, and the Arlberg technique in skiing was perfected there by Hannes Schneider, who was born at Stuben am Arlberg. A rail tunnel (built 1880–84 and 6.3 mi [10.2 km] long) carries the electrified railroad between Langen (Vorarlberg) and Sankt Anton (Tirol); the two towns were connected by a road tunnel, 8.7 mi in length, that opened in 1979.

Arlecchino: *see* Harlequin.

Arlen, Harold, original name HYMAN ARLUCK (b. Feb. 15, 1905, Buffalo, N.Y., U.S.), composer, arranger, pianist, and vocalist who contributed such popular songs as "Over the Rainbow," "Blues in the Night," "I Love a Parade," and "Stormy Weather" to Hollywood movies and Broadway musicals. Arlen was most prolific from 1929 through the 1950s.

The son of a cantor and a pianist, Arlen showed exceptional musical talent in childhood, but he rejected formal training to play piano in nightclubs. The composer Vincent Youmans encouraged him to notate a piano improvisation that, with lyrics by Ted Koehler, became the song "Get Happy." From the late 1920s until 1933, Arlen worked for J.H. Remick music publishers, and his songs, including "Between the Devil and the Deep Blue Sea" and "I've Got the World on a String," were featured in shows at Harlem's Cotton Club. Arlen's work for the Broadway stage included scores for the musicals *You Said It* (1931); *Life Begins at 8:40* (1934); *Hooray for What?* (1937); *Bloomer Girl* (1944); *St. Louis Woman* (1946) and *Saratoga* (1959), both with lyrics by Johnny Mercer; and *House of Flowers* (1954; lyrics by Truman Capote).

For Hollywood films, Arlen wrote, among other songs, "It's Only a Paper Moon," "Let's Fall in Love," Groucho Marx's theme song "Lydia the Tatoo'd Lady," and "That Old Black Magic." "Over the Rainbow" (lyrics by E.Y. Harburg), introduced by Judy Garland in *The Wizard of Oz* (1939) and used thereafter as her theme, won him a 1939 Academy Award, and he received an Academy Award nomination for "The Man that Got Away" (lyrics by Ira Gershwin), introduced by Garland in *A Star Is Born* (1954). Ira Gershwin also collaborated with Arlen on the film *The Country Girl* (1954), starring Bing Crosby. Arlen recorded as a vocalist with Leo Reisman and Cole Porter. He was widely honoured for his life achievements by both film and theatre societies, and his music was the subject of several television productions.

Arlen, Michael, original name DIKRAN KOUYOUMDJIAN (b. Nov. 16, 1895, Ruschuk, Bulg.—d. June 23, 1956, New York City), author whose novels and short stories epitomized the brittle gaiety and underlying cynicism and disillusionment of fashionable post-World War I London society. The phenomenal success of *The Green Hat* (1924)—a witty, sophisticated, but fundamentally sentimental novel about the "bright young things" of Mayfair, London's most fashionable romantic district—made him, almost overnight, the latest craze in Great Britain and the U.S.

The son of an Armenian merchant, he was brought up in England and took the name Michael Arlen in 1922, when he became a British subject and began his career as a writer. After 1928, when he married the beautiful Atalanta, a Frenchwoman who shared his love of the limelight, Arlen lived mainly in the south of France, feted and photographed wherever he went, and on visits to the U.S. treated like royalty. He never repeated the triumph of *The Green Hat.*

Arles, city, Bouches-du-Rhône *département,* Provence-Alpes-Côte-d'Azur region, southeastern France, on the Camargue plain where the Rhône divides to form its delta, northwest of Marseille. Already important in the days of the Ligurian tribes, Arles became a leading city (called Arelate) of the Western Roman Empire. St. Trophime in the 1st century AD founded the bishopric, which endured until 1790. The city fell to the Visigoths in the 6th century and then to Muslim invaders in 730. In the 10th century it became the capital of the kingdom of Burgundy, known later as the Kingdom of Arles, and in the 12th century emerged as an independent entity—much like the Italian republics—preeminent in commerce and navigation. In 1239 it was absorbed into Provence. Portions of the wall around the old town are Roman, and a Roman arena dating to the 1st century BC that seated more than 20,000 spectators is still used for bullfights and plays. Excavations at a Roman theatre have retrieved many art objects, including the "Vénus d'Arles" now in the Louvre. The church of Saint-Trophime was founded in the 7th century and was rebuilt several times; it is essentially 11th–12th-century Romanesque with 15th-century additions, a sculptured facade echoing antique Rome, and a sculpture-rich cloister, said to be the finest in France. The Museon Arlaten, which exhibits Provençal arts and crafts, was founded by the Provençal poet Frédéric Mistral, who gave most of his Nobel Prize money to its furtherance. The painter Vincent van Gogh entered into his first great productive period when he lived at Arles (1888–89).

The Roman arena at Arles, Fr.

By courtesy of Air France

A naval base under the Romans, Arles is still a river port, mainly for oil tankers via the Rhône and the Canal d'Arles à Port du Bouc. Industries include chemical, metal, and paper manufacture, but the economy is largely based on tourism and agriculture. Pop. (1982) 37,554.

Arles, Council of, the first representative meeting of Christian bishops in the Western Roman Empire. It was convened at Arles in southern Gaul in August 314 by Emperor Constantine I, primarily to deal with the problem of the Donatists, a schismatic Christian group in North Africa.

Attended by representatives of 43 bishoprics, this synod was held because the Donatists had denied the representative character of two earlier synods, at Rome and in Africa, at which they had been condemned. At Arles the Donatists were again condemned, but they rejected the decisions reached by the council and again appealed to Constantine to review their case.

Arletty, pseudonym of ARLETTE-LEONIE BATHIAT (b. May 15, 1898, Courbevoie, Fr.), Parisian actress whose stage work is overshadowed by her distinguished international reputation for her film characterizations.

Arletty became an artist's model, posing for Henri Matisse by the time she was 19 years of age. In 1920 she joined the Théâtre des Capucines and appeared there in innumerable revues as well as at other Parisian theatres in operettas (such as *Oui,* 1928) and comedies (such as *Fric Frac,* 1936).

Arletty made her film debut in a vaudeville about a dog (*Un Chien qui rapporte,* 1930) and played minor film roles for many years. Finally, when Marcel Carné cast her as the whore who longed for a better life, in *Hotel de Nord* (1938), she achieved star status. Similar roles in Carné's *Le Jour se lève* (1939) and *Les Visiteurs du soir* (1942) established her worldwide reputation as the interpreter of the quintessential Parisian *poule:* young yet old, foolish though sophisticated, and naive but world-weary. Arletty's most famous motion-picture role, however, was as the courtesan Garance in *Les Enfants du Paradis,* again directed by Carné (1945); it is this role that is favourably compared to Marlene Dietrich's in *The Blue Angel.*

Briefly jailed for collaboration at the end of the war, Arletty did not complete another film until 1949 (*Portrait d'un assassin*), the same year she also created the role of Blanche in the first French stage production of Tennessee Williams' *A Streetcar Named Desire.* The following year saw another stage success as the lead in *Revue de l'empire.* During the next 12 years Arletty continued to appear in plays and to make films, most notably playing the lesbian Inez in the screen version of Sartre's *No Exit* (*Huit Clos,* 1954) and a cameo role in one of the few films she made for a non-French company, *The Longest Day* (1961). Although by 1963 she had become almost blind, she eventually returned to the stage in the leading role in Jean Cocteau's *Les Monstres sacrés* (1966) and to films as a madam in Jean-Claud Brialy's *Les Volets fermés* (1972). An autobiography, *La Défense,* was published in 1971.

Arlington, urban town (township), Middlesex County, eastern Massachusetts, U.S., immediately northwest of Boston. Settled about 1630 as part of Cambridge, it was known as Menotomy (an Indian word meaning "swift waters") until separately incorporated as West Cambridge in 1807 and renamed for George Washington Parke Custis' Virginia estate in 1867. Its early economy was dependent on truck farming, the shipping of ice (cut from Spy Pond), and the manufacture of textile cards. The town developed as a residential suburb with the arrival of the railway from Boston in 1846. Light manufactures include textile machinery, electronic equipment, and boxes. Arlington's Jason Russell House (1680) was the scene of a fierce skirmish with the British in which 12 minutemen were killed on April 19, 1775. Their graves are marked in the Old Burying Ground of the town's Unitarian Church. The town includes the villages of East Arlington and Arlington Heights. Pop. (1980) 48,219.

Arlington, city, Tarrant County, northern Texas, U.S., between Fort Worth (west) and Grand Prairie and Dallas (east). The first settlement (1843), on an Indian council site, was called Bird's Fort and then Johnson's Station. In 1876 Arlington was laid out by railroad men and named for Gen. Robert E. Lee's home in Virginia. Primarily an industrial and commercial centre, it has automotive and aerospace industries that developed after 1950, with an accompanying rapid increase in population. It is the seat of the University of Texas at Arlington (1895) and the Arlington Baptist College (1939). Six Flags Over Texas, a large amusement park, and Arlington Stadium, home of the Texas Rangers baseball team, are located there. Inc. 1920. Pop. (1980) 160,123.

Arlington, urban county in northern Virginia, U.S., across the Potomac River (southwest) from Washington, D.C., with which it is connected by five bridges (Francis Scott Key, Arlington Memorial, George Mason, Theodore Roosevelt, and Rochambeau Memorial), and adjoining the city of Alexandria (south).

Established as Bellehaven (later Alexandria) County, it was ceded to the Federal Government in 1789 and became part of the District of Columbia; the county was returned to Virginia in 1846 and was renamed Arlington in 1920 for the former estate of the Custis-Lee families. Arlington has developed from a number of small villages (including Arlington, the county seat) into an integral part of metropolitan Washington. Governed as a unit, it has no incorporated places. One of the smallest counties in the nation, Arlington covers 24 sq mi (62 sq km) of which about 20 percent is federal property occupied by Arlington National Cemetery, Washington National Airport, Ft. Myer, and the Pentagon (Department of Defense) and other government offices. The county has become a residential and bustling business community with clusters of high-rise buildings and some light manufactures (electric components, scientific instruments, machinery). Housing developments include Ballston, Buckingham, Cherrydale, Clarendon, Columbia Pike, East Falls, Fairlington, Rosslyn, and Westover. Marymount College of Virginia for women (Roman Catholic) was founded (1950) in Arlington. Pop. (1980) 152,599.

Arlington, Henry Bennet, 1st earl of, also called (1663–72) BARON ARLINGTON (b. 1618, Little Saxham, Suffolk, Eng.—d. July 28, 1685, Euston, Suffolk), secretary of state under King Charles II of England from 1662 to 1674 and a leading member of Charles's "Cabal" ministry. Besides directing foreign policy for 12 years, Arlington, by creating the nucleus of a "court party" (the future Tories) in the House of Commons, helped to develop the party system in England.

Arlington, detail of an oil painting from the studio of Sir Peter Lely, 1665; in the collection of the Marquess of Bath

By courtesy of the Marquess of Bath; photograph, Courtauld Institute of Art

Bennet served as Charles's agent in Madrid while both were in exile after the English Civil War. As secretary of state, Bennet (created Baron Arlington in 1663 and given an earldom in 1672) survived parliamentary censure for the conduct and result of the second Anglo-Dutch War (1665–67). With the fall of the 1st Earl of Clarendon, the lord chancellor, in 1667, Arlington became in effect the chief minister of state.

A skeptic in religion (although on his deathbed he professed himself a Roman Catholic), he used the fear of popery to rouse popular feeling against France. In 1668, with Sir William Temple (one of the outstanding men whom Arlington brought into the King's service) as intermediary, he negotiated the Protestant Triple Alliance of England, the Dutch Republic, and Sweden. Because he was in the King's confidence, however, Arlington was ambiguously involved in Charles's pro-French and pro-Catholic policies that were embodied in the secret Anglo-French Treaty of Dover (1670), in which Charles agreed, among other things, to support Louis XIV of France in war against the Dutch Republic. Although Arlington supported measures intended to effectuate the Dover treaties (a second treaty having been signed openly later in 1670), he was thought to have taken bribes from the Dutch, with whom England concluded peace in 1673.

In 1674 Arlington, denounced by the 2nd Duke of Buckingham, was impeached for embezzlement, "betrayal of trust," and promoting Roman Catholicism. The charges failed, but Arlington resigned the secretaryship of state (Sept. 11, 1674) for the safer but lucrative position of lord chamberlain. He held that office until his death early in the reign of James II, whose exclusion from the succession to the throne Arlington may have proposed. See V. Barbour, *Henry Bennet, Earl of Arlington* (1914).

Arlington Heights, village, Cook County, northeastern Illinois, U.S. Settled in 1836, it was known as Dunton for Asa Dunton, the original settler, until the present name was adopted in 1874. The village has developed as a northwestern residential suburb of Chicago, and has some light industry. Arlington Park Race Track and Exposition Center are just west. The city is the site of a local historical centre, which includes reconstructed buildings. Inc. 1887. Pop. (1980) 66,116.

Arlington National Cemetery, American national burial ground in Arlington County, Virginia, U.S., on the Potomac River directly opposite Washington, D.C. It occupies a tract of more than 500 ac (200 ha) and is generally semicircular in shape; its central feature is the mansion built in 1802 on the estate of George Washington Parke Custis, adopted son of George Washington. The mansion is said to have been modelled after the Theseum in Athens. The portico, with its eight white columns, is a landmark visible from across the river. The mansion, now called Arlington House, serves as the Robert E. Lee Memorial.

When Lee, who had married Mary Anne Randolph Custis in the mansion in 1831, left Arlington (April 22, 1861) to command the Confederate troops in the Civil War, federal soldiers occupied the estate, converting the mansion into a headquarters and the grounds into a camp. Arlington became a military cemetery in 1864 by order of the secretary of war. After years of litigation George Washington Custis Lee, the residuary legatee, succeeded through the U.S. Supreme Court in declaring the government a trespasser. Eventually, in 1883, he sold the title to the U.S. for $150,000.

The first soldier buried there (May 13, 1864) was a Confederate prisoner who died in a local hospital. Some of the dead from every war in which the U.S. has participated, including a few officers of the American Revolution, have since been buried there. Many of the nation's military leaders and other outstanding individuals, including Gen. John J. Pershing, Adm. Richard E. Byrd, William Howard Taft, Robert E. Peary, Gen. Jonathan Wainwright, Gen. George C. Marshall, Robert Todd Lincoln, Maj. Pierre-Charles L'Enfant, William Jennings Bryan, John F. Kennedy, and Robert F. Kennedy, also are buried there.

The Tomb of the Unknown Soldier, first a memorial to the dead of World War I but now also considered a memorial to the dead of other wars, is located there. Nearby is the Memorial Amphitheatre, erected through the efforts of the Grand Army of the Republic as a place of assembly for Memorial Day services and dedicated May 15, 1920. The roofless, white marble structure, enclosing a natural amphitheatre, is copied after both the Theatre of Dionysus at Athens and the Roman theatre at Orange, Fr. The Fields of the Dead (interments now exceed 163,000), with their seemingly endless lines of plain stones, follow a pattern adopted in 1872 for use in all national cemeteries. The U.S. Marine Corps War Memorial (Iwo Jima flag-raising statue) is near the cemetery.

Arliss, George, original name AUGUSTUS GEORGE ANDREWS (b. April 10, 1868, London—d. Feb. 5, 1946, London), actor noted for his portrayal of historic personages in many motion pictures.

Arliss began his acting career in 1887 but did not have his first substantial success until

Arliss, 1938

By courtesy of the National Film Archive, London

he appeared with Mrs. Patrick Campbell in London during the 1900–01 season. In 1902 he played in *The Second Mrs. Tanqueray* in New York City and in 1911 played the title role in *Disraeli*.

Arliss was already established as a leading actor when he turned to films in 1920. His pictures included *The Green Goddess* (1930), *Old English* (1930), *Alexander Hamilton* (1931),

The House of Rothschild (1934), and *Cardinal Richelieu* (1935). He won an Oscar for best actor of 1929–30 for his role in the film version of *Disraeli*. Arliss wrote several plays and two autobiographical works: *Up the Years from Bloomsbury* (1927) and *My Ten Years in the Studios* (1940).

Arlit and Akouta, mine sites, Agadez *département*, northwestern Niger, West Africa, 155 mi (250 km) northwest of Agadez town. Situated in the Sahara (desert) at the western edge of the Aïr massif, the area is well-known for its rich uranium deposits. High-grade uranium was discovered in 1966 and exploitation by an amalgam of the French Atomic Energy Commission and French private companies known as Somair (Société des mines de l'Aïr) began in 1971. In 1974 the mines were nationalized and in 1977 an agreement with France increased Niger's share in the exploitation from 17 to 33 percent. In 1978 a second mine was opened at Akouta, six mi (10 km) southwest of Arlit, by a Japanese, French, and Spanish investment consortium known as Cominak (Compagnie Minière d'Akouta). Towns were created near both mines with educational, recreational, and health facilities. The population of the older Arlit town was 9,394 in 1977; newer Akokan town (adjacent to the Akouta mine) was expected to house 5,000 people in the early 1980s. Deep water drilling supplies the towns with water, and a thermal plant at Ânou Ararene (since 1981) supplies electricity. Uranium is concentrated in a processing plant at Arlit. The mines are connected by a 403-mi (648-km) all-weather "uranium road" (completed in 1980) to Tahoua in southern Niger. The proved reserves of 280,000 tons of uranium (1980) have placed Niger among the five major uranium producers in the world.

Arlon (French), Flemish AARLEN, capital of Luxembourg province, southeastern Belgium, at the foot of the southern end of the Ardennes Plateau near the source of the Semois River and the border of Luxembourg. It originated as the Roman Orolaunum, the oldest known settlement in Belgium, established on the road from Trèves to Reims and fortified in the 4th century. It became the seat of a countship in the 10th century. From its castle Richard I the Lion-Heart, who was also marquis d'Arlon, set out for the Third Crusade (1190). With Belgian independence, Arlon became the provisional capital of Luxembourg province (1830, confirmed 1839).

It has become an important livestock and agricultural market and a frontier station on the international Brussels-Namur-Luxembourg railway. There is some manufacturing, and part of its population is employed in steel plants across the borders in Luxembourg and in France.

Warfare during the 16th, 17th, and 18th centuries destroyed most of the relics of Arlon's past. Chief among the remains are the Tour Romaine (Roman Tower; from the 4th-century fortifications dismantled by the French in 1670) and the 17th-century Church of St. Donatus. Arlon's archaeological museum contains valuable Roman tomb reliefs. Associated with Arlon is the regional beverage, "Maitrank." Pop. (1983 est.) mun., 22,201.

Arlt, Roberto (b. April 2, 1900, Buenos Aires—d. July 26, 1942, Buenos Aires), novelist, short-story writer, dramatist, and journalist who emphasized the theme of the anger and disillusionment of the urban middle class. A first-generation descendant of German immigrants, Arlt was alienated by Argentine society. The world of his novels *El juguete rabioso* (1926; "The Rabid Toy"), *Los siete locos* (1929; "The Seven Madmen"), *Los lanzallamas* (1931; "The Flame Throwers"), and *El amor brujo* (1932; "False Love") is often grotesque and nightmarish. His *Aguafuertes porteñas* (1950; "Etchings from the Port") and *Nuevas aguafuertes porteñas* (1960), orginally published as articles in *El Mundo*, are picaresque sketches of the people of Buenos Aires. He follows the tradition begun by José Sixto Álvarez (1858–1903), known as Fray (Friar) Mocho, but with greater psychological perception and intense irony. Arlt's plays were produced under the auspices of El Teatro del Pueblo; *Trescientos millones* (1932; "Three Hundred Million") and *Saverio el cruel* (1936; "Saverio the Cruel," not staged until 1956) stand out. *Trescientos millones* is rich in its use of experimental techniques, and *Saverio* is notable for its treatment of reality along Pirandellian lines.

Arlt's complete fictional works were published in 1963.

Arluck, Hyman (composer): *see* Arlen, Harold.

arm, in zoology, either of the forelimbs or upper limbs of ordinarily bipedal vertebrates, particularly humans and other primates. The term is sometimes restricted to the proximal part, from shoulder to elbow (the distal part is then called the forearm); it also may denote the limb or the locomotive or prehensile organ of an invertebrate, such as the ray of a starfish, tentacle of an octopus, or brachium of a brachiopod.

The major extensor muscle of the arm is the triceps, which arises on the humerus and attaches to the ulna at the elbow; the brachialis and biceps muscles are the flexors. The pectoralis muscle, anchored in the chest, is important in the downward motion of the arm, and in quadrupeds pulls the limb backward in locomotion. In brachiating primates the arm is unusually long.

Arm-in-Arm Convention: *see* National Union Convention.

Armada, also called SPANISH ARMADA, or INVINCIBLE ARMADA, Spanish ARMADA ESPAÑOLA, or ARMADA INVENCIBLE, the fleet sent by Philip II of Spain, in 1588, to assist in an attempted invasion of England by a Spanish army from the Netherlands. Its defeat marked a revolution in the tactics of naval warfare and foreshadowed Spain's decline and England's emergence as a major world power.

The Armada sailed from Lisbon in May 1588 under the inexperienced Duque de Medina-Sidonia, a less able commander than Santa Cruz, who had died in February. The fleet consisted of 130 ships with about 8,000 sailors and 19,000 infantry. The ships, most of them slow and unwieldy, were armed with short-range heavy cannon and were designed for action at close quarters.

The larger English fleet, under the able command of Charles Howard, Baron Howard of Effingham, consisted of 197 ships with about 16,000 men, most of them experienced sailors. The ships were low-lying, manoeuvrable, and equipped with long-range light ordnance deployed broadside. The English captains, including Sir Francis Drake and Sir John Hawkins, were brilliant tacticians; daring and imaginative, they were able to employ their superior mobility to the best advantage.

The Armada was first sighted off Cornwall on July 29 (July 19, old style). The English fleet assembled at Portsmouth to secure the wind advantage and were nearly trapped in enclosed waters, only narrowly escaping across the prows of the Spanish ships. In three encounters (off Portsmouth, July 31 [July 21, O.S.]; off Plymouth, August 2 [July 23, O.S.]; and off the Isle of Wight, August 4 [July 25, O.S.]) the English harassed the Armada with their long-range guns, but their light shot could not seriously damage the enemy ships or break their tight defensive formation.

The Armada reached the Strait of Dover on August 6 (July 27, O.S.) and anchored off Calais. The invasion force from the Netherlands was not prepared, and now the entire Spanish strategy of a coordinated junction of land and sea forces appeared a monstrous blunder. The wind and the enemy prevented the Armada from retreating westward; it could only sail northward, away from Parma entirely, or eastward to suicide on the Zeeland banks. At midnight on August 7–8 (July 28–29, O.S.), the English launched six fire ships into the harbour at Calais, causing the Spanish ships to cut loose their anchors and irretrievably lose their formation. The English attacked off Gravelines on August 8, now able to inflict serious damage on the disorganized fleet. Only a sudden change of wind from northwest allowed the Spaniards to escape. They suffered further losses returning home northward around Scotland to Ireland and then across the open Atlantic. Only 76 ships reached Spain again. The English, on the other hand, lost no ships and fewer than 100 men during the fighting.

As the first gun duel between ships propelled exclusively by sail, the battle of the Armada was the prototype of all naval actions up to and including Trafalgar (1805).

armadillo, any of numerous mammals of the family Dasypodidae, order Edentata, related to sloths and anteaters. Armadillos are found in tropical and subtropical regions, primarily in South America; most species inhabit open areas, but some live in forests.

There are 9 genera and 20 species of armadillos. The three-, six-, and nine-banded armadillos (*Tolypeutes, Euphractus,* and *Dasypus*, respectively) are named for the number of movable bands in their armour. One species of nine-banded armadillo (*D. novemcinctus*) is

Nine-banded armadillo (*Dasypus novemcinctus*)
Appel Color Photography

the only armadillo to range into the United States. The pichi (*Zaedyus pichi*) is a common small resident of Argentinian Patagonia.

Armadillos are stout, short-legged animals with strong, curved claws and protective coverings of pinkish to brown armour. The armour is composed of solid, buckler-like plates separated by movable transverse bands. It covers most of the body, including the head and, usually, the tail. The coat ranges from a scattering of hairs in such forms as the nine-banded armadillos (*Dasypus*) to a comparatively dense coat of soft, white hair on the underparts and sides in the pink fairy armadillo, or lesser pichiciago (*Chlamyphorus truncatus*). Size varies considerably, from an overall length of about 16 centimetres (6.5 inches) in the pink fairy armadillo to about 1.5 metres (5 feet) in the giant armadillo (*Priodontes giganteus*).

Armadillos live alone, in pairs, or in small groups. Primarily nocturnal, they live in burrows and feed on termites and other insects, vegetation, small animals, and some carrion. Strong diggers, they are also good swimmers, swallowing air to make themselves buoyant in water. When threatened, armadillos retreat to their burrows or, if caught in the open, draw in their feet so the armour touches the ground. They may also run away, burrow, or claw at the attacker. The three-banded armadillos (*Tolypeutes*) are able to roll up into a ball. The pink fairy armadillo and Burmeister's armadillo (*Burmeisteria retusa*) have vertical armour plates on their hindquarters. The pink fairy armadillo uses this plate to plug the entrance to its burrow, and Burmeister's armadillo probably does the same.

Female armadillos bear one to 12 identical young, all of which develop from a single fertilized egg. The gestation period, not known for all armadillos, is about 65 days in one species of peludo, or hairy armadillo (*Chaetophractus villosus*); it is four months in one of the nine-banded armadillos (*Dasypus novemcinctus*), not including a delay of several months between fertilization of the egg and its implantation in the wall of the uterus.

armadillo lizard (*Cordylus cataphractus*), a South American member of the family Cordylidae, known for its defensive body posture. This lizard is about 25 centimetres (10 inches) long.

When danger threatens, it forms a ball by rolling on its back and taking its tail in its mouth. Protected by hard, bony scales and spines on the head and tail, the armadillo lizard remains in this position until the danger disappears.

Armagh, former (until 1973) county, Northern Ireland. It was bounded by Lough (lake) Neagh (north), former County Tyrone (northwest), former County Down (east), and by the Republic of Ireland (south and west). Its area was 512 sq mi (1,326 sq km).

From the fertile, low-lying northern part of the former county composed of Tertiary basalts, Pliocene deposits, Triassic rocks and Old Red Sandstone, the land rises southward to mountains of Ordovician and Silurian rocks. Farther south, the granite mountain core is revealed, whereas younger intrusive igneous rocks form Slieve Gullion (1,894 ft [577 m]). Vast numbers of drumlins (long oval mounds) and small lakes indicate the importance of glaciation in northern and central former County Armagh.

In late prehistoric times and at the dawn of history, Armagh was an important populated area in Ulster. At the beginning of the Christian Era, the fortress of Emain Mhacha, at the site known as Navan Fort, served as the centre of a kingdom of Ulster extending to the Rivers Shannon and Boyne in the west and south. Also associated with that period is an ancient frontier earthwork, Black Pig's Dyke. Following the decline of Ulster in the 4th century, Emain Mhacha lost its importance; and Ard Mhacha (now Armagh, the county town) became the political centre. It gained added importance after St. Patrick made it his metropolitan see in the 5th century. The area was later ravaged by Anglo-Norman and also Danish (841) invaders, but they made no permanent settlements.

Not until the 17th century did English influence become important in the county. Made shire ground in 1586 and included in the scheme for the Plantation of Ulster of the early 17th century, it was colonized mainly by landowners from England. Armagh's prosperity in the 18th century is attested to by many monuments and buildings. In the 1973 administrative reorganization of Northern Ireland, the county was divided into the district of Armagh and portions of Craigavon and Newry and Mourne districts.

Armagh, Irish ARD MHACHA, city, seat, and district (established 1973), formerly in County Armagh, Northern Ireland. The hill fort of Ard Mhacha, around which modern Armagh city developed, became important in the 4th century after the downfall of Emain Mhacha, the military centre of an ancient kingdom of Ulster. In the 5th century St. Patrick established his principal church in Ireland on the hill-fort site that later became a medieval ecclesiastical capital. Armagh's religious importance attracted the attention of marauding Danes in the 9th and 10th centuries and later that of Anglo-Normans. Its capture by English (Protestant) forces in the 16th century was followed by the opening of a number of educational institutions, including a Royal school (1627), a library, and an observatory (1765); more recently (1968) a planetarium opened there. The prosperity of the clergy and gentry in the 18th century is reflected in the city's many Georgian monuments and buildings. Contemporary Armagh is the seat of both the Church of Ireland (Anglican) and Roman Catholic archbishoprics, and the city is the market centre for the district and manufactures textiles, chemicals, optical items, and processed foods.

Armagh district covers an area of 261 sq mi (676 sq km) located south of Lough (lake) Neagh and is bordered by the districts of Dungannon to the northwest, Craigavon to the northeast, Banbridge to the east, Newry and Mourne to the southeast, and the Republic of Ireland to the southwest. Southern Armagh district is rugged terrain composed of Ordovician and Silurian rocks, which slope gradually down to more fertile lowlands in the north. Northern Armagh district is the main fruit-growing region on the island of Ireland, and the villages of Richhill and Loughhall are market centres for primarily apples and strawberries. Light industrial centres include Keady, Laurelvale, and Tanderagee in addition to Armagh city. Most formerly important linen mills in the district have closed or diversified into other synthetic fibres. Southern Armagh district and adjacent areas near the Irish Republic's border were continuing hotbeds of sectarian violence during the 1970s and early 1980s. Pop. (1971) city, 12,315; (1981 prelim.) district, 48,169.

Armagnac, historic region of southwestern France, now contained in the *département* of Gers.

A part of the duchy of Gascony in Merovingian and Carolingian times, Armagnac became a political unit during the feudal breakdown of the 10th century. From the 12th century it gained strategic importance as a buffer zone between lands controlled by the kings of France (Toulouse) and those controlled by the kings of England (Guyenne). Its counts used their position to shift allegiance and became highly independent. The Treaty of Calais (1360) during the Hundred Years' War (1337–1453) gave suzerainty over Armagnac to the English; an appeal by the count Jean I against English rule (1368) gave Charles V of France a pretext to resume the war.

During the 14th century, the counts greatly increased their holdings. By the beginning of the 15th century their lands reached from the Garonne to the Pyrenees and also included parts of the Massif Central.

The position of his holdings, along with the services of Gascon mercenaries, made it possible for the count Bernard VII to play a major role in France's internal conflicts of the early 15th century. The Armagnac party was formed in opposition to the Burgundians as a result of the murder of Louis, duc d'Orléans (brother of the mad king Charles VI), by John the Fearless, duke of Burgundy (1407). With the marriage of his daughter to the son of the victim, Bernard came to head what had been the Orleanist party. Because the Burgundians often aligned with the English, the Armagnacs seemed to be a national party but were basically a power-seeking group. They gained control of the mad king from 1413. Bernard was named constable, chief of the army, and governor of all finances. The Armagnacs led the resistance to the English king Henry V's invasion of France but suffered a setback in the Battle of Agincourt (1415). Profiting from discontent caused by the harsh government of the Armagnacs, the Burgundians entered Paris and killed Bernard and many of his followers in the summer of 1418. After 1418 the Armagnacs rapidly lost power as the new king Charles VII gained leadership and was reconciled with Charles the Bold, duke of Burgundy. In the late 15th century, Louis XI invaded the lands of the counts of Armagnac, captured their capital at Lectoure, and confiscated their territory.

Armagnac was permanently united to the French crown under Henry IV (1607). During the 17th and 18th centuries, it existed as an administrative division of the *gouvernement-général* of Guyenne-et-Gascogne.

Armah, Ayi Kwei (b. 1939, Takoradi, Gold Coast), novelist, short-story writer, and poet whose work deals with corruption and political repression in contemporary and historical Africa.

Armah was educated in local mission schools and at Achimota College before leaving for the United States in 1959 to complete his secondary education at Groton and his bachelor's degree at Harvard. Armah considered Paris his home, although he returned to Ghana in 1966 to teach English and become a script writer for Ghana Television; he also revisited the United States—first to accept a writing fellowship at Columbia and again in 1968 to lecture at the University of Massachusetts at Amherst—and Africa, in 1972, to teach at the University of Tanzania.

From his first work, *The Beautyful Ones Are Not Yet Born* (1968), Armah shows his deep concern for political corruption in independent Africa. At the centre is the Man, neither an outsider nor an activist but a witness to the moral decay around him. With *Fragments* (1970) the biographical nature is even more present, for here a young Ghanaian returns home after living in the United States. He is obviously disillusioned with what he sees, but his society seems to regard him from the start as an insane animal. The theme of return and disillusionment continues in *Why Are We So Blest?* (1971), but with a somewhat wider scope. Armah's view of the world changing for the worse is best seen in *Two Thousand Seasons* (1973), where language is borrowed from the African dirge and praise song to produce a kind of spoken chronicle. The African past is portrayed as having a certain romantic perfection about it before being destroyed by Arab and European despoilers.

All of Armah's works seem to be concerned with the widening moral and spiritual chasm that exists between appearance and reality, spirit and substance, and past and present. His overall contribution, however, has been his utilization of African folk forms in the novel and his use of local imagery, which, in the final analysis, gives promise of regeneration.

Armalite rifle, any of several lightweight, small-calibre assault rifles designed by the U.S. manufacturer Armalite, Inc. The first Armalite rifle, the AR-10, was a 7.62-millimetre, gas-operated weapon with a length of 40.5 inches (102.9 centimetres) and a weight of 9.2 pounds (4.2 kilograms). It did not survive its trials, but did pave the way for highly successful, similar designs, notably the AR-15, the U.S. Army rifle designated as the M16 (*q.v.*). The British firm of Sterling Armament Company, Ltd., produces a Sterling-Armalite AR-18 rifle that resembles and operates like the AR-15, but that was carefully redesigned to be easily manufactured with unsophisticated equipment in less-developed countries—although no such arrangement was actually made.

Arm'anskoje Nagor'e (Armenian S.S.R.): *see* Armenian Highland.

Armant (town, Egypt): *see* Hermonthis.

armature, in sculpture, an inner structure used for models that are made of soft materials and that are of sufficient size to require support. An armature can be made from any material that is damp resistant and rigid enough to hold such materials as moist clay and plaster, which are applied to and shaped around it. A few blocks of wood nailed together, a heavy lead pipe, or a galvanized iron pipe secured to a baseboard will serve as the armature for a life-sized head or similar sculptural unit. Larger pieces of sculpture are supported by more complicated armatures constructed of lead pipe, iron rods, or pipes and wood. A combination of these materials is used in the huge armatures required for monumental sculpture. Armatures for large models were used as early as the Renaissance.

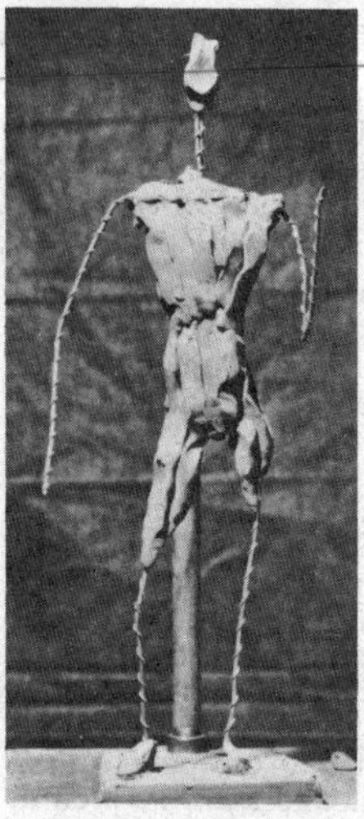

Armature for a standing male figure with some clay attached

From Louis Slobodkin, *Sculpture Principles and Practice*, © 1949, World Publishing Co.

Armavir, city, Krasnodar *kray* (territory), southwestern Russian Soviet Federated Socialist Republic, on the left bank of the Kuban River. Founded in 1839, Armavir became a town in 1914. It is a rail junction on the line from Rostov-na-Donu to Baku. A branch line runs southwestward to the Black Sea coast at Tuapse. Good communications and a rich agricultural development led to the growth of food-processing industries, including one of the largest meat-packing combines in the U.S.S.R. There is a wide range of machine-building and timber-working industries. Natural gas is obtained nearby. Pop. (1983 est.) 167,000.

Armco Inc., formerly (1948–78) ARMCO STEEL CORPORATION, or (1899–1948) AMERICAN ROLLING MILL COMPANY, U.S. corporation first incorporated, as the American Rolling Mill Company, on Dec. 2, 1899. It was newly incorporated on June 29, 1917, and renamed (using an acronym of the original) in 1948 and 1978 to reflect its diversified interests. Headquarters are in Middletown, Ohio.

Originally a manufacturer of sheet iron and steel, the company has diversified, and its activities now include the manufacture of steel mill products, including such support activities as the mining of iron and coal and the extraction of gas, oil, and other fuels; the fabrication of metal products; and the production of metal and plastic industrial equipment and materials, with related engineering and construction services and sales. Although most of the company's products and services originate in the United States, the sale of products by foreign subsidiaries has been substantial.

The company was founded by a group of investors led by George Matthew Verity (1865–1942), the company's president until 1930 and, thereafter, chairman of the board. The first steel mill, at Middletown, was completed in January 1901, and production started in February. In 1905 the company bought a second plant, in Zanesville, Ohio, and in 1914 began its first foreign plant operation, in Brazil. The company began to diversify in 1969, with the purchase of Hitco, a California-based manufacturer of plastics and other nonmetallic materials.

armed force, military organization designed to act in the name of legal authority against other political societies. Armed forces in this sense are to be distinguished from police forces and other armed groups such as brigands and rioters.

A brief treatment of armed forces follows. For full treatment, *see* MACROPAEDIA: War, The Theory and Conduct of.

All armed forces, regardless of their size, sophistication, or national allegiance, have several characteristics in common. They are all, first and foremost, agents of violent coercion or deterrence either directly (as invading armies) or by implication (as a show of strength and solidarity of purpose). Although armed forces have also served such adjunct functions as disaster relief agents, constructors of public works, sources of employment to and buyers in the public sector, etc., their primary function has always been the use of destructive force either to impose a political modus on an opponent or to prevent such an imposition on the host nation.

The second common characteristic is a structural and organizational likeness. This is due, in large part, to the inevitable degree of sameness that exists in any large, well-organized institution. It is due, further, to the fact that armed forces are usually deliberately designed and instituted according to patterns that date back to the Middle Ages. Unlike most social or business organizations that come into being as a response to an observed need (or the desire to create a need) which may then change or diminish over time, a military has almost always been a country's first order of priority. In fact, cases of a well-established military force preceding or even creating a nation are not uncommon.

The structure of any armed force, reduced to basics, consists of three main elements, which can be termed the strategic, the command, and the tactical. It is only through such a structure that the large numbers of personnel and materiel involved in a modern military will be adequately maintained, managed, and utilized.

The strategic element is the top-most echelon directly responsible for broad overall planning. In imperial armies such as that of ancient Rome, this function was (and still is) frequently usurped by a single individual who exercises it through force of character or demonstrated abilities or more simply by virtue of being the functional head of government. More commonly, however, strategy is the function of the highest ranking officers and the general staff, a group of officers without command authority who act as advisors. Outside the military, strategies are conceived by heads of state and their ministers, by full congresses or parliaments, and, in the latter half of the 20th century, in cooperation with so-called think tanks.

The command element is a middle-management sector. Its personnel (usually of the rank of colonel, major, captain, lieutenant, or their equivalents) are responsible for seeing that strategic goals are translated into operational terms: determining which units will be advanced and which held in reserve, ensuring that equipment and personnel levels are adequately maintained, etc.

The tactical element is, most basically, the fighting man and his immediate support team (usually of the rank of sergeant, corporal, private, or their equivalents). It is their responsibility to see to it that objectives formulated and defined in the upper echelons are carried out: battles fought, meals prepared, equipment cared for, etc.

It is interesting to note that, whereas in peacetime the military organization is usually quite rigid, in wartime a formal structure is regarded as perhaps a necessary evil, unavoidable to a point but often an actual hindrance to effective operations. This may be explained by the fact that an armed force is a somewhat artificial construct, achieving its full usefulness only in a situation, as in war, where a great degree of responsibility for initiative rests on the individual soldier rather than on the system as a whole. Indeed, the military vernacular includes many pejorative phrases describing a wartime soldier who, for reasons of lack of imagination or spirit, blindly adheres to a prescribed set of regulations. This difference is most clearly seen in attitudes toward rank. In a peacetime military, rank is almost an absolute condition, whereas in combat those men who demonstrate exceptional ability, though of lower rank, will frequently be accorded more respect and allegiance than their nominal superiors.

As with any other large, many-branched organization, the military is subject to money and manpower considerations. The size, strength, and sophistication of an armed force is ultimately dependent on two factors: (1) a nation's economic resources and (2) its population (more specifically, those between the ages of roughly 18 and 40).

As the military becomes more sophisticated, the cost of its operation and maintenance increases. It is estimated, for example, that the cost to the Roman Empire of killing a single enemy soldier ran to the equivalent of $5 (U.S.). By contrast, the U.S. action in Vietnam, fought with weapons systems of great complexity and requiring a large support system, cost approximately $22,000 per enemy soldier killed.

As important as an army's size is its emotional character. Because the number of people committed to the military as a career is usually a very small percentage of the whole, their numbers must be augmented, preferably with people who wholeheartedly agree to serve. It is obvious that an army of volunteers bound together by ideals such as patriotism would be an exceptional fighting force. Where this cannot be achieved (as it seldom is), a nation will usually resort to some form of conscription. Although this has never produced an army completely and passionately devoted to its goals, it usually does provide a body of soldiers who are at least willing to "do their part." A third class of soldier, the mercenary, has been effectively used, from time to time, by many nations. Their attitude of "being in it for the money," however, as opposed to loyalty to a national goal, has always made them the last choice.

The effect of a large armed force on a society goes beyond the cost of its upkeep and its demands on personnel and resources. It frequently extends into the direct political life of a nation. In less stable societies, for example, it is not unusual for an armed force to become disaffected from the government to the point where it actively takes control. Similarly, armed forces are not immune to being affected by prevailing societal attitudes. In the United States in recent years, studies have shown that the military closely reflects the attitudes of the general populace in areas such as drug use, sexual morality, and even submission to authority.

Armenia (Asia): *see* Urartu and Armenia, history of; Armenian Soviet Socialist Republic.

Armenia, a region and ancient kingdom of southwest Asia, roughly comprising what is now the northeastern part of Turkey and the Armenian Soviet Socialist Republic. At one time a nation powerful enough to challenge the Roman Empire, Armenia had a history marked by many struggles for independence and domination by many foreign powers.

A brief treatment of Armenia follows. For a full treatment, *see* MACROPAEDIA: Union of Soviet Socialist Republics.

The foundations of Armenian civilization were laid in the 6th century BC on the ruins of Urartu, an ancient kingdom that had been overrun by Scythians and Cimmerians in the wake of the conquest of Urartu's powerful ally Assyria by Babylonia and Media. Traces of Urartian civilization, particularly agricultural innovations, were probably extant when the Armenians—who called themselves the Hayk—moved into the area. The new occupants were quickly drawn into the Median Empire, which *c.* 550 BC became a province of Persia's Achamenian Empire. Local government was administered by village officials who paid tribute to the Persian king. In 331 BC Armenia was overrun by Alexander the Great, and in 301 it became part of the Seleucid Empire.

With Rome's conquest of the Seleucids in 190–189 Armenia was divided into two provinces, Greater Armenia and Sophene, and reunification did not take place until the reign of Tigran II the Great (*c.* 94–*c.* 56 BC). Under his rule Armenia reached the height of its power. It expanded to the south, bringing under its dominion Iberia, Albania, Atropatene, Syria, and part of Parthia. Armenia was briefly the strongest state in the Roman east. In 66 BC, however, Tigran was forced to cede territory and form an alliance with Rome, and Armenia subsequently became the focus of Roman and Parthian-Persian rivalry that lasted until the 3rd century AD.

A permanent break from Persia and the east was brought about by St. Gregory the Illuminator's introduction of Christianity and its acceptance as the official religion of the Armenian state in AD 300. About 390 the country was divided into Byzantine Armenia, which soon became part of the Byzantine Empire, and Persarmenia, which remained under Persian suzerainty. As Persian power declined Armenia was drawn into the Byzantine orbit. In 653 it came under Arab rule but was able to retain virtual autonomy.

The annexation of Armenia by the briefly revived Byzantine Empire in the 11th century was followed by the invasions of the Seljugs, and the last quarter of the 11th century found most of the country under Turkish domination. In the 13th century Armenia, much of which was then part of Georgia, was overrun by the Mongols. A migration into Cilicia following the Seljuq conquest had created the state of Little Armenia which in the period of the crusades became firmly allied to the West and absorbed much Frankish culture. During the 13th century Little Armenian rulers employed Mongol forces to help ward off invasions from Syria by the Egyptian Mamlūks, but the fall of the Little Armenian capital in 1375 brought the independence of the Armenian state to a close.

From the beginning of the 16th century Armenia was once more the object of contention between two hostile nations, the Ottoman Empire and Persia, a situation that continued—with a brief interlude of Armenian independence (1722–30)—through the 18th century. During this time the country became a trade link between the East and Europe.

The advance of Russia into the Caucasus early in the 19th century inspired a renewal of Armenian culture and initiated foreign concern over the situation of Armenians under Turkish rule. Following the Russo-Turkish war of 1877–78 and the Treaty of San Stefano, the issue grew into the "Armenian question." But attempts to effect reforms resulted only in a series of Turkish and Russian massacres of the Armenian populace, culminating in the Ottomans' virtually genocidal exile of 1,750,000 Turkish-Armenians to uninhabitable desert areas in 1915.

Following a Russian conquest in 1916, Armenia, with Georgia and Azerbaijan, formed a transcaucasian alliance; within a few months the alliance was dissolved. A series of political upheavals, including the brief appearance of an independent Armenian republic in 1920, eventually led to the reunion of the three states as the Transcaucasian Soviet Federated Socialist Republic, incorporated into the U.S.S.R. in 1922. In 1936 the new Soviet constitution gave Armenia the status of a republic of the U.S.S.R.

Articles are alphabetized word by word, not letter by letter

Armenia, capital (since 1966) of Quindío department, west central Colombia, on the western slopes of the Cordillera (mountains) Central at an altitude of 4,865 ft (1,483 m), between the Espejo and Quindío rivers. On the railway from Puerto Berrío to Popayán, it is the transfer point for road traffic to Bogotá via Ibagué (30 mi [50 km] southeast). Armenia (named after the ancient kingdom) was founded in 1889 by Jesús María Ocampo and Antonio Herrera. Coffee, corn (maize), beans, sugarcane, silk, and plantain are marketed, and there is some light manufacturing. Coal deposits are nearby. Armenia is the seat of the Universidad del Quindío (1962). Pop. (1984 est.) 156,670.

Armenia Minor: *see* Little Armenia.

Armenian, member of a people with a very ancient culture who originally lived in the

Armenian women and children
Marc Riboud—Magnum

region known as Armenia, which comprised what is now northeastern Turkey and the Armenian Soviet Socialist Republic. Although few remain in Turkey, more than 4,150,000 Armenians lived in the Soviet Union, of whom about 2,700,000 lived in the Armenian S.S.R. in the early 1980s, with more than 1,000,000 others living in the Azerbaijan and Georgian S.S.R.'s and other areas of the Caucasus and in the Middle East. Many emigrated to Europe and the Americas.

The Armenians are the descendants of a branch of the Indo-Europeans. The ancient Greek historians Herodotus and Eudoxus of Rhodes related the Armenians to the Phrygians—who entered Asia Minor from Thrace—and to the peoples of the ancient kingdom upon whom the Phrygians imposed their rule and language. Known to the Persians as Armina and to the Greeks as Armenioi, the people call themselves Hayq (singular, Hay) and their country Hayastan, and they look back to a folk hero, Hayk.

The Armenian language is Indo-European, but the phonetics and grammar have some features in common with the Caucasian languages. The Armenians are traditionally members of either the Monophysite Armenian Apostolic (Orthodox) Church or the Armenian Catholic branch of the Roman Catholic Church.

Until the early 20th century, the Armenians were primarily an agricultural people. Since 1930, however, considerable industrial development has taken place in the Armenian S.S.R.; by 1980, two-thirds of the population of the republic, which is nearly 90 percent Armenian, had become urbanized. This urban trend has also predominated among Armenians who have emigrated to Europe and the Americas.

The ancient Armenians had a highly developed and diversified culture that is most apparent in their architecture, painting, and sculpture. The periods of greatest artistic activity tended to correspond to those of national independence or semi-independence, but, for the most part, this activity had reached its high point by the end of the 14th century. Armenian literature continued to develop after that period and witnessed a strong revival during the 19th century in the face of Turkish and Russian domination. Armenian writers did much to awaken the national consciousness of the Armenians, who became increasingly impatient with foreign rule. Growing nationalism on the part of Armenians provoked massacres by the Turks and confiscations by the Russians. The greatest single disaster occurred with the outbreak of World War I. In 1915 the Turks, regarding the Armenians as a dangerous foreign element, decided to deport the entire Armenian population of about 1,750,000 to Syria and Palestine. An estimated 600,000 died of starvation or were killed en route. About one-third escaped deportation. Many later settled in the Soviet Union, Europe, and the Americas.

Armenian alphabet, script that was developed for the Armenian language in the 5th century AD and is still in use. It was probably derived from the Pahlavi alphabet of Persia, with some Greek influences. According to local tradition the Armenian alphabet was invented by St. Mesrob (Mashtots), aided by St. Sahak, supreme head of the Armenian Catholic Church, and by a Greek called Rufanos. St. Sahak founded a school of translators and had the Bible translated into Armenian in the new script. The oldest surviving documents in Armenian date from the 9th and 10th centuries AD.

The Armenian script is a system of 38 letters—31 consonants and seven vowels—well-adapted to the needs of the Armenian language. Although probably patterned after the Pahlavi script, a descendant of the widespread Aramaic alphabet (*q.v.*), Armenian script shows distinct Greek influence by the presence of letters for vowels and in the direction of writing (from left to right). As a means of stabilizing and formalizing Armenian speech, it was an important factor in the continued unity of the Armenian nation and church.

Armenian Apostolic Church, the Orthodox national church of Armenia. Its claim to the title Apostolic is based on the belief that Armenia was evangelized by the Apostles Bartholomew and Thaddaeus.

Christianity became the state religion of Armenia *c.* AD 300 with the conversion of the Arsacid king Tiridates III by St. Gregory the Illuminator. The new Armenian Church soon struck a course independent of the founding church at Caesarea in Cappadocia, though it developed in close relationship with the Syrians, who provided it with scriptures and liturgy and much of its basic institutional terminology. Its dependence on Syriac was ended in the 5th century, when St. Mashtots invented a national alphabet and carried out numerous translations.

In 506 at the Council of Dvin, the Armenian Church rejected the ruling of the Council of Chalcedon (451) that the one Person of Christ consists of two natures and became Monophysite (a view that claimed that Christ had only "one nature"). When the Georgian Church broke away from the Armenians and reunited with the Greek Orthodox in the early 7th century, the Armenians remained in communion with the Coptic and Syrian Jacobite churches, confessing the christological formula of St. Cyril of Alexandria, "one incarnate nature of the Word."

Gregory the Illuminator and his early successors had their residence at Echmiadzin. It was moved to Dvin from 485 to 927, then was located variously until 1293, when the catholicate (highest ecclesiastical administrative office) was transferred to the Cilician capital Sis, where it remained after the fall of Cilicia to the Muslim Mamlūks of Egypt. In the 15th century, Gregory IX Musabegian rejected efforts to transfer the see to East Armenia in order to withdraw it from Roman influence. A synod of 17 bishops deposed him, and the monk Kirakos was elected catholicos at Echmiadzin in 1441, initiating a long line of prelates bearing the title "Catholicos of All Armenians."

These historical events explain the existence in modern times of two catholicoi: the supreme catholicos of all Armenians, residing at Echmiadzin, and the catholicos of Sis, now residing at Anṭilyās, Lebanon. The catholicos at Echmiadzin is generally recognized as head of the whole church, the catholicos at Sis owing him spiritual allegiance, though retaining administrative autonomy. Relationships between the catholicates have on occasion been strained by political tensions. Whereas the supreme catholicos resides in Soviet Armenia, Armenian nationalists (Tashnaks) tend to support the see of Anṭilyās. This division is reflected among the Armenians of North America. The two Armenian patriarchates of Constantinople and Jerusalem are of comparatively recent origin and recognize the supremacy of Echmiadzin.

The Armenian Apostolic Church generally shares the doctrinal beliefs of the Eastern Orthodox Church, except on the Monophysite question, and retains traditional Armenian rites. It is seen by many as the custodian of Armenian national identity.

Armenian Catholic Church, an Eastern rite member of the Roman Catholic Church. The Armenians embraced Christianity *c.* AD 300, the first people to do so as a nation. About 50 years after the Council of Chalcedon (451), the Armenians repudiated the Christological decisions of the council and became the Armenian Apostolic (Orthodox) Church. There were Armenian Catholics, however, as early as the 12th century among the Armenians who fled from Muslim oppressors and established the kingdom of Cilicia. Although the kingdom collapsed in 1375, Armenian monks, known as the Friars of Unity of St. Gregory the Illuminator, laid the groundwork for the future Catholic Armenian Church under Dominican influence. The church came into being in 1740, when the Armenian bishop of Aleppo, Abraham Artzivian, already a Catholic, was elected patriarch of Sis, in Cilicia. In 1911 the Armenian Church was divided into 19 dioceses; but, during the persecution of the Armenians in Turkey (1915–18), several dioceses were abolished and the faithful left for other countries. In 1928 the hierarchical organization was revised, and new episcopal sees were successively erected. The Armenian patriarch of Cilicia now resides in Beirut and personally administers that diocese. There exist further three archdioceses (Aleppo, Baghdad, and Istanbul), three dioceses (Alexandria, Isfahan, and Kamichlie, Syria), one apostolic exarchy (Paris), and two ordinariates (Athens, and Gherla, Romania). The head of the Armenian Catholics is called "Patriarch of the Catholic Armenians and Katholikos of Cilicia" and has always taken the name Peter. The liturgy continues to be celebrated in the classical Armenian language.

Armenian chant, vocal music of the Armenian Church and the religious poetry that serves as its texts. Armenia was Christianized quite early by missionaries from Syria and Greek-speaking areas of the eastern Mediterranean and accepted Christianity as the state religion *c.* AD 300. The development of a distinctive Armenian liturgy was influenced by various factors. Toward the end of the 4th century, the Armenian Church proclaimed its independence from the archbishopric of Caesarea in Cappadocia, in Asia Minor. The great Armenian scholar St. Mesrob (Mashtots) invented the Armenian alphabet about 401 and carried out many important translations of religious literature from Syrian and Greek. The introduction of the new alphabet stimulated a flourishing literature, an important and prominent part of which was religious poetry. The earliest preserved examples date from the 4th century.

In the 12th century the catholicos (patriarch) Nerses IV Shnorhali ("the Gracious") is credited with musical reforms of the chant. He is said to have simplified the texts of the religious poetry and the melodies of the chant, bringing it closer to the style of Armenian folk music. Nerses also wrote a number of *sharakan* ("hymns"). The final form of the collection of *Sharakan,* containing nearly 1200 hymns, was obtained *c.* 1300 and has apparently remained unchanged.

In about 1820 an Armenian from Istanbul, Baba Hampartsoum Limondjian, proposed another reform and modernization of the musical notation along the lines of the contemporary notational reform in the Greek church (which allowed more precise indication of pitch). In its present-day performance, Armenian chant consists of intricate melodies with great rhythmic variety, and the melodies use many intervals not found in European music.

According to a long-standing tradition, the most reliable oral transmission of the chant occurs in the religious capital of Armenia, Echmiadzin, and in a few isolated monasteries. An important centre for Armenian musical studies is the Armenian Catholic monastery of San Lazzaro in Venice (founded 1717), where the traditional Armenian melodies are said to be fairly well preserved.

Armenian Highland, Russian ARMYANSKOYE NAGORYE, also spelled ARM'ANSKOJE NAGOR'E, mountainous region of Turkey, the Soviet Union, and Iran, covering almost 154,441 sq mi (400,000 sq km). In the Soviet Union, it occupies all of the Armenian Soviet Socialist Republic and parts of the Georgian and Azerbaydzhan Soviet Socialist republics. The average altitude is 5,000 to 6,500 ft (1,500 to 2,000 m), but several peaks exceed 14,000 ft. The highland is a segment of the Mediterranean alpine volcanic zone of folding and has a subtropical continental climate. It is rich in minerals including chromite, gold, and iron.

Armenian Language, a separate branch of the western group of Indo-European languages. It is the mother tongue of the Turkish Armenians and of the Armenians in the Armenian Soviet Socialist Republic and is also spoken by people in other parts of the Soviet Union. Armenian emigrants and refugees have taken their language with them all over Asia Minor and the Middle East and from there to many European countries (especially Romania, Poland, and France) and to America.

A brief treatment of the Armenian language follows. For full treatment, *see* MACROPAEDIA: Languages of the World.

Invaders from the northern Balkans introduced Armenian into the Transcaucasian region, probably in the latter part of the 2nd millennium BC. These invaders occupied the region on the shores of Lake Van. By the 7th century BC the Armenian language seems to have replaced the tongues of the native population.

In the beginning of the 4th century AD, the language was reduced to writing; the alphabet, of 38 letters, was invented, according to tradition, by the bishop St. Mesrob (Mashtots) in about AD 401 and is still used by Armenians all over the world. Grabar, the written language of the 5th century, the golden age of Armenian culture, is traditionally said to be based on the dialect of Tarawn on Lake Van. The language of the literature from the 5th to the 8th century is homogeneous, but by the 9th century the influence of the spoken dialects is noticeable. The best-known Middle Armenian variety of Grabar is the 12th- and 13th-century court language of the Armenian kingdom in Cilicia. More or less corrupted versions of Grabar continued as the literary language until the middle of the 19th century.

In the 1800s, Armenian nationalists attempted to reach the populace with nationalist propaganda. A national revival resulted, with a new literary language that was much closer to the spoken language. This is known in two varieties. East Armenian, now the official language of the Armenian Soviet Socialist Republic, is based on the dialect of the Ararat valley and the city of Yerevan; West Armenian has its foundation in the dialect of Istanbul. The differences between these two written forms of Modern Armenian are slight, constituting no barrier to mutual intelligibility. In addition, there are a great number of dialects, some of which are so different that the speakers cannot understand each other.

In the 19th century, the language was considered an Iranian dialect, but subsequent studies have shown Armenian to be an independent member of the Indo-European language family.

Phonetic developments in Armenian have radically changed the sound system of the Indo-European parent language. In particular, the pattern of the plosive consonants—the stops—has been reshuffled. In the central Armenian dialects, three series of stops are distinguished; in those of the periphery, these have been reduced to two. All Armenian dialects distinguish two types of *r,* one strongly trilled, one weakly trilled. Old Armenian also differentiated between two types of *l,* one of them neutral and the other velarized, that is, made by moving the back of the tongue nearer to the soft palate at the back of the mouth.

Both in the spoken dialects and in the two literary languages, a fairly complicated system of noun declension has been maintained. Characteristic of the changes in the Old Armenian verbal system is the general replacement of simple present tense forms by periphrastic expressions. These are groups of words, including auxiliaries, that take the place of a single word that is capable of being inflected to show tense or some other feature. The dialects are classified according to the various types of periphrastic forms. In Old and Modern Armenian, the main tense distinction is that between present, aorist (without reference to completeness or duration of the action), and periphrastic perfect tenses. The old subjective, still extant in classical Armenian, has been lost in the modern language.

To express future time, Old Armenian used the subjective forms; Modern Armenian uses periphrastic expressions, as English does in the future forms "I shall go" and "he will work." Also characteristic of Modern Armenian is the importance of the passive forms of the verb and the emergence of a negative conjugation with differing forms for verbs in instances like "I read" and "I don't read." Whereas Old Armenian was rather close to ancient Greek in many respects, Modern Armenian is typologically much closer to Turkish. The vocabulary of the written languages is purely Armenian, being based almost exclusively on that of Grabar, with very few loanwords from the neighbouring languages.

Armenian literature, body of writings in the Armenian language. There is evidence that a pagan oral literature existed in Armenia before the invention of the alphabet in the 5th century AD, but, owing to the zeal of the early Christian priests, little of this has been preserved. For about a century after their conversion to Christianity (*c.* 300), the Armenians had to rely on Greek and Syriac versions of the Bible and other religious books. These languages were unintelligible to the common people, and to remedy this St. Mesrob (Mashtots) invented the Armenian alphabet (*c.* 401). The *catholicos* Sahak (Isaac) the Great and St. Mesrob formed a school of translators who were reputedly sent to Edessa and to Constantinople to procure and translate Syriac and Greek copies of important works.

Much of the literary activity of the 5th century, the golden age of Armenian literature, was devoted to such translations. Original works, however, were not wanting, such as the histories of Eghishe and Ghazar of Pharp. The masterpiece of classical Armenian writing is the "Refutation of the Sects" by Eznik Koghbatsi. This was a polemic work, composed partly from Greek sources, in defense of orthodox Christian belief against—and thereby providing valuable information about—pagan Armenian superstitions, Iranian dualism, Greek philosophy, and the Marcionite heresy. Its pure classical style is unsurpassed in Armenian literature. The work of translation of such authors as SS. John Chrysostom and Cyril of Alexandria continued in the 6th–8th century. The so-called Hellenistic (Yunaban) school produced excessively slavish translations from Greek grammatical, theological, and philosophical works, including those of Plato, Aristotle, and Philo of Alexandria.

In the 10th and 11th centuries, which witnessed the maturity of the independent Bagratid kingdom of Armenia, the Artsruni kingdom of Vaspurakan, and the kingdom of Siuniq, Armenian literature, art, and architecture flourished more freely than at any time since the 5th century. The principal literary figure of the 10th century was St. Gregory Narekatzi, the first great Armenian poet, renowned for his mystic poems and hymns as well as for such prose works as the *Commentary on the Song of Songs.* Earlier in the same century, Thomas (Thovma) Artsruni wrote a *History of the House of Artsruni* which, in spite of its family bias, is the chief source of information on the history of Armenia down to 936; an anonymous writer continued the work to 1121. The *History of Armenia* by catholicos John VI Draskhanakertzi is of great value for its account of Arab relations with Armenia, for the author was himself an important participant in the later events he describes. At the turn of the 10th to 11th centuries Bishop Ukhtanes wrote a *History of Armenia* and a *History of the Schism between the Georgians and Armenians.* The beginning of the 11th century saw the completion of the reliable and well-written *Universal History* of Stephanos Asoghik. The *History of Armenia* by Aristakes Lastivertzi, relating the fall of the Bagratid kingdom (1045), the destruction of Ani (1064), and the victories of the Seljuks, is almost as much a prose elegy as a history.

After the political collapse of Greater Armenia (*c.* 1100) and the consequent shift southward of the cultural centre to Little, or Cilician, Armenia, the literature became divided into a western and an eastern branch. In both branches authors began to write in the spoken as well as the classical language. The Mamluk invasion of 1375 and the invasion by Timur (Tamerlane) in 1385 ushered in a long period of cultural and literary decline.

There were signs in the 17th century that the Armenians were emerging from the cultural decadence of the preceding centuries. The deeds of Turkish and Persian overlords figured prominently in histories by Araqel of Tabriz, Zaqaria the Deacon, and Eremia Chelebi Kömürjian, but there was some contact with Western scholars and works in Latin. Oskan of Erevan, born in 1614 in the newly founded trading colony of New Julfa, Isfahan, collaborated with the Dominican Pirandelli and printed the first Armenian Bible in Amsterdam in 1666. From the 13th century imaginative writing had been represented by a succession of popular troubadours, the most famous of these being Nahapet Kuchak (16th century), one of the rare Armenian poets to sing of physical love; Hovnatan Naghash (1661–1722); and in the following century, most famous of all, Aruthin Sayadian, called Sayat-Nova.

The 18th century witnessed an Armenian cultural and intellectual renaissance, and by the middle of the 19th century, the time was ripe for the development of a modern Armenian literature. The Armenian language, however, was in a chaotic state, and the question of which form should serve as the vehicle for new ideas led to controversies, both in Turkish and Russian Armenia, between champions of the old classical language and those of the modern spoken languages. Eventually the latter prevailed, with the result that the eastern literature became written in a modified form of the Erivan dialect (*rusahayeren*) and that of the west in a similarly modified form of the dialect of Istanbul (*dachgahayeren*). For their models, and for many of their ideals, Armenian writers looked to Europe. Among western authors, Hakob Paronian and Ervand Otian were outstanding satirical novelists, and Grigor Zohrab wrote realistic short stories; the theatre was best represented by Paronian, whose comedies (as *The Dowry, Master Balthazar, The Oriental Dentist*) still remain popular.

The novel, weak in western Armenian literature, was strongly represented in Russian Armenia, where it became a vehicle for Armenian moral, social, and political aspirations. Khachatur Abovean, "father of modern Armenian literature," wrote *Wounds of Armenia* in 1841. The most celebrated Armenian novelist was Hakob Meliq-Hakobian, or Raffi. Among eastern poets, Hovhannes Thumanian wrote lyric and narrative poems; and his masterpiece, a short epic, *Anush,* full of songs that have become traditional, was early adapted as an opera. The most outstanding Armenian dramatist was Gabriel Sundukian, whose comedies (*Hullabaloo, Pepo, The Broken Hearth*) portrayed the contemporary Armenian society of Tbilisi, in whose dialect most of them were written.

The rapid decline of Istanbul as the principal western Armenian literary centre (after massacres in the first quarter of the 20th century) brought about a new period of decadence in Armenian literature, although Armenians scattered abroad continued to write in Paris, Beirut, and Boston. Some Turkish Armenians fled to the east, where they enjoyed a certain degree of autonomy and where, after the foundation of the Armenian Soviet Socialist Republic in 1936, national literature was encouraged but was controlled by the state.

BIBLIOGRAPHY. E. Arch Dourian, *The History of Armenian Literature* (1933); H. Thorossian, *Histoire de la littérature arménienne* (1951).

Armenian massacres, series of brutal campaigns conducted against the Armenian subjects of the Ottoman Empire by Sultan Abdülhamid in 1894–96 and by the Young Turk government in 1915.

There were about 2,500,000 Christian Armenians within the Ottoman Empire by the late 1880s. The Armenians in the eastern provinces, encouraged by Russia, began promoting Armenian territorial autonomy. As the movement grew, various political groups were organized, culminating in the formation in 1890 of two revolutionary committees called Hënchak and Dashnaktzutiun. At the same time, Abdülhamid, intent on suppressing all separatist sentiments in the empire, aroused nationalistic feelings and resentment against the Armenians among the neighbouring Kurdish tribesmen. The resulting persecution by Kurds, coupled with a drastic increase in taxes, gave the Armenian radicals two pretexts to rise in revolt. When the Armenians in Sasum refused to pay the oppressive taxes, Turkish troops and Kurd ish tribesmen killed thousands of them and burned their villages (1894). In the hope of calling the attention of the European powers to their cause, the Armenian revolutionaries staged another demonstration two years later: they seized the Ottoman Bank in Istanbul. The repression of this action was again sanguinary; more than 50,000 Armenians were killed by mobs of Muslim Turks apparently coordinated by government troops.

The last of the massacres occurred during World War I (1914–18). Armenians from the Caucasus region formed volunteer battalions to help the Russian Army against the Turks. Early in 1915 these battalions organized the recruiting of Turkish Armenians from behind the Turkish lines. This led to the forcible deportation of those Armenians to Syria and Palestine, in the course of which large numbers died of starvation or were killed by Turkish soldiers and police. More than 1,000,000 Armenians died or were forced into exile as a result of this action.

Armenian rite, the system of liturgical practices and discipline observed by the Armenian Apostolic (Orthodox) Church and the Armenian Catholics, Eastern rite members of the Roman Catholic Church. The Armenians, who regard themselves as the "first Christian nation," were converted to Christianity by St. Gregory the Illuminator *c.* AD 300. The Liturgy of St. Gregory the Illuminator, used by both Apostolic and Catholic Armenians, is patterned after the Antiochene Liturgy of St. James and the Byzantine Liturgy of St. John Chrysostom and is usually divided into five parts: (1) the prayers of preparation in the sacristy; (2) the prayers of preparation in the sanctuary; (3) preparation and consecration of the gifts; (4) the liturgy of the catechumens; and (5) the liturgy of the faithful, culminating in Communion.

Churches of the Armenian rite, unlike Byzantine churches, are generally devoid of icons and, in place of an iconostasis (screen), have a curtain that conceals the priest and the altar during parts of the liturgy. The Communion itself is given in two species, as in other Orthodox churches. For its worship services the Armenian rite is dependent upon such books as the *Donatzuitz,* the order of service or celebration of the liturgy; the *Badaramaduitz,* the book of the sacrament, containing all the prayers used by the priest; the *Giashotz,* the book of midday, containing the Epistle and Gospel readings for each day; and the *Z'ama-*

girq, the book of hours, containing the prayers and psalms of the seven daily offices, primarily matins, prime, and vespers.

Armenian Soviet Socialist Republic, also called ARMENIA, Russian ARMYANSKAYA SOVYETSKAYA SOTSIALISTICHESKAYA RESPUBLIKA, or ARMENIYA, Akademiya Nauk romanization ARM'ANSKAJA SOVETSKAJA SOCIALISTIČESKAJA RESPUBLIKA, or ARMENIJA, union republic of the Soviet Union, smallest of the 15.

The following article summarizes the administrative history, geography, demographic patterns, economy, and culture of the modern Armenian S.S.R.; for additional treatment of its geography and history, *see* MACROPAEDIA: Union of Soviet Socialist Republics.

To the north and east Armenia is bounded by the Georgian and Azerbaijan S.S.R.'s, to the west by Turkey, and to the south by Iran. Armenia lies in the southern portion of the Soviet Union's Transcaucasian region. An ancient kingdom, Armenia was subjected to constant foreign incursions after losing its autonomy in the 14th century AD, which, together with centuries of rule by Ottoman and Persian conquerors, imperilled the very existence of the people in the early 20th century. The portion of historic Armenia lying within the former Russian Empire was incorporated into the U.S.S.R. in 1920. Its capital is Yerevan.

A mountainous country with an average elevation of 5,900 ft (1,800 m) above sea level, it has a dry and continental climate that changes drastically with elevation. The vegetation of the semidesert landscape includes drought-resistant plants, such as juniper, aloe, dog rose, and honeysuckle. At the lower elevations the extensive steppes are covered with drought-resistant grasses. The plains and foothills are sufficiently warm to permit cultivation of figs, pomegranates, peaches, and grapes. Higher up, tobacco, cereals and some fruits are raised, and grain crops, potatoes, and fodder grasses are found up to 8,000 ft; the mountain slopes are covered with juniper, and high meadows provide good summer pasture. A forest zone lying in the southeast and northeast occupies nearly 10 percent of the republic's territory. Wildlife includes the ubiquitous wildcat, and in the semi-desert, wild pig, jackal, and various snakes; Syrian bear is found in the forests.

Armenians constitute nearly 90 percent of the republic's population, including many emigrants repatriated after the Russian Revolution. There are also small populations of Azerbaijanis, Russians, Kurds, Ukrainians and other Soviet people in Armenia.

There is, as in most of the Soviet Union, increasing urbanization in Armenia and massive industrialization, though agriculture remains important. From its former status as a supplier of farm goods, copper, and cognac, Armenia has become a major supplier of chemicals, nonferrous metals, machinery, precision instruments, textiles, clothing, wines, and canned goods, and its economic expansion is unparalleled elsewhere in the U.S.S.R.

Agriculture still engages nearly half the population; they are dispersed among several hundred state farms (*sovkhozy*) and collective farms (*kolkhozy*). Wine grapes are the most important crop. There are also orchard crops, vegetables, tobacco, cotton, sugar beets, and livestock.

Mountainous terrain has made transportation difficult, but Armenia is served by railways and a dense network of motor roads. The hydroelectric potential of the mountain streams was a major factor in the industrial transformation.

The state structure of the Armenian S.S.R. is similar to that of the other union republics, with the Communist Party of Armenia choosing members of the Supreme Soviet, ratified by the voters every four years. The trade unions operate clubs, public libraries, and sport facilities but do not represent workers in disputes with management or negotiate wages or working conditions.

Education is compulsory and free of charge between the ages of 7 and 17. There is a system of general, trade, and secondary schools. Among the establishments of higher learning is Yerevan State University. Plentiful medical treatment in hospitals and clinics is free of charge for all citizens.

Armenian written literature began in the 5th century AD. The love songs of Sayat-Nova (d. 1795) are still popular. The modern Armenian composer Aram Khachaturian is known throughout the musical world. State publishing houses produce some 1,000 books a year, about two-thirds in Armenian. All news media are strictly controlled by the state and ultimately by the Party.

Among cultural institutions there are a State Academic Theatre of Opera and Ballet, several drama theatres, theatres for children, orchestras, and the Yerevan Film Studio, and the traditional folk arts are also flourishing. Area 11,500 sq mi (29,800 sq km). Pop. (1982 est.) 3,167,000.

Armentières, town, Nord *département*, Nord-Pas-de-Calais region, northern France, on the Lys River, near the Belgian frontier. It was entirely rebuilt after being destroyed in World War I, and its red brick buildings present a uniform appearance. Armentières was 2 mi (3 km) behind the battle line throughout World War I, and from April until September 1918 it was occupied by the Germans. The marching song about the mythical "Mademoiselle from Armentières" sung by British and U.S. troops dates from that period. During World War II the town was bombed and was again occupied by the Germans from May 1940 until September 1944.

Romans who were in the area in 57 BC raised cattle on the banks of the Lys. The Meadows of Hem are the only vestiges of the fields that pastured those herds. The name Armentières is derived from the Gallo-Roman *armentum*, meaning "cattle for ploughing" or, collectively, "herd."

Since the Middle Ages, Armentières has been noted for its linen, but the industry has had difficulties in recent years. Printing is important and other industries include dyes, clothing, beer, and machinery. Agriculture in the surrounding area is important, and flax was formerly one of the chief crops. Pop. (1982) 22,849.

Armfelt, Gustaf Mauritz (b. March 31, 1757, St. Mårtens, near Turku, Finland, Kingdom of Sweden—d. Aug. 19, 1814, Tsarskoye Selo, near St. Petersburg, Russia), Swedish statesman prominent both in diplomacy and in military affairs.

Appointed gentleman to Gustav III of Sweden in 1781, Armfelt made a brilliant career at the court. He was employed by Gustav III in the negotiations with Catherine II of Russia (1783) and with the Danish government (1787) and was one of his most trusted and active counselors during the war with Russia in 1788–90. In 1788 when the Danes invaded Sweden and threatened Göteborg, Armfelt, under the king's direction, organized the Dalarna levies. He remained faithful to Gustav when nearly all the nobility deserted him; he brilliantly distinguished himself in the later phases of the Russian war; and he was the Swedish plenipotentiary at the Peace of Värälä (1790). During Gustav III's last years his influence was paramount, though he protested against his master's headstrong championship of the Bourbons.

On his deathbed in 1792 Gustav III entrusted his son to Armfelt and made him a member of the council of regency; but the duke-regent Charles (afterward Charles XIII) sent Armfelt as Swedish ambassador to Naples to get rid of him. From Naples Armfelt communicated with Catherine II, urging her to make a military demonstration in favour of the Gustavians. The plot was discovered by the regent's spies, and Armfelt escaped only with the assistance of Queen Caroline of Naples (1794). He then fled to Russia. When Gustav IV Adolf attained his majority, Armfelt was rehabilitated and sent as Swedish ambassador to Vienna (1802), but he was obliged to quit that post two years later for attacking the Austrian government's attitude toward Napoleon Bonaparte. From 1805 to 1807 he was commander in chief of the Swedish forces in Pomerania, where he retarded the French conquest.

After the deposition of Gustav IV Adolf (1809), Armfelt was the most courageous supporter of the crown prince Gustav. Expelled from Sweden in 1811, he found refuge in Russia, where he obtained great influence over the emperor Alexander I. He contributed more than anyone else to the erection of the grand duchy of Finland as an autonomous state; and he participated in the planning of the Russian defensive campaigns against Napoleon and in the conference between Alexander and the Swedish crown prince (Bernadotte; the future Charles XIV John) at Turku in August 1812.

Armidale, city, northeastern New South Wales, Australia, on the valley slopes of Dumaresq Creek in the New England Range. Founded in 1839 by G.J. Macdonald, commissioner of crown lands, and named for his father's Scottish baronial estate on the Isle of Skye, it developed a pastoral–agricultural economy. It has become a regional cultural centre with Anglican and Roman Catholic cathedrals, a teachers' college, several private and state schools, and the University of New England (established 1954). The Hinton Benefaction Art Gallery contains a comprehensive collection of Australian paintings. For many years the community has been the main focus of a movement for a separate New England State. It became a town in 1845, a municipality in 1863, and a city in 1885. The city is linked by rail with Sydney, 230 mi (370 km) south, and has an airport. Pop. (1981) 18,922.

armillary sphere, early astronomical device for representing the great circles of the heavens, including in the most elaborate instruments the horizon, meridian, Equator, tropics, polar circles, and an ecliptic hoop. The sphere is a skeleton celestial globe, with circles divided into degrees for angular measurement. In the 17th and 18th centuries such models—either suspended, rested on a stand, or affixed to a

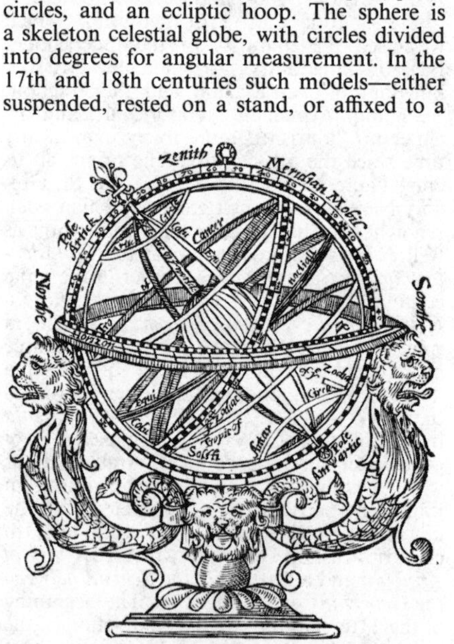

Armillary sphere from Thomas Blundeville's *Plaine Treatise . . . of Cosmographie*, 1594

By courtesy of the trustees of the British Museum; photograph, J.R. Freeman & Co. Ltd.

handle—were used to show the difference between the Ptolemaic theory of a central Earth and the Copernican theory of a central Sun.

The earliest known complete armillary sphere with nine circles is believed to have been the *meteōroskopion* of the Alexandrine Greeks (*c.* AD 140), but earlier and simpler types of ring instruments were also in general use. Ptolemy, in the *Almagest,* enumerates at least three. It is stated that Hipparchus (146–127 BC) used a sphere of four rings; and in Ptolemy's instrument, the *astrolabon,* there were diametrically disposed tubes upon the graduated circles, the instrument being kept vertical by a plumb line.

The Arabs employed similar instruments with diametric sight rules, or alidades, and it is likely that those made and used in the 12th century by Moors in Spain were the prototypes of all later European armillary spheres.

Armilus, in Jewish legends, an enemy who will conquer Jerusalem and persecute Jews until his final defeat at the hands of God or the true Messiah. His inevitable destruction symbolizes the ultimate victory of good over evil in the messianic era. Some sources depict Armilus as partially deaf and partially maimed, the frightful offspring of Satan or evil creatures. Parallel legends exist in the figures of Antichrist and of Ahriman, the Persian god of evil.

Arminianism, a theological movement in Christianity, a liberal reaction to the Calvinist doctrine of predestination. The movement began early in the 17th century and asserted that God's sovereignty and man's free will are compatible.

The movement was named for Jacobus Arminius, a Dutch Reformed theologian of the University of Leiden (1603–09), who became involved in a highly publicized debate with his colleague Franciscus Gomarus, a rigid Calvinist, concerning the Calvinist interpretation of the divine decrees respecting election and reprobation. For Arminius, God's will as unceasing love was the determinative initiator and arbiter of human destiny. The movement that became known as Arminianism, however, tended to be more liberal than Arminius.

Dutch Arminianism was originally articulated in the Remonstrance (1610), a theological statement signed by 45 ministers and submitted to the Dutch states general. The Synod of Dort (1618–19) was called by the states general to pass upon the Remonstrance. The five points of the Remonstrance asserted that: (1) election (and condemnation on the day of judgment) was conditioned by the rational faith or nonfaith of man; (2) the Atonement, while qualitatively adequate for all men, was efficacious only for the man of faith; (3) unaided by the Holy Spirit, no person is able to respond to God's will; (4) grace is not irresistible; and (5) believers are able to resist sin but are not beyond the possibility of falling from grace. The crux of Remonstrant Arminianism lay in the assertion that human dignity requires an unimpaired freedom of the will.

The Dutch Remonstrants were condemned by the Synod of Dort and suffered political persecution for a time, but by 1630 they were legally tolerated. They have continued to assert effective liberalizing tendencies in Dutch Protestant theology.

In the 18th century, John Wesley was influenced by Arminianism. In *The Arminian Magazine,* edited by him, he stated that "God willeth all men to be saved, by speaking the truth in love." Arminianism was an important influence in Methodism, which developed out of the Wesleyan movement. A still more liberal version of Arminianism went into the making of American Unitarianism.

Arminius, German HERMANN (b. 18 BC?—d. AD 19), German tribal leader who inflicted a major defeat on Rome by destroying three legions under Publius Quinctilius Varus in the Teutoburg Forest (southeast of modern Bielefeld, W.Ger.), late in the summer of AD 9. This defeat severely checked the emperor Augustus' plans, the exact nature of which is uncertain, for the country between the Rhine and Elbe rivers.

Arminius, bust; in the Capitoline Museum, Rome

Alinari—Art Resource/EB Inc.

Arminius was a chief of the Cherusci. In the service of the Romans he had obtained both citizenship and equestrian rank. Six years after the Teutoburg Forest Massacre, Germanicus Caesar engaged Arminius in battle, capturing his wife, Thusnelda, but in AD 16 Arminius skillfully survived a full-scale Roman attack. When Roman operations were suspended in 17, Arminius became involved in war with Maroboduus, king of the Marcomanni, and though successful he was subsequently murdered by his own people. The conception of Arminius as a German national hero reached its climax in the late 19th century. It could claim support from Tacitus' judgment of him as "unquestionably the liberator of Germany" (*liberator haud dubie Germaniae*); but it is clear that in Arminius' day a united "Germany" was not even an ideal.

Arminius, Jacobus, Dutch JACOB HARMENSEN or HERMANSZ (b. Oct. 10, 1560, Oudewater, Neth.—d. Oct. 19, 1609, Leiden), theologian and minister of the Dutch Reformed Church who opposed the strict Calvinist teaching on predestination and who developed his own system of belief known later as Arminianism.

His father died when Arminius was an infant, and one Theodore Aemilius adopted the child and provided for his schooling in Utrecht. On the death of Aemilius in 1575, Rudolf Snellius (Snel van Roijen, 1546–1613), a professor at Marburg and a native of Oudewater, became the patron for his further education at the universities of Leiden (1576–82), Basel, and Geneva (1582–86).

After brief stays at the University of Padua, in Rome, and in Geneva, Arminius returned to Amsterdam. He was ordained there in 1588. In 1603 Arminius was called to a theological professorship at Leiden, which he held until his death. These last six years of his life were dominated by theological controversy, in particular by his disputes with Franciscus Gomarus, his colleague at Leiden.

Considered a man of mild temperament, Arminius was forced into controversy against his own choice. He had earlier affirmed the Calvinist view of predestination, which held that those elected for salvation were chosen prior to Adam's fall, but he gradually came to have doubts. To him predestination seemed too harsh a position because it did not allow human decision a role in the achieving of salvation. Hence Arminius came to assert a conditional election, according to which God elects to life those who will respond in faith to the divine offer of salvation. In so doing, he meant to place greater emphasis on God's mercy.

After his death some of his followers gave support to his views by signing the *Remonstrance,* a theological dictum written by Johannes Uyttenbogaert, a minister from Utrecht, in 1610. Remonstrant Arminianism was debated in 1618–19 at the Synod of Dort (Dordrecht), an assembly of the Dutch Reformed Church at which all the delegates were supporters of Gomarus. Arminianism was discredited and condemned by the synod, the Arminians present were expelled, and many others suffered persecution.

In 1629, however, the works of Arminius (*Opera theologica*) were published for the first time in Leiden, and by 1630 the Remonstrant Brotherhood had achieved legal toleration. It was finally recognized officially in the Netherlands in 1795. In its emphasis on the grace of God, Arminianism influenced the development of Methodism in England and the U.S.

armistice, an agreement for the cessation of active hostilities between two or more belligerents. Generally, the terms, scope, and duration of an armistice are determined by the contracting belligerents. An armistice agreement may involve a partial or temporary cessation of hostilities—called a local armistice or truce—established for a variety of specific purposes, such as collecting the dead. Or it may involve a general armistice (*i.e.,* a total cessation of all hostilities) such as the French armistice agreement of 1940. Although a total cessation may appear to be tantamount to a de facto termination of the war, it is not recognized as such legally. Under international law the state of war still exists and with it the rights and duties of the belligerents and of the neutral parties. Thus, unless otherwise agreed, the warring parties may continue to maintain a blockade and conduct visitations of neutral ships. The more recent trend has been to broaden the scope of the armistice to give it the form and substance of a preliminary peace treaty such as the armistice agreement signed on July 27, 1953, ending the hostilities in Korea.

The general rules regarding an armistice were formulated at the Hague Peace Conference of 1907 and are contained in the Hague land war regulations (*see* Hague Peace Conferences). According to the provisions of these regulations, hostilities can be resumed in an indefinite armistice as a result of proper notification or serious violation of the armistice. Acts that constitute a serious violation include a deliberate advance, seizure of any point outside a party's line, and withdrawal of troops from an unfavourable or weak position.

The Armistice of Nov. 11, 1918, ending World War I between Germany and the Allied powers, departed from the usual form (1) in being preceded by negotiations between the belligerents, resulting in a so-called "prearmistice" agreement and (2) in including political and financial clauses in addition to the military terms. Its military terms made the resumption of hostilities virtually impossible for Germany, thus precluding the usual option in armistices.

Consult
the
INDEX
first

armlet, decorative band, usually of gold, silver, or other metal and sometimes featuring precious gems, worn for ornament around the arm, especially the upper arm. Armlets have been worn since ancient times: in Assyrian art, for instance, deities, monsters, and men are shown wearing armlets.

Several fine examples of armlets are included in the Oxus treasure, a collection of Persian art of the Achaemenidian period (6th–4th century BC) now in the British Museum, London. One of the armlets consists of a circular gold band with its two ends meeting in the form of finely worked griffins. Armlets are especially popular in the East, particularly in India, where a lavish display of jewelry over most of the body is common.

armoire, large cupboard, usually movable and containing shelves, hanging space, and sometimes drawers, and fitted with two doors. It was originally used for storing arms. The armoires designed by Andre-Charles Boulle, the cabinetmaker to Louis XIV in the late 17th century, are among the most sumptuous and imposing pieces of Western furniture.

The word, which sometimes denoted a cupboard set into the panelling of a room, was probably first used in the 16th century, when detailed carving based on Flemish design was characteristic of fine examples. In the following century geometrical designs in high relief became more common; also, in the

Oak armoire, French, 18th century; in the Metropolitan Museum of Art, New York City

By courtesy of the Metropolitan Museum of Art, New York, Rogers Fund, 1919

17th century the name was extended to cover wardrobes and clothespresses.

armor: *see* armour.

armorial ensign, flag with heraldic significance, distinguished by its shape and purpose. The principal armorial ensigns are the banner, the pennon, the guidon, the standard, and the pendant, or pennant.

Originally, the banner was restricted to magnates—peers, feudal barons, and knights bannerets, for example. A square or rectangular flag bearing personal or family insignia, it was carried in action before such royal and noble warriors. Today this most cherished ensign of medieval times is generally used by all armigerous persons throughout Europe except in Scotland, where it is restricted to magnates.

The ensign used by simple knights was a small triangular flag called a pennon. Flown from the lance, the pennon was used to terrorize the enemy as well as to indicate rank. All armigerous persons below banneret's rank may use it. On the field of battle, when promotion to the rank of knight banneret was made, the points of the knight's pennon were cut off, to make it an improvised banner.

Armorial ensigns: (A) banner of Haig of Bemersyde; (B) pennon of Sir John Chandos; (C) guidon of Mayster Compton; (D) standard of Bourbon of France

The guidon, a long, tapering flag, was the cavalry standard and was carried in battle by warriors below the rank of knight. In the hoist (the part nearest the staff to which the ensign was attached), the guidon usually had the national cross (St. George, St. Andrew, and so forth) and, in the fly (the part farthest from the staff), a principal (beast) badge, which, with the field, was in the livery colours.

The standard, half as long again as the guidon, was the largest form of armorial ensign and was intended to be stationary. It marked the carrier's position in battle, in a ceremony, or at a tournament. The flying of a standard often indicated the monarch's presence at a palace, castle, saluting base, or ship.

The pennant, or pendant, earlier called a streamer, was a long, tapering flag, from 20 to 60 yards (18 to 55 metres) in length and 8 yards wide, ending in two points. Used primarily at sea, in the 15th century it was flown from a pole rising above the fighting top and later from the yardarm or topmast. It came to distinguish the warship from the merchant ship. Hoisted when the captain assumes his command, the pennant is an indication of a warship in commission, as opposed to a warship laid up.

Armorica, also spelled AREMORICA (from Celtic *ar,* "on," and *mor,* "sea"), Latin name for the northwestern extremity of Gaul, now Brittany (*q.v.*). In Celtic, Roman, and Frankish times Armorica also included the western part of what later became Normandy (*q.v.*). In Julius Caesar's time it was the home of five principal tribes, the most important being the Veneti (*q.v.*). Under the Roman Empire it formed part of the province of Gallia Lugdunensis, but it was never thoroughly Romanized. It received many Celtic immigrants from the British Isles in the 5th century, during the time of the Saxon invasion.

Armoricain Massif, flattened erosional upland, or peneplain, encompassing the western French *départements* of Finistère, Côtes-du-Nord, Morbihan, and Ille-et-Vilaine and parts of Manche, Orne, Mayenne, Maine-et-Loire, Loire-Atlantique, and Vendée. The region has an area of approximately 25,000 sq mi (65,000 sq km) and is bounded by the Paris Basin and the Seine River to the north and by the lowlands of the Loire and its tributaries to the south. Crystalline schist from the Precambrian period (more than 570,000,000 years old) predominates and is interlaced with bands of gneiss. Mountains formed during the Hercynian orogeny (mountain-building episode) of the Carboniferous Period (280,000,000 to 345,000,000 years ago) have been largely worn down by erosion, and altitudes rarely exceed 1,300 ft (400 m). The mountain of Avaloirs in Orne reaches an altitude of 1,368 ft and is the highest point in the Massif Armoricain. Uplands include the hills of Arrée in Finistère and Côtes-du-Nord and Mené in Côtes-du-Nord. The basin of Châteaulin occupies much of Finistère and is drained by the Aulne River; the basin of Rennes dominates Ille-et-Vilaine. Erosion has carved out sharp *abers,* or gorges, in the north. The coastline is deeply indented.

The Gauls referred to the coastline as Armor, the land of the sea; the interior was known as Arcoat, the land of forests. Much of the interior has been deforested. Animal husbandry dominates agriculture, and the region is a leading producer of milk, cheese, beef, and pork. The cultivation of fodder is on the increase. Emigration from the countryside has resulted in the consolidation of farmland. The population is concentrated along the coast, which has grown at the expense of the hinterland.

Armory Show, formally INTERNATIONAL EXHIBITION OF MODERN ART, an exhibition of painting and sculpture held from Feb. 17 to March 15, 1913, at the Sixty-ninth Regiment Armory in New York City. The show, a decisive event in the development of American art, was originally conceived by its organizers, the Association of American Painters and Sculptors, as a selection of representational works exclusively by American artists, members both of the National Academy of Design and of the more progressive Ashcan School and The Eight. The election of Arthur B. Davies as president of the association changed this conception. A member of The Eight, Davies produced pleasant, Romantic paintings that enjoyed the respect of almost all of the American art establishment. He was also a man with a broad, highly developed taste, capable of appreciating trends in art far more radical than his own style, and he was aware of developments in Europe. Davies, with the help of Walt Kuhn and Walter Pach, spent a year, much of it in Europe, assembling a collection that was later called a "harbinger of universal anarchy." In New York City, Chicago, and Boston, where the exhibition travelled, an estimated 300,000 Americans saw the approximately 1,600 works included in the show. Of these, about one-third were European, and attention became focussed on them. The selection was almost a history of European Modernism. Beginning with J.-A.-D. Ingres and Eugène Delacroix, the exhibition displayed works by Impressionists, Symbolists, Postimpressionists, Fauves, and Cubists.

Although the sculpture section was weak and the Expressionists were poorly represented, the show exposed the American public for the first time to advanced European art. American art suffered by contrast.

Reactions to the show were varied. Marcel Duchamp's Cubist painting "Nude Descending a Staircase, No. 2" was popularly described as "an explosion in a shingle factory"; and Henri Matisse, Constantin Brancusi, and Walter Pach were hanged in effigy by Chicago art students. Yet this show became the basis of many important private American collections, and the Metropolitan Museum of Art purchased a work by Cézanne, becoming the first American museum to do so.

For American art, the show had results more difficult to gauge. Stuart Davis exemplifies one artist's reaction: "The Armory Show was the greatest shock to me—the greatest single influence I have experienced in my work. All my immediately subsequent efforts went toward incorporating Armory Show ideas into my work." The artists Joseph Stella, John Marin, Georgia O'Keeffe, and Arthur Dove were encouraged by the Armory Show to continue their avant-garde direction. American painting in general, however, continued to be dominated by the Realists—the Ashcan School and its successors, American Scene painting and Social Realism—until some 30 years later.

Partial view of the New York City installation of the International Exhibition of Modern Art (Armory Show), 1913

Photograph, courtesy of The Museum of Modern Art, New York City

armour, also spelled ARMOR, protective clothing with the ability to deflect or absorb arrows, spears, lances, swords, bullets, or whatever other kind of weapon might be used against its wearer.

A brief treatment of armour follows. For full treatment, *see* MACROPAEDIA: War, The Technology of.

The use of armour dates back to earliest times, and armour generally falls into one of three main categories: armour made of leather, fabric, or mixed layers of both, sometimes reinforced by quilting or felt; mail, made of interwoven rings of iron or steel; and rigid armour, made of metal, horn, wood, plastic, or some similar tough and resistant material. There are categories within categories, such as brigandine (plates sewn into a garment) and lamellar (small plates overlapping and held together with laces).

Presumably armour goes back beyond historical records, when primitive warriors protected themselves with leather hides and helmets. In the 11th century BC, Chinese warriors wore armour made of five to seven layers of rhinoceros skin. Ox hides were similarly used by the Mongols in the 13th century AD, and American Indians glued or sewed together several animal hides for protection. Fabric armour, too, has a long history: a Mycenaean grave of the 16th century BC held fragments of a garment made of 14 layers of linen, and in northern India quilted coats covered with velvet and sometimes studded with small gilt nails were used until the 19th century.

The heyday of armour was in the Middle Ages when knighthood was in flower. A complete suit of German armour from around 1510 shows a metal suit with flexible joints covering its wearer literally from head to toe, with only a slit for the eyes and small holes for breathing in a helmet of forged metal. Mail and jointed plates were used when necessary to give the wearer some mobility. A heavy lance rest was built into the breastplate just below the right armpit, indicating that one of the chief forms of combat for which this suit was built was jousting, in which two knights rode, lances poised for the strike, against each other, each attempting to knock the other out of the saddle.

In modern times the principal purpose of armour has been to stop or deflect bullets. Some use was made of bulletproof clothing in World War II, particularly to protect flying personnel, but it was never widespread. Today, however, serious efforts are being made to develop armour suitable for police and riot control forces and to develop plastic helmets to protect against rock-throwing.

Modern bulletproofing leans principally on the brigandine, or jack, type of armour. Small plates of alloy steel are sewn into pockets in a garment that covers at least the chest and groin. The plates are not joined together but secreted in the pockets and they give great freedom of movement as well as protection. Fibre glass or boron carbide sometimes replace the metal plates and tend to increase not only the protection but also the comfort of such garments.

Armour, Philip Danforth (b. May 16, 1832, Stockbridge, N.Y., U.S.—d. Jan. 6, 1901, Chicago), entrepreneur and innovator whose extensive Armour & Company enterprises helped make Chicago the meat-packing capital of the world.

Earning his first capital in California mining endeavours, Armour cofounded a grain-dealing and meat-packing business in Milwaukee in 1863. Anticipating a sharp decline in pork prices near the end of the U.S. Civil War (1861–65), he made nearly $2,000,000 buying pork at depressed rates and selling it for far more in New York City. He became involved in his brother Herman Ossian Armour's grain commission house in Milwaukee, to which

Philip Danforth Armour, portrait by an unknown artist, 1914

By courtesy of the Library of Congress, Washington, D.C.

he added a pork-packing plant in 1868. During the following decade the family's interests were concentrated in Chicago, and Philip Armour assumed leadership of the firm in 1875. He originated a number of slaughtering techniques, the use of waste products, and the sale of canned meat. When refrigeration was introduced in the 1880s, he established distributing plants in Eastern cities and began exporting meat products to Europe.

In his later years Armour employed part of his wealth, estimated at $50,000,000, for philanthropic purposes, founding the Armour Mission and the Armour Institute of Technology (1892, later the Illinois Institute of Technology), both in Chicago, and building the Armour flats for workingmen's families. He was, however, opposed to collective bargaining and unionization. His prestige was tarnished in the "embalmed beef" scandals of 1898–99 when his firm was accused, although guilt was never established, of selling tainted meat to the U.S. military.

After his death, Armour's firm continued to prosper under the leadership of his son, Jonathan Ogden Armour, at whose retirement in 1923 the company was the largest meat-packing firm in the world.

armoured mud ball, large ball of silt and clay, coated (armoured) with a poorly sorted mixture of gravel and sand. In many cases they are nearly spherical, with diameters ranging from a fraction of a centimetre to 50 centimetres (20 inches) but commonly 5–10 centimetres (2–4 inches). As the size increases, the grain size of the armour increases. The balls originate as clay chunks that are broken from a stream bank by erosion and then rolled downstream, acquiring armour as the sand and gravel grains press into the soft exterior until the surface is sufficiently covered to seal it off. Mud balls may be preserved by burial, and, when they occur in the geologic record, they give indications of the nature and properties of ancient streams.

armoured vehicle, motor vehicle running on tracks or wheels, protected with partial or complete armour and used to carry military personnel or as the motive power for self-propelled artillery pieces. The classification also embraces armoured cars used for military or civilian purposes, the latter including personal security for political leaders and, most common in urban places, the safe transportation of valuables.

The development of armoured cars predates the mass production of automobiles and trucks. As early as 1899, F.R. Simms in England fitted a powered quadricycle with a machine gun; at about the same time Maj. R.P.

Davidson in the U.S. devised a similar vehicle. By 1906 the French Société Charron, Girardot et Voigt developed an armoured car with a turret. The outbreak of World War I gave an initial impetus to the large-scale development and manufacture of military armoured cars, although the stalemate nature of trench warfare limited the value of the vehicles.

Armoured cars for civilian use were derived from the early military models not long after World War I, when an era of widespread robbery occurred in the United States. Armour was applied to truck bodies to enable banks and other interests to deliver payrolls and transport currency, negotiable securities, and other valuables without fear of loss to bandits. These vehicles began, as they remain, essentially as bulletproof chambers with armoured doors and gun ports and with space inside for valuables and armed guards, mounted on truck chassis. Late in World War I an armoured self-propelled field gun was developed as a tank destroyer (*q.v.*).

Early in the course of World War II Allied efforts to create a light tank that could be flown into battle set in motion a tendency toward building lightweight armoured vehicles to run on tracks or treads instead of the wheels which had been the norm. From the design program to create a cargo carrier able to make amphibious landings, the U.S. Marine Corps created the Landing Vehicle, Tracked, or LVT. Originally unarmoured, it was soon modified and appeared in two versions, both armoured, one carrying personnel, the other a turreted gun vehicle used for close support of landing troops.

Other self-propelled guns were developed by the Allies and the Axis forces, moving steadily toward turreted guns and away from the open gun mounts first favoured by the Germans. Personnel carriers using tracks in the rear for traction and wheels in front for steering were developed in World War II by both Germany and the United States; these were the so-called half-tracks. In postwar development, they gave way to fully tracked vehicles to gain improved performance on varied surfaces. Armoured vehicles are usually protected more lightly than tanks; their armour is, however, able to deflect machine-gun fire. *See also* tank.

Armoury Museum, Russian ORUZHEINAYA MUZEY, in Moscow, oldest museum in Russia. It is housed in a building between the Great Kremlin Palace and the Kremlin wall, was designed by K. Thon, and was built between 1844 and 1851. The museum was originally founded to house the treasures accumulated over the centuries by Russia and is Russo-Byzantine in style. It replaced the old armoury palace, which was started in the middle of the 16th century. The treasures of the Kremlin cathedrals and the Synodal Treasury were added to the museum after the Revolution.

Arms and armour include the armour of Boris Gudunov and the jewel-encrusted helmet of Tsar Michael. Russian gold and silver include a fine 16th-century round gold dish given by Ivan the Terrible as a wedding present to his second wife. Among the examples of enamel work, icons, and jewelry are some famous examples of the work of the Russian goldsmith Peter Fabergé, including a celebrated work, the Heliotrope Egg. There are also vestments and fabrics and European gold and silver, including one of the finest collections of 16th- and 17th-century English silver in the world and French porcelain from the Sèvres factory. The thrones include one of inlaid ivory that belonged to Ivan the Terrible and a gold throne presented to Boris Gudunov in 1604 by the Shah of Persia. The Russian state regalia including crowns and other precious objects is housed in the museum, as are examples of state carriages, saddlery, and various other items of historical interest.

arms, coat of, also called SHIELD OF ARMS, heraldic device dating back to 12th-century Europe, used primarily to establish identity in battle but evolving to denote family descent, adoption, alliance, property ownership, or profession—the oldest extant document being a copy of a roll of arms of the king of England, *c.* 1240. The coat of arms consists of a shield, or escutcheon, and surface or field. It is divided into nine parts (called points) in order to properly position bearings. It is further divided into chief and base, or top and bottom, and it is often ornamented with helmet, mantling, wreath, crest, badge, motto, supporters, crown, or coronet. The left, or sinister, side is to the observer's right; the right, or dexter, side to the left; and the entire display is designated the achievement. At first simply assumed, the coat of arms was later given under royal grant, the College of Arms being established in London in 1484 by Richard III.

Originally the coat of arms was a cloth tunic worn over, or occasionally to conceal, armour; or, in place of armour, it was padded and worn for protection but marked with the shield's identical emblem to aid identification. As shields themselves were artistically embellished to record personal or family history and conquest, they were chosen as emblems for organizations far removed from war—*i.e.*, schools, universities, guilds, churches, fraternal societies, and even modern corporations. Closely related to the science of heraldry and the study of genealogy, coat-of-arms design reflects historical tradition, relying on established patterns, positioning, symbols, and colours, often called tinctures: gold (or), white or silver (argent), blue (azure), green (vert), red (gules), purple, and black (sable).

arms, roll of, book listing and illustrating the arms of persons present at a particular battle or tournament. Not only of historical interest, they are excellent examples of heraldic art as well.

There has been no break in the compilation of rolls of arms for official purposes since their origin in mid-13th-century England. The official registers of heraldic administrations (such as the Lyon Court in Scotland) still maintain collections of rolls of arms recording armorial ensigns and insignia of historical import.

arms control, international limitation of development, testing, deployment, or use of weapons that, at the same time, accepts the inevitability of the continued existence of national military establishments. Arms control has two principal functions: to decrease the likelihood of all-out or total war by reducing certain risks inherent in the military situation and to increase the possibility that a policy of restraint will be followed when conflicts do arise. Arms control does not necessarily prohibit weapons production, but it may have an inhibiting effect. It differs from both disarmament and arms limitation.

Disarmament may be the penal destruction or reduction of the arms of a defeated country; or a bilateral or multilateral agreement applying to a specific geographical location (*e.g.*, the Rush–Bagot Agreement between the United States and Great Britain, which since 1817 has kept the Great Lakes and the U.S.–Canadian border disarmed); or disarmament may entail the abolition of all armaments.

Arms limitation is the reduction and limitation of national armaments by general international agreement. The possibility of arms limitation did not come before an international assembly until the Hague conventions (*q.v.*) of 1899 and 1907, which ended in failure. In early 1970, Strategic Arms Limitation Talks (SALT) began between the United States and the Soviet Union. Agreement about reducing nuclear armaments was hampered, however, by each country's insistence on bargaining from a position of strength.

Implied in arms control is some form of collaboration between generally antagonistic states in areas of military policy. Arms control can also encompass a decision by one state to encourage world security by decreasing unilaterally its war-making capability.

Many advocates of arms control continue to hope that there may eventually be moves toward total disarmament. Since the mid-1960s, however, there has been a shift in international policy toward arms control rather than total disarmament. The United States and the Soviet Union have taken the lead in that direction through the sponsorship of some international agreements of a limited risk character. The most notable has been the treaty (1963) banning tests of nuclear weapons in the atmosphere, in outer space, and underwater, in which 120 countries participated; France and the People's Republic of China abstained. That treaty limits testing of nuclear weapons by prohibiting the release of detectable radioactivity beyond the national borders of the country conducting the tests. By means of this restriction, the treaty has effectively limited the size of the bombs that can be detonated. In 1976 the U.S. and the Soviet Union further tightened the restriction by agreeing to limit underground testing to weapons of no more than 150 kilotons yield. The most substantial advance in international arms control was the Interim Agreement, the so-called SALT I, between the two superpowers in 1972 to limit the size of their strategic arsenals and their development of more advanced strategic weapons; the agreement was further defined and modified by the Vladivostok agreement in 1975. Although the 1977 expiration date of the Interim Agreement passed without a more definitive settlement, and although the SALT II treaty was not ratified by the U.S. Senate, intermittent negotiations have continued from time to time.

Armstrong, Edwin H(oward) (b. Dec. 18, 1890, New York City—d. Jan. 31/Feb. 1, 1954, New York City), U.S. inventor who laid the foundation for much of modern radio and electronic circuitry, including the regenerative and superheterodyne circuits and the frequency modulation (FM) system.

Early life. Armstrong was from a genteel, devoutly Presbyterian family of the old Chelsea district of Manhattan. His father was a publisher and his mother a former schoolteacher. Armstrong was a shy boy interested from childhood in engines, railway trains, and all mechanical contraptions.

At the age of 14, fired by reading of the exploits of Guglielmo Marconi in sending the first wireless message across the Atlantic, Armstrong decided to become an inventor. He built a maze of wireless apparatus in his family's attic, by then removed to the suburbs, and began the solitary, secretive work that absorbed his life. Except for a passion for tennis, acquired from his father, and later, for fast motor cars, he developed no other interest. Wireless was then in the stage of crude spark-gap transmitters and iron-filing receivers, producing faint Morse-code signals, barely audible through tight earphones. Armstrong joined in the hunt for improved instruments. On graduating from high school, he commuted to Columbia University's School of Engineering on a red motorcycle, a graduation gift from his father, to pursue his search.

In his junior year at Columbia, Armstrong made his first, most seminal invention. Among the devices investigated for better wireless reception was the then little understood, largely unused Audion, or three-element vacuum tube, invented in 1906 by Lee De Forest, a pioneer in the development of wireless telegraphy and television. Armstrong made exhaustive measurements to find out how the tube worked and devised a circuit, called the regenerative, or feedback, circuit, that suddenly, in the autumn of 1912, brought in signals with a thousandfold amplification, loud enough to be heard across a room. At its highest amplification, he also discovered, the tube's circuit shifted from being a receiver to being an oscillator, or primary generator, of wireless waves. As radiowave generator this circuit is still at the heart of all radio-television broadcasting.

Armstrong's priority was later challenged by De Forest in a monumental series of corporate patent suits, extending more than 14 years, argued twice before the Supreme Court, and finally ending—in a judicial misunderstanding of the nature of the invention—in favour of De Forest. But the scientific community never accepted this verdict. The Institute of Radio Engineers refused to revoke an earlier gold-medal award to Armstrong for the discovery of the feedback circuit. Later he received the Franklin Medal, highest of U.S. scientific honours, reaffirming his invention of the regenerative circuit.

This youthful invention that opened the age of electronics had profound effects on Armstrong's life. It led him, after a stint as an instructor at Columbia, into the U.S. Army Signal Corps laboratories in World War I in Paris, where he invented the superheterodyne circuit, a highly selective means of receiving, converting, and greatly amplifying very weak, high-frequency electromagnetic waves, which today underlies 98 percent of all radio, radar, and television reception. It brought him into early association with the man destined to lead the postwar Radio Corporation of America (RCA), David Sarnoff, whose young secretary Armstrong later married. Armstrong himself returned after the war to Columbia to become assistant to Michael Pupin, the notable physicist and inventor and his revered teacher. In this period he sold patent rights on his circuits to the major corporations, including RCA, for large sums in cash and stock. Suddenly, in the radio boom of the 1920s, he found himself a millionaire. But he continued to teach at Columbia, financing his own research, working along with Pupin, whose professorship he inherited, on the long-unsolved problem of eliminating static from radio.

Invention of FM broadcasting. In 1933 Armstrong secured four patents on advanced circuits that were to solve this last basic problem. They revealed an entirely new radio system, from transmitter to receiver. Instead of varying the amplitude or power of radio waves to carry voice or music, as in all radio before then, the new system varied or modulated the waves' frequency (number of waves per second) over a wide band of frequencies. This created a carrier wave that natural static—an amplitude phenomenon created by electrical storms—could not break into. As a result, FM's wide frequency range made possible the first clear, practical method of high-fidelity broadcasting.

Since the new system required a basic change in transmitters and receivers, it was not embraced with any alacrity by the established radio industry. Armstrong had to build the first full-scale FM station himself in 1939 at a cost of more than $300,000 to prove its worth. He then had to develop and promote the system, sustain it through World War II (while he again turned to military research), and fight off postwar regulatory attempts to hobble FM's growth. When FM slowly established itself, Armstrong again found himself entrapped in another interminable patent suit to retain his invention. Ill and aging in 1954, with most of his wealth gone in the battle for FM, he took his own life.

The years have brought increasing recognition of Armstrong's place in science and invention. FM is now the preferred system in radio, the required sound channel in all television, and the dominant medium in mobile radio, microwave relay, and space-satellite communications. Posthumously, Armstrong was elected to the pantheon of electrical greats by the Union Internationale des Télécommunications, to join such figures as the French physicist and mathematician André-Marie Ampère; Alexander Graham Bell, the inventor of the telephone; the English electrical pioneer Michael Faraday; and Marconi, the Italian developer of wireless telegraphy. (L.P.L.)

BIBLIOGRAPHY. L. Lessing, *Man of High Fidelity: Edwin Howard Armstrong* (1956; rev. paperback ed., 1969), the only definitive published biography; W.R. MacLaurin and R.J. Harman, *Invention and Innovation in the Radio Industry* (1949), inventive and industrial background.

Armstrong, Helen (singer): *see* Melba, Dame Nellie.

Armstrong, Henry, original name HENRY JACKSON (b. Dec. 12, 1912, Columbus, Miss., U.S.), only professional boxer to hold three world championships simultaneously.

Henry Armstrong (left) fighting Lou Ambers, 1938
UPI—EB Inc.

Armstrong fought as an amateur from 1929 to 1932. Early in his career he boxed under the name of Melody Jackson. He first won the featherweight (126-pound) title by knocking out Petey Sarron in six rounds, Oct. 29, 1937. On May 31, 1938, he took the welterweight (147-pound) championship from Barney Ross by decision, and on August 17 of that year he defeated Lou Ambers by decision to win the lightweight (135-pound) title. Late in 1938 he resigned the featherweight championship without having defended it, and on Aug. 22, 1939, he lost the lightweight crown in a 15-round return fight with Ambers.

Armstrong was a busy welterweight champion, successfully defending the title 19 times in somewhat over two years. On Oct. 4, 1940, he lost the championship when Fritzie Zivic outpointed him in 15 rounds. His attempt to regain the championship from Zivic on Jan. 17, 1941, resulted in his knockout in the 12th round by Zivic. On March 1, 1940, Armstrong attempted to win from Ceferino Garcia the New York State version of the middleweight (160-pound) title, which was then in dispute, but the decision was a draw, permitting Garcia to retain the championship.

Armstrong retired from the ring in 1945. He had fought 26 world title fights and from 1931 to 1945 had fought 175 bouts, winning 97 by knockouts. Intelligent and a fluent speaker, he turned to preaching and was ordained a Baptist minister in 1951.

Armstrong, Henry Edward (b. May 6, 1848, Lewisham, Kent, Eng.—d. July 13, 1937, Lewisham), organic chemist whose research in substitution reactions of naphthalene was a major service to the synthetic dye industry. He also pioneered in organic crystallography, contributed much to the understanding of the chemical composition of camphor and related terpene compounds, and devised a centric formula for benzene. In addition, Armstrong's contribution to research in water purification was instrumental in making typhoid fever a preventable disease.

Armstrong, John (b. Nov. 25, 1758, Carlisle, Pa.—d. April 1, 1843, Red Hook, N.Y., U.S.), soldier, diplomat, and politician who, as secretary of war during the War of 1812, was blamed for the British capture of Washington, D.C.

Armstrong fought in the U.S. War of Independence (1775–83) and, as an officer in the Continental Army, was apparently the author of the Newburgh Addresses attacking Congress. After the war, he entered politics in New York, serving briefly as U.S. senator, and from 1804 to 1810 was U.S. minister to France. When the War of 1812 began, he served as a brigadier general and, from February 1813 until September 1814, as secretary of war under Pres. James Madison, with whom he shared blame for failure to provide men and equipment to protect Washington, D.C., from British troops, who burned the Capitol on Aug. 24, 1814. Unpopularity forced him to resign his Cabinet position.

Armstrong, Louis (Daniel), byname SATCHMO (diminutive of Satchel Mouth) (b. July 4, 1900, New Orleans—d. July 6, 1971, New York City), the leading trumpeter in jazz history.

A prolifically gifted natural musician, Armstrong as a child followed the brass bands around the streets of New Orleans and came to know many of the pioneers of jazz. In his youth he played the trumpet in marching bands and on the Mississippi riverboats, but he did not really come into his own until, in 1922, his hero, King Oliver, then leading a band in Chicago, sent for him to play second trumpet. A series of recordings with Oliver's Creole Jazz Band resulted, with such pieces as "Dippermouth Blues," "Canal Street Blues," and other blues.

Until his advent, jazz had been based on a three-instrument front line of clarinet-trumpet-trombone, in which individual gifts were subordinated to the demands of the ensemble. It was evident, however, that as soon as individual virtuosity reached a certain peak and a player evolved the ability to create solos more

Louis Armstrong
AP/Wide World Photos

profound than anything the ensemble could offer, then this New Orleans convention was doomed. Armstrong, with his creativity, split the convention at the seams. The series of recordings he made between 1925 and 1928 with his Hot Five and Hot Seven ensembles established the preeminence of the virtuoso soloist. With these groups, Armstrong made records that included "Savoy Blues," "Potato Head Blues," and "West End Blues."

Harmonically, Armstrong was always one of

the clearest thinkers, and, despite the complex evolution of jazz after his youth, he remained rooted in the style that first established his reputation. With his beauty of tone, instrumental range, and gift for melodic variations, his extroverted style enabled him to bring jazz to audiences who cared little for the music. One of his most important contributions was to popularize a rhythmic approach in improvising that became known as jazz swing feeling. Another outcome of his burgeoning career was his invention of the "scat" vocal, in which the voice, by abandoning words in favour of conventional but meaningless syllables, reproduces the nuances of instrumental improvisation. Armstrong made many vocal records, and the scat vocal was imitated by jazz singers, including Ella Fitzgerald and Al Jarreau.

From the early 1930s on, he became something more than a jazz musician: he was bandleader, solo variety attraction, film star, and comedian. One of his most remarkable feats was his frequent conquest of the popular market with recordings that are in reality authentic jazz thinly disguised by its creator's contagious humour and delight in his own prowess.

As a composer, Armstrong is associated with such early jazz hits as "Dippermouth Blues" (with King Oliver), "Wild Man Blues" (with Jelly Roll Morton), "Gut Bucket Blues," and others.

Armstrong performed in a number of films, from *Diamond Lil* with Mae West to *Hello Dolly!* with Barbra Streisand. Armstrong autobiographies include *Swing That Music* (1936) and *Satchmo: My Life in New Orleans* (1954). *Louis*, a biography by Max Jones and John Chilton, was published in 1971.

Armstrong, Neil (Alden) (b. Aug. 5, 1930, Wapakoneta, Ohio, U.S.), astronaut, the first man to set foot on the Moon.

Armstrong became a licensed pilot on his 16th birthday and a naval air cadet in 1947. His studies in aeronautical engineering at Purdue University, West Lafayette, Ind., were interrupted in 1950 by the Korean War, in which he was shot down once and was awarded three Air Medals. In 1955 he became a civilian research pilot for the National Advisory Committee for Aeronautics (NACA), later the National Aeronautics and Space Administration (NASA). He flew more than 1,100 hours, testing various supersonic fighters as well as the X-15 rocket plane.

In 1962 he joined the space program with the second group of astronauts. On March 16, 1966, Armstrong, as command pilot of Gemini 8, and David R. Scott rendezvoused with an unmanned Agena rocket and completed the first manual space-docking manoeuvre. After the docking, a rocket-thruster malfunction forced them to separate from the Agena. Armstrong then regained control of the Gemini craft and made an emergency splashdown in the Pacific Ocean.

On July 16, 1969, Armstrong, along with Edwin E. Aldrin, Jr., and Michael Collins, blasted off in the Apollo 11 vehicle toward the Moon. Four days later, at 4:18 PM, Eastern Daylight Time (EDT), the "Eagle" lunar landing module, guided manually by Armstrong, touched down on a plain near the southwestern edge of the Sea of Tranquillity (Mare Tranquillitatis). At 10:56 PM EDT, July 20, 1969, Armstrong stepped from the "Eagle" onto the Moon's dusty surface with the words, "That's one small step for a man, one giant leap for mankind." During the 21 hours and 37 minutes that Armstrong and Aldrin spent on the Moon, they collected soil and rock samples, took numerous photographs, and deployed scientific instruments.

On July 21 they lifted off and began the voyage back to Earth. After splashdown in the Pacific at 12:51 PM EDT on July 24, the three astronauts spent 18 days in quarantine to guard against possible contamination by lunar microbes. During the days that followed and during a tour of 21 nations, they were hailed for their part in the opening of a new era in mankind's exploration of the universe.

Armstrong resigned from NASA in 1971. From 1971 to 1979 he was professor of aerospace engineering at the University of Cincinnati (Ohio), and from 1979 he was chairman of the board of Cardwell International, Ltd., of Lebanon, Ohio, suppliers of oilfield equipment.

Armstrong, Samuel Chapman (b. Jan. 30, 1839, Maui, Hawaii—d. May 11, 1893, Hampton, Va., U.S.) Union military commander of black troops during the Civil War and founder of Hampton Institute.

The son of American missionaries to Hawaii, Armstrong attended Oahu College for two years before going to the United States in 1860. He enrolled at Williams College; but, on the outbreak of the Civil War, he left school to accept a commission as captain in the 125th New York Regiment. He recruited and trained his own troops and led them in several battles, including Gettysburg.

First promoted to major and then to colonel, Armstrong was put in command of the 9th Regiment, a corps consisting entirely of black troops. Determined to show the full capabilities of black soldiers, he trained his men rigorously. By the end of the war, he held the rank of brigadier general, and the troops under his command had distinguished themselves on many occasions.

After the war, Armstrong became an agent of the Freedmen's Bureau and, in 1866, took charge of a huge camp of former slaves in Hampton, Va. Recognizing the need for those blacks to receive an education, Armstrong in 1867 convinced the American Missionary Association and a private benefactor to purchase land in Hampton and establish a vocational training institution there. Hampton Normal and Industrial Institute opened in 1868. For the next 25 years, Armstrong laboured to sustain and administer the school, which became a leading centre for both vocational training and academic education for Southern blacks.

Armstrong (of Cragside), William George Armstrong, Baron, also called (1859–87) SIR WILLIAM GEORGE ARMSTRONG (b. Nov. 26, 1810, Newcastle upon Tyne, Northumberland, Eng.—d. Dec. 27, 1900, Cragside, Northumberland), industrialist and engineer who invented high-pressure hydraulic machinery and revolutionized the design and manufacture of guns.

William George Armstrong, c. 1870
BBC Hulton Picture Library

Armstrong abandoned his Newcastle law practice in 1847 to devote full time to scientific experimentation. He founded an engineering works at Elswick-on-Tyne to build hydraulic cranes. Because his hydraulic machinery was dependent for power on water mains or reservoirs, he invented, in 1850, a hydraulic accumulator. It comprised a large water-filled cylinder with a piston that could raise water pressure within the cylinder and in supply pipes to 600 pounds per square inch (42 kilograms per square centimetre). Thus machinery such as hoists, capstans, turntables, and dock gates could be worked in almost any situation.

He next improved ordnance for the British Army. He shrank metal rings onto an inner steel barrel, later coiling a strip of wrought iron into a long helix and welding it to the barrel. This process, used by others, was most successfully developed by Armstrong. He also emphasized breechloading, rifled bores, and elongated projectiles. Armstrong was elected a fellow of the Royal Society in 1843 and created a baron in 1887.

army, a large organized force armed and trained for war and destined chiefly for land service. The term may be applied to a large unit organized for independent action, or it may be applied to the complete military organization of a nation for land warfare.

A brief treatment of armies follows. For full treatment, *see* MACROPAEDIA: War, The Theory and Conduct of; War, The Technology of.

The origin of armies cannot be dated. Nonetheless it may be assumed that the appearance of the city-states in Mesopotamia and Egypt, their continuous struggle for arable land and water rights, and the creation of fortifications and the expansions of the city-states into kingdoms and empires must have been paralleled in those focal areas of the ancient world by the appearance and growth of army organization. Four types of armed forces may be discerned in the history of the ancient world. Paramount was a warrior caste that formed the ruler's bodyguard and "ate before the king." Much scholarly debate revolves around the origins, in the various states of antiquity, of this caste system. In some cases, the warrior caste simply represented the retention of arms in the hands of a conquering people who had disarmed and reduced to serfdom an earlier group of inhabitants. In other cases the warrior caste appears to have been simply the product of birth or race. Next in importance to the guard attached to the person of the monarch were the provincial troops who served in districts outside the capital under a royal governor or great prince. A third class of soldiery common in antiquity were the mercenaries, sometimes slaves, as were the Nubians who served the first pharaohs, or freebooters such as the Philistines or the Germans who fought in the armies of the Roman Empire. Finally, there seems to have existed from the earliest times, and in all societies, the institution of the *corvée* or forced levy of troops from the ordinary population. This levy was often associated with public works but in wartime could augment the regular forces with lightly armed auxiliaries and road builders.

There was no general, long-service military class in feudal times. Each nobleman had his vassals for military duties in the short-lived campaigns of the early Middle Ages. The main business of the knights was agriculture. The annual 40 days of military service owed by vassals to their lords prevented warfare from being more than a desultory occupation and in no way qualified the feudal nobles as professional officers.

Professionalism took its most significant step in the 15th century, when free companies of Swiss, Italian, and German soldiers sold their services wherever they were needed. These mercenaries were international freebooters, and their captains were competent leaders who, to some extent, qualified as officers in the modern sense. Their livelihood was warfare; they made a business of fighting, contracting with various princes or dukes for professional service.

It was during the 17th and 18th centuries that the proprietary system replaced the obsolete combination of feudalism and free companies. Under this system the colonel was the proprietor of his regiment, the captain the proprietor of his company. The king accepted them as his officers and armed them with authority to raise men. Initially under this system armies were raised for each campaign and the regiments were made up from qualified volunteers. During the latter part of the 17th century, however, armies became permanent, or standing, and were kept up to strength by the regular influx of untrained recruits. The crown supplied the recruits and the money for maintaining the forces, the proprietorship of the colonels and captains being thus somewhat restricted.

Warfare itself was fought along conventional lines and the troops no longer plundered the countryside as the free companies had done in the past. Happily, too, the people of that time were as a whole less affected by war. It was the king's business and fought by professionals along regularly prescribed lines. Out of this orderly warfare of the standing armies came the next great development, that of the nation in arms. The middle-class revolt as a social phenomenon brought about a great change in armies.

The French Revolution entailed one of the greatest changes in the development of armies. The nation's call to arms produced in a few months more than 1,000,000 men, a number unknown in armies after the days of ancient Persia. That draft of manpower was a forerunner of the almost universal dependence on conscription as a basis of recruitment from that day forward.

This social phenomenon of the nation in arms induced tremendous changes in warfare. The tactics and strategy of the professional armies of the past needed revision to meet the new requirements of the conscripted armies. Another feature of the nation in arms was the appeal to patriotism and to the individualistic spirit of each citizen. The army was made up of men from all strata of society. The old differences between the nobility and the peasantry were broken down. Napoleon himself had risen from nowhere to become a general, and out of his experience he told his men that every man carried a baton in his knapsack. There was no insistence on noble ancestors, and many of Napoleon's marshals would never have been more than sergeants in the old French army.

In the 20th century, with the spread of both democratic and socialist types of government, permanent officer classes based on wealth or heredity have further tended to disappear. Except in states that have military dictatorships, the army is kept under the control of elected civilian officials. Officers are promoted from within the ranks or are trained at military schools.

In most modern armies the distinction is made between line officers and staff officers. Line officers are those in charge of the purely combatant section of an army. Staff officers are general officers who assist the commander of a military force. The United States, for instance, has a Department of the Army responsible to the president as commander in chief. The staff officers plan and coordinate the activities of an army in both peace and war.

The first such officer staff was the general staff established in Prussia in 1806 by Gen. Gerhard von Scharnhorst. With the unification of Germany it became the German General Staff, a highly effective model for all other command systems. By the start of World War I all major armies had command staffs. Since World War II the staffs of the separate military branches—army, navy, and air force—have been combined into a "joint staff" arrangement. The United States has a Joint Chiefs of Staff responsible to the secretary of defense and to the president. Other major military powers such as Great Britain, France, and the Soviet Union have similar military command structures.

Army, British: *see* British Army.

Army, United States: *see* United States Army, The.

Arnaud DANIEL: *see* Arnaut Daniel.

Arnauld FAMILY, French family of the lesser nobility that came to Paris from Auvergne in the 16th century and is chiefly remembered for its close connection with Jansenism (a Roman Catholic movement that propounded heretical doctrines on the nature of free will and predestination) and with the Jansenist religious communities of Port-Royal de Paris and Port-Royal des Champs.

The founder of the family, Antoine Arnauld (1560–1619), was born in Paris, the son of Antoine Arnauld, seigneur de La Mothe. Well known as an eloquent lawyer, he pleaded for the University of Paris against the Jesuits in 1594 and presented his case so forcefully that his speech on this occasion has been called "the original sin of the Arnaulds," as if it were the first cause of the Jesuits' animosity against the family. He married Catherine Marion de Druy, and they had 20 children, 10 of whom died young. All except one of the surviving children were in some way connected with Port-Royal. In 1629 Arnauld's widow became a nun at Port-Royal de Paris, where she died in 1641.

Perhaps the most notable of Arnauld's 10 surviving children were the youngest son, Antoine Arnauld (*q.v.*), called the Great Arnauld, who was the leading French Jansenist theologian of the 17th century; daughter Jacqueline-Marie-Angélique Arnauld (*q.v.*), called Mère Angélique, who, as abbess, transferred the community from Port-Royal des Champs (near Versailles) to Paris and made it a centre of Jansenism; and her younger sister, Jeanne-Catherine-Agnès Arnauld (*q.v.*), called Mère Agnès, who twice served as abbess of Port-Royal.

Robert Arnauld d'Andilly (1589–1674), the eldest surviving son, pursued a career in government service. In 1620, however, he made the acquaintance of the abbot of Saint-Cyran (*see* Duvergier de Hauranne, Jean), a founder of the Jansenist movement, and under Saint-Cyran's influence he eventually sought to retire from secular life. In about 1646 Arnauld d'Andilly at Port-Royal de Champs entered the ascetic religious community established earlier by several of his nephews, chiefly Antoine Le Maistre. Because of his connection with the French court, Arnauld d'Andilly was especially important in Jansenist political affairs. He was also a poet, a translator of religious texts, and the editor of Saint-Cyran's *Lettres chrétiennes et spirituelles* (1645). His *Mémoires* was published in 1734. Five of Robert Arnauld d'Andilly's daughters became nuns at Port-Royal des Champs.

Robert's younger brother, Henri Arnauld (1597–1692), left his diplomatic career for a life in the church. Ordained as a priest, he ultimately became bishop of Angiers. He played an important part in the Jansenist religious controversy, his sympathy lying with the Jansenists.

In addition to Mère Angélique and Mère Agnès, four more daughters of Antoine Arnauld eventually became nuns at Port-Royal. The most notable was Catherine Arnauld (1590–1651). She married Isaac Le Maistre, a king's counsellor, but, after his death, she too took religious vows and entered Port-Royal.

Antoine Le Maistre, (1608–58), Catherine's eldest son, abandoned worldly society and placed himself under the spiritual direction of Saint-Cyran. Thus guided, Le Maistre and several others—including two of his brothers—established the *solitaires* ("hermits"), a Jansenist ascetic group, at Port-Royal des Champs in about 1638. Early in 1656, as the anti-Jansenist campaign was gaining strength in France, Le Maistre went into hiding in Paris, along with his uncle, Antoine Arnauld, and the philosopher Blaise Pascal, who had been living at Port-Royal. Le Maistre collaborated in the composition of Pascal's *Les Provinciales* (1656–57), a series of letters written in defense of Arnauld, who was, at the time, on trial before the faculty of theology in Paris because of his Jansenist views.

Antoine Le Maistre's youngest brother—the fourth son of Catherine Arnauld—was Isaac-Louis Le Maistre de Sacy (1613–84). Le Maistre de Sacy, also a student and follower of Saint-Cyran, was ordained in 1649. He became the confessor to the nuns and *solitaires* of Port-Royal and was held in high esteem by the Jansenists as a spiritual director. He is best remembered, however, as the principal author of the translation of the New Testament known as the *Nouveau Testament de Mons* (1667). Fragments of his correspondence with Pascal are preserved in the famous *Entretien avec M. de Sacy* ("Conversation with M. de Sacy").

Arnauld, Antoine, byname THE GREAT ARNAULD (b. Feb. 6, 1612—d. Aug. 8, 1694, Brussels), leading 17th-century theologian of Jansenism, a Roman Catholic movement that held heretical doctrines on the nature of free will and predestination.

Arnauld was the youngest of the 10 surviving children of Antoine Arnauld, a Parisian lawyer, and Catherine Marion de Druy (*see* Arnauld family). He studied theology at the Sorbonne and, in 1641, was ordained into the Roman Catholic priesthood. Under the influence of the abbot of Saint-Cyran—a founder of Jansenism and spiritual adviser to several members of the Arnauld family—he published his treatise *De la fréquente communion* (1643; "On Frequent Communion"), defending controversial Jansenist views on the Eucharist and on penance. With his *Théologie morale des Jésuites* (1643), Arnauld launched his long polemical campaign against the Jesuits, in which Pierre Nicole, a young theologian from Chartres, was to be his collaborator. In 1655 Arnauld wrote two pamphlets in which he affirmed the substantial orthodoxy of Cornelius Otto Jansen (the Belgian theologian who initiated the movement). These works sparked a dispute that resulted in Arnauld's expulsion from the Sorbonne in 1656. It was this controversy that provoked the French philosopher Blaise Pascal to write his defense of Arnauld in the series of letters known as *Les Provinciales* (1656–57). During the period of the great persecution of the Jansenists (1661–69), Arnauld emerged as a leader of the resistance.

The so-called Peace of Clement IX (1669) brought Arnauld some years of tranquillity, beginning with the gracious reception accorded to him by Louis XIV, and he next turned to writing against the Calvinists and on subjects disputed between Protestants and Catholics. He then won such fame as a theologian that Pope Innocent XI is said to have considered making him a cardinal.

In 1679, the persecution of Jansenists was renewed and Arnauld sought refuge first in the Netherlands and then in Belgium. He settled permanently in Brussels in 1682, where he was to remain in voluntary exile until his death. Despite the precarious conditions in which he had to work, the amount of Arnauld's writing during his exile was enormous. He not only resumed his attack on the Jesuit casuists in the last six volumes of his *Morale pratique des*

Jésuistes (1689–94; the first two had appeared in 1669 and 1682) but also intervened in the dispute over the rights of the French monarch in the Gallican church. The major written works of Arnauld's later years were generated by his disagreements with the French philosopher and theologian Nicolas Malebranche and with Pierre Nicole, his ally in the earlier anti-Jesuit polemics.

Arnauld, Jacqueline-Marie-Angélique, byname MÈRE ANGÉLIQUE (b. 1591—d. Aug. 6, 1661, Port-Royal, Paris), monastic reformer who was abbess of the important Jansenist centre of Port-Royal de Paris. She was one of six sisters of the prominent Jansenist theologian Antoine Arnauld (the Great Arnauld).

Jacqueline Arnauld entered religious life as a child of 9, becoming abbess of the ancient Cistercian house of Port-Royal des Champs (near Versailles) when she was not yet 12. She had become a nun only by the decision of her parents and had had no vocation for a monastic life, but in 1608 she was converted by a visiting Capuchin friar's sermon. She then undertook to reform her monastery. After an arduous struggle, even against her own family, she succeeded, and Port-Royal became a house of deep spirituality. Mère Angélique was later engaged in the reform of several other convents, especially Maubuisson. From 1618 to 1622 she was under the guidance of St. Francis of Sales. It was she who, in 1625–26, transferred the community of Port-Royal des Champs to Paris. In 1635 she came under the influence of the abbot of Saint-Cyran, one of the founders of Jansenism, a Roman Catholic movement that propounded heretical doctrines on the nature of free will and predestination. The period of persecution of Jansenists in France (1661–69) was in its early stages when, from her deathbed, Mère Angélique wrote to the Queen Mother protesting the constraint that had been inflicted on the Port-Royal community.

Arnauld, Jeanne-Catherine-Agnès, byname MÈRE AGNÈS (b. 1593—d. 1671), abbess of the Jansenist centre of Port-Royal and author of the religious community's *Constitutions* (1665). She was one of six sisters of the prominent Jansenist theologian Antoine Arnauld (the Great Arnauld).

Like her older sister, the abbess Mère Angélique (Jacqueline-Marie-Angélique Arnauld), Jeanne Arnauld entered the cloister at an early age. From 1630 to 1636 she governed the Cistercian monastery of Tard, near Dijon. She then returned to Port-Royal, where she was twice elected abbess (1636; 1658). In August 1664, during the period of persecution of Jansenists in France (1661–69), she was removed to a convent at Chaillot and detained there in an attempt to force from her a statement condemning Jansenism. In 1665, with the other nuns from Port-Royal de Paris who had refused to subscribe to the anti-Jansenist formulary, Mère Agnès was transferred to the community's original house, Port-Royal des Champs, near Versailles. After the so-called Peace of Clement IX (1669), which suspended the persecutions, she lived peacefully and was held in general veneration. Mère Agnès was considered a spiritual writer of some distinction, although few of her works were published.

Arnauld d'Andilly, Robert, brother and follower of the prominent Jansenist theologian Antoine Arnauld. *See* Arnauld family.

Arnaut DANIEL, Arnaut also spelled ARNAUD (b. Ribérac?; fl. 1180–1200), celebrated Provençal poet, troubadour, and master of the *trobar ric*, a poetic style composed of complex metrics, intricate rhymes, and words chosen more for their sound than for their meaning.

A nobleman by birth, Arnaut was a highly regarded travelling troubadour. He is credited with inventing the sestina, a lyrical form of six six-line stanzas, unrhymed, with an elaborate scheme of word repetition. His skill with language was admired by Petrarch and in the 20th century by Ezra Pound and T.S. Eliot. His greatest influence, however, was on Dante, who imitated him and gave him a prominent place in Purgatory as a model for the vernacular poet. Arnaut's speech in Provençal is the only passage in the *Divine Comedy* not in Italian.

Arnaut DE MAREUIL (b. Mareuil, Perigord; fl. 1170–1200), Perigordian troubadour who is credited with having introduced into Provençal poetry the amatory epistle (*salut*) and the short didactic poem (*ensenhamen*).

Little is known of Arnaut's life. His early poems were dedicated to his patroness, Adelaide, the daughter of Count Raymond V of Toulouse and wife of Roger II, viscount of Bezières. After 1194 Arnaut was at the court of William VIII, count of Montpellier. Most of his extant work is passionate love poetry that combines conventional courtly love imagery (extravagant praise of his lady's beauty, despair at her cruel indifference) with unexpectedly delicate sentiment.

Arnd, Johann: *see* Arndt, Johann.

Arndt, Ernst Moritz (b. Dec. 26, 1769, Schoritz bei Gartz, Rügen, Swed.—d. Jan. 29, 1860, Bonn), prose writer, poet, and patriot who expressed the national awakening in his country in the Napoleonic era.

Arndt was educated at Stralsund, Greifswald, and Jena and qualified for the Lutheran ministry. At the age of 28 he rejected his clerical career and for 18 months travelled through Europe. On his return to Germany the sight of ruined castles along the banks of the Rhine River moved him to bitterness against the French who had destroyed them. He described the impressions of this journey in *Reisen durch einen Teil Deutschlands, Ungarns, Italiens, und Frankreichs in den Jahren 1798/99*, 6 vol. (1801–03; "A Journey Through Parts of Germany, Hungary, Italy, and France in 1798–99").

In 1800 Arndt settled in Greifswald as assistant lecturer in history and in 1803 published *Germanien und Europa*, in which he proclaimed his views on French aggression. His subsequent *Versuch einer Geschichte der Leibeigenschaft in Pommern und Rügen* (1803) is, as the title suggests, a history of serfdom in Pomerania and Rügen that resulted in its abolition three years later by the Swedish king Gustav IV. In 1806 Arndt was appointed to the chair of history at the University of Greifswald and published the first part of his *Geist der Zeit* (*Spirit of the Times,* 1808), in which he called on his countrymen to shake off the French yoke. To escape the vengeance of Napoleon, he took refuge in Sweden, from where he continued to communicate his patriotic ideals to his countrymen in pamphlets, poems, and songs.

Arndt returned to Germany in 1809. In 1812 he was summoned to St. Petersburg (now Leningrad) to assist in the organization of the final struggle against France. Meanwhile, he produced further patriotic songs and pamphlets. When, after the peace, the University of Bonn was founded in 1818, Arndt was appointed to the chair of modern history. In this year appeared the fourth part of his *Geist der Zeit,* in which he criticized the reactionary policy of the German powers. The boldness of his demands for reform offended the Prussian government, and in the summer of 1819 he was arrested. He was soon set free but was not allowed to teach. In 1840 he was reinstated and in 1841 was appointed rector of the university. After the revolutionary outbreak of 1848, he took his seat as one of the deputies to the national assembly at Frankfurt am Main. He took part in the deputation that offered the crown to Frederick William IV, but, indignant at the King's refusal to accept it, he retired from public life.

Not all of Arndt's lyrical poems were inspired by political ideas, nor was he a merely chauvinistic figure. Many of the *Gedichte* (1804–18, complete ed. 1860; "Poems") are religious poems of great beauty.

Other important works are his autobiography, *Erinnerungen aus dem äusseren Leben* (1840; "Recollections from the External Life"), the most valuable source of information for Arndt's life; and *Meine Wanderungen und Wandelungen mit dem Reichsfreiherrn Heinrich Karl vom Stein* (1858; "My Travels and Saunterings with the Baron Heinrich Karl von Stein"). A notable edition of his works is that of H. Meisner and R. Geerds, 16 vol. (1908). Studies on Arndt include A.G. Pundt's *Arndt and the National Awakening in Germany* (1935) and H. Scurla's *E.M. Arndt,* 2nd ed. (1952).

Where the same name may denote a person, place, or thing, the articles will be found in that order

---

Arndt, Johann, Arndt also spelled ARND (b. Dec. 27, 1555, Edderitz, Anhalt—d. May 11, 1621, Celle, Hanover), Lutheran theologian whose mystical writings were widely circulated in Europe in the 17th century.

Arndt studied at Helmstadt, Wittenberg, Strasbourg, and Basel. In 1583 he became a pastor at Badeborn, but in 1590 he was deposed for refusing to remove pictures from his church and to discontinue the use of exorcism in Baptism. Both were considered offenses against the Calvinist concept of strict purity and simplicity. Arndt found asylum in Quedlinburg the same year and in 1599 was transferred to St. Martin's Church at Brunswick.

The principal work among his many writings, which were inspired by the mystics St. Bernard, Johann Tauler, and Thomas à Kempis, is *Vier Bücher vom wahren Christentum* (1606–10; "Four Books on True Christianity"). Translated into most European languages and widely distributed in Arndt's time, it served as the foundation of many devotional books, both Roman Catholic and Protestant. Its publication aroused strong controversy among Lutherans. It was also a chief influence in the life of Philipp Jakob Spener (1635–1705), who was a founder of Pietism, a movement that stressed simple Christian living. Arndt held that to follow orthodox doctrine was not enough and that the Christian must undergo a moral purification through righteous living and communion with God.

The opposition aroused by his book caused difficulty for Arndt in Brunswick. In 1609 he moved to Eiseleben and in 1611 to Celle, where he remained until his death.

Arne, Thomas (Augustine) (b. March 12, 1710, London—d. March 5, 1778, London), composer, chiefly of dramatic music and song.

According to tradition, Arne was the son of an upholsterer in King Street, Covent Garden. Educated at Eton, he was intended for the law, but by secretly practicing he acquired such mastery of the violin and keyboard instruments that his father withdrew all objections to a musical career. Except for some lessons from Michael Festing, later leader of the Italian Opera orchestra, Arne was self-taught, and it was at the Opera (which he attended in a footman's livery to obtain free admission) that his musical taste was largely formed. He taught both his sister, later famous as the actress Mrs. Cibber, and his young brother to sing, and they appeared in his first stage work, *Rosamond* (1733). This opera, based

Arne, engraving after F. Bartolozzi (*c.* 1725–1815)
By courtesy of the National Portrait Gallery, London

on Joseph Addison's libretto of 1707, was set "after the Italian manner," and its bravura air "Rise, Glory, Rise" was sung for the next 40 years.

Arne was soon engaged to write musical afterpieces and incidental music for Drury Lane Theatre, and with *Comus* (1738), John Dalton's adaptation of Milton's masque, he became established as the leading English lyric composer. His light, airy, pleasing melodic style was apparent in *Alfred, a Masque* (notable for "Rule, Britannia") and *The Judgment of Paris,* both produced at the Prince of Wales's residence at Cliveden in 1740. Arne's settings of Shakespeare's songs, written for revivals of *As You Like It, Twelfth Night,* and *The Merchant of Venice* in 1740–41, provide the culmination of this early style.

In about 1744 Arne was engaged as composer to Drury Lane Theatre and Vauxhall Gardens, and during the next decade published a number of song collections. In 1759 he was made doctor of music at Oxford, and two years later his oratorio *Judith* was produced, followed by the opera *Artaxerxes* (1762), which held the stage until the early 19th century.

In the final decade of his life, Arne set Garrick's ode for the Stratford Shakespeare jubilee of 1769 and composed music for *The Fairy Prince* (1771), Mason's *Elfrida* (1772), and *Caractacus* (1776).

Arne's early melodic style was natural and elegant, owing something to Scots, Irish, and Italian sources. His later music became more Italianate and ornamented, though in his final years there emerged an opera buffa style that anticipates Sullivan. As the composer of such melodies as "Rule, Britannia," "Blow, Blow, Thou Winter Wind," and "Where the Bee Sucks," Arne, like Purcell, added substantially to the English heritage of song.

Arneth, Alfred, Ritter von (knight of) (b. July 10, 1819, Vienna—d. July 30, 1897, Vienna), historian important chiefly for his work in evaluating and publishing sources for Austrian history found in the Vienna state archives.

In 1841 Arneth was appointed by the Austrian statesman Klemens von Metternich to a post at the state archives, of which he became keeper in 1868. In 1879 he became president of the Imperial Academy of the Sciences, and in 1896 he was appointed chairman of the historical commission of the Bavarian Academy of the Sciences in Munich.

His chief publications concerned the 18th century and derived their value from the special facilities available to him. They include lives of Field Marshal Guido von Starhemberg (1853), Prince Eugene of Savoy (1858), and Maria Theresa (1863–79) and numerous collections of correspondence between Maria Theresa and Marie-Antoinette, Maria Theresa and Joseph II, Joseph II and Leopold, and Joseph II and Catherine of Russia. His early reminiscences, *Aus meinem Leben,* appeared in 1893.

Arneth had launched a political career as a member of the Frankfurt assembly in 1848, after which he served in the Lower Austrian Landtag (Diet) in 1861 and in the Herrenhaus (House of Lords) from 1869. He supported the liberal constitutional party.

Arngrímur THE LEARNED (Icelandic folk poet): *see* Jónsson, Arngrímur.

Arngrímur Jónsson (Icelandic historian): *see* Jónsson, Arngrímur.

Arnhem, German ARNHEIM, *gemeente* (municipality) and capital (1794), Gelderland *provincie* (province), eastern Netherlands, on the north bank of the Lower Rhine (Neder Rijn) River. Possibly the site of the Roman settlement of Arenacum, it was first mentioned in 893. Chartered and fortified in 1233 by Otto II, count of Geldern, it joined the Hanseatic League in 1443. As the residence of the dukes of Geldern, it was often attacked by their Burgundian rivals and in 1543 fell to Charles V, who made it the seat of the Council of Gelderland. It came under the United Netherlands in 1585, and the following year Sir Philip Sidney, the English poet, statesman, and soldier, died there after being wounded in the battle of Zutphen. Seized and dismantled by the French in 1672, Arnhem was refortified in the 18th century only to fall again to the French in 1793. Occupied by the Germans during World War II, it was the object of a heroic but unsuccessful attempt by British and Polish airborne troops to secure the Rhine bridges in September 1944. A British war memorial, cemetery, and museum in the suburb of Oosterbeek commemorate the battle.

Arnhem is a tourist centre and an industrial town. Industries include metallurgy, shipbuilding, and the manufacture of textiles, leather goods, electrical equipment, and chemicals.

Notable landmarks include a town hall (*c.* 1540), the Roman Catholic church of St. Walburgis (1422), the 15th-century Protestant Grote Kerk (St. Eusebius), and the modern provincial government house. The town has a municipal museum, and the aquarium and fish ponds of The Netherlands Society for Improving Moorland are in Sonsbeek Park. The Netherlands Open-Air Museum (1912), Hoge Veluwe National Park, Zuidelijke Veluwezoom National Park, and the Rijksmuseum Kröller-Müller (one of the major art collections in The Netherlands) are nearby. Pop. (1983 est.) *gemeenter,* 128,598; metropolitan area, 290,746.

Arnhem Land, historical region of northeastern Northern Territory, Australia, extending from Van Diemen Gulf southeastward to the Gulf of Carpentaria and Groote Eylandt. Never fully explored, it has a total area of about 37,000 sq mi (95,900 sq km) and includes a largely tropical plateau lying between the Roper and Victoria rivers. The name Arnhem Land is now used primarily for the large Aboriginal reserve in the area. It has been occupied by Aborigines since the late Pleistocene, and there are rock carvings at many sites. The northeast coast was visited in 1623 by the Dutch explorer Jan Carstensz, who named the region for his ship, "Arnhem" ("Aernem"). Since World War II bauxite and uranium mining have become important in the area.

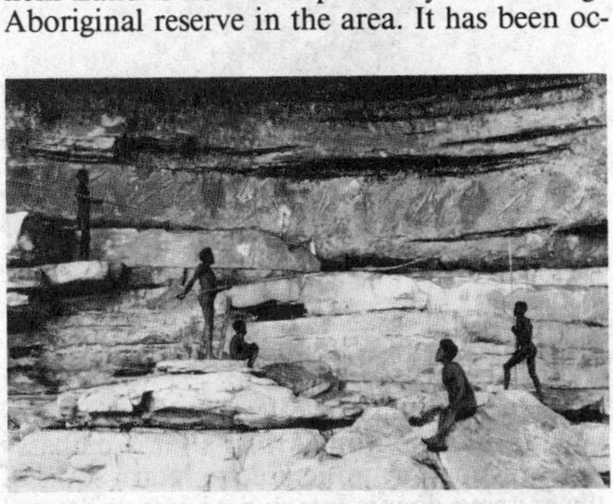

Aboriginal cave paintings, Arnhem Land, Northern Territory, Australia
By courtesy of the Australian Information Service

Árni Magnusson (Icelandic antiquarian): *see* Magnusson, Árni.

Arnica, genus of plants of the composite family (Asteraceae), most of whose approximately 50 species occur in northwestern North America. A typical species, *A. angustifolia,* of Arctic Asia and America, has narrow leaves and orange-yellow flower heads 5 to 7 centimetres (2 to 2.5 inches) across.

One of the most important species (*A. montana*) is a perennial herb of northern and central European highlands. It yields an essential oil formerly used in treating bruises and sprains.

Arniches (y Barrera), Carlos (b. Oct. 11, 1866, Alicante, Spain—d. April 16, 1943, Madrid), popular Spanish dramatist of the early 20th century, best known for works in the *género chico* ("lesser genre"): the one-act zarzuela (musical comedy) and the one-act *sainete* (sketch). These plays were based upon direct observation of the customs and speech of the lower class people of Madrid. He wrote some 270 of them and was considered a master of the genre, along with the Álvarez Quintero brothers. He spent the years of the Spanish Civil War (1936–39) in Buenos Aires and Paris.

Arnim, Achim von, byname of KARL JOACHIM FRIEDRICH LUDWIG VON ARNIM (b. Jan. 26, 1781, Berlin—d. Jan. 21, 1831, Wiepersdorf, Brandenburg), folklorist, dramatist, poet, and story writer whose collection of folk poetry was a major contribution to German Romanticism.

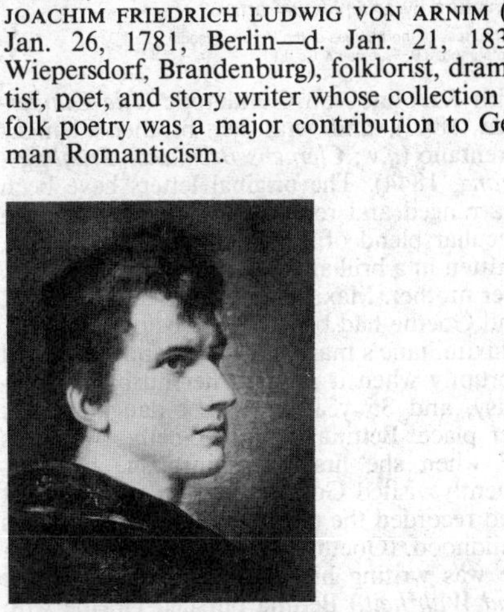

Achim von Arnim, oil painting by an unknown artist
Popperfoto

While a student at the University of Heidelberg, Arnim published jointly with Clemens Brentano a remarkable collection of folk poetry, *Des Knaben Wunderhorn* (*q.v.*; the title derives from the opening poem, which tells of a youth who brings the empress a magic horn). The first volume (published 1805, dated 1806) was dedicated to Goethe, who reviewed it appreciatively, though others criticized it for lacking philosophical accuracy. The collection was completed in 1808.

Arnim's numerous plays, poems, and novels are forgotten, but a few of his short stories—all strangely compounded of realism and fantasy—are notable contributions to German prose fiction. *See also* Arnim, Bettina von.

Arnim, Bettina von, byname of ELISABETH KATHARINA LUDOVICA MAGDALENA VON ARNIM, *née* BRENTANO (b. April 4, 1785, Frankfurt am Main—d. Jan. 20, 1859, Berlin), one of the outstanding women writers in modern German literature, memorable not only for her books but also for the personality they reflect. All of her writings, whatever their ostensible themes, are essentially self-portraits.

Gifted women played a prominent role in the German Romantic movement, and Bettina von Arnim was a Romantic par excellence. She was unconventional to the point of eccentricity; wayward, yet a loyal wife (she married Achim von Arnim [*q.v.*] in 1811) and a devoted mother to her seven children; susceptible and passionate, but jealous of her personal freedom; capable of enthusiastic devotion, yet absorbed in a cult of her own personality, which verged on narcissism. These paradoxes in her nature she projected into her books. Her three best known works purport to be records of her correspondence with Goethe (*Goethes Briefwechsel mit einem Kinde,* 1835; "Correspondence Between Goethe and a Child"),

Bettina von Arnim, engraving after Armgass von Arnim's copy of a miniature by an unknown artist

By courtesy of the trustees of the British Museum; photograph, J.R. Freeman & Co. Ltd.

with Karoline von Günderode (*Die Günderode,* 1840), and with her brother Clemens Brentano (*q.v.*; *Clemens Brentanos Frühlingskranz,* 1844). The original letters have been rearranged and retouched, the result being a peculiar blend of documentation and fiction, written in a brilliantly vivid, uninhibited style. Her mother, Maximiliane, *née* von La Roche, and Goethe had been friends before and after Maximiliane's marriage; this friendship ended abruptly when it aroused her husband's jealousy, and 35 years later her daughter took her place. Bettina idolized Goethe (who was 57 when she first met him); she had frequently visited Goethe's mother in Frankfurt and recorded the old lady's tales of the poet's childhood. (Goethe later used her notes when he was writing his autobiography, *Dichtung und Wahrheit.*) Bettina pursued Goethe with her attentions until in 1811 a public quarrel between her and Goethe's wife, Christiane, caused Goethe to disavow.

She stated her political views, which were sympathetic to the underprivileged, in two books written for the special benefit of the king of Prussia, Frederick William IV: *Dies Buch gehört dem König* (1843; "This Book Belongs to the King") and *Gespräche mit Dämonen* (1852; "Conversations with Demons"). Bettina was also a gifted sculptor and musician. In the diversity of her talents and interests, she exhibited the universality that has been regarded as the hallmark of the German Romantic spirit.

Arnim, Hans Georg von (b. 1581, Boitzenburg, Brandenburg— d. April 28 [April 18, old style], 1641, Dresden, Saxony), soldier and statesman prominent in German affairs during the Thirty Years' War. He served (1613–17) with the Swedes under Gustaf II Adolf, with the Poles (1621), with Wallenstein's imperial army (1626) as a field marshal, and with the Saxons (1631–35, 1638–41). A strict

Hans von Arnim, detail from an engraving by Martin Bernigeroth after an oil painting by an unknown artist

Archiv fur Kunst und Geschichte, West Berlin

Lutheran, Arnim resigned his imperial commission in protest against the Edict of Restitution (1629). Thereafter he worked for the creation of a "third party," under the Elector of Saxony, to hold the balance between the imperial court and the encroachment of Sweden, France, and Spain, and for a plan of general pacification. He left the Saxon Army in 1635 in protest over the Peace of Prague. Arrested by the Swedes (1637), he escaped and was reinstated in the Saxon Army (1638), but he died while preparing to oust the French and Swedes from German soil.

Arnim, Harry (Karl Kurt Eduard), Graf von (count of) (b. Oct. 3, 1824, Moitzelfitz, Pomerania—d. May 19, 1881, Nice, Fr.), Prussian diplomat whose opposition to Bismarck led to his prosecution and gave rise to the *Arnim Paragraphs*, an addition to the German criminal code that made unauthorized disclosures of official documents a criminal offense.

Arnim entered the diplomatic service in 1850 and served in Rome (1853–55), in Lisbon (1862), and as Prussian envoy to the Holy See (1864). At the first Vatican Council of 1869–70, he supported German bishops who opposed the doctrine of papal infallibility.

Arnim became Prussian envoy to France on Aug. 23, 1871, and ambassador on Jan. 9, 1872, arranging the Franco-German War reparations settlement in June. Soon he came into conflict with Bismarck.

In 1874 a Viennese newspaper published correspondence on the Vatican Council, including Arnim's confidential dispatches. The

Harry von Arnim

By courtesy of the Staatsbibliothek, West Berlin

subsequent inquiry revealed that more important documents from Arnim's Paris embassy were missing. Arnim refused to return some of the missing documents and so was suspected of keeping them in order to prove that his own French policy had been wiser than Bismarck's. Bismarck thereupon had him temporarily superannuated, then arrested (Oct. 4, 1874). Condemned to three months' imprisonment, Arnim appealed, but his sentence was increased to nine months.

Arnim went into exile and anonymously published *Pro Nihilo* (1875), a pamphlet attributing his disgrace to Bismarck's jealousy. Convicted of treason, of insulting the Emperor, and of libelling Bismarck, Arnim was sentenced in absentia to five years' penal servitude.

Arno, Peter, original name CURTIS ARNOUX PETERS (b. Jan. 8, 1904, New York City—d. Feb. 22, 1968, Port Chester, N.Y., U.S.), cartoonist whose satirical drawings, particularly of New York café society, did much to establish *The New Yorker* magazine's reputation for sophisticated humour.

While at Yale University (1922–24), Arno was particularly interested in music and organized his own band. He also decorated screens and panels for restaurants. After leaving Yale he went to New York City, where he joined the bohemian life of Greenwich Village and continued to do decorative painting. He was about to give up art to join a band when one of his cartoons was accepted by the newly established *New Yorker.* His association with the magazine lasted until his death.

In the late 1920s Arno's cartoons for *The New Yorker*, dealing with the city's aristocracy, became well known, and by 1931 he was the author of four cartoon books. In 1931 he was co-author of *Here Comes the Bride,* a musical satire produced in October of that year. A good-looking, sophisticated man, Arno played an active part in the world he satirized. Lecherous clubmen and sabled dowagers appeared frequently in his cartoons, collections of which include *Man in the Shower* (1944) and *Sizzling Platter* (1949).

Arno River, Italian FIUME ARNO, Latin ARNUS, principal stream of the Toscana (Tuscany) region, in central Italy. Rising on the slopes of Monte Falterona in the Tuscan Apennines, it flows for 150 mi (240 km) to the Ligurian Sea, receiving the Sieve, Pesa, Elsa, and Era rivers. Its drainage basin covers 3,184 sq mi (8,247 sq km). Navigation on the river is negligible. In its upper course the Arno flows generally south through the former lake basin called Casentino, to turn west and north at Arezzo. The fertile valley of its middle course is called the Valdarno.

Below Florence the river enters a gorge at Golfolina and begins its lower course westward past Empoli and Pisa to the sea, where the ancient delta has been reclaimed and the river reaches the sea through a single mouth. The valley of the Arno has been substantially modified by man: in its upper course the Val di Chiana now drains to the Tiber, and in its middle section are flood-control works (some designed by Leonardo da Vinci), though a sudden flood in 1966 inundated Florence.

Arnobius THE ELDER (fl. 4th century, Africa), early Christian convert who defended Christianity by demonstrating to the pagans their own inconsistencies.

Arnobius was born a pagan but had become a Christian by AD 300. He taught rhetoric at Sicca Veneria in Africa during the reign (284–305) of the Roman emperor Diocletian. Because of his former paganism, Arnobius was suspected, notably by the local bishop, and as a pledge of his conviction he composed the seven books *Adversus nationes* (*c.* 303; "Against the Pagans"). Nothing further is known about his life.

A general defense of Christianity from pagan calumnies (books 1 and 2) is followed by attacks on Neoplatonism, anthropomorphism, and heathen mythology (books 3–5), concluding with worship of images, temples, and ceremonials (books 6 and 7).

Arnold OF BRESCIA, Italian ARNALDO DA BRESCIA (b. *c.* 1100, Brescia, Rep. of Venice—d. *c.* June 1155, Civita Castellana or Monterotondo, Papal States), radical religious reformer noted for his outspoken criticism of clerical wealth and corruption and for his strenuous opposition to the temporal power of the popes. He was prior of the monastery at Brescia, where in 1137 he participated in a popular revolt against the government of Bishop Manfred. His proposals for reforming the clergy and for ending the church's temporal powers caused him to be condemned as a schismatic by Pope Innocent II in 1139.

Banished from Italy, Arnold went to France, where he became a supporter of the renowned theologian and philosopher Peter Abelard. Both were condemned as heretics at the Council of Sens, Fr., in 1141, through the influence of St. Bernard of Clairvaux. Though Abelard submitted, Arnold defiantly continued teaching in Paris until, through the insistence of Bernard, he was exiled by King Louis VII the Young of France in 1141. Arnold fled first to Zürich, then to Passau, Ger., where he was protected by Cardinal Guido, through whose mediation he was reconciled with Pope Eugenius III at Viterbo, Papal States, in September 1145.

Two years earlier the *renovatio senatus* ("renewal of the Senate"), seeking independence from ecclesiastical control, had expelled Innocent and the cardinals, revived the ancient senate, and proclaimed Rome a republic. Eugenius sent Arnold to Rome on a penitential pilgrimage. He soon allied himself with the insurgents and resumed his preaching against the Pope and cardinals. He was excommunicated in July 1148. Arnold's agitation for ecclesiastical reform vitalized the revolt against the Pope as temporal ruler, and he soon controlled the Romans. He also worked to consolidate the citizens' newly won independence.

Pope Adrian IV placed Rome under interdict in 1155 and asked the citizens to surrender Arnold. The Senate submitted, the republic collapsed, and the papal government was restored. Arnold, who had fled, was captured by the forces of the Holy Roman emperor Frederick I Barbarossa, then visiting Rome for his imperial coronation. Arnold was tried by an ecclesiastical tribunal, condemned for heresy, and transferred to the Emperor for execution. He was hanged, his body burned, and his ashes cast into the Tiber River.

Arnold's character was austere and his mode of life ascetic. His followers, known as Arnoldists, postulated an incompatibility between spiritual power and material possessions and rejected any temporal powers of the church. They were condemned in 1184 at the Synod of Verona, Rep. of Venice. Arnold's personality has been distorted through modern poets and dramatists and Italian politicians. He was foremost a religious reformer, constrained by circumstances to become a political revolutionary. G.W. Greenaway's *Arnold of Brescia,* with full bibliography, appeared in 1931.

Arnold, Benedict (b. Jan. 14, 1741, Norwich, Conn.—d. June 14, 1801, London), patriot officer who served the cause of the American Revolution until 1779, when he shifted his allegiance to the British; thereafter his name became an epithet for traitor in the U.S.

Upon the outbreak of hostilities at Lexington, Mass. (April 1775), Arnold volunteered for service and participated with Ethan Allen in the successful colonial attack on British-held Ft. Ticonderoga, N.Y., the following month. That autumn he was appointed by Gen. George Washington to command an expedition to capture Quebec. He marched with 700 men by way of the Maine wilderness, a remarkable feat of woodsmanship and endurance, and, reinforced by Gen. Richard Montgomery, attacked the well-fortified city. The combined assault (Dec. 31, 1775) failed, Montgomery was killed, and Arnold was severely wounded.

Promoted to the rank of brigadier general, Arnold constructed a flotilla on Lake Champlain and inflicted severe losses on a greatly superior enemy fleet near Valcour Island, N.Y. (Oct. 11, 1776). He returned a hero, but his rash courage and impatient energy had aroused the enmity of several other officers. When in February 1777 Congress created five new major generalships, Arnold was passed over in favour of his juniors. Arnold resented this affront, and only Washington's personal persuasion kept him from resigning.

Two months later he repelled a British attack on Danbury, Conn., and was made a major general, but his seniority was not restored and Arnold felt his honour impugned. Again he tried to resign, but in July he accepted a government order to help stem the British advance into upper New York. He won a victory at Ft. Stanwix (now Rome) in August 1777 and commanded advance battalions at the Battle of Saratoga that autumn, fighting brilliantly until seriously wounded. For his services he was restored to his proper relative rank.

Crippled from his wounds, Arnold was placed in command of Philadelphia (June

Benedict Arnold, engraving by H.B. Hall, 1865

By courtesy of the Library of Congress, Washington, D.C.

1778), where he socialized with families of Loyalist sympathies and lived extravagantly. To raise money, he violated several state and military regulations, arousing the suspicions and, finally, the denunciations of Pennsylvania's supreme executive council. These charges were then referred to Congress, and Arnold asked for an immediate court-martial to clear himself.

Meanwhile, in April 1779, Arnold married Margaret (Peggy) Shippen, a young woman of Loyalist sympathies. Early in May he made secret overtures to British headquarters, and a year later he informed the British of a proposed American invasion of Canada. He later revealed that he expected to obtain the command of West Point, N.Y., and asked the British for £20,000 for betraying this post. When his British contact, Maj. John André, was captured by the Americans, Arnold escaped on a British ship, leaving André to be hanged as a spy. The sacrifice of André made Arnold odious to Loyalists, and his reputation was further tarnished among his former neighbours when he led a raid on New London, Conn., in September 1781.

At the end of 1781 Arnold went to England, where he remained, inactive, ostracized, and ailing, for the rest of his life.

Arnold, Sir Edwin (b. June 10, 1832, Gravesend, Kent, Eng.—d. March 24, 1904, London), poet and scholar, best known as the author of *The Light of Asia* (1879), an epic poem that tells, in elaborate language, of the life and teachings of the Buddha. *The Light of the World* (1891), on the Christian theme, was less successful. From 1873 Arnold was chief editor of *The Daily Telegraph* of London. Before joining the *Telegraph,* he had

Sir Edwin Arnold, pencil drawing by A.-P. Cole, 1903; in the National Portrait Gallery, London

By courtesy of the National Portrait Gallery, London

been principal of the British government college at Poona (Pune), India. He was knighted in 1888.

Arnold, Harold De Forest (b. Sept. 3, 1883, Woodstock, Conn., U.S.—d. July 10, 1933, Summit, N.J.), physicist whose research led to the development of long-distance telephony and radio communication.

Arnold studied at Ohio Wesleyan University, Delaware, Ohio, and earned a doctorate at the University of Chicago in 1911. While working for the Western Electric Company, he developed and designed the manufacturing methods for reliable high-vacuum triodes (thermionic tubes) used to provide the amplification needed for transcontinental (1914) and intercontinental (1915) radio telephony.

Arnold also contributed to the development of new magnetic alloys (permalloy and permivar) used in sound reproduction and electroacoustics. In 1925 he was appointed the first director of research of the Bell Telephone Laboratories.

Arnold, Henry Harley, byname HAP ARNOLD (b. June 25, 1886, Gladwyne, Pa., U.S.—d. Jan. 15, 1950, Sonoma, Calif.), air strategist, commanding general of the U.S. Army Air Corps in World War II, who long and successfully advocated a separate air force ranking equally with the Army and the Navy.

Arnold graduated from the U.S. Military Academy at West Point, N.Y., (1907), and in 1911 received flying instruction from Orville Wright. He rose in the ranks of the Air Corps; becoming chief in 1938. Despite the isolationism then prevailing in the U.S., he urged increased appropriations for the air establishment and military aid to the Allies. During the war he commanded the U.S. Army Air

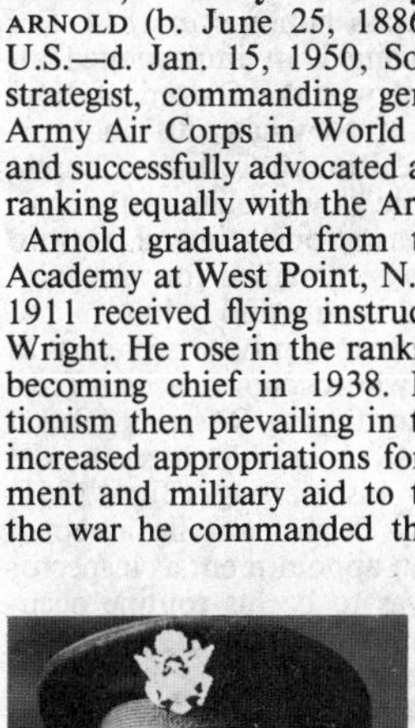

Gen. Hap Arnold

By courtesy of the Library of Congress, Washington, D.C.

Corps throughout the world and served as air representative on the U.S. Joint Chiefs of

Staff and the Allied Combined Chiefs of Staff, greatly influencing strategic air bombardment. In December 1944 he was promoted general of the Army (five stars; later general of the Air Force, the first to hold this rank). The National Defense Act of 1947 created the autonomous Air Force for which he had worked.

Arnold, Mary Augusta: *see* Ward, Mrs. Humphry.

Arnold, Matthew (b. Dec. 24, 1822, Laleham, Middlesex, Eng.—d. April 15, 1888, Liverpool), English Victorian poet and literary and social critic, noted especially for his classical attacks on the contemporary tastes and

Matthew Arnold, detail of an oil painting by G.F. Watts; in the National Portrait Gallery, London

By courtesy of the National Portrait Gallery, London

manners of the "Barbarians" (the aristocracy), the "Philistines" (the commercial middle class), and the "Populace." He became the apostle of "culture" in such works as *Culture and Anarchy* (1869).

Life. Matthew was the eldest son of the renowned Thomas Arnold, who was appointed headmaster of Rugby School in 1828. Matthew entered Rugby (1837) and then attended Oxford as a scholar of Balliol College; there he won the Newdigate Prize with his poem *Cromwell* (1843) and was graduated with second-class honours in 1844. For Oxford Arnold retained an impassioned affection. His Oxford was the Oxford of John Henry Newman—of Newman just about to be received into the Roman Catholic Church; and although Arnold's own religious thought, like his father's, was strongly liberal, Oxford and Newman always remained for him joint symbols of spiritual beauty and culture.

In 1847 Arnold became private secretary to Lord Lansdowne, who occupied a high Cabinet post during Lord John Russell's Liberal ministries. And in 1851, in order to secure the income needed for his marriage (June 1851) with Frances Lucy Wightman, he accepted from Lansdowne an appointment as inspector of schools. This was to be his routine occupation until within two years of his death. He engaged in incessant travelling throughout the British provinces and also several times was sent by the government to inquire into the state of education in France, Germany, Holland, and Switzerland. Two of his reports on schools abroad were reprinted as books, and his annual reports on schools at home attracted wide attention, written, as they were, in Arnold's own urbane and civilized prose.

Poetic achievement. The work that gives Arnold his high place in the history of literature and the history of ideas was all accomplished in the time he could spare from his official duties. His first volume of verse was *The Strayed Reveller, and Other Poems. By A.* (1849); this was followed (in 1852) by another under the same initial: *Empedocles on Etna, and Other Poems.* In 1853 appeared the first volume of poems published under his own name; it consisted partly of poems selected from the earlier volumes and also contained the well-known preface explaining (among other things) why *Empedocles* was excluded from the selection: it was a dramatic poem "in which the suffering finds no vent in action," in which there is "everything to be endured, nothing to be done." This preface foreshadows his later criticism in its insistence upon the classic virtues of unity, impersonality, universality, and architectonic power and upon the value of the classical masterpieces as models for "an age of spiritual discomfort"—an age "wanting in moral grandeur." Other editions followed, and *Merope*, Arnold's classical tragedy, appeared in 1858, and *New Poems* in 1867. After that date, though there were further editions, Arnold wrote little additional verse.

Not much of Arnold's verse will stand the test of his own criteria; far from being classically poised, impersonal, serene, and grand, it is often intimate, personal, full of romantic regret, sentimental pessimism, and nostalgia. As a public and social character and as a prose writer, Arnold was sunny, debonair, and sanguine; but beneath ran the current of his buried life, and of this much of his poetry is the echo:

From the soul's subterranean depth upborne
As from an infinitely distant land,
Come airs, and floating echoes, and convey
A melancholy into all our day.

"I am past thirty," he wrote a friend in 1853, "and three parts iced over." The impulse to write poetry came typically when

A bolt is shot back somewhere in the breast,
And a lost pulse of feeling stirs again.

Though he was "never quite benumb'd by the world's sway," these hours of insight became more and more rare, and the stirrings of buried feeling were associated with moods of regret for lost youth, regret for the freshness of the early world, moods of self-pity, moods of longing for

The hills where his life rose
And the sea where it goes.

Yet, though much of Arnold's most characteristic verse is in this vein of soliloquy or intimate confession, he can sometimes rise, as in "Sohrab and Rustum," to epic severity and impersonality; to lofty meditation, as in "Dover Beach"; and to sustained magnificence and richness, as in "The Scholar Gipsy" and "Thyrsis"—where he wields an intricate stanza form without a stumble.

In 1857, assisted by the vote of his godfather (and predecessor) John Keble, Arnold was elected to the Oxford chair of poetry, which he held for 10 years. It was characteristic of him that he revolutionized this professorship. The keynote was struck in his inaugural lecture: "On the Modern Element in Literature," "modern" being taken to mean not merely "contemporary" (for Greece was "modern"), but the spirit that, contemplating the vast and complex spectacle of life, craves for moral and intellectual "deliverance." Several of the lectures were afterward published as critical essays, but the most substantial fruits of his professorship were the three lectures *On Translating Homer* (1861)—in which he recommended Homer's plainness and nobility as medicine for the modern world, with its "sick hurry and divided aims" and condemned Francis Newman's recent translation as ignoble and eccentric—and the lectures *On the Study of Celtic Literature* (1867), in which, without much knowledge of his subject or of anthropology, he used the Celtic strain as a symbol of that which rejects the despotism of the commonplace and the utilitarian.

Arnold as critic. It is said that when the poet in Arnold died, the critic was born; and it is true that from this time onward he turned almost entirely to prose. Some of the leading ideas and phrases were early put into currency in *Essays in Criticism* (First Series, 1865; Second Series, 1888) and *Culture and Anarchy.* The first essay in the 1865 volume, "The Function of Criticism at the Present Time," is an overture announcing briefly most of the themes he developed more fully in later work. It is at once evident that he ascribes to "criticism" a scope and importance hitherto undreamed of. The function of criticism, in his sense, is "a disinterested endeavour to learn and propagate the best that is known and thought in the world, and thus to establish a current of fresh and true ideas." It is in fact a spirit that he is trying to foster, the spirit of an awakened and informed intelligence playing upon not "literature" merely but theology, history, art, science, sociology, and politics, and in every sphere seeking "to see the object as in itself it really is."

In this critical effort, thought Arnold, England lagged behind France and Germany, and the English accordingly remained in a backwater of provinciality and complacency. Even the great Romantic poets, with all their creative energy, suffered from the want of it. The English literary critic must know literatures other than his own and be in touch with European standards. This last line of thought Arnold develops in the second essay, "The Literary Influence of Academies," in which he dwells upon "the note of provinciality" in English literature, caused by remoteness from a "centre" of correct knowledge and correct taste. To realize how much Arnold widened the horizons of criticism requires only a glance at the titles of some of the other essays in *Essays in Criticism* (1865): "Maurice de Guérin," "Eugénie de Guérin," "Heinrich Heine," "Joubert," "Spinoza," "Marcus Aurelius"; in all these, as increasingly in his later books, he is "applying modern ideas to life" as well as to letters and "bringing all things under the point of view of the 19th century."

The first essay in the 1888 volume, "The Study of Poetry," was originally published as the general introduction to T.H. Ward's anthology, *The English Poets* (1880). It contains many of the ideas for which Arnold is best remembered. In an age of crumbling creeds, poetry will have to replace religion. More and more, we will "turn to poetry to interpret life for us, to console us, to sustain us." Therefore we must know how to distinguish the best poetry from the inferior, the genuine from the counterfeit; and to do this we must steep ourselves in the work of the acknowledged masters, using as "touchstones" passages exemplifying their "high seriousness," and their superiority of diction and movement.

The remaining essays, with the exception of the last two (on Tolstoy and Amiel), all deal with English poets: Milton, Gray, Keats, Wordsworth, Byron, and Shelley. All contain memorable things, and all attempt a serious and responsible assessment of each poet's "criticism of life" and his value as food for the modern spirit. Arnold has been taken to task for some of his judgments and omissions: for his judgment that Dryden and Pope were not "genuine" poets because they composed in their wits instead of "in the soul"; for calling Gray a "minor classic" in an age of prose and spiritual bleakness; for paying too much attention to the man behind the poetry (Gray, Keats, Shelley); for making no mention of Donne; and above all for saying that poetry is "at bottom a criticism of life." On this last point it should be remembered that he added "under the conditions fixed. . .by the laws of poetic truth and poetic beauty," and that if by "criticism" is understood (as Arnold meant) "evaluation," Arnold's dictum is seen to have wider significance than has been sometimes supposed.

Culture and Anarchy is in some ways Arnold's most central work. It is an expansion of his earlier attacks, in "The Function of Criticism" and "Heinrich Heine," upon the smugness, philistinism, and mammon worship of Victorian England. Culture, as "the study of perfection," is opposed to the prevalent "anarchy" of a new democracy without standards and without a sense of direction. By "turning a stream of fresh thought upon our stock notions and habits," culture seeks to make "reason and the will of God prevail."

Arnold's classification of English society into Barbarians (with their high spirit, serenity, and distinguished manners and their inaccessibility to ideas), Philistines (the stronghold of religious nonconformity, with plenty of energy and morality but insufficient "sweetness and light"), and Populace (still raw and blind) is well known. Arnold saw in the Philistines the key to the whole position; they were now the most influential section of society; their strength was the nation's strength, their crudeness its crudeness: Educate and humanize the Philistines, therefore. Arnold saw in the idea of "the State," and not in any one class of society, the true organ and repository of the nation's collective "best self." No summary can do justice to this extraordinary book; it can still be read with pure enjoyment, for it is written with an inward poise, a serene detachment, and an infusion of mental laughter, which make it a masterpiece of ridicule as well as a searching analysis of Victorian society. The same is true of its unduly neglected sequel, *Friendship's Garland* (1871).

Religious writings. Lastly Arnold turned to religion, the constant preoccupation and true centre of his whole life, and wrote *St. Paul and Protestantism* (1870), *Literature and Dogma* (1873), *God and the Bible* (1875), and *Last Essays on Church and Religion* (1877). In these books, Arnold really founded Anglican "modernism." Like all religious liberals, he came under fire from two sides: from the orthodox, who accused him of infidelity, of turning God into a "stream of tendency" and of substituting vague emotion for definite belief; and from the infidels, for clinging to the church and retaining certain Christian beliefs of which he had undermined the foundations. Arnold considered his religious writings to be constructive and conservative. Those who accused him of destructiveness did not realize how far historical and scientific criticism had already riddled the old foundations; and those who accused him of timidity failed to see that he regarded religion as the highest form of culture, the one indispensable without which all secular education is in vain. His attitude is best summed up in his own words (from the preface to *God and the Bible*): "At the present moment two things about the Christian religion must surely be clear to anybody with eyes in his head. One is, that men cannot do without it; the other, that they cannot do with it as it is." Convinced that much in popular religion was "touched with the finger of death" and convinced no less of the hopelessness of man without religion, he sought to find for religion a basis of "scientific fact" that even the positive modern spirit must accept. A reading of Arnold's *Note Books* will convince any reader of the depth of Arnold's spirituality and of the degree to which, in his "buried life," he disciplined himself in constant devotion and self-forgetfulness.

Arnold died suddenly, of heart failure, in the spring of 1888, at Liverpool and was buried at Laleham, with the three sons whose early loss had shadowed his life. (B.W./Ed.)

MAJOR WORKS. *Poetical works. Alaric at Rome* (1840; Rugby School prize poem); *Cromwell* (1843; Newdigate Prize poem); *The Strayed Reveller, and Other Poems. By A.* (1849); *Empedocles on Etna, and Other Poems. By A.* (1852); *Poems* (1853; including "Sohrab and Rustum," "The Forsaken Merman," and "The Scholar Gipsy"); *Poems, Second Series* (1855); *Merope* (1858; classical tragedy); *New Poems* (1867; including "Thyrsis" and "Dover Beach").

Prose works. The Popular Education of France with Notices of That of Holland and Switzerland (1861; revised text of the 1860 report prepared by Arnold for the Education Commission); *On Translating Homer* (1861); *On Translating Homer: Last Words* (1862); *A French Eton: or, Middle Class Education and the State* (1864); *Essays in Criticism* (1865; including "The Function of Criticism at the Present Time," "The Literary Influence of Academies," "Maurice de Guérin," "Eugénie de Guérin," "Heinrich Heine," "Joubert," "Spinoza," and "Marcus Aurelius"); *On the Study of Celtic Literature* (1867); *Schools and Universities on the Continent* (1868; reprinted from Arnold's report *On Secondary Education in Foreign Countries* of 1866); *Culture and Anarchy* (1869); *St. Paul and Protestantism* (1870); *Friendship's Garland* (1871); *Literature and Dogma* (1873); *God and the Bible* (1875); *Last Essays on Church and Religion* (1877); *Mixed Essays* (1879); *Irish Essays* (1882); *Discourses in America* (1885); *Essays in Criticism. Second Series* (1888; including "The Study of Poetry" and essays on Milton, Thomas Gray, Keats, Wordsworth, Byron, Shelley, Tolstoy, and Amiel); *Reports on Elementary Schools 1852–1882*, edited by Sir Francis Sandford (1889; new edition with added material and introduction by F.S. Marvin, 1908).

BIBLIOGRAPHY. A new and complete edition of Arnold's poems was published in "Oxford Standard Authors Series" (1950), ed. by C.B. Tinker and H.F. Lowry. *Arnold's Letters (1848–1888)*, collected and arranged by G.W.E. Russell (1895; 2nd ed., 1901); Arnold Whitridge (ed.), *Unpublished Letters* (1923); *Letters to Arthur Hugh Clough*, with an introductory study by H.F. Lowry (ed.) (1932, reprinted 1968). There is a complete edition (literary contents) of *The Note-Books of Matthew Arnold*, ed. by H.F. Lowry, K. Young, and W.H. Dunn (1952). An edition deluxe of Arnold's complete *Works*, 15 vol. (1903–04), includes a bibliography by T.B. Smart. For a more recent bibliography, see T.G. Ehrsam and R.H. Deily (comps.), *Bibliographies of Twelve Victorian Authors* (1936; suppl. by J.G. Fucilla in *Modern Philology*, 37:89–96, 1939).

It was Arnold's expressed desire that his biography should not be written; there are, however, a number of monographs and biographico-critical works, among them Lionel Trilling, *Matthew Arnold* (1939), the best full-length study; J. Dover Wilson, *Leslie Stephen and Matthew Arnold As Critics of Wordsworth* (1939); Sir E.K. Chambers, *Matthew Arnold: A Study* (1947); J.D. Jump, *Matthew Arnold*, "Men and Books Series" (1955); G. Robert Stange, *Matthew Arnold: The Poet As Humanist* (1967).

Arnold, Samuel (b. Aug. 10, 1740, London—d. Oct. 22, 1802, London), composer whose 36-volume edition of Handel (1786–97), although shown defective by later scholarship, was the earliest attempt to publish a composer's complete works.

Samuel Arnold, detail of a pencil drawing by G. Dance, 1795; in the National Portrait Gallery, London

By courtesy of the National Portrait Gallery, London

Educated at Chapel Royal, Arnold became composer to Covent Garden Theatre; his first annual production was *The Maid of the Mill* (1765). Subsequent positions were as music director of the Theatre Royal in the Haymarket (1777), organist and composer to the Chapel Royal (1783), and organist at Westminster Abbey (1793). His compositions include sonatas, symphonies, and oratorios, as well as ballad operas, farces, and pantomimes. His *Cathedral Music* (1790), a collection of service music, was an important supplement to William Boyce's *Cathedral Music*.

Consult the INDEX *first*

Arnold, Thomas (b. June 13, 1795, East Cowes, Isle of Wight, Eng.—d. June 12, 1842, Rugby, Warwickshire), educator who, as headmaster of Rugby School, had much influence on public school education in England. He was the father of the poet and critic Matthew Arnold.

Thomas Arnold was educated at Winchester and at Corpus Christi College, Oxford. He was elected a fellow of Oriel College, Oxford, in 1815. After ordination and marriage he settled at Laleham, Middlesex, in 1819 as a tutor to university entrants. In 1828 he became headmaster of Rugby and gradually raised it to the rank of a great public school.

Thomas Arnold, detail of an engraving by H. Cousins, 1840, after an oil painting by Thomas Philips

By courtesy of the trustees of the British Museum; photograph, J.R. Freeman & Co. Ltd.

Arnold was not an innovator in teaching method; his aim was to reform Rugby by making it a school for gentlemen. He used prefects more fully than any previous headmaster. Under the prefect system the older boys served as house monitors to keep discipline among the younger boys; this system was adopted in most English secondary schools. The Arnold tradition spread to other schools through Rugby pupils and masters, and many schools established after Arnold's death were modelled on Rugby.

Arnold was the author of five volumes of sermons, an edition of Thucydides, and a three-volume history of Rome. Arthur Penrhyn Stanley's *Life and Correspondence of Dr. Arnold*, 2 vol. (1844), was followed by Sir Joshua Fitch's *Thomas and Matthew Arnold, and Their Influence on English Education* (1897). Lytton Strachey included a sketch of Arnold in *Eminent Victorians* (1918).

Arnold Arboretum of Harvard University, major botanical research centre famous for its collection of ornamental trees and shrubs from the Orient. Founded in 1872 in Jamaica Plain, Boston, the 262-acre (106-hectare) arboretum has acquired and cultivated more than 6,000 species of woody plants. Of special importance are its Oriental cherries, forsythias, lilacs, honeysuckles, oaks, magnolias, conifers, dwarf evergreens, and Asiatic trees. The arboretum maintains an herbarium comprising more than 1,000,000 reference specimens, principally from eastern Asia and New Guinea. It also publishes the *Journal of the Arnold Arboretum* and *Arnoldia.*

Arnoldson, Klas Pontus (b. Oct. 27, 1844, Göteborg, Swed.—d. Feb. 20, 1916, Stockholm), politician, figured prominently in solving the problems of the Norwegian-Swedish Union, co-winner (with Fredrik Bajer) of the Nobel Peace Prize in 1908.

Arnoldson became a railway clerk and rose to stationmaster (1871–81) but then left the railway to devote himself entirely to politics and peace. In 1881 he was elected to the Riksdag, the Swedish parliament. A passionately devoted pacifist, Arnoldson supported the neutrality of the Nordic countries and in 1883 helped to found the Swedish Association for Peace and Conciliation.

From 1890, when the conflict between Norway and Sweden was critical, Arnoldson used all his powers, including his gift for inspiring oratory, to shape public opinion in both countries in favour of a peaceful settlement. In 1905 he saw the result of his work in the mutually agreed dissolution of the union.

Arnolfo DI CAMBIO (b. *c.* 1245—d. March 8, 1302, Florence), sculptor and architect, designer of the cathedral, or Duomo, in Florence, whose works embody the transition between the late Gothic and Renaissance architectural sensibilities. He was reputed in his own time to be the best architect in Tuscany.

Arnolfo studied painting under Cimabue and sculpture under Nicola Pisano. He served as assistant to Pisano in 1265–68 in the production of the pulpit for the Siena cathedral. Arnolfo went to Rome in 1277 as the protégé of Charles of Anjou, King of Sicily, at which time he may have produced the monument of Cardinal Annibaldi in S. Giovanni in Laterano (now disassembled) and the tomb of Pope Adrian V in the church of S. Francesco, Viterbo. In 1281 he executed a fountain at Perugia, figures from which survive in the Galleria Nazionale dell'Umbria. The following year he constructed a monument to Cardinal de Braye (died 1282) in S. Domenico at Orvieto and subsequently designed altar canopies for S. Paolo Fuori le Mura (1285) and Sta. Cecilia in Trastevere (1293) in Rome.

In 1296 Arnolfo returned to Florence to undertake his most important commission, the building of the Duomo and the carving of statues for its facade, now in the Museo dell'Opera del Duomo. Strongly influenced by antique art, he seems to have been responsible for imposing on Florentine Gothic sculpture and architecture the austere character it retained throughout the 14th century, exhibited in works traditionally credited to him, such as the design of the Palazzo Vecchio (Palazzo della Signoria), the church of Sta. Croce, and the choir of the Badia (Benedictine abbey).

Arnoul (French personal name): *see under* Arnulf.

Arnsberg, *Regierungsbezirk* (administrative district), east central Nordrhein-Westfalen *Land* (North Rhine-Westphalia state), north central West Germany. Arnsberg is bordered by Hessen (Hesse) *Land* to the east, Rheinland-Pfalz (Rhineland-Palatinate) *Land* to the southwest, and the *Regierungsbezirke* of Köln and Düsseldorf to the west and Münster and Detmold to the north. The largest of five districts in Nordrhein-Westfalen, it occupies an area of 3,088 sq mi (7,998 sq km) and is coextensive with the southern portion of the larger historic region of Westphalia (*q.v.*). Arnsberg district was created in 1816 and takes its name from that of its administrative seat.

The level, loess-covered Hellweg plateau, a historic routeway and zone of early settlement, runs east–west across northern Arnsberg between the Lippe (north) and Ruhr (south) rivers. The heavily industrialized Ruhr urban complex, and the immense Ruhr bituminous coalfield, extend east from Düsseldorf *Regierungsbezirk* across the western Hellweg to Hamm. Five cities in the Ruhr complex of Arnsberg—Dortmund (the largest city in the district), Bochum, Herne, Hamm, and Witten—have populations of more than 100,000. Population densities in these urban areas often exceed 7,800 persons per sq mi (3,000 per sq km). Dortmund is a major centre of heavy iron and steel processing. It is also a major manufacturer of heavy machine tools and is famous for its breweries. The eastern Hellweg is a fertile agricultural region centred on the Soester Börde. Sugar beets, vegetables, and fruits are the chief crops.

The Sauerland, the most northerly plateau of the Middle Rhine Highlands, comprises the southern three-quarters of Arnsberg. The region is bounded on the north by the Ruhr River and its tributary the Möhne and on the south by the Sieg River and the Westerwald (mountains). The chief city of the highly industrialized Sieg valley is Siegen, important for its production of special quality iron and steel. Northeast of Siegen the upwarped ridge of the heavily forested Rothaargebirge (mountains) rises to 2,759 ft (841 m) in altitude at the heath-covered Kahler Asten and forms a natural frontier with Hessen. From the Rothaargebirge the Sauerland plateau slopes gradually to the north and northwest and is increasingly dissected by the tributaries of the Ruhr and Rhine rivers. Numerous dams and reservoirs in the deep river valleys supply water to the Ruhr urban industrial complex. Population densities range from fewer than 130 persons per sq mi (50 per sq km) in the Rothaargebirge, Ebbegebirge, and Arnsberger Wald highlands to densities averaging about 2,600 persons per sq mi (1,000 per sq km) along the northern fringes near the cities of Hagen, Lüdenscheid, and Arnsberg. In the area of the former northwestern County of Mark, many medium and small towns specialize in the manufacture of machinery, hardware, and electrical equipment. Pasture farming and forestry occur in some of the lower valleys, and tourism is growing at a number of health and winter sports resorts, including Winterberg and Schmallenberg.

The majority of the population of Arnsberg *Regierungsbezirk* are descendants of the western Saxons and speak a Low German dialect. There is also a strong Frankish influence in regions of the Sauerland where the Ripuarian Franconian dialect is often spoken. More than 50 percent of the people are Protestants and about 40 percent are Roman Catholics. The predominant rural settlement pattern is one of dispersed farmsteads and small hamlets of half-timbered houses. Higher education in the district is centred at universities in Bochum, Dortmund, and Siegen. Pop. (1983 est.) 3,647,249.

Arnsberg, city, Nordrhein-Westfalen *Land* (North Rhine-Westphalia state), north central West Germany, on a loop of the Ruhr River, east of Iserlohn. Situated between wooded mountains and known as the Pearl of the Sauerland (southern land of Westphalia), it is a popular spa and summer resort. Arnsberg originated in the 11th century around a castle of the counts of Werl and was chartered in 1238. The countship of Arnsberg was under the jurisdiction of the electors of Cologne after the 12th century and was the main seat of the Westphalian fehmic courts (or Vehmgericht; medieval secret tribunals that usurped many functions of government). The ruins of the old castle and the 13th–14th century church of Wedinghausen Abbey are notable.

Industries include paper milling, woodworking, manufacture of metalware, and brewing. Pop. (1983 est.) 76,471.

Arnstadt, city, Erfurt *Bezirk* (district), southwestern East Germany, on the Gera River, at the northern edge of the Thüringer Wald (forest), just southwest of Erfurt city. First mentioned in 704 and chartered in 1266, it was bought in 1306 from the abbey of Hersfeld by the counts of Schwarzburg, who lived there until 1716. Their palace, Monplaisir (1703–07), survives, and the 12th–14th-century Liebfrauenkirche (Church of Our Lady) has many Schwarzburg graves. Several members of the Bach family worked in Arnstadt in the 17th century. J.S. Bach was organist of Boniface (now called Bach) Church from 1703 to 1707. The town hall dates from 1583–85. Northward rise the castle-crowned peaks, the Drei Gleichen (Three Alike).

Noted for its glove-manufacturing industries, Arnstadt also has glassworks, wood-finishing works, engineering works, leather-processing works, and foundries. There are many holiday and convalescent homes belonging to the Confederation of Free German Trade Unions. Pop. (1981 est.) 29,980.

Arnulf, also called ARNULF OF CARINTHIA, German ARNULF VON KÄRNTEN (d. Dec. 8, 899), duke of Carinthia, who deposed his uncle, the Holy Roman emperor Charles the Fat, and became king of Germany, later briefly wearing the crown of the emperor.

The illegitimate son of Charles the Fat's eldest brother, Carloman, and great-great-grandson of Charlemagne, Arnulf was chosen king by German leaders in 887, after Charles's failure to resist the Vikings vigorously enough. Ambitious for power, Arnulf acquired as vassals Odo, count of Paris, the new king of France; Berengar, marquis of Friuli, who was elected king of Italy; and Rudolph of Burgundy. In 889, when Berengar lost the throne of Italy to Guy of Spoleto, Pope Stephen V called on Arnulf to intervene; but, busy fighting the Slavs

Arnulf, seal, 9th century; in the Bayerisches Nationalmuseum, Munich

By courtesy of the Bayerisches Nationalmuseum, Munich; photograph, Foto Marburg

in Moravia, he was unable to respond, and in February 891 Guy was crowned emperor. Four months later Arnulf marched north to inflict a crushing defeat on the Vikings at the Dyle River, north of Brussels.

In 893, after reluctantly crowning Guy of Spoleto's son, Lambert, co-emperor, the new pope, Formosus, sought help against the Emperor from Arnulf, who invaded Italy in January 894, seizing Bergamo and quickly conquering Milan and Pavia. He next marched south to attack Guy, but defections among his troops forced him to abandon the campaign and withdraw across the Alps. His retreat was harassed by his own vassal, Rudolph of Burgundy; in retaliation, Arnulf sent his illegitimate son, Zwentibold, to pillage Burgundy.

When King Odo was deposed and the 13-year-old Charles the Simple was crowned king of France (893), Arnulf summoned Odo and Charles to Worms to end the civil war. Odo went; Charles refused. Arnulf threw his support to Odo, at the same time giving Zwentibold the crown of Lotharingia (now Lorraine).

After Guy of Spoleto's death in 894, Pope Formosus urged Arnulf to invade Italy once more. Crossing the Alps in October 895, Arnulf, although handicapped by bad weather, illness, and the absence of expected support from Berengar of Friuli, appeared before the walls of Rome. Rome fell, and in St. Peter's on Feb. 22, 896, Arnulf was crowned emperor by Formosus, who declared Lambert deposed. After a two-week stay in the city, Arnulf marched south to settle accounts with his rival at Spoleto, but en route he was suddenly taken ill and had to return to Germany. Lambert remained emperor despite the Pope's action.

The last three years of Arnulf's life, during which his illness continued, saw Germany invaded by Moravians and Hungarians, Lotharingia in revolt against Zwentibold, Italy lost, and France free of Arnulf's influence.

Arnulf I, byname ARNULF THE GREAT, or THE ELDER, French ARNOUL LE GRAND, or LE VIEUX, Dutch ARNULF DE GROTE, or DE OUDE (b. *c.* 900—d. March 27, 965), count of Flanders (918–958, 962–965), son of Baldwin II. On his father's death in 918, the inherited lands were divided between Arnulf and his brother Adolf, but the latter survived only a short time, and Arnulf succeeded to the whole inheritance. His reign was filled with warfare against the Norsemen, and he took an active part in the struggles in Lorraine between the emperor Otto I and Hugh Capet.

In 958 Arnulf placed the government in the hands of his son Baldwin (Baldwin III), and the young man, though his reign was a very short one, did a great deal for the commercial and industrial progress of the country, establishing the first weavers and fullers at Ghent and instituting yearly fairs at Ypres, Bruges, and other places. On Baldwin III's death in 962 the old count, Arnulf I, resumed control and spent the few remaining years of his life in securing the succession of his grandson Arnulf II the Younger (reigned 965–988).

Arnulf OF METZ, SAINT, French SAINT ARNOUL DE METZ (b. *c.* 580, near Nancy, Fr.—d. July 18, 640?, Remiremont; feast day August 16 or 19), bishop of Metz and, with Pepin I, the earliest known ancestor of Charlemagne. A Frankish noble, Arnulf gave distinguished service at the Austrasian court under Theudebert II (595–612) but in 613, with Pepin, led the aristocratic opposition to Brunhild that led to her downfall and to the reunification of Frankish lands under Chlotar II. About the same year he became bishop.

From 623, again with Pepin, now mayor of the Austrasian palace, Arnulf was adviser to Dagobert I, before retiring (629?) to become a hermit. Arnulf's son Ansegisel married Pepin's daughter Begga; the son of this marriage, Pepin II, was Charlemagne's great-grandfather.

Arnus (Italy): *see* Arno River.

Arochukwu, also spelled AROCHUKU, town, Imo State, southern Nigeria, on the road from Calabar to Umuahia. Arochukwu was the headquarters of the Aro, an Ibo subgroup that dominated southeastern Nigeria in the 18th and 19th centuries. It was the seat of the sacred Chuku shrine, the source of a much-feared oracle (called Long Juju by the Europeans) that acted as a judge for the Ibo supreme deity (Chuku) and that, as used by Aro middlemen, served as the major recruiter for the slaves sent to the port of Bonny (Ubani) for sale. The shrine and power of the oracle were destroyed by the British in their campaigns against the Aro in 1900–02. Arochukwu is a market centre and the site of a teacher-training college, a secondary school, and a hospital. It is the headquarters of the Arochukwu/Ohafia Local Government Council.

Aroe Eilanden (Indonesia): *see* Aru Islands.

aromatic compound, any of a large class of chemical compounds the molecular structure of which includes one or more planar rings of atoms joined by covalent bonds of two different kinds. The term aromatic was first applied in about 1860 to a group of hydrocarbons isolated from coal tar and distinguished by their odours, which are much stronger than those of other groups of hydrocarbons; in chemistry, aromaticity has come to denote the chemical behaviour, especially low reactivity, derived from the electronic structure of this class of molecules.

Many aromatic compounds are relatives of benzene (*q.v.*), an organic compound that contains a ring of six carbon atoms; in others, atoms of other elements, especially nitrogen, replace one or more of the carbon atoms. Every atom in the ring shares a pair of electrons with each of its two neighbours: each of these electron pairs is concentrated between the two atoms, forming a bond denoted σ (sigma). In addition, two regions of high electron density, parallel to the ring formed by the atoms, constitute a system of π- (pi-) bonds associated, not with any pair of atoms, but with the entire ring. The essential aspect of aromatic compounds is the number of electrons in the π-bond system, rather than the number or identity of the atoms in the ring. Most commonly, there are six electrons in the system, but there may be any number given by the expression $4n + 2$, in which $n = 1, 2, 3$, etc.

aron, also called ARON HA-QODESH (Judaism): *see* ark.

Aron, Raymond(-Claude-Ferdinand) (b. March 14, 1905, Paris—d. Oct. 17, 1983, Paris), sociologist, philosopher, and political commentator, known for his skepticism of ideological orthodoxies.

Aron received his doctorate in letters in 1930 from the École Normale Supérieure and taught at the University of Cologne (1930–31), the French Academic House in Berlin (1931–33), and the lycée in Le Havre (1933–34). He served as secretary of the Centre de Documentation Sociale at the École Normale Supérieure (1934–39), as professor of the normal school of Saint-Cloud (1935–39), and as professor of social philosophy at the University of Toulouse (1939).

During World War II, Aron served with the French Air Force and after the fall of France with the Free French forces of Gen. Charles de Gaulle in London, being editor of their organ, *La France Libre*. After the war he taught at the Institut d'Études Politiques at the Sorbonne and at the École Nationale d'Administration, and was professor of sociology in the Faculty of Letters of the Sorbonne (1955–68). In 1946–47 he wrote for the leftist *Combat* and in 1947 became a highly influential columnist for *Le Figaro*, a position he held for 30 years. He left *Le Figaro* in 1977, and from 1977 until his death, he wrote a political column for the weekly magazine *L'Express*.

In his earlier years Aron was a close colleague of Jean-Paul Sartre, but in *L'Opium des intellectuels* (1955; *The Opium of the Intellectuals,* 1957) he criticized Sartre and the Marxists for their unquestioning support of the Soviet Union. He became a strong supporter of the Western alliance. In *La Révolution introuvable* (1968; *The Elusive Revolution: Anatomy of a Student Revolt,* 1969) he castigated fellow academicians for supporting the French student revolt of 1968. Opposed to colonialism, he advocated French withdrawal from Algeria before the Algerian Revolution. He was a leading critic of Charles de Gaulle.

Among Aron's other works are *Introduction à la philosophie de l'histoire* (1938; *Introduction to the Philosophy of History,* 1961); *Les Guerres en chaîne* (1951; *The Century of Total War,* 1954); *Paix et guerre entre les nations* (1962; *Peace and War,* 1966); *Le Grand Débat* (1963; *The Great Debate: Theories of Nuclear Strategy,* 1965); *Les Étapes de la pensée sociologique* (1967; *Main Currents in Sociological Thought,* 2 vol., 1965–68); *République impériale: Les États-Unis dans le monde, 1945–1972* (1973; *The Imperial Republic: The United States and the World, 1945–1973,* 1974), and *Penser la guerre, Clausewitz* (1976; *Clausewitz, Philosopher of War,* 1983). His memoirs were published in 1983.

Aroostook War (1838–39), bloodless conflict over the disputed boundary between the U.S. state of Maine and the British Canadian province of New Brunswick. The peace treaty of 1783 ending the U.S. War of Independence had left unclear the location of a supposed "highlands," or watershed, dividing the two areas. Negotiators from Britain and the United States in subsequent years failed to come to an agreement, and the matter was referred to the King of The Netherlands, who in 1831 rendered a decision that the citizens of Maine objected to strenuously, forcing the U.S. Senate to reject it.

Meanwhile, settlers from New England and lumbermen from Canada were moving into the disputed Aroostook area, and in 1838–39 the conflict warmed up, with officials and bands of men from both sides making arrests and taking prisoners of "trespassers." In March 1839 British troops from Quebec reached Madawaska, the American sector of Aroostook; and the Maine legislature immediately voted $800,000, calling for 10,000 volunteer militiamen, who, within a week, were dispatched to Aroostook. The U.S. Congress voted for 50,000 men and $10,000,000; and Gen. Winfield Scott was ordered to Augusta, Maine, by Pres. Martin Van Buren to keep the peace. On March 21, 1839, he and the British negotiator, Sir John Harvey, arranged a truce and a joint occupancy of the territory in dispute until a satisfactory settlement could be reached. The boundary was later settled by the Webster–Ashburton Treaty (*q.v.*) of 1842.

Arosa, Alpine village, health resort, and winter sports centre, Graubünden canton, eastern Switzerland, on the Plessur River. The village, at an altitude of 5,689 ft (1,734 m), stretches along a wooded valley holding two small lakes, the Untersee and the Obersee, that are used for fishing, swimming, and boating in the summer. Arosa is noted as a fashionable winter-sports centre, particularly for horse racing on ice and snow. The ski slopes above the tree line are accessible by a network of ski lifts and linking ski runs. A cable car runs up the nearby Weisshorn (8,704 ft), and gondola cars reach up the Hörnli (8,200 ft). Curling, ice skating, and ice hockey are also popular. Arosa lies at the end of a road and rail spur from Chur. Pop. (1982 est.) 2,782.

Arouet, François-Marie: *see* Voltaire.

arousal (psychology): *see* activation.

Arp, Halton Christian (b. March 21, 1927, New York City), U.S. astronomer noted for challenging the theory that red shifts of quasars indicate their great distance.

Arp received a bachelor's degree from Harvard University in 1949 and a Ph.D. from the California Institute of Technology in 1953. He subsequently accepted a research fellowship to conduct post-doctoral studies at the nearby Mt. Wilson and Palomar Observatories. After he worked as a research associate at Indiana University from 1955 to 1957, Arp returned to Mt. Wilson, securing a post as an assistant astronomer on the observatory staff. He was appointed astronomer in 1969.

Arp became skeptical about the distance of quasars when he noticed that some of the galaxies that he had included in his *Atlas of Peculiar Galaxies* (1966) seemed to lie in the vicinity of quasars. Using photographic evidence, Arp tried to prove that the low-red-shift galaxies and the high-red-shift quasars not only appear close together but actually are connected by gaseous bridges, an impossibility if the quasars are billions of light-years further away than the galaxies. Arp theorized that the nuclei of galaxies may explode, ejecting quasars with a velocity great enough to account for their red shifts.

Arp, Jean, also called HANS ARP (b. Sept. 16, 1887, Strassburg, Ger. [now Strasbourg, Fr.]—d. June 7, 1966, Basel, Switz.), French sculptor, painter, and poet who was one of the leaders of the European avant-garde in the arts during the first half of the 20th century.

First trained as an artist in his native Strasbourg, he later studied in Weimar, Ger., and at the Académie Julian in Paris. In 1912 he went to Munich, where, through his friend Wassily Kandinsky, he became briefly associated with Der Blaue Reiter. He returned to Paris in 1914 and became acquainted with the artists Modigliani, Picasso, and Robert Delaunay, as well as with the writer Max Jacob. During World War I he took refuge in Zürich, where he became one of the founders of the Dada (*q.v.*) movement. It was there that he produced his first painted reliefs. After the war he lived in Germany until 1924, when he and his wife, the artist Sophie Taeuber, whom he had married in 1921, settled near Paris in the town of Meudon. During the 1920s he was associated with the Surrealists, and in 1930 he was a member of the Cercle et Carré group. This was also the year in which he made his first *papiers déchirés* ("torn papers"). In 1931 he participated in the Abstraction-Création movement. During World War II he again went to live in Zürich, where his wife died in 1943. While in Switzerland he did his first *papiers froissés* ("crumpled papers"). After the war Arp returned to Meudon, where he continued his experiments with abstract form and colour and wrote poetry. *Arp on Arp: Poems, Essays, Memories by Jean Arp* (1972) and Arp's *Collected French Writings* (1974) were edited by Marcel Jean.

Arpad, also called TALL RIF'AT, ancient city in northwestern Syria. Arpad is frequently mentioned in the Old Testament and in Assyrian texts.

Coming under Assyrian influence in the 9th century BC, Arpad regained its independence in 754, and it successfully sided with Sardur II of Urartu until the Assyrian king Tiglath-pileser III defeated both Urartu and Arpad. Tiglath-pileser made Arpad the capital of a province that included the western half of northern Syria. After an unsuccessful revolt against Sargon II in 720 BC, the city remained loyal to Assyria.

Árpád DYNASTY, rulers of Hungary from the late 9th century until 1301, under whom

Árpád dynasty

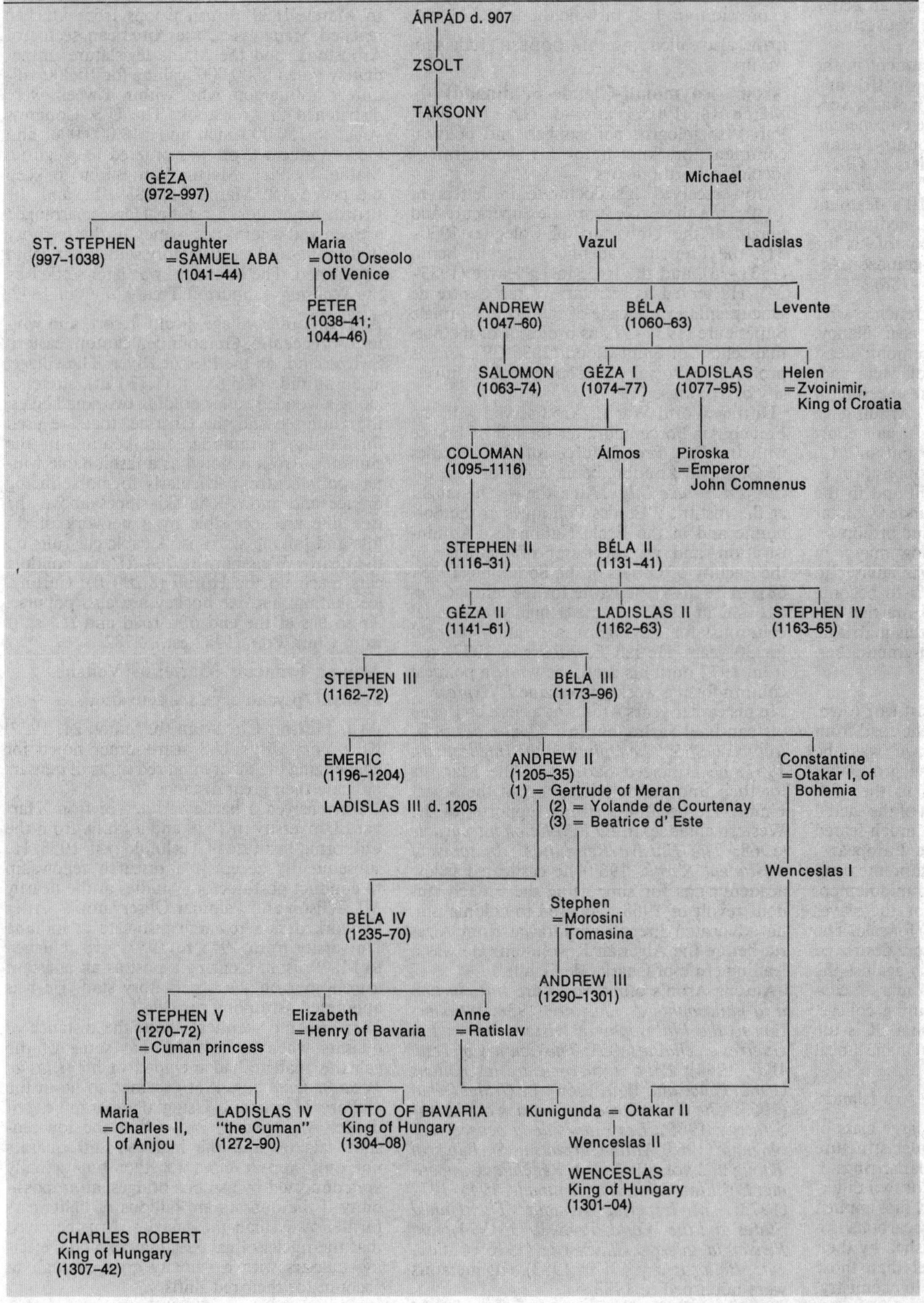

the Hungarian nation was transformed from a confederation of Magyar tribes into a powerful state of east central Europe. The dynasty was named after Árpád (d. 907), who was chosen by seven Magyar tribes to lead them westward from their dwelling place on the Don River (889). Having crossed the Carpathian Mountains (*c.* 896), the Magyars settled on the Pannonian, or Hungarian, Plain and for the next half century raided their neighbours and collected booty. But, after their defeat by Emperor Otto I (Battle of Lechfeld; Aug. 10, 955), they became less belligerent; during the reign of Géza (972–997), Árpád's great-grandson, they established cordial relations with the West and acknowledged the authority of their king before the authority of their chieftains.

Stephen (István; reigned 997–1038), expanding upon his father's accomplishments, officially converted his people to Christianity in the Western Church (1000), extended his control over Transylvania (1003), and replaced the tribal political structure with a system of counties, each one ruled by an appointed "count." Furthermore, by claiming all territory not occupied by freemen as property of the crown, Stephen laid the basis of the Hungarian monarchy's future wealth and power.

Although Stephen's successors were engaged in numerous struggles for succession, not only were they able to resist successfully the efforts of the Holy Roman emperor to dominate Hungary (especially in 1063 and 1074), but also King Ladislas (László; reigned 1077–95) and King Coloman (Kálmán; reigned 1095–1116) were able to extend Hungary's control over Croatia. In the 12th century it was the Byzantine emperor who gained significant influence in Hungary by intervening in the succession struggles of Ladislas II (László; reigned 1162–63) and Stephen IV (reigned 1163–65) against their nephew Stephen III (reigned 1162–72). But Béla III (reigned 1173–96), brother and successor of Stephen III, reestablished the independence and authority of the Hungarian monarchy.

During Béla's reign the Árpád dynasty achieved the peak of its power. Having derived great wealth from its crownlands, the dynasty gained control of Serbia and Galicia and made Hungary a large and formidable power in east central Europe. After Béla's death the monarchy suffered a decline. Emeric (Imre; reigned 1196–1204) and his brother Andrew II (Endre; reigned 1205–35), by making lavish land grants to their supporters, reduced the source of the monarchy's wealth and power. Andrew further weakened the strength of the monarchy by guaranteeing the liberties of the nobles (*see* Golden Bull of 1222) and allowing them to gain control of the county governments.

After the Mongols invaded and ravaged Hungary (1241–42), Béla IV (reigned 1235–70) encouraged reconstruction, but in the process he was forced to grant extensive privileges and authority to local magnates and thereby reduce the royal authority. His son Stephen V (reigned 1270–72) married a Cuman princess and was succeeded by their son Ladislas IV the Cuman (reigned 1272–90), and the prestige of the royal house declined even more. Ladislas left no legitimate heir; he was succeeded by Andrew III (reigned 1290–1301), grandson of Andrew II. But Andrew III also died without leaving an heir, and the Árpád dynasty, whose power had already significantly diminished, became extinct. Thereafter, the Hungarian throne became the object of contention among several foreign royal houses related by marriage to the House of Árpád.

Arpino, town, Frosinone province, Lazio (Latium) region, central Italy, on two hills 1,476 ft (450 m) above sea level, just east of the city of Frosinone. The town originated as Arpinum, a stronghold of the Volsci, who entered the area during the 5th century BC. During the 4th century BC it was held for a time by the Samnites, and it was finally conquered by the Romans in 305 BC, and Gaius Marius was born there. In the Middle Ages it was sacked by the Lombards, the Saracens, and the Hungarians; it passed to the papacy in 1215. The remains of the imposing cyclopean walls of the Volscian period, restored and added to in Samnite, Roman, and medieval times, surround the town. The 15th-century churches of S. Michele and S. Andrea contain paintings by the Mannerist Giuseppe Cesari, commonly known as the Cavalier d'Arpino.

Agriculture, woollen manufacturing, and the quarrying of coloured marbles are the chief occupations. Pop. (1981 prelim.) mun., 7,734.

arquebus (weapon): *see* harquebus.

Arrabal, Fernando (b. Aug. 11, 1932, Melilla, Spanish Morocco), Spanish-born French absurdist playwright, novelist, and filmmaker. Arrabal's dramatic and fictional world is often violent, cruel, and pornographic.

Arrabal worked as a clerk in a paper company, then studied law at the University of Madrid. He turned to writing in the early 1950s, and in 1955 he went to study drama in Paris, where he remained. The first volume of his plays was published in 1958, and the 1959 production of *Pique-nique en campagne* ("Picnic on the Battlefield"), an antiwar satire that contrasts the horrors of war with a cheerful family outing, brought him to the attention of the French avant-garde. Arrabal's most important play of this early period is probably *Le Cimitière des voitures* (1958; *Automobile Graveyard*, 1960), a parody of the Christ story. The characters in his plays are frequently childlike but seldom innocent; they are prostitutes, murderers, and torturers.

After the mid-1960s, Arrabal's plays became increasingly formal and ritualistic, evolving into what Arrabal called Théâtre Panique (Panic Theatre). Among the plays of this highly productive period are *L'Architecte et l'empereur d'Assyrie* (1967; *The Architect and the Emperor of Assyria*, 1969), in which the two characters assume each other's personae, and *Et ils passèrent des menottes aux fleurs* (1969; *And They Put Handcuffs on the Flowers*, 1973), more overtly political than his previous plays; its theme of freedom from oppression was inspired by the author's imprisonment while on a journey to Spain in 1967.

Arrabal's first novel, *Baal Babylone* (1959; *Baal Babylon*, 1961), dealt with his nightmarish childhood in Fascist Spain; in 1970 he adapted it into the screenplay *¡Viva la Muerte!* ("Long Live Death!") and directed its filming in Tunisia. An extremely prolific writer, he also, in addition to producing a dozen volumes of collected theatre pieces, wrote novels, filmscripts, poetry, political and other nonfictional texts, and two books on Chess.

Arrábida Highway Bridge, in Porto, Port., bridge (completed in 1963) spanning the gorge of the Douro River. The bridge carries a roadway 82 feet (25 metres) wide, supported 170 feet above the river; its overall length of 1,617 feet includes a reinforced-concrete arch 885 feet long, one of the largest in the world.

A list of the abbreviations used in the MICROPAEDIA *will be found at the end of this volume*

Arrah, also spelled ARA, town, administrative headquarters of Bhojpur district, Bihār state, northeastern India. The town is a major rail and road junction: agricultural trade and oilseed milling are carried on there. It is the site of three colleges affiliated with Magadh University. The Little House at Arrah is a building that was defended by the British against Kunwar Singh during the Indian Mutiny in 1857. Arrah was constituted a municipality in 1865. Pop. (1981) 125,111.

arraignment, in Anglo-American law, first encounter of an accused person with the court prior to trial, wherein he is brought to the bar and the charges against him are read. The accused usually enters a plea of guilt or innocence. If he chooses not to plead, a plea of not guilty will be entered for him. A guilty plea will usually result in the case's being handed over for judgment. Sometimes the court will permit a guilty plea to be withdrawn.

In civil-law countries arraignment does not exist, but accused parties must be brought before an investigating magistrate within a certain time, and the magistrate in turn must give his findings to the trial judge within a specified period. *See also* indictment.

Arraiolos rug, embroidered floor covering made at Arraiolos, north of Évora in Portugal. The technique is herringbone or cross-stitch on a linen cloth foundation. Early Arraiolos rugs utilized designs derived from the Persians, from whom the Portuguese learned the craft.

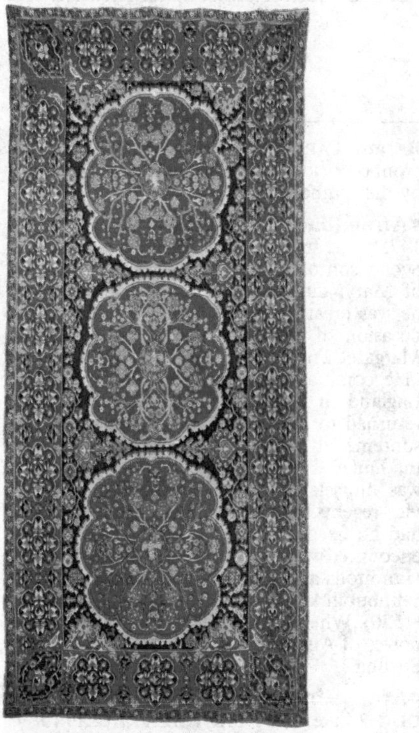

Arraiolos rug from Portugal, 17th century; in the Textile Museum, Washington, D.C.

Textile Museum Collection, Washington, D.C.; photograph, Otto E. Nelson—EB Inc.

Portuguese artisans soon replaced these Persian designs with Portuguese folk-art patterns in more limited colours, and most of the later rugs are much smaller and simpler. A fine collection of these rugs is displayed in the Museu Nacional de Arte Antiga in Lisbon. Arraiolos rugs are still being produced.

Arran, largest island in the district of Cunninghame, Strathclyde region (until 1975 in the county of Bute), Scotland, on the Atlantic coast at the mouth of the Firth of Clyde. Arran is approximately 20 mi (32 km) long and has a mean breadth of 9 mi and an area of about 165 sq mi (425 sq km).

Arran is called "Scotland in miniature" because of the beauty and variety of its scenery. The north of the island includes the most dramatic scenery, dominated by Goat Fell (2,868 ft [874 m]). The surrounding glens, notably Glen Rosa, Glen Sannox, and Glen Monamore, abound in hill and rock climbs and are well stocked with game, including grouse and red deer. In the south, the landscape is gentler and more pastoral and abounds in standing stones dating from approximately 2000 BC. Norse raiders inhabited Arran for a considerable period prior to the defeat of Haakon IV in 1263. The King's Caves, on the west coast, sheltered Robert I the Bruce in the early 14th century. In 1503 Arran was awarded by royal charter to Sir James Hamilton, whose castle dominates Brodick, the island's unofficial capital. Three miles south of Brodick in Lamlash Bay lies Holy Island, a cone of basaltic rock, 1,030 ft high, containing St. Molais' Cave, the cell of a hermit of the 6th century.

Because of its scenery and its accessibility to densely populated urban areas such as Glasgow, Arran has become an extremely popular holiday island and yet remains unspoiled. It is reached by steamer from Ardrossan, southwest of Glasgow. Pop. (1981) 4,726.

Consult the INDEX *first*

Arran, EARLS OF, titled Scottish nobility, grouped below chronologically and indicated by the symbol •.

• **Arran, James Hamilton, 1st earl of** (b. 1475?—d. July 1529, Kinneil, West Lothian, Scot.), son of James, 1st Lord Hamilton, and of Mary, daughter of James II of Scotland; he was created earl of Arran in 1503 on the occasion of the marriage of James IV with Margaret Tudor.

He commanded a naval expedition against England in 1513 but failed lamentably and returned to find his rival, the Earl of Angus, supreme at court. He therefore allied with the Duke of Albany, regent for James V, and was himself from 1517 to 1520 one of six vice-regents. But in the feuds of these years he had no fixed allegiance. His most spectacular encounter was the fierce fight between the Hamiltons and the Douglases in the streets of Edinburgh known as "Cleanse the Causeway" (1520). When James V freed himself from the power of Angus in 1528, Arran joined him at Stirling.

• **Arran, James Hamilton, 2nd earl of,** DUC (duke) DE CHÂTELHERAULT (b. *c.* 1517—d. Jan. 22, 1575, Hamilton, Lanarkshire, Scot.), earl of Arran who was heir presumptive to the throne after the accession of Mary Stuart in 1542 and was appointed her governor and tutor.

He negotiated for a marriage between Mary and Prince Edward (afterward Edward VI of England) but suddenly abandoned the project and joined the French party. He then agreed to the marriage of Mary with the dauphin of France, receiving the title of duc de Châtelherault at this time (1549); and he resigned office in 1554 in favour of the queen dowager, Mary of Lorraine. On the outbreak of the Scottish Reformation he joined the lords of the congregation (1559) and became the acknowledged leader of the Protestant party. He was exiled in 1565, but he returned to Scotland in 1569 to support the Queen's cause, not accepting the fact of Mary's abdication and the regency for her son James VI until 1573.

• **Arran, John Hamilton, earl of:** *see* Hamilton, John Hamilton, 1st marquess of.

• **Arran, James Hamilton, 3rd earl of** (b. 1537?—d. March 1609), earl of Arran who was twice considered as a husband both for Mary Stuart and for Henry VIII's daughter Elizabeth (afterward Elizabeth I). During his childhood these projects arose from his father's ambitions; later, when he had returned from commanding the Scots guards in France (1554–59) and had joined the lords of the congregation, the Protestants proposed him as suitor first for the hand of Elizabeth, and then, after December 1560, for that of Mary. He showed signs of insanity in 1562, and the rest of his life was spent in confinement.

• **Arran, James Stewart, earl of** (d. 1595, near Symington, Lanarkshire, Scot.), cousin of the 3rd earl, whose honours he claimed and for a short time legally enjoyed, from 1581 to 1585.

Both Stewart and his rival, Esmé, duke of Lennox, were deprived of office when the Protestant lords seized power by the raid of Ruthven (1582); but a year later they in turn were overthrown and driven into exile by Stewart. His tyranny and insolence, however, alienated many and caused his rapid fall from power. He was accused by Elizabeth I of England of the murder of Lord Russell on the border in July 1585 and was imprisoned; the banished lords returned and Stewart, proclaimed a traitor, fled in November 1585. From that time his movements are uncertain. He was ordered to leave Scotland in 1586 but may not have done so, and he returned to Edinburgh in 1592 and managed to have himself reinstated at court. He was assassinated near Symington by Sir James Douglas, nephew of the regent Morton, whose imprisonment and execution in 1581 Stewart had precipitated.

arrangement, in music, traditionally, any adaptation of a composition to fit a medium other than that for which it was originally written, while at the same time retaining the general character of the original. The word was frequently used interchangeably with transcription, although the latter carried the connotation of elaboration of the original, as in the virtuosic piano transcriptions of J.S. Bach's organ works by Franz Liszt, the Italian composer-pianist Ferruccio Busoni, and others. In later times the definitions were almost reversed, with arrangement connoting musical liberty in elaboration or simplification. In popular music and jazz, the word is often used synonymously with "score."

Arrangements of vocal compositions were crucial to the early history of instrumental music. Thus, vocal polyphony of the late Middle Ages and the Renaissance, including motets, chansons, and parts of the mass, was intabulated (transcribed so as to suggest finger positions rather than pitches) for the use of keyboard and lute players, permitting them to perform singly music written for several singers.

During the Baroque period (*c.*1600–1750), interest in arrangement declined, perhaps because of the increased importance of instrumental music and the waning significance of vocal writing. Bach, who arranged many of Antonio Vivaldi's violin concerti for harpsichord and organ, was a notable exception.

During the 19th century, with its stress on the piano, arrangements again became popular. Liszt transcribed Schubert songs as well as scenes from Wagner's music dramas. Brahms wrote for orchestra an arrangement of his own *Variations on a Theme by Haydn,* originally for two pianos, and of Bach's "Chaconne" from the *Partita in D Minor* for violin, which he recast as a piano study for the left hand. In the 20th century, Arnold Schoenberg in turn made elaborate orchestral arrangements of music by Bach, Georg Matthias Monn, and Brahms that amount to actual recompositions, quite unlike the popular Bach arrangements by Stokowski, Respighi, and others, which enjoyed a considerable vogue during the pre-World War II era.

Piano arrangements of opera and ballet scores, in particular, have long proven their value in the preparation of performances. Performance editions of problematically notated early scores often carry all the earmarks of highly subjective arrangements.

Arras, town, capital of Pas-de-Calais *département,* Nord-Pas-de-Calais region, former capital of Artois, northern France, on the Scarpe River, southwest of Lille. Of Gallo-Roman origin, it was the chief town (Nemetacum or Nemetocenna) of the Atrebates, one of the last Gallic peoples to surrender to Caesar. The woollen industry dates from the 4th century. The Middle Ages was a period of great material and cultural wealth, when Arras became the English word for tapestry hangings. The fortunes of the town followed those of troubled Artois, and it passed through many hands before being joined for the last time to France in 1659 by the Treaty of the Pyrenees. A peace treaty (1435) was signed there by Philip the Good of Burgundy and Charles VII of France. The Peace of Arras in 1482 fixed the northern frontiers of modern France. From 1479 to 1484 Louis XI, after razing the walls, ordered a mass deportation of citizens. Arras was the birthplace of Robespierre. The French Revolution and both world wars destroyed many of its ancient buildings. The town centres on two arcaded and gabled squares, the Grande and Petite. The reconstructed 16th-century Gothic Hôtel de Ville is on the Petite Place.

Tapestry making has long been extinct. Industry is diversified, the major employers representing the metallurgical, textile, and vegetable oil industries; the civil service is also a major employer. There is still an active agricultural market. Pop. (1982) 41,376.

The Gothic Hôtel de Ville (town hall) and belfry, Arras, Fr.

Editions "La Cigogne"—Hachette

Arras, Gautier d': *see* Gautier d'Arras.

Arras lace, bobbin lace made at Arras, Fr., from the 17th century onward and similar to that of Lille. Although Arras was known for its gold lace, its popularity rested on its exceptionally pure-white lace, stronger than Lille but with similar floral patterns. Arras lace was worn at the coronation (1714) of George I of England. In the 19th century Arras produced a light variety of lace called mignonette. After 1830 the industry declined.

arrastra, crude drag-stone mill for pulverizing ores such as those containing silver or gold or their compounds. *See* patio process.

Arrau, Claudio (b. Feb. 6, 1903, Chillán, Chile), Chilean-born U.S. pianist, regarded as one of the 20th century's most renowned performers.

After attending the Conservatory of Santiago for two years, Arrau went to Berlin, where he studied with Martin Krause, a pupil of Liszt, from 1912 to 1918. His serious career began with a recital in Berlin in 1914, and, during the next decade, he toured extensively in Europe, South America, and the United States. Between 1924 and 1940, he taught at Julius Stern's Conservatory in Berlin, and, in 1941, he moved permanently to the United States. He continued his frequent touring past his 80th birthday.

Arrau concentrated on the music of Liszt, Brahms, Chopin, Schumann, Debussy, and, above all, Beethoven. Regarded as one of the least ostentatious of the virtuoso pianists, Arrau developed a basically classical approach that exhibits an extreme concentration on detail, without sacrificing feeling.

Arrecifos (Caroline Islands): *see* Babelthuap.

arrest, placing of a person in custody or under restraint, usually for the purpose of compelling obedience to the law. If the arrest occurs in the course of criminal procedure, the purpose of the restraint is to hold the person for answer to a criminal charge or to prevent him from committing an offense. In civil proceedings, the purpose is to hold the person to a demand made against him.

In both common-law and civil-law jurisdictions, certain prerequisites must be met before there can be any interference with individual liberty. An arrest warrant may be issued by a court or judicial officer on a showing of probable cause that a criminal offense has been committed and that the person charged in the warrant is probably guilty. An arrest warrant may validly be served only by the person or class of persons to whom the warrant is addressed. In many states of the United States this can be a private citizen as well as a police officer.

More numerous and of greater practical importance are arrests without warrants. In general, the officer must believe a crime to have been committed and the person arrested to be the guilty party. In the United States an indictment provides sufficient warrant for arrest of the accused, because the return of an indictment by a grand jury constitutes a finding of "probable cause." The French *juge d'instruction* may recommend arrest at the end of his preliminary hearing; this proceeding is similar to an indictment proceeding. Arrests may be made of persons on probation or parole who have violated the conditions of their release, even though such violations do not involve commission of criminal acts. In many cases of minor offenses, the accused is not arrested but is notified of pending criminal proceedings by a summons.

Arrest in civil actions, when authorized, is an auxiliary remedy designed to (1) bring a person against whom a demand has been made within the jurisdiction of the court or (2) keep a person within the reach of the court's final process and obtain from him the satisfaction of the court's order, or judgment.

Arrest in civil cases is today regarded as a drastic remedy. In most jurisdictions it is available only in situations specified by statute and is regulated by procedures likewise specified. A judgment debtor may be arrested, for example, if there is reasonable ground for believing that he is about to abscond, destroy papers, or remove goods, or if he fails without good cause to attend any examination ordered by the court.

Arrest may also be authorized in connection with other specialized civil proceedings. The most prevalent instances of such arrests are of persons whose extreme mental disorders constitute a recognizable danger to themselves or to others.

Arrest, Heinrich Louis d' (b. July 13, 1822, Berlin—d. June 14, 1875, Copenhagen), German astronomer who, while a student at the Berlin Observatory, hastened the discovery of Neptune by suggesting comparison of the sky, in the region indicated by Le Verrier's calculations, with a recently prepared star chart. The planet was found the same night.

In 1851, while associated with the Leipzig Observatory, d'Arrest discovered a periodic comet, subsequently named for him. In that same year he published a book on the 13 asteroids known at that time and began his studies of the nebulae for which he received the Gold Medal of the Royal Astronomical Society in 1875.

Arrhenius, Svante (August) (b. Feb. 19, 1859, Vik, Swed.—d. Oct. 2, 1927, Stockholm), Swedish physical chemist best known

Arrhenius, 1918
By courtesy of the Kungl. Biblioteket, Stockholm

for his theory that electrolytes, certain substances that dissolve in water to yield a solution that conducts electricity, are separated, or dissociated, into electrically charged particles, or ions, even when there is no current flowing through the solution. In 1903 he was awarded the Nobel Prize for Chemistry.

Early training. Arrhenius is said to have taught himself to read at the age of three and to have become interested in mathematics from watching his father add columns of figures. He attended the Cathedral School at Uppsala and went on to the university, where he studied physics, mathematics, and chemistry. In pursuit of his doctorate he migrated to Stockholm to work on electrolysis under Erik Edlund. In 1883 he published his first paper and in May 1884, at Uppsala, defended his doctoral thesis containing in embryo the dissociation theory.

The thesis was greeted with incredulity and awarded the fourth class, a bare pass; the university in effect condemned an important and original thesis. The faculty at Uppsala were skeptical of hypotheses and devoted to accurate experimental work, while Arrhenius boasted (not quite truly) that he had never performed an exact experiment in his life; moreover, his subject fell awkwardly between chemistry and physics. Even to the sympathetic English physicist Sir Oliver Lodge, who in 1886 described the theory to the British Association for the Advancement of Science, Arrhenius seemed sometimes "to indulge in . . . manipulation of imaginary data," producing "a confusion" from which emerged so-called theoretical deductions. In reality, Arrhenius had a statistical sense and an ability to frame formulas to fit his facts, both of which were rare among chemists of his day. He had prudently sent copies of his thesis to the most prominent physical chemists of the day, who were able to understand it; and in August 1884 the German physical chemist Wilhelm Ostwald went from Riga to Uppsala to offer Arrhenius a post. He was at once given a lectureship in physical chemistry at Uppsala; and in 1886 Edlund got him a travelling fellowship from the Swedish Academy of Sciences.

Acceptance of his theory. Arrhenius spent from 1886 to 1890 working with other eminent scientists—Ostwald at Riga, F.W. Kohlrausch at Würzburg, Ludwig Boltzmann at Graz, and Jacobus van't Hoff at Amsterdam. During these years he refined his theory, which gradually began to win adherents. In 1891 he was offered a chair at Giessen, Ger., where Justus von Liebig, half a century earlier, had revolutionized the teaching of chemistry; but he wished to remain in Sweden and obtained a post at the Royal Institute of Technology in Stockholm. In 1895 he became professor of physics and, in 1896, rector of the school. Abroad, his reputation stood very high; but he was not elected to the Swedish Academy of Sciences until 1901, and even then with strong opposition. In 1902 he received the Davy Medal of the Royal Society of London, which in 1911 elected him a foreign member; and in 1903 his own countrymen made amends when he became the first Swede to be awarded a Nobel Prize.

In 1905 he was offered a chair at Berlin, then the most eminent position open to an academic chemist. On patriotic grounds, he refused; and the directorship of the Nobel Institute for Physical Chemistry at Stockholm was created for him. This gave him ample opportunity for research and writing, and his later years were contented.

In 1911 he visited the United States to receive the first Willard Gibbs Medal and to deliver the Silliman Lectures at Yale University, published as *Theories of Solutions* (1912).

Arrhenius was a genial, energetic man who made many friends on his visits abroad. His memory was excellent, he loved nature, but he was indifferent to the fine arts and literature. His range of scientific interests was very wide: over the years, he moved away from the study of solutions into immunology, where he made pioneering studies on toxins, and then into geology and cosmology. In *Worlds in the Making* (1908), he suggested that cool stars might collide and form nebulae from which new stars and planets would arise; and so the process would go on indefinitely, life being spread about the universe by bacteria propelled by light pressure. These speculations have not found their way into modern cosmology. (D.M.K.)

BIBLIOGRAPHY. The only full-length biography of Arrhenius is E.H. Riesenfeld, *Svante Arrhenius* (1931), in German. Brief English-language biographies may be found in the *Dictionary of Scientific Biography,* vol. 1, pp. 296–302 (1970), with a full bibliography; E. Farber (ed.), *Great Chemists* (1961); and J.R. Partington, *A History of Chemistry,* vol. 4 (1964).

Arrhenius equation, mathematical expression that describes the effect of temperature on the velocity of a chemical reaction, the basis of all predictive expressions used for calculating reaction-rate constants. In the Arrhenius equation, k is the reaction-rate constant, A and E are numerical constants characteristic of the reacting substances, R is the thermodynamic gas constant, and T is the absolute temperature. The equation is commonly given in the form of an exponential function,

$$k = A\exp(-E/RT),$$

and it predicts that a small increase in reaction temperature will produce a marked increase in the magnitude of the reaction-rate constant.

The Arrhenius equation was originally formulated by J.J. Hood on the basis of studies of the variation of rate constants of some reactions with temperature. The Swedish chemist Svante Arrhenius, for whom the equation is named, showed that the relationship is applicable to almost all kinds of reactions. He also provided a theoretical basis for the equation by an analogy with the expression for the thermodynamic equilibrium constant. Later, the numerical constants *A* and *E* were shown by the collision and transition-state theories of chemical reactions to represent quantities indicative of the fundamental process of chemical reactions; *i.e.*, *E* represents the energy of activation and *A* represents the frequency at which atoms and molecules collide in a way that leads to reaction.

Arrhenius theory, theory, introduced in 1887 by the Swedish scientist Svante August Arrhenius, that acids are substances that dissociate in water to yield electrically charged atoms or molecules, called ions, one of which is a hydrogen ion (H^+), and that bases ionize in water to yield hydroxide ions (OH^-). It is now known that the hydrogen ion cannot exist alone in water solution; rather, it exists in a combined state with a water molecule, as the hydronium ion (H_3O^+). In practice the hydronium ion is still customarily referred to as the hydrogen ion.

The acidic behaviour of many well-known acids (*e.g.*, sulfuric, hydrochloric, nitric, and acetic acids) and the basic properties of well-known hydroxides (*e.g.*, sodium, potassium, and calcium hydroxides) are explained in terms of their ability to yield hydrogen and hydroxide ions, respectively, in solution. Furthermore, such acids and bases may be classified as strong or weak acids and bases depending on the hydrogen ion or hydroxide ion concentration produced in solution. The reaction between an acid and a base leads to the formation of a salt and water; the latter is the result of the combination of a hydrogen ion and a hydroxide ion.

Arriaga (y Balzola), Juan Crisóstomo (Jacobo Antonio) (b. Jan. 27, 1806, near Bilbao, Spain—d. Jan. 17, 1826, Paris), Spanish composer of extraordinary precocity whose potential was cut short by his early death. Stylistically, his music stands between the Classical tradition of Haydn and Mozart and the Romanticism of Rossini and Schubert; it shows abundant invention, freshness, and technical resourcefulness.

After the success of his opera *Los ésclavos felices* (produced 1820, Bilbao) and of an octet for French horn, strings, guitar, and piano, he enrolled in the Paris Conservatoire, where by the age of 18 he became an assistant professor. His other compositions include three string quartets and a symphony.

Arrian, Latin in full FLAVIUS ARRIANUS (fl. 2nd century AD), Greek historian and philosopher born at Nicomedia in Bithynia, principally remembered as the author of a work describing the campaigns of Alexander the Great. Entitled *Anabasis,* presumably in order to recall Xenophon's work of that title, it describes Alexander's military exploits in seven books; an eighth, the *Indica,* tells of Indian customs and the voyage of Nearchus in the Persian Gulf.

Arrian is clearly a great admirer of his hero but is obsessed by the purely military aspect of the story he is telling. There is little to enlighten us about Alexander's motives for conquest or his ideal of the creation of a united world. The work, however, does contain some fine pieces of descriptive writing, such as the account of the siege and capture of Tyre in Book Two or the story in Book Seven of Alexander's grief at the death of his friend Hephaistion.

Arrian's other works include the *Encheiridion,* a manual of the teaching of Epictetus, the Stoic philosopher whose disciple Arrian was, and the *Diatribai,* which was a record of the philosopher's lectures. The first of these works was much used in the Middle Ages as a guide to the principles of the monastic life.

Arrian served in the Roman army and was appointed by the emperor Hadrian to be governor of the province of Cappadocia. After Hadrian's death (138), Arrian retired into private life to occupy himself with his literary work. He was archon, or chief magistrate, at Athens in 171 and died about the year 180.

Arron, Henck (Alphonsus Eugène) (b. April 25, 1936, Paramaribo, Dutch Guiana), prime minister of Suriname from 1973 until he was overthrown by a military coup in 1980.

Arron became prime minister by leading the National Party Alliance, a coalition of parties composed mainly of Creoles (Surinamese of African descent), to an election victory over the predominantly Hindustani Progressive Reform Party. The nation became independent in 1975, and, when reelected in October 1977, Arron declared that one of his goals was "to do something about the one-sided character of our economy, which has been primarily based on the bauxite industry." He was unsuccessful, however, and the high rate of unemployment, prompting the emigration to The Netherlands of approximately one-third of the country's population, was a major cause of his downfall. The coup was staged by army sergeants, discontented over pay and promotion opportunities, on Feb. 25, 1980. Arron was arrested in August 1980 but released in 1981.

arrow (weapon): *see* bow and arrow.

Arrow, Kenneth J(oseph) (b. Aug. 23, 1921, New York City), U.S. economist known for his contributions to welfare economics and to general economic equilibrium theory. He was co-winner (with Sir John R. Hicks) of the Nobel Prize for Economics in 1972. Perhaps his most startling thesis (using elementary mathematics) was the "impossibility theory," which deems that perfectly responsive representative government is impossible.

Arrow received his Ph.D. from Columbia University in 1951 and taught at the University of Chicago (1948–49) and Stanford University (1949–68). From 1968 to 1979 he was professor of economics at Harvard University, where he inspired the development of a first-rate school of economic theorists. In 1979 he returned to Stanford University.

Among his major publications are *Social Choice and Individual Values* (1951), *Essays in the Theory of Risk Bearing* (1971), and *The Limits of Organization* (1974). He was president of the American Economics Association in 1973.

Arrow Cross Party, Hungarian NYILASKERESZTES PÁRT, Hungarian Fascist organization that exercised varying degrees of influence before and during World War II and controlled the Hungarian government from October 1944 to April 1945. During the early 1930s many radical right-wing political groups were created in Hungary, including the Party of National Will founded by Ferenc Szálasi in March 1935. Szálasi's party was quite small and underwent numerous reorganizations: it merged with other rightist radical parties, broke away from them, was dissolved by the government, and reconstituted itself under new names, emerging early in 1939 as the Arrow Cross Party. In the May 1939 national elections it appeared as the second most popular party, receiving about 30 seats in parliament.

After World War II broke out, however, the Hungarian prime minister Pál Teleki (served February 1939–April 1941) suppressed the Arrow Cross Party, imprisoning many of its adherents, including members of parliament. When the Germans occupied Hungary and set up the collaborationist government of Döme Sztójay (March 1944), however, the Arrow Cross fortunes improved; the party received official approval from the new government and gained mass support from army officers, the middle class, and workers.

When the regent of Hungary Adm. Miklós Horthy began to seek a separate peace with the Allies (September 1944), the Germans decided to place Szálasi in power as prime minister (October 27), then as national leader (November 4). After the Soviet Union's Red Army seized Budapest in February 1945, it drove the Germans and their Arrow Cross allies out of Hungary.

arrow-poison frog, any of the closely related, poisonous frogs of the genera *Dendrobates* and

Arrow-poison frog (*Dendrobates*)
Joseph T. Collins, Museum of Natural History, University of Kansas

Phyllobates (family Dendrobatidae). These two genera include small, brightly coloured, terrestrial frogs of South and Central American forests. Their skins secrete a substance that is toxic to birds and small animals and used by Indians to coat their arrow tips. The vivid colours of arrow-poison frogs include red, orange, yellow, green, and pink.

Breeding behaviour in the two genera is similar. The fertilized eggs are attached to the back of the male, and, after hatching, the tadpoles cling to his back. The male later carries the young to a stream where they detach and complete their development into adults.

arrowhead, any freshwater plant of the genus *Sagittaria,* consisting of about 20 species distributed worldwide, having leaves resembling arrowpoints. Arrowhead is a perennial herb with fleshy, or tuberous, roots that grows in shallow lakes, ponds, and streams. The flowers have three rounded petals. The tubers of

Arrowhead (*Sagittaria*)
Kenneth and Brenda Formanek—EB Inc.

some North American species were eaten by Indians and were known to early settlers as duck, or swan, potatoes. The most common species in North America is the broad-leaved arrowhead (*S. latifolia*), introduced by man to improve feeding areas for birds. Leaves of this species vary from arrow-shaped to grasslike. The grass-leaved arrowhead (*S. graminea*) is found throughout eastern North America. *S. sagittifolia,* which grows in most of Europe, is cultivated in China for its edible tubers.

arrowroot, any of several species of the genus *Maranta,* members of the family Marantaceae (*q.v.*), the rhizomes, or rootstocks, of which yield an edible starch; the chief among these is *M. arundinacea,* the source of genuine, or West Indies, arrowroot. This herbaceous perennial, probably a native of Guyana and western Brazil, is cultivated throughout the West Indies, Southeast Asia, Australia, and South Africa. Its creeping rootstock has fleshy tubers (underground storage organs), and its many-branched stem, reaching a height of 5–6 feet (about 1.5 metres), bears numerous leaves, having long narrow sheaths and large spreading ovate blades, and a few short-stalked white flowers. Plants are harvested when the tubers are gorged with starch, just before the plant's dormant season. The roots are peeled and then grated in water. The resulting mixture is dried to a powder and purified by several washings.

Arrowroot, almost pure starch, supplies no vitamins and contains only 0.2 percent protein. In cookery, it is used as a thickener in soups, sauces, puddings, and desserts. When boiled in water, it yields a transparent, odourless, pleasant-tasting jelly. Its fine texture allows cooking at lower temperatures and for shorter periods than other starches, making it especially suitable for such egg preparations as custards, which are adversely affected by overcooking. Arrowroot is easily digested and is used in diets requiring bland, low-salt, and low-protein foods.

The name arrowroot is sometimes applied to starches obtained from other plants and used as substitutes for true arrowroot. Tous-les-mois, or Tulema arrowroot, a larger grained product, comes from another West Indies plant, a species of *Canna,* a genus allied to the *Maranta.* East India arrowroot is a product of several species of the genus *Curcuma,* of the

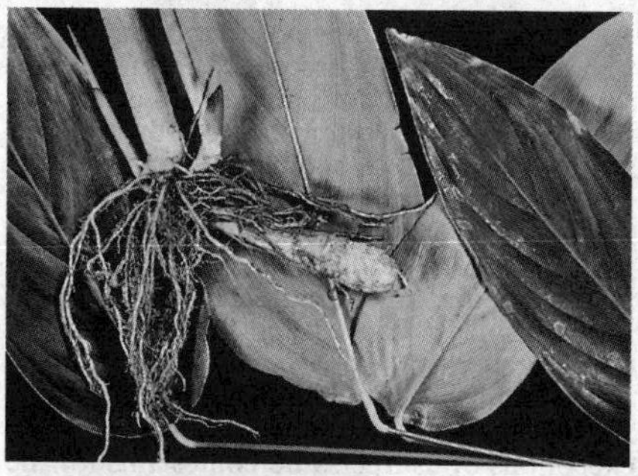

Arrowroot (*Maranta arundinacea*)
W.H. Hodge

family Zingiberaceae, chiefly *C. angustifolia,* native to central India. Brazilian arrowroot, from the cassava plant (*Manihot esculenta*), is the source of tapioca. Tacca, or Otaheite arrowroot, comes from the pia plant (*Tacca pinnatifida*) of the South Pacific islands. Portland arrowroot, once manufactured in Portland, Dorset, Eng., is derived from tubers of the common cuckoopint (*Arum maculatum*), and other *Arum* species are important food starch sources in hot countries. Potato farina, sometimes marketed as British arrowroot, has been used to adulterate more costly preparations.

Arrowsmith, Aaron (b. July 14, 1750, Winston, Durham, Eng.—d. April 23, 1823, London), British geographer and cartographer who engraved and published many fine maps and

Aaron Arrowsmith, engraving by T.A. Dean after a portrait by H.W. Pickersgill
By courtesy of the trustees of the British Museum; photograph, J.R. Freeman & Co. Ltd.

atlases based on the best available sources of the day.

Without a formal education Arrowsmith went to London *c.* 1770 and, after working as a surveyor, established himself as a mapmaker and publisher. His large world map (1790) established his reputation. A second such map published in 1794 was accompanied by an explanatory volume. Other notable works included a map of North America (1796), a chart of the Pacific Ocean (1798), and his *Atlas of South India* (1822).

After Arrowsmith's death, the business was carried on by his sons, Aaron and Samuel, who published geography manuals and a number of atlases. From 1839 the business was conducted by his nephew, John Arrowsmith, himself an eminent cartographer, who published the *London Atlas* 4 vol. (1834), the best set of maps then in existence. This work was followed by a long series of elaborate and carefully executed maps embodying the results of contemporary exploration. The maps of Australia, North America, Africa, and India were especially valuable.

arrowworm, also called CHAETOGNATH, any member of the invertebrate phylum Chaetognatha, a group of small wormlike marine animals with transparent to transluscent or opaque arrow-shaped bodies. The phylum consists of about seven extant genera and one fossil genus. There are more than 50 species, most of which are in the genus *Sagitta.* The size of arrowworms ranges from about 3 millimetres to more than 100 millimetres; species inhabiting colder waters generally are larger than those from tropical seas. Chaetognatha are hermaphroditic (having both male and female sex organs, or gonads). The body is divided into head, trunk, and tail by two transverse walls or membranes and has lateral fins and a tail fin. Respiratory, circulatory, and excretory systems are not properly developed.

Natural history. Arrowworms are protandric (*i.e.,* male gonads mature earlier than female gonads). Most arrowworms die after spawning, although some undergo cycles of maturity and often also growth. Cross-fertilization has been observed, the sperm passing from the storage organs called seminal vesicles, which open out to the exterior, to the seminal receptacle (tube along the female gonads) of another individual. The eggs are fertilized by the sperm either shortly before or as they are laid, in a part of the duct common to the oviduct and to the seminal receptacle. In several genera (*e.g., Eukrohnia,* and probably also in the genera *Bathyspadella, Krohnitta,* and *Heterokrohnia*), mature eggs and larvae are enclosed in a sac formed at the opening of oviducts. In *Pterosagitta,* eggs are laid in a capsule; in *Sagitta,* eggs are discharged into the surrounding water one at a time in several cycles; and in *Spadella,* eggs have an adhesive coat and a stalk and attach to any surface.

Arrowworms are voracious feeders; they consume copepods, euphausiids, fish larvae, medusae, other arrowworms, cladocerans, amphipods, appendicularias, and eggs and larvae of various animals. Arrowworms inhabit oceans, seas, and coastal lagoons. Although some species are cosmopolitan, others are restricted to a geographical region or an ocean. Southeast Asian seas have the largest number of species. Epiplanktonic species—*i.e.,* those within 200 metres of the water surface—increase in numbers from the poles to the

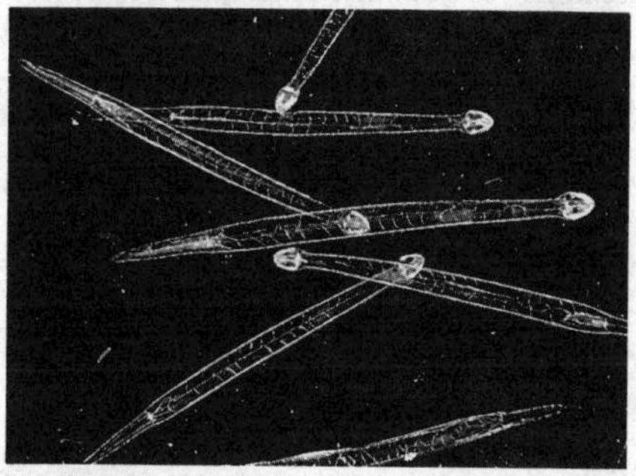

Arrowworm (*Sagitta*)
Douglas P. Wilson

Equator. Mature arrowworms inhabit deeper oceanic layers than do the young.

Form and function. The body of an arrowworm is covered by a cuticle of cells (called collarette when thickened). The head has hooks (curved, grasping spines) covered by a hood or thin fold of skin, which retracts when the arrowworm is catching prey. Head muscles control the movement of hooks, teeth, and mouth; body muscles are longitudinal with some transverse bands. Arrowworms swim with dartlike movements by contracting the longitudinal muscles and flapping the tail.

The nervous system consists of a large cerebral ganglion with sensory nerves (*e.g.,* optic, coronal). The cerebral ganglion is connected with the ventral ganglion by a pair of nerve cords. Additional ganglia and nerves spread along the body. Touch receptors, small, round, ciliated (hairlike) prominences, are scattered over the body.

There is evidence that regeneration of the head and the anterior part of the body occurs; during regeneration, the eyes appear first, then the mouth and hooks. The eyes contain a pigmented central cell, which encloses five clusters of photoreceptor cell processes (or ocelli). A conical body found in the photoreceptor cell either may guide the animal as it swims or act as a resonator. The pigmented central cell may have various shapes (*e.g.,* starlike) in different species. No pigment is present in most deep-sea dwelling species.

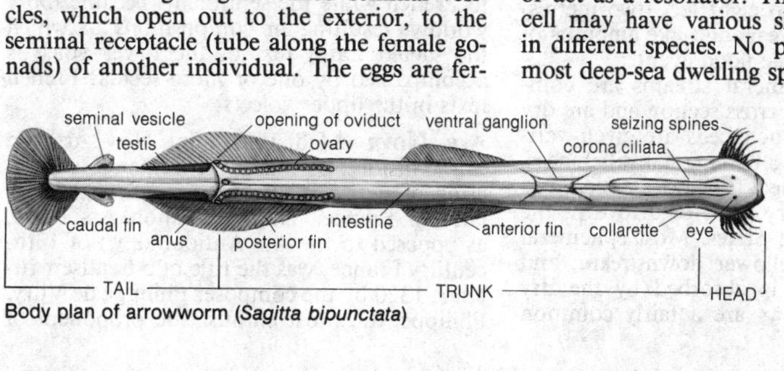

Body plan of arrowworm (*Sagitta bipunctata*)

The corona ciliata is an olfactory (smell) receptor or chemoreceptor peculiar to the phylum and is formed by a series of rows of ciliated cells forming a ring or elongated oval at the neck or extending toward the head and the trunk. The digestive tract, which is lined by glandular and absorptive cells, extends from the mouth to the anus and is supported by a mesentery. The central mesentery divides the trunk and tail into two cavities. Trunk and tail regions are filled with a colourless fluid that circulates forward along the body walls and backward in the medial region of the body.

Two ovaries, filled with rows of unfertilized eggs, extend along the trunk and are attached to the sides of the body by a mesentery. The seminal receptacle in the oviducts stores sperm after copulation. The testes are located in the tail cavities; a spermduct, or vas deferens, connects the testes with the seminal vesicles, which open out from the body. The ovaries in the trunk, therefore, are isolated from the testes in the tail, with no internal communication between male and female gonads. The seminal vesicles burst when filled with sperm, ejecting the spermatozoa into the surrounding waters or into the seminal receptacle of another individual.

Classification. The Chaetognatha is an isolated phylum in the animal kingdom; *i.e.,* comparative anatomy and embryology fail to link these animals with any other group. Arrowworms have been considered as worms, and attempts have been made to relate them to many animal groups (*e.g.,* Heteropoda, Annelida, Nematoda, Arthropoda). They also have been placed taxonomically between Annelida and Nematoda. Structure of the arrowworm eye, however, indicates a probable evolutionary relationship to echinoderms and chordates.

arroyo, also called WASH, DRY WASH, or COULEE, Arabic WADI, French OUED, a dry

Ephemeral stream (arroyo) in Big Bend National Park, Texas
Grant Heilman

channel lying in a semiarid or desert area and subject to flash flooding during seasonal or irregular rainstorms. Such transitory streams, rivers, or creeks are noted for their gullying effects, especially for their rapid rates of erosion, transportation, and deposition. There have been reports of up to eight feet (two metres) of deposition in 60 years and like amounts of erosion during a single flood event.

The beds of ephemeral streams are commonly almost flat in cross section and are dry most of the time. Such beds are given various names according to regional differences, such as wadi or oued in North Africa and Saudi Arabia and dry wash or arroyo in the southwestern United States. Most ephemeral streams become shallower downstream, and most of the water is absorbed by the dry stream bed; mudflows are a fairly common occurrence because sediment yields are high in arid and semiarid areas.

Arrupe, Pedro (b. Nov. 14, 1907, Bilbao, Spain), 28th superior general (1965–81) of the Society of Jesus.

He studied medicine at the University of Madrid but left to join the Jesuits in 1927. When the Spanish government dissolved the Jesuit order in Spain in 1932, he continued his studies elsewhere in Europe and in the United States. After his ordination in Cleveland, Ohio, he worked among Spanish and Puerto Rican immigrants in New York City.

In 1938 he went to Japan, where he spent the next 27 years as a missionary, giving aid in 1945 to the victims of Hiroshima. He later became vice provincial (1954–58) and the first Jesuit provincial in Japan (1958–65). Under his generalship the Jesuits extended their missions and educational work and became more active in the ecumenical movement, in civil rights activities, and in the communications field. He wrote eight religious works in Japanese and in 1965 published his memoirs in Spanish.

Ars, Jean-Baptiste-Marie Vianney, cure d': *see* Vianney, Saint Jean-Baptiste-Marie.

Ars Antiqua (Medieval Latin: Ancient Art), in music history, period of musical activity in 13th-century France, characterized by increasingly sophisticated counterpoint (the art of combining simultaneous voice parts), that culminated in the innovations of the 14th-century Ars Nova (*q.v.*). The term Ars Antiqua originated, in fact, with the Ars Nova theorists, some of whom spoke of the Ancient Art with praise, others with contempt. All of them, however, agreed upon a marked difference between the two styles, a difference rooted primarily in the profound rhythmic innovations of the Ars Nova. Those theorists limited the Ars Antiqua to the latter part of the 13th century, while modern music historians have broadened the term to encompass the entire century.

The authorship of most of the music of the Ars Antiqua is anonymous. Nevertheless, three important figures emerge from the general obscurity: Pérotin (flourished late 12th century), who succeeded the famed Léonin at Notre-Dame in Paris and who composed the earliest known music for four voices; Franco of Cologne (flourished mid-13th century), a theorist, whose *Ars cantus mensurabilis* ("The Art of Measured Song") served to organize and codify the newly formed mensural system (a more precise system of rhythmic notation, the direct ancestor of modern notation); and Pierre de la Croix (flourished last half of 13th century), whose works anticipate the Ars Nova style by virtue of their rhythmic fluency.

The most important form to originate in the Ars Antiqua is the motet, which retained its popularity for centuries. The essence of this form is its simultaneous presentation of more than one text. It seems to have begun with the addition of a new text to the upper voice(s) of a sacred polyphonic composition, the slower moving lower voice retaining its original sacred text. The next text—in Latin, like the original text—at first complemented or amplified the meaning of the original words. Later, the language of the added text changed to French while the sentiments became more worldly, resulting in compositions in which the sacred Latin text of the lower voice is accompanied by one or more secular French texts in the upper voice(s).

Ars Nova (Medieval Latin: New Art), in music history, period of the tremendous flowering of music in the 14th century, particularly in France. The designation Ars Nova, as opposed to the Ars Antiqua (*q.v.*) of 13th-century France, was the title of a treatise written *c.* 1320 by the composer Philippe de Vitry. Philippe, the most enthusiastic proponent of the New Art, demonstrates in his treatise the innovations in rhythmic notation characteristic of the new music.

These innovations, which were anticipated to a degree in the music of Pierre de la Croix (flourished last half of 13th century), are marked by the emancipation of music from the rhythmic modes (dominated by triple metre) of the preceding age and by the increased use of smaller note values. An important opponent of Philippe de Vitry's progressive ideas was the theorist Jacques de Liège, whose *Speculum musicae* ("The Mirror of Music") extolls the virtues of the older masters of the Ars Antiqua.

Some of the earliest examples of works in the new style may be found in the *Roman de Fauvel* (*c.* 1315), a narrative manuscript that contains compositions from both the Ars Nova and the Ars Antiqua. The most important composers of the Ars Nova are Philippe de Vitry and the composer and poet Guillaume de Machaut, whose work forms a substantial proportion of the surviving repertory. The production of polyphonic secular music, represented by the ballade, virelai, and rondeau (*qq.v.*), increased decidedly in the 14th century.

The term Ars Nova, specifically applicable to the French music of the 14th century, has been used less discriminately by a number of writers who refer to "Italian Ars Nova," which is also known as Italian *trecento* music. The most important theorist of this school is Marchettus of Padua, whose treatise *Pomerium* (in the early 14th century) outlines certain rhythmic innovations in Italian notation of the time. The most important composers of 14th-century Italy are Jacopo da Bologna, Francesco Landini, and Ghirardello da Firenze.

Ars poetica, English THE ART OF POETRY, verse epistle by the Roman poet Horace; one of the most influential texts (probably written 19/18 BC) of classical literary criticism. Urbane and sensible rather than profound, it established precepts for subject matter, decorum, and dramatic form that were highly esteemed up to the 19th century. It apparently was the poet's last work.

Arsaces, Iranian name borne by the Parthian royal house as being descended from Arsaces, son of Phriapites (date unknown), a chief of the seminomadic Parni tribe from the Caspian steppes. The first of his line to gain power in Parthia was Arsaces I, who reigned from *c.* 250 to *c.* 211 BC. (Some authorities believe that a brother, Tiridates I, succeeded Arsaces about 248 and ruled until 211; other authorities consider Arsaces I and Tiridates I to be the same person.)

All Parthian kings after Arsaces I used Arsaces as their throne name; and, with the rare exceptions of usurpers and contestants for the throne, all are so designated on their coins and in official documents. By historians they are generally called by their personal names. The Arsacid dynasty maintained itself, although not in unbroken succession, until its overthrow by Ardashīr in AD 224. During the time of the Parthian empire the Arsacids claimed descent from Artaxerxes II, probably to legitimate their rule over Achaemenid territories. From the Sāsānian chronicles they enter Persian epic under the name the Ashkanian (individual rulers as Ashak, Ashkan).

The name Arsaces was also borne by several kings of Armenia who were of Parthian royal blood.

Arsaces II (king): *see* Artabanus I.

Arsaces VI: *see* Mithradates I *under* Mithradates (Parthia).

Arsacid DYNASTY, also called ARSHAKUNI (247 BC–AD 224), ancient Iranian dynasty that founded and ruled the Parthian Empire. Members of the Parni tribe living east of the Caspian Sea, the progenitors of the dynasty entered Parthia (*q.v.*) shortly after the death of Alexander the Great (323 BC) and gradually gained control over much of Iran and Mesopotamia until, in AD 224, they were overthrown by the Sāsānians, an Iranian dynasty founded by Ardashīr I.

The first Arsacid to gain power in Parthia was Arsaces (reigned *c.* 250–*c.* 211 BC), but the Iranian plateau was not conquered in its entirety until the time of Mithradates I (reigned 171–138 BC). Two of the dynasty's most powerful rulers were Mithradates II (reigned 123–88 BC) and Phraates III (reigned 70–58/57 BC).

During the time of the Parthian Empire the Arsacids claimed descent from the Achaemenian king Artaxerxes II, probably to legitimize their rule over the former Achaemenian territories; in fact, in many of its outward forms the Parthian Empire was a revival of Achaemenian rule. The governmental organization, however, was based on that developed by the Hellenistic Seleucids. The Arsacids encouraged the development of Hellenistic cities and tolerated the formation of vassal kingdoms. Because the Arsacids and their vassals controlled almost all the trade routes between Asia and the Greco-Roman world, they became very wealthy, with the result that the Parthian period was one of intense building activity.

arsenate mineral, any of a group of naturally occurring compounds of arsenic, oxygen, and various metals, most of which are rare, having crystallized under very restricted conditions. At the mineralogically famous Långban iron and manganese mines in central Sweden, more than 50 species of arsenate minerals have been described, many peculiar to the locality. Such compounds occur in open cavities and resulted from the reaction of arsenic acid (H_3AsO_4) upon pyrochroite [manganese hydroxide; $Mn(OH)_2$] at moderate to low temperature. Arsenates at other localities are often oxidation products of arsenide ores and are deposited at low temperatures in late-stage veins and open cavities.

Only a few arsenate minerals have economic importance. Because the transition metals (*e.g.*, cobalt, copper, nickel) give brilliant colour to some of the arsenates, these can be used to advantage in prospecting; such arsenate oxidation products, or blooms, as erythrite (bright pink) and annabergite (green), are indicators of nickel and cobalt arsenide ores. Many of the nickel and cobalt deposits at Sudbury and Cobalt, Ont., were located in this manner.

The arsenate minerals, salts of arsenic acid, contain arsenate groups (AsO_4), in which four oxygen (O) atoms are arranged at the corners of a tetrahedron about a central arsenic (As) atom. Each arsenate tetrahedron has a net electric charge of −3, which is neutralized by large, positively charged metal ions (*e.g.*, calcium, manganese, or ferrous iron) outside the tetrahedron. Unlike the similar silicate tetrahedra, which link to form chains, sheets, rings, or frameworks, arsenate tetrahedra are insular.

The crystal structure of the arsenate minerals is very similar to that of the phosphate and vanadate minerals; indeed, many arsenate minerals form solid solutions with both the phosphates and the vanadates.

arsenic (As), a chemical element in the nitrogen family (Group Va of the periodic table), existing in both gray and yellow crystalline forms. Although compounds of arsenic were known as early as the 4th century BC, the element was not identified as such until 1649.

Occurrence, properties, and uses. Widely distributed in nature, arsenic occasionally is found uncombined, usually in association with such metals as antimony and silver. It also occurs combined in its sulfides realgar and orpiment; as arsenic oxide; and as a con-

Arsenic (gray) with realgar (red) and orpiment (yellow)

By courtesy of the Joseph and Helen Guetterman collection; photograph, John H. Gerard—EB Inc.

stituent of various metallic sulfides, of which arsenopyrite (*q.v.*) is the most abundant.

Although some forms of arsenic are metal-like, the element is best classified as a nonmetal. Gray, or metallic, arsenic, which is more stable and more common than the softer yellow form, is very brittle, tarnishes in air, and sublimes when heated strongly—*i.e.*, it passes directly into a vapour without melting and reverts to the crystalline solid without liq-

Arsenate minerals

name formula	colour	lustre	Mohs hardness	specific gravity	habit	fracture or cleavage	refractive indices	crystal system space group	remarks
erythrite $Co_3(AsO_4)_2 \cdot 8H_2O$	crimson or peach-red (erythrite); lightening to white, gray, and pale or apple-green (annabergite)	weakly adamantine; sometimes dull or earthy	1½–2½	3.0	radiating crystal groups; globular or reniform concretions; earthy or powdery masses	one perfect cleavage	anna eryth α = 1.622–1.629 β = 1.658–1.663 γ = 1.687–1.701	monoclinic $C\frac{2}{m}$	forms a solid solution series with annabergite in which nickel replaces cobalt in the molecular structure
mimetite $Pb_5(AsO_4)_3Cl$	olive-green; gray; yellow; brown to orange	resinous to subadamantine	3½–4	7.0	barrel-shaped prisms; globular, reniform, or botryoidal masses	uneven to subconchoidal fracture	ω = 2.041–2.144 ϵ = 2.030–2.131	hexagonal $C\frac{6_3}{m}$	forms solid solution series with pyromorphite in which phosphorus replaces arsenic, with vanadinite in which vanadium replaces arsenic, and with hedyphane in which calcium replaces lead in the molecular structure
pharmacosiderite $Fe_3(AsO_4)_2(OH)_3 \cdot 5H_2O$	olive-green to honey-yellow; yellowish brown; brown	adamantine	2½	2.8	transparent to translucent, striated cubes	one imperfect to good cleavage	n = 1.676–1.704	isometric $P\bar{4}3m$	weakly piezoelectric and pyroelectric
scorodite $FeAsO_4 \cdot 2H_2O$	various greens to grayish or liver-brown (scorodite); white to pale gray (mansfieldite)	strongly vitreous to subadamantine and subresinous	3½–4	3.0–3.3	irregular crystal aggregates or earthy masses (scorodite); crusts and porous masses (mansfieldite)	subconchoidal fracture	mans scor α = 1.622–1.784 β = 1.624–1.795 γ = 1.642–1.814	orthorhombic Pcab	forms solid solution series with mansfieldite in which aluminum replaces iron in the molecular structure
svabite $Ca_5(AsO_4)_3F$	colourless; yellowish white to gray; grayish green	vitreous to subresinous	4–5	3.5–3.8	brittle, transparent or translucent, short prisms	indistinct cleavage	ω = 1.703–1.709 ϵ = 1.695–1.701	hexagonal	forms a solid solution series toward fluorapatite with phosphorus partially replacing arsenic in the molecular structure

uefying upon cooling the vapour. In addition to gray and yellow arsenic, other forms (allotropes) have been reported.

Elemental arsenic has few practical uses, one of which is to impart more nearly spherical shape in the manufacture of lead shot. It is also used in certain alloys to increase strength at elevated temperatures, in bronzing, and in pyrotechnics. All naturally occurring arsenic consists of the stable isotope arsenic-75; the radioactive isotopes arsenic-72, -74, and -76 have been used in medical diagnostic procedures.

Principal compounds. Because arsenic has a range of oxidation states from −3 to +5, it can form a variety of different kinds of compounds. Among the most important commercial compounds are the oxides, the principal forms of which are arsenious oxide (As_4O_6) and arsenic pentoxide (As_2O_5). Arsenious oxide, commonly known as white arsenic, is obtained as a by-product from the roasting of the ores of copper, lead, and certain other metals as well as by the roasting of arsenopyrite and arsenic sulfide ores. Arsenious oxide provides the starting material for most other arsenic compounds. It is also utilized in pesticides and serves as a decolourizer in the manufacture of glass and as a preservative for hides. Arsenic pentoxide is formed by the action of an oxidizing agent (*e.g.,* nitric acid) on arsenious oxide. It comprises a major ingredient of insecticides, herbicides, and metal adhesives.

Arsine (AsH_3), a colourless poisonous gas composed of arsenic and hydrogen, is another familiar arsenic compound. The gas, also called arsenic hydride, is produced by the hydrolysis of metal arsenides and by the reduction by metals of arsenic compounds in acidic solutions. It has been used as a doping agent for semi-conductors and as a military poison gas. Arsenic compounds of particular importance in agriculture are arsenic acid (H_3AsO_4) and such salts as lead arsenate ($PbHAsO_4$) and calcium arsenate [$Ca_3(AsO_4)_2$], which are useful for sterilizing soils and controlling pests, respectively.

Arsenic also forms numerous organic compounds, as for example tetramethyldiarsine, $(CH_3)_2As{-}As(CH_3)_2$, used in preparing the common desiccant cacodylic acid. Several complex organic compounds of arsenic have been employed in the treatment of certain diseases, such as amebic dysentery, caused by microorganisms.

atomic number	33
atomic weight	74.9216
melting point (gray form)	814° C (1,497° F) at 36 atmospheres pressure
density	
(gray form)	5.73 g/cc at 14° C (57° F)
(yellow form)	2.03 g/cc at 18° C (64° F)
oxidation states	−3, +3, +5
electron config.	2-8-18-5 or $1s^2 2s^2 2p^6 3s^2 3p^6 3d^{10} 4s^2 4p^3$

arsenic poisoning, harmful effects of various arsenic compounds on body tissues and functions. Arsenicals are used in numerous products, including insect, rodent, and weed killers, some chemotherapeutic agents, and certain paints, wallpaper, and ceramics.

Arsenic poisoning in humans most often results from the ingestion or inhalation of insecticides containing arsenious oxide, copper acetoarsenite, or calcium or lead arsenate. Exposure may be accidental, especially among children, or may be an occupational hazard, especially among agricultural workers handling insecticidal sprays and dusts. The sprayed fruits and vegetables, if not washed, may also bear enough arsenic to be potentially toxic to the consumer. Among industrial workers, arsine may be a source of accidental poisoning. Poisoning may also result from prolonged treatment with such medications as Fowler's solution (potassium arsenate) and arsphenamine.

Arsenic is believed to exert its toxicity by combining with certain enzymes (the organic catalysts of the cell), thereby interfering with cellular metabolism.

Individual susceptibility to arsenic poisoning varies widely; some persons have been known to develop a tolerance to doses that would kill others. Poisoning may result from a single large dose (acute poisoning) or from repeated small doses (chronic poisoning). Symptoms of acute poisoning from swallowing arsenic include nausea, vomiting, burning of the mouth and throat, and severe abdominal pains. Circulatory collapse may occur and be followed by death within a few hours. In persons exposed to arsine, the outstanding effects are destruction of red blood cells and damage to the kidneys. With chronic exposure, the more common effects include gradual loss of strength; diarrhea or constipation; pigmentation and scaling of the skin, which may undergo malignant changes; nervous manifestations marked by paralysis and confusion; degeneration of fatty tissue; anemia; and the development of characteristic streaks across the fingernails. The criminal use of the colourless, tasteless compound arsenious oxide as a poison was common until chemical methods of detection were developed. Definitive diagnosis of arsenic poisoning is based on the finding of arsenic in the urine and in hair or nails.

The treatment of acute arsenic poisoning involves washing out the stomach and the prompt administration of dimercaprol (BAL).

arsenide, any member of a rare mineral group consisting of compounds of one or more metals with arsenic (As). The coordination of the metal is almost always octahedral or tetrahedral. In the former case, each metal ion occupies a position within an octahedron composed of six oppositely charged arsenic ions, whereas in the latter each of the metal ions is surrounded by six oppositely charged neighbours arranged tetrahedrally. Structurally the arsenides resemble the sulfides (*e.g.,* galena, sphalerite, and argentite) and one frequently included in that mineral group (*see* sulfide).

Two common arsenides are niccolite (NiAs) and skutterudite ($CoAs_3$). Niccolite is a low-temperature hydrothermal mineral with hexagonal symmetry that is usually associated with nickel, cobalt, and silver sulfides. Skutterudite, on the other hand, is an intermediate- to high-temperature hydrothermal mineral with cubic symmetry associated with arsenopyrite, native silver, and bismuth. Other arsenides include:

maucherite	$Ni_{11}As_8$
rammelskbergite	$NiAs_2$
smaltite	$(Co,Ni)As_{3-x}$
safflorite	$(Co,Fe)As_2$
löllingite	$FeAs_2$
arsenopalladinite	Pd_3As
dienerite	Ni_3As
oregonite	Ni_2FeAs_2
algodonite	Cu_6As
sperrylite	$PtAs_2$

All arsenides have a metallic lustre, are opaque, and have high specific gravity and intermediate to low hardness. The succession of arsenide minerals maucherite, niccolite, rammelsbergite, smaltite, skutterudite, safforite, and löllingite corresponds to the transition from a reducing to an oxidizing environment.

Arsenius THE GREAT, also called ARSENIUS OF ROME (b. *c.* 354, Rome—d. *c.* 455, Troe, Scete Desert, Egypt), Roman noble, later monk of Egypt, whose asceticism among the Christian hermits in the Libyan Desert caused him to be ranked among the celebrated Desert Fathers and influenced the development of the monastic and contemplative life in Eastern and Western Christendom.

Born of a Roman senatorial family, Arsenius probably was made a deacon by Pope Damasus. Recommended by Damasus *c.* 383, he was called to the court of Emperor Theodosius I the Great (ruled 379–395) in Constantinople and entrusted with the education of Theodosius' sons Arcadius and Honorius. After 11 years of tutoring, Arsenius retired to the eremitical life on Mount Scete in the Libyan Desert. Shortly afterward, he was forced to flee to Troe, near ancient Memphis, Egypt, in order to escape the devastating incursions of the Libyan Mazici tribesmen, whom he likened to the Goths and Huns who ravaged Rome. Following an odyssey of approximately 15 years throughout the Egyptian wilderness, he died in the desert of Scete. He was reputed to have lived for more than 100 years. His tall, lean appearance, as described by his biographer and monastic disciple, Daniel, reinforced his fame as an ascetic. Byzantine historians and monastic writers attribute various maxims and conferences to Arsenius, many of which are contained in the 5th-century anthology *Apophthegmata patrum* ("Sayings of the Fathers"). His principal works include the *Didaskalia kai parainesis* ("Instruction and Exhortation"), which was written as a guideline for monks and is evidence, according to 6th-century historians, that he was an abbot or spiritual leader of a religious community. His commentary on the Gospel According to Luke, *Eis ton peirastēn nomikon* ("On the Temptation of the Law"), in effect is also a treatise on asceticism and the contemplative life. These texts are contained in the series *Patrologia Graeca,* vol. 65–66 (1857–66), edited by J.-P. Migne.

Arsenius is honoured as a saint by the Greek Orthodox Church and the Syro-Maronites (an Eastern Syriac church in union with Rome). His feast day is July 19.

Arsenius Autorianus (b. *c.* 1200, Constantinople—d. 1273, Proconnesus, Tur.), patriarch of Constantinople, whose deposition caused a serious schism in the Byzantine Church. He took the name Arsenius on being appointed patriarch of Nicaea in 1255 by the Byzantine emperor Theodore II Lascaris. In 1259 he crowned John IV, Theodore's son and legitimate heir, and Michael VIII Palaeologus as co-emperors. Arsenius retired to a monastery when Michael extruded John from authority, but he was persuaded to return to office after Constantinople had been liberated from the Latins in 1261. When Michael banished and blinded John, Arsenius excommunicated the Emperor and was consequently deposed by him in 1265. He was exiled to Proconnesus, where he wrote a testament that has served as an important source of contemporary history.

After Arsenius' deposition, the empire was split into two factions known as the Arsenites (followers of Arsenius) and the Josephists (followers of Joseph, Arsenius' second successor). The Arsenites fanatically opposed Michael's pro-Latin policy, which culminated at the second Council of Lyon in 1274, when papal supremacy over the Greek Church was accepted by Michael's legates. The Arsenite schism continued after the council had been rejected by the Byzantines and officially abandoned as imperial policy, and it did not end until 1310, when the body of Arsenius was buried by Patriarch Niphon in Hagia Sophia, the primatial church in Constantinople.

arsenopyrite, also called MISPICKEL, an iron sulfoarsenide mineral (FeAsS), the most common ore of arsenic. It is most commonly found in ore veins that were formed at high temperatures, as at Mapimí, Mex.; Butte, Mont.; and Tunaberg, Swed. Arsenopyrite forms monoclinic or triclinic crystals with an orthorhombic shape; the physical appearance of these crystals is seldom an accurate method for determining their symmetry. A series of minerals in which cobalt partially replaces iron is called cobaltian arsenopyrites; those in which the Co:Fe ratio lies between 1:2 and 6:1 are called glaucodot (*see also* cobaltite). Weathering alters these sulfides to arsenates: arsenopyrite to scorodite, and glaucodot to erythrite. For detailed physical properties, *see* sulfide mineral (table).

Arses (d. June 336 BC), Achaemenid king of Persia (reigned November 338–June 336 BC); he was the youngest son of Artaxerxes III Ochus and Atossa. Arses had been placed on the throne by the eunuch Bagoas, who had murdered Arses' father and all his brothers. Little is known of Arses' short reign; the major external event was the invasion of Asia Minor by Philip II of Macedon, ostensibly because Arses refused to make reparation to Philip for Artaxerxes' aid to the city of Perinthus against Philip.

The young Arses objected to the tyrannical control by Bagoas and attempted to poison him. Instead, Arses and all his children were killed, and Bagoas gave the throne to a collateral heir, Darius III.

Arshakan (king of Parthia): *see* Sanatruces.

Arshakuni DYNASTY: *see* Arsacid dynasty.

Arsi, also spelled ARSSI, or ARUSI, province (*kifle hager*), south central Ethiopia, occupying 9,500 sq mi (24,600 sq km) just south of Shewa province (location of Addis Ababa). In the east is the spine of the Ahmar Mountains, including some of Ethiopia's highest peaks, such as Mt. Karra (14,239 ft [4,340 m]). The mountain nyala, a rare antelope unique to Ethiopia, lives there together with leopards, lions, and other wildlife. The western section of the province lies in the East African Rift System. Of the valley lakes developed for tourism since the 1960s, Lake Ziway, the northernmost, lies partly within Arsi.

Ethiopia's smallest province in area, Arsi is the second most densely populated, surpassed only by Shewa. The population, chiefly Oromo (Galla), engages in agriculture (both subsistence and cash crops) and cattle raising. Fertile hillside fields produce coffee, oilseeds, and legumes for market. Asela, the provincial capital and largest town, is connected to Addis Ababa by a major north–south road. Pop. (1982 est.) 1,212,700.

arsine, colourless, extremely poisonous gas composed of arsenic with hydrogen (*see* arsenic).

Arsinoe, also spelled ARSINOË, name of four queens of the Ptolemaic dynasty of Egypt, grouped below chronologically and indicated by the symbol •.

• **Arsinoe I** (fl. early 3rd century BC), queen of Egypt, daughter of Lysimachus, king of Thrace, and first wife of Ptolemy II Philadelphus. Although she bore Ptolemy three children, including his successor, she was unable to prevent him from repudiating her and marrying his sister, Arsinoe II.

Arsinoe I was married to Ptolemy around 282, as part of the alliance between Thrace and Egypt against Seleucus I Nicator of Syria. Three years later, Philadelphus' ambitious sister arrived in Egypt and, probably at her instigation, charges of conspiring to assassinate Ptolemy were soon brought against Arsinoe. She was banished to Coptos, a city of Upper Egypt near the Wadi Hammamat, while her rival married Ptolemy and adopted her children.

Arsinoe survived at Coptos, where a stela referring to her has been found; on it she is called King's wife, but her name is not enclosed in the royal cartouche (an oval figure on monuments enclosing a sovereign's name), as is customary for a queen.

• **Arsinoe II** (b. *c.* 316 BC—d. July 270 BC), daughter of Berenice and Ptolemy I Soter, founder of the Macedonian (Ptolemaic) dynasty in Egypt; as queen of Thrace and later wife of her brother, King Ptolemy II Philadelphus of Egypt, she ruthlessly used her two husbands to advance her own position and eventually wielded great power in both kingdoms.

In 300 BC Arsinoe was married to Lysimachus, the king of Thrace, who renamed Ephesus after her and gave her three cities on the Black Sea, as well as Cassandrea, a city in northern Greece. She strove to secure the succession of the Thracian kingdom for the eldest of her three sons by accusing the heir apparent, Agathocles, the King's son by an earlier marriage, of plotting to kill his father. When the old and suspicious King ordered him executed, an ally of Agathocles in Asia Minor, the governor of Pergamum, requested aid from the Seleucid ruler Seleucus I Nicator, and war broke out between Thrace and the Middle Eastern Seleucid kingdom. After Lysimachus' death in battle (281), Arsinoe fled to Cassandrea. After assassinating Seleucus, Ptolemy Ceraunus, Arsinoe's half brother, cajoled her into marrying him, but on entering Cassandrea, he promptly executed her two younger sons. Arsinoe escaped and eventually went to Alexandria (*c.* 279) to advance her fortune.

Soon after her arrival in Egypt, Ptolemy II's first queen was accused, probably at Arsinoe's instigation, of plotting his murder and was exiled. Arsinoe then married her own brother (*c.* 277), a customary practice in Egypt but scandalous to the Greeks. "Philadelphoi" (Brother-Loving) consequently was added to the names of Ptolemy and Arsinoe.

Arsinoe's influence in the Egyptian government grew very swiftly. She contributed to Ptolemy's victory in the First Syrian War (274–271 BC) between Egypt and the Seleucid realm. Argaeus, Ptolemy's brother, and a half brother were executed on the familiar charge of conspiracy.

Arsinoe shared all of Ptolemy's titles, appeared on the coinage alone and with her husband, and had her own throne name. Towns were named after her in Greece, and dedications to her were made at numerous places in Greece and Egypt.

According to Egyptian custom, which recognized the living rulers as deities in their own right, Arsinoe was probably deified within her lifetime. After her death in 270, her cult was established in numerous places, including Alexandria, the Ptolemaic capital, where a great shrine, the Arsinoeion, was dedicated to her. Toward the end of Ptolemy II's reign, a province, al-Fayyūm, southwest of Cairo, where the King had done much land reclamation, was renamed in her honour as the Arsinoite province.

• **Arsinoe III** (b. *c.* 235—d. *c.* 204 BC), daughter of Queen Berenice II and Ptolemy III Euergetes of Egypt, sister and wife of Ptolemy IV Philopator. Powerless to arrest the decline of the Ptolemaic kingdom under her debauched husband's rule, the popular queen was eventually murdered by the royal ministers.

In 217 Arsinoe accompanied her brother to Raphia in Palestine, reputedly encouraging the Egyptian troops before their victorious encounter with the army of the Middle Eastern Seleucid kingdom. Married to Ptolemy after the battle, she gave birth to the future Ptolemy V Epiphanes about 210. Thereafter she was sequestered in the palace, while Ptolemy's depraved male and female favourites ruined both King and government. Although Arsinoe apparently disapproved of the sordid state of the court, she was unable to exert any influence. Ptolemy IV Philopator died in 205 and his ministers, fearing retribution from Arsinoe, arranged her murder about a year later. Neither the King's nor the Queen's death was announced until the child Ptolemy had been

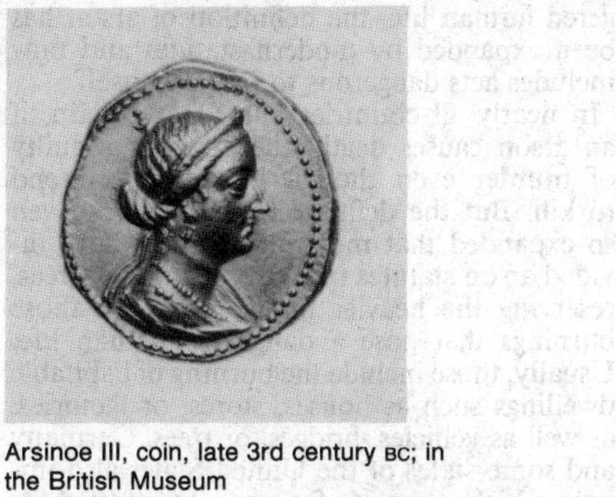

Arsinoe III, coin, late 3rd century BC; in the British Museum

By courtesy of the trustees of the British Museum; photograph, J.R. Freeman & Co. Ltd.

enthroned. Arsinoe had attained some popularity, and rioting followed the news of her assassination.

• **Arsinoe IV** (b. *c.* 63 BC—d. 41 BC), youngest daughter of the Macedonian king Ptolemy XII Auletes of Egypt, sister of Cleopatra VII and the kings Ptolemy XIII and XIV. During the Alexandrian war, Arsinoe attempted to lead the native forces against Cleopatra, who had allied herself with Julius Caesar.

Upon landing in Alexandria in 48, Caesar captured the members of the Ptolemaic royal family, but Arsinoe escape with the aid of Ganymedes, her mentor, and joined the Egyptian army led by Achillas. Following a feud between Ganymedes and the Egyptian commander, Arsinoe ordered Achillas executed. Ganymedes pressed Caesar's forces hard and negotiated an exchange of Arsinoe for Ptolemy XIII, but the Romans, with reinforcements, defeated the Egyptian army, and Arsinoe was sent to Rome to be led in Caesar's triumph. After this humiliation she found sanctuary in the Temple of Artemis at Ephesus, in Asia Minor, for she feared her ambitious sister; Cleopatra, after securing the affections of the Roman triumvir Mark Antony, in 41 persuaded him to execute Arsinoe.

Arsinoitherium, extinct genus of large, primitive, hoofed mammals found as fossils in Oligocene deposits in Egypt (the Oligocene Epoch began about 38,000,000 years ago and lasted approximately 12,000,000 years).

The animal, probably a swamp dweller, reached a length of about 3.5 metres (11 feet), and was about the size of a large rhinoceros.

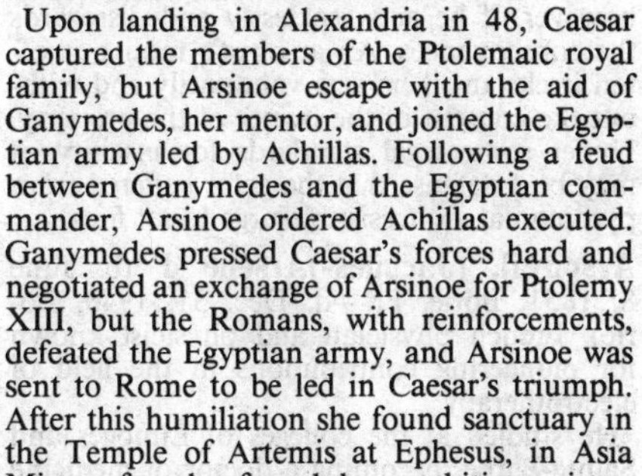

Arsinoitherium, detail of a painting by Charles R. Knight

By courtesy of the American Museum of Natural History, New York

It carried an enormous pair of horns on the nasal bones and an additional, smaller pair of horns on the frontal bones.

Arslantepe (Turkey): *see* Milid.

arson, crime commonly defined by statute as the malicious and voluntary burning of the property of another without his consent. Limited in English common law to the burning of dwellings under circumstances that endangered human life, the definition of arson has been expanded by modern statutes and now includes acts dangerous to property itself.

In nearly all countries but Great Britain, if an arson causes death, the arsonist is guilty of murder even though he did not intend to kill. But the definition of arson has been so expanded that most jurisdictions have divided arson statutes into two or more degrees, reserving the heavier punishments for those burnings that pose a danger to human life. Usually, those include the burning of habitable dwellings such as houses, stores, or factories, as well as vehicles, bridges, or trees. Germany and some states of the United States also impose a higher penalty for arson committed for the purpose of concealing or destroying evidence of another crime.

Lighter penalties are assigned to the new categories of arson endangering primarily property. Thus, it is arson to burn personal as well as real property or for a person to burn his own house to defraud an insurance company. Furthermore, modern statutes have forbidden burnings caused by newly invented incendiary devices.

A fire caused by accident or ordinary carelessness is not arson, because maliciousness is lacking. A person may be guilty of arson, however, if he acts recklessly and disregards the consequences. An arsonist's motive is often irrelevant if he acts voluntarily and without the consent of the owner of the property. Under some legal standards for insanity, it may be a defense that the actor suffered from pyromania, an irresistible urge to set fires.

Arsonval, (Jacques-)Arsène d' (b. June 8, 1851, Borie, Fr.—d. Dec. 31, 1940, Borie), French physician and physicist known for pioneering contributions in the field of electrotherapy.

He studied at the colleges of Limoges and Sainte-Barbe, becoming a doctor of medicine in 1877. In 1882, he was named director of the Laboratory of Biological Physics of the Collège de France, Paris, where he was appointed professor in 1894.

Arsonval's early research into animal heat, respiration, and electrophysiology led to his invention of devices used to treat diseases through electricity. He introduced the first reflecting moving-coil galvanometers used to measure weak electric currents (1882), invented mechanisms to obtain high-frequency currents used to treat diseases of the skin and mucous membranes ("d'Arsonvalization"; 1890), and demonstrated how a human being could conduct an alternating current strong enough to light an electric lamp (1892).

Arsouf, Battle of (1191): *see* Arsūf, Battle of.

arsphenamine, early chemotherapeutic drug, an arsenical (chemical agent containing arsenic) that was discovered by the founder of chemotherapy, the German bacteriologist Paul Ehrlich, and was marketed by him under the trade name Salvarsan. First prepared by Ehrlich in 1909, arsphenamine was the most effective drug for the treatment of syphilis until the discovery of the antibiotic penicillin in 1928. It has since been completely replaced in medicine by numerous other drugs less toxic to the human body.

Arssi (Ethiopia): *see* Arsi.

Arsūf, Battle of, Arsūf also spelled ARSOUF, famous victory won by the English king Richard I the Lion-Heart during the Third Crusade. Richard, having taken Acre in July 1191, was marching to Joppa (Jaffa), but was slowed by attacks from the Muslim army under Saladin. On September 7, after the crusaders had left Arsūf, the Muslim attacks became more intensive and were concentrated against the Hospitallers, Richard's rearguard, whom Richard forbade to counterattack until the evening. He then launched a general charge that overwhelmed Saladin's army, enabling the crusaders to occupy Joppa. It was not, however, a crushing blow to the Muslims, and Saladin was able to regroup his forces. From September 9 onward the Muslims renewed their harassing tactics, and Richard did not dare to push on to Jerusalem.

art, the expression of aesthetic ideas or purposes by the use of skill and imagination in the creation of objects, environments, or experiences that can be shared with others. The term art may also designate one of a number of modes of expression conventionally categorized by the medium utilized or the form of the product; thus we speak of painting, sculpture, filmmaking, dance, and many other modes of aesthetic expression as arts and of all of them collectively as the arts. The term art may further be used to distinguish a particular object, environment, or experience as an instance of aesthetic expression, allowing us to say, for example, that *that* drawing or tapestry is art.

Traditionally, the arts are divided into the fine and the liberal arts. The latter are concerned with skill of expression in language, speech, and reasoning. The fine arts, a translation of the French *beaux-arts,* are more concerned with purely aesthetic ends, or, in short, with the beautiful. Many forms of expression combine aesthetic concerns with utilitarian purposes; pottery, architecture, metalworking, and advertising design may be cited as examples. It may be useful to conceive of the various arts as occupying different regions along a continuum that ranges from purely aesthetic purposes at one end to purely utilitarian purposes at the other. This polarity of purpose is reflected also in the related terms artist and artisan, the latter understood as one who gives considerable attention to the utilitarian. This should by no means be taken as a rigid scheme, however. Even within one form of art, motives may vary widely; thus a potter or a weaver may create a highly functional work—a salad bowl, for example, or a blanket—that is at the same time beautiful, or he may create works that have no purpose whatever beyond being admired.

Another traditional system of classification, applied to the fine arts, establishes such categories as literature (including poetry, drama, story, and so on), the visual arts (painting, drawing, sculpture, etc.), the graphic arts (painting, drawing, design, and other forms expressed on flat surfaces), the plastic arts (sculpture, modelling), the decorative arts (enamelwork, furniture design, mosaic, etc.), the performing arts (theatre, dance, music), music (as composition), and architecture (often including interior design).

Art is treated in a number of articles in the MACROPAEDIA. For general discussions of the foundations, principles, practice, and character of art and the arts, *see* Aesthetics; Arts, Classification of the; Arts, Style in the; Arts, The Practice and Profession of the; Arts, Criticism of the; Philosophies of the Branches of Knowledge: *Philosophy of Art.*

For surveys of the traditional categories of art, *see* the articles referred to in the MICROPAEDIA entries architecture; dance; drawing; literature; music; painting; sculpture; theatre.

Other categories of art are treated in the MACROPAEDIA articles Folk Arts; Popular Arts. For discussions of other types of art, *see* Advertising: *Advertising Design;* Basketry; Broadcasting: *Broadcasting as a Medium of Art;* Enamelwork; Floral Decoration; Furniture and Accessory Furnishings; Glass Design, The History of; Interior Design; Lacquerwork; Masks; Metalwork; Mosaic; Motion Pictures; Photography; Pottery; Printmaking; Rhetoric; Rugs and Carpets; Stained Glass; Tapestry; Writing: *Calligraphy.* For treatments of the various arts as practiced by non-European peoples and cultures, *see* African Arts; American Indians; Central Asian Arts; East Asian Arts; Egyptian Arts and Architecture, Ancient; Islāmic Arts; Oceanian Arts; Prehistoric Peoples and Cultures; South Asian Arts; Southeastern Asian Arts. For special problems relating to the preservation of artworks, *see* Art Conservation and Restoration.

For a description of the place of art in the circle of learning and for a list of both MACROPAEDIA and MICROPAEDIA articles on the subject, *see* PROPAEDIA: Part Six.

Consult the INDEX *first*

art, academy of, in the visual arts, institution established primarily for the instruction of artists but often endowed with other functions, most significantly that of providing a place of exhibition for students and mature artists accepted as members. In the late 15th and early 16th centuries, a series of short-lived "academies" that had little to do with artistic training were founded in various parts of Italy. The most famous of these was the Accademia of Leonardo da Vinci (established 1498), which seems to have been simply a social gathering of amateurs meeting to discuss the theory and practice of art. The first true academy for instruction, the Accademia del Disegno, was established in 1562 in Florence by the duke Cosimo I de' Medici at the instigation of the

"The Royal Academy of Arts," mezzotint by Richard Earlom (1742/43–1822), after J. Zoffany
By courtesy of the Victoria and Albert Museum, London

painter and art historian Giorgio Vasari. The two nominal heads of the institution were Cosimo himself and Michelangelo. In contrast to the guilds, membership in the Accademia del Disegno was an honour conferred only on already recognized independent artists. When Vasari's academy fell into disorganization, his ideas were taken up by the Accademia di San Luca, founded in 1593 at Rome by the painter Federico Zuccari and Cardinal St. Charles Borromeo. With its emphasis on instruction and exhibition, the Accademia di San Luca was the prototype for the modern academy. Among its functions, much imitated in later academies, was the sponsorship of lectures given by members of the academy and later published and made available to the general public. Such discourses became the means by which academies fostered and gained public acceptance for particular aesthetic theories. The Accademia di San Luca was firmly established by 1635, having received support from the powerful Pope Urban VIII. All the leading Italian artists and many foreigners were members; the secondary aims of the institution—to obtain important commissions, to enhance the prestige of the members, and to practice exclusionary policies against those who were not members—were avidly pursued.

For the following two centuries, academicism dominated Italian artistic life. The decline of the church and then of aristocrats as patrons—those groups had formerly commissioned the painting of whole rooms at a time—resulted in the abandonment of the artist to an anonymous market of buyers who might commission one portrait or some other single easel painting at a time. This made exhibition essential to the artist's success. The state-supported academy, being the only institution financially able to provide this service on a large scale, came to control public taste, the economic fortunes of the artist, and ultimately the quality of his art by its determination of standards in the work it chose to show.

In France the Académie Royale de Peinture et de Sculpture was founded in 1648 as a free society of members all entitled to the same rights and granted admission in unlimited numbers. With the appointment of Jean Baptiste Colbert, powerful minister of Louis XIV, as vice protector in 1661, however, the Académie Royale began to function as an authoritarian arm of the state. As such it assumed almost total control of French art and began to exercise considerable influence on the art of Europe. For the first time, the concept of aesthetic orthodoxy obtained official endorsement. The Académie achieved a virtual monopoly in teaching and exhibition, beginning in 1667 the long-lived practices of annual Salons. Thus, the idea, born of the Enlightenment, that aesthetic matters could be universally subjected to reason led to a rigid imposition of a narrow set of aesthetic rules on all art that came within the Académie's jurisdiction. This approach found especially fertile ground in the Neoclassical style, which arose in the second half of the 18th century and which the Académie espoused with enthusiasm.

Meanwhile, numerous academies, usually state supported and similar in structure and approach to the French Académie, were established throughout Europe and in America. By 1790 there were more than 100 such institutions. One of the latest to be founded was the Royal Academy of Arts in London, established in 1768 by George III with Sir Joshua Reynolds as its first president. Although Reynolds gave the obligatory discourses on the importance of harmony and uplifting conceptions in painting, the Royal Academy never dominated art as completely as academies on the Continent.

The first important challenge to the power of the academies came with the rise of Romanticism, which saw the artist as an individual genius whose creative powers could not be taught or externally controlled. Although most notable Romantic artists were absorbed into the academic system in the first half of the 19th century, eventually almost all artists of significance found themselves excluded from official patronage, largely because of the widening gap between their achievements and the taste of the bourgeois public to which the academies catered. The blow that finally broke the power of the academy was struck in France. After a series of unsuccessful compromises (*e.g.,* the Salon des Refusés, established for painters excluded from the Académie in 1863 by Napoleon III), the Impressionists, who exhibited independently between 1874 and 1886, succeeded in winning the acceptance of the critics. In the 20th century the art academy has become an important source of instruction, synonymous with the modern art school.

art, popular: *see* popular art.

art, primitive: *see* primitive art.

art brut (French: "raw art"), designation by the French painter Jean Dubuffet in the 1940s for art that is crude, inexperienced, and

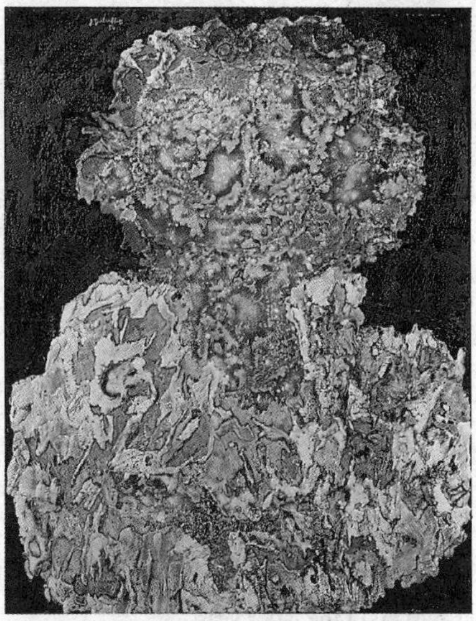

"Dame aux fourrures," art brut painting by Jean Dubuffet, oil, September 1954; in the Mr. and Mrs. Ralph F. Colin Collection, New York City

By courtesy of Mr. and Mrs. Ralph F. Colin, New York City

even indecent. Dubuffet, the most important French artist to emerge after World War II, became interested in the art of the mentally ill in mid-career, after studying *The Art of the Insane* by the Swiss psychiatrist Hans Prinzhorn. Dubuffet applied the name art brut to the drawings, paintings, and doodlings of the psychotic, the naive, and the primitive, works that he regarded as the purest forms of creative expression. Like the early Cubists' discovery of primitive Oceanian and African sculpture, Dubuffet's study of this type of art gave him the inspiration he sought for his own art, as it represented for him the most authentic expression of emotion and human values.

Originally inspired by the childlike art of the Swiss painter Paul Klee, from the 1940s on, Dubuffet's paintings emulated the sincerity and naiveté that he associated with real art brut. The first of these works shows a childlike vision of humanity and civilization, with bright, gay colours, and naive drawing. Later works, passionate and primitive, sometimes pathetic, sometimes obscene, incorporate forms derived from graffiti and psychotic art; painted in thick impasto or constructed in collage, these densely detailed and intensely expressive works convey teeming life and brutal force, often tempered with poetry and humour as well as passion.

art conservation, any attempt to repair and preserve works of sculpture, painting, drawing, architecture, and the decorative arts (furniture, glassware, metalware, textiles, ceramics, and so on) from the effects of negligence, willful damage, or, more usually, inevitable decay caused by the situations for which the objects are designed and the nature of the materials of which they are made. Ceramics, glassware, and gold are exceptionally durable, but artifacts in other materials are more susceptible to dampness, corrosion, and changes in atmosphere that cause warping and cracking; attacks by insects, fungi, and frost; tearing and staining; and the effects of simple aging or, if they are kept out of doors, weathering (likely to be compounded by the industrial atmosphere).

A brief treatment of art conservation follows. For full treatment *see* MACROPAEDIA: Art Conservation and Restoration.

Conservation deals with the maintenance, preservation, and restoration of art. Basically it consists of noticing decay and arresting it before it gets worse. Conservation, especially of painting, requires a peculiar combination of skills: manual dexterity, a knowledge of art history, and an understanding of materials and their chemistry. Noticing decay involves regular inspection, possibly including examination with a microscope and X-rays or other radiation, to provide a detailed diagnosis before treatment. Surfaces can be protected, for instance, with wax, or they can be more thoroughly sealed against damp and corrosion; weakened substances can be filled with a consolidating medium and impregnated with fungicides or insecticides; textiles, including the canvas support or backing of paintings, can be lined; and wooden, or other rigid supports can be backed.

Restoration, which may cover anything from cleaning to reconstruction, continues to be somewhat controversial. Opinions vary as to the proper degree of restoration; too much is interference, too little leaves the object in a state of disrepair. Then how obvious should restoration be?

To restore perfectly to the original state would leave no traces of restoration, but this would result in deception, or at least confusion, about how much of the object is authentic or how much aging it has undergone. Problems arise with paintings, for example, over whether to strip off old, darkened varnish, which may be disguising other effects of age that can only be remedied by complete repainting, such as fading colours, or an increased transparency of paint that reveals the underpainting. The patina of old metals provides another sort of difficulty; it is after all a form of corrosion, but may nevertheless be valued as an enhancing effect of age.

Ideals of restoration have followed a pendulum swing: a period in which restoration was carried to the point where only detailed examination would show which parts were original and which restored produced in reaction the practice of making the restored parts strikingly obvious. With time a middle course has prevailed; it is now common in restoring a broken pot, for example, to tint the restored areas with some colour that does not offer a glaring contrast to their surroundings but is still evident to a superficial examination. Similarly in painting, the retouched areas are distinguished by striation (the state of a surface where a stripe or line is distinguished from surrounding material by colour, texture or elevation).

Nowhere did these controversies rage more fiercely than in the 19th century in the field of architectural restoration. In the late 18th and early 19th century, its purpose was to impose unity of style—the style, in general, being Gothic. Where more than one medieval style was present, the architect would make a choice (commonly in favour of Decorated). This practice of replacing all styles later than that favoured by the restorer, came to be regarded by the middle of the 19th century as a falsification of history, and the British architect James Wyatt (1746–1813)—the restorer of the Durham, Hereford, Lichfield, and Salisbury cathedrals—was identified as one of the arch-culprits. A.W.N. Pugin and, later John Ruskin, agitated against restoration in their writings. William Morris joined the attack: in 1877 he helped found the Society for the Protection of Ancient Buildings, nicknamed Antiscrape. The society, through lectures, letters, articles, and reports kept the public aware of restoration and recruited hundreds of members. The society also formed a foreign committee to campaign against restoration on the continent, which lagged behind Great Britain in this respect. French restoration, in the second half of the century, still followed the practice of E.E. Viollet-le-Duc "to restore a building is to re-establish it to a completed state; which may never have existed at any given time." Gradually, however, the English creed "conserve, but not rebuild" prevailed in Europe; and by 1900 it had started to be enforced at home by acts of Parliament, the first of many being the 1882 Ancient Monuments Protection Act. Subsequent amendments and new acts enacted in the 20th century and the success of foundations such as the national trusts of Scotland and of England, Wales, and Northern Ireland to preserve historic buildings, reflect not only an increasing concern but an ever-widening view of the kind of building coming within the scope of such protection. In the United States both the National Trust for Historic Preservation and the National Park Service have somewhat similar functions.

Art Deco, also called STYLE MODERNE, movement in the decorative arts and architecture that originated in the 1920s and developed into the dominant style of the 1930s. Its name was derived from the Exposition Internationale des Arts Décoratifs et Industriels Modernes, held in Paris in 1925, where the style was first exhibited. Art Deco design represented modernism turned into fashion. Its products included both individually crafted luxury items and mass-produced wares, but in either case, the intention was to create a sleek and anti-traditional elegance that symbolized wealth and sophistication.

The distinguishing features of the style are simple, clean shapes, often with a "streamlined" look; ornament that is geometric or stylized from representational forms; and unusually varied, often expensive materials, which often include man-made substances (plastics, especially bakelite; vita-glass; and ferro-concrete) in addition to natural ones (jade, silver, ivory, obsidian, chrome, and rock crystal). Though Art Deco objects were rarely mass-produced, the characteristic features of the style reflected admiration for the modernity of the machine and for the inherent design qualities of machine-made objects (*e.g.,* relative simplicity, planarity, symmetry, and unvaried repetition of elements).

Among the formative influences on Art Deco were Art Nouveau, the Bauhaus, Cubism, and Sergey Diaghilev's Ballets Russes. Decorative ideas came from American Indian, Egyptian, and early Classical sources as well as from nature. Characteristic motifs included nude female figures, animals (especially deer, antelope, and gazelles), foliage, and sunrays, all in conventionalized forms.

Most of the outstanding Art Deco creators designed primarily individually crafted or limited-edition items. They included the furniture designers Jacques Ruhlmann and Maurice Dufrène; the architect Le Corbusier; metalsmith Jean Puiforcat; glass designer René Lalique; fashion designer Erté; artist-jewellers Raynmond Templier, Jean Fouquet René Robert, H.G. Murphy, and Wiwen Nilsson; and the figural sculptor Chiparus. The fashion designer Paul Poiret and the graphic artist Edward McKnight Kauffer represent those whose work directly reached a larger audience. New York City's Rockefeller Center (especially its interiors supervised by Donald Deskey), the Chrysler Building by William Van Alen, and the Empire State Building by Shreve, Lamb & Harmon are the most monumental embodiments of Art Deco. Although the style went out of fashion during World War II, beginning in the late 1960s there was a renewed interest in and revival of Art Deco design.

Art Gallery of New South Wales, in Sydney, Australia, government-maintained art museum founded in 1874 as the New South Wales Academy of Art. A new building was opened in 1972.

The original resolution of the gallery authorized buying in London and in Sydney, and English 19th-century paintings and contemporary British art are particularly well represented. Until the 1960s the museum was exclusively devoted to British art. Australian art later formed an important part of new acquisitions.

Art Institute of Chicago, museum of European, American, and Oriental sculpture, paintings, prints and drawings, and decorative arts, as well as photography and African and pre-Columbian American art. It was established in 1866 as the Chicago Academy of Design and took its current name in 1882. In 1893 it moved to the present building, designed by the architectural firm of Shepley, Rutan, and Coolidge.

The institute also includes the School of the Art Institute, the Ryerson Library (art), and the Burnham Library (architecture). The Goodman Theatre (founded 1925) presents productions of the Chicago Theatre Group (from 1977); the Goodman School of Drama, operated by the Art Institute from 1930 to 1978, became a school of DePaul University (Chicago) in the latter year.

Art Nouveau, ornamental style of art that flourished between *c.* 1890 and 1910, throughout Europe and the United States, characterized by a long, sinuous, organic line and employed most often in architecture, interior design, jewelry and glass design, posters, and illustration. It was a deliberate attempt to create a new style, free of the imitative historicism that dominated much of 19th-century art. Art Nouveau developed first in England and soon spread to the Continent, where it was called Jugendstil in Germany, Sezessionstil in Austria, Stile Floreale or Stile Liberty (from the London department store that exported Art Nouveau fabrics) in Italy, and Modernismo or Modernistà in Spain. The term Art Nouveau was coined by a gallery in Paris that exhibited much of the work.

In England the style grew out of a tradition of linearism, peripheral to the mainstream of English art, that began with the sinuous drawings of the poet and artist William Blake in the early 19th century. Its immediate precursors were the Aestheticism of the illustrator Aubrey Beardsley, who depended heavily on the expressive quality of organic line, and the Arts and Crafts Movement of William Morris, which established the importance of a vital style in the applied arts. On the Continent it was also influenced by experiments with expressive line by the painters Paul Gauguin and Henri de Toulouse-Lautrec. The movement was also partly inspired by a current taste for the abstract linear patterns of Japanese prints (Ukiyo-e).

The distinguishing ornamental characteristic of Art Nouveau is its undulating, asymmetrical line, often taking the form of flower stalks and buds, vine tendrils, insect wings, and other delicate and sinuous natural objects; the line may be elegant and graceful or infused with a powerful, rhythmic and whiplike force. In the graphic arts the line subordinates all other pictorial elements—form, texture, space, and colour—to its own decorative effect. In architecture and the other plastic arts the whole of the three-dimensional form becomes engulfed in the organic, undulating, linear rhythm, creating a fusion between structure and ornament. Architecture particularly shows this synthesis of ornament and structure; a liberal combination of materials—ironwork, glass, ceramic, and brickwork—was employed, for example, in the creation of unified interiors in which columns and beams became thick vines with spreading tendrils and windows were both openings for light and air and membranous outgrowths of the organic whole. This approach was directly opposed to the traditional architectural values of reason and clarity of structure.

There were a great number of artists and designers who worked in the Art Nouveau style. Some of the more prominent were the Scottish architect and designer Charles Rennie Mackintosh, who specialized in a predominantly geometric line and particularly influenced the Austrian Sezessionstil; the Belgian architects Henry van de Velde and Victor Horta, whose extremely sinuous and delicate structures influenced the French architect Hector Guimard, another important figure; the American glassmaker Louis Comfort Tiffany; the French furniture and ironwork designer Louis Majorelle; the Czechoslovakian graphic designer-artist Alphonse Mucha; the French jewelry designer René Lalique; the American architect Louis Henry Sullivan, who used plantlike Art Nouveau ironwork to decorate his traditionally structured buildings; and the Spanish architect and sculptor Antonio Gaudí, perhaps the most original artist of the movement, who went beyond dependence on line to transform buildings into curving, bulbous, brightly coloured, organic constructions.

After 1910, Art Nouveau appeared old-fashioned and limited and was generally abandoned as a distinct decorative style. The style was of great importance, however, in moving toward the 20th-century aesthetic of unity of design.

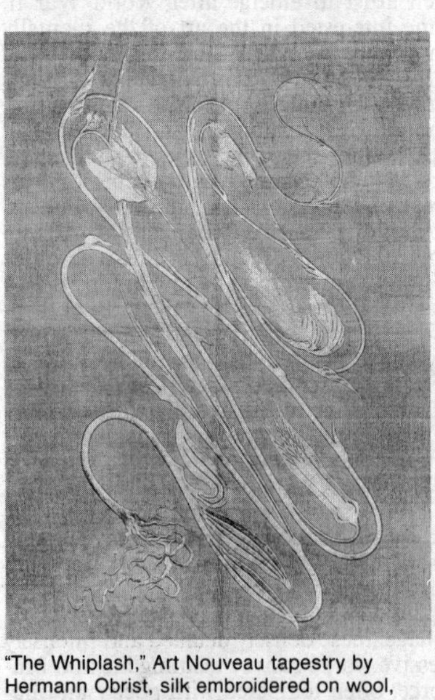

"The Whiplash," Art Nouveau tapestry by Hermann Obrist, silk embroidered on wool, 1895; in the Münchner Stadtmuseum, Munich

By courtesy of the Munchner Stadtmuseum, Munich

Art of Poetry, The (Horace): *see* Ars poetica.

Art Povera, conceptual art of several diverse forms produced in Europe and the United States beginning in the late 1960s, designed less to create an aesthetic object than to involve the viewer in the contemplation of an aesthetic idea or in the participation in an aesthetic act. Art Povera encompasses the very different conceptual activities of artists such as Richard Sierra, Robert Smithson, Robert Morris, Eva Hesse, Keith Sonnier, Bruce Nauman, and Walter de Maria, all of whom, however, rejected the traditional concept of art as object by producing not complete art works but works perpetually in a state of becoming. The special concern of these exponents of Art Povera was to involve the ordinary person in aesthetic experience, a goal that they pursued through radical means.

"Fifty-two Ton Granite Mass in Cement Depression, Silver Springs, Nevada," Art Povera sculpture by Michael Heizer, August 1969
Gianfranco Gorgoni

Art Povera grew out of the disillusionment of several young artists with what they saw as an increasing separation of art from life in Pop art, Minimal art (*qq.v.*), and other contemporary movements that seemed to them to be elitist because of the esoteric aesthetic principles from which they arose; they reacted especially against a contemporary tendency for works of art to become consumers' items rather than expressions of significant aesthetic or socially relevant ideas. The immediate antecedents of Art Povera, and of the whole conceptual art movement, were the music of the American composer John Cage and his followers, which in part involved "compositions of silence," through which the audience was forced to listen to the "music" of such mundane noises as its own coughing; and the "ideational art" of the American painter Ad Reinhardt and others, exemplified by Reinhardt's black on black paintings, which compelled the viewer to look beyond the art object and consider the problems of aesthetics that might have led to the production of such a work. Many of the forms that Art Povera took were inspired by these earlier works.

The principal art forms developed and named by Art Povera artists are "process art," in which the aesthetic experience consists of the transitory act of producing an art work rather than the completion or contemplation of that work; "earth art," gigantic, highly novel works, involving both nature and technology (such as the draping of a huge curtain across a valley), that may or may not be executed but that put forth, in their conception, an aesthetic idea in which the public participates by contemplating it; "body art, sculpture, or works," also called "corporal art," combining performance, sculpture, and conceptualism; the "art of antiform," involving the performance of everyday acts and the designation of these acts as aesthetic; "micro-emotive art," "aesthetic" acts performed with the emotions or the bodily functions (such as breathing); and "raw materialism," the aesthetic use of natural or industrial materials. Art Povera usually reaches the public through exhibits of photographs and other records that either document the execution of a work or describe its planning or even the work itself. All of these forms reflect the idea that everyone can participate in art, either by performing such easy "aesthetic" acts as walking down the street or by viewing the documentation of an earthwork or other work whose significance exists in terms of the viewer's personal aesthetic response to the documentation.

Some of the more notable examples of Art Povera are Christo's earthwork "Wrapping up the Coast of Australia," a feat that involved the use of vast quantities of plastic; Hans Haacke's documentary study of slum housing in New York City, which consisted of photographs of the buildings, a list of the landlords' names, and an invitation to the spectator to consider the slum-housing situation in aesthetic terms; the linguistic meditations of Joseph Kosuth, presented to spectators as a typescript consisting largely of visually pleasing words and sentences; and the artistic utterances of computers programmed by Michael Heizer and Douglas Huebler.

Árta, city and capital, *nomós* (department) of Árta, Ípiros (ancient Epirus) region, Greece, on the left bank of the Árakhthos Potamós north of the Gulf of Árta. The modern city is located on the site of Ambracia, an ancient Corinthian colony and the capital (from 294 BC) of Pyrrhus, king of Epirus. In 189 it was destroyed by the Romans. To commemorate his victory (31 BC) over Mark Antony at Actium, Octavian (later Augustus) founded the new town of Nicopolis Actia a few miles away; as a result, Ambracia declined.

Árta's modern history dates from the destruction of Nicopolis Actia in the 11th century AD by the Bulgars. A Byzantine bishopric, Árta survived a Norman seizure (1083) and the Greek despots of Epirus, passing in 1318 to the Orsini family of Cephalonia. It was captured by the Turks in 1449, but soon passed to Venice; after a brief period of French rule, it came again under the Turks. In the 16th and 17th centuries it was noted for its academic institutions. Several times during and after the War of Greek Independence (1821–29) it was fought over; but in 1881 it was ceded to Greece by Turkey, and after the Balkan Wars of 1912–13 it was incorporated into the Kingdom of Greece.

The seat of a metropolitan bishop, Árta is a prosperous agricultural town surrounded by groves of orange, lemon, and citron. It produces woollens, cottons, and embroidery. On the ancient acropolis are remains of a Byzantine fortress, and outside the town are several late 13th- and 14th-century churches with mosaics and glazed tiles and three 13th-century monasteries. Pop. (1981) city, 20,004; (1981) *nomós,* 80,044.

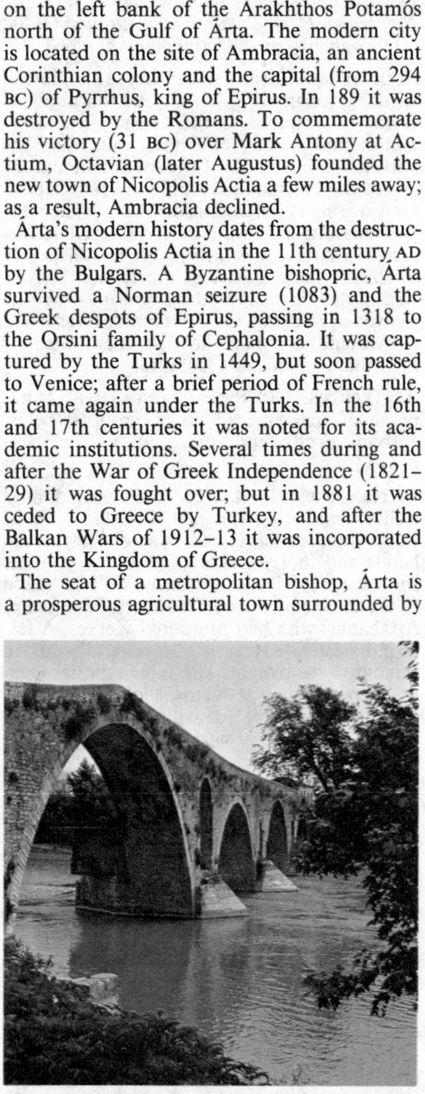

Seventeenth-century bridge over the Árakhthos Potamós (river), Árta, Greece
Babette and Marshall Druck—Photo Researchers

Árta, Gulf of, Modern Greek AMVRAKIKÓS KÓLPOS, deep inlet on the west coast of Greece. Almost landlocked by the peninsulas of Préveza on the north and Áktion on the south, it has access to the sea through the narrow strait called Stenón Prévezis.

The north shore of the gulf is formed by the combined deltas of the Loúros and Árakhthos rivers, with marshes and lagoons; the south shore has broad bays alternating with wooded, rocky headlands. The town of Amfilokhía lies at the southeast corner of the gulf, and the road linking Agrínion, Amfilokhía, and Árta skirts the gulf's eastern shore.

Artabanus, also called ARDABAN (d. 465/464 BC), minister of the Achaemenid king Xerxes I of Persia, whom he murdered in 465. According to one Greek source, Artabanus had previously killed Xerxes' son Darius and feared that the father would avenge him; other sources relate that he killed Xerxes first and then, pretending that Darius had done so, induced Darius' brother Artaxerxes I to avenge the "parricide." Artabanus was in control of the Achaemenid state for seven months and was recognized as king by Egypt. Finally, however, he was betrayed by his fellow conspirator Megabyzus and was killed by Artaxerxes.

Artabanus, also spelled ARDABAN, name of Parthian kings grouped below chronologically and indicated by the symbol •.

• **Artabanus I,** also called ARSACES II (fl. 3rd and 2nd centuries BC), king of Parthia (reigned 211–191 BC) in southwestern Asia. In 209 he was attacked by the Seleucid king Antiochus III of Syria, who took Hecatompylos, the Arsacid capital, the present location of which is uncertain, and Syrinx in Hyrcania; finally, however, Antiochus concluded a treaty with Artabanus, who after 206 lost much territory to Euthydemus, ruler of Bactria.

Artabanus I, coin, late 3rd–early 2nd century BC; in the British Museum
By courtesy of the trustees of the British Museum; photograph, J.R. Freeman & Co. Ltd.

• **Artabanus III** (fl. 1st century AD), king of Parthia (reigned *c.* AD 12–*c.* 38). At first king of Media Atropatene, he took the Parthian throne in AD 9 or 10 from Vonones and was proclaimed king about two years later in Ctesiphon, the Parthian capital on the Tigris. Vonones fled to Armenia, but Artabanus forced him to abdicate in AD 15 or 16. During the first part of Artabanus' reign there was peace with Rome. Although faced with internal unrest, he was apparently a strong king and helped restore the authority of the central government. A letter written by Artabanus in December 21 to the magistrates and the city of Susa is the only Arsacid royal document that has been preserved.

On the death of Artaxias III (Zeno) of Armenia (AD 34/35), Artabanus set his son, known only as Arsaces, on the Armenian throne. Two Parthian nobles, apparently restless at Artabanus' assertion of central authority, applied to the Roman emperor Tiberius for a king from among the descendants of an earlier king, Phraates IV. Thus, a grandson of Phraates, Tiridates III, arrived in Syria in AD

35 and was set on the Parthian throne by the Roman general Lucius Vitellius. Artabanus withdrew to Hyrcania, but within a year he was summoned by the anti-Roman party, returned, and won back his throne. The struggle had evidently weakened Parthia internally; large areas and some of the great commercial centres seem to have become independent of the crown. The general discontent drove Artabanus into flight again, and he took refuge with his vassal, Izates II of Adiabene, while a certain Cinnamus occupied the Parthian throne. Artabanus was restored by negotiation but died soon afterward.

• Artabanus V (fl. 3rd century), last king of the Parthian Empire (reigned *c.* AD 213–224) in southwest Asia. He was the younger son of Vologases IV, who died probably in 207, and was ruling the Median provinces at the time of his rebellion (*c.* 213) against his brother, Vologases V. By 216 he had apparently extended his power over the Mesopotamian part of the empire, although Vologases continued to strike coins at the Seleucia mint until 222 or 223. The Roman emperor Caracalla attacked Artabanus in 216, ravaging much of Media and desecrating the Parthian royal tombs at Arbela (modern ʿArbil, Iraq). In 217 Artabanus counterattacked; Caracalla was assassinated, and his successor, Macrinus, who was defeated at Nisibis (Nisibin), made peace with heavy indemnities. Meanwhile, however, Ardashīr the Sāsānian, who had begun his rule as petty king in the province of Persis in 208, had been steadily extending his domains and winning Iranian allies against Parthian overlordship. Revolt became general, and Artabanus was finally killed in battle against Ardashīr.

Artakhshathra (kings of Persia): *see* Ardashīr I; Ardashīr II; Artaxerxes I; Artaxerxes II; Artaxerxes III.

Artaud, Antonin (b. Sept. 4, 1896, Marseille—d. March 4, 1948, Ivry-sur-Seine, Fr.), French dramatist, poet, actor, and theoretician of the Surrealist movement who attempted to replace the "bourgeois" classical theatre with his "theatre of cruelty," a primitive ceremonial experience to liberate the human subconscious and reveal man to himself.

Artaud suffered from meningitis as a child, spent his youth in the Middle East, and became interested in mysticism. Lifelong mental disorders sent him repeatedly into asylums. He sent his Surrealist poetry *L'Ombilic des limbes* (1925; "The Navel of Limbo") and *Le Rèse-nerfs* (1925; "Nerve Scales") to the influential critic Jacques Rivière, thus beginning their long correspondence. After studying acting in Paris, he made his debut in Aurélien-Marie Lugné-Poe's Dadaist–Surrealist Théâtre de l'Oeuvre. Artaud broke with the Surrealists when their leader, the poet André Breton, gave their allegiance to Communism. Artaud, who believed the movement's strength was extrapolitical, joined another defecting Surrealist, the dramatist Roger Vitrac, in the short-lived Théâtre Alfred Jarry. Artaud appeared as a priest in Carl Dreyer's classic film *La Passion de Jeanne d'Arc* (1928).

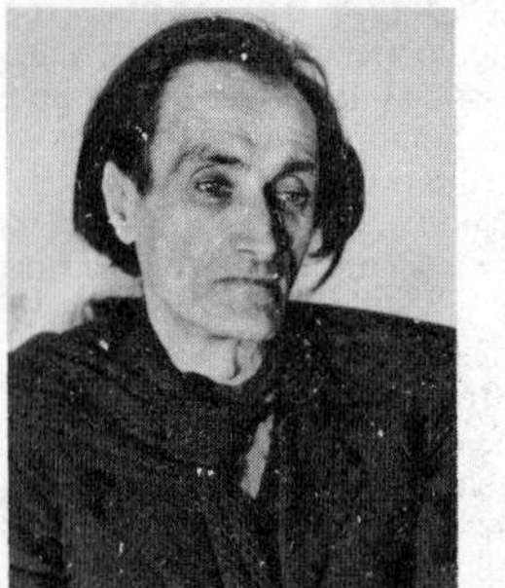

Artaud, 1948
Denise Colomb—J.P. Ziolo

Artaud's *Manifeste du théâtre de la cruauté* (1932) and *Le Théâtre et son double* (1938; *The Theatre and Its Double,* 1958) call for a communion between actor and audience in a magic exorcism; gestures, sounds, unusual scenery, and lighting combine to form a language, superior to words, that can be used to subvert thought and logic and to shock the spectator into seeing the baseness of his world.

Artaud's own works, less important than his theories, were failures. *Les Cenci,* performed in Paris in 1935, was an experiment too bold for its time. His vision, however, was a major influence on the Absurd theatre of Jean Genet, Eugène Ionesco, Samuel Beckett, and others and on the entire movement away from the dominant role of language and rationalism in contemporary theatre. His other works include *Mexico* (1936, written after a voyage there), *Van Gogh, le suicidé de la société* (1947), and *Heliogabalus, ou l'anarchiste couronné* (1934; "Heliogabalus, or the Crowned Anarchist").

Artavasdes II (fl. 1st century BC), king of Armenia (reigned 53–34 BC), the son and successor of Tigranes II the Great. Artavasdes was at first an ally of Rome, but when the Parthian king Orodes II invaded Armenia, he joined the Parthian side and gave his sister in marriage to Pacorus, Orodes' son. When the Romans under Mark Antony entered Armenia (36), Artavasdes again gave his allegiance to Rome. Later deserting the Roman forces, Artavasdes was captured by Antony when he reinvaded Armenia (34). Artavasdes was taken to Alexandria, where he was later killed by the Ptolemaic queen Cleopatra.

Artaxerxes, Old Persian ARTAKHSHATHRA, name of Achaemenid kings, grouped below chronologically and indicated by the symbol •.

• Artaxerxes I (d. 425 BC, Susa, Elam), Achaemenid king (reigned 465–425 BC); he was surnamed in Greek Macrocheir (Longhand) and in Latin Longimanus. A younger son of Xerxes I and Amestris, he was raised to the throne by the commander of the guard, Artabanus, who had murdered Xerxes. A few months later, Artaxerxes slew Artabanus in a hand-to-hand fight. His reign, though generally peaceful, was disturbed by several insurrections, the first of which was the revolt of his brother the satrap of Bactria. More dangerous was the rebellion of Egypt under Inaros, who received assistance from the Athenians. Achaemenid rule was restored by Megabyzus, satrap of Syria, after a prolonged struggle (460–454). In 448 fighting between the Achaemenids and the Athenians ended, and in the Samian and Peloponnesian wars Artaxerxes remained neutral; toward the Jews he pursued a tolerant policy. His building inscriptions at Persepolis record the completion of the throne hall of his father. The tomb of Artaxerxes is at Naqsh-e Rustam.

• Artaxerxes II (fl. late 5th and early 4th centuries BC), Achaemenid king of Persia (reigned 404–359/358); he was the son and successor of Darius II and was surnamed (in Greek) Mnemon, meaning "the mindful." When Artaxerxes took the Persian throne, the power of Athens had been broken in the Peloponnesian War (431–404), and the Greek towns across the Aegean Sea in Ionia were again subjects of the Achaemenid Empire. In 404, however, Artaxerxes lost Egypt, and in the following year his brother Cyrus the Younger began preparations for his rebellion. Although Cyrus was defeated and killed at Cunaxa (401), the rebellion had dangerous repercussions, for it not only demonstrated the superiority of the Greek hoplites used by Cyrus, but also led the Greeks to believe that Persia was vulnerable.

In 400 Sparta broke openly with the Achaemenids, and during the next five years its armies achieved considerable military success in Anatolia. The Spartan navy, however, was destroyed at Cnidus (394), thereby giving the Achaemenids mastery of the Aegean. The Greek allies (Thebes, Athens, Argos, and Corinth) continued the war against Sparta, but, when it became evident that the only ones to gain from the war were the Athenians, Artaxerxes decided to conclude peace with Sparta. In 386 Athens was compelled to accept the settlement known as the King's Peace, or the Peace of Antalcidas, by which Artaxerxes decreed that all the Asiatic mainland and Cyprus were his, that Lemnos, Imbros, and Scyros were to remain Athenian dependencies, and that all the other Greek states were to receive autonomy.

Elsewhere Artaxerxes met with less success. Two expeditions against Egypt (385–383 and 374) ended in complete failure, and during the same period there were continuous rebellions in Anatolia. There were also wars against the mountain tribes of Armenia and Iran.

By the King's Peace the Achaemenids had become the arbiters of Greece, and in the following wars all parties continually applied to them for a decision in their favour. After the Theban victory of Leuctra (371), an old alliance between the Achaemenids and the Thebans was restored. Achaemenid supremacy, however, was based on Greek discord; and, when this weakness became apparent, all the satraps (governors) of Anatolia rose in revolt (*c.* 366), in close alliance with Athens, Sparta, and Egypt, and Artaxerxes could do little against them. The satraps, however, were divided by mutual distrust, and the rebellion was finally put down by a series of treacheries. When the reign of Artaxerxes ended, Achaemenid authority had been restored over most of the empire—more from internal rivalries and discord than from his efforts.

Under Artaxerxes an important change occurred in the Persian religion. The Persians apparently did not worship images of the gods until Artaxerxes set up statues of the goddess Anāhitā in various large cities. Inscriptions by all former kings named only Ahura Mazdā, but those of Artaxerxes also invoked Anāhitā and Mithra, two deities of the old popular Iranian religion that had been neglected.

• Artaxerxes III (d. 338 BC), Achaemenid king (reigned 359/358–338 BC); he was the son and successor of Artaxerxes II and was called Ochus before he took the throne. Artaxerxes was a cruel but energetic ruler. To secure his throne he put to death most of his relatives. In 356 he ordered all the satraps to dismiss their mercenaries. He also forced Athens to conclude peace and to acknowledge the independence of its rebellious allies (355).

Artaxerxes then attempted to subjugate Egypt, which had been independent since 404. The failure of the first attempt (351) encouraged the Phoenician towns and the princes of Cyprus to revolt. At the beginning of 345, Artaxerxes collected a great army and marched against Sidon. Mentor of Rhodes, who had helped in the betrayal of Sidon, rose high in the King's favour and entered into a close understanding with the eunuch Bagoas, the King's favourite. Artaxerxes then advanced on Egypt with a great land and naval force and, at Pelusium in the Nile Delta, defeated the pharaoh Nectanebo II (343). A Persian satrap was placed over Egypt, the walls of its cities were destroyed, its temples were plundered, and Artaxerxes was said to have killed the Apis bull with his own hand.

After the King's return to Susa, Bagoas ruled the court and the upper satrapies, while Mentor restored the authority of the empire throughout the west. When Philip of Macedon attacked Perinthus and Byzantium (340), Artaxerxes sent support to those cities. In 338 Artaxerxes and his elder sons were killed by Bagoas, who then raised the King's youngest son, Arses, to the throne.

Artaxias, also spelled ARTASHES (fl. 2nd century BC) one of the founders of the ancient kingdom of Armenia (reigned 190–159 BC). After the defeat of the Seleucid king Antiochus III the Great by the Romans in the Battle of Magnesia (190), Artaxias and Zariadres, who were Antiochus' satraps (governors) in Armenia, revolted and established themselves with Roman consent as kings of Greater Armenia and its district of Sophene to the southwest, respectively. They united their efforts to enlarge their domains at the expense of neighbouring areas and are considered the creators of historical Armenia. Artaxias built his capital, Artaxata, on the Araxes (now Aras or Araks) River near Lake Sevan.

Arte de Cataluña, Museo de (Spanish: Museum of Catalonian Art), museum in the Palacio Nacional in Barcelona, housing one of the most important collections of medieval paintings in the world and also a fine and complete collection of Spanish ceramics. The Galerias Románicas comprise a series of reconstructions of church interiors with mural decorations brought from villages in the Pyrenees, transported to the museum in 1919. The exhibits include particularly fine examples of Romanesque architectural fragments such as capitals, stone carvings, and fragments from the cloister of S. Pere de les Puelles, Barcelona, the latter dating from the 12th century.

There are wall paintings, for example, from Argolell, Orcau, and San Quiricio de Pedret. Other important exhibits include paintings from the Sala Capitular of the Monastery of Sigena and five tombs from Santa Maria de Matallana, Valladolid. Thirteenth-century murals taken from the Aguilar Palace, Barcelona, depict the assault on Palma, Majorca (1229), by James I of Aragon and the battle of Porto-Pi. Important paintings of a later period include Zurbarán's "St. Francis of Assisi," El Greco's "Saints Peter and Paul" and "Christ Carrying the Cross," and "St. Paul" by Velázquez. The Ceramic Museum displays Spanish decorative pottery from the 13th century to the present. The lustreware of the 16th to 18th centuries is particularly noteworthy.

Arte Moderna, Galleria d' (Italian: Gallery of Modern Art), in Florence, museum of Italian painting and sculpture of the 19th and 20th centuries housed in a section of the Pitti Palace. It includes works from the Neoclassical and Romantic periods of the late 18th century.

Notable holdings include paintings by Pompeo Batoni and sculptures by Antonio Canova. The emphasis is on Italian artists, but representative works by those of other nationalities are included, including some fine French examples. One room contains the Diego Martelli collection of Macchiaioli painters. Artists represented include Giuseppe Abbati, Giovanni Boldoni, Silvestro Lega, and Giovanni Fattori.

Arte Moderna, Galleria Nazionale d' (Rome gallery): *see* Galleria Nazionale d'Arte Moderna.

Arte Moderno, Museo de (Spanish: Museum of Modern Art), gallery opened in Mexico City in 1964 to house works by modern artists. The museum's contemporary circular building features large domes and wedge-shaped exhibit areas. Until the early 1970s, the art was arranged according to historical periods; afterward the museum increasingly featured the paintings, sculptures, and other works of noted post-Revolutionary Mexican artists including Diego Rivera, José Clemente Orozco, David Alfaro Siqueiros, and Rufino Tamayo. Also shown are Mexican and international permanent collections.

A branch of the National Institute of Fine Arts, the Museum of Modern Art sponsors lectures, film showings, and discussions. The museum publishes a quarterly magazine, *Artes Visuales* (Visual Arts).

Artemidorus (fl. 100 BC, Ephesus, Lydia), Greek geographer whose systematic geography in 11 books was much used by the famed Greek geographer-historian Strabo (b. 64/63 BC). Artemidorus' work is based on his itineraries in the Mediterranean and on the records of others. The work is known only from Strabo's references to it and from fragments preserved by later authors and from the surviving part of an abridgement, dating possibly from the early 5th century AD, of his coastal guide to the Mediterranean and Euxine (Black) seas.

Artemidorus Daldianus (fl. 2nd century AD, Ephesus, Roman Asia), soothsayer whose *Oneirocritica* ("Interpretation of Dreams") affords valuable insight into ancient superstitions, myths, and religious rites. Mainly a compilation of the writings of earlier authors, the work's first three books consider dreams and divination generally; a reply to critics and an appendix comprise the fourth book. The author's surname, Daldianus, derives either from his mother's home, Daldis in Lydia, now in Turkey, or because he was an initiated votary of Apollo Daldiaios.

Artemis (Byzantine ruler): *see* Anastasius II *under* Anastasius (Byzantine Empire).

Artemis, in Greek religion, the goddess of wild animals, the hunt, and vegetation, and of chastity and childbirth; identified by the Romans with Diana (*q.v.*). Among the rural populace, she was the favourite goddess. Her character and function varied greatly from place to place, but, apparently, behind all forms lay the goddess of wild nature, who danced, usually accompanied by nymphs, in mountains, forests, and marshes.

Worship of Artemis probably flourished in Crete or on the Greek mainland in pre-Hellenic times. Many of Artemis' local cults, however, preserved traces of other deities, often with Greek names, suggesting that, upon adopting her, the Greeks identified Artemis with nature divinities of their own. Even where such syncretism is not discernible, non-Minoan influences may be seen.

Artemis as a huntress, classical sculpture; in the Louvre
Alinari—Art Resource/EB Inc.

Embodying as she did the sportsman's ideal, besides killing game she also protected it, especially the young; this was the Homeric significance of the title Mistress of Animals. Because she was the bow-carrying goddess, she sent sudden death to women through the "gentle darts." Her archer brother, Apollo, was responsible for the sudden deaths (off the battlefield) of men.

While the mythological roles of other prominent Olympians evolved in the works of the poets, the lore of Artemis developed primarily from cult. Dances of maidens representing tree nymphs (dryads) were especially common in Artemis' worship as goddess of the tree cult, a role probably derived from Minoan religion and especially popular in the Peloponnese. Throughout the Peloponnese, bearing such epithets as Limnaea and Limnatis (Lady of the Lake), Artemis supervised waters and lush wild growth, attended by nymphs of wells and springs (naiads). In parts of the peninsula her dances were wild and lascivious.

Outside the Peloponnese, Artemis' most familiar form was as Mistress of Animals. Poets and artists usually pictured her with the stag or hunting dog, but the cults showed considerable variety. For instance, the Tauropolia festival at Halae Araphenides in Attica honoured Artemis Tauropolos (Bull Goddess), who received a few drops of blood drawn by sword from a man's neck.

Many scholars have held that Artemis was originally a mother goddess, descended from a Cretan Mother of the Mountains similar to the Asian Magna Mater. Derived artistic types, however, do not necessarily impose the religious interpretations of their originals, and there are various difficulties in that equation. Although, as goddess of childbirth, Artemis was often identified with Eileithyia, and she was also at times called Kourotrophos (Nurse), midwife and nurse are not mother; lovemaking and probably conception, too, were Aphrodite's concern.

The frequent stories of the love affairs of Artemis' nymphs are supposed by some to have originally been told of the goddess herself, presumably as mother-goddess. The poets after Homer, however, stressed Artemis' chastity; Homeric hymn 5 attributes her immunity to Aphrodite to her delight in the hunt, dancing and music, shadowy groves, and the cities of just men. The reference to city life is unusual; but that the goddess of the unconquered wilderness should be free of sexual desire, a taming and subduing force, seems natural.

The wrath of Artemis is proverbial, for to it myth attributed wild nature's hostility to man. Yet Greek sculpture avoided Artemis' unpitying anger as a motif; in fact, the goddess herself did not become popular as a subject in the great sculptural schools until the relatively gentle 4th-century-BC spirit prevailed.

Artemis, Temple of, at Ephesus, one of the Seven Wonders of the World. The great temple was built by Croesus, king of Lydia, in about 550 BC and was rebuilt after being burned by a madman named Herostratus in 356 BC. The Artemesium was famous not only for its great size (over 350 by 180 feet [about 110 by 55 metres]) but also for the magnificent works of art that adorned it. The temple was destroyed by invading Goths in AD 262 and was never rebuilt. Little remains of the temple (though there are many fragments, especially of sculptured columns, in the British Museum), but excavation has revealed traces of both Croesus' and the 4th-century temple and of three earlier, smaller ones.

Copies survive of the famous statue of Artemis, an un-Greek representation of a mummy-like goddess, standing stiffly straight, with her hands extended outward. The original statue was made of gold, ebony, silver, and black stone, the legs and hips covered by a garment decorated with reliefs of animals and bees and the top of the body festooned with breasts; her head was adorned with a high-pillared headdress.

Reconstruction of the west front of the Temple of Artemis at Ephesus, first built *c.* 550 BC, drawing by Bluma Trell and Stuart Shaw; in the Metropolitan Museum of Art, New York City

By courtesy of the Metropolitan Museum of Art, New York City

Artemisa, city, western La Habana province, western Cuba; situated east of the Sierra del Rosario, it is a key commercial and processing centre of the region. Sugarcane, tobacco, and pineapples and other fruits are its major agricultural products. Liquor and soap are made in the city, and sugar refineries are nearby. Artemisa lies on the main highway and main railroad line between Havana and Pinar del Río. Pop. (1981 prelim.) 45,689.

Artemisia I (fl. first half of 5th century BC), queen of Halicarnassus, a Greek city in Caria, and of the nearby island of Cos *c.* 480. She ruled under the overlordship of the Persian king Xerxes (reigned 486–465) and participated in Xerxes' invasion of Greece (480–479). Despite her able command of five ships in the major naval battle with the Greeks off the island of Salamis near Athens, the Persian fleet suffered a severe defeat. Herodotus claims that Xerxes acted on her advice when he decided to retreat from Greece at once rather than to risk another engagement.

Artemisia II (d. *c.* 350 BC), sister and wife of King Mausolus (reigned 377/376–353/352) of Caria, in southwestern Anatolia, and sole ruler for about three years after the King's death. She built for her husband, in his capital at Halicarnassus (modern Bodrum, Tur.), the tomb called the Mausoleum, which was considered one of the Seven Wonders of the World. Artemisia was also known as a botanist and medical researcher; *Artemisia,* a plant genus, is named after her.

Artemisia II, statue by an unknown artist; in the Museo Archeologico Nazionale, Naples

Anderson—Mansell

Artemisium, Battle of (480 BC), during the Greco-Persian Wars, a Persian naval victory over the Greeks in an engagement fought near Artemisium, a promontory on the north coast of Euboea. The Greek fleet held its own against the Persians in three days of fighting but withdrew southwards when news came of the defeat at Thermopylae.

Artemovsk (Ukrainian S.S.R.): *see* Artyomovsk.

arteriosclerosis, also called HARDENING OF THE ARTERIES, arterial disease of three main types: intimal arteriosclerosis, or atherosclerosis, in which plaques of fatty deposits—atheromas—form in the lining of the blood vessels; medial sclerosis, or Mönckeberg's arteriosclerosis, involvement of the middle layer of the artery—the media—with calcium deposits; and arteriolar sclerosis, or sclerosis of the arterioles—small arteries. The formation of fatty deposits in intimal arteriosclerosis may be followed by development of scar tissue and calcification. The fatty deposits encroach upon the vessel channel and interfere with blood flow. Calcification causes loss of elasticity in the blood vessel, with increase in blood pressure.

Arteriosclerosis affecting the coronary arteries—the arteries that bring oxygen-rich blood to the heart muscle—may reduce the availability of oxygen to the heart and cause death of a section of the heart muscle (myocardial infarction). Arteriolar sclerosis of the retina causes blurring of vision and, if the blood pressure is not reduced, atrophy of the retina and of the optic nerve.

Arteriosclerosis affecting the cerebral vessels may interfere with blood flow to the brain and result in a "stroke," a loss of consciousness followed by some degree of paralysis. Treatment directed at prevention of such strokes includes administration of drugs that reduce the blood pressure. Arteriosclerosis affecting the peripheral arteries may reduce blood flow to the legs and cause intermittent claudication—lameness—and ulceration. There is also an increased possibility of infection in the feet and legs.

arteriovenous fistula, abnormal direct opening between an artery and a vein; it sometimes results from accidental penetration wounds or from vascular disease, or it may be congenital in origin. As a result of the defect, the arterial pressure is passed to the venous side of the fistula, and the pressure in the vein in the side of the fistula away from the heart increases, causing distension.

Affected persons complain of aching pain in or beyond the area of the injury, and the legs are usually puffy and frequently show distended veins. When there is an arteriovenous fistula, the pulse in the vein is diminished by direct compression of the supplying artery. By surgical repair normal flow can usually be reestablished.

arteritis, inflammation of the arteries. It may occur in any of a number of diseases, including syphilis; tuberculosis; disease of the pancreas; serum sickness, which is a reaction against a foreign protein; and lupus erythematosus, a systemic disease that has also been attributed to some form of immune reaction. Five varieties of arteritis not closely associated with systemic disease or disease of an organ outside the cardiovascular system have been described: thromboangiitis obliterans (*see* Buerger's disease); temporal, or cranial, arteritis; arteritis of the aged—also called senile arteritis and polymyalgia rheumatica; aortic arch arteritis (*see* aortic arch syndrome); and polyarteritis nodosa (*q.v.*).

Temporal, or cranial, arteritis, (also known as giant-cell artoritis), inflammation of the temporal arteries and of other arteries in the cranial area, is of unknown cause, although it is usually preceded by an infection. Most persons affected are in their 50s or older. The disease usually starts with a headache, which may be accompanied by pain in the scalp, face, jaws, and eyes. The affected person may find it difficult to move his jaws because of deficiency of blood flow to the jaw muscles. Paralysis of the eye muscles—ophthalmoplegia—may cause the affected person to see double, a condition called diplopia. Fluid may collect in the retina and in the optic disk, the point at which the optic nerve enters the eyeball; this condition may lead to blindness in one or both eyes. The disease may persist for as long as three years or may subside in a few months. The chief danger of temporal arteritis is its effect upon the eyes. Impairment of vision is combatted by administration of an adrenocorticosteroid hormone (a hormone secreted by the adrenal gland or a synthetic substitute).

Arteritis of the aged, which may be related to temporal arteritis, characteristically causes pain and wasting in the upper muscles of the limbs and in certain muscles of the neck. The condition usually develops rapidly, often after sensations of fatigue and loss of appetite. Adrenal steroids moderate the symptoms, but usually recovery occurs whether or not this medication is used.

artery, any of the vessels that, with one exception, carry oxygenated blood and nourishment to the tissues of the body. The exception, the pulmonary artery, carries oxygen-depleted blood to the lungs for oxygenation and removal of excess carbon dioxide (*see* pulmonary circulation).

For a depiction of many of the arteries in human anatomy; shown in relation to other parts of the body, *see* the colour Trans-Vision in the PROPAEDIA: Part Four, Section 421.

The arteries are classified by size into large, medium-sized, and small arteries. A small artery is ordinarily called an arteriole. All three types have walls with three layers, or coats. The innermost layer, or tunica intima, consists of a lining, a fine network of connective tissue, and a layer of elastic fibres bound together in a membrane pierced with many openings. The tunica media, or middle coat, is made up principally of smooth (involuntary) muscle fibres arranged in roughly spiral layers. The ends of the motor nerves, the impulses of which cause the muscle fibres to contract, are also in the middle coat. The outermost coat, or tunica adventitia, is a tough layer consisting mainly of collagen fibres (collagen is a white fibrous protein that is the main supporting element in the connective tissues). Minute blood vessels called vasa vasorum bring oxygenated blood to the medial wall of the artery (tunica media). The vasa vasorum originate in the artery itself, in a branch, or in a neighbouring artery. In the same way small veins carry oxygen-depleted blood from the artery wall to larger veins nearby.

The large arteries differ structurally from the medium-sized arteries in that they have a much thicker tunica media and a somewhat thicker tunica adventitia. The threadlike arterioles, the smallest of which have only a scattering of muscle fibres and connective tissue elements, carry blood from the larger arteries to the networks of microscopic vessels called capillaries that supply nourishment and oxygen to the tissues and carry away carbon dioxide and other products of metabolism. *See also* capillary; vein.

Consult the INDEX *first*

Artesia, city, Eddy County, southeastern New Mexico, U.S., near the Pecos River. It originated in 1890 as a stop (called Miller) on the old stagecoach route between Roswell and Carlsbad. As a livestock-shipping point on the Pecos Valley Southern Railway (completed 1894), it was known as Stegman. It adopted its present name in 1905 following the discovery of an underground artesian water basin.

Artesia is a trade centre and shipping point for irrigated farmlands (wool, cotton, alfalfa, feeds) and ranchlands. Nearby oil and gas fields (discovered in 1923) support refineries, extraction plants, and petrochemical industries. Potash mining is of economic importance. The College of Artesia was opened in 1967. The first underground school (Abo Elementary) in the United States, designed for safety against atomic radiation and fallout, was built within the city. Inc. village, 1905; city, 1930. Pop. (1980) 10,385.

artesian well, a man-made spring from which water flows under natural pressure without pumping. It is dug or drilled wherever a gently dipping, permeable rock layer (such as sandstone) receives water along its outcrop at a level higher than the level of the surface of the ground at the well site. At the outcrop the water moves down into the aquifer (water-bearing layer) but is prevented from leaving it by impermeable rock layers (such as shale) above and below it. Pressure from the water's weight (hydrostatic pressure) forces water to the surface of a well drilled down into the aquifer; the pressure for the steady upflow is maintained by the continuing penetration of water into the aquifer at the intake area.

In places where the overlying impermeable rocks are broken by joints or faults, water may escape through them to rise to the surface as artesian springs. In some areas, artesian wells and springs are a major source of water, especially in arid plains adjacent to mountain ranges that receive precipitation.

Artevelde, Jacob van, English JAMES VAN ARTEVELDE (b. *c.* 1295, Ghent—d. July 17, 1345, Ghent), Flemish leader who played a leading role in the preliminary phase of the Hundred Years' War (1337–1453). Governing Ghent with other "captains" from 1338, he aligned the Flemings with King Edward III of England and against both France and the Count of Flanders. He maintained his position as chief captain until he was murdered in a riot seven years later.

Life. Van Artevelde's profession is unknown, but he belonged to the wealthy bourgeoisie and owned land both in Ghent and in the surrounding area. His children's marriages indicate a connection with the nobility. His second wife, Kateline de Coster, took an active and capable part in public life. She travelled several times to England, in van Artevelde's name, to obtain payment of sums promised by the English king to the Flemish towns. One of their sons, Philip (born 1340), led a revolt against Count Louis II of Flanders in 1382. Van Artevelde had already reached middle age when he began to take part in public affairs. The only mention of him before 1338 is as a supporter of Louis I, count of Flanders, during a revolt against Louis in Ghent in 1325. But as relations between England and France worsened in the 1330s, tension arose between the Count and the Flemish towns. Louis, a vassal of the French king Philip VI, sided with France. The towns, although Philip offered them inducements, needed English wool for their textile industry and could not afford to alienate Edward III of England.

At that point, van Artevelde emerged as a leader. Early in 1338, the people of Ghent, under his leadership, declared their neutrality. Bruges and Ypres, the other major towns, followed suit. France was forced to acquiesce, and the vital trade with England was safeguarded.

Van Artevelde governed Ghent with a group of four other "captains." At least three of his colleagues were wealthy merchants. A dean of the weavers was also elected, and the extent of the power conferred on a member of the less prestigious artisan class was characteristic for the social aspect of van Artevelde's reforms.

Flanders remained neutral for only two years. At the beginning of 1340, it joined the English, thereby obtaining further commercial advantages and a promise by Edward III to help reconquer some Flemish areas under French control. To give the new situation some show of legality, the English king, probably on van Artevelde's initiative, let himself be proclaimed king of France in Ghent (Jan. 26, 1340). Edward overcame the French fleet near the Flemish port of Sluis and then, with van Artevelde, besieged the French city of Tournai.

Unlike his subjects, the Count of Flanders fought on the French side, and the Flemings, under van Artevelde, repudiated his authority. When a truce was declared after the siege of Tournai, the Count returned to Flanders, but he was subjected to the control of a council dominated by van Artevelde's supporters. When Louis extricated himself by flight, his relative Simon van Mirabello, a wealthy Lombard who had become a citizen of Ghent, was made regent by van Artevelde to replace him. Van Artevelde never made formal changes in institutions. His name never appears on an official document, but Edward III's correspondence shows that he exercised power. He owed his influence to the support of the great towns, whose interests he promoted. When necessary, he sacrificed the interests of the small towns and the rural population to this end.

Van Artevelde maintained his position unchallenged until the beginning of 1343, when an unsuccessful attempt to overthrow him was made by a onetime alderman, Jan van Steenbeke. A second attempt, in May 1345, was more successful. A conflict arose between the weavers and fullers, putting an end to the policy of balance among all classes, on which van Artevelde's authority rested. He lost his position as chief captain but retained the confidence of Edward III. That was fatal to him. In July 1345 Edward came to Sluis to negotiate the continuation of the alliance with Ghent's representatives. Van Artevelde quarrelled with his colleagues, who thought him too compliant. On his return to Ghent, he was murdered during a riot.

Assessment. Jacob van Artevelde long remained a controversial figure; more or less forgotten in the 17th and 18th centuries, his memory was resurrected by Belgian-nationalist historians in the 19th century. It is difficult to assess van Artevelde's personality. Most of the surviving information about him comes from his enemies. His only known writings are three letters, written in French during the winter of 1342–43 and addressed to the King of England, the Queen, and the Prince of Wales. They are businesslike in tone, without exaggerated compliments. It is possible to deduce from his actions some of the characteristics that made him stand out: a strong conviction about the needs of his people and how to secure them, a willingness to break with accepted values, and the ability to act without hesitation. His violent disposition, which led him to kill an opponent in a quarrel, was a quality he shared with many of his contemporaries. (H. van W.)

BIBLIOGRAPHY. N. de Pauw, *Cartulaire historique et généalogique des Artevelde* (1920), a nearly complete, but rather uncritical, collection of sources on Jacob van Artevelde and his family; H.S. Lucas, *The Low Countries and the Hundred Years' War, 1326–1347* (1929), an analytic description of van Artevelde's part in the Hundred Years' War in its first stage; Hans van Werveke, *Jacques van Artevelde* (1942), a synthetic view on his life and political career.

artha (Sanskrit: "wealth" or "property"), in Hinduism, the pursuit of wealth or material advantage, one of the four traditional aims in life. The sanction for *artha* rests on the assumption that—with the exclusion of the exceptional few who can proceed directly to the final aim of *mokṣa,* or spiritual release from life—material well-being is a basic necessity of man and is his appropriate pursuit while a householder, that is, during the second of the four life stages. Furthermore, *artha,* as the pursuit of material advantage, is closely tied to the activities of statecraft, which maintains the general social order and prevents anarchy. But, as the immoderate pursuit of material advantage would lead to undesirable and ruinous excesses, *artha* must always be regulated by the superior aim of dharma, or righteousness.

Artha, Leopold Hasner, Ritter von: *see* Hasner, Leopold, Ritter von Artha.

Artha-śāstra (Sanskrit: "Handbook of [the King's] Profit"), singularly important Indian manual on the art of politics, attributed to Kauṭilya (also known as Viṣṇugupta or Cāṇakya), who reportedly was chief minister to King Candragupta (*c.* 300 BC), the founder of the Maurya dynasty. Although it is unlikely that all of the text dates to such an early period, several parts have been traced back to the Mauryas.

The author is concerned with central control by the king of a realm of fairly limited size, and he speaks of the way the state's economy is organized, how ministers should be chosen and war conducted, and how taxation should be arranged and distributed. Great emphasis is placed on the importance of a network of runners, informers, and spies, which, in the absence of a ministry of public information and a police force, functioned as a surveillance corps for the king, focussing particularly on any external threats and internal dissidence.

Entirely practical in purpose, the *Artha-śāstra* presents no overt philosophy. But implicit is a complete skepticism, if not cynicism, concerning human nature and its corruptibility and the ways in which the king—and his trusted servant—can take advantage of such human weakness.

Unstated but apparent is the paradox that a king has to have complete confidence in the minister who is ruling his state. This paradox was dramatized by the playwright Viśākhadatta (*c.* 5th century AD), who was probably at the court of the Guptas, in his Sanskrit play *Mudrārākṣasa* ("Minister Rākṣasa and His Signet Ring").

arthāpatti (Sanskrit: "the incidence of a case"), in Indian philosophy, the fifth of the five means of knowledge (*pramāṇa*) by which man has correct cognitions of the world. *Arthāpatti* is knowledge arrived at by circumstantial implication. An example would be the knowledge, when it is day, that the sun is shining, even though it cannot be observed because of a cloud cover. By no means universally adopted, *arthāpatti* was especially advocated by Prabhākara (7th century), a thinker in the exegetic school (Pūrva-mīmāṃsā) of Hindu philosophy. *See also* pramāṇa.

A list of the abbreviations used in the MICROPAEDIA *will be found at the end of this volume*

arthritis, inflammation of the joints and its effects. In its acute form, arthritis is marked by pain, heat, redness, and swelling. There are three principal forms; *see* osteoarthritis; rheumatoid arthritis; septic arthritis.

Arthrobotrys, genus of soil-inhabiting, nematode- (roundworm-) trapping fungi (division Mycota) belonging to the Deuteromycetes (*q.v.*). A nematode is trapped on contact with a sticky fungal thread, and its tissues are invaded.

arthrodire, any of an order of extinct, armoured, jawed fishes, class Placodermi, found in Devonian freshwater and marine deposits. Early arthrodires, such as the genus *Arctolepis,* were well-armoured fishes with flattened bodies. They had hollow, backward-curved shoulder spines and may have used the long spines to anchor themselves or to move about on the bottom.

Later arthrodires, such as the Middle Devonian genus *Coccosteus,* tended toward marine habitats. They were less heavily armoured than *Arctolepis,* and the bony head and body shields were connected by a joint on each side that permitted free head movement. They were predators and had bony jaws with tusklike projections in front and cutting edges in back. The back of the body and the tail apparently were naked. The shoulder spine was shortened and in some forms was completely absent.

Arthrodires became extinct during the Late Devonian. The genus *Dinichthys* (sometimes included with *Dunkleosteus*), representative of this period, was similar to *Coccosteus* but grew much longer, about 9 metres (30 feet) against 0.6 metre (2 feet) for *Coccosteus.*

There were many arthrodire offshoots during the Devonian. Members of the genus *Phyllolepis* were specialized fishes that had lost most of the head armour. They were formerly considered ostracoderms. The ptyctodonts, relatives of the arthrodires, lived in the sea and possibly fed upon mollusks. Ptyctodonts have been thought of as ancestors of chimaeras, but evidence is inconclusive.

arthropod, any member of the phylum Arthropoda, the largest such division in the animal kingdom, consisting of at least 1,000,000 invertebrate species.

A brief treatment of arthropods follows. For full treatment, *see* MACROPAEDIA: Arthopods.

Almost 80 percent of all animals belong to this phylum, resulting in its tremendous diversity. About three-quarters of its members are insects ranging from cockroaches and crickets to butterflies and bees. Other important classes of arthropods include arachnids (*e.g.,* spiders, scorpions, ticks, and mites), crustaceans (shrimp, crabs, lobsters, crayfish, sand fleas, etc.), chilopods (centipedes), and diplopods (millipedes).

All the arthropods are bilaterally symmetrical, possessing a segmented body in which each segment may bear a pair of limbs. The most characteristic feature of the arthropods is a covering that, when thickened, forms an articulated armour (exoskeleton) over body and limbs. The head carries sense organs and the feeding apparatus. Among the several classes a variable number of trunk segments have been incorporated into the head, the head structure alone serving to differentiate the groups.

Arthropods are thought to have developed early in geological time. Abundant fossil remains of the now extinct trilobites, the oldest group of arthropods known, date back to the beginning of the Cambrian Period (about 600,000,000 years ago). Distributed worldwide, arthropods have successfully adapted to nearly all environments, both aquatic and terrestrial. A species of jumping spider, for example, is able to live permanently at latitudes above 6,000 metres (19,680 feet) on the upper slopes of Mount Everest. In contrast, a certain kind of blind crab thrives at depths of 2,500 m in the Galapagos Rift several hundred miles off the coast of Ecuador.

Arthur, name of rulers grouped below by country and indicated by the symbol •.

BRITAIN

• **Arthur,** legendary British king who appears in a cycle of medieval romances (known as the matter of Britain) as the sovereign of a knightly fellowship of the Round Table (*q.v.*). It is not certain how or where (in Wales or in

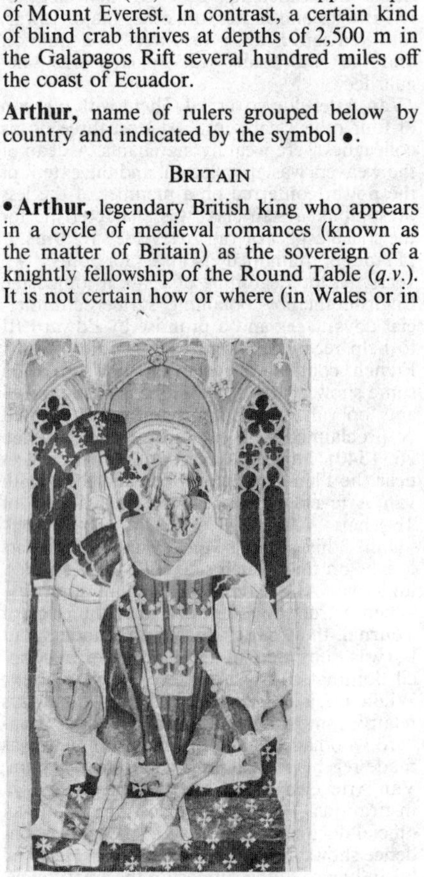

King Arthur, detail from "Christian Heroes," a French wool tapestry attributed to Nicolas Bataille, late 14th century; in the Cloisters, Metropolitan Museum of Art, New York City

By courtesy of the Metropolitan Museum of Art, New York, The Cloisters Collection, Munsey Fund, 1932

those parts of northern Britain inhabited by Brythonic-speaking Celts) these legends originated or whether the figure Arthur was based on a historical person. *See also* Arthurian legend.

Assumptions that a historical Arthur led Welsh resistance to the West Saxon advance from the middle Thames are based on a conflation of two early chroniclers, Gildas and Nennius, and on the *Annales Cambriae* of the late 10th century. The 9th-century *Historia Britonum* of Nennius records 12 battles fought by Arthur against the Saxons, culminating in a victory at Mons Badonicus. The Arthurian section of this work, however, is from an undetermined source, possibly a poetic text. The *Annales Cambriae* also mention Arthur's victory at Mons Badonicus (516) and record the Battle of Camlann (537), "in which Arthur and Medraut fell." Gildas' *De excidio et conquestu Britanniae* (mid-6th century) implies that Mons Badonicus was fought *c.* 500 but does not connect it with Arthur.

Another speculative view, put forward by R.G. Collingwood (*Roman Britain and the English Settlements,* 1936), is that Arthur was a professional soldier, serving the British kings and commanding a cavalry force trained on Roman lines, which he switched from place to place to meet the Saxon threat.

Early Welsh literature, however, quickly made Arthur into a king of wonders and marvels. The 12th-century prose romance *Culhwch and Olwen* associated him with other heroes, this conception of a heroic band, with Arthur at its head, doubtless leading to the idea of Arthur's court.

BRITTANY

• **Arthur I** (b. March 29, 1187, Nantes, Brittany—d. April 3, 1203?, Rouen or Cherbourg), duke of Brittany, a grandson of King Henry II of England; he was a rival of his uncle John (king of England from 1199) for several French provinces, both in his own interest and in that of King Philip II Augustus of France.

In October 1190 Arthur was recognized as heir presumptive to the English throne by another uncle, the childless King Richard I the Lion-Heart. Arthur was a posthumous child of Geoffrey, fourth of Henry II's five sons, and his wardship was a point of contention between Richard and Philip. From 1196 he was reared in Philip's household, causing Richard to disinherit the boy in favour of John, who, after Richard's sudden death, was accepted as king in England and Normandy. Philip, however, recognized Arthur's right to Brittany, Anjou, Aquitaine, and Maine and betrothed his daughter Mary to the young duke. The situation was complicated by Eleanor of Aquitaine, widow of Henry II, who wanted Aquitaine and Anjou for John. Captured in battle by John at Mirebeau-en-Poitou on Aug. 1, 1202, Arthur was imprisoned and, according to tradition, was murdered either by John himself or at his order.

• **Arthur II** (b. 1262—d. 1312, Château de l'Isle, near La Roche-Bernard, Brittany), duke of Brittany (1305–12), son of John II and Beatrice of England. By successive marriages before his accession, he acquired the viscounty of Limoges (1275) and the county of Montfort-l'Amaury (1292). During his short reign, the war between Edward I of England and Philip IV of France was ended by treaty, whereby France ceded Brittany to England; but Arthur, with the vigorous support of the Bretons, defied and aborted the transfer. Arthur was succeeded by his son, John III the Good.

• **Arthur III:** *see* Richemont, Arthur, constable de.

Arthur, village on the Douglas–Moultrie county line, east central Illinois, U.S. Founded in 1872 as a farming centre, it was originally called Glasgow and later renamed for the brother of Robert Hervey, president of the Paris and Decatur Railroad. Members of the Old Order Amish settlement, a conservative religious group in the area since 1865, have contributed to the character of the community. Horse-drawn buggies, the mode of travel for many Amish, share the country roads and village streets with automobiles. Agriculture (grain and livestock) is the mainstay of the economy, supplemented by some light industry, including a broomcorn processing plant. Inc. 1877. Pop. (1980) 2,122.

Arthur, Chester A(lan) (b. Oct. 5, 1830, Fairfield, Vt., U.S.—d. Nov. 18, 1886, New York City), 21st president of the United States

(1881–84). Elected vice president on the Republican ticket of 1880, he acceded to the presidency on the assassination of Pres. James A. Garfield.

Chester A. Arthur, photograph by C.M. Bell, 1882

By courtesy of the Library of Congress, Washington, D.C.

Admitted to the New York bar in 1854, Arthur was an ardent abolitionist and won an early reputation by successfully pleading the case of a slave who sued for his freedom on the ground that his master had brought him temporarily to the free state of New York. Joining the Republican Party in the 1850s, Arthur became active in local politics and was quartermaster general of state troops during the Civil War.

Resuming his law practice in 1863, he became closely associated with New York Republican boss Sen. Roscoe Conkling, and in 1871 he was appointed customs collector for the port of New York City by Pres. Ulysses S. Grant. The customhouse had long been conspicuous for some of the most flagrant abuses of the spoils system, and although Arthur conducted the business of the office with integrity, he continued the practice of overstaffing it with employees whose chief qualification was loyalty to Conkling. In 1877 the newly elected Pres. Rutherford B. Hayes, intent on reform of the civil service, demanded the resignation of Arthur and others in the New York City customhouse. With the support of Conkling, Arthur was able to resist Hayes for a time; but in July 1878 Hayes finally suspended him, and once again Arthur returned to the practice of law.

As a delegate to the Republican National Convention of 1880, Arthur worked with Conkling and the "Stalwart" faction for the renomination of Grant for a third term as president. With the triumph of James A. Garfield, Arthur was offered the vice presidency as a conciliatory gesture to the Stalwarts. His nomination was coldly received by the public, however, and when, during his first few months in office, he openly sided with Conkling in a bitter conflict with Garfield over New York patronage, the impression was widespread that he was too partisan for the nation's second highest office.

Acceding to the presidency on Sept. 19, 1881, in a period of intense factional controversy, Arthur is said to have been deeply wounded by public apprehension over the prospect of an administration in the hands of so confirmed an adherent of the spoils system. He did replace six of the seven members of Garfield's Cabinet with his own appointees, but his appointments were generally unexceptionable, and he displayed an unexpected independence by his veto in 1882 of an $18,000,000 rivers and harbours bill that contained ample funds for projects that could be used for political patronage. He particularly confounded his critics and dismayed his friends among the Stalwarts by his support of the Pendleton Act (1883), which created a civil service system with appointments and promotions based on merit in a limited number of specified offices. He was the first president since the Civil War to be interested in the Navy, and he and his secretary of the navy, William E. Chandler, recommended the appropriations which initiated the rebuilding of the U.S. Navy toward the strength it later achieved at the time of the war with Spain.

In 1884 Arthur, secretly suffering from an incurable disease, allowed his name to be presented for the Republican nomination. He was defeated by James G. Blaine and at the end of his term retired to New York City. A standard biography is George F. Howe, *Chester A. Arthur* (1934).

Arthur, Sir George, 1st Baronet (b. June 21, 1784, Plymouth, Devon, Eng.—d. Sept. 19, 1854, London), colonial administrator who, as governor of Van Diemen's Land (1825–36; now Tasmania), strove unsuccessfully to modify the tragic fate of the Tasmanian Aborigines; his efforts to reform the penal system and expand the island's economy, however, were remarkably successful.

After army duty in the Napoleonic Wars in Europe and Egypt (1804–14), Arthur served as lieutenant governor of British Honduras (1814–22). He was named lieutenant governor of Van Diemen's Land in 1823 and became governor two years later, when the colony was separated from New South Wales. That year (1825) he also helped the Van Diemen's Land Company to develop the northwest area of the island. He campaigned effectively against the bushrangers, rural outlaws who had robbed the settlers and fought the Aborigines. His attempt to restrict the Aboriginal population to the southeastern peninsula behind the so-called Black Line of armed settlers was a complete failure (*see* Black War). By 1835 the remaining Aborigines were persuaded to settle northeast of Tasmania on Flinders Island, where they soon died out; the last full-blooded Tasmanian perished in 1876.

Arthur established a penal settlement at Port Arthur (1832) and a model prison for boys at Point Puer (1835). He also helped to develop the colony's religious life and education. He antagonized the Tasmanian and Sydney press, however, by his autocratic administration and by his attempts at censorship.

In 1837 Arthur was appointed lieutenant governor of Upper Canada (now Ontario), arriving just after a rebellion against British rule had been suppressed. He was rewarded with a baronetcy for his help in uniting Upper Canada and Lower Canada (now Quebec) in 1841 and the following year was named governor of Bombay. He retired to England in 1846.

Arthur, J(oseph) C(harles) (b. Jan. 11, 1850, Lowville, N.Y., U.S.—d. April 30, 1942, Lafayette, Ind.), U.S. botanist who discovered basic facts about the life history of the parasitic fungi known as rusts.

Graduated from what is now Iowa State University, Ames, in 1872, he received the degree of doctor of science at Cornell University, Ithaca, N.Y., in 1886. In 1887 he became professor of botany at Purdue University, West Lafayette, Ind., where he served until 1915.

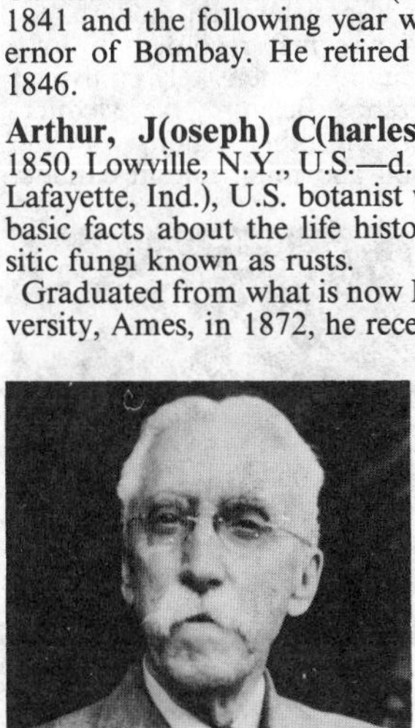

J.C. Arthur

By courtesy of the American Phytopathological Society and the Hunt Institute, Pittsburgh

During his professorship at Purdue he was also professor of vegetable physiology and pathology in the Indiana Agricultural Experiment Station, and it was during this period that he made his chief contributions on the life history of rusts. From 1882 to 1900 he was an editor of the *Botanical Gazette.*

Arthur wrote many articles on botanical subjects and published a *Handbook of Plant Dissection,* with Charles R. Barnes and John M. Coulter (1886); *Living Plants and Their Properties,* with Daniel T. MacDougal (1898); and *Manual of the Rusts in United States and Canada* (1934).

Arthur Kill Bridge, steel vertical-lift bridge, completed in 1959, spanning the Arthur Kill (channel) between Elizabeth, N.J., and Staten Island, N.Y. The movable section, suspended from two 215-foot (66-metre) towers, is 558 ft (170 m) long and can be raised 135 ft (41 m) above the water. It carries a single railroad track and, at its completion, was the longest and highest span of its type in the world.

Arthurian legend, the body of stories and medieval romances, known as the matter of Britain, centring on the legendary king Arthur (*q.v.*). Medieval writers, especially the French, variously treated stories of Arthur's birth, the adventures of his knights, and the adulterous love between his knight Sir Lancelot and his queen, Guinevere. This last and the quest for the Holy Grail (the vessel used by Christ at the Last Supper and given to Joseph of Arimathea) brought about the dissolution of the knightly fellowship, the death of Arthur, and the destruction of his kingdom.

Stories about Arthur and his court had been popular in Wales before the 11th century; European fame came through Geoffrey of Monmouth's *Historia regum Britanniae* (between 1135 and 1139), celebrating a glorious and triumphant king who defeated a Roman army in eastern France but was mortally wounded in battle during a rebellion at home led by his nephew Mordred. Some features of Geoffrey's story were marvellous fabrications, and certain features of the Celtic stories were adapted to suit feudal times. The concept of Arthur as a world conqueror was clearly inspired by legends surrounding great leaders such as Alexander the Great and Charlemagne. Later writers, notably Wace of Jersey and Layamon, filled out certain details, especially in connection with Arthur's knightly fellowship.

Using Celtic sources, Chrétien de Troyes (*q.v.*) in the late 12th century made Arthur the ruler of a realm of marvels in five romances of adventure. He also introduced the theme of the Grail into Arthurian legend. Prose romances of the 13th century began to explore two major themes: the winning of the Grail and the love story of Lancelot and Guinevere. An early prose romance centring on Lancelot seems to have become the kernel of a cyclic work known as the Prose *Lancelot*, or Vulgate cycle (*c.* 1225). The Lancelot theme was connected with the Grail story through Lancelot's son, the pure knight Sir Galahad, who achieved the vision of God through the Grail as fully as is possible in this life, whereas Sir Lancelot was impeded in his progress along the mystic way because of his adultery with Guinevere. Another branch of the Vulgate cycle was based on a very early 13th-century verse romance, the *Merlin*, by Robert de Boron, that had told of Arthur's birth and childhood and his winning of the crown by drawing a magic sword from a stone. The writer of the Vulgate cycle turned this into prose, adding a pseudo-historical narrative dealing with Arthur's military exploits. A final branch of the Vulgate cycle contained an account of Arthur's Roman campaign and war with Mordred, to which was added a story of Lancelot's renewed adultery with Guinevere and the disastrous war between Lancelot and Sir Gawain that ensued. A later prose romance, known as the post-Vulgate Grail romance (*c.* 1240), combined Arthurian legend with material from the Tristan romance (*q.v.*).

The legend told in the Vulgate cycle and post-Vulgate romance was transmitted to English-speaking readers in Thomas Malory's late 15th-century prose *Le Morte Darthur.* At the same time there was renewed interest in Geoffrey of Monmouth's *Historia,* and the fictitious kings of Britain became more or less incorporated with official national mythology. The legend remained alive during the 17th century, though interest in it was by then confined to England. Of merely antiquarian interest during the 18th century, it again figured in literature during Victorian times, notably in Tennyson's *Idylls of the King.* In the 20th century a U.S. poet, Edwin Arlington Robinson, wrote an Arthurian trilogy, and in England T.H. White retold the stories in a series of novels collected as *The Once and Future King* (1958). *Camelot* (1960), a musical by Alan Lerner and Frederick Loewe, was based on White's work. *See also* Grail, Holy.

Arthur's Pass, road through the Southern Alps, west central South Island, New Zealand. At an elevation of 3,038 ft (926 m) it is the lowest pass and the only crossing for motor traffic between Haast and Lewis passes. It crosses a mountain ridge between peaks 6,000 ft high and marks the divide of the watersheds of the Waimakariri (draining east) and Taramakau rivers. Site of a temporary settlement (Camping Flat) for Maoris, explorers, and miners, successively since the 1850s, the pass did not become a major route until gold was discovered in Westland in 1864. A road was put through two years later. The Otira Railway Tunnel, more than 5 mi (8 km) long, lies beneath the pass and is the only rail link across South Island. Arthur's Pass National Park (380 sq mi [980 sq km]) was created in 1929. The pass was named after the explorer Sir Arthur Dudley Dobson.

Arthus phenomenon, local swelling, redness, and tissue death following skin injection of soluble antigen into a subject previously immunized by a series of similar injections. Tissue damage is a result of the precipitation of antigen–antibody complexes in the walls of the blood vessels; the deposits are then ingested (phagocytosed) by neutrophilic white blood cells. The phenomenon is named for the French physiologist Maurice Arthus (1862–1945).

ārtī (Hindi), Sanskrit ĀRĀTRIKA, in Hindu and Jaina rites, the waving of lighted lamps before an image of a god or a person to be honoured. In performing the rite, the worshipper circles the lamp three times in a clockwise direction while chanting a prayer or singing a hymn. *Ārtī* is one of the most frequently observed parts of both temple and private worship (*see* pūjā). The god is honoured by the lighted ghee (clarified butter) or camphor and is protected by the invocation of the deities of the directions of the compass. In Indian households, *ārtī* is a commonly observed ritual treatment accorded specially honoured guests. It is also a part of many domestic ceremonies.

Artibonite River, French RIVIÈRE DE L'ARTIBONITE, Spanish RÍO ARTIBONITO, river, the longest on the island of Hispaniola. It rises in the Cordillera Central (Ciboa Mountains) of the Dominican Republic and flows southwest along the border with Haiti and then west and northwest into Haiti and through the fertile Artibonite Plain to enter the Golfe de la Gonâve (Gulf of Gonaïves) after a course of 150 mi (240 km). It is navigable upstream for about 100 mi by small craft. About 200,000 ac (80,000 ha) of land are being developed

Péligre Dam on the Artibonite River, Haiti
Adams and Adams

as part of the Artibonite Valley Agricultural Project, financed by international loans. The project includes a dam, the reclamation of eroded land, the teaching of better farm techniques, and the provision of agricultural credit and health and other social services. The dam was initiated in 1930 as a flood control project; its completion in 1956 resulted in the creation of a massive artificial lake (Lac de Péligre). The Péligre hydroelectric operation was finally completed in 1971, with a capacity of 31,400 kilowatts intended to supply power to the whole country.

artichoke, also called FRENCH, or GLOBE, ARTICHOKE, large, coarse, herbaceous, thistlelike perennial plant (*Cynara scolymus*) of the Asteraceae family. The fleshy parts of the immature flower heads are a culinary delicacy.

The aboveground parts die each year after flowers are formed; new shoots arise the next season to produce rosettes of deeply cut, woolly leaves up to a metre (over three feet) long; later, sturdy, branched flower stalks rise; flowers are purplish. After four to eight years the cluster of rosettes from a crown becomes crowded, and the size and quality of the heads become reduced. The plant is then renewed by planting divisions of the crown or rooted offshoots. The mature flower heads produce seeds, but the seedlings do not necessarily resemble the variety of the parent plant.

The artichoke is native to the western and central Mediterranean, whence it was carried to the eastern Mediterranean in ancient times. At that time the young leaves rather than the flower heads were eaten; the modern, edible-flower form was first recorded in Italy about 1400. Today it is extensively cultivated in California, France, Belgium, the Mediterranean countries, and other regions with the necessary rich soil and mild, humid climate.

Artichoke (*Cynara scolymus*)
Ingmar Holmasen

Flavour is delicate and nutlike, and smaller heads are usually the most tender. Artichoke leaves and heart are served as a hot vegetable with a sauce or as a cold salad or appetizer.

The Jerusalem artichoke (*q.v.*) is a tuber and does not resemble the artichoke.

Articles of Confederation: *see* Confederation, Articles of.

Articulatae (botany): *see* Sphenopsida.

articulation, in phonetics, a configuration of the vocal tract (the larynx and the pharyngeal, oral, and nasal cavities) resulting from the positioning of the mobile organs of the vocal tract (*e.g.*, tongue) relative to other parts of the vocal tract that may be rigid (*e.g.*, hard palate). This configuration modifies an airstream to produce the characteristic sounds of speech.

The main articulators are the tongue, the upper lip, the lower lip, the upper teeth, the upper gum ridge (alveolar ridge), the hard palate, the velum (soft palate), the uvula (free-hanging end of the soft palate), the pharyngeal wall, and the glottis (space between the vocal cords).

Articulations may be divided into two main types, primary and secondary. Primary articulation refers to either (1) the place and manner in which the stricture is made for a consonant or (2) the tongue contour, lip shape, and height of the larynx used to produce a vowel. The primary articulation may still permit some range of movement for other articulators not involved in its formation. For example, an "apico alveolar" articulation involves the tip of the tongue but leaves the lips and back of the tongue free to produce some degree of further stricture in the vocal tract. This latter is called a secondary articulation. Among the chief secondary articulations are palatalization, as in Russian and many other languages (the front of the tongue approaching the hard palate); velarization (the back of the tongue approaching the soft palate, or velum); labialization (added lip-rounding), glottalization (complete or partial closure of the vocal cords); and nasalization (simultaneous passage of air through the nasal and oral tracts).

artificial intelligence (AI), the capacity of a digital computer or computer-controlled robot device to perform tasks commonly associated with the higher intellectual processes characteristic of humans, such as the ability to reason, discover meanings, generalize, or learn from past experience. The term is also frequently applied to that branch of computer science concerned with the development of systems endowed with such capabilities.

Research on artificial intelligence began soon after the development of the modern digital computer (*q.v.*) in the 1940s. Early investigators quickly recognized the potential of computing devices as a means of automating thought processes. Over the years, it has been demonstrated that computers can be programmed to carry out very logically complex tasks—as, for example, theorem proving and chess playing—with remarkable proficiency. Their success at these activities, nevertheless, is attributable more to an ability to manipulate symbolic information iteratively at extremely high speeds than to one of the higher mental operations.

As of the early 1980s, no computer capable of approximating human intelligence had been developed. AI research, however, has yielded some results of immediate practical value, the most significant of which are related to decision making, natural language comprehension, and pattern recognition.

Knowledge-based software systems provide computers with the ability to make decisions for solving complicated non-numerical problems. These so-called expert systems consist of hundreds or even thousands of "if–then" logic rules formulated with knowledge gleaned from leading authorities in a given field. A notable example of such a heuristic program is MYCIN, which has been used to help physicians diagnose certain forms of bacterial blood infections and to determine suitable treatments. A computer programmed in MYCIN arrives at its recommendations by first making a plausible guess as to the patient's condition on the basis of observed symptoms and then determining how well that tentative diagnosis fits all known facts about the behaviour of the microorganism thought to be involved. Once the computer has identified the cause of the infection, it reviews the kinds of antibiotics available and makes its recommendation, offering, in most cases, several alternative forms of therapy.

Considerable progress also has been made in the development of programs that enable computers to comprehend commands in a natural language—*e.g.*, ordinary English. Most of the software systems of this type that have been produced so far are designed almost exclusively for querying data bases on specific subjects. They contain enormous amounts of information about the meaning of words pertaining to a narrowly defined subject, as well as information about grammatical rules and common violations of those rules.

The ability to identify graphic patterns or images is associated with artificial intelligence, since it involves both cognition and abstraction. In a system designed with this capability, a remote device linked to a computer scans, senses, and transforms images into patterns of digital pulses, which in turn are compared with pulse patterns stored in the computer's memory. The stored patterns represent the geometric shapes and forms that the computer has been programmed to identify. The computer processes the incoming digital pulse patterns in rapid succession, automatically isolating relevant features, filtering out unwanted signals, and adding to its memory any pattern whose deviation exceeds a specified threshold value and is thus perceived as a new entity.

Computerized pattern recognition and techniques based on the technology have found wide application in various kinds of scientific work. In astronomy, for example, such technology has been employed to enhance photographs of distant planets and other celestial objects taken by unmanned space probes. Also, robotic devices with pattern-recognition capability have been developed for industry, where they serve mainly to inspect or sort finished products.

Major advances both in microelectronics, most notably very large scale integrated circuitry (VLSI), and in programming have resulted in an intensification of AI research efforts, particularly in Japan and the United States. Many investigators believe that VLSI technology can provide the basis of the hardware needed to construct truly intelligent machines. They are convinced that such computers are attainable only through an internal structure that allows parallel processing—*i.e.*, the simultaneous execution of several separate operations (memory, logic, and control)—by means of numerous integrated circuits in which millions of CPU (central processing unit), memory, and input-output circuits are combined on a single, tiny silicon chip. Present-day digital computers perform their operations serially or sequentially: discrete input circuits feed data to individual memory cells, each of which in turn relays bits of information one at a time to a single CPU, with the results then being transmitted to an external output device. Although the fastest computers developed thus far are able to perform roughly 1,000,000,000 operations per second, they work much too slowly to approximate higher forms of human thought that entail making numerous associations and generalizations nearly instantly.

Other developments that may pave the way for intelligent computers are more sophisticated speech-processing software and voice-input devices capable of handling strings of spoken words, including terms with multiple meanings. Significant, too, are attempts to produce computer programs that can prepare other programs. Sophisticated versions of a programming language known as Lisp (List Processing) show promise as a means of effecting automated software of this type.

artificial jaundice: *see* carotenemia.

artificial organ, machine designed to replace the functions of an organ of the human body for varying periods of time, usually during surgery. The artificial kidney, heart-lung machines, and mechanical hearts are the leading examples of artificial organs.

Artificial kidney. The artificial kidney, or hemodialyzer, provides a means for removing certain undesirable substances from the blood or of adding needed components to it. By these processes the apparatus can control the acid-base balance of the blood and its content of water and dissolved materials. Another known function of the natural kidney—secretion of hormones that influence the blood pressure—cannot be duplicated. Modern hemodialyzers rely on two physicochemical principles, dialysis and ultrafiltration (*qq.v.*).

In dialysis two liquids separated by a porous membrane exchange those components that exist as particles small enough to diffuse through the pores. When the blood is brought into contact with one side of such a membrane, dissolved substances (including urea and inorganic salts) pass through into a sterile solution placed on the other side of the membrane. The red and white cells, platelets, and proteins cannot penetrate the membrane because the particles are too large. To prevent or limit the loss of diffusible substances required by the body, such as sugars, amino acids, and necessary amounts of salts, those compounds are added to the sterile solution; thus their diffusion from the blood is offset by equal movement in the opposite direction. The lack of diffusible materials in the blood can be corrected by incorporating them in the solution, from which they enter the circulation.

Although water passes easily through the membrane, it is not removed by dialysis because its concentration in the blood is lower than in the solution; indeed, water tends to pass from the solution into the blood. The dilution of the blood that would result from this process is prevented by ultrafiltration, by which some of the water, along with some dissolved materials, is forced through the membrane by maintaining the blood at a higher pressure than the solution.

The membranes first used in hemodialysis were obtained from animals or prepared from collodion; cellophane has been found to be more suitable, and tubes or sheets of it are used in many dialyzers. In the late 1960s hollow filaments of cellulosic or synthetic materials were introduced for hemodialysis; bundles of such filaments provide a large membrane surface in a small volume, a combination advantageous in devising compact dialyzers.

Hemodialysis—first used to treat human patients in 1945—replaces or supplements the action of the kidneys in a person suffering from acute or chronic renal failure or from poisoning by diffusible substances, such as aspirin, bromides, or barbiturates. Blood is diverted from an artery, usually one in the wrist, into the dialyzer, where it flows—either by its own impetus or with the aid of a mechanical pump—along one surface of the membrane. Finally the blood passes through a trap that removes clots and bubbles and returns to a vein in the patient's forearm. In persons with chronic kidney failure, who require frequent dialysis, repeated surgical access to the blood vessels used in the treatments is obviated by provision of an external plastic shunt between them.

Heart-lung machine. The heart-lung machine consists of an artificial lung (oxygenator) and a substitute heart (pump). For nearly a century, beginning about 1868, scientists attempted to develop a mechanical unit capable of restoring oxygen to blood depleted of this element in its movement through the tissues and removing the excessive carbon dioxide that accumulates during this same passage. Many of the same investigators worked also on the development of a pump to supplant heart action temporarily. Decades of animal investigation culminated in the first successful application of an artificial heart-lung machine to an operation on man, by John H. Gibbon, Jr., on May 6, 1953.

For intervals of an hour or more any one of the proven types of heart-lung machines can accept the entire venous return of a patient weighing as much as 100 kilograms (200 pounds). In such a case the blood is pumped back into the patient's arteries in a volume sufficient to maintain life at even the most distant parts of the patient's body as well as in those centres with the greatest requirements (brain and nervous tissue, liver, adrenals, kidneys). To do this, up to 5,000 millilitres (about 1 1/3 gallons) or more of blood must be moved each minute. While the heart is relieved of its pumping duties, it can be stopped by drugs or cooling and then started by warming or electrical means. Meanwhile, the surgeon can open this organ and repair or replace valves or close abnormal holes inside.

Mechanical hearts. Instruments capable of replacing the pumping action of the normal heart for prolonged periods of time, without excessively damaging either the fluid or the cellular elements of whole blood, are the goal of continuing research. On the way to this goal, several kinds of appliances have been tried; they are designed to reduce, rather than take over entirely, the total work load of a heart with impaired functional capacity.

In general these units consist of either counterpulsation (diastolic augmentation) equipment that pulses the blood during the heart's "resting" phase between beats or an auxiliary ventricle that substitutes temporarily by pumping a portion of the normal cardiac output. Use of these devices under experimental conditions has provided certain limited benefits to the circulation, including the heart; but the benefits are achieved at the expense of hazards to health with prolonged use. During the 1970s, synthetic materials were developed that overcame most of the medical drawbacks and greatly aided the development of artificial mechanical hearts. One such device, designed by Robert K. Jarvik, was implanted into a patient by William C. DeVries on Dec. 2, 1982. The device was powered by compressed air and monitored by computer. *See also* pacemaker.

artificial respiration, breathing induced by some manipulative technique when natural respiration has ceased or is faltering. Such techniques, if applied quickly and properly, can prevent some deaths from drowning, choking, strangulation, suffocation, carbon monoxide poisoning, and electric shock. Resuscitation by inducing artificial respiration consists chiefly of two actions: (1) establishing and maintaining an open air passage from the upper respiratory tract (mouth, throat, and pharynx) to the lungs and (2) exchanging air and carbon dioxide in the terminal air sacs of the lungs while the heart is still functioning. To be successful such efforts must be started as soon as possible and continued until the victim is again breathing.

The most widely used method of inducing artificial respiration is mouth-to-mouth breathing, which has been found to be more effective than the manual methods used in the past.

The person using mouth-to-mouth breathing places the victim on his back, clears his mouth of foreign material and mucus, lifts the lower jaw forward and upward to open the air passage, places his own mouth over the victim's mouth in such a way as to establish a leak-proof seal, and clamps the nostrils.

He then alternately breathes into the victim's mouth and lifts his own mouth away, permitting the victim to exhale. If the victim is a child the rescuer may cover both the victim's mouth and nose. The rescuer breathes 12 times each minute (15 times for a child and 20 for an infant) into the victim's mouth.

One method, the modified Sylvester chest-pressure–arm-lift technique, is used if mouth-to-mouth breathing is not possible. The victim is placed faceup, and the shoulders are elevated to allow the head to drop backward. The rescuer kneels at the victim's head, facing him, grasps the victim's wrists, and crosses them over the victim's lower chest. The rescuer rocks forward, pressing on the victim's chest, then backward, stretching the victim's arms outward and upward. The cycle is repeated about 12 times per minute.

artificial selection: *see* selective breeding.

Artigas, city and department, northwestern Uruguay. The city, which is also the capital of the department, lies on the Río Cuareim (Rio Quaraí in Brazil) across from Quaraí, Brazil, in the Cuchilla (hills) de Santa Ana (Coxilha de Santana in Brazil). Founded in 1852 as San Eugenio, it became the capital when the department was created in 1884. It is now a commercial and manufacturing centre for the surrounding agricultural and pastoral lands. Principal exports include cattle, jerked beef, wool, cereals, and fruit. The city has a television and a radio station. Artigas is linked by railroad and highway to Salto, and it has an airport.

The department is bounded on the north and east by Brazil and on the west by Argentina. Named in honour of José Gervasio Artigas, the national hero of independence, the territory, 4,605 sq mi (11,928 sq km), is the least densely populated department in the nation. The agate Cuchilla (hills) de Belén traverse the south. Like most of Uruguay, Artigas is ranching country. Its rolling, somewhat rocky pastures are good but subject to damaging droughts. There is some agriculture, with sugarcane, oranges, grapes, and corn (maize) being the principal crops. Black slaves were imported into northwestern Uruguay in the 18th and 19th centuries. When slavery was abolished in the 19th century, most of the slaves were sold to Brazil, and the few remaining did not form a distinct ethnic community. By 1850, due to intermarriage and warring with white settlers, the pure-blooded Indian population had also vanished. Pop. (1975) city, 29,256; department, 58,404.

Artigas, José Gervasio (b. June 19, 1764, probably Montevideo—d. Sept. 23, 1850, Ibiray, near Asunción, Paraguay), soldier and revolutionary leader who is regarded as the father of Uruguayan independence, although that goal was not attained until several years after he had been forced into exile.

As a youth Artigas was a gaucho, or cowboy, in the interior of the Banda Oriental region of present Uruguay. In 1797 he entered the Spanish military forces, which then were mainly engaged in exterminating bandits. Several years later (1810) he offered his services to the Buenos Aires junta that was leading an independence movement against Spain. After winning a brilliant victory at Las Piedras, he besieged Spanish-held Montevideo for a time. In the face of superior Portuguese forces (called in from Brazil by the Spaniards), Artigas led a dramatic withdrawal of about 16,000 people from the Banda Oriental into Argentine territory.

Artigas then became the champion of federalism against the efforts of Buenos Aires to assert centralized control over the whole Río de la Plata region. In 1814 this struggle became a civil war. At first Artigas ruled over about 350,000 square miles of what is now Uruguay and central Argentina. His hold, however, was weakened by his insistence on decentralized government and was finally broken by a Portuguese invasion, which he resisted for three years. From 1820 he lived in exile in Paraguay; the independence of his native Uruguay was finally achieved on Aug. 27, 1828.

artillery, crew-served, mounted big guns, howitzers, or rocket launchers used in modern warfare and having a calibre greater than that of small arms, or infantry weapons.

A brief treatment of artillery follows. For full treatment, *see* MACROPAEDIA: War, The Technology of.

The traditional dividing line between artillery and small arms has been calibre .60 (0.6 in. or 15 mm). Weapons with a bore diameter greater than calibre .60 have been considered artillery, and those with smaller bores have been considered small arms. But there have been many exceptions to the rule. Portable rocket launchers like the bazooka with its 2.36-in. (60-mm) bore or the larger 3.5 in. (89-mm) superbazooka and recoilless rifles of 57-mm and larger are sometimes classed as small arms because they are used by infantry troops and can be handled by one or two men. Small mortars also are often classed as infantry weapons rather than artillery. At the other end of the scale, the large rockets and guided missiles that emerged during and after World War II added a whole new category of weapons capable of performing an artillery function but operating on principles radically different from conventional guns and howitzers. Between these two extremes are rapid-firing aircraft weapons ranging from machine guns of calibre .30 and .50 up to larger pieces of 20 mm, 37 mm, and even 75 mm, plus aircraft rockets. With these aircraft weapons the distinction between infantry use and artillery use was, of course, not applicable. Though similar to their ground counterparts, these aircraft weapons are usually not designated as artillery but as aircraft armament, just as the big guns mounted on tanks are referred to as tank armament.

During World War II and the years that followed, artillery matérial was subject to various classifications. A simple method was to divide it into two basic groups: (1) mobile or field artillery, which was capable of comparatively quick transfer from one place to another, and (2) immobile artillery, or artillery of position, being heavy cannon that, once emplaced in a permanent seacoast or fortress defense, was rarely moved. Because World War II was a war of rapid movement over wide areas, mobile artillery assumed greater importance while immobile artillery of the old fixed-fortification type tended toward obsolescence. A new type came into service during the 1940s and took the name of self-propelled artillery. It consisted of guns or howitzers mounted on armoured tanklike carriages that moved under their own power instead of being towed by truck or tractor.

In field use there were many specialized classes of artillery such as mountain guns or howitzers, tank and antitank guns, and antiaircraft weapons. Each class had its own peculiar requirements and its own technique of fire. In terms of army organization, artillery was sometimes classed as battalion, regimental, divisional, corps, or army. As their names indicated, these classes steadily increased in calibre, range, and effectiveness from battalion up to corps, though army artillery was usually a composite of all types.

Another common practice was to classify artillery pieces as light, medium, or heavy. The lines dividing these classes differed among the armies of the world. The U.S. Army placed in the light category artillery weapons up to the 105-mm howitzer; in the medium category the 155-mm howitzer; and larger guns and howitzers in the heavy category.

Still another classification described the various types of artillery weapons as guns, howitzers, heavy mortars, or rocket launchers. Briefly, for arms of like calibre, the gun was a long-barrelled, long-range weapon with a relatively flat trajectory (path followed by the projectile); the howitzer had a shorter barrel and less range and followed a moderately arched trajectory; the mortar had a very short barrel, short range, and a hairpin-shaped trajectory because of the high angle at which it was fired. Intermediate types possessed some of the characteristics of both guns and howitzers and were referred to as gun-howitzers. Rocket launchers were simple tubes or guiding rails that held the rockets before firing and aimed them in the desired direction.

The advent of aircraft, long-range rockets, and guided missiles has further complicated classification, and there is now a new classification of guns into four dimensions: surface-to-surface, surface-to-air, air-to-surface, and air-to-air.

The term artillery also describes the personnel or artillerymen who transport and serve the weapons and the branch of the army to which such personnel are assigned.

Consult the INDEX *first*

Artin, Emil (b. March 3, 1898, Vienna—d. Dec. 20, 1962, Hamburg), Austro-German mathematician who made fundamental contributions to class field theory, notably the general law of reciprocity.

After one year at the University of Göttingen, Artin joined the staff of the University of Hamburg in 1923. He emigrated to the United States in 1937, where he taught at Notre Dame University (1937–38), Indiana University, Bloomington (1938–46), and Princeton University (1946–58). In 1958 he returned to the University of Hamburg.

Artin's early work centred on the analytical and arithmetic theory of quadratic number fields. He made major advances in abstract algebra in 1926 and the following year used the theory of formal-real fields to solve the Hilbert problem of definite functions. In 1927 he also made notable contributions in hypercomplex numbers, primarily the expansion of the theory of associative ring algebras. In 1944 he discovered rings with minimum conditions for right ideals, now known as Artin rings. He presented a new foundation for and extended the arithmetic of semi-simple algebras over the rational number field.

His theory of braids, set forth in 1925, was a major contribution to the study of nodes in three-dimensional space. Artin's books include *Geometric Algebra* (1957) and, with John T. Tate, *Class Field Theory* (1961). Most of his technical papers are found in *The Collected Papers of Emil Artin* (1965).

Artinskian Stage, uppermost stage or time of deposition of the Lower Permian Series of rock strata in the Soviet Union and a standard marine stage of the Permian Period for the world (the Permian Period began about 280,000,000 years ago and lasted about 55,000,000 years). Facies relationships exhibited by the Artinskian are similar to those developed in the earlier Sakmarian Stage. The Artinskian Stage is characterized by the biostratigraphic zones of the fusulinid genus *Parafusulina* and of the ammonoid genera *Metaperrinites* and *Perrinites*.

artiodactyl, a member of the mammalian order Artiodactyla, which consists of the even-toed ungulates. These large and medium-size herbivores, familiar from barnyard, field, and zoo, are distributed among nine families: pigs (Suidae), peccaries (Tayassuidae), hippopotamuses (Hippopotamidae), camels (Camelidae), chevrotains (Tragulidae), giraffes and okapi (Giraffidae), deer (Cervidae), pronghorn (Antilocapridae), and cattle, sheep, goats, and antelope (Bovidae).

A brief treatment of artiodactyls follows. For full treatment, *see* MACROPAEDIA: Mammals.

The artiodactyls were a distinct group by the end of the Eocene Epoch (38,000,000 years ago). They demonstrated skill at adapting to environmental changes during the Oligocene, which ended about 26,000,000 years ago, and have remained prominent ever since. The 150 living species of the order are widely distributed. Deer, originally Eurasian, have spread to the Americas. Their close cousins the giraffe and okapi are at home in Africa, as are the hippopotamuses. Various bovids (which number almost 100 species) and pigs flourish in the Western and Eastern hemispheres, and the two peccaries live in Central and South America. The larger camels are native to Asia and Africa, but smaller members of the family, such as llamas and vicuñas, are found in South America. Three of the chevrotains live in the tropical forests of Asia, and one lives in Africa. The pronghorn, not a true antelope, lives in the grasslands of western America. The value of these mammals to man has always been great. They provide food in the form of meat and milk as well as clothing in the form of hides and wool, and in parts of the world camels are still used for transportation.

The artiodactyls are distinguished from the perissodactyls—the odd-toed ungulates such as horses and rhinoceroses—by the weight-bearing axis of the leg, which extends through the third and fourth toes together. (There is a fifth toe, but no first.) In the five-toed perissodactyls, the axis passes through the third, or central, toe. Another basic characteristic that identifies artiodactyls is the astragalus, an ankle bone that has rounded articulations at both ends and no constricted neck. This arrangement provides greater thrust when the animal runs, and, together with long legs and the ability to contract muscles quickly, it adds to the speed of most artiodactyls. The evolutionary success of the artiodactyls may be attributed to this and other adaptations of skeletal structures for swift flight and to the ability of members of the order to swallow food quickly and, in many cases, regurgitate it and chew it later.

Antlers and horns are found in many members of the order. Antlers, the hard, branched outgrowths of bone in the skull, are common on most male deer and are found on female reindeer as well. Males use antlers, which are shed seasonally and regrown, to fight and to mark territory. Combatants usually seek to avoid inflicting serious injury. Bovids of both sexes often have horns, but they are not regenerated if lost. Hair or fur, the latter sometimes beautifully coloured or patterned, covers the bodies of all members of the order except the hippopotamuses.

Advanced members of the order can bolt their food and then regurgitate and chew it, or ruminate, at a time of their choosing, such as when a threat from predators has passed. Most of these ruminants, who graze a variety of vegetation, have evolved a complex stomach containing four parts. Swallowed food passes from one part, the rumen, back into the mouth for complete mastication and is then swallowed again, after which it passes through the three other chambers, specialized for the digestion of a largely cellulose diet.

Courtship among artiodactyls may be more or less elaborate, often beginning with the male sniffing the female's urine, perhaps to determine if she is in heat. Contact such as nuzzling or taps on the leg may precede mating. Gestation periods range from 4 to 14 months. A placenta joined to the mother's womb is the organ through which the fetus breathes, feeds, and eliminates waste. Single births are the rule, although some species of deer bear twins, and the number may range to five for the European wild pig.

Reliance on milk lasts at least a few months, but all young eventually join in the endless search for food, to which snow, fire, and competition from other herbivores pose the chief problems. Adaptations to the search for food include the snout and tusks of pigs and the thickened skin that protects the warthog foraging under low bushes. Chevrotains, frequenting the thick undergrowth near water, have added roots and tubers to their diet. Another dietary specialization is that of the reindeer, which prefer lichens during the winter. The preference of different species of herbivores for different plants permits a number of species to flourish in the same geographical area.

Some species have limited ranges, but others travel widely, frequently in seasonal migrations. Herds or solitary individuals may move from south to north or from low altitudes to the mountains as the snow recedes. Many species form herds, usually as protection from predators. Predation takes its heaviest toll among the young, the old, and the sick. Older members of the herd lead the way to food, water, and breeding sites. In general the herds consist of females, their offspring, and the older dominant males as guardians.

Artois, historic and cultural region encompassing most of the northern French *département* of Pas-de-Calais and coextensive with the former province of Artois.

The *gouvernement* of Artois in 1789

The following article summarizes the political history, geography, and modern culture of Artois; for additional treatment of its geography and history, *see* MACROPAEDIA: France.

The names of Artois and Arras, the capital, are derived from the Atrebates, who inhabited the district during Julius Caesar's time. From the 9th to the 12th century Artois belonged to the counts of Flanders. It passed to Philip II Augustus of France in 1180 and remained under French influence until 1329, when it entered a period of Burgundian domination. After being ruled by the Habsburgs from 1500, Artois was conquered by France during the Thirty Years' War (1616–48); French sovereignty in Artois was confirmed in the Treaty of the Pyrenees (1659) and in the treaties of Nijmegen (1678 and 1679) and Utrecht (1713).

The region separates Picardy, to the south, from the Flemish plain, to the north. From the high Middle Ages a prosperous trading and manufacturing region associated with the fortunes of Flanders, the region saw its historic fortune ended by the destruction brought by World War I. Numerous towns extensively damaged during World War I were entirely rebuilt after 1918. The population of these small towns has been further depleted by the emigration of young workers.

Artois is largely Roman Catholic, but less strongly so in the mining regions and the new neighbourhoods of Arras. Small Protestant parishes were established in the industrial towns during the early 20th century. The society of the *Rosati,* which was established in 1778 and saw a renascence in 1877, was instrumental in reviving regional literature.

Artois, Charles-Philippe, comte d' (count of): *see* Charles X *under* Charles (France).

Art'om (Russian S.F.S.R.): *see* Artyom.

Art'omovsk (Ukrainian S.S.R.): *see* Artyomovsk.

Artôt, (Marguerite-Joséphine-) Désirée (Montagney) (b. July 21, 1835, Paris–d. April 3, 1907, Berlin), Belgian mezzo-soprano, member of a famous family of musicians. Acclaimed in France as an opera singer, she suddenly married (1869) the Spanish baritone Mariano Padilla y Ramos (1842–1906) while briefly engaged to Tchaikovsky. Her daughter Lola Artôt de Padilla (1885–1933), a soprano whom she trained, became a prima donna with the Royal Opera, Berlin (1909–27).

Arts and Crafts Movement, English aesthetic movement of the second half of the 19th century that represented the beginning of a new appreciation of the decorative arts throughout Europe. By 1860 a few people had become profoundly disturbed by the level to which style, craftsmanship, and public taste had sunk in the wake of the Industrial Revolution and its mass-produced and banal decorative arts. Among them was the English reformer, poet, and designer William Morris, who, in 1861, founded a firm of interior decorators and manufacturers dedicated to recapturing the spirit and quality of medieval craftsmanship. Morris and his associates (among them the architect Philip Webb and the painters Ford Madox Brown and Edward Burne-Jones) produced hand-crafted metalwork, jewelry, wallpaper, textiles, furniture, and books. To this date many of their designs are copied by designers and furniture manufacturers.

"The Woodpecker Tapestry," designed by William Morris, one of the leaders of the Arts and Crafts Movement, 1881; in the William Morris Gallery, London

By courtesy of the William Morris Gallery, Walthamstow, London, E. 17

By the 1880s Morris' efforts had widened the appeal of the Arts and Crafts Movement to a new generation. In 1882 the English architect and designer Arthur H. Mackmurdo helped organize the Century Guild for craftsmen, one of several such groups established about this time. These men revived the art of hand printing and championed the idea that there was no meaningful difference between the fine and decorative arts. Many converts, both from professional artists' ranks and from among the intellectual class as a whole, helped spread the ideas of the movement.

The main controversy raised by the movement—as no one ever denied the quality or aesthetic appeal of the work produced—was whether or not it was practical in the modern world. The progressives claimed that the movement was trying to turn back the clock and that it could not be done, that the Arts and Crafts Movement could not be taken as practical in mass urban and industrialized society. On the other hand, a reviewer who criticized an 1893 exhibition as "the work of a few for the few" also realized that it represented a graphic protest against design as "a marketable affair, controlled by the salesmen and the advertiser, and at the mercy of every passing fashion."

In the 1890s approval of the Arts and Crafts Movement widened, and the movement became diffused and less specifically identified with a small group of people. Its ideas spread to other countries and became identified with the growing international interest in design, specifically with Art Nouveau (*q.v.*).

Arts Décoratifs, Musée de (French: Museum of Decorative Arts), in Paris, museum of Western and Oriental decorative arts. It was established in 1880 and is housed in a wing of the Louvre.

The collections of furniture and *objets d'art* date from the Middle Ages to modern times. They are chronologically arranged as complete room reconstructions.

Artsybashev, Mikhail Petrovich (b. Nov. 5 [Oct. 24, old style], 1878, Kharkov province, Ukraine, Russian Empire—d. March 3, 1927, Warsaw), Russian prose writer whose works were noted for their extreme pessimism and immorality.

The publication of the novel *Sanin* in 1907 brought Artsybashev widespread fame, or infamy. Following the failure of the Revolution of 1905, a wave of pessimism and cynicism overtook the Russian literary world. Its extreme expression was *Sanin.* The literary influence of Tolstoy is felt in this book, as in other works by Artsybashev, who dealt with metaphysical and moral problems; his position, unlike Tolstoy's, was a negation of everything except so-called primitive realities, which for him were sex and death. Conservative critics condemned him for immorality, and modernist critics found no merit in him. He enjoyed great popularity for a time, however, and some of his plays have literary value. Attacked by the Soviet critics for his decadence, Artsybashev was expelled from the Soviet Union in 1923, and *Sanin* and his other works were proscribed.

Artuqid DYNASTY, Turkmen dynasty that ruled the province of Diyār Bakr (northern Iraq) through two branches: at Ḥiṣn Kayfā and Āmid (1098–1232) and at Mardin and Mayyāfāriqīn (1104–1408).

Artuq ibn Ekseb, founder of the dynasty, was rewarded for his services to the Seljuq sultan Malik-Shāh and his brother Tutush with the grant of Palestine in 1086. Forced out of Palestine by the Fāṭimids of Egypt, Artuq's descendant Muʿīn ad-Dīn Sökmen returned to Diyār Bakr, where he took Ḥiṣn Kayfā (1102), Mardin, and several other northern districts. His brother Najm ad-Dīn Ilghāzī, meanwhile, returned to Seljuq service and was made governor of Iraq by the Seljuq sultan Muḥammad. Sent to Diyār Bakr *c.* 1107, Ilghāzī displaced one of Sökmen's sons at Mardin (1108); he then made it the capital of his line, leaving Ḥiṣn Kayfā to his brother's descendants.

The Artuqid's relations with the Seljuqs thenceforth steadily worsened. Ilghāzī organized a Turkmen coalition against the Seljuq governor of Mosul and was able to win control of all Diyār Bakr by 1118. The next year he defeated European crusaders who were threatening Aleppo. From 1113 the Artuqids were also expanding into the northeast, along the eastern Euphrates, where Ilghāzī's nephew Balak set up a state at Harput. It did not survive Balak's death in 1124, however, and was incorporated into the principality of Ḥiṣn Kayfā by Dā'ūd (reigned *c.* 1109–44).

The rise of the Zangids in Mosul and later in Aleppo during the reigns of Dā'ūd and his successor, Kara Arslan (1144–67), ended Artuqid expansion. The Artuqids were instead drawn into wars against the crusaders and the Byzantines by the Zangid Nureddin and, at his death in 1174, found themselves Zangid vassals. Their position in Diyār Bakr weakened further as Saladin, ruler of Egypt, gradually began to reconquer Nureddin's old kingdom. Muḥammad (reigned 1167–85) engineered a brief alliance with Saladin in 1183, for which he was given the city of Āmid, henceforth the new Artuqid capital. In 1185, however, Saladin took Mayyāfāriqīn, and the several ruling Artuqids, mostly young princes, soon submitted to him.

The Artuqids survived in Diyār Bakr for two more centuries as vassals of the Seljuqs of Rūm and the Khwārezm-Shāhs. In 1232 the Artuqid line in Ḥiṣn Kayfā, Āmid, and Harput was destroyed by the Seljuqs; but the Mardin branch continued under the Mongols until 1408, when it was finally displaced by the Turkmen federation of the Kara Koyunlu.

The artistic traditions of the Artuqid age had a strong Seljuq flavour. Contact with the West occasionally brought some Byzantine elements into the iconography. Several examples of Artuqid metalwork have survived. A bronze weight (Cabinet des Médailles, Paris) with depictions of two human-headed griffins, cast in rather high relief, and a border decorated with floriated script shows strong Seljuq influence. Artuqid textiles include delicate silks and heavier brocades. A typical tapestry features double eagles, repeated in rows, dominating the entire surface. Such a motif is reminiscent of the Būyid, or pre-Seljuq Persian, period, but the Artuqid stylization was original.

Little Artuqid architecture has survived. From recent excavations and historical descriptions, however, it is known that the palace at Diyār Bakr was splendid. It included the traditional elements of domed chamber tracts and long *eyvāns* (large, vaulted halls closed on three sides and open to a court on one). Mosaic decoration and polychrome stone floors have been excavated at the site where the building stood. The palace—with, reportedly, 50 rooms serving as living quarters—must have been the most monumental creation of the Artuqid era.

Artvin, city, capital of Artvin *il* (province), northeastern Turkey, on the Çoruh River near the Soviet border. A local market for agricultural and animal products, it is linked by road with its port of Hopa to the northwest, which is on the Black Sea, and with Erzurum to the south.

Artvin *il,* formerly called Çoruh *il,* with an area of 3,170 sq mi (8,210 sq km), is drained by the Çoruh and Bertasuyu rivers. In the early 19th century it formed part of the *sancak* (district) of Lazistan, with Batum (modern Batumi, U.S.S.R.) as its capital. Together with the neighbouring region of Kars, Artvin was ceded to Russia at the conclusion of the Russo-Turkish war of 1877–78. It was returned to Turkey by a treaty between Turkey and Soviet Russia, signed at Brest-Litovsk in 1918 and reconfirmed three years later. In 1945 Stalin unsuccessfully demanded the return to Russia of northeastern Turkey, including Artvin.

The *il* is forested and mountainous, with limited cropland. Major economic activities include livestock raising, agriculture (chiefly grains and high-value crops of tea and tobacco), and the extraction and smelting of copper from the mines at Murgul. The population includes many Georgians, Kurds, and Lazes. Pop. (1980) city, 14,307; (1982 est.) *il,* 227,324.

Artyom, also spelled ART'OM, city, Primorsky Kray (Maritime Territory), Far Eastern Russian Soviet Federated Socialist Republic. Founded in 1924, it became a city in 1938 and is a centre of lignite (brown coal) production that serves the regional power station. Factories produce building materials, porcelain, and pianos. The city was named in memory of the Soviet statesman and revolutionary F.A. Sergeyev (alias Artyom). Pop. (1983 est.) 71,000.

Artyomovsk, also spelled ART'OMOVSK, or ARTEMOVSK, formerly (until 1924) BAKHMUT, city, Donetsk *oblast* (administrative region), Ukrainian Soviet Socialist Republic, on the Bakhmut River. The town originated in the 17th century as a fort protecting the Russian frontiers against the Crimean Tatars. Peter I the Great established a salt industry there in 1701, but seven years later the fort was destroyed in the Bulavin revolt. It officially became a town in 1783. Salt operations were revived in the 19th century and are now the largest in the Soviet Union; they also gave rise to a chemical industry based similarly on local supplies of limestone and coke. There are also metalworking and light industries. Nearby is a hydroelectric station. Cultural amenities include an institute of the salt industry, various technical colleges, and medical, teacher-training, and musical schools. The city is also the headquarters of the Donets Geophysical Expedition. Pop. (1983 est.) 89,000.

Aru Islands, Bahasa Indonesia KEPULAUAN ARU, Dutch AROE EILANDEN, easternmost island group in Maluku Tenggara (Southeast Moluccas) district, Indonesia, in the Arafura Sea. Administratively they form part of Maluku *propinsi* (province). The main island, Tanabesar, 110 mi (177 km) long and 48 mi wide, is virtually subdivided into six separate islands (Warilau, Kola, Wokam, Kobroor, Maikoor, and Trangan) by five narrow channels. About 85 smaller islands bring the group's total area to 3,306 sq mi (8,563 sq km). Dobo, the capital, on the small Pulau Wamar, is the site of the principal harbour and a minor airport. All islands are low, covered with dense forest, and edged by swampy coastal areas. Vegetation includes screw pines, palm trees, kanari (Java almond), and tree ferns. Trangan has grassy plains. Fauna is Papuan with strong Australian affinities, particularly among the mammals, which are dominated by marsupials.

The inhabitants are of mixed Papuan and Malay stock and adhere to traditional animist religions; some Muslims and Christians inhabit the western islands, where the villages are coastal and nestle among clumps of trees. In the eastern islands the villages stand on high rocks. Houses are often built of rough wood, crowded together, and entered by a trapdoor in the middle of the floor. Crops include sago, rice, corn (maize), sugar, tobacco, and coconuts; little ground, however, is tilled except by the Christians and Muslims. Collecting trepang, pearls, mother-of-pearl, and tortoiseshells provides the islanders' main subsistence.

Visited in 1606 by the Dutch, the Aru Islands were occupied by the Japanese in 1942 and used as an air base. After World War II they reverted to The Netherlands, and they became part of Indonesia in 1949. Pop. (1971) 34,195.

Arua, town, administrative headquarters of Arua district and capital of Nile province, northwestern Uganda, East Africa, about 12 mi (19 km) east of the Zaire–Uganda border, at an elevation of 4,300 ft (1,310 m). Roads link it with Moyo and Nebbi, and it has an airstrip. A market town for cotton, tobacco, tea, coffee, cassava, and corn (maize), its industrial products include beverages, processed food, leather goods, soap, metal goods, wearing apparel, rope and twine, and oils and fats. Pop. (1980 prelim.) 9,663.

Aruba, island of the Benedenwindse Eilanden (Leeward Islands) of the Netherlands Antilles, at the southwestern extreme of the Lesser Antilles in the Caribbean Sea. It is situated some 50 mi (80 km) west of Curaçao and 15 mi north of the Venezuelan coast. Aruba has an area of 75 sq mi (193 sq km). The island is flat; its highest point is the 620-ft (189-m) Mt. Jamanota. The terrain contains immense boulders of diorite that appear to be precariously balanced. The average yearly temperature is 82° F (27° C), and the climate is extremely dry because the prevailing northeasterly trade winds drop their rain on the windward group of the Lesser Antilles. Rain, about 17 in. (430 mm) per year, is caught in dams and in rooftop basins, but most drinking water must be obtained from desalination of seawater. The distillation plant, completed in 1960, has a capacity of 5,500,000 gallons (20,800,000 litres) a day and is one of the largest such plants in the world. Aruba is entirely outside of the usual Caribbean hurricane range.

The island's earliest inhabitants were Arawak Indians, who left red drawings inside caves, along with clay pottery and stone tools. After Aruba was claimed by Spain in 1499, it became a centre of piracy and smuggling, but the Indians were not exterminated as they were elsewhere. Though the Dutch began to settle there in 1634, they did not come into official possession until 1816. The island has remained under Dutch control ever since, except for 10 years during the Napoleonic Wars. More than half the population is of Indian stock; the rest are descendants of the European settlers, recent immigrants from India and the Far East, and some political refugees from Central and South America. Because a plantation economy never developed, no black slaves were brought in. The official language is Dutch, but the language of daily affairs is Papiamento, a creole language based on Spanish.

The functions of the central government are administered by the legislative assembly (Staten) in the capital of the Netherlands Antilles, Willemstad, on Curaçao. All local affairs are handled by a separate island government composed of an Island Council, an Executive Council, and a lieutenant governor. In a referendum passed in 1977 the people voted overwhelmingly in favour of independence for Aruba, but no action resulted. Lack of water severely limits agriculture. An experiment in hydroponic farming did not succeed because prices could not compete with those of imported produce. Aruba does, however, continue to export aloes, which do not require irrigation. The economy depends almost entirely on the processing and storage of oil from Venezuela. The Lago Oil refining complex is among the world's largest and is the main source of employment. Two plants produce low-sulfur fuel oil, and a petrochemical plant produces ammonia. Gold was mined for a short time in the 19th century. The development of tourism is actively encouraged by the government's fiscal policies and is facilitated by the deepwater harbours for cruise ships and by an international airport. The long stretches of white sand and clear waters attract bathers and boaters. Pop. (1981 est.) 64,797.

Rock formations on the coast of Aruba, Netherlands Antilles
Bradley Smith, New York

Arum, genus of low-growing tuberous perennial plants in the family Araceae (order Arales). Of the 12 species generally recognized, only a few are grown for their showy spathe, a funnel-shaped bract surrounding the rodlike spadix (on which the tiny flowers are borne), and for their glossy, arrow-shaped leaves. The bitter taste (and burning sensation) of the sap may have led to the genus name *Arum,* from the Arabic word for fire (*ar*). The sap can be poisonous, especially as concentrated in the whitish tubers and the brilliant red berries. In most cases the spathe is a dull yellow-green outside, but it is variously coloured and marked and often curves back to expose the inner surface. The more colourful varieties are handsome plants for a shaded wild garden. They are not hardy much below freezing temperatures.

Cuckoopint (*Arum maculatum*)
G.E. Hyde—EB Inc.

Arun, district, county of West Sussex, England, named for the river Arun, which rises near the northern boundary of the county and flows south across it. With an area of 85 sq mi (221 sq km), the district includes the ancient borough of Arundel, with its great castle, and embraces a stretch of the South Downs and a section of the Channel coast that includes a line of holiday resorts; the largest of these are Littlehampton and Bognor Regis. Pop. (1982 est.) 120,200.

Arunāchal Pradesh, formerly NORTH EAST FRONTIER AGENCY, union territory in northeastern India. Arunāchal Pradesh stretches broadly from the Brahmaputra River plain in Assam northward to the main crestline of the Assam Himalayas and eastward to an irregular line passing through a series of lofty peaks, known as the "Hump" during World War II when supplies to China were carried over it by air. The territory covers an area of 32,270 sq mi (83,578 sq km), but the frontiers have never been surveyed in detail or marked out on the ground. The territorial capital is Itanagar.

The northern boundary is 550 mi (890 km) long; known as the McMahon Line, it was long in dispute between India and China. Representatives of Britain, China, and Tibet agreed at a conference in Simla (1914) that the frontier between Tibet and northeastern India should follow the crest of the Himalayas. Two days later China disavowed its representative and refused to sign a convention. Further disputes following the independence of India (1947) resulted in Chinese troops crossing the line on Aug. 26, 1959; they captured an Indian outpost, Longju, a few miles south but abandoned it in 1961. They crossed the line again in October 1962 and extended their attack along the whole frontier. The Chinese later withdrew and in 1963 returned the Indian prisoners of war. Arunāchal Pradesh was made a union territory in 1972; its name means "land of the rising sun." Pop. (1981) 631,839.

Arundel, parish (town), Arun district, county of West Sussex, England, in the valley of the River Arun where it cuts through the South Downs. The town occupies the hill slope between the river and Arundel Castle, built soon after the Norman Conquest (1066) to guard the route through the Arun Valley and along the coastal plain.

Arundel was a borough by prescription (without a written charter) and is first mentioned in 877. After the Norman Conquest, it became the head of one of the six rapes (administrative divisions) of Sussex, and the stone and flint castle replaced the earlier earthworks. In 1580 the earldom of Arundel passed to the Howards, who had been dukes of Norfolk and hereditary earls marshall of England since 1483. Successive dukes repaired and improved the castle. The 16th duke moved to a neo-Georgian house in Arundel Park.

Barbican towers of Arundel Castle, West Sussex
Jim Shaw—Vincent J. Kamin

Once a river port, Arundel is now a quiet country town with considerable tourist traffic in summer. An 18th-century coaching inn, the Norfolk Arms, dominates the High Street. Pop. (1981 prelim.) 2,235.

Arundel, EARLS OF, titled English nobility of several creations, notably in the families Fitzalan and Howard, grouped below chronologically and indicated by the symbol •.

• Arundel, Richard Fitzalan, 4th earl of, 10TH EARL OF SURREY (b. 1346—d. Sept. 21, 1397, London), one of the chief opponents of Richard II.

He began as a member of the royal council during the minority of Richard II and about

1381 was made one of the young king's governors. About 1385 he joined the baronial party led by the King's uncle, Thomas of Woodstock, duke of Gloucester, and in 1386 was a member of the commission appointed to regulate the kingdom and the royal household. As admiral of the west and south he gained a victory over the French and their allies off Margate in 1387.

Then came the King's futile attempt to arrest Arundel, which was the signal for the outbreak of hostilities. The Gloucester faction quickly gained the upper hand, and Arundel was again a member of the royal council. After a personal altercation with the King at Westminster in 1394, Arundel underwent a short imprisonment. In 1397 he was involved in a conspiracy against Richard II and was beheaded on Tower Hill.

• Arundel, Thomas Fitzalan, 5th earl of, 11TH EARL OF SURREY (b. Oct. 13, 1381—d. Oct. 13, 1415), only surviving son of Richard Fitzalan, the 4th earl, and a champion of Henry IV and Henry V of England.

King Richard II made him a ward of John Holland, duke of Exeter, from whose keeping he escaped about 1398 and joined his uncle, Archbishop Thomas Arundel, at Utrecht, returning to England in 1399 with Henry of Lancaster, afterward King Henry IV. In October 1400 he was restored to his father's titles and estates. Arundel joined the party of the Beauforts and was one of the leaders of the English army that went to France in 1411; then after a period of retirement he became lord treasurer on the accession of Henry V and was at the taking of Harfleur in 1415.

His wife was Beatrice (d. 1439), a natural daughter of John I, king of Portugal, but they left no children, and the lordship of Arundel passed to his second cousin, John.

• Arundel, Henry Fitzalan, 12th earl of (b. *c.* 1512—d. Feb. 25, 1580, London), prominent English lord during the reign of the Tudors, implicated in Roman Catholic conspiracies against Elizabeth I.

Son of William Fitzalan (1483–1544), the 11th earl, he succeeded to the earldom in 1544. He took part in the siege of Boulogne (1544) and was appointed lord chamberlain and a privy councillor in 1546. In June 1553 he alone of the council refused the "engagement" of the council to support Edward VI's "device" for the succession—which passed over his sisters, Mary and Elizabeth, as illegitimate, in favour of Lady Jane Grey. He did, however, sign the letters patent. On Edward's death, while pretending to support Northumberland, he secured the proclamation of Mary as soon as Northumberland had left London.

Under Mary I he held a series of high appointments, including the lord stewardship, which he retained under Elizabeth I. But as one of the leaders of the Catholic nobility he fell under suspicion, resigned his offices in 1564, and was more than once disgraced. In 1569 he was implicated in the intrigues of Thomas Howard, 4th duke of Norfolk, but, although he appears to have received money from Spain, the evidence against him was insufficient, and he was released in March 1570 and even recalled to the council. After the discovery of the Ridolfi plot he was once more arrested and liberated only after the execution of Norfolk in 1572. At his death the title passed through his daughter Mary, the wife of the beheaded Norfolk, to the Howards.

• Arundel, Philip Howard, 1st (or 13th) earl of, EARL OF SURREY (b. June 28, 1557, London—d. Oct. 19, 1595, London), first earl of Arundel of the Howard line, found guilty of Roman Catholic conspiracies against Elizabeth I of England.

Philip was the eldest son of Thomas Howard, 4th duke of Norfolk, executed for high treason in 1572, and of Lady Mary, daughter and heiress of Henry Fitzalan, 12th earl of Arundel. On the death of his maternal grandfather, the 12th earl, in February 1580 he became earl of Arundel.

In 1582 his wife Anne became a Roman Catholic and was committed to the charge of Sir Thomas Shirley by Queen Elizabeth. He was himself suspected of disloyalty and was regarded by the discontented Roman Catholics as the centre of the plots against the Queen's government and even as a possible successor. In 1583 he was with some reason suspected of complicity in Francis Throckmorton's plot and prepared to escape to Flanders, but his plans were interrupted by a visit from Elizabeth I at his house in London and by her subsequent order to confine himself there. In September 1584 he became a Roman Catholic and made another attempt to leave England. He was then brought before the Star Chamber and sentenced to a fine and imprisonment for life. He was released for a time but was again arrested on a charge of high treason and, in 1589, condemned to death. The sentence was not executed, and he died in the Tower of London. In 1929 he was beatified.

• Arundel, Thomas Howard, 2nd (or 14th) earl of, EARL OF SURREY, EARL OF NORFOLK (b. July 7, 1585—d. Oct. 4, 1646, Padua, Republic of Venice), English noble prominent during the reigns of James I and Charles I and noted for his art collections of marbles and manuscripts.

The son of Philip Howard, the first earl of the Howard line, he was educated at Westminster School and at Trinity College, Cambridge. On April 18, 1604, he was restored to his father's earldom of Arundel and to the baronies of his grandfather, Thomas, 4th duke of Norfolk. His fortunes fluctuated under James I and Charles I; he held many high offices and was more than once imprisoned. In 1641 as lord high steward he presided at the trial of the Earl of Strafford. This closed his public career. He again became estranged from the court, and in 1641 he escorted Marie de Médicis to Holland, remaining abroad, with the exception of a short visit to England in that winter, and taking up permanent residence at Padua. He contributed a sum of £54,000 to the King's cause and suffered severe losses in the Civil War. On June 6, 1644, he was created earl of Norfolk. He died at Padua when on the point of returning home.

The 2nd earl is best remembered for his patronage of the arts and for his magnificent collections. These were dispersed after his death, most of the marbles and statues being given to Oxford University in 1667 to become known later as the Arundel (or Oxford) marbles. The library was given to the Royal Society and to the College of Heralds, the manuscript portion of the Royal Society's moiety being transferred to the British Museum in 1831 and forming the present Arundel Collection.

Arundel, Thomas (b. 1353—d. Feb. 19, 1414), English statesman and archbishop of Canterbury who aided the opponents of King Richard II; during the reign of King Henry IV, Arundel vigorously suppressed the Lollards. His father was Richard Fitzalan, 3rd earl of Arundel, and his mother was a member of the powerful House of Lancaster. He became bishop of Ely in 1374, and during the early years of the reign of Richard II he sided with the nobles opposed to the King. This party forced Richard to make Arundel chancellor of England (1386) and archbishop of York (1388) until, in 1389, he was able to throw off control by the nobles and remove Arundel from office. After making peace with his opponents, Richard reappointed Arundel to the chancellorship in 1391, but Arundel resigned in 1396 to become archbishop of Canterbury. In the following year the King again deprived Arundel of his see and banished him from the kingdom. Arundel joined Henry of Bolingbroke in exile and returned to England in 1399 when Bolingbroke invaded the country, defeated Richard, and ascended the throne as Henry IV.

Resuming his duties at Canterbury, Arundel initiated against the Lollards (followers of John Wycliffe) a campaign that resulted in the burning of several of them; in 1413 he led proceedings against the Lollard leader Sir John Oldcastle, who was condemned to death. In addition, Arundel served as Henry's chancellor from 1407 to 1409 and in 1412–13.

Arundinaria, genus of grasses (Poaceae) native to Asia and America, characterized by woody, cylindrical stems, persistent leaf sheaths with stiff, rough bristles, and flower spikelets. There are about 300 species of these bamboos and canes.

Arundinaria gigantea—which is known as giant cane, southern cane, or canebrake bamboo—was once widely utilized as a forage plant in the southeastern United States, from eastern Texas and Oklahoma to the Atlantic coast and north to the Ohio River valley. It produces green leaves and stems throughout the year and is valued for winter forage along the coast of the Gulf of Mexico. Giant cane grows in thickets and canebrakes in moist, fertile soil and thrives especially along riverbanks and in bottomlands. The stems are also woven into baskets and mats and are used to make pipestems and fishing poles.

Arung Singkang, original name LA MA'DUKELLENG (b. *c.* 1700, Celebes—d. 1765, Peniki, Celebes), Buginese aristocrat who unified his southern Celebes people and created a state that held out against the Dutch for more than a century.

As a young man Arung Singkang was exiled to Borneo, where he gathered a following and in 1737 returned and won control of his native state, Wadjo. He also defeated Bone, another Buginese state, and created a Buginese federation headed by Wadjo. In February 1739 he set out against the Dutch in Macassar but was defeated (July 20) when part of his forces deserted him. A Dutch counterattack on Wadjo failed, however, and Wadjo retained its independence for more than 100 years. Arung Singkang was forced from power in 1754 after an internal dispute.

Arunta (Australian Aborigines): *see* Aranda.

arūpa-dhātu, in Buddhist thought, the realm of formlessness. *See* arūpa-loka.

arūpa-loka (Sanskrit and Pāli: "world of immaterial form"), in Buddhist thought, the highest of the three spheres of existence in which rebirth takes place. The other two are *rūpa-loka*, "the world of form," and *kāma-loka*, "the world of feeling" (the three are also referred to as *arūpa-dhātu*, *rūpa-dhātu*, and *kāma-dhātu*, the "realms" of formlessness, form, and feeling).

In *arūpa-loka,* existence depends on the stage of concentration attained, and there are four levels: the infinity of space, the infinity of thought, the infinity of nonbeing, and the infinity of neither consciousness nor nonconsciousness. The *rūpa-loka*, which is free from sensuous desire but is still conditioned by form, is inhabited by gods. It is also further subdivided into the spheres inhabited by Brahmā, by the luminous deities, by the blissful gods, and by the deities of great fruits. *Kāma-loka* includes the six heavens of the lesser gods and the five lower worlds (the worlds of men, demons, ghosts, animals, and purgatory).

As superior as is rebirth in the higher worlds, such an existence is nonetheless temporary, subject to change, and involves the fundamental conflicts of existence within the limits of transmigration. This can be broken only by further spiritual insight, resulting in Nirvāṇa and release from the cycle of rebirths.

Aruqtai (fl. early 15th century), chief of the As (or Alan) Mongols, who allied himself with Mahamu, chief of the Oyrat Mongols, and with him defeated Ugechi, whom the Ming dynasty had recognized as the chief of the Mongols. In 1423 Aruqtai proclaimed himself great khan of the Mongols, launching devastating raids into North China. He was finally defeated when Mahamu's son, Togon-temür, rebelled against him around 1425.

Arusha, formerly NORTHERN REGION, administrative region, northern Tanzania, East Africa. Established in 1963, it has an area of about 33,250 sq mi (86,100 sq km), including 950 sq mi of water area. It is bordered on the north by Kenya. The Serengeti Plain lies in the northwest, and the Masai Steppe, broken only by isolated gneiss hills, lies in the south. In the central area of the region are the Crater Highlands, bordering portions of the East African Rift System. Volcanic activity and faulting have created broad lava plains and volcanic massifs such as Mt. Meru (14,979 ft [4,566 m]) and the occasionally active Oldoinyo Lengai (9,442 ft). Rainfall varies from 70 in. (1,800 mm) annually on Mt. Meru to 20 in. on the semiarid plains. Terrain ranges from wooded savannas and montane forests to alpine areas.

Arusha is an important coffee-producing area. Other crops include grain, vegetables, cotton, pyrethrum, papain, sisal, and sunflower seeds. Magnesite and meerschaum are mined in the region; there are also salt, mica, saltpetre, and ochre deposits. Tourism is important, based upon the big-game areas of the Taranqire National Park, Ngorongoro and Ngurdoto craters, Olduvai Gorge, and Lake Manyara. The region's major ethno-linguistic groups include the Arusha, Meru, Iraqw, and

Tower marking the midpoint on the Cairo-to-Cape Town highway in Arusha town, Tanzania
Salmer/Plessner—Keystone

Masai. Arusha town, an important business centre, is the regional capital. Pop. (1978 prelim.) 928,478.

Arusi (Ethiopia): *see* Arsi.

Arvad (Syria): *see* Arwād, Jazīrat.

Arval Brothers, Latin FRATRES ARVALES, in ancient Rome, college or priesthood whose chief original duty was to offer annual public sacrifice for the fertility of the fields. The brotherhood, probably of great antiquity, was almost forgotten in republican times but was revived by Augustus and probably lasted until the time of Theodosius I. It consisted of 12 members, elected for life from the highest ranks, including the emperor during the principate. Literary allusions to them are scarce, but 96 of the *acta*, or minutes, of their proceedings, inscribed on stone, have been discovered in the grove of the Dea Dia near Rome.

Arve River, river in eastern France and Switzerland, rising in the Savoy Alps and flowing north into the Rhône River below Geneva. Over its 62-mi (100-km) course, the river passes by some of the finest and most varied Alpine scenery. Its upper section collects the drainage of the northwest face of the Massif du Mont Blanc and is a source of hydroelectric power. Below Bonneville, in the Faucigny district, it flows through the Arve Valley, which is low-lying and highly cultivated.

Consult the INDEX *first*

Arverni, ancient Celtic tribe inhabiting what is now the region of Auvergne, in central France; their chieftain Vercingetorix (*q.v.*) led a rebellion against Julius Caesar in 52 BC. Although rivalry between Arverni and Aedui for Gallic primacy weakened their coalition, the rebels were able to defeat Caesar at the Arverni capital, Gergovia (modern Gergovie), before Vercingetorix surrendered to the Romans. Under the empire the tribe was peaceful and prosperous. Their capital was moved to the new Roman city of Augustonemetum (modern Clermont-Ferrand).

Arwād, Jazīrat, Greek ARADOS, Phoenician ARVAD, island in the eastern Mediterranean off the Syrian coastal town of Ṭarṭūs. Originally settled by the Phoenicians in the early 2nd millennium BC, it formed an excellent base for their commercial operations, into both the Orontes Valley and the hinterland as far as the Euphrates, and also to Egypt. Arwadian soldiers fought against the Egyptians at the Battle of Kadesh (*c.* 1299 BC). From 1100 to 625 it was under Assyrian rule, passing to the Babylonians in 604 and to the Persians in 539. Its fleet fought against the Greeks at the Battle of Salamis in 480. It was not until Roman times that the island declined, losing its commercial power to Antaradus (Ṭarṭūs). In the 12th–13th century AD, the island was occupied and defended by the Templars. It finally fell to the Arabs, who razed the walls, in 1302. There is a Templar castle and an Arab castle, both dating from the 13th century, still to be seen on Arwād, which today is an entirely Arab island dependent for its livelihood on the fishing industry. Arwād can be reached by boat from Ṭarṭūs.

arya-pudgala (in Buddhism): *see* ariya-puggala.

Arya Samaj (Sanskrit: Society of Nobles), English SOCIETY OF ARYANS, vigorous reform sect of modern Hinduism, founded in 1875 by Dayananda Sarasvati (*q.v.*), whose aim was to reestablish the Vedas, the earliest Hindu scriptures, as revealed truth. He rejected all later accretions to the Vedas as degenerate but, in his own interpretation, included much post-Vedic thought, such as the doctrines of *karman* (effect of past deeds) and of rebirth.

The Arya Samaj has always had its largest following in West and North India. It is organized in local *samājas* ("societies") that send representatives to provincial *samājas* and to an all-India *samāja.* Each local *samāja* elects its own officers in a democratic manner.

The Arya Samaj opposes idolatry, animal sacrifice, ancestor worship, a caste system based on birth rather than on merit, untouchability, child marriage, pilgrimages, priestly craft, and temple offerings. It upholds the infallibility of the Vedas, the doctrines of *karman* and rebirth, the sanctity of the cow, the importance of the individual sacraments (*saṃskāras*), the efficacy of Vedic oblations to the fire, and programs of social reform. It has worked to further female education and intercaste marriages, has built missions, orphanages, and homes for widows, and has undertaken famine relief and medical work. It has also established a network of schools and colleges. From its beginning it was an important factor in the growth of nationalism. It has been criticized, however, as overly dogmatic and militant on occasion and as having exhibited an aggressive intolerance toward both Christianity and Islām.

Aryabhata, first unmanned Earth satellite built by India. It was named for a prominent Indian astronomer and mathematician of the 5th century AD. The satellite was assembled at Peenya, near Bangalore, but was launched from within the Soviet Union by a Russian-made rocket on April 19, 1975. Aryabhata weighed 794 pounds (360 kilograms) and was instrumented to explore conditions in the Earth's ionosphere, measure neutrons and gamma rays from the Sun, and perform investigations in X-ray astronomy. The scientific instruments had to be switched off during the fifth day in orbit because of a failure in the satellite's electrical power system. Useful information, nevertheless, was collected during the five days of operation.

Āryabhaṭa I (b. 476, Kusumapura, India—d. *c.* 550), astronomer and the earliest Hindu mathematician whose work and history are available to modern scholars. He was one of the first known to use algebra. In 499 he finished the *Āryabhaṭīya,* written in verse couplets and summarizing mathematics as known in his time. Most of this work deals with astronomy and spherical trigonometry; the remainder consists of 33 rules in arithmetic, algebra, and plane trigonometry. Perhaps its most important feature is the treatment of indeterminate equations by the application of continued fractions—substantially the modern method.

Āryabhaṭa gave an accurate approximation for pi (π), 3.1416, and introduced the versed sine function (that is, 1 minus the cosine of an angle) into trigonometry. He also taught that the apparent rotation of the heavens was attributable to the rotation of the Earth on its axis.

Aryan (from Sanskrit *ārya,* "noble"), a people who, in prehistoric times, settled in Iran and northern India. From their language, also called Aryan, the Indo-European languages of South Asia are descended. In the 19th century the term was used as a synonym for "Indo-European" and also, more restrictively, to refer to the Indo-Iranian languages (*q.v.*). It is now used in linguistics only in the sense of the term Indo-Aryan languages (*q.v.*).

During the 19th century there arose a notion—propagated most assiduously by the Comte de Gobineau and later by his disciple Houston Stewart Chamberlain (*qq.v.*)—of an "Aryan race," those who spoke Indo-European languages, who were considered to be responsible for all the progress that mankind had made and who were also morally superior to "Semites," "yellows," and "blacks." The Nordic, or Germanic, peoples came to be regarded as the purest "Aryans." This notion, which had been repudiated by anthropologists by the second quarter of the 20th century, was seized upon by Adolf Hitler and the Nazis and made the basis of the German government policy of exterminating Jews, Gypsies, and other "non-Aryans."

Aryan local race: *see* Indic local race.

aryballos, small, narrow-necked, spherical or globular Greek vase. Commonly used as a scent or oil bottle, particularly by athletes at the baths, the aryballos derives from the globular wine pourer (*oinochoe*) of the Geometric style (9th century BC), evolving its distinctive shape in the early Proto-Corinthian style (8th century BC). From the many aryballoi that have been found dating from the late 8th and 7th centuries BC, an evolution can be traced from a round to an ovoid shape, then to a pointed, top-heavy version, and finally to a round shape; the round, Corinthian type has a broad, disklike mouth, often nearly matching the circumference of the flask, and one small handle. Later aryballoi have a bell-shaped

Proto-Corinthian aryballos with mouth in the form of a lion's head, *c.* 650 BC; in the British Museum

By courtesy of the trustees of the British Museum

mouth, two handles with slight projections at the bases, and a flat bottom.

Arzamas, city and administrative centre of Arzamas region, Gorky *oblast* (administrative region), southwestern Russian Soviet Federated Socialist Republic, on the Tyosha River. First mentioned in a manuscript in 1366 and again in 1552, it was chartered in 1578. Agricultural equipment and food processing are the main economic activities, and there are two technical colleges devoted to agricultural studies. Between 1802 and 1862 the first Russian provincial school of painting existed there. Pop. (1983 est.) 101,000.

Arzamas society, Russian literary circle (flourished 1815–18), formed for the semiserious purpose of ridiculing the conservative "Lovers of the Russian Word," a group dominated by the philologist Aleksandr S. Shishkov, who wished to keep the modern Russian language firmly tied to Old Church Slavonic. The Arzamas circle included the poets Vasily A. Zhukovsky, Konstantin Batyushkov, and the youthful Aleksandr Pushkin, who were all advocates of recent Westernized language reforms. Though the activities of the club members were limited to composing burlesques of the archaic Slavonic style, their adoption of the new style in their subsequent works had a permanent effect on the formation of the modern Russian literary language.

Arzawa, ancient kingdom of western or southwestern Anatolia (its exact location is disputed). Although Arzawa was for long periods a rival of the Hittite kingdom, it was occasionally conquered and made a vassal by some of the more powerful Hittite kings, such as Labarnas I (*c.* 1680–*c.* 1650 BC). During the period of Hittite decline after the end of the Old Kingdom (*c.* 1500 BC), Arzawa's power and prominence reached its peak, and its king, Tarkhundaradu, corresponded with Amenhotep III (1417–1379 BC) of Egypt. It was later reconquered by the Hittite Mursilis II (1339–06 BC). During the reign of the Hittite king Arnuwandas III (1220–1190 BC), Arzawa was seized by a disloyal Hittite vassal, Madduwattas; it was never recaptured by the Hittites and gradually lost its political identity.

Arzew, also spelled ARZEU, town, port of Oran *wilāyah* (province, or *département*), Algeria, near the mouth of the Oued (stream) Mehgoun. Its natural Mediterranean harbour is sheltered by the mountainous promontory between the gulfs of Oran and Arzew. Arzew was an Almohad port in the 1100s. It was visited by Italian merchants in the 14th and 15th centuries and was captured and fortified by the Turks in the 16th. Occupied by the Algerian *amīr* Abdelkader in 1831, the town was taken by the French two years later and annexed to France by treaty in 1837. The walled town grew around the anchorage, with the Arab sector to the southwest near the ruined Roman settlement, Portus Magnus. Petrochemical products, esparto grass, salt (from Salines d'Arzew, 9 mi [11 km] south), wine, cereals, and cattle are exported, and there is some commercial fishing. Arzew is connected by pipelines with the Hassi R'Mel natural gas fields and the Hassi Messaoud oil fields. Industry includes a natural gas liquification plant, a fertilizer plant, and sulfur and oil refineries. Pop. (1977 prelim.) mun., 22,171.

Arzila (Morocco): *see* Asilah.

as if, philosophy of, name given by Hans Vaihinger to the system espoused in his major philosophical work *Die Philosophie des Als Ob* (1911), which proposed that man willingly accept falsehoods or fictions in order to live peacefully in an irrational world. Vaihinger, who saw life as a maze of contradictions and philosophy as a search for means to make life livable, began by accepting Immanuel Kant's view that knowledge is limited to phenomena and cannot reach to things-in-themselves. In order to survive, man must use his will to construct fictional explanations of phenomena "as if" there were rational grounds for believing that such a method reflects reality. Logical contradictions were simply disregarded. Thus in physics, man must proceed "as if" a material world exists independently of perceiving subjects; in behaviour, he must act "as if" ethical certainty were possible; in religion, he must believe "as if" there were a God.

Vaihinger denied that his philosophy was a Skepticism. He pointed out that Skepticism implies a doubting; but in his "as if" philosophy there is nothing dubious about patently false fictions which, unlike ordinary hypotheses, are not subject to verification. Their acceptance is justified as nonrational solutions to problems that have no rational answers. Vaihinger's "as if" philosophy was influenced by Arthur Schopenhauer, a voluntarist, and by Friedrich Lange, an antimaterialist, and is interesting as a venture in the direction of Pragmatism made quite independently of contemporary U.S. developments.

Asaba, town, Bendel State, southern Nigeria, on the west bank of the Niger River (opposite Onitsha) and on the road to Benin City. A traditional market centre (cassava, yams, palm oil and kernels, kola nuts) for the Ibo people, it was the place where Richard and John Lander, the British explorers of the Niger, were taken captive by the Ibos in 1830. It later became a trading post for Sir George Goldie's National African Company, and from 1886 to 1900 it served as the administrative headquarters of the territory governed by the Royal Niger Company. The town has been an entrepôt for palm produce and other agricultural exports carried by the Asaba-Onitsha ferry; it lies at the terminus of the 4,606-ft (1,404-m) bridge to Onitsha (completed in 1965), which serves as eastern Nigeria's only direct road link to Benin City and Lagos. Asaba has a textile factory, the only major industry in the town. It is also the site of a teacher-training college, secondary schools, several private trade schools, and a government hospital. Lignite deposits have been discovered in the vicinity. Pop. (1982 est.) 41,380.

asafetida, gum resin prized as a condiment in India and Iran, where it is used to flavour curries, meatballs, and pickles. It has been used in Europe and the United States in perfumes and for flavouring. Acrid in taste, it emits a strong onion-like odour because of its organic sulfur compounds. It is obtained chiefly from the plant *Ferula foetida* of the family Apiaceae (Umbelliferae). The whole plant is used as a fresh vegetable, the inner portion of the full-grown stem being regarded as a delicacy. The plant may grow as high as 7 feet (2 metres). After four years, when it is ready to yield asafetida, the stems are cut down close to the root, and a milky juice flows out that quickly sets into a solid resinous mass. A freshly exposed surface of asafetida has a translucent, pearly white appearance, but it soon darkens in the air, becoming first pink and finally reddish brown.

Asahi shimbun (Japanese: "Morning Sun Newspaper"), nationwide Japanese daily newspaper, one of the "big three" in influence and circulation, printed in Tokyo, Ōsaka, and several other regional centres and also as an English-language edition daily in Tokyo.

Founded in Ōsaka in 1879, *Asahi* has been in the hands of the Murayama and Ueno families since 1881. *Asahi* is particularly noted for its political coverage and its foreign news. It has correspondents in major cities in Europe, Asia, and the United States and subscribes to more than 20 international news services. Like the other two major Japanese newspapers, *Yomiuri* and *Mainichi, Asahi* publishes a much greater proportion of foreign news than is usual in the West. Its staff numbers more than 6,000 people, including reporters, photographers, and translators of foreign copy, and its daily circulation of morning and evening editions is one of the largest in the world. The main readership of the *Asahi* is drawn from the upper and middle classes.

Asahikawa, also spelled ASAHIGAWA, city, Hokkaido, Japan, on the Ishikari-gawa (Ishikari River), in the agriculturally important Kamikawa Basin. Settled in 1889 and organized as a village in 1893, Asahikawa became the railway, marketing, and industrial centre of northern Hokkaido. Industries include brewing and the manufacture of pulp, paper, wood chemicals, and cotton yarn. Asahikawa also serves as the entrance to Taisetsuzan National Park. It is linked to Sapporo by rail.

Ainu people dancing before a palace made of snow at the Asahikawa Snow Festival, Japan

FPG—EB Inc.

The Ainu reservation of Chikabuni is nearby. Pop. (1983 est.) 359,395.

Asaka, city, Saitama Prefecture (*ken*), Honshu, Japan, on the Kurume-gawa (Kurume River), northwest of Tokyo. It was a post town known as Hizaori during the Tokugawa era (1603–1867); its name was changed to Asaka in 1932. The city has been a centre of the copper-rolling industry since the late 19th century. Connected by rail with Tokyo, it is now a residential suburb of the Tokyo–Yokohama Metropolitan Area. Asaka is also the site of a large military base. Pop. (1980) 90,088.

Asalluhe, in Mesopotamian religion, Sumerian deity, city god of Ku'ar, near Eridu in the southeastern marshland region. Asalluhe was active with the god Enki (Akkadian Ea) in rituals of lustration magic and was considered his son. He may have originally been a god of thundershowers, as his name, Man-Drenching Asal, suggests; he would thus have corresponded to the other Sumerian gods Ishkur and Ninurta. In incantations Asalluhe was usually the god who first called Enki's attention to existing evils, perhaps surveying the world in the guise of a thundercloud. He was later identified with Marduk of Babylon.

Asam, Cosmas Damian and Egid Quirin (respectively b. Sept. 28, 1686, Benediktbeuren, Bavaria—d. May 10, 1739, Munich; b. Sept. 1, 1692, Tegernsee, Bavaria—d. April 29, 1750, Mannheim, Palatinate), principal late Baroque exponents of illusionist decoration in religious architecture. The Asam brothers were part of a generation of Germans educated in Rome in the Italian Baroque tradition. Their works, often produced in collaboration, are notable for their profound and dramatic intensity of religious feeling.

Cosmas Damian, primarily a painter, and Egid Quirin, an architect and a sculptor of stucco, were the sons of Hans Georg Asam, the first artist in Bavaria to practice illusionistic painting. The brothers studied in Rome with Gian Lorenzo Bernini, in about 1714, and their first religious commissions show Bernini's influence, especially in the concept of the *theatrum sacrum,* or sacred theatre, in which all decorative elements combine to involve the spectator in a vivid religious drama. In many of their creations, the complex weaving of architectural and decorative elements makes difficult any distinction of the brothers' individual contributions.

The beautiful Church of St. John of Nepomuk in Munich (1733–46), also known as the Asamkirche in honour of the brothers, is their masterwork. The high, narrow interior, mysteriously lit from above, is richly decorated with paint, stuccowork, sculpture, and gilt. The ceiling is decorated with painted figures ascending into a space that seems to transcend architectural boundaries.The building's relatively uncomplicated yet dramatic facade testifies to Egid Quirin's ability to generate a sense of movement in carved stone.

The brothers sometimes collaborated in the decoration of buildings designed by others, as in architect Johann Michael Fischer's noted Premonstratensian abbey church in Osterhofen (1726–29; decoration, 1730–35). Their other major works include the cloister church in the Benedictine abbey of Weltenburg (1716–21), where Egid Quirin's gilded sculpture "St. George and the Dragon" (1721), dramatically lit from behind, dominates the high altar, and the Ursuline church at Straubing (1736–41), in which the architectural plan is by Egid Quirin and the light, almost Rococo, interior, is the work of Cosmas Damian.

asana (tree): *see* narra.

āsana (Sanskrit: "sitting posture, seat"), in the Yoga system of Indian philosophy, immobile posture that the body assumes in an attempt to isolate the mind by freeing it from attention to bodily functions. It is the third of the eight prescribed stages intended to lead the aspirant to *samādhi,* the trancelike state of perfect concentration. Once the practitioner is able with ease to maintain a rigid, essentially unnatural posture, he has in a sense "concentrated" his body (the antithesis of its normal dispersed state, that of infinite mobility). As many as 32 or more different *āsana*s have been enumerated, of which perhaps the most common is the *padmāsana* ("lotus posture").

In the visual arts of India, *āsana* refers to the posture of a seated deity or figure or to the seat or throne on which he sits.

Asande (people): *see* Azande.

Asaṅga (fl. 4th–5th century AD, b. Puruṣapura, India), influential Buddhist philosopher who established the Yogācāra (Practice of Yogā) school of idealism. He was the eldest of three brothers who were the sons of a Brahman, a court priest at Puruṣapura, and who all became monks in the Sarvāstivāda order (which held the doctrine that "all is real"). Dissatisfied with the Hīnayāna concepts of *śūnyatā* ("emptiness") and *pudgala* ("person"), he turned to the Mahāyāna tradition and was credited also with winning over his brother, Vasubandhu, who made many important contributions to Mahāyāna scholarship.

Asaṅga's teacher in the Yogācāra doctrine was Maitreyanātha, who lived about 275–350. This school (also called Vijñānavāda, or Doctrine of Consciousness) held that the external world exists only as mental images that have no real permanence. A "storehouse" of consciousness (the *ālaya-vijñāna*) contains the trace impressions of the past and the potentialities of future actions. Asaṅga's great contribution was his development of Maitreyanātha's teaching, analysis of the *ālaya-vijñāna,* and setting forth of the stages (*bhūmi*) leading to Buddhahood. Among his important works is the *Mahāyāna-saṃgraha* ("Compendium of the Mahāyāna").

Asano Sōichirō (b. 1848, Etchū Province, Japan—d. 1930, Tokyo), Japanese businessman who founded the giant Asano *zaibatsu,* or industrial combine.

The son of a physician, Asano chose a career in business, but his first company failed. In 1871 he became a coal merchant in Tokyo. Five years later he developed methods for utilizing coke, until then a waste by-product of gas manufacture, in cement production, and this enterprise prospered. His business acumen interested Shibusawa Eiichi, a leading figure in Meiji era industrial development, who enabled Asano in 1883 to acquire a government cement plant being transferred to private ownership free of charge. It became the Asano Cement Company, cornerstone of the Asano *zaibatsu,* which eventually included shipping and shipbuilding, mining, gas and electricity, oil, iron and steel, and beer brewing. By 1929 it was the fifth largest such combine in Japan, with 17 wholly owned companies, 26 subsidiaries, 26 affiliates, and 6 associated concerns. The Allied Occupation authorities broke up the Asano *zaibatsu* into separate enterprises in 1947.

Asansol, town, Burdwān district, West Bengal state, northeastern India. Situated in the heart of the Rānīganj coalfield, it is the centre of the rapidly growing Kulti-Burnpur industrial complex. Connected by the Grand Trunk Road and by rail with Calcutta, Durgāpur, and Burdwān, it is an important coal-trading and railway centre, with large railway workshops and a railway colony. Major industries include textile, iron, and steel factories. Jaykaynagar, a suburb, has large aluminum works. Asansol was constituted a municipality in 1896 and has three colleges affiliated with the University of Burdwān. Pop. (1981) town, 187,039; metropolitan area, 366,424.

Steel mill, part of the Kulti-Burnpur industrial complex near Asansol in Burdwān district, West Bengal, India

Kaypix—Shostal/EB Inc.

Asante (people): *see* Ashanti.

Asante empire (West African history): *see* Ashanti empire.

āsava (Buddhist philosophy): *see* āsrāva.

Asbaje, Juana Inés de: *see* Cruz, Sor Juana Inés de la.

Asbest, city, Sverdlovsk *oblast* (administrative region), west central Russian Soviet Federated Socialist Republic, in the eastern foothills of the middle Ural Mountains. Developed from the settlement of Kudelka, founded in 1720 around the first Russian discovery of asbestos—from which it takes its name—it became a city in 1933. Asbestos production from the Bazhenovo deposit has been carried on since the 1880s. A century later the city was still the largest producer of asbestos in the U.S.S.R., contributing about 70 percent of Soviet output. There is a local factory for the concentration of asbestos, a medical institute, and a mining college. Pop. (1983 est.) 81,000.

Asbestos, town, Cantons-de-l'Est (Eastern Townships) region, southern Quebec province, Canada, near the Southwest Nicolet River, 95 mi (153 km) southwest of Quebec city. Its economy depends almost entirely on asbestos mining and the manufacture of asbestos products. One of the mines operated by the Canadian Johns-Manville Company—the Jeffrey open-pit mine—is said to be the largest asbestos mine in the world. Inc. village, 1899; town, 1937. Pop. (1981) 7,967.

asbestos, mineral fibre occurring in nature and obtained from certain types of asbestos rock, chiefly the chrysotile variety of the serpentine group of minerals, by mining or quarrying. Though valued since ancient times for its resistance to fire, asbestos fibre did not achieve commercial importance until the 19th century.

The fibre is freed by crushing the rock and is then separated from the surrounding material, usually by a blowing process. Only the longest of the fibres, at least 0.4 inch (1 centimetre), are suitable for spinning into yarn. Shorter fibres are used in such products as paper, millboard, and asbestos–cement building materials.

The brittle, smooth-surfaced fibres are difficult to spin, tending to slip past each other unless blended with a rough-surfaced fibre, such as cotton, which typically makes up 10–25 percent of the blend. Asbestos fibre usually has a whitish colour, although some varieties may be pale green, yellow, or blue. It cannot be dyed easily, and the dyed material is uneven and has poor colourfastness. In addition to its resistance to the effects of heat and fire, the fibre is resistant to acids and alkalies and is widely employed in working with chemicals.

Asbestos fibre is employed for applications requiring nonflammability and is chiefly of industrial importance, especially in the manufacture of brake linings, building construction materials, electrical equipment, and thermal insulation materials. Asbestos fabrics are used for safety apparel and for such items as theatre curtains and fire stop hangings in public buildings. Canada is the major source of asbestos fibre, and the United States leads in manufacture of asbestos products.

Reports of untoward effects of asbestos fibres on human health caused increasing concern beginning in the 1970s. The short fibres have been implicated in asbestosis, a lung disorder, and in mesothelioma, a rapidly fatal form of lung cancer. Once this became generally known, the widespread use of asbestos in construction and manufacturing since the turn of the century and the ubiquitous occurrence of asbestos "dust" in the air intensified concern and prompted attempts to limit its use. Contamination of water supplies by asbestos mine tailings presents another potential hazard, the extent of which is undetermined.

asbestosis, respiratory disease, a type of pneumoconiosis caused by inhalation of asbestos fibres, found primarily among workers whose occupations involve asbestos. Industries where asbestos exposure is common include mining; manufacture of insulation, fireproofing, cement products, and automobile brakes; and construction. The disease is not limited solely to asbestos workers but is also known among people living near mines, factories, and construction sites.

Asbestos fibres remain in the lungs for years and cause fibrosis, a stiffening of the lung that continues long after exposure ceases. Unlike other dust-associated respiratory disease, asbestosis can result from relatively little exposure. The first symptoms do not appear for many years after the initial exposure; shipyard workers exposed to asbestos during World War II began developing asbestosis in the 1960s and '70s. It is known that cigarette smoking aggravates the symptoms of asbestosis.

Persons suffering from asbestosis experience shortness of breath and, in more advanced cases, a dry cough. The stiffening of the lungs causes the heart to work harder and may induce a secondary heart disease; certain rare lung cancers also appear to be related to asbestosis. The incidence of asbestosis has been increasing since 1950, probably as a result of the increasingly widespread industrial use of asbestos.

Asbjørnsen, Peter Christen; and Moe, Jørgen Engebretsen (respectively b. Jan. 15, 1812, Christiania, Nor.—d. Jan. 5, 1885, Kristiania; b. April 22, 1813, Hole, Nor.—d. March 27, 1882, Kristiansand), collectors of Norwegian folklore. Their *Norske folkeeventyr* ("Norwegian Folktales") is a landmark in Norwegian literature and influenced the Norwegian language.

Closely united in their lives and work, they are rarely named separately. They met as youths in 1827 and became "blood brothers."

Asbjørnsen, the son of a glazier, became a private tutor in eastern Norway at the age of 20. There he began to collect folktales. Moe, the son of a rich and highly educated farmer, was graduated in theology from King Frederick's University, Christiania, in 1839; religious scruples, however, made him reject the ministry. He, too, became a tutor and spent holidays collecting folklore in southern Norway. Meanwhile, Asbjørnsen became a naturalist, and while making investigations along the fjords, he added to his collection of tales. They decided to pool their materials and publish them jointly.

At the time, the Norwegian literary style was too like that of Denmark to be suitable for national folklore, while the various dialects used by their oral storytellers were too local. Asbjørnsen and Moe solved the problem of style by adopting the Grimm brothers' principle of using simple language in place of the various dialects, yet maintaining the traditional form of the folktales. Some of the first tales appeared as early as 1837 in *Nor;* others were published as *Norske folkeeventyr* in 1841. Enlarged and illustrated collections appeared in 1842, 1843, and 1844. The whole was published with critical notes in 1852.

Accepted in Europe as a major contribution to comparative mythology, *Norske folkeeventyr* was widely translated. The first English translation in 1859 was followed by many more into the second half of the 20th century. In Norway it provided a stylistic model that substantially influenced the development of Bokmål, the literary language of modern Norway.

In 1856 Asbjørnsen became forest master and studied methods of timber preservation. He published a collection of fairy tales, *Norske huldreeventyr og folkesagn* (1845–48; "Norwegian Fairy Tales and Folk Legends"), and a translation of Darwin's *Origin of Species* (1860).

Moe's *Digte* (1850; "Poems") placed him among the finest Norwegian romantic poets. His *I brønden og i kjærnet* (1851; "In the Well and the Pond") is a Norwegian children's classic. In 1853 after experiencing a religious crisis, he was ordained and in 1875 became bishop of Kristiansand.

Asbury, Francis (b. Aug. 20, 1745, Hamstead Bridge, Staffordshire, Eng.—d. March 31, 1816, Spotsylvania, Va., U.S.), first bishop

Asbury, detail from an oil painting by Charles Peale Polk, 1794; in Lovely Lane Museum, Baltimore

By courtesy of the Methodist Historical Society, Baltimore

of the Methodist Episcopal Church consecrated in the United States. His efforts did much to assure the continuance of the church in the New World.

After limited schooling Asbury was licensed as a local preacher, and at the age of 21 he was admitted to the Wesleyan Conference. For four years he served as an itinerant preacher in England. In August 1771 he volunteered for service in North America.

Landing at Philadelphia the following October, he preached wherever he got a hearing, and he was soon made John Wesley's general assistant. To enforce Wesley's rules for his preachers and societies, Asbury required every preacher to travel a circuit. He favoured American independence and remained in the country when every other active preacher appointed by Wesley had departed for Britain. In 1778 he became a citizen of Delaware. At the organizing conference for the Methodist Episcopal Church (Baltimore, December 1784) Asbury refused to accept an appointment from Wesley as general superintendent of the church, insisting that the office be filled by a vote of the preachers. He was then elected by his peers, consecrated as superintendent, and in 1785 assumed the title of bishop.

Asbury crossed the Alleghenies 60 times and travelled an average of 5,000 miles a year on horseback. The early growth of the church was largely the result of his strenuous efforts; when he arrived in America there were only three Methodist meeting houses and about 300 communicants. By the time of his death there were 412 Methodist societies with a membership of 214,235. His life and work is discussed by Herbert Asbury in *A Methodist Saint: The Life of Bishop Asbury* (1927); his *Journal and Letters* were published in three volumes (1958).

Asbury Park, city, Monmouth County, northeastern New Jersey, U.S., on the Atlantic Coast. It was founded in 1871 by James A. Bradley, a New York manufacturer, who named it for the Rev. Francis Asbury, first American bishop of the Methodist Episcopal Church. A spectacular ship disaster (September 1934) killed 122 persons when the "Morro Castle" caught fire at sea and was grounded offshore. Its Convention Hall, 4,000-seat Auditorium, boardwalk, bathing pavilions, and fishing facilities have spurred its popularity as a resort and convention site. Lakes Sunset, Deal, and Wesley are within Asbury's boundaries. Nearby is the Long Branch Historical Museum, which contains relics of the period between the Civil War and World War I. Light manufactures include electronic equipment and textiles. Inc. borough, 1874; city, 1897. Pop. (1980) city, 17,015; metropolitan area (SMSA), 503,173.

Ascalon (Israel): *see* Ashqelon.

Ascanian DYNASTIES, branches of a German family influential from the 12th century to 1918. The name, adopted during the first quarter of the 12th century, was derived from Aschersleben, where the counts of Ballenstedt had a castle in the midst of possessions northeast of the Harz Mountains.

Albert the Bear (*see* Albert I *under* Albert [Brandenburg]) was the first to raise the family's rank from that of count to margrave. Having been invested with the North Mark in 1134, he extended it east of the Elbe to form the Mark of Brandenburg. These lands remained under the senior branch of the Ascanians until it became extinct in 1320.

In 1180, meanwhile, on the fall of Henry the Lion, duke of Saxony and Bavaria, Bernard (Bernhard; died 1212), one of Albert's younger sons, had obtained those of Henry's territories in the Elbe region which carried the title duke of Saxony. In 1260 these lands were divided into two duchies, Saxe-Lauenburg in the northwest and Saxe-Wittenberg in central Germany, for the sons of Bernard's son Albert. Saxe-Wittenberg, which secured the Saxon electoral title in 1356, passed in 1423, on the extinction of the Ascanian branch there, to the margraves of Meissen (of the House of Wettin). Thus the name Saxony, which originally belonged to a tribal land in the North German plain, was transferred to the southeast and to the upper Elbe. The Ascanians of Saxe-Lauenburg, however, lasted until 1689.

Yet another Ascanian principality was Anhalt, the basis of which was formed when the original possessions of the family (from Aschersleben to Zerbst and Dessau) passed to Bernard's elder son Henry in 1212. The Ascanians ruled in Anhalt until 1918.

Ascanius, in Roman legend, son of the hero Aeneas and traditional founder of Alba Longa, probably the site of the modern Castel Gandolfo, near Rome. In different versions, Ascanius is placed variously in time. Those set earlier cite the Trojan Creusa as his mother. After the fall of Troy, Ascanius and Aeneas escaped to Italy, where Aeneas subsequently founded Lavinium, the parent city of Alba Longa and Rome. Ascanius became king of Lavinium after his father's death. Thirty years after Lavinium was built, Ascanius founded Alba Longa and ruled it until he died.

In the Roman historian Livy's account, however, Ascanius was born after the founding of Lavinium and was the son of Aeneas and Lavinia, a daughter of King Latinus. Ascanius was also called Iulus, and through him by that name the gens Julia (including the family of Julius Caesar) traced its descent.

Ascari, Alberto (b. July 13, 1918, Milan—d. May 26, 1955, Monza, Italy), Italian automobile racing driver who was world champion driver in 1952 and 1953.

Ascari started racing on motorcycles, turning to cars in 1940, when he entered the Mille Miglia. He raced in Maseratis after World War II and in Ferraris from 1949 to 1954, when he joined the Lancia team. He won the Mille Miglia in 1954 and many Grand Prix. Like his father, Antonio Ascari, who also died at 36, Ascari was killed while testing a car.

ascariasis, infection of man and other mammals caused by the intestinal roundworm *Ascaris lumbricoides.* Infection follows the ingestion of Ascaris eggs that have contaminated foods or soil. In the small intestine the larvae are liberated and migrate through the intestinal wall, reaching the lungs, where they may produce a host sensitization that results in lung inflammation and fluid retention. About ten days later, the larvae pass from the respiratory passages into the digestive tract and mature into egg-producing worms, which grow to some 15 to 40 centimetres (6 to 16 inches) in length, in the small intestine. Serious, even fatal, complications of ascariasis result from the infiltration of the larvae into sensitive tissues, such as the brain, and from the migration of the adult worms into various body structures where they produce abcesses and toxic manifestations.

Ascariasis is worldwide in rural communities and is believed to affect some 660,000,000 persons. The sanitary disposal of human excreta is the most important preventive measure. Treatment is by chemotherapy.

Ascaris, any of a genus of worms (order Ascaroidea, class Nematoda) that are parasitic in the intestines of various terrestrial mammals, chiefly herbivores. They are typically large worms characterized by a mouth surrounded by three lips. The species *Ascaris lumbricoides* is probably the most familiar parasite in humans. An almost identical worm, often called *A. suum,* occurs in pigs. It is, however, not certain that this species is distinct from the one that infests humans.

The life cycle of *Ascaris* is direct. After the eggs are eaten by the host, the larvae migrate through the intestinal wall via the blood system to the lungs. In the lungs they undergo some development prior to being swallowed, and they finally develop to maturity in the intestines. An infestation with larvae can cause pneumonitis, and the presence of adult worms may produce malnutrition or even peritonitis. The adult worms can be removed by drugs such as piperazine.

Ascension (Caroline Islands): *see* Ponape.

Ascension, small British island of volcanic origin, South Atlantic Ocean, with an area of 34 sq mi (88 sq km). It is a dependency of the British colony of St. Helena, 700 mi (1,100 km) to the southeast. The island is barren, rocky, and almost without vegetation except for some 10 ac (4 ha) atop Green Mountain (2,817 ft [859 m]), where fruit and vegetables are grown and some livestock can be found. A heavy swell breaks on the island's lee shore with great violence. Average annual rainfall varies from 6 in. (150 mm) on the coast to 25 in. (635 mm) on Green Mountain. The prevailing winds are the southeast trades, and the climate is mild and healthful. Sea turtles and sooty terns breed there annually. No indigenous vertebrate land animals exist.

The island, discovered by the Portuguese navigator João da Nova Castella on Ascension Day, 1501, remained uninhabited until the arrival of Napoleon at St. Helena (1815), when some British troops were installed. The governor of St. Helena, of which Ascension has been a dependency since 1922, makes laws and is represented by an administrator. Ascension is an important telecommunications centre. Britain's first overseas satellite communications station was established there in 1966, and the British Broadcasting Corporation operates a powerful relay station.

Ascension Island from the top of Green Mountain
Picturepoint

Ascension was an important refueling base for British aircraft and ships during the Falkland Islands conflict between Britain and Argentina (1982). The United States maintains an air base that has a tracking station for missiles and facilities for tracking manned space flights and for conducting research into outer space. Pop. (1981) 1,038.

Ascension, in Christian belief, the ascent of Jesus Christ into heaven on the 40th day after his Resurrection. According to the first chapter of the Acts of the Apostles, after appearing to the Apostles on various occasions during a period of 40 days, Jesus was taken up in their presence and was then hidden from them by a cloud, a frequent biblical image signifying the Presence of God. Although belief in the Ascension is apparent in other books of the New Testament, the emphasis and the imagery differ. In the Gospel According to John, the glorification described by the Ascension story seems to have taken place immediately after the Resurrection. The imagery of the account in the Gospel According to Luke is similar to that of Acts, but there is no mention of a period of 40 days.

The meaning of the Ascension for Christians is derived from their belief in the glorification and exaltation of Jesus following his death and Resurrection, as well as from the theme of his return to the Father. Thus, the Gospel According to John uses both the sayings of Jesus and his post-Resurrection appearances to indicate a new relationship between Jesus and his Father and between him and his followers rather than a simple physical relocation from Earth to heaven.

The Ascension of Jesus is mentioned in the Apostles' Creed, a profession of faith used for Baptism in the early church. The feast of the Ascension has been celebrated 40 days after Easter in both Eastern and Western Christianity since the late 3rd or early 4th century. Prior to that time, the Ascension was commemorated as a part of the celebration of the descent of the Holy Spirit at Pentecost. In Christian art the Ascension is an old theme, appearing since the 5th century. The earliest version of the Ascension, which persisted in the West until the 11th century, shows Christ from the side, climbing to the top of the hill and grasping the hand of God, which emerges from a cloud above to pull him into heaven. The Apostles, assembled below, watch the event.

In the 6th century a different version of the Ascension was developed in Syria and was later adopted in Byzantine art. This version emphasizes Christ's divinity, showing him frontally, standing immobile in a mandorla, or almond-shaped aureole, elevated above the Earth and supported by angels. He holds a scroll and makes a gesture of benediction. A curious detail of this version is the regular inclusion of the Virgin Mary, who is not mentioned in the biblical account of the event, and St. Paul, who, on historical grounds, was not present. The inclusion of these figures has not been adequately explained, but they may represent, with the figure of St. Peter, an allegory of the church that Christ leaves behind. This type of the Ascension, which follows the Roman tradition of representing the apotheosis of an emperor, often figured prominently in the monumental decoration of Byzantine churches as the emblem of one of the principal church feast days. By the 11th century, the West had also adopted a frontal representation. In the Western version, however, the humanity of Christ is emphasized: he extends his hands on either side, showing his wounds. He is usually in a mandorla but is not always supported or even surrounded by angels; thus, he is no longer carried to heaven but ascends by his own power. In the 12th century this version of the Ascension had an especially prominent place in French Romanesque church decoration.

The Ascension continued to be important as a devotional subject in the art of the Renaissance and Baroque periods, both of which retained the iconography of Christ displaying his wounds.

Ascension of the Lord, Feast of the, also called ASCENSION DAY, the 40th day after Easter, commemorating the taking up of Jesus Christ into heaven, as witnessed by the Apostles. (*See* Ascension.) Ranking with Christmas, Easter, and Pentecost in the universality of its observance among Christians, the feast was celebrated as early as the end of the 4th century.

A distinctive feature of its liturgy in the Western churches is the extinguishing of the Paschal candle after the Gospel has been chanted, as a symbol of Christ's leaving the earth. Despite the idea of separation indicated in this act, which might be expected to set a note of sadness, the whole liturgy of Ascensiontide, through the 10 days to Pentecost, is marked by joy in the final triumph of the risen Lord.

In the Middle Ages the people's delight in the visual and dramatic found an outlet in various ritual practices that came to be associated with the feast. Popular customs included a procession, in imitation of Christ's journey with his Apostles to the Mount of Olives, as well as the raising of a crucifix or a statue of the risen Christ through an opening in the church roof.

asceticism (from Greek *askeō:* "to exercise," or "to train"), the practice of the denial of physical or psychological desires in order to attain a spiritual ideal or goal. Hardly any religion has been without at least traces or some features of asceticism.

The origins of asceticism. The origins of asceticism lie in man's attempts to achieve various ultimate goals or ideals: development of the "whole" person, human creativity, ideas, the "self," or skills demanding technical proficiency. Athletic *askēsis* ("training"), involving the ideal of bodily fitness and excellence, was developed to ensure the highest possible degree of physical fitness in an athlete. Among the ancient Greeks, athletes preparing for physical contests (*e.g.,* the Olympic Games) disciplined their bodies by abstaining from various normal pleasures and by enduring difficult physical tests. In order to achieve a high proficiency in the skills of warfare, warriors also adopted various ascetical practices. The ancient Israelites, for example, abstained from sexual intercourse before going into battle.

As values other than those concerned with physical proficiency were developed, the concept expressed by *askēsis* and its cognates was applied to other ideals—*e.g.,* mental facility, moral vitality, and spiritual ability. The ideal of training for a physical goal was converted to that of attaining wisdom or mental prowess by developing and training intellectual faculties. Among the Greeks such training of the intellect led to the pedagogical system of the Sophists—itinerant teachers, writers, and lecturers of the 5th and 4th centuries BC who instructed in return for fees. Another change in the concept of *askēsis* occurred in ancient Greece when the notion of such training was applied to the realm of ethics in the ideal of the sage who is able to act freely to choose or refuse a desired object or an act of physical pleasure. This kind of *askēsis,* involving training the will against a life of sensual pleasure, was exemplified by the Stoics (ancient Greek philosophers who advocated the control of the emotions by reason).

The view that one ought to deny one's lower desires—understood as sensuous, or bodily—in contrast with one's spiritual desires and virtuous aspirations, became a central principle in ethical thought. Plato believed that it is necessary to suppress bodily desires so that the soul can be free to search for knowledge. This view was also propounded by Plotinus, a Greek philosopher of the 3rd century AD and one of the founders of Neoplatonism, a philosophy concerned with hierarchical levels of reality. The Stoics, among whom asceticism was primarily a discipline to achieve control over the promptings of the emotions, upheld the dignity of human nature and the wise man's necessary imperturbability, which they believed would become possible through the suppression of the affective, or appetitive, part of man.

In a similar manner, the value of asceticism in strengthening an individual's will and his deeper spiritual powers has been a part of many religions and philosophies throughout history. The 19th-century German philosopher Arthur Schopenhauer, for example, advocated a type of asceticism that annihilates the will to live; his fellow countryman and earlier contemporary, the philosopher Immanuel Kant, held to a moral asceticism for the cultivation of virtue according to the maxims of the Stoics. Many factors were operative in the rise and cultivation of religious asceticism: the fear of hostile influences from the demons; the view that one must be in a state of ritual purity as a necessary condition for entering into communion with the supernatural; the desire to invite the attention of divine or sacred beings to the self-denial being practiced by their suppliants; the idea of earning pity, compassion, and salvation by merit because of self-inflicted acts of ascetical practices; the sense of guilt and sin that prompts the need for atonement; the view that asceticism is a means to gain access to supernatural powers; and the power of dualistic concepts that have been at the source of efforts to free the spiritual part of man from the defilement of the body and physically oriented living.

Among the higher religions (*e.g.,* Hinduism, Buddhism, and Christianity), still other factors became significant in the rise and cultivation of asceticism. These include the realization of the transitory nature of earthly life, which prompts a desire to anchor one's hope in otherworldliness, and the reaction against secularization that is often coupled with a belief that spirituality can best be preserved by simplifying one's mode of life.

Forms of religious asceticism. In all strictly ascetic movements, celibacy (*q.v.*) has been regarded as the first commandment. Virgins and celibates emerged among the earliest Christian communities and came to occupy a prominent status. Among the earliest Mesopotamian Christian communities, only the celibates were accepted as full members of the church, and in some religions only celibates have been permitted to be priests (*e.g.,* Aztec religion and Roman Catholicism). Abdication of worldly goods is another fundamental principle. In monastic communities there has been a strong trend toward this ideal. In Christian monasticism this ideal was enacted in its most radical form by Alexander Akoimetos, a founder of monasteries in Mesopotamia (died *c.* 430). Centuries before the activities of the medieval Western Christian monk St. Francis of Assisi, Alexander betrothed himself to poverty, and through his disciples he expanded his influence in Eastern Christian monasteries. These monks lived from the alms they begged but did not allow the gifts to accumulate and create a housekeeping problem, as occurred among some Western monastic orders, such as the Franciscans. In the East, wandering Hindu ascetics and Buddhist monks also live according to regulations that prescribe a denial of worldly goods.

Abstinence and fasting are by far the most common of all ascetic practices. Among the primitive peoples, it originated, in part, because of a belief that taking food is dangerous, for demonic forces may enter the body while one is eating. Further, some foods regarded as especially dangerous were to be avoided. Fasting connected with religious festivals has very ancient roots. In ancient Greek religion, rejection of meat appeared particularly among the Orphics, a mystical, vegetarian cult; in the cult of Dionysus, the orgiastic god of wine; and among the Pythagoreans, a mystical, numerological cult. Among a number of churches the most important period of fasting in the liturgical year is the 40 days before Easter (Lent), and among Muslims the most important period of fasting is the month of Ramaḍān. The ordinary fasting cycles, however, did not satisfy the needs of ascetics, who therefore created their own traditions. Among Jewish-Christian circles and Gnostic movements, various regulations regarding the use of vegetarian food were established, and Manichaean monks won general admiration for the intensity of their fasting achievements. Christian authors write of their ruthless and unrelenting fasting, and, between their own monks and the Manichaeans, only the Syrian ascetical virtuosos could offer competition in the practice of asceticism. Everything that could reduce sleep and make the resultant short period of rest as troublesome as possible was tried by Syrian ascetics. In their monasteries Syrian monks tied ropes around their abdomens and were then hung in an awkward position, and some were tied to standing posts.

Personal hygiene also fell under condemnation among ascetics. In the dust of the deserts—where many ascetics made their abodes—and in the blaze of the Oriental sunshine, the abdication of washing was equated with a form of asceticism that was painful to the body. With respect to the prohibition against washing, the Persian prophet Mani seems to have been influenced by those ascetic figures who had been seen since ancient times in India, walking around with their long hair hanging in wild abandonment and dressed in filthy rags, never cutting their fingernails and allowing dirt and dust to accumulate on their bodies. Another ascetic practice, the reduction of movement, was especially popular among the Syrian monks, who were fond of complete seclusion in a cell. The practice of restriction in regard to contact with human beings culminated in solitary confinement in wildernesses, cliffs, frontier areas of the desert, and mountains. In general, any settled dwelling place has been unacceptable to the ascetic mentality, as noted in ascetical movements in many religions.

Psychological forms of asceticism have also been developed. A technique of pain-causing introspection was used by Buddhist ascetics in connection with their practices for meditation. The Syrian Christian theologian St. Ephraem Syrus counselled the monks that meditation on guilt, sin, death, and punishment—*i.e.,* the pre-enactment of the moment before the Eternal Judge—must be carried out with such ardour that the inner life becomes a burning lava that produces an upheaval of the soul and torment of the heart. Syrian monks striving for higher goals created a psychological atmosphere in which continued fear and dread, methodically cultivated, were expected to produce continual tears. Nothing less than extreme self-mortification satisfied the ascetic virtuosos.

Pain-producing asceticism has appeared in many forms. A popular custom was to undergo certain physically exhausting or painful exercises. The phenomena of cold and heat provided opportunities for such experiences. The Hindu fakirs (ascetics) of India provide most remarkable examples of those seeking painful forms of asceticism. In the earliest examples of such radical forms of self-mortification that appeared in India, the ascetic stared at the sun until he went blind or held up his arms above the head until they withered. Syrian Christian monasticism was also inventive in regard to forms of self-torture. A highly regarded custom involved the use of iron devices, such as girdles or chains, placed around the loins, neck, hands, and feet and often hidden under garments. Pain-producing forms of asceticism include self-laceration, particularly castration, and flagellation (whipping), which emerged as a mass movement in Italy and Germany during the Middle Ages and is still practiced in parts of Mexico and the southwestern United States.

Variations of asceticism in world religions. In the primitive religions, asceticism in the form of seclusion, physical discipline, and the quality and quantity of food prescribed has played an important role in connection with the puberty rites and rituals of admission to the tribal community. Isolation for shorter or longer periods of time and other acts of asceticism have been imposed on medicine men, since severe self-discipline is regarded as the chief way leading to the control of occult powers. Isolation was and is practiced by young men about to achieve the status of manhood in the Blackfoot and other Indian tribes of the northwestern United States. In connection with important occasions, such as funerals and war, taboos (negative restrictive injunctions) involving abstinence from certain food and cohabitation were imposed. For the priests and chiefs these were much stricter. In Hellenistic culture (*c.* 300 BC–*c.* AD 300), asceticism in the form of fasting and refraining from sexual intercourse was practiced by communities of a religiomystical character, including the Orphics and Pythagoreans. A new impetus and fresh approach to ascetic practices (including emasculation) came with the expansion of the Oriental mystery religions (such as the cult of the Great Mother) in the Mediterranean area.

In India, in the late Vedic period (*c.* 1500 BC–*c.* 200 BC), the ascetic use of *tapas* ("heat," or austerity) became associated with meditation and *yoga,* inspired by the idea that *tapas* kills sin. These practices were embedded in the Brahmanic (ritualistic Hindu) religion in the *Upaniṣads* (philosophical treatises), and this view of *tapas* gained in importance among the Yogas and the Jainas, adherents of a religion of austerity that broke away from Brahmanic Hinduism. According to Jainism, liberation becomes possible only when all passions have been exterminated. Under the influences of such ascetic views and practices in India, Siddhārtha Gautama himself underwent the experiences of bodily self-mortification in order to obtain spiritual benefits; but since his expectations were not fulfilled, he abandoned them. But his basic tenet, which held that suffering lies in causal relation with desires, promoted asceticism in Buddhism. The portrait of the Buddhist monk as depicted in the *Vinaya* (a collection of monastic regulations) is of one who avoids extreme asceticism in his self-discipline. The kind of monasticism that developed in Hinduism during the medieval period also was moderate. Asceticism generally has no significant place in the indigenous religions of China (Confucianism and Taoism) and Japan (Shintō). Only the priests in Confucianism practiced discipline and abstinence from certain foods during certain periods, and some movements within Taoism observed similar rules. Shintō in Japan, however, does include ascetics.

Judaism, because of its view that God created the world and that the world (including man) is good, is nonascetic in character and includes only certain ascetic features, such as fasting for strengthening the efficacy of prayer and for gaining merit. Though some saw a proof of the holiness of life in some ascetic practices, a fully developed ascetical system of life has remained foreign to Jewish thought, and ascetic trends could, therefore, appear only on the periphery of Judaism. Such undercurrents rose to surface among the Essenes, a monastic sect associated with the Dead Sea Scrolls, who represented a kind of religious order practicing celibacy, poverty, and obedience. The archaeological discovery (1940s) of their community at Qumrān (near the Dead Sea in an area that was a part of Jordan) has thrown new light on such movements in Judaism.

In Zoroastrianism (founded by the Persian prophet Zoroaster, 7th century BC) there is officially no place for asceticism. In the Avesta, the sacred scriptures of Zoroastrianism, fasting and mortification are forbidden, but ascetics were not entirely absent even in Persia.

In Christianity all of the types of asceticism have found realization. In the Gospels asceticism is never mentioned, but the theme of following the historical Christ gave asceticism a point of departure. An ascetic view of the Christian life is found in the First Letter of Paul to the Corinthians in his use of the image of the spiritual athlete who must constantly discipline and train himself in order to win the race. Abstinence, fasts, and vigils in general characterized the lives of the early Christians, but some ramifications of developing Christianity became radically ascetic. Some of these movements, such as the Encratites (an early ascetic sect), a primitive form of Syrian Christianity, and the followers of Marcion, played important roles in the history of early Christianity. During the first centuries ascetics stayed in their communities, assumed their role in the life of the church, and centred their views of asceticism on martyrdom and celibacy. Toward the end of the 3rd century, monasticism originated in Mesopotamia and Egypt and secured its permanent form in cenobitism (communal monasticism). After the establishment of Christianity as the official religion of the Roman Empire (after AD 313), monasticism was given a new impetus and spread all over the Western world. In Roman Catholicism new orders were founded on a large scale. Though asceticism was rejected by the leaders of the Protestant Reformation, certain forms of asceticism did emerge in Calvinism, Puritanism, Pietism, early Methodism, and the Oxford Movement (an Anglican movement of the 19th century espousing earlier ecclesiastical ideals). Related to asceticism is the Protestant work ethic, which consists of a radical requirement of accomplishment symbolized in achievement in one's profession and, at the same time, demanding strict renunciation of the enjoyment of material gains acquired legitimately.

Islām in its beginnings knew only fasting, which was obligatory in the month of Ramaḍān. Monasticism is rejected in the Qur'ān (the Islāmic sacred scripture). Yet ascetic forces among Christians in Syria and Mesopotamia, vigorous and conspicuous, were able to exercise their influence and were assimilated by Islām in the ascetic movement known as *zuhd* (self-denial) and later in that of Ṣūfism, a mystical movement that arose in the 8th century and incorporated ascetic ideals and methods.

Asch, Sholem, Sholem also spelled SHALOM, or SHOLOM (b. Nov. 1, 1880, Kutno, Pol., Russian Empire—d. July 10, 1957, London), Polish-born U.S. novelist and playwright, the most controversial and widely known writer in modern Yiddish literature.

Asch
EB Inc.

One of the 10 surviving children of a poor family, Asch was educated at Kutno's Hebrew school. In 1899 he went to Warsaw, and in 1900 his highly praised first story—written, as was a cycle that followed, in Hebrew—was published. On the advice of the Yiddish writer and leader I.L. Peretz, however, he decided to write only in Yiddish, and with *Dos Shtetl* (1904; *The Little Town*, 1907) began a career outstanding for both output and impact. Tales, novels, and plays (32 volumes in a collected Yiddish edition by 1930) burst on the reading public of Europe and the U.S., stirring imagination by their vitality and opening up a new view of man as trekker, traveller, pilgrim, and sometime sleepwalker, a potential mover of mountains who often collapses just when about to gain new hope and courage. His works were soon widely translated; unlike his great Yiddish predecessors he was fortunate in having inspired translators—among them Edwin and Willa Muir and Maurice Samuel—through whom his work could enter the literary mainstream. (Subsequent titles and dates are of published English translations.)

Asch's work falls into three periods. In his first, the east European, he describes the tragicomedy of life in the small Jewish community torn between devotion to Orthodox Jewry and the urge toward emancipation. To this period belong the novels *Kiddush-Hashem* (1920) and *Mottke the Thief* (1935) and the play *The God of Vengeance*, produced in Berlin by Max Reinhardt in 1910 but banned elsewhere. To the American period (he visited the U.S. in 1910, returned in 1914, and was naturalized in 1920) belong *The War Goes On* (1936) and *Three Novels* (1938; includes *Uncle Moses, Chaim Lederer's Return*, and *Judge Not*). Throughout his career he spent much time in Europe and made long visits to Palestine. In his last, most controversial, period he attempted to unite Judaism and Christianity through emphasis upon their historical and theologico-ethical connections: *The Nazarene* (1939), a reconstruction of Christ's life as expressive of essential Judaism; *The Apostle* (1943), a study of St. Paul; *Mary* (1949), the mother of Jesus seen as the Jewish "handmaid of the Lord"; and *The Prophet* (1955), on the Second (Deutero-) Isaiah, whose message of comfort and hope replaces the earlier prophecies of doom. In the presentation of this unknown prophet, conjectures based on archaeology and theology are blended by Asch's depth of psychological insight.

But these last and most creative years, devoted to asserting a belief formulated when Asch visited Palestine in 1906—that Christianity is essentially a Jewish phenomenon, "one culture and civilization"—were tragic years. A number of his Orthodox coreligionists reviled him as an apostate.

Aščhabad (Turkmen S.S.R.): *see* Ashkhabad.

Aschaffenburg, city, Bayern *Land* (Bavaria state), south central West Germany, on the right bank of the canalized Main River near the mouth of the Aschaff River and at the foot of the forested Spessart (mountains), southeast of Frankfurt. Originally a Roman settlement, it came under the jurisdiction of the electors of Mainz *c.* 982 and was chartered in 1173. In 1292 a synod was held there, and in 1447 an imperial Diet (Assembly) there prepared the Aschaffenburg Concordat, a treaty between the empire and the papacy, which was later concluded in Vienna. The city became Bavarian in 1814. The Renaissance castle of Johannisburg (1605–14), on the site of an earlier castle and of a Roman castrum (fortification), was the summer residence of the electors of Mainz. The 12th-century abbey church of SS. Peter and Alexander contains the predella (altar platform) with the "Lamentation of Christ" by Matthias Grünewald, court painter to the electors, and a Romanesque crucifix. The municipal museum has a fine art collection, and there are many parks, of which the Schönbusch is particularly notable. Aschaffenburg's industries include the manufacture of clothing, coloured paper, machine and precision tools, metals, paint, cosmetics, and chemicals. Pop. (1983 est.) 59,643.

Ascham, Roger (b. 1515, Kirby Wiske, near York, Eng.—d. Dec. 30, 1568, London), British Humanist, scholar, and writer, famous for his prose style, his promotion of the vernacular, and his theories of education.

As a boy of 14 Ascham entered Cambridge, where he later took his M.A. and was elected a fellow of St. John's and appointed reader in Greek. The new Renaissance enthusiasm for the classics, especially Greek, was at its height.

Ascham's *Toxophilus* ("Lover of the Bow"), written in the form of a dialogue, was published in 1545 and was the first book on archery in English. In the preface Ascham showed the growing patriotic zeal of the Humanists by stating that he was writing "Englishe matter in the Englishe tongue for Englishe men." He became Princess Elizabeth's tutor in Greek and Latin (1548–50), then served for several years as secretary to Sir Richard Moryson, English ambassador to the Habsburg emperor Charles V, travelling widely on the Continent. Thereafter, he was appointed Latin secretary to Edward VI, a post he held until his death early in the reign of Queen Elizabeth I. He served her by composing her official letters to foreign rulers and by helping her pursue the study of Greek.

The *Scholemaster,* written in simple, lucid English prose and published posthumously in 1570, is Ascham's best known book. It presents an effective method of teaching Latin prose composition, but its larger concerns are with the psychology of learning, the education of the whole man, and the ideal moral and intellectual personality that education should mold.

aschelminth, phylum name ASCHELMINTHES, phylum of invertebrate animals distinguished by their possession of a pseudocoel (a space between the body wall and the gut), their exhibition of bilateral symmetry (in which the body is divided into mirror-image halves), and their lack of segmentation.

A brief treatment of aschelminths follows. For full treatment, *see* MACROPAEDIA: Aschelminths.

Comprising approximately 17,000 known species, aschelminths are divided into six diverse classes: Nematoda, Priapulida, Rotifera, Gastrotricha, Kinorhyncha (or Echinodera), and Nematomorpha (or Gordiacea).

Nematoda (eelworms, pinworms, threadworms, and roundworms) is the largest of the six classes, numbering approximately 13,000 species. Featuring both free-living and parasitic forms, the nematodes occur in saltwater, fresh water, sand, soil, plants, animals, and human beings, and they range in size from one millimetre (0.04 inch) to 20 centimetres (eight inches). The primary mode of nematode locomotion is similar to that of snakes, although some species are able to remain stationary by means of an adhesive cement formed by the caudal glands. The parasitic order *Filariida* is of medical importance to mankind.

Priapulida, with less than 10 known species, is the smallest of the six classes. They are warty, superficially segmented animals, which attain lengths of up to three inches. They are wholly carnivorous, and they are always found in marine environments, sometimes burying themselves in ocean mud at depths as great as 1,600 feet (500 metres).

Rotifera (wheel animalcules) numbers approximately 1,800 species, found primarily in freshwater environments, although a few forms are known to inhabit saltwater as well. Microscopic in size, rotifers generally feed on organic materials like bacteria, protozoans, and detritus, although a few species are carnivorous. Locomotion in nonsedentary forms is accomplished either by swimming or creeping.

Gastrotricha numbers approximately 1,800 known species, which are found primarily in freshwater bodies of water, although there are a few saltwater species as well. They are microscopic, wormlike animals that generally feed (like the rotifers) on small organic materials. Gastrotrichs move by gliding across a surface on cilia.

Kinorhyncha numbers approximately 100 known species, which are always found in marine environments. They are microscopic, wormlike animals that possess a retractable head and 13 or 14 superficial segments. Like rotifers and gastrotrichs, they feed on small organic materials. Kinorhynchs move by extending the head, anchoring it to a surface with hooked spines, and then pulling the rest of the body forward.

Nematomorpha (hairworms) numbers approximately 300 species, which are always found in freshwater environments, except for the saltwater genus *Nectonema.* They are long, thin, wormlike animals that can reach lengths of up to 30 inches (80 centimetres) and, before reaching maturity (when they become free-living adults), they are parasitic in such arthropods as crabs, millipedes, and centipedes.

Most aschelminths are wormlike, although a few species of rotifers are virtually spherical. All six classes, except for the kinorhynchs, have tails or tail-like structures which aid in such functions as locomotion, anchoring, and mating. Aschelminth heads are generally indistinct, although kinorhynchs have spherical heads that are extendable and retractable. Rotifer mouths are surrounded by a crown of cilia, while some adult species of nematomorphs have no mouths at all. Setae (bristles), scales, or spines are usually found on the body surfaces of the majority of aschelminths.

Internally, aschelminths are composed of three tubes enclosed within each other: the epidermis and cuticle (inner and outer layers of the body wall), the muscles, and the pseudocoelom. The cuticle may bear hooks and bristles in nematodes, wartlike structures in priapulids, external segments in kinorhynchs, and thick plates in rotifers. Musculature also varies from class to class, with nematodes and nematomorphs possessing only longitudinal muscles, priapulids possessing longitudinal muscles and circular muscles in the anterior end of the body, and rotifers, gastrotrichs, and kinorhynchs generally possessing longitudinal and circular transverse muscles. The digestive system comprises the pseudocoel, and in most aschelminths it runs the length of the body. While priapulids do possess a large body cavity, this space probably does not constitute a pseudocoel. Circulatory and respiratory systems are not well differentiated in this phylum.

Depending on the species, aschelminths may be either male, female, or hermaphroditic, with eggs fertilized inside the female and larval development outside. Male nematomorphs deposit sperm near the female cloaca (a reproductive and excretory duct), male nematodes release sperm into the female's vulva, and male rotifers inject sperm directly through the female's body wall. Priapulids, nematomorphs, kinorhynchs, and nematodes exhibit periodic shedding of the cuticle (molting) during larval development, though priapulids continue to molt throughout their lives. Nematomorphs first hatch into free-living larva, then they enter the body of some arthropod and undergo the parasitic phase of their life, and finally, after a period of weeks or months, they leave the host, molt once more, and become lethargic, free-living adults.

Aschersleben, city, Halle *Bezirk* (district), western East Germany, on the northern edge of the Unter Harz (Lower Harz) Mountains, southwest of Magdeburg. Probably founded in the 11th century by Count Esico von Ballenstedt, it was chartered in 1266 and was the ancestral seat of the Ascanians, an influential German family who derived their name (Latinized) from the town. It passed to the bishops of Halberstadt in 1315 and Brandenburg in 1648. It has the 15th-century Church of St. Stephen and a 16th-century town hall.

The centre of an extensive potash-mining region, it also has a lignite (brown-coal) mine to the north. Aschersleben is known for its seed raising and trade and manufactures machine tools, machinery, paper, sugar, and blankets. Pop. (1981 est.) 34,892.

Aschoff, Karl Albert Ludwig (b. Jan. 10, 1866, Berlin—d. June 24, 1942, Freiburg im Breisgau, Ger.), German pathologist who recognized the phagocytic (capable of engulfing bacteria and other substances) activity of certain cells found in diverse tissues and named them the reticuloendothelial system (1924). He also described (1904) the inflammatory nodule (called Aschoff's bodies, or nodules) in heart muscle characteristic of the rheumatic process.

Aschoff received his medical degree at Bonn in 1889 and in 1906 was appointed to the chair of pathology at Freiburg im Breisgau, where he spent the rest of his career. At Freiburg he established an institute of pathology that attracted students from all over the world.

ascidian (marine animal): *see* sea squirt.

ascites, accumulation of fluid in the peritoneal cavity, between the membrane lining the abdominal wall and the membrane covering the abdominal organs. The most common causes of ascites are cirrhosis of the liver, heart failure, tumour invasion of the peritoneal membranes, and escape of chyle (lymph laden with emulsified fats) into the peritoneal cavity. In patients having liver disease, the onset of ascites is usually preceded by accumulation of fluid in the ankles. The abdomen is often uncomfortably distended, and muscles become wasted.

Asclepiadaceae, the milkweed family of the flowering plant order Gentianales, including more than 280 genera and about 2,000 species of tropical herbs or shrubby climbers, rarely shrubs or trees. Most members of the family have milky juice, flowers with five united petals, podlike fruits, and, usually, tufted seeds. The silky-haired seeds are drawn out of their pods by the wind and are carried off. Male and female parts of each flower are united in a single structure. The pollen is massed in bundles called pollinia, pairs of which are linked by a yokelike bar of tissue contributed by the stigma of the pistil. Parts of the pollinia stick to the heads or bodies of visiting insects, which then carry them to other flowers. In some species the fertility is low, and many-flowered plants often produce few fruits.

(Top) Bloodflower (*Asclepias curassavica*); (bottom) wax plant (*Hoya carnosa*)

(Top) A to Z Botanical Collection—EB Inc., (bottom) Sven Samelius

Common milkweed (*Asclepias syriaca*) and bloodflower (*A. curassavica*) often are cultivated as ornamentals. Butterfly-weed (*A. tuberosa*) of North America has bright-orange flowers. *Hoya carnosa,* commonly called wax plant because of its waxy white flowers, often is grown indoors as a pot plant. Succulent plants of the family such as *Hoodia* and carrion flower (*Stapelia*) produce offensive odours, attracting flies, which then pollinate the plants. The pitcher plant (*Dischidia rafflesiana*), a climbing air plant native to Asia, has pitcher-shaped leaves that store rainwater. The plant absorbs the water through roots that grow into the pitcher. Ants sometimes drain a pitcher by puncturing the bottom, then fill the cavity with plant materials and use it as a nest for raising young. *See also* butterfly-weed; carrion flower.

Asclepiades OF BITHYNIA (b. 124 BC, Prusa, Bithynia—d. *c.* 40 BC, Rome), Greek physician who established Greek medicine in Rome. His influence continued until Galen began to practice medicine in Rome in AD 164.

He opposed the humoral doctrine of Hippocrates and instead taught that disease results from constricted or relaxed conditions of the solid particles, a doctrine derived from the atomic theory of the 5th-century philosopher Democritus. Asclepiades believed that harmony would be restored through fresh air, light, appropriate diet, hydrotherapy, massage, and exercise. A pioneer in the humane treatment of mental disorders, he had insane persons freed from confinement in the dark and treated them by using occupational therapy, music, soporifics (especially wine), and exercise.

Asclepius, Greek ASKLEPIOS, Latin AESCULAPIUS, Greco-Roman god of medicine, son of Apollo (god of healing, truth, and prophecy) and the nymph Coronis. The Centaur Chiron taught him the art of healing, but Zeus (the king of the gods), afraid that he might render all men immortal, slew him with a thunderbolt. Homer, in the *Iliad,* mentions him only as a skillful physician; in later times, however, he was honoured as a hero and eventually worshipped as a god. The cult began in Thessaly but spread to many parts of Greece. Since it was supposed that Asclepius effected cures or prescribed remedies to the sick in dreams, the practice of sleeping in his temples became common.

Festivals in honour of Asclepius are known to have been observed widely. The cult was introduced to Rome by order of the Sibylline Books (a collection of sibylline prophecies; 293 BC) to relieve a pestilence. Asclepius was frequently represented standing, dressed in a long cloak, with bare breast; his usual attribute was a staff with a serpent coiled around it. This staff is the only true symbol of medicine. The caduceus with its winged staff and intertwined serpents, frequently used as a medical emblem, is without medical relevance since it represents the magic wand of Hermes, or

Asclepius and his daughter Hygieia, classical sculpture; in the Vatican Museum, Rome

Anderson—Alinari from Art Resource/EB Inc.

Mercury, the messenger of the gods and the patron of trade.

ascocarp, fruiting structure of fungi (division Mycota) found in the class Ascomycetes. It arises from vegetative filaments (hyphae) after sexual reproduction has been initiated. The ascocarp (in forms called apothecium, cleistothecium [cleistocarp], or perithecium) contain saclike structures (asci) that usually bear four to eight ascospores. Apothecia are stalked and either disklike, saucer-shaped, or cup-shaped with exposed asci. The largest known apothecium, produced by *Geopyxis cacabus,* has a stalk 1 metre (40 inches) high and a cup 50 centimetres (20 inches) across. Cleistothecia are spherical and must rupture or disintegrate to release their ascospores. Perithecia are globular or flask-shaped with an apical opening for discharge of ascospores.

Ascoli, Graziadio Isaia (b. July 16, 1829, Gorizia, Venetia, Austrian Empire—d. Jan. 21, 1907, Milan), Italian linguist who pioneered in dialect studies, emphasized the importance of studying living vernaculars, and prepared a model classification of Italian dialects.

Ascoli did not receive any formal higher education, but he wrote his first major work, on Oriental languages, in 1854. Professor at the University of Milan (1860–1907), he made notable contributions to comparative linguistics, including Celtic, but his main work was in dialectology. In 1873 he founded the journal *Archivio glottologico italiano* ("Italian Linguistic Archives"), which he edited until 1907. In the first volume he published an essay on neglected Raeto-Romanic dialects and in the eighth his classification of Italian dialects.

Ascoli, Marchioness (writer): *see* Fuller, (Sarah) Margaret.

Ascoli Piceno, city, capital of Ascoli Piceno province, Marche region, central Italy, at the confluence of the Tronto and Castellano rivers. The ancient centre of the Picenes (early inhabitants of the Adriatic coast), it was conquered in the 3rd century BC by the Romans, who knew it as Asculum Picenum. After 1006 the city was ruled by its bishops and successive feudatories until it placed itself under papal protection in 1504. Carlo Crivelli started an art movement there *c.* 1486.

Extensive Roman remains include parts of the city wall, two bridges, and the ruins of a theatre, an amphitheatre, and a temple of Vesta. Notable medieval landmarks include the magnificent church of S. Francesco (begun 1262); the 7th-century cathedral, enlarged between 1481 and 1592; and, in the Piazza Arringo, the 13th-century Palazzo Comunale, formed by the union of two palaces, housing an art gallery. The 13th-century Palazzo del Popolo has become the civic museum. Walls and towers from the medieval fortifications still stand. Ascoli Piceno's chief industries are agricultural, but there are also chemical, textile, and electrical works. Pop. (1981 prelim.) mun., 54,193.

Ascomycetes, a class of fungi (division Mycota) known as the sac fungi. They are characterized by a saclike structure (ascus) containing four to eight ascospores in the sexual stage. The sac fungi are separated into subgroups based on whether asci arise singly or are borne in one of several types of fruiting structures, or ascocarps, and on the method of discharge of the ascospores. Many ascomycetes are plant pathogens, some are animal pathogens, a few are edible mushrooms, and many live on dead organic matter (as saprobes). The largest and most commonly known Ascomycetes include the morels (*see* cupfungus) and truffles (*q.v.*) and important plant pathogens such as powdery mildew of grape (*Uncinula necator*), Dutch elm disease (*Ophiostoma ulmi*), and the chestnut blight (*Endothia parasitica*). *Venturia inequalis,* the cause of apple scab, also attacks a number of other plants. Perhaps the most indispensable fungus of all is an ascomycete, the common yeast (*Saccharomyces cerevisiae*), whose varieties leaven the dough in bread making and ferment grain to produce beer or mash for distillation of alcoholic liquors; the strains of *S. cerevisiae* var. *ellipsoideus* ferment grape juice to wine.

Neurospora, a genus of about 12 widespread species produces bakery mold or red bread mold. It has been used extensively in genetic and biochemical investigations. Another genus, *Xylaria,* contains about 100 species of cosmopolitan fungi. *X. polymorpha* produces a club-shaped or fingerlike fruiting body (stroma), which resembles burned wood. They are common on decaying wood or injured trees.

Cordyceps, a genus of about 100 species within the order Clavicipitales (subclass Euascomycetidae), are commonly known as vegetable caterpillars or caterpillar fungi. *C. militaris* parasitizes insects. It forms a small, 3–4-centimetre (about 1⅓-inch) mushroom-like

(Top) *Xylaria hypoxylon;* (bottom) earth tongue (*Geoglossum fallax*)

(Top) H.R. Allen from Natural History Photographic Agency—EB Inc., (bottom) Donald Van Buskirk

fruiting structure with a bright orange head, or cap. A related genus, *Claviceps,* includes *C. purpurea* the cause of ergot of rye and ergotism in man and domestic animals. Earth tongue is the common name for the 10 *Geoglossum* species of the order Helotiales (subclass Euascomycetidae). They produce black to brown, club-shaped fruiting structures on soil or decaying wood.

ascorbic acid: *see* vitamin C.

Ascot, locality, Windsor and Maidenhead district, county of Berkshire, England, known

The parade to the post at the Royal Ascot meet, Ascot, Berkshire

Keystone Press Agency Ltd.

for its racecourse on Ascot Heath. The Royal Ascot meeting (initiated in 1711 by Queen Anne) lasts four days each June and is traditionally attended by the British sovereign. A major social and fashion event, it has lent its name to the ascot, a type of broad neck scarf. Its principal event is the Ascot Gold Cup, established in 1807 and run over 2½ mi (4 km) by horses more than three years old. Pop. (latest census) 7,799.

ascus, a saclike structure produced by fungi of the class Ascomycetes (sac fungi) in which sexually produced spores (ascospores), usually four or eight in number, are formed. Asci may arise from the fungal mycelium (the filaments, or hyphae, constituting the organism) without a distinct fruiting structure, as in the leaf curl fungi; or within a fruiting structure (ascocarp) that may be exposed, as in the molds and powdery mildew fungi, or be imbedded in a compact structure (stroma), as in the ergot and black knot fungi. In the case of yeasts, a single cell converts to an ascus.

Aseb, also spelled ASSAB, Red Sea port, Eritrea province, northeastern Ethiopia, at the entrance of Aseb Bay. Formerly a terminus of caravan routes across the Danakil Desert, the Aseb coastal strip was acquired by Italian shipping interests in 1869 and in 1882 became the first Italian colonial possession in Africa. The federation (1952) and incorporation (1962) of Eritrea with Ethiopia made possible the development of Aseb as a port for the southern half of the country.

Connected by road to Dese on the Addis Ababa–Asmera Highway, Aseb handles about one-third of Ethiopia's external trade. Besides the port's cold-storage facilities, the town has saltworks, a water distillation plant, an airfield, and Ethiopia's first oil refinery (1967). Pop. (1982 est.) 27,985.

Asela, also spelled ASELLA, or ASSELA, town, seat of Arsi province, south central Ethiopia, west of Mt. Chilalo on a high plateau overlooking Lake Ziway in the Great Rift Valley. The town is an important trading centre for the surrounding livestock and lumbering region. An all-weather road connects it with Nazret to the north. Pop. (1982 est.) 38,957.

Aselli, Gaspare, Aselli also spelled ASELLIO (b. *c.* 1581, Cremona, Italy—d. 1626?, Milan), physician in Milan and professor of anatomy and surgery at Pavia, who in 1622 contributed to knowledge of the circulation of body fluids by discovering the lymph vessels (lacteals) that take up the end products of fat digestion from the intestine. He called the new vessels *venae albae et lacteae* (white and lacteal veins) and described them in *De Lactibus sive Lacteis Venis*, published posthumously in 1627.

Aselli, detail of an engraving by Cesare Bassano, 1623

By courtesy of the trustees of the British Museum; photograph, J.R. Freeman & Co. Ltd.

Asen I (Bulgarian tsar): *see* Ivan Asen I.

Aseret Yeme Teshuva, English TEN DAYS OF PENITANCE, the first 10 days of the Jewish religious year. *See* yamim nora'im.

Aset (Egyptian religion): *see* Isis.

Asfi (Morocco): *see* Safi.

Asgard, Old Norse ÁSGARDR, in Norse mythology, the dwelling place of the gods, comparable to the Greek Mt. Olympus. Legend divided Asgard into 12 or more realms, including Valhalla, the home of Odin and the abode of heroes slain in earthly battle; Thrudheim, the realm of Thor; and Breidablik, the home of Balder.

Each important god had his own palace, and many Germanic peoples believed that these mansions were similar in design to those of their own nobility. Asgard could be reached from Earth only by the bridge Bifrost (the rainbow).

Ásgrímsson, Eysteinn (b. *c.* 1310—d. March 14, 1361, Helgisetr Monastery, Norway), Icelandic monk, author of *Lilja* ("The Lily"), the finest religious poem produced in Catholic Iceland.

In 1343 Ásgrímsson was imprisoned, probably for thrashing his abbot and perhaps for a breach of chastity as well. In 1349 he was made an official of the Skálholt bishopric and attended the bishop on a mission to Norway (1355–57). After that he was inspector of the Skálholt bishopric until excommunicated in 1360, when he returned to Norway, dying shortly thereafter. There is some doubt that the high church official and the unruly monk are the same person, but it is not unlikely under church conditions of the time. *Lilja* (Eng. trans., 1870) is a survey of Christian history from the Creation to the Last Judgment, followed by 25 stanzas on contrition and a prayer to the Virgin. By abandoning the circumlocutions of the skaldic poets, Ásgrímsson created a rapid, vivid narrative that remained the most popular of the Icelandic religious poems until the appearance of the Lutheran Passion hymns of Hallgrímur Pétursson in the 17th century.

ash, any tree of the genus *Fraxinus* of the olive family (Oleaceae), composed of about 70 species of Northern Hemisphere trees, many valuable for their timber and beauty. The leaves are opposite, usually deciduous, and compound with an odd number of leaflets, rarely one. The one-seeded fruits are winged. The bark contains glucoside fraxin that is used as a tonic. The flowers usually are inconspicuous, but some species have petalled blooms. The flowering ash (*F. ornus*) of southern Europe produces creamy white, fragrant flowers, has leaves with seven leaflets, and reaches 21 metres (about 70 feet). It is also known as manna ash for a laxative extracted from its gum.

Fruits and leaves of European ash (*Fraxinus excelsior*)

A to Z Botanical Collection—EB Inc.

F. cuspidata, from southwestern North America, has similar flowers, three to nine leaflets, and reaches 8 m. Among the taller ashes are *F. floribunda,* from the Himalayas (30 m), with 7 to 9 leaflets and producing clusters of petalled flowers 30 centimetres (1 foot) long; European ash (*F. excelsior*), about the same height, with 7 to 11 leaflets; and white ash (*F. americana*), not quite so tall, with 5 to 9 leaflets per compound leaf. There is a weeping form of the European ash.

Mexican ash (*F. uhdei*), a broad-crowned tree widely planted along Mexico City streets, is evergreen except in dry or freezing seasons. It reaches 18 m and has leaves with five to nine leaflets. The Arizona ash (*F. velutina*), also a mild-climate tree, reaches 13 m and has three to five narrow leaflets.

ash cone (volcanic deposits): *see* cinder cone.

ash-leaved maple: *see* box elder.

Ash Wednesday, in the Christian Church, the first day of Lent, occurring 6½ weeks before Easter (between February 4 and March 11, depending on the date of Easter). In the early church, the length of the Lenten celebration varied, but eventually it began 6 weeks (42 days) before Easter. This provided only 36 days of fast (excluding Sundays). In the 7th century, 4 days were added before the first Sunday in Lent to establish 40 fasting days, in imitation of Jesus Christ's fast in the desert.

It was the practice in Rome for penitents to begin their period of public penance on the first day of Lent. They were sprinkled with ashes, dressed in sackcloth, and obliged to remain apart until they were reconciled with the Christian community on Maundy Thursday, the Thursday before Easter. When these practices fell into disuse (8th–10th century), the beginning of the penitential season of Lent was symbolized by placing ashes on the heads of the entire congregation.

In the modern Roman Catholic Church, on Ash Wednesday the worshipper receives a cross marked on the forehead with the ashes obtained by burning the palms used on the previous Palm Sunday. Worship services are also held on Ash Wednesday in the Anglican, Lutheran, and some other Protestant churches. Orthodox churches begin Lent on a Monday and therefore do not observe Ash Wednesday.

Aʿshā, al- (Arabic: the Night-Blind), in full MAYMŪN IBN QAYS AL-AʿSHĀ (b. before 570, Durnā, Arabia—d. *c.* 625, Durnā), pre-Islāmic poet whose *qaṣīdah* ("ode") is included by the critic Abū ʿUbaydah (died 825) in the celebrated *Muʿallaqāt*, a collection of seven pre-Islāmic *qaṣīdah*s, each of which was considered by its author to be his best; the contents of the collection vary slightly, according to the views of several compilers.

Al-Aʿshā spent his youth in travels through Mesopotamia, Syria, Arabia, and Ethiopia. He continued to travel, even after becoming blind, particularly along the western coast of the Arabian Peninsula. It was then that he turned to the writing of panegyrics as a means of support. His style, reliant on sound effects and full-bodied foreign words, tends to be artificial.

aṣḥāb (Islām): *see* Companions of the Prophet.

Ashanti, also spelled ASANTE, people of southern Ghana and adjacent areas of Togo and Ivory Coast. Most of the Ashanti live in the Ashanti Region of Ghana, which comprises the metropolitan districts of the former independent Ashanti state. They speak a Twi language of the Kwa branch of the Niger-Congo family of African languages and constitute a section of the Akan peoples.

Although some Ashanti now live and work

The Omanhene, chief of the Ashanti village Berekum (in Ghana), sitting on his throne with an assistant chief to his left wearing the feathered headdress
Peter Buckley—Photo Researchers

in urban centres, they continue to be primarily a village people. They are agricultural, producing plantain, bananas, cassava, yams, and cocoyams for local markets, and cocoa for export.

The basis of Ashanti social organization is the matrilineage, a localized segment of a clan whose members claim descent from a common ancestress. Members of the lineage assist one another in such activities as building houses, farming, and clearing paths, and in funeral rites. Since the Ashanti believe every individual is made up of two elements—blood from the mother and spirit from the father—paternal descent is also recognized and governs membership in exogamous *ntoro* divisions that are associated with certain religious and moral obligations. The head of the lineage is chosen by its senior men and women; females are prohibited from holding this position because of menstrual taboos forbidding contact with sacred objects. The lineage head is responsible for internal peace and relations with other lineages and, as custodian of lineage stools, which embody the spirits of ancestors, is the mediator between its living and dead members. Every important lineage head also has a stool as a symbol of the office. The village chief is chosen from a particular lineage, which differs from village to village; his main task, with the advice of his council of elders, is to settle disputes within the community.

In the traditional Ashanti state, villages were grouped into territorial divisions; the chief of the capital village was the paramount chief of the division, and his village council served as the division council. The paramount chief of the national capital, Kumasi, was the chief of the confederation. The symbol of Ashanti unity was the Golden Stool, which reputedly descended from the sky and to which all chiefs acknowledged allegiance. The queen mother (more often actually the sister of the chief) advised him about his conduct and was regarded as the authority on kinship relations of the lineage; she nominated candidates to fill a vacant chief's stool. The chief's primary duties were religious and military, but in modern times the position has become increasingly secular, involving economic administration and the provision of social and welfare services. Although there are Christian and Muslim converts among the Ashanti, the traditional religion, based on belief in a distant supreme being, a pantheon of gods and lesser spirits, and the ever-present spirits of ancestors, remains the basis of the Ashanti conception of the universe.

Ashanti empire, Ashanti also spelled ASANTE, West African state that occupied what is now southern Ghana in the 18th and 19th centuries. Extending from the Komoé River in the west to the Togo Mountains in the east, the Ashanti Empire was active in the slave trade in the 18th century and unsuccessfully resisted British penetration in the 19th.

In their struggle against the suzerain state of Denkyera and lesser neighbouring states, the Ashanti people made little headway until the accession, probably in the 1670s, of Osei Tutu, who, after a series of campaigns that crushed all opposition, was installed as Asantehene, or king, of the new Ashanti state, whose capital was named Kumasi. His authority was symbolized by the Golden Stool (*sika 'dwa*), on which all subsequent kings were enthroned.

From the beginning of the 18th century, the Ashanti supplied slaves to British and Dutch traders on the coast; in return they received firearms with which to enforce their territorial expansion. After the death of Osei Tutu in either 1712 or 1717, a period of internal chaos and factional strife was ended with the accession of Opoku Ware (ruled *c.* 1720–50), under whom Ashanti reached its fullest extent in the interior of the country. Kings Osei Kwadwo (ruled 1764–77), Osei Kwame (1777–*c.* 1801), and Osei Bonsu (*c.* 1801–24) established a strong centralized state, with an efficient bureaucracy recruited by merit and a fine system of communications.

In 1807 Osei Bonsu occupied southern Fanti territory—an enclave around British headquarters at Cape Coast; in the same year Britain outlawed the slave trade. Declining trade relations and disputes over the Fanti region caused friction over the following decade and led to warfare in the 1820s. The Ashanti defeated a British force in 1824 but made peace in 1831 and avoided conflict for the next 30 years. In 1863, under Kwaku Dua (ruled 1834–67), the Ashanti again challenged the British by sending forces to occupy the coastal provinces. In 1869 the British took possession of Elmina (over which Ashanti claimed jurisdiction), and in 1874 an expeditionary force under Sir Garnet Wolseley marched on Kumasi. Though Wolseley managed to occupy the Ashanti capital for only one day, the Ashanti were shocked to realize the inferiority of their military and communications systems. The invasion, moreover, sparked numerous secessionary revolts in the northern provinces. The old southern provinces were formally constituted the Gold Coast colony by the British later in 1874. Ashanti's king Kofi Karikari was then deposed, and Mensa Bonsu (1874–83) assumed power. He attempted to adapt the agencies of Ashanti government to the changed situation. Though he reorganized the army, appointed some Europeans to senior posts, and increased Ashanti resources, he was prevented from restoring Ashanti imperial power by the British political agents, who supported the northern secessionist chiefs and the opponents of central government in Kumasi. The empire continued to decline under his successor, Prempeh I (acceded 1888), during whose reign, on Jan. 1, 1902, Ashanti was formally declared a British crown colony, the former northern provinces being on the same day separately constituted the Protectorate of the Northern Territories of the Gold Coast.

An Ashanti Confederacy Council was established under British rule in the 1930s, and the Asantehene was restored as a figurehead sovereign. *See also* Akan states.

Ashanti Region, administrative unit of Ghana, West Africa, once the core of the old kingdom of Ashanti annexed by the British in 1902. Bordered (north) by Brong-Ahafo Region (until 1959 part of Ashanti), it has an area of 9,417 sq mi (24,389 sq km). The Kwahu Plateau divides Ashanti into distinct halves.

The richly forested southern uplands, drained by tributaries of the Pra River and containing the sacred Lake Bosumtwi, slope southward from 1,000–500 ft (300–150 m), with scattered hills and ranges. The land is highly developed agriculturally, producing most of Ghana's export crops, including cocoa, corn (maize), oil palm, ginger, and rice. Local foodstuffs include plantain and cassava. There are timber and mineral-extraction industries; gold deposits are worked at Obuasi and Konongo and bauxite at Nyinahin. Kumasi (*q.v.*), the capital and seat of the Asantehene (Ashanti kingship), is the transportation and commercial centre. Most of the people, however, live in small rural settlements.

North of the Kwahu Plateau is undulating savanna land drained by the Volta River and with an altitude similar to that of the south. The harmattan (dry, interior wind) season from November to March creates periodic drought, and this area depends upon the cultivation of yams, rice, corn, and cassava. Its agricultural population is scattered because of tsetse infestation, poor soil, and lack of communication. Kujani Game Reserve is east of the Afram River, and Digya National Park is on Lake Volta, near Sumiso. Pop. (1980 est.) 1,996,821.

ʿĀshar min Ramaḍān, Madīnat al-, city, western al-Ismāʿīlīyah, *muḥāfaẓah* (governorate), southeastern delta, Lower Egypt. Construction of this industrial centre began in 1977 as part of the Egyptian government's program to shift population and industry away from Cairo and the cultivable lands of the Nile Valley.

Industries that have been established include factories that manufacture pharmaceuticals, plastics, electrical appliances, and medical furniture. There is also a wood treatment plant. A glass plant and a shale brick factory were under construction in the early 1980s.

Housing, schools, medical facilities, and mosques were built in the late 1970s. Madīnat al-ʿĀshar min Ramaḍān is located just north of the desert highway from Cairo to Ismailia.

Ashʿarī, Abū al-Ḥasan al- (b. 873/874, Basra, Iraq—d. *c.* 935/936, Baghdad), Muslim Arab theologian noted for having integrated the rationalist methodology of the speculative theologians into the framework of orthodox Islām. In his Maqālāt al-Islāmīyīn ("Theological Opinions of the Muslims"), compiled during his early period, al-Ashʿari brought together the varied opinions of scholars on Muslim theological questions. From about 912, he pursued a more orthodox study of theology through the Qurʾān (Islāmic sacred scripture) and the *sunnah* (the body of Islāmic custom and practice based on Muḥammad's words and deeds). He founded a theological school that later claimed as members such celebrated authors as al-Ghazālī and Ibn Khaldūn.

Al-Ashʿarī was born in the city of Basra, at that time one of the centres of intellectual ferment in Iraq, which, in turn, was the centre of the Muslim world and the seat of a world civilization. It is generally agreed that he belonged to the family of the celebrated Companion of the Prophet Abū Mūsā al-Ashʿarī (died 662/663), though some theologians opposed to his ideas contest the claim. Since this would have made him by birth a member of the Arab–Muslim aristocracy of the period, he must have received a careful education. A contemporary recorded that the wealth of al-Ashʿarī's family permitted him to devote himself entirely to research and study.

His works, especially the first part of *Maqālāt al-Islāmīyīn*, and the accounts of later historians record that al-Ashʿarī very early joined the school of the great theologians of that time, the Muʿtazilites. He became the favourite disciple of Abū ʿAlī al-Jubbāʾī, head of the Muʿtazilites of Basra in the final decades of the 3rd century AH (*anno Hegirae*, "in the year of the hijrah"), corresponding to the late 9th and early 10th centuries AD.

Despite the lacunae in the documentation concerning these theologians, certain characteristic traits of their culture and social position can be singled out. Anxious to mark the originality of Islām in contrast to all dualist doctrines and in contrast to Christianity and Judaism as interpreted by the Qurʾān, the Muʿtazilites concentrated their efforts on underlining the absolute transcendence of the one God. To accomplish this they drew principally from their own Arab-Muslim tradition and remained relatively impervious to the foreign cultures (especially Greek and Iranian) that invaded Baghdad from the beginning of the 3rd century AH. But the Arab-Muslim culture was not popular: during the period of al-Ashʿarī's studies, the rupture between the intellectual elite of Muʿtazilite theologians and the common people was all but complete.

A disciple of al-Ashʿarī describes that period of his master's life in this way: "Al-Ashʿarī was a disciple of Jubbāʾī. He faithfully went to hear him and take lessons from him, never leaving him for all of 40 years. In the sessions devoted to controversy, he showed his gift for argumentation and was bold in confronting his adversary; but he was not gifted for writing. When he took up a pen, at times he never finished, and at times what he wrote was not satisfactory."

That testimony, at least in its negative aspect, should be corrected by what Ibn ʿAsākir reports: "His works are very well organized, the expressions and the developments are very exact." In any case, it was during that period of his life that al-Ashʿarī, the brilliant and faithful disciple of the Muʿtazilites, undertook the composition of a work in which he gathered the opinions of the diverse schools on the principal points of Muslim theology. That work, the first volume of the current edition of the *Maqālāt*, is valuable for what it records of Muʿtazilite doctrines. It remains one of the most important sources for retracing the history of the beginnings of Muslim theology.

At the same period al-Ashʿarī composed *Risālah ilā ahl ath-thaghr* ("Treatise for the Men of the Frontier") for the Muslims of Bāb al-Abwāb (modern Derbent, between the Caucasus Mountains and the Caspian Sea). The occasion was the renewed interest of the central administration in the security of the northern frontier of the empire.

Later, at the age of 40, when he had become a specialist in theology and was well known for his oral controversies and his written works, al-Ashʿarī quit his master al-Jubbāʾī and abandoned Muʿtazilite doctrine. This conversion was spectacular. It made al-Ashʿarī the focus of attention of Basra for some time and merited a certain number of accounts, which, though impossible to confirm in their details, are certainly correct in their general lines. What happened was apparently this: following a crisis of conscience, accompanied, perhaps, by dreams, al-Ashʿarī saw clearly the limits of Muʿtazilism and was led back to a closer attachment to the sources of Muslim faith, the Qurʾān and the *sunnah.* Reading texts of his master, al-Jubbāʾī, it is possible to ascertain the defects that may have struck al-Ashʿarī. In those texts al-Jubbāʾī seems to have no particular audience in mind, nor does he try to convince; he only demonstrates. It appears that, for him, the reality of God as well as that of man has been so sterilized and desiccated that it has become little more than matter for rational manipulation.

Al-Ashʿarī, more conscious than all others of these limits and of the premature desiccation of Muʿtazilite theology, did not hesitate to proclaim his new faith publicly. Certain reports even speak of him dramatically declaring his new stand in the middle of the Friday prayer in the Cathedral Mosque of Basra. From that day, the former Muʿtazilite started combatting his colleagues of yesterday. He even attacked his old master, refuting his arguments in speech and writing. It was then, perhaps, that he took up again his first work, the *Maqālāt*, to add to the objective exposition rectifications more conformable to his new beliefs. In this same period, he composed the work that marks clearly his break with the Muʿtazilite school: the *Kitāb al-Lumaʿ* ("The Luminous Book").

It was not until his former master Abū ʿAlī al-Jubbāʾī died at Basra in 915 that al-Ashʿarī decided to make Baghdad his centre. Arriving in the capital, he soon became aware of the importance assumed by a group of faithful of the *sunnah*, the disciples of Ibn Ḥanbal. Their leader, al-Barbahārī, was a dynamic person with a touch of the demagogue. Al-Ashʿarī visited him to explain his doctrinal views, insisting on the fact that his previous theological formation enabled him to attack the Muʿtazilites with their own weapons, thus making his treatises models of apologetic in support of the truth. The response was disappointing: there was no encouragement, no approval, no acceptance into the ranks of the Ḥanbalites. Al-Barbahārī curtly replied that he had no interest in any of this; he had only one master—Ibn Ḥanbal.

It must have been after that interview that al-Ashʿarī composed, or perhaps put the last touches to, one of his most famous treatises, the *Ibānah ʿan uṣūl ad-diyānah* ("Statement on the Principles of the Religion"), which contains some passages venerating the memory of Ibn Ḥanbal.

In the years that followed, al-Ashʿarī, now installed in Baghdad, began to group around himself his first disciples. Focussing his theological reflection on certain positions of the mystic al-Muḥāsibī and of two theologians, Ibn Kullāb and Qalanisī, al-Ashʿarī laid the bases for a new school of theology distinct from both the Muʿtazilites and the Ḥanbalites. His three best known disciples were al-Bāhilī, aṣ-Ṣuʿlūkī, and Ibn Mujāhid, all of whom transmitted the doctrines of their master to what later became the flourishing school of Khorāsān.

Al-Ashʿarī died sometime around 932/933 but most probably in 935/936. He was buried at the southwest of the city in a place called the Wharf of the Water Jars. A mausoleum erected over his tomb was later destroyed by fanatic Ḥanbalites. The opposition that was first aroused by al-Ashʿarī himself through his spectacular conversion continued to assail his disciples, but through constant dialogue with their opponents they slowly disentangled the main lines of doctrine that became the stamp of the Ashʿarite school. (M.A.Al.)

BIBLIOGRAPHY. M. Allard, *Le Problème des attributs divins dans la doctrine d'al-Ašʿari et de ses premiers grands disciples* (1966), is a complete study of the life and works of al-Ashʿarī, including an exposition of his conception of God. An indispensable work for those who wish to read al-Ashʿarī is R.J. McCarthy (ed.), *The Theology of al-Ashʿarī* (1953), containing the texts of two of his theological treatises along with their English translation. W.M. Watt, *Islamic Philosophy and Theology* (1962), serves to situate al-Ashʿarī in the chronological development of Muslim thought.

Ashbee, Charles Robert (b. May 17, 1863, Isleworth, Middlesex, Eng.—d. May 23, 1942, Godden Green, Kent), architect, designer, writer, and metalworker; Ashbee was a founder of the Arts and Crafts Movement that flourished in England during the 1880s and 1890s and was one of many reform efforts protesting the social, moral, and cultural confusions that accompanied the Industrial Revolution. His Guild of Handicraft, founded in 1888, lasted 25 years and produced some of the finest works in the decorative arts. In his book *Should We Stop Teaching Art?* (1911), Ashbee gave the Arts and Crafts Movement its quintessential maxim: art education must recognize that machinery orders modern civilization. An exhibition of his works in Brussels in 1894 with those of William Morris and Aubrey Beardsley helped significantly in introducing the new trends of English art circles to the Continent, ultimately contributing to the whole of Art Nouveau. His house in Chelsea is one of the early 20th century's most harmoniously conceived domestic buildings and typifies the new British architectural tendencies of that time. He was one of the first Europeans to support Frank Lloyd Wright.

Ashbourne, parish (town), West Derbyshire district, county of Derbyshire, England. Ashbourne is a centre for the surrounding agricultural districts and for tourists visiting nearby Dovedale and the Manyfold Valley. Its buildings include the Church of St. Oswald, dating from 1241 and possessing an octagonal spire (212 ft [65 m]). The oldest of the famous almshouses there was founded in 1640. Small local industries include clock and fishing-tackle manufacture. The town has many associations with the lexicographer and author Samuel Johnson, who was a frequent visitor. Pop. (1981 prelim.) 5,960.

Ashburton, parish (town), Teignbridge district, county of Devon, England, lying on the southeastern margin of Dartmoor. It was designated a stannary (tin-mining) town in 1285. The priest of the Chantry Chapel of St. Lawrence kept a "free scole" which survived as a grammar school until 1938. The Church of St. Andrew was built of granite in the 15th century. The nearby village of Widecombe-in-the-Moor is known for an annual fair, commemorated in a folk song, while Buckfast Abbey (rebuilt 1806–38) made Ashburton serge famous in the 16th century. It now houses a Benedictine community. Pop. (1981 prelim.) 3,564.

Ashburton, John Dunning, 1st Baron (b. Oct. 18, 1731, Ashburton, Devonshire, Eng.—d. Aug. 18, 1783, Exmouth, Devonshire), jurist and politician who defended John Wilkes against charges of seditious and obscene libel (1763–64) and who is also important as the author of a resolution in Parliament (April 6,

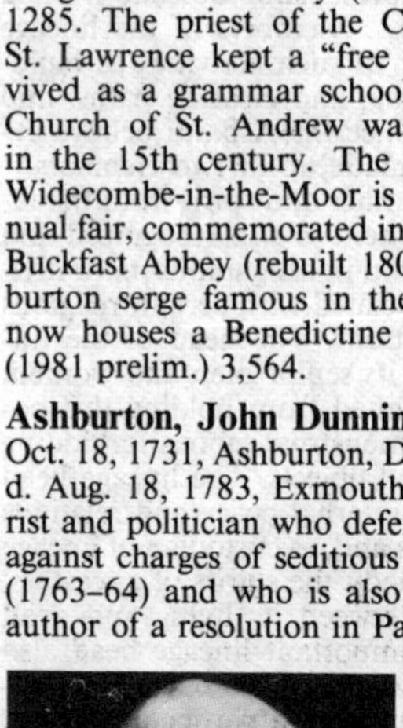

1st Baron Ashburton, detail of a portrait, studio of Sir Joshua Reynolds, *c.* 1768–73; in the National Portrait Gallery, London

1780) condemning George III for his support of Lord North's government despite the unpopularity of its policies during the American Revolution (1775–83).

Dunning was appointed solicitor general in 1768, probably at the instance of Lord Chancellor Camden, who as chief justice of common pleas had upheld Dunning's argument against general warrants (in Wilkes's case). In the same year Dunning's election to Parliament was secured by Lord Shelburne.

When Camden was dismissed (Jan. 16, 1770), Dunning resigned his office in protest and thenceforth was allied with the opposition. In 1778 he supported a bill to relieve Roman Catholics. In 1780 his motion against the King, which stated that the "influence of the crown has increased, is increasing, and ought to be diminished," was passed by a vote of 233 to 215. Shortly thereafter (April 24, 1780), he failed with a motion that the House of Commons should not be dissolved or prorogued until the constitutional balance favouring Parliament was restored.

In 1782, when the 2nd Marquess of Rockingham became prime minister, Dunning was raised to the peerage, accepting sinecures and pensions he had previously condemned.

Ashcroft, Dame Peggy, original name EDITH MARGARET EMILY ASHCROFT (b. Dec. 22, 1907, Croydon, London), distinguished British stage actress renowned for her appearances in both classic and modern plays.

After graduation from London's Central School of Dramatic Art, Ashcroft made her debut as Margaret in the Birmingham Repertory's production of *Dear Brutus* (1926). She made her initial London appearance in 1927, but her first important notices were for the role of Naomi in *Jew Süss* (1929).

Beginning in 1932 her appearances with the Old Vic Company established her reputation in the classics; in two years she portrayed, among other Shakespearean characters, Cleopatra, Rosalind, Portia, and Juliet. The latter role, repeated in John Gielgud's production (1935), established Ashcroft as perhaps the oustanding Juliet of the 20th century. Her debut in the U.S. was as Lise in Maxwell Anderson's *High Tor* (1936). Ashcroft created principal roles in more than 100 productions in England and on tour, receiving enthusiastic notices in classic and modern plays and displaying her versatility in comic and tragic roles. In addition to Juliet and Lise, other roles of particular note included Nina in *The Seagull* (1936), Cecily in *The Importance of Being Earnest* (1939 and 1942), the title role in *The Duchess of Malfi* (1945 and 1960), and Hester in *The Deep Blue Sea* (1952). She was a director of the Royal Shakespeare Company from 1968.

Ashcroft first appeared in films in 1933; her infrequent screen work includes the classic Alfred Hitchcock thriller *The Thirty-nine Steps* (1935) and *Sunday Bloody Sunday* (1971). Her first television was as Julia in *Shadow of Heroes* (1959), a role she created on the stage a year earlier; she subsequently translated several stage portrayals to radio and television.

Ashcroft received numerous awards for her acting, including the Ellen Terry Theatre Award for her role as Evelyn in *Edward, My Son* (1947). She was made Commander of the Order of the British Empire in 1951 and Dame Commander in 1956; in 1962 a new theatre in London was named in her honour.

Ashdod, city of southern Palestine, on the coastal plain of ancient Philistia; since 1948 it has been a city in southwest Israel and is one of its three international ports and chief industrial centres. In antiquity Ashdod was a member of the Philistine pentapolis (five cities). Although the Bible assigns it to the tribe of Judah (Joshua 15:47), the invading Israelites were unable to subdue it or its satellite towns. When the Ark of the Covenant was lost to the Philistines in battle (I Samuel 5), it was first taken to the Temple of Dagon at Ashdod. In the 8th century BC the city fell to King Uzziah of Judah (II Chronicles 26:6) but was soon captured by Assyria. According to the Greek historian Herodotus, Psamtik I, pharaoh of Egypt 664–610 BC, besieged Ashdod for 29 years. Nehemiah, governor of Judaea during the Persian monarchy (5th century BC), condemned the Jews of his time for intermarrying with the Ashdodites (Nehemiah 13). In Hellenistic times the city was known as Azotus. Pompey removed it from Jewish rule and annexed it to the province of Syria. In Byzantine times it was the site of a bishopric (4th–6th century AD), but declined to village status by the Middle Ages. The ancient city, under the mound of Tel Ashdod, had outports at Ashdod Yam (Greek: Azotus Páralios, and the Castellum Beroart of the crusaders) south of the modern city, and at Tel Mor, within the present city limits. Excavations there by American and Israeli archaeologists in the 1950s and 1960s have revealed remains dating back to the 17th century BC.

Modern Ashdod, founded in 1956 and incorporated 1968, is on the coast, 4½ mi (7 km) north-northwest of the ancient city ruins. The artificial port, enclosed by breakwaters, built there (beginning 1961), is southern Israel's only outlet to the Mediterranean Sea; much of the country's citrus crop is exported through Ashdod. There are large synthetic textile plants (nylon yarn, tire cord, acrilan); wool processing, vehicle assembly (buses), and frozen-food packing are also important. In addition, Ashdod has an oil refinery and one of Israel's major power plants. Pop. (1982 est.) 66,000.

Ashe, Arthur (Robert) (b. July 10, 1943, Richmond, Va., U.S.), U.S. tennis player, first black winner of a major men's singles championship.

Ashe began to play tennis at the age of seven in a neighbourhood park. He was coached by Walter Johnson of Lynchburg, Va., who had coached Althea Gibson. He moved to St. Louis, Mo., where he was coached by Richard Hudlin, before he entered the University of California at Los Angeles on a tennis scholarship. In 1963 Ashe won the U.S. hard-court singles championship; in 1965 he took the intercollegiate singles and doubles titles; and in 1967 he won the U.S. clay-court singles championship. In 1968 he captured the U.S. (amateur) singles and open singles championships. He played on the U.S. Davis Cup team (1963–70, 1975, 1977–78) and helped the U.S. team to win the Davis Cup challenge (final) round in 1968, 1969, and 1970. In 1970 he won 11 tournaments, and in September of that year he became a professional.

His criticism of South African apartheid racial policy led to denial of permission to play in that country's open tournament and as a consequence, on March 23, 1970, South Africa was excluded from Davis Cup competition. In 1975, when he won the Wimbledon singles and the World Championship singles, he was ranked first in world tennis. After retiring from play in 1980, he was captain of the U.S. Davis Cup team in 1981.

Asheboro, city, seat (1802) of Randolph County, central North Carolina, U.S., in the forested Uwharrie Mountains. It was founded in 1796 on land once the home of Keyauwee Indians. A prehistoric Indian burial ground nearby was excavated in 1936. The name (originally Asheborough), honoured North Carolina governor Samuel Ashe (1725–1813). The community was a rural trade centre until the first railroad arrived in 1889, connecting Asheboro with High Point, and several lumber plants, using waterpower furnished by the Deep and Uwharrie rivers, were established. Now industrialized, the city has large hosiery and knitwear mills and upholstery manufacturing plants. Lumbering and the manufacture of wood products are important. The North Carolina Zoological Park and the well-known Seagrove pottery settlement are nearby. Inc. 1843. Pop. (1980) 15,252.

Asher, one of the 12 tribes of Israel that in biblical times comprised the people of Israel who later became the Jewish people. The tribe was named after the younger of two sons born to Jacob (also called Israel) and Zilpah, the maidservant of Jacob's first wife, Leah. After the Israelites took possession of the Promised Land, Joshua assigned territory to each of the 12 tribes. The tribe of Asher apparently settled among the Phoenicians in the upper region of Palestine, beyond the tribe of Zebulun and west of the tribe of Naphtali.

Following the death of King Solomon (922 BC), the Israelites separated into the northern Kingdom of Israel (representing 10 tribes) and the southern Kingdom of Judah. When the northern kingdom was conquered by the Assyrians in 721 BC, the 10 northern tribes, including Asher, were partially dispersed. In time they were assimilated by other peoples and thus disappeared as distinctive units. Jewish legends refer to them as the Ten Lost Tribes of Israel.

Asher ben Jehiel, also called (by acronym) ROSH (for Rabbenu [Our Teacher] Asher) (b. *c.* 1250, Rhine District, Ger.—d. Oct. 24, 1327, Toledo, Spain), major codifier of the Talmud, the rabbinical compendium of law, lore, and commentary. His work was a source for the great codes of his son Jacob ben Asher (1269–1340) and of Joseph Karo (1488–1575).

When the German authorities began to persecute the Jews, Asher fled to France and then to Spain. With the help of Rabbi Solomon ben Adret, one of the most influential rabbis of his time, he was established as rabbi of Toledo, where he founded a yeshiva (school of advanced Jewish learning). He believed that the study of philosophy might endanger the Talmud's authority. Hence he, Rabbi ben Adret, and others signed a ban forbidding such study to those under 30. On Rabbi ben Adret's death, Asher was acknowledged as the leader of European Jewry.

His code, the *Piske Halakhot* ("Decisions on the Laws"; compiled between 1307 and 1314), based largely on the Palestinian Talmud (as distinct from the Babylonian Talmud), deals strictly with the Talmudic laws. Asher considered the Talmud a supreme authority and felt free to disregard the opinions of the most eminent Jewish authorities if their decisions were not based on the Talmud. His code has been reprinted with the Talmud continuously since its first issuance with the Bomberg Talmud in 1520 (a famous edition of the Talmud by the Flemish printer Daniel Bomberg).

Asherah, ancient West Semitic goddess, consort of the supreme god. Her full name was probably "She who walks in the Sea," but she was also called "holiness," and, occasionally, Elath, "the goddess." According to the texts from Ugarit (modern Ras Shamra), Asherah's

Asherah, detail from an ivory box from Mīnat al-Bayḍā' near Ras Shamra, Syria, c. 1300 BC; in the Louvre, Paris

Giraudon—Art Resource/EB Inc.

consort was El, and by him she was the mother of 70 gods. As mother goddess she was widely worshipped throughout Syria and Palestine, although she was frequently paired with Baal, who often took the place of El in practical cult; as Baal's consort, Asherah was usually given the name Baalat.

The word *asherah* in the Old Testament was used not only in reference to the goddess herself but also to indicate a wooden cult object associated with her worship.

Consult the INDEX *first*

Ashes, symbol of victory in the now biennial cricket Test (international) match series between select national teams of England and Australia, first staged in 1877. Its name stems from an epitaph published in 1882 after the Australian team had won its first victory over England in England, at the Oval, London. The epitaph lamented that English cricket was dead and that its body would be cremated and the ashes sent to Australia. The following year an urn containing the ashes of a wicket stump was presented to the captain of the touring English team in Australia. The urn is now kept at Lord's Cricket Ground, headquarters of the Marylebone Cricket Club, long the foremost British club. *See also* sporting record.

Asheville, city, seat of Buncombe County, west central North Carolina, U.S., in the Blue Ridge Mountains, at the junction of the French Broad and Swannanoa rivers. It is the eastern gateway to Great Smoky Mountains National Park and the Cherokee Indian Reservation and is the headquarters of the Croatan, Nantahala, Pisgah, and Uwharrie national

Biltmore House in Asheville, N.C.
Frank J. Miller

forests. Mt. Mitchell (6,684 ft [2,037 m]), the highest peak east of the Mississippi River, is nearby. Settled in 1794 by John Barton, who named it Morristown after Robert Morris, a financier of the Revolution, it was renamed to honour Gov. Samuel Ashe. The Western North Carolina Railroad arrived in 1880, and Asheville developed as a market for livestock and tobacco. Manufactures include textiles, furniture, and paper products. The city is also a vacation headquarters for the Blue Ridge Mountains.

Biltmore estate, the vast house and gardens established by George Vanderbilt, is located there. The University of North Carolina at Asheville was founded in 1927 as Asheville-Biltmore College. The birthplace of novelist Thomas Wolfe is preserved as a memorial, and a collection of his writings is in the Pack Memorial Library. His grave and that of short story writer O. Henry (William Sidney Porter) are in Riverside Cemetery. Inc. town, 1797; city, 1883. Pop. (1980) city, 53,281; metropolitan area (SMSA), 177,761.

Ashfield, district, county of Nottinghamshire, England, with an area of 42 sq mi (110 sq km). The name is ancient and appeared in the names of the two major towns within the district even before its formation. The two towns are the coal-mining centres of Kirkby-in-Ashfield and Sutton-in-Ashfield, forming, as does the whole district, part of the heavily industrialized western rim of the county, where it borders on Derbyshire. Pop. (1982 est.) 106,000.

Ashford, district (borough), county of Kent, England. It was established in 1974 from the former urban district of Ashford, rural districts of East and West Ashford, and metropolitan borough and rural district of Tenterden. It has an area of 224 sq mi (580 sq km). The old town of Ashford was granted a market in the 13th century that later became a stock market for the pastoral farms on nearby Romney Marsh. Modern Ashford developed as a railway centre with a locomotive works, and it manufactures agricultural implements, beer, and bricks. The eastern borough has been designated as an area for future expansion as mid-Kent reaches its optimum population. Pop. (1981 prelim.) town, 39,974; (1981) district, 85,968.

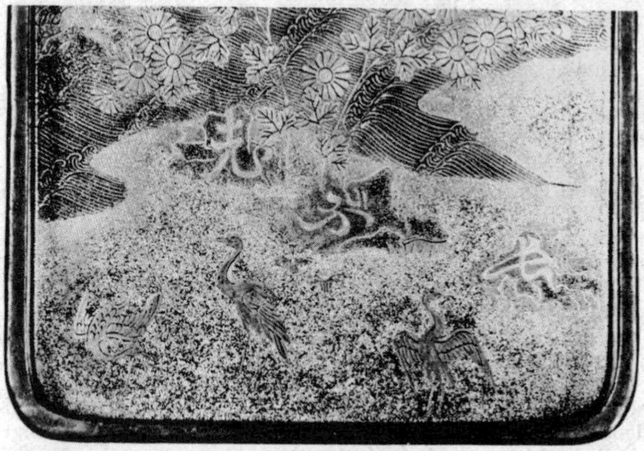

Detail of the inside cover of an ink-slab case with *ashide-e* writing signifying longevity
From Melvin and Betty Janss, *Inro and Other Miniature Forms of Japanese Lacquer Art;* Charles E. Tuttle Co.

Ashgill Series, uppermost series of Ordovician rocks (the Ordovician Period began about 500,000,000 years ago and lasted about 70,000,000 years), recognized on the basis of exposures in the Lake District of England. In the type area, the Ashgill Series is composed of the Applethwaite Beds and the overlying Ashgill Shales, from which the name of the series was derived. Two Ashgillian graptolite zones have been recognized: a lower zone of *Dicellograptus anceps* and an upper zone of *D. complanatus.* The Ashgill is also characterized by a distinctive trilobite (extinct marine arthropod) assemblage; many rare and unusual forms occur in Ashgill beds. About 155 metres (500 feet) of Ashgill rocks occur in South Wales; all are sedimentary, in contrast to lower Ordovician rocks, which contain extensive volcanic deposits. The Ashgill is predominantly mudstone; sandstones and conglomerates occur in central Wales. The Ashgill is sometimes grouped with the underlying Caradoc Series in the Bala Series.

Important Ashgill sections are found in the Oslo district, Norway, and in Bohemia. Ashgillian rocks have a wide distribution and occur in the Soviet Union, the Himalayas, southern China, Australia, and New Zealand.

Ashi ((b. *c.* AD 352—d. *c.* 427), preeminent Babylonian amora, or interpreter of the Mishna, the legal compilation that was the basis of the Talmud, the authoritative rabbinical compendium.

Ashi was head of the Jewish Academy at Sura, Babylonia, and was one of two chief editors who fixed the canon of the Babylonian Talmud. Under Ashi's leadership the Academy, which had been closed since 309, was revived, and the gigantic task of collating scattered notes, sayings, legislative opinions, and homiletic lore was conducted for more than 30 years. Ashi headed the Sura Academy for more than 50 years, and he also established the nearby city of Mata Mehasya as the focus of amoraic learning. One of his sons, Tabyomi, succeeded him at the Sura Academy. After an interruption of several decades, Ashi's work was completed by a staff of scholars from the academy. Arguments have been waged as to whether the Babylonian Gemara (Talmudic commentary on the Mishna) was actually redacted by Ashi or by others.

ashide-e (Japanese: "reed-script picture"), decorative, cursive style of Japanese calligraphy, the characters of which resemble natural objects, used to decorate scrolls, stationery, and lacquer ware. The typical *ashide-e* is a decorative representation of a poem, in which stylized characters serve as both text and illustration.

There are also *ashide-e* that do not represent a specific poem but a poetic sentiment. The *ashide-e* as a variety of poem-picture (*uta-e*) was often used on *maki-e* (lacquer ware decorated with gold or silver) such as ink-slab cases and letter boxes.

Ashihho (China): *see* A-ch'eng.

Ashikaga, city, Tochigi Prefecture (*ken*), Honshu, Japan, on the Watarase River. Ashikaga Takauji, who established the Ashikaga shogunate in the 14th century, was born there. Ashikaga was a post town on the Nikkō-kaidō (Nikkō Highway) during the Tokugawa era (1603–1867). It was a dyeing and weaving centre for several centuries, and after the national railway was opened in 1867 it flourished as a textile centre of the sericultural region in the northern Kantō Plain. Maintaining its traditional fibre industry as well as more recent manufacture of synthetic fibres, Ashikaga displays strong independence from the Keihin Industrial Region to the southeast. Other manufactures include metal products and machinery. In the southern, rural part of the city, flowers, strawberries, tomatoes, and cucumbers are raised for shipment to Ōsaka.

Ashikaga was the site of the former classical school, the Ashikaga Gakkō, founded in the 9th century; according to one tradition, its founder was the poet Ono Takamura. It was restored in 1432 by a nobleman, Uesugi Norizane, who engaged a Buddhist monk to head the school and imported a number of classical Chinese books; many of these are now housed in a library on the school grounds. The grounds also contain a 17th-century shrine dedicated to Confucius, and the city has two Buddhist temples. Pop. (1983 est.) 166,752.

Ashikaga period (Japanese history): *see* Muromachi period.

Ashikaga Tadayoshi (b. 1306, Japan—d. March 13, 1352, Kamakura, Japan), military and administrative genius who engineered many of the triumphs of his older brother, Ashikaga Takauji, the founder of the Ashikaga shogunate (military dictatorship) that dominated Japan from 1338 to 1573.

When in 1333 Takauji joined forces with the emperor Go-Daigo, Tadayoshi went with him, becoming a leading commander of the Imperial forces. In 1335, however, Tadayoshi revolted against the Imperial court, and when he had succeeded in rallying widespread support, Takauji joined his revolt, taking over the command of the rebel armies, which captured the Imperial capital at Kyōto in 1338. The Emperor fled the Yoshino Mountains, South of Naror, and Takauji installed in Kyōto an emperor who agreed to appoint him shogun.

Takauji proved to be inept at administrative matters, and for almost a decade Tadayoshi took charge of the government. Eventually, however, a feud erupted between Tadayoshi and some of Takauji's closest retainers, and Tadayoshi joined the followers of Go-Daigo, who had continued his rule in the area around Yoshino. Although Tadayoshi's forces immediately proved successful, his resources were limited; and he was eventually taken prisoner by Takauji, who had him confined in Kamakura, where he was allegedly poisoned.

Ashikaga Takauji (b. 1305, Japan—d. June 7, 1358, Kyōto), warrior and statesman who founded the Ashikaga shogunate, or hereditary military dictatorship, that dominated Japan from 1338 to 1573. Takauji established the shogunate by overthrowing the Imperial government; although the emperor continued to reign, he had little more than a symbolic role. Because of Takauji's usurpation of Imperial power, he was considered one of the major villains of Japanese history during the period of Imperial revival in the 19th century, but since World War II the emperor has been less revered, and Takauji's role has been reassessed.

The Ashikaga family became one of the most powerful in Japan during the Kamakura period (1199–1333); they provided leading retainers of the Hōjō regents who, with their capital at Kamakura, dominated the country during that time, relegating the emperors to a puppet role in the government. Finally, in 1331, the emperor Go-Daigo (ruled 1318–39) attempted to restore the status of the Imperial court by raising a revolt. The uprising was easily quashed, and the Emperor was banished, but two years later he escaped and again marshalled his forces, preparing to advance on the

Ashikaga Takauji, colour on silk by an unknown artist; in a private collection

By courtesy of the International Society for Educational Information, Tokyo

Imperial capital at Kyōto. Takauji was sent by the Hōjō government to reinforce Kyōto's defenses. By that time, however, the Hōjō government's control of the country outside Kamakura had declined. Encouraged by the strength of the Imperial forces, Takauji suddenly switched sides; returning to his own estate in Tamba province in eastern Japan, he raised an army against the Kamakura government.

Several other great warriors also switched sides, and the government of the Hōjō crumbled. Go-Daigo was able to establish the first Imperial government since the 10th century that controlled both political and military power. The new government, however, soon encountered difficulties; Go-Daigo was never able to gain complete control over the outlying countryside, and the warriors who had aided him soon became dissatisfied with their division of the spoils.

In July 1335 a member of the Hōjō family succeeded in raising an army and recapturing Kamakura. Taking advantage of this opportunity, Takauji requested that he be appointed shogun and put in charge of crushing the Hōjō uprising. Although this request was refused, he marched on Kamakura and defeated the enemy. The court then accused the Ashikaga family of murdering Prince Morinaga, the Emperor's son, who had been confined at Kamakura, and also of rewarding Ashikaga retainers without Imperial permission.

A battle ensued, and, with the help of his brother Tadayoshi, Takauji defeated the Imperial troops and captured Kyōto. The Imperial forces soon regrouped and drove Takauji from the city. In less than three months, Takauji returned again at the head of a large combined force and defeated the Emperor's forces. Declaring that Go-Daigo had forfeited the right to rule, he set up an emperor from another branch of the Imperial family and had himself appointed shogun. The former emperor fled to the Yoshino Mountains, south of Nara, declaring himself to be the true ruler; hostilities between the northern court at Kyōto and the southern court at Yoshino continued until 1392.

In later years the feud involving Takauji and his brother Tadayoshi so weakened Ashikaga family unity that Takauji was never able to fully consolidate his power. Not until the shogunate of his grandson Yoshimitsu did the office become completely established. Although the Ashikaga family held the title of shogun until 1573, it only briefly exercised effective control over all the feudal military leaders and powerful Buddhist monasteries scattered throughout the country.

Takauji was a highly cultured man, who composed waka (31-syllable poems) and renga (linked verse); he contributed to the development of the Zen sect, for which he built temples all over the country, including the Tenryū-ji at Kyōto.

Ashikaga Yoshiaki (b. Dec. 5, 1537, Japan—d. Oct. 19, 1597, Ōsaka), shogun (hereditary military dictator) of Japan who was the 15th and last of his family to hold the title. Yoshiaki had been a priest, but in 1568, with the aid of his protector, the general Oda Nobunaga, he deposed his cousin Yoshihide and took over the shogunate. Subsequently, rivalry developed between Yoshiaki and Oda, and the latter deposed Yoshiaki and banished him from Kyōto in 1573.

Ashikaga Yoshimasa (b. Jan. 20, 1436, Kyōto—d. Jan. 27, 1490, Kyōto), shogun (hereditary military dictator) who helped promote one of Japan's greatest cultural eras. His attempts to select an heir, however, brought on a dispute that caused the great Ōnin War (1467–77). This conflict not only laid waste the area around the capital at Kyōto and destroyed many of its great architectural treasures but also eliminated the fiction of central control over the outlying regions of the country, thus touching off a century of civil warfare.

Yoshimasa was proclaimed shogun in 1449 at the age of 13, at a time when central control over the countryside had begun to deteriorate, with starvation and misery rampant. When he was only 29 years old, unable to alter conditions, Yoshimasa decided to retire from the shogunate and name his younger brother as his successor. Before the succession could be effected, however, his wife bore a son (1465), whom she demanded be made the heir. In spite of Yoshimasa's attempts to settle the problem peacefully, in 1467 the difficulty became an excuse for war between two rival military factions serving the shogunate. Although the war dragged on until 1477 and ended in a stalemate, Yoshimasa finally abdicated in 1473 in favour of his son. After the boy's death in 1489, Yoshimasa appeased his brother by naming his brother's son as the new shogun.

Ineffective as shogun, Yoshimasa was a great patron of the arts. After his retirement he built the famous Ginkaku-ji (Silver Pavilion) in the Higashiyama, or Eastern Hills, area of Kyōto. There he practiced the Japanese tea ceremony, which he developed into a fine art, and sponsored many noted artists, potters, and Nō (classical dance-drama) performers. Today the Higashiyama period, as this cultural era became known, is considered one of the greatest in Japanese art history.

Ashikaga Yoshimitsu (b. Sept. 25, 1358, Kyōto—d. May 31, 1408, Kyōto), shogun (hereditary military dictator) of Japan, who achieved political stability for the Ashikaga shogunate, established in 1338 by his grandfather, Ashikaga Takauji (1305–58), and subsequently known as the Muromachi Period (for the district of Kyōto in which Yoshimitsu lived) until its end in 1573.

Proclaimed shogun in 1368, Yoshimitsu, in contrast to his father and grandfather, assumed an active role in the Imperial bureaucracy. In 1381 he became inner minister, later advancing to the position of minister of the left and, in 1394, minister of state. By the end of his reign he had accomplished a complete reorganization of the civil government.

In 1392 Yoshimitsu ended an Imperial division of Japan caused by Takauji's seizure of Kyōto, which had forced the emperor Go-Daigo (reigned 1318–39) and his adherents to flee to the Yoshino Mountains, south of Nara, where they established a court separate from that of the emperor designated by Takauji in Kyōto. Yoshimitsu concluded a truce with the southern court, promising that the position of emperor would alternate between the two Imperial lines if the Imperial Regalia would be returned to Kyōto. The promise was never kept. His hold over the countryside was not completely secure, however, and he had to deal with several serious revolts by provincial warrior groups during his reign. Nevertheless, by the beginning of the 15th century, Yoshimitsu was able to suppress the southwestern feudal lords, whose pirate ships were marauding the China coast, ending a 600-year lapse in formal trade with China.

The reopening of trade with China was symbolic of a 75-year cultural renaissance in Japan that began in 1392 under Yoshimitsu. Court life assumed a luxurious air; high positions in government went to Zen Buddhist monks, many magnificent temples and palaces were built, the most famous being the Golden Pavilion (Kinkaku-ji), put up on the northwestern outskirts of Kyōto after Yoshimitsu's retirement from the shogunate in 1394 in favour of his son.

Āshiq Pasha: *see* Aşık Paşa.

Ashiya, city, Hyōgo Prefecture (*ken*), Honshu, Japan, surrounded by the Rokkō-san-chi (Rokkō Mountains) and facing Ōsaka-wan (Ōsaka Bay). Located on railway lines and highways between Kōbe (west) and Ōsaka (east), it has been known for its beauty since the Heian period (794–1185), when court nobles and men of letters lived there. After the establishment of the first railway line in 1905, the city became a renowned residential area. One-third of its central area was destroyed during World War II, but it has since been rebuilt. Pop. (1980) 81,745.

Ashkelon (Israel): *see* Ashqelon.

Ashkenazi (from Hebrew *Ashkenaz*, Germany), plural ASHKENAZIM, any of the Jews who lived in the Rhineland valley and in neighbouring France before their migration to Slavic lands (*e.g.*, Poland, Lithuania, Russia) after the Crusades (11th to 13th century). Following the 17th-century persecutions in eastern Europe, large numbers settled in western Europe, where they assimilated, as they had done in eastern Europe, with other Jewish communities. In time, all Jews who had adopted the "German-rite" synagogue ritual were referred to as Ashkenazim to distinguish them from Sephardic (Spanish-rite) Jews. Ashkenazim differ from Sephardim in their pronunciation of Hebrew, cultural traditions, synagogue cantillation (chanting), widespread use of Yiddish (until the 20th century), and most especially in synagogue liturgy.

Today Ashkenazim constitute more than 80 percent of all the Jews in the world, vastly outnumbering Sephardic Jews in such countries as the United States, and the Soviet Union and in the nations of the Commonwealth of Nations. In the State of Israel, the chief rabbinate has both an Ashkenazi and a Sephardic chief rabbi on equal footing. All Reform and Conservative Jewish congregations belong to the Ashkenazi tradition.

Ashkenazy, Vladimir, original Russian VLADIMIR DAVIDOVICH ASHKENAZI (b. July 6, 1937, Gorky, Russian S.F.S.R.), Russian pianist and conductor whose extensive repertory included Mozart, Beethoven, the German Romantics, and 20th-century Russians.

Beginning piano lessons at the age of six, Ashkenazy studied for 10 years with Anaida Sumbatyan at the Moscow Central School of Music then entered Lev Oborin's piano class at the Moscow Conservatory in 1955. He attained international prominence when he won the gold medal at the Queen Elisabeth of Belgium International Music Contest in Brussels in 1956; he also claimed second prize at the fifth Warsaw International Chopin Competition in 1955 and shared first prize at the second Tchaikovsky Competition in 1962. In 1963 he emigrated to the West, assuming Icelandic citizenship in 1972 but residing in Switzerland. In the mid-1970s, he also became active as a conductor.

Ashkhabad, *oblast* (administrative region), Turkmen Soviet Socialist Republic, with an area of 36,800 sq mi (95,400 sq km). The *oblast* is mainly comprised of the Kara-Kum Desert. The Kopet-Dag Range extends along the southern border of the *oblast* and the Tedzhen and Ashkhabad oases lie at the foot of the mountains along the Kara-Kum Canal. The climate is continental and very dry, with moderately cold winters and long, hot summers. The economy is based on irrigated agriculture in the oases; cotton is the main crop, with grains and fodder occupying much of the remainder of the cultivated land. Vegetables, melons, potatoes, and some grapes are also grown. Karakul sheep are the most important livestock and there is also some cattle and camel raising. Rug making and silk production are the predominant industries.

Large areas of the Kara-Kum are unpopulated, and nearly all of the population is in the oases of the south. The only cities are Ashkhabad (the administrative centre), Bezmein, and Tedzhen. A railroad connects the *oblast* with the Caspian Sea and other parts of the republic. Pop. (1983 est.) 440,000.

Ashkhabad, also spelled AŠCHABAD, Turkmen ASHGABAT, formerly ASKHABAD and (1919–27) POLTORATSK, administrative centre of Ashkhabad *oblast* (administration region) and capital of the Turkmen Soviet Socialist Republic, in the Akhal oasis at the northern foot of the Kopet-Dag Range and on the edge of the Kara-Kum Desert, about 19 mi (30 km) from the Iranian frontier. It was founded in 1881 as a Russian military fort and took the name of the nearby Turkmen settlement of Askhabad (Arabic *ashk,* "love"; Persian *ābād,* "town"). It became the administrative centre of the Transcaspian *oblast* (administrative region) and, because of its position on the caravan routes and, from 1885, on the Transcaspian Railway, soon attracted a motley population that numbered more than 45,000 in 1911. Soviet rule was established in December 1917, but in July 1918 power was seized by the White Russians. The city soon was retaken and renamed Poltoratsk, after a local revolutionary. In 1924 it became the capital of the newly created Turkmen S.S.R., and in 1927 it reverted to its original name, now spelled Ashkhabad. The most violent earthquake yet registered in the Soviet Union virtually destroyed the city in October 1948; it was rebuilt on the same regular plan. A chronic water shortage was alleviated considerably when the Kara-Kum Canal reached the city in 1962.

Ashkhabad is now an administrative, industrial, transportation, and cultural centre. The city has glassworks, carpet-weaving and cotton mills and metalworking shops. Its spectacular natural setting has also made it a centre for the filmmaking industry. There are six institutions of higher education, including Turkmen State University, and polytechnic, agricultural, and medical institutes. The Turkmen S.S.R. Academy of Sciences, founded in 1951, includes the Desert Institute, the only institution of its kind in the U.S.S.R. Other amenities include an opera house and three theatres as well as museums of history, local lore, and the fine arts. Pop. (1983 est.) 338,000.

Ashland, city, Boyd County, northeastern Kentucky, U.S., on the Ohio River just below the mouth of the Big Sandy River, with Ironton, Ohio, and Huntington, W.Va., forms a tristate industrial complex. Settled in 1815 as Poage's Settlement, it was renamed (1854) after Henry Clay's home in Lexington, Va. Its proximity to coal and timber regions and iron-ore deposits (no longer mined) contributed to its growth as the state's major iron and steel centre (the continuous-sheet mill process was developed there). Ashland Community College (1937) is a branch of the University of Kentucky. The nearby "Traipsin' Woman's" cabin, which was the site of the annual America Folk Song Festival, is now a cornerstone of the Appalachian Cultural Park. Inc. town, 1856; city, 1876. Pop. (1980) 27,064.

Ashland, city, Jackson County, southwestern Oregon, U.S., on Bear Creek, in the southern reaches of the Rogue River Valley, at the base of the Siskiyou Mountains, just southeast of Medford. Settled in 1852 (during a gold rush) and laid out in 1860, it was named for Ashland County, Ohio, and known as Ashland Mills for its sawmills and gristmills. Located on the Siskiyou Toll Road (linking Sacramento, Calif., and Portland) and, after 1884, on the Oregon and California (now Southern Pacific) Railroad, it developed as a lumber town. Ashland adjoins Rogue River National Forest (containing Mount Ashland Ski Area), and tourism is a major source of income. It is the home of Southern Oregon State College (1826) and the site (since 1935) of the Oregon Shakespearean Festival (held annually in Lithia Park). Light manufacturing concentrates on wood products and fruit processing. Inc. 1874. Pop. (1980) 14,943.

Ashland, city, seat (1860) of Ashland County, extreme northern Wisconsin, U.S., 60 mi (97 km) east of Duluth, Minn.; it is a port on Chequamegon Bay of Lake Superior. A Jesuit mission was established there in 1665 by Claude-Jean Allouez, but not until 1854 did Asaph Whittlesey settle the site, which he named for Henry Clay's Kentucky estate. In 1877 Ashland became the terminus of the first railroad of northern Wisconsin and grew with iron mining and lumbering enterprises. Coal, iron ore, and black granite from the Penokee-Gogebic Range are shipped from the port (icebound December–April), and pulpwood from Canada is floated across the lake and moved by rail to mills at Wisconsin Rapids in the centre of the state. Manufactures include wood, paper, and metal products, explosives, and apparel. Ashland is the seat of Northland College (1892), site of a University of Wisconsin agricultural experimental station, and gateway to the Apostle Islands National Lakeshore (north). Inc. 1887. Pop. (1980) 9,115.

Shoreline on the Bayfield Peninsula from the Apostle Islands National Lakeshore, near Ashland, Wis.

By courtesy of the National Park Service; photograph, Richard Frear

Ashley (of Wimborne Saint Giles), Anthony Ashley Cooper, Baron: *see* Shaftesbury, Anthony Ashley Cooper, 1st earl of.

Ashley, Anthony Ashley Cooper, Lord: *see* Shaftesbury, Anthony Ashley Cooper, 7th earl of.

Ashley, William Henry (b. *c.* 1778, Powhatan, Va., U.S.—d. March 26, 1838, Cooper County, Mo.), U.S. congressman and fur trader who revolutionized the fur trade and hastened exploration of the American West when he introduced the rendezvous system as a substitute for traditional trading posts.

Having arrived in Missouri some time after 1802, Ashley prospered in mining, gunpowder manufacture, surveying, and land speculation, rose to general in the territorial militia, and served as the state's first lieutenant governor in 1820. Two years later, with experienced fur trapper Andrew Henry, he organized the Rocky Mountain Fur Company and travelled up the Missouri River to the mouth of the Yellowstone, where the party established a trading post. Indian hostility soon caused the partners to abandon the area in favour of the Central Rockies, where furbearing animals were so abundant that the only major concern was how to get the rich harvest out of the tramontane.

Ashley's solution was an annual rendezvous, or temporary wilderness market, where free trappers could bring their furs to him at the end of the season and purchase from him the supplies they needed for another year of trapping. The first such rendezvous was held on the Green River (in present Wyoming) in the spring of 1825. By 1827 Ashley had made a fortune, and he retired to devote the remainder of his life largely to politics. As a U.S. congressman from 1831, he was an effective champion of Western interests.

Ashmedai (Jewish legend): *see* Asmodeus.

Ashmolean Museum, one of the four museums of Oxford University and the oldest public museum of art, archaeology, and natural history in Great Britain. It was established to house collections donated to the university in 1675 by Elias Ashmole and was opened to the public in 1683 in a building designed by Thomas Wood. Initially the collection was primarily concerned with natural history, and it remained the centre of scientific studies at Oxford for 150 years. In the 19th century, the growth and variety of new acquisitions resulted in the dispersal and rehousing of the collections.

The present Ashmolean Museum was designed in the Neoclassical style by C.R. Cockerell and erected between 1841 and 1845. It houses the collection of art and archaeology, while the old Thomas Wood building has become the Museum of the History of Science.

Ashmore and Cartier Islands, external territory of Australia, in the Indian Ocean, 200 mi (320 km) northwest of Western Australia. The Ashmore Islands, comprising Middle, East, and West islands, are coral islets within a reef. Cartier Island, also lying within a reef, is more sandy in composition. Created in 1934, the territory was administratively linked to the Northern Territory of Australia from 1938 until 1978. When the Northern Territory became self-governing in 1978, administration of the islands passed to the national government. The islands are uninhabited, but there is an automatic weather station on West Island.

Ashmūnayn, al- (Egypt): *see* Hermopolis Magna.

Ashoka (Buddhist leader): *see* Aśoka.

Ashqelon, also spelled ASHKELON, classical ASCALON, or ASKALON, city on the coastal plain of Palestine, since 1948 in southwest Israel. The modern city is 1¼ mi (2 km) east-northeast of the ancient city site.

Traces of habitation extend back to 2000 BC; the city's name appears in Egyptian texts of about the 19th century BC. It is also mentioned in the Amarna Letters (from the 14th-century-BC pharaonic archives found at Tel el-Amarna); about 150 years later it was taken by the Egyptian pharaoh Merneptah II after a revolt. After Egyptian control waned in the mid-12th century BC, Ashqelon became a Philistine city and was a member of the Philistine pentapolis (five cities) throughout the period of the Judges and the early Israelite monarchy until it was subjected to Assyrian rule by Tiglath-Pileser III *c.* 735 BC. It was recaptured after revolting by Sennacherib in 701 BC. It remained tributary to Assyria until captured by Nebuchadrezzar, king of Babylon (reigned 605–562 BC), who deported many of its inhabitants to Babylon.

The city was conquered by Alexander the Great in 332. After Alexander's death (323) it was fought over by his successors, the Ptolemaic and Seleucid dynasties. During that period it became known by its Hellenized name of Ascalon, which it retained throughout the era of the Crusades. The tradition that Herod the Great, king of Judaea under Roman suzerainty (ruled 37–4 BC), was born there is probably untrue; he did, however, adorn the city with fine public buildings, some of which have been excavated. Ashqelon was conquered by the Arabs in 636. Captured by the crusaders after a 50-year struggle (1153), it became one of their principal ports and strongholds. It was eventually taken by Saladin, who destroyed its walls in 1191. A century later the city lay in ruins, and its site remained uninhabited until the mid-20th century. The ruins were excavated by the Palestine Exploration Fund in 1920–22. The site, now known as the mound of Tel Ashqelon, is protected by a national antiquities park.

Modern Ashqelon was originally an Arab settlement named al-Majdal. After the Arab–Israeli War (1948–49), the Arabs left the site, which was resettled with Jewish immigrants and renamed Migdal Gad, and later Migdal Ashqelon. The heart of the planned modern city was built to the west near the seacoast, beginning in 1950. Features include a tall central clock tower and shaded business malls. A factory was built there in the 1950s to produce prestressed concrete pipe for the National Water Plan. Manufactures now include textiles, plastics, and wristwatches. An industrial zone north of the city has plants that make automobile parts and process agricultural products. The trans-Negev oil pipeline from the Red Sea port of Elat reaches the Mediterranean there. It has also been developed as a resort centre, with hotels and campgrounds along the fine beaches. Pop. (1982 est.) 53,500.

Ashraf DYNASTY (Turkmen family): *see* Eşref dynasty.

ashram, Sanskrit ĀŚRAMA ("abode"), the hermitage of a religious leader, and often a retreat centre for his disciples. "Ashram" also signifies any of the four spiritual abodes, or stages of life, through which the "twice born" Hindu (belonging to one of the three upper *varṇas*, or social classes) ideally will pass. These are that of (1) the student (*brahmacārin*), marked by chastity, devotion and obedience to one's teacher, and religious study in preparation for the rest of life; (2) the householder (*gṛhastha*), requiring marriage, the begetting of sons, working to sustain one's family and to help support priests and holy men, and fulfilling duties toward gods and ancestors; (3) the hermit (*vànaprastha*), beginning when a man has seen the sons of his sons and consisting of withdrawal from concern with material things, solitude, ascetic and yogic practices, and living simply in the forest; (4) the homeless mendicant (*sannyāsin*), involving leaving the hermitage and renouncing all one's possessions to wander from place to place begging for food, concerned only with the eternal. The appropriate pursuits of a man during his stage as a householder are *kāma* (love, pleasure), *artha* (property, wealth), and *dharma* (religious and moral duties). Traditionally, *mokṣa* (spiritual liberation) should be the pursuit of a man only during the last two stages of his life. The dual ideals of living in accordance with one's *varṇa,* or social class, and with the appropriate ashram is called *varṇāśrama-dharma.*

Ashta Pradhan, also spelled AṢṬA PRADHĀD (Marathi: Council of Eight), administrative and advisory council set up by the Indian Hindu Marāthā leader Śivājī (died 1680), which contributed to his successful military attacks on the Muslim Mughal Empire and to the good government of the territory over which he established his rule. The senior member, the peshwa, or *mukhya pradhan* (the offices had both Persian and Marathi titles), was in charge of general administration and held the state seal. The *amātya,* or *mazumdār,* and the *pant sachir* dealt with finance, the *sumanta* with foreign affairs, and the *mantrī* with intelligence and police reports. The commander in chief (*senāpatī*) together with a legal member (*nyāyādhīśa*) and member for religious matters (*paṇḍit rāo*) completed the council.

All except the last two held military commands, their civil duties often being performed by deputies. These, with a staff of secretaries, formed the nucleus of the peshwa's bureaucracy, whose work survives in modern Indian administration in the peshwa's *daftar* at Pune (Poona). Śivājī's son Sambhājī (1680–89) scattered the council, but, when Marāthā power revived in the 18th century, the council members became hereditary with nominal powers except for the peshwas, who, in the persons of the Bhat family, became the actual controllers of the Marāthā state, nominally under the weaker descendants of Śivājī.

Ashtabula, city, Ashtabula County, northeastern Ohio, U.S., on Lake Erie, at the mouth of the Ashtabula River, 65 mi (105 km) northeast of Cleveland. Settled in 1801, its name, of Algonkian Indian origin, possibly means "river of many fish" and was applied to the township (1808). In the 1850s Hubbard Homestead and other houses in the city were stations on the Underground Railroad, an escape route for slaves. A St. Lawrence Seaway port, with a fine harbour, it handles with Conneaut (east) large quantities of coal and iron ore. It is also a trading centre for the Lake Erie resort area and manufactures a variety of products, including auto bodies and forgings, fibre glass, plastics, sheet metal boilers, corrugated boxes, farm tools, and leather. A regional campus of Kent State University is in the city. The county has several well-preserved covered bridges on its rural roads. Inc. village, 1831; city, 1891. Pop. (1980) 23,449.

Ashtart (goddess): *see* Astarte.

Ashton, Sir Frederick (William Mallandaine) (b. Sept. 17, 1906, Guayaquil, Ecuador), principal choreographer and director of England's Royal Ballet, the repertoire of which includes about 30 of his ballets.

Ashton studied dancing in London under Léonide Massine, Nicholas Legat, and Marie

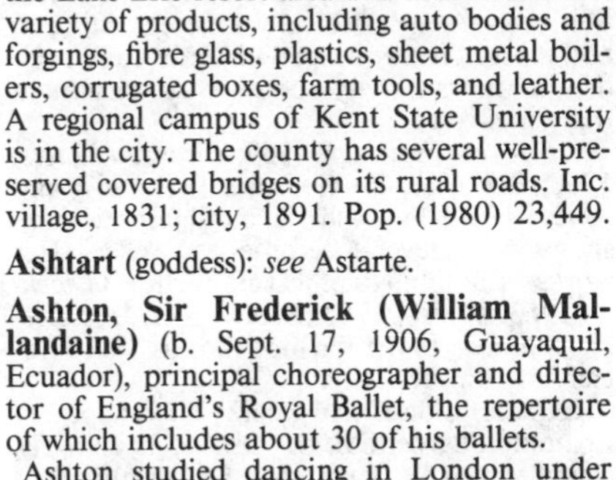

Ashton (left) and Robert Helpmann rehearsing their roles as the Ugly Sisters in *Cinderella,* 1965

Central Press—Pictorial Parade/EB Inc.

Rambert, who encouraged his first choreographic efforts, *The Tragedy of Fashion* (1926) and *Capriol Suite* (1930).

Ashton joined the Vic-Wells (later the Sadler's Wells and then the Royal) Ballet in 1933 and distinguished himself as a mime and character dancer in such roles as Carabosse in *The Sleeping Beauty* and the gigolo in *Façade* and as the versatile choreographer of ballets that include *Cinderella, Sylvia,* and *Daphnis and Chloë* and the film *Tales of Hoffmann* (1951). He was the Royal Ballet's principal choreographer from 1933 to 1970, during which time he also served as its associate director (1952 to 1963), and its director (1963 to 1970). In 1970 he retired from administration in order to devote his time exclusively to choreography.

In 1963 Ashton created *Marguerite and Armand* especially for the new partnership of Margot Fonteyn and Rudolf Nureyev. Others included *The Dream* (1964), a one-act ballet based on Shakespeare's *A Midsummer Night's Dream; Monotones* (Part I, 1965; Part II, 1966), to music of Erik Satie; *Jazz Calendar* (1968); *Enigma Variations* (1968); *A Month in the Country* (1976); and *Rhapsody* (1981), based on music by Sergey Rachmaninoff. In 1970 Ashton choreographed and danced in the motion picture *Tales of Beatrix Potter*. His major works include such enduring favourites as *Façade* (1931), *Les Rendezvous* (1933), *Les Patineurs* (1937), *Symphonic Variations* (1946), *Illuminations* (for the New York City Ballet, 1950), *Homage to the Queen* (1953), *Romeo and Juliet* (for the Royal Danish Ballet, 1955), *Birthday Offering* (1956), *Ondine* (1958), and *La Fille mal gardée* (1960). Ashton was knighted in 1962.

Ashton-Warner, Sylvia (Constance), married name SYLVIA HENDERSON (b. Dec. 17, 1908, Stratford, N.Z.—d. April 28, 1984, Tauranga), New Zealand educator and writer of fiction, nonfiction, and poetry. In the field of education, she became known for her innovative work in adapting traditional British teaching methods to the special needs of Maori children. Her aim was peace and communication between two radically different cultures, and most of her writing, both fiction and nonfiction, draws heavily upon her experiences in this endeavour.

Her novels (*Spinster,* 1959; *Incense to Idols,* 1960; *Bell Call,* 1964; *Greenstone,* 1967; and *Three,* 1970) met with favourable critical response, and several became best sellers. Her works of autobiographical nonfiction (*Teacher,* 1963; *Myself,* 1967; *Experiment: "Teacher" in America,* 1972) did not fare as well critically or commercially.

Her short stories and poems have appeared in numerous periodicals. One of her novels, *Spinster,* was the basis for a British film, *Two Loves* (1961).

Ashur, in Mesopotamian religion, city god of Ashur and national god of Assyria. In the beginning he was perhaps only a local deity of the city that shared his name. From about 1800 BC onward, however, there appear to have been strong tendencies to identify him with the Sumerian Enlil (Akkadian Bel) while under the Assyrian king Sargon II (reigned 721–705 BC), there were tendencies to identify Ashur with Anshar, the father of An (Akkadian Anu) in the creation myth. Under Sargon's successor Sennacherib, deliberate and thorough attempts were made to transfer to Ashur the primeval achievements of Marduk, as well as the whole ritual of the New Year festival of Babylon—attempts that clearly have their background in the political struggle going on at that time between Babylonia and Assyria. As a consequence, the image of Ashur seems to lack all real distinctiveness and contains little that is not implied in his position as the city god of a vigorous and warlike city that became the capital of an empire. The Assyrians believed that he granted rule over Assyria and supported Assyrian arms against enemies; detailed written reports from the Assyrian kings about their campaigns were even submitted to him. He appears a mere personification of the interests of Assyria as a political entity, with little character of his own.

Ashur, also spelled ASSUR, modern QAL'AT SHARQĀṬ, ancient religious capital of Assyria, located on the west bank of the Tigris River in Nīnawā (Nineveh) *muḥāfaẓah* (governorate) in northern Iraq. The first scientific excavations there were conducted by a German expedition (1903–13) led by W. Andrae. Ashur was a name applied to the city, to the country, and to the principal god of the ancient Assyrians.

The place was originally occupied *c.* 2500 BC by a tribe that probably had reached the Tigris River either from Syria or from the south. Strategically, Ashur was smaller and less well situated than Nimrūd (Kalakh) or Nineveh, the other principal cities of Assyria; but the religious sanctity of Ashur ensured its continuous upkeep until 614, when it was destroyed by the Babylonians. The inner city was protected by encircling walls nearly 2½ miles (4 kilometres) long. On the eastern side Ashur was washed by the Tigris, along which massive quays were first erected by Adad-nirari I (reigned *c.* 1307–*c.* 1275). On the north side an arm of the river and a high escarpment afforded natural defenses, which were augmented by a system of buttressed walls and by a powerful sally port named the *mushlalu*—a semicircular tower of rusticated stone masonry, built by Sennacherib and probably the earliest known example of this type of architecture. The southern and western sides were protected by a strong fortification system.

A catalog of Ashur's buildings inscribed during the reign of Sennacherib (704–681) lists 34 temples, although fewer than one-third of them have been found, including those of Ashur-Enlil, Anu-Adad, Sin-Shamash, and Ishtar and Nabu. Historically the most interesting temples are those devoted to the cult of the goddess Ishtar, or Inanna, as she was known to the Sumerians.

In addition to the temples, three palaces were identified. The oldest was ascribed to Shamshi-Adad I (*c.* 1813–*c.* 1781) and was later used as a burial ground. Many of the private houses found in the northwestern quarter of the site were spaciously laid out and had family vaults beneath their floors. The irregular planning of the town indicates a strict respect for property rights and land tenure. Other aspects of Assyrian law, particularly relating to women, are known from a series of tablets compiled between 1450 and 1250.

Although the sack of Ashur was extensive, a part of the city was later revived around the time of the Parthian conquest of Mesopotamia (140 BC).

Ashur-akh-iddina (Assyrian king): *see* Esarhaddon.

Ashur-uballit I (reigned *c.* 1365–30 BC), king of Assyria during Mesopotamia's feudal age, who created the first Assyrian Empire and initiated the Middle Assyrian period (14th to 12th century BC). With the help of the Hittites he destroyed the dominion of the Aryan Mitanni, a non-Semitic people from upper Iran and Syria who had subjugated Assyria, ravaged Nineveh (near present Mosul, Iraq), and sent off the image of Assyria's deity Ishtar to the Egyptian pharaoh (early 14th century). Later, allied with the Kassite successors in Babylonia, Ashur-uballit ended Hittite and Hurrian rule. By intermarriage he then influenced the Kassite dynasty and eventually dominated all of Babylonia, thus paving the way for the Neo-Assyrian mastery during the Sargonid dynasty (12th to 7th century).

'Āshūrā', Muslim holy day observed on the 10th of Muḥarram, the first month of the Islāmic year (Gregorian date variable). 'Āshūrā' was originally designated in AD 622 by Muḥammad, soon after the *hijrah,* as a day of fasting from sunset to sunset, patterned on the Jewish Day of Atonement, Yom Kippur. When Jewish–Muslim relations became strained, however, Muḥammad made Ramaḍān (*q.v.*) the Muslim month of fasting, leaving the 'Āshūrā' fast a voluntary observance, as it has remained among the Sunnah.

Among the Shī'ah, 'Āshūrā' is a major festival, the *ta'ziyah,* commemorating the death of Ḥusayn, son of 'Alī and grandson of Muḥammad, on the 10th of Muḥarram, AH 61 (Oct. 10, 680), in Karbalā' (present-day Iraq). It is a period of expressions of remorse and of pilgrimage to Karbalā'; passion plays are also presented, commemorating the death of Ḥusayn. *See also* ta'ziyah.

Ashurbanipal, also spelled ASSURBANIPAL, or ASURBANIPAL (fl. 7th century BC), last of the great kings of Assyria (reigned 668 to *c.* 627 BC), who assembled in Nineveh the first systematically organized library in the ancient Near East.

Early life. The life of this vigorous ruler of an empire ranging initially from the Persian Gulf to Cilicia, Syria, and Egypt can be largely

Ashurbanipal carrying a basket in the rebuilding of the temple, stone bas-relief from the Esagila, Babylon, 650 BC; in the British Museum

Reproduced by courtesy of the trustees of the British Museum

reconstructed from his autobiographical annals and royal correspondence. His father, Esarhaddon, appointed him crown prince of Assyria in May 672 BC to avert a dynastic struggle. Shamash-shum-ukin, a son of equal status by another wife, was appointed crown prince of Babylonia. Probably due to the influential queen mother Naqi'a-Zakutu, Ashurbanipal was given responsibility earlier.

Ashurbanipal was involved in administration and versed in the problems of controlling the northern hill tribes. His tutors were Nabu-shar-usur, a general, and Nabu-ahi-eriba, who interested him in history and literature. Like few Mesopotamian kings before him, he mastered all scribal and priestly knowledge and was able to read Sumerian and obscure Akkadian scripts and languages. His athletic powers were shown in hunting, archery, and horsemanship. Though there is little evidence of his experience on the actual battlefield, there is no reason to doubt Ashurbanipal's claim that his father favoured him for his bravery and intelligence.

He soon shouldered heavy responsibilities, having to command the court and nobles. No governor or prefect was appointed without consulting him, and he had authority over many state building projects. His reports to his father showed such qualities of statesmanship that he was left in charge of all affairs while his father was en route to Egypt. When Esarhaddon died at Harran in December 669 BC, Ashurbanipal transferred full power to himself without incident. The queen mother exacted an oath of allegiance from both family and courtiers.

Ashurbanipal's reign. Ashurbanipal's first concern was to quell a revolution in Egypt, where Taharqa (Tarku; biblical Tirhaka), an Egyptian king, had invaded the Nile Delta and won support. Swift Assyrian military action forced Taharqa's withdrawal, and Ashurbanipal appointed local princes supported by Assyrian garrisons. Some of the princes intrigued with Taharqa, and the Assyrians deported them to Nineveh. Keeping to his plan to have native administrators, Ashurbanipal chose Necho I as supreme ruler of the delta and made a treaty with him. Further pressure from Taharqa's successor, Tanutamon (Tandamane), led to another Assyrian intervention in 664–663, when the Assyrians seized control of Memphis and sacked Thebes. When Necho died in 663, Ashurbanipal held to his policy and accepted the succession of another local ruler, Psamtik (Psammetichus I); he was rewarded by a peace that enabled him to campaign elsewhere. In 654 BC the Assyrian garrisons were expelled from Egypt, but trade continued so that this loss resulted in little weakening of his position.

He next turned to the Phoenician city of Tyre, which had supported both Egyptian and Lydian bids for independence. A successful siege of Tyre led to the resubmission of the rulers of Syria and Cilicia and to a request for Assyrian help from Gyges of Lydia against Cimmerian intruders. Because Lydian mercenaries had assisted Egypt, this help was refused. A swift display of military might against the Mannaeans and an alliance with Madyes, the Scythian chief, repulsed Cimmerian advances and left Ashurbanipal free to attend to Babylonia, his southern neighbour.

Ashurbanipal had confirmed his half-brother Shamash-shum-ukin as local ruler of Babylonia, but with restricted powers. Assyrian garrisons and officials there continued to report to the Assyrian king, and he continued to appoint governors both in the Sealand (Persian Gulf) and in Ur. Babylonians petitioned him directly and received land grants. For 16 years, relations with his brother were peaceful. When Tept-Humban, a usurper in Elam, entered Assyrian territory and was killed, the Assyrian action was primarily in support of the Elamite princes Humbanigash and Tammaritu, who were given specific regions in Elam with no attempt at direct Assyrian rule. Ashurbanipal's actions probably aimed also to assist his own brother, whom he still trusted. Ashurbanipal received a deputation of Babylonians about this time, and he punished the Gambulu tribe for complicity in the Elamite affair.

Shamash-shum-ukin's long stay in Babylon had imbued him with the traditional local spirit of nationalism and resistance. He may have interpreted his brother's policy of appeasement as weakness and as an opportunity for him to increase his own status. In any event, he contrived a coalition with other outlying peoples of the Assyrian Empire—Phoenicia, Judah, Elam, Egypt, Lydia, and the Arab and Chaldean tribesmen—and had these groups risen simultaneously Assyria would have fallen. When Ashurbanipal discovered the plots, he appealed directly to the Babylonians and perhaps tested their loyalty by imposing a special tax; only upon their refusal did he take military action. He seemed to move in ways that avoided direct danger to his brother, and he worked more through siege warfare than through direct action; the Babylonian Chronicle records that for three years "the war went on and there were perpetual clashes." Elam, suffering from internal dissension, was unable to help the rebels; and gradually, through starvation, the Arabs who had retreated into Babylon deserted as the famine became intense. Shamash-shum-ukin committed suicide in his burning palace in 648 BC. Ashurbanipal's own feelings toward the city are shown by his work of restoration and by his appointment of a Chaldean noble, Kandalanu, as his viceroy there.

Ashurbanipal had to take further action to quell the rebellion. Raiding the Arab tribes, he defeated the Nabataean Uate and his allies and isolated the Qadar tribe. The struggle with Elam was harder; war there dragged on until 639 BC, when the Assyrians sacked Susa. That year Ashurbanipal celebrated his triumph; he had "the whole world" under his sway, and four captive kings drew his chariot in the procession.

The military action required to maintain order must not overshadow Ashurbanipal's ability as an administrator. The empire prospered economically despite the threatened closure of the northern and eastern trade routes due to Lydian and Median expansions. Unfortunately, the sources are too scanty to follow his reign after 631 BC. Ashurbanipal's death is nowhere recorded, but it seems that he followed his father's precedent in bringing his sons Ashur-etel-ilani and Sin-shar-ishkun into co-regency, each with a separately defined authority. It is no indictment of his rule that his empire fell within two decades after his death; this was due to external pressures rather than to internal strife.

Personality and significance. Ashurbanipal was a person of religious zeal. He rebuilt or adorned most of the major shrines of Assyria and Babylonia, paying particular attention to the "House of Succession" and the Ishtar Temple at Nineveh. Many of his actions were guided by the omen reports, in which he took a personal and informed interest. He celebrated the New Year Festival, and one of his reliefs, showing him dining in a garden with his queen Ashur-sharrat, may illustrate this event. His younger brothers were priests in Haran and Ashur.

Ashurbanipal's outstanding contribution resulted from his academic interests. He assembled in Nineveh the first systematically collected and cataloged library in the ancient Middle East (of which approximately 20,720 Assyrian tablets and fragments have been preserved in the British Museum). At royal command, scribes searched out and collected or copied texts of every genre from temple libraries. These were added to the basic collection of tablets culled from Ashur, Calah, and Nineveh itself. The major group includes omen texts based on observations of events; on the behaviour and features of men, animals, and plants; and on the motions of the Sun, Moon, planets, and stars. Lexicographical texts list in dictionary form Sumerian, Akkadian, and other words, all essential to the scribal educational system. Ashurbanipal also collected many incantations, prayers, rituals, fables, proverbs, and other "canonical" and "extracanonical" texts. The traditional Mesopotamian epics—such as the stories of Creation, Gilgamesh, Irra, Etana, and Anzu—have survived mainly due to their preservation in his library. The presence of handbooks, scientific texts, and some folk tales (*The Poor Man of Nippur* was a precursor of one of the *Thousand and One Nights* tales of Baghdad) show that this library, of which only a fraction of the clay tablets has survived, was more than a mere reference library geared to the needs of diviners and others responsible for the King's spiritual security; it covered the whole range of Ashurbanipal's personal literary interests, and many works bear the royal mark of ownership in their colophons.

The King was a patron of the arts; he adorned his new and restored palaces at Nineveh with sculptures depicting the main historical and ceremonial events of his long reign. The style shows a remarkable development over that of his predecessors, and many bas-reliefs have an epic quality unparalleled in the ancient world, which may well be because of the influence of this active and vigorous personality.

(D.J.W.)

BIBLIOGRAPHY. M. Streck, *Assurbanipal und die letzten assyrischen Könige bis zum Untergange Ninivehs* (1916), a reliable study and discussion of the historical, religious, and epistolary evidence for the King and his family; T. Bauer, *Das Inschriftenwerk Assurbanipals* (1933), further discussion with additional texts; A.C. Piepkorn (ed.), *Historical Prism Inscriptions of Ashurbanipal* (1933), a literary analysis of a historical text with English translation; S.S. Ahmed, *Southern Mesopotamia in the Time of Ashurbanipal* (1968), a study of Ashurbanipal's relations with his brother in Babylon; R.D. Barnett, *The Sculptures of Ashurbanipal* (1971), an illustrated presentation of the bas-reliefs from the palace at Nineveh depicting the royal campaigns, hunting, and other activities.

Ashurnasirpal, Assyrian ASSUR-NASIR-APLI (Ashur Is Guardian of the Son), name of Assyrian kings grouped below chronologically and indicated by the symbol •.

• Ashurnasirpal I (fl. 11th century BC), king of Assyria 1050–32 BC, when it was at a low ebb in power and prosperity caused by widespread famine and the pressure of western desert nomads, against whom Ashurnasirpal warred constantly. His father, Shamshi-Adad IV, a son of Tiglath-pileser I, was placed on the throne of Assyria by the Babylonian king Adad-apal-iddina. The few inscriptions of Ashurnasirpal I that survive reflect the unhappy situation in Assyria during his reign.

• Ashurnasirpal II (fl. 9th century BC), king of Assyria 883–859 BC, whose major accomplishment was the consolidation of the conquests of his father, Tukulti-Ninurta II, leading to the establishment of the New Assyrian

Ashurnasirpal II, relief from Nimrūd; in the British Museum
By courtesy of the trustees of the British Museum

Empire. Although, by his own testimony, he was a brilliant general and administrator, he is perhaps best known for the brutal frankness with which he described the atrocities committed on his captives. The details of his reign are known almost entirely from his own inscriptions and the splendid reliefs discovered in the ruins of his palace at Calah (now Nimrūd, Iraq).

The annals of Ashurnasirpal II give a detailed account of the campaigns of his first six years as king and show him moving from one corner of his empire to another, putting down rebellions, reorganizing provinces, exacting tribute, and meeting opposition with calculated ruthlessness. In the east, Ashurnasirpal early in his reign publicly flayed the rebel governor of Nishtun at Arbela (modern Irbil, Iraq), and, after brief expeditions in 881–880 BC, he had no further trouble there.

In the north, he thwarted Aramaean pressure on the Assyrian city of Damdamusa by storming the rebel stronghold of Kinabu and ravaging the land of Nairi (Armenia). He organized a new Assyrian province of Tushhan to control the border, and there he received tribute from his father's former opponent Amme-ba'ali. In 879 BC, however, the tribes in the Kashiari hills revolted and murdered Amme-ba'ali. The Assyrian revenge was swift and ruthless. In the west, he subdued the Aramaeans, extracting submission from the powerful state of Bit-Adini, and subsequently marched unopposed to the Mediterranean Sea by way of Carchemish and the Orontes River, receiving tribute along the way and from the cities of Phoenicia.

Ashurnasirpal used the captives from his campaigns to rebuild the city of Calah, which had been founded by Shalmaneser I (1274–45 BC), but was then only a ruin. By 879 BC the main palace in the citadel, the temples of Ninurta and Enlil, shrines for other deities, and the city wall had been completed. Botanical gardens and a zoological garden had been laid out, and water supplies were assured by a canal from the Great Zab River. In 1951 a stela was discovered at the site commemorating a feast lasting 10 days for 69,574 persons to celebrate the official opening of the city when the King moved there from Nineveh in 879 BC.

BIBLIOGRAPHY. E.A.T.W. Budge and L.W. King (eds.), *Annals of the Kings of Assyria,* vol. 1 (1902), and D.D. Luckenbill, *Ancient Records of Assyria and Babylonia,* vol. 1 (1926).

Ashvaghosa (Sanskrit poet): *see* Aśvaghosa.

ashvamedha, also spelled ASHWAMEDHA (religious rite): *see* aśvamedha.

Ashwell, Lena (Margaret), original name LENA MARGARET POCOCK (b. Sept. 28, 1872, on board ship in the River Tyne, Eng.—d. March 13, 1957, London), actress and theatrical manager well known for her work in organizing entertainment for the troops at the front during World War I. In 1917 she was awarded the Order of the British Empire for her services.

Educated in Canada, Ashwell studied music at Lausanne, Switz., and at the Royal Academy of Music, London. Her voice proved inadequate, however, and she turned to the stage in 1892. She established her reputation as an actress in Henry Arthur Jones's *Mrs. Dane's Defence* in 1900. Other notable successes were in a 1903 production of *The Darling of the Gods* and *Leah Kleschna* in 1905. She managed the Kingsway Theatre, London, from 1907 to 1915, after which she began organizing companies of entertainers for the troops in World War I. After the war she formed the Once-a-Week Players, later known as the Lena Ashwell Players, and produced drama at the Century Theatre, London, from 1924 to 1929.

Ashwell wrote about her war work in *Modern Troubadours* (1922) and also wrote an autobiography, *Myself a Player* (1936).

Asia, world's largest and most diverse continent, covering three-fifths of the land area on Earth, or approximately 17,225,709 sq mi (44,614,399 sq km). It is situated between latitude 85° N and 10° S and longitude 25° E and 170° W. The Asian mainland extends for about 6,000 mi (9,600 km) from east to west and 4,000 mi from north to south. The continent is bounded on the north by the Arctic Ocean, on the east by the Pacific Ocean, and on the south by the Indian Ocean; the western boundary, with Europe, runs roughly north-south along the eastern Ural Mountains, the Emba River, the Caspian Sea, the Kuma and Manych rivers, the Black Sea, the Aegean Sea, the Mediterranean Sea, and the Red Sea. The islands of Sri Lanka and Taiwan and the archipelagoes of Indonesia, the Philippines, and Japan also form part of Asia, the most populous of the continents. Its total population in 1981 was estimated at 2,665,412,000.

For additional information about Asia, *see* MACROPAEDIA: Asia.

The land. Elevations in Asia range from 29,028 ft (8,848 m) above sea level at Mt. Everest to 1,300 ft below sea level at the Dead Sea. Mountains and high plateaus predominate; approximately two-thirds of the land is above 1,600 ft, and about one-fifth is above 10,000 ft in elevation. The highest mountains (21,-000 to 24,000 ft), located in an 850,000-sq-mi area in Central Asia, can be grouped into two large belts. The first extends from the Chukchi Peninsula in the north to the mountains of southern Siberia (the Stanovoy Uplands and the Altai); the second belt comprises the highest mountain ranges in the world (the South Asian highlands, the Pamirs, the Karakorams, the Himalayas, and the Arakan Yoma). The Kunlun, Nan Shan, and the Tsinling mountains in the east and the Pamirs and the Armenian highlands in the west encompass the interior plateaus of Tibet, Iran, and Anatolia. The island chains in the east and southeast are also predominantly mountainous and are dotted with volcanoes.

Low plains occupy about one-fourth of Asia and include the plains of northern and western Siberia, Turan, Mesopotamia, northern India, and Southeast Asia. Tablelands and plateaus include the Arabian Plateau in the west, the Deccan Plateau in the south, and the Indo-Pacific Plateau in the east. Of the many desert regions, the largest ones are the Thar in India and Pakistan, the Takla Makan in China, the Rub' al-Khali in Saudi Arabia, and the Gobi in Mongolia and China.

Asia's hydrology is dominated by some of the longest rivers in the world, containing enormous hydroelectric reserves. Rivers, including the Euphrates, Tigris, Indus, Ganges, Brahmaputra, and Irrawaddy in the south, drain about half of the continent into the Indian Ocean; the Yangtze (Asia's longest river [3,716 mi]), Huang Ho, and Mekong drain into the Pacific Ocean. The size of these rivers varies considerably with the season, and flooding is a recurrent phenomenon. The Ob, Yenisey, and Lena rivers drain into the Arctic Ocean in the north, freeze over every winter, and flood every spring. Central and western parts of Asia are either drained into small inland basins or have no surface drainage. The largest inland basin is the Tarim Basin in China (164,000 sq mi); others are found in Afghanistan, Iran, and Jordan. The Caspian Sea is the world's largest body of inland water, covering 143,000 sq mi; the Aral and the Dead seas are Asia's other major saltwater lakes. All three have falling water levels as the surrounding nations develop rivers draining into them. The major freshwater lakes are Baikal and Wular.

Asia's climate is characterized by extreme annual temperature ranges. In the Gobi the temperature falls to −40° F (−40° C) in winter and climbs to 151° F (66° C) in summer. Temperatures also vary greatly according to regions and elevation. The average January temperature is below −4° F (−20° C) in most of Siberia (reaching −58° F [−50° C] in the Verkhoyansk region, one of the coldest in the world) and about 72° F (22° C) south of the Tropic of Cancer. The average July temperature ranges from more than 95° F (35° C) in parts of the southwest to less than 50° F (10° C) in the north. The Persian Gulf area is one of the hottest in the world, with summer (shade) temperatures reaching 122° F (50° C). About two-fifths of the continent (southwest and central) is dry, receiving less than 10 in. (250 mm) of annual rainfall, and about one-third (southeast), receives adequate rainfall of more than 45 in. annually. The maritime slopes of South and East Asia receive 80 to 120 in. of rainfall a year, and northeastern India (Cherrapunji receives 450 in. annually) is one of the wettest regions on Earth.

Vegetation types range from Arctic permafrost and tundra meadows along the northern coast and in Siberia to tropical rain forests in the southeast. Between these two extremes are extensive coniferous taiga forests (north), deciduous and mixed forests (south), vast steppes (central), and xerophytic vegetation (southwest). The fauna of Asia also varies by latitude and elevation. Migratory birds, caribou, fox, seal, walrus, and polar bear are found along the Arctic coast; elk, musk deer, brown bear, lynx, sable, and hare dwell in the taiga forests; antelope, wild sheep and goat, cheetah, hyena, jackal, and reptiles are characteristic of the steppes and deserts; the wild yak, snow leopard, marmot, and the Siberian wild dog abound in the Central Asian highlands; deer, raccoon, black bear, panda, tiger, and monkey dwell in eastern Asia; and elephant, rhinoceros, leopard, gibbon, crocodile, cobra, and peacock are found in South Asia. Wildlife in many areas, however, has become endangered because of encroaching development, slash-and-burn agriculture, poaching, and overhunting.

Despite large expanses of mountainous, Arctic, and desert wasteland, more than 10 percent of Asia's vast land area is arable. At least two-thirds of this is devoted to basic cereal and tuber crops (more than two-fifths to rice and wheat alone). About one-fifth of the continent is pasture or range land, supporting at least a third of the world's cattle, more than a fourth of its sheep, and nearly three-fifths of its goats. Despite afforestation and reforestation efforts by several countries, the overall size of forested and wooded areas remained a fairly constant 30 percent of the total land area throughout the 1970s because of overcutting in other nations.

Asia is well-endowed with nearly every mineral resource required by modern industrial society. In the early 1980s, the continent's reserves of antimony, magnesium, tin, and tungsten were estimated at more than half of world totals. Reserves of bismuth, cobalt, gold, titanium, iron, manganese, mercury, nickel, vanadium, and zirconium accounted for at least a third of their respective global reserves. These minerals are not evenly distributed throughout the continent, but are concentrated within one or two (and seldom more than three) countries. Because the Soviet Union has such a large proportion of the continent's mineral reserves within its national territory (much of which lies within Europe), reserve values are only roughly relevant to the Asian continent as a whole. Asia's fossil fuel endowment is immense, accounting for more than two-thirds of the global reserves of both petroleum and natural gas, and for as much as half of the coal resources; but their concentration is even more acute. Nearly 80 percent of the continent's petroleum reserves are located along the Persian Gulf, and almost 60 percent of its natural gas and half its economic reserves of coal are located in the Soviet Union.

The people. During the early 1980s Asia had more than half of the world's population.

The average annual growth rate for Asian countries is between 1.4 and 2.2 percent. At this rate, it is estimated that Asia's population will increase by 500,000,000 during the 1980s, possibly reaching a population of more than 3,000,000,000 by AD 2000. This will cause serious difficulties in terms of standards of living and economic development. The dependent age groups (younger than 15 and older than 60) are supported by a working-age group that consists of only slightly more than half of the population.

During the early 1980s Asia had the third highest birth rate in the world after Africa and the Americas. The average birth rate was 29 per 1,000 population, ranging from 13 per 1,000 in Japan to 49 per 1,000 in Oman. South Asia's birth rate was 37 per 1,000, and East Asia's was 21 per 1,000. Soviet Asia's birth rates remain high. In India, Sri Lanka, and some predominantly Muslim countries, males outnumber females in all age groups. The cause for this is unknown, but it might be related to the custom of early marriage in which young women have a high mortality rate in childbirth. Family planning programs have been effective in several Asian countries, notably Japan. Between 1950 and 1980 Asia's overall birth rate fell by 41 percent. A significant decline in the continent's death rate, which ranges from 29 deaths per 1,000 in Kampuchea to 3 per 1,000 in Kuwait, can be largely attributed to improved disease control.

Asia's average population density of 158 persons per sq mi (61 per sq km) is lower than Europe's (168 per sq mi), but regional population concentrations are extremely high. In South and East Asia the lowland populations exceed 2,000 persons per sq mi, and China's population density averages 250 persons per sq mi. Both the U.S.S.R. and China are conducting relocation programs from heavily populated areas.

Asian peoples have tended to settle in river valleys where soil is fertile. About 60 percent of the population is rural, but rapid migration from rural areas to industrial cities in the 20th century years has worsened urban slum conditions.

Southwest Asia, comprising a large part of the Middle East, is predominantly urban with more than 70 percent of the people living in cities in most of the countries. In East Asia more than 70 percent of the populations of Japan, Hong Kong, and Macao live in urban areas.

Distribution of ethnic groups has changed since the Soviet Union and China gained political and economic control over Siberia and Central Asia. Smaller ethnic groups have been absorbed into larger ones, as in the case of the Yukaghir and Kara Kirgiz of Siberia who were assimilated into Russian culture; and some have been relocated, as with the Ainu of northern Japan, who were gathered into "cultural villages" in the south that have become tourist attractions.

Patterns of ethnic groupings in southwestern Asia have been significantly altered with industrial modernization and with the impact of petroleum exploitation on the Arabian Peninsula. After the establishment of the state of Israel in 1948, 1,500,000 Jews migrated there from other parts of the world.

Traditionally, the eight basic language groups in Asia were Turkic, Slavic, Tungusic, Chinese, Tibeto-Burman, Indo-Aryan, Iranian, and Mongol. Russian and Chinese are becoming increasingly widespread, and Mandarin Chinese is the world's leading language by number of speakers. In India, regional languages effectively delineate political territories; Hindi and English are the official languages. The number of Tungusic speakers has decreased. Although many Paleo-Siberian (Paleo-Asiatic) languages are dying out, speakers of the Uzbek and Tadzhik languages are increasing in numbers.

The economy. Japan and Soviet Asia are the dominant economic powers of the continent, and together account for more than one-half of its economic output. Asia's aggregate gross national product (GNP) approached $2,300,000,000,000 in 1980; average per capita income for all of Asia exceeded $900, and ranged from less than $300 in Bhutan and surrounding countries to more than $20,000 in certain oil-exporting countries of the Persian Gulf. The economies of most Asian countries are not fully industrialized, and income tends to be unevenly distributed between the large mass of the poor and a small number of wealthy families. The economies of most Southwest Asian (Middle Eastern) countries are based largely on traditional agriculture and the production and export of petroleum; the manufacturing sector is limited in large part to traditional artisanship and petrochemical industries. Subsistence farming predominates in South Asia, whose manufacturing industries are of negligible importance outside India and Pakistan. Southeast Asia exports rice and cash crops such as rubber, copra, and kapok; most manufacturing industries centre on processing domestic raw materials and assembling consumer goods. Extensive land reform was implemented in Taiwan, China, North Korea, South Korea, and Japan after 1945 and was accompanied by rapid industrialization; the market economies of East Asia are heavily dependent on exports of manufactures. Industries in Soviet Asia are concentrated around the region's vast deposits of petroleum, natural gas, coal, and other minerals, and suffer from an acute shortage of manpower.

Agriculture employs more than 50 percent of the overall Asian work force; the percentage in Japan, Hong Kong, Singapore, Lebanon, Israel, and Kuwait is significantly lower and comparable to that in industrialized European countries. The abundance of cheap labour in most Asian countries has kept investments in agricultural machinery and fertilizers generally low. Arable land is scarce in Southwest Asia and is commonly worked by tenant farmers in small plots; domestic animals ordinarily graze on scrubland. Traditional patterns of pastoral nomadism persist in isolated regions of Southwest and Central Asia. Higher inputs of chemical fertilizer, irrigation, improved strains of seeds, and machinery have greatly increased agricultural yields in South Asia, but gains in production have been offset in large part by the rapid growth of the population. Land reform in Japan, Taiwan, and South Korea has primarily benefitted peasant families, who were allotted small private farms after 1945. Agriculture in North Korea, Vietnam, China, Mongolia, and Soviet Asia is collectivized.

Agricultural production meets domestic demand in most Asian countries, but fails to reach much of the population because rural roads are poorly maintained. Rice is the chief staple of southern Asia; wheat is widely cultivated in western India, Southwest Asia, Soviet Asia, and northern China. The productivity of Asian livestock tends to be extremely low because fodder is in short supply.

Fish are a major source of protein in Asia, and are landed primarily inshore. Offshore fisheries are exploited by Japan, China, India, South Korea, and Thailand, which maintain large fleets of trawlers. Aquaculture is highly developed in China, India, Japan, South Korea, Indonesia, the Philippines, Malaysia, Hong Kong, Singapore, Thailand, and Bangladesh. Relatively few Asian countries have the facilities to can or freeze large quantities of fish.

Soviet Asia, the countries of the Persian Gulf, China, and Indonesia produce up to one-half of the world's petroleum and up to one-third of its natural gas. Coal is mined principally in China (the world's largest producer of coal after the U.S. and the Soviet Union), Soviet Asia, India, and North Korea. Japan, which is attempting to reduce costly imports of petroleum, is the world's leading importer of coal. Malaysia, Thailand, and Indonesia are important producers of tin and belong to the International Tin Council. China is the world's largest producer and exporter of tungsten; large quantities of tungsten are also produced in South Korea, North Korea, and Thailand.

The manufacturing sector is relatively underdeveloped in most Asian countries and is dominated by light industries. Japan and Soviet Asia are fully industrialized; production of consumer and most capital goods meets domestic demand in China and India. South Korea, Taiwan, Hong Kong, Singapore, and the Philippines specialize in the manufacture of consumer goods for export. Southwest Asian countries must import most machinery and motor vehicles; Turkey, Iran, and Israel assemble motors and electrical machinery on a large-scale basis. Petrochemical industries are highly developed along the Persian Gulf.

Many Asian labour unions were formed to represent particular religious and ethnic groups; they often coalesced in association with nationalist movements. Most Arab unions are affiliated with the International Confederation of Arab Trade Unions (founded in 1956); Israeli unions are affiliated with various Asian regional unions. The Asian Regional Organization of the International Confederation of Free Trade Unions was established in 1951, and represents national unions in the non-Communist countries of Asia and Australia.

Public revenues in most Asian countries are derived largely from indirect taxes, which place a disproportionately high burden on the poor and limit public expenditures. Domestic savings have been kept low in most Asian countries by high rates of inflation. Foreign aid is an important source of public revenue in developing Asian countries, whose debt-service ratio (external debt service to exports) frequently exceeds 10 percent.

Administrative and social conditions. Non-democratic forms of government predominate, ranging from the absolute monarchies characteristic of Southwest Asia, to the military and martial law regimes found throughout the continent, to the one-party Communist states, notably the Soviet Union and the People's Republic of China. Multi-party parliamentary and presidential democracies are also common forms of government, operating in such countries as Israel, India, Sri Lanka, Malaysia, Indonesia, and Japan. The only remaining European colonial holdings in Asia are Hong Kong and Brunei (U.K.) and Macau (Portugal). The governments of Afghanistan and Kampuchea (Cambodia), the former supported by Soviet troops and the latter by Vietnamese troops, and the government of Taiwan, which claims to represent both the island and mainland China, are not recognized by the United Nations.

In the Islāmic countries, the legal code is based on Islāmic law, the Sharī'ah, while a number of countries derive their legal systems from their former colonial powers. In the Communist states, the judicial system is controlled and supervised by the party and the legal code is based on socialist principles; there is no equivalent to the Western concepts of habeus corpus and trial by jury.

There are some regional organizations, such as the Arab League, the Gulf Cooperation Council, and the Association of Southeast Asian Nations, that promote political and military cooperation. The Soviet Union and China are the dominant military powers of the continent and they or their proxies maintain troops in a number of Communist and non-Communist countries. Western powers also supply military training, arms, and troops to a number of Asian countries.

With the exception of the most developed countries, such as Japan and Israel, and most of the Communist states, most countries have not developed comprehensive social-welfare programs. Health conditions in Asian countries are generally poor; exceptions include Japan, Israel, Cyprus, Singapore, Taiwan, Brunei, Hong Kong, and the Soviet Union. As for the rest of the continent, already inadequate health services are generally concentrated in larger cities, leaving many Asians without access to modern medical care. Large investment in the construction of facilities and the training of medical personnel by the petroleum-rich countries and some of the Communist countries has produced a marked improvement in health services. Extremely poor sanitation throughout most of the continent contributes to a high incidence of infectious and parasitic diseases, particularly malaria, tuberculosis, gastrointestinal diseases, typhoid fever, influenza, pneumonia, bronchitis, and childhood diseases. Malnutrition is prevalent in the less developed countries. Average life expectancy ranges from 40 years in Afghanistan, Bhutan, and Nepal to 70 or more years in Cyprus, Japan, Taiwan, Hong Kong, and the Soviet Union. Infant mortality ranges from relatively high rates of 150 or more per 1,000 live births in Kampuchea, Afghanistan, Bhutan, and Nepal to relatively low rates of 20 or fewer in Japan, Singapore, Israel, Hong Kong, Cyprus, and Brunei.

Most Asian countries have introduced compulsory education, although some countries lack the facilities needed for its implementation. Though generally low, literacy tends to be higher in eastern than in western countries, where Islāmic traditions commonly produce still lower literacy among women. The Communist countries place a high priority on educational development, and school enrollment ratios are high, especially relative to their level of economic development.

The press and broadcast media of most Asian countries are government-controlled. Exceptions include Japan, Israel, India, Hong Kong, and Cyprus, whose media are free from government censorship, and Lebanon, Kuwait, Indonesia, and Taiwan, whose media exercise a limited degree of freedom.

Cultural life. The cultures of Southwest Asia are both Arabic and Islāmic. Literature, considered the preeminent art form, experienced a revival in the 19th century, when Western literary forms, the novel and short story, were added to the classical forms of poetry and formal prose. Visual arts are limited by Islāmic tenets to geometric, floral, and abstract designs and to calligraphy. Surviving traditional arts include basketweaving, brass and copper metalworking, pottery, and leatherwork.

The cultures of South Asia show similarities in music, dance, and literary ideals. Ancient sculpture and painting are seen in the colossal Buddhist images and temples. Theatre and dance stem principally from Indian traditions. Dance forms include the classical dance-drama, in which the actor dances out a story through a complex gesture language.

In Southeast Asia the performing and visual arts are among the most distinctive and original of the region's many artistic forms. In all areas drama, dance, mime, music, song, and narrative are integrated into composite forms, often with masks or in the form of puppetry.

Central Asian culture is an amalgamation of traditional and modern socialist elements. Buddhist monastic dances, known as 'Cham, and Buddhist morality plays contrast with the developing socialist and revolutionary literature.

East Asian cultures, long influenced by China, have inherited many ancient forms of literature, fine arts, and folk arts, such as calligraphy, Chinese opera, and the ceramics and lacquerwork. The literatures and graphic arts of China and North Korea embody the principles of Socialist Realism and do not depart from Party orthodoxy.

History. Asia, according to evidence discovered since the mid-20th century, has been displaced by sub-Saharan Africa as the cradle of mankind. Nevertheless, *Homo erectus* hominids appeared in East Asia some 500,000 to 200,000 years ago, followed by *Homo sapiens neanderthalensis* hominids, and subsequently by *Homo sapiens sapiens* (modern man) about 40,000 years ago. Migrations began possibly as early as 30,000 years ago in Southwest Asia, as peoples, primarily Caucasoid, travelled toward Europe and Central Asia. Mongoloid peoples began migrating first into North and South America during the glacial epochs, and later into Central Asia toward Europe from the region of North China and the Mongolian Plateau, mixing with Caucasoid inhabitants, and finally moving on from China toward Southeast Asia.

The origins, development, and diffusion of food production is complicated by contemporary evidence challenging the traditional view of the Middle East as the cultural hearth. Hunting and gathering gave way to farming and pastoralism in this region between 8500 and 7000 BC. Domesticated sheep, goats, and cattle appeared in eastern Turkey, Iraq, Iran, and Afghanistan between 9000 and 6000 BC along with early steps toward the cultivation of wild grains. Evidence of horticulture exists in Thailand (*c.* 10,000 BC) and on Taiwan (*c.* 9000 BC) in the form of slash-and-burn cultivation. Throughout East and Southeast Asia people were cultivating millet, buckwheat, beans, and probably rice by 2500 BC.

One of the earliest civilizations to use writing developed in the Tigris–Euphrates river valleys between 3500 and 3000 BC. Civilization in the Indus Valley and in northern Syria followed about 2500 BC. The South Chinese and Southeast Asians developed maritime skills, and by about 2500 BC sea trade probably extended as far west as Bengal. Chinese urban civilization began with the Shang or Yin dynasty (*c.* 1766–1122 BC) and continued under the Chou (*c.* 1122–221 BC), who marched in from the west, absorbed much of the Shang, and developed the Chinese social and cultural patterns still recognized today. Indo-European-speaking peoples (Aryans), introducing the horse, began to invade India from the west about 1700 BC, contributing to the destruction of the Bronze Age civilization of the Indus Valley; they also ruled as the Kassites of Mesopotamia. Developing the Vedic culture, they introduced iron to India around the 7th or 6th century BC. The Vedic period was succeeded by a plethora of dynasties and states, including the Mauryan Empire (*c.* 321–*c.* 185 BC).

Urban civilizations became firmly established, their economies based then as now primarily on agriculture. A succession of empires and charismatic tribal rulers united tribes and states, spreading their political mantles as far as military power, diplomacy and duplicity, and marital alliances could carry them. A few such individuals left lasting monuments—or ruins—on the landscape. Alexander the Great conquered the Persian Empire and smashed through Afghanistan, moving successfully into Central Asia and down the Punjab in the 4th century BC. Hellenism resulted; Greco-Bactrian and Indo-Greek kingdoms lasted well into the 1st century BC, and Buddhism, after being influenced by Greco-Roman humanism, spread along the Silk Road between China and the Mediterranean. Trade, by land and sea, prospered between East and West Asia during the period of Greek and Roman control of the Middle East. Christianity arose during this time in Palestine and spread. More influential in Asia was the rise of Islām in the 7th century AD, challenging the ideals and power of the Christian Byzantine Empire. In the 13th century Genghis Khan and his Mongol successors united most of Asia under their rule, controlling China, Central Asia, much of Southwest Asia, and parts of eastern Europe. In the 14th century Timur conquered an area that extended from Mongolia to the Mediterranean, and he fostered a cultural renaissance in Central Asia. China received cultural stimulation from its perennial conflicts with nomads beyond the Great Wall. In the 15th century Muslim Turks destroyed the remnants of the Byzantine Empire and established a Middle Eastern kingdom that endured into the 20th century.

Political insecurity, particularly after the Turco-Mongol invasions, interrupted commerce on the Silk Road and sent European navigators around the South African cape in search of new routes to the East. Beginning in the 19th century, European imperialism began to replace Asian imperialism, either by colonizing areas or by controlling them through zones of influence. Tsarist Russia drove to the Pacific Ocean, conquering the hunter-fishermen of Siberia and the ancient Muslim khanates of Central Asia; after the Russian Revolution, Communists replaced the Tsarists. The British gained control of the Indian subcontinent; the French moved into Indochina; the Dutch occupied the East Indies; and the Spanish ruled the Philippines until the U.S. took over after the Spanish-American War. China, culturally and politically introverted, was unable to resist foreign domination in the 19th and 20th centuries. Japan at first moved slowly from its self-imposed isolation, but it then moved rapidly to an imperialism that was ultimately ended by military defeat in World War II.

After the war European imperialism largely vanished as former colonies gained independence. (The U.S. had initiated in 1934 the process of independence for the Philippines, completed in 1946.) Asia has subsequently divided into pro-Western, Communist, and nonaligned groups. Competition developed within the Communist camp, first between China and the Soviet Union, and subsequently in Southeast Asia where Communist allies of the Chinese and Soviets came into conflict. The nonaligned countries included the Muslim and Arab states, India, and much of the East Indies, although the Soviet Union and U.S. competed for influence in many of these nations, and the Soviet Union imposed its direct control of Afghanistan in 1979. Pro-Western nations included the economic giant Japan and South Korea, Taiwan, and Thailand.

A list of the abbreviations used in the MICROPAEDIA *will be found at the end of this volume*

Asia, in antiquity, the first and westernmost Roman province in Asia Minor, stretching at its greatest extent from the Aegean coast in the west to a point beyond Philomelium (modern Akşehır) in the east and from the Sea of Marmara in the north to the strait between Rhodes and the mainland in the south. The province was first constituted when Attalus III, king of Pergamum, bequeathed his dominions to the Romans in 133 BC. At that time the province contained many different communities at different stages of development.

The province was rich in natural resources, and its dyestuffs and woollen textiles were famous. Under the Roman Republic, however, its prosperity was ruined by commercial exploitation, taxation, and war, so that its advance toward Hellenization and urbanization, begun under the Seleucid and Pergamene kings, was impeded.

Recovery under the empire was rapid. Asia was a peaceful province and was under senatorial jurisdiction, governed from Ephesus by a proconsul of consular rank (under the republic the governor had usually been a former praetor). The provincial assembly, called the *koinon* of Asia, to which the cities sent representatives, met annually in different cities, chose the officials known as Asiarchs, passed resolutions, made appeals, and sent deputations on provincial matters.

The great cities of Asia were leading educational and cultural centres. Important Christian communities and bishoprics grew up within the province, as did important heresies, such as Montanism. During the 3rd and 4th centuries AD the province lost much of its economic importance as the development of the Balkan provinces, military needs, and the founding of Constantinople turned the empire's main lines of communication away from the Aegean and toward the northwest. Yet the province's reserves of products and manpower and its relative immunity from devastation made it an important factor in the survival of the Eastern Roman Empire. Under Diocletian (reigned AD 284–305) it was divided into seven smaller provinces.

Asia Minor: *see* Anatolia.

Asian Development Bank (ADB), organization established under the auspices of ESCAP (the United Nations Economic and Social Commission for Asia and the Pacific) that entered into force in August 1966. Thirty "regional" countries of South and East Asia and the South Pacific and 14 "nonregional" countries of western Europe and North America constitute the membership. Each member appoints a governor and an alternate who combine to form the Board of Governors, which in turn selects a 12-member operating Board of Directors. ADB is the executive agency for the UN Development Programme authorized to supervise national and regional projects. The headquarters are in Manila.

ADB aims to foster economic growth within the region by administering direct loans or technical assistance to any member group. Such activities facilitate project preparation and implementation, policy formation, institutional building, and sectoral studies.

Asian flu: *see* influenza.

Asian Games, regional games sponsored by the International Amateur Athletic Federation (IAAF) for men and women athletes (track and field) from Asian countries affiliated with the IAAF. The International Olympic Committee also grants its patronage.

The first games were held in 1951 at New Delhi; from 1954 they were held every four years. The early Games had political difficulties: Pakistan objected to the site of the first Games, and the People's Republic of China objected to the participation of the Nationalist Chinese from Taiwan. The People's Republic objected again in 1962 to the inclusion of the Nationalist Chinese, and they were excluded; but the People's Republic did not participate. In the same games the Arab states objected to the participation of Israel, which was also excluded. In 1966 Israel competed, as did the Nationalist Chinese, in the games held in Thailand, and there was an Arab boycott; there were also riots at these games. In 1963 the Asian Communist countries had formed GANEFO (Games for the New Emerging Countries), which held games without IAAF approval in 1966 and 1969. In general, GANEFO performances were better than those of the Asian Games. In the 1970s the Communist countries rejoined the games. Throughout the history of the Asian Games, Japan has dominated the competition.

Asian geographical race: *see* Mongoloid geographical race.

Asiatic black bear, also called HIMALAYAN BEAR, TIBETAN BEAR, or MOON BEAR (*Selenarctos thibetanus*), Central and East Asian bear of the family Ursidae. It raids crops and occasionally attacks domestic animals, is considered sacred by Japanese aboriginals (Ainus), and is sought by the Chinese for the supposedly medicinal effects of its bone and flesh. It has a glossy black (sometimes brownish) coat,

Asiatic black bear (*Selenarctos thibetanus*)
Painting by Richard Ellis

with a whitish mark shaped like a crescent moon on the chest. Long, coarse neck and shoulder hair forms a modified mane.

The Asiatic black bear lives in forest and brushland. It ranges elevations up to 3,600 metres (11,800 feet) during the summer, becoming fat by fall. It spends the winter at an elevation of 1,500 m or less and may sleep for much of the time. The adult weighs about 110 kilograms (242 pounds); its length averages about 130–160 centimetres (52–64 inches), in addition to a 7–10-cm tail. A litter, normally of two cubs, follows the six-month gestation period.

Asiatic high: *see* Siberian anticyclone.

Asiatic low, large atmospheric low-pressure centre that develops over southwestern Asia in summer. The region's high summer temperatures cause the equatorial low-pressure belt to shift northward and form the Asiatic low; its average sea-level pressure in July is 999 millibars (29.5 inches of mercury). The low's counterclockwise circulation and its location northwest of India produce the summer monsoon winds from the southwest over the Indian subcontinent.

Asiatic Society of Bengal, society founded on Jan. 15, 1784, by Sir William Jones, a British lawyer and Orientalist, to encourage Oriental studies. At its founding, Jones delivered the first of a famous series of discourses.

The Asiatic Society had the support and encouragement of Warren Hastings, the governor general of Bengal (1772–85), though he declined its presidency. Until Jones's death (1794) it was the vehicle for his ideas about the importance of Hindu culture and learning and about the vital role of Sanskrit in the Aryan languages.

asiento de negros (Spanish: "Negroes' contract"), between the early 16th and the mid-18th century, an agreement between the Spanish crown and a private person or another sovereign power by which the latter was granted a monopoly in supplying African slaves for the Spanish colonies in the Americas. The contractor (*asentista*) agreed to pay a certain amount of money for the monopoly and to deliver a stipulated number of male and female slaves for sale in the American markets. The first such contractor was a Genoese company that in 1517 agreed to supply 1,000 slaves over an eight-year period. In 1528 an agreement was reached with a German firm to supply 4,000 slaves. For its monopoly the firm paid 20,000 ducats annually to the crown. Each slave was sold at a price not exceeding 45 ducats.

Until the 18th century individual Spaniards, as well as Portugal, France, and Great Britain, entered into such contracts. In spite of heavy taxation, government interference, and unsettled trade conditions, all of which greatly curtailed the profitability of *asientos,* foreigners, nevertheless, sought them because they provided the chance to share in the Spanish-American trade and, especially, to acquire some of the bullion produced by the slave trade.

The last and most notable *asiento* was that granted to the British South Sea Company, in 1713, by a provision in the Treaty of Utrecht. This contract entitled the company to send 4,800 slaves to Spanish America annually for 30 years and to send one ship (*navío de permiso*) each year to engage in general trade. The company found the enterprise unprofitable because war and other adverse conditions usually prevented importation to the American markets while an annual tax to the Spanish crown of £34,000 for the first 4,000 slaves had to be paid whether or not they were imported. Also, the legal trade was accompanied by illicit traffic that continually exacerbated Spanish–British relations, leading to the War of Jenkins' Ear in 1739. This disrupted the profitable British trade with peninsular Spain. Spain renewed the *asiento* at the Treaty of Aix-la-Chapelle in 1748, but two years later the British relinquished their rights in exchange for a payment of £100,000 from Spain. Between 1600 and 1750 an estimated 450,000 Africans were dispatched to Spanish America under the *asiento* system.

Aşık Paşa, in full ALÂEDDİN ALİ AŞIK PAŞA, also spelled ʿĀSHIQ PASHA (b. *c.* 1272—d. 1333, Kırşehir, Seljuq Empire), poet who was one of the most important figures in early Turkish literature.

Very little about his life is known. A wealthy and respected figure in his community, he apparently was also a very religious *shaykh* (mystic leader, hence his name, Aşık, which means lover, given to an ecstatic mystic; *i.e.,* a lover of God). Of the many legends about Aşık Paşa's life, one states that, although he was a rich man, he was, nevertheless, a devout Ṣūfī (Muslim mystic) at heart.

His most famous work is the *Gharībnāmeh,* a long didactic, mystical poem written in over 11,000 *maṣnavī* (rhymed couplets) and divided into 10 chapters, each with 10 subsections. Each of the chapters is associated with a subject in relation to its number. For example, the fifth chapter deals with the five senses; the seventh, with the seven planets; and so on. The underlying theme is a mystical, philosophical one, and there are many moral precepts supported by examples and quotations from the holy book of Islām, the Qur'ān, and the Ḥadīth (the sayings of the prophet, Muḥammad). Although the work is not considered great poetry, it is important as representing a staunch orthodox Muslim point of view during a period when a great number of heterodox Muslim sects flourished in Anatolia. In addition, it is an interesting document from a linguistic standpoint, because it is one of the earliest examples of an Ottoman Turkish work, written at a time when Turkish was beginning to emerge as a literary language in Anatolia.

The *Faqrnāmeh* ("The Book of Poverty") is also attributed to the poet. Introduced by the famous Ḥadīth "poverty is my pride," this poem of 160 rhymed couplets deals with poverty and humility, the ideal ethic of the Muslim mystic. Aşık Paşa at his death was a respected and revered figure, and his tomb has long been a magnet for pilgrims.

Aşıkpaşazâde, also called AŞIKI, original name DERVIS AHMET IBN ŞEYH YAHYA IBN ŞEYH SALMAN IBN AŞIK PAŞA (b. 1400, Amasya, Ottoman Empire—d. after 1484,

Constantinople), one of the most important early Ottoman historians. The great-grandson of the famous mystic poet of Anatolia, Aşık Paşa, Aşıkpaşazâde also had affiliations with a Muslim mystical order.

Very little is known about his early life. In 1413 he claimed to have met a certain Yahşi Fakih, whose early Ottoman history he utilized when writing his own many years later. In about 1437 he made the pilgrimage to Mecca, and, during the reigns of the Ottoman sultans Murad II (1421–51) and Mehmed II (1451–81), the historian took part in the Ottoman raids on Christian lands in the Balkans. Later, in Constantinople, he recorded the events he had either seen or heard about in his active and long life. His popular *Tevârih-i Âl-i Osman* ("The Chronicles of the House of Osman"), written in a vivid and simple narrative style, was meant, no doubt, to be read aloud. At the end of many chapters there are questions and answers as though to clarify the material for the listener. Although the source for the first half of the work is the history of the above-mentioned Yahşi Fakih and a continuation of that work, the rest is what Aşıkpaşazâde recorded from his own experience over the years.

Asilah, also called ARZILA, Spanish ARCILA, city on the Atlantic coast of western Morocco in Tétouan province. Built on the site of an ancient Phoenician-Carthaginian settlement (Zili), it later fell to the Romans. It passed to the Idrīsids, who in the early 11th century repulsed several attacks by Normans. From AD 972 on it was dominated by the Marīnids, until in 1471 the Portuguese occupied Asilah, which they fortified as a military base (the walls of which remain). The Spaniards followed the Portuguese (who in 1578 had been decimated by ʿAbd al-Malik at the Battle of the Three Kings) but ceded the town to Moulay Aḥmad al-Manṣūr in 1589. Thereafter, it was peopled by migrants from the Rif Mountains. In 1911 the Spaniards reoccupied the city, which remained part of Spanish Morocco until it was returned to the Moroccan kingdom in 1956. Asilah is now a fishing port and a trading centre for cereals, cattle, and sheep. Pop. (1971) 14,074.

Asimov, Isaac (b. Jan. 2, 1920, Petrovichi, Russia), U.S. biochemist and author, a highly successful and prolific writer of science fiction and of science books for laymen. He has published more than 200 volumes.

Asimov was brought to the United States at the age of three. He grew up in Brooklyn, N.Y., graduating from Columbia University in 1939 and taking a Ph.D. there in 1947. He then joined the faculty of Boston University, with which he remained associated thereafter, although, from 1958 on, his professorship was nominal, without stipend and without teaching or other duties.

He began contributing stories to science fiction magazines in 1939 and in 1950 published his first book, *Pebble in the Sky.* A trilogy, *Foundation, Foundation and Empire,* and *Second Foundation* (1951–53), won the Hugo award in science fiction. Other novels and collections of stories included *I, Robot* (1950), *The Stars Like Dust* (1951), *The Currents of Space* (1952), *The Caves of Steel* (1954), *The Naked Sun* (1957), and *Earth Is Room Enough* (1957). Among his books on various topics in science, written with lucidity and humour, are *The Chemicals of Life* (1954), *Inside the Atom* (1956), *The World of Nitrogen* (1958), *Life and Energy* (1962), *The Human Brain* (1964), *The Neutrino* (1966), *Science, Numbers and I* (1968), *Our World in Space* (1974), and *Views of the Universe* (1981).

Asimov also began writing his life story: *In Memory Yet Green: The Autobiography of Isaac Asimov, 1920–1954* appeared in 1979, followed the next year by *In Joy Still Felt: The Autobiography of Isaac Asimov, 1954–1978.*

Asinara Island, Italian ISOLA ASINARA, island lying in the Mediterranean Sea off the northwest coast of Sardinia. It has an area of 20 sq mi (52 sq km) and rises to 1,335 ft (407 m). The island is the site of one of Italy's top-security prisons. Pop. (1971) 453.

Asinius Pollio, Gaius: *see* Pollio, Gaius Asinius.

Asino, city, Tomsk *oblast* (administrative region), southeastern Russian Soviet Federated Socialist Republic. The city is located near the Chulym river, an important logging stream, and is the largest wood-processing centre in Western Siberia. It has a railroad spur which connects with the Trans-Siberian Railroad. Pop. (1970) 29,395.

Asir, Arabic ʿASĪR (Difficult Country), *minṭaqah* (province) and region of southwestern Saudi Arabia immediately north of the Yemen Arab Republic, comprising about 40,000 sq mi (100,000 sq km) of coastal plains, high mountains, and the upper valleys of the *wādīs* (seasonal watercourses) Bīshah and Tathlīth.

Asir was long a prosperous agricultural region under the protection of the ʿAbbāsid caliphs of Baghdad and the control of the Zaydī rulers of Yemen; it broke away from foreign domination in the 18th century only to be occupied again in 1872, this time by the Ottomans. During World War I, a revolt brought a local leader, Muḥammad ibn ʿAlī al-Idrīsī, to power. After his death in March 1923, the shaykhdom came under increasing pressure from Yemen. In an effort to thwart Yemeni designs, Shaykh Hasan ibn ʿAlī surrendered his external sovereignty in March 1926 to King Ibn Saʿūd, who four years later assimilated Asir into his kingdom.

Asir, which receives up to 20 in. (500 mm) of rain annually, has one of the kingdom's wetter—and more temperate—climates and is an important agricultural region. Crops, most of which are cultivated on steeply terraced mountainsides, include wheat, coffee, cotton, indigo, ginger, vegetables, and palms. Apart from agriculture, the economy is supported by the raising of cattle, sheep, goats, and camels throughout the region. The Asir mountains contain deposits, as yet unexploited, of nickel, copper, and zinc. Ancient *qasaba* ("towers") found in the province are almost unique to Asir architecture; they were used as lookouts or as granaries. The main towns include Abhā and Khamīs Mushayṭ. Pop. (1974) 682,000.

Asīrgarh, Indian fortress situated between the Tāpti and Narmada rivers a little to the north of the town of Burhānpur, in the former Central Provinces and the present state of Māharāshtra. The principal importance of the fortress lay in its command of the only easily accessible route from northern India to the Deccan in the southwest.

Asīrgarh was a stronghold of the Hindu Rājputs but fell to the Muslim sultanate of Delhi in the late 13th century. It was later held by the Fārūqī rulers of nearby Khāndesh, from whom it was taken after a long and historic siege (1600–01) by the Mughal emperor Akbar; his success opened the way for all the later Mughal operations in the Deccan. The fortress was later held by the Hindu Marāthās, whose lands lay to the west, from whom it was twice captured, in 1803 and 1819, by the British.

asity, either of two species of short-tailed, 15-centimetre (6-inch) birds of the family Philepittidae (order Passeriformes), inhabiting forests of Madagascar. The male of the velvet asity (*Philepitta castanea*) has yellow tips to its feathers when newly molted, but these wear off leaving the bird all black; at the same time a green wattle grows above the eye. The female is greenish. The male of Schlegel's asity (*P. schlegeli*) is yellow after molt, except for its black crown; and the wattle extends around the eye.

Velvet asity (*Philepitta castanea*)
Painting by H. Douglas Pratt

Velvet asities eat berries and other fruit in undergrowth, and they build hanging nests with a little roof over the entrance.

Asiut (Egypt): *see* Asyūṭ.

Askalon (Israel): *see* Ashqelon.

ʿAskarī, Jaʿfar al- (b. 1887, Baghdad—d. Oct. 30, 1936, Baghdad), Iraqi statesman, a strong supporter and servant of the kingdom of Iraq after its creation in 1921.

ʿAskarī was educated in Baghdad and in Istanbul and commissioned in the Turkish army in 1909. A burly, attractive figure and an accomplished linguist, he developed excellent diplomatic skills. He was sent in 1915 to join Turkish forces in Cyrenaica during World War I, but he was wounded and taken to Cairo as a prisoner by the British. After an attempted escape, ʿAskarī joined the Arab rebel movement against the Turks (1916), together with Nuri as-Said, his brother-in-law and lifelong close associate. In the Hejaz and later Syrian campaign of 1916–18 he rendered valuable services as the *amīr* Fayṣal's chief of staff and army commander, and during 1918–20 he served as Fayṣal's governor of Aleppo and in other posts. Moving to Iraq, he became, under the high commissioner Sir Percy Cox, defense minister in the first Iraqi cabinet and thus was a creator of the Iraqi army; from August 1921 he also became a pillar of the new monarchy. Thereafter until his murder by insurgent troops at Baghdad in 1936, he was repeatedly minister, prime minister, and Iraqi ambassador in London.

Askhabad (Turkmen S.S.R.): *see* Ashkhabad.

Askia DYNASTY, Muslim family that ruled the extensive Songhai empire of West Africa, centred around Timbuktu, in present Mali, from 1492 to 1591. Its members included the dynasty's founder, Mohammed I Askia (*q.v.*), Askia Musa (ruled 1528–31), and Askia Ismail (1537–39).

Askia Muḥammad: *see* Muḥammad I Askia *under* Muḥammad (Songhai Empire).

Askja, largest caldera in the Dyngjufjöl volcanic massif, in east central Iceland. It lies 20 mi (32 km) north of Vatnajökull, the island's largest ice field. Its rugged peaks, up to 4,954 ft (1,510 m) above sea level, encircle a 4¼-sq-mi (11-sq-km) lake that occupies the caldera (volcano's crater). Askja (Icelandic: Box) is the highest peak in the Dyngjufjöll; surrounding it is the Ódádhahraun, an extensive lava field covering 1,422 sq mi. The volcano erupted in 1875 and again in 1961.

Asklepios (Greek religion): *see* Asclepius.

Askr and Embla, in Norse mythology, the first man and first woman, respectively, parents of the human race. They were created from tree trunks found on the seashore by three gods—Odin and his two brothers, Vili and Ve (some sources name the gods Odin, Hoenir, and Lodur). From each creator Askr and Embla received a gift: Odin gave them breath, or life, Vili gave them understanding, and from Ve they received their senses and outward appearance.

Aṣmaʿī, al-, in full ABŪ SAʿĪD ʿABD AL-MALIK IBN QURAYB AL-AṢMAʿĪ (b. *c.* 740, Basra, Iraq—d. 828, Basra), noted scholar and anthologist, one of the three leading members of the Basra school of Arabic philology.

A gifted student of Abū ʿAmr ibn al-ʿAlāʾ, the founder of the Basra school, al-Aṣmaʿī became a member of the court of the ʿAbbāsid caliph Hārūn ar-Rashīd in Baghdad. Renowned for his piety and plain living, he was a tutor to the caliph's son and a favourite of the Barmakid viziers.

Al-Aṣmaʿī possessed an outstanding knowledge of the classical Arabic language. On the basis of the principles he laid down, most of the existing divans, or collections of the pre-Islāmic Arab poets, were prepared by his disciples. He also wrote an anthology, *al-Aṣmaʿīyāt,* displaying a marked preference for elegiac and devotional poetry. His method and his critical concern for authentic tradition are considered remarkable for his time. Some 15 monographs written by al-Aṣmaʿī, mainly on the animals, plants, customs, and grammatical forms in some way related to pre-Islāmic Arabic poetry, are extant, generally in recensions made by his students. The *Fihrist* ("Catalog") of an-Nadīm, the 10th-century Arabic bibliographer, lists 20 such works by al-Aṣmaʿī.

Asmar, Tall al- (Iraq): *see* Eshnunna.

Asmera, also spelled ASMARA, capital of Eritrea province, northern Ethiopia, on the Ethiopian Plateau at an altitude of 7,628 ft (2,325 m). It is the nation's second largest city after Addis Ababa. The municipality lies on the Eritrean Railway and is a major road junction; its international airport, built in 1962, is 2.5 mi (4 km) southeast, and its port on the Red Sea, Mitsiwa, is 40 mi northeast.

Formerly a hamlet of the Tigrai people, Asmera became the capital of the Italian colony of Eritrea in 1900 and remained a small colonial town until 1934. It was the main base for the Italian invasion of Ethiopia in 1935, and the town rapidly expanded as the leading city in Italian East Africa. Asmera was under British administration from 1941 until Eritrea's federation with Ethiopia in 1952 and was the site of Kagnew, a U.S. telecommunications base from 1942 to 1977.

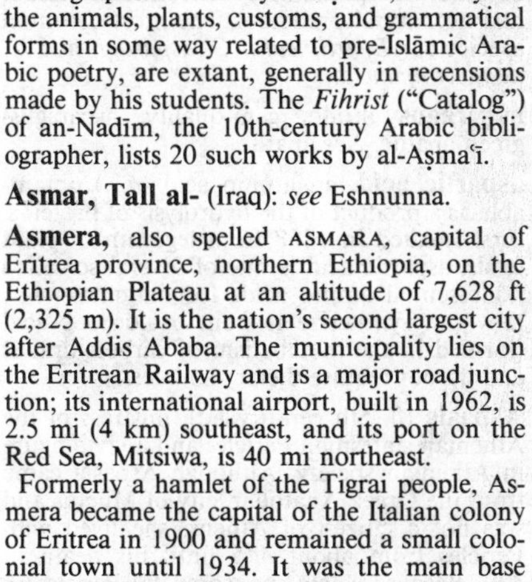

Ethiopian Orthodox churches (St. Mary's in background), Asmera, Eth.

Picturepoint, London

The city is well planned and converges on the palm-lined main street on which are located the Roman Catholic cathedral (1922) and the Grand Mosque (1937). Other notable structures include the former palace (now the residence of the administrator general), the former legislative assembly and the municipal buildings, and St. Mary's (the main Ethiopian Orthodox church). Also the seat of the University of Asmera (founded 1958, university status 1967), the city has a public library, numerous secondary schools, and specialized psychiatric and eye health facilities.

Asmera's chief manufactures include textiles, footwear, and soft drinks. The city is also a busy agricultural marketplace and a major tanning centre. The city's population is approximately half Christian and half Muslim. Pop. (1982 est.) 474,241.

Asmodeus, Hebrew ASHMEDAI, in Jewish legend, the king of demons. According to the apocryphal book of Tobit, Asmodeus, smitten with love for Sarah, the daughter of Raguel, killed her seven successive husbands on their wedding nights. Following instructions given to him by the angel Raphael, Tobias overcame Asmodeus and married Sarah.

The Talmud relates that Solomon captured the demon and pressed him into slave labour during the construction of the First Temple of Jerusalem. Other Haggadic legends depict Asmodeus as a more beneficent figure.

Asnam, el- (Algeria): *see* Cheliff, ech-.

Asnyk, Adam (b. Sept. 11, 1838, Kalisz, Kingdom of Poland—d. Aug. 2, 1897, Krakau, Austria-Hungary), Polish poet and playwright.

Asnyk was a member of the Polish revolutionary government in 1863, and after the failure of the insurrection he settled in Galicia (as Austro-Hungarian Poland was officially called). A disciple of the Polish Romantic poets, Asnyk adhered to the "positivist" school of political thinking, and in the 1880s he was recognized as a leading poet of the period. His first poetic volume, *Poezje* ("Poems"), appeared in 1869, followed by three others. In 1894 he published a cycle of 30 sonnets, *Nad głębi ami* ("Over the Depths"), in which he lays stress on the evolutionary character of nature; the struggle for survival is shown not as the law of the jungle but as a mutual interdependence and cooperation between human communities. Deprived of independence, doomed to a political death, Poland, according to Asnyk, will be reborn sooner or later because it refuses to commit "spiritual suicide." Asnyk also wrote comedies of manners, such as *Gałązka heliotropu* (1869; "A Sprig of Heliotrope"), and historical tragedies.

Aso-san (Japanese: Mount Aso), volcano, Kumamoto Prefecture (*ken*), Kyushu, Japan, rising to an altitude of 5,223 ft (1,592 m). It has the largest active crater in the world, measuring 71 mi (114 km) in circumference, 17 mi from north to south, and 10 mi from east to west. Its caldera (bowl-shaped volcanic depression) marks the original crater and contains the active volcano of Naka-dake and numerous hot springs. The crater is inhabited and is crossed by roads and railways. Its mountain pastures are used for cattle raising and dairy farming. The volcano is the central feature of Aso National Park.

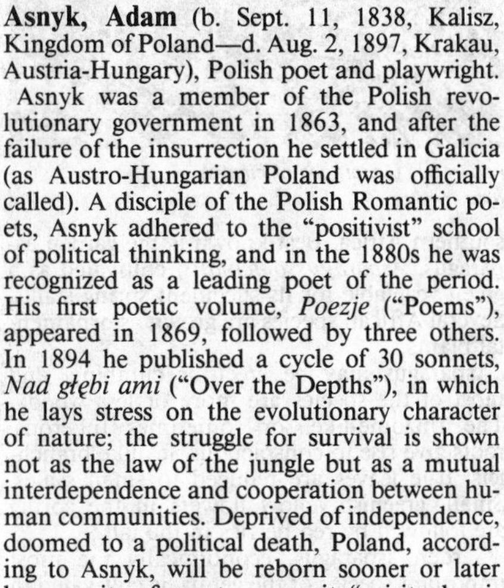

The caldera of Aso-san in central Kyushu, Japan

Kazumi Yahagi—Bon

Consult the INDEX *first*

Aśoka, also spelled ASHOKA (d. 238? BC, India), last major emperor in the Mauryan dynasty of India. His vigorous patronage of Buddhism during his reign (*c.* 265–238 BC; also given as *c.* 273–232 BC) furthered the expansion of that religion throughout India. Following his successful but bloody conquest of the Kaliṅga country on the east coast, Aśoka renounced armed conquest and adopted a policy he called "conquest by *dharma* (principles of right life)."

In order to gain wide publicity for his teachings and his work Aśoka made them known by means of oral announcements and also engraved them on rocks and pillars at suitable sites. From these inscriptions—the Rock Edicts and Pillar Edicts (*e.g.,* the lion capital of the pillar found at Sarnath, which has become India's national emblem)—mostly dated in various years of his reign and containing statements regarding his thoughts and actions, his life and acts are known. There is such a ring of frankness and sincerity in the utterances of Aśoka that they appear to be true.

According to his own accounts, Aśoka conquered the Kaliṅga country (modern Orissa state) in the eighth year of his reign. The sufferings the war inflicted on the defeated people moved him to such remorse that he renounced armed conquests. It was at this time that he came in touch with Buddhism and adopted it. Under its influence and prompted by his own dynamic temperament, he resolved to live according to, and preach, the *dharma* and to serve his subjects and all humanity.

By *dharma,* as Aśoka repeatedly declared, he understood the energetic practice of the socio-moral virtues of honesty, truthfulness, compassion, mercifulness, benevolence, nonviolence, considerate behaviour toward all, "little sin and many good deeds," nonextravagance, nonacquisitiveness, and noninjury to animals. He spoke of no particular mode of religious creed or worship, nor of any philosophical doctrines. He spoke of Buddism only to his co-religionists and not to others.

Toward all religious sects he adopted a policy of respect and guaranteed them full freedom to live according to their own principles, but he also urged them to exert themselves for the "increase of their inner worthiness." He, moreover, exhorted them to respect the creeds of others, praise the good points of others, and refrain from vehement adverse criticism of the viewpoints of others.

To practice the *dharma* actively Aśoka went out on periodical tours preaching the *dharma* to the rural people and relieving their sufferings; he ordered his high officials to do the same, in addition to attending to their normal duties; he exhorted administrative officers to be constantly aware of the joys and sorrows of the common folk and to be prompt and impartial in dispensing justice. A special class of high officers, designated "*dharma* ministers," was appointed to foster *dharma* work by the public, relieve sufferings wherever found, and look to the special needs of women, of people inhabiting outlying regions, of neighbouring peoples, and of various religious communities. It was ordered that matters concerning public welfare were to be reported to him at all times. The only glory he sought, he said, was for having led his people along the path of *dharma*. No doubts are left in the minds of readers of his inscriptions regarding his earnest zeal for serving his subjects. More success was attained in his work, he says, by reasoning with people than by issuing commands.

Among his works of public utility were the founding of hospitals for men and animals and the supplying of medicines; and the planting of roadside trees and groves, digging of wells, and construction of watering sheds and resthouses. Orders were also issued for curbing public laxities and preventing cruelty to animals. With the death of Aśoka the Maurya Empire disintegrated and his work was discontinued. His memory survives for what he attempted to achieve and the high ideals he held before himself.

Most enduring were Aśoka's services to Buddhism. He built a number of *stūpa*s (commemorative burial mounds) and monasteries and erected pillars on which he ordered inscribed his understanding of religious doctrines. He took strong measures to suppress schisms within the order (the Buddhist religious community) and prescribed a course of scriptural studies for adherents. Tradition recorded in the Ceylonese chronicle *Mahāvaṃsa* says that, when the church decided to send preaching missions abroad, Aśoka helped them enthusiastically and sent his own son and daughter as missionares to Ceylon. It is as a result of Aśoka's patronage that Buddhism, which until then was a small sect confined only to particular localities, spread throughout India and subsequently beyond the frontiers of the country.

A sample quotation that illustrates the spirit that guided Aśoka is: "All men are my children. As for my own children I desire that they may be provided with all the welfare and happiness of this world and of the next, so do I desire for all men as well." (A.Se.)

BIBLIOGRAPHY. Amulyachandra Sen (ed.), *Asoka's Edicts* (1956), deals with all aspects of Aśoka's life and work on the basis of archaeological and literary materials. D.R. Bhandarkar, *Asoka*, 3rd ed. (1955); and R.K. Mookergee, *Asoka*, 3rd ed. (1962), are studies based on historical materials.

asp, anglicized form of ASPIS, name used in classical antiquity for a venomous snake, probably the Egyptian cobra, *Naja haje* (*see* cobra). It was the symbol of royalty in Egypt, and its bite was used for the execution of favoured criminals in Greco–Roman times.

Cleopatra is said to have killed herself with an asp. For horned asp and for asp viper, often called asp, *see* viper.

Aspar, Flavius Ardaburius (d. 471), Roman general of Alani descent, influential in the Eastern Roman Empire under the emperors Marcian (ruled 450–457) and Leo I (ruled 457–474).

Aspar led an East Roman fleet in 431 to expel the Vandals from Africa, but he was defeated and was forced to withdraw in 434, in which year he served as consul. Although Aspar fought the Persians successfully in 441, the Huns under Attila triumphed over him outside Constantinople in 443. Aspar's influence increased; he was made a patrician after Marcian, who had formerly been in his service, became emperor in 450. When Marcian died Aspar had a protégé raised to the throne as Leo I (February 457). The general, head of a Gothic army devoted to him, was then at the height of his power. Leo, however, was not content to be Aspar's puppet. He began to rely increasingly on Isaurian supporters (from southern Anatolia), and for about four years a struggle for ascendancy took place in the Eastern Roman Empire between Aspar's Germans and the Isaurians led by Zeno. Aspar aroused intense resentment in Constantinople *c.* 470 by having the rank of caesar conferred on his son Patricius, though Patricius was an Arian Christian. A conspiracy organized by the Isaurians and Leo in 471 led to Aspar's murder, and German domination over Eastern Roman policy ended.

asparagine, an amino acid closely related to aspartic acid (*q.v.*), and an important component of proteins. First isolated in 1932 from asparagus, from which its name is derived, asparagine is widely distributed in plant proteins. It is one of several so-called nonessential amino acids in warm-blooded animals: they can synthesize it from aspartic acid.

Asparagus, genus of the lily family (Liliaceae) with about 300 species native from Siberia to southern Africa. Best known is the garden asparagus, *Asparagus officinalis,* cultivated as a green vegetable for its succulent spring stalks. Several African species are grown as ornamental plants.

Asparagus (*Asparagus officinalis*)
Walter Chandoha

Asparagus may be erect or climbing, and most of the species are more or less woody. The rhizome-like, or sometimes tuberous, roots give rise to conspicuous, leaflike branchlets; true leaves are reduced to small scales. Small, greenish-yellow flowers in the spring are followed by red berries in the fall.

Garden asparagus, economically the most important species of the genus, is cultivated in most temperate and subtropical parts of the world. As a vegetable it has been prized by epicures since Roman times; it is frequently served cooked, and the tips may be canned and used in salads and as garnishes. Asparagus is grown extensively in France, Italy, and the United States. Commercial plantations are not undertaken in regions where the plant continues to grow throughout the year, for the shoots become more spindly and less vigorous each year; a rest period is required. Where climate is favourable and with proper care, an asparagus plantation may be productive for 10 to 15 years or longer. Best soil types for asparagus are deep, loose, light clays, with much organic matter, and light, sandy loams. Asparagus will thrive in soils too salty for other crops, but acid soils are to be avoided. The asparagus cutting season varies from 2 to 12 weeks, depending on age of the plantation and on climate.

In parts of France, most notably at Argenteuil, asparagus is customarily grown underground to inhibit development of chlorophyll. This white asparagus is prized for its tenderness and delicate flavour.

The several poisonous species prized for their delicate and graceful foliage are: *A. plumosus,* the asparagus fern, or florists' fern (not a true fern), which has feathery sprays of branchlets often used in corsages and in other plant arrangements; and *A. sprengeri* and *A. asparagoides,* likewise grown for their attractive, lacy foliage.

asparagus beetle, any member of the *Crioceris* and *Lema* genera, important pests of the insect family Chrysomelidae (order Coleoptera). The adult beetle is red, yellow, and black in colour and about 7 millimetres (almost 0.3 inch) long. It feeds on and deposits its oval black eggs on young asparagus plants.

Asparagus beetle (*Crioceris duodecimpunctata*)
Grant Heilman—EB Inc.

This pest, which was brought to North America from Europe in about 1862, thrived and became widespread in a short time because it had no natural predators. The most common species are *L. trilineata, C. asparagi,* and *C. duodecimpunctata.*

asparagus stone, gem-quality, asparagus-green apatite. *See* apatite.

aspartic acid, an amino acid (*q.v.*) obtainable as a product of the hydrolysis of proteins. First isolated in 1868 from legumin in plant seeds, aspartic acid is one of several so-called nonessential amino acids for mammals; *i.e.,* they can synthesize it from oxaloacetic acid (formed in the metabolism of carbohydrates) and do not require dietary sources.

Aspasia (fl. 5th century BC), mistress of the Athenian statesman Pericles and a vivid figure in Athenian society. Although Aspasia came from the Greek Anatolian city of Miletus and was not a citizen of Athens, she lived with Pericles from about 445 until his death in 429. Because a law sponsored by Pericles in 451 required that for a person to be a citizen both parents must be citizens, their son, also named Pericles, was long excluded from civic participation. He was eventually made a citizen by special enactment and later became a general.

Aspasia was continually made the object of public attacks—particularly from the comedic stage—criticizing her private life and public influence. She was irresponsibly accused of urging Pericles to crush the island of Samos, Miletus' old rival, and to provoke war with Sparta. The Socratic philosopher Aeschines treated her more kindly in a dialogue bearing her name. Shortly before the Peloponnesian War she was acquitted of a charge of impiety.

Aspen, city, seat of Pitkin County, west central Colorado, U.S., on the Roaring Fork River at the eastern edge of the White River National Forest (altitude 7,907 ft [2,410 m]). Founded by prospectors *c.* 1878 and named for the local stands of aspen trees, it became a booming silver-mining town of 15,000 by 1887 but declined rapidly after silver prices collapsed in the early 1890s. Aspen's revival—as a recreational and cultural mecca—began in the late 1930s and was due in large part to the enterprise of Walter Paepcke, a Chicago industrialist. Nearby are some of the high points of the Rocky Mountains, including Capitol,

Creek, Snowmass, and Maroon peaks (all exceeding 14,000 ft [4,270 m]). Aspen's facilities for skiing and other winter sports make it a popular winter resort. The Aspen Music Festival and the Aspen Institute for Humanistic Studies are summer cultural attractions. Ballet West, Aspen Theatre Institute, and the Center of the Eye Photography School are in the city. Inc. 1881. Pop. (1980) 3,678.

aspen, any of three trees of the genus *Populus,* the willow family (Salicaceae), native to the Northern Hemisphere and known for the fluttering of leaves in the slightest breeze. Aspens grow farther north and higher up the mountains than other *Populus* species. An aspen rarely grows singly but soon sends up a thicket of sucker shoots.

Quaking aspen (*Populus tremuloides*)
Charles Hannum—EB Inc.

Aspens are useful in naturalistic landscaping. They all display a smooth gray-green bark, random branching, rich green leaves that turn brilliant yellow in fall, and catkins (male and female on separate trees) that appear before the leaves in spring.

The common European trembling aspen (*P. tremula*) and the American quaking aspen (*P. tremuloides*) are similar, reaching a height of 27 metres (90 feet); *P. tremuloides* is distinguished by its leaves, which have more pointed tips. The American big-tooth aspen (*P. grandidentata*), up to 18 m, has larger, somewhat rounded, coarse-toothed leaves.

Aspendus, Greek ASPENDOS, modern BELKİS, ancient city of Pamphylia, located in Antalya *il* (province), Turkey; it is noted for its Roman ruins. A wide range of coinage from the 5th century BC onward attests to the city's wealth, which was based on trade in salt, oil, and wool. Aspendus was occupied by Alexander the Great in 333 BC and later passed from Pergamene to Roman rule in 133 BC. According to Cicero, it was plundered of many of its artistic treasures by the provincial governor Verres. The hilltop ruins of the city include a basilica, an agora, and some rock-cut tombs of Phrygian design. A huge theatre, possibly the finest in the world, is carved out of the northeast flank of the hill. It was designed by the Roman architect Zeno in honour of the emperor Marcus Aurelius (reigned AD 161–180). Pop. (latest census) 515.

Aspenström, (Karl) Werner (b. Nov. 13, 1918, Norrbärke, Swed.), Swedish lyrical poet and essayist.

Aspenström's images are characterized by intensity and a rare lyrical quality. In the cycle *Snölegend* (1949; "Snow Legend"), *Litania* (1952; "Litany"), and *Hundarna* (1954; "The Dogs"), the poet treats his metaphysical and social concerns in a symbolic form. Aspenström also wrote a number of poetic dramas. He re-created the world of his childhood in *Bäcken* (1958; "The Brook"), a series of short stories. He wrote several collections of essays on current issues, including *Sommar* (1968; "Summer") and *Skäl* (1970; "Arguments").

Aspenström received several literary honours such as the Ovralid Prize (1958), the Prize of the Nine (1967), and the Small Nobel Prize (1969).

aspergillosis, infection common in birds and occurring less frequently in man, caused by the ubiquitous and usually saprophytic fungus *Aspergillus*, especially *A. fumigatus*. Human infection may be limited to the external ear (otomycosis); rarely, *Aspergillus* may produce a maduromycosis (infection arising from subcutaneous implantation). The most severe form of aspergillosis is primary bronchopulmonary infection, which is clinically similar to and sometimes mistaken for tuberculosis; characteristic symptoms include fever, severe cough, and purulent sputum occasionally tinged with blood and flecks of white or brownish mycelium (fungus material). This type of infection has been classed as an occupational disease among pigeon and squab handlers.

Aspergillus, genus of the Fungi Imperfecti (form-class Deuteromycetes, *q.v.*). Those species for which the sexual phase is known are placed in the Eurotiales. *A. niger* causes black mold of foodstuffs; *A. flavus, A. niger,* and *A. fumigatus* cause the disease aspergillosis in man. *A. oryzae* is used to ferment sake, and *A. wentii* to process soybeans. Three genera of the class Ascomycetes have *Aspergillus* type conidia (asexually produced spores): *Emericella, Eurotium,* and *Sartorya.*

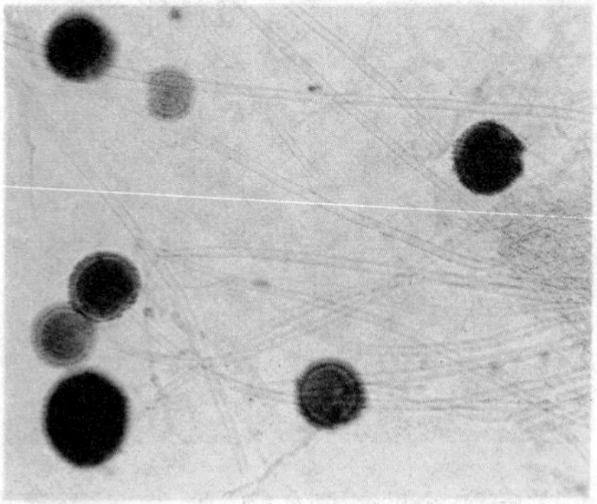

Aspergillus
Runk/Schoenberger from Grant Heilman—EB Inc.

asphalt, black or brown petroleum-like material that has a consistency varying from viscous liquid to glassy solid. It is obtained either as a residue from the distillation of petroleum or from natural deposits. Asphalt consists of compounds of hydrogen and carbon with minor proportions of nitrogen, sulfur, and oxygen. Natural asphalt (also called brea), which is believed to be formed during an early stage in the breakdown of organic marine deposits into petroleum, commonly contains minerals, while residual petroleum asphalt does not.

The use of asphalt is very old, dating back to its use as a water stop between brick walls of a reservoir at Mohenjo-Daro (about the 3rd millennium BC) in Pakistan. In the Middle East it was extensively used for paving roads and sealing waterworks, important applications even today. The Pitch Lake on the island of Trinidad was the first large commercial source, but natural sources have since declined in importance as petroleum became the major source. Gilsonite, wurzilite, and similar vein asphalts have special uses in heat-resistant enamels; they are hard and are mined like coal. Petroleum asphalt is produced in all consistencies from light road oils to heavy, high-viscosity industrial types.

Asphalt softens when heated and is elastic under certain conditions. The mechanical properties of asphalt are of little significance except when it is used as a binder or adhesive. The principal application of asphalt is in road surfacing, which may be done in a variety of ways. Light oil "dust layer" treatments may be built up by repetition to form a hard surface, or a granular aggregate may be added to an asphalt coat, or earth materials from the road surface itself may be mixed with the asphalt.

Other important applications include canal and reservoir linings, dam facings, and other harbour and sea works; asphalt so used may be a thin, sprayed membrane, covered with earth for protection against weathering and mechanical damage, or thicker surfaces, often including riprap (crushed rock). Asphalt is also used for roofs, coatings, floor tilings, soundproofing, waterproofing, and other building-construction elements and in a number of industrial products, such as batteries. For certain applications an asphaltic emulsion is prepared, in which fine globules of asphalt are suspended in water. *See also* bitumen.

asphalt tile, smooth-surfaced floor covering made from a mixture of asphalts or synthetic resins, asbestos fibres, pigments, and mineral fillers. It is usually about 1/8 or 3/16 inch thick, and is nonporous, nonflammable, fairly low in cost, and easily maintained.

Asphalt tile was developed for damp and alkaline conditions where linoleum did not fare well. It is resistant to fungal attack, mild acids, and oils and grease, and it can be used where floor temperature is less than 80° F (27° C).

asphaltite, any of several naturally occurring, hard, solid bitumens whose chief constituents, asphaltenes, have very large molecules. Asphaltites are dark brown to black in colour. They are insoluble in petroleum naphthas and thus require heating to release their petroleum content. Though related to asphalts, asphaltites differ from them both chemically and physically in various respects. Asphaltites, for example, contain little or no inorganic minerals, whereas asphalts may have a relatively large percentage of such matter. Also, unlike asphalts, asphaltites do not fuse readily.

Asphaltites are commonly classified into three groups: gilsonite, glance pitch (or manjak), and grahamite. These substances differ from one another basically in terms of specific gravity and temperature at which they soften. Gilsonite occurs chiefly along the Colorado–Utah border; glance pitch on Barbados and in Columbia; and grahamite in Cuba and Mexico, as well as in West Virginia and Oklahoma.

asphodel, any of several flowering plants belonging to the lily family (Liliaceae). It is a variously applied and thus much misunderstood common name. The asphodel of the poets is often a narcissus; that of the ancients is either of two genera, *Asphodeline* or *Asphodelus*, containing numerous species in the Mediterranean region.

They are hardy herbaceous perennials with narrow leaves and an elongated stem bearing a handsome spike of white, pink, or yellow flowers. *Asphodelus albus* and *A. fistulosus* have white to pink flowers and grow from 45 to 60 centimetres (1½ to 2 feet) high.

Bog asphodel (*Narthecium ossifragum*), also of the family Liliaceae, is a small herb growing in boggy places in Great Britain with rigid, narrow leaves and a stem bearing a raceme of small golden-yellow flowers. In the United States both the American bog asphodel (*N. americanum*), of the pine barrens of New Jersey and Delaware, and the western bog asphodel (*N. californicum*), of the coast ranges of California and Oregon, are rare plants.

In Greek legend the asphodel is the most famous of the plants connected with the dead and the underworld. Homer describes it as covering the great meadow, the haunt of the dead. It was planted on graves and is often connected with Persephone, daughter of the Greek god Zeus. Its general connection with death is probably associated with the grayish colour of its leaves and its yellowish flowers, which suggest the gloom of the underworld and the pallor of death. The roots were eaten by the poorer Greeks.

aspic, savoury clear jelly prepared from a stock (*q.v.*) made from the bones of beef, veal, chicken, or fish. The aspic congeals when refrigerated by virtue of the natural gelatin that dissolves into the stock from the tendons; commercial sheet or powdered gelatin is sometimes added to ensure a stiff set. Aspic is used to coat and glaze foods such as cold meats and fish, eggs, poached or roasted poultry, and vegetables; plain aspic chopped or cut into shapes garnishes cold dishes. Various foods can be combined with aspic in decorative molds. Mayonnaise or *sauce velouté* mixed with liquid aspic yields *chaud-froid*, a sauce that can be coloured and used to decorate cold foods; it is widely employed for formal buffet presentations.

Aspidistra, genus of ornamental foliage plants in the family Liliaceae, native to eastern Asia. The only cultivated species is a houseplant commonly known as cast-iron plant (*A. elatior* or *A. lurida*).

The cast-iron plant has long, stiff, pointed evergreen leaves that are capable of withstanding temperature extremes, dust, smoke, and other harsh conditions. The solitary, bell-shaped flowers, which are usually lilac in colour but sometimes brown or green, are borne at the base of the plant. The fruits of *Aspidistra* are small berries.

aspidium, ancient drug derived from the root or rhizome (underground stem) of the male fern (*Dryopteris felix-mas*) of Europe or of the marginal fern (*D. marginalis*) of North America. It still is used in medicine in the treatment of intestinal worm infestations. Aspidium oleoresin, which is extracted from the plant parts, is administered orally, often in the form of an emulsion; within a few hours after administration, a purgative is used to prevent absorption of the poisonous principles.

Aspidium was used in the time of the Greek physician Dioscorides (1st century AD) to treat tapeworm (such as *Taenia saginata*, beef tapeworm). It has been displaced largely by synthetic chemical anthelmintics (worming agents), such as quinacrine and hexylresorcinol, most of which are somewhat less toxic to the patient.

aspirate, the sound *h* as in English "hat." Consonant sounds such as the English voiceless stops *p, t,* and *k* at the beginning of words (*e.g.,* "pat," "top," "keel") are also aspirated because they are pronounced with an accompanying forceful expulsion of air. Such sounds are not aspirated at the end of words or in combination with certain consonants (*e.g.,* in "spot," "stop"). The voiced stops *b* and *d* in Sanskrit and Hindi also have aspirated forms that are usually transliterated in English as *bh* and *dh*.

aspirin: *see* acetylsalicylic acid.

Aspiring, Mount, mountain in the Southern Alps of west central South Island, New Zealand. It is a pyramid-shaped peak that rises from the small Bonar, Volta, Therma, and Iso glaciers. Its four ridges reach 9,960 ft (3,036 m), with thick rain forests clothing the western slopes. Sighted and named by the explorer-surveyor John Turbull Thomson in 1857, the peak was first scaled in 1909 by Maj. Bernard Head. It became the central feature of the 1,109-sq-mi (2,872-sq-km) Mount Aspiring National Park, created in 1964 and extending south from Haast Pass to the boundary of Fiordland National Park. It is accessible via the Haast Pass Highway.

Aspleniaceae, largest of 11 families in the fern order Polypodiales (in other classification systems one of five families of the order Aspidiales). Of worldwide distribution, the group contains about 3,000 species, including such well-known plants as the woodferns and shield ferns (*Dryopteris*), holly ferns (*Polystichum*), halberd ferns (*Tectaria*), lady ferns (*Athyrium*), marsh ferns (*Thelypteris*), chain ferns (*Blechnum* and *Woodwardia*), hart's-tongue ferns (*Phyllitis*), spleenworts and bird's nest ferns (*Asplenium*), and walking ferns (*Camptosorus*). The family is characterized by scaly creeping stems, or rootstocks (rhizomes), spore-producing structures (sporangia) with stalks and a ring of thickened cells (annulus or bow), the sporangia in clusters (sori) on the lower surfaces of the leaves and covered with shieldlike, kidney-shaped, oblong, or linear membranous protective structures (indusia). The spores are mostly bean shaped (bilateral).

(Top) Hart's tongue fern (*Phyllitis*); (bottom) maidenhair spleenwort (*Asplenium*)
(Top) J.E. Downward—EB Inc., (bottom) Thase Daniel

Chain fern (*Blechnum spicant*)
Ingmar Holmasen

Asplund, Erik Gunnar (b. Sept. 22, 1885, Stockholm—d. Oct. 20, 1940, Stockholm), architect whose work shows the historically important transition from Neoclassical to modern design.

Woodland Crematorium, Stockholm, by Asplund, 1935–40
Photoreporters

Asplund was educated at the Academy of Fine Arts in Stockholm. His exposure to classical architecture on a trip to Greece and Italy (1913–14) made a profound impression.

Among Asplund's significant early works are the charming Woodland Chapel in the Stockholm South Cemetery (1918–20); the Skandia Cinema (1922–23), which had considerable decorative detail; and the Stockholm City Library (1924–27), which emphasized geometrical simplicity. He planned the Stockholm Exposition of 1930, for which he designed a number of pavilions and the Paradise Restaurant. This exposition of housing and national arts and crafts gave international prominence to modern Swedish architecture and design.

Asplund's later work, particularly the Bredenberg Store (1933–35), the State Bacteriological Laboratory in Stockholm (1933–35), and the Göteborg Law Courts extension (1934–37), showed a continuing commitment to modern design. Asplund's Woodland Crematorium (1935–40) in Stockholm is considered one of the great monuments of modern architecture. The design makes extensive use of columns that, though starkly modern, convey a feeling of classical dignity and serenity.

Aspropótamos (Greece): *see* Achelous River.

Asquith, H(erbert) H(enry), 1st Earl of Oxford and Asquith (b. Sept. 12, 1852, Morley, Yorkshire, Eng.—d. Feb. 15, 1928, Sutton Courtenay, Berkshire), Liberal prime minister of Great Britain (1908–16), who was responsible for the Parliament Act of 1911, limiting the power of the House of Lords, and who led Britain during the first two years of World War I.

Asquith was the second son of Joseph

Asquith, a small businessman in the wool trade and an ardent Congregationalist, who died in 1860. Asquith was educated at the City of London School from 1863 to 1870, when he won a classical scholarship at Balliol College, Oxford. At Balliol he obtained the highest academic honours, and he became a fellow of his college in 1874. Deciding upon a legal career, he entered Lincoln's Inn and was called to the bar in 1876. The following year he married Helen Melland, daughter of a Manchester doctor, by whom he had four sons and one daughter. His early days at the bar were difficult, but from about 1883 onward he became highly successful.

A keen Liberal, Asquith entered the House of Commons for East Fife in 1886 and remained its member for 32 years. He commanded the attention of the House from the first, concentrating particularly upon the Irish question. In 1888 he achieved celebrity as junior counsel for the Irish leader Charles Stewart Parnell, when Parnell was accused, before a parliamentary commission, of condoning political murder. In 1892 Gladstone made Asquith home secretary. Before that, in 1891, his wife had died of typhoid fever, leaving him with a family of young children. Less than three years later he astounded the social and political world by marrying Margot Tennant, who was 12 years younger and the centre of social and intellectual circles far removed from those in which Asquith and his first wife had moved.

His three years as home secretary, though in general an unhappy period for the Liberals, established Asquith's reputation as an administrator and a debater. By 1895 he had become one of the leading figures of his party. Defeated at the polls, the party spent the next 11 years in opposition. Asquith earned during this time a large income at the bar, but the lack of any private means obliged him to refuse the party leadership when it was

Asquith
BBC Hulton Picture Library

offered to him in 1898, and Sir Henry Campbell-Bannerman succeeded instead. Asquith did not see eye to eye with the new leader on all questions of foreign and imperial policy. Their divergence became open and public during the South African War (1899–1902), when Asquith, along with Lord Rosebery, Sir Edward Grey, and R.B. Haldane, formed the Liberal League to advocate an imperial policy in support of the government's expansionism. The conflict was temporarily healed after the end of the war, and, following the Liberals' victory at the polls in 1906, Asquith served as chancellor of the Exchequer under Campbell-Bannerman.

Early in April 1908 Campbell-Bannerman resigned and died some days later. Asquith, generally regarded as his inevitable successor, became prime minister and was to hold the office for nearly nine years. He appointed David Lloyd George to the Exchequer and made Winston Churchill president of the Board of Trade. The chief problem confronting him at home was the opposition of the House of Lords to Liberal reforms, and the consequent danger of a rebellion from the frustrated radicals in his own party; abroad there was a growing naval competition with Germany. When Lloyd George endeavoured to raise money for naval increases and social services in his "radical budget" of 1909, the budget was vetoed by the House of Lords.

At this stage Asquith took over the conduct of a constitutional struggle. In 1910 he announced a plan to limit the powers of the upper house and, after two general elections, persuaded King George V to threaten to create enough new pro-reform peers to swamp the opposition. The resulting Parliament Bill, passed in August 1911, ended the Lords' veto power.

The three years between this episode and the outbreak of World War I were extremely harassing for the Prime Minister. Abroad, the international situation deteriorated rapidly; at home, controversy was caused by charges of corruption in his government, the disestablishment of the Anglican Church in Wales (1914), and the conflict between Home Rulers and Unionists in Ireland, which nearly led to civil war in 1914. Asquith's policies did little to improve the situation in Ireland.

Though convinced that a German victory over France would be disastrous to the British Empire, Asquith delayed Britain's entry into World War I until public opinion had been aroused by the German attack on Belgium. In war, he trusted his military experts and in general favoured the school that maintained that victory could be won only on the Western Front.

In May 1915 Asquith had to reconstruct his Cabinet on a coalition basis, admitting Unionists as well as Liberals, and appointing Lloyd George minister of munitions. The coalition was not successful under his leadership. The Dardanelles expedition failed, and there was no sign of a breakthrough in the west. At the end of 1915 Asquith substituted Sir Douglas Haig for Sir John French as British commander in chief in France and appointed Sir William Robertson as the new chief of the imperial general staff. But 1916 was an even unhappier year: the Easter Rising in Dublin caused a grave domestic crisis, and the Battle of the Somme led to a complete impasse on the Western Front. After a protracted struggle, conscription was belatedly introduced. But there was a general aura of dissatisfaction by the autumn, and Asquith was assailed by a strident press campaign. In December he resigned and was replaced by Lloyd George. He never held office again, though he remained leader of the Liberal Party until 1926. In this capacity he often opposed the policies of his successor.

Asquith accepted a peerage as earl of Oxford and Asquith in 1925 and was created a Knight of the Garter shortly afterward. In the last years of his life he was relatively impoverished and wrote a number of books to make money, the best known being *The Genesis of the War* (1923), *Fifty Years of Parliament* (1926), and *Memories and Reflections* (1928).

Asquith was a competent statesman, but not a great one. He had no original or innovating genius and lacked the sense of the dramatic needed to convince Britain that it was in good hands in a time of national crisis. (B.)

BIBLIOGRAPHY. J.A. Spender and Cyril Asquith, *Life of Herbert Henry Asquith, Lord Oxford and Asquith*, 2 vol. (1932), is the official biography, cautious, discreet, and highly favourable. The life by Roy Jenkins, *Asquith* (1964), is shorter and more critical than the official biography, though in general pro-Asquith. Robert Blake, *The Unknown Prime Minister: The Life and Times of Andrew Bonar Law, 1853–1923* (1955), gives the Conservative side of the period; Thomas Jones, *Lloyd George* (1951), and Frank Owen, *Tempestuous Journey* (1954), give the Lloyd Georgite point of view; Stephen Koss in *Asquith* (1976) offers a balanced judgment.

āśrama (Hinduism): *see* ashram.

āsrāva (Sanskrit: "what leaks out"), Pāli ĀSAVA, also called KLEŚA (Sanskrit: "affliction"), Pāli KILESA, in Buddhist philosophy, the illusion that ceaselessly flows out from internal organs (*i.e.*, five sense organs and the mind). To the unenlightened, every existence becomes the object of illusion or is inevitably accompanied by illusion. Such an existence is called *sāsrava.* Even if one leads a good life, it is still regarded as *sāsrava,* insofar as it leads to another existence in the world of transmigration. Through the effort of ridding oneself of *āsrāva,* one can attain *anāsrāva* (the Enlightenment), or freedom from the bond of illusion by undefiled wisdom.

Asroc, U.S. ship-launched, solid-propellant, acoustic-homing torpedo with a range of about six miles. It is usually launched from a surface ship. Its name is an acronym for anti-submarine rocket. An Asroc travels through the air until it arrives in the vicinity of an enemy submarine. It then plunges into the water and travels the remainder of its journey underwater.

ass, also called WILD ASS, either of two species of ass belonging to the horse family, Equidae, especially the African wild ass, *Equus asinus* (also, *Equus africanus*), often referred to as the true ass. The related Asiatic wild ass, often called the half-ass (*E. hemionus*), is usually known by the local names of its various races: *e.g.*, kulan (*E. h. hemionus*, Mongolia); kiang (*E. h. kiang*, Tibet); onager (*E. h. onager*, Iran and Turkmeniya); and khar (*E. h. khur,* India and Pakistan). The Syrian wild ass (*E. h. hemippus*) is probably extinct. The donkey (*q.v.*) is a domesticated descendant of *E. hemionus.*

Asses are small, sturdy animals, ranging from 90 to 150 centimetres (3 to 5 feet) high at the shoulder. The African wild ass is bluish gray to fawn; the half-ass, lighter in colour, is reddish to yellow-gray. Both have whitish muzzles and underparts, short, dark, erect manes lacking a forelock, and tufted tails. Most asses have a dark stripe from the mane back onto the tail, but only the Nubian ass (*E. a. africanus*) regularly has a prominent stripe across the shoulders, as does the donkey. The half-ass differs from the true ass in its extremely long, slender legs, shorter ears (intermediate between those of the horse and donkey), and relatively larger hooves. The bray of the half-ass lacks the alternating low tones heard in the "heehaw" of the true ass. The ass is a swift runner: kulans have been clocked at 64.4 kilometres per hour (40 miles per hour). In ancient times half-asses, especially the onager, were tamed

African wild ass (*Equus asinus*)
Tierbilder Okapia, Frankfurt am Main

and trained for work. These lighter-bodied animals were eventually rejected in favour of the sturdier donkey.

Desert dwellers, wild asses often inhabit very

arid regions that cannot support other large mammals. African wild asses are territorial, mature males (stallions) maintaining areas in which they are dominant over other asses. The only strong social bond is between the female and her foals, herds being formed only when individuals travel together casually. Kulans live in herds consisting of one stallion and several females with their young. These family groups join to form large herds in winter.

Both the Asiatic and African species are rare throughout their ranges as a result of hunting and competition with domestic stock. *E. asinus* and *E. h. khur* are considered endangered, and other local races are dwindling. Captive breeding programs have produced substantial zoo herds of several races.

Assab (Ethiopia): *see* Aseb.

Assad, Ḥafiz al- (b. 1928, Qardāḥa, Syria), president of Syria from 1971.

Assad was born in the Lataki province of Syria to a poor family of ʿAlawites, a minority Islāmic sect. He graduated from the Homs Military Academy in 1955 as a pilot officer and was sent to the Soviet Union in 1958 for training in night warfare. He was later promoted to squadron leader but was dismissed from the armed forces in 1961 because of his opposition to Syria's secession from the union with Egypt. He then devoted his activities to the Baʿath Party, which he had joined as a student in indignation against social conditions in Syria; and he became one of the key figures in the party's military wing when it took power in 1963. In 1964 he was made commander in chief of the Air Force, and in February 1966 he became minister of defense after the radical Baʿathists' overthrow of the moderate international Baʿath leadership in Syria. In 1969–70 he was involved in a power struggle with the party's civilian wing that came to a head after Syria's unsuccessful intervention (to which he was opposed) in the Jordanian civil war. When the civilian Baʿathists refused cooperation, he formed his own government and in March 1971 was elected president by a purported 99.2 percent of the votes cast in a national plebiscite.

As president, Assad initially took steps to liberalize the government in several areas and reduced Syria's isolation by improving relations with other Arab countries (although remaining hostile toward the rival Baʿathist regime in Iraq). His new alliance with Egypt culminated in their close collaboration in the October 1973 war against Israel, but differences over the cease-fire and the subsequent U.S.-sponsored disengagement agreements with Israel soon disrupted the alliance.

In 1976 Assad defied the opposition of most other Arab states and instituted a large-scale military intervention in Lebanon in an attempt to end the civil war; Syrian forces occupied most of the country for six years, until Israel invaded Lebanon in 1982 and drove them back to positions in the North and Northeast.

Assad's antagonism toward Iraq was evident in his decision in 1982 to close Syria's border with Iraq and to close its trans-Syrian pipeline. Simultaneously, he drew closer to the Iran of revolutionary fundamentalists, who supplied him with oil and other supplies. This was a far cry from the mood of 1979, when Assad had ambitions for a political union with Iraq. Assad also strengthened his ties with the Soviet Union.

At home, Assad's regime came under attack from dissidents, especially those belonging to the Muslim Brotherhood. Assad's reaction was extreme repression, climaxing in 1982 in the near-destruction of the city of Hamah, stronghold of the Brotherhood, and the killing of perhaps 10,000 rebels.

Assam, constituent state of the Republic of India, located in northeastern part of the country. It is bounded to the north and northeast by Bhutan and the union territory of Arunāchal Pradesh; to the east by the states of Nāgāland and Manipur; to the south by the union territory of Mizorām and Tripura state; and to the west by Bangladesh and the states of Meghālaya and West Bengal. To the northwest, a narrow corridor running through the foothills of the Himalayas in West Bengal connects Assam with India.

The following article summarizes the administrative history, geography, demographic patterns, economy, and culture of modern Assam; for additional treatment of its geography and history, *see* MACROPAEDIA: India.

In earliest times, the area was known as Kāmarūpa, and as far back as the first millennium BC boasted such renowned rulers as King Narakāsura and his son Bhagadatta. Various dynasties ruled Assam, but there was no stable government until the advent of the Ahoms from Burma in the 13th century. The power and prosperity of this group reached its zenith under King Rudra Singh (1696–1714). Internal strife brought the Burmese into Assam in 1817, and destruction and misery followed. The British eventually drove out the Burmese invaders and made the area part of British India in 1826. By 1842 the whole Assam Valley had come under British rule. Following Indian independence in 1947, Assamese territory shrank through cessions to Pakistan and the creation of a new Indian state from the Nāga Hills district and the union territory of Mizorām. In 1972 the capital was shifted from Shillong to Dispur, a suburb of Gauhāti, and again in 1984 to Prāgjyotiṣapura, near Gauhāti.

Except for the districts of Karbi Anglong and North Cāchār Hills, Assam is generally composed of plains and river valleys. Three physical regions stand out: the Brahmaputra Valley in the north, the Barāk Plain in the south, and the hilly regions lying between the two. The valley of the Brahmaputra is Assam's main physical feature. The average Brahmaputra Valley temperature in January—during the northeast monsoon, a time marked by fog and little rain—is 61° F (16° C). Assam's average temperature is moderate—about 84° F (29° C) in August, the hottest month. Earthquakes are common; one of the greatest in history occurred in 1950, and the resulting landslides and floods led to heavy losses in human life and property.

The people of Assam are mainly of Indo-Iranian and Mongoloid stock; about two-thirds are Hindus and one-quarter Muslims. Most of those of Mongoloid background speak dialects of Tibeto-Burman origin. There are Hindus of Bengali stock who have long resided there. More recent immigrants from Bangladesh were the object of riots and massacre in eastern Assam early in 1983.

Agriculture is basic to Assam's economy. Around 56 percent of the population is engaged in farming, with another 10 percent in related occupations. Rice grows on about 70 percent of the cultivated area; tea and jute are also important crops, their sale accounting for a major portion of Assam's income. Other crops include oilseeds, peas, beans, rape, and sugarcane. Assam also produces oranges, pineapples, and bananas.

Oil and coal are found in Upper Assam, and other mineral resources include natural gas, limestone, fireclay, and feldspar. Assam produces about one-half of the country's total petroleum and natural gas. Except for those industries based on tea and oil, however, Assam has few significant industrial facilities. The state has suffered industrially from a lack of capital, its isolation from the rest of India, and a poor transportation system. Extant industries include a fertilizer plant at Nāmrūp, a jute mill at Silghāt, a sugar mill at Dergaon, a paper mill at Jogighopa, a spun-silk mill at Jagiroad, and a cement factory at Bokajān. Numerous sawmills, along with plywood and match factories, utilize the state's forest resources. Assam has six airports, but these and the other (*i.e.,* road, rail, and water) transportation systems fail to serve the state's needs satisfactorily.

Social life in Assam is interwoven with the activities of a number of cultural institutions and religious centres. The most important social celebrations are the three Bihu festivals, originally agricultural fetes observed by villagers to mark different seasons of the year. The Bohāg Bihu in mid-April is the most important festival, celebrating the beginning of the new year. The Māgu Bihu, in mid-February, is a harvest featuring community feasting and bonfires. Kāti Bihu is observed in mid-October and is known as the "poor" festival, because at that time of year the houses of the poor are without food, the stock grain usually having been consumed before the next harvest.

Another important aspect of Assamese cultural life, particularly of women, is the weaving of fine silk and cotton cloths with various floral and other decorative designs. Every Assamese house—irrespective of caste, creed, and social status—has at least one handloom, and each woman is required to know the art of weaving. Assam has universities in Gauhāti, Jorhāt, and Dibrugarh. Area 30,318 sq mi (78,523 sq km) Pop. (1981 est.) 19,896,843.

Assam Himalayas, eastern section of the Himalayas, extending across Sikkim state (India), Bhutan, and into north Assam state (India) and along the Tibetan (Chinese) border. The mountains run eastward for 450 mi (720 km) from the upper Tista River in the west to the great bend of the Brahmaputra River in the east. Important peaks include Kula Kangri, Kangri, Chomo Lhāri, and Kangto, with the highest being Namcha Barwa (25,531 ft [7,782 m]) in Tibet. The Subansiri, Manās, Sankosh, Raidak, and Jaldhāka rivers rise in the mountains and flow southward to join the Brahmaputra. Main settlements in the region include Gangtok and Kālimpong in India, and Punakha and Paro in Bhutan. Important passes are Natu, Jelep, Tang, Pele, and Bum.

Assamese language, Indo-Aryan language of the northeast group, the official language of Assam state of India. The only indigenous Indo-Aryan language of the Assam Valley, Assamese has been affected in vocabulary, phonetics, and structure by its close association with Tibeto-Burman dialects in the region. Its grammar is noted for its highly inflected forms, and there are also different pronouns and noun plural markers for use in honorific and nonhonorific constructions. Assamese is also closely related to Bengali.

The language has an ancient literature most famous for its *buranji*s (historical works), which have been carefully preserved.

Assassin, one who murders by treacherous violence, originally referring to the Nizārī Ismāʿīlīyūn, a politico-religious Islāmic sect of the 11th–13th century that considered the murder of its enemies a religious duty. The term *hashishi* (assassin) is said to come from the terrorists' alleged practice of taking hashish to induce ecstatic visions of paradise before setting out to face martyrdom. This is, however, doubtful. The stories told by Marco Polo and others of the gardens of paradise into which the drugged devotees were introduced to receive a foretaste of eternal bliss are not confirmed by any known Ismāʿīlī source.

After the death of the Fāṭimid caliph al-Mustanṣir (1094), Ḥasan-e Ṣabbāḥ and some Persian allies captured the hill fortress of Alamūt near Kazvin, Iran. From this centre, by the end of the 11th century, Ḥasan, as grand master or leader of the sect, commanded a network of strongholds all over Persia and Iraq, a corps of devoted terrorists, and an unknown number of agents in enemy camps and cities, who claimed many victims among the generals and statesmen of the ʿAbbāsid caliphate, as well as some caliphs. At the beginning of the 12th century Assassin activities were extended to Syria. From Maṣyāf, the major castle in the Jabal Anṣarīyah, the Syrian grand master Rashīd ad-Dīn as-Sinān, the legendary *shaykh al-jabal,* ruled virtually independently of Assassin headquarters at Alamūt. Assassin power came to an end as the Mongols under Hülegü captured Assassin castles in Persia one by one until in 1256 Alamūt itself fell. The Syrian castles were gradually subjugated by the Mamlūk sultan Baybars I and placed under Mamlūk governors. Henceforth the sect stagnated as a minor heresy. Its followers are still to be found in Syria, Persia, and Central Asia, with the largest group in India and Pakistan, where they are known as Khōjās and owe allegiance to the Aga Khan.

assassin bug, any insect of the cosmopolitan family Reduviidae (order Heteroptera), containing about 4,000 species. The members of this family are easily recognized by the thin, necklike structure connecting the narrow head to the body; they range in size from 10 to 25 millimetres (0.4 to 1 inch). The short, three-segmented beak, which is curved and lies in a groove between the front legs, is used to suck the body fluids from victims. Although assassin bugs are generally black or dark brown, some species are brightly coloured. Most members of this family live outdoors and prey on

Assassin bug (*Narvesus carolinensis*)
Richard Parker

other insects; some, however, suck blood from vertebrates, including humans, and transmit diseases.

An important member of this family is the kissing bug (*Melanolestes picipes*). Its common name derives from the fact that it usually bites humans on the face around the mouth. This black-coloured insect is about 12 mm long and is usually found under stones and bark; it feeds on other insects.

The masked hunter (*Reduvius personatus*) is also known as the masked bedbug hunter or kissing bug. During the immature stages the body, legs, and antennae are covered with sticky hairs that catch pieces of lint and dust, camouflaging the insect as a ball of dust. The brownish-black adult, about 15 or 20 mm long, is commonly found in houses preying on insects, such as bedbugs and flies. It will also feed on man and has a painful bite. Though originally a central European species the masked hunter has spread throughout the southern parts of North America since its introduction into the port of New York.

One of the best known assassin bugs is the cone-nose bug (*Triatoma*), also known as the kissing bug, big bedbug, and Mexican bedbug. The adult is black with six red spots on each side of the abdomen and is about 25 mm long. The species *T. sanguisuga* is usually found in a bed, where it feeds on human blood. It has a painful, toxic, snakelike bite that may cause faintness, swelling, and vomiting. The South

Wheel bug (*Arilus cristatus*)
Richard Parker—The National Audubon Society Collection/Photo Researchers

American species *T. megista,* also known as the barber beetle, is the carrier of Chagas' disease and a trypanosome protozoal disease. Chagas' disease can also be transmitted by a related South American pest, *Rhodnius prolixus.* This bloodsucking assassin bug has been much used in insect physiology research.

T. rubrofasciata, found living in the debris on hut floors in southern Asia, may transmit kala-azar.

Pristhesancus papuensis is known as the bee killer. This bug waits on flowers to capture honey bees and other insects that frequent flowers; it sucks their body fluids.

The wheel bug (*Arilus cristatus*) is recognized by the notched crest on the top of the thorax. The adult is gray and quite large (about 25 mm); the nymph is red with black marks. Wheel bugs occur in North America, are predaceous on other insects, and have a painful bite. The venomous saliva is pumped into a victim through one channel in the wheel bug's beak. The digested body fluids of the prey are then pumped into the wheel bug's stomach through another channel in the beak.

The thread-legged bug (*Emesa brevipennis*) is about 33 mm long and is usually found on trees or in old buildings. It has long, thread-like middle and hindlegs; the shorter thicker front legs are modified into viselike grasping organs.

An oriental member of this family, *Ptilocerus ochraceus,* has a most unusual method of capturing prey. Tufts of red hair on its abdomen attract certain ants, which lick a glandular secretion from the hairs and become paralyzed. The assassin bug then pierces the ant with its beak and sucks out the body fluids.

The large assassin bug *Platymerus* has an effective means of protection. Its powerful salivary pump enables it to "spit" saliva as far as 30 centimetres. It has an accurate aim, and the saliva can cause blindness in humans.

Assateague Island, barrier reef off the Atlantic Coast of southeastern Maryland and eastern Virginia, U.S. Established as a national seashore in 1965, it is 37 mi (60 km) long, occupies 62 sq mi (160 sq km), about half land and half water, and is separated from the mainland by Chincoteague Bay, which is spanned by two bridges—one from Sinepuxent, Md., near the northern end, and the other from Chincoteague, Va., near the southern tip. The famous wild Chincoteague ponies (which are rounded up each July for auction), deer, small mammals, and waterfowl thrive in the pinelands and marshes of the Chincoteague National Wildlife Refuge at the southern end of the island. The refuge is also a bird sanctuary on the Atlantic Flyway. In sheltered bays and inlets, oysters and clams are harvested.

Assault (foaled 1943), U.S. racehorse (Thoroughbred), winner of the Triple Crown—the Kentucky Derby, the Preakness Stakes, and the Belmont Stakes—in 1946. A chestnut colt sired by Bold Venture (winner of the 1936 Kentucky Derby and Preakness) out of Igual, Assault was one of the smallest of the great racehorses, standing about 15 hands (60 inches). He had an exceptional season as a four-year-old, was injured in 1948, raced again in 1949–50, and then was retired to stud but never produced an offspring.

To make the best use of the Britannica, consult the INDEX *first*

assault and battery, related but distinct crimes, battery being the unlawful application of physical force to another and assault being an attempt to commit battery or an act that causes another reasonably to fear an imminent battery. These concepts are found in most legal systems and together with manslaughter and murder are designed to protect the individual from rude and undesired physical contact or force and from the fear or threat thereof.

No minimum degree of force is necessary to constitute a battery. A mere touch is sufficient. And force need not be applied directly. It is battery if one strikes a man's cane or horse, administers poison or drugs, or communicates a disease.

An accident or ordinary negligence that results in injury is not criminally punishable as battery unless it occurred during the commission of another unlawful offense. Generally, one does not commit battery unless he acts with intent to harm or with gross criminal negligence involving a high degree of carelessness. Even then such action may be justified if it is for the purpose of self-defense (*q.v.*).

Assault is a crime of attempt, the purpose of the law being to deter a possible battery by punishing conduct that comes dangerously close to achieving a battery. Although most courts in England and the United States consider an assault itself harmful in that it frightens the victim, in the U.S. one is guilty of assault even if the victim is ignorant of his peril.

As with most crimes of attempt, a clear line cannot be drawn between a criminal assault and conduct that is merely preparatory to an assault. There must be an intent to harm, but the intent is not sufficient if it produces the mere possibility of harm or the threat of battery in the distant future. Rather, the intent must be evidenced by an imminent danger, some overt act that threatens battery. Thus, words or intentions alone do not constitute assault.

England, the civil-law countries, and some American states define certain types of assault (such as assault with a deadly weapon) as "aggravated assault." The resulting battery is also called aggravated, and both crimes are assigned higher penalties than regular assault and battery.

assault gun: *see* tank destroyer.

assaying, in chemical analysis, process of determining proportions of metal, particularly precious metal, in ores and metallurgical products. The most important technique, still used today, grew largely out of the experiments of the ancient alchemists and goldsmiths in seeking to find or create precious metals by subjecting base metals and minerals to heat. More sophisticated methods, such as spectrographic analysis, are not suited to assaying precious metal ores because of the large sample required; precious metals tend to occur as scattered particles randomly distributed, so that a large sample of the ore must be taken. Such large samples—typically containing gold, silver, and lead—can be most economically assayed by the fire method, which usually consists of six steps:

1. Sampling: taking a representative proportion.
2. Fusion: melting the sample with suitable fluxes and other agents to produce a button—usually largely lead, containing the precious metal—and slag, which is discarded.
3. Cupellation: the button is melted in an oxidizing atmosphere, to oxidize impurities, including lead and other metals, and leaving a doré (gold-and-silver-alloy) bead.
4. Weighing: the bead is weighed to determine the total of gold and silver.
5. Parting: the bead is treated with hot dilute nitric acid to dissolve out the silver.
6. Weighing: the remnant of gold is weighed and subtracted from the gold–silver bead weight to give the weight of silver.

If platinum, palladium, or rhodium are present, they dissolve in the molten lead and are collected in the same manner as gold and silver. If iridium is present, it forms a black deposit that clings to the doré bead. Osmium and ruthenium, on the other hand, are largely lost during cupellation; if their presence is suspected, chemical methods instead of fire analysis are used.

Fire-assaying methods are also used to determine easily reducible base metals such as lead, bismuth, tin, antimony, and copper.

Assela (Ethiopia): *see* Asela.

Asselar man, extinct human known from a skeleton found in 1927 near the French military post of Asselar, French Sudan (now Republic of Mali), by M.V. Besnard and Théodore Monod. Asselar man is believed to belong to the Holocene or Recent era; some scholars consider it the oldest known skeleton of a Negro.

Asselian Stage, lowermost stage or time of deposition of the Lower Permian System of rock strata in the Soviet Union, especially well developed in the province of Perm (the Permian Period began about 280,000,000 years ago and lasted about 55,000,000 years). The Asselian also serves as the world standard for the lowermost Permian strata. Important fossil zones for the Asselian, as well as the succeeding Sakmarian Stage, are those of the fusulinid genus *Pseudoschwagerina* and the ammonoid genus *Properrinites,* permitting worldwide correlation of Lower Permian strata.

assemblage, in art, work produced by the incorporation of everyday objects into the composition. Although each non-art object, such as a piece of rope or newspaper, acquires aesthetic or symbolic meanings within the context of the whole work, it may retain something of its original identity. The term assemblage, as coined by the artist Jean Dubuffet in the 1950s, may refer to both planar and three-dimensional constructions.

Although artworks composed from a variety of materials are common to many cultures, assemblage refers to a particular form that developed out of intellectual and artistic movements at the beginning of the 20th century. The practice began about 1911–12 with the Cubist collages of Pablo Picasso and Georges Braques and sculptural assemblages by Futurists such as Umberto Boccioni and Filippo Tommaso Marinetti. One of the earliest examples is Picasso's "Still Life with Chair Caning" (1911–12; Picasso Collection), in which a piece of oilcloth with an imitation chair caning design was pasted onto the painting, and a rope was used to frame the picture. Subsequent art movements such as Dada (*q.v.*) and Surrealism (*q.v.*) explored the possibilities of assemblage. Marcel Duchamp, for instance, created "ready-mades" and "found objects" from industrial and natural objects; he elevated them into the realm of art simply by adding an inscription or by including them in an exhibition. In one canvas, he painted an illusionistic tear and then "mended" it with real safety pins, thus making a statement about the problem of representation and reality in art. Surrealists, such as Max Ernst, used material that suggested erotic and fantastic images to create symbolic assemblages. An exhibition at the Museum of Modern Art, New York City, in 1961, affirmed assemblage as a popular form in the United States and Europe. Artists of the late 1970s working in assemblage included Louise Nevelson and Robert Rauschenburg.

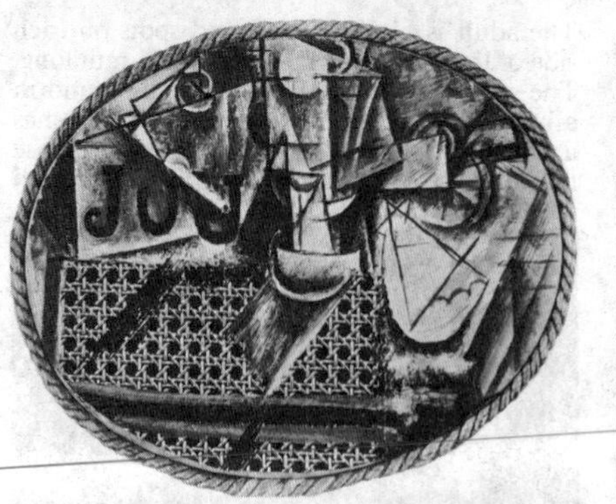

"Still Life with Chair Caning," assemblage with oilcloth chair caning and rope by Pablo Picasso, 1911–12; in the Picasso Collection

Because it obscured the traditional distinction between painting and sculpture by violating the picture plane with the introduction of three-dimensional, non-art media, assemblage was a significant development for the history of art. The form also laid open to question the historical role of the artist as the creator of permanent and valuable art objects.

assemblé, also called PAS ASSEMBLÉ (French: "step put together"), in classical ballet, a movement in which a dancer's feet or legs are brought together in the air and the dancer lands on both feet. It can be done front, back, dessus, dessous, and so on.

In a basic *assemblé,* the dancer brushes the working leg into the air while simultaneously pushing off the supporting leg, touches the feet or legs together in the air, and lands with the feet usually in fifth position *demi-plié* (feet crossed, knees bent). There are many variations of an *assemblé,* which can involve turning or travelling across the floor and executing small, *battu* ("beaten") steps.

assembled gem, cut jewel manufactured from two or three pieces of stone that are cemented together to create a larger stone with increased value. A doublet is composed of two pieces of material, usually cemented together at the girdle (the stone's widest part): if the two pieces are the same material, the gem is called a true doublet; if they are different, with the crown (above the girdle) being genuine and the pavilion (below the girdle) an inferior stone or glass, it is called a false doublet. True doublets may be detected by immersion in a liquid with an index of refraction nearly the same as that of the gem fragments; the layer of cement will appear as a dark line. Mounted false doublets will appear genuine because the crown will successfully withstand the usual tests that might be made upon it. False doublets may be exposed in the same manner as true doublets, but in this case the two halves of the stone will have a different appearance when immersed. Diamond doublets may have pavilions of colourless glass, zircon, topaz, quartz, or sapphire; ruby doublets of garnet, and beryl or garnet doublets of coloured glass. Sometimes, stones cut from one piece of glass will be called imitation doublets to increase their value.

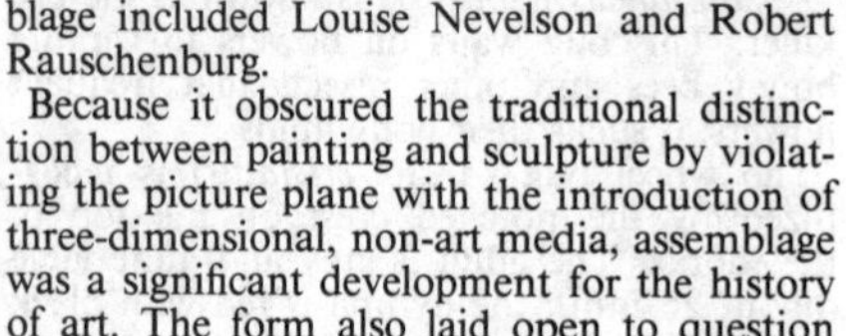

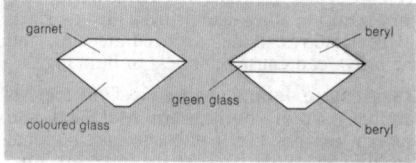

Assembled gems
(Left) Doublet; (right) triplet

From E.H. Kraus and C.B. Slawson, *Gems and Gem Materials;* copyright (1947); used with permission of McGraw-Hill Book Company

Triplets consist of a crown of stone and a lower portion (not necessarily the whole pavilion) of stone, sandwiching a layer of foil or other material to give the stone the desired colour.

Assemblée Législative (France): *see* Legislative Assembly.

Assemblies of God, Pentecostal denomination of the Protestant church, generally considered the largest such denomination in the United States, formed by a union of several small Pentecostal groups at Hot Springs, Ark., in 1914. The council of some 120 pastors and evangelists who effected this union among diverse regional associations adopted a simple kind of polity, an admixture of Congregational and Presbyterian elements. The council elected an Executive Presbytery to serve as the central administrative group; this organ was empowered to execute the mandates given it by the General Council and to act for the council in all matters that affected its interest when it was not in session.

Except for a pronouncement that "the Holy inspired Scriptures are the all-sufficient rule for faith and practice . . . and we shall not add to or take from them," that first General Council postponed action on the matter of a definitive doctrinal statement. Subsequently, however, a *Statement of Fundamental Truths* was adopted. The document demonstrated that the Assemblies of God are Trinitarian (believing in God as Father, Son, and Holy Spirit) and Arminian (accepting the doctrines of grace and free will as espoused by the 16th–17th-century Dutch theologian Arminius).

They also subscribed to two ordinances (Baptism by total immersion in water and the Lord's Supper), held a view of sanctification (becoming holy) that may be described as "progressive," or gradual, rather than "instantaneous" in regard to moral purity, and, finally, were strongly pre-millennial (believing in the doctrine of Christ's Second Advent before the 1,000-year reign of Christ and his saints).

From the outset, the Assemblies of God has been intensely missions-conscious. In addition to extensive foreign missions, the denomination conducts a diversified program of home missions among foreign language groups in America's urban centres, on Indian reservations, in prisons, and among the deaf and the blind.

The denomination operates the Gospel Publishing House at the church headquarters in Springfield, Mo., two fully accredited colleges of arts and science—Southern California College (Costa Mesa) and Evangel College (Springfield, Mo.)—and a number of regionally located Bible institutes. *See* Pentecostalism.

assembly, deliberative council, usually legislative or juridical in purpose and power. The name has been given to various ancient and modern bodies, both political and ecclesiastical. It has been applied to relatively permanent bodies meeting periodically, such as the ancient Greek and Roman assemblies, the Germanic tribal assemblies, the French National Assembly, the legislative houses called assemblies in certain states of the United States, and the UN General Assembly. It has also been applied to groups sitting only for special purposes and for limited periods, such as the Westminster Assembly, which met in 1643 to draft a new constitution for the Church of England.

assembly, unlawful: *see* unlawful assembly.

assembly line, industrial arrangement of machines, equipment, and workers for continuous flow of workpieces in mass-production operations.

An assembly line is designed by determining the sequences of operations for manufacture of each product component as well as the final product. Each movement of material is made as simple and short as possible with no cross flow or backtracking. Work assignments, numbers of machines, and production rates are programmed so that all operations performed along the line are compatible.

An automotive assembly line starts with a bare chassis; components are attached successively as the growing assemblage moves along a conveyor. Parts are matched into subassemblies on feeder lines that intersect the main line to deliver body parts, engines, and other assemblies. As the units move past, each worker along the line performs a specific function. Each part and tool is delivered to its point of use in synchronization with the line. A number of different assemblies are on the line simultaneously, but an intricate system of scheduling and control ensures that the appropriate body type and colour, trim, engine, and optional equipment arrive together to make the desired combinations.

Automated assembly lines consist entirely of machines run by machines. In such continuous-process industries as petroleum refining and chemical manufacture and in many modern automobile-engine plants, assembly lines are completely mechanized and consist almost entirely of automatic, self-regulating equipment.

Most products, however, are still assembled by hand because many component parts are not easily handled by a simple mechanism. The number of products automatically assembled is steadily increasing but at a low rate because a product must be designed for automatic assembly and must be accurately and consistently manufactured. Expensive and somewhat inflexible, automatic assembly machines are economical only if run at very high outputs. However, the development of versatile automatic machinery and industrial robots is increasing the flexibility of fully automated assembly operations.

Assen, *gemeente* (municipality) and capital, Drenthe *provincie* (province), northeastern Netherlands, at the northeastern end of the Drentsche Hoofd (also called Smilder) Canal. Founded in 1257 around a small convent, it was not chartered until 1807, when King Louis Bonaparte made it the provincial capital. An agricultural and dairy centre, it also has some light industry. It is a rail junction, and Eelde airport is 10 mi (16 km) north. The 13th-century Cistercian convent church remains and houses a museum of antiquities; in the vicinity of Assen are prehistoric stone monuments. Pop. (1983 est.) 45,906.

Asser (d. *c.* 909), Welsh monk, chiefly remembered as the friend, teacher, counsellor, and biographer of Alfred the Great. Born in Wales, he became a monk at St. David's Abbey, Pembrokeshire. In 886, eager to learn Latin, Alfred summoned Asser, who had acquired some reputation for learning, to his court in Wessex, and on St. Martin's Day (Nov. 11), 887, as Asser himself tells us, the Latin lessons began. Thereafter Asser divided his time between the court and his own community, and became Alfred's friend as well as his teacher. The king made him abbot of the monasteries of Congresbury and Banwell, Somerset, and later appointed him bishop of the diocese of Devon and Cornwall. At the time of his death he was bishop of Sherborne, Dorset.

Asser's *Life of King Alfred* follows Alfred's career from his birth to his accession in 871, and describes in detail his reign and his wars, stopping abruptly in 887, 12 years before Alfred's death. For historical events, it draws largely on the *Anglo-Saxon Chronicle.* Some scholars have suggested that, in whole or in part, the *Life of King Alfred* is not the work of Asser, but this view has not been widely accepted.

Asser, Tobias Michael Carel (b. April 28, 1838, Amsterdam—d. July 29, 1913, The Hague), Dutch jurist, co-winner (with Alfred Fried) of the Nobel Peace Prize in 1911 for his role in the formation of the Permanent Court of Arbitration at the first Hague peace conference (1899).

Asser was professor of commercial and private international law at the University of Amsterdam from 1862 to 1893. In 1869 Asser, along with two associates, started the *Revue de Droit International et de Législation Comparée* ("Review of International Law and of Comparative Legislation"). He was also a founder of the Institut de Droit International (Institute of International Law) in 1873.

Tobias Asser, 1911
By courtesy of the Nobel Foundation, Stockholm

In 1891 Asser prevailed upon the Dutch government to convoke the Hague Conference for the Unification of International Private Law, which first met in 1893 and later became a permanent institution, responsible, among other things, for the Hague treaties of 1902–05 concerning family law. In 1911–12 he presided over conferences for the unification of the law relating to international bills of exchange. In 1893 he became a member of the Dutch Raad van State (Council of State). Asser was a Netherlands delegate to the Hague peace conferences of 1899 and 1907.

assessment, process of setting a value on real or personal property, usually for the purpose of taxation. In most countries central government agencies do the assessing, but in some it is done by local officials.

Property is perhaps most commonly assessed on the basis of its annual rental value, as in Great Britain. In some countries, though, including the United States, West Germany, Austria, and Denmark, the tax base is the property's capital value. Methods of determining value include the analysis of market data to estimate the property's current market price, the estimation of the costs of reproducing the property minus the accrued depreciation, and the capitalization of the earnings of the property.

The last method seems most appropriate for the appraisal of commercial property and apartment buildings, whereas the second is well suited for appraising factories and other specialized properties. In practice, many assessing officers utilize an approach derived from all three methods, and the assessed valuation often is actually less than the property's current market value. Governments sometimes attempt to equalize effective assessed valuations by supplying a multiplying factor for various taxing districts based upon the degree to which their assessors undervalue.

assessor, in law, one called upon by the courts to give legal advice and assistance, and in many instances to act as judge in actual court cases. The term is also used in the United States to designate an official who evaluates property for the purposes of taxation.

Assessors were appointed in the late 19th and early 20th centuries throughout much of continental Europe as an attempt to limit the influence of the jury system, which had been introduced on the wave of egalitarianism that followed the French Revolution. Displeased with the freedom of the nonprofessional jury that was so contrary to the civil-law tradition of the professional judge, legislatures introduced assessors who would sit and decide cases alongside professional judges. In effect, the attempt at independence from state judges was more or less destroyed.

In France the jury of nine, which sits only in the assize courts, where only the most serious crimes are tried, is in reality a group of assessors who must decide in conjunction with three professional judges. It is possible for the jury to circumvent the judges, since a majority of eight votes is needed for conviction, but, in practice, the judges are often able to influence the jury and gain a majority.

In West Germany there are *Schöffen* (*see* Schöffe; lay jurists), who sit in groups of two at criminal cases. In specialized courts, such as labour courts, there are lay assessors who are representatives of the employers and employees. This latter type of assessor is found in England and the United States in maritime and admiralty courts, as well as in some other civil jurisdictions.

In the Soviet Union assessors replaced the jury after the October Revolution. In the local people's courts (*q.v.*), the assessors are chosen by the people, who meet in assemblies of workers, employers, or peasants. In the higher courts, however, they are elected by the soviets. Assessors sit with judges, but a majority of all those deciding is necessary for a verdict. Because the trial may be complex and the assessors untrained, they are under the influence of the professional judges, particularly on questions of law.

Assia Djebar: *see* Djebar, Assia.

assignat, paper bill issued in France as currency from 1789 to 1796, during the French Revolution. A financial expedient on the part of the Revolutionary government, the increasing issuance of the assignats resulted in inflation.

In December 1789, to pay its immediate debts, the National Assembly issued the assignat as a bond bearing 5 percent interest, with the recently nationalized church lands as security. By September 1790 the Assembly made the assignat into a paper currency, and the amount in circulation was increased from 400,000,000 livres to 1,200,000,000. The initial effect of the paper currency was beneficial, stimulating economic growth and eliminating a money shortage. But a deep public distrust of paper money and the fear that the currency would be worthless if the uncertain Revolutionary regime collapsed soon caused the assignat to depreciate.

The outbreak of war with the other European powers in 1792 caused a further decline in the value of the assignat. In 1796 the assignats were replaced by the mandats territoraux (land warrants) at the rate of one mandat for 30 assignats. The failure of the mandat to gain public confidence forced the Directory to return to a metallic currency (Feb. 4, 1797).

assigned counsel, lawyers appointed by the state to provide representation for indigent persons. Assigned counsel are private lawyers designated by the courts to handle particular cases; in some countries, particularly the United States, public defenders permanently employed by the government perform this function.

The right to counsel varies considerably from country to country. Until the late 19th century, access to counsel was almost entirely predicated upon an individual's ability to pay. If a person could afford a lawyer, he was entitled to one; if he was poor, he usually went unrepresented, except at times in capital cases. In the late 19th century, bar organizations and social-welfare groups banded together to supply legal aid (*q.v.*) to the indigent. By the mid-20th century, the governments of most European countries were participating in these programs in some fashion, either in their administration or funding or both.

Most countries have recognized the right of the indigent to have counsel in criminal cases, particularly the most serious types. The United States has taken the lead in this area, though Great Britain had legislated earlier (1949) to provide state legal aid. Beginning in 1963 the Supreme Court issued a series of decisions that upheld the rights of indigent persons accused of felonies to have counsel during trial, appeal, and even during police interrogation. Although this right has not yet been extended to cover misdemeanours, some jurisdictions and many public defender offices automatically give coverage in such cases.

In civil-law countries and in England, there has been a more limited advancement. In France, for example, anyone accused of a crime beyond a minor misdemeanour must have counsel at the preliminary hearing and the trial, but this right has not been extended to cover police interrogation. Japan requires counsel only for cases in which punishment may exceed a three-year prison term. In the Soviet Union there must be a defense counsel in any case in which a public prosecutor participates or any case in which the accused is incapable of handling his defense.

Many countries do not remunerate lawyers assigned to defend the poor in criminal cases. In the United States the salary is often considerably lower than what the attorney could get from a private client. In consequence, although many defenders and assigned attorneys are capable lawyers, they are often young and lack experience. In England, where the majority of lawyers volunteer to take indigent cases, an accused person has a somewhat better chance of obtaining experienced counsel in a criminal proceeding.

In civil cases there is an even greater disparity among countries as far as rights to counsel and the resultant quality of counsel are concerned. In England state aid has been granted in divorce and certain kinds of litigation since 1949. Only in 1971 did the United States begin to deal with the problem of civil litigation and then only in a limited fashion. The poor were given the right to sue for divorce without paying filing fees and court costs; the right to counsel in such cases was also indicated. But rights were not extended to other areas of civil litigation such as bankruptcy and eviction cases.

In civil-law countries the system of providing counsel for the indigent in civil cases is usually well organized but tends to employ young, inexperienced lawyers who usually serve without pay. This is the situation in both France and Italy. In West Germany, where the Federal Constitutional Court has upheld the right of the poor to counsel in civil actions, the compensation is adequate to appeal to experienced attorneys. Lawyers are appointed by the court and paid by the government.

assimilation, the process whereby individuals or groups of differing ethnic heritage are absorbed into the dominant culture of a society. Usually they are immigrants or hitherto isolated minorities who, through contact and participation in the larger culture, gradually give up most of their former culture traits and take on the new traits to such a degree that socially they become indistinguishable from other members of the society. Assimilation does not denote racial or other biological fusion, though such fusion may be related.

Complete assimilation rarely occurs, as evidenced, for example, by the great diversity of local and regional cultures in Europe, despite centuries of conquest and recurrent attempts to force assimilation. There have, nonetheless, been some notable instances of assimilation, particularly in the United States, the so-called melting pot of ethnic groups. Millions of European immigrants to the United States, through relocation, the influences of the public-school systems, and other forces in American life, became almost completely assimilated within two or three generations.

Assiniboia, region of western Canada, named for the Assiniboin Indians and the Assiniboine River, demarcated as a district in three different forms during the 19th and early 20th centuries.

Assiniboia was the official name of the Red River Settlement (*q.v.*) formed in 1811 by a grant from the Hudson's Bay Company; it included present-day southern Manitoba and (until 1818) the Red River Valley in what are now North Dakota and Minnesota. In 1835 the company reacquired the region and created the "District of Assiniboia," which comprised an area within a 50-mile radius of Ft. Garry (on the site of present-day Winnipeg, Man.). It was administered by a local governor and council appointed by the Hudson's Bay Company. When Manitoba was created in 1870, the district was incorporated into that province.

In 1882 the Canadian government created another District of Assiniboia as part of the old Northwest Territories. It extended westward from the boundary of Manitoba to the District of Alberta and was bounded on the north by the District of Saskatchewan and on the south by the Canada–United States border. In 1905 Assiniboia was divided between Alberta and Saskatchewan.

Assiniboin, also called STONIES, American Plains Indian people belonging to the Siouan linguistic stock who split from the Yanktonai Dakota before the 17th century and lived during their greatest prominence in the area west of Lake Winnipeg along the Assiniboin and Saskatchewan rivers, Canada. Their name is derived from the Ojibwa (Chippewa) tongue and means One Who Cooks with Stones (they are known as Stonies in Canada). They were closely allied with the Algonkian Cree, with whom they fought almost constantly against the Dakota.

The Assiniboin were great buffalo hunters known for their trading of pemmican (preserved buffalo meat) for firearms and other European goods brought in by traders on the Hudson Bay and along the upper Missouri. The encroachment of the British and French caused them to move continually westward into the plains of Canada, Montana, and North Dakota, bringing them into confrontation with the Blackfoot over control of the prairies.

The Assiniboin were divided into separate bands, each with its own chief and council. The bands moved their camps frequently in pursuit of the migrating buffalo; before the introduction of horses in the 18th century, they moved on foot and used dog-drawn travois. Women performed all work related to the lodges (tepees), including assembling and dismantling them. Prowess in war consisted of the taking of scalps and horses and of touching the enemy during battle. War-party leaders received their instructions in visions or dreams. In spite of their warrior tradition, the Assiniboin were exceptionally friendly with whites. The most significant religious ceremony was the sun dance, or medicine lodge dance.

Assiniboin, placating the spirit of a slain eagle, photograph by Edward S. Curtis, 1908; from *The North American Indian*

By courtesy of the Newberry Library, Chicago, Ayer Collection

The power and prominence of the Assiniboin were reduced severely in the 1820s and 1830s by recurrent smallpox epidemics during which thousands died. Their first treaty with the U.S. government was signed in 1851, after which they were placed on reservations. In the late 20th century the Assiniboin numbered more than 1,000 in Canada and were reported to exceed 4,000 in the United States.

Assiniboine River, river in southern Saskatchewan and Manitoba, Canada, a major tributary of the Red River. From its source in eastern Saskatchewan, it flows southeastward into Manitoba and thence eastward through a break in the Manitoba Cuesta, an escarpment, to the lowlands formed in ancient times by glacial Lake Agassiz; there it joins the Red River at Winnipeg, after a course of 665 mi (1,070 km). Explored by the French *voyageur* La Vérendrye, in 1736 the Assiniboine subsequently served as an important route for fur traders. It is named after the Assiniboine Indians (meaning "those who cook with hot stones"). Along with its two chief tributaries, the Qu'Appelle and Souris (*q.v.*) rivers, the Assiniboine drains one of Canada's major wheat-growing regions. Major riparian cities include Brandon, Portage la Prairie, and Winnipeg, which are in Manitoba.

Assiout (Egypt): *see* Asyūṭ.

Assis, city, in the highlands of west central São Paulo state, Brazil, at 1,847 ft (563 m) above sea level. It was given town status in 1915 and was made the seat of a municipality in 1938. Assis processes coffee, cotton, corn (maize), and rice and produces furniture and liquor. The city is easily reached by airplane, train, or automobile from São Paulo, the state capital, 250 mi (400 km) east-southeast. Pop. (1980 prelim.) 57,217.

Assisi, town, Perugia province, Umbria region, central Italy, situated on a spur of Monte

Subasio above the valleys of the Topino and Chiascio rivers, east of Perugia. Famous as the birthplace (1182) of St. Francis, the town developed from the Umbrian, Etruscan, and Roman town of Assisium, of which the temple of Minerva (now a church) is the most notable survival. Subject to the dukes of Spoleto in the early Middle Ages, Assisi became an independent commune in the 12th century and was involved in internal disputes and wars with Perugia before passing to the Papal States. It became part of the Italian kingdom in 1860.

The most notable landmark is the church and convent of S. Francesco, begun immediately after the canonization of the saint (died 1226) in 1228. The crypt in the lower church was added in 1818 when the tomb of St. Francis was opened. The upper and lower churches have numerous frescoes, most notably those depicting the life of St. Francis by Giotto and others by Giovanni Cimabue and Simone Martini. In the church of Sta. Chiara (St. Clare; 1257–65) is the tomb of St. Clare, who founded the Poor Clares, nuns who after 1212 lived in the convent and church of S. Damiano. The Eremo delle Carceri, or Prison Hermitage, given to St. Francis by Benedictine monks, and the church of Sta. Maria degli Angeli (1569), enshrining the tiny Romanesque church of the Porziuncola, the cradle of the Franciscan order, are both nearby.

Church and convent of S. Francesco, Assisi, Italy
SCALA—Art Resource/EB Inc.

Other monuments include the cathedral of S. Ruffino (1140) and La Rocca Maggiore fortress (1367).

The town has light manufacturing industries and derives considerable income from pilgrims and tourists. Pop. (1981 prelim.) mun., 24,440.

assistance, writ of, in English and American colonial history, a general search warrant issued by superior provincial courts to assist the British government in enforcing trade and navigation laws. Such warrants authorized customhouse officers (with the assistance of a sheriff, justice of the peace, or constable) to search any house for smuggled goods without specifying either the house or the goods. In common use since the reign of Charles II, the writs did not arouse controversy until a renewal attempt was made in 1761. Despite an eloquent attack on their constitutionality by James Otis, representing Boston merchants, the writs were continued after confirmation of their legality had been received from England in 1762. When similar warrants were expressly reauthorized by the Townshend Acts (1767), they were challenged for five years in every superior court in the 13 colonies and refused outright in 8 of them. Thus, writs of assistance became a major colonial grievance in the pre-Revolutionary period.

assize, in law, a session, or sitting, of a court of justice. It originally signified the method of trial by jury that superseded the barbarous judicial combat. During the Middle Ages the term was applied to certain court sessions held in the counties of England; it was also applied in France to special sessions of the Parlement of Paris (the High Court) that met in the provinces. The term also designated certain writs operable in such courts. In modern times, courts of assize are criminal courts that deal with the most serious crimes.

Originally, in England all writs of assize had to either be tried at Westminster in London or await trial in the locality of origin at the circuit of the justices every seven years. In order to remedy such delay and inconvenience, Magna Carta (1215) provided that certain writs of assize be tried annually by the judges in every county. By successive enactments, the civil jurisdiction of the justices of assize was extended, and the number of their sittings increased until it was no longer necessary to appear at Westminster; courts of assize were held regularly in the counties.

In France assizes were held regularly in the large towns and were run by the *prévôts* (*q.v.*), low-ranking royal judicial administrators, in conjunction with a group of local assessors (lay judges). The grand assizes met four times a year under the auspices of the area baron or count or his *bailli* (*see* bailiff), a high-ranking royal judicial officer in charge of the *prévôts.*

An important type of French assize was the *grand jour,* a meeting in a province of magistrates from the Parlement of Paris. The *grands jours* often were held at times of civil disruption in the area as a way of making the power and presence of the central government felt. They were held, for example, with some regularity during the Wars of Religion in the 16th century and after the Fronde rebellions in the 17th. In the Champagne, however, the *grand jour* was a more permanent fixture, although by the 16th century it met only irregularly. The *grands jours* dealt with cases of special interest and with appeals from the *bailli*'s courts.

In modern England, assizes (abolished in 1971) were periodical sessions of the High Court of Justice held in the counties; they dealt with issues such as the trying of prisoners who commit crimes in jail and regular cases of treason and murder. In France (and in Germany until 1975) the assize courts are criminal courts of first instance handling the most severe crimes.

Examples of writs of assize were those of *mort d'ancestor* and *novel disseizin.* The former was an action to recover lawfully inherited land taken by another before the heir was able to take possession; the latter was an action to recover lands of which the plaintiff had been dispossessed.

Associated Press (AP), cooperative news agency (wire service), the oldest and largest of those in the United States and long the largest and one of the preeminent news agencies in the world. Its beginnings trace to 1848, when six New York City daily newspapers pooled their efforts to finance a telegraphic relay of foreign news brought by ships to Boston, the first U.S. port of call for westbound transatlantic ships. In 1856 the service took the name of the New York Associated Press, a mutual, which sold its service to various regional newspaper groups. Pressure from the regional customers forced changes in its control, and in 1892 the modern AP was set up under the laws of Illinois. The *Chicago Inter Ocean,* a newspaper that did not have AP membership, brought an anti-monopoly suit in 1900, and AP moved to New York, where association laws permitted the group to continue its strict control of membership, including blackballing of applicants for membership by existing members. In the early 1940s, Marshall Field III, who had established the *Chicago Sun,* fought his exclusion from the AP service. Prosecution under the federal antitrust powers ended the AP's restrictive practices.

In the early 1980s, AP's annual operating budget, swollen by the cost of installing and maintaining electronic equipment for satellite relay of radioteleprinter and other services, exceeded $170,000,000, by far the largest of any such agency in the world. Its staff of some 2,500 reporters and correspondents, in bureaus in more than 100 U.S. and 50 world cities, collected and relayed to member papers news from about 100 countries. Staff efforts were augmented by those of more than 100,000 reporters of member papers. The agency had more than 6,500 newspaper clients in the early 1980s. For many years, AP leased more than 400,000 miles of telephone wire to carry its transmissions, but its use of radioteleprinters—begun in 1952—began mitigating the need for leased wires, a trend that increasing employment of satellite transmissions will carry on as subscribers install appropriate antennas.

Associated Talking Pictures, Ltd.: *see* Ealing Studios.

Associated Universities, Inc. (AUI), group of U.S. universities that administers the operation of two federally funded research facilities, one in nuclear physics and the other in radio astronomy. The member institutions are Columbia, Cornell, Harvard, Johns Hopkins, Massachusetts Institute of Technology, Pennsylvania, Princeton, Rochester, and Yale. AUI was incorporated in 1946 to manage the then new Brookhaven National Laboratory at Upton, Long Island, N.Y., for the Atomic Energy Commission. Brookhaven, now funded by the U.S. Department of Energy, carries out experiments in nuclear physics, chemistry, engineering, biology, and medicine. AUI was later chosen by the U.S. National Science Foundation to manage the National Radio Astronomical Observatory (NRAO), headquartered in Charlottesville, Va. The NRAO conducts extensive studies of cosmic sources of radio-frequency radiation.

association, general psychological principle originally closely linked with problems of recollection, or memory. The principle stated that when any past event or experience is recalled, the act of recollection tends to bring again into use other events and experiences that have become related to this event in one or more of certain specified ways. As time went on the application of this general principle was expanded. It was invoked to cover almost everything that could happen in mental life except original sensations, and associationism became a theoretical view embracing the whole of psychology.

Although the ancient Greek philosopher Aristotle had proposed three forms of association (similarity, contrast, and contiguity) and in doing so paved the way to much elaborate annotation and controversy, associationism is usually looked upon as a distinctively British doctrine. "Association of ideas" was first used by John Locke in *An Essay Concerning Human Understanding* (1690). David Hume maintained in *A Treatise of Human Nature* (1739) that the essential forms of association were by resemblance, by contiguity in time or place, and by cause and effect.

Following Hume the chief British exponents of associationism were David Hartley in the 18th century and James and John Stuart Mill, Alexander Bain, and Herbert Spencer in the 19th. There was much criticism and disagreement about both the number and the proper naming of the forms of association, but in general all the associationists are usually said to hold views that are sensationalist, mechanical, and atomistic. Knowledge is held to be acquired originally through one or more of the special senses. By repetitions occurring in the natural course of mental life, the original sensory data are interconnected and can be revived or reinstated as representative images or ideas. All human knowledge is built up from separate, simple, and particular experiences and is analyzable without remainder into these experiences.

During the 1880s a strong reaction in England against associationism was begun by the philosopher F.H. Bradley and the analytical psychologists James Ward and G.F. Stout, who denied that knowledge was founded solely on sensations and emphasized an inherent element of purpose in all mental activity.

In *The Principles of Psychology* (1890) the U.S. philosopher William James replaced association of ideas by an association of central nervous processes set up by overlapping or immediately successive stimuli. In 1903 the Russian physiologist Ivan P. Pavlov used purely objective methods to study what had been called association, and he arrived eventually at a complete and elaborate derivation of all behaviour from original and conditioned reflexes. The conditioned reflex theories and many of the behaviourist theories that grew up about the same time were an association psychology of conduct, making essentially the same claims as those doctrines of the association of ideas and open to the same criticism. This situation was true also of much of the stimulus-response psychology that became dominant in the United States and that persists in various forms. As experimenters who believed firmly in association as an explanatory principle designed and did more and more experiments, however, difficulties accumulated. Edward L. Thorndike of the U.S., for example, showed that mere repetition can do little or nothing to establish connections between stimulus and response. He himself considered most important the effect that followed action, and he thought of this effect chiefly in terms of pleasure or unpleasure (*The Fundamentals of Learning,* 1932). Others stressed an alleged direct effect of knowledge of results, and others, such as U.S. psychologist Clark Hull (*Principles of Behavior,* 1943), produced a complete account of learning mainly in terms of need reduction, or the strength of the drive linking stimulus and response under various empirical conditions.

All of these thinkers demanded not the rejection but some more or less radical reformulation of associationist principles. Others, including the Gestalt psychologists, called for total rejection of associationism so far as higher mental processes were concerned.

The end of criticisms of associationist theories as all-embracing explanatory principles in psychology is uncertain. Very few, if any, psychologists or students of the behaviour of animals other than man accord these theories the range and power once claimed for them. Most psychologists probably agree, however, that association remains a genuinely important and effective principle, active in all instances of learning through accumulated experience.

association, chemical: *see* chemical association.

association croquet, lawn game played with balls and a mallet on a court on which are set out six iron hoops and one central peg. It is played on an organized basis in the United Kingdom, New Zealand, Australia, and South Africa. (For the origins of the game and a general history, *see* croquet.)

In association croquet, the two sides alternate play, each side consisting of either one or two players. Four matched balls, made of compressed cork, are used, each side playing a different colour or colours; blue and black are always partners against red and yellow. The object of the game is to hit the ball through

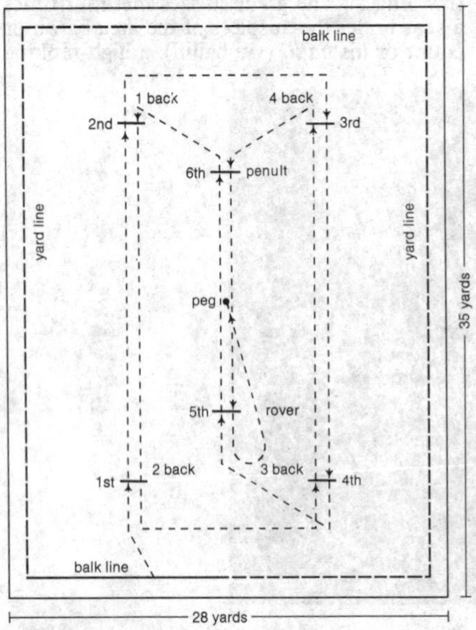

Association croquet court
Arrows indicate direction of play; hoop numbers indicate order of scoring

all of the hoops consecutively, in each direction, and then to hit the peg point. The peg may be hit from any direction; each side thus has 26 points to score, 13 with each ball. A game is won by the number of points that the loser has yet to make when the opponent has hit the peg with both balls. In singles, any ordinary turn may be played with either ball of the side, provided that no ordinary turn is played with the same ball again until all the balls are in play. In doubles, one partner plays throughout with one ball and his teammate plays with the other. When all four balls are in play, the sides alternate but the balls need not be played in sequence.

The association croquet court is rectangular, 35 yd (31.95 m) long by 28 yd (25.56 m) wide. Portions of the yard line, 13 yd (11.9 m) long, are the balk lines, from either of which each player starts his first turn. The inside of the white line is the actual boundary. A turn initially is comprised of one stroke; but if that stroke is a roquet—a move which strikes one of the other three balls—or if the ball passes through a hoop, the turn is extended. A player earns two additional strokes after a roquet: first, a croquet stroke, which is played by placing one's ball, fixed underfoot, in contact with the roqueted ball and then striking one's ball with the mallet, thereby driving the roqueted ball out of position; and secondly, one more ordinary stroke, called a continuation stroke. This second additional stroke also may roquet one of the other balls, but each ball may be roqueted only once in each turn, unless a hoop is scored (that is, the ball passes through the hoop).

Handicap games include bisques, extra turns that may be taken at any time during the game, and may be used defensively or offensively. A half-bisque is an extra turn in which no hoop may be scored; it is used to set up the balls in a break position. The number of bisques a player receives in a given game is contingent upon the handicap of his opponent.

In a modified version known as golf roquet, all balls are played for one hoop at a time, with the hoops played in order. A point is scored by the side whose ball first runs through each hoop.

In the United Kingdom, croquet tournaments are governed by the Croquet Association, founded in 1896, which sponsors the open championships; the men's, women's, and mixed-doubles championships; and invitational events, including the President's Cup. Separate governing bodies exist in Australia, New Zealand, and South Africa. In the 1970s, interest in association croquet arose in the United States, and the United States Croquet Association was founded in 1976.

association football, also called SOCCER, game popular throughout the world, played by two 11-member teams. The members of each team try to propel a ball into the opposing team's goal, using any part of the body except the hands and arms. Only the goalkeeper, who is restricted to the penalty area in front of the goal, is allowed to handle the ball. The team that scores the most goals is the winner.

A brief treatment of association football follows. For full treatment, *see* MACROPAEDIA: Sports, Major Team and Individual.

Soccer originated in England and was played by schoolboys under various rules. An attempt to standardize the rules was made at Cambridge University in 1843, but it was not until 1863, when the Football Association (FA) was created, that a uniform set of rules was established. The FA Cup was started in 1871, and professional leagues emerged, beginning with the English Football League in 1881. Other countries soon organized along similar lines.

In 1904 the Fédération Internationale de Football Association (FIFA) was organized, and it remains the world governing body of amateur competition. Soccer was officially included in the Olympic Games in 1908, and since 1930 the FIFA has sponsored the quadrennial World Cup competition, which is held between the Olympic Games. Prior to the formation of the FIFA, international matches were played by European and South American countries, but there were rule differences between the continents, particularly regarding the obstruction of a player who did not have possession of the ball, tackling from behind, and shoulder charging. These differences were gradually resolved, and by the late 1960s universal application of the rules was achieved.

Other major tournaments include the European Champions' Club Cup (begun 1956), the South American Copa de Libertadores (1960), and the European Cup–Winners' Cup (1963). An unofficial club championship is also played by the winners of the South American and European champions' cups.

See Sporting Record: *Football: Association football (soccer). See also* Olympic Games.

Association Internationale Africaine, English AFRICAN INTERNATIONAL ASSOCIATION, a society of explorers, geographers, and philanthropists formed in September 1876 at the instigation of Leopold II, king of the Belgians, to "civilize" Central Africa.

At its formation it was intended that the association, with headquarters in Brussels, should be divided into national committees, each of which was to be organized and financed by the country to which its committee members belonged. This plan was never fully implemented. Only Leopold had a strong investment in its success. Great Britain preferred to maintain friendly relations of correspondence with the Belgian and other committees without hampering itself "with engagements of an international nature." The French, too—preoccupied as always with their territories in Equatorial Africa and already active in the Congo Basin—were to act more as rivals to the association than as friends.

Belgium was the first to appoint a national committee, whose director—Leopold II himself—financed the organization from his private fortune. Sending an expedition from the east coast of Africa to Lake Tanganyika (1877) and authorizing Belgian officers to establish a fortified post at Karema (1879), he dreamed of establishing similar posts across the continent so that "our roads and posts will greatly assist the evangelization of the blacks and the introduction among them of commerce and modern industry." After H.M. Stanley's discovery of the Congo River in 1877, however, Leopold's attention became focussed on the Congo Basin and he lost interest in the association's broader goals. With the loss of Leopold's commitment, the association became inactive.

Association of ——: *see under* substantive word or words (*e.g.,* South East Asian Nations, Association of).

association test, test used in psychology to study the organization of mental life, with special reference to the cognitive connections that underlie perception and meaning, memory, language, reasoning, and motivation. In the "free association" test, the subject is told to give the first word that comes into his mind in response to a word, concept, or other stimulus. In "controlled association," a relation may be prescribed between the stimulus and the response (*e.g.,* the subject may be asked to give opposites). Though more complex analyses may be used for special purposes, the reaction time for each response and the words the subject gives are the basic data provided by the test.

Association tests also are a common procedure in psychoanalysis and are used to investigate personality and its pathology. In the latter the subject's reaction to emotionally charged memories and ideas provoked by certain of the test stimuli may produce atypical or revealing associations or, more often, unusually long or short reaction times.

associative law, in mathematics, either of two laws relating to number operations of addition and multiplication, stated symbolically: $a + (b + c) = (a + b) + c$, and $a(bc) = (ab)c$; that is, the terms or factors may be associated in any way desired. While associativity holds for positive or negative, integral or fractional, rational or irrational, or real or imaginary numbers, there are certain exceptions—as in nonassociative algebras, and nonadditivity of divergent series. *See also* commutative law; distributive law.

associative learning, any of many nonhuman learning processes that have in common the alteration of behaviour through behavioral responses to stimuli. Among the types of learning considered associative are conditioned response, trial-and-error learning, latent learning, insight learning, and imitation.

Conditioned response is the performance of behaviour appropriate for one stimulus, but in response to another, wholly different stimulus, it results from repeated exposure to both stimuli either simultaneously or in close succession. After a number of responses to both stimuli the animal responds to the second alone with action appropriate to the first. Although probably rare in nature, the conditioned response has been a valuable aid in laboratory studies of the nervous system since the classical work by Russian psychologist Ivan Pavlov (*q.v.*) in the late 19th century.

Trial-and-error learning occurs when an animal that is striving toward an objective accidentally performs the appropriate behaviour. If the situation is repeated and the solution is again found, it will gradually be incorporated into the animal's behaviour as a direct response to the situation. The number of repetitions that are necessary to fix the behaviour pattern varies with the type of animal and the individual.

Latent learning is the acquisition by an animal of information that is of no immediate use, but which is likely to prove useful in the future. The knowledge gained by an animal in exploring a territory, for example, may serve no purpose at the time of exploration but may save the animal's life should it be pursued by a predator.

Insight learning, the acquisition of a new behavioral response to a situation without trial and error, appears to require the ability of the animal to form a mental image of the solution in advance. This form of problem solving is difficult to demonstrate in wild animals but has been observed in the laboratory.

Imitative learning provides an animal with a new behaviour pattern through the observation of the performance of another individual. Social facilitation, in which the action imitated is already in the imitator's repertoire, is sometimes considered imitative learning, but most authorities restrict the term to situations in which the imitator acquires new behaviour. Thus defined, imitative learning apparently is found only in a few higher primates, including man.

assonance, in prosody, repetition of stressed vowel sounds within words with different end consonants, as in the phrase "quite like." It is unlike rhyme, in which initial consonants differ but both vowel and end-consonant sounds are identical, as in the phrase "quite right." Many common phrases, such as "mad as a hatter," "free as a breeze," or "high as a kite," owe their appeal to assonance. As a poetic device, internal assonance is usually combined with alliteration (repetition of initial consonant sounds) and consonance (repetition of end or medial consonant sounds) to enrich the texture of the poetic line. Sometimes a single vowel sound is repeated, as in the opening line of Thomas Hood's "Autumn":

I *saw* old *Au*tumn in the misty *morn*

Sometimes two or more vowel sounds are repeated, as in the opening lines of Shelley's "The Indian Serenade," which creates a musical counterpoint with long *i* and long *e* sounds:

I ar*i*se from dr*ea*ms of th*ee*
In the f*i*rst sw*ee*t sl*ee*p of n*i*ght

Assonance at the end of a line, producing an impure, or off, rhyme, is found in *La Chanson de Roland* and most French verses composed before the introduction of pure rhyme into French verse in the 12th century. It remains a feature of Spanish and Portuguese poetry. In English verse, assonance is frequently found in the traditional ballads, where its use may have been careless or unavoidable. The last verse of "Sir Patrick Spens" is an example:

Haf owre, haf owre to Aberdour,
It's fiftie fadom d*ei*p:
And thair lies guid Sir Patrick Spence,
Wi' the Scots lords at his f*ei*t.

Otherwise, it was rarely used in English as a deliberate technique until the late 19th and 20th centuries, when it was discerned in the works of Gerard Manley Hopkins and Wilfred Owen. Their use of assonance instead of end rhyme was often adopted by poets such as W.H. Auden, Stephen Spender, and Dylan Thomas.

assortative mating, in human genetics, a statement of the frequency at which individuals mate with persons of similar phenotype or, conversely, with persons of different phenotype (*see* phenotype). In the most general sense, assortative mating refers to a statement about the degree of phenotypic randomness of mating patterns in human beings; in a more specific sense the term can mean the selection of a mate on the basis of phenotype or with phenotype as one of the major criteria. For example, in the United States most people choose not to marry outside their own racial groups; this is an instance in which assortative mating is not random, in the first sense of the word, and in which assortative mating is in practice, in the second sense of the word. Positive assortative mating, or homogamy, exists when people choose to marry persons similar to themselves (*e.g.,* when white marries white, tall person marries tall person); this type of selection is very common. Negative assortative mating is the opposite case, when people avoid marrying persons similar to themselves; for example, the number of marriages between redheads—who presumably tend to avoid marrying other redheads—is lower than would be predicted by random marriage.

Assos (ancient city): *see* Assus.

Assouan, also spelled ASSUAN (Egypt): *see* Aswān.

assumpsit (Latin: "he has undertaken"), in common law, an action to recover damages for breach of contract. Originating in the 14th century as a form of recovery for the negligent performance of an undertaking, this action gradually came to cover the many kinds of agreement called for by an expanding commerce and technology.

The concept of assumpsit was first introduced in cases in which the defendant damaged goods entrusted to him by the plaintiff—*e.g.,* where the defendant had taken the plaintiff's horse in order to transport it across a river and negligently caused the ferry to overturn so that the horse drowned.

Assumpsit did not become a contractual remedy in the modern sense until two modifications occurred: (1) the emphasis shifted from the negligent act of the defendant to the defendant's failure to keep his promise; and (2) the action was made available as a remedy in situations where the defendant did something improperly or neglected to do something he had promised to do.

Assumption, in Roman Catholic and Eastern Christian theology, doctrine that Mary, the mother of Jesus, was taken (assumed) into heaven, body and soul, following the end of her life on Earth. There is no explicit mention of the Assumption in the New Testament, although various texts are frequently adduced to demonstrate the appropriateness of the doctrine, the imagery of which is related to the Ascension of Jesus into heaven. Theologically, the doctrine means that Mary's redemption involved a glorification of her complete personality and anticipated the state promised to the rest of mankind.

The doctrine's development is closely related to a feast devoted to Mary that passed from a general celebration in her honour to one celebrated on August 15 commemorating her dormition, or falling asleep. The feast, which originated in the Byzantine Empire, was brought to the West, where the term Assumption replaced the earlier title to reflect increased emphasis on the glorification of Mary's body as well as her soul. Although the dormition of Mary had been a frequent iconographic theme in the East, the theme of the Assumption was less prevalent there. An unwillingness to accept apocryphal (non-

"Assumption," oil painting by Titian, 1516–18; in Sta. Maria dei Frari, Venice

SCALA—Art Resource/EB Inc.

canonical and unauthentic) accounts of the Assumption caused some hesitation, but by the end of the Middle Ages there had been a general acceptance of the doctrine in both the East and the West.

The doctrine was declared a definitive doctrine (dogma) for Roman Catholics by Pope Pius XII in the apostolic constitution *Munificentissimus Deus* on November 1, 1950. The Assumption is not considered a revealed doctrine among the Eastern Orthodox and is considered an obstacle to ecumenical dialogue by many Protestants.

The Assumption as a theme in Christian art originated in western Europe during the late Middle Ages—a period when devotion to the Virgin Mary was growing in importance. Since the 13th century the Assumption has been widely represented in church decoration, and during the Renaissance and Baroque periods it became a popular subject for altarpieces. Characteristic representations of the Assumption show the Virgin, in an attitude of prayer and supported by angels, ascending above her open tomb, around which the Apostles stand in amazement. Until the end of the 15th century, she is represented surrounded by a mandorla (*q.v.*), or almond-shaped aureole; in the 16th century the mandorla was replaced by a cluster of clouds. The basic iconography of the theme, however, remained standard until its decline at the end of the 17th century.

Assur (ancient Assyrian city): *see* Ashur.

Assur-akh-iddina (king of Assyria): *see* Esarhaddon.

Assur-nasir-apli (kings of Assyria): *see under* Ashurnasirpal.

Assurbanipal (Assyrian king): *see* Ashurbanipal.

Assus, Greek ASSOS, Byzantine MACHRAMION, ancient Greek city of the Troad, located in modern Turkey, with the island of Lesbos lying about seven miles offshore to the south. Founded by Aeolic colonists from Methymna in Lesbos in the 1st millennium BC, the city was constructed on terraces, rising more than 700 feet (200 metres) above the sea. Assus had the only good harbour on the north shore of the Adramyttian Gulf (Gulf of Edremit) and commanded coastal traffic.

Assus came under the rule of the Persians and later of the Athenian Empire. It fell to Alexander the Great and subsequently was ruled by the Macedonian general Lysimachus, the kings of Pergamum, and Rome. In response to an invitation from Hermeias of Atarneus, tyrant of Assus, Aristotle founded a Platonic school there (348–345 BC). The Stoic philosopher Cleanthes was born there.

The site was quarried in the 19th century; nevertheless, much of the old city remains, including the submerged mole of the ancient harbour, parts of the fortifications, and ruins of the Doric Temple of Athena.

Assyria, kingdom of northern Mesopotamia that became the centre of one of the great empires of the ancient Near East. Located in present northern Iraq, in the area around Mosul, Assyria was a dependency of Babylonia and later of the Mitanni during most of the 2nd millennium BC. It emerged as an independent state in the 14th century BC, and in the subsequent period (that of the Old Assyrian Empire) it became a major power in Mesopotamia, Armenia, and sometimes in northern Syria. Assyrian power declined after the death of Tukulti-Ninurta I (*c.* 1208 BC). It was restored briefly in the 11th century BC by Tiglath-pileser I, but during the following period both Assyria and its rivals were preoccupied with the incursions of the semi-nomadic Aramaeans. The Assyrian kings began a new period of expansion in the 9th century BC, and from the mid-8th to the late 7th century BC, a series of strong Assyrian kings—among them Tiglath-pileser III, Sargon II, Sennacherib, and Esarhaddon—united most of the Near East, from Egypt to the Persian Gulf, in what is called the Neo-Assyrian Empire. The last great Assyrian ruler was Ashurbanipal, whose reign witnessed a notable flowering of the arts, but his last years and the period following his death, in 627 BC, are obscure. The state was finally destroyed by a Chaldean-Median coalition in 612–609 BC. Famous for their cruelty and fighting prowess, the Assyrians were also monumental builders, as shown by archaeological excavations at Nineveh, Ashur, Nimrūd, Khorsabad, and other sites.

Assyro-Babylonian language: *see* Akkadian language.

Aṣṭa Pradhād (Marāthā administrative council): *see* Ashta Pradhan.

Astaire, Fred, original name FREDERICK AUSTERLITZ (b. May 10, 1899, Omaha, Neb., U.S.), popular U.S. dancer of stage and motion pictures best known for the film musical comedies in which his partner was Ginger Rogers; these films not only were tremendous box-office hits but also contributed significantly to the development of the musical as a film genre.

Astaire studied dancing from the age of four. In 1906 he formed an act with his sister Adele that became a popular vaudeville attraction. On Broadway from 1917, Fred and Adele Astaire achieved international fame with stage hits that included *For Goodness Sake* (1922), *Funny Face* (1927), and *The Bandwagon* (1931). Astaire's initial film role was a small part in *Dancing Lady* (1933), and in the same year he made his first appearance with Ginger Rogers in *Flying Down to Rio.* It was followed by the series of films that included *The Gay Divorcee* (1934), *Roberta* (1935), *Top Hat*

Astaire in *Top Hat*, 1935

Penguin Photo Collection

(1935), *Swing Time* (1936), and *The Story of Vernon and Irene Castle* (1939). The sophisticated, intimate style, the grace and technical excellence, and the integration of plot and music in the Rogers–Astaire films revolutionized the musical comedy.

Astaire retired temporarily in 1946 but returned to the screen for *Easter Parade* (1948), with Judy Garland, and other hits, such as *The Barkleys of Broadway* (1949), *Daddy Long Legs* (1955), *Funny Face* (1957), and *Silk Stockings* (1957). In 1949 Astaire was honoured with a special Academy Award for his contributions to the musical film. Various television shows, among them *An Evening With Fred Astaire* and its sequel, earned him several "Emmy" awards, and non-dance dramatic roles in films added to his list of accomplishments. Astaire officially stopped dancing in 1971 but continued to make guest appearances in films and on television in the 1970s. In 1981 he co-starred in the motion picture *Ghost Story.*

aṣṭamaṅgala, eight auspicious symbols frequently represented on Jaina ritual objects. They are common to both the Śvetāmbara and Digambara sects and are found on 1st-century-AD votive slabs (*see* āyāgapaṭa) and in miniature paintings as well as being employed in Jaina worship today. In the modern Jaina

The *aṣṭamangalas*, or eight auspicious Jaina symbols, seen above and below the seated image of the Jina (saviour), miniature from the *Kalpa-sūtra*, 15th century; in the Freer Gallery of Art, Washington, D.C.

By courtesy of the Smithsonian Institution, Freer Gallery of Art, Washington, D.C.

temple they are seen carved on the offering stands. Women devotees also form the symbols out of uncooked rice when making an offering to the Jina images. Although there are various traditions, the eight symbols are usually considered to be (1) *darpaṇa* (mirror), (2) *bhadrāsana* (throne), (3) *vardhamānaka* (powder vase), (4) *kalaśa* (full water vessel), (5) *matsyayugma* (pair of fish), (6) *śrīvatsa* symbol, (7) *nandyāvarta* (an elaborated swastika), and (8) swastika.

aṣṭāṅgika-marga (Buddhism): *see* Eightfold Path.

Astarte, also spelled ASHTART, great goddess of the ancient Near East, chief deity of Tyre, Sidon, and Elath, important Mediterranean seaports. Hebrew scholars now feel that the goddess Ashtoreth mentioned so often in the Bible is a deliberate compilation of the Greek name Astarte and the Hebrew word *boshet*, "shame," indicating the Hebrew contempt for her cult. Ashtaroth, the plural form of the goddess's name in Hebrew, became a general term denoting goddesses and paganism.

Astarte, terracotta plaque, Late Bronze Age (*c.* 1550–*c.* 1200 BC), provenance unknown; in the Rockefeller Museum, Jerusalem

By courtesy of the Israel Department of Antiquities and Museums

King Solomon, married to foreign wives, "went after Ashtoreth the goddess of the Sidonians" (I Kings 11:5). Later the cult places to Ashtoreth were destroyed by Josiah. Astarte/Ashtoreth is the Queen of Heaven to whom the Canaanites had burned incense and poured libations (Jer. 44).

Astarte, goddess of love and war, shared so many qualities with her sister, Anath, that they may originally have been seen as a single deity. Their names together are the basis for the Aramaic goddess Atargatis.

Astarte was worshipped as Astarte in Egypt and Ugarit and among the Hittites, as well as in Canaan. Her Akkadian counterpart was Ishtar. Later she became assimilated with the Egyptian deities Isis and Hathor, and in the Greco-Roman world with Aphrodite, Artemis, and Juno, all aspects of the Great Mother.

astatine (At), radioactive chemical element, heaviest member of the halogen elements, or Group VIIa of the periodic table. Astatine, which has no stable isotopes, was first synthetically produced (1940) at the University of California by Dale R. Corson, K.R. MacKenzie, and Emilio Segrè, who bombarded bismuth with accelerated alpha particles (helium nuclei) to yield astatine and neutrons. Naturally occurring astatine isotopes have subsequently been found in minute amounts in the three natural radioactive decay series in which they occur by minor branching (astatine-218 in the uranium series, astatine-216 in the thorium series, and astatine-215 and astatine-219 in the actinium series). About 20 isotopes are known; astatine-210, with a half-life of 8.3 hours, is the longest lived.

Because of the short half-lives of astatine isotopes, only very small quantities have been available for study. By the use of astatine-210 and astatine-211 and the tracer methods of radiochemistry, some of the chemical properties of the element have been established. It generally resembles iodine (thus, like iodine, it concentrates in the thyroid gland of higher animals). It is somewhat soluble in water and much more soluble in benzene and carbon tetrachloride. Astatine can be reduced to the astatide ion, At^-, and has been oxidized to positive oxidation states that appear to be +1 (AtO^-) and +5 (AtO_3^-).

atomic number	85
stablest isotope	210
oxidation states	−1, +1, +3(?), +5, +7(?)
electronic config.	2-8-18-32-18-7 or $(Xe)4f^{14}5d^{10}6s^26p^5$

Astbury, John, byname ASTBURY OF SHELTON (b. 1688, England—d. 1743, Shelton, Staffordshire), pioneer of English potting technology and earliest of the great Staffordshire potters.

Although from 1720 several Astburys were working in Staffordshire, it is John who is credited with the important Astbury discoveries and creations. He allegedly masqueraded as an idiot in order to learn the craft from the potting brothers John Philip and David Elers, who in 1688 had emigrated from Holland. Establishing a factory at Shelton in the early 18th century, he succeeded in producing yellowish-glazed red earthenware decorated with bits of white pipe clay (which he was the first to import from Devonshire); his mode of decorating with such appliqués is called sprigging. Thus, some of the earliest Staffordshire figures in brown and white clay covered with a lead glaze have been attributed to him (a surviving example depicting the victory of Admiral Vernon at Porto Bello is dated 1739; Victoria and Albert Museum, London).

Astbury is credited with being the first (1720) Staffordshire potter to use flint for improving the quality of earthenware mixture by making it whiter. Figures now attributed to him reveal variously toned clays, as well as colours clouded to enrich them. He quite possibly originated the popular pew groups; *i.e.,* two or more rigidly posed, salt-glazed stoneware figures, some engaged in such activities as playing bagpipes, wearing stylized costumes and seated on stiff pews. Similar groups of musicians only have also been attributed to him. His other typical figure groups are soldiers and equestrians, rather crude in appearance, modelled by hand after being cast in simple molds. His utilitarian products include mugs, variously shaped bowls, and teapots. He also made agate and marbled wares.

Astbury's son Thomas experimented with the lead-glazed earthenware that was later called creamware and, improved by the great Josiah Wedgwood, eventually renamed Queen's ware. It was developed from the earlier white stoneware body and covered with a lead glaze. Astbury ware is now found primarily in museums and in renowned private collections. During the mid-20th-century renaissance of Staffordshire pottery, Astbury figures, particularly the pew groups, brought premium prices, some in the thousands of pounds.

Astbury ware, English earthenware produced by John Astbury and his son Thomas from about 1725; later a term for fine 18th-century Staffordshire earthenware until *c.* 1760. John Astbury (1688–1743) established a single-kiln pottery at Shelton in 1725; to him are ascribed productions that were markedly in advance of other potters' work. His ware was better formed, being finished on a lathe; better surfaced, with a coating of white pipe clay; and harder and lighter because of the introduction of calcined flint into the body. Astbury's red or buff earthenware was ornamented by white relief ships, figures, and fortifications.

Earthenware figure of a mounted dragoon of the Astbury type, Staffordshire, England, *c.* 1740; in the Victoria and Albert Museum, London

By courtesy of the Victoria and Albert Museum, London

Astbury products include agateware and tortoiseshell ware; black earthenware with relief ornament in white; glazed earthenware in various brown, fawn, and buff shades stamp-decorated with white pipe clay; salt-glazed stoneware; white and cream earthenware; terra-cotta, which was a hard red unglazed earthenware with geometric incised lathe-cut decoration; sgraffito (scratch-decorated) earthenware; and figures. The distinctive Astbury figures consisted of men, animals, and birds, singly or grouped, modelled in clay, slip-coated, and decorated in a coloured slip—later to be superseded by metallic oxide colours. Arbour groups (couples beneath a tree), musical groups of individual performers, equestrian figures, and Chinese figures are all represented.

Astbury-Whieldon ware, English pottery, principally earthenware, with applied decoration, produced from about 1730 to 1745 by two Staffordshire potters, John Astbury and Thomas Whieldon. Instead of the more common stamped relief decoration, the ornament was achieved by applying pre-molded relief motifs to the surface of the pottery object and connecting them by curled stems formed of threads of thinly rolled clay. The process was known as sprigging.

Astbury-Whieldon teapot, Staffordshire, England, *c.* 1740; in the Victoria and Albert Museum, London

By courtesy of the Victoria and Albert Museum, London; photograph, EB Inc.

Aṣṭchāp (Sanskrit: Eight Seals), group of 16th-century Hindi poets, four of whom were disciples of the Vaiṣṇava leader Vallabha, and four of his son and successor, Viṭṭhala. The greatest of the group was Sūrdās, a blind singer whose descriptions of the exploits of the child-god Krishna are the highlights of his collection of poetry called the *Sūrsāgar*, a work that is deeply loved throughout the Hindi-speaking areas of North India. It is particularly rich in its details of daily life and in its sensitive perception of human emotion, the parent for the child and the maiden for her lover. Other members of the Aṣṭchāp group were Paramānanddās, Nanddās, Kṛṣṇadās, Govindswāmī, Kumbhandās, Chitaswāmī, and Caturbhujdās.

aster yellows, plant disease once thought to be caused by a virus but now believed to be of mycoplasma (bacterial) origin found over much of the world wherever air temperatures do not persist much above 90° F (32° C). Some 300 species of plants in 48 families are susceptible including many wild and cultivated plants, both vegetables and garden plants. Typical symptoms include yellowing (chlorosis) of young shoots, stiff and erect bunchy growth, greenish and distorted or dwarfed flowers, and general stunting or dwarfing. Leafhoppers serve as transmitting agents when they feed on an infected plant and then a healthy one. No transmission occurs through leafhopper eggs or plant seed. The mycoplasma is perpetuated in overwintering weed and crop plants, propagative parts (bulbs, corms, tubers), and in leafhoppers in mild climates. The mycoplasma is destroyed in plants and leafhoppers subjected to temperatures of 100° to 108° F (38°–42° C) for two to three weeks; thus aster yellows is rare or unknown in many tropical regions.

Control is effected chiefly by excluding the leafhopper carriers, by promptly removing diseased crop and weed plants as well as all overwintering susceptible weeds, and by spraying or dusting with a contact insecticide. Oxytetracycline antibiotics effect remission of symptoms in new growth.

Asterābad (Iran): *see* Gorgān.

Asteraceae, also called COMPOSITAE, the aster, daisy, or composite family of the flowering plant order Asterales, with about 930 genera and between 15,000 to 20,000 species of herbs, shrubs, and trees, distributed throughout the world.

A brief treatment of the Asteraceae family follows. For full treatment, *see* MACROPAEDIA: Angiosperms.

It is one of the largest plant families and is important primarily for its many garden ornamentals, such as *Ageratum, Aster, Chrysanthemum, Cosmos, Dahlia,* marigold (*Tagetes*), and *Zinnia.* Other well-known garden plants and wildflowers include *Boltonia, Brachycome,* burdock (*Arctium*), butterbur (*Petasites*), *Calendula,* catsear (*Hypochoeris*), cudweed (*Filago* and *Gnaphalium*), *Gerbera,* hawksbeard (*Crepis*), *Inula, Matricaria,* and *Piqueria.*

Burdock (*Arctium pubens*)
G.E. Hyde—EB Inc.

Some genera include noxious weeds, such as dandelion (*Taraxacum*), ragweed (*Ambrosia*), and thistle (*Carduus, Cirsium,* and others). Artichoke (*Cynara*), endive (*Cichorium*), safflower (*Carthamus*), salsify (*Tragopogon*), lettuce (*Lactuca*), sunflower (*Helianthus*), and wormwood (*Artemisia*) are economically important for the products derived from their seeds, leaves, or tubers.

Members of the family have flower heads composed of many small flowers, called florets, that are surrounded by bracts (leaflike structures). Bell-shaped disk florets form the centre of each head; strap-shaped ray florets extend out like petals from the centre and are sometimes reflexed (bent back). Some species have flowers with only disk or only ray florets. The sepals have been reduced to a ring of hairs, scales, or bristles that is called the pappus on the mature fruit. The one-seeded fruit has a hard outer covering.

Asterales, order of flowering plants, containing one family, the Asteraceae, or Compositae, with about 950 genera and 15,000 to 20,000 species of herbs, shrubs, and trees, distributed throughout the world. *See* Asteraceae.

asterism, in mineralogy, starlike figure exhibited in light reflected or transmitted by some crystals. The stars shown by star sapphires, some phlogopite mica, rose quartz, and garnet are due to minute oriented crystals (often rutile) included within the mineral; several sets of inclusions are present, and each set produces its own ray. In minerals with hexagonal or pseudo-hexagonal symmetry (three equal axes at 120° all perpendicular to a fourth), three such rays produce a six-pointed star; and in those with isometric symmetry (three equal, mutually perpendicular axes), two rays produce a four-pointed star.

Articles are alphabetized word by word, not letter by letter

asteroid, also called MINOR PLANET, or PLANETOID, any of a host of small rocky astronomical objects found primarily between the orbits of Mars and Jupiter. Approximately 2,000 asteroids have so far been discovered in the solar system, some of which appear to be travelling in pairs.

A brief treatment of asteroids follows. For full treatment, *see* MACROPAEDIA: Solar System.

Asteroids are smaller than any of the nine major planets of the solar system. There are very few large asteroids; possibly seven have a diameter of more than 300 kilometres (186 miles). Ceres, the largest known minor planet, has a diameter of 1,020 km, and Pallas, the second in size, measures only 585 km across. Nearly 250 asteroids have a diameter of at least 100 km. It is estimated that millions of asteroids of boulder size exist in the solar system. These smaller objects are probably formed when larger asteroids collide. A few of them strike the Earth's surface in the form of meteorites (*see* meteorite).

The largest asteroids are massive enough for their gravity to have molded them into spheres during formation. This hypothesis is supported by the lack of regular variation in their brightness that would result if these objects were asymmetric in shape. Their rotation would manifest regularly a varying amount of reflecting surface area. Smaller asteroids may have a wide range of shapes. Icarus, for example, is nearly spherical, with a diameter of only 2 km. Eros, on the other hand, is more of a slab, having dimensions of approximately 10 × 15 × 30 km.

Asteroids such as Icarus and Eros, whose orbits bring them closer to the Sun than the Earth, are called Apollo asteroids. Only about two dozen of these asteroids have definitely been identified, but some 1,000 of them are thought to exist. Some astronomers would like to mount a full-scale search for such asteroids for two reasons. One is a fear that they may collide with the Earth. Knowing of their existence and calculating their orbits would afford a possibility of altering their motion away from the Earth. Collisions with larger asteroids are rare, but smaller ones are more numerous. It is estimated that three asteroids of 1-km diameter may collide with the Earth within a period of 1,000,000 years. If an asteroid of this size were to collide with the Earth, it would produce an explosion with as much force as several hydrogen bombs. The crater created by its impact would be about 13 km across. A short-term disturbance in the world's climate could result, and collision in the ocean could be catastrophic. During the extinction of the dinosaur some 65,000,000 years ago, it is believed by some investigators that many land and sea species were wiped out in a period of only a few years by the impact of either an asteroid or a comet on the order of 10-km diameter.

A second reason for seeking out Apollo asteroids is their potential as sources of important metals (most likely including iron, nickel, and magnesium). The energy and time required to travel to an Apollo asteroid would be far less than that needed to reach those within the asteroid belt between the orbits of Mars and Jupiter.

During the 1970s astronomers began to apply sophisticated analysis techniques to the reflecting spectra of asteroids to complement composition analysis of meteorites in the laboratory. Such efforts resulted in a better understanding of the composition of asteroids. These objects appear to be comprised of varying proportions of stony and metallic (principally iron) materials. Many of the primarily stony types contain chondrules, tiny spherical inclusions of olivine and pyroxene (iron and/or magnesium bound with silicates), and a large amount of carbon, which make them dark—albedoes of only 0.03–0.04. Such objects are called carbonaceous chondrites and are considered to have been the first materials to coalesce out of the primordial nebula from which the solar system is believed to have originated. They have avoided any subsequent alteration (*e.g.,* melting induced by heat from radioactivity within young asteroids or structural metamorphosis induced by meteoric impact). Recent laboratory studies of carbonaceous chondritic material have brought up the intriguing possibility that one or two nearby supernova explosions triggered the compression of the primordial nebula, which then went on to collapse by its own gravity to form the Sun and the planets.

No planet could have formed in the region between Mars and Jupiter because of the gravitational influence of the latter, which is the largest planet in the solar system and which resembles a star more than a planet. Its influence would have stirred up the pre-planetary material in the asteroid belt during the formation of the solar system, causing the material to crash and break up rather than coalesce to build up to a planet-sized object. It is theorized that if all of the asteroids were to fuse into one object, they would only form an object comparable in size to one of the larger satellites of the solar system such as the Moon or a Galilean satellite of Jupiter.

There are gaps in the orbital distances of the asteroids from the Sun because of Jupiter's gravitational influence. These interruptions, known as Kirkwood gaps, are a simple fraction (*i.e.,* $1/3$ and $1/2$) of the orbital period of Jupiter. This resonance phenomenon has the planet passing by any asteroid in the Kirkwood gaps every two or three asteroid years, depending on which gap. The repeated tugging induces an asteroid into larger, longer orbits closer to Jupiter. Eventually, however, an asteroid's resonance with Jupiter disappears as its orbit increases.

Jupiter's gravitational force has another effect. Because of its influence, a number of planetoids have become concentrated into two groups called the Trojan asteroids. One precedes Jupiter in its orbit at a 60° angle and the second follows at the same angle.

The discovery of the first asteroid (Ceres in 1801) came as no surprise because of Bode's law (*q.v.*), a scheme that yields a sequence of numbers analogous to the spacing of the planets. (The sequence breaks down for the later-discovered outer planets.) One of these numbers corresponded to a distance from the Sun between the orbits of Mars and Jupiter where there was no planet. Ceres, then, appeared to prove Bode's law, when it was observed to orbit at the very distance indicated by the sequence. The subsequent discoveries of Pallas in 1802, Juno in 1804, and Vesta in 1807, however, confused matters. Astronomers concluded that these objects resulted from the fragmentation of a major planet. This idea is no longer considered viable for three reasons. First, as discussed above, all the asteroids together do not comprise an object the size of a major planetary body. Second, Jupiter's gravitational influence would have prevented a sizable planet from forming. Third, astronomers have found that asteroids at different distances from the Sun differ in composition and density. With increasing distance away from the centre of the solar system, there is a progression from stony-metallic to watery, carbonaceous-stony material and an attendant decrease in density. This condition could not have resulted from the breakup or explosion of a planet because an occurrence of that type would have necessarily produced a random distribution of density and composition. By contrast, such a condition seems consistent with the process that, according to present theory, led to the formation of the solar system and corresponds to the trend observed in the major planets.

asthenia, a condition in which the body lacks or has lost strength either as a whole or in any of its parts. General asthenia occurs in many chronic wasting diseases, such as anemia and cancer, and is probably most marked in diseases of the adrenal gland. Asthenia may be limited to certain organs or systems of organs, as in asthenopia, characterized by ready fatigability of vision, or in myasthenia gravis, in which there is progressive increase in the fatigability of the muscular system. Those suffering from neurasthenia, or mental asthenia, have great difficulty in concentrating on a single topic. They can not keep their minds on a subject for any length of time; their thoughts wander. Neurocirculatory asthenia is a clinical syndrome characterized by breathing difficulties, heart palpitations, a shortness of breath or dizziness, and insomnia.

asthma, chronic disease characterized by sporadic attacks of shortness of breath, wheezing, and coughing, the result of muscular constriction of the bronchi and swelling of the bronchial mucosa, usually caused by an allergic reaction (extrinsic asthma), infection in persons with susceptible bronchi (intrinsic asthma), or malfunction of the autonomic nervous system. Asthma is common, shows a familial incidence, affects all races, and is of generally equal incidence in males and females.

Extrinsic asthma usually begins before age 30, but intrinsic asthma may have a later onset. Allergy may exist to materials such as pollen, mold spores, feathers, animal dander, and foods; established asthmatics may also experience attacks after exposure to sudden changes in temperature or humidity or both, exertion, emotional stress, strong odours, or smoke. Attacks usually last one-half hour to several hours; a person experiencing a prolonged attack resistant to drugs is said to be in status asthmaticus. Prolonged or frequent attacks of asthma may become dangerous if the sufferer is weakened by fatigue and inadequate nutrition, if oxygen consumption is too low, or if emphysema develops.

Some 35–40 percent of childhood asthma cases improve at puberty; a nearly equal number worsen, however, so that treatment of all childhood cases is necessary. Treatment consists in desensitization (*q.v.*); administration of epinephrine and other drugs and sometimes of oxygen; and avoidance, as far as possible, of all substances or situations that precipitate attacks.

Asti, city, capital of Asti province, Piemonte (Piedmont) region, northwestern Italy at the confluence of the Tanaro and Borbera rivers, southeast of Turin. The Hasta, or Colonia, of the Romans and the seat of a bishopric from AD 932, it reached its zenith as an independent commune in the 13th century, after which it fell to several overlords before coming under the House of Savoy in 1575. Notable landmarks include the cathedral (1309–48); the 13th-century collegiate church of S. Secondo, with a Romanesque campanile on a Roman base; the 13th-century Torre Troiana (Trojan Tower); the 10th-century Baptistery of S. Pietro; the 7th- and 8th-century crypts of S. Giovanni and S. Anastasius; and numerous medieval and Renaissance churches and palaces, including the Palazzo Alfieri, birthplace of the tragedian Vittorio Alfieri (1749–1803). Asti is an agricultural market known for fine wines, notably Asti spumante, and fruits. Industries include food canning, metallurgy, glassworks and brickworks, and the manufacture of chemicals. Pop. (1981 prelim.) mun., 76,950.

Astian Stage, uppermost major division of Pliocene rocks and time (the Pliocene Epoch began about 5,000,000 years ago and lasted about 2,500,000 years). Rocks of the Astian Stage were originally thought to overlie those of another stage of the Pliocene called the Piacenzian, but differences in the fossils of these two stages are now considered to be the result of differences in the habitats where the sediments were deposited, and so representative of the same period of time. The Astian Stage was named for the yellowish sands and gravels exposed near Asti, in northern Italy. The marine sands of the Astian are adjacent to continental deposits that have a distinctive group of mammalian fossils preserved in them, and these mammals are used to define the Villafranchian Stage (*q.v.*). The Astian corresponds in time to the lower and, possibly, middle Villafranchian.

astigmatism, lack of symmetry in the curvature of the cornea or, much less commonly, of the crystalline lens (the cornea is the transparent wall of the eye in front of the pupil and iris). The result is blurring of part of the image on the retina, the light-sensitive tissue lining the back and sides of the eyeball. The effect of astigmatism can also be produced by misalignment of the lens. Vision is corrected by means of cylindrical lenses—lenses with one side flat and the other either concave or convex in the shape of a cylinder wall.

āstika, in Indian philosophy, any orthodox school of thought, defined as one that accepts the authority of the Vedas (sacred scriptures of ancient India); the superiority of the Brahmins (the class of priests), who are the expositors of the law (*dharma*); and a society made up of the four traditional classes (*varṇa*). The six orthodox philosophic systems are those of Sāṃkhya and Yoga, Nyāya and Vaiśeṣika, and Mīmāṃsā and Vedānta.

The term *āstika* comes from the Sanskrit *asti,* which means "there is." Contrasted to the *āstika* systems are the *nā-stika* (Sanskrit: from *na asti,* "there is not"), the individuals and schools that do not accept the authority of the Veda, the system of the four classes, and the superiority of the Brahmins. Included among the *nāstika* schools are the Buddhists, Jainas, the ascetic Ājīvikas, and the materialistic Cārvākas.

Astilbe, genus of about 14 species of herbaceous perennials, in the family Saxifragaceae, native to eastern Asia and North America. They are often grown in gardens for their erect feather-like flower spikes of white, yellow, pink, magenta, or purple, which rise above clumps of fernlike leaves from mid- to late summer.

A. chinensis, up to 60 centimetres (2 feet) in height, has produced several hybrids with dwarf habit and more intense colours. The smaller *A. simplicifolia,* less than 30 cm, has starlike white flowers on slender spikes. *A. japonica* and its hybrids constitute the florist's spirea, some with variegated leaves and larger flowers, densely packed on the spikes.

Astipálaia, island, westernmost of the Greek Dodecanese Islands, Aegean Sea, between Amorgós and Cos (Kos). With an area of 37 sq mi (97 sq km), it comprises two mountain masses linked by a narrow isthmus that provided shelter for the ancient Roman fleet. The western hills rise to about 1,500 ft (450 m) and the eastern hills to about 1,200 ft. The coast is much indented, with high cliffs rising precipitously from the sea. Astipálaia, the capital (also known as Kastéllo), forms a commune with the port of Periyiálion on the west side of the Órmos (bay) Maltezána.

Perhaps a Cretan possession before 1400 BC, the island was colonized by Dorians from Epidaurus in the eastern Peloponnese (Argolís); the dialect spoken today reflects Argolian origins. In turn it was subject to Athens, Macedonia, and Egypt, but it remained largely independent during the Roman period. From AD 1207 to 1522 it was ruled by a Venetian family, but it then passed to Turkey, which held it except for two periods (1648–68; 1821–28) until 1912, when it became the first of the Dodecanese to be occupied by Italy. The island was restored to Greece after World War II. Pop. (1981) town, 800; island, 1,034.

Astley, Philip (b. Jan. 8, 1742, Newcastle-under-Lyme, Staffordshire, Eng.—d. 1814, Paris), English trick rider and theatrical manager who in 1770, in London, created Astley's Amphitheatre, considered the first modern circus ring.

A horseman with a British dragoon regiment from about 1759, Astley was at first the sole performer in the Amphitheatre, specializing in riding with one foot on the saddle and one on the horse's head while brandishing a sword. He gradually included other equestrians, acro-

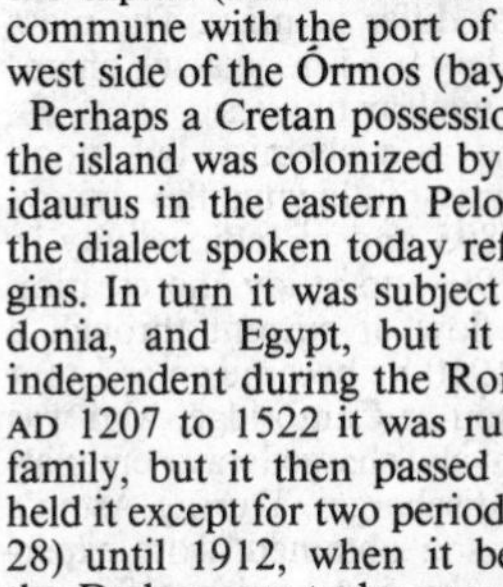

Philip Astley, engraving by J. Smith

By courtesy of the trustees of the British Museum; photograph, J.R. Freeman & Co. Ltd.

bats, rope dancers, aerialists, clowns, and the first recorded circus freak show.

The Amphitheatre suffered destruction by fire several times, and eventually it became The Royal Amphitheatre of Arts under the patronage of the Prince of Wales and the Duke of York in 1794. Beginning in 1772, Astley made numerous tours of European cities, including Paris, where he performed before the French king and royal court. He established the Astley Amphitheatre in Paris (1782) and 18 other permanent circuses in cities throughout Europe.

astome, any uniformly ciliated protozoan of the order Astomatida, commonly found in annelid worms and other invertebrates. As the name implies, this parasite has no mouth. Some astomes attach themselves to their hosts by suckers; others use various types of hooks or barbs. Asexual reproduction is by transverse fission. In some cases, chains of individuals form by repeated fission without separation of the cells. The sexual phenomenon of conjugation (nuclear exchange between individuals) also occurs. Representative genera are *Cepedietta,* which lives in the amphibian digestive system, and *Radiophrya,* an elongated parasite of various oligochaetes.

Aston, Francis William (b. Sept. 1, 1877, Harborne, Birmingham, Eng.—d. Nov. 20, 1945, Cambridge, Cambridgeshire), winner of the Nobel Prize for Chemistry in 1922 for his development of the mass spectrograph, a device that separates atoms or molecular fragments of different mass and measures those masses with remarkable accuracy, and for his discovery of a large number of nuclides, or nuclear species that differ in mass. The mass spectrograph is widely used in geology, chemistry, biology, and nuclear physics.

Aston was trained as a chemist, but, upon the rebirth of physics following the discovery of X-rays in 1895 and of radioactivity in 1896, he began (1903) to study the creation of X-rays by the flow of current through a gas-filled tube. In 1910 he became an assistant to Sir J. J. Thomson at Cambridge, who was investigating positively charged rays emanating from gaseous discharges. During Aston's assistantship Thomson obtained, from experiments with neon, the first evidence for isotopes (atoms of the same element that differ in mass) among the stable (nonradioactive) elements.

After World War I, Aston constructed a new type of positive ray apparatus, which he named a mass spectrograph. It showed that not only neon but also many other elements are mixtures of isotopes. Aston's achievement is illustrated by the fact that he discovered 212 of the 287 naturally occurring nuclides.

Astor FAMILY, wealthy American family whose fortune, rooted in the fur trade, came to be centred on real estate investments in New York City.

John Jacob Astor (1763–1848), the founder of the family fortune, is covered in a separate article: *see* Astor, John Jacob. His son, William Backhouse Astor (1792–1875), who inherited the major portion of the estate, continued his father's program of investing in Manhattan real estate, and greatly expanded the Astor Library. Stung by accusations that he was a slum landlord, he attempted to renovate some of the older tenements owned by the Astors. At the same time, he more than doubled the family fortune, leaving an estate valued at nearly $50,000,000.

John Jacob Astor (1822–90), son of William Backhouse Astor, increased the fortune to between $75,000,000 and $100,000,000. But he was a more active philanthropist than his predecessors, making substantial gifts to the Metropolitan Museum of Art and Trinity Church as well as to the Astor Library.

His son, William Waldorf Astor (1848–1919), was politically ambitious, but after a stint in the New York state legislature and three years as U.S. minister to Italy, he moved permanently to England in 1890. He became a British subject in 1899 and, in 1917, became 1st Viscount Astor, of Hever Castle. He used much of his wealth—aside from that spent building the Waldorf section of what eventually became the Waldorf-Astoria Hotel—restoring Hever Castle and funding conservative political causes in England.

John Jacob Astor (1864–1912) was a cousin of William Waldorf Astor and a great-grandson of the fur trader who founded the family fortune. An inventor and a science fiction novelist, he was also responsible for building several great New York City hotels: the Astoria (later combined with the Waldorf), the Knickerbocker, and the St. Regis. He served as a director on the boards of several major U.S. corporations, but his career was cut short when he perished in the mid-Atlantic aboard the "Titanic."

Waldorf Astor (1879–1952) and his wife, Nancy (1879–1964), are covered in separate articles: *see* Astor (of Hever Castle), Waldorf Astor, 2nd viscount, and Astor (of Hever Castle), Nancy Witcher Astor, Viscountess.

Vincent Astor (1891–1959), son of the John Jacob Astor who built the well-known hotels, departed markedly from Astor family conservatism. He sold some Astor-owned properties to New York City under generous terms so that they might be converted into housing projects. In addition, he backed the New Deal and supported other social reforms. He took an active role in managing the family real estate holdings, and during the last two decades of his life headed the corporation that published *Newsweek* magazine.

For John Jacob Astor (1886–1971), younger brother of Waldorf Astor, *see* Astor (of Hever, of Hever Castle), John Jacob Astor, 1st Baron.

Astor, John Jacob (b. July 17, 1763, Waldorf, Ger.—d. March 29, 1848, New York City), fur magnate and founder of a renowned family of Anglo-American capitalists, business leaders, and philanthropists. His American Fur Company is considered the first U.S. business monopoly.

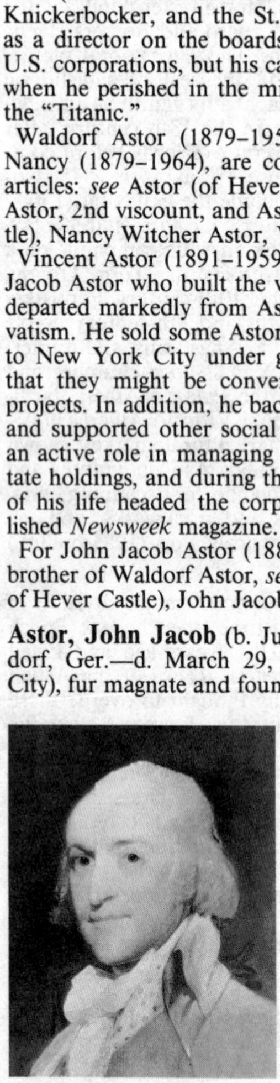
John Jacob Astor, detail of an oil painting by Gilbert Stuart, 1794; in the Brook Club, New York
By courtesy of the Frick Art Reference Library

Astor started a fur-goods shop in New York City about 1786 after learning about the fur trade from a fellow German immigrant aboard the ship that brought him to the U.S. Benefitting from a treaty between England and the U.S. (1794) that opened up new markets in Canada and the Great Lakes region, and from shrewd dealings with Indian tribes, he had by 1800 amassed $250,000 and become the leading figure in the fur trade. Given permission to trade in ports monopolized by the British East India Company, he made lucrative fur transactions in China (1800–17), but his plan to establish a network of fur-trading posts around Astoria (now in Oregon) failed when the British captured the post during the War of 1812.

At the same time, however, Astor invested in New York City real estate that became the foundation of the family fortune. His son, William Backhouse Astor (1792–1875), greatly expanded the family real estate holdings, building more than 700 stores and dwellings in New York City. The wealthiest person in the U.S. at the time of his death, the senior Astor bequeathed $400,000 for the founding of a public library, the Astor Library, in New York City, which was consolidated with others as the New York Public Library in 1895.

Astor (of Hever, of Hever Castle), John Jacob Astor, 1st Baron (b. May 20, 1886, New York City—d. July 19, 1971, Cannes, Fr.), British journalist and great-great-grandson of the U.S. fur magnate John Jacob Astor; as chief proprietor of *The Times* of London (1922–66) he maintained the newspaper's preeminent position in British journalism.

He was the second son of the 1st Viscount Astor (before his emigration to England) and Astor's first wife, Mary Dahlgren. Educated at Eton, the young Astor joined the First Life Guards in 1906, and, after serving as aide-de-camp to the Viceroy of India (1911–14) and in World War I, Astor entered Parliament in 1922 as a Unionist, holding his seat until 1945. Also in 1922 he bought nine-tenths ownership of *The Times* newspaper and established it as an independent political voice. In 1953 he was elected chairman of the Council of the British Press, a body created by Parliament to review recruitment, ethics, and pensions of journalists.

John Jacob Astor
By courtesy of *The Times*, London

Astor (of Hever Castle), Nancy Witcher Astor, Viscountess, *née* LANGHORNE (b. May 19, 1879, Danville, Va., U.S.—d. May 2, 1964, Grimsthorpe Castle, Lincolnshire, Eng.), first woman to sit in the British House of Commons, known in public and private life for her great energy and wit.

In 1897 she married Robert Gould Shaw of Boston, from whom she was divorced in 1903, and in 1906 she married Waldorf Astor, great-great-grandson of John Jacob Astor. When her husband succeeded to his father's viscountcy and thus relinquished his seat in

Lady Astor
Central Press Photos Ltd.

the House of Commons, Lady Astor, who had been his constant comrade-in-arms in his constituency at Plymouth, was adopted as Unionist candidate in his place and, after a stirring campaign, was elected by a substantial majority on Nov. 28, 1919. Lady Astor was returned for Plymouth at subsequent general elections until her retirement from Parliament in 1945.

Apart from questions relating exclusively to women, her chief parliamentary work was done for a progressive educational policy, for temperance, and for the extension of the Trade Boards Acts. She constantly advocated the raising of the school-leaving age and in 1923 carried through the Intoxicating Liquor (Sale to Persons under 18) Bill. She also maintained a continuous agitation for improved conditions in certain branches of the distributive and catering trades.

No less potent was her role as hostess at Cliveden, the Astor's country house near Taplow, Buckinghamshire, where she maintained a salon that exercised considerable influence in many fields, notably foreign affairs. Members of the group were called the "Cliveden set." Maurice Collis wrote *Nancy Astor: An Informal Biography* (1960).

Astor (of Hever Castle), Waldorf Astor, 2nd Viscount (b. May 19, 1879, New York City—d. Sept. 30, 1952, Cliveden, Buckinghamshire, Eng.), member of Parliament (1910–19) and agricultural expert whose Cliveden home was a meeting place during the late 1930s for Prime Minister Neville Chamberlain and supporters of his policy of "appeasement" toward Adolf Hitler.

He was the elder son of William Waldorf Astor, 1st Viscount Astor, and a great-great-grandson of the U.S. fur magnate John Jacob Astor. Waldorf Astor entered Parliament in 1910, acting as secretary to Prime Minister David Lloyd George in 1917. He retired from public office in 1919, his seat being taken by his wife, Nancy Witcher, Viscountess Astor, the first woman to sit in the British House of Commons. Astor was proprietor of *The Observer,* a London Sunday newspaper formerly owned by his father (to whose title he succeeded in 1919), from 1919 to 1945, when he turned it over to a trust.

Waldorf Astor
By courtesy of *The Times*, London

An authority on agricultural problems, Astor became chairman in 1936 of a committee that was the progenitor of the Food and Agriculture Organization of the United Nations.

Astorga, city, León province, in the provisional autonomous community (region) of Castile-León, northwestern Spain, on the left bank of the Río Tuerto on a spur of the Manzanal mountain chain. It originated as the Roman Asturica Augusta (called a "magnificent city" by Pliny) and was an important administrative and military centre. The see of a bishop since the 3rd century, Astorga decayed in the Muslim period from the time of the expulsion of the Berbers (*c.* 750) until the repopulation under Ordoño I of Leon (*c.* 860). It became a station on the road to Santiago de Compostela, a medieval pilgrimage centre, and a trade centre as well. During the Peninsular War, it was captured by the French in 1810 and retaken by Spanish troops in 1812. Historic landmarks include the Roman walls (a national monument); the Gothic cathedral (1471), with Plateresque and Baroque decorations; the 18th-century town hall; and the 19th-century Bishop's Palace, designed by Antonio Gaudí.

Modern Astorga is an agricultural trade centre, famous for its chocolates and cookies (biscuits). Its industries include flour and sawmilling, tanning, and meat processing. It is the centre of the so-called Maragatería, the district inhabited by the unique Maragato tribe, possibly of Germanic origin, who for centuries have interbred among themselves. Pop. (1981) 14,040.

Astoria, city, seat (1844) of Clatsop County, northwestern Oregon, U.S., on the south bank of the Columbia River (there bridged to Megler, Wash.) near its mouth on the Pacific. It is near the site of Oregon's first military establishment, Ft. Clatsop, built by the Lewis and Clark Expedition, which wintered there (1805–06); the reconstructed fort, 4½ mi (7.5

Interstate bridge spanning the Columbia River from Astoria, Ore., to Megler, Wash.
Ray Atkeson—EB Inc.

km) southwest, is a national memorial. In 1810–11 John Jacob Astor sent an expedition to establish a Pacific Fur Company trading post (Ft. Astoria); this was later sold to the North West Company. A British man-of-war took possession (1813) and renamed it Ft. George. It was restored to U.S. control in 1818 and was resettled in the 1840s. The area's natural resources attracted immigrants who developed fishing and lumber industries. A disastrous fire in 1922 temporarily reversed the city's economic growth. Possessing deep-water port facilities, Astoria has important salmon and tuna canneries; flour, lumber, aluminum, and dairy foods are also produced. It is a base for hunting and fishing and has seashore recreational facilities. Astor Column (1926), 125 ft (38 m) high on Coxcomb Hill, 700 ft above the river, commemorates the settlement of the Pacific Northwest. Ft. Astoria has been restored, and a maritime museum was opened in 1963. Clatsop Community College was established in 1958. Inc. 1865. Pop. (1980) 9,998.

Astoria Canyon, submarine canyon and fan-valley system of the Pacific continental margin, off the coast of Oregon, U.S. The canyon's head is in water about 330 ft (100 m) deep, 11 mi west of the mouth of the Columbia River. The canyon crosses the seaward half of the continental shelf in a westerly direction and trends sinuously down to the base of the continental slope and the apex of Astoria Fan at a depth of 6,840 ft, at which point it passes into Astoria Seachannel, a fan valley. The canyon is approximately 75 mi long. Along its upper reaches it has a U-shaped cross section; however, it is V-shaped near the shelf break, where the canyon has its maximum relief of 3,000 ft. It varies in width from 1.5 to 8.3 mi. The canyon is entered by 13 tributaries. It is believed to have been cut by the movement of Columbia River sediment down to the Astoria Fan. The sediment is distributed over the fan through Astoria Seachannel, a fan valley of low relief at least 70 mi long, with several distributaries. Astoria Seachannel, like other fan valleys, probably migrates laterally over the fan through time; its present position is the eastern portion of the fan, and its trend is southerly.

Astrakhan, *oblast* (administrative region), Russian Soviet Federated Socialist Republic, occupying an area of 17,027 sq mi (44,100 sq km) along the lower Volga River. The Volga and its parallel distributary, the Akhtuba, form the axis of the *oblast,* ending in a large delta. The majority of the population lives in the delta area around the city of Astrakhan, the administrative centre. Vegetables and fruit are grown on the fertile fields enriched by the Volga. Fishing is important along the rivers and Caspian shore, but it has suffered from pollution and the falling sea level. A major nature reserve in the delta protects the unique vegetation—including the lotus (*Nelumbium caspicum*)—and abundant birdlife—including pelicans and herons. Outside the floodplain and delta is an arid steppe–semidesert region, with sand dunes, saline soils and lakes, and a sparse sage vegetation; it is used only for extensive cattle and sheep raising and large-scale salt extraction at Lake Baskunchak. Pop. (1983 est.) 941,000.

Astrakhan, formerly KHADZHI-TARKHAN, city and administrative centre of Astrakhan *oblast* (region), southwestern Russian Soviet Federated Socialist Republic, in the delta of the Volga River, 60 mi (100 km) from the Caspian Sea. It lies on several islands on the left bank of the main, westernmost channel of the Volga. Astrakhan was formerly the capital of a Tatar khanate, a remnant of the Golden Horde, located on the higher right bank of the Volga, 7 mi from the present-day city. Situated on caravan and water routes, it developed from a village into a large trading centre. It was conquered by Timur (Tamerlane) in 1395 and captured by Ivan IV the Terrible in 1556. In 1558 it was moved to its present site. A cathedral and castle (kremlin, 1582–89) are still in existence. The great ethnic diversity of its population gives a varied character to Astrakhan. A city of bridges and water channels, it is an important river port, but because of the shallowness of the northern Caspian, seagoing craft have to transship about 125 mi by road from Astrakhan, which is reached by a dredged channel. The city is the base

The domes of the Cathedral of the Assumption and the kremlin wall, Astrakhan city, Russian S.F.S.R.
Novosti Press Agency

of a large fishing fleet and is important as a fish canning and caviar preserving centre. Other industries include clothing and footwear manufacture and ship repair. Astrakhan fur, from the karakul lamb of Central Asia, is so named because it was first brought to Russia by Astrakhan traders. There are medical and teacher-training institutes and a technical institute of fisheries and the food industry. Pop. (1983 est.) 481,000.

astreinte, in French law, procedural device used to enforce court decisions requiring the defendant to perform or not to perform a specific act. Whereas other civil-law countries include provisions for the enforcement of specific performance in their codes of civil procedure, France does not. *Astreinte* was developed in court cases and is one of the few instances in which a civil-law country has developed a procedure by case law. It was finally enacted by statute in 1972.

Astreinte carries the threat of a fine rather than imprisonment. It became truly effective when the penalty was allowed to exceed the amount of damages and when the court began to assess the penalty on a daily basis for nonperformance or disobedience.

astringent, any of a group of substances that tend to shrink mucous membranes and raw surfaces and to dry up secretions. Astringents are usually classed according to their mode of action into: (1) those that decrease the blood supply by narrowing the small blood vessels (*e.g.,* adrenaline and cocaine); (2) those that abstract water from the part (*e.g.,* glycerol and alcohol); and (3) those that coagulate the superficial layers into a crust (*e.g.,* metallic astringents, such as calamine or alum). Used in medicine to reduce swollen mucous membranes that result from inflammations of the nasal, alimentary, and urinary passages, astringents are also frequently employed to dry up excessive secretions and (in this connection often known as styptics) to stop the oozing of blood.

astrobiology: *see* exobiology.

astrobleme (from Greek roots meaning "star-wound"), remains of an ancient meteorite-impact structure on the Earth's surface, generally in the form of a circular scar of crushed and deformed bedrock. Because such telltale features as crater walls, fused silica glass, and meteorite fragments are heavily modified over time by erosion and weathering, the identification of astroblemes is chiefly based on the presence of subsurface shock structures known as shatter cones. These are conically shaped structures that form in the bedrock directly under the point of impact. They radiate in a distinctive pattern from the point of impact and are identifiable even in drill-core samples. The suddenness and intensity of the shattering precludes it from having taken place along pre-existing lines of weakness, and, because this type of shattering can be produced by no other natural means, it provides a useful criterion for recognizing astroblemes. Using this evidence, the Ashanti Crater in Ghana and the Vredefort Ring structure in the Republic of South Africa have been identified as probable astroblemes.

Astrodome, modern domed stadium built in Houston, Texas, in 1965. The largest previous covered sports arenas provided only limited performing space and seated no more than 20,000 persons. The Astrodome, however, built on the principle of the dome, completely protects a sports area suitable for baseball and football, with seating for 66,000 spectators in six tiers. The plastic-panelled dome, spanning 642 feet (196 metres), is supported by a steel lattice; the entire interior is air-conditioned at 74° F (23° C) and fully lighted with power from its own electric-generating system.

Astrodome, Houston, Texas, 1965

By courtesy of the Houston Sports Association, Inc.

astrogeology, scientific discipline that is concerned with all geological aspects of the Moon, the several solar planets, and such other bodies as asteroids, meteors, and comets, especially in terms of their effects on the Earth. The principal focus of astrogeology is now the production of geological maps of the lunar surface, analysis of Moon rock samples, and determining the nature of the Moon's interior and its thermal history. Investigations of Mars, Venus, and other planets are less advanced, but much insight can be gained from the analysis of surficial features that are visible on photos from satellites and space vehicles. Astrogeology requires knowledge of all of the terrestrial branches of the geological sciences for its application and advancement.

astrolabe, sometimes called the world's oldest scientific instrument, used by the ancients for observing the positions and altitudes of celestial bodies, may date to the 3rd century BC in Greece. In the late Middle Ages it became a navigational instrument by the addition of tables of the Sun's declination (angular distance north or south of the celestial equator), which permitted mariners to find their latitude. It was eventually replaced by the sextant.

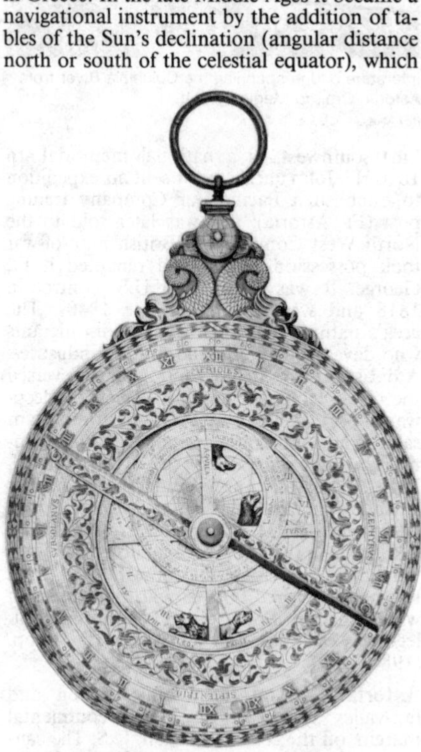

Rete side of an iron astrolabe made after 1582

By courtesy of the Peabody Museum of Salem; photograph, M.W. Sexton

In its earliest form the astrolabe consisted of a disk of wood suspended by a ring. Around the disk's edge were marked the degrees of the circle; a pointer, or alidade, along which the Sun or a star could be sighted, was pivoted on a centre pin. Later astrolabes were often of metal, frequently with a rete, consisting of a plate with a map of the stars and the circle of the zodiac on the reverse side. With the aid of this feature, the time of day could be determined; after measuring the Sun's altitude, its position was noted on the circle of the zodiac; a line drawn to a circle of hours showed the time.

astrology, the practice of interpreting the influence of planets and stars on earthly affairs in order to predict or affect the destinies of individuals, groups, or nations. At times regarded as a science, astrology has exerted an extensive or a peripheral influence in many civilizations, both ancient and modern. Astrology has also been defined as a pseudoscience and considered to be diametrically opposed to the theories and findings of modern science.

A brief treatment of astrology follows. For full treatment, *see* MACROPAEDIA: Occultism.

Astrology originated in Mesopotamia, perhaps in the 3rd millennium BC, but attained its full development in the Western World much later, within the orbit of Greek civilization of the Hellenistic period. It spread to India in its older Mesopotamian form. Islāmic culture absorbed it as part of the Greek heritage; and in the Middle Ages, when Western Europe was strongly affected by Islāmic science, European astrology also acquired an Arabian colour.

The Egyptians also contributed, though less directly, to the rise of astrology. They constructed a calendar, containing 12 months of 30 days each with five days added at the end of the year, that was subsequently taken over by the Greeks as a standard of reference for astronomical observations. In order that the starry sky might serve them as a clock, the Egyptians selected a succession of 36 bright stars whose risings were separated from each other by intervals of 10 days. Each of these stars, called *decans* by Latin writers, was conceived of as a spirit with power over the period of time for which it served; they later entered the zodiac (*q.v.*) as subdivisions of its 12 signs. The Greek term *hōroskopos* (literally, "hour-watcher"), from which the term horoscope (*q.v.*) derives, is, in one of its meanings, a synonym for "decan star."

In pre-Imperial China, the belief in an intelligible cosmic order, comprehended aspects of which would permit inferences on correlated uncomprehended aspects, found expression in correlation charts that juxtaposed natural phenomena with the activities and the fate of man. The transition from this belief to a truly astrological belief in the direct influence of the stars on human affairs was a slow one during which numerous systems of observation and strains of lore developed. When Western astronomy and astrology became known in China through Arabic influences in Mongol times, their data were also integrated into the Chinese astrological corpus. In the later centuries of Imperial China it was universal practice to have a horoscope cast for each newborn child by a professional diviner. These horoscopes were consulted and interpreted at all decisive junctures in life, particularly on the eve of a marriage.

Once established in the Classical world, the astrological conception of causation invaded all the sciences, particularly medicine and its allied disciplines. The Stoics, espousing the doctrine of a universal "sympathy" linking the microcosm of man with the macrocosm of nature, found in astrology a virtual map of such a universe.

Greek astrology was slow to be absorbed by the Romans, who had their own native methods of divination, but by the time of Augustus, the art had resumed its original role as a royal prerogative. Attempts to stem its influence on the populace met repeatedly with failure.

Throughout pagan antiquity the words astronomy and astrology had been synonymous; in the first Christian centuries the modern distinction between astronomy, the science of stars, and astrology, the art of divination by the stars, began to appear. As against the omnipotence of the stars Christianity taught the omnipotence of their Creator. To the determinism of astrology Christianity opposed the freedom of the will. But within these limits the astrological worldview was accepted. To reject it would have been to reject the whole heritage of classical culture, which had assumed an astrological complexion. Even at the centre of Christian history, Persian magi were reported to have followed a celestial omen to the scene of the Nativity.

Although various Christian councils condemned astrology, the belief in the world view it implies was not seriously shaken. In the late Middle Ages, a number of universities, among them Paris, Padua, Bologna, and Florence, had chairs of astrology. The revival of ancient studies by the Humanists only encouraged this interest, which persisted into the Renaissance and even into the Reformation.

It was the Copernican revolution of the 16th century that dealt the geocentric worldview of astrology its shattering blow. As a popular pastime or superstition, however, astrology continued into modern times to engage the attention of millions of people, this interest being catered to in the 20th century by articles in the daily press, by special almanacs, and by manuals, large and small, devoted to various aspects of the subject.

astronaut, person trained to pilot a spacecraft or to conduct scientific experiments during space flights. The term is commonly applied to those participating in U.S. space missions, as opposed to the designation cosmonaut used to refer to Soviet space travellers. Also, the U.S. Department of Defense awards the rating of astronaut to any military test pilot who has flown jet aircraft at altitudes of 50 miles (80 kilometres) or higher. Alan B. Shepard was the first U.S. astronaut to fly in space, undertaking a 15-minute suborbital flight in a Mercury spacecraft on May 5, 1961, less than a month after Soviet cosmonaut Yury A. Gagarin had made the first manned space flight (April 12).

From 1959 to 1980 the National Aeronautics and Space Administration (NASA), which manages the U.S. astronaut program, selected a total of 127 astronauts in nine groups. The criteria for choosing astronauts were modified through the years. Most of the individuals selected for the first three groups, primarily those assigned to the Mercury, Gemini, and early Apollo missions, were military pilots. From the fourth group onward, many persons who had no previous flight experience but who had advanced degrees in scientific disciplines such as physics, chemistry, and the earth sciences were appointed. This was particularly true of those selected for the space shuttle project, which included the first six women chosen for astronaut training. Such individuals serve as mission specialists whose primary responsibility is to perform scientific tasks on space missions.

Astronauts receive extensive training to prepare themselves both physically and psychologically for the rigours and complexities of a space mission. Although the training includes classroom study of varied technical subjects, much of it is conducted in computer-controlled simulators and full-size mock-ups of spacecraft. Some such devices are used to help astronauts become accustomed to living and working in the weightless environment of space by simulating conditions of zero gravity. Others enable astronauts to familiarize themselves with the control, communication, and life-support systems of any given spacecraft and to practice difficult flight operations. Mission specialists with no flight training are also required to spend a year learning to fly high-performance jet aircraft so that they acquire the basic skills needed for flight safety.

astronomical map, any cartographic representation of the stars, galaxies, or surfaces of the planets and the Moon. Modern maps of this kind are based on a coordinate system analogous to geographic latitude and longitude. In most modern cases, they are compiled from photographic observations made either with Earth-based equipment or instruments carried aboard spacecraft.

A brief treatment of astronomical maps follows. For full treatment, *see* MACROPAEDIA: Stars and Star Clusters; Solar System.

Representations of the celestial spheres have long been used for both navigational and scientific purposes. The earliest versions consisted of charts, globes, and drawings that grouped stars apparently close together in the sky into constellations, imaginative configurations of bright stellar bodies named after legendary or mythological beings that they supposedly resembled in form. Classical Greek astronomers are known to have employed maps and globes depicting constellations, but no examples survive. The ancient tradition was followed by the Alexandrian astronomer Ptolemy (Claudius Ptolemaeus) in compiling his *Almagest* (*c.* AD 150), the first important star catalog. The *Almagest* provides magnitudes and ecliptic coordinates for 1,028 stars (1,025 plus 3 duplicates) grouped into 48 constellations. For the next 1,400 years or so, Islāmic and European astronomers observed only those stars tabulated by Ptolemy with very few exceptions. The new catalogs that did appear were actually revisions of Ptolemy's work; examples of such include the 10th-century catalog of the Islāmic astronomer Al-Ṣūfī or the 13th-century Alfonsine tables. Other astronomical reference systems were developed independently in early antiquity, as exemplified by the lunar mansions, which are 28 divisions of the sky devised in China and India, and the Egyptian decans, which consisted of 36 star configurations circling the sky to the south of the ecliptic. The system that is used by modern astronomers, however, has grown out of that established by Ptolemy. Because no attempts were made in medieval Europe to refine or add to the existing information on the ancient constellations, the first maps produced were based wholly on the Ptolemaic star catalog.

The renaissance in science and the development of printing led to a widespread publication of astronomical maps, globes, and books during the 15th and 16th centuries throughout much of Europe. The first important printed star maps were published in 1515 by Albrecht Dürer. They consisted of two planispheres that depicted the classical constellation figures. Alessandro Piccolomini's *De Le Stelle Fisse Libro Uno* (1540) constituted the first book of printed star charts (as opposed to mere pictures of constellations) and introduced a lettering system for the stars. The star atlas published by Giovanni Paolo Gallucci in 1588 was the first to include coordinates. Ptolemy had used ecliptic coordinates, but most astronomers of the post-Renaissance period expressed positions in the equatorial coordinate system. Nearly all star maps are constructed on one or the other of these systems. The ecliptic coordinate system is based on the ecliptic, the apparent annual path of the Sun. Celestial longitude and latitude are defined with respect to the ecliptic and ecliptic poles. The equatorial system, on the other hand, is based on the celestial equator and poles. The equatorial coordinates are right ascension and declination; they are only applicable for a specific date, or epoch, because of the slow periodic change in the orientation of the Earth's axis of rotation.

Only those constellations listed in the *Almagest* were included in star charts produced until the end of the 1500s. Since that time 40 additional constellations, most notably those visible in the Southern Hemisphere, were introduced in celestial globes and star atlases. A definitive list of 88 constellations was established and the boundaries of these star groupings fixed in 1930 by the International Astronomical Union.

The idea of a photographic atlas of the entire sky was proposed as early as 1887, but it was not until 1914 that such a project was completed. This initial effort, the *Franklin-Adams Charts,* consisted of 206 prints of stars with a limiting photographic magnitude of 15. Improved equipment and techniques for photographic mapping of the skies have yielded various star atlases of superior quality since the early 1950s. Among these are the *National Geographic Society-Palomar Observatory Sky Survey* and *Norton's Star Atlas.*

In recent years astronomers also have prepared atlases of galaxies. In the future they expect to map the precise positions of cosmic sources of radio, infrared, ultraviolet, and X-ray emissions.

astronomical observatory, any structure containing telescopes and auxiliary instruments with which to observe celestial objects. Observatories can be classified on the basis of the part of the electromagnetic spectrum in which they are designed to observe. The largest number of observatories are optical; *i.e.*, they are equipped to observe in and near the region of the spectrum visible to the human eye. Some other observatories are instrumented to detect cosmic emitters of radio waves, while still others, known as orbiting astronomical observatories, consist of Earth satellites that carry special telescopes and detectors to study celestial sources of such forms of high-energy radiation as gamma rays and X-rays from high above the atmosphere.

Optical observatories have a long history. Predecessors of modern observatories of this type were monolithic structures, the most famous of which is the Stonehenge, constructed in England over the period from 2500 BC to 1700 BC. Not quite genuine observatories, their primary function apparently was to serve as a calendar for religious purposes. The motions of the Sun and the Moon were followed with the aid of properly placed rocks that composed the structures. At about the same time, astrologer-priests in Babylonia observed the motions of the Sun, Moon, and planets from atop their terraced towers known as ziggurats. No astronomical instruments appear to have been used. The Indians of the Yucatan Peninsula in Mexico carried out the same practice at El Caracol, a dome-shaped structure somewhat resembling a modern optical observatory. There is again no evidence of any scientific instrumentation, even of a rudimentary nature.

Perhaps the first observatory that utilized instruments for accurately measuring the positions of celestial objects was built about 150 BC on the island of Rhodes by the greatest of the pre-Christian astronomers, Hipparchus. There he discovered precession and developed the magnitude system used to indicate the brightness of celestial objects. Other notable pre-telescope observatories were the one at Samarkand, erected by the Tartar prince Ulugh Beg about AD 1420, and that at Uraniborg on the island of Hven, built by King Frederick of Denmark for Tycho Brahe in AD 1576.

The first optical telescope used to study the heavens was constructed in 1609 by Galileo Galilei, using information from Flemish pioneers in lens-making. The first major centres for astronomical study utilized a telescope movable only in one plane, with motion solely along the local meridian (the "transit," or "meridian circle"). Such centres were founded in the 18th and 19th centuries at Greenwich (London), Paris, Cape Town, and Washington, D.C. By timing the passage of stars as the local meridian was swept past them by the

Earth's rotation, astronomers were able to improve the accuracy of position measurements of celestial objects from a few minutes of arc (before the advent of the telescope) to less than a tenth of a second of arc.

One notable observatory built and operated by an individual was that of William Herschel, assisted by his sister Caroline, in Slough, England. Known as Observatory House, its largest instrument had a mirror made of speculum metal, with a diameter of 122 centimetres (48 inches) and a focal length of 17 metres (40 feet). Completed in 1789, it became one of the technical wonders of the 18th century.

Today, the site of the world's largest grouping of optical telescopes is atop Kitt Peak, near Tucson, in southern Arizona. Most of the telescopes are a part of the Kitt Peak National Observatory; the rest belong to the Steward Observatory of the University of Arizona, several other universities, and the National Radio Astronomical Observatory. Most notable among this array of instruments are the 4-m (157-in.) Mayall telescope and the McMath solar telescope, the largest of its type in the world.

The largest modern-day optical telescopes are the 6-m (236-in.) reflector on Mt. Pastukhov, in the Caucasus Mountains in the Soviet Union, and the 5-m (200-in.) Hale telescope on Palomar Mountain, near San Diego, Calif. Also noteworthy is the revolutionary Multiple-Mirror Telescope (*q.v.*) atop Mt. Hopkins, near Tucson, in southern Arizona; it has an aperture of 4.5 m (177 in.).

The ability to observe the universe in the radio region of the spectrum was developed during the 1930s. The U.S. engineer Karl Jansky detected radio signals from the centre of the Milky Way Galaxy in 1931 by means of a linear directional antenna. Soon thereafter, the U.S. engineer and astronomer Grote Reber constructed a prototype of the radio telescope, a bowl-shaped antenna 9.4 m (31 ft) in diameter.

Today's radio telescopes are capable of observing at most wavelength regions from a few millimetres to about 20 metres. They vary in construction, though they are typically huge movable dishes. The world's largest steerable dish is the 96-m (315-ft) telescope at Jodrell Bank, Cheshire, Eng. The largest single-unit radio telescope is located at Arecibo, P.R. Lying level in a rounded-out hollow in the mountains, the main antenna of this instrument has a diameter of 304 m (about 1,000 ft). Limited aiming capability is allowed by the Earth's motion and by some movement of the overhanging antenna. One other significant radio telescope is the Very Large Array (VLA), operated by the National Radio Astronomy Observatory. Located near Socorro, N.M., the VLA is composed of 27 individual 25-m- (81-ft-) diameter radio telescopes, which are not only steerable but also movable over railroad tracks in the shape of a large Y. Each arm of the Y is 21 km (13 mi) long. The purpose of the VLA is to obtain extremely high-resolution imaging of cosmic radio sources. The resolving ability of a telescope, whether radio or optical, improves with increasing diameter. The individual dishes of the VLA work in precise unison to fabricate a large radio telescope having an effective diameter of 27 km (16.7 mi).

With the advent of the space age, the capability of astronomical instruments to orbit above the Earth's absorbing and distorting atmosphere has enabled astronomers to build telescopes sensitive to regions of the electromagnetic spectrum besides those of visible light and radio waves. Since the 1960s, orbiting observatories have been launched to observe gamma rays (Orbiting Solar Observatory and the Small Astronomy Satellite-2), X-rays (Uhuru and the High Energy Astronomical Observatory), ultraviolet radiation (International Ultraviolet Explorer), and infrared radiation (Infrared Astronomical Satellite).

astronomical unit (a.u.), length of the semi-major axis of the Earth to the Sun, the value of which is 149,597,870 kilometres (about 92,560,000 miles). It also is often defined simply as the average distance from the Earth to the Sun.

The most obvious method for obtaining the value of the astronomical unit would seem to be to measure simultaneously from two places on the Earth the position of the Sun against the background of the distant stars. The two locations would have to be at opposite ends of the Earth to achieve the greatest parallax displacement. The angle subtended by the Earth's radius as viewed from the Sun is called the solar parallax. Its value is about 8.794 seconds of arc. Since the radius of the Earth is known, the distance to the Sun can thus be obtained in principle. This method, however, does not work, because the glare of the Sun's radiation drowns out the light from the stars against which the Sun would have to be projected.

Astronomers have found a way out of the dilemma. On the basis of the geometry of the motions and positions of the planets and of the Sun under Newton's inverse square law of universal gravity, a model for planetary positions and motions can be devised without the use of a scale. If at any time the distance from the Earth to a particular planet (or asteroid) can be determined, then the scale for the whole system is fixed and so is the astronomical unit. The planet Mars was used initially, but it proved to be too large and mountainous for precise measurements. The asteroid Eros, which at closest approach comes to within one-seventh of an astronomical unit to the Earth, was found to be ideal for the purpose. The close approach of Eros in 1932 yielded what seemed at the time a very precise value for the unit in kilometres.

Since 1958 even more precise values for the length of the astronomical unit have been obtained by timing radar reflections from Venus and by "laser ranging" of the Moon. The latter technique involves bouncing laser signals off a mirror placed on the lunar surface by U.S. Apollo astronauts. The timing of the return signal is so accurate that the distance between the observatory that transmits the signal and the reflecting surface on the Moon can be determined to within 2.5 centimetres (1 inch).

Astronomische Gesellschaft Katalog (in astronomy): *see* AG catalog.

astronomy, science that deals with the origin, evolution, composition, distance, and motion of all bodies and scattered matter in the universe. It includes astrophysics (*q.v.*), which focusses on the physical properties and structure of all cosmic matter.

A brief treatment of the discipline of astronomy follows. For full treatment, *see* MACROPAEDIA: Physical Sciences. The objects of astronomical study are treated in a number of articles in the MACROPAEDIA. For a treatment of astronomical bodies and their properties, *see* Cosmos; Eclipse, Occultation, and Transit; Galaxies; Gravitation; Light; Mechanics; Nebulae; Solar System; Stars and Star Clusters. For a treatment of the formation of chemical elements in stars, *see* Chemical Elements: *Origin of the Elements*. For a treatment of the principal tool for astronomical observation, *see* Telescope.

For a description of the place of astronomy in the circle of learning, and for a list of both MACROPAEDIA and MICROPAEDIA articles on the subject, *see* PROPAEDIA: Part One, Division III.

Astronomy is the most ancient of the sciences, having existed since the dawn of recorded civilization. Much of the earliest knowledge of the celestial bodies is often credited to the Babylonians. They are thought to have recognized a number of prominent constellations as early as 3000 BC and to have developed a calendar based on the regularity of certain astronomical events some centuries thereafter. The ancient Greeks introduced various influential cosmological ideas. During the 6th century BC Pythagoras proposed the notion of a spherical Earth and a universe populated by objects whose motions were governed by the harmonious relations of natural laws. Later Greek philosophers taught that the sky was a hollow globe surrounding the Earth and having the stars inlaid like jewels on its inner surface. The sky was supported on an axis thrust through the Earth; on this axis the sky rotated westward daily, causing the celestial bodies to rise and set. During the 2nd century AD Ptolemy (Claudius Ptolemaus), one of the most celebrated of the ancient Greek astronomers, put forth a conception of an Earth-centred (geocentric) universe that influenced astronomical thought for more than 1,300 years. In the Ptolemaic system, each planet moved in a small circle, the epicycle, in the period of its actual revolution around the heavens relative to the Sun's position. Meanwhile, the centre of this circle moved eastward around the Earth on a larger circle in the observed period of the planet's revolution relative to the stars.

During the 16th century the Polish astronomer Nicolaus Copernicus disposed of much of the complexity of the Ptolemaic system by assigning the central position to the Sun. In this revolutionary system the Earth, attended by the Moon, became one of the planets revolving around the Sun. Copernicus also proposed the daily axial rotation of the Earth from west to east, so that the daily circling of the heavenly bodies around the Earth results simply from its apparent motion. Published in *De revolutionibus orbium coelestium* (1543), the Copernican heliocentric theory ushered in the age of modern astronomy.

The 17th century witnessed several momentous developments that led to major advances in astronomy. These were the discovery of the principles of planetary motion by Johannes Kepler, the application of the telescope to astronomical observation by Galileo Galilei, and the formulation of the laws of motion and gravitation by Isaac Newton. Other significant contributions followed in rapid succession. In 1750 Thomas Wright, for example, postulated that the universe was made up of numerous galaxies. Later in the century another English astronomer, William Herschel, undertook the first thorough telescopic survey of the heavens and established the foundations of modern stellar astronomy.

Spectroscopy and photography were adopted for astronomical research in the 19th century. They enabled investigators to measure the quantity and quality of light emitted by stars and nebulae (clouds of interstellar gas and dust), making it possible for them to conduct studies of the brightness, temperature, and chemical composition of such cosmic objects. It was soon recognized that the properties of all celestial bodies, including the planets of the solar system, could only be understood in terms of the physics of their atmosphere and interior. The trend toward the application of physical laws to the interpretation of observational data gained impetus during the early 1920s, and many astronomers began referring to themselves as astrophysicists. This tendency continues to prevail.

The major areas of current interest—X-ray astronomy, gamma-ray astronomy, and radio astronomy—are all basically concerned with physics and engineering, the knowledge of the latter having utmost importance in the construction of observational instruments and auxiliary equipment. Technological advances such as electronic radar and radio units, high-speed computer systems, light-amplification systems, and Earth-orbiting observatories and long-range planetary probes have contributed greatly to broadening the scope of both theoretical and observational research on astronomical phenomena.

astronomy, infrared: *see* infrared astronomy.

astronomy, radio and radar: *see* radio and radar astronomy.

astronomy, ultraviolet: *see* ultraviolet astronomy.

astrophysics, branch of astronomy concerned primarily with the properties and structure of cosmic objects, including the universe as a whole. *See* astronomy.

Astruc OF **LUNEL**, original name ABBA MARI BEN MOSES BEN JOSEPH, also called DON ASTRUC, or HA-YAREAḤ (the Moon) (b. 1250?, Lunel, near Montpellier, Fr.—d. after 1306), anti-rationalist zealot who incited Rabbi Solomon ben Abraham Adret of Barcelona, the most powerful rabbi of his time, to restrict the study of science and philosophy, thereby nearly creating a schism in the Jewish community of Europe.

Although Astruc revered Maimonides, who had attempted to reconcile Aristotle's philosophy with Judaism, he deplored what he considered the excesses of Maimonides' followers, who, he believed, undermined the Jewish faith by interpreting the Bible allegorically. They even seemed to take as a religious guide Aristotle himself, whose teachings were often said by the anti-Aristotelians to be "a jar of honey about which a dragon is wrapped."

In a series of letters, Astruc persuaded Rabbi Adret to issue a ban in 1305 forbidding, on pain of excommunication, the study or teaching of science and philosophy by those under the age of 25. This ban provoked a counterban by other Jewish leaders against those who followed Adret's proscription. A threatened schism among the Jewish communities of France and Spain was averted only in 1306, when Philip IV expelled the Jews from France. Astruc then settled in Perpignan, mainland capital of the Kingdom of Majorca, and vanished from view. But he published his correspondence with Rabbi Adret, which primarily concerned the restrictions on studies. *Minḥat qenaot* ("Meal Offering of Jealousy"), as the collected correspondence is entitled, reveals much of the religious and philosophical conflicts of Judaism in that era. The epithet ha-Yareaḥ (the Moon) is derived from his polemical work *Sefer ha-yareaḥ* ("The Book of the Moon"), the title of which refers to the town of Lunel (French *lune,* meaning "moon").

Asturias, region of Spain, an autonomous governmental entity (*comunidad autónoma*) coextensive with the northwestern Spanish province of Oviedo.

The following article summarizes the administrative status and history, geography, demographic patterns, economy, and culture of modern Asturias; for fuller treatment of its geography and history, *see* MACROPAEDIA: Spain.

Asturias was an independent kingdom between 718 and 910 and was formed by Visigothic nobles and officials who had been displaced by the Muslim invasion of Spain. The Visigoths elected Pelayo as king and set up a capital at Cangas de Onís. The kingdom extended its frontiers to include Galicia to the southwest and Cantabria to the east before the end of the 8th century. The capital was transferred first to Pravia (*c.* 780) and in the 9th century to Oviedo, a strategically sited new city. During the reign of Alfonso III (866–910) the frontiers of Asturias were pushed south to the line of the Duero River from the Atlantic to Osma.

By the 10th century the kingdom had become too large to be controlled effectively from the mountain capital at Oviedo, and in 910 García I made Leon, to the south, his capital. García's successors styled themselves kings of Leon and Asturias, and eventually simply kings of Leon (*see* Leon, Kingdom of). John I of Castile (united with Leon from 1230) created his eldest son, Henry (later King Henry III), prince of Asturias; that title was applied to the crown princes throughout the years of the Spanish monarchy.

Mountains cover more than four-fifths of the land, effectively isolating the region from the provinces of Santander to the east, León to the south, and Lugo to the west. The region may be divided into several east–west zones. North to south, these include the plains and hills of the Atlantic coast, which occupy a narrow strip and recede into a range of coastal hills. These hills surround the central corridor, the valley of the Nalón River, in which most of the population and industries are concentrated. Structurally this is a longitudinal depression running between the centres of Cangas de Onis (east) and Oviedo (west). The Cantabrian Mountains rise to the south, with the glaciated Picos de Europa established as a national park. Valleys run north to south, but the col of Leitariegos is the only easily accessible pass into the neighbouring province of León to the south. Annual precipitation is high, exceeding 40 in. (1,000 mm), and much of the province is snowbound during the winter. The climate is oceanic, with relatively even precipitation throughout the year; temperatures are moderate and show little seasonal variation.

The Asturian population has doubled since 1900, but its proportion in the Spanish population has steadily declined, and emigration has left behind an aging population. Emigration to the industrialized regions of Spain and the European Economic Community has kept population growth below the national average. The declining agricultural sector has led to emigration from the countryside, with the province's present population increasingly concentrated in the industrial and urban triangle of Oviedo, Avilés, and Gijón.

Agriculture is poorly developed in the region. Traditional crops are wheat, millet, and kidney beans, and crop rotation has included corn (maize) and potatoes since the 18th century. Asturian agriculture has traditionally had a collective orientation, and the extensive pastures in the mountains were communal until the early 20th century. Pastures and the cultivation of fodder have spread dramatically since that time, establishing animal husbandry as the dominant agricultural activity. Swiss cattle, introduced in 1885, are the leading farm animals, and have steadily displaced sheep and horses.

Mining and metallurgy have dominated the industry of Asturias since the mid-19th century, when the foundries of Mieres, La Felguera, and Gijón were established. The government has been active in modernizing foundries and has sponsored major steelworks in Avilés and the valley of Veriña. Coal is mined principally in the valleys carved out by the rivers Nalón and Caudal; anthracite is found along the river Nacera. The province is a major producer of zinc, but production has fallen off considerably since the mid-19th century. Industries are not greatly diversified, although the manufacture of cement, glass, food and beverages, tobacco, leather, and textiles has increased.

The region's undeveloped infrastructure has hindered industrial expansion. Roads and railroads tend to run north to south, converging on the triangle of Oviedo, Avilés, and Gijón and largely bypassing points lying to the east and west. Shipping has increased, favouring the ports of Avilés, Gijón, and El Musel.

The traditional farmstead is the *caserio,* which is built of wood and stone and customarily features a balcony, gallery, and arcaded porch. The oval *pallaza* is the shepherd's hut and is built of rough stones; the roof is thatched and conical. The observance of Catholicism tends to be less intense in Asturias than in Castile, and the folklore preserves numerous superstitions. The *trasgu,* for example, is a mocking spirit and the *güestia* a nocturnal procession of troubled souls. The Dominicans and Jesuits undertook missions to the peasants of Asturias in the 16th and 17th centuries but had only limited success in the mountainous zones. Pop. (1981) 1,127,007.

Asturias, Miguel Ángel (b. Oct. 19, 1899, Guatemala City—d. June 9, 1974, Madrid), poet, novelist, and diplomat, winner of the Nobel Prize for Literature in 1967 and the Soviet Union's Lenin Peace Prize in 1966, whose writings, which combine the mysticism of the Mayas with an epic impulse toward social protest, are seen as summing up the social and moral aspirations of his people.

In 1923, after receiving his degree in law from the Universidad de Guatemala, Asturias settled in Paris, where he studied ethnology at the Sorbonne and became a militant Surrealist under the influence of the French novelist and literary theorist André Breton. His first major work, *Leyendas de Guatemala* (1930; "Legends of Guatemala"), describing the life and culture of the Mayas before the arrival of the Spanish, brought him critical acclaim in France as well as at home.

Asturias
Camera Press

On his return to Guatemala, Asturias founded and edited *El diario del aire,* a radio magazine. During these years he published several volumes of poetry, beginning with *Sonetos* (1936; "Sonnets"). In 1946 he embarked upon a diplomatic career, continuing to write while serving in several countries in Central and South America.

It was during this period that Asturias' talent and influence as a novelist emerged, beginning with *El señor presidente* (1946; *The President,* 1963), an impassioned denunciation of the Guatemalan dictator Manuel Estrada Cabrera. In *Hombres de maíz* (1949; *Men of Maize,* 1975), the novel generally considered his masterpiece, Asturias depicts the seemingly irreversible wretchedness of the Indian peasant. Another aspect of that misery—the exploitation of Indians on the banana plantations—appears in the epic trilogy comprised of the novels *Viento fuerte* (1950; *The Cyclone,* 1967), *El papa verde* (1954; *The Green Pope,* 1971), and *Los ojos de los enterrados* (1960; *The Eyes of the Interred,* 1973). From 1966 to 1970 Asturias served as Guatemalan ambassador in Paris, where he took up permanent residence.

Astyages, Akkadian ISHTUMEGU (fl. 6th century BC), the last king of the Median Empire (reigned 585–550 BC). According to Herodotus, the Achaemenian Cyrus the Great was Astyages' grandson through his daughter Mandane, but this relationship is probably legendary. According to Babylonian inscriptions, Cyrus, king of Anshan (in southwestern Iran), began war against Astyages in 553 BC; in

550 the Median troops rebelled, and Astyages was taken prisoner. Then Cyrus occupied and plundered Ecbatana, the Median capital. A

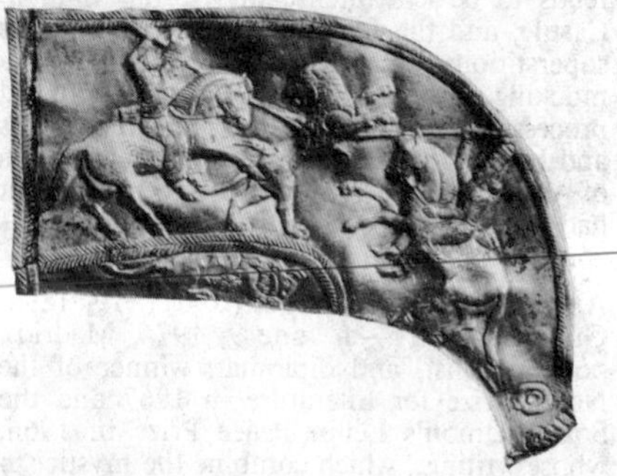

Astyages (left) spearing a lion, detail of a gold scabbard; in the British Museum
By courtesy of the trustees of the British Museum

somewhat different account of these events is given by the Greek writer Ctesias.

Astyanax, in Greek legend, prince, son of the Trojan prince Hector and his wife Andromache; he was also known as Scamandrius, after the River Scamander, near Troy. After the fall of Troy he was hurled from the battlements of the city by the Greek warrior Neoptolemus. According to medieval legend, however, he survived the war, established the kingdom of Messina in Sicily, and founded the line that led to Charlemagne.

Asuka period, in Japanese history and art, era from AD 552 to 645 that began with the introduction of Buddhism from Korea and culminated in the adoption of a Chinese pattern of government. Initially opposed by conservative clans, Buddhism found favour with the powerful Soga family which defeated its rivals in a succession dispute in 587. As Imperial regent, Shōtoku Taishi gave Buddhism official support, and his famous Seventeen Article Constitution, promulgated in 604, outlined moral precepts, largely Buddhist and Confucian in tone, for the establishment of a central government. Although the Soga were destroyed in 645, the reforms carried out from that year until 710 (called the Taika era reforms, *q.v.*) continued the institution of centralized rule.

Buddhist art found expression in the temples of the Asuka period, the first major one believed to be the Asuka-dera sponsored by the Soga. Prince Shōtoku founded the Hōryū-ji outside the city of Nara which, though later reconstructed, contains several examples of early Buddhist sculpture.

Asunción, city and capital of Paraguay, occupying a wooded promontory descending to the Paraguay River near its confluence with

The church of La Encarnación, Asunción, Paraguay
Art Resource—EB Inc.

the Pilcomayo. It lies 175 ft (53 m) above sea level.

The city was so named when a stockade was completed there on the Feast of the Assumption (August 15) in 1537. When Buenos Aires was evacuated in 1541 after an attack by the Pampa Indians, the inhabitants fled to Asunción. It was the headquarters of Spanish colonial activities in eastern South America for nearly half a century before Buenos Aires was refounded. In 1588 Jesuits established mission settlements on the Paraná River to convert the Guaraní Indian population. The Indians accepted the Spaniards, who introduced them to horseback riding and to coffee. Intermarriage of Indians and Spaniards contributed to the largely mestizo character of the present Paraguayans. After official separation from Buenos Aires in 1617, Asunción declined in importance. Partly because of its remoteness from Spain, nationalist and separatist movements began early in Paraguay: the Jesuits were expelled in 1767, and independence from both Spain and Argentina was declared in Asunción at midnight on May 14/15, 1811. The city's strategic position at the head of a great river system linking Argentina, Brazil, and Uruguay, its three enemies in the Paraguayan War (1864–70), led to Asunción's capture in 1868, and Brazil occupied and administered it until 1876.

Asunción has many beautiful large parks and flowering trees. Adjacent to the river, the buildings are colonial in style—one story with a patio—but the centre of town consists of modern high-rise buildings. The cathedral, presidential palace, and Pantheon of Heroes (a smaller replica of the Invalides in Paris), all built in the 19th century, and the ultramodern Hotel Guaraní, designed by the Brazilian architect Oscar Niemeyer, are among the notable buildings. As the seat of the national government, and of the archbishop of Paraguay, Asunción dominates social, cultural, and economic trends in Paraguay. Several institutions of higher education, including the Universidad Nacional de Asunción (1890) and the Universidad Católica "Nuestra Señora de la Asunción" (1960), are located in Asunción.

Asunción is the principal distributing and export centre of the most densely populated region of Paraguay. Cotton, sugarcane, corn (maize), tobacco, fruit, and cattle products from the rich agricultural and pastoral hinterland are processed in the capital. Industrial plants produce textiles, vegetable oils, footwear, flour, small river craft, and tobacco products. A piped water system was inaugurated in 1955. River steamers, mostly of foreign ownership, are the principal means of transporting freight. The city is also the terminus of the Ferrocarril (railway) Presidente Carlos Antonio López, which connects with the Argentine rail systems via a train ferry across the Paraná River at Encarnación. Another ferry connection across the Paraguay River provides trunk-road communication with Buenos Aires. Asunción also has an international airport. Pop. (1982 prelim.) 455,517.

Asunción, La, city, capital of Nueva Esparta state, northeastern Venezuela, on Isla de Margarita, in the Caribbean Sea, 12 mi (19 km) off the mainland. Lying in a fertile inland valley in the eastern portion of the island, La Asunción was first settled by Spaniards in 1524. Testimony to its prosperity during the colonial era is borne by the many remaining colonial buildings, most notably the Castle of Santa Rosa and the cathedral. The city is the commercial and manufacturing centre of the valley, in which cotton, sugarcane, cassava, and coconuts are grown. The principal industries include cotton ginning, corn and sugar milling, and the distilling of the alcoholic liquor aguardiente. Porlamar, the principal port and largest settlement of the island, lies approximately 10 mi to the south. Pop. (1971) 6,334.

asura, Iranian AHURA, in Hindu mythology, a class of titans or demons, the enemies of the gods and of men. In the Vedic age the *asuras* and the *devas* were both considered classes of gods, but gradually the two groups came to oppose each other, a development that was reversed in Iran. (There *asura*, or *ahura*, came to mean the supreme god and the *devas*, or *daevas*, became demons.) In Hindu mythology, the *asuras* and the *devas* together churned the milky ocean, in order to extract from it the *amṛta*, the elixir of immortality. Strife arose over the possession of the *amṛta*, a conflict that is never ending. *See also* deva.

Asurbanipal (Assyrian king): *see* Ashurbanipal.

Aśvaghoṣa, also spelled ASHVAGHOSA (b. AD 80?, Ayodhyā, India—d. 150?, Peshāwar), philosopher and poet who is considered India's greatest poet before Kālidāsa (5th century) and the father of Sanskrit drama; he popularized the style of Sanskrit poetry known as *kāvya* (*see* kāvya style).

Aśvaghoṣa was born a Brahman. Legend obscures the man, but it is known that he was an outspoken opponent of Buddhism until, after a heated debate with a noted Buddhist scholar on the relative merits of the Vedāntic (Hindu) religion and the middle path (Buddhism), he accepted the value of Buddhism and became a disciple of his erstwhile opponent.

While in Vārānasi (Benares), where Gautama Buddha had preached his first sermon, Aśvaghoṣa saw the city conquered by the Kushan (Kuṣāṇa) emperor Kaniṣka, a devout Buddhist. A huge war indemnity was demanded, and the ruler of Vārānasi handed over instead a symbolic tribute, a begging bowl said to have been used by both the Buddha and Aśvaghoṣa. Apparently the philosopher rose to the position of spiritual counsellor in Kaniṣka's court at Peshāwar.

A brilliant orator, Aśvaghoṣa spoke at length on Mahāyāna (Greater Vehicle) Buddhist doctrine at the fourth Buddhist council, which he helped organize. His fame lay largely in his ability to explain the intricate concepts of Mahāyāna Buddhism. Among the works attributed to him are the *Mahāyāna-śraddhotpāda-śāstra* ("The Awakening of Faith in the Mahāyāna"), the *Buddhacarita* ("The Life of Buddha") in verse, and the *Mahālaṅkara* ("Book of Glory").

Consult the INDEX *first*

aśvamedha (Sanskrit: "horse sacrifice"), also spelled AŚWAMEDHA, ASHVAMEDHA, or ASHWAMEDHA, grandest of the Vedic religious rites of ancient India, performed by a king to celebrate his paramountcy. The ceremony is described in detail in various Vedic writings, particularly the *Śatapatha Brāhmaṇa*. An especially fine stallion was selected and was allowed to roam freely for a year under the protection of a royal guard. If the horse entered a foreign country, its ruler had either to fight or to submit. If the horse was not captured during the year, it was victoriously brought back to the capital accompanied by the rulers of the lands it entered, and then sacrificed at a great public ceremony, which was accompanied by much feasting and celebration. The wandering horse was said to symbolize the Sun in its journey over the world and, consequently, the power of the king over the whole Earth. On successfully carrying out a horse sacrifice, the king could assume the title of *cakravartin* (universal monarch). The rite served not only to glorify the king but also to ensure the prosperity and fertility of the entire kingdom.

In historical times the practice was condemned by the Buddha and seems to have suffered a decline, but it was revived by Puṣyamitra Śuṅga (reigned 187–151 BC). He is said to have defeated, while protecting his horse, Greek warriors who had reached the Punjab. Samudra Gupta (c. AD 330–c. 380) issued coins in commemoration of his successful completion of an *aśvamedha,* and the rite is mentioned in connection with other Gupta and Cālukya monarchs. It may have continued as late as the 11th century, when it is said to have taken place in the Cōḷa Empire.

Aswān, also spelled ASSUAN, or ASSOUAN, *muḥāfaẓah* (governorate), Upper Egypt, embracing the Nile floodplain and immediately adjacent territories. Its area is 262 sq mi (679 sq km). Long and narrow in shape, it is the most southerly Egyptian *muḥāfaẓah* along the Nile; its short southern boundary forms part of the international frontier with The Sudan. The sandstone, granite, and diorite hills flanking the Nile are dissected by ancient, long dried-up streams; the hills reach a maximum elevation of 2,083 ft (635 m) near the Sudanese border and rise to more than 1,200 ft in several places farther north around Lake Nasser. At the capital of Aswān (*q.v.*) and at Wādī Ḥalfā, at the Sudanese frontier, the Nile flows through granite formations that, having eroded more slowly, have produced rapids and islands in the river, called cataracts. These presented obstacles to river traffic and were a factor in the location of the frontier at Aswān in pharaonic Egypt.

Just above the city of Aswān is the old Aswān Dam, completed in 1902. Some 4 mi (6 km) farther south is the Aswān High Dam (*q.v.*), one of the world's great engineering works, completed in 1970. South of the High Dam for nearly 150 mi to The Sudan border is a hilly, inhospitable desert wilderness without roads or railroads, with the original river valley flooded by Lake Nasser. The Nubian population was resettled in a reclaimed area near Kawm Umbū.

Since 1968, when the High Dam became operational, about 1,000,000 ac (400,000 ha) of former summer-irrigated lands have been converted to year-round irrigation, some of it in Aswān *muḥāfaẓah.* Sugarcane, lentils, corn (maize), and wheat are grown in the area north of Aswān city. Industry in the *muḥāfaẓah* is centred on the High Dam and in the larger towns of Kawm Umbū and Idfū, both of which have sugar refineries. Mineral deposits in the *muḥāfaẓah* include iron ore, gold, uranium, phosphates, and coal. Granite has been quarried around Aswān city since pharaonic times, and marble quarries opened in modern times.

Tourism is important as the governorate is rich in well-preserved ancient monuments. In the 1960s a massive international scientific effort excavated the area flooded by Lake Nasser, and the Nubian temples were moved to higher ground; the most complex efforts involved Abu Simbel and Philae. Pop. (1983 est.) 744,000.

Aswān, also spelled ASSUAN, or ASSOUAN, Greek SYENE, city, capital of Aswān *muḥāfaẓah* (governorate), Egypt, on the east bank of the Nile just below the First Cataract. It faces the island of Elephantine (*q.v.*; modern Jazīrat Aswān) with ruins of ancient Yeb, the southern frontier of pharaonic Egypt. Local quarries supplied granite for many monuments and are still operated; on the eastern bank was the site of the ancient city of Swen (ancient Egyptian: The Mart), whence came the Greek Syene and the Arabic Aswān. In the 5th century BC Swen contained a colony of Jewish mercenaries; it was later a Coptic Christian bishopric. It served as a frontier garrison post for the Romans, Turks, and British.

Aswān, on the Nile, in Egypt
Art Resource—EB Inc.

Modern Aswān is an administrative centre, winter resort, and commercial centre, receiving trade from The Sudan. It is also an industrial centre, with a copper- and steel-producing complex, a chemicals plant producing fertilizer, a cement plant, a sugar refinery, and a quarrying industry producing granite and marble. The old Aswān Dam (completed in 1902) rises about 3 mi (5 km) south of the city; the Aswān High Dam (completed in 1970) is about 7 mi (11 km) south of the city. The High Dam produces most of Egypt's electricity. Lake Nassar, which was created by the High Dam, supports a fishing industry, and construction of a refrigeration and processing plant started in the early 1980s. The Higher Industrial Institute is located in Aswān. A school for fisheries training opened in 1980. On Elephantine a museum contains antiquities from the *muḥāfaẓah.* There are many hotels in the city; it is the southern terminus of the Cairo–Aswān railway. There is also an international airport. Pop. (1983 est.) 174,000.

Aswān, Jazīrat (Egypt): *see* Elephantine.

Aswān High Dam, Arabic SAAD AL-ʿĀLI, rock-fill dam across the Nile River, at Aswān, Egypt, completed in 1970 (formally inaugurated in January 1971) at a cost of about $1,000,000,000. The dam, 364 feet (111 metres) high, with a crest length of 12,565 ft and a volume of 55,809,000 cubic yards (42,600,000 cubic metres), impounds a reservoir, Lake Nasser (*q.v.*), that has a gross capacity of 133,000,000 acre-feet (164,000,000,000 cubic metres). Of the Nile's total annual discharge, some 74,000,000,000 cu m of water have been allocated by treaty between Egypt and The Sudan, 55,500,000,000 to Egypt, and the remainder to The Sudan. Lake Nasser backs up the Nile about 200 miles (320 kilometres) in Egypt and almost 100 mi farther upstream (south) in The Sudan; creation of the reservoir necessitated the costly relocation of the temple complex of Abu Simbel, which would otherwise have been submerged. Ninety thousand Egyptian fellahin (peasants) and Sudanese Nubian nomads had to be relocated. Fifty thousand Egyptians were transported to the Kawm Umbū valley, 30 mi north of Aswān, to form a new agricultural zone called Nubaria; most of the Sudanese were resettled around Khashm al-Qirbah, The Sudan, near the Ethiopian frontier.

Aswān High Dam
Carl Frank

The Aswān High Dam yields enormous benefits to the economy of Egypt. For the first time in history, the annual Nile flood can be controlled by man. The dam contains floodwaters, releasing them when needed to maximize their utility on irrigated land, to water thousands of new acres, to improve navigation both above and below Aswān, and to generate electric power (capacity is 2,100 megawatts). The reservoir, which has a depth of 300 ft and averages 14 mi in width, supports a fishing industry; however, the dam has produced a negative effect on Egypt's Mediterranean coastal fishing grounds. The lake also has an enormous tourist potential.

Completed in 1902 and its crest raised in 1912 and 1933, an earlier dam 4 mi downstream from the Aswān High Dam holds back about 4,000,000 ac-ft of water from the tail of the Nile flood in the late autumn. Once one of the largest dams in the world, it is 7,027 ft long and is pierced by 180 sluices that can pass the whole Nile flood, with its heavy load of silt.

asylum, in international law, the protection granted by a state to a foreign citizen against his own state. The person for whom asylum is established has no legal right to demand it, while the sheltering state, which has the legal right to grant asylum, is under no obligation to give it. Asylum is thus a right of the state, not of the individual. The right of asylum falls into three basic categories: territorial, extraterritorial, and neutral asylum. Territorial asylum is granted within the territorial bounds of the state offering asylum and is an exception to the practice of extradition. It is designed and employed primarily for the protection of persons accused of such political offenses as treason, desertion, sedition, and espionage. It has become a widespread practice, however, to exclude from this category persons accused of the murder of a head of state, anarchism, collaboration with the enemy in time of war, crimes against peace, war crimes, and crimes against humanity. Extraterritorial asylum refers to asylum granted in legations, consulates, and warships and merchant vessels in foreign territory. It is therefore granted within the territory of the state from which protection is sought. It is most a matter of dispute when granted in embassies or legations and is then generally known as diplomatic asylum. Neutral asylum is used by a state, neutral in time of war, which is considered to have the right to offer asylum within its territory to troops of belligerent states, provided the troops submit to internment for the duration of the war.

In ancient times "asylum" meant a place of refuge or protection from which a person could not be removed forcibly without sacrilege—thus, a temple, altar, or statue of a god or, in later times, a Christian church (*see* sanctuary). Later it came to signify an institution for the protection or relief of some class of destitute or otherwise unfortunate persons; its commonest use in this sense was in "orphan asylum." *See also* safe-conduct.

asymmetric synthesis, any chemical reaction that affects the structural symmetry in the molecules of a compound, converting the compound into unequal proportions of compounds that differ in the dissymmetry of their structures at the affected centre. Such reactions usually involve organic compounds in which the symmetrical structural feature is a carbon atom bonded to four other atoms or groups of atoms, of which two are alike; in the asymmetric synthesis, one of the identical groups is preferentially modified or replaced, so that the product is a mixture of two dissymmetric compounds, one of which predominates.

Asymmetric reactions result from the influence of some dissymmetry in the reacting system, such as the presence of a dissymmetric centre in the molecule, a dissymmetric solvent or catalyst, or circularly polarized light, in which the plane of vibration of the electromagnetic fields rotates in either a right-handed or a left-handed sense.

Asymmetric syntheses often are called stereoselective; if one of the products forms exclusively, the reaction is called stereospecific.

asymmetrical parallel bars: *see* uneven parallel bars.

Asyūṭ, also spelled, ASIUT, or ASSIOUT, *muḥāfaẓah* (governorate) of Upper Egypt, along the Nile, between al-Minyā governorate to the north and Sawhāj governorate to the south. Its settled area is limited to the river valley, extending almost 100 mi (160 km) along the river and about 12 mi across, with an area of 600 sq mi (1,554 sq km), but it also extends into the Western Desert, with al-Jīzah governorate as its western boundary.

Its history dates to the Badarian prehistoric period, named after the site of al-Bādāri, where its remains were first excavated. The region was a battleground between the 10th and 11th dynasties in the First Intermediate Period (*c.* 2160–2040 BC); the frontier also lay at Cusae in the governorate during the Second Intermediate Period (1786–*c.* 1567 BC). Akhenaton (reigned *c.* 1379–1362 BC) moved his residence to the site of Tall al-Amarna, 50 mi downriver from Asyūṭ city on the eastern bank.

Agriculture is the main activity of the governorate; cotton, grains, vegetables, and lentils are the major crops, and chickens are raised. There are no major towns outside the governorate's capital, Asyūṭ (*q.v.*). The Baḥr Yūsuf Canal, branching off the Nile just north of the capital, flows in an old river channel on the western side of the valley and irrigates the agricultural land. Copts comprise a considerable part of the population of the *muḥāfaẓah*. Pop. (1983 est.) 2,059,000.

Asyūṭ, also spelled ASIUT, or ASSIOUT, capital of Asyūṭ *muḥāfaẓah* (governorate) and the largest settlement of Upper Egypt, lying on the west bank of the Nile, almost midway between Cairo and Aswān. The irrigated river valley is about 12 mi (20 km) wide at this point. The *muḥāfaẓah* extends into the Western Desert to include al-Wāḥat al-Farāfirah (Farafra Oasis).

Known as Syut in ancient Egypt, the city was a centre of worship of the jackal-headed god Wepwawet. In the Middle Kingdom (*c.* 2040–1786 BC) it was capital of the 17th nome (province) of Upper Egypt. While never able to challenge the power of Thebes, it was commercially prominent as a terminus of caravan routes traversing the Eastern and Western deserts, including the famous Darb al-Arbaʿīn. In Hellenistic times it was known as Lycopolis (Wolf City), an allusion to the worship of the jackal-headed god. It was the birthplace of the Neoplatonist philosopher Plotinus (*c.* AD 205–269/270).

Under Islāmic rule in the Middle Ages, Asyūṭ continued its commercial prominence, being noted for its quality textiles, which, with fine fruits and grain grown near the city, were exported to Dārfūr and elsewhere in the Sudan. Returning caravans brought slaves, ivory, and dyestuffs.

Continuing its ancient tradition, Asyūṭ is one of the few remaining places where silver appliqué-work shawls are still made; it also still makes fine pottery, inlaid woodwork, and rugs. There are also modern textile mills and a chemicals plant producing fertilizer. Just north of the city and its river port of al-Ḥamrā' is the Asyūṭ barrage (dam) across the Nile (1902), an open limestone weir 2,730 ft (832 m) long. It feeds the Baḥr Yūsuf (formerly Ibrāhīmīyah) canal, which parallels the Nile for about 200 mi to the north, irrigating much of Middle Egypt, with a westward branch to the oasis of al-Fayyūm. In the 1980s the barrage was improved, and a hydroelectric plant was added. Centres of higher education at Asyūṭ include a university (opened 1957) and a teacher training college. An important Coptic Catholic centre, the see of Asyūṭ is administered from Cairo by a metropolitan. The limestone hills rising southwest of the city have numerous rock tombs of the 12th dynasty (1991–1786 BC). Pop. (1983 est.) 259,300.

AT&T: *see* American Telephone and Telegraph Company.

Atacama, also called ATACAMEÑO, or CUNZA, extinct South American Indian culture of the Andean desert oases of northern Chile and northwestern Argentina. The last surviving groups of the Atacama have been assimilated by Spanish and Aymara culture.

In their widely scattered settlements the Atacama cultivated crops such as corn (maize), beans, quinoa, and squash with the aid of irrigation. They herded llama and alpaca and traded extensively between the coast and the interior, as well as with the neighbouring Diaguita and Peruvian Indians.

The arid climate limited settlements to the small and isolated oases. Each village was autonomous, made up of a group of related families under a chief. Villages were usually located on high ground, surrounded by defensive walls. The houses were built of stone and arranged along streets. Archaeological evidence shows that warfare was prevalent among the Atacama.

The language of the Atacama was called Cunza or Lincan Antai, of which a vocabulary of about 1,100 words has been recorded.

Atacama, region, northern Chile, bounded on the east by Argentina and on the west by the Pacific Ocean. Created as a province in 1843 and as a region in 1974, it has an area of 29,144 sq mi (75,482 sq km) and includes Chañaral, Copiapó, and Huasco provinces, and San Félix and San Ambrosio islands, which lie in the Pacific about 500 mi (800 km) west of Chañaral, the main port. The Atacama Desert covers much of the region. North of Copiapó (*q.v.*), the capital, a longitudinal valley lies between the coastal range and Andean volcanoes. South of Copiapó a complex series of intermontane basins is overshadowed by snowcapped Andean peaks up to 22,835 ft (6,960 m). Desert climate prevails throughout, and although some meteorological stations have never recorded a drop of rain, some rain falls in the south. Marine terraces and the Copiapó and Río Huasco valleys are irrigated for cultivation of fruits, olives, and alfalfa. Since the 18th century, however, gold, silver, copper, and iron mining, successively, have been the primary economic activities of Atacama. Communications are mainly north–south with the Pan-American Highway and a railroad running the length of the region. Pop. (1982 prelim.) 183,071.

Section of the Copiapó Valley in Atacama region, Chile

Peter L. Gould

Atacama Desert, Spanish DESIERTO DE ATACAMA, cool, arid region in northern Chile, 600 to 700 mi (1,000 to 1,100 km) long. Its limits are not exact, but it lies mainly within Antofagasta and Atacama administrative regions between the south bend of the Río Loa and the mountains separating the Salado–Copiapó drainage basins. To the north, the desert region continues into the Region of Tarapacá.

The desert consists mainly of salt pans at the foot of the Cordillera de la Costa to the west, and of alluvial fans sloping from the Precordillera ranges to the east; some of the fans are sandy and covered with dunes, but extensive pebble accumulations are more common.

Several parts of the Atacama Desert may be distinguished. Its western part includes a coastal chain of mountains 5,000 ft (1,500 m) or so in height with peaks reaching to 6,560 ft. There is no coastal plain; through much of their extent the mountains end abruptly in cliffs, some of them higher than 1,600 ft, making communication difficult between the coastal ports and the interior. The railroad from the port of Iquique, for example, must ascend about 2,300 ft before it passes through a valley to the interior.

In the interior a raised depression extends north and south and forms a high plain at an altitude of more than 3,000 ft. Farther to the east is the western range of the Andes, preceded by the Cordillera Domeyko. Here there are numerous volcanic cones, some exceeding 16,000 ft in altitude. Along Chile's north-eastern frontier with Argentina and Bolivia, between the western and eastern ranges of the Andes, is a high plateau more than 13,000 ft in altitude, called the Puna de Atacama.

The Atacama Desert forms part of the arid Pacific shoreline of South America. Moist air masses coming from the tropical Amazon Basin tend to be blocked by the Andes, making the desert one of the driest regions in the world. Some artesian waters exist, but their boron content makes them unsuitable for agriculture. In the Pampa del Tamarugal, to the north of the Río Loa, many salt beds have formed over subterranean waters.

On the coast the aridity is the consequence of the Peru (Humboldt) Current that brings cold water from the Antarctic, causing a thermal inversion—cold air at the surface of the ocean and warmer air higher up. This condition produces fog and stratus clouds, but no rain. Heavy rains fall in Iquique or Antofagasta only two to four times a century.

Temperatures in the desert are relatively low compared with those in similar latitudes elsewhere. The average summer temperature at Iquique is only 66°F (19°C) and at Antofagasta 65°F (18°C).

For many years in the 19th century, the desert was the object of conflicts among Chile, Bolivia, and Peru because of its valuable resources, particularly sodium nitrate deposits located northeast of Antofagasta and inland from Iquique. Much of the area belonged to Bolivia and Peru, but the mining industry was controlled by Chilean interests, which were strongly supported by the Chilean government. From the War of the Pacific (1879–83) between the three countries, Chile emerged victorious. The Treaty of Ancón (1884) gave Chile permanent ownership of sectors previously controlled by Peru and Bolivia, the latter losing its whole Pacific coastline.

The area proved to be one of the chief sources of Chile's wealth until World War I. Nitrate deposits in the central depression and in several basins of the coastal range were systematically mined after the middle of the 19th century. Ports were built at Iquique, Caldera, Antofagasta, Taltal, Tocopilla, Mejillones, and, farther north, Pisagua, and railroads penetrated the mountain barriers to the interior. Prior to World War I, Chile had a world monopoly on nitrate; in some years 3,000,000 tons were extracted, and the taxes on its export amounted to half the government's revenues. The development of synthetic methods of fixing nitrogen have since reduced the market to a regional one. Some sulfur is still mined in the high Cordillera. The region's chief source of revenue, however, is copper mining at Chuquicamata in the Andes and at Paposo on the coast.

Some farming is done in the desert, but this supports only a few thousand people. Lemons are grown at Pica, and a variety of products are cultivated on the shores of the salt marshes at San Pedro de Atacama. At Calama, near Chuquicamata, water from the Río Loa irrigates potato and alfalfa fields.

Atacama Plateau, Spanish PUNA DE ATACAMA, cold, desolate Andean tableland in northwestern Argentina and adjacent regions of Chile. It is about 200 mi (320 km) long (north to south) and 150 mi wide, and has an average elevation of 11,000 to 13,000 ft (3,300 to 4,000 m). The region may be defined as the southernmost portion of the Andean Altiplano (or Puno) and is separated from the Atacama Desert (west) by the Sierra Domeyko. The peaks of the Cordillera Oriental alternate with dry, sandy, clay-filled intermontane basins, the basins often occupied by salt pans or flats, called *salinas* in Argentina, of which the largest are the Antofalla, Hombre Muerto, Arizaro, Incahuasi, and Salinas Grandes. In Chile the Salar de Atacama is the largest such feature. Along the eastern margin the plateau has been dissected by streams into deep, narrow river valleys, as well as broader valleys known as *quebradas,* the latter historically important as colonial routes of penetration into the Argentine Andes. Peruvian and Chilean colonizers conducted expeditions through the Andean valleys in the latter half of the 16th century that led to the foundation of some of the oldest towns in Argentina at the eastern foot of the Andes. The Peruvians followed an old Inca road to settle Santiago del Estero, Tucumán Córdoba, Salta, La Rioja, and Jujuy. San Juan, Mendoza, and San Luis were established by Chileans.

Most of the region is dominated by a scanty growth of low shrub, 16–60 in. (40–150 cm) high, although a narrow belt of montane forest composed of a dense growth of broadleaf trees covers the east-facing edge. Temperatures average only 47–49° F (8.5–9.5° C).

The region is very sparsely populated with Indian and mestizo communities dependent on the valleys for corn (maize) and wheat. The northernmost portion of the Plateau is of the most economic value, salt being produced from the Salinas Grandes, and wool and skins from sheep and llama. Since 1948 a railroad has crossed the Plateau (east to west), linking Salta, Argentina, with the nitrate-mining communities of the Atacama Desert in Chile.

Atacama Trench (Pacific Ocean): *see* Peru-Chile Trench.

atacamite, green, brilliant halide mineral, basic copper chloride [$Cu_2(OH)_3Cl$]. It is a

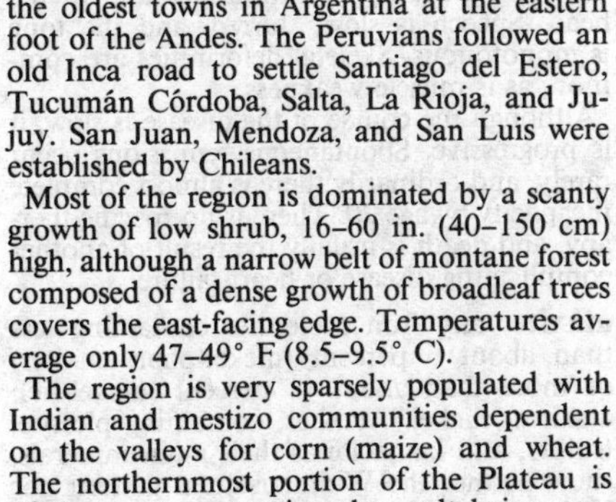

Atacamite from Wallaroo, South Australia

By courtesy of the Field Museum of Natural History, Chicago; photograph, John H. Gerard—EB Inc.

secondary mineral, formed by the oxidation of other copper minerals, particularly under arid conditions; it is widespread as brittle, transparent to translucent crystals in Atacama Province, Chile; in Boleo, Mex.; and in South Australia. For detailed physical properties, *see* halide mineral (table).

Consult
the
INDEX
first

Atahuallpa, also spelled ATAHUALPA (b. *c.* 1502—d. Aug. 29, 1533, Cajamarca, Inca Empire), 13th and last emperor of the Inca, who was victorious in a devastating civil war with his half brother, only to be captured, held for ransom, and then executed by Francisco Pizarro.

Atahuallpa was a younger son of the Inca ruler Huayna Capac and an Ecuadorian princess; although not the legitimate heir, he seems to have been his father's favourite. When the old Inca chief died (*c.* 1527), the kingdom was divided between Atahuallpa, who ruled the northern part of the empire from Quito, and Huáscar, the legitimate heir, who ruled from Cuzco, the traditional Inca capital.

Depicted by contemporary chroniclers as brave, ambitious, and extremely popular with the army, Atahuallpa was soon embroiled in a civil war with his older half brother for control of the empire. The war ravaged Incan cities, wreaked havoc on the economy, and decimated the population. Early in 1532, near Cuzco, Atahuallpa's army defeated the army of Huáscar in what was perhaps the greatest military engagement in Incan history. Huáscar and his family were captured and later executed under Atahuallpa's orders.

While Atahuallpa was enjoying the hot springs in the small Incan town of Cajamarca, preparatory to entering Cuzco in triumph, Francisco Pizarro entered the city with a force of about 180 men. On Nov. 15, 1532, Pizarro and Atahuallpa met in what was to prove one of the most fateful encounters in the New World. Invited by the Spaniard to attend a feast in his honour, the Inca chief accepted. The next day, he arrived at the appointed meeting place with several thousand unarmed retainers; Pizarro, prompted by the example of Cortés and Montezuma in Mexico, had prepared an ambush.

Atahuallpa rejected demands by the friar Vicente de Valverde, who had accompanied Pizarro, that he accept the Christian faith and the sovereignty of Charles V of Spain, whereupon Pizarro signalled his men. Firing their canons and guns and charging with their horses (all of which were unknown to the Inca), the conquistadores captured Atahuallpa and slaughtered thousands of his men. Perceiving the avarice of his captors, Atahuallpa offered to fill a room with gold as a ransom for his release. Pizarro and his men accepted the offer, and from all over the empire, Incas brought gold and silver statues, jewelry, and art objects. The Spaniards had the Indians melt it all down into bullion and ingots, accumulating 24 tons of gold and silver, the richest ransom ever received. Once the full amount was acquired, the conquistadores ordered Atahuallpa burned to death (Aug. 29, 1533).

When the Emperor was at the stake, Vicente de Valverde offered him the choice of being burned alive or dying by the more merciful garrote if he became a Christian. Atahuallpa, who had resisted proselytization throughout his captivity, agreed to the conversion and so died that day by strangulation. The execution of Atahuallpa, the last free reigning emperor, marked the end of the Inca civilization.

Atakpamé, town, Ōgou *préfecture,* Plateaux economic *région,* Togo, West Africa, on the railroad running north from Lomé, the capital, to Blitta. Atakpamé dates from the 19th century and was first settled by Ewe and Yoruba peoples. It developed as both a commercial centre on a major north–south caravan route and as a haven for refugees fleeing from Dahomean attacks. As a consequence, Atakpamé experienced numerous destructive assaults by the Kingdom of Dahomey. It is the centre of an important cotton-growing area and trades in both cocoa and coffee. It is the principal locale of the Plateaux *région.* Pop. (1977 est.) 21,800.

Atalanta, in Greek mythology, a renowned and swift-footed huntress, probably a by-form of the goddess Artemis; traditionally, she was the daughter of Schoeneus of Boeotia or of

Atalanta, Greek marble statue; in the Louvre

Giraudon—Art Resource/EB Inc.

Iasus and Clymene of Arcadia. Her complex legend includes the following incidents: at her father's instance she was left to die at birth but was suckled by a she-bear; she took part in the Calydonian boar hunt; she offered to marry anyone who could outrun her—but those whom she overtook she speared.

In one race Hippomenes (or Milanion) was given three of the golden apples of the Hesperides (*q.v.*) by the goddess Aphrodite; when he dropped them, Atalanta stopped to pick them up and so lost the race. Their son was Parthenopaeus, who later was one of the Seven who fought against Thebes after the death of King Oedipus. She and her husband, proving ungrateful to Aphrodite, were led to profane a shrine of the goddess Cybele (or of Zeus), for which Cybele (or Zeus) turned them into lions.

Atami, city, Shizuoka *ken* (prefecture), Honshu, Japan, on the northeastern coast of Izuhantō (Izu Peninsula), facing Sagami-nada (Sagami Gulf) of the Pacific Ocean. The city occupies the crater of the extinct volcano Atami-san (Mt. Atami). The surrounding hills are remnants of the crater wall, which has been drowned by the sea on the east. Atami's mild and warm climate, scenic seascape, and hot springs have made it a favoured resort since the 5th century AD. After the Meiji Restoration (1868) it also became a centre for artists and writers. Development of the city and its surrounding region as a recreational area was rapid after 1934, when the opening of Tanna Tunnel brought the Tōkaidō Line (railway) to the city. Overconstruction on mountainous land has caused landslides and traffic problems.

Of several attractions in the surrounding area, the Atami Tropical Garden contains hundreds of species of tropical plants and fish. An annual festival is held at the Atami Japanese-Apricot Garden. Atami Art Museum,

Twilight at Atami on Sagami-nada (Sagami Gulf), Japan
Satashi Ohkoshi—Orion Press from FPG/EB Inc.

on a hill overlooking the city, contains a fine collection of Japanese sculpture and painting. Pop. (1980) 50,082.

Atar, town, west central Mauritania, West Africa, capital of the arid Adrar administrative region. It is an oasis and a caravan stopping point. It lies on a road leading southwest to Nouakchott, the national capital. The oasis produces dates and grains and supports cattle, sheep, and goat grazing. Atar is the site of an airstrip; it also has a school for traditional

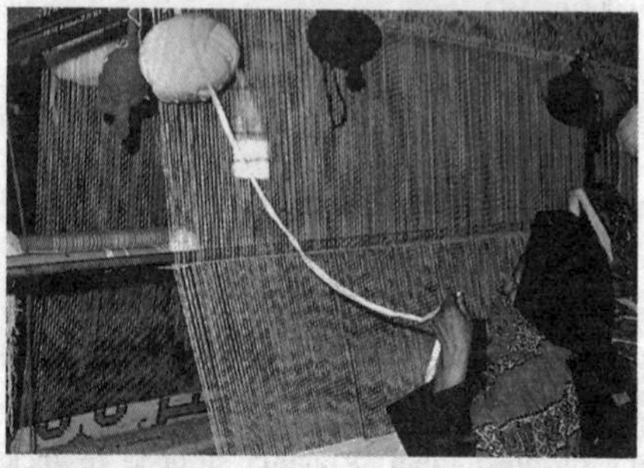

Traditional carpet weaving at Atar, Mauritania
Caracciolo-Banoun—M. Grimoldi

weaving, and it is an important source of rugs. Pop. (1977) 16,326.

Atargatis, great goddess of northern Syria; her chief sanctuary was at Hierapolis (modern Manbij), northeast of Aleppo, where she was worshipped with her consort, Hadad. Her ancient temple there was rebuilt about 300 BC by Queen Stratonice, and it was perhaps partly as a result of that Greek patronage that the cult, carried by Greek merchants and mercenaries, spread to various parts of the Greek world, where the goddess was generally regarded as a form of Aphrodite.

Her nature closely resembled that of her Phoenician counterpart, Astarte, though she also showed some kinship with the Anatolian Cybele. Primarily she was a goddess of fertility, but as the *baalat* ("mistress") of her city and people she was also responsible for their protection and well-being. Hence she was commonly portrayed wearing the mural crown and holding a sheaf of grain, while the lions who supported her throne suggest her strength and her power over nature.

ʿAtāsī, Hāshim al- (b. 1875, Homs, Syria—d. Dec. 5, 1960, Homs), nationalist politician and three-time president of Syria.

An official in the Ottoman administration of Syria in his early life, ʿAtāsī became a member of the Syrian Congress in 1919. The next year the Congress proclaimed Greater Syria an independent constitutional monarchy. One of the nationalist leaders opposing French occupation and mandate in the 1920s, he was elected president of the Constituent Assembly, which, because of its adherence to the 1920 proclamation, was dissolved by the French authorities in May 1930. In 1936 he headed a Syrian delegation to Paris that negotiated the Franco-Syrian treaty providing for Syrian independence; on his return he was elected president of the republic. Faced with the French government's refusal to ratify the treaty, he resigned in 1939.

In 1949, following a year of military uprisings, ʿAtāsī was called upon to form a provisional government and to hold elections for a Constituent Assembly. In December 1950 the Assembly, under a new constitution, elected him president, but he resigned the next year. With the fall of Adib ash-Shishakli's regime by a coup in 1954, he was recalled to complete his term of office. After the 1955 elections ʿAtāsī retired to private life in Homs.

Atatürk, Kemal (Turkish: Kemal Father of Turks), original name MUSTAFA KEMAL, also called MUSTAFA KEMAL PAŞA (b. 1881, Salonika, Greece—d. Nov. 10, 1938, Istanbul), soldier, statesman, and reformer, founder and first president (1923–38) of the Republic of Turkey. He modernized the legal and educational systems and encouraged adoption of a European way of life (with Turkish written in the Latin alphabet and with citizens adopting European-style surnames).

A brief account of the life and works of Kemal Atatürk follows; for a full biography, *see* MACROPAEDIA: Atatürk.

Mustafa Kemal's father, Ali Riza, died while his son was still in elementary school, and his mother, Zübeyde Hanim, reared him at her brother's home in the country. He was then sent to the Military Academy at Istanbul, from which he graduated in 1902. He advanced in the military and after World War I was appointed to a post in the Ministry of War. Supporting the idea of an independent Turkey, he resigned from the army (1919) and was chosen president of a National Congress. In 1920, when the British formally occupied Turkey and dissolved the Chamber of Deputies, he opened the first Grand National Assembly of Turkey; the assembly then assumed national sovereignty with Mustafa Kemal as president and prime minister of the state.

After consolidating his control of Anatolia, Mustafa Kemal proclaimed a republic and was elected its first president (1922). The peace treaty of 1923 established Turkey's independence. In 1924 Mustafa Kemal abolished the caliphate and began a sweeping reform of Turkish politics, law, and culture. In 1933 he was given the name Atatürk (Father of Turks) by the National Assembly.

Ataulphus, also spelled ATAWULF, or ATAULF (d. 415, Barcelona), chieftain of the Visigoths from 410 to 415 and the successor of his brother-in-law Alaric. In 412 he led the Visigoths, who had recently sacked Rome (410), from Italy to settle in southern Gaul. Two years later Ataulphus married the Roman princess Galla Placidia (sister of the emperor Honorius), who had been seized at Rome. Driven from Gaul, he retreated into Spain early in 415 and was in that year assassinated at Barcelona. The 5th-century historian Paulus Orosius records Ataulphus' statement that his original aim had been to overthrow the Roman Empire, but that later, recognizing the inability of his people to govern an empire, he desired to bolster Roman power by means of Gothic arms. His vision of an empire revitalized through a barbarian alliance was not realized.

ataxia, inability to coordinate voluntary muscular movements. In common usage, the term describes an unsteady gait.

Most hereditary ataxias of neurological origin are caused by degeneration of the spinal cord and cerebellum; other parts of the nervous system are also frequently involved. The commonest of these is Friedreich's ataxia, with a poorly understood mode of transmission. During the patient's first three to five years of life, only a few physical deformities (*e.g.,* hammertoe) may be present. Later, by adolescence, the unsteady gait begins—frequently interpreted as clumsiness—but, as the ataxia progresses, the unsteadiness becomes a broad-based, lurching gait, with sudden turns extremely difficult without falling. Tremors develop in the upper extremities and in the head. Speech is slow, slurred, and the tone is monotonous. Skeletal deformities are common, as is muscle weakness.

Although the course of the disease is slow, it is progressive. Spontaneous remissions occur rarely, and ordinarily there is almost complete incapacity by age 20. There is no specific therapy, and death is usually the result of another complicating disease or heart failure.

ataxite, any iron meteorite containing less than about 6 percent (nickel-poor ataxites) or more than about 11 percent (nickel-rich ataxites) nickel. Ataxites, containing plessite, troilite, and kamacite as their main minerals, show neither the Widmanstätten pattern nor Neumann lines. Nickel-poor ataxites generally have the same nickel content as hexahedrites but have a uniformly granular structure instead of large kamacite crystals. This structure is completely unrelated to that of the nickel-rich ataxites, which is a plessite-like intergrowth of taenite and kamacite; the ataxites that contain more than 27 percent nickel are composed of taenite instead of plessite.

Atbara River, Arabic NAHR ʿAṬBARAH, river joining the Nile as its last tributary at the town of ʿAṭbarah in The Sudan. It rises in the Ethiopian highlands north of Lake Tana and flows westward into The Sudan, turning north to receive the Angareb and Satīt (Takazē) rivers before heading northwestward to the Nile. It flows for a total of 500 mi (805 km). A dam at the rapids of Khashm al-Qirbah was built for storage and irrigation; past that point the river loses much water by evaporation and transpiration. During the dry season the water level sinks to pools in the riverbed. At flood, however, the Atbara is navigable and discharges at a rate of about 25,000 cu ft (700 cu m) per second (more than 20 percent of the total Nile discharge). It carries a heavy load of silt, and its banks are mainly badlands.

ʿAṭbarah, also spelled ATBARA, town, an-Nīl *mudīrīyah* (province), The Sudan, on the right (east) bank of the Nile River at the mouth of the seasonal Nahr (river) ʿAṭbarah. The junction of two major road and railway lines to Khartoum (from Wādī Ḥalfā and Port Sudan), it has become an important commercial and agricultural centre. The town's economy is based largely on railroad services and maintenance; The Sudan government railways, administrative headquarters, and workshops are located there; the town also has an airport. South of ʿAṭbarah is a large cement factory. Pop. (1980 est.) 110,000.

Atbasar, city, Tselinograd *oblast* (administrative region), Kazakh Soviet Socialist Republic, on the Zhabay River. It was founded as a Cossack settlement in 1846 and became the chief township of a district, known mainly for its annual fair. Atbasar is now a centre for processing locally produced grain and livestock and a railway junction. Pop. (1974 est.) 39,000.

ʿAtbāy (Egypt–The Sudan): *see* Itbāy.

Atbo (Egypt): *see* Idfū.

Atchafalaya Bay, arm of the Gulf of Mexico, extending southeastward along the southern coast of Louisiana, U.S., for 21 mi (34 km) from Point Chevreuil to Point Au Fer on Point Au Fer Island. The bay is 10 mi wide, and the Four League Bay extends another 11 mi southeast. On a long shell reef extending 25 mi northwest of Point Au Fer lies Eugene Island. The Lower Atchafalaya River links the bay with Morgan City (15 mi north), where the Gulf Intracoastal Waterway meets the Plaquemine–Morgan City Waterway and connects to the Mississippi River system. A comprehensive flood control project, the Atchafalaya Basin Floodway, to control overflows from the Mississippi was begun in the 1970s. The bay's reefs contain dead oyster shells, which provide road ballast and raw materials for making lime and cement at many coastal factories. There are also numerous gas and oil fields in the bay area. The name Atchafalaya is Choctaw Indian meaning "long river."

Atchafalaya River, distributary of the Red and Mississippi rivers in the U.S. It branches southwest from the Red River near a point in central Louisiana, where the Old River (about 7 mi [11 km] long) links the Red River with the Mississippi, and flows generally south for 225 mi to Atchafalaya Bay, an inlet of the Gulf of Mexico in southern Louisiana. Its drainage area is 95,105 sq mi (246,321 sq km). The river, winding a slow course through several lakes, including Grand Lake, threatened to capture, via the Old River, the major flow of the Mississippi until it was checked by a system of dams, locks, and guide levees. The damming of the Old River diverted waters from the Mississippi to the Atchafalaya and to floodways west and east of it. About halfway through the Atchafalaya Basin, the floodwaters converge to flow through a single floodway to the Gulf of Mexico. Below Grand Lake, at Morgan City, the river intersects the Gulf Intracoastal Waterway.

Atchison, city, seat (1855) of Atchison County, northeastern Kansas, U.S., on the Missouri River. It was founded in 1854 by a group of proslavery settlers and was named after their leader, David Rice Atchison, U.S. senator from Missouri. It developed as a focus for rail and river traffic, and in 1859 a charter was granted for the Atchison and Topeka Railroad (later Atchison, Topeka and Santa Fe Railway), which made Atchison an important railroad town. Atchison has mixed industry and is a shipping point for local agricultural products. It was the birthplace of the aviatrix Amelia Earhart (1898–1937). Benedictine College was founded (1971) in Atchison through the merger of St. Benedict's College (1858) and Mount St. Scholastica College (1863). Inc. 1855. Pop. (1980) 11,407.

Atchison, Topeka and Santa Fe Railway Company, one of the largest U.S. railroad systems, chartered in Kansas as the St. Louis and Topeka in 1859 and renamed in 1863. Its founder was Cyrus K. Holliday, a Topeka lawyer and business promoter, who sought to build a railroad along the Santa Fe Trail, a 19th-century trading route that ran from Independence, Mo., to Santa Fe, N.M. The railroad replaced merchants' covered wagons and U.S. mail coaches when its main line to the Colorado state line was completed in 1873.

The road was further expanded in the 1880s. In 1890 it acquired the St. Louis and San Francisco Railroad and the Colorado Midland Railroad to reach 9,000 mi (14,480 km)—the longest railroad in the world at that time—but it lost much of this mileage in a reorganization brought on by the financial crisis of 1893. Under the management of Edward Payson Ripley, its president from 1896 until 1920, the Santa Fe flourished and grew to over 11,000 miles of track. By 1941, it had over 13,000 miles of track even after shedding several unprofitable branch lines, but it has been shrinking gradually since then. In 1968 the company became a subsidiary of Santa Fe Industries, Inc., a holding company.

The Santa Fe covers 12 states, from Chicago to the Rocky Mountains, the Gulf of Mexico, and the Pacific Coast. Its freight revenues come principally from farm products, food products, chemicals, and industrial raw materials. The days of its famed passenger trains such as the Super Chief were largely over by 1970, and it sold its passenger service to the National Railway Passenger Corporation (Amtrak) in 1971.

Ate, Greek mythological figure who induced rash and ruinous actions by both gods and men; she made Zeus take a hasty oath that resulted in the Greek hero Heracles becoming subject to Eurystheus, ruler of Mycenae. Zeus thereupon cast Ate out of Olympus, after which she remained on earth, working evil and mischief. She was followed by the Litai (meaning Prayers), the old and crippled daughters of Zeus, who repaired the harm done by her. In works by some Elizabethan writers (*e.g.,* Edmund Spenser) she becomes a kind of fiend.

atelectasis, incomplete expansion of the lungs in the newborn infant or a lung's loss of ability to inflate, either partially or fully, because of specific respiratory disorders. There are three major types of atelectasis: congenital, compression, and obstructive atelectasis.

Congenital atelectasis is seen in stillborn infants who never breathe and in children living only a few days with breathing difficulties, whose lungs show areas in which the alveoli, or air sacs, are not expanded with air. These children usually suffer from a disorder called absorption atelectasis, in which the surface tension inside the alveolus is altered so that air continuously escapes through the walls, leaving the alveoli perpetually collapsed. Children with hyaline membrane disease, a disease of newborn infants associated with a failure to develop surfactant material in the lungs, experience atelectasis from blockage of the small ducts leading to the alveoli. When a duct is blocked, the trapped air left in the alveolus is slowly absorbed by the bloodstream until the alveolus finally collapses. When a sufficiently large area is obstructed in this manner, respiratory functions cease.

Compression atelectasis is caused by an external pressure on the lungs that drives the air out. Collapse is complete if the force is uniform or is partial when the force is localized. Local pressure can result from tumour growths, an enlarged heart, or elevation of the diaphragm. The ducts and bronchi leading to the alveoli are squeezed together by the pressure upon them, and air trapped in the alveoli is slowly absorbed by the blood.

Obstructive atelectasis may be caused by foreign objects lodged in one of the major bronchial passageways. It may also occur as a complication of abdominal surgery. The air passageways in the lungs normally secrete a mucous substance to trap dust, soot, and bacterial cells, which frequently enter with inhaled air. When a person undergoes surgery, the anesthetic stimulates an increase in bronchial secretions. Generally, if these secretions become too abundant they can be pushed out of the bronchi by coughing or strong exhalation of air. After abdominal surgery, the breathing generally becomes more shallow because of the sharp pain induced by the breathing movements, and the muscles beneath the lungs may be weakened. Mucus plugs can result that cause atelectasis. Massive collapse of the lungs may occur a few hours to a few days after the operation.

The symptoms in extreme atelectasis include laboured and painful breathing, a bluish tint to the skin, absence of respiratory movement on the side involved, displacement of the heart toward the affected side, and consolidation of the lungs into a smaller mass. If a lung remains collapsed for a long period, the respiratory tissue is replaced by fibrous scar tissue, and respiratory function cannot be restored.

The treatment is directed toward removal of any obstruction, control of the infection, removal of accumulated fluids, and reestablishment of the lost pressure.

Atellan play: *see* fabula Atellana.

Aten (Egyptian god): *see* Aton.

Aterian industry, stone tool tradition of the Middle and Late Paleolithic, found widespread in the late Pleistocene throughout northern Africa. The Aterian people are believed to have been the first to use the bow and arrow. Aterian stone tools are essentially an advanced African form of the European Levalloisian tradition, adapted to desert use. A distinctive Aterian sign is the formation of stems, or tangs, on tools to facilitate hafting; this was done on spearheads, arrowheads, scrapers, and other cutting tools. Bifacial spearheads were produced with a very fine pressure chipping technique, equivalent in difficulty to those used in later tool traditions such as the Mousterian. Leaf-shaped blades made by the Aterians have been likened to Solutrean blades; it has often been suggested that the Aterians may have entered the Iberian Peninsula during Solutrean times.

Ateso (people): *see* Teso.

Ateste, modern ESTE, an ancient town of northern Italy. In antiquity it occupied a commanding position beside the Adige River (which later changed course) and was for a time the capital of the Veneti (*q.v.*). After a period of complete abandonment, it was reoccupied in the Middle Ages, but it never regained its early importance.

Ateste was founded by Early Iron Age invaders, and its outstanding geographical position made it the chief centre of civilization in eastern Italy north of the Po River.

The archaeological remains at Ateste are conventionally divided into four periods. The remains of the first period are scanty and somewhat equivocal. The richest and most characteristic remains are those of the second and third periods, covering together the period from the early 7th to the middle of the 4th century BC. During the fourth period, after the Celtic invasion of northern Italy, the Veneti remained politically independent, but they had lost much of their individuality and local character.

The distinguishing feature of the material remains of pre-Roman Ateste is the burial of the cremated dead in flat urnfields, a characteristic that it shared with other contemporary cultures of central Italy (*see* Urnfield). The majority of the cemetery finds consist of pottery and decorative bronzework. Of the pottery, the most striking products are the cinerary urns, among which are vessels decorated with elaborate geometric designs of bronze studs (Period 2) and a very handsome group of wares painted with red ochre and graphite. The outstanding metalwork products are buckets (*situlae*) formed of sheet bronze that was rivetted into shape and sometimes richly decorated with geometric and figured designs, engraved or in relief.

The Gallic invasion of northern Italy marked the beginning of the decline of the Veneti, and about 200 BC they were peacefully absorbed by Rome. Already in the 3rd century BC Ateste had begun to be eclipsed by the rising prosperity of Patavium (Padua), and despite the establishment by the Roman emperor Augustus of a colony of veteran soldiers at Ateste, the Roman city was never important. It disappeared from history after the 3rd century AD.

Atget, (Jean-)Eugène(-Auguste) (b. Feb. 12, 1857, Libourne, near Bordeaux, Fr.—d. Aug. 4, 1927, Paris), French photographer whose pictures of Paris and its people made him one of the most influential photographers of the 20th century.

"Shop Window: Tailor Dummies" by Atget, *c.* 1910
George Eastman House Collection

Little is known of his early life. He was orphaned very young and lived with an uncle until he was old enough to go to sea as a cabin boy. After several voyages, he abandoned the sea for the stage. He soon fell in love with an actress much older than himself, and together they toured the provincial towns of France with an itinerant theatre company. Atget's ungainly appearance, however, relegated him to minor parts and low wages. By the time he was about 40 years old, neither he nor his companion was any longer able to earn a living by acting, and Atget was forced to begin a new career. For a short time, he tried to paint, and, about 1898, he decided to become a photographer.

The rest of Atget's life was spent recording everything he could that he considered picturesque or artistic in and around Paris. He made several series of photographs of iron grillwork, fountains, statues, and trees. He photographed shop fronts ("Basket and Broom Shop, Paris"; 1910), store windows ("Uniforms, Les Halles, Paris"; *c.* 1910), and poor tradespeople ("Lampshade Peddler"; *c.* 1910).

Atget's photographs were seldom simple or pedestrian statements. "Café 'La Rotonde,' Boulevard Montparnasse, Paris" (*c.* 1920) has a lyrical, human quality, even though it shows no people, and "The Giant, Fête du Trône, Paris" (*c.* 1910) reveals Atget's eye for strange, unsettling images. His main clients were museums and historical societies that bought his photographs of historic buildings and monuments.

During and after World War I, Atget was destitute. In 1921, however, he was given one of the few commissions he ever received, an assignment to document the brothels of Paris. For this he produced masterful photographic prints, such as "Brothel, Versailles" (*c.* 1921). In 1926 Man Ray (1890–1976), a U.S. artist and photographer living in Paris, saw such photographs as "Shop Window: Tailor Dummies" (*c.* 1910) and "Coiffeur, Avenue de l'Observatoire, Paris" (*c.* 1920). He was astonished by Atget's use of reflections on shop windows to achieve bizarre mixtures of images, and he published four of Atget's photographs in *La Révolution Surréaliste.* This publication was the only recognition Atget's work received during his lifetime.

During the last few years of his life, Atget produced little. After the turn of the century, he ate nothing but bread, sugar, and milk, being convinced that all other foods were poisonous. This spartan diet and years of hard work left him physically broken. After the death of his lifelong companion in 1926, he was alone and virtually helpless. Berenice Abbott, a U.S. photographer studying with Man Ray, and the New York art dealer Julien Levy bought his remaining collection upon his death. It is now at the Museum of Modern Art, New York City.

Athabasca, Lake, lake in Canada, astride the Alberta–Saskatchewan border, just south of the Northwest Territories. The lake, 208 mi (335 km) long by 32 mi wide, has an area of 3,064 sq mi (7,936 sq km) and a maximum depth of 407 ft (124 m). Fed from the southwest by the Peace and Athabasca rivers (the deltas of which have separated it from Lakes Claire and Mamawi), it is drained to the northwest by the Slave River, eventually reaching the Arctic Ocean via the Great Slave Lake and the Mackenzie River. The lake was explored (1771) by Samuel Hearne, who named it Lake of the Hills. Its present name (a Cree Indian term probably for "where there are reeds") was adopted by the North West Company when it built Ft. Chipewyan, a fur-trading post, on the southwestern shore in 1788. The only other significant settlement is Uranium City, which is important for its gold and uranium mines. The two settlements are connected (June–October) by steamer. The lake, which is economically important for commercial fishing (whitefish and lake trout), is immediately east of Wood Buffalo National Park.

Athabasca River, river in northern Alberta, Canada, forming the southernmost part of the Mackenzie River system. From its source in the Columbia Icefield (Canadian Rocky Mountains) near the Continental Divide, the river flows through Jasper National Park, site of the spectacular Athabasca Falls, northeastward across Alberta to its mouth and delta on Lake Athabasca. Its 765-mi (1,231-km) course is broken by rapids, so that navigation is limited above Fort McMurray (a major rail terminus and port serving the Mackenzie District). Chief tributaries include the McLeod, Pembina, Lesser Slave, and Clearwater rivers. Extensive petroleum deposits lie in oil-impregnated sands (known as the Athabasca Tar Sands) along a 70-mi stretch of the river near Fort McMurray; oil is recovered at the Great Canadian Oil Sands Plant.

Rapids on the Athabasca River, Alberta
Shostal—EB Inc.

Athabaska, District of, part of the original Northwest Territories in Canada. The district was created in 1882 and enlarged by an eastward extension in 1895. It was abolished in 1905. Its area comprised the northern parts of present Alberta and Saskatchewan and a small portion of northwestern Manitoba.

Athaliah, also spelled ATHALIA, in the Old Testament, the daughter of Ahab and Jezebel and wife of Jeham, king of Judah. After the death of Ahaziah, her son, Athaliah usurped the throne and reigned for seven years. She massacred all the members of the royal house of Judah (II Kings 11:1–3), except Joash. A successful revolution was organized in favour of Joash, and she was killed. The story of Athaliah forms the subject of one of Jean Racine's best tragedies, *Athalie.*

Athamas, in Greek mythology, king of the prehistoric Minyans in the ancient Boeotian city of Orchomenus. His first wife was Nephele, a cloud goddess. But later Athamas became enamoured of Ino, the daughter of Cadmus, and neglected Nephele, who disappeared in anger. Athamas and Ino incurred the wrath of the goddess Hera because Ino had nursed the god Dionysus (*q.v.*). Athamas went mad and slew one of his sons, Learchus; Ino, to escape, threw herself into the sea with her other son, Melicertes. Both were afterward worshipped as marine divinities—Ino as Leucothea, Melicertes as Palaemon. Athamas fled from Boeotia and finally settled at Phthiotis in Thessaly. The legend perhaps reflected a custom of human sacrifice among the Minyans.

Athanaric (d. 381), Visigothic chieftain from 364 to 376 who fiercely persecuted the Christians in Dacia (approximately modern Romania). The persecutions occurred between 369 and 372; his most important victim was St. Sabas the Goth. In 376 Athanaric was defeated by the Huns. He fled with a few followers to Transylvania (region in present-day Romania), but the bulk of his people, led by Fritigern, fled to the Roman Empire. Athanaric, too, took refuge there in 381 but died at Constantinople a fortnight after his arrival.

Athanasian Creed, also called QUICUMQUE VULT (from the opening words in Latin), a Christian profession of faith in about 40 verses. It is regarded as authoritative in the Roman Catholic and some Protestant churches. It has two sections, one dealing with the Trinity and the other with the Incarnation; and it begins and ends with stern warnings that unswerving adherence to such truths is indispensable to salvation. The virulence of these damnatory clauses has led some critics, especially in the Anglican churches, to secure restriction or abandonment of the use of the creed.

A Latin document composed in the Western

Church, the creed was unknown to the Eastern Church until the 12th century. Since the 17th century, scholars have generally agreed that the Athanasian Creed was not written by Athanasius (died 373) but was probably composed in southern France during the 5th century. Many authors have been suggested, but no definite conclusions have been reached. In 1940 the lost *Excerpta* of Vincent of Lérins (flourished 440) was discovered, and this work contains much of the language of the creed. Thus, either Vincent or an admirer of his has been considered the possible author.

The earliest known copy of the creed was included as a prefix to a collection of homilies by Caesarius of Arles (died 542). The creed's influence seems to have been primarily in southern France and Spain in the 6th and 7th centuries. It was used in the liturgy of the church in Germany in the 9th century and somewhat later in Rome.

Athanasius I (b. 1230, Adrianople—d. Oct. 28, 1310, Constantinople), Byzantine monk and patriarch of Constantinople, who directed the opposition to the reunion of Greek and Latin churches decreed by the Second Council of Lyon in 1274. His efforts in reforming the Greek Orthodox Church encountered opposition from clergy and hierarchy.

A monk who emigrated to a monastery in the hallowed region of Mt. Athos, Greece, Athanasius journeyed to the Holy Land and lived as a solitary on Mt. Galesios, Palestine, where he was ordained priest. Later he returned to Mt. Athos and founded a monastery. Because of his anti-unionist activities after the reunification decree of the Council of Lyon, he was compelled by the patriarch John XI Beccus (1275–82) to seek Palestinian refuge. With the accession of the anti-unionist emperor Andronicus II in 1289, however, Athanasius was chosen patriarch of Constantinople and initiated a sweeping ecclesiastical reform. He imposed strict discipline on the clergy, charged his bishops to live in their own dioceses, and restricted the wanderings of monks. Much of the source material on his reform effort, as well as on Byzantine social and economic conditions of the times, is recorded in a collection of 126 letters.

Athanasius' severe measures evoked opposition from the clergy, and Emperor Andronicus permitted his resignation. Popular support restored him to his patriarchal office; however, after his expulsion of the Latin Church's Franciscan monks from Constantinople in 1307, the unionist faction finally succeeded in forcing his retirement early in 1310 to the monastery of Xerolophus in Constantinople.

Athanasius, SAINT (b. *c.* 293, Alexandria—d. May 2, 373, Alexandria; feast day May 2), theologian, ecclesiastical statesman, and Egyptian national leader; he was the chief defender of Christian orthodoxy in the 4th-century battle against Arianism, the heresy that the Son of God was a creature of like, but not of the same, substance as God the Father. His important works include *The Life of St. Antony* and *Four Orations Against the Arians.*

Life and major works. Athanasius received his philosophical and theological training at Alexandria; in 325 he attended Bishop Alexander of Alexandria as deacon at the Council of Nicaea. A recognized theologian and ascetic, Athanasius was the obvious candidate to succeed Alexander when the latter died in 328. The first years of his episcopate were devoted to visitation of his extensive patriarchate, which included all of Egypt and Libya. During this time he established important contacts with the Coptic monks of Upper Egypt and their leader Pachomius. Soon began the struggle with imperialist and Arian churchmen that occupied much of his life. He used political influence against the Meletians, followers of the schismatic bishop Meletius of Lycopolis, who had gone back on the plans made at

St. Athanasius, detail of a 12th-century mosaic; in the Palatine Chapel, Palermo, Italy

Anderson—Alinari from Art Resource/EB Inc.

Nicaea for their reunion with the church; but he refuted specific charges of mistreatment of Arians and Meletians before a hostile gathering of bishops at Tyre (in modern Lebanon) in 335, which he refused to recognize as a general council of the church. When both parties met the emperor Constantine at Constantinople in 336, Athanasius was accused of threatening to interfere with the grain supply from Egypt, and without any formal trial Constantine exiled him to the Rhineland.

The Emperor's death in 337 allowed Athanasius to return to Alexandria, but Constantine's son Constantius, emperor in the East, renewed the order of banishment in 338. Athanasius took refuge at Rome under the protection of Constantius' brother Constans, emperor in the West. An Arian bishop, Gregory, was installed at Alexandria; Athanasius, however, kept in touch with his flock through the annual *Festal Letters* announcing the date of Easter. Pope Julius I wrote in vain on his behalf, and the general council called for 343 was no more successful—only Western and Egyptian bishops met at Sardica (modern Sofia, Bulg.), and their appeal for Athanasius was not accepted in the East. In 346, however, Constans' influence secured his return to Egypt, where he was welcomed as a popular hero. Athanasius' "golden decade" of peace and prosperity followed, during which he assembled documents relating to his exiles and returns in the *Apology Against the Arians.* Nevertheless, after the death of Constans in 350 and the following civil war, Constantius, as sole emperor, resumed his pro-Arian policy. Again political charges were brought against Athanasius, his banishment was repeated, and in 356 an attempt was made to arrest him during a vigil service. This time he withdrew to Upper Egypt, where he was protected in monasteries or friendly houses. In exile he completed his massive theological work *Four Orations Against the Arians* and defended his conduct in the *Apology to Constantius* and *Apology for His Flight.* The Emperor's persistence and reports of persecution at Alexandria under the new Arian bishop George led him, in the more violent *History of the Arians*, to treat Constantius as a precursor of Antichrist.

The death of Constantius, followed by the murder of the unpopular George in 361, allowed Athanasius to return triumphantly once more to his see. In 362 he convened a council at Alexandria during which he appealed for unity among those who held the same faith but differed in terminology. The way was thus prepared for the orthodox doctrine of the Trinity—"three Persons in one substance"—which stresses distinctions in the Godhead more than Athanasius usually had done. The new emperor, Julian the Apostate, rather petulantly ordered Athanasius to leave Alexandria, and he sailed up the Nile again, remaining in exile in Upper Egypt until Julian's death in 363. In 365 the emperor Valens, who favoured Arianism, ordered his exile once more, but this time the popular bishop merely moved to the outskirts of Alexandria for a few months until the local authorities persuaded the Emperor to reconsider. Finally, Athanasius spent a few years in peace before his death in 373.

Other works. Athanasius' two-part work of apologetics, *Against the Heathen* and *The Incarnation of the Word of God*, completed about 335, was the first great classic of developed Greek Orthodox theology. In Athanasius' system, the Son of God, the eternal Word through whom God made the world, entered the world in human form to lead men back to the harmony from which they had fallen away. Athanasius reacted vigorously against Arianism, for which the Son was a lesser being, and welcomed the definition of the Son formulated at the Council of Nicaea in 325: "consubstantial with the Father."

Among Athanasius' other important works are *The Letters* [*to Sarapion*] on the divinity of the Holy Spirit and *The Life of St. Antony*, which was soon translated into Latin and did much to spread the ascetic ideal in East and West. Only fragments remain of sermons and biblical commentaries; several briefer theological treatises are preserved, however, and a number of letters, mainly administrative and pastoral. Of special interest are the letter to Epictetus (bishop of Corinth), which anticipates future controversies in defending the humanity of Christ, and the letter to Dracontius, which urges a monk to leave the desert for the active labours of the episcopate. Precision of thought, tireless energy in defense of his convictions and the freedom of the church, and (within certain limits) breadth of understanding have given Athanasius an important place among the teachers and leaders of the church; and as an Egyptian patriot he is also a significant figure in the history of his country.

(E.R.Ha.)

BIBLIOGRAPHY. The great Benedictine edition of the works of Athanasius (1698), reprinted in J.P. Migne, *Patrologia Graeca*, vol. 25–28 (1857), is being replaced by that begun by H.G. Opitz (*Athanasius Werke*) in 1934; major works are translated in the "Post-Nicene Fathers," Series 2, vol. 4, *Select Writings and Letters of Athanasius* (1892)—the "Prolegomena" to this volume by A. Robertson remains the most complete life. For later discoveries and studies, see H.I. Bell (ed.), *Jews and Christians in Egypt* (1924); and the brilliant summary by F.L. Cross, *The Study of St. Athanasius* (1945). There are useful sketches in G.L. Prestige, *Fathers and Heretics* (1940, reprinted 1963); and in R.W. Thomson's edition of *Contra Gentes and De Incarnatione* (1971). For further references, see E.R. Hardy (ed.), *Christology of the Later Fathers* (1954); and J. Quasten, *Patrology,* vol. 3, pp. 20–79 (1960).

Athanasius THE ATHONITE, SAINT, also called ATHANASIUS OF TREBIZOND (b. *c.* 920, Trebizond, Asia Minor—d. *c.* 1000, Mt. Athos, Greece; feast day May 2), Byzantine monk who founded communal monasticism in the hallowed region of Mt. Athos, a traditional habitat for contemplative monks and hermits.

Originally named Abraham, he took the monastic name of Athanasius when he retired to Mt. Athos after forsaking the sophisticated, urban monastic life in Constantinople; there he had served as spiritual director to the general Nicephorus Phocas, later the emperor Nicephorus II Phocas.

In 963, with imperial support, Athanasius organized the scattered solitaries on Mt. Athos into the Great Laura (Greek *laura,* "monastery"). There, he introduced a *Typicon,* or rule, for cenobites (monks in community life) based on similar codes by the 4th-century monastic founder Basil of Caesarea and the 9th-century reformer Theodore Studites.

Various ecclesiastical and political factions opposed this monastic innovation and forced Athanasius to flee to Cyprus after the death of Nicephorus in 969. He returned to Mt. Athos, however, in response to a command he claimed to have received in a vision. Formal acceptance and financial assistance came from Nicephorus' successor, the emperor John I Tzimisces, who in 971–972 had settled the controversy by granting Athos its first charter. Athanasius died in the collapse of a building he was about to dedicate. His writings include a supplementary rule for monks (*Hypotyposis*), incorporating elements of Greek and Syriac monasticism; a detailed annotation (*Diatyposis*) of provisions for monastic transfer of authority; and a liturgical directory particularly for the Easter season.

Atharvaveda, collection of hymns and incantations that forms part of the ancient sacred literature of India known as the Vedas. *See* Veda.

atheism, the critique and denial of metaphysical beliefs in God or spiritual beings. As such, it is the opposite of theism, which affirms the reality of the divine and seeks to demonstrate its existence. Atheism is to be distinguished from agnosticism, which leaves open the question whether there is a god or not, professing to find the question unanswered or unanswerable; for the atheist, the nonexistence of God is a certainty.

A brief treatment of atheism follows. For full treatment, *see* MACROPAEDIA: Religious and Spiritual Belief, Systems of.

Atheism has emerged recurrently in Western thought. Plato argued against it in the *Laws*, while Democritus and Epicurus argued for it in the context of their materialism. In the 19th century, atheism was couched in the materialism of Karl Marx and others and pitted against the metaphysical position of spiritualism. Modern atheism takes many different forms other than that of materialism. The 18th century witnessed the emergence of atheism among the French Encyclopaedists, who combined British empiricism with René Descartes's mechanistic conception of the universe. Niccolò Machiavelli in the 16th century contributed to atheism in the political sphere by affirming the independence of politics from morals and religion. David Hume, in his *Dialogues Concerning Natural Religion* (1779), argued against the traditional proofs for the existence of God, as did Immanuel Kant. Neither Hume nor Kant were atheists, but their restriction of human reason to sense experience undercut natural theology and left the existence of God a matter of pure faith. In short, atheism has been rooted in a vast array of philosophical systems.

One of the most important 19th-century atheists was Ludwig Feuerbach (1804–72), who put forward the argument that God is a projection of man's ideals. Feuerbach associated his denial of God with the affirmation of man's freedom. The disclosure that God is mere projection liberates man for self-realization. Marx drew on Feuerbach's thesis that the religious can be resolved into the human, though he also held that religion reflects socio-economic order and alienates man from his labour product and, hence, from his true self. Marx sought the abolition of religion, defining it as the "sigh of the oppressed creature, the heart of a heartless world, and the soul of a soulless condition."

While Marx was professing atheism couched in socio-economic theory, Charles Darwin (1809–82), himself an agnostic, developed a scientific theory of natural history that challenged the Judeo-Christian concept of the Creator-God. Sigmund Freud (1856–1939) drew on Darwinian themes when he discussed religion in terms of the "primal horde." According to Freud, belief in God constitutes a regression to a childlike state in which helpless man projects upon nature the image of a comforting father-figure.

A third strain in modern atheism is the existentialist. Friedrich Nietzsche (1844–1900) proclaimed the "death of God" and the consequent loss of all traditional values. The only tenable human response, he argued, is that of nihilism—without God, there is no answer to the question of purpose and meaning in life. In Nietzsche's view, the death of God freed humanity to fulfill itself and find its own essence. In the 20th century Jean-Paul Sartre, Albert Camus, and others continued the theme that man is alone in the universe and free to determine his own values. Human freedom, according to Sartre, entails the denial of God, for God's existence would threaten man's freedom to create his own values through free ethical choice.

The philosophical movement known as logical positivism is also a major proponent of modern atheism. It holds that propositions concerning the existence or nonexistence of God are nonsensical or meaningless. This form of empiricist epistemology has its roots in the thought of Hume, Thomas Huxley, John Stuart Mill, and others who held that meaningful knowledge can be derived only from experience and observation. Positivists such as A.J. Ayer, in his book *Language, Truth and Logic* (1936), argued that atheism, along with theism and agnosticism, is simply an ungenuine position because all talk of the unverifiable God is nonsense. Positivists are not atheists in the sense that they think God can be disproven; they are atheists in the sense that they consider the very notion "God" impossible to discuss.

In the mid-20th century some Christian theologians, such as Paul Tillich, Karl Barth, and Rudolf Bultmann, responded to the challenge of atheism by asserting that the destruction of the metaphysical God permits man to encounter the living God through absolute faith.

Atheling (Old English title): *see* Aetheling.

Athelney, small eminence, formerly an island, rising above the drained marshes around the confluence of the Rivers Tone and Parrett in the county of Somerset, England. In 878 King Alfred sought refuge from the Danes in the marshes and constructed a stronghold at Athelney from where he broke out and won a decisive victory at Edington, near Chippenham. He later founded a monastery on the island as a thank-offering for his victory. The Alfred Jewel, an ornament inscribed with Alfred's name, was found at Athelney in 1693.

Athelstan (Danish king of East Anglia): *see* Guthrum.

Athelstan, also spelled AETHELSTAN, or ETHELSTAN (d. Oct. 27, 939), first West Saxon king to have effective rule over the whole of England.

On the death of his father, Edward the Elder, in 924, Athelstan was elected king of Wessex and Mercia, where he had been brought up by his aunt, Aethelflaed, Lady of the Mercians. Crowned king of the whole country at Kingston on Sept. 4, 925, he proceeded to establish boundaries and rule firmly. His dominion was significantly challenged in 937 when Constantine of the Scots, Owain of Strathclyde, and Olaf Guthfrithson, claimant of the kingdom of York, joined forces and invaded England. They were routed at Brunanburh.

Six of Athelstan's extant codes of law reveal stern efforts to suppress theft and punish corruption. They are notable in containing

Athelstan, detail of a manuscript illumination, 10th century; in the collection of Corpus Christi College, Cambridge (Corpus Christi Ms. 183)

By courtesy of the Master and Fellows of Corpus Christi College, Cambridge; photograph, Courtauld Institute Galleries, London

provisions intended to comfort the destitute and mitigate the punishment of young offenders. The form and language of his many documents suggest the presence of a corps of skilled clerks and perhaps the beginning of the English civil service.

Athena, also spelled ATHENE, in Greek religion, the city protectress, goddess of war, handicraft, and practical reason, identified by the Romans with Minerva (*q.v.*). She was essentially urban and civilized, the antithesis in many respects of Artemis, goddess of the outdoors. Athena was probably a pre-Hellenic goddess and was later taken over by the Greeks. Yet the Greek economy, unlike that of the Minoans, was largely military, so that

The Varakion, a Roman marble copy (c. AD 130) of the colossal gold and ivory statue of the Athena Parthenos by Phidias (438 BC); in the National Archaeological Museum, Athens

Alinari—Art Resource/EB Inc.

Athena, while retaining her earlier domestic functions, became a goddess of war.

Athena chose the Acropolis as her dwelling place, probably because the king's palace was there. She had no consort nor offspring. She may not have been described as a virgin originally, but virginity was attributed to her very early and was the basis for the interpretation of her epithets Pallas and Parthenos. Aphrodite could not affect Athena: as a war goddess Athena could not be dominated; as a palace goddess she could not be violated.

In the *Iliad,* Athena, as a war goddess, inspired and fought alongside the Greek heroes; her aid was synonymous with military prowess. Also in the *Iliad,* Zeus, the chief god, specifically assigned the sphere of war to Ares, the god of war, and Athena. Athena's moral and military superiority to Ares derived in part from the vastly greater variety and importance of her functions and in part from the patriotism of Homer's predecessors, Ares being of foreign origin. The qualities that led to victory were found on the aegis Athena carried when she went to war: fear, strife, defense, and assault, but not reason or prudence. Athena appears in the *Odyssey* as the tutelary deity of the king, and myths from later sources portray her similarly as helper of Perseus and Heracles (Hercules), perhaps originally Mycenaean monarchs, suggesting that her efforts were extended to all who held that office. Yet the kingship as such did not claim her protection; Athena guarded rather the king's person and in so doing became goddess of good counsel as well as of war.

In post-Mycenaean times the city, especially its citadel, replaced the palace as Athena's domain. She was widely worshipped, but in modern times she is associated primarily with Athens, to which she gave her name. Her emergence there as city goddess, Athena Polias (Athens Guardian of the City), accompanied the transition from monarchy to democracy. She was associated with birds, particularly the owl, which became famous as the city's own symbol, and with the snake. Her birth and her contest with Poseidon for the suzerainty of the city were depicted on the pediments of the Parthenon. Hesiod, in the *Theogony,* told how Athena, having no known mother, sprang from Zeus's forehead, and Pindar added that Hephaestus struck open his head with an ax. The contest between Athena and Poseidon shown on the Parthenon's west pediment featured her offer to the Athenians of the olive, his of the horse or a spring of water.

Athena's birthday festival, the Panathenaea, concerned the growth of vegetation. The similarly purposed Procharisteria celebrated the goddess' rising from the ground with the coming of spring. Athena's connection with vegetation, however, was only a by-product of her general civic duties.

Mythology made Erichthonius, who was believed to have instituted Athena's worship at Athens, the issue of an abortive attempt by Hephaestus upon Athena's virginity, the seed impregnating the ground instead. Athena's relationship with Hephaestus derived from the similar function of the smith god and the goddess of industry, Athena Ergane (Working, a common epithet). That she became ultimately allegorized to personify wisdom was a natural development of her patronage of skill.

Two Athenians, Phidias and Aeschylus, contributed significantly to Athena's spiritual development. She inspired three of Phidias' sculptural masterpieces, which traced her development from the warrior to the city goddess; and in Aeschylus' tragedy *Eumenides* she founded the Areopagus, and, by breaking a deadlock of the judges in favour of Orestes, the defendant, she set the precedent that a tied vote signified acquittal.

Athenaeus (fl. *c.* AD 200; b. Naukratis, Egypt), Greek grammarian and author of *Deipnosophistai* ("The Gastronomers"), a work in the form of an aristocratic symposium, in which a number of learned men, some bearing the names of real persons, such as Galen, meet at a banquet and discuss food and other subjects. It is in 15 books, of which 10 have survived in their entirety, the others in summary form. The value of the work lies partly in the great number of quotations from lost works of antiquity that it preserves, nearly 800 writers being quoted, and partly in the variety of unusual information it affords of all aspects of life in the ancient world.

Athenagoras (fl. 2nd century), Greek Christian philosopher and apologist whose treatise *Presbeia peri Christianōn* (*c.* 177; *Embassy for the Christians*) is one of the earliest works to use Neoplatonic concepts to interpret Christian belief and worship for Greek and Roman cultures and to refute early pagan charges that Christians were disloyal and immoral.

Identified by some early historians as a native of Athens and a Platonist who converted to Christianity, Athenagoras went to Alexandria and established the prototype for its celebrated Christian academy. He addressed the *Embassy,* an apology in 30 chapters, to the emperor Marcus Aurelius and his son Commodus as a response to the threefold indictment, levelled against the Jews in classical times, that by the 2nd century had been transferred to the Christians: atheism (disbelief in pagan deities), cannibalism (eating children at banquets), and incest. Athenagoras appealed to Greek and Roman rationality and claimed for Christians the same rights common to all citizens.

To the charges of atheism and child murder Athenagoras countered that Christians worship God in an unbloody manner. Unlike the degrading idolatry of the heathen submission to arbitrary and immoral deities (injecting an observation made by Plato), Christians, he asserted, reverence one perfect and eternal divinity whose threefold self-expression is not polytheistic. Athenagoras adduced the first rational apologetic for God's simultaneous unity and trinity by suggesting multiple persons in a single nature and potency.

By his account of the sometimes rigorous Christian moral code banning evil thoughts, second marriages, abortion, and the viewing of gladiator contests, while insisting on the duty of civil obedience and emphasizing an orientation toward the next life, Athenagoras refuted the allegation of sexual depravity.

A second work, the tract *Peri anastaseōs nekrōn* (*The Resurrection of the Dead*), is cautiously attributed to Athenagoras. Rejecting the Platonic tenet that the body is the prison of the soul, and affirming matter–spirit complementarity, he accepts bodily resurrection from the dead on the basis of God's omnipotence and purpose to manifest his image eternally.

Athenagoras I, original name ARISTOKLES SPYROU (b. March 25, 1886, Epirus, Greece—d. July 7, 1972, Istanbul), ecumenical patriarch and archbishop of Constantinople (modern Istanbul) from 1948 to 1972.

Athenagoras was the son of a physician. He attended the seminary on the island of Halki, new Constantinople, and was ordained a deacon in 1910. He then moved to Athens, where he served as archdeacon to the archbishop Meletios, who later became the ecumenical patriarch. From there, Athenagoras' career in the church progressed through successively higher offices. In 1922 he was consecrated bishop, and in 1931 he became archbishop of the Greek Orthodox Church of North and South America, with a membership of 150,000,000. While in that office, Athenagoras oversaw the establishment of many new parishes and schools, including a seminary for the training of Greek American priests.

In 1948 Athenagoras was elected ecumenical patriarch and proceeded to become, in the words of Pope Paul VI, "a great protagonist of the reconciliation of all Christians." At his own initiative, Athenagoras met with Pope Paul VI in Jerusalem in 1964, the first time the leaders of the Roman Catholic and Greek Orthodox churches had conferred since 1439. In 1965 the two leaders agreed to a revocation of the mutual excommunication decrees of 1054; this historic event was accomplished through simultaneous services in St. Peter's in Rome and the patriarchal church in Constantinople.

Athēnai (Greece): *see* Athens.

Athene (goddess): *see* Athena.

Athenodorus CANANITES, also called ATHENODORUS SON OF SANDON (b. *c.* 74 BC, Canana, near Tarsus, Cilicia—d. *c.* AD 7), Greek Stoic philosopher who was the teacher of the younger Octavian, who later became the emperor Augustus. He is to be distinguished from Athenodorus Cordylion, also a Stoic, who became keeper of the library in Pergamum. Athenodorus acquired a lasting influence over Octavian and probably followed him to Rome in 44 BC, later returning to Tarsus, where he remodelled the city's constitution, setting up a government of property owners favourable to Rome. None of his writing is extant, and Strabo and Cicero (whom he helped in the composition of the *De Officiis*) provide the main sources of information about him.

Athenry, Irish BAILE ÁTHA AN RÍ (Town of the King's Ford), market town, County Galway, Ireland. It was founded in the 13th century during the Anglo-Norman colonization. Much of the medieval town wall (1211) survives, together with the keep of the castle (1235) and part of the Dominican priory (founded 1241), which was specifically exempted from Henry VIII's dissolution of the monasteries. Pop. (1981) 1,479.

Athens, Modern Greek ATHÍNAI, ancient Greek ATHĒNAI, historic city and capital of Greece. Athens is generally considered to be the birthplace of Western civilization, and many of classical civilization's intellectual and artistic ideas originated there.

The following article treats briefly the modern city of Athens. Fuller treatment is provided in the following MACROPAEDIA articles. For history and contemporary life, *see* Athens; for additional perspective on the city in its national context, *see* Greece; for additional historical perspective, *see* Greco-Roman Civilizations, Classical.

Athens lies 5 mi (8 km) from the Bay of Phaleron, off the Aegean Sea, where its port, Piraeus (Piraiévs), is situated. The Imittós Mountains separate it from Petalion Bay to the east. The seasonal Kifisós River flows through western Athens and the Ilisós River crosses the eastern half. Greater Athens forms a *dhiamerisma* (administrative region) of modern Greece. The climate is temperate, with mild winters and hot, dry summers.

Athens is the hub of Greek mercantile business, both import and export. Tourism, shipping, and publishing are of major importance, as are the production of textiles, pottery, and alcoholic beverages. The mining of marble and bauxite is significant.

Athens is best known for its temples and public buildings of antiquity. Chief among these is the Parthenon, a columned, rectangular temple built for the city's patron goddess, Athena; it is considered to be the culmination of the Doric order of classical Greek architecture. Also located on the Acropolis are the Erectheum, originally the temple of both Athena and Poseidon, and the Propylaea, the entrance of which is through the wall of the Acropolis. At the foot of the Acropolis, to the south, are the theatres of Herodes and Dionysus, while to the northwest is the Agora, the ancient marketplace of the city. Other important ruins are situated on the Hill of the Pynx and in Zappion Park.

Old Athens is still evident in the streets near the excavated Agora and in the colourful Pláka district on the northern slope of the Acropolis. Near the Parliament Building is the National Garden and Síntagma (Constitution) Square, which caters to tourists with its luxury hotels and cafēs. Important museums include the Acropolis, the National Archeological, and the Byzantine museums; academic institutions include the University of Athens (refounded in 1837), the Greek Academy, and the National Library.

Athens has long been a mercantile centre, and all forms of transportation are well developed. Two rail lines extend southwest to Piraeus, the country's major port. Modern roads surround Athens, and the Ellinikon International Airport lies due south. Area city, 15 sq mi (39 sq km); metropolitan area, 167 sq mi (428 sq km). Pop. (1981 prelim.) city, 885,136; metropolitan area, 3,027,331.

Athens, city, seat (1819) of Limestone County, northern Alabama, U.S., in the Tennessee Valley. Settled after 1810 and named for Athens, Greece, it developed as an agricultural and timber centre. Athens State College was founded in 1822, originally as a female academy. During the Civil War, the town was occupied at intervals by Union troops until recaptured by the Confederate general Nathan Bedford Forrest in 1863. Cotton dominated the economy until 1934, when power from the Tennessee Valley Authority encouraged development of diversified industries. At Browns Ferry (10 mi [16 km] southwest) is a nuclear power plant. Inc. town, 1818; city, *c.* 1915. Pop. (1980) 14,658.

Athens, city, seat (1872) of Clarke County, northeastern Georgia, U.S., on the Oconee River. Founded in 1801 as the seat of the University of Georgia (chartered 1785), it was probably named for Athens, Greece. It grew with the university and became a trading centre of a rich agricultural area, which supports

The Taylor-Grady House, Athens, Ga.
Milt and Joan Mann from CameraMann

dairy and beef cattle and poultry. Industrial activities include poultry processing and the manufacture of apparel, textiles, clocks, and electric motors and transformers. Notable antebellum buildings survive, including the Lucy Cobb Institute, the Taylor-Grady House, and the Joseph Henry Lumpkin House. Athens is the site of the U.S. Navy Supply Corps School. Inc. 1806. Pop. (1980) city, 42,549, metropolitan area (SMSA), 130,015.

Athens, city, seat (1805) of Athens County, southeastern Ohio, U.S., on the Hocking River, 73 mi (117 km) southeast of Columbus. It was founded in 1800 by the territorial legislature as the seat of the American Western University, which was renamed Ohio University in 1804. Athens and the university campus were laid out by Gen. Rufus Putnam and the Rev. Manasseh Cutler. The village (incorporated in 1811) grew with the expansion of educational and research facilities and subsequently underwent planned industrial development with the establishment of facilities for the manufacture of business forms, printing machinery, tire molds, and tools. The surrounding region is mainly agricultural. Athens lies between segments of Wayne National Forest; and Lake Hope, within Zaleski State Forest, is 14 mi west. Inc. city, 1912. Pop. (1980) 19,743.

Athens, city, seat of McMinn County, southeastern Tennessee, U.S., in the Tennessee Valley, between the Great Smoky Mountains (east) and the Cumberland Plateau (west), 55 mi (89 km) southwest of Knoxville. It was founded in 1821 as a seat of justice, and the courts were moved there in 1823 from a temporary log courthouse that had been erected at Calhoun, 10 mi southwest on the Hiwassee River. Originally an agricultural community producing tobacco, beef cattle, and milk, it is now primarily industrial. The chief products are kitchen stoves, furniture, electric motors, farm machinery, clothing, and dairy foods. Athens is the site of Tennessee Wesleyan College (1857). Inc. 1868. Pop. (1980) 12,080.

atheriniform, any member of the order Atheriniformes, a group of bony fishes comprising such well-known marine forms as the flying fish as well as numerous freshwater species.

A brief treatment of atheriniforms follows. For full treatment, *see* MACROPAEDIA: Fishes.

Members of the suborder Exocoetoidei, which includes the flying fishes, halfbeaks, needlefishes, and sauries, are slender, elongated fish less than a metre (three feet) in length. The eggs of most species have adhesive filaments by which they adhere to aquatic plants. The dorsal and anal fins are set opposite each other and far back on the body. The bottom lobe of the caudal fin is larger than the top lobe and aids these fishes in rising above the water surface to escape predators.

The suborder Cyprinodontoidei consists of small, surface-oriented, omnivorous fishes with complex courtship and spawning patterns. They are highly adaptable and are able to tolerate extremes of heat, drought, and salinity. These fishes (*e.g.*, killifishes) are sometimes called topminnows, or toothed carp, because of the small teeth in their jaws. They have yearly life cycles, and the adults, before dying during the summer, leave behind eggs buried in the mud. With the return of the rain these eggs hatch, and the life cycle is repeated.

Several species of four-eyed fish are uniquely adapted to surface living. Their eyes are divided into upper and lower lobes with separate corneas and retinas so that they can see both above and below the water. Males and females have sex organs oriented either to the right or left. Because of this distinction, sinistral males can only mate with dextral females, and vice versa. In the live-bearers, the anal fins of the male have been modified into a copulatory organ called the gonopodium. Many species, including the guppies, mollies, and swordtails, give birth to live young.

Fishes that belong to the suborder Atherinoidei are small and elongated, with large eyes and two dorsal fins. This suborder includes the silversides, which are characterized by large silver scales and travel in schools near the shores of oceans and lakes. One of the best known species of Atherinoidei is the California grunion (*Leuresthes tenuis*). Each spring and sometimes long into the summer, these fish come out of the water to spawn during the full moon. During high tide, the grunions leave their eggs buried in the sand of the beaches. At the next high tide, about two weeks later, the young are swept out to sea.

Atherton, Gertrude Franklin, *neé* HORN (b. Oct. 30, 1857, San Francisco—d. June 14, 1948, San Francisco), U.S. novelist noted as an author of fictional biography and history.

Atherton began her prolific writing career to escape the restrictions of a stifling marriage. Her first work, *The Randolphs of Redwoods* (*c.* 1882), was published anonymously in *The Argonaut* (republished 1899 as a book, *A Daughter of the Vine*). It was based on a local story of a well-bred girl turned alcoholic, and its publication offended the Atherton family.

Atherton travelled extensively, and the information she thus accumulated lent vividness to her writing. Her work generally drew mixed reviews, with the notable exception of *The Conqueror* (1902), a novelized account of the life of Alexander Hamilton. Atherton did extensive research for this book, and the result won her critical acclaim as well as making the book a best-seller. Her controversial novel *Black Oxen* (1923), the story of a woman revitalized by hormone treatments and based on Atherton's own experience, was her biggest popular success.

Atherton wrote more than 40 novels in her long career, as well as many nonfiction works. Her work is uneven in quality, perhaps because of the rapidity with which she wrote, but at its best it displays strength and a talent for vivid description.

Consult the INDEX *first*

Atherton Plateau, also called ATHERTON TABLELAND, section of the Great Dividing Range (Eastern Highlands), northeastern Queensland, Australia, bounded by the Rivers Palmer (north) and Burdekin (south). The plateau has an area of 12,000 sq mi (31,000 sq km). Its average elevation of 2,000–3,000 ft (600–900 m) gives it a relatively high rainfall, which, in conjunction with rich volcanic soils, makes the plateau extremely fertile.

First settled in the 1870s, it had by 1890 been the scene of many mining ventures. As the ores were depleted, the workers turned to agriculture. The plateau yields tobacco, beef, peanuts (groundnuts), corn (maize), and dairy products, which are handled in the principal towns of Atherton, Herberton, and Mareeba. Liquid milk is shipped as far as Townsville, 830 mi (1,330 km) southeast. Lakes Eacham and Barrine, deep crater pools, lie on the plateau, which is the source of the Barron, Herbert, Johnstone, and Tully rivers.

Athesis (Italy): *see* Adige River.

athetosis, slow, purposeless, and involuntary movements of the hands and feet. The fingers are separately flexed and extended in an entirely irregular way. The hands as a whole are also moved, and the arms, toes, and feet may be affected. The condition is usually caused by malfunctioning of the basal ganglia of the cerebrum. The movements may or may not continue during sleep. They cannot be arrested for more than a moment by will power, and are aggravated by voluntary movements. *See also* cerebral palsy.

Athínai (Greece): *see* Athens.

athletics, also called TRACK-AND-FIELD ATHLETICS, a collection of sport competitions in running, walking, jumping, and throwing or pushing events.

History. Athletics is the oldest form of organized sports, having been a part of the Olympic Games (*q.v.*) from about 1370 BC to AD 393, and also of other less long-lived classical games. To the original running races of the Olympic Games were later added the sports of boxing and wrestling; and such athletic events as running, long (broad) jumping, discus throwing, and javelin throwing were combined with wrestling to form the ancient pentathlon (*q.v.*). According to legend, the Irish Tailleann Games, involving athletics and other sports, date back to the 19th century BC.

The events of the classical games no doubt arose from human prehistorical times when the activities of running, walking, jumping, and throwing were involved in hunting, one of man's earliest ways of feeding himself and his kin. The revival of organized athletics, first separately and then collectively, came only in the second half of the 19th century. There are no reports of athletics from the suspension of the Olympic Games in the 4th century until the 12th century, and in the period between that time and the 16th century athletics were frequently banned by royal decree, as were other sports, because it was thought that they interfered with archery, which was a vital military activity. In the 17th century noblemen frequently had footraces for their footmen and wagered on the outcome. Both sprint and distance racing persisted through the 18th century. Organized races were held in London in 1825, and after that both the public (private) schools and the universities promoted athletics, Eton from 1837. The first regular competition was held from 1849 at the Royal Military College at Woolwich; and Exeter College of Oxford University began regular competition in 1850. The first meet open to all amateurs was held by the West London Rowing Club in 1861, the club having originally taken up running for its members to keep themselves in condition during the off season. In 1866 the Amateur Athletic Club was founded and the first national championships were held. In 1880 the Amateur Athletic Association took over the governance of English athletics.

In North America development came more slowly, the first meet being held at Toronto in 1839. The San Francisco Olympic Club had an organized team in 1860. The New York Athletic Club (NYAC), founded in 1868, gave athletics a big impetus in the U.S., holding an "indoor" meet in that year at the Empire City Skating Rink. The runners used a dirt track with canvas walls enclosing a roofless arena. The NYAC was a leader in the formation of the National Association of Amateur Athletes (NAAA) in 1879, a combination of 14 clubs mainly from the New York–New Jersey area but with a Boston club and the San Francisco Olympic Club as members. NAAA meets were held through 1888. Because of alleged laxity in enforcing amateur rules, the Amateur Athletic Union of the United States (AAU) took over as the governing body and sponsor of championships from 1888, with outdoor meets being held annually thereafter and indoor meets from 1906. (Indoor meets became common in Europe only from the 1930s.)

Intercollegiate competition had begun in the United States under the supervision of the Intercollegiate Association of Amateur Athletes of America (ICAAA), with 10 schools from the northeastern section of the country as the charter members. The succeeding organization, the National Collegiate Athletic Association (NCAA), held its first championships in 1921 and continued thereafter. Disputes between the AAU and the NCAA over the regulation of amateurs, especially those in international competition outside the Olympic Games, led to the formation of the Athletics Congress (TAC) in 1979.

Between 1880 and 1890 national bodies for athletics were formed in France, New Zealand, Belgium, Canada, and South Africa. By the outbreak of World War I in 1914, 18 more national bodies had been formed in Europe, Australasia, South America, and the Pacific and Caribbean areas, and after the war dozens more were formed. The international governing body, the International Amateur Athletic Federation (IAAF), was founded in 1912 and thereafter governed international competition and validated world records, some as far back as 1870.

Women's participation in athletics was first marked by the formation in France of a national body in 1917. Women's competition in England began in 1919. The Fédération Sportive Feminine Internationale (FSFI) was formed in 1921 with groups from Great Britain, Czechoslovakia, France, Italy, Spain, and the United States as co-founders. World championships began in 1922. The International Olympic Committee refused to consider adding women's events for the 1924 Games, but five events under the joint control of the IAAF and the FSFI were included in the 1928 Games. The number of athletic events for women increased thereafter until in the 1980s the only men's events not duplicated for women were the longer distance running races (5,000 and 10,000 metres); the 110-m hurdles (the women's hurdle race is 100 m); the 3,000-m steeplechase; the 20,-000- and 50,000-m walks; the triple jump; the hammerthrow; and the decathlon (the corresponding women's event is the heptathlon). In 1936 the IAAF became the governing body of women's athletics, and the FSFI was dissolved. Thereafter international competitions increasingly included both men's and women's events.

The first international meet was held in 1895 between the NYAC and the London Athletic Club. In 1896 the Olympic Games were revived and held every four years thereafter, except for wartime. This furnished the focus that made athletics widely international in the 20th century. Other IAAF-regulated international games include the Commonwealth Games (*q.v.;* originally called the British Empire Games; from 1930); the European Championships (from 1934); the Pan-American Games (*q.v.;* from 1951); the Asian Games (*q.v.;* from 1951); and the African Games (*q.v.;* originally called the Pan-African Games; from 1965). From 1977 World Cup meets were held in years after the Olympic Games.

Events. Running, or track, events include the sprint (*q.v.*) races: 100, 200, and 400 m (in English-speaking countries the older equivalent distances, 100, 220, and 440 yards, have tended to disappear under the influence of the Olympic and international distances, which are all metric, save the marathon); the middle-distance races (*see* middle-distance running); the 800- and 1,500-m (the metric mile) races; and the 3,000-m steeplechase (English-speaking countries equivalent races are the 880-yd, or ½-mi race; and the 2-mi race; the steeplechase has been run at 2 mi); distance races (*see* long-distance running), the 5,000-, 10,000-, 20,000-, 25,000-, and 30,000-m races, and the marathon (*q.v.;* historically the distance run by a Greek runner bearing the tidings of a Greek victory at the Battle of Marathon, 26 mi, plus 385 yd added by the race conditions in the 1908 Olympics). Nonmetric racing distances are the 3-, 6-, 10-, and 15-mi races. The IAAF also lists a world record for the one-hour run. Cross-country (*q.v.*) is an off-season adjunct of track-and-field athletics. The walk races (*see* walking) are 20 and 50 kilometres long. Earlier discontinued events include the 10-mi and 3,500-km walks. Marathon races and walking events are usually held off the track.

Relay races (*see* relay race) include the 400-m (4 × 100) and the 1,600-m (4 × 400) races. Nonmetric equivalent races are the 440-yd (¼-mi) and 1-mi relays. An early mile medley relay race in which successive runners covered 440, 220, 220, and 880 yd was the only relay race in the English national championships from 1911 through 1926.

Hurdle races (*see* hurdling) include the 110-, 200-, and 400-m races for men and the 100-m (formerly 80-m) and 400-m (formerly 200-m) races for women.

Jumping events include the high jump, long jump (broad jump), triple jump (hop-skip-and-jump), and pole vault (*qq.v.*). Earlier, now discarded, events included a standing high jump and a standing long jump.

Throwing, or pushing, events include the shot put, discus throw, hammer throw, and javelin throw (*qq.v.*)

Meets and equipment. Early races were run on the grass, a public way (paved or unpaved), or whatever course was at hand. As track-and-field sports became more organized in the 19th century, however, tracks came to consist of cinders or a mixture of clay and cinders. Indoor tracks were mainly wooden. By the 1960s tracks were increasingly covered with synthetic materials.

The track is a 400-m (440-yd) oval for running events, and the enclosed area is the site of throwing and jumping events. The track is marked into lanes, and runners in races from 100 to 400 m must start and finish in their own lanes. Where the race involves a curve or curves, runners are placed for the start at staggered intervals to equalize the actual distance run. Longer races are started in lanes, but a runner can come to the inside at any time or in any way that does not interfere with other runners. In races of from 100 to 800 m, runners usually start from a crouched position, one foot back, the other just behind the starting mark, the fingers of each hand touching the ground to maintain balance. In early days, sprinters dug starting holes to give their feet purchase for the starting drive. Since the 1930s starting blocks have been used. Runners in longer races use a standing start. Running shoes have been traditionally spiked, but with the synthetic running surfaces the spikes are of plastic instead of metal as they were earlier. Runners in the longer races generally use smooth-soled shoes. Jumpers have a choice, depending on the surface of the approach. The throwing events are performed in smooth-soled shoes. The starter of a race gives the runners the commands, "On your marks," and "Set," and the start comes with the firing of a shot from the starter's gun. If a runner "jumps the gun," the race is restarted, the signal for a new start being another shot. Repeated false starts may disqualify a runner. Races were originally timed with a stopwatch, more than one timer usually being used; but since the 1960s electrical timing has been used, allowing records to be expressed in hundredths of a second.

Records. All world outdoor track records are validated by the IAAF. There are no official indoor world records. Records, kept from 1913 but going back in some cases to 1896, have been continually bettered, especially since the 1950s. By the 1980s, no record standing in the 1950s remained unbroken. The mile record was long thought to have a physical limit, called the four-minute barrier; but after Roger Bannister broke the barrier in 1954, the record was lowered 12 times by 1980 and 3 more times in 1981 alone. For Olympic champions, *see* Olympic Games, and for world records, *see* Sporting Record: *Track-and-field sports.*

Professional and amateur. There was much professional running in the early days of organized athletics, and isolated pockets remain, especially in road races in Great Britain and Australia. Attempts to organize professional athletics have been made, in the 1930s and as recently as the 1960s, but they have not been successful. The cost of international competition has somewhat relaxed rules for the payment of expense money to amateur runners. Allegations of money paid under the table to athletes have persisted. Athletes in the Soviet and Communist-bloc systems are state-supported and trained and thus defy ordinary standards of amateurism. In the second half of the 20th century, general interest in athletics was greatly increased by the popularity of jogging (*q.v.*), or slow running, and by the proliferation of marathons, in which runners from world-class rank and anyone else meeting minimal qualifications competed side by side.

Athlone, Irish BAILE ÁTHA LUAIN, urban district, County Westmeath, Ireland, on the River Shannon. Located at a major east–west crossing of the Shannon, it has always been an important garrison town. In the 12th century the site, previously fortified by the kings of Uí Maine and Connaught (Connacht), was seized by the Anglo-Normans. Their motte (palisade) castle was replaced in 1210, and the first walls were erected in 1257. It was besieged several times during the 17th century.

Athlone is an important regional fair and market centre. Industries include wool and cotton textiles, machinery, electrical cable, and plastics. It is a centre for pleasure cruising, and there is a regional technical college. Pop. (1981) 9,444.

Atholl, mountainous traditional region (approximately 450 sq mi [1,165 sq km]) in Perth and Kinross district, Tayside region, Scotland. Enclosed by mountains exceeding 3,000 ft (900 m), the Atholl Basin (floor level 1,500 ft) is entered by the passes of Drumochter in the north and Killiecrankie in the south. Glen Garry and Glen Tilt are the principal valleys, and Lochs Rannoch and Tummel, the latter with its hydroelectric stations, are the chief lakes. Pasture and cultivation are centred on the lower valleys. The population is concentrated mainly in Blair Atholl and Pitlochry. Blair Atholl, on the River Garry, is the site of Blair Castle (built 1269), the ancient seat of the dukes of Atholl.

Atholl, EARLS, MARQUESSES, AND DUKES OF, titled Scottish nobility, of several creations, in the families Stewart and Murray, grouped below chronologically and indicated by the symbol •.

• Atholl, John Stewart, 4th earl of (d. April 24/25, 1579, Kincardine Castle, near Auchterarder, Perthshire, Scot.), Catholic Scottish noble, sometime supporter of Mary, Queen of Scots.

The son of John Stewart, the 3rd earl of Atholl in the Stewart line (whom he succeeded in 1542), Atholl was particularly trusted by Mary Stuart; but after the murder of Lord Darnley in 1567 he joined the Protestant lords against her and on her abdication was included in the regent's council for her son James VI. But he was again advocating her cause by 1569. He failed to prevent the Earl of Morton's appointment to the regency in 1572 but succeeded, with the Earl of Argyll, in driving him from office in March 1578, when James dissolved the regency and Atholl was appointed lord chancellor. Morton, however, regained his guardianship of James two months later. Atholl and Argyll, who were seeking assistance from Spain, then advanced to Stirling with a force of about 7,000 men, whereupon a compromise was arranged, the three earls being all included in the government.

After a banquet held on April 20, 1579, to celebrate the reconciliation, Atholl became suddenly ill and his death on April 24 or 25 may have been caused by poison. On the death in 1595 of his son John, 5th earl of Atholl, the earldom in default of male heirs reverted to the crown.

• Atholl, John Murray, 2nd earl and 1st marquess of (b. May 2, 1631—d. May 6, 1703), a leading Scottish Royalist and defender of the Stuarts from the time of the English Civil War until after the accession of William and Mary.

The son of the 1st Earl of Atholl in the Murray line, Atholl was the chief supporter of the Earl of Glencairn's rising in 1653 but was obliged to surrender a year later to George Monck, the Commonwealth commander in chief in Scotland. At the Restoration, Atholl received many high offices in Scotland, including being raised to a marquessate in 1676, but later he joined in a remonstrance to the King against the severities inflicted on the Covenanters and, although he was made vice admiral of Scotland in 1680 and president of Parliament in 1681, he was passed over for the chancellorship which became vacant in that year. Appointed lord lieutenant of Argyll in 1684, he had by 1685 become master of that region and at Inchinnan in June captured the Earl of Argyll, who was leading an invasion in favour of the Duke of Monmouth.

In the Revolution of 1688–89 he acted indecisively, although he took part in the proclamation of William and Mary as king and queen at Edinburgh. During Dundee's Rising he retired to Bath to "take the waters," but became implicated in the Jacobite plot of Sir James Montgomery (1690) and subsequently in further similar intrigues. He received a pardon in June 1691 and acted later for the government in the pacification of the Highlands.

He married Amelia, daughter of James Stanley, 7th earl of Derby, through whom the later dukes of Atholl acquired the sovereignty of the Isle of Man (1736).

• Atholl, John Murray, 2nd marquess and 1st duke of (b. Feb. 24, 1660, Knowsley, Lancashire, Eng.—d. Nov. 14, 1724, Huntingtower, Perth, Scot.), a leading Scottish supporter of William and Mary and of the Hanoverian succession.

Son of the 1st Marquess of Atholl, he favoured the accession of William and Mary in 1689 but was unable, during his father's absence, to prevent the majority of his clan under the command of his brother, Lord James Murray, from joining Dundee's Rising. After he was made duke of Atholl in 1703, an attempt was made in 1703–04 by Simon, Lord Lovat, to implicate him in a plot against Queen Anne; but the intrigue was exposed, and Atholl sent an explanation to the Queen.

Between 1705 and 1707 he vehemently opposed the union of England and Scotland, but on the score of illness, real or feigned, he took no part in the Jacobite invasion of 1708 and was kept under close watch in his castle at Blair (Perthshire). When the Tories came to power in 1710 Atholl returned to office and was high commissioner for Scotland from 1712 to 1714. He was dismissed on the accession of George I (1714), but at the rebellion of 1715, while three of his sons joined the Jacobites, he supported and assisted the government. He captured, on June 4, 1717, Rob Roy (Robert MacGregor), who succeeded, however, in escaping.

Athos, Mount, Modern Greek ÁTHOS, also called ÁYION ÓROS, English HOLY MOUNTAIN, mountain in northern Greece, site of a semi-autonomous republic of Greek Orthodox monks inhabiting 20 monasteries and dependencies (*skítes*), some of which are larger than the parent monasteries. It occupies the easternmost of the three promontories of the Chalcidice (Khalkidhikí) Peninsula, which projects from Macedonia into the Aegean Sea. The Aktí promontory, 30 mi (50 km) long and 6.5 mi wide at its broadest point, has a mountainous spine thickly wooded on the north and culminating in the marble peak of Athos (6,670 ft [2,033 m]), which rises abruptly from the sea at the southern tip. The capital and only town of the subdivision of 130 sq mi (336 sq km) is Kariaí (Karyaes).

In the 5th century BC the Persian king Xerxes I, to avoid taking his fleet around the treacherous cape, cut a 1.5-mi-long canal through Aktí's neck, traces of which are still visible.

Although hermits inhabited Athos before

Monastery of St. Gregorius, Mt. Athos, Greece
Annan Photo Features

AD 850, organized monastic life began in 963 when St. Athanasius the Athonite, with the help of his Byzantine imperial patron, Nicephorus II Phocas, founded the first monastery, the Great Laura. Despite objections by the hermits to organized community monasticism, the rule of St. Athanasius was imposed upon them by the emperor John I Tzimisces, who granted Athos its first charter (*Typikon*). A traditional prohibition bars women and female animals from the Holy Mountain. Several more monasteries were built in the 11th century. With the endowment of monasteries by Russia and other Slavic countries, the peninsula took on an almost pan-Orthodox character. By 1400, the number of monasteries had reached 40, of which 20 survive; the last to be built was Stavronikita, in 1542.

In the 15th century some of the monasteries abandoned the strict regimen of the community under the rule of an abbot for a more liberal system in which monks could possess personal property and be governed by two annually elected trustees (*epitropoi*).

When the Turks captured Thessaloníki (Salonika) in 1430, the monks submitted to Turkish rule, a relation that led to the rapid decline and impoverishment of the monasteries and increased adoption of the more liberal system of governance. In reaction, the first *skítes*, or ascetic settlements, were founded in the 16th century, grouped around a common church as dependencies of the monasteries. In 1783 the patriarch Gabriel IV introduced successful reforms with a new charter. The Athos community suffered greatly from Turkish depredations during the War of Greek Independence (1821–29), when entire libraries were burned. By contrast, the patronage of the tsars in the 19th century brought about the expansion of the Russian monasteries and their properties.

The community's present constitution dates from 1924 and is guaranteed by the Greek constitution of 1975. The Greek government is represented by a governor (*dioikitís*) appointed by the Ministry of Foreign Affairs to underline the mountain's semi-autonomy, but actual administration is in the hands of the Holy Council (*Ierá Sýnaxis*), comprising one representative of each of the 20 monasteries. Executive power is vested in the Epistasia, composed of four representatives by annual rotation. Eleven of the monasteries are presently conservative, and nine are liberal; discipline and fasting are much stricter in the former. Most of the monasteries hug the coast and consist of a quadrangle of buildings enclosing a church. The churches contain some of the most important examples of Byzantine art, icons, and treasures. The surviving libraries hold a vast number of classical and medieval manuscripts, most of which have been cataloged. Pop. (1981) 1,472.

Athyr (Egyptian goddess): *see* Hathor.

Atīśa, also called DĪPAṄKARA (b. 982—d. 1054), Indian Buddhist reformer whose teachings formed the basis of the Tibetan Bka'-gdams-pa (Those Bound by Command) sect of Buddhism, founded by his disciple 'Brom-ston.

Travelling to Tibet in 1038 or 1042 from Nālandā, a centre of Buddhist studies in India, Atīśa established monasteries there and wrote treatises emphasizing the three schools of Buddhism: the Theravāda (exclusive belief in the Gautama Buddha), the Mahāyāna (belief that Gautama Buddha is one of many Buddhas), and the Vajrayāna (which emphasizes yoga). He taught that the three stages follow in succession and must be practiced in that order. He died at Nyethang monastery, where his tomb still exists.

Atitlán, Lake, Spanish LAGO DE ATITLÁN, Sololá department, southwestern Guatemala, in the central highlands about 5,125 ft (1,562 m) above sea level. The lake, 1,049 ft (320 m) deep, is 12 mi (19 km) long and 6 mi (9.6 km) wide, with an area of 49.3 sq mi (127.7 sq km). It occupies a valley dammed by volcanic ash; on its borders are three cone-shaped volcanoes: Atitlán, Tolimán, and San Pedro.

Lake Atitlán with volcanos Tolimán and Atitlán, in the Central Highlands of Guatemala
Ernst Jahn

The shores of the spectacular lake are dotted with Indian villages; the inhabitants engage in fishing and weaving cotton and woollen textiles. The main towns, including Panajachel, Atitlán, and San Lucas, cater to the tourist trade. It is located about 90 mi (145 km) by road west of Guatemala City.

Atjeh (Indonesia): *see* Aceh.

Atjehnese (people): *see* Achinese.

Atka mackerel, fish species of the greenling (*q.v.*) group.

Atkins Museum of Fine Arts: *see* Nelson Gallery of Art and Atkins Museum of Fine Arts.

Atkinson, Sir Harry (Albert) (b. Nov. 1, 1831, Broxton, Cheshire, Eng.—d. June 28, 1892, Wellington, N.Z.), statesman who, as prime minister of New Zealand in the depression-ridden 1880s, implemented a policy of economic self-reliance and austerity in government spending.

Atkinson left England for Taranaki Province, N.Z., in 1853 and attained distinction as a soldier in the wars of 1860 and 1863 against the native Maoris. As minister of defense (1864–65) in the administration of Sir Frederick Weld, he advocated reliance on the colony's own troops in fighting the Maoris. On returning from a trip to England, he reentered Parliament in 1872 and became a leading figure in the "continuous ministry" of Sir Julius Vogel (*q.v.*) He was prime minister (1876–77) when the act of abolition of the provincial governments was passed.

As colonial treasurer (1879–82, 1882–83) and again as prime minister (1883–84, 1887–90), he combatted a persisting economic depression by reducing government expenditures and increasing taxation, reversing the expansionist policies of Vogel. He also tried to stimulate domestic industry by installing a protective tariff (1888) and by encouraging land settlement for farming. After being defeated in the election of December 1890, he served as speaker of the legislative council. Many of his ideas for social legislation were implemented in the Liberal ministry of John Ballance (1891–93). He was knighted in 1888.

Atl, Doctor, pseudonym of GERARDO MURILLO (b. 1875, Guadalajara, Mex.—d. Aug. 15, 1964, Mexico City), painter, writer, and revolutionary who was one of the pioneers in Mexico of the movement for artistic nationalism (*Mexicanismo*) and of the mural painting renaissance.

Educated in Mexico City, Rome, and Peru, he founded *Action d'Art* in Paris in 1913 and edited it for three years. Returning to Mexico he founded the *Acción Mundiale* in 1916 and became its editor. He was made head of Mexico's Department of Archaeological Monuments in 1923 and director of the Department of Fine Arts in 1930.

From his student days at the Academia de San Carlos in Mexico City Murillo was passionately interested in the native art of Mexico, the creation of an indigenous modern artistic style of expression, and with the depiction of the Mexican landscape—his most famous paintings and drawings being of the Valley of Mexico and the volcanoes of Popocatépetl and Ixtacihuatl. Murillo is most commonly known by his Aztec name Atl (the Náhuatl word for "water"), which he adopted as a repudiation of his Spanish heritage and as a demonstration of his pride in his Mexican Indian ancestors and their culture. Atl colours, a type of crayon made of wax, resin, oil, and pigment, were invented and used by him for both drawings and murals.

Aṭlāl Bābil (city): *see* Babylon.

Atlanta, city, capital of Georgia, U.S., and seat (1853) of Fulton County (but also partly in De Kalb County), in the foothills of the Blue Ridge Mountains, just south of the Chattahoochee River. The state's largest city, it owes its existence to railroads. In 1837 a spot, near what is now Five Points, was selected for the southern terminus of a railroad to be built northward toward Chattanooga, Tenn. The location was first known as Terminus and then as Marthasville (1843; to honour the daughter of Gov. Wilson Lumpkin); at its incorporation as a city in 1845, it was named Atlanta for the Western and Atlantic Railroad.

Peachtree Center, Atlanta, Ga., with the "Early Mace" sculpture in the foreground
© Carl Purcell

During the Civil War, Atlanta, as a key Confederate supply depot, became the military objective of Gen. William Tecumseh Sherman's invasion of Georgia from Chattanooga (*see* Atlanta Campaign). It fell to Federal troops on Sept. 1, 1864, and was converted into a military camp. On November 15, Sherman departed on his famous "march to the sea," but not before a large part of the city had been burned. During Reconstruction, Atlanta was a centre of federal government activities. In 1867 it became headquarters for the 3rd Military District under Gen. John Pope. It was the site of the convention that drew up the Georgia constitution of 1868, and under the Republican state administration it became the state capital (chosen permanently by popular referendum, 1877). Atlanta came to epitomize the spirit of the "New South," having risen from the ashes of the Civil War, advocating reconciliation with the North in order to restore business. This spirit was dramatized by three Atlanta expositions: the International Cotton (1881), the Piedmont (1887), and the Cotton States and International (1895). At the latter, Booker T. Washington made his historic declaration (the Atlanta Compromise), urging blacks to seek economic security before political or social equality.

Apart from its position as a communications hub, many economic factors have combined to impel Atlanta's growth as a regional service centre and a leading national city. It is the financial and commercial capital of the Southeast and is an important distribution, manufacturing, educational, and medical centre. It is the home of Coca-Cola, developed by Asa G. Candler, a pharmacist, who was also an Atlanta builder. Besides being regional headquarters for many national industries, it is the focus of federal government activity in the Southeast; it is the headquarters of the Sixth Federal Reserve District. The Centers for Disease Control (a division of the U.S. Public Health Service), Ft. McPherson, Dobbins Air Force Base, and a federal penitentiary are in or near the city. Hartsfield-Atlanta International Airport is 8 mi (13 km) southwest of downtown Atlanta.

Within the metropolitan area are more than 20 degree-granting institutions, including Atlanta University (1865), Clark College (1869), Emory University (1836), Georgia Institute of Technology (1888), Georgia State University (1913), Morehouse College (1867), and Oglethorpe University (1835). Notable buildings include the State Capitol (1889); the Cyclorama (in Grant Park), containing a gigantic painting of the Battle of Atlanta; and the Wren's Nest (home of Joel Chandler Harris, creator of the folk character Uncle Remus). The Atlanta Memorial Arts Center (1968) includes a museum, a symphony hall, an art school, and a theatre.

The spirit of the city tends to be liberal within the framework of Southern conservatism. Attractions tend to be traditional rather than exotic, and customs have been influenced by the predominantly Protestant church tradition in the Bible Belt. Martin Luther King, Jr. (the assassinated leader of the Southern Christian Leadership Conference, headquartered in Atlanta), is buried in the Ebeneezer Baptist Churchyard. In 1973 Atlanta became the first major city in the South to elect a black mayor. Pop. (1980) city, 425,022, metropolitan area (SMSA), 2,029,618.

Atlanta Campaign, in the U.S. Civil War, important series of battles in Georgia (May-

September 1864), most ending in draws, that eventually cut off a main Confederate supply centre and influenced the Federal presidential election of 1864. By the end of 1863, with Chattanooga and Vicksburg firmly under the control of the North, Atlanta became the logical point for Union forces to attack in their western campaign. Distant from earlier fighting, Atlanta had become an important Confederate railroad, supply, and manufacturing centre and a gateway to the lower South. Southern defenders of the strategic city were led by Lt. Gen. John Bell Hood. After seesaw battles lasting over several months, the Union Gen. William Tecumseh Sherman forced Confederate evacuation of Atlanta (August 31–September 1). This Union victory presented Pres. Abraham Lincoln with the key to reelection in the fall of 1864.

Atlanta Compromise, classic statement of the views on race relations of Booker T. Washington, leading black educator in the U.S. in the late 19th century, in a speech at the Atlanta Exposition (Sept. 18, 1895). In a time of serious racial tensions, Washington asserted that vocational education, which gave blacks an opportunity for economic security, was more valuable to them than social advantages or political office. In one sentence he summarized his concept of race relations appropriate for the times; "In all things that are purely social we can be as separate as the fingers, yet one as the hand in all things essential to mutual progress."

White leaders in both the North and South greeted Washington's speech with enthusiasm, but it disturbed black intellectuals who feared that Washington's philosophy would doom blacks to indefinite subservience to whites. That fear led to the Niagara Movement (*q.v.*) and later to the founding of the National Association for the Advancement of Colored People.

Atlanta Constitution, morning daily newspaper published in Atlanta, Ga., generally regarded as the "voice of the New South," thanks to a succession of outstanding editors: Henry Grady, Clark Howell, and Ralph McGill. The *Constitution* is usually counted among the great newspapers of the United States.

It was founded in 1868, early in the Reconstruction era, and soon became a leader among Southern papers because of its general balance. In the late 1870s and the 1880s, the *Constitution* became famous for the editorials of Henry W. Grady and for the breadth of its coverage. In the same period, the *Constitution* developed an outstanding staff of correspondents. The paper was liberal in its editorial policies from the time of Grady, although it did, under the editorship of Clark Howell, support American intervention in Cuba before the Spanish–American War of 1898. Howell was the son of Evan P. Howell, president and editor in chief from 1876 to 1897, and was in turn succeeded by his son, Clark Howell, Jr., in 1938. In the early 1900s the senior Clark Howell had won wide political influence, and Joel Chandler Harris of the *Constitution* gained national fame as a political columnist. Ralph McGill became executive editor in 1938 and editor in 1942. Under McGill the *Constitution* fought McCarthyism in the early 1950s and antiblack bias in the next two decades.

In 1950 the paper was purchased by James M. Cox, who already owned the evening *Atlanta Journal* (founded in 1883) and other papers. The *Constitution* continued its nonsensational coverage of local, national, and international news and its informed editorial comment.

atlantes: *see* atlas.

Atlantic, Battle of the, in World War II, contest between Great Britain (and from December 1941 the United States) and Germany for the control of sea routes.

The first phase of the ensuing battle for the Atlantic lasted until the fall of France in June 1940. During this period the Anglo-French coalition drove German merchant shipping from the Atlantic and maintained a fairly effective long-range blockade. The battle took a radically different turn following conquest of the Low Countries, the fall of France, and Italy's entry into the war in May–June 1940. Britain lost French naval support at the very moment when its own sea power was seriously crippled by losses incurred in the retreat from Norway and the evacuation from Dunkirk. The sea and air power of Italy, reinforced by German units, imperilled and eventually barred the direct route to Suez, forcing British shipping to use the long alternative route around the Cape of Good Hope. This cut the total cargo-carrying capacity of the British merchant marine almost in half at the very moment when German acquisition of naval and air bases on the English Channel and on the west coast of France foreshadowed more destructive attacks on shipping in northern waters.

At this critical juncture, the United States, though still technically a nonbelligerent, assumed a more positive role in the battle for the Atlantic. Fifty U.S. destroyers were turned over to Great Britain to make good previous naval losses. In return, the United States received long-term leases for ship and plane bases in Newfoundland, Bermuda, and numerous points in the Caribbean. U.S. units were also deployed in Iceland and Greenland.

Early in 1942, after the United States had become a full belligerent, the Axis opened a large-scale submarine offensive against coastal shipping in American waters. German U-boats also operated in considerable force along the south Atlantic ship lanes to India and the Middle East. The Allied campaign (1942–43) to reopen the Mediterranean depended almost entirely upon seaborne supply shipped through submarine-infested waters. Allied convoys approaching the British Isles, as well as those bound for the Russian ports of Murmansk and Archangelsk, had to battle their way against savage air and undersea attacks. It was publicly estimated at the close of 1942 that Allied shipping losses, chiefly from planes and U-boats, exceeded those suffered during the worst period of 1917. And a considerable weight of Allied naval power had to be kept constantly available in northern waters in case Germany's formidable surface raiders, especially the superbattleship "Tirpitz," should break into the Atlantic shipping lanes as the "Bismarck" had done briefly in 1941.

On the other side of the ledger was the ever tightening Allied blockade of Axis Europe and perceptible, if slow, progress in combating the Axis war on shipping. With more and better equipment, the convoy system was strengthened and extended. Unprecedented shipbuilding, especially in U.S. yards, caught up and began to forge ahead of losses, though the latter still remained dangerously high. Bombing raids on Axis ports and industrial centres progressively impaired Germany's capacity to build and service submarines and aircraft. The occupation of virtually all West African ports, including the French naval bases at Casablanca and Dakar, denied to Axis raiders their last possible havens in southern waters. By these and other means the Atlantic Allies thwarted Axis efforts to halt the passage of American armies and material to Europe and North Africa, to prevent supplies reaching Britain and the U.S.S.R., and to break up the blockade of Axis Europe.

Atlantic, The, monthly journal of literature and opinion, published in Boston, one of the oldest and most respected of U.S. reviews. The *Atlantic* was founded in 1857 by Moses Dresser Phillips of Boston. It has long been noted for the quality of its fiction and general articles, contributed by a long line of distinguished editors and authors that included James Russell Lowell, Ralph Waldo Emerson, Henry Wadsworth Longfellow, and Oliver Wendell Holmes. In 1869, *The Atlantic* created a magazine sensation when it published an article by Harriet Beecher Stowe about Lord Byron and his salacious personal life. She intended the article to "arrest Byron's influence upon the young," but it fascinated young readers, whose outraged parents cancelled 15,000 subscriptions.

In the early 1920's, *The Atlantic* expanded its scope to political affairs, featuring articles by such figures as Theodore Roosevelt, Woodrow Wilson, and Booker T. Washington. The high quality of its literature—including serialized novels, best-sellers among them—and its literary criticism have preserved the magazine's reputation as a lively literary periodical with a moderate world view. In the 1970s, increasing publication and mailing costs, far outstripping revenues from subscriptions and its meagre advertising, nearly shut the magazine down. It was purchased in 1980 by Mortimer B. Zuckerman.

Atlantic Charter, joint declaration issued on Aug. 14, 1941, during World War II, by the British prime minister, Winston Churchill, and Pres. Franklin D. Roosevelt of the still non-belligerent United States, after five days of conferences aboard warships in the North Atlantic.

A propaganda manifesto of common aims, the charter stated that (1) neither nation sought any aggrandizement; (2) they desired no territorial changes without the free assent of the peoples concerned; (3) they respected every people's right to choose its own form of government and wanted sovereign rights and self-government restored to those forcibly deprived of them; (4) they would try to promote equal access for all states to trade and to raw materials; (5) they hoped to promote worldwide collaboration so as to improve labour standards, economic progress, and social security; (6) after the destruction of "Nazi tyranny," they would look for a peace under which all nations could live safely within their boundaries, without fear or want; (7) under such a peace the seas should be free; and (8) pending a general security through renunciation of force, potential aggressors must be disarmed.

The Atlantic Charter was subsequently incorporated by reference in the Declaration of the United Nations (Jan. 1, 1942).

Atlantic City, resort, Atlantic County, southeastern New Jersey, U.S., on the Atlantic Ocean. It lies on the low, narrow, sandy Absecon Island, 8.1 mi (13 km) long, which is separated from the mainland by a narrow strait and several miles of meadows partly covered with water at high tide. Development of the island as a summer resort was first envisioned by Jonathan Pitney, who arrived in 1820 to practice medicine. He later headed a group that persuaded the Camden and Atlantic Railroad to make the place its eastern terminus. Its success spurred construction of another line, the Narrow Gauge Railroad, in 1877.

Atlantic City's mild winter climate, tempered by the Gulf Stream, made it a popular resort. The first Boardwalk (8 ft [2 m] wide) was built in 1870 (later extended to a width of 60 ft and a length of 5 mi). Other innovations enhancing the resort's reputation included the rolling chair (1884) in which guests were wheeled about, the introduction from Germany of the picture postcard (1895), and saltwater taffy. Amusement piers, jutting from the Boardwalk into the ocean, brought a carnival atmosphere with their vendors, shows, and exhibits. The largest, Steel Pier, is 2,000 ft (610 m) long. Construction of Convention Hall (1929, new wing completed in 1972), with its 41,000-seat auditorium, made Atlantic City a popular convention site. The Miss America Pageant, held annually in September, was established in 1921, discontinued in 1928, and revived in 1935.

Atlantic City's resort trade declined in the post-World War II period. In hopes of reviving the city's stagnating economy, a statewide referendum legalizing gambling in Atlantic City was passed in 1976. Thus a new dimension was added to the city's activities when the first legal gambling casino in the United States located outside the state of Nevada opened on the Boardwalk in May 1978. The development of gambling resorts provided an influx of jobs and money, but much of Atlantic City beyond the Boardwalk remained blighted and impoverished. This situation fostered political resentment, and in March 1984 the citizens of Atlantic City recalled their mayor in mid-term and replaced him with the city's first black chief executive.

Atlantic City is a trade and shipping centre for agricultural products and seafood and has light manufactures (textiles, candy, glassware, and china). The Absecon Lighthouse State Historic Site (the lighthouse was in service from 1857 to 1933) is nearby. The Historic Towne of Smithville, 7 mi west, has restored 18th-century buildings including a general store, gristmill, and three inns. Greater Atlantic City embraces the down-beach communities of Ventnor, Margate, and Longport and the mainland communities of Absecon, Pleasantville (site of a racetrack), Northfield, Linwood, and Somers Point. Inc. 1854. Pop. (1980) city, 40,199; metropolitan area (SMSA), 194,119.

Atlantic Climatic Interval, division of the Holocene climatic chronology (the Holocene Epoch began about 10,000 years ago and continues to the present). The Atlantic Climatic Interval followed the Boreal and preceded the Sub-Boreal climatic intervals; the Atlantic is included in the Hypsithermal Climatic Interval together with the Boreal and the Sub-Boreal. Atlantic climates were warm and humid, and during them mixed oak forests dominated the land, as indicated by fossil pollen studies. In Europe, the Atlantic Climatic Interval is contemporaneous with the marine transgression of the Litorina Sea.

Atlantic Coast Conference (ACC), U.S. collegiate athletic organization formed in 1953 as an offshoot of the Southern Conference. Member schools are Clemson University, Duke University, the University of Maryland, the University of North Carolina, North Carolina State University, Wake Forest University, the University of South Carolina, and the University of Virginia.

The Southern Conference had been organized in 1921 to promote and govern intercollegiate athletics. By 1923 the conference had 23 member schools, and the number continued to increase. By 1953 some of the member schools felt the conference had become too large and unwieldy for competitive athletic scheduling. At the conference's spring meeting seven schools withdrew and formed the ACC. Virginia, which had not been a member of the Southern Conference, also joined the new organization.

Atlantic Intracoastal Waterway, shipping route paralleling the East Coast of the U.S., serving ports from Boston to Key West, Fla. It is part of the Intracoastal Waterway (*q.v.*).

Atlantic Ocean, body of salt water covering approximately one-fifth of the Earth's surface and separating the continents of Europe and Africa to the east from the Americas to the west.

A brief treatment of the Atlantic Ocean follows. For full treatment, *see* MACROPAEDIA: Oceans.

The Atlantic Ocean and its marginal seas constitute the world's second largest ocean after the Pacific and have an area of 41,100,000 sq mi (106,460,000 sq km); the Atlantic alone has an area of 31,830,000 sq mi. The average depth is 10,150 ft (3,330 m). The Atlantic Ocean is somewhat shallower than the Pacific and Indian oceans because of extensive continental shelves in the north and the shallowness of its marginal seas. These seas include the Baltic, North, Black, and Mediterranean seas to the east and Baffin Bay, Hudson Bay, the Gulf of St. Lawrence, the Gulf of Mexico, and the Caribbean Sea to the west. The Atlantic becomes broader south of the Equator and is bordered by simple coasts almost without islands.

Topographically the Atlantic floor is dominated by the tectonically and volcanically active Mid-Atlantic Ridge, which extends down the centre of the ocean from north to south and divides the ocean into two principal structural troughs. These two troughs comprise a number of smaller basins, usually separated from each other by continental shelves, oceanic rises or ridges, or other submarine relief features. The basins east of the Mid-Atlantic Ridge include (north to south) the Lofoten, Norwegian, West European, Canary, Cape Verde, Guinea, Angola, Cape, and Agulhas basins. Those west of the ridge include the Labrador, Newfoundland, North American, Guiana, Ceara, Brazil, and Argentina basins. Most mid-Atlantic islands are volcanic in origin because of the influence of the Mid-Atlantic Ridge; these include Iceland, the Azores, Ascension, St. Helena, Tristan de Cunha, Gough, and Bouvet, all closely adjoining the Mid-Atlantic Ridge. The Atlantic has relatively few seamounts, and long stretches of its coasts are devoid of fringing reefs. The continental slope around the Atlantic is cut by submarine canyons that funnel sediments from continental sources to the continental rise.

Most of the bottom of the Atlantic is covered with foraminiferal ooze, a calcareous deposit consisting mainly of the shells of dead unicellular organisms. Calcareous deposits give way to red clay at depths below 16,400 ft. Airborne material from the deserts of Africa accumulates off the western coast of Africa; detritus borne on ice is an important component of sediments in high latitudes. As a result of excess evaporation, salinity is highest in the surface waters of the North Atlantic and lowest in the Baltic Sea and other areas where precipitation is high and where admixture of fresh water from large rivers is substantial.

The surface currents of the Atlantic correspond to the system of prevailing winds and are modified by such factors as bottom and tidal friction, the Earth's rotation, regional excesses of evaporation or precipitation, and regional differences in cooling or heating. Trade winds in the North Atlantic maintain a fairly steady equatorial current from east to west. Much of the water carried by this current continues into the Caribbean and through the Strait of Yucatán into the Gulf of Mexico, from which it emerges as a warm and swift current to form the Gulf Stream off the eastern coast of the United States. The North Atlantic Current is a direct extension of the Gulf Stream that branches into the Irminger Current south of Iceland, the East Greenland Current, and the Canary Current between the Azores and Spain. The Canary Current flows southwest and joins the North Equatorial Current. Southeast trade winds in the South Atlantic maintain the South Equatorial Current, much of which is diverted northward by the coast of South America. No current in the South Atlantic is as powerful as the Gulf Stream.

Deep and bottom water in the North Atlantic is derived from surface water sinking between Iceland and Greenland and in the Labrador Sea. Water from the Mediterranean spreads out at depths between 3,000 and 6,500 ft and extends as far south as latitude 40° S. Intermediate water from the Antarctic flows as far north as 20° N; large quantities of Antarctic bottom water and intermediate water mix with North Atlantic deep water, return southward, and rise toward the surface between 50° and 60° S.

Atlantic Provinces (Canada): *see* Maritime Provinces.

Atlantic Richfield Company (Arco), U.S. petroleum corporation created in 1966 by the merger of Richfield Oil Corporation and Atlantic Refining Company. A further merger in 1969 brought in Sinclair Oil Corporation. Atlantic Richfield has petroleum operations in all parts of the United States and also has operations in Indonesia, the North Sea, and the South China Sea. The company also owns and operates transportation facilities for liquid petroleum, including pipelines and tankers; produces and sells chemicals, coal, and metal products; and is involved in the development of solar energy products and in other energy-related activities. Headquarters are in Los Angeles.

In 1977 the Anaconda Company—miner and processor of copper, aluminum, and uranium and manufacturer of copper and aluminum products—became a wholly owned subsidiary, though as a result of this merger Anaconda was forced to divest some of its copper interests.

Atlantic Refining, whose predecessor firms date back to the 1850s, was incorporated in 1870 and, after 1892, became one of the eastern companies of the Standard Oil Trust (*see* Standard Oil Company and Trust); after the U.S. Supreme Court's dissolution of the Standard Oil group in 1911, Atlantic Refining again became independent. Richfield, the product of several mergers in the first two decades of the 20th century, formally began in 1911 as a refining company financed jointly by the Los Angeles Oil and Refining Company and the Kellogg Oil Company (two of the several companies that were to merge under the Richfield name). Sinclair was formed in Kansas in 1916 by Harry F. Sinclair (1876–1956), who had made his first big oil strike in Oklahoma in 1907.

Atlantic salmon (*Salmo salar*), oceanic trout of the family Salmonidae, a highly prized game fish. It averages about 5.5 kilograms (12 pounds) and is marked with round or cross-shaped spots. Found on both sides of the Atlantic, it enters streams in fall to spawn. After spawning, adults are called kelts and may live to spawn again. The young enter the sea in about two years and mature in about four. The ouananiche (*Salmo salar ouananiche*) of rivers and the sebago, or lake, salmon (*S.s.*

Atlantic salmon (*Salmo salar*)

Tom Dolan—EB Inc., painted under the supervision of Loren P. Woods, Chicago Natural History Museum

sebago) are smaller, landlocked forms of Atlantic salmon, also prized for sport. The Atlantic salmon has also been successfully introduced into the Great Lakes of the United States. (*See also* salmon.)

Atlántico, department, northwestern Colombia, located on the Caribbean coastal plain and bounded east by the Río Magdalena. The department was established in 1905. Although it is one of Colombia's smallest departments, with an area of 1,308 sq mi (3,388 sq km), Atlántico's position at the mouth of one of the continent's major rivers is of strategic importance. Almost three-fourths of the population lives in the department capital of Barranquilla (*q.v.*), one of Colombia's most active ports, 15 mi (24 km) upstream from the mouth of the Magdalena. Cotton and sesame are the principal commercial crops, cattle are raised, and fishing is important. Pop. (1981 est.) 1,404,283.

Atlántida, department, northwestern Honduras, bounded on the north by the Caribbean Sea. Except for the southern portion, the department, of 1,641 sq mi (4,251 sq km), consists chiefly of fertile coastal and alluvial plains, on which most of the population resides.

Agriculture, producing cassava, sweet potatoes, rice, corn (maize), beans, and livestock, forms the economic mainstay; the Standard Fruit Company raises bananas, citrus fruits, and coconuts on plantations around La Ceiba for export. Forest products also are an important industry. Tela and La Ceiba (*q.v.*), the departmental capital, are important seaports and are also the chief industrial cities of Atlántida. The department is traversed by highways that are linked to the national road network; there is also a narrow-gauge railroad. Black Caribs, of Indian and African ancestry, who were deported by the English from St. Vincent in the Leeward Islands in 1796, live along the coast, most in either of the two major ports or on the plantations in the department. Pop. (1983 est.) 242,235.

Atlantis II Deep, submarine basin, the largest in the Red Sea, located at 21°23′ N and 38°04′ E. The Atlantis II Deep attains a maximum depth of 7,160 feet (2,170 m) and is noteworthy because it is one of the areas containing hot brines, with water temperatures ranging to 133° F (56° C) and salinities to as much as $7^{1}/_{2}$ times that of normal seawater. Metallic trace elements, such as zinc, copper, and cobalt, are present in concentrations exceeding those of normal seawater by about 1,000 times. The upper 33 ft of sediment in the Atlantis II Deep contains billions of dollars worth of economic metal deposits. Similar but somewhat smaller basins known to exist in the Red Sea are Chain Deep and Discovery Deep, with maximum depths of 6,778 and 7,283 ft, respectively.

Atlas, in Greek mythology, son of the Titan Iapetus and the nymph Clymene (or Asia) and brother of Prometheus (creator of mankind). In the works of Homer, Atlas seems to have been a marine creation who supported the pillars that held heaven and earth apart. These were thought to rest in the sea immediately beyond the most western horizon, but later the name of Atlas was transferred to a range of mountains in northwestern Africa. Atlas was subsequently represented as the king of that district, turned into a rocky mountain by the hero Perseus, who, to punish Atlas for his inhospitality, showed him the Gorgon's head, the sight of which turned men to stone. According to the Greek poet Hesiod, Atlas was one of the Titans who took part in their war against Zeus, for which as a punishment he was condemned to hold aloft the heavens. In works of art he was represented as carrying the heavens or the celestial globe.

atlas, plural ATLANTES, in architecture, male figure used as a column to support an entablature, balcony, or other projection, originating in the Classical architecture of antiquity. Such figures are posed as if supporting great weights (*e.g.,* Atlas bearing the world). The related telamon of Roman architecture, the male counterpart of the caryatid (*q.v.*), is also a weight-bearing figure but does not usually appear in an atlas pose.

Romanesque-style atlas on the cathedral of Sta. Maria Assunta, Spoleto, Italy, 1198
By courtesy of Thames and Hudson

The earliest known examples of true atlantes occur on a colossal scale in the Greek temple of Zeus (*c.* 500 BC) at Agrigentum (Agrigento), Sicily. Atlantes were used only rarely in the Middle Ages but reappeared in the Mannerist and Baroque periods.

atlas, collection of maps or charts, usually bound together. The name derives from a custom—initiated by Gerardus Mercator in the 16th century—of using the figure of the Titan Atlas, holding the globe on his shoulders, as a frontispiece for books of maps. In addition to maps and charts, atlases often contain pictures, tabular data, facts, and indexes of place-names. They may be either world or regional in coverage. Special subject atlases provide information on boundaries, climate, economy, geology, history, languages, population, religions, resources, or other data.

Atlas, Charles, original name ANGELO SICILIANO (b. Oct. 30, 1893, Acri, Calabria, Italy—d. Dec. 24, 1972, Long Beach, N.Y., U.S.), Italian-born U.S. bodybuilder and physical culturist who, with Charles P. Roman, created and marketed a highly popular mail-order bodybuilding course.

Atlas at the age of 10 immigrated to the United States with his parents. The legendary sand-kicking episode used in his later advertisements actually occurred at Coney Island when Atlas was still the skinny Angelo Siciliano: a brawny lifeguard kicked sand on him and stole away his girlfriend. Thereafter he built up his body—to the extent that Bernarr Macfadden, the publisher in the 1920s of many popular magazines, dubbed him "America's Most Perfectly Developed Man" at a physical culture exhibition in 1922 at the original Madison Square Garden. He had also changed his name, after seeing a statue of Atlas; and in 1929 he and a young advertising man, Roman, decided to incorporate and build up a business of Atlas home-study programs of isotonic exercises and nutrition tips. During his heyday, three generations of pulp comic books carried his advertisement—of a barrel-chested man with amazing strength and physique and a large smile.

Atlas Mountains, series of mountain ranges, northwestern Africa, running generally northeast to southwest through the three countries of the Maghrib—Morocco, Algeria, and Tunisia.

The following article summarizes information about the Atlas Mountains; for full details, *see* MACROPAEDIA: Africa.

The Atlas system takes the shape of an extended oblong, enclosing a complex of plains and plateaus, and contains distinct northern and southern ranges named the Atlas Tellien (Tell Atlas) and Atlas Saharien (Saharan Atlas), respectively. The ranges rim the extensive Hauts Plateaux (High Plateaus) of eastern Morocco and northern Algeria. To the east in Tunisia they join together in the Tébessa and Medjerda mountains, while to the west in Morocco they merge into the long folds of the Moyen Atlas (Middle Atlas) and the high, rugged peaks of the Haut Atlas (High Atlas). The Anti-Atlas extends southwestward from the Haut Atlas to the Atlantic Ocean. Geologically, the Atlas Tellien is a young, folded mountain range related to the Alpine system of Europe. The southern Atlas Saharien, however, belongs to a distinct structural grouping, that of the vast, ancient plateaus of the African continent.

The Atlas Mountains are a meeting place of two different kinds of air masses—the humid and cold polar air masses that come from the north and the hot and dry tropical air masses that move up from the south. Winter in the Atlas is hard, imposing severe living conditions upon the inhabitants. These include principally the Berber race, which has survived there, preserving its own language, traditions, and beliefs. The great Maghribian wadis, the Moulouya and the Chelif, issue from the Atlas Mountain ranges. There is considerable erosion aggravated by the sparseness of vegetation. The clearance of land for agriculture has also resulted in the disappearance of oak, pine, and cedar forests in the Atlas ranges. The geological formations are rich in minerals, the most important of these being lead, zinc, copper, iron, manganese, and phosphate. Length 1,200 mi (2,000 km); maximum elevation 13,665 ft (4,165 m) at Jebel Toubkal.

Atlas rocket, booster for space vehicles, particularly the U.S. Mercury spacecraft series, designed originally as an intercontinental ballistic missile (ICBM). Atlas is equipped with three engines—two boosters that are jettisoned after about $2^{1}/_{2}$ minutes of operation and a sustainer that operates until orbital ve-

Atlas D rocket launching U.S. astronaut L. Gordon Cooper, Jr., into orbit, May 15, 1963
UPI—EB Inc.

locity is attained. Atlas can lift about 5,800 pounds (2,600 kilograms) to about a 350-mile (560-kilometre) orbit. Coupled with Agena, the combined Atlas–Agena rocket is used for launching lunar and planetary probes, as well as Earth-orbiting satellites, such as Seasat, where the Agena is also the spacecraft. Atlas–Centaur, or Centaur, combines the first-stage Atlas, which burns kerosene, with a second stage fueled with liquid hydrogen; it was the first rocket to use liquid hydrogen as fuel.

Atlas Saharien (Africa): *see* Saharan Atlas.

Atlas Tellien (Africa): *see* Tell Atlas.

Atli, Lay of, Norse ATLAKVIDA, heroic poem in the Norse *Poetic Edda* (*see* Edda), an older variant of the tale of slaughter and revenge that is the subject of the German epic *Nibelungenlied* (*q.v.*), from which it differs in several respects. In the Norse poem, Atli (the Hunnish king Attila) is the villain, who is slain by his wife, Gudrun, to avenge her brothers.

In *Atlakvida,* Gudrun's brothers Gunnar and Hogni are lured to Atli's court so that Atli can learn the secret of their treasure. Gunnar and Hogni refuse to tell. Atli has Hogni's heart cut out while Gunnar laughs in scorn. Gunnar is thrown into a snake pit, then put to death. Gudrun, "the sweet-faced delight of the shield-folk," takes her revenge by serving the murderers dainties (actually the roasted hearts of Atli's sons). Then she stabs the wine-weary Atli and burns down his hall, allowing only the dogs to escape. In the German epic the characters of Atli, Gudrun, Gunnar, and Hogni are represented, respectively, by Etzel, Kriemhild (*q.v.*), Gunther, and Hagen.

Atlixco, city, southwestern Puebla state, south central Mexico. It lies at 6,171 ft (1,881 m) above sea level in a fertile valley irrigated by the Río Molinos, which descends through the volcanic axis from the southeastern slopes of Ixtacihuatl volcano. Founded in 1579 as Villa de Carrión, after its founder, Alonso Díaz de Carrión, Atlixco is a commercial, manufacturing, and industrial centre. Wheat, corn (maize), beans, fruits, and other crops are processed in and distributed from the city. Cotton and woollen textile mills, distilleries, and soft-drink plants are also located in Atlixco. The main highway linking Puebla city, the state capital, 19 mi (30 km) to the northeast, and Oaxaca passes through Atlixco, as does the narrow-gauge Mexico City–Río Balsas railroad. The city also has an airfield. Pop. (1970) 41,967.

ātman, one of the most basic concepts in Hindu philosophy, describing that eternal core of the personality that survives after death and that transmigrates to a new life or is released from the bonds of existence. While in the early Vedic texts it occurred mostly as a reflexive pronoun (oneself), in the later *Upaniṣads* it comes more and more to the fore as a philosophic topic: *ātman* is that which makes the other organs and faculties function and for which indeed they function; *ātman* underlies all the activities of a person, as Brahman (the absolute) underlies the workings of the universe; to know it brings bliss; it is part of the universal Brahman, with which it can commune or even fuse. So fundamental was the *ātman* deemed to be that certain circles identified it with Brahman. Of the various systems (*darśana*) of Hindu philosophy, the schools of Sāṃkhya and Yoga (which use the term *puruṣa* to convey the idea of *ātman*), and the orthodox school of Vedānta particularly concern themselves with the *ātman,* though the interpretation varies in accordance with each system's general world views.

atmosphere, the mantle of gases, also known as the air, that envelops the Earth. It consists principally of nitrogen, oxygen, argon, carbon dioxide, and small amounts of several other gases. At sea level it exerts an average pressure of 1.033 kilograms per square centimetre (14.7 pounds per square inch), equivalent to that of 760 millimetres (29.92 inches) of mercury.

A brief treatment of the atmosphere follows. For full treatment, *see* MACROPAEDIA: Atmosphere.

The depth of this mantle of air may be somewhat arbitrarily placed at about 1,000 kilometres (620 miles). It is impossible to be precise about this because the atmosphere thins progressively with altitude, exhibiting no sharp boundary, so that at great heights there are no more than traces of atmospheric gases. Half of the atmosphere, by weight, lies in the first 5.5 km (3.4 mi) above the Earth and more than 99 percent within 40 km (25 mi). At 100 km there is what at the surface would be considered a near-vacuum, with only one-millionth of the pressure at sea level.

The atmosphere is made up of two types of gases: the permanent gases, principally nitrogen (78 percent), oxygen (21 percent), argon (0.9 percent), plus carbon dioxide, neon, helium, krypton, xenon, hydrogen, and others in very small quantities; and the variable gases whose concentrations vary in both space and time, including carbon monoxide, sulfur dioxide, and the two most important, ozone and water vapour. Ozone, found mainly from 30 to 80 km, is vital to atmospheric processes and to life on Earth since it absorbs harmful ultraviolet radiation from the Sun. Water vapour, by contrast, is almost entirely concentrated in the first 10 to 15 km of the atmosphere. If it were all condensed and precipitated, it would amount to about 25 mm (1 in.) of rain over the entire Earth. Evaporation of water vapour from and precipitation to the Earth are in balance for the Earth as a whole, although not for individual points of the Earth's surface.

The thermal stratification of the lower atmosphere was first demonstrated at the end of the 19th century by the French meteorologist Teisserenc de Bort, who used balloons to carry recording instruments to about 15 km above Paris. He found that the temperature generally decreased up to about 11 km and then began to increase. The region of progressive decrease in temperature is called the troposphere, which varies in height above the surface from about 8 km above polar regions to 17 km above the Equator. At a boundary known as the tropopause the temperature begins to increase and continues to do so to about 50 km through a second layer of the atmosphere called the stratosphere. The troposphere and the stratosphere possess quite distinct systems of circulation, and exchange of air between the two regions takes place only very slowly. Although most weather processes of consequence to the Earth occur in the troposphere, the lower stratosphere appears to play some part in these processes.

At the top of the stratosphere, where ozone absorbs ultraviolet radiation, temperatures are roughly the same as those at the surface. Beyond this thermal maximum at the stratopause, temperatures begin to fall rapidly again with height. Through the region of the mesosphere the temperature falls to a minimum of about −100° C (−150° F) at about 85 km. Above the mesosphere and the mesopause is the thermosphere, through which the temperature again rises, this time to as high as 1,750° C. The atmosphere here contains significant amounts of atomic oxygen, the result of the dissociation of molecular oxygen by ultraviolet radiation, as well as helium and hydrogen. The outer fringes of the atmosphere above about 400 km are sparsely populated by neutral and charged atoms.

Other regions of the atmosphere may be identified according to parameters other than temperature gradient. The ionosphere (*q.v.*) is a region characterized by the presence of large numbers of ions; it begins at a height of about 55 km and extends upward a distance of several Earth radii. The region from the surface up through the mesosphere is referred to as the homosphere because, owing to the action of eddy convection, the distribution of component gases is even and stable. Above the homosphere is the heterosphere, in which molecular diffusion processes override eddy convection owing to the enormous decrease in density; the result is gradients for the abundances of constituent gases, notably an increase in atomic oxygen with altitude until it becomes the principal constituent of the atmosphere above 250 km. Beyond the thick blanket of atomic oxygen lie belts of helium and then hydrogen. At a height of from 400 to 800 km (for neutral gases) or 2,000 to 3,000 km (for ionized gases) lies a critical zone, which marks the transition to the exosphere, a region in which the density of the atmosphere is so low that molecular collisions are no longer common and hence the concept of temperature loses its usual meaning. In the exosphere light atoms, as of hydrogen and helium, may acquire sufficient velocity to escape the Earth's gravitational pull entirely.

atmosphere, unit of pressure, nearly equal to the mean atmospheric pressure naturally existing at sea level on the surface of the Earth; or to the pressure exerted by a vertical column of mercury (as in a barometer) 760 millimetres (29.9213 inches) high, used in meteorology. It is defined as 101,325 newtons of force per square metre (approximately 14.7 pounds per square inch). *See also* millibar.

atmospheric circulation, large-scale wind systems arranged in several east–west belts that encircle the Earth. In the subtropical high-pressure belts near latitudes 30° N and 30° S (the horse latitudes), air descends and causes the trade winds to blow westward and Equatorward at the Earth's surface. These merge and rise in the intertropical convergence zone near the Equator and, as the antitrades, blow eastward and poleward at altitudes of 2 to 12 kilometres (1 to 7 miles). Part of the antitrade flow descends in the subtropical high-pressure belts, and the remainder merges at high altitudes with the mid-latitude westerly winds farther north. Between latitudes 15° N and 15° S, a layer of high-speed winds, the Krakatoa winds, blow 20 to 40 kilometres (12 to 25 miles) above the surface.

The descending air in the subtropical high-pressure belts diverges near the surface; the air that does not flow Equatorward flows eastward and poleward as the mid-latitude westerlies. These extend to great altitudes and contain jet streams, high-velocity air currents around the 10-kilometre (6-mile) level in both hemispheres. Poleward of 60° N and 60° S, the winds generally blow westward and Equatorward as the polar easterlies. In the northern polar regions, where water and land are interspersed, the polar easterlies give way in summer to variable winds.

The zonal wind belts are much more uniform and constant in the Southern Hemisphere because there is little land to disturb the circulation. In the Northern Hemisphere, a number of large, semipermanent high- and low-pressure centres exist over the continents and oceans during various parts of the year; their winds prevent the zonal wind belts from extending continuously around the world.

atmospheric corona, set of one or more coloured rings that sometimes appear close to the Sun or Moon when viewed through a thin cloud composed of water droplets. They are caused by the diffraction of light around the edges of the droplets, with each colour being deviated through a slightly different angle, giving rise to the colour separation of the rings. The colour purity of the corona is never as great as for the rainbow, however, because the diffraction process does not concentrate the colours into as narrow a direction as do the processes giving rise to the rainbow. Furthermore, the wider the range of drop sizes present, the poorer will be the colour separation; and under conditions of a very broad range of droplet sizes, the colours will completely overlap one another, giving rise to the aureole. The colour sequence of the corona is from blue on the inside to red on the outside. *See also* halo.

atmospheric electricity, electrical phenomena that occur in the lower atmosphere, usually the troposphere—*e.g.,* the production, transport, and loss of free electrical charges; the change in electrical potential from point to point in the atmosphere; and the atmosphere's electrical conductivity. The term is not applied to phenomena in the ionosphere. Major fields of study within the subject are the mechanisms of charge separation in electrified clouds, especially thunderclouds; the properties of lightning strokes; global thunderstorm activity; the rate of production of ions in the troposphere by cosmic rays and background radioactivity; and the electrical properties of the atmosphere in fair and disturbed weather.

atmospheric optics, study of optical characteristics and phenomena associated with the interaction of visible sunlight with atmospheric gases, particulates, and water vapour. Refraction, diffraction, Rayleigh scattering (*qq.v.*), and polarization of light are within the compass of atmospheric optics; the phenomena studied include rainbows, halos, atmospheric corona, mirages, and sundogs (*see* parhelion).

atmospheric perspective (visual arts): *see* aerial perspective.

atmospheric pressure, also called BAROMETRIC PRESSURE, force per unit area exerted by an atmospheric column; that is, the entire body of air above the specified area. Atmospheric pressure usually is measured with a mercury barometer (hence the commonly used synonym barometric pressure), which indicates the height of a column of mercury that exactly balances the weight of the column of atmosphere the base of which coincides with that of the mercury column. Also, it may be measured using an aneroid barometer, in which the sensing element is one or more hollow, partially evacuated corrugated metal disks supported against collapse by an inside or outside spring; the change in the shape of the disk with changing pressure can be recorded using a pen arm and a clock-driven revolving drum.

Atmospheric pressure is expressed in several different systems of units: inches (or millimetres) of mercury, pounds per square inch (psi), dynes per square centimetre, millibars (mb), or atmospheres. Standard sea-level pressure, by definition, equals 29.92 inches (760 millimetres) of mercury, 14.70 pounds per square inch, 1013.25×10^3 dynes per square centimetre, 1013.25 millibars, or one atmosphere. Variations about these values are quite small; for example, the highest and lowest sea-level pressures ever recorded are 32.01 in. (in the middle of Siberia) and 25.90 in. (in a typhoon in the South Pacific). The small variations in pressure that do exist largely determine the wind and storm patterns of the Earth.

Near the Earth's surface the pressure decreases with height at a rate of about 3.5 mb for every 100 feet (30 metres). The pressure at 885,830 ft (10^{-6} mb) is comparable to that in the best man-made vacuum attainable. At heights above 5,000 to 10,000 ft (1,500 to 3,000 m) the pressure is low enough to produce mountain sickness and severe physiological problems unless careful acclimatization is undertaken.

At sea level the barometric pressure is subject to typical time and space variations. At many locations, for example, especially in low latitudes, the pressure varies diurnally as a result of atmospheric tides induced by the Sun, with maxima at 10:00 AM and PM local time, and minima at 4:00 AM and PM. The maximum range between high and low values is 3 mb near the Equator.

atmospheric refraction, change in the direction of propagation of electromagnetic radiation or sound waves in traversing the atmosphere. Such changes are caused by gradients in the density of the air. *See* refraction.

atmospheric turbulence, irregular air movement in which the wind constantly varies in speed and direction. Turbulence is important because it churns and mixes the atmosphere and causes water vapour, smoke, and other substances, as well as energy, to become distributed at all elevations.

Atmospheric turbulence near the Earth's surface differs from that at higher levels. Within a few hundred metres of the surface, turbulence has a marked diurnal variation, reaching a maximum around midday. When solar radiation heats up the surface, which in turn warms the air, the warm, light air rises, and cooler, denser air descends to replace it. That movement of air, together with disturbances around surface obstacles, makes low-level winds extremely irregular. At night, the surface cools rapidly, chilling the air near the ground; when that air becomes cooler than the air above it, a stable temperature inversion is created. Under that condition, the wind's speed and gustiness both decrease sharply. When the sky is overcast, the low-level air temperature varies much less between day and night, and turbulence remains nearly constant.

At altitudes of several thousand metres or more, the frictional effect of surface topography on the wind is greatly reduced, and the small-scale turbulence characteristic of the lower atmosphere is absent. Although upper-level winds usually are relatively regular, they sometimes become turbulent enough to affect aviation. Under certain conditions, including strong surface heating and high humidity, large masses of air rise to form huge cumulus clouds; often thunderstorms result. *See also* clear-air turbulence.

Atokan Series, major division of Pennsylvanian rocks and time in the United States (the Pennsylvanian Period, roughly equivalent to the Upper Carboniferous, began about 325,000,000 years ago and lasted about 45,000,000 years). It was named for exposures studied in the region of Atoka, Okla., where it is characterized by about 945 metres (3,100 feet) of sandstones and shales; the sandstones often contain natural gas. In Ohio and Pennsylvania, rocks correlated with the Atokan consist of repetitive alternations of sandstones, shales, coal beds, and thin marine limestones; these seem to indicate cyclically fluctuating terrestrial, freshwater, and marine depositional environments. Rocks of the Atokan Series overlie those of the Morrowan and underlie rocks of the Desmoinesian Series.

atoll, coral reef enclosing a lagoon. Atolls consist of ribbons of reef that may not always be circular but whose broad configuration is a closed shape up to dozens of kilometres across, enclosing a lagoon that may be approximately 50 m (160 ft) deep or more. The continuity of the reef may be broken in places by channels, sometimes as deep as the lagoon, through which boats may pass.

A brief treatment of atolls follows. For full treatment, *see* MACROPAEDIA: Oceans.

Most of the reef itself is a submarine feature, rising from the abyssal floors of the ocean to just beneath high-tide level, but around the rim along the top of the reef there are usually low, flat islands or more continuous strips of low, flat land. These islands, especially the smaller ones, are susceptible to damage or even outright destruction by storms, but they have nevertheless been settled by oceanic peoples like the Maldivians, Polynesians, and Micronesians for many centuries.

The origin of atolls has always fascinated sailors and naturalists, who early appreciated that, although reef-building organisms inhabit only the shallowest depths of the sea (about 100 m), the reefs rose from much deeper down. The modern explanation of atolls incorporates the theory of Charles Darwin, who suggested that atolls represented the final stage of a continuing upgrowth of reef around a sinking extinct volcanic island that had long since disappeared from view.

The reasons for subsidence are related to the geological nature of ocean floors, but the origin of oceanic volcanoes is not yet fully understood. One possible model for the larger atoll and reef archipelagoes is that of the Hawaiian Islands' "hot spot," a continuously active region in the Earth's mantle that generates volcanoes as the ocean floor crust passes slowly over it. Ocean floor crust subsides as it moves away from midocean ridges where it forms, so any feature that rises from the ocean floor, such as the Hawaiian chain or any reef-capped extinct volcano, will also subside with the ocean floor as a whole while also being borne along laterally.

Reefs tend to grow outward from a fringing reef stage toward the better conditions of open water and also grow upward if the foundations beneath are sinking. After thousands of years the actively growing reef structure becomes separated from the volcanic shoreline by an intervening stretch of lagoon water. This is the barrier reef stage. The volcanic island eventually subsides from view, leaving a reef whose uppermost part is like a saucer whose rim reaches up to sea level and whose deeper central area is a lagoon.

Different kinds of reefs and volcanic islands are found together in the tropical oceans, related to each other in such a way that they can be interpreted as representing the progressive stages postulated by the subsidence theory. Stronger direct evidence for subsidence has come from geological drilling of atolls (first at Enewetak Atoll in 1952), which revealed the presence of volcanic rock about 1,400 m below the modern reef top.

Changes in sea level complicate the subsidence model. These have been relatively frequent during the last 2,000,000 years or more and mostly result from cycles of glaciation. Foundation subsidence accounts for reef thicknesses of hundreds of metres, but the uppermost 150 m or so of a reef structure have also been affected by these sea level changes. Low sea levels exposed the reefs to weathering, which probably also enhanced their saucerlike shape while sculpturing numerous smaller-scale features such as canyons and pinnacles. Rising sea levels have drowned these subaerial features, and the renewed coral growth during the last 10,000 years has been especially active along the rims, where reef-building organisms are in the most direct contact with open ocean water.

While it is known that ocean floor subsidence and sea level changes have actually occurred, it is not so easy to determine which of these has been more important in causing particular features of atolls and other reefs. Reef patches can develop as upward growths from a preexisting shallow marine platform of any kind in response to rising sea levels alone, without any foundation subsidence, and they may possibly acquire an atoll-like form. Subsidence alone, however, explains the great thickness of reef limestone below most atolls.

atom, smallest unit of a chemical element that retains its chemical identity. It can exist either alone or in combination.

A brief treatment of atoms follows. For full treatment, *see* MACROPAEDIA: Atoms: Their Structure, Properties, and Component Particles.

The earliest well-authenticated expressions of the view that the ultimate structure of matter is discrete rather than continuous are commonly ascribed to Leucippus and his disciple Democritus, two Greek philosophers of the 5th century BC. Their atomic hypothesis was adopted and incorporated into a materialistic philosophy of life two centuries later by Epicurus, another Greek philosopher. His views were eloquently transmitted to posterity by the Roman poet Lucretius in *De rerum natura* (*On the Nature of Things*), a work written during the lst century BC. Here are found assertions that matter is composed of invisible atoms, that all changes in matter are simply changes in the grouping of atoms, and that the properties of objects are due to differences in the size and shapes of the atoms.

The atomism of the ancient Greeks was echoed many centuries later by such prominent thinkers as Giordano Bruno, Francis Bacon, and René Descartes. All of the principal scientific figures of the 17th century, including Galileo, Newton, and Huygens, also seem to have been strong advocates of the atomic concept of matter. Finally, in 1808, the English chemist and physicist John Dalton succeeded in crystallizing modern scientific thought on the issue with his formulation of the atomic theory, the thesis that all elements consist of indestructible microscopic particles which are identical in weight and in every other property.

By the early 1900s any doubts that might have persisted about the reality of atoms had been swept away, and individual atoms were being counted and weighed. The two events that did the most to bring about this advance were the discovery of the electron (*q.v.*) and the discovery of radioactivity (*q.v.*).

Later findings established that every atom has a small nucleus around which orbit the electrons. Roughly 4,000 times as massive as all of the electrons of an atom taken together, the nucleus comprises more than 99.9 percent of the mass of the entire atom. This core consists of protons with a single positive electric charge and neutrons with no charge. The number of protons in the nucleus is the atomic number of any given element. The number of neutrons varies, and atoms with the same atomic number but different numbers of neutrons are isotopes of that element (*see* isotope). The sum of the neutrons and protons is the atomic mass number. The nucleus is surrounded by as many electrons as there are protons. Because each of the electrons carries a single negative charge, they balance exactly the positive charge of every proton, making the atom as a whole electrically neutral.

The electrons associated with a nucleus are localized, or concentrated, in various specific regions of space known as atomic orbitals. Depending on their energy and on rules dictated by quantum mechanics, orbitals are arranged in shells, or families, the more massive atoms having seven such shells. The total energy of each electron varies with its position in the structure, and each position is defined in terms of the number of the shell in which it occurs (the numbers proceeding outward from the nucleus), followed by a letter—*s,p,d,f*—representing different classes of orbitals within the shells. As a result of receiving more energy an electron may move from one orbital to another, as from a $3s$ to a $3p$ orbital. The number of electrons in each orbital is customarily given as a superscript following the orbital designation; thus the notation $4s^24p^1$ means that the atoms of a particular element carry two *s* electrons and one *p* electron in their fourth shell. The way in which the electrons occupy the various atomic orbitals available to them is the electronic structure, or configuration, of an atom. This structure determines the way the atom interacts with other atoms; it thus governs not only chemical processes but also most of the physical properties of bulk matter. *See also* ion.

atomic bomb, weapon with large explosive power that results from the sudden release of energy upon the splitting of the nuclei of certain heavy elements such as the isotopes plutonium-239 or uranium-235. The fission is provoked by a bombardment of the fissionable material by neutrons in a very rapid chain reaction (*see* nuclear fission). An atomic bomb is immensely more powerful than a bomb of the same size containing chemical explosive, and in addition to shock and blast, releases heat, light, and lethal radiation.

The first atomic bombs were built in the United States during World War II under a program called the Manhattan Project. Two different types were produced. One, using plutonium, was successfully tested at Alamogordo, N.M., on July 16, 1945. The other type, using uranium, was dropped over Hiroshima, Japan, on Aug. 6, 1945, devastating most of the city. A second plutonium bomb was dropped over Nagasaki on August 9, again producing widespread devastation. Since the development of the thermonuclear bomb (*q.v.*) in the early 1950s, atomic bombs and weapons have been relegated mainly to tactical rather than strategic missions in the arsenals of the nuclear powers.

A list of the abbreviations used in the MICROPAEDIA *will be found at the end of this volume*

---

atomic clock, chronometer that utilizes certain resonance frequencies of atoms or molecules to keep time with especially great accuracy. Cesium atoms are frequently used, leading to the term cesium clock. In fact, in 1967 the 13th General Conference on Weights and Measures redefined the second in terms of atomic standards: "The 'second' is the duration of 9,192,631,770 periods of the radiation corresponding to the transition between the two hyperfine levels of the ground state of the cesium-133 atom."

atomic energy: *see* nuclear energy.

Atomic Energy Commission (AEC), U.S. federal civilian agency established by act of Congress, signed (Aug. 1, 1946) by Pres. Harry S. Truman, to control the development and production of nuclear weapons and to direct research and development of peaceful uses of nuclear energy. The AEC on Dec. 31, 1946, succeeded the Manhattan Engineer District of the U.S. Army Corps of Engineers, which had developed the atomic bomb during World War II.

By the Energy Reorganization Act of 1974, the AEC was disbanded; in 1975 its functions were transferred to two new agencies, the Energy Research and Development Administration (ERDA; disbanded in 1977 when the Department of Energy was created) and the Nuclear Regulatory Commission (NRC).

atomic mass, the quantity of matter contained in an atom of an element, expressed as a multiple of one-twelfth the mass of the carbon-12 atom, 1.9924×10^{-23} g, which is assigned an atomic mass of 12 units. In this scale, 1 atomic mass unit (amu) corresponds to 1.6603×10^{-24} g.

The observed atomic mass is slightly less than the sum of the masses of the protons, neutrons, and electrons that make up the atom. The difference, called the mass defect, is accounted for during the combination of these particles by conversion into binding energy, according to an equation in which the energy (E) released equals the product of the mass consumed (m) and the square of the velocity of light in vacuum (c); thus $E = mc^2$. *See also* atomic weight.

atomic number, the number of a chemical element in the periodic system, whereby the elements are arranged in order of increasing number of protons in the nucleus. Accordingly, the number of protons, which is always equal to the number of electrons in the neutral atom, is also the atomic number. An atom of iron has 26 protons in its nucleus; therefore the atomic number of iron is 26.

In the symbol representing a particular nuclear or atomic species, the atomic number may be indicated as a left subscript. An atom or a nucleus of iron (chemical symbol Fe), for example, may be written ${}_{26}Fe$.

atomic radius, half the distance between the nuclei of identical neighbouring atoms. An atom has no rigid spherical boundary, but it may be thought of as a tiny, dense positive nucleus surrounded by a diffuse negative cloud of electrons. The value of atomic radii depends on the type of chemical bond in which the atoms are involved (metallic, ionic, or covalent bond). When the neighbouring atoms are not alike, as in sodium chloride, part of the observed distance between atoms is assigned to one kind of atom and the rest to the other kind.

The metallic radius of sodium atoms bonded together in a chunk of sodium metal is larger than the ionic radius of sodium in the compound sodium chloride. In sodium chloride, each sodium atom has lost an electron to become a sodium ion (charged atom) of unit positive charge. On the other hand, each chlorine atom has gained one electron to become a chloride ion of unit negative charge. The ionic radius of chlorine is nearly twice as great as the radius of a neutral chlorine atom. The bond between the pair of chlorine atoms in a chlorine molecule and between the carbon atoms in diamond are examples of covalent bonds. In these and similar cases, the atomic radius is designated as a covalent radius.

The distances between atoms and ions have been determined very accurately, for example, by X-ray diffraction analysis of crystals. Typical atomic radii have values of about one or two angstrom units. (One angstrom, 1 Å, equals 10^{-10} metre.)

atomic theory, ancient philosophical speculation that all things can be accounted for by innumerable combinations of hard, small, indivisible particles (called atoms) of various sizes but of the same basic material; or the modern scientific theory of matter that the chemical elements that combine to form the great variety of substances consist themselves of aggregations of similar subunits (called atoms) possessing nuclear and electron substructure characteristic of each element. The ancient atomic theory was proposed (5th century BC) by the Greek philosophers Leucippus and Democritus and was revived (1st century BC) by the Roman philosopher and poet Lucretius. The modern atomic theory, which has undergone continuous refinement, began to flourish at the beginning of the 19th century with the work of the English chemist John Dalton.

atomic time, time scale generated by atomic clocks, which furnish time more accurately than was possible with previous astronomical means (measurements of the rotation of the Earth and revolution about the Sun). Independent atomic clocks, now maintained at about 50 places around the world, remain in agreement within a few parts in 10^{11}; that is, their readings would differ by less than one second after an interval of 3,000 years. International Atomic Time (abbreviated TAI, from the name in French) is based on this system of clocks, which transmit signals to the International Time Bureau at Paris. That agency, in turn, uses the signals to standardize its own broadcasts of Coordinated Universal Time (UTC), the basis of standard time observed in 24 zones around the world.

Astronomical observations have shown that the Earth's speed of rotation is decreasing. The number of mean solar seconds in one year (one revolution of the earth about the Sun) decreases but not the number of atomic seconds. The atomic second was defined so that the numbers were the same in about 1900. In 1980 there was about one more atomic second per year. *See also* atomic clock.

atomic weapon: *see* nuclear weapon.

atomic weight, ratio of the average mass of a chemical element's atoms to some standard. Since 1961 the standard unit of atomic mass has been 1/12 the mass of an atom of the isotope carbon-12 (an isotope is one of two or more species of atoms of the same chemical element that have different atomic masses). The atomic weight of carbon is 12.011, the average that reflects the typical ratio of natural abundances of its isotopes.

The concept of atomic weight is basic to chemistry, because most chemical reactions take place in accordance with simple numerical relationships among atoms. Since it is almost always impossible to count the atoms directly, chemists measure reactants and products by weighing and reach their conclusions through calculations involving atomic weights.

The quest to determine the atomic weights of elements occupied the greatest chemists of the 19th and early 20th centuries. Their careful experimental work became the key to chemical science and technology.

Reliable values for atomic weights serve an important purpose in a quite different way, when chemical commodities are bought and sold on the basis of the content of one or more specified constituents. Ores of costly metals such as chromium or tantalum and the industrial chemical soda ash are examples. Content of the specified constituent must be determined by quantitative analysis. The computed worth of the material depends on the atomic-weight values used in the calculations.

Atomic-weight scales. The original standard of atomic weight, established in the 19th century, was hydrogen, with a value of 1. From about 1900 until 1961, oxygen was used as the reference standard, with an assigned value of 16. The unit of atomic mass was thereby defined as 1/16 the mass of an oxygen atom. In 1929 it was discovered that natural oxygen contains small amounts of two isotopes slightly heavier than the most abundant one and that the number 16 represented a weighted average of the masses of the atoms of the three isotopic forms of oxygen as they occur in nature. This situation was considered undesirable for several reasons, and, since it is possible to determine the relative masses of the atoms of individual isotopic species, a second scale was soon established with 16 as the value of the principal isotope of oxygen rather than the value of the natural mixture. This second scale, preferred by physicists, came to be known as the physical scale, and the earlier scale continued in use as the chemical scale, favoured by chemists, who generally worked with the natural isotopic mixtures rather than the pure isotopes.

Although the two scales differed only slightly, the ratio between them could not be fixed exactly, because of the slight variations in the isotopic composition of natural oxygen from different sources. It was also considered undesirable to have two different but closely related scales dealing with the same quantities. For both of these reasons, chemists and physicists established a new scale in 1961. This scale, based on carbon-12, required only minimal changes in the values that had been used for chemical atomic weights.

Chemical methods of determining atomic weights. In the late 19th century, chemists differed among themselves on the merits of two scales of atomic weights, one based on hydrogen with the assigned relative mass of 1 and the other on oxygen with the assigned integral value of 16. Values on these two scales differed by nearly 1 percent, and much effort was directed toward fixing the relationship between the scales more exactly by determining the combining-weight ratio of the two elements. The first results on this ratio had been published in 1821, and other measurements had followed at intervals, until the American chemists E.W. Morley in 1895 and W.A. Noyes in 1907 published their elaborate and definitive studies. Their results did not quite agree with each other, but the mean of the two investigations agrees well with that derived from more recent physical determinations of the relative atomic weights of the two elements.

In 1912 two American chemists, G.P. Baxter and C.R. Hoover, reduced weighed amounts of carefully prepared ferric oxide in a current of hydrogen and weighed the residue of pure iron. Their investigation yielded 55.8456 as the atomic weight of iron, in excellent agreement with the currently accepted value, 55.847 ± 0.003.

The relative ease of preparing highly pure metallic silver, together with the stability of silver chloride and silver bromide, led many investigators to determine the equivalence ratios

Atomic weights, 1984

(based on the assigned relative atomic mass of $^{12}C = 12$)

The values given here apply to elements as they exist in materials of terrestrial origin and to certain artificial elements. When used with due regard to the footnotes they are considered reliable to ± 1 in the last digit, or ± 3 if that digit is in boldface. Atomic weights of elements with no stable isotope are given as mass numbers, in parentheses, of the most stable isotope.

name	symbol	atomic number	atomic weight	name	symbol	atomic number	atomic weight
Actinium	Ac	89	(227)	Manganese	Mn	25	54.9380*
Aluminum	Al	13	26.98154*	Mendelevium	Md	101	(258)
Americium	Am	95	(243)	Mercury	Hg	80	200.5**9**
Antimony	Sb	51	121.7**5**	Molybdenum	Mo	42	95.94
Argon	Ar	18	39.94**8**†‡§ ‖	Neodymium	Nd	60	144.2**4**
Arsenic	As	33	74.9216*	Neon	Ne	10	20.17**9**‡
Astatine	At	85	(210)	Neptunium	Np	93	237.0482†¶
Barium	Ba	56	137.3**3**	Nickel	Ni	28	58.7**1**
Berkelium	Bk	97	(247)	Niobium	Nb	41	92.9064*
Beryllium	Be	4	9.01218*	Nitrogen	N	7	14.0067†‡
Bismuth	Bi	83	208.9804*	Nobelium	No	102	(255)
Boron	B	5	10.81‡§♀	Osmium	Os	76	190.2
Bromine	Br	35	79.904‡	Oxygen	O	8	15.999**4**†‡§
Cadmium	Cd	48	112.41	Palladium	Pd	46	106.4
Calcium	Ca	20	40.08	Phosphorus	P	15	30.97376*
Californium	Cf	98	(251)	Platinum	Pt	78	195.0**9**
Carbon	C	6	12.011†§	Plutonium	Pu	94	(244)
Cerium	Ce	58	140.12	Polonium	Po	84	(209)
Cesium	Cs	55	132.9054*	Potassium	K	19	39.098**3**
Chlorine	Cl	17	35.453‡	Praseodymium	Pr	59	140.9077*
Chromium	Cr	24	51.996‡	Promethium	Pm	61	(145)
Cobalt	Co	27	58.9332*	Protactinium	Pa	91	231.0359*¶
Copper	Cu	29	63.54**6**‡§	Radium	Ra	88	226.0254*¶ ‖
Curium	Cm	96	(247)	Radon	Rn	86	(222)
Dysprosium	Dy	66	162.5**0**	Rhenium	Re	75	186.2
Einsteinium	Es	99	(254)	Rhodium	Rh	45	102.9055*
Element 106δ	none	106	(263)	Rubidium	Rb	37	85.467**8**‡
Element 107□	none	107	...	Ruthenium	Ru	44	101.0**7**
Element 108□	none	108	...	Rutherfordium	Rf	104	(260)
Element 109□	none	109	...	Samarium	Sm	62	150.4
Erbium	Er	68	167.2**6**	Scandium	Sc	21	44.9559*
Europium	Eu	63	151.96	Selenium	Se	34	78.9**6**
Fermium	Fm	100	(257)	Silicon	Si	14	28.0855§
Fluorine	F	9	18.998403*	Silver	Ag	47	107.868‡
Francium	Fr	87	(223)	Sodium	Na	11	22.98977*
Gadolinium	Gd	64	157.2**5**	Strontium	Sr	38	87.62 ‖
Gallium	Ga	31	69.72	Sulfur	S	16	32.06§
Germanium	Ge	32	72.5**9**	Tantalum	Ta	73	180.947**9**†
Gold	Au	79	196.9665*	Technetium	Tc	43	98.9062¶
Hafnium	Hf	72	178.4**9**	Tellurium	Te	52	127.6**0**
Hahnium	Ha	105	(260)	Terbium	Tb	65	158.9254*
Helium	He	2	4.00260†‡	Thallium	Tl	81	204.3**7**
Holmium	Ho	67	164.9304*	Thorium	Th	90	232.0381*¶
Hydrogen	H	1	1.0079†§	Thulium	Tm	69	168.9342*
Indium	In	49	114.82	Tin	Sn	50	118.6**9**
Iodine	I	53	126.9045*	Titanium	Ti	22	47.9**0**
Iridium	Ir	77	192.2**2**	Tungsten (wolfram)	W	74	183.8**5**
Iron	Fe	26	55.84**7**	Uranium	U	92	238.029†‡♀
Krypton	Kr	36	83.80	Vanadium	V	23	50.941**4**†‡
Lanthanum	La	57	138.9055†	Xenon	Xe	54	131.30
Lawrencium	Lr	103	(257)	Ytterbium	Yb	70	173.0**4**
Lead	Pb	82	207.2§ ‖	Yttrium	Y	39	88.9059*
Lithium	Li	3	6.94**1**‡§♀	Zinc	Zn	30	65.38
Lutetium	Lu	71	174.97	Zirconium	Zr	40	91.22
Magnesium	Mg	12	24.305‡				

. . . Not available. *Mononuclidic element. †Element with one predominant isotope (about 99–100% abundance). ‡Element for which the atomic weight is based on calibrated measurements. §Element for which variation in isotopic abundance in terrestrial samples limits the precision of the atomic weight given. ‖ In some geological specimens this element has a highly anomalous isotopic composition, corresponding to an atomic weight significantly different from that given. ¶Most commonly available long-lived isotope. ♀Element for which users are cautioned against the possibility of large variations in atomic weight due to inadvertent or undisclosed artificial isotopic separation in commercially available materials. δNo name proposed as yet. □Element whose existence has not yet been confirmed, and which has not yet been named, either for reasons of recency or duplication of discovery; no symbol, accordingly, has been assigned.

(relationship between quantities of reacting chemical species) of various soluble chlorides and bromides with silver and the corresponding silver salts. The experimental procedures involved in such measurements were brought to a high degree of perfection in the laboratories of T.W. Richards and G.P. Baxter at Harvard University and of O. Hönigschmid at the University of Munich, and it can now be said that the observed ratios of silver to chlorine, bromine, and oxygen were in error by no more than 0.001 percent, 0.002 percent, and 0.003 percent, respectively. Such determinations made major contributions during the period up to 1940 to the reliability of the International Table of Atomic Weights.

It seems probable that a principal source of the errors now known to have affected the halide–silver ratios was the virtual impossibility of achieving true equilibrium between a precipitate of silver chloride or bromide and the solution in which it was formed (equilibrium: a state of balance between all reactants and products in a reversible chemical reaction, attained when two opposing reactions go on at equal rates). If the equivalence point (where each reaction has the same rate) can be determined for two substances that react in solution without forming a precipitate, attainment of equilibrium is more assured. An example is provided by combining the ratio of sodium carbonate to iodine pentoxide (which forms iodic acid when dissolved in water) with that resulting from the dissociation of iodine pentoxide to iodine and oxygen. Combining these ratios cancels an apparent minute deviation of the iodine pentoxide from its nominal proportionate composition, and values then derived for sodium, carbon, and iodine are consistent within 0.001 percent of presently accepted values.

Physical methods of determining atomic weights. Physical measurements are rapidly increasing in diversity and precision. The gradual change from atomic-weight values based on chemical determinations to values based on physical measurements is expected to run its course to completion, but it is difficult as yet to predict which physical methods will be the most accurate.

Basically, two types of physical measurements should be distinguished. First, there are those in which the atomic weight of an element is determined directly as an average appropriate for the isotopic composition of that element. Historically the most important technique of this kind is that of gas-density ratios depending on Avogadro's rule. The most promising method of this first type is the X-ray-diffraction method in which, ideally, the macroscopic density of a pure, perfect crystal is compared with the density of the atomic-scale-pattern unit, dimensionally determined by X-ray diffraction.

In the second type of physical determinations the atomic masses of nuclides are first measured. This can now be done with great accuracy by mass spectroscopy, the technique in which charged particles are separated according to their atomic masses, and from the energy changes in nuclear reactions. For elements composed of only one nuclide, extremely accurate atomic-weight values are thus directly available. The isotopic composition must be separately measured, however, for the great majority of the elements before their atomic weights can be calculated from the nuclidic masses. Mass spectroscopic measurements, calibrated by synthetic mixtures of isotopes, are generally superior to chemical and to other physical methods for elements with two or at most three isotopes. Thus, for some time to come mass spectroscopy is likely to remain the technique on which a large number of atomic-weight values are based.

Atomic-weight tables. The table of atomic weights here reproduced, with minor editorial changes, is published and biennially revised by the Commission on Atomic Weights of the International Union of Pure and Applied Chemistry. The Table sets out values intended to be as accurate as possible, so accurate as not to discard reliable knowledge; however, atomic-weight values are not carried to more decimal places than are justified by the variability of isotopic composition and uncertainty in determination. The Table is also intended to warn of some kinds of processed materials that need to be more closely characterized before published atomic-weight values can be applied with confidence; *e.g.,* lithium, which may have been subjected to isotopic separation in commercially available materials.

(H.S.P./E.Wi./Ed.)

Atomism (from Greek *atoma:* "things that cannot be cut or divided"), the philosophical doctrine that explains complex phenomena in terms of aggregates of fixed unitary factors and the scientific view that the material universe is composed of relatively simple and immutable particles too minute to be visible. The various visible forms in nature are thus traced to differences in these particles and their configurations.

A brief treatment of Atomism follows. For full treatment, *see* MACROPAEDIA: Philosophical Schools and Doctrines.

In order to understand the historical development of Atomism and, especially, its relation with modern atomic theory, it is necessary to distinguish between Atomism in the strict sense and other forms of Atomism. Atomism in the strict sense, as propounded by the Greek philosophers Leucippus and Democritus in the 5th century BC, should be regarded as an attempt to reconcile with the data of sensory experience the thesis of Parmenides that matter is unchangeable. Parmenides rejected the possibility of change on rational grounds; change seemed to him to be unintelligible.

Democritus agreed with Parmenides on the unintelligibility and impossibility of qualitative change, but did not agree with him on the impossibility of quantitative change. This type of change, he maintained, is subject to mathematical reasoning and therefore possible. By the same token, Democritus denied the qualitative multiplicity of visible forms, but accepted a multiplicity based on purely quantitative differences. Consequently, the only differences between atoms, according to Democritus, must consist in their size and figure. The infinite variety of observable things could be explained by the different shapes and sizes of the atoms which constituted them and by the different ways in which the atoms were combined. Observable changes were based on a change in combinations of the atoms. During such combinations or separations, however, the atoms themselves remained intrinsically unchanged.

Other forms of Atomism differed from that conceived by Democritus mainly in two points. First, some Atomists, notably Anaxagoras, did not restrict the differences between the atoms to purely quantitative ones, but accepted also differences in quality. Secondly, some Atomists regarded atoms as divisible, whereas Democritus had regarded them as indivisible.

In Greek philosophy there were also transitions between qualitative and quantitative forms of Atomism. Plato characterized the atoms of the four elements by different mathematical forms. Examples of qualitative atomism, based upon the doctrine of the four elements, are also found in Indian philosophy.

In evaluating the importance of Greek Atomism in the light of modern atomic theories, it should be borne in mind that in Greek thought philosophy and science still formed a unity. Greek Atomism, then, was inspired as much by the desire to find a solution for the problems of mutability and plurality in nature as by the desire to provide scientific explanations for specific phenomena. While it is true that some of the Greek Atomists' ideas can rightly be considered as precursors of later physics, the main importance of the old Atomistic doctrine for modern science does not lie in these primitive scientific anticipations. The great achievement of the Greek Atomists was that they took a general view of nature as a whole, which made a scientific attitude possible. To this both the quantitative and the qualitative Atomism contributed, the former by drawing attention to the mathematical aspects of the problem, the latter by drawing attention to the empirical.

While Democritus' influence was eclipsed by that of Aristotle, there were a few adherents of Democritean Atomism in later times, notably Epicurus and the Roman poet Lucretius, whose *De rerum natura* ("On the Nature of Things") of *c.* 60 BC constitutes one of the most exhaustive extant accounts of the theory. The general tenets of Atomism were revived under the influence of Arabic philosophers during the medieval period and Pierre Gassendi and others in the 17th century. The concept of monads proposed by G.W. Leibniz *c.* 1695 reflects the influence of Atomism on other philosophical systems.

Atomism, Logical (philosophy): *see* Logical Atomism.

Aton, also spelled ATEN, in ancient Egyptian religion, a sun god, depicted as the solar disk emitting rays terminating in human hands, whose worship briefly was the state religion. The pharaoh Akhenaton (ruled 1379–62 BC) reinstituted the supremacy of the sun god (*see* Re) with two startling innovations: the Aton was to be the only god, and he was intangible.

King Akhenaton (left) with his wife, Queen Nefertiti, and three of their daughters under the rays of the sun god Aton, altar relief, *c.* 1360 BC; in the Staatliche Museen zu Berlin

Foto Marburg—Art Resource/EB Inc.

In opposition to the Amon-Re priesthood of Thebes (*see* Amon), Akhenaton built the city Akhetaton (now Tell el-Amarna) as the centre for Aton's worship.

The most important surviving document of the heretical religion is the Aton Hymn, a prayer preserved in several versions in the tombs of Akhetaton. The hymn opens with the rising of the sun: "Men had slept like the dead; now they lift their arms in praise, birds fly, fish leap, plants bloom, and work begins. Aton creates the son in the mother's womb, the seed in men, and has generated all life. He has distinguished the races, their natures, tongues, and skins, and fulfills the needs of all. Aton made the Nile in Egypt and rain, like a heavenly Nile, in foreign countries. He has a million forms according to the time of day and from where he is seen; yet he is always the same. During the day Aton causes everything to flourish for the sake of his son Akhenaton and Akhenaton's consort Nefertiti." The Hymn to the Aton has been compared in form and imagery to Psalm 104 ("Bless the Lord, O my soul").

Akhenaton devoted himself to the worship of Aton at the expense of other duties and the subsequent loss of unprotected border lands. The new religion was too different and complex for the general populace to grasp. After Akhenaton's death the old gods were reestablished, and the new city was abandoned.

atonality, in music, the absence of functional harmony as a primary structural element. The reemergence of purely melodic–rhythmic forces as major determinants of musical form in the Expressionist works of Arnold Schoenberg and his school prior to World War I was a logical, perhaps inevitable consequence of the weakening of tonal centres in 19th-century post-Romantic music; by the time of Richard Wagner's *Tristan und Isolde*, for example, the emphasis on expressive chromaticism had caused successive chords to relate more strongly to each other than to a common tonic firmly established by intermittent harmonic cadences. Eventually, the chromatic scale of 12 equidistant semitones superseded the diatonic scale, the inseparable partner of functional harmony, to the extent that melodic–rhythmic tensions and resolutions took the place of the harmonic cadences and modulations that had determined the structure of Western music for centuries.

Atonality, although well suited for relatively brief musical utterances of great rhetorical or emotional intensity, proved unable to sustain large-scale musical events. It was in an attempt to resolve this vexing dilemma that Arnold Schoenberg devised the method of composing with 12 tones related only to each other, a method predicated on purely polyphonic considerations of the sort that had been largely abandoned during the Classical and Romantic eras but had, by the same token, been typical of pre-tonal and early tonal music. *See also* chromaticism; polytonality; twelve-tone music.

atonement, a recurring theme in the history of religion and theology, the process by which a person removes obstacles to reconciliation with God. Rituals of expiation and satisfaction appear in most religions, whether primitive or developed, as the means by which the religious person reestablishes or strengthens his relation to the Holy. Atonement is often attached to sacrifice, both of which often connect ritual cleanness with moral purity and religious acceptability.

The term atonement developed in the English language in the 16th century by a combination of "at onement" meaning to "set at one" or "to reconcile." It was used in the various English translations of the Bible, including the King James Version (1611), to convey the idea of reconciliation and expiation, and it has been a favourite way for Christians to speak about the saving significance attributed to the death of Jesus Christ on the Cross. Various theories of the meaning of the Atonement of Christ have arisen: satisfaction for the sins of the world; redemption from the devil or from the wrath of God; a saving example of true, suffering love; the prime illustration of divine mercy; a divine victory over the forces of evil. In Christian orthodoxy there is no remission of sin without "the shedding of [Christ's] blood" (Heb. 9:26).

In Judaism vicarious atonement has little importance. For a traditional Jew, atonement is expiation for his own sin in order to attain God's forgiveness. He may achieve this in various ways, including repentance, payment for a wrong action, good works, suffering, and prayer. Repentance and changed conduct are usually stressed as the most important aspects of atonement. The ten "days of awe," culminating in the Day of Atonement (Yom Kippur), are centred on repentance.

Atonement, Day of (Judaism): *see* Yom Kippur.

Atoni, predominant population of Timor, easternmost of the Lesser Sunda Islands, Indonesia, inhabiting the central and western plains and mountains of the island and numbering 530,000 in 1978. Of Proto-Malay and Melanoid stock, they speak a Malayo-Polynesian dialect called Timorese. Atoni legend claims they fled to their present location when Tetum (Belu) princes migrated to inner Timor. They cultivate corn (maize) and rice, raise pigs, and collect honey, beeswax, and sandalwood for trade. Unlike other ethnic groups on Timor, the Atoni do no fishing. Their agricultural cycle determines the rhythm of life, and a strict division exists between male and female roles in the agricultural process. Organized into patrilineal descent groups, Atoni families consist of a husband and wife, unmarried children, married sons, as well as married daughters until the bride-price is fully paid. The local political authority is the village headman. Although Christianity was introduced by missionaries after 1910, traditional animism and religious rites of passage (such as marriage and death) continue to be important. They honour a Lord of Heaven and a Lord of Earth, plus ancestor spirits and forces of the hidden world.

atopic dermatitis, allergic disorder of infants, children, and young adults. It is characterized by a redness, thickening, and scaling of the skin in patches, typically on the face, neck, hands, and feet, in the crook of the elbow, or behind the knee. The cause of atopic dermatitis is not known, but it shows a familial tendency and is more common in persons with other allergic manifestations. Atopic dermatitis often appears a few weeks after birth, lasting until about age two; remission then often lasts until puberty. Thereafter most cases run a fluctuating course until the mid-20s, when inflammation tends to disappear permanently.

atopy, type of hypersensitivity characterized by immediate reaction, with movement of fluid from the blood vessels into the tissues, upon exposure to allergen. Atopy occurs mainly in persons with a familial tendency to allergic diseases; reaginic antibodies (*see* reagin) are found in the skin and serum of atopic persons. Atopy may be contrasted with the condition called delayed hypersensitivity, in which allergic symptoms take hours or days to develop. *See also* hypersensitivity.

ATP: *see* adenosine triphosphate.

Atrato River, Spanish RÍO ATRATO, river in northwestern Colombia, rising in the western slopes of the Cordillera (mountains) Occidental of the Andes and flowing generally northward to empty into the Golfo (gulf) de Urabá of the Caribbean. Its upper course passes through Chocó department, and the river then forms the border between Chocó and Antioquia departments. The river is only 416 mi (670 km) long, but its large discharge of no less than 175,000 cu ft (5,000 cu m) of water per second, together with a very large quantity of sediment, is rapidly filling the gulf. Navigable by small boats as far upstream as Quibdó, the Atrato has been considered a feasible route for a transisthmian canal.

atresia and stenosis, absence, usually congenital, of a normal passage or cavity (atresia) or narrowing of a normal passage (stenosis). Most such malformations must be treated soon after birth. Almost any cavity or passage may be affected; some of the more important disorders are:

1. Anal atresia (imperforate anus), a malformation of the intestinal tract (about one out of every 6,000 births in the United States) with varying degrees of congenital absence of the anus and lower end of the bowel. It is often associated with other anomalies of development. Surgery is required to produce a functional anal sphincter.

2. Esophageal atresia, a disorder in which only part of the esophagus develops and often connects with the trachea. Surgery may repair the defect.

3. Bile duct atresia, a condition that is always accompanied by severe jaundice and that limits the person's capacity to digest fatty foods. Survival for a few years is possible, and in a small but increasing number of cases surgery is effective.

4. Intestinal atresia, which occurs about twice as frequently as intestinal stenosis; there is a total incidence of one out of every 3,000 births, with a disproportionately high incidence in the duodenum (the uppermost portion of the small intestine). Vomiting and complete obstruction dictate early surgery.

5. Aortic arch and heart valve atresias, which cause serious difficulty in early life but can sometimes be repaired by surgery.

6. Ureteric and urethral atresias and stenoses, which cause distension of the urinary tract above the obstruction, with impairment of kidney function and often infection.

7. Pyloric stenosis, a spasmodic narrowing of the opening between the stomach and the duodenum. It is a relatively common cause of illness in newborns, occurring four times more often in males than in females and more frequently in Caucasians than in Negroes. The defect requires prompt surgical care.

8. Aortic, pulmonary, and heart valve stenoses, all of which cause mild to severe circulatory difficulty in early life but can be repaired by surgery. *See also* agenesis.

Atreus, in Greek legend, son of Pelops of Mycenae and his wife, Hippodamia, elder brother of Thyestes, and king of Mycena. The story of his family—the House of Atreus—is virtually unrivalled in antiquity for complexity and corruption.

A curse, said to have been pronounced by Myrtilus, a rival who died by Pelops' hand, plagued the descendants of Pelops. His sons Alcathous, Atreus, and Thyestes set upon a bloody course with the murder of their stepbrother Chrysippus, the son of Pelops' union with a nymph. After the crime the three brothers fled their native city of Pisa; Alcathous went to Megara, and Atreus and Thyestes stopped at Mycenae, where Atreus became king. But Thyestes either contested Atreus' right to rule or seduced Atreus' wife, Aërope, and thus was driven from Mycenae. To avenge himself, Thyestes sent Pleisthenes

The House of Atreus

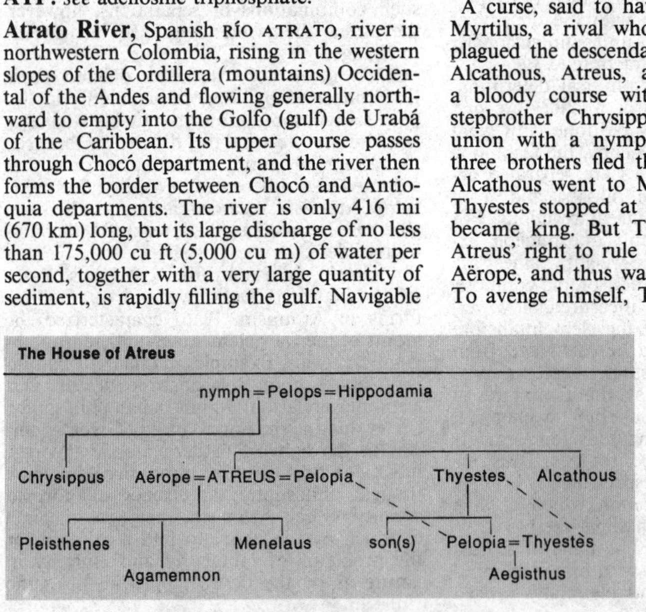

(Atreus' son, whom Thyestes had brought up as his own) to kill Atreus, but the boy was himself slain, unrecognized by his father.

When Atreus learned the identity of the boy, he recalled Thyestes to Mycenae in apparent reconciliation. At a banquet Atreus served Thyestes the flesh of Thyestes' own son (or sons), whom Atreus had slain in vengeance for the death of Pleisthenes. Thyestes fled in horror to Sicyon; there he impregnated his own daughter Pelopia in the hope of raising one more son to avenge himself. Atreus subsequently married Pelopia, and she afterward bore Aegisthus. Atreus believed this child to be his own, but Aegisthus was in fact the son of Thyestes.

Later, Agamemnon and Menelaus—sons of Atreus and Aërope—found Thyestes and imprisoned him at Mycenae. Aegisthus was sent to murder Thyestes, but each recognized the other because of the sword that Pelopia had taken from her father and given to her son. Father and son slew Atreus, seized the throne, and drove Agamemnon and Menelaus out of the country (*see also* Agamemnon; Menelaus).

Atreus, Treasury of, also called TOMB OF AGAMEMNON, BEEHIVE TOMB, or THOLOS, tomb built *c.* 1300 to 1250 BC at Mycenae, Greece. This surviving architectural structure of the Mycenaean civilization is a pointed dome built up of overhanging (*i.e.,* corbeled) blocks of conglomerate masonry cut and polished to give the impression of a true vault. The diameter of the tomb is almost 50 feet (15 metres); its height is slightly less. The enormous monolithic lintel of the doorway weighs 120 tons and is 29½ ft long, 16½ ft deep, and 3 ft high. It is surmounted by a relieving triangle decorated with relief plaques.

A small side chamber hewn out of the rock contained the burials, whereas the main chamber was probably reserved for ritual use. Two engaged columns of Minoan type (now in the British Museum, London) were secured to the facade, which was approached by a *dromos*, or ceremonial passageway, revetted with cyclopean blocks of masonry and open to the sky.

Atri, town, Teramo province, Abruzzi region, central Italy, northwest of Pescara, on a hill overlooking the Adriatic Sea 7.5 mi (12 km) to the east and the Gran Sasso d'Italia mountain group to the west. Atri originated as Hatria, a town of the Picenes, an ancient Italic people. In 282 BC it became the Roman colony of Hadria, which was later celebrated for heavy copper coins and for pottery. The family of the emperor Hadrian came from Hadria. In the Middle Ages, Atri passed from the popes to the Swabian imperial house and then to the Angevin dynasty before becoming, in 1393, the feudal estate of the Acquaviva family, whose descendants bear the title of dukes of Atri. Notable buildings are the 13th-century cathedral and the 15th-century palace of the dukes of Acquaviva.

The main industries are agricultural and include the raising of cattle and the production of wine, olive oil, grain, cattle, cheese and eggs, flour, macaroni, and terra-cotta. Pop. (1981 prelim.) mun., 11,215.

Atria (Italy): *see* Adria.

atrial fibrillation, irregular and uncoordinated rhythm of contraction of the muscles of the atria, the upper chambers of the heart. The most common of the major irregularities in heart rhythm (cardiac arrhythmics), atrial fibrillation may occur in spasms as a consequence of chest surgery, after blockage of a pulmonary blood vessel by a blood clot or some other type of embolism, or in association with serious infections or extreme fever. Otherwise, it is rarely present except in persons who have some form of physical defect, or disease, of the heart. Defects, for example, of the mitral valve—which functions between the upper and lower chambers of the left side of the heart—usually cause atrial fibrillation if they are severe enough to prevent the heart from pumping adequate quantities of blood into the circulatory system, a condition called congestive heart failure.

A possible complication of continued atrial fibrillation is the formation of blood clots in the atria. The clots get into the circulation and may, by blocking of blood vessels, cause death of tissue in essential organs.

A common form of treatment of atrial fibrillation when accompanied by ventricular paroxysmal tachycardia (rapid beating of the heart's lower chambers) is administration of the drug digitalis, which slows the heart's action. The fibrillation is sometimes stopped by administering electric shocks. *See also* ventricular fibrillation.

atrial septal defect, congenital opening in the partition between the two upper chambers (atria) of the heart. The most common atrial septal defect is persistence of the foramen ovale, an opening in this partition that is normal before birth and that normally closes at birth or shortly thereafter. The opening in the atrial septum results in the flow of blood from the left atrium to the right, causing enlargement of the right atrium and ventricle and of the main pulmonary artery. The usual treatment, the surgical closure of the defect, is sometimes made hazardous by serious disease of the pulmonary vessels.

Atriplex, genus of herbs and shrubs in the goosefoot family (Chenopodiaceae), containing about 100 species, often found on saline

Saltbush (*Atriplex*)

Kitty Kohout from Root Resources—EB Inc.

soils throughout temperate and subtropical areas of the world. The leaves of many species often are white and look scurfy or mealy. Several species are salt-tolerant shrubs of western North America, especially four-wing saltbush, or chamiso (*A. canescens*), and spiny saltbush (*A. confertifolia*). Young leaves of the garden orach (*A. hortensis*) are eaten. Orach (*A. patula*), sometimes called lamb's quarters, is a pale-green weed common on dry soils.

atrium, in architecture, originally an open central court of a Roman house and later of a Christian basilica. In domestic and commercial architecture the concept of the atrium experienced a revival in the 20th century.

In Roman times the hearth was situated in the atrium. With the developing complexity of the domus (a more capacious residence), however, the kitchen and hearth were removed

Atrium with impluvium and compluvium of the "House of the Silver Wedding," Pompeii, Italy, *c.* 1st century AD

Anderson—Alinari from Art Resource/EB Inc.

to other positions, and the atrium began to function as a formal reception room and as the official centre of family life. By the end of the Roman Republic, one or more colonnaded courts were added in the larger houses, removing from the atrium the last vestiges of family life. During the Roman Empire, the room virtually became the office of the owner of the house. Traditionally, the atrium held the altar to the family gods, the Lares. The atrium was designed either with or without columns; it had, universally, a marble basin known as the impluvium, which was situated in the centre of the room under the opening in the roof called the compluvium.

The term atrium is used in a generic sense (like the English "hall") for both consecrated and unconsecrated buildings such as the Atrium Vestae, where the vestal virgins lived, and the Atrium Libertatis, the residence of the Roman censor. In Rome the word atrium also signified any open court surrounded by porticoes placed in front of a temple. The concept of an atrium was also adopted by the early Christians. An open court, or atrium, surrounded by colonnades or arcades was often built in front of a Christian basilica (*q.v.*). The churches of S. Clemente at Rome, S. Ambrogio at Milan, and the Basilica Eufrasiana

Atrium of the basilica of S. Ambrogio, Milan, 1088–1128

Alinari—Art Resource/EB Inc.

of Parenzo (Poreč) in Istria (Yugoslavia) still retain their atria.

atrium, in vertebrates and the higher invertebrates, heart chamber that receives blood into the heart and drives it into a ventricle, or chamber, for pumping blood away from the heart. Fishes have one atrium; amphibians, reptiles, birds, and mammals, two.

For a depiction of the left atrium in human anatomy, shown in relation to other parts of the body, *see* the colour Trans-Vision in the PROPAEDIA: Part Four, Section 421.

In man the atria are the two upper chambers of the heart. Each is roughly cube-shaped except for an ear-shaped projection called an auricle. (The term auricle has also been applied, incorrectly, to the entire atrium.) The right atrium receives from the veins blood low in oxygen and high in carbon dioxide; this blood is transferred to the right lower chamber, or ventricle, and is pumped to the lungs. The left atrium receives from the lungs blood high in oxygen and low in carbon dioxide; this blood flows into the left ventricle and is pumped through the arteries to the tissues. The major openings in the walls of the right atrium are (1) the points of entrance for the superior and inferior venae cavae (the great veins that return blood from the bodily tissues), and for the coronary sinus, the dilated terminal part of the cardiac vein, bearing venous blood from the heart muscle itself; and (2) the opening into the right ventricle. The principal openings into the left atrium are the points of entry of the pulmonary veins, bringing oxygenated blood from the lungs, and the opening into the left ventricle. *See also* ventricle.

atrophy, decrease in size of a body part, cell, organ, or tissue. The term implies that the atrophied part was of a size normal for the individual, considering age and circumstance, prior to the diminution. In atrophy of an organ or body part, there may be a reduction in the number or in the size of the component cells, or in both.

Certain cells and organs normally undergo atrophy at certain ages or under certain physiologic circumstances. In the human embryo, for example, a number of structures are transient and at birth have already undergone atrophy. The adrenal glands become smaller shortly after birth because an inner layer of the cortex has shrunk. The thymus and other lymphoid tissues atrophy at adolescence. The pineal organ tends to atrophy about the time of puberty; usually calcium deposits, or concretions, form in the atrophic tissue. The widespread atrophy of many tissues that accompanies advanced age, although universal, is influenced by changes of nutrition and blood supply that occur during active mature life.

The normal cyclic changes of female reproductive organs are accompanied by physiologic atrophy of portions of these organs. During the menstrual cycle, the corpus luteum of the ovary atrophies if pregnancy has not occurred. The muscles of the uterus, which enlarge during pregnancy, rapidly atrophy after the delivery of the child; and after completion of lactation the milk-producing acinar structures of the breast diminish in size. After the menopause the ovaries, uterus, and breasts normally undergo a degree of atrophic change.

Whole body atrophy. Atrophy in general is related to changes in nutrition and metabolic activity of cells and tissues. A widespread or generalized atrophy of body tissues occurs under conditions of starvation, whether because food is unavailable or because it cannot be taken and absorbed due to the presence of disease. The unavailability of certain essential protein components and vitamins disturbs the metabolic processes and leads to atrophy of cells and tissues. Under conditions of protein starvation, the body protein is broken down into constituent amino acids, which serve to provide energy and help maintain the structure and cells of the most essential organs. The brain, heart, adrenals, thyroid, pituitary, gonads, and kidneys show less atrophy, relatively, than the body as a whole; whereas the fatty stores of the body, liver, spleen, and lymphoid tissues diminish relatively more than the body as a whole. The brain, heart, and kidneys, organs with abundant blood supply, appear to be the least subject to the wasting effects of starvation.

Associated with the widespread atrophy due to lack of protein is the atrophy of certain tissues that is due to deficiencies of specific vitamins. Atrophic changes of the skin increase because of the lack of vitamin A, and atrophy of muscle increases because of the unavailability of vitamin E.

After a growth period of human metabolism, there sets in a gradual decline: slow structural changes other than those due to preventable diseases or accidents occur. Aging eventually is characterized by marked atrophy of many tissues and organs, with both a decline in the number of cells and an alteration in their constitution. This is reflected eventually in the changed, diminished, or lost function characteristic of old age and eventuates in death. The changes in senescence are affected by both inherited constitution and environmental influences, including disease and accident.

Atrophic changes of aging affect almost all tissues and organs, but some changes are more obvious and important. Arteriosclerosis—the thickening and hardening of arterial walls—decreases the vascular supply and usually accentuates aging processes.

Atrophy in old age is especially noticeable in the skin, characteristically flat, glossy or satiny, and wrinkled. The atrophy is due to aging changes in the fibres of the true skin, or dermis, and in the cells and sweat glands of the outer skin. Wasting of muscle accompanied by some loss of muscular strength and agility is common in the aged. In a somewhat irregular pattern, there is shrinkage of many individual muscle fibres as well as a decrease in their number. Other changes have been observed within the muscle cells.

Increase of the pigment lipofuscin is also characteristic in the muscle fibres of the heart in the aged in a condition known as brown atrophy of the heart. Wasting of the heart muscle in old age may be accompanied by increase of fibrous and fatty tissue in the walls of the right side of the heart and by increased replacement of elastic tissue with fibrous tissue in the lining and walls of coronary arteries within the heart muscle. Abnormal deposits of the protein substance amyloid also occur with greater frequency in the atrophic heart muscle in old age.

Atrophy of the liver in the aged is also accompanied by increased lipochrome pigment in the atrophied cells.

The bones become progressively lighter and more porous with aging, a process known as osteoporosis. The reduction of bone tissue is most marked in cancellous bone—the open-textured tissue in the ends of the long bones—and in the inner parts of the cortex of these bones. In addition to changes in and loss of osteocytes, or bone cells, there is decreasing mineralization, or calcium deposit, with enhanced fragility of the bones.

Atrophy of the brain in old age is shown by narrowing of the ridges, or gyri, on the surface of the brain and by increased fluid in the space beneath the arachnoid membrane, the middle layer of the brain covering. There is shrinkage of individual nerve cells, with an increase in their lipochrome pigment content, as well as a decrease in their number. Sometimes the nerve fibrils have degenerated, and deposits called senile plaques may be found between the nerve cells, particularly in the frontal cortex and hippocampus (a ridge in the wall of an extension, or horn, of the lateral ventricle, or cavity, of the brain). Similar atrophic changes are seen in the brain in Alzheimer's disease, a condition of unknown cause most likely to occur in older patients. The mental deterioration (senile dementia) of the aged is the clinical manifestation of these changes. Senile atrophy may be increased and complicated by the presence of arteriosclerosis.

Simmonds' disease is a chronic deficiency of function of the pituitary gland that leads to atrophy of many of the viscera including the heart, liver, spleen, kidneys, thyroid, adrenals, and gonads.

A destructive or atrophic lesion affecting the pituitary glands with loss of hormones leads to atrophy of the thyroid, adrenal glands, and gonads and in turn brings atrophic changes to their target organs and the viscera. The decrease in size of the endocrine glands may be extreme.

Atrophy of muscle or of muscle and bone. Local atrophy of muscle, bone, or other tissues results from disuse or diminished activity or function. Although the exact mechanisms are not completely understood, decreased blood supply and diminished nutrition occur in inactive tissues. Disuse of muscle resulting from loss of motor nerve supply to the muscle (*e.g.,* as a result of poliomyelitis) leads to extreme inactivity and corresponding atrophy. Muscles become limp and paralyzed if there is destruction of the nerve cells in the spinal cord that normally activate them. The shrinkage of the paralyzed muscle fibres becomes evident within a few weeks. After some months, fragmentation and disappearance of the muscle fibres occurs with some replacement by fat cells and a loose network of connective tissue. Some contracture may result.

The skeletal tissues forced to inactivity by paralysis (*e.g.,* of a limb as a result of poliomyelitis) also undergo disuse atrophy. If there is a tendency for bone to become lighter and more porous in some particular area, a condition known as local osteoporosis, this can be recognized by X-rays within a few weeks. The cortex of the long bones becomes considerably thinned or atrophic, with decreased mineral content. Disuse as a result of painfully diseased joints, as in rheumatoid arthritis, results in a similar but lesser degree of atrophy of muscles concerned with movement of the involved joint; and local atrophy may also occur in the bone in the neighbourhood of the joint. A local osteoporosis of bone known as Sudeck's atrophy sometimes develops rapidly in the area of an injury to bone.

Severe or prolonged deficits of blood sugar deprive the nervous system of needed sources of energy and as a rare event result in degeneration of cells of the brain and peripheral nerves. The disuse atrophy of muscle or bone that may result is fundamentally similar to the other disuse atrophies of these tissues.

Persistent pressure will cause atrophy of a compressed cell, organ, or tissue, presumably because of interference with the nutrition and metabolic activity of the affected part. Cells in a local area (*e.g.,* in the liver) atrophy from the pressure of materials such as amyloid deposited around them. The pressure of an expanding benign tumour causes atrophy of adjacent normal structures. The pressure of a localized dilatation of an artery (aneurysm) will cause atrophy of tissues, even bone, on which it impinges.

Bulging of an intervertebral disk or growth of a tumour sometimes brings pressure on nerves near their point of exit from the spinal cord; if the pressure is prolonged, the muscles normally controlled by these nerves may atrophy. Most often the calf muscles are affected. Pressure as a result of involvement of the vertebrae at the level of the neck, or from compression of the network of nerves called the brachial plexus by the *scalenus anticus* muscle, produces similar effects in the upper chest and arms.

Simple disuse of muscle or bone, as, for example, from the immobilization produced when a limb is put in a cast or sling, results in atrophy of these tissues. In the case of muscle, the degree of atrophy is generally less severe than that caused by injury to a nerve, although the nature of the change is similar.

Localized atrophies of leg and arm muscles may result from hereditary or familial diseases in which the nerves of the spinal cord that supply them are inactivated or destroyed. In Charcot-Marie-Tooth disease, the atrophy involves mainly the peroneal muscles, at the outer side of the lower legs, and sometimes the muscles of the hand as well. It commonly begins in childhood or adolescence. Peroneal muscle atrophy is also seen in the hereditary spinal cord degenerative disease known as Friedreich's ataxia.

Atrophy of nerve tissue. Atrophy of brain or spinal cord tissue may be brought about by injuries that directly affect a localized area or that interfere with the blood supply to an area. When peripheral nerves are severed, degenerative and eventually atrophic changes ensue in the part beyond the injury. This type of atrophy is known as Wallerian degeneration. If conditions do not allow regeneration of nerve fibres from the proximal fragment of the cut nerve, atrophy is the eventual fate of the nerve tissue distal to the injury. Retrograde atrophy also occurs from disuse and affects the ganglion cells of the injured nerve.

Prolonged pressure brings about atrophy in the central nervous system as elsewhere. The pressure of an expanding tumour of the membranes covering the brain results in localized atrophy of the adjacent brain substance on which it impinges. In hydrocephalus more widespread atrophy of brain tissue results from the abnormal amounts of fluid confined within the rigid bony compartment of the skull. Increased pressure within the skull may force a portion of the brain through the *foramen magnum,* the bony opening at the base of the skull, and, if prolonged, results in a localized atrophy of cerebellar tissue pressed against the bony wall.

The late stages of chronic infections may be characterized by atrophy of the brain. A striking example of this is the variety of syphilitic infection of the nervous system known as general paresis in which the brain is shrunk and reduced in weight, the atrophy affecting mainly the cortex of the brain, particularly or most markedly in the frontal area. Occasionally the atrophy is local or affects only one side of the brain. The shrinkage of the brain tissue is mainly due to loss of many nerve cells of the cortex.

Atrophy of fatty tissue. Atrophy of adipose tissue of the body occurs as a part of the generalized atrophy of prolonged undernutrition. Localized atrophy of adipose tissue—lipodystrophy—may be the result of injury to the local area; *e.g.,* repeated insulin injections cause atrophy of fatty tissue at the site of the injections. Progressive lipodystrophy is a disease of unknown cause in which the fatty tissue atrophies only in certain regions of the body. It occurs mainly in women and often begins in childhood; the progressive wasting of adipose tissue affects mainly the face, arms, and trunk. In the affected areas, the specialized fat-holding cells of adipose tissue disappear.

Atrophy of skin. A widespread atrophic change in the skin has been noted as a prominent part of the aging process. Similar atrophic changes in the skin appear to be brought about or enhanced by excessive exposure to sunlight. While a number of abnormal conditions of the skin may include localized atrophic changes in the epidermis or dermis as a part of their lesions, certain generalized diseases of the skin are particularly characterized by such changes. The hardening of the skin known as scleroderma may occur in a localized, or circumscribed, form called morphea or as a more diffuse and severe disease. Advanced stages of scleroderma are characterized by marked atrophy of the tissue and appendages of the true skin. Atrophic thinning of the overlying epidermis also may occur, and the underlying fatty tissue and muscle may atrophy as well. The chronic form of the disease discoid lupus erythematosus also is characterized by atrophy. In advanced stages atrophy occurs particularly in the epidermis in focal areas. The thinned layer of epidermis may be a prominent feature of the microscopic appearance of the skin.

Atrophy of glands. Endocrine glandular tissues may undergo atrophy when an excess of their hormonal product is present as a result of disease. An example is seen in connection with a hormone-producing tumour of the cortical tissue of one adrenal gland, which may be accompanied by marked atrophy of the cortical tissue of the opposite adrenal gland. This probably results from disturbance of the delicate mechanism of hormonal stimulation via the pituitary gland.

Various endocrine organs (thyroid, adrenals, gonads) depend for their activity on endocrine stimulation by hormones of the pituitary gland. A severe general failure of production of the pituitary hormones results in the widespread endocrine atrophy of Simmonds' disease, as has been noted. Lesser degrees of pituitary functional disturbance may disturb a delicate balance, involving mainly one type of stimulating hormone of the pituitary, and may result in selective atrophy of the adrenal cortical tissue or of the gonads.

Glands that release their secretions through a duct (*e.g.,* salivary glands, pancreas) may become atrophic as a result of obstruction of the duct. In the pancreas, a complete obstruction of its duct results in atrophy of the glandular tissue, except for the insulin-producing islets of Langerhans, the secretion of which is absorbed into the bloodstream. Factors of both disuse and increased pressure may be present in the atrophy resulting from obstruction of the outlet channel. Similarly, rapid and complete obstruction of a ureter is followed by atrophy of the corresponding kidney.

Chemical-induced atrophy. Atrophy resulting from chemical injury is not common. In chronic arsenic poisoning, degenerative changes occur in peripheral nerves, resulting in weakness and atrophy in the tissues (usually legs or arms) to which the nerves are distributed. Similar results may follow the peripheral neuropathy of chronic lead poisoning.

atropine, poisonous, crystalline substance belonging to a class of compounds known as alkaloids and used in medicine. Its chief use is in ophthalmology, in which it is applied locally to the eye to dilate the pupil in the examination of the retina or to break up or prevent adhesions between the lens and the iris. It gives symptomatic relief from hay fever and head colds by drying up nasal and lachrymal secretions.

Because atropine relaxes intestinal spasms resulting from stimulation of the parasympathetic portion of the autonomic nervous system, it is prescribed in certain types of bowel distress and is included in a number of proprietary cathartics. It is used in the treatment of childhood bedwetting and is occasionally employed to relieve ureteral and biliary spasms. Atropine is no longer used as a respiratory stimulant. In the treatment of bronchial asthma to relax bronchial spasms, it has been largely replaced by epinephrine.

Specific effects of atropine include the arrest of secretion of sweat, mucus, and saliva; inhibition of the vagus nerve, which results in an increased heart rate; dilation of the pupil and paralysis of accommodation of the lens of the eye and relaxation of bronchial, intestinal, and other smooth muscles. Central effects include excitement and delirium followed by depression and paralysis of the medulla oblongata, a region of the brain continuous with the spinal cord.

The ubiquitousness of the effects of atropine is a distinct disadvantage in its clinical use; as a result, a number of synthetic substitutes with more specific effects have been introduced. Homatropine, for example, has a more transient action in the eye and little or no effect on the central nervous system; trasentine and syntropan, on the other hand, have the antispasmodic action of atropine without producing dilation of the pupil, dryness of the mouth, or an increase in heart rate.

Atropine, which does not occur in appreciable amounts in nature, is derived from levo-hyoscyamine, a component of plants such as belladonna, henbane, thorn apple, and *Scopolia,* all of the family Solanaceae; the best source is Egyptian henbane (*Hyoscyamus muticus*). It forms a series of well-crystallized salts, of which the sulfate is principally used in medicine. Both atropine and hyoscyamine have been synthesized from tropine.

Atrypa, genus of extinct brachiopods, or lamp shells, that has a broad time range and occurs abundantly as fossils in marine rocks from the Middle Silurian through the Lower Mississippian (the Silurian Period began 430,000,000 years ago and the Mississippian Period ended 325,000,000 years ago). Many species of *Atrypa* have been described. The genus is easily recognized by its distinctive concentric growth lines and peculiar outgrowths of the shell. It is unusual that in some Devonian exposures the abundant remains of only the pedicle (foot) valves of *Atrypa* occur; the brachial (upper) valves are rare or absent—apparently because of some sort of selective ocean current action.

Atrypa spinosa, of Middle Devonian age, from Erie County, N.Y.

By courtesy of the Buffalo Museum of Science, Buffalo, N.Y.

'Atshanah (Turkey): *see* Alalakh.

Atsina, also called GROS VENTRES OF THE PRAIRIE, an offshoot of the Algonkian-speaking Arapaho tribe of North American Indians, from which they may have separated as early as 1700; they were living in what is now northern Montana and adjacent regions of Canada in late historic times and were culturally similar to other Plains tribes. Together with the Assiniboin, they were settled on Fort Belknap Reservation, Montana, where the combined population totalled fewer than 2,000 in the late 20th century. *See also* Arapaho.

Atsugewi: *see* Achomawi and Atsugewi.

Atsugi, city, Kanagawa Prefecture (*ken*), Honshu, Japan, in the Sagami Valley, at the confluence of the Sagami-gawa (Sagami River) and the Nakatsu-gawa. Until the late 19th century, it flourished as a river port, post town and centre for sericulture. Now an important communication and commercial centre for the surrounding agricultural region, the city has convenient road and railway connections with Tokyo. Industries include the manufacture of automobile parts and electric communications equipment. Atsugi also serves as a tourist base for the Nakatsu and Tsukui valleys. The Sagami-gawa is renowned for its sweetfish, which attract numerous fishermen in season. Pop. (1983 est.) 165,349.

Atsunobu (Japanese philosopher): *see* Kaibara Ekiken.

Atsuta, ward (*ku*), Nagoya city, Aichi Prefecture (*ken*), Japan. A port and early religious centre, Atsuta in the Tokugawa era (1603–1867) was one of the most prosperous post towns on the Tōkaidō (Eastern Sea Highway) between Kyōto and Tokyo. Based on a pre-World War II munitions industry, the city currently produces automobiles, glass, musical instruments, rubber, and cedar products. A highlight of the city is the Shintō Atsuta Shrine, containing a sword, sacred since ancient times. Pop. (1980) 65,553.

attachment, in law, a writ issuing from a court of law to seize the person or property of a defendant. In several of the older states in the United States, attachments against property are issued at the commencement of suits to secure any judgment that may be entered for the plaintiff. In other states, attachments before a judgment are issued only against the property of nonresidents or upon specific statutory grounds relating to fraud or the like. In such cases, the plaintiff is commonly required to post an indemnity bond. An attachment may also be issued after a judgment, the term frequently being used to designate a levy upon a bank account, wages, or other intangible assets of the debtor. *See also* garnishment.

attack aircraft, also called GROUND ATTACK AIRCRAFT, or CLOSE SUPPORT AIRCRAFT, a type of military plane used during and since World War II primarily to support ground troops by low-level bombing and strafing attacks on enemy ground forces, vehicles, and installations on and near battlefields. Thus, the Douglas B-26 Invader, a piston-engine light bomber first flown in 1942 and used extensively in World War II, continued in service after the war, variously labelled B-26 and A-26. In improved and modernized variations, it filled a counterinsurgency role in the Vietnam War. Another World War II airplane, the North American F-51 Mustang, remained in service well into the 1970s in several countries. The Douglas A-1 Skyraider, first flown in 1945, was produced (3,180 in all variants) until 1957. It was used extensively in Vietnam. Both the F-51 and the A-1 are piston-engine aircraft.

Since World War II more sophisticated jet aircraft have been developed for the attack mission. The Grumman A-6 Intruder, first flown in 1960, is a two-engine, two-seat, carrier-based, long-range strike aircraft of the U.S. Navy. Variants have been developed as refuelling tankers, for finding targets at night in Vietnam, and for electronic countermeasures operations. The U.S. Navy's McDonnell Douglas A-4 Skyhawk, first flown in 1954, is a single-seat, single-engine aircraft that has been used both for carrier and (by other countries) for land-based operations. More than 2,700 had been delivered by 1975. The British Hawker Siddeley Harrier is the world's first V/STOL (vertical and short take-off and landing) fighter, first flown in 1967. It is in service with the Royal Air Force, the Royal Navy, and the U.S. Marine Corps. The Ling-Temco-Vought A-7 Corsair II, first flown in 1965, was developed by the U.S. Navy for carrier operations, and subsequently it was used also by the U.S. Air Force; it has night target-finding and all-weather capability. It replaced the A-4 Skyhawk. The Fairchild A-10A, a two-seat, twin-engine aircraft first flown in 1972, became in the mid-1970s the principal close-support attack aircraft of the U.S. Air Force.

European members of the attack aircraft family include the Sepecat Jaguar, a twin-engine, single-seat, tactical strike fighter developed jointly by the United Kingdom and France. It is also produced as a two-seat trainer, and another of its several roles is as the Panavia MRCA (Multi-Role Combat Aircraft), a two-seat, twin-engine, Mach 2 multi-purpose fighter developed jointly by the United Kingdom, West Germany, and Italy. The Jaguar entered service for the United Kingdom and France in 1972–73; the MRCA went into service for its three countries in the late 1970s.

The Soviet Union's attack aircraft, like its interceptor fighters, are of evolutionary design, many dating back to the 1950s and early 1960s. Its current standard ground attack fighter is the Sukhoy SU-7 Fitter, a single-seat, single-engine aircraft that originally entered service in the late 1950s and has been progressively improved. A variable-wing version was introduced in 1967. The SU-7 also serves in the air forces of Czechoslovakia, Egypt, East Germany, Hungary, India, and Poland.

Attaignant, Pierre (b. *c.* 1480—d. 1552, Paris), one of the most prominent music printers and publishers of the Renaissance and one of the earliest to use single-impression printing. (Earlier printers printed the staff and the notes in separate impressions.) Before 1527 he began using a newly invented movable music type, in which a fragment of a musical staff was combined with a note on each piece of type. He used the new type in a book of chansons, *Chansons Nouvelles* . . . (1528). In 1538 he was music printer and bookseller to the king. His printings represent more than 150 of the outstanding composers of his day and include chansons, dance collections, masses, motets, psalms, and Passions. His 111 surviving publications are a rich source of information for early 16th-century music.

attainder, in English law, the extinction of civil and political rights (attaint) resulting from a sentence of death or outlawry after a conviction of treason or a felony. The most important consequences of attainder were forfeiture and corruption of blood. For treason, the offender's lands were forfeited to the king. For felony, they were forfeited to the king for a year and a day and then escheated (*see* escheat) to the lord from whom the offender held his tenure, a result of the concept that felony was a breach of the feudal bond. Subsequently, in Magna Carta, the crown renounced its claim to forfeiture in the case of felony. Even harsher was the doctrine of corruption of blood, by which the person attainted was disqualified from inheriting or transmitting property, and his descendants were forever barred from any inheritance of his rights to title. All forms of attainder except the forfeiture that followed indictment for treason were abolished during the 19th century.

As a result of the English experience, the planners of the U.S. Constitution provided that "Congress shall have Power to declare the Punishment of Treason, but no Attainder of Treason shall work Corruption of Blood, or Forfeiture except during the Life of the Person attainted."

Historically, a legislative act attainting a person without a judicial trial was known as a bill of attainder, or, if punishment was less than death, as a bill of pains and penalties. The power of Parliament to declare guilt and impose punishment by such measures was well established by the 15th century. During the Wars of the Roses, bills of attainder were used by rival factions to rid themselves of each other's leaders, and Henry VIII induced both houses of Parliament to pass such bills against ministers whom he had ceased to trust. Unlike impeachment, a judicial proceeding in the House of Lords on charges made by the House of Commons, a bill of attainder was a legislative act adopted by both houses with the formal consent of the king. The offenses charged in such bills were usually characterized as treason but did not have to satisfy established legal definitions of that or any other crime. Thus, bills of attainder have generally been deplored not only because they deprived the accused of a fair trial but also because of their typically ex post facto quality. The dominant faction of the legislature could make any past conduct that it found offensive into a crime. In England, the last bill of attainder was that against Lord Edward Fitzgerald, who was condemned to death by act of Parliament for leading the 1798 rebellion in Ireland. The last bill of pains and penalties, introduced in 1820, led to a legislative trial of Queen Caroline, George IV's wife, on charges of adultery, but the bill was not passed.

Acts of attainder or of pains and penalties were passed by some of the American colonial legislatures until the Constitution of the United States forbade them. In applying these prohibitions, the Supreme Court has expanded the historical conception of attainder. It invoked these clauses in 1867 in *Cummings* v. *Missouri* and *Ex parte Garland* to strike down test oaths passed after the Civil War to disqualify Confederate sympathizers from practicing certain professions. Similarly, in *United States* v. *Lovett* in 1946, the court invalidated as a bill of attainder a section of an appropriation bill forbidding the payment of salaries to named government officials who had been accused of being subversive. Later decisions, however, have declined to treat requirements of loyalty oaths as bills of attainder, although they have invalidated such requirements on other grounds.

Attalia (Turkey): *see* Antalya.

Attalus, Greek ATTALOS, name of three kings of the Attalid dynasty of Pergamum, grouped below chronologically and indicated by the symbol •.

• Attalus I SOTER (Preserver) (b. 269 BC—d. 197 BC), ruler of Pergamum from 241 to 197, with the title of king after around 230. He succeeded his uncle, Eumenes I (ruled 263–241), and by military and diplomatic skill created a powerful Pergamene kingdom.

Attalus' mother, Antiochis, was a princess of the Seleucid house, a dynasty founded in Syria by one of the successors of Alexander the Great. Shortly before 230 Pergamum was attacked by the Galatians (Celts who had settled in central Anatolia in the 3rd century BC) because Attalus had refused to pay them the customary tribute. Attalus crushed his enemy in a battle outside the walls of Pergamum, and, to mark the success, he took the title of king—the first of the Attalids to do so—and the cult name Soter. Next, he defeated the Seleucid king Antiochus Hierax in three battles and thereby gained control (228) over all the Seleucid domains in Anatolia except Cilicia in the southeast. But by 222 the Seleucids had won back almost all of this.

Attalus then turned to checking the expansionist ambitions of the Macedonian king Philip V (ruled 221–179). He fought against Philip with help from Rome and the Aetolians of south central Greece during the inconclusive First Macedonian War (214–205). In 201 he took the side of the inhabitants of Rhodes in their war with Philip, and with them he brought about, by diplomatic approaches in Rome, a new Roman intervention against Macedonia (Second Macedonian War, 200–196). Shortly before the final defeat of Philip,

Attalus died. The Pergamene ruler had also gained renown as a generous patron of the arts.

• **Attalus II** PHILADELPHUS (Brotherly) (b. 220 BC—d. 138), king of Pergamum, in northwest Anatolia, from 159 until his death. He was the second son of King Attalus I Soter (ruled 241–197) and brother of Eumenes II (ruled 197–159), whom he succeeded. Before his accession he had been a loyal assistant to his brother, commanding the Pergamene forces that were fighting beside the Romans in campaigns in Galatia (189) and Greece (171). Attalus' frequent ambassadorial missions to Rome earned him a favourable reputation there, and he maintained close ties with the Romans after becoming king. They helped him hold his own in his struggle (156–154) against Prusias II, the aggressive king of Bithynia in northern Anatolia, and they conspired with him to aid the pretender Alexander Balas in overthrowing the Seleucid king Demetrius I in 150.

• **Attalus III** PHILOMETOR EUERGETES (Loving-his-mother Benefactor) (b. *c.* 170 BC—d. 133), king of Pergamum from 138 to 133 who, by bequeathing his domains to Rome, ended the history of Pergamum as an independent political entity. He was the son of Eumenes II (ruled 197–159) and nephew of Attalus II Philadelphus (ruled 159–138). Little is known of his reign. Attalus is said to have behaved tyrannically at first, but he evidently settled down to a quiet and studious life. His motives for bequeathing Pergamum to Rome are obscure. In 129 Rome organized the kingdom into the province of Asia.

Attapu, also spelled ATTOPEU, town and *khouèng* (province), southern Laos, bordering Kampuchea (Cambodia) and southern Vietnam. The town, the provincial seat, is on the Xé Kong, a tributary of the Mekong River. Most of the province of 4,600 sq mi (11,900 sq km) lies in the western slopes and foothills of the Chaîne Annamitique (Annamite Chain). Alluvial gold deposits have been found in the province. The region is occupied by the Lao-Theng (Lao-Theung; a Kha or Mountain Mon-Khmer people), who constitute some 70 percent of the provincial population and practice shifting cultivation. Much of the remainder are Lao-Tai, who practice rice culture on the limited wetlands. From 1963 Attapu was a major staging area for the Ho Chi Minh Trail, the Vietnamese Communist supply route through eastern Laos to the south, during the Vietnam War. Pop. (latest est.) town, 3,000; (1973 est.) province, 99,000.

attapulgite, fibrous clay mineral found at Attapulgus, Georgia, belonging to the palygorskite group. *See* palygorskite.

ʿAṭṭār, Farīd od-Dīn (Moḥammad ebn Ebrāhīm), also called FARĪD OD-DĪN ABŪ ḤAMĪD MOḤAMMAD (b. *c.* 1142?, Nīshāpūr, Iran—d. *c.* 1220, Mecca), Persian poet who was one of the greatest Muslim mystical poets and thinkers, writing at least 45,000 distichs (couplets) and many brilliant prose works. As a young man Farīd al-Dīn travelled widely, visiting Egypt, Syria, Arabia, India, and Central Asia, finally settling in his native town, Nīshāpūr, in northeastern Persia, where he spent many years collecting the verses and sayings of famous Ṣūfīs (Muslim mystics). His name, ʿAṭṭār, may indicate that either he, his father, or his grandfather was an apothecary, physician, or perfumer. In modern Ṣūfī circles the name of ʿAṭṭār has a kabbalistic or initiatory significance. There is much controversy among scholars concerning the exact details of his life and death as well as the authenticity of many of the literary works attributed to him.

The greatest of his works is his well-known *Manṭeq oṭ-ṭeyr* (*The Conference of the Birds,* 1955). This is an allegorical poem describing the quest of the birds (*i.e.,* Ṣūfīs) for the mythical Sīmorgh, or Phoenix, whom they wish to make their king (*i.e.,* God). In the final scene the birds that have survived the journey approach the throne contemplating their reflections in the mirror-like countenance of the Sīmorgh, only to realize that they and the Sīmorgh are one.

Other important works of this prolific poet are the *Elāhī-nāmeh* ("Divine Book") and the *Moṣībat-nāmeh* ("Book of Affliction"), both of which are mystical allegories similar in structure and form to *Manṭeq oṭ-ṭeyr*. Other works include his *Devān* ("Collected Poems") and the famous prose work *Tadhkirat al-Awliyāʾ*, an invaluable book for information on the early Ṣūfīs (abridged Eng. trans., *Biographies of the Saints,* 1961). From the point of view of ideas, literary themes, and style, ʿAṭṭār's influence was strongly felt not only in Persian literature but also in other Islāmic literatures.

attar of roses, also called OTTO OF ROSE, ESSENCE OF ROSE, or ROSE OIL, fragrant, colourless or pale-yellow liquid essential oil distilled from fresh petals of *Rosa damascena* and *R. gallica* and other species of the rose family Rosaceae. Rose oils are a valuable ingredient of fine perfumes and liqueurs. They are also used for flavouring lozenges and scenting ointments and toilet preparations.

In Bulgaria, roses are grown in humid valleys, and their subsequent distillation has become an important, modernized state enterprise. Turkish Anatolia also produces some attar commercially. In the south of France and in Morocco, rose oil is obtained partly by distilling but principally by extracting the oil from the flower petals of centifolia roses, *Rosa centifolia,* by means of a suitable solvent. One ounce of richly perfumed attar may be produced from about 250 pounds of roses. Rose water is a by-product of distillation.

The principal odorous constituents are geraniol and citronellol. *See also* essential oil.

attention, the concentration of awareness on some phenomenon to the exclusion of other stimuli.

A brief treatment of attention follows. For full treatment, *see* MACROPAEDIA: Attention.

In everyday waking life, attention, or the awareness of here and now, is discontinuous; periods of absentmindedness and reverie remove one from the immediacy of one's experience. Attention is selective, focussed on only a small set of the wide range of stimuli presented, and is partly determined by motivational states. Severe pain, for example, may be ignored during the exigencies of battle or heroic acts.

Early notions. One of the 19th-century pioneers of psychology, Wilhelm Wundt, distinguished between the *Blinkfeld* and the *Blinkpunkt,* the wide field of awareness and the restricted point of attention, respectively. Wundt suggested that the *Blinkpunkt* could include about six items or groups, and speculated that attention is based in the frontal lobes of the brain. William James proposed a similar notion; for him, attention involved the active selection of the mind on certain stimuli, thereby making them clearer to the mind.

Other late 19th- and early 20th-century theories of attention concentrated on behaviour. In his famous experiments Ivan Petrovich Pavlov found that dogs that had been fed after hearing a signal would eventually salivate on hearing the signal alone, even before sensing their food. This indicates that the dogs had "paid attention" to the signal and had learned to associate the signal with food. Building on Pavlov's work, John Broadus Watson tried to eliminate the concept of attention. Watson's behaviouristic theory challenged the existence of "inner" mental states like awareness; what mattered instead were behavioral responses to sensory stimuli. Attention, then, was seen not in terms of a concentration of awareness, but rather in terms of responses to narrowly specified stimuli. Because behaviourism could not account for situations involving competing stimuli, researchers have turned to richer theories of attention.

Current notions. Current views of attention consider it against a background of "preattentive processes," *i.e.,* unfocussed awareness that can be focussed when necessary. While a person is learning a task, such as knitting, the actions involved require close attention. But the knitter, as competence grows, can easily pay attention to something else, such as a television program or a conversation. The person's attention is called back to the activity only when a special situation arises, such as having to change yarn, or after having made a mistake. This indicates that once the skill is learned it is carried out preattentively.

Various factors may trigger shifts from preattention to full attention, including inborn or acquired tendencies and drives; interests and prejudices; a stimulus' novelty, significance, or complexity; and a person's social role.

Physiological changes related to attentiveness may include an increase in pulse rate, arrested respiration, increase in muscle tension, and a drop in skin resistance. Often, however, the only signs of attention are in the brain itself. Stimulation of any sense organ relays nerve impulses to various regions of the cerebral cortex. Electrical responses of the cortex evoked by these sensory signals can be detected by the electroencephalograph (EEG; *see* electroencephalography).

Experiments have shown that when a person is given a signal that indicates a second signal will follow shortly, the EEG readings show a slow change in the negative voltage of the brain's cortex. This change is called the CNV, for contingent negative variation, and is considered to be the most clear-cut physical correlate of attention. The CNV is at its highest when an individual must make a decision based on new information and hence needs to attend closely to a certain set of incoming messages. Correspondingly, the CNV is at its lowest when attention is split over information from a variety of messages. Thus, it is theorized that the function of the CNV is to make parts of the brain more sensitive to messages expected from the senses. How the CNV increases brain sensitivity—and how the CNV is itself produced—are matters involving extremely complex chemical reactions. Consequently, chemical changes in the body induced by drugs, lack of oxygen, and other causes often adversely affect the mechanisms of attention.

The development of computers has stimulated theorists to propose analogies between attention and the way machines handle information. Such an approach, known as information theory, focusses on mechanisms of the neural system which may impose order on the raging flood of incoming information, allowing it to be attended to selectively. Such mechanisms, which seem to be located in various parts of the brain, deal with many sorts of information by means of different criteria of selection. The complexity of this model is heightened by the fact that attention is at least partly subject to voluntary control.

See also biofeedback; learning; motivation.

Atterbom, Per Daniel Amadeus (b. Jan. 19, 1790, Åsbo, Swed.—d. July 21, 1855, Stockholm), leader in the Swedish Romantic movement; a poet, literary historian, and professor of philosophy, aesthetics, and modern literature. While a student at Uppsala he founded, with some friends, the society Musis Amici (1807; renamed Auroraförbundet, 1808). Publishing in the group's periodical,

Phosphorus, and in *Svensk Literatur Tidning* ("Swedish Literary News"), he became the leading poet and essayist of the new school of

Atterbom, oil painting by J.G. Sandberg, 1841; in Gripsholm Castle, Sweden
By courtesy of the Svenska Portrattarkivet, Stockholm

Swedish writers. He also contributed polemical articles against the old, pseudoclassical school in *Polyfem,* the organ of the Stockholm Romantics.

His greatest poetic work is the fairy-tale play *Lycksalighetens ö,* 2 vol. (1824–27; "The Isle of the Blessed"), which, on the literal level, deals with King Astolf, who deserts his northern kingdom for the temptations of sensual beauty, and, on the symbolic level, with the beguiling power of imagination in the history of poetry. Other works are *Blommorna* (1812; "The Flowers"), a cycle of poems envisioning eternal life beyond death; the unfinished *Fågel blå* (1814; "The Blue Bird"); and *Svenska siare och skalder* (1841–55; "Swedish Prophets and Poets"), a book that earned Atterbom the rank of Sweden's first great literary historian. In this six-volume work, distinguished for its style and erudition, Atterbom shows an appreciation for the writings he had recklessly attacked in his youth.

Atterbury, Francis (b. March 6, 1663, Milton, Buckinghamshire, Eng.—d. March 4, 1732, Paris), Anglican bishop, a brilliant polemical writer and orator who was a leader of the Tory High Church Party during the reign of Queen Anne (1702–14); later, he was a prominent Jacobite supporting Stuart claims to the English throne.

Educated at Oxford University, Atterbury took holy orders in 1687 and soon earned renown as a preacher in London. He led the campaign for the renewal of convocations (assemblies of Anglican churchmen), which were resumed in 1701. In 1704 Atterbury was made dean of Carlisle, and in 1710 he helped defend the High Church preacher Henry Sacheverell, who was impeached by Parliament for undermining the principles of the English Revolution of 1688–89. Queen Anne appointed Atterbury bishop of Rochester in 1713, and he associated closely with Viscount Bolingbroke, but his Jacobite sympathies cost him the favour of Anne's Hanoverian successor, King George I (ruled 1714–27). By 1717 he was in correspondence with the exiled Stuart claimant, James Edward, the Old Pretender. Five years later Atterbury was arrested for alleged complicity in a Jacobite plot against George. Exiled, he spent most of the rest of his life in James's service.

Atterbury befriended many major English writers of his day, including the poet Alexander Pope and the satirist Jonathan Swift. His own literary contribution lay in his topical polemical writings. H.C. Beeching's *Francis Atterbury* was published in 1909; see also G.V. Bennett, *The Tory Crisis in Church and State* (1975).

aṭṭhakathā (Pāli: "explanation"), commentaries on the Pāli Buddhist canon that provide much information on the society, culture, and religious history of ancient India and Ceylon (Sri Lanka). The earliest commentaries, written in Pāli, may have reached Ceylon along with the canon itself by the 3rd century BC. Between then and the 1st century AD they were translated into Sinhalese, and others were written in that language. In the 5th century the greatest commentator, Buddhaghosa, produced a reworking in Pāli of much of the earlier material plus Dravidian commentaries and Sinhalese traditions. Within a century or two, others, notably Dhammapāla, produced similar works on parts of the canon that Buddhaghosa had not covered.

The earlier *aṭṭhakathā* have not survived, but the works of Buddhaghosa and his successors are mines of information on the development of life and thought in the Theravāda Buddhist community and provide much secular and legendary material as well. Doctrinally orthodox and stylistically elegant, they offer section-by-section philological and exegetical commentary, a critical comparison of various authorities, and lucid narrative.

These commentaries were themselves the subject of later commentaries known as *ṭīkā* ("commentary"), and these in turn by others called *anuṭīkā* ("further commentary"). The earlier *aṭṭhakathā* also served as sources for the epic chronicles of Ceylon, the *Dīpavaṃsa* ("History of the Island") and *Mahāvaṃsa* ("Great History").

To make the best use of the Britannica, consult the INDEX *first*

attic, in architecture, story immediately under the roof of a structure and wholly or partly within the roof framing. Originally, the word denoted any portion of a wall above the main cornice. Utilized by the ancient Romans principally for decorative purposes and inscriptions, as in triumphal arches, it became an important part of the Renaissance facade,

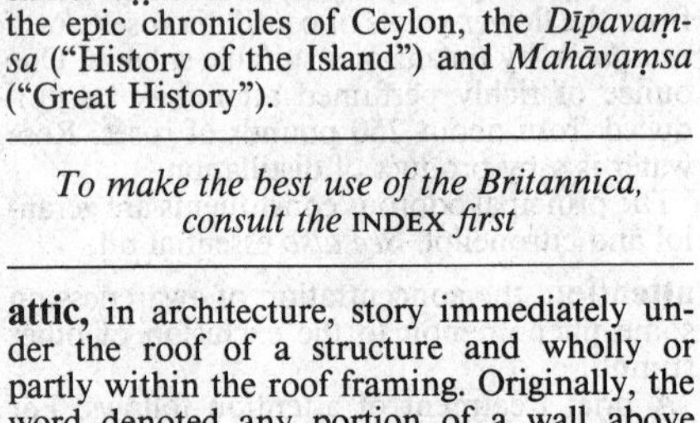

Inscribed attic surmounting the main cornice of the Arch of Titus, Rome, AD 81
A.F. Kersting

often enclosing an additional story, the windows of which became part of the decoration.

Attica, Greek ATTIKĒ, modern ATTIKÍ, ancient district of east central Greece; Athens was its chief city. Bordering the sea on the south and east, Attica attracted maritime trade. In early times there were several independent settlements there, centring on Eleusis, Athens, and Marathon. Athens may have been paramount in the Mycenaean age, but in the historical period it did not completely control Attica until the 7th century. The modern department (*nomós*) of Attica has its administrative centre at Athens and extends farther west than the ancient district, taking in Megara on the Isthmus of Corinth.

Atticus, Herodes: *see* Herodes Atticus.

Atticus, Titus Pomponius (b. 109 BC, Rome—d. 32 BC), Roman *eques* ("knight"), Epicurean, and patron of letters, best remembered for his connection with Cicero, with whom he was educated. His name was Titus Pomponius, that of Atticus being given him later from his long residence in Athens (88–65 BC) and his intimate acquaintance with Greek literature and language; he assumed the name of Quintus Caecilius Pomponianus when his rich uncle, Quintus Caecilius, died in 58.

Pomponius transferred himself and his fortune to Athens in 88 in order to escape the civil war. He lived quietly, devoting himself to study and business interests, and on his return to Rome he kept aloof from political life. His most intimate friend was Cicero, whose correspondence with him extended over many years.

Of his writings none is extant, although he wrote a history, in Greek, of Cicero's consulship, a Roman history down to 54 BC, and genealogical works. His most important work was the edition of the letters addressed to him by Cicero.

Attikē (ancient Greek district): *see* Attica.

Attikí, English ATTIKA, ancient Greek ATTIKE, *nomós* (department) of east central Greece. The *nomós* is bounded on the northwest by Boeotia, on the west by Kórinthos, on the south by the Gulf of Corinth and the Saronic Gulf, and on the north and east by the Aegean Sea. The name derives from the word *akte* ("promontory"), describing the district's position on the Greek mainland. It embraces an area of 1,303 sq mi (3,375 sq km), excluding Athens, its administrative centre and the national capital of Greece. Attikí *nomós* is made up of four arable plains watered by mountain streams flowing from nearby ranges. Geographically the plain of Attikí lies in a triangle formed by the sea coast and terminates in Cape Soúnion. The department of Attikí also administers the islands of Aígina, Hydra and Kethira. From early times Attikí attracted maritime trade, centring on several independent settlements: Elevsís (near ancient Eleusis), Athens, and Marathon—the latter where the Greeks were victorious over the Persians in 490 BC. Athens was paramount among these littoral cities by the 13th century BC but did not completely control Attikí until the 5th century BC. Attikí *nomós* is at the centre of much of Greek history and its historical monuments, such as the ruins of Eleusis, the remains of the temple of Demeter, and the Telesterium, the great hall of mysteries, are reminders of this heritage. The central region is rich in olives, vineyards (producing Kokkineli, a resinated rosé wine), figs, cotton, and aromatic shrubs. At Lávrion, near Cape Soúnion, silver, zinc, iron, and lead have been mined since ancient times. On Mount Parnassus bauxite has been found. Elevsís is a centre of heavy industry. Mount Hymettus and Mount Pentelikon are the sites of marble quarries. In the districts around Athens there is dairy farming, and poultry and vegetables are produced for the markets of the city. Sheep, goats, and cattle are raised on the pastures of the foothills. Pop. (1981) 342,093.

Attila, byname FLAGELLUM DEI (Latin: Scourge of God) (d. 453), king of the Huns from 434 to 453 (ruling jointly with his elder brother Bleda until 445). He was one of the greatest of the barbarian rulers who assailed the Roman Empire, invading the southern Balkan provinces and Greece and then Gaul and Italy. In legend he appears under the name Etzel in the *Nibelungenlied* and under the name Atli in Icelandic sagas.

Attacks on the Eastern Empire. The empire that Attila and his elder brother Bleda inherited seems to have stretched from the Alps and the Baltic in the west to somewhere near the Caspian Sea in the east. Their first known action on becoming joint rulers was the negotiation of a peace treaty with the Eastern Roman Empire, which was concluded at the city of Margus (Požarevac). By the terms of the treaty the Romans undertook to double the subsidies they had been paying to the Huns and in future to pay 700 pounds (300 kilograms) of gold each year.

From 435 to 439 the activities of Attila are unknown, but he seems to have been engaged in subduing barbarian peoples to the north or east of his dominions. The Eastern Romans do not appear to have paid the sums stipulated in the treaty of Margus, and so in 441, when their forces were occupied in the west and on the eastern frontier, Attila launched a heavy assault on the Danubian frontier of the Eastern Empire. He captured and razed a number of important cities, including Singidunum (Belgrade). The Eastern Romans managed to arrange a truce for the year 442 and recalled their forces from the West. But in 443 Attila resumed his attack. He began by taking and destroying towns on the Danube and then drove into the interior of the empire toward Naissus (Niš) and Serdica (Sofia), both of which he destroyed. He next turned toward Constantinople, took Philippopolis, defeated the main Eastern Roman forces in a succession of battles, and so reached the sea both north and south of Constantinople. It was hopeless for the Hun archers to attack the great walls of the capital; so Attila turned on the remnants of the empire's forces, which had withdrawn into the peninsula of Gallipoli, and destroyed them. In the peace treaty that followed, he obliged the Eastern Empire to pay the arrears of tribute, which he calculated at 6,000 pounds of gold, and he trebled the annual tribute, henceforth extorting 2,100 pounds of gold each year.

Attila's movements after the conclusion of peace in the autumn of 443 are unknown. About 445 he murdered his brother Bleda and thenceforth ruled the Huns as an autocrat. He made his second great attack on the Eastern Roman Empire in 447, but little is known of the details of the campaign. It was planned on an even bigger scale than that of 441–443, and its main weight was directed toward the provinces of Lower Scythia and Moesia in southeastern Europe—*i.e.,* farther to the east than the earlier assault. He engaged the Eastern Empire's forces on the Utus (Vid) River and defeated them, but he himself suffered serious losses. He then devastated the Balkan provinces and drove southward into Greece, where he was only stopped at Thermopylae. The three years following the invasion were filled with complicated negotiations between Attila and the diplomats of the Eastern Roman emperor Theodosius II. Much information about these diplomatic encounters has been preserved in the fragments of the *History* of Priscus of Panium, who visited Attila's headquarters in Walachia in company with a Roman embassy in 449. The treaty by which the war was terminated was harsher than that of 443; the Eastern Romans had to evacuate a wide belt of territory south of the Danube, and the tribute payable by them was continued, though the rate is not known.

Invasion of Gaul. Attila's next great campaign was the invasion of Gaul in 451. Hitherto, he appears to have been on friendly terms with the Roman general Aetius, the real ruler of the West at this time, and his motives for marching into Gaul have not been recorded. He announced that his objective in the West was the kingdom of the Visigoths (a Germanic people who had conquered parts of the two Roman empires) centred on Tolosa (Toulouse) and that he had no quarrel with the Western emperor, Valentinian III. But in the spring of 450, Honoria, the Emperor's sister, sent her ring to Attila, asking him to rescue her from a marriage that had been arranged for her. Attila thereupon claimed Honoria as his wife and demanded half the Western Empire as her dowry. When Attila had already entered Gaul, Aetius reached an agreement with the Visigothic king, Theodoric I, to combine their forces in resisting the Huns. Many legends surround the campaign that followed. It is certain, however, that Attila almost succeeded in occupying Aurelianum (Orléans) before the allies arrived. Indeed, the Huns had already gained a footing inside the city when Aetius and Theodoric forced them to withdraw. The decisive engagement was the Battle of the Catalaunian Plains, or, according to some authorities, of Maurica (both places are unidentified). After fierce fighting, in which the Visigothic king was killed, Attila withdrew and shortly afterward retired from Gaul. This was his first and only defeat.

In 452 the Huns invaded Italy and sacked several cities, including Aquileia, Patavium (Padua), Verona, Brixia (Brescia), Bergomum (Bergamo), and Mediolanum (Milan); Aetius could do nothing to halt them. But the famine and pestilence raging in Italy in that year compelled the Huns to leave without crossing the Apennines.

In 453 Attila was intending to attack the Eastern Empire, where the new emperor Marcian had refused to pay the subsidies agreed upon by his predecessor, Theodosius II. But during the night following his marriage, Attila died in his sleep. Those who buried him and his treasures were subsequently put to death by the Huns so that his grave might never be discovered. He was succeeded by his sons, who divided his empire among them.

Priscus, who saw Attila when he visited his camp in 448, described him as a short, squat man with a large head, deep-set eyes, flat nose, and a thin beard. According to the historians, Attila was, though of an irritable, blustering, and truculent disposition, a very persistent negotiator and by no means pitiless. When Priscus attended a banquet given by him, he noticed that Attila was served off wooden plates and ate only meat, whereas his chief lieutenants dined off silver platters loaded with dainties. No description of his qualities as a general survives, but his successes before the invasion of Gaul show him to have been an outstanding commander. (E.A.T.)

BIBLIOGRAPHY. The only comprehensive history of Attila in English is that of E.A. Thompson, *A History of Attila and the Huns* (1948); but the sources for his life and times are translated from the Latin and Greek by C.D. Gordon in *The Age of Attila* (1960). For what appear to be the archaeological remains of the Huns, see J. Werner, *Beiträge zur Archäologie des Attila-Reiches,* 2 vol. (1956).

Attis, also spelled ATYS, mythical consort of the Great Mother of the Gods (*q.v.*; classical Cybele, or Agdistis); he was worshipped in Phrygia, Asia Minor, and later throughout the Roman Empire, where he was made a solar deity in the 2nd century AD. The worship of Attis and the Great Mother included the annual celebration of mysteries on the return of the spring season. Attis, like the Great Mother, was probably indigenous to Asia Minor, adopted by the invading Phrygians and blended by them with a mythical character of their own. According to the Phrygian tale, Attis was a beautiful youth born of Nana, the daughter of the river Sangarius, and the hermaphroditic Agdistis. Having become enamoured of Attis, Agdistis struck him with frenzy as he was about to be married, with the result that Attis castrated himself and died. Agdistis in repentance prevailed upon Zeus to grant that the body of the youth should never decay or waste. Other versions also exist, but they all retain the essential etiological feature, the self-castration.

Attis was fundamentally a vegetation god, and in his self-mutilation, death, and resurrection he represents the fruits of the earth, which die in winter only to rise again in the spring. In art Attis was frequently represented as a youth, with the distinctive Phrygian cap and trousers.

attitude, in social psychology, a predisposition to classify objects and events and to react to them with some degree of evaluative consistency. While attitudes logically are hypothetical constructs (*i.e.,* they are inferred but not objectively observable), they are manifested in conscious experience, verbal reports, gross behaviour, and physiological symptoms.

The concept of attitude arises from attempts to account for observed regularities in the behaviour of individual persons. One tends to group others around him into common classes; he may assign people of a given skin colour to a single class and behave similarly toward all of them. In such case he is said to hold an attitude specific to that ethnic or racial group. He may lump together the rich or the pious or the lame and so is assumed to bear a particular attitude toward each group. Individuals also classify such objects as paintings or such events as battles and therefore may be considered to have distinctive attitudes toward nonobjective art or toward war.

The quality of one's attitudes is judged from the observable, evaluative responses he tends to make. He might react to everyone of the same ethnic background with expressions of dislike, with derogatory comments about their honesty or intelligence, or he may advocate repressive, exclusionary public policies against them. On the evidence of such negative responses he is said to have an unfavourable attitude toward that ethnic group. Someone who uniformly praises nonobjective paintings, who frequently attends museums that exhibit them, and who hangs their reproductions on his walls is judged to hold a favourable attitude toward nonobjective art.

Attitudes held by others are not directly observable; they must be inferred from behaviour. While one might consult his inner experiences as evidence of his own attitudes, only his public behaviour can receive objective study. Thus, investigators heavily depend on behavioral indexes of attitudes—*e.g.,* on what people say, on how they respond to questionnaires, or on such physiological signs as changes in heart rate.

Some authorities see the critical distinction between attitudes and a number of other terms to reside in their relative inclusiveness. Attitudes can be arranged in a hierarchy based on their degree of specificity or exclusiveness. "Values" are said to represent very broad tendencies of this type, "interests" being slightly less inclusive, and "sentiments" narrower still; "attitudes" are viewed as still more narrow predispositions, with "beliefs" and "opinions" being progressively the most specific members of this hierarchy. According to this terminology the difference is one of degree rather than of kind.

Other investigators consider one's attitude toward any class to be the intensity with which he expects that group to serve his own values. For example, he may be asked to rate the extent to which he prizes given values (such as health, safety, independence, justice). Then he estimates the degree to which that class (say, politicians) tends to facilitate or impede each value. The sum of the products of these two ratings provides a measure of the individual's attitude toward the group. Thus, if he highly prizes justice, and judges that politicians severely interfere with it, his attitude toward that class is taken to be negative.

Attitudes sometimes are regarded as underlying predispositions, and opinions as their overt manifestations. A rarer distinction equates attitudes with unconscious and irrational tendencies and opinions with conscious and rational activities. Others refer to attitudes as meaningful and central and to opinions as more peripheral and inconsequential. A still more popular distinction refers attitudes to matters of taste (*e.g.,* liking a certain country or type of music) and opinions to questions of fact (*e.g.,* whether Zeus exists).

Some apply the term knowledge to what are held to be certainties and attitudes to what is uncertain, even using them to mean "true" and "false" beliefs, respectively. Another suggestion is that attitudes refer to beliefs that impel action and that knowledge is more intellectual and passive.

There are many confusing alternative conventions for distinguishing attitudes from such related concepts as values, opinions, and knowledge. This tends to generate unnecessary dispute and mere proliferation of language. Generally accepted terminology is lacking, and investigators often accept or discard distinctions as they judge them to be useful.

BIBLIOGRAPHY. A succinct overview of this subject is found in W.J. McGuire, "The Nature of Attitudes and Attitude Change," in G. Lindzey and E. Aronson (eds.), *Handbook of Social Psychology,* 2nd ed., vol. 3 (1969). A fuller discussion of the nature of attitudes and their effects on human behaviour and conscious experience may be found in M.J. Rokeach, *Beliefs, Attitudes and Values* (1968); and in D.T. Campbell, "Social Attitudes and Other Acquired Behavioral Dispositions," in S. Koch (ed.), *Psychology: A Study of a Science,* vol. 6 (1963).

Attius, Lucius: *see* Accius, Lucius.

Attleboro, city, Bristol County, southeastern Massachusetts, U.S., just northeast of Pawtucket and Providence, R.I. Settled in 1669, it was part of the adjacent town of Rehoboth until separately incorporated as a town (township) in 1694 and named for Attleborough, Eng. In 1887 it was divided by the creation of North Attleborough. Jewelry-making became an early enterprise (1780), followed by leather and textile manufacturing. The completion (1836) of the Boston–Providence Railroad stimulated the town's development. The jewelry industry (including costume jewelry, silverware, and plated ware) remains the chief source of employment, augmented by the production of machine tools, electronic components, and other light manufactures. Inc. city, 1914. Pop. (1980) 34,196.

Attlee, Clement (Richard), 1ST EARL ATTLEE OF WALTHAMSTOW, VISCOUNT PRESTWOOD (b. Jan. 3, 1883, Putney, London—d. Oct. 8, 1967, Westminster, London), British Labour Party leader from 1935 to 1955, and prime minister from July 26, 1945, to Oct. 26, 1951, who presided over the establishment of the welfare state in Great Britain and over the most important step—the granting of independence to India—in the conversion of the British Empire into the Commonwealth of Nations.

The son of a prosperous lawyer, Attlee himself practiced law briefly after studying at Oxford but soon became primarily interested in social reform. From 1907 to 1922 (except for the period of his World War I service) he lived in a settlement house in the impoverished East End of London. In 1907 he joined the

Attlee, photograph by Yousuf Karsh
©Karsh—Woodfin Camp and Associates

Fabian Society and in 1908 the Independent Labour Party. Entering East End politics after the war, he became mayor of the borough of Stepney in 1919 and a member of Parliament from Limehouse in 1922. In the first Labour government (1924) he served as undersecretary of state for war and, in the second Labour ministry (1929–31), he was successively chancellor of the duchy of Lancaster and postmaster general. When the Labour prime minister Ramsay MacDonald formed a national coalition government in 1931, Attlee repudiated him, and in the same year he became deputy leader of the Labour Party under George Lansbury. In 1935 he succeeded Lansbury, who was forced to relinquish the party leadership because of his uncompromising pacifism.

Although approving of the British declaration of war in September 1939, he refused to take office in Neville Chamberlain's government. In May 1940 he supported the prime ministry of Winston Churchill and, during the war, served in the war Cabinet as lord privy seal (1940–42), deputy prime minister (1942–45), secretary of state for the dominions (1942–43), and lord president of the council (1943–45). In May 1945 he led the Labour Party out of the coalition, and, after the decisive defeat of Churchill's Conservatives in the election of July 1945, he was appointed prime minister.

Attlee assumed office during the final conference of the Allies in World War II (at Potsdam, Ger., July 17–Aug. 2, 1945). After accepting the U.S.-inspired European Recovery Program (1948; the Marshall Plan), Great Britain joined the North Atlantic Treaty Organization for mutual defense (1949) as well as the Council of Europe for unity of the European peoples (1949). At home, a program of economic "austerity" was rigorously administered by Sir Stafford Cripps, Attlee's chancellor of the exchequer and minister of economic affairs (1947–50). Major British industries were nationalized, including coal, steel, railways, civil aviation, telegraph services, and the Bank of England. The government created the National Health Service and put into effect other features of the comprehensive welfare scheme advocated (1942) by the economist William Henry Beveridge.

During Attlee's tenure, independence within the Commonwealth was granted to India, a measure (in which he took great pride) that established the separate Muslim nation of Pakistan. Great Britain also conceded independence to Burma and Ceylon and relinquished control of Egypt and of Palestine, where the nation of Israel was founded.

In April 1951 Attlee's already weak position (the Labour majority in the House of Commons had been reduced to six) further deteriorated when two Labour leaders, Aneurin Bevan and Harold Wilson (afterward prime minister), resigned from the government over the introduction of health-service charges. When the Conservatives narrowly won the election of October 1951, Attlee resigned. On yielding the party leadership in December 1955, he was created an earl. In 1937 he published *The Labour Party in Perspective* and in 1954 his memoirs, *As It Happened.*

Attock, formerly CAMPBELLPORE, district in Rāwalpindi division, Punjab province, Pakistan. It has an area of 4,148 sq mi (10,743 sq km), consisting of arid, rocky mountain tracts broken only by the fertile Chach plain to the north and by the southern portion of the central plain, which is irrigated by tributaries of the Soān River. The chief crops are wheat, corn (maize), sugarcane, vegetables, and tobacco; horse breeding is widespread. The district contains woollen mills and oil fields; deposits of limestone, marble, and gypsum are worked. Pop. (1981 prelim.) 1,140,000.

Attopeu (Laos): *see* Attapu.

attorney, power of, authorization to act as agent or attorney for another. Common-law and civil-law systems differ considerably with respect to powers of attorney, and there is also considerable diversity among the civil law systems themselves. Many of the general powers of attorney that are important in civil-law countries come under the powers of trust in common-law countries.

In England, for example, one may be given the general power to carry out all of a certain type of act, such as carrying on a business after the owner's death, or one may be given the power to carry out some very specific act. In France a general authorization must specify the types of transactions the agent may engage in, whereas in West Germany a general grant of power carries no such limitation. Requirements for registration and formalization also may vary among countries. In Italy, for example, powers of attorney must be verified by specific formalities, whereas in France they may be authorized by mere verbal agreement.

attorney general, the chief law officer of a state or nation and the legal adviser to the chief executive, common in almost every country in which the legal system of England has taken root.

The office of attorney general dates from the Middle Ages, but it did not assume its modern form before the 16th century. Initially, king's attorneys were appointed only for particular business or for particular cases or courts, but by the 15th century an attorney general for the crown was a regular appointee. In time, he acquired the right to appoint deputies and became a figure of great influence as the medieval system broke down and new courts and political institutions evolved.

Today, the attorney general, who with his assistant, the solicitor general, is the crown's representative in the courts and the legal adviser to the sovereign and the sovereign's ministers, is a member of the government, but not of the Cabinet. He is consulted on the drafting of all government bills, advises government departments on matters of law, and has a wide range of duties in relation to the courts.

By virtue of his position as a law officer of the crown, the attorney general, who continues to practice as a barrister with the crown as his only client, is recognized by the bar as the leader of the profession. He has control of the office of public prosecutions, which gives advice on and often conducts criminal prosecutions. Certain offenses can be prosecuted only with the consent of either the attorney general or the director of public prosecutions. The attorney general also has the right to stay criminal proceedings in the superior courts.

The office of attorney general of the United States was created by the Judiciary Act of 1789 that divided the country into districts and set up courts in each one, along with attorneys with the responsibility for civil and criminal actions in their districts. The attorney general, a member of the Cabinet, is head of the Department of Justice. As such, much of his time must be devoted to administration.

The U.S. solicitor general has charge of the government's litigation in the Supreme Court. He decides, after consultation with the attorney general, whether to seek review in the higher courts of cases that the government has lost in lower courts. The decisions on which important cases should be prosecuted in the various districts and which should be appealed are not made without the approval of the president; the U.S. attorney general does not have the freedom from political influence of his British counterpart.

Every U.S. state has an attorney general, who is an elected official with duties similar to those of the federal attorney general. *See also* prosecutor.

Attucks, Crispus (b. 1723?—d. March 5, 1770, Boston), leader and martyr of the colonial action that precipitated the Boston Massacre. Attucks' life prior to the day of his death is still shrouded in mystery. Most historians say he was black, others argue he was an American Indian, while still others contend his ancestry was both black and Indian.

In the fall of 1750, a resident of Framingham, Massachusetts, advertised for the recovery of a runaway slave named Crispus—usually thought to be the same Crispus who became the first casualty of the American Revolution. In the 20-year interval between his escape from slavery and his death at the hands of British soldiers, Attucks probably spent a good deal of time aboard whaling ships.

On the evening of March 5, 1770, he led a group primarily composed of sailors—probably 50 to 60 in all—from Dock Square to the British garrison in King Street. According to John Adams, in his subsequent defense of the British soldiers, Attucks grabbed a Redcoat's bayonet after attempting to strike at Captain Preston with a long stick. Samuel Adams, on the other hand, maintained that Attucks did nothing to provoke the attack.

The soldiers fired their muskets, killing three of the Americans instantly and mortally wounding two others. Crispus Attucks was the first to fall. His body was carried to Faneuil Hall, where it lay in state until March 8, when all five victims were buried in a common grave. In 1888 the Crispus Attucks monument was unveiled in the Boston Common.

Attwood, Thomas (b. Oct. 6, 1783, Halesowen, Worcestershire, Eng.—d. March 6, 1856, Great Malvern, Worcestershire), British economist and leader in the electoral reform movement.

Attwood entered his father's banking firm in Birmingham in 1800. After his election, in 1811, as high bailiff of the city, he showed increasing concern with currency questions and

Attwood, detail of an engraving by Charles Turner, 1864, after a painting by G. Sharples

By courtesy of the trustees of the British Museum; photograph, J.R. Freeman & Co. Ltd.

sought more equitable representation for middle- and lower-income groups in the House of Commons. He founded, in January 1830, the Birmingham Political Union, regarded as the political organization most effective in exerting pressure on the government for passage of the Reform Bill of 1832. Attwood formed the union because of widespread economic distress, particularly after 1826. Through its action, working class protest was strengthened by middle class agitation for parliamentary reform to secure currency reform. The union's structure and methods were applied in many parts of the country. After passage of the Reform Bill, Attwood was elected a member of Parliament for Birmingham, for which he sat until 1839.

Atum, also called TEM, or TUM, in ancient Egyptian religion, one of the manifestations of the sun-creator god, and originally a local deity of Heliopolis. Atum's myth merged with that of the great sun god Re, giving rise to the deity Atum-Re. When distinguished from Re, Atum was apparently believed to have been

Atum, wearing the double royal crown, worshipped by the deceased Lady Ta-Chenat; painted stela, Third Intermediate Period; in the Louvre, Paris

By courtesy of the Musee du Louvre, Paris; Cliche Musees Nationaux, Paris

the sun god's first form, living inside Nu, the primordial waters of chaos, as an immaterial spirit until by the force of his own will he manifested himself in concrete form as Re. Thus in the legends of the sun he is identified with the setting sun and the sun after it has returned to the bowels of the earth to be "reborn" at dawn, while Re is recognized as the sun at its zenith.

Atwater, Wilbur Olin (b. May 3, 1844, Johnsburg, N.Y., U.S.—d. Sept. 22, 1907, Middletown, Conn.), U.S. scientist who developed agricultural chemistry.

Upon completing his undergraduate work at Wesleyan University in Middletown, he continued his studies at Yale, where his Ph.D. thesis discussed for the first time how chemical techniques could be applied to food. After further study in Germany, he began to teach at Wesleyan, where he was professor of chemistry for the rest of his life. In 1875 he was instrumental in persuading the Connecticut legislature to set up the first state agricultural research station in the United States, at Middletown, and in 1887, again at his prodding, Congress passed the Hatch Act, providing funds for agricultural experiment stations in all the states. He was the first director of the Office of Experiment Stations (1888).

He then turned his attention to calorimetry, and with E.B. Rosa, professor of physics at Wesleyan, constructed the Atwater-Rosa calorimeter (1892–97), which proved the law of conservation of energy in human beings and made it possible to calculate the caloric values of different foods. The tables Atwater devised in 1896 continued to be used throughout the world.

Atwood, Margaret (Eleanor) (b. Nov. 18, 1939, Ottawa), poet, novelist, critic, and champion of her Canadian heritage and her sex.

The writer's own resourcefulness and self-assurance may be traced to her early life experience; her family was continually on the move because of her entomologist father's work, which often took the Atwoods into northern, sparsely settled bush country. She began writing at age five and resumed her efforts, more seriously, a decade later.

In her early poetry collections, *Double Persephone* (1961), *The Circle Game* (1964, revised in 1966 and winner of a Governor General's award in that year), and *The Animals in That Country* (1968), Atwood ponders the knowability of man, celebrates the natural world he lives in, and condemns his materialism. Role reversal and new beginnings are recurrent themes in her novels, all of them centred on women seeking their identity: the surreal *The Edible Woman* (1969), *Surfacing* (1972), *Lady Oracle* (1976), *Life Before Man* (1979), and *Bodily Harm* (1981).

She taught English literature at the University of British Columbia (1964–65), Sir George Williams University, Montreal (1967–68), and York University, Toronto (1971–72); was writer-in-residence at the University of Toronto (1972–73); and became active in Amnesty International, the Writers' Union of Canada, and the Canadian Civil Liberties Association.

Atys (ancient deity): *see* Attis.

Atzcapotzalco, also spelled AZCAPOTZALCO, city and delegation (administrative subdivision), northwestern Federal District, central Mexico. Situated approximately 7,350 ft (2,240 m) above sea level in the Valley of Mexico, the city was founded in the 12th century and given the Aztec name meaning "anthill" because of its large population. It became famous for its slave market and the skill of its craftsmen in working precious metals. Cortés later set up smelters there to melt Mexican treasure into bullion. The Spaniards also destroyed the Aztec temple, and on its site there is a Dominican convent with a 17th-century church and an 18th-century Rosary chapel.

The modern delegation is the Federal District's principal livestock-raising and dairying region, supplying Mexico City. With the growth of the federal capital, Atzcapotzalco has become part of the Mexico City metropolitan area. Among its numerous and varied industries are textile mills, automobile and bus assembly plants, and a petroleum refinery. Paper, matches, metal furniture, and phonograph records are also manufactured there. Highways and a railroad lead to central Mexico City, 9 mi (15 km) to the south-southeast. A campus of the Autonomous Metropolitan University is located in Atzcapotzalco. Pop. (1970) city, 8,287; delegation, 534,554.

Aubagne, town, Bouches-du-Rhône *département,* Provence-Alpes-Côte-d'Azur region, Provence, southeastern France, east of Marseille. It was the site of the Gallo-Roman Pagus Lucreti and derived its name from its health springs (Ad Bainea). An agricultural marketing centre, it has a brick and pottery industry dating from the 18th century and specializes in Provençal *santons* (folkloric and religious figurines). The French writer Marcel Pagnol was born there (1895) and the town has a museum of the French Foreign Legion. Pop. (1982) 28,438.

Aube, *département,* Champagne-Ardennes region, north central France, in the old province of Champagne, southeast of Paris. It has an area of 2,317 sq mi (6,002 sq km). The dry chalk platform of Champagne is traversed (southeast–northwest) by the converging Aube and Seine valleys, which cut through Côte des Bars, a region of scarped limestone hills. Agricultural improvements have made the chalk region fertile, but it is sparsely populated, most of the people living in the well-watered valleys. The trade fairs of Champagne, especially at Troyes, were famous in the 12th and 13th centuries. Sheep breeding and wool spinning have given way, except in the Pays d'Othe, to mixed farming and textiles woven of man-made fibres. Hosiery manufacture is widespread, the major mills being at Troyes.

Cities that head *arrondissements* are Troyes (the capital), Bar-sur-Aube, and Nogent-sur-Seine. The Aube Valley, in the southeastern corner of the *département,* is site of the historic abbey of Clairvaux. Pop. (1982) 289,300.

Aube River, river, north central France, navigable tributary of the Seine, which it joins above Romilly. The Aube and its tributary, the Aujon, rise on the Langres Plateau, flowing northwest for 154 mi (248 km) in trenchlike valleys across the dry oolitic limestone country. In front of the Côte des Bars escarpment, the valleys open out as stone gives way to clay at Montigny-le-Roi and Châteauvillain. As they enter the Aube *département* the two rivers join at Clairvaux. Moving toward Brienne, the river receives many small tributaries. After it passes Brienne on its way to the Seine, few surface tributaries add to the volume, and the country is flat alluvial earth on the Champagne chalk platform.

Auber, Daniel-François-Esprit (b. Jan. 29, 1782, Caen, Fr.—d. May 12, 1871, Paris), composer who was prominent in the development of opera containing spoken as well as sung passages (opéra comique). The great contemporary success of his works was due in part to the expertly tailored librettos of Eugène Scribe and in part to Auber's spirited musical settings, which were influenced by Rossini and well suited to French taste. One of the most successful and still familiar works in this popular, romantic vein is *Fra Diavolo* (1830; *Brother Devil*).

The collaboration between Auber and Scribe produced 38 stage works between 1823 and 1864. The spectacular *Muette de Portici* (*Mute Girl of Portici,* also known as *Masaniello,* 1828) has been regarded as the archetype of grand opera. It greatly impressed Richard Wagner, who modelled his *Rienzi* after it. In addition to anticipating the works of Meyerbeer, *Le Philtre* (1831) provided the dramatic basis for Donizetti's *Elisir d'amore* (*The Elixir of Love*), and *Gustave III* (1833) gave Verdi his story for *Un ballo in maschera* (*A Masked Ball*).

As a child Auber composed instinctively and later became a pupil of Luigi Cherubini. His life, almost entirely devoted to opera, was uneventful. His religious cantatas and motets were written between 1852 and 1855 and are little known. He was elected to the Académie Française (1829), was appointed director of the Paris Conservatoire (1842), and became

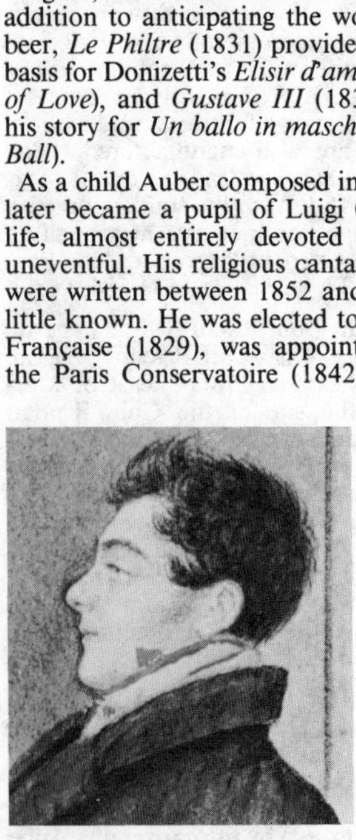

Auber, detail of an aquarelle by an unknown artist; in the André Meyer Collection

By courtesy of the Andre Meyer Collection

chapelmaster to Napoleon III (1857). Auber's music is also thought to have influenced Richard Strauss, Charles Gounod, and Jules Massenet.

aubergine: *see* eggplant.

Aubert, Étienne (pope): *see* Innocent VI.

Aubignac, François Hédelin, abbé d' (b. Aug. 4, 1604, Paris—d. July 25, 1676, Nemours, Fr.), associate of the statesman Cardinal de Richelieu, playwright, and critic who influenced French 17th-century writing and encouraged dramatic standards based on the classics. He wrote plays, fiction, translations of Homer and Ovid, and, most important, studies of dramatic technique and presentation.

Although trained as an advocate, Aubignac soon turned to the Church (1628) and was named tutor to Richelieu's nephew. Encouraged by the Cardinal, he wrote several prose tragedies, three of which survive: *Cyminde* (published 1642), *La Pucelle d'Orléans* (1642;

Aubignac, engraving, 1673

By courtesy of the trustees of the British Museum; photograph, J.R. Freeman & Co. Ltd.

"The Maid of Orleans"), and *Zénobie* (1647). His polemical writings include four critical essays on the plays of Pierre Corneille and several other critical commentaries, some of which offended members of the Académie Française. When, in consequence, he was not admitted to membership, he founded his own academy in 1654; despite his political connections, however, he was unable to enlist the king's support for it, and the group disbanded not long after Aubignac's death.

His major work, *La Pratique du théâtre* (1657; *The Whole Art of the Stage,* 1684), was commissioned by Richelieu and is based on the idea that the action on stage must have credibility (*vraisemblance*) in the eyes of the audience. Aubignac proposed, among other things, that the whole play should take place as close as possible in time to the crisis, that audiences should not be asked to imagine changes of scene or character, and that the number of actors be restricted so there is no confusion. Despite the *Pratique*'s small sale, it was probably a force in the formation of French Classical taste as put into practice by Corneille and Racine. Another work, *Projet pour le rétablissement du théâtre français* ("Plan for Reorganizing the French Theatre"), published after the *Pratique,* called for the establishment of a general directorship over all public theatres in order to raise comedies, in particular, from disrepute. He adamantly opposed the idea that advances in theatre were harmful to religion.

Aubigné, Françoise d': *see* Maintenon, Françoise d'Aubigné, marquise de.

Aubigné, Théodore-Agrippa d' (b. Feb. 8, 1552, Pons, Fr.—d. April 29, 1630, Geneva), major late 16th-century poet, renowned Huguenot captain, polemicist, and historian of his own times. After studies in Paris, Orléans, Geneva, and Lyon, he joined the Huguenot forces and served throughout the Wars of Religion on the battlefield and in the council chamber. He was *écuyer* ("master of horse") to Henry of Navarre. After Henry's accession to the French throne as Henry IV (1589) and his abjuration of Protestantism, Aubigné withdrew to his estates in Poitou. Under the regency of Marie de Médicis, his intransigence estranged him from his Huguenot brethren.

Aubigné, detail of an oil painting by Bartholomaus Sarburgh, 1622; in the Öffentliche Kunstsammlung, Basel, Switz.

By courtesy of the Offentliche Kunstsammlung, Basel, Switz.

Proscribed in 1620, he took refuge in Geneva, where he remained until his death. His closing years were clouded by the disreputable conduct of his son Constant—father of Madame de Maintenon, second and secret wife of Louis XIV.

Among Aubigné's prose works, the *Confession catholique du sieur de Sancy,* first published in 1660, is a parody, ironically dedicated to Cardinal Duperron, of the tortuous explanations offered by Protestants who followed Henry IV's example of abjuration. His comment on life and manners ranges more widely in the *Adventures du baron de Faeneste* (1617), in which the Gascon Faeneste represents attachment to outward appearances (*le paraître*) while honest squire Ënay, embodying the principle of true being (*l'être*), tries to clear Faeneste's mind of cant. The *Histoire universelle* deals with the period from 1553 to 1602, with an appendix to cover the death of Henry IV (1610); an unfinished supplement was meant to bring the story up to 1622. The chief interest of the *Histoire* lies in its eyewitness accounts and in the liveliness of Aubigné's writing.

His major poem in seven cantos, the *Tragiques,* begun in 1577 (published 1616), celebrates the justice of God, who on the Day of Doom will gloriously avenge his slaughtered saints. The subject matter, the sectarian bias, and the uneven composition and expression are offset by many passages of great poetic power, often lyrical in their Biblical language and noble in the despairing intensity of their invective. The scope of the design confers epic grandeur on the work. Modern research on Baroque literature has awakened interest in Aubigné's youthful love poetry, collected in the *Printemps* (1570–73, unpublished). It remained in manuscript until 1874. In these poems the stock characters and phraseology, modelled on Petrarch, are transmuted into a highly personal style, full of tragic resonances, by Aubigné's characteristic vehemence of passion and force of imagination.

Aubigny, Louise-Renée de Kéroualle, duchesse d' (duchess of): *see* Portsmouth, Louise-Renée de Kéroualle, duchess of.

Aubray, Marie-Madeleine-Marguérite d': *see* Brinvilliers, Marie-Madeleine-Marguérite d'Aubray, marquise de.

Aubrey, John (b. March 12, 1626, Easton Piercy, Wiltshire, Eng.—d. June 1697, Oxford), antiquarian and writer, best known for his vivid, intimate, and sometimes acid biographical sketches of his contemporaries. Educated at Oxford at Trinity College, he studied law in London at the Middle Temple. He early displayed his interest in antiquities by calling attention to the prehistoric stones at Avebury, Wiltshire. His literary and scientific interests won him a fellowship of the Royal Society in 1663. Meanwhile, in his travels in England and Europe, he became entangled in love suits and lawsuits (from which he was never free

Aubrey, pen-and-ink drawing by William Faithorne, 1666; in the Bodleian Library, Oxford

By courtesy of the curators of the Bodleian Library, Oxford

until he sold the remainder of his estates in 1670) and avoided creditors. His easy, equable temper won him many friends, among them the architect Sir Christopher Wren and the philosopher Thomas Hobbes.

In 1667 Aubrey met the historian and antiquarian Anthony à Wood and began gathering materials for Wood's projected *Athenae Oxonienses,* a vast biographical dictionary of Oxford writers and ecclesiastics. He also continued gathering antiquities. His *Miscellanies* (1696), a collection of stories of apparitions and curiosities, was the only work that appeared during his lifetime. After his death, some of his antiquarian materials were included in *The Natural History and Antiquities of... Surrey* (1719) and *The Natural History of Wiltshire* (1847).

His biographies first appeared as *Lives of Eminent Men* (1813). The definitive presentation of Aubrey's biographical manuscripts, however, is *Brief Lives* (2 vol., 1898; edited by Andrew Clark). Though not biographies in the strict sense of the word, Aubrey's *Lives,* based on observation and gossip, are profiles graced by picturesque and revealing detail that have found favour with later generations. They also convey a delightful impression of their easy-going author.

Articles are alphabetized word by word, not letter by letter

Auburn, city, Lee County, eastern Alabama, U.S., adjacent to Opelika. Founded in 1836 by settlers from Georgia, its name was inspired by the "sweet Auburn" of Oliver Goldsmith's *Deserted Village.* Auburn University, since its foundation as East Alabama Male College (Methodist) in 1856, has been the main factor in the city's development. The economy is supplemented by planned industrial development. Chewacla State Park and Tuskegee National Forest are southwest. Inc. 1839. Pop. (1980) 28,471.

Auburn, city, seat (1854) of Androscoggin County, southwestern Maine, U.S., on the Androscoggin River, opposite Lewiston, and part of the Lewiston–Auburn metropolitan area. Settled in 1786, Auburn was separated from Minot in 1842 and is supposed to have been named for the Auburn of Oliver Goldsmith's poem *The Deserted Village.* The manufacture of shoes is the city's chief industry. The Androscoggin Historical Library and Museum has exhibits derived from local history. Recreational facilities include the nearby Lost Valley Ski Area, Lake Auburn, and Taylor Pond. Inc. town, 1842; city, 1869. Pop. (1980) 23,128.

Auburn, city, seat (1805) of Cayuga County, west central New York, U.S., at the north end of Owasco Lake, in the Finger Lakes region, 22 mi (35 km) southwest of Syracuse. Founded in 1793 by Capt. John Hardenberg on the site of a Cayuga village called Wasco, it was first known as Hardenberg's Corners. It developed around Auburn State Prison (1816) and Auburn Theological Seminary (founded 1822, merged 1939 with Union Theological Seminary, New York City). Industry, attracted by abundant waterpower and the former practice of using cheap prison labour, includes the manufacture of shoes, rope, rugs, plastics, diesel engines, and electronic equipment. Cayuga County Community College was established there in 1953. The home (1816–17) of William H. Seward (governor of New York [1839–43], senator and secretary of state under Presidents Lincoln and Johnson) is maintained as a museum. Seward is buried in Fort Hill Cemetery and his records, books, and Indian relics are in the Cayuga Museum of History and Art. Harriet Tubman, the Abolitionist and former slave, died (1913) in Auburn and her house is preserved. Inc. village, 1815; city, 1848. Pop. (1980) 32,548.

Auburn, city, King County, west central Washington, U.S., in the White River Valley, 10 mi (16 km) northeast of Tacoma. It was laid out in 1887 by Levi W. Ballard, an early local settler, and named for W.A. Slaughter, an army officer killed in the Indian wars. In 1893 it was renamed for Oliver Goldsmith's *Deserted Village:* "Sweet Auburn, loveliest village of the plain." The city developed as an agricultural trade centre and as a division point for the Northern Pacific Railway (now Burlington Northern). Manufacturing, chiefly the production of aircraft parts, is important. A Federal Aviation Administration air traffic control centre to serve Idaho, Alaska, and Washington, was established there in 1962. The city is regional headquarters for General Services Administration distribution point for overseas shipment. A state salmon hatchery is nearby. The city is the site of Green River Community College (1967). Just north of Auburn a monument marks the site of the White River Massacre (Oct. 28, 1855), in which nine members of three pioneer families were killed by Indians. Inc. 1914. Pop. (1980) 26,417.

Auburn system, penal method of the 19th century in which persons worked during the day and were kept in solitary confinement at night, with enforced silence at all times. The silent system evolved during the 1820s at Auburn Prison in Auburn, N.Y., as an alternative to and modification of the Pennsylvania system of solitary confinement, which it gradually replaced in the United States. Later innovations at Auburn were the lockstep (marching in single file, placing the right hand on the shoulder of the man ahead, and facing toward the guard), the striped suit, two-foot extensions of the walls between cells, and special seating arrangements at meals—all designed to insure strict silence. The Auburn and Pennsylvania systems were both based on a belief that criminal habits were learned from and reinforced by other criminals. *See also* Pennsylvania system.

Aubusson, town, Creuse *département,* Limousin region, central France, on the Creuse River near the northern edge of the Plateau de Millevaches (highest part of the Monts du Limousin), northeast of Limoges. In the Middle Ages it was the seat of a viscounty from whose rulers descended Pierre d'Aubusson, grand master of the Order of the Hospital of St. John of Jerusalem, defender of Rhodes against the Turks. Since at least the 16th century, Aubusson has been famed for its manufacture of carpets and tapestries. A national school of decorative arts founded in 1869 maintains high standards of hand looming, still the principal occupation of the town. There is also a small electrical manufacturing industry. Pop. (1982) 5,326.

Aubusson, Pierre d' (b. 1423, Monteil-au-Vicomte, Fr.—d. July 3, 1503, Rhodes), grand master of the military-religious Order of St. John of Jerusalem, known for his defense of Rhodes against the Turks.

Aubusson, detail of an engraving

By courtesy of the Bibliothèque Nationale, Paris

The son of French nobility, Aubusson joined the Knights of St. John *c.* 1453. The Knights, with their headquarters at Rhodes, held the island as a bar to Ottoman expansion in the Aegean. Aubusson became grand master of the order in 1476 and in 1480 gained widespread fame in Europe for successfully defending Rhodes against Sultan Mehmed II's fleet.

Later, when Cem (Jem), brother of Mehmed's successor Bayezid II, took refuge in Rhodes, Aubusson, despite his promise to Cem of safe conduct, accepted a bribe from Bayezid and had Cem imprisoned. After six years, Aubusson turned Cem over to Pope Innocent VIII, who had been vying with the kings of Hungary and Naples for the possession of so valuable a political weapon as the Sultan's brother. In return, Innocent made Aubusson a cardinal (1489) with the power to confer all benefices connected with the order without the sanction of the papacy. As cardinal, Aubusson reformed the Order of St. John, strengthened its authority in Rhodes, and eliminated Judaism from the island by expelling all adult Jews and forcibly baptizing their children.

Two years before his death, Aubusson failed in trying to organize a large international crusade against the Turks.

Aubusson carpet, floor covering, usually of considerable size, handwoven at the villages of Aubusson and Felletin, in the *département* of Creuse in central France. Workshops were established in 1743 to manufacture pile carpets primarily for the nobility, to whom the Savonnerie court production was not available. Carpets were, however, also made for the royal residences. Soon after the production of carpets began at Aubusson, the pileless tapestry technique previously in use in this district was adopted for so many of the carpets that the word Aubusson has become synonymous with a flat-woven French carpet, and it is not generally realized that piled rugs in numbers have been made there.

Many of the early Aubussons were in modified Oriental designs, some resembling Ushak medallion carpets. Taste soon changed to a range of Renaissance floral and architectural patterns similar to those in use at the Savonnerie and continued to reflect court and republican fashions up to the modernistic painterly concepts of the 20th century.

Aucassin et Nicolette, early 13th-century French *chantefable* (a story told in alternating sections of verse and prose, the former sung, the latter recited). Aucassin, "endowed with all good qualities," is the son of the Count of Beaucaire and falls in love with Nicolette, a resourceful captive Saracen turned Christian. The lovers are imprisoned but manage to escape and after many vicissitudes (including flight, capture, and shipwreck) are able to marry. This theme was also treated in the romance of *Floire et Blancheflor* (*q.v.*), with which *Aucassin et Nicolette* is thought to share common Moorish and Byzantine sources.

The author of the *chantefable* may have been a professional minstrel from northeastern France, in whose dialect the work was written. He vividly depicted the ardour of young love but showed comparatively little skill in narrative. *Aucassin et Nicolette* is preserved in a single manuscript, kept in France's Bibliothèque Nationale.

Aucella, genus of clams characteristically found as fossils in marine rocks of the Jurassic Period (between 136,000,000 and 190,000,000 years old). The shell has a distinctive teardrop shape and is ornamented with a concentric pattern of ribs; the apex of one valve (shell half) is often curved over the other. A distinctive and commonly found Jurassic species is *Aucella piochii.*

Aucella, from the Jurassic Period

By courtesy of the trustees of the British Museum (Natural History); photograph, Imitor

Auch, town, capital of Gers *département,* Midi-Pyrénées region, southwestern France, ancient capital of Gascony and of Armagnac, built on and around a hill on the west bank of the Gers River, west of Toulouse. Capital of the Celtiberian tribe of Ausci, it became important in Roman Gaul as Elimberris and, after Christianity was established, became the metropolis of Novempopulani. In 732, to protect against Muslim raiders, the city was moved across the river to its present site. Seat of the dukes of Armagnac in the 10th century, it became capital of Gascony in the 18th. Its upper and lower quarters are joined by flights of steps. The Gothic cathedral of Sainte-Marie (1489–1662) has a 16th–17th-century facade, carved Renaissance choir stalls, and a renowned 17th-century organ. The prefecture is installed in the old palace of the archbishops of Auch.

The Escalier Monumental (steps) leading to the Tour d'Armagnac (Armagnac Tower) and the old section of Auch, Fr.

APA—POUX

There is a printing industry, and tile and tobacco are manufactured, but the chief trade is in celebrated regional foods: poultry, foie gras, wine, and Armagnac brandy. Pop. (1982) 19,543.

Auckland, administrative region, northwestern North Island, New Zealand. With an area of about 16,400 sq mi (42,400 sq km), it includes the statistical areas of Central and South Auckland and the Bay of Plenty. It is surrounded by several fine harbours of which the Kaipara and Manukau are the largest. Major rivers include the Waihou, Waikato, and Waipo.

When Europeans arrived in the early nineteenth century, Auckland was densely populated by Maoris. European settlements were predominantly around the shores of Hauraki Gulf or near the present site of Auckland city. The colonists introduced new crops and farming techniques to the Maoris, and during 1845–60 wheat, corn (maize), and potatoes were exported to Australia. In 1853 Auckland province was established; it had nearly 10,000 European settlers at the time and the city of Auckland soon became an administrative, military, and trading centre for the entire hinterland. The province of Auckland was abolished in 1876; Auckland Regional Authority was created in 1963.

Much of the region has been cleared for agriculture, although dairying and sheep raising are also important. Manufacturing includes sawmilling, food processing, steel mills, and allied industries. Pop. (1983 est.) 1,370,400.

Auckland, city, New Zealand, the country's second largest after Christchurch and its largest port, occupying a narrow isthmus of North Island between Waitemata Harbour (east) and Manukau Harbour. It was established in 1840 by Gov. William Hobson as the capital of the colonial government and was named for George Eden, earl of Auckland, British first lord of the admiralty and later governor general of India. Incorporated as a borough in 1851, it remained the capital until superseded by the city of Wellington in 1865. It was made a city in 1871. Auckland has the largest concentration of indigenous Maoris in New Zealand, and also large numbers of Polynesians from other islands in the South Pacific.

A focal point of road and rail transportation, the urban area is also served by New Zealand's leading international airport at Mangere. Auckland's most important feature is Waitemata Harbour, a 70-sq-mi (180-sq-km) body of water with maximum channel depths of 33 ft (10 m), serving overseas and intercoastal shipping. Principal exports include iron, steel, dairy products, and meat and hides. Petroleum, iron and steel products, sugar, wheat, and phosphates are imported. Other industries of the Auckland area are engineering and metal trades; textiles, clothing, leather, and timber and allied products; car assembly, boatbuilding, paint, glass, footwear, plastic, chemical, and cement; and fishing, food processing, brewing, and sugar refining. A large iron and steel mill was opened at Glenbrook (20 mi [32 km] south) in 1969. The Auckland Harbour Bridge (1959) links the city with the rapidly growing, primarily residential, North Shore suburbs and with Devonport, the chief naval base and dockyard for New Zealand. A natural gas pipeline running from Maui field to Auckland was completed in 1977.

Major institutions within the urban area include the War Memorial Museum, the Museum of Transport and Technology, the Auckland City Art Gallery, the public library, the University of Auckland (1957; from 1882 to 1957, Auckland University College, a constituent part of the University of New Zealand), the town hall, and three teachers' training colleges. Also in the locality are swimming and surfing beaches, several extinct volcanic cones, golf courses, sporting grounds, and parks and reserves. Pop. (1983 est.) city, 144,100; urban area, 800,100.

Town hall, Civic Square, Auckland, N.Z.

Robin Smith—Photographic Library of Australia

Auckland, George Eden, earl of, also called (1814–39) 2ND BARON AUCKLAND (b. Aug. 25, 1784, Eden Farm, near Beckenham, Kent, Eng.—d. Jan. 1, 1849, The Grange, near Alresford, Hampshire), governor general of India from 1836 to 1842, when he was recalled after participation in British setbacks in Afghanistan.

Succeeding to his father's barony in 1814, Auckland, a member of the Whig Party, served as Board of Trade president and as first lord of the admiralty before being selected in 1835 by his friend, the new Tory prime minister, Lord Melbourne, as governor general of India. He arrived in Calcutta in February of the following year with instructions to gain for Britain the friendship of buffer states between India and Russia, then expanding eastward with emissaries already in Afghanistan. Desiring expanded British trade and influence in central Asia, he sought a commercial treaty with the Afghan ruler Dōst Moḥammad. Hindered by Russian and Persian efforts there, Auckland replaced Dōst Moḥammad with his rival, Shāh Shojāʿ, who then depended strongly on British support.

Auckland firmly secured his influence in Afghanistan with threats and a disregard of treaties, and by 1839 Shojāʿ controlled Kābul and Qandahār. For his efforts, Auckland was created an earl in 1839, and Shojāʿ's power lessened in Afghan administration as Auckland's grew. His public reforms and orders to cut tribal allowances (to reduce the drain on India's treasury) created local unrest that led to attacks on British forces, resulting in the death or capture of 5,000 troops during the 1841 winter retreat from Kābul. With affairs at their worst for the British, Auckland was recalled in 1842. Facing government blame and public censure, he accepted the situation with composure and saw his successor in Calcutta depose Shojāʿ and restore Dōst Moḥammad, thus securing temporary stability in Afghanistan.

An excellent administrator as governor general, Auckland extended irrigation, inaugurated famine relief, and fought for the vernacular in education; he expanded training in the professions as the most practical measure for India's progress. In 1846 he again became first lord of the admiralty.

Auckland Islands, outlying island group of New Zealand, in the South Pacific Ocean, 290 mi (467 km) south of South Island. Volcanic in origin, they comprise six islands and several islets, with a total land area of 234 sq mi (606 sq km), and have a cool, humid, and windy climate. Soils are generally poor, and shrub forests cover lower elevations. Animal life includes birds, wild cattle, fur seals, sea lions, and sea elephants. Auckland Island, the largest (179 sq mi), rises to about 2,000 ft (600 m); it has a steep east coast, indented by Carnley Harbour and Port Ross.

Discovered in 1806 by Abraham Bristow, a whaling captain, they were later named after the Earl of Auckland, governor general of India. A whaling station was established there but was abandoned in 1852. Cattle and sheep were introduced in the 1890s, but the venture met with only limited success. There is a large bird population, particularly petrels and penguins. The Aucklands are under the administration of the New Zealand commissioner for crown lands and are presently uninhabited.

auction, buying and selling of real and personal property through open public bidding. The traditional auction process involves a succession of increasing bids or offers by potential purchasers until the highest bid is accepted by the auctioneer (usually an agent of the seller). Buyers are usually permitted to examine the items for sale beforehand. At a so-called Dutch auction, however, the seller offers property at successively lower prices until one of his offers is accepted or until the price drops so low as to force the withdrawal of the offered property.

Auctions are an important part of the assembly and selling operations in the agricultural markets of many countries, for they have traditionally provided a rapid and effective means of disposing of goods, especially perishable products. Auctions are also frequently used to sell products directly to consumers, especially if the value cannot readily be precisely determined, as in the case of works of art or antiques. Auction selling is also employed on stock and commodity exchanges.

Auction Bridge, card game played as early as the late 1890s, although generally believed to have been introduced in 1904. It was the third step in the historical progression from Whist to Bridge Whist to Auction Bridge to Contract Bridge. Like its precursors and successors, it is a four-handed game with partnerships of two. By 1910, Auction Bridge had supplanted Bridge Whist in Europe and the United States. Its major innovation was the addition of competitive bidding for the right to name the trump suit and by above- and below-line scoring. In the 1920s it became the most popular card game ever known; it still has a substantial, but declining, following.

The establishment of trump suit through competitive bidding allows one of the four players to become the declarer. A bid of 1 spade means a player expects to make one-odd (six tricks, comprising a book, plus one—tricks over six are called odd tricks), with spades as trump. Players may pass if they please. Succeeding bids must name a greater number of odd tricks or the same number in a higher suit (suits rank from high to low, no-trump, spades, hearts, diamonds, clubs). Bids may be doubled and redoubled; overcalling (*i.e.,* defensive bidding after an opponent has opened) is permitted whether bids have been doubled or not. The auction continues until three consecutive passes occur. The partner of the declarer becomes dummy and tables his hand face up after the opening lead.

It is possible to win a game by taking enough overtricks, which favours underbidding. Each odd trick taken above six, whether or not bid, scores 10 at no-trump, 9 in spades, 8 in hearts, 7 in diamonds, 6 in clubs. These values are multiplied by two if the contract is doubled, by four if it is redoubled. Odd tricks count below the line on a bridge scorepad toward game: game is 30 or more trick points. A rubber is won by winning two out of three games, and bonus for a rubber is 250, scored above the line.

Other above-the-line point bonuses go to the declarer's side for winning a doubled contract (50) or a redoubled contract (100); also awarded are 50 per overtrick doubled or 100 redoubled. If the declarer's side does not win its contract, the opponents score 50 above the line for each undertrick (100 if doubled, 200 redoubled). A winner of a small slam (all tricks but one) gets 50 above the line, 100 for a grand slam (all tricks). Elaborate scores for honours (ace, king, queen, jack, 10 of trumps, or aces only at no-trump) are scored above the line and include, at no-trump, 100 for four aces in one hand, 40 for four aces divided between two partners, and 30 for three, whether divided or not; in a suit, the value of the trump suit is multiplied by 10 for five honours in one hand; 9 if split four–one; 8 for four only but in one hand; 5 for five split two–three; 4 for four divided; and 2 for three, whether divided or not.

The side scoring the greater total of honours plus trick points in a rubber is the winner by the difference between the two total scores.

Auction Pitch (card game): *see* Pitch.

Audaghost, also spelled AWDAGHOST (fl. 9th–11th century), Berber town in the southwest Sahara, northwest of Timbuktu; an important terminus of the medieval trans-Saharan trade route. Primarily a centre where North African traders could buy gold from the kings of ancient Ghana, it was first an independent market town, and later a tributary satellite of Ghana. It was captured from Ghana *c.* 1054–55 by the Ṣanhajah wing of the Muslim Almoravid movement and thereafter declined in importance. Its location is not certain, but it probably occupied the site of what is now Tegdaoust, Mauritania.

Aude, *département,* Languedoc-Roussillon region, southern France, formed in 1790 from part of Languedoc and covering an area of 2,406 sq mi (6,232 sq km). From the Mediterranean Gulf of Lion on the east it reaches inland to the Gate of Carcassonne, which lies between the Pyrenees (maximum elevation 11,000 ft [3,400 m]) and the Massif Central (6,000 ft). Most of the *département* is within the Aude River drainage basin, but its westward reaches extend into the Garonne basin. The Canal du Midi (1685) crosses the region to connect the Atlantic with the Mediterranean; one of its branches, the Canal de la Robine, serves Narbonne, but both canals are archaic and now almost abandoned. Behind the coastal sand dunes are extensive lagoons, notably Sigean and Leucate.

The lowland, warm in winter, hot and dry in summer, produces vast quantities of cheap wine. Minerals are scarce, with some sulfur mined at Malvési and iron ore at Leucate on the coast. Quillan, in the foothills of the southwest, has an important plastics industry. Carcassonne, the capital, contains a

Towers and ramparts of the 12th-century citadel overlooking a residential street in Carcassonne, Aude *département*, France
W. Suschitzky

picturesque citadel with its restored medieval fortifications and buildings. It, like Narbonne and Limoux, heads an *arrondissement.* Aude *département* is under the jurisdiction of the court of appeals and *académie* (educational division) at Montpellier in the *département* of Hérault. Pop. (1982) 280,686.

Auden, W(ystan) H(ugh) (b. Feb. 21, 1907, York, Yorkshire, Eng.—d. Sept. 29, 1973, Vienna), poet and man of letters who achieved early fame in the 1930s as a hero of the left during the Great Depression. Most of his verse dramas of this period were written in collaboration with Christopher Isherwood. In 1939 Auden settled in the U.S., becoming a U.S. citizen.

Life. In 1908 Auden's family moved to Birmingham, where his father became medical officer and professor in the university. Since the father was a distinguished physician of broad scientific interests and the mother had been a nurse, the atmosphere of the home

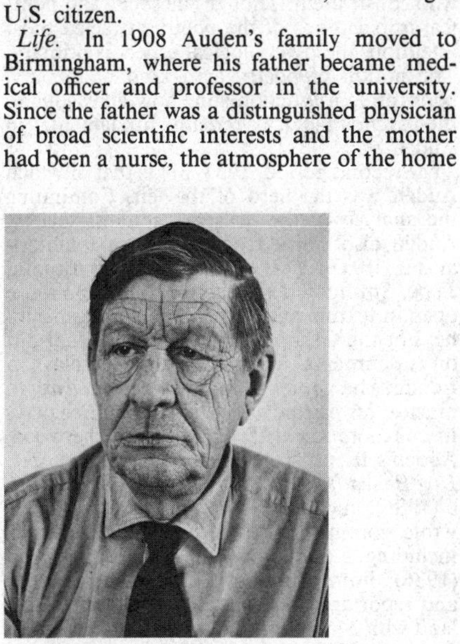

Auden, 1965
Horst Tappe

was more scientific than literary. It was also devoutly Anglo-Catholic, and Auden's first religious memories were of "exciting magical rites." The family name, spelled Audun, appears in the Icelandic sagas, and Auden inherited from his father a fascination with Iceland.

His education followed the standard pattern

for children of the middle and upper classes. At eight he was sent away to St. Edmund's preparatory school, in Surrey, and at 13 to a public (private) school: Gresham's, at Holt, in Norfolk. Auden intended to be a mining engineer and was interested primarily in science; he specialized in biology. By 1922 he had discovered his vocation as a poet, and two years later his first poem was published in *Public School Verse.* In 1925 he entered Oxford (Christ Church), where he established a formidable reputation as poet and sage, having a strong influence on such other literary intellectuals as C. Day Lewis (named poet laureate in 1968), Louis MacNeice, and Stephen Spender, who printed by hand the first collection of Auden's poems in 1928. Though their names were often linked with his as poets of the so-called Auden generation, the notion of an "Auden Group" dedicated to revolutionary politics was largely a journalistic invention. Upon graduating from Oxford in 1928, Auden, offered a year abroad by his parents, chose Berlin rather than the Paris by which the previous literary generation had been fascinated. He fell in love with the German language and was influenced by its poetry, cabaret songs, and plays, especially those by Bertolt Brecht. He returned to become a schoolmaster in Scotland and England for the next five years.

In his *Collected Shorter Poems* Auden divides his career into four periods. The first extends from 1927, when he was still an undergraduate, through *The Orators* of 1932. The "charade" *Paid on Both Sides,* which along with *Poems* established Auden's reputation in 1930, best reveals the imperfectly fused but fascinating amalgam of material from the Icelandic sagas, Old English poetry, public-school stories, Karl Marx, Sigmund Freud and other psychologists, and schoolboy humour that enters into all these works. The poems are uneven and often obscure, pulled in contrary directions by the subjective impulse to fantasy, the mythic and unconscious, and the objective impulse to a diagnosis of the ills of society and the psychological and moral defects of the individuals who constitute it. Though the social and political implications of the poetry attracted most attention, the psychological aspect is primary. The notion of poetry as a kind of therapy, performing a function somehow analagous to the psychoanalytical, remains fundamental in Auden.

The second period, 1933–38, is that in which Auden was the hero of the left. Continuing the analysis of the evils of capitalist society, Auden also warned of the rise of totalitarianism. In *On This Island* (1937; in Britain, *Look, Stranger!,* 1936) his verse became more open in texture and accessible to a larger public. For the Group Theatre, a society that put on experimental and noncommercial plays in London, he wrote first *The Dance of Death* (a musical propaganda play) and then three plays in collaboration with Christopher Isherwood, Auden's friend since preparatory school: *The Dog Beneath the Skin* (1935), *The Ascent of F 6* (1936), and *On the Frontier* (1938). He also wrote commentaries for documentary films, including a classic of that genre, *Night Mail* (1936); numerous essays and book reviews; and reportage, most notably on a trip to Iceland with MacNeice, described in *Letters from Iceland* (1937), and a trip to China with Isherwood that was the basis of *Journey to a War* (1939). He visited Spain briefly in 1937, his poem *Spain* (1937) being the only immediate result; but the visit, according to his later recollections, marked the beginning both of his disillusion with the left and of his return to Christianity. In 1936 he married Erika Mann, the daughter of the German novelist Thomas Mann, in order to provide her with a British passport. When he and Isherwood went to China, they crossed the United States both ways, and on the return journey they both decided to settle there. In January 1939, both did so.

In the third period, 1939–46, Auden became a U.S. citizen and underwent decisive changes in his religious and intellectual perspective. *Another Time* (1940) contains some of his best songs and topical verse, and *The Double Man* (containing "New Year Letter," which provided the title of the British edition; 1941) embodies his position on the verge of commitment to Christianity. The beliefs and attitudes that are basic to all of Auden's work after 1940 are defined in three long poems: religious in the Christmas oratorio *For the Time Being* (1944); aesthetic in the same volume's *Sea and the Mirror* (a quasi-dramatic "commentary" on Shakespeare's *Tempest*); and social-psychological in *The Age of Anxiety* (1947), the "baroque eclogue" that won Auden the Pulitzer Prize in 1948. Auden wrote no long poems after that.

The fourth period began in 1948, when Auden established the pattern of leaving New York each year to spend the months from April to October in Europe. From 1948 to 1957 his summer residence was the Italian island of Ischia; in the latter year he bought a farmhouse in Kirchstetten, Austria, where he then spent his summers. In *The Shield of Achilles* (1955), *Homage to Clio* (1960), *About the House* (1965), and *City Without Walls* (1969) are sequences of poems arranged according to an external pattern (canonical hours, types of landscape, rooms of a house). With Chester Kallman, a U.S. poet and close friend who lived with him for more than 20 years, he rehabilitated the art of the opera libretto. Their best known are *The Rake's Progress* (1951), for Igor Stravinsky, *Elegy for Young Lovers* (1961) and *The Bassarids* (1966), for Hans Werner Henze, and *Love's Labour's Lost* for Nicolas Nabokov. They also edited *An Elizabethan Song Book* (1956). In 1962 Auden published a volume of criticism, *The Dyer's Hand,* and in 1970 a commonplace book, *A Certain World.* He spent much time on editing and translating, notably *The Collected Poems of St. John Perse* (1972). In 1972 Auden transferred his winter residence from New York to Oxford, where he was an honorary fellow at Christ Church College. Of the numerous honours conferred on Auden in this last period, the Bollingen Prize (1953), the National Book Award (1956), and the professorship of poetry at Oxford (1956–61) may be mentioned.

Assessment. In the early 1930s W.H. Auden was acclaimed prematurely by some as the foremost poet then writing in English, on the disputable ground that his poetry was more relevant to contemporary social and political realities than that of T.S. Eliot and William Butler Yeats, who previously had shared the summit. By the time of Eliot's death in 1965, however, a convincing case could be made for the assertion that Auden was indeed Eliot's successor, as Eliot had inherited sole claim to supremacy when Yeats died in 1939.

Auden was a counterpart to Eliot not only in transatlantic migration (Auden assuming United States citizenship as Eliot had British) but in his long and controversial career as critic and man of letters as well as poet. He was, as poet, far more copious and varied than Eliot and far more uneven. He tried to interpret the times, to diagnose the ills of society and deal with intellectual and moral problems of public concern. But the need to express the inner world of fantasy and dream was equally apparent, and, hence, the poetry is sometimes bewildering. If the poems, taken individually, are often obscure—especially the earlier ones—they create, when taken together, a meaningful poetic cosmos with symbolic landscapes and mythical characters and situations. In his later years Auden ordered the world of his poetry and made it easier of access; he collected his poems, revised them, and presented them chronologically in two volumes: *Collected Shorter Poems 1927–57* (1967) and *Collected Longer Poems* (1969). A religious poet who is also a clown, a virtuoso who is incorrigibly didactic, a satirist who is also a supreme lyricist is a problem for critics; and most useful criticism of Auden is recent.

(M.K.Sp.)

MAJOR WORKS. *Poetical works. Poems* (1928, privately printed by Stephen Spender); *Poems* (1930), including the verse play *Paid on Both Sides,* subtitled "A Charade"; *The Orators* (1932); *Look, Stranger!* (1936; U.S. title, *On This Island,* 1937); *Spain* (1937); *Another Time* (1940); *New Year Letter* (U.S. title, *The Double Man*; includes sonnet sequence "The Quest," 1941); *For the Time Being* (1944), containing *The Sea and the Mirror,* subtitled "A Commentary on Shakespeare's The Tempest" and *For the Time Being,* subtitled "A Christmas Oratorio"; *The Age of Anxiety,* subtitled "A Baroque Eclogue" (1947); *Nones* (1951); *The Shield of Achilles* (1955); *Homage to Clio* (1960); *Aoout the House* (1965); *City Without Walls and Other Poems* (1969). *Collected Poems* (1976) includes all the poems the poet wished to preserve.

Plays. The Dance of Death (1933); written in collaboration with Christopher Isherwood: *The Dog Beneath the Skin* (1935); *The Ascent of F 6* (1936); and *On the Frontier* (1938).

Libretti (in collaboration with Chester Kallman). Igor Stravinsky's *Rake's Progress* (1951); Hans Werner Henze's *Elegy for Young Lovers* (1961) and *The Bassarids* (1966).

Travel books and criticism (in collaboration with Louis MacNeice). *Letters from Iceland* (1937), contains the long piece of light verse "Letter to Lord Byron"; with Christopher Isherwood: *Journey to a War* (1939), includes the sonnet sequence "In Time of War," later called "Sonnets from China"; *The Enchafed Flood,* subtitled "The Romantic Iconography of the Sea" (1950); *The Dyer's Hand and Other Essays* (1962); *Secondary Worlds* (T.S. Eliot Memorial Lectures) (1968); *A Certain World: A Commonplace Book* (1970).

BIBLIOGRAPHY. Full information about criticism of Auden (as well as about the publication of Auden's own works) may be found in B.C. Bloomfield, *W.H. Auden: A Bibliography* (1964); and a selection, with introduction, in M.K. Spears (ed.), *Auden: A Collection of Critical Essays* (1964). The most useful books are John Fuller, *A Reader's Guide to W.H. Auden* (1970); the interpretations by Herbert Greenberg, *Quest for the Necessary* (1968); and John G. Blair, *The Poetic Art of W.H. Auden* (1965). M.K. Spears, *The Poetry of W.H. Auden* (1963, in paperback with added preface, 1968), remains the most critical comprehensive account. Earlier books still worth consulting are Richard Hoggart, *Auden: An Introductory Essay* (1951), the first full-length study (together with the same author's pamphlet of 1957, "W.H. Auden"); and Joseph W. Beach, *The Making of the Auden Canon* (1957), an analysis of Auden's procedure in compiling his *Collected Poetry* (1945) and *Collected Shorter Poems* (1950). In Edward Mendelson (ed.), *The English Auden: Poems, Essays, and Dramatic Writings,* the works are given in order of composition. Mendelson's *Early Auden* (1980) is a history and interpretation of the poet's beliefs about the proper role of the poet, based on his writings before he went to the United States. Charles Osborne, *W.H. Auden: The Life of a Poet* (1979); and Humphrey Carpenter, *W.H. Auden: A Biography* (1981), are the fullest biographies.

Audenarde (Belgium): *see* Oudenaarde.

Audiberti, Jacques (b. March 25, 1899, Antibes, Fr.—d. July 10, 1965, Paris), poet, novelist, and, most importantly, playwright whose extravagance of language and rhythm shows the influence of Symbolism and Surrealism.

A former clerk for the justice of the peace in Antibes, he began his writing career as a journalist, moving to Paris in 1925 to write for *Le Journal* and *Le Petit Parisien.* Later, he wrote more than 20 plays on the theme of conflicting good and evil.

Audiberti's drama often treats the supernatural and becomes an "accepted delirium" full of vigour and rhetoric. In *Quoat-Quoat* (1946) a young passenger on a French ship bound for Mexico accepts death rather than loss of identity, and *Le Mal court* (1947; "Evil Is in the Air"), which takes place in an 18th-century, fairy-tale setting, deals with innocence corrupted by experience. *La Hobereaute* (1956; "The Falcon") is an attack on religion. Among Audiberti's verse collections are *Race des hommes* (1937; "The Race of Men") and *Des tonnes de semence* (1941; "Tons of Seed"); his novels include *Abraxas* (1938), *Carnage* (1942), and *Monorail* (1964).

audiencia, in the kingdoms of late medieval Spain, a court established to administer royal justice; also, one of the most important governmental institutions of Spanish colonial America. In Spain the ordinary judges of audiencias in civil cases were called *oidores* and, for criminal cases, *alcaldes de crimen*. The presiding officer of the audiencia was called *gobernador* or *regente*. From the reign of Philip II (1556–98) the decisions of audiencias were final, except when the death penalty was decreed or in civil cases when the amount of money involved exceeded a certain sum. In these instances appeals could be made to a higher court, the *chancillería*.

During the 16th century, audiencias were established in the various administrative districts (viceroyalties, captaincies general) of Spanish America. They were empowered to hear complaints against viceroys and captains general (executive officers) and to take appropriate actions to curb abuses of power. Audiencias were charged by the crown with safeguarding the rights of Indians, and two days a week were allotted to hearing cases involving them. Their primary function was still judicial. They had both civil and criminal jurisdiction, and appeals in major cases could be made from their decisions to the Council of the Indies in Madrid. The presiding officer of the audiencia was the viceroy or captain general, but unless he was learned in the law he was excluded from its strictly judicial functions. Three to five *oidores* and the presiding officer constituted the less important audiencias, whereas the number of judges of the audiencia of Mexico City, founded in 1527 with four *oidores,* had risen to 10 by the 18th century.

The first audiencia in the New World was that of Santo Domingo, set up in 1511, with jurisdiction over the Caribbean islands. The audiencia of Mexico embraced much of the present-day republic of Mexico and the Gulf of Mexico coastal region and Florida. The audiencias of Lima and Guatemala were set up in 1542 and 1543, respectively, and by *c.* 1550 three more had been constituted. By the end of the colonial era a total of 13 had been established within the four viceroyalities. *See also* Indies, Laws of the; residencia.

audion, elementary form of radio tube invented in 1906 by Lee De Forest of the U.S. It was the first vacuum tube in which a control grid as well as a cathode and an anode was incorporated. Valuable as a radio detector, radio and telephone amplifier, and oscillator, it was first manufactured in great quantities during World War I. It is also known as a three-element tube, or triode.

audiovisual education, use of supplementary teaching aids, such as recordings, transcripts, and tapes; motion pictures; radio and television; and computers, to improve learning.

Audiovisual education has developed rapidly since the 1920s by drawing on new technologies of communication, most recently the computer. Throughout history, however, man has shown a natural inclination to learn and to teach with pictures, specimens, demonstrations, and the like. John Amos Comenius (1592–1670), a Bohemian educator, was one of the first to propose a systematic method of audiovisual education. His *Orbis Sensualium Pictus* ("Picture of the Sensual World"), published in 1658, was profusely illustrated with drawings, each playing an important role in teaching the lesson at hand. Comenius was followed by other great educators, including Jean-Jacques Rousseau, John Locke, and J.H. Pestalozzi, who advocated the use of sensory materials to supplement teaching.

Audiovisual aids were widely used by the armed services during and after World War II. Educators drew on this experience, and in the years since the war much research has been done on the effectiveness of different audio-visual aids. This research indicates that, skillfully used, audiovisual aids can lead to significant gains in recall, thinking, interest, imagination, and personal growth. Best results are achieved when audiovisual materials are combined with printed materials, follow-up experiences, and good teaching.

audit, examination of the activities, records, and reports of an enterprise by accounting specialists other than those responsible for their preparation. Public auditing by independent accountants has acquired professional status and become increasingly common with the rise of large business units and the separation of ownership from control. The public accountant performs tests to determine whether the management's statements fairly present the firm's financial position and operating results; such independent evaluations of management reports are of interest to actual and prospective shareholders, bankers, suppliers, lessors, and government agencies.

In English-speaking countries, public auditors are usually certified, and high standards are encouraged by professional societies. Most European and Commonwealth nations follow the example of Great Britain, where government-chartered organizations of accountants have developed their own admission standards. Other countries follow the pattern in the United States, where the states have set legal requirements for licensing. Most countries have specific agencies or departments charged with the auditing of their public accounts (*e.g.,* the General Accounting Office in the United States and the Cour des Comptes in France).

Internal auditing, designed to evaluate the effectiveness of a business' accounting system, is relatively new. Perhaps the most familiar type of auditing is the administrative audit, or pre-audit, in which individual vouchers, invoices, or other documents are investigated for accuracy and proper authorization before they are paid or entered in the books.

auditorium, that part of a specialized building constructed for visual and auditory spectacles or experiences in which the audience sits, distinct from the stage area, where the performers produce the show. In a large theatre an auditorium includes a number of floor levels frequently designed as stalls, private boxes, dress circle, balcony or upper circle, and gallery. A sloping floor allows the seats to be arranged to give a clear view of the stage. The walls and ceiling usually contain concealed light and sound equipment and air extracts or inlets and may be highly decorated.

The term is also applied commonly to a large lecture room in a college, to a reception room in a monastery, and, rarely, to the audience area in a religious building.

auditory meatus, external: *see* external auditory canal.

auditory nerve: *see* vestibulocochlear nerve.

auditory ossicle: *see* ear bone.

auditory tube: *see* eustachian tube.

Audley (of Walden), Thomas Audley, Baron (b. 1488, Earls Colne, Essex, Eng.—d. April 30, 1544), lord chancellor of England from 1533 to 1544 who helped King Henry VIII break with the papacy and establish himself as head of the English church. Historians have viewed him as an unprincipled politician completely subservient to Henry's will.

Trained in law, Audley rose in politics to become speaker of the House of Commons

Audley of Walden, detail of an engraving by P.W. Tomkins, *c.* 1792, after a painting by Hans Holbein

By courtesy of the trustees of the British Museum; photograph, J.R. Freeman & Co. Ltd.

in 1529. Because he gained Parliament's acceptance of Henry's anti-papal policies, the King made him lord keeper of the great seal (1532) and lord chancellor (1533). As chancellor Audley presided at the trials of Bishop John Fisher and Sir Thomas More; he had both defendants executed for refusing to repudiate papal supremacy in England. Although he worked with Thomas Cromwell to establish the supremacy of statute law in England, he played a leading role in securing the attainder of Cromwell (1540) as well as of Henry's fifth wife, Catherine Howard (1542). In 1538 he was created Baron Audley of Walden, and four years later he founded Magdalene College, Cambridge.

Audubon, John James (b. April 26, 1785, Les Cayes, Haiti—d. Jan. 27, 1851, New York City), naturalist and artist who in the early 19th century painted all known species of North American birds.

The illegitimate son of a French naval officer and planter, Jean Audubon, he developed an interest in drawing birds during his boyhood in France. At 18 he was sent to the U.S. to enter business. By 1820, after several unsuccessful business ventures, he concentrated on his steadily growing interest in drawing birds. To

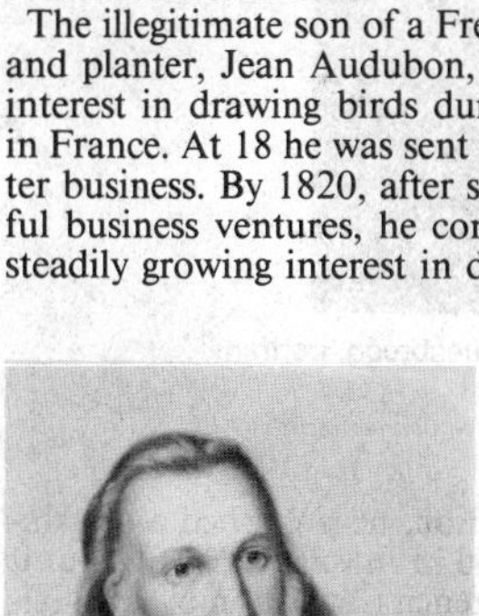

Audubon, detail of a portrait by his sons John and Victor, late 1840s; in the American Museum of Natural History, New York

By courtesy of the American Museum of Natural History, New York

support himself he painted portraits and taught drawing, while his wife worked as a governess.

By 1826 he had enough drawings to consider publication and went to Europe in search of patrons and publishers. The engraver Robert Havell of London undertook publication of his illustrations as *The Birds of America* (435 hand-coloured plates, 4 vol., 1827–38). William MacGillivray helped write the accompanying text, *Ornithological Biography* (5 vol., octavo, 1831–39), and *A Synopsis of the Birds of North America* (1 vol., 1839), which serves as an index. Until 1839 Audubon divided his time between Europe and the U.S., gathering material, completing illustrations, and financing publication through subscription. He then settled in New York City and prepared a smaller edition of his *Birds of America* (7 vol., octavo, 1840–44) and a new work, *Viviparous Quadrupeds of North America*, 150 plates (3 vol., 1845–48), and the accompanying text (3 vol., 1846–53), written with the aid of his sons and the naturalist John Bachman.

Aue, city, Karl-Marx-Stadt *Bezirk* (district), southern East Germany, in the western Erzgebirge (Ore Mountains), at the confluence of the Schwarzwasser and Zwickauer Mulde rivers, near the Czechoslovak frontier. A market village in the 15th century, it was chartered in 1629. Iron, cobalt, bismuth, nickel, and tin were worked there in the 16th and 17th centuries. After World War II Aue became the centre of Erzgebirge uranium mining based on extensive local deposits of pitchblende, a uranium ore. There are also metal, engineering, and woven-goods enterprises. The Romanesque church of the former Klösterlein Zelle, or Zell Maria, monastery (founded 1173) is still standing. Pop. (1981 est.) 29,186.

Auenbrugger von Auenbrugg, Leopold (b. Nov. 19, 1722, Graz, Austria—d. May 17, 1809, Vienna), physician who devised the diagnostic technique of percussion (the art of striking a surface part of the body with short, sharp taps to diagnose the condition of the parts beneath the sound). In 1761, after seven

Auenbrugger von Auenbrugg, portrait by an unknown artist

By courtesy of the Bild-Archiv, Osterreichische Nationalbibliothek, Vienna

years of investigation, he published a description of the method in *Inventum Novum,* but it was not until a French translation by Jean-Nicolas Corvisart des Marets, personal physician to Napoleon, appeared in 1808 that the method gained worldwide acceptance. It remains a fundamental procedure in diagnosis.

Auer, Carl: *see* Welsbach, Carl Auer, Freiherr von.

Auer, Leopold (b. June 7, 1845, Veszprém, Hung.—d. July 15, 1930, Loschwitz, near Dresden, Ger.), violinist especially renowned as a teacher who numbered among his pupils such famous performers as Mischa Elman, Jascha Heifetz, Efrem Zimbalist, and Nathan Milstein. He studied under the celebrated virtuoso Joseph Joachim. From 1868 he was professor of violin at the St. Petersburg Conservatory, Russia, and in 1883 became a Russian subject. While living in St. Petersburg he also taught in London and Dresden. In 1918 he settled in New York. Tchaikovsky originally dedicated his violin concerto to Auer, but, disappointed because Auer regarded the work as unplayable, he changed the dedication. Later Auer changed his mind, and the concerto occupied a prominent place in his extensive repertory. He wrote *Violin Playing As I Teach It* (1921); *My Long Life in Music* (1923); and *Violin Master Works and Their Interpretation* (1925).

Auerbach, Berthold (b. Feb. 28, 1812, Nordstetten, near Horb, Württemberg—d. Feb. 8, 1882, Cannes, Fr.), German novelist noted chiefly for his tales of village life.

Auerbach prepared for the rabbinate, but, estranged from Jewish orthodoxy by the study of the Dutch philosopher Benedict de Spinoza, he turned to literature. Spinoza's life formed the basis of his first novel (1837); a transla-

Berthold Auerbach, engraving

Bavaria-Verlag

tion of Spinoza's works followed in 1841. In 1843 he began publishing the *Schwarzwälder Dorfgeschichten* (*Black Forest Village Stories,* 1869), and there later appeared novels in the same genre, among them *Barfüssele* (1856; *Little Barefoot,* 1873) and *Edelweiss* (1861). These works found a wide public and many imitators. They are not realistic studies of rural life and owed some of their popularity to Auerbach's philosophical reflections and romanticism.

Auerbach, Erich (b. Nov. 9, 1892, Berlin—d. Oct. 13, 1957, Wallingford, Conn., U.S.), educator and scholar of Romance literatures and languages.

After gaining a doctorate in philology at the University of Greifswald in 1921, Auerbach served as librarian for the Prussian State Library. From 1927 to 1947 he was professor of Romance philology at the University of Marburg and at the Turkish State University in Istanbul. He joined the faculty at Yale in 1947, becoming Sterling professor of Romance philology in 1956. In 1949–50 he was a member of the Institute for Advanced Study at Princeton.

His foremost work was *Mimesis: The Representation of Reality in Western Literature* (1953, from the original German edition of 1946), which presents the development of Western literature in terms of the historical qualities of each era.

Consult the INDEX *first*

Auerbach, Red, byname of ARNOLD JACOB AUERBACH (b. Sept. 20, 1917, Brooklyn, N.Y., U.S.), U.S. professional basketball coach whose National Basketball Association (NBA) Boston Celtics won nine NBA championships and 1,037 games against 548 losses.

Auerbach was captain of his Eastern District (Brooklyn) High School and George Washington University (Washington, D.C.) teams. He began coaching at St. Alban's Preparatory School (1940) and Roosevelt High School (1940–43), both in Washington, D.C. He served during World War II in the U.S. Navy (1943–46) and after the war coached the Basketball Association of America Washington Capitals and Tri-City teams before becoming coach of the Celtics in 1950. He retired in 1966 as coach and became president and general manager of the Celtics; he retired as general manager in 1984. His trademark as a Celtics coach was that when he thought his team had the game in hand, he lit up a cigar, an act that delighted Celtic fans and infuriated the fans of their opponents. Auerbach was elected to the Basketball Hall of Fame in 1968.

Red Auerbach: Winning the Hard Way, which he wrote with Paul Sann, was published in 1966, and his autobiography, written with Joe Fitzgerald, was published in 1977.

Auersperg, Anton Alexander, Graf von (count of): *see* Grün, Anastasius.

Auerstädt, Battle of (1806): *see* Jena, Battle of.

Auerstedt, Louis-Nicolas Davout, duc d': *see* Davout, Louis-Nicolas.

Aufbau principle (German *Aufbauprinzip,* "building-up principle"), rationalization of the distribution of electrons among energy levels in the ground (most stable) states of atoms. The principle, formulated by the Danish physicist Niels Bohr around 1920, is an application of the laws of quantum mechanics to the properties of electrons subject to the electric field created by the positive charge on the nucleus of an atom and the negative charge on other electrons that are bound to the nucleus. The building-up denoted by the name of the principle is a hypothetical process in which the electrons are regarded as entering, one by one, this electric field and assuming their most stable conditions with respect to it. *See also* electronic configuration.

Aufklärung (German: Enlightenment), in Germany, the 17th- and 18th-century philosophical movement that emphasized rationalism. *See* Enlightenment.

Aufwuchs (German: "growth"), the community of plants and animals that are attached to or move about on the surfaces of submerged stems, leaves, rocks, sticks, or debris but do not penetrate the surface. The term periphyton is sometimes used to indicate organisms that attach themselves to submerged plant leaves or stems.

Augeas, also spelled AUGEIAS, or AUGIAS, in Greek legend, king of the Epeians in Elis, a son of the sun god Helios. He possessed an immense wealth of herds, and King Eurystheus imposed upon the Greek hero Heracles the task of clearing out all of Augeas' stables unaided in one day. Heracles did so by turning the Alpheus River through them. Although Augeas had promised Heracles a 10th of the herd, he later refused, alleging that Heracles had acted only in the service of Eurystheus. Heracles thereupon led an army against him and slew Augeas and his sons. *See also* Heracles.

auger, tool (or bit) used with a carpenter's brace for drilling holes in wood. It looks like a corkscrew and has six parts: screw, spurs, cutting edges, twist, shank, and tang. The screw looks like a tapered wood screw and is short and small in diameter; it centres the bit and draws it into the work. At the working end of the twist there are two sharp points called spurs, which score a circle equal in diameter to the hole, and two radial cutting edges that cut shavings within the scored circle. The twist is helical and carries the shavings away from the cutters. The tang is square and tapered and fits in the chuck on the brace. Expansive auger bits have adjustable blades with cutting edges and spurs that can be extended radially to cut large holes. Metal-cutting twist drills can drill holes in wood but they cannot produce as clean a hole as an auger bit nor as large a hole as an expansive auger.

Much larger augers are used to bore holes in soil for the emplacement of fence posts, telephone poles, and the like; horizontal augers as much as 96 inches in diameter are used in coal mining.

Auger effect, in atomic physics, a spontaneous process in which an atom with an electron vacancy in the innermost shell readjusts itself to a more stable state by ejecting one or more electrons instead of radiating X-rays. It is named after the French physicist Pierre-Victor Auger, who discovered it in 1925.

All atoms consist of a nucleus and concentric shells of electrons. If an electron in one of the inner shells is removed by electron bombardment, absorption into the nucleus, or in some other way, an electron from another shell will jump into the vacancy, releasing energy that is promptly dissipated either by producing an X-ray or through the Auger effect. In the Auger effect, the available energy expels an electron from one of the shells with the result that the residual atom then has two electron vacancies. The process may be repeated as the new vacancies are filled, otherwise X-radiation will be emitted. The same effect is called auto-ionization when it occurs in the optical rather than the X-ray-energy region. The probability that an Auger electron will be emitted is called the Auger yield for that shell. The Auger yield decreases with atomic number (the number of protons in the nucleus or the number of the element in the periodic table), and at atomic number 30 (zinc) the probabilities of the emission of X-rays from the innermost (*K*) shell and of the emission of Auger electrons is about equal. The Auger effect is useful in studying the properties of elements and compounds, nuclei, and the fundamental particles called muons.

auger mining, method for recovering coal by boring into a coal seam at the base of strata exposed by excavation. Normally one of the lowest cost techniques of mining, it is limited to horizontal or slightly pitched seams that have been exposed by geologic erosion. Augering is usually associated with contour strip-mining, recovering coal for a limited depth beyond the point where stripping becomes uneconomical because the seam of coal lies so far beneath the surface.

Augereau, Pierre-François-Charles, DUC (duke) DE CASTIGLIONE (b. Oct. 21, 1757, Paris—d. June 12, 1816, La Houssaye, Fr.), army officer whose military genius won for France a series of brilliant victories in Italy under Napoleon's command.

Augereau, detail of a portrait by J.E. Heinsius; in the Musée Carnavalet, Paris

Giraudon—Art Resource/EB Inc.

The son of a poor Parisian servant, Augereau turned to a military career at the age of 17, served in several foreign armies, and returned to France in 1792. He quickly advanced in rank and by 1793 headed a division in the eastern Pyrenees. In 1795 he was named lieutenant in the Italian campaign, and his victory at Castiglione (Aug. 5, 1796) convinced Napoleon of his indispensability. He executed the coup d'etat of 18 Fructidor (Sept. 4, 1797) and later was made commander of VII Corps of the Rhine Army by the Directory, the revolutionary executive. Elected deputy and secretary of the Assembly in 1798, he opposed Napoleon's coup d'etat of 18 Brumaire (Nov. 9, 1799), although he later vowed his support.

Augereau's mercurial loyalty to Napoleon caused the Emperor to grant him the minor command of the French and Dutch army. Replaced in 1801, he was later made head of a division in Germany, where he conducted several decisive manoeuvres against the Austrians. At the Battle of Eylau (Feb. 7–8, 1807), his corps, misdirected in a snowstorm, lost half its numbers. Nevertheless, in 1808 Napoleon named him duc de Castiglione and gave him a new command in Catalonia, in Spain, where he was soon defeated. Recalled to France in 1810, he was given a small post in Russia in 1812. He continued fighting in Germany the following year, but after the losses at Leipzig he returned to France.

Augereau had grown weary of the war by 1810. After another defeat at Lyon, in 1814, he bitterly attacked Napoleon and declared himself a royalist after the First Restoration of the Bourbon monarchy (1814). Louis XVIII rewarded him for his anti-Napoleonic sentiments; when he again offered his services to Napoleon in 1815, he was ignored. After the Battle of Waterloo the King gave him no command, and he retired to his estate at La Houssaye.

Aughrabies Falls, also spelled AUGRABIES FALLS, series of separately channelled cataracts and rapids on the Orange River in arid, northwestern Cape Province, South Africa. The falls, which form the central feature of Aughrabies Falls National Park (established in 1966), occur where the Orange River leaves a plateau formation of resistant granite. The main fall of water is 305 ft (93 m); and the total drop is about 625 ft. At the bottom the depth of the plunge pool probably exceeds 140 ft. The width of the falls at floodtime extends over some miles with 19 separate waterfalls tumbling into an 11-mi-long ravine.

Augier, (Guillaume-Victor-) Émile (b. Sept. 17, 1820, Valence, Fr.—d. Oct. 25, 1889, Croissy-sur-Seine), popular dramatist who wrote comedies extolling the virtues of middle-class life under the Second Empire and who shared with Dumas *fils* and Victorien Sardou mastery of the French stage. Didactic in purpose, his verse play *Gabrielle* (1849) attacks the Romantic belief in the divine right of passion, while his *Le Mariage d'Olympe* (1855) opposes the idea of the rehabilitation of a prostitute by love, as expressed in Dumas's *La Dame aux Camélias*. An unbending moralist and a champion of the institution of marriage, Augier satirized adultery in *Les Lionnes pauvres* (1858) and saw in greed the root of evil. His best known play, *Le Gendre de Monsieur Poirier* (1854), written in collaboration with Jules Sandeau, advocated fusion of the new prosperous middle class and the dispossessed nobility.

augite, dark-coloured pyroxene mineral (a silicate of calcium, magnesium, iron, titanium, and aluminum) that commonly occurs as dark, squatty crystals in igneous rocks, particularly gabbros, dolerites, and basalts. Iron-rich varieties are known as ferroaugites; they usually occur only in ferrogabbros, iron-rich dolerites, and their pegmatites; in syenites; and in acidic volcanic glass. Titaniferous varieties are called titanaugites; they are typical of basic alkaline rocks. For chemical formula and detailed physical properties, *see* Table under pyroxene.

Because there is a continuous chemical variation between the diopside–hedenbergite series and augite, these minerals are nearly indistinguishable from one another, even by optical methods. For this reason, the term

Augite from Ontario

By courtesy of the MacFall collection; photograph, Mary A. Root—EB Inc.

augite sometimes is used to designate any pyroxene with monoclinic symmetry (three unequal crystallographic axes with one oblique intersection).

Augmentations, Court of, in Reformation England, the most important of a group of financial courts organized during the reign of Henry VIII; the others were the courts of General Surveyors, First Fruits and Tenths, and Wards and Liveries. All of these were essentially common-law courts as distinct from the Tudor prerogative courts (*e.g.,* Star Chamber), which did not rely on established common-law procedures. These common-law courts were instituted so that the crown might gain more organized control over its lands and finances.

The Court of Augmentations was instituted in 1535 to handle the various financial and property problems brought on by the dissolution of the monasteries after Henry broke away from the Church of Rome: monks had to be placed in positions elsewhere or granted pensions, and debts owed by the community had to be paid; the property itself had to be assessed and then disposed of by sale or lease.

The machinery of the Court of Augmentations was modelled after that of the duchy of Lancaster, the lands of which were administered separately from the mass of crown lands. Augmentations as such became both a court and a department of revenue, as was the case with the other financial courts, which owed their creation to Henry's minister Thomas Cromwell, the person most responsible for replacing the medieval household administration with a modern state administration dependent upon a civil service.

The court had a chancellor and treasurer as well as lawyers and auditors; in addition, there were receivers who had charge of the monastic lands within a particular county. Their primary responsibility was the collection of rents.

In 1547 the Court of Augmentations was joined with the Court of General Surveyors, a court that had been established in 1542 out of the old household surveyors department to administer crown lands, handle cases, and register leases.

The remaining financial courts had very specific functions. The Court of First Fruits and Tenths was established in 1540 to collect from clerical benefices certain monies that had previously been sent to Rome. First fruits were the first year's profits owed by the new holder of a benefice; tenths were 10 percent of the annual income, due each year. The Court of Wards was established in 1540 (in 1542, as Wards and Liveries) to deal with monies owed to the king by virtue of his position as a feudal lord; it was also empowered to protect certain rights of marriage and wardship. In 1554 under Queen Mary, the functions of Augmentations, General Surveyors, and First Fruits and Tenths were absorbed by the Exchequer.

The Court of Wards and Liveries remained separate until it was abolished in 1660.

Augrabies Falls (South Africa): *see* Aughrabies Falls.

Augsburg, city, Bayern *Land* (Bavaria state), southern West Germany, at the junction of the Wertach and Lech rivers, on the northern tip of the Lechfeld (the river's plain). Traces of an Early Bronze Age settlement have been found at the site. Founded as a Roman colony (Augusta Vindelicorum) by Nero Claudius Drusus, younger brother of Tiberius (later emperor), in 15 BC, it was the seat of a bishopric by 739. The invading Hungarians were decisively defeated by King Otto I in 955 on the Lechfeld to the south. Augsburg became an imperial free city in 1276 and joined the Swabian League in 1331. The business houses, headed by the Fugger and Welser merchant families, were responsible for its development in the 15th and 16th centuries as a major European banking and commercial centre, encouraging both the arts and the sciences. The artists Hans Holbein, the Elder and the Younger, and Hans Burgkmair were natives of the town. At the Diet of 1530 the Augsburg Confession was read, at that of 1555 the religious Peace of Augsburg was concluded, and the League of Augsburg was decided in 1686. The city declined in the 17th century during the Thirty Years' War and fell to Bavaria in 1806.

Rotes Tor (tower), part of the old town wall, and the Church of SS. Ulrich and Afra (left), Augsburg, W.Ger.
Toni Schneiders—Bruce Coleman

Although considerably damaged in World War II, many of Augsburg's historic landmarks survived. The cathedral's west end and crypt date from 994 to 1065 and the Gothic additions from 1331 to 1432; its chief monuments are the 11th-century bronze doors, five Romanesque stained-glass windows in the nave, the bishop's throne, and the altarpieces by Holbein the Elder and Christoph Amberger. The Church of SS. Ulrich and Afra (1474–1604) contains a late-Gothic statue of the Madonna (*c.* 1500), stained-glass windows in the vestry, and a Baroque wrought-iron gate (1712). The town hall (1615–20) and the famous Fuggerei (1519), the oldest housing settlement for the poor in the world, were damaged in World War II. Both have been restored, but the famous Golden Hall in the town hall was destroyed. There are other medieval churches, three 16th-century fountains on the main street, a town museum, two art galleries, and a municipal library with a collection of archives, manuscripts, and drawings. The house of Leopold Mozart, father of the composer Wolfgang Amadeus Mozart, is now a Mozart museum. The University of Augsburg was founded in 1970; other educational establishments include three colleges of music and the Rudolph Diesel polytechnic, named after the inventor of the diesel engine.

In 1974 Augsburg annexed the neighbouring cities of Göggingen and Haunstetten. An important traffic junction, Augsburg is also one of southern Germany's busiest industrial centres. There are heavy-engineering, textile, metal, chemical, and electrical plants; and automobiles, airplanes, paper, and shoes are manufactured. Many commodities are exported, particularly diesel engines and printing machinery. Pop. (1983 est.) 247,148.

Augsburg, Peace of, first permanent legal basis for the existence of Lutheranism as well as Catholicism in Germany, promulgated on Sept. 25, 1555, by the Diet of the Holy Roman Empire assembled earlier that year at Augsburg.

The emperor Charles V's provisional ruling on the religious question, the Augsburg Interim of 1548, had been overthrown in 1552 by the revolt of the Protestant elector Maurice of Saxony and his allies. In the ensuing negotiations at Passau (summer 1552), even the Catholic princes had called for a lasting peace, for fear that otherwise the religious controversy would never be settled. The Emperor, however, was unwilling to recognize the religious division in Western Christendom as permanent and granted a peace only until the next imperial Diet.

The Diet, which opened at Augsburg on Feb. 5, 1555, was proclaimed by Charles V, but not wishing to take part in the inevitable religious compromises, he refused to attend the proceedings and empowered his brother Ferdinand (the future emperor Ferdinand I) to settle all questions.

The Diet determined that in the future no member of the empire should make war against another on religious grounds and that this peace should remain operative until the denominations were peacefully reunited. Only two denominations were recognized, the Roman Catholics and the adherents of the Confession of Augsburg—*i.e.,* the Lutherans. Moreover, in each territory of the empire, only one denomination was to be recognized, the religion of the prince's choice being thus made obligatory for his subjects. Any who adhered to the other denomination could sell his property and migrate to a territory where it was recognized. The free and imperial cities, which had lost their religious homogeneity a few years earlier, were exceptions to the general ruling. Protestant and Catholic citizens in these cities remained free to exercise their religion as they pleased. The same freedom was furthermore extended to Protestant knights and to towns and other communities that had for some time been practicing their religion in the lands of ecclesiastical princes of the empire. This last concession provoked vehement Catholic opposition, and Ferdinand circumvented the difficulty by deciding the matter on his own authority and including the clause in a separate article.

Ecclesiastical lands taken by Lutherans from prelates who were not immediate vassals of the emperor were to remain with the Lutherans if continuous possession could be proved from the time of the Treaty of Passau (Aug. 2, 1552), but, to ensure the permanence of the remaining ecclesiastical territories, the Catholics gained the condition that in the future any ecclesiastical prince who became Protestant should renounce his office, lands, and revenues. Because the Protestants would not accept this ecclesiastical reservation and the Catholics would not yield, Ferdinand incorporated the clause on his own authority with a note that agreement had not been reached on it. In fact, Protestants were in many cases able to nullify its effect.

The wish for a lasting settlement was so strong that the compromise peace, which satisfied no one completely and had many loopholes, was accepted. In spite of its shortcomings, the Peace of Augsburg saved the empire from serious internal conflicts for more than 50 years.

Augsburg, War of the League of: *see* Grand Alliance, War of the.

Augsburg Confession, Latin CONFESSIO AUGUSTANA, the basic confession of the Lutheran churches, presented June 25, 1530, in German and Latin at the Diet of Augsburg to the emperor Charles V by seven Lutheran princes and two imperial free cities. The principal author was the Reformer Philipp Melanchthon, who drew on earlier Lutheran statements of faith. The purpose was to defend the Lutherans against misrepresentations and to provide a statement of their theology that would be acceptable to the Roman Catholics in the Holy Roman Empire. On August 3 the Catholic theologians replied with the so-called Confutation (*q.v.*). The Emperor refused to receive a Lutheran counter-reply offered on September 22, but Melanchthon used it as the basis for his Apology of the Augsburg Confession (1531; *q.v.*). The unaltered 1530 version of the Confession has always been authoritative for Lutherans, but proponents of the eucharistic doctrine of Zwingli and Calvin received a modified edition prepared by Melanchthon (the *Variata* of 1540).

The Unaltered Augsburg Confession contains 28 articles. The first 21 set forth the Lutherans' overall doctrine in order to demonstrate that "they dissent in no article of faith from the Catholic Church." The remaining articles discuss abuses that had crept into the Western Church in the centuries immediately preceding the Reformation: Communion under one kind (the people received the bread only), enforced priestly celibacy, the mass as an expiatory sacrifice, compulsory confession, human institutions designed to merit grace, abuses in connection with monasticism, and the expanded authority claimed by the bishops.

The Confession was translated into English in 1536 and was a definite influence on the Thirty-nine Articles of the Anglicans and the Twenty-five Articles of Religion of the Methodists.

Augsburg Interim, temporary doctrinal agreement between German Catholics and Protestants, proclaimed in May 1548 at the Diet of Augsburg (1547–48), which became imperial law on June 30, 1548. It was prepared and accepted at the insistence of the Holy Roman emperor Charles V, who hoped to establish temporary religious unity in Germany until differences could be worked out in a general council of the Catholic Church.

Consisting of 26 articles, the Augsburg Interim primarily reflected a Catholic viewpoint. It did, however, allow clerical marriage and communion in both kinds (bread and wine) for the laity.

Several Protestant electors objected to the Catholic emphasis of the Augsburg Interim and refused to abide by it. Charles attempted to force its acceptance, an action that led the Protestants to adopt the Leipzig Interim, which upheld Protestant doctrines, at the Diet of Leipzig in December 1548. Neither interim was fully accepted, and a German religious settlement was not brought about until the Peace of Augsburg (1555).

augury, prophetic divining of the future by observation of natural phenomena—particularly the behaviour of birds and animals and the examination of their entrails and other parts, but also by scrutiny of man-made ob-

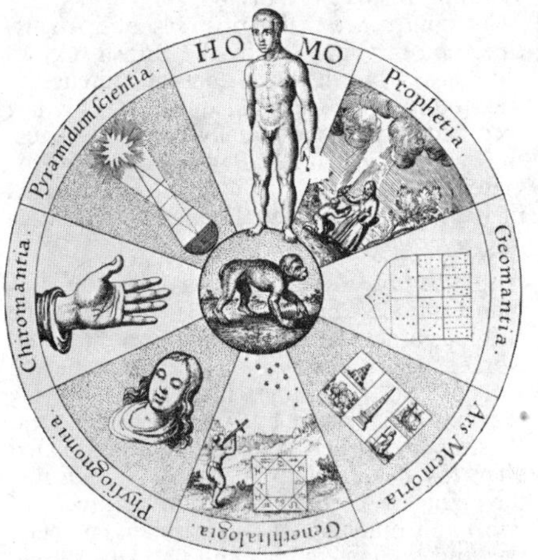

Synopsis of the diviner's arts, from *Utriusque Cosmi . . . Historia* by Robert Fludd, 1617–21
Ronan Picture Library and E.P. Goldschmidt & Co. Ltd.

jects and situations. The term derives from the official Roman augurs, whose constitutional function was not to foretell the future but to discover whether or not the gods approved of a proposed course of action, especially political or military. Two types of divinatory sign, or omen, were recognized: the most important was that deliberately watched for, such as lightning, thunder, flights and cries of birds, or the pecking behaviour of sacred chickens; of less moment was that which occurred casually, such as the unexpected appearance of animals sacred to the gods—the bear (Artemis), wolf (Apollo), eagle (Zeus), serpent (Asclepius), and owl (Minerva), for instance—or such other mundane signs as the accidental spilling of salt, sneezing, stumbling, or the creaking of furniture.

The prophetic art is age-old; the practice of augury is well substantiated in the Bible. Cicero's *De divinatione* (*Concerning Divination*), dated probably 44 BC, provides the best source on ancient divinatory practices. Both he and Plato distinguish between augury that can be taught and augury that is divinely inspired in ecstatic trance. In China for millennia many have sought the counsel of the *I Ching* ("Book of Changes") before taking important action. This book interprets the hexagram created by the tossing of yarrow stalks. Among the vast number of sources of augury, each with its own specialist jargon and ritual, were atmospheric phenomena (aeromancy), cards (cartomancy), dice or lots (cleromancy), dots and other marks on paper (geomancy), fire and smoke (pyromancy), the shoulder blades of animals (scapulimancy), entrails of sacrificed animals (haruspicy), or their livers, which were considered to be the seat of life (hepatoscopy).

August (German, Polish, etc., personal name): *see under* Augustus.

August, eighth month of the Gregorian calendar. *See* month.

Augusta, in full MARIA LUISE AUGUSTA KATHARINA (b. Sept. 30, 1811, Weimar, Saxe-Weimar—d. Jan. 7, 1890, Berlin), queen consort of Prussia from 1861 and German empress from 1871, the wife of William I.

The younger daughter of Charles Frederick, grand duke of Saxe-Weimar-Eisenach, she was married to the future king and emperor on June 11, 1829. She was jealously devoted to her children, Frederick William (later king and emperor as Frederick III) and Louise (grand duchess of Baden from 1856); her strong antagonism toward Otto von Bismarck was aroused in 1848, when he tried to persuade her husband to renounce his right of succession to the Prussian throne in favour of the youthful Frederick William, who would have been a figurehead under Bismarck's control.

Augusta was well-disposed toward liberals and Roman Catholics and was a friend of Queen Victoria of Great Britain.

Augusta, town, Siracusa province, Sicily, Italy, north of the city of Syracuse; it lies on a long sandy island off the southeast coast between the Golfo (gulf) di Augusta and the Ionian Sea and is connected by two bridges with the mainland. The town was founded near the site of the ancient Dorian town of Megara Hyblaea in 1232 by Emperor Frederick II for the rebellious people of Centuripe and Montalbano, towns that were destroyed because of their disaffection. Frederick called it Augusta Veneranda, and it became one of his favourite resorts. The town was rebuilt after the earthquake of 1693. It was chosen by the Knights of Malta to be a supply repository at the beginning of the 19th century. In 1861 Augusta (also spelled Agosta) became part of the Kingdom of Italy. In World War II it was one of the ports of disembarkation of the Anglo-American forces for the invasion of Sicily on July 10, 1943. Notable landmarks include the Swabian castle (now a prison), the cathedral (1769), and the Palazzo Comunale (1699).

The traditional industries are agriculture (cereals, olives, grapes, market produce), salt mining along the coast, fishing, and the preserving of anchovy. Long a naval station, Augusta has become a principal Sicilian trading port, with industrial growth on its extensive waterfront, including an oil refinery and a large chemical complex, which have caused severe environmental pollution problems. Pop. (1981 prelim.) mun., 38,900.

Augusta, city, river port, and seat (1777) of Richmond County, eastern Georgia, U.S., on the Savannah River, on the Fall Line where the Piedmont Plateau meets the Coastal Plain. The area was explored in 1540 by Hernando de Soto, but not until 1735 was a fortified fur-trading post established on the site (now marked by a Celtic cross) by James Oglethorpe, the founder of Georgia. The ensuing settlement was named for Princess Augusta, mother of England's George III.

During the Revolutionary period, Augusta saw bitter fighting and bloody reprisal, changing hands several times between the British and Americans. Twice during the struggle it served briefly as temporary capital of Georgia, and then was the capital again from 1786 to 1795. The Georgia state convention ratified the U.S. Constitution there on Jan. 2, 1788. During the Civil War the largest gunpowder factory in the Confederacy was located in Augusta; its 176-ft (54-m) chimney remains as a memorial to the war dead. Many well-preserved buildings of Georgian and Classic Revival design, notably MacKay House (*c.* 1760) and Ware Mansion (1818) stand along tree-shaded streets.

One of the early milling towns of the South, and still a centre for cotton trading, it is an important textile manufacturing centre. From local deposits of high-grade kaolin, firebrick and related products are made. Manufactures are highly diversified, and agricultural industries are important. The Clark Hill Dam, one of a series of 11 above Augusta for power production and flood control, helps insure water levels in the river port below the city.

Augusta College was founded in 1925, and the city is also the home of the Medical College of Georgia (founded as the Medical Academy in 1828) and Paine College (1882). Augusta is the home of the National Golf Club, host to the annual Masters Tournament. Ft. Gordon, an army military reservation, is 11 mi (18 km) southwest of the city. Inc. town, 1789; city, 1798. Pop. (1980) city, 47,532; metropolitan area (SMSA), 327,372.

Augusta, capital (1832) of Maine, U.S., seat (1799) of Kennebec County, at the head of navigation on the Kennebec River, 57 mi (92 km) northeast of Portland. The city's establishment and early prosperity, which began with the arrival of traders from the Plymouth Colony of Massachusetts in 1628, can be attributed to its location on navigable tidewater, 39 mi (63 km) from the Atlantic Ocean. A trading post was established on a site the Canibas Indians called Koussinoc. The first permanent structure, Ft. Western, was built there in 1754 for protection against Indian attacks. (In 1919 the fort was restored as a historic monument and museum.) In 1797 the settlement was incorporated as the town of Harrington; the present name (for Pamela Augusta, daughter of Revolutionary War general, Harry Dearborn) was adopted later that year.

Light industry and state government operations augmented by the University of Maine at Augusta (opened 1965) are the economic mainstays; manufactures include paper, textiles, food products, and shoes. The State House (1829–32) was originally designed by Charles Bulfinch, with a 185-ft dome topped

Augusta, Maine, on the Kennebec River
Gordon A. Reims

by a statue of Wisdom created by W. Clark Noble. The Executive Mansion was the former home of James G. Blaine, unsuccessful presidential candidate in 1884. A 2,100-ft (640-m) bridge of cantilever deck truss design (1950) spans the river in the heart of the city. With the Belgrade chain of lakes 15 mi north and the Kennebec River reaching south to the sea, Augusta is one of the state's leading vacation centres. Inc. town, 1797; city, 1849. Pop. (1980) 21,819.

Augusta, Julia: *see* Livia Drusilla.

Augustan Age, one of the most illustrious periods in Latin literary history, from approximately 43 BC to AD 18; together with the preceding Ciceronian period (*q.v.*), it forms the Golden Age (*q.v.*) of Latin literature. Marked by civil peace and prosperity, the age reached its highest literary expression in poetry, a polished and sophisticated verse generally addressed to a patron or to the emperor Augustus and dealing with themes of patriotism, love, and nature. One decade alone, 29 to 19 BC, saw the publication of Virgil's *Georgics* and the completion of the *Aeneid*; the appearance of Horace's *Odes*, Books I–III, and *Epistles*, Book I; the elegies (Books I–III) of Sextus Propertius, a member of a group of promising young poets under the patronage of Gaius Maecenas; and Books I–II of the elegies of Tibullus, who was under the patronage of Messalla. During those 10 years also, Livy began his monumental history of Rome, and another historian, Pollio, was writing his important but lost history of recent events. Ovid, the author of *Metamorphoses,* a mythological history of the world from the creation to the Augustan Age, was the last great writer of the Golden Age; his death in exile in AD 17 marked the close of the period.

By extension, the name Augustan Age also is applied to a "classical" period in the literature of any nation, especially to the 18th century in England and, less frequently, to the 17th century—the age of Corneille, Racine, and Molière—in France. Some critics prefer to limit the English Augustan Age to a period covered by the reign of Queen Anne (1702–14), when writers such as Alexander Pope, Joseph Addison, Sir Richard Steele, John Gay, and Matthew Prior flourished. Others, however, would extend it backward to include John Dryden and forward to take in Samuel Johnson.

Augustan History, Latin HISTORIA AUGUSTA, a collection of biographies of the Roman emperors (Augusti) from Hadrian to Numerian (117–284), an important source for the history of the Roman Empire.

The work is incomplete in its surviving form (it probably originally began with one of Hadrian's predecessors, Nerva or Trajan), and its original title is unknown. Its authorship and date of composition are also matters of argument. The names of six authors of the early 4th century are given in the manuscript itself, but some scholars regard these as spurious and believe that the *History* was written in the late 4th century. Its point of view is consciously pagan, and the author or authors may have been trying to counteract the growing dominance of Christianity, perhaps influenced by the paganism of the emperor Julian (reigned 361–363).

The first part of the work, from Hadrian to Caracalla, is thought to be based on reliable sources and is of great historical value; the remainder is considered to be generally less reliable.

Augustana Evangelical Lutheran Church, church organized by Norwegian and Swedish immigrants in 1860 in Jefferson Prairie, Wis., as the Scandinavian Augustana Evangelical Lutheran Synod. Tufve Nilsson Hasselquist, an ordained minister in the Church of Sweden, was the first president. It took its name from Confessio Augustana, the Latin name for the Augsburg Confession, written in 1530 by German Lutheran Reformers. After its Norwegian membership withdrew in 1870, the church was composed primarily of Swedish immigrants and their descendants. The first congregations were organized in New Sweden, Iowa (1848), served by a lay pastor, and in Andover, Ill. (1850), served by Lars P. Esbjörn, the pioneer Swedish missionary pastor to the Swedish immigrants of the Middle West. Under the leadership of Esbjörn and Hasselquist, many congregations were started, and Augustana College and Theological Seminary, Rock Island, Ill., was organized, with Esbjörn as its first president.

A member of the General Council of the Evangelical Lutheran Church of North America, an association of Lutheran synods organized in 1867, Augustana withdrew when that group became part of the United Lutheran Church in America in 1918. In 1962, however, the Augustana Church (with more than 600,000 members) merged with the United Lutheran Church in America, the American Evangelical Lutheran Church, and the Finnish Evangelical Lutheran Church (Suomi Synod) to form the Lutheran Church in America.

Augustine, SAINT, also called SAINT AUGUSTINE OF HIPPO, Augustine also spelled AUGUSTIN, original Latin name AURELIUS AUGUSTINUS (b. Nov. 13, AD 354, Tagaste, Numidia—d. Aug. 28, 430, Hippo Regius), bishop of Hippo in Roman Africa from 396 to 430 and the major Christian theologian of the early Western Church. His best known works are the *Confessions* and *The City of God.*

A brief account of the life and works of Saint Augustine follows; for a full biography, *see* MACROPAEDIA: Augustine.

Augustine recounted the story of his restless youth and his conversion in the *Confessions.* Though his mother, Monica, was a devout Christian, Augustine was not baptized in infancy. As a 19-year-old student at Carthage he read a treatise of Cicero that directed him to philosophy. His first discovery was Manichaeism, a materialistic dualism. At the age of about 28, he went to Rome and then to Milan, where he met the bishop Ambrose. Disillusioned with Manichaeism, he turned to Neoplatonism, in which he found solutions to his problems about the being of God and the nature and origin of evil. He was converted to Christianity in 386 and was baptized by Ambrose in 387.

Augustine returned to Africa, was ordained priest in 391, and became bishop of Hippo in 396. He served as pastor, teacher, preacher, and civil judge. He wrote extensively, especially in controversy with heretical groups (the Manichaeans, Donatists, and Pelagians) and in commentary on the scriptures. His masterpiece was *The City of God,* which espoused a religious philosophy of predestination.

Augustine OF CANTERBURY, SAINT, also called AUSTIN (b. Rome?—d. May 26, 604/605, Canterbury, Kent, Eng.; feast day, England and Wales, May 26; elsewhere May 28), first archbishop of Canterbury and the apostle of England, who founded the Christian Church in southern England.

Probably of aristocratic birth, Augustine was prior of the Benedictine monastery of St. Andrew, Rome, when Pope St. Gregory I the Great chose him to lead an unprecedented mission of about 40 monks to England, which was then largely pagan. They left in June 596, but, arriving in southern Gaul, they were warned of the perils awaiting them and sent Augustine back to Rome. There Gregory encouraged him with letters of commendation (dated July 23, 596), and he set out once more.

The entourage landed in the spring of 597 on the Isle of Thanet, off the southeast coast of England, and was well received by King Aethelberht (Ethelbert) I of Kent, who gave the missionaries a dwelling place in Canterbury and the old St. Martin's Church, where he allowed them to preach. With Aethelberht's support, their work led to many conversions, including that of the King. In the following autumn Augustine was consecrated bishop of the English by St. Virgilius at Arles.

Thousands of Aethelberht's subjects were reportedly baptized by Augustine on Christmas Day 597, and he subsequently dispatched two of his monks to Rome with a report of this extraordinary event and a request for further help and advice. They returned in 601 with the pallium (*i.e.,* symbol of metropolitan jurisdiction) from Gregory for Augustine and with more missionaries, including the celebrated SS. Mellitus, Justus, and Paulinus. Gregory, with whom Augustine corresponded throughout his apostolate, directed him to purify pagan temples for Christian worship and to consecrate 12 suffragan bishops; thus, he was given authority over the bishops in Britain, and the evangelization of the Kingdom of Kent began.

Augustine founded Christ Church, Canterbury, as his cathedral and the monastery of SS. Peter and Paul (known after his death as St. Augustine's, where the early archbishops were buried), which came to rank as the second Benedictine house in all Europe. Canterbury thus was established as the primatial see of England, a position maintained thereafter. In 604 he established the episcopal sees of London (for the East Saxons), consecrating Mellitus as its bishop, and of Rochester, consecrating Justus as its bishop.

At a conference with British bishops, Augustine tried in vain to unify the British (Celtic) churches of North Wales and the churches he was founding. A second conference, his last recorded act, proved equally fruitless. Augustine was buried at SS. Peter and Paul. F.A. Gasquet's *Mission of St. Augustine* appeared in 1924, followed by M. Deanesly's *Augustine of Canterbury* in 1964.

Augustinian, also called AUSTIN, in the Roman Catholic Church, member of any of the religious orders and congregations of men and women whose constitutions are based on the Rule of St. Augustine, instructions on the religious life written by Augustine, the great Western theologian, and widely disseminated after his death, AD 430. More specifically, the name is used to designate members of two main branches of Augustinians, namely, the Augustinian Canons and the Augustinian Hermits, with their female offshoots.

The Augustinian Canons, or Austin Canons (in full, the Canons Regular of Saint Augustine), were, in the 11th century, the first religious order of men in the Roman Catholic Church to combine clerical status with a full common life. The moral impulse emanating from the Roman synods of 1059 and 1063 and the Gregorian Reform led many canons to give up private ownership and to live together according to monastic ideals. By 1150 the adoption of the Rule of St. Augustine by these canons was almost universal. The order grew and flourished until the Protestant Reformation, during which time many of its foundations perished. The French Revolution also put an end to a number of its houses. Modern emphasis has been on mission, educational, and hospital work.

The Augustinian Hermits, or Austin Friars (in full, the Order of the Hermit Friars of Saint Augustine; O.S.A.), were one of the four great mendicant orders of the Middle Ages. Dispersed by the Vandal invasion of northern Africa (*c.* 428), a number of congregations of hermits who had been following the Rule of St. Augustine founded monasteries in central and northern Italy. These remained independent of one another until the 13th century, when Pope Innocent IV in 1244 established them as one order and when Alexander IV in 1256 called them from their solitary seclusion as hermits to an active lay apostolate in the cities. The order spread rapidly throughout Europe and took a prominent part in university life and ecclesiastical affairs; perhaps its most famous member was the Protestant Reformer Martin Luther in the 16th century. Its members now dedicate themselves to several activities, including foreign missions, as well as to the advancement of learning by teaching and scholarly research.

An offshoot of the Augustinian Hermits are the Augustinian Recollects (O.A.R.), formed in the 16th century by friars who desired a rule of stricter observance and a return to the eremetic ideals of solitude and contemplation. In 1588 the monastery at Talavera de la Reina in Spain was designated for the Recollects, and Luis de León was directed to devise constitutions for their government; but the movement proved so popular that soon it required four monasteries. In 1602 the Recollects were established as a distinct province of the Augustinians and in 1912 as an independent order. They now engage in high school and college teaching, administer parishes, and conduct retreats and missions.

Among nuns, the term Second Order of St. Augustine applies only to those nuns who are jurisdictionally dependent upon the Augustinian Friars. They were founded in 1264 and, until 1401, remained strictly cloistered, but at that date they began to accept third order affiliates—women who desired to perform apostolic works outside the cloister, in schools, hospitals, and missions.

A distinct group is the Hospital Sisters of Hôtel-Dieu and Malestroit. Sisters following the Rule of St. Augustine were staffing the Hôtel-Dieu, in Paris, at least from about 1217. They not only survived the French Revolution but were even allowed to continue their work. Though expelled in 1907, they managed to open other hospitals and today maintain several institutions.

Augustinus, Aurelius: *see* Augustine, Saint.

Augustulus, Romulus: *see* Romulus Augustulus.

Augustus, name of rulers grouped below by country and indicated by the symbol •.

Foreign-language equivalents:

German	August
Latin	Augustus
Polish	August

POLAND

• **Augustus I:** *see* Sigismund II Augustus *under* Sigismund (Poland).

• **Augustus II,** also called AUGUSTUS FREDERICK, byname AUGUSTUS THE STRONG, Polish AUGUST FRYDERYK, or AUGUST MOCNY, German AUGUST FRIEDRICH, or AUGUST DER STARKE (b. May 12, 1670, Dresden, Saxony—d. Feb. 1, 1733, Warsaw), king of Poland and elector of Saxony (as Frederick Augustus I). Though he regained Poland's former provinces of Podolia and the Ukraine, his reign marked the beginning of Poland's decline as a European power.

The second son of Elector John George III of Saxony, Augustus succeeded his elder brother John George IV as elector in 1694. After the death of John III Sobieski of Poland (1696), Augustus became one of 18 candidates for the Polish throne. To further his chances, he converted to Catholicism, thereby alienating his Lutheran Saxon subjects and causing his wife, a Hohenzollern princess, to leave him. Shortly after his coronation (1697) the "Turkish War," which had begun in 1683 and in which he had participated intermittently since 1695, was concluded; by the Treaty of Carlowitz in 1699, Poland received Podolia, with Kamieniec (Kamenets) and the Ukraine west of the Dnepr River from the Ottoman Empire.

Seeking to conquer the former Polish province of Livonia, then in Swedish hands, for his own Saxon house of Wettin, Augustus formed an alliance with Russia and Denmark against Sweden. Although the Polish Diet refused to support him, he invaded Livonia in 1700, thus beginning the Great Northern War (1700–21), which ruined Poland economically. In July 1702 Augustus' forces were

Augustus II, oil painting by Louis de Silvestre; in the State Collections of Art in the Wawel, Kraków, Pol.

By courtesy of the Panstwowe Zbiory Sztuki na Wawelu, Krakow, Pol.

driven back and defeated by King Charles XII of Sweden at Kliszów, northeast of Kraków. Deposed by one of the Polish factions in July 1704, he fled to Saxony, which the Swedes invaded in 1706. Charles XII forced Augustus to sign the Treaty of Altranstädt (September 1706), formally abdicating and recognizing Sweden's candidate, Stanisław Leszczyński, as king of Poland (*see* Altranstädt, treaties of). In 1709, after Russia defeated Sweden at the Battle of Poltava, Augustus declared the treaty void and, supported by Tsar Peter I the Great, forced the Diet to restore him as king of Poland (1710).

When Russia intervened (1716–17) in an internal dispute between Augustus and dissident Polish nobles (Confederation of Tarnogród; *q.v.*) and, in 1720, annexed Livonia, the King saw the danger of Russia's growing influence in Polish affairs. He tried unsuccessfully to create a hereditary Polish monarchy transmissible to his one legitimate son, Frederick Augustus II (eventually king of Poland as Augustus III), and to secure other lands for his many illegitimate children. But his hopes of establishing a strong monarchy came to naught. By the end of his reign, Poland had declined from a major European power to a protectorate of Russia, and when he died the War of the Polish Succession broke out. A man of extravagant and luxurious tastes, he did much to develop Saxon industry and trade and greatly embellished the city of Dresden.

• **Augustus III,** also called AUGUSTUS FREDERICK, Polish AUGUST FRYDERYK, German AUGUST FRIEDRICH (b. Oct. 17, 1696, Dresden, Saxony—d. Oct. 5, 1763, Dresden), king

Augustus III, detail of an oil painting by Louis de Silvestre; in the State Collections of Art in the Wawel, Kraków, Pol.

By courtesy of the Panstwowe Zbiory Sztuki na Wawelu, Krakow, Pol.

of Poland and elector of Saxony (as Frederick Augustus II), whose reign witnessed one of the greatest periods of disorder within Poland. More interested in ease and pleasure than in affairs of state, this notable patron of the arts left the administration of Saxony and Poland to his chief adviser, Heinrich von Brühl, who in turn left Polish administration chiefly to the powerful Czartoryski family.

The only legitimate son of Frederick Augustus I of Saxony (Augustus II of Poland), he followed his father's example by joining the Roman Catholic Church in 1712. In 1719 he married Maria Josepha, daughter of the Holy Roman emperor Joseph I. He became elector of Saxony on his father's death (February 1733). As a candidate for the Polish crown, he secured the support of the emperor Charles VI by assenting to the Pragmatic Sanction of 1713, designed to preserve the integrity of the Habsburg inheritance, and that of the Russian empress Anna by supporting Russia's claim to Courland. Chosen king by a small minority of electors on Oct. 5, 1733, he drove his rival, the former Polish king Stanisław I Leszczyński, into exile. He was crowned in Kraków on Jan. 17, 1734, and was generally recognized as king in Warsaw in June 1736.

Augustus gave Saxon support to Austria against Prussia in the War of the Austrian Succession (1742) and again in the Seven Years' War (1756). His last years were marked by the increasing influence of the Czartoryski and Poniatowski families, and by the intervention of Catherine the Great of Russia in Polish affairs.

ROMAN EMPIRE

• **Augustus, Caesar,** also called (until 27 BC) OCTAVIAN, original name GAIUS OCTAVIUS, adopted name GAIUS JULIUS CAESAR OCTAVIANUS (b. Sept. 23, 63 BC—d. Aug. 19, AD 14, Nola, near Naples), first Roman emperor, introduced an autocratic regime known as the principate (of which he was the *princeps,* or first citizen) which enabled him, working through institutions that were republican in outward form, to overhaul every aspect of Roman life, and to bring stability and prosperity to the Greco-Roman world. One of the great administrative geniuses of history, he centralized the power of the Roman empire of his day in Rome itself, and established the Pax Romana.

A brief account of the life and works of Augustus follows; for a full biography, *see* MACROPAEDIA: Augustus.

Octavian was born of a prosperous family and was named adoptive son and heir of Julius Caesar (his great-uncle) at age 18. In the power struggle that followed Caesar's death, he became (together with Mark Antony and Lepidus) one of three triumvirs governing a reconstituted Roman state (43 BC). After defeating Caesar's assassins, Brutus and Cassius, at Philippi (42), Octavian and Antony partitioned the empire, with Octavian receiving the west as his portion. Octavian then overcame various rivals, including Lepidus (in 32), and Antony and the queen of Egypt, Cleopatra (in 31), thus becoming ruler of the Greco-Roman world. From 31 to 23 he ruled as consul, thus preserving republican forms of government, but in 27 he accepted the title Augustus. In 23 he received imperial power (to be exercised in contingencies), as well as the power of tribune. He gradually reformed the administrative structure of the empire and added new territories, especially in Europe. By the time of his death, his adoptive son Tiberius had already become his successor in all but name. After death he was deified.

SAXONY

• **Augustus** (b. July 31, 1526, Freiberg, Saxony—d. Feb. 12, 1586, Dresden, Saxony), elector of Saxony and leader of Protestant Germany who, by reconciling his fellow Lutherans with the Roman Catholic Habsburg Holy

Augustus, portrait by Lucas Cranach the Younger; in the Gemäldegalerie, Dresden, E.Ger.

By courtesy of the Staatliche Kunstsammlungen Dresden, E.Ger.; photograph, Deutsche Fotothek Dresden

Roman emperors, helped bring the initial belligerency of the Reformation in Germany to an end. Under his administration Saxony enjoyed economic and commercial prosperity at a time when commerce in Germany as a whole was decaying.

Augustus succeeded to the electorate of Saxony and the leadership of Germany's Protestant princes on the death of his brother Maurice in 1553. Almost immediately a change in Saxon policy took place. While his brother had been an active opponent of the Habsburgs in the Schmalkaldic League and sought to make his house (the Albertine branch of the Wettin dynasty) a great power in central Germany, Augustus was content to consolidate and develop his holdings. By so doing, he split the Protestant leadership. In 1555 he accepted the Peace of Augsburg, which stopped hostilities on religious grounds between Catholic and Lutheran princes in Germany.

Augustus originally followed the religious doctrines of the Lutheran reformer Philipp Melanchthon. When he began to suspect several of his advisers of Calvinist leanings, however, he reacted with harsh and swift punishment. His hatred of Calvinism was strong, and from 1574 Saxony followed an orthodox form of Lutheranism. He waged a constant struggle for *Glaubensreinheit* (purity of religious belief) in his territories.

With the active encouragement and assistance of his wife, Princess Anna of Denmark (1532–85), Augustus transformed Saxony into a model state. His reorganization of the tax structure and reform of justice increased the state's efficiency and solvency. Saxon wealth was further enhanced by his encouragement of production and trade. The development of mining and the manufacturing skills of Dutch Protestant immigrants did much to promote the state's economic well-being.

Augustus' altar of peace: *see* Ara Pacis.

Auhausen, Union of (Germany): *see* Protestant Union.

Aujeszky's disease: *see* pseudorabies.

auk, in general, any of the 22 species (21 living) of the family Alcidae (order Charadriiformes), but especially three species, the great auk (*q.v.*; *Pinguinus impennis*), extinct since 1844; the little auk, or dovekie (*q.v.*; *Plautus alle*); and the razorbill, or razor-billed auk (*q.v.*; *Alca torda*). Auks are diving birds of the northern seas.

Birds of the auk family, often called alcids, range in length from about 15 to 40 centimetres (6 to 16 inches), though the great auk was about 75 cm (30 in.) long. They have short wings and legs, and webbed feet. Limited in distribution to Arctic, subarctic, and north temperate regions (with a few species south to Baja California), they nest colonially on ledges of cliffs and in rock crevices or burrows adjacent to the sea, and many spend the stormy winter months far from land. Auks are wholly dependent upon the sea for their food, which consists of fish, crustaceans, mollusks, and plankton. Although great auks could not fly, the living species can.

The true auks are black and white, and stand erect on land, as do the penguins of the Antarctic. A related smaller bird is the auklet (*q.v.*). *See also* guillemot; murre; murrelet; puffin.

auklet, also called SEA SPARROW, any of six species of small seabirds of the family Alcidae (order Charadriiformes). They breed primarily in the Bering Sea and the North Pacific; some winter as far south as Japan and Mexico. Auklets in breeding plumage differ from the related murrelets in having plumes and other head ornaments, including brightly coloured bill plates like those of their relatives the puffins. They nest in crevices near the sea, laying a single egg. The young remain in the nest until fully fledged.

Crested auklet (*Aethia cristatella*)
Jean Bedard

The smallest member of the entire family is the least auklet (*Aethia pusilla*), about 15 centimetres (6 inches) long. It winters far north in rough waters. The plainest and grayest species is Cassin's auklet (*Ptychoramphus aleuticus*), a common resident from the Aleutians to Baja California.

Aukrust, Olav (b. Jan. 21, 1883, Gudbrandsdalen, Nor.—d. Nov. 3, 1929, Gudbrandsdalen), regional poet whose verse has contributed to the development of Nynorsk (an amalgam of rural Norwegian dialects) as a literary language.

Aukrust was a teacher and later headmaster at a folk high school. As a young man he was an eager student of the language spoken in the countryside and received a government stipend to study Gudbrandsdalen dialects, in which all his verse is written. He drew inspiration from the folk legend, natural surroundings, and peasant life of his native area. As a result, although he wrote about matters of universal interest, he remained a poet of that region. The mystical poem *Himmelvarden* (1916; "Cairn of Heaven") is considered his most important work.

aula regis (Latin: "king's court"): *see* curia regis.

Aulacorhynchus (bird): *see* toucanet.

Aulard, François-Alphonse (b. July 19, 1849, Montbron, Fr.—d. Oct. 23, 1928, Paris), one of the leading historians of the French Revolution, noted for the application of the rules of historical criticism to the revolutionary period. His writings dispelled many of the myths surrounding the Revolution.

Aulard obtained his doctorate in 1877 and until 1884 taught French literature in various provincial universities. In 1879 he began his study of the French Revolution; his first publications concerned parliamentary oratory: *Les Orateurs de l'Assemblée constituante,* 2 vol. (1882; "The Orators of the Constituent Assembly") and *Les Orateurs de la Législative et de la Convention* (1885; "The Orators of the Legislative Assembly and the Convention").

Appointed to the new chair of the history of the French Revolution at the University of Paris (1887), Aulard specialized in the scientific documentation of the revolutionary period. He edited many large collections, among them *Recueil des actes du comité de salut public,* 16 vol. (1889–1904; "Collection of Acts by the Committee of Public Safety"); *La Société des Jacobins,* 6 vol. (1889–97; "The Jacobin Society"); and *Paris pendant la réaction thermidorienne et sous le directoire,* 5 vol. (1898–1902; "Paris During the Thermidorian Reaction and Under the Directory"). The important periodical *La Révolution française* was published under his supervision as well as various editions of memoirs written by men of the Revolution.

He also wrote works of broader scope: *Histoire politique de la Révolution française, origines et développement, de la démocratie et de la république, 1789–1804,* 4 vol. (*The French Revolution, a Political History, 1789–1804,* 1910) is especially valuable for its analyses of the currents of public opinion, description of party organization, and explanation of the mechanism of government. His *Taine, historien de la Révolution française* (1901; "Taine, Historian of the French Revolution") is a critique of Taine's work.

Also active politically, Aulard was a founder and president of the League of the Rights of Man, formed during the Dreyfus affair, and cofounder of *Quotidien,* an independent democratic journal. He became president of the Société de l'Histoire de la Révolution Française (1904) and presided at the International Congress of the League of Nations in Berlin (1927).

Aulis, ancient Greek town in Boeotia, separated from Chalcis (on the island of Euboea) three miles to the north by the Euboean Channel. Aulis was traditionally held to be the port from which the Greek fleet set off to the siege of Troy and the scene of the related sacrifice of Iphigenia, the eldest daughter of Agamemnon, king of Mycenae.

Aulne, Anne-Robert-Jacques Turgot, baron de l': *see* Turgot, Anne-Robert-Jacques.

Aulnoy, Marie-Catherine Le Jumel de-Barneville, comtesse d' (countess of), Aulnoy also spelled AUNOY (b. 1650/51, near Honfleur, Fr.—d. Jan. 14, 1705, Paris), writer of fairy tales and of novels of court intrigue, whose personal intrigues were commensurate with those described in her books.

Shortly after her marriage as a young girl in 1666, Marie d'Aulnoy conspired with her mother and their two lovers to accuse falsely

Comtesse d'Aulnoy, detail of an engraving by Basan after a painting by Élisabeth Chéron
By courtesy of the Bibliotheque Nationale, Paris

Marie's husband, a middle-aged financier, of high treason. When the plot miscarried, she was forced to spend the next 15 years out of the country, leading a peripatetic existence in Spain, the Netherlands, and England before returning to Paris and beginning her literary career in 1685. Her best remembered works are *Contes de fées* (1697; "Fairy Tales") and

Les Contes nouveaux ou les fées à la mode (1698; "New Tales, or the Fancy of the Fairies"), written in the manner of the great fairy tales of Charles Perrault but laced with her own sardonic touch. Her pseudo-historical novels, which were immensely popular all over Europe, include *Hippolyte, comte de Douglas* (1690; *Hippolitus, Earl of Douglas,* 1708), *Memoires de la cour d'Espagne* (1690; *Memoirs from the Court of Spain,* 1692), and *Relation du voyage d'Espagne* (1691; *Travels into Spain,* 1692). An English-translation collection of her works, in four volumes, was published in 1707, including the fairy tales, which were frequently reprinted throughout the 16th century.

aulos, Roman TIBIA, in ancient Greek music, a single- or double-reed pipe, classically played in pairs (*auloi*), postclassically played singly. Under a variety of names it was the principal wind instrument of most ancient Middle Eastern peoples and lasted in Europe up to the early Middle Ages. When played in pairs,

Auloi player with *phorbeia,* and dancer with *krotala,* detail from kylix signed by Epictetus, found at Vulci, Italy, *c.* 520–510 BC; in the British Museum, London
By courtesy of the trustees of the British Museum, London

the two pipes, of cane, wood, or metal, were held one in each hand and sounded simultaneously. In classical times the pipes were equal in length, each having three or four finger holes. Later, lengths became unequal and the number of holes increased.

The Greeks usually used double reeds of cane held in the pipes by bulbous sockets. A leather strap (*phorbeia;* Latin *capistrum*) was often tied across the cheeks to support them in the powerful blowing necessary to sound the pipes. The technical details mentioned by classical authors are too few and too obscure in meaning to explain further how the instrument was played or for what musical purpose it was designed. Typologically similar are the modern Sardinian *launeddas,* a triple pipe sounded by single reeds, and a host of double pipes, mostly parallel with single reeds, played as folk instruments in the Mediterranean area and the Middle East.

Where the same name may denote a person, place, or thing, the articles will be found in that order

---

Aulus (ancient Roman personal name, or praenomen): *see under* gens or family name or honorific (*e.g.,* under Vitellius for Aulus Vitellius).

Aumale, Henri-Eugène-Philippe-Louis d'Orléans, duc d' (duke of) (b. Jan. 16, 1822, Paris—d. May 7, 1897, Zucco, Sicily), fourth son of King Louis-Philippe of France, colonialist, and a leader of the Orleanists (*q.v.*), supporters of constitutional monarchy.

He entered an army career at age 17 and distinguished himself in Algerian campaigns; in 1847 he became lieutenant general and governor of France's African possessions. An exile in England after the Revolution of 1848, he returned to France in 1871 and served as an Orleanist deputy. In 1873 he presided at the trial of Gen. Achille Bazaine (*q.v.*). Retiring from public life in 1883, he spent the rest of his life in research and writing.

Aung San (b. 1914?, Natmauk, Burma—d. July 19, 1947, Rangoon), Burmese nationalist leader and assassinated hero who was instrumental in securing Burma's independence from Great Britain. Before World War II he was actively anti-British, then allied with the Japanese during World War II, but switched to the Allies before leading the Burmese drive for autonomy.

Born of a family distinguished in the resistance movement after the British annexation of 1886, he became secretary of the students' union at Rangoon University and, with U Nu, led the students' strike there in February 1936. After Burma's separation from India in 1937 and his graduation in 1938, he worked for the nationalist Dobama Asi-ayone (We-Burmans Association), becoming its secretary general in 1939.

While seeking foreign support for Burma's independence in 1940, Aung San was contacted in China by the Japanese. They then assisted him in raising a Burmese military force to aid them in their 1942 invasion of Burma. Known as the "Burma Independence Army," it grew with the advance of the Japanese and tended to take over local administration of occupied areas. Serving as minister of defense in Ba Maw's puppet government (1943–45), he became skeptical of Japanese promises of Burmese independence, even if an unlikely Japanese victory were to occur, and was displeased with their treatment of Burmese forces. Thus, in March 1945, Maj. Gen. Aung San switched his Burma National Army to the Allied cause.

After the Japanese surrender in August 1945, the British sought to incorporate his forces into the regular army, but he held key members back, forming the People's Volunteer Organization. This was ostensibly a veterans' association interested in social service, but it was in fact a private political army designed to take the place of his Burma National Army and to be used as a major weapon in the struggle for independence.

Having helped form the Anti-Fascist People's Freedom League (AFPFL), an underground movement of nationalists, in 1944, Aung San used that united front to become deputy chairman of Burma's Executive Council in late 1946. In effect he was prime minister but remained subject to the British governor's veto. After conferring with the British prime minister Clement Attlee in London, he announced an agreement (Jan. 27, 1947) that provided for Burma's independence within one year. In the election for a constitutional assembly in April 1947, his AFPFL won 196 of 202 seats. Though Communists had denounced him as a "tool of British imperialism," he supported a resolution for Burmese independence outside the British Commonwealth.

On July 19, the Prime Minister and six colleagues, including his brother, were assassinated in the council chamber in Rangoon while the executive council was in session. His political rival, U Saw, interned in Uganda during the war, was later executed for his part in the killings.

Aungerville, Richard: *see* Bury, Richard de.

Aungzeya (Burmese king): *see* Alaungpaya.

Aunis, ancient province (*pays*) of western France, corresponding to the northern part of the modern *département* of Charente-Maritime with the southern part of Deux-Sèvres. Subjected, from the 10th century on, to the counts of Poitiers, Aunis shared the political fortunes of neighbouring Poitou. In the pre-Revolutionary period it constituted, together with the

The *gouvernement* of Aunis in 1789

islands of Ré and Oléron, a military *gouvernement* with headquarters at La Rochelle.

Aunoy, Marie-Catherine Le Jumel de Barneville, comtesse d' (countess of): *see* Aulnoy, Marie-Catherine Le Jumel de Barneville, comtesse d'.

Aurangābād, town, administrative headquarters of Aurangābād district, Mahārāshtra state, western India, on the Kaum River. Originally known as Khadki, it was founded by Malik ʿAmbār in 1610. Its name was changed by the Mughal emperor Aurangzeb, who built the Bibika Makbara tomb, an imitation of the Tāj Mahal, in the town. Aurangābād remained the headquarters of the independent Niẓāms, but it

Tomb of the emperor Aurangzeb at Khuldābād in Aurangābād district, Mahārāshtra, India
Rapho/Photo Researchers

declined when the capital was moved to Hyderābād. With the accession of Hyderābād state, it became part of the Indian Union in 1947. Aurangābād is known for its artistic silk fabrics, particularly shawls. Seat of Marāthwādā University (1958), it is a prominent educational centre containing several branch colleges.

Aurangābād district occupies 6,255 sq mi (16,200 sq km) in the upper Godāvari River basin. Flanked by the Ajanta Hills (north) and the Bālāghāt Range (south), it is crossed by the Godāvari River and two of its tributaries, the Dudna and the Pūrna. The fertile soils are excellent for cotton growing; other important crops are millet and peanuts (groundnuts). Industry is little developed and mainly consists of the spinning and weaving of cotton and wool and oil processing. More important are the tourist centres, which attract great crowds throughout the year; they include the cave temples at Ellora and Ajanta, the tomb of Aurangzeb at Khuldābād, the fort at Daulatābād, and the temples at Ghrishneshwar and Paithan. Pop. (1981) town, 284,607; metropolitan area, 316,421; district, 2,433,-420.

Aurangzeb, also spelled AURANGZIB, Arabic AWRANGZĪB, kingly title ʿĀLAMGĪR, original name MUḤĪ-UD-DĪN MUḤAMMAD (b. Nov. 3 [Oct. 24, old style], 1618, Dhod, Mālwa, India—d. March 3 [Feb. 20, O.S.] 1707), last of the great Mughal emperors of India (reigned 1658–1707). Under him the Mughal Empire

Aurangzeb, Mughal miniature, 17th century; in the Metropolitan Museum of Art, New York City

By courtesy of the Metropolitan Museum of Art, New York, bequest of George D. Pratt, 1945

reached its greatest extent, although his policies helped lead to its dissolution.

Early life. Aurangzeb was the third son of the emperor Shāh Jahān and Mumtāz Maḥal (for whom the Tāj Mahal was built). Given the name Muḥī-ud-Dīn Muḥammad, he grew up as a serious-minded and devout youth, wedded to the Muslim orthodoxy of the day and free from the royal Mughal traits of sensuality and drunkenness. He early showed signs of military and administrative ability; and these qualities, combined with a taste for power, brought him into rivalry with his eldest brother, the brilliant and volatile Dārā Shukōh, who was designated by their father as his successor to the throne. From 1636 he held a number of important appointments, in all of which he distinguished himself. He commanded troops against the Uzbeks and the Persians with distinction (1646–47) and, as viceroy of the Deccan provinces in two terms (1636–44, 1654–58), reduced the two Muslim Deccan kingdoms to near-subjection.

When Shāh Jahān fell seriously ill in 1657, the tension between the two brothers made a war of succession seem inevitable. By the time of Shāh Jahān's unexpected recovery, matters had gone too far for either son to retreat. In the struggle for power (1657–59), Aurangzeb showed tactical and strategic military skill, great powers of dissimulation, and ruthless determination. Decisively defeating Dārā at Samugarh in May 1658, he confined his father in his own palace at Āgra. In consolidating his power he caused one brother's death and had two other brothers, a son, and a nephew executed. The war became a legend that found its way to Europe.

Emperor of India. Aurangzeb's reign falls into two almost equal parts. In the first, which lasted until about 1680, he was a capable Muslim monarch of a mixed Hindu–Muslim empire and as such was generally disliked for his ruthlessness but feared and respected for his vigour and skill. During this period he was much occupied with safeguarding the northwest from Persians and Central Asian Turks and less so with the Marāṭhā chief Śivājī, who twice plundered the great port of Surat (1664, 1670). He applied his great-grandfather Akbar's recipe for conquest: defeat one's enemies, reconcile them, and place them in imperial service. Thus Śivājī was defeated, called to Āgra for reconciliation (1666), and given an imperial rank. The plan broke down, however; then Śivājī fled to the Deccan and died, in 1680, as the ruler of an independent Marāṭhā kingdom.

After about 1680, Aurangzeb's reign underwent a change of both attitude and policy. The pious ruler of an Islāmic state replaced the seasoned statesman of a mixed kingdom; Hindus became subordinates, not colleagues, and the Marāṭhās, like the southern Muslim kingdoms, were marked for annexation rather than containment. The overt sign of the first change was the reimposition of the *jizya*, or poll tax, on non-Muslims in 1679 (a tax that had been abolished by Akbar). This in turn was followed by a Rajput revolt in 1680–81, supported by Aurangzeb's third son, Akbar. Hindus still served the empire, but no longer with enthusiasm. The Deccan kingdoms of Bijāpur and Golconda were conquered in 1686–87, but the insecurity that followed precipitated a long-incipient economic crisis, which in turn was deepened by the Marāṭhā war. Śivājī's son Sambhājī was captured and executed in 1689 and his kingdom broken up. The Marāṭhās, however, then adopted guerrilla tactics, spreading all over South India amid a sympathetic population. The rest of Aurangzeb's life was spent in laborious and fruitless sieges of forts in the Marāṭhā hill country.

Aurangzeb's absence in the south prevented him from maintaining his former firm hold on the north. The administration weakened, and the process was hastened by pressure on the land by Mughal grantees who were paid by assignments on the land revenue. Agrarian discontent often took the form of religious movements, as in the case of the Satnamis and the Sikhs in the Punjab. In 1675 Aurangzeb arrested and executed the Sikh guru (spiritual leader) Tegh Bahādur, who had refused to embrace Islām; and the succeeding guru was in open rebellion for the rest of the reign. This was the real beginning of the still-existing Sikh–Muslim feud. Other agrarian revolts, such as those of the Jāts, were largely secular.

In general, Aurangzeb ruled as a militant orthodox Sunnī Muslim, who put through increasingly puritanical ordinances that were vigorously enforced by *muḥtasib*s, or censors of morals. The Muslim confession of faith, for instance, was removed from all coins lest it be defiled by unbelievers; courtiers were forbidden to salute in the Hindu fashion. In addition, Hindu idols, temples, and shrines were often destroyed.

Aurangzeb maintained the empire for nearly half a century and in fact extended it in the south as far as Tanjore (Thanjāvūr) and Trichinopoly (Tiruchchirāppalli). Behind this imposing facade, however, were serious weaknesses. The Marāṭhā campaign continually drained the imperial resources. The militancy of the Sikhs and the Jāts boded ill for the empire in the north. The new Islāmic policy alienated Hindu sentiment and undermined Rājput support. The financial pressure on the land strained the whole administrative framework. When Aurangzeb died, after a reign of nearly 49 years, he left an empire not moribund but confronted with a number of menacing problems. The failure of his son's successors to cope with them led to the collapse of the empire in the mid-18th century. (T.G.P.S.)

BIBLIOGRAPHY. J.N. Sarkar, *History of Aurangzib*, 5 vol. (1924–30), the standard work by a leading Indian historian; *Anecdotes of Aurangzib*, 3rd ed. (1949), contains translated excerpts about Aurangzeb from contemporary works in Persian; S.M. Edwardes and H.L.O. Garrett, *Mughal Rule in India* (1930), a reliable background book of 17th-century India; K.R. Qanungo, *Dara Shekoh*, 2nd ed. (1952), a well-documented study of Aurangzeb's chief rival for the throne.

Aurasius Mons (mountains, Africa): *see* Aurès.

Auratus: *see* Dorat, Jean.

Auray, Breton ALRE, town, Morbihan *département,* Bretagne region, northwestern France, on the Auray Estuary 7.5 mi (12 km) from the Atlantic, southwest of Rennes. Its château (demolished 1558) was a residence of the dukes of Brittany. Outside its walls in 1364 the War of the Breton Succession was ended by the victory of Jean de Montfort and his English allies over Montfort's cousin, Charles de Blois. The battle involved two French military folk-heroes, Bertrand du Guesclin and Olivier de Clisson. The church erected on the battleground by Montfort is now a school for deaf-mutes. In 1795 on the nearby Champ des Martyrs, 952 Chouans, local antirevolutionary guerrillas, were killed.

The quarter of Saint-Goustan, in which Benjamin Franklin, as a member of the American

The basilica of Sainte-Anne d'Auray, Auray, Fr.

Editions "La Cigogne"—Hachette

Commission, stayed in 1776, is a picturesque neighbourhood of 15th-century houses. Auray's Gothic-Renaissance basilica of Sainte-Anne d'Auray is a noted place of pilgrimage in Brittany.

The chief industry is furniture making, and the oyster beds, among the biggest in Europe, are renowned. Pop. (1982) 9,357.

Aurelia, genus of marine jellyfish of the order Semaeostomeae (class Scyphozoa, phylum Cnidaria) found in coastal waters, particularly of North America and Europe. The adult may grow as large as 40 centimetres (16 inches) in diameter. Its medusoid body is bell-shaped, and from the dishlike underside hangs a short tube at the tip of which is the mouth. The edges of the tube form four frilly projections called mouth, or oral, arms. Four crescent- to circular-shaped gonads, situated at the base of the stomach, are visible near the centre of the gelatinous dish and are coloured pink through magenta to blue. The rim of the undersurface is similarly coloured and bears numerous short tentacles. Like other schyphozoan jellyfishes, the *Aurelia* goes through a sessile (attached) stage before taking on its adult free-swimming form. Only one species, *Aurelia aurita,* is known to exist, though several others have been proposed.

Aurelian, Latin in full LUCIUS DOMITIUS AURELIANUS (b. *c.* 215—d. 275, Caenophrurium, Anatolia), Roman emperor from 270 to 275. By reuniting the empire, which had virtually disintegrated under the pressure of invasions and internal revolts, he earned his self-adopted title *restitutor orbis* ("restorer of the world").

Aurelian, probably a native of the Balkan Peninsula, had established himself as an army officer when, about 260, from outside pressure and internal fragmentation of authority, the frontiers of the empire suddenly collapsed. With his compatriot Claudius, Aurelian led the cavalry of the emperor Gallienus (253–268), and, upon Gallienus' assassination in 268, Claudius became emperor. The new ruler quickly suppressed the rebellion of the usurper Aureolus, but after a reign of 18 months, Claudius died. His brother Quintillus ruled about three months, died or was killed, and in May 270, Aurelian succeeded as emperor.

Aurelian quickly set about restoring Roman authority in Europe. He turned back invaders from Pannonia (in present-day central Europe) and after a series of battles expelled the Juthungi from northern Italy. Returning to Rome, he quelled a revolt at the imperial mint. For protection against tribal incursions, the Emperor ordered the construction of a new city wall, 12 miles long and 20 feet high, much of which still stands.

In 271 Aurelian marched to the east. He defeated the Goths on the Danube and withdrew Roman occupants from Dacia to an area south of the Danube. Evidently he realized that the empire had overextended its resources and must contract if it was to survive. At the same time, he sought to recover the eastern provinces, which for ten years had obeyed the rule of the princes of Palmyra. He besieged Palmyra and captured Septimia Zenobia, regent for her young son Vaballathus; shortly afterward the capital surrendered. When Palmyra revolted a second time, Aurelian recaptured and destroyed the city (273).

In 274 he returned west to confront Tetricus, the rival emperor, who controlled Gaul, Spain, and Britain. Beset by a German invasion and by internal conspiracies, Tetricus concluded a secret treaty with Aurelian, deserting to him at the Battle of Châlons. The leaderless army of the Rhine was swiftly defeated, and Tetricus was rewarded with the governorship of Lucania. Thus the vast empire was again ruled by a central authority.

Aurelian was an outstanding general and a severe and uncompromising administrator. By increasing the distribution of free food at Rome, he did more for the plebeians than almost any other emperor. His attempt to reform the coinage, however, met with only limited success. The Emperor sought to subordinate the divergent religions of the empire to the cult of the Unconquered Sun (Sol Invictus).

Early in 275, while marching to open a campaign against Persia, Aurelian was murdered by a group of officers who had allegedly been misled by his secretary into believing themselves marked for execution. The government was continued in the name of Aurelian's widow, Ulpia Severina, until, after six months, the Senate appointed the elderly M. Claudius Tacitus to the throne.

Aurelian's Wall, rampart of imperial Rome, constructed in the second half of the 3rd century AD. It was begun by the emperor Aurelian, completed by his successor, Probus, and restored by Theodoric the Great in the 6th century and by several medieval popes.

Aurelian's Wall, near the Porta San Paolo, Rome
The Mansell Collection

It was constructed of tufa concrete, with a facing of triangular bricks, and was 60 feet (18 metres) high and about 12 miles (19 kilometres) long, with 18 fortified gates. Much of it survives.

Aurelianus, Caelius: *see* Caelius Aurelianus.

Aurelianus, Lucius Domitius: *see* Aurelian.

Aurelius, Lucius Aelius: *see* Commodus.

Aurelius Valerius Constantius: *see* Constantius I Chlorus.

Aureol, Peter: *see* Petrus Aureoli.

aureole, brightly illuminated area surrounding an atmospheric light source, such as the Sun, when the light is propagated through a medium containing many sizes of particles or droplets that are large compared to the wavelength of the light. Because the wavelength of visible light is about 0.00005 centimetre (0.5 micron), particles of size greater than about 0.0001 centimetre (one micron) will give rise to aureoles. Physically, aureoles are caused by the diffraction of large amounts of the incident light around the edges of the particles in directions deviating only slightly from that of the light source. In the atmosphere, aureoles may frequently be observed when a thin cloud passes between the Sun or Moon and the observer. If the cloud is composed of a wide range of droplet sizes, then the aureole will be observed. It is generally white in colour, but a brownish outer ring and bluish inner edge may sometimes be observed. Dense atmospheric haze also produces an easily observable solar aureole, apparent as a very bright region immediately surrounding the Sun, with a gradual tapering off of brightness with an increasing angle from the Sun.

Aurès, Latin AURASIUS MONS, mountains, part of the Atlas Saharien in northeastern Algeria, North Africa, fronted by rugged cliffs in the north and opening out in the south into the two parallel fertile valleys of the Oudiet (wadies) Abiod and 'Abdi, facing the Sahara. The highest peaks, which are snow capped during winter, include Djebel Chélia (7,638 ft [2,328 m]), the highest point in northern Algeria, and Djebel Mahmel (7,615 ft). The upper slopes are covered with pine, cedar, and oak forests that give way to xerophytic (dry-climate) vegetation on the lower slopes. A railroad and highway cross the mountains at el-Kantara pass, near the town of Batna. Many ancient Roman ruins are at Tazoult-Lambese (Lambèse). Long inhabited by semi-nomadic Berber tribes, the mountains have gradually become settled by a majority of Arab nomads from the Sahara. The people practice seasonal migration based on villages regulated by collective granaries.

Well-defined *balcons* (escarpments) in the Aurès Massif, Algeria
Transafrica—FPG/EB Inc.

aureus, basic gold monetary unit of ancient Rome and the Roman world. It was first named *nummus aureus* ("gold money"), or *denarius aureus*, and was equal to 25 silver denarii; a denarius equalled 10 bronze asses. (In 89 BC, the sestertius, equal to one-quarter of a denarius, replaced the bronze ass as a unit of account.) In Constantine's reform of AD 312, the aureus was replaced by the solidus as the basic monetary unit.

Aurgelmir, also called YMIR, in Norse mythology, the first being, a giant who was created from the drops of water that formed when the ice of Niflheim met the heat of Muspelheim. Aurgelmir was the father of all the giants; a male and a female grew under his arm, and his legs produced a six-headed son. A cow, Audumla, nourished him with her milk. Audumla was herself nourished by licking salty, rime-covered stones. She licked the stones into the shape of a man; this was Buri, who became the grandfather of the great god Odin and his brothers. These gods later killed Aurgelmir, and the flow of his blood drowned all but one frost giant. The three gods put Aurgelmir's body in the void, Ginnungagap, and fashioned the earth from his flesh, the seas from his blood, mountains from his bones, stones from his teeth, the sky from his skull, and clouds from his brain. Four dwarfs held up his skull. His eyelashes (or eyebrows) became the fence surrounding Midgard, or Middle Earth, the home of mankind.

Auric, Georges (b. Feb. 15, 1899, Lodève, Fr.—d. July 24, 1983, Paris), French composer, best known for his film scores and ballets. In these and other works, he was among those who reacted against the Impressionism of Debussy.

Auric studied under Vincent d'Indy and Albert Roussel in Paris, and in 1920 the critic Henri Collet included him in "Les Six," the group of young French composers under the informal patronage of Erik Satie and Jean Cocteau. He wrote music criticism for *Marianne, Paris-Soir,* and *Nouvelles Littéraires* and was artistic director of the Paris Opéra and Opéra-Comique (1962–68).

Auric's works are characterized by a type of musical irony, mingling popular tunes with sophisticated harmony. His most notable compositions are the ballet *Les Matelots* (1925; "The Sailors") and his film scores for René Clair's *À nous la liberté!* (1931) and for the film biography of Toulouse-Lautrec, *Moulin Rouge* (1952), which included the popular hit "Where Is Your Heart?" ("The Song from *Moulin Rouge*"). His other works include ballets produced by Diaghilev, Barrault, and Cocteau, film scores, an "overture" for orchestra (1938), songs, and chamber music.

aurichalcite, a mineral composed of the hydroxide carbonate of zinc and copper $(Zn, Cu)_5(OH)_6(CO_3)_2$. It is commonly found with malachite in the oxidized zone of zinc and

Aurichalcite from New Mexico

By courtesy of the Illinois State Museum; photograph, John H. Gerard—EB Inc.

copper deposits as at Tomsk, Siberia; Santander, Spain; and Bisbee, Ariz., U.S. Its pale blue-green feather-like form distinguishes it from malachite; and, because it is a weathered product of zinc-rich ores, it can serve as a guide to zinc deposits. For chemical formula and detailed physical properties, *see* carbonate mineral (table).

auricle, in anatomy of the ear, the visible portion of the external ear—*i.e.,* pinna or flap, notably, the point of striking difference between the human ear and that of other mammals. The auricle in man is almost rudimentary and generally immobile and lies close to the side of the head. It is composed of a thin plate of yellow fibrocartilage covered by a tight-fitting skin. The external ear cartilage is molded into shape and has well defined hollows, furrows, and ridges that form an irregular shallow funnel. The deepest depression in the auricle, called the concha, leads to the external auditory canal or meatus. The one portion of the auricle that has no cartilage is the lobule—the fleshy lower part of the auricle. The auricle has several small basic muscles that connect it to the skull and scalp. Generally nonfunctional in human beings, they are capable of limited movement in some people.

auricular style, also called KNORPELWERK, a 17th-century ornamental style based on parts of the human anatomy. Invented in the early 17th century by a Dutch silversmith, Paulus van Vianen, who was inspired by anatomy lectures he attended in Prague, it was adopted

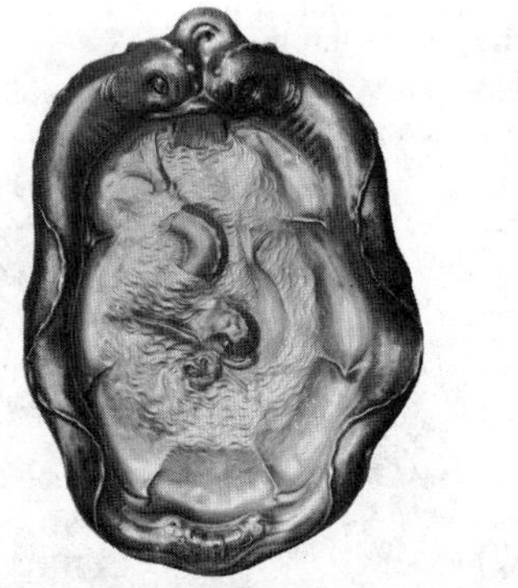

Silver dish representing an early development of the auricular style by Christian van Vianen of Utrecht, 1635; in the Victoria and Albert Museum, London

By courtesy of the Victoria and Albert Museum, London

by cabinetmakers and carvers in the Low Countries and Germany.

Applied to chair backs, frames, cupboards, and other surfaces, the gruesome, curving motifs consisting of bones, membranes, and cartilage were arranged in arabesques, particularly in forms that suggested the human ear, after which the style is named. The flabby, fleshy forms were sometimes contorted into masks, as shown in the *Neues Zieratenbuch* ("New Ornamentation Book") of the Mannerist designer Friedrich Unteutsch of Frankfurt am Main.

Aurignacian culture, toolmaking industry and artistic tradition of Upper Paleolithic Europe that followed the Mousterian industry, was contemporary with the Perigordian, and was succeeded by the Solutrean. The Aurignacian culture was marked by a great diversification and specialization of tools, including the invention of the burin, or engraving tool, that made much of the art possible.

The Aurignacian differs from other Upper Paleolithic industries mainly in a preponderance of stone flake tools rather than blades. Flakes were retouched to make nosed scrapers, carinate (ridged) scrapers, and end scrapers. Blades and burins were made by the punch technique and came in several sizes. Bones and antlers were made into points and awls by splitting, sawing, and smoothing; split-base

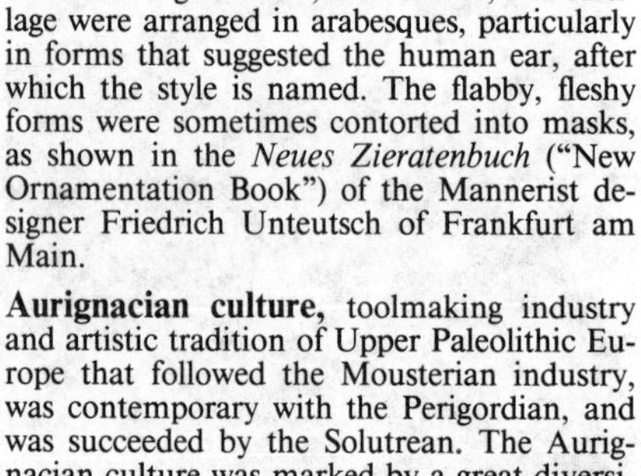

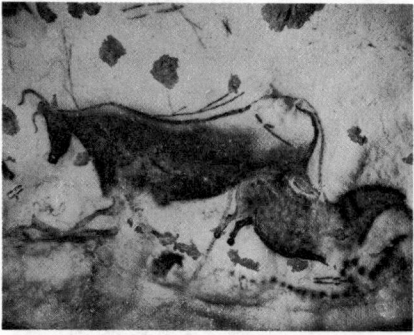

Cave painting of a bull and horse, Lascaux, Fr., Aurignacian Period

Hans Hinz, Basel

and biconical points provide evidence for hafting.

The art of the Aurignacian culture represents the first complete tradition in the history of art, moving from awkward attempts to a well-developed, mature style. The earliest examples of the small, portable art objects produced during this period are from western Europe and consist of pebbles with very simple engravings of animal forms. Later, animals were carved in pieces of bone and ivory. At the same time a tradition of true sculpture in the round grew up in eastern Europe, with vividly realistic, though simple, clay figurines of animals and highly stylized statuettes of pregnant women, the so-called Venus figures, presumably fertility figures. In the later part of the Aurignacian Period, a fusion of Eastern sculptural and Western linear traditions occurred in the west, resulting in small carvings of greatly increased naturalism; the engraved details show attempts at foreshortening and shading with cross-hatched lines.

Cave art was produced almost exclusively in western Europe, where, by the end of the Aurignacian Period, hundreds of paintings, engravings, and reliefs had been executed on the walls, the ceilings, and sometimes the floors of limestone caves. Probably the first paintings are stencillings outlined in colour of actual hands held against the cave walls. The stencillings were succeeded by the development of figural painting. A characteristic feature of these early pictures, which persisted throughout the Aurignacian Period, is their "twisted perspective," which shows, for example, the head of the animal in profile and its horns twisted to a front view. One of the finest examples of Aurignacian art is represented by paintings of animals, such as horses and bulls, on the walls and ceilings of the cave at Lascaux, in southwestern France. These impressive figures, painted in vivid polychrome red, yellow, brown, and black, with solid, closed outlines, show the lively naturalism, close observation of nature, and linear, one-dimensional approach that characterized mature Aurignacian art.

Aurigny (Channel Islands): *see* Alderney.

Aurillac, capital of Cantal *département,* Auvergne region, south central France, on the Jourdanne River, 2,040 ft (622 m) above sea level, southwest of Clermont-Ferrand. Gerbert, the first French pope (known as Sylvester II), was educated at Saint-Géraud abbey (founded 894). In the Religious Wars of the 16th century, a general massacre of Huguenots was answered by a Huguenot sack and burning of Aurillac and the slaughter of Catholics. The modern city encircles the old town of narrow, twisting streets. The Gothic church of Notre-Dame-aux-Neiges (1339) stands in the main square. The castle, now used as a school, has an 11th-century dungeon. The commercial and tourist centre of Haute-Auvergne, Aurillac is largely a cattle and dairy market specializing in two cheeses, Fourme and Bleu d'Auvergne. Light industry, especially furniture, umbrellas, food processing, and pharmaceuticals, has fostered recent growth of the city. Pop. (1982) 29,704.

Aurine, Alpi (Austria–Italy): *see* Zillertal Alps.

Auriol, Pierre: *see* Petrus Aureoli.

Auriol, Vincent (b. Aug. 25, 1884, Revel, Fr.—d. Jan. 1, 1966, Paris), first president of the Fourth French Republic, who presided over crisis-ridden coalition governments between 1947 and 1954.

After studying law at the University of Toulouse, Auriol was elected to the French Chamber of Deputies in 1914; he soon emerged as a prominent figure in the Socialist Party, leading its parliamentary delegation between 1919 and 1935. He served as the French

Auriol, *c.* 1947
H. Roger-Viollet

premier Léon Blum's minister of finance in 1936–37, voted against granting full administrative powers to Marshal Philippe Pétain as head of the Vichy regime in 1940, and was imprisoned between 1940 and 1943.

As minister of state in Charles de Gaulle's Cabinet in 1945, Auriol became known as a mediator of the right and left wings. His conciliatory policy was continued during his presidency, but the stresses in France at the end of the war proved to be overwhelming. Economic depression, factional political disputes, and the French Indochina War provided a basis for consistent attacks from both the Communists and the Gaullists. Auriol refused renomination in 1954 and removed himself from politics entirely in 1960.

Aurobindo, Śrī, original name AUROBINDO GHOSE, Aurobindo also spelled ARAVINDA (b. Aug. 15, 1872, Calcutta—d. Dec. 5, 1950, Pondicherry, Pondicherry Union Territory), seer, poet, and Indian nationalist who originated the philosophy of cosmic salvation through spiritual evolution.

His education began in a Christian convent school in Darjeeling, and then, still a boy, he was sent to England for further schooling. He entered Cambridge, where he became proficient in two classical and three modern European languages. After returning to India in 1892, he took various administrative and professorial posts in Baroda and Calcutta, and then turned to his native culture and began the serious study of yoga and Indian languages, including classical Sanskrit.

The years from 1902 to 1910 were stormy ones for Aurobindo, as he embarked on a course of action to free India from the British raj (rule). As a result of his political activities and revolutionary literary efforts, he was imprisoned in 1908. Two years later he fled British India to refuge in the French colony of Pondichéry (modern Pondicherry) in southeastern India, where he devoted himself for the rest of his life solely to the development of his unique philosophy. There he founded an *āśrama* (retreat) as an international cultural centre for spiritual development, attracting students from all over the world.

According to Aurobindo's theory of cosmic salvation, the paths to union with Brahman are two-way streets, or channels: Enlightenment comes from above (thesis), while the spiritual mind (supermind) strives through yogic illumination to reach upward from below (antithesis). When these two forces blend, a gnostic individual is created (synthesis). This yogic illumination transcends both reason and intuition and eventually leads to the freeing of the individual from the bonds of individuality and, by extension, all mankind will eventually achieve *mukti* (liberation). Thus, Aurobindo created a dialectic mode of salvation not only for the individual but for all mankind.

His voluminous, extremely complex, and sometimes chaotic literary output includes philosophical pondering, poetry, plays, and other works. Among his works are *The Life Divine* (1940), *The Human Cycle* (1949), *The Ideal of Human Unity* (1949), *On the Veda* (1956), *Collected Poems and Plays* (1942), *Essays on the Gita* (1928), *The Synthesis of Yoga* (1948), and *Savitri: A Legend and a Symbol* (1950).

aurochs, also spelled AUROCH (*Bos primigenius*), extinct wild ox of Europe, family Bovidae (order Artiodactyla), from which cattle are probably descended. The aurochs survived in central Poland until 1627. The aurochs was black, stood 1.8 metres (6 feet) high at the shoulder, and had spreading, forwardly curved horns. Some German breeders claim that since 1945 they have re-created this race by crossing Spanish fighting cattle with longhorns and cattle of other breeds. Their animals, however, are smaller and, though they resemble the aurochs, probably do not have similar genetic constitutions.

The name aurochs has sometimes been wrongly applied to the European bison, or wisent (*Bison bison*).

Aurora (Roman mythology): *see* Eos.

Aurora, city, Adams and Arapahoe counties, north central Colorado, U.S.; it is an eastern suburb of Denver. Founded during the silver boom of 1891 and named Fletcher after its Canadian-born founder, Donald Fletcher, it flourished as a mining centre until 1893, when a silver panic closed the mines. In 1902 Adams County was created from Arapahoe County, and the division line split the community, placing it in two counties. Fletcher was incorporated and renamed Aurora in 1907. The city is mainly residential but has some light manufactures (including fishing tackle and sporting goods, electronic equipment, luggage, and precision metal products). Fitzsimmons Army Medical Center and Buckley Air National Guard Base are in Aurora. Pop. (1980) 158,588.

Aurora, city, Kane County, northeastern Illinois, U.S., on the Fox River. Founded as a trading point and mill site near a Potawatomi Indian village in 1834, the town was laid out in 1836. Aurora developed as both a residential and an industrial city. Many of its residents commute to Chicago, 39 mi (63 km) east. Its manufactures include tractors, road-paving machinery, belt conveyors, steel furniture, ball bearings, and telephone equipment. Aurora College, founded in 1893 at Mendota by the Advent Christian Church of America, was moved to Aurora in 1912. Waubonsee Community College, named for a local Indian chief, was established in 1966 in Sugar Grove, 4 mi west. The city's name means "dawn." The historical society museum includes among its exhibits locally excavated mastodon bones. Inc. 1857. Pop. (1980) 81,293.

Aurora (Vanuatu): *see* Maéwo.

aurora, luminous phenomenon of the upper atmosphere that occurs in high latitudes of both hemispheres; auroras in the Northern Hemisphere are called Aurora Borealis, or northern lights; in the Southern Hemisphere, Aurora Australis, or southern lights.

A brief treatment of auroras follows. For full treatment, *see* MACROPAEDIA: Atmosphere.

Auroras are caused by the interaction of energetic particles (electrons and protons) from outside the atmosphere with atoms of the upper atmosphere. Such interaction occurs in zones, some 2,000 kilometres (1,200 miles) in diameter, surrounding the geomagnetic poles. During periods of great solar activity the Aurora Borealis has been seen as far south as Mexico, the Aurora Australis as far north as Samoa.

Auroras take many forms, including curtains, arcs, rays, bands, and fan-shaped coronas. The uniform arc is the most stable form of aurora, sometimes persisting for hours without noticeable variation. But in a great display, or auroral substorm, other forms appear, commonly undergoing dramatic variation. The lower edges of the arcs and folds are usually much more sharply defined than the upper parts. Greenish rays may cover most of the sky polewards of the magnetic zenith, ending in an arc that is usually folded and sometimes edged with a lower red border, that may ripple like drapery. The display ends with a poleward retreat of the auroral forms, the rays gradually degenerating into diffuse areas of white light.

The mechanisms that produce auroral displays are not completely understood. It is known, however, that charged particles arriving in the vicinity of Earth as part of the solar wind are captured by the Earth's magnetic field and conducted downward toward the magnetic poles. At heights of several hundred kilometres or less they collide with oxygen and nitrogen atoms, knocking away electrons to leave ions in excited states. These ions emit radiation at various wavelengths, creating the characteristic colours of the aurora.

aurresku, Basque folk dance of courtship, in which the men perform spirited acrobatic displays for their partners; one of the most elaborate European folk dances of this type. It begins as a chain dance for men, in which the leader and last man break off, dance competitively, and rejoin the chain. Each later dances before his partner, and finally all bring their partners into the line, which eventually breaks into a fandango for couples.

Aurresku, detail of an engraving by C. Llobet, 1929
By courtesy of the Biblioteca Nacional, Madrid

Aurunci, ancient tribe of Campania, in Italy; exterminated by the Romans in 295 BC as the culmination of 50 years of Roman military campaigns. The Aurunci occupied a strip of coast between the Volturnus and Liris (Volturno and Liri) rivers in the modern province of Caserta, with their capital at Suessa (modern Sessa Aurunca). No written record of their language survives, but the frequency of the use of the "-co" suffix in that part of the coast suggests that they spoke the same Italic dialect as their northern neighbours, the Volsci. Ausones, the Greek form of the name Aurunci, came to denote the inhabitants of the whole of Latium and Campania.

Auschwitz (Poland): *see* Oświęcim.

Auschwitz, Polish OŚWIĘCIM, also called AUSCHWITZ-BIRKENAU, Nazi Germany's largest concentration camp and extermination camp (*qq.v.*), located near the Polish town of Oświęcim in Galicia. Heinrich Himmler ordered the establishment of the first camp on April 27, 1940, and the first transport of Polish political prisoners arrived on June 14. This small "Auschwitz I" throughout its history was reserved for political prisoners, mainly Poles and Germans. It was supplemented in October 1941 by "Auschwitz II," or Birkenau, located outside the nearby village of Brzezinka (Birkenau in German). There the SS later developed a huge extermination complex—including *Badeanstalten* ("bathhouses") used for gassing, *Leichenkeller* ("corpse cellars") used for storage of bodies, and *Einäscherungsöfen* ("cremating ovens")—all for the "final solution," the annihilation of European Jews. Another camp, near the village of Dwory, later called "Auschwitz III," became in May 1942 a slave-labour camp supplying workers for the large chemical and synthetic-rubber works of IG Farben nearby. From 1940 to 1945 the commandant of all the Auschwitz camps was *SS-Hauptsturmführer* (Captain) Rudolf Franz Hoess.

Upon arrival in freight cars, Jewish prisoners were subjected to a *Selektion* ("selection"): able young men and women were sent to the forced-labour camp, while the aged, the weak, and children and their mothers were killed. The forced labourers too were periodically "selected," to weed out those weakened by overwork, disease, or hunger. Many prisoners were also selected for medical experiments, such as testing for cheap and quick methods of sterilization or killing and performing autopsies on twins in search of means of increasing the Aryan breed. The notorious camp doctor Josef Mengele conducted the latter experiments and supervised the *Selektionen.*

As Soviet armies advanced, Auschwitz was gradually abandoned, most of the remaining prisoners leaving on Jan. 17, 1945, and being transported to Dachau, Mauthausen, and other German camps; 7,650 prisoners left behind were found 10 days later by arriving Soviet troops.

Estimates of the total numbers who died at Auschwitz from all causes vary greatly, usually cited as between 1,000,000 and 2,500,000 but sometimes reaching 4,000,000. *See also* Holocaust.

auscultation, diagnostic procedure in which the physician listens to sounds within the body to detect certain defects or conditions, such as heart-valve malfunctions or pregnancy. Auscultation originally was performed by placing the ear directly on the chest or abdomen, but it has been practiced mainly with a stethoscope since the invention of that instrument in 1819.

The technique is based on characteristic sounds produced, in the head and elsewhere, by abnormal blood circuits; in the joints by roughened surfaces; in the lower arm by the pulse wave; and in the abdomen by an active fetus or by intestinal disturbances. It is most commonly employed, however, in diagnosing diseases of the heart and lungs.

The heart sounds consist mainly of two separate noises occurring when the two sets of heart valves close. Either partial obstruction of these valves or leakage of blood through them because of imperfect closure results in turbulence in the blood current, causing audible, prolonged noises called murmurs. In certain congenital abnormalities of the heart and the blood vessels in the chest, the murmur may be continuous. Murmurs are often specifically diagnostic for diseases of the individual heart valves; that is, they sometimes reveal which heart valve is causing the ailment. Likewise, modification of the quality of the heart sounds may reveal disease or weakness of the heart muscle. Auscultation is also useful in determining the types of irregular rhythm of the heart and in discovering the sound peculiar to inflammation of the pericardium, the sac surrounding the heart.

Auscultation also reveals the modification of sounds produced in the air tubes and sacs of the lungs during breathing when these structures are diseased.

Auseklis (Latvian), Lithuanian AUŠRINĖ, in Baltic religion, the morning star and deity of the dawn. The Latvian Auseklis was a male god, the Lithuanian Aušrinė a female.

Related in name to the Vedic Uṣas and the Greek Eos, goddesses of dawn, Auseklis is associated in Latvian solar mythology with Mēness (Moon) and Saule (Sun), being subordinate to the former and along with him a rival suitor of Saule's daughter, Saules meita.

According to Lithuanian traditions Aušrinė had an adulterous relationship with the moon god, Mėnuo, for which Mėnuo was punished by the god Perkūnas (Latvian, Pērkons).

Auserre Apopis (king of Egypt): *see* Apopis I.

Ausgleich (German: Compromise), the compact, finally concluded on Feb. 8, 1867, that regulated the relations between Austria and Hungary and established the Dual Monarchy, Austria-Hungary (*q.v.*).

Ausi (king of Israel): *see* Hoshea.

Ausonius, Decimus Magnus (b. *c.* 310, Burdigala, Gaul—d. *c.* 395, Burdigala), Latin poet and rhetorician interesting chiefly for his preoccupation with the provincial scene of his native Gaul. He taught in the famous schools of Burdigala (now Bordeaux, Fr.), first as a grammarian and then as a rhetorician, so successfully that Valentinian I called him to Trier to tutor Gratian, who, on his accession, elevated Ausonius to the prefecture of Africa, Italy, and Gaul and to the consulship in 379. After Gratian's murder, in 383, Ausonius returned to his estates on the Garonne to cultivate literature and pursue his many friendships with eminent persons through a lively exchange of letters, often poetic epistles. Although he was a Christian, he wrote mainly in the pagan tradition, but, by the sheer volume of his preserved work, he was one of the forerunners of Christian Latin literature and of the literature of his own country. His last years were saddened by the action of his favourite and most outstanding pupil, Paulinus of Nola (later bishop and saint), in deserting literature for a life of Christian retirement. Ausonius' pleading, pained letters to Paulinus continued until his death.

An incorrigible trifler and a victim of what he called "the poetic itch," Ausonius left few works of any consequence. A characteristic piece of trifling is the *Technopaegnion* ("A Game of Art"), a set of poems in which each line ends in a monosyllable. His longest poem, on the River Mosella, has flashes of an almost Wordsworthian response to nature, with descriptions of the changing scenery as it moves through the country. Ausonius produced the useful autobiographical *Praefatiunculae* ("Prefaces"); *Eclogae,* mnemonic verses on astronomy and astrology; *Ordo nobilium urbium* ("Order of Noble Cities"); *Ludus septem sapientum* ("Play of the Seven Sages"), a forerunner of the morality play; and many epigrams, including adaptations from the *Greek Anthology.* His sentimental fondness for old ties is seen in *Parentalia,* a series of poems on deceased relatives, and *Professores Burdigalenses,* on the professors of Burdigala; these are delightful portraits that give a valuable picture of provincial Gallic life.

Aušrinė (Baltic deity): *see* Auseklis.

Aussee (Austria): *see* Bad Aussee.

Aussig (Czechoslovakia): *see* Ústí nad Labem.

Aust-Agder, *fylke* (county), southern Norway. With an area of 3,557 sq mi (9,212 sq km), it extends 120 mi northwestward into the mountains from the coastline on the Skagerrak (strait between Norway and Denmark). The landscape is broken and uneven, with the Setesdal (valley) in the west bounded by steep coniferous-forested mountains rising to 3,500 ft (1,070 m); branching valleys in the middle of the county are divided by smaller hills. Most of the inhabitants live in coastal towns that until the mid-19th century were timber ports; they are now small, diversified commercial centres supporting a flourishing tourist trade. There are many burial mounds and excavation sites from the Stone and Iron ages and the Viking period throughout the *fylke.* Nickel and low-grade iron ore are mined in the area. Horticulture and forestry are the economic mainstays inland. The Setesdal region supports livestock. The county seat is Arendal (*q.v.*), other important towns being Risør, Grimstad, and Lillesand. Pop. (1982 est.) 92,751.

austausch coefficient, also called EXCHANGE COEFFICIENT, EDDY COEFFICIENT, or EDDY DIFFUSIVITY, in fluid mechanics, particularly in its applications to meteorology and oceanography, the proportionality between the rate of transport of a component of a turbulent fluid and the gradient of the component. In this context, the term component signifies not only material constituents of the fluid, such as dissolved or suspended substances, but also constituents of its energy, such as heat and momentum.

In a fluid reacting to mechanical stress by undergoing laminar flow, the shearing motion of adjacent layers past one another is impeded by friction arising from the migration of individual molecules between the different layers. That is, a fast-moving layer is slowed down by the arrival of molecules from a slower layer, and vice versa. The magnitude of this internal molecular friction, called the viscosity, can be identified as the proportionality between the magnitude of the shearing stress and the rate at which momentum is transported between adjacent layers (*i.e.,* in directions perpendicular to that of the stress and the flow). The flow becomes turbulent if the stress exceeds a certain limit, and the layers become disrupted by the formation of eddies, in which erratic motions of large, multi-molecular aggregates of the fluid are superimposed on the bulk flow. In this condition, the rate of transport of momentum and other components greatly exceeds that calculated from the value of the viscosity, and its proportionality to the shear stress is represented by the austausch.

Austen, Jane (b. Dec. 16, 1775, Steventon, Hampshire, Eng.—d. July 18, 1817, Winchester, Hampshire), English writer who first

Jane Austen, pencil and watercolour portrait by C. Austen, *c.* 1810; in the National Portrait Gallery, London

By courtesy of the National Portrait Gallery, London

gave the novel its distinctly modern character through her treatment of ordinary people in everyday life. She created the comedy of manners of middle-class life in the England of her time in such novels as *Sense and Sensibility* (1811), *Pride and Prejudice* (1813), *Mansfield Park* (1814), *Emma* (1815), and *Northanger Abbey* and *Persuasion* (published posthumously, 1817).

Family and upbringing. Jane Austen was born in the Hampshire village of Steventon, where her father, the Rev. George Austen, was rector. She was the second daughter and seventh child in a family of eight: six boys and two girls. Her closest companion was her elder sister, Cassandra, who also remained unmarried. Her formal education began in about 1782, when the sisters were sent to be tutored by a Mrs. Cawley at Oxford; and, in 1783 or 1784, they moved to the Abbey School, Reading, where they remained until about 1787. Thereafter, their education continued at home. Their father was a scholar who, before entering the church, had been a fellow of St. John's College, Oxford; and he encouraged the love of learning in his children. His wife, Cassandra (*née* Leigh), was a woman of ready wit, famed for her impromptu verses and stories. The great family amusement was acting. A Steventon dramatic company was recruited from the Austens and their neighbours; and the rectory barn was converted into a little theatre for productions in the summer holidays, while at Christmas, plays were performed in the house. The repertoire was not restricted and included even the broader kind of 18th-century comedy.

Although Jane Austen's early life was unmomentous and at a distance from the social and political upheavals of the time, a lively and affectionate family circle provided a stimulating context for her writing. Moreover, her experience was carried far beyond Steventon rectory by an extensive network of relationships by blood and friendship. It was this world—of the minor landed gentry and the country clergy, in the village, the neighbourhood, and the country town, with occasional visits to Bath and to London—that she was to use in the settings, characters, and subject matter of her novels.

Literary development. Her earliest known writings date from about 1787, and between then and 1795 she wrote a large body of material that has survived in fair copy in three manuscript notebooks: *Volume the First, Volume the Second,* and *Volume the Third.* In all, these contain 21 items: plays, verses, short novels, and other prose. They are the product of an analytical mind engaged in parody of existing literary forms, notably sentimental fiction. Her passage to a more serious view of life from the exuberant high spirits and extravagances of her earliest writings was announced finally in *Lady Susan*, a short novel-in-letters written about 1793–94. This, the portrait of a woman bent on the exercise of her own powerful mind and personality to the point of social self-destruction, is, in effect, a study of frustration and of woman's fate in a society that has no use for woman's stronger, more "masculine," talents.

Jane's first recorded romantic association was a flirtation early in 1796 with Tom Lefroy, a handsome young Irishman, nephew of the rector of a village near Steventon. In 1798 or 1799 she may have refused Samuel Blackall, a fellow of Emmanuel College, Cambridge, who was then staying with the Lefroys. In November 1802 it seems likely that she agreed to marry Harris Bigg-Wither, the 21-year-old heir of a Hampshire family: but next morning she changed her mind. Then there are a number of mutually contradictory stories connecting her with someone (sometimes a naval officer, sometimes an army officer, sometimes a clergyman) with whom she fell in love but who died very soon after.

Since Jane Austen's novels are so deeply concerned with love and marriage, there is some point in attempting to establish the facts of these relationships. Unfortunately, the evidence is unsatisfactory and incomplete. Cassandra was a jealous guardian of her sister's private life, and after Jane's death she (and other members of the family) censored the surviving letters, destroying many and cutting up others. Stories in the family memoirs and documents are confused; and Jane Austen's own references in her letters are always ironic and evasive. The novels, however, provide indisputable evidence that their author understood the experience of love and of love disappointed.

This observation relates most obviously to her last novel, *Persuasion.* Yet it has some relevance, too, to the earlier novels, on which she was working during the period of the recorded romances. The earliest, *Sense and Sensibility*, was begun about 1795 as a novel-in-letters called "Elinor and Marianne," after its heroines. Between October 1796 and August 1797 she completed the first version of *Pride and Prejudice*, then called "First Impressions." In November 1797 her father wrote to inquire from the London publisher Thomas Cadell about the possibilities for its publication, but there was no answer. *Northanger Abbey*, the last of the early novels, was written about 1798 or 1799, probably as "Susan."

Up to this time the tenor of life at Steventon rectory had been propitious for Jane Austen's growth as a novelist. The family provided an appreciative audience. There was all the variety of the neighbourhood society, with a much-loved home to return to after long visits to friends, relatives, and married brothers (Edward, the Austens' third son, adopted as heir by wealthy cousins, opened his home at Godmersham, Kent, to his sisters and later provided them with 11 motherless nieces and nephews to console and entertain; and Henry, living in London, often claimed their company). This stable pattern ended in 1801, when George Austen, then aged 70, handed on his parish duties to his eldest son, James, and retired to Bath with his wife and daughters. For eight years Jane Austen had to put up with a succession of temporary lodgings or visits to relatives, in Bath, London, Clifton, Warwickshire, and, finally, Southampton, where the Austens lived from 1805 to 1809.

Meanwhile, in 1803, the manuscript of "Susan" had been sold to the publisher Richard Crosby for £10. He took it for immediate publication, but although it was advertised, unaccountably it never appeared. In 1804 she began *The Watsons* but soon abandoned it. It is an unhappy work. Its social picture is one of unrelieved bleakness; its central character is the most assailed of her heroines in distress. Its satire is sharp to the point of cruelty. It signals a failing of generosity, a loss of creative power, perhaps the consequence of disappointment in love and other sorrows. In December 1804 her dearest friend, Mrs. Anne Lefroy, died suddenly; on Jan. 21, 1805, her father died in Bath.

Critical acclaim. Eventually, in 1809, Edward provided his mother and sisters with a large cottage in the village of Chawton, his Hampshire property, not far from Steventon, where they were joined by a close friend who had lived with them in Southampton. The prospect of settling at Chawton had already given Jane Austen a renewed sense of purpose. In April she wrote to Crosby to sound his intentions about "Susan," and, once installed at the cottage, she began to prepare *Sense and Sensibility* and *Pride and Prejudice* for publication. Two years later Thomas Egerton agreed to publish *Sense and Sensibility*, with the author's guarantee against loss. It came out, anonymously, in November 1811. Both of the leading reviews, the *Critical Review* and the *Quarterly Review*, welcomed its blend of instruction and amusement. Meanwhile, in February 1811, she had begun *Mansfield Park*, finished in the summer of 1813 and published in 1814. By then she was an established (though anonymous) author; Egerton had published *Pride and Prejudice* in January 1813; in November there were second editions of *Pride and Prejudice* and *Sense and Sensibility.* Between January 1814 and March 1815 she wrote *Emma*, which appeared in December 1815. In February 1816 there was a second edition of *Mansfield Park*, published, like *Emma*, by Byron's publisher, John Murray ("a rogue, of course, but a civil one," Jane Austen commented). *Persuasion* (written August 1815–August 1816) was published posthumously, with *Northanger Abbey*, in December 1817.

The years after 1811 seem to have been the most rewarding of her life. She had the satisfaction of seeing her work in print and well reviewed and of knowing that the novels were widely read. They were so much enjoyed by the Prince Regent (later George IV) that he had a set in each of his residences; and *Emma*, at a discreet royal command, was "respectfully dedicated" to him. The reviewers praised the novels for their moral entertainment, admired the character drawing, and welcomed the homely realism as a refreshing change from the romantic melodrama then in vogue.

For the last 18 months of her life, she was busy writing. Early in 1816 she set down the burlesque *Plan of a Novel, According to Hints from Various Quarters* (first published in 1871). Until August 1816 she was occupied with *Persuasion.* She looked again at the manuscript of "Susan" (*Northanger Abbey;* to which she was now referring as "Miss Catherine").

In January 1817, she began what was to be her last work, *Sanditon* (so named by the family), writing and revising more than 24,000 words in less than eight weeks. It was finally put aside on March 18. This may have been a race against time, for her health had been in decline since early 1816. She supposed that she was suffering from bile. But the symptoms make possible a modern clinical assessment that she was suffering from Addison's disease. Her condition fluctuated. A final burst of energy seems to have gone into *Sanditon*, with its robust and self-mocking satire on health resorts and invalidism. In April she made her will. In May she was taken to Winchester to be under the care of an expert surgeon. On the morning of July 18, at 4:30 AM, she died. Six days later she was buried in Winchester cathedral.

Her authorship was announced to the world at large by her brother Henry, who supervised the publication of *Northanger Abbey* and *Persuasion* and contributed a "Biographical Notice of the Author," paying tribute to his sister's qualities of mind and character and recording her final words: in answer to a question about her last wants, she replied, with characteristic decorum and economy, "I want nothing but death."

During her lifetime there had been a solitary response in any way adequate to the nature of her achievement: Sir Walter Scott's review of *Emma* in the *Quarterly Review* for March 1816, where he hailed this "nameless author" as a masterful exponent of "the modern novel" in the new Realist tradition. After her death, there was for long only one significant essay, the review of *Northanger Abbey* and *Persuasion* in the *Quarterly* for January 1821 by Richard Whately, the theologian, logician, and political economist, later archbishop of Dublin. Together, Scott's and Whately's essays provided the foundation for serious criticism of Jane Austen: their insights were appropriated by critics throughout the 19th century.

Modern critics remain fascinated by the commanding structure and organization of the novels, by the triumphs of technique that enable the writer to lay bare the tragicomedy of existence in stories of which the events and settings are apparently so ordinary and so circumscribed. (B.C.So./Ed.)

MAJOR WORKS. *Novels. Sense and Sensibility* (1811); *Pride and Prejudice* (1813); *Mansfield Park* (1814); *Emma* (published December 1815, dated 1816); *Northanger Abbey* and *Persuasion* (published together, posthumously, December 1817, dated 1818).

Unfinished works and juvenileia. The early novel-in-letters, *Lady Susan* and *The Watsons* (unfinished), were first published in the 1871 edition of J.E. Austen-Leigh's *Memoir of Jane Austen. Lady Susan* was republished from the original autograph by R.W. Chapman (1925), and *The Watsons,* also by R.W. Chapman (1927). *Sanditon* (left unfinished; extracts published in the 1871 *Memoir*) was first published in full from the original autograph by R.W. Chapman (1925). Three manuscript notebooks, *Volume the First, Volume the Second,* and *Volume the Third*, containing juvenilia written *c.* 1787–95, were first published in full by R.W. Chapman (*Volume the First*, 1933; *Volume the Third*, 1951) and B.C. Southam (*Volume the Second*, 1963). *Volume the Second* contains *Love and Friendship* (first published 1922).

BIBLIOGRAPHY. *Bibliographies:* Geoffrey L. Keynes, *Jane Austen: A Bibliography* (1929, reprinted 1977), places emphasis on the early editions. Robert W. Chapman, *Jane Austen: A Critical Bibliography*, 2nd ed. (1969), lists critical works as well as original and early editions. B.C. Southam, "Jane Austen," in the *New Cambridge Bibliography of English Literature,* vol. 3 (1969), and, in the *Shorter New Cambridge Bibliography of English Literature* (1981), lists collections, editions, letters, and critical and biographical books and articles.

Editions: The Oxford Illustrated Jane Austen, 6 vol. (1923–54; several revisions by B.C. Southam, 1963 through 1980), is a definitive, standard edition of the works. The Everyman's Library edition of the six novels, edited by Mary M. Lascelles, 5 vol. (1961–64), provides a sound working text. R.W. Chapman, *Jane Austen's Letters to Her Sister Cassandra and Others*, 2 vol. (1932; 2nd ed. with corrections and additional indexes, 1952; reprinted 1979), is a complete edition.

Biography and criticism: James E. Austen-Leigh, *A Memoir of Jane Austen* (1870; reprint of 1882 ed., 1979), written in old age by her favourite nephew, draws on family letters and personal recollections. It should be supplemented by William and Richard A. Austen-Leigh, *Jane Austen: Her Life and Letters* (1913, reissued 1965), which provides a more complete account of her life. Lord Brabourne (ed.), *Letters of Jane Austen*, 2 vol. (1884), provides an edition of letters, mainly to her sister, Cassandra, with a biographical introducton based on recollections. Constance Hill, *Jane Austen: Her Homes and Her Friends* (1902, reprinted 1978), is an informal but knowledgeable account, drawing on family papers now unlocatable. R.W. Chapman, *Jane Austen: Facts and Problems* (1948, reprinted 1970), is not a full biography, but it provides a scholarly and authoritative examination and evaluation of the evidence. Marghanita Laski, *Jane Austen and Her World*, rev. ed. (1975), is an illustrated, introductory biography. Mary Lascelles, *Jane Austen and Her Art* (1939; corrected 1941, 1951; reprinted 1970), is an account of the novelist's art and contains an introductory biographical chapter. Douglas Bush, *Jane Austen* (1975), is a critical biography of her life and works. Other biographies include Marilyn Butler, *Jane Austen and the War of Ideas* (1975); and David Cecil, *A Portrait of Jane Austen* (1980). B.C. Southam, in *Jane Austen: The Critical Heritage* (1968), collects and discusses the contemporary reviews and criticism from 1811 to 1870, and his *Critical Essays on Jane Austen* (1968) is a collection of modern critical approaches.

austenite, solid solution of carbon and other constituents in a particular form of iron known as γ (gamma) iron. This is a face-centred cubic structure formed when iron is heated above 910° C (1670° F); gamma iron becomes unstable at temperatures above 1,390° C (2530° F). Austenite is an ingredient of a kind of stainless steel used for making cutlery, hospital and food-service equipment, and tableware.

Austerlitz, Battle of, also called BATTLE OF THE THREE EMPERORS (Dec. 2, 1805), the first engagement of the War of the Third Coalition and one of Napoleon's greatest victories; his 68,000 troops defeated almost 90,000 Russians and Austrians nominally under Gen. M.I. Kutuzov, forcing Austria to make peace with France (Treaty of Pressburg) and keeping Prussia temporarily out of the anti-French alliance.

The battle took place near Austerlitz in Moravia (now Slavkov u Brna, Czech.) after the French had entered Vienna on November 13 and then pursued the Russian and Austrian allied armies into Moravia. The arrival of the Russian emperor Alexander I virtually deprived Kutuzov of supreme control of his troops. The allies decided to fight Napoleon west of Austerlitz and occupied the Pratzen Plateau, which Napoleon had deliberately evacuated to create a trap. The allies then launched their main attack, with 40,000 men, against the French right (south) to cut them off from Vienna. While Marshal Louis Davout's corps of 10,500 men stubbornly resisted this attack, and the allied secondary attack on Napoleon's northern flank was repulsed, Napoleon launched Marshal Nicolas Soult, with 20,000 infantry, up the slopes to smash the weak allied centre on the Pratzen Plateau. Soult captured the plateau and, with 25,000 reinforcements from Napoleon's reserve, held it against the allied attempts to retake it. The allies were soon split in two and vigorously attacked and pursued both north and south of the plateau. They lost 15,000 men killed and wounded and 11,000 captured, while Napoleon lost 9,000 men. The remnants of the allied army were scattered. Two days later Francis I of Austria agreed to a suspension of hostilities and arranged for Alexander I to take his army back to Russia.

Austin: *see* Augustinian.

Austin, city, seat (1857) of Mower County, southeastern Minnesota, U.S., on the Cedar River, in a farming area specializing in corn and livestock. It was settled in 1853, laid out in 1856, and named for its first settler, Austin R. Nicholas. Austin Community College (1940) and the Mower County Historical Center are there. George A. Hormel and Company's meat-packing and food-processing plant is the economic mainstay, supplemented by diversified manufactures including cartons, concrete products, and truck bodies. The Hormel Institute (1960), affiliated with the University of Minnesota, conducts research on the connection of fats and oils with heart disease. Several agricultural shows are held each year. Inc. city, 1873. Pop. (1980) 23,020.

Austin, city, capital of Texas, U.S., and seat (1840) of Travis County. Located where the Colorado River (of Texas) crosses the Balcones Escarpment in the south central part of the state, it originated as the riverside village of Waterloo, which in 1839 was selected by scouts as the site for the permanent capital of the Republic of Texas and renamed to honour Stephen F. Austin, father of the republic. By 1840 Austin was incorporated, with 856 residents. When Mexican invasion threatened in 1842, the government moved to Houston. Citizens, determined to keep Austin the capital, staged the Archives War, forcibly retaining government records. The government returned to Austin in 1845, the year in which Texas was admitted to the United States. The pink granite State Capitol (1888), modelled after the U.S. Capitol, succeeded an earlier wooden structure (burned 1881); it houses museums of the Texas Confederacy and republic.

The city flourished as a trading centre for ranchers and farmers after the arrival of the Houston and Texas Central Railroad in 1871. With the harnessing of the Colorado River for flood control and power in the early 20th century, industry began to develop. Austin has expanded as a research and development centre for defense and consumer industries; its educational resources, particularly the University of Texas at Austin (1881), have contributed to that growth. Other institutions include the Huston–Tillotson College (1876), St. Edwards University (1885), Concordia Lutheran College (1926), The Episcopal Theological Seminary of the Southwest (1951), and Austin Community College (1972). At dusk the central city is lighted by "artificial moonlight" from mercury vapour lamps atop 27 tall towers (erected in 1894). The O. Henry (William Sydney Porter) Museum was the author's residence from 1885 to 1895, and the Elisabet

Confederate monument on the State Capitol grounds, Austin, Texas
Meisel–Monkmeyer

Ney Museum houses a collection of her sculpture. The French Legation (1841) dates from the days of the Republic of Texas. The Lyndon Baines Johnson Library (1971), on the campus of the University of Texas, contains archives and documents of the President's public career.

The hill country west of Austin is a recreational region with the chain of Highland Lakes (including Town Lake and Lake Austin, which wind through the city) impounded by dams along the Colorado River. Unusual rock outcrops, caverns, and springs are found in the area. Bergstrom Air Force Base is immediately southeast. Pop. (1980) city, 345,496; metropolitan area (SMSA), 536,450.

Austin OF CANTERBURY, SAINT: *see* Augustine of Canterbury, Saint.

Austin, Alfred (b. May 30, 1835, Leeds, Eng.—d. June 2, 1913, Ashford, Kent), successor of Alfred, Lord Tennyson, as poet laureate who could write simply in praise of the English and Italian countryside, and who could claim to represent popular feeling, but who lacked the gift of transforming it into true poetry.

Before his official appointment, Austin studied law and was called to the bar, tried to enter politics, and practiced journalism.

Austin, Herbert Austin, Baron (b. Nov. 8, 1866, Little Missenden, Buckinghamshire, Eng.—d. May 23, 1941, near Bromsgrove, Worcestershire), founder and first chairman of the Austin Motor Company, whose Austin

Lord Austin, 1937

By courtesy of British Leyland Motor Corp. Ltd., Austin Morris & Manufacturing Group

Seven model greatly influenced British and European light-car design. An engineer and engineering manager in Australia (1883–90), he became manager and later director of the Wolseley Sheep-Shearing Company in England. In 1895 he designed the first Wolseley car—a three wheeler—and in 1900 drove the first Wolseley four-wheeled car, also of his design. He began production of his own cars at the Longbridge Works, Birmingham, in 1906. Knighted in 1917, he was a Conservative member of the House of Commons from 1919 to 1924 and was created a baron in 1936.

Austin, John (b. March 3, 1790, Creeting Mill, Suffolk, Eng.—d. December 1859, Weybridge, Surrey), English jurist whose writings, especially *The Province of Jurisprudence Determined* (1832), advocated a definition of law as a species of command and sought to distinguish positive law from morality. He had little influence during his lifetime outside the circle of Utilitarian supporters of Jeremy Bentham. His authority came posthumously.

Life. Austin began to study law in 1812 after five years in the army and from 1818 to 1825 practiced unsuccessfully at the chancery bar. His powers of rigorous analysis and his uncompromising intellectual honesty deeply impressed his contemporaries, and in 1826, when University College, London, was founded, he was appointed its first professor of jurisprudence, a subject that had previously occupied an unimportant place in legal studies. He spent the next two years in Germany studying Roman law and the work of German experts on modern civil law whose ideas of classification and systematic analysis exerted an influence on him second only to that of Bentham. Both Austin and his wife, Sarah, were ardent Utilitarians, intimate friends of Bentham and of James and John Stuart Mill, and much concerned with legal reform. Austin's first lectures, in 1828, were attended by many distinguished men, but he failed to attract students and resigned his chair in 1832. In 1834, after delivering a shorter but equally unsuccessful version of his lectures, he abandoned the teaching of jurisprudence. He was appointed to the Criminal Law Commission in 1833 but, finding little support for his opinions, resigned in frustration after signing its first two reports. In 1836 he was appointed a commissioner on the affairs of Malta. The Austins then lived abroad, chiefly in Paris, until 1848, when they settled in Surrey, where Austin died in 1859.

Work. Austin's best known work, a version of part of his lectures, is *The Province of Jurisprudence Determined*, published in 1832. Here, in order to clarify the distinction between law and morality, which he considered to be blurred by doctrines of Natural Law, he elaborated his definition of law as a species of command. According to Austin, commands are expressions of desire that another shall do or forbear from some act and are accompanied by a threat of punishment (the "sanction") for disobedience. Commands are laws "simply and properly so-called" when they prescribe courses of conduct, not specific acts, and are "set" by the "sovereign" (*i.e.*, the person or persons to whom a society renders habitual obedience and who render no such obedience to others). This is the mark distinguishing "positive law" both from the fundamental principles of morality, which are the "law of God," and from "positive morality," or manmade rules of conduct, such as etiquette, conventional morality, and international law, which do not emanate from a sovereign. *The Province* also contains a version of Utilitarianism in which "utility" is regarded as the index of God's commands and the test of the moral quality of general rules of conduct rather than of particular actions.

Austin viewed the doctrines in *The Province* as "merely prefatory" to the study that he termed "general jurisprudence": the exposition and analysis of the fundamental notions forming the framework of all mature legal systems. He devoted the main part of his lectures (published in 1863) to an analysis of such "pervading notions" as those of right, duty, persons, status, delict, and sources of law. Austin distinguished this general, or analytical, jurisprudence from the criticism of legal institutions, which he called the "science of legislation"; he thought both were important parts of legal education.

Assessment. Bouts of nervous illness and self-distrust prevented Austin from fully utilizing his great powers; his life, as his widow wrote, was one of "unbroken disappointment and failure," in ironic contrast with his posthumous fame and influence. A long succession of English writers have echoed or elaborated his doctrines or, when opposing them, have accepted his conception of the analysis of legal concepts as the central concern of jurisprudence. In the United States jurists such as J.C. Gray and Oliver Wendell Holmes welcomed his bold distinction between law and morality as a major clarification.

The reaction to Austin's work at the turn of the century was severe. His command theory was condemned as a misidentification of all law with the product of legislation and a distortion of many types of legal rule. The severance of a purely analytical jurisprudence from moral criticism of law was criticized as sterile verbalism obscuring the social function of law and the judicial process. Some critics consider that Austin's doctrine of sovereignty confuses the ideas of legal authority and political power; others hold "legal positivism" responsible for subservience to state tyranny or absolutism.

Some of these criticisms are well founded, but even so Austin's work is of permanent value. The rigour and clarity of his analysis have demonstrated the complexity of many important legal and political concepts and the perennial need for just such an analytical study as he proposed, and repeated efforts to show precisely where his simple distinctions between law and morality are wrong have increased the understanding of both.

(H.L.A.H.)

BIBLIOGRAPHY. John Stuart Mill, "Austin on Jurisprudence," in *Dissertations and Discussions*, vol. 4, pp. 157–226 (1874); R.A. Eastwood and G.W. Keeton, *The Austinian Theories of Law and Sovereignty* (1929); E.M. Campbell, *John Austin and Jurisprudence in Nineteenth Century England* (1959).

Austin, John Langshaw (b. March 28, 1911, Lancaster, Lancashire, Eng.—d. Feb. 8, 1960, Oxford), British philosopher best known for his individualistic analysis of human thought derived from detailed study of everyday language.

After receiving early education at Shrewsbury School and Balliol College, Oxford, he became a fellow at All Souls College (1933) and Magdalen College (1935), where he studied traditional Greco-Roman classics, which later influenced his thinking. After service in the British intelligence corps during World War II, he returned to Oxford and eventually became White's professor of moral philosophy (1952–60) and an influential instructor of the ordinary-language movement.

Austin believed that linguistic analysis could provide many solutions to philosophical riddles, but he disapproved of the language of formal logic, believing it contrived and inadequate and often not as complex and subtle as ordinary language.

Although linguistic examination was generally considered only part of contemporary philosophy, the analytical movement that Austin espoused did emphasize the importance of language in philosophy. Austin's theoretical essays and lectures were published posthumously in *Philosophical Papers* (1961), *Sense and Sensibilia* (1962), and *How to Do Things with Words* (1962).

Austin, Louis Winslow (b. Oct. 30, 1867, Orwell, Vt., U.S.—d. June 27, 1932, Washington, D.C.), physicist known for research on long-range radio transmissions. He was educated at Middlebury College, Vermont, and the University of Strasbourg, Germany. In 1904 he began work on radio transmissions for the U.S. Bureau of Standards. In 1908 Austin became head of a naval radiotelegraphy laboratory at the bureau (later to become the Naval Research Laboratory) and from 1923 until 1932 was chief of the bureau's Radio Physics Laboratory.

Austin's work involved long-range transmission experiments, most notably a study, conducted in 1910, that tested radio contact between ships travelling between the United States and Liberia. This work helped Austin and his collaborator Louis Cohen to develop the Austin–Cohen formula for predicting the strength of long-distance radio signals. Austin's later work centred on the study of radio atmospheric disturbances.

Austin, Mary, *née* HUNTER (b. Sept. 9, 1868, Carlinville, Ill., U.S.—d. Aug. 13, 1934, Santa Fe, N.M.), novelist and essayist who wrote on American Indian culture and social problems.

Austin graduated from Blackburn College, Carlinville, Ill., in 1888, taught for a time, and then moved to California, where she became the friend and chronicler of the nearby Indian tribes. Her first book, *The Land of Little Rain*

Mary Austin

By courtesy of the Museum of New Mexico, Santa Fe

(1903), a description of desert life in the West, won her immediate fame, and was followed by two collections of short stories, *The Basket Woman* (1904) and *Lost Borders* (1909), and a play, *The Arrow Maker* (1911).

A prolific writer, she published 32 volumes and about 200 articles in her lifetime. Her "problem" novels include *A Woman of Genius* (1912). In her essays she discussed socialism, feminism, and the various social problems she encountered through her association with the group of artists and writers surrounding Mabel Dodge Luhan in New Mexico.

Austin, Stephen Fuller (b. Nov. 3, 1793, Austinville, Va., U.S.—d. Dec. 27, 1836, Austin, Texas), founder in the 1820s of the principal settlements of English-speaking people in Texas, when that territory was still part of Mexico.

Raised on the Missouri frontier, Austin was educated at Transylvania University in Lexington, Ky., and served in the Missouri territorial legislature (1814–19). The economic panic of 1819 led his father, Moses Austin (1767–1821), to leave his lead-mining business in Missouri and embark upon a scheme of colonization in Texas. Moses obtained a grant of land from the Mexican government, but died soon thereafter, and in 1821 Stephen went to Texas to carry out his father's project. He founded a colony (1822) of several hundred families on the Brazos River, and for some years thereafter, as the migration of U.S. citizens to Texas increased, he was a major figure in the struggle between Mexico and the U.S. for possession of the territory.

A skillful diplomat, Austin served the interests of Anglo-American slaveholders by defeating an effort to ban slavery in Texas. He tried to induce the Mexican government to make Texas a separate state in the confederation so that the American settlers might have the liberty and self-government they considered indispensable. When this attempt failed, however, he recommended in 1833 the organization of a state without waiting for the consent of the Mexican congress, and was thrown in prison. He was released in 1835, and when the Texas revolution broke out in October of that year, he went to the U.S. to secure help. Returning in June 1836, he was defeated by Sam Houston for the presidency of the new Republic of Texas and served briefly as secretary of state until his death.

Consult the INDEX *first*

Austral Islands, French ÎLES AUSTRALES, also called TUBUAI ISLANDS, southernmost archipelago of French Polynesia. Volcanic in origin, they are part of a vast submerged mountain chain (probably a southeasterly extension of the Cook Islands) in the central South Pacific. Scattered for 800 mi (1,300 km), they comprise five inhabited islands—Raivavae (6 sq mi [16 sq km]), Rapa (15 sq mi), Rimatara, (3 sq mi), Rurutu (11 sq mi), and Tubuai (18 sq mi)—as well as the uninhabited Marotiri Rocks and Maria Island. Four of the islands were sighted by Capt. James Cook: Rimatara and Rurutu in 1769, and Raivavae and Tubuai eight years later. In 1791 George Vancouver sighted the southernmost island, Rapa, the broken rim of a former volcano curved around the harbour of Ahurei Bay. The whole group, brought under French protection between 1880 and 1889, now forms a *circonscription* (administrative division) of French Polynesia.

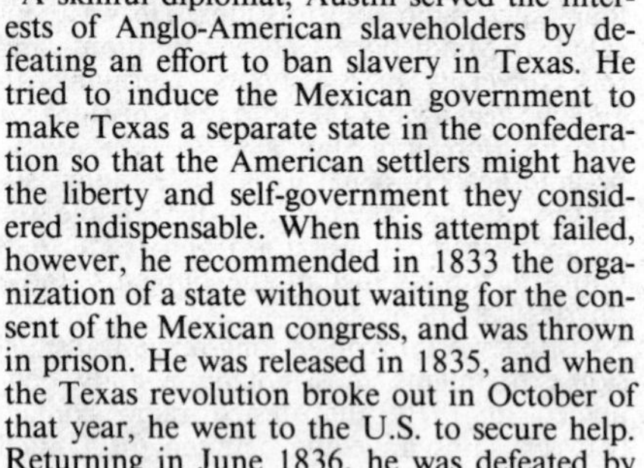

Ahurei village on Ahurei Bay, Rapa, Austral Islands, French Polynesia
Pierre Souhaite

Major settlements include Mataura (the *circonscription* headquarters) on Tubuai, Amaru on Raivavae, Ahurei on Rapa, and Moerai on Rurutu. The inhabitants are predominantly Protestant. Polynesian traditions are unusually well preserved in the Australs because of their comparative isolation. Principal resources are fish, coffee, taros, copra, and oranges. Pop. (1981 est.) 5,600.

Australia, officially COMMONWEALTH OF AUSTRALIA, the smallest continent and the sixth largest country on Earth, lying between the Pacific and Indian oceans in the Southern Hemisphere and covering an area, including Tasmania, of 2,966,144 sq mi (7,682,300 sq km). The capital is Canberra. The continent is bounded by latitudes 10° and 44° S (about 2,450 mi [3,940 km] from Cape York Peninsula in the north to Tasmania in the south) and by longitudes 112° and 154° E (about 2,700 mi from east to west). Australia is separated from Indonesia in the northwest by the Timor and the Arafura seas; from Papua New Guinea in the northeast by the Torres Strait; from the Coral Sea Islands Territory (in the Coral Sea), also in the northeast, by the Great Barrier Reef; from New Zealand in the southeast by the Tasman Sea; and from Antarctica to the south by the Indian Ocean. The population in 1981 was estimated to be 15,054,000.

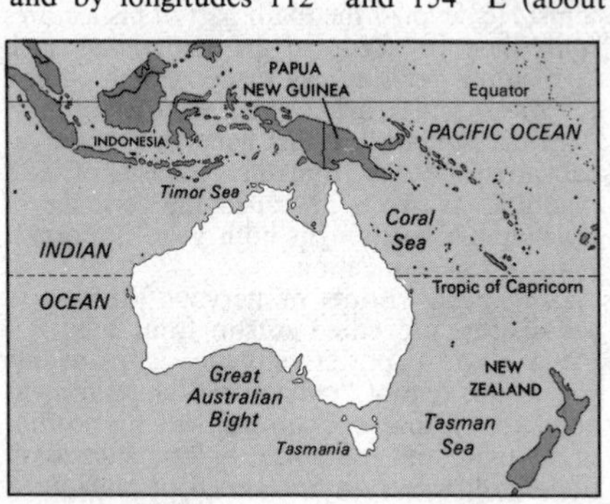

Australia

The article that follows is a summary of significant detail about Australia. Fuller treatment is provided in the MACROPAEDIA articles named below. For its geography and history, and its peoples and their traditional cultures, *see* Australia. For information about its major cities, *see* Melbourne; Sydney. For information about aspects of Australia's literary history, *see* Australia and New Zealand, The Literatures of.

For current history and for statistics on society and economy, *see* the article "World Affairs" and BRITANNICA WORLD DATA, respectively, in the *Britannica Book of the Year.*

The land. The largest of Australia's four major physiographic regions, more than half of its land area, is the Western Craton, or Western Shield. Its elevation averages between 1,300 and 2,000 ft (400 and 600 m) above sea level, with plateaus rising above the generally level landscape to heights of about 5,000 ft. The most conspicuous of these outcrops are the Arnhem Land and Kimberley blocks in the northwest, the Pilbara Block in the west, and the Macdonnell Ranges in the east. A second region, the Great Artesian Basin, lies east of the shield region and extends from the Gulf of Carpentaria in the north to the mouth of the Murray River in the south. It consists of three smaller basin areas, the Carpentaria Basin along the northern coast; the Eyre Basin, the largest, near the centre of the country; and the Murray Basin in the extreme south, with an area of some 90,000 sq mi. The third major region, the Great Dividing Range, or the Eastern Uplands, is a complex series of high ridges, high plains, plateaus, and basins extending from Cape York Peninsula in the north to Bass Strait in the south and extending into Tasmania. Australia's relief is generally low. Only 7,400 ft separates the elevation of its highest peak, Mt. Kosciusko (rising to only 7,316 ft), from that of its lowest point at Lake Eyre (46 ft below sea level). The country's fourth region, sandwiched between the Western Shield and the basin regions along the southern coast, is the Flinders–Mt. Lofty ranges, a minor divide between the Murray River basin to the south and the Lake Eyre basin to the north. Australia's volcanoes are no longer active, but there is much seismic activity in the eastern and the western highland areas.

Most of the Western Shield and the Great Artesian Basin regions receive annual rainfall of less than 17 in. (425 mm), with less than 10 in. falling in more than a third of the country's area. In the extreme southwest, in western Tasmania and along the northern and eastern coasts, there are generally ample supplies of water, with rainfall averaging as much as 80 in. Between the extremely arid southwest and the well-watered coasts lies a wide belt with average annual precipitation (though unreliable from year to year) of about 30 in. The catchment area of the Murray-Darling basin, the country's largest, and its water supply for irrigation purposes were greatly increased in 1974 with the diversion of the Snowy River from its normal southeastward course to flow northwestward into the Murray River. In the Great Artesian Basin local water supplies are provided by thousands of wells.

Tasmania and the Mt. Kosciusko area have snow fields in winter. Elsewhere, Australia is generally hot and in summer (December through February) has frequent heat waves with daytime temperatures exceeding 100° F (38° C). Most of Australia's arable land lies along the eastern coast (where sugarcane and cotton are grown) and in the southwest and southeast (where wheat is a major crop). About 18 percent of Australia is forested, mostly lying along the ranges of the Great Divide. Much of the continent's animal life is unique; best known are its distinctive marsupials, such as the koala and kangaroo, and the even more distinctive duck-billed platypus.

Although Australia is rich in several mineral resources, its bauxite reserves (estimated in the early 1980s at about 4,000,000,000 metric tons) and its high-grade iron ore reserves (35,000,000,000 tons, an average of about 55 percent containing iron) were among the world's largest. Its energy resources included more than 80,000,000,000 metric tons of coal (more than half was high-quality black coal), nearly 220,000,000 metric tons of petroleum, 18,700,000,000,000 cu ft (530,000,000,000 cu m) of natural gas, and nearly 300,000 tons of uranium, or 18 percent of global reserves.

The people. In 1981 Australia had a population of 15,054,000, spread thinly over the continent (density was only 4.9 persons per sq mi [1.9 persons per sq km]). The Australian population is remarkably homogeneous, as a result of the strict enforcement of a *de facto* white Australia policy. Yet Australia has one nonwhite minority, the Aborigines. Official policy is to help the Aborigines become an integral part of Australian community life. Nevertheless, many remain poorly trained and educated, caught at the lowest socioeconomic level of Australian society. In the late 20th century, however, public opinion has become more concerned at the plight of the Aborigines, and the federal and state governments have since the mid-1960s taken several measures, including granting full rights of Australian citizenship and improved educational facilities, that give some hope of improvement. The principal religion is Christianity, with Anglicans and Roman Catholics predominating; there is a considerable Protestant minority. In the late 1970s the birth rate was 15.4 per 1,000 and the death rate 7.4 per 1,000. The natural rate of increase was, thus, only 8 per 1,000, although immigration raised the overall national rate to 1.2 percent. The infant mortality rate was 11.4 per 1,000 for that same period. Australia's substantial population growth during the post-World War II period was in large measure attributable to immigration.

The economy. Australia has a basically free enterprise economy in structure. The gross national product (GNP) was estimated (1980) at U.S. $142,240,000,000, about $9,820 per capita. Its real average annual growth (1970–79) was 1.4 percent; it originates primarily from trade, manufacturing, and services.

Arable land totals about 6 percent of the total area; of that, about one-third requires irrigation. Agriculture produces 7 percent of the GNP and occupies an equal proportion of the labour force. Sugarcane is the leading crop, followed by wheat, barley, oats, rice, potatoes, cotton, sunflower seeds, and tomatoes. Fruits include grapes, primarily for wine, and oranges, apples, pineapples, and bananas.

Rangeland and pastures occupy about three-fifths of the land area; on this are raised the world's second largest number of sheep, producing more wool than any other country. Other livestock include cattle, about one-twelfth for dairying, and pigs. Beef and cattle hides are important products.

Australia is almost self-sufficient in lumber production. Some three-quarters of roundwood production is broadleaved, and timber plantations account for about one-fifth of the lumber output.

Most fishing in Australia is marine, about equally divided between the Indian and Pacific oceans. More than two-fifths of the annual catch consists of crustaceans, and tuna is important.

Mining and quarrying account for about one-twentieth of the GNP and employ about 2 percent of the labour force. Bituminous and lignite coal are the leading energy minerals followed by petroleum and natural gas. Australia leads the world in bauxite and zirconium concentrate production; other metallic minerals include iron ore, manganese ore, titanium oxide, zinc, lead, copper, nickel, tin, silver, gold, platinum, cobalt, cadmium, antimony, bismuth, and tungsten. The principal nonmetallic minerals include limestone, sand and gravel, brick clay, shale, salt, sulfur, and industrial diamonds.

Manufacturing is well diversified and has expanded to about one-fourth of the GNP. The principal manufactures include crude steel; pig iron; metal manufactured products; refined petroleum products; cement and concrete products; cotton, woollen, and man-made textiles and clothing; electrical and electronics equipment and machinery; agricultural equipment; road and railroad vehicles; aircraft; ships; domestic appliances; bricks; ceramic tiles; chemicals; fertilizers; plastics; synthetic rubber and tires; wooden building materials and furniture; leather goods; and beef and mutton. More than four-fifths of electrical production is from thermal power plants, the remainder from hydroelectric plants.

Construction generates 7 percent of the GNP and occupies about an equal proportion of the labour force. Major projects under construction in the early 1980s included coal mining facilities and aluminum smelting plants in New South Wales; a gas development project and diamond mining facilities in Western Australia; a high-level concrete box girder bridge in Brisbane; and modernization of various industrial plants.

Tourist attractions include Pacific coast beaches and deep-sea fishing, diving along the Great Barrier Reef, and winter sports in Australia's mountains. By the early 1980s about 1,000,000 tourists visited Australia annually, generating more than U.S. $700,000,000 in income.

Australia's labour force was more than two-fifths of the population in the early 1980s, principally employed in trade, manufacturing, and services. Unemployment rose to 7 percent, but some industries reported a shortage of skilled labour. Most unions, organized by industry, are affiliated to the Australian Council of Trade Unions.

Except for part of the railway system, industry is privately owned; many of Australia's large companies are subsidiaries of multinational corporations. The government regulates the economy mainly through monetary policy and taxation; in the early 1980s the goal was to restrain growth and inflation, but a massive inflow of foreign capital kept inflation at about 11 percent annually.

The Australian dollar ($A) is subdivided into 100 cents. Government spending cuts achieved a balanced budget in 1981 after deficits throughout the 1970s. The principal revenue sources are income taxes, excise and sales taxes, corporate taxes, and nontax revenue. The principal expenditures are for social security and assistance, state government transfers, health, defense, and economic sectors.

The Reserve Bank of Australia, located in Sydney, is the central bank with a separate department for commodity market finance. The Commonwealth Banking Corporation controls its member development, savings, and trading banks. There are branch banks throughout Australia. The Australian Associated Stock Exchange, located in Sydney, has member exchanges in the six state capitals.

The Australian National Railways Commission incorporates the Commonwealth railways and the South Australian and Tasmanian state railways; other railways are operated by the state governments. About one-fourth of the road network is paved, and only one-tenth of the remainder is unimproved. Major port facilities are located in Adelaide, Brisbane, Darwin, Freemantle, Gladstone, Gove (Melville Bay), Launceton, Melbourne, Newcastle, Sydney, Townsville, and Westernport, and numerous small ports serve mining and industrial towns. Most of the 5,200 mi of inland waterways are accessible only to small, shallow-draft vessels. Australia had more than 550 merchant vessels in 1982 larger than 100 gross tons. The busiest international airports are at Sydney, Melbourne, Brisbane, and Adelaide.

Australia achieved a foreign trade balance or slight surplus annually in the late 1970s and early '80s. Major exports were metal ores and scrap, wheat, coal, meat, and wool, principally to Japan and the United States. Major imports were machinery, crude petroleum, miscellaneous manufactured products, and transport equipment, primarily from the United States, Japan, the United Kingdom, and Saudi Arabia.

Administrative and social conditions. Australia is a federal state governed by a constitution adopted in 1900, entrusting the central government with power over defense, external affairs, foreign trade, immigration, customs and excise, and the Post Office. All residual powers are left to the country's six states.

Symbolic executive power is vested in the British monarch, who is represented throughout Australia by the governor-general. The highest political authority rests with the democratically elected Parliament, which consists of a 125-member House of Representatives and a 64-member Senate. The leader of the party or coalition that wins a majority in the House becomes the prime minister and appoints a cabinet. Both the prime minister and the cabinet are responsible to the Parliament. Three political parties usually dominate parliamentary elections: the Australian Labor Party, the Liberal Party, and the National Country Party. The country's judicial system is headed by the seven-member High Court of Australia, which has the power of constitutional review. Australia participates in three collective security organizations: the British Commonwealth Strategic Reserve, the Southeast Asia Treaty Organization (SEATO), and ANZUS (Australia–New Zealand–U.S. treaty).

Australia's social welfare system provides family allowances, work injury and unemployment benefits, and old-age, disability, and widow's pensions. In addition, the federal government operates a health insurance program that covers all residents.

Health conditions in Australia compare

Prime ministers of Australia

	party or parties	term
Edmund Barton (from 1902, Sir Edmund Barton)		1901–03
Alfred Deakin (*1st time*)	Liberal-Labor	1903–04
John Christian Watson	Labor	1904
George Houston Reid (from 1909, Sir George Houston Reid)		1904–05
Alfred Deakin (*2nd time*)	Liberal-Labor	1905–08
Andrew Fisher (*1st time*)	Labor	1908–09
Alfred Deakin (*3rd time*)	Liberal-Conservative	1909–10
Andrew Fisher (*2nd time*)	Labor	1910–13
Joseph Cook (from 1918, Sir Joseph Cook)	Liberal	1913–14
Andrew Fisher (*3rd time*)	Labor	1914–15
William Morris Hughes (*1st time*)	Labor	1915–16
William Morris Hughes (*2nd time*)	Nationalist	1916–23
Stanley Melbourne Bruce (from 1947, 1st Viscount Bruce of Melbourne)	Nationalist-Country	1923–29
James Henry Scullin	Labor	1929–32
Joseph Aloysius Lyons	United Australia	1932–39
Earle Page (from 1938, Sir Earle Page)	Country-United Australia	1939
Robert Gordon Menzies (*1st time*)	United Australia	1939–40
Robert Gordon Menzies (*2nd time*)	United Australia-Country	1940–41
Arthur William Fadden	Country-United Australia	1941
John Curtin	Labor	1941–45
Francis Michael Forde	Labor	1945
Joseph Benedict Chifley	Labor	1945–49
Robert Gordon Menzies (from 1963, Sir Robert Gordon Menzies) (*3rd time*)	Liberal-Country	1949–66
Harold Holt	Liberal-Country	1966–67
John McEwen	Liberal-Country	1967–68
John Grey Gorton (from 1977, Sir John Grey Gorton)	Liberal-Country	1968–71
William McMahon	Liberal-Country	1971–72
Gough Whitlam	Labor	1972–75
Malcolm Fraser	Liberal-National Country	1975–83
Robert Hawke	Labor	1983–

favourably with those found in the most advanced Western nations. High levels of nutrition, sanitation, disease control, and medical technology prevent the development and spread of infectious diseases. The country has a high proportion of doctors and hospital beds to population, a low infant mortality rate, and a life expectancy rate of more than 70 years.

Responsibility for education lies primarily with the states; the federal government administers education in the national territories. Free education at government schools is provided at the primary and secondary levels, though there are numerous schools run by the churches and a few private grammar schools. Education is compulsory between the ages of 6 and 15. Australia has 19 universities, the largest of which are the universities of New South Wales and Queensland.

The press in Australia is free from direct government censorship. The constitution does not guarantee press freedom, however, and the existence of a number of federal and state laws regulating the press sometimes has the effect of forcing Australian newspapers and magazines to practice self-censorship.

Cultural life. The figures and motifs of a 40,000-year-old tradition of Aboriginal art are seen throughout Australia, and the oral art of the Aboriginal storyteller reaches back to the dimmest times of the "Dreaming," before the white man arrived.

A number of Australian artists have gained international renown. Sidney Nolan, Russell Drysdale, and Arthur Boyd are famous for having developed an original school of Australian painting. Major writers include Thomas Keneally, Morris West, and Nobel Prize winner Patrick White, author of *The Tree of Man* (1955), *Voss* (1957), and *Riders in the Chariot* (1961). During the late 1970s and early 1980s several Australian filmmakers established themselves as world-class artists: Peter Weir, Bruce Beresford, Gillian Armstrong, George Miller, and Fred Schepisi. The history of music in Australia includes world figures such as Dame Nellie Melba, Percy Grainger, and Dame Joan Sutherland; the most visible monument to the musical arts is the astonishing Sydney Opera House, dominating that city's skyline. Although Australia reserves some of its strongest enthusiasms for sports (football, horse racing, swimming and surfing, tennis), relatively few sports are professionalized, and gambling, though widespread, has had little effect on a long tradition of amateurism.

History. The settlement of Australia by the Aborigines is at least 25,000 and perhaps 40,000 years old. They immigrated from Southeast Asia and numbered approximately 300,000 when Europeans arrived in the 18th century. There is some evidence of a Chinese landing at the site of Darwin in 1432, but widespread European knowledge of Australia only began with the explorations of the 17th century.

The Dutch landed in Australia in 1616 and, under such notable seamen as Abel Tasman, continued their explorations until 1644, when Australia became known as New Holland.

The British arrived in 1688 under William Dampier, but they did not launch a large-scale expedition until James Cook's historic voyage of 1770 that resulted in Britain's claim to Australia and formal possession of New South Wales with the establishment of the small colony of Sydney Cove within Port Jackson (1788). From the outset, British convicts were transported to the colony.

Tasmania, the next settlement, received settlers from Sydney as early as 1803, and colonists arrived in Western Australia in 1827. By 1859 the colonial nuclei of all of Australia's six states had been formed. Colonization with shiploads of convicts continued well into the 19th century

The discovery of copper in 1842 and gold in 1851 spurred economic growth and development. Likewise, the development of sheep grazing helped establish Australia's wool industry but caused widespread displacement among the Aborigines whose native habitats fell into the hands of pastoralists.

A concern for national defense and for intercolonial free trade and a desire to control European and Asian immigration (Australian-born comprised 64.5 percent of the population in 1901) led to the federation movement of the late 1800s. Popular referenda were held in 1898–99 and the Commonwealth of Australia was officially proclaimed on Jan. 1, 1901. Canberra was designated the federal capital in 1908.

Australia fought alongside Britain in World War I, notably with the Australia and New Zealand Army Corps (ANZAC) in the Dardanelles campaign (1915); the day of the landing at Gallipoli—April 25—became a major day of national reverence.

Prosperous years followed the end of the war until the worldwide depression of the 1930s brought deteriorating trading conditions. Also during this time, reserves were established for Aborigines to serve as a buffer between them and white Australians because of maltreatment and reciprocal violence.

World War II brought Australia closer to the United States; ties with Britain diminished and after 1942, the British Royal Navy ceased defending Australia. Australia joined SEATO in 1954 and fought with the U.S. in Vietnam (1965–71).

The Labor government of the 1970s attempted to strengthen ties with the non-Communist East. Papua New Guinea, formerly consisting of two territories administered by Australia, achieved complete independence in 1975. In 1981 the Pitjantjatjara Aborigines were given freehold title to 102,630 sq mi in South Australia, the first deeding of land in the country to its original inhabitants. A deteriorating economy in the early 1980s led to widespread strikes.

Australia, Church of England in: *see* Anglican Church of Australia.

Australian Aboriginal languages, a group of approximately 260 interrelated languages whose speakers occupied the entire Australian continent as well as the western islands of Torres Strait, but apparently not Tasmania. These languages are not known to be related to any outside language. The great majority of them were either extinct or nearing extinction in the late 20th century. Still-vigorous languages have, for the most part, only a few hundred speakers each. The languages with the most speakers are Mabuiag, the language of the Western Torres Strait islands, and the Western Desert language.

A brief treatment of the Australian Aboriginal languages follows. For full treatment, *see* MACROPAEDIA: Languages of the World.

The most recent classification of the Australian languages subdivides them into 28 families, of which 27 are located in the north and northwest, covering about one-eighth of the continent, and a single family, Pama-Nyungan, occupies the remaining seven-eighths of Australia. This skewed distribution is assumed to be the result of the spread of a language form referred to as Common Australian (dated at about 5,000-6,000 years ago) from somewhere in northwestern Australia throughout most of the continent except north and northwest regions.

The Australian languages are characterized by great similarities in their sound systems and considerable agreement in grammar but often by markedly few similarities in vocabulary. Nevertheless, a number of common words are found in a great many languages all over the continent, thus constituting a Common Australian element.

The Australian languages generally show considerable grammatical complexity. Inflection is chiefly by affixation. Prefixes and suffixes are found in northern and northwestern Australia, and suffixes, for the most part, are used elsewhere. A characteristic feature of many languages is the suffixing of markers onto the first word of the sentence or onto special particles not connected with the verb in order to indicate the subject and object of the verb. Another widespread feature is an ergative or agentive suffix, attached to nouns and pronouns, that indicates the actor of an action referred to by a transitive verb. A number of languages, mainly northern ones, have gender and noun class systems, with adjectives, numerals, and demonstratives showing special forms for each of the classes of nouns and often, also, for their number.

The sound systems of the Australian languages are extremely similar. Most of them have parallel series of stop consonants and nasal consonants at from four to six different points of articulation. In addition, most show no distinction between voiced and voiceless stops and have no fricative consonants. A three vowel system (*a, i, u*) is common.

Australian Aborigine, also called ABORIGINAL, any member of the indigenous Australoid geographical race (*q.v.*) of Australia and Tasmania, which at the time of European colonization in the late 18th century is thought to have numbered 300,000 and to have been divided into some 500 tribes, each with its recognized territory and its distinct language or dialect. As a result of European contact, most aspects of the traditional culture have been severely modified.

A brief treatment of Australian Aboriginal cultures follows. For full treatment, *see* MACROPAEDIA: Australia.

The archaeology of Australia shows a human occupation of between 25,000 and 40,000 years. The Aborigines, whether in one or several periods, probably arrived either by way of the now submerged Sahul Shelf or, where land connections were absent, by rafts and canoes. At some point in the immigration they introduced the dingo, a species of dog. There are apparent surviving pockets of a common Australian language, not necessarily the original, in Cape York Peninsula and northeast Arnhem Land. The Aborigines were not gardeners and Australia provided no animals suitable for herding, so they lived by food-gathering and hunting, in which activities they were limited by distance from fresh water. With increase of numbers, subgroups set out to find other waters: "paths" of mythological heroes and "trade" routes indicate the directions of the migrations.

An Aboriginal tribe consisted of several local groups which, food permitting, associated for most of the year. The territory of each group, membership of which was in the male line, was focussed upon a watering place where the group's ancestors originally settled and where the preexistent spirits of its members were believed to have sojourned ever since, waiting for incarnation and reincarnation. Founders of secondary settlements and their descendants were forever kinsfolk of the primary group and its descendants, regardless of how far they were separated in space, time, and customs. A system of classifying everyone as a relation codified reciprocal behaviour based on recognized indirect kinship links (if any), on apparent generation level, on membership of clans, and on ritual affiliation.

In much of Australia, relations were divided into two, four, or eight groups, which were correlated with rules of marriage and descent and were normally exogamous. Such divisions persisted among traditional groups in modern times.

The Aborigines possessed detailed knowledge of each tribal territory and when and where food could be obtained. This is summarized in the traditional reckoning of seasons, which vary from five to eight in different regions, each being marked by the normally expected climatic conditions and by the kinds of procurable foods.

Aborigines faced the recurrence of droughts and food failures by regarding natural species and the rain as part of man's social and moral order and by entering into ritual relations with them. Each group within a traditional tribe consists not only of men and women but also of several species, so that all are relations. The group (clan) bears the name of one of these, its totem. Further, the men are divided into lodges, each of which is custodian of the mythology, ritual, sites, and symbols associated with one or more natural species and with ancestral heroes. Through ritual reenactment the creative past becomes operative in the present and the life of species and man is assured. The myths and ritual constitute the Dreaming (*q.v.*), signifying continuity of life unlimited by space and time. Only the old men have full knowledge of the Dreaming and therefore authority in ritual and matters of social behaviour.

Except in the case of infants and old persons, or when caused by a weapon, death is traditionally attributed to sorcery and only the medicine man, the "clever fellow," can extract the "badness" and restore confidence and the will to live. A psychic expert and a good psychologist, he comes in his "training" into association with the dead, with some totem spirits, and with the sky-world. If he fails to cure, it is because he has been called too late, or the sorcery is too strong (as in fat and blood extraction), or the victim deserves his fate.

Aboriginal myth and ritual are expressed in art, poetry, music, and dance. The myths are preserved in chants that are poetic in expression, rhythmic in structure, and linguistically and musically complex. Sacred objects and even weapons such as the boomerang (*q.v.*) are painted and engraved to express myths, which are also chanted "into" them. The actors' bodies are painted in ritual, and mythological designs are engraved or painted on stone, on bark, and on the ground, the painting and engraving being themselves rites. Painting is also done for pleasure, just as singing and dancing take place at the camp-social corroboree as well as on the secret ground. There are regional schools of art and music and also regional differences in the form and decoration of implements and weapons. The content of some major religious cults also varies regionally.

Contact with Europeans, from the bloody "pacification by force" policy of 19th-century colonialists to the urban assimilation of the present day, has radically altered Aboriginal culture. It was for some time believed that the Aborigines would eventually die out, and reserves were established in the late 1920s and early 1930s. No Aborigines exist who have not had some contact with modern Australian society, and all are now Australian citizens. Recent decades have seen the emergence of more articulate part-Aboriginal groups in the south, who insist on integration rather than assimilation—that is, on retaining Aboriginal identity as a unique status symbol marking them off from other Australians. In the north, the focus has been on questions of land ownership and control, including compensation (and not merely royalties) for and a share in the mineral exploitation that is occurring on Aboriginal reserves.

Australian Alps, mountain mass, a segment of the Great Dividing Range (Eastern Highlands), occupying the southeasternmost corner of Australia, in eastern Victoria and southeastern New South Wales. In a more local sense, the term denotes the ranges on the states' border forming the divide between the watersheds of the Murray River system, flowing west, and the Snowy and other streams flowing southeastward directly to the Pacific. The name Alps is applied there not because of special structural features but for the general characteristics of massiveness and of being snow clad for five to six months each year. The mountains are the highest on the continent, reaching 7,310 ft (2,228 m) at Kosciusko (*q.v.*); yet the loftiest peaks are rather unremarkable prominences set upon a broad, gently undulating highland surface. The timberline lies at 5,000 ft. Because of strong vertical movements of the Earth in this region, many of the streams there have eroded "valley in valley" forms. These valleys and basins and lower uplands are used for grazing. The rocks of the highlands are extensively, if not richly, mineralized, and there have been many small scattered mining ventures in the past. More recently, tourism and winter sports have developed. National parks in the area include Kosciusko National Park, Gudgenby Nature Reserve, Cobberas-Tingaringy, and Wabonga Plateau. All development, however, is overshadowed by the Snowy Mountains (*q.v.*) hydroelectricity project, a joint undertaking of the commonwealth and the two states. A complex system of dams and tunnels feeds water from the Snowy River across the divide, supplying more than 30 generating stations and adding to the irrigation facilities of the Murray Basin. Cooma, the project's centre, and its suburbs and the city of Canberra, in the Australian Capital Territory, are the major urban centres of the Alpine district.

Mount Carruthers in the Kosciusko Snowfields of the Australian Alps
By courtesy of the Australian Information Service

Australian Antarctic Territory, external territory of Australia. Created in 1933, it encompasses all islands and lands south of latitude 60° S and between longitude 160° E and 45° E, with the exception of Adélie Coast, which is claimed by France. The territory's total area is 2,400,000 sq mi (6,200,000 sq km). Several research stations are located there.

Australian Ballet, leading ballet company of Australia. In 1962 the Australian Ballet Foundation, founded by art patrons interested in promoting a national ballet, sponsored the Australian Ballet company. It was formed mainly with native talent from the former Australian Borovansky Ballet.

Peggy van Praagh became the artistic director (1963); she was joined two years later by Sir Robert Helpmann as co-director. After Van Praagh retired in 1974 and Helpmann in 1976, Anne Woolliams was appointed artistic director. Since 1965 the company has made periodic tours of Europe and the U.S. with a repertoire of classical and original works.

Australian Ballot, the system of voting in which voters mark their choices in privacy on uniform ballots printed and distributed by the government or designate their choices by some other secret means. South Australia was the first state to introduce secrecy of the ballot (1858) and for that reason the secret ballot is referred to as the Australian Ballot. The system spread to Europe and America to meet the growing public and parliamentary demand for protection of voters. The means for securing secrecy vary considerably.

Arrangements found in the Federal Republic of Germany are typical of continental Europe. The voting urns are required to be four-cornered, of certain dimensions, and closed, the only aperture being a small slit at the top. These urns are examined before the poll begins and cannot be opened until the count begins. The voter indicates his choice by marking his ballot and placing it into an officially stamped envelope. The latter is given to him by an official, and no other envelope is legally valid. The envelope is made of opaque paper of a legally determined size. The voter places his ballot into the envelope in a special stall or voting booth so arranged as to preserve secrecy. The envelope containing the ballot is then given by the voter to the returning officer, who takes the name of the voter, verifies his right to vote, and then puts the vote into the urn.

In Great Britain the secret ballot was finally introduced for all parliamentary and municipal elections by the Ballot Act of 1872. In the United Kingdom, as in the Commonwealth generally, the ballots are officially provided and issued from a counterfoiled volume, but no envelope is provided and the voter marks his ballot with an impersonal "X" and casts it directly into the box.

Until 1913 the French system was full of defects; the candidates circulated the ballots even outside the polling sections, and the voter merely folded the paper and gave it to the presiding official to put into the ballot box. After 1913 the envelope system was adopted. After October 1919 also, the state printed the ballots, though at the expense of the candidates, sending them to the voters by mail under an official stamp. No voter could be offered ballots on election day except from the returning officer's staff inside the polling station.

Before 1884 the general practice in the United States was either open voting or, where this rudimentary and clumsy process had been superseded, voting by ballot. After the presidential elections of 1884 the Australian Ballot system was extensively adopted: ballots were printed at the public expense, distributed in the polling stations, and secretly marked and folded and were in some states officially numbered and identifiable by reference to the counterfoil retained by the official. Increasing use was also made of voting machines or ballots in the form of punched cards which assure a greater speed and honesty in counting.

In countries where large numbers of illiterates vote, special voting arrangements have to be made. In parts of India voting is done by tokens and each candidate has his own ballot box in each voting booth which is identified by a symbol placed on the outside. Each voter puts the token in the box of the candidate he wishes to support.

Australian Capital Territory, formerly YASS-CANBERRA, separate political entity of the Commonwealth of Australia consisting of the national capital, Canberra, and some surrounding country. The territory is situated in the Southern Tablelands district within the confines of New South Wales. Primarily a rolling plain (1,900-ft [580-m] elevation) known as the Canberra Basin, it is surrounded by ranges of the Australian Alps (rising to more than 6,000 ft) and is bisected from southeast to northwest by the Murrumbidgee River.

The area was explored in 1820 by Charles Throsby, who named it Limestone Plains. In 1901, under the urging of King O'Malley, a politician, it was stipulated in the commonwealth constitution that a land tract of at least 100 sq mi (260 sq km) in area and not less than 100 mi (160 km) from Sydney be set aside from New South Wales and reserved as a capital district. The Limestone Plains site was selected in 1908. Jurisdiction of 911 sq mi of land was transferred to the commonwealth in 1911, and 28 sq mi of territory at Jervis Bay (85 mi east) were added in 1915 for possible development as a federal seaport. Of the total land area, 170 sq mi are reserved from occupation as the catchment area of the Cotter River, 156 sq mi are for public purposes (parks, schools), and 12 sq mi are for the city of Canberra. The remaining acreage, which may be only leaseheld, is devoted primarily to commercial softwood and hardwood forests.

There is some market gardening and dairy, wheat, wool, and beef farming in the territory. Rural activities, however, are very modest in comparison with urban affairs, as is reflected in the population ratio (more than 98 percent urban). The territory is the site of both the Royal Military College (1911) and the Royal Australian Naval College at Jervis Bay. Pop. (1981) 221,609.

Australian Christmas tree (*Nuytsia floribunda*), parasitic tree of the mistletoe family (Loranthaceae), native to western Australia. The tree may grow to 10 metres (about 33 feet) or more and produces many yellow-orange flowers during the Christmas season. Its dry fruits have three broad, leathery wings.

Australian Christmas tree (*Nuytsia floribunda*)
W.H. Hodge

The Australian Christmas tree forms connections (haustoria) to the roots of small plants, such as grasses, through which it obtains water and nutrients. These connections may damage underground cables by forming constricting rings around them. New Christmas trees may sprout from roots at some distance from the original plant.

Australian Colonies Government Act (August 1850), the popular designation for the legislation of the British House of Commons separating the southeastern Australian district of Port Phillip from New South Wales and establishing it as the colony of Victoria. It was passed in response to the demand of the Port Phillip settlers, who felt inadequately represented in the New South Wales Legislative Council (self-governing since 1842) and who resented their revenues being channelled to the New South Wales area. The act, which took effect in July 1851, provided for a legislative council of 20 elected members and 10 members appointed by the governor. This body was given jurisdiction over all but crown lands and could pass any legislation not in conflict with English law. The act also recognized the desire for progress toward self-government elsewhere in Australia, and similar constitutional provisions were applied to Tasmania and South Australia.

Australian Democratic Labor Party (ADLP), right-wing political party in Australia founded in 1956–57 by Roman Catholic and other defectors from the Australian Labor Party. Militantly anti-Communist, the ADLP supported Western and other anti-Communist powers in Oceania and Southeast Asia and strongly backed Australia's involvement in the Vietnam War. The party was only nominally "labor" and occasionally supported the Liberal-Country coalition governments just to keep its parent, the Australian Labor Party, out of power. Electorally it occasionally won a few seats in the Senate but never won seats in the House of Representatives. The decline of the "Red" issue and the improved vitality of the Australian Labor Party tended to diminish the influence of the ADLP after 1970.

Australian Democrats, centrist political party founded in 1977 and supported by those dissatisfied with the major Australian parties, the Liberals on the right and the Australian Labor Party on the left. Its support is especially strong among professionals and small businessmen concerned with inflation, rising labour costs, environmental degradation, and polarization between right and left in Australia. Their most controversial stand has probably been their opposition to the export of uranium.

The party founder, Donald Leslie Chipp (b. 1925), was a Liberal minister who bolted after being denied a post in the 1975 Liberal-National Party government. The Australian Democrats won 9 percent of the vote in 1977 and elected two senators. Thanks to proportional representation, they elected five senators in 1980 and in 1983, and this success gave them the balance of power in the upper chamber.

Australian Encyclopedia, The, national encyclopaedia published in Sydney, emphasizing distinctive features of the country, particularly geography, natural history, and the Aborigines.

It was originally brought out by Angus and Robertson in 2 volumes (1925), and the second edition was expanded to 10 volumes in 1958. The encyclopaedia was sold to the Grolier Society of Australia in 1962, and thereafter, five reprintings, with generally minor alterations, were undertaken up to 1972. A third and completely new edition, comprising six volumes, was published in 1977, treating all aspects of Australian life and taking into account the country's enormous development of the preceding 20 years. In addition to more than 1,700 biographies of notable Australians, which clearly reflect the increasing role of women in Australia, there is extensive coverage of the continent's geographical features and mineral resources. There are more than 2,400 illustrations, many in colour, including photographs, original plates, maps, and diagrams and charts.

Australian External Territories, group of non-self-governing dependencies of Australia located variously on the Antarctic continent and in surrounding areas of the southern Pacific and Indian oceans. They comprise the Australian Antarctic Territory, Christmas Island, the Cocos (Keeling) Islands, Norfolk Island, the Heard and McDonald Islands, and the Coral Sea Islands (*qq.v.*). Only Christmas, Norfolk, and the Cocos Islands have permanent inhabitants. The external territories formerly included Nauru (granted independence 1968), Papua (administered directly as an external territory), and New Guinea (administered as a United Nations trust territory). The latter two achieved independence as the single country, Papua New Guinea, in 1975.

Australian geographical race: *see* Australoid geographical race.

Australian Labor Party (ALP), one of the major Australian political parties. The first significant political representation of labour was achieved during the 1890s; in 1891, for example, candidates endorsed by the Sydney Trades and Labor Council gained 86 out of 141 seats in the New South Wales legislature. The entry of labour into national politics came with the first federal elections in 1901, when labour candidates associated in a loose federal organization gained 16 seats in the House of Representatives and 8 in the Senate, giving them the balance of power. The state organizations finally adopted the name Australian Labor Party in 1918.

The early labour parties were moderately Socialist in their policies, which called for such reforms as removal of property qualifications for the franchise, removal of legal restrictions on union activity, establishment of the principle of employer liability for industrial accidents and diseases, and compulsory industrial arbitration. They were, however, extremely disciplined, well organized, and militant, setting a pattern of party organization that other political groups were forced, to some extent, to imitate.

The first majority federal Labor government was established in 1910, and by mid-1915 Labor also held power in all the states except Victoria. During World War I, however, the party split over the issue of conscription, the Labor Party proper going out of office until 1929. Many pro-conscription members remained in power for some years as members of the wartime Nationalist Party, formed from an alliance of pro-conscription Labor and the Liberal Party.

Despite a sweeping electoral victory in 1929, Labor split over economic policy regarding the Depression and, following a general election of December 1931, went out of office for 10 years. Between 1944 and 1949 the party enacted major welfare legislation.

From its defeat in 1949 until the election of Gough Whitlam as prime minister in 1972, the Labor Party remained out of office. Its weakness can be ascribed to an anti-Communist crusade of the 1950s that split the right and left wings of the party; to a certain amount of general hostility toward organized labour; and to two decades of prosperity, which resulted in electoral satisfaction with the ruling Liberal–Country coalition. Under Whitlam the Labor Party began a wide-ranging reform movement that touched upon Australia's economy, foreign policy, and social structure. In December 1975, however, the party was voted out of office when the governor general forced early elections by dismissing the government under highly controversial circumstances. Two years later Whitlam resigned as parliamentary leader of the party after a second electoral defeat and was replaced by a less reform-minded leadership. In 1983 the Labor Party returned to power under Robert J.L. Hawke.

A list of the abbreviations used in the MICROPAEDIA *will be found at the end of this volume*

Australian literature, the body of writing produced in English in Australia.

A brief account of the literature of Australia follows. For full treatment, *see* MACROPAEDIA: Australia and New Zealand, Literatures of.

For the first two generations after British settlement in 1788, Australian literature was sparse and derivative. William Charles Wentworth's poem *Australasia* (1819) marks the first significant native-born response to the environment. The first novels, Henry Savery's *Quintus Servinton* (1830–31) and Alexander Harris's *The Emigrant Family* (1849), drew on autobiographical material. After the gold rushes of the 1850s, a surer use of Australian background was made by novelists such as

Henry Kingsley (*The Recollections of Geoffry Hamlyn,* 1859), Marcus Clarke (*For the Term of His Natural Life,* 1874), and Rolf Boldrewood (*Robbery Under Arms,* 1888). As with the poets Charles Harpur, Adam Lindsay Gordon, and Henry Kendall the Australian bush was perceived ambivalently as hostile to alien intrusion and yet as the authentic environment of colonial Australians.

The Bulletin, founded in Sydney (1880), stimulated the publication of much popular verse and fiction and reinforced the nationalism of the era of federation. "Banjo" Paterson wrote bush ballads such as "The Man from Snowy River" (1895) and "Waltzing Matilda" (1895), which passed into national currency. Henry Lawson, a more socially conscious but probably a lesser versifier, achieved a Chekhovian greatness in the finest of his short stories such as the series *Joe Wilson and His Mates* (1899–1902). By far the foremost novel of this school was the sprawling, Shandyesque *Such Is Life* (1903) by Joseph Furphy.

Between 1900 and 1935 Australian writing took few new directions apart from the knockabout vitalism of writers such as Hugh McCrae and Norman Lindsay. Intellectually sophisticated writers lacked a supportive milieu. Some, such as the outstanding Symbolist poet Christopher Brennan, chose to remain in Australia. Others—such as the novelists Henry Handel Richardson (pseudonym of Ethel Florence Lindesay Robertson), author of the trilogy *The Fortunes of Richard Mahony* (1917–29), and Martin Boyd, author of *The Montforts* (1928) and its successors—moved to Europe. Both looked at the plight of the exile between two cultures.

Revival came in the 1930s with novelists such as Eleanor Dark, Katherine Susannah Pritchard, Barnard Eldershaw (a composite authorship of Marjorie Barnard and Flora Eldershaw), and the later works of Miles Franklin. Two major literary quarterlies, *Southerly* (founded 1939) and *Meanjin* (founded 1940), were flanked by the nationalist Jindyworobak movement (which believed in going back to aboriginal sources for cultural inspiration) and the avant-garde Angry Penguins group. The 1940s saw a major flowering of poetry in which national and international influences at last merged. A.D. Hope and James McAuley gained strength from classical traditions; Judith Wright explored the interaction of women, men, and the environment with tough-minded sensitivity. Later poets of note included Bruce Dawe, Les Murray, Thomas W. Shapcott, Chris Wallace-Crabbe, and Peter Porter.

Among novelists, Patrick White, a Nobel Prize winner in 1973, came to prominence with *The Aunt's Story* (1948). Later novels such as *Voss* (1957) and *The Twyborn Inheritance* (1979) confirmed his reputation as a profoundly subtle and innovative writer. Others to win international recognition included Randolph Stow, author of *Tourmaline* (1963) and *The Merry-go-round by the Sea* (1965), and the prolific and versatile Thomas Keneally, best known for *The Chant of Jimmie Blacksmith* (1972) and *Schindler's Ark* (1982), which won the prestigious British literary award the Booker Prize that year.

Australian drama grew slowly after 1945. Despite such harbingers as Sumner Locke-Elliott's *Rusty Bugles* (1948) and Ray Lawler's *Summer of the Seventeenth Doll* (1955), it was only during the late 1960s and '70s that dramatists such as David Williamson, Alexander Buzo, and Dorothy Hewett found receptive audiences in a movement that spilled over into the renaissance of Australian film during the late 1970s and '80s.

Australian National University, state-subsidized university in Canberra, Australia. Founded in 1946, the university was originally confined to graduate study. In 1960, when Canberra University College (1929) became part of the university, undergraduates were admitted for the first time. Affiliated with the university are the Institute of Advanced Studies, the unit responsible for doctoral degrees, and research schools of medicine, physical and biological sciences, social sciences, and Pacific studies.

Australian Patriotic Association (1835–42), group of influential Australians of New South Wales that sought a grant of representative government to the colony from the British House of Commons; their efforts aided significantly in the passage of the Constitution Act of 1842 and the incorporation of the city of Sydney as a municipality with a broadly based franchise. The APA stood as a champion of the rights of the less well-to-do and of former convicts (Emancipists). Among its leaders were W. C. Wentworth, the son of a convict woman and the publisher of the influential newspaper the *Australian;* Sir John Jamison; and a prominent Emancipist doctor, William Bland. The group had representatives in England to put their case before the British government, which was then considering a new constitution for New South Wales and municipal incorporation for Sydney. The efforts of the APA were unsuccessfully opposed by another, more conservative, group of colonists which, while favouring representative government, sought to exclude Emancipists from political participation. With its goals achieved, the APA disbanded in 1842.

Australian pitcher plant: *see* fly-catcher plant.

Australian region, one of the six major land areas of the world defined on the basis of its characteristic animal life. It coincides with the Notogaean realm and encompasses Australia and the outlying islands of Tasmania, New Guinea, New Caledonia, New Zealand, Melanesia, Micronesia, and Polynesia. It includes such animals as the birds of paradise, the duck-billed platypus, spiny anteaters, and the world's concentration of pouched mammals such as kangaroos and their kin. The vegetational division roughly corresponding to this region is called the Australian kingdom. Conspicuous among the plants of the region are the eucalypts, myrtles, acacias, and casuarinas.

Australian rules football, Australian version of football, developed in Melbourne, Victoria, about 1858 by H.C.A. Harrison (1836–1929). It has been described as a mixture of soccer and rugby and Gaelic football. It is played with an oval ball with circumferences of 57 and 74 centimetres (29.1 and 22.4 inches) on an oval field with a greatest width of about 110–155 metres (120.2–169.5 yards) and a length of 135–185 m. Three of the 18 players on each team move freely, while the others guard certain zones and opponents. Play consists mostly of kicking or punching the ball; players may run with the ball no more than 9.1 m without bouncing it on the ground. Throwing the ball is illegal, and there is no offside rule.

Australian rules football at the Melbourne Cricket Ground (Richmond Tigers versus Melbourne Demons)
By courtesy of the Australian Information Service

Four posts 6.09 m high are set up in a straight line 6.4 m apart at each end of the field. Any punt, placekick, or dropkick that goes between the two inner posts without being touched by a defender scores a goal, worth six points; any kick that goes between inner and outer posts or between the inner posts after being touched scores a "behind," worth one point. The four posts are distinctive of Australian rules football. A match consists of four 25-minute quarters. The game is governed by the Australian National Football Council and is especially popular in Victoria, South Australia, and Western Australia.

Australian terrier, one of the newer terrier breeds. First exhibited in 1885 as the Australian rough terrier, the perky breed can be traced back to an extinct British breed, the broken-haired, black-and-tan Old English terrier, but includes in its heritage a number of other terriers, among them possibly the Dandie Dinmont, Skye, Scottish, cairn, and Yorkshire terriers. The Australian terrier stands about 10 inches (25 centimetres) and weighs about 11 to 15 pounds (5 to 7 kilograms). It is a rather long-bodied dog, with a harsh coat and a softer topknot. The coat may be blue-black or silver-black, with tan on the head and legs, or sandy or reddish brown.

Australian terrier
Sally Anne Thompson—EB Inc.

Australoid geographical race, also called AUSTRALIAN GEOGRAPHICAL RACE, a group of human populations indigenous to Australia and Tasmania. Because of European migration since the 18th century, the Australoid population declined substantially in Australia and became extinct in Tasmania in 1876. Characteristics of the Australoid race are heavy skin pigmentation, wavy to curly hair (sometimes blond or reddish in childhood), linear (slender) body build, very large teeth, pronounced browridges and projecting jaws, moderate to heavy body hair, high frequencies of male pattern balding with associated balding of the calves of the legs, very low frequencies of blood type B (ABO system), remarkably high frequencies of blood type N and absence of type S (MNSs blood group system), and, as opposed to African populations, no evidence of abnormal hemoglobins or glucose-6-phosphate dehydrogenase (G-6-PD) deficiency.

Australopithecus ("southern ape"), genus of fossil hominids found in southern and eastern Africa and dating from between the end of the Miocene Epoch (about 8,000,000 years ago) and the end of the Early Pleistocene (about 1,500,000 years ago). This genus is often considered to be related, if not ancestral, to modern human beings.

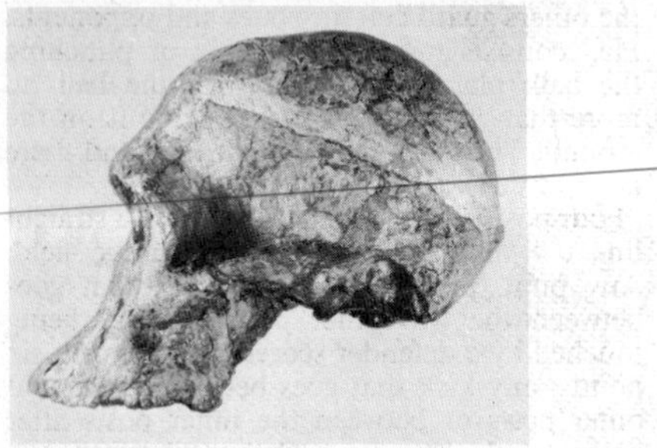

Lateral view of skull of *Australopithecus africanus* found at Sterkfontein, S.Af.
By courtesy of the Transvaal Museum, Pretoria, S.Af.

A brief treatment of the genus *Australopithecus* and its species follows. For full treatment, *see* MACROPAEDIA: Evolution, Human.

It has been postulated from fossil evidence that the emergence of australopithecines (as the early hominids are sometimes collectively known) occurred about 8,000,000 years ago, although the fossil record beyond 3,500,000 years ago is inconclusive; for purposes of comparison, it may be noted that *Homo erectus* ("upright man") is thought to have appeared some 1,500,000 years ago. The australopithecines are distinguished from the apes by their anatomical structure, which clearly indicates that they walked at least moderately upright. Their brains were small, not very different from those of the apes, and their teeth were like those of humans. Many anthropologists make a distinction between the smaller, light-bodied, or so-called gracile, australopithecines, classified as *Australopithecus africanus* (or related subspecies), and a heavier, more robust form, called *Australopithecus robustus*. Other species, including *A. boisei*, are sometimes included in the genus.

Australopithecus africanus. The name *Australopithecus* was first applied, along with the species name *africanus,* to a fossil found by Raymond Dart in 1924 at Taung, S.Af. The Taung fossil, also known as the "Taung skull," or "Taung baby," was determined to be the remains of an immature or juvenile specimen. It consisted of a face; mandible (jawbone); skull base, with brain cast; and full deciduous dentition and first permanent molars. Dart thought this fossil represented a hitherto unknown species that was intermediate between man and ape. But because of the immaturity of the specimen and because it was the first of its kind to be discovered, scientists were initially skeptical of this interpretation.

During the next 30 years, however, many other South African sites, notably Sterkfontein, Swartkrans, Kromdraai, and Makapansgat, yielded additional remains of similar light-bodied hominids that were eventually designated as *Australopithecus africanus.* Among these were *Plesianthropus transvaalensis,* discovered by Robert Broom (1937) at Sterkfontein, and *Australopithecus prometheus,* a small slender australopithecine from Makapansgat discovered by Dart (1948). In 1954 J.T. Robinson proposed that these gracile specimens be classified as a subspecies of *Australopithecus africanus;* Robinson named them *A. africanus transvaalensis* and further differentiated the Taung fossil, classifying it *A. africanus africanus.* As work in Africa continued into the middle and late 20th century, new discoveries of closely related species were made in Tanzania, Kenya, and Ethiopia.

Australopithecus robustus. In 1938 and a decade later, Robert Broom discovered at Kromdraai and Swartkrans, S.Af., hominid specimens that he initially judged to represent a separate genus from the *Australopithecus* remains found earlier in the same region by Dart. Broom named his first specimen *Paranthropus robustus* and the second *Paranthropus cressidens.* This classification was hotly debated among paleontologists for several years. Some believed with Broom that *Paranthropus* was a different genus, while others believed that it was a part of the genus *Australopithecus,* though with some differences that mark it as a later development.

The specimens found included enough dentition to reveal some major differences in teeth and jaw. The molars and premolars of *Paranthropus* are considerably larger than those of *A. africanus.* On the other hand, the incisors and canines in the two specimens are similar. It was suggested that the differences indicate that *Paranthropus* was a vegetarian hominid close to apes, while *Australopithecus* was meat-eating.

Later discoveries of additional fossils led Broom to reclassify his *Paranthropus* specimens as a single species of *Australopithecus, A. robustus.* He estimated its weight to have been about 150 pounds (68 kilograms), as compared with the estimated 80–100 pounds of *A. africanus.* Subsequent data have verified Broom's conclusion that the *robustus* remains are about 1,000,000 years later than *africanus.*

So far, no evidence has been uncovered that *A. robustus* used any tools. The brain of this creature is no larger than that of a modern ape, about 435 to 530 cubic centimetres (26 to 32 cubic inches). While *robustus* stood erect and was clearly not an ape, it is generally believed that this species is not in the line of evolution to modern man. Other fossil finds at Swartkrans reveal that *Homo erectus,* the direct ancestor of modern man, lived in the same region at the same time as *robustus,* and it has been suggested that the latter species simply became extinct because of competition from *Homo erectus.*

Australopithecus boisei. The robust australopithecine type designated *A. boisei,* originally called *Zinjanthropus boisei,* is represented by a fossil found in Olduvai Gorge, Tanzania, in 1959 by Mary D. Leakey. It has been dated by isotropic methods to 1,750,000 years ago. The massive adult skull, almost complete, was associated with Oldowan stone tools and a rich vertebrate fauna on an extensive occupation surface representing the shore of an ancient lake. *A. boisei* was contemporaneous with another early hominid designated *Homo habilis.* The relationship of *A. boisei* to other robust australopithecines is a subject of disagreement among anthropologists. Many remains of *A. boisei* have been found elsewhere in northern Kenya and southern Ethiopia.

Austrasia (from a Germanic word meaning "east"), the eastern Frankish kingdom in the Merovingian period (6th–8th century) of early medieval Europe, as distinct from Neustria, the western kingdom. Its mayors of the palace, leading household and government officials under the king, were ancestors of the Carolingian dynasty. Covering present northeastern France and areas of western and central Germany, the kingdom included the old homeland of the Ripuarian (Rhineland) Franks. Ruled from 561 to 613 by Sigebert I and his descendants, it was briefly reunited with the other Frankish kingdoms in the early 7th century. From 634, when Dagobert, sole king of the Franks from 629, gave to the Austrasians his son Sigebert III as their separate king, Austrasia had its fixed capital at Metz and its own mayor of the palace. Ascendancy over the other Frankish kingdoms was assured when the Carolingian Austrasian mayor of the palace, Pepin II, defeated the Neustrians at Tertry in 687. His grandson, Pepin III the Short, in 751 deposed the last Merovingian king and was himself elected king instead.

Austria, officially REPUBLIC OF AUSTRIA, German REPUBLIK ÖSTERREICH, mountainous, landlocked country of south central Europe, covering an area of 32,375 sq mi (83,850 sq km). The capital is Vienna. The country is 185 mi (300 km) from north to south and about 350 mi from east to west. Austria is bordered on the west by Switzerland and Liechtenstein, on the northwest by West Germany, on the north by Czechoslovakia, on the east by Hungary, on the southeast by Yugoslavia, and on the southwest by Italy. The population in 1982 was estimated at 7,571,000.

Austria

The article that follows is a summary of significant detail about Austria. Fuller treatment is provided in the following MACROPAEDIA articles: for geography and history, *see* Austria; for information about the country, its history, and its peoples in their regional setting, *see* Europe; Holy Roman Empire; for information about its capital city, *see* Vienna.

For current history and for statistics on society and economy, *see* the article "World Affairs" and BRITANNICA WORLD DATA, respectively, in the *Britannica Book of the Year.*

The land. Austria can be divided into three physiographic regions. The Austrian Alpine region, which shares the European Alps with Germany, Liechtenstein, Switzerland, and Italy, occupies about 64 percent of Austria's territory, making Austria the most mountainous major country in Europe. Several mountains are higher than 10,000 ft (3,000 m) above sea level; the Grossglockner, rising to 12,457 ft, is the country's highest peak. The Bohemian Massif, a forested highland region covering about 10 percent of the total land area, is part of a more general highland region that extends north into Czechoslovakia; elevations generally do not exceed 4,000 ft. The lowland region of Austria, including the Vienna Basin, lies almost entirely in the eastern fourth of the country. It supports the main agricultural activities although, at elevations of between 500 and 1,300 ft, it is quite hilly.

The Danube River and its Austrian tributaries drain nearly the entire country. Numerous streams and steep topography provide a large potential for hydroelectric development. During the 1970s hydroelectric power capacity expanded by nearly 65 percent.

The humid continental climate (cold winters and warm or hot, humid summers) characterizes the northeastern part of Austria and contrasts with the Alpine climate in the southern and western mountains. The wetter western parts of Austria have a yearly rainfall in excess of 39 in. (1,000 mm), and the eastern agricultural region has somewhat less. Median temperature in the lowlands and the hilly eastern region ranges between 30.4° F (−0.9° C) in January and 68.6° F (20.3° C) in July. The mountains above 10,000 ft are snow-covered all year. Austria's arable land in the east is characterized by very fertile soils—especially thick black chernozems.

The nature and distribution of Austria's pastureland (25 percent of total land area) and forested areas (40 percent) are primarily determined by elevation. In addition to altitude, the warm, dry south wind (the *föhn*) common to Austrian mountain valleys also affects vegetation and land use: south-facing mountain slopes tend to be settled, cleared, and used for crops and as pasture, whereas the north-facing slopes tend to remain forested.

Austria is the most densely forested nation in central Europe. The forests are mostly spruce, with some larch, beech, and oak. Wild animals include roe deer in the plains and low hills and red deer at higher elevations. The ibex and chamois, once abundant, are rigidly protected, and the latter have begun to increase.

Austria produces about one-tenth of the world's magnesite, a principal source of magnesium. The country has moderate reserves of petroleum, natural gas, and lignite and brown coal. Iron ore production cannot keep pace with domestic steel production. Austria has shortages of numerous other minerals essential for industry, and these must be imported or recycled when possible.

The people. Austria had an annual growth rate of only 0.06 percent from 1971 to 1981, a rate characteristic of its aging population; in the early 1980s less than one-fifth were under 15 years of age and almost one-fifth were older than 60. The population is 99 percent German-speaking; in general, the language is spoken here in a softer, more drawling and melodious manner than in West or East Germany. In terms of religion, the population is about 89 percent Roman Catholic, with a little more than 6 percent Protestant.

Austria experienced a distinct population shift from east to west during the decades following World War II. Emigration resulted in some losses in national population during the troubled post-World War II years, although a stream of persons expelled from eastern European countries, including refugees from Hungary in 1956, helped to make up some of the deficit. In the early 1980s the growing urban population accounted for about 54 percent of the country's total.

The economy. Austria has a developed mixed free market and government-operated economy based on manufacturing and commerce. The gross national product (GNP) in 1981 was U.S. $77,120,000,000, about $10,210 per capita. Annual growth of the real GNP (1970–80) was 3.4 percent. The GNP originated primarily from manufacturing, followed by commerce, restaurants, and hotels; administration and defense; and finance and insurance. Much of the arable land is cropped in cereals, primarily barley and wheat, but also corn (maize), rye, and oats. Cattle, including a substantial number of dairy cattle, and pigs are the principal livestock; overall, Austria's agriculture is well diversified, supplying more than 90 percent of domestic needs and exporting dairy products. Grape growing is the basis of a thriving wine industry that also provides an important export. Pastures are divided between open pasture in eastern Austria and Alpine pastures in the west.

Besides producing natural gas, petroleum, iron ore, lignite and brown coal, and magnesite, Austria extracts sand and gravel, quartz sand, graphite, gypsum and anhydrite, clays (illite and kaolin), quartz and quartzite, talc, manganese, zinc, and tungsten. Austria has good hydroelectric potential in its mountain streams, and nearly 70 percent of the country's electricity is produced by hydroelectric power stations.

Manufacturing is the strongest sector of the economy and is well diversified. The principal products are refined petroleum products, cement, crude steel, pig iron, coke, and paper including newsprint.

The construction industry generates about 8 percent of the GNP and is involved in housing, road, and industrial building projects. Important projects under construction in the early 1980s were a concrete box girder bridge over the Danube River at Vienna and the Karawanken Tunnel at Rosenbach in southern Austria, jointly with Yugoslavia.

Tourism is an important sector of the economy and has reduced the impact of increased foreign trade deficits incurred by higher energy import costs. Good skiing facilities abound in western Austria, and Vienna's cultural features draw additional visitors.

About one-fourth of Austria's industries are nationalized, including mining, energy production, and most heavy-manufacturing industries; since 1970 these have been controlled by the Austrian Nationalized Industries Holding Company. The nationalized sector contributed about one-fifth of the total industrial output in 1980.

The Austrian monetary unit is the schilling, subdivided into 100 groschen. Austria's inflation rate was among the lowest in Europe during the 1970s; it was rising, however, about 6.0 percent annually in the early 1980s.

The revenue in the Austrian budget originates primarily from social security taxes (36 percent), sales taxes (25 percent), and income and corporate taxes (20 percent). Expenditures go primarily to social security 39 percent, followed by health, education, and public services. Austria is a member of the European Free Trade Association (EFTA) and has a bilateral trade agreement (1973) with the European Economic Community (EEC), even though it is not an official member.

The Austrian transportation network is well developed. Railroads are about four-fifths government owned. About 62 percent of the road network is paved. The country has two principal Danube River ports, Vienna and Linz, and there are six international airports.

Exports in 1980 consisted primarily of basic manufactures (36 percent) and machinery and transport equipment (28 percent). West Germany is the principal importer of Austrian products, followed by Italy and Switzerland. Imports lead exports in value and consist primarily of machinery and transport equipment (29 percent), basic manufactured products (19 percent), and mineral fuels and lubricants (15 percent). The principal import source is West Germany.

Administrative and social conditions. Austria is a democratic federal republic governed on the national level by a bicameral legislature known as the Federal Assembly (Bundesversammlung). The lower house of this body is the National Council (Nationalrat), elected by popular vote on the basis of proportional representation. The Federal Council (Bundesrat), Austria's upper house, has 65 members elected by the legislatures of the country's nine states (*Bundesländer*). This body is restricted to reviewing and, in some cases, delaying legislation passed by the National Council. Austria's president, elected by popular vote for a term of six years, acts as head of state with primarily ceremonial functions. He appoints the chancellor (who heads the Council of Ministers) from the party with the strongest representation in the National Council. The Austrian Socialist Party, a social-democratic party, is the major political organization in the country; the Austrian People's Party (Christian Democrats) constitutes the principal opposition. The country's constitution, adopted in 1920 and amended in 1929, divides the functions of judicial power among three high courts.

The social welfare system provides earnings-related benefits for old age, permanent disability, death, illness, maternity, and work injury. Special programs also offer unemployment insurance, family allowance, and benefits for war victims. Health conditions in most of Austria are excellent, and doctors are in abundance, except in the rural Alpine areas. Life expectancy stands at 68 years for men and 75 years for women; as in most other highly developed countries, the most common causes of death are heart and circulatory diseases and cancer.

Education in Austria is free and compulsory for children between the ages of 6 and 15 years. Children devote their first four school years to primary education in a *Volksschule.* Upon graduation they must choose between two different types of secondary schools leading eventually to either vocational training or university education. About 110,000 Austrians attend colleges and universities, the oldest of which, the University of Vienna, was founded in 1365.

The news media in Austria operate without government censorship or other restrictions. Four Viennese daily newspapers, *Neue Kronen-Zeitung, Kurier, Arbeiter-Zeitung,* and *Kleine Zeitung,* account for about 75 percent of the country's newspaper sales. Radio and television broadcasting are the responsibility of the publicly owned Austria Broadcasting Company, and a special broadcasting law prohibits political interference in radio and television programming.

Cultural life. The contemporary cultural milieu of Austria has a rich heritage; in architecture and poetry this goes back to the Middle Ages, and in medicine and science it can be traced to the 18th and 19th centuries. Similarly, Vienna's art galleries are among the most famous in Europe because of their wealth of old masters. Austria's most highly recognized cultural contribution has been in the field of music, and this tradition persists. Great Austrian composers include Haydn, Mozart, Schubert, and the Johann Strauss family. Arnold Schoenberg, Alban Berg, and Anton von Webern rank among the founders of modern music. Although in literature Austria had often been considered a backwater of German culture, writers such as Franz Grillparzer, Johann Nestroy, and Ferdinand Raimund in the 19th-century postclassic era and Hugo von Hofmannsthal and Arthur Schnitzler in the early 20th century displayed distinctive Austrian traits. In the later 20th century, writers of international reputation included Stepan Zweig, Robert Musil, and Peter Handke. Oskar Kokoschka and Alfred Kubin are among Austria's foremost creators of modern painting. The Vienna Staatsoper (State Opera), completely rebuilt after World War II, ranks with La Scala in Milan and the Hamburg and Munich operas. The Vienna Philharmonic Orchestra has played in the musical capitals of the world.

History. Settlement within the boundaries of present-day Austria extends back to Early Paleolithic times. The existence of an Early Iron Age site near Hallstatt has given that name to the Iron Age culture generally in existence in western and central Europe about 3,000 years ago. Illyrians were probably the main inhabitants. The Celts invaded Austria around 400 BC and established a kingdom known as Noricum. The Romans, attracted by Austria's iron ore deposits, began to arrive after 200 BC. By 15 BC they had occupied the entire area and created the three provinces of Raetia, Noricum, and Pannonia. Prosperity followed and the indigenous population became romanized. Repeated incursions (AD 167–180) into Roman territory by Germanic peoples residing north of the Danube were repelled by the emperor Marcus Aurelius. With the fall of Rome in the 5th century, numerous Germanic tribes crossed the region, and its final ethnic composition was established in the 6th century when the Bavarians and the Slavic Avars settled there. The Bavarians and the Slavs were not necessarily enemies, but the Franks considered the Avars dangerous. Charlemagne subdued the independent-minded Bavarians and proceeded to destroy the Avars, after which the area became fully Christianized and ethnically Germanic.

After a half-century struggle with the Magyars to the east, the distinct political entity that would become Austria emerged in 976 with Leopold I of the House of Babenberg as margrave. By 1156 Austria had become a duchy under the Babenbergs and flourished economically and culturally. When Duke Frederick II died without an heir in 1246, the Austrian nobility elected the Bohemian prince, Přemysl Otakar II, duke of Austria. He was defeated in 1278 by Rudolf IV of Habsburg, later Rudolf I of the Holy Roman Empire, and the Habsburg rule of Austria, which was to last until 1918, began. In the ensuing centuries the Habsburgs created a central kingdom centred on Austria, Bohemia, and Hungary. They crushed the Protestant movements within their borders; and maintained the struggle against Turkish encroachment.

The Napoleonic wars of the early 1800s brought about the dissolution of the Holy Roman Empire and the creation of the Austrian Empire. Its chief minister, Metternich, tried to assure Austrian supremacy among the German states, but his conservative support of the old order, belief in autocracy, and undemocratic practices contributed directly to the short-lived Revolution of 1848, which racked the empire. Prussia had been increasing in strength, and the various ethnic minorities within the Austrian Empire brought extreme pressure on a government unfit to meet the challenge of a modern multinational state. When the Austrians lost a small war with Prussia in 1866, Prussia's role as the primary German state was assured and Austria was forced to divide its empire. In 1867 the dual monarchy of Austria-Hungary was formed.

Rising nationalist sentiment continued to plague the kingdom, and when the archduke Ferdinand was assassinated by a Serbian nationalist in Sarajevo in 1914, World War I, which would destroy the Austrian Empire, began.

After World War I, Austria-Hungary was carved into several independent states, Austria becoming an independent republic. Although some Austrians favoured union with Germany, the League of Nations forbade it, and for the next two decades Austria struggled to keep its independence despite the increasing Nazi menace from Germany. In 1938 Hitler annexed Austria.

The republic was restored in 1945 after World War II, but the Allied occupation forces remained until 1955 and then left only when Austria promised to maintain neutrality, not to confederate with either West or East Germany, and not to restore the Habsburgs. By 1966 the Austrian Socialist Party had become the dominant party, continuing Austria's prosperous and stable economy.

Austria, HOUSE OF: *see* Habsburg, House of.

Austria, Lower: *see* Niederösterreich.

Austria, Upper: *see* Oberösterreich.

Austria-Hungary, also called AUSTRO-HUNGARIAN EMPIRE, or AUSTRO-HUNGARIAN MONARCHY, byname DUAL MONARCHY, German ÖSTERREICH-UNGARN, ÖSTERREICHISCH-UNGARISCHES REICH, or ÖSTERREICHISCH-UNGARISCHE MONARCHIE, or DOPPELMONARCHIE, the Habsburg empire from the constitutional Compromise (*Ausgleich*) of 1867 between Austria and Hungary until the empire's collapse in 1918.

A brief treatment of the history of Austria-Hungary follows. For full treatment, *see* MACROPAEDIA: Austria.

The empire of Austria, as an official designation of the territories ruled by the Habsburg monarchy, dates to 1804, when Francis II, the last of the Holy Roman emperors, proclaimed himself emperor of Austria as Francis II. Two years later the Holy Roman Empire came to an end. After the fall of Napoleon (1814–15), Austria became once more the leader of the German states; but the Austro-Prussian War of 1866 resulted in the expulsion of Austria from the German Confederation and caused Emperor Francis Joseph to reorient his policy toward the east and to consolidate his heterogeneous empire. Even before the war the necessity of coming to terms with the rebellious Hungarians had been recognized. The outcome of negotiations was the *Ausgleich* concluded on Feb. 8, 1867.

The agreement was a compromise between the Emperor and Hungary, not between Hungary and the rest of the empire. Indeed the peoples of the empire were not consulted, despite Francis Joseph's earlier promise not to make further constitutional changes without the advice of the imperial parliament, the Reichsrat. Hungary received full internal autonomy, together with a responsible ministry, and, in return, agreed that the empire should still be a single great state for purposes of war and foreign affairs. Francis Joseph thus surrendered his domestic prerogatives in Hungary, including his protection of the non-Magyar peoples, in exchange for the maintenance of dynastic prestige abroad. The "common monarchy" consisted of the emperor and his court, the minister for foreign affairs, and the minister of war. There was no common prime minister (other than Francis Joseph himself) and no common cabinet. The common affairs were to be considered at the delegations, composed of representatives from the two parliaments. There was to be a customs union and a sharing of accounts, which was to be revised every 10 years. This decennial revision gave the Hungarians recurring opportunity to levy blackmail on the rest of the empire.

The *Ausgleich* came into force when passed as a constitutional law by the Hungarian parliament in March 1867. The Reichsrat was only permitted to confirm the *Ausgleich* without amending it. In return for this the German liberals, who composed its majority, received certain concessions: the rights of the individual were secured and a genuinely impartial judiciary was created; freedom of belief and of education were guaranteed. The ministers, however, were still responsible to the emperor, not to a majority of the Reichsrat.

The official name of the state shaped by the *Ausgleich* was Austria-Hungary. The kingdom of Hungary had a name, a king, a history of its own. The rest of the empire was a casual agglomeration without even a clear description. Technically it was known as "the kingdoms and lands represented in the Reichsrat" or, more shortly, as "the other Imperial half." The mistaken practice soon grew of describing this nameless unit as "Austria" or "Austria proper" or "the lesser Austria"—names all strictly incorrect until the title "empire of Austria" was restricted to "the other Imperial half" in 1915. These confusions had a simple cause: the empire of Austria with its various fragments was the dynastic possession of the House of Habsburg, not a state with any common consciousness or purpose.

Austrian Hunting Carpet, Persian floor covering of silk, enriched with gold and silver, made in Kāshān, Iran, in the last half of the 16th century. Its design, apparently following the cartoon of a master miniaturist, shows horsemen in pursuit of deer, and winged gods chasing lions and buffaloes.

Its border, showing angels in paradise, is remarkable in being unlike that of any other classical Persian carpet. It was the gift of Peter the Great to the Austrian emperor and is now displayed in the Österreichisches Museum für Angewandte Kunst, Vienna.

Austrian Netherlands (1713–95), provinces located in the southern part of the Low Countries (roughly comprising present Belgium and Luxembourg) which made up what had been the major portion of the Spanish Netherlands (*q.v.*).

Following the death of the Habsburg Charles II of Spain (1700), Spain and the Spanish territories had passed to the Bourbon grandson of Louis XIV, Philippe d'Anjou (Philip V). None of the other major powers in Europe—the Habsburgs, the Dutch Republic, and the English—would accept French succession: the War of the Spanish Succession ensued. When the Spanish possessions were divided in the Treaties of Utrecht in 1713, the Spanish Netherlands fell to the Holy Roman emperor Charles VI. It was known as the Austrian Netherlands until 1795.

The Treaty of Antwerp (also known as the Treaty of the Barriers, 1715) further provided that the Austrian administration of the southern Low Countries would remain essentially unchanged from the Spanish rule; the official organ of the region was simply transferred from Madrid to Vienna. As the natural prince of the Austrian Netherlands, Charles VI was subject to the same agreements as his predecessors. The autonomy of the cities and states and the ascendancy of the Roman Catholic Church were to remain intact. The one exception to this continuance of conditions was the quartering of Dutch troops against French invasion.

Charles's initial attempt to improve the economy of the region—the establishment of a trading company—was blocked by the Dutch and the English. He eventually dissolved the company and turned his attentions to the problem of Habsburg succession. Despite his efforts on his daughter's behalf, Maria Theresa was challenged as soon as she took up the sceptre (1740). The French took advantage of the Prussian challenge to Maria Theresa and invaded Flanders in 1744. Soon all the Austrian Netherlands except Limburg and Luxembourg fell to the French. They were restored to Austria in 1748.

During the rule of Maria Theresa, the Austrian Netherlands again began to prosper as it had during the first half of the Spanish regime. Still, the Austrians were unused to the republican spirit of the southern provinces. When Joseph II succeeded his mother to the throne in 1780, he attempted to force his Enlightenment ideas on the people. In 1783 he abolished contemplative orders, declaring them useless. In 1786 individual religious fraternities were regrouped into a single entity. Seminaries were disbanded and replaced with state schools. In 1787 Joseph negated the centuries-old privileges he had sworn to uphold and eliminated the ruling councils and judiciary bodies on which the people had come to depend. The people were outraged at his interference. Their objection caused some of his edicts to be suspended, but the spirit of the acts remained. When certain rebellious leaders were castigated, a revolution led by Brabant erupted.

The revolution was for a time successful. A republic was proclaimed by the rebels, but it was unable to withstand internal conflicts and external pressures. Regardless of revolutions, the peasants continued to support the Emperor. The republic fell within a year. In 1790 Joseph died and the new emperor, Leopold II, offered a restoration of all rights. When for various reasons his offer was refused, the Austrian resorted to military action. Into this confusion rode the French Revolutionaries in 1792, and they were welcomed as liberators.

Austrian rule held sway in 1792–93, but the French were determined to stay. On Oct. 1, 1795, after a period of arbitrary rule, the Austrian Netherlands was annexed to France. After the French Revolutionary and Napoleonic wars, it was merged with the Dutch provinces to become the Kingdom of the Netherlands (1815). An independent Belgium was established in 1831.

Austrian school of economics, body of economic theory developed in the late 19th century by Austrian economists who, in determining the value of a product, emphasized the importance of its utility to the final consumer. Carl Menger published the new theory of value in 1871, the same year in which William Stanley Jevons independently published a similar theory in England.

Menger's concept of value was completely subjective: the source of a product's value was its ability to satisfy human wants. The actual value depended on the utility derived by the consumer from the product in its least important use (marginal utility). If the product existed in abundance, it could be used in relatively inessential ways; as it became scarcer, however, the inessential uses would be abandoned, and the utility derived from the new least important use would increase.

The theory of marginal utility was applied to production as well as to consumption. Friedrich von Wieser derived the value of productive resources from their contribution to the final product, recognizing that changes in the amount used of one productive factor would alter the productivity of other factors. He also introduced the concept of opportunity cost, viewing the cost of a factor of production as determined by its utility in some alternative use—*i.e.,* an opportunity foregone. It was in von Wieser's work that marginal utility analysis was most fully presented.

Eugen von Böhm-Bawerk developed marginal utility analysis into a theory of price. He is best known, however, for his work on capital and interest, in which he emphasized the importance of the role of time in valuing goods. He viewed interest as the charge for the use of capital, a compensation to the owner for abstaining from present consumption. The rate of interest was determined by the size of the labour force, the amount of a community's capital, and the possibility of increasing productivity through more elaborate or roundabout methods of production.

Austrian Succession, War of the (1740–48), general name for several related wars, two of which developed directly from the death of Charles VI, Holy Roman emperor and head of the House of Habsburg, on Oct. 20, 1740. These related wars were the war for the Austrian succession itself, in which France unsuccessfully supported the dubious claims of Bavaria, Saxony, and Spain to parts of the Habsburg domain and supported the claim of Charles Albert, elector of Bavaria, to the imperial crown, all with the overall aim of crippling or destroying Austria, France's long-standing continental enemy; the First and Second Silesian Wars, in which Frederick II the Great of Prussia, allied with France, wrested the province of Silesia from Austria and held on to it; and the continuation of the wars between France and Britain over colonial possessions in India and North America (*see* Jenkins' Ear, War of; King George's War).

The war began on Dec. 16, 1740, when Frederick of Prussia invaded Silesia, one of the richest Habsburg provinces. His army defeated the Austrians at Mollwitz in April 1741 and overran Silesia. His victory enhanced the suspicion in Europe that the Habsburg dominions were incapable of defending themselves and thus insured that the war would become general. Within a month France's Charles-Auguste Rouquet, comte (later marshal and duc) de Belle-Isle, constructed an alliance with Bavaria and Spain and, later, with Saxony and Prussia against Austria. Maria Theresa's main foreign support came from Britain, which feared that, if the French achieved hegemony in Europe, the British commercial and colonial empire would be untenable. Thus, the War of the Austrian Succession was, in part, one phase of the struggle between France and Britain that lasted from 1689 to 1815.

The invasion of Austria and Bohemia by the French and Bavarian forces fell apart for lack of unity of purpose and military capability. Austria temporarily neutralized Prussia by allowing it to retain Silesia in July 1742, drove the French and Bavarians out of Bohemia (1742), and overran Bavaria. Austria's allies, the British, Hanoverians, and Hessians, defeated the French at the Battle of Dettingen (June 27, 1743) in Bavaria. In September 1743 Savoy joined the Austrians, and the French withdrew toward their own borders. In January 1745 the emperor Charles VII (Charles Albert of Bavaria), who was also chief claimant to the Austrian succession, died. His son Maximilian III Joseph gave up these claims and pledged to support Francis Stephen at the imperial election in return for Austria's restoration of its conquests to Bavaria. Frederick now feared the growing Austrian power, and he reentered the war. This Second Silesian War (1744–45) was concluded by the Treaty of Dresden (*see* Dresden, Treaty of) in December 1745. It confirmed Prussian possession of Silesia. The last major French success was Marshal Maurice de Saxe's conquest of the Austrian Netherlands (1745–46), which followed his great victory at the Battle of Fontenoy on May 11, 1745. From 1746 to 1748 the war dragged on indecisively. The British had withdrawn their army to England to oppose the French-supported efforts of the young pretender, Charles Edward, to win the thrones of Scotland and England for the Stuarts. The financial burden finally pushed the powers to the conference table. The Treaty of Aix-la-Chapelle (*see* Aix-la-Chapelle, Treaties of) in October 1748 preserved the bulk of the Austrian inheritance for Maria Theresa, but Prussian possession of Silesia was confirmed. None of the colonial or other conflicts between France and Britain was resolved.

Austric languages, hypothetical language grouping that includes the Austro-Asiatic and Austronesian (Malayo-Polynesian) language families. The languages of these two families are spoken in an area extending from the island of Madagascar in the west to Easter Island in the east and as far northward as the Himalayas. The existence of an Austric language family, proposed in 1906 by the German priest and anthropologist Wilhelm Schmidt, is not generally accepted.

Austro-Asiatic languages, a family of about 150 languages spoken in Southeast Asia and eastern India. Vietnamese, Khmer, and Mon are culturally the most important of these, and have the longest recorded history. Khmer is spoken primarily in Cambodia (Kampuchea), Mon in Thailand and Burma. Vietnamese and Khmer, with the largest number of speakers, are the only national languages of this group; speakers of minority languages in these two countries are under pressure to become bilingual.

A brief treatment of the Austro-Asiatic languages follows. For full treatment, *see* MACROPAEDIA: Languages of the World.

The three main subdivisions of the Austro-Asiatic family are Munda, spoken in eastern India; Nicobarese, spoken in the Nicobar Islands of the Andaman Sea; and Mon-Khmer, spoken in Southeast Asia. The Austro-Asiatic languages show great diversity. The Mon-Khmer subfamily has 12 branches, the Nicobarese group has four, and Munda has three. Yet despite this variety, the underlying unity of the Austro-Asiatic languages is well established through recent scholarship. It is difficult to estimate the date at which the three subfamilies separated from the protolanguage. Statistical measurement techniques of glottochronology applied to Mon-Khmer alone indicate that the division of Mon-Khmer into its 12 branches took place 3,000 to 4,000 years ago.

Many attempts have been made to relate Austro-Asiatic to other language families. Wilhelm Schmidt in 1906 was the first to propose an "Austric" superfamily, comprising Austro-Asiatic and Austronesian. Because such a theory reaches so far back into prehistory, its validity is difficult to demonstrate.

The subclassification of Austro-Asiatic has also been much discussed. Schmidt did not include Vietnamese in this family; others did not accept the Munda group. Recent studies have demonstrated, however, that both are indeed members of the Austro-Asiatic family. The numerous Austro-Asiatic languages were once grouped and classified with regard to geographical distribution alone; this revealed little as to their genetic relationship. Current work in classification is now based on the linguistic similarities measured by glottochronology.

Many of the less widely spoken languages have never been written; others have been recorded only recently. Letter shapes and writing principles for Mon and Khmer were borrowed from Indian alphabets once used in Southeast Asia. These were modified by each language to serve its special needs. The earliest inscriptions are from the 6th century AD (Old Mon) and the early 7th century (Old Khmer). Many monuments in Burma, Thailand, and Cambodia bear inscriptions from this time. The Khmer letters were later borrowed by the Thai, and the Burmese chose Mon letters in developing their writing system. Vietnam was a Chinese province for 1000 years, and Chinese was used for official purposes. So when Vietnamese first came to be written, modified Chinese characters were employed. These were gradually replaced by a Latin alphabet, introduced in 1650, representing the distinctive sounds and tones of Vietnamese.

Munda and Vietnamese, strongly influenced by Indian languages and Chinese respectively, have acquired features which make them very different from the other Austro-Asiatic languages. They are therefore to be excluded from generalizations regarding the structure of Austro-Asiatic.

The sound systems of Austro-Asiatic languages are unusual in containing large major vowel inventories: 30–35 different vowels may be found in a language. These vowels may have distinctive length; that is, a normal vowel and a shorter vowel of the same quality will contrast. Also typical of these languages is a contrast between two sets of vowels that differ in voice quality, or register. A vowel may be spoken in a "creaky" register, a "breathy" register, or a normal voice. Some languages have a series of aspirated consonants. Mon-Khmer has implosives, sounds made by drawing in air and creating a suction. Nasals and liquids preceded by glottal stops are also found.

The Austro-Asiatic languages are abundant in prefixes and infixes; suffixes are absent, except in Nicobarese. The same prefix may have a variety of functions. Austro-Asiatic languages also have a special word class called "expressives." These are sentence adverbials describing sensory impressions and emotions, often with a symbolism reminiscent of synesthesia (*i.e.,* the perception by one sense of a stimulus to another). Subtle wordplay lends further variety to this impressionistic language use.

Syntactic characteristics include the lack of the copula "be" and the common use of ergative constructions (where the agent of the action is not expressed as the subject). There are also sentence-final particles indicating degree of respect or familiarity or of the speaker's opinion, expectations, or intentions.

The vocabulary of each language reflects its history. Liberal borrowing characterizes all but the most isolated of them. Vietnamese borrowed from Chinese, Mon and Khmer from Sanskrit and Pali. Much of the original Austro-Asiatic vocabulary has been lost in these languages. It has been better preserved in languages of more isolated jungle and mountain regions, but these languages undergo change as well. Wordplay and expressive derivations extend the lexicon, and borrowing from nearby majority languages may take place. The vocabulary also continues to change in response to taboos. Nicknames or metaphors are used, for example, to refer to an animal whose true name may not be spoken. The new expression will eventually become stigmatized, and a new name invented once again. This can cause closely related languages, like those of Nicobarese, to have widely different lexicons.

Austro-Hungarian Empire, also called AUSTRO-HUNGARIAN MONARCHY: *see* Austria-Hungary.

Austro-Prussian War (1866): *see* Seven Weeks' War.

Austronesian languages, also called MALAYO-POLYNESIAN, family of languages spoken in most of Malaysia and the Indonesian Archipelago; all of the Philippines; parts of Vietnam, Cambodia, Taiwan, and Madagascar; and all of the main island groups of the Central and South Pacific (except for Australia and much of New Guinea). The family is divided into (1) Western Austronesian, or Indonesian, containing about 200 languages; and (2) Eastern Austronesian, or Oceanic, with about 300 languages.

A brief treatment of the Austronesian languages follows. For full treatment, *see* MACROPAEDIA: Languages of the World.

In pre-Columbian times the Austronesian languages were the most widespread language family, extending from the Malagasy of Madagascar to the Rapanui of the Easter Islanders. The vast majority of speakers today are in the Philippines and Indonesia, the island of Java containing somewhat more than half. There are four large countries in which a Malayo-Polynesian language is the official language or one of the official languages: Malay in Malaysia, Indonesian in the Republic of Indonesia, Pilipino in the Republic of the Philippines, and Merina in the Malagasy Republic.

Malay and the Polynesian languages do have relatively uncomplicated phonemic systems, but their grammatical structures are not particularly simple. On the other hand, a language like that of Yap shows complicated phonemic and grammatical structures.

The Austronesian languages were once a single language. The original undifferentiated language became diversified locally, and the hundreds of Austronesian languages are the result. The features of the original language, called Proto-Austronesian, can only be inferred by comparing the modern forms.

Although the classification of the members of the family is still debated, some close relationships seem to be observable. Most of the Philippine languages appear to be closely related to one another. The languages of western Indonesia (*e.g.,* Malay, Achinese, Minangkabau, Toba-Batak, Sundanese, Javanese, Balinese, and some of the languages of Borneo) seem closely related to one another, to the Cham languages of southern Vietnam and to Malagasy. Since these two groups share characteristics, some linguistics put them in the Western Austronesian group. Another group, the Eastern Austrasian, or Oceanic, group, consists of the languages of Polynesia, Melanesia, Micronesia, and parts of New Guinea. This classification is controversial also. The languages of eastern Indonesia and of New Guinea are not clearly of either subgroup.

Not all of the languages in the vast island area demarcated above are Austronesian. Most of the languages of New Guinea are not. The Austronesian area is limited to a large region near the isthmus connecting the northwest peninsula with the main body of New Guinea and the northern (both of the northwest peninsula and the main body) and eastern coasts. Non-Austronesian languages are spoken in the northern two-thirds of Halmahera, and in Timor in Indonesia, and in the Solomon Islands in Melanesia.

There is no generally accepted hypothesis regarding the origin of the Austronesian languages, but evidence increasingly points to Indonesia and New Guinea. The island of Madagascar was probably settled from Borneo in the first part of the 1st millennium AD.

Autant-Lara, Claude (b. Aug. 5, 1901, Luzarches, Fr.), motion-picture director who won an international reputation with his film *Le Diable au corps* (1947; *Devil in the Flesh*) nearly 30 years after entering the film industry. He became known for his leftist and atheistic views, which he often expressed in his films in the form of attacks on the military, religion, and the middle class. In return he was frequently attacked by official pressure and censorship.

Autant-Lara's mother, a strong pacifist, was self-exiled in England during World War I and took her young son with her. After several years of schooling in London he returned to France to study art. At 16 years of age he painted the sets for Marcel L'Herbier's film *Le Carnaval des vérités* (1919; "Carnival of Truths") and assisted Jean Renoir and other directors as a set decorator and costume designer.

Autant-Lara's first short avant-garde film, *Faits Divers* (1923; "Diverse Facts"), was made while he was a second assistant director to René Clair. After directing two other brief films, *Vittel* (1926) and *Construire un feu* (1927), he accepted a job in Hollywood directing French versions of American films. It was not until 1933, however, that he directed his first feature film, *Ciboulette,* an operetta, which was followed by a number of poorly received films. Two films completed in 1942, however, *Le Mariage de Chiffon* ("The Marriage of Chiffon") and *Lettres d'amour* ("Love Letters"), were light entertaining films that foreshadowed his most famous work, *Le Diable au corps.* His later films included *En cas de malheur* (1958; "In Case of Emergency," *Love Is My Profession*), *Le Journal d'une femme en blanc* (1965; *A Woman in White*), and *Gloria* (1977).

autecology, also called SPECIES ECOLOGY, the study of the interactions of an individual organism or a single species with the living and nonliving factors of its environment. Autecology is primarily experimental and deals with easily measured variables such as light, humidity, and available nutrients in an effort to understand the needs, life history, and behaviour of the organism or species. *Compare* synecology.

auteur theory, in the criticism of cinematography, the point of view that the director so totally dominates the making of a motion picture that he is considered to be its author. The French director and film critic François Truffaut first proposed the theory in 1954 in the film magazine *Cahiers du Cinéma.* The basic assumption was that the director, in close touch with all the technical and artistic aspects of a film, can place his personal stamp on the motion picture in the same way that an author places his stamp on a poem or a novel.

Principal support for the *auteur* theory came from the U.S. film critic Andrew Sarris. In 1962 he explained the presuppositions underlying it: (1) the director's competence is a criterion for judgment, (2) the director's personality is evident in his method, and (3) the tension created between the director's personality and the material he is working with bring out the interior meaning of the material. The technique, personal style, and intentions of the director, therefore, are starting points for evaluating a film. The *auteur* critic also considers the director's current reputation, the place a particular film held in the whole body of his work, and his contribution to the evolution of the film as an art form. Critics have applied the theory not only to independent directors such as Erich von Stroheim and Ingmar Bergman but also to directors working under the Hollywood studio system in which specialization and commercial pressure lessen the director's control.

Opponents of the *auteur* theory object to the resulting cult of the director, in which the original screenplay is of little significance. Collections of screenplays published under the directors' names with only fine-print credit given to the writers is a manifestation of this point of view. Critics also point to the danger of rejecting a film of a particular director because he might be unfashionable at the moment and to that of slighting a single masterpiece in focussing principally on the body of a director's work.

authigenesis, process of chemical reorganization within a sediment in which minerals in the sediment react with one another or with the fluid in the pore spaces. Sometimes new minerals are formed by these reactions, but grains of existing minerals also may be enlarged or otherwise altered. Reduction, hydration, and dehydration are among the processes involved; among the reactions between solid and liquid phases are the alteration of various minerals by addition of iron, magnesium, and potassium. Quartz, chalcedony, feldspar, calcite, dolomite, siderite, mica, rutile, gypsum, anhydrite, barite, pyrite, marcasite, and tourmaline are common authigenic minerals.

authoritarianism, system of government that concentrates power in a leader or small elite and is not constitutionally responsible to the people. It is the opposite of constitutional democracy. Rule without law has been justified by conquest, by the need of a people for absolute government, by superior qualities of the ruler, or, in the form of a temporary dictatorship, by emergency conditions.

Aristotle in the *Politics* defines rule by the wealthy few as oligarchy, a corruption of aristocracy. Aristocracy is also rule by the few but in accordance with virtue. Plato and Aristotle place aristocracy next in preference to the rule of the philosopher-king. Tyranny, according to Aristotle, is a corruption of monarchy: "the tyrant looks to his own advantage, the king to that of his subjects." Aside from the ancients' point that a superior person should rule inferiors in an absolute manner, Hobbes and Hegel present modern arguments for the necessity of absolute government: "[Their] point is rather that the very nature of government and the state requires a unified repository of absolute power" (*Syntopicon of Great Books of the Western World*: "Monarchy" [1952]).

Other views sharply differ. The authors of *The Federalist* and Jefferson held that both absolute and limited monarchies were undesirable and were fundamentally opposed in kind, not in degree, to the spirit of republican institutions. John Stuart Mill observed that constitutional government is to be preferred even to rule by a philosopher-king, assuming one could be found, because self-government is a good in itself: "passivity is implied in the very idea of absolute power. . . . What sort of human beings," Mill asks, "can be formed under such a regimen?"

The 20th century saw a rise in the number of authoritarian regimes, many led by generals and strong men in Latin America and Asia and by leaders of new states of post-colonial Africa. Authoritarian states may be distinguished from totalitarian states, though civil liberties are suppressed under both. The authoritarian state may be aligned with an established social class or may identify with a perceived system of values. A totalitarian regime ruthlessly imposes a new value system. *See also* checks and balances; dictatorship; monarchy; totalitarianism.

autism, an extreme self-preoccupation usually accompanied by withdrawal from reality, absorption in fantasy life, and unrelatedness to other people. Reverie, flights of fancy, and daydreaming are common examples of autistic thinking. Autism becomes pathological when the person loses contact with reality and retreats into a private world of delusion and hallucination as a means of escape. Autism is characteristic of a variety of behaviour disorders, particularly schizophrenia.

A childhood psychosis termed early infantile autism was first described by the German-born psychiatrist Leo Kanner. Whether infantile autism is related to schizophrenia is a subject of controversy. The disorder shows onset before 30 months of age, and is characterized by a lack of responsiveness to people, an obsessive desire to prevent environmental change, major deficits in language development and peculiar speech patterns, and frequently, rhythmic body movements such as rocking. Although in some cases children outgrow the illness to lead normal lives, in most cases it is chronically disabling.

Autlán, in full AUTLÁN DE NAVARRO, city, southwestern Jalisco state, west central Mexico. In the western foothills of the Sierra Madre Occidental, 3,291 ft (1,003 m) above sea level, it is an important regional centre of commerce, agriculture (oranges, lemons, guavas, and other fruits), livestock raising, and mining (iron and manganese). Since its founding during the colonial era, it has been a way station on the road from the Pacific port of La Barra de Navidad, 63 mi (101 km) to the south-southwest, and Guadalajara, the state capital, 122 mi to the northeast. Pop. (1970) 20,398.

auto-da-fé (Portuguese: "act of faith"), Spanish AUTO DE FÉ, a public ceremony during which the sentences upon those brought before the Spanish Inquisition were read. The first auto-da-fé took place at Seville in 1481; the last, in Mexico in 1850. The ceremonies, which became increasingly elaborate and spectacular, were normally staged in the city plaza, often in the presence of royalty. They usually comprised a lengthy procession, a solemn mass, an oath of obedience to the Inquisition, a sermon, and the reading of the sentences. The victims were most often apostate former Jews and former Muslims, then Alumbrados (followers of a condemned mystical movement) and Protestants, and occasionally those accused of such crimes as bigamy and sorcery. Life imprisonment was the extreme penalty that the inquisitor could impose; the death penalty was imposed and carried out by the civil authorities. Generally, neither punishment nor the handing over of condemned persons to the secular power took place on the occasion of an auto-da-fé.

auto sacramental (Spanish: "sacramental act"), Spanish dramatic genre that reached its height in the 17th century with *autos* written by the playwright Pedro Calderón de la Barca. Performed out of doors as part of the Corpus Christi feast day celebrations, *autos* were short allegorical plays in verse dealing with some aspect of the mystery of the Holy Eucharist, which the feast of Corpus Christi solemnly celebrated. They derived from tableaus which had been part of the procession that accompanied the Eucharist as it was carried through the streets at Corpus Christi. The tableaus became animated, then developed a dramatic form, and finally were detached from the Eucharistic procession to form one of their own. Mounted on carts, they were pulled to selected places in the municipality, and the actors presented their *autos,* one after another, much as the scriptural plays of the Netherlands and northern England had been presented on pageant wagons during the Middle Ages. Expenses for these superbly set and dressed *autos* were paid by the municipality.

These little plays had begun to appear in the late 16th century, but were at first rough and primitive, a rustic form of pious entertainment. Important names in the development of the *autos* into works of polished art were a bookseller from Valencia, Juan de Timoneda, and the playwrights Jose de Valdivielso (*c.* 1560–1638) and his contemporary, Lope de Vega. It was Calderón, however, who seized the opportunity that they offered for allegory to cover a wide range of nonsacramental subjects. He took the *auto* form to new heights of artistic achievement.

Accused of displaying irreverence toward the sacrament during the 18th century, their performance was in 1765 prohibited by royal decree. Some 20th-century poets have imitated their form and have written secularized versions of the old *autos.*

autoallergic disease, also called AUTOIMMUNE DISEASE, any of a group of disorders affecting single organs or the whole body, characterized by having autoantibodies (antibodies produced by the individual against his own tissues) in the circulation. The presence of the autoantibodies suggests a correlation between autoallergic disease and the immune system but, as far as is known, does not indicate that abnormality of the immune system is the cause of the disease or that the autoantibodies are responsible for the symptoms characteristic of the disease.

Autoimmune diseases that affect a single organ (*e.g.,* lymphadenoid goitre, pernicious anemia, idiopathic adrenal insufficiency [Addison's disease], encephalomyelitis) are believed to be the result of recent contact of formerly isolated (*i.e.,* usually isolated from the circulatory system, such as the lens of the eye) body tissue with a healthy immune system. Because the tissues were isolated, the immune system has not become tolerant of them during maturation and, on contact, recognizes them as foreign tissue and forms antibodies against them.

The mechanism in the case of systemic autoallergic disease (*e.g.,* systemic lupus erythematosus, rheumatoid arthritis) is believed to involve the breakdown of immune tolerance established by the immune system in childhood, with resultant failure of recognition of "self" tissues and generalized production of autoantibodies. Some autoallergic diseases are both organ specific and systemic, such as ulcerative colitis, primary liver cirrhosis, and acquired hemolytic anemia. The organ or organ system involved in autoallergic diseases often shows a familial tendency to disease of other kinds.

autoantibody, type of antibody produced by an individual against his own tissues. The suggested explanation of the phenomenon is that there is a body system that maintains immune tolerance—that is, the recognition of body constituents as "self" and not foreign. Should this system not function, antibodies to "self" may be formed.

Autoantibodies are of several kinds, including cold, which react below normal body temperature; warm, which react at body temperature; and those developed against cell nuclei, deoxyribonucleic acid (DNA), or the cell membrane. Some autoantibodies are common and without harmful effects, including antibody to complement (a component of blood plasma) and antinuclear antibodies. Autoantibodies can pass through the placenta to the fetus during pregnancy; this may result in transient symptoms in the child like those of the mother. *See also* autoallergic disease; autoimmunity.

Autobahn (German: "automobile road"), plural AUTOBAHNEN, high-speed, limited-access highway, the basis of the first modern national expressway system. Planned in Germany in the early 1930s, the Autobahnen were extended to a national highway network (*Reichsautobahnen*) of 1,310 miles (2,108 kilometres) by 1942. East and West Germany resumed construction of this system in 1957, and by 1981 the length attained was 5,700 mi.

autocatalysis, acceleration of a chemical reaction by one of its products. The reaction becomes faster as the quantity of the catalytic product increases. Some examples of autocatalysis include the combination of hydrocarbon compounds with oxygen (autoxidation) catalyzed by the resulting organic peroxides; and the decomposition of the gaseous compound germane (GeH_4) to hydrogen and solid germanium, germanium being a catalyst for the reaction.

autocephalous church, in the modern usage of Eastern Orthodox canon law, church that enjoys total canonical and administrative independence and elects its own primates and bishops. The term autocephalous was used in medieval Byzantine law in its literal sense of "self-headed" (Greek *autokephalos*), or independent, and was applied in church law to individual dioceses that did not depend upon the authority of a provincial metropolitan. Today the Orthodox archbishopric of Mount Sinai, with the historic monastery of St. Catherine, still enjoys this privilege.

Most modern Orthodox autocephalies are national churches, but some are limited only geographically and include the territories of several states. The autocephalous churches maintain canonical relations with each other and enjoy communion in faith and sacraments. There is between them a traditional order of precedence, with the ecumenical patriarchate of Constantinople (modern Istanbul) enjoying the first place. Throughout history, their borders have varied greatly, following political and social changes, while their numbers have been subject to increase or reduction by Byzantine emperors and individual patriarchs. The question of how and by whom new autocephalous churches are to be established is still a matter of debate in modern Eastern Orthodoxy.

The heads of individual autocephalous churches bear different titles: patriarch (Constantinople, Alexandria, Antioch, Jerusalem, Moscow, Georgia, Serbia, Romania, Bulgaria), archbishop (Athens, Cyprus), or metropolitan (Poland, Czechoslovakia, America).

Autocephalous Orthodox Church of Poland: *see* Orthodox Church of Poland.

autoclave, vessel, usually of steel, able to withstand high temperatures and pressures. The chemical industry uses various types of autoclaves in manufacturing dyes and in other chemical reactions requiring high pressures. In bacteriology and medicine, instruments are sterilized by being placed in water in an autoclave and heating the water above its boiling point under pressure.

In 1679 Denis Papin invented the steam digester, a prototype of the autoclave that is still used in cooking and is called a pressure cooker.

The name autoclave indicates a self-closing vessel with internal pressure sealing its joints, but many autoclaves are kept closed by external mechanical means.

autogiro, also spelled AUTOGYRO, rotary-wing aircraft, superseded after World War II by the more efficient helicopter; it employed a propeller for forward motion and a freely rotating rotor for lift. In searching for an aircraft that could be slowed down in flight and landed vertically, experimenters built many prototypes that were difficult to control in flight.

Small British-built autogiro, c. 1935

By courtesy of Pitcairn-Larsen Autogiro Co., Inc.

By 1923 the Spaniard Juan de la Cierva had discovered how to articulate (hinge) the rotor blades at the hub, thus allowing them to respond differentially to the aerodynamic and centrifugal forces involved in rotation. This made autogiro flight possible for the first time and led to later development of the helicopter. An autogiro must taxi for takeoff; it requires forward airspeed to drive its rotor. By contrast, a helicopter, with its engine-driven rotor, is capable of both vertical takeoff and landing. The gyroglider is an unpowered autogiro designed to glide freely on the rotary wings after release from towing.

autograph (manuscript): *see* manuscript, literary; manuscript, musical.

Autoharp (trademark), musical string instrument, similar to a zither and popular for accompaniment in folk music and country and western music. Players strum the strings while operating button-controlled bars that damp all strings except those of the chords selected. The number of chords varies from as few as 5 to as many as 15. It has been used for teaching simple harmony in the United States and Germany (German *Akkordzither*).

In 1881 a U.S. patent for the Autoharp was granted to C.F. Zimmermann, who had emigrated from Germany. His interests were later acquired by Alfred Dolge (1848–1922), a New York City piano-equipment manufacturer, who promoted wide sales in the 1890s through door-to-door travellers and through mail-order houses.

In the 1920s Ernest "Pop" Stoneman developed an Appalachian folk style and began making recordings, and the instrument was also made popular by Maybelle Carter, affiliated after World War II with the Grand Ole Opry in Nashville, Tenn.

autohelmsman: *see* automatic pilot.

autohypnosis, also called SELF-HYPNOSIS, hypnosis that is self-induced. Though feasible and possibly productive of useful results, it is often a sterile procedure because the autohypnotist usually tries too hard to direct *consciously* the activities that he wishes to take place at the hypnotic level of awareness, thus nullifying the effort. A form of self-hypnosis, or trancelike experience, is familiar to anyone who has been so absorbed in an activity that a moment or two is necessary to reorient to the existing environment. Studies conducted with individuals who have reported having such intense, absorbing experiences have shown that these persons tend to be highly susceptible to a deeper form of hypnosis when induced by an experienced hypnotist. *See also* hypnosis.

autoimmune disease: *see* autoallergic disease.

autoimmunity, state of being immune, or allergic, to oneself. The immune system serves a surveillance function—identifying and disposing of materials foreign to the body (*e.g.,* mutant cells newly produced in the body, invading microorganisms, dust). It matures late in the embryonic period and during childhood, well after most other organ systems are developed.

It is believed that those tissues formed before the immune system matures are accepted by it as "self" and do not provoke antibody formation; the immune system is said to be tolerant of such tissues. Those that the system contacts after maturity are recognized as foreign and stimulate antibody production. If, for some reason, the immune system can no longer distinguish self from foreign protein, antibodies are produced against the body's own tissues and a state of autoimmunity exists.

Three mechanisms have been proposed to explain why failure of the surveillance function should occur; all three are equally valid, as far as is known, and apply in different situations. (1) Tissues composing organ systems that mature later than the immune system (*e.g.,* sperm in the reproductive system) and tissues that develop in relative isolation from the immune system (usually circulatory isolation, as lens of eye, brain) may provoke antibody formation upon contact with the immune system, which has not developed tolerance to such tissues. (2) If normal cell characteristics, such as the surface protrusions, are altered, as by drugs, infections, or X-rays, the immune system may fail to recognize them as self and may develop antibodies against them. Such autoimmunity is often transient, lasting only as long as the drug or infective agent is in the body. (3) If, for reasons poorly understood, tolerance developed during the embryonic period fails or is lost later in life, antibodies, usually to a generalized tissue such as connective tissue, may be formed. Autoimmunity to one or more tissues is not uncommon but probably results in overt disease or disability in only a minority of cases. *See also* autoallergic disease; autoantibody.

autokinetic effect, illusory movement of a single still object, usually the stationary pinpoint of light used in psychology darkroom experiments. As one stares at a fixed point of light, his eye muscles become fatigued, causing a slight eye movement. Without the usual reference points available in the everyday environment, the movement of the image on the retina is perceived as its actual movement in space.

The autokinetic effect has been used by social psychologists to study suggestibility. Although the amount of apparent movement reported by observers in a group can vary considerably, each individual tends to allow the group's average reported movement to influence his own perception. This would indicate that people depend heavily on the judgment of others when objective standards are lacking.

Autolycus, in Greek mythology, the father of Anticleia, the mother of the hero Odysseus. Later authors made him the son of the god Hermes. He lived at the foot of Mt. Parnassus and was famous as a thief and swindler. On one occasion Sisyphus (the son of Aeolus), during a visit to Autolycus, recognized his stolen cattle. It is said that on that occasion Sisyphus seduced Autolycus' daughter Anticleia, and that Odysseus was really the son of Sisyphus, not of Laertes, whom Anticleia afterward married.

The object of the story probably was to establish the close connection between Hermes, the god of theft and cunning, and the three persons—Sisyphus, Odysseus, and Autolycus—who were the incarnate representations of that practice and quality.

automata: *see* automaton.

Automatic Picture Transmission station, in meteorology, any of several hundred installations, located in most of the countries of the world, that can receive and display the weather-forecasting data that is continuously transmitted by orbiting artificial satellites launched by the United States. The information gathered by the sensing equipment in the satellites is received in the form of facsimile visible and infrared pictures of cloud formations, snow and ice cover, and the sea surface, from which weather conditions can be inferred. The system began operation in the mid-1960s, employing the TIROS series of Earth satellites.

Improvements in the sensing equipment carried by the satellites have made it possible for the stations to receive information concerning the temperatures of the surface and the cloud tops and the temperature variation within the atmosphere at intervals up to 50 kilometres (31 miles). The temperature data have been found useful in extending the time interval for which reliable predictions of the weather can be made.

automatic pilot, also called AUTOPILOT, or AUTOHELMSMAN, device for controlling an aircraft or other vehicle without constant human intervention.

The earliest automatic pilots could do no more than maintain an aircraft in straight and level flight, and they are still used most often to relieve the pilot during routine cruising. Modern automatic pilots can, however, execute complex manoeuvres or flight plans, bring aircraft into approach and landing paths, or make possible the control of inherently unstable aircraft (such as some supersonic aircraft) and of those capable of vertical takeoff and landing. Automatic pilots are also used to steer surface ships, submarines, torpedoes, missiles, rockets, and spacecraft.

Automatic pilots consist of four major elements: (1) a source of steering commands (a computerized guidance program, radio receiver, etc.), (2) motion and position sensors (such as gyroscopes, accelerometers, altimeters, and airspeed indicators), (3) a computer to compare the parameters specified in the guidance program with the aircraft's actual position and motion, and (4) servomotors that actuate the craft's engines and control surfaces to alter its flight when corrections or changes are required.

Automatic pilots for manned aircraft are designed as fail-safe, or soft-fail, *i.e.,* no failure in the automatic pilot can be allowed to prevent effective manual override. Excessive accelerations are prevented by the automatic pilot through its numerous feedback loops. Automatic approach and landing employs microwave beams aimed from the runway and acquired aboard the aircraft by appropriate receivers.

Aboard spacecraft, automatic attitude-control systems compensate for the minor disturbances caused by micrometeorites, radiation pressure from the Sun, and minor irregularities in the gravitational fields of nearby planetary bodies. Instead of the aerodynamic control surfaces used by vehicles in Earth's atmosphere, automatic pilots on spacecraft control orientation with reaction controls (small rockets), electromagnets that couple to planetary magnetic fields, or gyroscopes.

automatic pistol, handgun that utilizes either recoil or blowback to discharge the empty cartridge after each shot, reload, and cock the piece. The automatic pistol dates from the very late 19th century, when developments in ammunition made possible cartridges and bullets that would not be deformed by their handling in automatic loading, as well as smokeless powder that burned evenly to provide smooth action.

Although there are a few automatic pistols that are fully automatic, the term ordinarily refers to a semiautomatic or autoloading pistol; a fully automatic weapon continues to fire as long as the trigger is depressed. Unlike automatic rifles and shotguns, automatic pistols are virtually never operated by combustion gases. In relatively low-powered pistols, the blowback mode of operation may be employed. In this system, the breechblock or bolt does not remain locked in firing position until the bullet has left the barrel, but is free to be thrust backward by the same burst of energy that propels the bullet forward; because it is many times heavier than the bullet, it moves much more slowly. The rearward thrust removes the spent cartridge from the chamber and ejects it, meanwhile storing energy in a spring; the spring projects the bolt assembly forward and injects a fresh shell into the chamber.

In the recoil method of operation, the breechblock is locked to the barrel at the moment of firing. Thus, when the recoil of the gun forces the barrel rearward, the breechblock moves with it. As soon as the pressure of gases in the barrel has diminished to a safe level, the breechblock is unlocked from the barrel and continues moving backward; meanwhile, the barrel stops its movement. The rearward motion removes and ejects the spent cartridge and loads a spring, which pushes the breechblock assembly forward again, thereby loading, cocking, and locking the piece to fire again.

Automatic pistols are valued because they can hold more ammunition in clips than revolvers in their cylinders, and because of their rapidity of fire. Except for target guns, however, their accuracy is significantly less than that of revolvers in most hands. Also, it is not possible to tell at a glance whether an automatic pistol is loaded, as is possible with a revolver.

Automatic pistols are chambered in sizes ordinarily ranging from .22 to .45 calibre and their metric equivalents. *See* revolver; automatic rifle.

automatic rifle, rifle that utilizes either its recoil or a portion of the gas propelling the projectile to remove the spent cartridge case, load a new cartridge, and cock the weapon to fire again. Automatic rifles (and pistols) are called autoloaders and are actually semiautomatic. Full automatic fire—firing repeatedly as long as the trigger is held down until the magazine is exhausted—is achieved by the submachine gun. This distinction is more a convention than a differentiation, however, and is most often applied to sporting weapons. A semiautomatic rifle needs only an adjustment (simple to a gunsmith) to convert it to full automatic functioning. Moreover, modern infantry rifles, while not called submachine guns, actually have full automatic fire capabilities.

Most automatic rifles are gas operated. A port near the muzzle of the gun allows a small portion of the combustion gases to escape the barrel into a cylinder. There a piston and spring combination operate the gun's bolt, pushing it backward to remove the spent cartridge after the bullet has left the barrel, ejecting it, moving the bolt forward again to impel a fresh round of ammunition into the chamber, cocking the gun, and locking the bolt in closed position. For information about military automatic rifles, *see* assault rifle; *see also* machine gun; submachine gun.

automatic shotgun, shotgun that is loaded automatically after each shot is fired by gases from the previous shot. The loading mechanism and procedure of automatic shotguns are the same as those of the automatic rifle (*q.v.*). A special design problem in automatic shotguns is that of handling the various weights of different-sized loads of shot in shotgun shells. This is solved by a different approach to the recoil brake, part of the mechanism.

Consult the INDEX *first*

automatic transmission, arrangement of gears, brakes, clutches, a fluid drive, and governing devices that automatically changes the speed ratio between the engine and the rear wheels of an automobile. Since its introduction in 1939, the fully automatic transmission has become optional or standard equipment on all modern American passenger cars. When the transmission is in the drive position, the driver has only to depress the accelerator pedal, and as the car gathers speed the transmission will shift automatically through its entire forward range from low to high (ratios of the speeds of drive shaft and engine shaft) until the two shafts are directly connected through the oil in the fluid drive, which may be either a two-element fluid coupling or a three-element torque converter. When the car loses speed the transmission automatically shifts back from high to low. Most modern cars have a torque converter in which an engine-driven pump or impeller directs fluid against the vanes of a stator that redirects the fluid from the impeller to the vanes of a turbine, connected through transmission gears to the automobile drive shaft. The three elements work together in a fluid-filled housing. At low turbine speeds the stator is fixed to the housing and multiplies the impeller (engine) torque by a factor of about two. At high speeds the stator rotates and the unit operates like a fluid coupling with no torque multiplication but a high efficiency. The transmission gears provide reverse motion and at low turbine speeds increase the torque delivered to the drive shaft so that the car can be more easily started from rest.

All automatic transmissions contain at least one planetary gear set because the gears in such sets are always in mesh, and it is easy to obtain suitable gear ratios under all driving conditions. There are three elements in a simple planetary gear set: the sun gear, the carrier on which the planet gears are mounted so that they can rotate freely, and the ring gear. The planet gears mesh with both the sun gear and the teeth on the inside of the ring gear. All three elements can rotate about the central axis. Any one of the elements—carrier, sun gear, or ring gear—can be locked, and the other two utilized as input and output. In this way two forward speed ratios and a reverse can be obtained or the three elements can be locked together and rotate as a unit. The fluid drives and the planetary gear sets are the main parts in an automobile automatic transmission—the other parts control their operation. One successful transmission contains three multiple-disk clutches, two one-way roller clutches, several valves, two brake bands, and a gear-type pump that provides working oil pressure to operate valve controls and the friction elements and to charge the torque converter. There are six positions on the gear-selector quadrant of most cars, and, because these are taken manually, the truly automatic nature of the transmission is displayed only in the D, or drive, range. On the transmission treated previously, the forward clutch is engaged when the transmission is in first gear; forward and intermediate clutches are engaged in second gear; all three clutches are engaged in third gear (direct drive). These automatic changes are brought about by the pressure in the engine intake manifold. Under light load the pressure is low (high vacuum) while at full throttle or heavy load the vacuum is low.

automatic writing, in spiritualism, writing produced involuntarily when the subject's attention is ostensibly directed elsewhere. The phenomenon may occur when the subject is in an alert waking state or in a hypnotic trance, usually during a séance (*q.v.*). What is produced may be unrelated words, fragments of poetry, epithets, puns, obscenities, or well-organized fantasies. During the late 19th century, at the height of popular interest in the phenomenon, inspiration for automatic writing was generally attributed to external or supernatural forces. Since the advent, around 1900, of theories of personality that postulate unconscious as well as conscious motivation, the inspiration for automatic writing has been assumed to be completely internal.

Modern psychodynamic theories of personality propose that traits, attitudes, motives, impulses, memories, and even partially developed talents and skills that are incompatible with maintenance of security in significant interpersonal relationships may be dissociated from awareness and rarely expressed overtly in the course of normal waking behaviour. These elements may be revealed, however, in the content of automatic writing. *See also* automatism.

automation, the application of machines to tasks once performed by human beings or, increasingly, to tasks that would otherwise be impossible. While the term mechanization is often used to refer to the simple replacement of human labour by machines, automation generally implies the integration of machines into a self-governing system. Automation has revolutionized those areas where it has been introduced, and there is scarcely an aspect of modern life that has been unaffected by it. Although the difference between automation and mechanization may be difficult to draw in practice, the difference between an automated and a mechanized society is more clearly apprehended; the introduction of automation has brought about a new and distinct stage in the development of industrial civilization.

A brief treatment of automation follows. For full treatment, *see* MACROPAEDIA: Automation.

Human beings have striven to transfer some of the burden of labour to mechanical devices for as long as they have worked. Remnants of pulleys, winches, and lifting devices have been found dating from the third millennium BC. However, widespread mechanization and the rudimentary incorporation of machines into a system did not take place until the beginning of the Industrial Revolution in the 18th century. The development of factories that produced interchangeable parts for products such as rifles paved the way, as did the complementary development of division of labour, the restriction of the activity of each labourer to one specific task to be repeated over and over. It was then a simple step to develop machines to perform these tasks, powered by the newly perfected steam engine and later by electricity. Assembly lines represented another step toward automation. First used on a large scale by Chicago meat-packers in the 1870s, the assembly line utilized a conveyor belt or similar device to move a job in stages from one worker or group of workers to another. Automatic transfer systems were developed during World War II that combined assembly lines with mechanization. These systems consisted of groups of machines linked by a conveyor belt; a workpiece was operated on and passed to subsequent production stages independent of human intervention.

True automation, as distinct from mechanization, did not come about until the development of feedback systems; it is the presence of these systems, more than anything else, that serves to distinguish the two. Feedback refers to the ability of a machine to regulate itself. Through a feedback system or loop, a machine monitors its own output, compares it with a set of standards stored, along with instructions, as a control program, and adjusts its performance accordingly.

The equipment needed for this kind of operation may be classified into three types: sensing, decision, and control elements. An automated machine must be equipped with sensing elements to take measurements of some property of the output. Photoelectric cells, thermocouples, X-ray machines, and electrical meters are typical sensing elements, and the properties they may measure include dimensions, weight, temperature, pressure, colour, or electrical resistance. The decision element compares the data supplied by the sensing elements with standards stored in the program; this step is often carried out by a computer. If discrepancies exist, the decision element generates the appropriate commands to activate the control elements. The control elements then act to bring the performance of the machine into line with the programmed values. The control elements may consist of switches, valves, or other mechanisms. When the sensing, decision, and control elements are operating properly, a machine is able to regulate its behaviour in a wide variety of circumstances that need not have been foreseen in detail. An airplane autopilot is a classic example of a self-regulating device; it uses information obtained from flight instruments to make continuous adjustments to the controls, keeping the craft on its preset course. A modern automated factory may have hundreds or even thousands of interconnected feedback loops.

Automation has been introduced into areas as diverse as office equipment, petroleum refining, and the flight of space vehicles. The launch of a spacecraft requires the continuous, instantaneous, and precise readjustment of controls in a degree impossible for a human operator. One of the most significant developments in automation is computer-aided design (CAD) and computer-aided manufacture (CAM). CAD systems permit an engineer to design models and to perform experiments and tests on them using a computer graphics terminal, making possible an evaluation of the model before production. CAM systems utilize computers to regulate the actual manufacturing process. The computer may direct a particular machine to select a metal part, machine it according to specifications, test it, and pass it on to other machines. Integrated computer-aided design and manufacture (ICAM) systems combine both features, so that CAD-produced designs are fed directly into CAM systems.

In certain areas progress in automation has been much slower than in others. Activities such as shape identification, alignment of two unequal bodies, and word recognition, easy for a human being, have proved to be unexpectedly complex and hence difficult to break down into a series of simple steps that can be performed by a machine. Nevertheless, automation has already increased not only productivity but also safety in certain areas. Complex tasks in situations hazardous for human beings, such as in nuclear reactor cores and in deep-sea mining sites, can be accomplished by automated machinery at no risk of harm.

The effects of automation extend beyond the increase in industrial productivity to society itself. Early predictions of an automation-induced increase in unemployment have been unfulfilled. Automation has, however, introduced large changes in the nature and kinds of jobs offered by society by replacing many unskilled jobs with skilled or semiskilled jobs in the field of creating and maintaining computerized and automated devices. The great demand for computer programmers is one example. Automation has also played a role in fostering a new generation of management methods to control the enormously complex projects it has made possible.

Automatism, technique used by Surrealist painters (*see* Surrealism) since 1924 to express the creative force of the unconscious in art. André Masson, Arshile Gorky, and Max Ernst (*qq.v.*), in particular, experimented with fantastic or erotic images spontaneously recorded, in a kind of visual free association, without the artist's conscious censorship; the images were either left as originally conceived or consciously elaborated upon by the artist. Related to Automatic drawing are the techniques devised by Ernst to involve chance in

"Automatic Drawing," ink drawing by André Masson, 1924; in the William S. Rubin Collection

By courtesy of the William S. Rubin Collection; photograph, Malcolm Varon, New York City

the creation of a picture. Among them were "frottage," rubbing canvas or paper, placed over different materials such as wood, with graphite to make an impression of the grain; "grattage," scratching the painted surface of the canvas with pointed tools to make it more tactile; and "decalcomania," pressing liquid paint between two canvases and then pulling the canvases apart to produce ridges and bubbles of pigment. The chance forms created by these techniques were then allowed to stand as incomplete, suggestive images or were completed by the artist according to his instinctive response to them.

Between 1946 and 1951 a group of Canadian painters—including Paul-Émile Borduas, Albert Dumouchel, Jean Paul Mousseau, and Jean-Paul Riopelle—was known as "Les Automatistes" and practiced Automatism. From about 1950 a group of U.S. artists called Action painters (*see* Action painting) adopted Automatic methods, some under the direct influence of Masson, Gorky, and Ernst, all of whom had moved to the United States. Seeking pictorial equivalents, for the most part nonobjective, for states of mind, Jackson Pollock, Willem de Kooning, Franz Kline, Jack Tworkov, and Bradley Walker Tomlin variously experimented for a brief time, before going on to something quite different, with chance dripping of paint on the canvas and free, spontaneous brushstrokes. This approach was seen as a means of stripping away artifice and getting to more basic creative instincts deep within the artist's personality. For the Action painters, in fact, the creative interaction of the artist and his materials that was involved in the Automatic technique was the primary work of art and the finished painting only a secondary product. Some of the later Automatic art reflects the influence of Zen philosophy.

automatism, in spiritualism, the spontaneous performance of certain physical acts without the conscious control of the agent. In automatism a message is purportedly conveyed, usually through a spiritualist medium speaking in a trance during a séance (French: "sitting"), through automatic writing or through a joint experiment involving several persons (*e.g.,* using a ouija board). Though the message may appear to come from the spirit world, spiritualists concede that automatism may be the result of subliminal thoughts or feelings that are released and given free expression in certain favourable situations. *See also* automatic writing; medium; ouija board; séance; trance.

automaton, plural AUTOMATONS, or AUTOMATA, any of various mechanical objects that are relatively self-operating after they have been set in motion. Automatons are generally designed to arouse interest through their visual appeal and then to inspire surprise and awe through the apparent magic of their seemingly spontaneous movement. The majority of automatons are direct representations of creatures and plants or of kinetic aspects of natural phenomena. Imitations of such natural phenomena as the moving water of streams and waterfalls, for instance, can be simulated with twisted rods of glass. A mechanical device can be used to make a flower open its petals to imitate blooming or to make a figure walk. Some purely capricious automatons consist of complete scenes in which caricature personages perform in a humorous manner. Not all automatons, however, are mimetic. Some offer only visual fascination, such as spinning roundels set with gems to make flashing patterns of color and light.

Automatons can be classified into two groups: those that are ancillary to a functional article and those that in themselves are fanciful objects, solely for decoration and pleasure. Clocks and watches, which lend themselves to displays of motion, are the most common type of functional object with automatons. Throughout the ages, most automatons have been objects of fancy that are purely decorative in concept and function. The most complicated are the androids: figures in human form that can be made to walk about, play music, write, or draw. They are mostly of fairly large size and intended for public display. At the other end of the scale are exquisitely finished, pocket-sized objects such as trick pistols that

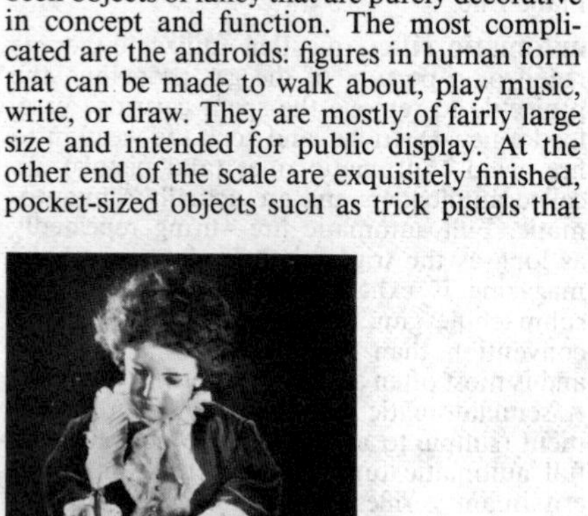

Android of a child writing by Pierre Jaquet-Droz, c. 1772; in the Musée d'Art et d'Histoire, Neuchâtel, Switz.

By courtesy of Musee d'Art et d'Histoire, Neuchatel, Switz.

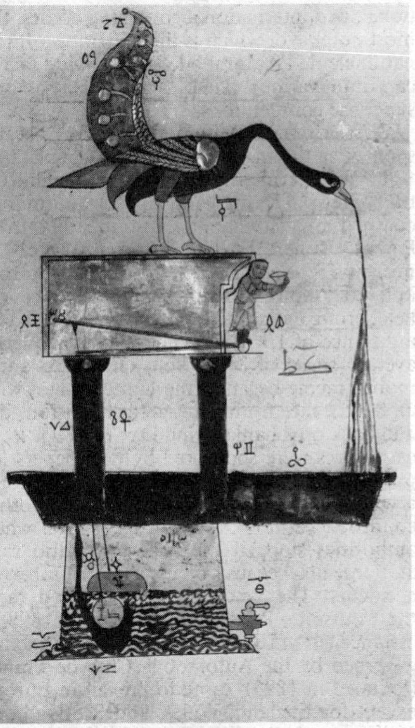

Automated peacock fountain from the treatise of al-Jazarī, Mesopotamian, 13th century AD; in the Museum of Fine Arts, Boston

By courtesy of the Museum of Fine Arts, Boston

were the speciality of the Rochat brothers, Ami-Napoléon and Louis, both of whom were among the finest 19th-century designers and craftsmen of automatons.

Few examples of automatons made prior to the 16th century remain, but numerous documents record their one-time existence. Among the earliest references is one to a wooden model of a pigeon constructed by Archytas of Tarentum (fl. 400–350 BC), a Greek friend of Plato. The bird was apparently suspended from the end of a pivoted bar, and the whole apparatus revolved by means of a jet of steam or of compressed air. More complete information about other devices is found in the writings of Hero of Alexandria (fl. 1st century AD), who described devices actuated by water, falling weights, and steam.

Accounts of automatons in China date from as early as the 3rd century BC, during the Han dynasty, when a mechanical orchestra was made for the emperor. By the Sui dynasty, in the 6th and 7th centuries AD, automatons had become widespread, and a book entitled the *Shui shih t'u Ching* ("Book of Hydraulic Elegancies") was published. In the T'ang period, from the 7th to the 10th centuries AD, automatons continued to be popular with imperial circles. There are records of flying birds, an otter which caught fish, and figures engaged in numerous activities ranging from a monk begging to girls singing. After the Yüan period (1279–1368), the creation of automatons seems to have waned.

During the Middle Ages in the Islāmic world, there were a number of inventors active from about the 9th century. Best documented are the water-operated automatons, many of moving peacocks, invented and made by al-Jazarī, who worked in the 13th century for princes of the Urtugid dynasty in Mesopotamia. References to automatons devised by western Europeans in the Middle Ages cite such distinguished names as Roger Bacon and Albertus Magnus, both of whom are credited with constructing androids—Bacon, a talking head, and Albertus, an iron man. Decorative mechanical objects for ecclesiastical use are illustrated by the Gothic architect Villard de Honnecourt in his famed sketchbook (1235).

In the early 16th century there was renewed interest in the manufacture of automatons, largely stemming from the influence of Eastern examples brought to Europe through trade with the Orient and the translation from the ancient Greek of the 1st century AD writings on mechanical objects by Hero of Alexandria. Intricate fountains emphasizing spectacular and trick effects became highly fashionable among the wealthy. Notable among them were the mid-16th century fountains and waterworks built for the gardens of the Villa d'Este at Tivoli, Italy.

With the use of coiled tempered steel spring from the mid-15th century, a truly portable source of motion became available in the Renaissance. It was used, for instance, in some of the nefs, table ornaments in the form of sailing ships. Largely dating from the second half of the 16th century, nefs probably originated in the gold and silversmithing centres of Germany, namely, Augsburg and Nürnberg, with such important masters of mechanical construction and the jeweler's craft as Hans Schlottheim. Among the most celebrated nefs is the "Ship of Charles V" (Musée de Cluny, Paris).

It was in the later 18th and early 19th centuries that the most intricate automatons made their appearance. Typical are the objects made by the Rochat brothers, who specialized in the manufacture of miniature singing birds. The mechanical songbirds were devised to appear suddenly from beneath hinged panels in snuffbox tops or to operate in cages that were suspended so that a clock under the base was visible. Perhaps the most intriguing of small-size automatons were the so-called magician boxes. A disk engraved with a question is inserted in a slot in the box, upon which the tiny figure of a magician comes to life and points with his wand at a space where the answer appears. Among the more elaborate mechanical devices popularized in the 18th century were *tableaux mécaniques,* or mechanical pictures. These framed painted landscapes, in which figures, windmills, and so forth spring to life by means of hidden clockwork, remained popular through the 19th century. A tableau designed for Mme de Pompadour (1759; Conservatoire National des Arts et Métiers, Paris) is a prime example of this type of automaton. Closely related to the *tableaux mécaniques* are mechanical theatres, the most extravagant of these having been built in the gardens of Hellbrunn near Salzburg. Consisting of 113 hydraulically operated figures, it was assembled between 1748 and 1752.

"Ship of Charles V," nef, 16th century; in the Musée de Cluny, Paris

Giraudon—Art Resource/EB Inc.

With the exception of a few works by Peter Carl Fabergé (d. 1920), the production of costly artistic automatons virtually ceased in the late 19th and early 20th centuries because of the diminishing number of skilled craftsmen, as well as rich patrons to support them. Collecting, therefore, is reserved for only the most wealthy. This expensive hobby is still served by the dealer who locates increasingly rare examples of historic automatons and by a small corps of highly skilled craftsmen whose dearly priced services keep the objects in working order.

automobile, a usually four-wheeled automotive vehicle designed primarily for passenger transportation and commonly propelled by an internal-combustion engine using a volatile fuel.

The following article treats briefly automobiles. Fuller treatment is provided in the following MACROPAEDIA articles. For treatment of historical and technical aspects, *see* Transportation; for manufacturing technology, *see* Manufacturing Industries.

Although by the mid-15th century the idea of a self-propelled vehicle had been put into practice, with the development of experimental vehicles powered by springs, clockworks, and the wind, Nicolas-Joseph Cugnot of France is considered to have built the first true automobile in 1769. The vehicle, designed as an artillery carriage, was a steam-powered tricycle that carried four passengers for 20 minutes at 2.25 miles (3.6 kilometres) per hour. In Britain, during the first half of the 19th century, steam-powered vehicles, although noisy, smelly, and dangerous because of the possibility of boiler explosions, were used on several routes for public transportation. Despite the development of the four-stroke gasoline-powered engine in 1876 by the German engineer Niklaus August Otto, steam and electricity remained the most widespread forms of automotive power until the beginning of the 20th century. Gasoline-powered engines eventually prevailed, however, as they allowed vehicles to travel at higher speeds and for longer distances than electricity and were safer and less troublesome than steam.

The pioneers of automobile manufacturing in Europe were Gottlieb Daimler and Carl Benz of Germany, who began, separately, to make cars in the 1880s (their companies were later merged). In the United States Ramson Eli Olds and Alexander and James Packard were among the first builders of automobiles. In 1898 there were 50 automobile-manufacturing companies in the United States, a number that rose to 241 by 1908. In that year Henry Ford revolutionized the manufacture of automobiles with his assembly-line style of production and brought out the Model T, a car that was inexpensive, versatile, and easy to maintain. The introduction of the Model T transformed the automobile from a plaything of the rich to an item that even people of modest income could afford; by the late 1920s the car was commonplace in modern industrial nations.

Automobile manufacturers in the 1930s and 1940s refined and improved on the principles of Ford and other pioneers. Cars were generally large, and many were still extremely expensive and luxurious; many of the most collectible cars date from this time. The increased affluence of the United States after World War II led to the development of large, gas-consuming vehicles while most companies in Europe made smaller, more fuel-efficient cars. Since the mid-1970s the rising cost of fuel has increased the demand for these smaller cars, many of which have been produced in

Japan as well as in Europe and the United States.

An average automobile is made of roughly 14,000 parts, which can be divided into several structural and mechanical subsystems.

The most basic of these is the body of the automobile, which contains the passenger and storage space as well as the engine compartment. It is usually classified according to the number of doors and the type of roof it has (*e.g.*, two-door hardtop) and is made of molded steel, which is painted and treated to retard corrosion. The body sits upon the chassis, a steel frame that also supports the engine, wheels, axle assemblies, transmission, steering mechanism, brakes, and suspension members.

The internal-combustion gasoline engine, with reciprocating pistons and a four-stroke cycle, is the most widely used power plant. In the United States in the 1940s engines were developed in size and design from four cylinders to the more powerful configuration of eight cylinders in a "V" shape. Since the 1970s, however, the trend has been toward smaller, less powerful, and yet more efficient engines. A transmission—comprised of shafts, gears, and a clutch—is installed between the engine and the driving wheels to allow the engine to be disconnected when the engine is started and idling and to make the most efficient use of the engine's power under varying loads. Transmissions are of two types: those in which the gears are shifted manually by the driver and those where the gears are shifted automatically by such a device as a hydraulic torque converter.

To control it once it is in motion, a car is equipped with steering and braking systems. The steering system consists of a series of linkages and gears that transmit the movement of the steering wheel to the front wheels. One braking system employs two semicircular "shoes" at each wheel that when activated press outward against the inner surfaces of drums attached to each wheel. More recently disk brakes, in which a clamp squeezes a disk attached to the wheel, have been used.

Automobiles have complex electrical systems that consist of a storage battery, alternator (alternating-current generator), devices for starting the engine and for vehicle operation (*e.g.*, headlights and windshield wipers), and such accessories as heaters and radios. The battery provides enough power to engage the starting motor and to activate the ignition system. Once the engine is started, the alternator continually recharges the battery and supplies power to the other electrical equipment.

There are several other important subsystems. The fuel system provides storage space for the fuel, transports it to the engine, and mixes it with air for combustion in the engine. The exhaust system vents exhaust gases by way of a muffler, which helps reduce engine noise. The lubrication system keeps friction from wearing out moving parts. Relatively lightweight motor oils are used in the engine, and heavier weight oils and greases are used in such parts as transmissions and wheel bearings. The cooling system keeps the engine from overheating, generally by means of liquid coolant, although many engines are air cooled. The suspension system, comprised of coil or leaf springs and shock absorbers, is combined with the tires to cushion the vehicle from the shock caused by driving over irregular surfaces. In addition, tires come in a variety of tread designs to provide traction in all driving conditions.

Manufacturing an automobile is a complex process involving first a number of subassembly steps—such as manufacturing engines and transmissions, stamping body parts, and procuring batteries and tires—and culminating in the assembly of the vehicle on a production line. Generally there are two lines, body and chassis. The stamped body parts are first welded together and painted, and such items as windows and the instrument panel are installed. Meanwhile, on the chassis line, the suspension, brake, and exhaust systems, the power train (engine, transmission, drive shaft, and differential), and tires are installed. The body is then joined with the chassis, and the finish work, including seat and wiring installation, is performed. After a series of adjustments and tests, the completed car is ready to be shipped.

automobile club, an organization of automobile owners. Begun as social clubs in which persons with an interest in motoring and motor racing could meet, such clubs later also developed into service organizations that provide members with emergency road service, assistance with planning trips and making reservations, auto insurance, and related services. Some clubs also continued to sponsor and organize motor sport competitions.

The first automobile club was the Automobile Club de France, formed in 1895 in Paris. Similar groups soon appeared in Great Britain and Belgium, and reciprocal arrangements between the French and British clubs were established by 1898. National clubs were formed in Germany, Austria, and Switzerland by 1900. The American Automobile Association (AAA) was established in 1902, consolidating nine earlier auto clubs. By the last quarter of the century there were more than 100 national auto clubs and associations affiliated throughout the world, linked by reciprocal agreements.

Many clubs have actively promoted highway construction and safety and lobbied for legislation and programs in the interests of motorists. The Automobile Club of Switzerland, for example, developed a form, the triptyque, that exempted motorists from paying customs duties on their autos when crossing national borders. Britain's Royal Automobile Club (RAC) and Automobile Association (AA) pioneered nationwide patrols, first by bicycle and later on motorbikes. The first roadside telephone box for motorist assistance was installed by the RAC in 1919. After World War II, insurance companies, oil companies, and national retailers formed auto clubs. Clubs were also formed by owners of types of vehicles and models. *See also* veteran car club.

automobile racing, also called MOTOR RACING, professional and amateur automobile sport practiced throughout the world in a variety of forms on roads, tracks, or closed circuits. It includes Grand Prix racing, speedway racing, stock-car racing, sports-car racing, drag racing, midget-car racing, and karting (*qq.v.*), as well as hill climbs and trials (*see* hill climb; *see also* rally driving; gymkhana). Local, national, and international governing bodies, the most notable of which is the Fédération Internationale de l'Automobile (FIA), divide racing cars into various classes and subclasses and supervise competitions.

Early history. Automobile racing began soon after the invention of the gasoline- (petrol-) fuelled internal-combustion engine in the 1880s. The first organized automobile competition, a reliability test in 1894 from Paris to Rouen, Fr., a distance of 32 km (50 mi), was won with an average speed of 16.4 kph (10.2 mph). In 1895 the first true race was held, from Paris to Bordeaux, Fr., and back, a distance of 1,178 km. The winner made an average speed of 24.15 kph. Organized automobile racing began in the United States with an 87-km race from Chicago to Evanston, Ill., and back on Thanksgiving Day in 1895. Both early races were sponsored by newspapers for promotional purposes. In Europe, town-to-town races in France, or from France to other countries, became the norm until 1903 when authorities stopped the Paris-to-Madrid race at Bordeaux because of the large number of accidents. The first closed-circuit road race, the Course de Périgueux, was run in 1898, a distance of 145 km on one lap. Such racing, governed by the Automobile Club de France (founded in 1895), came to prevail in Europe except for England, Wales, and Scotland. By 1900 racers had achieved speeds of more than 80.46 kph. Danger to spectators, racers, and livestock on roads not built for the automobile, let alone racing, ultimately caused road races to decrease in number. A notable exception was the Mille Miglia (*q.v.*).

International racing in the modern sense began after James Gordon Bennett, owner of *The New York Herald,* offered a trophy to be competed for annually by national automobile clubs, racing three cars each that had been built of parts made in the respective countries. The Automobile Club de France organized the first Bennett Trophy races in 1901, 1902, and 1903. The event was later held at the Circuit of Ireland (1903), the Taunus Rundstrecke in Germany (1904), and the Circuit d'Auvergne (1905). The unwillingness of French manufacturers to be limited to three cars led to their boycott of the Bennett Trophy Race in 1906 and the establishment of the first French Grand Prix Race at Le Mans in that year, the cars being raced by manufacturers' teams. The first Targa Florio was run in Sicily the same year and thereafter except during wartime at distances varying from 72 to 1,049 km.

William K. Vanderbilt, the New York sportsman, established a trophy raced for on Long Island from 1904 through 1909 (except for 1907) at distances ranging from 450 to 482 km. Thereafter the race was run at Savannah, Ga.; Milwaukee; Santa Monica, Calif.; and San Francisco until its discontinuance in

The Vanderbilt Cup Race of 1906
PHOTOWORLD—FPG

1916. Later Vanderbilt Cup races were run in 1936 and 1937 at Roosevelt Raceway, Long Island, New York.

In early racing, in both Europe and the United States, competing race cars were usually prototypes of the following year's models. After World War I, racing became too specialized for the use of production cars, though occasionally high-performance touring cars were stripped of their bodies and fitted with special seats, fuel tanks, and tires for racing. Still later stock-car racing in 1939 started with standard models modified for racing.

Speedway racing. The first speedway was built in 1906 at Brooklands, near Weybridge, Surrey, Eng. The track was a 4.45 km circuit, 30 m (100 ft) wide, with two curves banked to a height of 8.5 m. Sprint, relay, endurance, and handicap races were run at Brooklands, as well as long-distance runs (1,600 km) in 1932. Races for 24 hours were held in 1929–31. Brooklands closed in 1939. The first road racing allowed in England was at Donington Park, Lancashire, in 1932, but the circuit did not survive World War II. Oval, banked speedways on the Continent included Monza (outside Milan, 1922) and Montlhéray (outside Paris, 1924), both of which were attached to road circuits, using only half the track as part of Grand Prix racing. Montlhéray was also the site of many long-distance speed records.

Possibly the best known speedway is the 4 km Indianapolis Motor Speedway at Speedway, near Indianapolis, Ind., which opened as an unpaved track in 1909 but was paved with brick for the first Indianapolis 500 (*q.v.*) in 1911, the race continuing thereafter except during wartime. Oval, banked board tracks, first used before World War I, were popular in the United States throughout the 1920s. Both before and after that decade unpaved (dirt) tracks of half-mile and mile lengths were in use.

American, European, and international racing. After the first Grand Prix race in France in 1906 and the first Indianapolis 500 race in 1911, automobile racing was essentially different in Europe and in North America until in the 1950s Grand Prix racing was organized worldwide. Racing in the United States was essentially speedway track racing, the tracks varying mainly from half-mile dirt tracks to the 2½-mi track for the Indianapolis 500. Stock-car racing arose in the 1930s on the beach at Daytona Beach, Fla., then moved to tracks, and the major governing body, the National Association for Stock Car Racing, was founded in 1947. Hot-rod racing, particularly drag racing, a fast acceleration contest on a quarter-mile strip, originated in the United States in the 1930s in the southern California desert. Hot-rod cars originally were modified stock cars, but the racing cars ultimately became, like others, highly specialized. Hot-rod racing spread rapidly after World War II, and in 1951 the National Hot Rod Association was founded. The sport spread to Australia, New Zealand, Canada, England, Germany, Italy, Japan, and Sweden and in 1965 was recognized by the FIA. Racing with midget cars began in the United States in the 1940s and with even smaller cars, called karts, in the 1950s. Karts were also later raced in England, throughout the rest of Europe, and in Australia, New Zealand, and Japan, with international competition from the 1960s. Sports-car racing, both amateur and professional, became popular in the United States in the late 1930s, the earliest cars being European-made. The U.S. governing body, the Sports Car Club of America (founded 1944), and the Canadian Automobile Sports Committee (founded 1951) cooperate closely. Amateur members mainly compete in local rallies and gymkhanas, but general public interest is mainly in the professional races. Off road racing (*q.v.*), held in the western deserts of the United States from the 1960s and in Baja California, Mexico, is notable for the Baja 500 and the Mexican 1000 (mile) races.

Unlike most European and other countries, the United States has no single automobile racing body. The governing bodies noted above for various kinds of racing are members of the Automobile Competition Committee for the United States-FIA, basically an advisory and liaison organization.

Grand Prix racing. After the first French Grand Prix race of 1906 at Le Mans, a frequent early venue and also the site of the Le Mans 24-hour Grand Prix d'Endurance, run from 1923, the race was run in 1907 and 1908 and then not again until 1912. The first Italian Grand Prix was run in 1908. When racing resumed after World War I, the French and Italian Grand Prix were held in 1921. The Belgian Grand Prix began in 1925, the German in 1926, and that at Monaco in 1929. The national clubs had formed a governing body in 1904, the Association Internationale des Automobiles Clubs Reconnus (renamed the Fédération Internationale de l'Automobile in 1946). Cars were painted in national colours: French, blue; Italian, red; German, white; and British, green. Entries were made by manufacturers, usually two or three cars, and drivers were professional. Races were on closed circuits of 5 or 6 km to a lap with total distances of from 250 to 650 km. Through 1934 French and Italian manufacturers won most frequently, but throughout the rest of the 1930s, German manufacturers dominated. Racing resumed in 1947, and from the late 1950s British-made cars were dominant. In 1950 a world championship for drivers was instituted, usually involving Grand Prix races of Monaco, Belgium, The Netherlands, France, Great Britain, Germany, Italy, Mexico, South Africa, Canada, and the United States. A championship for Formula I car constructors was begun in 1955.

Rally driving. Racing over specified routes, the driver being kept on course by a navigator between checkpoints, began in 1907 with a Peking-to-Paris race of about 12,000 km. The Monte Carlo rally from various starting points began in 1911 and continued thereafter except for wartime interruptions. Rallies became very popular after World War II in Europe and elsewhere with European and international championships being instituted by the FIA. Weekend rallies came to be common worldwide, ranging from those held by local auto clubs to those sponsored by larger organizations. The longest rally held regularly, the East African Safari, as long as 6,234 km, began in 1953. The longest rally was the London-to-Sydney rally, in 1977, a distance of about 31,107 km.

Speed. In almost all kinds of racing, speed has been the preeminent goal, although concern for safety by governing bodies has prevented a steady climb in speeds. Nevertheless, speed has risen from 120.04 kph in the 1911 Indianapolis 500 to nearly 260 kph in the late 1970s. In Grand Prix racing, where courses vary, speed has risen from 101.20 kph in 1906 to more than 200 kph in Grand Prix racing by the 1960s.

In the 1920s, land-speed record attempts deserted the tracks and courses for special desert or beach strips, and cars were designed for the record alone. Jet engines later came into use, and in one case a three-wheeled vehicle attempting a new record had to be certified by the Fédération Internationale Motorcycliste, the FIA having refused certification.

For winners of major races, championship drivers and constructors, and speed records, *see* Sporting Record: *Automobile racing.*

automorphism, in mathematics, an assignment that associates to every element in a set one and only one other element (perhaps itself) and for which there is a companion assignment such that one assignment followed by the other produces the assignment in which every element is associated with itself. Furthermore, operations such as addition and multiplication, if they exist, must be preserved; for example, if $\sigma(a)$ is the element associated to a, then $\sigma(a+b) = \sigma(a) + \sigma(b)$ and $\sigma(ab) = \sigma(a) \cdot \sigma(b)$ for any a, b.

autonomic nervous system, also called VEGETATIVE, or VISCERAL, NERVOUS SYSTEM, in vertebrate animals, the part of the nervous system that controls and regulates the internal organs without any conscious recognition or effort by the organism. It is composed of two antagonistic sets of nerves, the sympathetic and parasympathetic nervous systems. The former connects the internal organs to the brain by spinal nerves. When stimulated, these nerves prepare the organism for stress: the heart rate increases, and blood flow to the muscles is increased and that to the skin is decreased. The nerve fibres of the parasympathetic nervous system are the cranial nerves, especially the vagus, and the lumbar spinal nerves. When stimulated, they increase digestive secretions and reduce the heartbeat.

autopilot: *see* automatic pilot.

autopsy, also called NECROPSY, POSTMORTEM, or POSTMORTEM EXAMINATION, dissection and examination of a dead body and its organs and structures to determine the cause of death, to observe the effects of disease, and to establish the sequences of changes and thus establish evolution and mechanisms of disease processes.

The early Egyptians did not study the dead human body for an explanation of disease and death, though some organs were removed for preservation. The Greeks and the Indians cremated their dead without examination; the Romans, Chinese, and Muslims all had taboos about opening the body; and human dissections were not permitted during the Middle Ages.

The first real dissections for the study of disease were carried out around 300 BC by the Alexandrian physicians Herophilus and Erasistratus, but it was the Greek physician Galen, in the late 2nd century AD, who was the first to correlate the patient's symptoms (complaints) and his signs (what can be seen and felt) with what was found upon examining the "affected part of the deceased." This was the great leap forward that eventually led to the autopsy and broke an ancient barrier to progress in medicine.

It was the rebirth of anatomy during the Renaissance, as exemplified by the work of Andreas Vesalius (*De Humani Corporis Fabrica,* 1543) that made it possible to distinguish the abnormal, as such (*e.g.,* an aneurysm), from normal anatomy. Leonardo da Vinci dissected 30 corpses and noted "abnormal anatomy"; Michelangelo, too, performed a number of dissections. Earlier, in the 13th century, Frederick II ordered that the bodies of two executed criminals be delivered every two years to the medical schools, one of which was at Salerno, for an "Anatomica Publica," which every physician was obliged to attend. The first forensic or legal autopsy, wherein the death was investigated to determine presence of "fault," is said to have been one requested by a magistrate in Bologna in 1302. Antonio Benivieni, a 15th-century Florentine physician, carried out 15 autopsies explicitly to determine the "cause of death" and significantly correlated some of his findings with prior symptoms in the deceased. Théophile Bonet of Geneva (1620–89) collated from the literature the observations made in 3,000 autopsies. Many specific clinical and pathologic entities were then defined by various observers, thus opening the door to modern practice.

The autopsy came of age with Giovanni Morgagni, the father of modern pathology, who in 1761 described what could be seen in the body with the naked eye. In his voluminous work *On the Seats and Causes of Diseases as Investigated by Anatomy,* he compared the symptoms and observations in some 700 patients with the anatomical findings upon examining their bodies. Thus, in Morgagni's work the study of the patient replaced the study of books and comparison of commentaries.

With Karl von Rokitansky of Vienna (1804–78), the gross (naked eye) autopsy reached its apogee. Rokitansky utilized the microscope very little and was limited by his own humoral theory. The French anatomist and physiologist Marie F.X. Bichat (1771–1802) stressed the role of the different generalized systems and tissues in the study of disease. It was the German pathologist Rudolf Virchow (1821–1902), however, who introduced the cellular doctrine—that changes in the cells are the basis of the understanding of disease—in pathology and in autopsy. He warned against the dominance of pathologic anatomy—the study of the structure of diseased tissue—alone as such and stressed that the future of pathology would be physiologic pathology—study of the functioning of the organism in the investigation of disease.

The modern autopsy has been expanded to include the application of all knowledge and all of the instruments of the specialized modern basic sciences. The examination has been extended to structures too small to be seen except with the electron microscope, and to molecular biology to include all that can be seen as well as what still remains unseen.

Procedure. The autopsy procedure itself has changed very little during the 20th century. The first step is a gross examination of the exterior for any abnormality or trauma and a careful description of the interior of the body and its organs. This is usually followed by further studies, including microscopic examination of cells and tissues.

The main incisions in the body remain the same. For the torso, a Y-shaped incision is made. Each upper limb of the "Y" extends from either the armpit or the outer shoulder and is carried beneath the breast to the bottom of the sternum, or breastbone, in the midline. From this point of juncture at the bottom of the sternum the incision is continued down to the lower abdomen where the groins meet in the genital area.

There are different schools as to procedure beyond this point. In one method, each organ is removed separately for incision and study. In the so-called en masse methods the chest organs are all removed in a single group and all of the abdominal organs in another for examination. The great vessels to the neck, head, and arms are ligated—tied off—and the organs removed as a unit for dissection. The neck organs are explored *in situ* only or removed from below. Dissection then proceeds usually from the back, except where findings dictate a variation in the procedure. Usually groups of organs are removed together so that disturbances in their functional relationships may be determined. After study of the brain in position, it is freed from its attachments and removed *in toto.* The spinal cord also can be removed.

The dissector proceeds to examine the external and cut surface of each organ, its vascular structures, including arteries, lymphatics, fascial or fibrous tissue, and nerves. Specimens are taken for culture, chemical analysis, and other studies. Immediately upon completion of the procedure, all of the organs are returned to the body and all incisions carefully sewn. After the body's proper restoration, no unseemly evidence of the autopsy need remain.

After the gross examination of the body the findings are balanced one against another and a list of pathological findings is compiled; this list comprises the tentative or "provisional anatomical diagnoses." Such diagnoses are grouped and arranged in the order of importance and of sequence. On occasion a quick microscopic study is done to confirm a diagnosis so as to assure its proper listing.

Finally the examiner lists as the cause of death the one lesion without which death would not have occurred. Though obviously all-important in forensic cases, this aspect of the autopsy analysis is also required in cases not required by law. After all studies—histological, chemical, toxicological, bacteriological, and viral—are completed, any errors of the provisional anatomical diagnoses are corrected and the final anatomical diagnoses and the final cause of death are listed. A statement of analysis of the autopsy that correlates the findings with the clinical picture, the "clinical pathological correlation," concludes the record of the autopsy.

Forensic autopsy. The forensic pathologist goes beyond the mere cause of death; he must establish all the facts, both lethal and nonlethal, with any potential bearing whatsoever on the criminal or civil litigation. The cause of death is not automatically revealed when the body is opened; it is not an isolated tangible and delimited entity; it is a *concept*—an opinion—as to mechanism or happening and as such is subject occasionally to differences in interpretation. The legal autopsy requires meticulous detailed descriptions, measurements, and documentation.

Experience in the investigation of the scene of a death in medicolegal cases is important, for the evaluation of circumstances of death may be critical in establishing the mode of death—*e.g.,* suicide. The autopsy may not be able, of itself, to determine intent, whereas the scene and the circumstances may provide unmistakable evidence. Photographic documentation is important in the medicolegal autopsy. The medicolegal postmortem examination must always be complete to rule out any other potential contributory cause of death and therefore must never be limited to a partial study. The identification of the deceased and of all specimens taken from the body is critical; the time of death and the blood grouping must, if possible, be established. In all autopsies, but especially in forensic cases, findings must be dictated to a stenographer or recording instrument during the actual performance of the procedure. The record often becomes legal evidence and therefore must be complete and accurate.

Purposes. The autopsy deals with the particular illness as evidenced in one individual and is more than simply a statistical average. Every autopsy is important to expose mistakes, to delimit new diseases and new patterns of disease, and to guide future studies. Morbidity and mortality statistics acquire accuracy and significance when based on careful autopsies; they also often give the first indication of contagion and epidemics. Nor can the role of the autopsy in medical education be understated. It is the focal point at which the profession learns to assess and to apply medical knowledge. Thus, the autopsy does more than merely determine the cause of death. While the medicolegal autopsy in particular has this important primary objective, most autopsies have a larger purpose.

autostrada (Italian: "automobile road"), plural AUTOSTRADE, national Italian expressway system built by the government as toll roads. The first, from Venice to Turin, was begun in 1924; construction was continuing in the early 1980s. The *autostrada* has three undivided lanes on a 33-foot (10-metre) roadway with 3-ft shoulders. Access is limited, with restrictions on commercial vehicles.

autotomy, also called SELF-AMPUTATION, the ability of certain animals to release part of the body that has been grasped by an external agent. A notable example is found among lizards that break off the tail when it is seized by a predator. The phenomenon is found also among certain worms, salamanders, and spiders. The cast-off part is sometimes regenerated.

Where the same name may denote a person, place, or thing, the articles will be found in that order

autumn, season of the year between summer and winter during which temperatures gradually decrease. It is often called fall in the U.S. because leaves fall from the trees at that time. Autumn is usually defined in the Northern Hemisphere as the period between the autumnal equinox (day and night equal in length), September 22 or 23, and the winter solstice (year's shortest day), December 22 or 23; and in the Southern Hemisphere as the period between March 20 or 21 and June 21 or 22. The autumn temperature transition between summer heat and winter cold occurs only in middle and high latitudes; in equatorial regions, temperatures generally vary little during the year. In the polar regions autumn is very short. For physical causes of the seasons, *see* season.

The concept of autumn in European languages is connected with the harvesting of crops; in many cultures autumn, like the other seasons, has been marked by rites and festivals revolving around the season's importance in food production. Animals gather food in autumn in preparation for the coming winter, and those with fur often grow thicker coats. Many birds migrate toward the Equator to escape the falling temperatures. A common autumn phenomenon in the central and eastern U.S. and in Europe is Indian summer (*q.v.*), a period of unseasonably warm weather that sometimes occurs in late October or November.

Autun, town, Saône-et-Loire *département,* Bourgogne region, central France, on the Arroux River, southwest of Dijon. Augustodunum (Autun) succeeded Bibracte as the Gallic *oppidum,* and was an important Roman city renowned for its schools of rhetoric. Much of the Roman wall, with two 3rd-century gates, remains, as well as a Roman theatre. The church of Saint-Lazare (1130), once the chapel of the dukes of Burgundy, is known for its Romanesque sculpture, particularly that of Gisleberte, whose work greatly influenced the succeeding age. Autun is a

Saint-André Gate, 3rd-century, Autun, Fr.
Editions "La Cigogne"—Hachette

market for the livestock of the Morvan highlands and is a centre for leather, furniture, and metal industries. Shale oil is extracted on a small scale from the Épinac coalfield. Pop. (1982) 19,129.

autunite, phosphate mineral, hydrated calcium and uranium phosphate [$Ca(UO_2)_2(PO_4)_2 \cdot 10–12H_2O$], that is an ore of uranium. It forms translucent to transparent, yellow to pale-green crystals, scaly masses, or crusts in

Autunite from Spokane, Wash.

By courtesy of the MacFall Collection; photograph, Mary A. Root—EB Inc.

hydrothermal veins and pegmatites, where it occurs as an alteration product of uraninite. It has been found in Cornwall, Eng.; Katanga, Zaire; and New England. For detailed physical properties, *see* phosphate mineral (table).

Auvergne, planning region (French *région de programme*), encompassing the central French *départements* of Allier, Puy-de-Dôme, Cantal, and Haute-Loire. The capital is Clermont-Ferrand. The region has an area of 10,034 sq mi (25,988 sq km) and is bounded by the *départements* of Cher and Nièvre to the north, Saône-et-Loire to the northeast, Loire and Ardèche to the east, Lozère and Aveyron to the south, Lot to the southwest, and Corrèze and Creuse to the west.

The following article summarizes the political history, geography, demographic patterns, and economy of modern Auvergne; for additional treatment of its geography and history, *see* MACROPAEDIA: France.

The Arverni, a powerful confederation under the chieftain Vercingetorix, inhabited the region during Julius Caesar's time; later the Romans made Arvernia part of Aquitania Prima. After 913 the viscounts of Clermont (now Clermont-Ferrand) adopted the hereditary title of counts of Auvergne. In the 12th and 13th centuries three other great countships developed in the region: the Dauphiné d'Auvergne, the Terre d'Auvergne, and the episcopal countship of Clermont. Charles, duc de Bourbon, united the Terre d'Auvergne and the Dauphiné d'Auvergne in 1503; these Bourbon domains were later confiscated by King Francis I, who gave them to his mother, Louise of Savoy, for the rest of her life, after which they were annexed to the kingdom of France (1532).

The *gouvernement* of Auvergne in 1789

The countship of Auvergne, having passed in 1422 to the house of La Tour, descended to Catherine de Médicis, who also got possession of Clermont in 1551. These domains were annexed to the crown by 1610.

Auvergne belongs to the Massif Central; the Paris Basin extends into Allier. A humid climate prevails in the west, which is open to Atlantic influences; a continental climate prevails in the east.

The region is sparsely populated and the population has shown only modest growth since 1946. It is increasingly concentrated in the plains of Allier, which have grown at the expense of the mountains to the south. The population of Cantal and Haute-Loire remains predominantly rural; approximately one-half of the population is urban. Emigration has left behind an aging population, with the result that the birthrate lags behind the national average.

Animal husbandry predominates in the mountains. The rich plains of Limagnes in Haute-Loire and Puy-de-Dôme produce wheat and fodder. Viticulture is in decline. Small farms predominate in the crystalline massif of the east and largely produce rye. Capital from emigrants and the cities has helped to finance the spread of tree farms.

Traditional artisanship has largely disappeared, although cutlery continues to be produced in Thiers in Puy-de-Dôme. Manufacturing is concentrated in Clermont-Ferrand, which emerged as a major industrial centre in the late 19th century, and in Allier, which has benefitted from its proximity to Paris. The Michelin plant in Clermont-Ferrand is France's largest producer of tires; the industrial complex of Montluçon-Commentry in Allier manufactures tires, computers, and machines. Spas are important: the thermal springs of Vichy, Néris-les-Bains, Bourbon-l'Archambault, Royat, Châtelguyon, La Bourboule, Saint-Nectaire, Vic-sur-Cère, and Claudes-Aigues draw large numbers of visitors. Pop. (1982) 1,332,678.

Auversian Stage, major division of Eocene rocks and time (the Eocene Epoch began about 54,000,000 years ago and lasted about 16,000,000 years). The Auversian was originally considered a distinctive stage between the Bartonian Stage and the Lutetian Stage, other major divisions of the Eocene Epoch. Many now regard the Auversian to be the lowest substage of the Bartonian Stage (*q.v.*). The Auversian was named for rock exposures near Auvers, in the Paris Basin of France, which consist primarily of marine lagoonal strata, especially marine sands containing a characteristic invertebrate fauna. Because the fauna of the Auversian is not strictly open marine, it has been difficult to correlate with other stages, causing it to be regarded as a stage and substage. In the London Basin, England, the Auversian is represented by the Upper Bagshot Beds and in the Hampshire Basin by the Upper Bracklesham Beds.

Auwers, (Georg Friedrich Julius) Arthur von (b. Sept. 12, 1838, Göttingen, Hanover—d. Jan. 24, 1915, Berlin), German astronomer who is best remembered for the meticulous observations and calculations that allowed him to develop extremely accurate star catalogs. As part of this process, Auwers researched solar and stellar parallaxes, making a new reduction of James Bradley's observations and measurements of star distances. Auwers is also remembered for his observations of double stars and especially for accurately computing the orbits of the companion stars of Sirius and Procyon before improved telescopes made it possible to observe them.

From 1881 to 1889 Auwers was president of the Astronomische Gesellschaft (Astronomical Society). He also served as permanent secretary of the Academy of Science in Berlin and was elected to the French Académie des Sciences.

Aux Cayes (Haiti): *see* Les Cayes.

Auxerre, town, capital, Yonne *département,* Bourgogne region, central France, on the Yonne River. The town, which flourished in pre-Roman and Roman days, became the seat of a bishop and a *civitas* (provincial capital) in the 3rd century. It was united to France by Louis XI in the 1400s. The cathedral of Saint-Étienne (13th–16th-century Gothic) has three sculptured doorways and a rose window on the west front. A massive tower rises in the northwest corner. The early Gothic choir and the apsidal chapel contain some of the best 13th-century stained glass in France. The church of Saint-Eusèbe (founded 7th century) shows styles from the 12th to the 16th century. Below the church of Saint-Germain, crypts of the 9th century contain tombs of the bishops of Auxerre. The town is a commercial and industrial centre; its industries include food processing, wood working, and batteries; another chief product of Auxerre is wine, especially Chablis, from the surrounding vineyards. Pop. (1982) 36,504.

The cathedral of Saint-Étienne in Auxerre, Fr., on the Yonne River

Peyto Slatter—Shostal/EB Inc.

auxiliary, in grammar, a helping element, especially a verb, that adds meaning to the basic meaning of the main verb or other predicate in a sentence. Auxiliaries can convey information about tense, mood, person, and number. An auxiliary verb occurs with a main verb that is in the form of an infinitive or a participle.

English has a rich system of auxiliaries. English auxiliary verbs include the modal verbs, which may express such notions as possibility ("may," "might," "can," "could") or necessity ("must"). In "Sam should write to his mother," the modal verb "should" adds the sense of obligation to the main verb "write." Other English auxiliaries are "will" and "shall," which often indicate futurity, and "would," which usually indicates desire or intent.

Some auxiliary verbs condition an associated change in or addition to the main verb, such as the English expanded form in "Mary is washing her hair now," in which the auxiliary verb "is" occurs with the present participle "washing." Another example is the French past indefinite form, as in *il a donné* and its English equivalent "he has given," in which there is not only an independent auxiliary verb (French *avoir,* English "have") but also a change of the main verb to the past participle.

auxin, any of a group of hormones that regulate plant growth, particularly by stimulating cell elongation in stems and inhibiting it in roots. For example, auxins influence the growth of stems toward light (phototropism) and against the force of gravity (geotropism). Auxins also play a role in cell division and differentiation, in fruit development, in the formation of roots from cuttings, in the inhibition of lateral branching (apical dominance), and in leaf fall (abscission). The most important naturally occurring auxin is beta-indolylacetic acid.

auxochrome, a group of atoms and electrons forming part of an organic molecule and modifying the absorption of light by an adjacent chromophore (*q.v.*) so as to intensify and alter the colour of the substance. The most potent auxochromes are amino groups, halogen atoms, and hydroxyl and alkoxyl groups, although none of these substituents alone confers colour on a compound.

The essential component of an auxochrome is at least one pair of electrons not involved in covalent bond formation; such unshared electrons are usually provided by an electronegative atom such as nitrogen, oxygen, sulfur, or one of the halogens. Combination of an auxochrome with a chromophore creates an electron system that absorbs a greater amount of light than the chromophore alone, and the light absorbed is of longer wavelength. As a result, the colour is more intense and has a deeper shade.

In older usage, the term auxochrome included groups such as sulfonic acid ($-SO_3H$) and carboxyl ($-CO_2H$) that are now recognized as influencing the solubility of a dye or its affinity for textile fibres, but not its colour.

Av, Ninth Day of (Judaism): *see* Tisha be-Av.

AV-8 (aircraft): *see* Harrier.

Ava, ancient capital of Burma, in Sagaing Division (*taing*), central Upper Burma, on the left bank of the Irrawaddy River at the Myitnge confluence. It is linked by a road and rail bridge, 5,894 ft (1,796 m) long, to the town of Sagaing; this is the only place where the Irrawaddy is bridged. Its name is a corruption of the Burmese Inwa, meaning "entrance to the lake." The site was chosen in 1364 by the Shans who succeeded the Pagan dynasty. The location allowed the Shans to control the rice supply from the Kyaukse irrigated area to the south, which became vital after the traditional rice-growing area in Lower Burma had been lost to a Mon kingdom. Ava flourished until destroyed by a rival group of Shans in 1527. In 1634 it again became the Burman capital under the Toungoo dynasty. Although it fell to the Mons in 1752, Alaungpaya, the Burman leader, recovered it; but he chose Shwebo (60 mi [100 km] north) as his capital. When Alaungpaya founded the Konbaung dynasty, Ava served as capital (1765–83 and 1823–37). Although the dynasty frequently changed capitals and built Amarapura (1783) and Mandalay (1857), its seat was always referred to by outsiders as the "Court of Ava." From the 15th century, Europeans used the term Ava as a synonym for Upper Burma. Little remains at the site except for a monastery.

ava (ritual beverage): *see* kava.

Avadāna (Sanskrit: "Noble Deeds"), legendary material centring on the Buddha's explanations of events by a person's worthy deeds in a previous life. The Pāli cognate of the term is *Apadāna* (*q.v.*). *Avadāna* designates both the class of such stories scattered within the *Vinaya Piṭaka* ("Basket of Discipline") and separate collections based upon them. Among the latter is an important anthology of the Sarvāstivāda (Doctrine That All Is Real) school given the modern title *Divyāvadāna* ("Divine Avadāna"), consisting of 38 legends, including some about the great Buddhist emperor Aśoka. The most famous and largest work classified as *Avadāna* is the *Mahāvastu* ("Great Story"), a compilation from the Mahāsaṅghika (Great Community) school of ancient Buddhism of miraculous events in the life and former lives of the Buddha himself.

avadavat, also called RED AVADAVAT, RED MUNIA, or LAL (*Amandava,* or *Estrilda, amandava*), plump, 8-centimetre- (3-inch-) long bird of the waxbill (*q.v.*) group (order Passeriformes), a popular cage bird. The avadavat is abundant in marshes and meadows of southern Asia (introduced in Hawaii). The male, in breeding plumage, is bright red with brown mottling and white speckling, hence another name, strawberry-finch.

Avadavat (*Estrilda amandava*) in non-breeding plumage
John Markham—Bruce Coleman Inc.

avahi (*Avahi laniger*), long-legged, arboreal primate belonging to the Madagascan family Indriidae. The avahi is grayish brown with reddish hands and feet and is about 35 centimetres (14 inches) long, excluding the furry, reddish, 39-cm tail. It has short arms, a short muzzle, and a round head with small ears hidden in the woolly fur. Nocturnal and apparently vegetarian, the avahis live in the rain forests in small groups and typically vertically cling to the trees. A single young is born after about five months' gestation. Of the two subspecies that inhabit the eastern and western forests of Madagascar, the western form faces extinction from the destruction of its habitat.

avalanche, large mass of rock debris or snow that moves rapidly down a mountain slope, sweeping and grinding everything in its path. An avalanche begins when a mass of material overcomes frictional resistance of the sloping surface, often after its foundation is loosened by spring rains or is rapidly melted by a foehn (warm, dry wind). Vibrations caused by loud noises, such as artillery fire, thunder, or blasting, can start the mass in motion.

Large rock avalanches (rockfalls) have dammed rivers and buried towns. They are commonly composed of bedrock fragments a few centimetres (an inch or so) in diameter and include much soil and dust. Rock avalanches are thought to ride on a cushion of compressed air that allows them to travel long distances. A debris avalanche usually occurs in unconsolidated earth materials when weakened by moisture.

Some snow avalanches develop during heavy snowstorms and slide while the snow is still falling, but more often they occur after the snow has accumulated at a given site. One of the causes of snow avalanches is the slow formation of depth hoar (hexagonal cuplike ice crystals that begin to form at ground level) under the snow pack. Depth hoar crystals develop in loose array from the evaporation of the original snow particles and the simultaneous vapour deposition of larger, denser ice crystals near the ground; thus a zone of weakness occurs within the snowpack near the ground, the particles of which act as a lubricant when the upper layers of the snow start sliding down the mountain.

The wet avalanche is perhaps the most dangerous because of its great weight, heavy texture, and tendency to solidify as soon as it stops moving. The dry type is also very dangerous because its entraining of great amounts of air makes it act like a fluid; this kind of avalanche may flow up the opposite side of a narrow valley. Avalanches carry a considerable amount of rock debris with the snow and therefore are significant geological agents; in addition to transporting unsorted materials to the bottoms of slopes, they may, if repeated, effect an important amount of erosion, as in some mountains of the western United States.

Considerable attention is given to the dangers presented by avalanches to mountain climbers, skiers, travellers, and residents of mountainous terrain. Much of the pioneering research and the testing of protective devices was conducted in Switzerland at the Snow and Avalanche Research Institute. Despite the construction of avalanche-protection works in most parts of Switzerland, destructive avalanches still occur following periods of intense snowfall. In some older Swiss towns, buildings in open areas likely to be swept by avalanches are built like the prows of ships to divert the flowing snow.

In the U.S., avalanche danger is monitored by the Forest Service of the Department of Agriculture because most of the ski areas in mountainous regions are located within national forests. Rangers, specially trained in avalanche forecasting and control, monitor the ski resort areas and mountain slopes where avalanches might endanger highways or other structures. Much of the control at present consists of lobbing explosives into the upper reaches of the avalanche zones, intentionally causing the snow to slide before accumulations become very great. Most large ski areas subject to the danger are now continuously patrolled by avalanche experts.

avalanche effect, in physics, a sudden increase in the flow of an electrical current through a nonconducting or semiconducting solid when a sufficiently strong electrical force is applied. The ability of most nonmetallic solids to carry an ordinary electrical current is limited by the scarcity of electrons free to move in the presence of an externally applied electric field. A sufficiently strong electrical force can break free a large number of electrons from the atoms that form the structure of the solid so that a large current can flow through the material. This avalanche effect is responsible for the phenomenon of breakdown in insulators and in semiconductors, where it is called the Zener effect. Because avalanche requires a specific electrical force for each type of substance, it can be used for precise control of voltages in electrical circuits, as in a device called the Zener diode.

At room temperature, even an insulator has

a few free electrons. Strong electrical forces cause these electrons to move through the solid rapidly and, if the free electron is moving rapidly enough, it may knock an electron away from an atom in the solid. This ejected electron (referred to as excited) can move freely through the solid and excite other electrons in the same way, in a process resembling an avalanche in which each rolling rock frees others.

When the electrical force is removed, the newly freed electrons are recaptured by the atoms of the solid, which once again becomes a poor conductor of electricity. Such sudden, large currents may alter or even melt the solid.

Avalokiteśvara (Sanskrit *avalokita,* "looking on"; *īśvara,* "lord"), Chinese KUAN-YIN, Japanese KANNON, the *bodhisattva* ("Buddha-to-be") of infinite compassion and mercy, possibly the most popular of all Buddhist deities, beloved throughout the Buddhist world. He supremely exemplifies the *bodhisattva's* resolve to postpone his own Buddhahood until he has helped every being on earth achieve emancipation.

Avalokiteśvara, bronze figure from Kurkihār, Bihār, 9th century; in Patna Museum, Patna, Bihār

By courtesy of Patna Museum, Patna (Bihar); photograph, Royal Academy of Arts, London

His name has been variously interpreted as "the lord who looks in every direction" and "the lord of what we see" (that is, the actual, created world). In Tibet he is known as Spyan-ras gzigs (With a Pitying Look) and in Mongolia as Nidü-ber üjegči (He Who Looks With the Eyes). The title invariably used for him in Indochina and Thailand is Lokeśvara (Lord of the World).

Avalokiteśvara is the earthly manifestation of the self-born, eternal Buddha, Amitābha, whose figure is represented in his headdress, and he guards the world in the interval between the departure of the historical Buddha, Gautama, and the appearance of the future Buddha, Maitreya. Avalokiteśvara protects against shipwreck, fire, assassins, robbers, and wild beasts. He is the creator of the fourth world, which is the actual universe in which we live.

According to legend, his head once split with grief at realizing the number of wicked beings in the world yet to be saved. Amitābha Buddha caused each of the pieces to become a whole head and placed them on his son in three tiers of three, then the 10th, and topped them all with his own image. Sometimes the 11-headed Avalokiteśvara is represented with thousands of arms, which rise like the outspread tail of a peacock around him. In painting he is usually shown white in colour (in Nepal, red). His female consort is the goddess Tārā. His traditional residence is the mountain Potala, and his images are frequently placed on hilltops.

The height of the veneration of Avalokiteśvara in northern India occurred in the 3rd–7th century. His worship (as Kuan-yin) was introduced into China as early as the 1st century AD and had entered all Buddhist temples by the 6th century. Representations of the *bodhisattva* in China prior to the Sung dynasty (960–1126) are unmistakenly masculine in appearance. Later images display attributes of both genders. One interpretation of this development contends that the *bodhisattva* is neither male nor female but has transcended sexual distinctions, as he has all other dualities in the sphere of *saṃsāra* (the temporal world). According to this opinion, the flowing drapery and soft contours of the body seen in statues and paintings have been intentionally combined with a visible moustache to emphasize the absence of sexual identity. Furthermore, the *Lotus Sūtra* relates that Avalokiteśvara has the ability of assuming whatever form is required to relieve suffering and also has the power to grant children. Another point of view, while accepting the validity of this philosophical doctrine, holds that from at least the 12th century the popular devotional cult of Kuan-ying has superimposed onto the *bodhisattva* qualities of a mother-goddess. A centre of the personal worship of the saviour Kuan-yin is the island of P'u-t'o near Ning-po (associated with the traditional mountain residence of the *bodhisattva* Potala).

Among the followers of the Pure Land sect, who look to rebirth in the Western Paradise of the Buddha Amitābha (Chinese O-mi-t'o-fo; Japanese Amida), Kuan-yin forms part of a ruling triad, along with Amitābha and the *bodhisattva* Mahasthāmaprāpta (Chinese Tai-shih-chih). Images of the three are often placed together in temples, and Kuan-yin is shown in painting welcoming the dead to the Western Paradise. This cult of Kuan-yin is based on scriptures of the Pure Land school that were translated into Chinese between the 3rd and 5th centuries.

The *bodhisattva* was introduced into Tibet in the 7th century, where he quickly became the most popular figure in the Lamaist pantheon, successively reincarnated in each Dalai Lama. He is credited with introducing the prayer formula *om maṇi padmehūṃ!* (frequently translated "the jewel is in the lotus") to the people of Tibet.

The cult of Kuan-yin probably reached Japan (there called Kannon) by way of Korea soon after Buddhism was first introduced into the country; the earliest known images at the Hōryū-ji (*ji,* "temple") in Nara date from the mid-7th century. The worship of the *bodhisattva* was never confined to any one sect and continues to be widespread throughout Japan.

As in China, some confusion exists about Kannon's gender. In Japan Kannon's ability to assume innumerable forms has led to seven major representations: (1) Shō Kannon, the simplest form, usually shown as a seated or standing figure with two hands, one of which holds a lotus; (2) Jū-ichi-men Kannon, a two-or four-handed figure with 11 heads; (3) Senju Kannon, the *bodhisattva* with 1,000 arms; (4) Jun-tei Kannon, one of the least common forms, represented as a seated figure with 18 arms, sometimes related to the Indian goddess Cuntī (mother of 700,000 Buddhas); (5) Fukū-kenjaku Kannon, a form popular with the Tendai sect, whose special emblem is the lasso; (6) Ba-tō Kannon, shown with a fierce face and a horse's head in the hairdress, probably related to the Tibetan protector of horses, Hayagrīva (*q.v.*); (7) Nyo-i-rin Kannon, shown seated, with six arms, holding the wish-fulfilling jewel.

The virtues and miracles of Avalokiteśvara are accounted in many Buddhist *sūtras* (scriptures). The *Avalokiteśvara-sūtra* was incorporated into the widely popular *Saddharma-puṇḍarīka-sūtra,* or *Lotus Sutra,* in the 3rd century AD, though it continues to circulate as an independent work in China and is the main scripture of his cult worship there.

He is the only Mahāyāna Buddhist deity commonly worshipped in Theravāda (Way of the Elders) countries that base their worship on the Pāli canon and do not normally recognize the concept of *bodhisattvas*. In Sri Lanka he is known as Nātha-deva (often mistakenly confused with Maitreya, the Buddha yet to come).

Avalon, island to which Britain's legendary king Arthur was conveyed for the healing of his wounds after his final battle. It is first mentioned in Geoffrey of Monmouth's *Historia regum Britanniae* (*c.* 1136), while the same author's *Vita Merlini* (*c.* 1150) described it as "the island of apples ['Insula pomorum'], called fortunate." It was ruled by the enchantress Morgan le Fay and her eight sisters, all of them skilled in the healing arts.

Geoffrey may have been attempting to connect his "island of apples" with Celtic mythology's traditions of an elysium; and the name Avalon is certainly close to the Welsh word for apple, *afal.* Sir John Rhys, however (*Studies in the Arthurian Legend,* 1891), preferred to link the name Avalon with that of Aballach, a (hypothetical) dark Celtic divinity. Avalon has been identified with Glastonbury in Somerset, and this may be connected with Celtic legends about an "isle of glass" inhabited by deceased heroes. It is equally likely to have been an attempt by the monks of Glastonbury to exploit the Arthurian legend for the benefit of their own community. *See also* Arthurian legend.

Avalon Peninsula, peninsula in southeastern Newfoundland, Canada; it is joined to the main part of the island by a 4-mi- (6-km-) wide isthmus between Placentia and Trinity bays and extends for about 110 mi with a maximum width of 60 mi. Its high point is about 1,000 ft (300 m) on the Atlantic coast south of St. John's, and it is deeply indented by Conception Bay (north) and St. Mary's Bay (south). Probably first visited in 1497 by the navigator John Cabot, the peninsula was named after the Arthurian Isle of Avalon by Sir George Calvert (later Lord Baltimore), who obtained a charter for a part of it in 1623. In 1866 the first successful transatlantic cable was landed at Heart's Content on Trinity Bay, and in 1941, on board a ship anchored in Placentia Bay off Argentia, the Atlantic Charter was signed by Franklin D. Roosevelt and Sir Winston Churchill.

Offshore islands at Tors Cove, Avalon Peninsula, Newfoundland

C.L. Barron—Shostal/EB Inc.

The Avalon Peninsula, the most densely populated part of Newfoundland, has more than 40 percent of the province's population. Fishing, lumbering, and manufacturing are the chief sources of employment. Its major settlements, mostly around the northern coast, include St. John's (the provincial capital), Wabana, Harbour Grace, and Carbonear.

Avalonian orogeny, a mountain-building event that affected the eastern portion of the Appalachian Geosyncline in Late Precambrian time (575,000,000 to 600,000,000 years ago). Evidence for the orogeny consists of igneous intrusions, folding of strata, and the development of angular unconformities in the Avalon Peninsula of Newfoundland, the eastern portion of the Maritime Provinces of Canada, and the southeastern coastal area of New England. Thick sequences of Late Precambrian clastic sedimentary rocks in the Blue Ridge and Piedmont provinces of the central and southern Appalachians may also be a reflection of the Avalonian orogeny in these areas.

Avalos, Fernando Francesco de: *see* Pescara, Fernando Francesco de Avalos, marchese di.

Avanti, kingdom of ancient India, in the territory of present Madhya Pradesh state. The area was for a time part of the historic province of Mālwa. In *c.* 600 BC the Avanti capital was Māhiṣmatī (probably modern Godarpura on the Narmada River), but it was soon moved to Ujjayinī (near modern Ujjain). The kingdom was on the overland trade routes between northern and southern India and to the port of Bharukaccha (modern Bharuch) on the Arabian Sea.

By the lifetime of the Gautama Buddha (*c.* 563–*c.* 483 BC), Avanti was one of the four powers of northern India; it was strong enough at that time, under King Pradyota the Fierce, to threaten the empire of Magadha. In the same period there was also an Avanti-dakṣiṇāpatha (Sanskrit: Avanti of the South; perhaps modern Nimār), of which Māhiṣmatī may have been the capital.

In the 4th century BC Candragupta Maurya of Magadha conquered and annexed Avanti to his dominions. Ujjayinī, one of the seven holy cities of the Hindus, renowned for its beauty and wealth, became a centre of early Buddhism and of Jainism.

After 50 BC, in the Magadha Empire's decline, Avanti was fought over by the Śuṅgas, Andhrabhṛtyas, and Śakas; and in the 2nd century AD Ujjayinī, under Rudradāman I, was the prosperous capital of the western Śaka satrapy. About AD 390 Candra Gupta II (who may have been the fabled Vikramāditya, hero and patron of the poet Kālidāsa) expelled the Śakas and held court at Ujjayinī. The name of the Mālava tribe (which had moved to Avanti at an uncertain date) gradually replaced that of the Avantis as the designation of this land.

Avar, one of a people of undetermined origin and language, who, playing an important role in eastern Europe (6th–9th century), built an empire in the area between the Adriatic and the Baltic Sea and between the Elbe and the Dnepr rivers (6th–8th century). Inhabiting an area in the Caucasus region in 558, they intervened in Germanic tribal wars, allied with the Lombards to overthrow the Gepidae (allies of Byzantium), and established themselves in the Hungarian plain between the Danube and the Tisza rivers (550–575). This area became the centre of their empire, which reached its peak under its khagan Bayan at the end of the 6th century.

The Avars engaged in wars against Byzantium, almost occupying Constantinople in 626, and against the Merovingians; they also were partly responsible for the southward migration of the Serbs and the Croats. In the second half of the 7th century, internal discord resulted in the expulsion of about 9,000 dissidents from the Avar Empire. The state, further weakened by a revolt that was caused by the creation of the Bulgarian state in the Balkans (680), survived until 805 when it submitted to Charlemagne.

Avar-Ando-Dido languages, spoken in western and central Dagestan A.S.S.R. and in part of the Azerbaijan S.S.R., include the Avar language, the Andi languages (Andian, Botlikh, Godoberi, Chamalal, Bagulal, Tindi, Karata, and Akhvakh), and the Dido languages (Dido or Tsez, Khvarshi, Hinukh, Bezhta, and Hunzib or Kapucha). Avar, or Avarish, the only one in the group with a written form, is also used for intertribal communication by native users of the Andi and Dido languages. All of these languages are often classified together with those of the Lakk-Dargwa and Lezgian groups as the Dagestanian languages. *See also* Dagestanian languages.

Avataṃsaka-sūtra, in full MAHAVAIPULYA-BUDDHĀVATAṂSAKA-SŪTRA (Sanskrit: "Discourse on the Great and Vast Buddha Garland"), also called GARLAND SŪTRA, voluminous Mahāyāna Buddhist text that some consider the most sublime revelation of the Gautama Buddha's teachings and that scholars value for its revelations about the evolution of thought from primitive Buddhism to fully developed Mahāyāna.

The *sūtra* speaks of the deeds of the Buddha and of their resulting merits that blossom much like a garland of flowers. The discourse begins with the Buddha's Enlightenment, attended by an anthem chorus of *bodhisattvas* (those destined to become enlightened) and divine beings as numerous as the atoms of all the worlds. There follows a great assembly in the palace of the god Indra, whom Buddha instructs, and similar assemblies in other celestial regions accompanied by manifestations of great glory. In such settings the Buddha teaches that all beings have the Buddha nature, that all phenomena are mutually originating and interdependent, and that, finally, all is Buddha.

Several versions of the text seem to have existed, one reputedly containing as many as 100,000 verses. A translation entitled *Hua-yen Ching* first appeared in China around 400. There it gave rise in the 6th century to the Avataṃsaka school, otherwise known as the Hua-yen, or Hsien-shou, sect—a movement that reached its climax, as the Kegon school, in 8th-century Japan. The text has also given rise to a large number of commentaries.

avatar, Sanskrit AVATĀRA ("descent"), in Hinduism, the incarnation of a deity in human or animal form to counteract some particular evil in the world. The term usually refers to these 10 appearances of Vishnu: Matsya (fish), Kūrma (tortoise), Varāha (boar), Narasiṃha (half man, half lion), Vāmana (dwarf), Paraśurāma (Rāma with the axe), Rāma (hero of the *Rāmāyaṇa* epic), Krishna (the divine cowherd), Buddha, and Kalkin (the incarnation yet to come). The number of Vishnu's avatars is sometimes extended or their identities changed, according to local preferences. Thus, Krishna is in some areas elevated to the rank of a deity, and his half brother, Balarāma, included as an avatar. One formulation of the doctrine is given in the religious poem the *Bhagavadgītā*, when charioteer Lord Krishna tells Arjuna: "Whenever there is a decline of righteousness and rise of unrighteousness then I send forth Myself. For the protection of the good, for the destruction of the wicked, and for the establishment of righteousness, I come into being from age to age."

Ave Maria (Roman Catholic prayer): *see* Hail Mary.

Avebury, parish, Kennet district, county of Wiltshire, England, partly within one of the largest and best known prehistoric sites in Europe, enclosing 28.5 ac (11.5 ha). The village lies on the River Kennet at the foot of the rolling Marlborough Downs.

A Neolithic (New Stone Age) structure there consists of a circular bank of chalk 1,400 ft (425 m) in diameter and 20 ft high, faced by chalk blocks quarried from a ditch within, which is 30 ft deep. Within the bank, a circle of more than 100 sandstone (sarsen) pillars, up to 50 tons in weight, surrounds two smaller adjoining stone circles, each consisting of about 30 uprights and each approximately 350 ft in diameter, and part of a third smaller circle. At the centre of the southern small circle stood a tall stone surrounded by smaller boulders. The middle smaller circle contained a central U-shaped stone structure. Part of a northern circle, apparently demolished to make way for the main ditch and bank, has also been found. The Ring Stone, a huge stone perforated by a natural hole, stood within the earthworks and main stone circle at the southern entrance.

East of the entrance causeway, excavations have revealed a socket for a large timber post, and on either side there are additional stone holes. These suggest a continuation of a route called the Kennet Avenue into the interior of the great circle. The Kennet Avenue, 50 ft wide, consists of stones 80 ft apart, arranged in pairs. It linked Avebury with a temple, the Sanctuary, on Overton Hill, 1 mi (1.6 km) southeast. Burial sites were found beside four of the Kennet Avenue stones. The circles at Avebury and the wooden structure on Overton Hill were all probably built at the same time by Neolithic communities, one of whose habitation sites was crossed by the Kennet Avenue, but dates remain uncertain.

The village of Avebury and a museum now are run by the National Trust, a conservation body. Pop. (1971) 537.

Avedon, Richard (b. May 15, 1923, New York City), one of the leading photographers of the mid-20th century, noted for his portraits and fashion photographs.

He began to photograph at the age of 10 and was immediately drawn to portraiture. His first sitter was the Russian pianist-composer Sergey Rachmaninoff, who lived then in the same New York City apartment building as Avedon's grandparents.

Richard Avedon, 1970
Doon Arbus

Avedon studied photography in the U.S. merchant marine and at the New School for Social Research. He turned professional in 1945 and became a regular contributor to the fashion magazine *Harper's Bazaar* (1946–65) and later a staff photographer for *Vogue* (1966–70).

Avedon's fashion photographs are characterized by strong patterns of stark black and white that create effects of austere sophistication. In his portraits of celebrities, he emphasizes the sitter's personality with dramatic graphic effects. Many of his photographs were collected in *Observations* (1959), with a text by Truman Capote, *Nothing Personal* (1974), text by James Baldwin, *Portraits* (1976), and *Avedon: Photographs, 1947–1977* (1978).

Avedon also directed a number of special television programs and served as visual consultant for the motion picture *Funny Face* (1957), which was based on his own life.

Aveiro, capital and port, Aveiro district, northwestern Portugal, on a lagoon at the mouth of the Rio Vouga, south of Porto. During the 16th century it was a port for Newfoundland (Grand Bank) cod-fishing fleets but declined after 1575 when sand blocked its lagoon. Aveiro (the Roman Talabriga) became a city in 1759 and an episcopal see in 1774. In 1808 it was linked by canal (Barra Nova) to the Atlantic; its facilities were improved in 1933, but Aveiro remained basically a fishing port for tuna, mackerel, sardines, whiting, pargo, and sea bream. Industries produce footwear, furniture, and tomato paste. Salt is extracted from the lagoon, which has been partly diked and reclaimed for agriculture. The Convento de Jesus, now a regional museum, contains medieval art treasures, including spectacular examples of Portuguese woodworking (*talhadourada*). The Universidade de Aveiro (1973) is located there.

The district has an area of 1,046 sq mi (2,708 sq km). It produces agricultural products, wine, salt, and pine lumber. Coal and lead are mined in the area. Pop. (1981) city, 28,625; (1981 prelim.) district, 622,988.

Avellaneda, formerly BARRACAS AL SUR (Spanish: Huts to the South), *cabecera* (principal built-up area) and *partido* (political subdivision) of Gran (Greater) Buenos Aires, Argentina, immediately southeast of the city of Buenos Aires, in Buenos Aires province, on the Río de la Plata estuary. In the late 19th and early 20th centuries the area was an industrial slum, slaughterhouse, and port district, separated from Buenos Aires by the Río Riachuelo. Early settlers were Spanish, Italian, and Polish immigrants. The *partido* was formally established in 1852, when the governor of Buenos Aires province, Vicente Lôpez, expropriated land from the existing *partido* of Quilmes. The *cabecera* and *partido* were renamed in 1914 in honour of Nicholás Avellaneda, former president of Argentina (1874–80). The *partido* covers 21 sq mi (55 sq km) and is bordered by the *partidos* of Quilmes (southeast) and Lanús (southwest). Besides the *cabecera*, Avellaneda, the major localities are Sarandí, Wilde, and Gerli. The *partido* experienced rapid commercial development in the 20th century, based on the processing and marketing of hides, wool, and meat.

During the mid-1940s Avellaneda became a centre of Peronist activity. In 1945 the *descamisados* ("shirtless ones"), rural migrants to the area, demonstrated in Perón's behalf, demanding his return from exile.

Port facilities at Avellaneda are utilized mostly for coastal and river trade, and continue to concentrate mostly on the handling of wool, hides, and other animal produce. The density of settlement is the fifth highest among Gran Buenos Aires' *partidos*, and total population has remained about the same since 1960. Pop. (1980) *partido,* 334,145.

Avellino, city, capital of Avellino province, Campania region, southern Italy, on the Sabato River surrounded by the Apennines, east of Naples. Its name is derived from Abellinum, a stronghold of the Hirpini (an ancient Italic people) and later a Roman colony, the site of which lies just to the east of the modern city. Conquered by the Lombards in the 8th century and destroyed by the Holy Roman emperor Otto I the Great, Avellino passed in turn to the princely families of Balzo, Filangieri, and Caracciolo. In the rising of 1820, the first attempt was made to obtain a constitution from the king of Naples. The city became part of the Italian kingdom in 1860. Avellino is largely modern, for it has suffered from numerous earthquakes in its history, the most recent in 1980. Notable landmarks are the 12th-century cathedral, which was rebuilt in 1868; the provincial archaeological museum; and the ruins of the Lombard castle where in 1130 the antipope Anacletus II conceded the titles of king of Sicily, Apulia, Calabria, and Capua to the Norman Roger II of Altavilla, duke of Calabria. On the nearby Monte Vergine is the famous Benedictine monastery and sanctuary of Montevergine, founded in 1119 and visited by thousands of pilgrims annually.

An agricultural trade centre, Avellino manufactures food products, wine, felt hats, and woollen cloth. Sulfur is mined in the district. Pop. (1981 prelim.) mun., 56,120.

Avempace, also called IBN BĀJJAH, in full ABŪ BAKR MUḤAMMAD IBN YAḤYĀ IBN AS-SĀYIGH AT-TUJĪBĪ AL-ANDALUSĪ AS-SARAQUSṬĪ (b. *c.* 1095, Zaragoza, Spain—d. 1138/39, Fès, Mor.), earliest known representative in Spain of the Arabic Aristotelian–Neoplatonic philosophical tradition and forerunner of the polymath scholar Ibn Ṭufayl and of the philosopher Averroës.

Avempace's chief philosophical tenets seem to have included belief in the possibility that the human soul could become united with the Divine. This union was conceived as the final stage in an intellectual ascent beginning with the impressions of sense objects that consist of form and matter and rising through a hierarchy of spiritual forms (*i.e.,* forms containing less and less matter) to the Active Intellect, which is an emanation of the deity. Many Muslim biographers consider Avempace to have been an atheist.

Avempace's most important philosophical work is *Tadbīr al-mutawaḥḥid* ("The Regime of the Solitary"), which he was unable to complete before his death. He also wrote a number of songs and poems and a treatise on botany; he is known to have studied astronomy, medicine, and mathematics.

Aven, John Hamilton, Lord: *see* Hamilton, John Hamilton, 1st marquess of.

Avenarius, Richard (Heinrich Ludwig) (b. Nov. 19, 1843, Paris—d. Aug. 18, 1896, Zürich), German philosopher who taught at Zürich and founded the epistemological theory of knowledge known as empiriocriticism, according to which the major task of philosophy is to develop a "natural concept of the world" based on pure experience. Traditional metaphysicians believed in two categories of experience, inner and outer, and held that outer experience applies to sensory perception, which supplies raw data for the mind, and that inner experience applies to the processes that occur in the mind, such as conceptualization and abstraction. Avenarius, in his most noted work, *Kritik der reinen Erfahrung,* 2 vol. (1888–1900), argued that there is no distinction between inner and outer experience, but only pure experience.

Avencebrol (Hebrew poet): *see* Ibn Gabirol.

Avennasar (Muslim philosopher): *see* Fārābī, al-.

avens, any of various perennial, flowering plants of the genus *Geum,* within the rose family (Rosaceae).

Most of the approximately 50 species occur in the northern or southern temperate zones or in the Arctic. Several species are cultivated for their white, red, orange, or yellow flowers. As a rule the plants grow no more than 60 centimetres (2 feet) tall. The leaves are chiefly basal (*i.e.,* arise from the base of the stem) and are compound or deeply lobed or cut. The flowers, commonly 2–3 cm (about an inch) in diameter, are solitary or in small clusters.

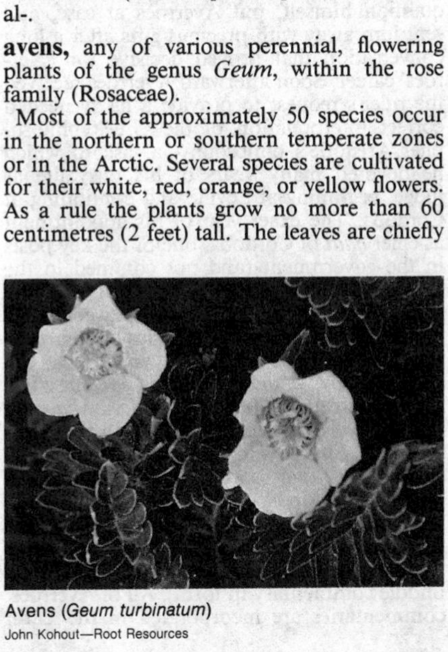

Avens (*Geum turbinatum*)
John Kohout—Root Resources

Aventinus, original name JOHANNES TURMAIR (b. July 4, 1477, Abensberg, Bavaria—d. Jan. 9, 1534, Regensburg), Humanist and historian sometimes called the "Bavarian Herodotus."

A student at the universities of Ingolstadt, Vienna, Kraków, and Paris, Aventinus served as tutor (1509–17) to the younger brothers of Duke William IV of Bavaria, during which

Aventinus, detail from an engraving by T. Stimmer
By courtesy of the Staatliche Graphische Sammlung, Munich

time he published a Latin grammar and a history of the Bavarian dukes. In his famous *Annales Boiorum* (1517–21; "Bavarian Annals"), his anticlericalism and attachment to the Holy Roman Empire are clearly revealed. Aventinus never fully accepted Protestantism. His sympathy with the reformers and their teachings and his open disapproval of monasticism, however, was enough to cause his imprisonment for a short time in 1528.

aventurine, also spelled AVANTURINE, either of two gem minerals, one a plagioclase feldspar (*see* sunstone) and the other quartz. Both have a sparkling reflection from oriented minute inclusions of mica or hematite.

Most aventurine quartz is silvery, yellow, reddish brown, or green. Extensive beds in mica schist occur in the Urals and near Kolivan, in the Soviet Union. Green aventurine, coloured by a chrome mica, has been found in the state of Tamil Nadu (formerly Madras), India; in China; and in Rutland, Vt. Aventurine quartz is used for jewelry, for vases and bowls (sometimes very large), and for other ornamental objects.

aventurine (Japanese lacquerwork): *see* nashiji.

Avenzoar: *see* Ibn Zuhr.

ʿavera, also spelled AVERAH (Hebrew: "a crossing over"), plural ʿAVEROT, or AVEROTH, in Judaism, a moral transgression (or sin) against God or man. It may vary from grievous to slight and is the opposite of *mitzwa* (commandment), understood in the broad sense of any good deed. Whereas Jews are taught to prefer death to the willful commission of any of the three major *ʿaverot* (idolatry, the shedding of innocent blood, and adultery and incest), they may commit lesser *ʿaverot* (*e.g.,* violate the sabbath) to preserve human life. On Yom Kippur, the Day of Atonement, one atones only for those *ʿaverot* against God, while those against a fellow man must be remedied in person as soon as possible.

average, in maritime law, loss or damage, less than total, to maritime property (a ship or its cargo), caused by the perils of the sea. An average may be particular or general. A particular average is one that is borne by the owner of the lost or damaged property (unless he was insured against the risk). A general average is one that is borne in common by the owners of all the property engaged in the venture.

The basic idea of general average (the more important form) pertains to property that is voluntarily sacrificed to preserve the remainder of the property from destruction (as by throwing cargo overboard or cutting away masts to preserve the ship in a storm); the owners of the property saved must contribute to the owners of the property sacrificed in such an amount that all will have contributed proportionately to the aggregate value of the lost property.

Such a custom of contribution was firmly established in Roman law by the 6th century AD. What is now called the law of general average thus has an ancient lineage, and the doctrine has been admitted by all seafaring nations as part of their maritime laws. Repeated attempts to draft international conventions in the field of general average, however, have met with failure.

averah (Judaism): *see* ʿavera.

Averescu, Alexandru (b. April 22, 1859, Izmail, Bessarabia, Moldavia, Ottoman Empire—d. Oct. 3, 1938, Bucharest), military leader and politician who three times served as premier of Romania and was the chief executor of the official suppression of the peasant revolt of 1907.

After serving in the Romanian war of independence against Turkey (Russo-Turkish War, 1877–78), Averescu was sent to Italy for military training. As an army general and newly appointed minister of war during the peasant uprising of March–April 1907, he balanced the land reforms with a ruthless campaign of suppression that within three days claimed the lives of perhaps 10,000 peasants. As Romanian chief of staff, he directed military operations against Bulgaria in the Second Balkan War (1913); and during World War I he conducted the successful resistance to the Germans at Mărăşeşti (July 1917).

The idol of the soldiery, Averescu was appointed premier in March 1918 to conclude peace with the Central Powers (the coalition of Germany, Austria-Hungary, Bulgaria, and Turkey), but he resigned before the Treaty of Bucharest was concluded with them in May 1918. Later, as head of the newly created People's Party, he again served as premier (March 1920–December 1921), introducing a much diluted measure of the long-awaited land redistribution. Between March 1926 and June 1927, Averescu again formed a government. His domestic policies were generally conservative and authoritarian; his foreign policies favoured Italian interests.

Averlino, Antonio di Pietro: *see* Filarete.

Averno, Lake of, Italian LAGO D'AVERNO, Latin LACUS AVERNUS, crater lake in Napoli province, Campania region, southern Italy, in the Campi Flegrei volcanic region, west of Naples. It is 7 ft (2 m) above sea level, 118 ft deep, and nearly 2 mi (more than 3 km) in circumference, with no natural outlet. Its Greek name, Aornos, was interpreted as meaning "without birds," giving rise to the legend that no bird could fly across it and live because of its poisonous sulfurous vapours. Surrounded by dense forests in ancient times, it was represented by the poet Virgil as the entrance to Hades (hell). The Carthaginian general Hannibal made a pilgrimage to it in 214 BC. Agrippa, the Roman statesman, in 37 BC cut down the forest (now replaced by vineyards) and converted the lake into a naval harbour, the Portus Iulius, which was linked to the sea by a canal via the Lago di Lucrino and to Cumae by a tunnel more than 1/2 mi long, the world's first major road tunnel. The canal was soon blocked because of a gradual rise of the shore, but the tunnel, now called the Grotta di Cocceio (or della Pace), remained usable until it was damaged during World War II. The so-called Grotta (or pseudo-Grotta) della Sibilla is a rock-cut passage, possibly part of the works connected with the naval harbour. Impressive Roman ruins include the remains of baths, temples, and villas.

Consult the INDEX *first*

ʿaverot, also spelled AVEROTH (Judaism): *see* ʿavera.

Averroës, medieval Latin AVERRHOËS, also called IBN RUSHD, Arabic in full ABŪ AL-WALĪD MUḤAMMAD IBN AḤMAD IBN MUḤAMMAD IBN RUSHD (b. 1126, Córdoba—d. 1198, Marrakech, Almohad Empire), influential Islāmic religious philosopher who integrated Islāmic traditions and Greek thought. At the request of the caliph Ibn aṭ-Ṭufayl he produced a series of summaries and commentaries on most of Aristotle's works (1162–95) and on Plato's *Republic*, which exerted considerable influence for centuries. He wrote the *Decisive Treatise on the Agreement Between Religious Law and Philosophy (Faṣl), Examination of the Methods of Proof Concerning the Doctrines of Religion (Manāhij),* and *The Incoherence of the Incoherence (Tahāfut) at-tahāfut*, all in defense of the philosophical study of religion against the theologians (1179–80).

Early life. Averroës was born into a distinguished family of jurists at Córdoba and died at Marrakesh, the North African capital of the Almohad (al-Muwaḥḥidūn) dynasty. Thoroughly versed in the traditional Muslim sciences (especially exegesis of the Qurʾān—Islāmic scripture—and Ḥadīth, or Traditions, and *fiqh*, or Law), trained in medicine, and accomplished in philosophy, Averroës rose to be chief *qāḍī* (judge) of Córdoba (Qurṭubah), an office also held by his grandfather (of the same name) under the Almoravids (al-Murābiṭūn). After the death of the philosopher Ibn Ṭufayl, Averroës succeeded him as personal physician to the caliphs Abū Yaʿqūb Yūsuf in 1182 and his son Abū Yūsuf Yaʿqūb in 1184. In 1169 Ibn Ṭufayl introduced Averroës to Abū Yaʿqūb, who, himself a keen student of philosophy, frightened Averroës with a question concerning whether the heavens were created or not. The caliph answered the question himself, put Averroës at ease, and sent him away with precious gifts after a long conversation that proved decisive for Averroës' career. Soon afterward Averroës received the ruler's request to provide a badly needed correct interpretation of the Greek philosopher Aristotle's philosophy, a task to which he devoted many years of his busy life as judge, beginning at Seville and continuing at Córdoba. The exact year of his appointment as chief *qāḍī* of Córdoba, one of the key posts in the government (and not confined to the administration of justice), is not known.

Commentaries on Aristotle. Between 1169 and 1195 Averroës wrote a series of commentaries on most of Aristotle's works (*e.g.*, the *Organon, De anima, Physica, Metaphysica, De partibus animalium, Parva naturalia, Meteorologica, Rhetorica, Poetica*, and the *Nicomachean Ethics*). He wrote summaries, and middle and long commentaries—often two or all three kinds on the same work. Aristotle's *Politica* was inaccessible to Averroës; therefore he wrote a commentary on Plato's *Republic* (which is both a paraphrase and a middle commentary in form). All of Averroës' commentaries are incorporated in the Latin version of Aristotle's complete works. They are extant in the Arabic original or Hebrew translations or both, and some of these translations serve in place of the presumably lost Arabic originals; *e.g.*, the important commentaries on Aristotle's *Nicomachean Ethics* and on Plato's *Republic*.

Averroës' commentaries exerted considerable influence on Jews and Christians in the following centuries. His clear, penetrating mind enabled him to present competently Aristotle's thought and to add considerably to its understanding. He ably and critically used the classical commentators Themistius and Alexander of Aphrodisias and the *falāsifah* (Muslim philosophers) al-Fārābī, Avicenna (Ibn Sīnā), and his own countryman Avempace (Ibn Bājjah). In commenting on Aristotle's treatises on the natural sciences, Averroës showed considerable power of observation.

Averroës' defense of philosophy. His own first work is on *General Medicine* (*Kulliyāt*, Latin *Colliget*), written between 1162 and 1169. Only a few of his legal writings and none of his theological writings are preserved. Undoubtedly his most important writings are three closely connected religious–philosophical polemical treatises, composed in the years 1179 and 1180: the *Faṣl* with its *Appendix: Manāhij*; and *Tahāfut at-tahāfut* in defense of philosophy. In the two first named Averroës stakes a bold claim: only the metaphysician employing certain proof (syllogism) is capable and competent (as well as obliged) to interpret the doctrines contained in the prophetically revealed law (Sharʿ or Sharīʿah), and not the Muslim *mutakallimūn* (dialectic theologians), who rely on dialectical arguments. To establish the true, inner meaning of religious beliefs and convictions is the aim of philosophy in its quest for truth. This inner meaning must not be divulged to the masses, who must accept the plain, external meaning of Scripture contained in stories, similes, and metaphors. Averroës applied Aristotle's three arguments (demonstrative, dialectical, and persuasive—*i.e.*, rhetorical and poetical) to the philosophers, the theologians, and the masses. The third work is devoted to a defense of philosophy against his predecessor al-Ghazālī's telling attack directed against Avicenna and al-Qārābī in particular. Spirited and successful as Averroës' defense was, it could not restore philosophy to its former position, quite apart from the fact that the atmosphere in Muslim Spain and North Africa was most unfavourable to the unhindered pursuit of speculation. As a result of the reforming activity of Ibn Tūmart (*c.* 1078–1130), aimed at restoring pure monotheism, power was wrested from the ruling Almoravids, and the new Berber dynasty of the Almohads was founded, under whom Averroës served. In jurisprudence the emphasis then shifted from the practical application of Muslim law by appeal to previous authority to an equal stress on the study of its principles and the revival of independent legal decision on the basis of Ibn Tūmart's teaching. Of perhaps even more far-reaching significance was Ibn Jūmart's idea of instructing the heretofore ignorant masses in the plain meaning of the Sharīʿah so that practice would be informed with knowledge. These developments were accompanied by the encouragement of the *falāsifah*—"those who," according to Averroës' *Faṣl*, "follow the way of speculation and are eager for a knowledge of the truth"—to apply demonstrative arguments to the interpretation of the theoretical teaching of the Sharīʿah. But with the hands of both jurists and theologians thus strengthened, Averroës' defense of philosophy continued to be conducted within an unfavourable atmosphere.

Averroës himself acknowledged the support of Abū Yaʿqūb, to whom he dedicated his *Commentary on Plato's Republic*. Yet Averroës pursued his philosophical quest in the face of strong opposition from the *mutakalli-*

mūn, who, together with the jurists, occupied a position of eminence and of great influence over the fanatical masses. This may explain why he suddenly fell from grace when Abū Yūsuf—on the occasion of a *jihād* (holy war) against Christian Spain—dismissed him from high office and banished him to Lucena in 1195. To appease the theologians in this way at a time when the caliph needed the undivided loyalty and support of the people seems a more convincing reason than what the Arabic sources tell us (attacks on Averroës by the mob, probably at the instigation of jurists and theologians). But Averroës' disgrace was only short-lived—though long enough to cause him acute suffering—since the caliph recalled Averroës to his presence after his return to Marrakesh. After his death, Averroës was first buried at Marrakesh, and later his body was transferred to the family tomb at Córdoba.

It is not rare in the history of Islām that the rulers' private attachment to philosophy and their friendship with philosophers goes hand in hand with official disapproval of philosophy and persecution of its adherents, accompanied by the burning of their philosophical writings and the prohibition of the study of secular sciences other than those required for the observance of the religious law. Without caliphal encouragement Averroës could hardly have persisted all his life in his fight for philosophy against the theologians, as reflected in his *Commentary on Plato's Republic*, in such works as the *Faṣl* and *Tahāfut at-tahāfut*, and in original philosophical treatises (*e.g.*, about the union of the active intellect with the human intellect). It is likely that the gradual estrangement of his two masters and patrons from Ibn Tūmart's theology and their preoccupation with Islāmic law also helped him. That Averroës found it difficult to pursue his philosophical studies alongside the conscientious performance of his official duties he himself reveals in a few remarks scattered over his commentaries; *e.g.*, in that on Aristotle's *De partibus animalium*.

Contents and significance of works. To arrive at a balanced appraisal of Averroës' thought it is essential to view his literary work as a whole. In particular, a comparison of his religious–philosophical treatises with his *Commentary on Plato's Republic* shows the basic unity of his attitude to the Sharīʿah dictated by Islām and therefore determining his attitude to philosophy, more precisely to the *nomos*, the law of Plato's philosopher-king. It will then become apparent that there is only one truth for Averroës, that of the religious law, which is the same truth that the metaphysician is seeking. The theory of the double truth was definitely not formulated by Averroës, but rather by the Latin Averroists. Nor is it justifiable to say that philosophy is for the metaphysician what religion is for the masses. Averroës stated explicitly and unequivocally that religion is for all three classes; that the contents of the Sharīʿah are the whole and only truth for all believers; and that religion's teachings about reward and punishment and the hereafter must be accepted in their plain meaning by the elite no less than by the masses. The philosopher must choose the best religion, which, for a Muslim, is Islām as preached by Muḥammad, the last of the prophets, just as Christianity was the best religion at the time of Jesus, and Judaism at the time of Moses.

It is significant that Averroës could say in his *Commentary on Plato's Republic* that religious law and philosophy have the same aim and in the *Faṣl* that "philosophy is the companion and foster-sister of the Sharīʿah." Accepting Aristotle's division of philosophy into theoretical (physics and metaphysics) and practical (ethics and politics), he finds that the Sharīʿah teaches both to perfection: abstract knowledge commanded as the perception of God, and practice—the ethical virtues the law enjoins (*Commentary on Plato's Republic*). In the *Tahāfut* he maintains that "the religious laws conform to the truth and impart a knowledge of those actions by which the happiness of the whole creation is guaranteed." There is no reason to question the sincerity of Averroës. These statements reflect the same attitude to law and the same emphasis on happiness. Happiness as the highest good is the aim of political science. As a Muslim, Averroës insists on the attainment of happiness in this and the next life by all believers. This is, however, qualified by Averroës as the disciple of Plato: the highest intellectual perfection is reserved for the metaphysician, as in Plato's ideal state. But the Muslim's ideal state provides for the happiness of the masses as well because of its prophetically revealed law, which is superior to the Greek *nomos* (law) for this reason. The philosopher Averroës distinguishes between degrees of happiness and assigns every believer the happiness that corresponds to his intellectual capacity. He takes Plato to task for his neglect of the third estate because Averroës believes that everyone is entitled to his share of happiness. Only the Sharīʿah of Islām cares for all believers. It legitimates speculation because it demands that the believer should know God. This knowledge is accessible to the naive believer in metaphors, the inner meaning of which is intelligible only to the metaphysician with the help of demonstration. On this point all *falāsifah* are agreed, and all recognize the excellence of the Sharīʿah stemming from its divinely revealed character. But only Averroës insists on its superiority over the *nomos*.

Insisting on the prerogative of the metaphysician—understood as a duty laid upon him by God—to interpret the doctrines of religion in the form of right beliefs and convictions (like Plato's philosopher-king), he admits that the Sharīʿah contains teachings that surpass human understanding but that must be accepted by all believers because they contain divinely revealed truths. The philosopher is definitely bound by the religious law just as much as the masses and the theologians, who occupy a position somewhere in between. In his search for truth the metaphysician is bound by Arabic usage, as is the jurist in his legal interpretations, though the jurist uses subjective reasoning only, in contrast to the metaphysician's certain proof. This means that the philosopher is not bound to accept what is contradicted by demonstration. He can, thus, abandon belief in the creation out of nothing since Aristotle demonstrated the eternity of matter. Hence creation is a continuing process. Averroës sought justification for such an attitude in the fact that a Muslim is bound only by consensus (*ijmāʿ*) of the learned in a strictly legal context where actual laws and regulations are concerned. Yet, since there is no consensus on certain theoretical statements, such as creation, he is not bound to conform. Similarly, anthropomorphism is unacceptable, and metaphorical interpretation of those passages in Scripture that describe God in bodily terms is necessary. And the question whether God knows only the universals, but not the particulars, is neatly parried by Averroës in his statement that God has knowledge of particulars but that his knowledge is different from human knowledge. These few examples suffice to indicate that ambiguities and inconsistencies are not absent in Averroës' statements.

The *Commentary on Plato's Republic* reveals a side of Averroës that is not to be found in his other commentaries. While he carried on a long tradition of attempted synthesis between religious law and Greek philosophy, he went beyond his predecessors in spite of large-scale dependence upon them. He made Plato's political philosophy, modified by Aristotle, his own and considered it valid for the Islāmic state as well. Consequently, he applied Platonic ideas to the contemporary Almoravid and Almohad states in a sustained critique in Platonic terms, convinced that if the philosopher cannot rule, he must try to influence policy in the direction of the ideal state. For Plato's ideal state is the best after the ideal state of Islām based on and centred in the Sharīʿah as the ideal constitution. Thus, he regrets the position of women in Islām compared with their civic equality in Plato's *Republic*. That women are used only for childbearing and the rearing of offspring is detrimental to the economy and responsible for the poverty of the state. This is most unorthodox.

Of greater importance is his acceptance of Plato's idea of the transformation and deterioration of the ideal, perfect state into the four imperfect states. Muʿāwiyah I, who in Muslim tradition perverted the ideal state of the first four caliphs into a dynastic power state, is viewed by Averroës in the Platonic sense as having turned the ideal state into a timocracy—a government based on love of honour. Similarly, the Almoravid and Almohad states are shown to have deteriorated from a state that resembled the original perfect Sharīʿah state into timocracy, oligarchy, democracy, and tyranny. Averroës here combines Islāmic notions with Platonic concepts. In the same vein he likens the false philosophers of his time, and especially the *mutakallimūn*, to Plato's sophists. In declaring them a real danger to the purity of Islām and to the security of the state, he appeals to the ruling power to forbid dialectical theologians to explain their beliefs and convictions to the masses, thus confusing them and causing heresy, schism, and unbelief. The study of *The Republic* and the *Nicomachean Ethics* enabled the *falāsifah* to see more clearly the political character and content of the Sharīʿah in the context of the classical Muslim theory of the religious and political unity of Islām.

Leaning heavily on the treatment of Plato's political philosophy by al-Fārābī, a 10th-century philosopher, Averroës looks at *The Republic* with the eyes of Aristotle, whose *Nicomachean Ethics* constitutes for Averroës the first, theoretical part of political science. He is, therefore, only interested in Plato's theoretical statements. Thus he concentrates on a detailed commentary on Books II–IX of *The Republic* and ignores Plato's dialectical statements and especially his tales and myths, principally the myth of Er. He explains Plato, whose *Laws* and *Politikos* he also knows and uses, with the help, and in the light, of Aristotle's *Analytica posteriora, De anima, Physica,* and *Nicomachean Ethics.* Naturally, Greek pagan ideas and institutions are replaced by Islāmic ones. Thus Plato's criticism of poetry (Homer) is applied to Arab pre-Islāmic poetry, which he condemns.

Averroës sees much common ground between the Sharīʿah and Plato's general laws (interpreted with the help of Aristotle), notwithstanding his conviction that the Sharīʿah is superior to the *nomos.* He accepts al-Fārābī's equation of Plato's philosopher-king with the Islāmic *imām*, or leader and lawgiver, but leaves it open whether the ideal ruler must also be a prophet. The reason for this may well be that, as a sincere Muslim, Averroës holds that Muḥammad was "the seal of the prophets" who promulgated the divinely revealed Sharīʿah once and for all. Moreover, Averroës exempts Muḥammad from the general run of prophets, thus clearly rejecting the psychological explanation of prophecy through the theory of emanation adopted by the other *falāsifah.* No trace of this theory can be discovered in Averroës' writings, just as his theory of the intellect is strictly and purely Aristotelian and free from the theory of emanation. In conclusion, it may be reiterated that the unity of outlook in Averroës' religious–philosophical writings and his commentary on *The Republic* gives his political philosophy a distinctly Islāmic character and tone, thereby adding to his significance as a religious philosopher. (E.I.J.R.)

BIBLIOGRAPHY. Léon Gauthier, *Ibn Rochd (Averroès)* (1948), a balanced overall picture of his life and works, and *La Théorie d'Ibn Rochd (Averroès) sur les rapports de la religion et de la philosophie* (1909), an indispensable work that was the basis for the author's later study cited above; G.F. Hourani, *(Averroës) On the Harmony of Religion and Philosophy* (Eng. trans. 1961); E.I.J. Rosenthal, "The Place of Politics in the Philosophy of Ibn Rushd," *Bulletin of the School of Oriental and African Studies,* vol. 15, no. 2 (1953), a discussion of Averroës' political philosophy within the context of his life and writings reprinted in *Studia Semitica et Orientalia* II (1971), *Averroës' Commentary on Plato's Republic,* 3rd ed. (1969), Hebrew text, Eng. trans. and notes, giving Averroës' Greek and Arabic sources, and "Ibn Rushd: The Consummation," in *Political Thought in Medieval Islam,* 3rd ed., ch. 9 (1968); S. van den Bergh, *Averroës' Tahāfut altahāfut: The Incoherence of the Incoherence,* 2 vol. (1954), Eng. trans. with important notes tracing Averroës' sources, especially Aristotle.

Averroism, Latin: *see* Latin Averroism.

Aversa, town and episcopal see, Caserta province, Campania region, southern Italy, in the fertile Campanian plain north of Naples. Founded in 1030 by the Normans, who made it the capital of the first Norman county in Italy, it became a centre of culture, noted for its grammar schools, and a diocese of the Holy See. It became part of the Kingdom of Italy in 1860. Notable landmarks include the 11th-century cathedral and the Norman castle, both rebuilt in the 18th century. The composer Domenico Cimarosa was born at Aversa in 1749.

Aversa is an important rail junction; its main industries are shoemaking, agriculture, and viticulture; and it markets asprino wine, mozzarella cheese, and dairy produce. Pop. (1981 prelim.) mun., 50,525.

aversion therapy, psychotherapy designed to cause a patient to reduce or avoid an undesirable behaviour pattern by conditioning him to associate the behaviour with an undesirable stimulus. The chief stimuli used in the therapy are electrical and chemical. In the electrical therapy, the patient is given a lightly painful shock whenever the undesirable behaviour is aroused; this method has been used in the treatment of sexual deviations. In the chemical therapy, the patient is given a drug that produces unpleasant effects, such as nausea, when combined with the undesirable behaviour; this method has been common in the treatment of alcoholism, the therapeutic drug and the alcohol together causing the nausea.

Averulino, Antonio di Pietro: *see* Filarete.

Avery, John (b. *c.* 1653, Cat Down, Plymouth, Eng.—d. after 1696, Bideford, Devonshire), one of Britain's most renowned pirates of the late 17th century, the model for Daniel Defoe's hero in *Life, Adventures, and Pyracies, of the Famous Captain Singleton* (1720).

Avery served in the Royal Navy and on merchantmen, as well as on buccaneer and slave ships, before beginning a life of piracy about 1691. In 1694, joining a ship in the service of Spain, he helped plot a mutiny and was elected captain of his new pirate ship, renamed the "Fancy." During the following year, after preying on various ships en route around Africa, he reached the mouth of the Red Sea, where he established himself and levied tolls on all ships, especially those of Mughal India and the East India Company, that passed in or out. The following year he sailed to the West Indies, where his ship was either sold or driven ashore in a storm and destroyed (various stories were told). Thereafter the crew broke up, several being captured and hanged; and Avery returned to England, where he was cheated by some Bristol merchants and subsequently died in poverty.

Avery, Milton (Clark) (b. March 7, 1893, Altmar, N.Y., U.S.—d. Jan. 3, 1965, New York City), painter noted in his later years for depicting the human figure as a contoured flat pattern in vivid colours. In 1905 his family moved to Hartford, Conn., where he studied briefly (1913) at the League of Art Students, but he was largely self-taught. He presented his first one-man show in New York City in 1928.

Milton Avery, photograph by Arnold Newman, 1961
© Arnold Newman

Avery painted many landscapes, particularly seashores; his daughter, March, was a frequent subject. His treatment of these themes is reminiscent of the French painter Henri Matisse in the use of colour, elimination of detail, and depiction of the figure and landscape as interwoven flat shapes.

Avery, Oswald (Theodore) (b. Oct. 21, 1877, Halifax, Nova Scotia, Can.—d. Feb. 20, 1955, Nashville, Tenn., U.S.), bacteriologist whose research on pneumococcus bacteria made him one of the founders of immunochemistry and laid the foundation for later discoveries that launched the science of molecular genetics.

In 1913 Avery joined the staff of the Rockefeller Institute Hospital, New York City, where he began to take part in the research then being done on lobar pneumonia. One of the first developments of the investigation was the discovery that the bacteria causing pneumonia produce a capsular envelope consisting of a specific chemical substance, later shown to be a polysaccharide (complex carbohydrate). Avery demonstrated that the polysaccharide envelope varied according to the virulence and immunological specificity of the bacteria. This research established the fact that virulence and immunity could be analyzed in terms of the biochemical components of cells and thus helped to establish the basis for immunochemistry.

Later, Avery investigated a phenomenon known as transformation, a process by which the formation of capsules in bacteria lacking them could be brought about by exposing the cells to minute amounts of material from capsule-containing bacteria. This change was heritable—*i.e.,* it was passed on to succeeding generations of the transformed cells. Avery and his coworkers reported in 1944 that the substance that caused the transformation was deoxyribonucleic acid (DNA), implicating it as the basic genetic material of the cell. Until this time, most authorities had expected that proteins would turn out to be the genetic material. Avery's discovery thus opened the door to the elucidation of the genetic code.

Avery, Samuel Putnam (b. March 17, 1822, New York City—d. Aug. 11, 1904, New York City), artist, connoisseur, art dealer, and philanthropist best remembered for his patronage of arts and letters.

Beginning as an engraver on copper (he worked for the American Bank Note Company), he became a skilled wood engraver and illustrated numerous books. In 1865 he established himself as an art dealer. Two years later he was U.S. commissioner at the International Exposition at Paris. In memory of his son, a distinguished architect, he established the Avery architectural library at Columbia University and, in memory of a daughter, the Teachers' College library, also at Columbia. He was one of the founders of the Metropolitan Museum of Art in New York, and he presented a collection of prints to the New York Public Library. Avery Hall, commemorating both father and son, was built at Columbia to house a valuable collection of works on architecture and decorative art.

The diaries of the father, edited by Madeleine Fidell Beaufort, and others, were published in 1979.

Aves: *see* bird.

Aves Island, Spanish ISLA AVES, or ISLOTA AVES (Caribbean Sea): *see* Bird Island.

Avesta, industrial town, in the southeastern corner of the *län* (county) of Kopparberg, central Sweden, on Dalälven (Dal River) at the Storforsen and Lillforsen rapids. It lies within the ore-producing Bergslagen region. Avesta was first chartered in 1641 but lost its charter privileges in 1686 and was not rechartered until 1919. Its copper refinery began operation in 1636; in 1644 a mint was established in the town that produced all of Sweden's copper coins until 1831. The first ironworks opened in 1823, and iron and steel quickly displaced copper as the major industry. Today Avesta's steelworks manufacture stainless steel with a worldwide reputation. Pop. (1983 est.) mun., 25,750.

Avesta, also called ZEND-AVESTA, sacred book of Zoroastrianism containing its cosmogony, law, and liturgy, the teachings of the prophet Zoroaster (Zarathushtra). The extant Avesta is all that remains of a much larger body of scripture, apparently Zoroaster's transformation of a very ancient tradition. The voluminous manuscripts of the original are said to have been destroyed when Alexander the Great conquered Persia. The present Avesta was assembled from remnants and standardized under the Sāsānian kings (3rd–7th century AD).

The Avesta is in five parts. Its religious core is a collection of songs or hymns, the *Gāthās*, thought to be in the main the very words of Zoroaster. They form a middle section of the chief liturgical part of the canon, the *Yasna,* which contains the rite of the preparation and sacrifice of *haoma.* The *Visp-rat* is a lesser liturgical scripture, containing homages to a number of Zoroastrian spiritual leaders. The *Vendidad*, or *Vidēvdāt*, is the main source for Zoroastrian law, both ritual and civil. It also gives an account of creation and the first man, Yima. The *Yasht*s are 21 hymns, rich in myth, to various *yazata*s (angels) and ancient heroes. The *Khūrda Avesta* (or Little Avesta) is a group of minor texts, hymns, and prayers for specific occasions.

Zend-Avesta literally means "interpretation of the Avesta." It originally referred to the commonly used Pahlavi translation but has often been used as the title of Western translations.

Avestan alphabet: *see* Pahlavi alphabet.

Avestan language, also called (incorrectly) ZEND LANGUAGE, eastern Iranian language of the Avesta, the sacred book of Zoroastrianism. Avestan falls into two strata, the older being that of the *Gāthās*, which reflects a linguistic stage (dating from *c.* 600 BC) close to that of

Vedic Sanskrit in India. The greater part of the Avesta is written in a more recent form of the language and shows gradual simplification and variation in grammatical forms. When the canon of the Avesta was being fixed (4th to 6th century AD), Avestan was a dead language known only to priests. It probably ceased to be used as an everyday spoken tongue *c.* 400 BC, but the sacred word was passed down through oral tradition. Avestan was written in a script evolved from late Pahlavi writing, which, in turn, derived from Aramaic.

Aveyron, *département,* Midi-Pyrénées region, southern France, encompassing the southwest sector of the Massif Central; formed from the old province of Guyenne, it has an area of 3,371 sq mi (8,735 sq km) comprising a series of crystalline and limestone plateaus, extending westward from the Cévennes across the Causses to the Aquitaine lowlands, and bordered (northeast) by the volcanic highlands of Aubrac. The plateaus, with large areas between 2,500 and 4,000 ft (750 and 1,200 m), are deeply cut by the Lot, Aveyron, and Tarn rivers, which often flow in gorges 1,500 ft deep. Along the margins softer rock has been hollowed into warm, sheltered depressions where, as in the low valleys, orchards and vineyards prevail. The climate is wetter and more severe on the plateaus, which are pastoral. The lower plateaus of the west, traditionally devoted to cultivation, were known as *chataigneraies* (from chestnut plantings) or *ségalas* (planted to rye). Now their small enclosed fields support cattle, fodder, and potatoes. Some wheat is grown in the dry, thin soil of the Causses, but sheep dominate the economy, their milk being used for making Roquefort cheese, matured in limestone caves. Millau is a glove-making centre. In the vicinity of Aubin and Décazeville are a small coalfield and some iron, zinc, glass, and chemical works. The valley of the Truyère is the site of a hydroelectric power plant. The Tarn gorges attract tourists.

Aveyron is rich in dolmens and was settled in Roman times. Unremitting grazing and deforestation have desolated much of the region, and since 1900 depopulation has been more rapid there than in most of rural France.

The *département* of Aveyron corresponds roughly to the ancient countship of Rouergue, which was united to Toulouse in the 11th century, and its history is also linked with Guyenne. After the devastation of the Albigensian Crusade, new colonists were implanted in Aveyron, and among the towns (*bastides*) established were Villefranche and Sauveterre. In the north the monastery and Romanesque church of Conques are among the architectural treasures of France. Espalion, Najac, and Sylvanès also have noteworthy castles and churches.

Rodez, the capital, on the Aveyron River; Millau, chief town for the Causses, at the outlet of the Tarn gorges; and Villefranche-de-Rouergue give their names to the three *arrondissements.* The court of appeal is at Montpellier, the educational centre at Toulouse. Pop. (1982) 278,654.

Limestone gorges at Causse Méjean in Aveyron *département*, France

Editions "La Cigogne"—Hachette

Avezzano, town, L'Aquila province, Abruzzi region, central Italy, south of L'Aquila city. Built on the reclaimed Fucino Basin (*q.v.*), it was destroyed in 1915 by an earthquake, of which it was the epicentre, and was subsequently rebuilt. In World War II it was heavily damaged. Only the ruins remain of the castle of the Orsini family (15th century). It is now an agricultural centre, producing timber and food products. Pop. (1981 prelim.) mun., 33,509.

avian pneumoencephalitis (bird disease): *see* Newcastle disease.

aviary, a structure for the keeping of captive birds, usually spacious enough for the aviculturist to enter. Aviaries range from small enclosures a metre or so on a side to large flight cages 30 metres (100 feet) or more long and as much as 15 metres (50 feet) high. Enclosures for birds that fly only little or weakly (*e.g.,* rails, pheasants) are often only one metre high. The private aviary often consists of a room or porch set aside for birds. In cold climates the aviary is usually enclosed and heated, depending on the types of birds being maintained, though sometimes the birds are merely driven into a smaller, heated enclosure at night. Although wire is usually less attractive than glass, it is usually employed for the sides, and sometimes for the roof, of the enclosure, because many birds tend to injure themselves by flying against glass.

Most aviculturists prefer to place birds in natural, planted surroundings. Depending on the bird species, plants can usually be chosen that are compatible with captive birds, the density and type of birds being critical factors. Large arboreal birds may break plants by their weight, and some others may destroy plants by eating the leaves. Droppings are ruinous for most plants, but their impingement on leaves can often be prevented by careful placement of perches.

Many aviaries are maintained for pleasure by private aviculturists; others, especially the large ones, are found in zoos—where their primary purpose is to exhibit birds—or in research institutions.

Avicebron (Hebrew poet): *see* Ibn Gabirol.

Avicenna, Arabic IBN SĪNĀ, in full ABŪ ʿALĪ AL-ḤUSAYN IBN ʿABD ALLĀH IBN SĪNĀ (b. 980, Bukhara, Iran—d. 1037, Hamadan), Persian physician, the most famous and influential of the philosopher-scientists of Islām. He was particularly noted for his contributions in the fields of Aristotelian philosophy and medicine. He composed the *Kitāb ash-shifāʾ* ("Book of Healing"), a vast philosophical and scientific encyclopaedia, and the *Canon of Medicine,* which is among the most famous books in the history of medicine.

Early years. Avicenna, a Persian who spent his whole life in the eastern and central regions of Persia, received his earliest education in Bukhara under the direction of his father, who was an Ismāʿīlī (a member of an Islāmic religious and political movement, the theology of which drew on a popularized form of Neoplatonism). Avicenna himself, however, was never attracted to the Ismāʿīlīyah. Since the house of his father was a meeting place for learned men, from his earliest childhood Avicenna was able to profit from the company of the outstanding masters of his day. A precocious child with an exceptional memory that he retained throughout his life, he had memorized the Qurʾān and much Arabic poetry by the age of 10. Thereafter, he studied logic and metaphysics under teachers whom he soon outgrew and then spent the few years until he reached the age of 18 in his own self-education. He read avidly and mastered Islāmic law, then medicine, and finally metaphysics. Particularly helpful in his intellectual development was his gaining access to the rich royal library of the Sāmānids—the first great native dynasty that arose in Persia after the Arab conquest—as the result of his successful cure of the Sāmānid prince, Nūḥ ibn Manṣūr. By the time he was 21 he was accomplished in all branches of formal learning and had already gained a wide reputation as an outstanding physician. His services were also sought as an administrator, and for a while he even entered government service as a clerk.

But suddenly the whole pattern of his life changed. His father died; the Sāmānid house was defeated by Maḥmūd of Ghazna, the Turkish leader and legendary hero who established Ghaznavid rule in Khorāsān (northeastern Iran and modern western Afghanistan); and Avicenna began a period of wandering and turmoil, which was to last to the end of his life with the exception of a few unusual intervals of tranquillity. Destiny had plunged Avicenna into one of the tumultuous periods of Persian history, when new Turkish elements were replacing Persian domination in Central Asia and local Persian dynasties were trying to gain political independence from the ʿAbbāsid caliphate in Baghdad (in modern Iraq). But the power of concentration and the intellectual prowess of Avicenna was such that he was able to continue his intellectual work with remarkable consistency and continuity and was not at all influenced by the outward disturbances.

Avicenna wandered for a while in different cities of Khorāsān and then left for the court of the Būyid princes, who were ruling over central Persia, first going to Rayy (near modern Tehrān) and then to Qazvīn, where as usual he made his livelihood as a physician. But in these cities also he found neither sufficient social and economic support nor the necessary peace and calm to continue his work. He went, therefore, to Hamadan in west central Persia, where Shams ad-Dawlah, another Būyid prince, was ruling. This journey marked the beginning of a new phase in Avicenna's life. He became court physician and enjoyed the favour of the ruler to the extent that twice he was appointed vizier. As was the order of the day, he also suffered political reactions and intrigues against him and was forced into hiding for some time; at one time he was even imprisoned.

Writings. This was the period when he began his two most famous works. *Kitāb ash-shifā'* is probably the largest work of its kind ever written by one man. It treats of logic, the natural sciences, including psychology, the *quadrivium* (geometry, astronomy, arithmetic, and music), and metaphysics, but there is no real exposition of ethics or of politics. His thought in this work owes a great deal to Aristotle but also to other Greek influences and to Neoplatonism. His system rests on the conception of God as the necessary existent: in God alone essence, what he is, and existence, that he is, coincide. There is a gradual multiplication of beings through a timeless emanation from God as a result of his self-knowledge. *The Canon of Medicine* (*al-Qānūn fī aṭ-ṭibb*) is the most famous single book in the history of medicine in both East and West. It is a systematic encyclopaedia based for the most part on the achievements of Greek physicians of the Roman imperial age and on other Arabic works and, to a lesser extent, on his own experience (his own clinical notes were lost during his journeys). Occupied during the day with his duties at court as both physician and administrator, Avicenna spent almost every night with his students composing these and other works and carrying out general philosophical and scientific discussions related to them. These sessions were often combined with musical performances and gaiety and lasted until late hours of the night. Even in hiding and in prison he continued to write. The great physical strength of Avicenna enabled him to carry out a program that would have been unimaginable for a person of a feebler constitution.

The last phase of Avicenna's life began with his move to Isfahan (about 250 miles south of Tehrān). In 1022 Shams ad-Dawlah died, and Avicenna, after a period of difficulty that included imprisonment, fled to Isfahan with a small entourage. In Isfahan, Avicenna was to spend the last 14 years of his life in relative peace. He was esteemed highly by ʿAlāʾ ad-Dawlah, the ruler, and his court. Here he finished the two major works he began in Hamadan and wrote most of his nearly 200 treatises; he also composed the first work on Aristotelian philosophy in the Persian language and the masterly summary of his "Book of Healing" called *Kitāb an-najāt* ("Book of Salvation"), written partly during the military campaigns in which he had to accompany ʿAlāʾ ad-Dawlah to the field of battle. During this time he composed his last major philosophical opus and the most "personal" testament of his thought, *Kitāb al-ishārāt wa at-tanbīhāt* ("Book of Directives and Remarks"). In this work he described the mystic's spiritual journey from the beginnings of faith to the final stage of direct and uninterrupted vision of God. Also in Isfahan, when an authority on Arabic philology criticized him for his lack of mastery in the subject, he spent three years studying it and composed a vast work called *Lisān al-ʿarab* ("The Arabic Language"), which remained in rough draft until his death. Accompanying ʿAlāʾ ad-Dawlah on a campaign, Avicenna fell ill and, despite his attempts to treat himself, died from colic and from exhaustion.

Besides fulfilling the role of the master of the Muslim Aristotelians, Avicenna also sought in later life to found an "Oriental philosophy" (*al-ḥikmat al-mashriqīyah*). Most of his works directly concerning this have been lost, but enough remains in some of his other works to give an indication of the direction he was following. He took the first steps upon a path toward mystical theosophy that marked the direction that Islāmic philosophy was to follow in the future, especially in Persia and the other eastern lands of Islām.

Avicenna's influence. In the Western world, Avicenna's influence was felt, though no distinct school of "Latin Avicennism" can be discerned as can with Averroës, the great Spanish-Arabic philosopher. Avicenna's "Book of Healing" was translated partially into Latin in the 12th century, and the complete *Canon* appeared in the same century. These translations and others spread the thought of Avicenna far and wide in the West. His thought, blended with that of St. Augustine, the Christian philosopher and theologian, was a basic ingredient in the thought of many of the medieval Scholastics, especially in the Franciscan schools. In medicine the *Canon* became *the* medical authority for several centuries, and Avicenna enjoyed an undisputed place of honour equalled only by the early Greek physicians Hippocrates and Galen. In the East his dominating influence in medicine, philosophy, and theology has lasted over the ages and is still alive within the circles of Islāmic thought. (S.H.N.)

BIBLIOGRAPHY. Translations and commentaries on Avicenna's works include: M. Achena and H. Masse, *Le Livre de science*, 2 vol. (1955–58); O.C. Gruner, *A Treatise on the Canon of Medicine of Avicenna* (1930); M. Horten (ed.), *Das Buch der Genesung der Seele: Eine philosophische Enzyklopädie Avicennas*, vol. 4, *Die Metaphysik, Theologie, Kosmologie und Ethik* (1908); H. Jahier and A. Noureddine, *Poème de la médicine* (1956); A.F. Mehren, *Traités mystiques d'Avicenne*, 3 vol. (1889–91); F. Rahman, *Avicenna's Psychology* (1952).

General studies include: S.M. Afnan, *Avicenna: His Life and Works* (1958); H. Corbin, *Avicenne et le récit visionnaire*, 2nd ed., 2 vol. (1954; *Avicenna and the Visionary Recital*, 1960); S.H. Nasr, *An Introduction to Islamic Cosmological Doctrines* (1964), and *Three Muslim Sages* (1964), locating Avicenna within the context of Islāmic intellectual tradition; M.H. Shah, *The General Principles of Avicenna's Canon of Medicine* (1966), an analysis from the point of view of modern medical theory and practice; G.W. Wickens (ed.), *Avicenna: Scientist and Philosopher* (1952), a collection of essays; Y. Mahdavi, *Bibliographie d'Ibn Sina* (1954).

aviculture, raising and care of wild birds in captivity, for the breeding of game stock, the perpetuation of declining species, or for display and education. The simulation of natural conditions is a necessary goal of aviculturists, allowing them to study aspects of mating and breeding behaviour that may not be easily observed in the wild. As a result of such study, a number of species, rare or endangered in the wild, have been kept from extinction by captive breeding. Some, such as the néné, or Hawaiian goose (*Branta sandvicensis*), and the whooping crane (*Grus americana*) are bred and restored to the wild to help build up their native populations. Other rare species, such as the golden pheasant (*Chrysolophus pictus*) and the Chinese silver pheasant (a subspecies of *Lophura nycthemera*), are maintained primarily in aviaries and zoos, where they are abundant.

Avidius Cassius, Gaius (b. Syria—d. July 175), usurping Roman emperor for three months in 175.

The son of a high civil servant of the emperor Hadrian (ruled 117–138), Avidius directed operations in Rome's war against the Parthians (161–165). In 164–165 Avidius advanced into Mesopotamia and then sacked Ctesiphon, Parthia's capital, and Seleucia—both located in present-day central Iraq. Soon he was made commander of all Roman military forces in the Eastern provinces, and in 172 he suppressed an agrarian revolt in Egypt. In April 175 Avidius suddenly proclaimed himself emperor. He had apparently acted after hearing a false rumour of the death of the emperor Marcus Aurelius (ruled 161–180), who was campaigning on the Danube. Marcus set out for the East, but before the two rivals could confront each other, Avidius was assassinated by one of his own soldiers.

avidyā (Sanskrit), in the Buddhist chain of dependent origination, the ignorance that fetters man to transmigration. *See* pratītya-samutpāda.

Avignon, city, capital of Vaucluse *département,* Provence-Alpes-Côte-d'Azur region, southeastern France, at a point on the east bank of the Rhône River where the narrow valley opens into a broad delta plain, northwest of Nîmes. A stronghold of the Gallic tribe of Cavares that became the Roman city of Avennio, it was a much-fought-over prize, although never of primary importance until it became the capital of the papacy in 1309.

At that time, Avignon was not on French soil but belonged to vassals of the pope. Avignon was bought by Clement VI, the fourth of seven Avignon popes, in 1348 from Queen Joan of Provence and remained papal property until the French Revolution. The Avignon papacy, derisively referred to as the "second Babylonian captivity" of the popes, lasted from 1309 to 1377.

Palais des Papes (papal palace), Avignon, Fr.

By courtesy of the French Government Tourist office; photograph, Lucien Viguier

Avignon was especially detested by Italians of the papal court. Petrarch described it as where the winter mistral winds blow bitterly, "a sewer where all the muck of the universe collects." The papal territory was a place of sure asylum, and the city harboured heretics and criminals, its taverns and houses of pleasure making it a byword for debauch. Avignon was often swept by the plague. Sometimes the *routiers* (private armies that lived by pillage between mercenary engagements) would descend upon the city, departing only after receiving a papal blessing and large sums of money.

Papal legates continued to govern the city until 1791, when the French National Assembly annexed it. In its seizure, there was bloodshed and the interior of the Palais des Papes was wrecked. The palace, a formidable eight-towered fortress on a rock 190 ft (58 m) above the town, was used as a barracks from 1822 to 1906.

One of the largest *châteaux-forts* still standing, it is really two buildings. The Palais Vieux (1334–42) is austere, the Palais Nouveau (1342–52) rich with architectural devices and embellishment. There are numerous small chapels and three large chapels decorated with 14th-century frescoes. Alongside the palace is the Romanesque cathedral (12th century) of Notre-Dame-des-Doms, burial place of two of the popes. In the town below there are 16th- and 17th-century houses and six churches dating from the 14th to the 17th century. Two of these are chapels of *pénitents noirs*, lay groups of 14th-century flagellants who marched hooded and barefoot through the streets and whose membership included kings of France. The ramparts built by the popes still gird the town, 3 mi (5 km) in circuit, with machicolated battlements (projecting turrets), towers, and gates. The walls are now encircled by boulevards.

Four arches of the famed Saint-Bénézet bridge (of the song "Sur le pont d'Avignon") still reach out from the town, its Romanesque St. Nicholas Chapel still perched on the second pier. The Rhône currents had defied bridging until St. Bénézet and his disciples built this one in 1177–88. Broken several times, it was abandoned in 1680. People did dance there, as in the song—not on it, but underneath it, on the Île de la Barthelasse. A suspension bridge and span now cross the Rhône downstream.

Avignon has an active local market and diversified industries that include wine, flour, oil, leather, soap, and fabrics. Madder, a dye source, was introduced in 1756 and was for many years the area's important money crop; it is still cultivated.

The house in which John Stuart Mill wrote his essay *On Liberty* is near Cimetière de Saint-Veran, where he lies buried. The summer arts festival includes plays acted out of doors at the papal palace, and *son et lumière* ("sound and light") spectacles recounting Avignon's history. Pop. (1982) 75,178.

Avignon papacy, designation for the period 1309–77 when the popes took up residence at Avignon instead of at Rome, primarily because of the current political conditions. Distressed by factionalism in Rome and pressed to come to France by Philip IV, Pope Clement V moved the papal capital to Avignon, which at that time belonged to vassals of the pope. In 1348 it became direct papal property. Although the Avignon papacy was overwhelmingly French in complexion (all seven of the popes during the period were French, as were 111 of the 134 cardinals created), it was not so responsive to French pressure as contemporaries assumed or as later critics insisted. During this time the Sacred College of Cardinals began to gain a stronger role in the government of the church; a vast reorganization and centralization of administrative offices and other agencies was effected; reform measures for the clergy were initiated; expanded missionary enterprises, which reached as far as China, were stimulated; university education was promoted; and numerous attempts were made by the popes to settle royal rivalries and to establish peace. Nevertheless, the antagonism, especially within England and Germany, to the residency at Avignon damaged the prestige of the papacy.

After Gregory XI succeeded in slipping the suffocating embrace of the French ruler and returned to Rome, cardinals of the Sacred College selected a second pope, who assumed the vacant Avignon seat. This marked the onset of the Great Schism. A succession of such "antipopes" were selected, and the Great Schism was not healed until 1417. The increased power and ambitions of the cardinals led no doubt to the Great Schism and to the subsequent emergence of conciliarism (*q.v.*).

Avignon school, a body of late Gothic painting, not necessarily of a single stylistic evolution, produced in and around the city of Avignon in southeastern France from the second half of the 14th century into the second half of the 15th. Subject to both Italian and Flemish influences—in contrast to the contemporary art of northern France, which was entirely Flemish in character—the art of Avignon, with that of nearby Aix-en-Provence and other centres in the surrounding region of Provence, represented some of the most vital developments in French Gothic painting.

The Avignon school had its beginnings during the period of the "Babylonian Captivity" (1309–77), when the papal court resided at Avignon under a series of French popes, the only period of its history in which the papacy was not centred at Rome. The immensely advantageous papal patronage attracted many artists, mainly Italians; the most prominent of these was the Sienese master Simone Martini, who worked at Avignon between 1335 and 1340. Under his direction and that of his successor, Matteo di Giovanetti da Viterbo (in Avignon 1342–53), the papal palace at Avignon and a number of secular buildings in nearby towns were decorated with frescoes that firmly established in Provence the Italian, and specifically Sienese, pictorial tradition: decorative elegance of outline and detail, easy, harmonious handling of numbers of solidly modelled, graceful figures, and, most important, a monumentality in the treatment of figures, born of classicism, that was completely foreign to the highly linear, precious elegance of current French painting, inspired as it was by the miniature arts of manuscript illumination and stained glass. The strong Italian tradition established at Avignon was in fact one of the more important means by which Italian monumental classicism was transmitted to the north before 1400, in anticipation of the monumental Flemish painting of the 15th century.

After the departure of the popes in 1377, Avignon and Aix maintained their positions as important artistic centres. Early in the 15th century, Flemish influences, already entrenched in northern France, began to reach Avignon. The precise realism with its intense interest in detail, the crisp, rhythmic line, and the sensitive colour of Flemish painting fused with the Italian tradition, which tended to neutralize the tension and angularity typical of Flemish art; these two influences are seen in varying proportions in the work of a number of artists painting in Avignon. Despite the strength of the two traditions, these artists also maintained an independent approach that remained typical of French art and was expressed in spacious monumentality of composition (in contrast with Sienese overcrowding), individuality of iconographic types, and a freshness and grace in the treatment of detail that revealed a particularly strong love of nature. The most prominent 15th-century artists of the Avignon school were Enguerrand Charonton, Simon de Chalons, and Nicolas Froment. The masterpiece of the school, however, is the anonymous "Avignon Pietà" (Louvre, Paris), painted before 1457 at Villeneuve-lès-Avignon and attributed by some to Charonton. This highly original work is an intensely spiritual combination of monumentality and penetrating realism.

In the second half of the 15th century, increasing virtuosity replaced the original vigour of the school. The forces that were at work at Avignon, however, influenced the mainstream of French painting in the late 15th and 16th centuries.

avijjā (Pāli), in the Buddhist chain of dependent origination, the ignorance that fetters man to transmigration. *See* pratītya-samutpāda.

Ávila, province, in the provisional autonomous community (region) of Castile-León, central Spain, on the plateau of Old Castile. It has an area of 3,107 sq mi (8,048 sq km) and is separated from Madrid province (east) by the Sierra de Guadarrama, and from Toledo province (south) by the Sierra de Gredos. Agriculture predominates on the level ground in the north, but the soils are poor, resting on outwash from the central sierras. To the south, sierras rise steplike from the plateau to the Sierra de Gredos and are separated from each other by longitudinal valleys, the most important of which are Alberche, Adaja, and Tiétar. There is little industrial development, and agriculture predominates throughout the province. The raising of stock, especially of Merino sheep, is the principal occupation; the forests, mostly pine, are still economically important in places. Wheat, with and without irrigation, is increasing in acreage. Rye, barley, oats, corn (maize), and tobacco are also grown. Modern methods are widely adopted; production of cereals exceeds consumption, and a surplus is exported to other parts of Spain. Agricultural processing is largely confined to the provincial capital, Ávila (*q.v.*), and the chief market is the town of Arévalo. The vine flourishes only in such areas as the Tiétar and Alberche valleys, which produce wines of some repute; olive cultivation is confined to a few sheltered localities (Arenas de San Pedro, Cebreros) with very high yield. The sierras formerly abounded in game; the diminution of the ibex (wild goat) of the Sierra de Gredos led to the creation of an ibex sanctuary in 1905. Pop. (1982 est.) 165,427.

Ávila, in full ÁVILA DE LOS CABALLEROS, capital of Ávila province, in the provisional autonomous community (region) of Castile-León, central Spain. It lies on the Río Adaja,

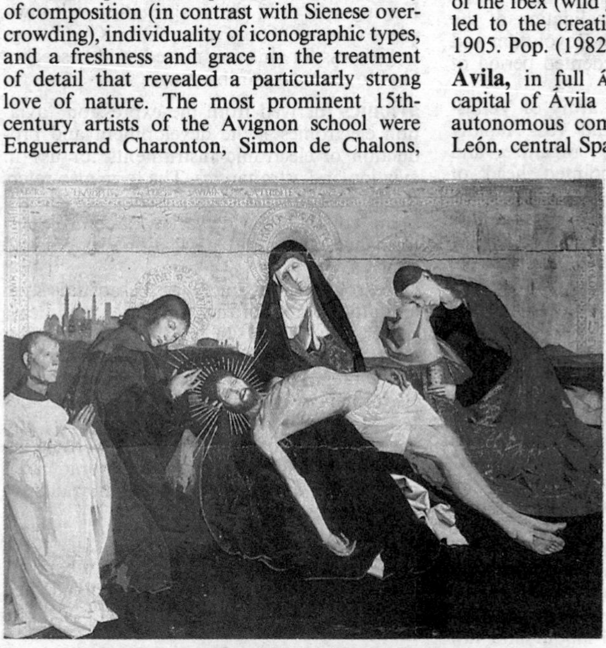

"Avignon Pietà," oil painting by an anonymous artist of the French school, 15th century; in the Louvre, Paris
EDI Studio, Barcelona

at 3,715 ft (1,132 m) above sea level and is surrounded by the lofty Sierra de Gredos (south) and the Sierra de Guadarrama (east), 54 mi (87 km) west of Madrid. A pre-Roman settlement on the site became part of Roman Lusitania and was known as Abula or Avela before falling (*c.* 714) to the Moors. Recaptured for the Christians by Alfonso VI in 1088, its walls, in polygonal form and extending 8,202 ft (2,500 m), were built in the 12th century and encompassed the whole of ancient Ávila; the modern part of the city lies outside. With the expulsion of the Moriscos (people of Moorish descent) in 1607–10, the city's commerce declined.

Ávila has been called the "finest medieval remnant in Spain" and is a noted tourist centre. Historic landmarks include the Gothic cathedral (begun *c.* 1091, completed 13th–15th century), in which the work of the goldsmith Juan de Arfe y Villafén (16th century) is preserved; the Convento de Santo Tomás (1482–93), containing the tombs of Tomás de Torquemada, who was the first grand inquisitor of Spain, and of Don Juan, the only son of Ferdinand and Isabella; the Romanesque Basilica of San Vicente; and the Encarnación convent, built on the site of the house of the mystic St. Teresa, a native of Ávila.

The walled city of Ávila, Spain, with the Río Adaja in the foreground

Josef Muench

Commercial activities now include tanning, flour milling, liquor distilling, and the manufacture of soft drinks and meat by-products. Pop. (1982 est.) 37,340.

Ávila Camacho, Manuel (b. April 24, 1897, Teziutlán, Mex.—d. Oct. 13, 1955, Mexico City), soldier and moderate statesman ever responsive to public opinion, whose presidency (1940–46) saw a consolidation of the social reforms of the Mexican Revolution and the beginning of an unprecedented period of friendship with the U.S.

Ávila Camacho joined the army of Venustiano Carranza in 1914 and rose rapidly through the ranks. A skilled organizer and administrator, he was appointed head of the Ministry of War and Navy under Pres. Abelardo Rodríguez and minister of national defense under Pres. Lázaro Cárdenas (1937). Resigning from his post in 1939, he won the nomination of the government party, the PRM (Partido de la Revolución Mexicana), and was elected president in a government-controlled election in 1940.

As president, Ávila Camacho pursued domestic policies of moderation and steady progress. He pacified the Roman Catholic Church by a public announcement of his own faith, expanded the school system, built hospitals, sponsored social security legislation, and supported limited land reform. His administration was noted primarily, however, for the new relationship it established with the hated neighbour to the north, the United States. The long-standing dispute over the expropriated U.S. oil properties was settled; Mexico supplied needed agricultural labour and raw materials for the Allied war effort, and it declared war on the Axis powers in 1942, even sending pilots to serve in the Pacific.

After the long years of disorder following the Mexican Revolution (1910–17), the regime of Ávila Camacho represented a turn to the right, a stabilizing of the thrust of reform, and an institutionalizing of social advances. Retiring from the presidency in 1946, Ávila Camacho remained an important political force for the rest of his life.

Avilés, city, Oviedo province, (autonomous community [region] of Asturias), northwestern Spain, on the Ría (inlet) de Avilés, an inlet of the Bay of Biscay. A summer resort with beaches at nearby Salinas, the city has an iron and steel industry and a fishing fleet, and it exports coal from the Asturias mines. Avilés is rich in medieval architecture, its outstanding examples including the Gothic churches of San Nicolás and San Francisco. The church of San Tomás contains the tomb of Pedro Menéndez de Avilés, founder of St. Augustine, Fla. The Fuero de Avilés (1155), a statute by which Alfonso VII of Castile freed the city from its feudal ties, was significant in the development of medieval Spanish law. Pop. (1981) 86,584.

Avinu Malkenu (Hebrew: Our Father, Our King), the opening words of each verse of a Jewish litany of supplication that is recited in synagogues with special devotion during the Ten Days of Penitence (except on the sabbath), which mark the beginning of the new religious year. Reform Jews recite the prayer only on Rosh Hashana and Yom Kippur, the first and last day of the 10-day observance.

The great rabbi Akiba (*c.* AD 40–135) is said to have composed the basic verses on a Jewish fast day to relieve a disastrous drought. The prayer is, thus, also part of the liturgy on Jewish fast days (except on the ninth day of Av). Praying as a unit, the congregation acknowledges God as "Our Father, Our King," begs forgiveness for sins committed, and beseeches God to grant certain blessings.

avionics (derived from the expression "aviation electronics"), the development and production of electronic instruments for use in aviation and astronautics. The term also refers to the instruments themselves. Such instruments consist of a wide variety of control, performance, and radio navigation devices and systems.

Control apparatus includes the attitude gyro and any number of instruments that indicate power, such as the tachometer (in propeller craft), torquemeter (in turboprops), and exhaust pressure ratio indicator (in turbojets). Performance instruments include the altimeter, Machmeter, turn and slip indicator, and varied devices that show airspeed, vertical velocity, and angle of attack. Electronic radio navigation equipment ranges from radar to instrument landing systems.

Avison, Charles (baptized Feb. 16, 1709, Newcastle upon Tyne, Northumberland, Eng.—d. May 9, 1770, Newcastle upon Tyne), composer, organist, and writer on musical aesthetics.

Little is known of Avison's life until he took positions as organist at St. John's and St. Nicholas' churches in Newcastle in 1736.

Avison, detail of a portrait by an unknown artist; in the Cathedral Church of St. Nicholas, Newcastle upon Tyne, Eng.

By courtesy of the Cathedral Church of St. Nicholas, Newcastle upon Tyne, Eng.

He also taught harpsichord, violin, and flute and conducted the newly founded subscription concerts, among the first such concerts in England. His "Essay on Musical Expression" (1752) evoked a pamphlet, published anonymously, from William Hayes, professor of music at Oxford (1753), to which Avison replied in an enlarged edition of the "Essay." Avison lived all his life in Newcastle, refusing appointments at York, Dublin, Edinburgh, and London. In 1757 he assisted the composer John Garth in an English edition of Benedetto Marcello's *Psalms.* The virtuoso violinist Francesco Geminiani, who may have been his teacher, visited him in 1760. As a composer, Avison was a representative of the last phase of the late Baroque style. Among his works are compositions for piano and string quartet, and sonatas for harpsichord and two violins. His "Essay" and other writings throw considerable light on 18th-century methods of performance.

Avitus, in full FLAVIUS MACCILIUS EPARCHUS AVITUS (d. 456), Western Roman emperor (455–456).

Born of a distinguished Gallic family, he was a son-in-law of the Christian writer Sidonius Apollinaris. By taking advantage of his great influence with the Visigoths who were settled at Toulouse, Avitus was able in 451 to persuade their king, Theodoric I, to join the Roman general Aetius in repelling the invasion of Gaul by the Huns under Attila. Avitus was appointed *magister utriusque militiae* ("master of both services") by the Western emperor Petronius Maximus (ruled 455). When Maximus was killed, the Goths proclaimed Avitus emperor at Toulouse, and this claim was upheld by the Gallo-Romans at Arles. The new emperor proceeded to Rome but was forced by Ricimer to abdicate (Oct. 17, 456) and to become bishop of Placentia.

AVNOJ: *see* Anti-Fascist Council of National Liberation of Yugoslavia.

avocado, also called ALLIGATOR PEAR, fruit of *Persea americana* of the family Lauraceae, a tree native to the mainland of the Western Hemisphere from Mexico south to the Andean regions. The tree, tall or spreading, has leaves elliptic to egg-shaped in form and 100–300 millimetres (4–12 inches) in length. The small, greenish flowers, borne in dense racemes, are devoid of petals and have six perianth lobes, nine stamens arranged in three series, and a one-celled ovary. The fruit is exceedingly variable in shape, size, and colour, with certain Mexican races no larger than hen's eggs and those of other races sometimes one to two kilograms (two to four pounds) in weight. The form varies from round to pear-shaped with a long, slender neck, and the colour ranges from green to dark purple. The single large seed, with two cotyledons, is round to conical. The fruit's outer skin is sometimes no thicker than that of an apple and sometimes is coarse and woody in texture. It protects the greenish or yellowish flesh, buttery in consistency and with a rich, nutty flavour. In some varieties the flesh contains as much as 25 percent of unsaturated oil. It is often eaten in salads, whence the name salad fruit. Mashed avocado is the principal ingredient of guacamole, a characteristic sauce in Mexican cuisine. Avocados provide thiamine, riboflavin, and vitamin A.

Avocados were widely cultivated in tropical America as individual seedling trees before the Spanish conquest but did not receive serious horticultural attention until about 1900, when horticulturists found that production of grafted trees was simple and allowed perpetuation of superior seedlings and the establishment of orchards producing fruit of uniform size, appearance, and quality.

Flourishing industries developed in Florida and California, in South Africa, and on a somewhat smaller scale in Chile, Brazil, Hawaii, Australia, and some islands of the Pacific. Mexico, where avocados are extremely popular, produces large quantities annually; commercial plantings have been made in Israel, and there are numerous trees in other countries around the Mediterranean.

Horticulturally, avocados are divided into the Mexican, West Indian, and Guatemalan races. The Mexican, considered a distinct species, *Persea drymifolia,* by some botanists, is native to Mexico and is characterized by the anise-like odour of the leaves and by small (90–240 grams [3–8 ounces]), thin-skinned fruits

Avocado (*Persea americana*)
S.A. Scibor—Shostal/EB Inc.

of rich flavour and excellent quality. Mexican avocados are the hardiest, valuable in regions too cold for other types. The Guatemalan, native to the highlands of Central America, is slightly less frost-resistant than the Mexican and produces fruits of medium to large size (240–1000 g), characterized by thick, woody skins and a ripening season different from that of the others. Cultivation of the West Indian, the most tropical in character, is limited in the U.S. to southern Florida. These fruits are frequently of large size and excellent quality. Natural crossing among the three races has resulted in numerous varieties of mixed character, some commercially important.

avocet, any of several large shorebirds belonging to the genus *Recurvirostra,* family Recurvirostridae. Avocets have boldly contrasting plumage, long bluish legs, and a long black bill upturned at the tip. They inhabit fresh and salt marshes that have areas of open shallow water and mud flats, and they feed by sweeping the bill, held partly open, back and forth in the shallows. Often they wade

American avocet (*Recurvirostra americana*)
Mildred Glueck from Root Resources—EB Inc.

together in line to corral minnows and crustaceans, and in deeper water they may upend like ducks. The nest, on the ground in open colonies, may be built up if flooding occurs.

Four species occur discontinuously in temperate and tropical regions, worldwide. The Old World avocet (*R. avosetta*) has the crown and hindneck black, the wings black and white. It breeds in central Asia and in scattered localities in Europe. Many winter in Africa's Rift Valley. The slightly larger American avocet (*R. americana*), about 45 centimetres (18 inches) long including the bill, differs chiefly in having the head and neck pinkish brown in breeding season, white in winter. It nests in western North America and winters from California and Texas to Guatemala. The Andean avocet (*R. andina*), with a primarily white body, black back and wings, is confined to alkali lakes of the high Andes. The red-necked, or Australian, avocet (*R. novaehollandiae*) is black and white with red-brown head and neck.

Avogadro's law, a statement that under the same conditions of temperature and pressure, equal volumes of different gases contain an equal number of molecules. This empirical relation can be derived from the kinetic theory of gases under the assumption of a perfect (ideal) gas. The law is approximately valid for real gases at sufficiently low pressures and high temperatures.

The specific number of molecules in one gram-mole of a substance, defined as the molecular weight in grams, is 6.023×10^{23}, a quantity called the Avogadro constant. For example, the molecular weight of oxygen is 32.00, so that one gram-mole of oxygen has a mass of 32.00 grams and contains 6.023×10^{23} molecules.

The volume occupied by one gram-mole of gas is about 22.4 litres at standard temperature and pressure (0° C, 1 atmosphere) and is the same for all gases according to Avogadro's law.

The law was first proposed in 1811 by Amedeo Avogadro, a professor of higher physics at the University of Turin for many years, but it was not generally accepted until after 1858, when the Italian chemist Stanislao Cannizzaro constructed a logical system of chemistry based on it.

avoidance, zone of, region near the Milky Way Galaxy where clouds of cosmic dust particles obscure from direct view virtually all distant galaxies. It was so called by the U.S. astronomer Edwin P. Hubble.

The zone of avoidance can only be penetrated by observations made in the far infrared end of the electromagnetic spectrum. It is entirely a local Milky Way effect. Millions of external galaxies are thought to lie beyond it.

avoidance behaviour, type of activity seen in animals exposed to adverse stimuli, in which the tendency to flee or to act defensively is stronger than the tendency to attack.

A brief treatment of avoidance behaviour follows. For full treatment, *see* MACROPAEDIA: Behaviour, Animal.

A threatening sight most often produces avoidance behaviour. Many small birds, for example, will react to the sight of an owl or, more particularly, to its characteristic wide-set eyes. This reaction is innate; birds raised in laboratories also display an avoidance reaction at the sight of an artificial owl with prominent eyes. The reaction of many people to the sight of snakes suggests that this too is an instinctive avoidance, albeit one that can be overcome.

Sound may also be as important as sight. An animal that spies a predator can warn its fellows with a cry that will produce in them instinctive avoidance responses even before the enemy is sighted. Also, what is instinctive to one species can be learned by another; a mixed colony of birds will react to the alarm cry of any of its constituent species. With some animals the danger signal is a chemical; ants, for example, emit a hormonelike substance into the air that induces other members of the nest either to take up defensive positions or to flee.

Once a warning has been received, the responses range from rapid flight to feigning death in expectation that the predator is interested only in living prey. A cat may end up on a high branch so insecure that it has difficulty descending when the danger is past. A burrowing animal will never lose sight of or stray too far from one of the many entrances to its underground warren, and some spiders make trapdoors they can close behind them. A squid will propel itself away from the source of danger, leaving behind an inky cloud to hinder pursuit. Noises and visual signs that serve to keep a group in contact will also be suppressed during flight. Thus, an antelope in flight will fold its tail to conceal the normally visible fluffy white patch.

When an animal cannot run away from danger, it may turn to face the predator with a threatening posture. A monkey, for example, will grimace, showing as many teeth as possible. Hair may stand on end to increase an animal's apparent size; an arched back—as seen in a cornered cat—further exaggerates the threat. An animal may discourage pursuit in other ways, as when a skunk leaves behind a cloud of noisome odour.

When no form of active avoidance or discouragement is available, the animal may have to rely on one of the totally passive means nature has devised; *i.e.,* the shell of a clam, the carapace of a turtle, the plates of an armadillo, or the quills of a porcupine.

avoidance relationship, in human societies, the institutionalized, formal avoidance of one individual by another, usually involving persons of opposite sexes standing in definite kinship relationship to one another. A classic example—and one found in numerous and diverse societies—is the culturally prescribed avoidance of a mother-in-law by her son-in-law. Similar patterns of avoidance have been noted in brother–sister, father–daughter, and father-in-law–daughter-in-law relations.

Formal rules for avoidance have generally been interpreted by anthropologists as a sign of respect rather than of bad feelings. Where the potential for strain is evident, however, the avoidance of contact serves to prevent, or at least to minimize, socially undesirable events or situations. Thus, in many groups, avoidance relationships are practiced by persons of the opposite sex between whom marital or sexual relations are forbidden. *See also* joking relationship.

avoirdupois weight (from French *avoir de pois,* "goods of weight"), traditional European system of weight incorporated into the British Imperial System and the U.S. Customary System of weights and measures. The avoirdupois pound is divided into 16 ounces, the ounce into 16 drams; the pound is equivalent to 7,000 grains and thus to about 1.22

apothecaries' or troy pounds. Since 1959 the avoirdupois pound has been officially defined in most English-speaking countries as 0.45359237 kilogram.

The avoirdupois pound and its subdivisions originated in the Middle Ages for weighing goods other than precious metals (for which troy weight was used) and drugs and medicines (for which apothecaries' weight was used).

Avola, town, Siracusa province, southeastern Sicily, Italy, southwest of Syracuse. Rebuilt after an earthquake in 1693, the town has several fine churches dating from the 18th century. Sugar refining and almond packing are the main industries. Pop. (1981 prelim.) mun., 29,173.

Avon, county, southwestern England, bordering the Severn Estuary and the Bristol Channel. Born out of the local government reorganization of 1974, it comprises parts of the historic counties of Gloucestershire and Somerset to the north and south respectively. With an area of 520 sq mi (1,346 sq km), the county is divided into the following administrative districts: Bath, Bristol, Kingswood, Northavon, Wansdyke, and Woodspring.

The county is a low-lying basin bordered on the east and northeast by the Cotswold Hills and on the south by the Mendip Hills. Both these uplands are classified as Areas of Outstanding Natural Beauty, and the Avon Gorge, through which the Bristol Avon passes on its way to the Bristol Channel, is a national nature reserve.

Prehistoric man was largely restricted to the uplands. During the Roman era major roads were built across the county, and Bath became renowned for its medicinal waters. Roman remains of considerable interest, including the baths themselves, are preserved in the city. From the 7th century, when Avon was incorporated into the Saxon kingdom of Wessex, until the 18th, the area played but a small part in national affairs. Bristol then became the main British terminal for the triangular trade between West Africa, the West Indies, and Britain, and Bath again became fashionable as a spa.

For many years the area has been relatively prosperous. The quality of housing is high, and slum clearance problems are small compared with many other areas. Avon has one of the greatest number of automobiles per capita in the country, a fact that to some extent accounts for the lack of local public transportation facilities. The county has a diversified employment structure. About 80 percent of the land is taken up with agriculture. Dairy farming is particularly important, and a limited amount of arable land, producing mainly cereals, is found on the bordering uplands. Limestone, clay, and fuller's earth are worked in the south and east of the county. Food, drink, tobacco, paper, publishing and printing, and aircraft construction are the principal manufacturing industries. Tourism, particularly at Weston-super-Mare and Bath, plays an important role in the economy. Both Bristol and Bath have universities, and there are also a number of other colleges of higher education. Pop. (1981) 915,176.

Avon, also called EAST AVON, or HAMPSHIRE AVON, river that rises 3 mi (5 km) east of Devizes, Wiltshire, England, on the north side of the Vale of Pewsey and flows generally southward for 48 mi to the English Channel. It has a drainage area of 1,132 sq mi (2,932 sq km) and a fall of 500 ft (150 m). From Upavon southward to Salisbury, the river meanders considerably among meadowlands of the Salisbury Plain in a narrow valley with many villages and much evidence of early settlement. Below Salisbury the valley is wider, with several watercourses in places, but there are few towns near the river banks. It enters the English Channel through the nearly landlocked Christchurch harbour. The main tributaries are the Bourne (from the east) and the Wylye (from the west) at Salisbury and the Stour (from the west) just above Christchurch. The river is navigable to Salisbury and probably was well travelled in prehistoric times. It has salmon fisheries and a variety of coarse fish.

Avon, (Robert) Anthony Eden, 1st earl of: *see* Eden, Anthony.

Avon, Lower, also called BRISTOL AVON, river that rises on the southeastern slope of the Cotswolds, England, and flows through Gloucestershire, Wiltshire, and Avon (formerly Somerset). With a drainage area of 891 sq mi (2,308 sq km), it has a fall of more than 500 ft (150 m) and a length, excluding minor sinuosities, of 75 mi (120 km). It flows eastward and southward in a wide curve through a broad valley, past Chippenham and Melksham, and it turns abruptly westward to Bradford-on-Avon. There the river enters a narrow, gorge-like valley as it swings northwestward through the Cotswolds past Bath. At Bristol the Avon has a straight channel, which was excavated in the 19th century to provide access for seagoing vessels. Below Bristol the river has cut through a limestone ridge to form the picturesque Clifton gorge, which is noted for its wooded cliffs and its suspension bridge. The Avon enters the Severn River estuary at Avonmouth, the ocean port of Bristol. Important tributaries are the Somerset Frome, joining the river from the south near Bradford-on-Avon, and the Bristol Frome, entering from the north in Bristol. The Kennet and Avon Canal (now abandoned) is linked to the river by a ladder of seven locks at Bath.

A list of the abbreviations used in the MICROPAEDIA *will be found at the end of this volume*

Avon, Upper, also called WARWICKSHIRE AVON, river, eastern tributary of the River Severn that rises near Naseby in central England and flows generally southwestward for 96 mi (154 km) through the counties of Northamptonshire, Leicestershire, Warwickshire, and Hereford and Worcester. It has a total fall of about 500 ft (150 m). The river valley widens through the Vale of Evesham, especially below Warwickshire, where its fertile soil supports extensive agriculture. The river is known for its scenic beauty, notably in the Vale of Evesham, which is flanked by the Cotswold Hills on the south and by the wooded Arden district on the north. The river, which abounds in coarse fish, has locks (now decayed) and formerly carried some trade; now it is used only by pleasure boats. Important towns along the river include Rugby, Leamington Spa, Warwick, Stratford, and Evesham. The river has literary associations with William Shakespeare, who was born and died at Stratford.

Avonian Stage, lowermost division of Carboniferous rocks and time in Great Britain, named for exposures studied in the Avon Gorge region near Bristol. (The Carboniferous Period began about 345,000,000 years ago and lasted about 65,000,000 years.) The Avonian consists of about 805 metres (2,460 feet) of fossiliferous limestones and has been subdivided into two formations: Lower Limestone Shales and the overlying Main Limestone. Six fossil zones, representing shorter spans of time, are recognized on the basis of characteristic brachiopod and coral genera. The Avonian is equivalent to the Dinantian Stage of worldwide usage.

Avraham, also spelled AVRAM (Jewish patriarch): *see* Abraham.

Avranches, town and port, Manche *département,* Basse-Normandie region, northwestern France, on a hill (341 ft [104 m]) overlooking the Sée Estuary. The celebrated sanctuary of Mont-Saint-Michel (*q.v.*) is on a rock in the bay. Important under the Romans, Avranches retained its position under the Norman dukes.

In 1172 the excommunicated Henry II of England received absolution in Avranches for the murder of Thomas Becket, archbishop of Canterbury, and made public penance before the cathedral (razed as unsafe in 1794). The paving stone on which he knelt is marked by chains on a little square locally called La Plate-forme. In 1639 Avranches was the centre of the peasants' Nu-Pieds (Barefoot) revolt against the salt tax. The museum contains incunabula and 8th- and 15th-century manuscripts from the abbey on Mont-Saint-Michel.

In July 1944 the U.S. 3rd Army under Gen. George S. Patton broke out of the Normandy "pocket" there. A monument to Patton stands on soil and amid trees brought from America. Avranches, centre for the marketing of the region's cattle, sheep, and fish, also manufactures knit goods and copperware. Pop. (1982) 9,462.

avunculate, special relationship between a man and his sister's children, particularly her sons, which prevails in many societies, notably those characterized by matrilineal descent. The term is derived from the Latin *avunculus,* meaning "uncle." It typically involves for the uncle a measure of authority over his nephews, coupled with specific responsibilities in their upbringing, initiation, and marriage. The nephew, in turn, often enjoys special rights against his uncle's property, frequently taking precedence in inheritance over his uncle's children. Not infrequently, a nephew has a preferential right or obligation to marry a daughter of his maternal uncle—a form of cross-cousin marriage.

In many matrilineal societies, an arrangement known as "avunculocal residence" obtains, in which boys leave their natal homes during adolescence and join the household of one of their mother's brothers. Girls remain at home until they marry, at which time they move to their husbands' households. Hence, in a long-established avunculocal joint family, a man dwells with his wife, his unmarried daughters and preadolescent sons, some of his sisters' adolescent sons, and some of his sisters' married sons with their wives, preadolescent sons, and daughters.

Avvakum Petrovich (b. 1620/1621, Grigorovo, Russia—d. April 14, 1682, Pustozersk), archpriest, leader of the Old Believers, conservative clergy who brought on one of the most serious crises in the history of the Russian Church by separating from the Russian Orthodox Church to support the "old rite," consisting of many purely local Russian developments. He is also considered to be a pioneer of modern Russian literature.

In 1652 he went to Moscow and joined in the struggle against Patriarch Nikon, whose high-handed methods and brutal treatment of dissidents made unpopular his reforms of adopting Greek Church customs in an effort to unite the entire Orthodox Church. Under Nikon's regime, Old Believers were excommunicated and severely persecuted. Avvakum himself was twice banished and finally imprisoned. It was during his imprisonment in Pustozersk that he wrote most of his works, the greatest of which is considered to be his *Zhitiye* ("Life"), the first Russian autobiography. Distinguished for its lively description and for its original, colourful style, the *Zhitiye* is one of the great works of early Russian literature. A council of 1682 against the Old Believers condemned Avvakum to be burned at the stake, and the sentence was carried out.

AWACS, abbreviation of AIRBORNE WARNING AND CONTROL SYSTEM, long-range radar surveillance and control centre for air defense. The system, as developed by the U.S. Air Force, is mounted in specially modified Boeing 707 aircraft. Its main radar antenna is mounted on a turntable housed in a circular rotodome 30 feet (9 metres) in diameter, elliptical in cross-section, and 6 ft deep at its centre. The radar system can detect, track, and identify low-flying aircraft at a distance of 200 nautical miles (370 kilometres) and high-level targets at much greater distances. It also can track maritime traffic, and it operates in any weather over any terrain. An airborne computer can assess enemy action and keep track of the location and availability of any aircraft within range. The communications system, enabling the control of friendly aircraft in pursuit of enemy planes, operates over a single channel, secure from enemy interception, that is also relatively immune to jamming because of its high speed.

The U.S. Air Force uses the AWACS, which it designates as E-3A, as a command and control centre for units of its Tactical Air Command, and also for command and control activity in its North American Air Defense Command (NORAD). NATO also uses the system, and the United Kingdom and the Soviet Union were developing their own similar systems in the 1980s. It has a maximum takeoff weight of 325,000 lb.

Awadh (India): *see* Ayodhyā.

Awaji-shima (Japanese: Awaji Island), island, Hyōgo *ken* (prefecture), Japan, at the eastern end of the Inland Sea. The narrow straits of Akashi (north) and Kii (southeast) separate it from Honshu, while Naruto-kaikyō (Naruto Strait; southwest), well known for its whirlpools, separates it from Shikoku. Most of the island's area of 229 sq mi (593 sq km) consists of low mountains. The one major plain bisects Awaji-shima from east to west and contains the bulk of the population and agricultural land, the main city of Sumoto, and the only railway line. Dairy products, vegetables, flowers, fruit, and ceramic tiles are produced mainly for the Ōsaka-Kōbe markets. Previously there was abundant fishing along the east and west coasts, but overfishing caused the industry to decline, and it has been replaced by freshwater fish cultivation.

The island is linked to Kōbe by hydrofoil boat. Rich in myths and historical monuments, Awaji-shima is considered to be the birthplace of the Japanese puppet play. Pop. (1980) 9,082.

ʿAwālī, municipality in the state and emirate of Bahrain, on central Bahrain island, in the Persian Gulf. Founded in the 1930s by the Bahrain Petroleum Company (Bapco), it is situated just north of Bahrain's oil fields and southwest of the country's oil refinery, one of the largest in the world, with a capacity of about 300,000 barrels a day. The municipality was built to house the main offices, headquarters staff, and foreign executives and employees of Bapco. ʿAwālī (Arabic: High Places) was laid out in the pattern of a Western small town or suburban development, with trees and gardens in the midst of the hostile desert. The expense and difficulty of maintaining such surroundings is emphasized by the fact that all water must be piped from sources several miles away. Furthermore, the settlement is built on a rocky outcrop; in order to plant a tree, a pneumatic drill must be used to penetrate the overlying rock strata. The population of ʿAwālī decreased sharply in the 1960s and early 1970s as the company replaced the expatriate Westerners, who resided there, with Bahrainis living elsewhere in the country. Oil production from the South ʿAwālī field peaked in 1970 and has been diminishing ever since. Pop. (1981) 1,769.

Awan, ancient city and region of the land of Elam, prominent throughout early Mesopotamian history and especially in the second half of the 3rd millennium BC. Although it was probably situated near Susa, in southwestern Iran, Awan's exact location is unknown. A coalition of four rulers of southwestern Persia, led by the King of Awan, provided vigorous resistance to the eastern campaigns of King Sargon of Akkad (reigned 2334–2279 BC). The coalition was eventually defeated, however, and it was perhaps at that time that the centre of Elamite power was transferred from Awan to Susa.

Awangarda Krakowska, avant-garde Polish literary movement, launched in 1922 at Kraków, that led to a regeneration of poetic technique and a renewed interest in Polish folklore and pre-17th-century Polish literature. Influenced by revolutionary trends in poetry, particularly Futurism, in France, Italy, and Spain, the movement opposed the emphasis on lyricism and anti-intellectualism of the contemporary Skamander group. Associated with the Awangarda were Julian Przyboś, one of the outstanding poets of the post-World War II period; Adam Ważyk, poet, essayist, prose writer and brilliant translator; and Józef Czechowicz, who assimilated traditional and regional elements to the new style.

Awarua (New Zealand): *see* Bluff.

Awash River, formerly HAWASH RIVER, river in eastern Ethiopia. It rises on a steep northern escarpment of the Great Rift Valley, fed by lakes Shala, Abayita, Langano, and Ziway. Parts of its northeasterly course form parts of the Shewa–Arsi and Shewa–Hararge provincial boundaries. Cotton is grown in the fertile Awash Valley, and dams (notably the Koka Dam, 1960) supply hydroelectric power. Herds of antelope and gazelle live in the Awash National Park and the Awash West Game Reserve. The river ends in a chain of salt lakes in the Danakil Desert, after a course of about 750 mi (about 1,200 km).

Awdaghost (ancient Africa): *see* Audaghost.

awdl (pl. *awdlau*), in Welsh verse, a long ode written in *cynghanedd* (a complex system of alliteration and internal rhyme) and in one or more of the 24 strict bardic metres, though only 4 bardic metres are commonly used. The *awdl* was, by the 15th century, the vehicle for many outstanding Welsh poems. It remains the predominant form in the annual national eisteddfod (bard and minstrel competition), at which it is awarded the chair or chief honour. Despite the criticism advanced by some that the form is obsolete, *awdlau* of high poetic merit are still occasionally written.

Awe, Loch, longest (24 mi [39 km]) lake in Scotland, situated in Strathclyde region, 117 ft (36 m) above sea level. At the northern end the scenery is rugged and grand, dominated by Ben Cruachan (3,695 ft); but at the southern end it is much softer. The loch's shores have been the scene of afforestation and hydroelectric power developments.

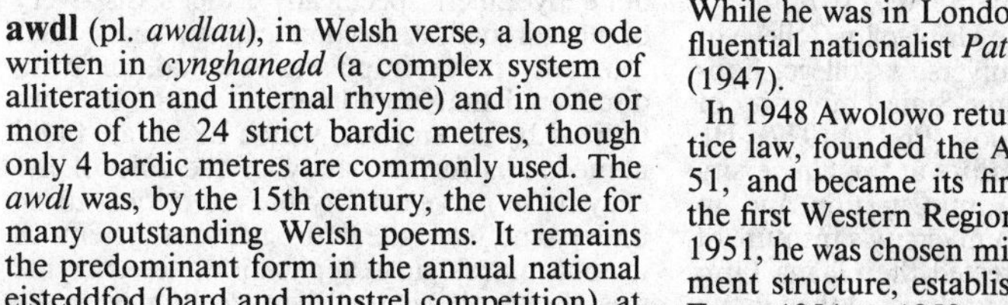

Loch Awe with Kilchurn Castle, Strathclyde
A.F. Kersting

Awemba (people): *see* Bemba.

Awka, town, Anambra State, southern Nigeria, on the roads from Owerri, Umuahia, Onitsha, and Enugu. Formerly covered with tropical forest, the area around Awka is now mostly wooded grassland. South of the town on the slopes of the Awka-Orlu Uplands are some examples of soil erosion and gullying. Awka is the traditional home of the Ibo blacksmiths; early bronze artifacts have been discovered in the vicinity, and the town's artisans are still noted for their metalworking and wood carving. In the 19th century, Awka's Agballa oracle, which was subservient to the supreme Ibo oracle (Chuku) at Arochukwu, was an active instrument of the hinterland slave trade. An agricultural trade centre (yams, cassava, taro, corn [maize], palm oil and kernels) for the Ibo people, it is also the site of an advanced teacher-training college, a branch of the Anambra State University of Technology, secondary schools, and a government hospital. Pop. (1983 est.) 80,350.

Awolowo, Obafemi (b. March 6, 1909, Ikene, Ijebu Remo, Nigeria), Nigerian nationalist politician and, in addition, leader of one of the country's three main ethnic groups, the Yoruba.

Son of a peasant, he first studied to be a teacher and later worked as a clerk, trader, and newspaper reporter while organizing trade unions in his spare time. He went to London to study law in 1944, and while there he founded the Egbe Omo Oduduwa (Society of the Descendants of Oduduwa), a Yoruba cultural society, which later was the basis for a Yoruba political party, the Action Group. While he was in London he also wrote his influential nationalist *Path to Nigerian Freedom* (1947).

In 1948 Awolowo returned to Ibadan to practice law, founded the Action Group in 1950–51, and became its first president. Winning the first Western Region (Yoruba) elections in 1951, he was chosen minister for local government structure, establishing elective councils. From 1954 to 1959, as premier of the Western Region, he worked to improve education, social services, and agriculture. Meanwhile, he also tried to build the Action Group into an effective nationwide party, making alliances with minority groups in other regions. After a disappointing showing in the hard-fought 1959 elections and after the two other major parties had formed a coalition, he became leader of the Opposition in the Federal House of Representatives. After independence in 1960 he became more left wing, turning to Socialism and advocating a neutralist rather than his earlier pro-Western stance in foreign relations.

Meanwhile, dissension was growing in his own party over both ideology and appointments to key positions. Awolowo managed to prevail at the annual party conference in 1962, but in 1963 he was tried and convicted of conspiracy to overthrow the government and was sentenced to 10 years in prison. He was released after the July 1966 army coup, and in the confused events of the next year and after some indecision, he eventually threw his support behind the federal government against the Ibos in the southeast. During the Biafran War he was federal commissioner for finance and vice president of the Federal Executive Council. In 1978, with the lifting of the 12-year ban on political activity and return to civilian rule, Awolowo emerged as the leader of the Unity Party. He ran for president in the elections of 1979 and 1983 but was defeated both times by Shehu Shagari. Following a military coup on Dec. 31, 1983, the Unity Party was banned and Awolowo was required to surrender his passport to the new government.

Awoonor, Kofi, original name GEORGE KOFI AWOONOR WILLIAMS (b. March 13, 1935, Weta, Gold Coast), Ghanaian novelist and poet, whose verse has been widely translated and anthologized. His major themes—Christianity and death are important among them—are enlarged from poem to poem by repetition of key lines and phrases and by use of extended rhythms. Each poem in *Rediscovery and Other Poems* (1964) records a single moment in a larger pattern of recognition and rediscovery, moments sometimes glorious and sometimes pedestrian. Subsequent volumes include *Night of My Blood,* published in 1971, and *The House by the Sea,* 1978.

Awoonor studied at the University College of Ghana (B.A., 1960), University College, London (M.A., 1970), and the State University of New York at Stony Brook (Ph.D., 1972). He lectured in English literature at the University of Ghana School of Administration and in African literature at the university's Institute of African Studies. He directed the Ghana Film Corporation, founded and directed the Ghana Playhouse, travelled to China as a guest of its writers' union, and served as an editor of the literary journal *Okyeame* and as an associate editor of *Transition.* Fellowship aid (1967–69) enabled him to study English and linguistics at the universities of London and California. A course that he initiated in African literature at the State University of New York at Stony Brook led to his appointment as chairman of the department of comparative literature there in the early 1970s. He returned to Ghana in August 1975 to teach at the University College of Cape Coast, but on December 31 he was arrested on charges of harbouring an army officer accused of initiating an attempt to overthrow the government. He was found guilty, but his sentence was remitted in October 1976, and he resumed his teaching post.

Awoonor's belief in the importance of incorporating African vernacular traditions into modern writing is evident in his poetry. He also published a novel, *This Earth, My Brother* (1971), and was co-editor (with G. Adali-Mortty) of a verse collection, *Messages: Poems from Ghana* (1970). *The Breast of the Earth: A Survey of the History, Culture, and Literature of Africa South of the Sahara* appeared in 1975.

Awrangzīb (emperor of India): *see* Aurangzeb.

ax, also spelled AXE, hand tool used for chopping, splitting, chipping, and piercing. Stone Age hand axes originated in simple stone implements that acquired wooden hafts, or handles, about 30,000 BC. Copper-bladed axes appeared in Egypt about 4000 BC and were followed by axes with blades of bronze and eventually iron; blades were fastened to hafts by a variety of means—*e.g.,* lashed into a wooden sleeve, bound into a split of wood, inserted in a bone socket. The development of the iron-bladed felling ax in the Middle Ages made possible the vast forest clearance of northwestern Europe and the development of medieval agriculture. The ax played a similar role in land clearance in eastern Europe, Scandinavia, North and South America, and elsewhere. In modern times the ax, now with a blade or bit of steel, sometimes double-bitted or sharpened on both ends, has lost much of its historic role to powered saws and other machinery, although it remains a widely used tool with a wide variety of uses.

Axelrod, Julius (b. May 30, 1912, New York City), U.S. biochemical pharmacologist who, along with the British biophysicist Sir Bernard Katz and the Swedish physiologist Ulf von Euler, was awarded the Nobel Prize for Physiology or Medicine in 1970. Axelrod's contribution was his identification of an enzyme that inhibits nerve impulses.

A graduate of the College of the City of New York (B.S., 1933), New York University (M.A., 1941), and George Washington University (Ph.D., 1955), Axelrod worked as chemist in the Laboratory of Industrial Hygiene (1935–46), became research associate at New York University, and joined the research division of Goldwater Memorial Hospital (1946), leaving in 1949 to join the staff of the section on chemical pharmacology at the National Heart Institute in Bethesda, Md. In 1955 he moved to the staff of the National Institute of Mental Health, where he became chief of the pharmacology section of the Laboratory of Clinical Sciences.

Axelrod's achievement grew out of work done by Euler, specifically Euler's discovery of noradrenaline, a chemical substance that transmits nerve impulses. Axelrod, in turn, discovered that noradrenaline could be neutralized by an enzyme, which he isolated and named. His further study of the role of the enzyme in nerve activity proved critical to an understanding of the entire nervous system. In its pharmacological application, the enzyme was shown to be useful in dealing with the effects of certain psychotropic drugs and in research on hypertension and schizophrenia.

Axelrod, Paul: *see* Akselrod, Pavel Borisovich.

Axholme, Isle of, part of an area of about 80 sq mi (210 sq km), west of the River Trent, Boothferry district, county of Humberside, England. Until 1974 it was part of Lincolnshire. A tract of low flatland less than 100 ft (30 m) above sea level, it was formerly surrounded by fens. Drainage works begun in the 17th century by Cornelius Vermuyden and subsequently extended and improved have transformed the area into one of high fertility. The chief settlement is Epworth, the birthplace of John and Charles Wesley, founders of Methodism, whose father was rector of the parish; the church survives, and the restored rectory is maintained as a museum. Pop. (1973 est.) 15,070.

axinite, borosilicate mineral that occurs most commonly in contact metamorphic rocks and also in basic igneous rocks. Particularly beautiful crystals occur at Le Bourg d'Oisans, Isère, France, and in San Diego County, Calif., U.S. Transparent axinite of the usual clove-brown colour is sometimes cut as a gem. For chemical formula and detailed physical properties, *see* silicate mineral (table).

axiology (Greek *axios,* "worthy"; *logos,* "science"), also known generally as theory of value, the philosophical study of goodness, or value, in the widest sense of these terms. Its significance lies (1) in the considerable expansion it has given to the meaning of the term value; and (2) in the unification it has provided for the study of a variety of questions—economic, moral, aesthetic, and even logical—that had often been considered in relative isolation.

The term value originally meant the worth of something, chiefly in the economic sense of exchange value, as in the 18th-century political economist Adam Smith. A broad extension of the meaning of value to wider areas of philosophical interest occurred during the 19th century under the influence of a variety of thinkers and schools: the Neo-Kantians Rudolf Hermann Lotze and Albrecht Ritschl; Friedrich Nietzsche, author of a theory of the transvaluation of all values; Alexius Meinong and Christian von Ehrenfels; and Eduard von Hartmann, philosopher of the unconscious, whose *Grundriss der Axiologie* (1909; "Outline of Axiology") first used the term in a title. Hugo Münsterberg, often regarded as the founder of applied psychology, and Wilbur Marshall Urban, whose *Valuation, Its Nature and Laws* (1909) was the first treatise on this topic in English, introduced the movement to the U.S. Ralph Barton Perry's book *General Theory of Value* (1926) has been called the magnum opus of the new approach. A value, he theorized, is "any object of any interest." Later, he explored eight "realms" of value: morality, religion, art, science, economics, politics, law, and custom.

A distinction is commonly made between instrumental and intrinsic value—between what is good as a means and what is good as an end. John Dewey, in *Human Nature and Conduct* (1922) and *Theory of Valuation* (1939), presented a pragmatic interpretation and tried to break down this distinction between means and ends, though the latter effort was more likely a way of emphasizing the point that many actual things in human life—such as health, knowledge, and virtue—are good in both senses. Other philosophers, such as C.I. Lewis, Georg Henrik von Wright, and W.K. Frankena, have multiplied the distinctions—differentiating, for example, between instrumental value (being good for some purpose) and technical value (being good at doing something) or between contributory value (being good as part of a whole) and final value (being good as a whole).

Many different answers are given to the question, "What is intrinsically good?" Hedonists say it is pleasure; Pragmatists, satisfaction, growth, or adjustment; Kantians, a good will; Humanists, harmonious self-realization; Christians, the love of God. Pluralists, such as G.E. Moore, W.D. Ross, Max Scheler, and Ralph Barton Perry, argue that there are any number of intrinsically good things. Moore, a founding father of Analytic philosophy, developed a theory of organic wholes, holding that the value of an aggregate of things depends upon how they are combined.

Since "fact" symbolizes objectivity and "value" suggests subjectivity, the relationship of value to fact is of fundamental importance in developing any theory of the objectivity of value and of value judgments. Whereas such descriptive sciences as sociology, psychology, anthropology, and comparative religion all attempt to give a factual description of what is actually valued, as well as causal explanations of similarities and differences between the valuations, it remains the philosopher's task to ask about their objective validity. The philosopher asks whether something is of value because it is desired, as subjectivists such as Perry hold, or whether it is desired because it has value, as objectivists such as Moore and Nicolai Hartmann claim. In both approaches, value judgments are assumed to have a cognitive status, and the approaches differ only on whether a value exists as a property of something independently of human interest in it or desire for it. Noncognitivists, on the other hand, deny the cognitive status of value judgments, holding that their main function is either emotive, as the Positivist A.J. Ayer maintains, or prescriptive, as the analyst R.M. Hare holds. Existentialists, such as Jean-Paul Sartre, emphasizing freedom, decision, and choice of one's values, also appear to reject any logical or ontological connection between value and fact.

axiom, in logic, according to Aristotle, an indemonstrable first principle from which all demonstrative sciences must start. In addition, each particular science has its own particular first principles on which it builds. Elsewhere, axioms are characterized as the common opinions from which all demonstration proceeds and as those things that anyone must hold who is to learn anything at all. An example would be: "Nothing can both be and not be at the same time and in the same respect."

In Euclid's *Elements* the first principles were listed as postulates and common notions. The former are principles of geometry and seem to have been thought of as required assumptions because their statement opened with "let there be demanded" (*ētesthō*). The common notions are evidently the same as Aristotle's axioms; and indeed Proclus, the last important Greek philosopher ("On the First Book of Euclid"), stated explicitly that the two terms are synonymous. The principle distinguishing postulates from axioms, however, does not seem certain. Proclus debated various accounts of it, among them that postulates are peculiar to geometry whereas axioms are common either to all sciences that are concerned with quantity or to all sciences whatever.

In modern times, mathematicians have often used the words postulate and axiom as synonyms. Some recommend that the term axiom be reserved for the axioms of logic and postulate for those assumptions or first principles beyond the principles of logic by which a particular mathematical discipline is defined. *Compare* theorem.

axiomatic method, in logic, a procedure by which an entire system (*e.g.*, a science) is generated in accordance with specified rules by logical deduction from certain basic propositions (axioms or postulates), which in turn are constructed from a few terms taken as primitive. These terms and axioms may either be arbitrarily defined and constructed or else be conceived according to a model in which some intuitive warrant for their truth is felt to exist.

The oldest examples of axiomatized systems are Aristotle's syllogistic and Euclid's geometry. Early in the present century Bertrand Russell and Alfred North Whitehead attempted to formalize all of mathematics in an axiomatic manner. Scholars have even subjected the empirical sciences to this method, as J.H. Woodger has done in *The Axiomatic Method in Biology* (1937) and Clark Hull (for psychology) in *Principles of Behaviour* (1943). *See also* axiom.

Axiós River (Greece): *see* Vardar River.

axis, in crystallography, any of a set of lines used to describe the orderly arrangement of atoms in a crystal. If each atom or group of atoms is represented by a dot, or lattice point, and these points are connected, the resulting lattice may be divided into a number of identical blocks, or unit cells. The intersecting edges of one of these unit cells are chosen as the crystallographic axes, and their lengths are called lattice constants. The relative lengths of these edges and the angles between them place the solid into one of the six crystal systems.

The position of an atom within a unit cell is given in terms of the crystallographic axes, and planes in the crystal are described using the axes. Although five of the crystal systems are described in terms of three crystallographic axes, the hexagonal system may be represented by four.

axis deer: *see* chital.

Axis Powers, the coalition headed by Germany, Italy, and Japan that opposed the Allied Powers in World War II. The alliance originated in a series of agreements between Germany and Italy, followed by the proclamation of an "axis" binding Rome and Berlin (Oct. 25, 1936) and then by the German-Japanese Anti-Comintern Pact against Soviet Russia (Nov. 25, 1936). The connection was strengthened by a full military and political alliance between Germany and Italy (the Pact of Steel, May 22, 1939), and the Tripartite Pact signed by all three powers on Sept. 27, 1940.

Axis Sally (propagandist): *see* Gillars, Mildred.

axle: *see* wheel and axle.

Axminster, parish (town), East Devon district, county of Devon, England, on the River Axe. Founded *c.* 705 at the intersection of two Roman roads, Portway and Fosse Way, it was one of the earliest Saxon settlements in Devon. Carpet making, for which it is famous, was established in 1755 and is continued in a modern factory. The Axminster carpet has a thick, soft pile tuft in a mixture of colours and textures. Little remains of the great Cistercian abbey of Newenham, which was pulled down after 1536. Pop. (1971) 4,515.

Axminster carpet, floor covering made originally in a factory founded at Axminster, Devon, England, in 1755 by the cloth weaver Thomas Whitty. Resembling somewhat the Savonnerie carpets produced in France, Axminster carpets were Ghiordes knotted in wool on woollen warps and had a weft of flax or hemp. Like the French carpets, they featured Renaissance architectural or floral patterns. Similar carpets were produced at the same time in Exeter and in the Moorfields section of London and, shortly before, at Fulham in Middlesex.

The Whitty factory closed in 1835 with the advent of machine-made carpeting. The name Axminster, however, survived as a generic term for machine-made carpets the pile of which is produced by techniques similar to those used in making velvet or chenille.

Axminster carpet from England, 1765–70; in the Henry Francis du Pont Winterthur Museum, Winterthur, Del.

By courtesy of the Henry Francis du Pont Winterthur Museum, Winterthur, Del.

axolotl (*Ambystoma* [or *Siredon*] *mexicanum*), salamander belonging to the family Ambystomatidae (order Urodela), notable for its permanent retention of larval features, such as external gills. It is found in lakes near Mexico

Axolotl (*Ambystoma tigrinum*)

Jacques Six

City, where it is considered edible. The name axolotl is also applied to any full-grown larva of the genus *Ambystoma* that has not yet lost its external gills.

Ambystoma mexicanum grows to about 25 centimetres (10 inches) long and is dark brown with black speckling. Both albino and white mutants, as well as other colour mutants, are common. The legs and feet are rather small, but the tail is long. A fin extends from the back of the head to the tip of the tail. A lower fin extends from between the hind legs to the tip of the tail. Laboratory specimens sometimes change into a gill-less form resembling the adult tiger salamander (*Ambystoma tigrinum*).

axon, also called NERVE FIBRE, extension of a nerve cell (neuron, *q.v.*) that carries nerve impulses away from the cell body. A neuron typically has one axon, which is rarely branched. The axon of a motor neuron may be quite long, reaching, for example, from the spinal cord down to a toe. Most axons of vertebrate animals are enclosed in a myelin sheath (or fatty membrane), which increases the speed of impulse transmission. A large, sheathed axon may transmit impulses at 200 metres (650 feet) per second, while small, unsheathed fibres conduct at only millimetres per second.

Axum (town, Ethiopia): *see* Aksum.

Axum, Kingdom of (Ethiopia): *see* Aksum, Kingdom of.

Axworthy (foaled 1892), U.S. harness racehorse (Standardbred), founder of one of the two dominant male lines of trotting horses. (Peter the Great founded the other.) Sired by Axtell out of Marguerite, Axworthy was a descendant of George Wilkes, a son of Hambletonian. He showed speed as a trotter, but, having been lamed, he was retired to stud in 1897.

Ay, also called KHEPERKHEPRURE AY, king of Egypt (reigned *c.* 1352–48 BC) who rose from the ranks of the civil service and the military to become king after the death of Tutankhamen, the last king of the 18th dynasty.

Ay began his career either by his prestige as a son of the parents of Queen Tiy, wife of Amenhotep III, or else with the aid of his own wife, who was the nurse of Nefertiti, Akhenaton's queen. As Akhenaton's courtier, he became very close to the royal family, as shown by his title, "god's father," and it has been suggested that he was Nefertiti's father. He also held an important army post and was the King's secretary.

After Akhenaton's death, Ay's prestige and influence increased as he became King Tutankhamen's closest adviser. Ay guided Tutankhamen's reconciliation with the priesthood of Amon, which Akhenaton had persecuted. During this reign he acquired another military title, a very high religious office, and the posts of chancellor and vizier. Nonetheless, he remained loyal to the royal family that had promoted him. There is no clear evidence that he became Tutankhamen's co-regent, but when the young king unexpectedly died, Ay officiated at his funeral as his successor.

When Tutankhamen's widow, Ankhesenamen, sought from the Hittite king, in Anatolia, a son whom she might marry and make king, it is not known whether she acted alone or on advice. The unfortunate prince, however, was intercepted and murdered.

A ring with Ay's and Ankhesenamen's names, seen in 1932 in Cairo, has been construed as indicating that Ay became king through marriage with the heiress. Nonetheless, Ay's original wife remained his chief queen, as illustrated in his royal tomb.

In Egypt, Ay built a fine funerary temple at Thebes, which incorporated innovations that later became standard. To his credit, he continued tolerance of the Aten as had Tutankhamen. Ay was already an old man at his accession, and he ruled only four years; lacking a son, he was succeeded by the general Horemheb.

Ayacucho, landlocked department (formed 1822) in the highlands of south central Peru. It has an area of 17,058 sq mi (44,181 sq km) and is chiefly a region of high plateaus interspersed with valleys. The region is drained by the Río Apurímac and its tributaries. Subsistence farming and herding are prevalent, but, in the north, cash crops such as sugarcane and cotton are grown. Mineral resources include silver, nickel, cobalt, copper, manganese, sulfur, and asphalt. Industrial activity is concentrated in the capital and largest city, Ayacucho (*q.v.*). Roads link the department with major highland and coastal cities. Pop. (1984 est.) 566,200.

Ayacucho, capital of Huamanga province and of Ayacucho department, south central Peru. It lies in a fertile valley on the eastern slopes of the Andean Cordillera Occidental at 9,007 ft (2,746 m) above sea level and has a pleasant and invigorating climate. Founded in 1539 by the conquistador Francisco Pizarro and called Huamanga until 1825, its present name comes from the surrounding plain of Ayacucho (a Quechua Indian word meaning "corner of the dead"), where revolutionaries defeated royalist forces in 1824 and secured Peru's independence from Spain. Many colonial buildings survive. The seat of an archbishopric, it has a 17th-century cathedral and many churches and is known for its Holy Week celebrations. Two universities—San Cristóbal de Huamanga (founded 1677, closed 1886, reopened 1957) and the private "Víctor Andrés Belaúnde" (founded 1967)—are located there. The economy is based on agriculture and light manufactures, including textiles, pottery, leather goods, and filigree ware. The city is a popular stop for tourists. Ayacucho can be reached by highway from Lima and Cuzco, as well as by air. Pop. (1981) city, 69,533; (1981 prelim.) province, 127,846.

The cathedral and San Cristóbal de Huamanga University on Plaza de Armas, Ayacucho city, Peru
Walter Aguiar—EB Inc.

Ayacucho, Battle of (Dec. 9, 1824), during the Latin-American wars of independence, patriot victory over royalists on the high plateau near Ayacucho, Peru; it freed Peru and ensured the independence of the nascent South American republics from Spain. The revolutionary forces, numbering about 6,000 men—among them Venezuelans, Colombians, Argentines, and Chileans, as well as Peruvians—were under the leadership of Simón Bolívar's outstanding lieutenant, the Venezuelan Antonio José de Sucre. The Spanish army numbered about 9,000 men and had 10 times as many guns as their foe. Just before the battle, large numbers of officers and troops crossed over to embrace their friends and brothers in the opposing battle lines.

Sucre opened the attack with a brilliant cavalry charge led by the daring Colombian José María Córdoba, and in a short time the royalist army had been routed, with about 2,000 men killed. The Spanish viceroy and his generals were taken prisoner. The terms of surrender stipulated that all Spanish forces be withdrawn from both Peru and Charcas (Bolivia); the last of them departed from Callao, the port of Lima, in January 1826.

āyāgapaṭa, any of numerous votive slabs found in association with such Jaina sites as Kaṅkālī Ṭīlā in Mathura (India) of about the 1st century AD. The slabs are decorated with some object of Jaina veneration such as the *stūpa* (relic mound), *dharmacakra* (wheel of law), *tri-ratna* (three jewels), *aṣṭamaṅgala* (eight auspicious symbols), *caityavṛkṣa* (sacred tree), or an image of a Jina or of a venerable monk. They bear a close resemblance to earlier *śilāpaṭas*, or stone slabs placed under trees in connection with the worship of *yakṣa* (nature deities) and tree spirits, and suggest to some authorities the close connection between the Jaina religion and the ancient non-Aryan folk traditions. The *āyāgapaṭa* was apparently set up on a platform underneath a tree, as an object of worship or possibly as an aid to meditation.

Ayala, Francisco (b. 1906, Granada, Spain), Spanish novelist and sociologist.

He received a law degree from the University of Madrid in 1929, having already published a novel—*Tragicomedia de un hombre sin espíritu* (1925)—which showed him to be a master of psychological and macabre effects. While studying in Berlin in 1930, he married a Chilean, Etelvina Silva Vargas. He received a second law degree from the University of Madrid in 1931, and in 1932 he joined that university's law faculty and published *El derecho social en la Constitución de la República Española.* He was outside Spain on a lecture tour when the Civil War broke out in 1936 but managed to return briefly. In 1937 he became secretary of the Republic's legation in Prague. When the Republic fell in 1939, he went to Argentina, where he taught, published a sociological textbook, *La realidad de sociología* (1947), and wrote short fiction—notably *El Hechizado* (1944), a macabre story of the 17th-century Spanish Empire, and *La cabeza del cordero* (1949), a novel about the past's influence on the present. He founded the magazine *Realidad* in 1947.

In 1949 he joined the faculty of the University of Puerto Rico and helped to organize its basic studies program. He founded the magazine *La Torre* in 1953. In 1958 he began a professional career in the United States. He continued to write in Spanish, developing, as in *Tecnología y libertad* (1959), his ideas on reconciling individual consciences to society and on restating ancient moral values for modern times. Relations between persons and societies were also themes in his two long novels, *Muertes de perro* (1958) and *El fondo del vaso* (1962), and collections of short fiction, such as *El jardín de delicias* (1971).

aʿyān (title): *see* ʿayn.

āyatana (Sanskrit: "field, base"), in Buddhist philosophy, the field of cognition. Human physical existence consists of 12 *āyatana*s, the six cognitive faculties (five sense organs and the mind) and the six corresponding categories of objects. This classification of the elements of the world is based on human experience and is used by Buddhist philosophers to explain that everything in this world is transient, painful, and nonsubstantial.

Aybak, ʿIzz ad-Dīn Abū al-Manṣūr (d. 1257), first Mamlūk sultan of Egypt (1250–57). The senior Mamlūk military commander, he became generalissimo and regent of Egypt after the assassination of Sultan Tūrān-Shāh. Although he shared his reign with a co-sultan, Musa, Aybak wielded all real power.

Aydın, city, capital of Aydın *il* (province), southwestern Turkey, near the Menderes River (Büyükmenderes Nehri; the ancient Maeander). It is an important trading centre on the

Afyon Karahisar–İzmir highway and rail line. Nearby is the site of ancient Tralles, said to have been founded by the Argives. Aydın was called Güzelhisar (Beautiful Castle) under the Turkmen Menteşe emirs in the 13th century. Renamed for the 14th-century ruling dynasty of Aydın, it was annexed to the Ottoman Empire around 1390. Timur (Tamerlane), who conquered it in 1402, reestablished the principality of Aydın; but it was soon recaptured by the Ottomans. The city was heavily damaged in September 1922 when the retreating Greeks set it afire as a final gesture before they surrendered to the Turkish nationalists. Historical buildings include mosques and a theological school. A Roman gymnasium (4th century BC), a marble column, and the theatre are the only remains of Tralles.

Densely populated Aydın *il,* 3,212 sq mi (8,319 sq km) in area, is bordered on the north by the Aydın Dağları (mountains) and on the southwest by the Aegean Sea. It contains the greater part of the Menderes Valley, drained by the Menderes and Akçay rivers, and is an important agricultural area of Turkey, producing tobacco, wheat, millet, cotton, figs, grapes, olives, and olive oil. Its mineral products include copper, emery, lignite, and mercury. The province's textile industry is centred in Nazilli. Pop. (1980) city, 74,021; (1982 est.) *il,* 677,430.

Aydın DYNASTY, Turkmen dynasty (*c.* 1308–1425) that ruled in the Aydın-Izmir region in western Anatolia.

Mehmed Bey (reigned *c.* 1308–34) founded the dynasty in territories he conquered in the Aegean region, including Birgi, Ayasoluk (modern Selçuk, Tur.), Tyre, and Izmir. His son and successor, Umur Bey (Umur I; reigned 1334–48), organized a fleet and led expeditions to the Aegean islands, the Balkans, and the Black Sea coasts, intervening in dynamic quarrels and assisting John VI Cantacuzenus in the neighbouring Byzantine Empire.

A crusade was organized against him under Pope Clement VI; it included Venice, Genoa, and the King of Cyprus. Umur Bey lost his fleet and the fortress of the Izmir to the crusaders in 1344, and he was killed in battle against them in 1348. His death marked the decline of the principality.

Situated in the prosperous coastal region, the Aydın principality was active in the Mediterranean trade, and as a frontier state it had a monopoly in providing mercenary troops to rival Byzantine factions and offered leadership to the *gazis* (warriors for the Islāmic faith) in their excursions into Byzantine lands.

Under Umur's successors, a treaty signed Aug. 18, 1348, gave the Latin crusader states commercial advantages over Aydın; the principality lost its political significance as a frontier state to the Ottomans and was annexed by the sultan Bayezid I in 1390. Its independence was restored by the Central Asian conqueror Timur (Tamerlane) in 1402. Cunayd, the last prince of Aydın (reigned 1405–25), after continual interference in Ottoman dynastic struggles, was captured and executed by Sultan Murad II, who then permanently annexed the principality.

aye-aye (*Daubentonia madagascariensis*), rare, squirrel-like primate, the sole living representative of the family Daubentoniidae, found in Madagascan rain forests. The aye-aye is about 40 centimetres (16 inches) long excluding the bushy, 55- to 60-cm tail; and it is covered with long, coarse, dark-brown or black fur. It has a broad, rounded head; short face; large eyes; and rodent-like, ever-growing incisors. Its hands are large, and its fingers, especially the third, are long and slender. All fingers have pointed claws, as do all toes except the large, opposable, flat-nailed great toes. The aye-aye is nocturnal, solitary, and arboreal. It constructs a large, ball-like nest of leaves in a fork in the tree branches and

Aye-aye (*Daubentonia madagascariensis*)
Tony and Liz Bomford—Ardea London

feeds mainly on insects and fruit. It locates wood-boring insect larvae by tapping with the long third finger, and it uses this finger to extract the insects. It also uses the third finger to dig the pulp out of fruit. The female bears a single young.

The aye-aye is listed as critically endangered in the *Red Data Book* and is protected by law.

Ayer, Francis Wayland (b. Feb. 4, 1848, Lee, Mass., U.S.—d. March 5, 1923, Meredith, N.Y.), U.S. advertising pioneer who founded N.W. Ayer & Son and revolutionized that industry by making the advertising firm an active agent for the advertiser, rather than a middleman selling a newspaper's space to the advertiser.

Francis Ayer was a member of an old Massachusetts family, the son of a lawyer who gave up his practice to teach school. Francis taught for five years himself, then attended the University of Rochester, N.Y., for a year. He moved with his father to Philadelphia, where the elder Ayer opened a girls' school.

Ayer took a temporary job as an advertising solicitor for a religious journal in Philadelphia in 1868. He quickly recognized the possibilities in advertising, and convinced his father to close his new school and set up an advertising agency with him in 1869 in the name of N.W. Ayer & Son. The company thrived. In 1875 Ayer introduced the open contract, which put the agency to work explicitly for the client for a given period of time. Prior to this, agencies had bought newspaper and magazine space for as little as possible and sold it to clients for as much as possible. Ayer brought advertising a new respectability and stability. He attracted such clients as American Telephone & Telegraph Company, W.K. Kellogg Company, Steinway & Sons, and E.R. Squibb & Sons, and pioneered in the refinement of copywriting and the development of advertising campaigns.

Ayers Rock, giant monolith, one of the tors (isolated masses of weathered rock) in southwestern Northern Territory, Australia; the others are the Olgas (Olga Rocks) and Mt. Conner, near Lake Amadeus. The monolith, which the Aborigines of the region call Uluru, is composed of conglomerate, which changes colour according to the attitude of the Sun. Rising 1,143 ft (348 m) above the surrounding desert plain (2,845 ft above sea level), it is oval in shape, 1.5 mi (2.5 km) long by 1 mi wide. The lower slopes have become fluted by the erosion of weaker rock layers, while the top is scored with gullies and basins that produce giant cataracts after infrequent rainstorms. Shallow caves at the base of the rock, which is within Uluru National Park (first established, in 1950, as the Ayers Rock-Mount Olga National Park), are sacred to several Aboriginal tribes and contain carvings and paintings. Sighted in 1872 by Ernest Giles, the rock was named for former South Australian premier Sir Henry Ayers. Visitors come to the rock via Alice Springs, 280 road mi northeast.

Áyion Óros (Greece): *see* Athos, Mount.

Aylesbury, town, Aylesbury Vale district, county of Buckinghamshire, England, at the centre of a rich clay vale. It was once an important market town for ducks and dairy produce but is now an expanding centre of industry, which includes food processing, light engineering, and especially printing. The market square in the centre of the old town is surrounded by such historic buildings as the county hall (1723–40) and the King's Head Inn (15th century). The 15th-century grammar school is now part of the County Museum. Pop. (1981 prelim.) 48,159.

Aylesbury Vale, district, in the northern part of the county of Buckinghamshire, England. The name comes from the rich clay Vale of Aylesbury between the ridges of the Cotswolds and the Chiltern Hills. With an area of 349 sq mi (904 sq km), the district includes both Aylesbury, the county town (seat), and Buckingham, 16 mi (26 km) farther north, and their surrounding rural countryside. Pop. (1982 est.) 134,700.

Ayllón, Lucas Vazquez de (b. *c.* 1475, Toledo, Spain—d. 1526, present South Carolina), Spanish explorer and first European colonizer of what is now South Carolina.

Going to the West Indies in 1502, he became judge in the colonial administration of Hispaniola (Santo Domingo). In 1520 he went to Mexico to mediate the dispute between the Spanish commanders Hernán Cortés and Diego Velázquez. An expedition sent by him under the command of Francisco Gordillo made a landfall near Cape Fear, N.C., in 1522; in 1523 Ayllón was authorized by the Holy Roman emperor Charles V (King Charles I of Spain) to explore that area, especially to find a strait to the Spice Islands. In the early summer of 1526 Ayllón sailed from Hispaniola to found a settlement called San Miguel de Guadalupe, probably at the mouth of the Pee Dee River (Winyah Bay), in South Carolina. (Little credence can be given to the claim that the settlement was made at Jamestown, Va., 81 years before the English arrived there.) The colony was abandoned a few months later, after Ayllón and many others had died in a fever epidemic.

Aylmer, John (b. 1521, Tivetshall St. Mary, Norfolk, Eng.—d. June 3, 1594, London), Anglican bishop of London in the reign of Elizabeth I, known for his vigorous enforcement of the Act of Uniformity (1559) within his Church of England diocese. His harsh treatment of all (whether Puritan or Roman Catholic) who differed with him on ecclesiastical questions caused him to be attacked in the anti-episcopal Marprelate Tracts (1588–89) and to be characterized as "Morrell," the bad shepherd, in Edmund Spenser's *Shepheardes Calender* (1579).

Aylmer served as chaplain to Henry Grey (later the duke of Suffolk) and as tutor to Grey's daughter, Lady Jane Grey. During Queen Mary's vigorous restoration of Roman Catholicism, Aylmer, who had been given an archdeaconate in 1553, lost his post because of his opposition to the doctrine of transubstantiation. While living in exile in Strassburg and then in Zürich, he wrote a reply, entitled *An Harborowe for Faithfull and Trewe Subjectes* (1559), to John Knox's famous *First blast of the trumpet against the monstruous regiment of women.* Knox had argued that by both natural law and revealed religion, women were unfit to rule. After the accession of the

Protestant queen Elizabeth I, he returned to England.

Aylmer became archdeacon of Lincoln in 1562 and was appointed a member of the convocation that reformed and settled the doctrine and discipline of the Church of England. He was consecrated as bishop of London in 1577. His vindictiveness toward personal as well as doctrinal enemies aroused so much opposition that he attempted to be transferred to a quieter see. Although Elizabeth is thought to have considered such a move, he remained in London until his death.

Aymara, large South American Indian group living in the vast windy Titicaca plateau of the central Andes in modern Peru and Bolivia. They speak languages of the Aymaran group. In colonial times the Aymara tribes were the Canchi, Colla, Lupaca, Collagua, Ubina, Pacasa, Caranga, Charca, Quillaca, Omasuyo, and Collahuaya. In addition, the Aymaran language was anciently spoken in portions of southern Bolivia, northern Chile, and southern Peru. The modern Aymara of Peru, Bolivia, and neighbouring sections of Argentina, numbered 1,500,000—2,000,000 in the mid-1970s.

Aymara Indians making reed boats on Lake Titicaca
Loren McIntyre—Woodfin Camp Associates

Basically agriculturalists and herders, the Aymara live in an area of poor soil and harsh climate. Coarse grass gives pasturage for llama and alpaca herds. Staple crops include potatoes, oca (*Oxalis tuberosa*), ullucu (*Ullucus tuberosus*), quinoa (*Chenopodium quinoa*), corn (maize), beans, barley, and wheat. Fishing is done from giant totora-reed rafts.

Before they were conquered by the Incas, the Aymara had a number of independent states, the most important being those of the Colla and the Lupaca. About 1430 the Inca emperor Viracocha Inca began conquests southward from his capital at Cuzco. Aymara territories ultimately formed a major part of the Inca Empire, against which the Aymara continually revolted.

The Spanish conquest, beginning in 1535, brought seekers of gold and Indian labour, followed by Dominican and Jesuit friars in search of converts. The colonial agrarian economy was based on the systematic exploitation of the Aymara in agriculture, in the mines, as household servants, and on the coca plantations in the jungles. A period of rebellion began in 1780, during which the Indians killed large numbers of Spaniards, and continued until Peruvian independence from the Spanish crown was proclaimed in 1821.

The Aymara have passed through several stages of acculturation, first under the Incas, then under the Spaniards, and subsequently in the course of modernization. The Inca strengthened local Aymara dynasties as part of their imperial system and introduced new religious cults and myths, a greater variety of foods, and new art styles. The Spaniards introduced new domesticated animals and plants, plow agriculture, and iron tools. They suppressed native religious institutions but effected only a superficial conversion to Christianity. Today, the Aymara maintain their beliefs in a multi-spirit world, have many categories of magicians, diviners, medicine men, and witches, but are Christian in their beliefs about the afterworld. Independence and economic development brought changes in social organization and a decline in traditional arts and crafts.

Aymara clothing copies in crude homespun earlier Spanish colonial models. Men wear conical, ear-flapped, knit wool *gorros;* women wear round, native-made wool derbies, with wool wimples in cold weather. The single-room, rectangular, gabled Aymara house, about 8 by 10 feet (2.5 by 3 metres) in size, is made of turf, thatched with wild grass over pole rafters; it contains a family sleeping platform of mud at one end and a clay stove near the door.

The basic social unit is the extended family, consisting of a man and his brothers, their wives, sons, and unmarried daughters, living in a cluster of houses within a compound. The political unit is the *ayllu,* or *comunidad,* composed of several extended families. It has little resemblance to the aboriginal *ayllu.*

Aymaran languages, a group of South American Indian languages spoken over a fairly large region in the southern Peruvian highlands and adjacent areas of Bolivia. Some scholars classify the Aymaran group and the Quechuan group together in the Quechumaran stock. *See* Quechuan languages.

Aymé, Marcel (b. March 29, 1902, Joigny, Fr.—d. Oct. 14, 1967, Paris), novelist, essayist, and playwright, long considered a secondary writer whose extravagant creations could not be taken seriously, who belatedly was recognized as a master of light irony and storytelling.

He grew up in the country among farmers, in a world of close-knit families bounded by the barnyard on one side, the schoolhouse on the other. Aymé drew most of his characters from this setting. After a short-lived attempt at a career in journalism, he launched into writing. His first novels, *Brûlebois* (1926) and *La Table-aux-crevés* (1929; *The Hollow Field,* 1933; Prix Théophraste-Renaudot) are comedies on rural life. The broad Gallic wit of *La Jument verte* (1933; *The Green Mare,* 1938) runs through his next novels, *La Vouivre* (1943; *The Fable and the Flesh,* 1949) and *Le Chemin des écoliers* (1946; *The Transient Hour,* 1948). In these works the universe of Aymé takes shape. Through the familiar sites of town and field, strange denizens roam unquestioned, side by side with normal beings who, in turn, often act in absurd ways. This counterpoint of fantasy and reality finds its perfect format in the short story. "Le Nain" (1934; "The Dwarf") is about a dwarf who starts growing at 30, and "Le Passe-muraille" (1943; "The Man Who Could Pass Through Walls") deals with a timid clerk who walks through walls and mystifies the police. *Les Contes du chat perché,* which appeared in three series in 1939, 1950, and 1958, delighted a vast public of children from "4 to 75" with its talking farm animals that include an ox that goes to school and a pig that thinks it is a peacock. Selections were published in English as *The Wonderful Farm* (1951).

Aymé, 1967
Keystone

Aymé made a late debut in the theatre with *Lucienne et le boucher* (1947; "Lucienne and the Butcher"). *Clérambard* (1950) begins with St. Francis of Assisi appearing to a country squire. The initial absurdity is developed with rigorous logic in the manner of the Theatre of the Absurd. The mood in *La Tête des autres* (1952; "The Head of Others"), an indictment of the judicial corps, is one of savage humour. Though Aymé's theatrical works are often cruel and heavy-handed, the wit, wisdom, and morality of his short stories places them in the tradition of the fables of La Fontaine and the fairy tales of Charles Perrault.

ʿayn (Arabic: "notable"), plural Aʿyān, in Islāmic countries, an eminent person. Under the Ottoman regime (*c.* 1300–1923) the term at first denoted provincial or local notables, but in the 18th and early 19th century it was applied to a class of landlords who exercised political functions and were accorded official status.

Many *aʿyān* during the 17th century acquired lifelong leases on tax farms and prospered financially. During the 1768–74 Russo-Turkish War, the Ottoman government turned to the *aʿyān* for military and financial assistance and in return officially recognized them as the chosen representatives of the people. In 1786 the central government, suspicious of the *aʿyān*'s growing influence, attempted to exclude them from provincial government; but, when war with Russia broke out again (1787), it once more turned to them for assistance and (1790) restored their provincial authority.

During the reigns of Selim III (1789–1807) and Mahmud II (1808–39), the *aʿyān* in Rumelia (the Balkan section of the empire) played an important part in Ottoman affairs, often defying the central authority. Of these Ali Paşa of Jannina (now in Greece), Pasvanoğlu of Vidin (now in Bulgaria), and İsmail Bey of Seres (now Sérrai, Greece) maintained their own private armies, levied taxes, and dispensed justice. The *ʿayn* of Rusçuk (now in Bulgaria), Bayrakdar Mustafa Paşa, although he failed to restore Selim III, led a successful coup and brought Selim's nephew Mahmud II to the throne. Bayrakdar subsequently became grand vizier and convened (1808) a conference of *aʿyān* and *derebey*s ("valley lords," hereditary and virtually independent feudatories in Anatolia) in Istanbul, where they and representatives of Mahmud II signed a mutual assistance pact that recognized and confirmed their status. Soon after, however, Mahmud succeeded in breaking the power of the *aʿyān* and the *derebey*s and established his rule over most of the empire.

ʿAyn, al-, also spelled AL-AIN, principal town in al-Buraymī oasis, southeastern Abu Dhabi emirate, United Arab Emirates. The oasis town consists of houses of dried earth in a large palm grove; it also has a modern mosque and many gardens. Al-ʿAyn is situated in a large expanse of fertile land at the foot of Jabal (mount) Ḥafīt. Grave mounds at al-ʿAyn have tombs with figures of animals and people carved from stone and dating to about 2700 BC. Across the desert from the oasis town stands the fort of al-ʿAyn erected by shaykh ibn-Zayd in 1910; a museum is nearby. In 1952, the Saudis occupied a neighbouring village in al-Buraymī oasis. Al-ʿAyn was assigned to Abu Dhabi emirate under an agreement with Oman in 1953. The Saudis withdrew their small force from al-Buraymī oasis in 1955, after being defeated by the forces of the Sultan of Abu Dhabi and the dispute was settled by an agreement signed in 1974.

Agriculture is the traditional economic activity; fodder and market garden crops are produced. An experimental farm (1967) at al-ʿAyn concentrates on intensive stock-raising and more than 1,200 ac (480 ha) of land have been reclaimed from the desert. Commercial poultry farming is also economically important. A network of roads radiates from al-ʿAyn, connecting it with Abu Dhabi, the national capital. The town also has an airport. There are a number of industries including a cement factory, a cable and electric wire plant, a sheet metal plant, a glass and ceramic factory, a flour mill, and a brickwork. A university was established at al-ʿAyn in 1977. Pop. (1980 prelim.) 101,663.

ʿAyn Jālūt, Battle of, ʿAyn Jālūt also spelled AIN JALUT (Sept. 3, 1260), decisive victory of the Mamlūks of Egypt over the invading Mongols, which saved Egypt and Islām and halted the westward expansion of the Mongol Empire.

Baghdad, the capital city of the ʿAbbāsid caliphate, had fallen to the Mongols under the Il-Khan Hülegü in 1258, and the last ʿAbbāsid caliph had been put to death. In 1259 the Mongol army, led by the Christian Turk Kitbuga, moved into Syria, took Damascus and Aleppo, and reached the shores of the Mediterranean Sea.

The Mongols then sent an envoy to Cairo in 1260 to demand the submission of Quṭuz, the Mamlūk *sulṭān*, whose reply was the execution of the envoy. The two powers then prepared for battle.

Kitbuga and his Mongol army of about 10,000 men were lured into a trap at ʿAyn Jālūt (Spring of Goliath), near Nazareth, in Palestine, by a Mamlūk force of 120,000 men commanded by Baybars. The Mongols were completely destroyed and Kitbuga was captured and killed. The Mamlūk victory was followed up by Muslim Syria, which then drove out its Mongol garrisons. Hülegü was unable to take reprisals, as he was preoccupied with an internal struggle for power within the Mongol Empire, forcing him and much of his army to return to inner Asia. The Mongol Empire was thus contained in Iran and Mesopotamia, leaving Egypt secure in Muslim Mamlūk hands.

Ayodhyā, also called OUDH, or AWADH, town, Faizābād district, Uttar Pradesh state, northern India, on the Ghāghara (Gogra) River. An ancient city, Ayodhyā is regarded as one of the seven holy places of the Hindus. According to traditional history, it was the early capital of the kingdom of Kośala, while in

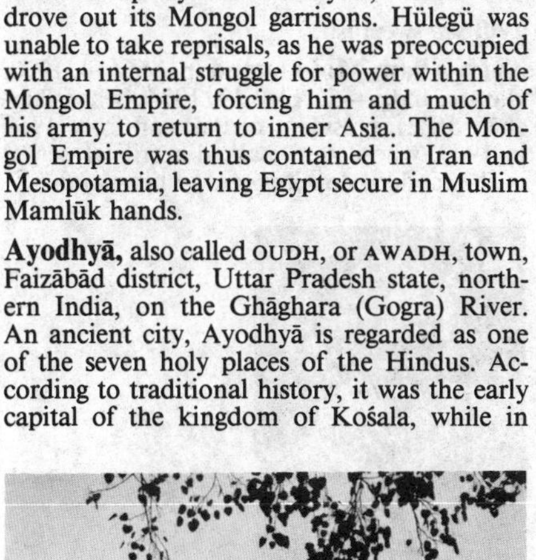

Mosque at Rāma's birthplace, Ayodhyā, Uttar Pradesh, India
Vidyavrata

Buddhist times (6th–5th century BC), Śrāvasti became the kingdom's chief city. Scholars generally agree that Ayodhyā is identical with the city of Saketa, where the Buddha is said to have resided for a time. Its later importance as a Buddhist centre can be gauged from the statement of the Chinese Buddhist monk Fa-hsien in the 5th century AD that there were 100 monasteries there. There were also a number of other monuments, including a *stūpa* (shrine) reputed to have been founded by Aśoka (3rd century BC). Ayodhyā is revered by Hindus because of its association, in the great Indian epic poem *Rāmāyaṇa*, with the birth of Rāma and with the rule of his father, Daśaratha. According to this source, the city was prosperous and well fortified and had a large population.

The Kanauj kingdom arose in Oudh during the 11th and 12th centuries. The region was later included in the Delhi sultanate, the Jaunpur kingdom, and, in the 16th century, the Mughal Empire. Oudh gained a measure of independence early in the 18th century but became subordinate to the British East India Company in 1764. In 1856 it was annexed by the British; the annexation and subsequent loss of rights by the hereditary land revenue receivers provided one of the causes of the Indian Mutiny in 1857. Oudh was joined with the Āgra Presidency in 1877 to form the North-Western Provinces and later the United Provinces of Āgra and Oudh, now Uttar Pradesh state.

There are few surviving monuments of any antiquity. Rāma's birthplace is marked by a mosque, erected by the Mughal emperor Bābur in 1528 on the site of an earlier temple. The numerous Vaiṣṇava shrines and bathing *ghāṭs* are of no great age. Close to the modern town are several mounds marking the site of ancient Ayodhyā that have not yet been adequately explored by archaeologists. Pop. (1981) 30,500.

Ayr, town, northeastern Queensland, Australia, on the delta of the Burdekin River. The settlement was surveyed and gazetted in 1881. Declared a town in 1882 and named after the Scottish birthplace of Sir Thomas McIllwraith, then state premier, it became a shire in 1903. On the north coast rail line and the Bruce Highway to Townsville (45 mi [70 km] northwest) and Brisbane (657 mi southeast), it is the centre of the lower Burdekin irrigation area, which produces sugarcane, rice, corn (maize), and beef cattle. There are several sugar mills in the area. A 3,619-ft (1,103-m) bridge is part of a road leading 7 mi south to the town of Home Hill. Pop. (1981) 8,787.

Ayr, also called AYRSHIRE, former county, southwestern Scotland, since the reorganization of 1975 divided among the four districts of Kyle and Carrick, Cumnock and Doon Valley, Kilmarnock and Loudoun, and Cunninghame, of Strathclyde region.

The county had a concave western coastline and rose to its eastern boundary in the Southern Uplands at about 2,000 ft (600 m). Rivers divide it into three ancient regions: Cunninghame, north of the River Irvine; Kyle, between the Irvine and Doon; and Carrick, south of the Doon. Inland is high, windswept moorland, with a heavy annual rainfall of 60–100 in. (1,500–2,500 mm) and a poor peat and heather vegetation. Along the coast is undulating lowland, between 100 and 1,000 ft overlying coal-yielding rocks, especially in the central areas. A mild, damp climate (rainfall 40–50 in.) results in luxuriant pastures. Coastal postglacial, raised beaches (about 25–100 ft) provide warm, well-drained soils for the intensive cultivation of such produce as early potatoes and strawberries.

Minor prehistoric finds indicate that Ayr had been occupied for about 6,000 years. One Roman fort, AD 79–84, survives at Loudoun Hill. In the 11th century, Ayr was part of the rudimentary kingdom of Scotland, and its king Duncan became the first ruler of all Scotland. Invading Norwegians were defeated at the Battle of Largs (1263); and in 1297 at Ayr, Sir William Wallace began the struggle to regain Scotland's independence. From Turnberry Castle (1307) Robert I the Bruce began his fight for the Scottish throne, and in 1315 he held Parliament in Ayr; there Oliver Cromwell later built a citadel (1654) to control southwestern Scotland.

Scotland's first deep coal mines were sunk in Ayr in 1780, and ironworks and textile industries followed rapidly. Simultaneously the agricultural revolution brought enclosures, draining, and crop rotation, and Ayr became an important and highly developed agricultural area, its lush lowland pastures having the heaviest stock-carrying capacity in Scotland. The main industrial areas are Irvine and Garnock, in which textiles of all kinds are produced.

Ayr, Gaelic AR, or AD'HAR, Atlantic coast seaport and former county town (seat) of Ayr, Scotland, and centre of the region associated with the national poet, Robert Burns. The town lies on the southern bank of the River Ayr, which is still crossed by the 13th-century Auld Brig, immortalized in Burns's poem "The Brigs of Ayr." Ayr was created a royal burgh in 1202 (the original charter is preserved in the Town Hall) and became the garrison and court town of the administrative entity known as the Sheriffdom of Ayr. During medieval times it was the chief Scottish port on the western coast until it was superseded by the developing River Clyde ports to its north. Surviving medieval relics include Loudoun Hall (16th century, restored), the town house of the Loudouns, a family that long supplied the sheriffs of Ayr. In the 18th century Ayr was a small town concentrated around the High Street, Sandgate, and the adjoining Vennels, but by the 19th century it had become a social centre and watering place for the Scottish gentry. Much of Ayr's heavy engineering, metalworking, and textile industry dates from this period, having been stimulated by the completion of a rail link with the city of Glasgow in 1840. Ayr still depends on the influx of people, both as a popular holiday resort, with the added attraction of regular horse racing meetings, and as an important local commercial centre and weekly cattle market. In addition to being a fishing port, Ayr exports coal across the North Channel to nearby Northern Ireland and imports phosphates and timber. Of the town's educational establishments, Ayr Academy (founded 1233) is the most notable. More recently, Craigie College of Education (1965) and Ayr Technical College have been opened.

Robert Burns was born at Alloway (3 mi [5 km] south), now a residential suburb of Ayr and an annual place of pilgrimage for thousands of tourists. Pop. (1981) 49,522.

ayre, also spelled AIR, genre of solo song with lute accompaniment that flourished in England in the late 16th and early 17th centuries. The outstanding composers in the genre were the lutanist John Dowland, whose "Flow, my teares" ("Lachrimae") became so popular that a large number of continental and English instrumental pieces were based on its melody; and the poet and composer Thomas Campion. Other leading composers included John Danyel, Robert Jones, and Michael Cavendish.

Generally, ayres are graceful, elegant, polished, often strophic songs (*i.e.,* having the same music for each stanza), typically dealing with amorous subjects. Many, however, are lively and animated, full of rhythmic subtleties, and others are deeply emotional songs that gain much of their effect from bold, expressive harmonies and striking melodic lines.

The ayre developed during a European trend toward accompanied solo song (in place of songs for several voices). Chansons, madrigals, and other polyphonic songs were frequently published in versions for voice and lute, and books of ayres often provided for optional performance by several singers, by having, opposite the solo and lute version, the three additional voice parts printed so that they could be read from three sides of a table. *See also* air de cour.

Ayrer, Jakob (b. March? 1543, Franconia—d. March 26, 1605, Nürnberg), dramatist who incorporated elements of Elizabethan plays (*e.g.,* spectacular stage effects, violent action, histrionic bombast, the stock figure of the clown) into his own plays, particularly his *Fastnachtsspiele,* the farces performed at Shrovetide.

A lawyer by profession, Ayrer spent his last 12 years as a city council member and imperial notary in Nürnberg, where he witnessed the plays of the Englische Komödianten, English acting troupes that toured Germany in the late 16th and early 17th centuries. Although not as talented as his master, Hans Sachs, Ayrer was very prolific. He wrote more than 100 comedies, tragedies, historical dramas, *Fastnachtsspiele,* and *Singspiele.* The last—vaudeville plays in which strophic texts are sung to traditional tunes—is a genre he first popularized, and it represents his greatest artistic achievement. Sixty-nine of his plays are preserved in his *Opus Theatricum* (1618; "Works of the Theatre"), of which *Comedia von der schönen Sidea* (*c.* 1600; "Comedy of the Beautiful Sidea") is often cited for the affinities it bears to Shakespeare's *Tempest.*

Ayres, Anne (b. Jan. 3, 1816, London—d. Feb. 9, 1896, New York City), the first American Protestant sister in the Protestant Episcopal Church.

Ayres migrated with her family to the United States in 1836 and began a career as a tutor soon thereafter. In 1845 she heard the preaching of William Augustus Muhlenberg, an Episcopal clergyman, and was moved to commit herself to a religious vocation. Later that year Muhlenberg consecrated her a "sister of the Holy Communion"; there had been no previous Protestant orders for women in the United States or England, because religious communities for women were abolished during the Reformation in the 16th century.

The sisterhood was formally organized in 1852, with Ayres as the "first sister." The sisters conducted a parish school and infirmary and later served St. Johnland, a religious and charitable community on Long Island, N.Y. (In 1940 the Sisterhood of the Holy Communion was disbanded.)

Ayres wrote several books, including *Practical Thoughts on Sisterhoods* (1864), *Evangelical Sisterhoods* (1867), and *The Life and Work of William Augustus Muhlenberg* (1880).

Ayrshire, breed of hardy dairy cattle originating in the county of Ayr, Scotland, in the latter part of the 18th century and considered to be the only special dairy breed to have originated in the British Isles. The body colour varies from almost pure white to nearly all cherry red or brown with any combination of these colours; black or brindle are considered undesirable. The beef qualities of the breed are of secondary importance. The distribution of the breed is wide, and exportations have been made to many countries. It is most strongly represented in the United Kingdom, Canada, and the United States.

Ayrshire whitework, in embroidery, 19th-century name for a kind of drawn thread work done in white thread on white material. Although similar work had been executed earlier and in other centres (for example, in 13th- and 14th-century Germany) and other examples are known from the intervening period, whitework became associated with the

Detail of fabric decorated with Ayrshire whitework, Scottish, first quarter of the 19th century
Tom Scott, Edinburgh—EB Inc.

county (shire) of Ayr in Scotland after 1780, when it became a centre for the manufacture of muslin. Fine muslin was the material par excellence for this work, in which a variety of drawn fabric stitches were combined with floral sprigs and formal decorative motifs in satin and other stitches. The effect was somewhat akin to lace.

Aysén (Chile): *see* Aisén.

Aytmatov, Chingiz, Aytmatov also spelled AITMATOV (b. Dec. 12, 1928, Sheker, Kirgiz A.S.S.R.), author, translator, and journalist, who began his literary career in 1952 and in 1959 became a *Pravda* correspondent in Kirgiz.

He achieved major literary recognition with his collection of short stories, *Povesti gor i stepey* (1962; *Tales of Mountains and Steppes,* 1969), for which he was awarded the Lenin Prize in 1963. His most important works include: *Trudnaya pereprava* (1956; "A Difficult Passage"), *Litsom k litsu* (1957; "Face to Face"), *Proshchay, Gulsary!* (1966; *Farewell, Gulsary!,* 1970), *Bely parokhod* (1970, *The White Ship,* 1972), and *Pervy uchitel* (1976; "The First Teacher").

Although Aytmatov composed in both Russian and Kirgiz, most of his works, predominantly long short stories or novelettes, were originally written in the latter language. His major themes were love and friendship, the trials and heroism of wartime, and the emancipation of Kirgiz youth from restrictive custom and tradition. Aytmatov was elected a member of the Presidium of the Kirgiz Writers' Union in 1958 and first secretary of the Kirgiz Union of Cinematography Workers in 1962. He was made a member of the Supreme Soviet of the U.S.S.R. in 1966. In 1967 he became a member of the Executive Board of the Writers' Union of the U.S.S.R., and he was awarded the Soviet state prize for literature in 1968.

To make the best use of the Britannica, consult the INDEX *first*

Ayton, Sir Robert, Ayton also spelled AYTOUN (b. 1570, Kinaldy, Fife, Scot.—d. *c.* Feb. 28, 1638, London), one of the earliest Scottish poets to use standard English as a literary medium.

Educated at the University of St. Andrews, in the county of Fife, he came into favour at court for a Latin panegyric on the accession of James VI to the English throne. He was knighted in 1612 and subsequently held various lucrative offices; he was private secretary to the queens of James I and Charles I. Although Ayton wrote poems in Latin, Greek, and French, as well as English, and enjoyed a considerable literary reputation, he never considered himself a poet. A poem, "Old Long Syne," that is ascribed to Ayton may possibly have been the inspiration for the famous "Auld Lang Syne" by Robert Burns.

Aytoun, William Edmondstoune (b. June 21, 1813, Edinburgh—d. Aug. 4, 1865, Elgin, Moray, Scot.), poet famous for parodies and light verse that greatly influenced the style of later Scottish humorous satire.

Born into a literary family, Aytoun learned from his mother to love Scottish ballads and history. He was educated at the University of Edinburgh and in Germany, and in 1840 was called to the Scottish bar. That same year he first collaborated with Theodore Martin in a series of humorous and satirical papers for *Blackwood's Magazine,* later published as the *Bon Gaultier Ballads* (1845); these include Aytoun's parodies "The Queen in France," based on "Sir Patrick Spens," and "The Massacre of the Macpherson," both of which were models for later writers, especially for W.S. Gilbert in the *Bab Ballads* (1869).

Aytoun joined the staff of *Blackwoods* in 1844, contributing political as well as miscellaneous articles. The following year he was appointed professor of rhetoric and belles lettres at Edinburgh. Shortly afterward he published *Lays of the Scottish Cavaliers* (1848), a set of Jacobite ballads that achieved wide popularity. In 1854, reverting to light verse, he published *Firmilian: . . . a Spasmodic Tragedy,* in which the writings of the spasmodic school (*q.v.*) were brilliantly ridiculed.

In 1858 Aytoun published the *Ballads of Scotland,* 2 vol., and a translation made with Martin of the *Poems and Ballads of Goethe.* His *Norman Sinclair* (1861) pictures Scottish manners in the early 19th century.

ayu: *see* sweetfish.

Ayub Khan, Mohammad (b. May 14, 1907, Hazāra, India—d. April 19, 1974, near Islāmābād, Pak.), president of Pakistan from 1958 to 1969, whose rule marked a critical period in the modern development of his nation.

Mohammad Ayub Khan
By courtesy of the Pakistan Information Department

After studying at Alīgarh Muslim University, in Uttar Pradesh, India, and at the British Royal Military College, at Sandhurst, he was commissioned an officer in the Indian Army (1928). In World War II he commanded a battalion in Burma, and after the 1947 partition of British India he was rapidly promoted in the army of the new Muslim state of Pakistan: from major general (1948) to commander in chief (1951). In addition, Ayub became minister of defense (1954) for a brief period.

After several years of political turmoil in Pakistan, in 1958 Pres. Iskander Mirza, with army support, abrogated the constitution and appointed Ayub as chief martial law administrator. Soon after, Ayub had himself declared president, and Mirza was exiled. Ayub reorganized the administration and acted to restore the economy through agrarian reforms and stimulation of industry. Foreign investment was also encouraged.

Ayub introduced the system of "basic democracies" in 1960. It consisted of a network of local self-governing bodies to provide a link between the government and the people. Primary governing units were set up to conduct local affairs; their members were elected by constituencies of 800–1,000 adults. A national referendum among all those elected confirmed Ayub as president. He was reelected under this system in 1965, against a strong challenge from an opposition united behind Fatima Jinnah, the sister of Mohammed Ali Jinnah, the creator of Pakistan.

When the United States began to rearm India after China's invasion of northern India in 1962, Ayub established close relations with China and received substantial military aid from it. In the meantime, Pakistan's dispute with India over Jammu and Kashmir worsened, culminating in the outbreak of war in 1965. After two weeks of fighting, both sides agreed to a UN-called cease-fire and came to a boundary settlement.

The failure to gain Kashmir, and student unrest over suffrage restrictions, intensified internal turmoil to such an extent that at the end of 1968 Ayub announced he would not stand for reelection. Riots continued, and he resigned his office on March 26, 1969, to be succeeded by Gen. Yahya Khan, commander in chief of the army.

Ayuthia, also spelled AYUTTHAYA (Thailand): *see* Phra Nakhon Si Ayutthaya.

ʿayyār (Arabic: "vagabond," "scoundrel"), Arabic plural ʿAYYĀRŪN, Persian plural ʿAYYĀRĀN, warrior common to Iraq and Iran in the 9th–12th centuries, often associated in *futūwah*, medieval Islāmic urban organizations.

Though *ʿayyārūn* were found fighting for Islām on the frontiers of Inner Asia, the most thorough documentation of these warriors describes their activities in Baghdad in the 10th–12th centuries, a picture that may not be typical of *ʿayyārūn* in other areas. The Baghdad of this period, ruled by the Būyids (945–1055), was an especially lawless city, troubled by violent battles between members of the Sunnī and Shīʿī sects of Islām. *ʿAyyārūn* terrorized the city, extorting taxes on roads or at markets, burning wealthy quarters and markets, and looting the homes of the rich at night. For several years (1028–33), al-Burjumī and Ibn al-Mawṣilī, leaders of the *ʿayyārūn*, virtually ruled the city in the face of an ineffectual government.

Although the *ʿayyārūn* have been commonly labelled thieves and robbers, modern historians point out that their activities multiplied only when the central government was weak or in times of civil war, when their services were sought by many of the conflicting parties. Under strong rulers their lawlessness subsided, and, with the appearance of the Seljuqs in the 12th century, it ceased. The *ʿayyārūn*, in reaction to social injustice, warred against the government and the wealthy, the police and the merchant classes.

Outside Baghdad, from Inner Asia to Mesopotamia, the *ʿayyārūn* identified more closely with the middle class, who depended on them to support the local dynasty or displace it. They even succeeded in setting up a dynasty of their own, the Ṣaffārids (867–*c.* 1495), in eastern Iran.

Ayyūbid DYNASTY, Sunnī Muslim dynasty, founded by Saladin (Ṣalāḥ ad-Dīn), that ruled over Egypt and what became upper Iraq, most of Syria, and Yemen in the late 12th and early 13th centuries.

Saladin's father, Ayyūb (in full, Najm ad-Dīn Ayyūb ibn Shādhī), for whom the Ayyūbid dynasty is named, was a member of a family of Kurdish soldiers of fortune who in the 12th century took service under the Seljuq Turkish rulers in Iraq and Syria. Appointed governor of Damascus, Ayyūb and his brother Shīrkūh united Syria in preparation for war against the crusaders. After his father's death in 1173, Saladin displaced the Shīʿī Fāṭimid dynasty, further mobilized Muslim enthusiasm to create a united front against the Crusades, and made Egypt the most powerful Muslim state in the world at that time. The solidarity maintained under Saladin disappeared just before his death (1193): following his distribution of his territories among vassal relations who enjoyed autonomous internal administration of their provinces, the Ayyūbid regime became a decentralized, semifeudal family federation. The strain of Frankish–Ayyūbid relations was relaxed under the reigns of al-ʿĀdil and al-Kāmil, Saladin's brother and nephew; Jerusalem was restored to the Christians; and Ayyūbid factionalism was quieted. With al-Kāmil's death (1238), however, old family disputes revived, and the Ayyūbid decline was ended by Mamlūk accession to power in 1250.

The Ayyūbids, zealous Sunnī Muslims seeking to convert Muslim Shīʿīs and Christians, introduced into Egypt and Jerusalem the *madrasah*, an academy of religious sciences. Culturally an extension and development of the Fāṭimids, the Ayyūbids were great military engineers, building the citadel of Cairo and the defenses of Aleppo.

ʿAyzarīyah, al- (Jerusalem): *see* Bethany.

Azad Kashmir, quasi-state in the Pakistani-held sector of Jammu and Kashmir, in the northwestern part of the Indian subcontinent. Azad (Free) Kashmir, established in 1947 after the partion of India, is neither a province nor an agency of Pakistan but has a government of its own that is regarded by Pakistan as "independent," even though it is protected by and economically and administratively linked to Pakistan. It has an area of about 650 sq mi (1,680 sq km) and consists of an arc-shaped stretch of territory bordering the Indian-held state of Jammu and Kashmir on the east, the Pakistani states of Punjab on the south and southwest and North-West Frontier Province on the west, and the Gilgit and Baltistān agencies of Pakistan on the north. Azad Kashmir is administratively divided into four districts: Muzaffarābād, Pūnch, Kotli, and Mīrpur.

Northern Azad Kashmir comprises foothills of the Himalayas rising to Jamgarh peak (15,531 ft [4,734 m]); south of this are the northwestern reaches of the Pir Panjāl Range, with an average crest line of 12,500 ft. The Jhelum River and its upper tributaries, including the Pūnch River, have cut deeply incised and terraced valleys through these mountain ranges; the Jhelum also forms most of the western boundary of Azad Kashmir. The southern part of the territory consists of a narrow zone of plains country in the Pūnch region that is characterized by interlocking sandy alluvial fans. Thorn scrub and coarse grass are the dominant forms of vegetation in the south; this scrubland gives way to pine forests at higher elevations in the north.

Wheat, barley, corn (maize), millet, and livestock are raised in the lower valleys and support relatively high population densities. In the more sparsely settled upper valleys, corn, cattle, and forestry are the economic mainstays. There are deposits of marble near Muzaffarābād and Mīrpur, graphite at Mohriwali, and other reserves of bauxite, silica, chalk, zircon, and low-grade coal. Household industries produce carved wooden objects, textiles, and Durri carpets. The government of Azad Kashmir has its headquarters at Muzaffarābād, which is linked by road with Abbottabād to the southwest. Mīrpur is the major town in the southern part of the territory.

Azaïs, Pierre-Hyacinthe (b. March 1, 1766, Sorèze, Fr.—d. Jan. 22, 1845, Paris), philosopher whose optimism was rooted in the idea that human experience is imbued with a natural and harmonious balance between joy and sadness and that it is in this balance that meaning can be discovered. He advocated the idea in the work that first brought him fame, *Des compensations dans les destinées humaines*, 3 vol. (1809). In a following work, *Système universel*, 8 vol. (1809–12), he further developed the same idea and related it to certain cosmological concepts. At the core of this voluminous work is the notion that all experience (past, present, and future) can be understood in terms of an interaction between expansive and compressive forces.

Later, Azaïs moved into politics and was appointed to minor administrative posts in France. When the Bourbons were restored to power in France he was dismissed and eventually sank into poverty. Years later he was granted a government pension, and with his wife, Sophie Cotton, a novelist, he turned to fiction and assisted her in writing *L'Ami des enfants*, 12 vol. (1816), a sequel to a collection of children's stories by Arnaud Berquin.

Azak (Russian S.F.S.R.): *see* Azov.

azalea, any of a certain species of *Rhododendron* (*q.v.*), of the family Ericaceae, formerly given the generic name *Azalea*. Neither the shape of the corolla (ring of petals) nor other characteristics are sufficiently constant to serve as a means of separating these plants into two distinct genera, although azaleas are typically deciduous while rhododendrons are evergreen. Azalea flowers are funnel-shaped, somewhat two-lipped, and often fragrant. Rhododendrons, on the other hand, are bell-shaped and usually odourless. Azalea flowers typically have only 5 projecting stamens. Intermediate forms, however, do occur. Cultivated varieties have been bred from species native to the hilly regions of Asia and North America.

Well-known North American kinds include the smooth, or sweet, azalea (*R. arborescens*), a fragrant white-flowering shrub 3 to 6 metres (about 10 to 20 feet) high; the flame azalea (*R. calendulaceum*) a shrub 0.5 to 2 m high; and the pinxter flower (*R. periclymenoides*), a shrub 1 to 2 m high, with pink to whitish

Azalea
Gretchen Garner—EB Inc.

flowers. Hundreds of horticultural forms have been bred from the Ghent azalea (*R. gandavense*); the molle azalea (*R. molle*); the Yodogawa azalea (*R. yedoense*); and the torch azalea (*R. kaempferi*).

Azalī, any member of the Bābī movement (followers of a 19th-century Iranian prophet, the Bāb) who chose to remain faithful to the Bāb's teachings and to his chosen successor, Mirza Yaḥya, given the religious title Ṣobḥ-e Azal, after a split in the movement occurred in 1863. For about 13 years after the Bāb's execution (1850), his followers acknowledged Ṣobḥ-e Azal as their lawful leader. In 1863, when Ṣobḥ-e Azal's half-brother Bahāʾ Ullāh privately declared himself "him whom God shall manifest"—a new prophet foretold by the Bāb—the Bābī community polarized. The

Azalīs rejected the divine claims of Bahā' Ullāh as premature, arguing that the world must first accept Bābī laws in order to be ready for "him whom God shall manifest." Most Bābīs, however, favoured Bahā' Ullāh and, after the public manifestation of his mission in 1867, began the development of a new religion, the Bahā'ī faith.

The Azalīs have retained the original teachings of the Bāb's *Bayān* ("Revelation") and supplemented them with the instructions of Ṣobḥ-e Azal. Numerically they have remained considerably outnumbered by the Bahā'īs. *See also* Bāb, the.

Azamgarh, town, administrative headquarters of Azamgarh district, Uttar Pradesh state, northern India, on the Tons River, a tributary of the Ghāghara, north of Vārānasi (Benares). Founded in 1665 by A'ẓam Khān, a local chief for whom it is named, the compact town is enclosed on three sides by the river, which occasionally floods. Principal industries are sugar milling and cotton weaving. The town is served by the Northeastern Railway.

Azamgarh district, 2,200 sq mi (5,700 sq km) in area, comprises a stretch of level plain that is bordered (north) by the Ghāghara River. Rainfall is plentiful, and the land is fertile; crops include rice, wheat, and sugarcane. The town of Maunath Bhanjan (short form, Mau) is noted for its handloomed cloth. Pop. (1981) town, 66,523; district, 3,544,130.

Azaña y Díaz, Manuel (b. Jan. 10, 1880, Alcalá de Henares, Spain—d. Nov. 4, 1940, Montauban, Fr.), Spanish minister and president of the Second Republic.

Azaña y Díaz, detail of an oil painting by J.M. López Mezquita, 1937; in the Hispanic Society of America collection

By courtesy of the Hispanic Society of America, New York

Azaña studied law in Paris and became a civil servant, journalist, and writer, figuring prominently in the Madrid literary Ateneo. He translated George Borrow's *The Bible in Spain* and was awarded the national prize for literature in 1926 for his biography of the novelist Juan Valera. His novel *El jardín de los frailes* (1927; "The Garden of the Monks") was a vehicle for his anticlericalism.

In 1930 he organized a republican party in opposition to the dictatorship of Gen. Miguel Primo de Rivera and was one of the signatories of the Pact of San Sebastián (August 1930), an alliance of republicans, socialists, and the Catalan left calling for the abdication of Alfonso XIII. When Alfonso left after the municipal elections of April 1931, this group became the provisional government. As minister of war, Azaña drastically reduced the army establishment and forced through the anticlerical clauses of the new constitution. This caused the resignation of the prime minister Niceto Alcalá Zamora (October 1931). Azaña succeeded him.

Azaña held office until September 1933, pushing through a draconian Law for the Defense of the Republic (1931) and severely repressing disorders. Reforms, some long overdue, were hastily adopted. Azaña's Acción Republicana was a small party, and he depended on the Socialists and Catalan left. His parliamentary defeat was followed by elections that showed a general rejection of his radicalism. In 1934 the Socialists rebelled in Asturias and the Catalan left rebelled in Barcelona, and Azaña was arrested for incitement, but acquitted at trial. In 1935 he formed the Popular Front in imitation of Léon Blum's French coalition—which admitted Communists. In the elections of February 1936 this alignment, led by Azaña, was successful, and he again formed a government. However, the Cortes decided to remove Pres. Alcalá Zamora, and Azaña was elected to succeed him (May 1936). He and his friends had not intended the president to be more than a figurehead, and he now found himself unable to check the deteriorating public order or the outbreak of civil war (July 1936). With the victory of Gen. Francisco Franco, he went into exile in France, where he died.

Azande, also spelled ASANDE, or ZANDE, also called NIAM-NIAM, people of central Africa who speak a language of the Adamawa-Eastern branch of the Niger-Congo family. Extending across the Nile–Congo divide, they live partly in The Sudan, partly in Zaire, and partly in the Central African Republic. Their country, savanna in the north and rain forest in the south, is mostly suitable for agriculture and hunting. They had a reputation for cannibalism in the past. The Azande are fine craftsmen in iron, clay, and wood.

They are ethnically very mixed. In the 18th century a people calling themselves Ambomu and living on the Mbomu River began, under the leadership of their ruling Avongara clan, to conquer vast stretches of territory to the south and east, overpowering many peoples, some of whom have preserved their languages while others have been completely assimilated. This amalgam is the Azande people of today. During their conquests, scions of the royal clan carved out kingdoms for themselves, and wars between kingdoms were frequent.

The traditional distribution of the Azande is in widely scattered family homesteads. Polygyny is practiced, and in the past many men, especially the nobles, had so many wives that it was difficult for the younger men to marry. Adultery could be heavily punished. Marriage was contracted by the gift of about 20 spears by the bridegroom to the family of the bride. Girls were married very young and sometimes affianced a few hours after birth. While commoners will not marry into their own clans, nobles often marry kinswomen, even their paternal half-sisters and their own daughters. Patrilineal clans are numerous but widely dispersed. These clans are totemic, and it is believed that at a man's death the body-soul, one of the two souls the Azande credit themselves with, becomes a totemic animal of his clan.

Azande religion is an ancestor cult, the conception of a god being vague and relatively unimportant. Witchcraft is more significant for them, however, than the cult of ancestors.

Āzārbāijān-e Gharbī, English WEST AZARBAIJAN, or AZERBAIJAN, *ostān* (province), northwestern Iran, bounded by Āzārbāijān-e Sharqī *ostān* and Lake Urmia on the east, and by Kordestān *ostān* on the south. It borders Iraq and Turkey on the west-northwest and the U.S.S.R. on the north and covers an area of 15,141 sq mi (39,216 sq km). Zoroaster, according to tradition, was born in Orūmīyeh (formerly Rezā'īyeh), now the capital of the *ostān*. The Arabs controlled the region in the 7th century and the Mongols in the 13th century. The constant wars between the Osmanlis and the Iranians over the province for more than 200 years (15th to 18th century) led eventually to the invasion of the Turks and subsequently the Russians before Nāder Shāh took control of the region about 1740. The area was again occupied by Turks during World War I and by the Soviet Union during World War II. The short-lived Kurdish Republic was set up at Mahābād in 1946 by the U.S.S.R. until the Iranian Army occupied the region in 1947. During the Iranian Revolution in 1979–80 the Kurds held demonstrations in Mahābād, and fighting broke out between Shī'ah and Kurds.

Āzārbāijān-e Gharbī province composes part of the Zagros Mountains, with a series of irregular tablelands at an average elevation of 5,000 to 6,000 ft (1,500 to 1,800 m). Elevation is greater in the extreme north and west and lower towards the south and east. The overall effect is of a stair-step topography emphasized by fault scarps defining a number of basins and the lowland around Khūy. Rainfall is relatively heavy over much of the plateau. Deeply incised, perennial streams have cut gorge-like valleys. The streams are maintained throughout the rainless summer and early autumn by melting snow and flowing springs. The climate is warm in summer and very severe in winter; the mountains are snow clad for seven to eight months of the year.

The population consists mainly of Turks, together with Kurds and Armenians. The Kurds are few in number and inhabit the area from the Aras River on the north to near Khūy on the south. The Armenians are thinly scattered in the northwest. Most of the population are Shī'ī Muslims. Agriculture, the mainstay of the economy, is concentrated in the fertile Orūmīyeh basin, and barley, wheat, rice, potatoes, sugar beets, walnuts, almonds, fruits, and vegetables are grown. Livestock, including sheep and goats, is raised. Industries include sugar mills, a cold-storage plant, food-processing units, and textile mills. Coarse carpets and rugs are woven, and metalware is produced on a small scale. Coal, salt, and building stone are worked. A railway line runs through the centre of the province, and roads link Orūmīyeh with Mahābād, Khūy, Makū, Mīāndowāb, Salmās (formerly Shāhpūr), and Pīrānshahr. There is much traffic ferried across Lake Urmia between Āzārbāijān-e Gharbī and Āzārbāijān-e Sharqī. Pop. (1983 est.) 1,688,000.

Āzārbāijān-e Sharqī, English EAST AZARBAIJAN, or AZERBAIJAN, *ostān* (province), northwestern Iran, bordering the U.S.S.R. on the north and northeast and Lake Urmia on the west. It is bounded by the *ostān* of Āzārbāijān-e Gharbī on the south and southeast. It has an area of 25,910 sq mi (67,102 sq km).

The region was occupied by the Arabs in the 7th century, and according to tradition, the wife of Caliph Hārūn ar-Rashīd settled in Tabrīz, now the capital of the *ostān,* in 791. The region suffered greatly from the Mongol invasions in the 13th and 14th centuries, but it became the centre of an empire extending from Syria to the Oxus River. Tabrīz, the capital, became a centre of cultural and commercial life. Tabrīz was also the capital of the Turkman dynasties of the Kara Koyunlu and Ak Koyunlu (1378–1502). The Russians invaded the area in the early 18th century and again during the brief Russian–Iranian war of 1826–28. The Turks occupied it during World War I in the wake of the Bolshevik Revolution in Russia in 1917. During World War II Soviet troops occupied the region, and with Soviet support the Tudeh (Communist) Party proclaimed the Sovereign Republic of Azerbaijan, with Tabriz as its capital; Iranian forces regained the province in 1947.

Āzārbāijān-e Sharqī *ostān* is generally mountainous; the eastern Zagros Mountains run north–south through the whole *ostān.* Large volcanic cones, such as Sabalān (14,000 ft [4,270 m]) and Sahand (12,138 ft), are found on the high plateau, and the region is subject to earthquakes. Steppeland, such as the Dasht-e Moghān on the southern bank of the

Aras River, is the dominant feature of the landscape; villages are located mostly in the foothills. The major rivers are the Aras on the north, with its tributary, the Qareh Sū; the Kizil Uzun on the east, with its tributaries, the Qarāngū and Aidughmish; and the Jaghātū. The climate is hot in summer, the winter lasts long, but the spring is temperate and delightful. The region is populated mainly by Turks, Armenians (who are Christians), and a few Chaldeans. The Turks are Shīʿī Muslims who speak Azerbaijani and use Arabic script. Agriculture is the principal occupation of the people; crops include barley, wheat, rice, indigo plants, fruits, and vegetables. Sheep, goats, and poultry are raised. Industries produce tractors, factory machinery, cement, textiles, electrical equipment and tools, animal fodder, turbines, motorcycles, clocks and watches, processed foods, and agricultural implements. Copper, arsenic, kaolin, lead, and salt are mined. A network of roads and railways link Tabriz with Marāgheh, Ardabīl, Ahar, Mīāneh, Marand, and Sarab. An oil pipeline runs through the *ostān* from Tabriz to Tehrān. Pop. (1983 est.) 3,679,000.

Azare, town and traditional emirate, Bauchi State, northeastern Nigeria, located in the northern extension of the state. The town and emirate are peopled by the Hausa, Fulani, and Beriberi, who are predominantly Muslim. The First Prime Minister of Nigeria, Sir Abubakar Tafawa Balewa, was born in the emirate. The area is chiefly agricultural, the principal crops consisting of cotton and peanuts (groundnuts). In addition to a teacher-training college for women, the town has a state-run advanced teachers college for the preparation of secondary level teachers. Azare town is served by a general hospital. Pop. (1963) 27,445.

Azariah (king of Judah): *see* Uzziah.

Azariah, The Prayer of, apocryphal insertion into the Book of Daniel in the Greek (Septuagint) and subsequently included in the Latin (Vulgate) Bible and the Roman Catholic biblical canon.

The Prayer of Azariah and the accompanying Song of the Three Young Men form part of chapter three and embellish the story of Shadrach, Meshach, and Abednego, three Jews who were bound and thrown into a fiery furnace for defying Nebuchadrezzar's order to worship an idol. The Prayer of Azariah (original Hebrew for Abednego) is a song of lamentation following a liturgical style popular after the 4th century BC: an introductory section of praise to God, a confession of Israel's sin, a plea for mercy, and a doxology. The Song of the Three Young Men is a hymn of thanksgiving for their escape by Azariah and his two companions. Its arrangement is similar to the repetitive refrains in Psalm 136. It takes its liturgical theme from Psalm 148.

Azariah, Vedanayakam Samuel (b. Aug. 17, 1874, Vellalanvillai, India—d. Jan. 1, 1945, Dornakal), first Indian bishop of the Anglican Church in India.

He was the son of an Indian clergyman and was educated at the Madras Christian College. In 1896 he became a travelling secretary for the Young Men's Christian Association and in 1906 secretary of the National Missionary Society of India, founded to evangelize India. He was ordained a priest in 1909. In 1912 he was made bishop of Dornakal, where he worked to create an indigenous Indian church using Indian postures, poetry, and idioms. During his episcopate the Christians in his diocese grew from 50,000 to 250,000. He led the Joint Committee on Church Union in South India that brought about in 1947, after his death, the merger of the Anglican Church in South India with other Protestant bodies.

azathioprine, immunosuppressive drug used in treating leukemia, rheumatoid arthritis, and other systemic inflammations. Azathioprine decreases the number of single-nucleus cells and granulocytic cells that can migrate to inflammatory sites.

Azathioprine and its metabolite, 6-mercaptopurine, are beneficial in maintaining transplanted kidneys and other tissues. Leukopenia is the major undesirable side effect, although anemia and bleeding may also occur. When used with allopurinol, its pharmacological effect is increased. Azathioprine is readily absorbed after oral administration.

Azay-le-Rideau, town, Indre-et-Loire *département,* Centre region, central France, midway on the 30-mi (48-km) road from Tours to Chinon, where it crosses the Indre River. Originally the site of a Roman villa, the town was known in the 12th century as Azayum, and in 1213 the chatelain was Hugues-le-Ridel. When the Dauphin (later Charles VII) was insulted by the Burgundian guard as he passed through in 1418, he had the captain and his 350 soldiers executed and the town put to the torch. For the next 100 years it was known as Azay-le-Brûlé (Azay the Burnt).

The splendid château, part of which extends out over the river, was built (1518–29) by Gilles Berthelot, whose wife, Philippa, directed the work. State owned since 1885, it is furnished as a Renaissance museum. The parish church in one corner of the park dates from about 1000. The town, at the foot of a hill by

The château at Azay-le-Rideau on the Indre River, France
Jean Feuillie

the river, is a maze of narrow, twisting streets. The bottom land produces wine, pears, and, particularly, apples. Veneer work, panelling, and boxes for dairy produce are made there. Pop. (1982) 1,955.

Azazel, in Jewish legends, a demon or evil spirit to whom, in the ancient rite of Yom Kippur (Day of Atonement), a scapegoat was sent bearing the sins of the Jewish people. Two male goats were chosen for the ritual, one designated by lots "for the Lord," the other "for Azazel" (Leviticus 16:8). After the high priest symbolically transferred all the sins of the Jewish people to the scapegoat, the animal was driven into the wilderness and cast over a precipice to its death. Azazel was thus the personification of uncleanness and in later rabbinic writings was sometimes described as a fallen angel.

Azcapotzalco (Mexico): *see* Atzcapotzalco.

Azeglio, Massimo Taparelli, marchese d' (marquess of) (b. Oct. 24, 1798, Turin, Piedmont—d. Jan. 15, 1866, Turin), aristocrat, painter, author, and statesman who was a leader of the movement that advocated a national revival (Risorgimento) by the expulsion of all foreign influences from the then-divided Italian states. His political influence far outweighed his artistic achievements.

After a youth dedicated to painting (1820–30 at Rome), D'Azeglio wrote two obscurely political novels, *Ettore Fieramosca* (1833) and

D'Azeglio, detail of an oil painting by F. Hayez, in the Brera, Milan
Alinari—Brogi from Art Resource

Niccolò de'Lapi (1841). These marked him as a relatively moderate leader of the Risorgimento. His chief work, *Gli ultimi casi de Romagna* (1846; "The Last Chances for Romagna"), is a trenchant political critique of the papal government of Romagna; it demanded that its populace renounce local revolts and show confidence in the Piedmontese king of Sardinia, Charles Albert, who would head a liberal Italian federation.

D'Azeglio fought against the Austrians in the Italian liberation movement of 1848. When Charles Albert, defeated by the Austrians first at Custoza (1848) and then at Novara (1849), abdicated to his son Victor Emmanuel II, D'Azeglio was named prime minister, on May 7, 1849. His most important piece of legislation, the Siccardi laws of 1851, abolished ecclesiastical courts and immunities. He resigned Oct. 30, 1852, because of a long-standing disagreement with his finance minister, Count Cavour. He retired from public life and served only in minor political roles thereafter. He continued to write articles that fostered a consciousness of the Italian nation among the people. During his last years he wrote his memoirs, *I miei ricordi,* unfinished and published posthumously in 1867.

azeotrope, in chemistry, a mixture of liquids that has a constant boiling point because the vapour has the same composition as the liquid mixture. The boiling point of an azeotropic mixture may be higher or lower than that of any of its components. The components of the solution cannot be separated by simple distillation.

Azerbaijan, East (Iranian province): *see* Azārbāijān-e Sharqī.

Azerbaijan, West (Iranian province): *see* Azārbāijān-e Gharbī.

Azerbaijan Soviet Socialist Republic, also called AZERBAIJAN, Russian AZERBAYDZHANSKAYA SOVETSKAYA SOTSIALISTICHESKAYA RESPUBLIKA, or AZERBAIJAN, Akademiya Nauk romanization AZERBAJDŽANSKAJA SOVETSKAJA SOCIALISTIČESKAJA RESPUBLIKA, or AZERBAJDAN, union republic of the Soviet Union, one of 15.

The following article summarizes the administrative history, geography, demographic patterns, economy, and culture of the modern Azerbaijan S.S.R.; for additional treatment of its geography and history, *see* MACROPAEDIA: Union of Soviet Socialist Republics.

Azerbaijan lies on the southeastern flanks of the Caucasus Mountains against the Caspian Sea. Its area includes the Nakhichevan Autonomous S.S.R. and the Nagorno-Karabakh Autonomous Oblast. Its capital city is Baku. The Azerbaijan S.S.R. is the easternmost of the three republics (the others are Armenia and Georgia) that occupy the southern flanks of the Caucasus Mountains. To the south of the Azerbaijan S.S.R. lies the Iranian region of Azerbaijan, and to the east the waters of the Caspian Sea. The Azerbaijan S.S.R. is characterized by a variety of landscapes. More than 40 percent of its territory is taken up by lowlands, about half lying at altitudes of from 1,300 to 4,900 ft (400 to 1,500 m). Areas above 4,900 ft occupy a little more than 10 percent of the total area.

The slopes of the mountains are covered with beech, oak, and pine, and the animal life includes Caucasian deer, roe deer, wild pig, brown bear, lynx, European bison (wisent), chamois, and leopard. Typical birds include the Caucasian grouse and stone partridge. The dry subtropical climate prevailing in eastern and central Azerbaijan is characterized by a mild winter and a long (four to five months), very hot summer.

Increasing emphasis on heavy industry has resulted in a considerable expansion of the petroleum and natural gas industries, but the machinery- and equipment-manufacturing and food-processing industries are of growing importance.

At the turn of the 20th century, Azerbaijan was the world's leading producer of petroleum and was one of the birthplaces of the oil-refining industry. Its other natural resources include iodo-bromide waters, lead, zinc, iron, copper ores, nepheline syenites, common salt, and various building materials. Most electric energy is produced at thermal stations.

Power generation, manufacturing, and chemical production predominate in Azerbaijan's diversified industrial base. Sumgait is the major centre of ferrous metallurgy and of the refining industry, whose products include mineral fertilizers, fuels, herbicides, industrial oils, synthetic rubber, and plastics. Light industrial manufactures include cotton and woollen manufactures, footwear, and other consumer goods.

Little of Azerbaijan's land is arable, but it nevertheless accounts for a tenth of the agricultural output of the entire Soviet Union. Azerbaijan is a leading producer of cotton; tobacco is its second most valuable crop; and grapes (for wine) and tea are also important. With few navigable rivers, Azerbaijan carries most of its freight by rail. Baku on the Caspian Sea, however, is one of the busiest seaports in the Soviet Union.

The Supreme Soviet of Azerbaijan is selected from a single slate of candidates—chosen by the Communist Party of Azerbaijan and ratified by voters—and sits for a four-year term. The Supreme Soviet selects a presidium and a cabinet to run the government. The Communist Party of Azerbaijan is the only authorized political organization.

The Azerbaijanis combine in themselves a Turkic strain dating from the Oguz Seljuq migrations of the 11th century with mixtures of older inhabitants, including Iranians and others who had lived in Transcaucasia since ancient times. In the Nakhichevan A.S.S.R., virtually all the inhabitants are Azerbaijanis, whereas more than four-fifths of the people in the Nagorno-Karabakh Autonomous Oblast are Armenians. Russians make up the largest minority in Azerbaijan (about 10 percent in 1970).

Health standards are very good, and the people are long-lived, particularly the Armenians, many of whom are reported to have life spans exceeding 100 years.

Illiteracy has been largely eradicated and there are 13 institutions of higher education in the republic. Education at all levels is free and supported by taxes and is compulsory between ages 7 and 17.

Azerbaijan has a long cultural history, which includes notable contributions by a number of medieval scientists and philosophers. The people of Azerbaijan have preserved their long traditions in science and music. In music, the art of the *ashugs*, who improvise songs to their own accompaniment on a stringed instrument called a *kobuz*, continues to be extremely popular. *Mugams*, vocal and instrumental compositions, also are widely known. Area 33,400 sq mi (86,600 sq km). Pop. (1983 est.) 6,399,000.

Azerbaijani, Turkic people living chiefly in the Azerbaijan Soviet Socialist Republic of the Soviet Union and in the provinces of Āzārbāijān-e Gharbī and Āzārbāijān-e Sharqī (West and East Azerbaijan) in Iran. In the late 1970s there were some 5,500,000 in the Soviet Union and about 3,000,000 in Iran. They are mainly sedentary farmers and herders, although some of those in the Soviet Union have found employment in industry. Most Azerbaijani are Shīʿī Muslims. A branch of the Kizilbash (*q.v.*) of Afghanistan, called the Afshari, is reported to be bilingual, retaining a dialect of their original Azerbaijani. They number only a few thousand.

Azevedo, Aluízio (b. April 17, 1857, São Luís, Maranhão, Braz.—d. Jan. 21, 1913, Buenos Aires), novelist who established the pattern for the Naturalistic novel in Brazil and anticipated the 20th-century novelists of social protest.

He studied at the school of fine arts of Rio de Janeiro and became a journalist. His works, modelled on the experimental novels of Zola and imbued with antislavery, anticlerical, and anti-bourgeois sentiments, closely document aspects of Brazilian life of his day. His first success, *O Mulato* (1881; "The Mulatto"), deals with racial prejudice. Two other memorable novels, *Casa de Pensão* (1884; "The Boarding House") and *O Cortiço* (1890; *A Brazilian Tenement*, 1926), provide detailed accounts of the emergent society of Rio de Janeiro. Azevedo abandoned his literary career at 37 and entered the diplomatic service, being a consul in Argentina at his death.

Azharī, Ismāʿīl al- (b. Oct. 30, 1900, Omdurman, Sudan—d. Aug. 26, 1969, Khartoum), statesman and Sudanese prime minister in 1954–56, who was instrumental in achieving his country's independence.

Educated at Gordon Memorial College at Khartoum and at the American University of Beirut, al-Azharī became president of the Graduates' General Congress in 1940. At first concerned primarily with educational and social reforms, the congress later opposed British administration and supported union with Egypt. In 1943, following a split within the congress, al-Azharī organized the Ashiggāʾ (Brothers) party; his opposition to the British proposal for self-government in the Sudan brought about his arrest in December 1948.

In 1952 he was made president of the National Unionist Party (NUP), which won an overwhelming victory in the elections of 1953. Al-Azharī became prime minister in January 1954. It became clear to him that union with Egypt could be achieved only at the risk of a civil war, given the anti-union opposition in the Sudan. In May 1955 he therefore pledged to work for complete independence. Shortly after The Sudan gained independence (Jan. 1, 1956), however, al-Azharī's power collapsed because of factional rivalries within the NUP. In 1958 a military government took power. In 1964 he re-emerged as the head of the NUP and in 1965 was appointed president of the Supreme Council of The Sudan (*i.e.*, head of state). He was overthrown in a military coup on May 25, 1969.

azide, any of a class of chemical compounds containing three nitrogen atoms as a group, represented as ($-N_3$). Azides are considered as derived from hydrazoic acid (HN_3), an inorganic salt such as sodium azide (NaN_3), or an organic derivative in which the hydrogen atom of hydrazoic acid is replaced by a hydrocarbon group as in alkyl or aryl azide (RN_3), or by an acyl (carboxylic acid) group as in acyl azide.

Most azides are unstable substances highly sensitive to shock. Some inorganic azides and alkyl azides are used as initiating explosives in detonators and percussion caps. Chemically, the azides behave like halogen compounds; they react rapidly with other substances by displacement of the azide group and can give rise to many types of compounds.

Acyl azides are prepared by reaction of nitrous acid and acid hydrazides or by reaction of an acyl chloride with sodium azide. They are generally more stable than the inorganic and alkyl azides. When heated they undergo molecular rearrangement (Curtius rearrangement), forming isocyanates. In the presence of water the isocyanate is converted to an amine containing one less carbon atom than the acyl azide.

Azīdī (religious sect): *see* Yazīdī.

Azikiwe, Nnamdi (b. Nov. 16, 1904, Zungeru, Nigeria), president of Nigeria (1963–66), founder of a nationalist political party, and perhaps the figure who best typified southern Nigerian (and certainly Ibo) nationalism; his crowded career has also included journalism and banking.

Azikiwe gained much of his early education and experience in the United States (1925–34). He attended several colleges and did graduate work at the University of Pennsylvania and Lincoln University. In 1934 he went to the Gold Coast, where he worked as a newspaper editor before returning to Nigeria in 1937. There he founded a chain of newspapers and also became directly involved in politics, first with the Nigerian Youth Movement and later (1944) as a founder of the National Council of Nigeria and the Cameroons (NCNC). Two years later, with the backing of the NCNC, he was elected to the Nigerian Legislative Council. After 1951, when the Yoruba Action Group (a western Nigerian party) was established, the NCNC became increasingly identified with the Ibo in the southeast. After the election of 1953 he became chief minister and later premier of the Eastern Region.

In 1956 Azikiwe was accused of investing government money in a bank in which he had considerable personal shares. Although he was found partly guilty by a tribunal, his popular support generally remained high. Despite some opposition within the party, he led a unified NCNC into the important 1959 federal elections, which preceded independence. He was able to form a temporary coalition with the powerful Northern Peoples Congress, but its leader, Abubakar Tafawa Balewa, took the key post of prime minister. Azikiwe received the largely honorary posts of president of the Senate, then governor general, and finally president.

In the Biafran Civil War (1967–70) Azikiwe first backed his fellow Ibo, travelling extensively in 1968 to win recognition of Biafra and help from other African countries. In 1969, however, he threw his support to the federal government, leading to some criticism of his "successive sincerities." Thereafter, he was one of the leaders opposing the ruling party and ran unsuccessfully for president in 1979 as a candidate of a newly formed Nigerian People's Party.

An articulate and charismatic figure, he has written extensively on African nationalism. Perhaps his most influential book was one of his earliest, *Renascent Africa* (1937).

Azilal, village, *commune rurale,* and province (established 1975), Centre region, central Morocco. Azilal village, the provincial capital, is situated on the northwestern side of the Haut (High) Atlas mountains between the Tadla plain and the Haut Atlas peaks (that rise 10,000 to 13,000 ft [3,000 to 4,000 m]) at an elevation of 4,460 ft above sea level. It is a market centre for the Ouled Outferkal, a local Berber group.

Azilal province is bounded by the provinces of Beni Mellal (north), er-Rachidia (east), Ouarzazate (south), and el-Kelaa des Srarhna and Marrakech (west). It embraces an area of 3,880 sq mi (10,050 sq km), comprised mostly of a rugged high plateau and mountainous area of the Haut Atlas with many chasms and ravines cutting into the granite massif. Berber semi-nomads build their homes, often clustered around a *tighremt* (fortified communal storehouse) on cliffside terraces. Non-irrigated subsistence agriculture produces cereals, sheep and goats are grazed, and olives and fruits are grown at lower elevations.

Azilal province constitutes a water catchment area; two dams (Bine el-Ouidane, built by the French in 1948–55 and Aït Adel, built by the Moroccan government in 1966–71) produce hydroelectricity and have turned the western and northern part of the semiarid Tadla plain into an area of intensive cultivation. Land that is irrigated by diverting water from *oueds* (streams) yields two crops a year, namely cereals in winter and vegetables in summer. Pop. (1971) *commune rurale,* 17,868; (1981 est.) province, 415,000.

Azilian industry, tool tradition of Late Upper Paleolithic and Early Mesolithic Europe, especially France and Spain, preceded by the richer and more complex Magdalenian industry, and more or less contemporary with such industries as the Tardenoisian, Maglemosian, Ertebølle, and Asturian. Stone tools of the Azilian were mostly extremely small, called microliths, and made to fit into a handle of bone or antler. Projectile points with curved backs and end scrapers were used; bone tools included punches, "wands" (of uncertain use), and flat harpoons often made of red deer antler. Art was confined to geometric drawings made on pebbles using red and black pigments. The big game of the Fourth Glacial Period had disappeared, and the Azilian people and their contemporaries ate mollusks, fish, birds, and small mammals that were probably trapped and snared.

azimuth: *see* altitude and azimuth.

ʿAzīz, al-, in full AL-ʿAZĪZ BI'LLĀH NIZĀR ABŪ MANṢŪR (b. May 10, 955—d. Oct. 14, 996, Bilbays, Egypt), caliph under whom the Fāṭimid Empire attained its greatest extent.

The first of the Fāṭimids to begin his reign in Egypt, where the caliphate was later centred, al-ʿAzīz succeeded his father, al-Muʿizz, in 975. Ambitious to expand his domains at the expense of the Byzantine Empire and of the rival ʿAbbāsid Caliphate, for most of his reign he was involved in military and political ventures in northern Syria, where he and the Byzantine emperor Basil II at length reached a stalemate. Al-ʿAzīz, who had a Christian wife, was known for his favourable attitude toward Christians and Jews, and he began the practice of employing Turkish mercenaries, who later came to dominate Egypt. He died as he was preparing to lead a great expedition against the Byzantines.

azlon, man-made textile fibre composed of protein material derived from natural sources. It is produced, like other man-made fibres, by converting the raw material to a solution that is extruded through the holes of a device called a spinneret and then stretched to improve the alignment of the chains of molecules making up the fibres.

Protein substances from both animal and vegetable sources have been employed, including casein, a by-product of skim milk; zein, derived from corn (maize); keratin, a horny substance obtained from such materials as chicken feathers; collagen, derived from leather and hide wastes; egg albumin, a by-product of commercially dried eggs; and the protein of cotton seed, peanuts (groundnuts), and soybeans.

Azlon has had little commercial success because it is especially low in strength when wet and can be stretched to a great extent but does not readily resume its original length. Although more flammable than wool, it is less so than rayon or acetate. Used in apparel fabrics, azlon is soft and warm to the wearer. It absorbs moisture, does not accumulate static electricity, and does not become matted. It is chiefly used in blends with other fibres, contributing soft hand (characteristics perceived by handling) to fabrics for such apparel as coats, suits, and knitwear.

Azo DEI PORCI: *see* Azzone dei Porci.

azo compound, any organic chemical compound in which the azo group ($-N=N-$) is part of the molecular structure. The atomic groups attached to the nitrogen atoms may be of any organic class, but the commercially important azo compounds, those that comprise more than half the commercial dyes, have the benzene group or its derivatives as the attached groups (aromatic azo compounds).

Most aromatic azo compounds are prepared by the reaction of a diazonium salt with an organic substance that contains easily replaced hydrogen atoms. The synthesis of azobenzene from nitrobenzene by treatment with certain oxygen-removing reagents is an example of an alternate method useful for symmetrical azo compounds.

Azo compounds in which the attached groups are aliphatic organic groups are usually made by dehydrogenation of the corresponding hydrazo compounds (containing the group $-HN-NH-$) made from hydrazine, N_2H_4. An important reaction of the aliphatic azo compounds is their decomposition by heat into nitrogen and free radicals; the latter often are employed to initiate polymerization reactions.

azo dye, any of a large class of synthetic organic dyes that contain nitrogen as the azo group $-N=N-$ as part of their molecular structures; more than half the commercial dyes belong to this class. Depending on other chemical features, these dyes fall into several categories defined by the fibres for which they have affinity or by the methods by which they are applied.

The oldest methods for applying azo dyes to cotton involved successive treatments with solutions of two chemical components that react to form the dye within the fibre or on its surface. Dyes applied in this way are called developed dyes; para red and primuline red are members of this group that were introduced in the 1880s.

The most easily applied azo dyes are those designated as direct: they contain chemical substituents that make them soluble in water, and they are absorbed from solution by cotton. The first direct dye was Congo red, discovered in 1884; it has been largely replaced by dyes with superior resistance to acids and to fading.

The acid azo dyes possess affinity for wool and silk and are applied by essentially the same procedure used for the direct class. Tartrazine is a yellow acid azo dye discovered in 1884 and still in common use.

Other azo dyes contain chemical groups that bind metal ions. Among numerous metal salts used with these dyes, chromium and copper are most common; often, the metal ion also unites with the fibre, improving the resistance of the dye to washing. The presence of the metal sometimes produces important changes in shade.

A few of the anthraquinone vat dyes and some disperse dyes are also azo compounds; the latter are not water-soluble but can be suspended in water by soap and in that state are adsorbed from the suspension by cellulose acetate fibres.

Azogues, capital of Cañar province, south central Ecuador, in a high Andean valley. Its economy is based on agricultural trade, and grains and fruit are cultivated. Important local industries include flour milling and leather tanning. The city takes its name from the Spanish *azogue,* meaning "mercury," which is a local resource. Nearby also are silver and copper mines and asphalt and ruby deposits, but exploitation of these resources is minimal. The city is on the Pan-American Highway and on the southern spur of the Guayaquil–Quito railway, northeast of Cuenca. Pop. (1983 est.) 13,840.

Azolinus Porcius: *see* Azzone dei Porci.

Azores, Portuguese in full ARQUIPÉLAGO DOS AÇORES, archipelago composed of nine major islands, in the North Atlantic Ocean; they are a part of Portugal. The islands, occupying 868 sq mi (2,247 sq km), are divided into three widely separated groups: the eastern group consists of São Miguel, Santa Maria, and the Formigas islets; the central, of Faial, Pico, São Jorge, Terceira, and Graciosa; and the northwestern, of Flores and Corvo.

The nearest continental land is Cabo (cape) da Roca, Portugal, which lies 740 mi (1,190 km) east of São Miguel. Thus, the Azores are farther from mainland Europe than any other eastern Atlantic islands. In general characteristics, all the islands are similar, rising steeply from shores lined with rock and pebble debris (scree or talus) to heights reaching 7,713 ft (2,351 m) in Pico. Their volcanic nature is indicated by the numerous earthquakes and basaltic eruptions that have taken place since their discovery. In 1522 the town of Vila Franca do Campo, then capital of São Miguel, was buried during a massive convulsion, and as recently as 1957–58 the Capelinhos eruption enlarged the Ilha do Faial.

The islands were reputedly discovered in about 1427 by Diogo de Senill (or Sevilha), a pilot of the king of Portugal. No traces of human habitation or visitation were found on any of them. Settlement began on Santa Maria, on about 1432, under Gonçalo Velho Cabral, a Portuguese official. São Miguel was settled on 1444 and Terceira some years later. A few Flemings, under Jobst van Heurter, were allowed to settle on Faial at the request of Isabella, duchess of Burgundy and sister of Henry the Navigator (Infante Don Henrique). By the end of the 15th century all the islands were inhabited, and trade with Portugal became well established. From 1580 until 1640 the Azores, like the rest of Portugal, were subject to Spain. The islands were the rendezvous for the treasure fleets on their voyages home from the West Indies; hence, they became a theatre of the maritime warfare between the English under Elizabeth I and Spain and Portugal, the peninsular powers. Except for a time during the Spanish occupation, there was no central government in the Azores until 1766, when the Marquês de Pombal installed a governor and captain general for the whole group at Angra do Heroísmo, Terceira, to halt abuses by the local administrators. A new constitution was established in 1832, and the islands were grouped into three administrative districts, which in 1895 were given limited autonomous administration.

The Azores still have no central government and remain organized as three districts with the same status as those of continental Portugal but with special autonomous Junta Geral exercised in each by a *junta geral* (general council). The principal seaports, which give their names to the districts, are Angra do Heroísmo (or Angra), Ponta Delgada, and Horta.

The trade of the Azores was long a Portuguese monopoly, but later, before World War II, it was shared by Great Britain, the United States, and Germany; textiles are imported from Portugal and coal from Great Britain. Other imports are automobiles, mineral oils, petroleum products, and machinery. Exports include hand embroideries, pineapples, canned fish, and wine.

Lajes and Santa Maria became important air bases and centres of communication between the United States and Europe during World War II, and since 1951, by agreement with Portugal, the United States has maintained a NATO airbase. Before the advent of weather satellites, meteorological data compiled and transmitted from the Azores were essential to European weather forecasting. Pop. (1981) 243,410.

Azores high, large atmospheric high-pressure centre that develops over the North Atlantic Ocean in summer. It is a subtropical high-pressure cell that has moved northward and intensified. Sometimes it divides, and a second cell, the Bermuda high, forms to the west; this high-pressure centre often is associated with warm, humid weather in the eastern United States.

Azorín, pseudonym of JOSÉ MARTÍNEZ RUIZ (b. June 8/11, 1874, Monóvar, Spain—d. March 2, 1967, Madrid), man of letters and the foremost Spanish literary critic of his day. He was one of a group of writers who were

Azorín, detail of an oil painting by Joaquín Sorolla y Bastida, 1917; in the collection of the Hispanic Society of America

By courtesy of the Hispanic Society of America

engaged at the turn of the 20th century in a concerted attempt to revitalize Spanish life and letters. Azorín was the first to identify this group as the Generation of '98—a name that prevails.

Both through the clarity of his own style and through the principles set forth in his criticism, he repudiated the imposing rhetoric of the 19th century.

He studied law at Valencia, Granada, and Salamanca, but later he went to Madrid to be a journalist, only to find that his outspokenness closed most doors. He wrote a trilogy of novels, *La voluntad* (1902; "Volition"), *Antonio Azorín* (1902), and *Las confesiones de un pequeño filósofo* (1904; "The Confessions of a Minor Philosopher"), which broke away from the traditional form of the novel and are actually little more than impressionistic essays written in dialogue. This trilogy operated with unifying force on the Generation of '98. Animated by a deep patriotism, Azorín tirelessly sought through his work to bring to light what he believed was of lasting value in Spanish culture. *El alma castellana* (1900; "The Castilian Soul"), *La ruta de Don Quijote* (1905; "The Route of Don Quixote"), and *Una hora de España 1560–1590* (1924; *An Hour of Spain, 1560–1590*; 1933) carefully and subtly reconstruct the spirit of Spanish life, directing the reader's sensibility by the suggestive power of the prose. Azorín's literary criticism, such as *Al márgen de los clásicos* (1915; "Marginal Notes to the Classics"), helped to open up new avenues of literary taste and to arouse a new enthusiasm for the Spanish classics at a time when a large portion of Spanish literature was virtually unavailable to the public.

Interested in keeping Spain aware of current foreign thinking, Azorín edited the periodical *Revista de Occidente* ("Magazine of the West") from 1923 to 1936. He spent the period of the Spanish Civil War in Paris writing for the Argentine newspaper *La Nación* but returned to Madrid in 1949. After his death a museum including his library was opened at Monóvar.

Azov, formerly AZAK, or TANA, town, southwestern Russian Soviet Federated Socialist Republic, on the left bank of the Don River, 4 mi (7 km) east of the Sea of Azov. The Greek colony of Tanais, the first known major city in the region, was founded there in the 6th century BC. It changed hands and was renamed several times over the ensuing centuries. It became the Genoese colony Tana (established 1316–22), which in 1471 was captured by the Turks and held as a fortress; it fell to Peter I the Great in 1696. The town he founded in 1708 was lost to the Turks but regained in 1739. The town has since silted up and lost its functions to nearby Rostov-na-Donu. Azov's industries include fish processing, lumber milling, and light manufacturing. Pop. (1983 est.) 78,000.

Azov, Sea of, Russian AZOVSKOYE, or AZOVSKOE, MORE, inland sea of the Atlantic Basin, situated on the southern shores of the European portion of the Soviet Union. Separated on the south from the Black Sea by the Kerch and Taman peninsulas, it meets the Black Sea at the Kerch Strait. The Sea of Azov has an area of about 15,000 sq mi (38,000 sq km). With a maximum depth of about 46 ft (14 m), it is the world's shallowest sea. Into the Sea of Azov flow the great rivers Don and Kuban and many lesser ones such as the Mius, the Berda, the Obitochnaya, and the Yeya.

The geological history of the Sea of Azov is inseparably connected with that of the Black Sea. The Sea of Azov formed in the Middle Miocene Epoch (16,000,000 years ago) as part of a wide basin. In the Early Pliocene (beginning 7,000,000 years ago), the basin of the Black Sea and the Sea of Azov were isolated from the ocean. In the subsequent period, connections with the Caspian Sea were formed and broken several times. At the beginning of the Quaternary Period (2,500,000 years ago) the Sea of Azov acquired roughly the outline it has today. Toward the end of this period a connection between the Black Sea and the Mediterranean Sea was established (a stage known as the Karangats Basin).

The climate of the Sea of Azov is continental and temperate. In the winter, northeast and east winds predominate, bringing cold air from the mainland. Under the influence of cyclones, heavy frosts often alternate with thaws, and there are frequent fogs. July is the warmest month.

The hydrological regime is determined by the continental situation of the sea, the climate, the influx from the rivers, and the water exchange with the Black Sea, as well as by the water-related human activities in the basin. As a result of a freshwater surplus the mean salinity is generally low but may vary in certain years, because of changes in the water turnover through the Kerch Strait and changes in the river influx. Sivash Lake is particularly noted for salinity.

Currents in the Sea of Azov flow in a counterclockwise rotation, but under the influence of winds they may occasionally reverse. The mean water level of the sea varies as much as 13 in. (33 cm) from year to year, according to the river influx. Tidal oscillations of the water level may reach 18 ft. In summer, during extended calms, the oxygen on the bottom may dissipate entirely through oxidation, causing the fish to die.

There is an extraordinarily high level of biological productivity, resulting from the sea's shallowness, the excellent mixing and even warming of the water, and the input of great quantities of nutrient material by the rivers. The varieties of phytoplankton found in the sea total 188, and 25–30 varieties of macrophytes are found. Among flowering plants zostera is common. The sea's fauna includes more than 300 invertebrate species and 79 species of fish, including sturgeon, perch, bream, herring, sea-roach, gray mullet, minnow, shemaja, and bullheads. Sardines and anchovies are particularly abundant.

The Sea of Azov handles much freight and passenger traffic, although the progress of heavy oceangoing craft is hampered by shallowness at some points. Icebreakers assist in winter navigation. Principal ports are Taganrog, Zhdanov, Yeysk, and Berdyansk.

Azov Upland, Russian PRIAZOVSKAYA VOZVYSHENNOST, hilly region, Zaporozhye and Donets *oblasti* (administrative regions), southeastern Ukrainian Soviet Socialist Republic. Part of the Ukrainian Crystalline Shield, the Azov Upland is an area of denuded mountains, extending southeastward from the Dnepr River for 100 mi (160 km) to the Donets Ridge. The highest point is Mt. Mogila-Belmak (1,063 ft [324 m]), 65 mi southwest of Donetsk. The soil cover, which is extensively cultivated, is of the Chernozem type, and sheep fescue and feather grass are found on the slopes of the mountains. The Berda, Molochnaya, and Obitochnaya rivers have their sources in the upland.

Azraq, al-Baḥr al- (Africa): *see* Blue Nile River.

Aztec, Nahuatl-speaking people who in the 15th and early 16th centuries ruled a large empire in what is now central and southern Mexico, so called from Aztlán (White Land), an allusion to their origins, probably in northern Mexico. They were also called the Tenochca, from an eponymous ancestor, Tenoch, and the Mexica, probably from Metzliapán (Moon Lake), the mystical name for Lake Texcoco. From "Tenochca" was derived the name of their great city, Tenochtitlán, and from "Mexica" came the other name for the city and the surrounding valley, which was applied later to the whole Mexican nation. They referred to themselves as Culhua-Mexica, to link themselves with Colhuacán, the centre of the most civilized people of the Valley of Mexico.

A brief treatment of the Aztec follows. For a full treatment, *see* the MACROPAEDIA article Pre-Columbian Civilizations.

The origin of the Aztec people is uncertain, but elements of their own tradition suggest that they were a tribe of hunters and gatherers on the northern Mexican plateau before their appearance in Middle America in perhaps the 12th century; Aztlán, however, may be legendary. It is possible that their migration southward was part of a general movement of peoples that followed, or perhaps helped trigger, the collapse of the Toltec civilization. They settled on islands in Lake Texcoco and in AD 1325 founded Tenochtitlán, which remained their chief centre. The basis of their success in creating a great state and ultimately an empire was their remarkable system of agriculture, which featured intensive cultivation of all available land and elaborate systems of irrigation and reclamation of swampland. The high productivity gained by these methods made for a rich and populous state.

Under the ruler Itzcóatl (1428–40), Tenochtitlán formed alliances with the neighbouring states of Texcoco and Tlacopan and became the dominant power in central Mexico. Later, by commerce and conquest, Tenochtitlán came to rule an empire of 400 to 500 small states, comprising by 1519 some 5,000,000 to 6,000,000 people spread over 80,000 square miles (207,200 square kilometres). At its height, Tenochtitlán itself covered more than 5 sq mi (13 sq km) and had upwards of 140,000 inhabitants, making it the most densely populated settlement ever achieved by a Middle American civilization. The Aztec state was a despotism in which the military arm played a dominant role. Valour in war was, in fact, the surest path to advancement in caste- and class-divided but nonetheless vertically fluid Aztec society. The priestly and bureaucratic classes were involved in the administration of the empire, while at the bottom of society were classes of serfs, indentured servants, and outright slaves.

Aztec religion was syncretistic, absorbing elements from many other Middle American cultures. At base, it shared many of the cosmological beliefs of earlier peoples, notably the Maya, such as that the present Earth was the last in a series of creations and that it occupied a position between systems of 13 heavens and 9 underworlds. Prominent in the Aztec pantheon were Huitzilopochtli, god of war and the sun; Tlaloc, god of rain; and Quetzalcóatl, the Feathered Serpent, who was part deity and part culture hero. Human sacrifice, particularly in the form of offering the victim's heart to the sun god, was commonly practiced, as was bloodletting. Closely entwined with Aztec religion was the calendar, on which was based the elaborate round of rituals and ceremonies that occupied the priests. The Aztec calendar (*q.v.*) was the one common to much of Middle America, and it comprised a solar year of 365 days (consisting of 18 months of 20 days, plus 5 unlucky days) and a sacred year of 260 days (13 cycles of 20 days); the two yearly cycles running in parallel produced a larger cycle of 52 years.

The Aztec Empire was still expanding, and its society still evolving, when its progress was halted in 1519 by the appearance of Spanish explorers. The last emperor, Montezuma II (ruled 1502–20), was taken prisoner by Hernán Cortés and died in custody. The empire was rapidly conquered by the better armed Europeans.

Aztec calendar, dating system that combines the *tonalpohualli*, a ritual cycle of 260 days, with the solar year of 365 days. Like the Mayan calendar (*q.v.*) from which it was derived, the Aztec calendar consisted of a ritual cycle that was divided into 13 periods of 20 days each and a civil cycle that was divided into 18 months of 20 days plus an additional 5 days, called *nemontemi,* considered to be very unlucky. Again like the Mayan calendar, the Aztec ritual and civil cycles returned to the same positions relative to each other every 52 years, an event celebrated as the Binding Up of the Years, or the New Fire Ceremony. In preparation, all sacred and domestic fires were allowed to burn out. At the climax of the ceremony, priests ignited a new sacred fire, after which the Aztecs rekindled their hearth fires and began feasting.

A circular calendar stone measuring 3.7 metres (about 12 feet) in diameter and weighing some 25 tons was uncovered in Mexico City in 1790 and is currently on display in the Museo Nacional de Antropología. The face of the Aztec sun god, Tonatiuth, appears at the centre of the stone, surrounded by four square panels honouring previous incarnations of the deity. Circumscribing these are signs that represent the 20 days of the Aztec month.

Aztec City (plant): *see* tiger-flower.

Aztec language: *see* Nahua language.

Aztec Ruins National Monument, archaeological site in northwestern New Mexico, U.S., on the Animas River, just north of the city of Aztec, established in 1923 upon an area of 27 ac (11 ha). The site, mistakenly called Aztec by early white settlers, actually contains the excavated ruins of a 12th-century Pueblo Indian town built of masonry and timber. Many Indian artifacts are displayed at the visitor centre.

Azteco-Tanoan languages, a major grouping (phylum or superstock) of American Indian languages that includes the large Uto-Aztecan language family and the small Kiowa-Tanoan language family of New Mexico and Oklahoma. The Uto-Aztecan languages (*q.v.*) are widely spoken in Mexico and, by fewer numbers, in California, the Great Basin, and Arizona. The Kiowa-Tanoan languages are four in number: Kiowa, Tiwa, Tewa, and Towa.

Azua, province, southwestern Dominican Republic, on the Caribbean Sea. Established in 1845, it has lost territory through the years, until it now consists of only 938 sq mi (2,430 sq km), much of which lies in the Sierra de Ocoa. Despite low rainfall, agricultural production has been made abundant by irrigation. Coffee, corn (maize), plantains, bananas, and peanuts (groundnuts) are cultivated. Lumbering of hardwoods and livestock raising are also significant. Gold and silver are found near Pueblo Viejo. Azua (*q.v.*) city is the provincial capital. Pop. (1981) 142,770.

Azua, in full AZUA DE COMPOSTELA, city, capital of Azua province, southwestern Dominican Republic. Founded in 1504 on the Caribbean coast, the original town was destroyed by an earthquake; the town was reestablished 3 mi (5 km) inland at its present site at the foot of the Sierra de Ocoa. It is one of the leading cities in the region, trading mainly in agricultural products: sugarcane, coffee, rice, corn (maize), fruits, and timber. The city lies on the paved highway linking Santo Domingo, the national capital, with Comendador, near the Haitian border. Pop. (1981) 31,481.

Azuay, province of southern highland Ecuador, in the Sierra, the Andean mountain section of the country. Its area is 3,211 sq mi (8,316 sq km). The mountains occasionally give way to fertile intermontane basins, the most important of which is the basin of Cuenca (about 8,500 ft [2,600 m] above sea level).

Early inhabitants of the area were primitive farmers, the ruins of whose civilization date from approximately 1000 BC. In pre-Columbian times, the Cara Indian Empire flourished, finally being conquered by the Incas in the 15th century. The Incan capital, Tumipampas, was occupied by the Spaniards in 1530. The provincial capital, Cuenca (*q.v.*), was founded on the site in 1557.

In the Cuenca Basin, wheat, barley, potatoes, and corn are grown. Sugarcane, coffee, and cotton are cultivated at lower elevations throughout the province. There is extensive pasture of dairy cattle; on higher ground, sheep are grazed. Poultry raising is becoming of increasing economic importance. Panama hats are made in towns throughout the province. The Pan-American Highway crosses the province from north to south.

The Andean Mission was created in 1951, through the combined efforts of the International Labour Organisation and the governments of Ecuador, Peru, and Bolivia, for the purpose of raising living standards among highland Indian populations; its Ecuadorian activities, now in the hands of the government, began after 1954 in Azuay province. Pop. (1983 est.) 468,533.

Azuchi-Momoyama period, also called MOMOYAMA PERIOD (1574–1600), in Japanese history, age of political unification under the daimyo Oda Nobunaga and his successor Toyotomi Hideyoshi, who finally brought all provinces under the control of the central government. In contrast to the restraint of the preceding Muromachi, or Ashikaga, period (1338–1573), it was an age of magnificence and ostentation. The building of great castles and mansions replaced temple architecture. Indeed, the period is named for two castles, Azuchi, built by Oda on the shore of Lake Biwa, and Momoyama, built by Hideyoshi in Kyōto. Castles were decorated by masters of the Kanō school with gorgeous large-scale paintings on sliding panels and folding screens. The period ended in 1600 and was succeeded by the Tokugawa, or Edo, period (1603–1867), after Hideyoshi's successor, Tokugawa Ieyasu, had established his capital at Edo (modern Tokyo).

Azuela, Mariano (b. Jan. 1, 1873, Lagos de Moreno, Mex.—d. March 1, 1952, Mexico City), writer whose 20 novels chronicle almost every aspect of the Mexican revolution.

He received an M.D. degree in Guadalajara in 1899 and practiced medicine, first in his native town and after 1916 in Mexico City. His best known work, *Los de abajo* (1916; *The Under Dogs,* 1929), depicting the horrors of the revolution, was written at the campfire during forced marches while he served as army doctor with Pancho Villa, in 1915. Forced to flee across the border to El Paso, Texas, he first published the novel as a newspaper serial (October–December 1915). It received little notice until it was "discovered" in 1924. It widely influenced other Mexican novelists of social protest and was translated into several languages.

Returning from Texas to Mexico City in 1916, Azuela, disillusioned with the revolutionary struggle, wrote novels critical of the new regime: *Las moscas* (1918) and *Los caciques* (1917; together translated as *Two Novels of Mexico: The Flies. The Bosses,* 1956); *Las tribulaciones de una familia decente* (1918; with *Los de abajo, Two Novels of the Mexican Revolution: The Trials of a Respectable Family and The Underdogs,* 1963). Later works experimented with stylistic devices later incorporated in the "new novel": *La malhora* (1923; "The Evil Hour"), *El desquite* (1925; "Revenge"), and *La luciérnaga* (1932; "The Firefly"). His complete works appeared in three volumes in 1959–60. English translations of *Las tribulaciones de una familia decente, Los de abajo,* and *La luciérnaga* were published in *Three Novels* (1979).

Articles are alphabetized word by word, not letter by letter

Azuero Peninsula, Spanish PENÍNSULA DE AZUERO, physical region in southwestern Panama, protruding south into the Pacific Ocean between the Gulf of Panama to the east and the Gulf of Montijo to the west. It measures 60 mi (100 km) from east to west and 55 mi from north to south. It attains a maximum elevation of 3,068 ft (935 m) at Mt. Canajagua, southwest of Las Tablas. The peninsula includes Herrera and parts of Los Santos and Veraguas provinces. The main towns of the region are Chitré and Las Tablas, both of which are linked by road to the Pan-American Highway.

azulejo, Portuguese AZULÊJO (from Arabic *az-zulayj*: "little stone"), Spanish and then principally Portuguese tiles produced from the 14th century onward. At first the term denoted North African mosaics, but it became the accepted word for an entirely decorated tile about 5 to 6 inches (13 to 15 centimetres) square. In the 15th and 16th centuries, Portugal imported azulejo tiles from Spain, and their use was widespread in religious and private architecture, particularly on facades, such as that of Coimbra cathedral (1510). About 1550 Flemish artists in Lisbon attempted the production of tiles, and the industry developed during the reigns of Philip II, III, and IV to become independent of Spain, which virtually ceased to manufacture them in the 18th century. Portuguese exports of tiles to the Azores, Madeira, and Brazil began in the 17th century; azulejos produced in Puebla, Mex., later were to be the most outstanding in the New World.

Azulejos from Seville, late 16th century; in the Museum Boymans-van Beuningen, Rotterdam
By courtesy of Museum Boymans-van Beuningen, Rotterdam

Initially, one-colour versions of the tiles were used in Portugal in decorative chessboard patterns. Variations included polychrome designs; scenes with military or religious themes; and humorous *singeries,* which depicted monkeys in human roles. During the height of the azulejo's popularity, from about 1690 to 1750, many exterior and interior walls were faced by complex continuous picture tiles.

azurite, also called CHESSYLITE, basic copper carbonate [$Cu_3(OH)_2(CO_3)_2$]. It is ordinarily found with malachite in the oxidized zone of copper lodes. Notable deposits are Tsumeb, South West Africa/Namibia; Chessy, Fr.; and Bisbee, Ariz., U.S. Azurite was used as a blue pigment in ancient Eastern wall painting and, from the 15th to the middle of the 17th century, in European painting. For detailed physical properties, *see* carbonate mineral (table).

ʿAzza (Gaza Strip): *see* Gaza.

ʿAzza, Rezuʿat: *see* Gaza Strip.

Azzone DEI PORCI, also called AZZONE SOLDANUS, Latin AZOLINUS PORCIUS, Azzone also spelled AZO, or AZZO (b. *c.* 1150, Bologna or Casalmaggiore, Italy—d. 1230), a leader of the Bolognese school of jurists, one of the few to write systematic summaries (*summae*) rather than textual glosses of Roman law as codified under the Byzantine emperor Justinian I (6th century AD). A professor of civil law at Bologna from 1190, he was a pupil of one noted jurist, Joannes Bassianus, and teacher of another, Franciscus Accursius. Much of the Roman material used by the English jurist Henry de Bracton (died 1268) in his *De legibus et consuetudinibus Angliae* ("On the Laws and Customs of England") was derived from Azzone's summaries. The legal historian F.W. Maitland edited *Select Passages from the Works of Bracton and Azo* (1895).

B-17, also called FLYING FORTRESS, U.S. heavy bomber used during World War II. The B-17 was designed by the Boeing Aircraft Company to specifications written in 1934. A prototype flew in 1935 and the craft was in small-scale production in 1937. The seventh substantial variation of the original design, the B-17G, was equipped with superchargers to allow it to cruise at 35,000 feet (10,675 metres) at a maximum speed of 287 miles per

U.S. B-17, or Flying Fortress
By courtesy of Boeing Co.

hour (462 kilometres per hour). It was called the Flying Fortress because of the .50-calibre machine guns, 13 in all, that bristled from every corner. It could carry 6,000 pounds (2,724 kilograms) of bombs in its bomb bays and more on racks under the wings. With production augmented at two other plants, Douglas and Lockheed, Boeing turned out 12,731 Flying Fortresses, nearly all of which were used by the U.S. Air Force for high-level daylight bombing over Europe. The airplane's formidable arsenal led to the development of a highly effective defensive tactic: on a bombing mission, B-17s would form a large square, enabling their gunners to pour withering crossfire on intruding fighters.

B-24, also called LIBERATOR, long-range heavy bomber used during World War II by the U.S. and British air forces; 19,000 of them were produced, more than any other U.S. aircraft in the war. The B-24 first flew in 1939 and was operational in the Royal Air Force in 1941. The "Lib" was effective in antisubmarine warfare (dropping depth charges) and was widely converted to transport service later, but primarily it was a high-level bomber with a range of 1,540 miles (2,465 kilometres; 40 percent longer than that of the B-17), a maximum speed of 297 miles per hour (475 kilometres per hour), and a ceiling of 28,000 feet (8,540 metres).

The Liberator's appearance was distinctive; it had a twin tail assembly and a boxlike fuselage slung low beneath its high wing. It had a retractable tricycle landing gear. The craft normally carried a crew of 10 and was armed with 10 .50-calibre machine guns mounted in pairs in the nose, tail, dorsal, and ventral turrets and singly in two waist ports. Its bomb bay accommodated four 2,000-pound (908-kilogram) bombs and one 4,000-lb bomb could be mounted under each wing. The wing, which spanned 110 ft, contained 18 separate self-sealing fuel tanks. Of the 19,000 B-24s built between 1940 and 1945, 10,000 were made by the craft's designer, Consolidated-Vultee, and the others by Ford Motor Company, Douglas Aircraft, and North American Aviation. The B-24 saw service in Europe, Africa, and the Pacific, where, because of its range, it virtually replaced the B-17.

B-29, also called SUPERFORTRESS, U.S. heavy bomber used in World War II. It was the airplane that was used to firebomb Tokyo and other Japanese cities and that dropped atomic bombs on Hiroshima and Nagasaki, Japan, on Aug. 6 and 9, 1945, respectively.

The Superfortress was designed to meet Army Air Corps specifications written in January 1940, then modified to provide heavier armament and bomb load. First flown in September 1942, the bomber was built at five plants around the United States and was operating in the Pacific theatre in flights of as many as 500 planes within two years. Armament was 10 .50-calibre machine guns and one 20-millimetre cannon, four of the gun turrets operated by remote control from various of five sighting stations. Bomb capacity was 10 tons, and the crew varied from 10 to 14. When production ended in 1946, 3,960 B-29s had been built, many of which were subsequently converted to tankers for in-flight refueling.

B-52, also called STRATOFORTRESS, U.S. long-range heavy bomber, first flown in 1952; various modifications have kept its capabilities aligned with changing strategic requirements, and as a result the airplane is remarkable for its longevity: U.S. Air Force expectations are that 300 or more of the B-52s will be in or capable of service for the remainder of the 20th century. Between 1954 and 1962, 744 of the bombers were produced in eight versions. The B-52 has a wingspan of 185 ft (56.39 m) and a length of 160 ft 10.9 in. It is powered with eight turbojet engines (turbofans in the last model, the B-52H), each delivering (in the B-52H) 17,000 lb of thrust. Maximum speed at high altitude is Mach 0.9, or 595 mph (957 kph); its ceiling is 55,000 ft. It is armed with up to 20 air-to-air short-range attack missiles (SRAM's), and in a tail turret four .50-calibre machine guns or a single multi-barrel 20-mm cannon, either of which is remote-controlled by an automatic fire-control system or by radar or closed circuit television.

The B-52H can carry 84 500-lb bombs (either nuclear or high-explosive) in its weapons bay and an additional 24 750-lb bombs under its wings. Adapted, it can also carry cruise missiles in place of bombs. With a full load of fuel it can fly 10,000 miles without refueling. It is equipped with highly sophisticated navigational, weapons-control, and electronic-countermeasures (ECM) systems. It has a crew of six. It was widely used for conventional bombing in the Vietnam War and remains a major component of the U.S. strategic deterrent force.

B Cassiopeiae: *see* Tycho's Nova.

ba, in ancient Egyptian religion, with *ka* and *akh,* a principal aspect of the soul; the *ba* appears in bird form, thus expressing the mobility of the soul after death. Originally written with the sign of the jabiru bird, and thought to be an attribute of only the god-king, the *ba* was later represented by a man-headed

Ba hovering over a dead man, from a papyrus of the Book of the Dead; in the British Museum
By courtesy of the trustees of the British Museum

hawk, often depicted hovering over the mummies of king and populace alike. Graves were frequently provided with narrow passages for visitation by the *ba.*

Ba, Oumar (b. *c.* 1900, Mauritania), African historian and poet whose works dealing with the cultures of the people of the Senegal River constitute a major contribution to the sociological, historical, and literary studies of the Fulani.

Ba received his doctorate in letters and social sciences in France. He subsequently held several academic and administrative positions, serving as a Mauritanian representative at UNESCO and as director of the Mauritanian section of the French Institute of Black Africa, in Senegal. He also taught history at the University of Dakar.

Using various approaches (oral tradition, linguistics, and comparative sociology), Ba presented the first scientific account of an early Fulani presence in the region of the Senegal River (now encompassing parts of the republics of Mauritania and Senegal). His book *Le Fouta Toro au carrefour des cultures* (1977; "The Futa Toro at the Crossroads of Cultures"), a presentation of his research on the Fulani, was dedicated to Leopold Senghor, poet and statesman of Negritude (a black African and Caribbean literary movement), with whom Ba shared an equal concern about the development of the French language as a means of unification.

Ba was also a man of letters whose poetry is closely linked with Fulani oral and written lyrics and ballads. *Poèmes peuls modernes* (1965; "Modern Peul Poems"), *Dialogue ou D'une rive à l'autre* (1966; "Dialogue, or, From One Bank to the Other"), and *Paroles plaisantes au coeur et à l'oreille* (1977; "Words Pleasant to the Heart and Ear") are probably his most widely read works. In the field of linguistic studies, Ba published several distinguished works in the Fulani language, a dictionary of Mande words in Fulani, and several dictionaries of expressions in Fulani.

Ba Jin (Chinese author): *see* Pa Chin.

Ba Maw (b. Feb. 8, 1893, Maubin, Burma—d. May 29, 1977, Rangoon), politician who in 1937 became the first Burmese premier under British rule; he later was head of state in the pro-Japanese government during World War II (August 1943–May 1945).

Ba Maw was educated at Rangoon College, Calcutta University, the University of Cambridge, the University of Bordeaux, Fr., where he received a doctorate in 1924. Admitted to the English bar the same year, he first came into prominence as defense lawyer for the Burmese rebel leader Saya San in 1931.

In 1930 the Simon Commission, which was examining the Indian constitution, recommended that Burma be separated from India. (Since the annexation, Burma had been under the jurisdiction of the Indian viceroy.) Ba Maw, believing that a separate Burma would receive a much smaller measure of self-rule than India, then organized a campaign against separation. In 1934, however, he reversed his position, agreeing to support the pro-separationists in a coalition government. That year he was made minister of education for Burma. In 1936 he founded his own political party, the Sinyetha Wunthanu (Proletarian Party), advocating land-reform measures. When the new constitution, providing for separation of Burma from India, went into effect on April 1, 1937, he became the first premier, and he held office until he was defeated by a coalition in February 1939.

After his defeat, Ba Maw allied with U Nu (Thakin Nu) and Aung San to form the "freedom bloc." In August 1940 he was arrested for sedition and remained in prison until the Japanese invasion in 1942. During the Japanese occupation (1943–45), he was *adipati* (head of state) of a theoretically independent Burma, although the country was actually a Japanese satellite. Even though certain of his colleagues revolted against the Japanese, he fled to Japan when the Allies reentered Burma. After a brief time in an Allied prison, he returned and attempted to reenter politics as leader of the Mahabamma (Great Burma) Party. He later retired to private life.

Ba Swe, U (b. Oct. 7, 1915, Onbinkwin, Burma), leader of the Burma Socialist Party and prime minister from June 1956 to June 1957.

Early in his youth Ba Swe developed strong anti-imperialist sentiments. While at the University of Rangoon, he was strongly influenced by Marxist ideas and was secretary of the powerful Students' Union in 1937–38. He organized his own political party, the Burma Revolutionary Party, with a paramilitary branch, the Steel Corps.

During World War II, Ba Swe served in the pro-Japanese government of a nominally independent Burma but later joined the underground Anti-Fascist Organization and worked in the resistance against the Japanese. After the war he participated in the popular-front government of the Burma Anti-Fascist People's Freedom League and became general secretary of the Socialist Party, which remained loyal to the government after the Communists went underground in 1946–48. Ba Swe was minister of defense in U Nu's government and served for a year as prime minister when U Nu stepped down in 1956.

Ba Xian (in Taoism): *see* Pa Hsien.

Baader, Franz Xaver von (b. March 27, 1765, Munich—d. May 23, 1841, Munich), Roman Catholic layman who became an influential mystical theologian and ecumenicist.

Abandoning a profitable career as a mining engineer in 1820, he turned his attention to a study of politics and religion. His earlier efforts to achieve ecumenical and political unity contributed to the formation in 1815 of the Holy Alliance, a security pact among Russia, Austria, Prussia, and France. Drawn up at the conclusion of the Napoleonic Wars, the alliance sought to inaugurate a world community of Christian nations resolved to prevent the recurrence of large-scale conflicts. Although the alliance eventually failed, Baader has subsequently been considered one of the founders of modern ecumenical activity.

In 1826, after further theological study, he was appointed professor of philosophy and speculative theology at the new University of Munich. There, with other Catholics who had formed the "Munich circle," he founded the journal *Eos* (Greek: "dawn"). Despite his eminence as a professor, he was not permitted after 1838 to lecture on religion because of a ministerial decree reserving that area to the clergy. Baader's mystical philosophy, often expressed through obscure aphorisms and symbols, sought to correlate the realm of reason with the realms of authority and revelation. Economically and politically conservative, he viewed the ideal state as a community ruled by a universal, or catholic, church, although he rejected the papacy as an essential ingredient in church governance. Baader's *Sämtliche Werke* ("Collected Works") were published in 16 volumes (1851–60).

Baader-Meinhof Gang: *see* Red Army Faction.

Baal, god worshipped in many ancient Near Eastern communities, especially among the Canaanites, who apparently considered him a fertility deity and one of the most important gods in the pantheon. As a Semitic common noun *baal* (Hebrew *ba'al*) meant "owner" or "lord," although it could be used more generally; for example, a *baal* of wings was a winged creature, and, in the plural, *baalim* of arrows indicated archers. Its original religious usage was probably as an appellative in denoting the god of a given place or object. Yet, such fluidity in the use of the term *baal* did not prevent it from being attached to a god of distinct character. As such, Baal designated the universal god of fertility, and in that capacity his title was Prince, Lord of the Earth. He was also called the Lord of Rain and Dew, the two forms of moisture that were indispensable for fertile soil in Canaan. In Ugaritic and Old Testament Hebrew, Baal's epithet as the storm god was He Who Rides on the Clouds. In Phoenician he was called Baal Shamen (Aramaic Baal Shemin), Lord of the Heavens.

Knowledge of Baal's personality and functions derives chiefly from a number of tablets uncovered from 1929 onward at Ugarit (modern Ras Shamra), in northern Syria, and dating to the middle of the 2nd millennium BC. The tablets, although closely attached to the worship of Baal at his local temple, probably represent Canaanite belief generally. Fertility was envisaged in terms of seven-year cycles. In the mythology of Canaan, Baal, the god of life and fertility, locked in mortal combat with Mot, the god of death and sterility. If Baal triumphed, a seven-year cycle of fertility would ensue; but, if he were vanquished by Mot, seven years of drought and famine would ensue.

Ugaritic texts tell of other fertility aspects of Baal, such as his relations with Anath, his consort and sister, and also his siring a divine bull calf from a heifer. All this was part of his fertility role, which, when fulfilled, meant an abundance of crops and fertility for animals and mankind.

But Baal was not exclusively a fertility god. He was also king of the gods, and, to achieve that position, he was portrayed as seizing the divine kingship from Yamm, the sea god.

The myths also tell of Baal's struggle to obtain a palace comparable in grandeur to those of other gods. Baal persuaded Asherah to intercede with her husband El, the head of the pantheon, to authorize the construction of a palace. The god of arts and crafts, Kothar, then proceeded to build for Baal the most beautiful of palaces which spread over an area of 10,000 acres. The myth may refer in part to the construction of Baal's own temple in the city of Ugarit. Near Baal's temple was that of Dagon, given in the tablets as Baal's father.

The worship of Baal was popular in Egypt from the later New Kingdom *c.* 1400 to its end (1085 BC), and, through the influence of the Aramaeans, who borrowed the Babylonian pronunciation Bel, he ultimately became known as the Greek Belos, identified with Zeus.

Baal was also worshipped by various communities as a local god. The Old Testament speaks frequently of the Baal of a given place or refers to Baalim in the plural, suggesting the evidence of local deities, or "lords," of various locales. It is not known to what extent that the Canaanites considered those various Baalim identical, but the Baal of Ugarit does not seem to have confined his activities to one city, and doubtless other communities agreed in giving him cosmic scope.

In the formative stages of Israel's history, the presence of Baal names did not necessarily mean apostasy or even syncretism. The judge Gideon was also named Jerubbaal (Judges 6:32), and King Saul had a son named Ishbaal (I Chronicles 8:33). For those early Hebrews, "Baal" designated the Lord of Israel, just as "Baal" farther north designated the Lord of Lebanon or of Ugarit. What made the very name Baal anathema to the Israelites was the program of Jezebel, in the 9th century BC, to introduce into Israel her Phoenician cult of Baal in opposition to the official worship of Yahweh (I Kings 18). By the time of the prophet Hosea (mid-8th century BC) the antagonism to Baalism was so strong that the use of the term Baal was often replaced by the contemptuous *boshet* ("shame"); in compound proper names, for example, Ishbosheth replaced the earlier Ishbaal.

ba'al shem, also spelled BAALSHEM, or BALSHEM (Hebrew: "master of the name"), plural BA'ALE SHEM, BAALESHEM, or BALESHEM, in Judaism, title bestowed upon men who reputedly worked wonders and effected cures through secret knowledge of the ineffable names of God. Benjamin ben Zerah (11th century) was one of several Jewish poets to employ the mystical names of God in his works, thereby demonstrating a belief in the efficacy of the holy name long before certain rabbis and Kabbalists (followers of esoteric Jewish mysticism) were popularly called *ba'ale shem.* During the 17th and 18th centuries there appears to have been a proliferation of *ba'ale shem* in eastern Europe. Travelling the countryside, these men were said to have performed cures by means of herbs, folk remedies, and the tetragrammaton (four Hebrew letters signifying the ineffable name of God). They also inscribed amulets with the names of God to assist in their cures and were reported to have been especially efficacious in exorcising demons. Because the *ba'ale shem* of this period, especially in Poland and Germany, combined faith healing with practical Kabbala (use of sacred formulas and amulets), they frequently clashed with physicians, against whom they competed. They were, moreover, constantly ridiculed both by rabbinic authorities and by followers of the Jewish Enlightenment (Haskala).

Preeminent among the *ba'ale shem* was Israel ben Eliezer, commonly called Ba'al Shem Ṭov (or simply the Beshṭ), founder of the social and religious movement known as Ḥasidism. He was not, like many others, merely a magician or exorcist but an effective religious leader whose message won a large and lasting following.

Ba'al Shem Ṭov (Hebrew: Master of the Good Name), byname of ISRAEL BEN ELIEZER, also called by acronym BESHṬ (b. *c.* 1700, probably Tluste, Podolia, Pol.—d. 1760, Medzhibozh), charismatic founder (*c.* 1750) of Ḥasidism, a Jewish spiritual movement characterized by mysticism and opposition to secular studies and Jewish rationalism. He aroused controversy by mixing with ordinary people, renouncing mortification of the flesh, and insisting on the holiness of ordinary bodily existence. He was also responsible for divesting Kabbala (esoteric Jewish mysticism) of the rigid asceticism imposed on it by Isaac ben Solomon Luria in the 16th century.

Life. The Beshṭ's life has been so adorned with fables and legends that a biography in the ordinary historical sense is not possible. He came from humble and obscure beginnings in a village known to contemporary Jews as Okop or Akuf, depending on the Hebrew vocalization. As a young orphan he held various semi-menial posts connected with synagogues and Hebrew elementary religious schools. After marrying the daughter of the wealthy and learned Ephraim of Kuty, he retired to the Carpathian Mountains to engage in mystical speculation, meanwhile eking out his living as a lime digger. During this period his reputation as a healer, or *ba'al shem,* who worked wonders by means of herbs, talismans, and amulets inscribed with the divine name, began to spread. He later became an innkeeper and a ritual slaughterer and, about 1736, settled in the village of Medzhibozh, in Podolia. From this time until his death, he devoted himself almost entirely to spiritual pursuits.

Though the Beshṭ gained no special renown as a scholar or preacher during his lifetime, he made a deep impression on his fellow Jews by going to the marketplace to converse with simple people and by dressing like them. Such conduct by a holy man was fiercely condemned in some quarters but enthusiastically applauded in others. The Beshṭ defended his actions as a necessary "descent for the sake of ascent," a concept that eventually evolved into a socio-theological theory that placed great value on this type of spiritual ministration.

While still a young man, the Besht had become acquainted with such figures as Rabbi Naḥman of Gorodënka and Rabbi Naḥman of Kosov, already spoken of as creators of a new life, and with them he regularly celebrated the ritual of the three sabbath meals. In time it became customary for them to deliver pious homilies and discourses after the third meal, and the Besht took his turn along with the others. Many of these discourses were later recorded and have been preserved as the core of Ḥasidic literature. When the Besht's spiritual powers were put to a test by other members of the group—an indication that he probably was not yet recognized as the "first among equals"—he reportedly recognized a mezuzah (ritual object affixed to a doorpost) as ritually "unfit" by means of his clairvoyant powers.

The Besht gradually reached the point where he was prepared to renounce the strict asceticism of his companions. In words recorded by his grandson Rabbi Baruch of Medzhibozh, he announced:

> I came into this world to point a new way, to prevail upon men to live by the light of these three things: love of God, love of Israel, and love of Torah. And there is no need to perform mortifications of the flesh.

By renouncing mortification in favour of new rituals, the Besht in effect had taken the first step toward initiating a new religious movement within Judaism. The teaching of the Besht centred on three main points: communion with God, the highest of all values; service in ordinary bodily existence, proclaiming that every human deed done "for the sake of heaven" (even stitching shoes and eating) was equal in value to observing formal commandments; and rescue of the "sparks" of divinity that, according to the Kabbala, were trapped in the material world. He believed that such sparks are related to the soul of every individual. It was the Besht's sensitivity to the spiritual needs of the unsophisticated and his assurance that redemption could be attained without retreat from the world that found a ready response among his listeners, the common Jewish folk. He declared that they were, one and all, "limbs of the divine presence."

The Besht and his followers were fiercely attacked by rabbinical leaders for "dancing, drinking, and making merry all their lives." They were called licentious, indifferent, and contemptuous of tradition—epithets and accusations that were wild exaggerations, to say the least.

An understanding of the Besht's view of the coming of the Messiah depends to a great extent on the interpretation of a letter attributed to, but not signed by, the Besht. It affirms that the author made "the ascent of the soul," met the Messiah in heaven, and asked him when he would come. The answer he received was: "when your well-springs shall overflow far and wide"—meaning that the Besht had first to disseminate the teaching of Ḥasidism. According to one view, the story indicates that the messianic advent was central in the Besht's belief; according to another, it effectively removes messianic redemption from central spiritual concern in the life that must be lived here and now.

Influence. During his lifetime, the Besht brought about a great social and religious upheaval and permanently altered many traditional values. In an atmosphere marked by joy, new rituals, and ecstasy, he created a new religious climate in small houses of prayer outside the synagogues. The changes that had occurred were further emphasized by the wearing of distinctive garb and the telling of stories. Though the Besht never did visit Israel and left no writings, by the time he died, he had given to Judaism a new religious dimension in Ḥasidism that continues to flourish to this day.

Among the Besht's most outstanding pupils was Rabbi Jacob Joseph of Polonnoye, whose books preserve many of the master's teachings. He speaks with holy awe of his religious teacher in tones that were echoed by other disciples, such as Dov Baer of Mezrechye, Rabbi Nahum of Chernobyl, Aryeh Leib of Polonnoye, and a second grandson, Rabbi Ephraim of Sydoluvka, who was but one of many to embellish the image of his grandfather with numerous legends. (R.S.-U.)

BIBLIOGRAPHY. Dov Baer, *Shivḥé ha-Besht* (1814), is the earliest collection of legends (in Hebrew) about the Ba'al Shem Ṭov. Dan Ben-Amos and Jerome R. Mintz (eds. and trans.), *In Praise of Baal Shem Tov* (1970), offers an English translation of Dov Baer's legends, based upon the 1814 edition. Meyer Levin, *The Golden Mountain* (1932); and Martin Buber, *Die Legende des Baalschem* (1932; *The Legend of the Baal-Shem,* 1955), retell with literary flair the legends of the Ba'al Shem Ṭov. Salomo Birnbaum, *Leben und Worte des Baalschem* (1920; *The Life and Sayings of the Baal Shem,* 1933), contains excerpts from the writings and teachings of the Ba'al Shem Ṭov. (S.Z.L.)

Baalat, also spelled BA'ALAT, or BA'ALATH (from West Semitic *ba'alat,* "lady"), often used as a synonym for the special goddess of a region; also, the chief deity of Byblos. Very little is actually known of Baalat, "the Lady [of Byblos]," but because of the close ties between Byblos and Egypt, she was often represented with a typically Egyptian hairstyle, headdress, and costume, and by the 12th dynasty (1991–1786 BC) she was equated with the Egyptian goddess Hathor. To the Greeks Baalat was a form of the goddess Astarte.

Baalat, bronze statuette plated with silver; in the Louvre, Paris

By courtesy of the Musee du Louvre, Paris; cliche des Musees Nationaux

Baalbek, Arabic BA'LABAKK, Greek HELIOPOLIS (City of the Sun), principal town and agricultural centre of al-Biqā' *muḥāfaẓah* (governorate), Lebanon, and site of the ruins of the Roman town.

Nothing is known of Baalbek earlier than the Greek conquest of Syria (332 BC). After the death of Alexander the Great (323), the region fell to the Ptolemaic dynasty of Egypt, under which the town was called Heliopolis, probably after its Egyptian namesake. In 200 it was conquered by the Seleucid Antiochus the Great and remained a Seleucid possession until the fall of that dynasty (64 BC), at which time it came under Roman control. Baalbek passed under Arab domination in AD 637. From then until the 20th century, it was administered by the various Muslim rulers of Syria. After World War I the French mandatory authorities included Baalbek in Lebanon.

Ruins of the Temple of Jupiter, Baalbek, completed 3rd century AD

Manoug from Yervant Sarrafian, Beirut

European attention was first directed to the ruins at Baalbek in the 16th century, but it was not until 1898–1903 that a German expedition excavated the two huge Roman temples there. Extensive clearings and repairs were accomplished under the French mandate, and the Lebanese government has undertaken considerable restoration work, but in the mid-1970s it became a stronghold of Palestinian and Syrian forces in Lebanon.

One of the principal remains is the Temple of Jupiter. It is entered by a propylaea, or entranceway, leading to a hexagonal forecourt and then to a rectangular main court (343 ft by 338 ft [104.5 m by 103 m]), which was surrounded by elaborately decorated exedrae (semicircular benches) and opened onto a portico whose 84 granite columns were brought from Aswān in Upper Egypt. On a high terrace at the western end of the court stood the sanctuary, a Corinthian building with 10 columns on each front and 19 on each flank, each 62 ft high and 7.5 ft in diameter. The temple was dedicated to three deities: the Syrian thunder god Hadad, equated with Jupiter; the Syrian nature goddess Atargatis, equated with Venus; and a youthful god, probably a vegetation spirit, equated by the Greeks with Hermes the shepherd, hence by the Romans with Mercury. Originally a purely agricultural cult was practiced there; later it seemed to have developed aspects of a personalistic mystery religion, worship of the youthful god apparently having acquired orgiastic features.

The Temple of Bacchus, almost entirely preserved, is also Corinthian with 8 columns on each front and 15 on each flank. Its symbolic decoration shows that it was dedicated to the same agricultural gods as the great temple, but the prevalence of bacchic symbols in the interior probably indicates instead the practice of a salvational mystery religion. Other ruins include a round Temple of Venus, remains of the town walls, traces of a temple dedicated to Hermes, important Roman mosaics from private homes, a ruined mosque with reemployed antique material, and extensive Arab fortifications. Pop. (1982 est.) 14,000.

Baarle-Hertog (Flemish), French BAERLE-DUC, municipality, Antwerp province, Belgium, enclave (2.7 sq mi [7 sq km]) in Noord-Brabant province, southern Netherlands, 4 mi

(6 km) north of the Belgian border. It has been a separate commune since 1479, when the town of Baarle was divided into Baarle-Hertog and Baarle-Nassau for purposes of noble inheritance. The status of the enclave was confirmed after Belgian independence by the Belgium-Netherlands Separation Treaty (1839). The enclave was an important information centre for the Allies in World War I because of its nearness to occupied Belgium; during World War II, however, it was damaged. It is a market for the surrounding agricultural area. Pop. (1983 est.) mun., 2,101.

Baʿath Party: *see* Baʿth Party.

Bāb, the, byname of MĪRZĀ ʿALĪ MOḤAMMAD OF SHĪRĀZ (b. Oct. 20, 1819, or Oct. 9, 1820, Shīrāz, Iran—d. July 9, 1850, Tabriz), merchant's son whose claim to be the Bāb (Gateway) to the hidden *imām* (the perfect embodiment of Islāmic faith) gave rise to the Bābī religion and made him one of the three central figures of the Bahāʾī faith.

The shrine of the Bāb on Mt. Carmel, Haifa, Israel
David Harris

At an early age, ʿAlī Moḥammad became familiar with the Shaykhī school of the Shīʿī branch of Islām and with its leader, Sayyid Kāẓim Rashtī, whom he had met on a pilgrimage to Karbalāʾ (in modern Iraq). ʿAlī Moḥammad borrowed heavily from the Shaykhīs' teaching in formulating his own doctrine, and they, especially Sayyid Kāẓim's disciple Mullā Ḥusayn, seem to have encouraged his proclamation of himself as the Bāb. Traditionally, the Bāb had been considered to be a spokesman for the 12th and last *imām,* or leader of Shīʿī Islām, believed to be in hiding since the 9th century; since that time, others had assumed the title of Bāb. Such a proclamation fit in well with the Shaykhīs' interest in the coming of the *mahdī*, or messianic deliverer.

It was on May 23, 1844, that ʿAlī Moḥammad, in an inspired fervour, wrote and simultaneously intoned a commentary, the *Qayyūm al-asmāʾ*, on the *sūrah* ("chapter") of Joseph from the Qurʾān. This event prompted ʿAlī Moḥammad, supported by Mullā Ḥusayn, to declare himself the Bāb. The same year he assembled 18 disciples, who along with him added up to the sacred Bābī number 19, and were called *ḥurūf al-ḥayy* ("letters of the living"). They became apostles of the new faith in the various Persian provinces.

The six-year career of the Bāb, who had popular support, was marked by a struggle for official recognition and by a series of imprisonments. He was suspected of fomenting insurrection, and some of his followers engaged in bloody uprisings. He had to do battle with the *mujtahid*s and mullahs, members of the religious class, who were unreceptive to the idea of a Bāb who would supersede their authority and provide another avenue to the Truth. Accordingly, his missionaries were arrested and expelled from Shīrāz, and the Bāb was arrested near Tehrān and imprisoned in the fortress of Māhkū (1847) and later in the castle of Chehrīq (1848), where he remained until his execution. Assembling at the convention of Badasht in 1848, the Bāb's followers declared a formal break with Islām.

The personality of the man was such that he could win over the Shāh's envoy who was sent to investigate the movement, as well as the governor of Isfahan, who protected him in that city, and even the governor of the fortress of Māhkū, where he was first confined. Nonetheless, a committee of *mujtahids* decided he was dangerous to the existing order and demanded his execution. On the first volley from the firing squad he escaped injury; only the ropes binding him were severed, a circumstance that was interpreted as a divine sign. On the second volley he was killed and his body disposed of in a ditch. Several years later it was buried by the Bahāʾīs in a mausoleum on Mt. Carmel, in Palestine.

Late in his active period, ʿAlī Moḥammad had abandoned the title Bāb and considered himself no longer merely the "gateway" to the expected 12th *imām* (*imām-mahdī*), but to be the *imām* himself, or the *qāʾim.* Later he declared himself the *nuqṭah* ("point") and finally an actual divine manifestation. Among his followers, Bābīs and later Azalīs, he is known as *noqṭey-e ūlā* ("primal point"), *ḥazrat-e aʿlā* ("supreme presence"), *jamāl-e mobārak* ("blessed perfection"), and even *ḥaqq taʿālā* ("truth almighty"). The Bahāʾīs assign him the position of a forerunner of Bahāʾ Ullāh—the founder of the Bahāʾī faith—but they suppress all his titles except Bāb.

The Bāb wrote a great many works not only in his native Persian but also in Arabic. Among the most important and most sacred are the Arabic and the longer Persian versions of his *Bayān.* Although these are the holy books of Bābī revelation, all the writings of the Bāb and his successors are considered divinely inspired and equally binding.

Bāb-ilim, also spelled BAB-ILU (city): *see* Babylon.

Baba, Meher (Indian religious leader): *see* Meher Baba.

Baba-Jaga: *see* Baba-Yaga.

Bābā Ṭāher, byname ʿARYĀN (b. *c.* 1000, Luristan or Hamadan, Iran—d. after 1055, Hamadan), one of the most revered early poets in Persian literature.

Most of his life is clouded in mystery. He probably lived in Hamadan. His nickname, ʿAryān (the Naked), suggests that he was a wandering dervish, or mystic. Legend tells that the poet, an illiterate woodcutter, attended lectures at a religious college, where he was ridiculed by the scholars and students because of his lack of education and sophistication. After experiencing a vision in which philosophic truths were revealed to him, he returned to the school and spoke of what he had seen, astounding those present by his wisdom. His poetry is written in a dialect of Persian, and he is most famous for his *do-baytī* (double distichs), exhibiting in melodious and flowing language a sincerity and spirituality with profound philosophical undertones. Bābā Ṭāher is highly revered even now by the Iranians, who have erected a magnificent mausoleum for him in Hamadan. Many of his poems have been translated into English in E. Heron-Allen's *The Laments of Baba Tahir* (1902), A.J. Arberry's *Poems of a Persian Ṣūfī* (1937), and in Mehdi Nakhosteen's *The Rubáiyyát of Bábá Táhir Oryán* (1967).

Baba-Yaga, also called BABA-JAGA, in Russian folklore, an ogress who steals, cooks, and eats her victims, usually children. A guardian of the fountains of the water of life, she lives with two or three sisters (all known as Baba-Yaga) in a forest hut which spins continually on birds' legs; her fence is topped with human skulls. Baba-Yaga can ride through the air—in an iron kettle or in a mortar that she drives with a pestle—creating tempests as she goes. She often accompanies Death on his travels, devouring newly released souls.

Babahoyo, capital of Los Ríos province, west central Ecuador, on the southern shore of the Río Babahoyo, a major branch of the Río Guayas. A processing and trade centre for the surrounding agricultural region, the city handles rice, sugarcane, fruits, balsa wood, and tagua nuts (vegetable ivory). Rice and sugar are milled, and there is also a government-owned distillery making alcohol, ether, and perfume. A technical university was established in 1971. Pop. (1983 est.) 42,583.

Babalola, S(olomon) Adeboye (b. Dec. 17, 1926, Nigeria), poet and scholar known for his illuminating study of Yoruba *ìjalá* (a form of oral poetry) and his translations of numerous folk tales. He devoted much of his career to collecting and preserving the oral traditions of his homeland.

Babalola received his education in Nigeria, Ghana, and Cambridge, Eng., and earned a Ph.D. at the University of London. On his return to Nigeria he held such positions as lecturer at the Institute of African Studies, University of Ife; principal of Igbobi College, Lagos; and professor of African languages and literatures at the University of Lagos. His *Content and Form of Yoruba Ijala* (1966) provides both a critical introduction to this vernacular poetic form and an annotated anthology of *ìjalá* poems (hunters' songs), with English translations. His writings are considered among the best recent efforts of scholars to conserve African oral traditions.

Bābar (emperor of India): *see* Bābur.

Babar Island, Bahasa Indonesia PULAU BABAR, island and island group in the Banda Sea, Maluku *propinsi* (province), Indonesia. Located between Timor to the west and the Tanimbar Islands to the east, the group consists of Babar, the largest island, surrounded by the five islets of Wetan, Dai, Dawera, Daweloor, and Masela, and the six cover an area of about 314 sq mi (822 sq km). Babar is roughly circular, about 20 mi (32 km) in diameter and mostly hilly, rising to about 2,733 ft (833 m) in the centre of the island. Rainfall is heavy and unevenly distributed, with a markedly dry season. The hillslopes are covered with teak and liana. A number of streams flow seaward through the fertile coastal strips.

The island group is sparsely populated, and the main agricultural products are sago and corn (maize). The chief towns are Tepa and Tutuwawang, both on Babar island.

babassu palm (*Orbignya martiana, O. oleifera,* or *O. speciosa*), tall palm tree with feathery leaves that grows wild in tropical northeastern Brazil. The kernels of its hard-shelled nuts are the source of babassu oil, similar in properties and uses to coconut oil and used increasingly as a substitute for it. Babassu oil is used as a food in cooking and as a fuel and a lubricant; the soap and cosmetic industries also take a major part of the oil produced. The press cake remaining after oil is extracted from the kernels is fed to animals.

Because babassu trees grow in dense jungles, the collection and transport of the nuts is difficult. Nevertheless, the tree has been exploited and the originally extensive natural forests have been thinned out. Machines have been developed to crack the hard shell and remove the kernels from the nut, but most of the kernel removal is still done by hand.

Like the coconut palm, the babassu palm has many uses. The fruit may be used when

Babassu palm (*Orbignya speciosa*)

Walter Dawn

green in the smoking of rubber. When ripe, it is eaten as a nutritious food. Stalks serve as timbers, and the leaves as coverings and partitions in dwellings. Leaves are also used domestically for making baskets and other plaited objects. A liquid contained in the fruit stalk, or peduncle, is fermented and drunk as an alcoholic beverage, much prized locally. Fibre is taken from the epicarp, or outer layer of the fruit, and used for various purposes. Nutritious beverages similar to chocolate drinks may be made from the mesocarp, or main portion of the fruit. Buttons are made of the endocarp, or inner layer.

The fruits, or nuts, are oblong, rusty in colour, and range in length up to about 15 centimetres (6 inches). They are borne in bunches of as many as 600 and contain 2 to 6 kernels each. Kernels are 65 to 68 percent oil but less than 10 percent of the weight of the nut.

Babbage, Charles (b. Dec. 26, 1792, Teignmouth, Devon, Eng.—d. Oct. 18, 1871, London), mathematician and inventor who is credited with having conceived the first automatic digital computer.

In 1812 Babbage helped found the Analytical Society, whose object was to introduce developments from the European continent into English mathematics. In 1816 he was elected a fellow of the Royal Society of London. He was instrumental in founding the Royal Astronomical (1820) and Statistical (1834) societies.

Babbage, detail of an oil painting by Samuel Lawrence, 1845; in the National Portrait Gallery, London

By courtesy of the National Portrait Gallery, London

The idea of mechanically calculating mathematical tables first came to Babbage in 1812 or 1813. Later he made a small calculator that could peform certain mathematical computations to eight decimals. Then in 1823 he obtained government support for the design of a projected machine with a 20-decimal capacity. Its construction required the development of mechanical engineering techniques, to which Babbage of necessity devoted himself. In the meantime (1828–39) he served as Lucasian professor of mathematics at Cambridge University.

During the mid-1830s Babbage developed plans for the so-called analytical engine, the forerunner of the modern digital computer. In this device he envisioned the capability of performing any arithmetical operation on the basis of instructions from punched cards, a memory unit in which to store numbers, sequential control, and most of the other basic elements of the present-day computer. The analytical engine, however, was never completed, largely because precision techniques of fabricating metal components to close tolerances had not yet been developed. Babbage's design was forgotten until his unpublished notebooks were discovered in 1937.

Babbage made notable contributions in other areas as well. He assisted in establishing the modern postal system in England and compiled the first reliable actuarial tables. He also invented a type of speedometer and the locomotive cowcatcher.

Babbitt, Irving (b. Aug. 2, 1865, Dayton, Ohio, U.S.—d. July 15, 1933, Cambridge, Mass.), critic and teacher, leader of the movement in literary criticism known as the "New Humanism," or Neohumanism.

Babbitt was educated at Harvard and at the Sorbonne in Paris and taught French and comparative literature at Harvard from 1894 until his death.

A vigorous teacher, lecturer, and essayist, Babbitt was the unrestrained foe of Romanticism and its offshoots, Realism and Naturalism; instead, he championed the classical virtues of restraint and moderation. His early followers included T.S. Eliot and George Santayana, who later criticized him adversely, and his major opponent was H.L. Mencken.

Irving Babbitt

The Bettmann Archive

Babbitt extended his views beyond literary criticism: *Literature and the American College* (1908) opposes vocationalism in education and calls for a return to the study of classical literatures; *The New Laokoön* (1910) deplores the confusion in the arts created by Romanticism; *Rousseau and Romanticism* (1919) criticizes the effects of Rousseau's thought in the 20th century; *Democracy and Leadership* (1924) studies social and political problems; *On Being Creative* (1932) compares the Romantic concept of spontaneity adversely with classic theories of imitation.

Babbitt, Isaac (b. July 26, 1799, Taunton, Mass., U.S.—d. May 26, 1862, Somerville, Mass.), inventor of a tin-based alloy (Babbitt's metal) widely used for bearings.

Trained as a goldsmith, Babbitt made the first britannia ware in the United States (1824) to compete with imports of utensils manufactured from the alloy, similar to pewter and then very popular. Ten years later he went to Boston as superintendent of the South Boston Iron Company, and, in addition to making the first brass cannon in the United States, in 1839 he produced one of the types of alloys known as Babbitt's metals, or white metals. The alloy he invented contained tin and a small percentage of antimony and copper, although the name also has come to be used for similar alloys involving other ingredients. For his invention, the U.S. Congress awarded him $20,000. He then became a manufacturer of this alloy and of soap.

Babbitt, Milton (b. May 10, 1916, Philadelphia), composer and theorist known as a leading proponent of total serialism—*i.e.,* musical composition based on prior arrangements not only of all 12 pitches of the chromatic scale (as in 12-tone music) but also of dynamics, duration, timbre (tone colour), and register as well.

Babbitt attended public schools in Jackson, Miss., and later studied at New York University and Princeton. His teachers included the U.S. composer Roger Sessions. Babbitt became a member of the music faculty at Princeton in 1938; he also taught mathematics, an interest evident both in his elaborate theories of composition and in his works themselves. He taught also at the Berkshire Music Center and at the Darmstadt (in West Germany) Internationale Ferienkurse and was elected to the National Institute of Arts and Letters (1959 award). His interest in electronic music brought him the directorship of the Columbia–Princeton Electronic Music Center.

Milton Babbitt

Babbitt's *Composition for Synthesizer* displayed his interest in establishing precise control over all elements of composition; the machine is used primarily to achieve such control rather than solely to generate novel sounds. *Philomel* (1964) combines synthesizer with the voices of live and recorded soprano. More traditional in medium is the 1957 *Partitions for Piano.* Babbitt wrote chamber music (*Composition for Four Instruments;* 1948) and film tracks (*Into the Good Ground;* 1949) as well as solo pieces and electronic works and published many articles on 12-tone and electronic music.

Babbitt's metal, alloy invented by Isaac Babbitt in 1839 as a bearing material for steam engines or any alloy rich in tin and containing copper and antimony. Some or most of the tin may be replaced by lead. Babbitt used a two-phase alloy consisting of hard particles, which supported the load, and a soft matrix, which wore down, leaving channels for supply of lubricant.

babbler, also called CHATTERER, family name TIMALIIDAE, any of more than 250 Old World songbirds (order Passeriformes); they are treated by many authorities as a subfamily of the Muscicapidae (*q.v.*). Noted for their continual and rapid vocalizations, babblers are sometimes called babbling thrushes or chatterers. The name babbler is often used in compound form suggesting habitat, appearance, or behaviour: jungle-babbler; rail-babbler; scimitar-babbler; song-babbler; tit-babbler; wren-babbler (*qq.v.*).

Babcock, Harold Delos (b. Jan. 24, 1882, Edgerton, Wis., U.S.—d. April 8, 1968, Pasadena, Calif.), astronomer who with his son Horace Welcome Babcock invented (1951) the solar magnetograph, an instrument allowing detailed observation of the Sun's magnetic field. With their magnetograph the Babcocks demonstrated the existence of the Sun's general field and discovered magnetically variable stars. In 1959 Harold Babcock announced that the Sun reverses its magnetic polarity periodically. He was on the staff of Mt. Wilson Observatory, California, from 1909, being semi-retired from 1948.

Babcock, Horace Welcome (b. Sept. 13, 1912, Pasadena, Calif., U.S.), astronomer who with his father, Harold Delos Babcock, invented the solar magnetograph.

Horace Babcock worked at the Massachusetts Institute of Technology and at the California Institute of Technology, Pasadena, before joining the staff of Mt. Wilson and Palomar Mountain observatories in 1946; he served as director of the observatories from 1964 to 1978. His work has included studies of stellar magnetism, the glow of the night sky, and the rotation of galaxies, as well as telescope design.

Babcock, Stephen Moulton (b. Oct. 22, 1843, near Bridgewater, N.Y., U.S.—d. July 2, 1931, Madison, Wis.), agricultural research chemist, often called the father of scientific dairying chiefly because of his development of

Babcock

By courtesy of the University of Wisconsin News and Publications Service

the Babcock test, a simple method of measuring the butterfat content of milk. Introduced in 1890, the test discouraged milk adulteration, stimulated improvement of dairy production, and aided in factory manufacture of cheese and butter.

Babcock took degrees both in the U.S. and Germany, where he earned a Ph.D. in 1879. After working as a teacher and chemist in New York, he joined the staff of the University of Wisconsin, where he remained for the next 43 years. The laboratory he established there carried out pioneering research in nutrition and in the chemistry of vitamins.

Babel (city): *see* Babylon.

Babel, Isaak Emmanuilovich (b. July 13 [July 1, old style], 1894, Odessa, Russia—d. March 17, 1941, Russia), Soviet short-story writer noted for his war stories and Odessa tales. He was considered an innovator in the early Soviet period and enjoyed a brilliant reputation in the early 1930s.

Born into a Jewish family, Babel grew up in an atmosphere of persecution that is reflected in the sensitivity, pessimism, and morbidity of his stories. His first works, later included in his *Odesskiye rasskazy* ("Odessa Tales"), were published in 1916 in St. Petersburg (now Leningrad) in a monthly edited by Maksim Gorky; but the tsarist censors considered them crude and obscene. Gorky praised the young author's terse, naturalistic style, at the same time advising him to "see the world." Babel proceeded to do so, serving in the Cossack First Cavalry Army and in the political police (Babel's daughter has denied this), working for newspapers, and holding a number of other jobs over the next seven years. Perhaps his most significant experience was as a soldier in the war with Poland. Out of that campaign came the group of stories known as *Konarmiya* (1926; *Red Cavalry,* 1929). These stories present different aspects of war through the eyes of an inexperienced, intellectual young Jew who reports everything with naive precision and Goyaesque graphicness. Though senseless cruelty often pervades the stories, they are lightened by a belief that joy and happiness must exist somewhere, if only in the imagination.

The "Odessa Tales" were published in collected book form in 1931. This cycle of realistic and humorous sketches of the Moldavanka—the ghetto suburb of Odessa—vividly portrays the life-style and jargon of a group of Jewish bandits and gangsters, led by their "king," the legendary Benya Krik.

Babel wrote other short stories, as well as two plays (*Zakat,* 1928; *Mariya,* 1935). In the early 1930s his literary reputation in the Soviet Union was high, but in the atmosphere of increasing Stalinist cultural regimentation Communist critics began to question whether his works were compatible with official literary doctrine. On an official visit to Paris in 1935 Babel refused to exploit the opportunity to become an expatriate. He returned to the Soviet Union, living in silence and obscurity. His last published work in the Soviet Union was a short tribute to Gorky in 1938. His powerful patron had died in 1936; in May 1939 he was arrested, and he died in a prison camp in Siberia. After Stalin's death in 1953, Babel was rehabilitated, and his stories were again published in the Soviet Union.

Babel, Tower of, in biblical literature, structure built in the land of Shinar (Babylonia) some time after the Deluge. The mythical story of its construction is given in Gen. 11:1–9 and appears to be an attempt to explain the existence of diverse human languages. According to Genesis, the Babylonians wanted to make a name for themselves by building a mighty city and a tower "with its top in the heavens." God disrupted the work by so confusing the language of the workers that they could no longer understand one another. The tower was never completed and the people were dispersed over the face of the Earth. The myth may have been inspired by the Babylonian tower temple north of the Marduk temple, which in Babylonian was called Bab-ilu ("Gate of God"); Hebrew form Babel, or Bavel. The similarity in pronunciation of Babel and *balal* ("to confuse") led to the play on words in Gen. 11:9: "Therefore its name was called Babel, because there the Lord confused the language of all the earth."

Consult the INDEX *first*

Babelthuap, also called PALAU, BABERUDAOBU, OR ARRECIFOS, largest of the Caroline Islands within the United Nations Trust Territory of the Pacific Islands and part of the Republic of Palau (internally self-governing in 1981). It has an area of 143 sq mi (370 sq km) and lies in the western Pacific, 550 mi (885 km) east of the Philippines. Partly elevated limestone and partly volcanic in origin, Babelthuap measures 27 mi by 8 mi; it is fertile and wooded and rises to 713 ft (217 m).

Sighted (1543) by the Spanish navigator Ruy López de Villalobos, it possesses stone ruins and sculptures of an ancient culture in addition to decaying remnants of Japanese occupation during World War II. Subsistence agriculture is the main activity, but there have been attempts to cultivate cacao for export. The island has unexploited deposits of manganese and iron ore, bauxite, and low-grade coal. Pop. (1980) 3,346.

Babemba (people): *see* Bemba.

Babenberg, HOUSE OF, Austrian ruling house in the 10th–13th centuries. Leopold I of Babenberg became margrave of Austria in 976. The Babenbergs' power was modest, however, until the 12th century, when they came to dominate the Austrian nobility. With the death of Duke Frederick II in 1246, the male line of the Babenbergs ended, and the family's power declined rapidly.

Bāber (emperor of India): *see* Bābur.

Babergh, district, county of Suffolk, England. Extending across the southern part of the county, it has an area of 230 sq mi (595 sq km). It includes much of the "Constable country"—the area made familiar by the paintings of John Constable (1776–1837), who was born within the district at East Bergholt and whose family owned mills there and at Flatford. It also includes a group of small towns—Lavenham, Lindsey, and Kersey—whose history and prosperity were bound with the region's medieval woollen industry; they still preserve the splendid churches and many of the period houses of their great days. Pop. (1982 est.) 74,800.

"The Tower of Babel," oil painting by Pieter Bruegel the Elder, 1563; in the Kunsthistorisches Museum, Vienna

By courtesy of the Kunsthistorisches Museum, Vienna

babesiasis, also called PIROPLASMOSIS, any of a group of tick-borne diseases of domestic animals caused by species of *Babesia*, protozoans that destroy red blood cells and thereby cause anemia. Cattle tick fever, from *B. bigemina*, occurs in cattle, buffalo, and zebu. Other *Babesia* species attack cattle, sheep, horses, donkeys, swine, and dogs. Mortality depends on the pest species and the resistance of the host; native animals often contract mild cases and recover with immunity. Various drugs can be used to clear the blood of the parasites. Tick control plays an important role in reducing incidence.

Babeuf, François-Noël, byname GRACCHUS BABEUF (b. Nov. 23, 1760, Saint-Quentin, Fr.—d. May 27, 1797, Vendôme), early political agitator in Revolutionary France whose tactical strategies provided a model for left-wing

Babeuf, engraving by an unknown artist, 18th century

By courtesy of the Bibliotheque Nationale, Paris

movements of the 19th century and who was called Gracchus for the resemblance of his agrarian reforms to those of the 2nd-century-BC Roman statesman of that name.

The son of a tax farmer, Babeuf worked after 1776 as a land surveyor, but his increasing distaste for feudal agricultural duties led him to begin an active career as a political journalist (1788–92). In 1789 he was appointed to help prepare for the States General the *cahier* of Roye (in Picardy), a list of grievances demanding the abolition of feudal rights. The same year he went to Paris and founded a journal, *Le Correspondant Picard.* Although imprisoned briefly, he became in 1792 administrator and archivist for the *département* of the Somme. During the rightist Thermidorian reaction that followed the collapse of Robespierre's radical-democratic Jacobin regime in July 1794, Babeuf returned to Paris and founded a new journal, *Le Tribun du Peuple*, in which he at first defended the Thermidorians and attacked the Jacobins. When he began to attack the Thermidorians, he was arrested (Feb. 12, 1795).

During his brief imprisonment, Babeuf formulated his egalitarian doctrines, advocating an equal distribution of land and income, and after his release he began a career as a professional revolutionary. He quickly rose to a position of leadership in the Society of the Pantheon, which sought political and economic equality in defiance of the new French Constitution. After the society was dissolved in 1796, he founded a secret inner Committee of Six to plan an insurrection.

On May 8, 1796, a general meeting of Babouvist, Jacobin, and military insurrectionary committees took place in order to plan the raising of a force of 17,000 men and a return to the Constitution of 1793, which the committee members considered the document most legitimately sanctioned by popular deliberation. On May 10, however, the conspirators were arrested after an informant revealed their plans to the government. The trial took place between Feb. 20 and May 26, 1797. All conspirators were acquitted except Babeuf and his companion, Augustin Darthé, both of whom were guillotined.

BIBLIOGRAPHY. P. Buonarroti, *Buonarroti's History of Babeuf's Conspiracy for Equality* (1836; reprinted as *Babeuf's Conspiracy for Equality*, 1965); Colloque International de Stockholm, *Babeuf et les problèmes du Babouvisme* (1963); Claude Mazauric, *Babeuf et la conspiration pour l'Égalité* (1962); and David Thomson, *The Babeuf Plot* (1947).

Babi Yar (Nazi persecution): *see* Baby Yar.

Babia Góra (Polish), Czech BABÍ HORA, highest mountain (5,659 ft [1,725 m] at Diablok) peak in the Beskid Mountains, on the Czechoslovakia–Poland border and one of the highest peaks in Poland. It is 12 mi (19 km) north-northeast of Námestovo, Czech., and 12 mi (19 km) south-southwest of Sucha Beskidzka, Pol. The site of a 6½-sq-mi (17-sq-km) Polish national park, the mountain attracts thousands of visitors to the resort facilities in Sucha.

Bābil, formerly AL-ḤILLAH *muḥāfaẓah* (governorate), central Iraq, formerly a *liwā'* (province). With an area of 2,035 sq mi (5,270 sq km), it is Iraq's second smallest *muḥāfaẓah.* The Euphrates River splits into two branches within the *muḥāfaẓah,* which consists of level, agriculturally rich land. Despite this, it is not densely populated. Dates, barley, and wheat are among the crops grown there. The capital, al-Ḥillah (*q.v.*), lies on a rail line and a main road that cross it northward to Baghdad. Bābil contains the ruins of the famous ancient cities of Babylon, Kish, and Borsippa (Birs Nimrud). Pop. (1977) 592,016.

Babington, Anthony (b. October 1561, Dethick, Derbyshire, Eng.—d. Sept. 20, 1586, London), English conspirator, a leader of the unsuccessful "Babington Plot" to assassinate Queen Elizabeth I and install Elizabeth's prisoner, the Roman Catholic Mary Stuart, Queen of Scots, on the English throne.

The son of Henry Babington of Derbyshire, he was brought up secretly a Roman Catholic. As a youth he served at Sheffield as page to the Earl of Shrewsbury, keeper of Mary Stuart, for whom he early felt an ardent devotion. In 1580 he went to London, attended the court of Elizabeth I, and joined the secret society supporting the Jesuit missionaries. In 1582, after the execution of Edmund Campion, he withdrew to Derbyshire and later went abroad. He became associated at Paris with Mary's supporters, who were planning her release with the help of Spain, and on his return he was entrusted with letters for her. In May 1586 he was joined by the priest John Ballard in the plot which generally bears his name. The conspiracy, in its general purpose of destroying the government, included many Roman Catholics and had ramifications all over the country. Philip II of Spain promised immediate assistance with an expedition after the assassination of the Queen was effected. Babington wrote to Mary explaining his plans, but his letters and her reply were intercepted by the spies of Elizabeth's secretary Sir Francis Walsingham. On August 4 Ballard was seized and betrayed his comrades, probably under torture. Babington had already applied for a passport abroad, for the ostensible purpose of spying upon the refugees but, in reality, to organize the foreign expedition and secure his own safety. The passport being delayed, he offered to reveal to Walsingham a dangerous conspiracy, but the latter sent no reply, and meanwhile the ports were closed.

Shortly afterward, Babington is said to have observed a memorandum of Walsingham's concerning himself while in the company of the minister's servants. Thereupon he fled to St. John's Wood and, after disguising himself, succeeded in reaching Harrow, where he was sheltered by a Roman Catholic convert. Toward the end of August he was discovered and imprisoned in the Tower of London. On September 13–14 he was tried with Ballard and five others by a special commission; he confessed his guilt but strove to place all the blame upon Ballard. All were condemned to death for high treason. On September 19 he wrote to Elizabeth praying for mercy and, the same day, offered £1,000 for procuring his pardon; the next day he was executed with great barbarity in Lincoln's Inn Fields. Mary Stuart was put to death on Feb. 8, 1587.

The historical significance of the Babington Plot lies in its implication of Mary Stuart. The only positive documentary proof that Mary had knowledge of the intended assassination of Elizabeth is in a postscript to her final answer to Babington. The authenticity of this postscript has been challenged, but it is argued that Mary's circumstances, together with the tenor of her correspondence with Babington, place her complicity beyond all reasonable doubt.

Babinski–Fröhlich syndrome: *see* Fröhlich's syndrome.

babirusa (*Babirousa babyrussa*), wild East Indian swine, family Suidae (order Artiodactyla), of Celebes and the Molucca islands.

The stout-bodied, short-tailed babirusa stands 65–80 centimetres (25–30 inches) at the shoulder. It has a rough, grayish hide and is almost hairless. Its most notable feature is the exaggerated development of the upper and lower canine teeth, or tusks, of the male. Those of the upper jaw grow upward from their bases so that they pierce the skin of the muzzle and curve backward, eventually almost touching the forehead.

The babirusa is a docile, retiring, night-hunting animal of dense jungle. It is a fast runner and swims readily. When foraging, it roots

Babirusa (*Babirousa babyrussa*)

W. Suschitzky

in soft soil near rivers and in swamps. The babirusa is considered good to eat and is often hunted locally.

Bābism, religion that developed in Iran around Mīrzā 'Alī Moḥammad's claim to be a bāb (Arabic "gateway"), or divine intermediary, in 1844. *See* Bāb, the.

Babits, Mihály (b. Nov. 26, 1883, Szekszárd, Hung., Austria-Hungary—d. Aug. 4, 1941, Budapest), poet, novelist, essayist, and translator who, from the publication of his first volume of poetry in 1909, played an important role in the literary life of his country.

Babits studied Hungarian and classical literature at the University of Budapest and was a teacher in provincial secondary schools until forced to resign during World War I because of his pacifist views. Thereafter, he devoted all his energies to literature. He belonged to the literary circle that included Endre Ady, Zsigmond Móricz, and Dezső Kosztolányi, whose works were published in the periodical *Nyugat*

("The West"; founded 1908), one of the most important critical reviews in Hungarian literary history. Babits became its editor in 1929.

Babits was an intellectual poet whose verse is difficult to understand. Self-centred and withdrawn in his early period, he later turned his attention to contemporary social problems. Among his novels, *Halálfiai* (1927; "The Children of Death"), a sympathetic portrayal of the decaying middle class, is outstanding. His translations include plays of Sophocles, Dante's *Divina Commedia,* medieval Latin hymns, and works by Shakespeare and Goethe.

Babiy Yar (Nazi persecution): *see* Baby Yar.

Bābol, also spelled BĀBUL, formerly BĀRFURUSH, chief town of a populous county, Māzandarān *ostān* (province), Iran, on the Bābol River, about 15 mi (24 km) from the Caspian Sea. The town gained importance during the reign (1797–1834) of Fatḥ ʿAlī Shāh, though ʿAbbās I (died 1629) had laid out a pleasure garden and summer palace there. Bābol has paved streets, large and crowded bazaars, well-built houses, and small, handsome mosques and funeral towers. There are some manufacturing activities, but larger plants are at nearby Shāhī.

Meshed-e Sar, now called Bābol Sar, was formerly the port of Bābol on the Caspian, but it lost its function after the water level dropped. It is now a fashionable resort and has an airport. Pop. (1976) 67,790.

baboon, large, robust monkey belonging to the family Cercopithecidae, found in Arabia and in Africa south of the Sahara. The five species are commonly placed in the genus *Papio;* some authorities, however, consider this name invalid and use *Chaeropithecus.*

Olive baboon (*Papio anubis*)
Norman Myers—Photo Researchers

Baboons are quadrupedal monkeys with large heads, large cheek pouches, and long, naked, doglike muzzles bearing the nostrils at the tip. Depending on species, they weigh about 14–40 kilograms (30–88 pounds) and are about 50–115 centimetres (20–45 inches) long without the 45–70-cm tail, which is carried in a characteristic arch. Male baboons are about twice the size of females.

Mainly found in drier savanna and rocky districts, baboons move about both on the ground and in the trees. They feed on a variety of plants and animals, including occasional small mammals, birds, and birds' eggs. They are very destructive to crops and, because of their enormous canines and powerful limbs, are dangerous adversaries, especially since they generally associate in large troops. Members of a troop form a cohesive society and are led and guarded by one or more dominant males. Females as well as males rank within social hierarchies. Baboons are noisy animals and have a number of calls with definite meanings. Alarm is given by a doglike bark. Individuals also communicate by posturing and tail signalling. Baboons are considered highly intelligent and educable.

Coat colour varies, but the texture of the fur is always harsh. Adult males tend to have capes of long hair over the shoulder. The underparts, hands, feet, face, and buttocks (often vividly coloured) are naked. Normally one young is born at a time; gestation lasts seven months.

Of the known species the largest baboon is the blackish gray common or chacma (*P. ursinus* or *P. comatus*); the smallest is the reddish Guinea baboon (*P. papio*). The most spectacular is the hamadryas (*q.v.*), or sacred baboon (*P. hamadryas*).

The name "baboon" in a wider sense includes the related drill and mandrill (*qq.v.*) and has been applied to the Celebes black ape (*q.v.*), certain species of macaque (*q.v.*), and to the gelada (*q.v.*). In the Guianas it is colloquially given to the red howler (*see* howling monkey).

Babrius, in full (?) VALERIUS BABRIUS (fl. probably 2nd century AD), author of the oldest surviving collection of fables in Greek. Nothing is known of the author. The fables are for the most part versions of the stock stories associated with the name of Aesop. Babrius has rendered them into the scazon, or choliambic metre, which had already been adopted from the Greek by the Roman poets Catullus and Martial.

Most of the Babrius fables are the beast stories typical of the genre. In language and style they are very simple, but the satirical element suggests that the stories are the product of sophisticated urban society. The fables, with those of Phaedrus, were edited with English translation by Ben Edwin Perry and published in 1965.

Bābul (Iran): *see* Bābol.

Bābur (Arabic: Tiger), also spelled BĀBAR, or BĀBER, original name ẒAHĪR-UD-DĪN MUḤAMMAD (b. Feb. 15, 1483, principality of Fergana—d. Dec. 26, 1530, Āgra, India), emperor (1526–30) and founder of the Mughal dynasty of India, a descendant of the Mongol conqueror Genghis Khan and also of Timur (Tamerlane). He was a military adventurer and soldier of distinction and a poet and diarist of genius, as well as a statesman.

Early years. Bābur came from the Barlas tribe of Mongol origin, but isolated members of the tribe had become Turks in language and manners through long residence in Turkish regions. Hence Bābur, though called a Mughal, drew most of his support from Turks, and the empire he founded was Turkish in character. His family had become members of the Chagatai clan, by which name they are known. He was fifth in direct male descent from Timur and 13th, through the female line, from Genghis Khan, the first of the great Mongol conquerors. Bābur's father, ʿUmar Shaykh Mīrzā, ruled the small principality of Fergana to the north of the Hindu Kush (mountains). Because there was no fixed law of succession among the Turks, every prince of the Timurids—the dynasty founded by Timur—considered it his right to rule the whole of Timur's dominions. These territories were vast, and, hence, the princes' claims led to unending wars. The Timurid princes, moreover, considered themselves kings by profession, their business being to rule others without observing too precisely whether any particular region had actually formed a part of Timur's empire. Bābur's father, true to this tradition, spent his life trying to recover Timur's old capital of Samarkand, and Bābur followed in his footsteps. The qualities needed in this jungle of dynastic warfare were the abilities to inspire loyalty and devotion, to manage the turbulent factions often rent by family feuds, and to draw revenue from the trading and agricultural classes. Bābur eventually mastered them all, but he was also a commander of genius.

Bābur, inspecting a garden, portrait miniature from the *Bābur-nameh,* 16th century; in the British Library (MS. Or 3714)
By courtesy of the trustees of the British Library

For 10 years (1494–1504) Bābur sought to recover Samarkand and twice occupied it briefly (1497 and 1501). But, in Muḥammad Shaybānī Khān, a descendant of Genghis Khan and ruler of the Uzbeks beyond the Syrdarya (Jaxartes) River, he had an opponent more powerful than even his close relatives. In 1501 Bābur was decisively defeated at Sar-e Pol and within three years had lost both Samarkand and his principality of Fergana. There was always hope at that time, however, for a prince of ability with engaging qualities and powers of leadership. In 1504 Bābur seized Kābul with his personal followers, maintaining himself there against all rebellions and intrigues. His last unsuccessful attempt on Samarkand (1511–12) induced him to give up a hopeless quest and to concentrate on expansion elsewhere. In 1522, when he was already turning his attention to Sind and India, he finally secured Qandahār, a strategic site on the road to Sind.

When Bābur made his first raid into India in 1519, the Punjab was part of the dominions of Sultan Ibrāhīm Khān Lodī of Delhi, but the governor, Dawlat Khān Lodī, resented Ibrāhīm's attempts to diminish his authority. By 1524 Bābur had invaded the Punjab three more times but was unable to master the tangled course of Punjab and Delhi politics sufficiently to achieve a firm foothold. Yet it was clear that the Delhi sultanate was rent with dissension and ripe for overthrow. After mounting a full-scale attack there, Bābur was recalled by an Uzbek attack on his Kābul kingdom, but a joint request for help from ʿĀlam Khān, Ibrāhīm's uncle, and Dawlat Khān encouraged Bābur to attempt his fifth, and first successful, raid.

First victory in India. Setting out in November 1525, Bābur met Ibrāhīm at Pānīpat, 50 miles (80 kilometres) north of Delhi, on April 21, 1526. Bābur's army was estimated at no more than 12,000, but they were seasoned followers, adept at cavalry tactics, and were aided by new artillery acquired from the Ottoman Turks. Ibrāhīm's army was said to number 100,000 with 100 elephants, but its tactics were antiquated, and it was rent with dissension. Bābur won the battle by coolness under fire, his use of artillery, and effective Turkish wheeling tactics on a divided, dispirited enemy. Ibrāhīm was killed. With his usual speed Bābur occupied Delhi three days later and reached Āgra on May 4. His first action there was to lay out a garden by the river Yamuna, now known as the Ram Bagh.

This brilliant success must have seemed at the time to be little more than one of his former forays on Samarkand. His small force, with the unaccustomed Indian hot weather upon them and 800 miles from their base at Kābul, was surrounded by powerful foes. All down the Ganges Valley were militant Afghan chiefs, in disarray at the moment but with a formidable military potential. To the south were the kingdoms of Mālwa and Gujarāt, both with large resources, while in Rājasthān, Rānā Sāngā of Mewār (Udaipur) was head of a powerful confederacy threatening the whole Muslim position in northern India. Bābur's first problem was that his own followers, suffering from the heat and disheartened by the hostile surroundings, wished to return home as Timur had done. By employing threats, reproaches, promises, and appeals, vividly described in his memoirs, Bābur diverted them. He then dealt with Rānā Sāngā, who, when he found that Bābur was not retiring as his Turkish ancestor had done, advanced to the attack with an estimated 100,000 horses and 500 elephants. With most of the neighbouring strongholds still held by his foes, Bābur was virtually surrounded. He sought divine favour by abjuring liquor, breaking the wine vessels, and pouring the wine down a well. His followers responded both to this act and his stirring exhortations and stood their ground at Khānua, 37 miles west of Āgra, on March 16, 1527. Bābur used his customary tactics—a barrier of wagons for his centre, with gaps for the artillery and for cavalry sallies, and wheeling cavalry charges on the wings. The artillery stampeded the elephants, and the flank charges bewildered the Rājputs, who, after 10 hours, broke, never to rally under a single leader again.

Bābur had now to deal with the defiant Afghans to the east, who had captured Lucknow while he was facing Rānā Sāngā. Other Afghans had rallied to Sultan Ibrāhīm's brother Maḥmūd Lodī, who had occupied Bihār. There were also Rājput chiefs still defying him, principally the ruler of Chanderi. After capturing that fortress in January 1528, Bābur turned to the east. Crossing the Ganges, he drove the Afghan captor of Lucknow into Bengal. He then turned on Maḥmūd Lodī, whose army was scattered in Bābur's third great victory, that of the Ghāghara, where that river joins the Ganges, on May 6, 1529. Artillery was again decisive, helped by the skillful handling of boats.

The Mughal Empire. Bābur's dominions were now secure from Qandahār to the borders of Bengal, with a southern limit marked by the Rājput desert and the forts of Ranthambhor, Gwalior, and Chanderi. Within this great area, however, there was no settled administration, only a congeries of quarrelling chiefs. An empire had been gained but had still to be pacified and organized. It was thus a precarious heritage that Bābur passed on to his son Humāyūn.

In 1530, when Humāyūn became so ill that his life was despaired of, Bābur is said to have offered his life to God in exchange for Humāyūn's, walking seven times around the bed to complete the vow. Humāyūn recovered, and, from that time, Bābur declined, dying within the same year.

Assessment. Bābur is rightly considered the founder of the Indian Mughal Empire, even though the work of consolidating the empire was performed by his grandson Akbar. Bābur, moreover, provided the glamour of magnetic leadership that inspired the next two generations.

Bābur was a military adventurer of genius, an empire builder of good fortune, and an engaging personality. He was also a Turki poet of considerable gifts that would have won him distinction apart from his political career. He was a lover of nature who constructed gardens wherever he went and complemented beautiful spots by holding convivial parties. Finally, his prose memoirs, the *Bābur-nāmeh,* have become a world classic of autobiography. They were translated from Turki into Persian in Akbar's reign (1589) and into English (1921–22). They portray a ruler unusually magnanimous for his age, cultured, witty, convivial, and full of good fellowship and adventurous spirit, with a sensitive eye for natural beauty.

(T.G.P.S.)

BIBLIOGRAPHY. Bābur's own autobiography, the *Bābur-nāmeh* in the original Turki, is available in English as the *Memoirs of Bābur,* 2 vol. (1921–22). J.F. Grenard, *Baber, fondateur de l'empire des Indes* (1930; *Baber, First of the Moguls,* 1931, reprinted 1971), is a good interpretive study. The standard work in English is William Erskine, *A History of India Under the Two First Sovereigns of the House of Taimur, Bâber and Humâyun,* 2 vol. (1854). A condensed but valuable study is by E. Denison Ross in *The Cambridge History of India,* vol. 4, ch. 1 (1963). For further information, see *The Encyclopaedia of Islam,* new ed., vol. 1 (1960).

Baburen, Dirck van, original name THEODOR BABUREN, Theodor also spelled THEODOOR (b. before 1590, Utrecht, Neth.—d. 1624, Utrecht), painter who was a leading member of the Utrecht school influenced by the Italian painter Caravaggio.

After studying painting with a portraitist and history painter in Utrecht, Baburen travelled to Rome about 1612. His most important Italian commission was the decoration of a chapel in the church of S. Pietro in Montorio, Rome (1615–20), which included his "Entombment" (1617).

"The Procuress," oil painting on canvas by Dirck van Baburen, 1622; in the Museum of Fine Arts, Boston

By courtesy of the Museum of Fine Arts, Boston

In 1620 Baburen returned to Utrecht, where he shared a studio with Hendrick Terbrugghen in about 1622–23. The influence of Caravaggio may be seen in his "Christ Crowned with Thorns" (two versions, at the Franciscan House, Weert, Neth., and at Drury-Lowe Collection, Locko Park, Eng.), based on a lost painting by the master. Baburen was especially fond of genre scenes or subjects from everyday life, such as "The Procuress" (1622; Museum of Fine Arts, Boston). A certain coarseness in conception, irregular compositional rhythms, and less atmospheric quality distinguish Baburen's art from that of his greater contemporaries.

Babuyan Islands, island group, a northerly extension of the Philippine archipelago, in the Luzon Strait, south of the Batan Islands and Balintang Channel. Administered by the province of Cagayan, they lie 20 mi (32 km) north of Luzon across the Babuyan Channel. With a total area of 230 sq mi (600 sq km), they comprise 24 volcanic-coralline islands, the chief of which are Babuyan, Camiguin, Calayan, Fuga, and Dalupiri. The inhabitants are fishermen and farmers with strong cultural ties to Luzon. Root crops, particularly sweet potatoes, are widely grown, and the surplus supports a small livestock industry. Calayan is the largest town and only port with regular interisland shipping service from Aparri and Manila, but this link is frequently broken from September to February during the typhoon season. Cattle, hogs, goats, and lumber are exported. Pop. (1980) 8,969.

A list of the abbreviations used in the MICROPAEDIA *will be found at the end of this volume*

Baby Elephant, also called BABY JACK (shot-putter): *see* Torrance, Jack.

baby tooth: *see* primary tooth.

Baby Yar, also spelled BABIY YAR, or BABI YAR, large ravine on the northern edge of Kiev in the Ukrainian S.S.R., the site of a mass grave of more than 100,000 victims, mostly Jews, who were killed by the German Nazis between 1941 and 1943. The site became a symbol to Soviet Jews of their Nazi martyrdom.

The German army took Kiev on Sept. 19, 1941. Earlier that year, Hitler had ordered special SS squads to follow the regular army into Russia and to exterminate all Jews and Soviet officials. Morever, a few days after the fall of Kiev, an explosion rocked the German command post in the city, killing many German soldiers and intensifying Nazi outrage against the Jews, whom they wrongly blamed for the explosion. When the SS *Sonderkommandos* entered the city, the Jews were marked for destruction. On September 19–20, over a 36-hour period, nearly 34,000 Jews were marched in small groups to the outskirts of the city, stripped naked, and machine-gunned into the ravine, which was immediately covered over, with several of the victims still alive. Over the next two years the gravesite was swelled with thousands of other victims, primarily Jews, but also including Communist officials and Russian prisoners of war. As the German armies retreated from the Soviet Union, the Nazis attempted to hide the evidence of the slaughter. During August and September 1943, the bodies were exhumed by slave labour and burned in large pyres.

The massacre was described in detail by eyewitnesses and is vividly depicted in novels by Ilya Ehrenburg (*The Storm,* 1948) and Anatoly Kutzenov (*Babi Yar: A Documentary in the Form of a Novel;* Eng. trans. 1971). However, Baby Yar came to world attention with the publication in September 1961 of Yevgeni A. Yevtushenko's moving poem *Babiy Yar,* written in protest against plans to build a sports stadium on the site. Dmitry Shostakovich set the poem to music as part of his choral 13th Symphony, first performed in Moscow in December 1962.

Both Yevtushenko and Shostakovich were reprimanded for their "cosmopolitanism" by the Soviet authorities, who refused to acknowledge the special Jewish significance of a site where other Russians had been killed. A small obelisk was constructed at Baby Yar in 1966, and in 1976 a 50-foot (15-metre) memorial statue was unveiled. Neither the statue nor the obelisk, however, makes any reference to the Jewish dead.

Babylon, Babylonian BAB-ILU, Old Babylonian BĀB-ILIM, Hebrew BAVEL, or BABEL, Arabic AṬLĀL BĀBIL, one of the most famous cities of antiquity. It was the capital of southern Mesopotamia (Babylonia) from the early 2nd millennium to the early 1st millennium

BC and capital of the Neo-Babylonian (Chaldean) Empire in the 7th and 6th centuries BC, when it was at the height of its splendour. Its extensive ruins on the Euphrates River about 55 miles (88 kilometres) south of Baghdad lie near the modern town of al-Ḥillah, Iraq.

History. Though traces of prehistoric settlement exist, Babylon's development as a major city was late by Mesopotamian standards, no mention of it occurring before the 23rd century BC. After the fall of the 3rd dynasty of Ur, under which Babylon had been a provincial centre, it became the nucleus of a small kingdom established in 1894 BC by the Amorite king Sumuabum, whose successors consolidated its status. The sixth and best known of the Amorite dynasts, Hammurabi (1792–50 BC), conquered the surrounding city-states and raised Babylon to the capital of a kingdom comprising all southern Mesopotamia and part of Assyria (northern Iraq). Its political importance, together with its favourable geographical position, made it henceforth the main commercial and administrative centre of Babylonia, while its wealth and prestige made it a target for foreign conquerors.

After a Hittite raid in 1595 BC, the city passed to the control of the Kassites (*c.* 1570), who established a dynasty lasting more than four centuries. Later in this period, Babylon became a literary and religious centre, the prestige of which was reflected in the elevation of Marduk, its chief god, to supremacy in Mesopotamia. In 1234 Tukulti-Ninurta I of Assyria took Babylon, though subsequently the Kassite dynasty reasserted itself until 1158, when the city was sacked by the Elamites. Babylon's acknowledged political supremacy is shown by the fact that the dynasty of Nebuchadrezzar I (1124–03) made it their capital, although they did not originate there. This dynasty endured for more than a century.

Just before 1000, pressure from Aramaean immigrants from northern Syria brought administrative dislocation inside Babylon. From this period to the fall of Assyria in the late 7th century BC, there was a continual struggle between Aramaean or associated Chaldean tribesmen and the Assyrians for political control of the city. Its citizens claimed privileges, such as exemption from forced labour, certain taxes, and imprisonment, which the Assyrians, with a similar background, were usually readier to recognize than were immigrant tribesmen. Furthermore, the citizens, grown wealthy by commerce, benefitted by an imperial power able to protect international trade but suffered economically from disruptive tribesmen. Such circumstances made Babylon usually prefer Assyrian to Aramaean or Chaldean rule.

From the 9th to the late 7th century Babylon was almost continuously under Assyrian suzerainty, usually wielded through native kings, though sometimes Assyrian kings ruled in person. Close Assyrian involvement in Babylon began with Tiglath-pileser III (744–727 BC) as a result of Chaldean tribesmen pressing into city territories, several times usurping the kingship. Disorders accompanying increasing tribal occupation finally persuaded Sennacherib (704–681 BC) that peaceful control of Babylon was impossible, and in 689 he ordered destruction of the city. Esarhaddon (680–669 BC) rescinded Sennacherib's policy, and, after expelling the tribesmen and returning the property of the Babylonians to them, undertook the rebuilding of the city; but the image of Marduk, removed by Sennacherib, was retained in Assyria throughout his reign, probably to prevent any potential usurper from using it to claim the kingship. In the mid-7th century, civil war broke out between the Assyrian king Ashurbanipal and his brother who ruled in Babylonia as sub-king. Ashurbanipal laid siege to the city, which fell to him in 648 after famine had driven the defenders to cannibalism.

After Ashurbanipal's death, a Chaldean leader, Nabopolassar, in 626 made Babylon the capital of a kingdom that under his son Nebuchadrezzar II became a major imperial power. Nebuchadrezzar undertook a vast program of rebuilding and fortification in Babylon, labour gangs from many lands increasing the mixture of the population. Nebuchadrezzar's most important successor, Nabonidus, campaigned in Arabia for a decade, leaving his son Belshazzar as regent in Babylon. Nabonidus failed to protect property rights or religious traditions of the capital and attempted building operations elsewhere to rival Marduk's great temple of Esagila. When the Persians under Cyrus attacked in 539 BC, the capital fell almost without resistance; a legend (accepted by some as historical) that Cyrus achieved entry by diverting the Euphrates is unconfirmed in contemporary sources.

Under the Persians, Babylon retained most of its institutions, became capital of the richest satrapy in the empire, and, according to Herodotus, the world's most splendid city. A revolt against Xerxes I (482) led to destruction of its fortifications and temples and the melting down of the golden image of Marduk.

In 331 Babylon surrendered to Alexander the Great, who confirmed its privileges and ordered the restoration of the temples. Alexander, recognizing the commercial importance of the city, allowed its satrap to issue coinage and began construction of a harbour to foster trade. In 323 Alexander died in the palace of Nebuchadrezzar; he had planned to make Babylon his imperial capital. Alexander's conquest brought Babylon into the orbit of Greek culture, and Hellenistic science was greatly enriched by the contributions of Babylonian astronomy. After a power struggle among Alexander's generals, Babylon passed to the Seleucid dynasty in 312. The city's importance was much reduced by the building of a new capital, Seleucia, on the Tigris, to which part of Babylon's population was transferred in 275.

The ancient city. Evidence of the topography of ancient Babylon is provided by excavations, cuneiform texts, and descriptions by the 5th-century Greek historian Herodotus and other classical authors. The extensive rebuilding by Nebuchadrezzar has left relatively little archaeological data in the central area earlier than his time, while elsewhere the water table has limited excavation in early strata. The reports of Herodotus largely relate to the Babylon built by Nebuchadrezzar.

Nebuchadrezzar's Babylon was the largest city in the world, covering 2,500 acres (1,000 hectares). The Euphrates, which has since shifted its course, flowed through it, the older part of the city being on the east bank. There the central feature was Esagila, the great temple of Marduk, with its associated ziggurat (a tower built in several stages) Etemenanki. The latter, popularly known as the Tower of Babel, had a base 100 yards on a side, and its seven stages, the uppermost a temple in blue glaze, reached to a height of 300 feet (91 metres). Four other temples in the eastern half of the city are known from excavations and a larger number from texts. Along the Euphrates, particularly in the neighbourhood of Esagila, were quays for trading vessels, and textual evidence that Babylon was an entrepôt for trade with south Babylonia points to the existence of warehouses. The river was spanned by a bridge on brick piles, with stone capping, to the western half of the city. The streets were laid out on a grid, with the main axis parallel to the river. From Esagila northward passed the paved Processional Way, its walls decorated with enamelled lions. Passing through the Ishtar Gate, adorned with enamelled bulls and dragons, it led to the Akitu House, a small temple outside the city, visited by Marduk at the New Year festival. West of the Ishtar Gate, one of eight fortified gates, were two palace complexes that covered about 40 acres with their fortifications.

East of the Processional Way lay an area that since the time of Hammurabi had contained private dwellings built around central courtyards. A powerful double wall, reinforced by a fosse (ditch), enclosed the city on both sides of the Euphrates. Beyond the city walls to the east an outer rampart of triple construction, 11 miles long, met the Euphrates south and north of the city, at its northern junction enclosing another palace. Between the inner and outer defenses was irrigated land with a network of canals, some going back to the time of Hammurabi. Greek tradition refers to the Hanging Gardens, a simulated hill of vegetation-clad terracing over a vaulted substructure that in Hellenistic times was deemed one of the Seven Wonders of the World. The German archaeologist R. Koldewey identified the base of this early in the 20th century AD with a part of the palace complex, though the tradition could have arisen from the existence of trees on the ziggurat.

The present site. The present site, an extensive field of ruins, contains several prominent mounds. The main mounds are (1) Babil, the remains of Nebuchadrezzar's palace in the northern corner of the outer rampart; (2) Qasr, comprising the palace complex (with a

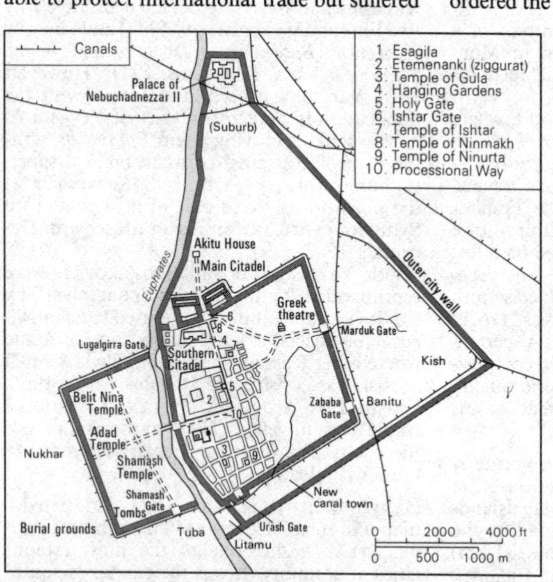

Babylon during the reign of Nebuchadrezzar II

Adapted from *Westermann Grosser Atlas zur Weitgeschichte*, Georg Westermann Verlag, Braunschweig building added in Persian times), the Ishtar Gate, and the Emakh temple; (3) Amran ibn Ali, the ruins of Esagila; (4) Merkez, marking the ancient residential area east of Esagila; (5) Humra, containing rubble removed by Alexander from the ziggurat in preparation for rebuilding, and a theatre he built with material from the ziggurat; and (6) Ishin Aswad, where there are two further temples. A depression called Sahn marks the former site of the ziggurat Etemenanki. An over-life-size basalt lion, probably of Hittite origin and brought to Babylon in antiquity, stands north of the Ishtar Gate.

Archaeology. After minor surveys and excavations by the British scholar C.J. Rich (1811 and 1817), and the English diplomat A.H. Layard (1850), the French orientalist F. Fresnel, the German assyriologist J. Oppert (1852–54), and others, a major archaeological operation began under R. Koldewey of the Deutsche Orient-Gesellschaft in 1899, continuing unbroken until 1917. In the course of his excavation of the structures mentioned, Koldewey also discovered cuneiform inscriptions, statues, steles (pillars), terra-cotta reliefs, cylinder seals, pottery, glassware, and jewelry. Further brief investigations were made by the Deutsches Archäologisches Institut in 1956 under H.J. Lenzen at the Greek theatre, and in 1966 under H.J. Schmidt at the site of Etemenanki. Restoration of the Emakh temple, and of part of the Ishtar Gate, the Processional Way, and the palace complex was begun in 1958 by the Iraq Department of Antiquities, which has also built a half-size model of the complete Ishtar Gate at the entrance to the site. (H.W.F.S.)

BIBLIOGRAPHY. The principal excavator's own account of his results is given in a good popular form by R. Koldewey, *Das wieder erstehende Babylon,* 4th ed. (1925; *The Excavations at Babylon,* 1914). H.W.F. Saggs, "Babylon," in D. Winton Thomas (ed.), *Archaeology and Old Testament Study,* pp. 39–56 (1967), gives a summary of medieval and early modern investigations of the site of Babylon, together with an account of the results of the excavations there, and related evidence, oriented to its biblical interest. H.W.F. Saggs, *Everyday Life in Babylonia and Assyria* (1965), popular account of particular aspects of Babylonian life, pp. 156–180 dealing with the Babylon of Nebuchadrezzar.

Babylon, town (township), Suffolk County, southeastern New York, U.S., on southern Long Island and Great South Bay, east of Freeport. Established in 1872 after separation from Huntington (founded 1653), it includes the villages of Babylon (incorporated 1893), Amityville (1894), and Lindenhurst (1923), and the unincorporated communities of Deer Park, Copiague, and Wyandanch. Guglielmo Marconi erected (1900–01) the first wireless station in the United States (preserved at Rocky Point) at Babylon village, and Lawrence Sperry experimented with early guided missiles at Amityville in 1918.

The town developed as a summer yachting resort, but experienced rapid population and diversified industrial growth after World War II. Pop. (1950) 45,556; (1970) 203,570; (1980) 203,483.

Babylonia, ancient cultural region occupying southeastern Mesopotamia between the Tigris and Euphrates rivers (modern southern Iraq from around Baghdad to the Persian Gulf). Because the city of Babylon was the capital of this area for so many centuries, the term Babylonia has come to refer to the entire culture that developed in the area from the time it was first settled, *c.* 4000 BC. Before Babylon's rise to political prominence (*c.* 1850 BC), however, the area was divided into two countries: Sumer in the southeast and Akkad in the northwest.

The history of Sumer and Akkad is one of constant warfare. The Sumerian city-states fought one another for the control of the region and rendered it vulnerable to invasion from Akkad and from its neighbour to the east, Elam. Despite the series of political crises that marked their history, however, Sumer and Akkad developed rich cultures. The Sumerians were responsible for the first system of writing, cuneiform; the earliest known codes of law; the development of the city-state; the invention of the potter's wheel, the sailboat, and the seed plow; and the creation of literary, musical, and architectural forms that influenced all of Western civilization.

This cultural heritage was adopted by the Sumerians' and Akkadians' successors, the Amorites, a western semitic tribe that had conquered all of Mesopotamia by *c.* 1900 BC. Under the rule of the Amorites, which lasted until *c.* 1600 BC, Babylon became the political and commercial centre of the Tigris-Euphrates area, and Babylonia became a great empire, encompassing all of southern Mesopotamia and part of Assyria to the north. The ruler largely responsible for this rise to power was Hammurabi (died 1750 BC), the sixth king of the 1st dynasty of Babylon, who forged coalitions between the separate city-states, promoted science and scholarship, and promulgated his famous code of law.

After Hammurabi's death, the Babylonian empire declined until 1595 BC, when the Hittite invader Mursil I unseated the Babylonian king Samsuditana, allowing the Kassites from the mountains east of Babylonia to assume power and establish a dynasty that lasted 400 years.

During the last few centuries of Kassite rule, religion and literature flourished in Babylonia, the most important literary work of the period being the *Enuma Elish*, the Babylonian epic of creation. During this same time, however, Assyria broke away from Babylonian control and developed as an independent empire, threatening the Kassite dynasty in Babylonia and on a few occasions temporarily gaining control. Elam, too, grew powerful and ultimately conquered most of Babylonia, felling the Kassite dynasty (*c.* 1159 BC).

In a series of wars, a new line of Babylonian kings, the 2nd dynasty of the city of Isin, was established. Its most outstanding member, Nebuchadrezzar I (reigned *c.* 1124–1103 BC), defeated Elam and successfully fought off Assyrian advances for some years.

For several centuries following Nebuchadrezzar I's rule, a three-way struggle developed among the Assyrians and Aramean and Chaldean tribesmen for control of Babylonia. From the 9th century to the fall of the Assyrian empire in the late 7th century BC, Assyrian kings most frequently ruled over Babylonia, often appointing sub-kings to administer the government. The last ruling Assyrian king was Ashurbanipal, who fought a civil war against his brother, the sub-king in Babylon, devastating the city and its population.

Upon Ashurbanipal's death, a Chaldean leader, Nabopolassar, made Babylon his capital and instituted the last and greatest period of Babylonian supremacy. His son Nebuchadrezzar II (reigned 605–562) conquered Syria and Palestine; he is best remembered for the destruction of Judah and Jerusalem in 587 BC and for the ensuing Babylonian captivity of the Jews. He also revitalized Babylon, constructing the wondrous hanging gardens and rebuilding the Temple of Marduk and its accompanying ziggurat.

The Persians, under Cyrus the Great, captured Babylonia from Nebuchadrezzar's last successor Nabonidus in 539 BC. Thereafter, Babylonia ceased to be independent, passing eventually in 331 to Alexander the Great, who planned to make Babylon the capital of his empire and who died in Nebuchadrezzar's palace. After Alexander's death, however, the Seleucids eventually abandoned Babylon, bringing an end to one of the greatest empires in history.

Babylonian calendar, chronological system used in ancient Mesopotamia, based on a year of 12 synodic months; *i.e.*, 12 complete cycles of phases of the Moon. This lunar year of about 354 days was more or less reconciled with the solar year, or year of the seasons, by occasional intercalation of an extra month. From about 380 BC the beginning of the first month of the year, Nisanu, was maintained near the onset of spring by use of a regular cycle (similar to the Greek Metonic cycle) of intercalations.

Babylonian Exile, also called BABYLONIAN CAPTIVITY, the forced detention of Jews in Babylonia following the conquest of the Kingdom of Judah in 598/7 and 587/6 BC. The Exile formally ended in 538 BC, when the Persian conqueror of Babylonia, Cyrus the Great, gave the Jews permission to return to Palestine. Historians agree that several deportations took place (each the result of uprisings in Palestine), that not all Jews were forced to leave their homeland, that returning Jews left Babylonia at various times, and that some Jews chose to remain in Babylonia—thus constituting the first of numerous Jewish communities living permanently in the Diaspora (*q.v.*).

Many scholars cite 597 BC as the date of the first deportation, for in that year King Jehoiachin was deposed and apparently sent into exile with his family, his court, and thousands of workers. Others say the first deportation followed the destruction of Jerusalem by Nebuchadrezzar in 586; if so, the Jews were held in Babylonian captivity for 48 years. Among those who accept a tradition (Jer. 29:10) that the exile lasted 70 years, some choose the dates 608 to 538, others 586 to *c.* 516 (the year when the rebuilt Temple was dedicated in Jerusalem).

Although the Jews suffered greatly and faced powerful cultural pressures in a foreign land, they maintained their national spirit and religious identity. Elders supervised the Jewish communities, and Ezekiel was one of several prophets who kept alive the hope of one day returning home. This was possibly also the period when synagogues were first established, for the Jews observed the sabbath and religious holidays, practiced circumcision, and substituted prayers for former ritual sacrifices in the Temple. The degree to which the Jews looked upon Cyrus the Great as their benefactor and a servant of their God is reflected at several points in the Hebrew Bible, *e.g.*, at Isa. 45:1–3, where he is actually called God's anointed.

Babylonian Talmud, also called TALMUD BAVLI, one of two compilations of Jewish religious teachings and commentary that was transmitted orally for centuries prior to its compilation by Jewish scholars in Babylon. The other such compilation, produced in Palestine, is called the Palestinian Talmud, or *Talmud Yerushalmi. See* Talmud.

baby's breath, two species of herbaceous plants of the genus *Gypsophila*, of the pink family (Caryophyllaceae), having profuse small blossoms. Both *G. elegans*, an annual, and *G. paniculata*, a perennial, are cultivated for their fine misty effect in rock gardens and flower borders and in floral arrangements. They are native to Eurasia.

Annual baby's breath, up to 50 centimetres (20 inches) tall, is much branched, with narrow bluish-green leaves. It is widely planted, especially the varieties such as 'Carminea,' with deep rose-red flowers; 'Grandiflora Alba,' with large white flowers; and 'Rosea,' with rose pink flowers.

Perennial baby's breath, up to 100 cm tall, is similar in appearance to *G. elegans* but has a stout storage rootstock and white to pinkish flowers. Popular varieties include 'Compacta,' dense growing; 'Flore Pleno,' with double flowers; and 'Grandiflora,' with larger flowers.

Bac Lieu, town and provincial seat, Minh Hai *tinh* (province), Ca Mau Peninsula, southern Vietnam. It has a hospital and a commercial airport and is linked by highway to Ho Chi Minh City (formerly Saigon), 120 mi (195 km) to the northeast. In addition to rice growing, there is mat making, and, on the coast, salt is obtained by evaporation. There is also a fishing industry. The government has moved people into the area from Ho Chi Minh City-Cho Lon. Pop. (1971 est.) 65,678.

Bac Thai, *tinh* (province), north central Vietnam. The Song (river) Cau flows east and then south through the province, which has an area of 2,521 sq mi (6,530 sq km). It is bounded by the provinces of Cao Bang on the north, Lang Son on the east, Ha Bac and Vinh Phu on the south, and Ha Tuyen on the west. Part of Viet Bac autonomous region until 1976, the mountainous province has forest enterprises, including a paper mill, and iron-ore mines. An iron and steel complex and industrial centre with factories under central government control are located at Thai Nguyen, the provincial seat. There are coal mines and a steel-rolling mill at Gai Sang. Since 1976, vegetables and tea have been grown. Major arteries of transportation are by road to Hanoi and by river steamboat to Haiphong. Pop. (1979) 815,105.

Bacab, in Mayan mythology, any of four gods, thought to be brothers, who, with upraised arms, supported the multilayered sky from their assigned positions at the four cardinal points of the compass. (The Bacabs may also have been four manifestations of a single deity.) The four brothers were probably the offspring of Itzamná, the supreme deity, and Ixchel, the goddess of weaving, medicine, and childbirth. Each Bacab presided over one year of the four-year cycle. The Maya expected the Muluc years to be the greatest years, because the god presiding over these years was the greatest of the Bacab gods. The four directions and their corresponding colours (east, red; north, white; west, black; south, yellow) played an important part in the Mayan religious and calendrical systems.

Bacan, also spelled BACHAN, or BATJAN, island, Maluku Utara *kabupaten* (North Molucca regency), Maluku *propinsi* (province), Indonesia, one of the northern Moluccas in the Molucca Sea, southwest of Halmahera. The islands of Kasiruta to the northwest, Mandioli to the west, and about 80 other islets compose the Kepulauan (islands) Bacan group. With an area of about 700 sq mi (1,800 sq km), Bacan is mountainous in the south, rising to 6,926 ft (2,111 m), relatively level and lower in the centre, and volcanic in the north, with some sulfurous springs. Gold, copper, and brown coal, or lignite, deposits exist. Products include spices, copra, timber, and mother-of-pearl, with tobacco and rice raised for local consumption. Labuha, the principal city and port, has the only airport.

Bacan has fine trees, a great variety of soils, and a number of small navigable streams. Its rich animal life includes the crested Celebes black ape, an eastern opossum, a pigmy flying phalanger, the great Indian civet, a bird of paradise, and several bats. Other birds are a red lory, little lorikeet, green parrot with red bill and head; golden-capped sunbird, racquet-tailed kingfisher, a rare goatsucker, and a large and handsome fruit pigeon with metallic-green and rust plumage.

The Bacanese are believed to have come originally from Halmahera. Other inhabitants include the Serani (Christian with some Portuguese blood), Makasarese, and Malays. A small fort was built by the Portuguese and captured (1609) and renamed Barneveld by the Dutch, who put the island's sultan under the suzerainty of the sultan of Ternate. The Bacan sultanate continued to exist until the end of the 19th century. The Japanese occupied Bacan during World War II. Pop. (1971) 29,137.

Bacău, *judeţ* (district), eastern Romania, occupying an area of 2,549 sq mi (6,603 sq km). The Eastern Carpathians and the sub-Carpathians rise above the settlement areas that are situated in intermontane valleys and lowlands. The district is drained southeastward by the Siret River and its tributaries. It was formerly included in feudal Moldavia. Manufactures of Bacău (*q.v.*) city, the district capital, include military airplanes, metal products, textiles, and timber. Gheorghe Gheorghiu-Dej city, located in the Trotuş Valley, was designated an industrial area in 1955 and has oil-processing, chemical, and synthetic-rubber factories. Agăş and Comăneşti are timber centres. Oil wells operate in Moineşti, Zemeş, Solonţ, and Lucăceşti. Coal mines are worked near Comaneşti and Asău towns, and salt is mined near Tîrgu Ocna. Borzeşti village was the birthplace of Stephan (Ştefan) the Great, who declared Moldavia's independence from the Turks in 1503. The regional museum, located in Bacău city, contains Neolithic idols and Dacian pottery and money found in the surrounding area. Several hydroelectric plants are located on the Bistriţa River, north of Bacău city. Railway lines and highways usually parallel the district's river courses. An airport is located near Bacău city. Pop. (1982 est.) 695,693.

Bacău, city, capital of Bacău *judeţ* (district), eastern Romania, near the confluence of the Bistriţa and Siret rivers, 150 mi (240 km) northeast of Bucharest. Bacău was an early customs post, where trade routes came together at a ford over the Bistriţa. It was first mentioned in documents in 1408. It is an important road and rail junction and is on the main railway from Bucharest to Chernovtsy, in the Ukrainian S.S.R. The manufacture of fighter airplanes in collaboration with Yugoslavia has become the most important industry. Other industries include a paper mill, a footwear factory, and several cloth and textile factories, in addition to wood processing. Foodstuffs and building materials are also produced. It is a cultural centre, with a state theatre, a symphony orchestra, and museums. Pop. (1982 est.) 151,795.

Baccarat, also spelled BACCARA, bank card game of Italian origin played in European casinos, having been introduced to France late in the 15th century. The game may go back to the 15th century, but its popularity in France and England dates from the mid-1800s. It is now played around the world.

The game is played with three to six 52-card decks shuffled together. Cards are dealt from a dealing box called a shoe. Players aim for a count of 9, or as close as they can get, in a hand of two or three cards. Face (court) cards and 10s are counted as zero; all others take their number values. The cards in each hand are added to obtain the value, but only the last digit is significant. Thus, if the two cards in a hand are 8 and 5, the count is not 13 but 3. A competing hand with a face card (0) and a 6 wins, because it is closer to 9.

The player with the most capital, or funds with which to accept bets, is declared the banker. The banker deals three hands of two cards each, face down, from the shoe. These hands are for two players, called punters, one to the right and one to the left, and for the dealer himself. Other players at the table may bet on either hand (cheval) or both to beat the banker's hand. If a punter declares banco, it means he is betting the total value of the bank's funds; all lesser bets are then withdrawn for that hand.

When the two-card deal is completed, the players examine their hands. A count of 8 or 9 is a natural and an automatic winner unless the banker also has a natural. In a tie, bets are called off. If a player has a count less than 8 or 9, he may stand (saying "*non*") or get one more card face up (saying "*carte*"). Punters must stand on a 6 or 7, draw a card if they have 4 or less, and do as they wish (*à volonté*) with 5. The banker is not restricted. When the full hands are compared, the banker settles all bets. Casinos usually take a small percentage of the bank and bets as their fee for the game. Late in the 1950s, Baccarat-Chemin de Fer was introduced at Las Vegas and became popular, as it is in Latin-American casinos.

To make the best use of the Britannica, consult the INDEX *first*

Baccarat glass, glassware produced by an important glasshouse founded in 1764 at Baccarat, Fr. Originally a producer of soda glass for windows, tableware, and industrial uses, Baccarat was acquired by a Belgian manufacturer of lead crystal in 1817 and since then has specialized in producing this type of glass. In 1823 the firm won its first gold medal in an international exposition for glass, and a showing of its works at the 1925 Exposition des Arts Decoratifs helped shape the Art Deco (*q.v.*) style. Among the many artistically significant works it has produced are the pieces by Émile Gallé (*q.v.*).

Baccarat began production of paperweights in 1846. Although they exhibited virtually all techniques of ornamental glassmaking, including millefiori, cameo, sculpture, engraving, and casings, the Baccarat paperweights were relatively inexpensive and became great favourites with collectors. Today Baccarat manufactures many lines of tableware in historical patterns.

Bacchanalia, also called DIONYSIA, in Greco-Roman religion, any of the several festivals of Bacchus (Dionysus), the wine god. They probably originated as rites of fertility gods. The most famous of the Greek Dionysia were in Attica and included the Little or Rustic Dionysia, characterized by simple, old-fashioned rites; the Lenaea, the chief rites of which were a festal procession and dramatic performances; the Anthesteria, essentially a drinking feast; the City or Great Dionysia, accompanied by dramatic performances in the theatre of Dionysus, which was the most famous of all; and the Oschophoria (Carrying of the Grape Clusters).

Introduced into Rome from lower Italy, the Bacchanalia were at first held in secret, attended by women only, on three days of the year. Later, admission was extended to men, and celebrations took place as often as five times a month. The reputation of these festivals as orgies led in 186 BC to a decree of the Roman Senate that prohibited the Bacchanalia throughout Italy, except in certain special cases. Nevertheless, Bacchanalia were not suppressed in the south of Italy for many years.

Bacchelli, Riccardo (b. April 19, 1891, Bologna, Italy), Italian poet, dramatist, literary critic, and novelist who championed the literary style of Renaissance and 19th-century masters against the innovations of Italian experimental writers.

Bacchelli attended the University of Bologna but left without a degree in 1912. He became a contributor to literary journals. Bacchelli published a notable volume of *Poemi lirici* ("Lyric Poems") in 1914, when he began service in World War I as an artillery officer. After the war, as a collaborator on the Roman literary periodical *La Ronda,* he attempted to discredit contemporary avant-garde writers by holding up as models the Renaissance masters and such fine 19th-century writers as Giacomo Leopardi and Alessandro Manzoni. Somewhat later he was drama critic for the Milanese review *La fiera letteraria*.

His first outstanding novel, *Il diavolo al pontelungo* (1927; *The Devil at the Long Bridge*, 1929), is a historical novel about an attempted Socialist revolution in Italy.

Bacchelli's strongest works are historical novels, and his masterpiece, with the general title *Il mulino del Po* (1938–40; Eng. trans., vols. 1 and 2, *The Mill on the Po*, 1950, vol. 3, *Nothing New Under the Sun*, 1955), is among the finest Italian works of that genre. Against the background of Italy's political struggles from the time of Napoleon to the end of World War I, *Il mulino del Po* dramatizes the conflicts and struggles of several generations of one family, owners of a mill on the banks of the Po River. The first volume, *Dio ti salve* (1938; "God Bless You"), covers the period from Napoleon's 1812 Russian campaign to the revolutionary events of 1848; the second, *La miseria viene in barca* (1939; "Misery Comes to a Boat"), continues the story during the Risorgimento, the 19th-century Italian struggle for political unity, stressing its terrible economic and social effect on the lower classes; and the third, *Mondo vecchio sempre nuovo* (1940), ends with the battle of Vittorio Veneto in World War I.

Il mulino del Po has been called an "epic of the common man," and its great value is its balanced humanism and compassion for the suffering of the little man caught in the great, impersonal web of political events.

Of Bacchelli's later historical novels, *I tre schiavi di Giulio Cesare* (1958; "The Three Slaves of Julius Caesar") is outstanding. Among his critical works are *Confessioni letterarie* (1932; "Literary Declarations") and a later work on two literary figures he greatly admired, *Leopardi e Manzoni* (1960). Bacchelli's early novels have been collected in *Tutte le novelle, 1911–51* (1952–53).

Bacchus: *see* Dionysus.

Bacchus, SAINT: *see* Sergius and Bacchus, Saints.

Bacchus Marsh, town in southern Victoria, Australia. It is located 32 mi (51 km) northwest of Melbourne (to which a growing proportion of its residents commute daily) on the east bank of the Werribee River in the La Trobe Valley. In 1838, Capt. William Henry Bacchus founded the town, and it grew as a stopping place for Cobb and Company coaches travelling from Melbourne to the Ballarat goldfields. Bacchus Marsh is situated in a fruit-growing, grazing, dairying, and mixed farming area and is also a centre of light manufacturing that produces hardboard, plastic goods, clothing, and engineering equipment. Maddingley opencut mine provides much of the state's supply of brown coal. A park, nearby Werribee and Lerderderg gorges, and an elm-tree lined entrance to the town are tourist attractions. The Manor, originally Bacchus' home, is one of the oldest colonial-period buildings in Victoria. Inc. shire, 1856. Pop. (1981) 6,224.

Bacchylides (fl. 5th century BC), Greek lyric poet of the Aegean island of Ceos, nephew of the poet Simonides and a younger contemporary of the Boeotian poet Pindar, whom he rivalled in the composition of epinician poems (odes commissioned by victors at the major athletic festivals). Little was known of Bacchylides' work until the discovery in Egypt of papyrus fragments that reached the British Museum in 1896 and were published in the following year. Of the 21 poems wholly or partially restored, 14 are epinician odes and the remainder are dithyrambs (originally choric songs in honour of Dionysus that became the subject of a choral competition at the Athenian festival of the Dionysia). Other fragments, supplemented by later papyrus finds, include passages from paeans (hymns in honour of Apollo and other gods) and encomiums (songs in honour of distinguished men, performed as part of an after-dinner entertainment).

A firm date is provided by Ode 5, an epinician ode written to celebrate the victory of Hieron I, ruler of Syracuse, in the horse race at the Olympian games of 476 BC. The poem implies that Bacchylides had already visited Syracuse before this date as a guest of Hieron, whose later victories in the Pythian horse race of 470 and the Olympian chariot race of 468 he celebrated in Odes 4 and 3, respectively. This brought him into direct competition with Pindar, who also celebrated two, if not all three, of these victories in *Olympian i* and *Pythian i* and *ii.* Pindar's uncomplimentary remarks about rival poets have been taken as referring to Bacchylides and Simonides. Bacchylides' style is simpler, if less sublime, than Pindar's; he excels in narrative and in clarity of expression. Like Simonides, Bacchylides wrote dithyrambs for the Dionysian festival at Athens, notably the unique Ode 18, which is semi-dramatic, taking the form of a dialogue between Theseus' father, Aegeus, and an answering chorus of followers. Literary historians differ as to how this literary form is related to the development of the Attic drama.

The best text is that of B. Snell (8th ed., 1961). There is also a commentary by R.C. Jebb (1905), and a translation by Robert Fagles of the complete poems was published in 1961.

Baccio D'AGNOLO, byname of BARTOLOMEO D'AGNOLO BAGLIONI (b. May 15, 1462—d. March 6, 1543, Florence), wood-carver, sculptor, and architect who exerted an important influence on the Renaissance architecture of Florence. Between 1491 and 1502 he did much of the decorative carving in the church of Sta. Maria Novella and in the Palazzo Vecchio in Florence. He helped restore the Palazzo Vecchio and in 1506 was commissioned to complete the drum of the cupola of Sta. Maria del Fiore; but, because of adverse criticism by Michelangelo, the work was not carried out. Baccio d'Agnolo also planned the Villa Borghese and the Bartolini palace and designed the campanile of S. Spirito. His studio was frequented by Michelangelo, Jacopo da Sansovino, Raphael, and other notable artists of the day.

Baccio DELLA PORTA: *see* Bartolomeo, Fra.

Bach, Carl Philipp Emanuel (b. March 8, 1714, Weimar, Saxe-Weimar—d. Dec. 14, 1788, Hamburg), second surviving son of J.S. and Maria Barbara Bach, and the leading composer of the pre-Classical period.

A precocious musician who remained successful, C.P.E. Bach was his father's true successor and an important figure in his own right. In his autobiography he writes: "For composition and keyboard-playing, I have never had any teacher other than my father." He studied law, taking his degree at Frankfurt in 1735, although he probably never had any intention of a career other than music.

In 1740 he was appointed harpsichordist to Frederick II of Prussia. Frederick was a good flutist and so fond of music that he had his court orchestra accompany him in concerti every night except Mondays and Fridays, which were opera nights. The subservience that he required from his distinguished harpsichordist grew irksome, but it was not until 1767 that Bach was able to resign his Berlin post to take up an appointment as music director at Hamburg. Meanwhile, he had married (1744), published his *Versuch über die wahre Art das Klavier zu spielen* (1753–62; *Essay on the True Art of Playing Keyboard Instruments*, 1948), and acquired an enviable reputation, as a composer, performer, and teacher.

Unlike his elder brother Wilhelm Friedemann, C.P.E. Bach was successful in assimilating the powerful influence of their father and in making the transition into the new style then evolving. This represented a break with the past such as has occurred in very few other periods of musical development. The monumental character of Baroque music gave way to a mercurial Romanticism, for which the favourite contemporary description was "sensitivity" (*Empfindsamkeit*). Bach became a leader of that movement but retained the advantage of a solid craftsmanship and assurance for which he always gave full credit to his father's teaching and example.

C.P.E. Bach, engraving by A. Stöttrup
By courtesy of Haags Gementemuseum, The Hague

C.P.E. Bach's numerous compositions include religious music (*e.g.*, a *Magnificat*, 22 Passions), symphonies, concerti (for flute, harpsichord, piano, harpsichord and piano, organ, oboe), organ sonatas, chamber music, and songs. The music of his Berlin period is comparatively old-fashioned, because of the conventional preferences of his royal employer. In Hamburg he developed a more adventurous vein, and his work there did as much as any to open up future musical styles. Particularly influential were his symphonies, concerti, and keyboard sonatas in the evolution of classical sonata-allegro form. His influence on Haydn, Mozart, and even Beethoven was freely acknowledged, and it is interesting that having influenced Haydn, C.P.E. Bach later allowed himself to be influenced by the younger composer, just as Haydn later influenced and was influenced by Mozart.

As a performer, Bach was famous for the precision of his playing, for the beauty of his touch, and for the intensity of his emotion. "He grew so animated and possessed," wrote Charles Burney (*Present State of Music in Germany*..., 1773), "that he looked like one inspired. His eyes were fixed, his underlip fell, and drops of effervescence distilled from his countenance."

The influence of C.P.E. Bach's *Essay on Keyboard Instruments* was unsurpassed for two generations. Haydn called it "the school of schools." Mozart said, "He is the father, we are the children." Beethoven, when teaching the young Karl Czerny, wrote "be sure of procuring Emanuel Bach's treatise." It is, indeed, one of the essential source books for understanding the style and interpretation of 18th-century music. It is comprehensive on thorough bass, on ornaments and fingering, and is an authentic guide to many other refinements of 18th-century performance.

Bach, Johann Christian (b. Sept. 5, 1735, Leipzig—d. Jan. 1, 1782, London), composer called the "English Bach," youngest son of J.S. and Anna Magdalena Bach and prominent in the pre-Classical period.

J.C. Bach received his early training from his father and, probably, from his father's cousin Johann Elias Bach. After his father's death

(1750) he worked with his half-brother, C.P.E. Bach, in Berlin.

At the age of 20 he made his way to Italy and in 1756 became a pupil of Padre Martini in Bologna. Having a grace and tactfulness of manner notably lacking in older generations of Bachs, he found a generous patron; his compositions, though immature, were in a serious style and largely liturgical. Having become a Catholic convert, he was appointed organist of Milan cathedral in 1760. His conversion was thought cynical and reprehensible by his strongly Lutheran family, from whom he became somewhat estranged. His taste next turned to opera, and he was thought to have neglected his official organist's duties.

In 1762 he became composer to the King's Theatre in London and wrote a number of successful Italian operas for it. He also produced much orchestral, chamber, and keyboard music, and a few cantatas. He started his fashionable series of concerts two years

Johann Christian Bach, detail of a portrait by Thomas Gainsborough; in the Civico Museo Bibliografico Musicale, Bologna, Italy
Fotofast, Bologna, Italy

later with the celebrated viola da gamba player Karl Friedrich Abel. Receiving a lucrative appointment as music master to Queen Charlotte and her children, he became a social as well as a musical success. In 1772 he was invited to write an opera for the German elector at Mannheim.

J.C. Bach's music reflects the pleasant melodiousness of the *galant*, or Rococo, style. Its Italianate grace influenced composers of the Classical period, particularly Mozart, who learned from and greatly respected Bach. His symphonies, contemporary with those of Haydn, were among the formative influences on the early Classical symphony; his sonatas and keyboard concerti performed a similar role. Nevertheless, his early success apparently relieved him of any urgent pressure to continue developing; although he never grew to be a profound composer, his music was always sensitive and imaginative.

Bach, Johann Christoph Friedrich (b. June 21, 1732, Leipzig—d. Jan. 26, 1795, Bückeburg, Prussia), longest surviving son of J.S. and Anna Magdalena Bach.

Probably educated by his father's cousin Johann Elias Bach, J.C.F. Bach became a chamber musician to Count Wilhelm at Bückeburg in 1750, and was appointed concertmaster *c.* 1758. His career was steady and his output of compositions extensive. He made a successful transition from the late Baroque style into the pre-Classical style. His compositions were well received, and although they did not lead their times, they kept successfully abreast of them. He is at his best in his later symphonies, similar in style to those of Haydn. He also composed motets, oratorios (some in collaboration with the poet Johann Gottfried von Herder), piano sonatas, chamber cantatas, and instrumental chamber works.

Bach, Johann Sebastian (b. March 21, 1685, Eisenach, Thuringia, Ernestine Saxon Duchies—d. July 28, 1750, Leipzig), composer of the Baroque era, the most celebrated member of a large family of northern German musicians. Though he was considered old-fashioned in his lifetime and his works were neglected after his death, Bach was recognized in the 19th century as one of the greatest composers of the Western world, a preeminence that continues undiminished.

A brief account of the life and works of Johann Sebastian Bach follows; for a full biography, *see* MACROPAEDIA: Bach, Johann Sebastian.

After the death of his parents when he was 10, Bach was looked after and taught by his eldest brother, Johann Christoph. He became a choirboy at the Michaelskirche, Lüneburg, when he was 15. In 1703 he was appointed organist at the Neukirche, Arnstadt, where he remained for four years, after which he moved to a similar post at Mühlhausen and about the same time married his cousin, Maria Barbara Bach.

A year later he became court organist at Weimar, staying there until 1717, when he went into the service of Prince Leopold of Köthen as musical director. There in 1721 he completed his Brandenburg Concertos. His first wife died in 1720, and at the end of the following year he married Anna Magdalena Wilcken. In 1728 he was appointed musical director for the city of Leipzig, where he had to supply performers for four churches. In May 1747 he played before Frederick II the Great of Prussia at Potsdam. Two years later his eyesight began to fail, and he became blind shortly before his death in 1750.

In the course of his various duties, Bach wrote an enormous amount of sacred choral music, including more than 200 cantatas, his noble *Mass in B Minor,* and three settings of the Passion story (one of which is lost). He also wrote extensively and significantly for the organ and harpsichord, the latter works including the great 48 Preludes and Fugues called *The Well-Tempered Clavier* (Book I, 1722; Book II, 1744) and the *Goldberg Variations* (1742). Among his many instrumental works are some 20 concertos and 12 unaccompanied sonatas for violin and cello.

Bach, Wilhelm Friedemann (b. Nov. 22, 1710, Weimar, Saxe-Weimar—d. July 1, 1784, Berlin), eldest son of J.S. and Maria Barbara Bach, composer during the period of transition between Baroque and Rococo styles.

W.F. Bach's musical instruction was primarily from his father (who wrote for him, when he was ten, the charming *Klavier-büchlein vor Wilhelm Friedemann Bach* of keyboard pieces). He also studied the violin. He matriculated at Leipzig University in 1729. In 1733, already composing extensively, he was appointed organist to the Church of St. Sophia in Dresden. In 1746 he moved to the Liebfrauenkirche at Halle. At about this time, or perhaps later, after his father's death in 1750, he seemed to begin to have personality difficulties, evidenced by excessive drinking and other lapses. After a late marriage in 1751, he became restless and applied unsuccessfully for a change of post in 1753 and 1758. In 1762 he won an appointment to the Darmstadt court but did not take it up. Resigning his old post in Halle in 1764, for 20 years he sought in vain for regular employment. He became touchy and unreliable, and although his talents were never doubted, he imagined that they were. In 1774 he moved to Berlin, where he lived meagrely by giving recitals and teaching.

Of his compositions, keyboard works and cantatas form the larger part; he also composed several symphonies and chamber works

Wilhelm Friedemann Bach, drawing by P. Gulle, 1783; in the Staatsbibliothek, West Berlin
By courtesy of the Staatsbibliothek, West Berlin

and an opera. His music vacillated between the Baroque style of his father and the newer *galant*, or Rococo, style. His compositions, few for his many years, are often impassioned, often unpredictable in their use of melody, harmony, and rhythm.

Bach Long Vi, island of northern Vietnam in the Gulf of Tonkin, halfway between the mouth of the Red River (Song Hong) near Nam Dinh and the Chinese island of Hainan. The island is a plateau that rises abruptly to 190 ft (58 m) above sea level and is fringed with precipitous cliffs. Fishing resources are abundant in the surrounding gulf of the South China Sea.

Bachan (Indonesia): *see* Bacan.

Bachčisaraj (Ukrainian S.S.R.): *see* Bakhchisaray.

Bacheller, Irving (Addison) (b. Sept. 26, 1859, Pierpont, N.Y., U.S.—d. Feb. 24, 1950, White Plains, N.Y.), journalist and novelist whose books, generally set in upper New York State, are humorous and full of penetrating character delineations, especially of rural types.

Bacheller graduated from St. Lawrence University, Canton, N.Y., in 1882 and entered journalism. In 1883 in Brooklyn, N.Y., he founded the first modern newspaper syndicate and through its services distributed fiction by such writers as Joseph Conrad, Rudyard Kipling, and Stephen Crane, as well as nonfiction material. From 1898 to 1900 he was editor of the *New York World.* Bacheller became extremely popular for *Eben Holden: A Tale of the North Country* (1900), which sold more than 1,000,000 copies. This novel about a hired man gives an authentic picture of 19th-century farm life and character in upper New York State. *D'ri and I* (1901), a novel about the Battle of Lake Erie in the War of 1812, was also popular. His own favourites were *The Light in the Clearing* (1917) and *A Man for the Ages: A Story of the Builders of*

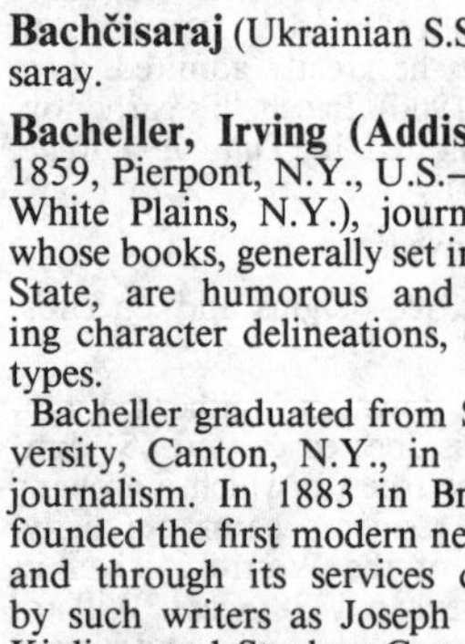

Bacheller
By courtesy of the Library of Congress, Washington, D.C.

Democracy (1919), the latter a story of Lincoln. *Opinions of a Cheerful Yankee* (1926); *Coming up the Road, Memories of a North Country Boyhood* (1928); and *From Stores of Memory* (1938) were autobiographical.

Bachman, John (b. Feb. 4, 1790, Rhinebeck, N.Y., U.S.—d. Feb. 24, 1874, Columbia, S.C.), naturalist and Lutheran minister who helped write the text of works on North American birds and mammals by the renowned U.S. naturalist and artist John James Audubon.

Ordained in 1814, Bachman obtained a parish in Charleston, S.C., the following year. Long a natural history enthusiast, Bachman published studies of Southern animals and works on botany and agriculture. He met Audubon in 1831 and helped him write the text of *The Birds of America* (1840–44). After visiting the German naturalist and explorer Alexander von Humboldt at the University of Berlin in 1838, Bachman did much of the writing and edited all of Audubon's *Viviparous Quadrupeds of North America* 3 vol., (1845–49). In 1850 he wrote *The Unity of the Human Race,* in which he insisted correctly that all mankind constitutes a single species.

As a clergyman, Bachman founded the Lutheran Synod of South Carolina, served as its first president, and founded the state's Lutheran theological seminary. He responded to local Roman Catholic criticism with *A Defense of Luther and the Reformation* (1853).

Bachofen, Johann Jakob (b. Dec. 22, 1815, Basel, Switz.—d. Nov. 25, 1887, Basel), jurist and anthropologist whose book *Das Mutterrecht* (1861; "Mother Right") is regarded as a fundamental contribution to modern social anthropology.

Bachofen was a professor of the history of Roman law at the University of Basel (1841–45) and also a judge of the Basel criminal court (1842–66). After writing two works on Roman civil law (1847 and 1848), he travelled to Italy and Greece and began earnestly to study the symbolism of ancient tombs, thereby gaining significant insights into primitive man, his laws, and his religion.

In *Das Mutterrecht,* Bachofen presented the first attempt to advance a scientific history of the family as a social institution and suggested that mother right preceded father right. Though he based his theorizing on Greek and Roman classics, his previously unpublished manuscripts in his *Gesammelte Werke* (10 vol., 1943 ff.; "Collected Works"), show that in 1869 he planned to revise *Das Mutterrecht* on the basis of wider evidence and had begun 15 years of study of nearly every known culture. From 1872 he increasingly adopted the views of U.S. anthropologist Lewis Henry Morgan on kinship.

Bacia do Cabo Verde (Atlantic Ocean): *see* Cape Verde Basin.

Baciccia, byname of GIOVANNI BATTISTA GAULLI (b. May 8, 1639, Genoa—d. April 2, 1709, Rome), leading Roman Baroque painter of the second half of the 17th century.

At Genoa, Baciccia was a student of Luciano Borzone but was also influenced by Van Dyck and Bernardo Strozzi. He moved to Rome about 1660, visiting Parma (1669) to study the frescoes of Correggio. His chief influence was Bernini, who befriended him and introduced him to his circle of Roman patrons.

Baciccia's principal works are his fresco decorations in the Roman churches Sta. Agnese (1668–71), the Gesù (finished 1684), and SS. Apostoli (1707). In these, and particularly in the Gesù, he combined an ecstatic religious figure-style, derived from Bernini, and a melting, sensual treatment of the heads, derived from Correggio, with his own masterly organization of masses of light and shade and an attractive bravura of execution. He also painted altarpieces and was well known as a portraitist of the papal circle.

Bacillariophyta, division of algae the members of which are commonly known as diatoms. *See* diatom.

bacillite (geology): *see* crystallite.

Bacillus, genus of rod-shaped bacteria of the family Bacillaceae widely found in soil and water. With few important exceptions (*B. anthracis* and *B. thuringiensis*) *Bacillus* species are harmless to man and other animals. All *Bacillus* are microbiologically characterized as gram-positive and can develop dormant cells, or endospores. The largest species are about 2 μm (micrometres; 1 μm = 10^{-6} metre) across by 7 μm long and frequently occur in chains. As endospores they are resistant to heat, chemicals, and sunlight and are constantly present on dust particles almost everywhere. The term bacillus in a general sense is applied to all cylindrical or rodlike bacteria.

Bacillus cereus, abundant in soil, sometimes causes spoilage in canned foods. *B. subtilis,* also widely disseminated, is a common contaminant of laboratory cultures (it plagued Louis Pasteur in many of his experiments) and is often found on human skin. Of importance as disease agents are *B. anthracis,* cause of anthrax (*q.v.*) in man and domestic animals, and *B. thuringiensis,* cause of a disease of caterpillars and exploited commercially in its sporulating form as an insecticide harmless to vertebrates but specific for many caterpillar plant pests. Medically useful antibiotics are produced by *B. subtilis* (bacitracin) and *B. polymyxa* (polymixin B).

Back, Sir George (b. November 1796, Stockport, Cheshire, Eng.—d. June 23, 1878, London), naval officer who helped to trace the Arctic coastline of North America. He twice accompanied the British explorer John Franklin to Canada's Northwest Territories (1819–22 and 1825–27) and later conducted two expeditions of his own to the same region.

Back; detail of a pencil and chalk drawing by W. Brockedon, 1824–29; in the National Portrait Gallery, London
By courtesy of the National Portrait Gallery, London

The first of these expeditions, in 1833, was to search for another British explorer, John Ross, who had disappeared on an Arctic voyage in 1829. The venture resulted in the exploration of the Great Fish River, now the Back River. In 1836 he returned to explore the coastal region east from the mouth of the Back. His writings include *Narrative of the Arctic Land Expedition to the Mouth of the Great Fish River* (1836) and *Narrative of Expedition in H.M.S. Terror* (1838). He was knighted in 1839.

back swimmer, any insect of the family Notonectidae (order Heteroptera), containing approximately 200 species. These relatively small insects occur worldwide. Most are less than 15 millimetres (0.6 inch) in length. Their long, oarlike legs are used when they swim on their backs, which are shaped like the keel and sides of a boat. The back swimmer has an oval head and an elongated body. It is a good example of countershading: its light-coloured back, seen from below, blends into the water surface and sky. The rest of the body is darker and, when seen from above, blends with the bottom of the body of water in which it lives.

Because the back swimmer is lighter than water, it rises to the surface after releasing its hold on the bottom vegetation. Once at the surface it may either leap out of the water and fly or get a fresh supply of air, which is stored under its wings and around its body, and dive again. The back swimmer is often seen floating on the water surface, with its legs extended, ready to dart away if disturbed. It preys on insects, tadpoles, and fishes, which are often larger than itself, sucking their body fluids with its strong beak.

The genus *Notonecta,* distributed worldwide, may be quite destructive to fishes and tadpoles. It will bite humans when handled, the bite feeling somewhat like a bee sting. Its eggs are deposited either on or in the plant tissue of pond vegetation.

The black-and-white back swimmer, *N. undalata,* found in North America, can often be seen swimming under the ice during the winter. The genus *Buenoa,* which usually floats or swims some distance below the surface, appears reddish or pinkish in colour because of the pigment (hemoglobin) contained in certain cells.

Plea, usually less than 3 mm (0.12 in.) long, is found in tangled aquatic plants. It feeds on small crustaceans.

backbone: *see* vertebral column.

Backbone Mountain, highest point (3,360 ft [1,024 m]) in Maryland, U.S., on a ridge of the Allegheny and Appalachian mountains, located in Garrett County, 10 mi (16 km) south of Oakland. The ridge, 35 mi long, extends southwest into Tucker County, W.Va.

backcross, the mating of a hybrid organism (offspring of genetically unlike parents) with one of its parents or with an organism genetically similar to the parent. The backcross is useful in genetics studies for isolating (separating out) certain characteristics in a related group of animals or plants. In animal breeding, a backcross is often called a topcross. Grading usually refers to the mating of average or "grade" females to a superior male, then backcrossing the female offspring to the same or a similar sire.

Backgammon, game played by moving counters on a board or table, the object of the game being a race to a goal, with the movement of the counters being controlled by the throw of two dice. Elements of chance and skill are nicely balanced in Backgammon so that each is usually essential to victory. The game became highly popular worldwide in the 1970s.

Precursors of Backgammon are among the most ancient of all games and may date from as early as 3000 BC. The ancient Romans played a game, Ludus Duodecim Scriptorum (Twelve-lined Game), which was identical, or nearly so, with modern Backgammon. The game is still most generally played in the eastern Mediterranean countries.

Backgammon is played by two persons. The board comprises four sections, or tables, each marked with six narrow wedges, or points, in two alternating colours. A vertical line called the bar divides the board in half, separating the "inner" and "outer" tables. There are 15 white and 15 black pieces, often called stones. Opposing stones are moved from point to point in opposite directions around the board, the exact number of points shown on the dice. The two numbers may be applied separately to two different stones or, in turn, to one. Doublets (identical numbers on the two dice) are taken twice over; *e.g.,* two 6s count as four 6s, making a total of 24 points traversed.

A point occupied by two or more stones of one colour is "made" by that player and cannot be occupied by the opponent. A single stone on a point is a "blot," liable to be "hit" by an adverse stone landing on that point. If hit, a blot is picked up and placed on the bar, and the owner may make no other move until it is reentered. Reentry must be made in the adverse inner table upon an open point of the same number as is cast with either dice.

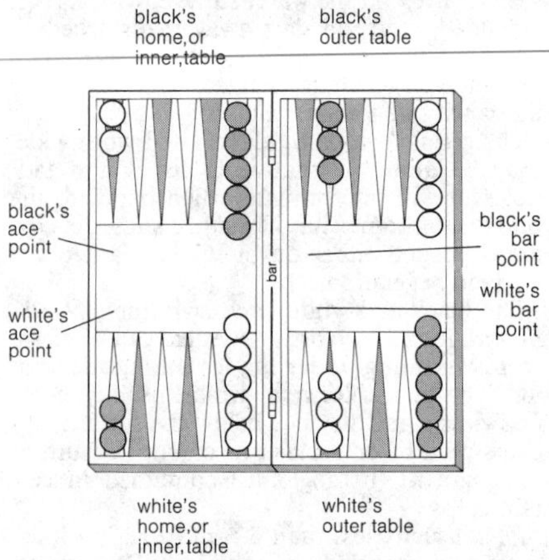

Backgammon board at beginning of play

On getting all 15 of his stones into his own home (inner) table, a player may begin "bearing off"—moving his stones to an imaginary point beyond the edge of the board. The player who first bears off all 15 stones wins the game. If the loser has borne off at least one stone, the game is a single; if he has borne off none, it is a gammon and counts double; and if in addition he has any stone left in the winner's inner table, it is a backgammon and counts triple.

background radiation, random radiation, either electromagnetic or particulate, that gives counts or signals in measuring devices and that originates in the surroundings (including the device itself), rather than in the radiation source being examined. For example, the use of a Geiger counter to measure beta radiation from a substance undergoing radioactive decay is complicated by the fact that the counter registers not only the radiation from the substance but also cosmic rays, which cannot be excluded from the apparatus. In practice, the sample is isolated and the background is counted alone so that it can be subtracted from the gross count to give a net count representing the sample alone. The intensity of the background imposes a lower limit on the intensity of the radiation that can be measured accurately. Analogous situations include the impossibility of seeing the stars during the daytime, when the light from the Sun constitutes an intense background; or the difficulty of hearing one individual in the midst of a noisy crowd.

Sometimes background radiation is referred to as noise.

Backhaus, Wilhelm (b. March 26, 1884, Leipzig—d. July 5, 1969, Villach, Austria), German pianist best known for his interpretation of the works of Beethoven.

Backhaus studied piano in Leipzig and in Frankfurt am Main. His first concert appearance took place when he was eight years of age, and in 1905 he won the Rubinstein prize in Paris. He held teaching appointments at the Royal Manchester College of Music (1905), at Sondershausen (1907), and at the Curtis Institute, Philadelphia (1925). After World War II, he settled in Lugano, Switz., but continued to tour and make recordings. His style was described as severe and articulate, yet not without warmth and the most scrupulous regard for the score.

backpacking, sport of hiking while carrying clothing, food, and camping equipment in a pack on the back. Originally in the early 20th century practiced in the wilderness as a means of getting to areas inaccessible by car or by day hike, backpacking demands physical conditioning and practice, knowledge of camping and survival techniques, and selection of equipment of a minimum weight consistent with safety and comfort. In planning his trip, the backpacker must take into consideration food and water, terrain, climate, and weather.

Packs hang from the shoulders or are supported by a combination of straps around shoulders and waist or hips. Types range from the frameless rucksack, hung from two straps, and the frame rucksack, in which the pack is attached to a roughly triangular frame hung on the shoulder straps, to the contour frame pack, with a frame of aluminum or magnesium tubing bent to follow the contour of the back. The Kelty-type pack, used with the contour frame, employs a waistband to transfer most of the weight of the pack to the hips.

Clothing is weatherproof and insulating, including shell parkas, insulating underwear, down clothing, windpants, ponchos, sturdy waterproof boots with soles designed for maximum traction, and heavy socks. Tents may be a simple tarpaulin, a plastic sheeting tube, or a two-person nylon mountain tent. Sleeping bags of foam, dacron, or down, and air mattresses or foam pads may be carried. Lightweight pots and pans and stoves are specially designed for backpacking; dehydrated food provides stew-type one-pot dishes.

Backpackers must be able to read topographic maps and find their way with a compass; they must also carry emergency food and first aid equipment and be acquainted with survival techniques.

Later, backpacking became associated with travel, especially by students, outside the wilderness; and in urban centres backpacks replaced satchels, book bags, and other hand luggage for many students and informally inclined young adults.

Backus, Isaac (b. Jan. 9, 1724, Norwich, Conn.—d. Nov. 20, 1806), controversial religious leader and historian.

Backus did not attend a college or religious seminary, but he was awarded an honorary degree by Rhode Island College (now Brown University) in 1797. In religious disputes and as an itinerant preacher in Massachusetts and Connecticut, he carried on his fight for religious freedom. He became the leading spokesman for the Baptist Church. He wrote *A History of New England, With Particular Reference to the Denomination of Christians Called Baptists* (1777–96).

Bacolod, chartered city, capital of Negros Occidental province, northwestern portion of the island of Negros, Philippines. On a coastal plain washed by Guimaras Strait, it lies opposite Guimaras Island and has been called the Philippine sugar capital because of its central location within the nation's most important sugar-producing area. Bacolod's growth began after 1800, when it was first used as a convenient gathering point for traffic bound for Iloilo, on the island of Panay. With subsequent development of the sugar plantations, it became Negros' most populous urban area and a regional trade centre. Its outport, Pulupandan, lies to the south along the main coastal highway and is a major fishing port.

The city's rectangular street pattern is unusual among Philippine coastal communities. Seasonal and permanent population growth has led to an acute housing shortage. Bacolod is served by a major airport, the provincial hospital, and the private University of Negros Occidental-Recolestos (1941). The nearest sugar central (mill) is 1.5 mi (2.4 km) inland. The large provincial capitol building is set amid spacious landscaped grounds, and an old stone church and convent are in the central square. Imposing residences of wealthy planters are on the city's outskirts. Inc. city, 1938. Pop. (1980) 262,415.

bacon (from German *bachen,* "wild pig"), originally, pork, especially salt pork; in modern times, usually a side of a pig after removal of the spare ribs and after curing, either dry or in pickle, and smoked. Some varieties, notably Canadian bacon, are cut from the loin portion of the pork, which is more lean.

Bacon was for centuries the staple meat of the Western European peasantry. Varieties distinguished by cut of meat or curing process became standardized in association with particular countries or regions, such as the Irish or various Italian styles. The relatively long storage life of bacon made it the only meat to gain importance as an international trade commodity in the late 19th century.

In the United States in the 20th century, bacon is generally marketed in five standard styles: slab, regular sliced, thin sliced, thick sliced, and ends and pieces. Slab bacon is taken from the side or belly of a hog that has been cured for 10–14 days under refrigeration, then cooked and smoked; it contains streaks of lean and fat, and one side is usually covered with skin. Sliced bacon is cut from the slab; it is usually shingled for packaging, with the outer skin removed.

Bacon has an extremely high fat content, and is therefore not an especially nutritious meat. By weight, raw American-style bacon contains only about 8.5 percent protein. Also, most bacon, like other commercially cured meats, contains the additive sodium nitrite, the possible carcinogenic properties of which generated controversy in the late 1970s.

Despite the limited nutritional value of bacon, it is widely enjoyed for its unique, smoky flavour. Bacon is a favourite with eggs and is used in the preparation or garnishment of a wide variety of dishes.

Bacon, Francis (b. Oct. 28, 1909, Dublin), British painter whose powerful images express isolation and terror.

The son of a horse trainer, Bacon was educated mostly by private tutors at home. His only professional art instruction was acquired through his friendship with the Australian painter Roy de Maistre. Bacon painted without recognition until 1945, at which time his original and powerful style won him almost instant notoriety. Many of his paintings are based on photographs, films, or paintings by other artists, which he distorts for his own expressive purposes. Examples of themes recurring in his work are the screaming nanny from Eisenstein's film *Potemkin*, Velázquez' "Portrait of Pope Innocent I," and studies of the human figure in motion by the 19th-century photographer Eadweard Muybridge. Most of Bacon's pictures show isolated figures, often framed, and in violent colours. He is admired for his skill in using oils, whose fluidity and mysteries he exploits to express images of anger, horror, and excitement. As he destroyed many of his works, only a few examples can be found, mainly in American and European museums.

Bacon, Francis, VISCOUNT ST. ALBANS, also called (1603–18) SIR FRANCIS BACON, or (1618–21) BARON VERULAM (b. Jan. 22, 1561, York House, London—d. April 9, 1626, London), lord chancellor of England (1618–21), philosopher, and man of letters whose *Essays* and other writings mark him as a master of English prose.

A brief account of the life and works of Francis Bacon follows; for a full biography, *see* MACROPAEDIA: Bacon, Francis.

Bacon attended Trinity College, Cambridge, and then went to Paris (1576). Recalled abruptly after the death of his father (1579), he took up residence at Gray's Inn, an institution for legal education, and became a barrister in 1582. He progressed through several legal positions, becoming a member of Parliament in 1584, but had little success in gaining political power. About 1591 Robert Devereux, 2nd earl of Essex, a favourite of Queen Elizabeth, became his patron. By 1600, however, Bacon was the Queen's learned counsel in the trial of Essex, and in 1601 he drew up a report denouncing Essex as a traitor.

With the accession of James I in 1603, Bacon sought anew to gain influence by means of unsparing service in Parliament, persistent letters of self-recommendation, and the help of important associates. He was engaged in a series of conflicts with Sir Edward Coke, the great jurist, in an effort to safeguard the royal prerogative. After a succession of legal posts, he was appointed lord chancellor and Baron Verulam in 1618; in 1620/21 he was created Viscount St. Albans. Between 1608 and 1620 he prepared at least 12 draftings of his most celebrated work, the *Novum Organum,* in which he presented his scientific method; he developed his *Instauratio Magna,* a plan to reorganize the sciences; and he wrote several minor philosophical works.

Bacon fell from power in 1621 following charges of bribery. He spent his final years writing some of his most valuable works.

Bacon, Henry (b. Nov. 26, 1866, Watseka, Ill., U.S.—d. Feb. 14, 1924, New York City), architect, best known as the designer of the Lincoln Memorial, Washington, D.C.

Bacon studied briefly at the University of Illinois, Urbana (1884), but left to begin his architectural career as a draftsman, eventually serving in the office of McKim, Mead & White (New York City), probably the most widely known architectural firm of their time. Bacon's works of that period were in the late classical revival and Beaux-Arts modes associated with the firm's creations. His more important works include the Danforth Library, Paterson, N.J. (1906); the train station in Naugatuck, Conn., built as an Italian villa; the Observatory and other buildings at Wesleyan University; and the Union Savings Bank, New York.

The Lincoln Memorial, Washington, D.C., designed by Henry Bacon, 1911
Authenticated News

Bacon was very active as a designer of monuments and settings for public sculpture. He collaborated with the sculptors Augustus Saint-Gaudens and Daniel French. It was the latter who carved the huge statue of Abraham Lincoln that sits within Bacon's last and most famous work, the Lincoln Memorial (dedicated May 18, 1923).

Bacon, John (theologian): *see* Baconthorpe, John.

Bacon, John (b. Nov. 24, 1740, London—d. Aug. 4, 1799, London), Neoclassical sculptor who perfected certain sculpturing techniques.

In 1754 Bacon was apprenticed in a porcelain works at Lambeth, London. There he was at first employed in painting small ornamental pieces of china, but he soon became modeller to the works. During his apprenticeship he improved the method of working statues in artificial stone, an art that he afterward carried to perfection. Bacon first attempted working in marble about 1763 and improved the method of transferring the form of the model to the marble by the invention of a more perfect instrument for the purpose. This instrument was more exact, took a correct measurement in every direction, was contained in a small compass, and could be used upon either the model or the marble. In 1769 he won the first gold medal for sculpture given by the Royal Academy, his work being a bas-relief representing the escape of Aeneas from Troy. In 1770 he exhibited a figure of Mars, which gained him the gold medal of the Society of Arts and his election as associate of the Royal Academy. Some of his best works are found among the monuments in Westminster Abbey.

Bacon, Nathaniel (b. Jan. 2, 1647, Suffolk, Eng.—d. October 1676, Virginia Colony), Virginia planter and leader of Bacon's Rebellion. His wife's disinheritance (her father opposed her marriage) and his involvement in a plan

Nathaniel Bacon, detail of an engraving
By courtesy of the Library of Congress, Washington, D.C.

to defraud a neighbour of his inheritance contributed to Bacon's decision to migrate to North America. Financed by his father, Bacon acquired two estates along the James River in Virginia. Less than a year after his arrival in the colony he was appointed to Gov. William Berkeley's council. When a dispute with Berkeley, who was his cousin by marriage, arose over the Indian policy, Bacon, a proponent of unlimited territorial expansion, organized an expedition against the Indians (1676). The governor, fearing a large-scale war, denounced Bacon's activities as rebellion. In turn, Bacon directed his forces against Berkeley and for a time controlled practically all of Virginia. At the height of his power, however, Bacon died, and the rebellion collapsed.

Bacon, Sir Nicholas (b. 1510, Drinkstone, Suffolk, Eng.—d. Feb. 20, 1579, London), high official in the government of Queen Elizabeth I and father of the renowned philosopher Francis Bacon.

Admitted to the bar in 1533, Bacon was made attorney of the court of wards and liveries in 1546. Notwithstanding his Protestant sympathies, he retained his office during the reign of the Roman Catholic queen Mary I (1553–58). Upon the accession of Elizabeth, Bacon was made lord keeper of the great seal, in which capacity in January 1559 he began to exercise the full judicial authority of lord chancellor.

In this position he worked with Elizabeth's chief minister, Sir William Cecil (later Lord Burghley), to maintain the relatively moderate Protestantism of the Elizabethan church. At the same time Bacon advocated policies designed to undermine the power of Catholics in Europe. He was temporarily dismissed from court after a misunderstanding with the Queen in 1564, but he soon regained his former influence. Bacon's distrust of the Catholic Mary

Sir Nicholas Bacon, detail of an oil painting by an unknown artist, 1579; in the National Portrait Gallery, London
By courtesy of the National Portrait Gallery, London

Stuart, who was imprisoned in England, led him in 1570 to oppose effectively a plan to reinstate her on the Scottish throne.

Bacon, Roger, byname DOCTOR MIRABILIS (Latin: Wonderful Teacher) (b. *c.* 1220, Ilchester, Somerset, or Bisley, Gloucester?, Eng.—d. 1292, Oxford?), English Franciscan philosopher and educational reformer who was a major medieval proponent of experimental science. Bacon studied mathematics, astronomy, optics, alchemy, and languages. He was the first European to describe in detail the process of making gunpowder, and he proposed flying machines and motorized ships and carriages. Bacon (as he himself complacently remarked) displayed a prodigious energy and zeal in the pursuit of experimental science; indeed, his studies were talked about everywhere and eventually won him a place in popular literature as a kind of wonder worker. Bacon therefore represents a historically precocious expression of the empirical spirit of experimental science, even though his actual practice of it seems to have been exaggerated.

Early life. Bacon was born into a wealthy family; he was well versed in the classics and enjoyed the advantages of an early training in the quadrivium (geometry, arithmetic, music, and astronomy). He boasted that he had frequently "heard" and "read" the works of Aristotle. Inasmuch as he later lectured at Paris, it is probable that his master of arts degree was conferred there, presumably not before 1241—a date in keeping with his claim that he saw the Franciscan professor Alexander of Hales (who died in 1245) with his own eyes and that he heard the master scholar William of Auvergne (died 1249) dispute twice in the presence of the whole university.

University and scientific career. In the earlier part of his career, Bacon lectured in the faculty of arts on Aristotelian and pseudo-Aristotelian treatises, displaying no indication, however, of his later preoccupation with science. His Paris lectures, important in enabling scholars to form some idea of the work done by one who was a pioneer in introducing the works of Aristotle into western Europe, reveal an Aristotelianism strongly marked by Neoplatonist elements stemming from many different sources. The influence of Avicenna on Bacon has been exaggerated.

About 1247 a considerable change took place in Bacon's intellectual development. From that date forward he expended much time and energy and huge sums of money in experimental research, in acquiring "secret" books, in the construction of instruments and of tables, in the training of assistants, and in seeking the friendship of savants—activities that marked a definite departure from the usual routine of the faculty of arts. The change was probably caused by his return to Oxford and the influence there of the great scholar Robert Grosseteste, a leader in introducing Greek learning to the West, and his student Adam de Marisco, as well as that of Thomas Wallensis, the bishop of St. David's. From 1247 to 1257 Bacon devoted himself wholeheartedly to the cultivation of those new branches of learning to which he was introduced at Oxford—languages, optics, and alchemy—and to further studies in astronomy and mathematics. It is true that Bacon was more skeptical of hearsay claims than were his contemporaries, that he suspected rational deductions (holding to the superior dependability of confirming experiences), and that he extolled experimentation so ardently that he has often been viewed as a harbinger of modern science more than 300 years before it came to bloom. Yet research on Bacon suggests that his characterization as an experimenter may be overwrought. His originality lay not so much in any positive contribution to the sum of knowledge as in his insistence on fruitful lines of research and methods of experimental study. As for actual experiments performed, he deferred to a certain Master Peter de Maricourt (Maharn-Curia), a Picard, who alone, he wrote, understood the method of experiment and whom he called *dominus experimentorum.* Bacon, to be sure, did have a sort of laboratory for alchemical experiments and carried out some systematic observations with lenses and mirrors. His studies on the nature of light and on the rainbow are especially noteworthy, and he seems to have planned and interpreted these experiments carefully. But his most notable "experiments" seem never to have been actually performed; they were merely described. He suggested, for example, that a balloon of thin copper sheet be made and filled with "liquid fire"; he felt that it would float in the air as many light objects do in water. He seriously studied the problem of flying in a machine with flapping wings. He was the first person in the West to give exact directions for making gunpowder (1242); and, though he knew that, if confined, it would have great power and might be useful in war, he failed to speculate further. (Its use in guns arose early in the following century.) Bacon described spectacles (which also soon came into use); elucidated the principles of reflection, refraction, and spherical aberration; and proposed mechanically propelled ships and carriages. He used a camera obscura (which projects an image through a pinhole) to observe eclipses of the Sun.

Career as a friar. In 1257 another marked change took place in Bacon's life. Because of ill health and his entry into the Order of Friars Minor, Bacon felt (as he wrote) forgotten by everyone and all but buried. His university and literary careers seemed finished. His feverish activity, his amazing credulity, his superstition, and his vocal contempt for those not sharing his interests displeased his superiors in the order and brought him under severe discipline. He decided to appeal to Pope Clement IV, whom he may have known when the latter was (before his election to the papacy) in the service of the Capetian kings of France. In a letter (1266) the Pope referred to letters received from Bacon, who had come forward with certain proposals covering the natural world, mathematics, languages, perspective, and astrology. Bacon had argued that a more accurate experimental knowledge of nature would be of great value in confirming the Christian faith, and he felt that his proposals would be of great importance for the welfare of the church and of the universities. The Pope desired to become more fully informed of these projects and commanded Bacon to send him the work. But Bacon had had in mind a vast encyclopaedia of all the known sciences, requiring many collaborators, the organization and administration of which would be coordinated by a papal institute. The work, then, was merely projected when the Pope thought that it already existed. In obedience to the Pope's command, however, Bacon set to work and in a remarkably short time had dispatched the *Opus majus* ("Great Work"), the *Opus minus* ("Lesser Work"), and the *Opus tertium* ("Third Work"). He had to do this secretly and notwithstanding any command of his superiors to the contrary; and even when the irregularity of his conduct attracted their attention and the terrible weapons of spiritual coercion were brought to bear upon him, he was deterred from explaining his position by the papal command of secrecy. Under the circumstances, his achievement was truly astounding. He reminded the Pope that, like the leaders of the schools with their commentaries and scholarly summaries, he could have covered quires of vellum with "puerilities" and vain speculations. Instead, he aspired to penetrate realms undreamed of in the schools at Paris and to lay bare the secrets of nature by positive study. The *Opus majus* was an effort to persuade the Pope of the urgent necessity and manifold utility of the reforms that he proposed. But the death of Clement in 1268 extinguished Bacon's dreams of gaining for the sciences their rightful place in the curriculum of university studies.

Bacon projected yet another encyclopaedia, of which only fragments were ever published, viz., the *Communia naturalium* ("General Principles of Natural Philosophy") and the *Communia mathematica* ("General Principles of Mathematical Science"), written about 1268. In 1272 there appeared the *Compendium philosophiae* ("Compendium of Philosophy"). In philosophy—and even Bacon's so-called scientific works contain lengthy philosophical digressions—he was the disciple of Aristotle and not of St. Augustine or the Persian philosopher Avicenna; even though he did incorporate Neoplatonist elements into his philosophy, his thought remains, nevertheless, Aristotelian in its main lines.

Sometime between 1277 and 1279, Bacon was condemned to prison by his fellow Franciscans because of certain "suspected novelties" in his teaching. The condemnation was probably issued because of his bitter attacks on the theologians and scholars of his day, his excessive credulity in alchemy and astrology, and his penchant for millenarianism under the influence of the prophecies of Abbot Joachim of Fiora, a mystical philosopher of history. How long he was imprisoned is unknown. His last work (1292), incomplete as so many others, shows him as aggressive as ever.

(T.Cr.)

BIBLIOGRAPHY. Andrew G. Little (ed.), *Roger Bacon* (1914), comprehensive and critical essays contributed by various eminent scholars on the occasion of the commemoration of the seventh centenary of Bacon's birth, is a collection that still retains its value. Two works that are complementary and contain fresh biographical insights and extensive bibliographies are Theodore Crowley, *Roger Bacon: The Problem of the Soul in His Philosophical Commentaries* (1950), presenting his philosophical positions; and Stewart C. Easton, *Roger Bacon and His Search for a Universal Science: A Reconsideration of the Life and Work of Roger Bacon in the Light of His Own Stated Purposes* (1952). Erich Heck, *Roger Bacon: Ein mittelalterlicher Versuch einer historischen und systematischen Religionswissenschaft* (1957), contains a critical survey of previous work and detailed studies of Bacon's approach to the scientific study of religion. A.C. Crombie, *Robert Grosseteste and the Origins of Experimental Science, 1100–1700,* pp. 139–162 (1953), is a balanced account of Bacon's contributions to science.

Baconian method, careful and methodical observation of facts as a means of interpreting nature or of studying natural phenomena. This essentially empirical method was formulated early in the 17th century by Francis Bacon, an English philosopher, as a scientific substitute for fanciful guessing and the mere citing of authorities to establish truths of science. After first dismissing all prejudices and preconceptions, Bacon's method, as explained in *Novum Organum* (1620; "New Instrument"), consisted of three main steps: first, a description of facts; second, a tabulation or classification of those facts into three classes—instances of the presence of the characteristic under investigation, instances of its absence, or instances of its presence in varying degrees; third, the rejection of whatever appears, in the light of these tables, not to be connected with the phenomenon under investigation and the determination of what is connected with it.

Bacon may be credited with recognizing, in their essence, the method of agreement, the joint method, and the method of concomitant variations. His emphasis on the exhaustive cataloguing of facts, however, has since been replaced as a scientific method (*q.v.*), for it provided no means of bringing investigation to an end or of insightful delimitation of the problem by creative use of hypotheses.

A list of the abbreviations used in the MICROPAEDIA *will be found at the end of this volume*

Baconthorpe, John, also called JOHN BACON, JOHANNES DE BACONTHORPE, or JOHANNES DE ANGLICUS, byname DOCTOR RESOLUTUS (b. *c.* 1290, Baconsthorpe, Norfolk, Eng.—d. 1346?, London), theologian and philosopher who, although he did not subscribe to the heterodox doctrine of the great Muslim philosopher Averroës, was regarded by the Renaissance Averroists as *Princeps Averroistarum* ("the prince of the Averroists"), and who strongly influenced the Carmelite scholastics for two centuries.

Reared in the Carmelite monastery of Blakeney, Norfolk, Baconthorpe studied at Oxford and at Paris and then taught at Cambridge and possibly at Oxford. He was provincial of the English Carmelites from 1329 to 1333 and thereafter devoted his life to study.

A learned and sharp critic of such theologians as St. Thomas Aquinas, John Duns Scotus, and Henry of Ghent, he failed to oppose them with constructive work. He was, however, familiar with and an excellent commentator on the works of Aristotle and Averroës, favourably interpreting them even though he dissented on fundamentals. Averroism, which was subsequently attacked by orthodox Christian thinkers for advocating the superiority of reason and philosophy over faith and knowledge founded on faith, retained a stronghold in northern Italy, and Baconthorpe's interpretations of Averroës were treasured by the Renaissance Averroists.

Baconthorpe also wrote commentaries on the *Sentences* of the theologian Peter Lombard, bishop of Paris (first published in Paris, 1484); on *De Trinitate* ("On the Trinity") and *De civitate Dei* (*The City of God*) of St. Augustine of Hippo; on *De incarnatione Verbi* ("On the Incarnation of the Word") and *Cur Deus homo* ("Why God Man . . .") of St. Anselm of Canterbury; and on Matthew and the Pauline Letters. His *Quodlibeta* ("Miscellanies") was first published in Venice, 1527.

Bács-Kiskun, *megye* (county), south central Hungary. The country's largest *megye,* it has an area of 3,229 sq mi (8,363 sq km) and extends eastward from the Danube River to the Tisza. Wheat, corn (maize), and vegetables are grown throughout the county, and in the northeast, around Kecskemét (*q.v.*), the *megye* seat, in an area of mixed sandy and loess soils, fruits (peaches, cherries, grapes, apricots) are grown. Major towns, apart from Kecskemét, are Baja, Kiskunhalas, and Kiskunfélegyháza. The latter has a large factory producing mining machinery. Tass, in the northeastern corner of the *megye*, is a centre for fishing and aquatic sports on the Danube; Kalocsa is known for its traditional folk art and culture. Pop. (1983 est.) 566,000.

bacteria, singular BACTERIUM, group of microscopic organisms that are procaryotic (*i.e.*, lacking a membrane-bound nucleus and organelles). Bacteria may have spherical, rodlike, or spiral unicellular or noncellular bodies. Bacteria are often aggregated into colonies but may be motile by means of flagella. They live in virtually all environments, including soil, water, organic matter, and the bodies of plants and animals. Autotrophic, saprophytic, or parasitic in nutrition, bacteria perform significant biochemical transformations that may be either beneficial or harmful to humans.

A brief treatment of bacteria follows. For full treatment, *see* MACROPAEDIA: Bacteria.

All bacterial cells have an outer cell membrane surrounded by a rigid cell wall. Beyond this, some species have a capsule of gelatinous material. Some species of bacteria possess whiplike flagella. Others are covered with short, spikelike projections known as pili. Many bacteria can assume a dormant state as a spore; in this state they may be highly resistant to heat, dryness, or other unfavourable conditions.

Growth in bacteria refers to the growth of population (or reproduction) rather than that of an individual microorganism. Bacteria usually reproduce through binary fission (an asexual process in which one cell divides into two new cells), multiplying in geometric progression, with generation times that range from 15 minutes to 16 hours. In some higher orders, bacteria reproduce through budding, chains of spores, segmentation of elementary units, or, in a few instances, by conjugation, a form of genetic exchange analogous to sexual reproduction.

The presence of intestinal (coliform) bacteria in water indicates that the water has been polluted with fecal matter and may contain pathogens. Water purification plants are designed to destroy these and other microorganisms. Bacteria from domestic and industrial wastes that appear in a community's used water supply also may act as pollutants. Conversely, they may act as cleansers, and treatment facilities utilize bacteria to break down organic matter in sewage.

The extent and nature of bacteria in the air depend largely on the particular environment and circumstances. A city street after heavy rain is relatively free of bacteria, as is air at an altitude of 10,000 feet (3,000 metres). A single sneeze or cough disperses huge numbers of bacteria which remain suspended in air for a while as droplet nuclei.

A variety of bacteria can contaminate foods and, when allowed to grow, can cause food poisoning—bringing about a reaction that may range from an upset stomach to death, as can happen with botulism. Just as water purification treats bacteria in water, pasteurization treats bacteria in milk, though milk taken from a healthy cow has relatively few bacteria; it is not sterile, however, and careless handling procedures can cause additional contamination.

There are numerous other ways, both physical and chemical, to sterilize materials and products, among them high temperature, radiation, ethylene oxide, and other antiseptics and germicides.

The ability of a bacterium to cause a disease is called virulence. Contributing factors to virulence are not clearly understood except in cases where the pathogen is known to secrete a toxin, as in the case of the diphtheria bacteria, which establish themselves in the human upper respiratory tract and cause cell death. Most pathogenic bacteria, however, do not kill their host.

Some pathogens have a specificity for various parts of the body: meningococcal bacteria infect the brain membranes, and tubercule bacteria infect the lungs. Some are slightly more generalized: staphylococcal bacteria can infect the skin, causing boils; the bloodstream, causing blood poisoning; and the bones, causing the condition known as osteomyelitis.

Although human interest in bacteria frequently focusses on the harmful effects of some of these microorganisms, it is important to remember that most bacteria are harmless to human beings, and a good many of them are extremely beneficial. Saprophytic bacteria, for example, perform an ecologically indispensable role in the breakdown of dead organisms and organic wastes; without such decomposition, the cycling of various elements vital to living organisms (including nitrogen, carbon, and phosphorus) would cease.

In addition to the role of saprophytic bacteria in the cycling of nitrogen, other bacteria are capable of nitrogen fixation—*i.e.*, the conversion of atmospheric nitrogen into a form that can be used by plants. Many of these nitrogen-fixing species live in nodules on the roots of leguminous plants.

Bacteria also form beneficial associations with animals. For instance, the bacterial inhabitants of the ruminant stomach break down cellulose; this enables cows, sheep, and other ruminants to digest grass. Humans also harbour beneficial bacteria, such as those in the lower intestinal tract that synthesize vitamin K.

Bacteria are also utilized in various industrial processes, especially in the food industry. The production of buttermilk, yogurt, cheeses, pickles, and sauerkraut are all dependent upon bacterial action.

The classification of bacteria is unsettled, particularly at the higher taxonomic levels. Traditionally, bacteria were grouped as a class (Schizomycetes) within the plant kingdom. Most authorities now place the bacteria—along with the blue-green algae, which are also procaryotic—within a separate kingdom (usually either Kingdom Procaryotae or Kingdom Monera). Within this procaryotic kingdom, the bacteria are grouped into one or several divisions, depending on the authority consulted.

bacterial virus: *see* bacteriophage.

bacteriology, the study of bacteria. It is a branch of microbiology, and its formal beginnings date from the researches of Ferdinand Cohn, a German botanist who published a classification of bacteria in 1872. The cultivation of bacteria, however, began with the crude experiments of the Italian physiologist Lazzaro Spallanzani in 1776.

Modern bacteriology is important for its applications in medicine and agriculture, industry (*e.g.*, certain alcohols, acids, and antibiotics are produced by bacteria), and molecular biology, including genetics research.

bacteriophage, also called PHAGE, or BACTERIAL VIRUS, a group of viruses that infect bacteria. Used extensively to study the chemistry of heredity, phages are usually designated by laboratory code names consisting of numbers, Roman or Greek letters, or combinations of these, which are related to the order in which they were isolated or to certain growth characteristics. Designations include T1, T3, T7, λ, MS2 (male-specific 2), φX174, and fd.

Bactria, also called BACTRIANA, or ZARIASPA, ancient country lying between the Hindu Kush (Paropamisus) Mountains and the Amu Darya (Oxus) River in what is now part of Afghanistan and of the Uzbek S.S.R. and Tadzhik S.S.R. in the Soviet Union; it was especially important between about 600 BC and about AD 600, serving for much of that time as a meeting place not only for overland trade between East and West but also for the crosscurrents of religious and artistic ideas. Bactria's capital was Bactra, also called Bactra-Zariaspa (probably modern Balkh, ancient Vahlika).

Bactria was a fertile country, and a profusion of mounds and abandoned water channels testifies to its ancient prosperity. Recent settlement begins with Iron Age deposits at Balkh and Khulm (Tāshkurghān); those may date from *c.* 750 BC and appear to be the remains of an Eastern Iranian-speaking people who settled there at that time.

The first written records of Bactria are Achaemenian. The region was probably subdued by Cyrus II the Great in the 6th century BC and remained an Achaemenian province for the next 200 years. When Alexander the Great defeated Darius III, the Bactrian satrap, Bessus, tried unsuccessfully to organize resistance in the East. Upon the death of Alexander (323 BC) Bactria passed under the rule of Seleucus I Nicator.

Around 250 BC either Diodotus, the Seleucid satrap of Bactria, or his son of the same name founded an independent kingdom. The Seleucid king Antiochus III the Great defeated their successor, the usurper Euthydemus, but continued to recognize his independence. Euthydemus' successors advanced into the Hindu Kush and northwestern India, where they established the Indo-Greek branch of the kingdom. At the height of their power they ruled almost all of what is now Afghanistan, parts of Soviet Central Asia, and a large area in Pakistan. Consequently, Hellenistic influence on the culture of Central Asia and northwestern India has been considerable. Hellenistic traditions are especially evident in art, architecture, coinage, and script.

Sometime before 128 BC Greek rule north of the Hindu Kush was challenged by a people known to the Chinese as Yüeh-chih. By 128 BC the Greeks had become Yüeh-chih tributaries, and soon afterward the Yüeh-chih occupied Bactria. They probably were an Iranian people and included the Tochari, whose name was subsequently applied to the whole area (Tocharian kingdom). In the 1st century AD the new rulers of Bactria extended their rule into northwestern India; that movement is associated with a group known as the Kushāns, under whom the country became a centre of Buddhism. In the latter half of the 4th century the Hephthalites (originally a tribe of the Yüeh-chih) settled in Bactria, and for almost two centuries they engaged in wars with the Sāsānians. In AD 565 the western Turks overthrew the Hephthalites and ruled the area until the Muslim conquest in the middle of the 7th century.

Bactrites, genus of extinct cephalopods (animals related to the modern squid, octopus, and nautilus) found as fossils in marine rocks from the Ordovician to the Permian periods (between 225,000,000 and 500,000,000 years ago). The shell consists of a linear series of chambers, each successively occupied by the body of the animal. *Bactrites* fed on animals it caught in its tentacles. It is possible that *Bactrites* gave rise to more advanced cephalopods of later geologic periods, notably the ammonoids and the belemnoids.

Baculites, genus of extinct cephalopods (animals related to the modern squid, octopus, and nautilus) found as fossils in Upper Cretaceous marine rocks (the Cretaceous Period began 136,000,000 years ago and lasted 71,000,000 years). *Baculites,* restricted to a narrow time range, is an excellent guide or index fossil for Upper Cretaceous time and rocks.

Baculites, collected from Sage Creek, South Dakota
By courtesy of the Buffalo Museum of Science, Buffalo, N.Y.

The distinctive shell begins with a tightly coiled portion that becomes straight in form, with a complex, ammonite sutural pattern.

baculum, also called OS PENIS, or OS PRIAPI, the penis bone of certain mammals. The baculum is one of several heterotropic skeletal elements; *i.e.,* bones dissociated from the rest of the body skeleton. It is found in all insectivores (*e.g.,* shrews, hedgehogs), bats, rodents, and carnivores and in primates except man. Such wide distribution suggests that it appeared early in mammalian evolution.

Bad Aussee, town, *Bundesland* Steiermark (federal province of Styria), central Austria, in the Traun Valley, southeast of Bad Ischl. The former centre of the Salzkammergut (salt region), it has the 15th-century Kammerhof (old offices of the salt administration) and two 14th- to 15th-century churches. Anna Plochl (1804–85), the wife of Archduke Johann, was born in Bad Aussee. Salt mining is still important. The town is well known as a health (brine baths) and summer resort and winter-sports centre in an area of picturesque lakes. Pop. (1981) 5,047.

Bad Dürkheim, also called DÜRKHEIM, city, Rheinland-Pfalz *Land* (Rhineland-Palatinate state), southwestern West Germany, on the eastern slope of the Haardt Mountains at the entrance of the Isenach Valley, north of Neustadt an der Weinstrasse. Originally a dependency of the Benedictine abbey of Limburg (founded in 1030 by the emperor Conrad II), the city came under the counts of Leiningen-Hartenburg, who built a castle there in the 14th century. The ruins of Limburg abbey lie to the southwest, and the city hall and casino occupy the site of the castle (destroyed by the French in 1794). The castle's church survives. Well-known as a health resort, it has saline and arsenious springs, a saltworks, and a brisk wine trade. Pop. (1983 est.) 15,494.

Bad Ems, also called EMS, city, Rheinland-Pfalz *Land* (Rhineland-Palatinate state), western West Germany, on the Lahn River, just east of Koblenz. It is one of the oldest spas in Europe, its mineral springs having been known to the Romans, and it was mentioned as a thermal spa in 1172. While vacationing there in 1870, King William I of Prussia (later emperor of Germany) had a fateful interview with the French ambassador and reported it to Otto von Bismarck in the telegram that touched off the Franco-German War.

Bad Ems remains a much frequented health and tourist resort, and its mineral water is exported. Industry includes a chemical factory. Pop. (1983 est.) 10,241.

Bad Gandersheim, also called GANDERSHEIM, city, Niedersachsen *Land* (Lower Saxony state), northeastern West Germany, in the Leine River Valley. It is remarkable for the 11th-century convent church containing the tombs of famous abbesses and for the former abbey, moved there in 852 by the Duke of Saxony, whose daughters were the first two abbesses. Louis III granted a privilege by which the office of abbess was to continue in the ducal family of Saxony as long as any member of the family was found willing and competent to accept it. Otto III gave the abbey a market, a right of toll, and a mint. It was ultimately recognized as a holding of the Holy Roman Empire, and its abbess was given a vote in the imperial Diet. The conventual estates were extensive, and its feudatories included the elector of Hanover and the king of Prussia. Protestantism was introduced in 1568, and the last Roman Catholic abbess, Augusta Dorothea of Brunswick, died in 1589; but the Protestant abbesses enjoyed imperial privileges until Gandersheim was incorporated into the duchy of Brunswick in 1803.

The memory of Gandersheim will long be preserved by its literary memorials. Hrosvitha (*q.v.*), the German poet and dramatist, was a member of the sisterhood in the 10th century, and the rhyming chronicle of Eberhard of Gandersheim is probably the earliest historical work composed in Low German.

Saline baths northeast of the city attract tourists. Manufactures include toys, cigars, aluminum products, chemicals, and glass. Pop. (1983 est.) 11,363.

Bad Godesberg, southern district, Bonn, Nordrhein-Westfalen *Land* (North Rhine-Westphalia state), western West Germany, on the left bank of the Rhine opposite the Siebengebirge (Seven Hills), a scenic natural park. The village that developed around a castle (the Godesburg), founded by Archbishop Dietrich of Cologne (Köln) in 1210, was developed in the late 19th century as a modern spa town and was chartered in 1935. In 1969 it was annexed to Bonn, along with seven other suburbs. Historic buildings include the ruined castle (destroyed in 1583 by the Bavarians); the Muffendorf Foundation (1254), former headquarters of the Order of German Knights; and La Redoute, a Rococo mansion and former pump room, the scene of diplomatic receptions held by the federal government. There is a 5½-mi (9-km) promenade along the Rhine. A large number of ministries, foreign legations, and scientific and industrial associations are headquartered at Bad Godesberg, and it is a popular resort for conferences. Its principal industry is the manufacture of pharmaceutical products.

Bad Harzburg, city, Niedersachsen *Land* (Lower Saxony state), northeastern West Germany, located on the northern slope of the Oberharz (Upper Harz mountains), at the entrance to the Radau River Valley just southeast of Goslar. It developed around a castle built in about 1066 by Emperor Henry IV on the nearby Grosser Burgberg (1,585 ft [483 m]). The ruins of the castle remain, and there are also remnants of an altar (now in the museum at Goslar) dedicated to the pagan god Krodo (Crodo). The city is now a winter-sports resort and a fashionable spa. Industries include the manufacture of pharmaceuticals, textiles, toys, and leather and wood products. Pop. (1983 est.) 24,472.

Bad Hofgastein, town, *Bundesland* (federal province) Salzburg, in west central Austria, on the Gasteiner Ache (Gastein Stream) below Badgastein. In the 16th century it was the richest town, after Salzburg, in Salzburg principality, because of its gold and silver mines. Until 1936 it was called Hofgastein. It is now a winter-sports and health resort with thermal waters piped from Badgastein. Pop. (1981) 5,960.

Bad Homburg, in full BAD HOMBURG VOR DER HÖHE, city, Hessen *Land* (Hesse state), central West Germany, at the foot of the wooded Taunus Mountains, just north of Frankfurt am Main. First mentioned in records of the 12th century, it changed hands often, passing to the house of Hesse in 1521 and later becoming the independent city and landgraviate of Hesse-Homburg (1622–1866).

In 1834 the rediscovery of the Elisabeth mineral spring and other springs known first to the Romans led to the founding of a casino (1841) and the building of the new city. It became an internationally fashionable spa; in the 1890s Edward, prince of Wales (later Edward VII of England), borrowed the headgear of a local militiaman and popularized the soft-felt Homburg hat. The landgraves' palace (1680–85, with a 12th-century tower) and the modern casino dominate the city; nearby is the Saalburg, a Roman frontier fortress excavated and reconstructed in the 1800s. After 1918 Bad Homburg expanded into a residential town with industries (machinery, biscuits, textiles, and leather goods). In 1972 two neighbouring towns were annexed and the enlarged city made the seat of the new Obertaunus county. Pop. (1983 est.) 50,877.

Bad Ischl, also called ISCHL, town, *Bundesland* Oberösterreich (federal province of Upper Austria), central Austria, at the confluence of the Traun and Ischler Ache rivers, southeast of Salzburg. First mentioned in records of 1262, it received municipal status in 1940. The centre of the Salzkammergut (*q.v.*) resort region, it has saline, iodine, and sulfur springs and has been a much-frequented spa since 1822. It became internationally known as the summer residence of Emperor Francis Joseph I from 1854 to 1914 and was frequented by the composers Franz Lehar, Johannes Brahms, Anton Bruckner, and Richard Strauss. The Imperial Villa is open to the public, and Lehar's home is a museum. Shoes, skis, clothing, and metalware are manufactured. Pop. (1981) 13,027.

Bad Kreuznach, also called KREUZNACH, city, Rheinland-Pfalz *Land* (Rhineland-Palatinate state), southwestern West Germany, on the Nahe River, a tributary of the Rhine, southwest of Mainz. The site of a Roman fortress and later (819) of a Carolingian palace (Cruciniacum), it fell to the bishops of Speyer in 1065 and to the counts of Sponheim in 1241 and was chartered in 1290. The city became part of the Palatinate in 1565, suffered heavily in the Thirty Years' War, and was destroyed by the French in 1689. It was ceded to Prussia in 1815 and became a popular spa with warm saline springs, the chief of which is on the island of Badewörth.

Historic landmarks include the ruined Sponheim Castle and the 13th-century church of St. Nikolaus. Quaint 15th-century houses—one reputed to have been the home of Dr. Faust—have survived. A centre of the wine trade, the city manufactures optical instruments, leather, and machinery. Pop. (1983 est.) 40,584.

Bad Mergentheim, city, Baden-Württemberg *Land* (state), southern West Germany, on the Tauber River, southwest of Würzburg. An ancient settlement, it became the property of the Knights of the Teutonic Order in 1219 and was the residence (1525–1809) of the grand master of the order. The city was chartered in 1340. The Baroque castle of the knights survives, and there are two 14th-century churches and numerous medieval houses.

Mineral springs, known in the Bronze and Iron ages but forgotten after they had silted up, were rediscovered in 1826, and the city developed as a health resort. Clothing and wood products are manufactured. Pop. (1983 est.) 19,140.

Bad Reichenhall, city, Bayern *Land* (Bavaria state), southeastern West Germany, in the Alpine Saalach River Valley, southwest of Salzburg. It is a noted health and winter resort surrounded by mountains, including the Predigtstuhl (5,413 ft [1,650 m]), ascended by cable railway. An important salt-extracting centre in Roman and medieval times, it prospered particularly under Charlemagne (*c.* 800). Although salt is still produced, the thermal saline springs (up to 24 percent content) are now used primarily by the health resort. The city was almost completely rebuilt after a fire in 1834. The nearby Romanesque Basilica of St. Zeno (altered 1512–20) was the church of a former Augustinian abbey founded in 1136. Pop. (1983 est.) 17,744.

Baḍaga, most numerous of the peoples of the Nīlgiri Hills of Tamil Nādu state in southern India. They have increased very rapidly, from fewer than 20,000 in 1871 to about 105,000 in the 1970s. Their language is a Dravidian dialect closely akin to Kannada as spoken in Karnātaka state to the north of the Nīlgiris. The name Baḍaga means "northerner," and it is clear that they came into the Nīlgiris from the north, perhaps impelled by economic or political pressures. The time of their migration was after the founding of the Liṅgāyat Hindu sect in the 12th century, because some of them apparently came as Liṅgāyats. It was before the first recorded observation of them, by a Roman Catholic missionary in 1602, when they were well established and maintaining symbiotic relations with the other Nīlgiri peoples.

The Baḍaga are divided into six endogamous groups that were ranked in ritual order. The two highest were vegetarians; the lowest provided servants for the other five. Their traditional religion and economy depended on goods and services supplied by the Nīlgiri peoples—Kota, Toda, and Kurumba.

The Baḍaga generally have taken to education and have vigorously advanced their community. In addition to grain, they now grow large crops of potatoes and vegetables. At the same time most have altered their traditional religious and social practices. Improved agriculture, local and national policies, high-caste Hindu tradition—these matters now engross many Baḍaga. In all, the Baḍaga are one of those indigenous groups who have turned their circumstances in the 20th century to success for their community.

Badagara, town and port, Kozhikode district, northern Kerala state, southwestern India. Located on the Arabian Sea northwest of the town of Kozhikode, Badagara is a fishing port and trade centre for pepper, copra, timber, and other products. It is served by a coastal road and a rail line. Pop. (1981) 64,174.

Badagry, also spelled BADAGRI, town and lagoon port in Lagos State, southwestern Nigeria. It lies on the north bank of Porto Novo Creek, an inland waterway that connects the national capitals of Nigeria (Lagos) and Benin (Porto-Novo), and on a road that leads to Lagos, Ilaro, and Porto-Novo. Founded in the late 1720s by Popo refugees from the wars with the Fon people of Dahomey, it was, for the next century, a notorious exporter of slaves to the Americas. A British trading post was established there in the 1820s, and Badagry developed as a palm-oil port for Egbaland to the north and as an importer of European cloth. In the 1830s it attracted freed slaves from Freetown (Sierra Leone), and, in 1842, it became the site of the first European mission (Methodist) in Nigeria. Although the trade route to Abeokuta (56 mi [90 km] north-northeast) was controlled by unfriendly Dahomeyans (whose frequent raids had almost destroyed the town in the late 18th century), Badagry remained a leading port and mission centre—a Yoruba mission (Anglican) was also established in the early 1840s—until the attack in 1851 by the army of Lagos. That attack, plus the constant threat of the Fon and the poor sandy soils in the vicinity, led to a general exodus of the town's traders, missionaries, and farmers.

Coconut plantations were first established in the vicinity in the 1880s, and modern Badagry exports coconuts, copra, coir, fish, vegetables, and cassava to Lagos (34 mi east). After the establishment in 1966 of a factory that makes bags for packing farm products, the collection of kenaf, cultivated for its fibres, became increasingly important. Local trade is primarily in fish, palm oil and kernels, cassava, corn (maize), and coconuts.

Badagry is the seat of a local government council and is mainly inhabited by Popo and Gun (Egun; a subgroup of the Yoruba) peoples. Badagry rapidly became a major residential suburb of Lagos after the opening in 1976 of the Lagos–Badagry Expressway. The town has an automotive assembly plant and it is the site of a college, a secondary school, several hospitals, and a health office. Pop. (1972 est.) 10,648.

Badajoz, province in the provisional autonomous community (region) of Extremadura, the largest province in Spain. Badajoz borders on Portugal and has an area of 8,362 sq mi (21,657 sq km). It represents 4.3 percent of the country's total area, and with the province of Cáceres comprises the historic region of Extremadura. The climate is characterized by long, hot, dry summers. The terrain is almost entirely flat but rises in the south and southwest near the Sierra Morena, and in the north it joins the foothills of the mountains of Toledo. It is crossed from east to west by the Río Guadiana, the most important tributary of which is the Zújar. Typifying the central plain is the Tierra de Barros, the largest cereal-, wine-, and oil-producing region of Extremadura; its main centre is Almendralejo. Other regions in the province produce wool, and livestock raising is important. Industry, primarily agricultural processing, is concentrated in Badajoz (*q.v.;* the provincial capital), Mérida, Almendralejo, and Villanueva de la Serena. The province's extensive forests are only minimally exploited.

In 1952 the Spanish government promoted a project known as the Plan Badajoz, which considerably raised the standard of living, productivity, and agriculture, and intensified development and industrialization in the area. Irrigation was undertaken using the waters of the Guadiana and Zújar, controlled by six dams. The plan provided for new agriculturally based industries, chiefly the production of flour, cotton, and olive oil, and for vegetable preserving. Electrification was also increased, and communications were improved. The Instituto Nacional de Colonización (The National Institute of Colonization) created new towns and resettled thousands of people to whom land grants were made. A nuclear power plant was under construction at Valdecaballeros in 1980. Pop. (1982 est.) 572,798.

Badajoz, city, capital of Badajoz province, in the provisional autonomous community (region) of Extremadura, southwestern Spain, on the south bank of the Río Guadiana, near the Portuguese frontier; it lies on a low range of hills crowned by a ruined Moorish castle. It originated as Pax Augusta (Pacensis Colonia), a small Roman town, and later flourished as the Baṭalyaws of the Moors. Freed from Moorish control by Alfonso IX of León in 1229, Badajoz (the ancient capital of Extremadura) was known as the key to Portugal, and it played strategic roles in both the Peninsular (1811–12) and Spanish Civil (1936–39) wars. Badajoz was the birthplace of Manuel Godoy, duke of Alcudia, of the painter Luis Morales, "the divine," and of the New World conquistador, Pedro de Alvarado. A bastioned wall with moat and outworks and forts on the surrounding heights gives the city an appearance of great strength. The river, which flows between the castle hill and the fort of San Cristóbal, is crossed by a granite bridge built in 1596 and rebuilt in 1833. With its massive walls, the cathedral of San Juan (1234–84) resembles a fortress.

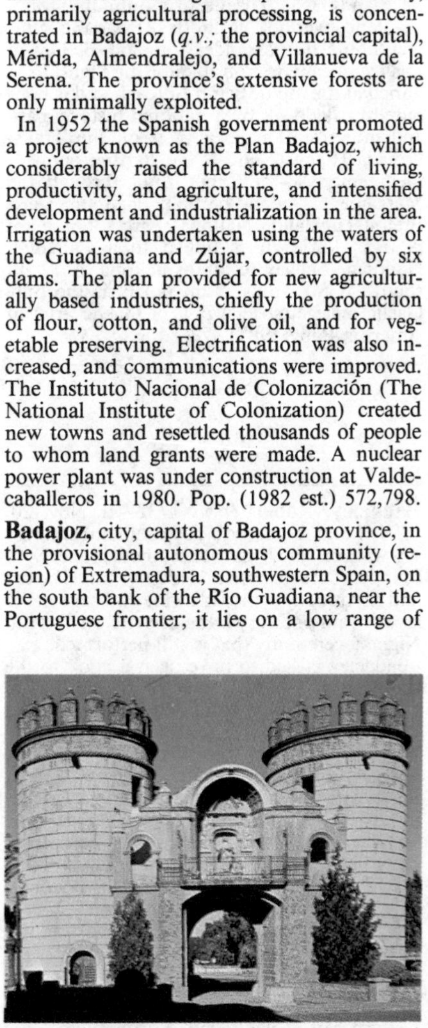

Puerta de las Palmas, ancient entrance gate to city, Badajoz, Spain
C.I.R.I.—EDISTUDIO

Badajoz has a considerable transit trade with Portugal; its principal industries are food processing and the production of alcoholic and other drinks, basketwork, blankets, and wax. Pop. (1982 est.) 102,615.

Badakhshan, *velāyat* (province), northeastern Afghanistan, bounded by the Tadzhik S.S.R. to the north and northeast, Pakistan to the southeast, the *velāyāt* of Konarhā and Laghmān to the south, Kāpīsā to the southwest, and Takhār to the west. Badakhshan's narrow eastern panhandle, called Vākhān, is situated in the extreme northeast of Afghanistan and borders the Sinkiang Uighur Autonomous Region, China. The province (area 18,299 sq mi [47,393 sq km]) is mostly mountainous, encompassing the northern spurs of the Hindu Kush, and is drained by the Kowkcheh and Vākhān rivers. Glaciers and glacial lakes are found in the eastern part of the province. Towns include Feyẕābād (*q.v.*; the provincial capital), Zībāk, Eshkāshem, and Jorm.

The name Badakhshan first appears in Chinese writings of the 7th and 8th centuries AD, before which the area was ruled successively by Hephthalites, Turks, and Arabs. From the 13th century, after several changes of possession, a local dynasty claiming descent from Alexander the Great ruled until the Timurids took over in the 15th century. In 1584 the Uzbeks conquered Badakhshan, and it remained under local Uzbek *mīr*s ("leaders") until 1822, when Morād Beg of Kondūz overran it. In 1859 Badakhshan became tributary to Kābul, and its autonomy ended in 1881. A British-Russian accord (1895) delineated the Panj River as part of the Russo-Afghan border separating Afghan Badakhshan from Russian Badakhshan in the Pamirs. After the Russian Revolution (1917), this Pamir region became the Gorno-Badakhshan *avtonomnaya oblast* (autonomous region), part of the Tadzhik S.S.R. In the 1979 Soviet military intervention, Feyẕābād and Eshkāshem were captured from Afghan guerrillas, and in 1980 the Soviets established a military command at Feyẕābād. The Soviet army occupied the Vākhān (Wakhan Corridor) in eastern Badakhshan in mid-1981, and most of the Vākhān's residents fled to Pakistan.

Agriculture is the chief occupation in Badakhshān. Irrigation in the valleys permits the growing of rice, wheat, corn (maize), and cotton, while barley and legumes are produced in the hills. Grapes, fruit trees, and nuts are also grown, and livestock are raised for wool and skins. The province has some mineral wealth, including unexploited sulfur deposits, and precious stones, including lapis lazuli, which has been mined for more than 4,000 years at Shar Shākh. Pop. (1982 est.) settled pop. 520,620, mainly Tadzhik.

Badalona, town, Barcelona province, in the autonomous community (region) of Catalonia, northeastern Spain. It is a northeastern industrial suburb of Barcelona, lying on the Mediterranean coast at the mouth of the Río Besós. Manufactures include chemicals, textiles, leather goods, liquor, motors, and perfumes. Some agricultural processing is carried on. The town's outstanding landmark is the 15th-century monastery of San Jerónimo de la Murtra. The local museum preserves relics from Roman times when Baetulo, an important centre before the foundation of Barcelona, occupied the site. Pop. (1981) 227,744.

Bādāmi, town, Bijāpur district, Karnātaka (formerly Mysore) state, southwestern India. The town was known as Vātāpi in ancient times and was the first capital of the Cālukya kings. It is the site of important 6th- and 7th-century Brahmanical and Jaina cave temples. Dug out of solid rock, the temples contain elaborate interior decorations. Pop. (1981) 15,023.

Badarian culture, Egyptian predynastic cultural phase, first discovered at al-Badārī, its type-site, on the east bank of the Nile in Asyūṭ *muḥāfaẓah* (governorate), Upper Egypt. British excavations there during the 1920s revealed settlements and cemeteries dating to about 4000 BC.

Tools and utensils from al-Badārī, *c.* 4000 BC; in the British Museum
Thames and Hudson

Although the Badarians apparently continued the agricultural and pastoral practices of the Tasians (*see* Tasian culture), whom some scholars consider to be their immediate predecessors, their artistic and technical skills were greatly improved. Their pottery, often distinguished by a black top, was extremely thin-walled, well baked, and often decorated with a burnished ripple; many regard it as the best ever made in the Nile Valley. Other remains include combs and spoons of ivory, slate palettes, female figurines, and copper and stone beads. Badarian materials have also been found at Jazīrat Armant, al-Ḥammāmīyah, Hierakonpolis (modern Kawm al-Aḥmar), al-Maṭmār, and Tall al-Kawm al-Kabīr.

Badā'ūnī, ʿAbd al-Qādir (b. 1540, Toda, India—d. *c.* 1615, India), Indo-Persian historian, one of the most important writers on history of the Mughal period in India. As a young boy he lived in Basāvar and studied at Sambhal and Āgra. In 1562 he moved to Badaun (hence his name) and then to Patiāla, where he entered the service of a local prince, Husayn Khān, with whom he remained for nine years. After leaving this post, he continued his education, studying with various Muslim mystics. In 1574 he was presented to the Mughal emperor Akbar, who appointed him to a religious office at the court and gave him a pension.

Of the many works he wrote on commission from the Emperor, the most highly regarded were the *Kitāb al-Ḥadīth* ("Book of Ḥadīth"), the sayings of the Prophet Muḥammad, no longer extant; a section of the *Tārīkh-e alfī* ("History of the Millennium"), commissioned by Akbar to celebrate the millenary of the *hijrah* in 1591/92, on which more than 10 authors collaborated; and a summary translation of the work of the great historian Rashīd ad-Dīn, *Jāmiʿ at-tawārīkh* ("Universal History"). His most important work, however, was the *Muntakhab at-tawārīkh* ("Selection from History"), often called *Tārīkh-e Badā'ūnī* ("Badā'ūnī's History"), a history of Muslim India containing additional sections on Muslim religious figures, physicians, poets, and scholars. It aroused discussion because of its hostile remarks about Akbar and his religious practices and apparently was suppressed until the reign of Jahāngīr in the early 17th century. In addition to these works, Badā'ūnī also was commissioned to translate many Sanskrit tales and the Hindu epics the *Rāmāyaṇa* and the *Mahābhārata.*

Badawī (member of a people): *see* Bedouin.

Baddeck, unincorporated place, seat of Victoria county, northeastern Nova Scotia, Canada, in the centre of Cape Breton Island, on the north shore of Bras d'Or Lake. Settled in the late 18th century, its name probably derives from a Micmac Indian term meaning "place at the backward turn" in reference to its position on the Baddeck River. Now a fishing and yachting resort with farming and lumbering interests, 27 mi (43 km) west of Sydney, it was the site of the first public airplane flight in the British Empire (made [1909] in the "Silver Dart" by J.A.D. McCurdy). Nearby Beinn Bhreagh (Gaelic: "beautiful mountain"), on a headland overlooking the lake, was the summer home of Alexander Graham Bell, who was technically responsible for the flight; he is buried at the top of Beinn Bhreagh and is honoured in Baddeck by a national historic park and museum. The locality is on the Trans-Canada Highway and is the starting point of the scenic 184-mi Cabot Trail through the Margaree Valley and partially encircling Cape Breton Highlands National Park (366 sq mi [950 sq km]). It is linked to a Canadian National Railway terminus at Iona, *c.* 12 mi south. At St. Ann's, 8 mi north, is the only Gaelic college (specializing in Gaelic arts) in America. Pop. (1981) 972.

Consult the INDEX *first*

Baddeley, Robert (b. *c.* 1732—d. Nov. 20, 1794, London), actor chiefly remembered for his will, in which he bequeathed property to found a home for aged and impoverished actors and also money to provide wine and cake in the green room of Drury Lane Theatre on Twelfth Night, a ceremony that is still performed.

Baddeley is said to have been a cook to the actor Samuel Foote. Later, as a valet, he acquired a familiarity with foreign languages and manners that made him especially successful in "broken English" parts. In 1761, described as "of Drury Lane Theatre," he was seen at the theatre in Smock Alley, Dublin, as Gomez in Dryden's *Spanish Fryar.* Two years later he was a regular member of the Drury Lane company in London. He remained at Drury Lane and the Haymarket until his death. Baddeley was the original Moses in Sheridan's *School for Scandal,* which had its first performance at Drury Lane in May 1777.

Baden, former state on the Rhine River in the southwestern corner of Germany, now the western part of the Baden-Württemberg *Land* (state) of the Federal Republic of Germany.

The following article treats briefly the former German state of Baden. For additional treatment of Baden's geography and history, *see* MACROPAEDIA: Germany.

The title margrave of Baden originated in 1112. In 1218 the margraves, members of the House of Zähringen, acquired part of the countship of Breisgau and later added other lands west of the Rhine. In 1535 their territory was divided into the margraviates of Baden-Baden and Baden-Durlach. Both became Protestant during the Reformation, but Baden-Baden returned to Catholicism in the 1570s. Their dynastic rivalry further weakened them vis-à-vis neighbouring German states. The towns of Pforzheim, Durlach, and Baden were destroyed during the expansionist wars of Louis XIV of France in the late 17th century. Louis William I, margrave of Baden-Baden from 1677 to 1707, was a distinguished commander in the imperial army in wars against the Turks and against the French; he built the palace of Rastatt. Charles III William, margrave of Baden-Durlach from 1709 to 1738, founded Karlsruhe as his capital. Baden was reunited under his grandson Charles Frederick, who was margrave of Baden-Durlach from 1738 to 1811 and of Baden-Baden from 1771, when its line became extinct. He was constrained into an alliance with Revolutionary France in 1796 and had to cede it territory west of the Rhine. Between 1803 and 1806, the French compensated their ally by extending its territory north as far as the Main River and south to Lake Constance (Bodensee). In 1803 Baden was made an electorate of the Holy Roman Empire and in 1806, upon the empire's dissolution, a grand duchy and a member of Napoleon's Confederation of the Rhine.

Baden as a unified state was recognized as a sovereign member of the newly formed German Confederation by the Congress of Vienna in 1814–15. In 1836 it joined the Prussian Zollverein, or Customs Union. In 1818 the Grand Duke issued a constitution that made Baden one of the first German states to establish a representative assembly; however, later liberal reforms under Leopold, grand duke from 1830 to 1852, did not keep pace with radical demands that precipitated revolution, led by Friedrich Hecker and Gustav von Struve in 1848. Prussian military force suppressed the revolutionary government and restored Leopold in 1849. Frederick I, grand duke from 1852 to 1907, was an ally of Prussia (except in the Seven Weeks' War in 1866) and helped to found the German Empire. Under the constitution of 1919, Baden ceased to be a grand duchy and became a *Land* of the German Reich. The *Land* of Baden-Württemberg (*q.v.*) was formed after World War II.

Baden, also called BADEN BEI WIEN, spa, *Bundesland* Niederösterreich (federal province of Lower Austria), on the Schwechat River, at the eastern edge of the Wiener Wald, south of Vienna. Settled in prehistoric times, it was a Roman watering place, or *aquae,* and was recorded in 869 as the seat of a Frankish imperial palace. Chartered in 1480, it was destroyed by the Turks in 1529 and 1683. It is famous for its warm (73° to 97° F [23° to 36° C]), radioactive sulfur-chlorine springs, which were visited every summer (1811–34) by Emperor Francis Joseph I. Beethoven, Mozart, Franz Schubert, Johann Strauss, and other composers spent parts of their working lives in Baden. It was the headquarters of the Soviet occupation zone from 1945 to 1955. The Roman spring has supply pipes dating from the 1st century AD. Other historic landmarks are the 15th-century Gothic parish church of St. Stephan and the town hall (1815). Textiles are manufactured there. Pop. (1981) 23,235.

Baden, town, Aargau canton, northern Switzerland, on the Limmat River, northwest of Zürich. The hot sulfur springs, mentioned as early as the 1st century AD by the Roman

Covered bridge over the Limmat River at Baden, Switz.
Photo Research International

historian Tacitus, still attract large numbers of people. The town, founded by the Habsburgs in 1291, was conquered in 1415 (with Aargau) by the Swiss Confederation. The Diet of the Swiss Confederation met at Baden from 1424 to 1712 in the old town hall (rebuilt 1497). Baden was the capital (1798–1803) of the former canton Baden. The town is dominated on the west by the ruined castle of Stein, a former Habsburg stronghold. To the northwest of the baths is a modern industrial quarter with electrical-engineering works and other factories. The population is predominantly German-speaking and Roman Catholic. Pop. (1983 est.) 13,997.

Baden, Treaty of (Sept. 7, 1714): *see* Rastatt and Baden, treaties of.

Baden-Baden, city, Baden-Württemberg *Land* (state), southwestern West Germany, on the middle Oos River in Schwarzwald (Black Forest), one of the world's great spas. Its Roman baths (parts of which survive) were built in the reign of Caracalla (AD 211–217) for the garrison of Strasbourg. The town fell into ruins but reappeared in 1112 as the seat (until 1705) of the margravate of Baden. Almost entirely destroyed in 1689, it revived as an asylum for refugees of the French Revolution. In the 19th century it became a fashionable

Trinkhalle, or Pump Room, Baden-Baden, W.Ger.
Schuster—De Wys Inc.

resort for European nobility and society. Notable buildings include the casino, the modern baths, the Stiftskirche (founded 7th century, rebuilt 1753, and now the parish church) with tombs of the margraves, and the 15th-century Neues Schloss, the former castle-residence of the margraves and later of the grand dukes of Baden, now housing the historical museum. Nearby are the ruins of the Altes Schloss, the Lichtental Convent (founded 1254), and the Greek Chapel (1863). The resort is frequented for its thermal saline and radioactive waters, and its establishments are open all year. Pop. (1983 est.) 48,886.

Baden-Powell (of Gilwell), Robert Stephenson Smyth Baden-Powell, 1st Baron, also called (1922–29) SIR ROBERT BADEN-POWELL, 1ST BARONET (b. Feb. 22, 1857, London—d. Jan. 8, 1941, Nyeri, Kenya), British army officer who became a national hero for his 217-day defense of Mafeking in the South African War of 1899–1902; he later became famous as founder of the Boy Scouts and Girl Guides.

In 1884–85 Baden-Powell became noted for his use of observation balloons in warfare in Bechuanaland and the Sudan. From Oct. 12, 1899, to May 17, 1900, he defended Mafeking, holding off a much larger Boer force until the siege was lifted. After the war he recruited and trained the South African constabulary. On returning to England in 1903, he was appointed inspector general of cavalry, and the next year he established the Cavalry School, Netheravon, Wiltshire. He was promoted to lieutenant general in 1907.

Having learned that his military textbook *Aids to Scouting* (1899) was being used for training boys in woodcraft, Baden-Powell ran a trial camp on Brownsea Island, off Poole, Dorset, in 1907, and he wrote an outline for the proposed Boy Scout movement. Scout

Baden-Powell, oil painting by S. Slocombe, 1916; in the National Portrait Gallery, London
By courtesy of the National Portrait Gallery, London

troops sprang up all over Britain, and for their use Baden-Powell's *Scouting for Boys* was issued in 1908. He retired from the army in 1910 to devote all his time to the Boy Scouts, and in the same year he and his sister Agnes (1858–1945) founded the Girl Guides (in the U.S., Girl Scouts from 1912). His wife, Olave, Lady Baden-Powell (1889–1977), also did much to promote the Girl Guides. In 1916 he organized the Wolf Cubs in Great Britain (Cub Scouts in the U.S.) for boys under the age of 11. At the first international Boy Scout Jamboree (London, 1920), he was acclaimed chief scout of the world.

A baronet from 1922, Baden-Powell was created a baron in 1929. He spent his last years in Kenya for his health. His autobiography, *Lessons of a Lifetime* (1933), was followed by *Baden-Powell* (1942, 2nd ed. 1957), by Ernest Edwin Reynolds.

Baden-Württemberg, *Land* (state), southwestern Federal Republic of Germany. It has an area of 13,804 sq mi (35,751 sq km) and is bordered by France, Switzerland, and a small portion of Austria (west and south), as well as the *Länder* (states) of Rheinland-Pfalz and Hessen (northwest and north). Theodor Heuss, the first president of the Federal Republic of Germany, called his native Baden-Württemberg "the model of German possibilities," and by the late 20th century there were several indications that the possibilities were becoming realized in this very young West German state. By that time, Baden-Württemberg ranked third in both area and population among the West German states, having grown more than any other in the period following World War II. Formed under post-World War II occupational rule, and confirmed by a December 1951 referendum, the *Land* consists of three former *Länder:* Württemberg-Baden (in the American zone), Südwürttemberg-Hohenzollern and Südbaden (both in the French zone). The merger took effect in 1952. The capital is at Stuttgart.

The land. Within the 1,026-mi- (1,651-km-) long border of Baden-Württemberg lies one of the most geographically varied territories of the German Federal Republic, with the forests of the upland regions alternating with fertile highlands, green meadows, lakes, and marshes, giving the landscape a unique character. The geographical boundaries of the *Land* are the waters of the Bodensee (Lake Constance) and the upper Rhine in the south, the widening Rhine Valley in the west, the River Main in the north, and the River Iller in the east. In addition, the source of the River Danube is at Donaueschingen, a popular excursion point, and the river cuts through the eastern part of the state on the first part of its journey across the European continent. The Danube is the main drainage basin south of the European water divide, which bisects the *Land.*

Using criteria from physical and human geography, it is possible to divide Baden-Württemberg into the following eight regions.

Before the Roman conquest of western Europe, the upper valley of the Rhine River was one of the main trading arteries on the Continent, and this region also included immense hardwood forests, most of which have fallen prey to floods and the timber industry over the ensuing centuries. The fertile southern part of the upper Rhine Valley now has many vegetable orchards, and the sun-drenched vineyards around Mount Kaiserstuhl produce wine that ranks among the finest of all wines produced in the German Federal Republic.

West Germany's largest continuous forest area, the Black Forest spreads westward to the banks of the Rhine River. Idyllic valleys break its uniformity, and over the years, low-lying portions have filled with water, with many small lakes now contributing to the forest's enchanting, if somewhat foreboding, scenery. The highest point is the Feldberg, 4,898 ft (1,493 m). The Black Forest edges into the Hotzenwald (Hotzen Forest) in the south, where many lakes and reservoirs feed the numerous power stations. Typical of this area is the so-called *Schwarzwaldhaus,* or Black Forest house, with its roof jutting far beyond its sides and its driveway leading straight up into the hayloft under the roof of the barn. The owners of these small holdings live predominantly from cattle breeding, the timber industry, and tourism.

The Alpenvorland (alpine foreland) is a deep trough at the edge of the Alps stretching from the formerly volcanic area of the Hegau Mountains in the west to the meadows of the Allgäu in the east. Within its area lies the famous Bodensee and numerous, apparently irregular, rolling hills, with many lakes and marshes, which give the region a distinct appearance. The marshy ground is used for therapeutic baths, hence the number of health spas in this area. Here, too, small holdings predominate, with a solitary main building containing living quarters in the front, barn and hayloft in the back, threshing floor in the middle, and stables lining both sides. The farmers' main income is derived from cattle breeding and dairy products. The Allgäuer cheese is internationally famous.

The Schwäbische Alb (Swabian Alb), emerging from the flats of the Alpenvorland but sectioned off from it by the Danube Valley, covers the area between the Black Forest and the Fränkische Alb (Franconian Alb). In the north its mountains fall abruptly into the valley of the Neckar River. Chalk formations and depleted forests make the Schwäbische Alb a barren terrain and Baden-Württemberg's poorest district. The weaving of linen textiles and sheep raising were the main sources of income for the population before the onset of synthetic textiles curtailed the breeding of sheep and forced many farmers to seek additional income in the cities of Heidenheim, Ulm, Reutlingen, or Balingen.

The fertile Neckarland region belongs among the most densely populated areas in the entire Federal Republic. There is a profusion of vineyards along the Neckar and its many tributaries; other produce grown in the region includes potatoes, sugar beets, and a variety of fruit and vegetables, together with some grain. The many medieval castle ruins have left a distinctive mark on the partly forested landscape, which is also broken by occasional cornfields. Small villages used to line the local highways, but since the end of World War II new high buildings have pushed city and town limits further and further into these surrounding rural districts.

The granary of Baden-Württemberg, the Hohenlohic district, lies around the old free city of Schwäbisch Hall and extends all the way to the borders of Bavaria at Rothenburg ob der Tauber. Unlike the custom of the Alb region, where holdings were divided among heirs, the laws of primogeniture (inheritance by the first-born) in this area resulted in a preservation of large estates. A bad effect of this has been that the many young people who do not inherit any land at all have had to find work somewhere else. The numerous, often well preserved, castles in this area are nevertheless ample evidence of the wealth of Hohenlohe in past centuries.

The Odenwald (Oden Forest) is often called *Badisch-Sibirien* (the "Siberia of Baden"). This hilly region unites Baden-Württemberg with the *Land* of Hessen, in the north. Its location outside the main traffic arteries as well as its raw climate prevented any cultural or economic growth for centuries, and only in the years since 1950 has a developing small industry created extra income possibilities for the local small farmer.

Located between the Rhine and Neckar rivers, the fertile Kraichgau district is the site of wheat, corn (maize), tobacco, and fruit culture. The Schwetzinger asparagus of this area is famous far beyond its borders. The castles of Schwetzingen and Bruchsal, reconstructed since World War II, complement the many castles around the cities of Karlsruhe and Mannheim.

The climate of Baden-Württemberg varies greatly among the regions of the *Land.* The upper Rhine Valley is the warmest area, with a yearly mean average of 48°–50° F (9°–10° C) whereas the Alb—the "raw Alb"—is the most inhospitable, with a mean average of about 40°–44° F (4.5°–7° C). Here, and in parts of the Black Forest, there is a yearly average of two months of frost. As a rule, spring comes to the southern part of the upper Rhine Valley before April 20 but does not reach the highest regions of the Alb until after May 25. The latter region also has the highest amount of precipitation in the *Land,* because of the westerly winds that drive ocean cloud formations across France to discharge over the slopes of the Black Forest and the Alb. The annual rainfall in the upper Rhine Valley is 26 in. (650 mm), compared with 79 in. (2,000 mm) on the Feldberg, a favourite ski resort. The average precipitation in the Alb district is 40 in. (a little over 1,000 mm), but in the valley of the Neckar River and in the valley of the Tauber River, lying further east, the amount is often less than 24 in. (600 mm), and most of this is summer rain.

A characteristic feature of Baden-Württemberg is the great number of urban settlements; the urban density is two to three times that of northern West Germany. By the late 20th century, more than 60 of these settlements, many of which had been founded by the Staufers (one of the numerous lesser rulers who governed this area at one point or another in its long history), had populations less than 2,000. Such towns as Ludwigsburg, Rastatt, and Öhringen still retain their typical residential character. The garrison towns, such as Ulm and Münsingen, are of more recent date. Heidelberg, Tübingen, and Freiburg im Breisgau, university centres dating back to the Middle Ages, have been joined in recent years by new universities in Konstanz and Ulm.

The people. The northern West German regards the people of Baden-Württemberg with some contempt. The nickname *Schwaben,* or even *Spätzle-Schwaben,* is often used. *Spätzle,* a local variety of homemade dumplings, is the favourite staple dish of local residents. The term *Schwaben* is a misnomer, since most of the native Swabians, descendants of the Suabi, an ancient Germanic tribe, live only in the southeast of the state. The people in the west and southwest of Baden-Württemberg are Alemanni, blood relatives of the French Alsatians and the neighbouring Swiss Alemanni. The influence of the Palatinate population is very strong in the northwest of Baden-Württemberg, whereas the Franconians pushed their way into the centre of the state from the northeast. The linguistic boundary between Franconians and Swabians runs approximately from Baden-Baden in the west, through the Stuttgart area, to Crailsheim in the east.

The geographical boundary between religions has no connection with the origin of the people. Catholics outnumber other denominations in the predominantly Alemannic Südbaden and Südwürttemberg; Protestants and Evangelists constitute the majority in the more Franconian Nordwürttemberg, and both faiths are more or less equally represented in Nordbaden. Historical developments within the state account for these differences: some ruling houses were Catholic, others, Lutheran Protestant, and each left its mark on the local subjects. In addition to these two main religions, there is a great variety of sects and free churches, especially in Württemberg, most of them a part of the Pietistic movement or of other Protestant origin.

Baden-Württemberg's great post-World War II expansion owed much to the fact that almost a quarter of its population is composed of people who moved to the *Land* as fugitives or displaced persons from the east. Their influx is partially explained by ancestral links between them and the states of Baden and Württemberg in previous centuries. In addition, many simply saw opportunities for a new start in this part of Germany, which had been spared the brunt of wartime destruction. From 1945 to 1950, the rural areas of the state provided the best prospects for housing and employment, but the following years saw a return of the working force to the industrial centres—so much so that many a local farmer's son or daughter got caught up in the ensuing migration from rural areas to the cities. The capital, Stuttgart, witnessed a spectacular growth, and there was severe depopulation of many rural districts. By the late 20th century, only the high rents in the cities apparently kept even more people from moving to the locality in which they worked. Many preferred to build their own home on cheaper ground in small dormitory villages, and to commute instead. Stuttgart alone has more than 100,000 commuters daily, almost one-quarter of the total working force, and a quarter of the entire working force of the *Land* are daily commuters.

The economy. Baden-Württemberg may be regarded as the one West German *Land* in which economic life is dominated by middle-class businessmen and small farmers. Although such world-famous firms as Daimler-Benz started as small workshops in Stuttgart and Mannheim, there is no heavy industry in the region. On the other hand, Baden-Württemberg is the centre for highly specialized mechanical and textile industries. The lack of valuable mineral and other deposits in Baden-Württemberg forces the population to earn its livelihood by the manufacture, improvement, and finishing of goods. Baden-Württemberg produces the majority of all clocks, watches, and custom jewelry in the country. Substantial amounts of West Germany's leather goods, musical instruments, medical instruments, food and produce, cigars, and hardware are produced in Baden-Württemberg.

The industrial centres are concentrated in the Neckar Valley between Esslingen, Stuttgart, and Heilbronn, and this area accounts for more than half the total production of the *Land.* Other industrial areas are found on the banks of the Rhine near Mannheim—the *Land*'s second largest city after Stuttgart—and near Karlsruhe and Ulm. More recently, the border district of the upper Rhine has gained in economic importance; close to the French and Swiss borders and in the centre of the European Economic Community, it has become the preferred site for new branch offices of German, as well as French and Swiss, companies.

During the late 20th century, the majority of all those gainfully employed in Baden-Württemberg worked in the production industry, with a shrinking proportion in agriculture and forestry. Trade and commerce, and other fields of the economy employed the remaining workers.

Agriculture continues to pose problems as farm holdings of less than 12 ac (about 5 ha) of arable land apiece are numerous. Their economic survival was seen to depend on their ability to buy or lease additional land. Similarly, several thousand farmers with slightly larger holdings had to specialize—in animal breeding, produce, or wine production—if they, too, were not to become bankrupt. Of the state's total number of farms, a small proportion were larger than 72 ac (30 ha) of land. Most of the small farmers were therefore forced to earn their livelihood in industry, returning to their farms in the afternoon, and taking their factory vacations during harvest time.

Many of the farmers of the late 20th century added to their income by converting either their own homes, or other nearby property, to tourist use. The well-known spas of Baden-Baden, Wildbad, and Badenweiler provided additional tourist facilities, while many other smaller spas had been enlarged and improved considerably with financial help from the *Land* authorities.

Lacking natural resources, and forced to depend mainly on commerce and trade, Baden-Württemberg pays particular attention to its transportation system. As early as 1955 the government prepared a general plan that, by the late 20th century, had been twice improved and adapted to more recent technological developments. The plan called for three express highways (*Autobahn*), traversing the state from north to south, and four more running from west to east. These were to be supported by an extensive system of improved four-lane smaller highways, together with appropriate railway developments. The Rhine and Neckar have been improved as waterways, augmenting this intricate network. By 1971, the Neckar had been canalized as far as Plochingen, and the Rhine could be used for shipping as far as Rheinfelden. Finally, Baden-Württemberg has one international airport near Stuttgart and many smaller airfields.

Administrative and social conditions. Since 1952 the state assembly (Landtag) of Baden-Württemberg has had 120 members, distributed in proportion to the population of the four administrative districts of Nordwürttemberg (capital Stuttgart), Südwürttemberg-Hohenzollern (capital Tübingen), Südbaden (capital Freiburg), and Nordbaden (capital Karlsruhe). Seventy members are elected by direct popular vote, the remainder by proportional representation. The *Land* entered the late 20th century as the only one in the Federal Republic still governed by the "grand coalition" of the Union of Christian Democrats (CDU) and the Social Democrats (SPD). The smaller Free Democrats (FDP/DVP) also retained representation, but the Union of Refugees and Disowned (Bund der Heimatvertriebenen und Entrechteten; BHE) and the Communists lost their minor representation of the 1950s in the ensuing decade, which, from 1968 onward, saw the rise of the right-wing National Democrats. As a rule, the strongest faction in the state assembly chooses the president after the elections; after majority confirmation, he in turn appoints his ministers, choosing within and outside of the assembly. In the late 20th century, the left-centre SPD, the strongest party in Baden-Württemberg in terms of organization, had over 50,000 members; the CDU had slightly more than 45,000 members; and the FDP/DVP had a little more than 10,000 members.

The *Land* is divided into two judicial districts: those of the supreme assize courts of Baden and Württemberg, each including several provincial courts and many local courts. The local courts were extensively reorganized into larger districts in the late 20th century. A peculiarity of Baden-Württemberg is its community courts, in which lay officials may settle civil rights disputes within the village or community. The local notary office is also a unique feature among the German *Länder.*

The Centre for the Clearing of National Socialist Crimes (Zentrale Stelle zur Aufklärung nationalsozialistischer Verbrechen) in Ludwigsburg has gained an international reputation, sifting thousands of documents from foreign archives concerning atrocities committed by Germans under the Third Reich. It has also started court proceedings against former Nazis.

The West German supreme courts are located in Karlsruhe; the Federal Constitutional Court (Bundesverfassungsgericht) settles constitutional questions, and the Federal Court of Justice (Bundesgerichtshof) is the highest court of appeal for criminal and civil law in the Federal Republic.

At the end of World War II, the greater part of Baden-Württemberg was occupied by American troops, and United States military headquarters have continued to be located in Heidelberg, with many American garrisons in the cities and towns of northern Württemberg and northern Baden. The headquarters of the limited French forces are in Baden-Baden, while the commander of the Federal German forces for Baden-Württemberg has his headquarters in Stuttgart.

Baden-Württemberg has more universities than any of the other *Länder* of the Federal Republic. In addition to the old classical universities of Heidelberg, Freiburg, and Tübingen, there are technical universities at Stuttgart and Karlsruhe, an agricultural university in Stuttgart-Hohenheim, and a university in Mannheim that specializes in economics. The Ulm University for medicine and natural sciences and the reform University of Konstanz were both founded in the 1960s. There are also many other institutions of higher education.

Approximately two-thirds of the three- to six-year-olds in the *Land* are enrolled in kindergartens, which obtain most of their support from churches and similar organizations. There also is a substantial enrollment in other branches of primary and secondary education, in which structure follows the national pattern.

From the 1950s onward, the *Land* government has been greatly concerned with the social welfare of its citizens. It has produced a hospital plan, a plan for the aged, a plan for youth, and an extensive social report. As a result, medical services were extensively improved during the late 20th century, with many specialized hospitals having been constructed, with further enlargement and modernization of many additional existing hospitals.

It is not surprising that living costs, wages, and rents differ greatly in the various parts of the state because of its diverse economic structure, with the rural areas being low in living costs and wages and the cities offering high wages, often with excessively high rents. Generally, the level of earning power in Baden-Württemberg exceeds that of other *Länder* in the German Federal Republic.

Cultural life. Baden-Württemberg is strong in architectural monuments. Gothic churches abound in Ulm and Freiburg; and baroque churches in Weingarten (Kreis Ravensburg), Birnau, Steinhausen, Zwiefalten, and Mannheim, together with the former Kaiserpfalz (Kaiser Palace) in Wimpfen and the castle of Rastatt, are popular sightseeing attractions. The state theatres in Karlsruhe and Stuttgart have an international reputation, particularly marked in the case of the Stuttgart ballet. Of the provincial and city theatres, the Mannheimer Nationaltheater merits special mention; Friedrich Schiller's *Die Räuber* (*The Robbers*) had its world premiere on this stage. The chamber orchestra of Stuttgart (Stuttgarter Kammerorchester) has a growing reputation. Such poets and writers as Friedrich Schiller, Friedrich Hölderlin, and Hermann Hesse, together with the great philosophers Georg Friedrich Wilhelm Hegel and Martin Heidegger, are among the *Land's* most famous sons. The sculptor Otto Dix made an important contribution to the German Expressionist movement.

Two of the radio broadcast stations in the *Land,* the Süddeutsche Rundfunk in Stuttgart and the Südwestfunk in Baden-Baden, have well-known popular orchestras, and each broadcasts three different program services. In addition to five or more important regional newspapers, the *Stuttgarter Zeitung* is of national significance.

The Baden-Württembergian is particularly likely to be a member of a club or society, and membership in such bodies is far above the average of the other *Länder* in the Federal Republic of Germany. Singing, sports, and gardening clubs abound throughout the *Land,* which is also a leader in the number of local historical and archaeological societies. The Schwäbische Albverein (Swabian Alb Walking Club) is the largest in the whole Federal Republic. Like the Schwarzwaldverein (Black Forest Walking Club), it concerns itself mainly with wildlife preservation.

The numerous adult education clubs and the many university extension courses in the *Land* testify to the continuing importance of education tradition in the region. Since 1970 all branches of public adult education have been brought together and are now a separate unit, the Fortbildungswerk.

Next to the city states of Berlin, Hamburg, and Bremen, Baden-Württemberg is the state with the highest proportion of students in all age groups. In the late 20th century, this was combined with a high number of car owners, and the second lowest rate of unemployment per 1,000 inhabitants. A government report of this period was not necessarily unjustified in concluding with a quotation from Theodor Heuss, "I believe that the daring prophecy that a self-reliant state could evolve there has been fulfilled." Pop. (1983 est.) 9,270,608.

BIBLIOGRAPHY. Eberhard Konstanzer, *Die Entstehung des Landes Baden-Württemberg* (1969), is a history of southwest Germany, with emphasis on the period from 1945 to the present; earlier history is treated in Ernst Muller, *Kleine Geschichte Württembergs* (1949). See also H. Gardiner Barnum, *Market Centers and Hinterlands in Baden-Württemberg* (1966), for commerce; and W.M. Schede, *Baden-Württemberg: A Panorama in Color* (1965), for a description of the area.

Badeni, Kasimir Felix, Graf von (count of), Polish KAZIMIERZ FELIKS, HRABIA (count) BADENI (b. Oct. 14, 1846, Surochów, Galicia—d. July 9, 1909, near Krasne), Polish-born statesman in the Austrian service, who, as prime minister (1895–97) of the Austrian half of the Austro-Hungarian Dual Monarchy, sponsored policies to appease Slav nationalism within the empire but was defeated by German nationalist reaction.

One of the richest Galician landowners, Badeni was appointed governor of Galicia (Austrian Poland) in 1888, where he acquired the reputation of a tough administrator. Appointed prime minister on the recommendation of the army, he had to face problems of suffrage and tax reform and the German–Czech language dispute in Bohemia and Moravia. His suffrage reform (May 1896) added a fifth electoral category to the existing system of indirect election but failed to please the partisans of equal and direct suffrage. In addition, his conciliatory policies toward the Czechs won him the enmity of the German minority parties. Two ordinances of April 1897, increasing linguistic concessions to the Czechs, precipitated strong opposition by German nationalists. New standing orders (the Falkenhayn laws), enacted to restore order to the Reichsrat, further aggravated the situation, as libertarian Social Democrats, denouncing the arbitrary legislation, now joined

Badeni, detail from an engraving after a photograph

By courtesy of the Bild-Archiv, Osterreichische Nationalbibliothek, Vienna

the German nationalists in opposition. The expulsion of some obstreperous members under the Falkenhayn ordinances (Nov. 26–27, 1897) triggered noisier protests in the Reichsrat and mass demonstrations in the streets of Vienna. Unabated disorder prompted Badeni's resignation on Nov. 28, 1897.

Badenoch and Strathspey, district, Highland region, northern Scotland; created by the reorganization of 1975 from the former counties of Inverness, Banff, and Moray. The district, area 1,003 sq mi (2,598 sq km), includes Strathspey, the valley of the River Spey, and part of the Cairngorm Mountains, rising more than 4,000 ft (1,200 m). The moors contain deer and grouse. Crofting (subsistence farming), forestry, and the raising of cattle and sheep are the chief occupations. Aviemore is a winter-sports centre. Kingussie is the seat of the district authority. Pop. (1982 est.) 9,971.

Badgastein, also called GASTEIN, town, *Bundesland* (federal province) Salzburg, in the Gastein Valley of west central Austria, on the Gasteiner Ache (river). Its radioactive thermal springs have been visited since the 13th century, and royal and other eminent patrons brought it world renown in the 19th century. Now one of Austria's most important spas and health resorts, it is also known as an international winter-sports centre and is the site of two magnificent waterfalls with drops of 207 ft (63 m) and 280 ft. The town was the site of the Convention of Gastein, under which (1865) Austria gained control of Holstein and Prussia of Schleswig. Pop. (1981) 5,600.

badger, any of several stout-bodied carnivores of the family Mustelidae. The eight species (in six genera) differ in size, habitat, and coloration; but all possess anal scent glands, powerful jaws, and large, heavy claws on their forefeet. Known for their burrowing ability, badgers dig for food and construct underground homes and escape routes. They are nocturnal and feed on small animals (especially rodents) and, in some species, on plant material. Because of delayed implantation of the fertilized egg in the wall of the uterus, the gestation period lasts about 183–240 days. Litters consist of one to seven young.

Badgers have been tamed as pets and hunted for their pelts (used in the manufacture of brushes and as fur trim). In an English sport (outlawed around 1850), a badger was placed in a barrel and defended itself from attacking dogs with its savage fighting instincts.

For the honey badger (*Mellivora capensis*), a related animal, *see* ratel.

The eight known badger species are:

American badger (*Taxidea taxus*), only New World species, usually found in open, dry country of western North America; generally solitary; a powerful animal and a rapid burrower; fierce when cornered; coat is grayish with blackish face and feet and white middorsal stripe extending from nose to back; shoulder height, 23 centimetres (9 inches); length, 42–76 cm, excluding the 10–16-cm tail; weight, 3.5–11.5 kilograms (7.7–25 pounds).

Eurasian badger (*Meles meles*), also called true, or typical, badger; Old World species of wooded regions; gregarious, omnivorous, and

American badger (*Taxidea taxus*)

Alvin E. Staffan—The National Audubon Society Collection/Photo Researchers

a tenacious fighter; lives in groups in an extensive network of burrows (sets); coat, grayish with large black-and-white facial stripes; black underparts, legs, feet, claws, and throat; shoulder height, 30 cm; length, 56–81 cm, excluding the 12–20-cm tail; weight, 10–22 kg.

Ferret badgers, *Melogale* (including *Helictis*), also called tree badgers and pahmi; three species: Chinese, or common; Burmese, or large-toothed; and Javan; confined to grasslands and forests in Southeast Asia; able to climb trees; muzzle, long; coat, brownish to blackish gray above, paler below; white markings on the face, throat, and sometimes on the back; length, 33–43 cm, excluding the 12–23-cm tail.

Hog badger (*Arctonyx collaris*), also called hog-nosed, or sand, badger; pale-clawed species of both low and mountainous regions in Southeast Asia; snout, mobile and piglike; coat, gray to black with darker undersides and feet, a black-and-white striped head pattern, and white throat, ears, and tail; length, 55–70 cm, excluding the 12–20-cm tail; weight, 7–14 kg.

Malayan stink badger (*Mydaus javanensis*), also called skunk badger and teledu; island-dwelling form of Southeast Asia, usually living in mountainous areas; secretion of anal glands strong smelling and offensive; coat, brown to black with white on the head and sometimes as a dorsal stripe; length, 38–51 cm, excluding the 5–8-cm tail; weight, 1–4 kg.

Palawan, or Calamanian, stink badger, *Suillotaxus* (formerly *Mydaus*) *marchei*, little-known badger from Palawan, in the Philippines, and neighbouring islands; scent very strong, offensive.

Badger (Soviet aircraft): *see* TU-16.

Bādghīsāt, also called BADGHIS, *velāyat* (province), northwestern Afghanistan, 8,438 sq mi (21,854 sq km) in area, with its capital at Qal'eh-ye Now. Created in 1964 out of the northwestern part of Herāt province, it is bounded by the Turkmen S.S.R. (northwest) and by the *velāyāt* of Fāryāb (north), Ghowr (east), and Herāt (south). Lying between the Selseleh-ye Band-e Torkestān (Torkestān Range) to the north and the Selseleh-ye Safīd Kūh (Paropamisus Range) to the south, the province is essentially a large valley drained by the Morghāb River.

Agriculture is the principal activity, with cereal grains, cotton, and pistachio nuts as the chief agricultural products. The population is chiefly Pashtun, with Baluchis and Ḥazāras among the ethnic groups. Pop. (1982 est.) settled pop. 244,346.

Badī ʿaz-Zamān Abū al-Faḍl Aḥmad ibn al-Ḥusayn al-Hamadhānī: *see* Hamadhānī, al-.

Badīn, town and administrative headquarters of Badīn district, Hyderābād division, Sind province, Pakistan. The town, founded in 1750, lies in swampy deltaic land east of the Indus River. Rice is the major crop in the region. Badīn town has a sugar mill and rice mills and is the terminus of the Hyderābād-Badīn railway.

Badīn district, formerly part of Hyderābād district, consists of a flat alluvial plain to the north and is swampy in the south. Rice, wheat, gram (legumes), cotton, and fruit are the main crops. Industry consists mostly of rice, flour, and sugar milling. Pop. (1981 prelim.) town, 23,000; district, 769,000.

Badings, Henk (b. Jan. 17, 1907, Bandung, Java), Dutch composer best known for his music featuring electronic sounds and the compositional use of tape recorders. He studied mining engineering before turning to music and began to compose without any formal training. He later studied composition (1930–31) with Willem Pijper.

After composing in nearly all traditional genres, he began in the 1950s to attract international attention for his electronic music and his pioneering work with tape recording. His later style is exemplified in such works as the radio operas of this period, particularly *Orestes* (1954). Many of his works use electronic sounds in combination with conventional instruments. Badings was director (1941–44) of the Royal Conservatory at The Hague.

Bādiyat ash-Shām (Asia): *see* Syrian Desert.

Badjok (people): *see* Chokwe.

badlands, also spelled (as singular) BADLAND, area cut and eroded by many deep, tortuous gullies with intervening sawtoothed divides. The gullies extend from main rivers back to tablelands about 150 metres (500 feet) and higher. The gully bottoms increase in gradient from almost flat near the main rivers to nearly vertical at the edges of the tablelands. Because the rocks are not uniform in character, differences in erosion result in stair-step profiles. The joining and separating of the gullies cause many isolated irregular spires, small flat-topped buttes, or mesas, and produce a landscape of jagged, fluted, and seemingly inaccessible hills.

Badlands develop in arid to semi-arid areas where the bedrock is poorly cemented and rainfall generally occurs as cloudbursts. The dry, granular surface material and light vegetation is swept from the slopes during showers, leaving the gullies bare.

The term badland was first applied to a part of southwestern South Dakota, which the French-Canadian trappers called the *mauvaises terres pour traverser* ("the bad lands to cross"); later the term was applied to other areas with similarly eroded topography. The South Dakota Badlands comprise an area of approximately 5,200 square kilometres (2,000 square miles) that stretches east and west for 160 kilometres (100 miles) along the Jackson–Washabaugh and Pennington–Shannon county lines. The Badlands National Monument (*q.v.*) embraces most of the rugged terrain in Jackson and Pennington counties.

Badlands National Monument, rugged, eroded area (243,508 ac [98,548 ha]) of nonporous clay that washes into gullies, buttes, and saw-toothed divides, in southwestern South Dakota, U.S. It was established as a national monument in 1939 and lies between the Cheyenne and White rivers, 40 mi (65 km) southeast of Rapid City.

The monument contains numerous fossil beds that have yielded the remains of such animals as the three-toed horse, camel, sabre-toothed tiger, and rhinoceros. The region is devoid of vegetation and is inhabited only by coyotes, prairie dogs, and jackrabbits.

Badminton, also called GREAT BADMINTON, parish, Northavon district, county of Avon, England. Until 1974 it was in Gloucestershire. Badminton House, seat of the dukes of Beaufort, stands in a large park.

The present ducal mansion was built in 1682 in Palladian style on the site of an old manor house. The game of badminton derives its name from the village. The park is also well known for its horse trials. Pop. (1971) 322.

badminton, court or lawn game played with lightweight rackets and a shuttlecock, a small, cork hemisphere with 14 to 16 feathers attached weighing about 80 grains (12.4 ounces; 5 grams). A nylon shuttlecock with the apron furnished by feathers is also used. The game is named for Badminton, the country estate of the English duke of Beaufort, where it supposedly originated about 1873. It was probably derived from an old children's game, battledore and shuttlecock. It was first popularized by army officers in India who played it out-of-doors. The International Badminton Federation, world governing body of the sport, was formed in 1934.

The game is usually played indoors because even light winds affect the course of the shut-

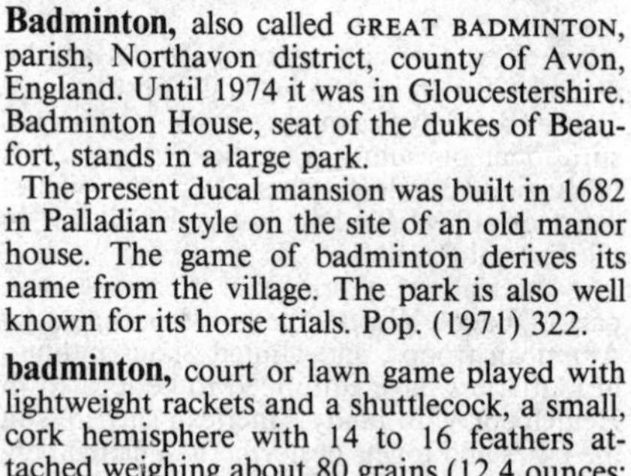

Men's Doubles Final in the All-English Badminton Championship, Wembley, Eng., 1971

Graham Habbin

tlecock. The court is 44 ft (13.4 m) long and 17 ft wide for singles (one against one), 20 ft for doubles (two against two). A net 5 feet high stretches across the width of the court at its centre. For international competition the minimum height of the court is 26 ft. Many national organizations require 30 ft. A clear space of 4 ft around the court is needed. Play consists entirely of volleying—hitting the shuttlecock back and forth across the net without letting it touch the floor or ground within the boundaries of the court. *See* Sporting Record: *Badminton.*

Badoglio, Pietro (b. Sept. 28, 1871, Grazzano Monferrato, Italy—d. Nov. 1, 1956, Grazzano Badoglio, formerly Grazzano Monferrato), general and statesman whose career reached its height during the dictatorship of Benito Mussolini (1922–43) and who successfully extricated Italy from World War II in arranging an armistice with the Allies in September 1943.

Badoglio
Keystone

From second lieutenant of the artillery in 1890, he rose to chief of the general staff in 1919. He distinguished himself during World War I by planning and directing the capture of Monte Sabotino on Aug. 6, 1916. Although his forces suffered defeat in the Battle of Caporetto on Oct. 24, 1917, he emerged from the war a general and conducted the armistice talks for the Italians. Initially lukewarm to Mussolini, Badoglio remained outside of politics for one year after the march on Rome (1922). He then served one and a half years in Rio de Janeiro as ambassador to Brazil before he was recalled to Italy to resume his military career. Mussolini named him chief of staff once again on May 4, 1925, and made him field marshal on May 26, 1926.

He governed Libya from 1928 to 1934, with the title of marquis of Sabotino. He assumed command of Ethiopian operations in 1935, capturing Addis Ababa, the capital, where he remained for a short time in 1936 as viceroy of Ethiopia. He later received the title of duke of Addis Ababa.

During 1940 he differed with Mussolini over Italy's preparations for entering World War II. On Dec. 4, 1940, in the midst of Italy's disastrous campaign in Greece, he resigned as chief of staff and disavowed responsibility for Mussolini's acts. It is not clear, however, whether his objections were moral or military. In any case, he headed the government that took power after Mussolini's downfall on July 25, 1943, and arranged for an armistice with the Allies on September 3. In June 1944 he resigned to allow the formation of a new cabinet in liberated Rome and retired to his familial home in Grazzano Badoglio.

Badr, Battle of (624), first military victory of the Islāmic Prophet Muḥammad. It seriously damaged Meccan prestige, while strengthening the political position of Muslims in Medina and establishing Islām as a viable force in the Arabian Peninsula.

Since their emigration from Mecca (622), the Muslims in Medina had depended for economic survival on constant raids on Meccan caravans. When word of a particularly wealthy caravan escorted by Abū Sufyān, head of the Umayyad clan, reached Muḥammad, a raiding party of about 300 Muslims, to be led by Muḥammad himself, was organized. By filling the wells on the caravan route near Medina with sand, the Muslims lured Abū Sufyān's army to battle at Badr, near Medina, in March 624. Despite the superior numbers of the Meccan forces (about 1,000 men), the Muslims scored a complete victory, and many prominent Meccans were killed. The success at Badr was recorded in the Qur'ān as a divine sanction of the new religion: "It was not you who slew them, it was God . . . in order that He might test the Believers by a gracious trial from Himself" (8:17). Those Muslims who fought at Badr became known as the *badrīyūn* and make up one group of the Companions of the Prophet.

Badr Khānī Jāladat (b. 1893, Maktala, Syria—d. 1951, Damascus), Kurdish nationalist leader and editor who was one of the chief 20th-century spokesmen for Kurdish independence.

Jāladat, like his elder brother Surayyā, devoted his life to the cause of establishing a unified Kurdish state in the Middle East. Educated in Istanbul, he emigrated in 1912 to avoid persecution and during World War I actively supported the British. Disappointed that the British did not support the formation of a unified Kurdish state after the breakup of the Ottoman Empire, Jāladat settled in Syria (1919), where he joined the Kurdish émigrés. In 1927 he was appointed the first president of the *Khoybun* (Kurdish National League) and three years later participated in the unsuccessful Kurdish rebellion in Turkey. He became the first editor (May 1932) of the bilingual Kurdish-French review *Ḥawār* ("Summons"), which, together with his later illustrated publication *Runahi* ("Light"), promoted understanding among the diverse and often conflicting elements of the Kurdish nationalist movement and contributed to the growth of a Kurdish popular literature.

Badrīnāth, uninhabited village and shrine in Garhwāl district, Uttar Pradesh state, northern India. In the Himalayas on a headstream of the Ganges River, it lies at an altitude of about 10,000 ft (3,050 m). Badrīnāth Peak (23,420 ft) is 17 mi (27 km) west.

Main entrance to the temple at Badrīnāth, Uttar Pradesh, India
Vidyavrata

Badrīnāth is the site of a temple that contains a shrine of Badrīnātha, or Vishnu, and has been a well-known pilgrimage centre for more than 2,000 years. Pilgrims believe that the long, arduous route to the shrine enhances the journey's spiritual merits.

Badulla, town, capital of Uva Province, southeastern Sri Lanka (Ceylon), southeast of Kandy, on the Badulu Oya (river). It is surrounded by mountains and is the site of two large and wealthy temples and a marketplace for the agricultural products of the villages, terraced rice paddies, and tea estates in the area. Limestone quarries are worked near the town, and it is linked by rail with Colombo. Badulla was at times the seat of a prince under various kingdoms. Pop. (1981 prelim.) town, 32,954; district, 665,000.

Badw (people): *see* Bedouin.

Baeck, Leo (b. May 23, 1873, Lissa, Posen, Ger.—d. Nov. 2, 1956, London), Reform rabbi and theologian, the spiritual leader of German Jewry during the Nazi period, and

Baeck, *c.* 1948
Picture in the archives of the Leo Baeck Institute, New York

the leading liberal Jewish religious thinker of his time. His magnum opus, *The Essence of Judaism,* appeared in 1905. His final work, *This People Israel: The Meaning of Jewish Existence* (1955), was written in part while Baeck was in a Nazi concentration camp.

Life. Baeck studied for the rabbinate in Breslau and Berlin, received his Ph.D. in philosophy at the University of Berlin in 1895, and was ordained in 1897 by the progressive Hochschule in Berlin. He immediately displayed his courage and personal independence of thought by being one of the two rabbis within the German Rabbinical Association who refused to condemn the Zionist leader Theodor Herzl (1860–1904) and the First Zionist Congress then meeting in Basel.

Baeck first served as rabbi in Oppeln Silesia (1897–1907), then Düsseldorf (1907–12), and finally Berlin (1912–42). In 1901 Baeck challenged the Protestant theologian and church historian Adolf von Harnack (1851–1930), whose lectures on *The Essence of Christianity* then presented essential original Christianity as a liberal faith that appeared at a unique moment of history and was unrelated to the Jewish tradition. Striving to show the originality of Jesus' teachings, Harnack denigrated the Pharisees and the Judaism they represented and committed lapses of scholarship singled out by the young Baeck.

Baeck's philosophy. Baeck's own masterpiece, *The Essence of Judaism* (1905), established him as the leading liberal Jewish theologian. In contrast to Harnack, Baeck stressed the dynamic nature of religion, the ongoing development that is man's response to the categorical "Ought," the Divine Imperative. The influence of the German-Jewish philosopher Hermann Cohen (1842–1918) and Neo-Kantianism (German philosophical movement, 1870–1920) is visible, but behind it stands the ethical rigorism of traditional rabbinic thought. The next edition of this work (1922), greatly expanded, moved on toward Baeck's "religion of polarity" with its dialectical movement between the "mystery" of the divine presence in life and the "commandment" of the ethical imperative that comes to man in his encounter with God. Baeck expressed the twofoldness of religious experience in the concept of *toladot* "generations," the chain of generations that is Jewish history and that made the Jewish people the vehicle of a continuous revelation that became that people's mission. "A light to the nations," it had to teach the revelation by living these teachings. Judaism was seen as the supreme expression of morality, a universal message expressed through the particular existence of Israel.

The dialogue between Christianity and Judaism was brought to greater clarity and intensity by Baeck's refusal to use evasions in his criticism. Traditional Jews disliked Baeck's early (1901) claim that Jesus was a profoundly Jewish figure and his view in *The Gospel as a Document of Jewish Religious History* (1938) that the Gospels belonged with the contemporary works of rabbinical literature. Christians, on the other hand, felt challenged by his definition of Judaism as the "classic" rational faith confronting a "romantic" Christianity of emotion, in his essay "Romantic Religion" (1922). The American philosopher Walter Kaufmann views this work as Baeck's greatest achievement next to *The Essence of Judaism.* Yet one cannot ignore Baeck's final work, written in the concentration camp, *This People Israel: The Meaning of Jewish Existence* (1955), which moves from the essence of an "ism" to the concrete existence of a people and creates an approach to Jewish life that must be set alongside the thought of the great 20th-century Jewish religious philosophers Martin Buber (1878–1965) and Franz Rosenzweig (1886–1929). Its full implications emerge only when the work is placed into the life of the author.

Role as Jewish leader. Baeck's life was his work, revealing his concept of polarity: an army chaplain in World War I, he became a pacifist; a non-Zionist, he became head of the German Keren Hayesod (Foundation Fund for Palestine land purchases). Baeck was the president of the German B'nai B'rith (Sons of the Covenant, the main Jewish fraternal and service organization); the chairman of the Rabbinical Association he had once defied; and taught Midrash (interpretative rabbinical literature) and homiletics at the Berlin Lehranstalt. He was called away from this to preside over the end of the 1,000-year-old German Jewish community.

In 1933 German Jewry's organizations united in the Reichsvertretung der Juden in Deutschland (National Agency of Jews in Germany) under Leo Baeck and Otto Hirsch (1885–1941), the jurist and community leader who was killed in the Mauthausen concentration camp. Under constant attack, this group took charge of Jewish life in Germany. Millions of dollars were spent annually in clearly defined fields: emigration, economic help, charity, education, and culture. Meanwhile, at the conference table with the Nazis, Baeck and the others battled for time so that lives could be saved. Later critics have felt that all resources should have been focussed on emigration; but the extermination camps were inconceivable to the German Jewish community of the 1930s. It planned to survive Hitler behind ghetto and prison walls—a tragic error of judgment but scarcely avoidable. Negotiating with Nazis always carried dangers of corruption, but Baeck was untouched by this. As late as 1939, he brought a trainload of children to England—and then returned to Germany. In both public and private, his life was a pattern of moral resistance that, after five arrests, brought Baeck to the Theresienstadt (Terezín) concentration camp.

Theresienstadt was a "model" camp, sometimes shown to outsiders. Its inmates were killed by neglect or illness or sent on to the extermination camps. Out of the 140,000 Jews sent to Theresienstadt less than 9,000 survived. The Nazis confused the death of a Rabbi Beck of Moravia with Leo Baeck; the latter became Number 187,894 and, incredibly, survived. Baeck set up classes inside the camp: more than 700 persons would press into a small barracks to listen to lectures on Plato and Kant. This, too, was a way of resistance. There were also Christian inmates whom Baeck served as pastor. Once more, the miasma of evil surrounded him but could not touch him. Critics have said that he was too aloof, or too liberal, but the only criticism to be taken seriously deals with Baeck's decision not to pass on rumours that the "resettlement" trains led to the death camps. The eminent Protestant theologian Paul Tillich (1886–1965), who admired Baeck, asserted that "Baeck should have spoken out . . . the full existential truth must always be made available." Baeck, however, thought the helpless victims should not be deprived of the hope keeping many alive.

On May 8, 1945, the day before Baeck was to be executed, the Russians liberated Theresienstadt, and Baeck stopped the inmates from killing the guards. He survived for a number of years, settling in England, and becoming a British subject; he taught and lectured in Britain and the United States, including a term at Hebrew Union College in Cincinnati, Ohio. His final writings, notably *Individuum Ineffabile* (1948) and *This People Israel*, continued to express hope in man and the human situation as the area of the revelation. In his life, Baeck summarized the greatness and perhaps also some of the flaws of German Jewry, which placed all of its hopes and commitments in western European civilization. In his teachings Baeck gave perhaps the clearest systematic exposition of liberal Jewish religious thought in the 20th century. (A.H.F.)

BIBLIOGRAPHY. Important works of Leo Baeck include: *Das Wesen des Judentums* (1905, 6th ed. 1932; Eng. trans., *The Essence of Judaism*, 1948), a classic text of modern Judaism; *The Phasees and Other Essays,* with an introduction by Krister Stendahl (Eng. trans. 1966), a text covering basic historical questions concerning Jewish life at the time of the emergence of Christianity; *Judaism and Christianity,* with an introduction by Walter Kaufmann (Eng. trans. 1958), a collection of the more polemical writings of Baeck clearly defining Judaism's disagreements with Christianity; and *Dieses Volk; Jüdische Existenz* (1955; Eng. trans. by A.H. Friedlander, *This People Israel,* 1966), Baeck's final work, covering 3,000 years of Jewish history. Full-length biographical studies include A.H. Friedlander, *Leo Baeck: Teacher of Theresienstadt* (1968), containing an exposition of Baeck's teachings and an extensive bibliography; and Leonard Baker, *Days of Sorrow and Pain: Leo Baeck and the Berlin Jews* (1978).

Baeda THE VENERABLE, SAINT: *see* Bede the Venerable, Saint.

Baedeker, Karl (b. Nov. 3, 1801, Essen, Duchy of Oldenburg—d. Oct. 4, 1859, Koblenz, Prussia), founder of a German publishing house known for its guidebooks.

Baedeker was the son of a printer and bookseller. In 1827 he started a firm at Koblenz and two years later brought out a guidebook to the town. It was in the second edition of a guide to the Rhine from Mainz to Cologne (which had appeared in 1828) that Baedeker evolved the system on which he based his series. His aim was to give the traveller the practical information necessary to enable him to dispense with paid guides. He checked the reliability of his publications by making incognito journeys and by consulting the best sources and experts. A notable feature of Baedeker's guides was the use of "stars" to indicate objects and views of special interest, as well as to designate reliable hotels. By the time of his death much of Europe had been covered by his guidebooks.

Karl Baedeker, oil painting by an unknown artist
Popperfoto

Under the ownership of his sons, Ernst (1833–61), Karl (1837–1911), and, especially, Fritz (1844–1925), the firm expanded still more. The first French edition appeared in 1846, and the first English one followed in 1861. The house moved to Leipzig in 1872, to Hamburg in 1948, and to Freiburg im Breisgau in 1956.

Consult the INDEX *first*

Baekeland, Leo Hendrik (b. Nov. 14, 1863, Ghent—d. Feb. 23, 1944, Beacon, N.Y., U.S.), U.S. industrial chemist who helped found the modern plastics industry through his invention of Bakelite, the first thermosetting plastic (a plastic that does not soften when heated).

Baekeland received his doctorate *maxima cum laude* from the University of Ghent at the age of 21 and taught there until 1889, when he went to the U.S. and joined a photographic firm. He soon set up his own company to manufacture his invention, Velox, a photographic paper that could be developed under artificial light. Velox was the first commercially successful photographic paper. In 1899 Baekeland sold his company and rights to the paper to the U.S. inventor George Eastman for $1,000,000.

Baekeland's search, begun in 1905, for a synthetic substitute for shellac led to the discovery of Bakelite, a condensation product of formaldehyde and phenol that is produced at high temperature and pressure. Though the material had been reported earlier, Baekeland was the first to find a method of forming it into the thermosetting plastic. Baekeland received many honours for his invention and served as president of the American Chemical Society in 1924.

bael fruit: *see* bel fruit.

Baer, Karl Ernst, Ritter von (knight of), EDLER (lord) VON HUTHORN (b. Feb. 29, 1792, Piep, Estonia, Russian Empire—d. Nov. 28, 1876, Dorpat, Estonia), Prussian–Estonian embryologist who discovered the mammalian ovum and the notochord and established the new science of comparative embryology alongside comparative anatomy. He was also a pioneer in geography, ethnology, and physical anthropology.

Baer, one of 10 children, spent his childhood with an uncle and aunt before he returned at the age of seven to his own family. His parents, of Prussian descent, were first cousins. After private tutoring Baer spent three years at a school for members of the nobility. In

1810 he entered the university at Dorpat to study medicine, receiving his medical degree in 1814.

Dissatisfied with his medical training, Baer studied in Germany and Austria from 1814 to 1817. The crucial year of his education was the academic year 1815–16, when his training in comparative anatomy at the University of Würzburg with Ignaz Döllinger introduced him to a new world that included the study of embryology.

In 1817 Baer began his teaching in Königsberg, where he remained until 1834. In 1820 he married Auguste von Medem of Königsberg, by whom he had six children. Although Döllinger had suggested that Baer begin a study of chick development, he was unable to meet the expense of purchasing the eggs and paying an attendant to watch the incubators. This work was done instead by Baer's more affluent friend Christian Pander, who in 1817 described the early development of the chick in terms of what are now known as the primary germ layers—that is, ectoderm, mesoderm, and endoderm.

From 1819 to 1834 Baer devoted most of his time to embryology, extending Pander's concept of germ-layer formation to all vertebrates. In so doing Baer laid the foundation for comparative embryology. He made many important technical discoveries. In 1827 he described his discovery of the mammalian ovum (egg) in his *De Ovi Mammalium et Hominis Genesi* ("On the Mammalian Egg and the Origin of Man"), thereby establishing that mammals, including human beings, develop from eggs. He opposed the popular idea that embryos of one species pass through stages comparable to adults of other species. Instead, he emphasized that embryos of one species could resemble embryos, but not adults of another, and that the younger the embryo the greater the resemblance. This was in line with his epigenetic idea—basic to embryology ever since—that development proceeds from simple to complex, from homogeneous to heterogeneous.

One of the most important books in embryology is Baer's *Über Entwickelungsgeschichte der Thiere* (vol. 1, 1828; vol. 2, 1837; "On the Development of Animals"), in which he surveyed all existing knowledge on vertebrate development and from which he derived his far-reaching conclusions. He identified the neural folds as precursors of the nervous system, discovered the notochord, described the five primary brain vesicles, and studied the functions of the extra-embryonic membranes. This pioneering work established embryology as a distinct subject of research, at least in its descriptive aspects. He marked out the main lines of descriptive and comparative study that had to be accomplished before the modern approach—the causal analysis of development—could emerge.

In 1834 Baer moved to St. Petersburg, Russia, where he became a full member of the Academy of Sciences; he had been a corresponding member since 1826. His first duties were as librarian of the foreign division, but he eventually served the Academy in a variety of administrative positions. He retired from active membership in 1862 but continued to work as an honorary member until 1867. After moving to Russia, Baer abandoned embryology. Particularly interested in the Russian north, he became a courageous explorer there; he was the first naturalist to collect specimens from Novaya Zemlya, which was then uninhabited. During his extensive travels throughout Russia, Baer developed a great scientific and practical interest in its fisheries. He made significant discoveries in geography, including one concerning the nature of the forces responsible for the configuration of riverbanks in Russia.

Baer's travels also increased his long-standing interest in ethnography. He contributed to the Academy at St. Petersburg by establishing an extensive skull collection. As a result of his interest in skull measurements, he called a

Karl Ernst, Ritter von Baer, detail of a lithograph by Rudolf Hoffmann, 1859, after a photograph

By courtesy of the Hunt Botanical Library, Carnegie-Mellon University, Pittsburgh

meeting of craniologists in Germany in 1861, which led to the establishment of the German Anthropological Society and to the founding of the journal *Archiv für Anthropologie.* He was responsible also for the founding of the Russian Geographical Society and the Russian Entomological Society, of which he was the first president.

In his early days as an embryologist Baer had begun to consider possible relationships, in terms of kinship, between animals. In 1859, the year that Darwin's *Origin of Species* appeared, Baer published a work on human skulls suggesting that stocks now distinct might have originated from one form; the ideas of the two men were formulated completely independently. Baer, however, was no strong adherent to the doctrine of transformation (the pre-Darwinian term for evolution). Although he believed that some very similar animals, such as goats and antelopes, might be related, he was vehemently against the concept expressed in the *Origin of Species* that all living creatures might have evolved from one or a few common ancestors.

In his philosophical writings—and all his embryological writings were philosophical to some degree—Baer saw nature as a whole, even though not in terms of modern evolutionary theory. He viewed the development of organisms and of the cosmos in the same light, and his all-encompassing view of the universe brought together what might otherwise have seemed diverging threads in his thought.

(J.M.O.)

BIBLIOGRAPHY. Baer's autobiography is *Nachrichten über Leben und Schriften,* 2nd ed. (1886). Two biographies in German (there are none in English), both entitled *Karl Ernst von Baer,* are by L. Stieda, 2nd ed. (1886); and by B.E. Raikov (1968), both with extensive bibliographies. Baer's *Entwickelungsgeschichte der Thiere, Beobachtung und Reflexion,* 2 vol. (1828–37), embodies his major discoveries and concepts in embryology; see also Jane Oppenheimer, "Baer, Karl Ernst von," in the *Dictionary of Scientific Biography,* vol. 1 (1970), for an analysis of his scientific contributions.

Baer, Max, byname of MAXIMILIAN ADELBERT BAER (b. Feb. 11, 1909, Omaha, Neb., U.S.—d. Nov. 21, 1959, Hollywood), professional boxer who won the world's heavyweight championship by knocking out Primo Carnera in 11 rounds in New York City on June 14, 1934. He lost the title to James J. Braddock on a 15-round decision at Long Island City, N.Y., on June 13, 1935.

Perhaps Baer's finest performance was a 10-round knockout of former heavyweight champion Max Schmeling on June 8, 1933. During Baer's boxing career (1929–41) he won 65 of 79 fights, 50 of them by knockouts, and was considered one of the hardest right-hand punchers in boxing history. After his retirement he appeared in films and on television.

Baerle-Duc (Belgium): *see* Baarle-Hertog.

Bærum, *herredskommune* (rural municipality), southeastern Norway, in Akershus *fylke* (county), at the head of Oslofjorden. It adjoins the national capital of Oslo on the west. Although officially classified as rural, Bærum is an agglomeration of populated places, which, taken as a unit, constitute the largest suburban *herredskommune* of Oslo. It has a broad frontage on Oslofjorden and also extends inland for several miles.

Important settlements within Bærum are Lysaker, a small coastal port with paper- and wood-products factories, and Sandvika, a commercial centre. There are fine beaches and residential sections, as well as many summer villas of Oslo residents. Fornebu, Oslo's international airport, is also in Bærum. Pop. (1983 est.) 80,947.

Baetic Cordillera (Spain): *see* Penibético Mountain System.

baetylus, also spelled BAETULUS, in Greek religion, a sacred stone or pillar; the word is of Semitic origin (*-bethel*). Numerous holy, or fetish, stones existed in antiquity, generally attached to the cult of some particular god and looked upon as his abiding place or symbol. The most famous example is the holy stone at Delphi, the omphalos ("navel"), that reposed in the Temple of Apollo and marked the exact centre of the universe. A second stone at Delphi was said to have been the one that the Titan Cronus swallowed; it was thought to be Zeus himself in his symbolic, or baetylic, form.

"Omphalos" (Greek: "navel") at Delphi, marble sculpture; in the Archaeological Museum, Delphi, Greece

Alinari—Art Resource/EB Inc.

Sometimes the stones were made into a more regular shape by forming them into pillars or into groups of three pillars. Such columns were sometimes placed before a shrine; others were used as mileposts and often shaped into human form. The baetylus became the parent form for altars and iconic statuary.

Baeyer, (Johann Friedrich Wilhelm) Adolph von (b. Oct. 31, 1835, Berlin—d. Aug. 20, 1917, Starnberg, near Munich), organic research chemist who synthesized indigo

(1880) and formulated its structure (1883). He was awarded the Nobel Prize for Chemistry in 1905. Notable among his many achievements

Baeyer, 1905
Historia-Photo

were the discovery of the phthalein dyes and his investigations of uric acid derivatives, polyacetylenes, and oxonium salts. He proposed a "strain" (*Spannung*) theory concerning the stability of certain cyclic organic compounds, as well as a centric formula for benzene.

Baeyer studied with Robert Bunsen, but August Kekule exercised a greater influence on his development. He took his Ph.D. at Berlin (1858), became a lecturer (*Privatdozent*) in 1860, and headed the chemistry laboratory at the Berlin *Gewerbeinstitut* until 1872. After holding a professorship at Strasbourg, he succeeded Justus von Liebig as chemistry professor at Munich (1875), where he stressed research. In 1881 the Royal Society of London awarded him the Davy medal for his work with indigo. To celebrate his 70th birthday a collection of his scientific papers was published in 1905.

Báez, Buenaventura (b. 1810, Azua de Compostela, Hispaniola—d. 1884, Puerto Rico), politician who served five terms as president of the Dominican Republic and is noted principally for his attempts to have the United States annex his country.

Báez was a member of a wealthy and prominent family in the Dominican Republic. He was educated in Europe and began his political career in 1843 by helping lead the revolt that established the independence of the Dominican Republic from Haiti, with which it shares the island of Hispaniola. At this time, Báez believed that his nation could maintain its independence only by becoming a French protectorate, and to secure that end he was sent to Europe in 1846; the French, however, were not interested.

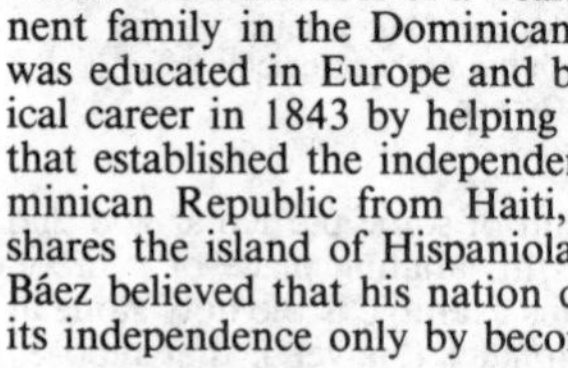

Báez, engraving
By courtesy of the Library of Congress, Washington, D.C.

Báez served his first term as president in 1849–53, and in 1850 he tried unsuccessfully to have his country annexed by the United States. His second term (1856–58) ended when his government was overthrown by a coup d'état because of his involvement in corrupt financial transactions. He then invited Spain to occupy the Dominican Republic, and in return he was exiled to a comfortable life in Europe, financed by the Spaniards. When Spain abandoned the Dominican Republic in 1865, Báez returned to begin a third presidential term, but in May 1866 he was removed by another coup. In 1868 he was again made president, this time determined to gain annexation by the United States. He even succeeded in persuading the U.S. to send warships, ostensibly to protect his country from Haiti; in reality he sought to protect his own business interests. The warships were soon removed, however, and in 1874 Báez again was forced to leave office. He served his last term in 1876–78 and was then exiled permanently to Puerto Rico.

Báez has been described as a thoroughly corrupt tyrant who had no regard for either the lives or the property of his people.

Baez, Joan (b. Jan. 9, 1941, Staten Island, New York City), U.S. folk singer and political activist, who interested large, young audiences in folk music during the 1960s.

The daughter of a physicist whose teaching and research took him to various communities in New York, California, and elsewhere, Baez moved often and acquired little formal musical training. Her soprano voice, usually accompanied only by her own guitar arrangements, was sometimes criticized as too pretty. However, she was in the forefront of the 1960s folk song revival, popularizing traditional songs through her performances in coffeehouses, at music festivals, and on television and through her record albums, which were best-sellers from 1960 through 1964 and remained popular into the 1970s.

An active participant in the 1960s protest movement, Baez made free concert appearances for UNESCO, civil rights organizations, and anti-Vietnam war rallies. In 1964 she refused to pay federal taxes that went toward war expenses, and she was jailed in October and December 1967. Her autobiography, *Daybreak,* was published in 1968.

Bafatá, region, north central Guinea-Bissau, West Africa, bordered by Senegal on the north, and by the regions of Gabú on the east, Oio on the west, and Quinará and Tombali on the south. It has an area of 2,266 sq mi (5,810 sq km). The Rio Gêba flows east–west through the northern half of the region and empties into the Atlantic Ocean; it is navigable to Bafatá town, the regional capital. The Rio Corubal flows east–west forming the southern border with Quinará and Tombali regions and empties into the Rio Gêba; it is navigable throughout the Bafatá region. The Planalto (Plateau) de Bafatá, rising to about 500 ft (150 m) above sea level, is located in central Bafatá between the Rio Gêba and the Rio Corubal. The northern and southern parts of the region contain timber resources, which have potential as export products. Peanuts (groundnuts) are intensively cultivated around Bafatá town and are grown in the north all the way to the Senegal border. In the northern savanna-covered part of the region, cattle, sheep, and goats are raised. Subsistence agricultural crops include millet, rice, sorghum, and corn (maize). Near Bafatá town is a major agricultural development project, and the cultivation of cotton was introduced to the area surrounding Gêba town in central Bafatá region in the early 1980s. Gold in small quantities is found near Taibatà town in the southwest. From Bafatà town, roads run north to Senegal, east to Gabú, west to Mansabá, and south to Bambadinca. The Fulani peoples are the dominant ethnic group, and the Balante and Malinke constitute most of the remainder. Pop. (1979) 117,202.

Bafatá, town, capital of Bafatá region, Guinea-Bissau, West Africa, on the Rio Gêba, which is navigable to this point. Bafatá is an important trading centre for the interior regions of Guinea-Bissau. There also is intensive agriculture around the town. It produces peanuts (groundnuts) for export and livestock for domestic consumption. Roads connect the town with Senegal to the north and the towns of Gabú (east), Mansabá (west), and Bambadinca (south). Pop. (1979) 13,429.

Baffin, William (b. *c.* 1584, London?—d. Jan. 23, 1622, Persian Gulf, off the island of Qeshm), navigator who searched for the Northwest Passage and gave his name to Baffin Island, now part of the Northwest Territories, Canada, and to the bay separating it from Greenland. His determination of longitude at sea by observation of the Moon is said to have been the first of its kind on record.

The earliest mention of Baffin (1612) was as a member of Capt. James Hall's expedition in search of the Northwest Passage. Aboard the "Discovery" with Capt. Robert Bylot (1615), he explored Hudson Strait, which separates Canada from Baffin Island. In 1616 Baffin again sailed as pilot of the "Discovery" and penetrated the bay some 300 miles (483 kilometres) farther than the English navigator John Davis had sailed in 1587. In honour of the patrons of his voyages, he named Lancaster, Smith, and Jones sounds, the straits radiating from the head of the bay. There seemed to be no hope, however, of discovering a passage to India by that route.

Next, in service to the East India Company, he made surveys of the Red Sea and the Persian Gulf. In 1622, during his final voyage to the Gulf, he was killed in an Anglo-Persian attack on Qeshm.

Baffin Bay, arm of the North Atlantic Ocean with an area of 266,000 sq mi (689,000 sq km), extending southward from the Arctic for 900 mi (1,450 km) between the Greenland coast (east) and Baffin Island (west) with a width varying between 70 and 400 mi. Davis Strait (south) leads to the Atlantic, whereas Nares Strait (north) leads to the Arctic Ocean. A pit at its centre, the Baffin Hollow, plunges to a depth of 7,000 ft (2,100 m), and the bay, although little exploited by man because of its hostile environment, is of considerable interest to geologists studying the evolution of the North American continent.

The first European visitor of the bay was Robert Bylot, an English sea captain, in May 1615, but his supposedly mutinous tendencies prevented his name from being given to the entity, and the honour went instead to his lieutenant, William Baffin. Even the latter's discoveries came to be doubted until the later explorations of Capt. (later Sir) John Ross, in 1818. The first scientific investigations since Bylot's mapping of the shores were conducted in 1928 by a Danish and also by an American expedition, followed by another, more extensive, survey in the 1930s. Patrol vessels, now aided by aircraft, have long investigated ice distribution in the region, and after World War II a Canadian expedition undertook complex investigations.

Baffin Bay's oval floor is fringed by the submarine shelves of Greenland and Canada and by ledges at the mouths of sounds. Apart from the central pit, depths range from 800 ft in the north to 2,300 ft in the south. The bottom sediments are mostly terrigenous (originating on land) and include gray-brown homogeneous silts, pebbles, and boulders. Gravel lies everywhere.

The climate is severe, especially in winter, when northeast winds blow off Baffin Island (in the south) and in the bay's northern sector. Northwesterly and southwesterly winds predominate in summer. Easterlies blow off the Greenland coast, and storms are frequent, notably in the winter. January temperatures average −4° F (−20° C) in the south and −18° F (−28° C) farther north, but the warm, dry foehn winds that sweep down from the valleys containing Greenland's glaciers occasionally cause winter thaws. In July the temperature on the shores averages 45° F (7° C), with some snow. Overall, the annual precipitation off Greenland amounts to 4–10 in. (100–250 mm), reaching twice this amount off Baffin Island.

Icebergs are dense even in August: the ice cover is formed from Arctic pack ice entering through the northern sounds, from local sea ice, and from icebergs that have broken off adjacent glaciers. By late October icefields reach Hudson Strait (between Baffin Island and the Quebec mainland), a region where coastal ice has already been thickening, mostly near Greenland, where prevailing easterly winds make for sheltered conditions. The centre of Baffin Bay is covered with compounded ice in winter, but in the north there is actually a permanent ice-free area (the "northern water") that may be related to the warming effect of the West Greenland Current.

The salinity of Arctic waters flowing into Baffin Bay ranges from 30.0 to 32.7 parts per thousand (‰), and their temperature warms up to 41° F (5° C) on the surface in summer, cooling in winter to 29° F (−2° C). The layers 1,300–2,000 ft deep reach 34° F (1° C) and a salinity of 34.5‰. Below 3,300 ft in the central regions, the water—probably Atlantic in origin—reaches 31° F (−0.5° C) and has a salinity of 34.4‰.

Tides are an important and interesting feature. Near Baffin Island and the shores of Greenland the tidal range is about 13 ft, reaching as much as 30 ft where the water is forced through narrow passages. The tidal rate varies between 0.6 and 2.3 mph and the direction of the tides varies by as much as 180°. This phenomenon produces unequal pressure on the fields of floating ice and results in the churning together and crushing of fresh, old, and pack ice.

The dissolution of salts in the water and the warming effect of southerly currents make Baffin Bay a haven for myriad life-forms. The numerous single-cell algae nourish small invertebrates, notably euphausiids (an order of small, shrimplike crustaceans), and these in turn are food for larger invertebrates, fish, birds, and mammals. Baffin Bay contains Arctic flounder, four-horned sculpin (a spiny, large-headed, broad-mouthed fish), polar cod, and capelin (a small fish of the smelt family). Migrant fish from Atlantic waters include cod, haddock, herring, halibut, and grenadier (a tapering-bodied, soft-finned fish). Wildlife also includes ringed seals, bearded seals, harp seals, and—in the north—walrus, dolphins, and whales (including killer whales). Coastal birds include gulls, ducks, geese, eiders, snowy owls, snow buntings (a type of finch), ravens, gyrfalcons, linnets, and sea eagles.

Plant cover, too, is remarkably varied, with about 400 types represented. Shrubs include birch, willow, and alder, and also halophytic plants (*i.e.,* those adapted to salty soils), as well as lyme (or tussock) grass, mosses, and lichens. These provide food for rodents and the splendid caribou of the area. Polar bears and Arctic foxes also abound. Large-scale fishing remains undeveloped because of the perils of the heavy ice cover, but local residents—who are mainly Eskimos—carry on some fishing and hunting, often with traditional methods.

Baffin Island, island, between Greenland (north), from which it is separated by Baffin Bay, and the Labrador-Ungava (Canadian) mainland (southward across the Hudson Strait). It is administered as part of Baffin Region in Franklin District, Northwest Territories, Canada. The Arctic island, believed to have been visited by Norse explorers in the 11th century and sighted by Sir Martin Frobisher during his search for a Northwest Passage (1576–78), was named after William Baffin, a 17th-century English navigator. A glacier-laden mountainous backbone with peaks up to 6,750 ft (2,057 m) in height extends throughout most of its 950-mi (1,500-km) length. The island, 195,928 sq mi (507,451 sq km) in area and indented by numerous fjords, is uninhabited except for a few small coastal settlements, including Frobisher Bay (*q.v.*). In 1972 Auyuittuq National Park (8,290 sq mi) was created on the Cumberland Peninsula (east coast) to preserve an Arctic wilderness of jagged mountain peaks, deep valleys, spectacular fjords, and marine coastal wildlife. Iron ore deposits have been found in the north, and Nanisvik at its northwestern tip is the site of the world's northernmost mining activity (silver, lead, zinc).

Baffin Island Current, also called BAFFIN CURRENT, surface oceanic current, a southward-moving water outflow along the west side of Baffin Bay, Canada. The Baffin Island Current, flowing at a rate of about 11 mi (17 km) per day, is a combination of West Greenland Current inflow and the outflow of cold Arctic Ocean water from the channels of the Canadian Arctic Archipelago.

Bafing River, river in West Africa, rising in the Fouta Djallon massif of Guinea and flowing generally northeast for about 200 mi (320 km). After passing the town of Bafing Makana in Mali, its only important riparian settlement, it curves around to flow approximately north-northwest, to form the Sénégal River at its confluence with the Bakoye River just south of Bafoulabé, Mali. It is approximately 350 mi long and unnavigable. It courses down from the massif via the intermediate sandstone Monts (hills) Mandingues to the Sénégal River Valley.

Bafoussam, capital of West province and of Mifi department, Cameroon, west central Africa, north-northeast of Douala. A trading centre of the Bamiléké peoples, it lies in a densely populated region where coffee, kola nuts, tobacco, tea, cinchona (from which quinine is made) and are grown and pigs and poultry are raised. The town has a trade school, coffee-processing plants, wood and construction industries, a hospital, and an airfield. Pop. (1981) 75,832.

Baga, people who inhabit the swampy coastal region between Cap Verga and Conakry in Guinea. They speak a language of the West Atlantic branch of the Niger-Congo family.

The women cultivate rice; the men fish and tend palm and kola trees. Some Baga are employed as wage labourers in the bauxite mines of the Los Islands off Conakry. Houses are typically cylindrical mud structures with thatched-straw roofs, grouped in compounds that may adjoin to form small villages. There is little formal political organization, authority traditionally having been wielded by petty paramount chiefs.

Although most Baga are Muslim, it is thought that some remote groups along the Rio Nunez and Rio Pongo have remained animist. The dead are exposed, before burial, in a sacred grove; their houses and certain possessions are burned.

Bagamoyo, town, historic seaport of eastern Tanzania, East Africa, on the Zanzibar Channel, 45 mi (75 km) northwest of Dar es-Salaam. The town was formerly a slave-trading depot at the terminus of Arab caravan routes from Ujiji on Lake Tanganyika. The town also served as the first capital of the German East Africa Company (1887–91). Pop. (1978) 16,272.

Baganda (people): *see* Ganda.

bagasse, also called MEGASS, fibre remaining after the extraction of the sugar-bearing juice from sugarcane. The word bagasse, from the French *bagage* via the Spanish *bagazo,* originally meant "rubbish," "refuse," or "trash." Applied first to the husks of olives, palm nuts, and grapes after pressing, use of the word was extended to mean residues from other processed plant materials such as sisal, sugarcane, and sugar beets. In modern use, the word is limited to the end product of the sugarcane mill.

Bagasse may be used as fuel in the sugarcane mill or as a source of cellulose for manufacturing animal feeds. Paper is produced from bagasse in several Latin-American countries, in the Middle East, and in all sugar-producing countries that are deficient in forest resources. Bagasse is the essential ingredient for production of pressed building board, acoustical tile, and other construction materials.

bagatelle, game, probably of English origin, variations being the cannon game, Mississippi, and sans égal, similar to billiards and probably a modification of it. It is played on an oblong board or table varying in size from 6 by 1½ feet (183 by 46 centimetres) to 10 by 3 feet, with nine numbered cups at its head, eight arranged in a circle and the ninth in its centre.

Billiard cues and nine balls—one black, four red, and four white—are used. The black ball is placed upon a spot about 9 inches (23 centimetres) in front of hole number one. A line (the balk) is drawn across the board, from behind which the players shoot. Any number may play. Each player in turn plays all eight balls up the table, no score being allowed until a ball has touched the black ball. The object of the game is to play as many balls as possible into the holes, the black ball counting double. The game is decided by the aggregate score made in an agreed number of rounds.

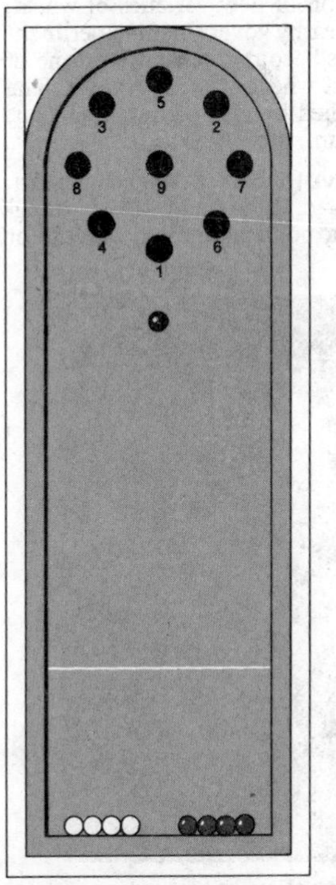

Bagatelle board; the game is played with billiard cues and nine balls

By courtesy of Messrs. Thurston and Co., Ltd.

Sans égal is a French form of the game. Two players take part, one using the red and one the white balls. The leader plays at the black, forfeiting a ball if he misses. His opponent then plays at the black if it has not been touched, otherwise any way he likes. They then play alternately, the object being to hole the black and the player's own balls. If a player holes one of his opponent's balls, it is scored for his opponent.

The cannon game, as in billiards, requires three balls—a cue ball and two object balls, one black and one white. The object of the game is to make cannons (caroms), in which the cue ball strikes both object balls. Balls played into holes at the same time count the number of the holes, but, if a ball falls into a hole during a play in which no cannon is made, the score counts for the adversary. A cannon counts two; missing the white object ball scores one to the adversary; missing the black, five to the adversary.

Mississippi is played with a bridge pierced with nine or more arches, according to the size of the table, the arches being numbered from one upward. All nine balls are usually played, though the black is sometimes omitted, each player having a round, the object being to send the balls through the arches. This may not be done directly, as the balls must strike a cushion first. A ball, lying in front of the bridge, may be sent through by the cue ball if the latter has struck a cushion. If a ball falls into a cup, the striker scores the value of the cup as well as of the arch.

Bagdad (Iraq): *see* Baghdad.

Bagé, city, south central Rio Grande do Sul state, Brazil, lying at 732 ft (223 m) above sea level amid gently rolling hills covered with tall prairie grass. It was founded in 1811 and given city status in 1859. Located southwest of Pôrto Alegre, the state capital, and 25 mi (40 km) north of the Uruguayan border, Bagé has long had military importance. In 1825 and 1827 it was occupied by Uruguayan and Argentinian forces. The surrounding country is used chiefly for cattle and sheep ranching, and the city is a meat-packing centre and wool depot. With the adoption of new varieties of wheat, developed at a nearby government experiment station, Bagé has become the centre of one of the state's largest wheat-growing regions. The city can be reached by rail, highway, and air. Pop. (1980 prelim.) 66,743.

Bagehot, Walter (b. Feb. 3, 1826, Langport, Somerset, Eng.—d. March 24, 1877, Langport), economist, political analyst, and editor of *The Economist,* who was one of the most influential journalists of the mid-Victorian period.

Bagehot, mezzotint by Norman Hirst, after a photograph

By courtesy of the trustees of the British Museum; photograph, J.R. Freeman & Co. Ltd.

Bagehot's father's family had been general merchants for several generations, whereas his mother—who was a great beauty but was 10 years older than his father and had had a tragic first marriage—was a sister of Vincent Stuckey, the head of the largest bank in the west of England. It was the opinion of his relations that his acute political sense derived from his father, whereas the sparkle and originality of his mind came from his mother, even though she became partly insane as she grew older.

Bagehot had the severe schooling of an early Victorian. As a child he went to Langport Grammar School, which had a famous headmaster who had been a friend of the poet Wordsworth; at 13 he was sent to Bristol College, one of the best schools in Great Britain. There he received a grounding in philosophy, mathematics, literature, the classics, and the new natural sciences, of an intensity that no English child today would be thought capable of assimilating.

The obvious university to choose was University College, London, because his father was a Unitarian, and Oxford and Cambridge in those days were dogmatically Anglican. He was a "lanky youth, rather thin and long in the legs with a countenance of remarkable vivacity and characterised by the large eyes that were always noticeable," wrote Sir Edward Fry, one of his friends at Bristol. He had a rather sardonic manner that did not endear him to all of his contemporaries, but he did make a number of lasting friends at University College, notably Richard Holt Hutton, who was for the latter part of the century the distinguished editor of *The Spectator;* William Roscoe, the grandson of the famous historian of the Medicis; Arthur Hugh Clough, the poet; and, of an older generation, Henry Crabb Robinson, who had been the friend of Goethe, Schiller, and Coleridge, and *The Times* correspondent in the Napoleonic Wars. In 1846 Bagehot took his bachelor's degree with first-class honours, despite bad health, and in 1848 his master's degree with the university's gold medal in moral and intellectual philosophy.

For three years after graduation, he studied at the bar, but he never liked it, and it was chance that took him into literature. He happened to be in Paris at the end of 1851, when Louis Napoleon's coup d'etat took place, and he wrote a series of articles in the leading Unitarian weekly journal of the day describing the coup at firsthand and defending Napoleon. These articles caused much controversy because the coup was widely disapproved of in England. But they convinced Bagehot that he could write, and he settled down to work in his uncle Stuckey's bank, writing in the next six or seven years a series of literary essays on Milton, Shakespeare, Gibbon, Sir Walter Scott, Pierre-Jean de Béranger, together with studies of leading political figures of the past century—Henry St. John Bolingbroke, William Pitt, Sir Robert Peel, and others—that are still widely quoted.

His entry into professional journalism was also accidental. In his role as a banker, he had written various economic articles that had attracted the attention of James Wilson, the man who had founded *The Economist* in 1843 and who was then an influential member of Parliament and financial secretary to the treasury in Lord Palmerston's government. Wilson asked Bagehot to stay, and he immediately fell in love with Eliza, the eldest of Wilson's six daughters. They were married in April 1858, but they had no children, and it is doubtful if Eliza's rather cold personality really suited the warmth and vigour of her husband's.

He went back to manage the Bristol branch of Stuckey's bank. But a year later Wilson was asked to go to India to reorganize the finances of the Indian government, and he died in Calcutta in 1860, leaving Bagehot in charge of *The Economist.* For 17 years he wrote the main article and improved and expanded the statistical and financial sections that have made it the leading business journal and one of the leading political journals of the world for more than 100 years. More than that, he humanized its political approach with a greater emphasis on social problems. As the American political scientist Walt Rostow has commented, "*The Economist* was not simply the hard bitten advocate of the mid-Victorian capitalist."

Bagehot described himself as a conservative Liberal or "between size in politics." Unlike many Liberals, he had grown up in the deep countryside, and he had a strong feeling for the social problems that rapid industrialization and urbanization were creating in Britain. He was also an acute observer of international affairs, with an instinctive affection for France and an equal distrust of Otto von Bismarck's Germany. His early years at *The Economist* coincided with the American Civil War, on whose development he wrote nearly 20 articles; instinctively, he was a Confederate like many of his British contemporaries, but his reason made him a supporter of Abraham Lincoln, of whom he wrote on the day the news of his assassination reached England:

> We do not know in history such an example of the growth of a ruler in wisdom as was exhibited by Mr. Lincoln. Power and responsibility visibly widened his mind and elevated his character. Difficulties, instead of irritating him as they do most men, only increased his reliance on patience; opposition, instead of ulcerating, only made him more tolerant and determined.

In 1867 he published *The English Constitution,* which was an attempt to look behind the facade of the British system of government—crown, Lords, and Commons—in order to see how it really operated and where true power lay. He was one of the first to observe the overriding power of the Cabinet in a party that commanded an effective majority in the House of Commons. He cultivated a number of close political friendships, notably with William Ewart Gladstone, who became the first Liberal prime minister in 1868; with Lord Carnarvon among the Conservatives (the author of the British North America Act, the constitution of Canada); and with William Edward Forster (the author of the first public education act in Britain).

Bagehot never succeeded, however, in entering politics himself. He tried at Manchester, at Bridgwater near his Somerset home (a district that had a notorious reputation for corruption), and in 1867 for London University. But he was a poor speaker and failed each time.

In 1872 Bagehot published *Physics and Politics,* which was an attempt to apply the new discoveries in anthropology to the development of societies and nations themselves. It is largely forgotten by reason of the vigour acquired by sociological investigation in the 20th century, largely under the stimulus of Karl Marx and Max Weber. But one of its central points, the process of unconscious imitation as a molding force in the development of nations—what Bagehot called "the cake of custom"—had a considerable influence on such philosophical sociologists as William James and Graham Wallas.

All this time, Bagehot and his wife were living in London, and he was editing a weekly of growing influence. In his 40s, he became increasingly frail, and such energy as he had was concentrated on professional economic studies. In 1873 he published *Lombard Street,* which, though really a tract arguing for a larger central reserve in the hands of the Bank of England, in fact contains the germ of the modern theory of central banking and exchange control. He was working on a major series of economic studies when pneumonia struck him down at the age of 51. The economist John Maynard Keynes, two generations later, paid tribute to his insight into business psychology.

But the greatest tribute to Bagehot's lively style, humanity, and insight is that his books have been read, republished, and subjected to a continuous stream of critical essays ever since his death. He once made fun of Thomas Macaulay for seeking posthumous fame but has, nevertheless, received a good measure of it himself.

Walter Bagehot has been described as Victorian England's most versatile genius. He wrote a series of literary essays that have been continually republished throughout the 20th century, a book on British politics that remains a widely read classic, and one of the earliest sociological studies to apply the concept of evolution to societies themselves; in addition, he made an important contribution to the theory of central banking. "Had I command of the culture of men," wrote U.S. president Woodrow Wilson, "I should wish to raise up for the instruction and stimulation of my nation more than one sane, sagacious, critic of men and affairs like Walter Bagehot." "Those who have the good fortune to know him still remember him as perhaps the most original mind of his generation," wrote Lord Bryce, British ambassador in Washington and the author of *The American Commonwealth.*

(A.F.B.)

BIBLIOGRAPHY. *Biographies.* Emilie I. Barrington (ed.), *The Love-Letters of Walter Bagehot and Eliza Wilson, Written from 10 November, 1857 to 23 April, 1858* (1933); Alastair Buchan, *The Spare Chancellor: The Life of Walter Bagehot* (1959), a short, critical biography dealing with all aspects of Bagehot's life, work, and thought; Norman St. John-Stevas, *Walter Bagehot* (1959), a selection of Bagehot's political studies with a biographical introduction and a useful bibliography.

Collected works. Emilie I. Barrington (ed.), *The Works and Life of Walter Bagehot,* 10 vol. (1915), series containing his books, most of his essays, and more than 50 of his *Economist* articles; *The Collected Works of Walter Bagehot,* ed. by Norman St. John-Stevas (1966–68), a more comprehensive edition containing considerably more journalistic material. Vol. 1 and 2, *The Literary Essays,* with an introduction by Sir William Haley, and vol. 3 and 4, *The Historical Essays,* with an introduction by Jacques Barzun.

Critical works. John Maynard Keynes, "The Works of Bagehot," *Economic Journal,* 25:369–375 (1915), an estimate of Bagehot as an economic writer by the greatest economist of his day; Sir Herbert E. Read, "Bagehot," in *The Sense of Glory: Essays in Criticism* (1929), a sensitive critique of Bagehot as a litterateur; Woodrow Wilson, "A Wit and a Seer," *Atlantic Monthly,* 82:527–540 (1898), one of the earliest works drawing attention to Bagehot's gifts and versatility by one of his greatest American admirers; George M. Young, "The Greatest Victorian," in *Today and Yesterday: Collected Essays and Addresses* (1948), an excellent brief portrait.

Baggara (people): *see* Baqqārah.

Baggesen, Jens (Immanuel) (b. Feb. 15, 1764, Korsør, Den.—d. Oct. 3, 1826, Hamburg), leading Danish literary figure in the transitional period between Neoclassicism and Romanticism.

In 1782 he went to Copenhagen to study theology. Three years later he had an unprecedented success in Denmark with his first poems, *Comiske fortællinger* (1785; "Comical Tales"). Later, after his libretto to the first Danish opera, *Holger Danske,* received adverse criticism, mainly because of its supposed lack of nationalism, Baggesen travelled through Germany, Switzerland, and France. The journey became the basis of his most important book, the imaginative prose work *Labyrinten* (1792–93; "The Labyrinth"), a "sentimental journey" reminiscent of the 18th-century English novelist Laurence Sterne's work. Baggesen was variously a Germanophile, a great admirer of Jean-Jacques Rousseau, an ardent supporter of the French Revolution, a disciple of Kant, and a Romanticist and early admirer of Denmark's foremost Romantic poet, Adam Oehlenschläger. Late in life he vigorously opposed Romanticism, carrying on a seven-year feud with Oehlenschläger.

Baggesen, engraving by Gilles-Louis Chrétien

By courtesy of the Royal Danish Ministry for Foreign Affairs, Copenhagen

Baghdād, also spelled BAGDAD, *muḥāfaẓah* (governorate), central Iraq. Its capital, Baghdad, is the national capital. The *muḥāfaẓah,* 1,988 sq mi (5,150 sq km) in area, comprises flat floodplain on both sides of the Tigris River and on part of the eastern bank of the Euphrates River. Much of the land is irrigated; dates, fruit, millet, and sesame are grown, and livestock raising is important. The area around Baghdad has been the location for many ancient capital cities, all of them built on new sites. Sargon of Akkad built the first, his capital Agade, in the mid-3rd millennium BC. It is presumed to lie within the environs of modern Baghdad. Seleucia on the Tigris was built by Seleucus I as his eastern capital in the 2nd century BC. It is located about 20 mi (30 km) southeast of Baghdad. The Parthian and later Sāsānian capital of Ctesiphon, begun in the 3rd century AD, is located just across the Tigris from Seleucia. In 762 the Arab conqueror al-Manṣūr, the second ʿAbbāsid caliph, began constructing his new capital, which grew into modern Baghdad. The Sumerian city of Sippar and the city of Sāmarrāʾ, built by the caliph al-Muʿtaṣim, which was briefly the ʿAbbāsid capital (836–892), are both located in Baghdād *muḥāfaẓah.* Pop. (1978 est.) 3,205,645.

Baghdad, also spelled BAGDAD, largest city and capital of modern Iraq and of Baghdad *muḥāfaẓah* (governorate). Located on both banks of the Tigris River in north central Iraq, about 350 mi (560 km) northwest of the Persian Gulf at the intersection of major historic trade routes, Baghdad was the foremost city of ancient Mesopotamia.

The following article treats briefly the modern city of Baghdad. Fuller treatment is provided in the following MACROPAEDIA articles. For history and contemporary life, *see* Baghdad; for additional perspective on the city in its national context, *see* Iraq.

The site of Baghdad is at the centre of a broad alluvial plain at the nearest approach of the Tigris to the Euphrates. Summers are dry and intensely hot, with prevailing winds, known as *shamāl*s, bringing some relief. Winters are mild.

Iraq's oil wealth is reflected in Baghdad's vigorous economic life. The import and manufacture, as well as distribution, of capital and consumer goods are important. Most Iraqi industries are located in the city; products include leather, silk, cotton textiles and clothing, bricks, cement, tobacco, and alcoholic beverages. The country's financial services are also centred there.

Modernization has dramatically changed the physical character of Baghdad, although many old buildings, cafés, and bazaars have been spared. Effective control of Tigris flooding has permitted the outward expansion of the city. The new city plan is circular in shape, encompassing both banks of the river; bridges link the city with large suburbs to the west and north.

Surviving 13th-century architecture includes the ʿAbbāsid palace and the Mustanṣirīyah law college (1232), both restored as museums. Many mosques and minarets have also remained through the centuries, and the royal mausoleum of King Fayṣal I, founder of the former monarchy, is a notable monument. Much of the cultural life centres on the Sunnī and Shīʿah sects of Islām. The University of Baghdad (1958) and several historical and ethnographic museums are located in the city. Libraries include the al-Awqāf (1929), with collections of Arabic history and literature, and the Central Library of the University of Baghdad.

The three major Iraqi railway lines meet in Baghdad, and the city is linked to Europe by a line that runs across Syria to Istanbul. Highways link the capital to other major Iraqi cities and to Damascus. The city has an international airport. Area city, 328 sq mi (850 sq km); *muḥāfaẓah,* 1,988 sq mi (5,150 sq km). Pop. (1970 est.) city, 2,183,760; (1978 est.) *muḥāfaẓah,* 3,205,645.

Baghdad Pact Organization: *see* Central Treaty Organization.

Baghdad Railway, major rail line connecting Istanbul with the Persian Gulf region. Work on the first phase of the railway, which involved an extension of an existing line between Haidar Pasha and Ismid to Ankara, was begun in 1888 by the Ottoman Empire with German financial assistance. In 1902 the Ottoman government granted a German firm the concession to lay new track eastward from Ankara to Baghdad. Financial difficulties and the technical problems of tunnelling through the Taurus mountains made progress extremely slow. Because of its potential strategic importance, work on the line was accelerated after the empire entered World War I on the side of Germany and the other Central Powers. By the end of the war in 1918 the line had been extended from the Bosporus to Nusaybin, several hundred miles short of Baghdad. This remaining stretch and a subsequent extension to the port of Basra near the Persian Gulf were eventually completed by Syria and Iraq, which had been formed after the dismemberment of the Ottoman Empire.

Baghdad school, important stylistic movement of Islāmic manuscript illustration, founded in the late 12th century (though the earliest surviving works cannot be dated before the 13th century). The school flourished in the period when the ʿAbbāsid caliphs had reasserted their authority in Baghdad. Characterized by the depiction of expressive, individualized faces rather than facial types, a suggestion of movement, and attention to the details of everyday life, work of this school continued to appear for some 40 years following the destruction of the city by the Mongols in 1258.

Early examples of Baghdad-school miniatures are illustrations from an Arabic translation of Dioscorides' medical treatise, *De materia medica,* dated 1224 (the manuscript is scattered among several private collections and museums). The paintings embody the traditional elements of the Baghdad school—strong colours, a well-developed sense of design, and expressive facial features. Frames do not appear; the miniatures illustrate the text and often appear between lines of it.

The miniatures made to illustrate manuscripts of the *Maqāmāt* of al-Ḥarīrī, between 1225 and the fall of the city to the Mongols in 1258, were among the finest works in all Arab painting; the finest, most complete, and best preserved of these manuscripts is that of the Bibliothèque Nationale of Paris, dated 1237.

The frontispiece to a book, "The Epistles of the Sincere Brethren," dated 1287, demonstrates that the main stylistic elements of the Baghdad school survived to the last. This illustration, in the Mosque of Süleyman in Istanbul, again shows realism in detail while maintaining an overall decorative quality. The authors of the book are depicted with their scribes, and attention is drawn to the faces. By the early 1300s, the school had died out, and painting in the area began to take on many characteristics of the Mongol schools.

Baghelkhand, historic region, eastern Madhya Pradesh state, central India. The area is divided into two natural regions by the Kaimur Range. To the west lie elevated plains; to the east is a rough, hilly tract intersected by a succession of parallel forested ridges of the Vindhya Range. The Tons and Son rivers and their tributaries drain the area. The population consists chiefly of tribal Goṇḍs and Kōḷs.

Known as Ḍāhala before the Muslims, Baghelkhand was held by the warlike Kalacuri dynasty (6th–12th century), whose stronghold was at Kālinjar. With the advent of the Baghelā Rājputs (warrior caste) in the 14th century, after whom the tract is named, it was absorbed into Rewa state. Baghelkhand Agency, a subdivision of the British Central India Agency, was created in 1871 and included Rewa and several other states, with headquarters at Satna. It merged with Bundelkhand Agency in 1931 and formed the eastern half of Vindhya Pradesh, created at Indian independence in 1947.

Bāgherhāt, town, Khulna district and division, Bangladesh, just south of the Bhairab River. The capital of Hazrat Khān Jahān Ali—the 15th-century pioneer of the Sundarbans—it contains the ruins of his mausoleum and

The Sāt Gumbaz Mosque, Bāgherhāt, Bangladesh
Frederic Ohringer from the Nancy Palmer Agency—EB Inc.

large audience hall (Sāt Gumbaz). The town is now a cotton textile centre, connected by road and rail with Khulna. It has two colleges affiliated with the University of Rājshāhi. Pop. (1981 prelim.) 38,539.

Bagheria, town, Palermo province, northwestern Sicily, Italy, just east-southeast of Palermo (city). A resort of wealthy Palermitans, it is noted for several historic villas. The best known are Villa Palagonia (1715), containing more than 60 Byzantine statues of beggars, dwarfs, monsters, and other oddities; the Villa Butera, with wax figures of monks wearing the Carthusian habit (1639); and the Villa Valguarnera (1721). Formerly called Bagaria, the town is in a fruit-growing area, principally of citrus and grapes. Pop. (1981 prelim.) mun., 39,867.

Baghkiriya (Russian S.F.S.R.): *see* Bashkir Autonomous Soviet Socialist Republic.

Baghlān, *velāyat* (province) in northeastern Afghanistan, 6,605 sq mi (17,106 sq km) in area, surrounded by the *velāyat* of Kondūz on the north, Takhār on the northeast, Parvān and Kāpīsā on the south, and Bāmīān and Samangān on the west. Topographically Baghlān is a mountainous area. It is drained northward by the Qondūz River and its tributaries, except for the relatively flat northern part, where Baghlān city, the capital, is located. Sugar beets, rice, wheat, and cotton rank as important agricultural products. The main road from Kondūz near the Soviet Union's border to Kābul crosses the province from north to south; following their military intervention in late 1979, Soviet forces began widening the portion of this road over the Sālang Pass. Pop. (1982 est.) settled pop. 516,921, predominantly Tadzhik.

Baghlān, capital of Baghlān *velāyat* (province), northeastern Afghanistan, near the Qondūz River, at an elevation of 1,650 ft (500 m). Baghlān is the centre of beet-sugar production and has a sugar refinery. Cotton textiles are also manufactured. The city's industrial development has led to rapid population growth. Recently built major highways link Baghlān with Kābul, the nation's capital, 130 mi (210 km) south, and with other commercial, industrial, and administrative centres of Afghanistan.

About 20 mi southwest of Baghlān is Āteshkadeh-ye Sorkh Kowtal, site of the ruins of a Zoroastrian fire temple, believed to have been built in the 1st century AD by the Kushān emperor Kaniṣka I. The population is predominantly Tadzhik. Pop. (1982 est.) 41,240.

Bāghmati River, river in eastern Nepal and northern Bihār State, northeastern India, rising in several headstreams in the lowland area of Nepal and flowing southward through the Siwālik Range, southernmost range of the Himalayas. It continues across the plains of Tarai into Bihār and then flows southeastward to enter the Burhi Gandak River after a course of 225 mi (360 km).

Bagirmi, also spelled BAGUIRMI, people of mixed origin living on the southern fringe of the Sahara, close to the region of Bornu. The Bagirmi are a mixture of Arab, Berber, and Negro. Most speak dialects of the Fulani language, called Fulfulde, which belongs to the West Atlantic branch of the Niger-Congo family.

In the old Bagirmi kingdom the Bagirmi exercised political dominance over many other peoples, and waves of invading peoples kept the Bagirmi almost constantly beleaguered.

When King Idris Alawma of Bornu conquered the Bagirmi in about 1600, Islām was introduced; it made scant headway, however, and most people retained their traditional beliefs.

The Bagirmi practice hoe cultivation, growing chiefly millet and sorghum. They also keep cattle, goats, sheep, dogs, and chickens. North African influence can be seen in the use of milk, butter, and cheese, as well as in the practices of irrigation and fertilization with manure.

The complex social stratification of the Bagirmi includes a privileged nobility headed by a royal family.

Bagirmi, Kingdom of, historic African state founded in the 16th century in the region just southeast of Lake Chad. Its king, called the Mbang, ruled from the capital city of Massenya (now in Chari-Baguirmi *préfecture,* Chad). The Bagirmi kings converted to Islām in the 17th century and prospered from the slave trade. Bagirmi became a pawn in the conflicts between the rival empires of Bornu to the west and Wadai to the east. A vassal of Bornu in the 17th and 18th centuries, it fell to Wadai early in the 19th century and became that empire's main source of skilled artisans. In both 1806 and 1870, troops from Wadai sacked Massenya and carried off thousands of weavers and metalworkers as slaves. The Sudanese armies of al-Mahdī overran Bagirmi in 1893 and incorporated it into the Mahdist state.

Bagley, William Chandler (b. March 15, 1874, Detroit—d. July 1, 1946, New York City), U.S. educator, author, and editor who, as a leading "Essentialist," opposed many of the practices of progressive education.

Bagley received his undergraduate degree in 1895 from the Agricultural College of the State of Michigan (East Lansing; now Michigan State University). He taught briefly at a one-teacher school in rural Michigan and then took graduate courses at the University of Chicago and the University of Wisconsin (Madison); he earned a doctorate in psychology and education from Cornell University, Ithaca, N.Y., in 1900.

After a year as principal of a St. Louis elementary school, he was appointed professor of psychology and education at Montana State Normal College in Dillon, where he became vice president of the college and superintendent of public schools at Dillon.

After briefly superintending teacher training at the New York State Normal School in Oswego (1907–08), Bagley became professor of education at the University of Illinois in Urbana-Champaign, and in 1917 he accepted a similar post at Teacher's College, Columbia University, where he stayed until his retirement in 1940.

Bagley's lifelong professional commitment was to the improvement of public education, largely through improved teacher training. He became a leading spokesman of the "Essentialists"—a group of professional educators who advocated European-style emphasis on a rigorous curriculum of traditional subjects, in opposition to the approach of many progressive-education circles. He was an outspoken proponent of equality in educational opportunity and vigorously opposed restricting such opportunity on the basis of intelligence-test scores. He was an early experimenter in the use of radio for instruction. His voluminous literary output included works with Charles A. Beard, *The History of the American People* (1918) and *Our Old World Background* (1922), and a work with Beard and Roy F. Nichols, *America, Yesterday and Today* (1938). Other collaborators included John A.H. Keith, Stephens S. Calvin, William Learned, and James Smith. Among his own titles are *Craftsmanship in Teaching* (1911), *School Discipline* (1914), *Determinism in Education* (1925), *Education, Crime, and Social Progress* (1931), *Education and Emergent Man* (1934), and *A Century of the Universal School* (1937). Bagley also founded and edited many professional journals.

To make the best use of the Britannica, consult the INDEX *first*

Baglioni FAMILY, related Umbrian nobles, many of whom were fierce and skillful condottiere, who dominated Perugia between 1488 and 1534. They were constantly challenged by other nobles and by the papacy.

The ascendancy of the family began with Malatesta (1389–1437), who joined with Bracchio Fortebracchi, tyrant of Perugia, in opposing Martin V. Wounded and imprisoned in 1424, Malatesta won his release by promising to persuade Perugia's populace to submit to Martin. He was rewarded with the seigneury of Spello (1425) and several other small territories. Although never formally created lord, Malatesta became the virtual ruler of Perugia. His son Bracchio (1419–74?) succeeded him.

Successful in expelling the rival Oddi family in 1488, the Baglioni created the Dieci dell'Arbitrio, a council of 10 family members, as a device through which they hoped to govern Perugia. The period was marked by excessive violence, especially within the Baglioni family. One episode was the so-called great betrayal of 1500, during which Carlo and Grifonetto Baglioni attempted a mass assassination of the other members of the family. Giampaolo (or Giovan Paolo; *c.* 1470–1520), one of the few to escape execution, exacted a harsh retribution and emerged as the sole leader of Perugia.

Preferring the life of a condottiere, Giampaolo left administrative matters to the just and able Morgante, who died in 1502; soon afterward the Baglioni were forced to flee the city. Giampaolo and his cousin Gentile retook Perugia after a brief but fierce battle in 1503. Julius II, elected pope later that year, determined to control Perugia, and in 1506 the Baglioni acknowledged his overlordship.

Giampaolo continued to play an important role in the power struggles of the time until he was lured to Rome and killed by order of Leo X. Gentile, who was implicated in Giampaolo's death, remained in power as a tool of the church until he was expelled by Malatesta (1491–1531) and Orazio. Malatesta, condottiere employed by both the Venetian and Florentine republics, is known for his betrayal of Florence, which he first defended against Clement VII in 1529, only to hand it over to Clement the following year. Malatesta ruled Perugia until his death. His successor, Rodolfo (1518–54), was defeated by Paul III, who banished the Baglioni in 1534. The Baglioni continued to furnish captains of war until, in the 17th century, the several branches of the family declined or disappeared.

Baglioni, Bartolomeo d'Agnolo: *see* Baccio d'Agnolo.

Bagnold, Enid, married name LADY RODERICK JONES (b. Oct. 27, 1889, Rochester, Kent, Eng.), novelist and playwright who was known for her broad range of subject and style.

Bagnold, the daughter of an army officer, spent her early childhood in Jamaica and attended schools in England and France. She served with the British women's services during World War I; her earliest books—*A Diary Without Dates* (1917) and *The Happy Foreigner* (1920)—describe her wartime experiences. In 1920 she married Sir Roderick Jones (1877–1962), who for 25 years was chairman of the news agency Reuters, Ltd.

Bagnold's best known work is the novel *National Velvet* (1935), which tells the story of an ambitious 14-year-old girl who rides to victory in Great Britain's Grand National steeplechase on a horse bought for only £10; a motion picture of the same title was made from the novel in 1944. Two quite different novels are *The Squire* (1938; U.S. title, *The Door of Life*), which conveys the mood of expectancy in a household awaiting the birth of a child, and *The Loved and Envied* (1951), a study of a woman facing the approach of old age. As a playwright, Bagnold achieved great success with *The Chalk Garden* (1955); a motion-picture version was produced in 1964. Bagnold's other works for the stage include *Four Plays* (1970) and *A Matter of Gravity* (1975).

Bagnold, Ralph Alger (b. April 3, 1896, Devonport, Devonshire, Eng.), geologist, a leading authority on the mechanics of sediment transport and on eolian (wind-effect) processes. He organized and led numerous desert explorations—particularly of the Libyan Desert—from 1929 to 1938. Bagnold researched the processes of sediment transport by wind and water; he studied the origins of sand dunes and classified them according to shape and method of growth. He served as a consultant and adviser to private industry, governments, and scientific study organizations. His published works include *Libyan Sands* (1935), *Movement of Desert Sand* (1936), *Physics of Blown Sand and Desert Dunes* (1941), *Motion of Waves in Shallow Water* (1946), and *Flow of Cohesionless Grains in Fluids* (1956).

Bago, chartered city, Negros Occidental province, western portion of the island of Negros, Philippines. On Guimaras Strait at the mouth of the Bago River, it lies between Bacolod and its outport, Pulupandan. Bago is in an agricultural area that produces rice and sugarcane. Sugar milling is the principal industry. There are road connections to Bacolod (the provincial capital) and the other cities of Negros Occidental. Pop. (1980) 99,631.

Bagoas (fl. 4th century BC), confidential minister of the Achaemenid king Artaxerxes III of Persia. His name was the Greek form of an Old Persian name often used for eunuchs.

Bagoas was commander in chief of the Achaemenid forces in the conquest of Egypt (343 BC) and gained wealth by selling back to the priests at an exorbitant price the sacred writings looted from Egyptian temples. He worked in close partnership with Mentor of Rhodes and rose to such power that he became the real master of the Achaemenid Empire, Artaxerxes doing nothing without his advice. In 338 Bagoas murdered Artaxerxes and all the King's sons except Arses, whom he placed on the throne. Two years later he murdered Arses and made a collateral heir, Darius III, king. When Darius asserted his independence, Bagoas attempted to poison him, but the King had been warned and forced Bagoas to drink the poison himself.

bagpipe, wind instrument consisting of two or more single or double-reed pipes, the reeds being set in motion by wind fed by arm pressure on a skin bag. The pipes are held in wooden sockets (stocks) tied into the bag, which is inflated either by the mouth (through a blowpipe with a leather nonreturn valve) or by bellows strapped to the body. Melodies are played on the finger holes of the melody pipe, or chanter, while the remaining pipes, or drones, sound single notes tuned against the chanter by means of extendable joints. The sound is continuous; to articulate the melody and to reiterate notes the piper employs gracing—*i.e.,* rapidly interpolated notes outside the melody, giving an effect of detached notes.

Bagpipes were alluded to in Europe as early as the 9th century; earlier evidence is scarce but includes four Latin and Greek references of *c.* AD 100 and, possibly, an Alexandrian terra-cotta of *c.* 100 BC (at Berlin). In the earliest ones the bag is typically a bladder or a whole sheepskin or goatskin, minus the hindquarters; later, two pieces of skin were cut to shape and sewn together. Bagpipes have always been folk instruments, but after the 15th century some were used for court music, and others have survived as military instruments.

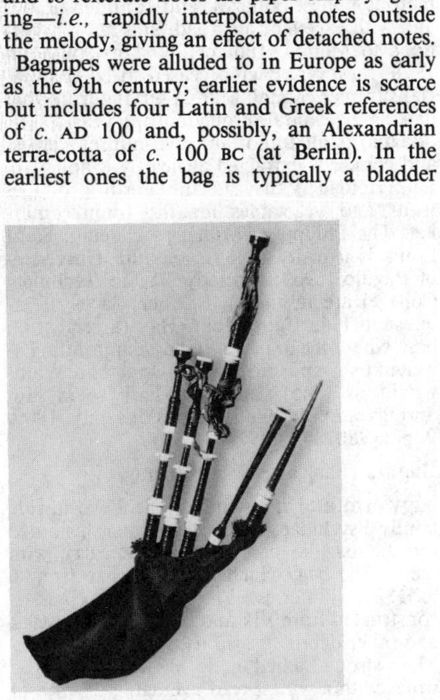

Highland bagpipe, Scottish, 19th century; in the Metropolitan Museum of Art, New York City

By courtesy of the Metropolitan Museum of Art, New York City, the Crosby Brown Collection of Musical Instruments, 1889

For the chanter, two single-reed cane pipes are placed parallel, one pipe often sounding a drone or other accompaniment to the other pipe. Most have cowhorn bells, being bag versions of hornpipes; they are found in North Africa, the Arabian Peninsula, the Aegean, the Caucasus, and among the Cheremis in the Soviet Union. Other double chanters in eastern Europe (Serbia, Hungary, the Ukraine, and elsewhere) are made of a single piece of wood with two cylindrical bores (as in cane pipes) and primitive single reeds of cane or elder. There is also a separate bass drone tuned, like most bass drones, two octaves below the chanter keynote. The Bulgarian *gaida* and the Czecho-Polish *dudy* (*koza*) have a single chanter, and in the *dudy,* the chanter and drone each carry a huge cowhorn bell.

In western European bagpipes the chanter typically is conically bored and sounded by a double reed; drones are cylindrical with single reeds, as in bagpipes found elsewhere. The Scottish Highland bagpipe has two tenor drones and a bass drone, tuned an octave apart; its scale preserves traditional intervals foreign to European classical music. It was once, like other bagpipes, a pastoral and festive instrument; its military use with drums dates from the 18th century. The Scottish Lowland bagpipe, played *c.* 1750–1850, was bellows-blown, with three drones in one stock, and had a softer sound. Akin to this were the two-droned bagpipes played up to the 18th century in Germany, the Netherlands, Ireland, and England. The modern two-droned Irish war pipe is a modified Highland bagpipe revived *c.* 1905. Other instruments resembling the Highland bagpipe are the *gaita gallega* of northwestern Spain (usually with bass drone only) and the Breton *biniou,* a half-sized version played in duet with the *bombarde* (Breton shawm).

The cornemuse of central France is distinguished by a tenor drone held in the chanter stock beside the chanter. Often bellows-blown and without bass drone, it is characteristically played with the *vielle à roue* (hurdy-gurdy). The Italian *zampogna* is unique, with two chanters—one for each hand—arranged for playing in harmony, often to accompany a species of *bombarde* (especially at Christmas); the chanters and two drones are held in one stock, and all have double reeds.

The bellows-blown musette (*q.v.*), fashionable in French society under Louis XIV, had one, later two, cylindrical chanters (the second extending the range upward) and four tunable drones bored in a single cylinder. Partly offshoots of the musette are the British small pipes (*c.* 1700), of which the Northumbrian small pipe is played today. Its cylindrical chanter, with seven keys, is closed at the bottom, so that when all holes are closed it is silent (thus allowing true articulation and staccato). The four single-reed drones are in one stock and are used three at a time.

A complex instrument of similar date is the bellows-blown Irish union pipe. Its chanter is stopped on the knee both for staccato and to jump the reed to the higher octave, giving this bagpipe a melodic compass of two octaves (in contrast to the more common compass of nine tones). The three drones are held in one stock with three accompanying pipes, or regulators. These resemble the chanter in bore and reeds but are stopped below and have four or five keys that are struck with the edge of the player's right hand to sound simple chords.

Bagradas (river, North Africa): *see* Majardah, Wādī.

Bagratid DYNASTY, princely and royal dynasty founded in Armenia and Georgia during the 9th century by the Bagratuni family. The Bagratid kings kept Armenia independent of both the Byzantine Empire and the ʿAbbāsid Caliphate.

With the decline of the previously ruling Mamikonian dynasty, the Bagratids emerged as one of the most powerful noble families in Armenia. The Arabs' choice in 806 of Ashot Bagratuni the Carnivorous to be prince of Armenia marked the beginning of the establishment of his family as the chief power in the land. The Bagratids were more diplomatic than the Mamikonians in their dealings with their foreign overlords. The governor Smbat Ablabas Bagratuni remained loyal to the caliph.

The election of Smbat's son Ashot I the Great, who had been accepted as "prince of princes" by the Arabs in 862, to be king of Armenia in 885 was recognized by both the caliph and the Byzantine emperor, and it was he who by his successful defense of his country against local Arab chieftains laid the foundations of a new golden age of Armenian history. Throughout the 10th century, art and literature flourished. Ashot III ("the Merciful," 952–977) transferred his capital to Ani (near modern Anipemza) and began to transform it into one of the architectural gems of the Middle Ages.

Another Bagratid, Adarnase IV, became king of Georgia in 888, and his line ruled there intermittently until 1505.

The Bagratids of Ani bore the title of *shahanshah* ("king of kings"), which was first conferred by the caliph in 922 upon Ashot II the Iron. In 961 Mushegh, the brother of Ashot III, founded the Bagratid kingdom of Kars. By the 11th century, the combined invasions of the Seljuk Turks and Byzantine conquests in the west destroyed what remained of the Bagratids and the Armenian kingdom.

Bagration, Pyotr Ivanovich, Knyaz (Prince) (b. 1765, Kizlyar, Russia—d. Sept. 24 [Sept. 12, old style], 1812, Sima, Vladimir *gubernaya*), general who distinguished himself during the Napoleonic Wars.

Bagration was descended from the Georgian branch of the Bagratid dynasty. He entered the Russian army in 1782 and served several years in the Caucasus. During the Russo-Turkish War of 1787–92 he participated in the siege of Ochakov, a fortress near the mouth of the Knepr River, and he helped suppress the Polish uprising (1794) after the second partition of Poland (1793).

He achieved prominence, however, by capturing Brescia during Gen. Aleksandr Suvorov's victorious campaign against Napoleon in Italy and Switzerland (1799). He further enhanced his reputation in 1805, when he assured the safe retreat of the main Russian army into Moravia by holding back a French force of 30,000 men with his 6,000 troops at Hollabrunn. He subsequently participated in a series of unsuccessful battles: Austerlitz (Dec. 2, 1805), Eylau (Feb. 7–8, 1807), Heilsburg (June 10, 1807), and Friedland (June 14, 1807), but, after Russia formed an alliance with France (Treaty of Tilsit; July 7, 1807) and engaged in a war against Sweden, Bagration marched across the frozen Gulf of Finland and captured the strategic Åland Islands (1808). He was then transferred to the south (1809) and placed in command of a force fighting the Turks in Bulgaria (Russo-Turkish War of 1806–12). When Russia and France renewed their hostilities (1812), he was given command of the 2nd Russian Army in the West. Although his troops were defeated by the French at Mogilyov and separated from the main Russian army in July, he saved them from destruction and rejoined the main force in August. On Sept. 7, 1812, at the Battle of Borodino, near Moscow, Bagration commanded the left wing of the Russian forces and was fatally wounded. A monument was erected in his honour by Emperor Nicholas I on the battlefield of Borodino.

Bagritsky, Eduard Georgiyevich, pseudonym of EDUARD GEORGIYEVICH DZYUBIN, or DZIUBIN (b. Nov. 3 [Oct. 22, old style], 1895, Odessa, Russia—d. Feb. 16, 1934, Moscow), Soviet poet known for his revolutionary verses and for carrying on the romantic tradition in the Soviet period.

Bagritsky, the son of a poor Jewish family of tradesmen, learned land surveying at a technical school. He enthusiastically welcomed the Revolution of 1917; he served in the Civil War as a Red guerrilla and also wrote propaganda poetry. The rigours of war left Bagritsky in ill health, and he turned to writing as a full-time career.

Bagritsky's first poems were in imitation of the Acmeists, a literary group of the early 1900s that advocated a concrete, individualistic Realism, stressing visual vividness, emotional intensity, and verbal freshness. Before long, however, he began writing in a style of his own, publishing *Duma pro Opanasa* (1926; "The Lay of Opanas"), a skillful poetic narrative set during the Revolution with a Ukrainian peasant named Opanas as its hero. Although his later works expressed accord with the aims of the Soviet regime, Bagritsky nevertheless retained his Romantic style despite the official preference for Socialist Realism. Bagritsky's poetry exhibits great metrical variety and reveals influences from classicism to Modernism; but his works have in common a positive, optimistic attitude toward the world.

Baguio, chartered city, Benguet province, west central Luzon, Philippines. After U.S. occupation of the archipelago (1898), Gov. William Howard Taft and other officials proposed the pleasant site nestled in pine-clad hills at about 4,900 ft (1,500 m) to serve as the summer capital of the Philippines. The idea was adopted by the Filipinos, and Baguio became the country's foremost resort, with numerous hotels, cottages, and summer homes and with excellent air, road, and rail connections to Manila, 160 m (260 km) south. In 1976, however, Baguio ceased to be the official summer capital, Manila serving from that date as the capital throughout the year.

Baguio is an important gold-mining centre, and copper is extracted at nearby Mankayan. La Trinidad Valley to the north produces fruits and vegetables for the Manila market. The Philippine Military Academy, Saint Louis University (1963), and the University of Baguio (1969; formerly Baguio Technical College) are in the city. Other places of interest include Camp John Hay (a recreation base where the Japanese Gen. Yamashita Tomoyuki surrendered to Gen. Jonathan Wainwright in 1945), Burnham Park, Asin Hot Springs, and Mt. Santo Tomas. Inc. city, 1909. Pop. (1980) 119,009.

Bagura (Bangladesh): *see* Bogra.

bagworm moth, any insect of the worldwide family Psychidae (order Lepidoptera), named for the baglike cases the larvae carry with them. The bag, which ranges in size from 6 to 152 millimetres (1/4 to 6 inches) and is constructed from silk and bits of leaves, twigs, and other debris, is also used as a pupal case.

The strong-bodied male has broad, fringed wings with a wingspread averaging 25 mm (1 in.). The wormlike female lacks wings; it may remain in the bag during mating and then deposit eggs there. The female evergreen bagworm (*Thyridopteryx ephemeraeformis*) dies after mating, and the eggs are retained in her body until they hatch. Bagworm larvae are often destructive to trees, especially evergreens.

Winged male bagworm moth (*Thyridopteryx meadi*) atop bag containing female bagworm

William E. Ferguson

Bagyidaw (d. October 1846), king of Burma (1819–37), seventh monarch of the Konbaung, or Alaungpaya, dynasty, which was defeated in the First Anglo-Burmese War (1824–26). As a result of his defeat, the provinces of Arakan and Tenasserim were lost to the British.

Bagyidaw was the grandson of King Bodawpaya (reigned 1782–1819), who had narrowly avoided war with the British over the frontier between Bengal and Arakan. Bagyidaw was an ineffectual king, but his general, Maha Bandula, influenced him to follow Bodawpaya's policy of aggressive expansion in northeastern India. He conquered Assam and Manipur, making them Burmese tributaries. The border with British India extended from Arakan on the Bay of Bengal to the foot of the Himalayan Mountains. The British, angered over Burmese border raids in pursuit of rebel forces, launched a war on March 5, 1824.

Bagyidaw's armies were driven out of Assam, Arakan, and Manipur. British forces occupied Lower Burma and advanced toward the capital, Amarapura (near present-day Mandalay). On Feb. 24, 1826, Bagyidaw's government signed the Treaty of Yandabo; its terms included cession of Tenasserim and Arakan to the British, payment of an indemnity equivalent to £1,000,000, and renunciation of all Burmese claims in Assam and Manipur, which became British protectorates.

During the remaining years of his reign, Bagyidaw attempted to mitigate the harsh terms of the treaty. In 1826 the King negotiated a commercial treaty with the British envoy, John Crawfurd, but refused to establish formal diplomatic relations unless he could deal on an equal basis with the British sovereign, rather than through the East India Company at Calcutta. Bagyidaw failed to persuade the British to give Tenasserim back to Burma, but a deputation that he sent to Calcutta in 1830 successfully reasserted the Burmese claim to the Kale-Kabaw Valley, which had been occupied by the Manipuris. After 1831 Bagyidaw became increasingly susceptible to attacks of mental instability, and in 1837 he was succeeded by his brother, Prince Tharrawaddy Min.

Bahāʾ ad-Dīn: *see* Ibn Shaddād.

Bahāʾ ad-Dīn Zuhayr, in full ABŪ AL-FAḌL ZUHAYR IBN MUḤAMMAD AL-MUHALLABĪ (b. Feb. 28, 1186, Mecca—d. Nov. 2, 1258, Cairo), Arab poet attached to the Ayyūbid dynasty of Cairo.

Bahāʾ ad-Dīn Zuhayr studied at Qūṣ, a centre of trade and scholarship in Upper Egypt, and eventually moved to Cairo. There he entered the service of the Ayyūbid prince aṣ-Ṣāliḥ Ayyūb, serving as the prince's secretary on a campaign in Syria in 1232. During an Ayyūbid family dispute in 1239, aṣ-Ṣāliḥ Ayyūb was imprisoned at Nābulus, Palestine, and Bahāʾ ad-Dīn Zuhayr remained nearby. He became vizier the following year, when aṣ-Ṣāliḥ Ayyūb was brought to power in Egypt, but the poet fell from favour in the last year of the Sultan's life. Rebuffed also by the Ayyūbid ruler of Damascus and Aleppo, he lived in Cairo in obscurity during his last years.

Bahā' ad-Dīn's Zuhayr's *dīwān* (collection of poems) was published in an Arabic edition with an English translation by E.H. Palmer, *The Poetical Works of Behā-ed-Dīn Zoheir*, 2 vol. (1876–77). Among his poems are *qaṣīdah*s (odes) of praise to a member of the Ayyūbid dynasty or an official; other poems are devoted to love found and lost and to friendship.

Bahā' Ullāh, also spelled BAHĀ' ALLĀH (Arabic: Glory of God), original name MĪRZĀ ḤOSEYN ALĪ NŪRĪ (b. Nov. 12, 1817, Tehrān—d. May 29, 1892, Acre, Palestine), founder of the Bahā'ī faith upon his claim to be the manifestation of the unknowable God.

Mīrzā Ḥoseyn was a member of the Shī'ī branch of Islām. He subsequently allied himself with Mīrzā 'Alī Moḥammad of Shīrāz, who was known as the Bāb (Gate) and was the head of the Bābī, a Muslim sect professing a privileged access to final truth. After the Bāb's execution by the Persian government for treason (1850), Mīrzā Ḥoseyn joined Mīrzā Yaḥyā (also called Ṣobḥ-e Azal), his own half brother and the Bāb's spiritual heir in directing the Bābī movement. Mīrzā Yaḥyā later was discredited, and Mīrzā Ḥoseyn was exiled by orthodox Sunnī Muslims successively to Baghdad, Kurdistan, and Constantinople. There, in 1867, he publicly declared himself to be the divinely chosen *imām-mahdī* ("rightly guided leader"), whom the Bāb had foretold. The resulting factional violence caused the Ottoman government to banish Mīrzā Ḥoseyn to Acre.

At Acre, Bahā' Ullāh, as he was by then called, developed the formerly provincial Bahā'ī doctrine into a comprehensive teaching that advocated the unity of all religions and the universal brotherhood of man. Emphasizing social ethics, he eschewed ritual worship and devoted himself to the abolition of racial, class, and religious prejudices. His place of confinement in Acre became a centre of pilgrimage for Bahā'ī believers from Persia and the United States.

bahada (landform): *see* bajada.

Bahādur Shāh I (b. Oct. 14, 1643, Burhānpur, India—d. Feb. 27, 1712, Lahore), Mughal emperor of India in 1707–12.

As Prince Mu'aẓẓam, the second son of the emperor Aurangzeb, he was prospective heir apparent after his elder brother defected to join their father's brother and rival, Shāh Shujā'. Prince Mu'aẓẓam was sent to represent his father in the Deccan Plateau region of south and central India in 1663. He led an army in 1683–84 against the Marāthās in the Portuguese enclave of Goa, south of Bombay, but, lacking Portuguese support, made a disastrous retreat. After being persecuted for eight years, he was appointed governor of Kābul (now in Afghanistan) in 1699 by his father; when his father died, Prince Mu'aẓẓam destroyed his two brothers to become master of the empire. During his short reign as Bahādur Shāh I, he encountered opposition from the Marāthās and Rājputs, and in 1710–12 he drove the followers of the Sikh religion into the hills of the Punjab, subduing but not capturing their leader, Bandā Singh Bahādur.

Bahādur Shāh II (b. Oct. 24, 1775, Delhi—d. Nov. 7, 1862, Rangoon), the last Mughal emperor of India (reigned 1837–58). He was a poet, musician, and calligrapher, more an aesthete than a political leader.

He was the second son of Akbar Shāh II and Lāl Bāī. For most of his reign he was a client of the British without real authority. He figured briefly, and unwillingly, in the Indian Mutiny of 1857; during the mutiny rebel troops from the city of Meerut seized Delhi and compelled him to accept nominal leadership of the revolt. At the age of 82, in fear of his life, he acquiesced. After the rebellion was put down by the British, he was exiled to Burma with his family.

Bāhādurpur, Battle of (Feb. 24, 1658), conflict that helped decide the war of succession among the sons of Shāh Jahān, Mughal emperor of India (reigned 1628–57/58). When Shāh Jahān fell ill in 1657, his four sons—Dārā Shikōh, Shāh Shujā', Aurangzeb, and Murād Bakhsh—fought for power.

Shujā', the second son—who had quickly set himself up as the independent governor of Bengal—was defeated at Bāhādurpur, five miles northeast of Vārānasi (Banāras) in Uttar Pradesh, by Dārā's son Sulaymān Shikōh. Shikōh was later captured and executed by his uncle Aurangzeb, who in June 1658 imprisoned his father and a month later crowned himself emperor. He also defeated Dārā, Murād, and Shujā' (who became a fugitive and died in Burma in 1660).

Bāḥah, al-, town and capital of al-Bāḥah *minṭaqah* (province), 'Asīr region, southwestern Saudi Arabia. The town is situated at an elevation of 7,014 ft (2,138 m) and is surrounded by terraced hillsides, which are covered with juniper. It is known as the gateway to the 'Asīr region, a prosperous agricultural area just north of Yemen (Ṣan'ā'). Al-Bāḥah lies on the main road from aṭ-Ṭā'if to Jīzān.

Al-Bāḥah province is the smallest *minṭaqah* in Saudi Arabia, and it is on a high mountainous plateau. It is bounded by the *manāṭiq* (provinces) of Makkah to the north, west, and south and 'Asīr to the east. Al-Bāḥah is an important agricultural region. Pop. (1974) province, 186,000.

Bahā'ī faith, religion founded in the mid-19th century by Mīrzā Ḥusayn Alī, known as Bahā' Ullāh (*q.v.;* Glory of God). Bahā' Ullāh was a follower of the Bāb (*q.v.*) who, some years after the Bāb's execution in 1850, claimed leadership of his community. In 1867 (or 1863) Bahā' Ullāh publicly proclaimed himself "him whom God should manifest," a divine spirit foretold by the Bāb. The Bahā'īs believe Bahā' Ullāh to be the latest of a series of past and future divine manifestations that include Jesus, Muḥammad, Zoroaster, and the Buddha. His teachings are believed to initiate a new dispensation for our age.

The cornerstone of Bahā'ī belief is the conviction that the Bāb and Bahā' Ullāh are manifestations of God, who in his essence is unknowable. The Bāb was the forerunner who announced a greater one to come. When Bahā' Ullāh proclaimed himself, the Bāb's short dispensation was fulfilled. The third important figure in the Bahā'i faith was 'Abd ol-Bahā' (Servant of the Glory; 1844–1921), eldest son of Bahā' Ullāh and the perfect exemplar and infallible interpreter of his teachings. The writings and spoken words of these three central figures of the Bahā'ī faith form its sacred literature.

Bahā' Ullāh's literary legacy of more than 100 works includes *al-Kitāb al-Aqdas* ("The Most Holy Book"), the repository of his laws; the *Ketāb-e Īqān* (*The Book of Certitude*), an exposition of essential teachings on the nature of God and religion; *The Hidden Words,* a collection of brief utterances aimed at the edification of men's "souls and the rectification of their conduct"; *The Seven Valleys,* a mystic treatise that "describes the seven stages which the soul of the seeker must needs traverse ere it can attain the object of its existence"; "Epistle to the Son of the Wolf," his last major work; as well as innumerable prayers, meditations, exhortations, and epistles. The Bahā'īs believe that the writings of Bahā' Ullāh are inspired and constitute God's revelation for this age.

Principal among Bahā'ī teachings are the unity of religions and the unity of mankind. Bahā'īs believe all the founders of the great religions to have been manifestations of God and agents of a progressive divine plan for the education of the human race. Despite their apparent differences the great religions, according to Bahā'īs, teach an identical truth. Bahā' Ullāh's peculiar function was to overcome the disunity of religions and establish a universal faith. Similarly, the Bahā'īs believe in the brotherhood of all men and devote themselves to the abolition of racial, class, and religious prejudices.

Membership in the Bahā'ī community is open to all who profess faith in Bahā' Ullāh and accept his teachings. There are no initiation ceremonies, no sacraments, and no clergy. Every Bahā'ī, however, is under the spiritual obligation to pray daily; to fast 19 days a year, going without food or drink from sunrise to sunset; to abstain totally from narcotics, alcohol, or any substances that affect the mind; to practice monogamy; to obtain the consent of parents to marriage; and to attend the Nineteen Day Feast on the first day of each month of the Bahā'ī calendar. The Nineteen Day Feast, originally instituted by the Bāb, brings together the Bahā'īs of a given locality for prayer, the reading of scriptures, the discussion of community activities, and for the enjoyment of one another's company. The feasts are designed to ensure universal participation in the affairs of the community and the cultivation of the spirit of brotherhood and fellowship. Eventually, Bahā'īs in every locality plan to erect a house of worship around which will be grouped such institutions as a home for the aged, an orphanage, a school, and a hospital. In the early 1980s, houses of worship existed in Wilmette, Ill.; Frankfurt am Main; Kampala, Uganda; Sydney; and Panama City; others were planned or under construction. In the temples there is no preaching; services consist of recitation of the scriptures of all religions.

The Bahā'īs use a calendar established by the Bāb and confirmed by Bahā' Ullāh, in which the year is divided into 19 months of 19 days each, with the addition of 4 intercalary days (5 in leap years). The year begins on the first day of spring, March 21, which is a holy day. Other holy days on which work is suspended are the days commemorating the declaration of Bahā' Ullāh's mission (April 21, April 29, and May 2), the declaration of the mission of the Bāb (May 23), the birth of Bahā' Ullāh (November 12), the birth of the Bāb (October 20), the passing of Bahā' Ullāh (May 29), and the martyrdom of the Bāb (July 9).

The Bahā'ī community is governed according to general principles proclaimed by Bahā' Ullāh and through institutions created by him that were elaborated and expanded by 'Abd ol-Bahā'. These principles and institutions constitute the Bahā'ī administration order, which the followers of the faith believe to be a blueprint of a future world order. The governance of the Bahā'ī community begins on the local level with the election of a local spiritual assembly. The electoral process excludes parties or factions, nominations, and campaigning for office. The local spiritual assembly has jurisdiction over all local affairs of the Bahā'ī community. On the national scale, each year Bahā'īs elect delegates to a national convention that elects a national spiritual assembly with jurisdiction over the entire country. All national spiritual assemblies of the world periodically constitute themselves an international convention and elect the supreme governing body known as the Universal House of Justice. In accordance with Bahā' Ullāh's writings, the Universal House of Justice functions as the supreme administrative, legislative, and judicial body of the Bahā'ī commonwealth. It applies the laws promulgated by Bahā' Ullāh and legislates on matters not covered in the sacred texts. The seat of the Universal House of Justice is in Haifa, Israel, in the immediate vicinity of the shrines of the Bāb and ʿAbd ol-Bahā', and near the shrine of Bahā' Ullāh at Bahjī near ʿAkkā.

There also exist in the Bahā'ī faith appointive institutions, such as the Hands of the Cause of God and the continental counsellors. The former were created by Bahā' Ullāh and later assigned by ʿAbd ol-Bahā' the functions of propagating the faith and protecting the community. The Hands of the Cause appointed by Shoghi Effendi in his lifetime now serve under the direction of the Universal House of Justice. The continental counsellors perform the same functions as the Hands of the Cause but are appointed by the Universal House of Justice. Assisting the counsellors in advising, inspiring, and encouraging Bahā'ī institutions and individuals are auxiliary boards appointed by the counsellors and serving under their direction.

Bahā'ī temple, in the Bahā'ī faith, house of worship open to adherents of all religions. *See* mashriq al-adhkār.

Bahamas, The, officially THE COMMONWEALTH OF THE BAHAMAS, archipelago and state on the edge of the West Indies, consisting of about 700 islands and cays and almost 2,400 low, barren rock formations, located off the southeastern coast of Florida, U.S. Spread across the Tropic of Cancer and about 90,000 sq mi (233,000 sq km) of ocean in the western Atlantic, the archipelago has a total land area of 5,353 sq mi. The capital is Nassau on New Providence—the most important island; Andros (104 mi long and 40 mi wide) is the largest. The population in 1982 was estimated at 240,000.

The article that follows is a summary of significant detail about The Bahamas. Fuller treatment is provided in the following MACROPAEDIA articles. For geography and history, *see* West Indies. For information about associated physiographic features in their continental setting, *see* Caribbean Sea; North America. For information about regional aspects of The Bahamas' history, *see* Latin America, The History of.

For current history and for statistics on society and economy, *see* the article "World Affairs" and BRITANNICA WORLD DATA, respectively, in the *Britannica Book of the Year.*

The land. Geologically composed of coral and other marine organisms, the archipelago lies mostly only a few feet above sea level and is generally flat. The highest point is Mt. Alvernia (formerly Como Hill), which rises 206 ft (63 m) on Cat Island. Most of the islands are long and narrow, each rising from the eastern shore to a low ridge, beyond which lie lagoons and mangrove swamps; coral reefs mark the shorelines. There are no rivers in The Bahamas.

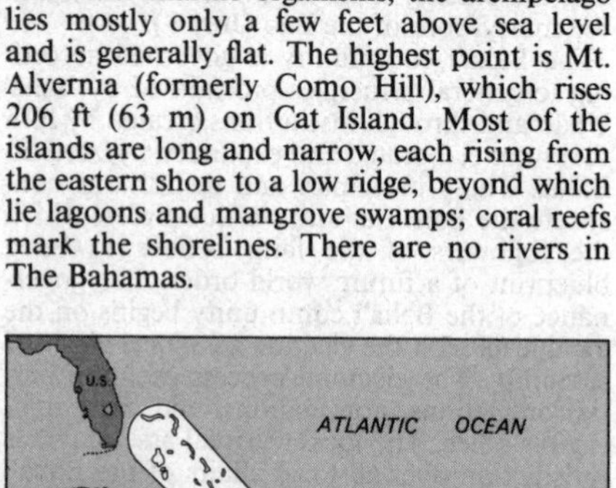

The Bahamas

The mild subtropical climate of The Bahamas, with two seasons (winter [December–April] and summer [May–November]), is greatly influenced by the Gulf Stream and Atlantic Ocean breezes. The average temperature varies from 70° F (21° C) during the winter to 81° F (27° C) during the summer; average annual rainfall is about 46 in. (1,170 mm). Hurricane season lasts from mid-July to mid-November.

The islands abound in tropical flora, including bougainvillea, jasmine, orchid, and oleander. Caribbean pine forests occur on some islands. Native trees include the black olive, cork tree, and several species of palm; mahogany, casuarina, and cedar trees have been planted on some islands. Animal life is dominated by frogs, lizards, and snakes; mosquitoes, sandflies, and termites are widespread. There are numerous species of bird, including the flamingo, the national bird. The Inagua National Park (287 sq mi) on Great Inagua Island is the home of more than 50,000 West Indian flamingoes, the largest such flock in the world. Domesticated livestock such as sheep and horses have been introduced from Europe. Salt is the only commercially important mineral, produced largely by solar evaporation from salt beds on Great Inagua and Long Island.

The people. The people of The Bahamas are a blend of European and African, the latter a legacy of the slave trade. Only about 22 of the islands and cays are inhabited. During the 1970s there was significant rural-to-urban interisland migration, mostly directed to the already densely populated islands of New Providence, where three-quarters of the populace lives, Grand Bahama, and Abasco. Long Cay had only 33 inhabitants in 1980. Average population density for the country is 44 persons per sq mi (17 per sq km). Population density has been diminishing in the older centre city areas as residents move to the suburbs.

The growth rate of The Bahamas was a high 3.7 percent during the late 1970s, mostly because of the substantial birth rate of 25 per 1,000 population; consequently, almost half of the populace is younger than 15 years. The death rate was only 5 per 1,000 population. English is the official language.

The economy. The Bahamas has a predominantly market economy heavily dependent on tourism and international financial services. The gross national product (GNP) totalled U.S. $800,000,000 in 1980; the GNP per capita, which had declined during the 1970s, was $3,300.

Agriculture accounts for less than one-tenth of the GNP and employs a comparable fraction of the work force. The government has had only limited success in increasing agricultural output, and large quantities of food continue to be imported from the United States. The sunny climate favours the cultivation of pineapple, mango, guava, sapodilla, soursop, grapefruit, and sea grape.

Mineral industries are limited to the production of salt and cement. Imported petroleum is refined and reexported to the United States on Grand Bahama. Manufacturing industries centre on the production of pharmaceuticals and rum and other liquors. The Industries Encouragement Act offers manufacturers relief from tariffs and various taxes. Production of electricity totalled 2,561,000,000 kW-hr in 1980 and was generated entirely from imported fuels.

Tourism accounts for as much as four-fifths of the GNP and employs two-thirds of the work force. It centres on New Providence and Grand Bahama; most tourists come from the U.S. Several hundred banks and trust companies have been attracted to the Bahamas because there are no income taxes and because the secrecy of financial transactions is guaranteed. Public expenditures are constrained by the government's dependence on indirect taxes, which are levied primarily on tourism and external trade. The U.S. is The Bahamas' principal trading partner and exempts certain Bahamian products from duties under the generalized system of preferences.

Administrative and social conditions. The Bahamas is an independent, democratic state within the Commonwealth of Nations. According to the country's 1973 constitution, ceremonial executive power is vested in the English monarch (represented in The Bahamas by a governor general). Real political power, however, lies with the House of Assembly, a legislative body consisting of 38 members elected by popular vote for five-year terms. The House appoints a prime minister, who wields the country's executive power. The other, less important legislative body is the Senate, with 12 members appointed by the prime minister and 4 by the leader of the largest opposition party in the House of Assembly. The Progressive Liberal Party dominated Bahamaian politics during the 1970s and early 1980s. Opposition parties include the Social Democratic Party, the Free National Democratic Movement, and the Vanguard Socialist Party. The judiciary is headed by a Supreme Court and a Court of Appeal, but certain appeals may be sent to the Judicial Committee of the Privy Council in the United Kingdom.

The social welfare system in The Bahamas offers sickness, maternity, and retirement benefits, as well as widow's pensions and social assistance payments. Most of the country's doctors and health facilities are located in the Nassau area. There is a Flying Doctor Service, which sends doctors to islands lacking adequate health care. For the most part, however, Bahamians are relatively free from debilitating diseases. In 1980, life expectancy in the country was 66 years. Infant mortality is relatively high at 27.7 per 1,000 live-born (1977).

Schooling is free and compulsory from 5 to 14 years of age. There is little illiteracy. Bahamians pursuing degrees in higher education study abroad or at the College of the Bahamas, which offers two-year degree programs.

The country has four daily newspapers, and they enjoy freedom of the press. The government-owned broadcasting corporation operates the broadcast media.

Cultural life. Outstanding among traditional group activities is the Junkanoo parade on Boxing Day and New Year's Day. The main thoroughfare is given over to hundreds of gaily bedecked celebrants who, with clanging cow bells and beating drums, march and dance to a goombay rhythm of African origin. In Nassau, amateur choral, dramatic, and dancing groups provide entertainment with much local flavour. Bahamians have contributed in modern times to the development of painting and literature.

History. The Bahamas were originally inhabited by a group of Arawak Indians known as Lucayan. Originally from the South American continent, some of the Arawak had been driven north into the Caribbean by the Carib. Unlike their Carib neighbors, the Lucayan were generally peaceful, more involved in fishing than agriculture, and non-cannibalistic.

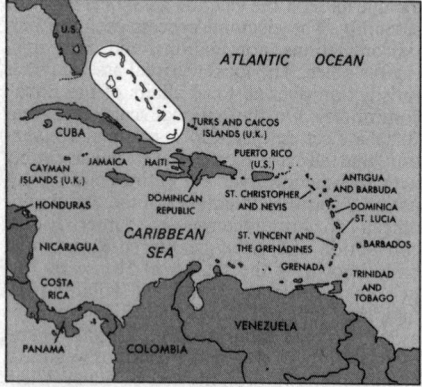

When Columbus reached the New World in 1492, he is thought to have landed on San Salvador in the Bahamas. The Spaniards made no attempt to settle but operated slave raids, on the peaceful Arawak, that depopulated the islands, and by the time the English arrived the Bahamas were uninhabited.

In 1629 Charles I of England granted the islands to one of his ministers, but no attempt at settlement was made. In 1648 William Sayle led a group of English Puritans from Bermuda to, it is thought, Eleuthera Island. This settlement met with extreme adversity and did not prosper, but other Bermudan migrants continued to arrive. New Providence was settled in 1656. By 1670 the Bahamas were given to the Duke of Albermarle and five others as a proprietary colony. The proprietors were mostly uninterested in the islands, and few of the settlements prospered. Piracy became a way of life for many.

The colony reverted to the crown in 1717 and serious efforts were made to end the piracy. The first royal governor, Woodes Rogers, succeeded in controlling the pirates but mostly at his own expense. Little monetary and military support came from England. Consequently, the islands remained poor and susceptible to Spanish attack.

Held for a few days by the U.S. Navy in 1776, and for almost a year by Spain in 1782–83, the islands reverted to England in 1783 and received a boost in population from loyalists and their slaves who fled the U.S. after the American Revolution. For a time, cotton plantations brought some prosperity to the islands, but when the soil gave out and slavery was abolished in 1834, the Bahamas' endemic poverty returned.

Two other periods of prosperity followed: the years 1861–65, when the Bahamas became a centre for blockade runners during the American Civil War, and in 1920–33, when bootlegging became big business during the years of American Prohibition. But these were economic accidents; not until the tourism industry was developed after World War II did any form of permanent prosperity come to the islands.

Racial animosity and segregation practices led to the formation of the Progressive Liberal Party (PLP), which was able to form a government in 1967. The PLP worked to end segregation and secure independence for the islands, granted in 1973. Among the problems with which it was greeted on independence were drug trafficking in the Out Islands and the illegal entry of many Haitian refugees.

Bahār, Muḥammad Taqī (b. 1885, Mashhad, Iran—d. April 22, 1951, Tehrān), poet who is considered to be one of the greatest poets of early 20th-century Iran.

Bahār succeeded his father, Sabūrī, as court poet of the reigning monarch, Muẓaffar ad-Dīn Shāh (1896–1907). Gradually, however, Bahār broke away from the court and became a sympathizer with the revolution. As editor of a liberal democratic newspaper in Mashhad, and later in Tehrān, called *Now bahār* ("The New Spring"), he wrote in praise of the new Iranian constitution. After spending a year in Istanbul (1915–16), he returned to Iran to lead an active political life as a deputy of the Iranian Parliament and became head of a literary group called *Dānishkadeh* (The Place of Knowledge). The group published a journal by the same name in which Bahār expressed his conservative literary tastes, upholding the classical style against that of the avant-garde poets. He retired from politics in 1921, and, except for a brief period as minister of national education in 1946, he devoted himself mainly to teaching and cultural projects. His poetry, although written in essentially classical Persian style, was unique in his expression of modern social ideas and criticism of his country and government, often in biting satire. He also wrote essays on literary style and grammar, translations from Pahlavi, or Middle Persian, a novel, and treatises on the works of great Persian poets and historians.

Baharampur, also spelled BERHAMPUR, or BERHAMPORE, town, administrative headquarters of Murshidābād district, West Bengal state, northeastern India, just east of the Bhāgīrathi River. Baharampur was founded and fortified in 1757 by the English East India Company and continued as a cantonment until 1870. It was the scene of the first overt act of the Indian Mutiny of 1857.

With major rail and road connections, the town is an important agricultural trade centre. Silk weaving, rice and oilseed milling, ivory carving, and gold, silver, and brass working are important industries. Constituted a municipality in 1876, it is the site of a hospital, the Bengal Silk Technological Institute, and four colleges affiliated with the University of Calcutta. Kasimbāzār, now an industrial suburb, was an important town in the 18th century, with a flourishing silk industry; it contains the palace of the maharaja of Kasimbāzār. Pop. (1981) town, 92,889; metropolitan area, 102,311.

Bahasa Indonesia: *see* Indonesian language.

Bahāwalnagar, town and district, Bahāwalpur Division, Punjab Province, Pakistan. The town, the district headquarters, lies just east of the Sutlej River. It is a market distributing centre connected by road with Multān and Bahāwalpur and also by rail with the latter. Amenities include two government colleges affiliated with the University of the Punjab.

Bahāwalnagar District (area 3,428 sq mi [8,878 sq km]) was created in 1955 in the division of the princely state of Bahāwalpur, and it is composed primarily of an alluvial tract lying for the most part in the lowlands of the Sutlej Valley. Wheat, rice, sorghum, and cotton are the chief crops. Pop. (1981 prelim.) town, 74,000; district, 1,371,000.

Bahāwalpur, city, district, and division of Punjab Province, Pakistan. The nawabs of Bahāwalpur originally came from Sind; they formed a princely state and assumed independence in 1802.

The old palace of the Nawab, Bahāwalpur, Pak.
Frederic Ohringer from the Nancy Palmer Agency—EB Inc.

The city, which is the divisional headquarters, just south of the Sutlej River, was founded in 1748 by Muḥammad Bahāwal Khān and was incorporated as a municipality in 1874. It is the site of the Adamwahan (Empress) Bridge, the only railway bridge over the Sutlej River in Pakistan, and has rail links with Peshāwar and Karāchi. Two palaces of the nawabs (the Nur Mahal and Gulzar Mahal) are located there as well as a library, hospitals, a zoological garden, and a museum. Dring stadium, a major Asian athletic facility, is supplemented by a nearby swimming pool, and there are several colleges affiliated with the University of the Punjab. The city is the seat of Islamia University (1975) and the Qā'id-e A'ẓam Medical College and is also an important agricultural training and educational centre. Soapmaking and cotton ginning are important enterprises; cotton, silk, embroidery, carpets, and extraordinarily delicate pottery are produced. Factories producing cottonseed oil and cottonseed cake were built in the 1970s.

Bahāwalpur District (area 9,587 sq mi [24,830 sq km]) is mostly desert, still inhabited by nomads. Irrigated agriculture and small-scale cottage industries are the chief activities. Bahāwalpurī, the language, is identical with Multānī. There are many historical sites in the area, including Uch, southwest of Bahāwalpur, an ancient town dating from Indo-Scythian (Yüeh-chih) settlement (*c.* 128 BC to AD 450).

Bahāwalpur Division was constituted in 1955 and embraces Bahāwalpur, Bahāwalnagar, and Rahīmyār Khān districts. Occupying an area of 17,602 sq mi, it covers a strip about 300 mi (480 km) in length, with an average width of 40 mi, and is divided lengthwise into three sections. The western, called Sind, is a fertile alluvial tract in the river valley, irrigated by floodwaters, planted with groves of date palms, and thickly populated. The central, called Pat, or Bār, is considerably higher than the adjoining valleys; it is chiefly desert irrigated by the Sutlej inundation canals and yields crops of wheat, cotton, and sugarcane. The eastern, called Rohi, or Cholistān, is a barren desert tract, bounded on the north and west by the Hakra depression with mound ruins of old settlements along its high banks. About four-fifths of the cultivated area of the division (about 4,000,000 ac [1,600,000 ha]) is irrigated. The chief crops are wheat, gram, cotton, sugarcane, and dates. Sheep and cattle are raised for export of wool and hides. The principal inhabitants are Jāṭ and Baluchi peoples. Bahāwalpur state acceded to Pakistan after independence in 1947. Pop. (1981 prelim.) city, 178,000; metropolitan area, 695,000; district, 1,447,000; division, 4,652,000.

Bahia, *estado* (state) of eastern Brazil. It is bounded on the northwest by Piauí, north by Pernambuco, northeast by Alagoas and Sergipe, east by the Atlantic Ocean, southeast by Espírito Santo, south by Minas Gerais, and west by Goiás. Bahia has an area of 216,613 sq mi (561,025 sq km). The capital, Salvador, a port commanding an inlet of the Atlantic Ocean, was once commonly known also as Bahia (Bay), whence the state derives its name.

On All Saints' Day, November 1, 1501, Portuguese explorers entered the bay on which Salvador now stands: they therefore named it Bahia de Todos os Santos, or All Saints' Bay. The subsequent occupation of the vicinity by the Portuguese led, in 1549, to the merging of four captaincies under the first governor general of Brazil, Tomé de Sousa, who in the same year founded Salvador as the seat of his government.

The colonization of the territory began in the Recôncavo—that is, in the coastal region—where sugarcane and tobacco were grown for export and other crops for the settlers' food. In the semiarid interior, cattle raising was considerably stimulated in the 18th century, when the discovery of gold and gems in the Diamantina Highland attracted more settlers.

When the Empire of Brazil was proclaimed in 1822, Bahia was still controlled by forces loyal to Portugal; but on July 2, 1823, Brazilian troops occupied Salvador, and Bahia became a province of the empire. In 1889, under the republic, Bahia became a state of the Brazilian Federation.

During the 19th century there was a revival of agriculture: it was the golden age for sugarcane; coffee also was grown on a large scale; cotton production went up; and the forests of the south were turned into profitable plantations of cacao. Rubber plantations were developed at the beginning of the 20th century.

The Diamantina Highland and its northern extension, the Serra do Tombador, run longitudinally across Bahia from the borders of Minas Gerais and constitute the line of greatest elevation, the Diamantina reaching its maximum elevation in Pico das Almas, which is 6,068 ft (1,850 m) in height. From this dorsal ridge descend the Western and Eastern plateaus, which vary in altitude between about 650 and 2,600 ft and are characterized by inselbergs (isolated eminences left by erosion). The Eastern Plateau ends with the heights overlooking the coastal plain.

The major river is the São Francisco, which rises in Minas Gerais and flows north across western Bahia before turning eastward in a great curve to form the frontier between

Bahia and Pernambuco and between Bahia and Alagoas, on its long way down to the Atlantic. The second most important river is the Paraguaçu, which has its sources in the Diamantina Highland and flows eastward into All Saint's Bay. Its basin is a cattle-raising zone, with small areas of agriculture, in an otherwise arid region.

Along Bahia's coastline there are areas with an annual rainfall exceeding 55 in. (1,400 mm), as well as sandy stretches on which the Brazilian coconut and the *mangabeira* rubber tree flourish, while the mud of the estuaries favours mangroves. In the broad-leaved tropical forest, where the annual rainfall exceeds 60 in. and where the coldest month has an average temperature of 64° F (18° C), the sandy clay soil supports an evergreen vegetation. In the zone of transitional forest there is a deciduous vegetation of shrubs and smaller plants. In the extensive *caatinga,* or zone of drought (nearly 60 percent of the state's territory lies within what Brazil's geographers call "the Polygon of Droughts"), the rainy season is irregular, and the annual rainfall never exceeds 24 in. The landscape is open and bare, and plants such as cactus predominate.

Peccary, tapir, and the two-toed sloth live in the forests. In open country the giant armadillo, the scarlet ibis, and the king vulture can be found.

Bahia's population consists of a mulatto majority, with sizable black and white minorities. Population density varies considerably. The greatest concentrations of Bahia's population reside in the cities and towns of its northern coastal area, particularly in the region known as the Recôncavo. Salvador (the capital), Ilhéus, Itabuna, Feira de Santana, and Vitória da Conquista are the major cities. The arid interior, on the other hand, is sparsely populated and has few towns. Of the total population, more than half live in rural areas.

The language of the people is Portuguese, but it is influenced to some extent by African idiom and slightly by various Indian languages. Roman Catholicism is professed by the overwhelming majority of the population. Protestantism, Spiritualism, and other beliefs claim small minorities of the population. Many people practice the rituals of candomblé, a syncretist religious sect, but declare themselves Roman Catholics.

The standard of living is low. Hygiene is defective, even in urban areas, and illiteracy is widespread, despite efforts to improve medical services and sanitation and to expand schooling. Salvador has two universities, the Federal and the Católica do Salvador.

Bahia's mineral resources include petroleum, natural gas, lead, copper, chrome, tin, barite, manganese, magnesite, titanium, hematite, quartz, kaolin, marble, asbestos, and amethyst. There is also a hydroelectric potential: the São Francisco River has been harnessed by the Paulo Afonso Dam at its major waterfall.

The most important crops are cacao, tobacco, vegetable oils, piassava, and sisal. Timber is also obtained from the forests. Cattle yield leather and skins. Heavy industry is represented by the Landulfo Alves petroleum refinery and by cement works and ironworks. Salvador, Feira de Santana, and Aratu are industrial centres. Energy is mostly hydroelectric, especially from the Paulo Afonso project. The state's roads and railway mostly serve the Recôncavo.

Prominent among cultural institutions are the Academia de Letras da Bahia, the Instituto Geográfico e Histórico da Bahia, and the Instituto de Musica da Bahia. Pop. (1980 prelim.) 9,597,393.

Bahia (Brazil): *see* Salvador.

Bahía, Islas de la, English BAY ISLANDS, group of small islands constituting the Islas de la Bahía department of Honduras. They have an area of 101 sq mi (261 sq km) and lie about 35 mi (56 km) offshore in the Caribbean Sea. The main islands were discovered in 1502 by Columbus and were settled in 1642 by English buccaneers. Between 1650 and 1850 Spain, Honduras, and England intermittently contested the islands, and Carib Indians from St. Vincent in the Leeward Islands were deported to a penal colony on Roatán. The islands were annexed to Great Britain in 1852 but ceded to Honduras in 1859. Roatán (*q.v.*), the departmental capital, is located on Roatán island. The chief activities are raising bananas, cassava, coconuts, and sweet potatoes; rearing livestock; and fishing; on Guanaja refrigeration and electronics plants have been built. Tourism grew in importance in the 1970s. An airport on Utila links the islands to the mainland and to an airstrip on the island of Guanaja. The inhabitants are English-speaking Protestants descended from settlers and from Caribs deported from St. Vincent. Pop. (1981 est.) 17,910.

Bahía Blanca, city and major port of Argentina, located near Bahía (bay) Blanca of the Atlantic Ocean in the southwestern part of Buenos Aires province. The bay forms a natural harbour for the city, which is located 4 mi (6.5 km) upstream on the shallow Arroyo (stream) Napostá Grande. Explorers in the 18th century named the area Bahía Blanca (White Bay), but the settlement that grew up around a military outpost, established in 1828 as a protection against Indian attacks and foreign encroachments, was first called Nueva Buenos Aires. It was chartered in 1895 as Bahía Blanca and developed as a commercial centre after the completion of the first rail connection with Buenos Aires in 1884. It has several subsidiary ports with modern facilities for handling grains, meat, fruits, and petrochemicals from the southwestern Pampa and northern Patagonia. Puerto Belgrano serves as a naval base. Construction of a petrochemical complex was a major project of the late 1970s and early 1980s.

Bahía Blanca is the site of the National University of the South (1956; formerly a technical institute), the Bernardino Rivadavia Library, and various museums. The atmosphere of growth and commercialism that characterized early 20th-century Bahía Blanca inspired Roberto Payró to write *Pago Chico* (1908), a novel about the city. Pop. (1980 prelim.) 202,601.

Bahmanī SULTANATE, Muslim state (1347–1518) in the Deccan in India. It was founded in 1347 by ʿAlā'-ud-Dīn Bahman Shāh, supported by other military leaders in rebellion against the sultan of Delhi, Muḥammad ibn Tughluq. Its capital was Aḥsanābād (Gulbarga) between 1347 and *c.* 1425 and Muḥammadābād (Bīdar) thereafter. Bahmanī attained the peak of its power during the vizierate (1466–81) of Maḥmūd Gāwān.

The Bahmanī sultanate's main foes in its efforts to extend itself securely over the Deccan tableland were the Hindu rulers of Vijayanagar, Telingāna, and Orissa and the Muslim rulers of Khāndesh, Mālwa, and Gujarāt. In the north, a *modus vivendi* with Mālwa had been achieved by 1468. In the south, war with Vijayanagar over the fertile Raichūr doab between the Krishna and Tungabhadra rivers was endemic until Krishna Deva Rāya, king of Vijayanagar, succeeded (1510–20) in incorporating it into his dominions. In the east, the Bahmanīs often warred with the Hindu chiefs of Telingāna, who were usually allied with the rajas of Orissa. In the west the Bahmanīs were unable to control the Western Ghāts, although Maḥmūd Gāwān temporarily occupied Sangameshwar and Goa in 1471–72.

The political domination of Muslim groups in a predominantly Hindu area was facilitated by mutual noninterference among the various religious communities. The Bahmanī sultans often encouraged a fusion of Deccan cultures. The division of the Bahmanī sultanate into four *ṭaraf* (provinces) encouraged an autonomy that the reforms of Maḥmūd Gāwān failed to combat. Between 1490 and 1518 the Bahmanī sultanate dissolved into the five successor powers of Bijāpur, Ahmadnagar, Golconda, Berār, and Bīdar.

Bahnaric languages, group of languages spoken chiefly in Vietnam, divided into North, South, and West Bahnaric categories. They are members of the Mon-Khmer language group affiliated with the Austro-Asiatic language family.

North Bahnaric, primarily Vietnamese, includes languages spoken in areas of Laos; its largest language is Bahnar. South Bahnaric is found in Vietnam and eastern Kampuchea, and its Ko'ho language has approximately 100,000 speakers. West Bahnaric, composed of smaller languages, is spoken in northeastern Kampuchea and Laos.

Bahoruco, province, southwestern Dominican Republic. Created in 1943 from the western part of Barahona province, it was later reduced in size by the formation of Independencia province. Its remaining 531 sq mi (1,376 sq km) extend from the high Sierra de Neiba in the north to the basin of Lago (lake) Enriquillo below sea level. Large, irrigated sugarcane plantations account for one-third of the cultivated area; other significant crops include plantains, bananas, coffee, corn (maize), and beans. Neiba (*q.v.*) is the provincial capital. Pop. (1981) 78,636.

Bahr, Hermann (b. July 19, 1863, Linz, Upper Austria—d. Jan. 15, 1934, Munich), Austrian author and playwright, whose keen interest in cultural movements makes his career a guide to literary developments in Austria during his lifetime.

After studying at Austrian and German universities, he settled in Vienna, where he worked on a number of newspapers. The early critical works *Zur Kritik der Moderne* (1890; "On Criticism of Modernity") and *Die Überwindung des Naturalismus* (1891; "Overcoming Naturalism") illustrate the first phase of his career, in which he attempted to reconcile naturalism with romanticism. In 1907 he published *Wien*, a remarkable essay on the soul of Vienna, which, however, was banned. Later, under the influence of Maurice Maeterlinck, Bahr became a champion of mysticism and Symbolism. His comedies, including *Wienerinnen* (1900; "Viennese Women"), *Der Krampus* (1901), and *Das Konzert* (1909), are superficially amusing.

In 1903 Bahr was appointed director of the Deutsches Theater, Berlin, and in 1918 he was for a short time director of the Vienna Burgtheater. During World War I, under the influence of Catholicism, his novel *Himmelfahrt* (1916; "The Ascension") represented the staunchly Catholic school of thought in his country. His later critical works, which show his interest in the social effect of creative art, including *Dialog vom Marsyas* (1904) and *Expressionismus* (1914).

Baḥr al-Abyaḍ, al-, English WHITE NILE, *mudīrīyah* (province), Central Region, central Sudan, bounded by the provinces of al-Kharṭūm on the north, Kurdufān ash-Shamālīyah and Kurdufān al-Janūbīyah on the west, Aʿālī an-Nīl on the south, and al-Jazīrah and an-Nīl al-Azraq on the east. It covers an area of 16,149 sq mi (41,825 sq km) and was created in 1975 from part of former an-Nīl al-Azraq province. The White Nile almost bisects the province from north to south and has more the appearance of a lake than a river in some places. Tropical clay soils, mainly derived from ancient alluvium, support short grass scrub.

About 1550 BC the region was occupied by the 18th Egyptian dynasty. In 750 BC the area came under the control of the 25th, or Kushite Egyptian dynasty, which ruled the region for about 1,000 years. Subsequently it passed under Axumite rule in the 14th century AD and became largely Christianized. In 1504 the province was conquered by the Funj dynasty of Sennār. In 1821 it was conquered by Muḥammad ʿAlī, ruler of Egypt. The Mahdists rebelled against the Egyptians and conquered the province in 1881. In 1898 the Mahdists were defeated by invading Anglo-Egyptian forces under General Kitchener; the province remained under joint Anglo-Egyptian rule until The Sudan's independence in 1956.

Agriculture dominates the provincial economy and produces cotton, cereals, oilseeds, peanuts (groundnuts), pulses, wheat, *durra* (sorghum), and vegetables. Industries include a meat cannery, sugar refineries, mills producing oils from sesame seeds and peanuts, and soap factories. Ad-Duwaym, the provincial capital, is linked by road with Kūstī and Tandaltī, which are connected by the Kassalā–Nyala railway. The population is mainly comprised of Arabs and Islām is the dominant religion. Pop. (1976 est.) 1,251,000.

Baḥr al-Abyaḍ, al- (The Sudan): *see* White Nile River.

Baḥr al-Aḥmar, al-, *muḥāfaẓah* (governorate) of Egypt, comprising much of the Eastern Desert east of the Nile Valley to the Red Sea; its name means "red sea." It extends from approximately 29° N southward to the frontier of The Sudan. On the west it is bounded from north to south by the *muḥāfaẓāt* of the Nile Valley of Upper Egypt. Its total area is 78,643 sq mi (203,685 sq km), about one-fifth of the area of the country.

The well-dissected Eastern Desert consists of a rolling limestone highland that falls away abruptly in bluffs on the Nile and extends southward to a point roughly opposite Qinā, where it breaks up into cliffs about 1,600 ft (488 m) high, deeply scored by wadis (seasonal watercourses). From east of Qinā southward the Nubian sandstone prevails, deeply indented by ravines and wadis. Small semi-nomadic settlements are scattered throughout. From 50 to 85 mi (80 to 137 km) east of the Nile the desert highland merges into a series of volcanic, arid mountain chains generally trending north–south, rising to 6,000–6,500 ft in the south. The northern boundary of al-Baḥr al-Aḥmar is near the southern extreme of the Jabal Jalālah al-Baḥrīyah, which rises to 4,183 ft in southern as-Suways (Suez) *muḥāfaẓah.* The next group south are the Jabal al-Jalālat al-Qiblīyah, which rise to a peak of 4,839 ft. Just west-northwest of the peak is the Christian monastery of St. Anthony (Arabic Dayr al-Qaddīs Anṭūn); across the crest of the range to the southeast is the monastery of St. Paul.

The Eastern Desert has no artesian wells and possesses only a few mountain springs, but it receives occasional rainfall. Where the mountains fall away to the Red Sea there is a coastal plain, which supports most of the sedentary population. Nomadic desert dwellers live by herding and trading with the mining and petroleum camps; others make up fishing communities on the Red Sea.

In the 1960s mineral deposits began to be exploited in al-Baḥr al-Aḥmar. Offshore and onshore oil fields, of which the largest is the al-Morgan field, located about 125 mi south of Suez, have produced most of Egypt's petroleum since the 1970s, and additional fields in the Gulf of Suez have started production. The Eastern Desert also yields asbestos, manganese, phosphates, uranium, and gold. Al-Quṣayr, the main Egyptian port in the Red Sea proper south of Suez (because coral reefs fringe most of the coast), has large phosphate deposits and a plant that processes the mined phosphates for shipment. The capital of the governorate is al-Ghurdaqah (*see* Ghurdaqah, al-), a major oil centre and site of an oil field. Other industrial sites or ports are Būr Safājah, Ḥamrāwein, and ʿAyn Sukhnah, the Gulf of Suez terminal of an oil pipeline to the Mediterranean Sea. From the mountains of the Eastern Desert, alabaster, porphyry, granite, and sandstone are still mined as in pharaonic times. A highway along the Red Sea coast links Suez and the Sudanese frontier, and four highways lead across the desert to the Nile Valley. Pop. (1983 est.) 68,000.

Baḥr al-Aḥmar, al-, English RED SEA, *mudīrīyah* (province), Eastern Region, northeastern Sudan, bounded by the Red Sea on the east, Egypt on the north, an-Nīl province on the west, and Kassalā province and Ethiopia on the south. Covering an area of 8,490 sq mi (21,990 sq km), the province was formed in 1975 from the northern part of the former Kassalā province. The Nubian Desert lies in the west of the province, drained by Wādī Jabjabah along its northwestern boundary and by a number of smaller intermittent streams including the ʿAmūr, Rabeida, Elei, and Moglal wadis. In the eastern half of the province rise the discontinuous Red Sea Hills to an elevation of about 6,560 ft (2,000 m). Along the uplifted western coast of the Red Sea rift valley are the east-facing scarplands, overlooking the Coastal Plain and its fringe and coastal indentations and coral reefs.

There were scattered settlements in the region after 5000 BC and prior to the establishment of Egyptian rule in the 15th to 14th centuries BC. Around 750 BC the region came under the rule of the 25th, or Kushite, Egyptian dynasty, which ruled the province for about 1,000 years. Muslim traders settled in the coastal areas in the 8th century AD and later more Arabs were attracted by the gold mines and growing importance of Red Sea ports. In the 16th century the people of the province converted to Islām, when the region was conquered by the Funj dynasty of Sennār with Arab assistance. The Funj continued to rule until 1821 when they were conquered by Muḥammad ʿAlī's Egyptian army. The province became part of the Anglo-Egyptian Condominium in 1899 and part of independent Sudan in 1956.

The Red Sea Hills in the eastern part of the province have only scanty vegetation on their western slopes; because of the winter rainfall a thicker growth of tall trees exists on their eastern slopes. In the Ṭawkar delta, situated south of Sawakin, cotton, and *durra* (sorghum) are grown. The Beja peoples in the east raise camels, sheep, and goats, and are engaged in the primary processing of hides and other animal products. Iron ore, gypsum, manganese, chromium, asbestos, talc, and gold are mined in the Red Sea Hills. Port Sudan, the provincial capital, is linked by road and railway with ʿAṭbarah and Kassalā. An oil pipeline, about 530 mi (850 km) in length, between Port Sudan and Khartoum, passes through the province. Pop. (1976 est.) 505,000.

Baḥr al-ʿArab, also spelled BAHR EL-ARAB, intermittent river of southwestern Sudan, rising northeast of the Massif du Tondou (Bongo), near the border with the Central African Republic. It flows 500 mi (800 km) east-southeast to join the Baḥr al-Ghazāl, a tributary of the Nile, at Ghābat al-ʿArab. It is not navigable and is subject to floods in summer.

Baḥr al-Ghazāl, also spelled BAHR EL-GHAZAL, *mudīrīyah* (province), Southern Region, southwestern Sudan, bounded by the provinces of Dārfūr al-Janūbīyah and Kurdufān al-Janūbīyah on the north, al-Buḥayrah on the east, al-Istiwāʾīyah al-Gharbīyah on the south, and by the Central African Republic on the west. It has an area of 51,960 sq mi (134,576 sq km) and was formed in 1975 from the western part of the former Baḥr al-Ghazāl province. Baḥr al-Ghazāl comprises part of the Ironstone Plateau, which dominates the northwestern part of the province with an average elevation of 1,200 ft (365 m). The plateau gradually merges with the southern clay plains of south central Sudan to the east and is cut by the valleys of the Raga, Sopo, Kuru, and Pongo rivers, all affluents of the Baḥr al-Ghazāl. Rainfall is sufficient to sustain woodland and savannah.

The region, inhabited by Nilotic-speaking Dinka peoples, was entered by European and Egyptian traders seeking ivory, beginning in the 1850s. But ivory became difficult to obtain, and slave raiding proved a profitable alternative. The slave trade was controlled by al-Zubayr Raḥma Mansūr, who was made provincial governor in 1872 to check his activities as a slave merchant. The Mahdists rebelled in 1881 and extended their control over the province; they were defeated in 1898 by the Anglo-Egyptian forces. In 1899 the province became part of the Anglo-Egyptian Condominium and part of independent Sudan in 1956.

Most of the population in the province is engaged in sedentary and shifting cultivation of cereals, root crops, cassava, millet, corn (maize), *durra* (sorghum), and pulses. The nomads in the north raise cattle. Household industry comprises leather and woodworking, blacksmithing, and the processing of hides and other animal products. Wāw, the provincial capital, is linked by road and railway with Uwayl to the northwest. The Nilotic Dinka, who migrate seasonally with their herds, are the most numerous group of people; the remainder are Sudanic-speakers. Pop. (1976 est.) 866,000.

Baḥr al-Ghazāl, also spelled BAHR EL-GHAZAL, English GAZELLE RIVER, river, The Sudan, chief western affluent of the Nile. It is 445 mi (716 km) long and joins the upper Nile (Baḥr al-Jabal) through Lake No, from which it flows eastward as the White Nile (Baḥr al-Abyaḍ). Vaguely known to early Greek geographers, the river was mapped in 1772 by the French geographer Jean-Baptiste Bourguignon d'Anville. It is known as the Baḥr al-Ghazāl only after joining with its main affluents (the Jur, Tonj, and Baḥr al-ʿArab). The river has a catchment area of 328,750 sq mi (851,459 sq km) extending as far west as the Central African Republic (the watershed of the Chari River) and Zaire. Its tributaries cut valleys across the Ironstone Plateau before reaching the clay plain of the Baḥr al-Ghazāl. The evaporation and transpiration due to passage through the swamps of as-Sudd so reduce the water flow that the seasonal discharge into Lake No ranges from nothing to 1,700 cu ft (48 cu m) per second.

Baḥr al-Jabal, also spelled BAHR EL-JEBEL, English MOUNTAIN NILE, that section of the

The Baḥr al-Jabal, near Jūbā, The Sudan

Nile River between Nimule near the Uganda border and Malakāl in south central Sudan. Below Nimule the river flows northward over the Fula Rapids, past Jūbā (the head of navigation), and through as-Sudd, an enormous, papyrus-choked swamp where half its water is lost. It receives the Baḥr al-Ghazāl at Lake No, and then turns east to join with the Sobat River of western Ethiopia above Malakāl, thereafter forming the White Nile. Much of the river's 594-mi (956-km) course winds between walls of high papyrus, reeds, and elephant grass, which, during the dry season, provide grazing for cattle.

Baḥr az-Zarāf, also spelled BAHR EL-ZARAF, English GIRAFFE RIVER, river, an arm of the Nile in as-Sudd region of south central Sudan. It is formed in the swamps north of Shambe, diverting water from the Baḥr al-Jabal (Mountain Nile), and flows 150 mi (240 km) north, past Fangak, to join the Baḥr al-Jabal, 35 mi west of Malakāl. It is not navigable but is permanently connected to the Baḥr al-Jabal by two cuts dredged where the streams are close together.

Baḥr Fāris (Asia): *see* Persian Gulf.

Bahraich, town, administrative headquarters of Bahraich district, Uttar Pradesh state, northern India, located on a tributary of the Ghāghara River and on a rail line between Lucknow and Nepālganj, Nepal. Bahraich is a centre of trade (agricultural products and timber) with Nepal; there is also some sugar processing. The tomb of Sayyid Sālār Mas'ūd, an Afghan warrior-saint who died there in 1033, is visited by Muslim and Hindu pilgrims. The ruins of a Buddhist monastery are located west of the town.

Bahraich district, 2,653 sq mi (6,871 sq km) in area, is a wedge-shaped territory between the Nepal border and the Ghāghara River. It consists of the Rāpti River Basin (east) and part of the Ghāghara Plain (west), separated by a highland area. The economy is agricultural (rice, corn [maize], wheat, and gram [chick-pea]). The area's history is little known before Sayyid Sālār Mas'ūd's invasion in 1033. It subsequently changed hands several times, finally becoming part of British India. Pop. (1981) town, 99,889; district, 2,216,245.

Bahrain, officially STATE OF BAHRAIN, Arabic DAWLAT AL-BAḤRAYN, country occupying an archipelago consisting of Bahrain Island and about 30 smaller islands, lying along the Arabian Peninsula in the Persian Gulf and covering 258 sq mi (669 sq km). The capital is Manama (al-Manāmah). The main island is about 30 mi (48 km) from north to south and about 10 mi from east to west and lies some 100 mi south of Iran, in the Gulf of Bahrain, midway between Saudi Arabia to the west and the Qatar Peninsula to the east. The population in 1982 was 371,000.

The article that follows is a summary of the significant detail about Bahrain. Fuller treatment is provided in the MACROPAEDIA articles named below. For geography and history, *see* Arabia; for information about the country and its major physiographic features in their regional setting, *see* Asia; for information about regional aspects of Bahrain's history, *see* The Islāmic World. For information about Bahrain's major cultural manifestations, *see* Muḥammad and the Religion of Islām; Ancient Middle Eastern Religions; Islāmic Art.

For current history and for statistics on society and economy, *see* the article "World Affairs" and BRITANNICA WORLD DATA, respectively, in the *Britannica Book of the Year.*

The land. Bahrain Island accounts for seven-eighths of the country's total area and, together with al-Muḥarraq and Sitrah, just off its northeastern coast, constitutes the population

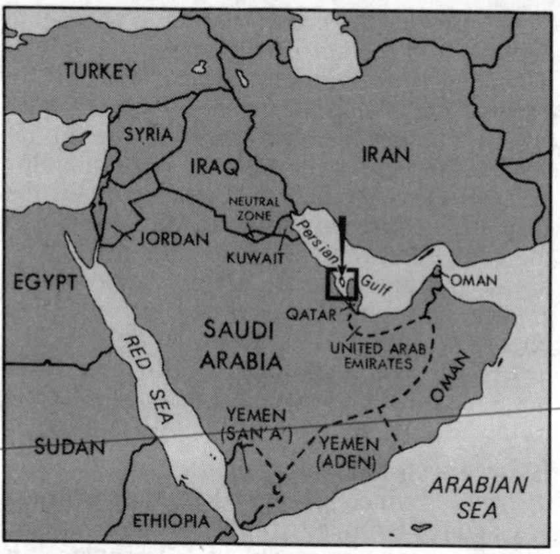

Bahrain

and economic centre of the country. Geologically, Bahrain is an elongated dome that rises to 443 ft (135 m) above sea level at Jabal ad-Dukhān, at the centre of the island. The lowlands in the south and the southwest are composed of sandy plains and salt marshes. Along a narrow coastal area in the north and northwest, the freshwater aquifers (which are tapped by artesian wells) and numerous springs provide water for irrigating date and vegetable gardens.

The climate is characterized throughout the year by high humidity. Summer temperatures (May until October) exceed 83° F (28° C), and rainfall then is nearly nonexistent. The winter temperatures average below 70° F (21° C), and those months provide almost all of the country's 3-in. (76-mm) annual average rainfall. Even with the island's extreme lack of precipitation, some 200 species of plants can be found, along with such mammals as the gazelle, hare, jerboa (desert rat), and mongoose (probably imported from India).

Bahrain's only significant natural resources are its petroleum and natural gas reserves.

The people. The majority of the population is native born, and more than one third of it is less than 30 years of age. The ratio of males to females is 106 to 100. Because the population is almost entirely urban, its density is 1,359 persons per sq mi (525 persons per sq km.) The Muslim population is almost equally divided between the Sunnī and Shī'ī sects. Arabic is the official language, but English is widely understood. For the years 1975–80 the birth rate was 34.4 per 1,000 and the death rate 8 per 1,000; infant mortality was 57 per 1,000 live births. The rate of natural increase was 2.8 percent. In 1981 almost one-third of the population was foreign born. Manama had a population of 108,684 (1981) and al-Muḥarraq 46,061.

The economy. Bahrain has a developing mixed state and private-enterprise economy. The gross national product (GNP) was (1980) U.S. $3,592,000,000, about $8,510 per capita. Average annual growth of the real GNP (1970–79) was 0.7 percent. The GNP originates primarily from petroleum and natural gas production, refining (25 percent and of increasing importance), banking and financial services, and social services.

Only about 3 percent of the total land area is arable, most of it near the springs of northern Bahrain Island. Agriculture is of minimal economic importance and produces only a fraction of Bahrain's food requirements, mainly in fruits and vegetables.

About one-twentieth of the land is in pasture, supporting a few thousand sheep, cattle, and goats.

Manufacturing is growing as the government strives to diversity in the face of dwindling petroleum reserves; together with utilities, it employs 11 percent of the labour force. The principal nonpetroleum industrial products include aluminum (from a smelter set up in the early 1970s) and various aluminum products, tiles and cement blocks, plastics, asbestos pipe, matches, wheat flour, and soft drinks. Electrical energy production (1980) was 1,290,000,000 kW-hr, all from thermal power plants.

Nearly three-fifths of Bahrain's labour force in the early 1980s was foreign born. The principal sectors of employment were community, personal, and social services (29 percent); construction (25 percent); and trade, restaurants, and hotels (12 percent). Trade unions are not allowed.

The Bahraini government is owner or part owner of all petroleum, natural gas, and heavy industries. Light industry, construction, trade, and finance are left to the private sector. Foreign investment is encouraged, but by law Bahrainis must retain at least 51 percent ownership of all enterprises.

The monetary unit is the Bahrain dinar (BD), subdivided into 1,000 fils. Three-fourths of the budgetary revenue is principally from petroleum and natural gas revenues, together with customs duties and port taxes, and loans and financial aid. Expenditures are principally for infrastructure development, social services, and housing. By 1982 Bahrain had more than 60 offshore banks; they may not engage in local banking services but may accept deposits from the government and large financial institutions and may extend loans to Bahraini and regional capital projects. With excellent telecommunications facilities and a computer services company, Bahrain has become the Persian Gulf's preeminent financial centre.

The road network includes about 60 mi of paved highways and interisland causeways. The principal port, Mīnā' Salmān, near Manama on Bahrain Island, offers container and roll-on–roll-off facilities and a ship-repair dry dock. Bahrain has 50 merchant ships larger than 100 gross tons. There is an international airport on al-Muḥarraq Island. Low landing fees have made it the busiest airport in the Persian Gulf area.

Exports, slightly greater in value than imports, are principally petroleum and natural gas products (89 percent) and aluminum products. Major importers of Bahrain's exports are the United Arab Emirates, Japan, and Singapore. Imports are mainly crude petroleum for refining, machinery and transport equipment, and manufactured products. Major sources for imports were Saudi Arabia (petroleum), the United States, and Japan.

Administrative and social conditions. Bahrain is a constitutional monarchy governed by the Āl (family) Khalīfah. Power is centred in the *amīr,* who, under the 1973 constitution, makes all the country's major decisions. He appoints a Council of Ministers to administer the government's day-to-day affairs. There was a popularly elected legislature, the National Assembly, but in 1975 the Amīr disbanded it, charging some of its members with subversive activity. The Khalīfah family, who are Sunnī Muslims, has encountered limited opposition to its rule from the country's Shī'īs.

Bahrain is to a large extent a welfare state, offering free and comprehensive medical care to all, including expatriates. It also provides free education and administers benefits programs for the old and the disabled.

Health conditions have greatly improved since the country's independence in 1971. Most tropical diseases have been eradicated, and life expectancy has risen to 64 years for men and 68 for women, among the highest rates in the Middle East. There are three levels of education in Bahrain: six-year primary school, two-year intermediate school, and three-year secondary school. Secondary graduates may attend one of two teacher-training colleges or the Gulf Technical College.

Most of the press in Bahrain is privately owned. Although it is not subjected to formal censorship, the press refrains from criticizing the ruling family and its policies.

Cultural life. In spite of its recent rapid economic development, Bahrain remains, in most respects, essentially Arab in its culture and life-style. The state radio station broadcasts mainly in Arabic, and television transmissions are received from Saudi Arabia. The traditional sports of falconry, gazelle and hare coursing, and horse and camel racing are still practiced by wealthier Bahrainis.

History. Burial mounds in the north of Bahrain Island suggest a period of Sumerian influence in the 3rd millennium BC. The island has been identified with the ancient Dilmun (Telmun) of *c.* 2000 BC, a lively and prosperous trading centre linking Sumeria with the Indus Valley. Written records of the archipelago exist in Assyrian, Persian, Greek, and Roman sources.

Bahrain may have been under mainland Arab domination when Shāpūr II annexed it, together with eastern Arabia, into the Persian Sāsānian empire in the 4th century AD. By the time of the Islāmic invasion, in the 7th century, Bahrain was being governed for Persia by a Christian Arab; Syrian Christian records suggest Bahrain had its own Nestorian bishop. The ʿAbbāsids took Bahrain in the 8th century, and it remained under Arab control until 1521, when Portugal seized it. In 1602, after 80 years of unrest, the Persians took Bahrain and held it against assaults by the Portuguese and the Omanis. In 1783 Aḥmad ibn Āl Khalīfah ousted the Persians, and his family has ruled Bahrain ever since.

During the 19th century, Britain intervened several times to suppress piracy by the Bahrainis and to defeat attempts by neighbouring Arabs to assert dominion over the islands. In a series of treaties from 1820, Britain gained extensive control over Bahrain. After Britain's decision in 1968 to withdraw all forces from the Persian Gulf, Shaykh ʿIsā ibn Sulmān Āl Khalīfah proclaimed Bahrain independent in August 1971. After independence, tensions between the Shīʿī and Sunnī communities increased, and Shīʿī Muslims, emboldened by Iran's revolution in 1979, continued to press for greater participation in government.

Articles are alphabetized word by word, not letter by letter

Bahrām, also called VARAHRAN, or VERETHRAGHNA, name of Sāsānian kings, grouped below chronologically and indicated by the symbol •.

• **Bahrām I** (fl. 3rd century), Sāsānian king (reigned 273–276).

A son of Shāpūr I, during his father's reign he governed the province of Atropatene. His succession to his brother Hormizd I strengthened the position of the Zoroastrian clergy and their high priest Kartēr, and at their insistence Bahrām imprisoned Mani, the founder of the anti-materialist, ascetic religion of Manichaeism. Subsequent religious persecution was directed not only at Manichaeans but at Christians and Buddhists as well. Bahrām, distinguished by his characteristic radiate crown, is portrayed on a rock sculpture at Bishāpūr (in southern Iran), although his name in the inscription was later erased by the Sāsānian king Narses.

Bahrām I, coin, 3rd century; in the British Museum

By courtesy of the trustees of the British Museum; photograph, J.R. Freeman & Co. Ltd.

• **Bahrām II** (fl. 3rd century), Sāsānian king (reigned 276–293), the son and successor of Bahrām I.

Soon after becoming king, he was forced to defend his position against a brother, Hormizd, viceroy of the eastern provinces. In 283, exploiting Bahrām's preoccupations, the Roman emperor Carus invaded Mesopotamia unopposed and entered Ctesiphon, the Sāsānian capital. Carus' sudden death, however, forced the Romans to withdraw, and soon thereafter the overthrow of Hormizd made Bahrām secure. Numerous southern Persian rock sculptures depict Bahrām wearing his winged crown, and several include his queen.

Bahrām II, coin, late 3rd century; in the British Museum

By courtesy of the trustees of the British Museum; photograph, J.R. Freeman & Co. Ltd.

Because female portraits are rare in Sāsānian art, she is thought to have been a major dynastic personage.

• **Bahrām IV** (fl. late 4th century), Sāsānian king (reigned AD 388–399). One of the sons of Shāpūr II, he first served as governor of Kermān before succeeding his brother Shāpūr III on the throne. Although the partition of Armenia with Rome is often ascribed to Bahrām, it probably occurred in 387, during the reign of his brother Shāpūr.

• **Bahrām V,** also called BAHRĀM GŪR (fl. 5th century), Sāsānian king (reigned 420–438). He was celebrated in literature, art, and folklore for his chivalry, romantic adventures, and huntsmanship.

He was educated at the court of al-Mundhir, the Lakhmid Arab king of al-Ḥira, in Mesene, whose support helped him gain the throne after the assassination of his father, Yazdegerd I. He was apparently also supported by Mihr-Naresh, chief minister of Yazdegerd's last years, to whom Bahrām later delegated much of the governmental administration.

Bahrām carried on an inconclusive war with the Romans (421–422), and in 427 he crushed an invasion in the east by the nomadic Hephthalites, extending his influence into Central Asia, where his portrait survived for centuries on the coinage of Bukhara (in modern Uzbek S.S.R.).

• **Bahrām VI Chūbīn** (fl. 6th century), Sāsānian king (reigned 590–591). A general and head of the house of Mihran at Rayy (near modern Tehrān), he performed, in gaining the throne, a feat exceptional for one not of Sāsānian royal blood. Prominent as master of the household in the Byzantine wars of the Sāsānian king Hormizd IV, Bahrām later received the supreme command in Khorāsān and was able to repel a Turkish invasion. After a defeat by the Romans in 589, however, he was harshly treated by Hormizd. Bahrām, supported by his army, rebelled; in the disorder, Hormizd was assassinated, and Khosrow II, his successor, marched against the irreconcilable general. The royal troops, however, mutinied, and Khosrow fled to the Byzantines. Bahrām then proclaimed himself king. In 591, with Byzantine support, Khosrow regained the throne.

Bahrām VI Chūbīn, coin, 6th century; in the British Museum

By courtesy of the trustees of the British Museum; photograph, J.R. Freeman & Co. Ltd.

Bahrām escaped to Turkistan, where he was assassinated. His colourful career became the subject of a Middle Persian popular romance.

Bahram (foaled 1932), English racehorse (Thoroughbred), winner in 1935 of the British Triple Crown and never beaten in nine contests.

Foaled by Friar's Daughter and sired by Blandford, Bahram was owned by the Aga Kahn and bred at his Curragh Stud in Ireland. Trained by Frank Butters at Newmarket, Bahram always came in first, from his first race in 1934, which he won by a neck. In 1935, ridden by his usual jockey Freddie Fox, Bahram won the Two Thousand Guineas and the Derby; and Charlie Smirke rode him to victory in the Saint Leger to complete the Triple Crown. In 1936 he was retired from the racetrack and sent to stud at Newmarket. Not outstanding as a stallion, he was sold in 1939 to a U.S. syndicate, which sold him to an Argentinian syndicate in 1946. He sired Turkham, a winner of the Saint Leger, Big Game, and Persian Gulf.

Bahrān (Zoroastrian deity): *see* Verethraghna.

Baḥrī Miṣr (Egypt): *see* Lower Egypt.

baht (unit of measure): *see* bat.

Bāhubali, also called GOMMATEŚVARA, according to Jaina legends of India, the son of Ṛṣabhanātha, the first Tīrthaṅkara, or saviour. Tradition relates that he stood immobile, with feet straight ahead and arms held at his side, for an entire year meditating in the Yogic po-

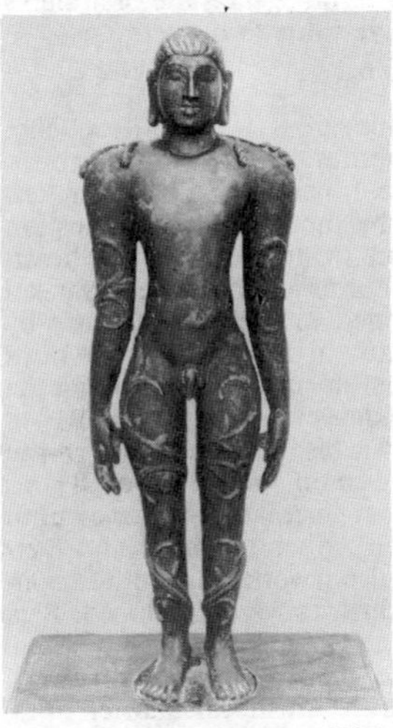

Bāhubali, bronze sculpture, Cālukya school, 9th century; in the Prince of Wales Museum of Western India, Bombay

By courtesy of the Prince of Wales Museum of Western India, Bombay sition of *kāyotsarga* ("dismissing the body"). He was so unmindful of the world around him that vines and creepers grew undisturbed up his arms and legs and anthills rose around his feet. Several works of sculpture depict Bāhubali, including an outstanding 9th-century bronze in the Prince of Wales Museum of Western India, Bombay. A colossal 10th-century sculpture stands on top of a hill at Sravana Belgola, a centre of the Digambara sect in Karṇāṭaka state. Cut out of a single block of gneiss, it stands 57 feet (17½ metres) high and is one of the largest free standing images in the world. Every 25 years the entire image is ceremonially bathed in curd, milk, and ghee.

Bahūtī, al-, in full SHAYKH MANṢŪR IBN YŪNUS AL-BAHŪTĪ, also called AL-BAHŪTĪ AL-MIṢRĪ (b. Bahūt, Egypt—d. July 1641, Cairo), teacher and the last major exponent in Egypt of the Ḥanbalī school of Islāmic law. Little is known about him except that he spent nearly all of his life teaching and practicing Ḥanbalī law. His legal writings, although not original, are noted for their clarity and are still used in Egypt.

Bahutu (people): *see* Hutu.

Bahya ben Joseph ibn Pakuda (fl. second half of the 11th century), dayyan—*i.e.*, judge of a rabbinical court—in Muslim Spain and author of a highly influential and popular work of ethical guidance. Around 1080 he wrote, in Arabic, *al-Hidāyah ilā-farā' id al-qulūb* ("Duties of the Heart"). In a rather inaccurate 12th-century translation into Hebrew by Judah ben Joseph ibn Tibbon, *Ḥovot ha-levavot*, it became a widely read classic of Jewish philosophic and devotional literature. An English translation, *Duties of the Heart* (1925–47; reprinted 1962), was completed by Moses Hyamson.

Via the Islāmic mystics, known as Ṣūfis, Bahya was influenced by Neoplatonism as to the nature of God and the soul's quest for him. From the Islāmic system of dialectical theology called *kalām* he borrowed proofs for the existence of God.

Critical of his predecessors who, of the two requirements of religion, had emphasized the "duties of the body" to the neglect of the "duties of the heart," Bahya wrote his book to restore the proper balance. The "duties of the body" are obligatory outward actions—religious ritual and ethical practice—while the "duties of the heart" are the attitudes and intentions that determine the state of a man's soul and alone give value to his acts.

Bai (people): *see* Pai.

Baia Mare, Hungarian NAGYBÁNYA, city, capital of Maramureş *judeţ* (district), northwestern Romania. It is in the Săsar River Valley, surrounded by mountains. This location affords protection from the cold northeastern winds and sustains a quasi-Mediterranean vegetation. Founded in the 12th century by Saxon immigrants, it was first known as Neustadt. The first document mentioning the name Baia Mare dates from 1329. Until 1948 it was the see of a bishop of an Eastern-rite church in communion with Rome. It was a mining centre of fluctuating fortunes until after World War II, when chemical and metallurgical works, lead works, and other nonferrous heavy industries were developed. Baia Mare contains a 14th-century Gothic-style clock tower (also named Stephen's Tower), which dominates the medieval quarter. Pop. (1982 est.) 119,973.

Baiae, Italian BAIA, ancient city of Campania, Italy, located on the west coast of the Gulf of Puteoli (Pozzuoli), traditionally named after Baios, the helmsman of Ulysses. In early Roman times it was called Aquae Cumanae because of its curative sulfur springs.

Its mild climate and luxuriant vegetation made it popular, and many magnificent villas were built there, including those of Julius Caesar and Nero. Baiae was devastated by Muslim raiders in the 8th century AD and entirely deserted because of malaria in 1500.

BAIB excretion (metabolic process): *see* beta-aminoisobutyric acid excretion.

Baibars I (Egyptian sultan): *see* Baybars I.

Baicheng (China): *see* Pai-ch'eng.

Baida (Libya): *see* Zāwiyat al-Bayḍā'.

Baie-Comeau, town, seat of Côte-Nord (North Shore) region, east central Quebec province, Canada, on the north bank of the St. Lawrence River, near the mouth of the Manicouagan River. Named after Napoléon-Alexandre Comeau, a local author, it was founded in 1936 at the instance of Robert R. McCormick, publisher of the *Chicago Tribune,* as a pulp and newsprint milling centre. The town is a busy deepwater port and industrial centre with an aluminum plant and grain-export facilities contributing to its economy. Baie-Comeau was unified with neighbouring and slightly larger Hauterive in 1983. The town is served by a paved highway to Quebec city (255 mi [410 km] southwest), an airport, and ferry service to Rimouski. Inc. 1937 (Baie-Comeau); 1983. Pop. (1981), including Hauterive, 26,861.

Baïf, Jean-Antoine de (b. 1532, Venice—d. October 1589, Paris), most learned of the seven French poets who constituted the group known as La Pléiade.

He received a classical education and in 1547 went with Pierre de Ronsard to study under Jean Dorat at the Collège de Coqueret, Paris, where they planned, with Joachim du Bellay, to transform French poetry by imitating the ancients and the Italians. To this program Baïf contributed two collections of Petrarchan sonnets and Epicurean lyrics, *Les Amours de Méline* (1552) and *L'Amour de Francine* (1555). In 1567 *Le Brave, ou Taillebras,* Baïf's lively adaptation of Plautus' *Miles gloriosus,* was played at court and published.

Baïf—who was the natural son of Lazare de Baïf, Humanist and diplomat—enjoyed royal favour and received pensions and benefices from Charles IX and Henry III. His *Euvres en rime* (1573; "Works in Rhyme") reveal great erudition: Greek (especially Alexandrian), Latin, neo-Latin, and Italian models are imitated for mythological poems, eclogues, epigrams, and sonnets. His verse translations include Terence's *Eunuchus* and Sophocles' *Antigone.*

Baïf was a versatile, inventive poet and experimenter; *e.g.,* he invented and used a system of phonetic spelling. With the musician Thibault de Courville, Baïf founded a short-lived Académie de Poésie et de Musique to promote certain Platonic theories on the union of poetry and music. His metrical inventions included a *vers baïfin* of 15 syllables. His theories were exemplified in *Etrénes de poezie fransoèze en vers mezurés* (1574; "Gifts of French Poetry in Quantitative Verse") and in his little songs, *Chansonnettes mesurées* (1586), with music written by Jacques Mauduit. His *Mimes, enseignements et proverbes* (1576; "Mimes, Lessons, and Proverbs") is considered to be his most original work.

Baïf was a personal poet whose gifts were inferior to his genius for invention of form and language; but he had a talent for vivid, realistic description, particularly in scenes of country life and in satire.

Baikal, Lake, Russian OZERO BAYKAL, also spelled OZERO BAJKAL, lake, located in the southern part of eastern Siberia within the Buryat Autonomous Soviet Socialist Republic and the Irkutsk (Irkutskaya) *oblast* (administrative region) of the Russian Soviet Federated Socialist Republic. It is the deepest continental body of water on Earth, having a maximum depth of 5,314 ft (1,620 m). Its area is 12,200 sq mi (31,500 sq km), with a length of 395 mi (636 km) and an average width of 30 mi. It contains about one-fifth of the fresh

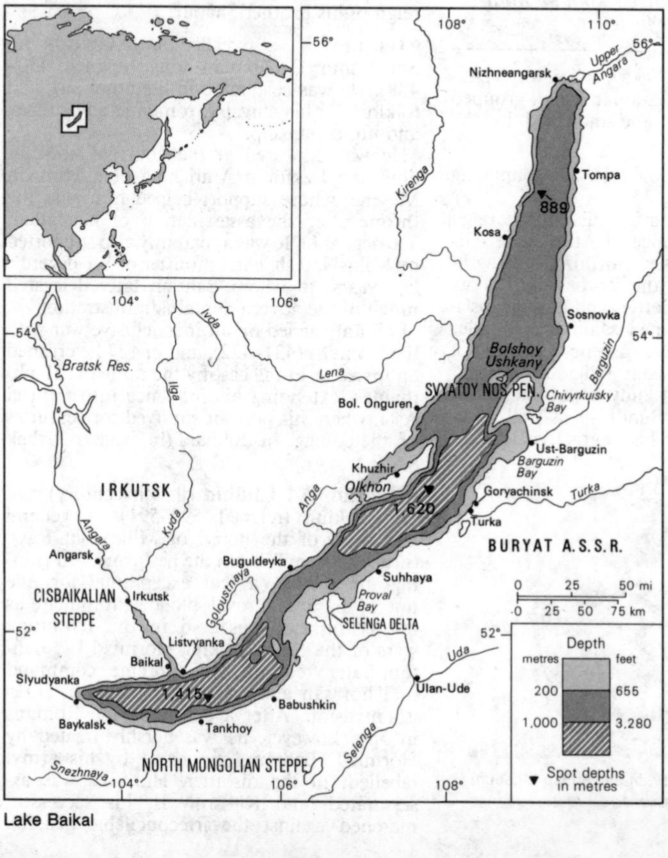

Lake Baikal

water on the Earth's surface and four-fifths of that in the U.S.S.R., or 5,500 cu mi (23,000 cu km). Into Lake Baikal flow 336 rivers and streams, of which the largest are the Selenga, Barguzin, Upper (Verkhnyaya) Angara, Turka, and Snezhnaya.

Baikal lies in a deep structural hollow surrounded by mountains, some of which tower 6,560 ft above it. The area is formed predominantly of metamorphic, sedimentary, and magmatic rock more than 500,000,000 years old. The sedimentary strata on the floor of the lake may be as much as 20,000 ft thick. Near the shore are remains of extinct volcanoes. Earth movements still continue, and there are occasional severe earthquakes; in 1862 a quake inundated 77 sq mi in the northern Selenga River Delta, creating a new bay in Baikal known as Proval Bay. Breaks in the Earth's crust continue to produce hot mineral springs.

The lake hollow is not symmetrical, having steep slopes on the western shores and gentler slopes on the eastern. About 8 percent of the floor consists of shallows 160 ft deep. The meandering shoreline runs for 1,300 mi, with large indentations at the bays of Barguzin, Chivyrkuysky, and Proval and at Ayaya and Frolikha inlets; the Svyatoy Nos Peninsula juts out into the lake from the southeastern shore. Baikal contains 27 islands, of which 5 are periodically submerged; the largest are Olkhon (280 sq mi) and Bolshoy Ushkany (more than 3 sq mi). The influx of water into the lake is primarily from rivers, chiefly the Selenga, while some comes from precipitation and subterranean sources. Most of the outflow is through the Angara River, a tributary of the Yenisey. The water level varies during the year by two or three feet, being highest in August–September and lowest in March–April.

Baikal's climate is much milder than that of the surrounding territory. January–February air temperatures average −2° F (−19° C), and the August temperatures average 52° F (11° C). The lake freezes in January and thaws in May. The water temperature at the surface in August is about 55° F (13° C) and reaches 68° F (20° C) in the offshore shallows. Waves sometimes measure more than 15 ft. The water is very clear down to 130 ft, containing few minerals. Its salinity is low.

Plant and animal life in the lake are rich and various. There are more than 1,200 animal species at different depths, and about 600 plant species live on or near the surface. About three-quarters of the species are peculiar to Baikal. There are some 50 species of fish, belonging to seven families; the most numerous of these are the 25 species of bullheads of the family Cottidae. The omul salmon is heavily fished; also important are the grayling and the lake whitefish. The largest of the fishes is the sturgeon, some of which may attain 71 in. (180 cm) in length and weigh up to 265 lb (120 kg). The one mammal is the Baikal seal. Unique to the lake is a fish called the golomyanka, of the family Comephoridae, which gives birth to live young. There are 326 bird species in the Baikal area.

Industries on the shores of Baikal include mining (mica and marble), cellulose and paper, shipbuilding, fisheries, and timber. There are many mineral springs, and visitors come to Goryachinsk and Khakusy for the curative properties of the waters. The lake is navigated from May to October by wooden rafts.

The Soviet government has begun to concern itself with the conservation of Baikal and its resources. A government decree concerning measures for the protection and rational use of those resources, and the prevention of polluting emissions from cellulose and other industrial plants, was adopted in June 1971.

The Limnological Institute of the Siberian Department of the Soviet Academy of Sciences and the Baikal Sanatorium are located in the town of Listvyanka, and the hydrobiological station of Irkutsk A.A. Zhdanov State University is in Bolshiye Koty.

Baikalsky Nature Reserve, natural area set aside for research in the natural sciences, on the southern shore of Lake Baikal, southeastern Russian Soviet Federated Socialist Republic. The reserve was established in 1969 and has an area of 418,350 ac (169,300 ha). It includes part of the Khamar-Daban mountain range. The park's vegetation includes poplar forests in the lowlands; taiga of spruce, fir, and larch on the mountain slopes; and thickets of dwarf Siberian pine and birch in the higher meadows. Among the wildlife are brown bear, wild pig, musk and roe deer, badger, stoat, lynx, wolverine, and birds such as the swan goose, rock ptarmigan, crested honey buzzard, and the great bustard. Scientific research on the ecosystem of southern Lake Baikal and the Khamar-Daban range is carried on in the reserve.

Baikie, William Balfour (b. Aug. 27, 1825, Kirkwall, Orkney Islands, Scot.—d. Dec. 12, 1864, Sierra Leone), explorer and philologist whose travels into Nigeria helped open up the country to British trade.

Educated in medicine, he entered the Royal Navy as an assistant surgeon and joined an expedition up the Niger River. On the death of the ship's captain, Baikie took command of the expedition (1854). With a crew made up chiefly of Africans, he explored the Benue River, the main tributary of the Niger, penetrating 250 miles farther than any European had before. He published his *Narrative* of this expedition in 1856.

Baikie, detail from an engraving, 1864

The Mansell Collection

In 1857, with the rank of consul, Baikie embarked on another Niger expedition, but his steamer was wrecked in a rapids. At Lokoja, where the Benue joins the Niger, he founded a trading settlement, where he practiced medicine, compiled African vocabularies, and translated parts of the Bible into the Hausa language. In 1862 he ventured some 250 miles northward to Kano.

bail, procedure by which a judge or magistrate sets at liberty one who has been arrested or imprisoned, upon receipt of security to ensure the released prisoner's later appearance in court for further proceedings. Release from custody is ordinarily effected by posting a sum of money or a bond, although originally bail included the delivery of other forms of property, such as title to real estate. The principal use of bail in modern legal systems is to secure the freedom, pending trial, of one arrested and charged with a criminal offense. Subject to jurisdictional variations, its use in civil cases has diminished along with the decline of imprisonment for debt.

The purposes of bail pending trial in criminal cases are to avoid inflicting punishment upon an innocent person (who may be acquitted at trial) and to encourage the unhampered preparation of his defense. The amount of bail is generally set in relation to the gravity of the offense charged, although some magistrates take into account other factors, such as the strength of the evidence, the character of the accused, and his financial ability to secure bail. Failure to consider financial ability has generated much controversy in recent years, for bail requirements may discriminate against poor people and certain minority groups who are thus deprived of an equal opportunity to secure their freedom pending trial. Some courts now give special consideration to indigent accused persons who, because of their community standing and past history, are considered likely to appear in court. A few jurisdictions make it a separate criminal offense to forfeit bail instead of appearing as required.

In legal systems that have a bail procedure, its operation is highly discretionary. If an accused is charged with an offense committed while free on bail or if the arrested person requires police protection or if evidence reasonably establishes that he committed murder or treason, bail may not be granted. Alternatively, bail may be set unusually high. *See also* recognizance.

Baila (people): *see* Ila.

Bailey, Sir Donald Coleman (b. Sept. 15, 1901, Rotherham, Yorkshire, Eng.), British engineer who invented the Bailey bridge, of great military value, especially in World War II.

After graduating from the University of Sheffield, he worked for a time in railroading, but then in 1929 he joined the staff of the Experimental Bridging Establishment of the Ministry of Supply. When World War II broke out, he had already developed an idea for a military bridge, and in late 1940, at a conference on the problem of providing temporary spans capable of taking heavy loading, his concept of a strong but relatively light steel truss that could be prefabricated in sections was at once approved. The characteristics of the Bailey bridge were standardization and simplicity of panels, readiness of assembly in the field, capacity for additional strengthening by doubling or tripling the truss girders, and adaptability to long spans with the aid of pontoons. A Bailey pontoon bridge over the Maas River in The Netherlands spanned 4,000 feet (1,200 metres).

Bailey was knighted in 1946.

Bailey, Florence Augusta Merriam *née* MERRIAM (b. Aug. 8, 1863, Locust Grove, N.Y., U.S.—d. Sept. 22, 1948, Washington, D.C.), U.S. ornithologist and author of popular field guides.

While attending Smith College, Northampton, Mass. (1882–86), Bailey became interested in ornithology and wrote articles that were later collected in her first book, *Birds Through an Opera Glass* (1889). During the next 40 years she published numerous articles and books, including such popular studies of American bird lore as *Birds of Village and Field* (1896) and a field guide that became a standard reference work, *Handbook of Birds of the Western United States* (1902). Working with the U.S. Biological Survey, Bailey also published the first comprehensive study of birds in the Southwest, *Birds of New Mexico* (1928). In 1908 a form of chickadee, *Parus gambeli baileyae,* was named after her.

An avid promoter of the Audubon Society, Bailey was also interested in social welfare issues, and actively participated in playground and recreation reform organizations. She was married in 1899 to Vernon Bailey, a naturalist who also served in the U.S. Biological Survey.

Bailey, Frederick Augustus Washington: *see* Douglass, Frederick.

Bailey, Gamaliel (b. Dec. 3, 1807, Mount Holly, N.J., U.S.—d. June 5, 1859, at sea en route to Europe), journalist and a leader of the Abolition Movement prior to the U.S. Civil War.

He graduated from the Jefferson Medical College in Philadelphia in 1827; in 1834 he was a lecturer on physiology at the Lane Theological Seminary, Cincinnati, Ohio. The Lane Seminary debates on slavery stirred him to become an ardent Abolitionist. In 1836 he joined James G. Birney in editing the Cincinnati *Philanthropist*, the first anti-slavery organ in the west. Later, as sole proprietor, he persisted even though his printing office was repeatedly wrecked by pro-slavery mobs. In 1843 he launched a daily paper, the *Herald.*

In January 1847 Bailey became editor of *The National Era,* established in Washington, D.C., by the American and Foreign Anti-Slavery Society. With its considerable circulation, this paper exerted a strong political and moral influence. Among its contributors were Nathaniel Hawthorne, John Greenleaf Whittier, and Theodore Parker; in its pages Harriet Beecher Stowe's *Uncle Tom's Cabin* first appeared as a serial in 1851–52.

Bailey died while making a voyage to Europe for his health.

Bailey, Hannah Clark Johnston, *née* JOHNSTON (b. July 5, 1839, Cornwall-on-the-Hudson, N.Y., U.S.—d. Oct. 23, 1923, Portland, Me.), U.S. reformer who was a leading advocate of the peace movement in the late 19th and early 20th centuries.

In 1868 she was married to Moses Bailey, a Maine manufacturer, who died in 1882. In 1883 Bailey joined the Woman's Christian Temperance Union. From 1888 to 1916 she headed its International Department of Peace and Arbitration; she published two widely circulated monthly periodicals, the *Pacific Banner* and the *Acorn*, and also distributed hundreds of thousands of pacifist leaflets.

Bailey travelled widely throughout the United States to promote pacifism, temperance, and woman suffrage. In 1892 she met with Pres. Benjamin Harrison to present a popular protest against military involvement in Chile. Bailey also crusaded against lynching, and she opposed military conscription, military drills, and military toys.

Bailey, James A(nthony), original name JAMES ANTHONY MCGINNES (b. July 4, 1847, Detroit—d. April 11, 1906, Mt. Vernon, N.Y., U.S.), U.S. impresario credited with the great success of the Barnum & Bailey Circus.

As a boy, Bailey travelled with an itinerant circus. In 1872 he became a partner in James E. Cooper's Circus, later called the Great International Circus, which made a profitable two-year tour of the United States, Australia, New Zealand, Java, and several countries of South America. From 1876 called Cooper,

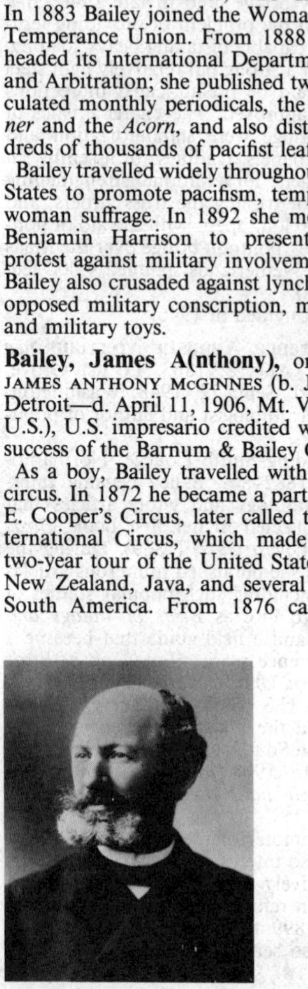

James A. Bailey

By courtesy of the Joe E. Ward Circus Collection, Hoblitzelle Theatre Arts Library, Humanities Research Center, the University of Texas at Austin

Bailey and Co.'s Circus, it became a serious competitor of P.T. Barnum's "Greatest Show on Earth," and merged with it in 1881. Bailey's managerial astuteness complemented Barnum's abilities as a promoter and made their circus the most successful enterprise of its kind in the United States. After Barnum's death in 1891, the circus made several triumphant tours of Europe under Bailey's sole leadership. It became the Ringling Bros. and Barnum & Bailey Combined Circus in 1919.

Bailey, Liberty Hyde (b. March 15, 1858, near South Haven, Mich., U.S.—d. Dec. 25, 1954, Ithaca, N.Y.), botanist whose systematic study of cultivated plants transformed U.S. horticulture from a craft to an applied science and had a direct influence on the development of genetics, plant pathology, and agriculture.

He served as an assistant to the U.S. botanist Asa Gray at Harvard University (1882–84) and as professor of horticulture and landscape gardening at Michigan State Agricultural Col-

Liberty Hyde Bailey, *c.* 1915

By courtesy of Bailey Hortorium, Cornell University, Ithaca, New York, and the Hunt Institute, Pittsburgh

lege (now Michigan State University), East Lansing (1884–88), where he established the first distinctively horticultural laboratory in the United States (1888).

At Cornell University, Ithaca, N.Y., where he served as professor of botany and horticulture (1888–1903), Bailey soon established botanical science as the basis of horticultural research, teaching, and practice; he invited physiologists and chemists to investigate problems of plant culture and production, encouraged geneticists to work with cultivated plants, and introduced to botanical education methods of "in-the-field" instruction that largely superseded exclusive emphasis on expository classroom teaching. Also dean of the New York State College of Agriculture, Cornell (1903–13), and an authority on the genera *Carex* (of the sedge family), *Rubus* (of the rose family), *Brassica* (of the mustard family), and tropical American palms, Bailey founded and directed (1935–51) the Bailey Hortorium, now a division of the college.

His prolific literary output (700 scientific papers and 66 books) included several landmark encyclopaedic works: *Cyclopedia of American Horticulture* (4 vol., 1900–02); *Cyclopedia of American Agriculture* (4 vol., 1907–09); and *The Standard Cyclopedia of Horticulture* (6 vol., 1914). The last work, condensed to three volumes (1925), and his *Manual of Cultivated Plants* (1923), through revised editions, remain the principal works in the field.

bailiff, a minor court official with police authority to protect the court while in session and with power to serve and execute legal process. In earlier times it was a title of more dignity and power.

In medieval England there were bailiffs who served the lord of the manor, while others served the hundred courts and the sheriff. The bailiffs of manors were, in effect, superintendents; they collected fines and rents, served as accountants, and were, in general, in charge of the land and buildings on the estate. Bailiffs who served the hundred courts were appointed by the sheriff; they assisted judges at assizes (sessions of the royal court held twice a year in each shire), acted as process servers and executors of writs, assembled juries, and collected fines in court.

In France the *bailli* had much greater power; from the 13th to the 15th century they were the principal agents of the king and his growing central administration for countering feudalism. The *bailli* was part of this central administration, appointed by the king and required to give account to him, and stood between a *prévôt* (*q.v.*) and the central royal court. In the south, *sénéchalux,* who had originally been feudal officers of the crown, assumed the same functions as the *baillis.* The position of a *grand bailli* in a district was equal to that of the English sheriff.

Like the *prévôts,* the *baillis* represented the king in many kinds of business. As administrators, they were in charge of lesser officeholders, maintaining public order, publishing the king's ordinances, and carrying out his orders. In military affairs the *bailli* called men for service, collected taxes paid in place of service, were in charge of troops assembled by the *prévôts,* and were responsible for the general defense of the area. As financial agents of the crown they were administrators of the royal domain, paid salaries to local officials, and gave over the funds received from various taxes, fines, and fees to the royal treasury. The *baillis'* judicial responsibilities were, perhaps, the most important. They held court at local assizes made up of royal officials and prominent bourgeois (later, judicial officers and lawyers) who gave their opinion of which local customary law should be applied in the cases before the court. The *baillis'* court had original jurisdiction over cases concerning the nobility, and appellate jurisdiction over cases originally heard by the *prévôts* and some seignorial courts. The *baillis* also had jurisdiction over cases that affected the king's domain and his rights.

With the consolidation of much feudal land into the domain of the crown, it was obvious that no one man could handle so many jobs. As a result, other officers were created to ease the burden of the *bailli,* and eventually they stripped him of much of his power. By the early 14th century, receivers were appointed who took over the administration of finances. With the creation of a permanent army and its own officers (15th century), the *bailli* lost his military powers. His judicial functions disappeared gradually over a period of centuries. As early as the late 13th century, lieutenants were created to serve under the *baillis;* often they served in their place. Eventually, the lieutenants were required to have legal degrees, and by the 16th century they had completely superseded the *baillis,* who were no longer allowed to participate in judicial decisions. In the 17th century the *baillis'* administrative responsibilities were completely taken over by the *intendants* (*q.v.*), thus removing the last of their real powers. Even though their offices were purchasable and hereditary, and they could not be removed, they became mere figureheads.

Baillie OF JERVISWOOD: *see* Baillie, Robert.

Baillie, Lady Grizel (b. Dec. 25, 1665, Redbraes Castle, Berwickshire, Scot.—d. Dec. 6, 1746), Scottish poet remembered for her simple and sorrowful songs.

The eldest daughter of Sir Patrick Hume (Home), later earl of Marchmont, she carried letters from her father to the imprisoned Scottish conspirator Robert Baillie of Jerviswood. After Baillie's execution (1684) the family fled to Holland, where they remained until it was safe to return to Scotland. In 1692 Lady Grizel married George Baillie, Robert Baillie's son.

Although Lady Grizel wrote several songs, only two are extant. "The ewe-buchtin's bonnie" may have been inspired by her father's hiding in Polwarth church after he had spoken in Baillie's defense; the well-known "And werena my heart licht I wad dee" first appeared in *Orpheus Caledonius* (1725) and was included in Allan Ramsay's *Tea Table Miscellany,* 4 vol. (1724–37).

Baillie, Joanna (b. Sept. 11, 1762, Hamilton, Lanark, Scot.—d. Feb. 23, 1851, Hampstead, London), poet and prolific dramatist whose plays, mainly in verse, were highly praised at a period when serious drama was in decline. Her *Plays on the Passions,* 3 vol. (1798–1812),

Joanna Baillie, engraving by H. Robinson after a portrait by Sir William Newton

By courtesy of the trustees of the British Museum; photograph, J.R. Freeman & Co. Ltd.

brought her fame but have long been forgotten. She is remembered, rather, as the friend of her countryman Sir Walter Scott and for a handful of lyrics in *Fugitive Verses* (1790), her first published work, that catch the authentic note of Lowland Scots folk song.

Baillie, Matthew (b. Oct. 27, 1761, Shots Manse, Lanarkshire, Scot.—d. Sept. 23, 1823, Duntisbourne, Gloucestershire, Eng.), Scottish pathologist whose *Morbid Anatomy of Some of the Most Important Parts of the Human Body* (1793) was the first publication in English on pathology as a separate subject and the first systematic study of pathology ever made.

A nephew of the great anatomists John and William Hunter, Baillie was educated at Oxford (M.D., 1789) and soon after became a fellow of the Royal College of Physicians and of the Royal Society. After the publication of his book, he devoted himself to his medical practice, which by 1800 was the largest in London.

Baillie, Robert (b. 1599—d. July 1662, Glasgow), Presbyterian minister and theological scholar who led the movement in Scotland to reject (1637) the Church of England's *Book of Common Prayer.* He was a member of the Glasgow Assembly (1638), at which the Church of Scotland broke away from English episcopacy. Baillie became professor of divinity at Glasgow (1642) and in 1661 was made principal of the university. His *Letters and Journals,* edited by D. Laing (1841–42), are of considerable historical importance.

Baillie, Robert, byname BAILLIE OF JERVISWOOD (b. *c.* 1634, probably Lanarkshire, Scot.—d. Dec. 24, 1684, Edinburgh), Scottish Presbyterian executed for allegedly conspiring to assassinate King Charles II of Great Britain. The evidence against him was inconclusive, and Scottish nationalist sentiment has regarded him as a martyr for the cause of religious liberty.

By 1676 Baillie had become involved in the struggle to free Scottish Presbyterianism from domination by the Anglican Church of England. Frustrated in these efforts, he planned to emigrate to South Carolina in 1683, but the scheme fell through. Baillie then travelled to London and met a group of Charles II's political opponents, headed by James Scott, duke of Monmouth, and Lord William Russell. Implicated with these men in the alleged Rye House Plot to murder Charles and his brother James, duke of York (later King James II), Baillie was arrested, imprisoned in London for six months, and then sent to Edinburgh. There he was found guilty of treason and hanged and drawn and quartered.

Baillou, Guillaume de, Latin BALLONIUS (b. 1538, Paris—d. 1616, Paris), physician, founder of modern epidemiology, who revived Hippocratic medical practice in Renaissance Europe. Dean of the University of Paris medical faculty (1580), he compiled a clear account of epidemics between 1570 and 1579, the first comprehensive work of its kind since Hippocrates. He was probably the first to describe whooping cough (1578) and to define the term rheumatism in its modern sense. His descriptions of plague, diphtheria, and measles and

Baillou, detail of an oil painting by an unknown artist, *c.* 1580

Giraudon—Art Resource/EB Inc.

works on epidemiology, especially *Epidemiorum,* 2 vol. (1640; "Of Epidemics"), may have influenced the great 17th-century Hippocratic physician Thomas Sydenham.

Bailly, Jean-Sylvain (b. Sept. 15, 1736, Paris—d. Nov. 12, 1793, Paris), French astronomer noted for his computation of an orbit for Halley's Comet (1759) and for his studies of the four satellites of Jupiter then known. He was also a statesman who took part in the revolutionary events of his age.

Bailly began his study of Halley's Comet in 1759. One year later he established an observatory where he could undertake observations of Jupiter's satellites. He was elected to the Académie des Sciences in 1763. His major works include *Essai sur la théorie des satellites de Jupiter* (1766; "Essay on the Theory of Jupiter's Satellites") and *Mémoires sur les inégalités de la lumière des satellites de Jupiter* (1771; "Memoirs on the Uneven Illumination of Jupiter's Satellites").

The French Revolution interrupted his studies. Elected deputy from Paris to the States General, he was chosen president of the third estate on May 5, 1789, and led the famous proceedings in the Tennis Court on June 20. He was proclaimed the first mayor of Paris

Bailly, detail of an engraving by P.-M. Alix, 1791

By courtesy of the trustees of the British Museum; photograph, J.R. Freeman & Co. Ltd.

on July 15, 1789. He was reelected mayor in August 1790 but lost popularity, particularly after his order to the national guard to disperse a riotous crowd led to the massacre of the Champ de Mars on July 17, 1791. Bailly retired on Nov. 16, 1791, and went to Nantes in July 1792, where he composed *Mémoires d'un témoin de la Révolution* ("Memoirs of a Witness of the Revolution"), an incomplete narrative of the extraordinary events of his public life. Late in 1793 Bailly went to Melun to join his friend Pierre-Simon Laplace, but was recognized, arrested, and taken before the revolutionary tribunal at Paris on November 10. He was subsequently guillotined.

bailment, in Anglo-American property law, delivery of specific goods by one person, called the bailor, to another person, called the bailee, for some temporary purpose such as storage, transportation, deposit for sale, pawn or pledge, repair or loan for use, with or without compensation. Formerly the bailee's responsibility for goods varied with the benefit he derived from the bailment. In present-day law, it is generally held that the bailee owes such duty of care as becomes the reasonably prudent man "under the circumstances." The purpose and advantage anticipated from the bailment are considered as circumstances governing the extent of care owed by the bailee.

Common types of bailment have been similar under most systems of law, and they were designated by specific names in Roman law. Some of them have characteristic legal consequences; *e.g.,* the bailee for repairs is entitled to retain possession until he has been paid for his service.

Baily, Francis (b. April 28, 1774, Newbury, Berkshire, Eng.—d. Aug. 30, 1844, London), astronomer who detected the phenomenon called "Baily's beads" during an annular

Baily, detail from an engraving by Thomas Lufton after a portrait by Thomas Phillips

By courtesy of the trustees of the British Museum; photograph, J.R. Freeman & Co. Ltd.

eclipse of the Sun on May 15, 1836. His vivid description aroused new interest in the study of eclipses.

Baily retired from a successful business career in 1825 and turned his energies to science. He had already, in 1820, taken a leading part in the foundation of the Royal Astronomical Society, which awarded him its Gold Medal in 1827 for his preparation of the society's catalog of 2,881 stars. His protests regarding the *British Nautical Almanac,* then notorious for its errors, were instrumental in bringing about its reform. Baily revised several star catalogs, repeated Henry Cavendish's experiments to determine the density of the Earth, and measured its elliptical shape.

Baily's beads, arc of bright spots seen during a total eclipse of the Sun. They are named for Francis Baily, an English astronomer, who first called attention to them. Just before the Moon's disk completely covers the Sun, the narrow crescent of sunlight may be broken in several places by irregularities (mountains and valleys) on the edge of the Moon's disk; the resulting array of spots roughly resembles a string of beads.

baimiao (Chinese painting): *see* pai-miao.

Bain, Alexander (b. June 11, 1818, Aberdeen, Aberdeen, Scot.—d. Sept. 18, 1903, Aberdeen), philosopher who advanced the study of psychology with his work on mental processes and who strove to improve education in Scotland. Soon after college graduation in 1840 he began to contribute to *The Westminster Review,* thus becoming acquainted with the philosopher John Stuart Mill and his circle in London. There Bain served as secretary of the board of health (1848–50) and for the next 10 years was variously employed in the civil service and as an educator. From 1860 to 1880 he taught logic and English literature at the University of Aberdeen, where he advocated the reform of teaching methods in Scotland. During this period he wrote several books on grammar and rhetoric and a two-volume work on *Logic* (1870) containing a detailed account of the application of logic to the natural sciences. He also devoted himself to the study of psychology, adopting a rigorously scientific approach. Bain sought to find physical correlatives for such abstract concepts as "idea" and "mind" and stressed the need for further investigation of the processes of the brain and the nervous system.

Bain founded the first journal devoted to psychology, *Mind,* in 1876. Among his works in psychological theory are *On the Study of Character* (1861), *Mental and Moral Science:*

Bain, detail of an oil painting by Sir George Reid; in the collection of the University of Aberdeen, Scotland

By courtesy of the University of Aberdeen, Scotland

A Compendium of Psychology and Ethics (1868), and *Mind and Body: The Theories of Their Relation* (1873). His other writings include *John Stuart Mill: A Criticism, with Personal Recollections* (1882), and an *Autobiography* (1904).

Bainbridge, city, seat (1823) of Decatur County, southwestern Georgia, U.S., on the Flint River, near the Florida border. The city was founded in 1823 near Ft. Hughes, an earthwork defended by the troops of Andrew Jackson during the Indian wars of 1817–21. The site was named for Capt. William Bainbridge, commander of the frigate "Constitution," and developed as a lumbering town and river port. Downriver, the Jim Woodruff Lock and Dam (1957) impounds Lake Seminole (southwest), provides hydropower, and controls navigation channels from the Gulf Intracoastal Waterway. This navigational system makes Bainbridge Georgia's first inland barge port (handling bulk cargoes such as industrial chemicals and minerals) with services along the Mississippi routes. Bainbridge Junior College was opened in 1970. Inc. 1829. Pop. (1980) 10,553.

Bainbridge, William (b. May 7, 1774, Princeton, N.J.—d. July 27, 1833, Philadelphia), naval officer who captured the British frigate "Java" in the War of 1812.

He commanded merchant vessels from 1793 to 1798, when he became an officer in the newly organized U.S. Navy. He served in the war with the Barbary States (1801–05) and was in command of the frigate "Philadelphia" when she was captured by the Tripolitans (1803). Imprisoned for a time, he returned to the merchant marine upon his release (1805). At the outbreak of the War of 1812 he was again

William Bainbridge, engraving

By courtesy of the Library of Congress, Washington, D.C.

commissioned in the U.S. Navy and was given command of the famed frigate "Constitution." His capture of the "Java" off the Brazilian coast was one of the notable U.S. naval victories of the war and, according to some, helped earn for his ship the sobriquet "Old Ironsides."

Baines, Thomas (b. 1822, King's Lynn, Norfolk, Eng.—d. May 8, 1875, Durban, Natal), artist, explorer, naturalist, and author who spent most of his life in southern Africa.

Love of adventure took him in 1842 to Cape Colony, where he served as an artist during the Eighth Frontier War (1850–53). His success as an artist led to his joining an expedition to northern Australia in 1855 and an invitation to take part in a Zambezi expedition under David Livingstone in 1858. In 1861 Baines accompanied the British hunter and explorer James Chapman in his travels from South West Africa to Victoria Falls, a journey on which his drawings and his book *Explorations in South-West Africa* (1864) were based. With his fame established, he opened a studio in London in 1865. Returning to Africa in 1868, he led an expedition to explore the goldfields of Matabeleland, where he won mining concessions that later were acquired by Cecil Rhodes. Baines's accurate map, scientific data, and illustrations of the scenery and people were published posthumously in *The Gold Regions of South-Eastern Africa* (1877).

Bainville, Jacques (b. Feb. 9, 1879, Vincennes, Fr.—d. Feb. 9, 1936, Paris), political writer and historian, a leading exponent of conservative ideals between World Wars I and II. He particularly stressed German influences in French history and warned of the menace of a strong Germany.

Although born into a family of republican sympathies, Bainville, under the influence of the royalist propagandists Maurice Barrès and Charles Maurras, early embraced the cause for the restoration of the monarchy. After being associated with the royalist papers *Action Française* and *Gazette de France,* he published his first book, *La République de Bismarck, ou Origines allemandes de la Troisième République* (1905; "The Republic of Bismarck: German Origins of the Third Republic"), in which he emphasized Bismarck's support of French Republicanism.

Bainville, 1936

Popperfoto

During World War I Bainville wrote several works on Russia, Italy, and Germany; notable is his *Histoire de deux peuples* (1915; "History of Two Nations"), an anti-German work dealing with the recurrent German invasions of France. In 1920 he published *Les Conséquences politiques de la paix* (1920; "The Political Consequences of the Peace"), in which he attacked the Treaty of Versailles and predicted the danger of a unified Germany. His *Histoire de France* (1924) was later republished with other studies under the title *Heur et malheur des français* ("The Fortunes and Misfortunes of the French"). His *Napoléon* (1931) is an excellent psychological study. In his later years Bainville, concerned with the rising German threat, wrote *Les Dictateurs* (1935) and *La Troisième République 1870–1935* (1935; *The Third Republic,* 1936), in which he predicted what he saw as two inevitable events: a German attack on France and a national revolution. He also published works on German and English history and literary essays.

Bainville was elected to the Académie Française (1935).

Baird, Bil and Cora, bynames of WILLIAM BRITTON BAIRD and CORA EISENBERG (respectively b. Aug. 15, 1904, Grand Island, Neb., U.S.; b. Jan. 26, 1912, New York City—d. Dec. 6, 1967, New York City), puppeteers who led the 20th-century revival of puppet theatre in the United States.

For five years, after studying stage design at the Chicago Academy of Fine Arts, Bil Baird

Bil and Cora Baird, 1956

By courtesy of the Bil Baird Collection; photograph, Nat Messik worked under Tony Sarg (*q.v.*), and in 1933 presented his first independent commercial production at the Century of Progress Exposition in Chicago. He married Cora Eisenberg, who had acted under the name of Cora Burlar, four years later. In the following years, they made their own puppets, built scenery, wrote scripts, and composed music. A few of the Bairds' creations became classic puppet figures: Bubbles La Rue, the marionette striptease dancer; the singing frogs; Snarky Parker, the master of ceremonies; and Heathcliff, the talking horse.

In the 1950s they produced several television programs. In the 1960s they performed at the New York World's Fair and later toured India and the Soviet Union and made educational films. In 1967 a permanent marionette theatre, the Bil Baird, was opened in New York City.

Baird, John Logie (b. Aug. 13, 1888, Helensburgh, Dunbarton, Scot.—d. June 14, 1946, Bexhill-on-Sea, Sussex, Eng.), Scottish engineer, the first man to televise pictures of objects in motion.

Educated at Larchfield Academy, the Royal Technical College, and the University of Glasgow, he produced televised objects in outline in 1924, transmitted recognizable human faces in 1925, and demonstrated the televising of moving objects in 1926 at the Royal Institution, London. The German post office gave him facilities to develop a television service in 1929. When the British Broadcasting Corporation (BBC) television service began in 1936, his system was in competition with one promoted by Marconi Electric and Musical Industries, and in February 1937 the BBC adopted the Marconi EMI system exclusively. Baird demonstrated colour television in 1928 and was reported to have completed his researches on stereoscopic television in 1946.

Baird, Spencer Fullerton (b. Feb. 3, 1823, Reading, Pa., U.S.—d. Aug. 19, 1887, Woods Hole, Mass.), naturalist, vertebrate zoologist, and in his time the leading authority on North American birds and mammals.

Spencer Fullerton Baird

By courtesy of the Smithsonian Institution, Washington, D.C.

A meeting in 1838 with John J. Audubon, who gave Baird part of his own collection of birds, turned the young naturalist's interest to ornithology. He was appointed professor of natural history at Dickinson College, Carlisle, Pa., in 1845 and five years later accepted the post of assistant secretary of the Smithsonian Institution in Washington, D.C., becoming secretary in 1878. The following year Congress authorized the construction of a building to house his vast collection of North American faunal materials assembled from government expeditions and private collectors. He prepared numerous volumes of reports on the Smithsonian collections, and he also prepared volumes on birds, mammals, and reptiles. His monographs were recognized as significant contributions to systematic zoology.

Through Baird's efforts Congress established in 1871 the U.S. Commission of Fish and Fisheries, which he headed at the request of Pres. Ulysses S. Grant. The commission made many studies on the distribution and behaviour of fishes, and its hatcheries increased the availability of fish for commercial use, introducing foreign species into the U.S. His work on fish culture helped make his laboratory at Woods Hole world famous.

Baird's publications include *North American Reptiles* (1853), with Charles Girard; *Mammals* (1857); *Catalogue of North American Birds* (1858); *Review of American Birds* (1864–66); and *A History of North American Birds* (1874), with T.M. Brewer and R. Ridgway.

Where the same name may denote a person, place, or thing, the articles will be found in that order

---

Baire, René-Louis (b. Jan. 21, 1874, Paris—d. July 5, 1932, Chambéry, Fr.) mathematician whose study of irrational numbers and whose concept to divide the notion of continuity into upper and lower semi-continuity greatly influenced the French school of mathematics.

Baire graduated from the l'École Normale Supérieure in 1895 and, the same year, became professor of mathematics at the Lycée Nancy. Four years later he received his Ph.D. from l'École Normale Supérieure. His doctoral thesis on the theory of functions of real variables led to the solution of the problem of the characteristic property of limited and continuous functions and helped establish the theory of functions of real variables.

In 1902 Baire joined the faculty at the University of Montpellier and three years later the faculty at Dijon. He wrote *Théories Générales de l'analyse* (1907); *Théorie des Nombres Irrationnels* (1912) and was a member of the French Academy of Science.

Bairnsdale, town, southeastern Victoria, Australia, at the mouth of the Mitchell River on Lake King, a lagoon. Development dates from the late 19th century, when the town served initially as a port for the east Gippsland goldfields; ship services have now been replaced by rail and road transport. At the intersection of the Prince's and Omeo highways, Bairnsdale is connected to Melbourne (171 mi [275 km] west) by rail. It is a marketing centre for an area supporting cattle, sheep, fisheries, fruit, and timber and has factories producing butter, cordials, leather, clothing, and sawn lumber. There is also a thriving tourist trade based on the nearby Gippsland Lakes and the Ninety Mile Beach. Pop. (1981) 9,459.

Bairnsfather, (Charles) Bruce (b. July 9, 1888, Murree, India—d. Sept. 29, 1959, Worcester, Worcestershire, Eng.), cartoonist best known for his grimly humorous depiction of British soldiers in the trenches of World War I.

The son of a soldier, Bairnsfather attended the United Services College at Westward Ho, north Devon, but after a short period in the army he decided on an art career. He studied art briefly but, unable to find work in the field, joined a firm of electrical engineers, for which he eventually became a representative. In August 1914 he rejoined his regiment and later that year went to France. He began sketching in the trenches, and in 1915 his first cartoons about army life appeared in *The Bystander,* where they were an immediate success. Wounded in action, he had further opportunity to sketch during his convalescence. Collections of his drawings enjoyed wide popularity. His most famous character was Old Bill, a middle-aged Cockney with a walrus moustache; and his most famous cartoon (Nov. 24, 1915) showed Old Bill and a comrade in a shell hole during a barrage, with a caption reading, "Well, if you knows a better 'ole, go to it."

In December 1916 Bairnsfather joined the intelligence department of the War Office as an officer cartoonist and was sent to various fronts. After the war he drew for a number of publications in England and the U.S. but did not maintain his earlier popularity. During World War II he served as an official cartoonist with the U.S. Army in Europe. In his later years he was active as a lecturer.

Bais, chartered city and port, Negros Oriental province, southeastern Negros island, Philippines. Fronting the Tanon Strait on the east, the port accommodates oceangoing vessels and is the shipping centre for sugar refined in Bais. The Sacred Heart Academy, a Roman Catholic liberal arts college, was founded in 1947. A pulp and paper mill is the other principal industry in Bais. Inc. city, 1968. Pop. (1980) 49,301.

Baise (China): *see* Pai-se.

Baius, Michael, Baius also spelled BAJUS, also called MICHAEL DE BAY (b. 1513, Melin, Hainaut—d. Sept. 16, 1589, Louvain, Brabant), theologian whose work powerfully influenced Cornelius Jansen, one of the fathers of Jansenism.

He was educated at the University of Louvain, where he studied philosophy and theology and held various university appointments. About 1550, with the theologian Jan Hessels, he began to advance revolutionary doctrines of grace and justification based on a new, rigid, and pessimistic interpretation of Augustine of Hippo. Baius' numerous short treatises on theological subjects incurred censures by ecclesiastical authorities; in 1567, Pope Pius V condemned 79 propositions in the bull *Ex Omnibus Afflictionibus*. Baius submitted, but indiscreet utterances by him and his supporters led to a new condemnation in 1580 by Pope Gregory XIII. Baius, however, kept his professorship and became chancellor of Louvain in 1575.

The most distinctive features of Baius' system, which are found also in some Protestant writers, concern the Fall of man. Baius held that the innocence of Adam and Eve was part of their nature, so that the first sin destroyed intrinsic principles of human nature. His principal works were published by the Maurists in Cologne in 1696, edited by G. Gerberon.

Baj Baj (India): *see* Budge Budge.

Baja (people): *see* Baya.

Baja, town, Bács-Kiskun *megye* (county), south central Hungary, east of the Danube mainstream, on the banks of the Kamarás-Danube (known locally as Sugovica). It is a river port and boating centre and has some industry (farm machinery, furniture, and chemicals). Formerly the chief port for the Bačka farming region (now part of Yugoslavia), it is still an important market centre for agricultural produce and livestock. Road and rail lines cross the Danube west of the town. Baja has several Baroque churches. Béke (Peace) Square is lined with old houses. There is a Serbian minority in the population. Pop. (1983 est.) 40,000.

Baja California, English LOWER CALIFORNIA, peninsula, northwestern Mexico, bounded north by the United States, east by the Gulf of California, and south and west by the Pacific Ocean. The peninsula is approximately 760 mi (1,220 km) long and 25 to 150 mi wide, with a total area of 55,518 sq mi (143,790 sq km). Politically, it is divided into the Mexican states of Baja California Norte and Baja California Sur.

The basic geological feature is a fault block rising precipitously on the gulf side and dropping gently into the Pacific, crowned by a chain of rugged peaks trending in a northwest–southeast direction. The granitic Juárez and San Pedro Mártir mountains, the latter rising 10,154 ft (3,095 m) above sea level, form the divide in the north, with lower parallel ranges much interrupted by erosion along both coasts. The centre of the peninsula is dominated by volcanoes and vast lava flows extending westward in a subpeninsula. Volcanoes include Las Tres Vírgenes (6,548 ft), last reported active in 1746. In the vicinity of La Paz the mountains disappear in a low, narrow isthmus, after which they reemerge in a final, lofty (7,100 ft) granite range. The most extensive plains are along the Pacific shore in the south, from near La Paz to Ojo de Liebre (Scammon's) Lagoon. At the head of the gulf is a delta formed by the alluvium of the Colorado River.

Baja California has 2,038 mi of coastline, with many islands on both sides. There are sheltered deepwater harbours on the western coast as well as on the gulf. With the exception of the Colorado River, surface water is confined to a few permanent streamlets in the northwest and extreme south and to rare springs forming oases elsewhere.

Three zones of climate determine the region's plant and animal life. The northwestern corner receives winter cyclonic cold fronts bringing rain and fog from the north; vegetation and fauna are similar to those of southern California in the United States. Southward from El Rosario and east of the Juárez–San Pedro Mártir mountains is an excessively arid zone extending through the waist of the peninsula to La Paz, where forests adapted to growth in arid regions are common. The region south of La Paz receives late summer tropical rains, with desert shrub in the lowlands and semi-deciduous forests in the more humid mountains.

Humans first moved into Baja California from the north perhaps 9,000 or 10,000 years ago, when the climate was more humid and huge Pleistocene mammals roamed the area. When the Spaniards landed in 1533, they found what were among the most primitive cultures in the Americas. An estimated 60,000 to 70,000 Indians lived at that time in small groups, each exploiting a definite territory for hunting, fishing, and gathering wild plants. Attempts to colonize the peninsula were fruitless until Jesuit missionaries established the first of a number of permanent settlements at Loreto in 1697. In 1768 the Jesuits were replaced by Franciscans, who left the peninsular missions to the Dominican order five years later. Independence from Spain, recognized in Baja California in 1822, was little noticed. The missions were gradually abandoned, and the Indians were replaced by a sparse population of mestizo farmers and cattlemen. After the Mexican War (1846–48), the Treaty of Guadalupe Hidalgo divided the two Californias between Mexico and the United States.

The construction and improvement of highways, harbour facilities, and airfields began in the 1960s and continued during the 1970s with completion of a 1,061-mi (1,708-km) highway running the length of the peninsula between Tijuana and Cabo San Lucas. Baja California's isolation began to be alleviated. Agriculture and mining have expanded, and industries have developed.

Baja California Norte, formerly (until 1974) BAJA CALIFORNIA, state, northwestern Mexico, bounded north by the United States, east by the Gulf of California, west by the Pacific Ocean, and south by the state of Baja California Sur. Its territory (26,997 sq mi [69,921 sq km]), occupying the Baja California peninsula north of latitude 28° N, consists of rugged granitic mountains, the Sierra de Juárez and the Sierra San Pedro Mártir. Coastal plains are narrow except in the extreme northeast, where the Colorado River forms a delta.

Although Baja California Norte has long been inhabited, settlement of the area remains sparse. In 1887 it was made a federal district, with its capital first at Ensenada and subsequently at Mexicali (*q.v.*). It was redesignated a federal territory in 1931 and was made a state in 1952; it was renamed Baja California Norte in 1974 to distinguish it from the newly created state of Baja California Sur.

Since the 1950s the state, and especially the border cities of Tijuana and Mexicali and, to a lesser extent, Ensenada, have experienced phenomenal growth. This has been partly due to proximity to U.S. markets, though production has been increasingly directed toward central Mexico. Expanded agriculture (predominantly cotton, followed by wheat, grapes, and olives) and industry (cottonseed and food processing, fish packing, and the manufacture of beer, wine, and soap) have absorbed many immigrants, but a large, idle surplus of unskilled workers, formerly employed seasonally in the United States but denied entry beginning in the late 1960s, has remained a problem. Wages and the cost of living, while higher than in the rest of Mexico, are lower than in the United States, and foreign companies have established factories in the border region.

The virtual absence of communications isolated all of Baja California for centuries. Since the late 1960s, however, paved roads have connected the principal cities in the north, and both a railroad and a good highway unite Mexicali with Sonora and the rest of Mexico. A new road to Baja California Sur, originating at Tijuana, was completed in the mid-1970s, extending southward for 1,061 mi (1,708 km). There are harbour facilities at Ensenada. Airlines provide frequent service to the largest cities. Pop. (1950) 226,965; (1960) 520,165; (1980) 1,178,000.

Baja California Sur, state, northwestern Mexico, bounded north by the state of Baja California Norte, east by the Gulf of California, and west and south by the Pacific Ocean. The central and eastern parts of its 28,369-sq-mi (73,475-sq-km) territory are dominated by volcanoes.

The area, declared a federal district in 1887, redesignated a federal territory in 1931, and made a state in 1974, is sparsely populated and remains relatively neglected. Much new acreage of cotton, irrigated by deep wells, has been planted near La Paz (*q.v.*), the capital, and on the Magdalena plain around Villa Constitución. Olives and sugarcane are also produced. Industry has been confined to processing of cotton by-products, fish-packing plants, and saltworks. The Boleo copper deposits at Santa Rosalía, exploited by a French company (1884–1953), are being worked on a reduced scale with government subsidy. Cattle raising and subsistence agriculture are the mainstays in isolated areas. Tourism is an important source of income.

Improved communications are slowly alleviating the isolation of the state. A road extending the entire length of the state connecting Tijuana and Cabo San Lucas was opened in the mid-1970s. A paved road north from La Paz to Ensenada was opened in the late 1970s, and a car ferry between La Paz and Mazatlán, across the gulf in the state of Sinaloa, was inaugurated earlier, in 1965. Harbour facilities were improved at Magdalena Bay (Puerto San Carlos) and La Paz (Pichilingui Harbour). La Paz is served by domestic airlines. Pop. (1980) 215,139.

Baja Verapaz, department, central Guatemala, bounded on the northwest by the Río Salinas. It has an area of 1,206 sq mi (3,124 sq km). The department lies in the valley drained by the Polochic River, there called the Río Panimá, and extends over the intervening Sierra de Chuacús and Sierra de las Minas to

The Sierra de Chuacús in Baja Verapaz department near Rabinal, Guatemala

Carl Frank

the Motagua River Valley. Its few inhabitants raise corn (maize), beans, coffee, sugarcane, and fruit. Formerly Salamá (*q.v.*), the departmental capital, and other settlements were accessible only with difficulty. A road now leads southwestward to Guatemala City. Pop. (1981 prelim.) 115,206.

bajada (Spanish: "slope"), also spelled BAHADA, broad slope of debris spread at the bottoms of mountains by descending streams, usually found in arid or semi-arid climates; the term was adopted because of its use in the U.S. Southwest. A bajada is often formed by the coalescing of several alluvial fans. The repeated shifting of a debouching stream from one side of a fan to the other spreads the sediment widely and almost uniformly. As these eventually grow together, the slope may extend several kilometres from the mountain front. A bajada is usually composed of gravelly alluvium and may even have large boulders interbedded in it. The slope is usually less than 7°. In humid climates, landforms of this nature are usually referred to as piedmonts.

Bājah, also spelled BÉJA, capital at Bājah, *wilāyah* (governorate), northern Tunisia. The town, lying in the hills on the northern edge of the Majardah (Medjerda) Valley, is built on the site of ancient Vacca (or Vaga)—a Punic town and Roman colony. An important agricultural market since the 1st century BC, it was conquered by the Vandals and rebuilt in part by Justinian in the 6th century AD. The town was made an administrative and military centre by the Turks in the 16th century. Bājah is the centre of the Majardah Valley grain-growing region. In addition to flour milling, the town has sugar refineries and is the site of an agricultural research station. It is linked by road and rail with Tūnis, 62 mi (100 km) east.

Hay-making in the Bājah region, Tunisia

F. Botts—M. Grimoldi

Bājah *wilāyah* embraces a diverse area of 1,374 sq mi (3,558 sq km) extending from the wet coastal plain along the Mediterranean Sea southeastward across the cork- and oak-covered highlands to the fertile Majardah Valley. It is an important wheat-growing and livestock-raising region and includes the towns of Nafzah, centre of the Nafzah plain, and Mājaz al-Bāb, a grain market on the site of ancient Membressa. Pop. (1975) town, 39,226; (1982 est.) *wilāyah*, 275,900.

Bājaur, agency, a special tribal area in North-West Frontier Province, Pakistan. The federally administered agency is bounded by Dīr district to the northeast, Malākand agency to the east, Mohmand agency to the southwest, and Afghanistan to the west. It comprises a mountainous region in the foothills of the Himalayas, drained by the Swāt River. Livestock are raised and wheat, rice, corn (maize), and vegetables are grown. The agency is inhabited by Pashtun tribes including the Utmān Khēl and Mahmand peoples. Pop. (1981 prelim.) 287,000.

Bajer, Fredrik (b. April 21, 1837, Denmark—d. Jan. 22, 1922, Copenhagen), Danish reformer and politician, co-winner (with Klas Pontus Arnoldson) of the Nobel Peace Prize in 1908.

Bajer entered the army but was discharged when it was reduced after the 1864 war with Prussia. He then started working for the emancipation of women, the peace movement, and for Scandinavian cooperation. He was a founder of the Danish Women's Association in 1871 and established in 1882 the Association for the Neutralization of Denmark, re-

Bajer
By courtesy of the Royal Danish Ministry of Foreign Affairs

named the Danish Peace Association in 1885, and the Danish Nations Association, or the Danish Peace Association, after World War II.

A left-wing liberal member of the Danish Parliament (1872–95), Bajer advocated international arbitration treaties and considerably influenced the development of the Danish neutrality policy. He was a prominent delegate to the first Scandinavian peace conference (1885) and provided great impetus for the formation of the International Peace Bureau in Bern in 1891; he was president of the Bureau until 1907.

Bajío, basin, or plains, region on the Mexican Plateau, west central Mexico, bounded north by the Sierra de Guanajuato, south by the volcanic axis marking the southern edge of the plateau, east by the hills separating the valleys of Celaya and Querétaro, and west by the Sierra de Pénjamo. Occupying southern Guanajuato and northern Michoacán states, the Bajío region ranges in elevation from approximately 5,100 ft (1,550 m) to 5,900 ft above sea level. The Lerma River and its major tributaries (the Laja, Turbio, and Apaseo rivers) have channelled through lacustrine deposits and volcanic tuff and basaltic rocks separating the series of lakes lying at the foot of the volcanic axis to create a single drainage basin. Fertile soil, temperate climate, and adequate rainfall make the Bajío an important agricultural region, known as the granary of Mexico. Wheat, corn (maize), chick-peas, beans, and various fruits are the principal crops. Numerous cities, including Celaya, Irapuato, Valle de Santiago, and Salamanca, lie in the densely populated Bajío.

Bajkal, Ozero (Siberia): *see* Baikal, Lake.

Bajkonur (Kazakh S.S.R.): *see* Baykonyr.

Bajocian Stage, lowermost division of Middle Jurassic rocks and time. (The Jurassic Period began about 190,000,000 years ago and lasted about 54,000,000 years.) Rocks of the Bajocian overlie those of the Toarcian and underlie those of the Bathonian Stage. They exhibit great variation and include coral reef limestones, oolitic deposits, and crinoidal limestones. Nine ammonite cephalopod zones (shorter spans of time characterized by fossil mollusks) have been recognized, aiding worldwide correlation with rocks elsewhere.

Bajokwe (people): *see* Chokwe.

Bajor, Gizi, Bajor also spelled BAYER (b. 1893, Budapest—d. Feb. 12, 1951, Budapest), Hungarian actress known not only for her magnetic charm and attractiveness but for her craftsmanship and versatility.

Bajor graduated into the National Theatre from the Academy of Theatrical Art in 1914 and was associated with that theatre throughout her career, becoming a life member in 1928.

Bajor excelled in a wide range of roles in both classic and modern plays; she received, for example, excellent notices for her portrayals of the title role in both George Bernard Shaw's *Saint Joan* and Gotthold Ephraim Lessing's *Minna von Barnhelm.* Under the direction of Sandor Hevesi, the plays of William Shakespeare, Lope de Vega and Victorien Sardou were part of her repertoire, as were the scripts of such contemporary Hungarian writers as Jenö Heltai, Zsigmond Móriez, Ferencz Herczeg, and Lajos Zilahy. In 1950 she was honoured as an Artist of the People of the Hungarian Republic.

Bajus, Michael: *see* Baius, Michael.

Bakahonde (people): *see* Kaonde.

bakeberry, also called BAKED APPLE BERRY: *see* cloudberry.

Bakel, town, Sénégal Oriental *région,* eastern Senegal, on the Sénégal River along the Mauritanian border. A fort built in 1818 marks the approach to the town; it is a vestige of the time when Bakel was one of three French-governed districts in Senegal (Saint-Louis and Gorée were the other two). Bakel is a market centre for the agricultural hinterland. The house of René Caillié, a Frenchman who was the first European to return from Timbuktu and who published an account of his travels in 1830, is a Bakel landmark. Pop. (1976) 6,300.

Bakelite, trademarked name of PHENOL–FORMALDEHYDE RESIN, synthetic resin used in many industrial applications as an electrical insulator, in molding and casting operations, as an adhesive, and in paints and baked enamel coatings. Phenol–formaldehyde resins are indispensable in manufacturing chemical equipment, machine and instrument housings, bottle closures, and many machine and electrical components.

The production method for manufacturing this plastic was devised in 1909 by L.H. Baekeland in the United States, and the name Bakelite is a registered trademark of the Union Carbide Corporation. It displaced celluloid for nearly all its applications early in the 20th century.

Bakema, Jacob B(erend) (b. March 8, 1914, Groningen, Neth.), Dutch architect who, in association with J.H. van den Broek, was particularly active in the reconstruction of Rotterdam after World War II.

He studied architecture and hydraulic engineering at Groningen, then studied advanced architecture at the Academy of Architecture, Amsterdam. For several years he worked under Cor van Eesteren in the City Architect's office in Amsterdam. In 1947 he designed the art centre called 't Venster in Rotterdam. The next year he entered into partnership with J.H. van den Broek. Van den Broek and Bakema were responsible for the Lijnbaan Shopping Centre, Rotterdam (1953). Later projects included schools, office buildings, department stores, and churches.

Baker, city, seat (1868) of Baker County, northeastern Oregon, U.S., on the Powder River, in the Baker Valley, between the Blue Mountains (west) and the Wallowa Mountains (east). On the old Oregon Trail and settled during the Oregon gold rush (1861–62), it was laid out in 1865 and named for U.S. Sen. Edward D. Baker. Headquarters for the Wallowa-Whitman National Forest, it has developed dairy, lumber, and tourist industries and is a trading point for cattle and mining interests. The U.S. National Bank in the city has the state's largest gold nugget display. Inc. 1874. Pop. (1980) 9,471.

Baker, Augustine (b. Dec. 9, 1575, Abergavenny, Monmouthshire, Eng.—d. Aug. 9, 1641, London), Benedictine monk who was an important writer on ascetic and mystical theology.

Educated at Broadgate's Hall (now Pembroke College), Oxford, Baker was a Roman Catholic convert who evolved an ascetical doctrine based on his reading and personal experiences. His doctrine was not original but yet was vigorously attacked—more for his explicit "method" of mortification and prayer than for his teaching on the ascetic life. Baker was criticized even more severely by some for professing that spiritual guidance came to the soul directly from God and was to be sought and found in prayer.

Baker wrote his ascetical treatises after being appointed (1624) spiritual director of the English Benedictine nuns at Cambrai, Fr. For those dedicated to the contemplative life in the cloister, he found "method" more hindering than helpful and advised beginning with "affective" prayer. As a help to those who sought his counsel or were entrusted to his care, he recommended especially two 14th-century English works: the anonymous *Cloud of Unknowing* and Walter Hilton's *Ladder of Perfection.*

Sixteen years after his death of the plague, his *Sancta Sophia,* a systematic work compiled from his treatises, was published. It covers the entire range of ascetic and mystic theology. His other writings available in print are *Secretum,* a commentary on the *Cloud of Unknowing,* in which the first section is somewhat of a spiritual autobiography (published under the title *The Confessions of Venerable Fr. A.B.,* 1922); an exposition of the *Cloud* (ed. by J. McCann, 1924); and *The Inner Life and Writings of Dame Gertrude More* (2 vol., 1910).

BIBLIOGRAPHY. P. Salvin and S. Cressy, *The Life of Fr. A.B.* (1933); N. Sweeney, *Life and Spirit of Fr. B.* (1861).

Baker, Sir Benjamin (b. March 31, 1840, Keyford, Somerset, Eng.—d. May 19, 1907, Pangbourne, Berkshire), civil engineer, chief designer of the railway bridge over the Firth of Forth, Scotland. In 1862 he became an assistant to the consulting engineer Sir John Fowler and, in 1875, his partner.

Baker was responsible in 1869 for the construction of the London Underground District Railway from Westminster to the City. He also served as consultant for the building of other London underground lines, all bored deep in the London clay. His other projects included the docks at Avonmouth and Hull and the ocean transport of Cleopatra's Needle from Egypt and its re-erection in London.

In 1867 Baker had written a series of articles,

"Long Span Bridges," discussing the application of cantilevers, which were later used in his bridge over the Firth of Forth (1882–90). At the completion of that bridge Baker was knighted. He served on numerous government

Sir Benjamin Baker, engraving, 1890
The Mansell Collection

commissions and boards and, among other assignments as a consultant, implemented William Willcocks' plans for the Aswān Dam (built 1898–1902). In the U.S. he was consulted by James B. Eads on the construction of the St. Louis bridge over the Mississippi River, and when the first Hudson River tunnel threatened to fail, Baker was called in to design a tunnelling shield that allowed work to be completed.

Baker was president of the Institution of Civil Engineers in 1895–96, contributed papers to its *Proceedings*, and was a vice president of the Royal Society from 1896.

Baker, Carlos (Heard) (b. May 5, 1909, Biddeford, Maine, U.S.), U.S. teacher, novelist, and critic known for his definitive, unbiased biographies of Percy Bysshe Shelley and Ernest Hemingway.

Baker received his Ph.D. from Princeton (1940) and became professor of English there in 1951. His book *Shelley's Major Poetry: The Fabric of a Vision* (1948) dwells on Shelley's inner self as visible in his poetry and largely ignores the exterior circumstances of the poet's life. Baker examines Shelley's work within a literary chronology and traces the poet's personal changes through his poems, revealing a many-faceted man. His widely acclaimed *Hemingway: The Writer as Artist* (1952) is regarded as one of the definitive works on the writer. It provides a portrait of an artist and his generation and a critique of Hemingway's novels in moral and aesthetic terms. Baker wrote two additional critical works on Hemingway and edited an anthology of criticism on him. He also edited Hemingway's letters into a comprehensive volume.

Baker, George: *see* Divine, Father.

Baker, George Fisher (b. March 27, 1840, Troy, N.Y., U.S.—d. May 2, 1931, New York City), financier, bank president, and philanthropist who endowed the Graduate School of Business Administration at Harvard.

George Fisher Baker
By courtesy of the Library of Congress, Washington, D.C.

When the national banking system was created in 1863, Baker joined with John Thompson and sons to establish the First National Bank of New York City. Beginning as a teller and small stockholder, he was the active head of the bank by the age of 25. By 1909, when he became chairman of the board, he ranked with J.P. Morgan and James Stillman as a force in U.S. finance and served as director of many corporations. In addition to his gift of $6,000,000 to Harvard, he made large gifts to other institutions including New York City's Metropolitan Museum of Art and the American Red Cross.

Baker, George Pierce (b. April 4, 1866, Providence, R.I., U.S.—d. Jan. 6, 1935, New York City), teacher of some of the most notable U.S. dramatists, among them Eugene O'Neill, Philip Barry, Sidney Howard, and S.N. Behrman. Emphasizing creative individuality and practical construction (he guided students' plays through workshop performances), Baker fostered an imaginative realism. The critic John Mason Brown and the novelists John Dos Passos and Thomas Wolfe also studied under Baker, who appears as Professor Hatcher in Wolfe's *Of Time and the River.*

Baker was graduated from Harvard in 1887 and remained there to teach. In 1905 he started his class for playwrights, "47 Workshop" (named after its course number), the first of its kind to be part of a university curriculum. He concerned himself not only with writing but also with stage design, lighting, costuming, and dramatic criticism.

George Pierce Baker, detail of an oil painting by Deane Keller, 1933; in the Yale University Art Gallery
By courtesy of the Yale University Art Gallery, gift of the Department of Drama

Baker's annual lecture tours, following a lectureship at the Sorbonne in 1907, introduced many Americans to European ideas of theatre art. His university productions pioneered advanced staging techniques in the U.S.

From 1925 until he retired in 1933, Baker was professor of the history and technique of drama at Yale University, founding a drama school there and directing the university theatre. Many innovative techniques in theatre, motion-picture, and television production had their origins in his work at Yale. Of his writings, the best known are *The Development of Shakespeare as a Dramatist* (1907) and *Dramatic Technique* (1919).

Baker, Dame Janet (Abbott) (b. Aug. 21, 1933, Hatfield, Yorkshire, Eng.), English operatic mezzo-soprano, known for her vocal expression, stage presence, and effective projection of words. As a recitalist she was noted for her interpretations of Gustav Mahler, Sir Edward Elgar, and Johann Sebastian Bach.

She studied voice in London until 1956 when she won second prize in the Kathleen Ferrier Award. After a period of study at the Mozarteum in Salzburg, Austria, she made her operatic debut in 1956 at the Oxford University Opera Club as Roza in Bedřich Smetana's *The Secret,* and also sang Eduige in *Rodelinda,* the first of many memorable performances of George Frideric Handel and preclassical operatic roles at the Barber Institute in Birmingham.

In 1962 Baker sang the female lead in Henry Purcell's *Dido and Aeneas* and Polly in Benjamin Britten's *The Beggar's Opera.* In 1971 she created the role of Kate Julian, written especially for her, in Britten's *Owen Wingrave,* first for television and then for the stage. She also won the Hamburg Shakespeare Prize that year. She performed successfully in the Raymond Leppard revivals of early Italian operas, notably as Penelope in Claudio Monteverdi's *Il Ritorno d'Ulisse in Patria* in 1972. She sang the 1975 premiere performance of Dominick Argento's song cycle *From the Diary of Virginia Woolf,* which won the Pulitzer Prize. In the following year she was made a Dame of the British Empire.

Baker, Josephine (b. June 3, 1906, St. Louis, Mo., U.S.—d. April 12, 1975, Paris), dancer and singer who symbolized the beauty and vitality of black American culture, which took Paris by storm in the 1920s.

As a child Baker developed the taste for the flamboyant that was later to make her famous. As an adolescent she became a dancer, touring at 16 with a dance troupe from Philadelphia. In 1923 she joined the chorus of a show in Boston; she then moved to New York City, where she advanced steadily through the show *Chocolate Dandies* on Broadway and the floor show of the Plantation Club in Harlem. In 1925 she went to Paris to dance at the Théâtre des Champs-Élysées in *La Revue nègre* and introduced *le jazz hot* to France. She continued her career in Paris and became a French citizen in 1937. She sang professionally for the first time in 1930, made her screen debut as a singer four years later, starred in a light opera, and made several more films before World War II.

During the German occupation of France, Baker worked with the Red Cross and the Résistance, and as a member of the Free French forces she entertained troops in Africa and the Middle East; she was later awarded the Croix de Guerre and the Légion d'Honneur with the rosette of the Résistance. After the war much of her energy was devoted to Les Milandes, her estate in southwestern France, from which she began in 1950 to adopt babies of all nationalities in the cause of what she defined as "an experiment in brotherhood"

Josephine Baker
H. Roger-Viollet

and her "rainbow family." She retired from the stage in 1956, but to maintain Les Milandes she was later obliged to return, starring in *Paris* in 1959. She travelled several times to the U.S. during the 1960s to participate in civil rights demonstrations, and in 1973 made a triumphant return to the New York City stage.

In 1949 *Les Mémoires de Joséphine Baker*

was published, and in 1976 a biography by Steven Papich, *Remembering Josephine Baker.*

Baker, LaFayette Curry (b. Oct. 13, 1826, Stafford, N.Y., U.S.—d. July 3, 1868, Philadelphia), chief of the U.S. Federal Detective Police during the Civil War and director of Union intelligence and counterintelligence operations.

In 1848 he left his family home in New York and worked at a variety of occupations in the West. In 1856 Baker joined the San Francisco Vigilance Command (known as the Vigilantes), a group of self-appointed police whose operations were characterized by arbitrariness and lack of due process. In the next four years he was often employed in an undercover capacity and became adept at deception and disguise. When the Civil War broke out in 1861, he went to Washington, D.C., and offered his services to Gen. Winfield Scott. Sent to reconnoitre the Richmond, Va., area, he was arrested as a spy, but Confederate president Jefferson Davis, after a personal interview, accepted his cover and gave him permission to practice his supposed trade of photography.

Baker later worked as a detective in the War Department, the State Department, and the Post Office before succeeding Allan Pinkerton as head of the federal secret service in November 1862. Baker soon penetrated every area of the military and the civil government of the Union as well as the Confederacy, using hundreds of agents and detectives deployed in two forces whose members were unknown to each other.

Baker adopted the motto "Death to Traitors" for himself and his service. He maintained a headquarters and a prison in the Old Capitol building, where he detained many citizens on flimsy evidence or mere suspicion and subjected them to intensive interrogation to extract confessions and information. In 1863 he raised a battalion of cavalry, officially known as the 1st District of Columbia Cavalry but more widely called Baker's Rangers. The unit was used primarily as a counter-guerrilla force against J.S. Mosby and his raiders and was expanded to a full regiment before the war was over.

In 1864 Baker personally uncovered a major fraud in the Treasury Department, broke up the "Northwest Conspiracy," a plan by Confederate terrorists to carry the war to the cities of the North by arson and other means, and uncovered acts of trading with the enemy by prominent Union officials. After Lincoln was assassinated in April 1865, Baker personally planned and managed the pursuit and capture of John Wilkes Booth and his accomplice, D.C. Herold. Baker was accused of negligence in Lincoln's death, but, in fact, had no direct responsibility for the President's protection and was on duty in New York when the assassination occurred. His quick response won him a long-sought promotion to brigadier general.

After the Civil War Baker continued his police and intelligence activities, paying particular attention to a large trade in pardons for former Confederates that reached into the White House. One pardon broker, Lucy Cobb, who bragged of her access to Pres. Andrew Johnson, was trapped by Baker using marked bills and detained on a charge of influence peddling. Cobb in turn had Baker indicted for false imprisonment. He was convicted, but the presiding judge found the violation to be merely technical and fined him the sum of one dollar and costs. Baker, whose disdain for due process frequently left him open to political attack, resigned his post and his secret service was disbanded when Congress refused it further funding. Baker later testified at Johnson's impeachment trial, making sensational but undocumented charges against the President. In 1867 he published *The History of the U.S. Secret Service.*

Baker, Newton D(iehl) (b. Dec. 3, 1871, Martinsburg, W.Va., U.S.—d. Dec. 25, 1937, Cleveland), lawyer, political leader, and U.S. secretary of war during World War I.

In 1897 he began to practice law in his home-town, moving later to Cleveland, where he served two terms (1912–16) as mayor.

Newton D. Baker, 1915

By courtesy of the Library of Congress, Washington, D.C.

Baker, who had played an important role in Woodrow Wilson's nomination in the Democratic National Convention of 1912, was appointed secretary of war by President Wilson and remained in the Cabinet to the end of Wilson's term of office. Although he was, as he himself said, so much of a pacifist that "he would fight for peace," he soon submitted to Congress a plan for universal military conscription, and he presided over the mobilization of more than 4 million men during World War I.

In 1928 he was appointed by Pres. Calvin Coolidge to the Permanent Court of Arbitration at The Hague, and in 1929 Pres. Herbert Hoover made him a member of the Law Enforcement Commission. His book, *Why We Went to War,* was published in 1936. A biography is C.H. Cramer's *Newton D. Baker* (1961).

Baker, Norma Jean (screen actress): *see* Monroe, Marilyn.

Baker, Ray Stannard, pseudonym DAVID GRAYSON (b. April 17, 1870, Lansing, Mich., U.S.—d. July 12, 1946, Amherst, Mass.), journalist, popular essayist, literary crusader for the League of Nations, and authorized biographer of Woodrow Wilson.

A reporter for the *Chicago Record* (1892–98), he became associated with *Outlook, McClure's*, and the "muckraker" *American Magazine* (1906). He explored the situation of black Americans in *Following the Color Line* (1908). As David Grayson he published *Adventures in Contentment* (1907), the first of his several collections of homely, widely read essays. From 1910, when he first met Woodrow Wilson, Baker became an increasingly fervent admirer. At Wilson's request, Baker served as head of the American Press Bureau at the Paris peace conference (1919), where the two were in close and constant association. Despite prolonged ill health, Baker wrote *Woodrow Wilson: Life and Letters* (8 vol., 1927–39). He was awarded the Pulitzer Prize for the work in 1940.

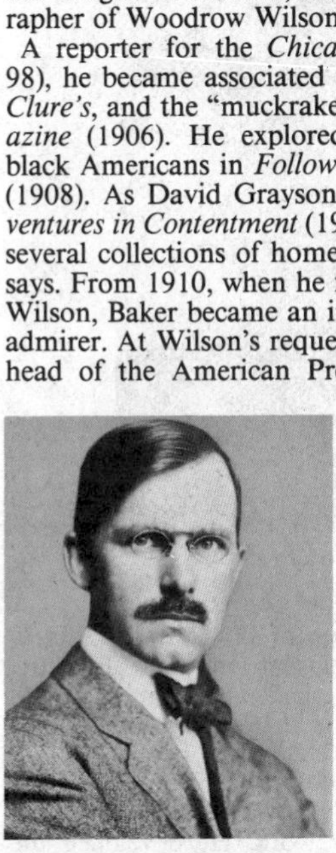

Ray Stannard Baker

By courtesy of the Library of Congress, Washington, D.C.

Baker, Sir Samuel White (b. June 8, 1821, London—d. Dec. 30, 1893, Sanford Orleigh, Devon, Eng.), explorer who, with John Hanning Speke, helped to locate the sources of the Nile.

The son of a merchant, he lived on the Indian Ocean island of Mauritius (1843–45) and in Ceylon (1846–55) before travelling through the Near East (1856–60). In 1861, with Florence von Sass (who later became his second wife), he went to Africa and for about a year explored the Nile tributaries around the Sudan and Ethiopia border. Using maps supplied by Speke, the Baker expedition set out in February 1863 to find the source of the Nile. In March 1864 Baker determined the source to be a lake, which he named Albert Nyanza (Lake Albert), lying between modern Uganda and Zaire. He was knighted in 1866, the year after he returned to England.

In 1869 the Ottoman viceroy of Egypt, Ismāʿīl Pasha, asked Baker to command a military expedition to the Nile equatorial regions. There the explorer helped to put down the slave trade and annexed territories of which he was appointed governor general for four years.

Sir Samuel Baker

BBC Hulton Picture Library

His books include *The Rifle and the Hound in Ceylon* (1854) and *The Nile Tributaries of Abyssinia* (1867). Biographies include *Baker of the Nile* (1949) by Dorothy Middleton, and *Lovers on the Nile* (1980) by Richard Hall.

Baker, Sara Josephine (b. Nov. 15, 1873, Poughkeepsie, N.Y., U.S.—d. Feb. 22, 1945, New York City), physician who contributed significantly to public health and child welfare in the United States.

After earning an M.D. from the Women's Medical College of the New York Infirmary for Women and Children in 1898, Baker began working for the New York City Health Department, becoming assistant commissioner in 1907. Her concern with the city's high infant mortality rate led to the establishment the next year of the Division of Child Hygiene—the first public agency solely devoted to child health and a model for similar agencies around the world.

As the division's first director, Baker developed pioneering programs that drew public attention to the value of preventive medicine. Her achievements include the introduction of public school health measures, midwife training schools, and baby health stations that dispensed both milk and advice. In 1909 Baker helped to found the American Child Hygiene Association, and in 1911 she organized the Babies Welfare Association, later the Children's Welfare Federation of New York.

In 1917 Baker earned from New York University the first doctorate ever awarded to a woman in the field of public health. After her retirement in 1923, she became a consultant to the federal Children's Bureau and a representative on child health issues to the League of Nations.

Her publications comprise over 250 popular and scholarly articles and five books on child hygiene. Her autobiography, *Fighting for Life*, was published in 1939.

Baker, Theodore (b. June 3, 1851, New York City—d. Oct. 13, 1934, Dresden, Ger.), American music scholar and lexicographer.

Trained as a young man for business, Baker preferred to study music and went to Germany in 1874 for that purpose. He became a pupil of Oskar Paul at the University of Leipzig and received his Ph.D. there in 1882. His dissertation, based on field research among the Seneca Indians in New York, was the first serious study of American Indian music and provided themes for Edward MacDowell's *Second (Indian) Suite for Orchestra.*

Baker lived in Germany until 1890, returning to the United States the following year and becoming (1892) the literary editor and translator for the publishing house of G. Schirmer, Inc. He remained at Schirmer until his retirement in 1926, when he returned again to Germany.

In addition to his many English translations of books, librettos, and articles (especially those appearing in the *Musical Quarterly,* a Schirmer publication), Baker compiled a useful and popular *Dictionary of Musical Terms* (1895), and *Baker's Biographical Dictionary of Musicians* (1900), the work for which he is best known. This last volume included the names of many musicians never previously mentioned in musical reference works. A second edition was published in 1905 and the dictionary underwent several revisions before the 6th edition of 1978 under the supervision of Nicolas Slonimsky.

Baker Island, formerly NEW NANTUCKET, or PHOEBE ISLAND, unincorporated territory of the U.S. in the South Pacific Ocean, 1,650 mi (2,650 km) southwest of Honolulu. A coral atoll rising to 25 ft (8 m), it measures 1 mi long by 0.7 mi wide and has a land area of about 0.6 sq mi (1.5 sq km). The uninhabited island is arid and is fringed by a reef.

Sighted (1832) by an American mariner, Capt. Michael Baker, the island was claimed (1857) along with nearby Howland Island by the U.S. under the Guano Act of 1856, but its guano deposits are now exhausted. In the 1930s, rising interest in transpacific aviation prompted the U.S. to strengthen its claim on Baker by colonizing it from Hawaii. In 1936 it came under the administration of the U.S. Department of the Interior. Evacuated in early 1942, the island was reoccupied by U.S. forces in late 1943, and an air base was built.

Baker v. Carr (1962), U.S. Supreme Court case that forced the Tennessee legislature to reapportion itself on the basis of population. Traditionally, particularly in the South, rural areas had been overrepresented in legislatures in proportion to urban and suburban areas. Prior to the Baker case, the Supreme Court had refused to intervene in apportionment cases; in 1946 in *Colegrove* v. *Green* the court said apportionment was a "political thicket" into which the judiciary should not intrude. In the Baker case, however, the court held that each vote should carry equal weight regardless of the voter's place of residence. Thus the legislature of Tennessee had violated the constitutionally guaranteed right of equal protection (*q.v.*). Chief Justice Earl Warren described this decision as the most important case decided after his appointment to the court in 1953.

Citing the Baker case as a precedent, the court held in *Reynolds* v. *Sims* (1964) that both houses of bicameral legislatures had to be apportioned according to population. It remanded numerous other apportionment cases to lower courts for reconsideration in light of the Baker and Reynolds decisions. As a result, virtually every state legislature was reapportioned, ultimately causing the political power in most state legislatures to shift from rural to urban areas.

Bākerganj, also called BARISĀL, district, Khulna division, Bangladesh, lying west of the Meghna River, forming part of the Ganges Delta. With an area of 2,792 sq mi (7,231 sq km) it is drained by the Meghna, Madhumati, Ariāl Khān, and Bishkhāli rivers.

The southern part of the district, between the Madhumati and Meghna rivers, is forested and forms part of the Sundarbans (*q.v.*). It is important for agriculture, especially rice, sugarcane, jute, pulses, and oilseeds. Rivers form the most important means of communication and steamer service connects Barisāl, the administrative headquarters, with Khulna, Dhākā, Chittagong, Patuākhāli, and Madaripur. Other important towns in the district are Bākerganj, Pirojpur, Bhola, Chakhar, and Swarupkāti. Pop. (1981 prelim.) 4,667,673.

Bakersfield, city, seat (1875) of Kern County, south central California, U.S., in the San Joaquin Valley. Founded in 1869 by Thomas Baker, it became a service point for the gold mines of the Sierra Nevada and Owens Valley. With the advent of the Southern Pacific (1874) and the Santa Fe (1898) railroads, an extensive irrigation system (based on the Kern River) was developed. The discovery of the Kern River oil fields (1899) brought petroleum-based industries to the city. The economy is now well balanced between manufacturing, agriculture (cotton, grain, and grapes), and tourism. Nearby vineyards produce 25% of California wine. Bakersfield (junior) College was founded in 1913. Inc. 1898. Pop. (1980) city, 105,611; metropolitan area (SMSA), 403,081.

Bakewell, Robert (b. 1725, Dishley, Leicestershire, Eng.—d. Oct. 1, 1795, Dishley), agriculturist who revolutionized sheep and cattle breeding in England by methodical selection, inbreeding, and culling. Bakewell's father was

Bakewell, detail of an engraving
The Mansell Collection

a farmer, with a farm of 440 acres at Dishley. Bakewell, as a young man, travelled about the country learning agricultural techniques and returned to the farm of his ailing father (who died in 1760). There Bakewell became one of the first to breed both sheep and cattle for meat; previously the animals were bred primarily for wool or work. He developed the Leicestershire longhorn cattle into good meat producers, but they were poor suppliers of milk and were later supplanted by the Shorthorns bred by Charles Colling.

Bakewell had more permanent success in developing the Leicester sheep, a barrel-shaped animal that produced long, coarse wool and also provided a good yield of high-quality meat. The first to establish on a large scale the practice of letting animals for stud, he made his farm famous as a model of scientific management.

Bakewell glass, glassware produced at the factory completed in 1808 in Pittsburgh by Benjamin Bakewell, an Englishman from Derby who became known as the father of the flint-glass industry in the United States. Pittsburgh Flint Glass Manufactory, then Bakewell & Company, and later Bakewell & Page, operated until 1882. In 1810 the factory began to produce both cut and engraved glass, and from the outset the firm was noted for quality and for the brilliance of its cutting. Since American cut glass was both a novelty and a luxury, the firm attracted much attention, and until about 1819 Bakewell's factory was the only one making cut and engraved tablewares; among its important early commissions was a comprehensive service of engraved glassware for Pres. James Monroe (1817). Early Bakewell glass is characterized by its elaborate decoration and by its use of shapes and cutting patterns adapted from contemporary Irish glass. Around 1824 a number of cut glass tumblers were produced that had embedded in their bases a bas-relief ceramic profile of an outstanding American (*e.g.*, George Washington, Benjamin Franklin, Andrew Jackson).

The first known patent for pressing glass by mechanical means was granted to John P. Bakewell in 1825 to make pressed glass knobs for furniture. This invention led to the mass production of glass, and for the first time glass tableware and ornamental glass became economical for all income levels.

Bakhchisaray, also spelled BACHČISARAJ, city, Crimea *oblast* (administrative region), Ukrainian Soviet Socialist Republic, in the Churuk-Su Valley on the Simferopol–Sevastopol railway. Before passing to Russia in 1783, it was the capital of the Crimean khanate. The city has many buildings of historical and architectural interest, including the palace of the Tatar khans built in 1519. Pop. (1970) 15,912.

Bakhmut (Ukrainian S.S.R.): *see* Artyomovsk.

Bakht Khan (b. *c.* 1797—d. 1859), commander in chief of rebel forces in the early stages of the anti-British Indian Mutiny (1857).

Related on his mother's side to the ruling house of Oudh (deposed by the British in 1856), Bakht Khan served for a number of years as a field battery commander in the army of the British East India Company. When the rebellion broke out in May 1857, he led his troops to Delhi, where he emerged as the dominant figure in the independent Indian government proclaimed by the rebels. To control the figurehead Mughal emperor, he established a court of administration, the members of which were elected by the army and the government departments. Forced out of Delhi by the British in September, he is said to have been killed in battle during the last days of the Mutiny.

Bakhtarān, *ostān* (province), western Iran, with an area of 9,138 sq mi (23,667 sq km). It stretches across the Zagros Mountains and is bounded on the west by the Iraqi frontier, on the north by Kordestān (Kurdistan) *ostān,* on the east by Hamadān *ostān,* on the southeast by Lorestān *ostān,* and on the south by Ilān *ostān.* Climatically it consists of the warm, fertile land of the western piedmont and lower valley bottoms; the cultivated upland valley bottoms, with hot summers and cold, snowy winters;

and the higher uplands, suffering long, harsh winters and providing summer grazing. Rainfall (20–35 in. [500–900mm] annually) allows grain crops (rice, barley, wheat) in many parts. The province is one of the richest agricultural areas of Iran; its agriculture is now mostly mechanized. Irrigation is largely used in the upland valleys. Cereals, cotton, oilseeds, fruit, and vegetables are the main crops, and the hills provide good pasturage; a livestock-breeding centre is located in the province. Industries produce textiles, processed food, metalware, sugar, woven carpets, animal feed, electrical equipment and tools, and alcoholic beverages. The inhabitants are mainly Kurds of many different tribes, most of whom settled in urban areas after World War II. Iraqi planes attacked the Iranian military bases in the *ostān* during Iran–Iraq hostilities in 1980.

Prehistoric sites are located at Harsīn, Alishtār, and Khorramābād. There are many rock carvings of Achaemenid (559–330 BC) and Sāsānid (*c.* AD 226–651) origin, such as those at Ṭāq-e Bostān, representing the investiture of Ardashīr II (379–383). Bīsitūn has two bas-reliefs, one representing Mithridates II (123–88 BC) receiving tribute from four dignitaries, and the other commemorating the victory of Gotarzes II over his rival Meherdates in AD 50. Pop. (1983 est.) 1,225,000.

Bakhtarān, formerly KERMANSHAH, city and capital, Bakhtarān *ostān* (province), western Iran, in the fertile valley of the Qareh Sū (river) and situated on the ancient caravan route between the Mediterranean Sea and central Asia. It was founded in the 4th century AD by Bahrām IV of the Sāsānian dynasty. Conquered by the Arabs in 640, the town was called Qirmasin (Qirmashin). Under Seljuq rule in the 11th century, it was the chief town of Kordestān. The Ṣafavids (ruled 1501–1736) fortified the town, and the Qājārs repulsed an attack by the Turks during Fatḥ ʿAlī Shāh's rule (1797–1834). Occupied by the Turkish Army in 1915 during World War I, it was evacuated in 1917. The construction of a road in the 1950s over the age-old Khorāsān track added considerably to the importance of the city. It is now a fairly important industrial centre; industries include textile manufacturing, food processing, oil refining, carpet making, sugar refining, and the production of electrical equipment and tools. It is connected by road to Tabriz, Hamadan, and Qazvin and has an airport. Pop. (1976) 290,861.

Bakhtiari rug, also spelled BAKHTYĀRĪ, handwoven pile floor covering made under Bakhtyārī patronage in certain villages of the Chahār district southwest of Isfahan in central Iran. Bakhtiari rugs are Ghiordes-knotted on a foundation of cotton.

Bakhtiari rug from Iran, 20th century; in a New Jersey private collection

In a New Jersey private collection; photograph, Otto E. Nelson—EB Inc.

The colouring and patterns of these rugs are bold. The field is usually divided into compartments that may be rectangular or produced by an ogival lattice. Occasionally there are tree or medallion decorative schemes. The palette is strong to the point of harshness, with much use of yellow.

Bakhtyārī, also spelled BAKHTIYĀRĪ, one of the nomad peoples of Iran; its chiefs were among the greatest tribal leaders in Iran and were long influential in Persian politics. The Bakhtyārī population of approximately 570,000 occupies roughly 25,000 square miles (65,000 square kilometres) of plains and mountains in the Khuzistan and Chahār Maḥāll-e Bakhtīārī regions of western Iran. They speak the Lurī dialect of Persian and are Muslims.

The Bakhtyārī consist of two groups, the smaller of which is mainly nomadic, the other, mostly sedentary. The nomadic, pastoral tent dwellers are dependent on their flocks of sheep, goats, and cattle and migrate 150 miles each year between their winter pastures in the plains and the summer pastures of the mountains. Agricultural products are mainly obtained by trade or as tax from dependent villages. There has been some urbanization resulting from the oil industry.

The Bakhtyārī are subdivided into sections under hereditary chiefs. Until 1949 these tribal leaders were united under one paramount chief, the *īl-khān*; he and his deputy, the *īlbeg,* were elected by the chiefly families.

Bakhtyārī women have long enjoyed a high degree of freedom. Unlike urban elite Muslim women elsewhere, pastoral and village women are not required to cover their faces with veils, except possibly when strangers appear. The daughters of tribal leaders are normally given at least an elementary education.

Bakhuis Gebergte, range of hills, west central Suriname, running north–south, about 70 mi (110 km) in length and separating the basins of the Kabalebo and Nickerie rivers (west) from that of the Coppename River (east). The range is relatively low-lying, comprising a northward continuation of the higher Wilhelmina Gebergte, to the south; it reaches a maximum height of 3,369 ft (1,027 m). The Wilhelmina Gebergte is the site of Suriname's largest bauxite deposit.

Bâkî, also spelled BĀQĪ, in full MAHMUD ABDÜLBÂKİ (b. 1526, Constantinople—d. April 7, 1600, Constantinople), one of the greatest lyric poets of the classical period of Ottoman Turkish literature.

The son of a muezzin, he lived in Constantinople. After an apprenticeship as a saddler, he entered a religious college, where he studied Islāmic law. He also came into contact with many famous men of letters and began to write poetry. In 1555 Bâkî submitted a *qaṣīdah* (ode) to the Ottoman sultan, Süleyman I, thereby gaining an entrée into court circles. At the Sultan's death he wrote an elegy that won him great acclaim. Later Bâkî resumed his religious career, aspiring unsuccessfully to the position of *shaykh al-Islām,* the highest religious office in the empire. He wrote several religious treatises, but his *Divan* ("Collected Poems") is considered his most important work. He is especially known for his *ghazal*s (lyrics), which lament the ephemeral nature of this world and urge the reader to enjoy the pleasures of love and wine. A witty man of the world in his private life, Bâkî rejuvenated Ottoman lyric poetry, breaking with the strict laws of classical prosody and instilling a freshness and vitality of both form and imagery that won for him the coveted title of *sulṭān ash-shuʿarā* ("king of poets") in his own lifetime.

baking, process of cooking by dry heat, most often (but not necessarily) in some kind of oven. Bakery products comprise a wide variety of foods, including bread, rolls, cookies, pies, pastries, and muffins.

A brief treatment of baking and baking products follows. For full treatment, *see* MACROPAEDIA: Food Processing.

Baking dates, in its most rudimentary form, to prehistoric times. At first it involved nothing more than the simple drying of grain seeds in the sun. Eventually the seeds came to be cooked in water, and the resulting gruel was baked on a hot stone, producing a kind of flat bread that was in many ways similar to the tortilla.

The process of leavening—that is, making bread lighter, thicker, and more flavourful—developed slowly. The Egyptians, it is believed, were the first to consciously use leavening in their baking and also were the first to use ovens. By the middle of the 3rd century BC, the Egyptians had developed baking methods in many ways similar to those in use today.

During the centuries following, no major advances in baking methods were made, although the Romans introduced some minor technological improvements. Only with the Industrial Revolution of the mid-19th century did the technology of baking begin to advance rapidly. The quality of ingredients improved, and automation began to replace the time-consuming manual process; both developments led to the establishment of a baking industry that in the 20th century produces a wide variety of goods with highly elaborate and efficient machinery.

While some baked products are still unleavened (such as pie crusts, tortillas, and the similar chapatis from India), many modern baked goods employ leavening, which is central to both their taste and their texture. Only wheat and rye flours have the qualities necessary for the expansion of an initial dough or batter, and wheat is more satisfactory. Although various flours are used in baking, some amount of wheat flour must be added if any significant degree of leavening is desired. Protein in the flour, known as gluten, combines with water to produce an elastic and porous web capable of trapping gas bubbles released by the action of a leavening agent.

In bread and in some other sweeter rolls and pastries, baker's yeast (composed of living cells of the *Saccharomyces cerevisiae* yeast strain) is used to create the leaven. It ferments sugars present in the flour and in other ingredients, giving off carbon dioxide and ethanol. Another leavening method is the use of sourdough, a type of dough that contains an acid-generating bacteria that ferments the sugars. Sourdough has a distinctive flavour and is often used in the making of rye bread. Salt-rising bread, with its sharp odour and taste, uses both yeast and sourdough as fermenting agents.

Such sweeter bakery products as layer cakes, biscuits, cookies, and muffins make use of chemical reactions rather than fermentation for leaven. Sodium bicarbonate (baking soda) is most commonly used, but it must be properly combined with counteracting acids in order to release a sufficient amount of carbon dioxide. Such a combination is provided in baking powder, whose formula also serves to regulate the timing of the gas's release. These bakery products generally employ a softer flour, containing less gluten than that used in yeast-leavened goods. Thus, the dough is not able to trap as much gas, and these products are generally denser.

Another important method of leavening batters is the mixing in of air bubbles from the outside atmosphere. This can be accomplished only by the inclusion of an ingredient (often egg whites) that can easily be beaten into a foam that can hold air bubbles. This method produces a particularly light and delicate product (for example, angel food or sponge cake), but must be executed very gently and with extreme care.

Important ingredients for baking other than flour, water, and leavening agents are shortening (fats, butter, oils, lard), eggs, milk, and sugars. Shortening tends to make doughs more easily workable and the final product more tender, while also, in many cases, adding flavour. Egg whites, as mentioned, are often used to produce a light, airy texture, and yolks contribute to the colour, flavour and texture of baked products. Milk is used for flavouring, and sugars to sweeten and to aid fermentation.

Commercial bakeries employ a variety of techniques ranging from the use of simple home baking methods by smaller companies to the use of highly complex and automated equipment in large commercial operations. Even in many larger bakeries, however, the basic steps of baking in batches remain the same; the ingredients are simply used in much larger quantities. Measured accurately by computers, the ingredients are first mixed into dough or batter, sometimes in large horizontal machines with revolving bars that work the mixture into a uniform structure, and other times in giant mixing bowls similar, except in size, to those found in the home. With yeast-leavened goods, mixing is often done in two stages, permitting an interim period of fermentation and a chance for more control over the variability that some ingredients exhibit from batch to batch. When the ingredients are mixed (and in the case of yeast leavening, the dough properly fermented), an elaborate series of machines that vary with the product separate and shape the dough or batter into individual units and prepare these for final baking. The batch is then placed in an oven and cooked to specifications.

Continuous baking, an alternative to the batch method, substitutes a steady flow of dough or batter through processing machines in place of the discrete amount of mixtures handled in batches. The ingredients are mixed and fermented in a liquid or semiliquid state and are then cooled into a continuous piece of dough or stream of batter. This dough or batter is pushed out through an opening of the mixing machine at a steady rate and is sliced into uniform pieces or poured into standardized containers and passed slowly on a conveyer belt through an open-ended oven.

baking powder, leavening agent (*q.v.*) used in making baked goods.

Bakkah (Saudi Arabia): *see* Mecca.

baklava, rich Middle Eastern and Greek pastry of filo (phyllo) dough and nuts. Filo is a simple flour and water dough that is stretched to paper thinness and cut into sheets, a process so exacting that it is frequently left to commercial manufacturers. For baklava, 30 or 40 sheets of phyllo, each brushed liberally with melted butter, are layered in a baking pan with finely chopped walnuts, pistachios, or almonds. After the pastry is baked it is drenched with a syrup of honey and lemon juice. Cinnamon, ground cloves, cardamom, or rosewater may flavour either the filling or the syrup.

Bakongo (people): *see* Kongo.

Bakony Mountains, mountain range in northwest central Hungary, covering about 1,500 sq mi (4,000 sq km) between Lake Balaton and the Little Alfold and running southwest–northeast for 70 mi (110 km) from the Zala River. The range forms the major component of the highlands of Dunántúl, or Transdanubia (the Bakony, Vértes, Gerecse, Budai and Pilis, and Visegrád mountains). The Keszthely and Balatoni Felvidék mountain groups are separated from the main Bakony by the Tapolca basin and a fault, respectively. The road and rail lines follow the main fault line from Székesfehérvár to Veszprêm to Devecser. Lake Balaton occupies a large tectonic depression south of the Bakony. The mountains consist of flat-topped or undulating fragments of a step-faulted range rising toward the north. Limestone and dolomite constitute most of the Bakony, which range from 700 ft to 2,300 ft (210 m to 700 m); Kőrishegy is 2,310 ft. In western and southern Bakony are sheets of basalt. Deposits of lignite, bauxite, and manganese in the Bakony have stimulated industrial development, as at Veszprêm and Ajka. New large deposits of bauxite were discovered in the 1970s near the village of Inarkúl. The formerly dense forest cover has been partially removed to provide farmlands in the basins and on the lower flattops. Precipitation is moderate (31 in. [800 mm] on the highest parts); most of this seeps through the limestone to emerge as springs on the mountain perimeter. The south-facing slopes overlooking Lake Balaton support a thriving wine industry.

Bakool, also spelled BAKOL, *gobolka* (administrative region), south central Somalia, East Africa. Part of the Italian-administered former United Nations Trust Territory of Somalia until 1960, the region was created from the northeastern part of the former Alto Giuba (Upper Juba) region in 1973. Bounded by the *gobollada* (administrative regions) of Gedo (west), Bay (south), Hiiraan (east), and Bale province of Ethiopia (north), the region encompasses 10,425 sq mi (27,000 sq km). The physiography of this hot (average annual temperature 81° F [27° C]) and dry (annual rainfall 17 in. [427 mm]) region is dominated by an upland plateau (average elevation 1,500 to 2,200 ft [455 to 670 m] above sea level). Vegetation is mostly thorn tree savanna, with grass providing pasturage for livestock. The population is mostly of the Rahanweyn ethnic group who are chiefly semi-nomadic pastoralists engaged in the raising of sheep, goats, camels, and cattle and in subsistence farming of sorghum, sesame, peanuts (groundnuts), and beans. Xuddur (Oddur), the regional capital, is connected by road with Muqdisho (Mogadishu) and Baydhabo (Baidoa) in the south and Beled Weyne in the northeast. Pop. (1975) 100,097.

Bakoye River, river in West Africa, rising in the Fouta Djallon massif of Guinea and flowing generally northeast through the sandstone Monts (hills) Mandingues to the Mali border. It then flows north-northwest through less elevated terrain to be fed by the Baoulé River. It turns west down a river valley until, at Bafoulabé, Mali, it merges with the Bafing River to form the Sénégal River. The Bakoye is about 250 mi (400 km) long and is unnavigable. It is the only river rising in the area around Siguiri, Guinea, that does not flow into the Niger. Guinea gold from Bouré, on the Bakoye's headstreams, was once an important export.

Bakr, Aḥmad Ḥassan al- (b. 1914, Tikrīt, Iraq—d. Oct. 4, 1982, Baghdad), president of Iraq, 1968–79.

Al-Bakr entered the Iraqi Military Academy in 1938 after spending six years as a primary school teacher. He was a member of the Ba'th Socialist Party and was forced to retire from the army for revolutionary activities in 1958. He supported the revolution of 1963 and replaced Pres. ʿĀrif ʿAbd ar-Raḥma in the coup of July 17, 1968. His truculent foreign policy effectively isolated him from his Muslim neighbours and his total opposition to any diplomatic solution to the Arab–Israeli dispute brought him into conflict with the Egyptian presidents Gamal Abdel Nasser and Anwar el-Sadat as early as 1970.

Al-Bakr's border claims against Iran made it impossible to bring the Iraqi Kurds under control until an agreement was reached in 1975. His economic policy began with a cautious continuation of the former regime's five-year plan but turned toward industrial expansion as oil revenues increased. After suffering a heart attack in 1976 al-Bakr delegated most administrative matters to Saddam at-Takrītī Hussein, who succeeded him on July 17, 1979.

Baksar (India): *see* Buxar.

Baksar, Battle of, Baksar also spelled BUXAR (Oct. 22, 1764), conflict between the East India Company's forces, commanded by Maj. Hector Munro, and those of the Mughal emperor, Shāh ʿAlam; the Mughal governor of Oudh, Shujāʿ ud-Dawlah; and the dispossessed governor of Bengal, Mīr Qāsim. This decisive battle confirmed the British in the control of Bengal and Bihār after their initial success of Plassey in 1757.

The battle marked the end of the attempt to rule Bengal through a puppet nawab; thenceforth the company took control. In 1765 it was granted the power to collect revenues in Bengal; and Robert Clive began his second govenorship, which continued until 1767.

Bakst, Léon, original name LEV SAMOYLOVICH ROSENBERG (b. Feb. 8, [Jan. 27, old style], 1866, St. Petersburg—d. Dec. 28, 1924, Paris), Russian artist who revolutionized theatrical design both in scenery and costume, emphasizing unity of impression.

Bakst attended the Imperial Academy of Arts at St. Petersburg but was expelled after painting a too-realistic "Pietà." He tutored the children of Grand Duke Vladimir and became a court painter. He began to design scenery in 1900, first at the Hermitage court theatre and then at the Imperial theatres. He designed sets for the tragedies of Sophocles in the spirit of the Greek theatre, copying the style of sculptures of the temple of Aphaea at Aegina. Visiting Greece and Crete, he wrote an account of his voyage and produced a painting, "Terror Antiquus," that expressed his vision of ancient Greece. In 1906 he exhibited at the Salon d'Automne in Paris and two years later achieved his greatest fame as chief set designer for the ballets produced by Diaghilev, painting sets for *Cléopâtre, Scheherazade,* and *Daphnis et Chloé.* Returning to Russia, he founded a progressive school of painting. Later he settled in Paris where he designed sets for the tragedies of D'Annunzio and a play by Émile Verhaeren, painted scenery and designed costumes for a London production of Tchaikovsky's *Sleeping Beauty* in 1921, and produced several plays at the Paris Opéra.

Baku, city, capital of the Azerbaijan Soviet Socialist Republic, on the western shore of the Caspian Sea and the southern side of the Apsheron Peninsula, around the wide, curving sweep of the Bay of Baku. The bay, sheltered by the islands of the Baku Archipelago, provides the best harbour of the Caspian, while the Apsheron Peninsula gives protection from the violent northerly winds (*Khazri*). The name Baku is possibly a contraction of the Persian *bad kube* ("blown upon by mountain winds"). It is one of the Soviet Union's largest cities and derives its importance from its oil industry and administrative functions.

The first historical reference to Baku dates from AD 885, although archaeological evidence indicates a settlement there several centuries before Christ. By the 11th century AD, Baku was in the possession of the Shīrvān-Shāhs, who made it their capital in the 12th century, although for a period in the 13th and 14th centuries it came under the sway of the Mongols. In 1723 Peter I the Great captured

Fountain in the town square, Baku, Azerbaijan S.S.R.

Luba Paz—Pictorial Parade/EB Inc.

Baku, but it was returned to Persia in 1735; Russia captured the town finally in 1806. In 1920 it became capital of the Azerbaijan republic.

The core of present-day Baku is the old town, or fortress, of Icheri-Shekher. Most of the walls, strengthened after the Russian conquest in 1806, survive, as does the 90-ft (27-m) tower of Kyz-Kalasy (Maiden's Tower, 12th century). The old town is highly picturesque, with its maze of narrow alleys and ancient buildings. These include the palace of the Shīrvān-Shāhs, now a museum, the oldest part of which dates from the 11th century. Also of the 11th century is the Synyk-Kala Minaret and Mosque (1078–79). Other notable historic buildings are the law court (Divan-Khan), the Dzhuma-Mechet Minaret, and the mausoleum of the astronomer Seida Bakuvi.

Around the walls of the fortress, the regular streets and imposing buildings of modern Baku rise up the slopes of the amphitheatre of hills surrounding the bay. Along the waterfront an attractive park has been laid out. Most industrial plants are located at the eastern and southwestern ends of the city. Greater Baku, divided into 11 districts, encompasses almost the entire Apsheron Peninsula and 48 townships. Among these are townships on islands off the tip of the peninsula and another built on stilts in the Caspian Sea, 60 mi (100 km) from Baku.

The basis of Baku's economy is petroleum. The presence of oil has been known since the 8th century, and by the 15th century oil for lamps was obtained from surface wells. Modern commercial exploitation began in 1872, second only to Ploeşti in Romania. The Baku oil field at the beginning of the 20th century was the largest in the world, and it remained the largest Soviet field until the 1940s. Today much of the oil has been exhausted, and, although some wells remain in the city itself, drilling has had to extend to 16,700 ft (5,090 m) underground and outward across the Apsheron Peninsula and into the sea. Many derricks stand in the gulf facing the city. Most of the subordinate townships are drilling centres, linked by a network of pipelines to the local refineries and processing plants. From Baku oil is piped to Batumi on the Black Sea or sent by tanker across the Caspian and up the Volga River. Besides oil processing, Baku is one of the largest Soviet centres for the production of equipment for the oil industry, in which 20 factories are engaged. Other engineering industries are shipbuilding and repair and the manufacture of electrical machinery. Chemicals, cement, textiles, footwear, and foodstuffs are also produced.

Baku is also a major cultural and educational centre, with a university and eight other institutions of higher education, including one specializing in the oil and chemical industries. The Azerbaijan S.S.R. Academy of Sciences comprises numerous scientific-research establishments. The city has a number of theatres and museums as well. Azerbaijanis are the largest ethnic group (46 percent), but there are also large numbers of Russians and Armenians (in 1979, respectively 28 and 16 percent). Pop. (1983 est.) 1,071,000.

Baku rug, also called CHILIA RUG, handwoven floor covering made near Baku in the eastern Caucasus. It is a variety of Dagestan rug in modified Persian design, the ground pattern usually bearing rows of the pear or leaf forms of the Seraband rugs but larger in scale and more geometric and complex in form. Stepped medallions and stepped cornerpieces may show a toothed outline, resembling the corners of the field of many Ferahan carpets, producing a raylike effect. The border may display a myriad of narrow diagonal stripes, as in some of the rugs from the Shīrāz area. The colour scheme may be more muted than is usual in the Caucasus, presumably a concession to the taste of Russian customers. These rugs, with warps and pile of wool, are apt to have wefts of cotton.

Sometimes also ascribed to Baku are certain finely woven Dagestan prayer rugs with rows of pears or leaves, each of which has a serrated outline, as if it were on fire. In these prayer rugs, the warp and weft may show combinations of cotton and silk or wool and cotton strands plied together.

Baku rug from the Caucasus, 19th century; in a private collection in New York state

In a New York state private collection; photograph, Otto E. Nelson—EB Inc.

Bakuba (people): *see* Kuba.

bakufu (Japanese history): *see* shogunate.

Bakunin, Mikhail Aleksandrovich (b. May 30 [May 18, old style], 1814, Premukhine, Russia—d. July 1 [June 19, O.S.], 1876, Bern), chief propagator of 19th-century anarchism, a prominent Russian revolutionary agitator, and a prolific political writer. His quarrel with Karl Marx split the European revolutionary movement for many years.

Bakunin was the eldest son of a small landowner in the province of Tver (now Kalinin). He grew up in idyllic surroundings, romantically devoted to four sisters who were nearer to him in age than his younger brothers. His lifetime of revolt began when he was sent to the Artillery School in St. Petersburg and later was posted to a military unit on the Polish frontier. In 1835 he absented himself without leave and resigned his commission, narrowly escaping arrest for desertion. For the next five years he divided his time between Premukhine, where he plunged into the study of the German philosophers Johann Fichte and Hegel, and Moscow, where he moved in the literary circles of the critic V.G. Belinsky, the novelist Ivan Turgenev, and the publicist Aleksandr Herzen. In 1840, his opinions still in a state of fluid turbulence, he journeyed to Berlin to complete his education. There he fell under the spell of the Young Hegelians, the radical followers of Hegel, and, having moved to Dresden, in 1842 published in a radical journal his first revolutionary credo, ending with the now-famous aphorism: "The passion for destruction is also a creative passion." This brought him a peremptory order to return to Russia and, on his refusal, the loss of his passport. After brief periods in Switzerland and Belgium, Bakunin settled in Paris, where he consorted with French and German Socialists, including Pierre-Joseph Proudhon and Karl Marx, and with numerous Polish émigrés who inspired him to combine the cause of the national liberation of the Slav peoples with that of social revolution. The February Revolution of 1848 in Paris gave him his first taste of street fighting; and after a few days of eager participation he travelled eastward in the hope of fanning the flames in Germany and Poland. In Prague in June 1848, he attended the Slav congress, which ended when Austrian troops bombarded the city; and later in the year, in the secure retreat of Anhalt-Köthen, in Germany, he wrote his first major manifesto, *An Appeal to the Slavs.* He denounced the bourgeoisie as a spent counterrevolutionary force; he called for the overthrow of the Habsburg Empire and the creation in central Europe of a free federation of Slav peoples; and he counted on the peasant and especially on the Russian peasant, with his tradition of violent revolt, as the agent of the coming revolution.

Bakunin

EB Inc.

Tired of inaction, Bakunin once more plunged into revolutionary intrigues and, engaging in the Dresden insurrection of May 1849, failed this time to escape arrest. The

Saxon authorities handed him over to Austria and Austria, after a further period of incarceration, to Russia. In May 1851 he was back on Russian soil in the Peter-Paul Fortress in St. Petersburg. There, at the invitation of the chief of police, he wrote an enigmatic *Confession*, which was not published until 1921. Much of it consists of expressions of repentance for misdeeds and abject appeals for mercy. But it includes some gestures of defiance and plays heavily on Bakunin's devotion to the Slavs and hatred of the Germans—sentiments that were noted with interest and approval by the Tsar. They did not, however, help the prisoner. He remained for three years in the Peter-Paul Fortress and for three further years in another fortress, the Schlisselburg, in conditions of rapidly deteriorating health. Finally, in 1857 he was released to live in Siberia. There he contracted a marriage, which was not consummated, with the daughter of a Polish merchant. The governor of Eastern Siberia was a cousin of Bakunin's mother, and it was probably through this connection that he obtained permission in 1861 to travel down the Amur, ostensibly on commercial business. Having reached the coast in a Russian ship, he transferred to an American vessel bound for Japan and travelled via the United States to Great Britain.

Bakunin's arrival in London at the end of 1861 reunited him with Herzen, whom he had last seen in Paris in 1847 and who now occupied a preeminent position among Russian émigrés as editor of *Kolokol* ("The Bell"). Bakunin's 14-month stay in London led to an irretrievable rift with Herzen, who had shed some of the revolutionary ardour of his youth and had already crossed swords with the critic and novelist Nikolay Chernyshevsky and other extreme radicals of the rising Russian generation. He now found Bakunin's financial, as well as political, irresponsibility hard to bear. When the Polish insurrection broke out early in 1863, Bakunin eagerly embarked with a shipload of Polish volunteers for the Baltic. He got only as far as Sweden, where he spent a fruitless summer. At the beginning of 1864 he established himself in Italy, which became his residence for four years. It was there that he framed the main outlines of the anarchist creed that he preached with unsystematic but unremitting vigour for the rest of his life. It was there, too, that he began to weave that complex network, part real, part fictitious, of interlocking secret revolutionary societies that absorbed his energies and bewildered the followers whom he enrolled in them.

The most famous episode of Bakunin's later years was his quarrel with Marx. In 1868, then settled in Geneva, he joined the First International, a federation of working-class parties aiming at transforming the capitalist societies into Socialist commonwealths and their eventual unification in a world federation. At the same time, however, he enrolled his followers in a semisecret Social Democratic Alliance, which he conceived as a revolutionary avant-garde within the International. The same organization could not hold two such powerful and incompatible personalities; and at The Hague congress in 1872 Marx, by an intrigue that had little relation to the causes of the quarrel, secured the expulsion of Bakunin and his followers from the International. The breach split the revolutionary movement in Europe for many years to come. Two of Bakunin's major writings, *L'Empire knouto-germanique et la révolution sociale* (1871) and *Staat en anarchie* (1873), directly reflected his conflict with Marx. Bakunin was as uncompromising a revolutionary as Marx and never ceased to preach the overthrow of the existing order by violent means. But he rejected political control, centralization, and subordination to authority (while making an unconscious exception of his own authority within the movement). He denounced what he regarded as characteristically Germanic ways of thought and organization and opposed to them the untutored spirit of revolt that he found embodied in the Russian peasant. Bakunin's anarchism took final shape as the antithesis of Marx's communism.

During his last years, which he spent in penury in Switzerland, Bakunin reverted to his preoccupation with central and eastern Europe. He was compromised by a short-lived enthusiasm for S.G. Nechayev, a young Russian nihilist who paraded his contempt for conventional morality, achieved notoriety by murdering a fellow conspirator whom he suspected of intending to betray or desert the cause, and for this crime was eventually extradited to Russia by the Swiss authorities. Bakunin consorted with Russian, Polish, Serb, and Romanian émigrés, among whom he found eager disciples; drafted proclamations; and planned revolutionary organizations. His health grew worse; his financial embarrassments became ever more acute, and he depended on the bounties of a few Italian and Swiss friends. But he never wholly lost the resilience of his revolutionary convictions.

Proudhon and Bakunin rank as the founding fathers of 19th-century anarchism. Bakunin formulated no coherent body of doctrine. His voluminous and vigorous writings were often left incomplete. But his fame and personality inspired a large and widely dispersed following. Small anarchist groups existed in Great Britain, Switzerland, and Germany, whereas the powerful anarcho-syndicalist wing of the French trade unions owed more to Proudhon than to Bakunin. Anarchist movements owing allegiance to Bakunin continued to flourish in Italy and especially in Spain, however, where as late as 1936 the anarchists were the strongest revolutionary party. (E.H.C.)

BIBLIOGRAPHY. The first collection of Bakunin's writings was published in six volumes in French between 1895 and 1913; a complete Russian edition of writings and letters was planned, but only the first four volumes down to 1861 were published (1934–36). A complete edition of the later writings, edited by Arthur Lehning, began publication in 1961 by the Instituut voor Sociale Geschiedenis, Amsterdam. Selected works in English translation were published in G.P. Maximoff (ed.), *Political Philosophy of Bakunin* (1953); Sam Dolgoff (ed.), *Bakunin on Anarchy* (1972); and S. Cox and O. Stevens (eds.), *Selected Writings* (1974, from the Lehning edition). Bakunin has not been well served by biographers: Max Nettlau's manuscript biography (in German), *Michael Bakunin*, 3 vol. (1896–1900), based on a large mass of documents, was distributed to the main European libraries; Y. Steklov's biography (in Russian), 4 vol. (1926–27), is unfriendly and Marxist; E.H. Carr, *Michael Bakunin* (1937), is the best in English.

Bakwanga (Zaire): *see* Mbuji-Mayi.

Bala, Welsh Y BALA, market town, Meirionnydd district, Gwynedd county, Wales, within Snowdonia National Park, at the northern end of mountain-girt Bala Lake (Llyn Tegid), the largest natural lake in Wales. The town was founded under a charter of 1324. In the 18th century it became famous both for its knitted stockings and for its huge Methodist revival meetings; it was the home of the Methodist preacher and organizer Thomas Charles. The town has remained small, though it enjoys a thriving tourist trade; the lake offers facilities for angling and yachting. Pop. (1981 prelim.) 1,848.

Balaam, a non-Israelite prophet described in the Old Testament (Num. 22–24) as a diviner who is importuned by Balak, the king of Moab, to place a malediction on the people of Israel, who are camped ominously on the plains of Moab. Balaam states that he will utter only what his god Yahweh inspires, but he is willing to accompany the Moabite messengers to Balak. He is met en route by an angel of Yahweh, who is recognized only by Balaam's ass, which refuses to continue. Then Balaam's eyes are opened, and the angel permits him to go to Balak but commands him not to curse but to bless Israel. Despite pressure from Balak, Balaam remains faithful to Yahweh and blesses the people of Israel.

Balabac, island, southwestern Palawan province, extreme southwestern Philippines. Located about 19 mi (30 km) southwest of the southern tip of Palawan island, and hardly twice that north of Borneo, Balabac rises to an elevation of about 1,890 ft (576 m) and has swamps on its northwestern coast. There are coral reefs off its western coast, and the island is particularly noted for its rare glory-of-the-seas cone shells. Philippine territory ends at the southwestern corner of the island, where small motorized canoes operated by Balabac Muslims make frequent border crossings to the nearby islands in Sabah state (Malaysia) off Borneo's northern coast. Coconuts are a major crop on Balabac. Its people are mostly Muslim (Moros). Balabac town is the main centre of settlement. Pop. (1980) 15,044.

Baʿlabakk (Lebanon): *see* Baalbek.

Balaclava, Battle of: *see* Balaklava, Battle of.

Balādhurī, al-, in full AḤMAD IBN YAḤYĀ AL-BALĀDHURĪ (d. *c.* 892), Arabic historian best known for his history of the formation of the Arab Muslim empire.

Al-Balādhurī lived most of his life in Baghdad and studied there and in Syria. He was for some time a favoured visitor at the Baghdad court of the ʿAbbāsid caliphs. His chief extant work, a condensation of a longer history, *Futūḥ al-buldān* (*The Origins of the Islamic State,* 1916, 1924), tells of the wars and conquests of the Muslim Arabs from the time of the Prophet Muḥammad. It covers the conquests of lands from Arabia west to Egypt, North Africa, and Spain and east to Iraq, Iran, and Sind. Al-Balādhurī drew on oral history and on the few earlier biographies and campaign accounts, giving variants and authorities for them. His history, in turn, was much used by later writers. *Ansāb al-ashrāf* ("Lineage of the Nobles"), also extant, is a biographical work in genealogical order devoted to the Arab aristocracy, from Muḥammad and his contemporaries to the Umayyad and ʿAbbāsid caliphs. It contains histories of the reigns of rulers.

Consult the INDEX *first*

Bālāghāt, town, administrative headquarters of Bālāghāt district, Madhya Pradesh state, central India, just east of the Wainganga River. A major road and rail junction, the town is an agricultural trade and manganese-mining centre. Sugar milling is important. The town has two colleges affiliated with the University of Saugar. Formerly called Burha, Bālāghāt was constituted a municipality in 1877.

Bālāghāt district has an area of 3,570 sq mi (9,245 sq km) and comprises a plateau of the Sātpura Range to the north and lowlands to the south. It is divided from the Chhattīsgarh Plain to the east by the Maikala Range. In the Wainganga Valley in the south and southwest, rich soil areas are extensive. Rice, millet, and pulses are the chief crops; cattle are raised on the plateau near Baihar. Manganese, bauxite, mica, copper, and red-ochre deposits are worked. Gonds form one-third of the district's population. There is also a small community of Baiga tribesmen who are skilled woodsmen. Pop. (1981) town, 49,564; metropolitan area, 53,183; district, 1,147,810.

Bālāghāt Range, series of hills in western Mahārāshtra state, western India. Originating in the Western Ghāts at the Harishchandra Range, it extends southeastward for about 200 mi to the border of Mahārāshtra and Karnātaka states. The width of the range varies from 3 to 6 mi. Higher in the west, the Bālāghāt has an altitude of 1,800–2,700 ft (550–825 m), gradually diminishing eastward until it terminates at the Bhīma River. The flat-topped hills are separated by saddles, which become progressively wider toward the east. The range forms the watershed between the Godāvari River (north) and the Bhīma (south). In the rainier west the hills bear vegetation, but they are barren and stony in the east. Shepherds occupy the entire range, and sheep trails connect the small villages and occasional hilltop temples. Traversing the Bālāghāt are a highway from Pune (Poona) to Nāsik and the railway from Dhond to Manmād.

Balaguer (y Ricardo), Joaquín (Vidella) (b. Sept. 1, 1907, Villa Bisonó, Dominican Republic), lawyer, writer, and diplomat who served as vice president of the Dominican Republic (1957–60) during the regime of Pres. Hector Trujillo and as president (1960–62 and 1966–78).

Between 1932 and 1957, Balaguer held numerous executive and diplomatic posts in the Dominican government. As secretary of education under Hector Trujillo, brother of dictator Gen. Rafael Trujillo, he established free universities and expanded educational and library facilities. He was sworn in as president when Hector Trujillo resigned because of illness. As Gen. Rafael Trujillo still held all power, Balaguer, only the nominal president, could effect little real change or reform. After Rafael Trujillo's assassination in 1961 Balaguer tried to liberalize the government and did convince the Organization of American States (OAS) to lift the economic sanctions that had been imposed during Trujillo's dictatorship, but his changes went too fast for the *trujillistas* and not fast enough for those who demanded immediate restoration of civil liberties and a more equitable distribution of wealth. The country disintegrated into violence, and a short-lived military coup forced Balaguer to resign in 1962 and take refuge in the United States.

Balaguer returned to the Dominican Republic during the U.S. military intervention of 1965 and ran successfully for president in 1966, campaigning on a platform of land reform and economic recovery. His first term was relatively stable, and he made great progress in expanding educational opportunities, but his last two terms were wracked by political violence, assassinations, inflation, and alleged electoral fraud. By 1971 a group of junior officers known as La Banda ("The Gang"), reportedly working in conjunction with the police, had thoroughly terrorized the population of Santo Domingo by their acts of violence against government opponents. Members were eventually brought to trial but released for lack of evidence. Balaguer lost the 1978 presidential race (the first election since 1966 to have the major opposition party represented) to Silvestre Antonio Guzmán. The election was marred by Balaguer's attempts to falsify the election results and delay the transfer of power once it was shown that he had lost.

Balaguer earned a law degree from the University of Santo Domingo and a Ph.D. from the University of Paris. He wrote numerous books on history, politics, and literature, including *La Realidad Dominica* (1947; Eng. trans. *Dominican Reality*, 1949) and *Historia de la Literatura Dominica* (1955).

Balakirev, Mily (Alekseyevich) (b. Jan. 2, 1837 [Dec. 21, 1836, old style], Nizhni Novgorod, Russia—d. May 29 [May 16, O.S.], 1910, St. Petersburg), composer of orchestral music, piano music, and songs and dynamic leader of the Russian nationalist group in the third quarter of the 19th century.

Balakirev, portrait by Léon Bakst, *c.* 1900–10
Novosti Press Agency

His early musical education was received from his mother. He also studied with John Field's pupil Alexander Dubuque and with Karl Eisrich, music director to A.D. Ulibishev, a wealthy landowner who published well-known books on Mozart and Beethoven. Balakirev had the use of Ulibishev's music library and at 15 began to compose and was allowed to rehearse the local theatre orchestra. From 1853 to 1855 he studied mathematics at the University of Kazan and wrote, among other things, a piano concerto.

During 1857 to 1859 Balakirev made a number of appearances as a concert pianist, composed an *Overture on Russian Themes* and music to *King Lear,* and became the mentor of two young composers, César Cui and Modest Mussorgsky. During 1861 and 1862 his circle of disciples was joined by Nikolay Rimsky-Korsakov and Aleksandr Borodin, forming the group known as "The Five." In 1862 he threw himself into a new venture, the Free School of Music, opened by G. Ya. Lomakin in opposition to the St. Petersburg Conservatory, and soon became principal conductor of its public concerts.

During the 1860s Balakirev was at the height of his influence. He collected folk songs up and down the Volga and introduced them in a *Second Overture on Russian Themes,* which ultimately became the symphonic poem *Russia;* he spent summer holidays in the Caucasus, gathering themes and inspiration for his brilliant piano fantasy *Islamey* (1869) and his symphonic poem *Tamara* (1867–82); he published the works of Glinka and visited Prague to produce them; and for a time (1867–69) he conducted the symphony concerts of the Russian Music Society.

His despotic nature and his tactlessness made him innumerable enemies, so that even his friends and disciples came to resent his tutelage; and a series of personal and artistic misfortunes led to his almost complete withdrawal from the world of music (1871–76) and his taking a humble post as a railway clerk. He had passed through a period of acute depression 10 years earlier; now he underwent a more severe crisis from which he emerged a totally changed man, a bigoted and superstitious Orthodox Christian. He gradually returned to the musical world, resumed the directorship of the Free School, and from 1883 to 1894 was director of the imperial chapel. He also resumed composition, completing works, including a symphony, abandoned many years before, and wrote new ones, including his *Piano Sonata* (1905), a *Second Symphony* (1908), and numerous piano pieces and songs. The last decade of his life was spent in almost complete retirement.

It has been said that it was Balakirev, even more than Glinka, who set the course for Russian orchestral music and lyrical song during the second half of the 19th century. He developed an idiom and technique that he imposed on his disciples (above all on Rimsky-Korsakov and Borodin, and to some extent on Tchaikovsky) not only by example but by constant autocratic supervision of their own earlier works. His music is superbly colourful and imaginative, but his creative personality was arrested in its development after 1871 and his later work is couched in the idiom of his youth.

Balaklava, Battle of, Balaklava also spelled BALACLAVA (Oct. 25 [Oct. 13, old style], 1854), indecisive military engagement of the Crimean War, best known as the inspiration of the English poet Alfred, Lord Tennyson's "Charge of the Light Brigade." In this battle, the Russians failed to capture Balaklava, the Black Sea supply port of the British, French, and Turkish forces in the southern Crimea; but the British lost control of their best supply road connecting Balaklava with the heights above Sevastopol, the major Russian naval centre that was under siege.

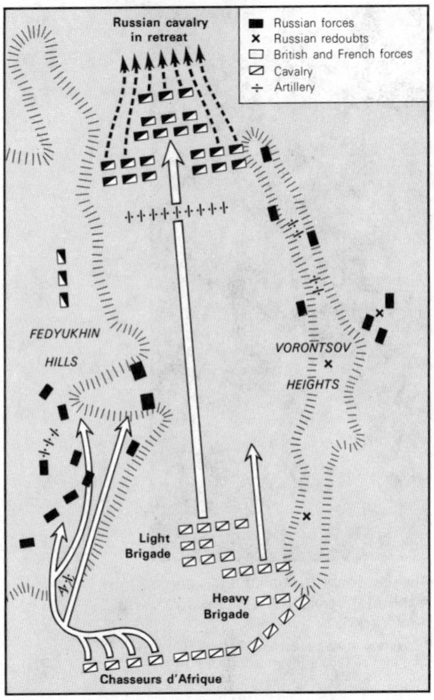

The charge of the Light Brigade at Balaklava
From C. Falls, *A Hundred Years of War* (1961); Duckworth

Early in the battle the Russians occupied the Fedyukhin and the Vorontsov (Causeway) heights, bounding a valley near Balaklava, but they were prevented from taking the town by Gen. Sir James Scarlett's Heavy Brigade and Sir Colin Campbell's 93rd Highlanders, who beat off two Russian cavalry advances. Lord Raglan and his British staff, based on the heights above Sevastopol, however, observed the Russians removing guns from the captured artillery posts on the Vorontsov heights and sent orders to the Light Brigade to disrupt them. The final order became confused, however, and the brigade, led by Lord Cardigan, swept down the valley between the heights rather than toward the isolated Russians on the heights. The battle ended with the loss of 40 percent of the Light Brigade. Tennyson's "Charge of the Heavy Brigade at Balaclava," never popular, is unknown except to literary scholars.

Balakovo, city, Saratov *oblast* (administrative region), southwestern Russian Soviet Federated Socialist Republic, on the left bank of the Volga River. Founded in 1762, it long remained a small agricultural town. Its growth was greatly stimulated by the construction in 1967–70 of the Saratov hydroelectric station on the Volga. Balakovo is also the site of construction of a nuclear power station. A major chemical industry, developed in the 1960s and still expanding in the 1980s, produces cord for tires, sulfuric acid, superphosphates, and carbon bisulfide. A factory for the manufacture of road-building machines was under construction in the early 1980s. Pop. (1983 est.) 170,000.

balalaika, Russian stringed musical instrument of the lute family. It was developed in the 18th century from the *dombra,* or *domra,* a round-bodied, long-necked, three-stringed lute played in Russia and Central Asia. The balalaika is made in six sizes, from piccolo to double bass, and has a flat back and a triangular table, or belly, that tapers to the fretted neck. The frets are movable, and there is a small, round sound hole in the narrow end of the belly. The three strings, usually gut, are end hitched and strung over a violin-like, or pressure, bridge. They are normally plucked with the fingers, although metal strings are also plucked with a leather plectrum.

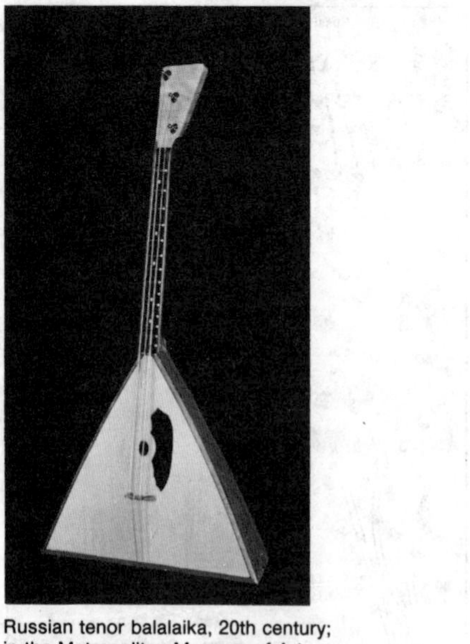

Russian tenor balalaika, 20th century; in the Metropolitan Museum of Art, New York City

By courtesy of the Metropolitan Museum of Art, New York City, the Crosby Brown Collection of Musical Instruments, 1889

The instrument was used in folk music but was also employed in large balalaika orchestras in the 20th century. The representative size, called the prime, or treble, is usually tuned E–E–A in the octave above middle C.

Consult
the
INDEX
first

balance, instrument for comparing the weights of two bodies, usually for scientific purposes, to determine the difference in mass. The invention of the equal-arm balance dates back to the time of the ancient Egyptians, possibly as early as 5000 BC. In the earliest types, the beam was supported at the centre and the pans were hung from the ends by cords attached through vertical holes in the beam. This design was improved by drilling the holes so that the end cords were pulled tightly against the ends of the beam by the loads on the pans. A later improvement in design was the use of a pin through the centre of the beam for the central bearing, introduced by the Romans about the time of Christ. The invention of knife-edges in the 18th century led to the development of the modern precision balance. By the end of the 19th century the balance had been developed in Europe into one of the world's most precise types of measuring devices.

The balance consists, essentially, of a rigid beam that oscillates on a horizontal central knife-edge as a fulcrum and has the two end knife-edges parallel and equidistant from the centre. The loads to be weighed are supported on pans hung from bearings, usually planes, supported by the end knife-edges. For the best design, two or more additional knife-edges should be located between the end bearing and the pan, one to prevent tilting of the plane and another to fix the centre of load at a particular point on the end knife-edge. An arresting mechanism prevents damage during loading by separating the knife-edges from their bearings. The deflection of the balance may be indicated by a pointer attached to the beam and passing over a graduated scale or by reflection from a mirror on the beam to a distant scale.

Many models of balances have mechanisms for interchanging the loads on the pans without opening the balance case. In some models, the controls can be operated from a distance by means of rods. In each case, the rest point of the beam is determined from readings of turning points on the image of a distant scale reflected into a telescope by a fixed prism and a mirror on the beam.

The most obvious method of using a balance is known as direct weighing. The material to be weighed is put on one pan, with sufficient known weights on the other pan such that the beam will be in equilibrium. The difference between the zero reading and the reading with the pans loaded indicates the difference between loads in scale divisions. This difference may be evaluated by comparison with the deflection resulting from a small known weight being added to one of the loads. Such a direct weighing requires that the arms be of equal length. New analytical balances are often required to have the two arms equal within one part in 100,000. With such balances, weighings within a precision of about one part in 100,000 can be made by direct weighing methods. The accuracy of the balance can be improved by means of the rider, a piece of wire that can be moved to a suitable position on the rider scale by a hook on the end of a rod projecting through the balance case.

When the error resulting from unequal arms is greater than the required precision, the substitution method of weighing may be used. In this method, counterpoise weights are added to one pan to balance the unknown load on the other. Then, known weights are substituted for the unknown load. This method requires only that the two arms of the beam maintain the same lengths during the weighing. Any effect of inequality is the same for both loads and is therefore eliminated.

Since the balance will respond to any force acting on the beam or pans, the observer must, as a part of the weighing procedure, assure himself that any extraneous forces have smaller effects than the required precision. Causes of such disturbances include air currents, heating effects, changes in relative humidity, magnetic influences, vibration, air-buoyancy effects, arrestment and release, and swinging of the pans. For precise work the balance should, therefore, be mounted on a rigid support free from vibration in a room with constant atmospheric conditions.

Under ideal conditions, the highest obtainable precision with the best balances is a little better than one part in 100,000,000 with loads of about 1 kg. The highest relative precision is less than this for both larger and smaller loads. With loads of 20 kg, a precision of about one part in 20,000,000 has been obtained. With loads of 1 g, the limit seems to be about one or two parts in 10,000,000. Such precision can be obtained only with balances of the best designs and under the best conditions. In other cases, the possible precision may be restricted by lack of ideal weighing conditions and by improper design.

Small quartz microbalances with capacities of less than a gram have been constructed with a reliability much greater than is ordinarily found with small assay-type balances having a metal beam with three knife-edges. Microbalances are used chiefly to determine the densities of gases, particularly of gases obtainable only in small quantities. Both the torsion-type and the knife-edge type of quartz balance have been used with success. The balance usually operates in a gas-tight chamber, and a change in weight is measured by the change in the net buoyant force on the balance due to the gas in which the balance is suspended, the pressure of the gas being adjustable and measured by a mercury manometer connected with the balance case.

In one successful design, the beam is suspended from two vertical quartz fibres that take the place of the fulcrum knife-edge used in some earlier types. Such a device is capable of detecting differences in weight of only 0.25×10^{-6} mg in a load of 250 mg.

The ultramicrobalance is any weighing device that serves to determine the weight of smaller samples than can be weighed with the microbalance—*i.e.,* total amounts as small as one or a few micrograms (1 microgram = 1 $\gamma = 0.001$ mg $= 10^{-6}$ g). It must show a detectable response to a weight of 00.1 γ or less. The ordinary methods of constructing delicate laboratory balances of the knife-edge type, already discussed, are not satisfactory in the ultramicro range and have been entirely replaced by designs based on other principles. A knife-edge narrow enough to yield necessary sensitivity would have so small an area of contact as to preclude any known material for its construction.

The principles on which ultramicrobalances have been successfully constructed include elasticity in structural elements, displacement in fluids, balancing by means of electrical and magnetic fields, and combinations of these.

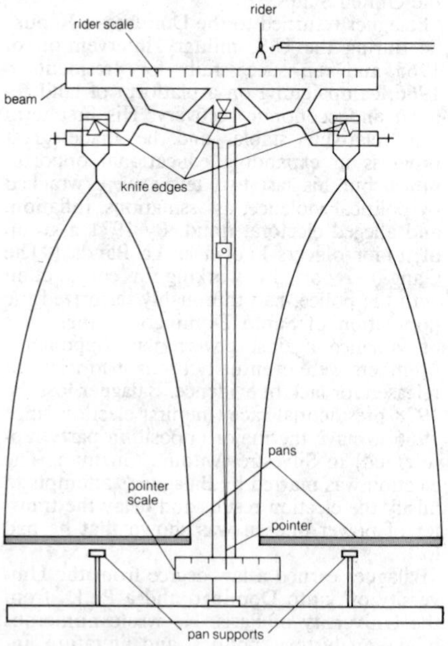

Rider analytical balance

From *McGraw-Hill Encyclopedia of Science and Technology,* Copyright (1971); used with permission of McGraw-Hill Book Co.

Measurement of the effects produced by the minute masses weighed has been made by optical, electrical, and nuclear radiation methods of determining displacements and by optical and electrical measurements of forces used to restore a displacement caused by the sample being weighed.

The preponderance of successful balances has been based on the elastic properties of certain suitable materials, especially quartz fibres, which have great strength and elasticity and are relatively independent of the effects of temperature, hysteresis, and inelastic bending. Glass fibres are also useful and were employed before fused quartz became generally available. Elastic balances are advantageous because of their inherent simplicity and sensitivity and because they measure the weight directly and independently of geographical variations in the gravitational field at the Earth's surface.

In 1901 E. Salvioni described a very simple elastic balance constructed from a single glass fibre, mounted horizontally with one end held rigidly and with a tiny pan suspended from the other (free) end. The application of a load on the pan caused bending of the fibre the amount of which was measured against a stationary scale. Modern modifications of this simple design tend to employ a quartz fibre heavy enough to yield a small amount of bending, the magnitude of which is determined sensitively with a microscope. The weighing range of the Salvioni-type balance is always restricted by the fact that the weight of the pans is usually considerably greater than the weight of the sample. The unloaded pan will then cause a deflection greater than the additional deflection produced by adding the sample to the pan. The subtraction of the large initial deflection from the total deflection leaves only a comparatively small range for the sample, with corresponding difficulty in reading the small movement accurately. The deflection of the fibre caused by its own weight is also quite significant and greater as the length is increased or the diameter reduced.

Quartz fibres, much longer than are practical with the simple design of Salvioni, are often wound into a helix or spring. By increasing both the diameter of the fibre, to increase the possible load, and its length, to increase the sensitivity, greater range of weighing may be achieved.

The most successful and practical ultramicrobalances have been based on the principle of balancing the load by applying torque to a quartz fibre. A simple design described by H.V. Neher utilizes a rigid fibre as a horizontal beam, supported at its centre by a stretched horizontal quartz torsion fibre sealed to it at right angles. On each end of the beam a pan is suspended, one counterbalancing the other. The deflection of the beam caused by adding the sample to one pan is restored by rotating the end of the torsion fibre until the beam is again in its horizontal position and the full range of torsion in the suspending fibre can be applied to the measurement of the load added to one pan. The amount of torsion necessary for restoration is read by means of a dial attached to the end of the torsion fibre. The weight is obtained by calibrating the balance against known weights and reading the value from the calibration chart of weight versus torsion. Unlike direct displacement balances that rely only on the elasticity of the structural members, the torsion balance allows gravity to balance the largest component of the load, *i.e.*, the pans, and results in greatly increased load capacity. *See also* spring balance.

Balance (constellation): *see* Libra.

balance beam, gymnastics apparatus used in women's competition, a wooden beam 5 m (16 ft 5 in.) long, 10 cm (4 in.) wide, and raised 120 cm (3 ft 11 in.) from the floor. The performer begins the exercise by mounting the beam by either a vault or a jump and executes movements that must include steps, running, jumps, turns, sitting, and lying positions, and some held, or posed, positions. The duration of the exercise is 80 to 105 seconds. *See* Sporting record: *Gymnastics: World Championships: Women. See also* Olympic Games.

Balance beam
Novosti—Sovfoto

balance of ———: *see under* substantive word (*e.g.*, payments, balance of).

Balanchine, George, original name GEORGY MELITONOVICH BALANCHIVADZE (b. Jan. 22 [Jan. 9, old style], 1904, St. Petersburg, Russia—d. April 30, 1983, New York City), most influential choreographer of classical ballet in the U.S. in the 20th century. His works, characterized by a cool neoclassicism, include *Serenade* (first performed 1935), *The Nutcracker* (1954), and *Don Quixote* (1965), the latter two pieces choreographed for the New York City Ballet, of which he was a founder (1948), the artistic director, and the chief choreographer. He was also a pioneer in choreography for the musical theatre and motion pictures.

The European years. Georgy Balanchivadze, a Georgian, was one of a generation of dancers who spent the World War I years at the Imperial School of Ballet at the Mariinsky Theatre. The theatre closed for some months in 1917, and, until the Imperial School reopened in 1918 as the Soviet State School of Ballet, he had to support himself with unskilled jobs or by playing piano in a cinema. After three more years of study, he was graduated. The son of a composer, he had also studied music at the Petrograd (St. Petersburg) Conservatory (1921–24).

Balanchine instructing Allegra Kent, *c.* 1960
Martha Swope

As a student Balanchivadze had already tried choreography. His first work, as early as 1920, was a short piece danced to Anton Rubinstein's *Nuit.* He also choreographed works for evenings of experimental ballet performed by himself and his colleagues at the State School of Ballet. The school's directors discouraged this activity, however. He mounted some new and experimental ballets for the Mikhailovsky Theatre in Petrograd. Among them were *Le Boeuf sur le toit* (1920) by Jean Cocteau and Darius Milhaud and a scene for *Caesar and Cleopatra* by George Bernard Shaw.

Balanchivadze was one of the first ballet dancers to leave the Soviet Union, initially to tour with a small group, the Soviet State Dancers, which also included Aleksandra Danilova, Tamara Gevergeva (later Geva), and Nicolas Efimov. They toured Germany, London, and Paris, where in June 1925 he joined Sergey Diaghilev's Ballets Russes. (It was Diaghilev who at that time simplified Balanchivadze to Balanchine.)

It was as a choreographer that Diaghilev envisaged Balanchine—Bronisława Nijinska had recently left Diaghilev, and Balanchine assumed her duties—and in 1925 the Ballets Russes danced Balanchine's *Barabau,* the first of 10 ballets Balanchine was to mount for Diaghilev. Of the ballets he choreographed for Diaghilev, two survive notably in the world repertoire: *Apollo* (1928), the first example of his individual neoclassical style, and *Le Fils prodigue* (*The Prodigal Son,* 1929).

When Diaghilev died in 1929, Balanchine was sufficiently established to have little difficulty in continuing as a choreographer and ballet master. He worked successively with the Royal Danish Ballet and with the Ballet Russe de Monte Carlo, adding significantly to his reputation by composing *La Concurrence* (1932) and *Cotillon* (1932). In 1933 he was one of the founders of the avant-garde company Les Ballets 1933, whose work so enormously impressed the American dance enthusiast Lincoln Kirstein that he invited Balanchine to organize the School of American Ballet and the American Ballet company (of which Kirstein was cofounder and director), thus beginning the association of "Mr. B.," as the ballet world knows him, and ballet in the United States.

The U.S. years. The American Ballet became the resident ballet company at the Metropolitan Opera in New York City, and, while there, Balanchine produced among other works *Le Baiser de la fée* (1937; *The Fairy's Kiss*). He was also creative in a totally different sphere, as pioneer choreographer for Broadway musicals and Hollywood motion pictures, including the celebrated *Slaughter on Tenth Avenue* ballet in *On Your Toes* (1936).

The end of the largely unsatisfactory association between the American Ballet and the Metropolitan Opera came in 1938. Kirstein founded Ballet Caravan in 1936, with a repertoire of ballets by American choreographers. In 1941 this company and what remained of the American Ballet were united for a Latin-American tour, for which Balanchine composed *Concerto barocco* and *Ballet Imperial.* During the World War II period, Balanchine worked in the U.S. for the Original Ballet Russe, for Ballet Russe de Monte Carlo, and in Hollywood or on Broadway. In 1947 he was guest ballet master at the Paris Opéra.

Kirstein's determination, however, to establish American ballet under Balanchine's artistic direction never faltered. In 1946 he succeeded in founding the Ballet Society, which developed in 1948 into the New York City Ballet. First centred at the New York City Center and later at the New York State Theatre at Lincoln Center, this company became particularly identified with Balanchine. A prolific creator in various styles, he was responsible for most of the New York City Ballet's extensive repertoire, having created more than 150 works for the company. Among the works choreographed for the company were the full-length versions of *The Nutcracker* and *Don Quixote*.

In 1964 the U.S. dance world was stirred when the Ford Foundation, having granted nearly $8,000,000 to strengthen professional ballet in the United States, presented the entire amount to the New York City Ballet, its affiliated School of American Ballet, and six other ballet companies—all under the direct or indirect influence of Balanchine. He continued as artistic director and ballet master of the New York Ballet until late in 1982, when ill health forced him to relinquish his duties.

Although he worked mainly in the U.S., Balanchine was an international choreographer, and almost every leading ballet company in the world has mounted at least one of his ballets. Best known abroad are his interpretations of musical compositions, either in a serious vein, such as Brahms' *Liebeslieder Walzer* (1960), or broadly comic, such as Hershy Kay's *Western Symphony* (1954), or richly Romantic, such as "Robert Schumann's David bündlertänze" (1980).

Balanchine had a special artistic relationship with the composer Igor Stravinsky. Stravinsky's connection with the ballet started with Diaghilev, and Balanchine's first association with his music was in choreographing a new version of *Le Chant du rossignol* (*The Song of the Nightingale*) for the Ballet Russe in 1925. A long series of Stravinsky–Balanchine ballets followed; some of them were composed in collaboration. In 1972, a year after Stravinsky's death, the New York City Ballet staged a Stravinsky Festival. Ten years later, in 1982, a second Stravinsky Festival was held during the centenary of the composer's birth. Balanchine choreographed 4 of the 14 Stravinsky works performed. Other modern composers whose music Balanchine set to dance are Arnold Schoenberg (*Opus 34*) and Charles Ives (*Ivesiana*).

Balanchine studied his scores intensively as a preliminary to composition and began dance creation only at the first rehearsal. He said that his ideas came from working with his dancers, but he rarely discussed his ideas with them. He invented rapidly and without indulging in fits of temperament. This approach, together with a predominating impression of cool intellectuality rather than warm emotion in the body of his work, established Balanchine, to an outside view, as a slightly remote and superhuman personality. The other side of the coin showed a man who enjoyed working with every kind of musical entertainment in the theatre and in motion pictures. (K.S.W.)

BIBLIOGRAPHY. An autobiographical chapter is contained in George Balanchine and Francis Mason, *Balanchine's Complete Stories of the Great Ballets*, rev. and enl. ed. (1977). See also Bernard Taper, *Balanchine*, rev. and updated ed. (1974), a full and interesting, if slightly adulatory, account of the man and his work; and Anatole Chujoy, *The New York City Ballet* (1953, reprinted 1981), an account of publications of Balanchine and his company.

Balanopales, order of dicotyledonous flowering plants comprising the family Balanopaceae, with a single genus (*Balanops*) and 12 species of trees and shrubs that have simple, alternately positioned or somewhat whorled leaves. The plants are further characterized by flowers that lack showy parts (sepals and petals). The male and female flowers occur on separate plants (*i.e.*, the plants are dioecious), the male in catkins (elongated, dangling clusters) and the female solitary. Each female flower consists of a single ovule-bearing structure (pistil) composed of two or three carpels, or structural units, and containing two or three imperfectly separated chambers (locules), each with two ovules. The upper part of the pistil is formed into two short processes (styles), each terminated by two long, tapering stigmas, or pollen-receptive surfaces. The pistil is seated in a basal whorl (involucre) of many overlapping, scalelike bracts forming a cupule that persists in the mature fruit, giving it an acorn-like appearance.

The order is distributed mainly in New Caledonia, with populations occurring also in Vanuatu (formerly the New Hebrides), Fiji, and limited tropical areas of Queensland, Australia. The order is an ancient group whose evolutionary position is controversial but thought to be closest to the beech order (Fagales); both are considered to have a common ancestor.

Balanophoraceae, the balanophora family of flowering plants, which includes about 18 genera containing more than 100 species of root parasites that are distributed primarily throughout the tropics. The Balanophoraceae are sometimes placed in their own order, Balanophorales, although they are usually considered to be members of the sandalwood order (Santalales).

The club-shaped flower spikes of balanophora plants resemble fungi in their appearance and also in their emergence from the soil. The unisexual flowers range in colour from pale yellow to deep purple. The unlobed, scalelike leaves lack the chlorophyll necessary for food production, and thus the plants must obtain their nourishment by parasitizing other plants. Balanophoraceae species attach their tuberous rhizomes (underground stems) to the roots of host trees by means of highly modified roots (haustoria), through which water and nutrients pass from host to parasite. Plants of the genera *Balanophora* and *Langsdorffia* contain an inflammable waxy material, and the stems have been used as candles in South America. The rhizomes of these plants are sometimes processed to produce wax, but the plants are not abundant enough for commercial wax production.

Balantidium, genus of ovoid protozoans of the holotrichous order Trichostomatida. Uniformly covered with longitudinal rows of minute, hairlike projections (cilia), *Balantidium* exists as a parasite in the intestines of pigs, apes, and other animals. The species *B. coli* can, in rare cases, infect humans and cause balantidiosis (balantidial dysentery), a relatively severe disease causing formation of intestinal ulcers. The disease is most often reported in the Philippines. *Balantidium,* which feeds on red blood cells, cell fragments, and cell debris, is transmitted to new hosts by rounded cysts passed in excrement and subsequently ingested by a new host.

Balao, oil port, Esmeraldas province, northwestern Ecuador, on the Pacific Ocean, adjacent to Esmeraldas city. Its development is entirely due to its choice as the terminus for the Trans-Ecuadorian Pipeline, built 1970–72 to exploit the rich petroleum deposits of Ecuador's Napo province, in El Oriente region, the tropical rain forest of the headwaters of the Amazon east of the Andes. Balao's terminal, opened August 1972, is the seaward end of the 313-mi (504-km) oil transportation system, one of the world's highest major pipelines, which crosses the Andes at a maximum elevation of over 13,300 ft (4,054 m).

The port accommodates 100,000-ton tankers, and special installations have been built to guard against pollution of Pacific waters from possible spillages. The port, pipeline, and oil fields were developed by local subsidiaries of Texaco, Inc. and Gulf Oil Corp., international producers with headquarters in the United States. By 1977 Ecuador owned the major share of its petroleum industry. Pop. (1974) 2,326.

Balarāma, in Hindu mythology, the elder half-brother of Krishna, with whom he shared many adventures. Sometimes Balarāma is considered one of the 10 *avatāra*s (incarnations) of the god Vishnu, particularly among those members of Vaiṣṇava sects who elevate Krishna to the rank of a principal god. Other legends identify him as the incarnation in human form of the serpent Śeṣa, and he may originally have been an agricultural deity. As early as the 2nd–1st century BC he is depicted holding a plowshare and a pestle with a snake canopy above his head and may be among the earliest Brahmanic gods to be given sculptural representation. In painting he is always shown with fair skin, in contrast to Krishna's blue complexion. The stories associated with him emphasize his love of wine and his enormous strength. He was rarely worshipped independently.

Balard, Antoine-Jérôme (b. Sept. 30, 1802, Montpellier, Fr.—d. March 30, 1876, Paris), chemist who in 1826 discovered the element bromine, determined its properties, and studied some of its compounds. Later he proved the presence of bromine in sea plants and animals.

In studying salt marsh flora from Mediterranean waters, Balard, after crystallizing sodium chloride and sodium sulfate from the seawater, saturating the residue with chlorine,

Balard

Boyer—H. Roger-Viollet

and distilling the product, discovered the only liquid nonmetallic element, bromine.

An exponent of the potential value of the sea as a source of chemicals, Balard taught at Montpellier École de Pharmacie, from which he had graduated in 1826. He became professor of chemistry at the Sorbonne (1842) and at the Collège de France, Paris (1851).

balas ruby, variety of the gemstone ruby spinel (*q.v.*).

Balāsh, also spelled VALĀKHSH (fl. late 5th century), Sāsānian king (reigned 484–488), succeeding his brother Fīrūz I. Soon after he ascended the throne, Balāsh was threatened by the dominance of invading Hephthalites, a nomadic eastern tribe. Supported by Zarmhir, a feudal chief, Balāsh suppressed an uprising by his rebel brother Zareh. Later, however, he was abandoned by Zarmhir, and shortly afterward he was deposed and blinded. The crown was given to a son of Fīrūz, Kavadh I.

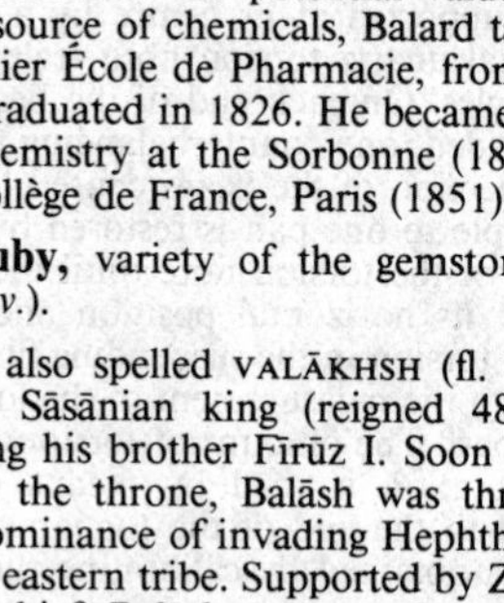

Balāsh, coin, 5th century

By courtesy of the trustees of the British Museum; photograph, J.R. Freeman & Co. Ltd.

Balashikha, also spelled BALAŠICHA, city, Moscow *oblast* (administrative region), western Russian Soviet Federated Socialist Republic, 15 mi (25 km) east of Moscow on the Pekhorka River. Balashikha developed in the 19th century, first as the site of a cloth factory and later as a centre for papermaking. In Soviet times it underwent rapid growth and was incorporated in 1939. It is now a heavy-industrial centre, specializing in machine building. Balashikha's 19th-century townscape contrasts markedly with the newer sections. Pop. (1983 est.) 125,000.

Balasore, also called BĀLESHWAR, town, administrative headquarters of Balasore district, northeastern Orissa state, eastern India. The town lies on the Burhābalang River, 7 mi (11 km) from the Bay of Bengal. It was the site of a British settlement in 1633; Dutch, Danish, and French merchants followed later in the 17th century. The Dutch and Danish settlements were ceded to the British in 1846, but the French holding remained until 1947. In the 18th century Balasore became important in rice trading and the salt industry. Besides rice, the town now trades in fish, hardware, and other products; other economic activity includes rice milling, light manufacturing, fish curing, and weaving. The town has several colleges affiliated with Utkal University. Good road and rail links exist to Calcutta and to other Orissa towns.

Balasore district is a strip of alluvial land on the Bay of Bengal, 2,469 sq mi (6,394 sq km) in area and crossed by six rivers. The principal crop is rice, and fishing and weaving are important. Chandīpur, the only port in the district, is used mainly by Indian coastal steamers. Pop. (1981) town, 65,779; district, 2,252,808.

Balassi, Bálint, Balassi also spelled BALASSA (b. Oct. 20, 1554, Zólyom, Hung.—d. May 30, 1594, Esztergom), the outstanding Hungarian lyric poet of his time, remaining unrivalled in his native literature until the end of the 18th century.

He was born into one of the richest Protestant families of the country and lived an adventurous life, fighting against the Turks and against his own relatives, who sought to despoil him of his heritage. At first his poetry was conventional, but his powerful personality soon found original expression. He wrote vividly about the beauties of the countryside and the rough pleasures of warfare. His love poems show genuine feeling. Balassi was the inventor of a stanza form that was copied by later poets. His conversion to Catholicism led to a religious poetry in which he exhibited a strong, masculine spirituality. He died of wounds received during the siege of Esztergom.

Balat (ancient city, Turkey): *see* Miletus.

balata, also called GUTTA BALATA, hard rubberlike material made by drying the milky juice produced principally by the bully tree (*Manilkara bidentata*) of Guyana and the West Indies. The tree is tapped by cutting zigzag gashes in the bark and collecting the latex in cups, to be coagulated in trays. Like gutta-percha, balata is inelastic, tough, leathery, and water-resistant, and it softens when heated. It is often used as a substitute for the more expensive gutta-percha, chiefly in the manufacture of golf balls and machine belting.

Balaton, Lake, largest lake of central Europe, located in central Hungary about 50 mi (80 km) southwest of Budapest. It has an area of 230 sq mi (596 sq km) and extends for 48 mi along the southern foothills of the Bakony Mountains of Hungary. At its widest point, Lake Balaton measures about 9 mi across. Its maximum depth is 37 ft (11 m). The Zala River provides the largest inflow of water. Water outflow is through the sluice gates of Siófok, toward the eastern end of the lake, and the entire contents of the lake are replenished about every two years.

The bed of the Balaton is relatively young; it was formed at the end of the Pleistocene Epoch, less than 1,000,000 years ago. Originally, there were five small lakes that extended in a north–south chain, but these coalesced when erosion broke down the dividing ridges. Traces of these former lakes can still be seen in the configuration of Lake Balaton today, and the Tihany Peninsula—which projects from the northern shore narrowing the lake to a width of 1 mi—is the remnant of one of the dividing ridges.

The climate of the region is rather continental, with warm and sunny weather prevailing from May to October. In winter the lake is covered with a sheet of ice about 8 in. (20 cm) thick. As the prevailing winds are from the northwest, the southeastern shore of the lake is subject to erosion of its banks by wave action. Oscillations in the levels of the water surface known as seiches, the product of local variations of atmospheric pressure aided by currents in the water, increase the erosive effect. In the Tihany Narrows, the water currents flows with a speed of up to 5 ft per second.

The chemical composition of the lake differs greatly from that of most central European lakes. The predominant anions, of negatively charged chemical components, are carbonate and sulphate; while the corresponding cations or positive components, are magnesium, calcium, and sodium. Their interaction has given the lake its sulfo-carbonate character.

The regions around the lake are inhabited by a rich and interesting variety of plant and animal life. There is a wildlife reserve in the Tihany Peninsula, and another one in the extensive reedbeds near Keszthely, where rare water birds nest. The southern border of the lake is very fertile, and the volcanic soils to the northwest form the basis of a noted wine-growing region.

Agriculture nevertheless declined in significance as a result of the development of the tourist industry in the second half of the 20th century. A number of watering places sprang up, notable among which were Siófok, on the southern shore, and Balatonfüred, on the northern shore. The town of Balatonfüred was also traditionally known for its medicinal springs. The oldest and best known settlement is Tihany, noted for its museum and biological station.

Balatonfüred, resort town, Veszprém *megye* (county), central Hungary, on the north shore of Lake Balaton. The town has been known for at least 250 years as a health spa and resort. In the town centre is Gyógy Tér (Healing Square) where the waters of volcanic springs rise up under a pavilion. There are 11 medicinal springs said to have a stimulating effect on the heart and nerves. The foothills of the Bakony Mountains to the north protect the town from cold winds and help make the district one of the most celebrated wine-growing regions of Hungary. Pop. (1983 est.) 14,000.

Balbases, Ambrogio di Filippo Spinola, marqués de los (marquess of): *see* Spinola, Ambrogio di Filippo.

Balbinus, Decimus Caelius Calvinus (d. 238), Roman emperor in 238.

A patrician, he was a Salian priest, twice a consul, and proconsul in Asia. In 238, when the Senate led a rebellion of the Italian cities against Maximinus (emperor 235–238), it placed the government in the hands of a board of 20, one of whom was Balbinus, and then chose Balbinus and Pupienus Maximus to be joint emperors. Maximus, a former city prefect, was extremely unpopular with the people of Rome. When the enraged populace besieged the Senate and emperors in the Capitol, Balbinus and Maximus extricated themselves by appointing as caesar the young Gordian, grandson of the original leader of the revolt.

Balbinus remained in Rome while Maximus advanced to defeat Maximinus. When Maximus returned, Balbinus, fearing his colleague intended to make himself sole ruler, quarrelled with him. The Praetorian Guards in the city took advantage of the dispute to kidnap both emperors; the two were murdered as their captors tried to escape from the German guards. Gordian was thereupon proclaimed sole emperor.

Balbinus, marble bust; in the Villa Albani, Rome
Alinari—Art Resource/EB Inc.

Balbo, Cesare, Conte (count) (b. Nov. 27, 1789, Turin, Piedmont—d. June 3, 1853, Turin), Piedmontese political writer, a liberal but cautious constitutionalist who was influential during the Italian Risorgimento and served as the first prime minister of Sardinia–Piedmont under the constitution of March 5, 1848.

Balbo grew up while Piedmont was annexed to France and began his career by entering the Napoleonic bureaucracy, wherein he acquired a wide knowledge of Italy. When the House of Savoy was restored to the kingdom of Sardinia in 1814, Balbo's service to Napoleon was held against him; although he had little respect for the regime of Victor Emmanuel I and was friendly with liberals in Turin, he disapproved of revolution and remained loyal to the dynasty. Nevertheless, he fell into official disgrace because of his association with some leaders of the revolution in March 1821 and his attempt to persuade the future king Charles Albert to lead the constitutionalist movement. Balbo left Turin for several years and devoted himself to writing.

Balbo's most famous book, *Delle speranze d'Italia* (1844; "The Hopes of Italy"), showed the anti-revolutionary nature of his patriotism and liberalism. He wrote that the independence of Italy from Austria was desirable, but Austria should be compensated with territory in the Balkans; that the interests of the papacy should be safeguarded; and that a confederation might be the best political organization for Italy. In *Lettere di politica e letteratura edite ed inedite* (1847), Balbo called for a specifically moderate Italian party.

Encouraged by Charles Albert's grant of the constitutional *statuto* in 1848, Balbo accepted the office of prime minister on March 13. Alarmed by the democratic agitation in Italy, he resigned in July 1848, later served as Piedmontese emissary to Pope Pius IX, and refused the premiership in 1852.

Balbo, Italo (b. June 6, 1896, near Ferrara, Italy—d. June 28, 1940, Tobruk, Libya), airman and Fascist leader who was decisive in developing Benito Mussolini's air force.

After studying at Florence University and the Institute of Social Science in Rome, Balbo served as an officer in the Alpine Corps during World War I. An early Fascist, he led the Blackshirt militia in the March on Rome (October 1922). In rapid succession Mussolini made him a general of militia (1923), under-

Italo Balbo
By courtesy of the Istituto Italiano di Cultura, New York; photograph, Agenzia Giornalistica Italia, Rome

secretary of state for air (1926), air minister (1929), and air marshal (1933).

Upgrading military as well as commercial aviation, Balbo became famous for his promotion of mass international flights to demonstrate Italy's air power. Though he was one of Fascism's best salesmen, his pro-British sentiment and his rising popularity among Italians may have caused Mussolini to remove him from the limelight by appointing him governor of Libya. Balbo was killed when his plane, it was stated, failed to give correct recognition signals and was shot down by Italian guns in Tobruk harbour.

Balboa, Pacific terminal port in Panamá province, central Panama, at the southern end of the Panama Canal. It lies between the canal docks and Ancón Hill, which separates it from Panama City. Founded in 1914 and named for Vasco Núñez de Balboa, European discoverer of the Pacific, it has extensive harbour

Monument to George Washington Goethals, builder of the Panama Canal, in Balboa, Panama
Douglas Faulkner—Photo Researchers

installations, drydocks, marine and railroad repair shops, warehouses, and a coaling plant. Balboa is noted for its orchid gardens, with more than 400 orchid varieties.

The former Canal Zone (*q.v.*) was administered from Balboa Heights, on a hill overlooking the town of Balboa. Pop. (1980) 1,952.

Balboa, Vasco Núñez de (b. 1475, Jerez de los Caballeros, or Badajoz, Extremadura province, Castile—d. Jan. 12, 1519, Acla, near Darién, Panama), Spanish conquistador and explorer, who was head of the first stable settlement on the South American continent (1511) and who was the first European to sight the Pacific Ocean (on Sept. 25 [or 27], 1513, from "a peak in Darién").

Career in the New World. Balboa came from the ranks of that lower nobility whose sons—"men of good family who were not reared behind the plow," in the words of the chronicler Gonzalo Fernández de Oviedo y Valdés—often sought their fortunes in the Indies. In 1500 he sailed with Rodrigo de Bastidas on a voyage of exploration along the coast of present-day Colombia. Later, he settled in Hispaniola (Haiti), but he did not prosper as a pioneer farmer and had to escape his creditors by embarking as a stowaway on an expedition organized by Martín Fernández de Enciso (1510) to bring aid and reinforcements to a colony founded by Alonso de Ojeda on the coast of Urabá, in modern Colombia. The expedition found the survivors of the colony, led by Francisco Pizarro, but Ojeda had departed. On the advice of Balboa the settlers moved across the Gulf of Urabá to Darién, on the less hostile coast of the Isthmus of Panama, where they founded the town of Santa María de la Antigua, the first stable settlement on the continent, and began to acquire gold by barter or war with the local Indians. The colonists soon deposed Enciso, Ojeda's second in command, and elected a town council; one of its two alcaldes, or magistrates, was Balboa. With the subsequent departure of Enciso for Hispaniola, Balboa became the undisputed head of the colony. In December 1511 King Ferdinand sent orders that named Balboa interim governor and captain general of Darién.

Balboa meanwhile had organized a series of gold- and slave-hunting expeditions into the Indian chiefdoms of the area. His Indian policy combined the use of barter, every kind of force, including torture, to extract information, and the tactic of divide and conquer by forming alliances with certain tribes against others. The Indians of Darién, less warlike than their neighbours of Urabá and without poisoned arrows, were not formidable foes and often fled at the approach of the Spaniards. The Spanish arsenal included their terrible war dogs, sometimes used by Balboa as executioners to tear Indian victims to pieces.

The Spaniards were told by Indians that to the south lay a sea and a province infinitely rich in gold—a reference to the Pacific and perhaps to the Inca Empire. The conquest of that land, their informants declared, would require 1,000 men. Balboa hastened to send emissaries to Spain to request reinforcements; the news they brought created much excitement, and a large expedition was promptly organized. But Balboa was not given command. Charges brought against him by his enemies had turned King Ferdinand II against him, and, as commander of the armada and governor of Darién, the King sent out the elderly, powerful nobleman Pedro Arias Dávila (usually called Pedrarias). The expedition, numbering 2,000 persons, left Spain in April 1514.

Discovery of the Pacific. Meanwhile, Balboa, without waiting for reinforcements, had sailed on Sept. 1, 1513, from Santa María for Acla, at the narrowest part of the isthmus. Accompanied by 190 Spaniards and hundreds of Indian carriers, he marched south across the isthmus through dense jungles, rivers, and swamps and ascended the cordillera; on Sept. 25 (or 27), 1513, standing "silent, upon a peak in Darién," he sighted the Pacific. Some days later he reached the shore of the Gulf of San Miguel and took possession of the Mar del Sur (South Sea) and the adjacent lands for the king of Castile. He then recrossed the isthmus, arriving at Santa María in January 1514. His letters and those of a royal agent who had been sent to Darién to prepare the ground for the coming of Pedrarias, announcing the discovery of the "South Sea," restored Balboa to royal favour; he was named *adelantado* (governor) of the Mar del Sur and of the provinces of Panamá and Coiba but remained subject to the authority of Pedrarias, who arrived in Darién, now a crown colony and renamed Castilla del Oro, in June 1514.

Relations between the two men were, from the first, troubled by the distrust and jealousy of the ailing, ill-natured Pedrarias toward the younger man. The first bishop of Darién, Juan de Quevedo, sought to act as peacemaker and arranged a temporary reconciliation; in a turnabout Pedrarias by proxy betrothed his daughter María in Spain to Balboa. But the underlying causes of friction remained. The suspicious Pedrarias pursued a tortuous policy designed to frustrate Balboa at every turn; but he at last gave Balboa grudging permission to explore the South Sea. By dint of enormous efforts Balboa had a fleet of ships built and transported in pieces across the mountains to the Pacific shore, where he explored the Gulf of San Miguel (1517–18). Meantime, the stream of charges of misconduct and incapacity levelled against Pedrarias by Balboa and others had finally convinced the crown of Pedrarias' unfitness to govern; news arrived in Darién of his imminent replacement by a new governor who would subject Pedrarias to a *residencia* (judicial review of his conduct in office). Pedrarias doubtless feared that Balboa's presence and testimony would contribute to his total ruin and decided to get rid of his rival. Summoned home on the pretext that Pedrarias wished to discuss matters of common concern, Balboa was seized and charged with rebellion, high treason, and mistreatment of Indians, among other misdeeds. After a farcical trial presided over by Gaspar de Espinosa, Pedrarias' chief justice, Balboa was found guilty, condemned to death, and beheaded with four alleged accomplices in January 1519. (B.K.)

BIBLIOGRAPHY. The standard biography in English, well-documented and well-written, is Kathleen Romoli, *Balboa of Darién: Discoverer of the Pacific* (1953), which also contains an extensive bibliography of sources. There is a judicious survey of Balboa's career in Amando Melón y Ruiz de Gordejuela, *Los primeros tiempos de la colonización. Cuba y las Antillas. Magallanes y la primera vuelta del mundo* (1952). For a discussion of Balboa's route to the Pacific, see Angel Rubio, *La ruta de Balboa y el descubrimiento del Océano Pacífico* (1965). All modern accounts take as their points of departure the great chronicles of Pietro Martire d'Anghiera, *De orbe novo,* trans. by Francis A. MacNutt, 2 vol. (1912, reprinted 1970); Gonzalo Fernández de Oviedo y Valdés, *Historia general y natural de las Indias,* ed. by Juan Pérez de Tudela Bueso, 5 vol. (1959); and Bartolomé de las Casas, *Historia de las Indias,* ed. by Augustin Millares Carlo and preliminary study by Lewis Hanke, 2nd ed., 3 vol. (1965). See also C.L.G. Anderson, *Life and Letters of Vasco Núñez de Balboa* (1941).

Balbuena, Bernardo de (b. 1568, Valdepeñas, Spain—d. Oct. 11, 1627, San Juan, P.R.), poet and first bishop of Puerto Rico, whose poetic descriptions of the New World earned him an important position among the greatest poets of colonial America.

Balbuena, taken to Mexico as a child, studied there and in Spain. Returning to the New World, he held minor church offices in Jamaica (1608) and became bishop of Puerto Rico (1620), remaining there until his death.

Balbuena is best remembered for two epic poems, *La grandeza mexicana* (1604; "The Greatness of Mexico") and *El Bernardo o la victoria de Roncesvalles* (1624; "Bernardo; or, The Victory at Roncesvalles"), and for a collection of eclogues, *El siglo de oro en las selvas de Erífile* (1608; "The Golden Age in the Jungles of Erífile"). Much of his work was lost when his library was destroyed by the Dutch in the attack on San Juan in 1625.

Balbus, Lucius Cornelius (fl. 1st century BC), wealthy Roman, originally from Gades (modern Cádiz, Spain), who exerted influence on the major Roman political figures of the last years of the republic.

Gnaeus Pompey conferred Roman citizenship on Balbus and his family for his services against the rebel Quintus Sertorius in Spain.

Becoming friendly with all political parties in Rome, Balbus had the determining role in the formation of the "first triumvirate" (60) and was one of the city's chief financiers. He won the favour of Julius Caesar, accompanying the general as chief of staff to Spain (61) and Gaul (58). In 56, however, Balbus' enemies had him prosecuted for illegally assuming the rights of a Roman citizen, a charge directed as much against the "triumvirs" as against the defendant. With Cicero, Pompey, and Marcus Licinius Crassus speaking on his behalf, Balbus was acquitted. At the beginning of the Civil War (49–45) he attempted to persuade Cicero to mediate between Caesar and Pompey. Balbus then became Caesar's private secretary; he attached himself to Octavian after Caesar's murder in 44. He was consul—the first time for a provincial—in 40. Balbus published a diary, now lost, of the chief events of his life.

Balch, Emily Greene (b. Jan. 8, 1867, Jamaica Plain, now part of Boston—d. Jan. 9, 1961, Cambridge, Mass., U.S.), U.S. sociologist, political scientist, economist, and pacifist, a leader of the women's movement for peace during and after World War I; she received the Nobel Prize for Peace in 1946 jointly with John Raleigh Mott. She was also noted for her sympathetic and thorough study of Slavic immigrants in the United States.

A member of the first graduating class at Bryn Mawr (Pennsylvania) College, she taught at Wellesley (Massachusetts) College from 1897. She founded a settlement house in Boston and served on the Massachusetts commissions on industrial relations (1908–09) and immigration (1913–14) and the Boston city planning board (1914–17). To prepare *Our Slavic Fellow Citizens* (1910), she lived in Slavic-American neighbourhoods in various cities and travelled to eastern Europe for firsthand knowledge of the Slavic homelands.

A member of the Society of Friends (Quakers), she was a delegate to the International Congress of Women, The Hague (1915), and

Emily Greene Balch
By courtesy of the Emily Greene Balch Papers, Swarthmore College Peace Collection

she helped found the Women's International League for Peace and Freedom, of which she was secretary-treasurer (1919–22, 1934–35). For opposing U.S. entry into World War I, she was dismissed from her professorship at Wellesley in 1918. Realizing the intractability of Nazi Germany and Japan, she approved U.S. participation in World War II. Her writings on peace include *Approaches to the Great Settlement* (1918).

Balchaš (Kazakh S.S.R.): *see* Balkhash.

Balchaš, Ozero (lake, Soviet Union): *see* Balkhash, Lake.

Balchin, Nigel (Marlin) (b. Dec. 3, 1908, Wiltshire, Eng.—d. March 17, 1970, London), novelist who achieved great popularity with novels of men at work.

After studying natural science at the University of Cambridge, Balchin divided his time between research work in science and industry (as an industrial psychologist) and writing. During World War II he was deputy scientific adviser to the Army Council.

In *The Small Back Room* (1943), his best known novel, he describes the conversation, behaviour, and intrigues for position and power of the "backroom boys" with whom he worked during the war. Almost as successful is *Mine Own Executioner* (1945), a study of a psychiatrist unable to cure his own neuroses and of the tensions created in his marriage by his lack of self-confidence. The problems of the psychologically and physically disabled are a recurrent theme: the hero of *A Sort of Traitors* (1949) is a former pilot who has lost both arms; *The Fall of a Sparrow* (1955) explores the mental processes of a psychopath.

Balcon, Sir Michael (b. May 19, 1896, Birmingham, Warwick, Eng.—d. Oct. 17, 1977, Hartfield, East Sussex), motion-picture producer, a leader in the British cinema industry.

He began his career as a producer in 1922, founded and directed Gainsborough Pictures, Ltd., in 1928, and became the director of production for Gaumont-British Pictures, Ltd., in 1931. From 1936 to 1938 he worked as producer for Metro-Goldwyn-Mayer and from

Balcon, 1970
By courtesy of Sir Michael Balcon

1938 to 1959 as executive producer of Ealing Films, Ltd. In 1959 he became an independent producer. He was knighted in 1948.

Balcon believed that British films should be designed for a specific home market, as opposed to those who wanted to compete with Hollywood in the international market, resulting in Ealing's production of patriotic adventure films during World War II. After the war Balcon produced at Ealing a series of witty comedies (many of them starring Alec Guinness) reflecting the social conditions of postwar Britain, such as *Passport to Pimlico* (1949), *Kind Hearts and Coronets* (1949), and *The Lavender Hill Mob* (1951); they found an international audience.

balcony, external extension of an upper floor of a building, enclosed up to a height of about three feet (one metre) by a solid or pierced screen, by balusters (*see also* balustrade), or by railings. In the medieval and Renaissance periods, balconies were supported by corbels made out of successive courses of stonework, or by large wooden or stone brackets. Since the 19th century, supports of cast iron, reinforced concrete, and other materials have become common.

The balcony serves to enlarge the living space and range of activities possible in a dwelling without a garden or lawn. In many apartment houses the balcony is partly recessed to provide for both sunshine and shelter or shade. (In Classical architecture a balcony that is fully recessed or covered by its own roof is described as a loggia; [*q.v.*].) In hot countries a balcony allows a greater movement of air inside the building, as the doors opening onto it are usually louvered.

From classical Rome to the Victorian period, balconies on public buildings were places from which speeches could be made or crowds exhorted. In Italy, where there are innumerable balconies and loggias, the best known is that at St. Peter's in Rome from which the pope gives his blessing.

In Islāmic countries the faithful are called to prayer from the top balcony of a minaret. In Japanese architecture, based on wooden structures, a balcony is provided around each, or part of each, story.

Internal balconies, also called galleries, were constructed in Gothic churches to accommodate singers. In larger halls during the Middle Ages they were provided for minstrels. With the Renaissance development of the theatre, balconies with sloped floors, allowing more and more spectators to have a clear view of the stage, were built in the auditorium.

bald crow (bird): *see* rockfowl.

bald cypress, either of two species of ornamental and timber conifers constituting the genus *Taxodium* (family Taxodiaceae), native to swampy areas of southern North America. The name bald cypress, or swamp cypress, is used most frequently as the common name for *T. distichum,* economically the most important species.

A young bald cypress is symmetrical and pyramidal; as it matures, it develops a coarse, wide-spreading head. Its tapering trunk is usually 30 metres (about 100 feet) tall and one metre in diameter. The reddish-brown bark weathers to an ashy gray. An old tree is usually hollow and is known as pecky, or peggy, cypress in the lumber trade, because of small holes in the wood caused by a fungus. A tree growing in wet soil is strongly buttressed about the base, and its horizontal roots often send conical, woody projections called "knees" above the waterline. The knees, thought to be air-obtaining organs and stabilizers for the submerged roots, are popular household ornaments.

The smaller pond, or upland, cypress of the southeastern U.S., a variety of the bald cypress, sometimes is considered to be a separate species (*T. ascendens*). It has erect branches and shorter, more scalelike leaves.

Bald cypress (*Taxodium distichum*)
Alan Pitcairn from Grant Heilman—EB Inc.

The closely related Montezuma or Mexican cypress (*T. mucronatum*) is native to the southwestern U.S., Mexico, and Guatemala. It is distinguished from the bald cypress by its shorter, persistent leaves and larger cones.

bald eagle (*Haliaetus leucocephalus*), bird of the family Accipitridae, the only eagle solely native to North America. Since 1782 the bald eagle has been the U.S. national bird. It is a sea eagle that commonly occurs inland, along rivers and large lakes. The adult, about one metre (40 inches) long, is dark brown with white head and tail. Beak, eyes, and feet are yellow. The immature bird, all brown but showing some white in tail and wing linings, may not attain full adult plumage until the seventh year.

Bald eagles follow seabirds to locate fish. They rob the osprey of fish catches and also eat carrion. They nest in lone trees, often on islands in rivers. The species is threatened by river pollution, pesticides, and loss of nesting sites. It is protected in the United States under the National Emblem Act (1940), but Alaska was long exempted because eagles perched on fish traps and scared away the salmon (an annoyance eventually overcome by fitting the traps with devices to discourage perching); Alaskan bounty hunters killed more than 100,000 eagles in the periods 1917–40 and 1949–52 (no bounty having been offered in the interim). Now the bald eagle is protected in all states. The northern subspecies, which has declined throughout the area from Maine to the Pacific Northwest, is still widespread in Alaska and nearby regions of Canada. The southern bald eagle (*H. l. leucocephalus*) is an endangered species. It is numerous now only in Florida, where breeding sanctuaries are maintained. *See also* eagle.

Bald eagle (*Haliaetus leucocephalus*)
Alexander Sprunt, IV

baldachin, also spelled BALDACHINO, or BALDAQUIN, also called CIBORIUM, in architecture, the canopy over an altar or tomb, supported on columns, especially when freestanding and disconnected from any enclosing wall. The term originates from the Spanish *baldaquin,* an elaborately brocaded material imported from Baghdad that was hung as a canopy over an altar or doorway. Later it came to stand for a freestanding canopy over an altar.

Early examples of the baldachin are found in Ravenna and Rome. The usual form consists of four columns supporting entablatures, which carry miniature colonnades topped by a pyramidal or gabled roof. In Romanesque work, arches generally replaced the entablatures; and gables frequently topped the four sides, as in S. Ambrogio in Milan. Few baldachins of the Gothic period remain, and their use outside Italy seems to have been intermittent; there is, however, a rich Gothic example in the Sainte-Chapelle at Paris (1247–50), reconstructed by Viollet-le-Duc in the 19th century. In the Renaissance the use of the baldachin became commoner, and during the 17th century elaborate structures were built, probably as a result of the influence of the enormous bronze baldachin that Gian Lorenzo Bernini designed for the altar of St. Peter's in Rome.

Baldachin, St. Peter's, Vatican City, by Gian Lorenzo Bernini, 1624–33
SCALA—Art Resource/EB Inc.

Baldad (Old Testament): *see* Bildad.

Balder, Old Norse BALDR, in Norse mythology, the son of the chief god Odin and his wife Frigg. Beautiful and just, he was the favourite of the gods. Most legends about him concern his death. Icelandic stories tell how the gods amused themselves by throwing objects at him, knowing that he was immune from harm. The blind god Höd, deceived by the evil Loki, killed Balder by hurling mistletoe, the only thing that could hurt him. After Balder's funeral, the giantess Thökk, probably Loki in disguise, refused to weep the tears that would release Balder from death.

Some scholars believe that the passive, suffering figure of Balder was influenced by that of Christ. The Danish historian Saxo Grammaticus (*c.* 1200), however, depicts him as a warrior engaged in a feud over the hand of a woman.

Baldinucci, Filippo (b. *c.* 1624, Italy—d. Jan. 1, 1696), first art historian to make full use of documents and to realize the importance of drawings in the study of painting. Working for Cardinal Leopoldo de' Medici, Baldinucci advised on the acquisition of the great collection of drawings now in the Uffizi in Florence. His *Notizie dei professori del disegno da Cimabue in qua . . .* (1681–1728; "Report on Drawing Teachers from Cimabue to the Present") is his most notable work, often correcting and completing Vasari.

baldness, also called ALOPECIA, lack or loss of hair, of two primary types: permanent hair loss from destruction of, and temporary hair loss from transitory damage to, hair germ centres. The first category includes the common patterned baldness occurring to some degree in up to 40 percent of some male populations. Hair loss progresses gradually, beginning with a characteristic recession of the hairline at the front or thinning of the crown hair and proceeding, in extreme cases, until only a thin rim of hair is left at the sides and back of the head (the "Hippocratic wreath").

Pattern balding has a hereditary basis; it varies in degree and tends to be dependent on male-hormone levels in the blood. Usually seen in persons with comparatively heavy body and facial hair, male pattern balding is characteristically frequent in people with origins in the European and Australian geographical races. In Australian Aborigines it is often accompanied by balding of the calves of the legs, and it is rare among Asians, American Indians, and Africans. Other causes of permanent baldness include many scar-producing skin diseases and injuries, inborn lack of hair development, and severe injury to hair germ centres by chemical or physical agents.

Temporary loss of hair occurs fairly commonly after conditions accompanied by high fever but may also be produced by X-rays, ingestion of metals (such as thallium, tin, and arsenic) or drugs, malnutrition, some inflammatory skin diseases, chronic wasting diseases, and endocrine disorders. Alopecia areata, a fairly common disorder of unknown cause characterized by sharply outlined patches of sudden complete baldness, is also usually temporary. The breaking of hairs close to the skin surface, which causes the appearance of baldness, may be attributable to disorders of the hair shaft, fungus infections, or mechanical damage.

Baldovinetti, Alesso, Alesso also spelled ALESSIO (b. Oct. 14, 1425?, Florence—d. Aug. 29, 1499, Florence), painter whose work, though seldom innovative, assimilated and proficiently exemplified the careful modelling of form and the accurate depiction of light characteristic of the most progressive style of Florentine painting during the last half of the 15th century. At the same time he contributed importantly to the fledgling art of landscape painting.

"Madonna and Child," oil on canvas by Alesso Baldovinetti, *c.* 1465; in the Louvre, Paris
Giraudon—Art Resource/EB Inc.

He is presumed to have been an assistant to Domenico Veneziano, whose influence is reflected in the clear, pervasive light of his earliest surviving works: "The Baptism of Christ," "Marriage at Cana," and "The Transfiguration" (Museo di San Marco, or Museo dell'Angelico, Florence). He achieved his fully mature style in his masterpiece, "The Nativity" (1460–62), a fresco in the church of SS. Annunziata, Florence. Although Baldovinetti's technical experiments led to the fresco's rapid decay, it shows the pale colours, atmospheric light, and integration of detail with large-scale design that characterized most of his later works, such as "Madonna and Child" (*c.* 1465; Louvre, Paris). Both "The Nativity" and "Madonna" include views of the Arno River Valley and are among Europe's earliest paintings of actual landscapes.

Baldovinetti also did two strips of mosaic decoration over Lorenzo Ghiberti's doors on the Baptistery in Florence (1453–55) and a St. John the Baptist over the south doorway of Pisa cathedral (1462). He also prepared designs for intarsias, or wood inlays, and for stained glass.

baldpate, popular North American game duck, also known as the American wigeon. *See* wigeon.

Baldung-Grien, Hans (b. *c.* 1484, Schwäbisch Gmünd, Württemberg—d. 1545, Imperial Free City of Strasbourg), painter and graphic artist, one of the most outstanding figures in northern Renaissance art. He was an assistant to Albrecht Dürer, whose influence is apparent in his early works, although the demonic energy of his later style is closer to that of Matthias Grünewald.

His work is extensive and varied. It ranges from religious paintings and secular portraits to designs for tapestries and stained glass. He is noted for representations of the Virgin Mary, in which he combined landscapes, figures, light, and colour with an almost magical serenity. His portrayals of age, on the other hand, have a sinister character and a mannered virtuosity. His best known work in painting is the High Altar of the cathedral at Freiburg im Breisgau, W.Ger., for which he also designed the stained-glass choir windows.

Baldung-Grien's paintings are equalled in importance by his extensive body of drawings, engravings, and woodcuts of an intense vitality. The *Todentanz* ("dance of death") and the "death and the maiden" theme occur frequently in his graphic works. An early supporter of the Reformation, he executed a woodcut in which Martin Luther is protected by the Holy Spirit in the form of a dove.

Baldung-Grien was a member of the Strasbourg town council, as well as official painter to the episcopate. His works also appear in the church at Elzach and the museums of Basel, Karlsruhe, Cologne, Freiburg, and Nürnberg.

Baldwin, name of rulers grouped below by country and indicated by the symbol •.

Foreign-language equivalents:
Dutch .... Boudewijn
French .... Baudouin

BELGIUM

• **Baldwin I:** *see* Baudouin I.

CONSTANTINOPLE

• **Baldwin I** (b. 1172—d. 1205), count of Flanders (as Baldwin IX) and of Hainaut (as Baldwin VI), a leader of the Fourth Crusade, who became the first Latin emperor of Constantinople.

The son of Baldwin V, count of Hainaut, and Margaret of Alsace, countess of Flanders, he was an ally of the English royal house of the Plantagenets, fighting at the side of Richard I against Philip II Augustus of France. During the Fourth Crusade, which was conceived by Pope Innocent III in 1199 and was fought not against the Muslims but against the Byzantine Christians, he took part in the capture of Constantinople and the installation of the pro-Latin Alexius IV Angelus as emperor in 1203; after Alexius and his father, Isaac II, were deposed in February 1204, the crusaders and their Venetian allies seized power, and Baldwin, with Venetian support, was chosen as ruler of a new Latin state. He was crowned emperor on May 16, 1204, in the church of the Hagia Sophia. The Pope, although initially shocked at the crusaders' pillage of Constantinople and disconcerted by their failure to consult him on the partition of the empire, quickly recognized the Latin emperor.

Baldwin created a new government, based on the western European feudal model, to replace the traditional hierarchy of the Byzantine Empire. In October 1204 he enfeoffed 600 knights with lands formerly held by Greek nobles.

A Byzantine revolt in Thrace provided the Bulgarian tsar Kaloyan with a pretext for invasion. Baldwin led a small force to confront him at Adrianople in March 1205. Defeated, taken prisoner, and executed by the Bulgars, he was succeeded by his brother Henry.

• **Baldwin II** PORPHYROGENITUS (Born to the Purple), byname BALDWIN OF COURTENAY, French BAUDOUIN PORPHYROGÉNÈTE, or BAUDOUIN DE COURTENAY (b. 1217, Constantinople—d. October 1273, Foggia, Kingdom of Sicily), the last Latin emperor of Constantinople, who lost his throne in 1261 when Michael VIII Palaeologus restored Greek rule to the capital.

The son of Yolande, sister of Baldwin I, the first Latin emperor of Constantinople, and Peter of Courtenay, the third Latin emperor, he came to the throne after the death of his brother Robert, the fourth emperor, in 1228. In his minority the regency was entrusted to John of Brienne, the titular king of Jerusalem. During this time, invasions by the Greeks under the emperor John III Ducas Vatatzes at Nicaea and by the Bulgars under Tsar John Asen II substantially reduced the territory of the empire, leaving only the area around Constantinople to the Latins. In 1236 and 1245 Baldwin went to western Europe to solicit funds and military aid; his treasury was empty, and he was forced to break up parts of the imperial palace for firewood. He sold a large number of alleged relics that had been kept at Constantinople, including Jesus' crown of thorns and a large portion of the True Cross, to the French king Louis IX, who placed them in the Sainte-Chapelle in Paris. When Michael VIII Palaeologus captured Constantinople on July 25, 1261, Baldwin fled through Greece to Italy and France. In May 1267 he persuaded Charles of Anjou, king of Naples and Sicily, to pension him and sign a treaty for the reconquest of the empire; in October 1273 he married his son Philip to Charles's daughter Beatrice. Nothing came of this alliance, however, for Baldwin died a few days later.

FLANDERS

• **Baldwin I,** byname BALDWIN IRON-ARM, French BAUDOUIN BRAS-DE-FER, Dutch BOUDEWIJN DE IJZERE ARM (d. 879), the first ruler of Flanders. A daring warrior under Charles II the Bald of France, he fell in love with the King's daughter Judith, the youthful widow of two English kings, married her (862), and fled with his bride to Lorraine. Charles, though at first angry, was at last conciliated, and made his son-in-law margrave (*Marchio Flandriae*) of Flanders (864), which he held as a hereditary fief. The Norsemen were at this time continually devastating the coastlands, and Baldwin was entrusted with this outlying borderland in order to defend it. He was the first of a line of strong rulers, who early in the 10th century exchanged the title of margrave for that of count.

• **Baldwin II,** byname BALDWIN THE BALD, French BAUDOUIN LE CHAUVE, Dutch BOUDEWIJN DE KALE (d. 918), second ruler of Flanders, who, from his stronghold at Bruges, maintained, as his father Baldwin I before him, a vigorous defense of his lands against the incursions of the Norsemen. On his mother's side a descendant of Charlemagne, he strengthened the dynastic importance of his family by marrying Aelfthryth, daughter of Alfred the Great, of Wessex, Eng.

• **Baldwin IV,** byname BALDWIN THE BEARDED, French BAUDOUIN LE BARBU, Dutch BOUDEWIJN DE SCHONE BAARD (b. *c.* 980—d. May 30, 1035), count of Flanders (988–1035) who greatly expanded the Flemish dominions. He fought successfully both against the Capetian king of France, Robert II, and the Holy Roman emperor Henry II. Henry found himself obliged to grant to Baldwin IV in fief Valenciennes, the burgraveship of Ghent, the land of Waes, and Zeeland. The count of Flanders thus became a feudatory of the empire as well as of the French crown. The French fiefs are known in Flemish history as Crown Flanders (*Kroon-Vlaanderen*), the German fiefs as Imperial Flanders (*Rijks-Vlaanderen*). Baldwin's son—afterwards Baldwin V—rebelled in 1028 against his father at the instigation of his wife Adela, daughter of Robert II of France; but two years later peace was sworn at Oudenaarde, and the old count continued to reign until his death.

• **Baldwin V,** also called BALDWIN OF LILLE, French BAUDOUIN DE LILLE, Dutch BOUDEWIJN VAN RIJSEL (d. Sept. 1, 1067), count of Flanders who became one of the most influential figures of 11th-century Europe. He was an active, enterprising man and greatly extended his power by wars and alliances. He obtained from the Holy Roman emperor Henry IV the territory between the Scheldt and the Dender as an imperial fief, as well as the margravate of Antwerp. So powerful had he become that on the decease of Henry I of France he was appointed regent during the minority of Philip I (1060–66). Before his death he saw his eldest daughter Matilda (d. 1083) sharing the English throne with William the Conqueror; saw his eldest son, Baldwin of Mons, in possession of Hainaut in right of his wife Richilde, heiress of Regnier V (d. 1036); and saw his second son, Robert the Frisian, regent (*voogd*) of the county of Holland.

• **Baldwin IX:** *see* Baldwin I *under* Baldwin (Constantinople).

HAINAUT

• **Baldwin VI:** *see* Baldwin I *under* Baldwin (Constantinople).

JERUSALEM

• **Baldwin I,** byname BALDWIN OF BOULOGNE, French BAUDOUIN DE BOULOGNE (b. 1058?—d. April 2, 1118, al-ʿArīsh, Egypt), king of the crusader state of Jerusalem (1100–18), who expanded the kingdom and secured its territory, formulating an administrative apparatus that was to serve for 200 years as the basis for Frankish rule in Syria and Palestine.

Son of Eustace II, count of Boulogne, and Ida d'Ardenne, Baldwin was the younger brother of Godfrey of Bouillon (*q.v.*), whom he accompanied on the First Crusade (1096–99). While Baldwin was campaigning against the Seljuq Turks in Anatolia, Ṭoros, the Christian prince of Edessa (Urfa, Tur.), promised to make him his heir in return for military aid. Baldwin forced Ṭoros to abdicate and took possession of Edessa in 1098. He consolidated his new principality and strengthened its ties with the native Armenians by marrying Arda, the daughter of an Armenian noble.

In July 1100 his brother Godfrey died in Jerusalem, and Baldwin was summoned by the nobles to succeed him as *Advocatus Sancti Sepulchri* (Defender of the Holy Sepulchre). After leading a campaign in the south to impress the Egyptian Fāṭimids with his strength, and after subduing the opposition of the crusader nobles, he was crowned king of Jerusalem in December.

Once he had consolidated his strength at home, Baldwin seized the coastal cities of Arsuf (Tel Arshaf, Israel) and Caesarea (Ḥorbat Qesari, Israel) in 1101; by 1112 he had captured all the coastal cities except Ascalon and Tyre. In 1115 he built the castle of Krak de Montréal to protect the kingdom in the south.

In 1113 Baldwin forced his wife to enter a convent and married Adelaide of Saona, countess dowager of Sicily. He died without an heir and was succeeded by Baldwin du Bourg, a cousin whom he had named count of Edessa in 1100.

• **Baldwin II,** byname BALDWIN OF BOURG, French BAUDOUIN DU BOURG (d. August 1131, Jerusalem), count of Edessa (1100–18), king of Jerusalem (1118–31), and crusade leader whose support of the religious–military orders founded during his reign enabled him to expand his kingdom and to withstand the attacks of Seljuq Turks.

A son of Hugh, count of Réthel, in the Ardennes region of France, he held the castle of Bourg as a feudal domain and was at first referred to as Baldwin du Bourg. He accompanied his cousins Godfrey of Bouillon and

Baldwin, later King Baldwin I of Jerusalem, to Palestine with the First Crusade (1096). In 1100 he was named count of Edessa (Urfa, Tur.) by Baldwin I when the latter became king of Jerusalem. The Seljuq Turks moved against Edessa in 1104, capturing Baldwin on May 7. Ransomed in 1108, he fought his way into Edessa to reclaim his principality from the regent, Tancred, and later recovered most of the lost territory.

On April 14, 1118, Baldwin was crowned king of Jerusalem. Though captured by the Turks and held hostage from 1123 until 1124, in subsequent years he succeeded in expanding his territory and directing attacks against Muslim Damascus with the aid of the Hospitallers and the Templars, crusading religious-military orders. Having had only daughters from his Armenian wife, Morfia, Baldwin married his daughter Melisend to Fulk V, count of Anjou and Maine, in 1129 and named them as his successors.

•**Baldwin III** (b. 1131—d. Feb. 10, 1162, Beirut), king of the crusader state of Jerusalem (1143–62), military leader whose reputation among his contemporaries earned him the title of "ideal king."

Son of King Fulk of Jerusalem (1131–43) and of Melisend, the daughter of Fulk's predecessor, Baldwin II, Baldwin and his mother were corulers from 1143 to 1151. During the period of their joint rule, the Latin colonies in Palestine were strengthened by the Second Crusade from the West (1147).

In 1151 Baldwin, following his assumption of sole rule, had to suppress a civil war that broke out between his supporters and those of his mother. He intervened frequently in the affairs of the Christian states of Tripoli and Antioch and captured Ascalon from the Egyptian Fāṭimids in August 1153, but he failed to prevent the capture of Damascus by the Muslim leader Nureddin (*q.v.*) the following year.

In 1158 Baldwin married Theodora Comnenus, niece of the Byzantine emperor Manuel I Comnenus. He and Manuel planned a joint attack against Nureddin, but it failed to materialize.

Baldwin III was highly respected by his contemporaries. Well educated, he imposed his authority on his barons without resorting to force, and he avoided imposing oppressive taxes. His qualities gained him the love of his subjects and the esteem of his enemy Nureddin.

•**Baldwin IV,** byname BALDWIN THE LEPER, French BAUDOUIN LE LÉPREUX (b. 1161—d. March 1185, Jerusalem), king of Jerusalem (1174–85), called the "leper king" for the disease that afflicted him for most of his short life. His reign saw the growth of factionalism among the Latin nobility that weakened the kingdom during the years when its greatest adversary, the Muslim leader Saladin, extended his influence from Egypt to Syria.

Educated by William, archdeacon of Tyre, Baldwin was crowned four days after his father died. Too young at age 13 to rule the kingdom, he was assisted by his kinsman Raymond III, count of Tripoli, who acted as his regent until 1177. Baldwin's health steadily deteriorated, requiring periodic appointment of other regents and contributing to power struggles among the nobility.

In November 1177 Saladin marched from Egypt to attack Ascalon, and Baldwin rushed to the aid of the city. Trapped within its fortifications, he broke out and defeated Saladin near Mont Gisard. A two-year truce was arranged in 1180, but soon after it expired Saladin captured Aleppo (June 1183), thus completing the encirclement of Jerusalem.

In an attempt to keep the succession to the throne in his family, the childless Baldwin crowned his nephew king as Baldwin V in November 1183, naming Raymond of Tripoli and Jocelin III of Courtenay the boy's guardians.

•**Baldwin V** (b. 1177, Jerusalem—d. August 1186, Acre), nominal king of Jerusalem who reigned from March 1185 until his death a year and a half later.

The son of William of Montferrat and Sybil, the sister of King Baldwin IV, Baldwin V came to the throne when his uncle died of leprosy at the age of 24. The able knight Raymond III, count of Tripoli, acted as regent for the young king, managing to obtain with Saladin, in 1185, a four-year truce that gave the kingdom of Jerusalem a much needed respite from Muslim attacks; trade in grain was revived between the coastal cities of Acre and Tyre and the interior, and a famine was consequently avoided.

A boy of delicate health, Baldwin died and was buried in the Church of the Holy Sepulchre in Jerusalem, the last Latin king to have that distinction. He was succeeded by Guy de Lusignan, Sybil's second husband.

Baldwin, Frank Stephen (b. April 10, 1838, New Hartford, Conn., U.S.—d. April 8, 1925, Denville, N.J.), inventor best known for his development of the Monroe calculator.

His first calculator, the arithmometer (patented 1875), could add, subtract, multiply, and divide. Economic conditions, however, prevented its immediate manufacture. The Baldwin computing engine (1890) was followed by the Baldwin calculator (1902), but not until 1912 (patent date, 1913), in association with Jay Monroe, did he perfect the Monroe calculator. He remained research director of the Monroe Calculating Machine Company until his death.

Consult the INDEX *first*

Baldwin, Henry (b. Jan. 14, 1770, New Haven, Conn., U.S.—d. April 21, 1844, Philadelphia), associate justice of the United States Supreme Court (1830–44).

Baldwin graduated with honours from Yale University in 1797 and studied law under Alexander J. Dallas before opening his practice in Pittsburgh and building up reputedly one of the finest law libraries in the West. He was elected to the first of three terms to the U.S. House of Representatives in 1816. He was a supporter of protective tariffs and played a leading role in Florida treaty negotiations before ill health forced him to resign in 1822.

An ardent supporter of Pres. Andrew Jackson, he hoped to be named secretary of the treasury but was instead appointed to the U.S. Supreme Court. Initially, his respect for Chief Justice John Marshall allied him to the liberal interpreters of the Constitution, but he gradually moved to a middle ground between them and the strict-construction school. He attempted to put his judicial principles in a systematic framework in *A General View of the Origin and Nature of the Constitution and Government of the United States* (1837), but his decisions on the Court were unpredictable. His most important opinion was handed down in the Florida Land Case, *United States* v. *Arredondo* (1832), which made strict adherence to treaties a basic element of public land policy.

Baldwin, James (Arthur) (b. Aug. 2, 1924, New York City), novelist, essayist, and playwright who became an important interpreter of black-white relations in the U.S. and a spokesman for blacks.

The eldest of nine children, he grew up in poverty in the Harlem Negro ghetto in New York. From 14 to 16 he was active during out-of-school hours as a preacher in a small revivalist church, a period he wrote about in his semi-autobiographical first, and perhaps finest, novel, *Go Tell It on the Mountain* (1953), and in his play about a woman evangelist, *The Amen Corner* (performed in New York, 1965).

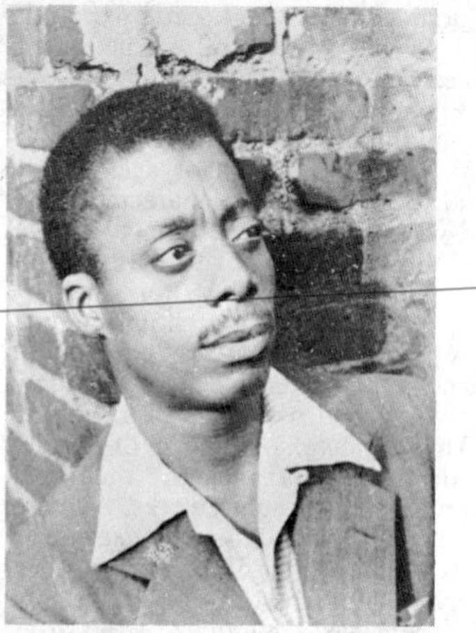

James Baldwin
UPI—EB Inc.

After graduation from high school, he began a restless period of ill-paid jobs, self-study, and literary apprenticeship in Greenwich Village, the bohemian quarter of New York. He left in 1948 for Paris, where he lived for the next eight years. His second novel, *Giovanni's Room* (1956), deals with the white world and concerns an American in Paris torn between his love for a man and his love for a woman. Between the two novels came his collection of essays, *Notes of a Native Son* (1955).

In 1957 he returned to the U.S. and became an active participant in the civil rights struggle that swept the nation. His book of essays, *Nobody Knows My Name* (1961), explores the complex ramifications of black-white relations in the U.S. This theme also was central to his novel *Another Country* (1962), which examines the sexual as well as the racial complications of its characters in a New York setting.

The New Yorker magazine gave over almost all of its Nov. 17, 1962, issue to a long article by Baldwin on the Black Muslim separatist movement and other aspects of the civil rights struggle. The article became a best-seller in book form as *The Fire Next Time* (1963). His bitter play about racist oppression, *Blues for Mister Charlie* ("Mister Charlie" being a black term for a white man), played on Broadway to mixed reviews in 1964. The next year his *The Amen Corner,* which he had written 10 years earlier, also was staged in New York. *Going to Meet the Man,* a collection of short stories, appeared in 1965, and the novels *Tell Me How Long the Train's Been Gone* in 1968, *If Beale Street Could Talk* in 1974, and *Just Above My Head* in 1979.

Baldwin, James Mark (b. Jan. 12, 1861, Columbia, S.C., U.S.—d. Nov. 8, 1934, Paris), philosopher and theoretical psychologist who exerted a notable influence on U.S. psychology during its formative period in the 1890s. Concerned with the relation of Darwinian evolution to psychology, he favoured the study of individual differences, stressed the importance of theory for psychology, and was critical of narrow experimentalism.

During a year of study in Berlin and at the University of Leipzig (1884–85), Baldwin became acquainted with the new experimental psychology and its founder, Wilhelm Wundt. To answer the need for English textbooks in the new psychology, he wrote a *Handbook of Psychology* (2 vol., 1889–91). In 1889 he became professor of philosophy at the University of Toronto, where he established a psychological laboratory. Later, as professor of psychology and philosophy at Princeton University

(1893–1903), where he established another laboratory, he published two works advancing evolutionary principles in psychology, *Mental Development in the Child and the Race* (1895) and *Social and Ethical Interpretations in Mental Development* (1897). With James McKeen Cattell, he founded the *Psychological Review* (1894), from which other publications also developed, including the *Psychological Index* and the *Psychological Bulletin*.

Baldwin edited the contributions of some 60 philosophers and psychologists in his *Dictionary of Philosophy and Psychology* (3 vol., 1901–05), the final volume of which was a 1,200-page bibliography by Benjamin Rand. Associated with Johns Hopkins University, Baltimore (1903–09), he then spent five years in Mexico City as an adviser to the National University of Mexico. During this period he completed *Genetic Logic* (3 vol., 1906–11), which examined the nature and development of thought and meaning. Settling in Paris (1913), he lectured at various provincial universities and in 1919 became professor at the École des Hautes Études Sociales in Paris.

Baldwin, Matthias William (b. Dec. 10, 1795, Elizabethtown, N.J., U.S.—d. Sept. 7, 1866, Philadelphia), manufacturer whose significant improvements of the steam locomotive included a steam-tight metal joint that permitted his engines to use steam at double the pressure of others.

Originally trained as a jeweller but experienced in industrial design and manufacture, he was approached in 1832 by the Philadelphia and Germantown Railroad, which needed a locomotive. The commission proved to be the start of the Baldwin Locomotive Works. During its founder's lifetime, the plant built more than 1,500 locomotives.

Among Baldwin's philanthropies was education for Negro children. His Abolitionist sympathies led to a Southern boycott of his engines shortly before the Civil War.

Baldwin, Ralph B(elknap) (b. June 6, 1912, Grand Rapids, Mich., U.S.), geologist and astrophysicist whose book *The Face of the Moon* (1949) presented such an extensive array of evidence about lunar and terrestrial craters that it persuaded the majority of scientists that lunar craters were created by meteoritic impact rather than by volcanic eruption, as many scientists had believed. That book and his later works *The Measure of the Moon* (1963) and *A Fundamental Survey of the Moon* (1965) are particularly noted for their syntheses of all aspects of the history of the Moon.

Baldwin, Robert (b. May 12, 1804, York, Upper Canada—d. Dec. 9, 1858, Toronto), statesman who was joint leader with Louis Hippolyte Lafontaine of the first and second Liberal administrations in Canada, which established the principle of responsible, or cabinet, government in Canada.

Robert Baldwin
By courtesy of the Public Archives of Canada

Called to the bar in 1825, Baldwin began his political career as a member (1829–30) of the Legislative Assembly of Upper Canada for York (as of 1834, Toronto). In 1836 he served briefly on the Executive Council of Upper Canada and supported the union of Canada, condemning the Rebellion of 1837. He served (1840) on the Executive Council under Charles Poulett Thomson (later Baron Sydenham) but resigned, joining the opposition.

In 1842, under the governor generalship of Sir Charles Bagot, Baldwin and Lafontaine formed a Liberal administration and held office until Bagot's successor, Sir Charles Metcalfe, caused several ministers to resign. In the 1843 election the governor generalship was narrowly sustained, but in 1848 the Liberals were returned to power. Under James Bruce, 8th earl of Elgin, Baldwin and Lafontaine saw the accomplishment of their aim of responsible government and the enactment of other reforms, including municipal self-government for Canada West (Upper Canada, now in Ontario) and the freeing of the University of Toronto from sectarian control.

Feeling increasingly out of sympathy with the advanced reformers in his party and offended by an attempt to abolish the Court of Chancery in Canada West, which he had personally helped to establish, Baldwin resigned in 1851. He was not reelected to Parliament by Toronto, largely because of his uncommitted attitude toward the Clergy Reserves question, regarding the secularization of the one-eighth of crown lands in Canada set apart for the support of a Protestant clergy. In 1858 the coalition Liberal–Conservative Party invited him to stand for a seat in the upper house, but disassociated from the radicals, he could not identify with the conservative element of the Liberal Party either. In retirement he devoted himself to the improvement of Anglo-French relations in Canada.

Baldwin, Stanley, 1st Earl Baldwin of Bewdley, Viscount Corvedale of Corvedale (b. Aug. 3, 1867, Bewdley, Worcestershire, Eng.—d. Dec. 14, 1947, Astley, Lancashire), British Conservative politician, three times prime minister between 1923 and 1937; he headed the government during the General Strike of 1926, the Ethiopian crisis of 1935, and the abdication crisis of 1936.

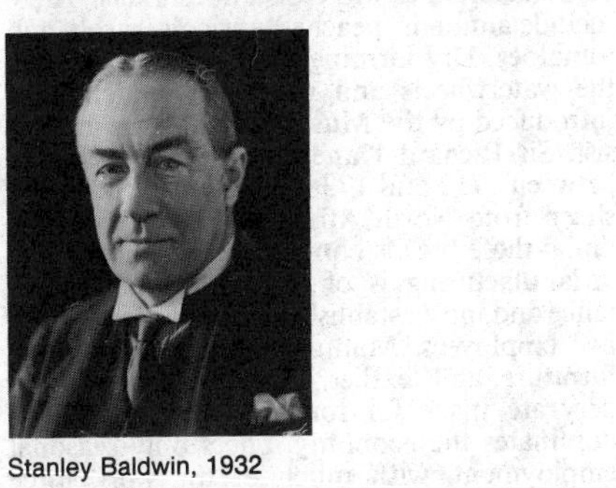

Stanley Baldwin, 1932
Bassano and Vandyk

A relative of the author Rudyard Kipling and the painter Sir Edward Burne-Jones, Baldwin managed his father's diversified heavy industries for several years. From 1908 to 1937 he was a member of the House of Commons. In December 1916 he became parliamentary private secretary to Andrew Bonar Law, chancellor of the exchequer in David Lloyd George's World War I coalition ministry. From 1917 to 1921 he served as financial secretary of the treasury, and then he became president of the Board of Trade. In October 1922, Bonar Law and Baldwin induced a majority of the Conservative members of Parliament to repudiate Lloyd George's coalition. Baldwin was then appointed chancellor of the exchequer in the new Conservative government headed by Bonar Law. Sent to Washington, D.C., in January 1923 to settle the British World War I debt to the U.S., he was widely criticized for negotiating terms less favourable to Great Britain than had been expected. When ill health forced Bonar Law to quit the premiership, it nonetheless was Baldwin whom King George V asked, on May 22, 1923, to form a government. His first ministry ended Jan. 22, 1924, after the voters had rejected his protective tariff policy.

Baldwin returned to office Nov. 4, 1924, following the downfall of the first Labour prime minister, Ramsay MacDonald. When deteriorating economic conditions resulted in a general strike by British workers (May 4–12, 1926), Baldwin proclaimed a state of emergency, organized volunteers to maintain essential services, and refused to negotiate further with labour until the strike was called off. The following year he secured passage of the antiunion Trade Disputes Act.

A Conservative electoral defeat over the issues of unemployment and the Trade Disputes Act caused Baldwin to resign June 4, 1929. Returning to the government in 1931 as lord president of the council in MacDonald's national coalition ministry, he promoted the 10 percent ad valorem tariff and the Ottawa agreements of 1932, which established economic protectionism and impelled numerous Liberal ministers to resign. Upon Adolf Hitler's rise to power in Germany in 1933, Nazism first became recognized as an international threat. Because Baldwin feared the domestic political consequences of British rearmament and a firm foreign policy to meet that threat, he later said, "My lips were sealed."

From June 7, 1935, to May 28, 1937, Baldwin once more was prime minister. In view of the Italian conquest of Ethiopia, the unopposed German reoccupation of the Rhineland, and German–Italian intervention in the Spanish Civil War, he began to strengthen the military establishment while showing little outward concern. His government faced public outrage over the agreement (December 1935) between Sir Samuel Hoare, the British foreign secretary, and Pierre Laval, the French premier, to permit Fascist Italy to have its way in Ethiopia. At home, the determination of the new king, Edward VIII, to marry a U.S. divorcée, Wallis Warfield Simpson, endangered the prestige of the monarchy and perhaps the unity of the British Empire. Baldwin procured Edward's abdication (Dec. 10, 1936) and satisfied public opinion. Five months later he resigned in favour of Neville Chamberlain, accepted an earldom, and retired from politics.

Baldy Mountain, highest peak in Manitoba, Canada, in the southeastern part of Duck Mountain Provincial Park, 36 mi (58 km) northwest of Dauphin. At 2,729 ft (832 m) above sea level, it is also the highest peak in the 350-mi-long Manitoba Escarpment.

Bale, province (*kifle hager*) of southern Ethiopia, between Hararge and Sidamo. It borders Arsi province in the mountainous northwest and Somalia in the low southeast. The mountains are the source of several rivers that flow southeast into Somalia and eventually into the Indian Ocean. The Shebeli River forms Bale's boundary with Arsi and Hararge; the Genale forms most of its boundary with Sidamo; and the Weyib flows through the centre of Bale. The southeastern part of the province is an arid extension of the Ogaden region of Hararge. With an area of about 49,500 sq mi (128,300 sq km), Bale is one of Ethiopia's largest provinces, second only to Hararge. In population density Bali ranks lowest in the country. The dry land between the rivers, in the southeast, is home only to Somali-speaking nomads and their cattle. Unrest in the 1970s led many of them to leave for Somalia (*see* Ogaden). At the other end of the province Goba, the capital and largest town (pop. [1982 est.] 24,326), lies among mountains that rise to 14,130 ft (4,307 m) at Mt. Batu. Bale Mountains National Park (about 1,160 sq mi) features the rare mountain nyala, an antelope found only in this part of the world. The Bale Game Reserve occupies about 800 sq mi. A limestone cave with stalactites extends two miles into the earth. Pop. (1982 est.) 927,500.

Bâle (Switzerland): *see* Basel.

Bale, John (b. Nov. 21, 1495, Cove, Suffolk, Eng.—d. November 1563, Canterbury, Kent), bishop, Protestant controversialist, and dramatist whose *Kynge Johan* is asserted to have been the first English history play. He is notable for his part in the religious strife of the 16th century and for his antiquarian studies, including the first rudimentary history of English literature.

Bale was educated at a Carmelite convent in Norwich and at Cambridge. He was the prior of Carmelite convents at Maldon, Doncaster, and Ipswich at various times but became a Protestant and at some date (probably 1533) left his order, married, and became rector of Thorndon, Suffolk. Frequently attacked and once imprisoned for his religious views, he took refuge on the Continent from 1540 to 1548 and from 1553 until after the accession of Elizabeth in 1558. In 1560 he was appointed to the staff of Canterbury cathedral.

Bale's voluminous writings are characterized by a fiercely partisan spirit, crude but vigorous satire, and frequent scurrility. His plays, only five of which survive, are thought to belong to the early 1530s. They employ the old forms of miracle and morality play as vehicles of Protestant propaganda.

His most ambitious effort was three biographical catalogs of English writers: the *Illustrium majoris Britanniae scriptorum* (1548); the revised and much expanded *Scriptorum illustrium majoris Britanniae catalogus* (1557–59; reprinted 1977); and the autograph notebook, first published in 1902 by R.L. Poole and M. Bateson as *Index Britanniae Scriptorum Quos Collegit J. Baleus*. Though marred by inaccuracy, this early literary history is invaluable to students of the medieval and early Tudor periods.

Bâle-Campagne (Switzerland): *see* Basel-Landschaft.

Bâle-Ville (Switzerland): *see* Basel-Stadt.

Balearic Islands, Spanish ISLAS BALEARES, archipelago in the western Mediterranean Sea, and a province of Spain with a provisional autonomous government (*comunidad autónoma*).

The following article summarizes the administrative status and history, geography, demographic patterns, economy, and culture of the modern Balearic Islands; for additional treatment of their geography and history, *see* MACROPAEDIA: Spain.

The Balearics were conquered by the Vandals in 526 and fell to the Byzantines in 554. The Muslim occupation of the islands was complete by 903. James I of Aragon conquered the islands of Majorca and Ibiza between 1229 and 1235, and Minorca fell to his descendant, Alfonso III, in 1287. The Balearics were established as an autonomous kingdom in 1298 and rejoined the Crown of Aragon in 1349. The British captured Mahón in 1708, and the Treaties of Utrecht in 1713 ceded Minorca to the British, who occupied it until 1802. The Balearics were established as a Spanish province in 1833.

A regionalist movement emerged in the late 19th century but failed to consolidate. A statute of autonomy was proposed in 1931.

Palma is the capital as well as the military, judicial, and ecclesiastical centre of the province. The provisional autonomous government encompasses the insular councils of Majorca, Minorca, and Ibiza-Formentera.

The archipelago lies 50 to 190 mi (80 to 300 km) east of the Spanish mainland and has a land area of 1,936 sq mi (5,014 sq km). There are two groups of islands. The eastern and larger forms the Balearics proper and includes the principal islands of Majorca (Spanish Mallorca) and Minorca (Menorca) and the small island of Cabrera. The western group is known as the Pitiusas (ancient Pityusae) and includes the islands of Ibiza and Formentera. The archipelago is an extension of the sub-Baetic mountains of peninsular Spain, and the two are linked by a sill near Cape Nao in the province of Alicante. The Balearics exhibit a varied terrain, with undulating hills, plateaus, and lowlands. Minorca has extensive plains. Annual precipitation is low, rarely exceeding 18 in. (450 mm), concentrated in the autumn and spring.

The raids of the Barbary pirates discouraged settlement along the coast until the 19th century. The spread of tourism since the mid-19th century has led to the concentration of the population along the coastal areas and the depopulation of the hinterland. The population grew only moderately between 1900 and 1970, reflecting high emigration and a low birth rate, but subsequently has grown at a rate well above the national average. The population of Majorca and Minorca is heavily concentrated in the larger cities, while that of the islands of Ibiza and Formentera tends to be dispersed. Farmland is often subdivided into *minifundios* (small landholdings), the number of *latifundios* (large landholdings) having declined sharply since 1920.

Emigration from the hinterland has sharply reduced the agricultural work force. The traditional Mediterranean crops of wheat, grapes, and olives predominated until 1830, when improved transport allowed new cash crops to be transported to more distant markets. These include almonds, peaches, apricots, carob, and tomatoes. Dry farming predominates, though the waterwheels and windmills, which were introduced by the Muslims for irrigation, persist. Sir Richard Kane, governor of Minorca between 1712 and 1736, introduced cattle and sheep from North Africa and pigs from Sardinia; these breeds continue to be raised.

Manufacturing is of relatively little importance and most establishments have fewer than five employees. Manufactures include shoes, furniture, and textiles. Fine lace and embroidery are made for tourists. Tourism, which dominates the economy, offers only seasonal employment, with much of the work force idle during the winter. More than 1,000,000 tourists visit the Balearics each year.

Varied civilizations have left their marks on the islands, and although the prehistoric talayotic civilization, so termed from its characteristic rough stone towers called talayots, seems to have continued without much modification, the focal position of the islands in the Mediterranean laid them open to continued influence from civilizations centred farther to the east, as many archaeological finds attest. Important discoveries of bronze swords and single and double axes, antennae swords, and heads and figures of bulls and other animals all bear witness to foreign influence over long periods of time. Pottery, mostly of the native talayotic types, seems to have persisted with little change until the Roman occupation. Historical evidence points to at least 2,600 years of settlement, for the islands were successively ruled by Carthaginians, Romans, Vandals, Moors, and Spaniards, all of whom have left their mark on the physical and cultural landscape. *See also* Majorca; Minorca; Ibiza. Pop. (1982 est.) 669,101.

baleen whale, also called TOOTHLESS WHALE, any of several whales of the family Balaenopteridae, distinguished from other groups by a specialized feeding structure, the baleen, or whalebone. Whalebone was once widely used for stays in women's corsets and is still used in some industrial brushes.

The baleen, which is used to strain plankton and small crustaceans from the water, consists of two horny plates attached to the roof of the mouth. Each plate is composed of a series of parallel slats with fringes that mat together to form a sieve. There are about 300 slats in each triangular-shaped plate, which may be as long as 3.6 metres (12 feet) in the right whale.

For more information on baleen whale species and groups, *see* blue whale; fin whale; gray whale; humpback whale; right whale; sei whale.

Balenciaga, Cristóbal (b. Jan. 21, 1895, Guetaria, Spain—d. March 24, 1972, Valencia), dress designer who created elegant ball gowns and other classic designs.

He began seriously studying dressmaking at the age of 10, when the death of his father, a sea captain, made it necessary for his mother to support the family by sewing. His first trip to Paris at 15 inspired him to become a couturier, and by the time that he was 20 he had his own dressmaking establishment at the fashionable summer resort of San Sebastián in Spain.

In the next 15 years Balenciaga became the leading couturier of Spain. In 1937, when the Spanish Civil War disrupted his business, he moved to Paris. For the next 30 years his collections featured sumptuously elegant dresses and suits. Considered a master of construction and a "prophet of the silhouette," he produced designs that were expertly cut and fitted. Harmonious balance and dramatic effect were achieved by colour, cut, and studied ornamentation.

Balenciaga helped popularize the trend toward capes and flowing clothes without waistlines in the late 1950s and the use of plastic for rainwear in the mid-'60s. In 1968 the house of Balenciaga, with its branches in Spain, closed, and the master couturier retired.

baler, largest living snail, a species of conch (*q.v.*).

Bales, Peter, also called PETER BALESIUS (b. 1547, London—d. 1610?), English calligrapher who devised one of the earliest forms of shorthand, published in his book *Arte of Brachygraphie* (1590). Remarkably skilled as a copyist, he gained renown for his microscopic writing, producing a Bible roughly the size of a walnut. He inscribed a number of texts within a circumference about that of a penny, mounted this example of dexterous penmanship on a ring, and presented it to Elizabeth I, who greatly admired it. His skill in imitating handwriting was used for secret state purposes by Elizabeth's principal secretary, Sir Francis Walsingham, and helped to uncover Anthony Babington's plot to assassinate the Queen. He was head of a penmanship school in 1590, when he published *Writing Schoolemaster, in Three Parts*.

Bāleshwar (India): *see* Balasore.

Balewa, Sir Abubakar Tafawa (b. 1912, Bauchi, Northern Nigeria—d. January 1966, near Ifo), Nigerian politician, leader in the Northern Peoples Congress (NPC), and the first federal prime minister. A commoner by birth, an unusual origin for a political leader in the NPC, Balewa was both a defender of northern special interests and an advocate of reform and Nigerian unity.

Balewa was a teacher by profession and was one of the first Northern Nigerians to be sent to London University Institute of Education (1945). On his return in 1946 he was elected to the House of Assembly of the Northern Region and in 1947 was one of five representatives to the Central Legislative Council in

Lagos. He was reelected to the assembly in 1951 despite the hostility of some conservative *amīrs* of the generally Muslim north.

From 1952 until his death Balewa served in the federal government: he was minister of works and of transport in the middle 1950s, and then, as leader of the NPC in the House of Representatives, he was made the first prime minister of Nigeria. After the preindependence elections of 1959, he again became prime minister in a coalition government of the NPC and Nnamdi Azikiwe's National Council of Nigeria and the Cameroons. As prime minister of independent Nigeria, he was sharply circumscribed in his powers by those delegated to regional premiers. He proved unable to mitigate the growing tensions of 1964–66, manifested by a partial boycott of the election in 1964, army unrest, and outbreaks of violence in the Western Region. He was killed in the first of two Nigerian army coups in 1966.

Balfe, Michael William (b. May 15, 1808, Dublin—d. Oct. 20, 1870, near Ware, Hertfordshire, Eng.), singer and composer, best

Balfe, lithograph by F. Salabert

By courtesy of the trustees of the British Museum; photograph, J.R. Freeman & Co. Ltd.

known for the facile melody and simple vocal effects of his opera *The Bohemian Girl.*

Balfe appeared as a violinist at the age of nine and began composing at about the same time. In 1823 he went to London, where he played in the orchestra at Drury Lane Theatre, and in 1825 was taken to Rome by Count Mazzara, a wealthy patron. Between 1827 and 1833 he sang leading baritone roles in operas by Rossini, Meyerbeer, and others in Paris and Italy. His own early operas were written on Italian librettos and produced at Palermo, Pavia, and Milan between 1829 and 1833, after which he returned to London. His first English opera, *The Siege of Rochelle,* was produced at Drury Lane in 1835. His popularity was established; in 1838 he sang Papageno in the first English performance of *The Magic Flute,* and with *Le Puits d'amour* (Paris, 1843) he began a series of French operas.

The Bohemian Girl (Drury Lane, 1843) was the most successful of all his operas and was produced in many countries, in French, German, Italian, and Russian. Two of the ballads from it, "When Other Lips" and "I Dreamt That I Dwelt in Marble Halls," have been published in many arrangements.

Balfe produced several other operas in London; essayed managing and conducting with little success; and between 1849 and 1864 travelled in France, Germany, Italy, and Russia.

Balfour (of Whittingehame), Arthur James Balfour, 1st earl of, VISCOUNT TRAPRAIN (b. July 25, 1848, Whittinghame, East Lothian, Scot.—d. March 19, 1930, Woking, Surrey, Eng.), British statesman who maintained a position of power in the British Conservative Party for 50 years; he was prime minister from 1902 to 1905, and as foreign secretary from 1916 to 1919 he is perhaps best remembered for his World War I statement (the Balfour Declaration) expressing official British approval of Zionism.

The son of James Maitland Balfour and a nephew of Robert Cecil, 3rd marquess of Salisbury, Balfour was a member of a highly intellectual, wealthy, and aristocratic circle. He was educated at Eton and at Trinity College, Cambridge, and, upon leaving Cambridge, he entered Parliament as a Conservative member for Hertford. In 1879 he published his *Defence of Philosophic Doubt* in which he endeavoured to show that scientific knowledge depends just as much as theology upon an act of faith. In the great Victorian struggle between science and religion, Balfour was on the side of religion. He continued to take a keen interest in scientific and philosophical problems throughout his life.

Balfour was president of the Local Government Board in his uncle's first government (1885–86). In the second Salisbury ministry (1886–92), he was secretary for Scotland and then chief secretary for Ireland, with a seat in the Cabinet. An implacable opponent of Irish Home Rule, he earned the name "Bloody Balfour" because of his severity in suppressing insurrection. At the same time he opposed the evils of English absentee landlordism in Ireland and made various concessions for the purpose of "killing home rule by kindness."

Known as a formidable parliamentary debater, Balfour became (1891) leader of the House of Commons and first lord of the treasury, thus being second in command to Lord Salisbury. During W.E. Gladstone's last Liberal ministry (1892–94), he led the opposition in the House of Commons. In the last of Salisbury's three governments (1895–1902), Balfour became more powerful as his uncle's health declined. Although he disapproved of the policies that resulted in the South African (Boer) War (1899–1902), he insisted that the British win the war decisively.

After Salisbury's retirement, Balfour served as prime minister from July 12, 1902, to Dec. 4, 1905. He sponsored and secured passage of the Education Act (Balfour Act; 1902), which reorganized the local administration of elementary and secondary schools. The Wyndham Land Purchase Act (1903) encouraged the sale of land to tenant farmers in Ireland. The Committee of Imperial Defense (created 1904) made possible a realistic worldwide British strategy. None of these measures was especially popular with the voters. Balfour also decided to meet a shortage of miners in South Africa by importing large numbers of indentured Chinese, a decision that was condemned by humanitarians and by British organized labour. After a Cabinet crisis in 1903, Balfour regained prestige in the completion of negotiations for the Anglo-French agreement (Entente Cordiale; 1904), a major change in British foreign policy, by which the supremacy of Great Britain in Egypt and of France in Morocco was recognized. Increasing Conservative disunity over the question of abandoning free trade finally caused him to resign, although he remained the official party leader until November 1911.

On May 25, 1915, when H.H. Asquith formed a wartime coalition ministry, Balfour succeeded Winston Churchill as first lord of

Arthur James Balfour, *c.* 1900

Bassano and Vandyk

the Admiralty. In the political crisis of December 1916, he ceased to support Asquith and turned to David Lloyd George, in whose new coalition he became foreign secretary. In that office he had little to do with the conduct of World War I or with the peace negotiations.

His most important action occurred on Nov. 2, 1917, when, prompted by the Zionist leaders Chaim Weizmann and Nahum Sokolow, he wrote a letter to Baron Rothschild, head of the English branch of the Jewish banking family, that contained the so-called Balfour Declaration. This declaration, pledging British aid for Zionist efforts to establish a home for world Jewry in Palestine, gave great impetus to the establishment of the state of Israel.

After the war Balfour served twice (1919–22, 1925–29) in the Cabinet post of lord president of the council. He was largely responsible for the negotiations that led to the definition of relations between Great Britain and the dominions—the Balfour Report (1926)—which was to be expressed in the Statute of Westminster in 1931. In 1922 he was created an earl. His *Chapters of Autobiography* (1930) was edited by B.E.C. Dugdale, who also wrote *Arthur James Balfour,* 2 vol. (1936).

Balfour, Francis Maitland (b. Nov. 10, 1851, Edinburgh—d. July 19, 1882, near Martigny-Ville, Switz.), British zoologist, younger brother of the statesman Arthur James Balfour, and a founder of modern embryology.

Francis Maitland Balfour, engraving

The Mansell Collection

His interest in the subject was aroused by the lectures of the British physiologist Michael Foster, and, after graduation from Cambridge in 1873, Balfour obtained one of the university's chairs at the Stazione Zoologica in Naples, an international centre for marine biological research. During the next five years, he made many original observations about the embryonic development of vertebrate urogenital organs (*e.g.,* kidneys, sex organs) and the origin of spinal nerves. These discoveries, along with his descriptions of the initial changes in the ovum after fertilization and of the early stages of the embryo, provided crucial information on the evolution of invertebrates to vertebrates.

He returned to Cambridge in 1876 to lecture on animal morphology and there published *A Treatise on Comparative Embryology* (1880–81), which laid the foundations of modern embryology. Such was his fame that he was invited to succeed the eminent biologists George Rolleston at Oxford and Sir Charles Wyville Thomson at Edinburgh, but he refused both offers to remain at Cambridge, where in 1882 a special professorship in animal morphology was created for him. Before he could assume his new position, however, he died in a fall while attempting to scale the unconquered Aiguille Blanche of Mont Blanc.

Balfour Declaration (Nov. 2, 1917), statement of British support for "the establishment in Palestine of a national home for the Jewish people." It was made in a letter from Arthur James Balfour, the British foreign secretary, to Lionel Walter Rothschild, 2nd Baron Rothschild, a leader of British Jewry.

The Balfour Declaration, issued through the continued efforts of Chaim Weizmann and Nahum Sokolow, Zionist leaders in London, fell short of the expectations of the Zionists, who had asked for the reconstitution of Palestine as "the" Jewish national home. The declaration specifically stipulated that "nothing shall be done which may prejudice the civil and religious rights of existing non-Jewish communities in Palestine." Nevertheless, it aroused enthusiastic hopes among Zionists and seemed the fulfillment of the aims of the World Zionist Organization.

The British government hoped that the declaration would rally Jewish opinion, especially in the United States, to the side of the Allies and that the settlement in Palestine of a Jewish population attached to Britain by ties of sentiment and interest might help to protect the approaches to the Suez Canal and hence the route to India.

The Balfour Declaration was endorsed by the principal Allied Powers, and through its acceptance by the Conference of San Remo in 1920 it became an instrument of British and international policy. Together with various provisions dealing with facilitating Jewish immigration, it was further included in the British mandate over Palestine, approved by the League of Nations on July 24, 1922.

Bali (India): *see* Bally.

Bali, island and *propinsi* (province) in the Lesser Sunda Islands, Indonesia, 1 mi (1.6 km) east of the island of Java. Visited by Chinese traders and Indian literati, the Balinese had embraced Hinduism by the 7th century AD. Mahendradatta, the mother of Airlangga (who ruled Java from 1019 to *c.* 1049), married Udayana, the Balinese king, and many Javanese Hindus immigrated to Bali. In 1284 Kertanagara, last king of Tumapel (Singhasāri) in Java, captured Bali; upon his death in 1292, the island regained its independence. Bali came under the rule of the Majapahit Empire of eastern Java in 1343 and continued under the Majapahits until the empire was overthrown in 1478 by Muslims. The Dutch first visited Bali in 1597, when the island was divided among a number of warring Muslim states. The Dutch annexed the northern Balinese states of Buleleng and Jembrana in 1882, and in the 1894 Dutch invasion of nearby Lombok Island, Anak Agung Ktut, the Balinese prince, was killed. In 1906 the Dutch attacked Denpasar, massacred about 3,600 Balinese, and captured the whole island. Bali was occupied by the Japanese during World War II. In 1946 a battle was fought between Dutch troops and Indonesian revolutionary forces at Marga in western Bali. The island became part of the Republic of Indonesia in 1950.

Rice paddies on Bali, Indonesia
Shostal—EB Inc.

Most of Bali's 2,147 sq mi (5,561 sq km) is mountainous (essentially an extension of the central mountain chain in Java), the highest point being Mount Agung, or Bali Peak, 10,308 ft (3,142 m) in height and known locally as the "navel of the world." It is an active volcano that erupted in March 1963, killing more than 1,500 persons and leaving thousands homeless. The main lowland is south of the central mountains. The period of the southeast monsoon (May to November) is the dry season. Bali's flora (mostly hill tropical rain forest) and fauna resemble those of Java. Some teak grows there, and the giant banyan (*waringin*) trees are held sacred by the Balinese. Tigers are found in the west, and deer and wild pigs are numerous.

The two major towns are Singaraja and Denpasar, the provincial capital; others include Klungkung, a centre of wood carving and gold and silver industries; Gianyar, with a lively market; Kuta, a centre of the increasingly important tourist trade; and Ubud, in the foothills, a centre for European and U.S. artists, with a fine art museum. All Balinese villages have temples and an assembly hall, usually located on a square that serves for festivals and markets. Each family lives in its own compound surrounded by earthen or stone walls. Population density in the lowlands is more than 1,500 per sq mi (580 per sq km).

When Islām triumphed over Hinduism in Java (16th century), Bali became a refuge for many nobles, priests, and intellectuals. Today it is the only remaining stronghold of Hinduism in the archipelago, and Balinese life is centred on religion—a blend of Hinduism (especially that of the Śaivite sect), Buddhism, Malay ancestor cult, and animistic and magical beliefs and practices. Places of worship are numerous and widespread, and there is a firm belief in reincarnation. Caste is observed, though less strictly than is the case in India, since nine-tenths of the population belong to the Śūdra, the lowest caste. The nobility is divided into priests (Brahmin), the military and ruling royalty (Kṣatriya), and the merchants (Vaiśya). Some Muslims and Chinese live in northern and western Bali, and there are few Christians. The Balinese language is distinct from that of eastern Java, but the upper-class form contains many Javanese and Sanskrit words.

The Balinese are fond of music, poetry, dancing, and festivals; are extraordinarily able in arts and crafts; and are passionately fond of betting games, especially cockfighting. A typical Balinese gamelan (orchestra) consists of various percussion instruments, a two-string violin, and a flute; and every village has its gamelan club. Stage plays, and especially dancing, are an integral part of Balinese life, serving magico-religious purposes or telling stories by pantomime. The artistic temperament is also evident in sculpture, painting, silverwork, and wood carving and bone carving and in the animal-shaped wooden coffins in which corpses are carried to the cremation ground.

Balinese farmers, raising principally rice, are organized into cooperative water-control boards. The average farm is 2.5 ac (1 ha). About one-quarter of the agricultural acreage is irrigated, the remainder being used for yams, cassava, corn (maize), coconuts, fruits, and, occasionally, oil palm and coffee plantings. A large cattle population is supplemented by smaller livestock. There are several meat-processing plants; fishing is only a minor occupation. Food must be imported because of the growing population, but exports include beef, pork, coffee, copra, and palm oil. The tourist industry and the sale of craft articles are important to the economy. There is an airport on the south central coast near Denpasar. Pop. (1980) 2,469,930.

Bali, Piek van (Indonesia): *see* Agung, Mount.

Bali cattle: *see* banteng.

Balıkesir, city, capital of Balıkesir *il* (province), northwestern Turkey, situated on rising ground above a fertile plain that drains to the Sea of Marmara. It lies at or near the site of the Roman town of Hadrianutherae, named after its founder, the emperor Hadrian (reigned AD 117–138); but no trace of the ancient town remains. In the early 14th century, Balıkesir was an important town of the Turkmen Karası emirate, which was soon absorbed in the Ottoman Empire. The old town and its bazaar, which occupy the upper slopes, contain numerous inns and mosques dating from the early Ottoman period. Below the old town are the modern administrative buildings, the railway station, a teacher-training school, and residential districts. The centre of a rich agricultural province, Balıkesir is linked by rail with İzmir and Ankara by way of Kütahya. Industries produce cotton textiles, flour, rugs, and leather goods.

Balıkesir *il,* 5,837 sq mi (15,119 sq km) in area, extends from the Kapı Dağı Peninsula on the Sea of Marmara to Edremit on the Aegean coast. With a milder climate than that of inner Anatolia, the *il* is well forested; and its rich soil produces a varied crop of cereals, beans, fruits, vegetables, sesame, cotton, tobacco, and olives. It is also rich in minerals: iron, lead, zinc, antimony, chromium, lignite, and boracite. Bandırma (*q.v.*), on the Sea of Marmara, is the province's chief port; and Erdek, one of the most attractive ports on the Marmara, is a growing tourist resort. The province has many ancient historical and archaeological sites, including those at Edremit, Gönen, and Kaz Dağı (ancient Mount Ida). On 130 ac (52 ha) on the northeastern shore of Manyas Gölü (lake), south of Bandırma, is located a bird sanctuary, which was established as a national park in 1959; in spring, when the water in the lake is at its highest point, thousands of herons nest in the inundated reeds and willows. Pop. (1980) city, 124,051; (1983 est.) *il,* 890,000.

Balikpapan, bay and seaport, Kalimantan Timur *propinsi* (East Borneo province), Indonesia, on the eastern coast of Kalimantan (Indonesian Borneo), facing the Makasar Strait. It is the site of a major oil refinery that processes both imported and local crude oils. There are producing oil fields, which are operated, though they are no longer controlled, by British–American–Dutch interests, that have been in operation there since 1899 as well as in the coastal region stretching about 60 mi (100 km) toward the northeast. The refinery was destroyed in 1942 as part of a "scorched-earth" policy, in the face of the Japanese invasion, but it was rebuilt after World War II. Pop. (1980) 279,852.

Baline, Israel: *see* Berlin, Irving.

Balinese, people of the island Bali, Indonesia. They differ from other Indonesians in adhering to the Hindu religion, though their culture has been heavily influenced by the Javanese. Their language belongs to the Austronesian (Malayo-Polynesian) linguistic family.

In the Balinese village each family lives in its own compound, surrounded by earthen or stone walls. The shady courtyard is usually divided into three sections containing, respectively, the rice granaries and cattle sheds, the sleeping quarters and kitchen, and the house temple. The living quarters have walls of clay and roofs of thatch or palm leaves. All villages have temples and an assembly hall, usually located on a square that serves for festivals and markets.

Balinese life centres upon religion, which is

Hindu Śaivism (Shaivism) fused with Buddhism, ancestor cults, and belief in spirits and magic. The Balinese believe in reincarnation, and the dead are cremated in order to liberate their souls for the onward journey.

Caste practices exist, but, since most of the population belong to the lowest caste, there is little formality among the villagers. As in Java, there are different modes of speech to reflect differences in social rank.

Each village is a self-contained community, venerating common ancestors and usually subdivided into cooperative societies whose members assist each other in temple maintenance, festivals, and family rites.

Family relationships are reckoned through the male line. Marriage is often limited to members of the same *dadia*, or kinship organization.

Rice is the main crop; others include yams, sweet potatoes, cassava, and corn (maize).

Baliol FAMILY: *see* Balliol family.

Baliol, Edward de: *see* Edward *under* Edward (Scotland).

Baliol, John de: *see* John *under* John (Scotland).

Balkan confederation, proposed federation of Communist Balkan republics. The plan, conceived by Balkan social-democratic parties at the beginning of the 20th century, was fostered immediately after World War II by Tito of Yugoslavia and Georgi Dimitrov of Bulgaria. To implement the plan, Yugoslavia supported the establishment of a Communist regime in Albania and provided aid to the Communists fighting for control in Greece. But U.S. support of the anti-Communist Greeks and Soviet dissatisfaction with Tito forced the abandonment of the scheme.

Balkan Entente, also called BALKAN PACT, mutual defense agreement between Greece, Turkey, Romania, and Yugoslavia, signed on Feb. 9, 1934, to guarantee the signatories' territorial integrity and political independence against attack by another Balkan state (*i.e.*, Bulgaria or Albania). The agreement provided for a Permanent Council, composed of the members' foreign ministers, that would coordinate legislation and foster economic cooperation.

But despite professions of unity, the entente was ineffective against growing German economic and political influence in the Balkans (1934–39) and against actual Axis aggression during World War II, when Albania had already fallen to the Italians. It likewise offered no security to Romania against the territorial claims of either the Soviet Union or Hungary.

Treaties signed by Yugoslavia, Greece, and Turkey (Feb. 28, 1953, and Aug. 9, 1954) after the break between Stalin and Tito ostensibly created a new Balkan Entente, calling for political, social, and economic collaboration and for mutual defense for 20 years. National rivalries and ideological conflicts, however, prevented the implementation of these treaties.

Balkan grippe: *see* Q fever.

Balkan League (1912–13), alliance of Bulgaria, Serbia, Greece, and Montenegro, which fought the First Balkan War against Turkey (1912–13). Originally intended to limit increasing Austrian power in the Balkans, the league was formed at the instigation of Bulgaria and Serbia with the aid of Russian diplomacy. During 1912, however, the alliance became more anti-Turkish than anti-Austrian; hoping to expel the Turks from the Balkans, the Allies declared war on the Ottoman Empire (October 1912). The league was victorious, but it disintegrated when its members quarrelled over the division of their territorial spoils. This dispute resulted in the Second Balkan War, against Bulgaria, in 1913 (*see* Balkan Wars).

The term Balkan League also refers to an alliance organized in 1866–68 by the Serbian prince Michael III (Mihailo Obrenović). Including Serbia, Romania, Montenegro, Greece, and a Bulgarian revolutionary society, it tried to drive the Turks from the Balkans and to unite the South Slavs in a single state. The league planned a coordinated rebellion against the Turks, but the assassination of Prince Michael (June 10, 1868) prevented the fulfillment of the plans and destroyed the league.

Balkan Mountains, Bulgarian STARA PLANINA (Old Mountains), Latin HAEMUS, chief range of the Balkan Peninsula and Bulgaria and an extension of the Alpine–Carpathian folds. The range extends from the Timok Valley near the Yugoslav border, spreading out eastward for about 330 mi (530 km) into several spurs, rising to 7,795 ft (2,376 m) at Botev peak and breaking off abruptly at Nos (cape) Emine on the Black Sea. They form the major divide between the Danube (north) and Maritsa (south) rivers and are crossed by about 20 passes, notably Shipka Pass, by three railway lines, and by the Iskŭr River. Mineral resources include bituminous and anthracite coal, graphite, and metallic ores, and there are thermal and mineral springs. High alpine meadows descend to coniferous and deciduous forests. Mountain towns such as Veliko Tŭrnovo served as focusses for early Bulgarian nationalist movements.

Although no longer a barrier to movement, except in winter, when snow cover is deep, the range is a climatic barrier between the continental climate of the Danube and the transitional continental climate south of the mountains. Rainfall exceeds 40 in. (1,000 mm) on the range, with long, severe winters. The valleys and basins are suitable for agriculture, and there is a small tourist industry.

Balkan Peninsula, most easterly of the three southern peninsulas of Europe, the others being the Iberian and the Italian. Its boundaries are commonly considered to be the lower Danube and Sava rivers on the north, the Black Sea on the east, the Aegean Sea on the southeast, the Mediterranean Sea on the south, the Ionian Sea on the southwest, and the Adriatic Sea on the west. Politically, the Balkan Peninsula includes Albania, Bulgaria, Greece, Romania, Turkey (in Europe), and most of Yugoslavia (*qq.v.*). The long, frequently turbulent history of the peninsula has affected events in Europe and the world.

Balkan Wars (1912–13), two successive military conflicts that increased tension in the Balkans just before the outbreak of World War I. The first war, between the members of the Balkan League—Serbia, Bulgaria, Greece, and Montenegro—and the Ottoman Empire, began with Montenegro's declaration of war against the Turks on Oct. 8, 1912, and the entrance of its three allies into the war 10 days later. The Balkan states were victorious, and under the treaty signed in London on May 30, 1913, the empire lost almost all its European territory; Albanian independence was agreed on in principle, and the remainder of the territory was to be divided among the Balkan powers. In the second war, which opened in July 1913, Serbia, Greece, and Romania quarrelled with Bulgaria over the distribution of the conquests in Macedonia, the Turks, in the meantime, recovering part of Thrace. The Bulgarian forces were defeated, and peace was concluded at Bucharest on Aug. 10, 1913.

Balkans, the easternmost of Europe's three great southern peninsulas and, collectively, the countries there. The name has been in use since the early 19th century; *balkan* is Turkish for "mountains." The Balkan Peninsula is defined physiographically by the lower Danube and Sava rivers (north), the Black Sea (east), the Aegean Sea (southeast), the Mediterranean Sea (south), the Ionian Sea (southwest), and the Adriatic Sea (west). Its area within these limits is about 195,000 sq mi (505,000 sq km).

Politically the Balkans extend beyond those limits to include all of Yugoslavia and Romania (*i.e.*, those areas formerly belonging to the Ottoman Empire) and comprise Albania, Bulgaria, Greece, Romania, the European part of Turkey, and Yugoslavia. The population of the peninsula so defined in the early 1980s was approximately 71,500,000; its area was about 305,000 sq mi.

The article that follows is a summary of significant detail about the Balkans. Fuller treatment is provided in the following MACROPAEDIA articles: for geography and history, *see* Balkans; for information about each country, its history, and its people, *see* Albania, Bulgaria, Greece, Romania, Yugoslavia, and the relevant portions of Turkey and Anatolia.

For current history and for statistics on society and economy, *see* the article "World Affairs" and BRITANNICA WORLD DATA, respectively, in the *Britannica Book of the Year*.

The land. Most of the Balkan Peninsula is mountainous. The principal ranges are the Carpathian Mountains in Romania, the Balkan (Stara Planina) and Rhodope Mountains in Bulgaria, and the Pindus Mountains in Greece. The Dinaric Alps stretch through the region along the Adriatic coast from the Julian Alps in Slovenia to the Yugoslav border with Albania, rising to 8,000 ft (2,400 m) above sea level. Branches of the Dinaric Alps extend inland toward the Morava-Vardar basin in the centre of the peninsula and through Albania, continuing as the Pindus Mountains down the centre of the Greek Peninsula. The latter reach elevations of 6,000 ft and impede rain-bearing winds rising from the Mediterranean on the west in their passage toward the fertile basin of Thessaly to the east. The Carpathian Mountains extend southward from Romania, dividing the alluvial Wallachian and Moldavian plains from the less fertile upland basin of Transylvania to the west. The lower half of the range curves southward across the Danube River and turns eastward across Bulgaria to continue as the Balkan Mountains. The Balkan Mountains stretch southward with several appendages from southeastern Yugoslavia and southwestern Bulgaria into northern Greece. The Rhodope Mountains extend along the Bulgaria–Greece border and follow an east–west alignment.

The north–south mountain barriers limit annual rainfall on much of the peninsula to 20 in. (500 mm). The heaviest precipitation generally occurs during the winter months, except for some northern and central parts where it occurs during summer. Droughts are frequent in eastern Greece, Bulgaria, and Romania. Generally a Mediterranean type of climate prevails throughout the peninsula, although variations are caused by elevation and degree of wind exposure. The climate of the northern and central regions resembles the continental climate of central Europe. The average winter temperature is 45° F (7° C), and summer averages 70° F (21° C).

The Danube River connects the eastern Balkan countries with the Black Sea. In Yugoslavia the Sava River in the north and the Morava in the east are tributaries of the Danube; the Neretva in the west flows southward into the Adriatic Sea. Other important rivers in the Balkans are the Maritsa in Bulgaria, the Drin in Albania, and the Vardar in Greece, all flowing south and east. Several small lakes are scattered through northern Greece, and the large lakes Ohrid and Prespa are located near the borders of Albania, Greece, and Yugoslavia.

In the northern and central parts of the peninsula forests are deciduous up to about

5,000 ft and coniferous above that, and at elevations higher than about 6,000 ft the forest gives way to scrub, herb, and mat associations. In the southern and western coastal areas evergreen and various Mediterranean woods and brush are common, with oak and conifer forests at higher elevations. Throughout the peninsula much of the woody vegetation has been destroyed by human occupance.

Among the Mediterranean mammals found in the southern and western coastal areas are the jackal, the wild goat (bezoar), the porcupine, and several kinds of bat. Lynx, wildcat, marten, wolf, fox, and bear are among the central European mammals found in the interior. Mediterranean birds include the cuckoo and various warblers; central European forms include the chaffinch, creepers, some thrushes, birds of prey such as the golden imperial eagle, and various vultures. The fishes of lakes and rivers include carp, barbel, small salmon, and wels. The harmful plant insects are tussock moths and several species of locust.

Brown coal or lignite is abundant in Yugoslavia, Bulgaria, Greece, and Romania. Petroleum and natural gas are primarily exploited in Romania, but deposits have also been found in Yugoslavia, Albania, and Turkey. Bauxite is mainly extracted in Greece. Gold is produced in small amounts in Yugoslavia; copper in Yugoslavia, Bulgaria and Turkey; and nickel in Greece and Albania.

The people. Five major ethnic groups and several scattered minorities are found in the Balkan Peninsula. Southern Slavs, embracing Slovenes, Croats, and Serbs, are the most numerous. They live mainly in the west central and east central parts of the peninsula. In the northeast are Romanians; in the southeast Turks; in the southwest, Albanians; and in the south Greeks. Gypsies and Balkan Jews are minorities. The birth rate is about 20–25 per 1,000 population, and the death rates about 10 per 1,000. Albania and Turkey had the highest annual growth rate in the 1980s at about 2 percent. Largely because of the rural character of the population, the paucity of large towns, and the absence of industrial conurbations, the population density averages only about 235 persons per sq mi (90 sq km) throughout the Balkans, except for the Thrace region of Turkey, where it is about 490 per sq mi. The largest cities are Istanbul, 2,800,000; Bucharest, 1,950,000; Belgrade, 1,200,000; Sofia, 1,070,000; Athens, 886,000; and Zagreb, 770,000.

In addition to Greek and Turkish, the languages of the peninsula include Slavic languages spoken by the Bulgarians and southern Slavs of Yugoslavia; Albanian, a mixture of Illyrian, Thracian, Latin, Slavic, and Turkish elements; and Romanian, a Romance language. Before World War II a majority of the Balkan peoples belonged to the Greek Orthodox church, Roman Catholics were found mostly in eastern and northern Yugoslavia and northern Romania, and Muslims inhabited Albania and Turkey. After the war the suppression of religious practices in the Communist Balkan countries made religious distinctions less important, but about half of Yugoslavia's people are Orthodox and a third Roman Catholics. Greek Orthodoxy and Islām still predominate in Greece and Turkey, respectively.

Economy. Greece and Turkey have market economies and Albania, Bulgaria, Romania, and Yugoslavia have planned economies. The aggregate gross national product (GNP) of the Balkans, excluding Albania, was about $256,240,000,000 in 1980. The GNP per capita was about $3,000. The agricultural sector averaged about 45 percent of the GNP and the industrial sector about 30 percent, with the services sector accounting for the remainder. The labour force is similarly apportioned.

The relatively poor soil of the mountains and foothills that characterize the Balkans accounts for the predominance of livestock over field crops in many regions. The principal meat animals are pigs, cattle, and sheep; poultry are also important. In low-lying land near water, domestic buffaloes are common. In the plains, various crops are grown, often under irrigation. These include corn (maize), wheat, barley, rye, cotton, tobacco, hemp, and flax. Bulgaria, Romania, and Yugoslavia specialize in the production of fruits and wines. Currants, grapes, olives, and citrus fruits are grown in Greece.

The major industries include textiles, food and wine, farm and other machinery, chemicals, petroleum products, and ship building. Bulgaria produces the largest amount of electricity per capita annually, followed by Romania, Greece and Yugoslavia, Albania, and Turkey. Half of the total energy produced in Albania, Turkey, and Yugoslavia, and about 10–15 percent of that in Greece and Romania, is hydroelectric. Tourism is a vital and growing sector for all the Balkan countries, especially Greece, Yugoslavia, and Turkey. Prices of hotels, restaurants, and related tourist services are relatively low.

From 1960 to 1980 there was a gradual shift of labour away from the agricultural sector toward industry and services. Government controls have slowed this process in Albania, Bulgaria, and Romania; but it has progressed more rapidly in Greece, Turkey, and Yugoslavia. Emigration from these same countries during the 1960s and '70s, mostly to West Germany, helped alleviate the problem of surplus labour in local industry, but labour-intensive industries in these countries now experience a shortage of workers.

Bulgaria, Albania, Romania, and Yugoslavia have state-operated banking systems. Greece and Turkey have central and commercial banks. Greece is a member of the European Economic Community (EEC) and Turkey is an associate member, and Bulgaria and Romania are members of the Council of Mutual Economic Assistance (Comecon); Yugoslavia is associated with both, and Albania with neither.

The Balkan Peninsula is a gateway between eastern and central Europe and the Middle East. On both sides of the peninsula, ports such as Constanța, Varna, and Istanbul on the Black Sea and Trieste, Rijeka, and Dubrovnik on the Adriatic are important for sea transportation. The Greek ports of Kavålla, Pátrai, Piraeus, and Thessaloníki in the south are also important. The Danube, the Maritsa, and the Vardar rivers are continously navigable. Major highways link Belgrade with eastern and western Europe, with Thessaloníki in the south and Istanbul in the east; local networks connect with the main international routes. Each country has its own government-operated railroad, and all have airports providing domestic and international services, except Albania which has international but no internal service.

Major exports include vegetables, fruits, wine, tobacco, cotton, textiles, machinery, and livestock. Principal imports are petroleum products, iron, machinery, tractors, combines, and transportation equipment. Greece and Turkey conduct about half of their international trade with the U.S. and only about one-tenth with socialist economies. Up to half of the trade of the communist countries is with other communist regimes.

Administrative and social conditions. Bulgaria, Romania, Yugoslavia, and Albania are socialist states dominated by their own Communist parties. Greece and Turkey are republics with some socialist tendencies. Each country has a constitution drafted after World War II. Judicial systems in the Balkans vary, but most have criminal and civil codes. Greece and Turkey are members of the North Atlantic Treaty Organization (NATO), Bulgaria and Romania are members of the Warsaw Pact, Albania has been relatively nonaligned since it broke ties with China after Mao Tse-tung's death in 1978, and Yugoslavia is aloof from Moscow and more or less independent.

The standard of living in the Balkans has improved considerably since the 1960s and is still rising. Life expectancy averages 70 years. Infant mortality ranges from 10 to 15 per 1,000 live births in Bulgaria and Greece, to 30 per 1,000 in Romania and Yugoslavia, and 90 to 130 per 1,000 in Albania and Turkey, respectively. The availability of medical care and health conditions are relatively good in most of the Balkan countries, but Turkey and Albania have considerably higher ratios of population to facilities and personnel. Major diseases in rural areas are gastrointestinal and infectious, while in the cities traffic accidents, cardiovascular diseases, and mental illnesses remain serious problems. In most of the Balkans housing is subsidized by the government, but in Greece and Turkey, and to some extent in Yugoslavia, there is both subsidized and private housing.

Education plays an important role in the Balkans. The average enrollment ratio in secondary schools is more than 80 percent, although Turkey's enrollment is only about half the average. More than four-fifths of the population of the region, on the average, is literate, although in Turkey, the fraction is much lower. Both Greece and Turkey suffer a drain of scientists and professionals to the United States, the United Kingdom, West Germany, and France. Social security systems are well developed in most of the Balkans, and provide housing, inexpensive or free medical services, child care, and pensions. The press is government-controlled except for Turkey and Greece. The broadcast media are government-operated throughout the Balkans as in most of Europe.

Balkan cultural life is greatly varied and each region has its traditional customs. Among shared traditions are music, dance, and slivovitz (plum brandy). Fine woodwork, ceramic ware, handicrafts, embroidery, and a variety of national costumes have long traditions. Architecture reflects the numerous influences—Slavic, Mediterranean, Asian, West European, Christian, and Muslim—that have borne on the region and can be seen in the many surviving cathedrals, churches, mosques, and other architectural splendours. Many of the ancient customs have survived through oral rather than literary tradition.

History. The Balkans emerge from prehistory in classical times, with records of civilization in Greece and contacts between various states and peoples of the central and northern regions of the peninsula. The latter were eventually incorporated into the Roman Empire, while the eastern half of the peninsula became the Byzantine Empire. The Slavs began to penetrate the peninsula at the end of the 5th century, the Avars made incursions southward beginning in the 6th century, and the Bulgars arrived from the Volga region in the 7th century. The 11th century saw further invasions by the Pechenegs and the Kumans.

At the beginning of the 13th century, Greek Byzantine rule was replaced by Roman, except in Epirus. The Ottoman Turks began their onslaught on the Balkans in the 14th century, and by the end of the 15th century they occupied the entire peninsula, except for some isolated coastal areas. Turkish power began to decline in the 18th century, and the partition of the Balkan dominions into local states or colonies of the great powers of Europe drew increasing international attention. Greece was recognized as independent in 1829, and the state of Serbia was created in 1830. In the half century after 1830 three new Balkan states appeared: Romania, Montenegro, and Bulgaria.

The Bulgarian occupation of eastern Rumelia

in 1885 was followed by the Serbo-Bulgarian war, and at the turn of the century the Balkans were increasingly the scene of international conflict. In 1908 Austria-Hungary annexed Bosnia-Hercegovina and in 1912–13 the Balkan league of Greece, Serbia, Bulgaria, and Montenegro attacked and defeated Turkey the first of two conflicts known as the Balkan Wars. As a consequence Ottoman rule and intervention by Austria-Hungary in the Balkans was effectively ended. After World War I, a Serb-Croat-Slovene kingdom of the South Slavs was constituted. Italy received the extreme northwest coast of the Balkan peninsula including Rijeka, as well as some of the Adriatic islands. Large population exchanges were carried out in an attempt to stabilize the new frontiers. Romania and Yugoslavia allied with Czechoslavakia in 1921 to counter foreign threats, and in 1934 a new Balkan Pact allied Greece, Yugoslavia, Turkey, and Romania.

After World War II the Allied peace treaty with Italy, Romania, and Bulgaria (concluded in Paris in 1947) introduced the present frontiers. Longtime Soviet support for local communist leaders and groups in the region was instrumental in the establishment of the post-war communist governments of Albania, Bulgaria, Romania, and Yugoslavia. Yugoslavia broke with the Soviet bloc in 1948, and in 1961 the Albanians expelled their Soviet advisers and allied themselves with China, an association that lasted until 1978. Bulgaria and Romania were founding members of Comecon in 1949. Greece and Turkey became members of NATO in 1952.

Balkh, *velāyat* (province) in northern Afghanistan, 4,569 sq mi (11,833 sq km) in area, with its capital at Mazār-e Sharīf. It is bounded by the Turkmen and Uzbek S.S.R.'s on the north and the *velāyāt* of Samangān on the east, and Jowzjān on the west. The province consists of two contrasting parts: the north is a flat plain, the south a mountainous area drained by the Balkh River. Agriculture

Shrine of Khvājeh Abū Naṣr Pārsā, 16th century, Balkh, Afg.

K. Horold—Bavaria Verlag

is the principal activity, with an irrigated, highly fertile district near the capital, producing grain, fruit, and cotton. There is some industry in Mazār-e Sharīf.

A few miles west of the capital is Balkh (Vazīrābād), a place of historic importance and generally agreed to represent the ancient Bactra, capital of Bactria (*q.v.*). As capital of Khorāsān under the ʿAbbāsids and Sāmānids, it was a noted centre of learning. Sacked by the Mongol invader Genghis Khan in 1220, and again, a century later, by the Turkic conqueror Timur (Tamerlane), it never regained its former glory. The shrine of Khvājeh Abū Naṣr Pārsā is a remnant of its historic past. Pop. (1982 est.) settled pop. 609,590, mainly Uzbek, with some Tadzhik and Turkmen.

Balkhash, also spelled BALCHAŠ, city, Dzhezkazgan *oblast* (administrative region), Kazakh Soviet Socialist Republic, a landing on the northern shore of Lake Balkhash. A major centre of nonferrous (copper, predominantly, and molybdenum) metallurgy, it came into being in 1937 in connection with the construction of large copper-smelting works for the Kounrad mines to the north. Fish canning is the second industry. There is a botanical garden of the Kazakh S.S.R. Academy of Sciences. Pop. (1983 est.) 80,000.

Balkhash, Lake, Russian OZERO BALKHASH, also spelled OZERO BALCHAŠ, lake, situated in the eastern part of the Kazakh Soviet Socialist Republic, U.S.S.R., contained in the vast Balkhash–Alakol Basin, 1,115 ft (340 m) above sea level and 600 mi (966 km) east of the Aral Sea. It is 376 mi long from west to east. Its area varies within significant limits, depending on the water balance. In years in which there is an abundance of water, as at the beginning of the 20th century and in the decade 1958–69, the area reaches 6,900 to 7,300 sq mi (18,000–19,000 sq km). In drought-afflicted periods, however (as at the end of the 19th century and in the 1930s and 1940s), the area of the lake decreases to 6,000–6,300 sq mi. Such changes in area are accompanied by changes in the water level of about 10 ft. Such variability is caused by the structure of the basin and the lake's location. Jutting far out into the lake is the Sarymsek Peninsula (Poluostrov), which divides Balkhash into two separate hydrological parts: a western part, wide and shallow, and an eastern part, narrow and relatively deep. Accordingly, the width of the lake changes from 46 to 17 mi in the western part and 6 to 12 mi in the eastern part. The depth of the western part does not exceed 36 ft, whereas the eastern part reaches 85 ft. The two parts of the lake are united by a narrow strait, the Uzynaral, with a depth of about 21 ft.

The large Ili River, flowing in from the south, spills into the western part of the lake and contributes 75–80 percent of the total influx into the lake. Only such small rivers as the Karatal, Aksu, Ayaguz, and Lepsa feed the eastern part of the lake. With almost equal areas in both parts of the lake, this situation creates a continuous flow of water from the western section to the eastern section. The water of the western part is almost fresh (total mineralization 0.74 gram per litre) and suitable for industrial use and consumption; the water of the eastern part, however, is salty (about five grams per litre).

The east bank of the lake bears traces of a historically recent union (perhaps occurring only two or three hundred years ago) of the Balkhash Basin with the basin of Ozero (Lake) Alakol in the Dzungarian Gate to the east. The similarity between the fauna of Lake Balkhash and that of the Tarim River Basin in Central Asia and the dissimilarity of the faunas of the Aral Sea and Lake Balkhash suggest that formerly Lake Balkhash, through Lakes Alakol and Ai-pi, went into the system of lakes that formerly filled the Turfan Depression in the T'ien Shan (Celestial Mountains) and had no connection with the Aral Sea to the west.

The north banks of the lake are high and rocky, with clear-cut traces of ancient terraces. Farther north a dry steppe passes into the undulating Kazakh Plain. The south banks are low and sandy, and wide belts of them are covered with thickets of reeds and numerous small lakes. The low-lying banks, periodically flooded by the waters of the lake, are being continually transformed into the desert sands of the Sary-Ishikotrau and, further away, into the foothills of the Dzhungarsky Alatau.

Extremely harsh continental conditions prevail and significantly affect the whole regime of the lake. The average (1930–67) air temperature in the western part is 44° F (7° C), with an annual range of from 80° F (June) to −1° F (Jan.; 27° C to −18° C) and, in the eastern part, 39° F (4° C) with a range of from 72° F (June) to −13° F (Jan.; 22° C to −25° C). The water temperature in the western part of the lake is 50° F (10° C); in the eastern part it is 48° F (9° C). Average precipitation is approximately 17 in. (430 mm). The predominant winds are from the northwest (in the west) and from the northeast (in the east). They are usually fairly strong, giving rise to constantly choppy water. The lake remains frozen from the end of November to the beginning of April.

Carbonates predominate in the ground deposits of the lake. The fauna of the lake is rich, especially in regions dense with reeds. Different types of gulls and ducks and a large number of cormorants are most frequently found here. Now and then one can spot swans and pink pelicans. Among the brushwood on the banks, pheasants and partridges can be seen. Wild boars still forage among the reeds, and wolves, foxes, and hares inhabit the thickets. In the past tigers were not infrequent here; the last one was killed in the 1940s.

Twenty species of fish inhabit the lake, of which six are peculiar to the lake itself. The remainder were introduced to the lake by man and include the sazan, sturgeon, eastern bream, pike, and the Aral barbel. The main food fish are the sazan, pike, and Balkhash perch. Bottom life is poor, and the most important sources of food for the fish are benthos (Chironomidae), zooplankton, and the larvae of Tendipedidae. Pollution is only a problem insofar as it results from natural biological processes or enters the lake via the rivers.

The economic importance of the lake has greatly increased during the 20th century. Most significant is the fishing and fish breeding begun in the 1930s and now rapidly developing. A regular shipping service with a large freight turnover has developed. Of great importance to the economic development of the region was the construction of the Balkhash copper-refining plant, around which the large city of Balkhash grew on the north shore of the lake. A railway line connects Balkhash with all the major centres of Kazakhstan and Central Asia. Cattle breeding and rice growing in the lower reaches of the Ili River are of major economic importance to the region. In 1970 the Kapchagay hydroelectric power station began operations on the Ili River. As its reservoir began to fill, the regime of Lake Balkhash began to change radically.

balkline billiards, group of billiard games played with three balls (red, white, and white with a spot) on a table without pockets, upon which lines are drawn parallel to all cushions and usually either 14 or 18 inches (36 or 46 centimetres) away from them. The object of the games is to score caroms by driving a cue ball against both object balls. The eight areas between the lines and cushions are called balks, and when both object balls are within one of them, a player may score only once or twice (depending on the game played) before driving at least one of the balls out of the balk. The large central area of the table is not a balk, and scoring there is unrestricted.

The balkline game was devised to prevent expert players from playing the balls into a corner and scoring indefinitely on a series of simple, soft shots. As a further precaution, squares (anchors) were drawn at the intersection of the balklines and the cushions. The anchors are treated as separate balks, and scoring within them is similarly restricted. This keeps a player from manoeuvring the object balls to a cushion and slightly to either side of a balkline, thus circumventing the balk rule and scoring easily.

Principal varieties of balkline billiards are 18.1 and 18.2—requiring lines 18 inches from the cushions and allowing one and two shots, respectively, within a balk—and 14.1 and 14.2, with 14-inch lines and the same restrictions on shots. Other games are played occasionally, such as 28.2, with one line down the centre of the table parallel to the long cushions and with lines parallel to each of the short cushions, thus marking the whole table into balks and allowing no free centre area.

ball, spherical or ovoid object for throwing, hitting, or kicking in various sports and games, used from prehistoric times. The ball is mentioned in the earliest recorded literatures and finds a place in some of the oldest graphic representations.

Greek ball players, relief on a statue base from Athens, *c.* 510 BC; in the National Archaeological Museum, Athens
By courtesy of the Athens National Archaeological Museum, TAP Service

Homer and other early writers reported that the ancient Greeks found ball play particularly appealing and that it came to be much valued as a means of giving grace and elasticity to the figure. Some form of ball game is portrayed on early Egyptian monuments. Even among the Romans, who disliked participation sports, ball play was extremely popular. The Roman baths set aside an apartment for ball play, and many gentlemen had ball courts in their private villas. The ancient Roman ball was usually made of leather strips sewn together and filled with various materials. The smallest, the *harpastum,* was a hard ball stuffed with feathers. The largest, the *follis,* contained an air-filled bladder, similar to a modern soccer ball or basketball.

In many early games the ball was simply thrown back and forth among a group of individuals, but there were also genuine team games and competitions among the ancient Greeks. Ball games were especially popular at Sparta.

One early Greek game known as *episkyros* involved two teams of equal numbers; between them a white line was laid out, and, at some distance behind each team, another line was marked. The play consisted in throwing the ball back and forth until one team in the exchange was finally forced back over its rear line.

Ball playing also is of great antiquity in western Europe, and an early form of lacrosse was well established among the American Indians before Columbus sailed the Atlantic.

As skills required in games using the ball alone, and more particularly in games involving the use of various implements for striking it, were developed and refined, balls became specialized and available in a multiplicity of types. The weight and circumference of various balls have been changed over the years as the other equipment and rules of the individual sports changed in order to increase the interest of the spectators. An example is the change made in the American football, with the popularization of the forward pass, from the egg-shaped rugby ball to a more elongated shape that was easier to throw with accuracy. This variation changed the sport from a running game to one in which the forward pass also played an exciting role.

Ball, Albert (b. Aug. 21, 1896, Nottingham, Nottinghamshire, Eng.—d. May 7, 1917, Annoeullin, near Lens, Fr.), British fighter ace during World War I who won 43 victories in air combat.

Ball was educated at Trent College, which he left in 1913. On the outbreak of World War I, he joined the army. During the summer of 1915 he learned to fly at his own expense at Hendon, Middlesex, obtaining his pilot's certificate in October 1915, and transferred to the Royal Flying Corps. Having served in France as an army cooperation pilot from February 1916, he was posted in June to No. 11 fighter squadron (flying Nieuport Scout airplanes) and later to No. 60 and 56 squadrons (flying S.E.5s). In spite of his skill and daring, Captain Ball was shot down and killed over Annoeullin, near Lens, in 1917, possibly by gunfire from the ground, but exactly how he was killed is not definitely known. He won the Victoria Cross and many other honours.

Ball, Sir Alexander John, 1ST BARONET (b. 1757, Gloucestershire, Eng.—d. Oct. 25, 1809, Malta), rear admiral, a close friend of Admiral Lord Nelson, who directed the blockade of Malta (1798–1800) and was civil commissioner (governor) of the island (1802–09).

Ball served under Adm. Sir George Rodney in the West Indies and was present at his great victory over the French off Dominica (April 12, 1782). Promoted to captain in 1783, he did not receive his first command until 1790. On May 20, 1798, he saved Lord Nelson's flagship from running ashore after being dismasted in a storm, and the two became close friends.

On Feb. 9, 1799, while he was blockading Malta, the island's legislature elected him president and commander in chief. After the French had surrendered Malta (September 1800), the British Admiralty withheld Ball from naval service, despite Nelson's plea in his favour. He was created a baronet in 1801 and then was made governor of Malta, where he remained the rest of his life. He was praised highly by Samuel Taylor Coleridge, who was his secretary on Malta in 1804.

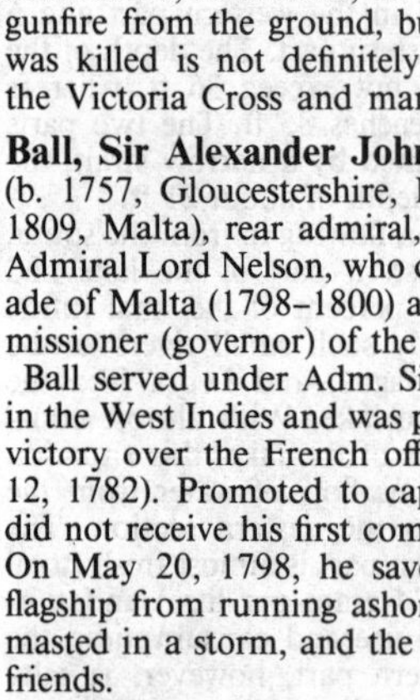

Sir Alexander Ball, detail of an oil painting by H.W. Pickersgill; in the National Maritime Museum, Greenwich Hospital Collection
By courtesy of the National Maritime Museum, Greenwich Hospital Collection

Ball, Hugo (b. Feb. 22, 1886, Pirmasens, Ger.—d. Sept. 14, 1927, St. Abbondio, Switz.), writer, actor, and dramatist, a harsh social critic, and an early critical biographer of German novelist Hermann Hesse (*Hermann Hesse, sein Leben and sein Werk,* 1927).

He studied sociology and philosophy at the universities of Munich and Heidelberg (1906–07) and went to Berlin (1910) to become an actor. He was a founder of the Dadaist movement in art.

A staunch pacifist, Ball left Germany during World War I and moved to neutral Switzerland (1916). His more important works include *Kritik der deutschen Intelligenz* (1919) and *Die Flucht aus der Zeit* (1927; "The Flight from Time").

Ball, John (d. July 15, 1381, St. Albans, Hertfordshire, Eng.), one of the leaders of the Peasant's Revolt in England, formerly a priest at York and at Colchester. Excommunicated *c.* 1366 for his inflammatory sermons advocating a classless society, Ball continued to preach in open marketplaces or wherever he could. After 1376 he was frequently imprisoned, and at the outbreak of the rebellion (June 1381) he was rescued from prison at Maidstone by Kentish rebels whom he accompanied to London. There he incited a crowd at Blackheath with the popular text, "When Adam dalf [dug] and Eve span [spun], Wo was thanne a gentilman?" An account in the *Anonimalle Chronicle,* given by a witness of the London events, states that he urged the killing of lords and prelates. After the collapse of the rebellion, he was tried and hanged at St. Albans. Knowledge of his career is derived almost entirely from prejudiced chroniclers. Froissart calls him the mad priest of Kent. Ball is the subject of William Morris' romance, *The Dream of John Ball.*

Ball, Lucille (Désirée) (b. Aug. 6, 1911, Jamestown, N.Y., U.S.), radio and motion picture actress and longtime comedy star of U.S. television. Her program "I Love Lucy" was a situation comedy series first telecast by the Columbia Broadcasting System (CBS) in 1951. In various guises the program was broadcast until 1956, and again in the periods 1961–65 and 1968–74.

Young Lucille set her mind early on a theatrical career, and in her teens she alternated between Broadway tryouts in New York City and returning home to western New York State to attend high school. She became a model, which, after several years, led to minor roles in motion pictures, beginning in 1933. After a decade of this more substantial parts materialized. In 1947 she took the part of a harebrained housewife in a radio series on CBS, and this brought her wide notice.

In 1940 Ball had married a popular bandleader, Desi Arnaz. She later helped create the television comedy series "I Love Lucy," in which she and Arnaz played a husband and wife constantly befallen by outlandish encounters and mishaps. The show was enormously popular, both in its network run and in reruns, and its influence on the situation comedy was felt for years thereafter.

Ball, Thomas (b. June 3, 1819, Charlestown, Mass., U.S.—d. Dec. 11, 1911, Montclair, N.J.), sculptor whose work had a marked influence on monumental art in the U.S., especially in New England.

Ball began his career as a wood engraver and miniaturist. An accomplished musician, his work includes many early cabinet busts of musicians. Among his best known works are an equestrian statue of George Washington (Public Garden, Boston), and the Lincoln "Emancipation" group (Washington, D.C.). He published his autobiography, *My Threescore Years and Ten,* in 1891.

ball-and-socket joint, also called SPHEROIDAL JOINT, in vertebrate anatomy, a joint in which the rounded surface of a bone moves within a depression on another bone, allowing greater freedom of movement than any other kind of joint. It is most highly developed in the large shouder and hip joints of mammals, including humans, in which it provides swing for the arms and legs in various directions and also spin of those limbs upon the more stationary bones.

To make the best use of the Britannica, consult the INDEX *first*

ball bearing, one of the two members of the class of rolling, or so-called antifriction, bearings (the other member of the class is the roller bearing). The function of a ball bearing is to connect two machine members that move relative to one another in such a manner that the frictional resistance to motion is minimal. In many applications one of the members is a rotating shaft and the other a fixed housing.

There are three main parts in a ball bearing: two grooved, ringlike races and a number of balls. The races are of the same width but different diameters; the smaller one, fitting inside the larger one and having a groove on its outside surface, is attached on its inside surface to one of the machine members. The larger race has a groove on its inside surface and is attached on its outside surface to the other machine member. The balls fill the space between the two races and roll with negligible friction in the grooves. The balls are loosely restrained and separated by means of a retainer or cage.

The most common ball bearing, with one row of balls, is usually classified as a radial ball bearing, but its capacity for carrying an axial, or thrust, load may exceed its radial capacity. The angular-contact bearing has one side of the outer-race groove cut away to allow the insertion of more balls, which enables the bearing to carry large axial loads in one direction only. Such bearings are usually used in pairs so that high axial loads can be carried in both directions. The clearances in a single-row ball bearing are so small that no appreciable misalignment of a shaft relative to a housing can be accommodated. One type of self-aligning bearing has two rows of balls and a spherical inner surface on the outer race. For pure thrust loads there are ball thrust bearings that consist of two grooved plates with balls between. The outstanding advantage of a ball bearing over a sliding bearing is its low starting friction. At speeds high enough to develop a load-carrying oil film, however, the friction in a sliding bearing may be less than in a ball bearing.

ball cactus, any of 25 species of the genus *Notocactus,* family Cactaceae, native in grasslands of South America. Small, globose to cylindroid, they are commonly cultivated as potted plants. *N. scopa* and *N. leninghausii,* silver ball and golden ball cacti respectively, are most common and are valued for their woolly hair. These and other hairy *Notocactus* species have small, often yellow to red flowers, sometimes only about 1 centimetre (1/2 inch) in diameter. Another group, not hairy, has larger flowers, to about 6 cm.

Ball cactus (*Notocactus*)
G.E. Nicholson

ball lightning, also called GLOBE LIGHTNING, aerial phenomenon that occurs as a moving luminous sphere several inches in diameter. It usually occurs near the ground during thunderstorms, may be red, orange, or yellow in colour, and is often accompanied by a hissing sound and distinct odour. It lasts only a few seconds and dies out suddenly, either silently or explosively. Ball lightning has been observed to cause damage by burning or melting. Its relation, if any, to common lightning is uncertain. Its causes are unknown, but among the explanations of ball lightning are the following: air or gas behaving abnormally; high-density plasma; an air vortex containing luminous gases; and microwave radiation within a plasma shell.

Balla, Giacomo (b. July 24, 1871, Turin, Italy—d. March 1958, Rome), artist and founding member of the Futurist movement in painting.

Balla studied art in Paris, where he was greatly influenced by the Pointillist painters. Settling in Rome in 1901, he gradually came under the influence of the Milanese poet Filippo Marinetti. In 1909 Marinetti launched the literary movement he called Futurism, an attempt to revitalize Italian culture by embracing the power of modern science and technology. In 1910 Balla and other Italian artists published the "Technical Manifesto of Futurist Painting," which adopted Marinetti's principles and urged painters to use art as a weapon to destroy the old social and cultural order.

"Dynamism of a Dog on a Leash," oil on canvas by Giacomo Balla, 1912; in the Buffalo Fine Arts Academy
By courtesy of George F. Goodyear and the Buffalo Fine Arts Academy

Unlike most Futurists, Balla was a lyrical painter, unconcerned with modern machines or violence. "The Street Light—Study of Light" (1909; Museum of Modern Art, New York City), for example, is merely a dynamic depiction of light. In later works, such as "Dynamism of a Dog on a Leash" (1912; Buffalo Fine Arts Academy, Buffalo), he established as his main concerns the principle of simultaneity (the rendering of motion by simultaneously showing many aspects of a moving object) along with the abstract treatment of rhythm, light, and colour.

During World War I Balla began to compose paintings with large, simple planes of colour. After World War I he remained faithful to the Futurist style long after its other practitioners had abandoned it. Gradually, however, he reverted to a more traditional style.

Ballaarat (Australia): *see* Ballarat.

ballad, form of short narrative folk song the distinctive style of which crystallized in Europe during the late Middle Ages. The ballad has been preserved as a musical and literary form up to modern times.

A brief treatment of the ballad follows. For full treatment, *see* MACROPAEDIA: Literature, The Art of.

Typically, the folk ballad (or standard ballad) tells a compact tale in a style that achieves bold, sensational effects through deliberate starkness and abruptness. Despite a rigid economy of narrative, it employs a variety of devices to prolong highly charged moments in the story and to thicken the emotional atmosphere, the most common being a frequent repetition of some key word, line, or phrase. Any consequent bareness of texture finds ample compensation in this dramatic rhetoric.

Because ballads have thrived among unlettered people, and are freshly created from memory at each performance, they are subject to constant variation in both text and tune; tradition has preserved them by re-creation, not by ossification. They exhibit fascination with supernatural happenings; with the fate of lovers (usually, though not always, tragic); with crime and its punishment; with apocryphal legends (the chief stuff of religious balladry); with historical disasters (usually matters of regional rather than national importance); with sensational acts of God and man; with the deeds of outlaws and badmen; and with the hazards of such occupations as seafaring and railroading.

The ballad genre in its present form can scarcely have existed before about 1100. The oldest ballad in Francis Child's definitive compilation, *The English and Scottish Popular Ballads* (1882–98), dates from 1300, but as an oral form the ballad did not need to be written down in order to be performed or preserved. Indeed, to ask for the date of a ballad displays a misunderstanding of the very nature of balladry. Behind each recorded ballad can be detected the workings of tradition upon some earlier form of the same work.

Some scholars have argued that ballads are the result of collective composition (the "communal school," led by F.B. Gummere and G.L. Kittredge), others that each is the work of an individual composer (the "individualist school," led by W.J. Courthope, Andrew Lang, Louise Pound). The tunes are based on the modes of medieval plainsong, not on the chromatic scales of modern music, and most consist of 16 bars with two beats per measure. Musical variation, however, is as frequent as textual variation, and since the singer performs solo, or plays the accompanying instrument, the performance need not keep rigidly to set duration or stress, and the balladeer may introduce grace notes to accommodate hypermetric syllables and may lengthen notes for emphasis.

There are significant balladries in England, Scotland, Ireland, the United States, France, Denmark, Germany, Russia, Greece, and Spain. Their formal characteristics vary from one area to another: British and U.S. ballads, for instance, are invariably rhymed and divided into stanzas (strophes). The Russian ballads (*byliny*) are unrhymed and unstrophic; the Spanish *romances* and the Danish *viser* employ assonance rather than rhyme, but the latter are strophic while the former are not.

In addition to folk ballads, other types may be mentioned that are more properly relevant to the history of poetry than to that of true balladry. Minstrel ballads call attention to themselves and to the performer in a way quite foreign to the strict impersonality of the folk ballads and are the work of professional entertainers employed in wealthy households from the Middle Ages until the 17th century. Many of these pieces glorify noble families. The older Robin Hood ballads, celebrating traditional yeoman virtues, are also examples of minstrel propaganda. Broadside ballads are urban adaptations of the folk ballad, and are the work of hack poets commemorating some sensational item of topical interest. They appeared on crudely printed handbills (called broadsheets or broadsides) in the 16th to 19th century. Sophisticated imitations of broadside ballads, usually penned for purposes of jocular satire, were popular in the 18th and 19th centuries, enjoying a special vogue after the publication in 1765 of Thomas Percy's *Reliques of Ancient English Poetry.* The modern literary ballad recalls in its rhythmic and narrative elements the traditions of folk balladry.

ballad horn (musical instrument): *see* mellophone.

ballad opera, characteristic English type of comic opera, originating in the 18th century and featuring farcical or extravaganza plots. The music was mainly confined to songs or interludes interspersed in spoken dialogue. It was based at first on ballads or folk songs to which new words were adapted; later, tunes were borrowed from popular operas, or music was occasionally newly composed.

One of the earliest and the most famous of ballad operas is *The Beggar's Opera* (1728), which is at once a spoof on Italian serious opera and a satire on the morality of contemporary politicians. Its text is by John Gay, with music adapted by John Pepusch. It had many imitators. Other composers adapting or writing music for ballad operas included Thomas Arne, Charles Dibdin, Stephen Storace, and, in the 19th century, Sir Henry Bishop.

The ballad opera developed into the light opera of Gilbert and Sullivan and, indirectly through musical comedy, into the modern musical. It also influenced the evolution of the similar German Singspiel in the 18th century. Several early ballad operas were successfully revived in the 20th century. Modern works directly influenced by the ballad opera include Vaughan Williams' opera *Hugh the Drover.*

ballad revival, the interest in folk poetry evinced within literary circles, especially in England and Germany, in the 18th century. Actually, it was not a revival but a new discovery and appreciation of the merits of popular poetry, formerly ignored or despised by scholars and sophisticated writers. The trend that began in England in 1711 with the publication of Joseph Addison's three *Spectator* papers cautiously defending "the darling Songs of the common People" crystallized in 1765 with the publication of Thomas Percy's *Reliques of Ancient English Poetry,* a collection of English and Scottish traditional ballads. The *Reliques* and a flood of subsequent collections, including Sir Walter Scott's *Minstrelsy of the Scottish Border* (1802), had great impact and provided the English Romantic poets with an alternative to outworn Neoclassical models as a source of inspiration. The impact was not reciprocal; literary ballads had no effect on the art or production of oral balladry, which was already in decline. In Germany the influential philosopher-critic Johann Gottfried von Herder conferred an almost mystical distinction on the ballad as the genuine expression of the spirit of the folk. The German collection of lyrical and narrative folk songs *Des Knaben Wunderhorn* (1805–08; "The Boy's Magic Horn"), edited by Clemens Brentano and Achim von Arnim, was the dominant influence on German poetry throughout the 19th century.

ballade, one of several *formes fixes* ("fixed forms") in French lyric poetry and song, cultivated particularly in the 14th and 15th centuries (*compare* rondeau; virelai). Strictly, the ballade consists of three stanzas and a shortened final dedicatory stanza. All the stanzas have the same rhyme scheme and the same final line, which thus forms a refrain (R). Each of the three main stanzas is built in three sections, the first two of which have the same rhyme scheme. The total form can be expressed:

I	II	III	E
a a b R	a a b R	a a b R	b R

The final dedicatory stanza is called the prince (because that is usually its first word) or the envoi. The *chanson royale* is similar to the ballade but has five main stanzas.

The general shape of the ballade is present in the poetry of many ages. The odes of the Greek poet Pindar (5th century BC) have the same stanza form with their strophe, antistrophe, and epode. Much of the art song of the 16th century in Germany is cast in a similar form, though normally without the envoi, or the refrain line; when in Richard Wagner's music drama *Die Meistersinger* (1868) Fritz Kothner defines a *Bar* (a poetic form) as consisting of several *Gesetze* ("stanzas"), each made up of two *Stollen* (*a a*) and an *Abgesang* (*b*), he is accurately describing a historical reality. But in its purest form the ballade is found only in France and England.

The immediate precursors of the ballade can be found in the songs of the troubadours (poet-musicians using the Provençal language), which frequently employ the *a a b* stanza pattern with an envoi. They normally have more than three stanzas, however, and the refrain line, if there is one, is often not the last line of the stanza. In the later 13th century the standard form appears more and more frequently in the French songs of the trouvères (the northern counterparts of the troubadours).

The songs of the trouvères and troubadours are monophonic (having one melody line or voice part). The history of the polyphonic ballade begins with Guillaume de Machaut, the leading French poet and composer of the 14th century. He wrote more songs in this than in any other form. In his work can be seen the gradual emergence of a standard manner of setting a ballade and in particular the convention of closing the second *a* section with a musical epilogue that is repeated at the end of the stanza.

The ballade was the most expansive of the *formes fixes,* and Machaut used it to express the loftiest emotions. The texts more often contained elaborate symbolism and classical references than did those of the other *formes fixes.* Later in the 14th century, the ballade was used for the most solemn and formal songs: the celebration of special patrons, the commemoration of magnificent occasions, the declarations of love in the highest style.

In the 15th century the form became less popular. The foremost Burgundian composer, Guillaume Dufay, wrote few ballades, almost all of which can be connected with specific occasions and all early in his life. Later in the century, musical ballades are rare except in the work of English composers. Among the two greatest songwriters of the later 15th century, Antoine Busnois wrote no ballades, and Jean d'Okeghem wrote just one—on the occasion of the death of another famed song composer, Gilles Binchois, in 1460.

The form gradually disappeared among the poets too, only to reappear spasmodically in the work of later writers as a conscious archaism. But there are fine examples from the 15th century among the work of Alain Chartier, Charles d'Orléans, and Molinet; and François Villon's best known poem is a ballade with the refrain line "Mais où sont les neiges d'antan?" ("But where are the snows of yester-year?").

Ballance, John (b. March 27, 1839, Glenavy, County Antrim, N.Ire.—d. April 27, 1893, Wellington, N.Z.), prime minister of New Zealand (1891–93) who unified the Liberal Party, which held power for 20 years; he also played a major role in the enactment of social welfare legislation.

After working as an ironmonger in Birmingham, Eng., the self-educated Ballance emigrated to Wanganui, N.Z., in 1865. There he was editor of the *Wanganui Herald* and fought against the native Maoris. Entering Parliament in 1875, he advocated abolition of provincial governments. As colonial treasurer in 1878, he introduced a land tax to raise revenue more equitably. As minister of lands, defense, and native affairs in 1884–87, he tried to shift land ownership from monopolists to small farmers and to retain crown land while preventing abuses in the sale of Maori land.

During his term as prime minister, Ballance imposed progressive land and income taxes and gained for the government the right to repurchase private land for development. He combatted the lingering depression by limiting government borrowing and won reduction of life membership in the upper house to a seven-year term, curtailing the power of his opponents. His Cabinet was noted for its distinguished ministers, including William Pember Reeves, who sponsored pioneering labour-protection legislation; John McKenzie, who fought against land monopolies; and Ballance's successor, Richard John Seddon.

Ballanche, Pierre-Simon (b. Aug. 4, 1776, Lyon—d. June 12, 1847, Paris), religious and social philosopher who made a considerable impact on the Romantic writers and played an important part in the development of French thought in the early decades of the 19th century. The Romantics were attracted by his rejection of 18th-century Rationalism and by the poetic and oracular style in which he expressed his religious and social theories.

Ballanche, portrait by an unknown artist

By courtesy of the Bibliotheque Nationale, Paris

Basically a Catholic, Ballanche read widely among the mystical authors of the past and of his own time. In *Du sentiment considéré dans ses rapports avec la littérature et les arts* (1801; "Sentiment Considered in Its Relationship to Literature and the Arts") he expressed views on the role of religious emotion in art that foreshadow Chateaubriand's influential landmark of Romanticism, *Le Génie du christianisme* ("The Genius of Christianity"). In the post-Revolutionary era he reconsidered the basis and functions of human society in the light of his religious opinions.

Ballantyne, John: *see* Bellenden, John.

Ballantyne, Robert Michael (b. April 24, 1825, Edinburgh—d. Feb. 8, 1894, Rome), British author chiefly famous for *The Coral Island;* all his stories are lively adventures whose heroes are endowed with self-reliance and moral uprightness. *Snowflakes and Sun-*

Robert Ballantyne, detail of a portrait by John Ballantyne, 19th century; in the National Portrait Gallery, London

By courtesy of the National Portrait Gallery, London

beams, or, The Young Fur Traders (1855) is based on his experiences with the Hudson's Bay Company. Annoyed by a mistake he had made in *The Coral Island* (1858) through lack of firsthand knowledge of the setting, he afterward travelled widely to research the background of his stories.

Ballarat, also spelled BALLAARAT, city, central Victoria, Australia, on the Yarrowee River. First settled (1838) by sheepherders, its name was derived from two Aboriginal words meaning "resting place." The area developed rapidly after the discovery of rich alluvial gold deposits in 1851. In 1854, two years after its founding, Ballarat was the scene of an armed rebellion known as Eureka Stockade, in which about 25 miners, demanding political reform and the abolition of licenses, were shot down by the military; the incident is commemorated by a memorial. The town became a municipality in 1855, a borough in 1863, and a city in 1870.

A rail and road centre, Ballarat is the largest inland city of Australia and includes the borough of Sebastopol and portions of the shires of Ballarat, Bungaree, Buninyong, and Grenville. It serves an agricultural and pastoral district. Although the alluvial gold was soon exhausted, underground mining continued until 1918. Manufacturing concerns produce woollens, agricultural and industrial machinery, bricks, chemicals, and furniture. Many public buildings date from the 1860s and 1870s, and there are Anglican and Roman Catholic cathedrals, a school of mines and industries, a botanical garden hosting an annual begonia festival, and a historical museum. Almost 20 percent of the city's area (including Lake Wendouree) is in recreational use. Cultural resources include the Ballarat College of Advanced Education, founded in 1967. Pop. (1981) 62,641.

Ballard FAMILY (fl. from mid-16th to mid-18th century, France), printers who from 1560 to 1750 virtually monopolized music printing in France.

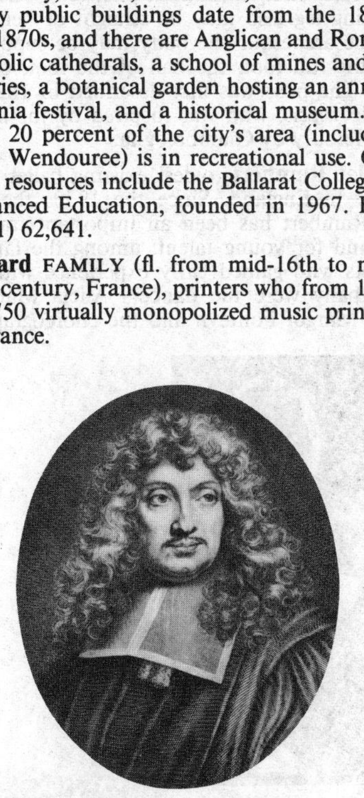

Robert Ballard, engraving by Claude du Flos, 1713, after a portrait by Lefevre

J.P. Ziolo

The founder of the dynasty was Robert Ballard (d. 1588), brother-in-law to the celebrated lutanist and composer Adrian Le Roy. These two used movable type, cut in 1540 by Robert's father-in-law, Guillaume Le Bé (or du Gué). Their first patent was granted in 1552 as sole music printers to Henry II. Robert's widow and son, Pierre (d. 1639), continued the business, and further patents were obtained from Henry IV and Louis XIII. Robert's grandson Robert II ran the firm from 1640 to 1679. He was succeeded by Christophe (d. 1715), Jean-Baptiste-Christophe (d. 1750), Christophe-Jean-François (d. 1765), and Pierre-Robert-Christophe (d. 1812), who carried on management until 1788. Throughout the history of the printers, the women of the family were often as active in the business as the men.

Ballard publications, both those with the early movable type and the later ones engraved on copper plates, were noted for their beauty and care of presentation. Their title pages were frequently superb examples of decorative engraving. The music published represented practically all the French composers of the period, among them Le Roy, Titelouze, Janequin, Goudimel, Lasso, Mersenne's *Harmonie universelle,* Campra, Couperin, Lalande, Montéclair, Philidor, Rameau, and Lully.

ballas, a variety of industrial diamond (*q.v.*).

Ballenden, John: *see* Bellenden, John.

ballet, theatrical dance in which a formal academic dance technique—the danse d'école—is combined with other artistic elements to provide a stage entertainment centred in the presentation of such dancing. The academic technique itself is also known as ballet.

A brief treatment of ballet follows. For full treatment, *see* MACROPAEDIA: Dance, The Art of.

Ballet developed out of the court spectacles of the Renaissance and the subsequent French ballet de cour, in which social dances performed by royalty and aristocracy were presented in harmony with music, speech, verse, song, pageant, decor, and costume. After some years of decline in dance standards in the 17th century, Louis XIV of France (1638–1715), a great devotee of dancing himself, in his concern to "reestablish the dance in its true perfection," established the Académie Royale de Danse in 1661—the same year that the first comédie-ballet (with text by Molière and music by Jean-Baptiste Lully), in which dances were separated by scenes of a play, was presented. In due course, this led to Lully's opéra-ballets and the establishment of a school to train professional dancers for them, attached to the Académie Royale de Musique (or the Opéra). The new professionals were trained in dance as a mirror of the noble deportment and manners. With the guidance of Lully and the ballet master Pierre Beauchamps (1631–1719), ballet emerged as a theatrical form.

The century that followed saw great advances in technical standards of ballet dancing and a new concern with ballet as a vehicle of drama. In the latter, Jean-Georges Noverre (1727–1810) was central: his *Lettres sur la danse et les ballets* (1760) was a major influence throughout Europe on the development of the ballet d'action, or dramatic ballet, as a summation and exploration of contemporary concerns. At the same time, the composer Christolph Gluck, in both opera and ballet, brought fresh vigour and drama to dance accompaniment. This was also the era of the three *genres.* According to physique, dancers were trained in different techniques—*noble,* or *sérieux*; *demi-caractère*; and *comique,* or *grotesque.* Thus stratified, ballet became a grand theatrical form like opera, performed in opera houses, as often it still is today; many operas contained ballet divertissements (suite of ballet numbers used as interludes).

Ballet of that time still reflected aristocratic attitudes, but the industrial, social, political, and artistic revolutions of the late 18th and early 19th centuries brought great alterations. Especially in France, the centre of style in ballet teaching, the ancien régime and its social dances ceased to be a model for dancers. The stage dancing of the early 19th century was given new artistic purpose in the Romantic ballet, particularly with the dancing of Marie Taglioni (1804–84) and Fanny Elssler (1810–84). With the introduction of pointe-work (position of balance on extreme tip of toe) to the dance vocabulary, the ballerina became a supreme or ideal stage figure. Scenarios for ballets began to be devised for the first time by professional writers or librettists, a method that became general in the 19th century. With the codification of ballet technique by such teachers as Carlo Blasis (1803–78), ballet dancing reached the basic form by which it may be recognized today—one essentially separate from social dance.

After the widespread enthusiasm for the Romantic ballet between 1830 and 1850, however, the art became regionalized with little international cross-fertilization. Artistic standards declined except in Russia and Denmark. Ballet masters such as August Bournonville (1805–79), Jules Perrot (1810–92), and Marius Petipa (1818–1910) gave new choreographic presentations of ballet. Petipa in particular helped to bring academic ballet to a new height in St. Petersburg in the last decades of the century, producing, to Peter Ilich Tchaikovsky's music, such enduring classics of the repertory as *The Sleeping Beauty* and, with his assistant Lev Ivanov (1834–1901), *Swan Lake.*

The 20th century saw Russia spreading ballet across the Western world to enormous acclaim and influence. Anna Pavlova (1881–1931), supreme ballerina, toured the world for 20 years; and the Ballets Russes of Serge Diaghilev (1872–1929), appearing in Europe for the last 20 years of his life, brought a new intensity of collaboration between choreographer, designer, and composer.

Diaghilev's influence on artists and audiences was immense. His five main choreographers—Mikhail Fokine (1880–1942), Vaslav Nijinsky (1888–1950), Leonide Massine (1895–1979), Bronislava Nijinska (1891–1972), and George Balanchine (1904–83)—all made major contributions to his work of revitalizing and redefining the art of ballet. The full-length ballet gave way to the one-act form; ballets could be plotless or could take the modern world as their subject. They could be set to arrangements of music not intended for dance or to commissioned scores with unconventional rhythms, harmonies, or everyday noises.

After the death of Diaghilev and with the emergence of other Ballets Russes companies in his wake, there were new steps taken to establish ballet in the West. New schools and companies were set up in order to give the art national identity and academic discipline. In Great Britain the Vic–Wells (later Sadler's Wells, then Royal) Ballet, founded in 1931 and directed by Ninette de Valois (b. 1898), with Sir Frederick Ashton (b. 1904) as resident choreographer, quickly achieved national importance; in the United States the School of American Ballet and the attached New York City Ballet, founded, respectively, in 1934 and 1948 and directed by Lincoln Kirstein (b. 1907) and the choreographer Balanchine, acquired comparable stature.

After World War II the Royal Danish Ballet and especially the Kirov and Bolshoi ballets of Leningrad and Moscow made tours abroad, having a profound impact. Today, no continent and few countries are without ballet companies and schools. Ballet is an artistic entertainment for a general public, and attendance is governed more by economic than by social circumstances. The art is even more complex and diverse than it was in Diaghilev's day, incorporating dance styles of all kinds into the danse d'école and collaborating with other arts in diverse ways. Performing to popular rather than classical music (or to silence), in minimal or practice dress, with no subject other than dancing itself are some of the directions the art has taken in recent years.

Ballet comique de la reine, court entertainment that is considered the first ballet. Enacted in 1581 at the French court of Catherine de Médicis by the Queen, her ladies, and the nobles of the court to celebrate the betrothal of her sister, it fused the elements of music, dance, plot (the escape of Ulysses from Circe), and design into a dramatic whole.

It is also the first ballet of which there is a printed account (libretto); it was published in 1582 as the *Balet comique de la royne* by Balthazar de Beaujoyeulx (or Baltazarini di Belgioioso), Catherine's director of court festivals. The *Ballet comique* was a brilliant success, and Beaujoyeulx's volume circulated to the courts of Europe, influencing the development of court ballet in France and the masque in England.

ballet d'action, ballet in which all the elements of production (*e.g.,* choreography, set design, and costuming) are subordinate to the plot and theme. John Weaver, an English ballet master of the early 18th century, is considered the originator of pantomime ballet, a drama in dance form that became formalized as the classical ballet d'action later in the century. The choreographers Angiolini, Franz Hilverding, van Wewen, and especially Noverre became its advocates. Noverre's *Lettres sur la danse, et sur les ballets* (1760) is the authoritative work on the ballet d'action.

ballet movement, in classical ballet, any of the formalized actions of a dancer that follow specific rules regarding the positions of the arms, feet, and body. Ballet choreography is based on combinations of these fundamental movements. Some movements, like the plié and battement, are training exercises designed to give strength and flexibility to the entire body while helping the dancer acquire perfect posture, or "placement," with the weight lightly balanced over the centre of gravity and the legs turned out from the hip sockets. Other movements are steps in a ballet. These may be jumping or leaping steps (*pas d'élévation*), like the entrechat (a jump beginning and ending in the fifth position, during which the feet are rapidly crossed) or the jeté (a jump in which the weight is transferred from one foot to the other); or they may be turns (*tours*), such as the pirouette (a turn on one foot) and the tour en l'air (a complete single, double, or triple, turn in the air).

See also assemblé; battement; brisé; cabriole; entrechat; fouetté en tournant; glissade; jeté; pas d'élévation; pirouette; plié; tour en l'air; ballet position.

ballet position, any of the five positions of the feet fundamental to all classical ballet. The term may also denote the various poses of the body. First used by Thoinot Arbeau in 1588, codified by Pierre Beauchamp *c.* 1680, and set down by Pierre Rameau in *Le Maître à danser* (1725; *The Dancing Master,* 1931), the positions are the starting and ending points for the intricate ballet movements (*q.v.*).

In all positions each leg is turned sideways from the hip, so that the toes extend out to each side and the feet form straight or parallel lines on the floor. Body weight is evenly distributed over both feet, which remain flat on the floor, rest on the balls of the feet (demi-pointe), or rest on the toes (pointe; women only). Corresponding positions of the arms and hands (port de bras) complete the perfect balance of the figure.

Arabesque executed by Natalya Bessmertnova, with Nikolay Fadeychev, of the Bolshoi Ballet; *Swan Lake*
Novosti—Sovfoto

In the first position, the heels are together, with toes turned out until the feet are in a straight line. In the second position, the feet are in a parallel line, separated by a distance of about 12 inches (30 centimetres) and both turned outward, with the weight equally divided between them. In second position *en l'air* ("in the air"), the weight is supported by one foot while the other is raised at the side. In the third position, the heel of one foot rests against the instep of the other; both are firmly turned out, and the weight is divided between them. Used extensively in 18th-century social dances such as the minuet and gavotte, this position has almost disappeared from theatrical usage. In the fourth position, one foot rests about 12 inches in advance of the other, both are turned out, and the weight is divided between them. Like the second position, fourth has its equivalent *en l'air.* In the fifth position, the feet are turned out and pressed closely together, the heel of the one foot against the toe of the other.

Attitude executed by Diana Weber of the American Ballet Theatre
Martha Swope

In addition to the five fundamental positions of the feet, there are two major body positions in classical ballet. The arabesque is a body position in which the weight of the body is supported on one leg, while the other leg is extended in back with the knee straight. One of the most graceful of ballet positions, the arabesque can be varied in many ways by changing the position of the arms, the angle of the body, and the height of the leg in the air. The dancer's body may be supported on the full foot, the ball of the foot (demi-pointe), or toe (pointe; women only), and the supporting leg may be straight or bent.

The attitude is a position similar to the arabesque except that the knee of the raised leg is bent. The raised leg is held at a 90° angle to the body in back or in front (*attitude an avant*); the knee may be either well bent or nearly straight (*attitude allongée*). The supporting leg also may be straight or bent. As in the arabesque the body may be supported on the full foot, the ball of the foot, or the toe. The pose was first described in 1829 by Carlo Blasis, who was inspired by the statue of Mercury by Giambologna.

Ballet Rambert, oldest existing ballet company in England. Since the 1930s the Ballet Rambert has been an important training ground for young talent; among the famous artists who gained early experience with the company were the dancers Alicia Markova and Margot Fonteyn and the choreographers

Ballet positions
(From left to right): First, second, third, fourth, and fifth positions
Martha Swope

Antony Tudor, Sir Frederick Ashton, Agnes deMille, Andrée Howard, Walter Gore, and Peggy van Praagh.

Inspired by Dame Marie Rambert, a former dancer with Diaghilev, the Rambert Dancers (performing from 1926) and the Ballet Club (established in 1930) staged small-scale Sunday afternoon productions that were mainly new ballets by unknown choreographers. During World War II the company toured factories, military camps, and outlying areas and later staged seasons in major London theatres. Its postwar tours include one of Australia and New Zealand (1947–48) that greatly stimulated interest there in ballet. The Ballet Rambert is a small company; in 1966 its repertoire was reformed to make it almost exclusively a forum for young talent. John Chesworth was appointed artistic director in 1974.

Ballet Russe de Monte Carlo, ballet company founded in Monte-Carlo in 1932. The name Ballets Russes had been used by the impresario Sergey Diaghilev for his company, which revolutionized ballet in the first three decades of the 20th century. Under the direction of Colonel W. de Basil, the Ballet Russe de Monte Carlo brought to audiences new compositions by Léonide Massine and George Balanchine, with such dancers as Aleksandra Danilova, Leon Woizikowki, and David Lichine. Ballet Russe de Monte Carlo divided into new competitive companies in 1938, one under de Basil, the other under Massine.

De Basil renamed his company the Royal Covent Garden Ballet Russe and finally the Original Ballet Russe (1939); the company toured internationally before dissolving in 1947.

Massine, with René Blum, formed another Ballet Russe de Monte Carlo with the dancers Danilova, Tamara Toumanova, Dame Alicia Markova, Mia Slavenska, Serge Lifar, Igor Youskevitch, and André Eglevsky and new choreography by Massine. This company performed principally in the U.S., produced traditional revivals and works by U.S. choreographers, and featured U.S. dancers, including Maria Tallchief. The company declined in the 1950s and ceased producing in 1963; its ballet school was maintained in New York City for a time. Massine and Sergei Denham organized the new Ballets de Monte Carlo in 1966 under the patronage of Prince Rainier III of Monaco.

Ballet Theatre, American: *see* American Ballet Theatre.

Ballets Russes, ballet company founded in Paris in 1909 by the Russian impresario Sergey Diaghilev. The original company included the choreographer Michel Fokine and the dancers Anna Pavlova and Vaslav Nijinsky; the choreographer George Balanchine joined in 1925. Music was commissioned of Rimsky-Korsakov and Stravinsky and designs of Picasso, Rouault, Matisse, and Derain. The company was dissolved after Diaghilev's death in 1929. *See also* Diaghilev, Sergey.

balletto, in music, genre of light vocal composition of the late 16th–early 17th centuries, originating in Italy. Dancelike and having much in common with the madrigal, a major vocal form of the period, it is typically strophic (stanzaic) with each of the two repeated parts ending in a "fa-la-la" burden, or refrain. It has a clear alternation of strong and weak beats, a quality common to the lighter forms of the time, such as the *canzonetta, villota, villanesca,* and *villanella.* The term was first applied to musical compositions by the Italian Giovanni Gastoldi in 1591 in his *Balletti a cinque voci . . . per cantare, sonare, et ballare* (*Balletti in Five Voices . . . to Sing, Play, and Dance*).

Although greatly influenced by the Italian model, the English composer Thomas Morley expanded its contrapuntal and harmonic dimensions in his *First Booke of Balletts* (1595). Morley's style influenced not only the English composers but also the German Hans Leo Hassler and his younger contemporaries who transformed the *balletto* in the early 17th century into a more instrumental and homophonic (chordal) style. The suites of the German Johann Hermann Schein as well as later 17th-century Italian instrumental works often contain such *balletti.* Both the Italian Girolamo Frescobaldi and, in the 18th century, J.S. Bach wrote instrumental movements entitled *balletto.* The name was also given to a form of dramatic choreography popular in 15th-century Italy.

Ballia, town, administrative headquarters of Ballia district, Uttar Pradesh state, northern India, on the Ganges River, northeast of Vārānasi (Benares). An ancient settlement, it has occasionally been moved northward because of changes in the river's course. It is an administrative, trade, and business centre, with some light industry. The town houses two colleges and an annual cattle fair. Ballia is connected by rail with Vārānasi and other northern Indian cities.

Ballia district, 1,229 sq mi (3,183 sq km) in area, comprises the eastern tip of Uttar Pradesh, jutting into Bihār state. It is a wedge of alluvial plain between the Ganges and Ghāghara rivers, at their confluence. The fertile land, frequently flooded by the rivers, supports various grains, sugarcane, and other crops. Pop. (1981) town, 61,704; district, 1,945,376.

Ballina, town and port, north coastal New South Wales, Australia, at the mouth of the Richmond River. Founded (1842–43) as the shipping outlet for the river valley, it was significantly affected by a gold rush in 1860. Proclaimed a town in 1856 and a municipality in 1883, Ballina was an important timber port by the 1880s but declined when forestry waned. It now functions as an outport for Lismore, 20 mi (30 km) upstream, and as a base for a large fishing fleet, as well as a service centre for an agricultural district (dairy produce, sugarcane, and tropical fruit). Industries include fish and fruit canneries and shipyards. Its name, derived from an Aboriginal word meaning "place where oysters are plentiful," refers to the nearby rich oyster beds. Ballina is at the junction of the Bruxner and Pacific highways, 376 mi northeast of Sydney and 105 mi south-southeast of Brisbane. Pop. (1981) 9,738.

Ballina, Irish BÉAL AN ÁTHA, urban district, County Mayo, Ireland, on the River Moy. The town, the largest in Mayo, has a modern Roman Catholic cathedral and the remains of an Augustinian friary founded about 1375. Salmon and trout fishing nearby are notable. Hand tools, drills, and medical products are manufactured there. Pop. (1981) 6,856.

Ballinasloe, Irish BÉAL ÁTHA NA SLUAIGHE, market town and urban district, County Galway, Ireland, on the River Suck and a northerly extension of the Grand Canal. Originally a small settlement beside the medieval castle guarding the important Suck crossing, the town was developed mainly in the 18th century. It is the main market town of east County Galway and is noted for its livestock fairs, the largest in Ireland, which reached a peak in the mid-19th century. The famous local quarries supplied the masonry for a street of shop fronts in New York City. It is also an important angling centre. Pop. (1981) 6,374.

Ballinger, Richard A(chilles) (b. July 9, 1858, Boonesboro, Iowa, U.S.—d. June 6, 1922, Seattle, Wash.), U.S. secretary of the interior (1909–11) whose anti-conservationist policy contributed to the rift between the conservative and progressive factions in the Republican party.

As the reform mayor of Seattle, Wash. (1904–06), Ballinger attracted the attention of the Theodore Roosevelt administration, and in 1907 he was appointed commissioner of the General Land Office. In 1909 he became secretary of the interior in the Cabinet of Pres. William Howard Taft. During his two years in that post Ballinger sought to make public resources more available for private exploitation and became embroiled in a highly publicized controversy with Gifford Pinchot, chief of the Division of Forestry in the Department of Agriculture. Citing evidence supplied by a public-land inspector, Pinchot charged that Ballinger had cooperated with private interests in a fraudulent scheme to plunder coal reserves in Alaska. Taft supported his secretary and dismissed both Pinchot and his informant, Louis Glavis. Although a Congressional investigation exonerated Ballinger, the episode left a residue of bitterness between the conservative Republicans led by Taft and the progressives loyal to Theodore Roosevelt.

Balliol FAMILY, also spelled BALIOL, medieval family that played an important part in the history of Scotland and came originally to England from Bailleul (Somme) in Normandy. Guy de Balliol already possessed lands in Northumberland and elsewhere during the reign of William II of England (1087–1100). Guy's nephew and successor, Bernard (d. *c.* 1167), built Barnard Castle and was the first of his family to receive lands in Scotland. He fought against David I of Scotland at Northallerton in 1138, and with King Stephen was captured by Matilda at Lincoln in 1141. His son Bernard (d. *c.* 1190) was present at the capture of King William I of Scotland at Alnwick in 1174. A descendant, Hugh (d. 1228), supported King John against the baronial party in England in 1215–16.

Hugh's son and successor John (d. 1268) married in 1233 Dervorguilla, daughter of Alan, the last "Celtic" lord of Galloway, and also an heiress of King William I of Scotland. His descendants were therefore able to have royal pretensions. John served (1251–55) as guardian of the young Scottish king Alexander III. His loyalty to King Henry III of England in the Barons' War (1264–67, against rebellious nobles led by Simon de Montfort, earl of Leicester) cost him the temporary loss of his lands and a period of imprisonment after his capture in the Battle of Lewes (May 14, 1264). About that time (perhaps in 1263) he began to support several students at Oxford, apparently as penance for a quarrel with the Bishop of Durham. After his death, his widow completed his endowment of scholars, and their house was formally chartered as Balliol College in 1282.

John was succeeded in turn by his three sons, Hugh (d. 1271), Alexander (d. 1278), and John de Balliol (*see* John *under* John [Scotland]). This last son, John, established the Scottish royal House of Balliol, which, however, lasted only a generation, ending with the resignation of John's son Edward (*see* Edward *under* Edward [Scotland]).

ballista, ancient heavy missile launcher designed to hurl long arrows or heavy balls. The Greek ballista was basically a huge crossbow fastened to a mount. The Roman ballista, however, was powered by torsion derived from two thick skeins of twisted cords through which were thrust two separate arms joined at their ends by the cord that propelled the missile. The largest ballistas were quite accurate in hurling 60-pound weights up to about 500 yards. *Compare* catapult.

ballistic pendulum, device for measuring the velocity of a projectile, such as a bullet. A large wooden block suspended by two cords serves as the pendulum bob. When a bullet is fired into the bob, its momentum is transferred to the bob. The bullet's momentum can be determined from the amplitude of the pendulum swing. The velocity of the bullet, in turn, can be derived from its calculated momentum. The ballistic pendulum has been largely supplanted by other devices for projectile velocity tests, but it is still used in classrooms for demonstrating concepts pertaining to momentum and energy.

ballistics, science of the propulsion, flight, and impact of projectiles. Modern ballistics grew from technical advances in weaponry during the 19th century. It is divided into several disciplines. Internal and external ballistics, respectively, deal with the propulsion and the flight of projectiles. The transition between these two regimes is called intermediate ballistics. Terminal ballistics concerns the impact of projectiles; a separate category encompasses the wounding of personnel.

A brief treatment of ballistics follows. For full treatment, *see* MACROPAEDIA: Mechanics: *Ballistics*.

The gun and the rocket motor are types of heat engine, partially converting the chemical energy of a propellant into the kinetic energy of a projectile. Propellants are unlike conventional fuels in that their combustion does not require atmospheric oxygen. Within a restricted volume, the production of hot gases by a burning propellant causes an increase in pressure. The pressure propels the projectile and increases the burning rate. The hot gases tend to erode the gun bore or rocket throat.

When the charge of propellant in a gun chamber is ignited, the combustion gases are restrained by the shot, so the pressure rises. The shot starts to move when the pressure on it overcomes its resistance to motion. The pressure continues to rise for a time and then falls, while the shot is accelerated to a high velocity. The rapidly burning propellant is soon exhausted and, in time, the shot is ejected from the muzzle: muzzle velocities up to 15 kilometres per second have been achieved. Recoilless guns vent gas through the rear of the chamber to counteract recoil forces.

A precursor blast, which precedes the exit of the shot, is followed by the main blast as the compressed gases behind the shot are released. The shot is briefly overtaken by the rapid gas outflow and so may suffer severe yawing. The blast shock wave, travelling outward at a speed greater than that of sound, is heard as gunfire. Heat generated near the muzzle causes flash, which in large guns is accompanied by flames. Devices can be affixed to the muzzle to suppress blast and flash by dispersing shock waves, and they can reduce recoil by deflecting the outflow.

A trajectory is the path of a shot, subject to the forces of gravity, drag, and lift. Under the sole influence of gravity, a trajectory is parabolic. Drag retards motion along the trajectory. Below the speed of sound, the drag is roughly proportional to the square of the velocity; streamlining of the shot tail is effective only at these velocities. At greater velocities, a conical shock wave emanates from the nose of the shot. The drag, which is largely dependent on the nose shape, is least for finely pointed shots. Drag can be reduced by venting gases from a burner in the tail.

Tail fins can be used to stabilize projectiles. Spin stabilization, provided by rifling, causes gyroscopic wobbling in response to aerodynamic tumbling forces. Insufficient spin permits tumbling, and too much prevents dipping of the shot nose as it traverses the trajectory. Drift of the shot arises from lift, due to yawing, meteorological conditions, and rotation of the Earth.

Rockets are propelled by reaction to the momentum of the gas efflux. The motor is designed so that the pressures generated are nearly constant during burning. Fin-stabilized rockets are sensitive to crosswinds, as resulting yaw causes thrust misalignment. Two or more motor nozzles canted from the line of flight can provide spin stabilization.

Targets are generally solid and are termed thick or thin according to whether or not the impact of the shot is influenced by underlying material. Penetration occurs when the stress intensities of impact exceed the yield stress of the target; it causes ductile and brittle failure in thin targets and hydrodynamic flow of material in thick targets. The shot may be subject to similar failure during impact. Penetration completely through the target is called perforation. Enhanced armour penetrators either detonate a squashed explosive against the target or explosively focus a jet of metal onto its surface.

Wound ballistics is mainly concerned with the mechanisms and medical implications of trauma caused by bullets and explosively driven fragments. Upon penetration, the momentum given to the surrounding tissues generates a large temporary cavity. The extent of local injury is related to the size of this transient cavity. Quantitative assessment of injury is problematic. Evidence suggests that physical injury is proportional to the projectile's velocity cubed, its mass, and its cross-sectional area. The wounding potential of a bullet is thus increased by tumbling or mushrooming upon impact. Further injury is often caused by fast-moving fragments of impacted bone. Studies of body armour seek to prevent projectile penetration and minimize injury.

ballistocardiography, graphically recording the stroke volume of the heart as a means of calculating cardiac output. The heartbeat results in motion of the body, which in turn causes movements in a suspended supporting structure, usually a special table or bed on which the subject is lying, and these movements are recorded photographically (ballistocardiogram, or BCG) as a series of waves. The BCG is one of the most sensitive measures of the force of the heartbeat, and an abnormality appearing in the BCG of an apparently healthy subject aged 40, or younger, may be suggestive of symptomatic coronary disease.

ballistospore, in fungi, a spore forcibly propelled from its site. The basidiospores of the mushrooms, produced on the gills and on the walls of the spores, are ballistospores. They are shot from the vertical walls of the fruiting structure and then drift down. In other fungi, including certain slime molds, they are propelled in other directions by various mechanisms.

Ballivián, Lake, predecessor to modern Lake Titicaca, on the Bolivia–Peru border during Pleistocene times (from about 10,000 to about 2,500,000 years ago). Its surface is thought to have been at least 330 ft (100 m) above the present surface of Lake Titicaca. As the lake drained, it formed two smaller lakes: Titicaca, in the northern portion of its basin, and Minchin, predecessor to modern Lake Poopó, in the southern.

Ballon, Jean: *see* Balon, Jean.

Ballonius: *see* Baillou, Guillaume de.

balloon, large airtight bag filled with hot air or a lighter-than-air gas, such as helium or hydrogen, to provide buoyancy so that it will rise and float in the atmosphere. Most balloons have a basket or container hung below for passengers or cargo.

Balloons were used in man's first successful attempts at flying. Experimentation with balloon-like craft may have begun as early as 1709 with the work of Bartolomeu Lourenço de Gusmão, a Brazilian priest and inventor. In 1783 Joseph and Étienne Montgolfier at Annonay, Fr., confirmed that a fabric bag filled with hot air would rise. On June 5 of that year they launched an unmanned balloon that travelled some 1.5 miles. At Versailles, they repeated the experiment with a larger balloon on Sept. 19, 1783, sending a sheep, rooster, and duck aloft.

Ascent of a Piccard balloon
UPI—EB Inc.

On Nov. 21, 1783, the first manned flight took place when Jean-François Pilâtre de Rozier and François Laurent, marquis d'Arlandes, sailed over Paris in a Montgolfier balloon. They burned wool and straw to keep the air in the balloon hot; their flight covered 5½ miles (almost 9 kilometres) in about 23 minutes. In December of that year the physicist J.-A.-C. Charles, accompanied by Nicolas-Louis Robert, flew a balloon filled with hydrogen on a two-hour flight. Shortly thereafter Charles made a solo 35-minute flight.

Military uses for balloons were soon developed. Anchored observation balloons were used by Napoleon in some of his battles and by both sides in the U.S. Civil War and World War I. The powered airship developed from balloons, but, while the airship was eventually supplanted by the airplane, balloons have continued to find useful applications. During World War II, balloons were anchored over many parts of Britain to defend against low-level bombing or dive-bombing.

Balloons have also proved enormously valuable to science. As early as 1911–12, V.F. Hess, an Austrian physicist, made a daring series of balloon ascensions as high as 5,000 metres (about 3 miles) to prove the existence of cosmic rays. Advances in weather science since 1900 have resulted in great part from intensive exploration of the upper air by instrumented free balloons, which have risen to an altitude of 30 kilometres (19 miles). Auguste Piccard, Swiss physicist and educator, set a world's altitude record in May 1931 in a balloon of his own design, which featured the first pressurized cabin used in flight. Jean-Felix Piccard, twin brother of Auguste, experimented with plastic balloons, and helped to design the polyethylene Skyhook series of high-altitude balloons with which the U.S. Air Force sent manned flights to more than 100,000 feet (30,000 metres) to collect data on the upper atmosphere. Sport ballooning has gained in popularity over the years.

balloon fly, also called SMALL-HEADED FLY, any insect of the family Acroceridae (order Diptera), so named because of its swollen abdomen. It is also characterized by an extremely small head and a humped back.

Adults that have a slender proboscis (feeding organ) feed from flowers; those lacking a proboscis probably do not feed in their adult stage. Their larvae are internal parasites of spiders.

balloon framing, framework of a wooden building in which the elements consist of small members nailed together. In balloon framing, the studs (vertical members) extend the full height of the building (usually two stories) from foundation plate to rafter plate, as contrasted with platform framing, in which each floor is framed separately.

Balloon framing is used primarily in Scandinavia and in the United States. Queen Anne and Shingle Style buildings are typical examples of balloon framing.

balloon vine, also called HEART PEA (*Cardiospermum halicacabum*), woody perennial vine, in the soapberry family (Sapindaceae), native to subtropical and tropical America. It is naturalized and cultivated widely as an ornamental for its white flowers and its nearly globular inflated fruits, about 2.5 centimetres (1 inch) across. The seeds are black with a heart-shaped white spot. The vine can reach an extension of 3 metres (10 feet) as a perennial but is usually grown from seed as an annual.

balloonflower, also called CHINESE BELLFLOWER (*Platycodon grandiflorum*), the only species of its genus, an East Asian perennial of the bellflower family (Campanulaceae). The balloonflower has balloon-like buds that become flaring, five-lobed, bell-shaped flowers with a thick, rubbery texture.

At maturity the fruit is a five-valved seedpod that opens at the top. The leaves are unstalked, pointed and oval, becoming narrow higher on the stems, which are 30 to 70 centimetres (1 to 2½ feet) long. The lavender-blue to white flowers have sharp-pointed lobes and are 5 to 7 cm across. Many varieties of balloonflower are cultivated as garden ornamentals and border plants.

Balloonflower (*Platycodon grandiflorum*)
Joan E. Rahn—EB Inc.

ballooning, unpowered balloon flight in competition or for recreation that became popular in the 1960s. The balloons used are of plastic, nylon, or polyethylene, filled with hydrogen, helium, methane, or hot air.

Although ballooning began in 1783 with the flight of the Montgolfier brothers in France, the earliest uses were scientific and military. Sport ballooning began in earnest in 1906, when the U.S. publisher James Gordon Bennett offered an international trophy for annual long-distance flights, won permanently by Belgians with victories in 1922–24. Belgium then offered the trophy until it was discontinued in 1939. This sport, like international yachting, was a rich man's sport.

Hot-air balloons in the 1965 U.S. National Championship balloon races at Reno, Nev.
Jim Larsen

The sport was revived after World War II following the introduction of new materials and the propane burner to provide hot air. Events include those for duration of flight, altitude, and distance. Hare-and-hound races entail a lead "hare" balloon that takes off and flies a certain distance, pursued by the "hound" balloons. The winner is the balloon landing first and closest to the "hound." The Fédération Aéronautique Internationale (FAI; International Aeronautical Federation) maintains international records for 10 classes of balloons, both gas and hot-air, ranging in volume from 250 to 16,000 cubic metres (8,829 to 565,035 cubic feet).

Ballooning clubs are mainly local, and world championships have not been highly successful, but out of the sport came the record transatlantic (1978), transcontinental (1980), and transpacific (1981) flights of Max Anderson, Ben Abruzzo, and Larry Newman; of Anderson and his son Kristian; and of Abruzzo, Newman, Rocky Aoki, and Ron Clark, respectively.

Ballou, Hosea (b. April 30, 1771, Richmond, N.H., U.S.—d. June 7, 1852, Boston), theologian who for more than 50 years was an influential leader in the Universalist Church.

Converted in 1789 to a belief in universal salvation, he began preaching that doctrine on a Calvinist basis, substituting for John Calvin's concept of salvation of the "elect" a concept of salvation that included all of mankind. Ballou reexamined Calvinist tenets further, however, under the influence of Ethan Allen's deistic *Reason the Only Oracle of Man* (1784), and in *A Treatise on Atonement* (1805) Ballou presented his own version of Universalist theology. In 1809 he became a pastor in Portsmouth, N.H.; in 1815 he moved to Salem, Mass.; and from December 1817 until his death he was pastor of the Second Universalist Church in Boston.

Stressing the use of reason in religious thinking, Ballou shifted Universalism from its belief in a three-person Godhead to a unitarian basis that did not see God as having separately personified attributes or functions. He also discarded the doctrines of original sin and vicarious atonement, believing that Christ died not to reconcile man to God but to demonstrate God's unchanging love for man. From 1817 Ballou held that punishment for sin is limited to earthly life and that at death the soul is purified by divine love and enters immortality. The ensuing controversy resulted in the secession of the Restorationists, who believed in a limited period of punishment in the afterlife; Ballou gave his views in this dispute in *An Examination of the Doctrine of Future Retribution* (1834).

Among his many other writings are some 10,000 sermons and numerous hymns and essays. He founded and edited *The Universalist Magazine* (1819) and *The Universalist Expositor* (1830). On the *Expositor* (later *The Universalist Quarterly and General Review*) he was assisted by his nephew, also named Hosea Ballou (1796–1861), who continued the work of the Universalist Church and was the first president of Tufts College, later Tufts University. Ernest Cassara's *Hosea Ballou and the Rise of American Religious Liberalism* (1958) was followed by *Hosea Ballou: The Challenge to Orthodoxy* (1961).

ballroom dance, western European and American social dancing performed by couples. It includes the standard repertory of dances such as the fox-trot, waltz, polka, and tango as well as various fad dances from the Charleston through the jitterbug, hustle, frug, and disco dancing. In Europe, in particular, ballroom dance contests, both amateur and professional, are organized on a national and international scale.

Bally, also spelled BALI, or BALY, town, Howrah district, West Bengal state, northeastern India, just west of the Hooghly River. A part of the Howrah urban agglomeration, it is connected by road and rail with Howrah, Kharagpur, and Burdwān and is a steamer station for traffic along the Hooghly. Major industries in the town include jute, paper, and bone milling, iron- and steel-rolling works, and the manufacture of chemical fertilizer, cotton cloth, bricks, and glass. The Bally Bridge across the Hooghly to Baranagar was opened in 1931. Constituted a municipality in 1883, Bally has a college that is affiliated with Rabindra Bhārati University in Calcutta. Pop. (1981) 54,859.

Ballycastle, Irish BAILE AN CHAISTIL, town, Moyle district (established 1973), formerly in County Antrim, Northern Ireland, on Ballycastle Bay, opposite Rathlin Island, where Robert Bruce, king of Scotland, is said to have hidden in a cave. Ballycastle is at the mouth of Glenshesk and close to Knocklayd (1,695 ft [517 m]). The town is a market centre, fishing harbour, and resort. Nearby are the ruins of Bunamargy Franciscan Friary and Dunaneanie Castle. In 1898 Guglielmo Marconi's first wireless system between a lighthouse and the mainland was installed at Rathlin and Ballycastle. Pop. (1981) 3,284.

Ballymena, Irish AN BAILE MEÁNACH, town, seat, and district (established 1973), formerly in County Antrim, Northern Ireland, in the River Main Valley about 24 mi (40 km) northwest of the city of Belfast. Ballymena town is the market centre for the surrounding countryside and has been long known for its production of linens and woolens; more recently, synthetic fibres have also been manufactured there.

Ballymena district covers an area of 55 sq mi (142 sq km) and borders the districts of Magherafelt to the west, Ballymoney and Moyle to the north, Larne to the east, and Antrim to the south. The desolate Antrim Mountains, which reach an altitude of more than 1,430 ft (435 m) above sea level, traverse the eastern part of the district north to south, sloping westward to the River Main Valley in central Ballymena. Cattle, pigs, and poultry are raised in the valley along with barley. Diatomite is extracted from the shores of Lough (lake) Beg in southwestern Ballymena district. The Antrim Mountains are popular with grouse hunters, and anglers enjoy the rivers and streams of the Main Valley. A national highway extension from Belfast facilitates travel through the valley. Pop. (1981) town, 28,166; district, 54,426.

Ballymoney, Irish BAILE MONAIDH, town, seat, and district (established 1973), formerly within County Antrim, Northern Ireland. The town of Ballymoney, located on the eastern side of the valley on a tributary of the River Bann, was the birthplace of James McKinley, grandfather of the U.S. president William McKinley. The town preserves a market place of 1775 and an old parish church (1637). Ballymoney town is now a thriving agricultural centre with textile and engineering industries as well as several bacon and ham processing plants.

Ballymoney district covers an area of 161 sq mi (418 sq km) and is bordered by the districts of Coleraine to the west, Moyle to the north and east, and Ballymena and Magherafelt to the south. From the eastern border of the district the Antrim Mountains gradually descend to the Bann Valley in the west. Significant quantities of potatoes, barley, and livestock (mostly pigs) are produced in the district. Primary roads connect Ballymoney town with the towns of Coleraine to the northwest and Ballymena to the southeast. Pop. (1981) town, 5,679; district, 22,873.

balm, any of several fragrant herbs of the mint family, particularly *Melissa officinalis,* also called balm gentle or lemon balm, and cultivated in temperate climates for its fragrant leaves, which are used as a scent in perfumery, and as a flavouring in foods such as salads, soups, sauces, stuffings, in liqueurs, and in wine and fruit drinks. It was used in medicinal teas, as a diaphoretic, and in wine drinks by the Greeks and Orientals in ancient times.

The name is also applied to *Melittis melissophyllum,* bastard balm; *Monarda didyma,* bee balm, or Oswego tea; *Collinsonia canadensis,* horse balm; *Glecoma hederacea* and *Satureja* (*Calamintha*) *nepeta,* field balm; and *Molucella laevis,* Molucca balm, or bells of Ireland. Aromatic exudations from species of *Commiphora* (trees and shrubs of the incense-tree family) may also be referred to as balm. Balm of Gilead, or balm of Mecca, is the myrrhlike resin from *Commiphora opobalsamum* of Arabia. The balsam fir (*Abies balsamea*) is sometimes called balm fir or balm of Gilead fir. The balm of Gilead poplar is related to the balsam poplar. Balm of heaven is the California laurel (*Umbellularia californica*).

Balmaceda, José Manuel (b. July 19, 1840, Santiago, Chile—d. Sept. 19, 1891, Santiago), liberal reformer and president of Chile (1886–91) whose conflict with his legislature precipitated a civil war.

Balmaceda was elected to the Chilean congress in 1870. While serving in the cabinet of Pres. Domingo Santa María (1881–86), he pushed anticlerical measures and promoted public works. As president he advanced public education and railroad construction but inherited the legislative revolt against the executive begun in the 1860s. His attempts to prevent congressional limitation of the presidential powers led to civil war in 1891. Congress, with navy support, defeated Balmaceda's forces within eight months. His defeat and subsequent suicide left parliamentary government entrenched until the mid-1920s.

Balmaceda
By courtesy of the Organization of American States

Balmain, Pierre(-Alexandre-Claudius) (b. May 18, 1914, Saint-Jean-de-Maurienne, Fr.—d. June 29, 1982, Paris), French couturier who founded a fashion house that made his name a byword for elegance during the post-World War II years. His clients included the Duchess of Windsor, the Queen of Belgium, and many of the leading film stars of the 1950s. But one of the first and most important was the U.S. writer Gertrude Stein, who encouraged him and publicized the House of Balmain when it opened in 1945.

Balmain had abandoned his architectural studies because of lack of money and in 1934 joined Edward Molyneux as a designer. In 1939 he went to Lucien Lelong, where he worked with Christian Dior, who was to become his main rival during their heyday in the postwar years. The House of Balmain was an immediate success, its clothes characterized by superb quality, particularly in evening wear, which combined femininity with an imposing elegance. He rapidly expanded, opening branches in New York City and Caracas and diversifying into perfume and accessories. He designed for films and for film stars, among them Marlene Dietrich, Katharine Hepburn, Sophia Loren, Ingrid Bergman, and Brigitte Bardot. As haute couture gave way to ready-to-wear, he opened boutiques and developed his ancillary interests in handbags, scarves, luggage, and even furniture.

He published his memoirs, *My Years and Seasons,* in 1964 and in 1978 was made an officer of the Legion of Honour.

Balmer, Johann Jakob (b. May 1, 1825, Lausanne, Switz.—d. March 12, 1898, Basel), Swiss mathematician who discovered a formula basic to the development of atomic theory and the field of atomic spectroscopy.

A secondary schoolteacher in Basel from 1859 until his death, he also lectured (1865–90) on geometry at the University of Basel. In 1885 he announced a simple formula representing the wavelengths of the spectral lines of hydrogen—the "Balmer series" (*see* spectral line series). Why the formula held true, however, was not explained until 1913, when Niels Bohr found that it fit into and supported his theory of discrete energy states within the hydrogen atom.

Balmes, Jaime Luciano (b. Aug. 28, 1810, Vich, Spain—d. July 9, 1848, Vich), ecclesiastic, political writer, and philosopher whose liberal ideas were strongly opposed by conservative Roman Catholics. Receiving a doctorate in civil and canon law from the University of Cervera, he returned to Vich and taught physics and mathematics. In Madrid he founded and edited a weekly newspaper, *El pensamiento de la nación* ("The Thought of the Nation").

He is best known for his *El protestantismo comparado con el catolicismo en sus relaciones con la civilización europea* (1842–44; *Protestantism and Catholicism Compared in Their Effect on the Civilization of Europe,* 1849), a defense of Catholicism against the accusation of being unsympathetic toward the spirit of progress. His philosophical works are *El criterio* (1845), called Balmes' logic; *Filosofía fundamental* (1846; *Fundamental Philosophy,* 1856); and *Curso de filosofía elemental* (1847). A critical edition of his complete works was published in 33 volumes at Madrid (1948–50).

Balmoral Castle, private residence of the British sovereign, on the right bank of the River Dee, Grampian region, Scotland, at 926 ft (282 m) above sea level. After its acquisition (1852) by Albert, the prince consort (husband of Queen Victoria, who reigned 1837–1901), the small castle then on the land was replaced 1853–56 by the modern granite building, designed in Scottish Baronial style. Queen Victoria and successive sovereigns have used the castle as a summer residence and for grouse shooting on the local moors, visiting the competitive Scottish sports assembly known as the Highland Games (held locally at Braemar), and attending the parish church of Crathie, 1.5 mi (2.5 km) to the east.

Balmoral Castle, Grampian region, Scotland, designed in Scottish Baronial style, 1853–56
Aerofilms, Ltd.—Ewing Galloway

Balnaves, Henry (b. *c.* 1512, Kirkcaldy, Fife, Scot.—d. February 1579, Edinburgh), politician and diplomat who was one of the chief promoters of the Reformation in Scotland.

Converted to Protestantism while on the Continent, he favoured an Anglo-Scottish alliance, ecclesiastical reform, and a vernacular Bible. After returning to Scotland, he held various offices, and in 1543, during the Protestant period of the Earl of Arran's regency, he rose to secretary of state and became one of the commissioners appointed to arrange a marriage treaty between Mary Stuart and Prince Edward (later Edward VI of England). He was instrumental in persuading Parliament to permit the reading of Scripture in the vernacular.

Imprisoned in Blackness Castle (November 1543) after Arran's reconciliation with Catholicism, Balnaves was released by English forces. Thereafter he acted as a paid agent for the English in Scotland until he was taken captive when a French expedition captured St. Andrews Castle (July 1547). While imprisoned by the French at Rouen, he wrote *The Confession of Faith,* reflecting Lutheran influence and published posthumously in 1584 with a preface by John Knox. Returning to Scotland in 1557, Balnaves was restored to his lands, took an active part in the religious rising of 1559, and was appointed an ordinary lord of session in 1564. On the fall of Mary Stuart he sided with the Protestant lords and by 1568 was a privy councillor.

Balochi (people): *see* Baluchi.

Balochi rug: *see* Baluchi rug.

Balodis, Jānis (b. Feb. 20, 1881, Trikata, Latvia, Russian Empire—d. Aug. 8, 1965, Saulkrasti, Latvian S.S.R.), army officer and politician, who was a principal figure in the foundation and government of independent Latvia as commander in chief of the army and navy in Latvia's war of independence and later as Cabinet member and vice president.

Graduated from the military academy at Vilnius in 1902 and commissioned an officer in the Russian Army, Balodis was decorated for his service in the Russo-Japanese War (1904–05). Wounded in action in East Prussia at the beginning of World War I and imprisoned by the Germans, he escaped and returned in November 1918 to Latvia. There the movement for national independence was asserting itself against both the Germans, to whom Bolshevik Russia had ceded the country in March 1918, and the Bolsheviks, who were now trying to reconquer it. Balodis took command of the Latvian national army on the death of Col. Oskars Kalpaks in March 1919 and was officially appointed commander in chief in October. He defended the newly founded national state against Bolshevik, German–Balt, German, and White Russian attacks.

In 1925 Balodis was elected to the Latvian Saeima (parliament), and in December 1931 he became the minister of war. Appointed deputy prime minister in the Cabinet of Kārlis Ulmanis on May 15, 1934, he became vice president when Ulmanis assumed the presidency on April 11, 1936. Shortly after the Soviet Army occupied Latvia, Ulmanis' government was deposed, and in July 1940 Ulmanis and Balodis were arrested and deported to the Soviet Union. After several years Balodis was permitted to return to Latvia and was allotted a small pension.

Balon, Jean, Balon also spelled BALLON (b. 1676, Paris—d. 1739, Paris), ballet dancer whose extraordinarily light, elastic leaps reputedly inspired the ballet term "ballon" used to describe a dancer's ability to ascend without apparent effort and to land smoothly and softly. The ballet term is also thought to derive from the French word *ballon* ("balloon"). Jean Balon, a popular virtuoso during the reign of Louis XIV, joined the Paris Académie (now Opéra) in 1691 and was a partner of Marie Subligny and Françoise Prévost. In 1708 he appeared with Prévost in *Les Horaces*, an early dance pantomime based on Corneille's play *Horace* and considered a forerunner of Jean-Georges Noverre's ballets d'action, or ballets with a plot.

Balovedu (people): *see* Lovedu.

Balquhidder, village, Stirling district, Central region, Scotland, near the east end of Loch (lake) Voil, famed as the burial place of the outlaw Rob Roy (Robert MacGregor), who died in 1734. His grave and those of some of his family are marked by three ancient carved stones. The ruined 17th-century church stands in front of a new church built in the 19th century. Pop. (1971) 556.

Balranald, town, southern New South Wales, Australia, on the Murrumbidgee River, near its junction with the Murray. Settled in 1847 and proclaimed a town in 1851, it was an important livestock ferrying point in the 1860s. Gazetted a municipality in 1882, it became a shire in 1957. Balranald serves a region of sheep, cattle, wheat, and irrigated fruit farming; lumbering and mining are also local activities. On the Sturt Highway, 418 mi (673 km) southwest of Sydney, it is served by the rail system of the state of Victoria. The closest rail link to the New South Wales system is at Hay (84 mi east). Pop. (1981) 1,442.

balsa (*Ochroma pyramidale,* or *lagopus*), tree of the bombax family (Bombacaceae), also called corkwood, native to tropical South America and noted for its exceedingly light wood (Spanish *balsa,* "raft" or "float"). The wood resembles clear white pine or basswood. Well-seasoned balsa weighs only 6 to 8 pounds (2.7 to 3.6 kilograms) per cubic foot, although wood from very slow growing trees may weigh more. Because of its buoyancy, about twice that of cork, balsa is admirably adapted for making floats for lifelines and life preservers. Its resiliency makes it an excellent shock-absorbing material for packing furniture and similar articles and also for foundation pads for machinery. Because of its insulating properties, it is used as a lining material for incubators, refrigerators, cold-storage rooms, and the like. Its lightness combined with high insulating power makes it a valuable construction material for transportation containers for solidified carbon dioxide. It is also used in the construction of passenger compartments for airplanes and in making model airplanes and boats.

Balsa seed fibre, known commercially as *édredon végétal* (plant eiderdown) or *pattes-de-lièvre* (rabbit's paws), is used as stuffing for mattresses and cushions. A floss mixture, composed of balsa fibre and several other seed fibres, is sold as *ouate végétale* (plant fibres).

balsam, aromatic resinous substance that flows from a plant, either spontaneously or from an incision; it consists of a resin dispersed in benzoic or cinnamic acid esters and is used chiefly in medicinal preparations. Certain of the more aromatic varieties have been incorporated into incense. Balsams are sometimes difficult to distinguish from oleoresins, which are resins dissolved in essential oils, but usually the oleoresins are slightly more fluid. Balsam of Peru, a fragrant, thick, deep brown or black fluid used in perfumery, is a true balsam, the produce of a lofty leguminous tree, *Myroxylon pereirae* growing in a limited area in El Salvador and introduced into Sri Lanka. It is mentioned in pharmacopoeias but has no medicinal value. Balsam of Tolu (Colombia), a brown balsam thicker than balsam of Peru, is used in perfumery and as a constituent in cough syrups and lozenges. It becomes solid on keeping. It also is a product of equatorial America.

Canada balsam and Mecca balsam, or balm of Gilead, are not true balsams.

balsam of fir: *see* Canada balsam.

Balsamo, Giuseppe: *see* Cagliostro, Alessandro, conte di.

Balsamon, Theodore (b. *c.* 1105, Constantinople—d. *c.* 1195, Constantinople), the principal Byzantine legal scholar of the medieval period and patriarch of Antioch (*c.* 1185–95). After a long tenure as law chancellor to the Patriarch of Constantinople, he preserved the world's knowledge of many source documents from early Byzantine political and theological history through his commentary (*c.* 1170) on the nomocanon, the standard annotated collection (since the 7th century) of Eastern Orthodox ecclesiastical and imperial laws and decrees.

A list of the abbreviations used in the MICROPAEDIA *will be found at the end of this volume*

Balsas River, Spanish RÍO BALSAS, river in southern central Mexico, one of that country's largest rivers. It rises as the Río Atoyac (Poblano) at the confluence of the San Martín and Zahuapan rivers in Puebla state and flowing southwestward and then westward through Guerrero state, in which it is the principal river and is locally known as the Mezcala. It forms the border between Guerrero and Michoacán states and empties into the Pacific Ocean at Mongrove Point. Although its 479-mi (771-km) course is unnavigable because it is frequently interrupted by rapids, the river is utilized extensively for generating hydroelectric power and for irrigation. Corn (maize), coffee, cotton, sugarcane, tropical fruits, and vegetables are the principal crops cultivated in its basin.

balshem (Judaism): *see* ba'al shem.

Balt, member of a people of the Indo-European linguistic family living on the southeastern shores of the Baltic Sea. (The name Balts, coined in the 19th century, is derived from the sea; Aestii was the name given these peoples by the Roman historian Tacitus.) In addition to the Lithuanians and the Latvians (Letts), several groups now extinct were included: the Yotvingians (Jatvians, or Jatvingians; assimilated among the Lithuanians and Slavs in the 16th–17th century); the Prussians (Germanized in the 18th century); the Curonians (Cours, or Kurs; Latvianized in the 16th century); and the Semigallians (Zemgalians) and the Selonians (Selians, extinct in the 14th century). Estonians, north of Latvia, are not Balts; they are members of the Finnic peoples (*q.v.*)

The prehistoric origin of the Balts, as of other Indo-Europeans, is obscure, but they arrived in the vast area of the eastern Baltic and west central Russia in the 3rd millennium BC, bringing with them knowledge of agriculture and cattle raising. Because of the inaccessibility of the western part of the area, bound in by sea, forest, and swamps, the Balts there—ancestors of Latvians and Lithuanians—maintained their individuality and paganism until the Middle Ages. Other Balts, however, were absorbed or displaced over the centuries; the eastern Baltic tribes, in particular, spread throughout Belorussia and western Russia and were Slavicized after the northward expansion of the Slavs from the 7th to the 13th century AD.

In the 13th century the historical record of the Balts really begins, for it was then that the Teutonic Order and the Order of the Brothers of the Sword conquered the Balts inhabiting the areas of Estonia and Latvia and converted them forcibly to Christianity. In reaction to the Teutonic pressures, the Lithuanians consolidated themselves into a powerful state and, allied with the Poles, checked the German expansion; by 1386, when Lithuania officially adopted Christianity, it had become a great empire. After the union between Lithuania and Poland in 1569, however, the Lithuanian aristocracy became decidedly Polish in language and politics; cultural decline and territorial shrinkage began, and by 1795 all Baltic lands were under Russian rule, which has persisted, except for a period of independence from 1917/18 to 1940.

Since Christianization, the Lithuanians traditionally have been mainly Roman Catholics, and the Latvians, since the Reformation, have been Lutherans (there are also small minorities of Greek Orthodox and other Protestants). In the past, all Baltic peoples were primarily agriculturalists and, especially among the Latvians, stock farmers. Originally land was held by individual peasants, but after the Baltic states were incorporated into the Soviet Union it was taken over by large state farms and collectives. At the same time the proportion of people working in agriculture and the position of agriculture in the economy steadily declined. There has been a considerable amount of industrial growth; engineering products, together with textiles, are of primary importance. Both the Lithuanians and the Latvians, despite heavy Germanic and Slavic influences, have retained a rich tradition of folktales, songs, and poetry.

Baltasar, also spelled BALTHASAR (co-regent of Babylon): *see* Belshazzar.

Balthus, pseudonym of BALTHAZAR KLOSSOWSKI, also spelled BALTHASAR KLOSSOWSKY (b. Feb. 29, 1908, Paris), reclusive French painter who, in the 20th century, reanimated the traditional categories of European painting—the landscape, the still life, the subject painting, and the portrait. His private, hallucinatory vision has, on occasion, been labelled surrealistic.

Balthus was born of artistic Polish parents, whose early married years were spent in Paris in an intellectual milieu that included Pierre Bonnard, André Gide, and André Derain. The family of his father—a painter, art historian, and stage designer—had left Warsaw in 1830 and settled in East Prussia, and that of his Jewish mother—also a painter—had moved from Minsk to Breslau, East Prussia, in 1873. Balthus was taken to Berlin by his parents in 1914 at the beginning of World War I, but after his parents separated in 1917 his time was divided for a number of years between war-torn Germany and Switzerland. Rainer Maria Rilke, a friend of Balthus' mother, encouraged the precocious youth to publish an early book of drawings about Mitsou, a lost cat, for which Rilke also contributed a preface. With the help of Gide, Balthus returned to Paris in 1924 and began studying and painting with financial aid raised on his behalf in part by Rilke. Balthus soon began to support himself by accepting commissions for stage sets and portraits, but after his first one-man show in Paris in 1934, he devoted most of his time to increasingly large and mysterious poetic interiors and austere, muted landscapes that were peopled with isolated and illusive nubile adolescents.

Balthus was given a successful show at the Museum of Modern Art in New York City in 1956, served as director of the French Academy in Rome from 1961 to 1977 (earning André Malraux's praise as France's "second ambassador to Italy"), and was honoured with huge retrospectives at the Georges Pompidou Center in Paris in 1983 and the Metropolitan Museum in New York City in 1984. His best known works include "The Street" (1933), "Guitar Lesson" (1934), "The Mountain" (1937), "Therese" (1938), "Patience" (1943), "The Méditeranée's Cat" (1949), "Le Passage du Commerce Saint-André" (1954), "Nude in Front of a Mantel" (1955), "Golden Afternoon" (1957), and "Card Players" (1973).

Baltic Entente, mutual defense pact signed by Lithuania, Latvia, and Estonia on Sept. 12, 1934, that laid the basis for close cooperation among those states, particularly in the conduct of their foreign affairs. Shortly after World War I, efforts were made to conclude a Baltic defense alliance among Finland, Estonia, Latvia, Lithuania, and Poland, all of which had recently broken away from the Russian Empire to form independent states, and feared the aggressive policies of Soviet Russia. But by the mid-1920s, when negotiations had failed to produce an agreement, the idea of a broad Baltic league was dropped in favour of a pact among Estonia, Latvia, and Lithuania. Latvia and Estonia had formalized a bilateral defense agreement in November 1923, and after they renewed it in February 1934 they invited Lithuania to join their alliance. On Sept. 12, 1934, the three nations signed the Treaty of Understanding and Cooperation at Geneva. Aimed primarily against Nazi Germany, which had replaced the Soviet Union as the most likely aggressor, the treaty, which was to last for 10 years, provided for mutual defense assistance in case of attack as well as for semi-annual foreign ministers' meetings to coordinate the signatories' foreign policies and diplomatic activities. The treaty also pledged the three countries not only to confer with each other on all foreign policy matters of mutual concern (excluding Lithuania's outstanding territorial disputes with Germany over Klaipėda [German Memel] and with Poland over Vilnius) but also to give each other diplomatic and political aid. As a result of this treaty, the three Baltic nations sent only a single representative to all international conferences, including the meetings of the League of Nations; in 1936 Latvia, as a representative of all three states, was elected a nonpermanent member of the League's council. The pact, which stimulated close cooperation in cultural and economic as well as foreign affairs, failed, however, as a means of defense. Notwithstanding their declaration of neutrality (1938), the Baltic pact members were not able to defend their independent status. Under the German-Soviet Pact of August 1939, the Baltic States were recognized as belonging to the Soviet sphere of interest; they were unable to prevent being annexed in 1940 by the Soviet Union.

Baltic languages, group of Indo-European languages, that includes modern Latvian and Lithuanian, spoken on the eastern shores of the Baltic Sea, and the extinct Old Prussian, Yotvingian, Curonian, Selonian, and Semigallian languages. The Baltic languages are related more closely to Slavic, Germanic, and Indo-Iranian than to other languages of the Indo-European family.

A brief treatment of the Baltic languages follows. For full treatment, *see* MACROPAEDIA: Languages of the World.

The Baltic languages form a branch of the Indo-European family of languages. The domain of the Baltic languages was far greater in the past, extending eastward from the Vistula River at least as far as the upper Dnepr Basin. Of the extinct Baltic languages, there are written records only for Old Prussian. Lithuanian and Latvian (East Baltic) are more closely related to each other than either is to Old Prussian (West Baltic).

The Baltic languages share a number of isoglosses with Slavic and Germanic and could thus be considered part of a north Indo-European dialect area. They are most closely related to the Slavic branch of Indo-European. Strong evidence for a period of Balto-Slavic unity is found in common lexical items: more than 100 words are common in their form and meaning to Baltic and Slavic alone. Morphological, tonal, and stress correspondences also demonstrate this relationship.

The question of the relationship between Baltic and Slavic is complicated by the fact that East Baltic and West Baltic each share a number of exclusive features with Slavic. As opposed to Old Prussian, for example, both East Baltic and Slavic have a genitive singular ending similar to that of Common Slavic. Old Prussian, on the other hand, agrees with Slavic in the formation of the possessive pronouns, while the East Baltic forms represented by Lithuanian *mãnas, tãvas, sãvas* are in basic agreement with forms found in other Indo-European languages. The original Balto-Slavic area was thus divided by a number of distinct isoglosses.

Of the East Baltic languages, Lithuanian is unusually conservative in its phonology. Certain Lithuanian words, for example, can serve as protoforms for Latvian and are often nearly identical with the forms posited for Proto-Slavic. Lithuanian is thus of particular importance for comparative Indo-European linguistics.

Latvian, by contrast, has undergone extensive sound change, including the development of the diphthongs *an, en, in, un* (preserved in Lithuanian) into *uo, ie, ī, ū;* the development of palatalized *k* and *g* (preserved in Lithuanian) into the affricates *c* and *dz;* the development of *š, ž,* resulting from the Indo-European palato-velars, into the dental spirants *s, z;* and the shortening of long vowels in final position and the loss of final short vowels.

Literary tradition among the Eastern Balts dates from the 16th century. The first book in Lithuanian is Martin Mažvydas's translation of Martin Luther's catechism (Königsberg, 1547). The first grammar of Lithuanian (1653 and 1654), written by Danielius Kleinas, and the poetry of Kristijonas Donelaitis (18th century) had a great influence on the formation and standardization of written Lithuanian in East Prussia. Literary tradition in the Grand Duchy of Lithuania begins with the translation from Polish of a catechism (1595) and a postilla, or collection of homilies (1599), by Mikalojus Daukša. The first dictionary of Lithuanian (1629) was compiled by Konstantinas Sirvydas and reflects the East and Central High Lithuania Lithuanian dialects.

The two major dialects of Lithuanian are Žemaičių, or Low Lithuanian, spoken in the western third of Lithuania, and Aukštaičių, or High Lithuanian. The Lithuanian standard language, established at the end of the 19th and beginning of the 20th centuries, is based on the highly conservative southern subdialect of West High Lithuanian.

The Lithuanian alphabet is based on the Latin alphabet, with the addition of diacritical marks. The "nasal" characters *ą, ę, į, ų* represent long pure vowels. In the linguistics literature, an acute is used for long stressed syllables with falling tone, and a circumflex marks long stressed syllables with a protracted or rising tone. The grave is used for short stressed syllables.

The Latvian literary tradition begins in 1585 with the publication of a translation of a Catholic catechism. The first Latvian dictionary, compiled by Georgius Mancelius, dates from 1638; and the first grammar, written by Johann Rehehausen, appeared in 1644. The language of the early texts differs little from the modern language.

Latvian is divided into three major dialects: Central Latvian (*vidus dialekts*), Livonian or Tahmian (*lībiskais dialekts*), and High Latvian *augšzemnieku dialekts*). The standard language is based on the Central dialect, which is phonologically the most conservative. A part of this dialect still distinguishes three phonemic tones: falling, protracted or rising, and broken, historically related to the rising tone. Unlike Lithuanian, which has free stress, the main word stress in Latvian has been generalized on the initial syllable.

The Latvian alphabet is based on the Latin alphabet, with added diacritical marks. The characters *ģ, ķ, ļ, ņ* represent palatal consonants.

The earliest text in Old Prussian is the so-called Elbing vocabulary, a German-Old Prussian vocabulary of 802 words, extant in a copy dating from about 1400. A second German-Old Prussian vocabulary of 100 words was compiled by Simon Grunau between 1517 and 1526. The most important Old Prussian written records are three 16th-century catechisms, translated from German. The language of these catechisms gives a distorted reflection of Old Prussian; the translations are excessively literal and contain numerous errors in language as well as inconsistencies in orthography. The texts, nevertheless, show that Old Prussian, which became extinct at the beginning of the 18th century, preserved a greater number of archaisms than either Lithuanian or Latvian.

Baltic Sea, German OSTSEE, Swedish ÖSTERSJÖN, Russian BALTIYSKOYE MORE, Finnish ITÄMERI, Polish MORZE BAŁTYCKIE, arm of the North Atlantic Ocean extending northward from the latitude of southern Denmark almost to the Arctic Circle, separating the Scandinavian peninsula from the rest of continental Europe.

The following article summarizes information about the Baltic Sea. For full treatment, *see* MACROPAEDIA: Europe.

The Baltic Sea is encircled by Norway, Sweden, Finland, the Soviet Union, Poland, East and West Germany, and Denmark. Covering an area of 160,000 sq mi (420,000 sq km), it is the largest expanse of brackish water in the world. Among its major affluents are the Vistula and the Oder rivers. The catchment area drained by the rivers bringing fresh water into the Baltic Sea is about four times as large as the sea itself. The Baltic Sea's major axis, from eastern Denmark to southern Finland, is about 1,000 mi (1,600 km) long, and its average width is approximately 120 mi. The western Baltic is connected to the North Sea by the channel known as the Skagerrak, a deep inlet that separates southern Norway from the tip of the Jutland peninsula; to the immediate east of the Skagerrak, but at a right angle to it, the shallower Kattegat separates northeastern Denmark from Sweden. The large islands of Bornholm (Denmark) and Öland and Gotland (Sweden) lie in the western Baltic, while the Åland Islands (Finnish Ahvenanmaa; Swedish Åland), farther north, rise from a narrows between Sweden and Finland and mark the entrance to the arm of the Baltic known as the Gulf of Bothnia (Swedish Bottenhavet). Just to the south of the Aland Islands, the narrow Gulf of Finland stretches eastward between Finland and the Soviet Union, with Leningrad at its head.

The Baltic is a shrunken remnant of the water-covered region that emerged as the melting Scandinavian Ice Sheet retreated toward the Arctic at the close of the Ice Age. The shallowest part of the Baltic is the continental shelf, from which rise the islands of the Danish archipelago. Here the Lille Bælt divides eastern Jutland from the island of Fyn (Funen), which is itself separated from Sjælland (Zealand) by the deeper Store Bælt. The narrow channel of The Sound (Danish Øresund) is too shallow for oceangoing vessels, so that Göteborg is the Swedish transatlantic shipping terminal on the coast of the Kattegat. The greatest deeps, more than 1,500 ft (457 m), lie off the southeastern coast of Sweden between Nyköping and the island of Gotland and also in the Gulf of Bothnia in the Aland Sea between Sweden and the Aland Islands. A deepwater channel also extends along most of the Gulf of Finland. The Baltic Sea proper contains a series of basins divided by shallow shelves.

Consult the INDEX *first*

Baltic Shield (Europe): *see* Fennoscandia.

Baltic War of Liberation (1918–20), military conflict in which Estonia, Latvia, and Lithuania fended off attacks from both Soviet Russia and Germany. Estonia, Latvia, and Lithuania had been part of the Russian Empire since the end of the 18th century, but after the Russian Revolution of 1917 they became independent states. After World War I ended, however, Soviet Russia, hoping to advance through the Baltic states in order to bring about a Socialist revolution in Germany, attacked in November 1918 and conquered three-quarters of Estonia's territory by the end of the year. In January the Red Army seized the capitals of Latvia and Lithuania, advanced to the Venta River in Latvia, and occupied northern and eastern Lithuania. The Estonians, who obtained weapons from the Allies and received naval support from the British and volunteers from Finland, were able to stop the Bolshevik advance, launch a counteroffensive (Jan. 3, 1919), and evict the Red Army from their land.

The Latvians and Lithuanians, however, were forced to rely upon the Germans, who wished not only to drive the Bolsheviks out of the Baltic states but also to establish their own hegemony in the area; they therefore prevented the Latvian and Lithuanian governments from organizing regular armies. They did help Lithuanian volunteers halt the Soviet advance in February 1919 and subsequently provided some military assistance as the Lithuanians slowly pushed the Red Army back. In addition, the Poles, who were at war with Soviet Russia, entered Lithuania (March 1919) and seized Vilnius from the Bolsheviks (April).

The commander of the German troops in Latvia, Gen. Rüdiger, Graf von der Goltz, sought to transform Latvia into a base for a new anti-Communist German–Russian force and to form Baltic regimes loyal to imperial Germany and pre-revolutionary Russia. Although his troops took Riga from the Red Army on May 22, 1919, they were stopped by the Estonian army and some 2,000 Latvian troops. The Germans were then compelled to abandon Riga, and the autonomous Latvian government was restored. Still hoping to dominate the Baltic region, General von der Goltz, who had retreated into Courland, joined forces in July with the anti-Communist West Russian army of Col. Pavel Bermondt-Avalov and participated in his attacks on Riga and on northwestern Lithuania. Bermondt's campaign, however, was unsuccessful, and by December 15 all German troops had finally abandoned Latvia and Lithuania.

While the Baltic forces subdued the Germans, the Bolshevik threat persisted. In August 1919 the Lithuanians expelled the Soviet army from northwestern Lithuania, and in November–December the Estonians repulsed a fresh invasion of the Red Army pursuing an anti-Bolshevik Russian force into Estonia. After the Latvians, aided by the Poles, drove the Bolsheviks from southeastern Latvia, the Soviets signed the treaties of Tartu (February 1920), Moscow (July 1920), and Riga (August 1920), thereby recognizing the independence of the Baltic states.

Baltiisk, also spelled BALTIJSK (Russian S.F.S.R.): *see* Baltiysk.

Baltimore, city, within but administratively independent of Baltimore County, north central Maryland, U.S., at the head of the Patapsco River estuary 15 mi (24 km) above Chesapeake Bay. The state's largest city and economic hub, it covers an area of 91.3 sq mi (236.5 sq km), about 14 percent of which is water. It was established in 1729 and named after the Irish barony of Baltimore (seat of the Calvert family, proprietors of the Colony of Maryland). The founders were seeking outlets for local tobacco, but slow development led to a search for more prosperous markets. At the outbreak of the American Revolution it was a bustling seaport and shipbuilding centre. Baltimore clippers plied the seas, and trade extended to the Caribbean. The U.S. Navy's first ship, "Constellation," launched in Baltimore, is now permanently moored in the city's harbour. After the British occupation of Philadelphia, the Continental Congress met in Baltimore (December 1776–March 1777). During the War of 1812 the successful defense (Sept. 13–14, 1814) of Ft. McHenry (now a national monument) was the inspiration for Francis Scott Key's "Star-Spangled Banner," the original manuscript of which is in the Maryland Historical Society quarters. In 1827 the nation's first railroad, the Baltimore and Ohio, started from the city's Mount Clare Station (preserved; now the site of a railroad museum). Though Maryland did not secede from the Union, many of its citizens had Southern sympathies. The state's first casualties of the Civil War occurred in Baltimore during a railway transfer of Federal troops six days after the Ft. Sumter engagement. The city was under martial law until the end of the war.

A fire on Feb. 7, 1904, razed most of the business district, but recovery was rapid. At the beginning of World War I, Baltimore began to develop industrially with the construction of steelworks, oil refineries, and related war industries. It is now a major seaport with extensive shipbuilding and repair facilities and a highly diversified economy. The National Social Security Headquarters is in the city, and industrial parks dot the surrounding area. The port, relatively free of shipping hazards, opens to the sea through Chesapeake Bay and the Chesapeake and Delaware Canal.

In the 1920s and early '30s Baltimore acquired an intellectual aura from the work of H.L. Mencken, essayist and editor, and his circle, including journalists on *The Sun* newspaper. Educational institutions in the Baltimore area include Johns Hopkins University (1876), Coppin State College (1900), Towson State University (1866), Loyola College (1852), College of Notre Dame of Maryland (1873), Morgan State University (1867), University of Maryland (1807), Maryland Institute College of Art (1826), Peabody (music) Institute (1868), and the University of Baltimore (1925). Cultural facilities include the Enoch Pratt Free Library (1884), Peale Museum (1813), Baltimore Museum of Art (1914), Walters Art Gallery (1931), and a symphony orchestra, civic opera, and stage theatre.

Baltimore was the first diocese of the Roman Catholic Church, and the Basilica of the Assumption of the Blessed Virgin Mary (1806–21) was the first Roman Catholic cathedral in the U.S.; St. Mary's Seminary was founded in 1791. Presbyterian Church cemetery contains the grave of Edgar Allan Poe. The Shot Tower (1829) is a 234-ft shaft that was used to manufacture round shot. The Washington

The Washington Monument (centre), Baltimore, Md.
Paul Conklin

Monument (1829), a 160-ft Doric shaft, is on a hilltop north of the city. Ft. Howard, Hampton National Historic Site, Aberdeen Proving Ground, and Pimlico Race Track (home of the Preakness Stakes) are nearby. The city's representatives in professional sports are the Orioles (baseball). The birthplace of Babe Ruth, the baseball great, is preserved as a shrine and museum. The Lacrosse Hall of Fame on Johns Hopkins University campus is testament to the popularity of the old Indian game in Baltimore. Baltimore's Friendship International Airport also serves Washington, D.C. The Harbor Tunnel Thruway (1957) and Francis Scott Key Bridge (1977) cross the Patapsco. Urban renewal projects were in various stages of development in the 1980s. Inc. town, 1745; city, 1797. Pop. (1980) city, 786,775; metropolitan area (SMSA), 2,174,023.

Baltimore, BARONS, titled English nobility in the family Calvert, grouped below chronologically and indicated by the symbol •.

• Baltimore, George Calvert, 1st Baron (b. 1580?, Kipling, Yorkshire, Eng.—d. April 15, 1632, London), British statesman who projected the founding of the North American province of Maryland, in an effort to find a sanctuary for practicing Roman Catholics.

A member of the English House of Commons, George Calvert gave up his seat in 1625 after he had declared himself a Roman Catholic and was created Baron Baltimore with extensive estates in Ireland. From then on he directed his main attention to colonial enterprise, having earlier been active in the Virginia Company (1609–20).

In 1621 Baltimore had sent Capt. Edward Wynne to Newfoundland to establish a small settlement named Ferryland; two years later he procured a charter for the colony under the name Avalon. In order to assure the prosperity of his holdings in the New World, Baltimore visited Avalon briefly in 1627 and returned with most of his family the following year. The climate proved too severe, however, taking its toll in death and illness among the settlers, and Lady Baltimore left the colony in 1628 for Virginia. Baltimore thereupon petitioned the king for a land grant in the more temperate Chesapeake Bay area and, without waiting for a reply, sailed for Jamestown to join his wife. He was, however, forbidden to settle in Virginia because of his religion. He therefore returned to England to plead his case for the Maryland charter, but died before a new cession could be secured.

• Baltimore, Cecilius Calvert, 2nd Baron (b. 1605—d. Nov. 30, 1675), founder of the colony of Maryland. He was the eldest son of the 1st Baron Baltimore, who had initiated the idea of a sanctuary for Roman Catholics in the Americas.

Cecilius Calvert studied at Trinity College, Oxford, and married Anne Arundell, daughter of the 2nd Baron Arundell of Wardour, a Roman Catholic peer. The charter for Maryland was issued on June 20, 1632, two months after his father's death, and he received it as the 2nd Baron Baltimore. He never visited the New World himself but instead entrusted the governorship of the colony to his younger brother, Leonard Calvert (1606–47). During this period the Calverts sought to establish freedom of conscience in the colony for both Catholics and Protestants who accepted the doctrine of the Trinity.

• Baltimore, Charles Calvert, 3rd Baron (b. Aug. 27, 1637, England—d. Feb. 21, 1715, London), British statesman who was commissioned governor of Maryland in 1661 and succeeded as proprietor of the colony in 1675.

Like his grandfather, George Calvert, 1st Baron Baltimore, Charles Calvert was a Roman Catholic, and anti-Catholic feeling was strong among Maryland's Protestant majority. Matters were further aggravated by the hostility of the Susquehanna Indians as well as by the need to defend his territorial jurisdiction against claims by William Penn to the north. Antagonism in the Maryland Assembly led Calvert in 1670 to restrict suffrage by property qualifications and occasionally to set aside acts of the legislature. Finally, after the English Revolution of 1688, he was deprived of the province. He returned to England and was later accused of taking part in two Catholic plots but was never arrested.

His son, Benedict Leonard Calvert, had conformed to the established church in 1713 and thereupon had the colony of Maryland restored to him.

Baltimore, David (b. March 7, 1938, New York City), U.S. virologist who shared the Nobel Prize in Physiology or Medicine in 1975 with his former professor, Renato Dulbecco, and another of Dulbecco's students, Howard M. Temin.

Baltimore and Temin discovered independently that some animal cancer viruses that are composed mainly of ribonucleic acid (RNA) can transfer their genetic information to deoxyribonucleic acid (DNA). This DNA alters the hereditary pattern of the cell infected by the virus, tranforming it into a cancer cell.

Baltimore and his wife, Alice Huang, showed that the virus causing vesicular stomatitis reproduced itself through the action of an enzyme that copies RNA by a process that does not involve DNA. Baltimore in 1970 tested two cancer viruses to see if they did anything similar. He found that both contained an enzyme that made DNA copies of the viral RNA, thereby reversing the common pattern of molecular biology, that is, that genetic information always passes from DNA to RNA.

After graduating from Swarthmore College in Pennsylvania, Baltimore was trained in virology at Rockefeller University (New York), where he obtained his Ph.D. in 1964, and at the Massachusetts Institute of Technology (MIT). He worked with Dulbecco at the Salk Institute in La Jolla, Calif. (1965–68), then returned to MIT to join its faculty.

Baltimore and Ohio Railroad (B&O), first steam-operated railway in the United States to be chartered as a common carrier of freight and passengers (1827). The B&O Railroad Company was established by Baltimore merchants to compete with New York merchants following the opening of the Erie Canal in 1825. A driving force in its early years was the Baltimore banker George Brown, who served as treasurer from 1827 until 1834 and had Ross Winans build the first real railroad car.

The first stone for the line was laid on July 4, 1828, by Charles Carroll, the revolutionary leader and last surviving signer of the Declaration of Independence. The first 13 mi (21 km) of line, from Baltimore to Ellicott's Mills, Md. (now Ellicott City), opened in 1830. Peter Cooper's steam locomotive, the "Tom Thumb," ran over this line and demonstrated to doubters that steam traction was feasible on the steep, winding grades.

The railroad was extended to Wheeling, Va. (now West Virginia), a distance of 379 miles, in 1853. In the 1860s and 1870s the railroad reached Chicago and St. Louis. In 1896 it went bankrupt. After it was reorganized in 1899, it grew further, reaching Cleveland and Lake Erie in 1901. In 1963 the B&O was acquired by the Chesapeake and Ohio Railway Company, and in 1980 became part of the newly formed CSX Corporation.

The B&O's long-distance passenger trains were discontinued in 1971 when the National Railroad Passenger Corporation (Amtrak) took over intercity passenger service, although it continued limited commuter service at Washington, D.C., and Pittsburgh. About one-quarter of the B&O's freight revenues come from its traditional haulage of bituminous coal from mines in the Allegheny Mountains. Other important freight includes motor vehicles and parts, and chemicals.

Baltimore Aquarium, one of the largest public aquariums in the United States. The aquarium, which opened in 1981 in the Inner Harbor area of Baltimore, was financed by the city but was officially designated a branch of the National Aquarium (*q.v.*), by the U.S. Congress. Of the more than 5,000 aquatic specimens maintained by the aquarium, many are marine mammals and birds. The marine-life exhibits are connected to a system of three large tanks that are used to circulate 1,900,000 litres (500,000 gallons) of salt water. Numerous freshwater life forms are also on display. The decor and effect of the aquarium are impressive. There is, for example, a 19-metre- (63-foot-) long skeleton of a finback whale suspended from the ceiling, and background sounds of the sea and sea life are audible throughout various sections of the facility.

The underlying theme of the exhibits is the concept that all life is dependent on water, whether in the atmosphere, in the soil, or in the lakes, rivers, and oceans. One of the more notable displays is of a tropical rainforest with waterfalls and dripping vegetation inside of an 18-metre (60-foot)-high glass pyramid.

Baltimore clipper, small, fast sailing ship developed by Chesapeake Bay (U.S.) builders in the 18th century. Its speed made it valuable for use as a privateer, for conveying perishables, and in the slave trade, and its hull design gives it claim as an ancestor of the larger

The "Tom Thumb," first American-built locomotive to operate in regular service

By courtesy of The Baltimore and Ohio Railroad Co.

Baltimore clipper "Ann McKim," drawing and lithograph by E. Armitage McCan

By courtesy of the Peabody Museum, Salem, Mass.

clipper ships of the 19th century. Most Baltimore clippers had two steeply raked masts that were rigged with various combinations of fore-and-aft and square sails.

Baltimore County, county in north central Maryland, U.S., almost surrounding Baltimore city, which was separately organized in 1851. It was named for the Barons Baltimore who founded Maryland. Its legal origin is not precisely known, although records date from 1659. Since no community within its boundary is incorporated, all local administration is by the county government under provisions of a 1956 charter. The county (area 638 sq mi [1,652 sq km]) was primarily rural until World War II, after which large tracts of farmland were developed as suburban industrial communities. These include Sparrows Point (site of a huge steel plant), Dundalk, Essex, Middle River, Pikesville, and Woodlawn–Woodmoor. Hampton National Historic Site, a restored 18th-century Georgian mansion, is near Towson (*q.v.*), the county seat. The Gunpowder River, impounded by Prettyboy and Loch Raven dams, supplies water to the area. Pop. (1980) 655,615.

Baltimore Incident: *see* Itata and Baltimore incidents.

Baltistān, agency and geographical region, in the Pakistani-held sector of Jammu and Kashmir, in the northwestern part of the Indian subcontinent. Drained by the Indus and Shyok rivers, Baltistān is situated on the high Ladākh Plateau and contains the loftiest peaks of the Karakoram Range—K2 (Mt. Godwin Austen; at 28,250 ft [8,611 m] the second highest mountain in the world), Gasherbrum I (26,470 ft), and Broad Peak (26,400 ft). Harsh in climate, Baltistān receives an average precipitation of only 6 in. (150 mm) per year, but it contains several glaciers. The valleys are at an elevation of 8,000 to 10,000 ft. The agricultural economy of the agency depends upon the melting ice and snow and on irrigation. The most abundant crops are barley and fruits. Baltistān is chiefly inhabited by Baltis, Muslim tribes of Tibetan origin who eke out a meagre living growing crops and raising fruit. Skārdu, in the Indus River Valley, is the administrative headquarters of the agency.

Baltit (Jammu and Kashmir): *see* Hunza.

Baltiysk, also spelled BALTIISK, or BALTIJSK, formerly (until 1946) PILLAU, city and port, Kaliningrad *oblast* (administrative region), northwestern Russian Soviet Federated Socialist Republic, at the entrance to the tip of the narrow peninsula separating Frisches Haff (lagoon) from the Baltic Sea. Originally the German East Prussian town of Pillau (1686–1946), Baltiysk is connected by canal to Kaliningrad and serves as its outport. It also has good railway connections with Lithuania, Belorussia, and the Ukraine. There are metal-working and light engineering industries and ship repairing. Pop. (1970) 20,300.

Baltiyskoye More (Europe): *see* Baltic Sea.

Balto-Slavic languages, hypothetical language group comprising the languages of the Baltic and Slavic subgroups of the Indo-European language family. Those scholars who accept the Balto-Slavic hypothesis attribute the large number of close similarities in the vocabulary, grammar, and sound systems of the Baltic and Slavic languages to development from a common ancestral language after the breakup of Proto-Indo-European. Those scholars who reject the hypothesis believe that the similarities are the result of parallel development and of mutual influence during a long period of contact.

Baltra Island, also called SOUTH SEYMOUR ISLAND, one of the smaller (area 8 sq mi [21 sq km]) of the Galápagos Islands, in the eastern Pacific Ocean, about 600 mi (965 km) west of Ecuador. Before volcanic faulting occurred, the island was a part of Santa Cruz (Indefatigable) Island. During World War II, when the island was nicknamed the "Achilles' Heel of the Panama Canal," Ecuador granted the United States permission to establish an air base (defunct since 1946) there. With the growth of tourism, the Ecuadorian government has renovated the airfield for commercial airline use.

Bałtyckie, Morze (Europe): *see* Baltic Sea.

Baluba (people): *see* Luba.

Balūchestān va Sīstān (*ostān* [province], Iran): *see* Sīstān-e Balūchestān.

Baluchi, also spelled BALOCHI, or BELUCHI, group of tribes speaking the Baluchi language and estimated at about 3,200,000 inhabitants of the province of Baluchistan in Pakistan and also neighbouring areas of Iran, Afghanistan, Bahrain, and Punjab (India). The Baluchi people are divided into two groups, the Sulaimani and the Makrani, separated from each other by a compact block of Brahui tribes.

The original Baluchi homeland lay probably on the Iranian plateau. They were mentioned in Arabic chronicles of the 10th century AD. The old tribal organization is best preserved among those inhabiting the Sulaimān Mountains. Each tribe (*tuman*) consists of several clans and acknowledges one chief, even though in some *tuman* there are clans in habitual opposition to the chief.

The Baluchi are traditionally nomads, but settled agricultural existence is becoming commoner; every chief has a fixed residence. The villages are collections of mud or stone huts; on the hills enclosures of rough stone walls are covered with matting to serve as temporary habitations. The Baluchi raise camels, cattle, sheep, and goats and engage in carpet making and embroidery. Their agricultural methods are primitive. They profess Islām.

Baluchi rug, Baluchi also spelled BALOCHI, or BELUCHI, floor covering woven by the Baluch people living in Afghanistan and east Iran. The patterns in these rugs are highly varied, many consisting of repeated motifs, such as the diagonal, evidently copied from other textile types. Some present a maze of intricately latch-hooked forms. Prayer rugs, with a simple rectangular arch-head design at one end (to indicate the direction of Mecca, the Holy City), are common. Normally, the field of these prayer rugs is filled with the leaves and stems of a highly stylized tree, and geometric small plants appear in the spandrels.

Frequently, the Baluchi rugs have long aprons at both ends, decorated with stripes and bands of brocading. The colour scheme of older rugs is a dark combination of reds and blues with touches of white. Many pieces, including those more poorly made, also make use of varying brown and tan shades, either of camel hair or material dyed to resemble it. Baluchi rugs are usually all wool, but their material may also include goat and camel hair, cotton for whites, and in some cases a few knots of silk.

Baluchi rug from Iran, 20th century; in a New York state private collection

In a New York state private collection; photograph, Otto E. Nelson—EB Inc.

The knotting is customarily Senna (Sehna). The rugs vary greatly in quality, the better ones usually being ascribed to the Khorāsān province of Iran. Baluchi rugs are frequently classed with the products of the Turkmens but show little relationship to them.

Baluchistan, also spelled BALŪCHISTĀN (Baluch: "place of the Baluch people"), westernmost province of Pakistan. It is bordered on the west by Iran; on the northwest by Afghanistan; on the northeast and east by Pakistani provinces of North-West Frontier, Punjab, and Sind; and on the south by the Arabian Sea.

While an indigenous population of the region passed through the Stone and Bronze Ages and was part of Alexander the Great's empire, the Baluch people themselves did not enter the region until the 14th century AD. The Baluch and Pashtun (Pathan) people constitute the two major and more distinct ethnic groups; the mixed ethnic stock, mainly of Sindhi origin, forms the third major group. Baluch, Brahui, Pashto, Sindhi, and Seraiki are the main languages. It was established as a separate province in its present form in 1970. Its capital, Quetta, is located in the north. It is the largest and most sparsely populated province in Pakistan.

The following article summarizes the political history, geography, and modern culture of the Baluchistan; for additional treatment of its geography and history, *see* MACROPAEDIA: Pakistan.

There are four major physical regions. The upper highlands of the central and northeastern areas are bounded by the Sulaimān Range to the east and the Toba Kākar Range to the northwest. The lower highlands include the eastern slopes of the Sulaimān Range; the lower ranges of the Makrān, Khārān, and Chāgai on the west; and the Pab and Kīrthar ranges on the southeast. The highland regions are primarily inhabited by nomadic herdsmen. Flat plains extend northward along the coast into the mountains; in the northwest an arid desert region consists of the Chāgai, Khārān, and Makrān deserts and the swamps of Lora and Māshkel. The upper highlands drain into the Indus, while the lower highlands drain northward into the swamps or southward into the Arabian Sea. Outside the influence of the Asian monsoon, most of the province is dry with continental extremes of heat and cold.

Agriculture is limited by the scarcity of water, power, and adequate transportation facilities. Wheat, *jowar* (sorghum), and rice are the major food crops, and fruits are the principal cash crops. Sheep raising employs the great majority of the population and occupies most of the land. The sheep provide a high-quality wool, part of which is exported. Almost all industry is small-scale and includes cotton and woollen manufacturing, food processing, carpet making, textile and leather embroidery, small machinery and appliance manufacturing, and handicrafts. The transportation network is poorly developed, but roads connect the major towns, and Quetta is connected by road to the ocean port of Karāchi in Sind province. Quetta is the centre of the railway network and its airport offers domestic service.

The University of Baluchistan was established in Quetta in 1970. The Baluchi Academy, the Brahui Adabī Dīwān, and the Pashto Academy, also in Quetta, promote the preservation of the traditional culture. Area 134,050 sq mi (347,188 sq km). Pop. (1981 prelim.) 4,305,000.

Baluchistan, Iranian, also spelled BALŪCHESTĀN, nonpolitical region, the greater part of which is in southeastern Sīstān-e Balūchestān *ostān* (province), southeastern Iran. With harsh physical and social conditions, the region is the least developed part of Iran. Precipitation, scarce and falling mostly in violent rainstorms, causes floods and heavy erosion, while heat is oppressive for eight months of the year. Its mountain chains, including the Bāga-e Band and Kūh-e Bāmpusht, run east-west, parallel to the Gulf of Oman, making access difficult. In the centre of the region there is abundant groundwater and streams, such as the Rūd-e Māshkīd and the Kunārī Rūd, that sometimes open out into valleys.

The Baluchi and Brahui nomads long resisted settlement. Sedentary groups include the descendants of old Iranian stock, Indians (Jāṭ), and remnants of an ancient primitive group. Camelback raiding and internal warfare were once common in the region.

In ancient times, Iranian Baluchistan provided a land route to the Indus Valley and the Babylonian civilizations. The region has also been called Mokran, Land of the Ichthyophagi (Fish Eaters), mentioned by Herodotus. The armies of Alexander the Great marched through Baluchistan in 326 BC on their way to the Hindu kush and on their return march in 325 experienced great hardships in the barren wastes inland along the entire length of Baluchistan. The Seljuq invasion of Kermān in the 11th century AD stimulated the eastward migration of the Baluchi. The Seljuq ruler Qāwurd (Kavurt) sent an expedition against the Kufichis (Qufs), Baluchi mountaineers whose banditry had long made the southern and eastern parts of the region insecure. After suppressing the Baluchi, the Seljuqs put watchtowers, cisterns, and caravansaries along the route through the desert to encourage trade with India. The Baluchi remained rebellious under Ṣafavid rule (1501–1736). Moḥammad Taqī Khān, governor of Fārs, led an expedition from Makran to Sind; his land forces were defeated by the Baluchi in 1740. The western part of Baluchistan was conquered by Persia during the 19th century, and its boundary was fixed in 1872. Russian and British colonialism consisted in part of instigating the local people to rebel against the Iranian government. In 1910 Baluchi cut telephone wires and killed officials of the Iranian government in remote outposts of the Indo-European Telegraph. The government began to assist settlement and economic development in the 1970s by constructing dams and thermoelectric power plants. In the wake of the Iranian Revolution there were disturbances by the Baluchi in the region in 1979.

Palm-tree oases in central Iranian Baluchistan contain orchards of oranges, pomegranates, mulberries, and bananas; grain, tobacco, rice, cotton, sugarcane, and indigo plants are grown. A road was opened from Zāhedān, capital of Sīstān-e Balūchestān *ostān,* to the port of Chāh Bahār. Zāhedān also is connected by rail with Pakistan, Zābol, and Tehrān; and it is a junction for roads east–west. There are airports at Zāhedān, Īrānshahr, and Jāsk.

Baluchitherium, extinct genus of giant browsing perissodactyls found as fossils in Asian deposits of late Oligocene and early Miocene age (the Oligocene Epoch preceded the Miocene Epoch and ended 26,000,000 years ago). *Baluchitherium,* related to the modern rhinoceroses but hornless, was probably the largest land mammal that ever existed, standing about 5.5 metres (18 feet) high at the shoulder. Its skull, small in proportion to its body, was more than four feet in length. *Baluchitherium* had relatively long front legs and a long neck; thus, it was probably able to browse on the leaves and branches of trees. Its limbs were massive and strongly constructed.

Baluchitherium, detail of a restoration painting by Charles R. Knight

By courtesy of the American Museum of Natural History, New York

A relative of *Baluchitherium* was *Indricotherium,* an animal restricted to the Oligocene of Asia.

Balue, Jean (b. *c.* 1421, Angles-sur-l'Anglin, Poitou, Fr.—d. 1491, Ancona, Italy), French cardinal, the treacherous minister of Louis XI.

Of humble parentage, he was first patronized by the bishop of Poitiers. In 1461 he became vicar-general of the bishop of Angers. His activity, cunning, and mastery of intrigue gained him the appreciation of Louis XI, who made him his almoner. In a short time Balue became a considerable personage. In 1465 he received the bishopric of Évreux; the King made him *le premier du grant conseil,* and, in spite of his dissolute life, obtained for him a cardinalate (1468). But in that year Balue was compromised in the King's humiliation by Charles the Bold, duke of Burgundy, at Péronne and excluded from the council.

Balue then intrigued with Charles against his master: their secret correspondence was intercepted, and on April 23, 1469, Balue was thrown into prison, where he remained 11 years, but not, as has been alleged, in an iron cage. In 1480, through the intervention of Pope Sixtus IV, he was set at liberty and from that time lived in high favour at the court of Rome. He received the bishopric of Albano and afterward that of Palestrina. In 1484 he was even sent to France as legate *a latere.*

Bālurghāt, town, administrative headquarters of West Dinājpur district, West Bengal state, northeastern India, just east of the Atrai River. Connected by road with English Bāzār (India) and Dinājpur and Rājshāhi (Bangladesh), it is the chief distributing centre for the district, trading mainly in rice, jute, sugarcane, and oilseeds. It was declared a municipality in 1951. Pop. (1981) 104,646.

balustrade, low screen formed by railings of stone, wood, metal, glass, or other materials and designed to prevent falls from roofs, balconies, terraces, etc.

Stairway and porch balustrades of Chiswick House, London, built by Lord Burlington and Colin Campbell, 1725

A.F. Kersting

The classic Renaissance balustrade consisted of a broad, molded handrail supported by a series of miniature columns of freely adapted traditional form. On building exteriors it was made of stone; in interiors, often of wood. These supporting columns are known as balusters and may be of shaped wood or metal and either decorated or not. In modern balustrades the uprights are frequently of metal and placed far apart to support horizontal rails of wood or panels of glass or plastic.

The pulpit balustrade in Siena cathedral, Italy, and the parapet of the Pitti Palace, Florence, are good examples of classic balustrades.

Baluze, Étienne (b. Nov. 24, 1630, Tulle, Fr.—d. July 28, 1718, Paris), French scholar, notable both as a historian and as the collector and publisher of documents and manuscripts.

At the Collège St. Martial at Toulouse, he studied chiefly ecclesiastical history and canon law, becoming in 1654 secretary to the Archbishop of Toulouse, a noted historian. After five years as secretary to the Bishop of Auch, in 1667 Baluze entered the service of Jean-Baptiste Colbert, the future minister of finances to Louis XIV, as his librarian, a post he was to hold for more than 30 years. In 1670 he received the additional appointment of professor of canon law at the Collège Royal.

He published his *Concilia Galliae Narbonensis* in 1668, following this with other important works, including *Capitularia regum Francorum* (1677), *Miscellanea* (1678–83), *Nova collectio Conciliorum* (1683, only one vol. published), and *Vitae Paparum Avenionensium* (1693). He also edited the works of many ecclesiastical writers. In 1700 he relinquished his position as librarian, having enormously enriched Colbert's collection of books, and in 1707 was appointed director of the Collège Royal. In 1708 appeared his *Histoire généalogique de la maison d'Auvergne,* undertaken at the request of the Cardinal de Bouillon. In this, which purported to trace the cardinal's descent from the counts of Auvergne in the 9th century, Baluze made use of documents already proved to have been forged. After Bouillon fled abroad, Baluze was deprived of all his offices and banished for some years from Paris. While in exile he completed his *Historia Tutelensis* (1717).

Baly (India): *see* Bally.

Balzac, Honoré de, original name HONORÉ BALSSA (b. May 20, 1799, Tours, Fr.—d. Aug. 18, 1850, Paris), French fiction writer, who produced a vast collection of novels and short stories called *La Comédie humaine* (*The Human Comedy*). He helped to establish the orthodox classical novel, with logically sequenced events, coherent characters, and strong dialogue.

Early career. Balzac was of southern peasant stock. His father had made a career in the civil service, mainly based in Paris, but he was in Tours from 1798 to 1814. He had no right to the aristocratic particle *de,* which first he, then his son, assumed. Honoré's mother was of bourgeois stock, her family being cloth makers. Of neurotic temperament, she never understood her son, but it was probably thanks to her that he became attached to the various kinds of pseudo-science and occultism—mesmerism, magnetism, somnambulism, physiognomy, phrenology, and Illuminism—that permeated his thought. His sister Laure (later de Surville) was his only childhood friend, and she became his first biographer.

He spent nearly six years at the Collège des Oratoriens at Vendôme. At Napoleon's downfall his family moved to Paris, where Honoré went to school for two more years and then spent three more as a lawyer's clerk. He aimed, however, at a literary career: as a writer of tragedy (*Cromwell,* 1819) he had no success. He turned to the novel: the results were sentimental and mystic. He turned out potboilers—gothic, humorous, historical novels—written under composite pseudonyms. He turned his attention to social skits—"physiologies" and "codes," parodies of scientific and legalistic compilations. Then he tried a business career as publisher, printer, and typefounder. By 1828 he was on the verge of bankruptcy and pulled out—the beginning of a lifetime of debt. He returned to writing, and his literary apprenticeship was over.

Two works of 1829 brought Balzac to the brink of success. *Les Chouans,* the first novel published under his own name, is a historical novel about Breton peasants called Chouans and their part in royalist guerrilla warfare

Honoré de Balzac, daguerreotype, 1848
J.E. Bulloz

in western France in 1799. The other, *La Physiologie du mariage* (*The Physiology of Marriage*), was anonymous and, on the surface, humorous and satirical: the subject was cuckoldry, encompassing both its causes and its cure. It betrayed a fundamental sympathy for and understanding of women that he was immediately to unfold in fiction and thereby began to establish his reputation.

Balzac's parents had retired to Versailles, while he himself spent most of his time in Paris: the man from Tours was already a Parisian and settled in a flat in the rue Cassini. A boisterous, somewhat vulgar person, avid for fame, fortune, and love, but above all conscious of genius, he decided to conquer not only the world of letters but also fashionable and artistic society. His knowledge of women was no longer secondhand. Of all his early loves, Madame de Laure Berny—"la Dilecta" ("The Beloved")—was, however, the most important. No doubt it was she who helped him come to an understanding of the mature woman, which inspired many of his novels.

Between 1828 and 1834 Balzac led a characteristically tumultuous existence, spending his earnings in advance as a dandy and man-about-town, exciting some general hilarity by his sartorial extravagances, his two-wheeler and groom, his gaudy walking stick, and other adornments. As a fascinating raconteur, he was fairly well received in society. But social ostentation then and later was, above all, a relaxation from phenomenal bouts of work—14 to 16 hours at his table in his white, quasi-monastic dressing gown, with his goose-quill pen and his exorbitant drinking of coffee. He was keen to make money but was already upbraiding his age for worshipping it. He was exigent with editors and publishers. Everything, however, was genuinely subservient to a tremendous creative urge within him and a desire to put his century to rights.

The reigns of Louis XVIII and Charles X witnessed an upsurge of polemical and satirical journalism. Cheap, small, and generally scurrilous sheets bent on attacking the increasingly reactionary ministries appeared, and Balzac wrote for some of these between 1829 and 1831 and even helped to found one, *La Caricature.* They were mostly liberal, but by this time Balzac was no longer liberal-minded. He moved over to the absolutist view and wrote in 1832 for the royalist *Le Rénovateur.* Furthermore, he began to restrict his journalistic writing to such reputable periodicals as *La Revue de Paris.* Even with these, however, he quarrelled repeatedly, and he began to nourish a rancour against journalism. His later scathing attacks on the periodical press are truly memorable.

Balzac worked at high pressure in his rue Cassini flat until in 1835 the pursuit of creditors drove him to a house in Chaillot, a suburb of Paris, where he adopted a series of ingenious schemes for evading writ servers. He looked upon the novel as a variety of drama, and between 1829 and 1830 he produced his first six *Scènes de la vie privée* ("Scenes from Private Life"). Two novels of this period of special importance are *Le Curé de Tours* (*The Vicar of Tours*) and *Eugénie Grandet,* which show him working toward a second kind of *scène*—that of provincial life.

"La Comédie humaine." The year 1834 marks a climax in Balzac's career, for by then he was totally conscious of his great plan to group his work so that it should form one whole. There were to be three general categories: *Études analytiques* ("Analytic Studies"), dealing with the principles governing human life and society; *Études philosophiques* ("Philosophical Studies"), revealing the causes determining human action; *Études de moeurs* ("Studies of Manners"), showing the effects of those causes, and now to be divided into six kinds of *scènes*—private, provincial, Parisian, political, military, and country life.

This entire project resulted in a total of 12 volumes (1834–37), the first volume of *Études philosophiques* (December 1834) being preceded by an explicative preface, of primary importance, which was written by a friend, Félix Davin. By 1837 Balzac had, naturally, written much more, and by 1840 he had hit upon a Dantesque title for the whole: *La Comédie humaine.* He negotiated with a consortium of publishers for an edition under this name, 17 volumes of which appeared between 1842 and 1848, including a famous foreword written in 1842. In 1845, having new works to include and many others in project, he began preparing for another complete edition. A "definitive edition" was published, in 24 volumes, between 1869 and 1876.

Also in 1834 the idea of using "reappearing characters" matured. He was to establish a pool of characters from which he would constantly draw, thus adding a sense of solidarity and coherence to the imaginary world he was superimposing on the real world. A certain character would reappear—now in the forefront, now in the background, of different fictions—in such a way that the reader could gradually form a full picture of him. He first applied the device in *Le Père Goriot,* a masterpiece of realism. It may perhaps be considered an artificial technique, but its effect is to give the reader a convincing sense of being in contact with human experience. Furthermore, Balzac's use of this device places him among the originators of the modern novel cycle.

The middle and final years. "My life-story," Balzac wrote in 1841, "is the story of my work." He must then be pictured continuing his threefold activities as writer, as social lion, and, more especially still, as collector of emotional experience. In 1832 he became friendly with Éveline Hanska, a Polish countess who was married to an elderly Ukrainian landowner. She, like many other women, had written to Balzac expressing admiration of his writings. They met twice in Switzerland in 1833, the second time in Geneva, where they became lovers; then again in Vienna in 1835. They agreed to marry when her husband died, and so they continued to correspond; the *Lettres à l'étrangère* ("Letters to a Foreigner"), which appeared posthumously (4 vol., 1889–1950), are an important source of information for the history both of Balzac's life and of his work. A striking feature of his work is the way he so ostensibly yet so subtly used his knowledge of specific people in conceiving his characters. In 1834 he met another woman who, notwithstanding his increasing devotion to Madame Hanska, was to be his mistress, friend, and patron for a number of years: Sarah

Frances Lowell, the English wife of an eccentric Italian, Count Guidoboni-Visconti—"la contessa." In 1835 he also made momentary contact with Jane Digby, Lady Ellenborough. It would be superfluous to complete the count of his loves, who caused Madame Hanska many transports of jealousy.

Further highlights in Balzac's life include his unsuccessful ventures as editor of *La Chronique de Paris* (1836) and *La Revue Parisienne* (1840); culturally profitable journeys to Italy in 1836 and 1837; an abortive expedition to Sardinia in 1838 on a mining quest: the building in 1838 of a fantastic house near Versailles called Les Jardies, which increased his debts and which he left in 1840, taking a house in Passy (now the Balzac Museum); from 1839 onward, renewed but frustrated bids for success in the theatre; efforts on behalf of authors' copyright as president of the Société des Gens de Lettres ("Society of Men of Letters"); vain attempts to save a former fellow journalist from the guillotine for murder; the signing of the contract for the *La Comédie humaine*; and failure to obtain election to the Académie Française.

In January 1842 Balzac learned of the death of Wenceslas Hanski. He now had good expectations of marrying Éveline, but there were many obstacles, not the least being his inextricable indebtedness. She in fact held back for many years, and the period of 1842–48 shows Balzac continuing and even intensifying his literary activity in the frantic hope of winning her, though he had to contend with increasing ill health. He joined her again in St. Petersburg in the summer of 1843. After that, his life, apart from his writing and wrangles with publishers or editors, was a story of new meetings and holidays together; of a longed-for paternity and miscarriage; of anxiety, anguish, and misgivings: the tragedy of an ailing man longing to find stability. His literary productivity, however, did not visibly flag: *Les Parents pauvres* (*Poor Relations*—consisting of *La Cousine Bette* and *Le Cousin Pons*) is among his greatest works.

In the autumn of 1847 he went to Madame Hanska's château at Wierzchownia and remained there until February 1848. He returned again in October to stay, mortally sick, until the spring of 1850. Then at last Éveline relented. They were married in March and proceeded to Paris, where Balzac lingered on miserably for the few months before his death.

Reputation. Until well into the 20th century, Balzac was chiefly regarded as the creator of realism, or naturalism, in the novel; as a man obsessed with the positive and sordid aspects of life; of limited vision, of too coarse a fibre to understand the aristocracy, leaving the working classes out of account though acutely perceptive of every aspect of bourgeois life from the professional classes downward; as giving a vivid picture of artistic and bohemian circles and a grim view of the peasantry; obsessed also with the power of money; intensely sympathetic with, though critical of, the young men of his time who were desperately struggling for recognition and success (as in *Le Père Goriot*). Balzac's reputation and influence have been worldwide. On the whole, readers have more appreciated his human understanding than his harsher critical qualities.

Balzac is openly acknowledged as one who established the technique of the orthodox classical novel, in which consequent and logically determined events are narrated by an all-seeing observer and characters are coherently presented. The study of Balzac, however, has taken a new turn. Less attention is now given to him as a scientifically minded determinist and more instead to Balzac the visionary: to the man claiming "second sight," the philosopher and the illuminate.

Certainly Balzac had exceptional powers of observation and a photographic memory, but he also had a sympathetic, intuitive capacity to get inside other people's skins. He was bent on illustrating the relation between cause and effect, background and character. This preoccupation explains the main feature of his novelistic technique: the long preparative descriptions of antecedents and environment—locality, architecture, houses, atmosphere, furniture, clothes, personal physiognomy—from which his characters emerge. His ambition was to "compete with the civil register," exactly picturing his contemporaries in their class distinctions and occupations. In this he succeeded; but he went even further in his efforts to show that the human spirit has power over men and events—to become, as he has been called, "the Shakespeare of the novel." The basic question to ask is how deep his understanding of human nature went. Most of his readers would answer that it plumbed the depths. (H.J.H./Ed.)

BIBLIOGRAPHY. Balzacian archives are kept at the museum at Chantilly. Charles V. Spoelberch de Lovenjoul, *Histoire des oeuvres de Honoré de Balzac* (1879, reissued 1968), is still indispensable for Balzacian research. See also William H. Royce, *A Balzac Bibliography* (1929, reprinted 1969); and Charles B. Osburn (comp.), *The Present State of French Studies* (1971). There are many excellent editions of complete works, including *La Comédie humaine*, ed. by Marcel Bouteron, 11 vol. (1935–59); *La Comédie humaine*, ed. by Pierre Citron, 7 vol. (1965–66); *Oeuvres complètes de Balzac* (1965–); and Pierre Barbéris, *Aux sources de Balzac: les romans de jeunesse* (1965). There are many special critical editions. The partly critical editions of the Classiques Garnier are especially useful. A complete, compact collection of Balzac's letters consists of Roger Pierrot (ed.), *Correspondence*, 5 vol. (1960–69), and *Lettres à Madame Hanska*, 4 vol. (1967–71). Biographies include V.S. Pritchett, *Balzac* (1973), a concise introduction; André Maurois, *Prometheus: The Life of Balzac* (1965; trans. from the French); Herbert J. Hunt, *Honoré de Balzac* (1957, reprinted 1969); and André Billy, *Vie de Balzac*, 2 vol. (1944). Classical presentations include Laure (de Balzac) Surville, *Balzac, sa vie et ses oeuvres* (1858); Théophile Gautier, *Honoré de Balzac* (1859, reissued 1980); Edmond Werdet, *Portrait intime de Balzac* (1859, reissued 1970), by Balzac's one-time editor; Leon Gozlan, *Balzac in Slippers* (1929; originally published in French, 1856); and Ferdinand Brunetière, *Honoré de Balzac: 1799–1850* (1906, reprinted 1970). Among general works are Diana Festa-McCormick, *Honoré de Balzac* (1979), an introductory critical survey; Christopher Prendergast, *Balzac: Fiction and Melodrama* (1978), a comparative study of his novels; Samuel Rogers, *Balzac and the Novel* (1953, reissued 1969), a thoughtful work; W. Somerset Maugham, *Ten Novels and Their Authors* (1954, reissued 1969; U.S. title, *The Art of Fiction*, 1955, reissued 1977); H.J. Hunt, *Balzac's Comédie Humaine* (1959, reissued 1964), a complete historical and analytical study that shows the work's expansion; Jules Bertaut (ed.), *Balzac* (1959), including an interesting tribute by Michel Butor; Philippe Bertault, *Balzac and The Human Comedy* (1963, originally published in French, 1946), a judicious general study by a great Balzacian scholar; Harry Levin, *The Gates of Horn: A Study of Five French Realists* (1963), a valuable assessment; Maurice Bardeche, *Une Lecture de Balzac*, 2nd ed. (1970), an introduction; Frederick W.J. Hemmings, *Balzac: An Interpretation of La Comédie Humaine* (1967), a perceptive analysis of Balzac in relation to his times; Stefan Zweig, *Balzac*, 2nd ed. (1970; originally published in German, 1946), an assessment.

Balzac, Jean-Louis Guez de (b. 1597, probably in Balzac, near Angoulême, Fr.—d. Feb. 18, 1654, Balzac), man of letters and critic, one of the original members of the Académie Française, who had a great influence on the development of Classical French prose.

After studies in the Netherlands at Leiden (1615), some youthful adventures, and a period in Rome (1620–22), he hoped for a political career and wrote in defense of Cardinal de Richelieu's administration. When he saw, however, that Richelieu would not offer him preferment, he retired to his country house, from which he maintained relations with Parisian literary circles, chiefly by letter. Elected to the Académie Française in 1634, he rarely attended its sessions. His reputation, high in his lifetime, declined rapidly after his death. Balzac's published works include *Le Prince* (1631), a political treatise, and *Le Socrate chrétien* (1652), a synthesis of Stoic and Christian ethics. Far more influential, however, were the *Lettres* (short dissertations on political, moral, and literary matters), which appeared in numerous editions and were continually expanded from 1624.

bama (shrine): *see* high place.

Bamako, capital city and district of Mali, West Africa, on the Niger River. When occupied for the French in 1880 by Capt. Joseph-Simon Gallieni, Bamako was a settlement of a few hundred inhabitants, grouped in villages. It became the capital of the former colony of French Sudan in 1908, four years after the Kayes–Bamako segment of the Dakar–Niger Railway (now the Regie des Chemins de Fer du Mali) was opened.

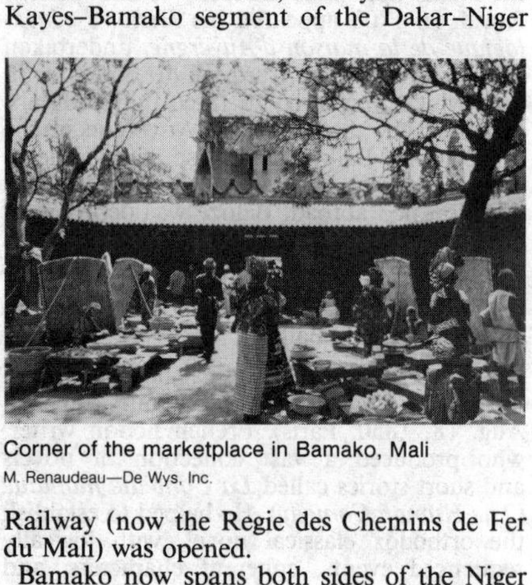

Corner of the marketplace in Bamako, Mali
M. Renaudeau—De Wys, Inc.

Bamako now spans both sides of the Niger River, which is navigable 225 mi (360 km) south, to Kouroussa, Guinea, from mid-June to mid-December. To the north a canal around the Sotuba Rapids has opened the northeastern section of the river to shipping as far as Gao (869 mi). Cement and petroleum products are shipped downstream from Bamako, with rice and groundnuts (peanuts) coming upstream for transshipment via the railway. A bridge was constructed over the Niger in 1960. The city is also served by an airport.

Bamako is a bustling city with a large market, botanical and zoological gardens, an active artisan community, and several research institutes. It also supports four colleges and houses the majority of Mali's industrial enterprises. The city more than tripled in size from 1960 to 1970, largely because of rural migration from drought-stricken areas of the countryside. A traditional character prevails, however, and mud brick buildings can still be seen throughout the city. Pop. (1980 est.) 477,750.

Bambara, ethnolinguistic group of the upper Niger region of Mali who speak a language called Bamana (or Bammana) of the Mande branch of the Niger-Congo family. The Bambara are to a great extent intermingled with other tribes, and there is no centralized organization. Each small district, made up of a number of villages, is under a dominant family, which provides a chief, or *fama.* The *fama* has considerable powers, deriving from his role as a representative of the original inhabitants of the region, and he is involved mystically in agricultural operations.

The Bambara are distinguished by their indigenous method of writing. They also have a remarkable system of metaphysics and cosmology, encompassing associated animistic cults, prayers, and myths. Religious sculpture in wood and metal is well developed.

Mid-20th-century changes have included the introduction of cash crops, such as peanuts (groundnuts), rice, and cotton, into the pattern of subsistence agriculture; and there has been substantial migration to the towns.

Bambara states, two separate West African states, one of which was based on Segu, between the Sénégal and Niger rivers, and the other on Kaarta, along the Middle Niger (in present-day Mali). According to tradition, Segu was founded by two brothers, Barama Ngolo and Nia Ngolo. Initially little more than marauding robber barons, the brothers settled sometime before 1650 near the market town of Segu, on the south bank of the Niger. The Bambara empire extended to include Timbuktu during the reign (*c.* 1652–82) of Kaladian Kulibali, but it disintegrated after his death.

Mamari Kulibali, known as "the Commander" (reigned *c.* 1712–55), is regarded as the true founder of Segu; he extended his empire to what is now Bamako in the southwest and to Djénné and Timbuktu in the northeast by forming a professional army and navy and conquering other Bambara rivals and fighting off the king of Kong (*c.* 1730).

Mamari Kulibali's death was followed by a period of instability in which several rulers rose and fell in quick succession. Finally, in 1766, Ngolo Diara seized power and restored order to the empire, which he ruled for almost 30 years. Under his son Mansong and his grandson Da Kaba, the Bambara directed their attention southward to the region of the Black Volta. In 1818 Bambara collapsed before the onslaughts of Shehu Ahmadu Lobbo of Macina.

Some of the rivals defeated by Mamari Kulibali fled to the Middle Niger region and founded (*c.* 1753) the city of Kaarta near Kumbi, the site of the last capital of ancient Ghana. There they created another group of Bambara states, which dominated the lands of the Middle Niger into the 19th century.

Bamberg, city, Bayern *Land* (Bavaria state), eastern West Germany, on the canalized Regnitz River, 2 mi (3 km) above its confluence with the Main, north of Nürnberg. First mentioned in 902 as the seat of the ancestral castle of the Babenberg family, Bamberg became the seat of a bishopric founded there by Emperor Henry II (Heinrich the Holy) in 1007; the bishops became princes of the empire in the mid-13th century. In 1459 the first book in the German language was printed here. Bamberg passed to Bavaria in 1802 after the secularization of the see. An archbishopric was established in 1817. The imperial cathedral (1004–1237) contains many notable statues, the tombs of Henry II, his wife Cunegund, and Pope Clement II, and a wooden altar carved by Viet Stoss. There are two bishops' palaces: the Alte Residenz, or old palace (1571–76), which houses a local history museum, and the splendid Neue Residenz (1695–1704), containing several notable art collections. Other historic buildings include the former Benedictine abbey and St. Michael's Church (consecrated 1015), the 12th-century St. Jacob's Church, St. Martin's (1685–93), the old town hall (1453; rebuilt 1744–56), the chapel of the ancient fortress on the Altenburg, and several Baroque patricians' houses. A former Jesuit university (1648–1803), later a theological academy, was united with a teachers college in 1972 to form a *Gesamthochschule* (a university-level institution for advanced technical training). Opposite the Civic Theatre is the E.T.A. Hoffmann house, where the poet and composer lived from 1808 to 1813. One of Bamberg's internationally known attractions is its symphony orchestra.

Rathaus (town hall) in Bamberg, W.Ger.

Karl Jung—ZEFA

Industries include the manufacture of electrotechnical equipment, clothing, shoes, machinery, pianos, and porcelain. There is extensive market gardening and brewing. Pop. (1983 est.) 70,878.

Bamberger, Ludwig (b. July 22, 1823, Mainz, Hesse—d. March 14, 1899, Berlin), economist and publicist, a leading authority on currency problems in Germany. Originally a radical, he became at least partly converted to Bismarckian anti-liberalism.

Bamberger, engraving by A. Neumann, *c.* 1890

Archiv fur Kunst und Geschichte, West Berlin

Born of Jewish parents, he was studying French law when the 1848 revolution inspired his radicalism. He became a newspaper editor, took part in the 1849 republican rising in the Palatinate, went into exile, and was condemned to death in absentia. Bamberger managed the Paris branch of a London bank until the amnesty of 1866 enabled him to return to Germany.

By then an admirer of Bismarck, Bamberger dissociated himself from all democratic groups. In 1870, at Bismarck's request, he participated in the Franco-German peace negotiations, and in 1871 he entered the Reichstag as a National Liberal.

Bamberger obtained standardization of the German coinage, adoption of the gold standard, and establishment of the Reichsbank. Although he supported Bismarck's outlawing of the Socialist Party and attempts to nationalize the railways, Bamberger from 1878 opposed the chancellor's policy of protective tariffs, state socialism, and colonial expansion. In 1880 Bamberger left the National Liberal Party and helped to found the splinter party called the Sezession. For some years afterward he was the trusted adviser of the crown princess Victoria (wife of the future German emperor Frederick III).

Bambocciati, group of relatively small, often anecdotal, paintings of everyday life, made in Rome in the mid-17th century. The word derives from the nickname "Il Bamboccio" (Large Baby) applied to the physically malformed Dutch painter Pieter van Laer (1592/95–1642). Generally regarded as the originator of the style and its most important exponent, van Laer arrived in Rome from Haarlem about 1625 and was soon well known for paintings in which his Netherlandish interest in the picturesque was combined with the pictorial cohesiveness of Caravaggio's dramatic tenebrist lighting. Because van Laer and his followers dared to paint nature as if seen through a window opening, or realistically rather than ideally as was the current fashion, their works were condemned by both court critics and the leading painters of the classicist-idealist school as indecorous and ridiculous. The painter Salvator Rosa was particularly savage in his comments about the later followers of the style, whom he criticized for painting "baggy pants, beggars in rags, and abject filthy things."

The influence of the Bamboccianti (painters of Bambocciati) has been considerable. Not only did their works revive and retain the influence of Caravaggio's stylistic innovations in Italy but also served to transport them to the Netherlands and to France as well. In the late 19th century, with the rise of Realism, the Bamboccianti enjoyed a belated reevaluation.

bamboo, any of the tall, treelike grasses comprising the subfamily Bambusoideae of the family Poaceae. More than 75 genera and 1,000 species have been proposed in botanical literature, but many names are synonymous and thus not considered legitimate.

Bamboos are distributed in tropical and subtropical to mild temperate regions, with the heaviest concentration and largest number of species in southeastern Asia and on islands of the Indian and Pacific oceans. The woody, hollow aerial stems (culms) of bamboo grow in branching clusters from a thick underground stem (rhizome). The culms often form a dense undergrowth that excludes other plants. Bamboo culms range in length from 10 to 15 centimetres (about 4 to 6 inches) to more than 40 metres (about 130 feet). The foliage leaves have stalked blades and are borne on branches; leaves on young culms arise directly from the stem. Most bamboos flower only after many years of vegetative growth and reproduction.

Bamboos are used for construction material, household implements, fishing poles, plant supports, and as ornamental plants and soil stabilizers. Cooked young shoots of some bamboos are eaten as vegetables. The pulp and

Bamboo

Sven Samelius

fibre of several species, especially *Dendrocalamus strictus* and *Bambusa arundinacea,* are used in the manufacture of paper products. The nearly solid culms of *D. strictus* and similar species, known as male bamboos, are used locally as walking sticks and lance shafts.

Bamboo Annals, Chinese (Wade–Giles romanization) CHU-SHU CHI-NIEN, Pinyin ZHUSHU JINIAN, set of records written on bamboo slips, from the state of Chin, one of the many small states into which China was divided during the late, or Eastern, Chou dynasty (770–221 BC). The Chin state was destroyed around the middle of the 5th century BC, and the state records were hidden in a tomb sometime later. Uncovered in the middle of the 3rd century BC, when the use of bamboo slips had already gone out of style, the records acquired the name under which they have since been known.

The *Bamboo Annals* contain one of the few written records of the earliest period in Chinese history, but the originals have been lost, and the later copies that survive have been proved to contain much spurious information.

bamboo rat, any of several burrowing Asiatic rodents of the genera *Rhizomys* and *Cannomys*, belonging to the family Rhizomyidae (order Rodentia). Bamboo rats are thickset, short-legged, and short-tailed, with gray, grayish brown, or reddish brown fur. Members of the genus *Rhizomys* are 25 to 40 centimetres (10 to 16 inches) long, exclusive of the tail. The lesser, or chestnut, bamboo rat (*C. badius*), is smaller, about 17 to 25 cm long without the tail. Bamboo rats burrow with their teeth and claws. They eat bamboo but also take fruit, seeds, and other plant material. Members of the genus *Rhizomys* are found in bamboo-covered areas of southeastern Asia and the Malay Peninsula. The lesser bamboo rat lives in gardens, forests, and grassy regions of southern and southeastern Asia.

Bamburgh, parish, Berwick upon Tweed district, county of Northumberland, Eng., dominated by Bamburgh Castle on its cliff, 150 ft (45 m) high. The fortress was founded in the 6th century by Ida, first monarch of the Anglo-Saxon kingdom of Bernicia, and subsequently remained the principal stronghold

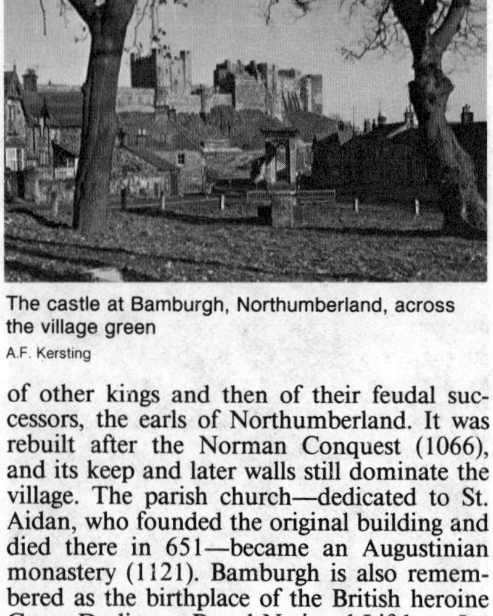

The castle at Bamburgh, Northumberland, across the village green
A.F. Kersting

of other kings and then of their feudal successors, the earls of Northumberland. It was rebuilt after the Norman Conquest (1066), and its keep and later walls still dominate the village. The parish church—dedicated to St. Aidan, who founded the original building and died there in 651—became an Augustinian monastery (1121). Bamburgh is also remembered as the birthplace of the British heroine Grace Darling: a Royal National Lifeboat Institution museum contains relics of her rescue (1838) of five people from the wrecked steamboat "Forfarshire." Pop. (1971) 458.

Bambuti (people): *see* Mbuti.

Bamenda, capital of Northwest province and of Mezam department, Cameroon, west central Africa, in the volcanic, bamboo-forested

The Bamenda highlands, Cameroon
Syndication International Ltd., London

Bamenda highlands. Although communications are difficult because of heavy rainfall and rugged relief, the town serves as a trade and export centre for local agricultural products such as hides, coffee, and tobacco. The Bamenda Museum displays specimens of local handicrafts: elaborate wood and ivory carving, clay modelling (especially pipes modelled in human form), raffia work, and brass jewelry and figures. The German fort (*c.* 1912) is a relic of the colonial period. A nurses' training centre and hospital serve the town, and the Cameroon College of Arts, Science, and Technology is located at nearby Bambili. Pop. (1981 est.) 58,697.

Articles are alphabetized word by word, not letter by letter

Bamford, Samuel (b. Feb. 28, 1788, Middleton, Lancashire, Eng.—d. April 13, 1872, Harpurhey, Lancashire), English radical reformer, who was the author of several widely popular poems (principally in the Lancashire dialect) showing sympathy with the condition of the working class. He became a working weaver and earned great respect in northern radical circles as a reformer; but he was moderate in policy and jealous of rivals.

Bamford formed a Hampden Club in Middleton in 1817 and met William Cobbett, Henry Hunt, William Benbow, and Sir Francis Burdett. The same year, although he was an opponent of violence, he was arrested and imprisoned. In 1819 he was arrested again as a result of attending and speaking at the Manchester meeting known as Peterloo (*see* Peterloo Massacre) and was sentenced to 12 months imprisonment. Bamford lost some of his popularity when he left his trade and became a journalist in London (*c.* 1826). He was also disliked for his work as a special constable during the Chartist riots. But he continued to press for reform of working-class conditions, on which his *Passages in the Life of a Radical* (1840–44) and *Early Days* (1849) are illuminating, although marred sometimes by personal prejudices. On his death, he was accorded a public funeral, attended by thousands.

Bāmīān, also spelled BĀMYĀN, *velāyat* (province) in central Afghanistan, 6,722 sq mi (17,411 sq km) in area, with its capital at Bāmīān city. It is surrounded by the *velāyāt* of Jowzjān, and Samangān (north); Baghlān, Parvān, and Vardak (east); Ghaznī (southeast); Orūzgān (southwest); and Ghowr (west). The province is comprised of narrow valleys situated between the Hindu Kush and the Selseleh-ye Kūh-e Bābā mountain ranges. The Band-e Amīr lakes, 3 hr west by road from the Bāmīān Valley, are noted for their scenic beauty. Agriculture is the principal activity, with wheat and barley the main crops. Pop. (1982 est.) settled pop. 280,859, mostly Ḥazāra.

Bāmīān, also spelled BĀMYĀN, capital of Bāmīān *velāyat* (province), central Afghanistan, northwest of Kābul, the nation's capital, with which it is connected by road. It lies in the Bāmīān Valley at an elevation of 8,495 ft (2,590 m).

Bāmīān is first mentioned in 5th-century-AD Chinese sources and was visited by the Chinese travellers Fa-hsien around AD 400 and Hsüan-tsang in AD 630; it was by that time a centre of commerce and of the Buddhist religion. The two great carved rock figures of Buddha there date from this period; the larger is 175 ft (53 m) high and the smaller is 120 ft; these, together with numerous ancient man-made caves in the cliffs north of the town, have made Bāmīān a major Afghan archaeological site. The town was ruled in the 7th century by princes, probably Hephthalite, but was subject to the Western Turks. The rulers first accepted Islām in the 8th century. The Ṣaffārid ruler Ya'qūb ebn Leyṣ captured Bāmīān in 871; after changing hands several times, it was destroyed in 1221 by the Mongol

The Bāmīān Valley, Afghanistan, showing the ancient caves
Richard Abeles

invader Genghis Khan and has never regained its former glory. In 1840 Bāmīān was the scene of fighting in the First Anglo-Afghan War.

The tourist traffic has prompted the building of a tourist centre and a government hotel. Pop. (1982 est.) 7,732.

Bamileke, any of about 90 West African peoples in the Bamileke region of Cameroon. They speak a language of the Benue-Congo branch of the Niger-Congo family. They do not refer to themselves as Bamileke but use the names of the individual kingdoms to which they belong.

Some of these kingdoms exhibited typical characteristics of African realms: divine kings, elaborate courts in capital cities, numerous officials and attendants, and a queen mother of great prestige and influence. Descent, succession, and inheritance are patrilineal. Polygyny is practiced, marriage often involving a substantial bride-price.

The Bamileke practice sedentary farming. Staple crops include maize, taro, and groundnuts (peanuts). Men clear the fields, build houses, and engage in crafts; while women do most of the cultivating. They have little livestock.

Settlement patterns typically take the form of neighbourhoods of scattered family homesteads. Their square houses have conical thatched roofs surmounting latticework walls, made of raffia poles with mud-filled interstices. Chief's houses are decorated with carved doorframes and house posts; a wide variety of articles was at one time skillfully carved from wood, ivory, and horn.

Ancestor worship is the dominant form of religion; the lineage head preserves the ancestral skulls and offers sacrifices to them. Charms and medicines are prepared by doctors, who also practice divination by interpreting an earth spider's manipulation of marked blades of grass. Some Bamileke have adopted Islām, especially in the north; and others have been converted to Christianity.

Bamingui-Bangoran, *préfecture*, northern Central African Republic. The well-watered *préfecture* (with 53 in. [1,350 mm] of rainfall per year) lies in the Chari River basin, draining northwest into Lake Chad. Its boundary with Chad follows the Aouk River, a major headstream of the Chari. The Bamingui and Koukourou rivers bound it on the southwest and the Kameur and Vakaga rivers on the northeast. Bamingui-Bangoran covers an area of 22,500 sq mi (58,200 sq km). The climate is warm, with temperatures averaging 80° F (27° C).

The prefectural seat is N'Délé, centrally located in the *préfecture* at an altitude of 1,673 ft (510 m). A road joins N'Délé and Bamingui (further south, on the Bamingui River) to Ouadda (east) and Mbrés (south). The transportation network is otherwise minimal in this sparsely populated region inhabited by Banda people. Sorghum is the staple subsistence crop. Ironwork, knives, weapons, and utensils are produced around N'Délé and diamonds are found to its south. Herds of elephants and other large animals roam the national parks of Saint-Floris in the east and Bamingui-Bangoran (park) in the west.

The region was designated a *préfecture* in the mid-1960s. It was previously the autonomous sub-prefecture of N'Délé. Pop. (1975) 25,943.

Bampton, John (b. 1690?—d. June 6, 1751), English clergyman who gave his name to one of Protestant Christendom's most distinguished lectureships, the Bampton lectures at Oxford University.

Bampton studied at Trinity College, Oxford, and was a prebendary of Salisbury Cathedral from 1718 until his death. The Bampton lectures were established in accordance with his will. They consist of eight lecture-sermons preached on Sunday mornings between the beginning of the last month in Lent term and the third week in Act term, upon specified topics of Christian doctrine. The lecturer is chosen by the heads of colleges during Easter term. Since 1895 the Bampton lectures have been given every other year.

Bamum, also spelled BAMOUN, also called MUM, a West African people speaking a language that is often used as a lingua franca and belongs to the Benue-Congo branch of the Niger-Congo family. Their kingdom, with its capital at Foumban (*q.v.*) in the high grasslands of Cameroon, is ruled over by a king (*mfon*).

Early in the 18th century the first *mfon,* Nchare, came from the territory of the neighbouring Tikar people, with whom the Bamum claim a common origin. The 11th *mfon,* Mbuembue, was the first to enlarge the kingdom. The 17th *mfon,* Njoya, became the most celebrated. Familiar with Arabic script from contact with Fulani and Hausa, Njoya about 1895 invented a system of writing with 510 pictographic characters. This was eventually reduced to a syllabary of 73 characters and 10 numerals. With the help of his scribes Njoya prepared a book on the history and customs of the Bamum, which has been published in a French translation. Njoya was converted to Islām in 1918, and it is estimated that more than half the Bamum have become Muslim.

The Bamum are noted craftsmen. The economy rests on sedentary agriculture, supplemented by fishing and hunting.

Bāmyān (Afghanistan): *see* Bāmiān.

ban, former Hungarian title denoting a governor of a military district (banat) and later designating a local representative of the Hungarian king in outlying possessions; *e.g.,* Bosnia and Croatia. Originally a Persian word, ban was introduced into Europe by the Avars. The Kingdom of Yugoslavia, divided into *banovine,* or provinces, revived the title and office of ban in October 1929 and used it until the German–Italian invasion of April 1941.

ban (South Africa): *see* banning.

Ban Biao (Chinese historiographer): *see* Pan Piao.

Ban Chao (Chinese general): *see* Pan Ch'ao.

Ban Don (Thailand): *see* Surat Thani.

Ban Gu (Chinese historian): *see* Pan Ku.

Ban Me Thuot (Vietnam): *see* Buon Me Thuot.

Ban Zhao (Chinese scholar): *see* Pan Chao.

Bāṇa, also called BĀṆABHAṬṬA (fl. first half of 7th century), one of the greatest masters of Sanskrit prose, famed principally for his chronicle, *Harṣacarita* ("Deeds of Harṣa"), depicting the court and times of the Buddhist emperor Harṣa (reigned *c.* 606–647).

Bāṇa gives some autobiographical account of himself in the early chapters of the *Harṣacarita.* He was born into an illustrious family of Brahmans; his mother died when he was a small child, and he was raised by his father with loving care. His father died, however, when Bāṇa was 14, and for some years he travelled adventurously, visiting various courts and universities with a colourful group of friends (including his two half brothers by a lower caste woman, a snake doctor, a goldsmith, a gambler, and a musician). At last he returned home and married; then one day he was called to the court of Harṣa. Treated coolly at first by the Emperor, perhaps because of some gossip about his wayward youth, in time he won the Emperor's high regard.

Bāṇa's life of Harṣa provides valuable information about the period, though with some obvious exaggeration in the Emperor's favour. Written in the ornate *kāvya* style (*q.v.*), involving extremely lengthy constructions, elaborate descriptions, and poetic devices, the work has great vitality and a wealth of detail, keenly observed. His second great work, the prose romance *Kādambarī,* involves narrative within narrative, related to a king by a parrot; it is remarkable for the freshness with which it deals with the emotions of love. Both works were left unfinished; the second was completed by the author's son, Bhūṣaṇabhaṭṭa.

Banaadir, also spelled BENADIR, also called MOGADISHU, or MUQDISHO, *gobolka* (administrative region), southern Somalia, East Africa. Part of the Italian-administered former United Nations Trust Territory of Somalia until 1960, the region was created from the central part of the formerly larger Benadir administrative region in 1973. Fronting the Indian Ocean (southeast) and bounded by the *gobollada* (administrative regions) of Shabeellaha Dhexe (north) and Shabeellaha Hoose (west), it is the smallest of Somalia's administrative regions and extends over only 386 sq mi (1,000 sq km). Banaadir is centred on Muqdisho (or Mogadishu), the capital of Somalia, and is the most industrially developed region of the country. It has a concentration of cotton ginning, food processing, soap making, textile and cigarette manufacturing, and vegetable-oil refining factories. Irrigated rice, cotton, and sugarcane are grown; salt deposits were under exploration in the early 1980s. A new port with modern shipping berths to handle most of the country's imports, was completed in 1971. Banaadir has the country's largest urban population, and it is the only region where almost all of the population is sedentary. Muqdisho is also the *gobolka* capital. Pop. (1975) 370,671.

Banaba, also called OCEAN ISLAND, coral and phosphate formation 250 mi (400 km) west of the nearest Gilbert Islands, part of Kiribati, in the west central Pacific Ocean. It has a circumference of 6 mi and an area of 2 sq mi (5 sq km). Sighted in 1804 by the British ship "Ocean," the island was annexed by Britain in 1900. In that same year the mining and shipping of phosphate began. By the early 1970s, annual production reached a high of 550,000 tons, but deposits were exhausted by 1979. Made part of the crown colony of the Gilbert and Ellice Islands in 1919, the island was occupied by Japanese forces from 1942 to 1945. The Japanese deported many of the local Micronesian inhabitants (including both Banabans and Gilbertese) to the Gilbert Islands and in 1945 massacred all but one of the remaining Gilbertese.

Many of the Banabans who had been deported to the Gilberts later elected to move to Rabi, a small island 1,300 mi southeast of Banaba, in Fiji, after wartime destruction at Banaba made living conditions there impossible. After 1965, Banabans received more adequate compensation from the phosphate company for the exploitation of their island. During the 1970s Banabans attempted to separate from the Gilbert Islands, which was nearing independence as part of Kiribati. Since independence (in 1979) they have been guaranteed ownership of Banaba, as well as dual citizenship in both Kiribati and Fiji. Tabiang is the administrative seat. Pop. (1983 est.) Banaba, 72; (1977) Rabi Island, Fiji (almost all Banabans), 2,426.

Banach, Stefan (b. March 30, 1892, Kraków, Austria-Hungary—d. Aug. 31, 1945, Lvov, Ukrainian S.S.R.), Soviet mathematician who founded modern functional analysis and helped develop the theory of topological vector spaces. A lecturer in mathematics at the Institute of Technology, Lvov, from 1919, he became a lecturer at the University of Lvov in 1922 and a full professor in 1927.

Banach contributed to the theory of orthogonal series and made innovations in the theory of measure and integration, but his most important contribution was in functional analysis. Of his published works, his *Théorie des opérations linéaires* (1932; "Theory of Linear Operations") is the most important.

Banana, port on the Atlantic coast in Bas-Fleuve subregion, Bas-Zaïre region, far southwestern Zaire, central Africa, at the mouth of the Congo (Zaïre) River. One of the nation's older towns, it was known as a trading centre in the 19th century, mainly during the slaving period. In the 1970s and 1980s its port was developed to increase its facilities as a deepwater port and a rail line was built to link Banana with Boma and Kinshasa, the national capital. Banana lies in deltaic mangrove forests, but northward along the coast lie some beaches, near which is Moanda, an offshore oil centre. Pop. (latest est.) 2,000.

banana, fruit of the genus *Musa,* of the family Musaceae, one of the most important

Banana (*Musa cavendishii*)
Ingmar Holmasen

food crops of the world, consumed extensively throughout the tropics, where it is grown, and also valued in the temperate zone for its flavour, nutritional value, and availability throughout the year. The plant, a gigantic herb springing from an underground stem, or rhizome, forms a false trunk 3–6 metres (10–20 feet) high, composed of the leaf sheaths and crowned with a rosette of 10 to 20 oblong to elliptic leaves sometimes attaining a length of 3–3.5 m and a breadth of 650 millimetres (26 inches).

The large flower spike, carrying numerous yellowish flowers, emerges at the top of the false trunk and bends downward to become bunches of 50 to 150 individual fruits, or fingers. These are grouped in clusters, or hands, of 10 to 20. After the plants have fruited, they die and are replaced by others (suckers) arising from the underground stem. The life of one stool, or clump, thus continues for many years.

There are hundreds of varieties of banana in cultivation; confusion exists because of diverse names applied to one and the same variety in different parts of the world. Consumption of the banana is mentioned in early Greek, Latin, and Arab writings. Alexander the Great saw bananas on an expedition to India. Shortly after the discovery of America, the banana was brought from the Canary Islands to the New World, where it was first established in Hispaniola, and soon spread to other islands and the mainland. Cultivation increased until it became a staple foodstuff in many regions, and in the 19th century it began to appear in the markets of the U.S.

Bananas, thriving naturally on deep, loose, well-drained soils in humid tropical climates, are grown successfully under irrigation in such semi-arid regions as the southern side of Jamaica. Suckers and divisions of the pseudobulb are used as planting material; the first crop ripens within 10 to 15 months, and thereafter production is more or less continuous.

Desirable commercial bunches of bananas consist of nine hands or more and weigh 22–65 kilograms (49–143 pounds). Three hundred or more such bunches may be produced annually on one acre of land. The ripe fruit contains as much as 22 percent of carbohydrate, mainly as sugar, and is high in potassium, low in protein and fat, and a good source of vitamins C and A. Though most commonly eaten fresh, bananas may also be fried or mashed and chilled in pies or puddings.

Cooking varieties, or plantains, differ from other bananas in that the ripe fruit is starchy rather than sweet. They are extensively cultivated and used in tropical regions and are marketed in large urban areas worldwide (*see* plantain). The U.S. imports more bananas than any other country; large quantities are also shipped to Great Britain and western Europe.

Even for local consumption, bananas are not allowed to fully ripen on the plant. For export, the desired degree of maturity attained before harvest depends upon distance from market and type of transportation. Frequently, ripening is artificially induced after shipment by exposure to ethylene gas.

Especially designed refrigerated ships operate between tropical countries and consumption centres in North America and Europe. Chief sources of production in Middle America and the West Indies include Costa Rica, Honduras, Guatemala, Mexico, Panama, the Dominican Republic, Guadeloupe, Jamaica, and Martinique; in South America, Brazil, Colombia, and Ecuador; in Africa, Spain's Canary Islands, Ethiopia, Cameroon, Guinea, and Nigeria; and in Asia, Taiwan.

banana fish: *see* bonefish.

banana wilt (plant disease): *see* Panama disease.

Bananal Island, Portuguese ILHA DO BANANAL, island, Goiás state, central Brazil, formed by Rio Araguaia, which for 200 mi (320 km) divides into major (western) and minor (eastern) branches. The major branch forms part of the boundary between Mato Grosso and Goiás states. Small boats navigate the minor branch. The island (maximum width 35 mi) is the habitat of babassu palms, tropical birds, and freshwater fish. Suyá Indians live on Bananal Island. It became the Araguaia National Park in 1959 and includes an airstrip.

bananaquit (*Coereba flaveola*), bird of the West Indies (except Cuba) and southern Mexico to Argentina. It is usually placed with honeycreepers in the family Emberizidae (order Passeriformes), but it may belong with woodwarblers (*q.v.*; Parulidae). About 11 centimetres ($4\frac{1}{2}$ inches) long, the bananaquit is blackish above and yellow below, with, generally, white stripes near the eyes and white patches on the wings. It uses its sharp curved bill to probe flowers for nectar; sometimes it eats insects and fruit. It uses banana-leaf fibre in making its domed nest.

Banāras (India): *see* Vārānasi.

Banaras, Treaties of (1773; 1775), two agreements regulating relations between the British government of Bengal and the ruler of the Muslim state of Oudh, Shujāʿ-ud-Dawlah. The defense of Shujā's state had been guaranteed in 1765 on the condition that he pay the cost of the necessary troops. The First Treaty of Banaras (1773) was the result of the Mughal emperor Shāh ʿĀlam's cession of Allāhābād and Kora to the warlike Marāthās as the price of their support. Warren Hastings, the British governor, ceded Allāhābād and Kora to Shujā and promised to support him against the menacing Afghan Rohillas in return for cash payments. This move, designed to strengthen Oudh as a buffer state between Bengal and the Marāthās, led to the Rohilla War of 1774, which later became a major factor in Hastings' impeachment (1788–95).

The Second Treaty of Banaras is otherwise known as the Treaty of Faizābād (1775). It was forced on the new vizier of Oudh by the company's governing council after the death of Shujā. The Vizier had to pay a larger subsidy for the use of British troops and to cede Banaras to the company. This treaty led to a revolt by the raja Chaith Singh of Banaras in 1781.

Banās Kāntha, district, northern Gujarāt state, west central India, bounded by Rājasthān state (north). Formed in 1949–50 from small Muslim and Rājput principalities and *jāgīrs* (feudal estates), it covers 4,904 sq mi (12,702 sq km). It extends from the Rann (marsh) of Kutch eastward to the Arāvalli Range and consists mainly of a sandy plain on the southern edge of the Great Indian (Thar) Desert. Some parts of the district are forested, and there are good pastures. Millet and wheat are the staple crops; corn (maize), potatoes, timber, wool, and handwoven cloth are produced for export. There are also quarries for building stone. Communications are generally poor, but Pālanpur (*q.v.*), the district headquarters, and a few other towns are on the Western Railway. Pop. (1981) 1,667,914.

Banās River, river in Rājasthān state, northwestern India, rising near Kūmbhalgarh, in Udaipur district, and cutting its way tortuously through the Arāvalli Range. It then flows down onto the plains and, on a generally northeasterly course, through portions of Chitorgarh, Bhīlwāra, and Tonk districts and into Sawai Mādhopur, where it joins the Chambal River, just north of Sheopur, after a course of 310 mi (500 km). The Banās (Sanskrit: The Forests), a seasonal river often dry in the hot months, provides a source of irrigation. Its main tributaries are the Berach and Kotari rivers.

Banat, ethnically mixed historic region of eastern Europe, which is bounded by Transylvania and Walachia in the east, by the Tisza River in the west, by the Mures River in the north, and by the Danube River in the south; after 1920 Banat was divided among the modern states of Romania, Yugoslavia, and Hungary. The name banat has its origin in a Persian word meaning lord, or master, and was introduced into Europe by the Avars; it came to mean a frontier province or a district under military governorship.

First occupied in prehistoric times, the Banat was later controlled by the Romans, Goths, Gepidae, Huns, and Avars. The Slavs settled there in the 5th century AD; and after the Magyars displaced them (9th century), the area became an integral part of Hungary and was organized as the Banat of Severin (Terra de Zevrino) by King Andrew II in 1233. In the 14th and 15th centuries many Serbs settled there; in the mid-16th century it was conquered by the Ottoman Turks, who retained it until 1718 when Austria acquired it (Treaty of Passarowitz).

Under Austrian military rule, the region was organized as the Temeser Banat (or Banat of Temesvár). Later a civil administration took control of the northern part of the area, and the Austrian rulers encouraged the settlement of colonists from the Rhineland, Lorraine, and Luxembourg. For most of the period 1779–

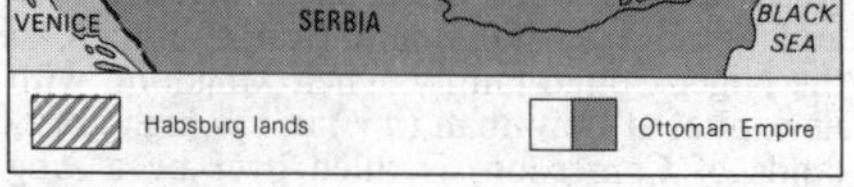

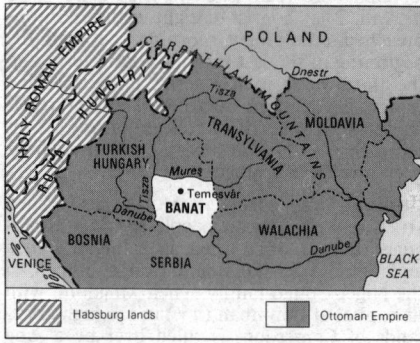

Banat in the mid-16th century

1920 the Banat was attached to Hungary. After World War I, the victorious Allies divided it by the Treaty of Trianon (June 4, 1920). Hungary retained the district of Szeged, Romania acquired the large eastern section, and the remainder went to the Kingdom of Serbs, Croats, and Slovenes (Yugoslavia).

Banbridge, Irish DROICHEAD NA BANNA, town, seat, and district (established 1973), formerly within County Down, N.Ire. Located on the River Bann, the town of Banbridge came into existence following the building of a stone bridge across the river in 1712. It is the main agricultural and population centre of the region; manufactures include linen, light footwear, and motor vehicle components. Much of the land in the surrounding area is utilized for crops, including oats, potatoes, and barley, or as pasture for livestock (mostly pigs). Primary roads connect the town of Banbridge with the towns of Lisburn to the north and Newry to the south.

Banbridge district has an area of 172 sq mi (445 sq km) and is bordered by the districts of Armagh to the west, Craigavon and Lisburn to the north, Down to the east, and Newry and Mourne to the south. Reaching an altitude of 1,745 ft (532 m) at Slieve Croob in eastern Banbridge district, the Legananny Hills slope gradually southwestward to rolling lowlands dissected by the River Bann and its tributaries in central Banbridge and then to Newry Canal

Valley in the western part of the district. Limestone is quarried in the northwest. Pop. (1981) town, 9,650; district, 29,885.

Banbury, town, Cherwell district, county of Oxfordshire, Eng., on the River Cherwell. For centuries Banbury was noted for its ale, cheese, and Banbury cakes, a spiced currant pastry. Part of the original 16th-century cake house remains, together with several timbered and stone houses. The original Banbury Cross, celebrated in the English nursery rhyme, was destroyed by Puritans in 1602 but was replaced in 1858. Banbury Castle (1125) was twice besieged by Parliamentarians during the English Civil War of the mid-17th century and was later demolished. Broughton Castle (14th–16th centuries) lies 2½ mi (4 km) to the southwest. Banbury market is noted for its cattle sales. The town is expanding as a centre for the overspill population of Greater London and is increasingly important for light industry, commerce, and tourism. Pop. (1981 prelim.) 35,796.

Banca (Indonesia): *see* Bangka.

Banchieri, Adriano (b. Sept. 3, 1568, Bologna, Papal States—d. 1634, Bologna), one of the principal composers of madrigal comedies, choral pieces that suggest plots and action to be imagined by the performers and listeners.

He spent almost his whole life at the monastery of San Michele in Bosco, near Bologna, becoming abbot in 1620. Banchieri was second only to Orazio Vecchi as a composer of madrigal comedies, a genre much in fashion shortly before the rise of opera. His *Il festino nella sera del giovedì grasso avanti cena* (1608; modern English edition, *The Animals Improvise Counterpoint,* 1937) contains some delightful characterizations.

Banco, Parc National du, national park, southeastern Ivory Coast, immediately north of Abidjan, the national capital. Declared a national park in 1953, Banco preserves both flora and fauna in *c.* 7,400 ac (3,000 ha). Gigantic rain-forest trees occupy most of the park; an arboretum displays trees (especially teak) and shrubs from all over the country. Animals roam the park in a natural environment—they live, reproduce, stalk prey, and die with little or no human interference. A few monkeys inhabit the park's small zoo. The park serves primarily as a recreational centre for the inhabitants of Abidjan.

Bancroft, village, Hastings County, in the hills of southeastern Ontario, Can., 60 mi (95 km) northeast of Peterborough. It originated as a farming settlement called York River in 1855 but later became a lumbering community and was renamed in 1878 for Phoebe Bancroft, wife of Sen. Billa Flint, a prominent Canadian politician of the late 1800s. It became a centre for rock hounds, with examples of about 80 percent of Canada's minerals found in the vicinity; the annual Bancroft Gemboree attracts many rock collectors. Economic activities focus on woollen milling, quarrying, lumbering, dairying, and tourism. Pop. (1981) 2,329.

Bancroft (Zambia): *see* Chililabombwe.

Bancroft, Edward (b. Jan. 9, 1744, Westfield, Mass., U.S.—d. Sept. 8, 1821, Margate, Kent, Eng.), secretary to the American commissioners in France during the American Revolution who spied for the British.

Although he had no formal education, Bancroft assumed the title and style of "Doctor." In 1769 he established his credentials as a scientist with the publication of his "Essay on the Natural History of Guiana." Around 1770 he went to England, where he became friendly with Benjamin Franklin during one of Franklin's early missions to London. Bancroft became an adherent of the American cause and returned to the colonies. As a result of his friendship with Franklin he accompanied Franklin and the two other American commissioners to France in 1776. In France Bancroft was contacted by Paul Wentworth, an American-born Loyalist who headed a ring of Loyalist spies for the British. By December of that year he had begun receiving a salary from the British. Between 1777 and 1783 he reported every movement of Franklin and the other Americans to the British, writing his reports in invisible ink and relaying them by means of a dead drop. Bancroft's information included the details of treaties and the movement of ships and troops from France to America. To avoid suspicion Bancroft made several trips to Britain ostensibly to spy on the British; they provided him with harmless or false information and once pretended to arrest him. In 1783 Bancroft moved to England, primarily to preserve his British citizenship and the pension due him for his secret service. He continued to correspond with Franklin, who never suspected him. He invented several processes for dyeing textiles and in 1794 wrote a work called "Experimental Researches concerning the Philosophy of Permanent Colors." He gained international fame as a chemist and was made a fellow of the Royal Society. Not until nearly 70 years after his death did his role as a British spy become public knowledge.

Bancroft, George (b. Oct. 3, 1800, Worcester, Mass., U.S.—d. Jan. 17, 1891, Washington, D.C.), U.S. historian whose comprehensive 10-volume study of the nation's origins and development caused him to be referred to as the "father of American history."

Bancroft's life presented a curious blend of scholarship and politics. Although he received an excellent education at Harvard and several German universities, he initially eschewed an academic career for an eight-year experiment

George Bancroft, photograph by Mathew Brady
By courtesy of the Library of Congress, Washington, D.C.

in elementary education at Round Hill, his private school for boys at Northampton, Mass. (1823–31). He then turned to Anti-Masonic and Democratic politics—the latter a particularly unpopular affiliation in Whig-dominated Massachusetts. He received his first patronage post as collector of the Port of Boston (1838) and became U.S. secretary of the navy (1845–46) and minister to England (1846–49). Though not an Abolitionist, Bancroft broke with the Democrats over the slavery issue in the 1850s and shifted his support to the Republican Party. As a result, he served as minister to Prussia (1867–71) and to the German Empire (1871–74). While in Germany he became closely identified with the German intellectual community.

Throughout his lifetime he fitted his research and writing around his political requirements, so that compilation of his *History of the United States* extended over a period of 40 years (1834–74). With a few exceptions, earlier U.S. historians had been collectors or annalists, concerned chiefly with state or Revolutionary War histories. Bancroft was the first scholar to plan a comprehensive study of the nation's past, from its colonial foundations through the end of its struggle for independence. Influenced by the nationalistic German school of historians, he approached his subject philosophically, molding it to fit his preconceived thesis that the U.S. political and social system represented the highest point yet reached in mankind's quest for the perfect state. He placed great emphasis on the use of original sources, building a vast collection of documents and hiring copyists to translate materials from European archives.

Many critics thought that, in the first three volumes (1834–40), the writer was too strongly influenced by the political attitudes of Pres. Andrew Jackson. Nevertheless, Bancroft's reputation as the country's leading historian was firmly established by 1850. Seven succeeding volumes were published between 1852 and 1874. A revised centenary edition (1876) reduced the number of volumes to six, but the author's basic approach to American history remained unchanged. A still later edition (1885) included a two-volume study, *The History of the Formation of the Federal Constitution* (1882).

Although Bancroft neglected economic and social forces in historical development and favoured political, military, and religious approaches, he was nevertheless the first to recognize the importance of the colonial period, foreign relations, and the frontier as forces in U.S. history.

Bancroft, Hubert Howe (b. May 5, 1832, Granville, Ohio, U.S.—d. March 2, 1918, Walnut Creek, Calif.), historian of the American West who collected and published a 39-volume *History of the Pacific States of North America* that remains one of the great sources of information on the West.

Born into a sternly religious and hard-working family, Bancroft abandoned formal education at the age of 16, after a brief enrollment in a local academy. His father went to California to pan for gold in 1850, and Bancroft followed him two years later. By 1856 he had opened a bookshop in San Francisco and had travelled extensively, both in America and in Europe. His firm became the largest bookselling business in the West. In 1859 he began to collect California materials, and he soon expanded his interest to include western America from Panama to Alaska. His collection eventually included some 60,000 volumes.

Around 1870 Bancroft conceived the idea of writing an encyclopaedic history of the American West, which he implemented by utilizing the skills of relatively untrained collaborators to index the massive documentation and work on special projects. Their combined effort resulted in the largest collection of information on the American West.

To himself Bancroft assigned the task of writing *The Native Races of the Pacific States of North America,* 5 vol. (1875–76), a description of indigenous ethnic groups, still useful to anthropologists. The remaining volumes include histories of the western Americas from Central America to Alaska, covering such various subjects as Mormonism in Utah and the colonization of Alaska by Russia.

After completing the first five volumes on *The Native Races* and the next 28 volumes on the settlement and history of the Western states, Bancroft wrote an additional five volumes on the history of California between 1769 and 1848, including the settling of San

Francisco, and a defense of vigilante committees in the West; the latter is considered one of his best monographs. The 39th volume in the set is *Literary Industries* (1890), his autobiography. Through an extensive publicity campaign, he achieved a gross return of more than $1,000,000. On Nov. 25, 1905, he sold his entire library to the University of California at Berkeley for $250,000. His writing included *The New Pacific* (1898), in which he argued in favour of U.S. imperialism in the West.

Although marred by a general lack of careful scholarship and editing, Bancroft's library made available to scholars a great amount of historical material, with a broad emphasis on cultural and social interchange in the origin and development of nations. Although he failed to identify his helpers, their contribution serves as a model for cooperative writing in large projects of historical research. Bancroft's histories are still considered a generally accurate and valuable source on the history of the Far West. Further biographical information may be found in his *Literary Industries* and in J.W. Caughey's *Hubert Howe Bancroft, Historian of the West* (1946).

Bancroft, Sir Squire (b. May 14, 1841, London—d. April 19, 1926, London), British actor and manager whose espousal of careful craft in the writing and staging of plays did much to lay the foundations of modern theatrical production.

Sir Squire Bancroft
BBC Hulton Picture Library

Left fatherless at an early age, Bancroft was educated privately in England and France. He first appeared on the stage in Birmingham in 1861 and played in the provinces before his London appearance in 1865. He married the theatre manager Marie Effie Wilton in 1867. At the Prince of Wales's Theatre they produced all the better known comedies of Thomas William Robertson, among them *Society* (1865) and *Caste* (1867). These productions swept away the old crude methods of writing and staging. Later they produced new plays and revivals, such as Bulwer-Lytton's *Money*, Dion Boucicault's *London Assurance*, and an adaptation of Sardou's *Théodora*, entitled *Diplomacy*. In 1880 they moved to the Haymarket Theatre and continued a brilliant career until their retirement from management in 1885. Bancroft played with Henry Irving in 1889 and was knighted in 1897. Together the Bancrofts wrote *Mr. and Mrs. Bancroft on and off the Stage* (1888) and *The Bancrofts: Recollections of Sixty Years* (1909). *Sir Squire's Empty Chairs* (1925) is a volume of his reminiscences.

band (from Middle French *bande*, "troop"), in music, an ensemble of musicians playing chiefly woodwind, brass, and percussion instruments, in contradistinction to an orchestra, which contains stringed instruments. Apart from this specific designation, the word band has wide vernacular application, from generalized usage (as in "dance band" and "jazz band") to the very specific (as in "harmonica band," "brass band," and "string band"). The term was first used in England to apply to the "king's band" of 24 violins at the court of Charles II (reigned 1660–85), a group modelled on Louis XIV's famous group of violins.

The wind, brass, and percussion ensemble that is called a band originated in 15th-century Germany, where ensembles consisting chiefly of oboes and bassoons formed part of the paraphernalia of military life. German musicians joined foreign groups, and wind bands spread eventually through France and England and to the New World. Toward the end of the 18th century, in the wake of the Turkish occupation of large parts of eastern Europe, a style of band music identified as Turkish, or Janissary, music (after the elite troops who, *c.* 1400–1826, guarded the Turkish sultans), became popular across the Continent. Its characteristically strident sound, produced in the original by shrill flutes and large drums, jangling triangles, cymbals, and Turkish crescents (jingling Johnnies), and its emphatic duple accent appealed to a growing taste for exoticism that led also to the employment of Negro drummers who marched brandishing their drumsticks in the manner of the later drum major. Janissary music inspired some of the greatest composers, including Haydn, in the second movement of his *Symphony No. 100 in G Major* (*The Military*); Mozart, in the "Rondo alla Turca" movement of his *Piano Sonata in A Major* K. 331; and Beethoven, in the incidental music for *The Ruins of Athens*.

By the end of the 18th century, the number of wind instruments had increased greatly, primarily under the impact of the large-scale outdoor ceremonies of the French Revolution, which featured bands of as many as 2,000 musicians. Haydn's marches written for the Derbyshire yeomanry were scored for trumpet, two horns, two clarinets, two bassoons, and serpent (the wooden precursor of the tuba). In Berlin in 1838, 1,000 wind instruments and 200 drummers were assembled by the organizer of Prussian military music to perform in honour of the Russian emperor.

In England the brass band (sometimes called silver band, referring to the metal alloy of many instruments) began to replace the earlier bands of the town "waits" (public musicians) and of village churches at the end of the 18th century. The formation of such bands was encouraged by employers in industrial areas, and the development of the cornopean, a predecessor of the cornet, and of a family of brass instruments, with similar fingering, invented by the French instrument builder Adolphe Sax, facilitated the adoption of brass instruments by amateur players. Among the earliest of the English brass bands were the Stalybridge Old Band (1814) and the famous Besses o' the Barn (all-brass by 1853). Groups were formed to represent towns, factories, religious and social organizations, and the Salvation Army; contests, notably at Bell Vue, Manchester, and Alexandra Palace, London, culminated in 1900 in the National Brass Band Festival. Composers such as Sir Edward Elgar, Sir Arthur Sullivan, Gustav Holst, and Benjamin Britten contributed to the band literature. Such works were usually scored for cornets, flugelhorns, horns, B♭ baritones, euphoniums, and basses.

In the U.S., professional bands such as the celebrated band of Patrick Sarsfield Gilmore (1829–92) competed in attracting virtuoso soloists. Gilmore, whose musical skill was matched by a flair for showmanship, was particularly influential in promoting technical skill and repertory of high quality. His true successor was John Philip Sousa (1854–32), bandmaster of the U.S. Marine Band and composer of such marches as *Semper Fidelis, The Washington Post*, and *The Stars and Stripes Forever*. The accomplishments of Gilmore and Sousa were to raise the art of the band to a distinguished level, making band music, in a sense, a very American musical genre. It remains a staple in parades and in the extravaganzas that form an important part of the entertainment incidental to sports events.

band, in cultural anthropology, theoretical type of human social organization consisting of a small number of nuclear families (usually no more than 30 to 50 persons in all) who are loosely organized for purposes of subsistence and security. They may also be integrated into a larger community, usually called a tribe (*q.v.*). Bands exist in sparsely populated areas and possess only primitive technologies, but there may be considerable variation in their habitats, as witness the desert-dwelling Australian Aborigines, the Pygmies of the Congo rain forests, and the Kaska Indians of the Yukon. Bands may occasionally coalesce for broader tribal ceremonies, hunting, or warfare.

band-pass filter, arrangement of electronic components that allows only those electric waves lying within a certain range, or band, of frequencies to pass and blocks all others. The components may be conventional coils and capacitors, or the arrangement may be made up of freely vibrating piezoelectric crystals (crystals that vibrate mechanically at their resonant frequency when excited by an applied voltage of the same frequency), in which case the device is called a crystal band-pass filter or a monolithic filter (*q.v.*).

The crystal band-pass filter makes it possible to send a great number of simultaneous telephone conversations over a single long-distance line, microwave radio system, or submarine cable, because it separates each voice channel from all others. *See also* multiplexing.

band theory, in solid-state physics, theoretical model describing the states of electrons in solid materials that can have values of energy only within certain specific ranges. The behaviour of an electron in a solid (and hence its energy) is related to the behaviour of all other particles around it. This is in direct contrast to the behaviour of an electron in free space where it may have any specified energy. The ranges of allowed energies of electrons in a solid are called allowed bands. Certain ranges of energies between two such allowed bands may be forbidden—*i.e.*, electrons within the solid may not possess these energies. The band theory accounts for many of the electrical and thermal properties of solids and forms the basis of the technology of such devices as transistors, heating elements, and capacitors.

The band of energies permitted in a solid is related to the discrete allowed energies—the so-called energy levels—of single, isolated atoms. When the atoms are brought together to form a solid, these discrete energy levels become perturbed interactions termed quantum mechanical effects, and the many electrons in the collection of individual atoms occupy a band of levels in the solid called the valence band. Empty states in each single atom also broaden into a band of levels that is frequently empty or nearly so, called the conduction band. Just as electrons at one energy level in an individual atom may transfer to another empty energy level, so electrons in the solid may transfer from one energy level in a given band to another in the same band or in another band, often crossing an intervening gap of forbidden energies. Studies of such changes of energy in solids interacting with photons of light, energetic electrons, X-rays, and the like confirm the general validity of the band theory and provide detailed information about allowed and forbidden energies.

A variety of ranges of allowed and forbidden energy gaps are found in pure elements, alloys, and compounds. Three distinct groups are usually described: metals, insulators, and semiconductors. In metals, forbidden bands do not occur in the energy range of the most energetic (outermost) electrons. Accordingly, metals are good conductors. Insulators have wide forbidden energy gaps—namely, several electron volts. Because electrons cannot move freely in the presence of an applied voltage, insulators are poor conductors. Semiconductors have relatively narrow forbidden gaps (roughly one electron volt), and so are intermediate conductors.

Banda, also called TOGBO, a people of the Central African Republic, some of whom also live in Zaire, Cameroon, and possibly in The Sudan. Banda speak a language of the Adamawa-Eastern subgroup of the Niger-Congo family that is related to that of their Baya and Ngbandi neighbours.

In the early 18th century some Banda occupied what is now southern Chad, while others in contact with the Islāmic Kingdom of Wadai converted to Islām and became known as Runga. In 1830 still other Banda, called Marba, joined Wadai warriors led by an exiled Bagirmi (Baguirmi) prince and founded Dar al-Kuti, which became a satellite of Wadai. The inhabitants of Dar al-Kuti and others began attacking nonallied Banda, who then fled to the west and south; most, however, settled in the Ouaka River area of what is now south central Central African Republic. Banda fought the Sudanese warriors of al-Mahdī in the 1880s, and active resistance continued until the Belgians (1892) and then the French (early 20th century) occupied the upper Oubangui (Ubangi).

The Banda observe patrilineal descent and live in hamlets of dispersed homesteads under the local governance of a headman. Southern Banda, in particular, are scattered in isolated settlements, each of which has a different dialect. Men and women often migrate to urban areas in search of employment. Rural Banda raise corn (maize), cassava, peanuts (groundnuts), sweet potatoes, and tobacco. Men hunt and fish while women gather wild foods and assist in farming. Banda craftsmen produce carved wooden ritual and utilitarian objects; they are best known for their large slit drums carved in the shape of animals.

The Banda have in their oral tradition a great chief, called Ngakola, and "mountain kings," yet they were a stateless people when encountered by Europeans; war chiefs were selected and remained active only during times of crisis. They used age grades and initiations called *semali* to assure unity in time of war; initiates received instruction in agricultural, social, and religious knowledge. Ele is the Banda supreme being, while Badagi is an important water spirit. Marriage traditionally required bridewealth, often in iron implements. Polygamy, although still practiced, has declined with the rise of a money economy.

Bānda, town, administrative headquarters of Bānda district, Uttar Pradesh state, northern India, near the Ken River (a tributary of the Yamuna). An agricultural marketplace, it lies at a road junction on a major rail line. The town's trade has been declining, and the road leading southward is no longer maintained. Bānda is noted for its agates from the Ken riverbed, which are exported. There are several mosques and Hindu temples; outside the town are the ruins of an 18th-century fort, Kālinjar. The town and the fort changed hands repeatedly during struggles between the Muslims, Marāṭhās, French, and British.

Bānda district, 2,952 sq mi (7,645 sq km) in area, lies between the Yamuna (Jumna) River (north) and the Vindhya Range (south) and is drained by the Ken. Predominantly agricultural, it produces wheat, rice, gram (chickpea), millet, and other crops; cattle and other animals are raised. Chitrakūt Dham, near Karwi, is a notable pilgrimage centre. The district contains a number of Stone Age archaeological sites. Pop. (1981) town, 72,379; district, 1,533,990.

Banda, H(astings) Kamuzu (b. *c.* 1902, near Kasungu, British Central Africa Protectorate), first president of Malaŵi (formerly Nyasaland) and the principal leader of the Malaŵi nationalist movement.

He was the son of a peasant and received his earliest education in a mission school. He attended college in the United States, where he received his medical degree in 1927. He then took another medical degree in London (1941) and practiced there until 1953.

Banda first became involved in African politics when white settlers in Central Africa demanded federation of the Rhodesias and Nyasaland in 1949. Banda and others in Nyasaland strongly objected to this extension of white dominance, but the Federation of Rhodesia and Nyasaland was nevertheless established in 1953. In 1953–58 Banda practiced medicine in Ghana, but from 1956 he was under increasing pressure from Nyasa nationalists to return; he finally did so, to a tumultuous welcome, in 1958. As president of the Nyasaland African Congress, he toured the country making anti-federation speeches and was held partly responsible by the colonial government for increasing African resentment and disturbances. In 1959 a state of emergency was declared, and he was imprisoned. He was released in 1960 and a few months later accepted British constitutional proposals granting Africans in Nyasaland a majority in the Legislative Council. He was minister of natural resources and local government in 1961–63, and he became prime minister in 1963, the year the federation was finally dissolved.

A ministerial crisis occurred in 1964, shortly after independence, when some of his younger ministers, angered by his growing authoritarianism and disagreeing with several of his decisions (such as his accommodation with the Portuguese colonies and with South Africa), either were dismissed or resigned. In 1965 a rebellion broke out, led by two of these former ministers, but it failed to take hold in the countryside. Malaŵi became a republic in 1966 under President Banda's austere, autocratic one-party regime. Banda gained firm command of his own country, being declared president for life in 1971, but his reputation in most of black Africa deteriorated as his trade and contacts with white South Africa grew.

Banda Aceh, *kotamadya* (city), capital of Aceh *daerah istimewa* (special district), located at the northwestern tip of Sumatra, Indonesia. Banda Aceh is known as the "doorway to Mecca," for historically it has been a stopping place for pilgrims journeying by ship to Mecca. Visited by Marco Polo in 1292 and by Ibn Baṭṭūṭah in 1345 and 1346, it became the capital of the sultanate of Aceh in the 17th century. Its ruler, Iskandar Muda, engaged in naval battles with the Portuguese in the Strait of Malacca. The Dutch occupied the city in 1873; the subsequent Aceh War between the Dutch and the Achinese continued until 1903. The city remained under Dutch control until it was occupied by the Japanese at the beginning of World War II.

The population of Banda Aceh is mostly Achinese, together with a mixture of Indians, Arabs, Turks, Chinese, Abyssinians, and Persians. Industries produce gold jewelry, cotton and silk fabrics, lamps, engraved copper bowls, brocades, and sword blades. The city is linked by road and rail with the eastern coastal cities of Lhokseumane, Langsa, and Medan; it also has an airport. Notable sites include a sports stadium; the Baturrachman Mosque; the Aceh Museum (with a giant Chinese bell and Achinese cultural items); the Gunongan, or Walking Palace, a series of baths and pleasure gardens on the banks of a river; and a fine beach. The Universitas Syiah Kuala was founded in 1959 as a faculty of economics and became a state university in 1961. Pop. (1980) 72,090.

Banda Islands, island group, Maluku *propinsi* (province), Indonesia, in the Banda Sea, southeast of Pulau Ambon (*pulau*, "island") and south of Seram. The largest of the nine islands, which have a total land area of 17 sq mi (44 sq km), is Pulau Banda Besar, or Great Banda. An inland sea, formed by three of the group, provides an outstanding harbour; the marine gardens beneath the sea are virtually unrivalled. Banda Besar has coral rock to a height of 400 ft (120 m), with lava and basalt up to 1,758 ft. Gunung Api (*gunung*, "mount"), one of the group, is an active volcano 2,200 ft in height; it caused extensive destruction in 1820 and 1852.

The islands' volcanic soil is well adapted to the growth of nutmeg, which is indigenous. Other products are cloves, coconuts, tapioca, fish, and tropical fruits and vegetables. Half the population of the islands lives in Bandanaira, the capital and port city of Bandanaira Island. The inhabitants are mostly descendants of Javanese, Makasarese, and people from neighbouring islands brought in as slaves to work the Dutch nutmeg plantations. Regular ship service connects Bandanaira and Ambon.

The Banda Islands were annexed by the Portuguese in 1512, but early in the 17th century the Dutch expelled the Portuguese. England and the Netherlands vied for the islands, which changed hands several times before 1814, when they were restored to the Dutch by the Treaty of Paris. Pop. (1971) 13,638.

Banda Sea, Bahasa Indonesia LAUT BANDA, portion of the western South Pacific, bounded by the southern islands of the Moluccas of Indonesia (Alor, Timor, Wetar, Babar, Tanimbar, and Kai on the south and Seram, Buru, and Sula on the north). It occupies a total of 180,000 sq mi (470,000 sq km) and opens to the Flores (west), Savu (southwest), Timor (south), Arafura (southeast), and Ceram and Molucca (north) seas. The sea's North Banda Basin, plunging to a depth of 19,000 ft (5,800 m), is separated from the South Banda Basin by a submarine ridge that has coral islands surmounting its highest peaks. The South Banda Basin, descending to 17,700 ft, holds Gunung Api, a volcano rising from 14,800 ft below sea level to 2,200 ft above. An arc of active volcanic islands stands on a second ridge dividing the South Banda Basin from Weber Basin, the deepest in the sea (24,409 ft). Surface currents in the Banda Sea trend east from December to February, reversing themselves during the remainder of the year. In the clear waters around many islands, notably the Banda group just south of Seram, corals flourish in spectacular beauty.

Bandā Singh Bahādur, also called LACHMAN DĀS, LACHMAN DEV, or MADHO DĀS (b. 1670, Rājauri, India—d. June 1716, Delhi), first Sikh military leader to wage an offensive, rather than defensive, war against the Mughal rulers of India, thereby temporarily extending Sikh territory.

As a youth, he early decided to be a *samāna* (ascetic), and until 1708, when he became a disciple of Gurū Gobind Singh, he was known as Madho Dās. After his initiation into the Sikh brotherhood, he took the name Bandā Singh Bahādur and became a respected, if not popular, general; his cold and impersonal character did not endear him to his men.

Bandā Singh set out in 1709 to attack the Mughals, conquering large tracts of territory. His pillaging and massacring in the Deccan area led the Mughal rulers finally to move against him in force. After an eight-month siege, the fortress town of Gurdas Nangal fell to the Mughals in 1715. Bandā Singh and his men were taken as prisoners to Delhi, where every day for six months a few of his men were taken out and executed. When his own turn came, Bandā Singh stated to the Muslim judge that this fate befell him justly because he had failed his beloved Gurū Gobind Singh. He was tortured to death with red-hot irons.

Bandama River, longest and, commercially, most important river in the Ivory Coast; with its major tributaries, the Bandama Rouge (Marahoué) and the Nzi, it drains half of the surface area of the country. It rises as the Bandama Blanc in the northern highlands and flows southward for 497 mi (800 km) to enter the Gulf of Guinea and the Tagba Lagoon near Grand-Lahou. Diamonds are extracted from its upper reaches in the savanna. A hydroelectric plant at Kossou, just north of the confluence with the Marahoué, provides power for the Ivory Coast. Kossou is the site of the largest dam in the country and major agricultural fishery projects, which have led to the formation of pilot villages. Kossou provides electric power to the southern part of the country and will be linked to Ghana's Akopombo project for power-sharing. Manganese and timber are shipped coastwise from the Tagba Lagoon and the river's lower section via the Asagny Canal to Abidjan for export. The Bandama is navigable for about 35 mi upstream from Grand-Lahou.

Bandar (India): *see* Masulipatam.

Bandar ʿAbbās, port on the Strait of Hormuz and capital of Hormozgān *ostān* (province); it is the main maritime outlet for much of southern Iran. It lies on the northern shore of Hormuz Bay opposite the islands of Qeshm, Lārak, and Hormuz. The inhabitants are mainly Arabs and African blacks. The summer climate is oppressively hot and humid, and many inhabitants move then to cooler places, but winter is pleasant. Trade includes oil products from Abadan. Imports, mainly manufactured goods, generally exceed exports, which include Kermān rugs and agricultural produce. The town has a cotton mill and a fish cannery. The roadstead is shallow and badly sheltered, and vessels must sometimes lie 4 mi (6.5 km) out. Port facilities are poor; a new harbour is under construction about 9 mi west of the existing port.

Bandar ʿAbbās (Port of ʿAbbās) was established in 1623 by Shāh ʿAbbās I to replace the city of Hormuz, captured by the Portuguese *c.* 1514. During the 17th century it was the main port of Persia, but it lost this status in the 18th century. From about 1793 it was under lease to the rulers of Muscat, but in 1868 Iran cancelled the contract and resumed direct control. Pop. (1976) 89,103.

Bandar Maharani (Malaysia): *see* Muar.

Bandar Penggaram (Malaysia): *see* Batu Pahat.

Bandar Seri Begawan, formerly (until 1970) BRUNEI TOWN, capital of Brunei, on the Sungai (river) Brunei near its mouth on Brunei Bay, an inlet of the South China Sea. It is an agricultural trade centre and river port. After suffering extensive damage during World War II, it was largely rebuilt; newer buildings include a royal palace, a sports stadium, and the Sultan Omar Ali Saifuddin mosque, largest in the Far East. The residents of the section known as Kampong Ayer, who live in houses built on stilts over the river, were unsuccessfully encouraged by the government to move ashore in the early 1970s. Bandar Seri Begawan lies on the main road running westward along Borneo's coast to Seria and Kuala Belait, and it is also served by a modern international airport. The Brunei Museum, a major cultural resource, is about 4 mi (6.5 km) away. Pop. (1982 est.) 51,649.

Bandaranaike, S(olomon) W(est) R(idgeway) D(ias) (b. Jan. 8, 1899, Colombo, Ceylon—d. Sept. 26, 1959, Colombo), statesman and prime minister of Ceylon (1956–59), whose election marked a significant change in the political history of modern Ceylon.

S.W.R.D. Bandaranaike
Camera Press

Educated at Oxford, he was called to the bar in 1925. After returning to Ceylon he entered politics and, in 1931, was elected to the newly formed legislative assembly, the State Council. In 1947, as a prominent member of the governing United National Party (UNP), he was elected to the new House of Representatives and appointed minister of health and local government. He resigned from the government and the Western-oriented UNP in 1951 and was re-elected in 1952 as the founder of the nationalist Sri Lanka (Blessed Ceylon) Freedom Party, becoming leader of the opposition in the legislature. Four years later he formed the Mahajana Eksath Peramuna (MEP; People's United Front), a political alliance of four nationalist-socialist parties, which swept the election; he was appointed prime minister on April 12, 1956.

The MEP advocated a neutralist foreign policy and strong nationalist policies at home. Sinhalese, the language spoken by the majority community, replaced English as the official language of the country, and Buddhism, the majority religion, was given a prominent place in the affairs of state. By amicable agreement the British relinquished their military bases on the island, and Ceylon established diplomatic relations with Communist states.

A disgruntled Buddhist monk, Talduwe Somarama, shot Bandaranaike Sept. 25, 1959, and he died the following day. After the 1960 elections, his widow, Sirimavo Ratwatte Dias Bandaranaike (*q.v.*), became prime minister.

Bandaranaike, Sirimavo Ratwatte Dias (b. April 17, 1916, Ratnapura, Ceylon), stateswoman who, upon her party's victory in the 1960 Ceylon general election, became the world's first woman prime minister.

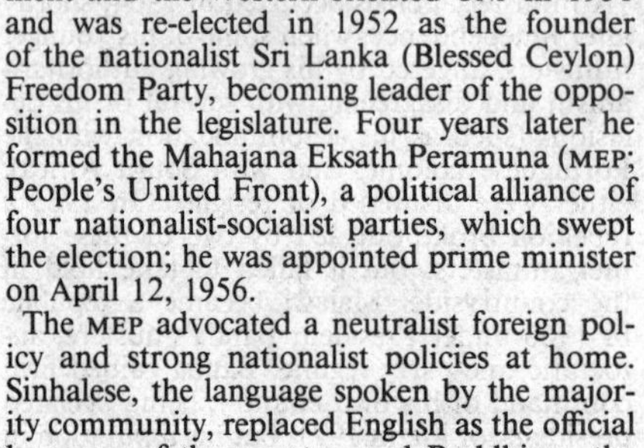

Sirimavo Bandaranaike, 1960
Keystone

In 1940 she married S.W.R.D. Bandaranaike (*q.v.*) and began to interest herself in social welfare. After her husband, who became prime minister in 1956, was assassinated in 1959, she was induced by his Sri Lanka (Blessed Ceylon) Freedom Party (SLFP) to become the party's leader. The SLFP won a decisive victory at the general election in July 1960, and she became prime minister.

She carried on her husband's policies of socialism, neutrality in international relations, and the active encouragement of the Buddhist religion and of the Sinhalese language and culture. In 1964 her coalition with the Marxist Lanka Sama Samaja Party (Ceylon Socialist Party) caused dissension in her government, which was subsequently defeated in the general election of 1965. In 1970, however, her Socialist coalition, the United Front, regained power, and as prime minister she pursued more radical policies. Her strategy, which included the nationalization of important industries, was nullified by repressive measures and failure to deal with ethnic rivalries and economic distress; in the election of July 1977 her party retained only eight of the 168 seats in the National Assembly, and she was replaced as prime minister.

banded anteater (marsupial mammal): *see* numbat.

banded-iron formation (BIF), chemical sediment, typically thin bedded or laminated, comprised of 25 percent or more iron of sedimentary origin and layers of chert, chalcedony, jasper, or quartz. Such formations occur on all the continents and are older than 1,700,000,000 years. They also are all highly metamorphosed. BIF's contain much iron oxides—magnetite and hematite with secondary goethite and limonite—and are commonly used as low-grade iron ore, as for example in the Lake Superior region of North America. Because BIF's apparently have not formed since the Precambrian era, special conditions are thought to have existed at the time of their formation. Considerable controversy exists over BIF origin and a number of theories have been proposed. Their formation has been variously ascribed to volcanic activity; rhythmic deposition from iron and silica solutions due to seasonal variations; oxidation of iron-rich sediments contemporaneous with deposition; and precipitation from solution as a result of special oxidation-reduction conditions.

bandeira, Portuguese slave-hunting expedition into the Brazilian interior in the 17th century. The *bandeirantes* (members of such expeditions) were usually *mamelucos* (of mixed Indian and Portuguese ancestry) from São Paulo who went in search of profit and adventure as they penetrated into unmapped regions. They thus helped establish Brazil's claim to the South American interior, beyond the line between Portuguese and Spanish possessions in the Americas that had been laid down in the Treaty of Tordesillas (1494).

The *bandeiras,* numbering anywhere from about 50 to several thousand men, were organized and tightly controlled by wealthy entrepreneurs. The expeditions would usually found settlements en route, build roads, and lay the basis for agriculture and ranching in the interior. They would often ally themselves with one Indian tribe against another and end by enslaving both weakened belligerents. The mission villages established by the Jesuits for the Indians were prime targets for *bandeira* slave raids. The first *bandeira,* organized by Antonio Raposo Tavares in 1628, raided 21 such villages in the upper Paraná Valley and captured about 2,500 Indians. Thus, the Jesuit missionaries were the chief opponents of the *bandeirantes* and tried to stave off their attacks by moving their villages farther south and west and by arming the mission Indians. Nevertheless, the *bandeiras,* the most famous of which was led by Fernão Dias Pais Leme, netted large profits in slaves and thus wreaked great injury on the Indians.

Bandeira (Filho), Manuel (Carneiro de Sousa) (b. April 19, 1886, Recife, Braz.—d. Oct. 13, 1968, Rio de Janeiro), poet, literary historian, translator, and educator who in a career of more than 50 years influenced two generations of Brazilian writers. After his death, his reputation as a poet was established.

Bandeira was educated in Rio de Janeiro and São Paulo, but in 1903 tuberculosis forced him to abandon his dream of becoming an architect. He spent the next several years in convalescence, reading widely and trying his hand at poetry. In 1913, still in search of health, he entered a sanatorium in Switzerland, where he became friendly with the French Symbolist poet Paul Éluard. Returning to Rio de Janeiro on the outbreak of World War I in 1914, he determined to pursue a literary career.

Bandeira's first books of poetry, *A Cinza das Horas* (1917; "Destruction of the Hours") and *Carnaval* (1919; "Carnival"), brought him recognition both as a strikingly personal and individual poet and as a representative of the new Modernist movement (*see* modernismo, Brazilian), which was attempting to liberate South American poetry from academicism and European influence. Sympathetic to the aesthetic principles of Modernism, Bandeira continued to affirm its methods—free verse, of which he was a master, the use of colloquial language and unconventional syntax, and themes based on Brazilian folklore—in his own work. He did so always as a means of personal expression, as in *Libertinagem* (1930; "Libertinism") and *Estrêla da Manhã* (1936; "Morning Star"), rather than as a literary device. He also translated Shakespeare, García Lorca, Rilke, and Jean Cocteau.

Bandeira taught literature in Rio de Janeiro from 1938 to 1943. He also wrote newspaper and magazine articles and published editions and anthologies of other poets in order to acquaint the public with the new Brazilian literature. For his students he wrote a history of world literature, *Noções de História das Literaturas* (1940; "Concepts of Literary History"); with characteristic modesty, he mentions his own name only once in the section on Brazilian literature, as a sympathizer with Modernism, "although preserving a certain personal independence."

Despite his immense popularity as a poet and a national figure among all sections of the Brazilian public, Bandeira led a quiet life in Rio and the nearby town of Petropólis, continuing to publish almost until his death at the age of 82. On his 50th birthday a group of Brazilian writers published *Homenagem a Manuel Bandeira* (1936; "Homage to Manuel Bandeira"), demonstrating their esteem for him both as a major influence and as a great poet in his own right.

Bandeira Mountain, Portuguese PICO DA BANDEIRA, peak, on the border of Espírito Santo and Minas Gerais states, eastern Brazil. In the Serra do Caparaó, it lies 100 mi (160 km) inland from Vitória on the Atlantic coast. Until 1962, when Neblina Peak was discovered, Bandeira Mountain (9,495 ft [2,890 m]) was considered to be the highest point in Brazil.

Bandelier, Adolph (b. Aug. 6, 1840, Bern—d. March 18, 1914, Seville), Swiss-American anthropologist, historian, and archaeologist who was among the first to study the Indian cultures of the southwestern United States, Mexico, and Peru–Bolivia; his works, particularly those relating to the Southwest and Peru–Bolivia, are still of considerable value.

Between 1873 and 1879, as an enthusiastic disciple of the U.S. ethnologist Lewis Henry Morgan, he tried to prove, in support of Morgan's evolutionary theories, that Aztec sociopolitical structure had been kin-based, democratic, and substantially similar to that of the Iroquois Indians of North America. These findings, published in three monographs, are now chiefly of historical interest.

Bandelier
By courtesy of the Southwest Museum, Los Angeles

In the period following 1880 he undertook archaeological, ethnographic, and documentary studies in the Southwest and Mexico. Works resulting from these efforts included *Final Report of Investigations Among the Indians of the Southwestern United States . . .* (1890–92) and a fictionalized Pueblo ethnography, *The Delight Makers* (1890). The most important work based on his studies in Peru and Bolivia (1892–1903) was *The Islands of Titicaca and Koati* (1910). Following his return to the United States, he held museum and teaching posts in New York City and Washington, D.C., before departing for Spain (1913) to continue documentary investigations on the Pueblo Indians. The Bandelier National Monument, containing prehistoric homes of the later Pueblo period, was established near Santa Fe, N.M., in 1916.

Bandelier National Monument, canyon containing many cliff and open pueblo ruins, in north central New Mexico, U.S., on the Rio Grande, 20 mi (32 km) west-northwest of Santa Fe. Established in 1916, it occupies an area of 46 sq mi (120 sq km) and was named for Adolph Bandelier, the Swiss-American archaeologist. The monument contains ruins, notably Tyuonyi and Tsankawi, of pre-Columbian Indians (mostly 15th-century) in the canyon of the Rito de los Frijoles and on the Pajarito Plateau. Kivas (ceremonial chambers), stone sculpture, and man-made caves have also been unearthed.

Bandello, Matteo (b. 1485, Castelnuovo Scrivia, Duchy of Milan—d. 1561, Agen, Fr.), Italian writer whose *Novelle* (stories) started a new trend in 16th-century narrative literature and had a wide influence in England, France, and Spain.

A monk, diplomat, and soldier as well as a writer, Bandello was educated at Milan and the University of Pavia. He frequented the courts of Ferrara and Mantua and knew Niccolò Machiavelli.

He was entrusted with the education of Lucrezia Gonzaga, to whom he dedicated a long poem. After the material for his *Novelle* was destroyed in the Spanish attack on Milan (1522), he fled to France. In 1550 he was made bishop of Agen and spent the remainder of his life in France writing the stories on which his reputation rests.

Bandello's *Novelle* (4 vol. containing 214 stories, 1554–73) provide an insight into the social intrigues of the Italian Renaissance. His style has been criticized, particularly for Lombardisms and Gallicisms, but it strengthened the establishment of the vernacular as the Italian literary language, opposing such classicists as Pietro Bembo who preferred the Florentine elegance of the 14th century.

His stories were translated into French as *Histoires tragiques extraictes des oeuvres italiennes de Bardel . . .* (1559) and into English as *Certaine Tragicall Discourses Written Oute of Frenche and Latin* (1567, 1579), the translators adding a severe moral tone to the tales. Shakespeare's *Romeo and Juliet* was based on one of Bandello's tales, *The Tragicall Historye of Romeus and Juliet* (1562). The stories of such other Shakespearean plays as *Much Ado About Nothing* and *Twelfth Night* are also in Bandello. Bandello's influence can also be discerned in French and Spanish literature.

bandeng: *see* milkfish.

bāndhanī work, Indian tie dyeing, or knot dyeing, in which parts of a silk or cotton cloth are tied tightly with wax thread before the whole cloth is dipped in a dye vat; the threads are afterward untied, the parts so protected being left uncoloured. The technique is used in many parts of India, but Gujarāt and Rājasthān produced, and are still noted for, the finest work. Although the technique is mentioned by Bāṇa, a Sanskrit author of the 7th century AD, who refers to material so treated as *pulaka-bandha* (tie-dyed), surviving examples do not predate the 18th century, making it difficult to trace its earlier history.

Detail of a *bāndhanī*-work sari from Gujarāt, 19th century; in the Prince of Wales Museum of Western India, Bombay
P. Chandra

The process is fairly laborious and largely confined to young working girls, who grow long fingernails with which they deftly handle the fabric. It consists of folding, tying, and dyeing the cloth in several stages; the final result is of a fabric with a red or blue field patterned with white and yellow dots. Geometrical ornament is most popular, but animal and human figures and flowers are also introduced in elaborate examples.

bandicoot, any of about 22 species of Australasian marsupial mammals comprising the

Bandicoot (*Perameles nasuta*)
Warren Garst—Tom Stack and Associates

family Peramelidae. (For Asian rodents of this name, *see* bandicoot rat.) Bandicoots are 30 to 80 centimetres (12 to 31 inches) long, including the 10- to 30-cm, sparsely haired tail. The body is stout and coarse haired, the muzzle tapered, and the hind limbs longer than the front. The toes are reduced in number; two of the hind digits are united. The teeth are sharp and slender. The pouch opens rearward and encloses 6 to 10 teats. Unlike other marsupials, bandicoots have a placenta (lacking villi, however). Most species have two to six young at a time; gestation takes 12–15 days.

Bandicoots occur in Australia, Tasmania, New Guinea, and nearby islands. They are terrestrial, largely nocturnal, solitary animals that dig funnel-like pits in their search for insect and plant food. Farmers consider them pests; some species are endangered, and all have declined.

The long-nosed bandicoot (*Perameles,* or *Thylacis, nasuta*), a vaguely ratlike brown animal whose rump may be black-barred, is the common form in eastern Australia. The three species of short-nosed bandicoots, *Isoodon* (incorrectly *Thylacis*), are found in New Guinea, Australia, and Tasmania. Rabbit-eared bandicoots, or bilbies, are species of *Thylacomys* (sometimes *Macrotis*); now endangered, they are found only in remote colonies in arid interior Australia. As the name implies, they have big narrow ears, long hind legs, and bushy tails. The 35-cm-long, pig-footed bandicoot (*Chaeropus ecaudatus*) of interior Australia has feet that are almost hooflike, with two toes functional on the forefoot, one on the hind foot. This herbivorous creature, resembling a little deer, is an endangered species and may well be extinct; it was last observed locally in the 1920s.

bandicoot rat (*Bandicota indica*), large, blackish-brown burrowing rat belonging to the family Muridae (order Rodentia), of India and Sri Lanka; sometimes called mole rat. The bandicoot rat has a short head, broad muzzle, and a scaly, almost hairless tail. It weighs 0.5 to 1.4 kilograms (1 to 3 pounds) and is 20 to 38 centimetres (8 to 15 inches) long, with the tail an additional 15 to 30 cm. An inhabitant of forest, cultivated land, villages, and towns, the bandicoot rat is destructive to crops, grain, and poultry. Litter size is probably large, since the female has 12 teats. An allied species, called the pest rat, short-tailed bandicoot, or mole rat (*Nesokia indica*), inhabits southwestern Asia. A large, burrowing rodent, it also is destructive to crops.

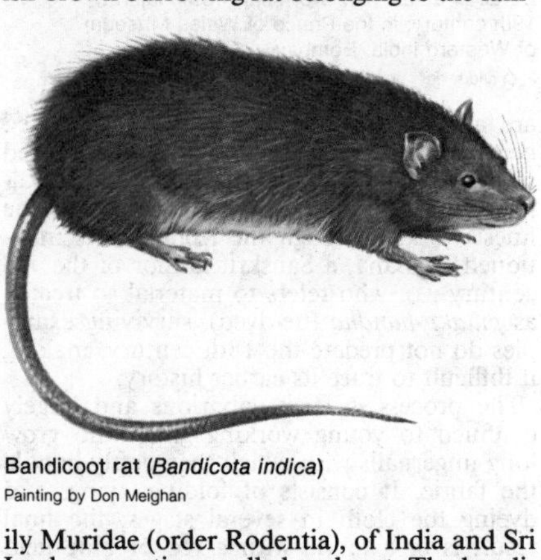
Bandicoot rat (*Bandicota indica*)
Painting by Don Meighan

The bandicoot rat is said to grunt like a pig, and a Telugu name *pandi-koku* (meaning "pig-rat") has been corrupted into "bandicoot." The name has since been applied to a family (Peramelidae) of Australian marsupials.

Bandiera, Attilio and Emilio (respectively b. May 24, 1810, Venice—d. July 23, 1844, Cosenza, Kingdom of the Two Sicilies; b. June 20, 1819, Venice—d. July 23, 1844, Cosenza), followers of Giuseppe Mazzini, who led an abortive revolt against Austrian rule in Italy and whose execution made a profound impression on the Italian revolutionary movement.

The sons of Baron Francesco Bandiera, an admiral in the Austrian Navy, Attilio and Emilio themselves became naval officers but were converted to the cause of Italian independence by Mazzini, carrying on correspondence with him and with members of his organization, Giovine Italia (Young Italy). In 1841, while serving in the war with Syria under their father's command, they founded a secret society, Esperia, devoted to the cause of freeing Italy. In 1843 they began to agitate among their fellow officers and sailors, trying to get them to join a Malta-based revolutionary group, the Legione Italiana, in its plan for stealing a warship and bombarding Messina. The plot was betrayed by a member of Esperia, and in 1844 the brothers were forced to flee to the island of Corfu off the coast of Greece.

Attilio Bandiera, oil painting by Molmenti Pompeo, *c.* 1840; in the Museo del Risorgimento, Venice
By courtesy of the Civici Musei, Venice

Hearing that the people of the Kingdom of Naples were only awaiting the appearance of a leader to rise en masse, the Bandieras gathered a band of about 20 young men and set sail for Calabria (the toe of Italy) on June 12, 1844. Landing at Cotrone four days later, they intended to march on nearby Cosenza, liberating political prisoners and issuing a proclamation of independence. Their expected support did not materialize, and they were betrayed by a Corsican member of their party, Pietro Boccheciampe. On July 23, 1844, the Bandieras and nine companions were executed, crying "Viva l'Italia!" as they fell.

Emilio Bandiera, oil painting by Molmenti Pompeo, *c.* 1840; in the Museo del Risorgimento, Venice
By courtesy of the Civici Musei, Venice

The execution had wide repercussions extending to England. Mazzini proved that his correspondence with the Bandieras had been systematically opened on the orders of the British home secretary, Sir James Graham. He charged the British Foreign Office with having forwarded their plans to the Austrians. That accusation was later disproved, but it gave Mazzini the opportunity of making an eloquent plea for his cause in a famous "Letter to Sir James Graham."

Where the same name may denote a person, place, or thing, the articles will be found in that order

---

Bandinelli, Baccio (b. Nov. 12, 1493?, Florence—d. Feb. 7, 1560, Florence), Florentine Mannerist sculptor whose Michelangelo-influenced works were favoured by the Medici in the second quarter of the 16th century.

Bandinelli was trained as a goldsmith by his father, Michele di Viviano de' Brandini, who was patronized by the Medici family. Showing marked predilection for sculpture, he worked under the sculptor Giovanni Francesco Rustici and became one of the principal artists at the court of Cosimo I de' Medici, grand duke of Tuscany. He founded an academy for artists in the Vatican (1531) and one in Florence (*c.* 1550). Accounts of Bandinelli given in Giorgio Vasari's *Lives* and in the *Autobiography* of Benvenuto Cellini represent him as jealous, malignant, and untalented. He assumed the surname Bandinelli in 1530.

Bandinelli's surviving works prove him to have been a more distinguished sculptor than his contemporaries allowed. His copy of the Laocoön (Uffizi, Florence), his statue of Hercules and Cacus (1534; Piazza della Signoria), and his reliefs on the choir screen of Florence Cathedral explain the vogue that his austere, rather arid work enjoyed at the Medici court. In later life he was supplanted in favour by Cellini and Bartolommeo Ammannati. Shortly before his death he and his son Clemente sculpted his own tomb (1554; SS. Annunziata, Florence), noted for its group of "Lamentation over the Dead Christ."

"Self-Portrait," oil on panel by Baccio Bandinelli, 1529–30; in the Isabella Stewart Gardner Museum, Boston
By courtesy of the Isabella Stewart Gardner Museum, Boston

Bandinelli, Rolando: *see* Alexander III *under* Alexander (papacy).

Bandırma, formerly PANDERMA, port and chief town of Bandırma *ilçe* (district), Balıkesir *il* (province), northwestern Turkey, on the Sea of Marmara. Known in antiquity as Panormos, it was used in the 13th century by the Latin crusaders as a base of operation against the Greeks of Asia Minor and was taken by the Ottomans in the next century. Its protected harbour is now an active transit port between Istanbul and İzmir. A commercial centre, it exports the varied products of the hinterland, including cereals, sheep and cattle, grain, and boracite. Bandırma has road and rail connections with İzmir, Ankara, and

Balıkesir. Manyas Gölü (lake), to the south, is a bird sanctuary and national park. Pop. (1980) town, 53,497; *ilçe,* 80,951.

Bandjarmasin (Indonesia): *see* Banjarmasin.

Bandoeng (Indonesia): *see* Bandung.

bandola (musical instrument): *see* bandurria.

Bandon, Irish DROICHEAD NA BANDAN, town, County Cork, Ireland, 17 mi (27 km) southwest of Cork. Founded in 1608 by Richard Boyle, later earl of Cork, Bandon was initially populated by English and Scottish settlers. Parts of the original town wall remain; the ruins of a 15th-century castle are nearby. Kilbrogan Church (1610), the first Protestant church built in Ireland, contains the town stocks. Bandon lies in the broad valley of the River Bandon, which has good salmon and trout fishing; it is an agricultural centre with distilleries, light engineering industries, breweries, and flour mills. Pop. (1981) 2,055.

Bandon, River, river in County Cork, Ireland, flowing in a valley cut in Carboniferous (280,000,000–345,000,000 years old) rocks but covered with glacial drift and alluvium. The river rises in the Maughanaclea Hills in western Cork and flows east to a point west of Caha Bridge where it turns south, before turning east again to the southeast of Dunmanway. It then flows in a broad fertile valley, with woodlands, to Bandon, and loops in an arc past Inishannon, where it flows southeast and then east, becoming an estuary reaching the sea in Kinsale Harbour, a distance of about 40 mi (64 km). The Bandon Estuary in the vicinity of the town of Kinsale is an important resort and fishing area.

Bandula, Maha, also spelled MAHABANDULA (b. 1780?—d. April 1, 1825, Danubyu, Burma), Burmese general who fought against the British in the First Anglo-Burmese War (1824–26).

In 1819 Maha Bandula served in the Burmese Army occupying Manipur, and two years later he commanded a second Burmese force in the conquest of Assam. King Bagyidaw subsequently appointed him governor of Assam and minister at the court of Ava. In January 1824, because of increased tensions along the Bengal–Arakan border, he was sent with 6,000 troops to Arakan. When the British declared war in March, he immediately invaded Bengal, occupying Ratnapallang and defeating a British force at Ramu. His objective was to seize Chittagong and Dacca in a lightning thrust and, with the aid of a second Burmese army marching from Assam, to expel the British from Bengal. His plan was frustrated, however, when the British landed a force at Rangoon in May. The opening of a second front obliged him to call off the campaign and make a difficult retreat over the Arakan Yoma to Ava.

After raising a large army in Upper Burma, Maha Bandula marched to Danubyu, on the Irrawaddy River, where he established his headquarters in October 1824. In December he attempted, unsuccessfully, to encircle the British, who were entrenched in the neighbourhood of Rangoon. When his headquarters fell to the British, he retreated to prepare for the defense of Danubyu.

In March 1825 the British attacked Danubyu, which Bandula defended courageously. After he was killed in battle, resistance collapsed, Danubyu fell, and the British advanced to Prome, signalling defeat for the Burmese.

Bandundu, region in southwestern Zaire, central Africa, bordering the Congo on the north and Angola on the south. Bandundu was for a while part of Kinshasa province. From 1963 to 1966 its present rural subregions, Kwilu, Kwango, and Maindombe, were separate and autonomous provinces. Bandundu region (area 114,154 sq mi [295,658 sq km]) was created in 1966 with its capital at Bandundu city. Bandundu city and Kikwit (*q.v.*) are cities or urban subregions; other major towns are Inongo and Kenge. The region is dominantly agricultural, producing palm oil and kernels, cocoa, sesame, manioc, livestock, poultry, peanuts (groundnuts), and vegetables. Its forests yield copal and timber. Fish are taken from Lake Mai-Ndombe (formerly Lake Leopold II), rivers, and swamps. Salonga National Park extends into Bandundu's northeastern sector. Pop. (1979 est.) 3,398,574.

Bandundu, formerly (until 1966) BANNINGVILLE, city, since 1972 the capital of Bandundu region, is southwestern Zaire, central Africa, at the junction of the Kwango and Kwilu rivers. It is a river port serving navigation on the Congo (Zaïre) River system from Kinshasa (the national capital, 186 mi [300 km] southwest). There are air links to Kinshasa and such eastern centres as Kikwit and Kananga. The locality is mainly agricultural, producing palm oil and kernels, peanuts (groundnuts), manioc, and fibrous plants (for rope making). Pop. (1976) 96,841.

Bandung, also spelled BANDOENG, *kotamadya* (city), *kabupaten* (regency), and capital of Jawa Barat *propinsi* (West Java province), Indonesia, in the interior of Java on the northern edge of a plateau nearly 2,400 ft (730 m) above sea level. The city, founded in 1810 by the Dutch, has a mild and pleasant climate. Beautiful scenery surrounds the city, with rice fields, waterfalls, and heights rising to nearly 7,050 ft. Bandung is a modern city, with wide, tree-lined streets and many buildings and residences built in Western style. Notable public buildings include the Merdeka and the Dwiwarna, site of the 1955 Bandung Conference of African and Asian nations, which took

The administration building of the Bandung Institute of Technology, Java, Indonesia; the Minangkabau roofs are typical of the local architecture

C. May—Shostal/EB Inc.

a strong stance against Western colonialism. Taman Sari, or Jubilee Park, is the finest of three large parks.

Bandung is the centre of Sundanese cultural life. The Sundanese, who compose the largest segment of Jawa Barat's population, differ significantly in customs and language from their Javanese neighbours to the east. In Bandung, Sundanese literature, dance, song, and theatre are preserved, studied, and renewed.

The city's prestigious Bandung Institute of Technology, which originated as a college of architecture and engineering in the Dutch period, today represents the faculties of mathematics and of the natural and applied sciences of the National University of Indonesia. Also located in Bandung are the Universitas Negeri Padyayaran (1957) and the private Universitas Katolik Parahyangan (1955). There are academies for plastic arts, physical education, and military affairs and a geological museum. The Observatorium Bosscha is in the Lembang highlands, to the north. A large area is devoted to the experimental cultivation of vegetables and flowers. The Nuclear Research Centre (1964) houses an atomic reactor.

The chief industry is textile manufacturing; other manufactures are quinine, rubber goods, and machinery. Industrial institutes conduct research on yarns, dyes, chemicals, and ceramic raw materials. Communications include a railway line, an airport, and a powerful radio station. Pop. (1980) city, 1,462,637; regency, 2,669,240.

Bandung Conference, a meeting of Asian and African states, organized by Indonesia, Burma, Ceylon (Sri Lanka), India, and Pakistan, which met April 18–24, 1955, in Bandung, Indon. In all, 29 countries representing more than half the world's population sent delegates.

The conference reflected the five sponsors' dissatisfaction with what they regarded as a reluctance by the Western powers to consult with them on decisions affecting Asia; their concern over tension between the People's Republic of China and the United States; their desire to lay firmer foundations for China's peaceful relations with themselves and the West; their opposition to colonialism, especially French influence in North Africa; and Indonesia's desire to promote its case in the dispute with The Netherlands over western New Guinea (Irian Jaya).

Major debate centred upon the question of whether Soviet policies in eastern Europe and Central Asia should be censured along with Western colonialism. A consensus was reached in which "colonialism in all of its manifestations" was condemned, implicitly censuring the U.S.S.R., as well as the West. The Chinese prime minister, Chou En-lai, displayed a moderate and conciliatory attitude that tended to quiet fears of some anti-Communist delegates concerning China's intentions. A 10-point "declaration on the promotion of world peace and cooperation," incorporating the principles of the UN charter and Jawaharlal Nehru's five principles, was adopted unanimously.

Consult the INDEX *first*

bandurria, also called BANDOLA, short-necked, pear-shaped, flat-backed stringed musical instrument of the lute family, native to Spain, where it is often used in outdoor music.

Bandurria by Hijos de González, Madrid, 1892; in the Smithsonian Institution, Washington, D.C.

By courtesy of the Smithsonian Institution, Washington, D.C.

Mentioned in the 14th century as the *mandurria* (the name it still bears in the Balearic Islands), it was originally both fretted and unfretted, with three to five strings.

The modern bandurria has six paired courses of gut and metal-spun silk strings that are tuned g♯–c♯′–f♯′–b′–e″–a″ (beginning with the G♯ below middle C) and hitched to a guitar-like (tension) bridge. There are 12 fixed metal frets on the fingerboard, and the instrument is played with a short, hard plectrum. The regular tuning in fourths throughout gives great facility and uniformity of fingering in chromatic passages.

bandwidth, in electronics, the range of frequencies occupied by a modulated radio-frequency signal, usually given in hertz (cycles per second) or as a percentage of the radio frequency. For example, an AM (amplitude modulation) broadcasting station operating at 1,000,000 hertz has a bandwidth of 10,000 hertz, or 1 percent (10,000/1,000,000). The term also designates the frequency range that an electronic device, such as an amplifier or filter, will transmit.

A list of the abbreviations used in the MICROPAEDIA *will be found at the end of this volume*

---

bandy, also called BANTY, a game similar to ice hockey. It is played almost exclusively in the Scandinavian countries, the Baltic countries, and Mongolia. A team is made up of from 8 to 11 players who wear skates and use curved sticks to hit a ball. Rink size varies but is usually larger than an ice hockey rink (about 100 by 55 metres [109 by 60 yards]). The goalie does not use a stick, but alone among the players can touch the ball with his hands. There are two halves of 45 minutes each, and play starts at the centre circle. Unlike hockey, no play is allowed behind the goals. Play begins with a "stroke off," and each team is confined to its own half of the rink. Use of a ball instead of a flat puck makes bandy faster than hockey. Free strokes are given for penalties, such as for going over the midline. Free substitution is allowed. There are six officials. Bandy originated in England in the late 18th century, and the modern game of ice hockey probably developed from it.

bandy-bandy (*Vermicella annulata*), Australian snake of the cobra family Elapidae, strikingly ringed with black and white or yellow. It is about 76 centimetres (30 inches) long and is venomous but inoffensive. Five species are recognized.

It has a small head and eyes and a slender, cylindrical body. To frighten off enemies the

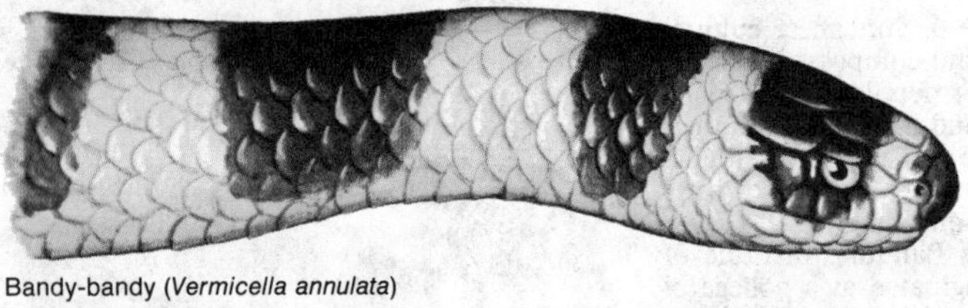

Bandy-bandy (*Vermicella annulata*)
Painting by David M. Dennis

bandy-bandy raises a few coils of its body vertically, presenting an unusual silhouette.

baneberry, also called COHOSH, or NECKLACEWEED, any of about eight species of perennial herbaceous plants constituting the genus *Actaea* of the buttercup family (Ranunculaceae); they are all native to North Temperate Zone woodlands.

The white baneberry (*A. pachypoda;* sometimes *A. alba*), native to North America, is 30 to 45 centimetres (12 to 18 inches) tall and bears white berries. The cohosh, or herb Christopher (*A. spicata*), native to Eurasia, is about 30 to 60 cm tall and bears pur-

White baneberry (*Actaea pachypoda*) showing (top) leaves and flowers, (bottom) fruit
(Top) Peter K. Nelson, (bottom) Nelson Groffman

plish-black berries that sometimes are used to make dye. The red baneberry, or red cohosh (*A. rubra*), native to North America, closely resembles *A. spicata*. Its fruits are red or ivory. The roots contain a violent purgative, irritant, and emetic. The plants are useful subjects for the shady wild garden.

Banér, Johan (b. July 3 [June 23, old style], 1596, Djursholm Castle, Sweden—d. May 20 [May 10, O.S.], 1641, Halberstadt, Magdeburg), Swedish field marshal who was one of the foremost soldiers in the Thirty Years' War.

His father, Gustaf Banér, a member of the King's Council, was executed in 1600 after the defeat of Sigismund III of Poland. Entering the Swedish Army in 1615, Johan Banér was greatly influenced by the military ideas of the young king Gustavus Adolphus: he served with distinction in Russia, Livonia, Poland, and Germany and early attained the rank of general. In 1634 he was appointed field marshal, with command of an army corps in Silesia and Bohemia; and when the main Swedish Army had been crushed at Nordlingen he was asked to take command of the whole Swedish Army in Germany.

In 1636 his great victory at Wittstock restored for some time Sweden's paramount influence in central Germany. In 1637, hard pressed by the enemy's armies and almost surrounded, he made a strategic retreat into northern Germany that provoked the contemporary comment that "the enemy had put him in the sack but had forgotten to tie it." By the end of 1638, however, Banér had collected reinforcements, with which he began a new offensive toward central and southern Germany. At Chemnitz (April 1639), he defeated the Emperor's army. Reinforced by French troops, he advanced toward southern Germany during the summer and autumn of 1640 but could not force the enemy to a battle. After a dangerous march through Bohemia in the winter, he died at Halberstadt of a pulmonary disease contracted during the winter campaign.

Banerjea, Sir Surendranath (b. Nov. 10, 1848, Calcutta—d. Aug. 6, 1925, Barrackpore, near Calcutta), one of the founders of modern India and proponent of autonomy within the British Commonwealth.

Born into a distinguished family of Kulin Brahmans, then the highest ranking level in the hereditary caste system, Banerjea, after graduation from college, applied in England for admission to the Indian Civil Service, which at that time had only one Hindu. Banerjea was rejected on the grounds that he had misrepresented his age. Charging racial discrimination, he won his appeal by arguing that he calculated his age according to the Hindu custom of reckoning age from the date of conception rather than from birth. He was appointed to Sylhet (now in Bangladesh) but was dismissed in 1874, in the midst of controversy and protests, following charges of procedural irregularities.

In a teaching career for the next 37 years, Banerjea founded Ripon College (Calcutta), later renamed after him, and developed his ideas on nationalism. In 1876 he helped found the Indian Association to bring Hindus and Muslims together for political action; three years later he purchased *The Bengalee,* a newspaper he edited for 40 years from his nationalist viewpoint. In 1883 he was imprisoned for two months for editorial criticism of a judge.

An effective speaker at the annual sessions of the Indian National Congress, which first met in 1885, he was twice elected its president in the years before the moderate–extremist split of 1917.

In London in 1909 Banerjea appealed to the British to modify the partition of Bengal, reinstitute habeas corpus, and grant India a constitution on the Canadian model. He believed firmly in representative government and constitutional progress by constitutional means. He advised Indians to "agitate, agitate, agitate—you have yet to learn the great art of grumbling," but he opposed the extreme methods advocated by the political leader B.G. Tilak and some of the non-cooperation tactics that were practiced by Mahatma Gandhi.

Elected in 1913 to both the Bengal and imperial legislative councils, Banerjea welcomed the principles of the Montagu–Chelmsford report of 1918, which recognized self-government as the goal of British policy in India. In 1921 he was knighted and accepted office as minister of local self-government in Bengal. Attacked by extreme nationalists as a turncoat, he was defeated in the 1924 dyarchy elections by a Swaraj (independence) candidate, whereupon he retired to write his autobiography, *A Nation in Making* (1925).

Banff, unincorporated place, southwestern Alberta, Canada, on the glacial-green Bow River, near the scenic Lake Louise and the

Banff Avenue in Banff, Alta.; in the background is Cascade Mountain
Shostal—EB Inc.

British Columbia border; it is the headquarters of Banff National Park (*q.v.*). Named by Lord Strathcona for the Scottish royal burgh of Banff, it developed as a resort after the arrival of the Canadian Pacific Railway (1883) and the establishment (1885) of Banff National Park. On the Trans-Canada Highway, it is a year-round tourist and convention centre, with hot sulfur springs, skiing facilities, a school of fine arts, a museum, and a sanitarium. Indian Days celebration (August) and a winter sports carnival are annual events. Light manufactures include pharmaceuticals, and coal is mined locally. Pop. (1981) 4,208.

Banff, also called BANFFSHIRE, former county, northeastern Scotland, since the reorganization of 1975 included largely in the districts of Banff and Buchan, Moray, and Gordon (*qq.v.*), of Grampian region.

Banff, ancient royal burgh and seat of the district of Banff and Buchan, Grampian region, Scotland, on the western bank of the River Deveron opposite its sister town Macduff (*q.v.*), to which it is connected by a bridge (1799).

By the 12th century Banff was a thriving port and a member of the Northern Hanseatic League. Its castle (the remains of which still exist), built originally as a defense against Viking raids, was then a royal residence and the town a royal burgh, whose charters date from 1163, 1324, and 1372 (still extant). Duff House, the town's architectural showpiece, was designed by William Adam (*c.* 1735) and presented to the burgh in 1906. Local industries include fishing, brewing, distilling, and iron founding. Pop. (1981) 3,938.

Banff and Buchan, district, Grampian region, northeastern Scotland; created by the reorganization of 1975, it covers part of the former counties of Banff and Aberdeen. The district, area 588 sq mi (1,523 sq km), faces the North Sea on the north and east and is a windswept coastal plain with sand dunes and outcroppings of higher ground. The raising of beef cattle, fishery, boat building at Peterhead and Fraserburgh, and some industry are the chief occupations. North Sea oil comes on shore at points near Peterhead. The town of Banff is the seat of the district authority. Pop. (1982 est.) 83,223.

Banff National Park, park in southwestern Alberta, Canada. Established in 1885 as the country's first national park, it is located on the eastern slopes of the Canadian Rocky Mountains and embraces several large ice fields and glacial lakes. It originally protected a 10-sq-mi (26-sq-km) area containing numerous hot mineral springs but has been expanded to 2,564 sq mi. Vegetation includes alpine meadows covered with flowers. The animals are typical Rocky Mountain fauna: bears, elk, deer, moose, and wild sheep and goats. There are campgrounds and trailer sites for visitors and hotels in nearby towns. The great influx of visitors has made difficult the maintenance of Banff National Park as a conservation area, and it has become principally a recreational area.

Moraine Lake and Valley of the Ten Peaks in Banff National Park, Alberta
Josef Muench

Banfora, town and seat of Banfora *cercle,* Comoé *département,* southwestern Burkina Faso (formerly Upper Volta), on a hilly, wooded site at the southern end of the Falaise de Banfora (Banfora Cliff). It has been designated a site for industrial growth and as the capital of a regional development organization. Food processing is the main industry. Sugar refineries, flour mills, and sawmills process materials from the surrounding area, considered by planners to be one of the country's most promising regions for rural development because of its rich soil, abundant rainfall, and low population density. Sugarcane and rice grow in irrigated fields; peanuts (groundnuts) and grains are also prevalent. Banfora has an airfield and lies on the railroad between Ouagadougou and the Atlantic port of Abidjan, Ivory Coast. Pop. (1980 est.) 13,000.

Bang, Bernhard Lauritz Frederik (b. June 7, 1848, Sorø, Den.—d. June 22, 1932, Copenhagen), veterinarian who in 1897 discovered *Brucella abortus* (Bang's bacillus), the causative agent of contagious abortion in cattle and of brucellosis (undulant fever) in human beings.

After obtaining his M.D. in 1880, Bang began teaching at the Royal Veterinary and Agricultural College in Copenhagen, later becoming its director. He also served as veterinary adviser to the Danish government.

Bang is known for his work on bovine tuberculosis, for which he developed a method of control, and for his research on smallpox vaccination and on bacillary diseases of animals.

Bang, Herman (b. April 21, 1857, island of Als, Den.—d. Jan. 29, 1912, Ogden, Utah, U.S.), novelist, one of Denmark's most important representatives of literary Impressionism. His work reflected the profound pessimism of his time.

Bang was the son of a clergyman. Rejected as an actor in 1877, he became a journalist and critic. His first novel, *Håblose slaegter* (1880; "Hopeless Generations"), was confiscated as immoral for its depiction of the life of a decadent homosexual writer. Although he also wrote plays, poetry, short stories, and criticism, Bang is best known for his novels, some of which have been translated into English: *Ludvigsbakke* (1896; *Ida Brandt,* 1928) and *De uden faedreland* (1906; *Denied a Country,* 1927).

The work he did from 1886 to 1890—including a collection of short stories, *Stille existenser* (1886; "Quiet Existences"), and the novels *Stuk* (1887; "Stucco") and *Tine* (1889)—is considered to be his best.

Bang died while on a lecture tour of the United States.

Bang Klang Thao, also spelled BANG KLANG HAO (Thai ruler): *see* Sri Indraditya.

Baṅgālā (Indian history): *see* Bengal.

Bangalore, city, capital (since 1830) of Karnātaka (formerly Mysore) state, southern India, and headquarters of Bangalore district. It is the nation's fifth largest city. It lies 3,113 ft (949 m) above sea level atop an east–west ridge in the Karnātaka Plateau in the southeastern part of the state, a cultural meeting point of the Kannaḍa-, Telugu-, and Tamil-speaking peoples. Pleasant winters and tolerable summers make it a popular place of residence, but

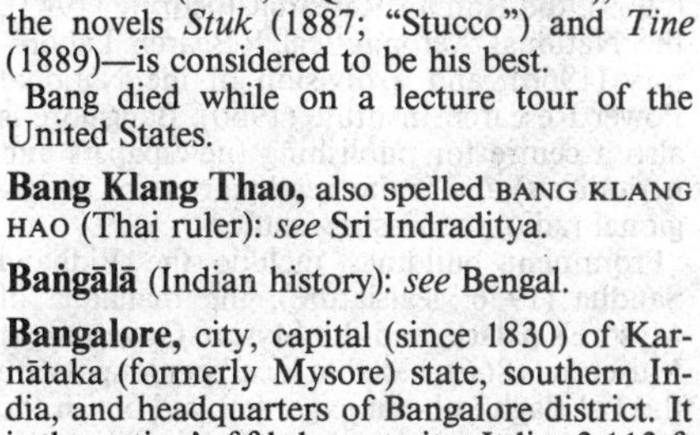

Vidhana Saudha (legislative building) in Bangalore, Karnātaka, India
Candida

water supply for its increasing industrial and domestic needs is a problem.

Its name is an Anglicization of the Kannada *bengaluru,* "village of boiled beans." The city consists of the closely built old town; a number of modern suburbs laid out on a gridiron pattern to the north and south, with many parks and wide streets; and a sprawl of military cantonments to the east. Its nucleus was a settlement around a mud fort, built (1537) by a petty chief, Kempe Gowda, and constructed of stone in 1761. Bangalore was the headquarters of the British administration from 1831 to 1881 when the raja was restored, but Britain retained an administrative and military presence there until 1947.

Aircraft, railway-coach, and machine-tool installations in the city are run by the federal government; and the state owns electrical and telephone industries and porcelain and soap factories. Privately owned concerns produce pharmaceuticals, textiles, radio parts, glassware, leather and footwear, agricultural implements, paper, and watches.

At the focus of South India's road system, Bangalore lies on the Vārānasi–Kanniyākumāri National Highway, is connected by major roads with Bombay and Madras, and is linked to Kerala via Mysore city, through the Nīlgiris (hills) and Pālghāt Gap. It is also a junction for the Southern Railway's broad-gauge line (from Madras) with an extensive metre-gauge system to the north and west. Hindustan Airport, 5 mi (8 km) east, has scheduled flights to and from Bombay, Madras, Mangalore, and Colombo (Sri Lanka).

Bangalore University (succeeding the branch of the University of Mysore, founded 1916) was opened in 1964 as was the University of Agricultural Sciences. The city also has several evening colleges and a public library and is the site of the Indian Institute of Science (1909), the Raman Research Institute (1943), the National Aeronautical Research Laboratory (1960), and a division of the National Power Research Institute (1960). Bangalore is also a centre for publishing (newspapers and periodicals) and is the headquarters of the regional radiobroadcasting station.

Prominent buildings include the Vidhana Saudha (1956; legislature), the maharaja of Mysore's palace, and the Mysore Government Museum (1866). Notable local scenic spots are the Lal Bagh (a botanic garden laid out in the 18th century), Hesaraghatta Lake, Chamaraja Sāgar Reservoir, and Nandi (Nandidrug) Hill Station, a summer resort 38 mi north, which is the site of two temples to the god Śiva (Shiva).

The district (3,090 sq mi [8,003 sq km] in area) is drained by the Arkavati and Kanva rivers, tributaries of the Cauvery, which forms its southern border. Millet and oilseeds are the main crops. Cattle and sheep are grazed. Besides Bangalore, the main towns are Channapatna, Closepet, Māgadi, and Hoskote. Pop. (1981) city, 2,628,593; metropolitan area, 2,921,751; district, 4,947,610.

Bangbu (China): *see* Pang-pu.

Banggai Islands, Bahasa Indonesia KEPULAUAN BANGGAI, archipelago consisting of two major islands and about 100 islets, constituting Luwuk Banggai *kabupaten* (regency), in Sulawesi Tengah *propinsi* (Central Celebes province), Indonesia, between the Kepulauan (islands) Sula and Celebes at the entrance to Teluk (gulf) Tolo. Peleng, the largest island, is well forested and mountainous; the bays affording anchorage have reefs. Chief town and port of the group is Banggai, on the western coast of Pulau (island) Banggai. The islands supply sea cucumbers, turtles, resin, rice, and sago starch. The people live mainly along the coasts. Pop. (1980) 268,203.

Banghāzī, also spelled BENGHAZI, Italian BENGASI, city and major seaport of northeastern Libya, on the Gulf of Sidra. It was founded by the Greeks of Cyrenaica as Hesperides (Euesperides) and received from Ptolemy III the additional name of Berenice in honour of his wife. After the 3rd century AD it superseded Cyrene and Barce as the chief centre of the province; but its importance waned, and it remained a small town until it was extensively developed during the Italian occupation (1912–42). In World War II, Banghāzī suffered considerable damage and after changing hands five times was finally captured by the British in November 1942.

Banghāzī, Libya's second largest city, is an administrative, commercial, and educational centre. It is the site of several national government buildings, as well as the Gar Younis University (formerly Benghazi; founded 1955). Local industries include salt processing, oil refining, food processing, cement manufacturing, and tanning, brewing, and fishing. Fresh water is provided by one of the world's largest desalinization plants. Benina International Airport is 20 mi (32 km) east of the city. Roads connect Banghāzī with other Libyan centres on the Mediterranean coast. Pop. (1979 est.) 267,700.

Bangka, also spelled BANKA, or BANCA, Bahasa Indonesia PULAU BANGKA, island and *kabupaten* (regency) of Sumatera Selatan *propinsi* (South Sumatra province), Indonesia, separated from the eastern coast of Sumatra by Selat (strait) Bangka and from Billiton Island by Selat Gaspar. Its area is 4,375 sq mi (11,330 sq km). The soil is somewhat dry and stony but is largely covered with tropical vegetation. Coastal areas, containing few anchorages, are generally swampy, but the interior is hilly, up to 2,313 ft (705 m). Many rivers are tidal and navigable for nearly 20 mi (32 km).

Bangka, which resembles the Malay Peninsula geologically, is composed of sandstones and slate, with irregular hills and ridges formed by granite outcrops. It is one of the world's chief tin-producing centres. The ore is found in many river alluvial deposits and in the alluvial strata on the slopes of small granitic hills; labourers of Chinese descent work in the mines under government contract and supervision. There are also deposits of lead, copper, tungsten, gold, iron, and manganese.

The aboriginal inhabitants consist of a few primitive hill tribes, probably of mixed Malay origin. Other inhabitants are mainly immigrant Malay peoples of the Muslim faith. Rice, pepper, gambier, coffee, and coconut palms are cultivated. There is an airport in the chief town, Pangkalpinang (on the eastern coast), and another in the chief port, Muntok (in the northeast). Pop. (1980) island, 399,855; regency, 399,986.

Bangkok, Thai KRUNG THEP ("City of Angels"), city, capital, and chief port of Thailand. As the only cosmopolitan city in a country of small towns and villages, it is Thailand's cultural and commercial centre.

The following article treats briefly the modern city of Bangkok. Fuller treatment is provided in the following MACROPAEDIA articles. For history and contemporary life, *see* Bangkok; for additional prespective on the city in its national context, *see* Thailand.

Bangkok is located on the delta of the Mae Nam Chao Phraya (Chao Phraya River), about 25 mi (40 km) from the Gulf of Thailand. In 1971 the original city merged with the former municipality of Thon Buri on the west bank of the Chao Phraya, and in 1972 the unified city was merged with other outlying areas to form a single city-province, Krung Thep Mahanakhon (Bangkok Metropolitan City).

The climate of Bangkok is hot throughout the year, with high humidity. The city has traditionally relied on a system of canals to drain its delta site, which annually receives 60 in. (1,520 mm) of rain. A principal and worsening problem of the city is subsidence of its deltaic site, which is exacerbated by filling of many canals.

The city's economy is centred on its port, which handles nearly all of the country's exports and imports, and on its commerce and industry. Principal industries include food processing and the production of textiles and building materials. Bangkok houses a majority of the country's bank deposits and also is the base for several insurance firms.

Bangkok has been expanding outward into surrounding agricultural areas. The inner city has become an institutional and commercial centre, while industrial and residential areas have been shifting to the port and suburbs. Governmental offices are located around the Grand Palace. The city houses various international agencies as well, including the headquarters of the United Nations Economic and Social Commission for Asia and the Pacific (ESCAP). The Chinese quarter of Sam Peng is the main commercial district. Though the city's residents are predominantly Thai, there are small concentrations of other Asians and of Westerners.

The *wat,* or Buddhist monastery, represents classic Thai architecture and is an important cultural feature. Ancient art relics and royal objects are housed in the National Museum. Jim Thompson's Thai House, a union of five traditional Thai houses, contains a major collection of Thai religious paintings assembled by the U.S. silk magnate and art collector. The National Library and the Thai National Documentation Centre are also located in Bangkok. Among the several universities are Chulalongkorn (1916) and Kasetsart (1943).

Inner-city traffic—consisting of three-wheeled taxis, private automobiles, and buses—is extremely congested. Some canals, remnants of the city's originally water-based transportation system, still exist. Highways and railways run north, east, and south, reaching Laos, Kampuchea (Cambodia), and Malaysia. The city's Don Muang airport is one of the busiest in Southeast Asia. Area (1980) Bangkok Metropolis, 604 sq mi (1,565 sq km). Pop. (1982 est.) Bangkok Metropolis, 5,407,100.

Bangkok Metropolitan City (province, Thailand): *see* Krung Thep Mahanakhon.

Bangladesh, officially PEOPLE'S REPUBLIC OF BANGLADESH, Bengali GANA PRAJATANTRI BANGLADESH, small coastal country of south central Asia, covering an area of 55,598 sq mi (143,998 sq km). The capital is Dhākā (formerly Dacca). The country lies between latitudes 20°30′ and 26°15′ N (about 390 mi [625 km]) from its extreme north and south extensions) and between longitudes 88°30′ and 92°15′ E (about 190 mi from east to west). Bangladesh, to the south, has an irregular coastline fronting the Bay of Bengal and is bordered on the southeast by Burma. The Indian states of West Bengal to the west and north and Assam to the north and east

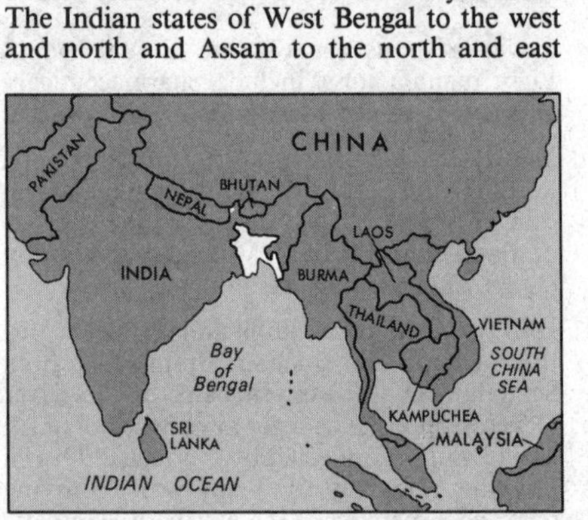

Bangladesh

comprise the border between Bangladesh and India. The population in 1981 was estimated at 89,940,000.

The article that follows is a summary of the significant detail about Bangladesh. Fuller treatment is provided in the MACROPAEDIA articles named below. For geography and history, *see* Bangladesh; for information about the country in its regional setting, *see* Asia: *Ganges River*; for information about regional aspects of Bangladesh's history *see* Pakistan; and for more information about Bangladesh's peoples and their traditional cultures, *see* Islāmic World.

For current history and for statistics on society and economy, *see* the article "World Affairs" and BRITANNICA WORLD DATA, respectively, in the *Britannica Book of the Year*.

The land. Bangladesh's landscape is dominated by the confluence of the Ganges (or Padma, as the united streams of the Ganges and Brahmaputra are known), the Brahmaputra (Jamuna), and the Meghna river systems. It may be divided into three major regions: one of highlands in the east and northeast, and two of lowlands in the west. The Dhākā–Rājshāhi lowland region in the northwestern part of the country comprises the area north of the Ganges-Padma and includes, from west to east, the Bhar Basin (the depression between the Ganges and Brahmaputra rivers), the Madhupur Tract (an elevated plateau north of the Padma River between the Brahmaputra and the Meghna rivers), and, in the southernmost part, Dhākā, the national capital. The Khulna lowland region in the southwestern part of Bangladesh lies generally southward from the Ganges (Padma) River, shares the coastal marshes and mangrove forests of the Sundarbans tract with India to the west, contains the estuary formed by the confluence of the Meghna and Padma rivers that empty into the Bay of Bengal in the southeast, and the densely populated lower Ganges agricultural area to the north. The highland region in the eastern and northeastern part of the country includes the Sylhet Hills in the northeast that rise to elevations of between 2,000 and 3,000 ft (600 and 900 m), providing the country's only striking relief, and the hilly Chittagong tract in the southeast. The country's highest peak, the Keokradong, rising to 4,034 ft, lies in the extreme southeast.

The climate and hydrology of Bangladesh are dramatically affected by the annual monsoon season (June through October); 75 percent of the country's precipitation, accounting for nearly 80 percent of the water discharged annually into the Bay of Bengal, occurs during this five-month period. The hydrology in the highland Chittagong is especially important because the power plant at the Kaptai dam (forming the Karnaphuli Reservoir) provides nearly two-thirds of the country's hydroelectric capacity. The annual rates of precipitation vary from a low of 40 to 80 in. (1,000 to 2,000 mm) in the western lowlands to more than 150 in. in the Sylhet Hills in the northeast. The temperature varies generally between 70° F (21° C) in the winter and 95° F (34° C) in the summer. In the early summer (April and May) and late in the monsoon season, high intensity storms, including cyclones with winds exceeding 100 mph (160 kmh) and waves with crests as high as 20 ft have frequently inundated the extensive coastal lowland areas. Since the early 18th century, when such records were first kept, many more than 1,000,000 people have been killed by such storms, 815,000 of them in three storms in 1737, 1876, and 1970.

More than two-thirds of Bangladesh's land is considered arable and lies primarily in the lowland regions; one-fifth is irrigated. Forests cover about one-sixth of the country. Plant and animal life is abundant and varied, and includes tigers, leopards, and Asian elephants, all endangered species.

The people. The bulk of the country's population are Bengali, an ethnic as well as linguistic group, who are primarily Muslims. More than 85 percent of the country's total population profess the religion of Islām. The Chittagong Hill Tracts in southeastern Bangladesh are inhabited mostly by tribal peoples, including the Chakmā, the Murung, the Tippera (Tipra), and the Mru, who are predominantly Buddhists. The country's annual growth rate is 2.4 percent. Bangladesh is one of the most densely populated areas in Asia, with 1,617 persons per sq mi (625 per sq km).

In 1977 the birth rate stood at 45 live births per 1,000 and the death rate was 17 per 1,000. The infant mortality rate was more than 140 per 1,000 live births in 1977. Life expectancy at birth is less than 50 years for both males and females. In rural areas of the country, maternal mortality is as high as 5.7 per 1,000 live births. The ratio of males to females is 106 to 100. The government of Bangladesh, with the help of UNICEF/WHO, has initiated rural health programs intended to reverse these negative statistics.

Bangladesh is one of the least urbanized areas in South Asia, and in the mid-1970s only about 9 percent of its population was urban. In 1981, Dhākā, the national capital and largest city, had a population of 3,458,-602; other major urban centres included Chittagong 1,388,475; and Khulna 623,184.

The economy. Bangladesh has a developing centralized economy, heavily based upon agriculture. The gross national product (GNP) was estimated in 1980 at U.S. $11,170,000,-000, about $120 per capita. Annual growth of the real GNP (1970–79) was a relatively low 0.8 percent. About half of the GNP originates primarily from agriculture, followed by commerce and trade; manufacturing; real estate, finance, insurance, and business services; and forestry and fishing.

Cereals, principally rice, are the main crops, occupying 87 percent of the cultivated land. Jute, pulses, fruits (bananas, mangoes, and pineapples), roots and tubers, sugarcane, and vegetables are also grown. Other crops include tobacco, sesame seed, and tea.

The principal livestock are cattle (including about one-tenth dairy cattle), water buffalo, asses, sheep, and goats. Bangladesh is nearly self-sufficient in timber production, but imports sawnwood and pulpwood.

Coastal waters of the Bay of Bengal offer excellent marine fishing, and Bangladesh's innumerable rivers, estuaries, and *bhils* are ideally suited for freshwater fishing, yielding about four-fifths of the total catch. About 3,200,000 acres (1,296,000 ha) are devoted to fisheries.

Natural gas is the country's richest mineral resource, and there are known deposits of crude petroleum. Other major minerals include salt (extracted from seawater), limestone, and kaolin. Mineral reserves include heavy mineral sands containing ilmenite, monazite, and zircon; coal; and peat. Other minerals needed to support petrochemical, metal, and ancillary industries must be imported. The manufacturing sector is largely concentrated on processing agricultural materials or imported raw materials. Important manufactures include refined petroleum, jute textiles, cement, urea fertilizer (partly derived from natural gas), rerolled steel products, crude steel ingots, nitrogen from ammonia, refined sugar, tea, cotton yarn and cloth, and newsprint and other paper. Electric power production (1980) was 2,587,000,000 kW-hr, three-fourths from thermal plants and the rest from hydroelectric power stations.

Bangladesh possesses the world's longest beach, 75 mi in length at Cox's Bāzār, and the cities of Chittagong and Dhākā also attract numerous foreign tourists.

After independence in 1971, Bangladesh nationalized most industries, but by 1980 almost all sectors of the economy had been returned to private control, leaving only tea, utilities, jute, and some textile mills under government control.

About 80 percent of the total work force is employed in agriculture, followed by manufacturing, and services. In the 1970s many Bangladeshis found overseas employment in Kuwait, Oman, Saudi Arabia, and the United Arab Emirates. Since 1976, all trade union federations have been banned by the government.

The monetary unit of Bangladesh is the *taka*, subdivided into 100 *paisa*, and was introduced in 1972 to replace the Pakistani *rupee*. The country is heavily dependent on foreign aid for its economic development. The World Bank and the United States have been the principal donors of aid. The cost of living roughly doubled between 1975 and 1980. One-third of the budgetary revenue originates from customs duties, excise duties, sales taxes, and income taxes (9 percent). Recurrent expenditures include defense (about one-fifth of the total), followed by administration, education and science; justice and police; and railways.

The railway system is government owned and operated, and there is also a government road transport corporation. Railways constitute about 2,500 mi of track. The road network is about 10 percent paved. Navigable inland waterways are well developed, and extend over some 5,200 mi; there are five principal river ports, and two seaports. Dhākā, Chittagong, and Kurmitola have international airports.

Exports, in value, are only about one-third of imports and consist primarily of raw jute, jute cuttings, and jute products (77 percent); hides, skins, and leather goods; tea; and fish. Major importers of Bangladesh's exports are the United States and Puerto Rico, the Soviet Union, the United Kingdom, Italy, and Japan. Imports consist primarily of basic manufactures (about one-fourth of the total); machinery and transport equipment; chemicals, drugs, and medicine; wheat; and mineral fuels and lubricants. The principal sources for imports were Japan, the United States and Puerto Rico, and the United Kingdom.

Adminstrative and social conditions. Bangladesh is an independent republic within the Commonwealth of Nations. The country's government is ostensibly democratic; according to Bangladesh's constitution, the president, elected by popular vote for a five-year term, heads the government. The president forms his Council of Ministers from the elected members of the parliament. In reality, however, democracy has had very little opportunity to function in Bangladesh, because of almost continual domination of the nation's politics by the military. When there have been elections, the outcomes have been dominated by a single party, the Bangladesh National Party (BNP), an organization incorporating several different political groups. The judiciary is headed by a Supreme Court, whose members are appointed by the president.

Severe overcrowding, an inadequate food supply (a daily per capita total of only 1,796 calories in 1977), and poor sanitary conditions have combined to help create extremely poor health conditions in Bangladesh. A significant number of citizens suffer from such serious diseases as malaria, cholera, and tuberculosis. Government efforts to significantly improve health conditions in Bangladesh have failed, mostly because of the country's shortage of physicians and modern medical facilities, and poor sanitation.

The government offers children free primary education for five years; however, the literacy rate in Bangladesh remains extremely low—only 25 percent for men and 13 percent for women. In 1980, the government took steps to eliminate illiteracy over a five-year period with the initiation of a special education program. There are six universities.

Bangladesh's news media have been under strict government control since the country achieved independence in 1971.

Cultural life. An important part of the Bengali cultural heritage is represented by literature. Rabindranath Tagore, winner of the Nobel Prize for Literature in 1913, wrote many of his poems and short stories about the beautiful Bengali countryside, most of all about the Ganges River. His song "Our Golden Bengal" became the national anthem of Bangladesh. Kazi Nazrul Islam, another renowned 20th-century writer, devoted his poetry to the subjects of social justice and Bengali nationalism. Bengalis have also made major contributions as playwrights. Following World War I, Musharraf Husain wrote the play *Zamindar Darpan* ("The Landlord Exposed"), thought to be the first drama of social consciousness by a Muslim.

History. Mention of a deltaic kingdom known as Vanga or Banga (hence, Bengal and Bangladesh) is found in the early Sanskrit literature of India (*c.* 1000 BC). By the 4th century BC, Bengal was part of the Indian Maurya Empire (*c.* 325–185 BC) and exposed to Buddhism. In the 4th century AD, it passed to the Gupta dynasty of the Magadha state in northeastern India. Two native Bengali dynasties, the Palas and Sena, ruled in succession from *c.* 750 to 1200. Despite the many years of Buddhist rule (only the Guptas were Hindu), Bengal was predominantly Hindu by the 10th century.

Muslim raids began on northern India at the close of the 10th century, and a dynasty known as the Slave, or Mamlūk, dynasty was founded at Delhi in 1206. In 1338, Bengal was able to separate itself from the Delhi sultanate and remain independent until its conquest by the Mughals in 1576.

During the Mughal rule the Europeans arrived as traders. In 1651 the British East India Company established a factory in Bengal. A decline in Mughal authority in Bengal corresponded with a rise in the company's concern for its Bengal operation. At the Battle of Plassey (1757), Robert Clive, acting for the company, defeated the *nawab* (ruler) of Bengal and placed in office a successor more sympathetic to British interests. By 1765 the British East India Company had secured the revenue rights (*diwani*) for Bengal which marked the beginning of the British Empire in India.

British policies caused much economic misery for the people of Bengal. Local handicraft industries, especially the muslin industry, were ruined by the introduction of British machine-made goods and much of the country's natural wealth was drained off to England. Enmity between Hindus and Muslims was exacerbated by British policies, and the British, responding to Muslim pressure, partitioned Bengal in 1905 and created a Muslim-dominated East Bengal. One year later, the Muslim League, a communal organization seeking to safeguard the rights of Indian Muslims, was formed in Dacca.

Hindu reaction to the partition was extreme and the British rescinded the partition in 1912, but the problem between the Hindus and Muslims festered. When the British left the subcontinent in 1947, East Bengal became East Pakistan, a part of the Muslim state of Pakistan, but separated from the dominant West Pakistan by a thousand miles, a different language, and a different culture.

Bengali nationalist sentiment increased. The Awami League, a political party, campaigned openly for Bengali autonomy. In 1970 the Awami League won a majority of seats in the National Assembly, but the Pakistan government postponed convening the Assembly. Violence erupted and guerrilla warfare resulted. Millions of refugees fled to India, which finally entered the war on the side of the Bengalis and insured Pakistan's defeat. On Dec. 16, 1971, an independent Bangladesh was established in Dhākā.

The destruction caused by the war was immense, and political stability was uncertain. Founding president Sheikh Mujibur Rahman was assassinated in 1975 as was his successor, Ziaur Rhaman, in 1981. In the presidential election that followed Abdus Sattar was elected.

Bangni (people): *see* Dafla.

Bangor, Irish BEANNCHAR, town, North Down district (established 1973), formerly in County Down, Northern Ireland, on the southern side of Belfast Lough (inlet of the sea). In about 555, St. Comgall founded a monastery at Bangor, which became a celebrated seat of learning. Incursions by Danes in the 9th century destroyed Bangor, which was partially rebuilt by St. Malachy in the 12th century. Part of his stone church remains. Bangor is a seaside resort with a small harbour serving as the headquarters of the Royal Ulster Yacht Club; it has some light industry. Pop. (1981) 46,585.

Bangor, city, seat (1816) of Penobscot County, east central Maine, U.S., port of entry at the head of navigation on the Penobscot River opposite Brewer. The site, visited in 1604 by Samuel de Champlain, was settled in 1769 by Jacob Buswell. First called Kenduskeag Plantation (1776) and later Sunbury (1787), it was incorporated as a town in 1791 and was supposedly named Bangor by the Rev. Seth Noble for his favourite hymn tune. It was briefly held by the British in the War of 1812. After 1830 it became a leading lumber port with shipbuilding yards. It is now mainly a commercial centre with varied manufactures including paper, electronic equipment, and footwear. The city is the seat of Bangor Theological Seminary (1814), Beal College (1891), Husson College (1898), and the Eastern Maine Vocational-Technical Institute (1966). Bangor International Airport occupies the former Dow Air Force Base. At Orono, 9 mi (14 km) upriver, is the parent campus of the University of Maine (1865). Inc. city, 1834. Pop. (1980) 31,643.

Bangor, cathedral city, seat of Arfon district, Gwynedd county, Wales. It commands the northern entrance to the Menai Strait, the narrow strip of water separating the Isle of Anglesey from the mainland. Bangor cathedral is dedicated to the Celtic St. Deiniol, who founded a church there in the 6th century; the community was a leading centre of Celtic Christianity. The cathedral later underwent a series of restorations after damage by invading Normans, the English king John, and the early 15th-century Welsh rebel leader Owen Glendower. The present structure was extensively restored in 1866.

The town, which grew up beside a Norman castle (few traces of which remain), is notable mainly as a cultural centre. It has the University College of North Wales (1884), a group of denominational theological colleges, and a museum of Welsh antiquities. Port Penrhyn nearby grew as an outlet for slates from the quarries near Bethesda. Penrhyn Castle, northeast of the town, is a modern copy, in Penmon marble, of a Norman castle. Bangor lies on major road and rail routes from London to northwest Wales and (via Holyhead, Anglesey) Ireland. Pop. (1981 prelim.) 12,174.

Bangui, capital of the Central African Republic, on the west bank of the Ubangi River. Administratively it is a commune, covering 26 sq mi (67 sq km), lying outside the boundaries of the country's 14 *préfectures.* Bangui is connected by an extended 1,100-mi (1,800-km) river and rail transport system with Pointe-Noire, on the west central African coast, and Brazzaville (both in the Congo).

Édouard-Renard Place in Bangui, Central African Republic
Picturepoint, London

Industries in Bangui include soapmaking and breweries, but the town is mainly commercial. The river port development includes a quay 1,300 ft (400 m) long and an oil port downstream. Cotton, timber, coffee, and sisal are shipped. There is also ferry service to Zongo, Zaire, and a network of roads connecting Bangui with Cameroon, Chad, and the upper Central African Republic.

Bangui is the site of the University of Bangui (1969), the National School of Arts (1966), several scientific and technological research institutes, the Boganda Museum, and the St. Paul Museum. Pop. (1982 est.) 387,143.

Bangweulu (Bantu: Large Water), shallow lake with extensive swamps in northeastern Zambia, East Africa, and part of the Congo (Zaire) River system. At an altitude of 3,740 ft (1,140 m), its waters, fluctuating with the rainy season, cover a triangular-shaped area of about 3,800 sq mi (9,800 sq km). There are three inhabited islands in the lake—Chisi, Mbabala, and Chilubi—and many low islands in the swamps, as well as the large Lunga (Sand) Bank. Excessive vegetation growth along the course of the Chambeshi River forms a swampland, acting as a check to floods; water seepage eventually issues as the Luapula River. A tall, common water reed, *Phragmites communis,* grows above mean water level, papyrus at water level, and floating hippo-grass in deeper water. Fish are caught, dried, and exported west to the copper belt. The explorer-missionary Dr. David Livingstone, the first European to visit the lake (1868), died on its southern shore (1873).

Consult the INDEX *first*

Banhā, also spelled BENHA, town, capital of al-Qalyūbīyah *muḥāfaẓah* (governorate), Lower Egypt, on the right bank of the Damietta Branch of the Nile, and on ar-Rayyāḥ (canal) at-Tawfīqī, in the delta area. It is about 30 mi (48 km) northwest of Cairo on the superhighway to Alexandria. Its Arabic name is derived from the Coptic Panaho. Since the early Middle Ages Banhā has been known for the production of quality honey. It is situated in the heart of a highly fertile cotton-growing district, and its industries include cotton ginning, manufacture of cotton and flax textiles, and vegetable processing. It is also well known for its oranges and grapes. Its historic position on the direct route from Cairo to Alexandria made it first a road centre and later a principal rail focus of Egypt. Lines from Banhā link Cairo to Ismailia on the Suez Canal (east) via az-Zaqāzīq and to Alexandria, via Ṭanṭā and

Damanhūr (northwest). Close by are mounds of the site of the ancient town of Athribis. Pop. (1983 est.) 109,600.

banhu (musical instrument): *see* pan-hu.

Baní, city, capital, Peravia province, southern Dominican Republic, situated in coastal lowlands 3 mi (5 km) from the Caribbean Sea. The city is a commercial and manufacturing centre for the fertile agricultural hinterland, whose main products are bananas, rice, and coffee. The city lies on the paved highway linking Santo Domingo, the national capital, with Commendador, near the Haitian border. Pop. (1981) 36,705.

Banī Ḥasan (Egypt): *see* Beni Hasan.

Bani River, principal affluent of the Niger River on its right bank in Mali, West Africa, formed by the confluence of the Baoulé and Bagoé headstreams 100 mi (160 km) east of Bamako. The Bani proper flows 230 mi northeast to the Niger at Mopti in the swampy Macina depression. It is navigable only in part. Within a savanna zone, the region derives its wealth from the cultivation of millet, rice, sorghum, and corn along the riverbanks and from cattle herding.

Banī Suwayf, *muḥāfaẓah* (governorate), lying along the Nile River in northern Upper Egypt, with an extension into the Western Desert at its southern end, with al-Fayyūm governorate to the west and north and al-Minyā to the south. Its cultivated, settled area consists mainly of a strip of the Nile River Valley floodplain, extending about 50 mi (80 km) north–south and 15 mi in width at its widest point, near Banī Suwayf city. It has a total settled area of 510 sq mi (1,322 sq km). Because the river throughout history has eroded away the eastern bank, it now embraces only a narrow, gravelly plain terminating abruptly below the bluffs of the Eastern Desert. In 1964 Banī Suwayf *muḥāfaẓah* pioneered a nationally supervised cooperative-farming scheme in which scattered land holdings were consolidated into large units. Cotton, grains, beans, and sugarcane are the principal crops, and chickens and pigeons are also raised. The capital, Banī Suwayf (*q.v.*), is a regional market. In the Eastern Desert alabaster is quarried, and there are iron-ore deposits in the desert to the west.

Among the *muḥāfaẓah*'s antiquities are the 3rd-dynasty (*c.* 2686–2613 BC) pyramid of Huni at Maydūm, and the ruins of ancient Heracleopolis lie near the village of Ihnāsiyat al-Madīnah, west of Banī Suwayf city near the Baḥr Yūsuf, an irrigation canal, which turns north of the site into al-Fayyūm governorate. The Cairo–Aswān railway stops at Banī Suwayf city, from where a branch runs into al-Fayyūm. Pop. (1983 est.) 1,347,000.

Banī Suwayf, also spelled BENI SUEF, city, capital of Banī Suwayf *muḥāfaẓah* (governorate), northern Upper Egypt. It is an important agricultural trade centre on the west bank of the Nile, 70 mi (110 km) south of Cairo.

In the 9th and 10th dynasties (*c.* 2160–2040 BC), Heracleopolis (modern Ihnāsiyat al-Madīnah), 10 mi west of the modern city, was the capital of kings who ruled Lower and Middle Egypt. During the first millennium BC a Libyan family settled there and gained sovereignty over all of Egypt, founding the 22nd dynasty (*c.* 950–*c.* 730 BC). Later, though losing political importance, it remained an important city. In later centuries Banī Suwayf became the chief town of the second province of Upper Egypt, attaining special prominence under the Turkish governor and the autonomous ruler Muḥammad ʿAlī (ruled 1805–48). Banī Suwayf's industries, mostly agriculturally related, include flour milling, cotton ginning, and textile manufacturing. Alabaster is quarried near the capital. Perennial irrigation water is supplied by the large Baḥr Yūsuf Canal. It is on the main rail line along the Nile; a branch railroad connects it to the al-Fayyūm oasis complex of agricultural settlements. The oldest mosque, Jāmiʿ al-Baḥr, has a shrine that is locally venerated. Pop. (1983 est.) 142,500.

Bania, also spelled BANIYĀ, (from Sanskrit *vāṇijya*, "trade"), Indian caste consisting generally of moneylenders or merchants, found throughout northern and western India; strictly speaking, however, many mercantile communities are not Banias, and, conversely, some Banias are not merchants. In the fourfold division of Indian society, the innumerable Bania subcastes, such as the Agarwālā (*q.v.*), are classed as members of the Vaiśya, or commoner, class. In religious affiliation they are generally Vaiṣṇavas (worshippers of the Hindu god Vishnu) or Jainas and tend to be strict vegetarians, teetotallers, and orthodox in observing ceremonial purity. The Indian leader Mahatma Gandhi belonged to a Gujarati Bania caste.

Banihāl Pass, pass in the Pīr Panjāl Range in the Indian-held sector of the state of Jammu and Kashmir in the northern part of the Indian subcontinent. Banihāl—a name that in Kashmīrī means "blizzard"—lies at an altitude of 9,290 ft (2,832 m) in the Doda district. It forms the main gateway to the Vale of Kashmir from the Indian plains. The Jammu–Srīnagar road enters the pass through the Jawahar Tunnel, which is occasionally blocked by snow in winter. Goods formerly crossed the pass on the backs of porters, who made the journey in a day.

Banim, John and Michael (respectively b. April 3, 1798, County Kilkenny, Ire.—d. Aug. 13, 1842, County Kilkenny; b. Aug. 5, 1796, County Kilkenny—d. Aug. 30, 1874, Booterstown, near Dublin), brothers who collaborated in novels and stories of Irish peasant life.

John studied drawing in Dublin and subsequently taught it in Kilkenny. Shortly afterward he went to Dublin, where he earned a living by journalism. In 1821 his blank verse tragedy, *Damon and Pythias,* was produced at Covent Garden; John married, moved to London, and continued to live by journalism. In 1825 there appeared *Tales, by the O'Hara Family,* written in collaboration with Michael, who had studied for the bar but had had to take over his father's business. All three *Tales*—two by John, *The Fetches* and *John Doe,* and one by Michael, *Crohoore of the Bill Hook*—are remarkable for their melodramatic invention and were immediately successful, John being dubbed "the Scott of Ireland." He followed them with *The Boyne Water* (1826), a novel about the Jacobite wars in Ireland, and in 1826 a second series of *Tales* appeared, containing *The Nowlans,* a story of passion, guilt, and religious fervour displaying a degree of insight that makes it possibly John's best novel. *The Croppy* (1828) is mainly by Michael, then an active supporter of Roman Catholic emancipation.

Despite a painful spinal malady, John continued to produce novels; but ill health eventually led to poverty, and in 1833 subscriptions were opened for him in England and Ireland. He returned to Kilkenny in 1835. *Father Connell,* the Banims' happiest book, published the same year, was almost entirely by Michael, who continued to write but in 1873 retired to Booterstown, near Dublin.

banishment: *see* exile and banishment.

Baniyā (Hindu caste): *see* Bania.

Banja Luka, also spelled BANJALUKA, city of northeast Bosnia and Hercegovina, Yugoslavia, on the Vrbas River at its confluence with the Vrbanja. Under the Turks, Banja Luka (Baths of St. Luke) was an important military centre and the original location (1583–1639) of the seat of the Bosnian *paşalik* (territory governed by a pasha). Commercial growth declined following fires and plagues in the 17th and 18th centuries. In the 19th century Banja Luka played an important part in the uprisings of the Bosnians against Turkey, as well as in the revolts of the Serbs. Again, during World War II, the city and district were a resistance centre while part of the Axis-created country of Croatia.

Since 1945 a new industrial section of the city has been developed. Industries include fruit and vegetable canning, tobacco processing, brewing, and the manufacture of machine tools, electrical appliances, clothing, pulp and paper, and synthetic fibres. It has road connections with Zagreb and with Jajce and Sarajevo, but it is south of Yugoslavia's main road and rail arteries. There are many Turkish mosques, notably the beautiful Ferhadija, or Ferhad-Pasha Mosque, built in 1583. Pop. (1981 prelim.) mun., 183,618.

Banjak (Indonesia): *see* Banyak Islands.

Banjarmasin, also spelled BANDJARMASIN, or BANJERMASIN, *kotamadya* (city), capital of Kalimantan Selatan *propinsi* (South Borneo province), Indonesia, on Tapas island between the Barito and Martapura rivers on the southern coast of Borneo. The rivers drain the largest plain on Kalimantan. To the east the Pegunungan (mountains) Meratus range, lacking roads, is largely inaccessible. Houses are raised on piles, gardens are walled and drained, and rivers and streams are used in place of roads, though there is an airfield. There is a good harbour, from which rubber, pepper, timber, rattan, cordage fibres, oil, gold, diamonds, coal, and iron are exported. The coal comes from the nearby town of Pengaron, lumber from Alalak and Cerucuk, and bricks and earthenware from Sungri Tabok. A sultanate was originally centred there, and, despite treaties signed with the Dutch East India Company in the 18th century, this sultanate was a centre of resistance against the Dutch government for most of the 19th century. Pop. (1980) 380,884.

banjo, stringed musical instrument of African origin, popularized in the U.S. by slaves in the

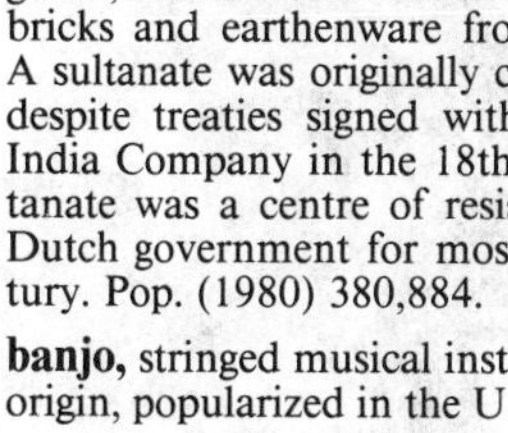

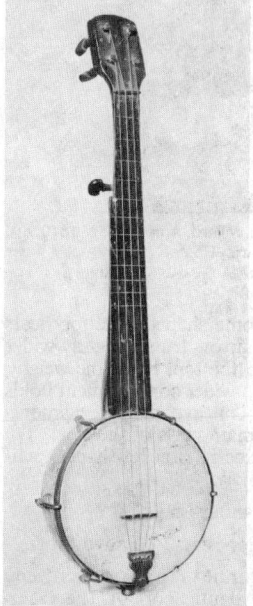

Five-string banjo; in the Metropolitan Museum of Art, New York City

By courtesy of the Metropolitan Museum of Art, New York City, the Crosby Brown Collection of Musical Instruments, 1889

19th century, then exported to Europe. Several African stringed instruments have similar names—*e.g., bania, banju.* The banjo has a tambourine-like body with a hoop and a screw that secure the vellum belly to the frame. Screw stretchers are used to vary the tension of the belly. The strings pass over a violin-type, or pressure, bridge and are hitched to a tailpiece. In the 1890s, frets were added to the long neck, and a machine head with screws replaced the tuning pegs.

The earliest banjos had four gut strings; later, from five to nine metal strings were used. The standard banjo has five metal strings. Four are tuned from the head, usually to C′–G′–B′–D″ upward from (notated) middle C. Preceding the C string is the chanterelle, or thumb string, a shorter string fastened to a screw midway in the banjo neck. It is tuned to the (notated) second G above middle C. The actual pitch is an octave lower than notated.

A plectrum banjo lacks the chanterelle and is played with a plectrum rather than with the fingers. On a zither banjo the vellum is suspended in a resonator that throws the sound forward; the chanterelle, tuned from the head, passes under the fingerboard to emerge at the fifth fret. The banjo is widely played in U.S. folk music and has also been used in jazz ensembles.

banjo clock, clock so named because its upper portion is shaped like an inverted banjo, patented by Simon Willard of Connecticut in 1802. The clock has a circular face with a narrow metal frame and bezel for the glass,

Banjo clock by Simon Willard, American, *c.* 1810; in the Museum of Fine Arts, Boston

By courtesy of the Museum of Fine Arts, Boston, M. & M. Karolik Collection

which is usually dome shaped. The top bears a finial. Below, a narrow trunk, slightly wider at the bottom than the top, holds the weight, and at the bottom a wider compartment holds the bob. Slender, concave metal ornaments connect the three main parts of the clock. On the finest banjo clocks, bracket-shaped pendants are added below.

banjo shark: *see* guitarfish.

Banjoewangi (Indonesia): *see* Banyuwangi.

Banjul, formerly (until 1973) BATHURST, city and capital, and Atlantic port of The Gambia, on St. Mary's Island, near the mouth of the Gambia River. It is the country's largest city. It was founded in 1816, when the British Colonial Office ordered Capt. Alexan-

The port of Banjul, near the mouth of the Gambia River, in The Gambia

Kjell Johansson—Ostman Agency

der Grant to establish a military post on the river to suppress the slave trade and to serve as a trade outlet for merchants ejected from Senegal, which had been restored to France. Grant chose Banjul Island (ceded by the chief of Kombo) as the site, which he renamed St. Mary's. He named the new settlement for Henry Bathurst, 3rd Earl Bathurst, then colonial secretary. It became the capital of the British colony and protectorate of Gambia and after 1947 was governed by a town council. With The Gambia's independence in 1965, the town was granted city status and became the national capital. The name was changed to Banjul in 1973.

Banjul is The Gambia's commercial and transportation centre. It has several peanut (groundnut) decorticating plants and oil mills; peanuts, peanut oil and meal, and palm kernels are exported. Tourism is of increasing importance, alleviating some of the urban unemployment problem and encouraging handicraft (wood carvings, filigree jewelry, hand-dyed cloth) industries. Banjul is connected with the interior and Senegal via a 3-mi (5-km) ferry northward across the Gambia River (to Barra) and by a road that joins the Trans-Gambia Highway just south of Mansa Konko. A regular steamer service operates to Basse Santa Su, 242 mi upstream. The Gambia's international airport is at Yundum, 14 mi southwest.

The nation's educational centre, Banjul has the Gambia High School (1958), two Roman Catholic secondary schools, a Muslim high school, a vocational school, and a public library. Associated with the city's Royal Victoria Hospital (1957) are the Gambia School of Nursing (1964), a mental hospital, a tuberculosis sanatorium, and a home for the infirm.

Almost half of the city's population is Wolof, but the Aku (descendants of freed slaves), Malinke (Mandingo), Mauritanian, and Lebanese communities are significant minorities. Banjul has a mosque and Anglican, Catholic, and Methodist churches. Pop. (1983 prelim.) 44,500.

Banjuwangi (Indonesia): *see* Banyuwangi.

bank, an institution that deals in money and its substitutes and provides other financial services. Banks accept deposits and make loans and derive a profit from the difference in the interest rates paid and charged, respectively. They also have the power to create money.

A brief treatment of banks follows. For full treatment, *see* MACROPAEDIA: Banks and Banking.

The two major classes of banks are commercial and central banks. Commercial banks accept savings and checking deposits, make loans and other investments, and offer financial services that facilitate the exchange of funds among individuals and institutions. In addition to the profit derived from the interest "spread," banks charge fees for various services. Central banks act as bankers to governments, as the agents and frequently the designers of monetary and credit policies, and as lenders of last resort to commercial banks in the case of a financial crisis. In addition to their essential technical activities, central banks play a significant psychological role as guarantors of the monetary system, supported by government bank insurance. Central banks frequently make healthy profits for governments through fees and security transactions.

Early banks only verified coinage or exchanged one jurisdiction's coins for another's. As trade routes extended in the early Renaissance, bankers devised means for their agents to make payments at a distance (at exchange rates profitable to the banker), without physically transferring any coins. Early banks accepted deposits of money or valuables for safekeeping. By the 17th century, London bankers had developed a system with most of the essentials of modern banking. They dealt in foreign exchange, paid interest to attract coin deposits, and, discovering that only a fraction of depositors would demand their cash at any one time, loaned the balance at interest. It became common for individuals and firms to exchange funds through bankers with written drafts—the origin of the modern check. Banks offered loans by granting overdraft privileges to checkwriters and by issuing bank notes. Both methods of extending credit had the practical effect of increasing the supply of money. Central banks eventually supplanted commercial banks as issuers of notes and currency in most countries.

The United States and Great Britain represent the extremes of national banking practice. The system in the U.S. is called unit banking; the British system, branch banking. The haphazard settling of the U.S. frontier, combined with a hostility toward concentrated financial power, led to a proliferation of local banks. For large and complex transactions, country banks came to depend on correspondent city banks. Although the strictures are gradually loosening, interstate branch-banking is restricted in the United States; some states even limit branching within their borders. The British banking system is dominated by four large banks, each with a great number of branches. This system evolved because of the small size of the country, the early development of efficient transportation and communications, and legislation encouraging joint-stock bank companies, which spread risks among a number of owners and limited the liability of stockholders in case of a failure. Most countries of the British Commonwealth (except India) have followed the branch model. India, Japan, and most European countries can be located on a spectrum between these two extremes.

The essential quality of banking is the creation of money, either through credit or government action. Financial institutions such as investment banks, home loan and savings banks, and finance companies cannot create money through credit; they can only lend deposits or funds they borrow from others. Commercial banks are required to keep only a portion of deposits as cash and near-cash. (Near-cash includes such short-term, safe, liquid instruments as treasury bills, commercial paper, and deposits at central or other commercial banks.) They make loans generally by crediting borrowers with an addition to their checking accounts, which are, effectively, approved overdrafts. These checks must be honoured by other banks, even if the funds were created by the bank through the loan. Since most payments generated by the loan return to the banking system as deposits, the creation of credit reinforces itself. Banking depends entirely on public confidence in the system's soundness, since no bank could pay all its depositors should all of them simultaneously demand cash, as may happen in a crisis. Commercial banks in most countries prefer to make short-term loans, since they involve less risk, although Japanese and West German banks provide long-term financing.

In the Soviet Union and other planned economies, banks do not create money but facilitate transactions among individuals and state enterprises, regulate business activity, and accept deposits and payments such as taxes and fees. Modest interest rates are charged to consumers and firms to cover the expense of processing the transaction. The Soviet system is highly centralized, held to the discipline of a central plan. Eastern European countries have experimented with semi-autonomous regional systems.

Central banks evolved in response to the recurrent financial crises of the 19th century that characterized the boom and bust cycles typical of market economies. The Bank of England was the first "banker's banker"; other countries followed its model, with the U.S. establishing its Federal Reserve System in 1913. Besides acting as banker to governments, central banks also have responsibility for the regulation of commercial banks, which they exercise by prohibiting excessively risky loans, auditing their books, supervising bank management, and lending money to banks facing a run on their cash resources. In recent decades central banks have become actively involved in economic policy, stabilizing foreign exchange markets, and controlling the growth of the supply of money and credit (*see* monetary policy). Central banks enjoy varying degrees of autonomy from direct government control; in the United States, for example, the president appoints the members of the Federal Reserve Board to long and staggered terms; the intention of this system is to immunize members from short-term political pressures.

bank, rocky or sandy submerged elevation of the seafloor with a summit less than 200 metres (650 feet) below the surface but not so high as to endanger navigation. Many banks are local prominences on continental or island shelves. Similar elevations with tops more than 200 metres below the surface are called oceanic plateaus. Banks whose tops rise close enough to the sea surface to be hazardous to shipping are called shoals. Some banks provide favourable conditions for marine life and are therefore important fishing grounds—*e.g.,* the Grand Banks of Newfoundland.

Bank Craps, also called LAS VEGAS CRAPS, dice game, the variant of Craps most played in Nevada gambling houses. A special table and layout are used, and all bets are made against the house. A player signifies his bet by placing chips or cash on the appropriate part of the layout before any roll. It is invariably required that the dice be thrown over a string or wire stretched a few inches above the surface of the table or that they strike a wall of the table and bounce back.

The shooter, or anyone wishing to bet that the shooter will win, places his bet "on the line" (in the area marked "Does Pass," "Line," or "Win" on various layouts). Anyone betting against the shooter places his bet in the area marked "Don't Pass." Anyone wishing to bet on a special contingency, such as that craps (2, 3, or 12) will or will not be thrown on the next roll, places his bet in the appropriate space on the layout; such bets are called proposition bets. The house maintains a mathematical advantage on all bets of about 1.4 percent, higher on certain layouts and special bets.

New York Craps is a version of Bank Craps popular in the eastern United States, the Bahamas, and England. The table and layout, called a double-end dealer, are slightly different from those used in Bank Craps.

bank holiday, in the United Kingdom, any of several days designated as holidays by the Bank Holidays Act of 1871 and a supplementary act of 1875 for all the banks in England, Wales, Northern Ireland, and Scotland. Though they are not statutory public holidays, their observance is no longer limited to banks.

Before 1830 the Bank of England closed on approximately 40 saints' days and anniversaries, but in that year the number was reduced to 18 days. In 1834 they were further reduced to four: Good Friday, May 1, November 1, and Christmas Day. By the act of 1871, the following were constituted bank holidays in England, Wales, and Ireland: Easter Monday; Whitmonday, the first Monday of August; December 26 if a weekday; and, by the act of 1875, December 27 when December 26 falls on a Sunday (*i.e.,* the first weekday after Christmas; Boxing Day). The Bank Holiday (Ireland) Act of 1903 designated March 17, St. Patrick's Day (or, if on a Sunday, the following Monday), as a bank holiday for Ireland. In England, Wales, and Northern Ireland, Christmas Day and Good Friday are bank holidays under common law.

In Scotland, New Year's Day and the day after, Christmas Day (or, if these days fall on Sunday, the following Mondays), Good Friday, Labour Day (May 1), and the first Monday of August are bank holidays.

The act of 1871 also made it lawful for any day to be officially proclaimed a bank holiday in the United Kingdom. In the 1980s the list for England, Wales, and Northern Ireland included New Year's Day, or the first Monday in January if January 1 falls on a Saturday or Sunday; Good Friday; Easter Monday; May 1 (Labour Day), or the first Monday in May if May 1 falls on a Saturday or Sunday; the last Monday in May; the last Monday in August; Christmas Day; and Boxing Day.

The term bank holiday is also used to refer to the period during which all banks in the U.S. were closed by proclamation of Pres. Franklin D. Roosevelt on March 6, 1933. The moratorium was made necessary by a series of major bank failures and runs on banks (in the eight days preceding March 4, $1,500,000,000 had been withdrawn by depositors) and the closing of banks by a number of states, beginning with Michigan in mid-February. Following passage by Congress of the Emergency Banking Act on March 9, sound banks were permitted to reopen.

Bank of ——— : *see under* substantive word (*e.g.,* England, Bank of), except as below.

Bank of Boston Corporation, U.S. bank holding company whose principal subsidiary is the First National Bank of Boston. Through this subsidiary and others located throughout the United States and abroad, the Bank of Boston Corporation offers its individual and commercial customers a complete range of financial, banking, and trust services. Headquarters for both are in Boston.

The bank, one of the oldest in the United States, was originally chartered in 1784 as the Massachusetts Bank. In 1903 it merged with the First National Bank of Boston (established in 1859 as the Safety Fund Bank) and assumed the latter's name. A number of other mergers and acquisitions preceded the present corporate relationship.

The Bank of Boston Corporation was formed in 1970 as the First National Boston Corporation. A reorganization followed that merged First National Bank of Boston and Old Colony Trust Company into the newly formed Massachusetts Bank NA, which then assumed the name First National Bank of Boston. The present corporate name was adopted in 1983.

Subsidiaries of the corporation provide numerous services, including lending, cash-management programs, payroll processing, equipment leasing, and data processing. They also offer money-market operations, trust and agency services, factoring, mortgage banking, venture-capital financing, and commercial finance.

bank rate: *see* discount rate.

Bank Street College of Education, privately supported coeducational teachers college in New York City offering graduate courses only, operating a laboratory school, and conducting basic research in education. Established in 1916 by Lucy Sprague Mitchell, first dean of women at the University of California and a disciple of John Dewey, the institution was at first called the Bureau of Educational Experiments; it incorporated a nursery school in which child development was studied. In 1930 the bureau opened an elementary school and a teacher-training school at 69 Bank Street, at which new curriculums were developed, classroom material was produced, and children's books were written.

In 1950 the school's name was changed to the Bank Street College of Education. In 1964 Bank Street helped launch the National Head Start Program for pre-school disadvantaged children; beginning in 1965 the school published the Bank Street Readers, an early contribution to multi-racial, urban-oriented teaching materials. It acted as a consultant for children's television and for school and child care facilities all over the world and developed mainstreaming programs for handicapped children.

Bank War, in U.S. history, the struggle between Pres. Andrew Jackson and Nicholas Biddle, president of the Bank of the United States, over the continued existence of the only national banking institution in the nation during the second quarter of the 19th century. The first Bank of the United States, chartered in 1791 over the objections of Thomas Jefferson, ceased in 1811 when Jeffersonian Republicans refused to pass a new federal charter. In 1816 the second Bank of the United States was created, with a 20-year federal charter.

In 1829 and again in 1830 Jackson made clear his constitutional objections and personal antagonism toward the bank. He believed it concentrated too much economic power in the hands of a small monied elite beyond the public's control. Biddle turned to the National Republicans—especially Henry Clay and Daniel Webster—for support, turning the issue into a political battle. On their advice, Biddle applied for a new charter even though the old charter did not expire until 1836.

The recharter bill easily passed both houses of Congress in 1832. Saying "The bank is trying to kill me, but I will kill it," Jackson issued a potent veto message. The fate of the bank then became the central issue of the presidential election of 1832 between Jackson and Clay. Jackson concluded from his victory in that election that he had a mandate not only to refuse the bank a new charter but to destroy what he called a "hydra of corruption" (many of his political enemies had loans from the bank or were on its payroll) as quickly as possible.

Jackson ordered that no more government funds were to be deposited in the bank. Existing deposits were consumed paying off expenses, while new revenues were placed in 89 state "pet banks." Biddle responded by calling in loans and thus precipitating a credit shortage and business downturn. Clay in 1834 pushed a resolution through the Senate censuring Jackson for removing the deposits.

Jackson held firm. Biddle was eventually forced to relax the bank's credit policies, and in 1837 the Senate expunged the censure resolution from its record. When the bank's federal charter finally expired, Biddle secured a state charter from Pennsylvania to keep the bank operating. But in 1841 it went out of business, the result of faulty investment decisions and national economic distress.

Banka (Indonesia): *see* Bangka.

BankAmerica Corporation, U.S. holding company incorporated on Oct. 7, 1968, which owns Bank of America National Trust and Savings Association (incorporated Nov. 3, 1930) and several subsidiaries engaged in financial services, insurance, real estate, investment management, computer leasing, and other banking-related services. Bank of America NT & SA has some 1,100 branches in California and operates subsidiary banks and financial institutions in several other U.S. states and in Europe, Latin America, and the Far East. It is one of the world's largest banks in assets. Headquarters for both BankAmerica Corporation and Bank of America NT & SA are in San Francisco.

Bank of America NT & SA resulted from the merger of two earlier banking systems, both founded by Amadeo Peter Giannini. On Oct. 17, 1904, in San Francisco he opened a small neighbourhood bank called the Bank of Italy, which became prosperous in the period of rebuilding following the great earthquake of 1906. In 1907 he opened his first branch bank; and by the end of 1918, mainly through purchases of existing banks, Bank of Italy had 24 branches in 18 California cities; by 1929 there were 292.

In 1927, in an effort to navigate through the new, more restrictive banking laws, Giannini began putting together another branch banking system, which, after a series of mutations, became known as the Bank of America of California; by the summer of 1930 it had 163 branches. On Nov. 3, 1930, in a complex merger and realignment of the two systems, with the addition of other individual California banks, he incorporated the Bank of America NT & SA (operating under U.S. federal authority) and Bank of America (operating under California authority); in 1934 the latter was absorbed by the former.

At the time, these and other banks and financial institutions principally developed by Giannini were owned predominantly by Transamerica Corporation, a holding company that he had created in 1928. In 1930, because of ill health, he turned control of the corporation over to some New York bankers, who soon, in face of the Great Depression, began liquidating the banking empire. Giannini, recovering from his illness, waged a proxy war, won back control, and stopped the liquidation. Between 1937 and 1952 Transamerica divested itself of all stock in Bank of America NT & SA.

Giannini and his son, Lawrence Mario Giannini, ruled Bank of America until their deaths in 1949 and 1952 respectively, when leadership passed to other executives. From the 1950s on, the company expanded vigorously both in the United States and overseas. In 1957 it acquired control of Banca d'America e d'Italia with 65 branches in Italy. In 1962 it purchased control of a Swiss company, the Financial Corporation for Overseas Countries, with interests in several banks in Africa. Over the years it developed international banking offices in major U.S. cities and major cities overseas. (By 1975, international earnings contributed more than 40 percent of BankAmerica's income, before securities transactions.) In 1983, BankAmerica received approval to buy Charles Schwab and Company, a major U.S. discount stockbroker. Later that year the company bought the Washington state bank Seafirst Corp. in what was the biggest U.S. interstate bank merger to date.

BankAmerica Corporation was organized in Delaware in 1968 as a holding company to acquire Bank of America NT & SA and other financial subsidiaries.

Bankers Trust Company, major U.S. commercial bank established in 1903 as a trust company for national and state banks, now the largest bank subsidiary of Bankers Trust New York Corporation (*q.v.*), a holding company.

Bankers Trust New York Corporation, U.S. bank holding company originally incorporated as BT New York Corporation in 1965. It took its current name in 1967. Headquarters are in New York City.

The corporation was organized mainly by acquiring banks and other financial institutions. The largest commercial bank in the organization is Bankers Trust Company, New York, established in 1903 as a trust company for national and state banks. It is an international banking network with branches, subsidiaries, affiliates, and representative offices in over 30 countries. During the early 1980s the bank placed its highest priority on wholesale commercial banking, phasing out its retail branches and credit card operations.

Bankers Trust has engaged in the sale of commercial paper since 1978. In 1981, Bankers Trust Company of Florida, N.A., commenced business as a trust company. The corporation also has credit, leasing, and investment advising affiliates.

bankruptcy, the status of a debtor who has been declared by judicial process to be unable to pay his debts.

A brief treatment of bankruptcy follows. For full treatment, *see* MACROPAEDIA: Business Law.

The terms bankruptcy and insolvency, although sometimes used indiscriminately, have distinct legal significations. Insolvency, as the term is used in the equity receivership courts in the United States, in state insolvency laws, and in the English and most European bankruptcy laws, means inability to meet debts as they mature; but in England, for example, there is no special procedure relating to one who is merely "insolvent." Insolvency as it is defined in the U.S. federal bankruptcy act means that the aggregate of the debtor's property, at a fair valuation, is insufficient to pay his debts. A debtor may be insolvent without becoming a bankrupt.

Conversely, because proof of insolvency is not required where the debtor files a voluntary petition in bankruptcy or where an involuntary petition filed by his creditors alleges the commission of certain acts of bankruptcy, a debtor may become a bankrupt without being insolvent. A bankruptcy adjudication is a legal declaration that the debtor has filed a proper voluntary petition or that creditors have filed and supported a proper involuntary petition against him. The adjudication initiates a statutory proceeding for the administration of the debtor's property, which is thereby taken out of his personal control.

The primary objects of bankruptcy legislation are to obtain justice while not pressing unduly on debtors, to discriminate between involuntary inability to meet obligations and willful refusal or neglect, and to secure to creditors an equitable share of the debtor's assets available for the payment of his liabilities. Another object has marked modern legislation, namely, the fostering of a higher tone of commercial morality and the protection of the trading community at large from the evils arising through the reckless abuse of credit and through unnatural trade competition. Because creditors have conflicting interests and are therefore incapable of acting together as a homogeneous body, it is necessary to obtain the aid of professional assignees or trustees, solicitors, and other agents, who make it their special business to deal with such matters, exercising both administrative and quasi-judicial functions, in return for the remuneration which they receive out of the property for their services.

In common-law countries today, rehabilitation of the bankrupt is a major concern, provided, of course, that his insolvency did not involve fraud. Such relief for honest debtors dates back as far as 1705 in England, when a statute was passed establishing that once a debtor complied with the court's decisions, he was released from obligation. Such a release, or discharge, may, however, be conditional. Modern attitudes in civil-law countries as well as in common-law countries regard liquidation as something to be avoided if possible, and efforts are made to enlist the creditors in plans to rehabilitate the estate.

Banks, Sir Joseph (b. Feb. 13, 1743, London—d. June 19, 1820, Isleworth, London), explorer and naturalist known for his patronage and promotion of science rather than for his own researches.

Sir Joseph Banks, engraving by Ridley, 1802
The Mansell Collection

After education at Harrow, Eton, and Oxford, he travelled, collecting plant and natural history specimens, to Newfoundland and Labrador (1766), around the world with Capt. James Cook (1768–71), and to Iceland (1772). He was interested in economic plants and their introduction into countries, was the first to suggest (1805) the identity of the wheat rust and barberry fungus, and was the first to show that the marsupial mammals were more primitive than the placental mammals. In his capacity as honorary director of the Royal Botanic Gardens at Kew, he sent many botanical collectors to various countries. His house became a meeting place for the exchange of ideas. After he became president of the Royal Society (1778) he improved the position of science in Britain and cultivated interchange with scientists of other nations. The title of Knight Commander of the Bath was bestowed upon him in 1795, and two years later he was admitted to the Privy Council.

Banks's herbarium, considered one of the most important in existence, and his library, a major collection of works on natural history, are now at the British Museum.

A biography, *Sir Joseph Banks*, by Hector C. Cameron, was published in 1952. *Banks' Florilegium,* a collection of copperplate engravings of plants compiled by Banks and based on drawings made by Daniel Solander during Cook's 1768–71 voyage, was published in 1978.

Banks, Nathaniel P(rentiss) (b. Jan. 30, 1816, Waltham, Mass., U.S.—d. Sept. 1, 1894, Waltham), U.S. politician and Federal general during the Civil War, who during 1862–64 commanded at New Orleans.

Banks received only a common school education and at an early age began work as a bobbin boy in a cotton factory. He subsequently edited a weekly paper at Waltham, studied law, and after being admitted to the bar, became active in politics. He served in the Massachusetts legislature (1849–53) and as president of the state constitutional convention in 1853. In that year he entered the U.S. Congress, holding the support of Democrats and Free-Soilers for a time, and later of the Know-Nothing Party. He joined the newly formed Republican Party in 1855 and in 1856, after a bitter and protracted contest, was elected speaker of the House of Representatives on the 133rd ballot. He served in Congress until elected governor of Massachusetts in 1858.

Although while governor he had been a strong advocate of peace, Banks was one of the earliest to offer his services to President Lincoln, who in 1861 appointed him a major general of volunteers. He served in the campaigns of early 1862 in the Shenandoah Valley, and later in the year was in command of the Department of the Gulf in New Orleans. Forces under his command laid siege to Port Hudson, La., which finally fell in July 1863. In 1863 and 1864 he organized a number of expeditions in Texas, but he proved unsuccessful as a tactician and his Red River expedition (March–May 1864) ended in disaster.

After the war Banks reentered politics, serving several more terms in Congress and as U.S. marshal for Massachusetts (1879–88).

Banks, The (North Carolina, U.S.): *see* Outer Banks.

Banks Island, westernmost island in the Canadian Arctic Archipelago, Franklin District, Northwest Territories; it lies northwest of Victoria Island and is separated from the mainland (south) by Amundsen Gulf. About 250 mi (400 km) long and 110–180 mi wide, it has an area of 27,038 sq mi (70,028 sq km). Its hilly terrain ranges from 1,100-ft (335-m) cliffs along the north shore to Durham Heights (2,500 ft) at the southern tip. The island is the habitat of Arctic fox, wolf, caribou, polar bear, and many birds. First sighted by Sir William Parry's expedition in 1820, it was named for Sir Joseph Banks. Vilhjalmur Stefansson explored the interior in 1914–17. Sachs Harbour on its southwest coast, with air

Eastern shoreline of Banks Island, Northwest Territories
Joe Rychetnik—Photo Researchers

service to Inuvik on the mainland, is a base for trappers (especially of white fox) and for oil exploration.

Banks Islands, volcanic group in Vanuatu, southwestern Pacific Ocean. They include the islands of Vanua Lava, Santa Maria (Gaua), Mota, and Mota Lava (Saddle), and numerous islets. First explored in 1793 by Capt. William Bligh of the British Navy and named by him after his patron, the naturalist Sir Joseph Banks, the group enjoys sufficient rainfall and is covered by forest. The northernmost islet, Uréparapara, is a volcanic cone that has been breached by the sea, thus creating Dives Bay in its east coast. Several of the islands have active volcanoes. The islands' Polynesian inhabitants cultivate copra and coffee for export. Pop. (1979) 4,614.

Banks Peninsula, peninsula in eastern South Island, New Zealand, extending 30 mi (48 km) into the Pacific Ocean. It is bounded by Pegasus Bay (north) and Canterbury Bight (south) and has a total land area of about 500 sq mi (1,300 sq km). Generally hilly, it rises as high as 3,012 ft (918 m) at Herbert Peak. The peninsula, originally an island formed by two contiguous volcanic cones, was joined to the mainland by sediments of the Waimakariri River. It was visited (1770) by Capt. James Cook, who named it after Sir Joseph Banks, and it was surveyed by John Stokes (1850). In the early 19th century, whalers and sealers made use of Lyttelton and Akaroa harbours, occupying the breached craters of the volcanoes. Later in the century, the peninsula was stripped of its forests. Agriculture (sheep, grass seed, and garden products) is the major activity. Christchurch, the largest city of South Island, lies just northwest of the peninsula.

Bānkura, town, administrative headquarters of Bānkura district, West Bengal state, north-

Farmland in Bānkura district, West Bengal, India
Kaypix—Shostal Assoc./EB Inc.

eastern India, just north of the Dhāleśwarī (Dhalkisor) River. As a major Grand Trunk Road and rail junction, Bānkura is an agricultural distributing centre. Rice and oilseed milling, cotton weaving, metalware manufacture, and railway workshops are the major industries. Constituted a municipality in 1869, Bānkura has five colleges, including a medical school, affiliated with the University of Burdwān.

Bānkura district (area 2,657 sq mi [6,881 sq km]) was constituted in 1835. It comprises a densely populated alluvial plain in the east and a portion of the eastern Choṭa Nāgpur plateau in the west. Susuniā Hill bears a 3rd-century-BC Aśokan inscription. The Dāmodar Valley projects provide irrigation for some 80,000 ac (32,400 ha) of land. Rice, wheat, corn (maize), and sugarcane are the chief crops; mica, china clay, iron-ore, lead, zinc, and wolframite deposits are worked. The area long remained a focus of Hindu culture based on the Mallabhūm kingdom, with its capital at Bishnupur (*q.v.*). Pop. (1981) town, 94,954; district, 2,374,815.

Bann, River, Irish AN BHANNA, river, the largest in Northern Ireland, falling into two distinct parts. The upper Bann rises in the Mourne Mountains and flows northwest to Lough (lake) Neagh. The lower Bann flows northward through Lough Beg and carries the waters of Lough Neagh to the sea below Coleraine. The total length is 80 mi (129 km). The lower river occupies a peaty depression in the basalt plateaus of Ballymena, Ballymoney, Coleraine, and Magherafelt districts. Upstream the waterpower from the river played an important part in the industrialization of the Ulster linen industry. The river has valuable salmon and eel fisheries, and its valley contains prehistoric remains of the Mesolithic and Neolithic periods. The chief town on the upper Bann is Portadown, near Lough Neagh.

Bannatyne, George (b. 1545, Newtyle, Angus, Scot.—d. 1608?), compiler of an important collection of Scottish poetry from the 15th and 16th centuries (the golden age of Scottish literature).

A prosperous Edinburgh merchant, he compiled his anthology of verse, known as the *Bannatyne Manuscript,* while living in isolation during a plague in 1568. It contains many of the best known poems of the courtly poets known as Scottish Chaucerians (*see* makaris); it also preserves work by such poets as Alexander Scott who otherwise would be virtually unknown; and it also includes much interesting anonymous verse. It influenced the 18th-century Scottish revival, when Allan Ramsay reprinted many of the poems (though often in altered form) in his *Ever Green* (1724). In 1823 the Bannatyne Club was founded in Edinburgh to promote the study of Scottish history and literature.

Bannatyne, John: *see* Bellenden, John.

Banneker, Benjamin (b. Nov. 9, 1731, Ellicott's Mills, Md.—d. Oct. 25, 1806, Baltimore), mathematician, astronomer, compiler of almanacs, inventor, and writer, one of the first important U.S. black intellectuals.

A free black who owned a farm near Baltimore, Banneker was largely self-educated in astronomy by watching the stars, and in mathematics by reading borrowed textbooks. In 1761 he attracted attention by building a wooden clock that kept precise time. Encouraged in his studies by a Maryland industrialist, Joseph Ellicott, he began astronomical calculations about 1773, accurately predicted a solar eclipse in 1789, and published annually from 1791 to 1802 the *Pennsylvania, Delaware, Maryland, and Virginia Almanac and Ephemeris.* Appointed to the District of Columbia Commission by Pres. George Washington in 1790, he worked with Andrew Ellicott and others in surveying Washington, D.C.

As an essayist and pamphleteer, Banneker opposed slavery and war. He sent a copy of his first almanac to Thomas Jefferson, then U.S. secretary of state, along with a letter asking Jefferson's aid in bringing about better conditions for U.S. blacks. Banneker's almanacs were acclaimed by European scientists to whom Jefferson made them known.

Banner System, Chinese (Wade–Giles romanization) CH'I-PING, Pinyin QIBING, the military organization used by the Manchu tribes of Manchuria (Northeast Provinces) to conquer and control China in the 17th century. The Banner System was developed by the Manchu leader Nurhachi (1559–1626), who in 1601 organized his warriors into four companies of 300 men each. The companies were distinguished by banners of different colours—yellow, red, white, and blue. In 1615 four more banners were added, using the same colours bordered in red, the red banner being bordered in white. As the Manchus increased their conquests, the size of the companies grew until each came to number 7,500 men divided into five regiments, divided, in turn, into four companies.

All of Nurhachi's followers, with the exception of a few Imperial princes, were organized into this Banner System, which also served an administrative function. Taxation, conscription, and registration of the population was carried out through the banner organization. The bannermen lived, farmed, and worked with their families during times of peace, and in times of war each banner contributed a certain number of fighting men.

As the Manchus began to conquer their Chinese and Mongol neighbours, they organized their captives into companies modelled after the banners. In 1634 eight Mongol banners were added to the Manchu system, and in 1642 eight Chinese banners were added. The new banners, which fought alongside the old, brought to 24 the total number of banner units. With these troops, the Manchus were able to conquer China and establish the Ch'ing dynasty (1644–1911/12).

After the establishment of the dynasty, a constabulary Army of the Green Standard was garrisoned throughout the country to quell minor disturbances; this army consisted mainly of former Ming remnants and local forces. The main Manchu force continued to be the 24 banners, which were garrisoned at the capital in Peking and in several selected strategic spots throughout the country, where they could be called quickly in the event of an emergency.

In the early Ch'ing period the emperor controlled only three of the eight Manchu banners, the others being under the rule of various Imperial princes. But when the emperor Yung-cheng ascended the throne in 1722, he took control of all eight banners to prevent his brothers from attempting to usurp the throne. Thereafter, the banners were the sole possession of the Ch'ing emperors and their greatest source of power.

The bannermen were considered a form of nobility and were given preferential treatment in terms of annual pensions, land, and allotments of rice and cloth. Manchu bannermen were on the whole treated better than their Mongol and Chinese counterparts, but all were prohibited from participating in trade and manual labour unless they petitioned to be removed from banner status. Moreover, those who broke the law were not tried before an ordinary civil magistrate but by a special Manchu general.

During the century and a half of peace following the establishment of the Ch'ing, the fighting qualities of the banner forces deteriorated, and their training was neglected. During the White Lotus Rebellion (1796–1804) and then again during the Taiping Rebellion (1850–64), the banners were unable to protect the dynasty, and the government eventually had to organize other forces. By the end of the 19th century the Banner System, with the exception of a few thousand bannermen trained in modern methods and weapons, had become totally ineffective.

banneret, a European medieval knight privileged to display in the field a square banner (as distinct from the tapering pennon of a simple knight). The term was used in countries of French and English speech from the 13th to the 16th century. In 13th-century England any commander of a troop of 10 or more lances who was not a count or an earl was usually a banneret. Later, in both England and France, the style became a title of honour, conferred for distinguished military service. There is no connection between the style of banneret and the baronetage (hereditary knighthood) established in England by King James I in 1611.

Bannerman, Henry: *see* Campbell-Bannerman, Sir Henry.

banning, in South Africa, an administrative action by which publications, organizations, or assemblies may be outlawed and suppressed and individual persons may be placed under severe restrictions of their freedom of travel, association, and speech.

The power to ban publications rests with the minister of the interior under provisions of the Publications and Entertainments Act of 1963. Under the act a publication may be banned if it is found by a Publications Control Board appointed by the minister to be "undesirable" for any of a number of reasons, including obscenity, moral harmfulness, blasphemy, bringing a section of the population into ridicule or contempt, causing harm to relations among sections of the population, or being prejudicial to the safety, general welfare, peace, or order of the state. The power to ban extends to publications produced locally or imported, in the latter case under customs law.

The banning of organizations or of individuals was originally authorized by the Suppression of Communism Act of 1950, with numerous subsequent amendments, notably the Internal Security Act of 1976, and the Riotous Assemblies Act of 1956; those and other laws were superseded by the Internal Security Act of 1982, which retained nearly all their provisions. Under the older laws the minister of law and order could ban an organization found to be promoting or aiding the objects of Communism, or to be likely to promote such objects, or to be engaged in any activity associated with another organization already banned. The definitions of Communism and of the objects of Communism are very broad, including not only revolutionary activity aimed at establishing a dictatorship of the proletariat but also any activity allegedly promoting disturbances, disorder, or unlawful activity likely to further the goal of revolution; promoting industrial, social, political, or economic change in South Africa; and encouraging hostility between whites and nonwhites in such a way as to promote change or revolution. The power to label an organization or individual as Communist or revolutionary rested with the minister. The principal organizations that were banned under these laws are the Communist Party of South Africa, the African National Congress, and the Pan-African Congress.

The banning of individuals in South Africa is a practice virtually unique among nations with legal systems derived from Roman or common-law traditions. At the order of the minister, a person deemed a Communist, a terrorist, a member of a banned organization, or otherwise a threat to the security and public order of the state may be confined to his home or immediate surroundings; prohibited from meeting with more than one person at a time (other than his family); forced to resign any offices in any organization; prohibited from speaking publicly or writing for any publication; and barred from certain areas or from certain buildings and institutions, such as law courts, schools, and newspaper offices. Moreover, the banned person may not be quoted in any publication. The effect is to render the banned person a public nonentity. The minister exercises wide discretionary power as to the terms and duration of a ban; the subject of banning has a right to certain administrative review procedures but no recourse at law.

Banningville (Zaire): *see* Bandundu (city).

Bannister, Sir Roger (Gilbert) (b. March 23, 1929, Harrow, Middlesex, Eng.), first athlete to run a mile in less than 4 minutes—3 min 59.4 sec—in a dual meet at Oxford, May 6, 1954. Breaking the world record (4 min 1.3 sec), held for nine years by Gunder Hägg of Sweden, was almost incidental to his successful defiance of the "psychological" barrier, the general belief in the impossibility of running a mile in less than 4 minutes. Bannister is said to have achieved his speed through scientific training methods and thorough research into the mechanics of running.

Bannister, 1951
EB Inc.

While a student at Oxford and at St. Mary's Hospital Medical School, London, he won British (1951, 1953–54) and Empire (1954) championships in the mile run and the European title (1954) in the 1,500-metre event. A neurologist, he wrote *First Four Minutes* (1955) and papers on the physiology of exercise, heat illness, and neurological subjects. He was knighted in 1975. He edited *Brain's Clinical Neurology* (5th ed., 1978).

Bannock, Indian tribe of the Great Basin area of North America. In historical times and probably before 1700 the Bannock ranged through southern Idaho, especially along the Snake River and its tributaries. Linguistically they were most closely related to the Northern Paiute of eastern Oregon, from whom they were separated by 200 miles (320 kilometres). According to both Paiute and Bannock legend, the Bannock went to Idaho to live among the Shoshoni and hunt buffalo.

The culture of the Bannock was very much the Plains type in its emphasis on buffalo, the horse, and a semi-nomadic life. Seasonal migrations carried them west during summer to the Shoshone Falls for salmon, small game, and berries, and northeast in the fall to hunt buffalo in the Yellowstone area of Wyoming and Montana. The latter expeditions allowed the band chief to acquire power over hunting and subsistence activities and also required a good deal of cooperation with the Shoshoni, among whom the Bannock lived and with whom they shared a common enemy in the fierce Blackfoot, who controlled the buffalo-hunting grounds in Montana.

The Bannock were not numerous, probably never reaching more than 2,000, but they had considerable influence in inciting their more pacific neighbours to revolts and raids against the whites. Famine, frustration over the disappearance of the buffalo, and insensitive reservation policy by the U.S. government led to the Bannock War in 1878, which was suppressed with a massacre of about 140 Bannock men, women, and children at Charles's Ford in what is now Wyoming.

The independence and cultural autonomy of the Bannock did not survive the confinement of reservation life; by 1900 there were only about 500 Bannock left, much intermarried with Shoshoni, their tribal identity and warrior traits extinguished.

bannock, flat, sometimes unleavened bread eaten primarily in Scotland. Although most commonly made of oats, bannocks of barley, ground dried peas, and a combination of grains are sometimes encountered. Selkirk bannock is made from wheat flour and contains fruit.

The word bannock derives from the Latin *panicum*, denoting an edible, millet-like grain. Special bannocks were once made for holidays and religious feasts, such as Beltane bannocks on the first of May and Lammas bannocks on the first day of autumn. Stirring the batter for bannocks counterclockwise was popularly thought to bring bad luck.

A well-known tale of King Alfred indicates that bannocks were once commonly eaten in England. The king, unrecognized, sought hospitality at a cottage during his campaign against the Danes. He was set to minding the bannocks that were baking at the hearth and was scolded by the mistress of the house when through inattention he allowed the cakes to burn.

Bannockburn, former town, now part of Stirling, central region, Scotland. With its original location slightly to the east of the famous battlefield to which it lent its name, Bannockburn (from Scots Gaelic *ban ochburn,* "white shining stream") was known in the 18th and 19th centuries for cottage weaving, tartan, and carpet manufacture.

The Battle of Bannockburn, fought June 23–24, 1314, was a decisive event in Scottish history. In 1964, on the 650th anniversary of the battle, an equestrian statue of Robert I the Bruce was unveiled on the site by Queen Elizabeth II.

Bannockburn, Battle of (June 23–24, 1314), decisive battle in Scottish history, whereby the Scots under Robert the Bruce defeated the English under Edward II, regained their independence, and established Bruce on his throne as Robert I. The battle was fought for possession of Stirling Castle (3 miles to the north of the town of Bannockburn), then the last stronghold of the English in Scotland.

The Scottish army, consisting almost entirely of pikemen, was outnumbered by at least three to one by the English foot soldiers and cavalry, but, by masterly use of the terrain, the Scots were able to overcome the superior numbers of the enemy. The English army, confined in a small, marsh-bordered area between the Bannock Burn and the River Forth, had insufficient room for their cavalry and men to manoeuvre effectively. Bruce took advantage of the enemy's confusion and attacked. The defeated English army was finally put to flight by a charge of about 2,000 Scots, probably mainly camp followers, who swept down from Gillies Hill, which overlooked the battlefield to the west. The subsequent slaughter was immense, and many of those who survived the wrath of the Scots perished in the Bannock Burn and the morasses beyond. Edward II escaped by a circuitous route to Dunbar and thence to England.

Exact estimates of the numbers engaged are impossible, but the English had probably about 3,000 horse and 20,000 foot, the Scots perhaps 10,000 altogether or even as few as 5,000. English losses in killed and prisoners included the earls of Gloucester and Hereford, more than 60 barons and bannerets, and many scores of knights; the Scots claimed to have lost only two knights but numerous pikemen. Scotsmen regard the battle as the culmination of their War of Independence.

Bannu, town, headquarters of Bannu District, Dera Ismāīl Khān Division, North-West Frontier Province, Pakistan, just south of the Kurram River. The nearby Akra mounds have revealed finds dating to *c.* 300 BC. In ancient and medieval times, the Kurram–Bannu route into the Indian subcontinent was used by invaders and colonizers from the northwest. Founded in 1848 by Lieut. (later Sir) Herbert Edwardes as a military base, the town was named Dalīpnagar (1848) and then Edwardesābād (1869). In 1903 its name was changed to Bannu after the district (area, 1,695 sq mi [4,390 sq km]), which was constituted in 1861.

Bannu District occupies a circular alluvial plain, hemmed in by low hills and drained by the Kurram River and its tributary, the Tochi (Gambila). The Kurram–Garhi Project (completed 1962) provides irrigation, power, and flood control. Wheat, corn (maize), and barley are the chief crops. It is a military station and commercial centre at the junction of roads running from the Indus River to Peshāwar and Wazīristān, and is connected with the Indus by rail. Local industries include a large woollen mill. Bannu is the seat of a college affiliated with the University of Peshāwar. Inhabitants are mainly Pashtun tribal people. Pop. (1981 prelim.) town, 43,000; district, 699,000.

Banpocun (Chinese site): *see* Pan-p'o-ts'un.

Bansang, town, MacCarthy Island division, east central Gambia, on the south bank of the Gambia River. A local trade centre in peanuts (groundnuts), rice, and fish among the Malinke (Mandingo), Fulani (Fula), and Wolof peoples, it is a port of call for the government steamer from Bathurst, 188 mi (303 km) downstream. Bansang is the site of the only government hospital in the interior; the associated Leprosy Village at Alla Tentu is 1½ mi northwest. Pop. (1973) 2,109.

banshee, Irish BEAN SIDHE, Scots Gaelic BAN SITH ("woman of the fairies"), supernatural being in Celtic folklore whose mournful keening, or wailing lamentation, at night was believed to foretell the death of a member of the family of the person who heard the spirit. In Ireland banshees were believed to warn only families of pure Irish descent; the Welsh counterpart, the *gwrach y Rhibyn* ("witch of Rhibyn"), visited only families of old Welsh stock. Sir Walter Scott mentions belief in a kind of banshee or household spirit in certain Highland families (*Letters on Demonology and Witchcraft,* 1830).

Banshee, from *Fairy Legends and Traditions of the South of Ireland* (1825–28), by Thomas Croker
By courtesy of the Folklore Society Library, University College, London; photograph, R.B. Fleming

Banská Bystrica, German NEUSOHL, Hungarian BESZTERCEBÁNYA, town, capital of Středoslovenský *kraj* (Central Slovakia region), Czechoslovakia, in the Hron River Valley, surrounded by mountains. It has been an important mining centre since the 13th century, when it was chartered. Gothic and Renaissance-style buildings, including burghers' houses and the castle group (in the heart of town), date from the 15th and 16th centuries, when the silver and copper mines supplied much of the European market. On Aug. 29, 1944, Banská Bystrica was the scene of the Slovak national uprising against the Germans. The Old Town Hall (1479) contains a museum commemorating this event. Since World War II, the town has developed as an industrial centre for the manufacture of textiles, paper, metal products, and cement. It is also a popular summer and winter resort. Pop. (1983 est.) 70,774.

Town square in Banská Bystrica, Czech.
FPG—EB Inc.

Banstead (England): *see* Reigate and Banstead.

Bānswāra, town, administrative headquarters of Bānswāra district, Rājasthān state, northwestern India. Bānswāra is an agricultural market centre. Its principal industries include cotton ginning, flour milling, handweaving, and woodwork. A walled city, it was founded in the early 16th century. A government college there is affiliated with the University of Rājasthān.

Bānswāra district (1,945 sq mi [5,037 sq km] in area) comprises two distinct regions. The western part is comparatively flat and fertile; the eastern part is covered with rugged hills and woodland and forms the extreme western region of the Mālwa Plateau. The principal river is the Mahi. Corn (maize), wheat, and gram (chick-pea) are the chief crops; iron-ore, lead, zinc, silver, and manganese deposits are worked.

The district was formerly the princely state of Bānswāra, founded *c.* 1530, of which the town of Bānswāra was capital. Earlier it formed part of the original Dūngarpur state. It merged with the union of Rājasthān in 1948. Pop. (1981) town, 46,749; metropolitan area, 48,-070; district, 886,600.

Bantam, Bahasa Indonesia BANTEN, former city and sultanate of Java, Indonesia, near the site of present-day Banten, on Teluk (bay) Banten, at the extreme northwest of the island, just north of Serang. Now in ruins, Bantam was the most important Javanese port for the spice trade with Europe from the 16th century until the end of the 18th, when its harbour silted up. Its site is now more than a mile from the sea. Ruined buildings include the Pakuwonan palace (1680), Ft. Speelwijk, and several mosques, the oldest of which dates from 1562. Under Dutch occupation Bantam was the westernmost residency of Java, comprising the districts of Pandeglang, Serang, and Lebak. The people of the region are still known for their fervid devotion to Islām. Bantam fowl were erroneously thought to have originated there.

banteng, also called BALI CATTLE (*Bos banteng*), species of wild Southeast Asian cattle, family Bovidae (order Artiodactyla), found in hill forests. A shy animal resembling a domestic cow, the banteng attains a shoulder height of about 1.5–1.75 metres (60–69 inches). It has a slight ridge on the back, a white rump, white "stockings" on the legs, and slender, curving horns. Bulls are dark brown or black, and cows and young are reddish brown. The banteng is kept as a domestic animal in some areas.

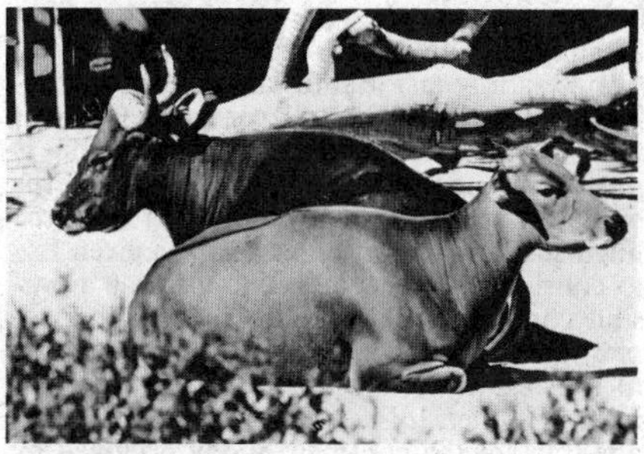
Banteng (*Bos banteng*)
Tom McHugh—Photo Researchers

Banting, Sir Frederick Grant (b. Nov. 14, 1891, Alliston, Ont., Can.—d. Feb. 21, 1941, Newfoundland), physician who, with Charles H. Best, was first to obtain (1921) a pancreatic extract of insulin. Working in the laboratories of the Scottish physiologist J.J.R. Macleod at the University of Toronto, they were able to isolate the hormone in a form consistently effective in treating diabetes. In 1923 Banting became head of the university's Banting and Best Department of Medical Research and was corecipient with Macleod of the 1923 Nobel Prize for Physiology or Medicine for the discovery of insulin. Banting voluntarily shared his portion of the award with Best, and he was created a knight of the British Empire in 1934. He was killed in a plane crash while on a war mission.

Bantry Bay, long inlet of the Atlantic Ocean, southwestern County Cork, Ireland. The bay has a maximum length of 30 mi (48 km) and is 10 mi wide at its broadest point; it separates the Caha peninsula to the north from the Sheep's Head peninsula to the south, and is surrounded by mountains. Bantry Bay was entered in 1689 and 1796 by French fleets attempting invasions of Ireland. On Whiddy Island there are 19th-century relics of a British naval station, and a large oil terminal. The town of Bantry is located near the head of the bay.

Bantu Homeland (South Africa): *see* black state.

Bantu languages, a group of the Benue-Congo branch of the Niger-Congo language family. The Bantu languages are spoken in a very large area, including most of Africa from the fifth parallel of north latitude (roughly, below the bulge into the Atlantic) to Cape Province in the Republic of South Africa, the southernmost tip. Four of the major Niger-Congo languages (Rwanda, Makua, Xhosa, and Zulu) are Bantu languages. Swahili (*q.v.*) is a Bantu lingua franca important both in commerce and in literature.

Bantu nouns usually consist of a stem preceded by a prefix that changes according to number. Nouns are grouped into categories (genders) on the basis of these prefixes. All or almost all the words in a Bantu sentence are usually marked by a prefix indicating the category to which the noun used as subject of the sentence belongs. Suffixes are also used, especially in the formation of verb stems and verb forms.

Bantu peoples, the approximately 60,000,000 speakers of the more than 200 distinct languages of the Bantu subgroup of the Niger-Congo family (*see* Bantu languages), occupying almost the entire southern projection of the African continent. The classification is primarily linguistic, for the cultural patterns of Bantu speakers are extremely diverse; the linguistic connection, however, has given rise to considerable speculation concerning a possible common area of origin of the Bantu peoples, the linguistic evidence pointing strongly to the region of the present-day Cameroon–Nigeria border. It is generally agreed that some one-third of the continent today occupied by Bantu-speaking peoples was, until approximately 2,000 years ago, the dominion of other groups, mainly Pygmies and San (Bushmen), and the causes and itinerary of the subsequent Bantu migration have attracted the attention of several anthropologists. George P. Murdock of the United States postulated that the expansion of the Bantu was associated with their acquisition of certain Malaysian food crops (banana, taro, and yam), which spread westward across the continent at about the time that the migration is thought to have begun. These crops, Murdock argued, enabled them to penetrate the tropical rain forest of equatorial Africa, whence they spread across the southern part of the continent. A more widely held view, however, is that the migratory route lay eastward, across the southern Sudan, and then south, past the great lakes of the northeast.

Bantu tribesman of Kenya
Camera Press

The economic, social, and political organization of the various Bantu-speaking peoples is extremely diverse, partly reflecting the wide range of habitats they occupy. The economy may, for example, be based on pastoralism, on sedentary agriculture, on a combination of agriculture, hunting, and gathering (particularly in the equatorial forest), or on fishing and river trade, as among some groups of the central equatorial region. Descent and kinship systems, religious practices, and political organization exhibit a similar range of diversity.

Bantustan (South Africa): *see* black state.

banty (game): *see* bandy.

Banū al-Aghlab DYNASTY: *see* Aghlabid dynasty.

Banū Ḥafṣ (dynasty): *see* Ḥafṣid dynasty.

Banū Marīn (dynasty): *see* Marīnid dynasty.

Banū Zayyān (dynasty): *see* ʿAbd al-Wādid dynasty.

Banū Zīrī (dynasty): *see* Zīrid dynasty.

Banville, (Étienne-Claude-Jean-Baptiste-) Théodore (-Faullain) de (b. March 14, 1823, Moulins, Fr.—d. March 13, 1891, Paris), a respected French poet of the mid-19th century who was a late disciple of the Romantics, a leader of the Parnassian movement, and an influence on the Symbolists. His first book of verse, *Les Cariatides* (1842), owed much to the style and manner of Victor Hugo, but Banville rejected the poor craftsmanship of much French Romantic poetry. His *Petit Traité de poésie française* (1872) shows his interest in the technicalities of versification, of which he became a master. He considered rhyme to be the single most important element in French verse. Following the lead of the critic Charles Sainte-Beuve, who had revived interest in the sonnet, Banville experimented with various fixed forms that had been neglected since the mid-16th century—*e.g.,* the ballade and the rondeau. The chief quality of his poetry is its technical virtuosity, but contemporaries also admired its delicate wit and fantasy. His best known collection is *Les Odes funambulesques* (1857).

Banville
Popperfoto

Banyak Islands, Bahasa Indonesia KEPULAUAN BANYAK, or BANJAK, group of more than 60 small islands, in Aceh *daerah istimewa* (special district), Indonesia. The largest of the islands are Great Banyak, or Pulau (island) Tuangku, and Pulau Bangkaru. With an area of 123 sq mi (319 sq km), the group lies north of Pulau Nias and 18 mi (29 km) west of Sumatra in the Indian Ocean. The population is a mixture of settlers from northern and central Sumatra and from Nias; most are Muslims. Agriculture—rice and root crops—is largely for subsistence, but copra is exported. Pop. (latest est.) 1,015.

Banyamwesi (people): *see* Nyamwezi.

banyan (*Ficus benghalensis,* or *F. indica*), unusually shaped tree of the fig genus in the mulberry family (Moraceae) native to tropical Asia. Aerial roots that develop from its branches descend and take root in the soil to become new trunks. The banyan reaches a height up to 30 metres (100 feet) and spreads laterally indefinitely. One tree may in time assume the appearance of a very dense thicket as a result of the tangle of roots and trunks.

Banyan (*Ficus benghalensis*)
Gerald Cubitt

Banyoro (people): *see* Nyoro.

Banyuwangi, also spelled BANJUWANGI, or BANJOEWANGI, city and *kabupaten* (regency), Jawa Timur *propinsi* (East Java province), Java, Indonesia. A major port on the Selat (strait) Bali, opposite Bali just to the east, it is located 120 mi (193 km) southeast of Surabaya, the capital of Jawa Timur. It is linked by railway and road with Jember to the west and by road with Situbondo to the northwest. Exports are copra, lumber, and rubber from the inland area. Industries include sawmilling, wood carving, paper making, leather tanning, and printing. The population is predominantly Javanese, and Islām, influenced by Hindu and Buddhist customs, is the dominant religion. About 50 mi south of Banyuwangi is the Sukameda beach; a wildlife preserve containing the Java tiger, and the Bawean Bird Park are located nearby. Banyuwangi is the terminus of cables from Australia and Singapore. Pop. (1980) city, 90,359; regency, 1,420,837.

Banzart, also spelled BIZERTA, or BIZERTE, capital of Banzart *wilāyat* (governorate), northern Tunisia. The town, situated on the Mediterranean coast at the mouth of a channel from Buḥayrat (lake) Banzart, originated as a Phoenician outpost and was known through Carthaginian and Roman times as Hippo Diarrhytus or Hippo Zarytus. Captured in AD 661 by Ibn al-Hadaij, it was given the name Bizerte. It was occupied by the Spanish from 1535 to 1572 but later became a privateering stronghold. During the 1890s a canal (5,000 ft [1,500 m] long, 787 ft wide, and 32 ft deep) was built (completed in 1895) from Buḥayrat Banzart to the sea to open up the naval port and arsenal of Sidi Abdallah (now Manzil Bū Ruqaybah [Menzel-Bourguiba]). This canal altered the layout of Banzart, as a new town was built on the canal's outlet. The old town (surrounded by an ancient wall) was on the mouth of the natural channel, which has since been filled in.

Banzart, which was an important military base during the French Protectorate (1881–1955), is now a seaport, beach resort, administrative centre, and regional market centre. Divested of its military function in 1963, Banzart now exports fish, phosphates, iron ore, and cereals. Oil refining, which was begun in 1964, is its main industry; fish canning is of lesser importance. The town is linked by road and rail with Tūnis and Ṭabarqah (Tabarka) and has an airport.

Banzart *wilāyat*, embracing much of Tunisia's wet northern coastal region, has an area of 1,423 sq mi (3,685 sq km). It includes the towns of Māṭir and Manzil Jamīl and encompasses areas of cork production (west), wheat growing and cattle ranching (central), and market gardening and viticulture (east).

Banzart, Tunisia, with its ancient wall
By courtesy of the Embassy of Tunisia

Iron ore is mined at Tāmirah and supplies the steel complex at Manzil Bū Ruqaybah near Bizerte town. Pop. (1975) town, 62,856; (1982 est.) *wilāyat*, 389,500.

Bánzer Suárez, Hugo, byname EL PETISO (Spanish: The Short One) (b. July 10, 1926, Santa Cruz, Bolivia), soldier, politician and president of Bolivia, 1971–78.

Bánzer was educated at the Bolivian Army Military College and in two United States Army training schools. He served as minister of education from 1964 to 1967 in the cabinet of Pres. René Barrientos and as military attaché in Washington from 1967 until 1969, when he returned to Bolivia to head the Military College. In successive governmental changes between right- and left-wing officers, the conservative Bánzer helped Gen. Rogelio Miranda overthrow Pres. Alfredo Ovando in September 1969; Bánzer himself overthrew the leftist Gen. Juan José Torres on Aug. 22, 1971. Bánzer's policies included encouragement of foreign investment. His restrictive policies regarding union activity and constitutional liberties led to opposition from labour leaders, clergymen, peasants, and students. All opposition was severely repressed. He survived a coup in 1974, but declined to run for president in the 1978 elections. Gen. Juan Pereda Asbún won the 1978 presidential election, amid universal charges of vote fraud (50,000 more votes were cast than there were eligible voters). Pereda himself ordered a new election, but before it could take place, he staged a coup, forcing Bánzer to resign on July 21, 1978. Exiled by Pereda to Argentina, Bánzer returned in March 1979 to enter the July 1 presidential elections. He finished a distant third, supported mainly by middle- and upper-class voters.

Bao Dai, original name NGUYEN VINH THUY (b. Oct. 22, 1913, Vietnam), the last reigning emperor of Vietnam (1926–45), who in his youth was a symbol of hope for the Vietnamese independence movement but who later became known as the "Playboy Emperor."

The son of Emperor Khai Dinh, a vassal of the French colonial regime, and a concubine of peasant ancestry, Nguyen Vinh Thuy was educated in France and spent little of his youth in his homeland. He succeeded to the throne in 1926 and assumed the title Bao Dai (Keeper of Greatness). He initially sought to reform and modernize Vietnam but was unable to win French cooperation.

During World War II the French colonial regime exercised a firm control over Bao Dai until the Japanese *coup de force* of March 1945, which swept away French administration in Indochina. The Japanese considered bringing back the aging Prince Cuong De from Japan to head a new quasi-independent Vietnamese state, but they finally allowed Bao Dai to remain as an essentially powerless ruler. When the Viet Minh seized power in their revolution of August 1945, Ho Chi Minh and his colleagues judged that there was symbolic value to be gained by having Bao Dai linked to them. The Viet Minh asked Bao Dai to resign and offered him an advisory role as "Citizen Prince Nguyen Vinh Thuy." Finding that the Viet Minh accorded him no role, and distrustful of the French, Bao Dai fled to Hong Kong in 1946. There he led a largely frivolous life, occasionally making appeals for international support against the reestablishment of French rule.

In 1949 the French accepted the principle of an independent Vietnam but retained control of its defense and finance. Bao Dai agreed to return to Vietnam in these circumstances in May 1949, and in July he became temporary premier of a tenuously unified and nominally independent Vietnam. Reinstalled as sovereign, Bao Dai continued his pleasure-seeking ways, leaving affairs of state to his various pro-French Vietnamese appointees, until October 1955 when a national referendum called for the country to become a republic. Bao Dai retired and returned to France to live.

To make the best use of the Britannica, consult the INDEX *first*

---

baobab (*Adansonia digitata*), tree of the bombax family (Bombacaceae) of the order Malvales, native to Africa. The barrel-like trunk may reach a diameter of 9 metres (30 feet) and a height of 18 m. The large, gourdlike, woody fruit contains a tasty mucilaginous pulp. A strong fibre from the bark is used locally for rope and cloth. The trunks are often excavated to serve as water reserves or temporary shelters.

So extraordinarily shaped is the baobab that an Arabian legend has it that "the devil plucked up the baobab, thrust its branches into the earth, and left its roots in the air." It is grown as a curiosity in areas of warm climate, such as Florida. A related species, *A. gregorii*,

Baobab (*Adansonia digitata*)
B.A. Barlow

occurs in Australia, where it is called baobab or bottle tree (the latter name being more correctly applied to the family Sterculiaceae).

Baoding (China): *see* Pao-ting.

Baoji (China): *see* Pao-chi.

baojia (Chinese custom): *see* pao-chia.

Baol, in the 14th century, a satellite state of the Wolof empire of West Africa; situated along the coast and inland to the south of Dakar in present Senegal, it was conquered some time after 1556 by the neighbouring state of Cayor, which controlled it until 1686. When, late in the 17th century, Wolof invaded Cayor, causing many of its inhabitants to flee to Baol, the positions of the two states were reversed. The rulers of Baol were able to withstand European attempts at conquest until the French occupied their territory in the mid-19th century.

Baotou (China): *see* Pao-t'ou.

Bapedi (people): *see* Pedi.

Baptism, a sacrament that admits a person to membership in the Christian Church. The forms and rituals of the various churches vary, but Baptism almost invariably involves the use of water and the Trinitarian invocation, "I baptize you: In the name of the Father, and of the Son, and of the Holy Spirit." (Some Eastern churches use the formula: "This servant of Christ is baptized in the name of the Father, and of the Son, and of the Holy Spirit.") The candidate may be wholly or partly immersed in water, the water may be poured over the head, or a few drops sprinkled or placed upon it.

During Jesus' lifetime Judaism practiced various baptismal rites, and according to the Gospels John the Baptist baptized Jesus. Although there is no actual account of the institution of Baptism by Jesus, the Gospel According to Matthew portrays the risen Christ issuing the "Great Commission" to his followers: "Go therefore and make disciples of all nations, baptizing them in the name of the Father and of the Son and of the Holy Spirit, teaching them to observe all that I have commanded you" (Matt. 28:19–20). Elsewhere in the New Testament, however, this formula is not used. Some scholars thus doubt the accuracy of the quotation in Matthew and suggest that it reflects a tradition formed by a merging of the idea of spiritual baptism (as in Acts 1:5), early baptismal rites (as in Acts 8:16), and reports of Pentecostalism after such rites (as in Acts 19:5–6).

Baptism occupied a place of great importance in the Christian community of the 1st century, but Christian scholars disagree over whether it was to be regarded as essential to the new birth and to membership in the Kingdom of God or to be regarded only as an external sign or symbol of inner regeneration. The Apostle Paul likened baptismal immersion to personal sharing in the death, burial, and Resurrection of Christ (Rom. 6:3–4). By the 2nd century, the irreducible minimum for a valid Baptism appears to have been the use of water and the invocation of the Trinity. Usually the candidate was immersed three times, but there are references to pouring as well.

Most of those baptized in the early church were converts from Greco-Roman paganism and therefore were adults. Both the New Testament and the Church Fathers of the 2nd century make it clear that the gift of salvation belongs to children, however. Tertullian seems to have been the first to object to infant Baptism, suggesting that by the 2nd century it was already a common practice. It remained the accepted method of receiving members in the Eastern and Western churches, except in the case of adult converts.

During the Reformation the Lutherans, Reformed, and Anglicans accepted the Catholic attitude toward infant Baptism. The radical Reformers, however, primarily the Anabaptists, insisted that a person must be sufficiently mature to make a profession of faith before receiving Baptism. In modern times the largest Christian groups that practice adult rather than infant Baptism are the Baptists and the Christian Church (Disciples of Christ).

Baptist, member of a group of Protestant Christians who share the basic beliefs of most Protestants but who hold as an article of faith that only believers should be baptized and that it must be done by immersion. The Baptists do not constitute a single church or denominational structure, but most of them adhere to a congregational form of church government.

A brief treatment of the Baptist movement follows. For full treatment, *see* MACROPAEDIA: Protestantism.

Two groups of Baptists emerged in England during the Puritan reform movement of the 17th century. While sharing the view that only believers should be baptized, the two groups differed with respect to the nature of Christ's atonement. Those who regarded the atonement as general (*i.e.*, for all persons) came to be called General Baptists. Those who interpreted it as applying only to the particular body of the elect acquired the name Particular Baptists.

The General Baptists trace their beginnings to the Baptist Church founded in London *c.* 1611 by Thomas Helwys and his followers. This group had returned to England from Amsterdam, where they had gone *c.* 1608 because of religious persecution of Separatists (those who wished to separate from the Anglican Church of England). While in Amsterdam, the group adopted the beliefs of their original leader John Smyth (Smith), who, by studying the New Testament, decided that only believers should be baptized. Through the work of the original London congregation, other General Baptist congregations were formed and the movement spread. In doctrine they were Arminians, believing in the general atonement; *i.e.*, that Christ's death was for all men and not only for the elect (those predestined to be saved). In the late 17th and 18th centuries, the General Baptists declined in numbers and influence. Churches closed and many members became Unitarians. The General Baptists were continued by a new group organized in 1770, the New Connection General Baptists, who had been influenced by the Methodist revival led by John Wesley.

Particular Baptists originated with a Baptist church established in 1638 by two groups who, in 1633 and 1638, left an Independent church (not part of the Church of England) in London. Members of the new church believed that only believers (not infants) should be baptized. In theology they were Calvinists, who held to the doctrine of a particular atonement, *i.e.*, that Christ died only for the elect.

The Particular Baptists grew more rapidly than the General Baptists, but growth subsequently slowed as the Particular Baptists emphasized their doctrine of salvation only for the elect and did not work to gain new members. After 1750, however, they were influenced by the Methodist movement, and new interests in evangelism and missions brought about renewed growth. Through the leadership of William Carey, the English Baptist Missionary Society was organized in 1792, and Carey went to India as the society's first missionary. Baptists were influential in the religious and political life of Great Britain during the 19th century, but their membership and influence declined after World War I.

The Baptist Union of Great Britain and Ireland was organized originally in 1813 by Particular Baptists. In 1891 the New Connection General Baptists merged into the Baptist Union. The strict Calvinism of the Particular Baptists had gradually been modified, and, although controversies occurred between conservatives and liberals, freedom of thought within denominational unity was generally acceptable to those in the Baptist Union.

Baptist origins in the United States can be traced to Roger Williams, who established a Baptist Church in Providence in 1639 after being banished by the Puritans from Massachusetts Bay. Williams soon abandoned his fold and leadership passed to John Clarke.

Though Rhode Island remained a Baptist stronghold, the centre of Baptist life in colonial America was Philadelphia. The first supra-congregational association was formed there in 1707, and the Philadelphia Baptist Association proceeded to sponsor new Baptist churches throughout the colonies.

Baptist growth was spurred by the Great Awakening of the mid-18th century. Increases were especially dramatic in the Southern colonies, where Shubael Stearns established a church at Sandy Creek, N.C., in 1755. From this centre revivalistic preachers fanned out across the southern frontier, establishing a Baptist dominance in the region which persists to the present. The membership of revivalistic Baptists continued to grow rapidly in the 19th century, assisted by lay preachers and a congregational church government well adapted to frontier settings.

Baptists in the United States were not united in a national body until 1814, when an increasing interest in foreign missions necessitated a more centralized organization. The General Convention was soon torn apart, however, by dissension over slavery. A formal split occurred in 1845 when the Southern Baptist Convention was organized in Augusta, Ga. and was confirmed when the Northern Baptist Convention was organized in 1907. Southern Baptists and Northern Baptists (later American Baptists) developed distinct regional characteristics following the Civil War and still exhibit different tendencies in theology, ecumenical involvement, missionary activity, and worship.

Black Baptist churches, now grouped primarily in two large conventions, constitute another major segment of Baptists in the United States. Organized by freed slaves after the Civil War, these churches have contributed enormously to the character of black life in America, often serving as the social and spiritual centre of the black community. Black Baptist churches and ministers, led by Martin Luther King, Jr., played a significant role in the Civil Rights Movement of the 1960s. These churches and ministers continued as vital elements of organization in black communities through the 1980s, as was evident in the presidential candidacy (1984) of the Rev. Jesse Jackson.

In the 20th century Baptists have experienced additional fragmentation, arising from theological controversy. There are now hundreds of independent Baptist churches, completely separated from all other bodies or loosely affiliated with other congregations in small, fundamentalist sects.

Through continuing missionary activity Baptists have established churches throughout the world. An important Baptist centre is the Soviet Union, where Baptists constitute the largest Protestant group.

Baptists maintain that authority in matters of faith and practice rests, under Christ, with the local congregation of baptized believers. These local congregations are linked voluntarily into state, regional, and national organizations for cooperative endeavors such as missions, education, and philanthropy. The larger organizations, however, have no control over the local churches. The separation of church and state has historically been a major tenet of Baptist doctrine.

Baptist worship is centred around the exposition of the scriptures in a sermon. Extemporaneous prayer and hymn-singing are also characteristic.

Early Baptists were characterized theologically by strong-to-moderate Calvinism, but this position was tempered considerably by the Evangelical revivals of the 18th and 19th centuries. Baptists in the 20th century have provided leadership for diverse theological movements, notably Walter Rauschenbusch in the Social Gospel movement, Harry Emerson Fosdick and Shailer Mathews in American Modernism, and Billy Graham in contemporary Evangelicalism. Baptists have generally been more concerned for religious experience and expression than precise theological formulations.

Baptist Federation of Canada, cooperative agency for several Canadian Baptist groups, organized in 1944 in Saint John, N.B., by the United Baptist Convention of the Maritime Provinces, the Baptist Convention of Ontario and Quebec, and the Baptist Union of Western Canada.

Baptist churches were organized in the Maritime Provinces in the latter half of the 18th century, primarily by Baptists who were loyal to England and who left New England because of the American Revolution. In 1846 the Baptist Convention of Nova Scotia, New Brunswick, and Prince Edward Island was organized. The name was changed in 1879 to the Baptist Convention of the Maritime Provinces. In 1905–06 this group and Free Baptists in New Brunswick and Nova Scotia merged to form the United Baptist Convention of the Maritime Provinces. In the 1960s it was renamed the United Baptist Convention of the Atlantic Provinces.

A few Baptist churches were organized in Ontario in the late 18th century, but, in the 19th century, many congregations were started in Ontario and Quebec by Baptists from the United States, England, and Scotland. The Ottawa Baptist Association, including churches in Quebec and eastern Ontario, was organized in 1836. Subsequently, other associations and mission societies were formed in these provinces, but various controversies delayed the union of these groups until 1888, when the Baptist Convention of Ontario and Quebec was organized.

Baptist missionaries from Ontario began working in western Canada in the 1870s, and congregations and associations were organized. In 1897 the Baptist Convention of British Columbia was established, and in 1909 the more inclusive Baptist Union of Western Canada was organized.

As early as 1900, efforts were made to unite the three Baptist conventions in Canada, but agreement could not be reached for many years. The groups did cooperate, however, in home and foreign missions and in educational activities. From 1931 to 1943, an Inter-Conventions Committee worked out the details of union, which was completed in 1944. The federation operates as a coordinating agency and does not supplant the area conventions.

Baptist General Conference, conservative Baptist denomination that was organized in 1879 as the Swedish Baptist General Conference of America; the present name was adopted in 1945. It developed from the work of Gustaf Palmquist, a Swedish immigrant schoolteacher and lay preacher who became a Baptist in 1852. He established the first Swedish Baptist Church in Rock Island, Ill., that same year. Palmquist and other Swedish Baptists worked in several Midwestern states among Swedish immigrants. The movement received assistance from the American Baptist Home Mission Society and the American Baptist Publication Society for several years, until the Swedish Baptists became self-supporting. After World War I, the Swedish language was gradually replaced by English in worship services, and persons other than Swedes became members of the church.

The Baptist General Conference is generally considered to be theologically conservative, although the right of individuals to differ in their beliefs is respected. Bethel College and Seminary in St. Paul, Minn., is owned and operated by the conference. The work of the denomination is carried out through several boards; a general conference is held annually. Headquarters are in Chicago.

Baptist Missionary Association of America, association of independent, conservative Baptist churches, organized as the North American Baptist Association in Little Rock, Ark., in 1950, as a protest to the American Baptist Association's policy of seating messengers at meetings who were not members of the churches that elected them. The present name was adopted in 1968. These churches cooperate in missions and have sent missionaries to several countries. An active publications department publishes Sunday school and other religious material, and a radio ministry produces programs that are heard in many places throughout the world.

The member churches of the Baptist Missionary Association of America are autonomous and share equally in the cooperative activities of the association. All of the churches, however, must subscribe to a strict Fundamentalist interpretation of Christian doctrine. They accept the statements of the Bible literally and expect the Second Coming of Christ. There is no cooperation or association with other groups who do not hold the same beliefs.

Baptist Union of Great Britain and Ireland, largest Baptist group in the British Isles, organized in 1891 as a union of the Particular Baptist and New Connection General Baptist associations. These groups were historically related to the first English Baptists, who originated in the 17th century.

The Baptist Union is a voluntary organization made up of area associations of churches, individual churches, colleges, and individual members. In the 20th century it has become more centrally organized. Its activities include education, ecumenical relations, missions, and social welfare, but it cannot interfere in the autonomy of the local churches. Headquarters are in London.

Baptist World Alliance (BWA), international advisory organization for Baptists, founded in 1905 in London. Its purpose is to promote fellowship and cooperation among all Baptists. It sponsors regional and international meetings for various groups for study and promotion of the gospel, and it works to safeguard religious liberty throughout the world.

World congresses of the BWA are held every five years; an executive committee meets annually. Headquarters are in Washington, D.C.

Baptiste, original name NICOLAS ANSELME (b. June 18, 1761, Bordeaux, Fr.—d. Nov. 30/ Dec. 1, 1835, Les Batignolles), one of the leading actors of sentimental comedy (*comédie larmoyante*) in France.

Baptiste, detail of a lithograph by F. Tomaszkiewicz
BBC Hulton Picture Library

After two provincial engagements Baptiste went to Paris in 1791. In 1793 he joined the Théâtre de la République and in 1799 the Comédie-Française, from which he retired in 1828. He was not successful in tragedy. Parisians of the Napoleonic era primarily associated him with the noble fathers in such plays as Beaumarchais's *Eugénie* (1767) and Diderot's *Père de famille* (1758). His greatest achievement was in the title role of Philippe-Néricault Destouches's masterpiece *Glorieux*. Known as Baptiste the Elder, he was survived by his brother Paul-Eustache Anselme (1765–1839), called Baptiste the Younger, who had made a name for himself as a comedian.

baptistery, hall or chapel situated close to, or connected with, a church, in which the sacrament of Baptism is administered. The form of the baptistery originally evolved from small, circular Roman buildings that were designated for religious purposes (*e.g.*, Temple of Venus, Baalbek [Ba'labakk], Lebanon, AD 273, and Mausoleum of Diocletian, Spalato [Split, Yugos.], AD 300); but because Baptism originally was performed on only three holidays, Easter, Pentecost, and Epiphany, enlargement of the

Battistero (baptistery) S. Giovanni, Florence, begun 7th century
Alinari—Art Resource/EB Inc.

older Roman buildings became necessary to accommodate the growing numbers of converts.

Baptisteries were among the most symbolic of all Christian architectural forms; and the characteristic design that was developed by the 4th century AD can be seen today in what is probably the earliest extant example, the baptistery of the Lateran palace in Rome, built by Sixtus III, pope between 432 and 440.

The baptistery was commonly octagonal in plan, a visual metaphor for the number eight, which symbolized in Christian numerology a new beginning. As eight follows the "complete" number, seven, so the beginning of the Christian life follows Baptism. Customarily, a baptistery was roofed with a dome, the symbol of the heavenly realm toward which the Christian progresses after the first step of Baptism. The baptismal font was usually octagonal, set beneath a domical ciborium, or canopy (*q.v.*), and encircled by columns and an ambulatory (*q.v.*)—features that were first used in the baptistery by the Byzantines when they altered Roman structures.

Baptisteries commonly adjoined the atrium, or forecourt, of the church and were often large and richly decorated, such as those at Pisa, Florence, Parma, and Nocera in Italy; el Kantara, Alg.; and Poitiers, Fr. After the 6th century they were gradually reduced to the status of small chapels inside churches. In the 10th century, when Baptism by affusion (pouring liquid over the head) became standard practice in the church, baptisteries, or baptismal chapels, were often omitted entirely.

In most modern churches the font alone serves for Baptism; something of earlier symbolism survives, however, in its usual location near the church door—an allusion to entering the Christian life.

Baqdash, Khalid, also spelled BEKDACHE (b. 1912, Damascus, Syria), Syrian politician who acquired control of the Syrian Communist Party in 1932 and remained its most prominent spokesman until 1958, when he went into exile.

As a young man Baqdash went to law school in Damascus but was expelled for illegal political activity. In 1930 he joined the Communist Party and began to acquire a reputation for skillful public debate, dedication to his political vision, and personal magnetism. Jailed in 1931 and 1932 by the French, he nevertheless succeeded in 1932 in ousting Fuad ash-Shamali from leadership of the Syrian Communist Party. He was soon forced to go underground and then left Syria. In 1935 he led the Syrian delegation to the Seventh Congress of the Communist International, which was meeting in Moscow, and remained there for a period of training.

In 1954 Baqdash was elected to a seat in the Syrian Parliament, becoming the first Communist deputy in the Arab world. He adopted alliances with the Socialist and the increasingly powerful Ba'th Party. He became Syria's apologist for the policies of the Soviet Union, and, when in August 1957 the Soviet Union signed a wide-ranging economic and technical agreement with Syria, his influence rose considerably.

Yet his position was threatened by widespread Syrian sentiment for some kind of union with Egypt, the president of which, Gamal Abdel Nasser, would not tolerate a Communist opposition. By 1957 he found himself increasingly at odds with the Ba'th, and, hoping to take the initiative, he demanded a total merger with Egypt. He expected Nasser to refuse such a prospect, leaving Baqdash a leading exponent of Arab Nationalism but free to continue his activities as Communist leader. On Feb. 1, 1958, however, union with Egypt was proclaimed; three days later Baqdash fled to eastern Europe, staying in Moscow from 1958 to 1966. He returned to Syria in April 1966, where he again became leader of the Syrian Communist Party.

Bāqī (Turkish poet): *see* Bâkî.

Baqqārah, also spelled BAGGARA (Arabic: Cattlemen), nomad Arabs who have been forced by circumstance to live in a part of Africa that will support the cow but not the camel—south of latitude 13° and north of latitude 10° from Lake Chad eastward to the Nile. Probably they are the descendants of Arabs who migrated west out of Egypt in the Middle Ages, turned south from Tunisia to Chad, and finally moved back eastward in the 18th or 19th century to settle below the now Islāmized sultanates of Kordofan, Dar Fur, and Wadai.

Herding cattle is the Baqqārah livelihood, requiring them to migrate south to the river lands in the dry season and north to the grasslands during the rains. During these seasonal treks, crops such as sorghum and millet as well as indigenous Sudanic crops are grown.

Association with local peoples such as the Fulani have given the Baqqārah a distinct dialect of Arabic.

Ba'qūbah, capital, Diyālā *muḥāfaẓah* (governorate), eastern Iraq. Located on the Nahr Diyālā (Diyālā River) and on a road and a rail line between Baghdad and Iran, it is a regional trade centre for agricultural produce and livestock. The name comes from the Aramaic *Bāya 'qūbā,* meaning "Jacob's house." The town is located on the site of a settlement dating back to pre-Islāmic times. Under the 'Abbāsid caliphate, it was a prosperous town known for its date and fruit orchards, and the surrounding country was populous and fertile with many villages. It was an important stop on the Baghdad–Khorasan road, part of the silk and spice route. Many Assyrian Christian refugees fled there during World War I. Pop. (1970 est.) 39,186.

Bar, port in Montenegro, Yugoslavia, on the Adriatic Sea at the base of 5,226-ft (1,593-m) Mt. Rumija. It comprises Stari (Old) Bar and Novi (New) Bar. Stari Bar was first mentioned in the 9th century, when it came under the control of the Byzantine Empire; it was frequently autonomous from the 11th to the 15th century. During the 14th century its archbishop acquired the title primate of Serbia. It was ruled from Venice (1443–1571), then by the Turks (1571–1878). Partly ruined in 1878 when the Montenegrins wrested it from the Turks, it was abandoned after gunpowder explosions in 1881 and 1912. The new town, the port and recreation centre, is connected with Belgrade by rail, providing a maritime outlet for landlocked Serbia. The port was further enlarged in the late 1970s to facilitate increased oil imports and exports. A ferry service runs to Bari, Italy. To the southeast is the port of Ulcinj, a tourist and health resort, while inland is Lake Scutari, largest lake in the Balkans. Pop. (1981 prelim.) mun., 32,535.

BAR (U.S. rifle): *see* Browning automatic rifle.

Bar, Confederation of, Polish BARSKA KONFEDERACJA (1768–72), league of Polish nobles and gentry that was formed to defend the privileges of the Roman Catholic Church and the independence of Poland from Russian encroachment; its activities precipitated a civil war, foreign intervention, and the First Partition of Poland.

After Russia had compelled the Polish Sejm (legislature) to abandon projects for internal reform, grant full political rights to religious dissenters (*i.e.,* members of the Protestant and Orthodox faiths), and make Poland a Russian protectorate (February 1768), Adam Krasiński, the bishop of Kamieniec, Józef Pułaski, and Michał Krasiński organized a confederation at the little fortress of Bar in Podolia (Feb. 29, 1768) to oppose both the Polish king Stanisław II August Poniatowski and Russia.

Forced to abandon Bar by the King's army, the confederates were generally checked in Poland's southeastern provinces (summer 1768) by Russian troops, who had been occupying Warsaw during the Sejm's session. Nevertheless, uprisings occurred in support of the confederation in all of the country's major cities; and under the military leadership of Ignacy Malczewski, Prince Karol Radziwiłł, and Kazimierz Pułaski, the confederates spread their rebellion throughout the country, gained the support of the Turks (who declared war on Russia on Oct. 8, 1768) and of the French (who sent advisers and some troops to the confederates), proclaimed the dethronement of Stanisław (Oct. 22, 1770), and refused to surrender to the Russians, whose continued military victories culminated in Gen. Aleksandr Vasilyevich Suvorov's triumph over the confederate army near Lanckorona (May 1771).

Although the Confederation of Bar stubbornly pursued its struggle until its last contingent was defeated at Częstochowa (Aug. 18, 1772), it failed to overthrow Stanisław or to end Russian domination over Polish affairs. Furthermore, its campaigns so devastated the country and weakened the government that Poland was defenseless when Prussia, and eventually Austria, agreed (Feb. 17 and Aug. 5, 1772) to partition Poland, which was compelled to cede almost one-third of its territory to the three partitioning powers.

Bar, François de (b. 1538, Seizencourt, near Saint-Quentin, Fr.—d. March 25, 1606, Abbey of Anchin, near Pecquencourt), historiographer and scholar of ecclesiastical law, whose church histories are considered the most detailed and complete of his time. Named prior of the Benedictine abbey of Anchin in 1576, Bar served during a time of religious and political power struggles. His main contribution, however, was the compilation of extensive documents on church history and law from the valuable library of the abbey. In addition to his historical and legal works, he cataloged and annotated many of the manuscripts in the Anchin library and wrote treatises on geography, cosmography, and church practices.

bar association, also called LEGAL ASSOCIATION, group of attorneys, local, national, or international, organized primarily to deal with issues affecting the legal profession. In general, bar associations are concerned with furthering the best interests of lawyers. This may mean the advocacy of reforms in the legal system, the sponsoring of research projects, or the actual regulation of professional standards.

Bar associations sometimes administer examinations requisite for admission to practice and supervise necessary apprenticeship programs. Membership requirements vary from country to country. In the United States, for example, law school graduates are admitted to a state bar association immediately after they pass a series of examinations, which are usually administered by examiners appointed by state courts; in Austria, on the other hand, it is necessary for a lawyer to have seven years' legal experience in order to be a member. Membership in the bar associations of many countries is often compulsory. In Japan, Nigeria, Israel, and France, and in more than half the states of the United States, for example, membership is required of all lawyers. On the other hand, in England, Norway, and Sweden, membership in such bar associations is voluntary.

Many bar associations have disciplinary powers over their members, but actual procedures for disbarment (*q.v.*), relieving an attorney of his license to practice, are usually carried on in court. In France, for example, the major responsibility for disciplining attorneys belongs to the Cour de Cassation.

There are many international associations of lawyers, the most prominent being the International Bar Association, a voluntary group of national bar associations and some individual lawyers, which is dedicated, among other things, to achieving uniformity in certain areas of law.

Bar Cochba: *see* Bar Kokhba.

Bar form, in music, the structural pattern *aab* as used by the medieval German minnesingers and meistersingers, poet-composers of secular monophonic (*i.e.,* having a single line of melody) songs. The modern term *Bar* form derives from a medieval verse form, the *Bar,* consisting of three stanzas, each having the form *aab.* The musical term thus refers to the melody of a single stanza, the *a* sections (called *Stollen*) having the same melody, and the *b* section (*Abgesang*) having a different melody.

The *Bar* form had important precedents in some Gregorian chants, in the canso of the Provençal-speaking troubadours, and in the ballade of the trouvères (their French-speaking counterparts). It was eagerly embraced by the meistersingers, bourgeois successors to the courtly minnesingers, and even influenced the structure of 15th- and early 16th-century German part-songs. In the 19th century Richard Wagner revived the *Bar* form in his neo-medieval music dramas (*e.g., Tannhäuser* and *Die Meistersinger*), causing Alfred Lorentz in the early part of the 20th century to speculate that it concealed the "secret" of Wagner's monumental structures at virtually every level.

Bar Harbor, coastal town, Hancock County, southern Maine, U.S., on Mount Desert Island, at the foot of Cadillac Mountain (1,532 ft [467 m]) facing Frenchman Bay, 46 mi (74 km) southeast of Bangor. Settled in 1763, it was incorporated in 1796 as Eden; the present name (for Bar Island in the main harbour) was adopted in 1918. Most of the town was destroyed by fire in 1947. Rebuilt Bar Harbor is the centre of a popular resort area verging on Acadia National Park (*q.v.*) and is a port of entry. It is linked to the mainland by bridge and is the terminus for the ferry service to and from Yarmouth, Nova Scotia. The College of the Atlantic opened there in 1969. The Jackson Laboratory for biological research is nearby. Pop. (1980) 4,124.

Bar Hebraeus, Arabic IBN AL-'IBRĪ (Son of the Hebrew), or ABŪ AL-FARAJ, Latin name GREGORIUS (b. 1226, Melitene, Armenia—d. July 30, 1286, Marāgheh, Iran), medieval Syrian scholar noted for his encyclopaedic learning in science and philosophy and for his enrichment of Syriac literature by the introduction of Arabic culture.

Motivated toward scholarly pursuits by his father, a Jewish convert to Christianity, Bar Hebraeus emigrated to Antioch (now Antakya, Tur.) and at the age of 17 became a hermit. Made a bishop at 20 and an archbishop at 26, he was by 1264 assistant patriarch (chief prelate) of the Eastern Jacobite Church, a schismatic group named after its founder, Jacob Baradaeus, who led its separation from the Orthodox Church in the 6th century in a dispute over the nature of the Person of Christ. Also called Monophysites (of one nature), the group maintained that Jesus' single divine nature virtually excluded his humanity, in contradistinction to the theory of the Antiochian school that Christ's humanity functioned integrally relative to his divine kinship (Nestorianism).

Travel to libraries throughout Syria and Armenia expanded Bar Hebraeus' erudition; he compiled collections of classical texts in philosophy and theology, ranging from astronomy and the nature of the universe to the existence of God, angels, and demons. His chief work was an encyclopaedia of philosophy, *Ḥē'wath ḥekkmthā* ("The Butter of Wisdom"), in which he commented on every branch of human knowledge in the Aristotelian tradition. Bar Hebraeus divided philosophy into two categories: theoretical (logic, natural science, metaphysics, and theology) and practical (ethics, economics, and politics). He wrote extensively, moreover, on spiritual counselling and biblical interpretation, collecting linguistic commentaries from Greek and Syrian churchmen.

Bar Hebraeus' scholarship and political tact significantly affected cultural exchange between the Christian and Muslim worlds. In the midst of 13th-century Muslim rule, he followed a conciliatory policy, seeking tolerance from the Arabs, whom he served as physician, and promoting rapport among disputing Christian groups. Undaunted by initial Arab harshness when he was imprisoned and his cathedral city sacked by Mongols, he later aided in Muslim–Christian relations by translating Arabic literature, law, and philosophy and rendering in Syriac and Arabic his own edition of *The Chronicle,* a record of the Middle East's secular and religious history from the time of creation.

bar Hiyya Hanasi, Abraham, also called ABRAHAM BAR HIYYA SAVASORDA: *see* Abraham bar Hiyya Savasorda.

Bar Kokhba, original name SIMEON BAR KOSBA, Kosba also spelled KOSEBA, or KOCHBA, also called BAR KOZIBA (d. AD 135), Jewish leader who led a bitter but unsuccessful revolt against Roman dominion in Palestine.

During his tour of the Eastern Empire in 131, Hadrian, the Roman emperor, decided upon a policy of Hellenization to integrate the Jews into the empire. Circumcision was proscribed, a Roman colony was founded in Jerusalem, and a temple to Jupiter Capitolinus was erected over the ruins of the Jewish Temple.

Enraged by these measures, the Jews rose in revolt the following year; and Simeon bar Kosba, an able and energetic leader, emerged as its head. According to later accounts, the revolt apparently enjoyed initial success, taking the form of guerrilla warfare. Rabbi Akiba ben Joseph, a highly esteemed teacher of the period, enthusiastically supported the rebels and conferred upon their leader the name Bar Kokhba (Son of the Star), a messianic allusion. Akiba also hailed him as the Messiah, and Bar Kokhba took the title nasi (prince) and struck his own coins.

Hadrian, exasperated by the protracted and dangerous war, sent heavy reinforcements and finally, in 134, summoned Gaius Julius Severus, governor of Britain. This general, utilizing small-unit tactics, gradually wore down the rebels and constricted their area of operation. In August 135 Bar Kokhba himself was killed at Bethar, his stronghold southwest of Jerusalem. The remnants of his army made a stand near the Dead Sea; but a Roman manhunt crushed the rebellion, and harsh policy drove the Jews from Palestine. With the failure of the revolt, Bar Kokhba was referred to by some as Bar Koziba, a pun referring to the Hebrew word for liar.

In 1960 letters of Bar Kokhba were found in a cave near the Dead Sea. They revealed his real name and suggest that he was a hard, tough commander.

Bar-le-Duc, capital of the Meuse *département,* Lorraine region, northeastern France, extending out along the narrow valley of the Ornain River, west of Nancy. To the northeast is the Canal de la Marne au Rhin, on the southwest the Canal des Usines. The valley is enclosed by wooded and vine-clad hills. From the 10th century Bar was the seat of a countship, later duchy. The remains of the château of the counts and dukes of Bar are in the upper town, along with the 15th–16th-century church of Saint-Etienne and medieval houses. The church of Notre-Dame (15th century) and the buildings housing municipal offices are in the lower town. In 1960 an industrial zone was set up to the east of the town. There is now some heavy industry and textile manufacture, although not enough to sustain any major growth of population. Pop. (1982) 18,406.

Bar Mitzvah, also spelled BAR MITZVA, or MITZWA (Hebrew: Son of the Commandment), plural BAR MITZVAHS, BAR MITZVOT, or BAR MITZWOT, widely observed Jewish religious celebration marking the religious adulthood of a boy on his 13th birthday. The boy, now deemed personally responsible for fulfilling all the commandments, may henceforth don phylacteries (religious symbols worn on the forehead and left arm) during the weekday-morning prayers and may be counted an adult whenever 10 male adults are needed to form a quorum (*minyan*) for public prayers.

The public act of acknowledging religious majority is being called up (*see* aliyah) during the religious service to read from the Torah. This event may take place on any occasion following the 13th birthday at which the Torah is read but generally occurs on the sabbath. The liturgy of the day thus permits the boy to read the weekly text from the prophets, called Haftarah. This is sometimes followed by a hortatory discourse, which in Orthodox groups becomes part of the family social dinner that takes place among all groups after the religious ceremony. Though records of the 2nd century mention 13 as the age of religious manhood, most elements of the Bar Mitzvah celebration did not appear until the Middle Ages.

Reform Judaism replaced Bar Mitzvah, after 1810, with the confirmation of boys and girls together, generally on the feast of Shavuot. In the 20th century, however, many Reform congregations restored Bar Mitzvah, delaying confirmation until the age of 15 or 16. Numerous Conservative and Reform congregations have instituted a separate ceremony to mark the adulthood of girls, called Bat Mitzvah.

Bar-Salibi, Jacob, also called DIONYSIUS BAR-SALIBI (d. Nov. 2, 1171), the great spokesman of the Jacobite (Monophysite) Church in the 12th century.

A native of Melitene (Malatya), Bar-Salibi was made bishop of Marash in 1154 and, a year later, of Mabbog as well. In 1166 he was transferred to the metropolitan see of Amid (Diyarbakır), where he remained until his death. His works include poems, prayers, homilies, liturgies, a commentary on the six *Centuries* of Evagrius with the text translated into Syriac, a treatise against heresies, expositions of the Syrian Eucharistic service and doctrine, and commentaries on the Old and New testaments. The Old Testament commentary, a compilation rather than an original composition, gives a material or literal exposition and a spiritual or mystical exposition. The New Testament commentary, less developed except on the Gospels, also deals with the text on two levels.

bar Sauma, Rabban (b. *c.* 1220, Chung-tu, China—d. January 1294, Baghdad), Nestorian Christian ecclesiastic whose important but little-known travels in western Europe as an envoy of the Mongols provide a counterpart to those of his contemporary, the Venetian Marco Polo, in Asia.

Born into a wealthy Christian family living in Chung-tu (now Peking) and descended from the nomadic Uighurs of Turkistan, bar Sauma became a monk at the age of 23. After living for seven years in a Nestorian monastery in Chung-tu, he went into the mountains outside the city for meditation and prayer, gaining fame as an ascetic and teacher of great wisdom. With his disciple Marcus he attempted a pilgrimage to Jerusalem, passing through Kansu and Khotan in western China, Khorāsān in Persia, and Azerbaijan before reaching Baghdad, the residence of the Catholicus, or head, of the Nestorian Church. Unable to reach Jerusalem because of local fighting, he stayed some time in Nestorian monasteries in Armenia before being called back to Baghdad by the Catholicus to head a mission to Abagha, the Mongol Il-khan ("regional khan") of Persia. Later he was appointed visitor general of the Nestorian congregations of the East, a post similar to that of archdeacon.

In 1287 bar Sauma was sent on a mission to the Christian monarchs of western Europe by Abagha's son Arghūn, a religious eclectic and Christian sympathizer who hoped to persuade the Christian kings to join him in expelling the Muslims from the Holy Land. Travelling to Constantinople, bar Sauma was received hospitably by the emperor Andronicus II Palaeologus, but when he reached Rome he learned that Pope Honorius IV had just died. He was interviewed by the Sacred College of Cardinals, who, less interested in his mission than in his theological tenets, asked him to recite the Nestorian creed. Reluctant to do so, as Nestorianism was considered a heresy in the West, he left Rome and travelled to Paris, where he stayed for a month at the court of King Philip IV, and to Bordeaux, where he met Edward I of England. Neither monarch was willing to commit himself to an alliance with Arghūn.

Leaving France, bar Sauma passed back through Rome and met the newly elected pope, Nicholas IV, before returning to Persia. Later he was appointed chaplain to the Il-khan's court and still later retired to Marāgheh in Azerbaijan to found a church. A perceptive traveller, he kept a diary in Persian that gives an unusual outsider's view of medieval Europe. An English translation is included in Sir Wallis Budge's *Monks of Kublai Khân.*

Bara, also called IBARA, a Malagasy people living in south central Madagascar. Bara lands are bounded by those of coastal people around the southern tip of Madagascar, while Betsileo lie to the north. The Bara speak a dialect of Malagasy, the West Indonesian language common to all Malagasy peoples.

Traditionally a bellicose people, the Bara lived in a great many independent groups based on lineage identity. Five main groupings exist, but these have never been unified. The Bara were never conquered by or assimilated into the central Merina kingdom, and when the French occupied Madagascar in 1895, they had difficulty uniting the Bara into administrative entities.

Chiefs of Bara clans are of Indian ancestry and were thus related to the nobles of the Sakalava and Betsileo. Like most Malagasy, Bara were traditionally socially stratified into four tiers, but the French dissolved the old "feudal" organization, and little of it exists in modern Madagascar.

The Bara grow rice as a staple crop, and cassava, yams, and bananas are also important. Cattle are kept; during the past they were stolen from neighbouring people during raids. Bara villages are densely concentrated and are separated from other settled areas by forest.

Bara, Theda, original name THEODOSIA GOODMAN (b. July 20, 1890, Cincinnati, Ohio, U.S.—d. April 7, 1955, Los Angeles), early silent-film star who was the first screen vamp who lured men to destruction. Her films set the vogue for sophisticated sexual themes in motion pictures and made her an international symbol of daring new freedom.

A brief stage career under the name Theodosia de Coppet preceded her going to Hollywood as a film extra. *A Fool There Was* (1915), her first important picture, was released with an intense publicity campaign that made her an overnight success. She was billed as the daughter of an Eastern potentate, her name an anagram for "Arab Death."

Theda Bara made more than 40 pictures within three years, mostly costume spectacles in which she played the irresistible, heartless woman who lived only for sensual pleasure. They include *Romeo and Juliet* (1916), *Under Two Flags* (1916), *Camille* (1917), *DuBarry* (1917), *Cleopatra* (1917), *Salome* (1918), and

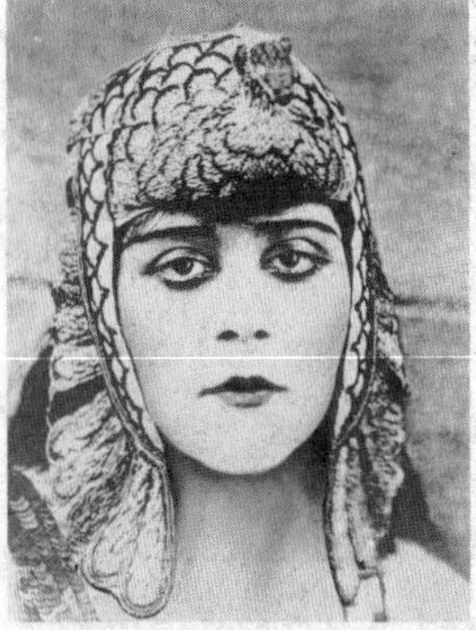

Theda Bara in the film *Cleopatra*

By courtesy of the Twentieth Century-Fox Film Corp., © 1917 William Fox, © renewed 1944 Twentieth Century-Fox Film Corporation. All rights reserved

Kathleen Mavourneen (1919). By the end of World War I, her popularity had declined. After an unsuccessful appearance on Broadway and an attempted Hollywood comeback, she retired from the screen in the late 1920s.

Bāra Banki, town, administrative headquarters of Bāra Banki district, Uttar Pradesh state, northern India, northeast of Lucknow and including the larger town of Nawābganj. Nawābganj is an agricultural market and cotton-weaving centre. The two towns are on a main road between Lucknow and Faizābād and on two railways.

Bāra Banki district, 1,707 sq mi (4,422 sq km) in area, comprises a stretch of alluvial plain bounded on the north by the Ghāghara River. Dotted with *jhīl*s, or marshy lakes, it is drained by the Gomati River. Some areas become waterlogged after heavy rainfall. Rice, gram (chick-pea), and wheat are the most important crops. Dewa houses the mausoleum of the Muslim saint Ḥājī Ḥāfiz Sayyid Shāh Wārris ʿAlī and is a place of pilgrimage. Annual fairs are held at Dewa and Bānsda. Pop. (1981) town, 10,322; metropolitan area, 62,216; district, 1,992,074.

Baraboo, city, seat (1840) of Sauk County, south central Wisconsin, U.S., 40 mi (64 km) northwest of Madison. It originated in the early 19th century as a trading post established by the French trapper Jean Baribault, who lived along the river that was named (somewhat phonetically) for him. Incorporated in 1882, the community developed as a distribution centre for dairy products. Baraboo is best known, however, as the original home of the five Ringling (Rüngeling) brothers (Charles, Albert, Alfred, Otto, and John) and the birthplace in 1883 of the Ringling Circus, which wintered there until 1918. The city's Circus World Museum, owned by the State Historical Society and occupying 33 ac (13 ha), displays circus wagons, an animated miniature circus, and other relics; in the summer it holds circus parades. Baraboo was also the home of the smaller Gollmar Brothers and the Burlington and Seils Sterling circuses. The city has acquired some manufacturing (housewares, industrial coils and transformers, and plastics), and a number of old circus buildings are now occupied by commercial establishments. A University of Wisconsin centre opened in 1968. Devil's Lake State Park with historic Indian mounds and the Ice Age National Scientific Reserve is 3 mi south. Pop. (1980) 8,081.

Baracaldo, industrial municipality, northern Biscay (Vizcaya) province, in the autonomous Basque Country, northeastern Spain, on the south bank of the Río Nervión. Baracaldo consists of the Bilbao suburbs of El Regato, San Vicente de Baracaldo, Iráuregui, and Alonsótegui. It is the terminus of a mining railway; the locality's primary economic activities include iron refining and the manufacture of steel tubing, machinery, and shipbuilding equipment. With Sestao (northeast), Baracaldo is the leading iron and steel centre of Spain. Pop. (1981) 117,422.

Baradā, Greek CHRYSORRHOAS, river of western Syria, rising in the Anti-Lebanon Mountains and flowing southward for 52 mi (84 km) through Damascus to the marshes of Buḥayrat (Lake) al-ʿUtaybah. The Baradā sets out peacefully on its course only to become within 20 mi a raging torrent, its volume almost doubled by the spring ʿAyn Fījah (this spring has recently been tapped to bring drinking water to Damascus). Without human intervention, the Baradā would have cut a deep bed through the Damascus Depression, wasting most of its water. Throughout history man has cut various channels at different levels parallel to the main branch of the river to divert its flow. The channels, of Nabataean, Aramaean, and especially Roman origin, fan out as they reach the edge of Damascus, irrigating an area of more than 145 sq mi (375 sq km). This system, kept in repair over time, has created the Ghūṭah Oasis, an artificial oasis of extreme fertility in what would otherwise have been an arid place.

barae (Shintō rite): *see* harai.

Baragwanathia, a genus of fossil plants from the Early Devonian Period (more than 345,000,000 years ago) of Australia, of interest as being perhaps the earliest club moss class (or subdivision) Lycopsida. The plants exceeded the size of present-day lycopsids, some being up to 28 centimetres (11 inches) long.

Barāhanagar (India): *see* Baranagar.

Barahona, province, southwestern Dominican Republic, on the Caribbean Sea. Established in 1888 as a maritime district and reduced to create Bahoruco province in 1943, the territory now comprises 976 sq mi (2,528 sq km). The high Sierra de Bahoruco separates a broad peninsula jutting into the Caribbean from a wide coastal lowland area to the north. The main crops are sugarcane in the alluvial lowland, irrigated by the Yaque del Sur River, and coffee in the mountains. Barahona also has rock salt, gypsum, granite, marble, and mahogany and other fine hardwoods. Bauxite is mined on the southern slopes of the Sierra de Bahoruco. Numerous secondary highways converge upon the port city of Barahona (*q.v.*), also the provincial capital. Pop. (1981) 137,160.

Barahona, in full SANTA CRUZ DE BARAHONA, city, capital of Barahona province, southwestern Dominican Republic, on Bahía de Neiba, off the Caribbean Sea, at the northeastern foot of the Sierra de Bahoruco. The gateway to the Dominican Republic's lake district, Barahona is an important port and fishing centre. Industrial and commercial activity centres on sugar; sugarcane, molasses, coffee, hardwoods, and fruits are the principal exports. Salt beds are located in the area. The city is accessible by air and secondary highway. Pop. (1981) 49,334.

Barahona de Soto, Luis (b. 1548?, Lucena, Spain—d. 1595), poet who is remembered for his *Primera parte de la Angélica* (1586; "The First Part of the Angelica"), more commonly known as *Las lágrimas de Angelica* ("The Tears of Angelica"), a continuation of the Angélica and Medoro episode in Ariosto's *Orlando furioso.*

After completing his education in Antequera and service as a soldier, Barahona began practicing medicine in the principal towns of Andalusia, including Madrid, where he met some of the leading literary figures of his day, including the lyric poet Fernando de Herrera and the novelist Miguel de Cervantes. The fame that the *Angélica* received was in part attributable to his friendship with Cervantes, who lavishly praised it in his *Don Quixote.*

barai (Shintō rite): *see* harai.

Baraita, also spelled BARAITHA (Hebrew: Outside Teaching, or Exclusion), plural BARAITOT, BARAITOTH, OR BARAITHOTH, ancient oral traditions of Jewish religious law that were not included in the Mishna (the first authoritative codification of such laws). The Baraitot that are found dispersed singly throughout the Palestinian and Babylonian Talmuds are often recognizable by such introductory words as "it was taught" or "the rabbi taught." Other Baraitot are found in independent collections, the best known of which is called Tosefta; in form and content it parallels the Mishna. Halakhic Midrashim (interpretations and commentaries on Oral Law) are another source of Baraitot. Since the Mishna was selective and concisely phrased, Baraitot preserved oral traditions that might otherwise have been lost. *See also* Halakha; Tosefta.

Barāk River (India): *see* Surma River.

Baraka, Imamu Amiri, original name (until 1968) (EVERETT) LEROI JONES (b. Oct. 7, 1934, Newark, N.J., U.S.), playwright, poet, novelist, and essayist who writes of the experiences and anger of black Americans with an affirmation of black life. He was also a leading black nationalist.

A graduate of Howard University (1953), Baraka published his first major collection of poetry, *Preface to a Twenty Volume Suicide Note* (1961), followed by *The Dead Lecturer* (1964) and *Black Magic* (1969). In *Blues People: Negro Music in White America* (1963) he wrote of black music in the context of American social history.

In 1964 Baraka's play *Dutchman,* about interracial hostility, appeared off-Broadway and won critical acclaim. The following year *The Slave* and *The Toilet* were also produced off-Broadway. He published an autobiographical novel, *The System of Dante's Hell* (1965); a collection of short stories, *Tales* (1967); and a collection of essays, *Home: Social Essays* (1966). He has also written numerous other plays.

Baraka founded the Black Arts Repertory Theatre in Harlem in 1965; in 1966 he moved this workshop to Spirit House in Newark, where it serves as a community centre. In 1968 he founded the Black Community Development and Defense Organization, a Muslim group committed to affirming black culture and to gaining political power for blacks. In the 1970s he turned to Marxism-Leninism. During his career Baraka was frequently arrested and jailed under circumstances indicating political motivations on the part of the authorities.

Barakah (Mongol ruler): *see* Berke.

Bārakzay DYNASTY, ruling family in Afghanistan in the 19th and 20th centuries. The Bārakzay brothers seized control of Afghanistan and in 1826 divided the region between them. Dōst Moḥammad Khān gained preeminence and founded the dynasty in *c.* 1837. Thereafter his descendants ruled in direct succession until 1929, when the reigning monarch abdicated and his cousin Moḥammad Nāder Khān was elected king.

Nāder Khān, on his assassination in 1933, was succeeded by his son Zahir Shah, who reigned until July 17, 1973, when he was deposed and a republic was proclaimed. The Bārakzay rulers, in chronological order, were Dōst Moḥammad Khān, Shīr ʿAlī Khān, Yaʿqūb Khān, ʿAbdor Raḥmān Khān, Ḥabībollāh Khān, ʿAmānollāh Khān, Nāder Khān, and Moḥammad Zahir Shah.

Baram, Batang, river in northern Sarawak state, East Malaysia, in northwestern Borneo. Rising in the Pegunungan Iran (Iran Mountains), it flows 250 mi (400 km) west and northwest, mostly through primary rain forest to the South China Sea at Tanjung Baram (Baram Point). Above the lowest 100 mi, gorges and rapids make upstream navigation difficult. The Baram is Sarawak's second longest river, its tributaries including the Bakong, Apoh, Palutan, and Patah.

Bāramūlla, town, administrative headquarters of Bāramūlla district, in the Indian-held sector of Jammu and Kashmir state, in the northern part of the Indian subcontinent.

Bāramūlla district occupies an area of 2,880 sq mi (7,458 sq km) and is bordered by the Pīr Panjāl Range of the Himalayas (west) and the Vale of Kashmir (east). Bāramūlla is drained by the Jhelum River and is essentially agricultural (rice, wheat, and barley). In addition to Bāramūlla, main towns include Sopur and Pattan. Pop. (1981) town, 33,945; district, 670,142.

Baranagar, also spelled BARĀHANAGAR, town, Twenty-four Parganas district, West Bengal state, northeastern India, just east of the Hooghly River, part of the Calcutta urban agglomeration. Originally a Portuguese settlement, it became the seat of a Dutch factory (trading station) and an important river anchorage for Dutch shipping; in 1795 it was ceded to the British. Constituted as the municipality of North Suburban in 1869, the town was renamed Baranagar in 1889. In 1899 it was divided, the northern half becoming Kāmārhāti (*q.v.*) municipality. Connected by road and rail with Calcutta, it is a major industrial centre engaged in jute and cotton milling, cotton ginning and baling, and the manufacture of chemicals, castor oil, matches, and agricultural and industrial machinery. Pop. (1981) 170,343.

Baranauskas, Antanas (b. Jan. 17, 1835, Anykščiai, Russian Lithuania—d. Nov. 26, 1902, Seinai), Roman Catholic bishop and poet who wrote one of the greatest works in Lithuanian literature, *Anykščių šilelis* (1858–59; *The Forest of Anykščiai,* 1956). The 342-line poem, written in East High Lithuanian dialect, describes the former beauty of a pine grove near his village and its despoliation under the Russians ("Hills with tree-stumps, bare slopes! Who would believe in your former beauty?"); it depicted in symbolic form the plight of Lithuania under the tsarist regime.

Baranauskas' interests included dialectology and mathematics, though his work in those disciplines was seriously compromised by his lack of training. Nevertheless, he provided the most detailed classification of Lithuanian dialects up to his time.

barangay, type of early Filipino settlement; the word is derived from *balangay,* the name for the sailboats that originally brought settlers of Malay stock to the Philippines from Borneo. Each boat carried a large family group, and the master of the boat retained power as leader, or *datu,* of the village established by his family.

Barangay villages sometimes grew to include 30 to 100 families, but the *barangay*s remained isolated from one another. Except on Mindanao, the part of the Philippines where Islām first got a foothold, no larger political grouping emerged. This fact greatly facilitated Spanish conquest of the Philippines in the 16th century, since resistance remained uncoordinated and sporadic. The Spaniards retained the *barangay* as their basic unit of local administration in the islands.

Baranī, Ẓiyā'-ud-Dīn, Baranī also spelled BARNI (b. 1285, India—d. after 1357), the first known Muslim to write a history of India; he resided for 17 years at Delhi as *nadīm* (boon companion) of Sultan Muḥammad ibn Tughluq.

Using mainly hearsay evidence and his personal experiences at court, Baranī in 1357 wrote the *Tārīkh-e Fīrūz Shāhī* ("History of Fīrūz Shāh"), a didactic work setting down the duties of the Indian sultan toward Islām. In his *Fatawā-ye jahāndārī* ("Rulings on Temporal Government"), influenced by Ṣūfī mysticism, he expounded a religious philosophy of history that viewed the events in the lives of great men as manifestations of Divine Providence. According to Baranī, the Delhi sultans from Ghiyāṣ-ud-Dīn Balban (reigned 1266–87) to Fīrūz Shāh Tughluq (reigned from 1351) who had followed his guidelines for the good Islāmic ruler had prospered, while those who had deviated from those precepts had failed.

Baranovichi, also spelled BARANOVIČI, Brest *oblast* (administrative region), Belorussian Soviet Socialist Republic, on the southern edge of the Novogrudok Hills. It developed from a small village in the late 19th century into a major railway junction, with lines to Moscow, Warsaw, and other eastern European centres. It has cotton, food-processing, and machine construction industries. Pop. (1983 est.) 144,000.

Barante, Amable-Guillaume-Prosper Brugière, baron de (b. June 10, 1782, Riom, Fr.—d. Nov. 21, 1866, Le Dorat), French statesman, historian, political writer, a liberal representative under the Bourbon restoration and a leading member of the narrative school of Romanticist historians who portrayed historical episodes with high literary style and in the vivid and intimate manner of a reportage of current events.

Educated at the École Polytechnique of Paris, Barante received his first civil service appointment in 1802. Named auditor to the council of state (1806), he went on several political missions to Germany, Poland, and Spain, later becoming subprefect of Bressuire (1807) and prefect of Vendée (1809). During the Hundred Days (1815), Barante took up the prefecture of Loire-Inférieure, and, with the second restoration of the Bourbons, he was made councillor of state and secretary general of the ministry of the interior. Created a peer in 1819, he used this position to promote liberal reforms but was subsequently removed by the Duc de Richelieu.

After the revolution of 1830, which brought Louis-Philippe to power, Barante was named ambassador at Turin (1830) and later ambassador at St. Petersburg (1835). Throughout Louis-Philippe's reign he remained a supporter of the government, withdrawing from political affairs, however, after the fall of the monarchy (1848).

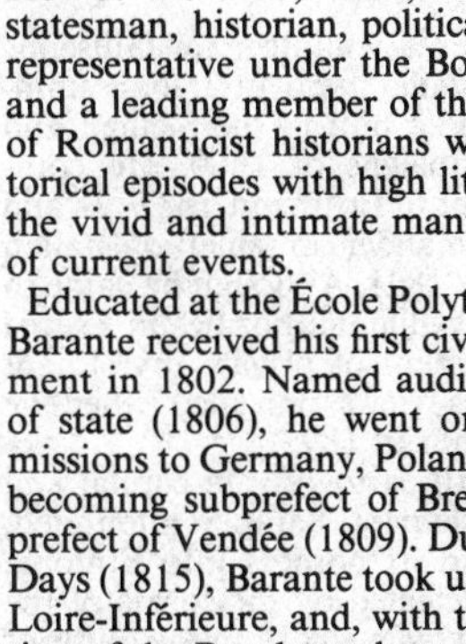

Barante, detail of a portrait by C. Fuhr
H. Roger-Viollet

Barante's most important historical work, *Histoire des ducs de Bourgogne* (1824–28; "History of the Dukes of Burgundy"), won him immediate admission to the Académie Française. Its moving narrative quality, purity of style, and brilliant use of local colour were highly praised; it exhibits, however, a lack of critical discernment and scientific scholarship. His other historical studies include *Histoire de la Convention Nationale,* 6 vol. (1851–53; "History of the National Convention"), and *Histoire du Directoire de la République française* (1855; "History of the Directory of the French Republic"). He also wrote biographies of Joan of Arc and other French historical figures, as well as a study of 18th-century French literature; he is furthermore known as a translator of Shakespeare and Schiller. Barante's political writings dealt with contemporary views on aristocracy and social organization.

A list of the abbreviations used in the MICROPAEDIA *will be found at the end of this volume*

Bárány, Robert (b. April 22, 1876, Vienna—d. April 8, 1936, Uppsala, Swed.), otologist who won the 1914 Nobel Prize for Physiology or Medicine for his work on the physiology and pathology of the vestibular (balancing) apparatus of the inner ear. His name is associated with tests for detecting vestibular disease and for examining activities of the cerebellum and their relation to disturbances of equilibrium.

Bárány was graduated in medicine in 1900. After study at German clinics he became assistant at the ear clinic of the University of Vienna and, in 1909, a lecturer on otological medicine. From 1917 until his death he taught at Uppsala University, where he was head of the ear, nose, and throat clinic.

Bárány, *c.* 1930
Archiv fur Kunst und Geschichte, West Berlin

Baranya, *megye* (county), southern Hungary, bounded to the south by the Drava River, and by the Mecsek Mountains in its northwestern area. Its area of 1,732 sq mi (4,487 sq km) is hilly, forested terrain. With adjacent Somogy *megye,* it is the least densely populated part of Hungary. The climate is semi-Mediterranean, and peaches, plums, sour cherries, grains, and vegetables are grown. Pigs and poultry are raised. Wines from the Villánykövesd district are well known. The Mecsek Mountains are quarried for building stone, limestone, and marls for industrial use. Although Pécs (*q.v.*) is the *megye* seat, it is a county-level city, administratively independent of Baranya. Komló, 8 mi (13 km) north of Pécs, is a planned coal-mining town with a full range of social services; its collieries have considerably expanded since World War II. Szigetvár is the site of a 16th-century fortress. In 1566 the Hungarian defenders of the fort blew themselves and the fort up rather than surrender to the Turks. At Siklós is a *c.* 13th-century castle with a fine Gothic and Renaissance interior. Pop. (1983 est.) 433,000.

Baranya Mountains (Hungary): *see* Mecsek Mountains.

Barāri Ghāt, Battle of (Jan. 9, 1760), in Indian history, one of a series of Afghan victories over the Marāthās in their war to gain control of the decaying Mughal Empire, which gave the British time in which to consolidate their power in Bengal. At the Barāri Ghāt (Ferry Station) of the Jumna (now Yamuna) River, 10 miles (16 kilometres) north of Delhi, the Marāthā chief Dattāji Sindhia, retreating from the Punjab before the Afghan army of Aḥmad Shāh Durrānī, was surprised by Afghan troops who, concealed by high reeds, crossed the river. Dattāji was killed and his army scattered. His defeat opened the way to the Afghan occupation of Delhi.

Bārāsat, town, Twenty-four Parganas district, West Bengal state, northeastern India. Connected by road and rail with Calcutta and Howrah, it is an important district trade centre for rice, legumes, sugarcane, potatoes, and coconuts; cotton weaving is the major industry. An annual fair held in honour of a Muslim saint is attended by both Muslims and Hindus. Bārāsat was constituted a municipality in 1869. Pop. (1981) 69,586.

barasingha, also called SWAMP DEER (*Cervus duvauceli*), graceful deer, family Cervidae (order Artiodactyla), found in open forests and

Barasingha, or swamp deer (*Cervus duvauceli*)
E. Hanumantha Rao—Photo Researchers

grasslands of India and Nepal. The barasingha stands about 1.1 metres (45 inches) at the shoulder. In summer, its coat is reddish or yellowish brown with white spots; in winter, its coat is heavier, particularly on the neck—brown with faint spots or none. The male has long antlers that branch into a number of tines. Formerly more widespread, the barasingha is now found only in scattered areas and in national parks and reserves. It is listed in the *Red Data Book* as an endangered species.

Barat, Saint Madeleine-Sophie (b. Dec. 12, 1779, Joigny, Burgundy, Fr.—d. May 25, 1865, Paris; canonized 1925; feast day May 25), nun and founder of the Society of the Sacred Heart.

Born of peasant stock, Madeline was expertly tutored by her brother Louis, deacon and master. After the French Revolution, she went to Paris with Louis, who had become a priest. His superior, Joseph Varin, appointed Madeleine to head an educational order dedicated to the Sacred Heart of Jesus. She made her first consecration in 1800. In 1801 the first Convent of the Sacred Heart was opened at Amiens, Fr., and she became superior in 1802.

In 1804 Madeleine journeyed to Grenoble, Fr., to found her second convent and to receive into the order Blessed Rose Philippine Duchesne, its first missionary. In 1806 Madeleine was elected superior general for life, and in 1815 the constitutions and rules of the order, drafted with Varin's help, were adopted. The Society of the Sacred Heart received ecclesiastical approval in 1826. During her lifetime the order spread from France to 11 other countries of Europe, Algeria, and North and South America. Under her guidance remarkable uniformity was established.

Barataria Bay, inlet of the Gulf of Mexico, about 15 mi (24 km) long by 12 mi wide, in southeastern Louisiana, U.S. Its entrance, largely blocked by the Grand and Grand Terre islands, is via a narrow Gulf channel navigable through connecting waterways into the Gulf Intracoastal Waterway system. The bay is indented and marshy with many islands. The surrounding low-lying Barataria Country, south of New Orleans and west of the Mississippi Delta, is noted for its shrimp industry (based on villages built on pilings above the coastal marshes), muskrat trapping, and gas and oil wells. It is sometimes called Laffite Country after the celebrated Jean Laffitte and his brother Pierre, who in 1810–14 organized a colony of pirates and smugglers around the Baratarian coast. The name Barataria is from the Spanish meaning "to deceive."

Baratieri, Oreste (b. Nov. 13, 1841, Condino, Lombardy, Austrian Empire—d. Aug. 7, 1901, Sterzing, Tyrol, Austria-Hungary), general and colonial governor who was responsible for both the development of the Italian colony of Eritrea and the loss of Italian influence over Ethiopia.

Baratieri had been a volunteer for Giuseppe Garibaldi, the popular hero of Italian unification, serving under him in the Sicilian and south Italian campaigns of 1860. He commanded a regiment in Eritrea in 1887–91 and was named commander in chief of Italian troops in Africa in 1891. Although he came in conflict with the civilian authorities in Eritrea for his encouragement of private investment in the colony, his views prevailed when he was named governor in 1893.

After opening Eritrea to private capital and extensive land settlement, Baratieri attempted, in 1895, to extend its borders into Ethiopia but was gravely defeated by the forces of the Ethiopian emperor, Menelik II, in the Battle of Adowa in 1896. This defeat led to the Italian recognition of full Ethiopian sovereignty and independence. Baratieri's court-martial for his rout at Adowa resulted in his acquittal. He was a deputy of the Italian legislature (1876–95) and author of *Memorie d'Africa* (1897).

Baratynsky, Yevgeny Abramovich, Baratynsky also spelled BORATYNSKY (b. March 2 [Feb. 19, old style], 1800, Mara, Russia—d. July 11 [June 29, O.S.], 1844, Naples),

Baratynsky, detail from an engraving by E. Ckomnukobz
Novosti Press Agency

foremost Russian philosophical poet contemporary with Aleksandr Pushkin, who combined an elegant precise style with spiritual melancholy in dealing with abstract idealistic concepts.

Of noble parentage, Baratynsky was expelled from the imperial corps of pages, entered the army, was commissioned, and retired in 1826. He married and settled at Muranovo, near Moscow. His early romantic lyrics are strongly personal, dreamy, and disenchanted. His narrative poems *Eda* (1826), *Bal* (1828; "The Ball"), and *Nalozhnitsa* (1831; "The Concubine"; rewritten as *Tsyganka,* "The Gypsy Girl," 1842) treat the emotions analytically. *Tsyganka* was attacked by critics of the time as "base" and "coarse." The poem *Na smert Gyote* (1832; "On the Death of Goethe") is one of his masterpieces. Tragic pessimism dominates his later poetry, which is mainly on philosophical and aesthetic themes. Modern critics value his thought more highly than did his contemporaries.

Barauni (India): *see* Bāruni.

Barb, also called BARBARY, native horse breed of the Barbary States of North Africa. It is related to, and probably an offshoot of, the Arabian horse but is larger, with a lower placed tail, and has hair at the fetlock (above and behind the hoof). The coat colour is usually bay or brown. Like the Arabian, it is noted for speed and endurance. A variety known as the Spanish-Barb is bred in small numbers in the United States.

barb, also called BARBEL, any of numerous freshwater fishes belonging to the genus *Barbus,* in the carp family, Cyprinidae. The barbs

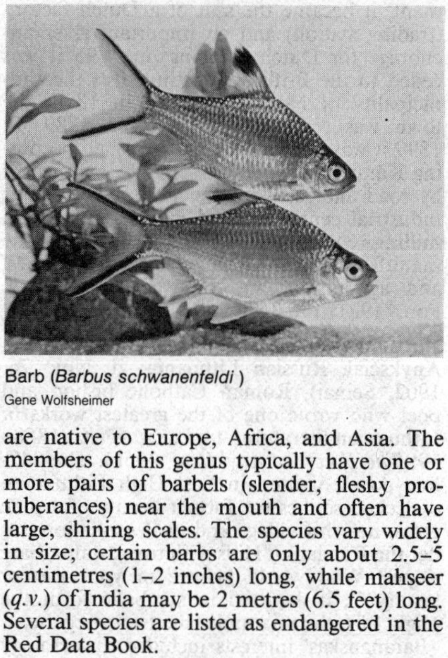

Barb (*Barbus schwanenfeldi*)
Gene Wolfsheimer

are native to Europe, Africa, and Asia. The members of this genus typically have one or more pairs of barbels (slender, fleshy protuberances) near the mouth and often have large, shining scales. The species vary widely in size; certain barbs are only about 2.5–5 centimetres (1–2 inches) long, while mahseer (*q.v.*) of India may be 2 metres (6.5 feet) long. Several species are listed as endangered in the Red Data Book.

The barbel (*B. barbus*) of central and western European rivers is a slender, rather elongate fish with a thick-lipped, crescent-shaped mouth and four barbels, which it uses to search out fish, mollusks, and other food along the river bottom. The barbel is greenish and usually attains a length and weight of about 75 centimetres (30 inches) and 3 kilograms (6.5 pounds). It is a good sport fish.

There are many African and Asian members of the genus *Barbus,* those of the East Indian region sometimes being placed in a separate genus, *Puntius.* Some of these African and Asian species, such as the mahseer, are esteemed food or game fishes, while several of the small species are the popular barbs of home aquariums. Following are some barbs well known to aquarists:

Cherry barb (*B. titteya*), to 3 centimetres long; male silver to cherry-red, female silver to pinkish; both sexes with a broad gold and black band on each side.

Clown barb (*B. everetti*), large, to 13 centimetres; pinkish with red fins and several large, dark spots on each side.

Rosy barb (*B. conchonius*), to 5–6 centimetres in aquariums, larger in nature; colour silvery rose with dark spot near tail; breeding male deep rose with black-edged dorsal fin.

Sumatra, or tiger, barb (*B. tetrazona*), about 5 centimetres long; silvery orange with four vertical black stripes on each side.

Two-spot barb (*B. ticto*), 5–16 centimetres long; silvery with black spot near head and tail; dorsal fin of male reddish with black spots; no barbels.

Barbacena, city, southeastern Minas Gerais state, Brazil, in the Serra da Mantiquera, at 3,727 ft (1,136 m) above sea level. The settlement was made the seat of a municipality in 1791 and elevated to city rank in 1840. It is now the trade and manufacturing centre for an agricultural region that raises corn (maize), *feijão* (beans), rice, coffee, and various fruits and vegetables. The largest of Barbacena's industries are two textile factories. Railroads and highways link the city to Belo Horizonte, Rio de Janeiro (130 mi [210 km] south), and neighbouring communities. Pop. (1980 prelim.) 69,675.

Barbados, independent island nation in the West Indies, situated east of the Windward Islands and about 270 mi (435 km) northwest of Venezuela in the western Atlantic Ocean, covering an area of 166 sq mi (430 sq km). The capital is Bridgetown, the only seaport of the country. Triangular in shape, Barbados extends at its maximum about 21 mi from northwest to southeast and about 15 mi from east to west. The population in 1981 was estimated at 253,000.

The article that follows is a summary of significant detail about Barbados. Fuller treatment is provided in the following MACROPAEDIA articles. For its geography and history, *see* West Indies. For information about associated physiographic features in their continental setting, *see* Caribbean Sea; North America. For regional aspects of Barbados' history, *see* Latin America, The History of.

For current history and for statistics on society and economy, *see* the article "World Affairs" and BRITANNICA WORLD DATA, respectively, in the *Britannica Book of the Year.*

The land. Geologically composed of coral accumulation (up to 300 ft [90 m] thick) on sedimentary rocks, Barbados is an island of low and flat relief, except in the north central part where the highest point is reached at Mt. Hillaby (1,115 ft above sea level). The land falls in a series of terraces to the west and declines sharply in the east and south.

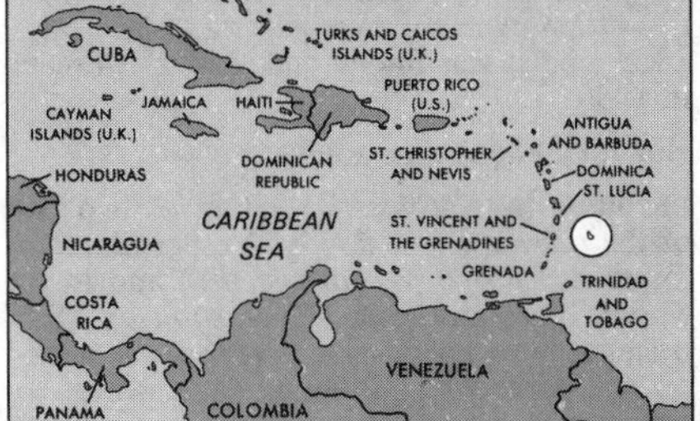

Barbados

The island is almost encircled with coral reefs. There is little surface water, but subterranean water, stored in the limestone beds, supports a few natural springs.

Barbados has a moderate tropical climate with only two seasons, dry (December–May) and wet (June–November). Average temperatures vary from 75° F (24° C) in February to 82° F (28° C) in September. Average precipitation is about 60 in. (1,525 mm), varying from 40 in. on the coasts to 90 in. in the hilly central area. The island lies in the Caribbean hurricane zone.

Tropical trees such as mahogany, palm, casuarina, frangipani, and flamboyant (poinciana) are found on the island; flowering shrubs (wild roses, carnations, lilies, and several varieties of cactus) are widespread. Most of the level terrain is under sugarcane cultivation (about seven-eighths of the total cultivated area); mangoes, avocados, citrus fruits, and guava are grown in orchards. Natural wildlife is limited to hare, mongoose, monkey, and a few birds, such as hummingbird, sparrow, dove, and blackbird. Small reserves of natural gas and petroleum exist in the southeast; some clay, limestone, and sand are quarried.

The people. About 90 percent of the population is black. The average annual growth rate (1975–79) of 0.5 percent remained relatively stable since the 1960s when family-planning services began. Birth and death rates were 16 and 7 per 1,000 population, respectively, during the late 1970s. Much emigration of males in search of employment also affected the growth rate; females outnumber males 110 to 100. About one-third of the population is younger than 15 years. English is the major language and Christianity the principal religion; 70 percent of the population adheres to the Anglican Church. Legal marriages are uncommon, and about 70 percent of the population is illegitimate. Barbados is one of the most densely populated countries in the world, with 1,600 inhabitants per sq mi (619 per sq km).

The economy. Barbados has a predominantly market economy based largely on tourism and the production and export of sugar. The gross national product (GNP) totalled U.S. $760,000,000 in 1980; the GNP per capita, which has grown more rapidly than the population, was $3,040.

Agriculture accounts for approximately one-tenth of the GNP and employs a comparable fraction of the work force. The production of sugar has declined as a result of slackening international demand, poor weather, and a shortage of arable land and was supplanted by tourism as the island's most important industry in 1969. The government has attempted to diversify agricultural production by promoting such crops as sea island cotton.

Limited quantities of petroleum and natural gas are produced. Manufacturing industries account for more than one-tenth of the GNP and employ a comparable fraction of the work force. Light industries predominate, and the government has encouraged investment in the production of pharmaceuticals, ceramics, glass, and electronics. Large quantities of molasses and rum are produced for export. Production of electricity exceeds 3,000,000,000 kW-hr and is generated from imported and domestic fuels.

Tourism accounts for as much as one-half of the GNP, and the government has shifted the burden of taxation from income to indirect taxes in an effort to benefit from tourist expenditures. Barbados joined the Caribbean Community and Common Market (Caricom) in 1973 and is a member of the Caribbean Development Bank, which is headquartered in Bridgetown. There has been an outflow of capital from Barbados as a result of higher interest rates offered abroad; the Offshore Banking Act (1980) guarantees low taxes and the confidentiality of accounts. The U.S. is Barbados' principal supplier of imports.

Administrative and social conditions. Barbados is an independent state within the Commonwealth of Nations. Under its 1966 Constitution the British monarch, represented by the governor general, is the head of state. Executive power is exercised by the prime minister, cabinet, and other appointed ministers, who are responsible to the parliament, where legislative power resides. The parliament is bicameral, consisting of the House of Assembly with 27 elected members, and the Senate, with 21 members appointed by the governor general, 12 on the advice of the prime minister, 2 on the advice of the leader of the opposition, and 7 at his own discretion. Members of both houses serve five-year terms. The major political parties are the Barbados Labour Party (BLP) and the Democratic Labour Party (DLP). The judicial system is headed by a High Court.

A social security system established in 1967 provides benefits for sickness and maternity and for old age, disability, and survivor pensions.

Modern medical facilities are generally accessible, and Barbadians are relatively free from malnutrition and infectious diseases. The average life expectancy is about 70 years and the infant mortality rate is about 30 per 1,000 live births.

Education is free in state schools and compulsory between the ages of 5 and 14. Higher education is available at the Barbados campus of the University of the West Indies and at Codrington College, the oldest degree-granting institution in the English-speaking Caribbean.

Cultural life. The culture is based on folk arts and tradition. Barbados has dramatic groups, schools of dancing, and art exhibitions. The country is internationally known in the game of cricket.

History. The early history of Barbados is obscure, but it was probably inhabited by Arawak Indians originally from South America. There is some evidence that Spaniards had landed by 1518, and, apparently, by 1536 no Indians remained on the island.

In 1624 or early 1625 John Powell led an expedition to the island, and in 1627 his younger brother, Capt. Henry Powell, landed a party of English settlers. Slaves were brought in from Africa to work the sugar plantations. Slavery was abolished in the British Empire in 1834, and the slaves on Barbados were totally freed by 1838. This shook but did not destroy the island's economy.

Widespread riots and disorders erupted in Barbados and the British West Indies in 1937–38, fueled by a rapidly growing population, the closing of emigration outlets, and economic depression. A British Colonial Welfare and Development Organization was subsequently established and provided large sums of money for Barbados and other colonies. In addition, there were changes in colonial policies in England; in Barbados, black reformers became active participants in politics.

In 1958 Barbados joined the West Indies Federation, and the chief minister of the island became the first prime minister of the federation. Between 1961 and 1965, however, the federation gradually dissolved, and Barbados sought and gained (1966) independence within the Commonwealth. In the first elections the DLP won a majority of seats in the House of Assembly. E.W. Barrow, leader of the party and subsequently reelected, became the first prime minister. In 1976 the BLP, led by J.M.G. Adams, came to power and continued to rule into the early 1980s. Since independence, the social and political objectives of the BLP and DLP have not differed significantly, as both parties have followed moderate Socialist philosophies.

Barbados cherry, also called WEST INDIAN CHERRY OR ACEROLA, common name for various tropical and subtropical trees and shrubs of the genera *Bunchiosa* and *Malpighia* (family Malpighiaceae), especially *M. glabra, M. punicifolia,* and *M. urens.*

The *Malpighia* species bear edible fruits, rich in vitamin C, that are used in preserves and commercial vitamin production. They are native to the West Indies and southern Texas southward to northern South America. *M.*

Barbados cherry (*Malpighia glabra*)
Douglas David Dawn

glabra, the species perhaps most often called Barbados cherry, grows about 3.6 metres (12 feet) tall. The flowers, which appear throughout the summer, are pink or rosy, 2 centimetres (nearly one inch) in diameter, and grow from the leaf axils in clusters of three to five. The tart, red fruit is the size of a cherry.

Barbados Ridge, submarine ridge of the Caribbean Sea rising from the southern end of the axis of the Puerto Rico Trench. The Barbados Ridge is paralleled on either side by a shallow trough. Negative gravity anomalies (observed gravity values less than theoretically calculated values because of a mass deficiency at depth in the Earth) associated with the Puerto Rico Trench extend over the Barbados Ridge, and thus structural continuity between these two features is established.

Barbara, SAINT (d. *c.* 200; feast day December 4), virgin martyr of the early church and patroness of artillerymen. According to legend, which dates only to the 7th century, she was the daughter of a pagan, Dioscorus, who kept her guarded to protect her beauty from harm. When she professed Christianity, he became enraged and took her to the provincial prefect, who ordered her to be tortured and beheaded. Dioscorus himself performed the execution and, upon his return home, was struck by lightning and reduced to ashes.

Some accounts name the ancient Egyptian city of Heliopolis, others Nicomedia or a town in Tuscany, as the scene of her sufferings. The original Greek accounts of her martyrdom are lost, but Syriac, Latin, and other versions are extant. Her story, reproduced in great detail in Jacobus de Voragine's *Legenda aurea* (1255–66; *Golden Legend*, 1483), was popular in the Middle Ages.

Venerated as one of the 14 Auxiliary Saints (Holy Helpers), she is invoked in thunderstorms. Because Barbara's authenticity is highly questionable and her legend is probably spurious, she was dropped from the church calendar in 1969.

Barbarelli, Giorgio (painter): *see* Giorgione.

Barbari, Jacopo de', Jacopo also spelled IACOPO, also known in the north as JAKOB WALCH (Jacob the Foreigner) (b. 1440—d. 1516), Venetian painter and engraver who probably painted the first signed and dated (1504) pure still life (a dead partridge, gauntlets, and arrow pinned against a wall). Until *c.* 1500 he remained in Venice. A large engraved panorama of the city is among the Venetian works attributed to him. An acquaintance of Albrecht Dürer, he moved to the north where he worked as a court painter in the German cities of Wittenberg, Nürnberg, and Frankfurt an der Oder and finally settled at the Dutch court. Like Dürer, who consulted him on technique, Barbari engraved on copper and made woodcuts.

Barbarossa: *see* Frederick I *under* Frederick (Germany/Holy Roman Empire).

Barbarossa (Redbeard), byname of KHAYR AD-DĪN, original name KHIḌR (d. 1546), Barbary pirate and later admiral of the Ottoman fleet, by whose initiative Algeria and Tunisia became part of the Ottoman Empire. For three centuries after his death, Mediterranean coastal towns and villages were ravaged by his pirate successors.

Khiḍr was one of four sons of a Turk from the island of Lesbos. Hatred of the Spanish and Portuguese who attacked North Africa between 1505 and 1511 encouraged Khiḍr and his brother ʿArūj to intensify their piracy. They hoped, with the aid of Turks and Muslim emigrants from Spain, to wrest an African domain for themselves and had begun to succeed in this design when ʿArūj was killed by the Spanish in 1518. Khiḍr, who had been his brother's lieutenant, then assumed the title Khayr ad-Dīn. Fearing he would lose his possessions to the Spanish, he offered homage to the Ottoman sultan and in return was granted the title *beylerbey* and sent military reinforcements (1518). With this aid Khayr ad-Dīn was able to capture Algiers in 1529 and make it the great stronghold of Mediterranean piracy. In 1533 he was appointed admiral in chief of the Ottoman Empire, and the next year he conquered the whole of Tunisia for the Turks, Tunis itself becoming the base of piracy against the Italian coast. The Holy

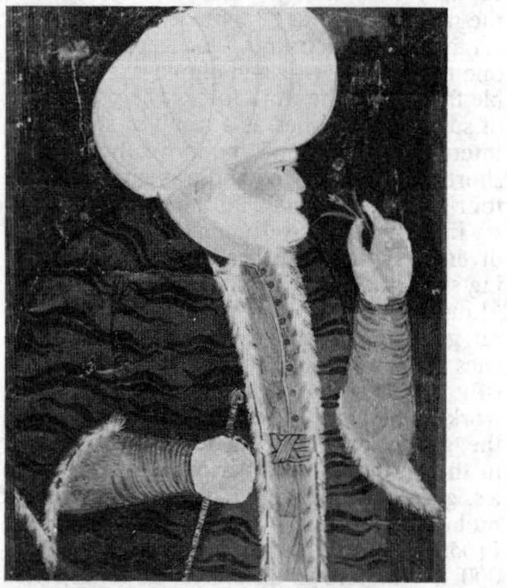

Barbarossa, watercolour miniature by Haydar Reis, middle of the 16th century; in the Topkapı Sarayı Museum, Istanbul
By courtesy of the Topkapi Sarayi Museum, Istanbul

Roman emperor Charles V led a crusade that captured Tunis and Goletta in 1535, but Barbarossa defeated Charles V's fleet at the Battle of Preveza (1538), thereby securing the eastern Mediterranean for the Turks (until their defeat at the Battle of Lepanto in 1571). Barbarossa remained one of the great figures of the court at Constantinople until his death.

Barbary, also called BARBARY STATES, former designation for the coastal region of North Africa bounded by Egypt (east), by the Atlantic (west), by the Sahara (south), and by the Mediterranean Sea (north), and now comprising Morocco, Algeria, Tunisia, and Libya. The name originates from that of the Berbers, the oldest known inhabitants of the region, and was for centuries associated with the coastal pirates who preyed upon Mediterranean shipping. The term was in use until occupation of the region by European powers in the 19th century (*see* Maghrib).

Barbary (horse): *see* Barb.

Barbary ape, also called MAGOT (*Macaca sylvana*), tailless, terrestrial macaque (*q.v.*) found in bands in Algeria, Morocco, and on the Rock of Gibraltar. The Barbary ape is about 60 centimetres (24 inches) long and has light yellowish-brown fur and a naked, pale-pink face. It is the only wild monkey in Europe

Barbary ape (*Macaca sylvana*)
Tom McHugh—Photo Researchers

and may have been taken westward during the Muslim Arab territorial expansion of the Middle Ages. According to legend, British dominion will end when the Barbary ape is gone from the British-held Rock of Gibraltar.

Barbary pirate, any of the Muslim pirates operating from the coast of North Africa, at their most powerful during the 17th century but still active until the 19th century. Captains, who formed a class in Algiers and Tunis, commanded cruisers outfitted by wealthy backers, who then received 10 percent of the value of the prizes. The pirates used galleys until the 17th century, when Simon Danser, a Flemish renegade, taught them the advantage of using sailing ships.

North African piracy had very ancient origins. It gained a political significance during the 16th century, mainly through Barbarossa (Khayr ad-Dīn), who united Algeria and Tunisia as military states under the Ottoman sultanate and maintained his revenues by piracy. With the arrival of powerful Moorish bands in Rabat and Tétouan (1609), Morocco became a new centre for the pirates and for the ʿAlawī sultans, who quickly gained control of the two republics and encouraged piracy as a valuable source of revenue. During the 17th century, the Algerian and Tunisian pirates joined forces, and by 1650 more than 30,000 of their captives were imprisoned in Algiers alone. Piratical practices were the cause of several wars between Tripolitania and the United States in the 19th century. The British made two attempts to suppress Algerian piracy after 1815, and it was finally ended by the French in 1830.

Barbary sheep: *see* aoudad.

barbastelle (*Barbastella*), either of two bats of the common bat family, Vespertilionidae, found in Europe (*B. barbastellus*) and in the Middle East and Asia (*B. leucomelas*). Barbastelles have short, wide ears that are joined on the forehead and long, dark, white- or gray-tipped fur. They are about 4–6 centimetres (1.6–2.4 inches) long without the 4–5.5-cm tail and weigh about 6–10 grams (0.2–0.3 ounce). Relatively heavy fliers, barbastelles live alone or in small groups and roost in trees or buildings. From fall to spring they hibernate in caves.

Barbauld, Anna Laetitia (b. June 20, 1743, Kibworth Harcourt, Leicestershire, Eng.—d. March 9, 1825, Stoke Newington, near London), miscellaneous writer, poet, and editor, whose best writings are on political and social themes. Her poetry belongs essentially in the tradition of 18th-century meditative verse.

Anna was the only daughter of John Aikin, and from the age of 15 to 30 she lived in Warrington, Lancashire, where her father taught at a Nonconformist Protestant academy. There she was encouraged by her father's friends and colleagues to pursue her education and literary talents. In 1774 she married Rochemont Barbauld, a French Protestant clergyman. Although she is probably best known for her hymn "Life! I Know Not What Thou Art," Anna's most important poems include "Corsica" (1768) and "The Invitation" (1773). She edited William Collins' *Poetical Works* (1794), and *The British Novelists,* 50 vol. (1810).

Barbé-Marbois, François, marquis de (b. Jan. 31, 1745, Metz, Fr.—d. Jan. 14, 1837, Paris), statesman who in 1803 negotiated the Louisiana Purchase.

After serving as a diplomat in Germany and with the American colonists, Barbé-Marbois was intendant of Santo Domingo (1785–89). Returning to France, he became a deputy in the Conseil des Anciens (1795–97) but was exiled later as a monarchist to French Guiana (1797–99). Recalled to France in 1800, he became minister of the treasury and, as such, negotiated the sale of Louisiana to the United States, getting a better price than had been expected. Napoleon dismissed him in 1806 because his excessive advances to contractors in 1805 had caused a grave financial crisis. He was, however, appointed first president of the Cour des Comptes (an administrative court handling public accounts of the country) in 1808 and was made a senator and a count in 1813. When Napoleon's fall became likely, Barbé-Marbois hastily and successfully attached himself to the Bourbons and was made a peer of France (1814), a marquis (1817), minister of justice (1815–16), and again president of the Cour des Comptes (1816–34). In 1834 he switched his loyalties to the July Monarchy of 1830.

barbecue, an outdoor meal, usually a form of social entertainment, at which meats, fish, or fowl, along with vegetables, are roasted over a wood or charcoal fire. The term also denotes the grill or stone-lined pit for cooking such a meal, or the food itself, particularly the strips of meat. The word barbecue came into English via the Spanish, who adopted the term from the Arawak Indians of the Caribbean, to whom the *barbacoa* was a grating of green wood upon which strips of meat were placed to cook, or to dry over a slow fire.

Barbecuing is popular throughout the United States, especially in the South, where pork is the favoured meat, and the Southwest, where beef predominates. Other foods barbecued are lamb or kid, chicken, sausages, and, along the Gulf and Atlantic coasts, seafood. Basting and marinating sauces also reflect regional tastes, vinegar-based sauces in the Carolinas, tomato-based in the Midwest, with the spiciest versions generally found in the Southwest.

barbed wire, fence wire usually consisting of two longitudinal wires twisted together to form cable and having wire barbs wound around either or both of the cable wires at regular intervals. The varieties of barbed wire are numerous, with cables being single or double, round, half-round, or flat, and of a range of gauges. The twisted double cable provides extra strength and permits contraction and expansion without breakage. Barbs are diagonally cut in order to provide sharper points; they may consist of one or two pieces (two or four points) and are generally spaced at intervals of four to five inches.

The first patents on barbed wire were taken out in the United States in 1867, but it was not until 1874, when Joseph Glidden of De

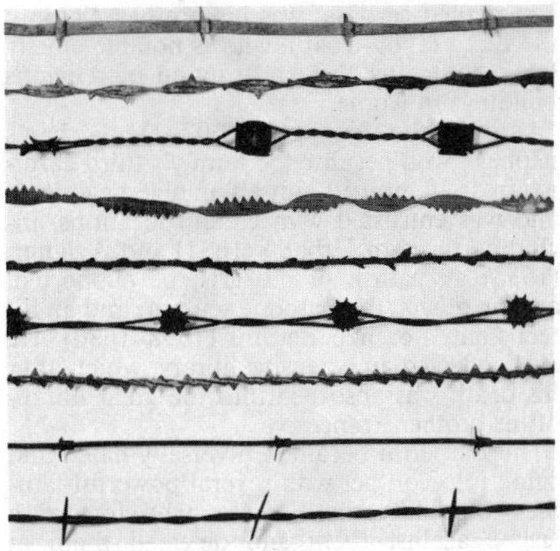

Barbed wire used for fencing, 19th century; from the collection of Jesse S. James

By courtesy of Jesse S. James, Maywood, Calif.

Kalb, Ill., invented a practical machine for its manufacture, that the innovation became widespread. By 1890, fenced pastureland had virtually replaced the open range.

Barbeitos, Arlindo (do Carmo Pires) (b. Dec. 24, 1940, Angola), African poet, many of whose works, written in Portuguese, portray in a subtle manner the struggle of his people for independence as well as the essential harmony between man and nature.

From 1965 to 1969 Barbeitos studied in West Germany. He returned home to teach at several bases of the Popular Movement for the Liberation of Angola during Angola's struggle for independence. He later returned to Europe for treatment of tuberculosis and continued his graduate studies in ethnology at the University of West Berlin.

Barbeitos' poetry includes *Angola, Angolê, Angolema* (1975) and *Nzoji* (1979; "Dream"). His poems are noted for their concentration and density of thought, tenderness of tone, and ultimate simplicity of style.

Barbellion, W.N.P.: *see* Cummings, Bruce Frederick.

barber, craftsman whose primary activities in the 20th century are trimming and styling the hair of men, shaving them, and shaping their beards, sideburns, and moustaches. Barbers, or hairdressers, often provide shampooing, manicuring, hair dying, permanent waves, and shoe polishing within their shops, or salons. *See also* hairdressing.

The barber shop was a familiar institution in ancient Greece and Rome and then, as now, was a centre for the exchange of gossip and opinion. The more prosperous citizens, however, particularly in Rome, had household barbers. The great houses of ancient Egypt also had barbers among their retainers and offered the services of these as part of their hospitality to guests.

For six centuries the barbers of Europe practiced surgery. This custom began with the papal decree of 1163 that forbade the clergy to shed blood. Monks were required to undergo bloodletting at regular intervals, and some of them had been performing this task, along with minor surgery. Now they turned these duties over to the barbers—familiar figures at the monasteries since 1092, when the clergy had been required to be clean shaven. This arrangement was satisfactory to the doctors of the era, who considered that bloodletting was necessary but beneath their dignity. They were also glad to relegate to the barbers other physical tasks such as the lancing of abscesses and treatment of wounds. At the beginning of his career, Ambroise Paré, one of the great pioneers of surgery, was among those who gave shaves and haircuts for a living.

In France a royal decree of 1383 declared that "the king's first barber and valet" was to be head of the barbers and surgeons of the kingdom, who had been organized in a guild in 1361. The barbers of London were first organized as a religious guild but were granted a charter as a trade guild in 1462 by Edward IV. This guild was amalgamated with that of the surgeons in 1540 under a charter granted by Henry VIII, and the members of the joint corporation were accorded the right to be addressed as "Master"—colloquially, "Mister." British surgeons still prefix their names with "Mr." instead of "Dr."

The barber-surgeons were sometimes called "doctors of the short robe" to distinguish them from university-trained physicians and surgeons, whose superiority was apt to be only in their knowledge of Latin and their title of "doctor of the long robe." In England the guild of surgeons was separated from that of barbers in 1745. The Royal College of Surgeons, however, did not receive its charter until 1800. The barber's trade was acquired only by a long apprenticeship until the 1890s, when schools for barbering were established.

Barber, Samuel (b. March 9, 1910, West Chester, Pa., U.S.—d. Jan. 23, 1981, New York City), composer who is considered one of the most expressive representatives of the lyric and Romantic trends in musical composition in the United States.

Barber studied the piano from an early age and soon began to compose. In 1924 he entered the Curtis Institute of Music in Philadelphia, where, in addition to piano and composition, he studied singing and conducting.

Barber

By courtesy of G. Schirmer, Inc.

After graduation in 1934, Barber devoted himself entirely to composition. He developed a distinctive style, absorbing some technical procedures of modern music but without indulging in experimentation for its own sake. He established his reputation with He established his reputation with his overture to *The School for Scandal,* Opus 5 (1933), based on Sheridan's comedy by that name, and with *Music for a Scene from Shelley,* Opus 7 (1935), inspired by Shelley's *Prometheus Unbound.*

Although many of Barber's works make literary allusions, his music is not programmatic in the strict sense. Significant in this respect are the two *Essays for Orchestra,* Opus 12 (1938) and Opus 17 (1942), which are intended as musical counterparts of the literary form. Structural considerations govern Barber's instrumental writing; there is great astringency in harmony, but the basic tonality remains secure; the rhythmic lines are very strong, without loss of coherence.

In 1936 Barber composed his *String Quartet,* Opus 11, the slow movement of which, arranged for string orchestra, was performed under the title *Adagio for Strings* by the NBC Symphony Orchestra under Arturo Toscanini in 1938 and acquired extraordinary popularity both in America and in Europe.

Barber's *First Symphony*, Opus 9 (1936; revised, 1942), is in the Romantic tradition. In the *Second Symphony*, Opus 19 (1944; revised, 1947), commissioned by the U.S. Army Air Forces (which he had joined in 1943), Barber introduced an electronic instrument imitating radio signals for air navigation, replaced in the revised version by an E-flat clarinet.

Barber also wrote a *Violin Concerto*, Opus 14 (1941), and a *Cello Concerto*, Opus 22 (1946). His *Piano Sonata*, Opus 26 (1949), is the most ambitious work in this form by an American composer. Other compositions are *Dover Beach*, Opus 3, for voice and string quartet (1931); three vocal works with orchestra, *Knoxville: Summer of 1915*, Opus 24 (1948), *Prayers of Kierkegaard*, Opus 30 (1954), and *Andromache's Farewell*, Opus 39 (1962); *Medea*, Opus 23 (1947); and the opera *Vanessa*, produced by the Metropolitan Opera Association, New York City, in 1958, which was awarded a Pulitzer Prize.

Barber's *Piano Concerto*, Opus 38 (1962), brought him new international success and another Pulitzer Prize (1963). His opera *Antony and Cleopatra* opened the new auditorium of the Metropolitan Opera Association at the Lincoln Center for the Performing Arts in 1966. After a period of creative inactivity, Barber resumed composing for orchestra. *The Lovers* and *Fadograph of a Yestern Scene* were first performed in 1971 and *Third Essay for Orchestra* had its premiere in 1980.

Barbera, Joseph (Roland): *see* Hanna, William (Denby); and Barbera, Joseph (Roland).

Barberi, Domenico, also called DOMINIC OF THE MOTHER OF GOD (b. June 22, 1792, Viterbo, Papal States—d. Aug. 27, 1849, Reading, Berkshire, Eng.), mystic and Passionist who worked as a missionary in England.

Born a peasant and raised without any formal education, Barberi entered the Passionist order as a lay brother and was ordained a priest in 1818. In 1821, when he had finished his studies, he became lecturer in theology at a Passionist college near Vetralla. In 1824 he moved to Rome, where he continued to teach. An early inspiration had convinced him that he should work for the conversion of England, but his appointments to Lucca, Italy (1831), and as provincial for southern Italy (1833) seemed to preclude his hopes, until in 1840 he was sent to Ere to found the first Passionist house in Belgium. English friends there aided him and in 1841 offered him a house at Aston, Staffordshire.

Barberi was already following the growth of the Tractarian movement, and in 1845 he received John Henry Newman (later Cardinal Newman) into the church. In Staffordshire, Barberi incurred insult and even violence with undaunted patience. He spoke English with difficulty but made converts among all classes. He founded four Passionist houses in England and made plans for one in Ireland, which was established after his death. He was declared venerable in 1911 and beatified in 1963. An account of his life appears in Denis Gwynn's *Father Dominic Barberi* (1948).

Barberini FAMILY, an aristocratic Roman family, originally of Barberino in the Else Valley; they later settled first in Florence and then in Rome, where they became wealthy and powerful.

Antonio Barberini defended Florence in 1530 and then went to Rome, to which in 1555 he summoned his nephew Francesco (1528–1600), the real founder of the Barberini dynasty. Francesco and his brother Raffaelo accumulated the riches and trade advantages that became the base of the Barberini power. Francesco (1597–1679) was the first cardinal nominated by his uncle Pope Urban VIII (October 1623). The second family member Urban named cardinal was his brother Antonio the Elder (1569–1646), who is notable chiefly for encouraging the construction of religious buildings in Rome.

Antonio the Younger (1607–71), Urban's nephew, who became the family's third cardinal in 1628, proved himself an able negotiator and was entrusted with certain legations, including those of Urbano (1631) and Avignon (1633). A patron of the arts, he supported, among others, the Baroque sculptor and architect Gian Lorenzo Bernini (1598–1680). He also collected an extensive library, which after his death was absorbed into the great library of his brother Francesco.

The Barberini became universally hated and came into conflict with several powerful families, especially the Farnese, who formed a league against them and defeated them at Lagoscuro (March 30, 1644). This defeat, together with the death of Urban, severely weakened the position of the Barberini.

When the newly elected Innocent X (pope 1644–55) began an investigation into charges of the Barberini's misuse of church funds, Taddeo, Francesco, and Antonio the Younger fled to Paris. Protected by the French cardinal Jules Mazarin, they enjoyed comfortable positions. With Mazarin's help, and with the arrangement of the marriage of Taddeo's son Maffeo to Olimpia Giustiniani, Innocent's protégée, the Barberini were reconciled to Innocent in 1653. Taddeo died in Paris, but both Francesco (1648) and Antonio (1653) returned to Rome and lived in the magnificent Barberini Palace in Rome, built under the supervision of Bernini.

The family retained power for some time, mainly through wise marriages, including that of Lucrezia, daughter of Taddeo, to Francesco II, duke of Modena. The Barberini died out in 1736, and their estate passed to the Colonna.

Barberini, Maffeo (pope): *see* Urban VIII.

barberry, any of almost 500 species of thorny evergreen or deciduous shrubs constituting the genus *Berberis* of the family Berberidaceae, mostly native to the North Temperate Zone, particularly Asia. Species of Oregon grape, previously included in *Berberis* but now assigned to the genus *Mahonia,* are sometimes called barberry (*see* Oregon grape).

Plants of the genus *Berberis* have yellow wood, yellow, six-petalled flowers, and usually three-branched spines at the base of leafstalks. The fruit is a red, yellow, blue, purple, or black berry, with one to several seeds. The fruits of several species are made into jellies. Yellow dyes are extracted from some South American and Asian barberry plants.

American barberry (*Berberis canadensis*)
Walter Chandoha

The American or Allegheny barberry (*B. canadensis*) is native to eastern North America. Japanese barberry (*B. thunbergii*) often is cultivated as a hedge or ornamental shrub for its scarlet fall foliage and bright-red, long-lasting berries. Several varieties with purple or yellow foliage, thornlessness, or dwarf habit are useful in the landscape. Another widely planted species is wintergreen barberry (*B. julianae*), an evergreen shrub with bluish-black berries. The cultivation of certain barberry species is prohibited in some regions because they harbour one of the spore stages of the fungus that causes black stem rust of wheat.

barbershop quartet, form of informal choral music performed in the United States, consisting of improvising harmonies to popular melodies. The phrase either dates from an era when barbershops formed social and musical centres for a neighbourhood's males or refers back to the British expression "barber's music," meaning extemporized performance by patrons waiting to be shaved and referring to barbers' traditional roles as musicians.

Barberton, city, Summit County, northeastern Ohio, U.S., just south of Akron, on the Tuscarawas River, there dammed to form the Portage Lakes. It was founded in 1891 by Ohio C. Barber as the new site of his match factory (later the Diamond Match Company), which had been established in 1867 in Akron. Manufactures now include chemicals, heavy boilers, rubber goods, metal and iron products, and insulators. A local deposit of limestone more than 345 ft (105 m) thick and 0.5 mi (0.8 km) below the surface of the Earth has one of the deepest mines of its kind in the world. Inc. city, 1892. Pop. (1980) 29,751.

barbet, any of about 75 species of tropical birds constituting the family Capitonidae (order Piciformes). Barbets are named for the bristles at the bases of their stout, sharp bills. They are big-headed, short-tailed birds, 9–30 centimetres (3.5–12 inches) long, greenish or brownish, with splashes of bright colours or white. The smallest barbets are known as tinkerbirds (*see* tinkerbird). The distribution of the family spans Central America to northern South America; sub-Saharan Africa; and Southeast Asia, eastward only to Borneo and Bali. All are nonmigratory.

Crimson-headed barbet (*Capito bourcieri*)
C. Laubscher—Bruce Coleman Inc.

Barbets sit stolidly in treetops when not feeding on insects, lizards, birds' eggs, fruit, and berries. Some climb like woodpeckers; all fly weakly. The nest is a hole, dug with the beak, high up in a rotting tree or in a termite nest.

Barbets call loudly, jerking the head or tail; a male and a female may call alternately or together. Some species, such as the coppersmith (*Megalaima haemacephala*) of Asia and the African tinkerbirds of the genus *Pogoniulus,* are noted for their ringing calls. Maddeningly vocal or repetitious species are sometimes called brain-fever birds.

Barbey d'Aurevilly, Jules-Amédée (b. Nov. 2, 1808, Saint-Sauveur-le-Vicomte, Fr.—d. April 23, 1889, Paris), French novelist and influential critic; he was an arbiter, in his day, of social fashion and literary taste. A member of the minor nobility of Normandy, he remained throughout his life proudly Norman in spirit and style, a royalist opposed to democracy and materialism and an ardent but unorthodox Catholic.

After study at the Collège Stanislas in Paris (1827–29) and, in law, at Caen (1829–33), Barbey d'Aurevilly established himself in Paris in 1837 and began to earn a precarious living by writing for periodicals. Despite poverty, he went to great lengths to establish himself as a dandy, and his sartorial splendours and magnificent attitudes became legendary. He took "Beau" Brummell as his model and in 1844 published a treatise, *Du dandysme et de Georges Brummell* (dated 1845). He had met Brummell in Caen, where the Englishman was consul.

Barbey d'Aurevilly, detail of an oil painting by Émile Lévy, 1881; in the Musée National de Versailles et des Trianons, France
J.E. Bulloz

Barbey d'Aurevilly was appointed, in 1868, to alternate with Sainte-Beuve as literary critic for *Le Constitutionnel,* and on Sainte-Beuve's death, in 1869, he became sole critic. Thenceforward, his reputation grew, and he came to be known as *le Connétable des Lettres* ("Lord High Constable of Literature"). Though he was often arbitrary, vehement, and intensely personal in his criticism, especially of Zola and the Naturalist school, many of his verdicts have stood the test of time; he recognized the attainments of Balzac, Stendhal, and Baudelaire when they were far from being fully appreciated.

His own novels reflect the influence of Sir Walter Scott and Lord Byron. Set in Normandy, they combine description of Norman daily life and history with an imaginative vision of the power of evil. Most of them are tales of terror in which morbid passions are acted out in bizarre crimes. Two of his best works are set against a background of the French Revolution: *Le Chevalier des Touches* (1864), dealing with the rebellion of the Chouans (bands of Norman outlaws) against the French Republic, and *Un Prêtre marié* (1865; "A Married Priest"), dealing with the sufferings of a priest under the new regime. *Les Diaboliques* (1874; *Weird Women,* 1900), a collection of six short stories written by one "who believes in the devil and his power over the world," is often considered his masterpiece.

Barbeyales, order of dicotyledonous flowering plants comprising the family Barbeyaceae. The single species within the family, *Barbeya oleoides*, is a tree of Ethiopia, Somalia, and the Arabian Peninsula having the general aspect of the olive tree but many botanical characteristics of the elms. Because of its latter affinity, *Barbeya* is usually included in the nettle order (Urticales), either as a member of the elm family or as a separate family; but many authorities regard it as sufficiently distinct to warrant ordinal status in its own right.

Barbeya has oppositely paired, simple, smooth-margined leaves that lack basal appendages (stipules) and are densely white-hairy on the lower surface. The male and female flowers are on separate plants. The flowers lack petals but have a three- or four-lobed calyx, or outer whorl, of floral parts that persists and enlarges with the fruit. Male flowers have six to nine stamens (pollen-producing structures) and are often covered with a rust-coloured fuzz. Female flowers have a superior (*i.e.*, positioned above the other floral parts) ovary composed of one carpel, or ovule-bearing structural unit, containing one ovule and having one terminal plumelike style, which is the pollen-receptive part of the female structure.

Barbie, Klaus, byname BUTCHER OF LYON, French BOUCHER DE LYON (b. Oct. 25, 1913, Bad Godesberg, near Bonn), Nazi leader, head of the Gestapo in Lyon from 1942 to 1944, held responsible for the death of some 4,000 persons and the deportation of some 7,500 others.

Barbie was a member of the Hitler Youth and joined the SD (Sicherheitsdienst, or Security Service), an elite branch of the SS, in 1935. After German forces overran western Europe in World War II, Barbie served in The Netherlands and then, in 1942, was made chief of Gestapo Department IV in Lyon. (The SD was closely related to the Gestapo, and personnel were frequently transferred from one to the other.) In this position he became especially active against partisans, promoting the torture and execution of thousands of prisoners. He personally tortured prisoners whom he interrogated. Among the more specific charges against him were that he ordered the death of Resistance leader Jean Moulin and the arrest of 41 Jewish orphans, aged 3–13, who later were delivered to the Auschwitz death camp.

After the war he was seized by U.S. authorities, who recruited him briefly for anti-Soviet intelligence work and then spirited him and his family out of Germany to South America (for which the U.S. government later officially apologized to France). In 1971 he was discovered in Peru, living under the name of Klaus Altmann. Accused of illegal financial manipulations there, he moved to Bolivia. After long negotiations, the Bolivian government extradited him to France in February 1983 to stand trial. (He had already been sentenced in absentia to death by a postwar French military tribunal.)

Barbier, Antoine-Alexandre (b. Jan. 11, 1765, Coulommiers, Fr.—d. Dec. 5, 1825, Paris), librarian and bibliographer who compiled a standard reference directory of anonymous writings and helped in preserving scholarly books and manuscripts during and after the French Revolution.

In 1794 Barbier became a member of the temporary commission of the arts and was charged with the duty of distributing among the various libraries of Paris the books confiscated during the Revolution. A few years later, under the Directory, he became a member of the council for the preservation of works in the arts and sciences. In the course of his work he discovered and saved the letters of Pierre-Daniel Huet, bishop of Avranches, and, more important, the manuscripts of the works of François Fénelon, the celebrated 17th-century author and theologian. Although Barbier had been ordained priest, his main passion was for books, and in 1801 he was released from his orders. He became librarian successively to the Directory, to the Conseil d'État, and, in 1807, to Napoleon, for whom he also researched scholarly answers to political and religious problems. His *Dictionnaire des ouvrages anonymes et pseudonymes* (1806–09; "Dictionary of Anonymous and Pseudonymous Works") is still a standard library reference. He had a share in the foundation of the libraries of the Louvre museum and those of the palaces of Fontainebleau, Compiègne, and Saint-Cloud. Under Louis XVIII he served as administrator of the King's private libraries until he was abruptly dismissed in 1822.

Barbieri, Giovanni Francesco: *see* Guercino, Il.

Barbirolli, Sir John (Giovanni Battista) (b. Dec. 2, 1899, London—d. July 28, 1970, London), English conductor and cellist of Italian parentage.

Barbirolli studied on scholarship at the Royal Academy and the Trinity College of Music. In his teens he established himself as orchestral and solo performer and took advantage of military service to conduct a voluntary orchestra. During his mid-20s he devoted himself to chamber work. He then turned to opera as a full-time conductor, taking seasons at Covent Garden and Sadler Wells and making appearances at the British National Opera. Early credits in the concert hall included the London Symphony Orchestra and the Scottish Symphony. Invited for the 1936–37 season of the New York Philharmonic, he won the permanent post in succession to Toscanini, holding it through that organization's memorable centenary season, 1941–42.

Subsequent appointments included conductorships with the Hallé Orchestra, Manchester (1943–58), and the Houston Symphony Orchestra (1961–67). A decade of deteriorating health did not prevent him from continuing guest conducting, recording, and world-wide touring with major orchestras. He was created a knight in 1949.

barbiturate, any of a class of organic compounds used in medicine as sedatives (to produce a calming effect), as hypnotics (to produce sleep), or as an adjunct in anesthesia. The barbiturates act by depressing the central nervous system. Most of them exert a sedative effect in small doses and a hypnotic effect in larger doses.

They are classified according to their duration of action. Long-acting barbiturates, such as barbital and phenobarbital, are used in conjunction with other drugs for the treatment of certain convulsive disorders (as epilepsy) where prolonged depressant action is desired. Barbiturates of intermediate duration of action, such as amobarbital and butabarbital sodium, are used to relieve insomnia; and short-acting barbiturates, such as pentobarbital and secobarbital, are used to overcome difficulty in falling asleep. Ultra-short-acting barbiturates, such as thiopental sodium and thiamylal, constitute the intravenous anesthetic agents, inducing unconsciousness smoothly and rapidly.

In order to prevent accumulation of barbiturates in the body, they must be used with caution in any condition associated with impaired liver function. Barbiturate poisoning resulting from accidental or intentional overdosage may be fatal as a result of brain damage caused by lack of oxygen or of other complications (such as pneumonia) incident to a prolonged inactive, depressed state.

Prolonged use of the barbiturates (especially secobarbital and pentobarbital) may in time cause the user to develop tolerance to them and require amounts of the drug much larger than the original therapeutic dose.

Denial of a barbiturate to the habitual user may precipitate a series of systemic reactions, described collectively as a withdrawal syndrome, indicative of physiological dependence on the drug. Such reactions may be fatal. Treatment of the barbiturate addict involves gradual withdrawal of the drug under medical supervision, followed by a program of rehabilitation.

barbituric acid, an organic compound of the pyrimidine family, a class of compounds with a characteristic six-membered ring structure composed of four carbon atoms and two nitrogen atoms, and regarded as the parent compound of the barbiturate (*q.v.*) drugs. It is used in the production of riboflavin, a nutritional factor (*see* vitamin B_2).

Barbizon school, mid-19th-century French school of painting, part of a larger European movement toward naturalism in art, that made a significant contribution to the establishment of realism in French landscape painting. Inspired by a search for solace in nature that was an outgrowth of Romanticism, the Barbizon painters nevertheless turned away from the melodramatic picturesqueness of established Romantic landscape painters as well as from the classical academic tradition, which used landscape merely as a backdrop for allegory and historical narrative: they painted landscape in realistic terms and for its own sake. They based their art on the works of 17th-century French and Dutch and contemporary English landscape painters, all of whom approached their subject with sensitive observation and a deep love of nature.

The name of the school was taken from the village of Barbizon, on the edge of the great forest of Fontainebleau near Paris, where the school's leaders, Théodore Rousseau and Jean-François Millet, driven from Paris by poverty and lack of success, settled in 1846 and 1849, respectively. They attracted a large following of landscape and animal painters, some coming to live at Barbizon, others visiting only infrequently; those of the group who were to become most notable were Charles-François Daubigny, Narcisse-Virgile Diaz de La Peña, Jules Dupré, Charles Jacque, and Constant Troyon, all of whom had had indifferent success.

"The Forest at Fontainebleau," Barbizon school painting by Théodore Rousseau, oil on canvas, *c.* 1848; in the Louvre, Paris

Giraudon—Art Resource/EB Inc.

Each Barbizon painter had his own style and specific interests. Rousseau's vision was melancholy, concentrating on vast sweeps of landscape and looming trees. Dupré's close-range, detailed scenes are suffused with foreboding. Daubigny favoured scenes of lush, verdant fields, and Diaz painted sun-dappled forest interiors. Troyon and Jacque painted placid scenes that featured livestock. Millet, the only major painter of the group for whom pure landscape was unimportant, made monumental paintings of peasants that celebrated the nobility of humble men living close to nature. All of these artists, in spite of their Romantic inspiration, emphasized the simple and ordinary rather than the terrifying and monumental aspects of nature. Unlike their English contemporaries, they had little interest in the surface effects of light and colour or in atmospheric variations. Instead, they emphasized permanent features, painting solid, detailed forms in a limited range of colours. Also concerned with mood, they altered physical appearance to express what they saw as the objective "character" of the landscape; instead of imposing the subjective emotion of earlier Romantics, they listened for the "voice" of each site.

Having suffered for some time from a total lack of recognition, the Barbizon painters began to gain popularity by midcentury. Their success increased, most winning official recognition from the French Academy and receiving large prices for their paintings; their work was particularly popular at the end of the century. Some of the Barbizon painters were masters of composition and description; others were less competent. But the historical importance of all of them is undeniable, for as a group they helped to establish pure, objective landscape painting as a legitimate genre in France.

Barbo, Pietro: *see* Paul II *under* Paul (papacy).

Barbon, Nicholas (b. *c.* 1640, London—d. 1698), English economist, widely considered the founder of fire insurance.

Barbon was probably the son of Praise-God Barbon (*q.v.*). He studied medicine at the University of Leiden, received his M.D. at Utrecht in 1661, and became an honorary fellow of the College of Physicians in 1664. The considerable part that he took in the rebuilding of London after the Great Fire of 1666 apparently roused his interest in selling fire insurance, and about 1680 he set up an office in London for that purpose.

Barbon's writings on economics to some extent anticipated the conclusions of Adam Smith on the division of labour and the theory of currency as expounded by David Ricardo. His works include *Apology for the Builder; or, A Discourse Showing the Cause and Effects of the Increase of Building* (1685); *A Discourse of Trade* (1690); and *A Discourse Concerning Coining the New Money Lighter* (1696).

Barbon, Praise-God, Barbon also spelled BAREBONE, or BAREBONES, Praise-God also spelled PRAISEGOD (b. *c.* 1596—d. 1679, London), English sectarian preacher from whom the Cromwellian Barebones Parliament derived its nickname.

By 1634 Barbon was becoming a prosperous leather seller and was attracting attention as the minister of a congregation that assembled at his own house, the "Lock and Key," on Fleet Street. His preaching, in which he advocated infant baptism, was attended by large audiences and was sometimes the occasion of riots. After Oliver Cromwell had dissolved the Long Parliament, Barbon was summoned

Praise-God Barbon, engraving

By courtesy of the trustees of the British Museum; photograph, J.R. Freeman & Co. Ltd.

by Cromwell to sit as a member for London in the new assembly of "godly" men who were nominated by the Independent congregations. This "Nominated Parliament" (July–December 1653), also derisively nicknamed the "Barebones Parliament" after Barbon, consisted largely of strict Puritans. Barbon himself played no significant role, though he did support radical legal reforms. In the 1650s he was active in the London Common Council.

Opposing the restoration of Charles II, Barbon presented in February 1660 a petition to Parliament deprecating any reconciliation with the Stuarts. He also circulated Marchamont Needham's pamphlet detailing anecdotes critical of Charles II's morals. After the Restoration (May 1660), Barbon publicly opposed the government and was imprisoned in the Tower of London (Nov. 26, 1661, to July 27, 1662) for his rashness.

Called a Brownist and an Anabaptist by his opponents, Barbon displayed in his writings a toleration unusual in a period of much acrimonious religious controversy.

Barbooth, also called BARBOTTE, or BARBUDI, dice game of Middle Eastern origin, used for gambling; in the U.S. it is played chiefly by persons of Greek ancestry. The shooter casts two dice. If he throws 3–3, 5–5, 6–6, or 6–5, he wins; if he throws 1–1, 2–2, 4–4, or 1–2, he loses. Other combinations are meaningless. A second player, the fader, sets stakes in betting against the shooter and alternates with him in casting the dice. Other players may make side bets on whether the shooter or the fader will win.

Barbosa, Jorge (Vera-Cruz) (b. May 25, 1902, Praia, Santiago, Cape Verde Islands—d. Jan. 6, 1971, Cova da Piedade), African poet who expressed in Portuguese the cultural uniqueness and the tragic nature of life on the African Cape Verdean islands, repeatedly besieged by droughts. He was one of the three founders of the literary journal *Claridade* ("Clarity") in the 1930s, which marked the beginning of modern Cape Verdean literature.

Barbosa spent his early years on the island of São Vicente, excluding his years of study at the Liceu Gil Vicente in Lisbon. He resided for many years on the island of Sal, working as a civil servant of the customhouse. His poetry was published as *Arquipélago* (1935), *Ambiente* (1941; "The Circle"), and *Caderno de um Ilheu* (1956; "An Islander's Notebook"). He died shortly after retiring from the civil service.

Barbotine ware, pottery decorated with a clay slip first employed on Rhenish pottery prior to the 3rd century AD. It was used to adorn the edges of flat dishes with such designs as small flowers. By the 3rd century it started to oust molded ornamentation. Application was by piping, as with icing on cakes. Ernest Chaplet began to experiment with this technique in the 1870s but had to abandon it because of firing difficulties that caused the slip to flake off.

Barbour, John, Barbour also spelled BARBERE, or BARBIER (b. 1325?—d. March 13, 1395, Aberdeen, Aberdeenshire, Scot.), author of a Scottish national epic known as *The Bruce,* the first major work of Scottish literature.

Records show that Barbour became archdeacon of Aberdeen while still a young man and in 1357 was granted a safe conduct by Edward III of England to study at Oxford. That same year he participated in the negotiations for ransoming King David II, who had been a prisoner in England after his capture in the Battle of Neville's Cross (1346). In 1364 and 1368 Barbour studied in France. Throughout his life he enjoyed royal favour and in 1388 as given a life pension.

rbour completed *The Actes and Life of the Victorious Conqueror, Robert Bruce King land,* a metrical historical romance in s, in 1376. The background of *The* he political history of the Scottish independence, from the death of I (1286) to the death of Douglas of Bruce's heart (1332). The s the chivalry and idealism of es and exhorts their succes- air nobill elderis." But the rn (1314) was still within ontemporaries, and *The* y realistic story of re- of the chansons de ce of chivalry. The rous, direct, and er. Barbour evi- llect firsthand kburn, which is narrative ottish bor-

y 25, 25, of)

and a gateway to the Daniel Boone National Forest. It was founded in 1800 and named for James Barbour, who donated land for the townsite. Union College was founded there by the Methodist Church in 1879. The Dr. Thomas Walker State Shrine, 6 mi (10 km) south, has a replica of the log cabin (the first house in Kentucky) built in 1750 by Walker, who explored the state and discovered the Cumberland Gap. Barbourville is an agricultural trading centre (tobacco, vegetables, sorghum) and has some light industry. A floodwall protects the city from the meandering Cumberland River. Pop. (1980) 3,333.

Barbudi (dice game): *see* Barbooth.

Barbusse, Henri (b. May 17, 1873, Asnières, Fr.—d. Aug. 30, 1935, Moscow), novelist, author of *Le Feu* (1916; *Under Fire,* 1917), a firsthand witness of the life of French soldiers in World War I. Barbusse belongs to an important lineage of French war writers who span the period 1910 to 1939, mingling war memories with moral and political meditations.

Barbusse, 1935
H. Roger-Viollet

Barbusse started as a neo-Symbolist poet, with *Pleureuses* (1895; "Mourners"), and continued as a neo-Naturalist novelist, with *L'En*- (1908; *The Inferno,* 1918). In 1914 he unteered for the infantry, was twice cited allantry, and finally was discharged be- of his wounds in 1917. Barbusse's *Le rnal d'une escouade,* awarded the Prix is one of the few works to survive ation of wartime novels. Its subti- *Squad,* reveals the author's dou- relate the collective experience (French soldiers') life in the lenounce war. The horror of truction led Barbusse to an as a whole. He became itant Communist and a l peace organizations. , 1919), his literary finite political ori- *line* (1935; Eng. en in the Soviet he time of his

BARCAS:

rom "), d - d in- n opera . The term hen the French ncluded a "Fête des e work (*Les Fêtes vé*- sequently, operas by Gio- Carl Maria von Weber, Daniel- nt Auber, Gioacchino Rossini, Giuseppe Verdi, and Johann Strauss, among others, featured barcaroles.

Without question, the most famous operatic specimen is the Barcarolle from Jacques Offenbach's *Tales of Hoffmann.* Chopin's *Barcarolle,* Opus 60, is possibly the best known of the 19th-century compositions, although other 19th-century composers from Mendelssohn to Liszt and Gabriel Fauré contributed a host of similar pieces. Barcaroles for various performance media were written by Franz Schubert (voice and piano), Johannes Brahms (women's chorus), and Sir William Sterndale Bennett (piano and orchestra).

Barce (Libya): *see* Marj, al-.

Barcelona, province, in the autonomous community (region) of Catalonia, northeastern Spain, formed in 1833 from a number of districts stretching between the Pyrenees and the Mediterranean coast. Its area is 2,986 sq mi (7,733 sq km). The province follows the axis of the Río Llobregat basin, from which its regions are symmetrically arranged. No province has a more diverse landscape; it is a cross section of many varied geological zones, namely, the Pyrenees, the scarps and basins of the interior of Catalonia, the Serralada interior, the central depression, the Serralada del Mar, and the coastal plains.

The economy is as varied as the landscape. In the mountainous northern tableland near Berga, lignite is mined, and cement, of which the province is Spain's leading producer, is manufactured. Southwest, in the Cardona Valley, salt has been exploited since Roman times; and there are important potash deposits (discovered in 1912) near Suria. The fertile plains of Vich and Barcelona (around the provincial capital of Barcelona) yield grapes, as does the area around Villafranca, in the south. Grains are cultivated throughout the central depression. The coastal plain area around the Llobregat river delta is Barcelona province's market garden, with more than 50,000 ac (20,200 ha) under intensive cultivation. Tourism is a growing economic concern because of the mild climate and the Mediterranean beaches.

Barcelona, long the principal Catalan province, is the heart of the greatest industrial concentration of Spain, and its main city is the

Monastery of Santa María de Montserrat, Barcelona province, Spain
J. Allan Cash—Rapho/Photo Researchers

chief seaport. It produces three-quarters of the textile manufactures and a high proportion of the output of the chemical and engineering industries. Exports include table and sparkling wines and manufactured goods. The province has utilized the hydroelectric power sources of the Pyrenees and its strategic location to good advantage. Pop. (1982 est.) 4,949,892.

Barcelona, city, seaport, and capital of Barcelona province and of Catalonia au-

n Barclay, engraving by Claude llan
courtesy of the trustees of the British Museum; otograph, J.R. Freeman & Co. Ltd.

tonomous region, Spain. Located in the northeastern part of the country, 90 mi (150 km) south of the French frontier, it is Spain's major Mediterranean port and commercial centre and is famed for its great individuality, cultural interest, and physical beauty.

The following article treats briefly the modern city of Barcelona. Fuller treatment is provided in the following MACROPAEDIA articles. For history and contemporary life, *see* Barcelona; for additional perspective on the city in its national context, *see* Spain.

Barcelona is built on a gentle slope facing southeast to the sea, in a fertile plain between the Besós and Llobregat rivers. The mountain-ringed city has a mild and agreeable climate.

Economic life centres on manufacturing, shipping, and tourism. Dominant industries produce automobiles, heavy machinery, chemicals, and textiles. As the hub of Catalonian industrial activity, Barcelona contributes greatly to Spain's economic output. The city has an active stock exchange and is an international banking and finance centre. More than 100 regular shipping lines link the city with other world ports.

The main axis of the old town is formed by the Ramblas, a series of spacious, tree-lined avenues, leading north to the commercial centre, Plaza de Cataluña, and south to the Paseo Marítimo and the seafront. To the north is the new town, the Ensanche (Extension). Industrial plants extend beyond the residential and commercial areas.

The oldest part of the city is built on a small hill, Monte Taber, and some of its Roman walls are still visible. Fine Gothic buildings remain, including the cathedral (built between 1289 and the late 15th century) with its 6th-century basilica, and the church of Santa Maria del Mar. Royal and episcopal palaces house the archives of the city and of the crown of Aragon. Monuments include a 197-ft (60-m) column built as a tribute to Christopher Columbus and the Templo Expiatorio de la Sagrada Familia (Church of the Holy Family), which was begun in 1882. Though unfinished, this huge and elaborate church features openwork spires that dominate the skyline and is the best known work of the Catalonian architect Antonio Gaudí.

The language of Catalonia, Catalan, has a long literary tradition and has deeply marked the political, social, and cultural history of the area. The University of Barcelona (1450) and the Autonomous University of Barcelona (1968) are among the city's educational and research institutions. Libraries include the Central Library of Catalonia, the University Library, and the Municipal Periodical Library. Outstanding museums include the Fine Arts Museum of Catalonia, the maritime museum, and the Picasso Museum.

City transportation is facilitated by an urban belt of rapid transit, including subways, tunnels, buses, cable cars, and freeways. Railways connect the city with the suburbs as well as with the rest of Spain and with France, while the Prat Airport serves international flights. The Barcelona harbour dates from the 17th century. Area city, 35 sq mi (91 sq km); metropolitan area, 184 sq mi (477 sq km). Pop. (1981 prelim.) city, 1,754,900; metropolitan area, 3,096,748.

Barcelona, city, capital of Anzoátegui state, northeastern Venezuela. On the west bank of the Río Neverí, 3 mi (5 km) inland from the Caribbean Sea and about 200 mi east of Caracas, it lies in the Barcelona Gap, through which the Llanos (plains) extend from the interior to the sea. Barcelona is an important cattle-shipping centre as well as an outlet for coffee grown in the high interior valleys and for the important oil fields nearest the northern Venezuelan coast. Although the city's commercial and industrial development has been erratic, it has prospered as a part of the Barcelona–Guanta–Puerto La Cruz industrial complex. The nation's principal coalfields (lignite and semibituminous) are nearby. Pop. (1981) 284,000.

Barcelona, Museo Arqueologica de (Barcelona museum): *see* Museo Arqueologica de Barcelona e Instituto de Prehistoria y Arqueología.

Barcelona chair, one of the finest and most elegant chairs of the 20th century. It was designed by Mies van der Rohe for the German Pavilion, which he also designed, at the International Exposition in Barcelona in 1929.

The framework consists of two connected pairs of crossed steel bars: the single curve of the back continues into the front legs, and the rear legs, which cross these, form a double

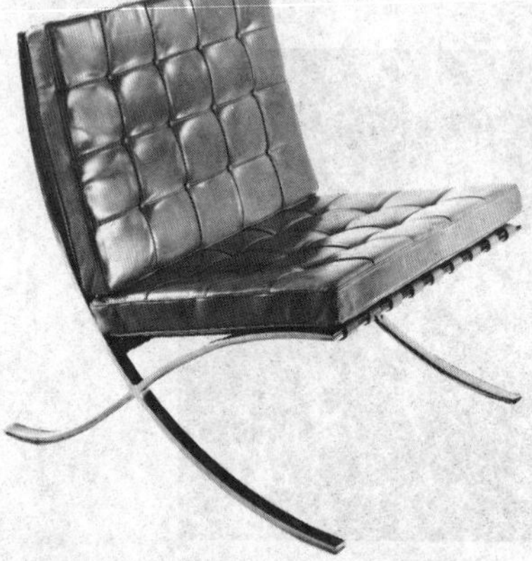

Barcelona chair, chrome-plated steel with leather cushions and supporting straps, designed by Mies van der Rohe, Germany, 1929; in the Museum of Modern Art, New York City

By courtesy of the Museum of Modern Art, New York, gift of Knoll Associates, Inc.

curve supporting the seat. The seat and back consist of leather straps supporting foam-rubber cushions covered with buttoned leather.

barchan, also spelled BARKHAN, crescent-shaped sand dune produced by the action of wind predominately from one direction. One of the commonest types of dunes, it occurs in sandy deserts all over the world. Barchans are convex facing the wind; the horns of the crescent point downwind and mark the lateral advancement of the sand. These dunes are markedly asymmetrical in cross section, with a gentle slope facing toward the wind and a much steeper slope facing away from the wind. Barchans may be 9–30 metres (30–100 feet) high and 370 m (1,214 ft) wide at the base measured perpendicular to the wind. They gradually migrate with the wind as a result of erosion on the windward side and deposition on the leeward side. The rate of migration ranges from about a metre to a hundred metres per year. Barchans usually occur as groups of isolated dunes and may form chains that extend across a plain in the direction of the prevailing wind.

Barchans are characteristic of open, inland desert regions such as Turkistan, where the name originated. The Russian naturalist Alexander von Middendorf is credited with introducing the word into scientific literature in 1881.

Barclay, Alexander (b. *c.* 1476—d. June 10, 1552, Croydon, Surrey, Eng.), poet who won contemporary fame chiefly for his adaptation of a popular German satire, *Das Narrenschiff*, by Sebastian Brant, which he called *The Shyp of Folys of the Worlde* (first printed 1509).

Barclay, possibly of Scottish birth, was by 1509 a chaplain at the College of St. Mary Ottery, Devon. He later became a Benedictine

Alexander Barclay (kneeling), woodcut from the frontispiece of the *Mirror of Good Manners*, 1523

By courtesy of the trustees of the British Museum; photograph, J.R. Freeman & Co. Ltd.

monk at Ely and still later a Franciscan
of Canterbury. He presumably conform
Protestantism, however, for after the
mation he retained livings (benefices) i
and Somerset held since 1546. In 1
became rector of All Hallows, Londo

Barclay also wrote (probably while
at Ely) the first formal eclogues i
filled with entertaining pictures of r

Barclay, John (b. Jan. 28, 15
Mousson, near Nancy, Fr.—d. Au
Rome), Scottish satirist and Lati
Argenis (1621), a long poem of
venture, had great influence o
ment of the romance in the 17

Barclay was a cosmopolitan
who travelled freely between
don. He remained in Lond
until 1616 as a minor c
settled permanently in Ro
phormionis Lusinini Saty
severe satire on the Jesui
fession, and contempora
cation, and literature, is
of Petronius Arbiter; it i
mixture of prose and ve
and rogues, it contri
velopment of the pica
most celebrated wo
outstanding exampl
Its political implica
many editions we
the characters and
persisted; it was r
during the 17th
such as William
Crashaw, and J
miliar with the

Joh
Me

By
p

Barclay, Robert (b. Dec. 23, 1648, Gordonstoun, Moray, Scot.—d. Oct. 3, 1690, Ury, Aberdeen), Quaker leader whose *Apology for the True Christian Divinity* (1678) became a standard statement of Quaker doctrines and whose friendship with James II, then duke of York, helped obtain the patent to settle the province of East Jersey, in the New World.

After returning to Scotland from his education in Paris, Barclay joined the Society of Friends (Quakers) in 1666. For a public debate at Aberdeen in 1675, he published *Theses Theologicae*, a set of 15 propositions of the Quaker faith. To amplify them further, he published the *Apology* three years later. This early and enduring exposition of Quaker beliefs defined Quakerism as a religion of the Inner Light. Arguing against both Roman Catholicism and traditional Protestantism, including Anglicanism, Barclay asserted that neither the church nor the Scriptures could claim completeness or ultimate authority and that both were secondary to the work of the Holy Spirit—the Inner Light—in the believer.

In 1677 Barclay and other Quaker leaders, including William Penn (1644–1718), visited Holland and northern Germany to promote the Quaker movement. Repeatedly imprisoned and persecuted at home, Barclay and Penn found a friend in the Duke of York. Their influence with him helped secure a patent for themselves and 10 other society members to settle in that area of present-day New Jersey then called East Jersey (not to be confused with the area in present Pennsylvania where Penn founded Philadelphia). The group emigrated to America in 1682. After serving from 1682 to 1688 as nominal governor of East Jersey, Barclay returned to Scotland and died at his estate at Ury.

Barclay de Tolly, Mikhail Bogdanovich, Knyaz (Prince) (b. Dec. 27 [Dec. 16, old style], 1761, Luhda-Grosshof, Livonia, Russian Empire—d. May 26 [May 14, O.S.], 1818, Insterburg, East Prussia), Russian field marshal prominent in the Napoleonic Wars.

He was a member of a Scottish family that had settled in Russia in the 17th century. Entering the Russian Army in 1786, he served against Turkey (1788–89), Sweden (1790), and Poland (1792–94). In the campaign of 1806–07 against Napoleon, Barclay distinguished himself in the Battle of Pultusk and was wounded in the Battle of Eylau, after which he was made lieutenant general. In 1808–09 he commanded Russian forces against the Swedes in Finland. From 1810 to 1812 he was Russian minister of war.

In 1812 Barclay took command of one of two Russian armies operating against Napoleon. His strategy of avoiding decisive action and retreating into Russia proved unpopular, and he was forced to resign his command in favour of General M.I. Kutuzov, who followed the same strategy.

Barclay was present at the Battle of Borodino, left the army soon afterward, and was recalled in 1813 for service in Germany. After the Battle of Bautzen he was made commander in chief of the Russian forces, and after the Battle of Leipzig he received the title of count from the emperor Alexander I. Barclay took part in the invasion of France in 1814 and while in Paris was promoted to field marshal. In 1815 he was commander in chief of the Russian Army that invaded France after Napoleon's return from Elba. He was made a prince at the end of that campaign.

Barclays Bank PLC, British banking and trust firm registered July 20, 1896, under the name Barclay & Co. Ltd. and assuming the name Barclays Bank Ltd. in 1917. It was converted into a public limited company in 1981. The largest commercial banking concern in the United Kingdom, it operates about 5,000 offices in England and Wales and overseas and has several subsidiaries in Britain and elsewhere. The group's overseas business is managed by Barclay Bank International Ltd., which has some 2,000 offices in over 70 countries. Headquarters are in London.

The bank, as created in 1896, merged the banking business of Barclay, Bevan, Tritton, Ransom, Bouverle & Co., Gurney & Co., and various other private banking concerns. Over the years it took over several other banks, mostly in Britain but also in Commonwealth nations, continental Europe, and other areas. In 1979 Barclays purchased American Credit Corporation and changed the name of that institution to Barclays American Corporation. Through this subsidiary, the bank embarked on a program of significant expansion in the United States in the early 1980s, purchasing numerous consumer finance companies and trust company operations.

Barclay Bank International Ltd.—called Barclays Bank D.C.O. until 1971 and Barclays Bank (Dominion, Colonial and Overseas) until 1954—was created in 1925 in the amalgamation of Colonial Bank, Anglo-Egyptian Bank, and National Bank of South Africa and became a wholly owned subsidiary of Barclays Bank Ltd. in 1971. The Colonial Bank had been founded in 1836 to carry on business in the West Indies and British Guiana and had been empowered by special acts of 1916–17 to conduct business anywhere in the world. The Anglo-Egyptian Bank had been created in 1864 to do business in Alexandria and, later, elsewhere in the Mediterranean, as in Malta. De Nationale Bank der Zuid-Afrikaansche Republiek (Beperkt) had been incorporated in the Boer republic in 1890 and renamed the National Bank of South Africa Limited in 1902, after British occupation.

Barcoo River (Australia): *see* Cooper Creek.

bard, in the original meaning, a Celtic composer of eulogy and satire; more generally, a tribal poet-singer gifted in composing and reciting verses on heroes and their deeds. As early as the 1st century AD, the Latin author Lucan referred to bards as the national poets or minstrels of Gaul and Britain. In Gaul the institution gradually disappeared, whereas in Ireland and Wales it survived. The Irish bard through his chanting has preserved a tradition of poetic eulogy. In Wales, where the word bard has always been used for poet, the bardic order was codified into distinct grades in the 10th century. Despite a decline of the order toward the end of the Middle Ages, the Welsh tradition has persisted and is celebrated in the annual eisteddfod (*q.v.*), a national assembly of poets and musicians.

Bardanes: *see* Philippicus Bardanes.

Bardeen, John (b. May 23, 1908, Madison, Wis., U.S.), co-winner of the Nobel Prize for Physics in both 1956 and 1972. He shared the 1956 prize with William B. Shockley and Walter H. Brattain for their joint invention of the transistor. With Leon N. Cooper and John R. Schrieffer he was awarded the 1972 prize for development of the theory of superconductivity.

Bardeen

By courtesy of University of Illinois at Urbana—Champaign

Bardeen obtained his Ph.D. in 1936 in mathematics and physics from Princeton University. A staff member of the University of Minnesota, Minneapolis, from 1938 to 1941, he served as principal physicist at the U.S. Naval Ordnance Laboratory in Washington, D.C., during World War II. After the war he joined Bell Telephone Laboratories, Inc., where he did research on the electron-conducting properties of semiconductors. This work led to the invention of the transistor, which replaced the bulkier vacuum tube in many applications and ushered in the age of microminiature electronic parts.

In 1951 Bardeen was appointed professor of electrical engineering and physics at the University of Illinois, Urbana (emeritus, 1978). The theory of superconductivity that is now called the BCS theory (from the initials of Bardeen, Cooper, and Schrieffer) was first advanced in 1957; all later theoretical work in superconductivity is based upon it. Bardeen was also the author of a theory explaining certain properties of semiconductors.

Bardesanes, also called BARDAISAN, or BAR DAIṢĀN (b. July 11, 154, Edessa, then in Syria, now Urfa, Tur.—d. *c.* 222, Edessa), a leading representative of Syrian Gnosticism. A pioneer of the Christian faith in Syria, he embarked on missionary work after his conversion in 179.

His chief writing, *The Dialogue of Destiny, or The Book of the Laws of the Countries,* recorded by a disciple, Philip, is the oldest known original composition in Syriac literature. Bardesanes attacked the fatalism of the Greek philosophers after Aristotle (4th century BC), particularly regarding the influence of the stars on human destiny. Mingling Christian influence with Gnostic teaching, he denied the creation of the world, of Satan, and of evil by the supreme God, attributing them to a hierarchy of deities.

Some authorities hold that the Christian Bardesanes, responding to heavy Gnostic pressure in Edessa, integrated a semi-Gnostic fatalism concerning life's external circumstances with the Christian notion of personal freedom in moral choice and belief in the saving power of God that brings knowledge. Aided by his son Harmonius, he wrote many of the first Syriac hymns to popularize his teachings. Their literary value earned for him renown in the history of Syriac poetry and music.

Bardhamān (India): *see* Burdwān.

Bardi FAMILY, an aristocratic Florentine family that successfully developed its financial and banking company to become one of the most influential European business powers between 1250 and 1345.

By coordinating its political activity with its financial interests the Bardi became the leading Florentine merchant house. Along with many other Florentine aristocratic families, their power was curtailed somewhat by ordinances of 1293 and 1295. Despite the loss of several estates in 1341, the family retained its prominent political position, until unwise financial ventures, including support of Edward III (king of England 1327–77) in the Hundred Years' War against France (1337–1453), and aid to Florence in a war with the rival city of Lucca, caused the bankruptcy of the banking company in 1345. This bankruptcy provoked resounding financial repercussions in Florence and Europe and toppled the Bardi from political power.

Bardi, Giovanni, CONTE (count) DI VERNIO (b. Feb. 5, 1534, Florence—d. 1612, Florence), musician, writer, and scientist, influential in the evolution of opera. In about 1580 he founded the Florentine Camerata, a group that sought to revive ancient Greek music and drama and whose participants composed the earliest operas. Among the members were the poet Ottavio Rinuccini, the theorist Vincenzo Galilei (father of Galileo), and the composers Giulio Caccini, Jacopo Peri, and Emilio del Cavaliere, with most of whom Bardi collaborated in court entertainments from 1579 to 1608.

Bardi's *Discorso mandato a Caccini sopra la Musica Antica* (1580; "Discourse to Caccini on Ancient Music") develops ideas similar to those of Caccini and Galilei: counterpoint obscures the words in musical settings and should be abandoned; music should consist of a single vocal line, lightly accompanied, exactly reflecting the rhythm and intonation of speech. These theories underlie the musical style of the early Florentine operas. Ironically, Bardi's only surviving compositions are two highly contrapuntal madrigals. Bardi also belonged to the Accademia della Crusca, a literary association, and in 1592 became a chamberlain to Pope Clement VIII.

Bardiya (king of Persia): *see* Smerdis.

Bardo, Treaty of, also called TREATY OF AL-QAṢR AS-SAʿĪD, or TREATY OF KASSER SAID (1881), agreement that established France's protectorate over Tunisia. A French expeditionary force of 36,000 men was sent to Tunisia in 1881 at the urging of the French foreign minister, Jules Ferry, ostensibly to subdue attacks of the Tunisian Kroumer tribe on the Algerian frontier. The French met little resistance from the bey, Muḥammad as-Ṣadiq, and on May 12, 1881, a treaty was concluded, authorizing indefinite French military occupation, restricting the bey's authority to domestic affairs, stipulating a reorganization of Tunisian finances, and providing for a French minister resident, who would act as liaison between French and Tunisian authorities.

Bardsey Island, Welsh YNYS ENLLI, small island (0.7 sq mi [1.8 sq km]) off the tip of the Lleyn Peninsula, Dwyfor district, Gwynedd county, Wales. It is separated from the mainland by a channel 2 mi wide, which has a strong tidal race. On this naturally protected site the earliest religious house in Wales was founded by the Celtic St. Cadfan in the early 6th century and was later superseded by an Augustinian abbey. A place of pilgrimage in the Middle Ages and later a haunt of pirates, it is now a major British bird nature reserve.

Bardstown, city, seat of Nelson County, in the outer Bluegrass region of central Kentucky, U.S., 39 mi (63 km) southeast of Louisville. Founded as Salem in 1778, it was later renamed to honour William Baird (Bard), one of the original landowners. During the Civil War it was occupied (September 1862) by Gen. Braxton Bragg's Confederate forces.

The city is the trade centre for a fertile agricultural area (tobacco, grain, livestock, and dairy products); its manufactures include bourbon whiskey, flour, and lumber. St. Joseph's Cathedral (1819), the oldest Catholic cathedral west of the Alleghenies, is in the city. Nearby is "Federal Hill" (1795; a Georgian house preserved as a shrine within a state park), where Stephen Foster is said to have composed the song "My Old Kentucky Home." Wickland (1813; home of three Kentucky governors), the Trappists' Abbey of Our Lady of Gethsemane (founded 1848), the Barton Museum of Whiskey History, and Bernheim Forest are in the vicinity. Inc. 1788. Pop. (1980) 6,155.

bareback bronc-riding, rodeo event in which a cowboy attempts to ride a bucking horse (bronco) for a specified time (usually eight seconds). The horse is equipped only with a surcingle—a rope belt about its midsection—which the rider may grip with one hand only. The rider must have his spurs in contact high on the horse's shoulders to begin the event, and he is disqualified if he is thrown off, touches the horse with his free hand, or al-

Bareback rider trying to ride bucking horse
E.W. Marugg Photography

lows the surcingle to slip off the horse. Horse and rider are scored separately for their performance, and the rider with the highest total is the winner.

Barebone, Praise-God, Barebone also spelled BAREBONES: *see* Barbon, Praise-God.

Barebones Parliament, also called LITTLE, or NOMINATED, PARLIAMENT (July 4–Dec. 12, 1653), a hand-picked legislative group of "godly" men convened by Oliver Cromwell following the Puritan victory in the English Civil Wars. Its name was derived from one of its obscure members, Praise-God Barbon. After Cromwell expelled the Rump Parliament (April 20, 1653), he prompted the army council to dispatch letters to the Congregational churches inviting suggestions of fit persons to sit in a new assembly. From the names submitted, the council chose 140 members—129 for England, 5 for Scotland, and 6 for Ireland. On July 4 the delegates met, assuming by a resolution of July 6 the name of Parliament. The zeal of this Nominated Parliament for reform, however, threatened to confuse rather than settle the war-weary nation. On December 12 conservative members of the Parliament accused their radical opponents of destroying the clergy, the law, and the property of the subject and, by a surprise motion, resolved upon the abdication of the Parliament. The majority thereupon waited on Cromwell and laid their resignation before him, while the recalcitrant minority was expelled from the house by the military. Next day Gen. John Lambert produced the "Instrument of Government," which after two days' discussion established the system of Protectorate government that lasted until May 1657.

Bareilly, town, administrative headquarters of Bareilly district, Uttar Pradesh state, northern India, on the Rāmganga River. Founded in 1537, the town was built largely by the Mughal governor Makrand Rāy. It later became the capital of the Rohillas, a migrant clan that gained control of the surrounding territory. In 1774 the ruler of Oudh conquered the area with British aid, and Bareilly was ceded to the British in 1801. It was a centre of the 1857 Indian Mutiny against British rule. Situated at a major rail and road junction, it is a trade centre for agricultural products and has a number of industries (sugar processing, cotton ginning and pressing). Bareilly College (1837) is in the town, and the Indian Veterinary Research Institute is in the suburb of Izatnagar. Bareilly contains a number of fine mosques and other ancient buildings and a fort (1657).

Bareilly district, 1,593 sq mi (4,125 sq km) in area, is a largely level region watered by the Rāmganga River and the Sārda Canal system. There is some jungle in the north. Rice, wheat, sugarcane, and other crops are grown. The ancient fortress city of Ahicchattrā, 21 mi (34 km) northwest of Bareilly, is believed to have been visited by Buddha. Pop. (1981) town, 386,734; metropolitan area, 449,425; district, 2,273,030.

Barents, Willem (b. *c.* 1550—d. June 20, 1597, the Arctic), Dutch navigator who searched for a northeast passage from Europe to Asia and for whom the Barents Sea was named. Because of his extensive voyages, accurate charting, and the valuable meteorological data he collected, he is regarded as one of the most important of the early Arctic explorers.

On his voyages of 1594 and 1595 he rounded northern Europe and reached the vicinity of the Novaya Zemlya archipelago, north of European Russia. On a third voyage (1596), he sighted Spitsbergen (now Svalbard), but upon rounding the north of Novaya Zemlya his ship became trapped in ice, and Barents was compelled to winter in the north. He lived only a week after he and his party were able to leave in open boats. The Arctic dwelling in which the party had wintered was found in 1871; many of its relics are preserved at The Hague. In 1875 a portion of his journal was found.

Barents Sea, Norwegian BARENTSHAVET, Russian BARENTSEVO MORE, outlying portion of the Arctic Ocean 800 mi (1,300 km) long and 650 mi wide and covering 542,000 sq mi (1,405,000 sq km). Its average depth is 750 ft (229 m), plunging to a maximum of 2,000 ft in the major Bear Island Trench. It is bounded by the archipelagoes of Svalbard and Franz Josef Land (north), the Norwegian and Soviet mainland (south), the Novaya Zemlya archipelago (east), and by the conventional border with the Greenland Sea (west), which runs from Spitsbergen to Norway's northernmost tip, North Cape, via Bear Island (Bjørnøya).

The sea was known to Vikings and medieval Russians as the Murmean Sea. It first appeared under its modern name in a chart published in 1853, honouring a 16th-century Dutch seeker of a northeast passage to Asia, Willem Barents.

The Barents Sea covers a relatively shallow continental shelf fringing the Eurasian landmass. The floor—covered by sands, silts, and a sandy-silt mixture—is cut from east to west by the major Bear Island Trench and the smaller South Cape, Northern, and Northeastern trenches. The Central and Perseus elevations provide shallower relief in the north, and there are fishing banks and shallows to the southeast. Also in the southeast is Kolguyev Island. The western mainland coast is abruptly elevated and pierced by fjords, while east of the Kanin Peninsula the coast is low-lying, with a number of shallow bays and inlets. The coasts of the northern archipelagoes are steep and high, with glaciers plunging down to the sea and accumulations of glacier-carried debris in the hollows.

The climate is sub-Arctic, with winter air temperatures averaging −13° F (−25° C) in the north and 23° F (−5° C) in the southwest; summer temperatures in the same regions average, respectively, 32° F (0° C) and 50° F (10° C). Annual precipitation is 20 inches (500 mm) in the south but only half that in the north.

The North Cape and Spitsbergen branches of the Norway Current bring warm currents into the sea, but heat is lost in mixing with colder waters. Despite the high salinity (34 parts per 1,000) ice forms in winter, but fields are thin and icebergs do not linger long. In summer, the edge of the ice retreats far to the north. The tidal amplitude and current direction varies greatly. Ice-free ports are Murmansk and Teribyorka (U.S.S.R.) and Vardø (Norway).

Fishing flourishes. Microscopic forms of phytoplankton feed deep-sea invertebrates, small, shrimp-like crustaceans, bivalves, and sponges, which in turn support such fish as cod, herring, salmon, plaice, and catfish. There are also sea mammals (seals and whales), land mammals (polar bears and Arctic foxes), sea gulls, and, in warm weather, ducks and geese. Underwater flora is very rich in the shallow southern regions; and brown, red, and green algae are widespread. Most of the coastline is rock and stone, but about 20 to 40 percent contains shrubs, mosses, and lichens. Grasses are rare.

Barère (de Vieuzac), Bertrand (b. Sept. 10, 1755, Tarbes, Fr.—d. Jan. 13, 1841, Tarbes), a leading member of the Committee of Public Safety that ruled Revolutionary France during the period of the Jacobin dictatorship (1793–94); his stringent policies against those suspected of royalist tendencies made him one of the most feared revolutionaries.

Reared in a middle-class family of lawyers and ecclesiastics, Barère studied law at the University of Toulouse and in 1777 became a magistrate at Tarbes. Travelling to Paris in 1788, he came into contact with liberal and republican ideas and came to support suppression of local Parlements and the creation of a popular national assembly.

In 1789 Barère helped draw up the *cahier* (a list of grievances demanding the abolition of feudal rights) of Bigorre, Tarbes, for which he served as deputy to the States General. By autumn 1789 he had joined the Club of the Jacobins and was serving on the Committee on Domains, organized to dispose of crown property. Prominent in Paris by 1790, he supported Robespierre and espoused a larger role for the Revolutionary government in 1791. After the mob attack on the Tuileries Palace, he was in agreement with the imprisonment of King Louis XVI, and by 1793 he was an outspoken regicide. In January 1793 he made

Barère, engraving by Louis-François Mariage, early 19th century, after a drawing by François Bonneville

By courtesy of the Bibliotheque Nationale, Paris

his "Report to the French Nation," supporting nationalism and war against the royalist powers of Europe as an extension of revolutionary principles. His political power reached its apex when he helped found the first Committee of Public Safety in April 1793, was elected its secretary, and formulated much of its propaganda on the "aristocratic conspiracy." By August he supported the confiscation of émigrés' estates, the expulsion of all Bourbon princes, the decree for mass conscription and a national army, and the Committee's policy of absolute economic and diplomatic control. The following spring he was appointed head of cultural propaganda.

After Robespierre's execution in July 1794, Barère's popularity diminished rapidly, and his arrest and deportation were ordered in 1795, although he escaped to Bordeaux. In 1799 Napoleon granted him amnesty and in 1803 made him "reporter of public opinion," but after the First Restoration of the Bourbon monarchy (1814), he shifted his loyalties to the crown. Elected deputy during Napoleon's Hundred Days, he was placed on the police list after the Second Restoration in 1815 and was forced to flee to Belgium. He returned to Paris in 1830 and was elected to the general council of the Hautes-Pyrénées in 1833.

BIBLIOGRAPHY. B. Barère de Vieuzac, *Mémoires* (1842–44); Leo Gershoy, *Bertrand Barère: A Reluctant Terrorist* (1962); and Robert Launay, *Barère de Vieuzac, l'Anacréon de la guillotine* (1929).

Bārfurush (Iran): *see* Bābol.

Barge Canal (New York, U.S.): *see* New York State Barge Canal.

bargeboard, also called VERGEBOARD, exposed board or false rafter running underneath

Gothic Revival style bargeboard on the New York Yacht Club House (currently in Mystic, Conn.), by Alexander Jackson Davis, 1846

Wayne Andrews

the slopes of a projecting gable roof. Such a board is often richly decorated with carved, cut out, or painted designs and patterns, particularly in late medieval Europe, in Tudor England, and in 19th-century Gothic Revival architecture in England and the United States.

Bargello, Museo Nazionale del (Italian: National Museum of the Bargello), art museum housed in the Palazzo del Bargello (or del Podestà), Florence, which dates from the 13th and 14th centuries. The museum was established in 1865 and is especially famous for its collection of Renaissance sculpture, including works by Donatello, Michelangelo, Pollaiuolo, Sansovino, and Verrocchio.

There is also a collection of some decorative arts, with displays of ivories, bronzes, majolica, medals, textiles, arms, and armour. The collection includes works by Luca Della Robbia and Cellini.

bargello work, also called FLORENTINE CANVAS WORK, kind of embroidery exemplified in

Bargello, or Florentine, work, detail of an American needlepoint upholstery, *c.* 1725; in the Metropolitan Museum of Art, New York City

By courtesy of the Metropolitan Museum of Art, New York, gift of Mrs. J. Insley Blair, 1950

the upholstery of a set of 17th-century Italian chairs at the Bargello in Florence and practiced from the 17th century till modern times. It consists of flat vertical stitches laid parallel with the canvas weave rather than crossing the intersections diagonally as in most canvas stitches. These stitches, in gradating tones of the same colour or in contrasting colours, are arranged in a wavy zigzag pattern. The characteristic stitch is variously called Florentine, cushion, or, in allusion to the flamelike gradation of colour, flame stitch; its 17th-century name was Hungarian stitch.

Bargest (folklore): *see* Barghest.

Barghash (ibn Saʿīd) (b. *c.* 1834—d. March 27, 1888, Zanzibar), sultan of Zanzibar (1870–88), a shrewd and ambitious ruler, who, for most of his reign, looked to Britain for protection and assistance but eventually saw his domains divided between Germany and his former protector.

Although not the first heir to the throne of his father, Saʿīd ibn Sulṭān, Barghash had made plans to seize the throne at his father's death in 1856; he was, however, forestalled by the rightful heir, his brother Mājid, and spent two years in exile in Bombay. Shortly after Barghash came to power (1870), his longtime friend John Kirk became British consul. Kirk, a strong advocate of British support of Zanzibar, forced Barghash to sign an anti-slavery treaty in 1873 and two further proclamations in 1876 to close additional slave-trade loopholes. The British government (despite Kirk's recommendations) was not prepared to support actively the extension of Barghash's authority in the interior, but British pressure did discourage Egyptian expansion along the East African coast in 1875.

Recognizing his political and military weakness, Barghash afterward looked to Britain both as a protector and as a source of technical and military aid. In the following years, with British help, he created a small but modern army and attempted to modernize his government. By 1882, however, he recognized the threat posed by Belgian king Leopold II's determination to control the rich ivory trade of the Congo Basin. At first Barghash tried to prevent that control by supporting the state-building efforts of the Arab trader Tippu Tib. But when Leopold's claims had been recognized by other European powers in 1885 and Germany was claiming most of present-day Tanzania, the disillusioned Barghash had no choice but to acquiesce in the dismemberment of his kingdom late in 1886.

Barghawāṭah, Berber tribal confederation that created a religio-political state in Morocco (8th–12th centuries). The Barghawāṭah, members of the Maṣmūdah family inhabiting the plain between the Moyen Atlas and the Atlantic, had joined the Miknāsah and Ghumārah Berbers in the Khārijite revolt against the Umayyad caliph in 740–742, seizing Tangier and defeating Umayyad armies from Spain in the Battle of the Nobles (740). Shortly afterward the rebellion was suppressed, but a new leader, Ṣāliḥ ibn Ṭarīf, emerged in 748–749 among the Barghawāṭah and presented himself as a prophet, teaching a mixture of Islāmic, pagan, and astrological beliefs. His successors propagated this doctrine throughout the confederation. In the reign of Abū Ghufayl (885–913) the confederation became firmly established in Barghawāṭah territory and aided in the creation of a highly defensive state that also proved to be commercially prosperous.

By the mid-10th century the Barghawāṭah were influential enough to maintain diplomatic relations with the Umayyads of Córdoba, despite the heretical beliefs of the Berbers and the rigidly orthodox position of the Muslim court. Relations between the two powers were strained by the end of the century, however, and the Barghawāṭah were beset by two invasions from Spain (977–978; 998–999), as well as an attack by an agent of the Fāṭimids from the east (982–983). The Barghawāṭah successfully countered these incursions, but, in the 11th century, they were conquered by their Berber neighbours, the Banū Ifran, allies of the Umayyads. The Almoravid invasion followed in 1059, and, although the Barghawāṭah killed the Almoravid spiritual leader ʿAbd Allāh ibn Yāsīn in battle, they themselves were soundly defeated. The remainder of the Barghawāṭah did not survive the Almohad assault and disappeared after their defeat in 1148–49.

Barghest, also spelled BARGUEST, or BARGEST, in folklore of northern England (especially Yorkshire), a monstrous, goblin dog, with huge teeth and claws, that appears only at night. It was believed that those who saw one clearly would die soon after, while those who

Barghest, drawing by Don Bolognese from *Dragons, Unicorns and Other Magical Beasts*, by Robin Palmer, 1966

caught only a glimpse of the beast would live on, but only for some months. The Demon of Tidworth, the Black Dog of Winchester, the Padfoot of Wakefield, and the Barghest of Burnley are all related apparitions. Their Welsh counterparts were red-eyed Gwyllgi, the Dog of Darkness, and Cwn Annwn, the Dogs of Hell. In Lancashire the monster was called Trash, Skriker, or Striker; its broad, sometimes backward-pointing feet made a splashing noise, and it howled horribly. In East Anglia, where it was thought to be amphibious, the dog had only one eye and was known as Black Shuck or Shock. It was called Mauthe Doog on the Isle of Man. The Manchester Barghest was said to be headless.

bargueño (cabinet): *see* vargueno.

Barguzinsky Nature Reserve, natural area set aside for research in the natural sciences, extending from the northeastern shore of Lake Baikal to the western slopes of the Barguzinsky Mountains, southeastern Russian Soviet Federated Socialist Republic. The reserve was established (1916) to protect the habitat of the Barguzin sable and has an area of 650,380 ac (263,200 ha). It covers 37 mi (60 km) of the Lake Baikal shoreline and adjacent lake waters, and part of the summit ridge of the Barguzinsky Mountains. The mountainous section is dissected by glacial cirques and lakes. Vegetation near the shore of Lake Baikal includes larch and rhododendron. At higher elevations there are taigas of cedar, larch, and fir. The upper elevations are dominated by tundra and lichen-covered rocks and cliffs. Wildlife includes pika, Siberian chipmunk, fox, elk, reindeer, brown bear, stoat, weasel, otter, moose, wolverine, Baikal hair seal (abundant along the lake shore), and musk and red deer. White-tailed eagle, ptarmigan, grouse, oriental cuckoo, warbler, and tit are the main bird species in the park.

Bari, people living near Juba in the southern Sudan. They speak an Eastern Sudanic language of the Chari-Nile branch of the Nilo-Saharan family. They live in small villages scattered across the hot, dry, flat countryside in the Nile Valley. Their staple crop is millet, and they also keep cattle. Their culture and language are shared by many other small tribes in the region, most important of these being the Kakwa, Mondari, Kuku, Fajulu, Nyangbara, and Nyepu.

The Bari are divided into freemen and serfs. Blacksmiths, professional hunters, and similar groups form inferior castes. Most of the 150 patrilineal clans are composed of freemen. Both men and women undergo initiation by the extraction of the lower incisors and by scarring. Men then enter age sets that have distinctive names and ornaments. The people have many "big men" rather than a single chief. These include ritual functionaries, the rainmakers, who are few in number but extremely powerful, and the "fathers of the earth," who are responsible for magic to ensure successful cultivation, hunting, and warfare. Both these offices are hereditary. The Bari believe in a god who has two aspects: a benevolent god who dwells in the sky and produces rain and a malevolent god who lives in the earth and is associated with cultivation. Sacrifices are made to the spirits of the dead.

Bari, Latin BARIUM, city, capital of Bari province and of Puglia (Apulia) region, southeastern Italy; it is a port on the Adriatic Sea, northwest of Brindisi. The site may have been inhabited since 1500 BC. Greek influence was strong, and under the Romans, who called it Barium, it became an important port, the harbour being mentioned as early as 180 BC. Fishing was also significant in Roman times. A Saracen stronghold in the 9th century AD, the city became the seat of the Byzantine governor of Apulia in 885. It was captured for the Normans by Robert Guiscard in 1071. Peter the Hermit preached the First Crusade there in 1096, and a large party of crusaders embarked from its port. Razed by William the Bad of Sicily in 1156, Bari acquired new greatness under Emperor Frederick II (reigned 1220–50). An independent duchy under a succession of rulers from the 14th century, it passed from the Sforza family to the Kingdom of Naples in 1558 and became part of the Italian kingdom in 1860.

S. Nicola basilica, Bari, Italy

SCALA—Art Resource/EB Inc.

Modern Bari consists of the old city on the peninsula dividing the old from the new harbours; the new city along the coast on either side; and the industrial area inland. The chief features of historic interest are in the old city, notably the 12th-century Romanesque cathedral; the Norman castle, rebuilt by Frederick II and later extended; and the basilica of S. Nicola, founded in 1087 to house the relics of St. Nicholas, the patron saint of Bari. The seat of an archbishop and of a university (founded 1924), the city has a provincial picture gallery and archaeological museum. The annual Fiera del Levante, an Occidental–Oriental trade fair, has been held since 1930.

On the east coast railway from Milan and Bologna to Brindisi, Bari has international air services from nearby Palese airport and steamer services to Adriatic ports, the Black Sea, and the Mediterranean. Bari is connected by motorway to other Adriatic cities and to Naples on Italy's western coast. The city is an agricultural centre; its industries include food processing, oil refining, textile milling, printing, and the production of tobacco, sulfide, building materials, machinery, aluminum, and ironwork. A busy centre for sea trade with the Balkans and the Middle East, the Porto Nuovo exports wine, olive oil, and almonds. Pop. (1981 prelim.) mun., 370,781.

Bari, *gobolka* (administrative region), northeastern Somalia, East Africa. Part of the former British Somaliland Protectorate until 1960, it is the largest of Somalia's regions and was created from the northern part of the former Migiurtin region in 1973. Its area of 27,027 sq mi (70,000 sq km) fronts the Gulf of Aden on the north and the Indian Ocean on the east, and is bounded by the *gobollada* (administrative regions) of Sanaag (west) and Nugaal (southwest and south). The extremely hot (average annual temperature of 86° F [30° C] at Boosaaso [or Bender Cassim]) and extremely arid northern and eastern coasts (receiving less than 1 in. [25 mm] of annual rainfall) rise to a semi-desert plateau in the interior. Temperatures range from below freezing in the plateau area in December to more than 120° F (49° C) in the coastal plains in July. The region was a major disaster area during the great drought of 1974–75. The northeasternmost tip of Somalia, the Caseyr (or Cape Guardafui), marking the entrance of the Gulf of Aden from the Indian Ocean, has a lighthouse built by the Italians in 1922. The salt deposits of Ras (point) Hafun on the eastern coast are among the world's largest. Coastal waters off Bari are rich in sardines, and excellent natural harbour facilities exist in the Hafun area; its development was one of the major development projects of the Somali government in the early 1980s. Boosaaso, the regional capital on the northwestern coast, is known for its hot springs. Pop. (1975) 154,352.

Bari, Siege of (1068–71), three-year blockade by Norman forces under Robert Guiscard that resulted (April 1071) in the surrender of the last important Byzantine stronghold in southern Italy. It brought an end to Byzantine domination on the Italian peninsula.

An Adriatic seaport and trading centre surpassed only by Venice, Bari commanded a strategic position on the crossroads between western Europe and the Byzantine east. Its well-fortified harbour had always protected it from attack by sea until Guiscard utilized the Norman fleet to blockade the harbour.

Barīd Shāhī DYNASTY, the rulers of the small state of Bīdar (now in Karnātaka in southwestern India) from *c.* 1487 until 1619. The Barīd family were ministers of the Muslim Bahmanī sultans of the Deccan, who in 1430 made their capital at Bīdar.

In about 1492 the Bahmanī kingdom disintegrated, but the sultans retained a small principality around Bīdar. Real power was by then in the hands of Amīr Qāsim Barīd, and his grandson ʿAlī Barīd assumed the royal title in 1542. The kingdom was absorbed by the larger Deccan kingdom of Bijāpur in 1619.

Bariloche (Argentina): *see* San Carlos de Bariloche.

Barīm Island (Yemen [Aden]): *see* Perim Island.

Barinas, state, western Venezuela, bounded north by Portuguesa and Cojedes states, east by the Río Guarico, south by the Río Apure, and west by Táchira and Mérida. Because the territory of 13,590 sq mi (35,200 sq km) lies in the Llanos (plains), it is plagued by alternate drought and flood. With control of malaria, development of all-weather highways, rapid growth of the petroleum industry and of manufacturing, and government investment in the Llanos, especially in irrigation works in the northwest, the economy of Barinas has developed and diversified beyond its original base of cattle raising. Barinas has continued to rank among Venezuela's most important states in cattle production, but agriculture is increasingly important. The greatest changes have resulted from the discovery of oil in 1948. A pipeline moves the oil some 200 mi (320 km) northward to a terminal at Puerto Cabello. The network of roads focusses on Barinas (*q.v.*), the state capital and a cattle-trading centre. Pop. (1983 est.) 331,458.

Barinas, city, capital of Barinas state, western Venezuela, on the Río Santo Domingo. On the Llanos (plains) at the foot of the Cordillera de Mérida in the northwestern part of the state, Barinas is the regional centre for a large cattle-raising area. Its main commodities are livestock products; the dairy industry is also prominent. Cacao and tobacco are cultivated in the hinterland. Barinas is on the highway that skirts the southern flanks of the Andes, 170 mi (270 km) northeast of San Cristóbal, capital of Táchira state, and 60 mi southwest of Guanare, capital of Portuguesa state. The city also has an airport. Pop. (1981) 90,900.

Bārind, region occupying parts of Dinājpur, Rangpur, Bogra, and Rājshāhi districts, Rājshāhi division, Bangladesh, and West Dinājpur and Mālda districts, West Bengal, India. It comprises the northwestern portion of the lower Gangetic Plain between the Padma (Ganges) and Jamuna (Brahmaputra) rivers and is drained mainly by the Tista, Karatoya, and Atrai rivers, tributaries of the Jamuna River. Bārind is a comparatively high, undulating region, with reddish and yellowish clay soils (*khiyar*); it is broken by ravines that vary from shallow lowland stretches to deeper depressions (*kharis*) resembling old riverbeds and sometimes containing water. *Bhils* (marshes) are numerous in the southern section. Much of Bārind has been cleared and reclaimed, but it still contains much scrub and degraded remnant forest land. Wheat, barley, tobacco, and a large proportion of the sugarcane, pulses, and oilseeds of Bangladesh are grown there.

Baring FAMILY, British family (of German ancestry) prominent in mercantile and financial enterprises since the second half of the 18th century. The family firm, originally named John & Francis Baring & Company, was founded in London in 1763, principally by the future Sir Francis Baring, lst Baronet (1740–1810). At first the partners were import and export commission agents for other merchants, but they soon began to buy merchandise for sale in their own name, to lend their credit in the form of trade acceptances, and to receive deposits of money from clients and personal friends. From 1792 the house of Baring helped to finance the British war effort against revolutionary France. In 1806 the firm was renamed Baring Brothers and Company. Francis Baring also underwrote marine insurance, and he was given a baronetcy for his part in managing the East India Company. He was a follower of the Scottish political economist Adam Smith, a friend of the utilitarian reformer Jeremy Bentham, and an adviser to numerous British politicians—notably, Prime Minister William Pitt the Younger.

On Sir Francis' death, the leadership of the firm passed to his second son, Alexander Baring, afterward 1st Baron Ashburton (1774–1848), who married Anne Bingham, a member of one of the wealthiest families in Pennsylvania, and who secured for Baring Brothers the leadership (until the U.S. Civil War, 1861–65) in financing U.S. foreign trade and selling U.S. bonds. As ambassador to the United States, Lord Ashburton negotiated with U.S. Secretary of State Daniel Webster the Webster-Ashburton Treaty (1842) concerning the boundary between Maine and New Brunswick.

After Lord Ashburton's death in 1848 the affairs of the house were managed by Thomas Baring (1799–1873), another son of Sir Thomas Baring. Thomas Baring represented Huntingdon in Parliament from 1844 until his death. His elder brother, Sir Francis Thornhill Baring (1796–1866), was a member of Parliament for Portsmouth from 1826 to 1865. From 1839 to 1841 he was chancellor of the exchequer, and from 1849 to 1852 first lord of the Admiralty. In 1866 he was created Baron Northbrook, the barony being converted in 1876 into an earldom in favour of his eldest son, Thomas George Baring (1826–1904; *see* Northbrook, Thomas George Baring, 1st earl of). The latter, the 1st earl of Northbrook, was occupied almost entirely with public affairs and filled at different times many important official positions. He is best remembered as viceroy of India, an office he held from 1872 to 1876, but his last public position was first lord of the Admiralty (1880–85).

With the death of Thomas Baring in 1873, Edward Charles Baring (1828–1897), son of Henry Baring and grandson of Sir Francis Baring, became head of the firm of Baring Brothers, and in 1885 he was raised to the peerage as Baron Revelstoke. The house of Baring then stood at the height of its prosperity. During the following years a large amount of English capital was advanced to the Argentine Republic, Barings undertaking the loans and guaranteeing the interest. Through the continued default of the Argentine government, Barings became seriously involved, their heavy obligations precipitating a general financial crisis. Toward the end of 1890 it became known that the firm was on the eve of suspending payment, with liabilities amounting to £21,000,000. The prompt action of the Bank of England, which in conjunction with the leading joint-stock banks of the United Kingdom took over these liabilities, averted further disaster, and the firm of Baring Brothers was subsequently reorganized as a limited company with a capital of £1,000,000. Given this respite, the company and individual members of the family paid the entire debt. During World War II the firm's managing director was entrusted with liquidating Great Britain's fixed assets in the United States.

Other members of the family were Evelyn Baring, 1st earl of Cromer (1841–1917; *see* Cromer, Evelyn Baring, 1st earl of), de facto ruler of Egypt as British agent and consul general (1883–1907), and Maurice Baring (1874–1945), man of letters.

The House of Baring in American Trade and Finance . . . 1763–1861, by Ralph Willard Hidy, was published in 1949.

Baringo, Lake, lake in west central Kenya, East Africa, situated 3,200 ft (975 m) above sea level in the northern section of the Great Rift Valley, between the Laikipia Escarpment (east) and the Kamasia Hills (west). The lake, with an area of 50 sq mi (129 sq km), is 11 mi (18 km) long and 5 mi (8 km) wide and has an average depth of 17 ft (5 m). A freshwater lake with no visible outlet, its waters seep into lavas at its northern end, where a rocky shore contrasts with the alluvial flat on its southern border. The Kamasya and Njamus peoples of the Baringo Basin catch *Tilapia* (a perchlike fish) in the lake, herd cattle, and raise crops (watered by the Perkersa Irrigation Project). The first European to reach the lake was Joseph Thomson in 1883.

Baripāda, town, administrative headquarters of Mayūrbhanj district, northeastern Orissa state, eastern India, on the Burhābalang River. Founded around 1800, the town is a trade centre for rice and other crops and for timber and other forest products, and it has some industry, including pottery making, distilling, and weaving. The former ruler's palace now houses Maharaja Purna Chandra College, and there is an archaeological museum. A narrow-gauge rail line links the town with the South-Eastern Railway along the coast. Pop. (1981) town, 40,314; metropolitan area, 52,989.

Barisāl (district, Bangladesh): *see* Bākerganj.

Barisāl, headquarters of Bākerganj (Barisāl) district, Khulna division, Bangladesh, lying in the Ganges Delta on the west bank of the Barisāl River, a tributary of the Ariāl Khān. Incorporated as a municipality in 1876, it is a jute and rice transshipment centre, linked by steamer with Dhākā (73 mi [117 km] north), and is a key port on the river–sea route to Chittagong. It has 15 colleges affiliated with the University of Dhākā and a public library and park.

Barisāl gives its name to a curious natural phenomenon known as Barisāl guns, thundering noises heard in the delta and apparently coming from the sea. The sounds have not been satisfactorily explained but may have a seismic origin. Pop. (1981 prelim.) town, 159,298.

barite, also called BARYTES, OR HEAVY SPAR, the commonest barium mineral, barium sulfate ($BaSO_4$). Barite occurs in hydrothermal ore veins, particularly those containing lead and silver; in sedimentary rocks such as limestone; in clay deposits formed by the weathering of limestone; in marine deposits; and in cavities in igneous rock. It commonly forms as large tubular crystals, as rosette-like aggregates of those crystals, or as divergent plates known as crested barite. It is abundant in Castile and Andalusia, Spain; Nordrhein-Westfalen, W. Ger.; and at various localities in the southern Appalachian and central states and in California in the United States. Commercially, ground barite is used in oil well and gas well drilling muds; in the preparation of barium compounds; as a body, or filler, for paper,

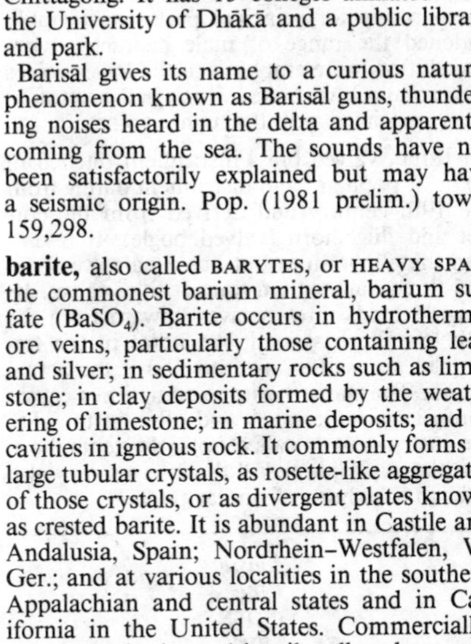

Sample of crested barite from Missouri

Joseph and Helen Guetterman collection; photograph, John H. Gerard—EB Inc.

cloth, and phonograph records; as a white pigment (*see* lithopone); and as an inert body in coloured paints. It forms a solid solution series with celestite, in which strontium replaces barium. For detailed physical properties, *see* sulfate mineral (table).

baritone (from Greek *barytonos,* "deep-sounding"), in vocal music, the most common category of male voice, between the bass and the tenor and with some characteristics of both. Normally, the baritone parts are written for a range of A to f′, but this may be extended in either direction, particularly in solo compositions or as a reflection of an accepted cultural tradition (*e.g.,* that of England, France, Italy, Germany, or Russia). In practice, the classification of voices is determined not only by range but also by the quality, or colour, of the voice and the purpose for which it is to be trained and used. A singer of oratorio, for example, might be comfortable as a tenor, whereas the harsher demands on a tenor in operatic roles might influence the singer to develop his baritone range instead. The term *baritonans* was first used in Western music toward the end of the 15th century, when composers, chiefly at the French court, explored the polyphonic sonorities made possible by the addition of lower pitched voices. Later choral singing, which evolved into the popular four-part writing (soprano, alto, tenor, bass), usually omitted the baritone. German composers seem to have been the first to focus on the use of the baritone as a solo voice, and the prominent use of baritone characters in Mozart's operas was regarded as a distinct innovation by his European contemporaries. The acceptance of the baritone for principal parts considerably widened the range of male character types and shifted more emphasis to the lower voices in hero and lover roles, which had heretofore been associated with the higher voices.

baritone, valved brass instrument pitched in B♭ or C, popular band instrument dating from the 19th century and derived from the cornet and flügelhorn (valved bugle). It resembles the euphonium but has a narrower bore and three, rather than four or five, valves. Its range extends three octaves upward from the E below the bass staff; the notes in the treble clef are written a ninth above the actual sound. The name baritone sometimes causes confusion; in Germany and often in the U.S. the instrument is called both the tenor horn and the euphonium. All three terms may also refer to a saxhorn of similar pitch.

Consult the INDEX *first*

barium (Ba), chemical element, one of the alkaline-earth metals of main Group IIa of the periodic table. The element is used in metallurgy, and its compounds in pyrotechnics, petroleum mining, and radiology.

Properties, occurrence, and uses. Barium, slightly harder than lead, has a silvery white lustre when freshly cut. In nature it is always combined with other elements. The Swedish chemist Carl Wilhelm Scheele discovered (1774) a new base (baryta, or barium oxide) as a minor constituent in pyrolusite and from this base he prepared some crystals of barium sulfate, which he sent to Johan Gottlieb Gahn, the discoverer of manganese. A month later Gahn found that the mineral barite is also composed of barium sulfate. Only after the electric battery became available could Sir Humphry Davy finally isolate (1808) the element itself by electrolysis.

Though barium minerals are dense, barium itself is comparatively light. Barium constitutes about 0.05 percent of the Earth's crust, chiefly as the minerals barite and witherite. Commercial production of barium depends upon the electrolysis of fused barium chloride or the reduction by aluminum of a mixture of barium monoxide and peroxide in an electrically heated vacuum furnace.

The metal is used as a getter in electron tubes to perfect the vacuum by combining with final traces of gases, as a deoxidizer in copper refining, and as a constituent in certain alloys. The alloy with nickel readily emits electrons when heated and is used for this reason in electron tubes and in spark plug electrodes. The presence of barium (atomic number 56) after uranium (atomic number 92) had been bombarded by neutrons was the clue that led to the recognition of nuclear fission (1939).

Naturally occurring barium is a mixture of seven stable isotopes: barium-138 (71.66 percent), barium-137 (11.32 percent), barium-136 (7.81 percent), barium-135 (6.59 percent), barium-134 (2.42 percent), barium-130 (0.101 percent), and barium-132 (0.097 percent). About twice this many radioactive isotopes have been prepared with mass numbers ranging from 126 to 143. In its compounds barium has an oxidation state of +2. The Ba^{2+} ion may be precipitated from solution by the addition of carbonate (CO_3^{2-}), sulfate (SO_4^{2-}), chromate (CrO_4^{2-}), or phosphate (PO_4^{3-}) anions. All soluble barium compounds are toxic.

Most barium compounds are produced from the sulfate via reduction to the sulfide. Barium sulfate ($BaSO_4$), a white, heavy powder that occurs in nature as the mineral barite, is one of the most insoluble salts known. It is widely used as a filler (*e.g.,* in paper and rubber) and finds an important application as an opaque medium in the X-ray examination of the gastrointestinal tract. Lithopone, a mixture of barium sulfate and zinc sulfide, is a brilliant white pigment.

A number of uses of barium compounds depend on the ready formation of the highly insoluble sulfate. Thus the compound barium carbonate ($BaCO_3$), perhaps the most important barium compound, is employed in removing sulfate from salt brines before they are fed into electrolytic cells (for the production of chlorine and alkali). The carbonate also is used to make other barium chemicals, as a flux in ceramics, and in the manufacture of optical glass, fine glassware, and ceramic permanent magnets for loudspeakers. Although barium carbonate is not soluble in water it dissolves in the hydrochloric acid of the stomach and thus is used in rat poisons.

Another barium compound, barium chloride ($BaCl_2 \cdot 2H_2O$), consisting of colourless crystals that are soluble in water, is utilized in heat-treating baths, in laboratories as a chemical reagent to precipitate soluble sulfates, and on a commercial scale with sodium sulfate to form a white filler and pigment (blanc fixe) for leather, rubber, cloth, and photographic paper. The oxygen compound barium peroxide (BaO_2) is used for both oxygen production and as a source of hydrogen peroxide. Volatile barium compounds impart a yellowish-green colour to a flame due to the emission of light of predominantly two characteristic wavelengths. Barium nitrate, formed with the nitrogen-oxygen group NO_3^-, and chlorate, formed with the chlorine-oxygen group ClO_3^-, are used for this effect in green signal flares and fireworks.

atomic number	56
atomic weight	137.34
melting point	725° C
boiling point	1,640° C
specific gravity	3.5 (20°C)
valence	2
electronic config.	2-8-18-18-8-2 or (Xe)$6s^2$

bark, in woody plants, tissues external to the vascular cambium (the growth layer of the vascular cylinder); the term bark is also used more popularly to mean all tissues outside the wood. The inner soft bark, or bast, is produced by the vascular cambium; it consists of secondary phloem tissue whose innermost layer conveys food from the leaves to the rest of the plant. The outer bark, mostly dead tissue, is the product of the cork cambium (phellogen). Layered outer bark, containing cork and old, dead phloem, is called rhytidome. The dead cork cells are lined with suberin, a fatty substance that makes them highly impermeable to gases and water. Gas exchange between the inner tissues of bark-covered roots and stems and their surroundings takes place through spongy areas (lenticels) in the cork.

Bark is usually thinner than the woody part of the stem or root. Both inner bark (secondary phloem) and wood (secondary xylem) are generated by the vascular cambium layer of cells: bark toward the outside where the oldest layers may slough off, and wood toward the inside where it accumulates as dead tissue. *See also* cork; cortex; periderm.

bark, also spelled BARQUE, sailing ship of three or more masts, the rear (mizzenmast) being rigged for a fore-and-aft rather than a square sail. Until fore-and-aft rigs were applied to large ships to reduce crew sizes, the term was often used for any small sailing vessel. In poetic use, a bark can be any sailing ship or boat.

"Eagle," U.S. Coast Guard Academy cadet training bark

By courtesy of the U.S. Coast Guard

bark beetle, also called ENGRAVER BEETLE, any member of the insect family Scolytidae (Ipidae, with more than 2,000 species) of the order Coleoptera. They are cylindrical, usually under 6 millimetres (1/4 inch) long, brown or black in colour, and often very destructive. The male and female—sometimes as many as

Bark beetle (*Dendroctonus valens*)

William E. Ferguson

60 females are found with each male—bore into a tree and form an egg chamber. The female deposits her eggs in niches along the sides of the chamber. After the eggs hatch, the larvae bore away from the chamber, forming a characteristic series of tunnels. Each larva pupates at the end of its tunnel and emerges as an adult through a hole bored in the bark.

Different species of bark beetles attack particular trees, damaging roots, stems, seeds, or fruits. Diseases are transmitted by some beetles. For example, the elm bark beetles (*see* elm bark beetle) of the genera *Scolytus* and *Hylurgopinus* carry the spores of the fungal Dutch elm disease. Most species of *Ips* and *Dendroctonus* attack pines, and the larvae of the clover root borer *Hylastinus obscurus* damage clover roots.

Other insects sometimes included in this family are the ambrosia beetles, also called timber beetles, which bore into the wood of trees, thereby destroying much timber. The female constructs a long central gallery, off of which are the egg chambers. On a pile of excrement and wood chips in the main chamber, she cultivates a fungus for food. The galleries of the ambrosia beetle are recognized by their uniform size and dark stain, which is caused by the fungus growing on the wall.

bark cloth: *see* bark painting.

bark-gnawing beetle, any member of the insect family Trogossitidae (Ostomidae), containing about 500 species, most of which are tropical. Bark-gnawing beetles range from 5 to 20 millimetres (0.2 to 0.8 inch) and are dark coloured.

Tenebrioides mauritanicus is found in granaries; its larvae, commonly known as cadelles, feed on both the grain and other insects in the grain. *Tennochilus virescens,* an eastern species, is blue-green in colour and has a ferocious bite.

bark painting, also called TAPA, or BARK CLOTH, nonwoven fabric decorated with figurative and abstract designs usually applied by scratching or by painting. The basic cloth-like material, produced from the inner bark, or bast, of certain trees (*see* bast fibre), is made by stripping off the bast, soaking it, and beating it to make the fibres interlace and to reduce thickness. The most popular material is the inner bark of the paper mulberry tree, although breadfruit and fig trees are also used. Hand-painted bark cloth is limited today primarily to northern Australia, New Guinea, and parts of Melanesia.

On the Australian mainland, style varies according to location: from the Kimberley region to Oenpelli in the west, a naturalistic rendering of human and animal forms prevails; in the east, a schematized style, relying heavily on the lozenge motif, dominates; between Oenpelli and Groote Eylandt in the Gulf of Carpentaria, the schematized and naturalistic styles coexist. In the Kimberley region, bark paintings frequently depict mythological beings known as Wondjinas (*see* wondjina style); it is not known whether these wondjina images on bark had a religious significance, as did those that appear on the walls of caves. In Arnhem Land, where the X-ray style—which shows the internal structures of animals—is concentrated, bark paintings are done in a style of schematic naturalism. In general, there are two kinds of paintings: those that can be viewed only by initiates and those that can be viewed by the entire community. The first group, the cult objects, depict the Aborigines' mythical ancestors. Some of the paintings in the second group, which contains historical, narrative subject matter, are associated with sorcery and the magical powers connected with hunting and fishing; others were created, irrespective of ritual, solely for the enjoyment of the artist and the community.

In New Guinea, animal motifs are predominant in the Danau Sentani–Teluk Kajo (Lake Sentani–Humboldt Bay) area; but in the art of the Gulf of Papua, where animal images are conspicuously absent, abstract motifs, such as the spiral and circle, and highly stylized representations of the human figure prevail. Bark painting rarely appears in the art of the Sepik River basin, and no examples have been found in the Asmat or Massim regions. In Melanesia the style and content of bark paintings varies from region to region.

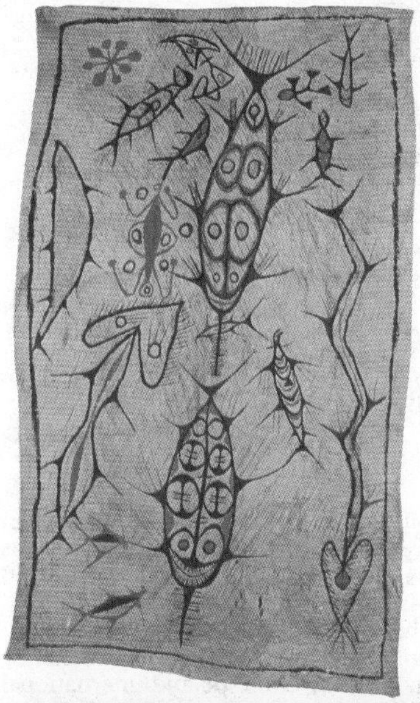

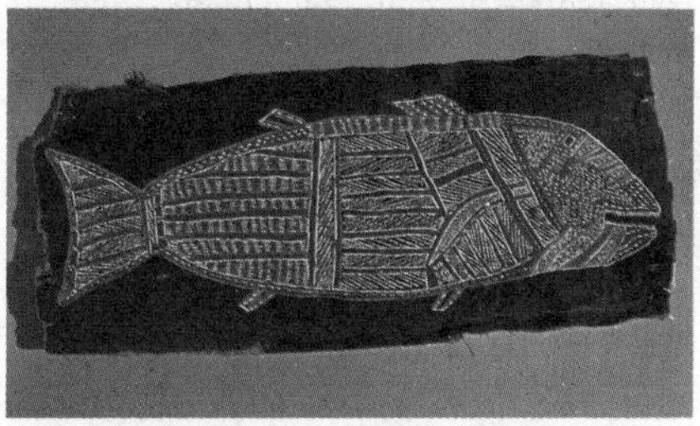

(Top) Tapa wall drapery painted with animal clan emblems, from the Teluk Jos Sudarso (Humboldt Bay) area, Irian Jaya (West New Guinea), Indonesia, in the Rijksmuseum voor Volkenkunde "Justinus van Nassau," Breda, Neth.; (bottom) bark painting of a freshwater fish, from Groote Eylandt, Gulf of Carpentaria, northern Australia, in the Charles P. Mountford Collection, St. Peters, South Australia

Holle Bildarchiv, Baden-Baden, W.Ger.

barkentine, also spelled BARQUENTINE, sailing ship of three or more masts having fore-and-aft sails on all but the front mast (foremast), which is square rigged. Because of the reduction of square sails, it required fewer crew members and was popular in the Pacific after its introduction about 1830.

"W.H. Diamond," a three-masted barkentine of the U.S. west coast

By courtesy of the Mariners' Museum, Newport News, Va., A.M. Barnes Collection

Barker, George (Granville) (b. Feb. 26, 1913, Loughton, Essex, Eng.), English poet largely concerned with the elemental forces of life. His first verses were published in the 1930s, and he became popular in the 1940s, about the same time as the poet Dylan Thomas, who was involved in voicing similar themes and whose reputation overshadowed Barker's.

He left school at 14 and worked at a variety of jobs before his first publications, the novel *Alanna Autumnal* and *Thirty Preliminary Poems* (both 1933). He taught English literature in Japan, the U.S., and England (1939–74).

Two of his important long poems are *Calamiterror* (1937) and *The True Confession of George Barker* (1950; rev. ed. 1957). His poems include the moving "Sonnet to My Mother."

Barker, Ma, byname of ARIZONA DONNIE BARKER, *née* CLARK (b. 1872, near Springfield, Mo., U.S.—d. Jan. 16, 1935, near Oklawaha, Fla.), matriarch of an outlaw gang of brothers and allies engaged in kidnapping and in payroll, post-office, and bank robberies in the 1920s and '30s. The activities of the gang, which included her sons, the "Bloody Barkers"—Herman (1894–1927), Fred (1902–35), and Arthur, known as "Doc" (1899–1939)—ranged throughout the midwestern United States from Minnesota to Texas. All met violent deaths. Ma Barker and Fred were killed at a Florida resort in a gun battle with the FBI; Arthur was killed in an attempted escape from Alcatraz; Herman, cornered by Kansas police, shot himself. A fourth brother, Lloyd (1896–1949), a loner, spent 25 years in Leavenworth prison (1922–47) and, after release, was killed by his wife. (The father of the Barker boys, George Barker, was never a gang member and was abandoned by Ma Barker in 1927.)

Barkerville, restored ghost town, east central British Columbia, Canada, in the western foothills of the Cariboo Mountains, just west of Bowron Lake Provincial Park and 55 mi (88 km) east of Quesnel. Once a boom town of nearly 10,000 inhabitants, which sprang up during the Cariboo gold rush, it was named after Billy Barker, a prospector who made an important strike locally at Williams Creek in 1862. It is now a provincial historical park (established 1959) and a tourist attraction. The 400-mi Cariboo Road from Yale at the head of navigation of the Fraser River to Barkerville was the major wagon route in the 1860s to the gold-mining region; it is now rebuilt and much extended as a modern highway.

barkhan (sand dune): *see* barchan.

Barkhausen, Heinrich Georg (b. Dec. 2, 1881, Bremen, Ger.—d. Feb. 20, 1956, Dresden), physicist who discovered the Barkhausen effect, a principle concerning changes in the magnetic properties of metal.

Barkhausen attended the universities of Munich and Berlin before earning his doctorate in 1907 from Göttingen. After working for the Siemens and Halske laboratories in Berlin, he accepted the world's first professorship in communication engineering, at the Technische Hochschule in Dresden (1911). There he worked on theories of spontaneous oscillation and nonlinear switching elements and formulated electron-tube coefficients that are still in use. He also experimented with acoustics, proposing methods for the subjective measurement of loudness.

His work in acoustics and magnetism led to the discovery in 1919 of the Barkhausen effect, which provided evidence that magnetization affects whole domains of a ferromagnetic material, rather than individual atoms alone.

In 1920 Barkhausen developed, with Karl Kurz, the Barkhausen–Kurz oscillator for ultrahigh frequencies (a forerunner of the microwave tube), which led to the understanding of the principle of velocity modulation. He is also known for experiments on shortwave radio transmissions.

Barkhausen effect, series of sudden changes in the size and orientation of ferromagnetic domains, or microscopic clusters of aligned atomic magnets, that occurs during a continuous process of magnetization or demagnetization. The Barkhausen effect offered direct evidence for the existence of ferromagnetic domains, which previously had been postulated theoretically.

Heinrich Barkhausen, a German physicist, discovered in 1919 that a slow, smooth increase of a magnetic field applied to a piece of ferromagnetic material, such as iron, causes it to become magnetized, not continuously but in minute steps. The sudden, discontinuous jumps in magnetization may be detected by a coil of wire wound on the ferromagnetic material; the sudden transitions in the magnetic field of the material produce pulses of current in the coil that, when amplified, produce a series of clicks in a loudspeaker. These jumps are interpreted as discrete changes in the size or rotation of ferromagnetic domains. Some microscopic clusters of similarly oriented magnetic atoms aligned with the external magnetizing field increase in size by a sudden aggregation of neighbouring atomic magnets; and, especially as the magnetizing field becomes relatively strong, other whole domains suddenly turn into the direction of the external field.

Barking and Dagenham, formerly BARKING, outer borough of Greater London, on the north bank of the Thames. It has an area of 13 sq mi (34 sq km).

Barking was an important fishing port until the coming of the railways, when such activities were replaced by market gardening. This, in turn, ceased with the building of the huge Becontree Estate by the London County Council in the 1920s and the associated large-scale influx of new industries. Important industries include the large Ford Motor Company works at Dagenham and the Barking power station. Pop. (1981) 149,786.

barking deer: *see* muntjac.

Barkla, Charles Glover (b. June 7, 1877, Widnes, Lancashire, Eng.—d. Oct. 23, 1944, Edinburgh), physicist awarded the Nobel Prize for Physics in 1917 for his work on X-ray scattering, which occurs when X-rays pass through a material and are deflected by the atomic electrons. This technique proved to be particularly useful in the study of atomic structures.

Educated at Trinity and King's colleges, Cambridge, he joined the faculty of Liverpool University in 1902, moved to the University of London in 1909, and became professor of natural philosophy at the University of Edinburgh in 1913. In 1906 Barkla and C.A. Sadler used X-ray scattering to determine the number of electrons in the carbon atom. At about the same time he was able to polarize X-rays (select X-ray waves that vibrate in the same plane), thus demonstrating that X-rays are transverse waves and hence like other electromagnetic radiations, such as light.

Barkley, Alben W(illiam) (b. Nov. 24, 1877, Graves County, Ky., U.S.—d. April 30, 1956, Lexington, Va.), 35th vice president of the United States (1949–53) under Pres. Harry S. Truman; one of the chief builders of the Democratic New Deal in the 1930s, he became a major symbol of party continuity as a member of Congress for almost 40 years.

Barkley began practicing law in 1898 at Paducah, Ky. An early participant in Democratic politics, he was elected in 1912 to the

Barkley
Paducah *Sun-Democrat*

U.S. House of Representatives, serving seven successive terms (1913–27). In 1926 he was elected to the U.S. Senate, in which he served until 1949. Increasing senatorial seniority enhanced his influence on the committees on foreign affairs and finance. He was a leading spokesman for the domestic and international policies of the administration of Pres. Franklin D. Roosevelt. An able parliamentary tactician, he served from 1937 to 1947 as Senate majority leader.

Barkley played important roles at every Democratic national convention he attended from 1932, and at the 1948 convention he was nominated for the vice presidency. He served steadfastly, if unspectacularly, for the next four years. He sought the presidential nomination in 1952 but withdrew when informed that many considered him too old for that office. He was reelected to the Senate in 1954, the same year his autobiography, *That Reminds Me,* was published.

Barkly, Sir Henry (b. 1815, Ross-shire, Scot.—d. Oct. 20, 1898, London), British colonial administrator who played a major role in the establishment of responsible governments in Victoria (Australia) and Cape Colony (South Africa).

The son of a merchant, Barkly was a member of Parliament for Leominster from 1845 to 1848 and then served appointments as governor of British Guiana (1848–53), Jamaica (1853–56), Victoria (1856–63), Mauritius (1863–70), and Cape Colony (1870–77). In 1870 he was named high commissioner to settle a dispute among the Transvaal, the Orange Free State, and the chief of the West Griqua tribe over border territory lately discovered to be rich in diamonds. He found for the Griquas but proclaimed Griqualand West a crown dependency in 1871. He was knighted in 1853.

Barkly Tableland, region of Australia, south of the Gulf of Carpentaria and extending southeastward about 350 mi (560 km) from Newcastle Creek, Northern Territory, to Camooweal, Queen. A grassy, undulating upland (average altitude 1,000 ft [300 m]), nourished by subartesian water and seasonal water courses, it embraces an area of about 50,000 sq mi (130,000 sq km). Cattle are bred on large open ranges. Visited in 1845 by Ludwig Leichhardt, it was named by William Landsborough in honour of Sir Henry Barkly, governor of Victoria (1856–63). It is crossed (east–west) by the Barkly Highway.

Barlach, Ernst (b. Jan. 2, 1870, Wedel, Ger.—d. Oct. 24, 1938, Güstrow, Ger.), outstanding sculptor of the Expressionist movement whose style has often been called modern Gothic. He was also a distinguished playwright whose most notable dramas, *Der tote Tag* (1912; "The Dead Day") and *Der Findling* (1922; "The Foundling"), combine symbolism and realism to present the tragic futility of existence. Similarly, his expressionistic graphic work is notable for its preoccupation with the sufferings of humanity.

He studied art in Hamburg and later in Dresden and Paris. Influenced early in his career by Jugendstil, Germany's Art Nouveau style, he vacillated between sculpture and decorative arts. In 1906 he travelled to Russia. The strong bodies and expressive faces of the Russian peasants stimulated the development of his mature style, which characteristically features heavy, massive figures in rigid drapery, animated by a single, forceful movement. This is exemplified by "The Avenger" (1922; private collection).

Barlach's interest in late Gothic German sculpture led to his preference for wood sculpture. Even when he worked with other materials, as in his bronze "Death" (1925; Ernst Barlach Haus, Hamburg), he often emulated the blocky, rough-hewn quality of wood sculpture to achieve a more brutal effect.

Barlach achieved great fame in the 1920s and early 1930s, when he executed, among other works, the celebrated war memorials in Magdeburg and Hamburg and the religious figures for the church of St. Katherinen in Lübeck. Although his work was removed from

"The Avenger," wood sculpture by Ernst Barlach, 1922; in the collection of Mrs. Herman Shulman, New York City
Andreas Feininger, © Time Inc.

the museums under the Nazi regime, after World War II his genius was once more recognized. A Barlach society was established in Hamburg and a small Barlach museum near Lüneburg.

Barlavento, Ilhas de (Cape Verde): *see* Windward Islands.

Barletta, city, Bari province, Puglia (Apulia) region, southeastern Italy, and port and resort on the Adriatic Sea, northwest of Bari. Originating as the ancient Barduli, it served as the port and bathing resort for Canusium (modern Canosa di Puglia; 14 mi [22 km] west-southwest) in Roman times. Captured by the Ostrogoths (5th century), the Byzantines (6th century), and the Lombards (6th century), it became part of the Kingdom of Naples in the 11th century. During a siege of Barletta by the French in 1503 a combat took place between 13 Italian and 13 French picked knights in which the Italians were victorious. An episcopal see, Barletta was the seat of the archbishops of Nazareth from 1291 to 1818.

Notable buildings of the old town include the Gothic cathedral (1150; extended 14th and 15th centuries); the Norman castle, extended by the emperor Charles V in 1532–37; and the 13th-century church of S. Sepolcro. There are several palaces and museums.

An agricultural centre, Barletta is noted for wines, olives, almonds, and fruits. The main industries are electrical, chemical, and automobile manufacture and sawmilling and leatherworking. The port is important for fishing as well as commerce. Pop. (1981 prelim.) mun., 83,719.

barley, cereal plant belonging to the genus *Hordeum* of the grass family Poaceae (Gramineae) and its edible grain. *Hordeum* comprises

Barley (*Hordeum vulgare*)
Grant Heilman

four sections, and all cultivated barleys belong to the section Cerealia. The three species within this section include *Hordeum vulgare,* a six-rowed type having its spike notched on opposite sides, with three spikelets at each notch, each containing a small individual flower, or floret, that develops a kernel; *Hordeum distichum,* a two-rowed type having central florets producing kernels and lateral florets that are normally sterile; and *Hordeum irregulare,* sometimes called Abyssinian intermediate, the least cultivated, with fertile central florets and varying proportions of fertile and sterile lateral florets.

Barley cultivation probably originated in the highlands of Ethiopia and in Southeast Asia in prehistorical times. It is believed to extend back to 5000 BC in Egypt, 3500 BC in Mesopotamia, 3000 BC in northwestern Europe, and 2000 BC in China. Barley was the chief bread plant of the Hebrews, Greeks, and Romans and of much of Europe through the 16th century.

Barley is adaptable to a greater range of climate than any other cereal, with varieties suited to temperate, sub-Arctic, or subtropical areas. Although it does best in growing seasons of at least 90 days, it is able to grow and ripen in a shorter time than any other cereal; cultivation is possible even in very short seasons such as those of the Himalayan slopes, although the yield there is smaller than in less harsh areas. Barley, with greater resistance to dry heat than other small grains, thrives in the near-desert areas of North Africa, where it is mainly sown in the autumn. Spring-sown crops are especially successful in the cooler, moist areas of western Europe and North America.

The annual world harvest of barley in the late 1970s was approximately 180,000,000 metric tons from about 246,000,000 acres (96,000,000 hectares). About half of the world's crop is used as livestock feed, the rest for human food and for malting. Most beer is made from malted barley, more than 10 percent of the world's crop being used for this purpose; malted barley is also used in the production of distilled beverages (*see* malt).

Barley has a nutlike flavour and is high in carbohydrates, with moderate quantities of protein, calcium, and phosphorus and small amounts of the B vitamins. Because it contains little gluten, an elastic protein substance, it cannot be used to make a flour that will produce a porous loaf of bread; barley flour is used to make an unleavened type, or flatbread, and to make porridge, especially in North Africa and parts of Asia, where it is a staple food grain. Pearl barley, the most popular form in many parts of the world, consists of whole kernels from which the outer husk and part of the bran layer have been removed by a polishing process. It is added to soups.

Barley has a soft straw, used mostly as bedding for livestock and as a feed providing bulk roughage.

barley-sugar column (architecture): *see* salomónica.

Barlow, Joel (b. March 24, 1754, Redding, Connecticut Colony—d. Dec. 24, 1812, Zarnowiec, Pol.), public official, poet, and author of the mock-heroic poem *The Hasty Pudding.*

A graduate of Yale, he was a chaplain for three years in the Revolutionary Army. In July 1784 he established at Hartford, Conn., a weekly paper, the *American Mercury.* In 1786 he was admitted to the bar. Along with John Trumbull and Timothy Dwight, he was a member of the group of young writers, known as the Connecticut, or Hartford, Wits, whose patriotism led them to attempt to create a national literature. Barlow's *Vision of Columbus* (1787), a poetic paean to America in nine books, brought the author immediate fame.

In 1788 Barlow went to France as the agent of the Scioto Land Company and induced the company of Frenchmen who ultimately founded Gallipolis, Ohio, to emigrate to America. In Paris he became a liberal in religion and an advanced republican in politics. In England he published various radical essays, including *Advice to the Privileged Orders* (1792), proscribed by the British government. In 1792 he was made a French citizen. Thomas Paine had become his friend in England, and during Paine's imprisonment in Paris Barlow effected the publication of *The Age of Reason.*

In 1795–97 he was sent to Algiers to secure a release of U.S. prisoners and to negotiate treaties with Tripoli, Algiers, and Tunis. He returned to the United States in 1805 and lived near Washington, D.C., until 1811, when he became U.S. plenipotentiary to France. He became involved in Napoleon's retreat from Russia and died in Poland of exposure.

Joel Barlow, detail of an engraving by A. Smith after a painting by R. Fulton, 1807
By courtesy of the Connecticut Historical Society

In addition to religious verse and political writings, Barlow published an enlarged edition of his *Vision of Columbus* entitled *The Columbiad* (1807), considered by some to be more mature than the original but also more pretentious. His literary reputation now rests primarily on *The Hasty Pudding* (1796), which has appeared in many anthologies. A pleasant and humorous mock epic inspired by homesickness for New England and cornmeal mush, it contains vivid descriptions of rural scenes.

Barlow, Peter (b. Oct. 13, 1776, Norwich, Norfolk, Eng.—d. March 1, 1862, Kent), optician and mathematician who invented two varieties of achromatic (non-colour-distorting) telescope lenses known as Barlow lenses.

Self-educated, he became assistant mathematics master at the Royal Military Academy, Woolwich, in 1801. He published numerous mathematical works, including *New Mathematical Tables* (1814). Later known as *Barlow's Tables,* this compilation of factors and functions of all numbers from 1 to 10,000 was considered so accurate and so useful that it has been regularly reprinted ever since.

In 1819 Barlow began work on the problem of deviation in ship compasses caused by the presence of iron in the hull. For his method of correcting the deviation by juxtaposing the compass with a suitably shaped piece of iron, he was awarded the Copley Medal of the Royal Society. He also conducted early investigations into the development and efficiency of the electric telegraph.

Barlow constructed (1827–32) his first achromatic telescope lens by enclosing liquid carbon disulfide between two pieces of glass. His second lens (1833) was a combination of flint and crown glass. The Barlow lens has come into general use for increasing the eyepiece power of any optical instrument.

Barmakids, also called BARMECIDES, Arabic AL-BARĀMIKA, or AL-BARMAK, priestly family of Iranian origin, from the city of Balkh in Khorāsān, who achieved prominence in the 8th century as scribes and viziers to the early ʿAbbāsid caliphs. Their ancestor was a *barmak,* a title borne by the high priest in the Buddhist temple of Nawbahār. The Barmakids were also known for their patronage of literature, philosophy, and science and for their tolerant attitude toward various religious and philosophical issues. They promoted public works—such as canals, mosques, and postal services—but also squandered money on building magnificent palaces by the Tigris.

When Balkh, the native town of the Barmakids, fell to the Arabs *c.* 663, Khālid ibn Barmak and his brothers moved to the garrison city of Basra in Iraq, where they converted to Islām.

Khālid ibn Barmak. Khālid ibn Barmak is the first Barmakid about whom much is known. He first appears in the mid-8th century as a supporter of the revolutionary movement that established the ʿAbbāsid caliphate. In 747 Khālid was put in charge of the distribution of spoils when the ʿAbbāsid army moved toward Iraq. Afterward, he was sent to Dayr Qunnā to administer the district. Under the ʿAbbāsid caliph Abū al-ʿAbbās as Saffāḥ, Khālid shared ministerial authority with Abū al-Jahm and was entrusted with the army and the collecting of the land tax.

Khālid's intimacy with the Caliph reached the extent that the latter entrusted him with the upbringing of his daughter. During the reign of al-Manṣūr, Khālid was appointed governor of Fars, and in 765 he was among the delegates to obtain Prince ʿIsā's renunciation of succession to the caliphate. Khālid then was nominated governor of Ṭabaristān, where coins were struck in his name between 767 and 771. There, he distinguished himself by capturing Ustūnā Wand and building a town called Manṣūrah. Because of political intrigues and rivalry, al-Manṣūr dismissed Khālid in 775 and imposed a heavy fine upon him. Al-Khayzurān, Prince al-Mahdī's wife, helped him to raise the money. Subsequently Khālid was sent to Mosul to suppress Kurdish disturbances while his son Yaḥyā was put in charge of Azerbaijan. The Barmakids were endowed with more privileges during al-Mahdī's reign, when Khālid, helped by his son Yaḥyā, was appointed governor of Fars.

Yaḥyā. Khālid died in 781/782. Yaḥyā, well trained by his father and already undertaking various administrative jobs, was nominated in 778 as secretary-tutor to the Caliph's son Hārūn. As secretary, he played a decisive role in ensuring the succession of his ward to the caliphate. In 779/780 the Caliph appointed Hārūn, accompanied by Yaḥyā, to lead the expedition against the Byzantines. On his return Hārūn was put in charge of the western provinces, with Yaḥyā as his adviser. In 781 Hārūn was proclaimed second in succession after his brother Mūsā, but a little later—and due to al-Khayzurān's and Yaḥyā's influence—the Caliph intended to deprive Mūsā of his rights as an heir apparent but died before accomplishing his scheme. Hārūn decided not to put up any opposition to the new caliph Mūsā al-Hādī. This wise decision, inspired by Yaḥyā, perhaps saved the empire from civil war.

Al-Hādī, in turn, confirmed Yaḥyā's position with Hārūn. This was, no doubt, a tactical error by al-Hādī, for when he decided to nominate his own son to the caliphate, Hārūn would have given in had Yaḥyā not objected. Yaḥyā tried in vain to convince the Caliph that the violation of an oath after so short a time would have disastrous consequences. Hārūn and Yaḥyā were jailed. At this point, however, al-Hādī suddenly died in obscure circumstances.

Thus Hārūn ar-Rashīd (786–809) was raised to power not by his own efforts but by the machinations of the queen mother al-Khayzurān and Yaḥyā the Barmakid. It was, therefore, no surprise that he put the whole administration in the hands of Yaḥyā and his sons. Yaḥyā received the title of *wazīr*, and his sons al-Faḍl and Jaʿfar were placed in charge of the Caliph's personal seal.

Al-Faḍl and Jaʿfar. Al-Faḍl and Jaʿfar also bore the title *wazīr*. Jaʿfar, the younger brother and ar-Rashīd's favourite, was known for his eloquence and for his love of pleasure and parties. He rarely left the court, but when, in 796, the Caliph sent him to control a disturbance in Syria, Jaʿfar succeeded in quieting the situation. On his return, he was appointed director of the bureaus (*dīwāns*) of the post, textiles, and mint. In the latter office Jaʿfar minted coins in his name in various provinces. Al-Faḍl, unlike his brother, distinguished himself by his competence and seriousness. When in 792 the ʿAlid Yaḥyā ibn ʿAbd Allāh rebelled in Daylam, al-Faḍl, through diplomacy and promises, persuaded him to give in. In 793 al-Faḍl was appointed governor of Khorāsān; he was able to put an end to the disturbances in Kābul. In 797 al-Faḍl took over the central government from his father, who resided at Mecca. Al-Faḍl, besides, was a tutor to ar-Rashīd's elder son and heir apparent, al-Amīn.

The fall of the Barmakids. The Barmakids' influence lasted 17 years, but they were extirpated at the peak of their power and fortune. Jaʿfar, only 36 years old, was executed in 803 and parts of his body displayed on the bridges of Baghdad. Other Barmakids, with the exception of Muḥammad ibn Khālid, were imprisoned and their property confiscated. Yaḥyā and al-Faḍl died in prison in 805 and 808, respectively. A number of their partisans were accused of heresy and executed.

The Barmakids' fall was sudden and brutal. Many accusations were made against them at the time, but the Barmakids' disgrace is to be attributed, first, to their overmighty influence in the court, administration, and society. Second, they seized every opportunity to enrich themselves (which accounts for their ostentatious generosity). Thirdly, they showed a certain degree of liberalism toward various religious and political sects, which the Caliph considered as a danger to his authority. The Barmakids' role ended but their fame survived. They became the subject of controversies among historians. Contradictory traditions, marred by the obvious flattery or prejudice by which they are inspired, represent an attempt by narrators to exalt or discredit the Barmakids' character, thus obscuring their true historical role. Late Muslim literature, especially Persian literature, is inclined to visualize the Barmakid period as an ideal period in the history of the caliphate. These traditions even consider the Barmakids Zoroastrian by faith and trace their descent to the Sāsānid period. Be that as it may, their downfall was to be considered the end of the theory that ministers were initiators of policy and not merely heads of administration; it also marked the Caliph's reaction against the liberal tendency current at the time.

The expression Barmecide feast, for an imaginary banquet, comes from "The Barber's Tale of His Sixth Brother" (*The Arabian Nights' Entertainment*), where a Barmakid has a series of empty dishes served to a hungry man to test his sense of humour. (F.Om.)

BIBLIOGRAPHY. The chief sources are the classical Arabic and Persian works such as at-Tabari, *Tārīkh* (1903); Yaʿqubi, *Tārīkh*, 2 vol. (1883); Al-Masʿudi, *Murūj* (French trans., *Les Prairies d'or*), 9 vol. (1861–77); Ibn Khallikan, *Wafayat al-aʿyān* (Eng. trans. by M. de Slane, 1961); and al-Jahshiyari, *Kitab al-wuzarā* (1938; German trans. 1958). See also Charles Henri Schefer, *Chrestomathie persane à l'usage des élèves de l'École Spéciales des Langues Orientales Vivantes,* 2 vol. (1833–85).

Modern works. Apart from general works on Islāmic history, see Lucien Bouvat, *Les Barmécides, d'après les historiens arabes et persans* (1912); W. Barthold, "Barmakids," in the *Encyclopaedia of Islam,* vol. 1, pp. 663–666 (1913); D. Sourdel, "al-Barāmika," *ibid.*, new ed., vol. 1, pt. 2, pp. 1033–1036 (1960); F. Omar, "Hārūn al-Rashīd," *ibid.*, new ed., vol. 3, pp. 232–234 (1971); Syed Nadvi, "The Origin of the Barmakids," *Islamic Culture,* 6:19–28 (1932); and Harry Phillby, *Hārūn al-Rashīd* (1933).

Barmen, Synod of, meeting of German Protestant leaders at Barmen in the Ruhr, in May 1934, to organize Protestant resistance to National Socialism (Nazism). The synod was of decisive importance in the development of the German Confessing Church (Bekennende Kirche). Representatives came from established Lutheran, Reformed, and United churches, although some of the church governments had already been captured by men loyal to Adolf Hitler, and others had decided to limit their activities to passive resistance. The Pastors' Emergency League, headed by Martin Niemöller, was the backbone of the active resistance. Various lay leaders and groups also rallied to the cause.

At Barmen the representatives adopted six articles, called the Theological Declaration of Barmen, or the Barmen Declaration, that defined the Christian opposition to National Socialist ideology and practice. The major theological influence was that of Karl Barth. The declaration was cast in the classical form of the great confessions of faith, affirming major biblical teachings and condemning the important heresies of those who were attempting to accommodate Christianity to National Socialism. It is treated as a confession by some denominations.

Bārmer, town, administrative headquarters of Bārmer district, Rājasthān state, northwestern India. Standing on a rocky hill crowned by a fort, the town is said to have been founded in the 13th century, when it was named Bahadamer (The Hill Fort of Bahada), after a local raja. The name has since been contracted to Bārmer. Connected by rail with Jodhpur, it is a trade mart for camels, sheep, wool, and salt. Handicraft products include millstones, camel fittings, and leather bags. The town has an observatory, a hospital, and a government college affiliated with the University of Rājasthān.

Bārmer district (10,960 sq mi [28,387 sq km] in area) chiefly comprises what was formerly the Mallani district of the princely state of Jodhpur—an expanse of sandy plain forming part of the Great Indian (Thar) Desert, watered only by the Lūni River in the south. Irrigation is mainly by means of deep wells, bajra (pearl millet) being the chief crop. The breeding of cattle, horses, camels, sheep, and goats is important to the economy; fuller's earth, bentonite, and gypsum deposits are worked. Pop. (1981) town, 55,554; district, 1,118,892.

barn, in agriculture, farm building for sheltering animals, their feed and other supplies, farm machinery, and farm products. Barns are named according to their purpose, as hog barns, dairy barns, tobacco barns, and tractor barns. The principal type in the United States is the general-purpose barn, used for housing horses and mules, cows, calves, and sheep and for storing hay and grain. Although the need for the general barn declined with the advent of tractors and electrical service, one or more barns are still found on the majority of North American and European farms. Many have been adapted to other uses.

Wood is the traditional barn material, but sheet steel and aluminum have been increasingly used since World War II, particularly on large farms. Barns usually consist of two stories, the first to shelter animals or machines and the second to store hay or grain, though one-story barns were gaining in popularity in the late 20th century.

barn, unit of area used to measure the absorption cross section of atomic nuclei in the study of interactions between the nuclei and other particles. It is equal to 10^{-24} square centimetre. The name, coined by U.S. scientists, is derived from the proverbial phrase "side of a barn," something easy to hit. *See* cross section.

barn owl, any of several species of nocturnal birds of prey of the genus *Tyto* (family Tytonidae). Barn owls are sometimes called monkey-faced owls because of their heart-shaped facial disks and absence of ear tufts. They are about 30 to 40 centimetres (12 to 16 in.) long, white to gray or yellowish to brownish orange. Their eyes are small in comparison with those of other owls and dark-coloured. Barn owls hunt mainly small rodents (such as mice and shrews), often in cultivated land. They nest in hollow trees, buildings, towers, and old hawk nests.

Common barn owl (*Tyto alba*)

Karl Maslowski—Photo Researchers

The common barn owl (*Tyto alba*) occurs worldwide except in Antarctica and Micronesia. Other species occur only in the Old World. Many inhabit open grasslands. Some are called grass owls (such as the common grass owl, *Tyto capensis*, of India, the South Pacific, Australia, and South Africa).

Barnabas, SAINT, original name JOSEPH THE LEVITE, OR JOSES THE LEVITE (b. Cyprus; fl. 1st century; feast day June 11), Apostolic Father, an important early Christian missionary.

Barnabas was a hellenized Jew who joined the Jerusalem church soon after Christ's crucifixion, sold his property, and gave the proceeds to the community (Acts 4:36–37). He was one of the Cypriots who founded (Acts

11:19–20) the church in Antioch, where he preached. After he called Paul from Tarsus as his assistant (Acts 11:25), they undertook joint missionary activity (Acts 13–14) and then went to Jerusalem in 48. Shortly afterward, a serious conflict separated them, and Barnabas sailed to Cyprus (Acts 15:39). There is no contemporary mention of his subsequent activity, except for a brief reference by Paul a few years later (I Cor. 9:6).

Nothing is known for certain about the time or circumstances of his death. Barnabas' alleged martyrdom and burial in Cyprus is described in the apocryphal *Journeys and Martyrdom of Barnabas,* a 5th-century forgery. Subsequent church tradition finds Barnabas in Alexandria, Egypt, and ascribes to him the *Letter of Barnabas* (an exegetical treatise on the use of the Old Testament) or pictures him in Rome and assumes that he wrote the *Letters to the Hebrews.* Barnabas' reputed tomb, discovered in 488, is near the Monastery of St. Barnabas, in the Cypriot city of Salamis, whose Christian community was founded by Paul and Barnabas.

Barnabas, Letter of, an early Christian work written in Greek by one of the so-called Apostolic Fathers, Greek Christian writers of the late 1st and early 2nd centuries. Ascribed by tradition to St. Barnabas, the Apostle, the writing dates possibly from as late as AD 130 and was the work of an unknown author who refers to himself in the letter as a teacher.

The *Letter of Barnabas* was essentially a treatise on the use of the Old Testament by Christians. Very anti-Jewish, the author believed that the Old Testament could not be understood by Jews and that its significance could be understood only by those who read it and searched for types or prefigurations of Jesus. At the end of the letter the author discusses the ways of light and darkness; *i.e.,* the way of good and of evil.

Evidently regarded as scriptural in Egypt, the *Letter of Barnabas* was included in the Codex Sinaiticus, a 4th-century Greek manuscript of the Bible, and it was also quoted by the influential presbyter Clement of Alexandria (died *c.* 215). It was less highly regarded elsewhere, however, and few Christians continued to read it.

Barnack, Oskar (b. Nov. 1, 1879, Lynow, Brandenburg—d. Jan. 16, 1936, Bad Nauheim, Ger.), designer of the first precision miniature camera available commercially, the Leica I, introduced in 1924 by the Ernst Leitz optical firm at Wetzlar, Hesse. Barnack had completed a prototype by 1913, but World War I and the postwar chaos in Germany delayed production. The success of the Leica I promoted the use of 35-mm and other small cameras. Barnack determined the standard 24 × 36-millimetre picture size for 35-mm film and was partly responsible for designing the Leitz Elmar lens.

barnacle, also called CIRRIPED, any of a majority of the 1,000 species of marine crustaceans of the subclass Cirripedia. Some authorities consider the Cirripedia to be a separate class. Adults of cirripeds other than barnacles are internal parasites of crabs, jellyfish, starfish, and some other marine invertebrates. They have no popular name.

A brief treatment of cirripeds follows. For full treatment, *see* MACROPAEDIA: Crustaceans.

As adults, typical barnacles are covered with calcareous plates and are cemented, head down, to rocks, pilings, ships' hulls, driftwood, or seaweed, or to the bodies of larger sea creatures, from clams to whales. They trap tiny particles of food by means of cirri—feathery retractile organs formed by metamorphosis of certain of their legs.

Adult cirripeds commonly are hermaphrodites (having male and female reproductive organs in the same individual). Hermaphroditic

Barnacle
Anthony Mercieca, from Root Resources—EB Inc.

forms sometimes have a minute, virtually formless complemental male attached to them; in the few species with separate sexes, a similar male is attached to a much larger, fully formed female. Cross-fertilization is usual, but self-fertilization does occur. The eggs mature within the mantle cavity, and the larvae emerge as free-swimming forms called nauplii, as in other crustacean subclasses. In typical barnacles about six naupliar stages precede formation of the cypris—the subadult, which has a bivalved shell of chitin (a hard protein substance), cement glands on the antennules (first antennae), and cirri. The cypris changes into an adult by body rotation and starts to produce shell plates.

Typical barnacles (order Thoracica) have six pairs of cirri and more or less complete shells. Pedunculate (stalked) forms include the common goose barnacle (genus *Lepas*), found worldwide on driftwood. Rock barnacles, also called acorn shells, are sessile (not stalked); their symmetrical shells tend to be barrel-like or broadly conical. This group includes *Balanus*, responsible for much of the fouling of ships and harbour structures. Wart barnacles, such as *Verruca,* have asymmetrical shells.

Burrowing barnacles (order Acrothoracica) are small, unisexual forms that lack shells and have fewer than six pairs of cirri. They burrow into hard limy material, such as clam shells and coral. *Trypetesa* is found only inside the snail shells worn by hermit crabs.

Parasitic cirripeds of the order Rhizocephala, such as *Sacculina,* lack appendages, shell, and gut, and resemble fungi. They parasitize decapod crustaceans (crabs and allies) by sending rootlike absorptive processes through the host's body; this intrusion inhibits the host's reproductive development (parasitic castration). Parasites of the order Ascothoracica, the most primitive of cirripeds, are cypris-like as adults. An example is *Laura,* found imbedded in cnidarians and echinoderms.

barnacle goose (*Branta leucopsis*), water bird of the family Anatidae (order Anseriformes); it resembles a small Canada goose, with dark back, white face, and black neck and bib. It winters in the northern British Isles and on the coasts of Denmark, Germany, and The Netherlands. During the Middle Ages people thought it hatched from barnacles; thus, the birds were considered "fish" and could be eaten on Fridays. The brent goose, or brant (*q.v.*), was called barnacle, or bernicle, in Ireland for the same reason.

Barnard, Chester Irving (b. Nov. 7, 1886, Malden, Mass., U.S.—d. June 7, 1961, New York City), business executive, public administrator, and sociological theorist who specialized in the nature of corporate organization. Although he was not himself an academician, his first book, *Functions of the Executive* (1938), was widely influential in the teaching of sociology and business theory.

An employee of the American Telephone and Telegraph Company from 1909, Barnard became president of an AT&T subsidiary, the New Jersey Bell Telephone Company, in 1927. During the depression of the 1930s, he directed the New Jersey state relief system. He later worked with the United Service Organizations (USO), of which he was president from 1942 to 1945. After World War II he helped to write the U.S. State Department's report on the international control of atomic energy (1946). When he retired from business, he served as president of the Rockefeller Foundation (1948–52) and chairman of the National Science Foundation (1952–54).

In his theoretical writing, Barnard stressed the cooperative nature of a business organization. In many of his papers—some of which were published in *Organization and Management* (1948)—he elaborated his observation that executives' ability to deal with practical matters tends to diminish when the same problems are presented in theoretical terms.

Barnard, Christiaan (Neethling) (b. Nov. 8, 1922, Beaufort West, S.Af.), surgeon who performed the first human heart transplant operation.

As a resident surgeon at Groote Schuur Hospital, Cape Town (1953–56), he was first to show that intestinal atresia, a congenital gap in the small intestine, is caused by an insufficient blood supply to the fetus during preg-

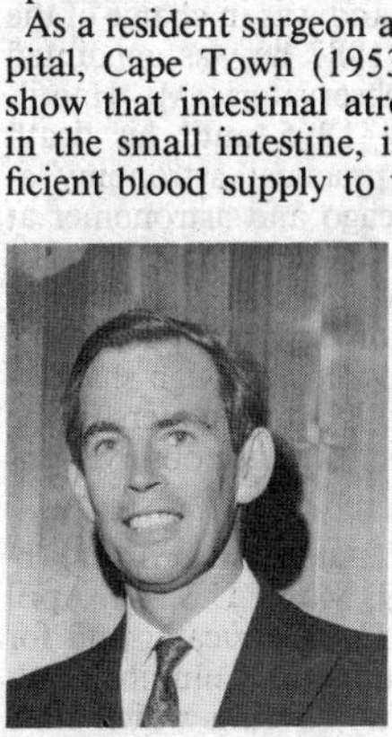
Christiaan Barnard, 1968
AP/Wide World Photos

nancy. This discovery led to the development of a surgical procedure to correct the formerly fatal defect. After completing doctoral studies at the University of Minnesota (1956–58), he returned to the hospital as senior cardiothoracic surgeon, introduced open-heart surgery to South Africa, developed a new design for artificial heart valves, and began extensive experimentation on heart transplantation in dogs.

In December 1967 Barnard led a team of 20 surgeons in replacing the heart of Louis Washkansky, an incurably ill South African grocer, with a heart taken from a fatally injured accident victim. Although the transplant itself was successful, Washkansky died 18 days later from double pneumonia, contracted after destruction of his body's immunity mechanism by drugs administered to suppress rejection of the new heart as a foreign protein.

Barnard's later transplant operations were increasingly successful; by the late 1970s a number of his patients had survived for several years. Barnard served as the head of the cardiac unit at Groote Schuur Hospital until 1983, at which time he retired from active surgical practice.

Barnard, Edward Emerson (b. Dec. 16, 1857, Nashville, Tenn., U.S.—d. Feb. 6, 1923, Williams Bay, Wis.), astronomer who pioneered in celestial photography and who was the leading observational astronomer of his time.

Edward Barnard

By courtesy of the Niels Bohr Library, American Institute of Physics, New York

In 1889 he began to photograph the Milky Way with large-aperture lenses, revealing much new detail. He discovered 16 comets and Jupiter's fifth satellite (1892). In 1916 he discovered the star (Barnard's star) that has the greatest known proper motion (motion of an individual star relative to the other stars). He published a catalog of dark nebulae in 1919.

From 1883 to 1887 he studied at Vanderbilt University, Nashville, and was in charge of the observatory there. In 1887 he was appointed astronomer at Lick Observatory, Mt. Hamilton, California. From 1895 until his death he was professor of practical astronomy at the University of Chicago and astronomer at Yerkes Observatory in Williams Bay, Wis. His eyesight was renowned. He observed Mars in a position that was not directly opposite the Sun, when detail is revealed through shadowing, and also observed Martian craters in the 1890s. He made neither of those observations public at the time.

Barnard, Frederick (Augustus Porter) (b. May 5, 1809, Sheffield, Mass., U.S.—d. April 27, 1889, New York City), educator and for nearly 25 years president of Columbia College in New York City, during which time Columbia was transformed from a small undergraduate institution for men into a major university.

Frederick Barnard, detail of an oil painting by an unknown artist, *c.* 1861; in the collection of the University of Mississippi, University, Miss.

By courtesy of the University of Mississippi, University, Miss.

Graduated from Yale in 1828, Barnard held several academic posts before becoming president and chancellor of the University of Mississippi from 1856 to 1861, when he resigned because of his Union sympathies.

Until Barnard went to Columbia in 1864, he had always defended the traditional prescribed curriculum of the classics and mathematics and had opposed vocational or professional subjects. At Columbia, Barnard changed his views, urging the college to expand its curriculum and introduce the elective system into the last two undergraduate years, to best develop advanced scholarship leading to graduate and professional education. He argued that this was the best way to attract more students. He was instrumental in establishing the School of Mines and opening the university to women. Barnard College, which bears his name, was founded as a "women's annex" in 1899 after the trustees had turned down his plan for coeducation at Columbia.

Barnard, George Grey (b. May 24, 1863, Bellefonte, Pa., U.S.—d. April 24, 1938, New York City), sculptor whose works were characterized by a vitality and individuality that brought him early fame.

After studying in Chicago and Paris, he exhibited at the 1894 Paris Salon, where his work (including the "Struggle of the Two Natures in Man," 1894; Metropolitan Museum of Art, New York City) created a sensation. Probably his best known work is a vigorous statue of

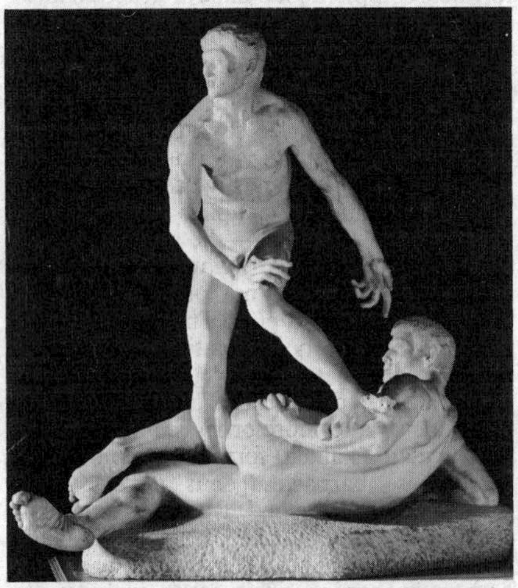

"Struggle of the Two Natures in Man," over-life-size marble sculpture by George Grey Barnard, 1894; in the Metropolitan Museum of Art, New York City

By courtesy of the Metropolitan Museum of Art, New York, gift of Alfred Corning Clark, 1896

Lincoln (Lytle Park, Cincinnati, Ohio), which was the centre of a storm of criticism when it was unveiled in 1917. Barnard made a collection of early Gothic sculpture and medieval architectural fragments that in 1925 was purchased by the Metropolitan Museum of Art in New York City.

Barnard, Henry (b. Jan. 24, 1811, Hartford, Conn., U.S.—d. July 5, 1900, Hartford), educator, jurist, and the first U.S. commissioner of education (1867). With Horace Mann he shared early leadership in improving the U.S. educational system.

Born into a wealthy family, Barnard graduated from Yale in 1830 and then studied law. As a Whig member of the Connecticut state legislature (1837–39), he was instrumental in legislation that created a state board of education. Serving as secretary of that board, he founded the *Connecticut Common School Journal and Annals of Education* (1838) and the first teachers' institute (1839).

In 1843 Barnard was called to Rhode Island to make a study of that state's schools, and in 1845 he became the state's first commissioner

Henry Barnard, detail of a portrait by an unknown artist; in the University of Wisconsin collection, Madison

By courtesy of the University of Wisconsin, Madison

of education. At his urging, appropriations were increased, teachers' wages were raised, buildings were repaired, and teaching and supervision were much improved. In 1851 he returned to his post in Connecticut as secretary of the school board. He instituted reforms similar to those in Rhode Island, but eventually the job proved too strenuous for him, and in 1855 he retired. In that same year he helped found the American Association for the Advancement of Education and the *American Journal of Education.* He edited 30 volumes of the *Journal,* spending so much of his fortune that he died a virtual pauper.

Barnard travelled widely to confer with writers and educators abroad, among them William Wordsworth, Thomas De Quincey, and Thomas Carlyle. He was chancellor of the University of Wisconsin, Madison (1858–61), and president of St. John's College, Annapolis, Md. (1866–67).

The scope of his activities and publications is shown in the *Bibliography of Henry Barnard* (1897) by W.S. Monroe and in *Henry Barnard, School Administrator* (1938) by A.L. Blair.

Barnard, Kate (b. May 23, 1875, Geneva, Neb., U.S.—d. Feb. 23, 1930, Oklahoma City, Okla.), Oklahoma welfare leader and the first woman to hold statewide elective office in the United States.

Barnard began her public career as an officer of the Provident Association, an Oklahoma benevolent organization. She soon became interested in such social legislation as compulsory education and the abolition of child labour. Those concerns led her to actively lobby for progressive issues at the Oklahoma constitutional convention in 1906. She was elected in 1907 to the state office of commissioner of charities and corrections, leading the state Democratic ticket while becoming the first woman in the world to hold such a post.

While state commissioner from 1907 to 1914, Barnard won national attention for her promotion of reform legislation on such issues as child labour, prison reform, Indian rights, and the improved care of the insane.

Barnard, Lady Anne, *née* LINDSAY (b. Dec. 8, 1750, Balcarres House, Fifeshire, Scot.—d. May 6, 1825, London), author of the popular ballad "Auld Robin Gray" (1771).

In 1763 she married Sir Andrew Barnard and accompanied him to the Cape of Good Hope when he became colonial secretary there in 1797. When the Cape was ceded to Holland (1802), they settled permanently in London. "Auld Robin Gray," written to the music of an old song, was first published anonymously; in 1823 she confided its authorship to her friend Sir Walter Scott, who in 1825 prepared an edition of the ballad.

Barnard Castle, parish (town), Teesdale district, county of Durham, England, on the north bank of the River Tees (there crossed by a medieval bridge). It developed around a Norman castle built by Bernard de Balliol, who gave the town its first charter *c.* 1178. The castle was the birthplace of John de Balliol, founder of Balliol College, Oxford, and father of John de Balliol, king of Scotland (1292–96). The town retains many Georgian buildings, including the town hall. The Bowes Museum, a former residence completed in 1892 in the style of a French château, has a notable art collection. In 1838 Charles Dickens was inspired to write *Nicholas Nickelby* (1839) while staying at the local King's Head Inn. Manufacture of stockings and carpets, the principal local activity in the early 19th century, has been superseded by other industries, including pharmaceuticals. Pop. (1981 prelim.) 5,016.

Ruins of Barnard Castle, Durham, above the River Tees where crossed by a medieval bridge
A.F. Kersting

Barnardo, Thomas John (b. July 4, 1845, Dublin—d. Sept. 19, 1905, Surbiton, Surrey, Eng.), pioneer in social work who founded more than 90 homes for destitute children. Under his direction, the children were given care and instruction of high quality despite the then unusual policy of unlimited admittance.

Barnardo
BBC Hulton Picture Library

Barnardo's father, of an exiled Spanish Protestant family, emigrated from Hamburg to Ireland. Barnardo himself went to London in 1866 to train as a Protestant medical missionary to China. While studying medicine he became superintendent of a "ragged school" (free school for poor children) in the East End of London, where, in 1867, he founded a juvenile mission. The first of "Dr. Barnardo's homes" for destitute boys was founded in 1870 and his first home for girls in 1876. The homes were chartered in 1899 as the National Incorporated Association for the Reclamation of Destitute Waif Children.

Barnard's star, second nearest star to the Sun, at a distance of about six light-years. It is named for Edward Emerson Barnard, the U.S. astronomer who discovered it in 1916. Barnard's star has the largest proper motion of any known star—10″.25 arc annually. It is a red dwarf star with a visual magnitude of 9.5; its intrinsic luminosity is only 1/2,300 that of the Sun.

Because of its high velocity of approach, 108 kilometres (67 miles) per second, Barnard's star is gradually coming nearer the solar system and by the year 11,800 will reach its closest point in distance—namely, 3.85 light-years. The star is of special interest to astronomers because its proper motion, observed photographically between the years 1938–81, has shown periodic deviations of one micron, or 0″.02 of arc. This "perturbation" is interpreted as being caused by the gravitational pull of two planetary companions having orbital periods of 13½ and 19 years, respectively, and masses of about two-thirds that of Jupiter. The existence of planetary bodies outside the solar system, however, remains unproved.

Barnato, Barney, original name BARNETT ISAACS (b. 1852, London—d. June 14, 1897, at sea), financier and diamond magnate who rivalled Cecil Rhodes in struggling for control in the development of the South African mining industry.

The son of a Jewish shopkeeper, Isaac Isaacs, in the East End of London, Isaacs followed his brother Henry to Kimberley, Cape of Good Hope, in 1873 to seek his fortune in the diamond rush. Adopting the name Barnato Brothers, which he and his brother had used in London as vaudeville entertainers, the two formed a diamond brokerage firm in 1874. Two years later "Barney" Barnato began the bold speculation in mining claims that led to the formation of the Barnato Diamond Mining Company (1880), which seriously challenged Cecil Rhodes's De Beers Mining Company. The struggle for control of the industry resulted in Rhodes's victory and the merger of the two companies as De Beers Consolidated Mines (1888), in which Barnato was made life governor. The same year he was elected to a seat in the Cape Parliament, which he held until his death. In 1889 he resumed speculating, buying up mining claims and real estate in the newly discovered Witwatersrand goldfields and floating Barnato Consolidated Mines and Barnato Bank. In ill health, however, Barnato committed suicide by jumping from a ship bound for England.

Barnaul, city and administrative centre, Altay *kray* (territory), south central Russian Soviet Federated Socialist Republic, on the left bank of the Ob River at its confluence with the Barnaulka. In 1738 a silver-refining works was established, the settlement becoming the hub of the Altay mining region. It was a major trade centre in the second half of the 19th century. Barnaul has excellent communications by the navigable Ob, by the South Siberian, Turk-Sib, and Omsk-Barnaul railways, and by roads to the Kolyvan–Rubtsovsk mining area and Novosibirsk. As a consequence, its industrial importance has increased steadily and its range of products grown wider. Today its engineering industries produce boilers, presses, diesel motors, and radios; other industries make cotton textiles, chemical fibres, cellophane, tires, and lumber and forest products. There is also a range of consumer-goods industries. Barnaul has a research institute of agriculture and livestock husbandry and institutes for agriculture, engineering, teacher training, and medicine. Pop. (1983 est.) 561,000.

Barnave, Antoine (-Pierre-Joseph-Marie) (b. Oct. 22, 1761, Grenoble, Fr.—d. Nov. 29, 1793, Paris), prominent political figure of the early French Revolutionary period whose oratorical skill and political incisiveness made him one of the most highly respected members of the National Assembly.

Of an upper bourgeois Protestant family, Barnave was privately trained in law. In 1789 he was elected Dauphiné's deputy to the last States General and quickly established a reputation as Mirabeau's chief rival in debates in the new National Assembly. Throughout 1790 he played an active role in formulating the Assembly's decrees, addresses, and resolutions, eventually becoming president of the National Assembly. At the same time, he joined his friends Adrien Duport and Alexandre de Lameth in the reorganization of the Club of the Jacobins.

In March 1790 he was elected to the Committee on Colonies and drafted several proposals supporting the interests of French trading monopolies in the West Indies, maintaining that their retention was vital to the needs of the French nation. His opponents, led by Jacques-Pierre Brissot, bitterly attacked his policies, and, as the anti-slavery campaign won favour in the increasingly radical Jacobin society, Barnave's influence waned considerably. The death of Mirabeau and the uprising of the Parisian populace in the spring of 1791 convinced him of the urgency of mobilizing

Barnave, detail of a portrait by J.-B. Audebert; in the Bibliothèque Nationale, Paris
By courtesy of the Bibliotheque Nationale, Paris

the wealthy propertied class in support of a strong constitutional monarchy. Louis XVI's abortive attempt to flee France in June 1791 led Barnave to believe that the King could be persuaded to accept the constitution as it stood and thus bring the Revolution to a close before its prolongation resulted in political anarchy. Thus he began his correspondence with Queen Marie-Antoinette, which became the source of later attacks against him.

On July 15, 1791, Barnave delivered his famous speech favouring the ultimate restoration of the King under a conservative monarchical constitutionalism, opposing republicanism as inappropriate to France's interests, and appealing for the end of the Revolution and its upheavals. When the National Assembly ended in September 1791, he retired to his home in Dauphiné, enrolled as an officer in the national guard, and began a project of correspondence and writing. His royalism, however, was systematically attacked after January 1792. He was arrested on Aug. 29, 1792, imprisoned at Grenoble, and on November 3 he was transferred to Paris, where he was tried (Nov. 28, 1793) and executed.

Barnave's *Introduction à la révolution française,* written during his imprisonment at Grenoble, is considered a major document of the Revolution. The work, in which he outlines the "natural history" of society's evolution toward the hegemony of the middle class, was one of the first attempts to place the French Revolution into a broad scheme of political, legal, and social history.

Barnburners: *see* Hunkers and Barnburners.

Barnes, Albert (b. Dec. 1, 1798, Rome, N.Y., U.S.—d. Dec. 24, 1870, Philadelphia), U.S. Presbyterian clergyman and writer.

Of Methodist parentage, he intended to study law but, while at Hamilton College, decided to enter the Presbyterian ministry. He attended Princeton Theological Seminary and became a pastor in Morristown, N.J. In 1830 he moved to the First Presbyterian Church in Philadelphia. At that time he became involved in the controversy between Old School Presbyterians, who held to traditional doctrine, and those of the New School, who wished to relax it. For a year he was suspended from the ministry on charges that he departed from the doctrines of the Westminster Confession, but he was reinstated by the Assembly of 1836.

The rest of his career was devoted to pastoral work and to writing numerous books on the Scriptures and on theology and ethics. He stood strongly against slavery, arguing that the Bible condemned it. He also lent his support to the Prohibition movement, to the development of the Sunday school, and to the New School Presbyterians. He was a director of the Union Theological Seminary. In 1870 the first assembly of reunited Presbyterians was held in his church.

Barnes, Barnabe (b. 1569?—d. 1609), Elizabethan poet known for *Parthenophil and Parthenophe*, a collection of love poetry containing sonnets, madrigals, elegies, and odes. It was published in 1593 on his return from the Earl of Essex's Normandy expedition. In 1598 Barnes was apprehended to stand trial before the Star Chamber on a charge of attempted poisoning, but he escaped from Marshalsea Prison to avoid the trial and fled to the north. His other works included *A Divine Centurie of Spirituall Sonnets* (1595), a prose work, and a play. He also acknowledged, in verse, his indebtedness to Sir Philip Sidney and to Petrarch.

Where the same name may denote a person, place, or thing, the articles will be found in that order

Barnes, Ernest William (b. April 1, 1874, Birmingham, Warwickshire, Eng.—d. Nov. 29, 1953), controversial Anglican bishop of Birmingham, a leader in the Church of England Modernist movement.

Barnes was educated at Trinity College, Cambridge, where he subsequently became fellow, lecturer in mathematics, and tutor. He was ordained in 1902. By 1915, when he was made master of the Temple, he had established a reputation for outspoken and provocative preaching, which he maintained as canon of Westminster (1918–24). Appointed bishop of Birmingham in 1924 on the recommendation of the prime minister, Ramsay MacDonald, he immediately attacked ritualistic practices and in 1929 evoked much protest by his refusal to install an Anglo-Catholic priest. His scientific approach to Christian dogma (exemplified in his Gifford lectures on *Scientific Theory and Religion*, 1933) brought him into open conflict with his fellow bishops; his controversial *The Rise of Christianity* (1947) was condemned by the archbishops of Canterbury and York. An uncompromising pacifist, he refused during World War II to take part in national days of prayer and later vigorously opposed German rearmament and the use of the atomic bomb.

Barnes, George Nicoll (b. Jan. 2, 1859, Dundee, Scot.—d. April 21, 1940, London), trade union leader, Socialist, one of the founders (1900) and chairman (1910) of the British Labour Party, and a member of David Lloyd George's coalition ministry during World War I.

A clerk in a jute mill at the age of 11, Barnes later became an engineer and was assistant secretary (1892–96) and general secretary (1896–1908) of the Amalgamated Society of Engineers. He led a nationwide strike (July 1897–January 1898) of the engineers, at that time the strongest labour union in Great Britain.

George Barnes, detail of an oil sketch by Sir James Guthrie; in the Scottish National Portrait Gallery, Edinburgh

By courtesy of the Scottish National Portrait Gallery, Edinburgh

Although forced to capitulate in its demands for an eight-hour working day, the union established the principle of collective bargaining over employment conditions.

Barnes sat in the House of Commons as a Labour member from 1906 until his retirement from politics in 1922. Under Lloyd George, he served as minister of pensions (1916–17) and minister without portfolio (1917–20), with a seat in the War Cabinet (1917–19). Late in 1918, when Labour withdrew its support of the coalition, he resigned from the party in order to retain office and take part in the peace treaty negotiations. He was responsible for establishing the International Labour Organisation (ILO) as an agency of the League of Nations.

Barnes, Robert (b. 1495, Lynn, Norfolk, Eng.—d. July 30, 1540, London), English Lutheran who was martyred after being used by King Henry VIII to gain support for his anti-papal campaign in England.

Barnes, a prior of the Austin Friars at Cambridge, was early influenced by reformist views and ruined a promising academic career when on Christmas Eve, 1525, he preached a sermon attacking clerical worldliness. Pressure from the university authorities caused him officially to abjure his heretical opinions, but in 1528 he escaped to Wittenberg, in Germany, where he formed an enduring friendship with Martin Luther. Beginning in 1531 Henry VIII's chief minister, Thomas Cromwell, obtained for Barnes safe conduct for frequent diplomatic trips between Germany and England. Henry and Cromwell seem to have had no respect for Barnes; instead they exploited his close contact with the Lutherans in order to bolster their drive to make the king, rather than the pope, the head of the church in England.

The fall of Cromwell in June 1540 removed Barnes's sole protector; in July he was burned as a heretic, though he had never been accorded a trial. Historians have generally viewed him as a sincere but rash and somewhat unstable man. His most important writings are *A Supplication to Henry VIII* (1531), *Vitae Romanorum Pontificum* (1535; "Lives of the Roman Pontiffs"), and *Confession of Faith* (1540).

Barnes, Thomas (b. Sept. 16, 1785, London—d. May 7, 1841, London), British journalist who as editor of *The Times* for many years established its reputation and founded a tradition of independent journalism.

The son of a solicitor, he was educated at Christ's Hospital and at Pembroke College, Cambridge. After studying in the chambers of Joseph Chitty, he abandoned the idea of being called to the bar and began writing on literature, theatre, and politics in his friend Leigh Hunt's *Reflector* and *Examiner* and in John Scott's *Champion,* to which he contributed literary portraits under the pseudonym "Strada." His political sketches in the *Examiner* were collected and published anonymously as *Parliamentary Portraits* in 1815. Meanwhile, he had also been contributing to *The Times*; and in 1817 he was appointed to the editorship, which he held until his death. Despite ill health and somewhat intemperate habits, Barnes brought *The Times* from comparative obscurity to the position of Britain's leading newspaper.

Barnes exerted his considerable influence in favour of the Reform bill and acquired for himself and his paper the nickname "the Thunderer." In 1834 he was described by Lord Chancellor Lyndhurst as "the most powerful man in the country." Barnes first collaborated but later quarrelled with Lord Brougham. Barnes sponsored Disraeli's "Letters to Statesmen," signed "Runnymede" (1836–39).

Barnes, William (b. Feb. 22, 1801, Bagber, near Sturminster Newton, Dorsetshire, Eng.—d. Oct. 7, 1886, Winterbourne Came), English dialect poet whose work gives a simple and sincere picture of the life and labour of rural southwestern England. A gifted philologist, his linguistic theories as well as his poetry influenced two major writers, Thomas Hardy and Gerard Manley Hopkins.

William Barnes, portrait by G. Stuckey, *c.* 1870; in the National Portrait Gallery, London

By courtesy of the National Portrait Gallery, London

After leaving school at 15, he worked for a solicitor, studied classics with local clergymen, opened a school in 1823, and was ordained priest in 1848. His first Dorset dialect poems were published in the Dorset *County Chronicle* (1833–34). His many books include an Anglo-Saxon primer, *An Outline of English Speech-Craft* (1878), *Poems of Rural Life in Common English* (1868), *Poems of Rural Life* (two series: 1844, 1862), and *Hwomely Rhymes* (1859).

Barnet, outer borough of Greater London, on the northwestern perimeter of the metropolis. It was formed by the amalgamation in 1965 of

Chipping Barnet Church in Barnet, London

A.F. Kersting

the former boroughs of Hendon and Finchley and the urban districts of Barnet, East Barnet, and Friern Barnet. These once formed separate manors and ecclesiastical parishes. The borough is now almost entirely residential, but some industry is concentrated along the Edgware Road, its western boundary. Before the advent of railways in the mid-19th century the area was almost entirely agricultural. The population then began to rise sharply, and estates and farms were replaced by brick Victorian villas. Development was accelerated during the 1920s and 1930s with the expansion of the London Underground (subway) network.

Few notable old buildings remain; but Chipping Barnet Church dates from 1250, and Monken Hadley parish church has a tower that was rebuilt in 1494. East Barnet parish church dates from 1100, and there are Norman traces in the Hendon parish church of St. Mary. The training college and driving school of the Metropolitan Police Force are near the former Hendon Military Airfield (closed 1957), which now houses the Royal Air Force Museum. There are two colleges of higher education, one at Barnet and a college of technology at Hendon. Barnet's grammar school dates from 1573. There are local history museums at Wood Lane, Barnet, and at Greyhound Hill, Hendon. The borough covers an area of 34 sq mi (89 sq km). Pop. (1982 est.) 294,800.

Barnet, Battle of (April 14, 1471), in the English Wars of the Roses, a momentous victory for the Yorkist king Edward IV over his Lancastrian opponents, the adherents of Henry VI. It was fought around Hadley Green, now in East Barnet, just north of London, on Easter Day. Edward, in power since 1461, had in 1470 been driven into exile when his main supporter, Richard Neville, earl of Warwick, changed sides and restored Henry VI. Returning to England in March 1471, Edward seized London and the person of Henry VI, and then moved north to meet Warwick's advance from Coventry. Warwick chose his positions on April 13. Edward, with his brother the Duke of Gloucester (afterward King Richard III), arrived later, spent the night close to the enemy, and attacked at dawn. Although Edward's left flank was routed, his right and his centre were victorious. Warwick, who had fought on foot to avert suspicion that he would desert his men, was killed while fleeing. The defeat a month later of an army led by Henry VI's queen, Margaret of Anjou, and their son at the Battle of Tewkesbury and Henry's death in captivity left Edward secure until his own death in 1483.

Barnett, Samuel A(ugustus) (b. Feb. 8, 1844, Bristol, Gloucestershire, Eng.—d. June 17, 1913, London), Anglican priest and social reformer who founded building programs and cultural centres (notably Toynbee Hall, 1884, which Barnett served as its first warden) in London's impoverished East End. In his teaching and writings he advanced a doctrine of Christian Socialism. Barnett House, Oxford, a centre for the study of social sciences, was founded in his memory. Among his works is *Practicable Socialism* (1888), written with the aid of his wife, Henrietta Octavia Rowland, who was also active in Barnett's social reform efforts.

Barni, Ẓiyā'-ud-Dīn: *see* Baranī, Ẓiyā'-ud-Dīn.

Barnsley, district (borough), metropolitan county of South Yorkshire, England, of which it is the administrative seat. It has an area of 127 sq mi (329 sq km). Situated on the River Dearne, a tributary of the Don, it is an old market town and had early wire-drawing and linen industries, but its major growth came in the 19th century as a coal-mining town in the heart of the Yorkshire coalfield. Local coal production was at its peak at the beginning of the 20th century, and, as mining employment was reduced, engineering, clothing, and other light industries have been promoted. Barnsley has a new mining and technical college and still functions as an agricultural market and district service centre. Pop. (1982 est.) 225,400.

Barnstable, town (township), seat (1685) of Barnstable County, southeastern Massachusetts, U.S., between Cape Cod Bay and Nantucket Sound, on the "upper arm" of Cape Cod. It was settled in 1638 by farmers attracted to the site by salt hay, found in the surrounding marshes. During the 18th century, Barnstable was a thriving port for the New England molasses and rum trade. Since 1900, its economy has depended on summer tourism supplemented by fishing, oyster culture, and cranberry farming. Several villages make up the town, including Hyannis Port (site of the Kennedy compound with the home of Pres. John F. Kennedy), and Hyannis (the business centre). The town is the site of the Sturgis Library (built in 1645 and one of the oldest library buildings in the U.S.), the Crocker Tavern (1745, now a museum), and the Donald G. Trayser Memorial Museum (Old Customs House, built in 1856). The West Parish Congregational Church (1717) and Cape Cod Community College (1961) are in West Barnstable. Barnstable is the birthplace of Revolutionary statesman James Otis, Jr. (1725), and the jurist Lemuel Shaw (1781). Inc. 1639. Pop. (1980) 30,898.

Barnstaple, parish (town), North Devon district, county of Devon, England, on the north bank of the Taw Estuary, about 10 mi (16 km) from the Bristol Channel. The Taw is spanned by a 15th-century stone bridge (widened in 1796 and 1962). The town was walled in the early 12th century and incorporated in 1557. Barnstaple imported wool from Ireland, which, together with local wool, was made into cloth. Silting of the estuary led to the decline of the port, but the town revived in the railway age. Barnstaple has a few light industries, including pottery manufacture, mainly for the tourist trade, and serves as the main service centre of the district. Pop. (1981 prelim.) 19,025.

Barnum, P(hineas) T(aylor) (b. July 5, 1810, Bethel, Conn., U.S.—d. April 7, 1891, Bridgeport, Conn.), celebrated American showman who employed sensational forms of presentation and publicity to popularize such amusements as the public museum, the musical concert, and the three-ring circus. In partnership with James A. Bailey, he made the American circus a popular and gigantic spectacle, the so-called Greatest Show on Earth.

Barnum was 15 years old when his father died, and the support of his mother and his five sisters and brothers fell largely upon his shoulders. After holding a variety of jobs, he became publisher of a Danbury, Conn., weekly newspaper, *Herald of Freedom.* Arrested three times for libel, he enjoyed his first taste of notoriety.

Barnum
By courtesy of the Library of Congress, Washington, D.C.

In 1829, at the age of 19, Barnum married a 21-year-old Bethel girl, Charity Hallett, who was to bear him four daughters. In 1834 he moved to New York City, where he found his vocation as a showman one year later when he successfully presented Joice Heth, a wizened black lady whom he advertised as the 161-year-old nurse to Gen. George Washington. This human relic, on her death, was exposed as a hoax.

Casting about for a legitimate undertaking, Barnum outmanoeuvred wealthier bidders to acquire John Scudder's American Museum, in New York City, a five-story marble structure filled with stuffed animals, waxwork figures, and similar conventional exhibits. The new owner rapidly transformed the museum into a carnival of live freaks, dramatic theatricals, beauty contests, and other sensational attractions. Although driven at the outset of his career by a desire for wealth and fame, Barnum may have been basically motivated by less selfish reasons. "This is a trading world," he wrote, "and men, women and children, who cannot live on gravity alone, need something to satisfy their gayer, lighter moods and hours, and he who ministers to this want is in a business established by the Author of our nature." Playing upon the public's interest in the unusual and bizarre, Barnum scoured the world for curiosities, living or dead, genuine or fake. By means of outrageous stunts, repetitive advertising, and exaggerated publicity, Barnum excited international attention and made his showcase of wonders a landmark.

Between 1842, when he took over the American Museum, and 1868, when he gave it up after fires twice had all but destroyed it, Barnum's gaudy showmanship enticed 82,000,000 visitors into his halls and to his other enterprises, among them Henry and William James, Charles Dickens, and Edward VII, then prince of Wales.

Barnum's first successful exhibit in the museum was the Feejee Mermaid, which had a seemingly human head topping the finned body of a fish and was, of course, found later to be a fake. Among the genuine curiosities were Chang and Eng, Siamese twins who were connected by a ligament below their breastbones. It was, however, Charles S. Stratton, a midget only 25 inches tall who was discovered by Barnum, that proved to be his most profitable exhibit. Ballyhooing his midget as General Tom Thumb, Barnum sold 20,000,000 tickets to the museum. After being received by Pres. Abraham Lincoln, Barnum and Tom Thumb enjoyed a triumphal tour abroad, during which the midget gave a command performance before Queen Victoria.

Eager to change his image from promoter of freaks to impresario of artistic attractions, Barnum risked his entire fortune by importing Jenny Lind, a Swedish soprano whom he had never seen or heard and who was almost unknown in the United States. Dubbing Lind "The Swedish Nightingale," Barnum mounted the most massive publicity campaign he had ever attempted. Jenny Lind's opening night in New York, before a capacity audience of 5,000, and her nine months of concerts across the United States earned immense sums.

At the peak of his career, Barnum's own appearance was nearly as familiar to the public as the exhibits he promoted. An impressive figure six feet two inches tall, semibald, with blue eyes, a bulbous nose, and potbelly, he called himself the "Prince of Humbugs." He dwelt in a three-story Oriental mansion, named Iranistan, on a 17-acre estate in Bridgeport, Conn., where he played host to such notables as Mark Twain, Horace Greeley, and Matthew Arnold. Close friends regarded him as good-natured, thoughtful, and kind, as well as parsimonious and egotistical.

His avocations were politics and writing. After serving two terms in the Connecticut state legislature, he was elected mayor of Bridgeport, in which post he fought prostitution and union discrimination against Negroes. In 1855 he published his autobiography, *The Life of P.T. Barnum, Written by Himself*; and because he frankly revealed some of the deceits he had employed, he was harshly taken to task by the majority of critics. Stung, Barnum continually modified the book in many revised versions, which, he claimed, sold a total of 1,000,000 copies. By 1884, more anxious for publicity than for profit, Barnum placed his autobiography in the public domain, allowing anyone to print and sell it without copyright infringement. Though the cynicism "There's a sucker born every minute" has long been attributed to Barnum, there is no proof that he ever wrote or spoke these words.

Barnum's family life was not entirely happy. One daughter had died in childhood; another was dropped from his will for committing adultery. Disappointed because he had no male heir, Barnum left a sizable bequest to a grandson on the condition that he agree to use the name of Barnum as part of his name. After 44 years of marriage, Charity Barnum died in 1873. The following year, Barnum, who was then 64, took the 24-year-old Nancy Fish, the daughter of a British admirer, for his second wife.

Although his name has been popularly linked with the circus, Barnum did not, in fact, become a circus showman until he was past the age of 60. Barnum did not invent the modern circus, but, in partnership with the retiring, efficient James A. Bailey, he did give the American spectacle its gigantic size, its most memorable attractions, and its widest popularity, attempting to make it what he called "the greatest show on earth." Barnum capped his circus career by purchasing a $6\frac{1}{2}$-ton elephant named Jumbo, who quickly earned back his purchase price during his first season under the big top.

In his 81st year, Barnum fell gravely ill. At his request, a New York newspaper published his obituary in advance so that he might enjoy it. Two weeks later, after inquiring about the box office receipts of the circus, Barnum died in his Connecticut mansion. *The Times* of London echoed the press of the world in its final tribute. ". . . He created the *métier* of showman on a grandiose scale. . . . He early realized that essential feature of a modern democracy, its readiness to be led to what will amuse and instruct it. . . . His name is a proverb already, and a proverb it will continue." (Ir.W.)

BIBLIOGRAPHY. Irving Wallace, *The Fabulous Showman: The Life and Times of P.T. Barnum* (1959); Neil Harris, *Humbug, the Art of P.T. Barnum* (1973); P.T. Barnum, *The Life of P.T. Barnum, Written by Himself* (1855), *Barnum's Own Story*, ed. by W.R. Browne (1927), *Struggles and Triumphs: or, The Life of P.T. Barnum, Written by Himself*, ed. by G.S. Bryan, 2 vol. (1927), the last two works combining material from all versions of Barnum's autobiographies.

barnyard grass (*Echinochloa crus-galli*), coarse annual grass of the family Poaceae (Gramineae) and one of about 20 species comprising the genus *Echinochloa*. The common name also applies to a similar species, *E. muricata*, not considered a separate species by some authorities.

Barnyard grass is distributed throughout

Barnyard grass (*Echinochloa crus-galli*)
J.C. Allen and Son

much of North America as a weed in moist cultivated and waste areas. It has been variously known as barn grass and barnyard millet.

Baro, town and river port, Niger State, west central Nigeria, on the Niger River, 400 mi (650 km) from the sea. Lying at the end of a 111-mi rail branch that joins the main Nigerian railway system at Minna, it also has road connections to Agaie and Bida. Originally a small village of the Nupe people, it was selected by the British as Nigeria's link between rail and river transport; its solid bank—rare along the Lower Niger—could be used for loading river craft with Northern Nigeria's cotton crop. Although the 350-mi Baro–Kano railway was completed in 1911, it was shortly eclipsed in importance by the railroad from Kano through Minna to Lagos that crossed the Niger at Jebba, 150 mi upstream. From July to March, however, Baro is still used to ship peanuts (groundnuts) and cotton downstream to the Niger Delta ports of Burutu and Warri.

Most of the town's local trade is in sorghum, yams, rice, millet, fish, palm oil, shea nuts, peanuts (groundnuts), and cotton. Swamp rice is cultivated commercially both by farmers in the vicinity and at the government's irrigated rice projects at Loguma (10 mi northwest) and Badeggi (35 mi northwest). Pop. (1972 est.) 5,148.

baro-otitis: *see* ear squeeze.

Barocci, Federico, Barocci also spelled BAROCCIO or BARROCIO, also called FIORI DA URBINO (b. *c.* 1526, Urbino, Duchy of Urbino, Papal States—d. 1612, Urbino), leading painter of the central Italian school in the last decades of the 16th century and an important precursor of the Baroque style.

Although he made two visits to Rome—one in about 1550 to study the works of Raphael, and another in 1560 when, with Federico Zuccari, he worked on the frescoes for Pope Pius IV's Casino in the Vatican Gardens—Barocci lived and worked all his life in Urbino and the surrounding small towns. He executed altarpieces and devotional paintings for local churches and patrons such as the Duke of Urbino and, in time, the cathedrals of Genoa and Perugia.

Barocci may have never seen an original Correggio, yet Correggesque motifs appear in his compositions. Warmth of feeling, tenderness of expression, and a painterly (as opposed to a draftsman-like) approach are common to the work of both artists. This is particularly evident in the many paintings by Barocci on the theme of the Madonna; two of the most famous are the "Madonna del Popolo" (1579) and the exquisitely beautiful "Nativity" (1597). Barocci was unusual in the Mannerist period for his numerous and extremely sensitive life drawings. His distinctive use of colour is central Italian in origin—pale, fugi-

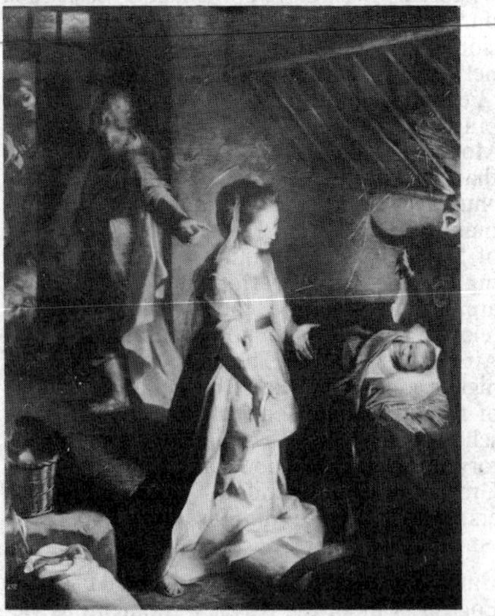

"Nativity," oil painting by Federico Barocci, 1597; in the Prado, Madrid
By courtesy of Museo del Prado, Madrid

tive colours blended chiefly from vermilion pinks, mother-of-pearl whites, and grays.

Baroda (India): *see* Vadodara.

Baroja (y Nessi), Pío (b. Dec. 28, 1872, San Sebastián, Spain—d. Oct. 30, 1956, Madrid), Basque writer who is considered to be the foremost Spanish novelist of his generation.

After receiving his medical degree, Baroja practiced medicine for a short time in a village in northern Spain, later returning to Madrid

Baroja
Archivo Mas, Barcelona

to work in the family bakery. As a member of the Generation of '98 (*q.v.*), Baroja revolted against the stultification of Spanish life. His first two books, a collection of short stories, *Vidas sombrías* (1900; "Sombre Lives"), and a novel, *La casa de Aizgorri* (1900; *The House of the Aizgorri,* 1958), clearly show the direction his later work would take. Attempting to arouse people to action, he wrote 11 trilogies dealing with contemporary social problems, the best known of which, *La lucha por la vida* (1904; *The Struggle for Life,* 1922–24), portrays the misery and squalor in the poor sections of Madrid. Himself a confirmed rebel and nonconformist, Baroja wrote at length about vagabonds and people who reflected his own thinking; *El árbol de la ciencia* (1911; *The Tree of Knowledge,* 1928) is considered to be basically autobiographical. Of the almost 100 novels he wrote, the most ambitious project was *Memorias de un hombre de acción* (1913–28; "Memoirs of a Man of Action"), a series of 14 novels and 8 volumes of shorter narratives dealing with a 19th-century insurgent and his era. One of his best novels, *Zalacaín el aventurero* (1909), is written in an intentionally abrupt style reflecting Baroja's vision of reality as disjointed.

Because of his anti-Christian views, his stubborn insistence on nonconformity, and a somewhat pessimistic attitude, Baroja's novels never achieved great popularity. His terse and unadorned style, which relied heavily upon understatement, is said to have had great influence on Ernest Hemingway.

barometer, device used to measure atmospheric pressure. Because atmospheric pressure changes with distance above or below sea level, a barometer can also be used to measure altitude. There are two main types of barometers: mercury and aneroid.

In the mercury barometer, atmospheric pressure balances a column of mercury, the height of which can be precisely measured. To increase their accuracy, mercury barometers are often corrected for ambient temperature and the local value of gravity. Common pressure units include pounds per square inch; dynes per square centimetre; newtons per square metre (the SI unit called the pascal); inches, centimetres, or millimetres of mercury; and millibars (1 millibar equals 1,000 dynes per square centimetre, or 0.75 millimetre of mercury). Normal atmospheric pressure is about 14.7 pounds per square inch, equivalent to 30 inches (760 millimetres) of mercury, 1,013.2 millibars, or 101,320 pascals.

Of the many different varieties of mercury barometers, most variations arise from different techniques for measuring the height of the mercury column. Though other liquids can be used in a barometer, mercury is the most common. Its density allows the vertical column of the barometer to be of manageable size. If water were used, for instance, the column would have to be 34 feet high.

A nonliquid barometer called the aneroid barometer is widely used in portable instruments and in aircraft altimeters because of its smaller size and convenience. It contains a flexible-walled evacuated capsule, the wall of which deflects with changes in atmospheric pressure. This deflection is coupled mechanically to an indicating needle. A mercury barometer is used to calibrate and check aneroid barometers. Calibration can be, for example, in terms of atmospheric pressure or altitude above sea level.

A barometer that mechanically records changes in barometric pressure over time is called a barograph. Though mercury barographs have been made, aneroid barographs are much more common. The motion of the aneroid capsule is magnified through levers to drive a recording pen. The pen traces a line on a graph that is usually wrapped around a cylinder driven by a clockwork mechanism.

barometric light, luminous glow appearing in the vacuum above the mercury in a barometer tube when the tube is shaken, first noticed in 1675 by a French astronomer, Jean Picard. The electrical discharge takes place with a variety of rarefied gases trapped in the tube (neon glows with its characteristic red light even at atmospheric pressure). The shaking is essential; electrification is probably produced both by the splashing of the mercury and by its movement over the glass surface. Impurities in the mercury considerably influence the phenomenon of barometric light, never exhaustively investigated. Francis Hauksbee in 1709 proved that the effect occurred in other than glass containers, did not require an extremely low pressure, and was similar to discharges produced by his electrical machine.

barometric pressure: *see* atmospheric pressure.

baron, feminine BARONESS, title of nobility, ranking in modern times immediately below a viscount or a count (in countries without viscounts). Originally, in the early Middle Ages, the term baron designated a tenant of whatever rank who held a tenure of barony direct from the king. Gradually, however, the word came to mean a powerful personage and, therefore, a magnate.

Baron, baroness
foreign-language equivalents

	masculine	feminine
Czech	baron	barónka
Danish	friherre	friherreinde
Dutch	vrijheer	vrijvrouw
French	baron	barone
German	Freiherr	Freifrau
Hungarian	báró	bárónö
Italian	barone	baronessa
Japanese	danshaku	danshaku-fujin
Latin	baro	baronissa
Norwegian	friherre	friherrinna
Polish	baron	baronowa
Portuguese	barão	baronesa
Romanian	baron	baroneasă
Russian	baron	baronessa
Serbo-Croatian	barun	barunica
Spanish	barón	baronesa
Swedish	friherre	friherrinna

France. In 12th-century France the term *baron,* in a restricted sense, was applied properly to all lords possessing an important fief, but toward the end of the 13th century the title had come to mean that its bearer held his principal fief direct from the crown and was therefore more important than that of count, since many counts were only mediate vassals. From this period, however, the title tended to sink in importance. In the 14th century the barons were ranked below counts and viscounts, though in power and possessions many barons were superior to many counts. In any case, until the 17th century the title of baron could be borne only by the holder of a territorial barony, and it was Louis XIV who first cheapened the title in France by creating numerous barons by royal letters. The creation of barons was later revived by the Emperor Napoleon, continued by Louis XVIII, Charles X, and Louis Philippe, and revived again on a generous scale by Napoleon III. Since 1870 the tolerant attitude of the French republican governments toward titles, which are not officially recognized, has increased the confusion by facilitating the assumption of the title on very slender grounds of right.

Germany. The German equivalent of baron, *Freiherr,* or "free lord" of the empire, originally implied a dynastic status, and many *Freiherren* held countships without taking the title of count (*Graf*). When the more important of them styled themselves counts, the *Freiherren* sank into an inferior class of nobility. The practice of conferring the title *Freiherr* by imperial letters—begun in the 16th century by the emperor Charles V—was later exercised by all the German sovereigns.

Italy. In the Middle Ages the Italian barons had extensive powers of jurisdiction within their domains and could inflict the death penalty. There was a right of appeal, but it was of little value and in Sicily and Sardinia was nonexistent. In the late Middle Ages the barons' powers became more extensive, especially in the south, and they had the right to mint money and wage private war. The title was recognized until 1945.

Spain. In early medieval Navarre and Aragon *barón* described the senior nobility but later, perhaps under the influence of Castilian practice, it was displaced by *ricos hombres* ("rich men"). In Catalonia a baron was simply a magnate but in the later Middle Ages achieved a distinct status even more important than the French barons. Some nobles retained the title until it was abolished by the *Cortes* of Cadiz in 1812.

England. In the 11th and early 12th centuries all English tenants in chief were known as barons and their reliefs regulated more or less according to the size of their estates. By the year 1200, however, the barons were coming to be regarded as a distinct class and were even roughly divided between "greater" and "lesser" baronies.

Thus far the barons' position was connected with the tenure of land. The great change in their status was effected when their presence in that council of the realm that became the House of Lords was determined by the issue of a writ of summons, dependent not on the tenure of land but only on the king's will. This change occurred under Edward I, although those who received such summons were not as yet distinguished from commoners by any style or title. The style of baron was first introduced by Richard II in 1387, when he created John Beauchamp, by patent, lord de Beauchamp and baron of Kidderminster. Such creations became common under Henry VI but "Baron" as a form of address could not evict "Lord." To this day a baron is addressed in correspondence as "the Lord *A*," although other peers under the rank of duke are spoken of as "lords," while they are addressed in correspondence by their proper styles. To speak of "Baron *A*" is an unhistorical and quite recent practice. When a barony, however, is vested in a lady, it is now the recognized custom to speak of her as baroness; *e.g.,* Baroness Berkeley.

Baron, Michel (b. Oct. 8?, 1653, Paris—d. Dec. 22, 1729, Paris), actor, from 1670 until his retirement in 1691 the undisputed master of the French stage.

The child of theatrical parents, he was orphaned at the age of 12 and joined the company of children known as the Petits Comédiens du Dauphin. He joined Molière's company in 1670 and was treated like a son by the master. He later became a member of the company at the Hôtel de Bourgogne and subsequently of the newly formed Comédie-Française. He created many of the leading roles in Racine's tragedies, besides those in two of his own comedies, *L'Homme à bonnes fortunes* (1686; "The Don Juan") and *La Coquette et la fausse prude* (1687; "The Flirt and the False Prude"). He retired in 1691 but in 1720 returned to the Comédie-Française.

His son Étienne-Michel Baron (1676–1711) was also an actor and left a son and two daughters, all of whom played at the Comédie-Française.

Barone, Enrico (b. Dec. 22, 1859, Naples—d. May 14, 1924, Rome), Italian mathematical economist who expanded on the ideas of economist Léon Walras regarding general equilibrium theory.

Barone spent much of his life as an army officer, only resigning from the army in 1907 after obtaining a professorship at the University of Rome. His main contributions, however, were largely made before that date. Walras proposed a mathematical model which demonstrated that products and prices automatically adjust in equilibrium. Barone further developed the general equilibrium structure of Walras to include variable combinations of inputs in production. Barone also worked on the marginal productivity theory of distribution independently of British economist Philip Wicksteed. However, he was persuaded by Vilfredo Pareto, the Italian economist and sociologist, that his approach to distribution was invalid.

In his treatment of general equilibrium Barone, though he was not personally sympathetic to Socialism, developed the theory of a Socialist economy as parallel to the Walrasian theory of a pure competitive economy. He believed he had solved the problems of attainment of equilibrium, at least in principle, by the introduction of the concept of a trial and error process to achieve correct prices. Barone also contributed to international trade theory.

baroness: *see* baron.

baronet, British hereditary dignity, first created by King James I in May 1611. The baronetage is not part of the peerage, nor is it an order of knighthood.

James I, desperate for funds like all the Stuarts, decided to institute by letter patent "a new dignitie between Barons and Knights." Because the money was ostensibly for support of the troops, candidates for the baronetage were required to pay the King £1,095 (the sum required to maintain 30 soldiers for three years), but such requirements were soon abandoned. In 1619 a baronetage of Ireland was also established, and in 1624 James planned another creation in connection with the plantation of Nova Scotia. This was carried out after his death by Charles I in 1625. The baronets of Scotland (or of Nova Scotia) were required to pay a total of £2,000 (the amount required to support six colonists) and to pay a fee of £1,000 to Sir William Alexander (afterward earl of Stirling), to whom the province had been granted in 1621. In return they received, as well as their title, 16,000 acres of land in Nova Scotia. The creation of baronets of Scotland ceased with that country's union with England in 1707; thereafter, until 1800, the new baronetcies were those of Great Britain. No more Irish baronets were created after the Irish Act of Union in 1801. From 1801 all creations were of baronets of the United Kingdom.

A baronet is styled, for example, Sir A.B., Bart. (or Bt.), to distinguish him from a knight; his wife is Lady B.

Barong, masked figure, usually representing an unidentified creature called *keket,* who appears at times of Balinese celebration. He is the symbol of health and good fortune, in opposition to the "black widow" witch, Rangda. In a dance-drama that includes the famous *kris* dance, in which the performers are in deep trance, Barong defeats Rangda in magic combat. Barong is "animated" by two dancers encased in an ornately decorated harness. From his mask hangs a beard of human hair, decorated with frangipani flowers, in which his magic power is thought to reside.

Baronius, Caesar (b. Oct. 31, 1538, Sora, Kingdom of Naples—d. June 30, 1607, Rome), ecclesiastical historian and apologist for the Roman Catholic Church.

He joined the Oratory in Rome in 1557, eventually succeeding Philip Neri as superior in 1593. Clement VIII, whose confessor he was, made him cardinal in 1596, and in the following year he became Vatican librarian.

His major work, the *Annales Ecclesiastici* (1588–1607), undertaken in reply to the *Centuriae Magdeburgenses* and under the inspiration of Philip, consists of 12 folios narrating the history of the church down to the year 1198. Hailed by Roman Catholic writers as the "father of ecclesiastical history," Baronius was scorned by Protestant critics for his ignorance of Hebrew and poor knowledge of Greek. It was claimed that he had made numerous factual errors. The chief merit of the *Annales* lies in its enormous accumulation of sources—some not previously published. The most useful edition of the *Annales* is by A. Theiner (37 vol., 1864–83).

Barons' War (1264–67), in English history, the civil war caused by baronial opposition to the costly and inept policies of Henry III. The barons in 1258 had attempted to achieve reform by forcing Henry to abide by the Provisions of Oxford (*see* Oxford, Provisions of). When, by the Mise of Amiens (1264), the Provisions of Oxford were declared invalid by Louis IX of France, some barons, led by Simon de Montfort, took up arms and, in May 1264, captured the King at the Battle of Lewes in the southeastern Downs. From then until his death at the Battle of Evesham in August 1265, Simon de Montfort largely controlled England and made important administrative and parliamentary experiments. A settlement was achieved by the Dictum of Kenilworth (1266) and finally by the Statute of Marlborough (1267), which remedied some of the baronial grievances.

baroque pearl, pearl that is irregularly or oddly shaped. Pearl formation does not always occur in soft-tissue areas, where the expanding pearl sac grows regularly because it encounters no appreciable resistance. Pearl cysts are sometimes lodged in muscular tissue, for example, where, unable to overcome the resistance of tough muscle fibres, they assume irregular or unusual shapes.

Baroque pearls were highly prized by Renaissance jewellers, who saw them not as misshapen products of sea mollusks but rather as unique and exquisite natural forms. They were often used in pieces of jewelry to form the bodies of figures. A superb example is a piece from the 16th century known as the Canning Jewel (Victoria and Albert Museum, London), in which a large baroque pearl is used for the torso of a sea figure having the body of a man and the tail of a fish, the whole mounted in enamelled gold set with pearls, rubies, and diamonds. *See also* pearl.

Baroque period, era in the history of the Western arts roughly coinciding with the 17th century. Its earliest manifestations, which occurred in Italy, date from the latter decades of the 16th century, while in some regions, notably Germany and colonial South America, certain of its culminating achievements did not occur until the 18th century.

The work that distinguishes the Baroque period is stylistically complex, even contradictory. In general, however, the desire to express emotional states in forms that appeal to the senses, often in dramatic ways, underlies its manifestations. The arts of the Baroque period are never narrowly austere or intellectual, although even these qualities may occasionally be recognized within the complex aesthetic. Some of the qualities most frequently associated with the Baroque are grandeur, vitality, movement, tension, expression of extreme and diverse emotional states and of perceptions of the infinite, and a tendency to blur distinctions between the various arts. Renaissance adulation of classical antiquity continued in the Baroque period and conditioned many of its artistic manifestations in varying degrees. This, together with the regulatory power of the concept of decorum, accounts for much of the dignified character of the arts in the Baroque period.

Although other theories have been advanced, the most commonly accepted notion of the origin of the word baroque is that it derives from the Portuguese *barroco* (Spanish *barrueco*), meaning "irregular," with specific reference to imperfectly shaped pearls. The French adjective *baroque* derived from the Iberian one, and the word passed directly into English from the French. Its original use in art criticism, occurring before the end of the 17th century, came from the generic sense of the word, as used to describe anything irregular, bizarre, and thus departing from established rules. By the 18th century the word was generally used pejoratively to indicate what was considered abandonment of the norms of nature and of classical antiquity. The name continued to be one of abuse rather than stylistic designation until the middle of the 19th century, and only with Heinrich Wölfflin's *Renaissance und Barock* (1888) was a systematic formulation of the characteristics of Baroque style achieved.

Because the arts present such diversity within the Baroque period, their unifying characteristics must be sought in relation to the era's broader cultural tendencies, of which three are most important for their effect on the arts. The first of these was the emergence of the Counter-Reformation and the expansion of its domain, both territorially and intellectually. Many monuments of the Baroque, particularly in the art and architecture of Italy, may be directly related to the newly propagandistic stance of the church or to the sensibility that position encouraged. Both Bernini's colonnades for the elliptical piazza at St. Peter's in Rome—which encircle a crowd as if embracing it—and Caravaggio's realistic depictions of religious narratives exemplify, in their disparate ways, the Counter-Reformation mentality. The second tendency was the consolidation of absolute monarchies, accompanied by a simultaneous crystallization of a prominent and powerful middle class, which now came to play a role in art patronage. Effects of these political and social developments on the arts may be seen in such different manifestations as the building of the palace and gardens of Versailles for the French royalty and the development of a picture market for the middle class; its taste for realism may be seen as an influence on the work of the brothers Le Nain and Georges de La Tour in France and on the varied schools of 17th-century Dutch painting. The third tendency was a new interest in nature, spurred by developments in science and by explorations of the globe. These simultaneously brought to man a new sense both of his own insignificance (particularly abetted by the Copernican displacement of the Earth from the centre of the universe) and of his own majesty, as great conquests in knowledge were achieved. The development of landscape painting, in which man plays only a limited, sometimes minute, role, may be linked to this polarized awareness of the human condition, as also may be depictions of physical power, as, in the military sense, Velázquez' "Surrender at Breda" displays, and, in the artistic sense, his "Las Meninas" shows, for there he portrays himself as a practicing artist in the midst of royalty. Overall, these tendencies and their reflection in the arts add up to what art historian Wolfgang Stechow has called "a basically new and optimistic equilibrium of religious and secular forces."

The style of the Baroque period in the visual arts was born of a reaction against the academic and abstract qualities of International Mannerism, which the new style opposed with a more relaxed naturalism. Chief among the early Baroque painters in Rome were Annibale Carracci (1560–1609) and Caravaggio (1573–1610). Annibale was a reformer who wished to purge art of the excesses of Mannerism through the study of nature and of the art of the High Renaissance and ancient masters. Caravaggio stripped away the artificialities that tradition had introduced in representations of the lives of Christ and the saints and populated his scenes with everyday people. The immediacy of his art, combined with a highly dramatic use of light, marked him as a revolutionary. The greatest of the Italian Baroque sculptor-architects was Gian Lorenzo Bernini (1598–1680). The huge bronze baldachin that he placed above the high altar of St. Peter's in Rome completely transformed the area of the previously static and confined High Renaissance interior into flowing space.

In 1665 Bernini was invited to Paris to sculpt Louis XIV's portrait and to design a new facade for the Louvre. The resultant portrait bust is one of the sculptor's finest achievements, but the Louvre project was rejected, for the Italian Baroque style was not compatible with the King's desire for a palace that would link his reign to that of the Roman Caesars. The Louis XIV style, the "official royal style," was, rather, a classicized version of the Italian Baroque. Nicolas Poussin (1594–1665), the greatest French painter of the century, had created works that were noble, serious, logical, orderly, and rational, thus establishing the allegiance to antiquity that characterized the French Baroque. Under Louis XIV the arts were controlled by the state, and they tended to glorify the king instead of the church.

In Flanders the Baroque can best be studied in the paintings of Peter Paul Rubens (1577–1640), who painted large altarpieces and mythological works and designed elaborate courtly and allegorical cycles, including one of 21 canvases, painted between 1622 and 1625, depicting events in the life of Marie de Médicis, queen mother of France. In Holland the Baroque style developed under a number of the earlier masters, several of whom, like Rubens, had studied in Italy and knew of the Italian Baroque style at firsthand. In addition to them, there were the genre painters—landscapists, still-life painters, seascape painters, portraitists, painters of domestic interiors, and painters of church interiors—and a few transcendant masters, such as Vermeer (1632–75) and Rembrandt (1616–69). Spain produced a noteworthy master in Velázquez (1599–1660). The Baroque style in England is best seen in the portraits painted by Sir Anthony Van Dyck (1599–1641) for Charles I and his court and in the architecture of Sir Christopher Wren (1632–1723) and Sir John Vanbrugh (1664–1726). In Germany the Baroque visual arts culminated in the 18th century, when the great, ornately decorated churches and palaces of the Asam brothers and of Balthasar Neumann (1687–1753) and Dominikus Zimmerman (1685–1766) were constructed.

One of the most dramatic turning points in the history of music occurred at the beginning of the 17th century, with Italy again leading the way. While the *stile antico,* the universal polyphonic style of the 16th century, continued, it was henceforth reserved for sacred music, while the *stile moderno,* or *nuove musiche*—with its emphasis on solo voice, polarity of the melody and the bass line, and interest in expressive harmony—developed for secular usage. The expanded vocabulary allowed for a clearer distinction between sacred and secular music as well as between vocal and instrumental idioms, and national differences became more pronounced. The Baroque period in music, as in other arts, therefore, was one of stylistic diversity. The opera, oratorio, and cantata were the most important new vocal forms, while the sonata, concerto, and overture were created for instrumental music. Claudio Monteverdi (1567–1643) was the first great composer of the "new music." He was followed in Italy by Alessandro Scarlatti (1660–1725) and Giovanni Pergolesi (1710–36). The instrumental tradition in Italy found its great Baroque composers in Arcangelo Corelli (1653–1713), Antonio Vivaldi (1678–1741), and Giuseppe Tartini (1692–1770). Jean-Baptiste Lully (1632–87), a major composer of opera, and Jean Philippe Rameau (1683–1764) were the masters of Baroque music in France. In England, the total theatrical experience of the Stuart masques was followed by the achievements in vocal music of the German-born, Italian-trained George Frideric Handel (1685–1759), while his countryman, Johann Sebastian Bach (1685–1750) developed Baroque sacred music in Germany. Other notable German Baroque composers include Heinrich Schütz (1585–1672), Dietrich Buxtehude (1673–1707), and Georg Philipp Telemann (1681–1767).

The literature that may specifically be called Baroque may be seen most characteristically in the writings of Giambattista Marino in Italy, Luis de Góngora in Spain, and Martin Opitz in Germany. English Metaphysical poetry, most notably much of John Donne's, is allied with Baroque literature. The Baroque period ended in the 18th century with a transition of its characteristic style into the lighter, less dramatic, more overtly decorative Rococo style.

barosinusitis: *see* sinus squeeze.

Barossa Valley, important wine-producing region of South Australia, located 30 mi (48 km) northeast of Adelaide in the Mt. Lofty Ranges. The valley, drained by the North Para River, is about 19 mi long and 5 mi wide. It was named in 1837 by its surveyor for a district of Andalusia, Spain, and was settled by Prussians and Silesians in 1838. It has an excellent climate with reliable winter rains and dry, sunny summers, and its subsoil is suited to viticulture. From its grapes are produced a substantial proportion of Australia's light table wines, and the valley holds a wine festival in odd-numbered years. Supplementary farming yields honey, olive oil, fruits, and citrus juices. Its principal towns are Tanunda, Nuriootpa, and Angaston. A second, smaller wine region is in the nearby Barossa Hills.

barotitis: *see* ear squeeze.

barotrauma, any of several disorders arising from changes in pressure upon the body. Man is adapted to live at an atmospheric pressure of 760 millimetres (the pressure at sea level). When he ventures under water or into the upper atmospheres of space, the surrounding pressure varies from that of his usual environment. Most body tissue is either solid or liquid and remains virtually unaffected by pressure changes; in certain cavities of the body, however, such as the ears, sinuses, lungs, and intestines, there are air pockets that either expand or contract in response to changes in pressure. Several complications arising from changes in pressure are commonly known as squeezes: ear squeeze; tooth squeeze; thoracic squeeze; sinus squeeze; intestinal squeeze (*qq.v.*). *See also* decompression sickness; nitrogen narcosis.

Barotse (people): *see* Lozi.

Barotseland (province, Zambia): *see* Western.

barouche (carriage): *see* calash.

Barozio, Giacomo, Barozio also spelled BAROZZI: *see* Vignola, Giacomo da.

Barqah (North Africa): *see* Cyrenaica.

barquentine (ship): *see* barkentine.

Barquisimeto, city, capital of Lara state, northwestern Venezuela. On a wide terrace of the Río Turbio, 1,856 ft (566 m) above sea level, Barquisimeto is swept by the drying trade winds but has a warm climate (mean average temperature, 75° F [24° C]). One of Venezuela's oldest cities, it was founded in 1552 by the Spanish interim governor Juan de Villegas, who named the city Nueva Segovia, after his home in Spain. Shortly after the city's founding, gold was discovered nearby at San Felipe and Los Teques; these mines were first worked by black slaves, who revolted and were suppressed by Diego de Losada y Quiroga when they threatened Barquisimeto, sometime prior to 1569. The local Jirajira Indians also revolted at about this time but were not defeated until 1628. The city was attacked in 1561 by the pirate Lope de Aguirre, but the attack failed when Aguirre's men accepted royal pardons, abandoning him and his daughter, both of whom died in the aftermath. Aguirre's name survives in the local *Tirano Aguirre,* an *ignis fatuus,* or ephemeral light seen at night in the savanna surrounding the city. The city was almost destroyed by an earthquake in 1812 and was further damaged in the war of independence and, later, by the civil wars of the 19th century.

Barquisimeto's rise among Venezuelan cities was because of its strategic position as the hub of transport and commerce between the central and western parts of Venezuela. It is also the centre of a large agricultural area producing sisal, cacao, cattle, sugarcane, and coffee, as well as subsistence crops. In the 1960s it gained industrial stature, manufacturing local raw materials into rope and twine, food products, cement, and other items. In the centre of the city's broad streets and tall buildings stands a 230-ft (70-m) tower built in 1952 to commemorate the city's 400th anniversary. The Universidad Centro-Occidental "Lisandro Alvarado" attained university status in 1968. Pop. (1981 est.) 504,000.

Barra, Atlantic island of the Outer Hebrides group, Scotland, about 5 mi (8 km) southwest of the neighbouring island of South Uist. Formed of gneiss (an ancient, hard rock), it is about 10 mi long and with its neighbouring islets covers about 35 sq mi (90 sq km). It reaches 1,260 ft (384 m) at Heaval. Castlebay, on the southeastern coast, is the chief settlement, with a pier and steamer connection with Mallaig and Oban. Aircraft can land on the beach of North Bay at low tide, and a road 14 mi long runs around the island. A lighthouse crowns the 630-ft-high rock of Barra Head at the top of Berneray, the southernmost islet. There are prehistoric stone circles, Viking duns (castles), and the medieval Kisimul Castle, stronghold of the Macneils, a Scottish clan. Gaelic is still spoken by the predominantly Roman Catholic population. Considerable emigration has accompanied the decline of herring fishing, which, with poor semisubsistence farming, was formerly the mainstay of the economy. Pop. (1981) 1,339.

Barra do Piraí, city, western Rio de Janeiro state, eastern Brazil, at the confluence of the Piraí and Paraíba do Sul rivers, 20 mi (32 km) east of Volta Redonda. Its varied industries include textile mills and metallurgical, chemical, and food-processing plants. Near the Rio de Janeiro–São Paulo axis, at 1,175 ft (358 m) above sea level, Barra do Piraí is easily accessible by train or automobile. Pop. (1980 prelim.) 51,214.

Barra Mansa, city, western Rio de Janeiro state, eastern Brazil, on the Rio Paraíba do Sul, at 1,234 ft (376 m) above sea level, just southwest of Volta Redonda. The largest of the city's varied industries is the Nestlé food and chocolate complex. Situated on the Rio de Janeiro–São Paulo axis, Barra Mansa is easily accessible by railroad and highway. Pop. (1980 prelim.) 123,421.

Barracas al Sur (Argentina): *see* Avellaneda.

Barracco, Museo (Italian: Barracco Museum), in Rome, museum devoted to ancient sculpture and comprising the collection formed by Giovanni Barracco (1829–1914). The collection was given to Rome in 1902. There are fine examples of Egyptian, Assyrian, and Phoenician art, including a bust from Roman Egypt of a priest wearing a diadem, formerly thought to be a portrait of Julius Caesar. Greek sculpture of the classical period is well represented. Among the finest examples is a head of Marsyas, a replica of the head of the famous statue by Myron. A head of Apollo Kitharoidos, after Praxiteles, is the best extant replica of that work. In addition there are excellent and valuable examples of Hellenistic sculpture and fine Roman portrait busts.

Barrackpore, also spelled BARRACKPUR, also called CHANAK, town, Twenty-four Parganas district, West Bengal state, northeastern India, just east of the Hooghly River, part of the Calcutta urban agglomeration. Connected by road and rail with Calcutta and Bhātpāra, it includes North and South Barrackpore and the central cantonment area. The name Barrackpore probably is derived from the fact that troops have been stationed there—in barracks—since 1772. Barrackpore Park contains the former suburban residence of the viceroy of India.

The town was constituted a municipality in 1869, but its area was curtailed by the separation of Titāgarh (*q.v.*) municipality in 1895 and Pānihāti (*q.v.*) municipality in 1900. Major industries include jute and rice milling, sawmilling, and hosiery manufacture. Barrackpore has a racecourse, an airfield for freight traffic, a government agricultural institute, and three colleges affiliated with the University of Calcutta. Pop. (1981) 115,516.

Barrackpore Mutiny (Nov. 2, 1824), incident during the First Anglo-Burmese War (1824–26), generally regarded as a dress rehearsal for the Indian Mutiny of 1857 because of its similar combination of Indian grievances against the British, caste feeling, and the ineptitude of its handling. During the war, Indian forces of the 47th regiment were ordered to march to Chittagong by land because caste taboo forbade high-caste men to go by sea. Under the regulations they had to transport their personal effects, also subject to caste rules, but had no bullocks available because the army had already engaged the supply. The men's complaints and petitions were disregarded, and their grievances increased when camp followers were offered higher pay than the troops themselves. When the regiment refused to march, it was surrounded on the parade ground, bombarded by the artillery, and forced to flee under fire.

The regiment's name was erased from the army list; the ringleaders were hanged, and others were imprisoned. The incident nearly led to the recall of the British governor general, Lord Amherst, and the military authorities were criticized for their rigidity and vindictive harshness.

barracuda, any of about 20 species of predacious fishes of the family Sphyraenidae (order Perciformes). Barracudas are found in all warm and tropical regions; some also range into more temperate areas. Swift and powerful, they are slender in form, with small scales, two well-separated dorsal fins, a jutting lower jaw, and a large mouth with many large, sharp teeth. Size varies from rather small to 1.2–1.8 metres (4–6 feet)—doubtfully more—in the great barracuda (*Sphyraena barracuda*) of the Atlantic, Caribbean, and western Pacific.

Barracudas are primarily fish eaters, preying on such smaller fishes as mullets, anchovies, and grunts. Esteemed as sport fishes, barracudas, especially the smaller forms, are also valued as food. In certain seas, however, they may become impregnated with a toxic substance that produces a form of poisoning known as ciguatera. Barracudas are often regarded as bold and inquisitive, and large ones are regarded as fearsome fishes, potentially dangerous to man. The threat, though probably exaggerated, is real; the great barracuda is known to have been involved in attacks on swimmers.

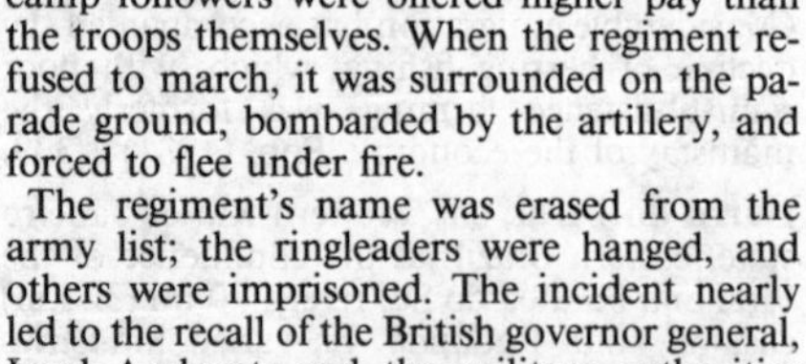

Barracuda (*Sphyraena*)
C. Leroy French—Tom Stack & Associates

barracudina, any of about 50 species of marine fishes of the family Paralepididae, found almost worldwide in deep waters. Barracudinas are long-bodied, slender fishes with large eyes, pointed snouts, and large mouths provided with both small and larger, fanglike teeth. Barracudinas grow to about 60 centimetres (2 feet) long. They are not often seen but are sometimes attracted to bright lights at the surface. It is thought that they may be an important food for larger fishes, such as tunas and swordfish.

Barrancabermeja, city, Santander department, north central Colombia, on the Río Magdalena. In 1536 a Spanish conquistador, Gonzalo Jiménez de Quezada, discovered the wooden-stockaded Indian settlement of La Tora. The Spaniards eventually renamed it Barrancas-Bermejas (Reddish Cliffs) after the nearby river bluffs. Barrancabermeja became a ranching town and marketed beef. The Mares Oil Concession (1921) and the development of the petroleum industry gave impetus to its growth. Networks of highways, railroads (including the Atlantic Railway linking Santa Marta and Bogotá), and oil pipelines appeared; a large oil refinery and an international airport were built. The Catedral del Sagrado Corazón de Jesús (Cathedral of the Sacred Heart of Jesus) is a notable landmark. Pop. (1973) city, 92,038; mun., 105,115.

Oil refinery at Barrancabermeja on the Magdalena River, Colombia
Loren McIntyre—AVP

Barranco, city and district, in the southern portion of the Lima–Callao metropolitan area, Peru, lying on the Pacific coast at an elevation of 213 ft (65 m) above sea level. Founded as a village beach resort in 1874, it became a town in 1893 and a city in 1901. In 1881, during the War of the Pacific, it was sacked and burned by Chilean forces. It is a middle- and high-income residential district, with public beaches, a large municipal park, and a zoo. The Pedro de Osma, a museum containing an extensive collection of colonial artifacts, and the national aviation school are in Barranco. Pop. (1981 prelim.) 46,388.

Barrande, Joachim (b. Aug. 11, 1799, Saugues, Fr.—d. Oct. 5, 1883, Frohsdorf, Austria), geologist and paleontologist whose studies of the fossil strata of Bohemia revealed the abundance and rich variety of life in the Early Paleozoic Era (from 395,000,000 to 570,000,000 years ago).

The tutor of the grandson of Charles X, the king of France, he joined the royal family in exile in 1830. They settled temporarily in Prague in 1832, and Barrande remained there. While working as an engineer, he became interested in the fossils of the region, and, when he realized the striking similarity between the strata of Britain, as described by the noted British geologist Sir Roderick I. Murchison, and the strata in Bohemia, he began an intensive geological study. His primary work, *Système silurien du centre de la Bohême* (1852–94; "Silurian System of Central Bohemia"), complete with excellent drawings, is still used as a reference work. In it he identified and analyzed more than 4,000 new fossil species.

Barranquilla, capital of Atlántico department, northwestern Colombia, in the Caribbean lowlands, 15 mi (24 km) upstream from the mouth of the Río Magdalena.

El Prado suburb of Barranquilla, Colom.
Carl Frank

Founded in 1629, it remained unimportant until the construction of a railroad to satellite ports on the Bahía (bay) de Sabanilla and the clearing of the river's mouth in the 1930s. Since World War II, the relative decline in traffic on the river and the growth of road transport have supported the development of the Pacific port of Buenaventura. Barranquilla, however, continues to handle much coffee and petroleum from the interior and cotton from the surrounding region. It is also the terminus of four natural-gas pipelines from fields in northern Colombia. Textiles, beverages, cement, shoes, clothing, cardboard, and chemicals are among its industrial products. Barranquilla houses Atlántico University (1941) and the University of the North (1966). The city is accessible by highway, possesses an international jet airport, and is a major gateway to tourism on the Caribbean coast. Pop. (1984 est.) 926,890.

Barras, Paul-François-Jean-Nicolas, vicomte de (viscount of) (b. June 30, 1755, Fox-Amphoux, Fr.—d. Jan. 29, 1829, Chaillot), one of the most powerful members of the Directory during the French Revolution.

A Provençal nobleman, Barras volunteered as gentleman cadet in the regiment of Languedoc at the age of 16 and, from 1776 to 1783, served in India. A period of unemployment in Paris left Barras disenchanted with the royal regime, and he welcomed the outbreak of the Revolution in 1789. He entered the Club of the Jacobins almost immediately after it was founded and returned to the *département* of Var in 1791 to make himself eligible for election to the Legislative Assembly. Although his fierce electoral campaign failed to gain him election to the Assembly itself, he was made an elector from Var.

In September 1792, Barras returned to Paris, where he was elected deputy to the National Convention. As commissar in the French Army of Italy, his first mission was to liberate the Var and Nice from royalist forces and to organize the new *département* of Alpes-Maritimes. After voting for the King's death, he was sent to the Alps to conquer anti-Jacobin forces at Toulon, where his successful campaign gained him new prominence in the Convention and where he first met Napoleon Bonaparte.

During the Reign of Terror of 1794, Barras refused to align himself with any particular group. Nevertheless, he shrewdly reasserted himself in the coup of 9 Thermidor (July 27, 1794), acting as one of the three key figures in the overthrow of the Jacobin leader Maximilien Robespierre, and he emerged as the commander of the Army of the Interior and the police. His fame and power quickly increasing, he held a number of high-level positions in the Convention and Committee of Public Safety between the summer of 1794 and the autumn of 1795, by which time he had helped crush a revolt of the Parisian populace, aggravated antiroyalist attacks in the Convention, and had begun an affair with Joséphine de Beauharnais, Napoleon's future wife.

Renamed general of the Army of the Interior on 13 Vendémiaire (Oct. 5, 1795), he and Napoleon defended the regime against an attempted royalist insurrection and brought about the establishment of the Directory. By engineering the elections, Barras made himself one of the new *directeurs,* emerging as the most popular of the five. In 1796 he became actively involved with Le Cercle Constitutionnel, a group of antiroyalist liberals that included Talleyrand, Joseph Fouché, Benjamin Constant, and Madame de Staël, who supported the less republican and more authoritarian structure of the Directory.

The coup of 18 Fructidor (Sept. 4, 1797), a purge of royalists in the Assembly, brought Barras to the apex of his power, but he fell from power in Napoleon's coup of 18 Brumaire (Nov. 9, 1799). He was placed under the constant surveillance of Fouché's spy network, and Napoleon's suspicion of his conspiratorial activities brought about his exile to Brussels between 1801 and 1805, when he was permitted to return to southern France. When Napoleon learned of his secret meetings there with the former Spanish king Charles IV, he sent him to Rome in 1813. Barras may have contacted Louis XVIII even before 18 Brumaire; in any event, after the Second Restoration of the Bourbon monarchy (1815) the King permitted him to live in peace at his estate at Chaillot.

BIBLIOGRAPHY. Barras, *Mémoires* (1895–96; reprinted 1968); A. Mathiez, *Le Directoire* (1934); and J. Vivent, *Barras, Le "Roi" de la République* (1938).

Barrault, Jean-Louis (b. Sept. 8, 1910, Vesinet, Fr.), French actor, director, and producer whose work with modern and classic plays won him international honours.

Barrault, a student of Charles Dullin, first appeared on the stage as a servant in Dullin's production of *Volpone* (1931). Barrault also studied mime with Étienne Decroux; indeed, Barrault's first independent production, *As I Lay Dying* (1935), was a mime play. Further production, which included Cervantes' *Numancia* (1937) and Shakespeare's *Hamlet* (1937), was interrupted by army service. In 1940 he joined the Comédie-Française at the instigation of Jacques Copeau, and it was there that he met his wife and working associate, the actress Madeleine Renaud. With the Comédie, Barrault directed and acted in numerous works, including *Phèdre, Antony and Cleopatra,* and *Le Soulier de Satin.*

In 1947 he and his wife formed their own company at the Théâtre Marigny under the name Compagnie M. Renaud–J.L. Barrault. They opened with *Hamlet* in a translation by André Gide (later performed at the Edinburgh Festival), followed by *Les Fausses Confidences* and *Baptiste* (a ballet pantomime) by Pierre Marivaux and by Armand Salacrou's *Les Nuits de la colère.* The combination of French and foreign classics with modern plays became the hallmark of the company's great success. Their productions included Georges Feydeau's farces as well as such modern scripts as Eugene Ionesco's *Rhinocéros* (1960), Christopher Fry's *A Sleep of Prisoners* (1955) and *The Dark is Light Enough* (1962), and works by Jean Anouilh, Jean-Paul Sartre, and Henry de Montherlant. Barrault continued his schedule of producing, directing, and acting lead roles throughout this period. In 1956 the company left the Marigny and took a long tour that included London and a return to New York City, where they had debuted with Molière's *Les Fourberies de Scapin* four years previously. Upon returning to France the company used the Théâtre Sarah-Bernhardt for a while and then moved to the Palais-Royal.

In 1959 Barrault was appointed director of the Odéon, which was renamed the Théâtre de France, and there he produced new plays by Samuel Beckett and François Billetdoux, as well as three Shakespearean plays in honour of the 400th anniversary of Shakespeare's birth. Barrault was also director of the Théâtre des Nations (1964–67, 1972–74) and founder-director of Théâtre D'Orsay (1974).

Barrault's extensive film work began with *Les Beaux Jours* in 1936 and includes, among many others, *La Symphonie Fantastique* (1942), *Les Enfants du Paradis* (1944), *La Ronde* (1950), and *The Longest Day* (1962). Among his publications are *Reflections on the Theatre* (1951), *The Theatre of Jean-Louis Barrault* (1961), and *Memories for Tomorrow* (1974). Barrault was named a chevalier of the Légion d'Honneur.

Barre, city, Washington County, central Vermont, U.S., just south of Montpelier, the state capital. The area, settled *c.* 1788, was organized as a town (township) in 1793 under the name of Wildersburgh but was soon renamed for Barre, Mass. The city was set off and incorporated in 1894. It is a centre of the nation's granite quarrying, which began after the War of 1812 and attracted Italian, Scottish, and Scandinavian stoneworkers. In 1975, a new operation, the Adams Quarry, opened at Barre. The manufacture of electrical equipment is also important. The surrounding Barre town (township) includes the villages of East Barre, South Barre, Graniteville (site of Rock of Ages Granite Quarry), and Websterville. Goddard College (1863) is 5 mi (8 km) north. East Barre Dam (1935) is part of the Winooski Flood Control Project. Groton State Forest is nearby. Pop. (1980) 9,824.

Granite quarry, Barre, Vt.
By courtesy of the Vermont Development Agency

barre, in ballet, the horizontal handrail, usually wooden, that is fixed to the walls of a ballet studio approximately 3½ feet (1 metre) from the floor. It is used by dancers as an aid to confidence and as a point of support during the preliminary exercises ("barre work") that have been an essential part of ballet training since the development of classical ballet in the 19th century.

Barre being used by students of the Moscow Academic School of Choreography of the Bolshoi Theatre
Tass—Sovfoto

barrel, large, bulging cylindrical container of sturdy construction traditionally made from wooden staves and wooden or metal hoops. The term is also a unit of volume measure, specifically 31 gallons of a fermented or distilled beverage, or 42 gallons of a petroleum product. According to the 1st-century-AD Roman historian Pliny the Elder, the ancient craft of barrel making, also called cooperage, was invented by the inhabitants of the Alpine valleys.

Slack barrels, made to hold dry products, may be made of pine or softwood and do not require precise workmanship. Smaller versions, usually called kegs, long were used to contain heavy bulk products such as nails. Tight barrels, made to hold liquids, must be constructed carefully of high-grade woods, such as white oak, with bungholes for filling and emptying.

Wood for barrel staves and headings is usually air-dried for at least a year, then kiln-dried for 10 to 20 days before being cut and planed to the needed size and finish. A crucial operation is the jointing of the edges of the staves and giving them the proper bilge (middle bulge) so that the joints will be tight and the circumference uniform. The bulge gives the barrel added resistance to internal pressure.

The most complex part of the operation is called raising the barrel. Staves are set vertically into a head truss ring, and a temporary hoop is placed over the other end. In this arrangement, the staves are passed through a steam tunnel to soften them for drawing into final shape and then dried again. Whisky barrels are charred on the inside at this point, so that they will develop flavour in the whisky as it ages. Beer, formerly stored and shipped in wooden barrels, now is placed in one-piece metal barrels. A machine called a crozer trims the ends of the staves and cuts the croze, the groove near the end of the stave where the head pieces fit. The temporary end rings are pulled off, the head pieces fitted, and permanent head hoops put in place. The temporary bilge hoops are removed, and the rest of the permanent hoops are put on.

Tight barrels have been superseded for the most part by metal drums and bulk-tank transportation, and slack barrels by paper-shipping sacks, corrugated paperboard cartons, and fibreboard drums.

barrel, unit of both liquid and dry measure in the British Imperial and U.S. Customary systems, ranging from 31 to 42 gallons for liquids and fixed at 7,056 cubic inches (105 dry quarts, or 115.65 litres) for most fruits, vegetables, and other dry commodities. The cranberry barrel, however, measures 5,826 cubic inches. In liquid measure, the wine barrel of 126 quarts (31.5 gallons, or 119.24 litres) and the ale and beer barrel of 144 quarts (36 gallons, or 136.27 litres) probably were defined by the traditional size of the actual wooden barrels used in these trades. In the United States a 40-gallon barrel for proof spirits has been legally recognized, and federal taxes on fermented liquors are calculated on a barrel of 31 gallons. A petroleum barrel of 42 gallons may have become standard in the American Southwest because casks of this capacity were readily available. Dry-weight barrels include the barrel of 200 pounds for fish, beef, and pork and that of 376 pounds for cement, among others.

barrel cactus, name for a group of more or less barrel-shaped cacti, family Cactaceae, native to North and South America. It is most often used for two large-stemmed North

Barrel cactus (*Echinocactus grusonii*)
Carlo Bevilacqua—SCALA from Art Resource/EB Inc.

American genera, *Ferocactus* and *Echinocactus.* Small barrels cacti include the genera *Sclerocactus, Neolloydia, Echinofossulocactus,* and *Thelocactus.*

Echinocactus usually grows to about 60 centimetres (2 feet) long and about 30 cm in diameter, and *Ferocactus* to about 3 metres (10 feet) long and about 60 cm in diameter. A large specimen may weigh several hundred pounds.

The stems of barrel cacti generally have strong stiff spines and prominent ribs. They endure the driest environments. Flowers, yellow to orange and purplish and sometimes fragrant, are up to 8 cm across. Long narrow fruit distinguishes *Echinocactus* from *Ferocactus. Echinocactus* contains about 16 species, *Ferocactus* 25.

Barrel cactus (*Sclerocactus parviflorus*)
Dorothea W. Woodruff—EB Inc.

Many authorities include *Astrophytum* and *Homalocephala* with *Echinocactus,* and *Hamatocactus* with *Ferocactus.* The eight or nine species of *Sclerocactus* have at least one hooked central spine. Their flowers are mainly pink, yellow, and cream. The Mojave Desert giant of the genus, *S. polyancistrus,* a cylindroid cactus up to 40 cm in height and 13 cm in diameter, has showy red and white spines and large flowers. Almost as large are the cacti of the commonest and least specialized group, the *S. parviflorus* complex of the Colorado Plateau. The remaining six species of small cacti grow in widely scattered colonies.

Neolloydia, with about 20 species, is native to the southwestern U.S. and south far into Mexico. Spiny and globose to cylindroid, *Neolloydia* species reach 40 cm in height and 12 cm in diameter. The genus is related to *Sclerocactus, Thelocactus,* and *Gymnocactus.*

Echinofossulocactus (formerly *Stenocactus*) comprises about 30 species native to Mexico. Plants are more or less globose, rarely exceeding 12 cm in diameter. The genus is distinguished primarily by its numerous wavy ribs, in one species numbering more than 100, giving the convoluted aspect of a "brain"; hence the common name brain cactus. One species, *E. coptonogonus,* otherwise fitting the genus, does not have this characteristic.

Thelocactus is a genus of a few to 30 species (depending on the authority) of small to medium-sized, more or less spiny plants with tubercles (protuberances) distinct or coalescent into ribs. *T. hexaedrophorus,* with large blue tubercles, is an unusual pot plant. Some species have showy white, pink, or purple flowers and colourful spines.

barrel organ, musical instrument in which a pinned barrel turned by a handle raises levers, admitting wind to one or more ranks of organ pipes; the handle simultaneously actuates the bellows. Ten or more tunes can be set on one barrel.

Italian barrel organ, early 19th century; in the Metropolitan Museum of Art, New York City
By courtesy of the Metropolitan Museum of Art, New York City, the Crosby Brown Collection of Musical Instruments, 1889

Barrel organs are valuable because they preserve old styles of musical ornamentation. They reached a peak of popularity in the late 18th and early 19th centuries; some played the psalms in village churches until well into the 20th century. They are sometimes confused with other handle-operated street instruments, including the barrel piano and the hurdy-gurdy.

barrel piano, also called STREET PIANO, stringed musical instrument (chordophone) in which a simple pianoforte action is worked by a pinned barrel turned with a crank, rather than by a keyboard mechanism. It is associated primarily with street musicians and is believed to have been developed in London early in the 19th century. The centre of its manufacture later moved to Italy.

European barrel piano, early 19th century; in the Metropolitan Museum of Art, New York City
By courtesy of the Metropolitan Museum of Art, New York City, the Crosby Brown Collection of Musical Instruments, 1889

It is sometimes confused with two older street instruments, the barrel organ and the hurdy-gurdy, as these are also operated by a crank. It is also wrongly referred to as a hand, or handle, organ.

barrel vault, ceiling or roof consisting of a series of semicylindrical arches. *See* vault.

Barrell, Joseph (b. Dec. 15, 1869, New Providence, N.J., U.S.—d. May 4, 1919, New Haven, Conn.), geologist who proposed that sedimentary rocks were produced by the action of rivers, winds, and ice, as well as by marine sedimentation.

Barrell worked with the United States Geological Survey in 1901 in Montana, where he conducted studies of the Marysville mining district, near Helena. Concluding that a new theory for the granite batholiths (great masses of igneous rock) of that area was necessary, he presented his ideas in *Geology of the Marysville Mining District, Montana* (1907). In this classic work on geology he proposed the then new concept that molten magma from the Earth's interior interacts with the crust to form fissures and create new surface features.

Before the publication of Barrell's papers on sedimentation, it was generally believed that almost all sedimentary strata were produced by oceans. A close study of the Triassic deposits (190,000,000 to 225,000,000 years old) of New Jersey and the Western deserts convinced Barrell that at least one-fifth of the land was covered by other types of sediments. In addition, he challenged the idea that the depth of sedimentary layers is directly related to the time necessary to produce them. In a pioneering work, "Strength of the Earth's Crust," published in the *Journal of Geology* (vol. 22 and 23, 1914–15), Barrell presented his own views on isostasy (the equilibrium forces involved in balancing mountains and basins in the Earth's crust) and tried to explain many geological phenomena by the interaction of two hypothetical crust layers.

Barremian Stage, standard, worldwide division of Lower Cretaceous rocks and time (the Cretaceous Period began about 136,000,000 years ago and lasted about 71,000,000 years). Rocks of the Barremian Stage overlie those of the Hauterivian Stage and underlie rocks of the Aptian Stage. The Barremian of Great Britain is represented by the upper portions of the Wealden Series, whereas in northern Europe it consists of portions of the thick Hils Clay. Sandstones and shales dominate the Barremian of North Africa, the Middle East, Australia, New Zealand, and Japan. The Barremian has been divided into three zones, smaller divisions of rocks and time, characterized by distinctive types of fossil ammonite cephalopods (mollusks).

Where the same name may denote a person, place, or thing, the articles will be found in that order

---

Barren Grounds, also called BARREN LANDS, sub-Arctic prairie (tundra) region of northern mainland Canada (Northwest Territories), extending westward from Hudson Bay to the Great Slave and Great Bear lakes, northward to the Arctic Ocean, and southward to latitude

The Barren Grounds of the Northwest Territories
George Hunter—National Film Board of Canada Phototheque

59° N along the Hudson Bay coastal plain. Its surface is a low (less than 1,000 ft [300 m]), glaciated, treeless plain covered with grasses, mosses, and lichens, interspersed with granitic outcrops, and dotted with innumerable lakes and streams, including the Coppermine, Back, Dubawnt, Kazan, and Thelon rivers. Everywhere the ground is permanently frozen to within a few inches of the surface, creating, in many areas, vast stretches of mosquito- and fly-infested swamp during the summer thaw. Caribou, musk-ox, fox, and bear inhabit the Barren Grounds, which is protected, in part, by Yellowknife and Thelon game sanctuaries. A few Inuit (Eskimo), living in the coastal areas, are the only human inhabitants.

The Barren Grounds was first explored by the Englishman Samuel Hearne, who crossed the area during his 1769–72 expedition.

Barrera, Carlos Arniches y: *see* Arniches (y Barrera), Carlos.

Barrès (Auguste-)Maurice (b. Aug. 19, 1862, Charmes-sur-Moselle, Fr.—d. Dec. 5, 1923, Paris), writer and politician whose individualism and fervent nationalism strongly influenced his generation.

After completing his secondary studies at the Nancy *lycée,* Barrès went to Paris to study

Barrès, 1906
H. Roger-Viollet

law but instead turned to literature, publishing a few essays critical of the historians Hippolyte Taine and Ernest Renan, the spiritual mentors of his day. Then he embarked on a solitary project of self-analysis, through a rigorous method described in *Le Culte du moi* (comprising *Sous l'oeil des Barbares,* 1888; *Un Homme libre,* 1889; and *Le Jardin de Bérénice,* 1891).

At 27 he embarked on a tumultuous political career. He ran successfully for deputy of Nancy on a platform demanding the return to France of Alsace-Lorraine and an end to the mutilation of French territory. From this patriotic stance he adopted an increasingly intransigent nationalism. This stage was minutely reported in a new trilogy, *Le Roman de l'énergie nationale* (*Les Déracinés,* 1897; *L'Appel du soldat,* 1900; *Leurs Figures,* 1902); in these works he expounded an individualism that included a deep-rooted attachment to one's native soil. With the doctrinaire author Charles Maurras, he blocked out the doctrines of the French Nationalist Party in the pages of two papers: *La Cocarde* and *Le Drapeau.* He took a passionate stand in all the most celebrated issues of the period before World War I, and his series entitled "Les Bastions de l'Est" (*Au service de l'Allemagne,* 1905; *Colette Baudoche,* 1909; Eng. trans., 1918) became grist for the propaganda mill of the war. In *La Colline inspirée* (1913; *The Sacred Hill,* 1929) he demonstrated how Catholicism and nationalism had been integrated.

At times, however, the artist may be found to supersede the politician in Barrès's writing. His travels in Spain, Italy, Greece, and Asia inspired the beautiful pages, free from ideology, of *Du sang, de la volupté et de la mort* (1894; completed in 1904 and 1909) and of *Un Jardin sur l'Oronte* (1922). He was elected to the Académie Française in 1906.

Barreto, Afonso Henriques de Lima: *see* Lima Barreto, Afonso Henriques de.

Barreto, Francisco (b. 1520, Faro, Port.—d. July 9, 1573, Sena, Mozambique), Portuguese soldier and explorer.

Barreto served in the East Indies, was governor of Portuguese India, and was probably instrumental in exiling Luís de Camões to Macau, after the poet had published criticisms of Portuguese administration in India. In 1569 Barreto was entrusted by King Sebastian of Portugal with an expedition to the empire of Mwene Matapa in southeastern Africa, to assert Portuguese authority over the area, capture the gold mines of Manica, and avenge the murder of a missionary. Barreto took the Zambezi valley route (1572); the following year the expedition was repeated, but Barreto became mortally ill and died at Sena.

Barretos, city, north central São Paulo state, Brazil, near the Rio Pardo at 1,713 ft (522 m) above sea level. Known at various times as Amaral dos Barretos, Espírito Santo de Barreto, and Espírito Santo dos Barretos, the settlement was given town status and was made the seat of a municipality in 1885. The site of the state's biggest cattle market, Barretos also serves an agricultural area producing rice and other grains, *feijão* (beans), cotton, and coffee. Its industries bottle mineral water, process crops, and manufacture shoes, furniture, and other goods. A railroad line runs to Ribeirão Prêto (80 mi [130 km] southeast), and Barretos is on the São Paulo–Uberlândia (Minas

Cathedral and main square at Barretos, Braz.
Plessner International

Gerais state) highway. The city also has an airfield. Pop. (1980 prelim.) 65,294.

Barrett, Elizabeth: *see* Browning, Elizabeth Barrett.

Barrett, Kate Harwood Waller, *née* KATHERINE HARWOOD WALLER (b. Jan. 24, 1857, Falmouth, Va., U.S.—d. Feb. 23, 1925, Alexandria, Va.), U.S. physician who directed the rescue-home movement for unwed mothers in the United States.

Barrett became interested in the issue of prostitution while helping her husband, Robert S. Barrett, a minister whom she married in 1876. She earned an M.D. from the Medical College of Georgia in 1892 in order to further her understanding of the problem of illegitimacy. The next year she opened a rescue home in Atlanta, which became affiliated with Charles Crittenton's national chain of Florence Crittenton homes for unwed mothers.

In 1897 Barrett became vice president of the Florence Crittenton Mission, which numbered over 50 homes nationwide, and from 1909 until her death she served as the organization's president. She guided the movement away from its focus on prostitute reformation and toward a concern with the social welfare of the unwed mother, a shift that helped to make the unwed mother an acceptable subject of philanthropy. Barrett also promoted vocational guidance and child care training, and she campaigned against the practice of separating illegitimate infants from their mothers.

Barrett, Lawrence (b. April 4, 1838, Paterson, N.J, U.S.—d. March 20, 1891, New York City), one of the leading actors of the 19th century, especially noted for his Shakespearean interpretations.

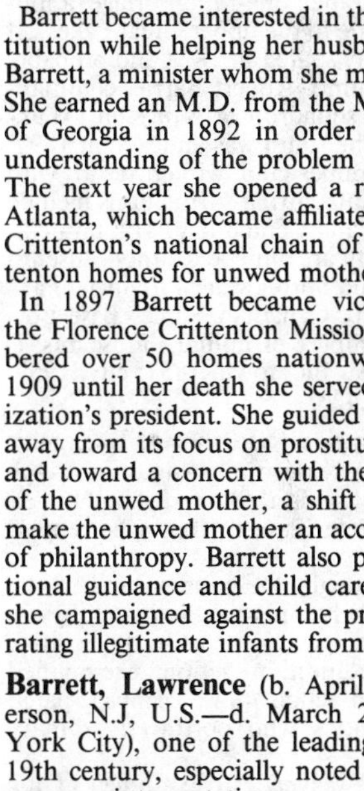

Barrett
BBC Hulton Picture Library

He made his stage debut at age 15 in Detroit in J. Talbot Haines's *French Spy,* and on Jan. 20, 1857, he first appeared in New York City at Burton's Chambers Street Theatre as Sir Thomas Clifford in James Sheridan Knowles's *Hunchback*. He played various leading roles in New York City and Boston until 1861, when the Civil War broke out; he served as a captain in the 28th Massachusetts Regiment until Aug. 8, 1862. After the war he acted in several cities, achieving national prominence. With John McCullough, he managed the California Theatre in San Francisco (1867–70). His many roles include Hamlet, Lear, Macbeth, Shylock, Richard III, and Cardinal Wolsey, as well as Lanciotto in George Henry Boker's *Francesca da Rimini* (probably his greatest popular success), and Harebell in William Wills's *Man o' Airlie.* He played Othello to Edwin Booth's Iago, and Cassius to Booth's Brutus. He acted in London a number of times between 1867 and 1884. Barrett also wrote a life of Edwin Forrest in the "American Actors" series (1881) and a sketch of Booth in *Edwin Booth and His Contemporaries* (1886).

Barri, Gerald de: *see* Giraldus Cambrensis.

Barri, Y (Wales): *see* Barry.

Barrie, city, seat (1837) of Simcoe County, southeastern Ontario, Canada, on Kempenfelt Bay, an arm of Lake Simcoe, 55 mi (90 km) north-northwest of Toronto. In 1812 a storehouse was probably built on the site, which during the War of 1812 was the landing and starting point of the Nine-Mile-Portage (a military supply route to the upper Great Lakes). It was permanently settled in 1828 and probably named for Commo. Robert Barrie, commander of a naval squadron at Kingston. Allandale village to the south was annexed in 1897. Barrie is a summer and winter resort with diversified manufacturing. Attractions include Brookdale Zoo and Centennial Park; immediately to the north are Simcoe County Museum and Archives and Springwater Provincial Park (116 ac [47 ha]). Canadian Forces Base Borden, with a complex of military museums, is a few miles west. Inc. town, 1851; city, 1959. Pop. (1981) 38,423.

Barrie, Sir James (Matthew), BARONET (b. May 9, 1860, Kirriemuir, Angus, Scot.—d. June 19, 1937, London), dramatist and novelist, creator of Peter Pan, the boy who refused to grow up.

Barrie also brought the supernatural to the stage at a time when it was dominated by social criticism and gave impetus to the Scottish sentimental tradition in fiction, exemplified by the Kailyard school (*q.v.;* "cabbage-patch school") of writers who portrayed ordinary cottage life.

The son of a weaver, Barrie studied at the University of Edinburgh and spent two years on the Nottingham *Journal* before settling in London as a free-lance writer in 1885. His first successful book was *Auld Licht Idylls* (1888), sketches of life in Kirriemuir. *The Little Minister* (1891), a novel in the same style, was a best-seller, and after its dramatization in 1897, most of his work was for the theatre.

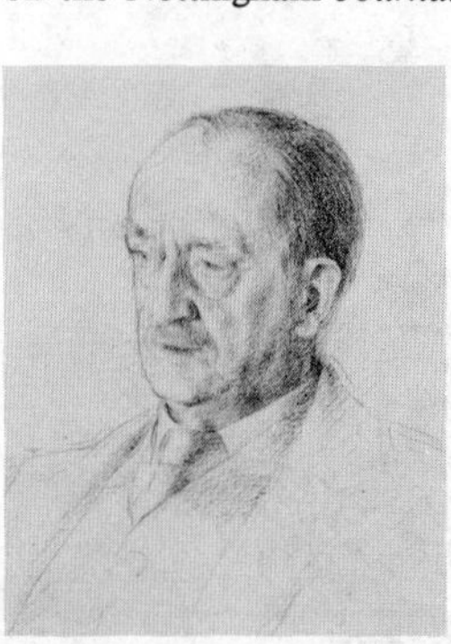

Barrie, pencil drawing by Walter T. Monnington, 1932; in the National Portrait Gallery, London
By courtesy of the National Portrait Gallery, London

His best known plays are *The Admirable Crichton, Peter Pan, Dear Brutus,* and *Mary Rose.* He also wrote a number of excellent one-act plays. Barrie was created a baronet in 1913 and awarded the Order of Merit in 1922; he became president of the Society of Authors in 1928 and chancellor of Edinburgh University in 1930.

Barrie never recovered from the shock he received at six from a brother's death and its grievous effect on his mother, who dominated his childhood and retained that dominance thereafter. He made her the heroine of the novel *Margaret Ogilvy* (1896), which describes her both as the mother of her family of 10 and as a "little mother" to her motherless brothers and sisters during her girlhood. His autobiographical novel, *Sentimental Tommy* (1896), again has a "little mother" heroine.

Barrie's marriage in 1894 to the actress Mary Ansell was childless and apparently unconsummated. In 1897 he found another "little mother" in Sylvia Llewellyn Davies. To her sons he told his first Peter Pan stories, some of which were published in *The Little White Bird* (1902). The play *Peter Pan* followed in 1904, and Barrie published the story in 1911 under the title *Peter and Wendy.*

His marriage ended in divorce in April 1910; Sylvia Davies, then a widow, died four months later; two of her sons, to whom Barrie acted as guardian, were killed.

Barrie took a disenchanted view of adult life, an attitude reflected in most of his writing. *The Admirable Crichton* (1902), *The Twelve Pound Look* (1910), *The Will* (1913), and *Dear Brutus* (1917) are usually considered the finest of his plays.

barrier penetration (quantum mechanics): *see* tunnelling.

barrier reef, a coral reef (*q.v.*) roughly parallel to a shore and separated from it by a lagoon or other body of water. A barrier reef is usually pierced by several channels that give access to the lagoon and the island or continent beyond it.

Barrin, Roland-Michel: *see* La Galissonière, Roland-Michel Barrin, marquis de.

Barringer Crater (Arizona): *see* Meteor Crater.

Barrington, town (township), Bristol County, eastern Rhode Island, U.S., on the eastern shore of Narragansett Bay just southeast of Providence; it occupies two peninsulas separated by the Barrington River. As early as 1632, Plymouth settlers had established a trading post in the area on Sowams, once the fishing and hunting grounds of Wampanoag Indians. The first European settlement was made by John Myles and his followers, who had left Rehoboth because of religious differences. In 1677 Myles's settlement, including Sowams, it was incorporated as Swansea. This section, in turn, was incorporated in 1717 as the Town of Barrington (named for Viscount Barrington, an English lawyer who advocated religious freedom) by the General Court of Massachusetts Bay Colony. In 1746 Barrington was transferred to Rhode Island Colony, forming a part of the Town of Warren. In 1770 the western part of Warren was separated and incorporated as Barrington. Barrington (including the village of West Barrington) is mainly residential, with a few light industries manufacturing textiles, foods, rubber, and plastics. Barrington College was founded (1900) in Dudley, Mass.; it was moved to Barrington in 1951. Pop. (1980) 16,174.

Barrington, George (b. May 14, 1755, Maynooth, County Kildare, Ire.—d. Dec. 27, 1804, Parramatta, New South Wales, Australia), Irish adventurer notorious for his activities as a pickpocket in England in the 1770s and 1780s; he was allegedly the author of several histories of Australia.

Barrington, detail of an engraving
BBC Hulton Picture Library

Barrington's father was a silversmith named Henry Waldron. About 1771 young Waldron joined a troupe of actors, taking the name George Barrington. They introduced him to the pickpocket's art, and in 1773 he entered London society as a gentleman of wit and breeding. He picked the pockets of the rich at races, theatrical performances, and state ceremonies. After his eighth conviction (1790) for these crimes he was deported to a prison settlement in Australia. There he reformed, obtained a pardon (1796), and eventually became superintendent of the convicts. He became insane shortly after retiring in 1800.

Although publishers used Barrington's name in advertisements for several histories—including *A Voyage to New South Wales* (1803) and *The History of New South Wales* (1802)—there is no evidence that Barrington wrote these works. In addition, he was said to have originated a well-known couplet concerning the exiled convicts:

True patriots all, for be it understood,
We left our country for our country's good.

These lines were actually written by an Englishman named Henry Carter in 1801 and included in a work ascribed to Barrington.

Barrington Island (Galápagos Islands): *see* Santa Fe Island.

Barrio Obrero Industrial, community of San Martín de Porres district, in the Lima–Callao metropolitan area, Peru, lying on the north bank of the Río Rímac at an elevation of 492 ft (150 m). Among the oldest and best developed of Lima's *pueblos jóvenes* ("young towns"), Barrio Obrero Industrial is primarily a working-class residential area. It contains numerous retail and service establishments, some light industry, educational and recreational facilities, and churches. The private university "San Martín de Porres" (1965) is located in the district. Pop. (1972) community, 90,645; (1981 prelim.) district, 403,445.

Barrios, Eduardo (b. Oct. 25, 1884, Valparaíso, Chile—d. Sept. 13, 1963, Santiago), writer best known for his psychological novels.

Barrios was educated in Lima and at the Chilean Military Academy, in Santiago. After working as a merchant, a rubber agent, and a prospector in several Latin-American countries, he settled in 1913 in Santiago, where he served as minister of public education and director of the National Library.

Barrios began his literary career under the influence of Zola, with a collection of naturalistic stories, *Del natural* (1907; "In the Naturalistic Style"). His later novels, which established his reputation, include *El niño que enloqueció de amor* (1915; "The Love-Crazed Boy"), a fictionalized diary of a boy obsessed with love for one of his mother's friends; *Un perdido* (1918; "A Down-and-Outer"), the story of a young boy with a deep inferiority complex; and *El hermano asno* (1922; *Brother Asno,* 1969), an unusual episode in the life of a mentally disturbed monk who attacks a girl in order to be despised by those who consider him a living saint. Barrios' most successful work was *Gran señor y rajadiablos* (1948; "Grand Gentleman and Big Rascal"), a best-seller in which the novelist portrayed life on a typical Chilean farm.

The author's personal experiences played an important part in all these novels, as well as in his other works: *Páginas de un pobre diablo* (1923; "Pages from a Poor Devil"), a series of autobiographical sketches; *Tamarugal* (1944), a novel about life in the northern mining region of Chile; and *Los hombres del hombre* (1950; "Men Within Man"), a novelistic study in human psychology.

Barrios, Justo Rufino (b. 1835, San Lorenzo, Guatemala—d. April 2, 1885, Chalchuapa, El Salvador), president of Guatemala from 1873 who carried out liberal domestic policies by dictatorial means and persistently advocated Central American unity, to be imposed by force if diplomacy proved inadequate.

Justo Barrios, portrait by an unknown artist
By courtesy of the Library of Congress, Washington, D.C.

Trained for the law, Barrios became Guatemalan army commander and the power behind the president, Miguel García Granados, in 1871, when the Conservative Party government was overthrown. After replacing Granados in 1873, Barrios became known as "the Reformer." He subjugated the local aristocracy; expelled the Jesuits and confiscated church property; enlarged and laicized the school system; built highways, railroads, and telegraph lines; encouraged the growing of coffee as the basis of the country's agriculture; and promulgated a new constitution (1876).

Barrios intervened repeatedly in the affairs of the other Central American republics in an effort to restore the five-nation federation that had collapsed in 1838. When his political persuasion failed, he invaded neighbouring El Salvador and was killed in battle.

His nephew José María Reina Barrios was president of Guatemala from 1892 until his assassination in 1898.

barrister, one of the two types of practicing lawyers in England, the other being the solicitor. In general, barristers engage in advocacy (trial work) and solicitors in office work, but there is a considerable overlap in their functions. The solicitor, for example, may appear as an advocate in the lower courts, whereas barristers are often called upon to give opinions or to draft documents.

Only barristers may appear as advocates before the High Court; they are known collectively as the bar, and it is from their ranks that the most important judicial appointments are made. To be a barrister it is necessary to be a member of one of the four Inns of Court (*q.v.*). A prospective barrister must pass a series of examinations established for the inns by the Council of Legal Education and must satisfy certain traditional requirements such as eating a certain number of dinners at the respective inn. In addition, the inns still stress the pupillage system, whereby a student or a young barrister reads with a practicing barrister for not less than a year.

The General Council of the Bar sets standards for the bar and acts in matters of general concern to the profession. A barrister is required to accept any case for a proper professional fee, for example, regardless of his personal feelings, except when there are circumstances of conflicting interests of clients. Furthermore, if a barrister does not receive payment for his work, he may not take action in court to obtain it. Barristers cannot form partnerships with other barristers or with solicitors nor can they carry on any other profession or business. Disciplinary power used to be in the hands of the governing body of each inn, the benchers (judges of the High Court or barristers), but this power was delegated to the Senate of the four Inns of Court set up in 1966. *See also* solicitor.

Barrois, ancient county, then duchy, on the western frontier of Lorraine, a territory of the Holy Roman Empire, of which Barrois was long a fiefdom or holding before being absorbed piecemeal by France. The centre and capital was the town that later came to be known as Bar-le-Duc, in the modern French *département* of Meuse.

Because of its location between France and Germany, the dukedom was for many years of uncertain loyalty. In 951 the German emperor Otto I gave the countship of Barrois (*i.e.,* the district of Bar), at the time a fief of the duchy of Lorraine, to Frederick of Ardenne. When Frederick's great-great-grandson Renaud (Reynald) inherited the countship, he founded the House of Bar. The counts of Bar increased their wealth and became the most powerful vassals of the dukes of Lorraine, with whom, however, they carried on endless struggles, usually fighting in the French ranks, while the dukes adhered to the Germans. Count Henry III made an alliance with Edward I of England and the German king Adolf of Nassau against France. Defeated in battle with the French, Henry III was forced in 1301 to do homage to the French king Philip IV for that part of the Barrois west of the Meuse River, which was claimed as being in the *mouvance,* or feudal dependency, of France and which from then on was called the "Barrois mouvant."

In 1354 Robert of Bar took the title of duke of Bar. In 1420 René of Anjou, who had inherited the dukedom, married Isabella, heiress of the Duke of Lorraine, so that on the death of the latter (1431) the Barrois and Lorraine were united. From then on the Barrois shared the fate of Lorraine, which was annexed to the French crown in 1766 on the death of Stanisław Leszczyński, the former king of Poland, to whom it had been granted in 1738.

Barron, Clarence W(alker) (b. July 2, 1855, Boston—d. Oct. 2, 1928, Battle Creek, Mich., U.S.), financial editor and publisher who founded *Barron's Financial Weekly.*

In 1875 he joined the staff of the Boston *Transcript,* holding positions as a reporter and as financial editor. Aware of the need for daily financial news in bulletin form, he established the Boston News Bureau in 1887, became its president, and in 1897 founded the Philadelphia News Bureau. In 1901 Barron acquired from Charles Dow the firm of Dow, Jones & Company, which became the principal financial news agency in the United States. At the same time, Barron acquired the firm's *Wall*

Barron, portrait by David MacIntosh
By courtesy of Dow Jones & Co., Inc.

Street Journal, the nation's leading financial newspaper. *Barron's Business and Financial Weekly,* which he founded in 1921, and the *Journal* both continue to be published by Dow, Jones & Company. Barron was the author of several books, including *The Federal Reserve Act* (1914), *War Finance* (1919), and *A World Remaking* (1920).

Barron River, river in northeastern Queensland, Australia, rising near Herberton in the Hugh Nelson Range of the Eastern Highlands and flowing north across the Atherton Plateau past Mareeba and then east and south through the Barron Gorge to enter the Pacific Ocean

The Barron River winding through the coastal plain of northeastern Queensland
Frederick Ayer—Photo Researchers

at Trinity Bay, just north of Cairns, after a course of 100 mi (160 km). The river, draining a basin of 835 sq mi (2,160 sq km), was named in 1870 after T.H. Barron, a chief clerk of the state police.

Fed by the Clohesy River and Mazzlin, Rocky, and Flaggy creeks, the Barron is dammed to form Tinaroo Reservoir (1958), which supplies irrigation water for a tobacco and mixed-farming area, and bisects Barron Falls National Park. The Barron Falls, 10 mi above the river's mouth, are accessible from the town of Kuranda; the series of cascades plunges 980 ft (300 m) to the coastal plain and has been harnessed for hydroelectric power.

Barros, João de (b. *c.* 1496, Viseu?, Port.—d. Oct. 20, 1570, São Lourenço), possibly the first great colonial historian, a pioneer Orientalist, one of the principal Portuguese Humanists, and an outstanding civil servant. He was called the "Portuguese Livy."

João de Barros, lithograph by Luiz after a portrait by Legrane
By courtesy of the Casa de Portugal, London

His precocious chivalresque romance *Crónica do Imperador Clarimundo* (1520) induced King Manuel I of Portugal to encourage Barros' idea of writing an epic history of the Portuguese in Asia, *Décadas da Ásia;* but, before that monumental work was published (1552), he had written several moral, pedagogical, and grammatical works that won him eminence as an educational innovator. His elementary ABC primer-*cum*-catechism (1539) became the prototype of all such works.

In 1522 the succeeding king John III sent Barros to Guinea; soon after his return he was appointed treasurer (1525–28) and then Casa da India e Mina (1533–67), a post corresponding to crown agent for the Portuguese colonies. It was in this period that he compiled his chronicle of the Portuguese discovery and conquest of the Orient until 1538. He finished the first draft in 1539; publication began in 1552 and the last (4th) volume appeared posthumously in 1615. The work, covering the years 1539 to 1616, was carried on by Diogo do Couto.

Barros procured Persian, Arabic, Indian, and Chinese manuscripts, engaging scholars of those nationalities to translate them. The manuscripts included the Arab chronicle on Kilwa in East Africa, of which Barros' version is the pre-10th-century primary source. His works on geography, commerce, and navigation disappeared after his death.

Barros Arana, Diego (b. Aug. 16, 1830, Santiago, Chile—d. Nov. 4, 1907, Santiago), historian, educator, and diplomat who is best known for his celebrated *Historia general de Chile,* 16 vol. (1884–1902; "General History of Chile").

Barros Arana came from a distinguished Chilean family. He originally studied for a legal career, but he gave up the law for his interests in history and literature, perhaps because of ill health. In 1859 the Chilean government exiled Barros Arana for writing inflammatory articles that demanded the reform of the country's political institutions. While in exile he visited Buenos Aires, Montevideo, and Rio de Janeiro, where he collected historical data, then went to Europe, where he explored the archives and libraries of France, England, and Spain. In Spain he discovered the manuscript of a celebrated 16th-century poem about Spanish wars against the Araucanian Indians.

In February 1863 a more liberal government allowed Barros Arana to return to Chile. He was made a dean of the humanities faculty at the University of Santiago, where he introduced several reforms in the curriculum, most notably in the fields of Latin literature and the experimental sciences, and fought for academic and religious freedom within the university. Barros Arana was made Chilean ambassador to Argentina and Uruguay in 1876 and, shortly thereafter, to Brazil. In the 1890s he played a prominent role in the settlement of boundary disputes between Chile and Argentina.

In the writing of history, Barros Arana preferred to give what he considered an objective account of the facts rather than a general interpretation, though his works are somewhat coloured with ideas of Chilean nationalism. Among his numerous historical works are *Las campañas de Chiloé; 1820–1826* (1856; "The Campaigns of Chiloé"); *Historia general de la independencia de Chile* (1854; "General History of the Independence of Chile"); *Elementos de literatura; historia literaria* (1869; "Elements of Literary History"); *Historia moderna y contemporánea* ("Modern and Contemporary History"); and *Historia de la guerra del Pacífico 1879–1880,* 2 vol. (1880–81; "History of the Pacific War").

Barrot, (Camille-Hyacinthe-) Odilon (b. July 19, 1791, Villefort, Fr.—d. Aug. 6, 1873, Bougival), prominent liberal monarchist under the July Monarchy in France (1830–48) and a leader of the electoral reform movement of 1847.

He began his career in 1814 as a barrister in the Court of Cassation. After making his name as a defender of liberals, he was elected

Barrot
By courtesy of the Bibliotheque Nationale, Paris

president of the society Aide-toi, le ciel t'aidera ("Heaven helps those who help themselves"), an organization for promoting resistance, by legal means, against the reactionary government of the Bourbon Restoration. During the July Revolution (1830), Barrot supported the proclamation of Louis-Philippe as king of the French and was one of the three commissioners of the new government who escorted the former king, Charles X, to Cherbourg on his way into exile.

From 1830 to 1848 Barrot, as deputy from Eure, was an active member of the opposition, directing the "dynastic left" in the Chamber of Deputies. During 1846–47 he was one of the managers of the "banquets" campaign, which attempted to pressure the government into extending the franchise.

The reforms did not come, but a republican revolution did. After the flight of Louis-Philippe in 1848, Barrot joined the moderate Republicans. He headed the first ministry called by Louis-Napoléon Bonaparte (December 1848) and also became minister of justice. Dismissed from the government in October 1849, Barrot was imprisoned briefly after the coup d'etat of Dec. 2, 1851, and then retired to private life. In 1871 he became vice president of the new Council of State.

Barrow (Alaska, U.S.): *see* Point Barrow.

barrow, in England, ancient burial place covered with a large mound of earth or stones. *See* burial mound.

Barrow, Clyde, and Parker, Bonnie (respectively b. March 24, 1909, Telico, Texas, U.S.—d. May 23, 1934, near Gibsland, La.; b. 1911, Rowena, Texas—d. May 23, 1934, near Gibsland, La.), small-time robber team that gained legendary fame in the United States through their flamboyant encounters with police and their promotion by the nation's newspapers. Bonnie and Clyde, as they were popularly known, robbed gas stations, restaurants, and small-town banks (their take never exceeded $1,500), chiefly in Texas, Oklahoma, New Mexico, and Missouri.

Clyde had been a young robber long before meeting Bonnie in January 1930. After arrest and 20 months in prison (1930–32), he teamed up with Bonnie, and they began their short 21-month career, often working with confederates, such as his brother, Buck Barrow, and Buck's wife, Blanche; Ray Hamilton; and W.D. Jones. Bonnie and Clyde at last were betrayed by a friend and bullet-riddled by police in a roadblock ambush.

Barrow, Henry (b. *c.* 1550, Shipdam, Norfolk, Eng.—d. April 6, 1593, London), lawyer and early Congregationalist martyr who challenged the established Anglican Church by supporting the formation of separate and independent churches.

After leading a dissolute life as a student at Cambridge, he was converted through the chance hearing of a sermon and became a strict Puritan. Becoming a friend of the Separatist John Greenwood, Barrow was persuaded by him to accept the Brownist position, named for Robert Browne (*c.* 1550–1633), who advocated the foundation of churches separate from secular governmental authority. Both Greenwood and Barrow were subsequently imprisoned after refusing to recant their beliefs. During a brief period of freedom in 1592, the two joined Separatists Francis Johnson and John Penry to form their own church.

Barrow defined his concept of the church as "a company of faithful people, separated from the unbelievers and heathen of the land, gathered in the name of Christ." Taking its government, worship, and discipline from the New Testament, his ideal church made no distinction between clergy and laity and stressed the sovereign autonomy of each congregation. Barrow was again imprisoned, however, and in 1593 he and Greenwood were tried before a civil court under the Act of 1581 against writers of seditious books. Barrow had earlier written in prison several works defending Separatism and congregational independency, including *A True Description out of the Word of God, of the Visible Church* (1589) and *A Brief Discovery of the False Church* (1590). On March 23, 1593, Barrow and Greenwood were sentenced to die on the scaffold together.

Barrow, Isaac (b. 1630, London—d. May 4, 1677, London), classical scholar, theologian, and mathematician who was the teacher of Isaac Newton. He developed a method of determining tangents that closely approached the methods of calculus, and he was first to recognize that the processes of integration and differentiation in calculus are inverse operations.

While his degree was granted in 1648, his academic appointment was delayed because of political unrest during the Cromwellian period. He was ordained an Anglican minister in 1660 and became a professor of Greek at Cambridge University (1660–63). Two years later he was also appointed professor of geometry at Gresham College, London. Of Barrow's early works, which dealt primarily with

Isaac Barrow, pencil drawing by David Loggan, 1676; in the National Portrait Gallery, London

By courtesy of the National Portrait Gallery, London

ancient Greek mathematics, the most notable is his translation of Euclid's *Elements: The Whole Fifteen Books* (1660), which was reissued six times in the early part of the 18th century.

As Lucasian professor of mathematics at Cambridge (1663–69), he devoted much of his time to the preparation of three lecture series concerning optics (1669), geometry (1670), and mathematics (1683). These lectures contain most of his contributions to science and mathematics. His *Lectiones Geometricae* (1670; "Geometrical Lectures") contained elements similar to the calculus later developed by Gottfried Leibniz of Germany, and it was known to both Leibniz and Newton.

The association between Newton and Barrow has often been disputed. Newton was Barrow's pupil, he did attend some of Barrow's later lectures, and he was influenced to an uncertain extent. They worked together for a short time in 1669. In that year Barrow resigned his chair in favour of Newton and thereafter devoted himself to the study of divinity. In 1670 he became chaplain to Charles II, in 1673 was appointed master of Trinity College, Cambridge, and in 1675 was chosen vice chancellor of Cambridge University.

Barrow, Joseph Louis (boxer): *see* Louis, Joe.

Barrow, River, Irish AN BHEARU, river rising in the Slieve Bloom mountain range in the centre of Ireland and flowing for about 120 mi (190 km) to Waterford harbour in the southeast, where it joins the Rivers Nore and Suir. From its upper mountain course in counties Leix and Offaly, it flows east across bogs and lowlands and then turns south into the lowland immediately east of the Castlecomer Plateau. In the last 15 mi before the confluence with the Nore, it flows through a steep, wooded gorge, which gives way to a wider lowland near New Ross. The Barrow was canalized to St. Mullins from 1759 on and linked to the Grand Canal from Dublin to the River Shannon, but barge traffic ceased in 1954. Market towns on the river include Athy, Carlow, and Graiguenamanagh.

Barrow Canyon, submarine canyon incised into the Arctic continental shelf off Alaska. From its head in the Chukchi Sea, about 95 mi (150 km) west of Point Barrow, in water depths of about 150 ft (45 m), the canyon trends northeast along the coast and crosses into the Beaufort Sea, north of Point Barrow. The canyon has a U-shaped cross section with a width of 3½ to 6 mi and depths of 165 to 330 ft on the Chukchi Shelf. It is poorly mapped in the Beaufort Shelf but is known to extend to the shelf edge. Barrow Canyon was used as a submarine entrance to the Arctic Basin in 1957, during the polar crossing of the U.S. Navy submarine USS "Nautilus."

Barrow-in-Furness, district (borough), county of Cumbria, England, on the seaward side of the Furness peninsula between the estuary of the River Duddon and Morecambe Bay. The district has an area of 30 sq mi (77 sq km). A narrow channel of the Irish Sea, now bridged, lies between the mainland and the low, elongated Isle of Walney, providing shelter for extensive shipyards. The rapid modern growth of Barrow dates from the 1840s, when ironworks were established, using local high-grade ore and coke brought by rail across the Pennines. Shipbuilding and repairing—for both Royal Navy and merchant vessels—subsequently developed and outstripped the steel industry in economic importance; the local ore supply is now almost exhausted. Submarines have become a noted product of the shipyards. Pop. (1981 prelim.) town, 61,704; (1982 est.) district, 73,800.

Barrow Island, Australian island in the Indian Ocean, 30 mi (50 km) off the northwest coast of Western Australia and 10 mi southwest of the Monte Bello Islands. Measuring 12 mi by 5 mi, it has an area of 78 sq mi (202 sq km). Geologically an extension of the Carnarvon Basin on the mainland, the island is characterized by its aridity and by its grass- and bush-covered sand hills, which rise steeply to heights of 270 ft (80 m). Once a turtle fishery, Barrow became the site of Western Australia's first commercial oil field in 1967 and is today one of Australia's richest oil fields. Oil is extracted through fracturing of rocks, and there are no derricks, but "Christmas tree" pipe structures dot the landscape. Because of the shallowness of the surrounding sea, the oil must be carried 6 mi offshore via a submarine pipe to a tanker-loading jetty. There are also oil deposits on Pasco Island, 4 mi south.

Barry, Welsh Y BARRI, Bristol Channel port town, seat of Vale of Glamorgan district, South Glamorgan County, Wales. Barry has associations with Baruch, a 7th-century Celtic monk, and with the Normans, who built a castle there in the 11th century; but its growth from a tiny village dates from 1889, when a new dock was opened there so that Barry could compete with nearby Cardiff in exporting coal. The trade of the port, which was almost entirely confined to coal exports, declined after World War I, but it revived after 1960 to handle more diversified cargoes including banana and oil imports.

Barry is a shopping and service centre and a popular seaside resort for southeast Wales, with sandy beaches and recreational facilities. Pop. (1981 prelim.) 43,828.

Barry, Sir Charles (b. May 23, 1795, London—d. May 12, 1860, London), one of the architects of the Gothic Revival in England and chief architect of the British Houses of Parliament (1840–60).

The son of the stationer, Barry was articled to a firm of architects until 1817, when he set out on a three-years' tour of Greece, Italy, Egypt, and Palestine to study architecture. In 1820 he settled in London. One of his first works was the church of Saint Peter at Brighton, in 1826. In 1831 he completed the Travellers' Club in Pall Mall, the first work in the Italian style built in London. In the same style and on a grander scale he built in 1837 the Reform Club. He was also engaged on numerous private mansions in London, the finest being Bridgewater House (1847). In Birmingham one of his best works, King Edward's School, was built in the Tudor style between 1833 and 1836. For Manchester he designed the Royal Institution of Fine Arts (1824) and the Athenaeum (1836), and for Halifax the town hall. He was engaged for some years in reconstructing the Treasury buildings, Whitehall. But his masterpiece, notwithstanding all unfavourable criticism, was the Houses of Parliament at Westminster, London (1840–60), on which Augustus W. Pugin assisted him. Barry was elected associate of the Royal Academy in 1840 and a royal academician in the following year and received many foreign honours. He was knighted in 1852 and, on his death, was buried in Westminster Abbey.

His son, Edward Middleton Barry (1830–80), also a noted architect, completed the work on the House of Parliament.

Barry, James (b. Oct. 11, 1741, Cork, County Cork, Ire.—d. Feb. 22, 1806, London), self-taught artist whose major work, "The Progress of Human Knowledge," is a series of six monumental paintings of historical and allegorical subjects done for the Great Room of the Royal Society of Arts, London.

Barry was an exponent of the "grand style" of Sir Joshua Reynolds; hence, he drew his subject matter from classical antiquity and from literary works. Stylistically, however, his linearity and undulating forms brought him closer to the work of the leaders of the English Neoclassical style, the sculptor John Flaxman and the poet-painter William Blake.

Barry, (Marie-) Jeanne Bécu, comtesse du (countess of) (b. Aug. 19, 1743, Vaucouleurs, Fr.—d. Dec. 8, 1793, Paris), last of the mistresses of the French king Louis XV (ruled 1715–74). Although she exercised little political influence at the French court, her unpopularity contributed to the decline of the prestige of the crown in the early 1770s.

She was born Marie-Jeanne Bécu, the illegitimate daughter of lower-class parents. After receiving a convent education, she took a job, under the name Jeanne Vaubernier, as a shop assistant in a fashion house in Paris. While there she became the mistress of Jean du Barry, a Gascon nobleman who had made a fortune as a war contractor. He introduced Jeanne into Parisian high society, and her beauty captivated a succession of nobly born lovers before she attracted the attention of Louis XV in 1768. She could not, however, qualify as official royal mistress (*maîtresse en titre*), a position vacant since the death of Madame de Pompadour in 1764, unless she was married to a noble. Hence, du Barry arranged a nominal marriage between Jeanne and his brother, Guillaume du Barry; in April 1769 she joined Louis XV's court.

The Comtesse immediately became a member of the faction that brought about the downfall of Louis XV's powerful minister of foreign affairs, the Duc de Choiseul, in December 1770; and she then supported the drastic judicial reforms instituted by her friend the chancellor René-Nicolas de Maupeou, in 1771. She spent much of her time on the estates that Louis had given her near Louveciennes, where she earned a reputation as a generous patron of the arts. On the death of Louis XV (May 1774) and the accession of Louis XVI, Madame du Barry was banished to a nunnery; from 1776 until the outbreak of the Revolution she lived on her estates with the Duc de Brissac. In 1792 she made several trips to London, probably to provide financial assistance to French émigrés. Condemned as a counter-revolutionary by the Revolutionary Tribunal of Paris in December 1793, she was guillotined.

Barry, John (b. 1745, County Wexford, Ire.—d. Sept. 13, 1803, Philadelphia), naval officer who won significant maritime victories during the U.S. War of Independence (1775–83); because he trained so many young officers who later became celebrated in the nation's history, he was often called the "Father of the Navy."

A merchant shipmaster out of Philadelphia at the age of 21, Barry outfitted the first Continental fleet at the outbreak of the Revolution. Commissioned captain of the brig "Lexington" in 1776, he early distinguished himself by capturing the British tender "Edward" after a short engagement. He fought with distinction in the campaign around Trenton, N.J. (1776), and was then commissioned captain of the frigate "Effingham," which he was forced to scuttle to avoid capture by the British.

John Barry, detail of an oil painting by Gilbert Stuart, *c.* 1801
By courtesy of the Oak Ridge Collection

In the winter of 1777–78 Barry commanded a spectacular boat foray that ran the British batteries at Philadelphia and raided enemy shipping in the Delaware River and Bay. Next commanding the frigate "Raleigh" out of Boston, he fought a vigorous but futile battle against superior enemy forces but managed to save most of his crew from capture. Commanding the frigate "Alliance" in 1780, he was assigned to convey Col. John Laurens on a diplomatic mission to France. En route he took several prizes and in returning engaged in a notable battle with two British sloops of war, eventually subduing them.

On the final cruise of the "Alliance" (beginning in 1782), Barry ranged the shipping lanes from Bermuda to Cape Sable and captured four British ships. He fought the last battle of the war (March 1783) in the Straits of Florida, where he beat off three British frigates seeking to intercept him.

After the war Barry was recalled to active service as senior captain of the new U.S. Navy. In the quasi-war with France (1798–1800), he was twice in command of all U.S. ships in the West Indies. By the end of his career he was senior officer of the navy.

A reliable biography is William Bell Clark's *Gallant John Barry* (1938).

Barry, Philip (b. June 18, 1896, Rochester, N.Y., U.S.—d. Dec. 3, 1949, New York City), U.S. dramatist best known for his comedies of life and manners among the socially privileged.

Barry was educated at Yale and in 1919 entered George Pierce Baker's 47 Workshop at Harvard. His *A Punch for Judy* was produced by the workshop in 1920. *You and I*, also written while Barry was a student, played 170 performances on Broadway in 1923. Over the next 20 years a succession of plays included such comedies as *Paris Bound* (1927), *Holiday* (1928), *The Animal Kingdom* (1932), and *The Philadelphia Story* (1939). They are characterized by witty and graceful dialogue and humorous contrasts of character or situation. Many of them use a triangle theme or conflicts between the generations to point up, with almost tender satire, various truths about human nature.

Philip Barry
By courtesy of the Library of Congress, Washington, D.C.

Barry's thoughtful approach to life is apparent in *White Wings* (1926), a fantasy considered by some critics Barry's best play; *John* (1927), a drama about John the Baptist; *Hotel Universe* (1930), a penetrating psychological study; and *Here Come the Clowns* (1938), an allegory of good and evil. His final play, *Second Threshold* (1951), revised by Robert E. Sherwood after Barry's death, combined his flair for social comedy and his preoccupation with more serious drama.

Barrymore, Ethel, original name ETHEL BLYTHE (b. Aug. 15, 1879, Philadelphia—d. June 18, 1959, Hollywood), U.S. stage and film actress whose distinctive style, voice, and wit made her to her public the "first lady" of the American theatre.

Ethel Barrymore, 1901
By courtesy of the Library of Congress, Washington, D.C.

The daughter of the actors Maurice and Georgiana Barrymore (*qq.v.*), she made her professional debut in New York in 1894 in a company headed by her grandmother, Louisa Lane Drew, a member of another prominent acting family. Her first success was scored in London in *The Bells* and *Peter the Great* (1897–98). She was starred for the first time on Broadway in *Captain Jinks of the Horse Marines* (1901).

Barrymore's notable plays include *Alice-Sit-by-the-Fire* (1905), *Mid-Channel* (1910), *Trelawny of the "Wells"* (1911), *Déclassée* (1919), *The Second Mrs. Tanqueray* (1924), *The Constant Wife* (1928), *Scarlet Sister Mary* (1931), *Whiteoaks* (1938), and *The Corn Is Green* (1942). In 1928 she opened the Ethel Barrymore Theater in New York, named in her honour, with *The Kingdom of God*.

She also appeared in vaudeville, on radio, and on television and made a number of motion pictures. Her outstanding films include *The Nightingale* (1914), and the most noteworthy were *Rasputin and the Empress* (1933), which was the only work in which she appeared with her brothers John and Lionel; *The Spiral Staircase* (1946); and *None but the Lonely Heart* (1944), for which she won an Academy Award. In her later motion pictures she was usually cast as an imperious but lovable matriarch. She published her reminiscences in *Memories, an Autobiography* (1955).

Barrymore, Georgiana, *née* GEORGIANA EMMA DREW (b. 1856, Philadelphia—d. July 2, 1893, Santa Barbara, Calif., U.S.), actress and, with Maurice Barrymore, founder of the famous stage and screen family Barrymore, who occupied a preeminent position in the U.S. theatre in the first half of the 20th century.

Georgiana was a member of the Drew family (*q.v.*) of theatrical fame, daughter of John and Louisa Lane Drew. Her father died when she was small, and she was raised in Philadelphia and trained for the theatre by her mother. She made her debut at the Arch Street Theatre, managed by her mother, in 1872. She followed her brother John Drew, Jr., into Augustin Daly's theatre company, where she met and married Maurice Barrymore. Their children, all major stars of stage and cinema, were Ethel, John, and Lionel Barrymore. She was an actress noted for her vivacity, quick wit, and comic sense.

Barrymore, John, original name JOHN BLYTHE (b. Feb. 15, 1882, Philadelphia—d. May 29, 1942, Hollywood), actor, called the "great profile," who is remembered both for his roles as a debonair leading man and for his interpretations of Shakespeare's Richard III and Hamlet.

The son of the stage actors Maurice and Georgiana Barrymore, he studied painting in Paris but returned to the United States to make his stage debut in 1903. He became a popular light comedian but scored his greatest stage triumphs in serious roles. Most important of these were in *Justice* (1916), *Peter Ibbetson* (1917), *The Jest* (1919), *Richard III* (1920), and *Hamlet* (New York, 1922; London, 1925).

He appeared in motion pictures from 1913 and gave notable performances in *Dr. Jekyll and Mr. Hyde* (1920), *Beloved Rogue* (1927), *Moby Dick* (1930), *Grand Hotel* (1932), *Dinner at Eight* (1933), *Counsellor-at-Law* (1933), *Romeo and Juliet* (1936), and *The Great Profile* (1940). Though his talents were prodigious, and he was considered one of the greatest, and handsomest, actors of the age, he became better known for his flamboyant and often outrageous behaviour than for his acting. John Kobler's biography *Damned in Paradise* was published in 1977.

Of the second generation of Barrymores (he was the brother of Ethel and Lionel), only John had children, and both of them turned to the stage. Diana (1921–60) was an actress whose promising career was frequently interrupted by alcoholism; she committed suicide.

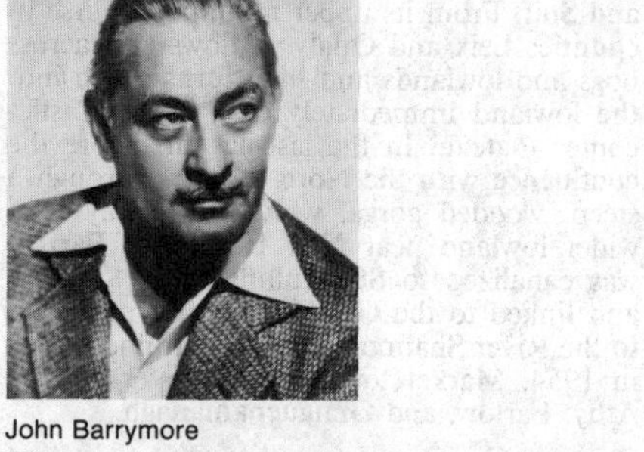

John Barrymore
EB Inc.

Her autobiography, *Too Much, Too Soon* (1957), was made into a motion picture in 1958. His son, John Blyth Barrymore, Jr. (b. 1932), known as John Drew Barrymore, was also a film actor. He is the father of Drew Barrymore (b. 1975), one of the child stars of the motion picture *E.T.* (1982).

Barrymore, Lionel, original name LIONEL BLYTHE (b. April 28, 1878, Philadelphia—d. Nov. 15, 1954, Van Nuys, Calif., U.S.), one of the most important character actors in the early 20th century.

The son of the stage actors Maurice and Georgiana Barrymore, founders of the celebrated family of actors, he originally studied

Lionel Barrymore
EB Inc.

painting in Paris for three years. On his return to New York, however, he established his reputation as an actor in such plays as *Peter Ibbetson* (1917), *The Copperhead* (1918), and *The Jest* (1919).

In 1926 he left Broadway permanently for Hollywood and began a long line of outstanding screen characterizations in such films as *The Mysterious Island* (1929), *A Free Soul* (1931), for which he won an Academy Award, *Grand Hotel* (1932), *Captains Courageous* (1937), and *Duel in the Sun* (1947). In the Dr. Kildare series, the first of which was released in 1938, he played Dr. Gillespie. In his older years he projected an image of an irascible (but usually lovable) curmudgeon, a role in which he exploited to the fullest his distinctive traits—a tall, stooped posture (though he usually performed in a wheelchair in his later years), shaggy eyebrows, and a hoarse, rasping voice. He was also a radio actor and is perhaps best remembered for his annual radio performance as Scrooge in Dickens' *Christmas Carol.*

We Barrymores (1951), by Lionel Barrymore as told to Cameron Shipp, is basically an autobiography but contains much information on his famous siblings John and Ethel.

Barrymore, Maurice, original name HERBERT BLYTHE (b. 1846, Fort Agra, India—d. March 26, 1905, Amityville, N.Y., U.S.), actor and sometime playwright, founder, with his wife, Georgiana Barrymore, of the renowned Barrymore theatrical family.

Herbert Blythe's father was a surveyor for the British East India Company, and the boy was sent back to England for education at Harrow and Oxford. To the dismay of his parents, who hoped he would practice law, in 1872 he became a champion amateur boxer and then went on the stage. Adopting the stage name Barrymore, he went to America in 1875. Though never a star, Barrymore was an excellent supporting actor and acted with many of the great names of theatre. He played with Augustin Daly's company, where he met Georgiana Drew, whom he married in 1876. He later joined Lester Wallack's company; on occasion he would be on the stage with his wife and son John. He took engagements in London and tried his hand at playwriting, with scant success, although (with much rewriting help) he did write original plays for Helena Modjeska and played in some of them.

James Kotsilibas-Davis' *Great Times, Good Times: The Odyssey of Maurice Barrymore* was published in 1977.

bars (game): *see* prisoner's base.

Barsento, Emilio Pucci, marchese di (marquess of): *see* Pucci, Emilio.

Barṣīṣā, in Islāmic legend, an ascetic who succumbed to the devil's temptations and denied God.

Barṣīṣā, a saintly recluse, is given care of a sick woman by her three brothers, who are going on a journey. At the devil's suggestion the hermit seduces the woman. When he discovers that she has conceived, Barṣīṣā kills her and buries her body to hide evidence of his sin. The devil, however, reveals the murder to the woman's brothers. Barṣīṣā, panic-stricken, again succumbs to the devil, renouncing God in return for safety, only to be mocked by Satan, in the words of the Qur'ān (59:16), "I am free of thee; I fear God, the Lord of the Worlds."

The legend of the recluse, who is nameless and is described variously as a Jewish ascetic or a Christian monk, appears first in aṭ-Ṭabarī's Commentary on the Qur'ān in the early 10th century. By 985 an author states that the recluse was called Barṣīṣā, an Aramaic name meaning "he of priestly regalia." Elements of the story are traced back to Coptic folklore, and the legend survived in the Islāmic world in several forms. By the end of the 18th century, it had made its way to England, where it became the subject of Matthew Gregory Lewis' book *The Monk.*

Barstovian Stage, uppermost major division of Miocene rocks and time in North America (the Miocene Epoch began about 26,000,000 years ago and lasted about 19,000,000 years). The Barstovian Stage follows the Hemingfordian Stage and precedes the Clarendonian Stage of the Pliocene Epoch. It was named for exposures studied near Barstow, Calif. The Barstovian contains a distinctive mammalian fauna.

Barstow, city, San Bernardino County, south central California, U.S., in the Mojave Desert. At a junction of pioneer trails, Barstow was founded (1880) in a silver-mining rush. First called Fishpond and then Waterman Junction, it was renamed (1886) to honour William Barstow Strong, then president of the Santa Fe Railroad. Mining declined, but Barstow endured as a railroad town (diesel repair shops) and tourist spot. Its growth was stimulated by the establishment nearby (in the 1940s) of a large Marine Corps supply depot and (now deactivated) Ft. Irwin (armour and desert training centre), and, in 1958, of Goldstone Tracking Station (operated by the Jet Propulsion Laboratory of California Institute of Technology), and Barstow Community College (1960). Agriculture (supported by artesian irrigation) and mining (agate, jasper, copper, salt) supplement the economy. The Mohave River Valley Museum in Barstow has displays devoted to the archaeology, minerals, and Indian lore of the area. Inc. 1947. Pop. (1980) 17,690.

Barstow, Stan, byname of STANLEY BARSTOW (b. June 28, 1928, Horbury, Yorkshire, Eng.), English novelist who achieved success with his first book, *A Kind of Loving* (1960; filmed 1962; stage play 1970).

Barstow grew up in a working-class environment and worked in the engineering industry until 1962. He was among a group of young British writers (including Alan Sillitoe, John Braine, and others) who achieved immediate success in the 1950s and '60s with their unsentimental depiction of working-class life. His later novels include *The Watchers on the Shore* (1966), *A Raging Calm* (1968), *A Season with Eros* (1971), *The Right True End* (1976), and *A Brother's Tale* (1980). He also wrote short stories and adapted several stories and novels for radio and television.

Bart, Jean, Bart also spelled BARTH (b. Oct. 21, 1650, Dunkirk, Fr.—d. April 27, 1702, Dunkirk), privateer and naval officer, renowned for his skillful and daring achievements in the wars of Louis XIV, king of France.

Descended from a family of fishermen and privateers, Bart entered naval service first under the Dutch admiral Michiel de Ruyter, but when war broke out between the French and the Dutch (1672–78) he returned to Dunkirk, where his knowledge of every detail of the coast enabled him to command a fleet of small privateering vessels with great success. He took 81 prizes in six battles and was rewarded by Louis XIV with the rank of lieutenant. In the War of the Grand Alliance (1689–97) he was taken prisoner by the English but escaped from Plymouth and rowed for 52 hours to the French coast. Promoted to captain, he commanded the "Alcyon" at the Battle of Beachy Head (1690) and afterward a division of ships at Dunkirk.

Bart, detail of an engraving by the studio of Nicolas Bonnart; in the Bibliothèque Nationale, Paris
By courtesy of the Bibliotheque Nationale, Paris

Bart defended Dunkirk during the English attacks of 1694–95. In June 1696, when France was facing famine, he engaged a Dutch squadron off the coast of the Netherlands and captured a convoy of 96 ships loaded with Russian and Polish wheat. For this exploit, the King made him a member of the nobility.

Given command of a squadron, Bart escorted the Prince de Conti (François-Louis de Bourbon), candidate for the Polish crown, to Danzig in 1697, slipping six frigates through a tight enemy blockade. By the end of the war his division had destroyed 30 warships and captured more than 200 merchant ships.

Bartas, Guillaume de Salluste, seigneur du (lord of) (b. 1544, Montfort, near Auch, Fr.—d. July 1590, Coudons), author of *La Semaine* (1578), an influential poem about the creation of the world.

Though he tried to avoid serving in the Wars of Religion, du Bartas was an ardent Huguenot and a trusted counsellor of Henry of Navarre. His aim was to use the new poetic techniques introduced into France by the literary group known as La Pléiade for the presentation of distinctively Protestant views. He was himself dissatisfied with his first biblical epic, *Judith* (1574). On the publication of *La Semaine,* however, du Bartas was hailed as a major poet. His prestige was all the greater because Pierre de Ronsard, his contemporary, had failed in his ambition to compose a first-class epic in French. *La Semaine* did not remain popular in France for long; its style is marred by numerous neologisms and ungainly compound adjectives, and the didactic intent is too obvious. In fact, the poem made a more lasting impression in England, where its Protestant teaching was more generally acceptable. Sir Philip Sidney, Edmund Spenser, and John Milton are among the English poets influenced by du Bartas.

Bartenstein, Johann Christoph, Freiherr von (baron of) (b. Oct. 23, 1689, Strasbourg, Alsace—d. Aug. 6, 1767, Vienna), Austrian statesman and trusted counsellor of Emperor Charles VI, he created the political system that was based upon the Pragmatic Sanction; it was intended to guarantee the peaceful accession of Charles VI's daughter Maria Theresa to the entire Habsburg inheritance. He became the most powerful minister in the Habsburg dominions when Charles died in 1740.

Joining the imperial chancellery in 1726, Bartenstein gradually won the confidence of Charles VI and was subsequently appointed secretary of state (1733). After 1735 his influence with the Emperor was paramount. His was the primary role in negotiating the marriage of Maria Theresa to Francis Stephen of Lorraine (later Emperor Francis I) and implementing the diplomacy required to promote her husband's eventual accession to the imperial title.

Bartenstein, detail from a portrait by an unknown artist

By courtesy of the Bild-Archiv, Osterreichische Nationalbibliothek, Vienna

As a chief adviser to Maria Theresa, Bartenstein steadily opposed concessions to Prussia and generally pursued an anti-English, pro-French foreign policy. He was finally displaced as chief minister in 1753 by Wenzel Anton von Kaunitz. Bartenstein's honesty and discretion were matched by his self-righteousness toward foreign diplomats and obsequiousness to his patrons; his efficiency and legal knowledge, however, made him an indispensable figure in Habsburg diplomacy.

barter, the direct exchange of goods or services—without an intervening medium of exchange or money—either according to established rates of exchange or by bargaining. Barter is common among nonliterate societies, particularly in those communities with some developed form of market.

Goods may be bartered within a group as well as between groups, although gift exchange probably accounts for most intragroup trade, particularly in small and relatively simple societies. Where barter and gift exchange coexist, as among the peoples of the Trobriand Islands of Melanesia, the simple barter of ordinary household items or food is distinguished from the ceremonial exchange, which serves other than economic purposes. *See also* gift exchange.

Barth, Heinrich (b. Feb. 16, 1821, Hamburg—d. Nov. 25, 1865, Berlin), German geographer and one of the great explorers of Africa.

Heinrich Barth

By courtesy of the Royal Geographical Society, London

Educated in the classics at the University of Berlin, he was a competent linguist, fluent in French, Spanish, Italian, English, and Arabic. He travelled the Mediterranean coastal areas that are now part of Tunisia and Libya (1845–47) and published his observations in 1849.

Early in 1850, with the explorer James Richardson and the geologist and astronomer Adolf Overweg, he set out from Tripoli across the Sahara on a British-sponsored expedition to the western Sudan (a term then in use for most of central West Africa). When Richardson died a year later in what is now northern Nigeria, Barth assumed command. He explored the area south and southeast of Lake Chad and mapped the upper reaches of the Benue River. Overweg died in September 1852, and Barth travelled to the city of Timbuktu, now in the Republic of Mali. He remained there for six months before returning, via Tripoli, to London (1855).

Despite ill health and the loss of his colleagues, he had travelled some 10,000 miles, laid down accurate routes by dead reckoning, and returned to Europe with the first account of the middle section of the Niger. His four large volumes, *Reisen und Entdeckungen in Nord- und Central-Afrika in den Jahren 1849 bis 1855* (1857–58; "Travels and Discoveries in North and Central Africa in the Years 1849–1855"), remain one of the most comprehensive works on the area and contain an immense amount of anthropological, historical, and linguistic information as well as the daily travel details he so assiduously recorded. His work was honoured and rewarded financially by the British government. Later travels took him to Turkey and Asia Minor as well as to Spain, Italy, and the Alps. He was appointed professor of geography at the University of Berlin (1863).

Barth, Jean (French privateer): *see* Bart, Jean.

Barth, John (Simmons, Jr.) (b. May 27, 1930, Cambridge, Md., U.S.), U.S. writer best known for novels that combine philosophical depth and complexity with biting satire and boisterous, often bawdy humour. Much of Barth's writing is concerned with the seeming impossibility of choosing the right action in a world that has no absolute values.

Barth grew up on the Eastern Shore of Maryland, the locale of most of his writing, and studied at Johns Hopkins University in Baltimore, where he graduated with an M.A. in 1952. The next year he began teaching at Pennsylvania State University; he moved in 1965 to the State University of New York at Buffalo as professor of English and writer in residence. He was appointed professor of English and creative writing at Johns Hopkins University in 1973.

Barth's first two novels, *The Floating Opera* (1956) and *The End of the Road* (1958), describe characters burdened by a sense of the futility of all action and the effects of these characters upon the less self-conscious, more active people around them. Barth forsook realism and modern settings in *The Sot-Weed Factor* (1960), a picaresque tale that burlesques the early history of Maryland and parodies the 18th-century English novel. All three novels appeared in revised editions in 1967.

Giles Goat-Boy (1966) is a bizarre tale of the career of a mythical hero and religious prophet, set in a satirical microcosm composed of vast, computer-run universities. His work *Lost in the Funhouse* (1968) consists of short, experimental pieces, some designed for performance, interspersed with short stories based on his own childhood. It was followed by *Chimera* (1972), a volume of three novellas, and *Letters* (1979), an experimental novel.

Barth, Karl (b. May 10, 1886, Basel, Switz.—d. Dec. 9/10, 1968, Basel), Swiss theologian, among the most influential of the 20th century, who initiated a radical change in Protestant thought, stressing the "wholly otherness of God" over the anthropocentrism of 19th-century liberal theology. His vigorous opposition to the National Socialism of Germany led to his suspension as chairman of theology at Bonn. Subsequently, at Basel, he continued work on his monumental *Church Dogmatics* (completing four volumes) and delivered more than 500 sermons.

Karl Barth, 1965

Horst Tappe—EB Inc.

Early life and career. He was born in Basel, the son of Fritz Barth, a Reformed professor of church history and New Testament at Bern, and Anna Sartorius. He attended the Free Gymnasium at Bern, where as a young student he displayed a keen interest in history and military matters. Although there is no account of his conversion, the pastor under whom he was confirmed suggested that he take up the study of theology. At the age of 18 he began his studies: first at Bern, then at Berlin, Tübingen, and Marburg—the last three in Germany—during which time he was greatly influenced by the leaders of liberal theology, notably Adolf von Harnack and Wilhelm Herrmann.

For two years Barth served as an assistant minister in Geneva (1909–11) and then from 1911 to 1921 as minister in the farming and working-class congregation in Safenwil (Aargau canton). In 1913 he married Nelly Hoffman, a talented violinist. Their children were a daughter, Franziska (1914); Markus (1915), a professor of New Testament; Christoph (1917), a professor of Old Testament; Mathias (1921), a theology student who died as a result of a mountain-climbing accident in 1941; and Hans Jakob (1925), a landscape architect. While at Safenwil, in close cooperation with Eduard Thurneysen, a lifelong friend and fellow theologian, Barth began to think through the situation of the church and theology burdened with the liberalism of 19th-century Protestantism.

Publication of Der Römerbrief. Shocked by the failure of the theology of his teachers in the face of social questions and World War I, he joined the Religious Socialist movement and sought to organize the workers of his congregation. Deeper reflection upon the real task of theology and the church led in 1919 to the publication of *Der Römerbrief* (*The Epistle to the Romans*), which, in six successive editions, shocked theologians of the early 1920s out of their complacency. During that period Barth stressed the "wholly otherness of God" in contrast to the rationalism, historicism, and psychologism that prevailed in liberal Protestantism.

The sensation created by this book brought the young Barth, who had never taken an earned doctoral degree, to the attention of academic theologians, and he was subsequently appointed to the chairs of theology at Göttingen (1921), Münster (1925), and Bonn (1930). Another result of the attention gained by the publication of *Der Römerbrief* was the formation of the "Dialectical school," composed of Thurneysen, Rudolf Bultmann, Friedrich Gogarten, Emil Brunner, and Georg Merz, all theologians who became influential in Protestantism and beyond, and the founding of the periodical *Zwischen den Zeiten* ("Between the Times"). Differences concerning the basis of evangelical theology began to appear among the members of the school, and a crisis eventually occurred with the rise of Adolf Hitler to power in January 1933.

Political concerns. From the outset Barth was a vigorous opponent of National Socialism and of the "German Christian" party within the German Evangelical Church. Through his pamphlet *Theologische Existenz heute* ("Theological Existence Today"), the first in a series under that name, he clarified the basic theological issues and rallied churchmen to resistance. With Martin Niemöller, an anti-Nazi church leader, and others he organized the Synod of Barmen (May 1934) at which was adopted the Barmen Declaration that became the confessional basis of the Confessing Church, which claimed to be the "evangelical church in Germany," in opposition to the established church that did not oppose National Socialism. The text of the declaration was almost entirely Barth's work. Its first article epitomized his theological position:

> Jesus Christ, as He is attested for us in Holy Scripture, is the one Word of God which we have to hear and which we have to trust and obey in life and in death.

Refusal to take an unconditional oath of allegiance to Hitler led to Barth's suspension at Bonn and was the occasion of his accepting a chair of theology at Basel. From there he continued his fight against Nazism. Prior to and during World War II he wrote letters of encouragement and admonition to the churches and their leaders in many lands and voluntarily enlisted for service in the Swiss Army.

Church Dogmatics. At Basel, Barth continued to work on *Church Dogmatics,* which he had begun at Bonn. Although never completed, it runs to four volumes (13 parts) of more than 9,000 pages. A truly ecumenical work, filled with new insights and a wealth of exegetical, historical, philosophical, and dogmatic material, it is regarded by many Protestant and Roman Catholic scholars as the classical theological work of the century. Basic to all his writings has been his concern with the task of the preacher who, from Sunday to Sunday, is called to proclaim not man's word but the Word of God. He delivered more than 500 sermons, most of which are yet to be published. In his later years he preached almost exclusively in the Basel prison as "a prisoner among prisoners."

Even before the collapse of the Third Reich near the end of World War II, Barth was among the first to champion friendship with defeated Germany. Symbolic of this friendship were lectures he delivered in 1946 and 1947 amid the ruins of the University of Bonn, but he did not withhold the sharpest criticism of the development of German history from Frederick the Great, king of Prussia in the 18th century, to Otto von Bismarck, founder and first chancellor of the German Empire in the 19th century, and to Adolf Hitler, founder of the Third Reich. Indeed, he declared that the German people "suffers from the legacy of the greatest Christian German: from the error of Martin Luther with respect to the relation of law and Gospel, of temporal and spiritual power, by which its natural paganism has not been so much limited and restrained as it has been ideologically transfigured, affirmed and strengthened."

Soon thereafter, Barth's polemic was directed against those inside and outside the church who were advocating what amounted to an "anti-Communist crusade." He took a stand for peace, for the abolition of the "iron curtain" between East and West, against equating the totalitarianism of the Soviet Union with that of Nazi Germany, and against the use of nuclear bombs—not because he had a love of Communism but because he had a penetrating insight into the Phariseeism (legalism and belief in a moral superiority) of anti-Communism.

International reputation and influence. Indicative of his international reputation and influence, as well as of the ecumenical significance of his work, Barth's travels took him to France, Italy, The Netherlands, England, Scotland, Hungary, Romania, Czechoslovakia, and, in 1962, the United States. In 1948 he delivered one of the major addresses at the opening of the first meeting (in Amsterdam) of the World Council of Churches and, following the second Vatican Council (1962–65), made a special trip to Rome in order to be better informed about the renewal of the Catholic Church. Barth was the recipient of honorary degrees from the universities of Münster, Glasgow, Edinburgh, St. Andrews, Oxford, Budapest, Geneva, Strasbourg, Paris, and Chicago and was honorary senator of the University of Bonn, honorary professor of universities in Hungary and Romania, an honorary member of the British and Foreign Bible Society and of the Académie des Sciences Morales et Politiques of the Institut de France, and holder of the British King's Medal for Service in the Cause of Freedom.

Characteristics of the man were an uncompromising devotion to the Gospel of Christ and kindliness even toward those with whom he sharply disagreed, an insatiable intellectual curiosity combined with a probing, critical mind, and a humility and cheerfulness born of a sense of the goodness of the Creator and his creation—reflected in a childlike enjoyment of the music of Mozart. For Barth, theology was "a peculiarly beautiful science" and a joyful task because its object is the indescribably good news of "the beauty of the Lord our God" in the humiliation and exaltation of Jesus Christ. And—in the words of Keats—"a thing of beauty is a joy forever; its loveliness increases." (A.C.C.)

MAJOR WORKS. *Theological writings. Das Wort Gottes und die Theologie* (1924; *The Word of God and the Word of Man,* 1957); *Die Theologie und die Kirche* (1928); *Fides quaerens intellectum: Anselms Beweis der Existenz Gottes* (1931; *Anselm: Fides quaerens intellectum,* 1960); *Kirchliche Dogmatik* (1932; *Church Dogmatics,* 1961); *Credo: Die Hauptprobleme der Dogmatik dargestellt im Anschluss an das Apostolische Glaubensbekenntnis* (1935; *Credo: A Presentation of the Chief Problems of Dogmatics with Reference to the Apostles' Creed,* 1936); *Evangelium und Gesetz* (1935); *Gotteserkenntniss und Gottesdienst nach reformatorischer Lehre* (1938; *The Knowledge of God and the Service of God According to the Teaching of the Reformation,* 1938); *Dogmatik in Grundriss* (1947; *Dogmatics in Outline,* 1949); *Christus und Adam nach Röm 5* (1952; *Christ and Adam: Man and Humanity in Romans 5,* 1957).

Biblical exegesis. His best known commentaries include *Der Römerbrief* (1919; *The Epistle to the Romans,* 1933); and *Erklärung des Philipperbriefes* (1927; *The Epistle to the Philippians,* 1962).

BIBLIOGRAPHY. Karl Kupisch, *Karl Barth in Selbstzeugnissen und Bilddokumenten* (1971), although only 156 pages in length, is a good account of Barth's life and work and is supplied with copious quotations from his letters and books, and with documentary pictures; E. Busch, *Karl Barth: His Life from Letters and Autobiographical Texts* (1976), not a critical biography but a picture of Barth in his own words, by the man who served as his last personal assistant. Georges Casalis, *Portrait de Karl Barth* (1960; Eng. trans. with an introduction by Robert McAfee Brown, 1963), a portrait of the man and his work. See also the articles on Barth by W. Matthias in *Evangelisches Kirchenlexikon,* vol. 1 (1956); and by G. Gloege in *Die Religion in Geschichte und Gegenwart,* 3rd ed., vol. 1 (1957). T.H.L. Parker, *Karl Barth* (1970), is an account of Barth's spiritual pilgrimage and of the development of his theological method. A definitive biography is being projected by the Karl Barth Foundation in Basel, together with some 40 volumes of unprinted material that Barth left to the executors of his literary estate. A complete edition of his works will run to some 70 volumes, exclusive of the *Church Dogmatics.*

Barth, Paul (b. Aug. 1, 1858, Baruth, Silesia, Prussia—d. Sept. 30, 1922, Leipzig), German philosopher and sociologist who considered society as an organization in which progress is determined by the power of ideas.

Barth was professor of philosophy and education in Leipzig from 1897. His *Philosophy of History of Hegel and the Hegelians* (1896) and his broad *Philosophy of History of Sociology* (1897) were outstanding works. He developed for the first time in German not only a history of the various sociological systems but also, in his critique of Hegel, the different philosophic systems of history (anthropological, political, individualist, collectivist, and ideological).

Barth edited the *Quarterly of Scientific Philosophy* from 1899 until 1916. His *Elements of Education and Teaching Based on Psychology and Philosophy* (1906; trans. into Italian, Spanish, and Russian) was concerned chiefly with moral education and was designed to replace the old textbooks based on Johann Herbart's philosophy. Barth also wrote *History of Education in the Light of Sociology and History of Ideas* (1911) and *The Necessity of a Systematic Moral Teaching* (1922).

A list of the abbreviations used in the MICROPAEDIA *will be found at the end of this volume*

Barthélemy-Saint-Hilaire, Jules (b. Aug. 19, 1805, Paris—d. Nov. 24, 1895, Paris), French philosopher, statesman, journalist, and essayist remembered for his 35-volume translation (1833–95) of Aristotle's works.

He worked briefly for the French government's Ministry of Finance (1825–28) before he became a journalist. Three days after the absolutist king Charles X ended freedom of the press (July 28, 1830), Barthélemy-Saint-Hilaire signed a journalists' protest, for which indiscretion he was imprisoned until August 2, when Charles abdicated in the midst of a brief revolution.

Under the more enlightened successor, Louis-Philippe, he continued to write, helping to found the paper *Le Bons Sens* ("Common Sense"). In 1838 he became professor of ancient philosophy at the Collège de France. Following the revolution that led to Louis-Philippe's abdication in 1848, Barthélemy-Saint-Hilaire was elected to the national Chamber of Deputies from the district of Seine-et-Oise but withdrew after the coup d'etat of 1851.

He worked briefly as a woodcutter until he joined the *Journal des savants.* He travelled to Egypt in 1855 with the diplomat Ferdinand Lesseps, promoter of the Suez Canal project, and was appointed secretary of the new canal construction company. Reelected deputy from Seine-et-Oise in 1869, Barthélemy-Saint-Hilaire aligned with the moderates against the dictatorial policies of Napoleon and joined in the proposal that Adolphe Thiers, a republican politician, become head of the executive power. Appointed an unpaid secretary to Thiers, Barthélemy-Saint-Hilaire also became senator for life in 1875, was vice president of the Senate (1880), and served as minister of foreign affairs under Premier Jules Ferry (1880–81). He wrote frequently in the areas of history, sociology, political economy, and languages; published a translation of the works of Marcus Aurelius (1876); and wrote several studies of Oriental religions.

Barthold, Wilhelm: *see* Bartold, Vasily V(ladimirovich).

Bartholdi, Frédéric-Auguste (b. April 2, 1834, Colmar, Alsace, Fr.—d. Oct. 4, 1904, Paris), sculptor of the Statue of Liberty in New York Harbor. Dedicated in 1886, the statue was titled in full, "Liberty Enlightening the World." His masterpiece, however, is the "Lion of Belfort" (in Belfort, France), which is generally regarded as the best of a number of patriotic sculptures inspired by the French defeat in the Franco-Prussian War.

Bartholin, Caspar Berthelsen, Latin BARTHOLINUS (b. Feb. 12, 1585, Malmö, Den.—d. July 13, 1629, Sorø, Zealand), physician, theologian, who wrote one of the most widely read Renaissance manuals of anatomy.

At the University of Padua (1608–10) he conducted anatomical studies under the famed Italian anatomist Hieronymus Fabricius ab

Caspar Bartholin, detail of a lithograph by Baerentzen after a contemporary portrait by an unknown artist, 1615

Archiv fur Kunst und Geschichte, West Berlin

Aquapendente. These formed the basis for his manual *Anatomicae Institutiones Corporis Humani* (1611; "Textbook of Human Anatomy"). A professor at the University of Copenhagen (1613–29), he was first to describe the olfactory nerve (associated with the sense of smell) as the first cranial nerve. He also identified the small lubricating gland—known as Bartholin's gland—located near the vaginal opening in female mammals.

Bartholin, Erasmus, Latin BARTHOLINUS (b. Aug. 13, 1625, Roskilde, Den.—d. Nov. 4, 1698, Copenhagen), physician, mathematician, and physicist who discovered the optical phenomenon of double refraction.

While professor of medicine (1657–98) at the University of Copenhagen, Bartholin observed that images seen through Icelandic feldspar (calcite) were doubled and that, when the crystal was rotated, one image remained stationary while the other rotated with the crystal. Perceiving that light passing through calcite was split into two rays, he called the stationary image the "ordinary beam" and the moving image the "extraordinary beam." Although Bartholin himself was unable to explain double refraction, it was recognized as a serious contradiction to Isaac Newton's optical theories.

Bartholin, Thomas, Latin BARTHOLINUS (b. Oct. 20, 1616, Copenhagen—d. Dec. 4, 1680, Copenhagen), anatomist and mathematician who was first to describe fully the entire human lymphatic system (1652). He and his elder brother, Erasmus Bartholin, were the sons of the eminent anatomist and theologian, Caspar Bartholin.

Thomas Bartholin, engraving, 1651

BBC Hulton Picture Library

A student of the Dutch school of anatomists, Bartholin supported the English physician William Harvey's theory of blood circulation. He taught at the University of Copenhagen (1646–61) and served as physician to King Christian V (1670–80).

Bartholomaeus ANGLICUS (Latin), English BARTHOLOMEW THE ENGLISHMAN (fl. *c.* 1220–40, England, Paris, and Germany), Franciscan encyclopaedist who was long famous for his highly esteemed encyclopaedia, *De proprietatibus rerum* ("On the Properties of Things"). He lectured in divinity at the University of Paris and became a Franciscan *c.* 1225.

Though primarily interested in Scripture and theology, he covered in his 19-volume encyclopaedia all the customary knowledge of his time and was the first writer to make conveniently available the views of Greek, Jewish, and Arabic scholars on medical and scientific subjects. The immense popularity of his work is shown by the very large number of manuscript copies of it found in European libraries and by the fact that it was regularly lent out to scholars at the University of Paris. It was translated into English by John of Trevisa and printed about 1495; it also appeared in other vernacular languages. Very popular reading in Tudor England, it influenced English thought and writing in the 16th century.

Bartholomäusee (West Germany): *see* Königssee.

Bartholomé, (Paul-) Albert (b. Aug. 29, 1848, Thiverval, Fr.—d. Oct. 31, 1928, Paris), sculptor whose works, particularly his funerary art, made him one of the best known of modern French sculptors.

Bartholomé began his career as a painter, studying at the Académie des Beaux-Arts. Wanting to construct a monument to his dead wife, he turned to sculpture in 1886. Though he had no formal training, he made a careful study of nature and of the masterpieces of the past. His reputation was established with the "Monument to the Dead" in the Père-Lachaise Cemetery, Paris, a piece of architectural sculpture on a grand scale. Composed of a number of mourning figures in differing postures of grief, it is non-Christian in feeling, though situated in a Christian cemetery. This success led to commissions for a number of funerary monuments. In his later period he tended toward a somewhat Rodin-like impressionistic sculpture. There is a great deal of modulated chiaroscuro and pictorial quality in his many female nudes.

Bartholomew, SAINT (fl. 1st century AD; d. traditionally Albanopolis, Armenia; Western feast day August 24, date varies in Eastern churches), one of the Twelve Apostles. Apart from the mentions of him in four of the Apostle lists (Mark 3:18, Matt. 10:3, Luke 6:14, and Acts 1:13), nothing is known about him from the New Testament. Bartholomew is a family name meaning son of (Hebrew *bar*) Tolmai or Talmai, so he may have had another personal name. For that reason and because he was always associated with the Apostle St. Philip in the Gospel lists, a 9th-century tradition identified him with Nathanael, who, according to John 1:43–51, was called with Philip by Jesus. Upon seeing Nathanael, Jesus said, "Behold, an Israelite indeed, in whom is no guile!" This identification sought to explain how the otherwise unknown Bartholomew could be mentioned in the Apostle lists, while Nathanael, whose call is explicitly described by John, does not figure in them. His full name would then be Nathanael bar Tolmai.

The 4th-century Bishop Eusebius of Caesarea in his *Ecclesiastical History* relates that when the 2nd-century teacher St. Pantaenus of Alexandria visited India, he found the Hebrew "Gospel According to Matthew," which had been left behind by Bartholomew. Traditionally, the Apostle was also a missionary to Ethiopia, Mesopotamia, Parthia (in modern Iran), Lycaonia (in modern Turkey), and Armenia. He is said to have been martyred by flaying and beheading at the command of the Babylonian king Astyages. His relics were supposedly taken to the Church of St. Bartholomew-in-the-Tiber, Rome.

Bartholomew THE ENGLISHMAN: *see* Bartholomaeus Anglicus.

Bartholomew, John George (b. March 22, 1860, Edinburgh—d. April 13, 1920, Cintra, Port.), cartographer and map and atlas publisher who improved the standards of British

"Monument to the Dead," stone sculpture by Bartholomé, 1895; in the Père-Lachaise Cemetery, Paris

Giraudon—Art Resource/EB Inc.

cartography and introduced into Great Britain the use of contours and systematic colour layering to show relief.

The eldest son of the Edinburgh map publisher John Bartholomew (1831–93), he concerned himself with producing new geographical works as well as with technical improvements in map production. He published major atlases of Scotland (1895) and England and Wales (1903) and initiated a great physical atlas, but only two volumes appeared, the *Atlas of Meteorology* (1899) and the *Atlas of Zoogeography* (1911). He also began compiling *The Times Survey Atlas of the World,* published in 1921 by his son John Bartholomew (1908–62), who also edited the new *Times Atlas of the World* (1955).

Barthou, (Jean-) Louis (b. Aug. 25, 1862, Oloron-Sainte-Marie, Fr.—d. Oct. 9, 1934, Marseille), French premier (1913), conservative statesman, and long-time colleague of Raymond Poincaré. He was assassinated with King Alexander of Yugoslavia during the latter's visit to France in 1934.

Barthou, *c.* 1922

H. Roger-Viollet—Harlingue

Trained as a lawyer and first elected a deputy in 1889, Barthou filled various posts in different ministries and, as premier from March to December 1913, secured the passage of a three years' compulsory military service bill (July 19, 1913). After serving in the cabinets of Paul Painlevé, Aristide Briand, and Raymond Poincaré, Barthou represented France at the Genoa Conference (1922), entered the Senate, and became chairman of the reparations commission. In July 1926 he became minister of justice under Poincaré. He was named foreign minister in the coalition ministry of Gaston Doumergue shortly before his death.

Bartica, capital, Mazaruni-Potaro district, north central Guyana, in tropical rain forests in which the Essequibo, Mazaruni, and Cuyuni rivers meet. A small commercial centre and transportation hub, Bartica is situated at the head of navigation by small oceangoing ships, on the Essequibo River 50 mi (80 km) inland from the Atlantic Ocean, and it is linked by air with Georgetown, the national capital. From Bartica, roads lead to the goldfields and diamond fields of the interior.

Bartle Frere, Mount, mountain in Bellenden-Ker Range, northeastern Queensland, Australia. It is the highest point in the state and rises to 5,287 ft (1,611 m) in an area reserved as a national park. Its slopes have the climate of a rain forest and provide cover for a variety of tropical plants, birds, and mammals. The peak was named in 1873 by George A.F.E. Dalrymple, a Scottish explorer, in honour of Sir Henry Bartle Edward Frere, governor of Bombay (1862–67).

Bartlesville, city, seat (1907) of Washington County, northeastern Oklahoma, U.S., on the Caney River. It was settled in the 1870s around Jacob Bartles' trading post. Growth was spurred by the discovery of oil in 1897 and the arrival of the Santa Fe Railway in 1899. A replica of the first commercial well (Nellie Johnstone No. 1) in Oklahoma is in Johnstone Park, site of the original tapping. Oil and gas production, zinc smelting, and the manufacture of oil-field equipment are the economic mainstays. A U.S. Bureau of Mines petroleum experimental station is in the city. Bartlesville Wesleyan College was founded in 1880. Woolaroc Museum, established by oilman Frank Phillips and housing a collection of Western art, is 14 mi (23 km) southwest. Tom Mix was deputy marshal of nearby Dewey before becoming a famous silent-screen movie star; his elaborate cowboy gear is displayed in a museum. Inc. 1897. Pop. (1980) 34,568.

Bartlett, Sir Frederic C(harles) (b. Oct. 20, 1886, Stow-on-the-Wold, Gloucestershire, Eng.—d. Sept. 30, 1969, Cambridge, Cambridgeshire), British psychologist best known for his studies of memory.

Through his long association with Cambridge University, Bartlett strongly influenced British psychological method, emphasizing a descriptive, or case study, approach over more statistical techniques. In 1922 he became director of the Cambridge Psychological Laboratory and in 1931 was appointed the university's first professor of experimental psychology, retaining that position until his retirement in 1952. Bartlett was elected to the Royal Society in 1932 and was knighted in 1948.

In his major work, *Remembering: A Study in Experimental and Social Psychology* (1932), Bartlett advanced the concept that memories of past events and experiences are actually mental reconstructions that are coloured by cultural attitudes and personal habits, rather than being direct recollections of observations made at the time. In experiments beginning in 1914, Bartlett showed that very little of an event is actually perceived at the time of its occurrence but that, in reconstructing the memory, gaps in observation or perception are filled in with the aid of previous experiences. A later work, *Thinking: An Experimental and Social Study* (1958), broke no new theoretical ground but added observations on the social character of human thinking.

Bartlett, John (b. June 14, 1820, Plymouth, Mass., U.S.—d. Dec. 3, 1905, Cambridge, Mass.), bookseller and editor best known for his *Familiar Quotations.*

John Bartlett

By courtesy of Little, Brown and Co.

At 16 he became an employee of the Harvard University bookstore, where he became so versed in book knowledge that the advice "Ask John Bartlett" became common on the Harvard campus. Eventually he came to own the store, and in 1855 he published the first edition of his *Familiar Quotations*, based largely on the notebook that he kept for the benefit of his customers. Later editions of the work were greatly expanded, and, from the fourth edition on, these were published by Little, Brown and Company, Boston, which Bartlett joined in 1863. The book went through nine editions in his lifetime and appeared in a centennial edition, the 13th, in 1955. Bartlett also wrote books on chess and angling and, after many years of labour, a *Complete Concordance to Shakespeare's Dramatic Works and Poems* (1894), a standard reference work that surpassed any of its predecessors in the number and fullness of its citations.

Bartlett, John Russell (b. Oct. 23, 1805, Providence, R.I., U.S.—d. May 28, 1886, Providence), bibliographer who made his greatest contribution to linguistics with his pioneer work, *Dictionary of Americanisms: A Glossary of Words and Phrases, Usually Regarded as Peculiar to the United States* (1848). It went through four editions and was translated into Dutch and German.

John Russell Bartlett

By courtesy of The Rhode Island Historical Society

Appointed commissioner for the survey of the boundary between the United States and Mexico in 1850–53, he wrote as a result *Personal Narrative of Explorations and Incidents in Texas, New Mexico, California, Sonora and Chihuahua . . . ,* 2 vol. (1854, reprinted 1965). Robert V. Hine, *Bartlett's West: Drawing the Mexican Boundary* (1965), assesses Bartlett's drawings and his stature as an interpreter of the West. As secretary of the state of Rhode Island he rearranged and classified the state records and prepared bibliographies and compilations on state history. Bartlett assisted John Carter Brown in acquiring and cataloging his noted book collection, now in the John Carter Brown Library on the campus of Brown University.

Bartlett Deep, also called BARTLETT TROUGH (Caribbean Sea): *see* Cayman Trench.

Bartmannkrug, also called BEARDED-MAN JUG, type of 16th-century German jug, characterized by a round belly and a mask of a

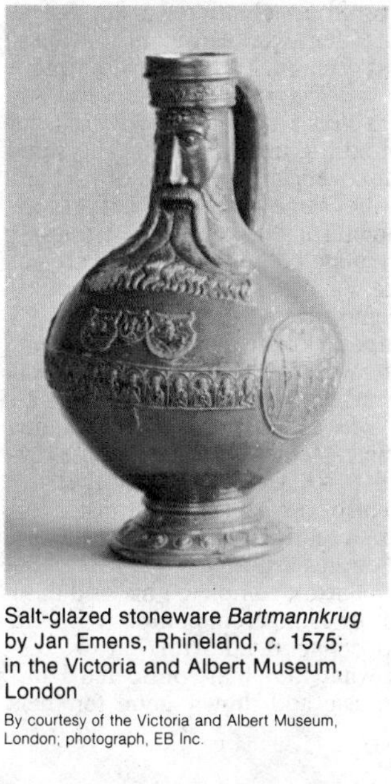

Salt-glazed stoneware *Bartmannkrug* by Jan Emens, Rhineland, *c.* 1575; in the Victoria and Albert Museum, London

By courtesy of the Victoria and Albert Museum, London; photograph, EB Inc.

bearded man applied in relief to the neck. This salt-glazed stoneware jug is associated particularly with Cologne and Frechen, where it was manufactured in considerable numbers. It was sometimes called a "Bellarmine," the mask being regarded as a satire on Cardinal (later Saint) Robert Bellarmine, a Roman Catholic cleric who opposed Protestantism.

The jugs were exported in large quantities to England, where they were known as "graybeards." The jug is usually finished in golden brown or blue and gray, and the mask descends from the rim of the neck so that the rectangular beard falls over the shoulder and onto the belly of the jug. Other raised designs were invariably added, including rosettes, medallions, leaves, ornamental friezes, or coats of arms.

Bartók, Béla (b. March 25, 1881, Nagyszentmiklós, Hung., Austria-Hungary—d. Sept. 26, 1945, New York City), composer, pianist, ethnomusicologist, and teacher, noted for the Hungarian flavour of his major musical works, which include orchestral works, string quartets, piano solos, several stage works, a cantata, and a number of settings of folk songs for voice and piano.

Bartók, photograph by Fritz Reiner
Mrs. Fritz Reiner

Career in Hungary. Bartók spent his childhood and youth in various provincial towns, studying the piano with his mother and later with a succession of teachers. He began to compose small dance pieces at the age of nine, and two years later he played in public for the first time, including a composition of his own in his program.

Following the lead of another eminent Hungarian composer, Ernő Dohnányi, Bartók undertook his professional studies at the Royal Hungarian Academy of Music in Budapest rather than in Vienna. He developed rapidly as a pianist but less so as a composer. After writing no music at all for two years, he resumed composing in 1902 under the stimulus of his discovery of the music of Richard Strauss. At the same time a spirit of optimistic nationalism was sweeping Hungary, inspired by Ferenc Kossuth and his Party of Independence. As other members of Bartók's generation demonstrated in the streets, the 22-year-old composer wrote a symphonic poem, *Kossuth,* portraying in a style that was reminiscent of Strauss, though with a Hungarian flavour, the life of the great patriot Lajos Kossuth, Ferenc's father, who had led the revolution of 1848–49. Despite a scandal at the first performance, occasioned by a distortion of the Austrian national anthem, the work was received enthusiastically.

Shortly after Bartók completed his studies in 1903, he and the Hungarian composer Zoltán Kodály, who collaborated with Bartók, discovered that what they had considered Hungarian folk music and drawn upon for their compositions was instead the dilettante music of city-dwelling Gypsies. A vast reservoir of authentic Hungarian peasant music was subsequently made known by the research of the two composers. The initial collection, which led them into the remotest corners of Hungary, was begun with the intention of revitalizing Hungarian music. Both composers not only transcribed many folk tunes for the piano and other media but incorporated into their original music the melodic, rhythmic, and textural elements of peasant music. Ultimately, their own work became suffused with the folk spirit.

Bartók was appointed to the faculty of the Academy of Music in 1907 and retained that position until 1934, when he resigned to become a working member of the Academy of Sciences. His holidays were spent collecting folk material, which he then analyzed and classified, and he soon began the publication of articles and monographs.

At the same time, Bartók was expanding the catalog of his compositions, with many new works for the piano, a substantial number for orchestra, and the beginning of a series of six string quartets that was to constitute one of his most impressive achievements. The first quartet (1908–09) shows few traces of folk influence, but in the others that influence is thoroughly assimilated and omnipresent. The quartets parallel and illuminate Bartók's stylistic development; in the second quartet (1915–17) Arab elements reflect the composer's collecting trip to North Africa; in the third (1927) and fourth (1928) there is a more intensive use of dissonance; and in the fifth (1934) and sixth (1939) there is a reaffirmation of traditional tonality.

In 1911 Bartók wrote his only opera, *Duke Bluebeard's Castle,* an allegorical treatment of the legendary wife murderer, with a score permeated by characteristics of old Hungarian folk song, especially in the speechlike rhythms of the text setting. The technique is comparable to that used by the French impressionist composer Claude Debussy in his opera *Pelléas et Mélisande* (1902), and Bartók's opera has other impressionistic qualities as well. A ballet, *The Wooden Prince* (1914–16), and a pantomime, *The Miraculous Mandarin* (1918–19), followed; thereafter he wrote no more for the stage.

Unable to travel during World War I, Bartók devoted himself to composition and the study of the collected folk music. During the short-lived proletarian dictatorship of the Hungarian Soviet Republic in 1919, he served as a member of the Music Council with Kodály and Dohnányi. Upon its overthrow Kodály was removed from his position at the Academy of Music; but Bartók, despite his defense of his colleague, was permitted to remain.

His most productive years were the two decades that followed the end of World War I in 1918, when his musical language was completely and expressively formulated. He had assimilated many disparate influences: in addition to those already mentioned—Strauss and Debussy—there were also the 19th-century Hungarian composer Franz Liszt and the modernists Igor Stravinsky and Arnold Schoenberg. Bartók arrived at a vital and varied style, rhythmically animated, in which diatonic and chromatic elements are juxtaposed without incompatibility. Within these two creative decades, Bartók composed two concerti for piano and orchestra and one for violin; the *Cantata Profana* (1930), his only large-scale choral work; and a number of important chamber scores, including the *Music for Strings, Percussion, and Celesta* (1936), and the *Sonata for Two Pianos and Percussion* (1937). The same period saw Bartók expanding his activities as a concert pianist, playing in most of the countries of western Europe, the United States, and the Soviet Union.

U.S. career. As Nazi Germany extended its sphere of influence in the late 1930s, and Hungary appeared in imminent danger of capitulation, Bartók found it impossible to remain there. After a second concert tour of the United States in 1940, he emigrated there later the same year. An appointment as research assistant in music at Columbia University enabled him to continue working with folk music, transcribing and editing for publication a collection of Serbo-Croatian women's songs, a part of a much larger recorded collection of Yugoslav folk music. With his wife, the pianist Ditta Pásztory, he was able to give a few concerts. His health, however, was never very strong and had begun to deteriorate even before his arrival in America.

Bartók's last years were marked by the ravages of leukemia, which often prevented him from teaching, lecturing, or performing. Nonetheless, he was able to compose the *Concerto for Orchestra* (1943), the *Sonata for Solo Violin* (1944), and all but the last measures of the *Third Piano Concerto* (1945). When he died, his last composition, a *Concerto for Viola and Orchestra,* was left an uncompleted mass of sketches.

During his life Bartók published several important book-length studies of Hungarian and Romanian folk music. His three-volume study of Romanian folk music was issued only in 1967; the first of three volumes on Slovakian folk music appeared in 1959. These contributions loom large in the field of musical ethnology, and it may be argued that they overshadow Bartók's legacy as composer. Though his music was infrequently performed outside Hungary during his lifetime, many of his compositions, including the string quartets and the *Concerto for Orchestra,* later entered the standard concert repertory. Bartók's compositions within a quarter century after his death were ranked among the classics of Western music.

(H.Ss.)

MAJOR WORKS. *Orchestral music. Kossuth,* symphonic poem (1903); *Suite No. 1,* op. 3, for large orchestra (1905); *Suite No.2,* op. 4, for small orchestra (1905–07); *Dance Suite* (1923); *Music for Strings, Percussion and Celesta* (1936); *Divertimento,* for string orchestra (1939); *Concerto for Orchestra* (1943). Concerti: *Violin Concerto No. 1* (1907–08), *No. 2* (1937–38); *Piano Concerto No. 1* (1926), *No. 2* (1930–31), *No. 3* (unfinished, 1945); *Viola Concerto* (unfinished, but completed by Tibor Serly, 1945).

Chamber music. String quartets: *No. 1,* op. 7 (1908–09); *No. 2,* op. 17 (1915–17); *No. 3* (1927); *No. 4* (1928); *No. 5* (1934); *No. 6* (1939). Miscellaneous: *Piano Quintet* (1904); *Sonatas for Violin and Piano No. 1* (1921), *No. 2* (1922); *Rhapsodies for Violin and Piano No. 1 and 2* (1928); *Forty-four Duos,* for two violins (1931); *Sonata for Two Pianos and Percussion* (1937; transcribed as *Concerto for Two Pianos and Orchestra,* 1940); *Contrasts,* for violin, clarinet, and piano (1938); *Sonata for Solo Violin* (1944). Piano solos: *Rhapsody,* op. 1 (1904; also arranged for piano and orchestra and for two pianos); *Fourteen Bagatelles,* op. 6 (1908); *For Children* (1908–09); *Allegro barbaro* (1911); *Sonatina* (1915); *Suite,* op. 14 (1916); *Sonata* (1926); *Out of Doors,* suite (1926); *Mikrokosmos,* 153 progressive pieces for piano (1926–39).

Vocal music. Stage works: *Duke Bluebeard's Castle,* op. 11, an opera, libretto by Béla Balázs (Budapest, 1918); *The Wooden Prince,* op. 13, ballet, libretto by Béla Balázs (Budapest, 1917); *The Miraculous Mandarin,* op. 19, pantomime, libretto by Menyhért Lengyel (Cologne, 1926). Canata: *Cantata Profana: The Nine Enchanted Stags,* for double mixed chorus, tenor and baritone soloists, and orchestra (1930). Songs: A large number of settings of Hungarian and other folk songs, including *Five Village Scenes,* for voice and piano (1924).

BIBLIOGRAPHY. A listing of the Bartók compositions and papers held by the Béla Bartók Archives in New York City appears in Victor Bator, *The Béla Bartók Archives: History and Catalogue* (1963). The composer's letters have been collected and edited by János Demény in *Bartók Béla levelek* (1948), and *Bartók Béla levelei* (1951 and 1955); in *Ausgewählte Briefe* (1960); and in *Bartók Letters* (1971). Halsey Stevens, *The Life and Music of Béla Bartók,* rev. ed. (1964), is a biographical study and critical examination of all published works, with a catalog of compositions and an extensive bibliography. Ferenc Bónis, *Bela Bartok: His Life in Pictures and Documents* (1972; 2nd ed. 1980) is available in Hungarian and English.

Bartold, Vasily V(ladimirovich), also called WILHELM BARTHOLD (b. Nov. 15 [Nov. 3, old style] 1869, St. Petersburg—d. Aug. 19, 1930, Leningrad, Russian), Russian anthropologist who made valuable contributions to the study of the social and cultural history of Islām and of the Tadzhik Iranians and literate Turkic peoples of Central Asia.

Bartold joined the faculty of the University of St. Petersburg in 1901 and for the remainder of his life devoted himself to teaching and research, interrupted by frequent, extended field trips. His studies ranged from broader questions, such as those of cultural history, to more delimited, specialized histories. The interaction of the individual with society was of particular interest to him, and he also devoted some attention to refining the theory of his colleague Vasily Radlov on the formation of Turkic states through usurpation of popular authority by a powerful individual. His major works were published in nine volumes; translations include *Four Studies on the History of Central Asia* (3 vol., 1956–62) and *Turkestan Down to the Mongol Invasion* (1928). Bartold contributed a number of articles to *The Encyclopaedia of Islam;* especially noteworthy are the portraits of peoples of the Caucasus and Asia, including the Kalmyks, Kazakhs, and Kirgiz.

Bartoli, Daniello (b. Feb. 12, 1608, Ferrara, Papal States—d. Jan. 12, 1685, Rome), Jesuit historian and Humanist who ranked among classic Italian writers.

Bartoli entered the Society of Jesus in 1623 and wrote the well-known and frequently translated *L'uomo di lettere difeso ed emendato* (1645; *The Learned Man Defended and Reformed,* 1660). In addition to writing a history of the Jesuits in Italian, *Istoria della Compagnia di Gesù* (1653–73), Bartoli was the biographer of such Jesuit saints as Ignatius Loyola, Francis Xavier, and Francis Borgia.

Bartoli, Matteo Giulio (b. Nov. 22, 1873, Albona d'Istria, Austria-Hungary—d. Jan. 23, 1946, Turin, Italy), linguist who emphasized the geographic spread of linguistic changes and their interpretation in terms of history and culture.

Having obtained his doctorate at the University of Vienna, Bartoli in 1907 became professor at the University of Turin, where he remained until his retirement. In an important early study, *Das Dalmatische* (1906; "Dalmatian"), he documented and analyzed the now extinct Romance dialect of the Adriatic island of Veglia (Krk, Yugos.). He later advanced his theories about language in *Introduzione alla neolinguistica* (1925; "Introduction to Neolinguistics") and *Saggi di linguistica spaziale* (1945; "Essays on Areal Linguistics"). In his view, there is a direct, causal connection between linguistic expansion and distribution, on the one hand, and linguistic change and its order of occurrence, on the other. Though his chief interest was in Romance languages, he also addressed himself to Proto-Indo-European languages.

Bartolo de Simone, Andrea di: *see* Castagno, Andrea del.

Bartolomeo, Fra, also called BACCIO DELLA PORTA (b. March 28, 1472, Florence—d. Oct. 31, 1517, Florence), painter who was the most prominent exponent in early 16th-century Florence of the classical idealism of the High Renaissance style. His early works, such as the

"God the Father with S.S. Catherine of Siena and Mary Magdalene," painting by Fra Bartolomeo, 1509; in the Pinacoteca Civica, Lucca, Italy
SCALA—Art Resource/EB Inc.

"Annunciation" (1497; Volterra cathedral), were influenced by the balanced compositions of the Umbrian painter Perugino and by the sfumato (smoky effect of light and shade) of Leonardo da Vinci. Saddened by the death of the Florentine Dominican religious reformer Girolama Savonarola, Bartolomeo joined the Dominican order in 1500 and gave up painting. He began painting again in 1504, and his "Vision of St. Bernard" (completed 1507; Accademia, Florence) shows that he had thoroughly assimilated the idealizing principles of High Renaissance art.

In 1508 Bartolomeo visited Venice. There he was much impressed by the later work of Giovanni Bellini, whose influence is visible in the thick, atmospheric light and monumental figures of his "God the Father with SS. Catherine of Siena and Mary Magdalene" (1509; Pinacoteca Civica, Lucca) and in the sombre colours of his "Mystic Marriage of St. Catherine" (1512; Uffizi, Florence), the composition of which was adapted from Bellini's enthroned madonnas.

Bartolomeo visited Rome in 1514, where he saw Raphael's mature work and Michelangelo's frescoes on the ceiling of the Sistine Chapel. The results of his journey may be seen in the colossal figures of "Jonah," "Isaiah" (both in the Uffizi, Florence), and "St. Mark" (Pitti Palace, Florence). The gigantic figures overflow the niches in which they are painted and twist in tense, unnatural poses. Michelangelesque violence, however, did not suit Bartolomeo's gentle temperament, and his "Pietà" (*c.* 1515; Pitti Palace, Florence) shows a return to his earlier restraint. Bartolomeo's art is, on the whole, conservative, and he painted religious subjects almost exclusively.

Bartolozzi, Francesco (b. Sept. 21, 1727, Florence—d. March 7, 1815, Lisbon), Florentine engraver in the service of George III of England. Bartolozzi, the son of a goldsmith, studied painting in Florence, trained as an engraver in Venice, and began his career in Rome.

In 1764 Bartolozzi was invited to London, where he remained for 40 years. For his patron, George III, he executed numerous engravings, including those after Holbein's drawings at Windsor. He also engraved many works after Italian masters and after his friends, the fashionable contemporary painters Giovanni Cipriani and Angelica Kauffmann. He was not the inventor of the red-chalk method of engraving, but he made it the fashion. In 1802 he was invited to Lisbon as director of the National Academy. His son, Gaetano Stephano (1757–1821), also an engraver, was the father of Madame Vestris.

Bartolus OF SAXOFERRATO (b. 1313/14, Sassoferrato, Papal States—d. 1357, Perugia), lawyer, law teacher at Perugia, and the most prominent of the post-glossators, or commentators, a group of north Italian jurists who, from the middle 14th century, wrote on the civil (Roman) law. They succeeded the glossators, who had worked chiefly at Bologna from *c.* 1125.

Bartolus and his colleagues generally dealt with broad legal conceptions (derived from the Corpus Juris Civilis of the 6th-century Byzantine emperor Justinian I and from canon law), rather than elucidating short passages or even single words, as the glossators had done. During Bartolus' tenure (from 1343), the law school at Perugia rivalled that of Bologna. In addition to a commentary on the Code of Justinian, he wrote treatises on evidence and procedure.

Barton, Clara, in full CLARISSA HARLOWE BARTON (b. Dec. 25, 1821, Oxford, Mass., U.S.—d. April 12, 1912, Glen Echo, Md.), humanitarian and founder of the American Red Cross, known as the "angel of the battlefield."

After 18 years as a schoolteacher in Massachusetts and New Jersey, Barton moved to Washington, D.C., and became a clerk in the U.S. Patent Office. At the outbreak of the Civil War she organized an agency to obtain and distribute supplies for the relief of wounded soldiers. In 1865, at the request of Pres. Abraham Lincoln, she set up a bureau of records

Clara Barton, 1860s
By courtesy of the American National Red Cross

to aid in the search for missing men. While she was in Europe for a rest (1869–70), the Franco-German War broke out, and she again distributed relief supplies to war victims.

In Europe she became associated with the International Red Cross, and in 1881 she established the American National Red Cross. In 1882 she succeeded in having the United States sign the Geneva Agreement on the treatment of the sick, wounded, and dead in battle and the handling of prisoners of war. She was the author of the American amendment to the constitution of the Red Cross, which provides for the distribution of relief not only in war but also in times of such other calamities as famines, floods, earthquakes, cyclones, and pestilence.

Barton conducted relief for sufferers from disasters in the 1880s and 1890s and served in Cuba during the Spanish–American War (1898). She served as president of the American Red Cross until 1904, when, under increasing criticism of her arbitrary leadership, she stepped down to avoid further dissension within the organization. She wrote several books, including *History of the Red Cross*

(1882) and *The Red Cross in Peace and War* (1899). Biographies are P.H. Epler, *Life of Clara Barton* (new ed., 1953), and Ishbel Ross, *Angel of the Battlefield: The Life of Clara Barton* (1956).

Barton, Derek H(arold) R(ichard) (b. Sept. 8, 1918, Gravesend, Kent, Eng.), British joint recipient, with Odd Hassel of Norway, of the 1969 Nobel Prize for Chemistry for research that helped establish conformational analysis (the study of the three-dimensional geometric structure of complex molecules) as an essential part of organic chemistry.

In 1945 Barton joined the staff of the Imperial College of Science and Technology, London, first as an assistant lecturer and later as a research fellow. While serving as a visiting professor at Harvard University in 1949–50, he began work that led to his seminal publication (1950) on conformational analysis, which immediately caught the attention of the scientific community and revolutionized organic chemistry.

A faculty member of Birkbeck College, University of London, from 1950, Barton served as professor of chemistry at the University of Glasgow (1955–57) and then became professor of organic chemistry at Imperial College. In 1960 he discovered the Barton reaction, a process that led to an easier means of synthesizing the hormone aldosterone.

Barton, Sir Edmund (b. Jan. 18, 1849, Sydney—d. Jan. 7, 1920, Medlow, New South Wales, Australia), statesman who guided the Australian federation movement to a successful conclusion and became the first prime minister of the resulting commonwealth in 1901.

Barton in 1879 entered the New South Wales Legislative Assembly, where he served as speaker (1883–87); he was attorney general in 1889 and 1891–93. In 1891 he assumed leadership of the federation movement and, in the federal convention of that year, helped shape the draft that became the foundation for the eventual commonwealth constitution. The constitution bill passed the assembly in 1893, and for the next four years Barton campaigned vigorously for its approval by the public. He led the federal convention of 1897–98 that drafted the final commonwealth constitution bill.

Barton went to England in 1900 to guide the new constitution through Parliament and returned to become prime minister later that year. (He was knighted in 1902.) Never thoroughly at home in the partisan atmosphere of the new Australian Parliament, he resigned his ministry in 1903 and became a senior judge on the High Court of Australia, serving until 1920.

Barton, Elizabeth, byname NUN OF KENT, or HOLY MAID OF KENT (b. *c.* 1506, Kent, Eng.—d. April 21, 1534, London), English ecstatic whose outspoken prophecies aroused public opinion over the matrimonial policy of King Henry VIII and led to her execution.

A domestic servant on the estate of William Warham, archbishop of Canterbury, she fell ill and about 1525 began to experience trances and to utter prophecies. Her fame spread, gaining for her a group of devotees, both clerical and lay. But her prophecies grew less mystical and more precise, and she began to threaten Henry VIII with dire consequences if he did not drop the projected annulment of his marriage to Catherine of Aragon and abandon Anne Boleyn. On one occasion she admonished the King in person.

After Henry's marriage to Anne, Elizabeth Barton's utterances approached the treasonable, and the new archbishop of Canterbury, Thomas Cranmer, began an investigation. Arrested and examined, she finally confessed to having feigned her trances and pretended her inspiration. She was condemned by Parliament and executed at Tyburn, outside London. It is not certain, however, that her confession—although extracted without torture—was the result of anything but confusion and fear, for she had no education and little intellect. If she was more a hysteric than a saint, it is probable that she was, in the main, sincere, more deluded than deluding.

Barton, Frances: *see* Abington, Fanny.

bartonellosis, also called CARRIÓN'S DISEASE, rickettsial infection limited to South America, caused by *Bartonella bacilliformis* of the order Rickettsiales. It is characterized by two distinctive clinical stages: Oroya fever, an acute febrile anemia of rapid onset, bone and joint pains, and a high mortality if untreated, and verruga peruana, a more benign skin eruption characterized by reddish papules and nodules, which usually follows the Oroya fever but may also occur in individuals without previous symptoms. The skin lesions are thought to be an expression of developing immunity in the affected persons; reinfection is extremely rare.

The disease is transmitted to man by the night-biting sand fly of the genus *Phlebotomus*, which propagates in the Andes mountains in parts of Peru, Ecuador, and Colombia. The disease responds well to certain antibiotics. Control measures are directed principally at the insect carrier, with the use of insecticides and insect repellents.

Bartonian Stage, division of Eocene rocks and time (the Eocene Epoch began about 54,000,000 years ago and lasted about 16,000,000 years). The Bartonian, considered to be middle or upper Eocene in age, is named for rock exposures near Barton, in the Hampshire Basin of Great Britain. This stage is represented by the Barton Beds, a sequence of clays and sands rich in the greenish, iron-bearing mineral glauconite that is formed only in a marine environment. Many kinds of marine fossils, especially those of the molluscan group, occur in abundance throughout much of the beds. They become rarer and are replaced by freshwater fossil forms in the upper parts of the beds, however. The Barton Beds mark the end of an Eocene marine transgression that was followed by a gradual freshening of the waters and a gradual return to dominantly terrestrial conditions.

Bartow, city, seat (1861) of Polk County, central Florida, U.S., near the Peace River and Lake Hancock, 12 mi (19 km) southeast of Lakeland. In 1851 the Readding Blount family built a stockade community known as Fort Blount on the site of an earlier settlement (Peas Creek). It was incorporated as a municipality (1867) and named for Francis S. Bartow, a Confederate general. Promoted by the stockman Jacob Summerlin, a former Confederate cattle agent, it was incorporated as a town in 1882 and became a city in 1893. Phosphate mining, citrus cultivation, and truck farming are now the economic mainstays. The nearby Bone Valley Phosphate Museum exhibits fossil remains and traces the history of the phosphate industry. Pop. (1980) 14,780.

Bartram, John (b. March 23, 1699, near Darby, Pa.—d. Sept. 22, 1777, Kingsessing, Pa., U.S.), naturalist and explorer considered the "father of American botany." Largely self-educated, Bartram was a friend of Benjamin Franklin and an original member of the American Philosophical Society. He was botanist for the American colonies to King George III.

The first North American experimenter to hybridize flowering plants, Bartram established near Philadelphia a botanical garden that became internationally famous. He also collected and exported seeds and plants that were in great demand abroad and thus established friendships with European botanists, among them Linnaeus, who esteemed him as a great "natural botanist."

Bartram made scientific forays into the Alleghenies, Carolinas, and other areas of North America, and in 1743 he was commissioned by the British crown to visit the Indian tribes of the League of Six Nations and to explore the wilderness north to Lake Ontario in Canada. In 1765–66 he explored extensively in Florida with his son William, also a naturalist, whose *Travels* (1791) greatly influenced English Romanticism.

Baruch, Apocalypse of, in full THE BOOK OF THE APOCALYPSE OF BARUCH THE SON OF NERIAH, a pseudepigraphal work (not in any canon of scripture), whose primary theme is whether or not God's relationship with man is just. The book is also called *The Syriac Apocalypse of Baruch* because it was preserved only in the 6th-century Syriac Vulgate. It was originally composed in Hebrew and ascribed to Baruch, a popular legendary figure among Hellenistic Jews, who was secretary to Jeremiah, the biblical prophet.

Passages in the book indicate that it was written after the destruction of Jerusalem in AD 70, probably around AD 100. Textual conflicts suggest possible multiple authorship but may be due to inaccurate translations and to the use of traditional materials from different historical periods that are not easily harmonized.

The question of divine justice that preoccupied the Jews after the fall of Jerusalem is discussed in the *Apocalypse* in a series of prayers and visions. The apparent unjust sufferings of the righteous are explained as God's method of sanctifying his chosen people. Unlike II Esdras, the *Apocalypse of Baruch* does not question the efficacy of the Mosaic Law as the means of ultimate salvation but emphasizes the necessity of obeying its legal precepts. Some scholars see in this an indication that rabbinic authors composed the text to refute II Esdras.

Baruch, Bernard (Mannes) (b. Aug. 19, 1870, Camden, S.C., U.S.—d. June 20, 1965, New York City), financier and adviser to U.S. presidents, who was instrumental after World War II in the formulation of policy at the United Nations regarding international control of atomic energy.

Graduated from the College of the City of New York (1889), Baruch then worked as an office boy in a linen business and later in Wall Street brokerage houses. Over the years he amassed a fortune as a stock market speculator. In 1916 he was appointed by President Wilson to the Advisory Commission of the Council of National Defense, and during World War I he became chairman of the War Industries Board. In 1919 he served as a member of the Supreme Economic Council at the Versailles Peace Conference and also as personal adviser to President Wilson on the terms of peace. As an expert in wartime economic mobilization, Baruch's advisory services were employed by President Roosevelt during World War II, although he did not hold an administrative position. The designation of "elder statesman" was applied to him perhaps more often than to any other American.

Baruch, Book of, ancient text still extant in Greek and in several translations from Greek into Latin, Syriac, Coptic, Ethiopic, *et al.*, purportedly written by Baruch, secretary and friend of Jeremiah, the Old Testament prophet. The book of Baruch is apocryphal to the Hebrew and Protestant canons but was incorporated in the Septuagint (*q.v.;* Greek version of the Hebrew Bible) and was included in the Old Testament for Roman Catholics.

The work is a compilation of several authors and is the only work among the apocrypha that was consciously modelled after the prophetic writings of the Old Testament.

A brief introduction reports that Baruch wrote the book five years after the destruction of Jerusalem by Babylonia in 586 BC. A long prayer (1:15–3:8) is a national confession of sins similar to the lamentation in Dan. 9. The original Hebrew text perhaps dates from the late 2nd century BC. In the next section, a poem identifies God with universal wisdom and names the Judaic Law as God's gift of wisdom to men (3:9–4:4). In poems of lamentation and consolation that follow (4:5–5:9), Jerusalem is personified as a widow who weeps for her lost children, and God speaks words of comfort to the Jews. These latter poems are possibly also of Jewish origin and perhaps date from the 1st century BC.

Barūjird (Iran): *see* Borūjerd.

Bāruni, also spelled BARAUNI, or BERUNI, town, Begusarai district, Bihār state, northeastern India, north of the Ganges River, part of the Begusarai urban agglomeration. Formerly called Jhuldabhaj, it merged with Phulwaria township in 1961. It has major highway, rail, and ferry connections and is an agricultural trade centre. Bāruni is chiefly an industrial complex, with an oil refinery and a thermal power plant. The town is the site of a college affiliated with Bhāgalpur University. Pop. (1981) 56,366.

Baruta, city, northwestern Miranda state, northern Venezuela, in the central highlands. Formerly a commercial centre in a fertile agricultural area producing coffee, cacao, and sugarcane, the city has become a residential suburb in the Caracas metropolitan area. An expressway links Baruta to Caracas, approximately 10 mi (16 km) to the north-northeast. Pop. (1981) 180,100.

Barwāni, town, West Nimār district, Madhya Pradesh state, central India, just south of the Narmada River. A major trade centre for agricultural produce and timber, it is heavily engaged in cotton ginning. Founded *c.* 1650, the town served as capital of the former Barwāni princely state, which merged with Madhya Bhārat in 1948. Nearby lies Chulgiri Hill, a pilgrimage site of special sanctity to the Jainas; on the face of the hill is carved a gigantic figure of the Jaina saint Bāhubali (Gommateśvara). Barwāni has a hospital and a government college affiliated with Vikram University. Pop. (1981) 27,769.

Bary, Heinrich Anton de (b. Jan. 26, 1831, Frankfurt am Main—d. Jan. 19, 1888, Strasbourg), botanist whose development of modern concepts concerning the roles of fungi and other agents in causing plant diseases earned him distinction as a founder of modern mycology and plant pathology.

A professor of botany at the universities of Freiburg im Breisgau (1855–66), Halle (1867–72), and Strasbourg (1872–88), de Bary determined the life cycles of many fungi, for which he developed a classification that has been retained in large part by modern mycologists. Among the first to study host-parasite interactions, he demonstrated ways in which fungi penetrate host tissues.

In his book *Untersuchungen über die Brandpilze* (1853; "Researches Concerning Fungal Blights"), de Bary correctly maintained that fungi associated with rust and smut diseases of plants are the cause, rather than the effect, of these diseases, and in 1865 he provided the first demonstration of heteroecism when he proved that the life cycle of wheat rust involves two hosts, wheat and barberry. First to show (1866) that lichens consist of a fungus and an alga in intimate association, he coined the term symbiosis in 1879 to mean an internal, mutually beneficial partnership between two organisms.

De Bary also did important research on slime molds and sexual modes of reproduction in algae, and he wrote *Vergleichende Anatomie der Vegetationsorgane der Phanerogamen und Farne* (1877; *Comparative Anatomy of Phanerogams and Ferns,* 1884).

Barye, Antoine Louis (b. Sept. 24, 1796, Paris—d. June 29, 1875, Paris), prolific French sculptor, primarily of animals, known as the father of the Animalier school.

The son of a jeweller, Barye was apprenticed to an engraver of military equipment at age 13; after completing service in the army he worked in the jewelry trade. Around 1817 he began to sculpt and was influenced by the Romantic paintings of Géricault. From 1823 to 1831 he worked with Fauconnier, a goldsmith.

Barye's talent for rendering dynamic tension and exact anatomical detail, refined during his tenure as a model maker at the Jardin des Plantes, is especially evident in his bronzes of wild animals struggling with or devouring their prey. He also produced many figures and groups of domestic animals.

Barye moved in and out of the dominant artistic circle during his turbulent career. He exhibited bronze portraits at the Salon in 1827 and in 1832 received the Légion d'Honneur. In 1834 he began to have conflicts with the controlling art establishment and did not exhibit again until 1851.

He produced two notable sculptures of Napoleon—an equestrian statue at Ajaccio and the pediment on the Pavillon de l'Horloge at the Louvre.

Barylambda, extinct genus of unusual and aberrant mammals found as fossils in late Paleocene deposits in North America (the Paleocene Epoch began about 65,000,000 years ago and lasted about 11,000,000 years). *Barylambda* was a relatively large animal, 2½ metres (about 8 feet) long, with an unusually massive body and legs. The very thick tail possibly was used as a support, allowing the animal to raise itself on its hind legs. The skull was relatively small and short. The feet were short and broad, with five digits. *Barylambda* retained clavicles, or collar-bones, a feature that is considered primitive in hoofed mammals. It is likely that *Barylambda* fed on plants that were rather soft and easily chewed. *Barylambda* was among the largest animals of its time.

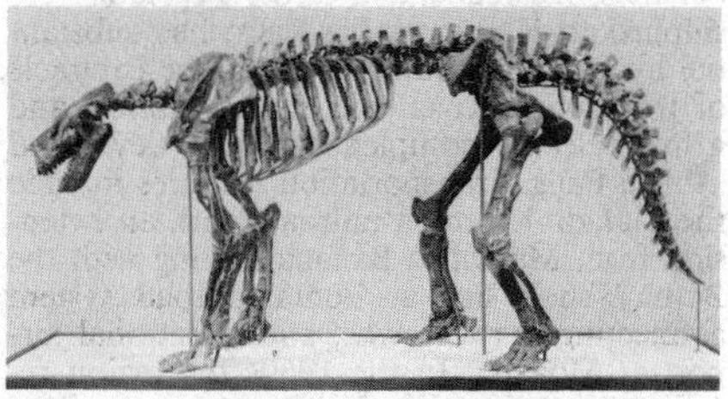

Barylambda faberi, from Colorado
By courtesy of the American Museum of Natural History, New York

baryon, any member of the class of heaviest subatomic particles that includes nucleons (protons and neutrons) and hyperons (lambda, sigma, xi, and omega particles). Their antiparticles are called antibaryons. Baryons are those fermions that participate in strong interaction, the force binding together neutrons and protons in atomic nuclei (*see* fermion). The baryon number, which for baryons is +1, for antibaryons −1, and for nonbaryons 0, remains the same in every particle reaction.

Baryshnikov, Mikhail (Nikolayevich) (b. Jan. 27, 1948, Riga, Latvian S.S.R.), Soviet-born U.S. ballet dancer of international acclaim and, from 1980, the artistic director of the American Ballet Theatre (ABT), in New York City.

Baryshnikov studied ballet in Leningrad with Aleksandr Pushkin, joined the Kirov Ballet at age 18, and soon rose to *premier danseur noble*. He defected from the Soviet Union in 1974 and became a member of the ABT. He left that company in 1978 to dance with the New York City Ballet under George Balanchine, but he returned to the ABT in 1980. In addition to his stage performances he played a leading role as dancer and actor in the motion picture *The Turning Point* (1976), and he made numerous appearances on television.

barytes (mineral): *see* barite.

baryton (brass wind instrument): *see* euphonium.

baryton, bowed, stringed musical instrument that enjoyed a certain vogue in the 18th century. It was related to the viol family, was about the size of a cello, and had six melody strings and a fretted fingerboard. Up to 40 sympathetically vibrating strings, some of which were plucked with the left-hand thumb, ran behind the wide neck.

German baryton; in the Museum of Fine Arts, Boston
Leslie Lindsay Mason Collection of Musical Instruments (formerly the Galpin Collection), Museum of Fine Arts, Boston

Haydn wrote 175 baryton compositions for his patron, Prince Miklós Esterházy, a skilled baryton player. "Baryton" also refers to an oboe pitched an octave below the ordinary oboe (*hautbois baryton*).

Barzānī, Mullah Muṣṭafa al- (b. 1904, Barzān, Iraq—d. March 1, 1979, Washington, D.C.), Kurdish military leader who for 50 years fought the Iraqi government in an unsuccessful attempt to win autonomy for the Kurds.

Al-Barzānī joined his brother Shaykh Ahmed in revolt in 1931 and became leader of the Barzānī tribe the following year. In 1943 he led more than 6,000 Kurds into Iran, where the Soviet Union established a Kurdish republic and made him a major general. When the Soviets withdrew in 1947, he fled to the U.S.S.R., where he studied at the Moscow Institute of Languages.

Al-Barzānī returned to Iraq after the revolution of 1959, formed another guerrilla army, called Pesh Merga (Forward to Death), and battled the government continuously until, in 1972, he was de facto ruler of all of Kurdish Iraq. When the Shah of Iran ceased supporting him in 1975 his troops were overrun by

Iraqi tanks. Al-Barzānī, in exile again, settled in northern Virginia in 1976.

Barzas-Breiz, in full BARZAS-BREIZ; CHANTS POPULAIRES DE LA BRETAGNE ("Breton Bardic Poems: Popular Songs of Brittany"), collection of folk songs and ballads purported to be survivals from ancient Breton folklore. The collection was made, supposedly from the oral literature of Breton peasants, by Théodore Hersart de La Villemarqué and published in 1839. It was later demonstrated that *Barzas-Breiz* was not an anthology of Breton folk poetry, but a mixture of old poems, chiefly love songs and ballads, that were rearranged by the editor or others; modern poems made to look medieval; and spurious poems about such romance figures as Merlin and Nominoë.

Nevertheless, *Barzas-Breiz* was extremely influential: the historical poems exalting the Breton's traditional struggle against oppression revived Breton pride in their language and heritage; it also led to the reawakening of Breton writers and stimulated further study of Breton folklore.

Barzizza, Gasparino da, original name GASPARINO DI PIETROBUONO (b. 1360?, Barzizza, near Bergamo, Italy—d. 1431, Milan), teacher noted for his ability to relate classical civilization to the Italy of his day. He was living at Bergamasco when he adopted the cognomen da Barzizza, or Barzizius.

Barzizza studied grammar and rhetoric at Pavia and stayed there to teach. He moved to Venice and then to Padua, where he won fame as a teacher of science and as a Humanist. He taught later at Ferrara and, from 1421, at Milan. Barzizza was known for his scholarship as well as for his teaching. His writings included works in epistolography, oratory, rhetoric, and literary and historical commentary, and he compiled a manual of Latin orthography. His *Book of Letters* (1470) was the first book produced by a printing press in France. His son Guimforte (*c.* 1406–63) became a noted teacher and author.

Barzun, Jacques (b. Nov. 30, 1907, Créteil, Fr.), French-born U.S. teacher, historian, and author who influenced higher education in the United States by his insistence that undergraduates avoid early specialization and instead be given broad instruction in the humanities.

Barzun moved to the United States in 1920. He became a lecturer in history at Columbia University in 1927, obtaining his Ph.D. from there in 1932. Remaining at Columbia, he rose to dean of faculties and provost in 1958 and became emeritus in 1967. He assisted in the development of a two-year course at Columbia for the reading and discussion of great books.

His works on education include *Teacher in America* (1945), essays; *The House of Intellect* (1959), a work that indicts the American educational system for producing counterfeit intellectuals; and *The American University: How It Runs, Where It Is Going* (1969). A related work is *Science: The Glorious Entertainment* (1964), in which he criticizes what he considers to be an overestimation of scientific thought. Noteworthy among his books on the arts are *Berlioz and the Romantic Century,* 2 vol. (1950; 3rd ed. 1969), *Pleasures of Music* (1951; reissued 1977), *The Energies of Art: Studies of Authors, Classic and Modern* (1956), *Classic, Romantic, and Modern* (1961), *On Writing, Editing, and Publishing* (1971), and *The Use and Abuse of Art* (1974). *Simple and Direct* (1975) is a rhetoric for writers.

Bas-Rhin, *département,* Alsace region, on the northeastern frontier of France. Formed from the northern half of Alsace, it has an area of 1,848 sq mi (4,787 sq km). French since the 17th century, it was lost to Germany in 1871–1919 and 1940–44. It includes the northern part of the plain of Alsace and the flanking highlands to the west. The Vosges Mountains rise in the southwest corner to 3,600 ft (1,100 m) in the Hochfeld Massif.

The plain has a sheltered climate. Where covered with loess, the terraces are exceptionally fertile and highly cultivated for corn (maize), sugar beets, fodder, and hops. Elsewhere are nonarable wooded tracts, the largest being Haguenau Forest.

The low-lying belts of damp alluvium are rich meadowlands. At the foot of the highlands is a rich zone of small towns and villages surrounded by orchards and celebrated vineyards. In the north of the plain was the Péchelbronn oil field, now exhausted.

Strasbourg, its old town originally sited on the Ill River (a Rhine tributary), is a terminal point for the Rhine–Rhône and Rhine–Marne canals, and an oil pipeline that connects Berre (near Marseille) and southern West Germany. Strasbourg, a university and cathedral city, is the departmental capital and also centre for an *arrondissement,* as are Erstein, Haguenau, Molsheim, Saverne, Sélestat, and Wissembourg. The court of appeal is in Colmar. Pop. (1982) 915,676.

Bas-Zaïre, English LOWER ZAIRE, region in western Zaire, central Africa, bordering the Congo on the north, the Angolan enclave of Cabinda on the northwest, and Angola on the south. Once joined with Bandundu (east) as Kinshasa province, Bas-Zaïre was separated in 1962 and now has an area of 20,819 sq mi (53,920 sq km). Administratively it is divided into two rural subregions, Bas-Fleuve and Cataractes, and two cities, Matadi and Boma. Matadi (*q.v.*; the regional capital) is a cargo and fishing port for maritime and Congo (Zaïre) River shipping; other river ports are Boma, 45 mi (72 km) downstream from Matadi, and Banana, in the estuary. Mbanza-Ngungu and Tshela are also important towns. The region produces timber, petroleum (at Moanda, on the Atlantic coast), cement, palm products, bananas, sugarcane, and cattle. Vegetables are shipped to Kinshasa. Bas-Zaïre has substantial hydroelectric potential along the cataracts of the Congo River and its tributaries, and a hydroelectric complex has been developed at Inga Falls. Transportation facilities include the Matadi–Kinshasa railroad, with an extension from Matadi to Banana linking with the Boma–Tshela line at Boma; a road system connecting major towns; and a national airport at Moanda. In the 1960s the region received heavy immigration from Angola. Pop. (1979 est.) 1,727,811.

basal metabolic rate (BMR), index of the general level of activity of an individual's body metabolism, determined by measuring oxygen intake in the basal state—*i.e.,* during absolute rest, but not sleep, 14 to 18 hours after eating. The higher the amount of oxygen consumed in a certain time interval, the more active is the oxidative process of the body and the higher is the rate of body metabolism. The BMR has been used in measuring the general metabolic state during therapy. It was formerly widely used to assess thyroid function, since the thyroid hormones are prime regulators of tissue oxidation and metabolism; but, since the advent of radioactive-isotope tests and thyroid hormone studies, BMR measurements have fallen into disuse.

Consult the INDEX *first*

basalt, extrusive igneous (volcanic) rock that is low in silica content, dark in colour, and comparatively rich in iron and magnesium.

Some basalts are quite glassy (tachylytes), and many are very fine-grained and compact; it is more usual, however, for them to exhibit porphyritic structure, with larger crystals (phenocrysts) of olivine, augite, or feldspar in a finely crystalline matrix (groundmass). Olivine and augite are the commonest porphyritic minerals in basalts. Porphyritic plagioclase feldspars, however, are also very common. Basaltic lavas are frequently spongy or pumiceous; the steam cavities become filled with secondary minerals such as calcite, chlorite, and zeolites.

Basalts may be broadly classified on a chemical and petrographical basis into two main groups: the calc-alkali and the alkali basalts. Calc-alkali basaltic lavas are characterized by basic plagioclase with augite, pigeonite or hypersthene, and olivine as the dominant mafic (basic) minerals; basalts without olivine are also well represented. Calc-alkali basalts which contain from 45 percent to 52 percent silica, include the tholeiites (basalts with calcium-poor pyroxene). They predominate among the lavas of mountain belts; their flows may build enormous plateaus, as in the northwestern United States, the Deccan of India, and the Paraná Basin of South America. The active volcanoes of Mauna Loa and Kilauea in Hawaii erupt tholeiitic lavas, and similar basalts occur in the lower portions of the volcanic pile of other extinct volcanoes of the Hawaiian group.

Normal alkali basalt contains olivine and, commonly, a diopsidic or titaniferous augite. Pigeonite and hypersthenic pyroxenes are typically absent. Alkali basalts predominate among the lavas of the ocean basins and are common among the basic lavas of the forelands and backlands of the mountain belts. In the Brito-Icelandic province the Tertiary lava flows of the Inner Hebrides, Antrim, and the Faeroe Islands include great successions of both calc-alkali and alkali basalts.

Minerals of the feldspathoid group occur in a large number of basaltic rocks belonging to the alkali group; nepheline, analcime, and leucite are the commonest, but haüynite is occasionally present. If nepheline entirely replaces feldspar, the rock is known as nepheline-basalt; if the replacement is only partial the term nepheline-basanite is used. Similarly, there are analcime- and leucite-basalts and leucite-basanites. Most nepheline-basalts are fine-grained, very dark coloured rocks and are of Tertiary age. They are fairly common in some parts of Germany and also occur in the United States (as in New Mexico) and in Libya, Asia Minor, the Cape Verde Islands, and elsewhere. Leucite-basalts are well known in the Eifel and other German volcanic districts, as well as in Czechoslovakia, Italy, Montana, and Java and Celebes in Indonesia. The young volcanic fields of the western rift of Equatorial Africa in southwestern Uganda and Zaire exhibit a series of undersaturated alkali basalts.

basaltes ware, also called BLACK BASALTES, basaltes also spelled BASALT, hard black vitreous stoneware, named after the volcanic rock basalt and manufactured by Josiah Wedgwood at Etruria, Staffordshire, Eng., from about 1768. Wedgwood's black basaltes ware was an improvement on the stained earthenware known as "Egyptian black" made by other Staffordshire potters.

The fine-grained basaltes stoneware reflected Wedgwood's Neoclassicism: its dense, uniform surface, requiring no glaze, was polished to a dull gloss; the ornament was usually intricate and well defined, often in complex geometric designs and either molded and applied or incised by turning on a lathe. Early productions included "bronze Etruscan" vases with faint gilding and copies of Greek vase painting in mat red and white encaustic enamels on the black ground. Classical relief medallions, cameos, and plaques were imitated in black basaltes, and even tea and coffee sets were made; small statues were fashioned as well as

Wedgwood basaltes ewer (one of a pair), Etruria, Staffordshire, Eng., *c.* 1775; in the Victoria and Albert Museum, London

By courtesy of the Victoria and Albert Museum, London; photograph, EB Inc.

important life-size "library" busts of classical and modern philosophers and authors. Some basaltes ware is essentially severe, with no decoration or added ornamentation.

Basanavičius, Jonas, Basanavičius also spelled BASSANOWICZ (b. Nov. 23, 1851, Ožkabaliai, Lithuania, Russian Empire—d. Feb. 16, 1927, Vilnius, Lithuania), physician, folklorist, and a leader of the Lithuanian national movement.

In 1873 Basanavičius went to Moscow to study history and archaeology but after a year changed to medicine. He was graduated in 1879 and spent most of the next 25 years practicing medicine in Bulgaria. He edited the first number of the important Lithuanian cultural and political magazine *Aušra* ("Dawn"), published 1883–86; it was printed in East Prussia and had to be smuggled into Lithuania because of the tsarist regime's ban on the printing of Lithuanian in the Latin alphabet. *Aušra* significantly influenced the development of the Lithuanian national movement.

From 1905 Basanavičius lived in Vilnius. Considered to be the moral president of the nation, he was chairman of the Great Assembly in Vilnius that in 1905 demanded autonomy for Lithuania; in 1917 he was president of the conference that elected him to the Lietuvos Taryba (Council of Lithuania), which on Feb. 16, 1918, proclaimed Lithuanian independence. Basanavičius' founding of the Lithuanian Scientific Society in 1907 was an outstanding contribution to Lithuanian learning. For 20 years he was president of the society, editor of its journal, and organizer of research in archaeology and folklore. His many publications are largely collections of Lithuanian folklore. He also wrote several studies expounding his hypothesis that the Lithuanians were descendants of the Thraco-Phrygians.

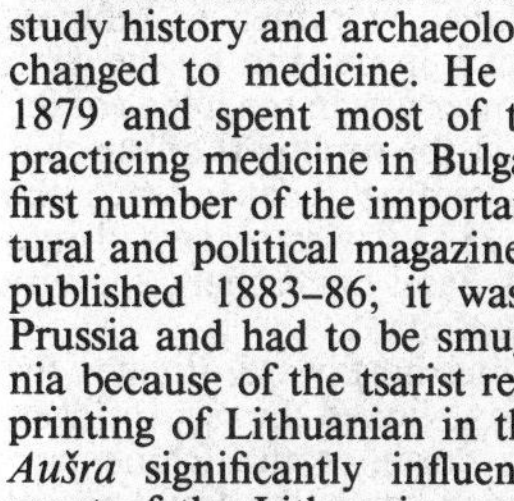

Basanavičius, portrait by A. Varnas; in the Istorijos Etnografijos Muziejus, Vilnius, Lithuanian S.S.R.

By courtesy of the Istorijos Etnografijos Muziejus, Vilnius, Lithuanian S.S.R.

basanite, extrusive igneous rock that contains calcium-rich plagioclase feldspar (usually labradorite or bytownite), feldspathoid (usually nepheline or leucite), olivine, and pyroxene (titanaugite). Basanite grades into tephrite, which contains no olivine.

In basanites and tephrites, the plagioclase occurs as large, single crystals (phenocrysts). The feldspathoid (nepheline) in nepheline-basanite and nepheline-tephrite occurs mainly in the matrix (groundmass), whereas that in leucite-basanite and leucite-tephrite (leucite) occurs abundantly in crystals as well. Olivine occurs as phenocrysts, as does the augite. Biotite, apatite, and titanium-rich magnetite are common accessories.

Basanites and tephrites occur as gray to black rocks in sheets and flows. Places where basanites are found include Czechoslovakia, Spain, Hungary, Italy, New Zealand, and the southwestern United States; tephrites are found in Germany, Italy, Portugal, Greenland, Uganda, and Colorado.

Basano, Manuel de Godoy, príncipe de (prince of): *see* Godoy, Manuel de.

Basarab, Matthew, Romanian MATEI BASARAB: *see* Matthew Basarab.

Basāsīrī, al- (d. Jan. 15, 1060), Islāmic military leader.

Al-Basāsīrī was born a Turkish slave, and his activities were first mentioned in about 1025. At the time, the weakened ʿAbbāsid caliphs at Baghdad, who represented Sunnī Islām, were under continuous pressure from the Faṭimid caliphs of Egypt, representing the Shīʿī sect, and the insurgent Turks commanded by Toghrïl Beg. Al-Basāsīrī, a veteran of many battles in these struggles, joined with Arab tribesmen in 1058–59 to attempt to defeat the ʿAbbāsid caliph al-Qāʾim in favour of the Fāṭimids. He was unsuccessful and was killed by the Turks in 1060. Toghrïl Beg seized Baghdad and reestablished under his control the supremacy of the ʿAbbāsids, and thereby favoured Sunnī over Shīʿī Islām.

Basava (fl. mid-12th century, South India), Hindu religious reformer, teacher, theologian, and administrator of the royal treasury of the Cālukya king Bijjala I (reigned 1156–67). Basava is the subject of the *Basava-Purāṇa*, one of the sacred texts of the Hindu Liṅgāyat sect (*see* Liṅgāyats). According to South Indian oral tradition, he was the actual founder of the Liṅgāyats, but study of Cālukya inscriptions indicates that rather than found a new sect he in fact revived an existing one. His life and doctrines were recorded in the *Basava-Purāṇa*, written by Bhīma Kavī (14th century) in the Kannada language and based on an earlier Telugu version by Pālkuriki Sōmanātha.

Basava helped to spread the Liṅgāyat sect by teaching and by dispersing funds to Liṅgāyat guilds. It was his uncle, a prime minister, who first used his influence at court to secure an appointment for his erudite relative. Basava was appointed chief of the treasury, and for several years he and his faction enjoyed a great deal of popularity. Buddhists and Jainas were apparently resentful of his power, and his enemies pointed out that he had depleted the treasury by excessive patronage of Liṅgāyat mendicants. As a result of these accusations, he fled the kingdom.

Basāvan (fl. 16th century, India), an outstanding Mughal painter, renowned as a superb colourist and as a sensitive observer of human nature. His name indicates that he may have been a member of the Ahīr, or cowherders' caste, in the region of modern Uttar Pradesh. He was most active between about 1580 and 1600, and his name appears on the margins of more than 100 paintings, most often as the designer, in collaboration with a second artist who applied the colour. A son, Manohar, became celebrated for his animal studies and portraits.

Abū-ul-Fazl ʿAllāmī, the emperor Akbar's historiographer, wrote of Basāvan: "In designing and portrait painting and colouring and painting illusionistically . . . he became unrivalled in the world." Basāvan was noted for his exploration of space, for the depth and richness of his glowing colours, and above all for his keen powers of observation and sensitive, often moving, characterizations. Among the handful of miniatures that can be definitely attributed as solely his work is an illustration of the prose and verse work *Bahārestān,* by the Persian poet Jāmī, showing a mullah, or religious leader, rebuking a dervish for pride (Bodleian Library, Oxford); and an illustration of the *Dārāb-nāmeh* ("Book of Darius") in the British Museum. Many of his compositions are found in the Jaipur *Razm-nāmeh* (the Persian name for the Indian epic the *Mahābhārata*), the Patna *Tīmūr-nāmeh* ("Book of Timur"), and the Victoria and Albert Museum's copy of Akbar's official history, the *Akbar-nāmeh.* Basāvan appears to have studied the European paintings that were brought to Akbar's court by Jesuit missionaries, though Western influence is never predominant in his work.

Bascio, Matteo da (*c.* 1495–1552): *see* Matteo (Serafini) da Bascio.

Bascom, Florence (b. July 14, 1862, Williamstown, Mass, U.S.—d. June 18, 1945, Northhampton, Mass.), educator and geological survey scientist who is considered to be the first U.S. woman geologist.

Bascom earned bachelor's and master's degrees at the University of Wisconsin, and she later received the first Ph.D. awarded to a woman at Johns Hopkins University, Baltimore (1893). Bascom then taught at Ohio State University (1893–95) before going to Bryn Mawr College, where she founded the department of geology; under her direction, it gained a national reputation. From 1896 to 1908, she was also associate editor of the *American Geologist.*

In 1896 Bascom was named assistant geologist with the U.S. Geological Survey—the first woman ever to receive that appointment. Her work on the Mid-Atlantic Piedmont region led to the contributions for which she is best known—U.S. Geological Survey Folios on Philadelphia (1909), Trenton (1909), Elkton-Wilmington (1920), Quakertown-Doylestown (1931), and Honeybrook-Phoenixville (1938). Bascom also wrote some 40 scientific articles on genetic petrography, geomorphology, and gravels.

Bascom, William R(ussell) (b. May 23, 1912, Princeton, Ill., U.S.—d. Sept. 11, 1981, San Francisco), U.S. anthropologist who served as chairman (1956–57) of the anthropology department and acting director of African studies (1953, 1957) at Northwestern University, Evanston, Ill.

Having held various official positions in British West Africa (1943–46), Bascom became a Fulbright research scholar (1950–51). In 1957 he was made professor and director of the Robert H. Lowie Museum at the University of California, Berkeley. A specialist in African folklore, Bascom, in his treatise on *Ifa Divination: Communication Between Gods and Men in West Africa* (1969), clarified the Yoruba divination system, which is orally transmitted by Ifa priests to apprentices. Other writings include *African Arts* (1967) and *The Yoruba of Southwestern Nigeria* (1969).

base, also called RADIX, in mathematics, an arbitrarily chosen number in terms of which any number can be expressed. *See* number system.

base, in chemistry, any substance that in water solution is slippery to the touch, tastes bitter, changes the colour of indicators (*e.g.,* turns red litmus paper blue), reacts with acids to form salts, and promotes certain chemical reactions (base catalysis). Examples of bases are the hydroxides of the alkali and alkaline earth metals (sodium, calcium, etc.) and the water solutions of ammonia or its organic derivatives (amines). Such substances produce hydroxide ions (OH^-) in water solutions (*see* Arrhenius theory).

Broader definitions of a base, to include substances that exhibit typical basic behaviour as pure compounds or when dissolved in solvents other than water, are given by the Brønsted–Lowry theory (*q.v.*) and the Lewis theory (*q.v.*). *Compare* acid.

base (game): *see* prisoner's base.

baseball, game played with bat, ball, and gloves between two teams of nine players each on a field on which four bases are laid out in a square. Teams alternate positions as batters and fielders, exchanging places when three members of the batting team are put out. As batters, players try to hit the ball out of reach of the fielding team and run a complete circuit around the bases for a run. The team that scores the most runs in nine innings (times at bat) wins the game.

A brief treatment of baseball follows. For full treatment, *see* MACROPAEDIA: Sports, Major Team and Individual.

Baseball is traditionally considered to be the national pastime of the United States. It was once thought to have been invented in 1839 by Abner Doubleday in Cooperstown, N.Y., but it is more likely that baseball developed from an 18th-century English game called rounders (*q.v.*). The innovation that runners be tagged with the ball rather than hit with it was among the rules adopted by Alexander J. Cartwright and a group of New York City players who established the modern game. The tag rule made possible the introduction of a smaller hard ball and a larger diamond-shaped field.

During the U.S. Civil War (1861–65), baseball became popular among the troops, and following the war professional players appeared from the ranks of amateur associations. A National Association of Professional Base Ball Players was formed in 1871 and became the National League of Professional Baseball Clubs in 1876. A rival American League was later organized, comprising cities outside of the National League. Since 1903 the winning teams of each league have played a postseason championship, known as the World Series.

The National and American leagues remain the two components of professional baseball in the United States. In the early 20th century there was a separate league for black athletes that produced many fine baseball players. Black players had briefly appeared in the short-lived American Association League during the 1880s, but it was only after Jackie Robinson began playing for the Brooklyn Dodgers in the 1940s that black players became integrated into major league baseball.

Each league now has an eastern and western division. The season extends from early April to early October and is concluded by division play-offs. Winners of these contests then contend for the World Series. Major league baseball in the United States is generally considered to be the apex of the sport as an organized profession, although the game is also played in Japan and in Latin-American countries. *See* Sporting Record: *Baseball.*

baseball, pocket-billiards game, named for the similarity in its scoring system to the American game played with bat and ball, in which players attempt to score runs by pocketing 21 consecutively numbered object balls, the number of runs scored corresponding to the total of the numbers on the balls pocketed. Players are allowed nine innings, in each of which they play until they foul or fail to score. As each player begins his innings, which are taken in succession, the balls are racked in a pyramid with the one ball at the apex, the two at the left point, the three at the right, and the nine near the centre. After the first (break) shot, players must call both the ball and the pocket aimed for before each shot.

For fouls, *see* pocket billiards.

Baseball Hall of Fame, in full NATIONAL BASEBALL HALL OF FAME AND MUSEUM, museum and honorary society at Cooperstown, N.Y., founded in 1936 and dedicated in 1939, the centennial of the supposed origination of baseball by Abner Doubleday. Players, umpires, and managers who have made outstanding contributions to the game are honoured with plaques in the hall.

Selections are made by the Baseball Writers' Association of America and a Hall of Fame Committee. Memorabilia of all eras of the game and an extensive baseball library are also housed in the hall and museum. *See* Sporting Record: *Baseball: Baseball Hall of Fame.*

Basedow, Johann Bernhard (b. Sept. 11, 1723, Hamburg—d. July 25, 1790, Magdeburg, Brandenburg), highly influential German educational reformer who advocated the use of realistic teaching methods and the introduction of nature study, physical education, and manual training into the schools. He also called for an end to physical punishment and to rote memorization in language learning.

The son of a wigmaker and a mother who was nearly mad, Basedow as a boy revolted against the harsh discipline of his school. He ran away from home and became the servant of a physician. Urged by the latter, he returned to school and in 1744 entered the University of Leipzig. Brilliant but undisciplined, he refused to study and instead wrote term papers for money, tutored wealthy students, and spent his earnings in dissipation.

In 1749 he became tutor to a difficult aristocratic child, and it was then that he began inventing games as aids to teaching. His success brought him an appointment in 1753 as a teacher of philosophy at the Danish Academy of Suro. There he fascinated his students with his lectures but alienated his colleagues by his riotous living and attacks on organized religion. Expelled from the academy, he obtained a similar post at the *Gymnasium* at Altona, but this time he failed to impress his students, who were mostly aristocratic and from conservative families.

In 1768 Basedow published a highly acclaimed monograph demanding educational reform and, more particularly, calling for the creation of a laboratory school for training teachers in his methods. Two years later, backed financially by the Prince of Anhalt, he set up a school, the famous Philanthropinum, in Dessau. The performances of his first pupils profoundly impressed observers from all over Europe, including Kant and Goethe. However, his heavy drinking and emotional outbursts drove away the better teachers and in 1784 Basedow severed his connection with the school.

Basedow was not an original thinker; his views were based on the writings of men such as Comenius, Locke, and Rousseau. Nonetheless, his sense realism was more expansive in its implications for education than that of any of his immediate predecessors in the field, and by the early 19th century sense realism had become a fundamental force in Germany's public school systems.

Basel, also spelled BASLE, French BÂLE, capital of the half canton of Basel-Stadt (with which it is virtually coextensive), northern Switzerland, on the Rhine, at the mouths of the Birs and Wiese rivers, where the French, West German, and Swiss borders meet, at the entrance to the Swiss Rhineland.

It was originally a Celtic settlement of the Rauraci tribe. The name Basilia seems first to have been applied to a Roman fortification mentioned in AD 374. At the beginning of the 5th century, the bishop of Augusta Raurica moved his see there. The city's university, the first in Switzerland, was founded in 1460 by Pope Pius II, who had been in Basel for the celebrated Ecumenical Council (1431–49). In 1501 Basel was admitted into the Swiss Confederation. With the Dutch scholar Erasmus teaching at the university (1521–29), the city became a centre of humanism and of the Reformation in Switzerland. The Counter-Reformation brought skilled workmen as refugees from other parts of Europe, and by the 18th century political power was in the hands of the trade guilds. In 1831 the rural part of the canton revolted, proclaiming independence the following year; in 1833 it was organized into the half canton of Basel-Landschaft, the city forming that of Basel-Stadt.

The Rathaus (town hall), Basel, Switz., fronted by market stalls

Photo Research International

The Rhine, bending northward, divides the city into two parts, linked by six bridges. Kleinbasel, to the north, is the Rhine port and industrial section, with the buildings of the annual Swiss Industries Fair. Grossbasel, the older commercial and cultural centre on the south bank, is dominated by the Romanesque and Gothic Münster (Protestant); consecrated in 1019, it was the cathedral until 1528 and has a monumental slab to Erasmus, who is entombed there. Other notable buildings are the late Gothic town hall (1504–21); the Church of St. Martin, the oldest religious foundation in Basel; and the former 14th-century Franciscan church, now housing the historical museum. There are three surviving medieval city gates, of which the 15th-century Spalentor (St. Paul's Gate) is one of the finest in Europe. The new university buildings were completed in 1939; the university library contains manuscripts of the religious reformers Martin Luther, Erasmus, Huldrych Zwingli, and Philipp Melanchthon and of acts of the Ecumenical Council. The public art gallery (Kunstmuseum Basel, founded 1662) has fine collections of works by Hans Holbein the Younger, Konrad Witz, and Arnold Böcklin, all of whom lived and worked in Basel; the gallery also contains works by Pablo Picasso.

An important distributing centre for foreign trade, producing one-third of the total Swiss Customs' revenue, and site of the Bank for International Settlements (1930), Basel is one of the nodal points of the railways of Europe and is an equally important river port. Regular air services operate from the international airport at Saint-Louis, in French territory 8 mi (13 km) northwest. Also a major industrial city, Basel is the centre of the Swiss chemical and pharmaceutical industries. Electrical engineering and banking and the manufacture of machinery and silk textiles are also important. The population is mainly German speaking and Protestant. Pop. (1983 est.) 179,684.

Basel, Confession of, moderate Protestant Reformation statement of Reformed doctrine composed of 12 articles. It was first drafted by John Oecolampadius, the Reformer of Basel, and was compiled in fuller form in 1532 by his successor at Basel, Oswald Myconius. In 1534 it was adopted by the Basel city authorities and two or three years later by the city of Muhlhausen in Alsace. It was used by the church of Basel into the 19th century. The Confession of Basel must be distinguished from the First Helvetic Confession, which is sometimes called the Second Confession of Basel.

Basel, Council of, a general council of the Roman Catholic Church held in Basel, Switz.; it was called by Pope Martin V a few weeks before his death in 1431 and then confirmed by Pope Eugenius IV. Meeting at a time when the prestige of the papacy had been weakened by the Great Schism (1378–1417), it was concerned with two major problems: the question of papal supremacy and the Hussite heresy. (The Hussites were followers of the Bohemian religious Reformer Jan Hus.)

The council was inaugurated on July 23, 1431; but, when the Pope's legate, Cardinal Giuliano Cesarini, arrived in September, he found few people there. In December, because of the sparse attendance, war, and the prospect of a council with the Greeks in Italy, the Pope adjourned the council. The council, however, refused to be dissolved and renewed the decree *Sacrosancta* of the Council of Constance (1414–18), which declared that a general council draws its powers immediately from God and that even the pope is subject to a council's direction. More delegates arrived at Basel, and, although the number of bishops and abbots was never large, the council proceeded to deal with the Hussites, the majority of whom were received back into communion by the Compactata of Prague in November 1436.

On Dec. 15, 1433, the Pope yielded and revoked his decree of dissolution. In the negotiations and discussions that followed, the council and the Pope could not agree, and the council gradually lost prestige. The council proposed several antipapal measures, and in 1437 Eugenius transferred the council to Ferrara, Italy, in order to consider reunion with the Greeks. Many of the bishops at Basel accepted the move to Ferrara, but several remained at Basel as a rump council. When the rump council suspended Eugenius, he excommunicated its members. The council, with only seven bishops present, then declared Eugenius deposed and in 1439 elected as his successor a layman, the duke of Savoy, Amadeus VIII, who took the name Pope Felix V. The next 10 years of this rump council are important only because the princes used it to strengthen their control over the churches in their own territories. On the death of Eugenius in 1447, his successor, Nicholas V, brought about the abdication of Felix V and ended the rump council in April 1449.

Basel-Landschaft (German), French BÂLE-CAMPAGNE, half canton, northern Switzerland, traversed by the Jura Mountains and drained by the Ergolz and Birs rivers. It was formed in 1833 by the division of Basel canton into two half cantons, or demicantons, and its early history is linked with Basel (*q.v.*) city. Its present constitution dates from 1892. Its capital is Liestal (*q.v.*). About one-third of its 165 sq mi (428 sq km) is forested. Fruit growing, dairy farming, and cattle breeding are important; textiles, metal products, and chemicals are manufactured. Watches are made in the Jura. The population is mainly German speaking and Protestant. Pop. (1983 est.) 221,203.

Basel-Stadt (German), French BÂLE-VILLE, half canton, northern Switzerland, consisting of the city of Basel (*q.v.*) and two small villages north of the Rhine. Occupying an area of 14 sq mi (37 sq km), it was formed in 1833 by the division of Basel canton into two half cantons, or demicantons. Its present constitution dates from 1889. The population is mainly German speaking and Protestant. Pop. (1983 est.) 201,242.

Basel Zoo, German ZOOLOGISCHE GARTEN BASEL, also called ZOLLI, privately owned zoological garden in Basel, Switz., noted for its outstanding work in the breeding of the Indian rhinoceros and the pygmy hippopotamus. The zoo was founded in 1874 for the purpose of exhibiting local wildlife (it opened with about 100 mammals and perhaps 400 birds, mostly European). Financial difficulties, however, forced zoo administrators to obtain exotic animals that would arouse greater public interest.

Today, the zoo maintains more than 4,000 specimens of nearly 600 species on its 13-hectare (32-acre) grounds. It uses at least three-quarters of the mammal species for breeding. Besides its excellent record for the Indian rhinoceros and pygmy hippopotamus, the zoo has had considerable success breeding the gorilla, bongo (broad-horned antelope), proboscis monkey, and Malayan tapir. The zoo works closely with local universities and emphasizes a scientific approach to the husbandry of its stock. It has also developed extensive educational programs for both schoolchildren and advanced students.

baselevel, in hydrology and geomorphology, limit below which a stream cannot erode. Upon entering a still body of water, a stream's velocity is checked and thus it loses its eroding power; hence, the approximate level of the surface of the still water body is the stream's baselevel. If a stream enters the sea, its baselevel is sea level; this is known as ultimate baselevel. If a stream enters a lake, the lake level acts as a temporary baselevel for all parts of the stream above that elevation. All continental areas tend to be eroded down to ultimate baselevel, or sea level, but uplifting of the Earth's crust and variations in sea level prevent this from happening except in rare, small areas.

Basellaceae, the Madeira-vine family of flowering plants in the order Caryophyllales, with 4 genera and 15 to 25 species of herbaceous perennial vines, distributed primarily in the New World tropics. Members of the family have fleshy, untoothed leaves, tuberous rootstocks, and red or white flowers in branched or unbranched clusters. Madeira-vine, or mignonette-vine (*Anredera cordifolia* or *Boussingaultia baselloides*), and Malabar nightshade (several species of *Basella*) are cultivated as ornamentals. Malabar spinach (*Basella alba*) is a hot weather substitute for spinach.

basenji, also called CONGO BUSH DOG, or BELGIAN CONGO DOG, ancient breed of hound dog native to central Africa, where it is used to point and retrieve and to drive quarry into a net. It is also known as the barkless dog, but it does produce a variety of sounds other than barks. A graceful animal, it is characterized by an alert expression typified by the finely wrinkled forehead, erect ears, and tightly curled tail. The short, silky coat is reddish brown, black, or black-and-tan; feet, chest, and tail tip are white. The basenji stands 16 to 17 inches (41 to 43 centimetres) and weighs 22 to 24 pounds (10 to 11 kilograms). It is characterized as a clean and gentle dog.

Basenji

Sally Anne Thompson—EB Inc.

BASF Aktiengesellschaft (German: BASF Limited-liability Company), West German chemical and plastics manufacturing company originally founded in 1865 and today operating in some 30 countries. The BASF Group produces oil and natural gas, chemicals, fertilizers, plastics, synthetic fibres, dyes and pigments, potash and salt, inks and printing accessories, electronic recording accessories, cosmetic bases, pharmaceuticals, and other related equipment and products. Headquarters are in Ludwigshafen am Rhein, W.Ger.

The company was founded in 1865 in Mannheim, as Badische Anilin- & Soda-Fabrik (Baden Aniline & Soda Factory), one of the first dyestuff manufacturers producing a full range of chemicals from basic materials to finished products. The principal founder was Friedrich Engelhorn (1821–1902), a former goldsmith and manufacturer of coal-tar dyes. In 1919 head offices moved across the Rhine to Ludwigshafen. From 1925 to 1945 the company was part of IG Farben (*q.v.*), the world's largest chemical concern; the latter was dissolved by the Allies in 1945, and Badische Anilin- & Soda-Fabrik, refounded in 1952, became one of the three successor firms. The shortened name, BASF Aktiengesellschaft, was adopted in 1973.

Bashan, country often cited in the Old Testament and later important in the Roman Empire, located mainly in the Darʿā *muḥāfaẓah* (governorate) in modern Syria. Bashan was the northernmost of the three ancient divisions of eastern Palestine, and in the Old Testament it was proverbial for its rich pastures and thick forests. In New Testament times, Bashan was one of the great granaries of the Roman Empire. Ashtaroth, Edrei, Golan, and Salchah were important Old Testament towns of Bashan. Bozrah (Roman Bostra) was an important Nabataean and Roman city.

The Israelites defeated Og, king of Bashan, at his frontier city Edrei (Num. 21:33 ff.) and assigned his land to half the tribe of Manasseh. From 84 to 81 BC Bashan was ruled by Alexander Jannaeus of Judaea, but the land to the east belonged to the Nabataeans. The Romans drove the Nabataeans southward (64 BC), and Bozrah and Salchah became the northernmost Nabataean towns. The Roman emperor Augustus made Herod the Great ruler of Bashan. In AD 106 Trajan brought the whole Nabataean kingdom under the empire in creating the province of Arabia with Bostra (Bozrah) as its capital. Bostra eventually became the ecclesiastical capital of the Hauran and a trading centre second only to Damascus. By AD 635 Damascus had fallen to the Muslims, and thereafter Bashan's prosperity declined.

bashi-bazouk, Turkish BAŞIBOZUK ("corrupted head," "leaderless"), mercenary soldier belonging to the skirmishing or irregular troops of the Ottoman Empire, notorious for their indiscipline, plundering, and brutality. Originally describing the homeless beggars who reached Istanbul from the provinces of the Ottoman Empire, the term bashi-bazouk was later applied to all Muslim subjects not members of the armed forces and so came to mean "civilian." Finally it was applied to units of irregular volunteers (both infantry and cavalry) attached to the army but under independent officers and providing their own weapons and horses. These forces became notorious for lawlessness. They appeared at the end of the 18th century and fought in Egypt against Napoleon. During the Crimean War the allied generals made fruitless attempts to discipline them. Their excesses during the Russo-Turkish War of 1877–78 at last forced the Ottoman government to abandon their use.

Bashīr Shihāb II (b. 1767, Ghazīr, Lebanon—d. 1850, Istanbul), Lebanese prince who established hegemony over Lebanon in the first half of the 19th century and ruled it under Ottoman and, later, Egyptian suzerainty from 1788 to 1840.

Although born into the princely Shihāb family, Bashīr grew up in poverty but married into great wealth. In 1788 the Lebanese *amīr* was forced to abdicate, and the local nobility selected Bashīr to fill the post. As *amīr*, Bashīr had to raise tribute for Aḥmad al-Jazzār, an official nominated by the Ottoman sultan to administer the district of Lebanon. After the death of al-Jazzār (1804), the financial demands were much less severe, and Bashīr was able to consolidate his position. With the notable exception of the Jānbulāṭs, he destroyed the power of the Druze princes, on whose support Lebanese *amīrs* had usually depended.

In 1821 Bashīr provided military support to the Pasha of Acre, who tried to draw the city of Damascus under his authority. But the Ottoman sultan declared the Pasha a rebel, and Bashīr fled to Egypt. Later, after the Pasha was pardoned, Bashīr returned to Lebanon, where, in his absence, Jānbulāṭ had plotted against him. By having Jānbulāṭ killed, Bashīr became the undisputed ruler of Lebanon.

When Muḥammad ʿAlī occupied the Fertile Crescent (exclusive of Iraq) in the 1830s, Bashīr cooperated fully with the new regime. Bashīr was concerned mainly with the military conscription and disarmament of the Druzes and the Lebanese Christians. In 1837 he armed 4,000 Christians to put down a rebellion that the Druzes had begun when threatened with conscription (hitherto Lebanese rulers had avoided direct clashes between the two groups). Two years later Bashīr tried to disarm the same Christians he had previously armed, clearly as a prelude to their conscription. The Christians were determined to resist, even if it meant cooperating with the Druzes. A Druze and Christian rebellion against Bashīr broke out in June 1840, supported by the British, who were intent on driving Muḥammad ʿAlī out of the Fertile Crescent. Bashīr could not reassert his authority, and in October he was forced into exile in Malta.

Bashkir, member of a Turkic people, numbering more than 1,370,000 in the 1980s, settled in the eastern part of the European U.S.S.R., between the Volga and the Urals, and beyond the Urals. Their main territory is the Bashkir Autonomous Soviet Socialist Republic, where they are far outnumbered by Russians.

The Bashkirs settled their land under the Mongol khanate of Kipchak from the 13th to the 15th century. In 1552 the area passed into the hands of the Russians, who founded Ufa in 1586 and thereafter began colonization of the area, dispossessing the Bashkirs. This led to many uprisings of the Bashkirs, which were severely repressed. In 1919 the Bashkir Autonomous Republic was set up, among the first such republics in the Soviet Union.

The Bashkirs were originally nomadic pastoralists, like other Turks, and their stock consisted of horses, sheep, and, to a lesser extent, cattle and goats. Mare's milk was made into koumiss, a fermented drink; sheep were raised for wool, skins, and meat; and cattle were milked. At one time the Bashkirs bred camels. During the 19th century, through pressure of Russian colonists and colonial policy, the Bashkirs settled, gave up nomadizing, and developed a primary dependence on agriculture for support. This is the case today; pastoralism plays a subordinate role in their economy.

In settling down they established themselves in fixed villages with houses of earth, sun-dried brick, or logs. They were formerly divided into patrilineal clans and tribes. These groups bore names that are remembered today but have lost most of their social significance. Formerly the Bashkirs were organized, reckoned kinship, ran their affairs, sought help, and regulated disputes within these clan and tribal structures. They do so no longer. The village and collective farm are the key social structures today. The religions of the Bashkir are Islām and the Eastern Orthodox rite.

Bashkir Autonomous Soviet Socialist Republic, also called BASHKIRIYA, administrative division of the Russian Soviet Federated Socialist Republic. Extending from the western slopes of the southern Ural Mountains in the east to the rolling hills of the Bugulma-Belebey Upland in the west, it covers an area of 55,450 sq mi (143,600 sq km).

From Mt. Yamantau, the highest peak in the southern Urals, elevation generally decreases southward and westward, with the heavily forested mountains giving way to open steppe interspersed with islands of mainly deciduous trees and to the floodplains of the Belaya (White) River. The largest tributary of the Kama and the main water route of the republic, the Belaya rises in the southern Urals, flows southwest and then northwest, and separates the mountainous east from the upland west. Cold Siberian air masses severely affect the humid, continental climate of the republic. Extreme temperatures of −49° F (45° C) in the winter and 97° F (36° C) in the summer may be recorded. The southern part of the republic suffers from the scorching and drought-producing *sukhovey* winds in late spring and summer. Rainfall varies from 16 to 20 in. (400 to 500 mm) in the steppe areas to 24 in. (600 mm) in the mountains.

Settled during the khanate of the Golden Horde by former steppe nomads, the Turkic Bashkirs, the area passed to Russia in 1552 after the overthrow of the Kazan Khanate by Tsar Ivan IV the Terrible. In 1574 the Russians founded Ufa (*q.v.*), now the capital and largest city of the republic. By the mid-18th century, copper and iron production had begun in the area, and it was made an autonomous republic in 1919.

Included in the Volga economic region of the U.S.S.R., Bashkiriya has developed both agriculturally and industrially. The republic's rich mineral resources provide many raw materials for its expanding industries. Oil and natural gas are extracted from oil fields near Ufa and near Neftekamsk in the northwest, at Belebey in the west, and at Ishimbay on the middle Belaya; iron ore and manganese are mined in the Urals, copper in the southeast, and salt near Sterlitamak (*q.v.*); and quarries provide materials for the glass and cement industries. Petroleum production, refining, and processing rank as the most important of the republic's industries. The main refineries at Ufa, Ishimbay, and Salavat are linked by a pipeline network with regional oil fields and those of the Tatar Autonomous Soviet Socialist Republic. Iron and steel centres at Beloretsk and Tirlyansky produce steel cables, wire, and sheet steel, used in the manufacture of machine tools, petroleum and mining equipment, motor engines, electric cables, telephones, and typewriters. The chemical industry uses oil and gas by-products, and the timber industry produces veneer, furniture, matches, and paper for manufacture. Large power plants are located at Ufa, Sterlitamak, Ishimbay, Kumertau, Salavat and Karmanovo.

Agriculture is most important in the Belaya Valley. The main agricultural products include rye, oats, corn (maize), flax, sugar beets, potatoes, and sunflowers; market gardening flourishes around Ufa and Sterlitamak, while stock raising (cattle, sheep, goats) predominates in the Urals. The area is famous for its breed of horses, and beekeeping, a traditional occupation, is widespread. Rail and motor roads radiate from Ufa, which also has an airport; one of the main trans-Urals railway routes passes through the capital, and branch lines from it lead to other industrial centres of the republic, to Magnitogorsk, and to the mountainous regions of Bashkiriya.

The Bashkir A.S.S.R.'s population comprises Russians, Tatars, Bashkirs, Chuvash, Mari, Ukrainians, and Mordvinians; 60 percent were urban in 1982. Sterlitamak and Salavat rank with Ufa as major cities. The republic has several institutes of higher education, more than 1,700 libraries, and a number of theatres, several of which perform in the Bashkir language. Pop. (1983 est.) 3,845,000.

Bashkirtseff, Marie, Russian in full MARIYA KONSTANTINOVNA BASHKIRTSEVA (b. Nov. 23, 1860, Gavrontsy, Poltava, Russian Empire—d. Oct. 31, 1884, Paris), Russian emigré best known for her sensitive and candidly girlish autobiography in French.

The daughter of Russian nobility, she spent her childhood wandering with her mother through Germany and on the Riviera until they settled in Paris. Her earliest artistic inclination, toward a singing career, was succeeded by an interest in art. She studied painting at the Robert-Fleury studio in Paris, and exhibited in the 1880 Salon. Just before her 24th birthday, she died of tuberculosis.

Bashkirtseff's diary, begun when she was 12, presents a frank picture of her artistic and emotional development. Unusual in its depiction of a young, gifted mind in the process of growth, the diary draws a surprisingly contemporary psychological self-portrait.

Bashō, in full MATSUO BASHŌ, pseudonym of MATSUO MUNEFUSA (b. 1644, Ueno, Iga Province, Japan—d. Nov. 28, 1694, Ōsaka), considered the greatest of the Japanese haiku

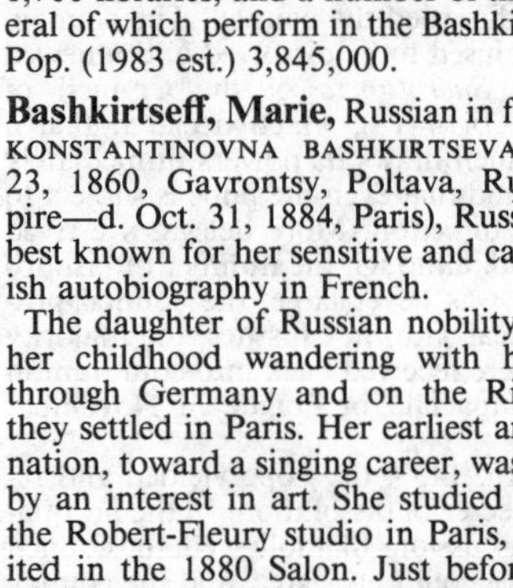

Bashō, detail of an India ink portrait by Morikawa Kyoroku; in a private collection

By courtesy of the International Society for Educational Information, Tokyo poets, who greatly enriched the meaning and tradition of the 17-syllable haiku form, embuing it with the spirit of Zen Buddhism and making it an accepted medium of artistic expression.

Interested in haiku from an early age, Bashō at first put his literary interests aside and entered the service of a local feudal lord. After his lord's death in 1666, however, Bashō abandoned his samurai (warrior) status to devote himself to poetry. Moving to the capital city of Edo (now Tokyo), he gradually acquired a reputation as a poet and critic. In 1679 he wrote his first verse in the "new style" for which he came to be known:

On a withered branch
A crow has alighted:
Nightfall in autumn.

The simple descriptive mood evoked by this statement and the comparison and contrast of two independent phenomena became the hallmark of Bashō's style. He attempted to go beyond the stale dependence on form and ephemeral allusions to current gossip that had been characteristic of haiku, which in his day had amounted to little but a popular literary pastime. Instead he insisted that the haiku must be at once unhackneyed and eternal. Following the Zen philosophy he studied, Bashō attempted to compress the meaning of the world into the simple pattern of his poetry, disclosing hidden hopes in small things and showing interdependence of all objects.

In 1684 Bashō made the first of many journeys that figure so importantly in his work. His accounts of his travels are prized not only for the haiku that record various sights along the way but also for the equally beautiful prose passages that furnish the backgrounds. *Oku no hosomichi* (1694; *The Narrow Road to the Deep North*, 1966), describing his visit to northern Japan, is one of the loveliest works of Japanese literature.

On his travels Bashō also met local poets and competed with them in composing the linked verse (*renga*), an art in which he so excelled that some critics believe his *renga* was his finest work. When Bashō began writing *renga* the link between successive verses had generally depended on a pun or play on words, but he insisted that poets must go beyond mere verbal dexterity and link their verses by "perfume," "echo," "harmony," and other delicately conceived criteria.

One term frequently used to describe Bashō's poetry is *sabi*, which means the love of the old, the faded, and the unobtrusive, a quality found in the verse

Scent of chrysanthemums . . .
And in Nara
All the ancient Buddhas.

Here the musty smell of the chrysanthemums blends with the visual image of the dusty, flaking statues in the old capital. Living a life that was in true accord with the gentle spirit of his poetry, Bashō maintained an austere, simple hermitage that contrasted with the general flamboyance of his times. On occasion he withdrew from society altogether, retiring to Fukagowa, site of his Bashō-an ("Cottage of the Plantain Tree"), a simple hut from which the poet derived his pen name. Later men, honouring both the man and his poetry, revered him as the saint of the haiku.

Basic English, simplified form of English developed between 1926 and 1930 by the British writer and linguist Charles Kay Ogden. Promoted by Winston Churchill with the support of Franklin Roosevelt in 1943, Basic English was intended for use as an international second language, but interest was not great and the language continues to be little used.

Basic English derives its vocabulary and grammar from English but reduces both to a remarkable extent: there are 850 basic vocabulary items, 600 of which are nouns and 150 of which are adjectives. The remaining 100 are operative words such as "can," "do," "across," "after," "to," "the," "all," "if," "not," and "very." Only 18 verbs are used, and these are conjugated as in standard English, but through combination with nonverbs these 18 verbs can replace about 4,000 standard English verbs (*e.g.,* "put together" for "assemble" or "combine"; "make up" for "invent"; "take pictures" for "photograph"). Other than rules for conjugating verbs, there are only a few rules concerned with formation of plurals, comparative degrees of adjectives, and use of such prefixes and suffixes as *un-, -er, -ing, -ed,* and *-ly.* Word order, compound words, and idioms are also dealt with in Ogden's books *Basic English, The Basic Words,* and *The ABC of Basic English.*

basic oxygen process, also called L–D PROCESS, method of converting iron to steel developed in Austria in 1952 that demonstrated important advantages over the Bessemer and open-hearth processes. The rapidity of the process and the low nitrogen content of steel made by using pure oxygen instead of air had long been recognized, but pure oxygen threatened destruction of the openings (tuyeres) in the furnace because of the high temperatures produced. Austrian steelmakers in Linz and Donawitz (hence the name L–D process) experimented with a pipe (lance) through which a supersonic jet of oxygen could be blown onto the surface of a mixture of molten pig iron and scrap in a vessel lined with a basic refractory such as magnesite. The lance position and oxygen velocity can be adjusted if the reaction becomes too violent.

A process in which oxygen is blown directly into the liquid metal from tuyeres in the bottom or sides of a vessel was developed in Germany and later modified in the United States. It differs from the Bessemer process in that the jet of oxygen is kept away from the refractory of the injection tuyere by a surrounding stream of fuel gas or steam.

These operations, carried out in cylindrical vessels slightly taller than they are wide, require 20 to 50 minutes to produce a batch, or heat, of 30 to 300 metric tons of steel. The oxygen combines with carbon, silicon, manganese, and part of the iron in the liquid charge to form carbon monoxide, which is carried off in the gas stream, and metal oxides that form a slag. Ferroalloys are added to adjust the composition of the steel as it is poured from the furnace.

In Japan virtually all steel is produced by the basic oxygen process, which also has been widely adopted in the steel industries of North America and Europe.

basic rock (geology): *see* acid and basic rocks.

basidiocarp, in fungi, a large sporophore, or fruiting body, in which sexually produced spores are formed on the surface of club-shaped structures (basidia). Basidiocarps are found among the members of the class Basidiomycetes (*q.v.*), with the exception of the rust and smut fungi. The largest basidiocarps include giant puffballs (*Calvatia gigantea*), which can be 1.6 metres (5¼ feet) long, 1.35 metres broad, and 24 centimetres (9½ inches) high and those of bracket fungi (*Polyporus squamosus*)—2 metres in diameter. The smallest are single cells of the yeast-like *Sporobolmyces.*

Basidiomycetes, a large and diverse class of fungi (division Mycota) including jelly, shelf, and bracket fungi; mushrooms, puffballs, and stinkhorns; and the rusts and smuts. The club-shaped spore-bearing organ (basidium) usually produces four sexual spores (basidiospores). Basidia are borne on fruiting bodies (basidiocarps), which are large and conspicuous in all but the rusts and smuts.

The common name bird's nest fungus includes species of the genera *Crucibulum, Cyathus,* and *Nidularia* of the order Nidulariales (about 60 species). The hollow fruiting body resembles a nest containing eggs (peridioles). The peridioles carry the spores when they disperse at maturity.

The 15 species of the order Exobasidiales do not form fruiting bodies. The species, parasitic on higher plants, cause leaf spots, witches'-broom (tufted growth), and galls (swellings). Particularly affected are azaleas and rhododendrons.

Jelly fungus (*Tremella mesenterica*)
Larry C. Moon—Tom Stack & Associates

Jelly fungus is the common name for several species of the cosmopolitan order Tremellales, including those of the genus *Tremella* (40 species), so-called because they have jelly-like fruiting bodies. Frequently brightly coloured (especially yellow and orange) or white, the fungi occur on decaying wood after heavy rains in late summer.

The ear fungus (*Auricularia auricula-judae*), also called Jew's ear fungus, is a brown gelatinous edible fungus found on dead tree trunks in moist weather in the autumn. One of 10 widespread *Auricularia* species, it is ear- or shell-shaped and sometimes acts as a parasite, especially on elder (*Sambucus*).

Ear fungus (*Auricularia*)
H.R. Hungerford

basidium, in fungi (division Mycota), the organ in the members of the class Basidiomycetes (*q.v.*) that bears sexually reproduced bodies called basidiospores. The basidium serves as the site of karyogamy and meiosis, functions by which sex cells fuse, exchange nuclear material, and divide to reproduce basidiospores.

Basie, Count, byname of WILLIAM BASIE (b. Aug. 21, 1904, Red Bank, N.J., U.S.—d. April 16, 1984, Hollywood, Fla.), U.S. pianist, composer, and one of the outstanding organizers of big bands in jazz history.

Basie studied music with his mother and was later influenced by the Harlem pianists James P. Johnson and Fats Waller. He began his professional career in vaudeville, in and around New York City, but developed his band style in Kansas City, Mo., during the 1930s with former members of the Bennie Moten and Walter Page bands. Though rooted in the riff style of the 1930s swing-era bands, the Basie band included soloists who reflected the styles of their own periods. In this way the band was a springboard for tenor saxophonist Lester Young, trumpeter Buck Clayton, trumpeter-composer Thad Jones, and others. Many musicians considered Basie's to be the major big band in jazz history, a model for ensemble rhythmic conception and tonal balance.

Count Basie, 1969
Ron Joy—Globe Photos

During the late 1930s the accompanying unit for the band (pianist Basie, rhythm guitarist Freddie Green, bassist Walter Page, and drummer Jo Jones) was unique in its lightness, precision, and relaxation, becoming the precursor for modern jazz accompanying styles. Basie's syncopated and spare but exquisitely timed chording, commonly termed "comping," became the model for what was expected from combo pianists in their improvised accompaniments for the next 30 years of jazz. Despite its influence on modern piano styles, Basie's solo technique had roots in the pre-swing-era style of Fats Waller, and Basie continued to display such a "stride style" in performances during the early 1980s.

Arrangements for the early Basie band were informally worked out and memorized. His hits "One O'Clock Jump" and "Jumpin' at the Woodside" were done this way. Arrangements used in the later years maintained a style developed for his 1950s bands by Neal Hefti and Ernie Wilkins. Raymond Horrick's *Count Basie and Orchestra* was published in 1957.

Basil (personal name): *see under* Vasily, except as below.

Basil, name of rulers grouped below by country and indicated by the symbol •.

Foreign-language equivalents:
Greek .... Basileios
Romanian............... Vasile
Russian .... Vasily, or Vasilii

BYZANTINE EMPIRE

• **Basil I,** byname BASIL THE MACEDONIAN (b. 826–835?, Thrace—d. Aug. 29, 886), Byzantine emperor (867–886), who founded the Macedonian dynasty and formulated the Greek legal code that later became known as the Basilica.

Basil came of a peasant family that had settled in Macedonia, perhaps of Armenian origin. He was a handsome and physically powerful man who gained employment in influential official circles in Constantinople and was fortunate enough to attract the imperial eye of the reigning emperor, Michael III. After rapid promotion he became chief equerry, then chamberlain, and finally, in 866, co-emperor with Michael. Quick to sense opposition, he forestalled the Emperor's uncle, the powerful Caesar Bardas, by murdering him (866) and followed this by killing his own patron, Michael, who had begun to show signs of withdrawing his favour (867).

From the mid-9th century onward, the Byzantines had taken the offensive in the age-long struggle between Christian and Muslim on the eastern borders of Asia Minor. Basil continued the attacks made during Michael III's reign against the Arabs and their allies, the Paulicians, and had some success. Raids across the eastern frontier into the Euphrates region continued, though Basil did not manage to take the key city of Melitene. But the dangerous heretical Paulicians on the borders of the Armenian province in Asia Minor were crushed by 872, largely owing to the efforts of Basil's son-in-law Christopher. In Cilicia, in southeast Asia Minor, the advance against the Emir of Tarsus succeeded under the gifted general Nicephorus Phocas the Elder. Though Constantinople had lost much of its former naval supremacy in the Mediterranean, it still had an effective fleet. Cyprus appears to have been regained for several years.

Basil's plans for Italy involved him in negotiations with the Frankish emperor Louis II, the great-grandson of Charlemagne. The Byzantine position in southern Italy was strengthened with the help of the Lombard duchy of Benevento, and the campaigns of Nicephorus Phocas the Elder did much to consolidate this. The region was organized into the provinces of Calabria and Langobardia. But key cities in Sicily, such as Syracuse in 878, still continued to fall into Muslim hands, an indication of the strength of Arab forces in the Mediterranean.

Another arm of Byzantine policy was the attempt to establish some measure of control over the Slavs in the Balkans. Closely allied to this was the delicate question of ecclesiastical relations between Constantinople and Rome.

Basil I, coin, 9th century; in the British Museum
By courtesy of the trustees of the British Museum

During Basil I's reign, the young Bulgar state accepted the ecclesiastical jurisdiction of Constantinople (870). This had significant results both for the Balkan principalities and for the Orthodox Church, as well as greatly strengthening Byzantine influence in the south Slav world. Basil had inherited a quarrel between Photius and Ignatius as to which was to be patriarch of Constantinople. This had international implications, since appeals had been made to Rome. Immediately on his accession, Basil attempted to win support at home and to conciliate Rome by reinstating the deposed patriarch Ignatius and excommunicating Photius. Eventually, Photius was restored by Basil on the death of Ignatius (877) and recognized by Rome in 879. Contrary to the belief that used to be held, no "second schism" occurred. Basil successfully resolved the tension between liberal and strict Byzantine churchmen and managed to maintain a show of peace between East and West despite Rome's displeasure at the marked extension of imperial influence in the new Balkan principalities.

Toward the end of his life, Basil seemed to suffer fits of derangement, and he was cruelly biassed against his son Leo. Basil died on the hunting field. The 11th-century historian Psellus wrote of his dynasty as "more blessed by God than any other family known to me, though rooted in murder and bloodshed." But Macedonian historians were understandably biassed in favour of the existing dynasty, to the detriment of the rulers it had supplanted. Recent historical research has raised the stature of Basil's predecessor, Michael III, and his regents. It is now generally agreed that the "new age" in Byzantine history began with Michael III in 842 and not with the Macedonian dynasty in 867. Basil's policies were largely determined, both at home and abroad, by factors not of his own making.

(J.M.H.)

BIBLIOGRAPHY. A good short outline of Byzantine history is G. Ostrogorsky, *Geschichte des byzantinischen Staates,* 3rd ed. (1963; *History of the Byzantine State,* 2nd ed., 1968). Views on Basil I, particularly in relation to his predecessor, Michael III, are presented in H. Gregorie, "The Amorians and Macedonians 842–1025," *Cambridge Medieval History,* new ed., 4:105–192 (1966).

• **Basil II,** byname BASIL BULGAROCTONUS (Greek: Basil, Slayer of the Bulgars) (b. 957/958—d. Dec. 15, 1025), Byzantine emperor (976–1025), who extended imperial rule in the Balkans (notably Bulgaria), Mesopotamia, Georgia, and Armenia and increased his domestic authority by attacking the powerful landed interests of the military aristocracy and of the church.

The reign of Basil II, widely acknowledged to be one of the outstanding Byzantine emperors, admirably illustrates both the strength and the weakness of the Byzantine system of government. His indomitable and forceful personality and his shrewd statesmanship were offset by the inherent weakness of an imperial autocracy that depended so much on the character of the ruler.

Basil was the son of Romanus II and Theophano and was crowned co-emperor with his brother Constantine in 960, but as minors both he and his brother remained in the background. After their father's death in 963, the government was effectively undertaken by the senior military emperors, first by Nicephorus II Phocas, their stepfather, and then by John I Tzimisces. On the latter's death (976) the powerful great-uncle of Basil II, the eunuch Basil the chamberlain, took control. His authority—and that of Basil II—was challenged by two generals who coveted the position of senior emperor. Both related to emperors, they belonged to powerful landed families and commanded outside support from Georgia and from the Caliph in Baghdad. After a prolonged struggle both were defeated by 989, though only with the help of Russians under Vladimir of Kiev, who was rewarded with the hand of Basil II's sister Anna on condition that the Kievan state adopted Christianity. Certain Russian soldiers remained in Basil II's service, forming the famous imperial Varangian guard. Eventually, Basil II asserted his claim to sole authority by ruthlessly eliminating the dominating grand chamberlain, who was exiled in 985.

Basil II aimed solely at the extension and consolidation of imperial authority at home and abroad. The main fields of external conflict were in Syria, Armenia, and Georgia on the eastern front, in the Balkans, and in southern Italy. He maintained the Byzantine position in Syria against aggression stirred up by the Fāṭimid dynasty in Egypt and on occasion made forced marches from Constantinople across Asia Minor to relieve Antioch. By aggression and by diplomacy he secured land from Georgia and from Armenia, with the promise of more to come on the death of the Armenian ruler. He is, however, best known for his persistent and ultimately successful campaigns against a revived Bulgarian kingdom under its tsar Samuel. This ruler centred his activities in Macedonia and established his hegemony in the west Balkans. From 986 until 1014 there was warfare between Byzantium and Bulgaria, interrupted from time to time by Basil II's intermittent expeditions to settle crises on the eastern front. Basil II enlisted Venetian help in protecting the Dalmatian coast and Adriatic waters from Bulgarian aggression. Year by year he slowly penetrated into Samuel's territory, campaigning in winter as well as summer. Finally, holding northern and central Bulgaria, he advanced toward Samuel's capital, Ochrida, and won the crushing victory that gave him his byname, "Slayer of the Bulgars." It was then that he blinded the whole Bulgarian army, leaving one eye to each 100th man, so that the soldiers might be led back to their tsar (who died of shock shortly after seeing this terrible spectacle). Thus the revived Bulgarian kingdom was incorporated into the Byzantine Empire. Basil II then looked further west and planned to strengthen Byzantine control in southern Italy and to regain Sicily from the Arabs. He attempted to establish a Greek pope in Rome and to unite in marriage the German (though by birth half Byzantine) ruler Otto III with Basil II's favourite niece, Zoe. Both schemes failed, but he was more successful in southern Italy, where order was restored, and at his death preparations were being made for the reconquest of Sicily.

The ruthlessness and tenacity that served Basil II in his military and diplomatic activities were displayed in his domestic policy as well. Its keynote was the strengthening of imperial authority by striking at his overpowerful subjects, particularly the military families who ruled like princes in Asia Minor. The by-product of this policy was the imperial protection of the small farmers, some of whom owed military service to the crown and paid taxes to the central exchequer. Title to land was rigorously inspected, and vast estates were arbitrarily confiscated. Thus, in spite of his costly wars, Basil left a full treasury, some of it stored in specially constructed underground chambers.

Both in near-contemporary history and in manuscript illustrations, Basil II is pictured as a short, well-proportioned figure, with brilliant light-blue eyes, a round face, and full, bushy whiskers, which he would twirl in his fingers when angry or while giving an audience. He dressed plainly and even when wearing the purple chose only a dark hue. An abrupt speaker, he scorned rhetoric yet was capable of wit. He has been described as mean, austere, and irascible, spending most of his time as though he were a soldier on guard. He knew only too well the danger of any relaxation. He showed no obvious interest in learning, but he did apparently commission works of religious art, and he had churches and monasteries rebuilt or completed in Boeotia and in Athens, though this may be accounted for by conventional piety. He seems never to have married or had children. On his death there was no able military aristocrat or other leader to take the situation in hand, and thus Basil II's work was rapidly undone. (J.M.H.)

BIBLIOGRAPHY. G. Schlumberger, *L'Épopée Byzantine*, vol. 1–2 (1896–1900), the classic narrative account, now in need of some revision; H. Gregoire, "The Amorians and Macedonians 842–1025," *Cambridge Medieval History*, new ed., vol. 4, pt. 1, pp. 105–192 (1966); G. Ostrogorsky, *Geschichte des byzantinischen Staates*, 3rd ed. (1963; *History of the Byzantine State*, 2nd ed., 1968), a good short outline with bibliography.

MOLDAVIA

• **Basil,** byname BASIL THE WOLF, Romanian VASILE LUPU (b. *c.* 1595—d. 1661, Constantinople), ambitious and enterprising prince of Moldavia (1634–53) who introduced the first written laws and printing press to his principality.

Albanian in origin, Basil acceded to the throne of Moldavia in the spring of 1634. He intrigued throughout his reign to acquire the Walachian throne as well, and in 1637 and 1639 led unsuccessful expeditions against the ruling prince of Walachia, Matthew Basarab. Basil's military expenses and payments to his Turkish overlords taxed his subjects; but his rule also brought important cultural improvements through the creation of Greek monastic schools, the first codification of Moldavian civil and criminal law (1646), and the establishment of the first printing press in the country at Iaşi. In 1653 he was briefly evicted from his throne by Matthew Basarab and the Prince of Transylvania, but regained his crown with the help of the cossacks of Bohdan Chmielnicki, hetman of the Ukraine and also his son-in-law. He subsequently pressed into Walachia, but was decisively beaten at Vinta (July 1653). Deposed by his own boyars, he fled to the Khan of the Tatars, and thence to Constantinople, where he died in prison. His reign was one of the longest in the history of Moldavia.

RUSSIA

• **Basil I–IV:** *see* Vasily I–IV.

basil, also called SWEET BASIL, spice consisting of the dried leaves of *Ocimum basilicum,*

Basil (*Ocimum basilicum*)
Walter Chandoha

an annual herb of the family Lamiaceae (Labiatae) native to India and Iran. A number of varieties are used in commerce including the small-leaf common basil, the larger leaf Italian basil, and the large lettuce-leaf basil. The dried large-leaf varieties have a fragrant aroma faintly reminiscent of anise, and a warm, sweet, aromatic, mildly pungent flavour. The dried leaves of the common basil are less fragrant and more pungent in flavour. Basil is widely grown as a kitchen herb and used fresh or dried to flavour meats, fish, salads, and sauces. Tea made from basil leaves is a stimulant. The essential oil content is 0.1 percent, the principal components of which are methyl chavicol and *d*-linalool.

The heart-shaped basil leaf is a symbol of love in Italy.

Basil OF ANCYRA (d. *c.* 364, Illyria), Greek theologian and bishop of Ancyra (now Ankara, Tur.) whose attempt to mediate a controversy in the Eastern Church was rejected by the heretical faction and brought about his exile.

Basil, a physician, was nominated bishop in 336 by the Semi-Arian party (*see* Semi-Arianism). In a *Synodal Letter* sent to all bishops summarizing the conclusions of a local council in Ancyra (358), Basil's clear enunciation of the Semi-Arian viewpoint established him as that group's intellectual leader.

Despite the efforts of Basil and his colleagues, the Arians (*see* Arianism) gained the support of the emperor Constantius II (ruled 337–361) and repudiated Basil's formula at two councils convened in 359. Basil's party was compelled by Constantius II in December 359 to sign the heretical Arian formula of Ariminum. The Arians, led by Bishop Acacius of Caesarea, met in synod at Constantinople in 360, deposed Basil, and banished him to Illyria.

Before his death, however, Basil recanted his signature of the Arian formula extorted from him by the Emperor. The orthodox party, represented by Athanasius of Alexandria and Hilary of Poitiers, acknowledged that Basil's formula approximated their own and urged others to seek a consensus with him.

Among Basil's other writings is a treatise on virginity, which suggests that this virtue can be secured on the basis of bodily harmony fostered by an ascetical life.

Basil THE BLIND: *see* Vasily II.

Basil THE CHAMBERLAIN (d. 985), eunuch minister of the Byzantine Macedonian dynasty.

After the death of the emperor John I, Basil the Chamberlain controlled the throne for his two grandnephews and co-emperors Constantine and Basil II. After engineering his uncle's downfall, Basil II was finally able to assume his own independent rule.

Basil THE GREAT, SAINT, Latin BASILIUS (b. *c.* AD 329, Caesarea Mazaca, Cappadocia—d. Jan. 1, 379, Caesarea; Western feast day January 2; Eastern feast day January 1), early Church Father who defended the orthodox faith against the heretical Arians. As bishop of Caesarea he wrote several works on monasticism, theology, and canon law. He was declared a saint soon after his death.

Early life and ecclesiastical career. Basil was born of a distinguished family of Caesarea, the capital of Cappadocia, which was a province of Asia Minor of special importance

Saint Basil, detail of a mosaic, 12th century; in the Palatine Chapel, Palermo
Alinari—Art Resource

in the 4th century due to its position on the military road between Constantinople and Antioch. The family had been Christian since the days of the persecutions of Christians, which ended early in the 4th century. One of Basil's uncles was a bishop, as later were two of his brothers (Gregory and Peter of Sebaste). He received a literary education, however, which would have fitted him to follow in his father's footsteps as lawyer and orator. He studied at Caesarea and Constantinople and, finally (*c.* 351–356), at Athens, where he developed his friendship with Gregory of Nazianzus. On returning home he began a secular career, but the influence of his pious sister Macrina, later a nun and abbess, confirmed his earlier inclination to the ascetic life. With a group of friends, he established a monastic settlement on the family estate at Annesi in Pontus. In 357 he made an extensive tour of the monasteries of Egypt, and in 360 he assisted the Cappadocian bishops at a synod at Constantinople. He had been distressed by the general acceptance of the Arian Creed of the Council of Ariminum the previous year and especially by the fact that his own bishop, Dianius of Caesarea, had supported it. Shortly before the death of Dianius (362), Basil was reconciled to him and later was ordained presbyter (priest) to assist Dianius' successor, the new convert Eusebius. Basil's abilities and prestige, as well as Eusebius' dislike of asceticism, led to tension between them, and Basil withdrew to Annesi. In 365 he was called back to Caesarea, when the church was threatened by the Arian emperor Valens. His theological and ecclesiastical policy thereafter aimed to unite against Arianism the former semi-Arians and the supporters of Nicaea under the formula "three persons (*hypostases*) in one substance (*ousia*)," thus preserving both unity and the necessary distinctions in the theological concept of the godhead. On Eusebius' death in 370, Basil became his successor, although he was opposed by some of the other bishops in the province.

Anti-Arian activities. As bishop of Caesarea, Basil was metropolitan (ecclesiastical primate of a province) of Cappadocia, and his own diocese covered the great estates of eastern Cappadocia, where he was assisted by a number of "country bishops" (*chorepiscopi*). He also founded charitable institutions to aid the poor, the ill, and travellers. When Valens passed through Caesarea in 371, Basil dramatically defied his demand for submission. But in 372 Valens divided the province, and Basil considered this a personal attack, since Anthimus of Tyana thus became metropolitan for the cities of western Cappadocia. Basil countered by installing supporters in some of the border towns—Gregory of Nazianzus at Sasima and his own brother Gregory at Nyssa. This tactic was only partially successful, but Basil escaped the attacks that Valens launched on orthodox bishops elsewhere. Meanwhile, Basil tried to secure general support for the former semi-Arian Meletius as bishop of Antioch (one of the five major patriarchates of the early church), against Paulinus, the leader of the strict Nicene minority, since he feared that the extreme Nicenes at this point were lapsing into Sabellianism, a heresy exaggerating the oneness of God. During Basil's lifetime, however, this was prevented by the recognition of Paulinus by the bishops of Alexandria and—in spite of a series of negotiations—after 375 by Pope Damasus of Rome.

Basil's numerous and influential writings stemmed from his practical concerns as monk, pastor, and church leader. The *Longer Rules* and *Shorter Rules* (for monasteries) and other ascetic writings distill the experience that began at Annesi and continued in his supervision of the monasteries of Cappadocia: they were to exert strong influence on the monastic life of Eastern Christianity. A notable feature is Basil's strong preference for the monastic life, in which brotherly love can be practiced, as opposed to that of the hermit. Basil's preserved sermons deal mainly with ethical and social problems. One of the best known, the *Address to Young Men,* defends the study of pagan literature by Christians (Basil himself made considerable critical use of Greek philosophical thought). In the *Hexaëmeron* ("Six Days"), nine Lenten sermons on the days of creation, Basil speaks of the varied beauty of the world as reflecting the splendour of God. *Against Eunomius* defends the deity of the Son against an extreme Arian thinker, and *On the Holy Spirit* expounds the deity of the spirit implied in the church's tradition, though not previously formally defined. Basil is most characteristically revealed in his letters, of which more than 300 are preserved. Many deal with daily activities; others are, in effect, short treatises on theology or ethics; several of his *Canonical Epistles,* decisions on points of discipline, have become part of the canon law of the Eastern Orthodox Church. The extent of Basil's actual contribution to the magnificent series of eucharistic prayers known as the *Liturgy of St. Basil* is uncertain. But at least the central prayer of consecration (setting apart the bread and wine) reflects his spirit and was probably in use at Caesarea in his own lifetime.

Basil's health was poor, perhaps because of the rigours of his ascetic life. He died soon after Valens' death in the Battle of Adrianople had opened the way for the victory of Basil's cause. Vigorous and firm and sure of his own position, in his own time he seems to have been admired rather than loved, even by his intimates. But he was widely mourned and was soon numbered among the saints.

(E.R.Ha.)

BIBLIOGRAPHY. The Benedictine edition of Basil's works is reprinted in J.P. Migne (ed.), *Patrologia Graeca,* vol. 29–32 (1857). There are modern editions in *Sources Chrétiennes* of *On the Holy Spirit,* 2nd ed. by B. Pruche, vol. 17 (1968); and the *Hexaëmeron,* 2nd ed. by S. Giet, vol. 26 (1968), with French translations; and of the *Letters* and *Address to Young Men* in the *Loeb Classical Library;* the *Hexaëmeron* and *Letters* are in *Nicene and Post-Nicene Fathers,* ser. 2, vol. 8 (1895), trans. by Blomfield Jackson. *The Ascetic Works* was translated by W.K.L. Clarke (1925).

The basic source for the life of St. Basil is the eulogy by Gregory of Nazianzus (Oration 43). E. Venables, "Basilius of Caesarea," in *Dictionary of Christian Biography,* vol. 1, pp. 282–297 (1877), is still important. Among modern sketches, see J. Quasten, "Basil the Great," in *Patrology,* vol. 3, pp. 204–235 (1960), with bibliography; J.W.C. Wand in *Doctors and Councils,* pp. 31–46 (1962); and Hans von Campenhausen in *The Fathers of the Greek Church,* pp. 84–100 (1963).

Basil THE MACEDONIAN: *see* Basil I *under* Basil (Byzantine Empire).

Basil THE WOLF: *see* Basil *under* Basil (Moldavia).

Basil, Colonel W. de, original name VASILY GRIGORIEVICH VOSKRESENSKY (b. 1888, Kaunas, Lithuania, Russian Empire—d. July 27, 1951, Paris), Russian impresario who in 1932 became codirector with René Blum of the Ballet Russe de Monte Carlo. He lost the celebrated premier danseur Léonide Massine and several other dancers to Blum, who, with a U.S. sponsoring agency (World Art), reorganized the Ballet Russe de Monte Carlo with Massine as director. De Basil then formed a troupe with dancers who did not go over to Massine and called it the Original Ballet Russe, managing it until it dispersed (1948).

Basil, Liturgy of Saint, a eucharistic service used by Eastern Orthodox and Eastern-rite Catholic churches 10 times during the year: January 1 (the feast of St. Basil), the first five Sundays in Lent, Holy Thursday, Holy Saturday, Christmas Eve, and the Eve of the Epiphany (unless Christmas or the Epiphany falls on Sunday or Monday).

The Liturgy of St. Basil, of which two versions—the Alexandrian and the somewhat longer Byzantine—are extant, was probably authored, in part at least, by St. Basil himself. Except for the anaphora (the central part of the liturgy), it is identical with the Liturgy of St. John Chrysostom, which is a shortened form in daily use.

Basilan, island, province, and chartered city, southern Philippines, in the Celebes Sea. Basilan island lies 5 mi (8 km) off the southern tip of the Zamboanga Peninsula of Mindanao, across the Basilan Strait. It is the largest (495 sq mi [1,282 sq km]) and northernmost island of the Sulu Archipelago. Most of the island consists of rugged or rolling forested uplands with several volcanic peaks exceeding heights of 2,000 ft (600 m). Short streams provide a roughly radial pattern of drainage. Since about 1900, lumber mills have operated in the tropical rain forest. The island's gentle, rolling slopes and its valleys have fertile soils and are largely under plantation agriculture. Rubber, the primary crop, is processed on the plantations and sold to Manila factories.

The inhabitants are Yakans, descendants of early Papuan settlers who were converted to Islām during the 14th century. Their culture includes many non-Muslim beliefs and customs. Unlike the Muslims of Jolo and Zamboanga, they are not beach dwellers and fishermen but live on higher lands and cultivate coconuts, rice, corn (maize), abaca, and coffee. In the

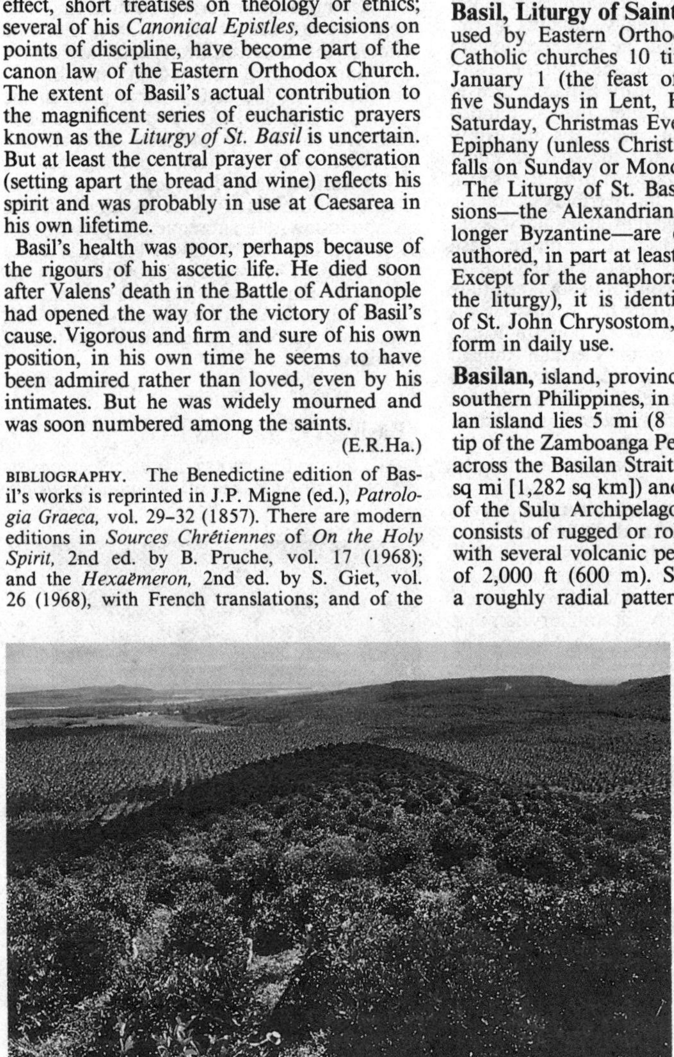

Coffee plantation, Basilan Island, Philippines
Ted Spiegel—Rapho/Photo Researchers

20th century, as more land was cleared by timber extraction, Christian Filipinos, mainly from the Visayan Islands, migrated to Basilan in considerable numbers. The University of the Philippines (at Diliman, Quezon City) owns a 10,000-ac (4,000-ha) land grant on the northern coast.

Basilan province has an area of 512 sq mi. In addition to Basilan Island, it includes several nearby small isles. Until 1973 the area was a part of Zamboanga del Sur province. The provincial capital is Isabela (also called Basilan City). Other important towns include Lamitan, in the north of Basilan Island, and Maluso, in the west. The province was one of the centres of the 1972 Muslim rebellion in southern Mindanao.

Basilan City is the headquarters of the Menzi Agricultural Corporation, which operates harvesting and processing facilities for the surrounding agricultural region. Important products include rubber latex, palm oil, and coffee. Pop. (1980) province, 201,407; Isabela mun., 49,891.

Articles are alphabetized word by word, not letter by letter

Basildon, district, county of Essex, England, about 25 mi (40 km) east of central London. After World War I many Londoners settled in the Billericay area of Essex, forming what became known as "rural slum" villages. The district, with an area of 43 sq mi (111 sq km), includes Billericay and Wickford as well as the new town of Basildon, so designated in 1949. Main industries are light engineering, chemicals, clothing, and printing. Pop. (1982 est.) 154,800.

Basildon, new town, Basildon district, county of Essex, England. Basildon new town was established in 1949. It was one of eight established 20 to 30 mi (32 to 48 km) from central London to help alleviate the city's acute post-World War II housing shortage. More than 230 factories have been built and nearly 400 shops, with more than 200 in the town centre. An ultimate population of 130,000 is planned. Basildon district occupies 43 sq mi (110 sq km). Pop. (1981 prelim.) new town, 93,913.

Basile, Giambattista (b. *c.* 1575, Naples—d. Feb. 23, 1632, Giugliano, Campania), Neapolitan soldier, public official, poet, and short-story writer whose *Lo cunto de li cunti,* 50 zestful tales written in Neapolitan, was one of the earliest such collections based on folktales and served as an important source both for the later fairy-tale writers Charles Perrault in France in the 17th century and the brothers Grimm in Germany in the 19th century, and for the Italian commedia dell'arte dramatist Carlo Gozzi in the 18th century.

Basile was a soldier as a young man and began a career in government after moving to Naples in 1608. He later was part of the Mantuan court of Ferdinando Gonzaga, and then moved on to become governor, successively, of several small Italian states.

Basile was most at home in Naples, and during his career he became fascinated with the folklore, customs, literature, music, and dialect of the Neapolitan people. He began serious study of things Neapolitan and began to collect fairy tales and folktales, setting them down in a lively Neapolitan style with much local flavour and all the ornament and flamboyance of his influential contemporary Giambattista Marino.

Basile's collection, *Lo cunto de li cunti* (1634; "The Story of Stories"; best Italian translation B. Croce, 1925; best English translation N.B. Penzer, *The Pentamerone,* 2 vol., 1932), was published posthumously under the anagrammatic pseudonym Gian Alesio Abbattutis and referred to by its first editor as *Il pentamerone* because of the similarity of its framework to that of Boccaccio's *Decameron.*

In *Lo cunto de li cunti,* a prince and his wife, a slave who has been posing as a princess, are entertained for 5 days by 10 women, who tell them 50 stories, among which are the familiar tales of Puss in Boots, Rapunzel, Cinderella, Snow White and Rose Red, the Three Oranges, and Beauty and the Beast. On the last day of storytelling, the real princess appears, tells her story, and ousts the deceptive slave.

Basile also wrote Italian and Spanish verse. *Le muse napolitane* (1635) was a series of satirical verse dialogues on Neapolitan mores.

Basileios (Greek personal name): *see under* Basil.

Basilian, member of any of several Christian monastic communities of the Byzantine Rite, so named because they claim St. Basil the Great as their spiritual father. (The Basilians is also the name of a Latin-rite congregation founded in France in 1822 and later active mainly in Canada, its members devoting themselves to the education of youth.)

St. Basil, theologian and archbishop of Caesarea in Cappadocia (modern Turkey), set down his monastic rule between 358 and 364, and possibly was influenced by the monasteries founded by St. Pachomius of the Thebaid. St. Basil's rule was simple but strict and called for his followers to live a life in common (cenobitism), in contrast to the followers of both St. Anthony of Egypt and St. Pachomius. Basil carefully avoided the extreme asceticism of the desert hermits. His rule, found in two forms, *Regulae fusius tractatae* (55 items) and *Regulae brevius tractatae* (313 items), follows a question-and-answer form and encourages ascetic practices as a means to the perfect service of God. The rule calls for community living under obedience with hours of liturgical prayer and with manual as well as mental work. Basil's rule implied vows of chastity and poverty, similar to those set down in Western monasticism at a later time. Basil also called for children to be trained in schools attached to the monastery, along with opportunities for testing the students' possible vocations to the religious life. The monks also were advised to take care of the poor. St. Theodore of Studios revised the rule of Basil in the 9th century.

Over the centuries, the Rule of St. Basil has wielded enormous influence in the Byzantine world and is comparable to St. Benedict's influence in Western monasticism. Among the best known Basilians are Cyril and Methodius, the apostles to the Slavic nations; St. John Damascene; and Maximus Confessor.

There are five major branches of the Order of St. Basil in the Byzantine Rite: (1) Grottaferrata in the Italo-Albanian Rite was restored in 1880 in its Greek traditions and controls monasteries in southern Italy and Sicily. Grottaferrata was once famous for creating religious art and illumination and for copying manuscripts. (2) St. Josaphat in the Ukrainian and Romanian Rite was introduced in Kiev in 1072 by St. Theodosius and became the model for the Ukrainian, White Russian, and Russian monasteries. In the 17th and 18th centuries, its special interest was the union of the Ukrainian and Roman churches. Reformed by Pope Leo XIII, these Basilians spread into Galicia, Ruthenia, Yugoslavia, and Romania and then followed immigrants into the United States, Canada, and Latin America. The present name dates from 1932. (3) St. Savior in the Melchite Rite was founded by the Archbishop of Tyre and Sidon in 1684 and placed under the rule of Basil in 1743. Members engaged in parochial ministry in Lebanon, Palestine, Egypt, and the city of Damascus prior to 1832. The Vatican approved their constitution in 1955, and they now have foundations in the United States as well. (4) The Basilian Order of St. John the Baptist, also known as the Order of Suwayr, or the Baladites, was founded in 1712 and added the vow of humility to the usual vows. Its motherhouse is in Lebanon, and the Vatican set its canonical status in 1955. (5) The Basilian Order of Aleppo separated from the preceding group in 1829 and was approved by the Vatican in 1832, with headquarters in Lebanon.

basilica, in the Roman Catholic and Greek Orthodox churches, a canonical title of honour given to church buildings that are distinguished either by their antiquity or by their role as international centres of worship because of their association with a major saint, an important historical event, or, in the Orthodox Church, a national patriarch. The title gives the church certain privileges, principally the right to reserve its high altar for the pope, a cardinal, or a patriarch, and special penitential privileges that remove the basilica from local geographical jurisdiction and give it international status.

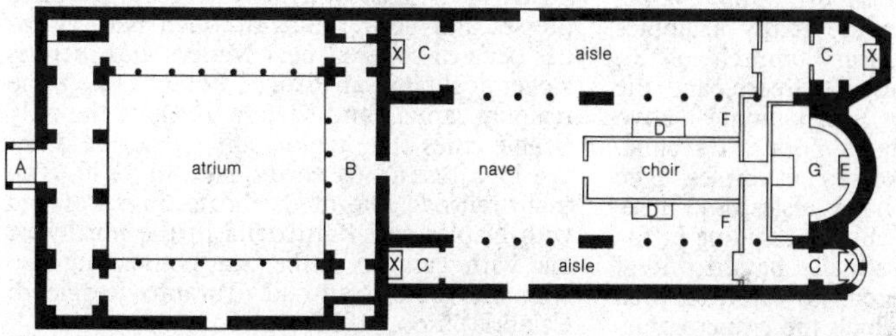

Plan of the basilican church of S. Clemente, Rome (1099–1108): (A) entrance, (B) narthex, (C) chapels, (D) ambos, (E) cathedra, (F) cancelli, (G) apse, (X) altars

From M.S. Briggs, *Everyman's Concise Encyclopaedia of Architecture;* E.P. Dutton & Co., Inc., and J.M. Dent Ltd.

In architecture, "basilica" in its earliest usage designated any number of large roofed public buildings in ancient Rome and pre-Christian Italy, markets, courthouses, covered promenades, and meeting halls. Gradually, however, the word became limited to buildings of a more or less definite form: rectangular walled structures with an open hall extending from end to end, usually flanked by side aisles set off by colonnades (in large buildings often running entirely around the central area), and with a raised platform at one or both ends. During the 1st century BC, when basilicas were increasingly used for judicial purposes, the raised platform became enclosed by an apse, or semicircular half-domed protrusion of the end wall, to accommodate the magistrate. The foundations of a number of very large basilicas have been excavated at several sites in Italy. The most impressive remains, however, are those of a basilica begun by Emperor Maxentius in the early 4th century AD in Rome and finished by his successor, Constantine the Great.

One type of smaller secular basilica had side aisles extending the length of the sides only and an apse at one end. It was this type that the early Christians adopted for their churches, possibly because similar halls in large private houses had been used for Christian worship before the religion was officially recognized by the Roman emperor Constantine in 313. Constantine himself commissioned the construction of three enormous Christian basilicas in Rome: St. Peter's, S. Paolo Fuori le Mura, and S. Giovanni in Laterano. He added a new feature, the transept, a lateral aisle crossing the nave just before the apse, and thus created the cross-shaped plan that became standard for churches in western Europe throughout the Middle Ages.

In the typical Early Christian basilica, the columns separating the nave from the side aisles carried either arches or an entablature (straight band of molding), and above these was a blank wall supporting the timber roof of the nave. Because the nave rose considerably higher than the side aisles, the wall that supported the nave roof stood above the level of the side aisle roofs and could thus be pierced at the top with windows to light the centre of the church. This high nave wall is called the clerestory. The side aisles themselves were either single or double. The apse opened from the nave by a great arch known as the triumphal arch. In some cases, if there was a transept, another triumphal arch separated the transept from the nave. At the entrance end a narthex, or vestibule, extended the entire width of the nave and aisles. This narthex was commonly fronted by a colonnade and, in many cases, opened onto a court surrounded by either colonnades or arcades. After the 10th century a round or square campanile, or bell tower, was added.

The exterior of such a building was simple and was rarely decorated. The simplicity of the interior, however, provided surfaces suitable for elaborate ornamentation.

Although the basilica is primarily characteristic of Rome, there are many examples elsewhere. The 5th-century church of St. Demetrius at Thessalonica, Greece, and the 6th-century churches of S. Apollinare Nuovo and S. Apollinare in Classe, both at Ravenna, are particularly noteworthy examples. The basilica plan, with its nave, aisles, and apse, remained the basis for church building in the Western Church. It gradually passed out of use in the Eastern Church, however, eclipsed by the radial plan on which the emperor Justinian I constructed the domed cathedral of Hagia Sophia at Constantinople.

Basilica (from Greek *basilikos,* "imperial"), 9th-century Byzantine code of law initiated by the emperor Basil I and completed after the accession of his son Leo VI the Wise.

The Justinian code of the 6th century, augmented by later imperial ordinances, had been the chief law source for the Roman world but was marred by much internal repetitiveness and inconsistency. Conflicting interpretations on how to select and apply elements of Justinian's works had contributed to uncertainty among imperial judges. Emperors Basil and Leo therefore had a commission of lawyers reexamine the code in order to abridge it, to cast out obsolescent, conflicting, and superfluous items, and to arrange the resultant provisions into orderly single titles. Basil's jurists apparently produced 40 books, which were enlarged to 60 under Leo.

The Basilica was written in Greek and was as much a collection of canon law as of civil and public law. It was far more systematically arranged than Justinian's code and comprised a single integrated work, unlike Justinian's four works, in which one subject might be treated in various places. The Basilica became the foundation of Byzantine jurisprudence.

In the 12th century an index for the Basilica was compiled. Because only about two-thirds of the Basilica survives, the index aids in rounding out knowledge of the contents. *See also* Justinian, Code of.

Basilica of Constantine (Rome): *see* Maxentius, Basilica of.

Basilicata, region, southern Italy, along the Golfo di Taranto (Gulf of Taranto), consisting of the provinces of Potenza and Matera, with a total area of 3,858 sq mi (9,992 sq km). Bounded by the regions of Puglia (north and east), Calabria (south), and Campania (west), Basilicata is roughly divided into a western mountainous section, dominated by the Appennino Lucano, and an eastern section of low hills and wide valleys, while along the Ionian Sea the sand and clay hills overlook narrow coastal plains. The extinct volcano of Monte Vulture (4,350 ft [1,326 m]) stands isolated from the Apennines in the north.

Known in ancient times as Lucania (*q.v.*), the region was under Lombard rule in the early Middle Ages. It was controlled by the dukes of Benevento and then by the princes of Salerno. After an interval of Byzantine control, the Normans took over and made Melfi (*q.v.*) the capital of one of their dominions. Until the fall of the Swabian Hohenstaufens (1254), Basilicata played a significant part in the affairs of southern Italy; afterward, passing through Angevin and Spanish hands, it followed the variable fortunes of the Kingdom of Naples until united with Italy in 1860. The region was coextensive with Potenza province until the establishment of Matera province in 1927.

The mainstay of the economy is agriculture, but yields are generally low because of poor soil and the rugged terrain. Crops include wheat, rye, grapes, and olives; sheep, goats, pigs, and an increasing number of beef and dairy cattle are raised. New crops introduced in the eastern and coastal areas include tobacco, vegetables, sugar beets, and flowers. Industry is virtually nonexistent except for olive presses and flour mills, although natural gas has been discovered near Matera and there is a chemical plant at Pisticci. Potenza (*q.v.*), the regional capital, and Matera (*q.v.*) are the only sizable cities. The region suffered severe damage in a disastrous earthquake in 1980. The main railroad line of Basilicata links Potenza with Naples and Battipaglia in the northwest and with Taranto in the east, connecting also with the Ionian railroad (Taranto–Reggio di Calabria). Pop. (1983 est.) 612,785.

Basilide (Ethiopian emperor): *see* Fasilides.

Basilides (fl. 2nd century AD, Alexandria), scholar and teacher, who founded a school of Gnosticism known as the Basilidians. He probably was a pupil of Menander in Antioch, and he was teaching in Alexandria at the time of the Roman emperors Hadrian and Antonius Pius.

Clement of Alexandria, a Christian theologian of the 3rd century AD, wrote that Basilides claimed to have received a secret tradition—on which he apparently based his gnosis, or esoteric knowledge—from Glaucias, an interpreter of the Apostle Peter. In addition to psalms and odes, Basilides wrote commentaries on the Gospels and also compiled a "gospel" for his own sect; only fragments of these writings have been preserved. Contradictory accounts of Basilides' theology have been provided by Clement, as well as by the theologians Hippolytus of Rome and Saint Irenaeus. While interpreters cite elements of Neoplatonism, the New Testament, and other Gnostic systems, description of the Basilidian system of belief remains incomplete.

Basilides was succeeded by his son, Isidore, and the Basilidian school still existed in Egypt in the 4th century. Its followers were the first to keep the day of Jesus' baptism on January 6 or 10, celebrating it with an all-night vigil.

Basílio da Gama: *see* Gama, Basílio da.

Basilios, also spelled BASILOS (b. 1891?—d. Oct. 12, 1970, Addis Ababa, Ethiopia?), religious leader who, on Jan. 14, 1951, became the first Ethiopian bishop to be consecrated *abuna*, or primate, of the Ethiopian Orthodox Church. From the 4th century the Ethiopian Church was headed by Egyptian *abuna*s appointed by the Alexandrian patriarch of the Coptic Church. As the result of reforms negotiated under Emperor Haile Selassie I, however, the Ethiopian Orthodox Church began in the late 1940s to gain independence. Following Basilios' consecration, the church achieved completely indigenous leadership by 1954. In 1959 it became an autocephalous (ecclesiastically independent) body, and Basilios was made its first patriarch.

Basiliscus (d. 477), usurping Eastern Roman emperor from 475 to 476. He was the brother of Verina, wife of the Eastern emperor Leo I (ruled 457–474).

In 468 Basiliscus was given supreme command of a vast Eastern Roman force that sought to expel the Vandals from Africa. When his incompetent leadership led to total defeat at the hands of the Vandal king Gaiseric off Mercurius (modern Cap Bon, Tunisia), Verina procured the Emperor's pardon for her brother. In January 475 Basiliscus executed a coup d'etat, which drove the new Eastern emperor, Zeno, from Constantinople. For the next 20 months Basiliscus held the power in the East. As emperor he stirred up discontent because he favoured the Monophysite heresy, which held that the human and divine elements in Christ's nature were inseparable. During his reign a disastrous fire in Constantinople destroyed much of the city along with many Greek works of art. When Zeno returned to the capital in August 476, Basiliscus was exiled to Cappadocia and there beheaded.

basilisk (legendary serpent): *see* cockatrice.

basilisk (*Basiliscus*), any of four species of lizards belonging to the family Iguanidae. The name is applied because of a resemblance to the legendary monster called basilisk.

Basilisks are found in trees near the rivers and streams of tropical America. The body is compressed from side to side, the tail is long and whiplike, and the rear of the head is extended into a flat lobe like a cock's comb. The outer edges of the toes have a wide fringe

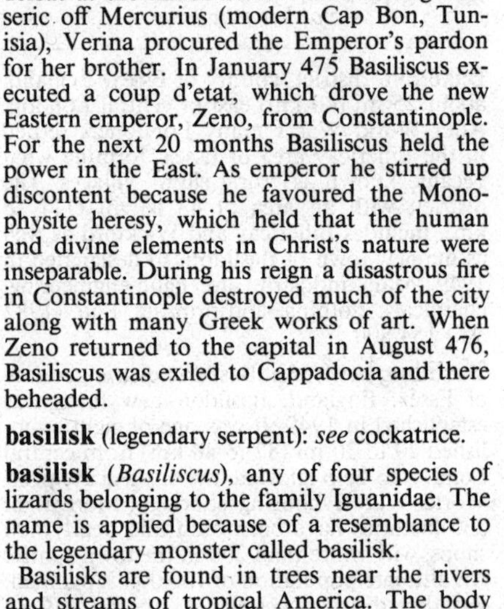

Basilisk (*Basiliscus basiliscus*)

Dade Thornton—The National Audubon Society Collection/Photo Researchers

of elongated scales. Males have a crest along the back, as deep as the body in two species. Basilisks can run across the surface of water on their hind limbs, the body being held almost upright.

Basilius THE GREAT, SAINT: *see* Basil the Great, Saint.

Basilosaurus, also called ZEUGLODON, extinct genus of primitive whales of the family Basilosauridae (suborder Archaeoceti) found in upper Eocene rocks in North America and northern Africa (the Eocene Epoch began about 54,000,000 years ago and lasted about 16,000,000 years). *Basilosaurus* had primitive dentition and skull architecture; the rest of the slender, elongated skeleton was well adapted to aquatic life. It attained a length of about 21 metres (about 70 feet), with the skull alone as much as 1.5 metres (5 feet) long. *Basilosaurus* was common throughout late Eocene seas.

Basin, Thomas (b. 1412, Caudebec, Fr.—d. Dec. 3, 1491, Utrecht, Neth.), bishop and historian noted for his opposition to King Louis XI of France.

After studying liberal arts at Paris and law at Pavia and Louvain, Basin travelled in Hungary and took part in the Council of Basel before returning to teach canon law at Caen. In 1447 he became bishop of Lisieux. After the French recovery of Normandy from the English (1450), he served Charles VII faithfully and was appointed one of the royal counsellors. His refusal to support the revolt of the dauphin Louis was a cause of the latter's animosity toward him when Louis finally became king (1461). Another reason was Basin's joining the League of the Public Weal against Louis in 1465. Basin went into exile and renounced his bishopric. In 1474, however, Pope Sixtus IV made him titular archbishop of Caesarea.

Basin's principal work, a history of the reigns of Charles VII and Louis XI, was written in Latin between 1471 and 1487 in a style imitating that of classical historians. It is a valuable testimony on his times but is marred to some extent by his dislike of Louis XI.

Basin and Range Province (in North American geology): *see* Great Basin.

Basingstoke and Deane, district (borough), county of Hampshire, Eng., west-southwest of London. With an area of 246 sq mi (637 sq km), the borough is largely rural but includes the market town of Basingstoke. Its 17th-century cloth industry has been reestablished, and it has a wide range of light industries. It has been designated for planned expansion to accommodate overspill population from Greater London. The countryside is important for agriculture, particularly for cereal production. Pop. (1982 est.) 132,000.

Basīrhāt, town, Twenty-four Parganas district, West Bengal state, northeastern India, just south of the Ichāmati (Upper Jamuna) River. Connected by road and rail with Bārāsat, it is a major district trade depot for rice, jute, mustard, legumes, dates, and potatoes; sugar milling and metalware manufacture are the chief industries. It has a college affiliated with the University of Calcutta. Basīrhāt was constituted a municipality in 1869. Pop. (1981) 81,040.

basisphenoid bone, in reptiles, birds, and many mammals, a bone located at the base of the skull. It is immediately in front of the bone that contains the opening through which the brainstem projects to connect with the spinal cord. In man the basisphenoid is present in the embryo but later fuses with the rest of the sphenoid. It contains the hollow in which the pituitary gland rests.

Baskerville, John (b. Jan. 28, 1706, Wolverly, Worcestershire, Eng.—d. Jan. 8, 1775, Birmingham, Warwickshire), printer and creator of a typeface of great distinction bearing his name, whose works are among the finest examples of the art of printing.

He became a writing master at Birmingham but in 1740 established a japanning (varnishing) business, whose profits enabled him to experiment in typefounding. He set up a printing house and in 1757 published his first work, an edition of Virgil, followed in 1758 by an edition of John Milton. Appointed printer to Cambridge University, he undertook an edition of the Bible (1763), which is considered his masterpiece. He published a particularly beautiful Horace in 1762; the success of a second edition (1770) encouraged him to issue a series of editions of Latin authors.

The bold quality of Baskerville's print derived from his use of a highly glossed paper and a truly black ink that he had invented. His typography was much criticized in England,

Baskerville, detail of a portrait after James Millar, 1774; in the National Portrait Gallery, London

By courtesy of the National Portrait Gallery, London

and after his death his types were purchased by the French dramatist Pierre-Augustin Caron de Beaumarchais. Their subsequent history is uncertain, but in 1917 the surviving punches and matrices were recognized, and in 1953 they were presented to Cambridge University. Baskerville type has been revived, its clarity and balance making it a good type for continuous reading.

basket chair, chair made from plaited twigs, or osiers, shaped on a warp of stiff rods. Basketmaking is one of the oldest crafts, and basket chairs are known to date back at least as far as Roman times. An early 3rd-century-AD stone relief in the Trier Museum, West Germany, shows a woman at her toilet seated in a basket chair that curves to fit the body. Similar chairs were still being made in the first decades of the 20th century.

Because furniture lacked upholstery during the Middle Ages, basket chairs were among the most comfortable. They achieved great popularity in Victorian times; padded with cushions or buttoned upholstery, they were used in both house and garden.

basket-flower (*Centaurea americana*), annual garden flower of the family Asteraceae,

Basket-flower (*Centaurea americana*)

L.N. and Anella Dexter

native to southwestern North America. The name basket-flower also is used for a species of spider lily (*Hymenocallis*) of another family. Basket-flower has oblong leaves and rose-coloured, compact heads of disk flowers that appear to be in baskets because the ray flowers around the head are enlarged.

Other plants of the genus *Centaurea* also are cultivated as garden ornamentals, especially cornflower (*C. cyanus*), dusty miller (*C. cineraria* and *C. gymnocarpa*), and sweet sultan (*C. moschata*). Knapweed (*C. nigra*) is a hairy perennial weed commonly found in temperate areas of the world.

basket-of-gold, also called GOLDEN TUFT ALYSSUM (*Aurinia,* or *Alyssum, saxatile*), ornamental perennial plant, of the mustard family (Brassicaceae), with golden-yellow clusters of tiny flowers and gray-green foliage. It is

Basket-of-gold (*Alyssum*)

G. Tomsich—Shostal/EB Inc.

native to sunny areas of central and southern Europe, usually growing in thin, rocky soils. It forms a dense mat, low to the ground. Several varieties are available, which are planted in rock gardens.

basketball, game played with an inflated ball between two teams of five players each on a rectangular court, usually indoors. Each team tries to score by passing the ball through the opponent's goal, an elevated, horizontally mounted hoop and net called a basket.

A brief treatment of basketball follows. For full treatment, *see* MACROPAEDIA: Sports, Major Team and Individual.

Basketball was introduced in 1891 by James Naismith, a physical education instructor at the Young Men's Christian Association Training School in Springfield, Mass. The game caught on quickly, and in 1896 the first college basketball game with five team members on a side was played at Iowa City, Iowa.

During the 1930s several rules were changed to speed up the game; *e.g.*, each team had 10 seconds in which to advance the ball beyond midcourt or lose possession of it, and a player could not stand inside the opposing team's foul area (in front of the basket) for more than three seconds. The centre jump was eliminated, and the adoption of the one-hand shot led to higher scoring games. The presentation of college games at large exhibition arenas in major cities contributed greatly to the popularity of basketball as a spectator sport, and with the inclusion of basketball in the Olympic Games in 1936, the game gained worldwide attention. The Fédération Internationale de Basketball Amateur was organized in 1932 to govern the international game.

Organized U.S. professional basketball began in 1898 with the creation of the National Basketball League. The Basketball Association of America, a second league, was organized in 1946, but in 1949 the two leagues were merged to form the National Basketball Association (NBA). A rival American Basketball Association (ABA) was set up in 1967 but was merged with the NBA in 1976.

U.S. basketball courts are slightly larger than international courts and measure 50 feet wide by 94 feet long (15 by 28 metres). A field goal is worth two points and a free throw, shot after a foul has been committed, one point. When the ABA was merged with the NBA, the ABA's three-point shot (in which three points are scored for field goals made from beyond a line 25 feet from the basket) was retained, although the distance was changed. Fouls are caused by contact between players when one player puts another at a disadvantage. A jump ball is held between two opposing players either to begin each of the periods (four of 8 minutes each in high school games and two of 20 minutes each in college) or when the possession of the ball is shared between two opposing players. There has been an effort to reduce the number of jump balls: in professional games only the first of the four 12-minute periods is begun by a jump ball, while in college play teams alternate throwing the ball into play in jump-ball situations (other than at the start of halves). After a team scores, the other team brings the ball into play.

The major annual U.S. basketball events are the NBA championship (for professionals), the National Collegiate Athletic Association (NCAA) championship, and the National Invitation Tournament, a postseason college competition.

See Sporting Record: *Basketball. See also* Olympic Games.

basketry, the art and craft of making interwoven objects, usually containers, from flexible vegetable fibres, such as twigs, grasses, osiers, bamboo, and rushes, or from plastic or other synthetic materials. The containers made by this method are called baskets.

Basketmaking may be considered one of Neolithic man's contributions to cultural history. Some of the techniques employed in Egyptian basketwork 5,000 years ago remain in wide use in 20th-century Africa.

A brief account of basketry follows. For full treatment, *see* MACROPAEDIA: Decorative Arts and Furnishings.

Basketry, on the whole, is a useful rather than a decorative art and has evolved to fulfill primarily utilitarian functions. Nevertheless, basketry has an aesthetic quality that is extremely varied and forms an important part of the art. Within the confines of the function of the object that he is making, the basket maker has considerable scope for artistic expression by means of colour, texture, pattern, form, and detail. Not all basketry products are receptacles or even exclusively useful objects. Mats such as the Japanese tatami mat, woven from flexible vegetable materials, are part of the art of basketry, as are the decorative and ritual masks and shields found in Micronesia. The art of basketry is ancient, and many myths describing the creation name basketry as one of man's earliest art forms.

Basketry is distinguished from weaving in that, in most techniques of basketry (matting being a notable exception), the flexible fibres are usually interwoven with rigid ones. Even when only flexible fibres, such as grasses, are used, they are frequently woven and intertwined in such a way as to produce a relatively large and rigid continuous surface, either flat or enclosed. The coiled forms of basketry begin with soft, flexible fibres that are plaited and coiled to form receptacles that emerge quite rigid, capable sometimes even of containing liquids. The woven forms are usually composed of a rigid framework of willows, twigs, or similar materials around and through which the flexible grasses or like fibres are twisted and woven.

The variety and type of vegetable material in a given geographical region determine the type of basketry feasible there. Certain materials, such as palms and other large-leaved plants found in tropical regions, require a plaiting technique somewhat different from that suitable to the dry straws and grasses of other regions. Most basketry materials are of vegetable origin and are soft and flexible, though they may range in hardness from grasses and leaves to bamboo and cane. The function of the basketry object will determine in part the materials to be used in its construction. A utensil designed to hold grain or liquid, for example, will of necessity be dense and closely woven, while a cage, net, or trap will be of openwork construction.

There are many varied techniques of basketry. The main distinction is between coiled construction, in which a single fibre is formed into a spiral of coils, stitched together in some way one upon another, and noncoiled construction, which includes the woven types such as wattle, lattice, and matting. The type of work known as wickerwork is of the wattle type of construction, in which stiff standards (framing elements) are interwoven with flexible threads. Matting is closest to textile weaving in construction, and all the materials are, at the outset, relatively soft and flexible.

Basketry lends itself to a great variety of decorative effects. The way in which the materials are interwoven gives texture and form, and the choice of differently coloured materials creates patterns and decorative effects. The characteristics of woven basketry have even sometimes been reproduced in harder materials, such as metal or porcelain.

Basketry may be classified in many different ways: by function, by technique, by appearance, or by geographical or cultural origin. It is such a widely known art as to occur virtually throughout the world.

Baskets are used as domestic utensils—such as breadbaskets, Japanese tea strainers, and Chinese bamboo steamers—or for storage of grains, nuts, or even personal possessions. Houses and furniture can be constructed using the techniques of basketry. Shoes and hats are sometimes made by basketry techniques. Baskets are used for hunting and for fishing, for winnowing grain, to transport people or objects, and for both large- and small-scale storage. There are even types of boats—such as the coracle of Great Britain, the balsa of Peru, and the gufa of Mesopotamia—made with basketry frames.

Basketry had its origin in prehistory. Certain cultures and regions have particularly excelled in basketry. These include the North American Indians, whose work is aesthetically pleasing as well as culturally useful and technically excellent. In Oceania and southern Asia the art of basketry has traditionally predominated over such "harder" arts as pottery and metalwork, owing largely to the abundance of available raw materials suitable for the craft. African basketry is exceptionally varied and refined, appearing widely throughout the continent. African regions particularly notable for their basketry include Chad and Cameroon.

Baskin, Leonard (b. Aug. 15, 1922, New Brunswick, N.J., U.S.), notable U.S. sculptor and printmaker who, after studying in the United States and Europe, had his first one-man show in New York City in 1939; he won a Tiffany fellowship for sculpture in 1947 and the Guggenheim fellowship for printmaking in 1953. From the latter year he taught at Smith College in Northampton, Mass.

Baskin designed monumental figures in bronze, limestone, wood, and relief. Among his subjects are poets ("Blake," 1955; "Barlach Dead," 1959) universal symbols ("Hanged Man," 1956; "Man with Owl," 1960), and biblical subjects ("Prodigal Son," 1976; "Ruth and Naomi," 1978). "Man of Peace" and "Everyman" are among his best known woodcuts. He used some of his cuts to illustrate books printed by the Gehenna Press, which he owned.

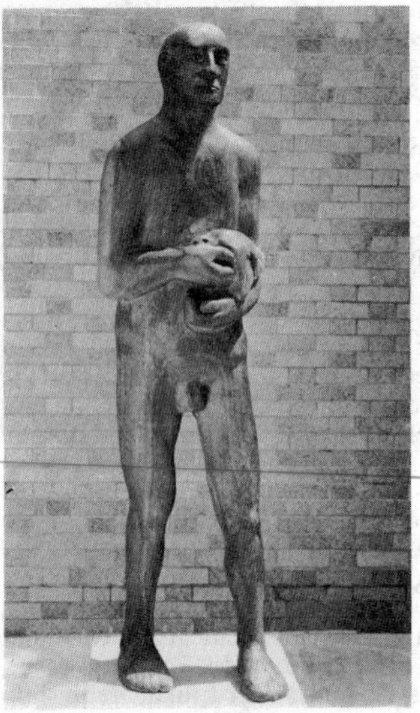

"Man with a Dead Bird," walnut sculpture by Leonard Baskin, 1951–56; in the Museum of Modern Art, New York City

By courtesy of the Museum of Modern Art, New York, A. Conger Goodyear Fund

basking shark, huge, sluggish shark of the family Cetorhinidae, usually classified as *Cetorhinus maximus* but possibly separable into more than one distinct species. Named for its habit of floating or slowly swimming at the surface, the basking shark inhabits northern and temperate regions of the Atlantic, Pacific, and Indian oceans. It is a giant, growing as long as 14 metres (46 feet), and is exceeded in size among fishes only by the whale shark. Despite its size, the basking shark feeds on plankton. It is a gray-brown or blackish shark, with tiny teeth and very long gill slits. It is generally inoffensive and is hunted sporadically for fish meal and liver oil. When found decaying on beaches, it is sometimes reported as a sea serpent.

Basking shark (*Cetorhinus maximus*)

Painting by Richard Ellis

Basle (Switzerland): *see* Basel.

Basmachi Revolt, Russian BASMACHESTVO, insurrection against Soviet rule in Central Asia, begun in 1917 and largely suppressed by 1926. An amalgam of Muslim traditionalists and common bandits, the Basmachi were soon widespread over most of Turkistan, much of which was under regimes independent of but allied to Soviet Russia.

In the early 1920s the revolt threatened the Soviet government with the permanent loss of much of Turkistan. But the Bolsheviks enjoyed military superiority, greater discipline, and a singleness of purpose. The Basmachi, on the other hand, were nearly as inclined to attack each other as to fight their common foe. By conciliating nationalist sentiment in Central Asia, the Soviet government defused the revolt and paved the way for successful incorporation of the area into the Soviet Union.

basmalah, also called TASMIYAH, in Islām, the formula-prayer: *bi'ṣm llāh ar-raḥmān ar-raḥīm*, "in the name of God, the Merciful, the Compassionate." This invocation, which was first introduced by the Qur'ān, appears at the beginning of every Qur'ānic *sūrah* (chapter) except the ninth (which presents a unique textual problem), and is frequently recited by Muslims to elicit God's blessings on their important actions. The *basmalah* also introduces all formal documents and transactions and must always preface actions that are legally required or recommended. An abbreviated version precedes certain daily rituals, such as meals. Magicians often use the *basmalah* in amulets, claiming that the prayer was inscribed in Adam's side, Gabriel's wing, Solomon's seal, and Jesus Christ's tongue.

Basohli painting, school of Pahari miniature painting that flourished in the Indian hill states during the late 17th and the 18th centuries, known for its bold vitality of colour and line. Though the school takes its name from the small independent state of Basohli, the principal centre of the style, examples are found throughout the region.

The origins of the school are obscure; one of the earliest examples so far discovered, a series

A musical mode, Basohli miniature painting, early 18th century; in a private collection
P. Chandra

of illustrations to the *Rasamañjarī* (*c.* 1690), exhibits a style already completely formed. An oblong format is favoured, with the picture space usually delineated by architectural detail, which often breaks into the characteristic red borders.

The stylized facial type, shown in profile, is dominated by the large, intense eye. The colours are always brilliant, with ochre yellow, brown, and green grounds predominating. A distinctive technique is the depiction of jewelry by thick, raised drops of white paint, with particles of green beetles' wings used to represent emeralds.

Basov, Nikolay Gennadiyevich (b. Dec. 14, 1922, Leningrad), Soviet physicist, winner of the Nobel Prize for Physics in 1964, with Aleksandr Mikhaylovich Prokhorov of the Soviet Union and Charles H. Townes of the United States, for fundamental research in quantum electronics that led to the development of both the maser and laser. These devices produce monochromatic, parallel, coherent beams of microwaves and light, respectively.

In the 1960s Basov served as a deputy director of the Lebedev Institute. In 1952 he and Prokhorov suggested the maser principle, for which they were awarded the Lenin Prize in 1959.

Basque, Spanish VASCO, or VASCONGADO, Basque EUSKALDUNAK, or EUSKOTARAK, member of a people who live in both Spain and France in areas bordering the Bay of Biscay and encompassing the western foothills of the Pyrenees. In the late 1970s probably about 850,000 true Basques lived in Spain and 130,000 in France; as many as 170,000

Basque shepherds, Navarra, Spain
Koldo Chamorro—Ostman Agency

Basques may live in emigrant communities outside Europe, mostly in South America and the United States. In Spain their home is the autonomous community of Vascongadas, including the provinces of Álava, Guipúzcoa, and Vizcaya (Biscay), with Navarra (Navarre). In France, Basques are the chief element in the *département* of Pyrénées-Atlantiques; the area mainly occupied by Basques is called informally the Pays Basque (Basque Country). In physique the Basques are not notably different from the other peoples of western Europe; their language, however, is not Indo-European (*see* Basque language).

The Basques were traditionally farmers of small acreages, shipbuilders and seafarers, and, it is said, smugglers of goods across the Franco-Spanish frontier. They have had a strong sense of family and a strong allegiance to Roman Catholicism. In most of the larger industrial towns, however, not only Basque customs but also the Basque language tend to be lost. It is still spoken in the zones of coastal humidity and in remote inland mountain areas. Today, virtually all Basques speak French or Spanish, whether or not they speak Basque. Curiously, the Basque ethnic identity in Barcelona strengthened in the 20th century as a correlative of civil disturbances in Spain.

The early history of the Basques remains a subject for speculation, but Roman authors record the presence of the tribe of Vascones in lands corresponding roughly to the province of Navarra. They appear to have resisted the Visigoths, the Franks, the Normans, and, on occasion, the Moors, who occupied the valley of the Ebro. By the end of the political turmoil of the Middle Ages, their provinces had become united with Castile and Aragon, though they retained, in France as well as in Spain, a degree of local autonomy. The *fueros*, or *fors* (bodies of traditional law by which they governed themselves), of the French Basques were abolished, however, by the Revolution at the end of the 18th century, and the *fueros* in Spain were erased later, in the 19th century, in reaction to rising Basque nationalism and Basque support of Carlism.

The advent of the Spanish Republic in 1931 divided the political aspirations of the Basques: Guipúzcoa, Vizcaya, and, to a certain extent, Álava were prepared to work for a status of relative autonomy within the republic, and for this reason they remained loyal to it in spite of its anti-Catholic policy; Navarra, on the other hand, was eager to see the republic overthrown and furnished one of the strong points of the rebellion in 1936 and some of its best troops. The city of Bilbao, which had always been a stronghold of liberalism, became at the same time the centre of republican government and also of Basque nationalism. The fighting lasted until September 1937 and outside Spain is chiefly remembered for the bombing, supposedly by German aircraft, of Guernica, the traditional assembly place of the province of Vizcaya and a symbol of the Basque nation in nationalist eyes. After the war, many Basques went into exile.

After the death of Francisco Franco and especially after the establishment of the liberal Spanish monarchy in 1975, the Basques engaged in vigorous demonstrations for local autonomy, which the Spanish government granted in some measure in 1978–79. The increased freedoms and home rule, however, did not satisfy the more militant separatists, such as the hard-line "military" wing of the ETA (Euzkadi Ta Azkatasuna—Basque for "Basque Homeland and Liberty"), a terrorist-liberation organization seeking Basque self-determination and secession from Spain. The Basques thus continued on an unsettled course in their relations with the dominant Spaniards.

Basque, Pays, cultural region, extreme southwestern France, bordering the western Pyrenees where they adjoin the Basque provinces of Spain, along the Bay of Biscay. The region extends from the Pic d'Anie, 8,215 ft (2,504 m), of the Pyrenees to the magnificent rock-bound coast around Biarritz and Saint-Jean-de-Luz on the Bay of Biscay. The climate is very wet, rainfall exceeding 120 in. (3,000 mm) per year in the mountains, and numerous rivers divide the landscape into countless verdant valleys that support both agriculture and forestry. The Basque people themselves speak a language that is among the oldest in Europe and are ethnically distinct from the peoples who surround them in France and Spain, having preserved their identity among the waves of migrants who have passed through the region since prehistoric times. Fishing and tourism are the economic mainstays of a coast known for the sweetness of its climate. The region has not experienced the problems associated with the Basque separatist movement in the Basque Provinces of Spain, but has provided a refuge for exiles of that and other conflicts in Spain.

Basque Country, Spanish PAÍS VASCO, Basque EUSKARDI, *comunidad autónoma* (autonomous region) of Spain, a governmental entity encompassing the Spanish Biscayan provinces of Álava, Guipúzcoa, and Vizcaya ratified by a regional referendum of Oct. 25, 1979. The government consists of a president, who serves for five years, and a parliament with an equal number of representatives from each province. Earlier, the turbulent region had seen the Basque separatist movement of the 1930s culminate in a Statute of Autonomy on Oct. 5, 1936. Gen. Francisco Franco suppressed Basque separatism the following year; the extremists of that movement subsequently conducted a campaign of terrorism against the Spanish central government.

The Pyrenees separate the Spanish region from a heavily Basque region of France to the northeast; the Cantabrian Mountains separate it from the province of Santander to the west. To the south the Pyrenees give way to the Ebro Basin and the Castilian provinces of Burgos and Logroño. To the east the Basque Country is bordered by the province of Navarre. The mountains of Vizcaya and Guipúzcoa are formidably jagged;

coastal hills ordinarily extend inland no more than 25 to 40 mi (40 to 60 km). Rivers are short and rapid, cutting sharp gorges through the mountains. Average annual precipitation reaches 47 in. (1,200 mm), exceeding 60 in. around San Sebastián and dropping to half that amount in the Ebro Basin. An Atlantic climate prevails in the northeast, characterized by relatively heavy and regular precipitation. A sub-Mediterranean climate prevails in the southern intermontane basin of Álava, linking the region to the climate and culture of Navarre and Aragón.

The population of the Ebro Basin is concentrated in small communal nuclei surrounded by open fields and vineyards. The population of the Pyrenees, by contrast, is more widely dispersed and centres on the individual farmstead, the *caserío*, allowing for intensive cultivation of small plots in the mountains. The *caseríos* in a locality form an informal community, the *etchalde* or *baserri*. The rapid industrialization of the region since the mid-19th century has undermined traditional patterns of settlement in the Pyrenees, causing such coastal cities as San Sebastián and Bilbao to grow at the expense of settlements in the hinterlands. Population density is highest along the coast: some four-fifths of the Basque population is concentrated in greater Bilbao. Álava is the least developed of the Basque provinces; Vitoria its only major city.

Aside from the forests of oak and beech lining its northern hills, Álava presents an open landscape suitable for the cultivation of cereals and grapes. The Alavese Rioja produces notable wines, while large modernized farms toward the centre of the province produce sugar beets and various fodder crops. Irrigation is widespread. The Basques of the Pyrenees have traditionally been herders, although the introduction of crops from the Americas (corn [maize] and potatoes) has resulted in the expansion and diversification of cultivation since the early modern period. Corn was widely cultivated by 1630, supplanting the traditional millet in crop rotation. The rotation of corn, wheat, and turnips allowed for two to three crops every two years, giving the countryside a new lease on life during the 17th and 18th centuries. The relative importance of agriculture declined sharply after the 19th century, until it accounted for only 5 percent of the region's domestic product while employing less than 10 percent of the work force outside Álava. Álava remains the most agricultural of the Basque provinces, though its city, Vitoria, has undergone considerable industrialization since the early 1950s.

Vizcaya and Guipúzcoa are heavily industrialized, having exploited their extensive resources of iron and timber since the late Middle Ages. The wars and fleets of the Habsburgs increased demand for Basque iron and timber, although these industries declined with the rise of English and Dutch naval power. Basque metalworking industries revived toward the middle of the 19th century. The foundry of Santa Ana de Bolueta was opened in 1841, and capital from France, Belgium, and Great Britain advanced the development of Bilbao's foundries in the 1870s. The Basque metallurgical industries are heavily concentrated in Bilbao and along the banks of the Nervión. Outside Bilbao the metallurgical, food-processing, and chemical industries tend to be dispersed, while the paper industry centres on Tolosa and the banks of the Oria. Industry accounts for one-half of the region's domestic product and employs a comparable fraction of the work force.

Service industries are highly developed in the Basque Country. The foundation of the Banco de Vizcaya in 1857 and of the Banco de Bilbao in 1902 established that metropolis as one of the leading financial centres of Spain. Since 1950, however, much of the region's capital has come from foreign sources, and many metallurgical industries have come under the management of multinational companies.

Traditional Basque culture centres on the *caserío*. The *caserío* houses a barn and family living quarters under one roof, and its isolation has led to a strong sense of family. The patriarch, the *etcheco jaun*, exercises complete control over his family, and his primary task is to preserve the patrimony intact. The Basques favour competitive sports, among them wood chopping, weight lifting, and boxing. The Basques were not converted to Christianity until the 10th century, and although they are now among the most observant of Spanish Catholics, animism survives in the folklore. Gravestones are disk-shaped and often feature swastikas. Traditional Basque culture has declined with the urban and industrial development of the region, and emigration to France and the Americas has sharply reduced the population living in *caseríos*. The terrorist acts of the ETA, the radical Basque separatist party, have nonetheless made Basque regionalism one of the most destabilizing forces in Spanish political life. The creation of the autonomous region of the Basque Country has failed to end the terrorism of the ETA. Modern Basque literature is limited and has served primarily as a vehicle for the expression of radical Basque nationalism. The poetry of Telesforo Monzón envisions a Basque nation encompassing the Basques of Spain and France, while the members of the ETA are seen as the continuation of the Basque soldiery who rose against Franco in 1936. Pop. (1981) 2,134,967.

Basque language, Basque EUSKARA, a language spoken by a largely bilingual people called Basques, or Euskaldunak, living either in the autonomous Basque country (which includes the Spanish province of Guipuzcoa, part of Vizcaya, and a corner of Álava) or in the western region of the French *département* of Pyrénées-Atlantiques. In all, the majority of Basque speakers are concentrated in narrow areas of approximately 10,000 square kilometers (3,900 square miles).

A brief treatment of the Basque language follows. For full treatment, *see* MACROPAEDIA: Languages of the World.

Basque has constantly struggled for survival against the more popular and widespread Spanish and French. In the pre-Christian era, Basque country stretched across the Pyrenees as far east as the Valle de Aran in northeastern Spain. During the Roman administration, however, the eastern Basque settlements were cut off from more populated Basque colonies to the west and were assimilated into Roman culture, abandoning the Basque language. In the Middle Ages, the influence of Basque, an unwritten language, steadily declined when it could not compete against the influx of literary Latin and its successors, Navarrese Romance and Provençal. The advent of the first printed Basque book in 1545, however, began a literary tradition that continues to the present.

The origin of the Basque language remains a mystery. The German philologist Hugo Schuchardt (1842–1927) hypothesized that Basque had a genetic connection with the now-extinct Iberian and that both languages evolved from the Hamito-Semitic (Afro-Asiatic) language group. The existence of a connection seems unlikely, however, since Basque and the Hamito-Semitic languages do not really share common linguistic characteristics. Although Basque and Iberian are similar, the knowledge of Basque could not help decipher ancient Iberian inscriptions discovered in eastern Spain and on the Mediterranean coast of France. This incongruity led to the theory that the similarities between the two languages arose from a close geographic proximity rather than a genetic linguistic tie. Basque is also linked with Caucasian, the ancient language spoken in the Caucasus region. Again, there are parallels between the two languages; but, without conclusive evidence of a tie, Basque remains a language without linguistic relatives.

Spoken Basque resembles Spanish most closely in sound. Similarities include the palatal *ñ*, which is similar to the *ny* sound in the English *canyon*, and the palatal *ll* which sounds like *l* + *y*, or the *lli* in *million*. Another similarity to Spanish is the pronunciation of the Basque *s* and *ts* which sound like the *s* in Castilian Spanish.

The hushing sibilants *x* and *tx* are voiced like English *sh* and *ch*. These, along with the above mentioned *ll* and *ñ*, denote an endearment or a diminutive. For example, *hezur* means "bone," while *hexur* means "little bone."

The phonology of some Basque dialects may be more complex than that of standard Basque. The dialect peculiar to the easternmost Souletin region has adopted a sixth oral vowel—the rounded *e* or *i*—in addition to the five (pure) vowels of standard Basque. Consonants in both dialectal and standard Basque consist of two sets of the stopped variety; *b, d,* and *g* are voiced; *p, t,* and *k* are voiceless.

Although some ancient prefixes are still apparent, modern Basque can be characterized as a "suffixing" language; that is, the case denoting the agent of the action is represented by a suffix. For example, the suffix "*-k*" is a marker for the subject of a transitive verb, while subjects of the intransitive verb remain unchanged. In the sentence *Sabelak jaten ez ba du, sabela bera ihartuko da* ("If the belly does not eat, the belly itself will fail"), *sabelak* (the belly) is the agent of a transitive verb and adopts the *-k*, while *sabela,* in the second clause, is the subject of the intransitive verb (fail) and, therefore, remains unaltered.

In Basque the finite verb may contain as many as three personal references for subject, direct object, and indirect object. The verb *da* ("is"), for example, declines to *du* ("he has it") and to *dio* ("he has it for him") in the sentence *Oinare ez dio eskuak kolperik emaiten* ("The hand does not give a blow to the foot"). Most verbs are conjugated by compounding the verb and the auxilliary: *erori da* ("he has fallen," or literally, "he is fallen") and *jaten du* ("he eats [is eating] it").

Although Basque remains unique, phrases and words from other languages, particularly Latin, have crept into common usage. *Bake* from the Latin *pax* and *pacis* ("peace"), *bike* from the Latin *pix* and *picis* ("pitch"), and *errege* from the Latin *rex* and *regis* ("king") are a few examples. Conversely, however, Spanish, Occitan, French, and English have acquired few Basque words or phrases.

Basra, Arabic AL-BAṢRAH, city and *muḥāfaẓah* (governorate), southern Iraq; the city of Basra is the capital of the *muḥāfaẓah* and is the metropolis of its region. Basra is situated

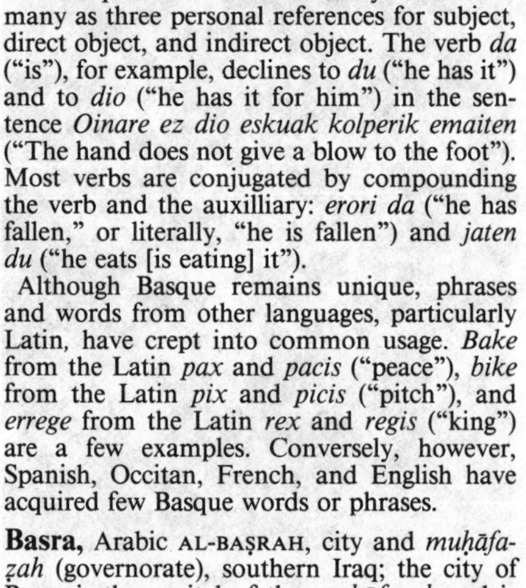

Part of the harbour at Basra, Iraq, on the Shatt al-Arab, with a date palm grove in the foreground
Diane Rawson—Photo Researchers

on the western bank of the Shatt al-Arab (formed by the union of the Tigris and Euphrates) at the exit from Hawr al-Ḥammār

(Ḥammār Lake), 70 mi by water above al-Fāw on the open Persian Gulf. From ancient times Basra was a centre of Arab letters, poetry, science, commerce, and finance. It was founded as a military encampment by the second caliph, ʿUmar I, in 638 about 8 mi (13 km) from the modern town of az-Zubayr, Iraq. Its proximity to the Persian Gulf and easy access to both the Tigris and Euphrates rivers and the eastern frontiers encouraged its growth into a real city, despite the hard climate and the difficulty of supplying the camp with drinking water. The first architecturally significant mosque in Islām was constructed there in 665.

Basran troops fought the Sāsānian Persians at Nahāvand (642) and conquered the western provinces of Iran (650), while the town itself was the site of the Battle of the Camel (656), an encounter between ʿĀʾishah, the Prophet Muḥammad's widow, and ʿAlī, Muḥammad's son-in-law and fourth caliph.

In the years during and after ʿAlī's caliphate (656–661), the Islāmic community split into three factions. While Basra remained essentially Sunnī—that is, in favour of the regular progression of Umayyad caliphs after ʿAlī—elements of the other two groups were also active in the city: the ʿAlid, or Shīʿī, faction, who accepted only ʿAlī's descendants as legitimate caliphs, and the Khārijites, who believed that any qualified Muslim could be caliph. This political friction was intensified by a volatile social situation. Whereas the Arab army constituted an aristocracy in Basra, the local and various migrant peoples who had settled there (Indians, Persians, Africans, Malays) were merely *mawālī,* or clients attached to Arab tribes. Basran history from the late 7th century is thus one of unrest and insurrection. The city was seized briefly by the forces of a claimant of the caliphate, ʿAbd Allāh ibn az-Zubayr (died 692), then became the centre of Ibn al-Ashʿath's revolt in 701 and al-Muhallab's revolt in 719–720. Conditions did not improve under the ʿAbbāsids, who took over the caliphate in 750. The uprisings continued: the Zoṭṭ, a Gypsylike Indian people, rose up in 820–835; the Zanj, African blacks brought into Mesopotamia for agricultural slave labour, rebelled (*c.* 869–883). The Qarmaṭians, an extremist Muslim sect, invaded and devastated Basra in 923, and thereafter the city declined, overshadowed by the prominence of the ʿAbbāsid capital, Baghdad. By the 14th century, neglect and the Mongol invasions left little of the original Basra standing, and by the turn of the 16th century it was relocated at the site of the ancient al-Ubullah, a few miles upstream.

Basra had been, however, a brilliant centre in its own right throughout the 8th and into the 9th century. It was the home of Sībawayh and Khalīl ibn Aḥmad, who formulated the earliest principles of Arab grammar; the renowned poets Bashshār ibn Burd and Abū Nuwās; the first Arabic prose writers, Ibn al-Muqaffaʿ, Sahl ibn Hārūn, and al-Jāḥiẓ; and such literary and religious scholars as Abū ʿAmr ibn al-ʿAlāʾ, Abū ʿUbaydah, and al-Aṣmaʿī. Islāmic mysticism was first introduced in Basra by al-Ḥasan al-Baṣrī, and the theological school of the Muʿtazilah developed there.

Basra's commercial achievements were no less impressive. Caravans and ships passed through its facilities; it was a bustling financial and industrial centre, and its large and varied date crop supported a lively agricultural trade.

The modern city of Basra is an agglomeration of three small towns, Basra, al-ʿAshār, and al-Maʿqil, and several villages clustered around Nahr al-ʿAshshār.

Al-Baṣrah *muḥāfaẓah,* 7,363 sq mi (19,070 sq km) in area, is Iraq's southeastern tip, at the head of the Persian Gulf. It is very productive agriculturally, despite its large swampy areas. Crops grown include dates, corn, rice, and millet. The *muḥāfaẓah* includes part of a large lake, Hawr al-Ḥammār. Pop. city (1970 est.) 333,684; *muḥāfaẓah* (1977 est.) 1,008,626.

bass, in music, the lowest part in a multi-voiced musical texture. In polyphony of the sort that flourished during the Renaissance, the bass formed one of several relatively independent or contrapuntal melodies.

During the figured bass era (17th and early 18th centuries), the thorough bass, or basso continuo, furnished a "base" for accompaniments played with relative freedom, though bound by certain conventions as well as shorthand instructions inserted in figures above the bass. In the homophonic, basically chordal, musical styles of the later 18th and 19th centuries, the bass was of crucial structural significance as the lowest of parts and, thus, the foundation of harmony.

In vocal music, the bass is the lowest male voice, with a typical range from the second E below middle C to F♯ above; the basso profundo is low and rich, while the basso cantante ("singing bass") is lighter and more lyric. Among instruments, the lowest pitch member of a family is referred to as the bass, for example, the bass recorder or bass viol.

bass, in zoology, any of a large number of fishes, many of them valued for food or sport. The name covers a range of fishes, but most are placed in three families of the order Perciformes: Serrandiae, including about 400 species of sea bass and grouper (*qq.v.*); Moronidae, sometimes considered a subfamily of the Serranidae and containing about 12 species, such as the striped and European basses; and Centrarchidae (sunfishes), including the black bass (*q.v.*), prized by fishermen.

Many other fishes are also known as bass; among them are the channel bass, a drum (*q.v.*); the rock bass, a sunfish (*q.v.*); and the calico bass, a crappie (*q.v.*).

Bass, George (b. Jan. 30, 1771, Aswarby, Lincolnshire, Eng.—d. 1803, at sea en route from Australia to South America), surgeon and sailor, who was important in the early coastal survey of Australia.

Bass was apprenticed as a surgeon and in 1789 accepted in the Company of Surgeons. He joined the Navy, where his proficiency in navigation and seamanship and interest in the Pacific explorers led to his transfer to the ship "Reliance," on which Matthew Flinders was mate. When the ship reached Port Jackson in 1795, Bass, Flinders, and Bass's personal servant William Martin explored the George's River and Botany Bay and recommended a settlement, which was made at Banks Town. In 1796 the three unsuccessfully sought a river south of Botany Bay and discovered and explored Port Hocking. Bass also studied the animals and plants of the region. In 1797 Bass explored the coast south of Sydney and confirmed reports of coal. Later in the year and in 1798 he determined the existence of a strait—which was named for him—between New South Wales and Van Diemen's Land. In 1799 Bass was elected to the Linnean Society of London for his field collections and writings on the wombat, the swan, and the albatross.

Bass then turned to commercial ventures, although he continued to chart wherever he sailed. In 1803 he sailed with a cargo from Sydney bound for South America and was never heard of again. In 1805 his widow was granted his naval pension. A biography by K.M. Bowden was published in 1952.

Bass, Sam (b. July 21, 1851, near Mitchell, Ind., U.S.—d. July 21, 1878, Round Rock, Texas), U.S. Western outlaw who was finally gunned down by the Texas Rangers.

Bass left his Indiana home at age 18 and drifted to Texas, where in 1874 he befriended Joel Collins. In 1876 Bass and Collins went north on a cattle drive but turned to robbing stagecoaches; in September 1877 in Big Springs, Neb., they and four others robbed a Union Pacific train of $65,000 in gold coin and other valuables. Returning to Texas, Bass collected a gang and began a less successful career of train robbery—with the Texas Rangers in pursuit. Finally, in July 1878, a former crony, Jim Murphy, tipped off the Rangers, who ambushed and wounded Bass, who was attempting a bank robbery in Round Rock. Bass died two days later, on his birthday. His career became the stuff of legend in a popular cowboy song, "The Ballad of Sam Bass."

bass drum, largest and deepest sounding military and orchestral drum. The military bass has two heads, tensioned by rope lacings or metal rods, and is struck on both heads. Most orchestral bass drums have only one head, rod-tensioned; two-headed ones normally are struck on one head only. Bass drums are usually played with a pair of large felt-headed sticks, although in modern popular-music bands the drum is commonly struck by one stick operated by a pedal. Bass drums may reach 40 inches (100 centimetres) in diameter and 20 inches (50 centimetres) in height. A larger form of one-headed bass drum is the gong drum, often used in British orchestras.

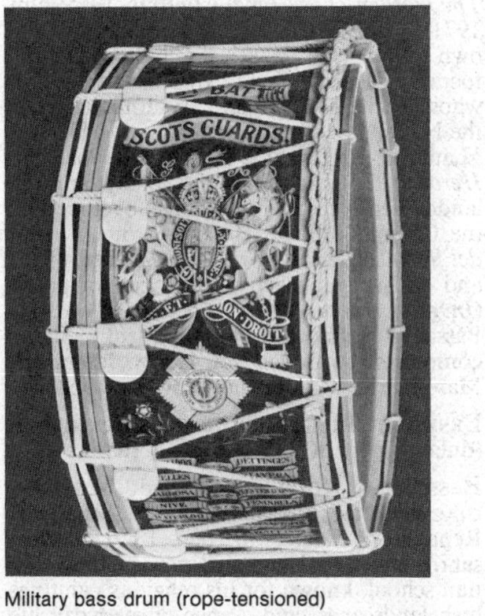

Military bass drum (rope-tensioned)

Messrs. H. Potter, Aldershot, Hampshire, Eng.

The bass drum was introduced into Europe in the 18th century as part of the vogue for Turkish music and for imitation of the music of the Turkish Janissary bands, and it typically appeared in combination with cymbals and triangle. It was at first known as the Turkish drum; the long drum was a deep-shelled instrument that resembled the *davul* of modern Turkey and the Balkans. Originally the bass drum was beaten with a stick in the right hand and a switch in the left; similarly, in modern regimental bands the right hand beats time with a larger stick than that used for the accompanying rhythms played by the left. The bass drum entered the orchestra in the 18th century, at first for special effect, as in Haydn's *Military Symphony* (1794).

Bass Strait, channel separating Victoria, Australia, from the island of Tasmania on the south. Its maximum width is 150 mi (240 km), its depth 180–240 ft (50–70 m). King Island and the Indian Ocean lie at its western extremity and the Furneaux Group are at its eastern end. Banks Strait is the southeastern opening to the Tasman Sea. Another small group, the Hunter Islands, is located off the northwestern tip of Tasmania. The strait was named in 1798 by the English navigator Matthew Flinders for the surgeon-explorer George Bass.

Development of the offshore petroleum resources of the strait began with the discovery in 1965 of natural gas at Barracouta and in 1967 of oil at the Halibut and Kingfish fields; production began in 1970.

Bassac (Laos): *see* Champasak.

Bassani, Giorgio (b. March 4, 1916, Bologna), Italian author and editor noted for his novels and stories examining individual lives played out against the background of modern history. The author's Jewish heritage and the life of the Jewish community in Ferrara, where he lived most of his life, are among his recurrent themes.

The collection *Cinque storie ferraresi* (1956; *Prospect of Ferrara,* 1962; reissued as *Dentro le mura,* 1973; "Behind the Wall"), in which five novellas describe the growth of Fascism and anti-Semitism, brought Bassani the Strega Prize and his first commercial success. The Ferrara setting recurs in Bassani's notable novel *Il giardino dei Finzi-Contini* (1962; *The Garden of the Finzi-Continis,* 1965; film, 1971). The narrator of this work contrasts his own middle-class Jewish family with the aristocratic, decadent Finzi-Continis, also Jewish, whose sheltered lives end in annihilation by the Nazis.

Later novels include *L'airone* (1968; *The Heron,* 1970), a portrait of a lonely Ferrarese landowner during a hunt. This novel received the Campiello Prize. He also wrote *L' odora del fieno* (1972; *The Smell of the Hay,* 1975); and he has published a collection of poems (*In gran segreto,* 1978; "In Great Secrecy"). Bassani's elegiac tone has frequently elicited comparison with that of Henry James and Marcel Proust, his acknowledged models.

Bassano, Hugues-Bernard Maret, duc de (duke of): *see* Maret, Hugues-Bernard.

Bassano, Jacopo, also called JACOPO, or GIACOMO, DA PONTE (b. *c.* 1517, Bassano, Republic of Venice—d. Feb. 13, 1592, Bassano), late Renaissance painter of the Venetian school, known for his religious paintings, lush landscapes, and scenes of everyday life. The son of a provincial artist, Francesco da Ponte, who adopted the name Bassano, he was the outstanding member of a thriving family workshop.

His early works, such as the "Susannah and the Elders" (1534–36) and the "Flight into Egypt" (*c.* 1536; both in the Museo Civico, Bassano, Italy), reveal the influence of his master, Bonifacio Vernese (Bonifacio di Pitati), a minor Venetian painter, as well as the outmoded anecdotal art of Lorenzo Lotto and the atmospheric light of Titian. As Bassano's art matured, his brushstrokes became looser and the forms and masses of his compositions became larger and more lively—a development that resulted in such fresco-like canvases as his "Calvary" (*c.* 1538–40; Fitzwilliam Museum, Cambridge, Eng.). Around 1540, he was greatly influenced by the elegance of the Florentine and Roman Mannerists. He especially admired the graceful attenuation of Parmigianino's figures, as can be seen in his "Adoration of the Shepherds" (Hampton Court, London). But the robust modelling, vibrant colour, and thick impasto of his "Rest on the Flight into Egypt" (*c.* 1545; Pinacoteca Ambrosiana, Milan) lend such works a vigour his Mannerist models lack.

"Pastoral," oil on canvas by Jacopo Bassano, *c.* 1560; in the Sammlung Thyssen-Bornemisza, Lugano, Switz.

By courtesy of the Sammlung Thyssen-Bornemisza, Lugano, Switz.

After 1560 Jacopo painted a large number of works, such as the "Madonna with SS. Roch and Sebastian" (Alte Pinakothek, Munich) and "The Adoration of the Magi" (Kunsthistorisches Museum, Vienna), characterized by an unearthly pale light, colours, and nervous, attenuated figures in affectedly sophisticated poses.

Landscape and genre subjects became particularly important about 1565–70, when his first paintings of rural life were produced. One of the finest is his "Pastoral" (Thyssen Collection, Lugano, Switz.). These works elaborated the genre and landscape elements that had been incidental in his religious works.

Jacopo's four sons were all painters, and Francesco the Younger (1549–92) and Leandro (1557–1622) were important in the continuity of the workshop; many Bassano paintings are the product of a family collaboration. Francesco the Younger had a predilection for the rural scenes begun by his father, and he developed this aspect of the workshop. He was entrusted with the Venetian branch of the workshop until his death by suicide in 1592. Leandro, who settled in Venice in 1582, was also successful there, receiving a number of commissions for canvases for the Doges' Palace. He is best known now for his portraits in a style based on that of Tintoretto.

Bassano del Grappa, town, Vicenza province, Veneto region, northern Italy, on the Brenta River at the foot of Monte Grappa, north of Padua. Between 1036 and 1259 the town became important under the Ezzelini family, who built the castle the walls of which enclose the often-renovated cathedral. Later disputed by Vicenza, Padua, and Verona, it flourished as a dependency of Venice from 1405 to 1796. It was famous in the 16th century as the home of the Da Ponte family of painters, surnamed Bassano, and from 1650 to 1850 for its printing and publishing works. Napoleon defeated the Austrians there in 1796, and the town was severely damaged during the heavy fighting on Monte Grappa in 1917–18 and again in World War II.

S. Francesco, a 13th-century Romanesque-Gothic church, is notable, and in the cloister of the old convent is the civic museum, which contains ceramics, wood blocks (*legni*), samples from the Remondini printing house, and works of art by Jacopo Bassano and others of his family, Antonio Canova, and Vittore Carpaccio. Since the late 18th century, the famous grappa (a kind of brandy) has been made in the town, which is also a commercial centre with metal and textile industries. Pop. (1981 prelim.) mun., 38,262.

Bassar, formerly BASSARI, town, Bassar *préfecture* in la Kara economic *région,* north central Togo, West Africa. The town lies in a major cotton growing area about 30 mi (50 km) northwest of Sokodé, Togo's second largest town. Bassar serves as an important centre for commercial trade among the country's economic *régions.* It has road links with Burkina Faso (formerly Upper Volta) to the north and the national capital of Lomé to the south. The Bassar people inhabit the town and surrounding area. Pop. (1977 est.) 17,500.

basse danse (French: "low dance"), courtly dance for couples, originating in 14th-century Italy and fashionable in many varieties for two centuries. Its name is attributed both to its possible origin as a peasant, or "low," dance and to its style of small gliding steps in which the feet remain close to the ground. Danced by hand-holding couples in a column, it was performed with various combinations of small bows and a series of walking steps completed by drawing the back foot up to the leading foot. The music was in the modern equivalent of $\frac{12}{8}$ time. The basse danse was typically followed by its afterdance, the saltarello.

Basse-Kotto, *préfecture,* south central Central African Republic, on the Ubangi River opposite Zaire. Its area of 6,750 sq mi (17,600 sq km) comprises three sub-prefectures—Mobaye in the southwest, Kembé in the southeast, and Alindao in the north—each named for its principal town and prefectural seat. Mobaye town, the capital of Basse-Kotto, lies on the Ubangi, where a bridge connects it with Mobayembongo, Zaire. The lower Kotto River flows in rapids southward along the eastern boundary of the *préfecture* to Limassa, where it empties into the Ubangi some 60 mi (95 km) above Mobaye. The Banguikété River flows through the *préfecture,* reaching the Ubangi below Mobaye.

Basse-Kotto is one of the more densely populated parts of the Central African Republic. The population includes nomadic Bororo-Fulani cattle-herders and sedentary Banda cultivators, as well as an ethnic mix (Sango, Yakoma, and Banziri) along the Ubangi River. Cassava is the staple food crop. Cash crops include cotton, grown throughout the *préfecture;* coffee, grown on the Ubangi plain in the south; and oil palms, grown near Mobaye. Pop. (1975) 161,997.

Basse-Normandie, planning region (French *région de programme*), encompassing the northwestern French *départements* of Orne, Calvados, and Manche and coextensive with western Normandy (*q.v.*). The capital is Caen. The region has an area of 6,789 sq mi (17,583 sq km) and is bounded by the *départements* of Ille-et-Vilaine, Mayenne, and Sarthe to the south and Eure-et-Loir and Eure to the east. Manche and Calvados face the English Channel. The uplands of the Massif Armoricain extend into Manche and western Calvados and Orne; eastern Calvados and Orne belong to the Paris Basin. A humid climate prevails, with annual precipitation in the Cotentin peninsula of Manche approaching 35 in. (900 mm).

Basse-Normandie is sparsely inhabited. The process of rural depopulation, which characterized much of France in the 19th and early 20th centuries, was especially pronounced in Basse-Normandie, whose population declined by more than 38 percent between 1851 and 1946. It has subsequently grown at a rate well below the national average, and most of the recovery has occuried in Calvados, which has benefitted from the growth of Caen. There is a large rural population.

Animal husbandry dominates agriculture. Grainfields around Caen have been converted to pastures for beef cattle, and the regions of Auge in Calvados and Perche in Orne are major producers of beef. Artificial insemination is widely used to improve dairy herds. Camembert cheese is produced in Orne; Pont-l'Évêque and Livarot in Calvados also produce fine cheeses. Large numbers of horses are raised in Manche. Port-en-Bassin-Huppain in Calvados and Cherbourg are major fishing ports.

Industries are concentrated around Caen, whose manufactures include electronic goods and Citroën automobiles. The production of iron, which is concentrated around Caen in

May-sur-Orne, Soumont, and Potigny, is in decline. Orne has benefitted from the decentralization of Parisian industries since 1950. Tourism is being developed along the coast of Calvados between Honfleur and Cabourg. Pop. (1982) 1,350,979.

Basse Santa Su, town, port, administrative headquarters of the Upper River division, eastern Gambia, on the south bank of the Gambia River. It is a branch banking centre, a market centre in peanuts (groundnuts), rice, and cattle among the Muslim Fulani (Fula), Malinke (Mandingo), and Wolof peoples, and the last port of call for the government steamer from Banjul, 244 mi (393 km) downstream. The Basse Health Centre is the largest in the interior. Pop. (1973) 2,899.

basse-taille (French: "low-cut"), an enamelling technique in which a metal surface, usually gold or silver, is engraved or carved in low relief and then covered with translucent vitreous enamel. This technique dramatizes the play of light and shade over the low-cut design and also gives the object a brilliance of

Gold cup of the kings of France and England decorated in basse-taille enamel, showing the life and martyrdom of St. Agnes, 1381; in the British Museum

By courtesy of the trustees of the British Museum

tone. Developed in Italy in the 13th century, basse-taille enamelwork was especially popular in Europe during the Gothic and Renaissance periods.

Basse-Terre (island): *see* Guadeloupe.

Basse-Terre, administrative capital of Guadeloupe (an overseas *département* of France), on the Caribbean island of Guadeloupe (Basse-Terre). The town, dating from 1643, is situated on the western coast of the island between the sea and the 4,868-ft (1,484-m) peak of Soufrière and is some 4 mi (6 km) from the island's southwestern tip. There is a deep-water anchorage but no harbour. Basse-Terre yielded commercial paramountcy to the town of Pointe-à-Pitre on Grande-Terre island in the late 18th century. The port of the town was destroyed by hurricanes in 1979, a serious blow to the efforts to expand and modernize the economy. Pop. (1982) 13,656.

Bassein, town, capital of Irrawaddy Division (*taing*), Lower Burma, on the Bassein River, the westernmost distributary of the Irrawaddy River and navigable by ships up to 10,000 tons. The town is a deepwater port and has several rice mills; rice is exported from there. It also has sawmills and machine shops and is known for its pottery and coloured umbrellas and sunshades. Linked by air and river launch to Rangoon, 100 mi (160 km) east, it is also on the railway that runs northeast to Henzada (where the Irrawaddy is crossed by ferry) and continues to Letpadan and Rangoon. Construction projects during the 1970s included a road to Rangoon and a road along the west bank of the Irrawaddy to Monya. Bassein College is affiliated with the Arts and Science University at Rangoon. There is also a training institute for elementary teachers and a large hospital. The Shwemoktaw pagoda (984) in the centre of town is considered one of the most venerable in Lower Burma. It was one of several built by the Mon king Samuddaghosa.

The nearby coastline along the Bay of Bengal is backed by the forested mountains of Arakan Yoma. Its eastern half is a vast rice-producing alluvial plain in the Irrawaddy Delta. The area is noted for its fishing grounds, the largest being Inyegyi Chaung (Inye Lake), 1½ mi long and 1 mi wide. Diamond Island, an offshore reef, is a popular bathing spot and the haunt of large turtles, whose eggs are collected for sale. Pop. (1973) 126,041.

Bassein, also called VASAI, town, Thāna district, Mahārāshtra state, western India, on the Arabian Sea coast, north of Bombay. Part of the territory of the Hindu Devagiri Yādavas until 1317, it later became a seaport for the Gujarāt Muslim kings. In 1526 the Portuguese established a fort (now in ruins) and trading station at Bassein, and the town became famous for its shipbuilding industry. After frequent but unsuccessful attacks by the Mughals in the 17th century, it fell to the Marāṭhās in 1739 and was later taken by the British. The town is a large-scale fishing centre and a wholesale exporter for agricultural produce. Its industries are silk and cotton handloom weaving and salt manufacture. Pop. (1981) town 34,940; metropolitan area, 52,398.

Bassein, Treaty of (Dec. 31, 1802), pact between Bājī Rāo II, the Marāṭhā peshwa of Pune (Poona) in India, and the British; it was a decisive step in the breakup of the Marāṭhā confederacy. The pact led directly to the East India Company's annexation of the Peshwa's territories in western India in 1818. The Marāṭhā confederacy was distracted by dissensions following the death in 1800 of the Peshwa's minister Nāna Fadnavis. The military chiefs Daulat Rāo Sindhia and Jaswant Rāo Holkar (Hulkar), both with disciplined forces at their back, contended for the control of the Peshwa. In October 1802 Holkar defeated Sindhia and the Peshwa and installed an adopted brother on the throne of Pune. Bājī Rāo fled to Bassein and appealed for British help.

By the Treaty of Bassein, the Peshwa agreed to maintain a British subsidiary force of six battalions, for whose upkeep territory was ceded; to exclude all Europeans from his service; to give up his claims on Surat and Baroda; and to conduct his foreign relations in consultation with the British. In return, Arthur Wellesley (later 1st duke of Wellington) restored the Peshwa to Pune in May 1803. The leading Marāṭhā state had thus become a client of the British. This treaty led to the Second Marāṭhā War (1803–05), between the British and the Marāṭhās, and to the defeat of the three other principal Marāṭhā powers.

Bassermann, Albert (b. Sept. 7, 1867, Mannheim, Baden—d. May 15, 1952, Zürich), stage and screen actor known as the finest German interpreter of Ibsen.

He began his career in Mannheim in 1887 and during engagements in several cities established himself in character roles from Shakespeare, Schiller, and Goethe. From 1890 to 1895 he was with the Meiningen court theatre and in 1899 joined Otto Brahm in Berlin, where he established his reputation in Ibsen. He was a member of Max Reinhardt's company from 1909 to 1915. After World War I, Bassermann worked in some of Leopold Jessner's Expressionist productions of the classics

Albert Bassermann, 1948

By courtesy of the National Film Archive, London

and in 1933 left Germany to protest the Nazi regime. He went to the U.S. in 1938 where he played in a variety of Hollywood films. Returning to Europe in 1946, he toured with his own company, whose repertory included Ibsen's *Ghosts* and Schiller's *Wilhelm Tell.* Bassermann was noted for his infinite care with the details of his characterizations, to which he gave an individual stamp, often in defiance of tradition.

Consult the INDEX *first*

Bassermann, Ernst (b. July 26, 1854, Wolfach, Baden—d. July 24, 1917, Baden-Baden), German politician, leader of the National Liberal Party through the last years of imperial Germany.

After achieving financial independence as a legal counsel and through other business interests, Bassermann joined the German National Liberal Party and in 1893 was elected to the Reichstag (national parliament), where, except for a brief period in 1903, he retained a seat for the rest of his life. A follower of the old National Liberal heroes—especially Eduard Lasker and Rudolf von Bennigsen—he was elected leader of the parliamentary party in 1898 and president of the party executive council in 1905. From 1906 to 1909, in the parliamentary coalition of Chancellor Bernhard von Bülow, he served as mediator between extreme factions but refused all overtures to form a political front with the Socialist leader August Bebel and the Social Democrats. His leadership of his own party—torn as it was by conflict from left and right and ever-diminishing membership—was occasionally challenged, but never successfully, and he maintained his control of party affairs until his death.

Basses-Alpes (France): *see* Alpes-de-Haute-Provence.

Basses-Pyrénées (France): *see* Pyrénées-Atlantiques.

basset horn, clarinet pitched a fourth lower than the ordinary B♭ clarinet, probably invented in about 1770 by A. and M. Mayrhofer of Passau, Bavaria. The name derives from its basset ("small bass") pitch and its original curved-horn shape (later supplanted by an angular form). Its bore is narrower than that of the E♭ alto clarinet, and it has a downward extension of compass to the low F of the bass voice (written as C). The boxwood instrument is usually built to order, in straight form with upturned bell.

Though primarily a German instrument, it was known in Paris by 1774 as a *contre-clarinette* and in London by 1789 as a *clara voce.*

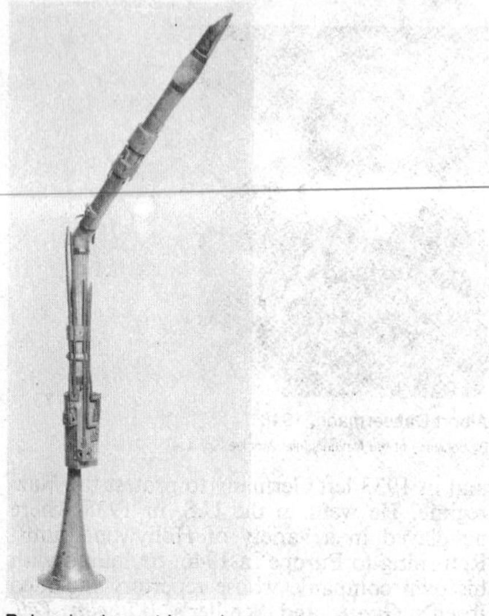

Bohemian basset horn, boxwood and brass, second half of the 18th century; in the Metropolitan Museum of Art, New York City

By courtesy of the Metropolitan Museum of Art, New York City, gift of the University Museum, University of Pennsylvania, 1953

It was employed notably by Mozart but had practically vanished by 1850. It was revived by Richard Strauss (*Elektra,* first performed 1909).

basset hound, breed of dog developed centuries ago in France and maintained for many years, chiefly in France and Belgium, as a hunting dog of the aristocracy. Originally used to trail hares, rabbits, and deer, it has also been used in hunting birds, foxes, and other game. It is characterized as a slow, deliberate hunter, with a deep voice and a "nose" second in keenness only to that of the bloodhound. Short-legged and heavy-boned, the basset hound has long, pendulous ears and a short coat in any combination of black, tan,

Basset hound

Sally Anne Thompson—EB Inc.

and white. It stands 12 to 15 inches (30 to 38 centimetres) and weighs 24 to 44 pounds (11 to 20 kilograms). There are several varieties within the breed, one of the most popular being the sad-eyed Le Couteulx.

Basseterre, chief town of St. Christopher island and capital of St. Christopher and Nevis (*q.v.*), a parliamentary federated state located in the eastern Caribbean. It lies on the island's southwestern coast, 60 mi (100 km) west of St. John's, Antigua. Founded in 1627 and rebuilt after being destroyed by fire (1867), it is St. Kitts's chief port and serves as a depot distributing merchandise to neighbouring islands. Sugar refining is the chief industry, and there is trade in sugar, molasses, cotton, salt, and fruit. Places of interest include St. George's Church, Government House, and a botanical garden. Golden Rock Airport provides air links with the Caribbean and other areas. Old Brimstone Hill Fort is nearby. Pop. (1980 prelim.) 14,283.

Bassetlaw, district, county of Nottinghamshire, England, with an area of 246 sq mi (637 sq km). The district occupies the northern quarter of the county. The name Bassetlaw previously applied to the Parliamentary Constituency that covers much the same area and earlier still was the name of one of the English "wapentakes," or territorial divisions, through which law was administered and defense organized. The court of this wapentake met on a hill called Bassetlaw. Pop. (1982 est.) 102,700.

Bassett, John Spencer (b. Sept. 10, 1867, Tarboro, N.C., U.S.—d. Jan. 27, 1928, Washington, D.C.), U.S. historian and founder of the *South Atlantic Quarterly,* influential in the development of historiography in the South.

A graduate of Trinity College (now Duke University), Durham, N.C., in 1888, he received a doctorate in 1894 from Johns Hopkins University, Baltimore, and taught history at Trinity College (1893–1906) and at Smith College, Northampton, Mass. (1906 until his death). During his tenure at Trinity he was

John Spencer Bassett

By courtesy of Smith College Archives, Northampton Mass.

actively engaged in collecting historical works on the South and by 1902 had launched the *South Atlantic Quarterly,* a literary periodical for scholars. Under his editorship, the *Quarterly* became one of the more liberal periodicals in the South; his own articles deplored racial injustice and provincial isolation.

In 1906 he organized the *Smith College Studies in History,* and in 1919 he was elected secretary of the American Historical Association. A prolific writer, he produced, among other works, *The Federalist System* (1906), *The Life of Andrew Jackson,* 2 vol. (1911), *Short History of the United States* (1913), *The Middle Group of American Historians* (1917), and *Makers of a New Nation* (1928).

Bassi, Agostino (b. Sept. 25, 1773, near Lodi, Italy—d. Feb. 8, 1856, Lodi), pioneer Italian bacteriologist, who anticipated the work of Louis Pasteur by 10 years in discovering that many diseases are caused by microorganisms.

In 1807 he began an investigation of the silkworm disease *mal de segno* (commonly known as muscardine), which was causing serious economic losses in Italy and France. After 25 years of research and experimentation, he was able to demonstrate that the disease was contagious and was caused by a microscopic, parasitic fungus. He concluded that the organism, later named *Botrytis paradoxa* (now *Beauvaria*) *bassiana,* was transmitted among the worms by contact and by infected food.

Bassi announced his discoveries in *Del mal del segno, calcinaccio o moscardino* (1835; "The Disease of the Sign, Calcinaccio or Muscardine") and proceeded to make the important generalization that many diseases of plants, animals, and man are caused by animal or vegetable parasites. Thus, he preceded both Pasteur and Robert Koch in formulating a germ theory of disease. He prescribed methods for the prevention and elimination of muscardine, the success of which earned him considerable honours.

Bassi, Ugo (b. Aug. 12, 1801, Cento, Papal States—d. Aug. 8, 1849, Bologna), Italian priest and patriot, who was a follower of Garibaldi in his fight for Italian independence.

Educated at Bologna, he became a novice in the Barnabite order at age 18, and after studying in Rome, he entered the ministry in 1833. He gained fame as a preacher with eloquent and genuinely enthusiastic sermons that attracted large crowds. Living chiefly at Bologna, he travelled all over Italy aiding and tending the poor.

At the outbreak of the revolutionary movements in 1848, when Pope Pius IX still appeared to be a liberal and a nationalist, Bassi joined, as an army chaplain, Gen. Giovanni Durando's papal force protecting the frontiers. His eloquence helped draw new recruits into the republican movement, and he exercised great influence over the soldiers and the people generally. When Pius discarded all connection with the nationalist movement, only Bassi was able to restrain the Bolognese in their indignation. He was wounded at Treviso in May 1848, but on his recovery marched unarmed at the head of the volunteers at Mestre.

After the Pope's flight from Rome in November and the proclamation of the Roman republic in early 1849, Bassi joined the forces of Garibaldi, fighting against French troops that were sent in to restore the temporal power. When Garibaldi was forced to leave Rome, Bassi followed him to San Marino; when the legion broke up, Garibaldi escaped but Bassi and a fellow patriot, Count Livraghi, were captured near Comacchio. Turned over to the Austrian authorities and taken to Bologna, they were charged with having been found with guns in their hands (Bassi had never borne arms) and executed.

Bassianus, Varius Avitus: *see* Elagabalus.

Bassianus Alexianus, Gessius, also called ALEXIANUS BASSIANUS (Roman emperor): *see* Severus Alexander.

Bassin (U.S. Virgin Islands): *see* Christiansted.

basso continuo (music): *see* thorough bass.

basso ostinato (music): *see* ground bass.

Bassompierre, François de (b. April 12, 1579, Castle of Harrouel, Lorraine—d. Oct. 12, 1646, Castle of Tillières, Normandy), French soldier and diplomat who left an influential autobiography, *Le Journal de ma vie* (1665; *The Journal of My Life*).

Bassompierre was descended from an old family which had for generations served the dukes of Burgundy and Lorraine and, after being educated with his brothers in Bavaria and Italy, was introduced to the court of Henry IV in 1598. He became a great favourite of the King and shared to the full in the dissipations of court life. In 1600 he took part in the brief campaign in Savoy, and in 1603 fought in Hungary for the Emperor against the Turks.

In 1614 he assisted Marie de Médicis in her struggle against the nobles but, upon her failure in 1617, remained loyal to King Louis XIII. His services during the Huguenot rising of 1621–22 won for him the dignity of marshal of France. He was with the army of the King during the siege of La Rochelle in 1628, and in 1629 distinguished himself in the campaign against the rebels of Languedoc; after a short campaign in Italy his military career ended. As a diplomat in Spain, Switzerland, and England, his career was undistinguished. Sometime between 1614 and 1630 he was secretly married to Louise-Marguerite of Lorraine, widow of François, prince of Conti, and through her became implicated in the plot to overthrow Richelieu on the "Day of Dupes," 1630. His share was only a slight one, but his wife was an intimate friend of Marie de Médicis, and her hostility to the Cardinal aroused his suspicions. By Richelieu's orders, Bassompierre was arrested at Senlis on Feb. 25, 1631, and put into the Bastille, where he remained until Richelieu's death in 1643. On his release his offices were restored to him, and he passed most of his time at the Castle of Tillières in Normandy until his death.

His *Mémoires,* which are an important source for the history of his time, were first published at Cologne in 1665. He also left an incomplete account of his embassies to Spain, Switzerland, and England (Cologne, 1668) and a number of discourses upon various subjects.

bassoon, French BASSON, German FAGOTT, principal tenor and bass instrument of the orchestral woodwind family. Its narrow conical bore leads from the curved metal crook, onto which the double reed is placed, downward through the wing joint (on which are the left-hand finger holes) to the butt joint (on which are the right-hand holes). The bore then doubles back, ascending through the butt to the long joint and bell, where the holes are controlled by keywork for the left thumb.

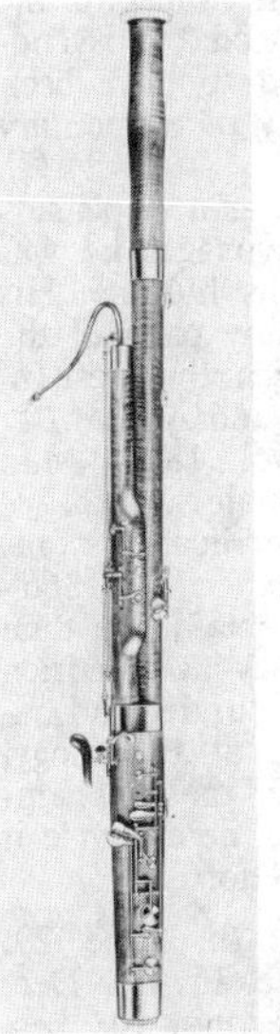

Bassoon

By courtesy of Conn Corporation, Oak Brook, Ill.

The bassoon is held on a sling aslant across the body. Its classical compass is three octaves upward from the B♭ below the bass staff, the most used melodic range coinciding with that of the tenor voice. Since the mid-19th century, the range has been extended up to treble E.

The bassoon is exceptionally difficult to play because the traditional placing of the finger holes is scientifically irrational; yet this is essential to the production of a tone quality that has been one of the primary orchestral colours from Handel's time. The reed is made by bending double a shaped strip of cane.

The bassoon is a 17th-century development of the earlier fagotto, or dulzian, known in England as the curtal (*q.v.*). It was first mentioned *c.* 1540 in Italy, with the descending and ascending bores contained in a single piece of maple or pear wood. Many examples survive in museums at Brussels, Berlin, Vienna, and elsewhere. The present construction in four separate joints is thought to have been developed in France by 1636, closely following the reconstruction of the shawm, which produced the oboe, to which the bassoon served as bass. During the 18th century the individuality of the bassoon became recognized not only in the orchestra (in which two have normally been since employed) but also as a solo instrument for concerti. Well into Mozart's time no mechanism was required beyond four keys, most of the semitones outside the natural scale of C having been well obtained by cross-fingerings opening the holes nonconsecutively. Leisurely addition of keys from *c.* 1780 led to Jean-Nicolas Savary's Paris models of *c.* 1840, which, with further improvements in bore and mechanism, became the 20-keyed French bassoon, made by the famous firm of Buffet-Crampon, that is used in France, Italy, and Spain and by some British players.

Although it has preserved and developed the sympathetic vocal sonority of the classical instrument, the French bassoon remains difficult to control, owing to inherent unevenness in the quality and steadiness of many notes. Alterations to minimize these defects were initiated in Germany in 1825 by Carl Almenräder. A reformed model was developed by the firm of Johann Adam Heckel and perfected in the German bassoon now standard everywhere except in France, Italy, and Spain. It is of European maple, with its own positions and sizes of the holes to give a more even and positive response throughout the compass. It can be more quickly learned, is easier to choose reeds for, and is in many respects more telling in a large orchestra. Research on old bassoons suggests that its tone quality, different from the French and considered by some to have sacrificed eloquence for expediency, may not represent as gross a deviation from classical tone as was hitherto believed.

The first useful contrabassoon, or double bassoon, sounding an octave lower than the bassoon and much employed in large scores, was developed in Vienna and used occasionally by the classical composers. The modern contrabassoon follows Heckel's design of *c.* 1870, with the tubing doubled back four times and often with a metal bell, pointing downward.

Bast, also called BASTET, or UBASTI, ancient Egyptian goddess worshipped in the form of a cat; she was essentially a goddess of the home, but in the New Kingdom (1567–1085 BC) many changes were made in the official religion, and Bast became equated with the lioness war goddess. Bast, however, never lost her feline identity or her hold on popular affection, as is shown by the number of small figures of the goddess evidently intended to be used in home worship or to be worn as amulets.

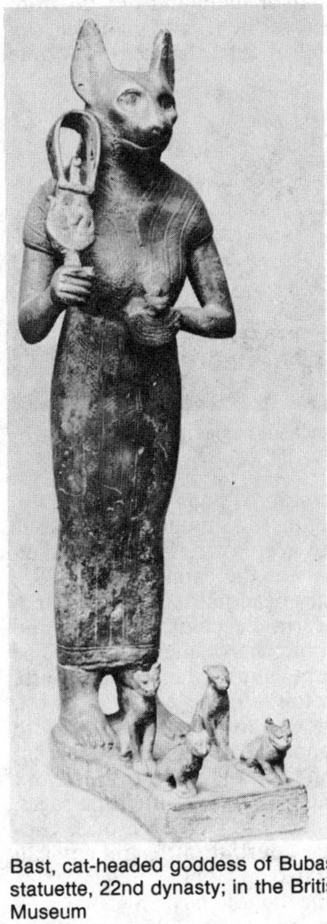

Bast, cat-headed goddess of Bubastis, statuette, 22nd dynasty; in the British Museum

Reproduced by courtesy of the trustees of the British Museum

Bast is represented as a woman with a cat's head: she carries an ancient percussion instrument, the sistrum, in her right hand; a so-called aegis, or breastplate (in Bast's case, surmounted with the head of a lioness), in her left hand; and a small bag over her left arm. Her cult was later carried to Italy by the Romans and traces of it have been found in Rome, Ostia, Nemi, and Pompeii.

bast (botany): *see* phloem.

bast fibre, soft, woody fibre obtained from stems of dicotyledonous plants (flowering plants with net-veined leaves, such as sunflowers, roses, most trees, and flax) and used for textiles and cordage. Such fibres, usually characterized by fineness and flexibility, are also known as "soft" fibres, distinguishing them from the coarser, less flexible fibres of the leaf, or "hard," fibre group. Commercially useful bast fibres include flax, hemp, jute, kenaf, ramie, roselle, sunn, and urena.

Fibre bundles, often several feet long, strengthen plant stems. Located beneath the epidermis, or bark surface, they are composed of many overlapping fibre cells, or true plant fibres, held together by gummy substances. Stalks are cut off close to the base or pulled up. The fibres are usually freed from the stalk by retting but are sometimes obtained by decortication, a manual or mechanical peeling operation. The released fibre bundles, called strands, are frequently used without additional separation, in which case they are called fibres. Flax and ramie strands, however, are usually separated into individual fibre cells, or true plant fibres.

Most bast fibres are quite strong and are widely used in the manufacture of ropes and twines, bagging materials, and heavy-duty industrial fabrics. In the early 1980s, jute, used mainly for sacking and wrapping purposes, led other fibres in world production but suffered from intense competition from synthetic fibres. Flax, traditionally valued as raw material for linen yarn and fine linen fabrics, is decreasing in importance for luxury textile applications as other fibres, both natural and man-made, become more plentiful.

Bastaard (people): *see* Baster.

Basṭām, also spelled BUSTAM, BISTAM, or BOSTUM, small historic town, Semnān *ostān* (province), Iran, just south of the Elburz Mountains in a well-watered plain. Clustered around the tomb of the poet and mystic Abū Yazīd al-Bisṭāmī (died 874) are a mausoleum, a 12th-century minaret and mosque wall, a superb portal (1313), and a 15th-century college. Nearby are interesting ruins, including a mosque and a cloister with fine stucco. Most of the constructions were ordered by two Mongol rulers, Haḥmūd Ghāzān (1295–1304) and Öljeitü (1304–16). Pop. (latest census) less than 5,000.

Bastar, district, Madhya Pradesh state, central India, occupying an area of 15,081 sq mi (39,060 sq km) and comprising the former Bastar and Kānker princely states, which merged in 1948. The largest district of the state, it consists chiefly of western outliers of the Eastern Ghāts; in the south the district is divided by the Bailādila (Bullock's Hump) Range. Toward the west the country falls away into the Godāvari Valley, while much of the east is a plateau at 1,500–2,000 ft (450–600 m). Less than one-tenth of the district is cultivated, and the villages are separated

Plowing a rice paddy at Nārāinpur in Bastar district, Madhya Pradesh, India
Syndication International London, Ltd.

by broad forest tracts. There are considerable undeveloped timber (sal and teak) and mineral resources. The Indrāvati and Mahānadi rivers drain the area. Rice and millet are the chief crops; hematite, mica, and corundum deposits are worked. The majority of the population are tribal Goṇḍs and Halbīs. The district headquarters is at Jagdalpur. Pop. (1981) 1,842,854.

bastard toadflax, any of several small annual or perennial herbs of the sandalwood family (Santalaceae) that have narrow leaves resembling those of true toadflax (*Linaria*). In North America, bastard toadflax refers to plants of the genus *Comandra.* They are sometimes parasitic on the roots of other plants and have creeping roots, small white flowers clustered at the top of each plant, and one-seeded fruits.

In Europe the name bastard toadflax is used for plants of the genus *Thesium,* which also has species distributed throughout Africa, Asia, and South America. The bisexual yellow or yellowish-green flowers are grouped in terminal clusters, and the one-seeded fruit is dry and green.

Bastarnae, in Hellenistic and Roman times, large tribe settled in Europe east of the Carpathian Mountains from the upper valley of the Dniester to the Danube Delta. The Bastarnae were used by the Macedonian kings Philip V and Perseus against their Thracian enemies and by Mithradates of Pontus against the Romans. The name Peucini, occasionally applied to the tribe, properly belonged only to part of it. Pliny and Tacitus as well as recent archaeological discoveries confirm the Germanic origins of the tribe. Subdued by the Roman general Marcus Licinius Crassus in 29 BC, the Bastarnae caused the Romans little trouble until the 3rd century AD, when they joined with other tribes in raiding Roman territory. The Roman emperor Probus then transplanted them to the southern bank of the Danube (AD 279–280).

Baster, formerly BASTAARD, member of a racially mixed group in South West Africa/Namibia and northwestern South Africa, most of whom are descendants of Afrikaner men and indigenous Nama women of southwestern Africa. They speak a language that is primarily Afrikaans and follow a western way of life.

The Basters were originally seminomadic pastoralists and hunters who gradually settled as pioneers in the northwestern frontier areas north of Cape Town. Largely through missionary work during the 19th century, they coalesced into fiercely independent, autonomous communities that maintained their identities even after being incorporated into the Cape Colony. Others moved further north into what is now South West Africa/Namibia in the late 1860s because of pressure from Boer settlers and eventually established a settlement that became known as Rehoboth.

The Rehoboth community remains the largest group of Basters. They practice subsistence farming and keep cattle, but they also rely heavily on the remittances of migrant labourers working at the port of Walvis Bay and in the diamond mines near the Orange River mouth at the South African border.

Bastet (Egyptian goddess): *see* Bast.

Bastī, town, administrative headquarters of Bastī district, Uttar Pradesh state, northern India, east of Faizābād on the Kuwāna River. Located on a national highway and a major rail line, it is an agricultural trade centre with some industry at nearby villages. Bastī consists of three sections—Old Bastī, extending east-west between the railway and the provincial road; Pukka Bāzār, a suburb just southwest with official and professional residences; and the "civil station," an administrative sector west of Pukka Bāzār, on the Kuwāna. The town has a college affiliated with Gorakhpur University. Bastī was small until 1865, when it became the district headquarters. Since then its population has greatly increased.

Bastī district, 2,822 sq mi (7,309 sq km) in area, is a stretch of alluvial plain between the Ghāghara River and the Nepal border. Crossed by the Kuwāna, Rāpti, and Ami rivers, it is poorly drained and contains a number of swamps and marshy lakes; Lake Chanda and Lake Badhanchh are the largest. Grains, sugarcane, and other crops are grown, in some places under irrigation. The district conducts some trade with Nepal. Pop. (1981) town, 69,465; district, 3,578,069.

Bastia, city, capital of Haute-Corse *département,* Corse region, France, on the northeastern coast, 22 mi (35 km) south of the island's northernmost point, the tip of Cap Corse. It is close to the Italian mainland (73 mi from Livorno) and across the Tyrrhenian Sea can be seen the island of Elba, flanked by Monte

Bastia, on the northeastern coast of Corsica
Marc Garanger

Cristo and Capraia. A poor fishing village, Marina di Cardo, in 1383 it changed its name after the Genoese keep, or *bastiglia,* was constructed there. It was the capital (until 1791) and still is military headquarters of the island. The old town (Terra Vecchia) is built in and around the central part of the harbour. The upper town (Terra Nuova) lies to the south, and the modern town to the north and west. One of the first towns to welcome union with France, it was opposed to the anticlericalism of the Revolution. The old town is a network of alleys connected by dark, vaulted passages. The classical facades of the church of S. Giovanni Battista, law court, theatre, and city hall are floridly decorated.

The town is the largest city in Corsica, a modern port city and, since 1976, capital of the newly created *département* of Haute-Corse. Bastia manufactures cigarettes, cigars, and preserves, and its exports include the celebrated wines of Cap Corse. Pop. (1982) 43,502.

Bastian, Adolf (b. June 26, 1826, Bremen, Ger.—d. Feb. 2, 1905, Port of Spain, Trinidad), ethnologist who theorized that there is a general psychic unity of mankind that is responsible for certain elementary ideas common to all peoples. Bastian proposed that cultural traits, folklore, myths, and beliefs of various ethnic groups originate within each group according to laws of cultural evolution

Bastian
Bavaria-Verlag

and are essentially the same, merely differing in form because of geographical environment. His views are thought to have influenced a number of prominent anthropologists, including Bronisław Malinowski. The concept of the collective unconscious advanced by psychoanalyst Carl Jung is believed to have been derived from Bastian's theory of elementary ideas.

In 1851 Bastian went to sea as a ship's surgeon on the first of many voyages he was to make in the course of his lifetime. His first venture took him to many parts of the world, including South America, the West Indies, Australia, China, India, and Africa. *Der Mensch in der Geschichte* (3 vol., 1860; "Man in History") is considered his major work. Five years in the Orient preceded publication of his *Die Völker des östlichen Asien* (6 vol., 1866–71; "The People of Eastern Asia"). He then became professor of ethnology at Friedrich Wilhelm University, Berlin. Founder and curator of the Royal Museum of Ethnology, Berlin, for many years one of the most important institutions of its kind, he enriched it with his own substantial collection.

Bastiat, (Claude-)Frédéric (b. June 29, 1801, Mugron, near Bayonne, Fr.—d. Dec. 24, 1850, Rome), French economist, best known for his journalistic writing in favour of free trade and the economics of the Scotsman Adam Smith. In 1846 he founded the Associations pour la Liberté des Échanges (Associations for Free Trade) and used its journal, *Le Libre-Échange,* to advance his antiprotec-

Bastiat, detail of an engraving
H. Roger-Viollet

tionist views. In a well-known satirical parable that appeared in his *Sophismes économiques* (1845; *Sophisms of Protection,* 1922) he concocted a petition brought by candlemakers who asked for protection against the Sun, suggesting that candlemaking and related industries would greatly profit if the Sun were eliminated as a competitor in furnishing light.

During the revolutionary years 1848–49 he wrote against the rise of socialism, which he identified with protectionism. It was primarily his campaign against socialism and communism that won for him a seat in the Constituent Assembly in 1849 and in the subsequent Legislative Assembly of the same year. Bastiat also carried on a vigorous, if unsystematic, polemic against Ricardian economics.

bastide, type of village or town built largely in the 13th and 14th centuries in England and Gascony and laid out according to a definite geometric plan. It is thought by some to have been an influence on English colonists when building such New World settlements as New Haven, Conn.

Edward I of England, also duke of Gascony, was one of the foremost rulers to lay out new towns. He did so for defensive, economic, and colonizing purposes. The lord of a manor with a successful bastide on it could expect an increase of revenue from the rents, fair and market tolls, justice profits, and trade tariffs. Most of the British bastides, especially those in Wales, had a marine-based economy, while the Gascon bastides were dependent on the production and exportation of wine.

With allowances made for local terrain, bastides were laid out according to a rectangular grid derived from ancient Roman town plans. The bastide was often built on a hilltop, with the streets dividing the town into rectilinear *insulae* ("islands" or "blocks"), which, in turn, were divided into *placae,* or house and garden lots. In order to facilitate rent collecting, the blocks were numbered in military fashion from right to left, top to bottom. The streets, as far as possible, met at right angles. A marketplace was always planned, which included arcaded shops (*cornières*) and sometimes a market hall.

The typical bastide is found in the ruins of New Winchelsea, Eng., a town that died because the sea on which it depended receded, leaving marshland. In Gascony the bastides were founded for security and colonization purposes in a heavily forested area. Bastides in Gascony include Lalinde, Beaumont-du-Périgord, and La Bastide Monestier.

Bastien-Lepage, Jules (b. Nov. 18, 1848, Damillers, Fr.—d. Dec. 10, 1884, Paris), French painter of rustic outdoor genre scenes widely imitated in France and England.

Bastien-Lepage studied under Alexandre Cabanel, first exhibited at the Paris Salon of

"The Hayfield," painting by Bastien-Lepage, 1878; in the Louvre, Paris
Eddy van der Veen

1870, and won a medal at the Salon of 1874 for "Spring Song," which stylistically owes a little to Édouard Manet. "The Hayfield" (1878; Louvre, Paris) follows in the tradition of Jean-François Millet and reveals the sentimental element that characterizes Bastien-Lepage's work. "Joan of Arc Listening to the Voices" (Metropolitan Museum of Art, New York City), which represents Joan as a Lorraine peasant, typifies his subject pictures. He was also a portraitist of note.

Bastille, medieval fortress on the east side of Paris that became, in the 17th and 18th centuries, a French state prison and a place of detention for important persons charged with miscellaneous offenses. The Bastille, stormed by an armed mob of Parisians in the opening days of the French Revolution, was a symbol of the despotism of the Bourbons and held an important place in the ideology of the Revolution.

With its eight towers, 100 feet high, linked by walls of equal height and surrounded by a moat more than 80 feet wide, the Bastille dominated Paris. The first stone was laid on April 22, 1370, on the orders of Charles V of France, who had it built as a *bastide,* or fortification (the name Bastille is a corruption of *bastide*), to protect his wall around Paris against English attack. The Bastille, in fact, was originally a fortified gate, but Charles VI turned it into an independent stronghold by walling up the openings. In 1557 its defensive system was completed on the eastern flank by the erection of a bastion. In the 17th century a transverse block was built, dividing the inner court into unequal parts.

The Cardinal de Richelieu was the first to use the Bastille as a state prison, in the 17th century; the yearly average number of prisoners was 40, interned by *lettre de cachet,* a direct order of the King, from which there was no recourse. Prisoners included political troublemakers and individuals held at the request of their families, often to coerce a young member into obedience or to prevent a disreputable member from marring the family's name. Under Louis XIV, the Bastille became a place of judicial detention in which the *lieutenant de police* could hold prisoners; under the regency of Philippe II, duc d'Orléans, persons being tried by the Parlement were also detained there. Imprisonment by *lettre de cachet* remained, however, in force, and prohibited books were also placed in the Bastille. The high cost of maintaining the building prompted talk of demolition in 1784.

On the morning of July 14, 1789, when only seven prisoners were confined in the building, a mob advanced on the Bastille with the intention of asking the prison governor, Bernard Jordan, marquis de Launay, to release the arms and munitions stored there. Angered by Launay's evasiveness, the people stormed and captured the place; this dramatic action came to symbolize the end of the ancien régime. The Bastille was subsequently demolished by order of the Revolutionary government.

Bastille Day, celebrated annually on July 14, was chosen as a French national holiday in 1880. It is celebrated with parades, speeches, and fireworks and with such slogans as *Vive le 14 juillet!* ("Long live the 14th of July!") and *À bas la Bastille!* ("Down with the Bastille!").

bastnaesite, also spelled BASTNÄSITE, a cerium fluoride carbonate, $CeCO_3(OH,F)$, found in contact metamorphic zones and pegmatites; cerium is commonly substituted by light rare earths, lanthanum, yttrium, and thorium. It ranges in colour from wax-yellow to reddish-brown. Bastnaesite is commonly associated with other rare-earth-bearing minerals such as allanite, cerite, and tysonite; it is often an alteration product of tysonite. Bastnaesite occurs in pegmatites near Pikes Peak, Colo. and with fluorite in Lincoln County, New Mexico; it is commercially mined at Mountain Pass, Calif. For detailed physical properties, *see* carbonate mineral (table).

Bastrop, city, Morehouse Parish, northeastern Louisiana, U.S., 29 mi (47 km) northeast of Monroe. Founded in 1846 as the parish seat, it experienced an industrial boom after 1916, when natural gas was discovered. Manufactures include wood products, carbon black, and chemicals. Bastrop is also an agricultural centre (cattle, cotton, corn, rice, and soybeans) and site of the North Louisiana Cotton Festival and Fair. Nearby are Chemin-A-Haut State Park and Bussey Brake Reservoir. Inc. city, 1952. Pop. (1980) 15,527.

Bastwick, John (b. 1593, Writtle, Essex, Eng.—d. September/October 1654), English religious zealot who opposed Roman Catholic ceremonial in the years before the outbreak of the English Civil War.

After a brief education at Cambridge, he wandered on the Continent and graduated in medicine at Padua, Italy. On his return he settled in Colchester. About 1633 he printed in the Netherlands two Latin treatises, entitled *Elenchus Religionis Papisticae* and *Flagellum Pontificis et Episcoporum Latialium;* and because William Laud and other English prelates thought themselves the target of the treatises, he was fined, excommunicated, and prohibited from practicing medicine; his books were burned, and he was consigned to prison. His counterblast was *Apologeticus ad Praesules Anglicanos* and another book, in English, *The Litany,* in which he charged the bishops with being the enemies of God and "the tail of the beast." Bastwick, William Prynne, and Henry Burton came under the lash of the Star Chamber court at the same time; they were all censured as turbulent and seditious persons and condemned to pay a fine of £5,000 each, to be set in the pillory, to lose their ears, and to undergo imprisonment for life in remote parts of the kingdom, Bastwick being sent to Scilly. The Parliament in 1640 reversed these proceedings and ordered Bastwick a reparation of £5,000 out of the estates of the commissioners and lords who had sentenced him. He joined the Parliamentary army but in later years showed bitter opposition to the Independents.

Basuku (people): *see* Suku.

bat, a member of any of some 900 species of flying mammals. Bats are the only mammals to have evolved true flight, and most species also possess an acute system of acoustic orientation, or echolocation.

A brief treatment of bats follows. For full treatment, *see* MACROPAEDIA: Mammals.

Most bats are insectivorous. As they consume immense quantities of insects, bats are important in the balance of insect populations and may even be instrumental in controlling some insect pests. Certain bats also feed on fruit, pollen, and nectar, and vampire bats in tropical America feed on the blood of mammals and large birds. These bats sometimes serve as carriers of rabies.

Bats are found worldwide. The United States is known to have 15 genera, totalling 40 species of bats. While in the West they are the subject of unfavourable myths, in the Orient bats are often considered to be good luck symbols. In the tropics, where they are particularly abundant, bats attract considerable attention by their noisiness, guano (droppings), and odor, as large colonies of bats can infest houses and public buildings.

Two suborders divide the bat order: the Megachiroptera (flying foxes and Old World fruit bats) and the Microchiroptera (distributed worldwide). The Megachiroptera are visually oriented—only one genus, *Rousettus,* possesses an acoustic orientation ability—and in many ways skeletally primitive. The Microchiroptera all possess the ability to orient and even hunt by acoustic means. It is not known whether the two have a common origin. Bats vary greatly in size. The largest of the flying foxes, *Pteropus vampyrus*, has a wingspread of as much as 1.5 meters (5 feet), while the wingspread of the Philippine bamboo bat (*Tylonycteris pachypus meyeri*) is not more than 15 millimetres (6 inches). Bats also display variety in colour, fur texture, and facial appearance.

The wings of bats are an evolutionary modification of the forelimbs. The fingers are greatly elongated, except the thumb, and joined by a membrane extending from the posterior border of the forearm and upper arm down the side of the body to the ankle or foot. The thumb ends with a claw. Most bats also have a membrane extending between their legs with two layers of darkly pigmented, naked skin similar to that of the wings.

The bat's head is its most striking feature. The external ear projects forward and is usually very large and often highly mobile. The bat's muzzle is often rodentlike or foxlike. Many bats also have a nose leaf, which consists of skin and connective tissue that either surrounds the nostrils or flaps above them. It is thought that the nose leaf influences sound production for echolocation. The bat's neck is short, the chest and shoulders well muscled and large, and the hips and legs slender. Except for the wing membranes, bats are well furred in shades of gray, tan, brown, or black on the back and in lighter shades ventrally. Among species that roost in the open, mottled or speckled fur and variations in coloration are common.

Bats affect the natural order not only through predation but also by pollination and seed dispersal, which they aid by their feeding habits. The vampire bats of tropical America are the only bats that pose a serious problem to man; among livestock they can transmit a cattle disease, and the small wounds they cause are often egg-laying sites for botflies. The guano deposits of insectivorous bats have long been used for agricultural fertilizer.

The sexual cycles of entire bat populations are synchronized so that most of the mating activity occurs over a period of a few weeks. Gestation ranges from six or seven weeks to five or six months. Pregnant female bats of many species migrate to special nursery roosts. Bats generally bear one young, although the big brown bat (*Eptesicus fuscus*) can bear twins and the red bat (*Lasiurus borealis*) bears a litter of one to four. Infants are born nude or with light fur and are often blind and deaf for a short period after birth. They nurse for five or six weeks or for as long as five months, depending on size and suborder. By two months of age most Microchiroptera are adult sized.

Nearly all bat species roost during the day and forage at night. This gives carnivorous bats, vampires, and perhaps fishing bats an advantage over sleeping prey and also protects bats from predators, sun, and high temperatures. Bats generally prefer isolated roosts such as caves, crevices, burrows, or buildings. Some bats, however, roost outdoors on trees or rocks. Usually bats are found in large clustered colonies. These groups can range from a few dozen to hundreds of thousands of individuals. The mortality rate for adult bats is very low. Predation is not a serious threat, and disease, starvation, and accidents appear to take small tolls. Some bats are known to have lived more than 20 years. Isolated roosts, nocturnal activity, and a generally colonial way of life are factors that contribute to the longevity of bats.

In those bats that use echolocation, short high-frequency sound pulses are produced that reflect from objects in the vicinity. The bats listen to the returning echoes and are able to locate prey and obstacles. Highly sensitive ears and greatly developed integration of vocal and auditory centres of the brain are required for this feat. The sound pulses may also be used for communication between bats.

bat, also spelled BAHT, or BATH, also called EPHAH, ancient Hebrew unit of liquid and dry capacity. Estimated at 37 litres (6.5 gallons) and approximately equivalent to the Greek *metrētēs*, the *bat* contained 10 omers, one omer being the quantity of manna allotted to each Israelite for every day of the 40-year sojourn in the desert recorded in the Bible.

bat bug, any blood-sucking insect of the family Polyctenidae (order Heteroptera), which numbers at least 18 species. Bat bugs are external parasites found in the fur of tropical bats. The adult (between 3.5 and 5 millimetres, or less than 0.2 inch, long) lacks eyes and wings. Its forelegs are short and thick, and its middle and hindlegs are long and slender.

As indicated by the family name, the bat bug has from one to many comblike rows of spines (ctenidia) on its body. The young are born alive in an advanced stage of development.

bat-eared fox, also called CAPE FOX, BIG-EARED FOX, or MOTLOSI (*Otocyon megalotis*), large-eared fox, belonging to the dog family (Canidae), found in open, arid areas of eastern and southern Africa. It has 48 teeth, 6 more than any other canid. The bat-eared fox is like the red fox in appearance but has unusually large ears. It is yellowish gray with black face and legs and black-tipped ears and tail. It grows to a length of about 80 centimetres (32 inches), including the 30-cm tail, and weighs from 3 to 4.5 kilograms (6.6–10 pounds). It lives alone or in small groups and feeds primarily on insects, especially termites. Litters contain two to five young; gestation lasts 60 to 70 days.

Bat-eared fox (*Otocyon megalotis*)

Mark Boulton—The National Audubon Society Collection/Photo Researchers

bat fly, any insect belonging to the two families Nycteribiidae and Streblidae (order Diptera). Members of the family Nycteribiidae are wingless, spiderlike insects with long legs and a small head that folds back into a groove in the thorax when at rest. They are external parasites of bats.

Members of the family Streblidae do not bend their heads back. Wings may be present, vestigial (reduced), or absent in members of this family.

bat parrolet, also called HANGING PARAKEET, small, short-tailed green parrot of the genus *Loriculus*, order Psittaciformes. *See* parakeet.

Bat Yam, city, west central Israel, on the Plain of Sharon and the Mediterranean coast just south of Tel Aviv–Yafo. Founded in 1926 as a suburban development called Bayit ve-Gan (Hebrew: House and Garden), it was abandoned during the Arab riots of 1929. Resettled, it developed as a seaside resort and residential suburb of Tel Aviv. In 1936 the name was changed to Bat Yam (meaning "daughter of the sea"), and the town received municipal status. After 1950 its population grew rapidly, as housing quarters were built for new Jewish immigrants. Bat Yam is a principal centre of Israel's printing and publishing industry; food processing (beer and light beverages) is also important. Inc. city, 1958. Pop. (1982 est.) 132,800.

Bat Zabbai (queen of Palmyra): *see* Zenobia.

Bata, capital of Río Muni province (also called Río Mbini), Equatorial Guinea, West Africa, lying on the Gulf of Guinea 18 mi (29 km) north of the Río Mbini. Because it has no natural harbour, a jetty was built to facilitate offshore handling of ships' cargoes; the principal exports are timber and coffee. Bata has air links with the Guinean capital, Malabo (formerly Santa Isabel), and to Libreville, Gabon.

After the anti-Spanish riots of 1969, there was a dramatic decrease in the number of resident Europeans in Bata, followed by severe economic stagnation extending into the early 1980s. Pop. (1974 est.) 10,000.

Bataan, province, central Luzon, Philippines; it occupies a 530-sq-mi (1,370-sq-km) peninsula extending southward and sheltering Manila Bay (east) from the South China Sea. Corregidor Island (*q.v.*) lies just off its southern tip at the entrance of the bay. About 30 mi (48 km) long and averaging 15 mi in width, Bataan is largely covered by jungle and is traversed north to south by steep mountains culminating in Mt. Natib (4,224 ft [1,287 m]) in the north and Mt. Bataan (4,701 ft) in the south.

After the Japanese invasion of the Philippines in December 1941 and the fall of Manila (Jan. 2, 1942), the defending Americans and Filipinos withdrew to Bataan, defeating Japanese efforts to split the forces of U.S. Gen. Douglas MacArthur. His troops fought a fierce delaying action until April 9, 1942, and remnants, led by Lieut. Gen. Jonathan M. Wainwright, escaped to Corregidor Island, where they surrendered about a month later. On Jan. 9, 1945, U.S. forces under MacArthur landed at Lingayen Gulf to the north and sealed off the Bataan Peninsula. Landings were then made at Mariveles Harbor in the south and on Corregidor Island, thus securing Manila Bay for the U.S. Navy.

The provincial capital is Balanga. Subic Bay in the northwest is the site of U.S. and Philippine naval bases. There are shipyards at Mariveles; a free trade zone was opened there in the 1970s. Because of the proximity of Manila, none of Bataan's five ports is open to overseas shipping. The towns of Orani, Samal, Abucay, Orion, and Limay are located along the eastern coastal plain, the principal agricultural (rice, corn [maize], sugarcane) district. Morong and Bagac are on the western coast. Hermosa in the north is the site of Roosevelt National Park (1933), a 3,296-ac (1,335-ha) area with hot springs and a game refuge. The Bataan National Park (1945), overlooking Manila Bay, is largely a World War II commemorative area of 77,593 ac. Pop. (1980) 323,254.

Bataan Death March, forced march of 70,000 American and Filipino prisoners of war captured by the Japanese in the Philippines in the early stages of World War II. Starting out from Mariveles, on the southern end of the Bataan Peninsula, on April 9, 1942, they were force-marched 55 miles to San Fernando, then taken by rail to Capas, from where they walked the final eight miles to Camp O'Donnell. They were starved and mistreated, often kicked or beaten on their way, and many who fell were bayonetted. Only 54,000 reached the camp; 7,000–10,000 died on the way and the rest escaped to the jungle.

After the war, the Japanese commander of

the invasion forces in the Philippines, Lieut. Gen. Homma Masaharu, was charged with responsibility for the death march and was tried by a U.S. military commission in Manila in January–February 1946. Convicted, he was executed on April 3.

Batabanó, Gulf of, Spanish GOLFO DE BATABANÓ, inlet of the Caribbean Sea, indenting southwestern Cuba. The gulf stretches from the shore of eastern Pinar del Río province approximately 80 mi (130 km) to the southwestern coast of Matanzas province and the Península de Zapata. At its northern edge lies La Habana province; 50 mi to the south is the Isla (island) de la Juventud. The shallow gulf, economically important for sponge fishing, is dotted with many smaller islands and keys.

Bataille, (Félix-)Henry (b. April 4, 1872, Nîmes, Fr.—d. March 2, 1922, Rueil-Malmaison), dramatist whose luxuriant plays of passionate love and stifling social conventions were extremely popular at the beginning of the 20th century.

Bataille's parents died when he was very young, and, having shown talent for both painting and poetry at school, he turned to writing by the age of 14. After several false starts his successful career began with *L'Enchantement* (1900), followed by such works as *Maman Colibri* (1904); *La Femme nue* (1908; "The Nude Woman"), considered by many his best play; and *La Vierge folle* (1910; "The Foolish Virgin"). The combination of sonorous, exaggerated language and explicit social messages soon dated his plays; critics also began to attack his "immorality." Even though his art evolved toward the theatre of ideas and, later, toward social drama, as in *La Chair humaine* (1922; "Human Flesh"), his later works were less successful. His theory of "indirect language," capable of betraying or concealing a character's subconscious desires, although largely unapplied in his own work, makes him a forerunner of Jean-Jacques Bernard and the "school of silence."

Bataisk, also spelled BATAJSK (Russian S.F.S.R.): *see* Bataysk.

Batak, also spelled BATTAK, or BATTA, several closely related ethnic groups of central Sumatra, Indonesia. They possess a written language of their own, consisting of several diverse dialects, belonging to the Austronesian family. The Batak are descendants of a powerful Proto-Malayan people who until 1825 lived in relative isolation in the highlands surrounding Lake Toba in Sumatra.

Batak village, Sumatra
Marc Riboud—Magnum

The Batak had felt Indian influences by the 2nd or 3rd century AD and had borrowed ideas of government, writing, elements of religion, arts, and crafts. They did not, however, develop a unified state and today are found in six cultural divisions. Within these are exogamous patrilineal clans known as *marga.* A price is paid for a bride, who then becomes a member of her husband's group. Among the Toba Batak a village consists of several clan houses, but in the Karo division all dwell in one or more longhouses.

Ancestors, plants, animals, and inanimate objects are considered to possess souls or spirits that can be coerced or enticed by male priests. These priests are aided by female mediums who, in trance, communicate with the dead. Cannibalism was once practiced, but victims were confined to prisoners and those guilty of incest.

Today most of the Toba Batak are literate, as is the case of many in the other groups. Many are Christians who occupy places of importance in trade and in the Indonesian government. Muslim missionaries have been active in regions to the north and south of the Toba. The estimated population of Batak lands is about 3,100,000, of which about one-third is Christian, one-third Muslim, and the balance still adherents of traditional beliefs.

After World War II there was a mass movement of Toba squatters into the rich plantation lands of the east coast, formerly owned by foreign investors. Their adjustment to a humid lowland jungle environment raised many complex problems.

Batak Protestant Christian Church, also called KRISTEN BATAK PROTESTANT (HKBP), church in northern Sumatra, Indon., organized as an independent church in 1930, and the largest Lutheran church in Asia. It developed from the work of missionaries of the Rhenish Mission Society, established in Barmen, Ger., in 1828. Under the leadership of the German Lutheran missionary Ludwig Ingwer Nommensen, the missionaries began working among the Batak people in Sumatra in 1862. Resistance to Christianity lessened slowly, and by 1880 entire tribes and villages began converting to Christianity. Nommensen translated Luther's Small Catechism, the New Testament (1878), and several other works into the Batak language and wrote hymns and a church order for the Batak church. By 1894 the entire Bible had been translated. Education was stressed, and many elementary schools were established in the villages. A Batak mission society extended the mission work among the people.

After the HKBP was organized in 1930, the foreign missionaries began withdrawing; the last of them departed in the 1940s, during World War II and the Indonesian war for independence from The Netherlands. The HKBP was accepted as a member of the Lutheran World Federation in 1952.

The church is divided into districts, each headed by a superintendent. The superintendents make up the church council headed by an *ephorus* (bishop), who is elected for a specified term of office.

Batāla, city, Gurdāspur district, Punjab state, northwestern India. Located northeast of Amritsar, Batāla is an agricultural marketplace and industrial centre. Cotton ginning, weaving, sugar refining, and manufacturing are the principal industries. Batāla has two colleges and is linked by road and rail with Amritsar and other cities in Punjab. Pop. (1981) city, 87,135; metropolitan area, 101,966.

Batalha, town and *concelho* (municipality), Leiria district, west central Portugal, just south of Leiria city. The town is dominated by the great Dominican abbey of Santa Maria da Vitória, also known simply as Batalha (Battle). In the Battle of Aljubarrota, fought on a plain 9 mi (14 km) southwest of the town, John I of Portugal defeated John I of Castile in 1385 and secured the independence of his kingdom. The abbey was probably founded in 1388 to commemorate the victory. The Founder's Chapel contains the tomb of the victor, John I, and Philippa of Lancaster, his English queen, as well as the tomb of Henry the Navigator, their son. Other monarchs are buried in the royal mausoleum. Only the royal cloister, church, and Founder's Chapel

Dominican abbey of Santa Maria da Vitória, Batalha, Port.
Inge Morath—Magnum

were included in the original design by Afonso Domingues, a native architect. The Capelas Imperfeitas (Unfinished Chapels) are among the best examples of Manueline architecture. This style of architecture, which was named for the monarch Manuel, who reigned from 1495 to 1521, and which flourished in the 16th century, employed decorative stonework, using nautical, angelic, and military motifs. The catastrophic earthquake of 1755 damaged the abbey, and the French sacked it in 1810. Secularized in 1834, it was declared a national monument in 1840 and was gradually restored. Pop. (1981) town, 519; *concelho,* 12,588.

Batanes, northernmost province of the Philippines, coextensive with the Batan Islands of the Luzon Strait, a north–south chain of 14 islands. It has an area of 81 sq mi (209 sq km) and is the smallest of the provinces. The Bashi (north) and Balintang (south) channels separate the group from Taiwan and the Babuyan Islands. Volcanic in origin, the islands are rugged, rocky, and windswept. Only the four largest (Itbayat, Batan, Sabtang, and Ibuhos) are inhabited. The frequency of destructive typhoons dictates both agricultural and architectural patterns. Root crops, particularly sweet potatoes, are the main food crop, and the surplus supports a small livestock industry. Fishing is a supplementary activity. Houses are built of stone and tile in the shelter of swales or trees.

The inhabitants are Roman Catholic and speak Ivatan, a local dialect. Population increase since 1900 has been very slight, since the islanders have steadily migrated to the kinder environment of Luzon. Basco, on northwestern Batan Island, is the provincial capital and the only national port; it is served by an airfield. Pop. (1980) 12,091.

Batangas, peninsula, province, and chartered city, southern Luzon, Philippines. Batangas Peninsula (about 7,010 sq mi [18,150 sq km] in area) stretches south of Manila and includes the provinces of Cavite, Laguna, and Batangas and the southern part of Quezon.

Batangas province has an area of 1,222 sq mi (3,166 sq km) and includes nearby Maricaban and Verde islands. It surrounds Taal Lake (*q.v.*). To the west lies the South China Sea. Balayan and Batangas bays are in the south, where Verde Island Passage separates the province from Mindoro. The province's fertile volcanic soil provides productive agricultural land; rice, sugarcane, and coconuts are the major crops. The province is known for its quality beef, and fishing is important. Petroleum refining and food processing are among the major industries. The provincial capital is Batangas City. Other important towns include Lipa, a chartered city, Bauan, Taal, Lemery, and Balayan, which is noted for piña cloth embroidery. Nearly all of the population is Roman Catholic.

Batangas City is connected with Manila by roads and shipping. It is also the northern terminus of ferry service to Calapan, in Oriental Mindoro province, and is the site of an oil refinery. The Pablo Borbon Memorial Institute of Technology was founded there in 1903. Pop. (1980) province, 1,174,201; city, 143,570.

Batavi, ancient Germanic tribe from whom Batavia, a poetic name for The Netherlands, is derived. The Batavi inhabited what is now the Betuwe district of The Netherlands, around Lugdunum Batavorum (Leiden), at the mouth of the Rhine River. Subjugated by Rome in AD 12, they became an "allied people" (*gens foederata*) and furnished troops for the Roman army until their rebellion under Gaius Julius Civilis (AD 69–70). In the 4th century the Salian Franks displaced the Batavi.

Batavia (Indonesia): *see* Jakarta.

Batavia, city, seat (1802) of Genesee County, northwestern New York, U.S., on Tonawanda Creek, midway between Buffalo (west) and Rochester (33 mi [53 km] east). The site, at the junction of ancient Indian trails and the Genesee Road, was laid out in 1801 by Joseph Ellicott for the Holland Land Company (whose office [1815] is maintained as a museum) and named for the Batavian (Dutch) Republic (set up 1795). It developed as a distribution point and trade centre for a dairy, poultry, and truck-farm region and has acquired some industry, including the manufacture of shoes, paper, die castings, and radio and television sets. A New York state school for the blind was established there in 1868. The Tonawanda Indian Reservation is 13 mi (21 km) northwest and Attica Correctional Facility, where a race-related riot in 1971 resulted in the deaths of 43 persons, is 11 mi south. Batavia was identified with the Anti-Masonic Party because William Morgan, who threatened to reveal Masonic secrets, lived there prior to his mysterious disappearance in 1826. Genesee Community College was opened in 1966. Inc. village, 1823; city, 1914. Pop. (1980) 16,703.

Batavian Republic, French RÉPUBLIQUE BATAVE, Dutch BATAAFSE REPUBLIEK, republic of the Netherlands, established after it was conquered by the French during the campaign of 1794–95. Set up in April 1798, it possessed a government patterned after that of the Directory (*q.v.*) in France and was bound to France by alliance. In March 1805 Napoleon changed the system of government once more: the Batavian Republic was renamed Batavian Commonwealth, and executive power was given to a kind of dictator called the council pensionary. In June 1806, however, the Batavian Commonwealth was replaced by the Kingdom of Holland under Napoleon's brother Louis; this monarchy lasted until July 1810, when Holland was incorporated into the French Empire.

Bataysk, also spelled BATAJSK, or BATAISK, city, Rostov *oblast* (administrative region), southwestern Russian Soviet Federated Socialist Republic, just south of Rostov-na-Donu. It is a transport centre in the northern Caucasus and a main rail junction, with railway shops and freight yards: more than 20 percent of the city's labour force is in transportation. Other important industries are metalworking and aircraft manufacture, and Bataysk functions also as a grain, livestock, and food centre. It became a city in 1938. Pop. (1983 est.) 94,000.

Batchelor, Joy: *see* Halas, John; and Batchelor, Joy.

Bătdâmbâng, also spelled BATTAMBANG, town and *khêt* (province), Northwest Zone (*phumipheak*), western Kampuchea (Cambodia). The second largest urban area in Kampuchea, on the Stœng (river) Sângkê northwest of Phnom Penh, the national capital, Bătdâmbâng, the provincial capital, had a substantial Chinese trading community until the Khmer Rouge government took control in 1975. From 1794 to 1904 and again from 1941 to 1946 the town was under Siamese sovereignty. Among its industries are a textile mill and rice mills; there is also a rice research station. Bătdâmbâng is linked to Phnom Penh both by railway and by flights from its major airfield. Cultural assets include the Buddhist temple Wat Poveal and 10th-century ruins of the Khmer Empire, including several temples.

The province borders Thailand to the west, and occupies part of a low-lying, mountain-enclosed basin west of the Tonle Sap (Great Lake), the largest freshwater body in Southeast Asia. The 7,407-sq-mi (19,184-sq-km) province is partially shielded from the southwest summer monsoon rains by the Chuŏr Phnum Krâvanh (Cardamom Mountains).

In the shielded area, annual rainfall averages from 50 to 75 in. (1,250 to 1,875 mm) and much of this area is also watered by the backflooding of the Tonle Sap basin from the Mekong River between June and October. The availability of water and particularly rich soils in many parts of the province makes Bătdâmbâng one of the richest rice-growing regions of Kampuchea in normal years. The natural fertility of the province was enhanced by a number of large-scale irrigation projects carried out during the middle and late 1970s, including the 17 January reservoir at Phnum Kâmping Puŏy, the Prayuth Dam on the Stœng Sângkê, the Trâpeăng Thmâ reservoir in Phnum Srŏk, the "77" reservoir at Phnum Bassac, and a pair of canals linking Stœng Moŭng with the Stœng Poŭthĭsăt in the neighbouring province of Poŭthĭsăt. The province also produces cotton, cassava, sweet potatoes, corn (maize), bananas, sugarcane, mulberry, hemp, beans, jute, coffee, and durian and ramboutan fruits, and salted fish (especially carp) from the Tonle Sap fisheries. Upland areas are rich in timber, including good quality hardwoods, such as wild date, bean trees, and mahogany. Pop. (1971 est.) town, 670,600.

Bate, W(alter) Jackson (b. May 23, 1918, Mankato, Minn., U.S.), author and literary biographer known for his studies of John Keats and Samuel Johnson.

Educated at Harvard University, Bate taught history and literature there from 1946 and was chairman of the department of English from 1956 to 1962.

In 1945 the Modern Language Association published Bate's *Stylistic Development of Keats.* His *John Keats* (1963) was awarded the Pulitzer Prize for Biography, the Christian Gauss Prize, and the Harvard Faculty Prize in 1964. In 1955, *The Achievement of Samuel Johnson* was awarded the Gauss Prize for literary history and criticism. *Samuel Johnson* (1977), a colourful account of Johnson's personality and a vivid portrayal of the times in which he lived, won the acclaim of scholars and critics and was awarded the 1978 Pulitzer Prize and the National Book Award.

Bate's other works include *From Classic to Romantic* (1946) and *Coleridge* (1968). He was also responsible for editing *Criticism: The Major Texts* (1952).

bateleur (*Terathopius ecaudatus*), small eagle of Africa and Arabia, belonging to the subfamily Circaetinae (serpent eagles) of the family Accipitridae. The name bateleur (French, "tumbler") comes from the birds' distinctive aerial acrobatics. About 60 centimetres (2 feet) long, the bateleur has glossy black head, neck, and underparts; a reddish-brown back; whitish to red-brown shoulders; a bare red face; and powerful red-orange feet. Its tail is only 10 cm (4 in.) long (longer in young birds), and its wings, black above and white beneath, are long, pointed, and exceptionally wide. A short full crest makes the bird's head appear large. One of the most familiar birds of the African skies, it is almost constantly on the wing. Often it turns somersaults in the air, claps its wings loudly, utters cawing or barking cries, and dives with a screaming sound. It hunts open country for small mammals, reptiles, eggs, grasshoppers, and carrion. It seems to favour snakes.

A leaf-lined stick nest is built in a low, spreading tree. The clutch is probably a single egg; the female incubates, for 40 days or more. The young do not fledge until three or four months after hatching. Maturity is reached in the fifth or sixth year. *See also* eagle.

Bateman, H(ezekiah) L(inthicum) (b. Dec. 6, 1812, Baltimore—d. March 22, 1875, London), actor and theatrical manager who made a great success touring the United States and England with two of his daughters, both child actresses.

Bateman made his stage debut in 1832 and acted in various repertory companies until 1849. Then he, his wife, Sidney Frances, and his two eldest daughters, Kate and Ellen, aged six and four, respectively, began to tour widely as stars. Later Ellen played Richard III, Shylock, and Macbeth to Kate's Richmond, Portia, and Lady Macbeth. In 1855 Bateman managed a St. Louis theatre and later, as Kate's manager, moved to New York City, where she was a hit in *Leah the Forsaken* (1863), Augustin Daly's version of Salomon Mosenthal's *Deborah.* The French company that Bateman presented in New York (1867–69) started a craze for light opera in the United States. In 1871 he leased the Lyceum Theatre, London, and engaged the actor Henry Irving, who won fame in Leopold Lewis' *Bells.*

Bateman's wife (1823–81), in addition to acting, also wrote plays, of which the most popular was *Self* (1857). After her husband's death, she managed the Lyceum and later Sadler's Wells Theatre. Ellen Bateman (1844–1936) married early and gave up the stage, but Kate (1842–1917) continued a long career of acting. She retired briefly in 1866 when she married George Crowe but returned in 1868, later playing Lady Macbeth and other roles with Irving.

Bateman, H(enry) M(ayo) (b. Feb. 15, 1887, Sutton Forest, N.S.W., Australia—d. Feb. 13, 1970, Malta), cartoonist known for narrative cartoons and cartoons of situations involving social gaffes.

After studying drawing and painting he began drawing for publication in 1906. Before World War I his work had appeared in *Punch* and other publications. A notable series of cartoons consisted of a wordless sequence of drawings. One, dating from 1916 and captioned "Prisoner when arrested, clung to the railing . . . ," showed the arrest of a soapbox orator; successive panels depicted increasingly forceful efforts to remove him from the fence railings, ending with the section of fence cut away and being carried off by the police with the orator still attached.

Another notable series involved the odd man out, a solitary figure that had just committed an unpardonable breach of convention, surrounded by an outraged crowd. One of these was captioned, "The Guest Who Called 'Pâté de Foie Gras' Potted Meat." His biography, *Man Who Drew the 20th Century,* by Michael Bateman, was published in 1969.

Bateman, Hester, *née* NEEDHAM (b. 1709, London—d. 1794, London), silversmith noted particularly for her domestic silver of elegant simplicity.

Her husband, John Bateman, who worked in gold and silver, particularly watch chains,

Silver coffee pot by Hester Bateman, 1773–74; in the Victoria and Albert Museum, London

By courtesy of the Victoria and Albert Museum, London

died in 1760. The next year she took over the family business, registering her mark at the Goldsmiths' Hall, London. Initially she was assisted by two of her sons, John and Peter, and an apprentice. Until 1774 little Bateman work is known, largely because the shop was busy with work commissioned by other silversmiths. Thereafter, her shop became well known and successful, specializing in tableware, such as spoons, sugar bowls, salt cellars, and teapots. Energetic and shrewd in business, she also possessed exceptional skill and taste. Working with graceful, refined shapes, she characteristically used restrained decoration, most often in the form of beaded edges. In addition to domestic silver, she executed some large presentation pieces. After her retirement in 1790, the business was continued by other members of the family who, for a time, also produced outstanding silver.

Batemans Bay, coastal town and inlet of the Tasman Sea, southeastern New South Wales, Australia. The inlet, an estuary of the Clyde River, measures 4 by 5 mi (6 by 8 km). Sighted in 1770 by Capt. James Cook, it was named by him after the captain of the ship "Northumberland." The town, founded early in the 19th century, is on the southwest shore. Serving a district producing timber, vegetables, cheese, oysters, and crayfish, it is linked to Sydney (136 mi northeast) via the Prince's Highway and is a convenient resort for Canberra, 65 mi west-northwest. Pop. (1981) 4,924.

Bates, Edward (b. Sept. 4, 1793, Goochland County, Va., U.S.—d. March 25, 1869, St. Louis, Mo.), lawyer and Whig politician who joined the Republican Party before the U.S. Civil War and served as Abraham Lincoln's attorney general.

Educated largely at home, Bates moved from Virginia to Missouri in 1814 and shortly thereafter began the study of law. By 1816 he was practicing law in St. Louis. Over the next decade he served in a number of territorial and state offices. Elected in 1826 to a term in the U.S. House of Representatives, Bates was defeated in a bid for a Senate seat by followers of Democrat Thomas Hart Benton. As a Whig in a strongly pro-Andrew Jackson state, Bates also lost his reelection attempt in 1828 for another term in the House.

Although his career in national politics was largely dormant for more than three decades, Bates served in the Missouri legislature, drew national attention as president of the River and Harbor Improvement Convention of 1847, and in 1850 declined appointment as secretary of war during the administration of Whig Millard Fillmore. After serving as president of the Whig convention of 1856, he broke with the party and joined the newly created Republican Party.

Bates had long been a free-soil advocate. He freed his own slaves, opposed the Kansas–Nebraska Bill, and spoke out against the admission of Kansas under the Lecompton constitution. As a Southern-born border-state politician, Bates attracted support for the 1860 Republican presidential nomination. His followers believed he could maintain party principles opposing the extension of slavery without alienating the South and provoking secession.

When Bates's presidential bid failed, the triumphant Lincoln offered his erstwhile rival a choice of Cabinet positions. Bates chose the attorney generalship and for a time exercised some influence in the administration. But he opposed the admission of West Virginia as a state, the subjugation of constitutional rights to military control, and the increasing power of the Radical Republicans. On Nov. 24, 1864—weary of a position in which he wielded little authority—Bates resigned as attorney general.

He returned to Missouri and fought the Radical Republicans in his home state by writing newspaper articles and letters to prominent citizens.

Bates, H(erbert) E(rnest) (b. May 16, 1905, Rushden, Northamptonshire, Eng.—d. Jan. 29, 1974, Canterbury, Kent), novelist and short-story writer of high reputation and wide popularity.

Bates gained his knowledge of rural English life as a country-town solicitor's clerk and sharpened his skill as a reporter of atmosphere and action as a provincial journalist. His early short stories, essays, and novels in the 1920s were highly praised, but he became well known as a writer about the countryside and the life of the agricultural labourer with *The Poacher* (1935); *A House of Women* (1936); *My Uncle Silas* (1940), widely enjoyed for its earthy, Rabelaisian humour; and *The Beauty of the Dead and Other Stories* (1941).

World War II made Bates famous. Commissioned as a writer for the Royal Air Force in 1941, as "Flying Officer X" he gained great popularity with *The Greatest People in the World* (1942) and *How Sleep the Brave* (1943), collections of stories that conveyed the feel of flying in wartime. Three novels published under his own name, *Fair Stood the Wind for France* (1944), about a British bomber crew forced down in occupied France, and two set in Burma during the Japanese invasion, *The Purple Plain* (1946) and *The Jacaranda Tree* (1948), earned Bates a new reputation as a novelist of power.

In his postwar novels and stories Bates reached the height of his powers. From *The Nature of Love* (1954) to *A Moment in Time* (1964) and *The Triple Echo* (1970), he developed consistently in subtlety, depth, and strength as a novelist, and in *The Darling Buds of May* (1958) he created a realistic, lovable farm family, the Larkins. *Colonel Julian* (1955) demonstrates his range in the short story, and the autobiographical *The Vanished World* (1969) and *The Blossoming World* (1971) show that he retained his power to capture the mood of the passing moment.

Bates, H(enry) W(alter) (b. Feb. 8, 1825, Leicester, Leicestershire, Eng.—d. Feb. 16, 1892, London), naturalist and explorer whose demonstration of the operation of natural selection in animal mimicry (the imitation by a species of other life forms or inanimate objects), published in 1861, gave firm support to Charles Darwin's theory of evolution.

In 1844 Bates introduced the subject of entomology to Alfred Russel Wallace, who in

H.W. Bates, lithograph by W. Purkiss, *c.* 1880

BBC Hulton Picture Library

1847 suggested a trip to tropical jungles to collect specimens to sell at home and to collect data that might help solve the problem of the origin of species. On May 28, 1848, they arrived at Pará, Braz., near the mouth of the Amazon River. Wallace returned to England in 1852; Bates remained 11 years, exploring the entire valley of the Amazon, where he collected about 14,712 species, mostly of insects, 8,000 previously unknown. On his return to England (1859), he began work on his huge collections and the preparation of his famous paper, presented in 1861 as "Contributions to an Insect Fauna of the Amazon Valley." In 1864 Bates was appointed assistant secretary of the Royal Geographical Society (London) and held the position until his death. He wrote *The Naturalist on the River Amazons,* 2 vol. (1863), and many papers on entomology.

Bates, Katharine Lee (b. Aug. 12, 1859, Falmouth, Mass., U.S.—d. March 28, 1929, Wellesley, Mass.), author and educator who wrote the text of the national hymn "America the Beautiful."

She was educated at Wellesley College, Wellesley, Mass., where she taught English literature from 1885 to 1925. Among her many works are *The College Beautiful and Other Poems* (1887), *English Religious Drama* (1893), and *The Pilgrim Ship* (1926). Her *America the Beautiful and Other Poems* was published in 1911.

Where the same name may denote a person, place, or thing, the articles will be found in that order

Batesian mimicry, a form of biological resemblance in which a noxious, or dangerous, organism (the model), equipped with a warning system such as conspicuous coloration, is mimicked by a harmless organism (the mimic). The mimic gains protection because predators mistake it for the model and leave it alone. This form of mimicry is named for its discoverer, the 19th-century English naturalist H.W. Bates. *Compare* Müllerian mimicry.

Bateson, William (b. Aug. 8, 1861, Whitby, Yorkshire, Eng.—d. Feb. 8, 1926, London), biologist who founded and named the science of genetics and whose experiments provided evidence basic to the modern understanding of heredity. A dedicated Darwinist, he cited embryo studies to support his contention in 1885 that chordates evolved from primitive echinoderms, a view now widely accepted. In 1894 he published his conclusion (*Materials for the Study of Variation*) that evolution could not occur through a continuous variation of species, since distinct features often appeared or disappeared suddenly in plants and animals. Realizing that discontinuous variation could be understood only after something was known about the inheritance of traits, Bateson began work on the experimental breeding of plants and animals.

William Bateson, drawing by Sir William Rothenstein, 1917; in the National Portrait Gallery, London
By courtesy of the National Portrait Gallery, London

In 1900, he discovered an article, "Experiments with Plant Hybrids," written by Gregor Mendel, an Austrian monk, 34 years earlier. The paper, found in the same year by Hugo de Vries, Carl Correns, and Erich Tschermak von Seysenegg, dealt with the appearance of certain features in successive generations of garden peas. Bateson noted that his breeding results were explained perfectly by Mendel's paper and that the monk had succinctly described the transmission of elements governing heritable traits in his plants.

Bateson translated Mendel's paper into English and during the next 10 years became Mendel's champion in England, corroborating his principles experimentally. He published, with Reginald Punnett, the results of a series of breeding experiments (1905–08) that not only extended Mendel's principles to animals (poultry) but showed also that certain features were consistently inherited together, apparently counter to Mendel's findings. This phenomenon, which came to be termed linkage, is now known to be the result of the occurrence of genes located in close proximity on the same chromosome. Bateson's experiments also demonstrated a dependence of certain characters on two or more genes. Unfortunately, he misinterpreted his results, refusing to accept the interpretation of linkage advanced by the geneticist Thomas Hunt Morgan. In fact, he opposed Morgan's entire chromosome theory, advocating his own vibratory theory of inheritance, founded on laws of force and motion, a concept that found little acceptance among other scientists.

Bateson became, at the University of Cambridge, the first British professor of genetics (1908). He left this chair in 1910 to spend the rest of his life directing the John Innes Horticultural Institution, London, transforming it into a centre for genetic research. His books include *Mendel's Principles of Heredity* (1902) and *Problems of Genetics* (1913).

Batesville, city, seat (1821) of Independence County, north central Arkansas, U.S., in the foothills of the Ozarks on the White River. Named for James W. Bates, a territorial judge and U.S. congressman, it was founded (1812) by John Reed, who built a trading post at the mouth of Poke (now Polk) Bayou, where a fork of the Southwest Trail crossed the river. Ferry service began in 1818, and in 1831 the settlement became a steamboat shipping point for farm products. Poultry processing, light manufactures, and lime and black marble quarries form its economic base. Arkansas College (1872; Presbyterian) was founded in 1836 as Batesville Academy. The White River Dam and Locks (1900) are nearby. Inc. town, 1841; city, 1846. Pop. (1980) 8,263.

batfish, any of about 60 species of fishes of the family Ogcocephalidae (order Lophiiformes), found in warm and temperate seas. Batfishes have broad, flat heads and slim bodies and are covered with hard lumps and spines. Some species have an elongated, upturned snout. Batfishes grow at most about 36 centimetres (14 inches) long. They are poor swimmers, and usually walk on the bottom on thickened, limblike pectoral and pelvic fins. Most live in the deep sea, but some inhabit shallow water.

Torpedo batfish (*Halieutaea retifera*)
Douglas Faulkner

Batfishes are members of the group known as anglerfish and are equipped with a "fishing pole," tipped with a fleshy "bait" to lure prey close enough to be eaten. The apparatus is located above the small mouth and, unlike that of other anglers, can be drawn into a tube when not in use.

Bath, district (city), county of Avon, England, on the River Avon in a natural amphitheatre of steep hills. It has an area of 11 sq mi (28 sq km). Built of local limestone, it is one of the most elegant and architecturally distinguished of British cities. Its 16th-century abbey church of St. Peter and St. Paul is late Perpendicular Gothic and is noted for its windows, but it is the wealth of classical Georgian buildings mounting the steep valley sides that gives Bath its distinction.

Royal Crescent, Bath, Avon
J. Allan Cash—EB Inc.

The hot mineral springs (120° F [49° C]) on the site attracted the Romans, who founded Bath as Aquae Sulis, dedicated to the deity Sul (Minerva). The Saxons built the abbey on the site at which Edgar, first king of all England, was crowned (AD 973). The Normans subsequently rebuilt the church between 1088 and 1122, transferring there the diocese they had founded at Wells. The bishop's throne returned to Wells in 1206, and there was a long rivalry between the canons of Wells and the monks of Bath, of which the bishop was titular abbot. The diocese is still styled Bath and Wells.

Incorporated by charter in 1189, medieval Bath shared in the west-of-England wool trade and later in the cloth trade, but the baths, although still used by royalty, were poorly maintained. When the Roman bath, lined with lead from the nearby Mendip Hills, was rediscovered in 1755, Bath had already revived as a spa. In its heyday as a fashionable resort—presided over by the social figure Richard "Beau" Nash, one of the greatest English dandies—the Elizabethan town was rebuilt and extended in Palladian style by the architects John Wood the Elder and Younger and their patron, Ralph Allen, who provided the stone from his local quarries and built the mansion of Prior Park (1735–43) outside the city. In 1769–74 Robert Adam built Pulteney Bridge to connect Bath with the new suburb of Bathwick across the River Avon.

Close to the abbey, in the entrenched valley of the River Avon, is the 18th-century Pump Room, giving access to the hot springs and Roman baths. Among some 140 historic terraces and individual buildings that grace the city are Queen Square, built by John Wood the Elder between 1728 and 1735; the Circus, begun by Wood in 1754 and completed by his son; the Royal Crescent, 1767–75; the Guildhall, 1775; Lansdown Crescent, built by John Palmer, 1796–97; and the 1795 pavilion in Sydney Gardens, Bathwick, which now houses the Holburne of Menstrie Museum of Arts collection. In 1942 the Assembly Rooms of 1771 were destroyed in an air raid from which the whole city suffered severely, but extensive reconstruction, as well as renovation, has since been carried out. The Assembly Rooms, reopened in 1963, now contain a comprehensive 18th- and 19th-century costume collection. Claverton Manor, 2 mi (3 km) outside the city, is an early 19th-century mansion housing the American Museum in Britain, a large museum of Americana.

As the leading centre of English high society outside London in the 18th and early 19th centuries, the city is rich in literary associations. The life of the time is graphically depicted in the novels of Tobias Smollett and in the plays of Richard Brinsley Sheridan. Jane Austen's novels *Northanger Abbey* and *Persuasion* (both 1817/18) portray with delicate satire and keen perception the fashionable life of Bath about 1800. Bath Olivers (biscuits that take their name from William Oliver, an eminent physician who founded what is now the Royal National Hospital for Rheumatic Diseases), Bath buns, Bath bricks, and Bath (invalid) chairs all derive their names from the city.

Although not primarily a manufacturing centre, Bath nevertheless has considerable printing and bookbinding, light engineering, and clothing industries. Pop. (1982 est.) 84,200.

Bath, city, port of entry (since 1789), seat (1854) of Sagadahoc County, southwestern Maine, U.S., on the Kennebec River near its mouth on the Atlantic coast, 36 mi (58 km) northeast of Portland. Settled *c.* 1670 and named for the English city, it was part of Georgetown until incorporated as a separate town in 1781. Its shipbuilding industry (exemplified in the Bath Marine Museum) dates from 1762, when Capt. William Swanton launched the "Earl of Bute." The Bath Iron Works (founded 1833 and the city's

The Bath Iron (shipbuilding) Works, Bath, Maine
Gordon A. Reims

main economic asset) has been building ships since 1889, reaching peak naval production during the world wars. At Popham Colony (Ft. St. George), 16 mi (26 km) south, the pinnace "Virginia"—first vessel to be built by colonists—was launched in 1607. Inc. city, 1847. Pop. (1980) 10,246.

Bath, town, Beaufort County, eastern North Carolina, U.S., on the Pamlico River estuary. The first proprietary grant in the area (1684) embraced the townsite then occupied by an Indian village called Pamticoe. Settled by the English (1695), it became the seat of old Bath

The Bonner House in Bath, N.C.
Milt and Joan Mann from CameraMann

County (formed 1696 and named for the Earl of Bath) and was the colony's first incorporated town (1705). Survivors of the Tuscarora (Indian) War (1711–13) found refuge there, and the pirate Edward Teach, known as Blackbeard, made it his headquarters. It served as the colony's first official port of entry. One of the first parish libraries in America was established there in 1700. Surviving colonial buildings include St. Thomas Episcopal Church (*c.* 1734) and the Bonner and Palmer–Marsh houses. The town was designated a state historic site in 1963. Pop. (1980) 207.

Bath (town, West Virginia, U.S.): *see* Berkeley Springs.

bath, process of soaking the body in some element other than air—such as mud, steam, sunshine, or water. The bath may have cleanliness or curative purposes, and it can have religious, mystical, or some other meaning (*see* ritual bath).

The bath as an institution has a long history. Writings from ancient biblical and other sources mention baths. Architectural remains from ancient Egypt indicate the existence of special bathrooms, and both vase paintings and restored ruins show that the Greeks of classical antiquity thought the bath important. Roman baths featuring a combination of steaming, cleaning, and massage appeared wherever the Romans made conquests. In Rome itself the aqueducts fed sumptuous baths such as those of Caracalla, which covered 28 acres.

By medieval times the luxurious baths of ancient Rome had given way to more primitive facilities that had purely curative or cleanliness purposes. Public baths were built as early as the 12th century. In the 14th and 15th centuries public bathhouses and garden baths or pools accommodated men and women together. In the 1600s many persons visited spas to take baths, sometimes remaining submerged for health purposes for days at a time.

Modern baths have taken many forms. In some cases they have combined features from many types of older baths, including the Turkish bath and the oriental tub bath, or *furo.* In the 1900s public baths frequently took the place of domestic facilities. In later decades the medicinal bath using a special tub or pool has developed separately from the home bathtub or shower stall. The medicinal bath may use special waters, such as carbonated or chemically treated waters, at high or low temperatures.

bath (unit of measure): *see* bat.

Bath, The Most Honourable Order of the, order of British knighthood established by King George I in 1725, conferred as a reward either for military service or for exemplary civilian merit. Like most chivalric orders, it has antecedents that exist much earlier in history than the date of its actual founding. Bathing as a purification ritual was probably introduced in a religious context with knighthood in the 11th century. From the coronation of Henry IV (1399), who traditionally has been made the founder of the order, to the coronation of Charles II (1661), it became customary to create a certain number of knights during royal occasions of great brilliance. The medieval "knights of the bath," as they were called, took precedence over knights bachelors, from whose ranks they had been promoted, but they never formed an order of chivalry. When George I, advised by his prime minister Robert Walpole, created the order, he believed that he was reviving an ancient order that had, in fact, never existed.

Originally membership comprised the British monarch, a great master of the order, and 36 knights. Membership regulations have undergone numerous changes over the centuries. Three classes of knights were instituted in 1815 to commemorate the end of the Napoleonic Wars. Corresponding civilian classes were added in 1847. The order currently includes the monarch, members of the royal family, foreigners (known as "honorary members"), and the classes of knights—115 knights or dames grand cross (G.C.B.), 328 knights or dames commanders (K.C.B. or D.C.B., respectively), and 1,815 companions (C.B.). Investiture into the two highest classes (knight/dame grand cross and knight/dame commander) means induction into knighthood. The officers of the order are the dean (usually the dean of Westminster), Bath king of arms, registrar, usher of the Scarlet Rod, and secretary. Women are admitted to all classes of the order.

The knights grand cross are allotted stalls in the order's chapel, Henry VII Chapel in Westminster Abbey, where their banners, crests, and coats of arms are affixed. The badge of the order depicts three crowns with the order's motto *Tria juncta in uno* ("Three joined in one"), as well as the Welsh motto *Ich dien* ("I serve"), and the emblems of England, Scotland, and Ireland (rose, thistle, shamrock).

Bath, Thomas Thynne, 1st marquess of, also called (1751–89) 3RD VISCOUNT WEYMOUTH (b. Sept. 13, 1734—d. Nov. 19, 1796, London), politician who, as Viscount Weymouth, held important office in the British government during two critical periods in the reign of George III. Although he was an outstanding orator, his dissolute habits (gambling and heavy drinking), indolence, and secretiveness concerning his official policies prevented him from realizing his potential as a statesman.

Appointed viceroy of Ireland in June 1765, Weymouth resigned two months later. In his first term as secretary of state for the southern department (1768–70), he had to maintain public order during the riots protesting the imprisonment of John Wilkes, politician and advocate of freedom of the press. For approving the use of troops leading to a massacre at St. George's Fields (May 10, 1768), he became extremely unpopular and was denounced by Wilkes himself and by the pseudonymous journalist "Junius." After four more years (1775–79) as secretary of state for the southern department, he retired because he opposed Prime Minister Lord North's Irish policy and Britain's role in the American Revolution. He was created marquess in 1789.

Bath's estate, Longleat, in Wiltshire, is a major work of the landscape gardener Lancelot ("Capability") Brown.

Bath, William Pulteney, 1st earl of (b. March 22, 1684, London—d. July 7, 1764, London), English Whig politician who became prominent in the opposition to Sir Robert Walpole (first lord of the treasury and chancellor of the exchequer, 1721–42), after being staunchly loyal to him for 12 years, up to 1717. Pulteney was himself three times in a position to form a government but failed to do so. A scholarly and versatile man and a brilliantly satirical orator, he conspicuously lacked the true statesman's willingness to assume responsibility.

A member of the House of Commons from 1705 to 1742 (when he was created an earl), Pulteney served as secretary at war (1714–17) in the first ministry in the reign of George I. When Walpole came to power in 1721, Pulteney was not given high office, and his subsequent failure (1724) to obtain the secretaryship of state greatly embittered him and prompted him to charge Walpole with corruption. As a leader of the anti-Walpole Whigs, he joined the 1st Viscount Bolingbroke in trying to form a united party of opposition and in publishing a political newspaper, *The Craftsman* (1726–36). Pulteney's journalism and brilliant parliamentary speeches encouraged the Whig and Tory factions opposed to Walpole to form an alliance, and he was considered largely responsible for Walpole's inability to enact a wine and tobacco excise bill in 1733.

Pulteney's career lost its momentum in 1735, when Bolingbroke retired from politics and the Whig–Tory combination against Walpole disintegrated. When Walpole fell from power in 1742, Pulteney declined two requests by King George II to form a government, accepting instead the first lordship of the treasury in the 1st Earl of Wilmington's ministry (1742–43) and the earldom of Bath, thus alienating many of his supporters. He left office when Wilmington died (July 2, 1743), and Henry Pelham, an old enemy of Bath, became prime minister. In 1746 Bath and John Carteret, Earl Granville, attempted to organize a government; their failure terminated Bath's political life.

bath chair, chair on wheels intended for use by ladies and invalids. It was devised by James Heath, of Bath, Eng., in about 1750. For the next three-quarters of a century it rivalled the sedan chair and ultimately superseded it as a form of conveyance in Great Britain. The commonest variety was supported on two wheels joined by an axle beneath the seat, with a small pivoting wheel in front supporting the footrest.

The chair could be pushed from behind and steered by a long curved rod connected to

Bath chair
By courtesy of the Bath Municipal Libraries, England

the front wheel and controlled by the occupant. The whole conveyance was designed on flowing lines. The bath chair was especially popular during Victorian times, when it was used at seaside resorts.

Baʿth Party, in full ARAB SOCIALIST BAʿTH PARTY, or ARAB SOCIALIST RENAISSANCE PARTY, Arabic ḤIZB AL-BAʿTH AL-ʿARABĪ AL-ISHTIRĀKĪ, Baʿth also spelled BAʿATH, Arab political party advocating formation of a single Arab Socialist nation; it has branches in many Middle Eastern countries and has been the ruling party in Syria and Iraq.

The Baʿth Party was founded in 1943 in Damascus by Michel ʿAflaq and Ṣalah ad-Dīn al-Bīṭār, adopted its constitution in 1947, and in 1953 merged with the Syrian Socialist Party to form the Arab Socialist Baʿth (Renaissance) Party. The Baʿth Party espoused nonalignment and opposition to imperialism and colonialism, took inspiration from what it considered the positive values of Islām, and attempted to ignore or transcend class divisions. Its structure was highly centralized and authoritarian.

The Syrian Baʿthists took power in 1963, but factionalism between "progressives" and "nationalists" was severe until 1970, when Hafez al-Assad of the "nationalists" secured control. In Iraq the Baʿthists took power briefly in 1963 and regained it in 1968. Differences between the Iraqi and Syrian wings of the Baʿth Party precluded unification of the two countries. Within both countries the Baʿthists formed fronts with smaller parties, including at times the Communists. In Syria the main internal threat to Baʿth hegemony stemmed from the Muslim Brotherhood, while in Iraq Kurdish and Shīʿite opposition was endemic.

In foreign policy al-Assad greatly enhanced Syrian Baʿth prestige by his successful opposition to American intervention in Lebanon and by his stubborn opposition to Israel. In Iraq the Baʿthists became bogged down in a war of attrition with Iran and turned more to the West for aid in the 1980s.

Bathiat, Arlette-Leonie: *see* Arletty.

Bathinda (India): *see* Bhatinda.

bathing suit: *see* swimsuit.

batholith, large body of igneous rock formed by the intrusion and solidification of magma. Its shape is equidimensional to elongate, but it is not tabular, as is typical of bodies called dikes. The surface outcrop of a batholith exceeds 100 square kilometres (40 square miles); it may be much larger. The contacts with the surrounding rock are vertical to very steep, and the available evidence suggests that the upper surfaces are quite irregular. Folding, faulting, and contact metamorphism of the country rock near the batholith are typically strongly developed. In older definitions, batholiths were said to extend to unknown depths, but more recent studies have shown that many of them have floors, indicating a limited thickness of perhaps several thousand feet. Acidic rocks often form batholiths, but complex zoning or evidence for several episodes of intrusion are commonly present.

Bathonian Stage, division of Jurassic rocks and time. (The Jurassic Period began about 190,000,000 years ago and lasted about 54,000,000 years.) Rocks of the Bathonian Stage overlie those of the Bajocian Stage and underlie the Callovian. They consist of limestones, marls, and some chalky beds in which mollusks such as clams and ammonites and brachiopods predominate. Several ammonite zones (shorter spans of time characterized by fossil mollusks) have been recognized and aid in correlation of Jurassic rocks throughout the world.

Báthory, Sigismund, Hungarian ZSIGMOND BÁTHORY (b. 1572—d. 1613, Prague), prince of Transylvania whose unpopular anti-Turkish policy led to civil war.

The son of Christopher Báthory (prince of Transylvania, 1575–81) and nephew of Stephen (István Báthory, king of Poland, 1575–86), Sigismund succeeded his father in 1581 and actually assumed control of government affairs in 1588. Acting on the advice of his foreign counsellor Alfonso Carrillo, Báthory reversed the traditional policy of Transylvania (*i.e.,* to play off the Ottoman sultan against the Holy Roman emperor and thereby preserve Transylvanian de facto independence) and adopted an anti-Turk position. Although this policy shift provoked a rebellion, which was not suppressed until 1595, he nevertheless joined the princes Aaron of Moldavia and Michael the Brave of Walachia in an alliance against the Turks in 1594 and conquered Walachia for Michael after defeating an Ottoman army at Giurgiu (in present-day Romania; Oct. 25–27, 1595).

Báthory, copper engraving by Egidius Sadler, 1607
By courtesy of the National Szechenyi Library, Budapest, Hungary

Báthory, a Roman Catholic, became increasingly active in the Counter-Reformation, to the dismay of the leading Transylvanian nationalists, most of whom were Protestant. In 1599 Báthory decided to take holy orders; he separated from his wife, the archduchess Christina of Austria, and gave up his throne, offering it to the Habsburg emperor Rudolf II (also king of Hungary) in exchange for the Silesian duchy of Oppeln (Opole). Rudolf, however, supported Michael the Brave, who defeated Báthory's son Andreas and declared himself prince of Transylvania. Although Báthory tried to recover his throne in 1600 and again in 1601, on both occasions he was driven out by Michael, and he died in obscurity.

Báthory, Stephen: *see* Stephen Báthory.

bathos (from Greek *bathys,* "deep"), unsuccessful, and therefore ludicrous, attempt to portray pathos in art, *i.e.,* to evoke pity, sympathy, or sorrow. Bathos may result from an inappropriately dignified treatment of the commonplace, the use of elevated language and imagery to describe trivial subject matter, or from such an exaggeration of pathos (emotion provoked by genuine suffering) as to become overly sentimental or ridiculous.

Even great poets occasionally lapse into bathos. Wordsworth's attempt to arouse pity for the old huntsman in "Simon Lee" is defeated by the following lines:

> Few months of life has he in store
> As he to you will tell,
> For still, the more he works, the more
> Do his weak ankles swell.

Bathsheba, also spelled BETHSABEE, in the Old Testament (II Sam. 11, 12; I Kings 1, 2), wife of Uriah the Hittite and later of King David, mother of King Solomon. She was a daughter of Eliam and was probably of noble birth. A beautiful woman, she was seduced by David and became pregnant. David then had Uriah killed and married her. The child died, but Bathsheba later gave birth to Solomon.

When David was dying, she successfully conspired with the prophet Nathan to block Adonijah's succession to the throne and to win it for Solomon. Strong-willed and fearless, she occupied an influential position as the queen mother.

Bathurst, city, east central New South Wales, Australia, on the south bank of the Macquarie River, west of the Blue Mountains. Founded in 1815 and named after the 3rd Earl Bathurst, then secretary of state for the colonies, it is the oldest settlement west of the Great Dividing Range. Charles Darwin, the British naturalist, visited Bathurst in 1836. Initially, its growth was slow, but the population increased rapidly following the discovery of gold in the vicinity in 1851. Declared a town in 1833, it was proclaimed a borough in 1862 and became a city in 1885. Bathurst is now the service centre of a district producing sheep, grains, timber, fruits, and vegetables; its industries include railway and precision-engineering works, flour mills, and canning, clothing, footwear, plastics, furniture, and ceramics plants. At the junction of the Mitchell and Mid and Great Western highways and on the main rail line to Sydney (100 mi [160 km] southeast), the city has Roman Catholic and Anglican cathedrals, a memorial carillon tower (focus of a March festival), and the Mitchell College of Advanced Education. An eisteddfod (Welsh festival of arts) is celebrated each October. Pop. (1981) 19,640.

Bathurst, city, seat (1826) of Gloucester County, northeastern New Brunswick, Canada, at the mouth of the Nepisiguit River, on Chaleur Bay, a southern arm of Bathurst Harbour, 127 mi (204 km) north-northwest of Moncton. The original French settlement, founded in 1619 by a French missionary, was called Nepisiguit and then St. Peters (from St.-Pierre, given to the area in 1671 by Richard Denys). After 1755 the British displaced the French, and in the 1820s the community was renamed to honour the 3rd Earl Bathurst, then secretary for war and the colonies. The city's economy is based mainly upon lumbering and fishing. A pulp mill was built in the early part of the 20th century, and the manufacture of pulp and boxboard continues to be the major industry. Since 1953, the mining of local base-metal ore deposits has been of growing significance. West Bathurst is the seat of the Université du Sacré-Coeur (1899). The Sacred Heart Church became a cathedral in 1942 after the episcopal see was transferred from Chatham. Youghal Beach, a popular summer resort on Nepisiguit Bay at the entrance to Bathurst Harbour, is about 7 mi (11 km) north. Inc. town, 1912; city, 1966. Pop. (1981) 15,705.

Bathurst (The Gambia): *see* Banjul.

Bathurst, Henry Bathurst, 3rd Earl (b. May 22, 1762—d. July 27, 1834), British statesman, elder son of the 2nd Earl Bathurst, who was a prominent Tory in the late 18th and early 19th centuries.

Bathurst was member of Parliament for Cirencester from 1783 until he succeeded to the earldom in 1794. Mainly as a result of his friendship with William Pitt, he was a lord of the Admiralty (1783–89), a lord of the Treasury (1789–91), and commissioner of the Board of Control for India (1793–1802). Returning to office with Pitt in May 1804, he became master of the mint and was president of the Board of Trade and master of the mint during the ministries of the Duke of Portland and Spencer Perceval, vacating these posts in June 1812 to become secretary for war and the colonies under the Earl of Liverpool. For two months during 1809 he was in charge of the Foreign Office. He was secretary for war and the colonies until Liverpool resigned in 1827 and deserves some credit for improving the conduct of the Peninsular War. As secretary for the colonies, Bathurst was closely concerned with the abolition of the slave trade. He was lord president of the council in the government of the Duke of Wellington from 1828 to 1830, favouring Roman Catholic emancipation but opposing the Reform Bill of 1832. He was made a knight of the Garter in 1817.

Bathurst Island, island in the Timor Sea, Northern Territory, Australia, separated from Melville Island to the east by Apsley Strait. Densely wooded, it is triangular in shape and has an area of about 1,000 sq mi (2,600 sq km). It was the site of an Aboriginal reserve and of a large Roman Catholic mission. In 1978, ownership of the island passed from the crown to the Tiwi Land Council of tribal representatives. Cattle and varied crops are raised. The island was the target of the first Japanese bombing attack against Australia in 1942. It was explored in 1818 by Phillip Parker King, who recommended it for settlement, and was named after the 3rd Earl Bathurst, secretary for war and the colonies (1812–27). Pop. (1981) 1,032.

Bathurst Island, one of the Parry Islands in Franklin District, Northwest Territories, Canada, in the Arctic Ocean between Cornwallis and Melville islands. Bathurst Island is 160 mi (260 km) long and 50–100 mi wide and has an area of 6,194 sq mi (16,042 sq km). The highest point is about 1,500 ft (457 m). Its northern coastline is deeply indented by Erskine and May inlets. The entire coastline is fringed with islets, and several islands stretch in a northwesterly direction from its western tip. Discovered in 1819 by Sir William Parry, it was named for the 3rd Earl Bathurst, then secretary for war and the colonies. The north magnetic pole is located off the island's northern coast (1980).

bathyal zone, marine ecologic realm extending down from the edge of the continental shelf to the depth at which the water temperature is 4° C (39° F). Both of these limits are variable; the shelf break occurs at an average depth of 133 metres (436 feet) but ranges between 20 and 550 m, and the 4° C isotherm lies anywhere between 1,000 and 3,000 m below the surface.

Photosynthesis does not occur in bathyal waters as a rule, the zone being characteristically dark except in the clear, virtually lifeless waters of the tropics, where small amounts of sunlight can penetrate as deeply as 600 m. Temperatures in high latitudes range from about 3° to −1° C. Elsewhere, normal temperatures range between 5° and 15° C, the western oceanic margins being warmer owing to the presence of currents from the Equator and the eastern margins receiving boreal currents and experiencing upwelling. Salinities typically range between 34 and 36 parts per thousand, varying with local conditions of water-mass formation. Bathyal fauna reflect the generally narrow ranges of temperature and salinity that occur.

At bathyal depths, currents are exceedingly slow, and in many areas bathyal waters deeper than 1,000 m are essentially stagnant, resulting in low oxygen concentrations and impoverished faunal levels.

Although upwelling and countercurrents may create favourable nektonic conditions and deep-fishing grounds in some middle- to high-latitude areas, the number of individuals in a bathyal faunal assemblage is generally only about half as large as in shallow-water fauna. It has been demonstrated, however, that single-habitat species diversity is higher for bathyal fauna. It has been suggested that this condition is caused by the constancy of the bathyal environmental conditions, especially its temperature. Bottom dwellers in areas with adequate circulation are adapted to local substrate conditions. Terrigenous bottoms near the continents support the most abundant suspension and mud-eating populations. Cold-water bathyal corals are found in sub-Arctic to equatorial regions.

Bathyal sediments are terrestrial, pelagic, or authigenic (formed in place). Terrestrial (or land-derived) sediments are predominantly clays and silts, commonly blue because of accumulated organic debris as well as bacterially produced ferrous iron sulfides. Coarser terrigenous sediments are also brought to the bathyal sea floor by sporadic turbidity currents originating in shallower areas. Where supplies of terrigenous materials are scarce, microscopic shells of phytoplankton (coccolithophorids) and zooplankton (foraminiferous and pteropods) fall through the water grain by grain, accumulating as white calcareous ooze deposits. Authigenic sediments result from the interaction of clay, feldspar, and volcanic glass particles with seawater, forming the minerals glauconite, chlorite, phillipsite, and palagonite. These sediments are generally green because of their chlorite and glauconite contents.

bathymetry, measurement of ocean depth. The earliest technique involved lowering a heavy rope or cable of known length over the side of a ship, then measuring the amount needed to reach the bottom. Tedious and frequently inaccurate, this method yielded the depth at only a single point rather than a continuous measurement; inaccuracies arose because the rope did not necessarily travel straight to the bottom but instead might be deflected by subsurface currents or movements of the vessel.

A more satisfactory approach, though not without problems, is echo sounding, widely used today, in which a sound pulse travels from the vessel to the ocean floor, is reflected, and returns. By calculations involving the time elapsed between generation of the pulse and its return and the speed of sound in water, a continuous record of sea-floor topography can be made. Most echo sounders perform these calculations mechanically, producing a graphic record in the form of a paper chart. Misleading reflections caused by the presence of undersea canyons or mountains plus variations in the speed of sound through water caused by differences in temperature, depth, and salinity limit the accuracy of echo sounding, though these problems can be met somewhat by crossing and recrossing the same area. Sonar has also been employed in bathymetric studies, as have underwater cameras.

bathyscaphe, navigable diving vessel developed by the Swiss educator and scientist Auguste Piccard (with assistance in later years from his son Jacques), designed to reach great depths in the ocean.

The first bathyscaphe, the "FNRS 2" built in Belgium between 1946 and 1948, was damaged during 1948 trials in the Cape Verde Islands. Substantially rebuilt and greatly improved, the vessel was renamed "FNRS 3" and carried out a series of descents under excellent conditions, including one of 4,000 m (13,000 ft) into the Atlantic off Dakar, Senegal, on Feb. 15, 1954. A second improved bathyscaphe, the "Trieste," was launched on Aug. 1, 1953, and dived to 3,150 m (10,300 ft) in the same year. In 1958 the "Trieste" was acquired by the United States Navy, taken to California, and equipped with a new cabin designed to enable it to reach the seabed of the great oceanic trenches. Several successive descents were made into the Pacific by Jacques Piccard, and on Jan. 23, 1960, Piccard, accompanied by Lieut. Don Walsh of the U.S. Navy, dived to a record 10,916 m (35,810 ft) in the Pacific's Mariana Trench.

The bathyscaphe consists of two main components: a steel cabin, heavier than water and resistant to sea pressure, to accommodate the observers; and a light container called a float, filled with gasoline, which, being lighter than

"FNRS 2," the first bathyscaphe, built between 1946 and 1948, designed by Auguste Piccard

Actualit

water, provides the necessary lifting power. The cabin and float are closely linked. On the surface, one or more ballast tanks filled with air provide enough lift to keep the bathyscaphe afloat. When the ballast tank valves are opened, air escapes and is replaced by water, making the whole device heavy enough to start its descent. The gasoline is in direct contact with the sea water and so is compressed at a rate almost exactly in proportion to the prevailing depth. Thus, the bathyscaphe gradually loses buoyancy as it descends, and the speed of its descent tends to increase rapidly. To slow down or to begin the reascent, the pilot releases ballast that consists essentially of iron shot stored in silos and held in place by electromagnets.

bathysphere, spherical steel vessel for use in undersea observation, provided with portholes and suspended by a cable from a boat. Built by the U.S. zoologist William Beebe and the U.S. engineer Otis Barton, the bathysphere made its first dives in 1930. On June 11, 1930, it reached a depth of 400 metres, or about 1,300 feet, and in 1932, Beebe and Barton reached 900 metres, or about 3,000 feet. Through these dives, the bathysphere proved its qualities but also revealed weaknesses. It was difficult to operate and involved considerable potential risks. A break in the suspension cable would have meant certain death for the observers; surface waves and resulting movement of the boat could have produced such a

William Beebe's bathysphere

By courtesy of the New York Zoological Society

fatal strain. In light of these disadvantages, the bathysphere was supplanted by the safer, more manoeuvrable mesoscaphe and bathyscaphe (*qq.v.*).

bathythermograph, any of various oceanographic devices containing temperature- and pressure-sensitive elements, and producing a continuous record of underwater temperature and pressure. Recoverable bathythermographs, lowered from a ship at rest or in motion, produce this record on a coated glass slide. Expendable types, often dropped from aircraft, radio back information from depths up to 300 metres (1,000 feet) and are frequently employed in making surveys of large areas.

Bathyuriscus, genus of trilobites (extinct arthropods) that provide a useful index fossil

Bathyuriscus, of Cambrian age

By courtesy of the trustees of the British Museum (Natural History); photograph, Imitor

for the Middle Cambrian of North America (the Cambrian Period began 570,000,000 years ago and lasted 70,000,000 years). In *Bathyuriscus* the head segment is well developed, and marginal spines are present. The tail region is large and has many well-developed segments. Several species of *Bathyuriscus* are recognized.

batik, method of dyeing in which patterned areas are covered with wax so they will not receive the colour. The method is used mainly on cottons and in the traditional colours of blue, brown, and red. Multicoloured and blended effects are obtained by repeating the

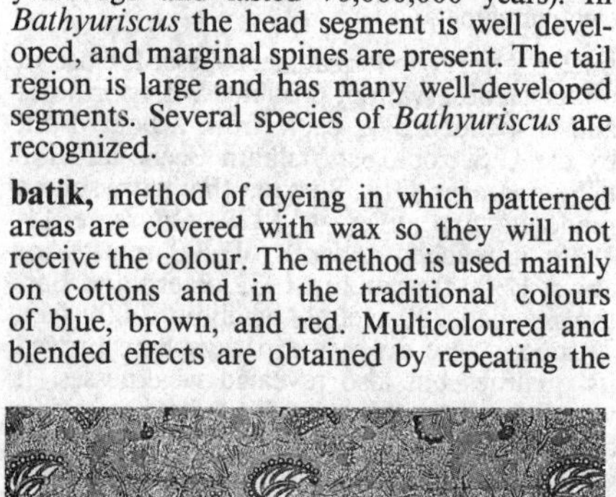

Batik work, traditional Javanese pattern

By courtesy of the Koninklijk Instituut voor de Tropen, Amsterdam

dyeing process several times, with the initial pattern of wax boiled off and another design applied before redyeing. The basic technique, originated at an unknown time, was apparently practiced widely in Southeast Asia with local variations, as in Celebes Island, where the wax was applied with bamboo strips. In Java, by the mid-18th century, a small copper crucible with a handle and narrow applicator spout for applying the wax came into use, producing a much more elaborately patterned cloth; a further Javanese innovation was the wood-block wax applicator introduced in the 19th century. The Dutch imported both the cloth and the technique to Europe. Present machines for applying wax in traditional Javanese patterns may reproduce such effects of the hand process as the staining caused by fissures in the wax. *See also* resist printing.

Bāṭinah, al-, *liwāʾs* (province) and narrow, well-populated coastal plain, northeastern Oman, fronting the Gulf of Oman for about 150 mi (240 km) and extending from Oman's border with the United Arab Emirates near Shināṣ southeast to as-Sīb. Although its boundaries have never been officially defined, the province is generally contiguous with the coastal plain. It varies in width between 10 and 30 miles, crossed by numerous wadis descending northeastward from the mountain chain of al-Ḥajar (the Stone); the upper courses of the wadis are densely populated. In the parts of the plain removed from the coast and the wadis, acacia trees give way to a barren, pebbly plain near the foothills of al-Ḥajar. Cultivation is intensive along the length of the coast for the first mile inland because of the ribbon of oases watered by wells and underground channels. Since early times the region has been known for its exports of dates, horses, dried limes, copper, and ambergris washed up on its shore. It was dominated by the Persians at various times and came under attacks by the Carmathians in the 10th century, the Turks in the 11th–12th centuries, and the Portuguese in the 16th century.

Al-Bāṭinah has vast plantations of date palms; papaya, lime, and mango trees are grown along the coast in irrigated gardens, which also produce vegetables and some cereal grains. Sheep and goats are raised, and fishing is important. The major towns of al-Bāṭinah (all on the coast) include al-Musanaʿa, as-Suwayq, al-Khābūrah, as-Ṣaham, Ṣuḥār, and Shināṣ. The inhabitants of the plain, comprising about one-third of Oman's total population, are a mixture of Arabs and Baluchi and are Muslims.

Bāṭiniyah, Muslim sects—the Ismāʿīlīyah, in particular—that interpreted religious texts exclusively on the basis of their hidden or inner meanings (Arabic *bāṭin*) rather than their literal (*ẓāhir*) meanings. This type of interpretation gained currency about the 8th century among certain esoteric Shīʿī sects, especially the Ismāʿīlīyah, a religiously and politically extremist and revolutionary group. The Ismāʿīlīyah believed that beneath every obvious or literal meaning of a sacred text lay a secret, hidden meaning, which could be arrived at through *taʾwīl* (allegorical interpretations); thus, every statement, person, or object could be scrutinized in this manner to reveal its true intent. They further stated that Muḥammad was only the transmitter of the literal word of God, the Qurʾān, but it was the *imām* (leader) who was empowered to interpret, through *taʾwīl,* its true, hidden meaning.

Speculative philosophy and theology eventually influenced the Bāṭinīyah, though they remained at all times on the side of esoteric knowledge; some Ṣūfīs (Muslim mystics) were also placed among the Bāṭinīyah for their insistence that there was an esoteric body of doctrine known only to the initiate. While the Ismāʿīlīyah had always acknowledged the validity of both *bāṭin* and *ẓāhir,* about the 12th century this balance was upset by the Nuṣayrīyah and the Druze, who accepted only the hidden meanings and exalted the *imām* over the Prophet himself.

Sunnī (traditionalist) Muslim scholars condemned the Bāṭinīyah for all interpretations that rejected the literal meaning and rightly criticized them for producing confusion and controversy through a multiplicity of readings; this in turn allowed ignorant or mischievous persons to claim possession of religious truths and thus deceive those who lacked the knowledge to expose them. The Bāṭinīyah were further labelled by the Sunnah as enemies of Islām and were often suspected of intrigues and secret propaganda to destroy the faith. *See also* tafsīr.

Batista (y Zaldívar), Fulgencio (b. Jan. 16, 1901, Banes, Cuba—d. Aug. 6, 1973, Marbella, Spain), soldier and dictator who twice ruled Cuba: first in 1933–44, when he gave the nation a strong, efficient government, and again in 1952–59 as a dictator, jailing his opponents, using terrorist methods, and making fortunes for himself and his associates.

The son of impoverished farmers, Batista worked in a variety of jobs until he joined the army in 1921, starting as a stenographer. He rose to the rank of sergeant and developed a large personal following. In September 1933 he organized the "sergeants' revolt"; it toppled the provisional regime of Carlos Manuel de Céspedes, which had replaced the dictatorial regime of Gerardo Machado y Morales. Batista thus became the most powerful man in Cuba.

An astute judge of men, Batista preferred to consolidate his control through patronage rather than terror. He cultivated the support of the army, the civil service, and organized labour. Ruling through associates the first few years, he was elected president in 1940. While greatly enriching himself, he also governed the nation most effectively, expanding the educational system, sponsoring a huge program of public works, and fostering the growth of the economy.

Retiring from office in 1944, he travelled abroad and lived for a while in Florida, where he invested part of the huge sums he had acquired in Cuba. The eight years he was out of power in Cuba witnessed the resurgence of corruption on a grand scale and the virtual breakdown of public services. His return to power through another army revolt in March 1952 was widely welcomed. But he returned as a brutal dictator, controlling the university, the press, and the Congress, and he embezzled huge sums from the soaring economy. His regime was finally toppled by the rebel forces led by Fidel Castro, who launched their successful attack in the fall of 1958. Faced with the collapse of his regime, Batista fled with his family to the Dominican Republic on Jan. 1, 1959. Later he went into exile on the Portuguese island of Madeira and finally to Estoril, near Lisbon.

Batiushkov, Konstantin Nikolayevich: *see* Batyushkov, Konstantin Nikolayevich.

Batjan (Indonesia): *see* Bacan.

Batlle Berres, Luis (b. Nov. 26, 1897, Montevideo—d. July 15, 1964, Montevideo), Uruguayan journalist who became active in politics and served as president of his country from 1947 to 1951 and chief executive officer from 1954 to 1956.

Nephew of former president José Batlle y Ordóñez, Batlle Berres was known as a champion of democracy and civil liberties and an outspoken critic of U.S. support of authoritarian Latin American regimes. He served as a representative from 1923 to 1933 and from 1942 to 1947, and was president of the Chamber of Representatives from 1943 to 1945. Elected vice president in 1946, he succeeded to the presidency when the incumbent, Tomás Berreta, died in office. His stable and peaceful administration attracted large amounts of foreign investment capital. After Uruguay adopted a form of government in which the executive branch consisted of a nine-man council, Batlle was elected head of the council in 1954 and remained a member after his two-year term as chief expired. Batlle founded the newspaper *Acción* in 1948, using it as a vehicle for his political opinions. He also owned the radio station, Ariel.

Batlle y Ordóñez, José (b. May 21, 1856, Montevideo—d. Oct. 20, 1929, Montevideo), statesman who, as president of Uruguay in 1903–07 and 1911–15, is generally credited with transforming his country from an unstable dictatorship into a viable democracy.

Batlle y Ordóñez

By courtesy of the Organization of American States

Batlle y Ordóñez was the son of Gen. Lorenz Batlle, a president of Uruguay, and a grandson of José Batlle y Carréo, a leading citizen of colonial Montevideo. He was educated at the University of Montevideo and at the Sorbonne. He began his political career on June 16, 1886, when he founded the newspaper *El Día.* Shortly thereafter he joined the Colorado Party, one of the two ruling political parties of Uruguay, and in 1890 he started work to transform his party into a nationwide democratic political organization. He was elected to the Uruguayan Chamber of Deputies in 1893 and to the Senate for Montevideo in 1896. He soon became president of the Senate and a member of his party's National Executive Commission. In 1900 he made an unsuccessful bid for the national presidency.

Batlle y Ordóñez was elected president in 1903, but by a narrow margin that produced tension with the opposition Blanco Party and led to a civil war in 1904. Batlle y Ordóñez and his followers emerged victorious in 1905, with the Colorado Party in undisputed control of the country. He held honest new presidential and legislative elections in 1905, which he and his party won. At the end of his term in 1907, he freely stepped down from the presidency, though he played a role in choosing his party's presidential candidate.

Following a triumphant tour of Europe, Batlle y Ordóñez was reelected president in 1911, and he continued the reforms he had started earlier. During his two periods in office, Batlle y Ordóñez inaugurated labour reforms, limited the profits of foreign-owned businesses, encouraged migration, nationalized and developed public works, ended the death penalty, and protected illegitimate children.

At the end of his presidency, fearing the power of a one-man executive, he sought to reform the Uruguayan constitution by creating a collegiate executive. This effort aroused great opposition throughout the country and even divided his own political party. As a result, a new constitution established in 1918 provided for a bifurcated executive—a president and national executive council—which was considered a defeat for Batlle y Ordóñez. Nevertheless, he agreed to serve as president of the council in 1920 and in 1926.

Batman, town, Siirt *il* (province), southeastern Turkey, in the centre of the nation's oil-producing region. It is located about 5 mi (80 km) west of Siirt town, the provincial capital, and lies in a region of broad plateaus. A government-owned refinery is located at Batman, and a pipeline extends for nearly 320 mi from the oilfields near Batman to the port of İskenderum on the Mediterranean Sea coast. Industries produce beverages, processed food, chemicals, furniture and fixtures, footwear, machinery, and transport equipment. There are road and railway links with Diyarbakir and Kurtalan, and it has an airport. Pop. (1980) 86,172.

Batna, *wilāyah* (province, or *département*), northeastern Algeria, established in 1974 from part of Aurès *wilāyah.* It embraces an area of 5,746 sq mi (14,882 sq km), and is bounded by the *wilāyāt* (provinces) of Oum el-Bouaghi and Sétif (north), Tébessa (southeast), Biskra (south), and M'Sila (west). The *wilāyah* consists mostly of the Aurès Massif, except for lower-lying high-plain areas in the west and northeast. The Aurès Massif, an area of steep cliffs and long, straight ridges, contains the highest peaks in the Atlas Mountains of Algeria, several of them rising more than 7,500 ft (2,280 m) above sea level. The main inhabitants are the Shawia (Chaouia), a Berber group that practices both subsistence cultivation of wheat and barley and pastoral nomadism. Industries produce textiles and woven carpets. Other major towns besides Batna, the *wilāyah* capital, include Barika, Râs el-Aïoun, and Aïn Touta (a zinc-mining centre). High-grade iron-ore deposits were discovered at Djebel (ridge) Bou Ari in 1975. Pop. (1980 est.) 648,228.

Batna, city, capital of Batna *wilāyah* (province, or *département*), Algeria, on the Oued (stream) Tilatou and a well-watered plain bounded on the south by the Aurès Massif and on the north by the Monts (mountains) de Batna. To the west, the cedar-forested Djebel (mount) Tougour (Pic des Cèdres) rises to 6,870 ft (2,094 m).

Batna originated in 1844 as a French military outpost, established to protect el-Kantara Pass between the Tell Atlas and the Sahara and to patrol the neighbouring mountains. The site was moved a short distance east to Râs el-Aïoun where the city was founded in 1848 as Nouvelle Lambèse; it was renamed Batna in 1849. Its original rectangular plan includes tree-lined avenues, a walled military quarter to the east, and less orderly recent additions. Batna trades in agricultural and forest products and is a tourist base for the Roman ruins at Tazoult-Lambese (*see* Lambessa) 7 mi (11 km) to the southeast and Timgad (*see* Thamugadi) 17 mi to the east-southeast. Pop. (1977 prelim.) mun., 112,095.

Batna, Alg., with the Monts de Batna in the background

Dominique Darbois

Batoche, unincorporated place, central Saskatchewan, Canada, on the east bank of the South Saskatchewan River, 40 mi (64 km) southwest of Prince Albert. The site was settled about 1870 by colonists from the Red River Settlement (founded in 1811–12 near the present city of Winnipeg, Man.). The settlement (named for a Métis trader, Xavier Letendre, whose nickname was Batoche) became the headquarters of Louis Riel, leader of the Métis (half-breeds) in the Riel (North West) Rebellion of 1885, and was the scene of the decisive and bloody battle (May 9–12) in which Canadian militia under Gen. Frederick Middleton defeated the rebels. The battlefield is now contained in Batoche National Historic Park; of special interest are the Métis Cemetery and Rectory (which houses historical exhibits).

Batoe Eilanden (Indonesia): *see* Batu Islands.

Baton Rouge, city, capital of Louisiana, U.S., seat (1811) of East Baton Rouge Parish, port at the head of deepwater navigation on the Mississippi River, in the southeast central part of the state. The French named the town for a red cypress post that marked a boundary between Indian tribes. They built and garrisoned a fort on the site in 1719. The area was ceded to Britain in 1763 at the end of the French and Indian Wars. During the American Revolution, the Spanish overpowered the British garrison there in the first battle of Baton Rouge (Sept. 21, 1779) and controlled the area for the next 20 years. In 1800 Spain ceded Louisiana to France, and at the time of the Louisiana Purchase (1803) by the U.S. Baton Rouge was claimed by Spain, along with the entire territory of West Florida. The city's inhabitants and the U.S.-born citizens of the surrounding parishes rebelled against Spanish rule in the second battle of Baton Rouge (Sept. 23, 1810) and established the West Florida Republic, which was annexed to the United States three months later. Baton Rouge was incorporated in 1817, and in 1849 it became capital of the state. On March 21, 1861, Louisiana joined the Confederacy; in 1862 Federal forces captured the city in the third battle of Baton Rouge and held it for the remainder of the war. During the war the seat of government was transferred to other towns but in 1882 was returned to Baton Rouge.

State Capitol, Baton Rouge, La.

Alan Pitcairn from Grant Heilman—EB Inc.

The old State Capitol (1847–49) was replaced (1931–32) during Gov. Huey P. Long's administration; constructed of marble and other stone brought in from various parts of the world, it is 34 stories high and has an ornate Memorial Hall and observation tower. Its grounds contain a sunken garden with Long's grave.

The city's growth as an industrial centre began with the building of the Standard Oil Company's giant refinery in 1909. Subsequently, many industries were established there, attracted by the proximity of the oil fields (in Texas, Oklahoma, and Louisiana), the economy of ocean and river transportation, and the abundance of natural gas and other natural resources. Dock facilities were expanded, and the Port Allen–Morgan City Cut-Off Canal constructed. Under the impetus of industries established during World War II, the city's population trebled in the decade 1940–50. Baton Rouge is the seat of Louisiana State University and Agricultural and Mechanical College (1860) and Southern University and Agricultural and Mechanical College (1880). Pop. (1980) city, 219,486; metropolitan area (SMSA), 493,973.

Batoni, Pompeo Girolamo, Batoni also spelled BATTONI (b. Jan. 25, 1708, Lucca, Tuscany—d. Feb. 4, 1787, Rome), Italian painter, who in his own time was ranked with Anton Raphael Mengs as a painter of historical subjects. Probably his portraits are now better known, as he invented the type of "grand tourist" portrait, very popular among the English, which shows the sitter at his ease among the ruins of antiquity. He also painted three popes and many princes. Sir Joshua Reynolds referred to him disparagingly in his 14th discourse, but, as a competitor for English sitters, Reynolds may not have been entirely disinterested. Most of Batoni's portraits are still in country houses, but there are examples at Cardiff and Dublin, at the National Portrait galleries of Edinburgh and London, and at Oxford.

Batoro (people): *see* Toro.

Batory, Stefan: *see* Stephen Báthory.

Baṭrā (ancient Arabia): *see* Petra.

Batrachospermum, genus of freshwater red algae ranging in colour from violet to blue-green. Its long, branched, threadlike filaments bear dense whorls of branchlets, the whorls themselves resembling beads on a string. Spores are formed in clusters around the base of the carpogonium (female sex organ) after fertilization. This macroscopic alga, found in streams and in the pools formed in sphagnum bogs, is one of the very few freshwater algae.

Consult the INDEX *first*

Batsányi, János (b. May 9, 1763, Tapolca, Hung.—d. May 12, 1845, Linz, Austria), Hungary's leading political poet and one of its chief arbiters of literary taste during the Enlightenment.

As editor of *Magyar Museum,* he organized the literature of national resistance. Writing little pure lyrical poetry, he concentrated on political poetry (the ultimate of its kind in Hungary), advocating revolution and freedom of the oppressed. After 1796 he moved to Vienna, where he married the Austrian poet Gabrielle Baumberg. Supporting Napoleon, he finally settled in Paris, where he was eventually seized by the allied powers. While imprisoned in Linz, he wrote some famous elegies; among his important volumes of verse are *A franciaországi váltózasokra* (1789; "On the Changes in France") and *Látó* (1793; "The Seer").

Batswana (people): *see* Tswana.

Battak, also spelled BATTA (people): *see* Batak.

battalion, a tactical military organization composed basically of a headquarters and two or more companies, batteries, or similar organizations and usually commanded by a field-grade officer. The term has been used in nearly every Western army for centuries and has had a variety of meanings. In the 16th and 17th centuries it denoted a unit of infantry forming part of a line of battle and was loosely applied to any large body of men. During the Napoleonic Wars the French developed an army organization in which the regiment was a unit of administration for its battalions serving as fighting units in the field. In this connection, the terms regiment and battalion often were used interchangeably, but in most modern armies the regiment is a higher unit than the battalion.

In the armies of the Commonwealth nations, infantry battalions, usually commanded by lieutenant colonels, are tactical units formed within regiments, the latter being not tactical but administrative parent organizations. The equivalent tactical artillery and armoured units, however, are called regiments. In most military forces the cavalry equivalent and aviation equivalent of the battalion is the squadron.

In the U.S. Army of the early years of the 20th century, a battalion usually numbered from 500 to 1,000 men and was normally commanded by a lieutenant colonel. After World War I the "square" infantry battalion of four companies was superseded by the "triangular" battalion of World War II and the Korean War, usually composed of three rifle companies, a heavy-weapons company, and a headquarters company. During World War II and in Korea, the infantry battalion often was used as the nucleus of a combat team in special operations, such as airborne or amphibious assaults, requiring decentralization of tactical control by higher echelons. Battalion combat teams included such reinforcements as attached artillery, tanks, engineers, and other special elements.

In 1957 the U.S. Army eliminated its infantry battalions and regiments, replacing them with "battle groups." Battalion organization was retained in most non-infantry commands.

A further reorganization, begun in 1961, called for the restoration of infantry battalions as administratively and tactically self-sufficient units of between 800 and 900 officers and men, normally divided into a headquarters company and three rifle companies. Armoured battalions were to be reorganized along similar lines. From two to five battalions were to form the combat manoeuvre elements attached to a tactical brigade.

In the Soviet Army the battalion was smaller than its U.S. counterpart. A typical rifle battalion of a rifle division consisted of 370 officers and men organized into three 78-man rifle companies plus machine-gun, artillery, mortar, and service units.

Battambang (Kampuchea): *see* Bătdâmbâng.

Battānī, al-, in full ABŪ ʿABD ALLĀH MUḤAMMAD IBN JĀBIR IBN SINĀN AL-BATTĀNĪ AL-ḤARRĀNĪ AS-ṢĀBIʾ, Latin as ALBATENIUS, ALBATEGNUS, or ALBATEGNI (b. *c.* 858, in or near Haran, near Urfa, Syria—d. 929, near Sāmarrāʿ, Mesopotamia), astronomer and mathematician who found more accurate values for the length of the year and of the seasons, for the annual precession of the equinoxes, and for the inclination of the ecliptic. He showed that the position of the Sun's apogee, or farthest point from the Earth, is variable and that annular (central but incomplete) eclipses of the Sun are possible. He improved Ptolemy's astronomical calculations by replacing geometrical methods with trigonometry. From 877 he carried out many years of remarkably accurate observations at ar-Raqqah in Syria.

He was the best known of Arab astronomers in Europe during the Middle Ages. His principal written work, a book of astronomical tables, was translated into Latin *c.* 1116 and into Spanish in the 13th century. A printed edition, titled *De motu stellarum* ("On Stellar Motion"), was published in 1537.

batte din (Judaism): *see* bet din.

battement (French: "beating"), in ballet, an extension of the leg to the front, side, or back, either repeatedly or as a single movement. Among representative types are *battement tendu* ("stretched beating"), in which one leg is extended until the point of the stretched foot barely touches the ground; *grand battement* ("large beating"), in which the leg is lifted to hip level or higher and held straight; *battement frappé* ("struck beating"), in which the ball of the foot brushes the floor as the working foot is briskly extended from a flexed position against the lower calf of the supporting leg; and *petit battement sur le cou-de-pied* ("small beatings on the instep"), in which the working foot touches the front and back of the instep of the supporting leg.

Grand battement, from George Balanchine's *Symphony in C,* performed by the New York City Ballet

Martha Swope

Battenberg FAMILY, English MOUNTBATTEN, a family that rose to international prominence in the 19th and 20th centuries, the name being a revival of a medieval title.

The first Battenbergs were a family of German counts, which died out about 1314 and whose seat was the castle of Kellerburg, near Battenberg, in Hesse. The title was revived in 1851, when Alexander (1823–88), a younger son of Louis II, grand duke of Hesse, contracted a morganatic marriage with the Polish lady, Countess Julia Theresa von Hauke (1825–95), who was then created countess of Battenberg. In 1858 the Countess and her children were all raised to the rank of prince or princess (*Prinz* or *Prinzessin*) of Battenberg.

In 1917 the eldest son of this union, Louis Alexander (1854–1921), who had become an admiral in the British navy, was created marquess of Milford Haven (*see* Milford Haven, Louis Alexander, 1st Marquess of); and, at the request of King George V, the members of the family who lived in England renounced, in 1917, the German title of prince of Battenberg and adopted the surname of Mountbatten.

Milford Haven was the father of Princess Alice (1885–1969), who married Prince Andrew of Greece (1882–1944); their only son, Prince Philip (1921–), took the surname Mountbatten and was created duke of Edinburgh when he became a British subject in 1947 and married Princess Elizabeth, who became Queen Elizabeth II in 1952. Milford Haven's younger daughter, Louise (1889–1965), became in 1923 the second wife of Crown Prince Gustav Adolf, who in 1950 became King Gustav VI Adolf of Sweden.

Milford Haven had three younger brothers. Alexander (1857–93) was ruling prince of Bulgaria from 1879 to 1886. Henry Maurice (1858–96) took British nationality on his marriage in 1885 to Queen Victoria's youngest daughter, Princess Beatrice, and was the father of Victoria Eugenie, or Ena (1887–1969), who in 1906 married King Alfonso XIII of Spain. Francis Joseph (1861–1924) married in 1897 Anna, daughter of Nicholas I, prince of Montenegro.

Battenberg, Louis Alexander, prince of: *see* Milford Haven, Louis Alexander Mountbatten, 1st marquess of.

Battenberg, Louis Francis Albert Victor Nicholas, prince of: *see* Mountbatten of Burma, Louis Mountbatten, 1st Earl.

batter, mixture of flour and liquid with other ingredients, such as leavening agents, shortening, sugar, salt, eggs, and various flavouring materials, used to make baked products.

Such mixtures—called doughs—are thick and flexible, allowing them to be shaped and rolled. Batters, however, contain higher proportions of liquids, are thinner than doughs, and can be stirred, poured, and dropped from a spoon. Batter products are mainly shaped by the form of the containers in which they are baked and include biscuits, muffins, scones, corn bread, pancakes, layer cakes, and angel food cakes. Angel food and sponge-cake batters, usually made without leavening ingredients, are leavened during baking by the expansion of the many small air bubbles incorporated in the batter by vigorous mixing or beating. Batters are also used as coatings for foods that are to be sautéed or fried.

battering ram, medieval weapon consisting of a heavy timber with a metal knob or point at the front. Such devices were used to batter down the gates or walls of a besieged city or castle. The ram itself, usually suspended by ropes from the roof of a movable shed, was swung back and forth by its operators against the besieged structure. The roof of the shed was usually covered with animal skins to protect the weapon's operators from bombardment with stones or fiery materials.

Battersea, area of Greater London, on the south bank of the River Thames, in the borough of Wandsworth. The riverside of the area is lined with factories and is dominated by an electric power station, a well-known London landmark. Battersea Park (200 ac [80 ha]), bordering the river between Albert and Chelsea bridges, was laid out (1858) as a municipal park and adapted as pleasure gardens with rides and other amusement devices for the Festival of Britain (1951). The home (founded 1860) on Battersea Park Road for stray and unwanted dogs and cats is also well known.

Battersea enamelware, type of painted enamelware considered the finest of its kind to be produced in England during the mid-18th century. It is especially noted for the high quality of its transfer printing. Battersea ware was made at York House in Battersea, a district in London, by Stephen Theodore Janssen between 1753 and 1756. This ware is variably composed of soft white enamel completely covering a copper ground. A design is applied to the white enamel either by painting by hand or by transfer printing, a process by which an impression from an engraved metal plate brushed with enamel colours is transferred to paper and then to the surface to be decorated. Transfer printing was used on a large scale for the first time at Battersea. Most of the articles produced there, small ornamental pieces such as snuffboxes and watchcases, were decorated in the Rococo style with mottoes, portraits, landscapes, or flowers. The shapes of the objects and the decorative motifs are often imitative of Meissen porcelain ware.

Battersea enamelware plaque, 1750–56; in the Victoria and Albert Museum, London

By courtesy of the Victoria and Albert Museum, London; photograph, A.C. Cooper Ltd.

battery (law): *see* assault and battery.

battery, in electricity and electrochemistry, any of a class of devices that convert chemical energy directly into electrical energy. Although the term battery, in strict usage, designates an assembly of two or more voltaic cells capable of such energy conversion, it is commonly applied to a single cell of this kind.

A brief treatment of batteries follows. For full treatment, *see* MACROPAEDIA: Energy Conversion.

The mechanism by which a battery generates an electric current involves the arrangement of constituent chemicals in such a manner that electrons are released from one part of the battery and made to flow through an external circuit to another part. The part of the battery at which the electrons are released to the circuit is called the anode, or the negative electrode; the part that receives the electrons from the circuit is known as the cathode, or the positive electrode. (In a device that consumes current—*e.g.*, electroplating cell, electron tube, etc.—the term anode is often applied to the positive electrode, while the negative electrode is called the cathode.)

The first battery appears to have been constructed about 1800 by Alessandro Volta, a professor of natural philosophy at the University of Pavia in Italy. This device, later known as the voltaic pile, was composed of a series of silver and zinc disks in pairs, each of which was separated with a sheet of pasteboard saturated in salt water. A current was produced when the uppermost disk of silver was connected by a wire to the bottom disk of zinc. In 1836 the English chemist John Daniell developed what is considered the classic form of the voltaic cell.

A voltaic cell is composed of two chemicals with different electron-attracting capabilities that are immersed in an electrolyte and connected to each other through an external circuit. These two chemicals are called an electrochemical couple. In a zinc-acid cell, for example, the electrochemical couple is a zinc–hydrogen ion couple. The reaction that occurs between an electrochemical couple in a voltaic cell is an oxidation–reduction reaction.

At rest, a voltaic cell exhibits a potential difference (voltage) between its two electrodes that is determined by the amount of chemical energy available when an electron is transferred from one electrode to the other and is thus subject to the chemical nature of the materials used in the electrode. The current that flows from a cell is determined by the resistance of the total circuit, including that of the cell itself. A low-resistance cell is required if extremely large currents are desired. This can be achieved by the utilization of electrodes with large areas. In short, the maximum current that can be drawn from a cell is dependent on the area of the electrodes. Whenever a current flows, the voltage of a cell decreases because of internal resistance of the cell and the slowness of the chemical process at the electrodes.

A voltaic cell has a limited energy content, or capacity, which is generally given in ampere-hours and determined by the quantity of electrons that can be released at the anode and accepted at the cathode. When all of the chemical energy of the cell has been consumed—usually because one of the electrodes has been completely exhausted—the voltage falls to zero and will not recover. The capacity of the cell is determined by the quantity of active ingredients in the electrode.

There are two major types of voltaic cells: primary batteries and secondary, or storage, batteries. (The latter are sometimes also called accumulators.) Primary cells are constructed in such a way that only one continuous or intermittent discharge can be obtained. Secondary devices, on the other hand, are constructed so that they can be discharged and then recharged to approximately their original state. The charging process is the reverse of the discharge process; therefore, the electrode reactions in these batteries must be reversible.

Primary batteries. Several varieties of primary cells are available. These include dry, wet, and solid electrolyte.

Dry cells are not actually dry but contain an aqueous electrolyte that is unspillable or immobilized. Many of these cells are sealed to prevent seepage of the electrolyte or reaction products. Common examples of such primary batteries are acidic dry cells (*e.g.*, carbon–zinc cells), used in flashlights, toys, and certain transistorized portable radios; alkaline dry cells, employed in cameras, tape recorders, and electric razors; and mercury cells, utilized in hearing aids and photographic flash guns.

Wet cells contain a free and mobile electrolyte. They are used when service requirements include large capacity and moderately high currents, as, for example, in telephone and telegraph circuits and in signal systems for marine, mine, highway, and railway use. The Lalande cell of zinc–copper oxide—sodium hydroxide and the zinc–air–sodium hydroxide cell have been widely employed for such applications. Often included among wet primary cells is the so-called reserve battery, in which either magnesium–silver chloride or magnesium–cuprous chloride serves as the electrode material. Because these compounds are readily attacked by electrolytes (either seawater or liquid ammonia), the battery is assembled with the electrolyte stored in a separate container. The electrolyte is added immediately before use. The reserve battery has been utilized primarily for military applications.

Solid electrolyte cells contain electrolytes of crystalline salts such as silver iodide or lead chloride that have predominantly ionic conductivity. They are suitable for long-term operations that require very low drain or for stand-by services. Miniature versions of solid salt electrolyte batteries have been developed for use in various kinds of electronic devices.

Secondary batteries. Such batteries consist of an assemblage of several identical voltaic cells. Of the various types of storage batteries available, the lead–acid type is the most widely used. It serves as the power source for the electrical systems of many kinds of motor vehicles, particularly automobiles and trucks. It is also commonly used to provide electricity for emergency lighting and communication circuits. The active constituents of a lead–acid battery are sulfuric acid and two sets of plates (electrodes)—one containing pure lead and the other lead dioxide. Each component cell consists of several of these plate pairs connected in parallel and is capable of delivering approximately two volts. Three or six cells are connected in series to make a 6- or 12-volt battery, respectively. The sulfuric-acid electrolyte in each of the cells is stored separately in its own compartment. During discharge, the plate materials are converted into lead sulfate and the sulfuric acid is depleted. Discharge stops before all component chemicals are exhausted, usually when the acid can no longer reach the active materials. Charging the battery by passing a direct current through it reverses the chemical changes, displacing the sulfate from the plates and causing a rise in the specific gravity of the sulfuric acid.

Another important type of storage battery is the nickel–cadmium battery, which operates much like the lead–acid variety but with different chemical ingredients. It consists of a nickel hydroxide cathode and a cadmium anode immersed in an electrolyte of potassium hydroxide solution. The nickel–cadmium battery is lighter in weight than are other storage batteries and can be hermetically sealed. Because of these features, nickel–cadmium cells are utilized in many kinds of cordless appliances and other portable equipment.

A third storage battery of significance is the silver–zinc type. The anode of this device is composed of a porous plate of zinc, the cathode of a silver screen pasted with silver oxide, and the electrolyte of a solution of potassium hydroxide saturated with zinc hydroxide. Silver–zinc batteries can only be charged and discharged a limited number of times because of the structure used to separate the electrodes. They do have, however, a high energy-to-weight ratio and are suitable for applications in which light weight is important.

Batthyány, Lajos, Gróf (Count) (b. Feb. 14, 1806, Pozsony, Hung., Austrian Empire—d. Oct. 6, 1849, Pest, Hung.), statesman who during the revolution of 1848 was premier of the first Hungarian parliamentary government and a martyr for Magyar independence.

The son of wealthy liberal landowners whose nobility dated to 1398, Batthyány entered the military but left it in 1827 to manage his estates and to take a law degree at the University of Zagreb. Travel in Western Europe acquainted him with advanced liberal ideas and capitalist business practices, which he applied successfully to his interests.

He became a member of Hungary's upper house in 1830, and in 1845 led the forces seeking independence from the Habsburg monarchy. At the same time, he continued his business activity and in 1843 headed the sugar industry trust. He went to Vienna in March 1848, as a member of the committee that presented Hungarian demands for parliamentary reform to the imperial court. The following month the emperor Ferdinand I (King Ferdinand V of Hungary) appointed Batthyány prime minister of the new parliamentary government, which took office on April 7. Despite his able leadership and the passing of important social legislation, his government found itself caught between the forces of the monarchy and the extreme separatist Hungarian elements.

In the ensuing civil war, Batthyány tried to mediate, but finally took the side of the revolutionaries. On October 11 he was wounded in battle, fell from his horse, and broke an arm. In attempting to negotiate with the Austrian forces, he was captured on Jan. 3, 1849, and sentenced to death by hanging. The night before the execution Batthyány tried, unsuccessfully, to kill himself with a knife. The next morning, badly wounded, he was shot for the crime of sedition. His death caused deep mourning across the nation and aligned European public opinion against Austria.

Batticaloa, town, capital of Eastern Province, Sri Lanka (Ceylon), on an island off the eastern coast. It is linked to the mainland by causeway, bridge, and ferry and by road and railway connections. Batticaloa is the trading centre for rice and coconuts from nearby plantations and for other agricultural products. It was captured by the Portuguese in 1622 and by the Dutch in 1638, and it was surrendered by them to the British in 1796. Ruined Portuguese and Dutch forts remain from the colonial period. Pop. (1981 prelim.) 42,934.

Battishill, Jonathan (b. May 1738, London—d. Dec. 10, 1801, Islington, London), composer of church music and popular songs.

Battishill was a chorister at St. Paul's Cathedral (1747) and later a harpsichordist at Covent Garden. He composed songs and choruses for plays, notably, *Almena* (1764), an opera produced at Drury Lane as the work of Battishill and Michael Arne. In 1764 he became organist at St. Clement Danes and St. Martin-in-the-Fields and wrote psalms settings and hymns, catches, glees, and madrigals. He ceased composing after his wife's elopement in 1777, devoting himself to his book collection.

Battle, parish (town), Rother district, county of East Sussex, England, just inland from Hastings. A ridge to the southeast, called Senlac, was the site of the famous battle in which William I the Conqueror defeated the English in 1066. Before the battle William vowed to build an abbey on the spot if victorious, and in 1094 its church was consecrated, with an altar standing where the English king Harold II fell. The great gateway, built in 1338, survives alongside the town, but after the Reformation the church was destroyed and the abbey converted into a mansion that is now occupied by a school. Pop. (1971) 4,987.

Battle Creek, city, Calhoun County, south central Michigan, U.S., at the juncture of Battle Creek with the Kalamazoo River, 23 mi (37 km) east of Kalamazoo and 49 mi southwest of Lansing. Settled in 1831 and named in 1933 for a "battle" that had taken place on the riverbank between two Indians and two members of a surveying party, it became a flour and woollen mill centre and the site of a Seventh-day Adventist colony. In 1866 the colony founded the Western Health Reform Institute (renamed Battle Creek Sanitarium, 1876, and Battle Creek Health Center, 1959). Under the direction (1876–1943) of John Harvey Kellogg, the sanitarium experimented with health foods, leading to the manufacture of ready-to-eat cereals, which became the city's main industry. The Cereal City Festival with "the world's longest breakfast table" is an annual (June) event. In addition to the Kellogg, Post, and Ralston Purina cereal plants, manufactures include auto parts, trucks, farm equipment, and paper products. Battle Creek's reputation as a "health city" was furthered in 1930 when the W.K. Kellogg Foundation was established to improve the well-being of children. The city is the site of Kellogg Community College (1956), the Post Cereal Art Gallery, and the Leila Arboretum and Kingman Museum of Natural History. The Kellogg Bird Sanctuary of Michigan State University is 13 mi northwest. Sojourner Truth (*c.* 1797–1833), the Negro civil rights pioneer, lived and is buried in Battle Creek (which was an active station on the underground railroad for escaped slaves). Inc. village, 1850; city, 1859. Pop. (1980) 35,724.

Battle Creek Health Center, Mich.
Milt and Joan Mann from CameraMann

battle cruiser, naval combat ship carrying the heavy guns of a battleship but with less armour and hence capable of higher speeds. *See* battleship.

battle fatigue: *see* combat fatigue.

Battle of ——— : *see under* substantive word (*e.g.*, Waterloo, Battle of), except as below.

Battle of Brunanburh, The, Old English poem of 74 lines included in the Anglo-Saxon Chronicle under the year 937. It relates the victory after a day-long battle of the Saxon king Athelstan over the allied Norse, Scots, and Strathclyde Briton invaders under the leadership of Olaf Guthfrithson, king of Dublin and claimant to the throne of York. The poem is basically the victors' bitter taunt of the defeated. It counts the dead kings and earls on the battlefield and pictures the Norsemen slinking back to Dublin in their ships while their dead sons are being devoured by ravens and wolves. The poem claims that this was the greatest battle ever fought in England.

Battle of Maldon, The, Old English heroic poem describing a historical skirmish between East Saxons and Viking (mainly Norwegian) raiders in 991. It is incomplete, its beginning and ending both lost. The poem is remarkable for its vivid, dramatic combat scenes and for its expression of the Germanic ethos of loyalty to a leader. The poem, as it survives, opens with the war parties aligned on either side of a stream (the present River Blackwater near Maldon, Essex). The Vikings offer the cynical suggestion that the English may buy their peace with golden rings. The English commander Earl Byrhtnoth replies that they will pay their tribute in spears and darts. When the Danes cannot advance because of their poor position, Byrhtnoth recklessly allows them safe conduct across the stream, and the battle follows. In spite of Byrhtnoth's supreme feats of courage, he is finally slain. In panic some of the English desert. The names of the deserters are carefully recorded along with the names and genealogies of the loyal retainers who stand fast to avenge Byrhtnoth's death. The 325-line fragment ends with the frequently quoted rallying speech of the old warrior Byrhtwold:

> Mind must be firmer, heart the more fierce,
> Courage the greater, as our strength
> diminishes . . . .

battledore and shuttlecock, children's game played by two persons using small rackets called battledores that are made of parchment, plastic, or rows of gut or nylon stretched across wooden frames, and shuttlecocks, made of a base of some light material, such as cork, with trimmed feathers fixed around the top. Players try to bat the shuttlecock back and forth as many times as possible without allowing it to fall to the ground. Battledore and shuttlecock has been popular in China, Japan, India, and Thailand for at least 2,000 years and has been played in Europe for centuries. Badminton is a further development of the game.

Battleford, town, western Saskatchewan, Canada, at the confluence of the Battle and North Saskatchewan rivers, opposite North Battleford. Established in 1876 as Ft. Battleford, an outpost of the North West Mounted Police, the settlement served as capital of the Northwest Territories until 1883. Battleford was partially burned in 1885 by the Crees, spurred on by the Riel (North West) Rebellion of Métis (half-breeds). It was resettled but after repeated flooding was forced to move to the north bank of the Battle River. When the Canadian National Railway bypassed it in 1903, a new settlement (North Battleford) was established on the north bank of the North Saskatchewan River. Aside from flour milling and its historical interest, highlighted by Fort Battleford National Historic Park (containing buildings of the original fort), Battleford is overshadowed commercially by its northern neighbour. Sweet Grass and other Indian reservations are nearby. Inc. village, 1899; town, 1910. Pop. (1981) 3,565.

battlement, the parapet of a wall consisting of alternating low portions known as crenels, or crenelles (hence crenellated walls with battlements), and high portions called merlons. Battlements were devised in order that warriors might be protected by the merlons and yet be able to discharge arrows or other missiles through the crenels. The battlement is an early development in military architecture; it is found in Chaldea, Egypt, and prehistoric Greece, as well as commonly in Roman fortifications. It was in the Middle Ages that the battlement received its highest development, crenels being narrowed and frequently given splayed sides, the merlons often having in the centre a thin slit sometimes cross-shaped to give the widest possible arc for the discharge of missiles. The developed medieval battlement was frequently bracketed out from the face of the wall, and holes in its floor were furnished to allow objects to be dropped directly upon attacking forces.

In actual siege use, the battlement was usually covered with a protecting shed of timber and hides. In the Saracen countries and in Italy, through Eastern influence, the battlement frequently took decorative shapes; and toward the end of the Gothic period, as the military necessity decreased, the battlement became merely decorative. A similar persistence of the battlement as a purely decorative form occurs in much late Gothic architecture throughout Europe, especially in the Perpendicular work in England, when it was richly ornamented with tracery and frequently pierced as well.

battleship, capital ship of the world's navies from 1860 to World War II, when its pre-eminent position was taken over by the aircraft carrier.

Battleships combined large-size, powerful guns, heavy armour, and underwater protection with fairly high speed, great cruising radius, and general seaworthiness. In their ultimate development they were able to hit targets with great precision at a range of more than 20 miles (30 kilometres) and to absorb an astonishing amount of damage while remaining afloat and continuing to fight.

The type had its genesis in the French oceangoing ironclad "Gloire," designed by Stanislas-Henri-Laurent Dupuy de Lôme and completed in 1859; the word battleship was not applied until some years later. In 1862 the "Prince Albert" became the first battleship equipped with a revolving turret. *See also* ironclad.

The American Civil War demonstrated the value of the ironclad fighting ship, though none of the vessels on either side was of the dimensions or seagoing capability of the new European ships. The first true battleships in the U.S. Navy were authorized by Congress in 1890: the "Indiana," the "Massachusetts," and the "Oregon."

The period before World War I witnessed a naval building race centring on battleship competition, which was intensified by the

USS "Alabama," navy battleship of World War II

By courtesy of the U.S. Navy

British introduction in 1906 of the all-big-gun battleship "Dreadnought." By 1914 the British fleet included 73 battleships and battle cruisers (a lighter, faster version), the largest displacing 33,000 tons, while the German fleet possessed 52. Yet in the war, battleship combat was limited to the inconclusive Battle of Jutland in 1916. After the war there was a general reaction against the enormous expenditures involved in maintaining such flotillas; the Washington Conference of 1922 brought sharp reductions in fleets, size limitations (35,000 tons for battleships), and a slowdown in construction that lasted until shortly before World War II. Size then rose once more, with the British building five battleships of the King George V class of 44,000 tons, Germany two of the Bismarck class of 52,600 tons, the U.S. four of the Iowa class of 58,000 tons, and Japan two of the Yamato class, which set the all-time battleship record at 72,000 tons.

Battleships saw considerably more action in World War II than in World War I, but the advantages of the aircraft carrier, revealed especially in the Japanese attack on Pearl Harbor, ended the dominance of the battleship. Construction of battleships stopped in 1945. In 1968–69 the U.S. Navy briefly employed the "New Jersey" to shell the Vietnamese coast, in what appeared to be the last combat mission for a battleship. In 1982, however, the "New Jersey" was recommissioned after a modernization program equipped it with cruise and other missiles and new guidance and radar electronic systems.

Despite its high cost and dubious military achievements, in its 100-year career the battleship spurred industry to improve steel and other metals. Its construction also contributed to advances in electronics and marine engineering.

Battoni, Pompeo Girolamo (Italian painter): *see* Batoni, Pompeo Girolamo.

Batu (d. *c.* 1255, Russia), grandson of Genghis Khan and founder of the Khanate of Kipchak, or the Golden Horde.

Batu conquered most of Russia and invaded central Europe. In 1235 he was elected commander in chief of the western part of the Mongol Empire and was given responsibility for the invasion of Europe. By 1240 he had conquered all of Russia. In the campaign in central Europe one Mongol army defeated Henry II, duke of Silesia (now in Poland), on April 9, 1241; another army led by Batu himself defeated the Hungarians two days later.

With Poland, Bohemia, Hungary, and the Danube Valley under his control, Batu was poised for the invasion of western Europe when he received news of the death of the head of the Mongol Empire, the great khan Ögödei (December 1241). In order to participate in the choice of a successor, Batu withdrew his army, saving Europe from probable devastation. He established the state of the Golden Horde in southern Russia, which was ruled by his successors for the next 200 years. In 1240 Batu's army sacked and burned Kiev, then the major city in Russia. Under the Golden Horde the centre of Russian national life gradually moved from Kiev to Moscow.

Batu Islands, Bahasa Indonesia KEPULAUAN BATU, Dutch BATOE EILANDEN, group of three major islands and 48 islets, part of the Nias *kabupaten* (regency) of Sumatera Utara *propinsi* (North Sumatra province), Indonesia, located west of Sumatra. The three largest islands are Pini, Tanahmasa, and Tanahbala; the total area is 6,370 sq mi (16,500 sq km). The administrative centre is Pulautelo on Pulau (island) Sibuasi. The islands are generally low and forested, notably with coconut palm; copra and forest products predominate. The natives are of Malay or Proto-Malay stock, akin to those of Pulau Nias. Only about 20 of the smaller islands are inhabited. Pop. (1971) 10,488.

Batu Pahat, also called BANDAR PENGGARAM, port, western Johor state, West Malaysia (Malaya), on the Strait of Malacca at the mouth of the Sungai (River) Batu Pahat. It is a fishing town and a distribution centre, and until the completion of a bridge in 1968, it was a ferry point for road traffic across the river. Rubber, coconuts, fruit, and especially sago palms are grown in the area. Batu Pahat ("carved rock") is also a petroleum depot. Iron is mined at Seri Medan to the northeast. There is a lighthouse at nearby Tanjung (Cape) Seginting. Pop. (1980) 64,727.

Batumi, city and capital of the Adzhar Autonomous Soviet Socialist Republic, Georgian Soviet Socialist Republic, on a gulf of the Black Sea about 9½ mi (15 km) north of the Turkish frontier. With a history dating from the Middle Ages, Batumi was ceded by

Tea plantation outside Batumi, Adzhar A.S.S.R., Georgian S.S.R.

Se-Hedin-Bild

Turkey to Russia in 1878. It is an important port. There is an oil refinery using petroleum piped from Baku. Other industries include a shipyard, machine building, zinc plating, and furniture factories, as well as a range of light industries. Although industrially developed, Batumi is an attractive city and popular resort. Its many gardens and its streets are lined with exotic plants; north of the city is the Batumi Botanical Garden, with a rich collection of subtropical and tropical plants. Tea plantations are on the city's outskirts. There are teacher-training and polytechnic institutes. Pop. (1983 est.) 129,000.

Batusi (people): *see* Tutsi.

Batwa (people): *see* Twa.

Baty, (Jean-Baptiste-Marie) Gaston (b. May 26, 1885, Pélussin, Loire, Fr.—d. Oct. 13, 1952, Pélussin), French playwright and producer who, as a disciple of Theatricalist movement in stage design, exerted a notable influence during the 1920s and 1930s on world theatre.

He studied stagecraft with Max Reinhardt and was influenced by both German and Russian theatre, favouring a nontraditional approach to staging in order to abolish barriers between performers and audience. In 1922 he helped found the Compagnons de la Chimère and, in the following year, its workshop, La Baraque de la Chimère. With its closing he worked at various theatres, including the Odéon and the Studio de Champs-Élysées in Paris. In 1930 he settled permanently at the Théâtre Montparnasse in Paris, where he presented his greatest productions, of which *Crime and Punishment* was perhaps the best. Possessing a superb pictorial sense for beautiful groupings and movement, he directed the delicate plays of Jean-Jacque Bernard, notably *Martine,* with admirable subtlety. He brought to the stage such unconventional plays as Jean Sarment's *Facilité,* August Strindberg's *The Dance of Death,* and Simon Gantillon's *Cyclone.* He also produced the works of Shakespeare, Goethe, George Bernard Shaw, and Eugene O'Neill. Among his own plays, the adaptation of Gustave Flaubert's *Madame*

Bovary (1936) and *Dulcinée* (1938), drawn from Cervante's *Don Quixote,* are particularly noteworthy. Baty was appointed one of the producers at the Comédie-Française in 1936.

Batyushkov, Konstantin Nikolayevich, Batyushkov also spelled BATIUSHKOV (b. May 29 [May 18, old style], 1787, Vologda, Russia—d. July 19 [July 7, O.S.], 1855, Vologda), elegiac poet whose sensual and melodious verses were said to have influenced the great Russian poet Aleksandr Pushkin.

Batyushkov's early childhood was spent in the country on his father's estate; when he was 10 he went to Moscow, where he studied the classics and learned French and Italian, languages that were to have an important influence on his style of writing. In 1802 he went to St. Petersburg, living for a time with an uncle, Mikhail Muravyov, a writer and poet. He served in the army during the campaigns of 1813–14 against Napoleon. Afterward, he became a prominent member of the Arzamas (a literary group formed by the followers of Nikolay Karamzin, who advocated the modernization of the Russian literary language).

Batyushkov's literary output was not large—a few elegies and lyrics and some free translations of amorous epigrams from the Greek—but his verses are unique in their Italianate quality, producing a musical softness and sweetness. His poetry, written between 1809 and 1812, brought him fame. His collected works appeared in 1817, and shortly afterward he ceased writing. Suffering from mental illness, he was sent abroad in hope of a cure. This was not achieved, and he remained insane the rest of his life.

Batz, Jean, baron de (b. Dec. 26, 1760, Goutz, Fr.—d. Jan. 10, 1822, Chadieu), royalist conspirator during the French Revolution.

Born of a noble family in Gascony, Batz entered the army at the age of 14, rising to the rank of colonel by 1787. Between 1789 and 1793 he was a member of each of the successive national revolutionary assemblies and served on the Committee on Finances. At the same time he engaged in financial speculation in France and England and conspired with King Louis XVI to subvert the Revolution. After his schemes were discovered late in 1793, 55 of his associates were executed (June 1794). Imprisoned briefly in 1795, he lived in obscurity at his estate at Chadieu until 1801. He was honoured for his "heroism" after the Second Restoration of the Bourbon monarchy in 1815.

Bau (Sumerian), also called NININSINA, Akkadian GULA or NINKARRAK, in Mesopotamian religion, city goddess of Urukug in the Lagash region and, under the name Nininsina, the Queen of Isin, city goddess of Isin, south of Nippur. Bau seems originally to have been goddess of the dog; as Nininsina she was long represented with a dog's head, and the dog was her emblem. Perhaps because the licking of sores by dogs was supposed to have curative value, she became a goddess of healing. She was a daughter of An, king of the gods, and the wife of Pabilsag, a rain god who was also called Ninurta or Ningirsu.

Bauchi, state, northeastern Nigeria, until 1976, a province in former North-Eastern State, that was part of the former Northern Region prior to 1967. With an area of 24,944 sq mi (64,605 sq km), Bauchi is bounded by the states of Kano on the northwest, Kaduna on the west, Plateau and Gongola on the south, and Borno on the east. The highlands in the southwestern part of the state are an extension of the Jos Plateau and slope eastward towards the basin of the Gongola River. The Gongola River, rising in the Jos Plateau, flows to the northeast then turns southward (almost parallel to the southern half of the state's eastern boundary) to merge with the River Benue in Gongola State. Bauchi State is inhabited by a large number of ethnic groups; the Tangale, Waja, Fulani, and Hausa are the major groups. The state also contains a number of traditional Muslim emirates. According to tradition, it was named for a hunter known as Baushe who settled in the region before the arrival of Yakubu, the first traditional ruler of Bauchi emirate (founded 1800–10). Agriculture dominates the economy and produces millet, sorghum, corn (maize), yams, rice, cassava, wheat, tobacco, tomatoes, and other vegetables. Bauchi is one of the country's main cotton producing states; coffee and peanuts (groundnuts) are the other cash crops. Cattle, goats, and sheep are raised. Alluvial tin and columbite mining provide minerals for export; gold, cassiterite, coal, limestone, iron ore, antimony, and marble comprise the other mineral resources. Cotton weaving and dyeing, tanning, and blacksmithing are traditional activities. Industries include meat-products processing and canning, peanut processing, vegetable oil milling, and cotton ginning; there is also an assembly plant for commercial vehicles and trucks, an asbestos factory, and a cement factory. Bauchi town, the state capital and largest urban centre, is an important collecting and shipping centre on the railway from Maiduguri to Kafanchan and is linked by roads with Toro, Darazo, and Gombe. The Yankari Game Reserve (opened 1972), with a hot spring at Wikki, and the wall of a cave with the drawings of domesticated animals dating from the Neolithic period in Bauchi town are the major tourist attractions. Pop. (1983 est.) 3,975,200.

Bauchi, town, capital of Bauchi State and traditional emirate, northeast central Nigeria. Bauchi town lies on the railroad from Maiduguri to Kafanchan, where it joins the line to Port Harcourt and has road connections to Jos, Kafin Madaki, Kari, Gombe, and Lere. The emirate was founded (1800–10) by Yakubu, the only one of the 14 *masu-tuta* ("flag bearers" who carried out the *jihād* ["holy war"] for Shehu [Sheikh] Usman dan Fodio) who was not a member of the Fulani people. Probably of Gerawa parentage, Yakubu, a former student of the *shehu,* conquered a sparsely wooded savanna region (the Bauchi High Plains and the adjacent lowlands of the Gongola Basin) mainly inhabited by non-Muslim peoples. After successful campaigns (*c.* 1802–09), he moved his headquarters a few miles to the west from Inkil to Warunje Hill, where he founded (1809) the town of Bauchi. Yakubu built the town's walls, the circumference of which measures 6.5 mi (10.5 km); and for many years after his death (1845) Bauchi was called Yakoba.

Several of the subject peoples successfully revolted under the rule of his son and successor, Emir Ibrahim ibn Yakubu. Emir Usman moved the capital to Rauta (35 mi northwest, where there are remains of the palace) in 1877; but Bauchi once again became the emirate headquarters when, in 1902, the British occupied the town and deposed Emir Umaru. The town served as the provincial capital from 1904 until 1911 and again from 1917 to 1924. In 1926 it became the headquarters of Bauchi province, and in 1975 capital of the newly created Bauchi State.

The coming of the railway in 1961 stimulated Bauchi's importance as a collecting point for peanuts (groundnuts) and cotton and as a trade centre in sorghum, millet, cowpeas, corn (maize), cassava, beans, rice, onions, potash, tobacco, cattle, goats, and sheep. Cotton weaving and dyeing, tanning, and blacksmithing are traditional activities. Industry includes an asbestos factory, a government meat-products processing plant and cannery, and one of the first Nigerian assembly plants for commercial vehicles and trucks. Bauchi is the headquarters of a local government council.

The town is the site of the University of Bauchi, a state College of Arts and Sciences, a federal polytechnic, and, at the secondary level, of a federal government women's college, several secondary schools, and several primary teacher-training colleges. It also has a school of agriculture and animal husbandry. A specialist hospital is located there, in addition to a number of other medical and health facilities. Pop. (1983 est.) town, 62,290.

Bauchi Plateau (Nigeria): *see* Jos Plateau.

Baucis (Greek mythology): *see* Philemon and Baucis.

Baudelaire, Charles(-Pierre) (b. April 9, 1821, Paris—d. Aug. 31, 1867, Paris), French poet and translator of the tales of Edgar Allan Poe. Prosecuted for obscenity and blasphemy, and long after his death still identified in the public mind with depravity and vice, Baudelaire has become above all others of his age the poet of modern civilization, seeming to speak directly to the 20th century. Rejecting the posing of the Romantics, he revealed himself in his often introspective poetry as a seeker of God without religious beliefs, searching in every manifestation of life—the colour of a flower, the frown of a prostitute—for the true significance. Both as poet and as critic he appeals to man's condition in the modern world; and modern, too, are his refusal to admit restriction in the poet's choice of theme and his assertion of the poetic power of symbols.

Baudelaire, photograph by Étienne Carjat, 1863
By courtesy of the Bibliotheque Nationale, Paris

Early life. Baudelaire's father, François Baudelaire, an elderly widower, in 1819 had married a young woman, without dowry, who had despaired of acquiring through marriage the luxury and security for which she longed. Baudelaire was their only child, and on him she lavished all the devotion of her ardent nature. His father, who had retired from his position in the civil service on a substantial pension, was a man of culture and an amateur painter of some merit. He taught his son, when only four or five, to appreciate the beauty of form and line, thus laying the foundation of the sureness of taste that was to make him one of the most interesting art critics of the 19th century.

François Baudelaire died in February 1827. In November 1828 his widow married Jacques Aupick, a soldier who already had risen in the ranks and was to become a general, an ambassador, and a senator. Anxious that his stepson should learn discipline, in 1832 he sent Charles as a boarder to the Collège Royal at Lyons. There, in spite of the strict military routine of the school, he seems to have been happy; and he won several prizes. He also began to show a feeling for language and to develop a literary style.

In 1836, when his stepfather was transferred

to Paris, he was sent to the Lycée Louis-le-Grand. There, instead of fulfilling Aupick's claim that he would "bring honour to the establishment," he proved troublesome and undisciplined. To his masters he seemed an example of precocious depravity, adopting what they called "affectations unsuited to his age" and cultivating his gifts for outrageous paradox. He developed a tendency to moods of intense melancholy, and he also became aware that he was by nature solitary.

After passing his *baccalauréat* examinations in 1839, he rejected his stepfather's offer of a post in the diplomatic service and, to his mother's alarm, announced that he meant to live by writing. His chief wish was for freedom, leisure to read what he liked and to enjoy the student life of the Latin Quarter. Like many future writers, he enrolled as a law student, remaining at the École de Droit, nominally at least, until 1840. It was probably at this time that he became addicted to opium and hashish and contracted the venereal disease from which he was to die.

In 1841, hoping to wean him from his friends in whose company he was leading a life of debauchery, his stepfather sent him on a voyage to India, intending him to stay there for at least two years. Baudelaire set sail on June 9 but, becoming bored, amused himself by scandalizing the other passengers by his unconventional behaviour, and at Mauritius, where the boat put in for repairs after a storm (in which Baudelaire had behaved with great courage), he declared that he would go no farther. Persuaded to go on to Réunion, he there insisted on taking the next boat home and arrived back in France in February 1842. The voyage, however, and his three weeks in Mauritius, had deepened and enriched his imagination and had given him a store of images on which he was to draw in his poetry. He never forgot this, his only experience of the East, but kept for it a nostalgic, mystical yearning that gives his poetry its characteristic quality. He had gone away a boy, still uncertain of himself and his future; he returned a man, his imagination on fire, determined as never before to become a poet.

On attaining his majority in April 1842, he gained control of the capital left him by his father and, leaving home, determined to satisfy his inherited taste for luxury. He spent his money recklessly on fine clothes and on rich furnishings for his apartment at the Hôtel Lauzun, in the Île Saint-Louis and lived the life of a typical "dandy" of the period. Knowing nothing of business or finance, he regarded his inheritance as a fortune and soon fell prey to cheats and moneylenders, thus laying the foundation for the pile of debts that were to cripple him for the rest of his life. It was while living at the Hôtel Lauzun that his reputation for eccentricity, affectation, and immorality was confirmed; in his desire to shock he did not, however, differ from most of the poets and artists of the Paris of his time.

By 1844 Baudelaire had formed an association with the mulatto woman Jeanne Duval, who was to bring him much unhappiness. For a time he loved her passionately, and even at the end, when her cruelty, treachery, and stupidity had driven him to attempted suicide, he still felt in some ways attached to her. She inspired his first cycle of love poems, the "Black Venus"; and these are among the finest erotic poems in the French language.

During those early years of leisure and freedom from anxiety, Baudelaire was composing many—perhaps most—of the poems that were to form part of *Les Fleurs du mal,* his one collection, which comprised the Lesbian poems, the poems of revolt and decay, and the great erotic poems. At this time, too, he became acquainted with many artists, among them Delacroix and Courbet, and so acquired the knowledge of painting that was to give his art criticism much of its distinction and originality.

When within two years he had run through half his inheritance, his family early in 1844 obtained a decree by which the remainder of his capital was placed in trust, and he received the income in monthly installments. Baudelaire was wounded that his mother should have consented to a step that put an end to his freedom. In attempting to secure his future, his family had misguidedly prevented him from recovering his independence; still heavily in debt, he was unable, out of the £ 75 a year allowed him, to clear off his debts without borrowing.

This sudden change in Baudelaire's circumstances ended his life of luxury and carefree leisure; in the future he was to know only straitened means and eventually real poverty. He began to be uncertain of his own gifts, and his bitterness against his family was deepened by doubts whether they were perhaps right to try to prevent him from following a literary career. The melancholy he had known in adolescence returned, and what he called his mood of "spleen" became more frequent. It was at this time that the first of his great poems of spleen were written. Among his friends were many more unfortunate than himself, and he developed a sympathy for suffering humanity. Attracted by the revolutionary idealism of many of his friends, he took part in the February revolution of 1848 that resulted in the establishment of a republic.

Determined to prove that he could live by his pen, he had meanwhile become a professional writer. His first published work was a piece of art criticism, a review of the Salon of 1845 that reveals a perceptive and farsighted judgment and shows that he had already formulated a conception of what modern art should be. His "Salon de 1846" is a landmark in aesthetic criticism: no longer content to give an account of the exhibition, he puts forward independent and original theories and gives the first hint of his later concept of the *correspondances* between nature and art, claiming that painting, like music, has its own harmony, of light and shade, and that in nature colour is melody. In 1845 and 1846 some of his poems were printed in avant-garde journals, to which he also contributed articles and reviews.

In 1847 he published his only novel, the autobiographical *La Fanfarlo.* Begun much earlier, it is of interest mainly for its analysis of his personality during the period when he was living in luxury at the Hôtel Lauzun.

What Baudelaire did between the June revolution of 1848, in which he took a minor part, and December 1849 is not known, nor is it certain why he was then in Dijon or how long he stayed there. By 1850 he was back in Paris, as destitute and unhappy as ever. His mother had refused to write to him until he showed signs of reformation; and although she intended to goad him into working regularly, his brief burst of activity had ended without conspicuous success, and he was further discouraged by her sternness. Many articles were planned but never written; many begun but never finished. But in these years of experience and suffering he had prepared himself for his great creative period. Spiritually, his nature had been enriched, and after Pres. Louis-Napoléon Bonaparte's coup d'etat of December 1851, which ended his active interest in politics, he was ready for the opening of his mature period.

Poe translations and Les Fleurs du mal. This began with his discovery early in 1852 of the writings of Edgar Allan Poe, and he set to work at once to translate them. His first article on Poe—the first in any foreign language—appeared in March and April in the *Revue de Paris* and was followed by several translations published in reviews, among them his only attempt at translating a poem, "The Raven." From 1852 to 1865 he was occupied in translating Poe and in writing critical articles on him. *Histoires extraordinaires* appeared in 1856; *Nouvelles Histoires extraordinaires* in 1857; *Aventures d'Arthur Gordon Pym* in 1858; *Eureka* in 1864; and *Histoires grotesques et sérieuses* in 1865. The first two had long critical introductions.

As translations these are, at their best, classics of French prose: Baudelaire's mother had been born in England the daughter of an émigré, and he had spoken English as a child. In Poe he found for the first time someone who belonged to his own spiritual family and who had already reached, independently, conclusions toward which he had been groping. Poe thus gave him confidence in his own aesthetic theories and ideals of poetry.

In April 1852 Baudelaire had left Jeanne Duval—though by no means, as it turned out, for good. He could not, however, live without the company of women; and seeking someone to love, he turned first to the actress Marie Daubrun, and when she rejected him, to Apollonie-Aglaé Sabatier, a well-known beauty and former artist's model and friend of many artists and writers whom he had known for many years. She was the inspiration of his cycle of the "White Venus." In 1854 he renewed his association with Marie Daubrun, who inspired the cycle of the "Green-Eyed Venus." In many of the poems in these two cycles he reaches the highest peak of his art.

Baudelaire's growing reputation as Poe's translator and as art critic at last enabled him to publish some of his poems; and in June 1855 the *Revue des Deux Mondes,* the bastion of conservative Romanticism, ventured to print a selection of 18, submitted by Baudelaire as representative and chosen because they were original and startling in expression and themes. Their publication brought him notoriety, and he was widely accused of obscenity. In the spring of 1857, however, nine more poems appeared in *La Revue Française* and three in *L'Artiste;* and in June *Les Fleurs du mal* was published. But as a result, Baudelaire, the publisher, his friend Poulet-Malassis, and the printers were prosecuted; and in a famous trial for obscenity and blasphemy, they were found guilty and fined. Six poems were banned—a ban lifted only in 1949. Although a few readers understood and appreciated Baudelaire's intention and consummate artistry, for several generations *Les Fleurs du mal* remained a byword for depravity, morbidity, and obscenity. Baudelaire published a second edition in 1861, greatly enlarged and enhanced but omitting the banned poems, which were first republished in Belgium in 1866 in the collection *Les Épaves.* A third edition, further enlarged, was being prepared in 1866 when Baudelaire became paralyzed; it was published posthumously by his friend Charles Asselineau, although probably not as Baudelaire had planned it. It contains, however, six "Nouvelles Fleurs du mal," first published in 1866 in *Le Parnasse Contemporain,* as well as some poems that do not belong to the plan of the collection.

The last years. The failure of *Les Fleurs du mal,* from which he had expected so much, was a bitter blow to Baudelaire, and the remaining years of his life were darkened by a growing sense of failure, disillusionment, and despair. His platonic relationship with Sabatier had ended sadly, and Jeanne Duval, from whom he had finally parted in 1861, remained a constant burden and anxiety. Although some of his finest works were written in these years, few were published in book form. Some appeared in periodicals—his "Salon de 1859" in *La Revue Française;* "Richard Wagner et Tannhäuser à Paris" in *La Revue Européene* (1861); "Le Peintre de la vie moderne" (the draftsman Constantin Guys) in *Le*

Figaro (1863); and his prose poems, intended to form part of the collection *Le Spleen de Paris,* in various papers. This last was a work of which Baudelaire was particularly fond and in which he had been engaged for many years—he was still working on it just before his final collapse. He had taken the idea from Aloysius Bertrand's *Gaspard de la nuit,* but the subject is that of his poems in verse of the same period, and in mood the work reflects the settled pessimism of the aging and deeply saddened Baudelaire. These poems in prose express even more poignantly than does *Les Fleurs du mal* his feeling for Paris, for the teeming modern city, and his compassion for the failures and outcasts in its streets.

In 1860 Poulet-Malassis published two studies of the effects of hashish and opium as *Les Paradis artificiels,* and in 1861, the second version of *Les Fleurs du mal.* In 1862 he was declared bankrupt; Baudelaire was involved in his publisher's failure, and his financial difficulties became desperate. To escape his creditors, and, in an attempt to dispose of the copyright of the works he had ready for publication, in 1864 he went on a lecture tour in Belgium. It proved a failure, and he was unsuccessful in negotiating a contract for his books. This was a bitter disappointment, for he had wished particularly to publish his critical works, in which he had defined his theory of aesthetics; he regarded his work as an organic whole and his critical prose therefore as important as his poetry. To appreciate his poetry fully it is necessary to understand his ideas of the nature of art. Each of his poems is a crystallization of his vision, and his criticism is a meditation on the nature of a work of art and on the principles that underlie it. Baudelaire believed that every great creative artist must in the end become also a critic; his criticism explains his poetry, and his poetry is an extension of his aesthetic theory.

In February 1866, while still in Belgium, at Namur, Baudelaire became seriously ill. Taken back to Paris, he died there in his mother's arms in August 1867. Of the many invited to give orations at his funeral, only Asselineau and the poet Théodore de Banville accepted; they were among his oldest friends.

Baudelaire died unrecognized, with many of his writings still unpublished and those that had been published out of print. Among poets, however, opinion soon began to change: the future leaders of the Symbolist movement who were at his funeral were already describing themselves as his followers. By the 20th century he had become widely recognized as one of the great French poets of the 19th century. His admirers even claimed that he revolutionized the sensibility and way of thinking and writing throughout western Europe, and that the formulation of his aesthetic theory marks a turning point in the history of poetry and, indeed, in the history of art. For it was in this theory that the Symbolist movement found its source. (En.S.)

MAJOR WORKS. *Verse. Les Fleurs du mal* (1857; 2nd enl. ed. 1861; definitive ed. 1868), notable among many translations are those by Roy Campbell, 1952, and Richard Howard, 1982; *Les Épaves* (1866), 23 poems, including 6 banned poems from *Les Fleurs du mal.*

Prose. La Fanfarlo (1847), autobiographical *nouvelle,* published in the *Bulletin de la Société des Gens de Lettres; Les Paradis artificiels* (1860), essays, including a study of and translation from Thomas De Quincey's *Confessions of an English Opium-Eater; Petits Poèmes en prose* (1869), later entitled, as intended by Baudelaire, *Le Spleen de Paris;* among translations are those by Arthur Symons (1905), Michael Hamburger (1946), and Louise Varèse (1951); *Curiosités esthétiques and L'Art romantique* (1868), critical essays, including "Salon de 1845," "Salon de 1846," "Salon de 1859," "Richard Wagner et Tannhäuser à Paris," and "Eugène Delacroix," translations by Jonathan Mayne in *The Mirror of Art* (1955), and *The Painter of Modern Life, and Other Essays* (1964).

Translations (from Edgar Allan Poe). *Histoires extraordinaires* (1856); *Nouvelles Histoires extraordinaires* (1857); *Aventures d'Arthur Gordon Pym* (1858); *Eureka* (1864); *Histoires grotesques et sérieuses* (1865).

BIBLIOGRAPHY. The first edition of Baudelaire's *Oeuvres complètes,* 7 vol. (1868–70), was edited by C. Asselineau, with a preface by Théophile Gautier. It does not contain the *Journaux intimes,* other posthumous works, or the correspondence. Fragments of the *Journaux intimes* were published in *Le Livre* in September 1884, and the first complete edition in 1909. *Lettres 1841–1866* were published in 1905, *Lettres inédites à sa mère* in 1918, and *Dernières lettres inédites à sa mère* in 1926. Some *Juvenilia* were published by Jules Mouquet in 1932. A complete edition of his entire works, including *Juvenilia, Oeuvres posthumes,* and *Correspondance générale,* was edited by Jacques Crépet (1922–53); a revised version of this, under the editorship of Georges Blin and Claude Pichois, began appearing in 1968. The best one-volume edition is that by Yves Le Dantec for the "Pléiade Series" (1950); a further volume contains translations from Poe. Robert Kopp's 1969 edition of *Petits poèmes en prose* may be considered definitive. The best edition of *L'Art romantique* is by L.J. Austin (1968). The first complete biography was included in *Oeuvres posthumes et correspondances inédites,* which was published in 1887 and revised and enlarged in 1907 by Eugène and Jacques Crépet. L.J. Austin, *L'Univers poétique de Baudelaire* (1956), evaluates the significance of Baudelaire in the development of French poetry in the 19th century; the title of W.T. Bandy (comp.), *Baudelaire Judged by His Contemporaries* (1845–1867) (1933), is self-explanatory. Leon Bopp, *Psychologie des "Fleurs du mal,"* 4 vol. (1964–69), is an extremely detailed investigation, based upon close study of the texts of *Les Fleurs du mal,* of the workings of Baudelaire's mind. Alison Fairlie, *Baudelaire: Les Fleurs du mal* (1960), is a short study intended for undergraduates: there is no better introduction to Baudelaire in English; André Ferran, *L'Esthétique de Baudelaire* (1933), contains a comprehensive account of Baudelaire's philosophy of art; P. Mansell Jones, *Baudelaire* (1952), is a sensitive and scholarly introductory work; F.W. Leakey, *Baudelaire and Nature* (1969), is an exhaustive study of an important aspect of Baudelaire, a work of synthesis as well as of analysis, with a full and up-to-date bibliography; C. Mauron, *Le Dernier Baudelaire* (1966), is a valuable contribution to the understanding of the *Petits poèmes en prose.* Jean Pommier, *La Mystique de Baudelaire* (1932), has become a standard general critical survey: his *Dans les chemins de Baudelaire* (1945) contains useful essays on Baudelaire's earlier works; François Porché, *Baudelaire, histoire d'une âme* (1945), adopts a biographical approach to Baudelaire's poetry; Jean Prévost, *Baudelaire* (1953), contains a fine account (in French) of the forces that influenced Baudelaire and discussions of themes and versification; Peter Quennell, *Baudelaire and the Symbolists,* 2nd rev. ed. (1954), is a study of Baudelaire and of his influence; Marcel Ruff, *L'Esprit du mal et l'esthétique baudelairienne* (1955), is a wide-ranging study of all aspects of Baudelaire; Jean-Paul Sartre, *Baudelaire* (1947; Eng. trans. 1950), is a thought-provoking, though controversial, work of criticism that takes biography as its starting point; Enid Starkie, *Baudelaire* (1957), is a critical biography that places Baudelaire's work in its cultural context. Robert Vivier, *L'Originalité de Baudelaire,* 2nd ed. (1952), contains a comprehensive and systematic study of Baudelaire's style and poetic technique. Additional titles may be found in R.T. Cargo, *Baudelaire Criticism, 1950–1967: A Bibliography with Critical Commentary* (1968).

Baudh Khondmāls, district, central Orissa state, eastern India. It has an area of 4,274 sq mi (11,070 sq km). The district comprises a plain in the north, across which flows the Mahānadi River, and the Khondmāl and Balliguda highlands in the south, part of which is cultivated by the Khond. The main products are rice, oilseeds, and timber. Irrigation works have been built, and such cash crops as jute and cotton are also cultivated. Phūlbani (*q.v.*) is the district headquarters. The only other town of any size, Baudh, lies on the Mahānadi River. It is notable for its huge 11th-century image of the Buddha. Gandharadi, just northwest, has twin temples built in the 9th century. Pop. (1981) 717,280.

Baudissin, Wolf Heinrich (Friedrich Karl), Graf von (count of) (b. Jan. 30, 1789, Copenhagen—d. April 4, 1878, Dresden, Ger.), man of letters who with Dorothea Tieck was responsible for many translations of Shakespeare and thus contributed to the development of German Romanticism.

Baudissin served in the diplomatic corps and travelled in Italy, France, and Greece. In 1827 he settled in Dresden, where he spent the rest of his life. The works he translated include Shakespeare, other Elizabethan drama (*Ben Jonson und seine Schule,* 2 vol., 1836; "Ben Jonson and His School"), Molière, Italian plays, and the Middle High German epics *Iwein* and *Wigalois.*

Baudot, Jean-Maurice-Émile (b. 1845, Magneux, Fr.—d. March 28, 1903, Sceaux), engineer who, in 1874, received a patent on a telegraph code that by the mid-20th century had supplanted Morse Code as the most commonly used telegraphic alphabet. In Baudot's code, each letter was represented by a five-unit combination of current-on or current-off signals of equal duration; this represented a substantial economy over the Morse system of short dots and long dashes. Thus, 32 permutations were provided, sufficient for the Roman alphabet, punctuation signs, and control of the machine's mechanical functions. Baudot also invented (1894) a distributor system for simultaneous (multiplex) transmission of several messages on the same telegraphic circuit or channel.

Modern versions of the Baudot Code usually use groups of seven or eight "on" and "off" signals. Groups of seven permit transmission of 128 characters; with groups of eight, one member may be used for error correction or other function. *See also* teleprinter.

Baudouin (French personal name): *see under* Baldwin, except as below.

Baudouin I (French), Dutch BOUDEWIJN I (b. Sept. 7, 1930, Stuyvenberg Castle, near Brussels), king of the Belgians from 1951, who helped restore confidence in the Belgian monarchy after the stormy reign of King Leopold III.

The son of Leopold III and Queen Astrid, Baudouin shared his father's internment by the Germans during World War II and his postwar exile in Switzerland. After Leopold

Baudouin I, 1960

stepped down, Baudouin acted as head of state from Aug. 11, 1950, until July 16, 1951, and the next day he became fifth king of the Belgians.

After unrest in the Belgian Congo in early 1959, Baudouin told the Belgian people on

January 13 that Congolese independence was imminent. He made a fact-finding tour of the colony in December 1959 and proclaimed its independence at Léopoldville (now Kinshasa, Zaire) on June 30, 1960.

On Dec. 15, 1960, Baudouin married a Spanish noblewoman, Doña Fabiola de Mora y Aragón. Because the royal couple were childless, the King's brother, Prince Albert, remained heir to the throne, followed in the line of succession by his son Prince Philippe.

Baudouin de Courtenay, Jan Niecisław (b. March 13, 1845, Radzymin, Pol., Russian Empire—d. Nov. 3, 1929, Warsaw), linguist who regarded language sounds as structural entities, rather than mere physical phenomena, and thus anticipated the modern linguistic concern with language structure. His long teaching career in eastern European universities began in 1871 and included professorships at the universities of St. Petersburg (now Leningrad; 1900–14) and Warsaw.

Although he was a specialist in comparative linguistics, Baudouin de Courtenay turned to general problems, including questions of language mixture, children's speech, and the effect of linguistic structure on world outlook. He introduced the linguistic term phoneme to denote a speech sound that distinguishes meaning; *e.g.,* the *b* in "bit" that distinguishes it from "pit," "fit," and "sit." Views expressed in his major work, *Versuch einer Theorie phonetischer Alternationen* (1895; "Essay on a Theory of Phonetic Alternation"), have become a part of modern linguistic science. *A Baudouin de Courtenay Anthology: The Beginnings of Structural Linguistics* (1972) was translated by Edward Stankiewicz.

Bauer, Georg (German scientist): *see* Agricola, Georgius.

Bauer, Gustav (Adolf) (b. Jan. 6, 1870, Darkehmen, East Prussia—d. Sept. 16, 1944, Berlin), German statesman, chancellor of the Weimar Republic (1919–20).

As a Königsberg office worker, Bauer in 1895 founded the Verband der Büroangestellten (Office Employees Association), over which he presided until 1908. Entrusted with the leadership of the Zentral-Arbeiter-Sekretariat der Freien Gewerkschaften (Central Workers' Secretariat of the Free Trade Unions) in Berlin (1903), he subsequently served as second chairman of the Generalkommission der Gewerkschaften (General Commission of Trade Unions) for all of Germany (1908–18). As a Social Democrat member of the Reichstag (imperial German parliament), he was appointed secretary of the new Labour Ministry in the last imperial Cabinet under Prince Max of Baden (October 1918), and later, under the Weimar constitution, he served as minister of labour in the government of Philipp Scheidemann (February–June 1919). He was raised to the chancellorship after the resignation of Scheidemann (June 1919) and was charged with the thankless task of securing ratification of what the Germans called "the peace of unjustice"—the Treaty of Versailles. Resigning the chancellorship shortly after an abortive anti-governmental coup (the Kapp Putsch of March 1920) during which the Cabinet, with the exception of the vice-chancellor, had left Berlin, he was subsequently retained in the governments of Hermann Müller and Joseph Wirth as minister of the treasury and vice-chancellor.

Bauer, Harold (b. April 28, 1873, Kingston-on-Thames, near London—d. March 12, 1951, Miami), pianist who introduced to the U.S. contemporary works by Debussy, Ravel, and Franck. His playing combined traits of both 19th-century Romanticism and 20th-century restraint and was noted for its sensitivity, free approach to the printed note, and lack of egocentricity.

He was originally a concert violinist until about age 19, when he began serious study of the piano; in both instruments he was almost completely self-taught. He toured widely from 1893 and became a U.S. citizen in 1921.

Bauer frequently appeared in trios, as with Pablo Casals and Fritz Kreisler, and in joint recitals, as with the violinist Jacques Thibaud. His extensive repertory included 17th- and 18th-century harpsichord and clavichord works as well as the standard piano works. He wrote an autobiography, *Harold Bauer: His Book* (1948), and transcribed many works for piano.

Bauer, Otto (b. Sept. 5, 1881, Vienna— d. July 4, 1938, Paris), theoretician of the Austrian Social Democratic Party and statesman, who proposed that the nationalities problem of the Austro-Hungarian Empire be solved by the creation of nation-states and who, after World War I, became one of the principal advocates of Austrian *Anschluss* (unification) with Germany.

Otto Bauer

By courtesy of the Bild-Archiv, Österreichische Nationalbibliothek, Vienna

A founder of the Socialist educational movement Die Zukunft (The Future) and contributor to various periodicals, Bauer became secretary to his party's parliamentary faction in 1904. His theoretical talents were revealed with the publication of *Die Nationalitätenfrage und die Sozialdemokratie* (1907; "The Nationalities Question and Social Democracy"), in which he viewed the conflict among the nationalities as a class struggle and foresaw many of the actual post-World War I developments in the Danubian region.

A soldier and prisoner of war in Russia during World War I, Bauer assumed leadership of his party's left wing on his return in 1917. He became Austrian foreign minister at the end of the war. On March 2, 1919, he signed the secret *Anschluss* agreement with Germany, which was later rejected by the Allies. Bauer deals with this period in his *Die österreichische Revolution* (1923; *The Austrian Revolution,* 1925). He resigned in July 1919, but he remained his party's guiding personality for the next two decades. A member of the Austrian National Council from 1929 to 1934, he went into exile after the abortive Viennese Socialist revolt in 1934, first to Czechoslovakia, then to France.

Bauer, Sebastian Wilhelm Valentin (b. Dec. 23, 1822, Dillingen, Bavaria—d. June 20, 1875, Munich), pioneer inventor and builder of submarines.

In 1850 Bauer built his first submarine, "Le Plongeur-Marin" ("The Marine Diver"), which in February 1851 sank in 50 feet (15 metres) of water during a test dive in Kiel Harbour, trapping Bauer and his two crewmen. Although Bauer realized the hatch could be opened when the pressure of the air inside the hull, compressed by water leaking into the submarine, matched the water pressure outside, he had difficulty preventing his crew from panicking. When the pressure was at last equalized, the hatch was opened and the men swam to the surface, emerging, after 7½ hours below, in the midst of their own funeral services.

In 1855, sponsored by Grand Duke Constantine of Russia, Bauer built the 52-foot iron submarine "Le Diable-Marin" ("The Marine Devil"), carrying a crew of 11, 4 of whom worked a treadmill that drove a screw propeller. Through windows in this submarine Bauer made what were probably the first underwater photographs. He also experimented with underwater sound for signalling and with a system for purifying the air in submerged craft.

Discouraged by conservative naval officers, Bauer left Russia in 1858 but was unable to find other sponsors. In 1869 ill health forced his retirement in Munich.

Bauernfeld, Eduard von (b. Jan. 13, 1802, Vienna—d. Aug. 9, 1890, Vienna), dramatist who dominated the Vienna Burgtheater for 50 years with his politically oriented drawing room comedies.

He studied philosophy and law at the University of Vienna before turning to the theatre. Active in the local liberal movement, he became friends with the composer Franz Schubert and the dramatist Franz Grillparzer; the latter had considerable influence on his style. Bauernfeld's comedies are witty portrayals of Viennese society; cleverly plotted and elegant in language, they also are concerned with the acute social and political questions of the day. His most successful works included *Das Liebes-Protokoll* (1834), *Die Bekenntnisse* (1834), *Bürgerlich und romantisch* (1835), *Grossjährig* (1846), *Krisen* (1852), and *Aus der Gesellschaft* (1867).

Bauer's test (medicine): *see* galactose tolerance test.

Baugh, Sammy, byname of SAMUEL ADRIAN BAUGH (b. March 17, 1914, Temple, Texas, U.S.), first outstanding quarterback in the history of U.S. professional football, who led the National Football League (NFL) in forward passing in 6 of his 16 seasons (1937–52) with the Washington Redskins. On two occasions (Oct. 31, 1943, and Nov. 23, 1947) he passed for six touchdowns in a single game. He also excelled as a punter and as a defensive halfback.

After graduation from Texas Christian University, Fort Worth, in 1937, Baugh joined the Redskins and also the St. Louis Cardinals baseball organization, for which he played shortstop in the minor leagues for a few years. Immediately successful in professional football, he led the NFL in passing in 1937, 1940, 1943, 1945, 1947, and 1949, and in average yards per punt in 1940–43. In 1945 he completed 70.3 percent of his passes (128 of 182), and in 1940 he averaged 51.3 yards per punt. As a defensive back he led the NFL in 1943 by intercepting 11 passes. He had a career record of 1,693 pass completions in 2,995 attempts (56.5 percent) for 21,886 yards and 186 touchdowns.

Baugh was head coach of two American Football League teams, the New York Titans (afterward Jets) in 1960–61 and the Houston Oilers in 1964. He was elected to the professional football Hall of Fame in 1963.

Bauhaus, in full STAATLICHES BAUHAUS (German: Public House of Building), school of design that existed in Germany from 1919 to 1933, based in Weimar until 1925, Dessau through 1932, and Berlin in its final months. The Bauhaus was founded by the architect Walter Gropius, who combined two schools, the Grand Ducal Saxon Academy of Arts and the Grand Ducal Saxon School of Arts and Crafts, into what he called the Bauhaus, or "house of building," a name derived by inverting the German word *Hausbau,* "building of a house." Gropius' "house of building" included the teaching of various crafts, which he saw as allied to architecture, the matrix of the arts. By training students equally in art and in technically expert craftsmanship, the Bauhaus sought to end the schism between the two.

Earlier, beginning in the mid-19th century, reformers led by William Morris (1834–96) had sought to bridge the same division by emphasizing high-quality handicrafts in combination with design appropriate to its purpose. By the last decade of that century, these efforts had led to the Arts and Crafts Movement. While extending the Arts and Crafts attentiveness to good design for every aspect of daily living, the forward-looking Bauhaus rejected the Arts and Crafts emphasis on individually executed luxury objects. Realizing that machine production had to be the precondition of design if that effort was to have any impact in the 20th century, Gropius directed the school's philosophy toward mass manufacture. On the example of Gropius' ideal, modern designers have since thought in terms of producing functional and aesthetically pleasing objects for mass society rather than individual items for a wealthy elite.

Before being admitted to the workshops, students at the Bauhaus were required to take a six-month preliminary course taught variously by Johannes Itten, Josef Albers, and Lászlô Moholy-Nagy. The workshops—carpentry, metal, pottery, stained glass, wall painting, weaving, graphics, typography, and stagecraft—were generally taught by two people: an artist (called the Form Master), who emphasized theory, and a craftsman. After three years of workshop instruction, the student received a journeyman's diploma.

The Bauhaus included among its faculty several outstanding artists of the 20th century. In addition to the above-mentioned, some of its teachers were Paul Klee (stained-glass workshop and painting class), Wassily Kandinsky (wall painting), Lyonel Feininger (graphic arts), Oskar Schlemmer (stagecraft), Marcel Breuer (interiors), Herbert Bayer (typography and advertising), Gerhard Marcks (pottery), and Georg Muche (weaving). A particular style—based on the cube, rectangle, and circle—has been considered characteristic of the Bauhaus, though in fact the works produced were richly diverse.

Although Bauhaus members had been involved in architectural work from 1919 (notably, the construction in Dessau of administrative, educational, and residential quarters designed by Gropius), the department of architecture, central to Gropius' program in founding this unique school, was not established until 1927; Hannes Meyer, a Swiss architect, was appointed chairman. Upon Gropius' resignation the following year, Meyer became director of the Bauhaus until 1930. He was asked to resign because of his extreme left-wing political views, which brought him into conflict with Dessau authorities. Ludwig Mies van der Rohe became the new director until the Nazi regime forced the school to close in 1933.

The Bauhaus had far-reaching influence. Its workshop products were widely reproduced, and widespread acceptance of functional, unornamented designs for objects of daily use owes much to Bauhaus precept and example. Bauhaus teaching methods and ideals were transmitted throughout the world by faculty and students. Today, nearly every art curriculum includes foundation courses in which, on the Bauhaus model, students learn about the fundamental elements of design. Among the best known of Bauhaus-inspired educational efforts was the achievement of Moholy-Nagy, who founded the New Bauhaus (later renamed the Institute of Design) in Chicago in 1937, the same year in which Gropius was appointed chairman of the Harvard School of Architecture. A year later Mies moved to Chicago to establish the department of architecture at the Illinois Institute of Technology (then known as the Armour Institute), and eventually he designed its new campus.

The Bauhaus school building at Dessau, E.Ger., designed by Walter Gropius, 1925–26

Bauhaus-Archiv, Darmstadt, W.Ger.

Bauhin, Gaspard, also called CASPER BAUHIN (b. Jan. 17, 1560, Basel, Switz.—d. Dec. 5, 1624, Basel), physician, anatomist, and botanist who introduced a scientific binomial system of classification to both anatomy and botany.

Gaspard Bauhin, detail from an engraving

By courtesy of the Ashmolean Museum, Oxford

A student of the Italian anatomist Fabricius ab Aquapendente at the University of Padua, Italy (1577–78), he spent most of his career at the University of Basel (M.D. 1581), where he was appointed professor of Greek (1582), anatomy, botany (1588), and medicine (1614). One of the first to describe (1588) the ileocecal (Bauhin's) valve, located between the large and small intestines, Bauhin wrote the *Theatrum anatomicum* (1605; *Microcosmographia, A Description of the Body of Man,* 1615), considered the finest comprehensive anatomy text to that time. In this work he replaced the ambiguous practice of numbering muscles, vessels, and nerves with a system that named parts according to their most salient features.

Refining the principles of systematic botanical classification developed by the 16th-century Italian botanist Andrea Cesalpino, Bauhin was first to clearly delineate botanical species and groups of species, or genera, utilizing the concept of natural relationships, or "affinities," as criteria for his classifications. In his *Pinax theatri botanica* (1623; "Illustrated Exposition of Plants"), the most celebrated of the early attempts to name and catalog all known kinds of plants, he listed and described briefly about 6,000 species, while introducing the practice of naming plants by their genus and species (binomial nomenclature), a system that found wide application by the botanists John Ray and Linnaeus.

Bauhin's brother Jean (1541–1613), also a physician and botanist, is known for his *Historia plantarum universalis* (1650–51; "General History of Plants"), in which he rendered elaborate descriptions of more than 5,000 species.

Bāul, member of an order of religious singers of Bengal known for their unconventional behaviour and for the freedom and spontaneity of their mystical verse. Their membership consists both of Hindus (primarily Vaiṣnavites, or followers of Lord Vishnu) and Muslims (generally Sufis, or mystics). Their songs frequently deal with the love between the human personality and a personal god, who resides within the individual. Little is known of the early history and development of the cult, as their songs began to be collected and written down only in the 20th century. Rabindranath Tagore was one of many Bengali authors who acknowledged an indebtedness of inspiration to Bāul verse.

Baule, people inhabiting the Ivory Coast between the Komoé and Bandama rivers; they are an Akan group, speaking a Twi language of the Kwa branch of the Niger-Congo family.

The ancestors of the Baule were a section of the Ashanti who emigrated to their present location under the leadership of Queen Awura Pokou in about 1750, following a dispute over the chieftaincy, and assimilated many of the indigenous peoples. After 1790, quarrels between important families destroyed the polit-

Baule carved wood male figure; in the Metropolitan Museum of Art, New York City

By courtesy of the Metropolitan Museum of Art, New York City, The Michael C. Rockefeller Memorial Collection of Primitive Art, gift of Nelson A. Rockefeller, 1969 ical unit of the Baule, though they continued to rule much of the Ivory Coast until the end of the 19th century.

The Baule live in compact villages divided into wards, or quarters, and subdivided into family compounds of rectangular dwellings arranged around a courtyard; the compounds are usually aligned on either side of the main village street.

The Baule are agriculturalists; yams are the staple, supplemented by fish and game; coffee and cocoa are major cash crops. The importance of the yam is demonstrated in an annual harvest festival in which the first yam is symbolically offered to the ancestors, whose worship is a prominent aspect of Baule religion.

The foundation of Baule social and political institutions is the matrilineal lineage; each lineage has ceremonial stools that embody ancestral spirits. Paternal descent is recognized, however, and certain spiritual and personal qualities are believed to be inherited through it. A headman and a council of elders representing the lineages handle village affairs.

The Baule are noted for their fine wooden sculpture, particularly for their ritual statuettes representing ghosts or spirits; these, as well as carved ceremonial masks, were formerly associated with the ancestor cult but are increasingly produced for commercial purposes.

Baule-Escoublac, La, also called LA BAULE, fashionable resort, Loire-Atlantique *département,* Bretagne region, France, on the Atlantic coast near the mouth of the Loire, west of Saint-Nazaire. Facing south, protected from the north wind by 1,000 ac (400 ha) of dune-stabilizing maritime pines, it is on a crescent-shaped bay in the centre of a fine sand beach 5 mi (8 km) long. Headlands at each end of the bay shelter the town from east and west winds. Created in 1879, it and Biarritz are the best known Atlantic resorts. Behind the line of the seafront hotels, luxurious villas are dotted among the pines. The town has a park, an open-air school, a casino, golf and tennis clubs, and a yacht harbour. Nearby are salt marshes. Pop. (1982) 13,151.

Seafront and the bay at La Baule-Escoublac, Fr.
Editions "La Cigogne"-Hachette

Baum, L(yman) Frank (b. May 15, 1856, Chittenango, N.Y., U.S.—d. May 6, 1919, Hollywood), writer known for his series of books for children about the imaginary land of Oz.

Baum began his career as a journalist, initially in Aberdeen, S.D., then in Chicago. His first book, *Father Goose* (1899), was a commercial success, and he followed it the next year with the even more popular *Wonderful Wizard of Oz.* A modern fairy tale, it tells the story of Dorothy, a Kansas farm girl who is blown by a cyclone to the land of Oz, where she is befriended by some memorable characters, including a Tin Woodman, a Scarecrow, and a Cowardly Lion. In 1901 it was produced as a musical spectacle in Chicago. Its film version, in 1939, became a cinema classic and was made familiar to later generations of children through frequent showings on television.

He wrote 13 more Oz books, and the series was continued by another after his death. Using a variety of pen names as well as his own, Baum was the author of some 60 books, the bulk of them juveniles, popular in their day.

Baumann, Pic, also called MONT AGOU, mountain in southwestern Togo, near the border with Ghana. An extreme western outlier of the Chaîne de l'Atacora of adjacent Dahomey, it rises to 3,235 ft (986 m), and is the highest point in Togo. It was named for Oskar Baumann (1864–99), an Austrian-African explorer, when Togo (then called Togoland) was a German colony (1880s to World War I).

Baumbach, Rudolf (b. Sept. 28, 1840, Kranichfeld, Thuringia—d. Sept. 21, 1905, Meiningen, Ger.), German writer of popular student drinking songs and of narrative verse.

Baumbach was a poet of the vagabond school and wrote, in imitation of Viktor von Scheffel, many excellent drinking songs, such as "Die Lindenwirtin," which endeared him to the German student world. His real strength, however, lay in narrative verse, especially concerning the scenery and life of his native Thuringia. Among his best known works are *Frau Holde* (1881), *Spielmannslieder* (1882; "Songs of a Troubadour"), and *Von der Landstrasse* (1882; "On the Highway").

Baumes Laws, several statutes of the criminal code of New York state, enacted on July 1, 1926—most notably, one requiring mandatory life imprisonment for persons convicted of a fourth felony. A "three-time loser" was thus one who had thrice been convicted of a felony and faced life imprisonment if convicted again.

In 1926 the New York State Crime Commission, chaired by Caleb H. Baumes, proposed a number of reforms and revisions of the criminal code to the state legislature. The most forceful recommendation was the Habitual Criminal Act. It provided for increasingly heavy sentences to repetitive felons. Although the clause providing for mandatory life imprisonment for a fourth felony had been a state statute since 1907, the Baumes Laws closed loopholes that had rendered the previous law ineffective. Baumes Laws, based on the principle that repression is the best method of eliminating crime, became a model for criminal-code reform in other states.

Baumgarten, Alexander Gottlieb (b. July 17, 1714, Berlin—d. May 26, 1762, Frankfurt an der Oder, Prussia), German philosopher and educator who coined the term aesthetics and established this discipline as a distinct field of philosophical inquiry.

As a student at Halle, Baumgarten was strongly influenced by the works of Leibniz and by Christian Wolff, a professor and systematic philosopher. He was appointed extraordinary professor at Halle in 1737 and advanced to ordinary professor at Frankfurt an der Oder in 1740.

Baumgarten's most significant work, *Aesthetica,* 2 vol. (1750–58), has never been reprinted or translated from Latin. The problems of aesthetics had been treated by others before Baumgarten, but he both advanced the discussion of such topics as art and beauty and set the discipline off from the rest of philosophy. His student G.F. Meier (1718–77), however, assisted him to such an extent that credit for certain contributions is difficult to assess. Immanuel Kant (1724–1804), who used Baumgarten's *Metaphysica* (1739) as a text for lecturing, retained Baumgarten's use of the term aesthetics to apply to the entire field of sensory knowledge. When combined with logic, aesthetics formed a larger discipline that he called "gnoseology," or theory of knowledge, which to other philosophers has been known as epistemology. Only later was the term aesthetics restricted to questions of beauty and of the nature of the fine arts.

In Baumgarten's theory, with its characteristic emphasis on the importance of feeling, much attention was concentrated on the creative act. For him it was necessary to modify the traditional claim that "art imitates nature" by asserting that artists must deliberately alter nature by adding elements of feeling to perceived reality. In this way, the creative process of the world is mirrored in their own activity.

In addition to his earlier work on aesthetic theory, *Meditationes Philosophicae de Nonnvillis ad Poema Pertinentibus* (1735), Baumgarten wrote *Ethica Philosophica* (1740), *Acroasis Logica* (1761), *Jus Naturae* (1763), *Philosophia Generalis* (1770), and *Praelectiones Theologicae* (1773). His brother, Siegmund Jakob Baumgarten, was an influential Wolffian theologian.

BIBLIOGRAPHY. Thomas Abbt, *A.G. Baumgartens Leben und Charakter* (1765); Bernard Poppe, *A.G. Baumgarten, seine Bedeutung und seine Stellung in der Leibniz-Wolffischen Philosophie und seine Beziehungen zu Kant* (1907); Albert Riemann, *Die Ästhetik A.G. Baumgartens* (1928).

Baunsgaard, Hilmar (Tormod Ingolf) (b. Feb. 26, 1920, Slagelse, Den.), Denmark's leading non-Socialist politician, who served as prime minister of a coalition government from 1968 until 1971.

Entering the Radical Party's youth organization in 1936, Baunsgaard rose to become its chairman in 1948. He remained in that office until 1957; then, after a successful career in the grocery industry, he entered Parliament. The recognized spokesman of the Radical Party, in 1961 he became minister of commerce in the Cabinet of Viggo Kampmann, continuing in that post until 1964. From 1964 to 1968 he served as director of an advertising firm, and in 1968 he became prime minister of a non-Socialist coalition government. His government, forced to increase taxes to cope with an economic crisis, resigned after losing its parliamentary majority in the September 1971 general election. During his term in office Baunsgaard successfully supported the abolition of the pornography laws as well as Danish entry into the European Economic Community (EEC).

Baur, Ferdinand Christian (b. June 21, 1792, Schmiden, near Stuttgart, Württemberg—d. Dec. 2, 1860, Tübingen), German theologian and scholar who initiated the Protestant Tübingen school of biblical criticism and who has been called the father of modern studies in church history.

Educated at the seminary at Blaubeuren and at the University of Tübingen, he became a professor of theology in 1817 at the seminary and in 1826 at the university, where he remained until his death. Influenced by the thought of the German philosopher G.W.F. Hegel, Baur began to develop a new perspective on the history of Christianity.

In general, Hegel saw history as a working out of opposing forces—thesis and antithesis—which interact and form a third force, known as the synthesis. In studying the New Testament's pastoral letters, Baur came to view early Christianity as the outcome of a conflict between Jewish Christianity (an amalgam of practices of the two faiths) and Gentile Christianity (which was viewed as free of Jewish influence). Baur held that Jewish Christianity was the thesis; the Gentile version was the antithesis, or reaction; and catholic Christianity constituted the Hegelian synthesis.

Baur, detail from an engraving by Conrad Kull, 1859

By courtesy of the Universitatsbibliothek Tubingen, West Germany

In his *Paulus, der Apostel Jesu Christi* (1845; *Paul, the Apostle of Jesus Christ*, 2 vol., 1873 and 1875), Baur applied the same principles to the life and thought of the Apostle Paul and concluded that Paul did not write all of the letters then attributed to him. Baur considered only the letters to the Galatians, Corinthians, and Romans to be genuinely Pauline. In addition, he believed that the author of Acts was post-apostolic; Acts appeared to him to synthesize and harmonize the conflict between Jewish and Gentile Christianity, hence could not have been written in the 1st century, when a portrayal of Jewish and Gentile Christianity would have shown more cleary the conflict between them.

Baur took a similar view of the authorship of the Gospels; his conclusions became known as the "tendency theory," for he asserted that the Gospels reveal a mediating, or conciliatory, *Tendenz* of their authors to overcome the Jewish–Gentile conflict. Baur posited the existence of an initial Gospel modified by later writers.

Later in life Baur concentrated on church history. His five-volume *Geschichte der christlichen Kirche* (1853–63; "History of the Christian Church") is still considered valuable, as are his works on the doctrines of the Atonement, the Trinity, and the Incarnation. Baur's methods helped to make Christianity subject to critical historical examination. His ideas were rejected at first, but both his methods and conclusions emerged in the 20th century as important contributions to biblical scholarship and the study of church history. Baur's work is discussed by Karl Barth in *Die protestantische Theologie im 19. Jahrhundert* (1947), and by Peter C. Hodgson in *Ferdinand Christian Baur on the Writing of Church History* (1968).

Bauria, extinct genus of advanced reptiles found as fossils in Early Triassic rocks in South Africa (the Triassic Period began 225,000,000 years ago and lasted 35,000,000 years). The skull of *Bauria* had several mammal-like features. A secondary palate separates air and

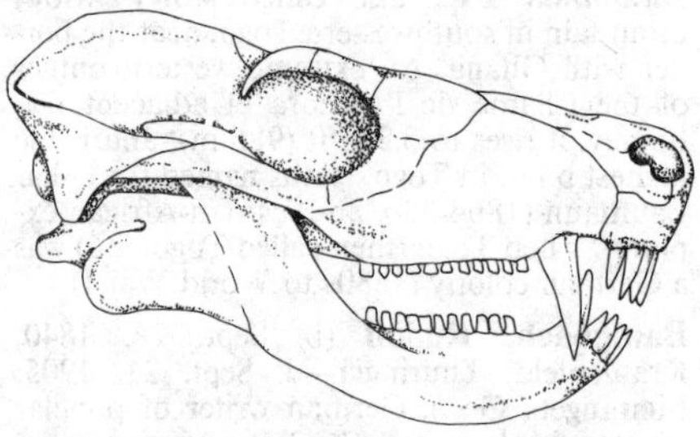

Skull of *Bauria*

Reprinted from *Vertebrate Paleontology* by A.S. Romer, by permission of the University of Chicago, copyright 1933, 1945, 1966; all rights reserved

food passages. The teeth show specialization and are differentiated into a set of incisor-like, canine-like, and molar-like cheek teeth. A single bone, the dentary, dwarfs the other lower jawbones, a trend toward the mammalian condition of only one bone, the dentary. *Bauria* and its relatives did not survive the Early Triassic.

Bauru, city, central São Paulo state, Brazil, lying near the Rio Batalha at 1,640 ft (500 m) above sea level. Formerly known as Divino Espírito da Fortaleza, it was given town status in 1887 and was made the seat of a municipality in 1896. Bauru is a trade centre for an agricultural region (coffee, cotton, peanuts [groundnuts], rice, *feijão* [beans], and corn [maize]). It is also a manufacturing centre producing textiles, ceramics, furniture, shoes, and other goods. An important railroad junction 190 mi (300 km) northwest of São Paulo, the state capital, Bauru is also accessible by highway and air. Pop. (1980 prelim.) 178,861.

Bauta, city, northwestern La Habana province, west central Cuba. It is a commercial and manufacturing centre for the surrounding agricultural lands, known primarily for their tobacco and sugarcane, although pineapples and various other fruits and vegetables also are grown. The city contains cigar factories and a cotton mill. Goods are shipped via the central highway to the urban markets in Havana, 15 mi (24 km) northeast. Pop. (1981 prelim.) 26,826.

Bautzen, city, Dresden *Bezirk* (district), southeastern East Germany, in the Oberlausitz (Upper Lusatia) region, on a granite elevation above the Spree River. It was originally the Slavic settlement of Budissin (Budyšin), and the Peace of Bautzen was concluded there in 1018 between the German king Henry II and the Polish king Bolesław I. Bautzen became German in 1033, passed to Bohemia in 1319 and to Saxony in 1635. The capital of the Federation of Lusatian cities in 1346, it was and is an important political and cultural centre of the Lusatian Sorbs, a West Slavic people also called the Wends or Domowina. Sorb traditions and customs are kept alive by the Bautzen Institute for Sorbian Folk Research and the Institute for Sorbian Studies, both located in the city. Bautzen gives its name to the hard-fought battle of May 20–21, 1813, in which French troops under Napoleon I defeated a Russo-Prussian army. Notable buildings include the Ortenburg Castle (1483–86) and St. Peter's Church (1220–1497), which has been shared since 1523 by both Roman Catholics and Protestants and has, since 1921, served as the Roman Catholic cathedral and seat of the bishop of Meissen.

A railway junction, Bautzen's industries include wagon and vehicle building, iron foundries, and the manufacture of electrotechnical equipment, machinery, paper, and textiles. It is also the site of the School of Conveyor Engineering. Pop. (1983 est.) 49,767.

Baux-de-Provence, Les, also called LES BAUX, village, Bouches-du-Rhône *département,* Provence-Alpes-Côte-d'Azur region, southeastern France, on a bare rock spur of the Chaînes des Alpilles rising abruptly from the valley floor, northeast of Arles. On this mountain spur, about 1,000 yd (900 m) long and 220 yd wide, are a ruined château and streets of abandoned houses, plus a church, a museum, and small modern tourist installations. In the Middle Ages this was the seat of the mighty lords of Baux, who in the 11th century held 72 towns and domains in Provence and the Dauphiné including the principality of Orange. In the 13th century their *cours d'amour* drew highborn ladies and troubadours. Over the centuries their struggles against the pope, the rulers of Provence, and the kings of France reduced the power of the house. In 1632 Louis XIII destroyed the château and city walls. Although the city later became a marquisate under the Grimaldis, its prominence was ended. At the church of Saint-Vincent shepherds still come with their animals to the midnight mass. The windmill (now a museum) that inspired Alphonse

The ruins of Les Baux, Fr.

Marc Garanger

Daudet's *Lettres de mon moulin* is at nearby Fontvieille. Bauxite, the mineral that is the raw material for the refining of aluminum, was named for Les Baux, near which it was discovered in 1821. Local deposits are still worked. Pop. (1982) 62.

bauxite, rock largely composed of a mixture of hydrous aluminum oxides; the principal ore of aluminum. Bauxites vary physically according to the origin and geologic history of their deposits: some deposits are soft, easily crushed, and structureless; some are hard, dense, and pisolitic, or pealike; still others are porous but strong or are stratified or largely pseudomorphic after parent rock. The laterite type is commonly pisolitic and mottled, with pisolites ranging in size from about 2.5 millimetre (0.10 inch) to 25 centimetres (10 inches) or more in diameter. Both pisolites and groundmass (matrix) may exhibit great colour variations; common colours are pink, cream, red, brown, yellow, and gray. Exposed surfaces of lateritic ore are rough, often lava-like, with a wormlike structure and variegated colours on vertical faces. Such material tends to harden or reconsolidate on exposure to air. Although terra-rossa types are granular and earthy, they also may possess pisolitic structures.

Bauxite from Elizabethton, Tenn.

By courtesy of the Field Museum of Natural History, Chicago; photograph, John H. Gerard—EB Inc.

Bauxite is formed by the thorough weathering of many different rocks. Clay minerals commonly represent intermediate stages, but some bauxites appear to be reworked chemical precipitates rather than simple alteration products. Bauxite may grade into laterite or clay, laterally or vertically.

Constituent minerals are rarely recognizable in hand specimens, and even in thin sections complete identification may be difficult. Combined petrography, X-ray diffraction, and differential thermal analysis have shown that gibbsite, boehmite, and diaspore, alone or in mixtures, are the constituent minerals. Clay minerals, hematite, magnetite, goethite, siderite, and quartz are common impurities. Most deposits contain rutile, anatase, zircon, and other minerals.

Bauxite is found in most countries but the larger deposits are found in the tropics. Monohydrate ores have been extensively mined, for example, in France, Italy, Yugoslavia, and Greece; and trihydrate ores in Arkansas, Suriname, Guyana, and Jamaica. Gibbsite-rich ores occur in Ghana, Guinea, India, and Brazil. Major deposits of gravels mixed with sand were discovered in Australia in the 1950s. Deposits in the Ural Mountains and in northern Asia are largely diaspore.

Bāvand DYNASTY, also spelled BĀVEND (665–1349), Iranian dynasty that ruled Ṭabaristān (now Gīlān and Māzandarān), in northern Iran.

The Bāvands ruled, sometimes independently and at other times as vassals of various Islāmic dynasties, over an area delimited by the Caspian Sea and the Elburz Mountains. The geographic isolation of Bāvand territories permitted a degree of historical continuity rare in Islāmic history.

The origins and early years of the dynasty are clouded by myth and legend. The Bāvands can be divided into three distinct lines: the Kā'ūsīyeh (665–*c.* 1006), the Espahbadīyeh (1074–1210), and the Kīnkhvārīyeh (*c.* 1238–1349).

The first line, the Kā'ūsīyeh, ruled independently over their mountainous kingdom. In 854 they were converted to Islām. In the 10th century their power weakened; they maintained their position by various marriage alliances with the Zeyārid dynasty of northern Iran, but from 1006 they became vassals of that dynasty.

The Espahbadīyeh line, centred at Sārī, was originally a tributary of the Seljuq dynasty. Rostam I (ruled 1140–63) reasserted the independence of the Bāvand dynasty, but soon afterward, with the assassination of Shams ol-Molk Rostam II (ruled 1206–10), the Espahbadīyeh line was vanquished by the Khwārezm-Shāh dynasty.

The third, or Kīnkhvārīyeh, line was founded by Ḥosām od-Dowleh (ruled 1238–49) and was centred at Āmol. It was a vassal of the Il-Khanid rulers of Iran. This line was finally extinguished with the assassination of Fakr od-Dowleh (ruled 1334–49).

Bavaria (West Germany): *see* Bayern.

Bavarian Alps, German BAYERISCHE ALPEN, northeastern segment of the Central Alps along the West German–Austrian border. The mountains extend east-northeastward for 70 mi (110 km) from the Lechtaler Alpen to the bend of the Inn River near Kufstein, Austria. Zugspitze (*q.v.*; 9,718 ft [2,962 m]) is the highest point in the range and in West Germany. Subranges include the Wettersteingebirge, Karwendelgebirge, and Nordkette; the Austrian portion is also known as the Nordtiroler Kalkalpen (North Tirol Limestone Alps). To the south the range's steep wall overlooks the Inn River Valley, whereas to the north its gentle slopes allow the grazing of cattle. The mountains hold lignite mines and petroleum deposits and are crossed at Scharnitz Pass (3,140 ft) by road and railway and at Achen Pass (3,087 ft) by road. Tourism and winter sports are the region's main activities. A large national park preserves the original Alpine landscape, plants, and animals from the steady encroachment of urbanization.

Neuschwanstein Castle in the Bavarian Alps, built in the late 19th century

By courtesy of Trans World Airlines

Bavarian cream, custard enriched with whipped cream and solidified with gelatin. Bavarian creams can be flavoured with chocolate, coffee, fruits, etc., and are usually molded in fancy shapes and garnished with fruits and sweet sauces. Its country of origin is either Bavaria or France.

Bavarian Forest (West Germany): *see* Bayerischer Wald.

Bavarian State Picture Galleries: *see* Bayerische Staatsgemäldesammlungen.

A list of the abbreviations used in the MICROPAEDIA *will be found at the end of this volume*

Bavarian Succession, War of the (1778–79), conflict in which Frederick the Great of Prussia blocked an attempt by Joseph II of Austria to acquire Bavaria.

After losing Silesia to the Prussians, the Austrian emperor Joseph II and his chancellor Prince Kaunitz wished to acquire Bavaria in order to restore Austria's position in Germany. When the Bavarian electoral line of the Wittelsbachs failed on the death of Maximilian Joseph on Dec. 30, 1777, a treaty was signed with his successor, Charles Theodore, the elector Palatine, ceding Lower Bavaria and the lordship of Mindelheim to Austria. However, Frederick II of Prussia declared war on July 3, 1778, in support of the claims to Bavaria made by Charles, duke of Zweibrücken. Austria's ally France refused to give aid, and Frederick with Saxony as his ally entered Bohemia, where he was opposed by an imperial army led by the Emperor himself. There was little fighting, because each force was concerned with cutting its opponent's communications and denying it supplies. Hence contemporaries nicknamed the war the "potato war" (*Kartoffelkrieg*).

Maria Theresa, whose consent to the occupation of Bavaria had been given very unwillingly, made peace proposals to Frederick II against Joseph II's wishes. With France and Russia acting as intermediaries between Austria and Prussia, the representatives of the two powers met at Teschen on March 10, 1779. On May 13, 1779, they reached an agreement whereby Austria was to receive the Inn district, a fraction of the territory originally occupied.

Bavel (city): *see* Babylon.

Bāvend DYNASTY: *see* Bāvand dynasty.

Bavli, David ha-: *see* Mukammas, David al-.

bawu, Chinese single free-reed wind instrument, an aerophone particularly popular in southwestern China. It is played in a manner similar to that of playing the flute except that all the air passes through a single, pointed reed at the mouth hole. The tone produced is a result of the coupling between the reed and the air column. The common F *bawu* has the lowest pitch and spans a compass of more than two octaves.

Bawu performance is characterized by colourful tonal contrast, glissandos, various tonguing and fingering techniques, and circular breathing.

Bax, Sir Arnold (Edward Trevor) (b. Nov. 8, 1883, London—d. Oct. 3, 1953, Cork, County Cork, Ire.), composer whose work is representative of the Neoromantic trend in music that occurred between World Wars I and II.

In 1900 he entered the Royal Academy of Music where he studied the piano. Influenced by the Celtic revival and Irish poetry, in 1909 he wrote the symphonic poem *In the Faëry Hills.* He spent the year 1910 in Russia. During the following years, under the pseudonym Dermot O'Byrne he published short stories and poems in Ireland, where he spent much time. In 1916 and 1917 he wrote three symphonic poems, *The Garden of Fand, Tintagel,* and *November Woods,* which established his reputation. His ballet, *The Truth About the Russian Dancers,* on a scenario by the playwright J.M. Barrie, was produced by Sergey Diaghilev in 1920. Between 1921 and 1939 he wrote seven symphonies dedicated to the musicians he admired, among them John Ireland

Bax, pen-and-ink drawing by P. Evans; in the National Portrait Gallery, London

By courtesy of the National Portrait Gallery, London

and Jean Sibelius. He also wrote numerous piano and chamber works, including a sonata for viola and harp (1928) and a nonet for winds, strings, and harp (1931). Living for long periods on the coasts of Ireland and Scotland, he wrote music that was romantically evocative and richly orchestrated. He was knighted in 1937 and in 1941 was appointed Master of the King's Musick.

Baxter, Andrew (b. 1686/87, Aberdeen, Scot.—d. April 23, 1750, Whittingehame, East Lothian), Scottish metaphysical rationalist who maintained the essential distinction between matter and spirit, resisting the more advanced British epistemology of his century. Having gone to Utrecht in the Netherlands as tutor to two young gentlemen in 1741, he went on an excursion to Spain in 1745 and there met John Wilkes, for whose intellect he conceived a fervent admiration subsequently expressed in a number of letters.

Baxter published anonymously *An Enquiry Into the Nature of the Human Soul* (1733; 3rd ed., 1745; *Appendix,* 1750) and *Matho, sive cosmotheoria puerilis* (1738), a compendium of scientific knowledge. *The Evidence of Reason in Proof of the Immortality of the Soul* (1779) was edited from his papers by John Duncan.

Baxter, George (b. July 31, 1804, Lewes, Sussex, Eng.—d. Jan. 11, 1867, Sydenham, Kent), engraver and printer who invented a process (patented 1835) of colour printing that made reproductions of paintings available on a mass scale.

George Baxter, detail of a pencil drawing by an unknown artist

By courtesy of the trustees of the British Museum; photograph, J.R. Freeman & Co. Ltd.

He was the son of John Baxter (1781–1858), printer and publisher at Lewes, who issued the popular illustrated "Baxter" Bible. George Baxter went to London in 1827. There he supplied colour illustrations to the publisher George Mudie and produced prints for the London Missionary Society. Although he sold his work to several highborn clients and was even summoned to visit Queen Victoria, he had little business sense and did not profit greatly from his invention, partly because he encountered competition from cheap coloured lithographs. Baxter used carefully etched plates, a handpress, a system of register points, and the finest colours, oils, and paper. He mixed the colours himself but left no record of their composition.

Baxter, James K(eir) (b. June 29, 1926, Dunedin, N.Z.—d. Oct. 22, 1972, Auckland), poet whose mastery of versification and striking imagery made him a central figure among New Zealand writers after World War II.

Educated in New Zealand and England, he first published *Beyond the Palisade* (1944), which displayed youthful promise. *Blow, Wind of Fruitfulness* (1948), superficially a less attractive collection, was more profound. *Recent Trends in New Zealand Poetry* (1951) was his first critical work, its judgments revealing a maturity beyond his years. Later verse collections include *The Fallen House* (1953), the satirical *Iron Breadboard* (1957), and *Pig Island Letters* (1968). He also published *Aspects of Poetry in New Zealand* (1968).

Baxter, Richard (b. Nov. 12, 1615, Rowton, Shropshire, Eng.—d. Dec. 8, 1691, London), Puritan minister who profoundly influenced 17th-century English Protestantism. Known as a peacemaker who sought unity among the clashing Protestant denominations, he was the centre of nearly every major controversy in England in his fractious age.

Baxter was ordained into the Church of England in 1638 after studying divinity. Within

Richard Baxter, detail from an oil painting after R. White, 1670; in the National Portrait Gallery, London

By courtesy of the National Portrait Gallery, London

two years, however, he had allied himself with Puritans in opposition to the episcopacy established by his church. During his ministry at Kidderminster (1641–60) he made this Worcestershire town of handloom workers into a model parish. Preaching in a church enlarged to accommodate the crowds he drew, he aimed to convert them to utter trust in God and then urged them to use that faith in a day-to-day life of Christian obedience. He was ill most of his life and claimed he preached as a "dying man to dying men." Pastoral counselling was as important to him as preaching; his program, which came to serve as a pattern for many other ministers, included everyone in the parish.

A believer in limited monarchy, Baxter attempted to play an ameliorative role during the Civil War. He served briefly as a chaplain in the parliamentary army but then helped to bring about the restoration of the King (1660). After the monarchy was reestablished, he fought for toleration of moderate dissent within the Church of England. He was persecuted for his views for more than 20 years and was imprisoned (1685) for 18 months. The Revolution of 1688, replacing James II with William and Mary, brought in its wake an Act of Toleration that freed Baxter from most of the encumbrances he suffered for his opinions.

Among his more than 200 works are devotional manuals, pastoral handbooks, and such highly controversial doctrinal writings as *Aphorismes of Justification* (1649). His best known works are *The Saints' Everlasting Rest* (1650) and *The Reformed Pastor* (1656). His autobiographical *Reliquiae Baxterianae, or Mr. Richard Baxter's Narrative of the Most Memorable Passages of his Life and Times* (1696), still of interest, gives an account of his inner spiritual struggles.

bay (title): *see* bey.

Bay, *gobolka* (administrative region), south central Somalia, East Africa. Part of the Italian-administered former United Nations Trust Territory of Somalia until 1960, the region was created from the southeastern part of the former Alto Giuba (Upper Juba) region in 1973. With an area of 15,058 sq mi (39,000 sq km), it is bounded by the *gobollada* (administrative regions) of Bakool (north), Gedo (west), Jubbada Dhexe (southwest), Shabeellaha Hoose (southeast), and Hiiraan (northeast). Situated in the middle of the Doi plain (between the Jubba and Shabeelle rivers), it is the main dryland farming area in the country. Its economy is chiefly based on the subsistence farming of sorghum, corn (maize), sesame, peanuts (groundnuts), and beans, supplemented by livestock raising. Uranium, iron-ore, and bauxite deposits were reported by a United Nations survey team in 1968 at Buur Hakaba (Bur Acaba) but had not been exploited into the 1980s. Baydhabo (or Baidoa), the regional capital, has the Bonka Farmers' Training Center and an airfield; it is connected by road with Afgooye (Afgoi) in the southwest. Pop. (1975) 302,054.

bay, concavity of a coastline or re-entrant of the sea, formed by the movements of either the sea or a lake. The difference between a bay and a gulf is not clearly defined, but the term bay will usually refer to a body of water somewhat smaller than a gulf. Numerous exceptions, however, are found throughout the world, such as the Bay of Bengal, larger than the Gulf of Mexico and about the same size as the Arabian Sea.

A brief treatment of bays follows. For full treatment, *see* MACROPAEDIA: Oceans.

The bay is usually located where more easily eroded rocks, such as clays and sandstones, are bounded by harder and more resistant formations made from igneous rocks, such as granite, or hard calcareous rocks, such as massive limestones, which are more resistant to the erosional forces of the land and sea or lake. The harder rocks therefore stand out as promontories projecting out to sea, often with caves that may in some cases link the two sides of the promontory, thus creating an island, perhaps with a natural bridge to the mainland. This bridge will later fall as a result of erosion and weathering and leave an island completely separated from the mainland.

The softer rocks between the promontories are subjected to more rapid erosion as lines of waves, originally moving at an angle to the coastline, are turned more parallel to the coast by the shallower waters immediately offshore, so that the end of the line of waves closest to shore moves forward more slowly than the end farther out to sea. In this way the lines of waves gradually turn as they move around the windward headland to sweep directly onshore in the bay. The erosion of the soft rocks of the bay is most rapid during storms, when material eroded just behind the line of breakers is thrown by the waves farther up the beach; in this way a series of ridges may mark a succession of storms, particularly where the beach material is mainly pebbles. The wind may then carry the finest beach material inland beyond the high-water mark, where it may be deposited in a zone of sand dunes. These may, if uncontrolled, move many miles inland. The most common practice is to encourage deep-rooted marram grass to colonize the dunes in order to stabilize them.

There are no defined dimensions for bays. Smaller bays may be only a few hundred metres wide, while others, such as the Bay of Biscay off Spain and France and Hudson Bay in Canada, are several hundred kilometres from side to side. Some of these larger bays may represent depressions in the ground, formed by vertical earth movements and/or glacial erosion by ice sheets. Hudson Bay is of this type. All bays are semicircular or nearly circular in shape, which distinguishes them from estuaries, which are elongated and funnel-shaped with a river running along the centre line and beaches mainly near the mouth of the estuary. Estuaries and some of the more enclosed and sheltered bays form excellent harbours, provided the seabed is deep enough and well scoured. They were popular sites for early settlements, and many of the larger coastal cities today have their original cores around a bay that provided protection for ships at anchor.

bay, in architecture, any division of a building between vertical lines or planes, especially the entire space included between two adjacent supports; thus, the space between two columns, or pilasters, or from pier to pier in a church, including that part of the vaulting or ceiling between them, is known as a bay.

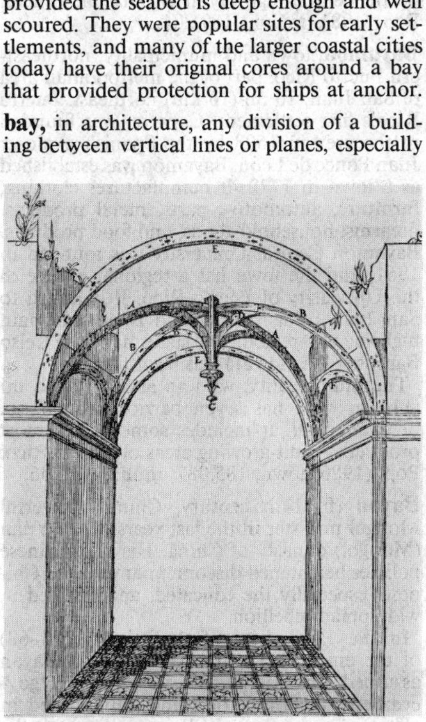

The area of a bay indicated in a reconstruction of a Gothic vault, from *Le Premier Tome de l'architecture de Philibert de l'Orme* (1567), by Philibert Delorme

By courtesy of the Royal Institute of British Architects, London

Bay, Laguna de, lake, the largest inland body of water in the Philippines, on Luzon just southeast of Manila. Probably a former arm or extension of Manila Bay cut off by volcanism, Laguna de Bay (Lake of the Bay) has a normal area of 344 sq mi (891 sq km) and is about 32 mi (51 km) long. Its shallow, crescent-shaped basin is poorly drained by many small, sediment-laden streams, and the surrounding low-lying plains are inundated during seasons of heavy rainfall. The Pasig River is its outlet to Manila Bay, 10 mi northwest. An important fishing area, with productive wet margins (rice), Laguna de Bay is broken by two peninsulas in the north and dotted by islands; densely settled Talim (9 mi long, 1 mi wide, and rising to 1,420 ft [433 m]) is the largest. Santa Cruz, Biñan, and Calamba are busy market and fishing towns on the lake's southern shore.

Bay, Michel de: *see* Baius, Michael.

Bay Bridge, in full SAN FRANCISCO–OAKLAND BAY BRIDGE, complex crossing that spans San Francisco Bay from the city of San Francisco to Oakland via Yerba Buena Island. One of the preeminent engineering feats of the 20th century, it was built during the 1930s under the direction of C.H. Purcell.

Bay Bridge with San Francisco skyline

Ewing Galloway

The 8-mile- (13-kilometre-) long double-deck crossing consists of two end-to-end suspension bridges of 2,310-foot (704-metre) main spans and 1,160-ft side spans, a half-mile-long tunnel of exceptionally large bore through the island, a cantilever bridge with a main span of 1,400 ft, and a long viaduct to the Oakland shore. The largest problem in its construction was the sinking to bedrock (265 ft deep) of the central anchorage for the two suspension bridges, accomplished by a multiple-dome caisson invented by Daniel Moran.

Bay City, city, seat (1857) of Bay County, east central Michigan, U.S., on the Saginaw River near its juncture with Saginaw Bay (Lake Huron), 13 mi (21 km) north of Saginaw. Settled in the 1830s, it was formed in 1857 after a series of consolidations of five villages, culminating in 1905 with the union of Bay City and West Bay City. The community thrived during the Michigan lumber boom (1850–90); but, when the local forests were depleted and the mills closed, it turned to soft-coal mining, commerical fishing, and beet-sugar refining. The city's economy is now geared toward both agriculture (potatoes, melons, and beets) and industry (notably the manufacture of power shovels, cement, auto and aircraft equipment, and petrochemicals). Shipbuilding is also important. With deepwater harbour facilities, it is a port for Great Lakes and ocean shipping. Bay City State Park is 5 mi north, and Delta (1961) and Saginaw Valley State (1963) colleges are in nearby University Center. Inc. city, 1865. Pop. (1980) 41,593.

Bay Islands (Honduras): *see* Islas de la Bahía.

bay leaf, also called LAUREL LEAF, leaf of the sweet bay tree, *Laurus nobilis,* an evergreen of the family Lauraceae, indigenous to countries bordering the Mediterranean. A popular spice used in pickling and marinating and to flavour stews, stuffings, and fish, bay leaves are delicately fragrant but have a bitter taste. They contain about 2 percent essential oil, the principal component of which is cineole. The smooth and lustrous dried bay leaves are usually used whole and removed from the dish after cooking; they are sometimes marketed in powdered form. Bay has been cultivated from ancient times; its leaves made up the wreaths of laurel that crowned victorious athletes in ancient Greece. During the Middle Ages bay leaves were used medicinally.

bay lynx: *see* bobcat.

Bay of ———: *see under* substantive word (*e.g.,* Biscay, Bay of), except as below.

Bay of Pigs invasion (April 17, 1961), abortive invasion of Cuba at the Bay of Pigs (Bahía de los Cochinos), on the southwestern coast by some 1,500 anti-Castro Cuban exiles. Because the invasion was financed and directed by the U. S. government, it aggravated already hostile United States–Cuban relations and intensified international Cold War tensions.

Within six months of Fidel Castro's overthrow of Fulgencio Batista's dictatorship in Cuba (January 1959), relations between Castro's government and the United States began to deteriorate. The new Cuban government confiscated private property (much of it owned by North American interests), sent agents to initiate revolutions in several Latin-American countries, and established diplomatic and economic ties with leading Socialist powers (beginning early in 1960), especially with the Soviet Union and the People's Republic of China. The former, in May 1960, promised to defend Cuba. Castro himself often and vociferously accused the United States of trying to undermine his government. When the French vessel "La Coubre," carrying arms from Belgium to Cuba, exploded in Havana Harbour in March 1960, killing about 70 seamen, Castro accused the United States of sabotage and rejected a U.S. denial, as he had rejected other U.S. notes. Several congressmen and senators, from early 1960, denounced Castro; and by June the U.S. Congress had passed legislation enabling Pres. Dwight D. Eisenhower to take retaliatory steps: the United States cut off sugar purchases from Cuba and soon thereafter placed an embargo on all exports to Cuba except food and medicine. Castro replied by accelerating the nationalization of North American properties. In January 1961, Eisenhower, in one of the final acts of his administration, broke diplomatic ties with Cuba after Castro had ordered a drastic cutback of U.S. embassy personnel in Havana.

An invasion of Cuba had been planned by the U.S. Central Intelligence Agency (CIA) since May 1960. The wisdom of proceeding with it had been debated within the newly inaugurated administration of Pres. John F. Kennedy before it was finally approved and carried out.

On April 15, 1961, three U.S.-made airplanes piloted by Cubans bombed Cuban air bases. Two days later the Cubans trained by the United States and using U.S. equipment landed at several sites. The principal landing took place at the Bay of Pigs on the south central coast. The invasion force was unequal to the strength of Castro's troops, and by April 19 its last stronghold had been captured, along with more than 1,100 men. In the aftermath of the invasion, critics charged the CIA with supplying faulty information to the new president and also noted that, in spite of Kennedy's orders, supporters of Batista were included in the invasion force, whereas members of the non-Communist People's Revolutionary Movement, considered the most capable anti-Castro group, were excluded. It was further charged that the Cuban government and even some U.S. newsmen had known of the plans for invasion in advance.

The captured members of the invasion force were imprisoned. From May 1961 the Kennedy administration unofficially backed attempts to ransom the prisoners, but the efforts of the Tractors for Freedom Committee, headed by Eleanor Roosevelt, failed to raise the $28,000,000 needed for heavy construction equipment demanded by Castro as reparations. The conditions for the ransom changed several times during the next several months; after painstaking negotiations by James B. Donovan, Castro finally agreed to release the prisoners in exchange for $53,000,000 worth of food and medicine. Between December 1962 and July 1965 the survivors were returned to the United States. Some critics thought that the United States had not been aggressive enough in its support of the Bay of Pigs invasion and had left an impression of irresolution. The incident was crucial to the development of the Cuban missile crisis of October 1962.

bay owl (*Phodilus badius*), uncommon and atypical Asian owl of the family Phodilidae (order Strigiformes) with a heart-shaped facial disk having two earlike extensions dorsally that aid sound reception. Bay owls are sometimes classified with the barn owls (Tytonidae)

Bay owl (*Phodilus badius*)
Ron Garrison—San Diego Zoo

and sometimes with the typical owls (Strigidae). The bay owl, found in southeastern Asia, is entirely nocturnal and retiring. The Congo bay owl of Africa, which is sometimes classified as a separate species, is even less familiar. Bay owls eat insects, lizards, frogs, and small mammals and birds.

Bay Psalm Book, byname of THE WHOLE BOOKE OF PSALMES FAITHFULLY TRANSLATED INTO ENGLISH METRE (1640), perhaps the oldest book now in existence that was published in British North America; it was prepared by Puritan leaders of the Massachusetts Bay Colony. Printed in Cambridge, Mass., on a press set up by Stephen Day (*q.v.*), it included a dissertation on the lawfulness and necessity of singing psalms in church.

Bay Saint Louis, city, seat (1860) of Hancock County, south central Mississippi, U.S., on the Mississippi Sound at the entrance to St. Louis Bay, 58 mi (93 km) northeast of New Orleans. The site was part of a 1789 Spanish land grant to Thomas Shields. By 1812 the village had become a resort for wealthy planters and, later, for tourists who arrived after the New Orleans, Mobile and Chattanooga Railroad was completed in 1869. Unofficially incorporated as Shieldsborough in 1858, it was officially incorporated as Bay St. Louis in 1882. The bay (named in 1699 for Louis IX of France) was the scene (1814) of the naval engagement against the British known as the Battle of Pass Christian. Manufactures include electrical appliances, steel and aluminum products, plastics, and leather goods. The Mississippi Test Facility of the National Aeronautics and Space Administration is 17 mi (27 km) west. Pop. (1980) 7,891.

bay tree, any of several small trees with aromatic leaves, especially the sweet bay, or bay laurel (*Laurus nobilis*), source of the bay leaf (*q.v.*) used in cooking. The California laurel (*q.v.; Umbellularia californica*) is an ornamental tree also called bay tree. The bay rum tree, or simply bay (*Pimenta racemosa*), has leaves and twigs that yield, when distilled, oil of bay, which is used in perfumery and in the preparation of bay rum.

bay window, window formed as the exterior expression of a bay within a structure, a bay being an interior recess made by the outward projection of a wall. The purpose of a bay window is to admit more light than would a window flush with the wall line.

A bay window may be rectangular, polygonal, or arc-shaped. If the last, it may be called a bow window. There has been a continuing confusion between bay and bow windows. Bay window is the older term and has become the generic form.

Bay windows are associated historically with mansions of the early English Renaissance. They are characteristically employed at the end of a great hall opposite the entrance and behind the raised dais on which the lord of the manor was served. Bay windows are used extensively in Hardwick Hall, Derbyshire, Eng. (1576–97), where towers are formed of the protruding bays.

In modern architecture the bay window emerged as a prominent feature of the Chicago School. The utilitarian program of William Le Baron Jenney, one goal of which was maximum admission of natural light, resulted in the creation of the cellular wall and a new emphasis on bay windows. An interesting example is Jenney's Manhattan Building (Chicago, 1890), which displays both polygonal bay windows and bow windows.

Baya, also spelled GBAYA, or GBEYA, a people of southwestern Central African Republic and east central Cameroon; most Baya live in the Haute-Sangha and Lobaye prefectures of the Central African Republic. They speak a language of the Adamawa-Eastern subgroup of the Niger-Congo family that is related to those of their Banda and Ngbandi neighbours.

Baya migrated southeastward from what is now the Hausa area of northern Nigeria early in the 19th century, fleeing the *jihād* (holy war) of Usman dan Fodio. The Baya, who were led by a war chief, Gazargamu, vanquished and assimilated or drove ahead of them the peoples they encountered. Contemporary Baya subgroups, which include the Bokoto, Kara, Buli, Kaka, and Bwaka, reflect this integration of defeated peoples. The Baya, in turn, were attacked annually by Fulani slavers from what is now northern Cameroon.

The Baya resisted French forces throughout the colonial period. They revolted in the early 1920s because of the brutal impressment of Baya men and women as porters and labourers. In 1929 the Baya began what became a three-year revolt in response to conscription for the Congo–Ocean Railway; a French "nightmare campaign" decimated the rebellious Baya to an extent that was still evident as late as the 1960s.

The Baya observe patrilineal descent and traditionally had a stateless society. In the past, war chiefs were selected only in times of crisis and were divested of their powers thereafter. Baya village chiefs were arbiters and symbolic leaders, but they were later made into administrative magistrates by the French colonizers. Baya clans were the primary identity group within which marriage, religious ceremonies, and trade with outsiders (*e.g.*, Arab caravanners) was regulated. Age groups called *labi* cut across clan identities and further assured solidarity in times of war; initiates received training in agricultural, social, and religious knowledge and skills.

Rural Baya grow corn (maize), cassava, yams, peanuts (groundnuts), and tobacco. They also hunt and fish. Coffee and rice, introduced by the French, are cash crops. The diamond rush of the late 1930s greatly disrupted traditional life of Baya in Haute-Sangha; diamond prospecting continues to be economically important.

Where the same name may denote a person, place, or thing, the articles will be found in that order

Bayamo, city, capital of Granma province, eastern Cuba. Lying on the Río Bayamo, it was founded as San Salvador de Bayamo in 1513. In colonial times it was one of Cuba's most important cities, and it has been the scene of several uprisings, including the independence movement of 1895. It is now an important manufacturing, commercial, and transportation centre for the surrounding countryside, in which cattle raising is widespread and the dairy and tanning industries are well developed; copper and manganese are mined in the area. Sugar, rice, coffee, and tobacco also are processed in the city, and tiles are manufactured. Bayamo is a railroad junction and lies on the central highway; it also has an airfield. Pop. (1981 prelim.) 109,201.

Bayamón, town and municipality, northeastern Puerto Rico, part of the metropolitan area of San Juan, 10 mi (16 km) northeast. Puerto Rico's first settlement, Caparra, was founded in the area in 1508 by the Spanish explorer Juan Ponce de León. Bayamón was established as a town in 1772. It manufactures clothing, furniture, automotive parts, metal products, firearms, household goods, and food products. Bayamón Central University was founded in 1961, and the town has a regional college of the University of Puerto Rico. It is linked to San Juan by a freeway and is on the main highway to Arecibo. The statesman José Celso Barbosa (1857–1921) was born there.

The municipality, with an area of 44 sq mi (114 sq km), has seven barrios (wards), six of them rural. It includes some of the most productive fruit-growing areas of Puerto Rico. Pop. (1980) town, 185,087; mun., 196,206.

Bayan (fl. 14th century, China), powerful Mongol minister in the last years of the Yüan (Mongol) dynasty of China. His anti-Chinese policies heightened discontent among the Chinese, especially the educated, and resulted in widespread rebellion.

In the early years of the reign (1333–68) of the emperor Toghōn Temür (*q.v.*), Bayan assumed almost complete control of the government, the Emperor being uninterested in affairs of state. Bayan's desire was to stop the absorption of the Mongols into Chinese culture and buttress their declining power within China. He suspended the civil service examinations and decreed that only Mongols could hold offices. He issued a number of other proscriptions making it illegal for Chinese to learn to read either Mongol or Arabic script, to wear certain colours, and to use certain ideographs, including those for long life and happiness. Finally he proposed that all Chinese with the surnames Chang, Wang, Liu, Li, and Chao be executed. Since these were among the commonest family names in China, the carrying out of this order would have caused the extermination of 90 percent of the population. Although this last proposal was not adopted, rebellions broke out repeatedly, and Bayan was finally deposed and banished by his nephew in 1339. It was possible to reverse his policies, but the deterioration of the dynasty had become irreversible. It was supplanted by the Ming in 1368.

Bayan Tumen (Mongolia): *see* Choybalsan.

Bayanhongor, also spelled BAYAN KHONGOR, town, administrative headquarters of Bayanhongor *aymag* (province), west central Mongolian People's Republic; it lies in the foothills of the Hangayn Mountains. The town was established in the 1930s. Its economy is dominated by animal husbandry, as the surrounding country contains some of Mongolia's best pasturelands. Sheep, goats, and cattle are the principal livestock.

Bayanhongor is connected by road to Ulaanbaatar, the Mongolian capital, 330 mi (530 km) west-southwest. Pop. (1979) 15,500.

Bayar, (Mahmud) Celâl (b. 1883, Umurbey, near Bursa, Ottoman Empire), third president of the Turkish Republic (1950–60), who initiated etatism, or a state-directed economy, in the 1930s and who after 1946, as the leader of the Democrat Party, advocated a policy of private enterprise.

The son of a *muftī* (Muslim jurist), Bayar attended a French school operated by the Alliance Israélite Universelle in Bursa, where he studied economics and finance. He then worked for the Bursa branch of the Deutsche Orient Bank. After the Young Turk Revolution of 1908, he became the secretary of the Smyrna branch of the Committee of Union and Progress (CUP) directed against Sultan Abdülhamid's autocratic rule. Following the collapse of the Ottoman Empire at the end of World War I, he joined the movement of Mustafa Kemal (later Atatürk) to resist the Allied occupation of Anatolia, organizing the national forces in the Smyrna and Bursa regions in western Anatolia. In January 1920 he was elected to the last Ottoman Parliament as deputy for Smyrna; when the Parliament was suppressed and the British arrested the nationalists, he escaped to Ankara, where Mustafa Kemal had convened the Grand National Assembly (GNA). Bayar served as minister of economy (1921–22) in the government of the GNA and for a time (1922–24) as minister of reconstruction and settlement for the new republic. He resigned to form the Iş (Work) Bank.

In 1932 Bayar, an exponent of a state-operated economy, became the minister of economy and contributed to the development of Turkey's industries and mines. In 1937 he became prime minister but resigned in January 1939 after Atatürk's death.

Bayar was deputy for Izmir between 1939 and 1945, when he resigned from Parliament and also from the Republican People's Party of Atatürk. In January 1946, with Adnan Menderes, Mehmed Fuad Köprülü, and Refik Koraltan, he helped organize the opposition Democrat Party, which won 62 seats in the general election of July 1946. Under Bayar's leadership the party won an overwhelming victory at the election of May 14, 1950, and he was elected president by the new Parliament. He was twice reelected (1954, 1957). Bayar was the architect of the government's economic policy, which gave priority to private enterprise and limited the state's functions to regulating and coordinating the forces participating in the economy.

Arrested during the military coup d'etat of May 27, 1960, he was subsequently tried, along with other leaders of the Democrat Party, on dubious charges of crimes against the state and sentenced to death (September 1961). Because of his advanced age, however, the sentence was commuted to life imprisonment. Released for reasons of health in 1964, he began publication of his memoirs, entitled *Ben de yazdim* ("I, Too, Have Written"). He was pardoned in 1966.

Bayard, Pierre Terrail, seigneur de (lord of) (b. *c.* 1473, near Pontcharra, Fr.—d. April 30, 1524, Italy), French soldier known as *le chevalier sans peur et sans reproche* ("the knight without fear and without reproach").

Born into a noble family, Bayard accompanied King Charles VIII of France into Italy in 1494 and was knighted after the Battle of Fornovo (1495). In Louis XII's wars he was

The chevalier Bayard, engraving by P. Mariette, 16th century

By courtesy of the Bibliotheque Nationale, Paris

the hero of numerous combats; on one occasion he is said to have defended a bridge over the Garigliano single-handed against about 200 Spanish troops, an exploit that brought him such renown that Pope Julius II sought unsuccessfully to entice him into the papal service. In 1508 he distinguished himself again at the siege of Genoa and, later, at the siege of Padua. Severely wounded at Brescia, he nevertheless hurried to join the Battle of Ravenna (1512).

On the accession of Francis I in 1515, Bayard was made lieutenant general of Dauphiné. When war broke out again between Francis I and the Holy Roman emperor Charles V, Bayard, with 1,000 men, held Mézières against an army of 35,000, and after six weeks he compelled the imperial generals to raise the siege. This stubborn resistance saved central France from invasion and gave Francis time to collect the army that drove out the invaders (1521). In 1523 Bayard was sent to Italy with Guillaume de Bonnivet. The latter, who was defeated at Robecco and wounded during his retreat, implored Bayard to assume command. Guarding the rear at the passage of the Sesia, Bayard was mortally wounded by a harquebus ball.

Bayard, Thomas Francis (b. Oct. 29, 1828, Wilmington, Del., U.S.—d. Sept. 28, 1898, Dedham, Mass.), U.S. statesman, diplomat, and lawyer. Bayard was admitted to the bar in 1851 and served for one year (1853–54) as U.S. attorney for Delaware. During the sectional crisis of 1860–61 he was instrumental in keeping Delaware in the Union. He served in the U.S. Senate (1869–85), succeeding his father, James Asheton Bayard, and was secretary of state in the first administration of Pres. Grover Cleveland (1885–89).

In 1893 Bayard was appointed ambassador to Great Britain, the first U.S. representative to Great Britain to hold that rank. As a champion of arbitration, he was critical of the aggressive position taken by Cleveland in the dispute with Great Britain over the Venezuelan boundary (1895). His critics thought him too pro-British, and he was censured by the U.S. House of Representatives.

Because of failing health, Bayard left London in 1897. His son, Thomas Francis Bayard (1868–1942), represented Delaware in the U.S. Senate in the 1920s.

Baybars I, in full AL-MALIK AẒ-ẒĀHIR RUKN AD-DĪN BAYBARS AL-BUNDUQDĀRĪ, or AṢ-ṢĀLIḤĪ, Baybars also spelled BAIBARS (b. 1223, north of the Black Sea—d. July 1, 1277, Damascus), most eminent of the Mamlūk (Slave) sultans of Egypt and Syria, which he ruled from 1260 to 1277. He is noted both for his military campaigns against Mongols and crusaders and for his internal administrative reforms. The *Sirat Baybars,* a folk account purporting to be his life story, is still popular in the Arabic-speaking world.

Al-Malik aẓ-Ẓāhir Rukn ad-Dīn Baybars was born in the country of the Kipchak Turks on the northern shores of the Black Sea. After the Mongol invasion of their country in about 1242, Baybars was one of a number of Kipchak Turks sold as slaves. Turkish-speaking slaves, who had become the military backbone of most Islāmic states, were highly prized, and eventually Baybars came into the possession of Sultan aṣ-Ṣāliḥ Najm ad-Dīn Ayyūb of the Ayyūbid dynasty of Egypt. Sent, like all the Sultan's newly acquired slaves, for military training to an island in the Nile, Baybars demonstrated outstanding military abilities. Upon his graduation and emancipation, he was appointed commander of a group of the Sultan's bodyguard.

Baybars gained his first major military victory as commander of the Ayyūbid army at the city of al-Manṣūrah in February 1250 against the crusaders' army led by Louis IX of France, who was captured and later released for a large ransom. Filled with a sense of their military strength and growing importance in Egypt, a group of Mamlūk officers, led by Baybars, in the same year murdered the new sultan, Tūrān Shāh. The death of the last Ayyūbid sultan was followed by a period of confusion that continued throughout the first years of the Mamlūk sultanate.

Having angered the first Mamlūk sultan, Aybak, Baybars fled with other Mamlūk leaders to Syria and stayed there until 1260, when they were welcomed back to Egypt by the third sultan, al-Muẓaffar Sayf ad-Dīn Quṭuz. He restored them to their place in the army and conferred a village upon Baybars.

Within a few months of Baybars' arrival, in September 1260, the Mamlūk troops defeated a Mongol army near Nābulus in Palestine. Baybars distinguished himself as the leader of the vanguard, and many Mongol leaders were slain on the field.

For his military achievement, Baybars expected to be rewarded with the town of Aleppo; but Sultan Quṭuz disappointed him. On the way home through Syria, Baybars approached Quṭuz and asked him for the gift of a captive Mongol girl. The Sultan agreed, and Baybars kissed his hand. On this prearranged signal the Mamlūks fell upon Quṭuz, while Baybars stabbed him in the neck with a sword. Baybars seized the throne to become the fourth Mamlūk sultan.

Baybars' ambition was to emulate Saladin,

the founder of the Ayyūbid dynasty, in the holy war against the crusaders in Syria. As soon as he was acknowledged as sultan, Baybars set about consolidating and strengthening his military position. He rebuilt all the Syrian citadels and fortresses that had been destroyed by the Mongols and built new arsenals, warships, and cargo vessels. To achieve unity of command against the crusaders, Baybars united Muslim Syria and Egypt into a single state. He seized three important towns from the Ayyūbid princes, thus ending their rule in Syria. From 1265 to 1271, Baybars conducted almost annual raids against the crusaders. In 1265 he received the surrender of Arsūf from the Knights Hospitallers. He occupied ʿAtlit and Haifa, and in July 1266 he received the town of Safed from the Knights Templar garrison after a heavy siege. Two years later, Baybars turned toward Jaffa, which he captured without resistance. The most important town taken by Baybars was Antioch (May 1268), which was followed by a number of minor Frankish fortresses. His seizure of additional strongholds in 1271 sealed the crusaders' fate; they were never able to recover from their territorial losses. Baybars' campaigns made possible the final victories won by his successors during the next decades.

Baybars' permanent goal was to contain the continued Mongol attacks on Syria from both north and east that threatened the very heart of the Islāmic East. During the 17 years of his reign, he engaged the Mongols of Persia in nine battles. Within Syria, Baybars dealt with the Assassins, a fanatical Islāmic sect. After seizing their major strongholds between 1271 and 1273, he wiped out the Syrian members of the group.

Baybars also took the offensive against the Christian Armenians, who were allies of the Mongols, devastating their lands and plundering their major cities. In 1276, having defeated the Seljuq troops and their Mongol allies, he personally seized Caesarea (modern Kayseri in Turkey) in Cappadocia. To secure Egypt on the south and west, Baybars sent military expeditions into Nubia and Libya, taking personal command in 15 campaigns and often endangering his life.

In the interest of good diplomatic relations with the Byzantine Empire, Baybars sent envoys to the court of Michael VIII Palaeologus in Constantinople. The Byzantine sovereign thereupon ordered the restoration of the ancient mosque and permitted the Egyptian merchants and ambassadors to sail through the Hellespont and Bosporus. One of Baybars' principal goals during his reign was to acquire more Turkish slaves to be used in the Mamlūk army; another was to contract an alliance with the Mongols of the Golden Horde in South Russia against the Mongols of Persia. In 1261 Baybars sent an ambassador to the Sicilian king Manfred. Other embassies to Italy followed, and in 1264 Charles of Anjou, later king of Naples and Sicily, sent an embassy with letters and gifts to Cairo, a remarkable testimony to Baybars' strength and influence. Baybars was also able to sign commercial treaties with such distant sovereigns as James I of Aragon and Alfonso X of León and Castile.

In a brilliant political move Baybars invited a fugitive descendant of the ʿAbbāsid dynasty of Baghdad to Cairo and established him as caliph—head of the Muslim community—in 1261. Baybars wished to legitimize his sultanate and to give preeminence to his rule in the Muslim world. The ʿAbbāsid caliphs in Cairo had no practical power in the Mamlūk state, however.

Baybars was, moreover, more than a military leader or a diplomatic politician. He built canals, improved harbours, and established a regular and fast postal service between Cairo and Damascus, one that required only four days. He built the great mosque and the school bearing his name in Cairo. He was also the first ruler in Egypt to appoint chief justices representing the four main schools of Islāmic law.

A sportsman as well as a warrior, Baybars was fond of hunting, polo, jousting, and archery. He was also a strict Muslim, a generous almsgiver, and watchful of the morals of his subjects—he issued a prohibition against the use of wine in 1271.

He died in Damascus after drinking a cup of poison intended for someone else and was buried in Damascus under the dome of the present aẓ-Ẓāhirīyah Library, which he had established. (H.Ra.)

BIBLIOGRAPHY. Two important primary sources for the career of Baybars I are the biographies of Muḥyī al-Dīn ibn ʿAbd al-Ẓāhir (d. 1292) and Muhammad ibn Shaddād (d. 1285). Unfortunately neither of these is fully extant. Part of the life of Baybars by Ibn ʿAbd al-Ẓāhir has been published by S.F. Sadeque, *Baybars I of Egypt* (1956). See also E.M. Quatremere (trans. and annotator.), *Histoire des sultans mamlouks de l'Égypte*, vol. 1 (1837); S. Lane-Poole, *A History of Egypt in the Middle Ages*, pp. 242–275 (1901, reprinted 1968); and G. Wiet, "Baybars I," in the *Encyclopaedia of Islam*, new ed., vol. 1 (1960).

bayberry, any of several aromatic shrubs and small trees of the genus *Myrica* in the bayberry family (Myricaceae), but especially *M. pennsylvanica*, also called candleberry, whose grayish waxy berries, upon boiling, yield the wax used in making bayberry candles. The California bayberry, or California wax myrtle (*M. californica*), is used as an ornamental on sandy soils in warm climates.

Bayḍā', al-, also spelled BEIDHA, or BEIDA, *liwā'* (province), extreme southeastern Yemen (Ṣanʿā'). The province embraces an area of 4,310 sq mi (11,170 sq km), and its eastern half consists of the easterly slopes of the Yemen Highlands; the western half is the highlands proper. The province is bounded by Maʾrib *liwā'* to the north, Yemen (Aden) to the east and south, and Dhamār *liwā'* to the west. The area was part of the former Aden Protectorate under the British. A 1934 treaty between the British and Yemen placed al-Bayḍā' in Yemen (Ṣanʿā'), and it was made a province in 1949. The main crops are teff (a cereal grain used as forage), millet, and *qāt* (a narcotic plant). Horses are raised extensively. Copper ore has been detected, but industry is based on handicrafts. Pop. (1980 est.) 182,132.

Bayḍā', al-, also spelled BEIDHA, or BEIDA, town, al-Bayḍā' *liwā'* (province), extreme southeast Yemen (Ṣanʿā'). It is situated on a high plateau near the disputed frontier with Yemen (Aden).

The town, formerly known as Bayḥān Umm Rusās, was the historic capital of the Sultanate of Bayḥān (Beihan), which ruled over a wide area from the lifetime of Muḥammad (7th century AD) to the 16th century. In modern times, before delimitation of the international frontier, the town and environs were considered to be part of the former British-controlled Aden Protectorate. On behalf of the rulers of the protectorate, the British concluded a treaty (1934) with Yemen, which provided that the frontier at the time of its signing should be accepted for a period of 40 years. Under the terms of this treaty, al-Bayḍā' became part of Yemen. There were frequent incursions from al-Bayḍā' into territory claimed by successive governments based at Aden, since the status quo line had never been demarcated on the ground.

The area was not a traditional province of Yemen (Ṣanʿā') but was set up in 1949, primarily for political reasons. After 1962 the town remained a provincial capital under the republican regime. Teff, a cereal grain introduced into southern Arabia from Ethiopia, is produced in the area and marketed in the town; al-Bayḍā' is also a horse-breeding centre. A road from Ṣanʿā' to al-Bayḍā' was completed in 1979. Pop. (1977 est.) 6,453.

Bayer, Friedrich (b. June 6, 1825, Barmen, Rhine Province, Prussia—d. May 6, 1880, Wurzburg, Ger.), founder of the well-known German chemical firm Bayer AG (*q.v.*).

Bayer served as an apprentice with a firm dealing in chemical products and quickly became the deputy of the owner. He soon established his own business in chemicals and dyewoods and took up the manufacture of dye extracts and dyestuffs. In 1863, together with Friedrich Weskott, Bayer founded a new firm producing triphenylmethane and azo dyestuffs and later also alizarin dyestuffs. At the time of his death, his business served textile firms throughout the world and the foundation for Bayer AG was already laid. After his death the management of the firm was taken over by his son, Friedrich Bayer (1851–1920), and H.T. von Böttinger.

Bayer, Gizi: *see* Bajor, Gizi.

Bayer, Herbert (b. April 5, 1900, Haag, Austria), graphic artist, painter, and architect, influential in spreading European principles of advertising in the United States.

Bayer was first trained as an architect, but, from 1921 to 1923, he studied typography and mural painting at the Bauhaus, then Germany's most advanced school of design. After spending a year (1923) as a house painter, he became a master of typography and advertising at the Bauhaus and simultaneously was an art director with *Vogue*, an American fashion magazine. In 1928 he moved to Berlin,

Herbert Bayer in his studio, 1969
Hans Graff Photo

where he worked in advertising, painting, exhibition design, typography, and photography until 1938, when he moved to New York City and concentrated on advertising design.

In 1946 Bayer became chairman of the department of design of the Container Corporation of America and design consultant for Aspen Development, a corporation that stages an annual festival of the arts in Aspen, Colo. In the latter capacity he designed many architectural projects, such as the Aspen Institute for Humanistic Studies (1962) and the Music Tent (1965) used during the annual festival. He also experimented in environmental sculpture (*e.g.*, "Marble Garden" [1955] and "Beyond the Wall" [1976]) while continuing his work in painting ("White Moon and Structure" [1959]) and the graphic arts. He received a gold medal for excellence from the American Institute of Graphic Arts in 1970.

Bayer, Johann (b. 1572, Rain, Bavaria—d. March 7, 1625, Augsburg), astronomer whose book *Uranometria* (1603) promulgated a system of identifying all stars visible to the naked eye.

Before Bayer's work, star charts were based on Ptolemy's star catalog, which was incomplete and ambiguous. Bayer updated Ptolemy's list of 48 constellations, adding 12 constellations newly recognized in the Southern Hemisphere. Based upon Tycho Brahe's determinations of stellar positions and magnitudes, Bayer assigned each visible star in a constellation one of the 24 Greek letters. For constellations with more than 24 visible stars, Bayer completed his listing with Latin letters. The nomenclature Bayer developed is still used today and has been extended to apply to about 1,300 stars.

Bayer AG, West German chemical and pharmaceutical company founded in 1863 by a chemical salesman, Friedrich Bayer (1825–80), and now operating plants in Germany and more than 30 other countries. Company headquarters, originally in Weppertal-Barmen, have been in Leverkusen, north of Cologne, since 1912.

The company was originally called Friedrich Bayer & Co. and manufactured dyestuffs; in 1881 it was incorporated as Farbenfabriken vormals Friedrich Bayer & Co. In 1912 Carl Duisberg (1861–1935), a chemist, became Bayer's general director and soon began spearheading the movement that would result in 1925 in the consolidation of Germany's chemical industries known as IG Farben (*q.v.*); Duisberg was IG Farben's first chairman, and Bayer remained within the cartel until it was dissolved by the Allies in 1945. In 1951 an independent Bayer was reestablished as Farbenfabriken Bayer Aktiengesellschaft; the current name was adopted in 1972. In 1981 Bayer acquired a controlling interest in the Agfa-Gevaert Group, a German and Belgian corporate group producing photographic equipment and film, magnetic tape, and photocopying and duplicating machines.

The company's trademark, the Bayer cross, is internationally famous. Scores of pharmaceuticals, dyes, acetates, synthetic rubbers, plastics, fibres, insecticides, and other chemicals were first developed by Bayer. Notably, it was the first developer and marketer of aspirin (1899); of the first sulfa drug, Prontosil (1935); and of polyurethane (1937), the base material for synthetic foams, paints, adhesives, fibres, and other goods.

Bayerische Alpen (West Germany–Austria): *see* Bavarian Alps.

Bayerische Julius-Maximilians-Universität Würzburg: *see* Würzburg, University of.

Bayerische Motoren Werke AG (BMW), West German automaker noted for quality sports sedans and motorcycles. Headquarters are in Munich.

The company was founded in 1929, and its motorcycles soon became famous for setting speed records. During World War II, BMW built the world's first jet airplane engines, used by the Luftwaffe, Germany's air force.

After the war, the company tried to move into the small-car market but found that it could not compete with Volkswagen's compact, inexpensive autos. By 1969 the company was on the verge of bankruptcy and owed the equivalent of U.S. $29,000,000 to the Bavarian government.

In that year BMW finally began to pull out of its financial slump when it introduced its new line of cars. The cars were of conventional design but drove, and were priced, like sports cars. At about the same time, the company introduced a new series of motorcycles, which were particularly popular in the United States.

Bayerische Staatsgemäldesammlungen (German: Bavarian State Picture Gallery), in Munich, museum composed of several collections, the major ones being the Neue Pinakothek, the Alte Pinakothek, and the Schack-Galerie. It also embraces, however, the Staatsgalerie moderner Kunst, the Olaf Gulbransson Museum in Kurpark, the Staatsgalerie im Neuen Schloss Schleissheim bei München, the Abteilung für Restaurierung und naturwissenschaftliche Untersuchungen, and subsidiary galleries in a dozen cities throughout West Germany.

The *Neue Pinakothek* (New Pinakothek), based on private picture collections of the Bavarian kings, is a collection noted for its works of European painting from the 18th through the 20th century and for its sculpture of the 19th–20th centuries. It is housed with the Neue Staatsgalerie in the Haus der Kunst, which was built in 1933–37.

The *Alte Pinakothek* (Old Pinakothek) is a museum specializing in European painting from the Middle Ages through the late 18th century. Its collection derives from accumulations made by several early electors palatine of Bavaria. The building in which it is now housed is a reconstruction of the 19th-century gallery, by Leo von Klenze, which was destroyed in World War II. It opened in 1957.

The *Schack-Galerie* collection of 19th-century, late Romantic German painting was acquired by the state in 1940 and represents the private collection of Graf Adolf Friedrich von Schack. It is housed in the former Prussian Embassy, built by Heilmann and Littman in 1907–09.

Bayerischer Wald, English BAVARIAN FOREST, mountain region in east central Bayern *Land* (Bavaria state), southeastern West Germany. The Bayerischer Wald comprises the highlands between the Danube river valley and the Böhmerwald (Bohemian Forest) along Bayern's eastern frontier with Czechoslovakia. Located largely in the *Regierungsbezirk* (administrative district) of Niederbayern (Lower Bavaria), the highlands parallel the southeasterly flowing Danube for about 90 mi (145 km) from the Cham and lower Regen rivers to the Austrian border east of Passau.

The Bayerischer Wald, composed mainly of granite and gneiss hills, is divided into two sections by a sharp quartz ridge known as the Pfahl. The ridge runs roughly along the Regen valley and ranges from 65 to 100 ft (20 to 30 m) in height. The Vorderer Wald, or Donaugebirge (Danube Hills), a rolling plateau situated to the southwest between the Danube and the Pfahl, seldom rises more than 3,300 ft above sea level. Meadow, isolated farmsteads, and small hamlets dominate the landscape; only the higher and steeper slopes are still wooded. Northeast of the Pfahl is the Hinterer Wald, a higher and almost continuously forested mountain region where human settlement is confined to a few longitudinal valleys. Its highest peaks include the Grosser Arber, with an elevation of 4,780 ft, and the Rachel, Lusen, Dreisesselberg, and Grosser Falkenstein.

The climate of the highlands is severe and wet, supporting only modest yields of rye, oats, and potatoes produced on small valley farms. Coniferous forest predominates, with spruce the main species at higher altitudes and a mixed woodland of spruce, silver fir, and beech found at lower levels. Lumbering, woodworking, and glass grinding are the principal industries. The tourist trade is expanding as the reputation of the Bayerischer Wald as a beautiful and uncrowded holiday resort area spreads. Each year many visitors explore the Bayerischer Wald National Park, where more than 98 percent of the park's 50.5-sq-mi (130.8-sq-km) area is tree-covered and many species of plants, birds, and small animals thrive. Principal towns of the mountain region are Regen, Zwiesel, Waldkirchen, and Grafenau.

To make the best use of the Britannica, consult the INDEX *first*

Bayern, English BAVARIA, largest *Land* (state) of the Federal Republic of Germany, with an area of 27,238 sq mi (70,547 sq km). Bayern comprises the eastern part of southern West Germany and is bounded on the west by the *Länder* of Baden-Württemberg and Hessen, on the north by the German Democratic Republic, on the east by Czechoslovakia, and on the south and southeast by Austria. Munich (München) is the capital.

The following article summarizes the political history, geography, demography, economy, and modern culture of Bayern; for additional treatment, *see* MACROPAEDIA: Germany.

History. The earliest known inhabitants in the area of present-day Bayern were the Celts. In the last decade BC they were pressed between Teutonic tribes in the north and the Romans in the south. The Romans divided the southern part into Raetia and Noricum and built fortifications along the northern boundary to keep out the Teutons. Flourishing Roman colonies arose in the south: Augsburg, Kempten, Regensburg, and Passau.

The Romans were overcome in the 5th century by repeated Germanic attacks. The lands were eventually settled by tribes from the Elbe area and from Bohemia, Moravia, and Hungary, who mixed with the remaining Celts and Romans. The tribe that gave the territory its name was the Baiuvarii (Bavarians), who settled in the south between AD 500 and 800. The southwest belonged to the Alemanni, while northern Bayern was in the hands of the Franks and Thuringians.

In the 7th and 8th centuries Bayern was Christianized by Irish and Scottish monks (St. Boniface, St. Korbinian, St. Emmeram, and St. Rupert). From about 555 to 758 the Bavarians were ruled by Frankish dukes of the Agilolfing family. The last of the family, Tassilo III, was deposed by Charlemagne, who incorporated Bayern into the Carolingian Empire.

After the partitioning of the empire in 817, the Duchy of Bayern became a central part of the territory of the East Franks, with its capital at Regensburg. In 1180 the Holy Roman emperor Frederick I Barbarossa gave Bayern to the count palatine Otto of Wittelsbach, whose family ruled it until 1918. At first the Wittelsbachs possessed only the southeastern part of present-day Bayern, the rest being fragmented into numerous imperial cities, monastic holdings, and family domains. In 1214 the Palatinate was added (which remained Bavarian until 1945). In the 14th and 15th centuries the power of the dukes was notably weakened by political divisions, until finally Albert IV (1467–1508) reunited Bayern, making Munich the capital.

William IV (1508–50) opposed the Protestant Reformation; under his successor, Albert V (1550–79), Bayern became a strictly Catholic territory. Maximilian I (1597–1651) fought on the side of the Habsburgs in the Thirty Years' War (1618–48), and by his leadership, increased Bayern's prestige, gaining territorial accessions and attaining for himself the title of elector. Throughout the 18th century Bayern was ravaged by the wars of the Spanish Succession, the Austrian Succession, and the Bavarian Succession.

In 1800, French Revolutionary armies occupied Munich. In the following year Bayern became an ally of France and was able to expand its territories at the expense of Austria, acquiring by 1806 approximately the boundaries it now has. In 1813, shortly before the Battle of Leipzig, Bayern rejected Napoleon and in 1815 joined the Germanic Confederation against him. The reigns of kings Maximilian I and Louis I saw the consolidation of the country and the establishment of the first constitution, a parliament, municipal autonomy, and tax reform. In 1848, however, Louis was forced to abdicate.

Maximilian II (ruled 1848–64) proceeded with domestic reform programs and also promoted the arts and learning. His successor,

Louis II (ruled 1864–86), refused Bismarck's proposal to incorporate Bayern into a German domain under Prussian leadership and sided with Austria in the Prussian–Austrian War of 1866. The quick victory of the Prussians and the moderation of their policies led Bayern to join Prussia in the Franco-German War of 1870 and afterward to share in the establishment of a German empire under William I, king of Prussia.

In the German constitution of 1871 Bayern retained an autonomous diplomatic service, military administration, postal service, and railways but otherwise cast its lot with the German Empire. At the end of World War I, King Louis III had to abdicate, and Bayern became a republic. The five years thereafter were filled with constant unrest: 1919 saw the murder of Kurt Eisner, the Socialist leader, and the establishment of a short-lived soviet republic; in 1920 and 1921 there were right-wing coups; and in 1923 Adolf Hitler and Gen. Erich Ludendorff attempted their unsuccessful *Putsch* in Munich.

After World War II Bayern became part of the American zone of occupation. The Palatinate was detached and joined to the new Rheinland-Pfalz state. Under the Basic Law (constitution) of West Germany of 1948, Bayern became a *Land* of the Federal Republic.

The land. Bayern is a country of high plateaus and medium-sized mountains. In the northwest are the wooded sandstone hills of the Spessart; in the north are basalt knolls and high plateaus. The northwest is drained by the Main River, which flows into the Rhine. To the southeast, the topography varies from the stratified land formations of Swabia-Franconia to shell limestone and red marl, the hill country of the Franconian-Rednitz Basin, and the limestone mountains of the Franconian Jura along the Danube, which divides Bayern north and south. On the eastern edge of Bayern, adjoining Czechoslovakia, is the Böhmerwald (Bohemian Forest), and, in the north, the Frankenwald (Franconian Forest). South of the Danube is a plateau upon which lies the capital, Munich, and beyond it the Bavarian Alps. Bayern's share of the Alps consists of wooded heights of several thousand feet, behind which rise steep ridges and high plateaus (in the west, the Allgäuer Alps; in the east, the Alps of Berchtesgaden). They reach their highest peak in the 9,718-ft (2,962-m) Zugspitze in Germany's Wettersteingebirge (Wetterstein Range). Bayern has a continental climate that is harsh for middle Europe, although there are some exceptions, such as the Lower Main Valley.

The people. The southeast is inhabited by an old Bavarian stock, the southwest by people of Bavarian–Swabian descent, and the north by descendants of the Franks. Traditional differences are still visible in their villages. The Franks built large village clusters and laid out their farms in narrow strips. The houses are partly sandstone, partly half-timbered. Row houses with paved floors appear in some areas. In old Bayern and Swabia there are both village clusters and one-street villages; most of the houses have wooden floors. The cities show even more marked differences. In the Swabian and, particularly, the Frankish areas, religious and secular landholders established a large number of towns, most of which remained small and were referred to as dwarf towns. These medieval towns were built compactly within protective walls. The churches, public buildings, and homes were lavishly decorated; the examples that remain are a constant delight to the tourist, notably in Rothenburg, Nördlingen, Dinkelsbühl, and sections of Nürnberg and Regensburg.

While nearly half of Bayern's inhabitants still live in places of less than 5,000 population, more than one-fifth live in towns of 100,000 or more. Munich is the third largest city in West Germany (excluding Berlin) and the largest city in Bayern.

After World War II there was an influx of refugees from the Sudetenland and eastern Europe, where many Germans had lived for centuries. About one-fifth of Bayern's population in the late 20th century was composed of these refugees. Beginning in the 1960s the industrial areas received large numbers of migrant workers from southern Europe.

Great changes took place in the religious composition of the population after the war, with a heavy influx of Protestants. In the late 20th century the vast majority of the Bavarians were Roman Catholics, having bishoprics in Munich-Freising, Augsburg, Regensburg, Passau, Bamberg, Eichstätt, and Würzburg. A substantial proportion were of Evangelical Lutheran faith, with centres in Munich, Augsburg, Regensburg, Nürnberg, Bayreuth, and Ansbach. The proportion of the population engaged in farming declined steadily since 1882, from a majority of the work force to less than one-fifth in the late 20th century. Industry and service sectors employ the largest number of workers.

The economy. More than half of the state's gross output in the late 20th century consisted of industrial and handicraft products. Trade, transportation, and services accounted for less than half, and agriculture and forestry for less than one-tenth.

Farms have grown larger and employ fewer hands. There has been a trend to specialization in crops and to production for specific markets. Most farms are family operated. Small units are common, and there are a few large landholdings manned by foreign workers. Rye, wheat, and barley take up more than half of the farmland; potatoes, sugar beets, and other vegetables less than one-fourth; and the rest is given to hay, hops, and vineyards.

The development of Bavarian industry was at first hampered by a lack of minerals and poor transportation. The natural disadvantages have been overcome by the development of hydroelectric power and more recently by the use of oil piped in from the Mediterranean ports of Marseilles, Genoa, and Trieste. Improved transportation has encouraged industries that manufacture and finish quality materials.

After World War II the government made great efforts to attract expanding industries, with the result that Bayern attained a higher rate of industrial growth than the rest of West Germany. In the late 20th century the leading industries were electronics, machinery, chemicals, textiles, automobiles, clothing, and foodstuffs; the range of industrial effort was too broad to give any industry a unique predominance.

Trade and commerce resemble that of the rest of West Germany, with the exception of the tourist trade, which has assumed particular importance in the Bavarian Alps. Bayern has several hundred thousand hotel beds, and three-fourths of them are in the Alpine area.

Begun in 1835, the Bavarian railroad system was heavily developed in the second half of the 19th century. All main lines either are electrified or use diesel engines. The most important waterway is the Main River, which is navigable as far as Bamberg. The Danube carries vessels as far upstream as Kelheim. Bayern has major airports at Munich-Riem and Nürnberg.

Cultural life. Under its constitution of 1946, Bayern is a free state with democratic parliamentary institutions. The voters are represented directly in a lower house, the Landtag, elected every four years. The Landtag chooses a minister-president and a Cabinet. There is also a Senate composed of representatives of economic, social, cultural, and religious organizations.

The predominant political party in Bayern since 1957 has been the Christian-Social Union (CSU). The other major parties are the Social Democratic Party and the Free Democratic Party. Universities include two in Munich and one each in Erlangen-Nürnberg, Würzburg, Regensburg, Bayreuth, Passau, and Augsburg. There are theatres in all the larger cities (including three state theatres in Munich alone), as well as numerous orchestras, museums, and art galleries. The libraries are excellent, particularly the Bavarian State Library in Munich. The Bavarian radio (broadcasting both radio and television programs) is a public, state-controlled system with headquarters in Munich. Pop. (1983 est.) 10,966,717.

BIBLIOGRAPHY. Statistical information on Bayern is available in the *Statistisches Jahrbuch für Bayern* (annual). Recent census material is contained in *Beiträge zur Statistik Bayerns* (1971). The most recent and comprehensive treatment of Bavarian history is Max Spindler, *Handbuch der bayerischen Geschichte,* 4 vol. (1967–). An historical atlas is *Bayerischer Geschichtsatlas* (1969). A classic geographical work on Bayern is Robert Gradmann, *Süddeutschland,* 2 vol. (1931). Other sources for climate and topography include Oskar Kuhn, *Geologie von Bayern* (1954); K. Rocznik, *Wetter und Klima in Bayern* (1960); K. Knoch (ed.), *Klima-Atlas von Bayern* (1952); and *Topographischer Atlas Bayern* (1968), which has maps of selected landscapes and towns with geographical essays. For the economy, see K. Schreyer, *Bayern: Ein Industriestaat* (1969), on the postwar development of Bavarian industry.

Bayes, Nora, original name DORA GOLDBERG (b. 1880, Joliet, Ill., U.S.—d. March 19, 1928, Brooklyn, N.Y.), singer in vogue in the early 1900s in vaudeville and musical revues, notably the *Ziegfeld Follies.* She was identified with the songs "Down Where the Wurzburger Flows" (1902) and "Shine on, Harvest Moon" (1908), which were written by her husband, Jack Norworth, who was her singing partner during their marriage (1908–13). During World War I Bayes introduced George M. Cohan's famous "Over There." In 1919 a New York theatre was named for her.

Consult the INDEX *first*

Bayes, Thomas (b. 1702, London—d. April 17, 1761, Tunbridge Wells, Kent, Eng.), theologian and mathmematician who was first to use probability inductively and who established a mathematical basis for probability inference (a means of calculating, from the frequency with which an event has occurred in prior trials, the probability that it will occur in future trials).

He set down his findings on probability in "Essay Towards Solving a Problem in the Doctrine of Chances" (1763), published posthumously. That work became the basis of a statistical technique, now called Bayesian estimation, for calculating the probability of the validity of a proposition on the basis of a prior estimate of its probability and new relevant evidence. Disadvantages of the method—pointed out by later statisticians—include the different ways of assigning prior distributions of parameters and the possible sensitivity of conclusions to the choice of distributions.

The only works Bayes is known to have published in his lifetime are *Divine Benevolence, or an Attempt to Prove That the Principal End of the Divine Providence and Government Is the Happiness of His Creatures* (1731) and *An Introduction to the Doctrine of Fluxions, and a Defence of the Mathematicians Against the Objections of the Author of The Analyst* (1736), which countered the attacks by Bishop Berkeley on the logical foundations of Newton's calculus.

List of Abbreviations

A	ampere
AB	Limited-liability Company (Swedish *aktiebolag, aktiebolaget*)
A.B.	bachelor of arts (Latin *artium baccalaureus*)
ac	acre(s); alternating current
Ac	actinium
ac-ft	acre-foot, acre-feet
A.C.T.	Australian Capital Territory
AD	in the year of our Lord (Latin *anno Domini*)
Adj. Gen.	Adjutant General
Adm.	Admiral
Afg.	Afghanistan
Ag	silver (Latin *argentum*)
AG	Limited-liability Company (German *Aktiengesellschaft*)
AH	in the year of the hijrah (hegira), or Muslim era (Latin *anno Hegirae*)
Al	aluminum, aluminium
Ala.	Alabama
Alb.	Albania
Ald.	Alderman
Alg.	Algeria
alt.	altitude
Alta.	Alberta
Am	americium
AM	before noon (Latin *ante meridiem*)
AM	amplitude modulation
A.M.	master of arts (Latin *artium magister*)
Ar	argon
Arg.	Argentina
Ariz.	Arizona
Ark.	Arkansas
As	arsenic
A.S.S.R.	Autonomous Soviet Socialist Republic
At	astatine
atm	atmosphere(s)
Au	gold (Latin *aurum*)
a.u.	astronomical unit(s)
Aug.	August
avdp	avoirdupois
b.	born
B	boron
Ba	barium
B.A.	bachelor of arts
Bar.	Baruch (Apocrypha)
bbl	barrel(s)
BC	before Christ
B.C.	British Columbia
BCE	before the Christian era, or Common Era
bd-ft	board-foot, board-feet
Be	beryllium
B.Ed.	bachelor of education
Bel.	Bel and the Dragon (Apocrypha)
Belg.	Belgium
Bi	bismuth
Bk	berkelium
BP	before the present
B.Ph.	bachelor of philosophy
Br	bromine
Braz.	Brazil
Brig. Gen.	Brigadier General
Brit.	British
B.S.	bachelor of science
BTU	British thermal unit(s)
bu	bushel(s)
Bulg.	Bulgaria
c.	about, approximately (Latin *circa*)
C	carbon; Celsius
Ca	calcium
cal.	calorie(s)
Cal.	kilocalorie(s)
Calif.	California
Can.	Canada
Capt.	Captain
cat.	catalog
Cb	columbium
Cd	cadmium
Ce	cerium
CE	Christian era, Common Era
cf.	compare (Latin *confer*)
Cf	californium
ch.	chapter
Chron.	Chronicles (Bible)
Cia.	Company (Italian *Compagnia*; Portuguese *Companhia*; Spanish *Compañia*)
Cie.	Company (French *Compagnie*)
Cl	chlorine
cm	centimetre(s)
Cm	curium
Co	cobalt
Co.	Company
col.	column
Col.	Colonel; Colossians (Bible)
Colo.	Colorado
Colom.	Colombia
cols.	columns
Comdr.	Commander
Comdt.	Commandant
Commo.	Commodore
comp.	compiled; compiler
comps.	compilers
Conn.	Connecticut
Cor.	Corinthians (Bible)
Corp.	Corporal; Corporation
cos	cosine
cot	cotangent
Cr	chromium
Cs	cesium
csc	cosecant
cu	cubic
Cu	copper (Latin *cuprum*)
Czech.	Czechoslovakia
d.	died
Dan.	Daniel (Bible)
dau.	daughter
dB	decibel(s)
dc	direct current
D.C.	District of Columbia
D.D.	doctor of divinity
Dec.	December
Del.	Delaware
Den.	Denmark
Deut.	Deuteronomy (Bible)
D.F.	Federal District (Spanish *Distrito Federal*)
dict.	dictionary
D.Litt.	doctor of letters (Latin *doctor litterarum*)
Dr.	Doctor
Dy	dysprosium
E	east
Eccles.	Ecclesiastes (Bible)
Ecclus.	Ecclesiasticus (Apocrypha)
ed.	edited; edition; editor
Ed.B.	bachelor of education
eds.	editors
e.g.	for example (Latin *exempli gratia*)
E.Ger.	East Germany
emf	electromotive force
encyc.	encyclopaedia
Eng.	England; English
enl.	enlarged
Eph.	Ephesians (Bible)
Er	erbium
Es	einsteinium
Esd.	Esdras (Apocrypha)
est.	estimate; estimated
Esth.	Esther (Bible)
et al.	and others (Latin *et alii*, or *aliae*)
et seq.	and following page(s) (Latin *et sequens, sequentes*, or *sequentia*)
etc.	and so forth (Latin *et cetera*)
Eth.	Ethiopia
Eu	europium
eV	electron volt(s)
Ex.	Exodus (Bible)
ex parte	on one side, or party, only (law)
Ezek.	Ezekiel (Bible)
F	Fahrenheit; fluorine
Fe	iron (Latin *ferrum*)
Feb.	February
ff.	and following pages
Fig.	Figure
Fin.	Finland
fl.	flourished (Latin *floruit*)
Fla.	Florida
Fm	fermium
FM	frequency modulation
fol.	and following page(s)
Fr	francium
Fr.	France
ft	foot, feet
Ft.	Fort
ft-lb	foot-pound(s)
g	gram(s)
Ga	gallium
Ga.	Georgia
gal	gallon(s)
Gal.	Galatians (Bible)
Gd	gadolinium
Ge	germanium
Gen.	General; Genesis (Bible)
Ger.	Germany
GmbH	Company with Limited Liability (German *Gesellschaft mit beschränkter Haftung*)
Gov.	Governor
Govt.	Government
H	hydrogen
ha	hectare(s)
Ha	hahnium
Hab.	Habakkuk (Bible)
Hag.	Haggai (Bible)
He	helium
Heb.	Hebrews (Bible)
Hdbk.	Handbook
Hf	hafnium
Hg	mercury (Latin *hydrargyrum*)
HMS	His, or Her, Majesty's Ship, or Service
HMSO	His, or Her, Majesty's Stationery Office
Ho	holmium
Hon.	Honourable
Hos.	Hosea (Bible)
hp	horsepower
hr	hour(s)
Hung.	Hungary
I	iodine
ibid.	in the same place (Latin *ibidem*)
Ice.	Iceland
i.e.	that is (Latin *id est*)
Ill.	Illinois
in.	inch(es)
In	indium
in re	in the matter of (law)
Inc.	Incorporated
Ind.	Indiana
Indon.	Indonesia
inf.	information
Ir	iridium
Ire.	Ireland
Isa.	Isaiah (Bible)
J	joule(s)
J.	Journal
Jam.	Jamaica
Jan.	January
Jer.	Jeremiah (Bible)
Josh.	Joshua (Bible)
Jr.	Junior
Judg.	Judges (Bible)
K	Kelvin; potassium (Latin *kalium*)
Kan.	Kansas
kg	kilogram(s)
KG	Limited Partnership (German *Kommandit Gesellschaft*)
kHz	kilohertz
KK	Limited-liability Company (Japanese *Kabushiki Kaisha*)
km	kilometre(s)
kph	kilometres per hour
Kr	krypton
kW	kilowatt(s)
kW-hr	kilowatt-hr(s)
Ky.	Kentucky
l	litre(s)
£	pound(s) sterling (Latin *libra*)
La	lanthanum
La.	Louisiana
Lam.	Lamentations (Bible)
lb	pound(s)
Lev.	Leviticus (Bible)
Li	lithium
Lieut.	Lieutenant
LL.B.	bachelor of laws (Latin *legum baccalaureus*)
LL.D.	doctor of laws (Latin *legum doctor*)
log	logarithm
Lr	lawrencium
Ltd.	Limited
Lu	lutetium
m	metre(s)
M	noon (Latin *meridies*)
M.A.	master of arts
Macc.	Maccabees (Apocrypha)
Maj.	Major
Mal.	Malachi (Bible)
Man.	Manitoba
Mass.	Massachusetts
Matt.	Matthew (Bible)
mbH	Limited, with Limited Liability (German *mit beschränkter Haftung*)
Md	mendelevium
Md.	Maryland
M.D.	doctor of medicine (Latin *medicinae doctor*)
Mex.	Mexico
mg	milligram(s)
Mg	magnesium
mHz	megahertz
mi	mile(s)
Mic.	Micah (Bible)
Mich.	Michigan
Mij	Company (Dutch *Maatschappij*)
min	minute(s)
Minn.	Minnesota
Miss.	Mississippi
ml	millilitre(s)
Mlle	Mademoiselle
mm	millimetre(s)
Mme	Madame
Mn	manganese
Mo	molybdenum
Mo.	Missouri
Mont.	Montana
Mor.	Morocco
MP	member of Parliament
mph	miles per hour
MS.	manuscript
M.S.	master of science
Msgr.	Monsignor
MSS.	manuscripts
Mt.	Mount; Mountain(s)
mun.	municipality
MV	Motor Vessel
N	newton(s); nitrogen; north
Na	sodium (Latin *natrium*)
NA	National Association
Nah.	Nahum (Bible)
Nat.	National
Nb	niobium
N.B.	New Brunswick

N.C.	North Carolina
n.d.	no date
Nd	neodymium
N.D.	North Dakota
Ne	neon
Neb.	Nebraska
Neh.	Nehemiah (Bible)
Neth.	The Netherlands
Nev.	Nevada
Nfd.	Newfoundland
N.H.	New Hampshire
Ni	nickel
N.Ire.	Northern Ireland
N.J.	New Jersey
N.M.	New Mexico
no.	number
No	nobelium
Nor.	Norway
nos.	numbers
Nov.	November
Np	neptunium
NS	Nuclear Ship
N.S.	new style (calendar)
N.S.W.	New South Wales
N.Terr.	Northern Territory
Num.	Numbers (Bible)
NV	Limited-liability Company (Dutch *Naamloze Vennootschap*)
N.W.Terr.	Northwest Territories
N.Y.	New York
N.Z.	New Zealand
O	oxygen
Obad.	Obadiah (Bible)
Oct.	October
Okla.	Oklahoma
Ont.	Ontario
op.	opus
op. cit.	in the work cited (Latin *opere citato,* or *opus citato*)
Ore.	Oregon
Org.	Organization
Os	osmium
O.S.	old style (calendar)
oz	ounce(s)
p.	page
P	phosphorus
pA	Limited (Italian *per Azioni*)
Pa	protactinium
Pa.	Pennsylvania
Pak.	Pakistan
Pb	lead (Latin *plumbum*)
Pd	palladium
P.E.I.	Prince Edward Island
Pet.	Peter (Bible)
pH	potential of hydrogen (acidity–alkalinity factor)
Ph.B.	bachelor of philosophy (Latin *philosophiae baccalaureus*)
Ph.D.	doctor of philosophy (Latin *philosophiae doctor*)
Phil.	Philippians (Bible); Philippines
Philem.	Philemon (Bible)
PLC	Public Limited Company
Pm	promethium
PM	afternoon (Latin *post meridiem*)
Po	polonium
Pol.	Poland
pop.	population
Port.	Portugal
pp.	pages
Pr	praseodymium
P.R.	Puerto Rico
Pr. Man.	Prayer of Manasseh (Apocrypha)
prelim.	preliminary
Pres.	President
Proc.	Proceedings
Prov.	Proverbs (Bible)
Ps.	Psalms (Bible)
pseud.	pseudonym; pseudonymous
pt	pint(s)
Pt	platinum
ptg.	printing
Pu	plutonium
Pvt.	Private
qq.v.	which see (plural; Latin *quae vide*)
qt	quart(s)
Que.	Quebec
Queen.	Queensland
q.v.	which see (singular; Latin *quod vide*)
R	rankine(s)
Ra	radium
Rb	rubidium
Re	rhenium
Rear Adm.	Rear Admiral
Rep.	Representative
rev.	revised; revision
Rev.	Revelations (Bible); Reverend
Rf	rutherfordium
Rh	rhodium
R.I.	Rhode Island
Rn	radon
Rom.	Romania; Romans (Bible)
rpm	revolutions per minute
Rt. Rev.	Right Reverend
Ru	ruthenium
S	south; sulfur
S.	Saint (*san, santo, santa, sant'*)
S. of III Ch.	Song of the Three Children (Apocrypha)
S. of Sol.	Song of Solomon (Bible)
SA	Limited-liability Company (French *Société Anonyme*; Italian *Società Anònima*; Portuguese *Sociedade Anónima*; Spanish *Sociedad Anónima*)
S.Af.	South Africa
Sam.	Samuel (Bible)
Sask.	Saskatchewan
S.Aus.	South Australia
Sb	antimony (Latin *stibium*)
Sc	scandium
S.C.	South Carolina
Scot.	Scotland
SCSA	standard consolidated statistical area
S.D.	South Dakota
Se	selenium
sec	secant; second(s)
sect.	section
sects.	sections
Sen.	Senator
Sept.	September
sess.	session
S.F.S.R.	Soviet Federated Socialist Republic
Sgt.	Sergeant
Si	silicon
sin	sine
Sm	samarium
SMSA	standard metropolitan statistical area
Sn	tin (Latin *stannum*)
SpA	Limited-liability Company (Italian *Società per Azioni*)
sq	square
Sr	strontium
Sr.	Senior
ss	Steamship
SS.	Saints; Saintliest, or Holiest (Italian *Santissimo, Santissima*)
S.S.R.	Soviet Socialist Republic
St.	Saint (*Sankt, Sint*)
Sta.	Saint (*Santa*)
Ste.	Saint (*Sainte*)
suppl.	supplement
Sus.	Susanna (Apocrypha)
Swed.	Sweden
Switz.	Switzerland
Ta	tantalum
tan	tangent
Tanz.	Tanzania
Tas.	Tasmania
Tb	terbium
Tc	technetium
Te	tellurium
Tech.	Technical
Technol.	Technological; Technology
Tenn.	Tennessee
Th	thorium
Thess.	Thessalonians (Bible)
Ti	titanium
Tim.	Timothy (Bible)
Tit.	Titus (Bible)
Tl	thallium
Tm	thulium
Tob.	Tobit (Apocrypha)
trans.	translated; translation; translator(s)
Tur.	Turkey
U	uranium
UHF	ultrahigh frequency
U.A.E.	United Arab Emirates
U.K.	United Kingdom
UN	United Nations
U.S.	United States
USGPO	United States Government Printing Office
USS	United States Ship
U.S.S.R.	Union of Soviet Socialist Republics
v.	versus (law)
V	vanadium; volt(s)
Va.	Virginia
VHF	very high frequency
Vic.	Victoria
Vice Adm.	Vice Admiral
Vice Pres.	Vice President
vol.	volume(s)
Vt.	Vermont
W	tungsten (wolfram); watt(s); west
Wash.	Washington
W.Aus.	Western Australia
W.Ger.	West Germany
Wis.	Wisconsin
Wisd. Sol.	Wisdom of Solomon (Apocrypha)
W.Va.	West Virginia
Wyo.	Wyoming
Xe	Xenon
Y	yttrium
Yb	ytterbium
yd	yard(s)
Yugos.	Yugoslavia
Zech.	Zechariah (Bible)
Zeph.	Zephaniah (Bible)
Zn	zinc
Zr	zirconium